# The
# Philosopher's
# Index

## An International Index to
## Philosophical Periodicals and Books

**1997 CUMULATIVE EDITION
VOLUME 31**

Published by:
**Philosopher's Information Center
1616 East Wooster Street
Bowling Green, OH 43402**

# THE PHILOSOPHER'S INDEX

## Publisher and Editorial Office

Philosopher's Information Center
1616 East Wooster Street
Bowling Green, OH  43402

## Phone Numbers

Voice: (419) 353-8830   or   (800) 476-8757
Fax:    (419) 353-8920   or   (800) 476-8784

## E-Mail Address

PhilIndex@wcnet.org

# THE PHILOSOPHER'S INDEX

## Editor

Richard H. Lineback

## Editorial Staff

Robert Goodwin, Assistant Editor
*Bowling Green State University*
Steven Laycock, Assistant Editor
*University of Toledo*
Fred Miller, Assistant Editor
*Bowling Green State University*

Frederick Rickey, Assistant Editor
*Bowling Green State University*
Mario Sáenz, Assistant Editor
*LeMoyne College*
Kartik Seshadri, Assistant Editor
*Cardiff, CA*

Robert Wolf, Assistant Editor
*Southern Illinois University*

## Table of Contents

## The Philosopher's Index

*The Philosopher's Index,* ISSN 0031-7993, is a subject and author index with abstracts. Philosophy books and journals in English, French, German, Spanish, and Italian are indexed, along with selected books and journals in other languages and related interdisciplinary publications. This periodical is published quarterly and cumulated annually as a service to the philosophical community. Suggestions for improving this service are solicited and should be sent to the Editor.

*Policies:* Each quarterly issue of the *Index* includes the articles of journals and books that are received in the months prior to its publication. The dates on the journals indexed vary due to dissimiliar publishing schedules and to delays encountered in overseas mailing.

The following factors are weighed in selecting journals to be indexed: 1) the purpose of the journal, 2) its circulation, and 3) recommendations from members of the philosophic community. Articles in interdisciplinary journals are indexed only if they are related to philosophy.

Most of the journal articles and books cited in *The Philosopher's Index* can be obtained from the Bowling Green State University Library, through the Inter-Library Loan Department. The library, though, requests that you first try to locate the articles and books through your local or regional library facilities.

*Subscriptions* should be sent to the Philosopher's Information Center, 1616 East Wooster Street, Bowling Green, OH 43402-3456. The 1998 subscription price for 4 quarterly issues is $209 (Individuals $62). The price of any single quarterly issue is $60 (Individuals $20). An annual Cumulative Edition of *The Philosopher's Index* is published in the spring following the volume year. The 1996 Cumulative Edition is $205 (Individuals $75); the 1997 Cumulative Edition is $225 (Individuals $82).

# Abbreviations of Periodicals Indexed

(*Journal is no longer indexed and/or published. The abbreviation is included here for use in conjunction with DIALOG.)

| | |
|---|---|
| Abraxas*.................... | Abraxas |
| Acorn ..................... | The Acorn: Journal of the Gandhi-King Society |
| Acta Analytica ............. | Acta Analytica: Philosophy and Psychology |
| Acta Phil .................. | Acta Philosophica: Ateneo Romano della Santa Croce |
| Acta Phil Fennica............. | Acta Philosophica Fennica |
| Aesthetics................. | Aesthetics |
| Agora*.................... | Agora: A Journal of the Humanities and the Social Sciences |
| Agora (Spain)............... | Agora: Papeles de Filosofía |
| Agr Human Values ........... | Agriculture and Human Values |
| Aitia...................... | Aitia: Philosophy-Humanities Magazine |
| Ajatus*................... | Ajatus: Yearbook of the Philosophical Society of Finland |
| Aletheia*.................. | Aletheia: An International Journal of Philosophy |
| Alg Log*.................. | Algebra and Logic |
| Alg Ned Tijdschr Wijs .......... | Algemeen Nederlands Tijdschrift voor Wijsbegeerte |
| Amer Cath Phil Quart........... | American Catholic Philosophical Quarterly (formerly The New Scholasticism) |
| Amer J Philo............... | American Journal of Philology |
| Amer J Theol Phil............. | American Journal of Theology & Philosophy |
| Amer Phil Quart ............. | American Philosophical Quarterly |
| An Cated Suarez ............. | Anales de la Cátedra Francisco Suárez |
| An Seminar Hist Filosof ........ | Anales del Seminario de Historia de la Filosofía |
| An Seminar Metaf............ | Anales del Seminario de Metafisica |
| Analisis Filosof ............. | Análisis Filosófico |
| Analogia .................. | Analogía Filosófica: Revista de Filosofía |
| Analysis .................. | Analysis |
| Ancient Phil ............... | Ancient Philosophy |
| Ann Esth*................. | Annales D'Esthétique |
| Ann Fac Lett Filosof........... | Annali della Facolta di Lettere e Filosofia |
| Ann Univ Mariae Curie-Phil....... | Annales Universitatis Mariae Curie-Sklodowska, Sectio I/Philosophia-Sociologia |
| Annals Math Log ............ | Annals of Mathematical Logic (see Annals Pure Applied Log) |
| Annals Pure Applied Log........ | Annals of Pure and Applied Logic (formerly Annals of Mathematical Logic) |
| Annu Soc Christ Ethics ......... | The Annual of the Society of Christian Ethics |
| Antioch Rev ................ | The Antioch Review |
| Anu Filosof ................ | Anuario Filosófico |
| Apeiron.................... | Apeiron: A Journal for Ancient Philosophy and Science |
| Applied Phil ................ | Applied Philosophy (see Int J Applied Phil) |
| Aquinas................... | Aquinas: Rivista Internazionale di Filosofia |
| Arch Begriff*............... | Archiv für Begriffsgeschichte |
| Arch Filosof*............... | Archivio di Filosofia |
| Arch Gesch Phil............. | Archiv für Geschichte der Philosophie |
| Arch Math Log* ............. | Archiv für Mathematische Logik und Grundlagenforschung |
| Arch Phil.................. | Archives de Philosophie |
| Arch Rechts Soz............. | Archiv für Rechts- und Sozialphilosophie |
| Arch Stor Cult............... | Archivio di Storia della Cultura |
| Arete..................... | Areté: Revista de Filosofía |
| Argumentation* .............. | Argumentation: An International Journal on Reasoning |
| Arion..................... | Arion: A Journal of Humanities and the Classics |
| Aris Soc .................. | The Aristotelian Society: Supplementary Volume |
| Asian J Phil................ | The Asian Journal of Philosophy |
| Asian Phil ................. | Asian Philosophy |
| Augustin Stud.............. | Augustinian Studies |
| Augustinus ................ | Augustinus |
| Auslegung ................ | Auslegung: A Journal of Philosophy |
| Austl J Phil................ | Australasian Journal of Philosophy |
| Behavior Phil .............. | Behavior and Philosophy (formerly Behaviorism) |
| Behaviorism ............... | Behaviorism (see Behavior Phil) |
| Berkeley News.............. | Berkeley Newsletter |
| Between Species ............ | Between the Species: A Journal of Ethics |
| Bigaku................... | Bigaku: The Japanese Journal of Aesthetics |
| Bijdragen ................. | Bijdragen, Tijdschrift voor Filosofie en Theologie |
| Bioethics.................. | Bioethics |
| Bioethics Quart ............. | Bioethics Quarterly (see J Med Human) |
| Biol Phil.................. | Biology & Philosophy |
| Boll Centro Stud Vichiani......... | Bollettino del Centro di Studi Vichiani |
| Boston Col Stud Phil*........... | Boston College Studies in Philosophy |
| Boundary 2*................ | Boundary 2: An International Journal of Literature and Culture |
| Brahmavadin*............... | Brahmavadin |
| Bridges................... | Bridges: An Interdisciplinary Journal of Theology, Philosophy, History, and Science |
| Brit J Aes ................. | The British Journal of Aesthetics |
| Brit J Hist Phil............... | British Journal for the History of Philosophy |
| Brit J Phil Sci............... | British Journal for the Philosophy of Science |
| Bull Hegel Soc Gt Brit .......... | Bulletin of the Hegel Society of Great Britain |
| Bull Santayana Soc ........... | Overheard in Seville: Bulletin of the Santayana Society |
| Bull Sec Log................ | Bulletin of the Section of Logic |

| | |
|---|---|
| Int J Moral Soc Stud. . . . . . . . . . . | International Journal of Moral and Social Studies |
| Int J Phil Relig . . . . . . . . . . . . . . | International Journal for Philosophy of Religion |
| Int J Phil Stud . . . . . . . . . . . . . . | International Journal of Philosophical Studies (formerly Philosophical Studies) |
| Int Log Rev . . . . . . . . . . . | International Logic Review |
| Int Phil Quart . . . . . . . . . . | International Philosophical Quarterly |
| Int Stud Phil . . . . . . . . . . . | International Studies in Philosophy (formerly Studi Internazionali di Filosofia) |
| Int Stud Phil Sci . . . . . . . . . | International Studies in the Philosophy of Science |
| Interchange* . . . . . . . . . . . . . . . | Interchange |
| Interpretation . . . . . . . . . . . . . . | Interpretation: A Journal of Political Philosophy |
| Iride . . . . . . . . . . | Iride: Filosofia e discussione pubblica |
| Irish Phil J . . . . . . . . . . | Irish Philosophical Journal |
| Isegoria . . . . . . . . . . | Isegoria: Revista de Filosofía Moral y Política |
| ITA Humanidades* . . . . . . . . . . . . | ITA Humanidades: Revista do Departamento de Humanidades do Instituto Tecnologica de Aeronautica |
| Itinerari Filosof . . . . . . . . . . . . . | Itinerari Filosofici: Rivista di Filosofia |
| Iyyun . . . . . . . . . . | Iyyun: The Jerusalem Philosophical Quarterly |
| J Aes Art Crit . . . . . . . . . . . | The Journal of Aesthetics and Art Criticism |
| J Aes Educ . . . . . . . . . . | The Journal of Aesthetic Education |
| J Agr Ethics . . . . . . . . . . | Journal of Agricultural Ethics (see J Agr Environ Ethics) |
| J Agr Environ Ethics . . . . . . . . . . | Journal of Agricultural and Environmental Ethics (formerly Journal of Agricultural Ethics) |
| J Amer Orient Soc* . . . . . . . . . . | Journal of the American Oriental Society |
| J Applied Phil . . . . . . . . . . | Journal of Applied Philosophy |
| J Brit Soc Phenomenol. . . . . . . . | The Journal of the British Society for Phenomenology |
| J Bus Ethics . . . . . . . . . . | Journal of Business Ethics |
| J Chin Phil. . . . . . . . . . . | Journal of Chinese Philosophy |
| J Clin Ethics . . . . . . . . . . | The Journal of Clinical Ethics |
| J Crit Anal* . . . . . . . . . . | The Journal of Critical Analysis |
| J Comp Syst* . . . . . . . . . . | Journal of Computing Systems |
| J Consciousness Stud . . . . . . . . . . | Journal of Consciousness Studies |
| J Dharma . . . . . . . . . . | Journal of Dharma |
| J Existent* . . . . . . . . . . | Journal of Existentialism |
| J Gen Phil Sci. . . . . . . . . . | Journal for General Philosophy of Science (formerly Z Allg Wiss) |
| J Hellen Stud . . . . . . . . . . | The Journal of Hellenic Studies |
| J Hist Ideas . . . . . . . . . . | Journal of the History of Ideas |
| J Hist Phil . . . . . . . . . . | Journal of the History of Philosophy |
| J Indian Acad Phil* . . . . . . . . . . | Journal of the Indian Academy of Philosophy |
| J Indian Counc Phil Res . . . . . . . . . | Journal of Indian Council of Philosophical Research |
| J Indian Phil . . . . . . . . . . | Journal of Indian Philosophy |
| J Infor Ethics . . . . . . . . . . | Journal of Information Ethics |
| J Liber Stud . . . . . . . . . . | The Journal of Libertarian Studies |
| J Log Lang Info . . . . . . . . . . | Journal of Logic, Language and Information |
| J Med Ethics. . . . . . . . . . | Journal of Medical Ethics: The Journal of the Institute of Medical Ethics |
| J Med Human . . . . . . . . . . | The Journal of Medical Humanities (formerly The Journal of Medical Humanities and Bioethics) |
| J Med Human Bioethics. . . . . . . . . | The Journal of Medical Humanities and Bioethics (formerly Bioethics Quarterly) |
| J Med Phil. . . . . . . . . . | The Journal of Medicine and Philosophy |
| J Mind Behav . . . . . . . . . . | The Journal of Mind and Behavior |
| J Moral Educ . . . . . . . . . . | Journal of Moral Education |
| J Neoplatonic Stud. . . . . . . . . . | The Journal of Neoplatonic Studies |
| J Non-Classical Log. . . . . . . . . . | The Journal of Non-Classical Logic |
| J Phenomenological Psychology* . . | The Journal of Phenomenological Psychology |
| J Phil. . . . . . . . . . | The Journal of Philosophy |
| J Phil Ass* . . . . . . . . . . | Journal of the Philosophical Association |
| J Phil Educ . . . . . . . . . . | Journal of Philosophy of Education (formerly Proceedings of the Philosophy of Education Society of Great Britain) |
| J Phil Log . . . . . . . . . . | Journal of Philosophical Logic |
| J Phil Res . . . . . . . . . . | Journal of Philosophical Research (formerly Philosophy Research Archives) |
| J Phil Sport . . . . . . . . . . | Journal of the Philosophy of Sport |
| J Prag . . . . . . . . . . | Journal of Pragmatics |
| J Relig Ethics . . . . . . . . . . | The Journal of Religious Ethics |
| J Semantics . . . . . . . . . . | Journal of Semantics |
| J Soc Biol Struct. . . . . . . . . . | Journal of Social and Biological Structures |
| J Soc Phil . . . . . . . . . . | Journal of Social Philosophy |
| J Speculative Phil. . . . . . . . . . | The Journal of Speculative Philosophy |
| J Sym Log. . . . . . . . . . | The Journal of Symbolic Logic |
| J Theor Crit Vis Arts* . . . . . . . . . | The Journal of the Theory and Criticism of the Visual Arts |
| J Theor Phil Psych . . . . . . . . . . | Journal of Theoretical and Philosophical Psychology |
| J Theor Soc Behav. . . . . . . . . . | Journal for the Theory of Social Behaviour |
| J Thought . . . . . . . . . . | Journal of Thought |
| J Value Inq . . . . . . . . . . | The Journal of Value Inquiry |
| J W Vir Phil Soc*. . . . . . . . . . | Journal of the West Virginia Philosophical Society |
| Jahr Hegelforschung . . . . . . . . . . | Jahrbuch für Hegelforschung |
| Jahr Recht Ethik. . . . . . . . . . | Jahrbuch für Recht und Ethik |
| Jahr Soz Gesch* . . . . . . . . . . | Jahrbuch für Soziologiegeschichte |
| Kantstudien . . . . . . . . . . | Kant-Studien: Philosophische Zeitschrift der Kant-Gesellschaft |
| Kennedy Inst Ethics J . . . . . . . . . | Kennedy Institute of Ethics Journal |
| Kennis Methode. . . . . . . . . . | Kennis en Methode: Tijdschrift voor Wetenschapsfilosofie en Wetenschapsonderzoek |
| Kierkegaardiana* . . . . . . . . . . | Kierkegaardiana |

# Key to Abbreviations

# List of Periodicals Indexed

(frequency of publication given in parentheses)

**The Acorn: Journal of the Gandhi-King Society**. No ISSN. (bi-ann) Box CB, St.Bonaventure University, St.Bonaventure, NY 14778, USA

**Acta Analytica**. ISSN 0353-5150 (bi-ann) Verlag Dr. Josef H. Röll, Postfach 9, D-97335 Dettelbach, Germany

**Acta Philosophica: Ateneo Romano della Santa Croce**. ISSN 1121-2179. (3 times per yr) Armando Armando s.r.1., Viale Trastevere, 236, 00153 Rome, Italy

**Acta Philosophica Fennica**. ISSN 0355-1792. (irr) Academic Bookstore, Keskuskatu 1, 00100 Helsinki, Finland

**Aesthetics.** ISSN 0289-0895. (bi-enn) Japanese Society for Aesthetics, c/o Institute of Aesthetics, Faculty of Letters, University of Tokyo, Hongo 7-3-1, Bunkyo-ku, Tokyo 113, Japan

**Agora: Papeles de Filosofía**. ISSN 0211-6642. (bi-ann) Servicio de Publicaciones, Universidad de Santiago de Compostela, Santiago de Compostela 15701, Spain

**Agriculture and Human Values**. ISSN 0889-048X. (q) Managing Editor, 370 ASB, University of Florida, Gainesville, FL 32611, USA

**Aitia: Philosophy-Humanities Magazine**. ISSN 0731-5880. (3 times per yr) Knapp Hall 15, SUNY at Farmingdale, Farmingdale, NY 11735, USA

**Algemeen Nederlands Tijdschrift voor Wijsbegeerte**. ISSN 0002-5275. (q) Van Gorcum, Postbus 43, 9400 AA Assen, The Netherlands

**American Catholic Philosophical Quarterly.** ISSN 1051-3558. (q) American Catholic Philosophical Assoc., The Catholic University of America, Washington, DC 20064, USA

**American Journal of Philology**. ISSN 0002-9475. (q) The Johns Hopkins University Press, 701 West 40th Street, Suite 275, Baltimore, MD 21211, USA

**American Journal of Theology & Philosophy**. ISSN 0194-3448. (3 times per yr) W. Creighton Peden, Editor, Dept. of Philosophy, Augusta College, Augusta, GA 30910, USA

**American Philosophical Quarterly**. ISSN 0003-0481. (q) Philosophy Documentation Center, Bowling Green State University, Bowling Green, OH 43403-0189, USA

**Anales de la Cátedra Francisco Suárez**. ISSN 0008-7750. (ann) Departamento de Filosofía del Derecho, Moral y Política, Facultad de Derecho, Plaza de la Universidad, 3, 18071 Granada, Spain

**Anales del Seminario de Historia de la Filosofía**. ISSN 0211-2337. (ann) Editorial Complutense, C/ Donoso Cortés, 65, E-28015 Madrid, Spain

**Anales del Seminario de Metafísica**. ISSN 0580-8650. (ann) Editor, Universidad Complutense, Noviciado 3, 28015 Madrid, Spain

**Análisis Filosófico**. ISSN 0326-1301. (bi-ann) Bulnes 642, 1176 Buenos Aires, Argentina

**Analogía Filosófica: Revista de Filsofía**. ISSN 0188-896X (bi-ann) Dr. Gabriel Chico O.P., Apartado 23-161; Xochimilco, 16000 México D.F., Mexico

**Analysis**. ISSN 0003-2638. (q) Blackwell Publishers, 108 Cowley Road, Oxford OX4 1JF, United Kingdom (or 238 Main St., Cambridge, MA 02142, USA)

**Ancient Philosophy**. ISSN 0740-2007. (bi-ann) Prof. Ronald Polansky, Duquesne University, Pittsburgh, PA 15282, USA

**Annales Universitatis Mariae Curie-Sklodowskiej, Sectio 1/Philosophia-Sociologia**. ISSN 0137-2025. (ann) Biuro Wydawnictw, Uniwersytet Marii Curie-Sklodowskiej, Pl. Marii Curie-Sklodowskiej, 5, 20-031 Lublin, Poland

**Annali della Facoltà di Lettere e Filosofia**. No ISSN. Pubblicazioni dell'Università di Studi di Bari, Palazzo Ateneo, 70100 Bari, Italy

**Annals of Pure and Applied Logic**. ISSN 0168-0072. (18 times per yr) Elsevier Science Publishers, Box 211, 1000 AE Amsterdam, The Netherlands

**The Annual of the Society of Christian Ethics**. ISSN 0732-4928. (ann) Georgetown University Press, P.O. Box 4866, Hampden Station, Baltimore, MD 21211, USA

**Antioch Review**. ISSN 0003-5769. (q) P.O. Box 148, Yellow Springs, OH 45387, USA

**Anuario Filosófico**. ISSN 0066-5215. Servicio de Publicaciones de la Universidad de Navarra, S.A. Edificio Bibliotecas, Campus Universitario, 31080 Pamplona, Spain

**Apeiron: A Journal for Ancient Philosophy and Science**. ISSN 0003-6390. (q) Academic Printing and Publishing, P.O. Box 4834, Edmonton, Alberta T6E 5G7, Canada

**Aquinas: Rivista Internazionale di Filosofia**. ISSN 0003-7362. (3 times per yr) Pontificia Università Lateranense, Piazza S. Giovanni in Laterano 4, 00120 Città del Vaticano, Vatican City State

**Archiv für Geschichte der Philosophie**. ISSN 0003-9101. (3 times per yr) Walter de Gruyter, Genthiner Str. 13, D-10785 Berlin, Germany

**Archiv für Rechts- und Sozialphilosophie**. ISSN 0001-2343. (q) Franz Steiner Verlag Wiesbaden GmbH, Postfach 101526, D-70014 Stuttgart, Germany

**Archives de Philosophie**. ISSN 0003-9632. 72 rue des Saints-Pères, 75007 Paris, France

**Archivio di Storia della Cultura**. (ann) Morano Editore S.P.A., Vico S. Domenico Maggiore, 9-80134 Napoli, Italy

**Areté: Revista de Filosofía**. ISSN 1016-913X. (bi-ann) Pontificia Universidad Católica del Perú, Fondo Editorial, Apartado 1761, Lima-100, Peru

**Argumentation**. ISSN 0920-427X. (q) Kluwer Academic Publishers, P.O. Box 322, 3300 AH Dordrecht, The Netherlands (or P.O.Box 358, Accord Station, Hingham, MA 02018-0358, USA)

**Arion: A Journal of Humanities and the Classics**. ISSN 0095-5809. (3 times per yr) 745 Commonwealth Avenue, Nr.435, Boston, MA 02215, USA

**The Aristotelian Society: Supplementary Volume**. ISSN 0309-7013. (ann) Members: The Aristotelian Society, Dept. of Philosophy, Birkbeck College, Malet Street, London WC1E 7HX, United Kingdom. Non- members: Blackwell Publishers, 108 Cowley Road, Oxford OX4 1JF, United Kingdom (or 238 Main St., Cambridge, MA 02142, USA)

**The Asian Journal of Philosophy**. No ISSN. (bi-ann) Prof. Tran Van Doan, Dept. of Philosophy, National Taiwan University, Roosevelt Road, Sec. 4, 10764 Taipei, Taiwan

**Asian Philosophy**. ISSN 0955-2367 (bi-ann) Carfax Publishing Co., P.O. Box 25, Abingdon, Oxfordshire OX14 3UE, United Kingdom

**Augustinian Studies**. ISSN 0094-5323. (ann) Tolentine Hall, P.O. Box 98, Villanova University, Villanova, PA 19085, USA

**Augustinus**. ISSN 0004-802X. (q) P. José Oroz Reta, General Dávila 5, Madrid 28003, Spain

**Auslegung: A Journal of Philosophy**. ISSN 0733-4311. (bi-ann) Editors, Dept. of Philosophy, University of Kansas, Lawrence, KS 66045, USA

**Australasian Journal of Philosophy**. ISSN 0004-8402. (q) Robert Young, Editor, Department of Philosophy, La Trobe University, Bundoora, Victoria 3083, Australia

**Behavior and Philosophy**. No ISSN. (bi-ann) Boyd Printing, 49 Sheridan Avenue, Albany, NY 12210, USA

**Berkeley Newsletter**. ISSN 0332-026X. (ann) The Editor, Dept. of Philosophy, Trinity College, Dublin 2, Ireland

**Between the Species: A Journal of Ethics**. No ISSN. (q) Schweitzer Center, San Francisco Bay Institute, P.O. Box 254, Berkeley, CA 94701, USA

**Bigaku: The Japanese Journal of Aesthetics**. ISSN 0520-0962. (q) The Japanese Society for Aesthetics, c/o Faculty of Letters, University of Tokyo, Bunkyo-Ku, Tokyo, Japan

**Bijdragen, Tijdschrift voor Filosofie en Theologie**. ISSN 0006-2278. (q) Administratie Bijdragen, Krips Repro B.V., Postbus 106, 7940 AC Meppel, The Netherlands

**Bioethics**. ISSN 0269-9702. (q) Blackwell Publishers, 108 Cowley Road, Oxford OX4 1JF, United Kingdom (or 238 Main St., Cambridge, MA 02142, USA)

**Biology & Philosophy**. ISSN 0169-3867. (q) Kluwer Academic Publishers, P.O. Box 322, 3300 AH Dordrecht, The Netherlands (or P.O.Box 358, Accord Station, Hingham, MA 02018-0358, USA)

**Bollettino del Centro di Studi Vichiani**. ISSN 0392-7334. (ann) Bibliopolis, Edizioni di Filosofia e Scienze, SpA, Via Arangio Ruiz 83, 80122 Napoli, Italy

**Bridges: An Interdisciplinary Journal of Theology, Philosophy, History, and Science**. ISSN 1042-2234. (bi-ann) Robert S. Frey, Editor, 5702 Yellow Rose Court, Columbia, MD 21045, USA

**The British Journal of Aesthetics**. ISSN 0007-0904. (q) Oxford University Press, Pinkhill House, Southfield Road, Eynsham, Oxford OX8 1JJ, United Kingdom

**British Journal for the History of Philosophy**. ISSN 0960-8788. (bi-ann) Thoemmes Press, 11 Great George Street, Bristol, BS1 5RR, United Kingdom

**British Journal for the Philosophy of Science**. ISSN 0007-0882. (q) Oxford University Press, Pinkhill House, Southfield Road, Eynsham, Oxford OX8 1JJ, United Kingdom

**Bulletin de la Société Française de Philosophie**. ISSN 0037-9352. (q) 12 rue Colbert, 75002 Paris, France

**Bulletin of the Hegel Society of Great Britain**. ISSN 0263-5232. (bi-ann) H. Williams, Dept. of International Politics, University College of Wales, Penglais Aberystwyth, Dyfed SY23 3DB, United Kingdom

**Bulletin of the Section of Logic**. ISSN 0138-0680. (q) Managing Editor, Grzegorz Malinowski, 8 Marca 8, 90-365 Lodz', Poland

**Bulletin of the Santayana Society**. (ann) Santayana Edition, Dept. of Philosophy, Texas A & M University, College Station, TX 77843-4237, USA

**The Bulletin of Symbolic Logic**. ISSN 1079-8986. (q) Assoc. of Symbolic Logic, Journals Division UIP, 1325 South Oak St., Champaign, IL 61820, USA

**Business Ethics Quarterly**. ISSN 1052-150X. (q) Philosophy Documentation Center, Bowling Green State University, Bowling Green, OH 43403-0189, USA

**Business & Professional Ethics Journal**. ISSN 0277-2027. (q) Center for Applied Philosophy, 243 Dauer Hall, University of Florida, Gainesville, FL 32611, USA

**Cadernos de História e Filosofia da Ciéncia**. ISSN 0101-3424. (bi-ann) Editor, Centro de Lógica-Unicamp, C.P. 6133, 13.081 Campinas, São Paulo, Brazil

**Cambridge Quarterly of Healthcare Ethics**. ISSN 0963-1801. (q) Cambridge University Press, The Edinburgh Building, Shaftesbury Road, Cambridge CB2 2RU, United Kingdom (or 40 West 20th Street, New York, NY 10011-4211, USA)

**Canadian Journal of Philosophy**. ISSN 0045-5091. (q) University of Calgary Press, 2500 University Drive NW, Calgary, Alberta T2N 1N4, Canada

**Canadian Philosophical Reviews**. ISSN 0228-491X. (m) Academic Printing and Publishing, Box 4834, Edmonton, Alberta T6E 5G7, Canada

**Il Cannocchiale: Rivista di Studi Filosofici**. No ISSN. (3 times per yr) Il Cannocchiale. C.P. 12014, Roma 00100, Italy

**Chinese Studies in Philosophy**. ISSN 0023-8627. (q) M.E. Sharpe, 80 Business Park Drive, Armonk, NY 10504, USA

**Christian Bioethics**. ISSN 1380-3603. (3 times per yr) Swets and Zeitlinger, P.O.Box 825, 2160 SZ Lisse, The Netherlands

**Clio: A Journal of Literature, History, and the Philosophy of History**. ISSN 0884-2043. (q) Indiana University-Purdue University, Fort Wayne, IN 46805, USA

**Communication and Cognition: An Interdisciplinary Quarterly Journal**. ISSN 0378-0880. (q) Blandijnberg 2, B-9000 Ghent, Belgium

**Communication and Cognition—Artificial Intelligence (CC-AI): The Journal for the Integrated Study of Artificial Intelligence, Cognitive Science and Applied Epistemology**. ISSN 0773-4182. (q) Blandijnberg 2, B-9000 Ghent, Belgium

**Conceptus: Zeitschrift für Philosophie**. ISSN 0010-5155. (3 times per yr) Verband der wissenschaftlichen Gesellschaften Oesterreichs, Lindengasse 37, A-1070 Vienna, Austria

**Conference: A Journal of Philosophy and Theory**. ISSN 1072-1894 (bi-ann) Conference, c/o Dept. of Philosophy, 139 Collins Hall, Fordham University, Bronx, NY 10458, USA

**Constellations: An International Journal of Critical and Democratic Theory**. ISSN 0260-8448. (3 times per yr) Blackwell Publishers, 108 Cowley Road, Oxford OX4 1JF, United Kingdom (or 238 Main St., Cambridge, MA 02142, USA)

**Contemporary Philosophy**. No ISSN. (bi-m) P.O. Box 1373, Boulder, CO 80306, USA

**Convivium: Revista de Filosofia**. No ISSN. (3 times per yr) Redacció Administració, Dept. de Filosofia Teorètica i Pràctica, Facultat de Filosofia, Universitat de Barcelona, Carrer Baldiri Reixac, 1, 08028 Barcelona, Spain

**Criminal Justice Ethics**. ISSN 0731-129X. (bi-ann) The Institute for Criminal Justice Ethics, CUNY, John Jay College of Criminal Justice, 899 Tenth Avenue, New York, NY 10019, USA

**Crítica: Revista Hispanoamericana de Filosofía**. ISSN 0011-1503. (3 times per yr) Apartado 70-447, 04510 México, DF, Mexico

**Critical Inquiry**. ISSN 0093-1896. (q) The University of Chicago, Wieboldt Hall 202, 1050 East 59th Street, Chicago, IL 60637, USA

**Critical Review: An Interdisciplinary Journal**. ISSN 0891-3811. (q) P.O. Box 14528, Dept. 26A, Chicago, IL 60614, USA

**Cuadernos de Etica**. ISSN 0326-9523. (bi-ann) Asociación Argentina de Investigación Etica, Tte. Gral. J. D. Perón 2395-3° "G", 1040 Buenos Aires, Argentina

**Cuadernos de Filosofía**. ISSN 0590-1901. (bi-ann) Prof. Margarita Costa, Editor, Instituto de Filosofía, 25 de Mayo 217, 1002 Buenos Aires, Argentina

**Cuadernos Sobre Vico**. ISSN 1130-7498 (ann) Secretariado de Publicaciones de la Universidad de Sevilla, c/ Valparaíso, 5, E-41003 Sevilla, Spain

**Daimon, Revista de Filosofía**. ISSN 1130-0507. (bi-ann) Secretario de Daimon, Departamento de Filosofía y Lógica, Universidad de Murcia, E-30071 Espinardo-Murcia, Spain

**Danish Yearbook of Philosophy**. ISSN 0070-2749. (ann) Museum Tusculanum Press, Njalsgade 94, DK 2300 Copenhagen S, Denmark

**Darshana International**. No ISSN. Anurag Atreya, Managing Editor, Moradabad 244 001, India

**Das Argument: Zeitschrift für Philosophie und Sozialwissenschaften**. ISSN 0004-1157. (bi-m) Argument- Verlag, Rentzelstr. 1, D-20146 Hamburg, Germany

**De Philosophia**. ISSN 0228-412X. Editor, Dept. of Philosophy, University of Ottawa, Ottawa, Ontario K1N 6N5, Canada

**Deutsche Zeitschrift für Philosophie**. ISSN 0012-1045. (m) Akademie Verlag GmbH, Mühlenstr. 33-34, D-13187 Berlin, Germany

**Dialectica: International Journal of Philosophy of Knowledge**. ISSN 0012-2017. (q) P.O. Box 5907, CH-3001 Bern, Switzerland

**Diálogo Filosófico**. ISSN 0213-1196. (3 times per yr) Apartado 121, 28770 Colmenar Viejo, Madrid, Spain

**Diálogos: Revista del Departamento de Filsofía Universidad de Puerto Rico**. ISSN 0012-2122. (bi-ann) Box 21572, UPR Station, Río Piedras, PR 00931, USA

**Dialogue: Journal of Phi Sigma Tau**. ISSN 0012-2246. (bi-ann) Phi Sigma Tau, Dept. of Philosophy, Marquette University, Milwaukee, WI 53233, USA

**Dialogue: Canadian Philosophical Review**. ISSN 0012-2173. (q) Peter Loptson, Editor, Philosophy Dept., University of Saskatchewan, Saskatoon, Saskatchewan S7N 0W0, Canada

**Dialogue and Humanism: The Universalist Journal**. ISSN 0324-8275. (q) Institute of Philosophy, Warsaw University, Krakowskie Przedmiescie 3, 00-047 Warsaw, Poland

**Diánoia**. ISSN 0185-2450. (ann) Instituto de Investigaciones Filosóficas, Dirección del Anuario de Filosofía, Circuito Mtro. Mario de la Cueva, Ciudad de la Investigación en Humanidades, Coyoacán 04510, México, DF, Mexico

**Diogenes**. ISSN 0392-1921. (q) Berg Publishers Ltd., 150 Cowley Road, Oxford OX4 1JJ, United Kingdom

**Dionysius**. ISSN 0705-1085. (ann) Dept. of Classics, Dalhousie University, Halifax, Nova Scotia B3H 3J5, Canada

**Diotima: Review of Philosophical Research**. (ann) Hellenic Society for Philosophical Studies, 40 Hypsilantou Street, Athens 11521, Greece

**Discurso: Revista do Departamento de Filosofia**. ISSN 0103-328X. (ann) Departamento de Filosofia-FFLCH, Universidade de São Paulo, 05508 São Paulo, Brazil

**Economics and Philosophy**. ISSN 0266-2671. (bi-ann) Cambridge University Press, The Edinburgh Building, Shaftesbury Road, Cambridge CB2 2RU, United Kingdom (or 40 West 20th Street, New York, NY 10011-4211, USA)

**Educação e Filosofia**. ISSN 0102-6801. (bi-ann) Revista "Educação e Filosofia", Universidade Federal de Uberlândia, Av. Universitaria, 155 C.P. 593, Campus Santa Monica, 38.400 Uberlândia MG, Brazil

**Educational Philosophy and Theory**. ISSN 0013-1857. (bi-ann) D.N. Aspin, Editor, Faculty of Education, Monash University, Clayton, Victoria 3168, Australia

**Educational Studies**. ISSN 0013-1946. (q) Richard LaBrecque, Editor, 131 Taylor Education Building, University of Kentucky, Lexington, KY 40506-0001, USA

**Educational Theory**. ISSN 0013-2004. (q) Education Building, University of Illinois, 1310 South 6th Street, Champaign, IL 61820, USA

**Eidos: The Canadian Graduate Journal of Philosophy**. ISSN 0707-2287. (bi-ann) Editors, Dept. of Philosophy, University of Waterloo, Waterloo, Ontario N2L 3G1, Canada

**El Basilisco: Revista de Filosofía, Ciencias Humanas, Teoría de la Ciencia y de la Cultura**. ISSN 0210-0088. (q) Apartado 360, 33080 Oviedo, Spain

**Environmental Ethics: An Interdisciplinary Journal Dedicated to the Philosophical Aspects of Environmental Problems**. ISSN 0163-4275. (q) Dept. of Philosophy, The University of North Texas, P.O. Box 13496, Denton, TX 76203-3496, USA

**Environmental Values**. ISSN 0963-2719. (q) The White Horse Press, 10 High Street, Knapwell, Cambridge CB3 8NR, United Kingdom

**Epistemologia: Rivista italiana di Filosofia della Scienza**. (bi-ann) Tilgher-Genova s.a.s., via Assarotti 52, 16122 Genova, Italy

**Epoche**. No ISSN. (bi-ann) c/o Philosophy Dept., Jesse Knight Humanities Building, Brigham Young University, Provo, Utah 84602-6279, USA

**Erkenntnis: An International Journal of Analytic Philosophy**. ISSN 0165-0106. (6 times per yr) Kluwer Academic Publishers, P.O. Box 322, 3300 AH Dordrecht, The Netherlands (or P.O.Box 358, Accord Station, Hingham, MA 02018-0358, USA)

**Escritos de Filosofía**. ISSN 0325-4933. (ann) Centro de Estudios Filosoficos, Academia Nacional de Ciencias, Av. Alvear 1711, 3er. Piso, 1014 Buenos Aires, Argentina

**Espíritu**. ISSN 0014-0716. (ann) Durán y Bas Nr 9, Apartado 1382, 08080 Barcelona, Spain

**Estetika**. ISSN 0014-1291. (q) Helena Lorenzová, Editor, Institute of History & Theory of Art, Czech Academy of Sciences, Husova 4, 110 00 Praha 1, Czech Republic

**Ethics: An International Journal of Social, Political, and Legal Philosophy**. ISSN 0014-1704. (q) University of Chicago Press, P.O. Box 37005, Chicago, IL 60637, USA

**Ethics & International Affairs**. ISSN 0892-6794. Carnegie Council on Ethics and International Affairs, 170 East 64th Street, New York, NY 10021-7478, USA

**Ethics and Behavior**. ISSN 1050-8422. (q) Journal Subscription Dept., LEA, 365 Broadway, Hillsdale, NJ 07642, USA

**Ethics and Medicine: An International Christian Perspective on Bioethics**. ISSN 0226-688X. (3 times per yr) Paternoster Periodicals, P.O. Box 11127, Birmingham, AL 35202, USA

**Etica & Animali**. Corso Magenta 62, 20123 Milano, Italy

**Etyka**. ISSN 0014-2263. (bi-ann) Instytut Filozofii i Socjologii PAN, Nowy Swiat 72, pok 243, 00-330, Warsaw, Poland

**Eurídice**. ISSN1131-6640. (ann) Secretario-Eurídice, Servicio de Publicaciones, UNED-Navarre, Apdo.409, E-31080 Pamplona (Navarre), Spain

**European Journal of Philosophy**. ISSN 0966-8373. (3 times per yr) Blackwell Publishers, 108 Cowley Road, Oxford OX4 1JF, United Kingdom (or 238 Main St., Cambridge, MA 02142, USA)

**Explorations in Knowledge**. ISSN 0261-1376. (bi-ann) David Lamb, Sombourne Press, 294 Leigh Road, Chandlers Ford, Eastleigh, Hants S05 3AU, United Kingdom

**Facta Universitatis**. ISSN 0354-4648. (ann) Facta Universitatis, University of Niš, TRG Bratsva i Jedinstva 2, 18000 Niš, Yugoslavia

**Faith and Philosophy: Journal of the Society of Christian Philosophers**. ISSN 0739-7046. (q) Michael Peterson, Managing Editor, Asbury College, Wilmore, KY 40390, USA

**Feminist Studies**. ISSN 0046-3663. (3 times per yr) Claire G. Moses, Women's Studies Program, University of Maryland, College Park, MD 20742, USA

**Fichte-Studien**. ISSN 0925-0166. (ann) Mr. Eric Van Broekhuizen, Editions Rodopi B. V., Keizersgracht 302-304, 1016 EX Amsterdam-Holland, The Netherlands

**Filosofia**. ISSN 0015-1823. (q) Piazza Statuto 26, 10144 Turin, Italy

**Filozofia**. ISSN 0046-385X. (bi-m) Frantisek Novosád, Editor, Klemensova 19, 813 64 Bratislava, Slovakia

**Filozoficky Casopis**. ISSN 0015-1831. (bi-m) Petr Horák, Editor, Institute of Philosophy & Sociology, Czech Academy of Sciences, Jilská 1, 110 00 Praha 1, Czech Republic

**Filozofska Istrazivanja**. ISSN 0351-4706. Editor, Filozofski Fakultet, D. Salaja 3, p.p. 171, 41000 Zagreb, Croatia

**Filozofski Vestnik**. ISSN 0353-4510. (bi-ann) Filozofski Vestnik, ZRC SAZU, Gosposka ul. 13, SL-61000 Ljubljana, Slovenia

**Franciscan Studies**. ISSN 0080-5459. (ann) St. Bonaventure University, St. Bonaventure, NY 14778, USA

**Franciscanum: Revista de las Ciencias del Espiritu**. ISSN 0120-1468. (3 times per yr) Universidad de San Buenaventura, Calle 73 No. 10-45, Apartado Aéreo No. 52312, Bogotà, Colombia

**Free Inquiry**. ISSN 0272-0701. (q) Paul Kurtz, Editor, Box 5, Central Park Station, Buffalo, NY 14215, USA

**Freiburger Zeitschrift für Philosophie und Theologie**. ISSN 0016-0725. (bi-ann) Editions St.-Paul, Perolles 42, CH-1700 Fribourg, Switzerland

**Fronesis: Revista de Filosofía Jurídica, Social y Política**. ISSN 1315-6268. Instituto de Filosofía del Recho "Dr. J. M. Delgado Ocando", Av. Guajira, Ciudad Universitaria "Dr. Antonio Borjas Romero", Facultad de Ciencias Jurídicas y Políticas, Universidad del Zulia, Maricaibo 4011, Venezuela

**Giornale Critico della Filosofia Italiana**. ISSN 0017-0089. (q) LICOSA, SpA, Subscription Dept., Via B. Fortini 120/10, 50125 Florence, Italy

**Giornale di Metafisica**. (3 times per yr) Tilgher-Genova s.a.s., via Assarotti 52, 16122 Genova, Italy

**Gnosis: A Journal of Philosophic Interest**. ISSN 0316-618X. (ann) Editor, Dept. of Philosophy, Concordia University, 1455 de Maisonneuve Boulevard West, Montreal, Québec H3G 1M8, Canada

**Graduate Faculty Philosophy Journal**. ISSN 0093-4240. (bi-ann) Editor, Dept. of Philosophy, New School for Social Research, 65 Fifth Avenue, New York, NY 10003, USA

**Grazer Philosophische Studien**. ISSN 0165-9227. (ann) Humanities Press International, Atlantic Highlands, NJ 07716, USA

**Gregorianum**. ISSN 0017-4114. (q) 4 Piazza della Pilotta, 1-00187 Rome, Italy

**The Harvard Review of Philosophy**. ISSN 1062-6239. (ann) Dept. of Philosophy, Harvard University, Emerson Hall, Cambridge, MA 02138, USA

**Hastings Center Report**. ISSN 0093-0334. (bi-m) The Hastings Center, Garrison, NY 10524-5555, USA

**Heidegger Studies**. ISSN 0885-4580 (ann) Duncker & Humblot GmbH, Postfach 41 03 29, D-12113 Berlin, Germany

**Hermathena: A Dublin University Review**. ISSN 0018-0750. (bi-ann) The Editor, Trinity College, Dublin 2, Ireland

**The Heythrop Journal: A Quarterly Review of Philosophy and Theology**. ISSN 0018-1196. (q) The Manager, 11 Cavendish Square, London W1M 0AN, United Kingdom

**History and Philosophy of Logic**. ISSN 0144-5340. (bi-ann) Taylor & Francis, 4 John Street, London WC1N 2ET, United Kingdom

**History and Philosophy of the Life Sciences**. ISSN 0391-9114. (bi-ann) Taylor & Francis, 1900 Frost Road, Suite 101, Bristol, PA 19007, USA (or Rankine Road, Basingstoke, Hants RG24 0PR, United Kingdom)

**History and Theory: Studies in the Philosophy of History**. ISSN 0018-2656. (q) Julia Perkins, History and Theory, Wesleyan Station, Middletown, CT 06457, USA

**History of European Ideas**. ISSN 0191-6599. (bi-m) Pergamon Press, Headington Hill Hall, Oxford OX3 0BW, United Kingdom

**History of Philosophy Quarterly**. ISSN 0740-0675. (q) Philosophy Documentation Center, Bowling Green State University, Bowling Green, OH 43403-0189, USA

**History of Political Thought**. ISSN 0143-781X. (q) Imprint Academic, 32 Haldon Road, Exeter EX4 4DZ, United Kingdom

**History of the Human Sciences**. ISSN 0952-6951. (q) Sage Publications, LTD, 6 Bonhill Street, London, EC2A 4PU, United Kingdom

**Hobbes Studies**. (ann) Van Gorcum, P.O. Box 43, 9400 AA Assen, The Netherlands

**Horizons Philosophiques**. ISSN 0709-4469. (bi-ann) Service de l'Edition, College Edouard-Montpetit, 945 chemin Chambly, Longueuil, Québec J4H 3M6, Canada

**Human Studies: A Journal for Philosophy and the Social Sciences**. ISSN 0163-8548. (q) Martinus Nijhoff Publishers, P.O. Box 322, 3300 AH Dordrecht, The Netherlands

**The Humanist: A Magazine of Critical Inquiry and Social Concern**. ISSN 0018-7399. (bi-m) Frederick Edwords, American Humanist Assoc., 7 Harwood Drive, P.O. Box 1188, Amherst, NY 14226-7188, USA

**Hume Studies**. ISSN 0319-7336. (bi-ann) Editor, Dept. of Philosophy, University of Western Ontario, London, Ontario N6A 3K7, Canada

**Husserl Studies**. ISSN 0167-9848. (q) Kluwer Academic Publishers, P.O. Box 322, 3300 AH Dordrecht, The Netherlands (or P.O.Box 358, Accord Station, Hingham, MA 02018-0358, USA)

**Hypatia: A Journal of Feminist Philosophy**. ISSN 0887-5367. (3 times per yr) Linda Lopez McAlister, Editor, University of South Florida, SOC 107, Tampa, FL 33620-8100, USA

**Idealistic Studies: An Interdisciplinary Journal of Philosophy**. ISSN 0046-8541. (3 times per yr) Walter Wright, Editor, Dept. of Philosophy, Clark University, Worcester, MA 01610, USA

**Ideas y Valores: Revista Colombiana de Filosofía**. ISSN 0120-0062. (3 times per yr) Departamento de Filosofía, Universidad Nacional de Colombia, Ciudad Universitaria, Bogotà, Colombia

**Il Protagora**. (bi-ann) via A. Gidiuli 19, 73100 Lecce, Italy

**The Independent Journal of Philosophy**. ISSN 0378-4789. (irr) George Elliott Tucker, Editor, 47 Van Winkle Street, Boston, MA 02124, USA

**Indian Philosophical Quarterly**. ISSN 0376-415X. (q) The Editor, Dept. of Philosophy, University of Poona, Pune 411 007, India

**Informal Logic**. ISSN 0824-2577. (3 times per yr) Assistant to the Editors, Dept. of Philosophy, University of Windsor, Windsor, Ontario N9B 3P4, Canada

**Inquiry: An Interdisciplinary Journal of Philosophy**. ISSN 0020-174X. (q) Universitetsforlaget, P.O. Box 2959, Tøyen, 0608 Oslo 6, Norway

**Inquiry: Critical Thinking Across the Disciplines**. No ISSN. (q) Institute for Critical Thinking, Montclair State University, Upper Montclair, NJ 07043, USA

**International Journal for Philosophy of Religion**. ISSN 0020-7047. (q) Kluwer Academic Publishers, P.O. Box 322, 3300 AH Dordrecht, The Netherlands (or P.O.Box 358, Accord Station, Hingham, MA 02018-0358, USA)

**International Journal of Applied Philosophy**. ISSN 0739-098X. (bi-ann) Indian River Community College, Fort Pierce, FL 34981-5599, USA

**International Journal of Moral and Social Studies**. ISSN 0267-9655. (3 times per yr) Journals, One Harewood Row, London NW1 6SE, United Kingdom

**International Journal of Philosophical Studies**. ISSN 0967-2559. (bi-ann) Professor Dermot Moran, Editor, Dept. of Philosophy, University College Dublin, Dublin 4, Ireland

**International Logic Review**. (bi-ann) Editor, via Belmeloro 3, 40126 Bologna, Italy

**International Philosophical Quarterly**. ISSN 0019-0365. (q) Vincent Potter, S.J., Fordham University, Bronx, NY 10458, USA

**International Studies in Philosophy**. ISSN 0270-5664. (3 times per yr) Scholars Press, P.O. Box 15288, Atlanta, GA 30333, USA

**International Studies in the Philosophy of Science**. ISSN 0269-8595. (3 times per yr) Carfax Publishing Co., P.O. Box 25, Abingdon, Oxfordshire OX14 3UE, United Kingdom

**Interpretation: A Journal of Political Philosophy**. ISSN 0020-9635. (3 times per yr) Hilail Gildin, Editor-in-Chief, King Hall 101, Queens College, Flushing, NY 11367-0904, USA

**Iride: Filosofia E Discussione Pubblica**. Strada Maggiore, 37, 40125 Bologna, Italy

**Irish Philosophical Journal**. ISSN 0266-9080. (bi-ann) Dr. Bernard Cullen, Editor, Dept. of Scholastic Philosophy, Queen's University, Belfast BT7 1NN, Northern Ireland, United Kingdom

**Isegoria: Revista de Filosofía Moral y Politíca**. ISSN 1130-2097. (q) Editorial Anthropos, Apartado 387, 08190 Sant Cugat del Valles, Spain

**Itinerari Filosofici: Rivista di Filosofia**. ISSN 1121-2772 (3 times per yr) Redazione di Itinerari Filosofici, Via Carlo Crivelli, 20, 20122-Milano, Italy

**Iyyun: The Jerusalem Philosophical Quarterly**. ISSN 0021-3306. (q) Manager, S.H. Bergman Centre for Philosophical Studies, Hebrew University of Jerusalem, Jerusalem 91905, Israel

**Jahrbuch fur Hegelforschung**. ISBN 3-88345-718-3. Academia Verlag, Postfach 16 63, D-53734 Sankt Augustin, Germany

**Jahrbuch fur Recht und Ethik**. ISSN 0944-4610. Institut fur Strafrecht und Rechtsphilosophie, Schillerstr. 1, D-91054 Berlin, Germany

**Journal for General Philosophy of Science**. ISSN 0925-4560. (bi-ann) Kluwer Academic Publishers, P.O. Box 322, 3300 AH Dordrecht, The Netherlands (or P.O.Box 358, Accord Station, Hingham, MA 02018-0358, USA)

**Journal for the Theory of Social Behavior**. ISSN 0021-8308. (q) Blackwell Publishers, 108 Cowley Road, Oxford OX4 1JF, United Kingdom (or 238 Main St., Cambridge, MA 02142, USA)

**The Journal of Aesthetic Education**. ISSN 0021-8510. (q) University of Illinois Press, 54 East Gregory Drive, Champaign, IL 61820, USA

**The Journal of Aesthetics and Art Criticism**. ISSN 0021-8529. (q) Philip A. Alperson, Editor, University of Louisville, Louisville, KY 40292, USA

**Journal of Agricultural and Environmental Ethics**. ISSN 0893-4282. (bi-ann) Room 039, MacKinnon Building, University of Guelph, Guelph, Ontario N1G 2W1, Canada

**Journal of Applied Philosophy**. ISSN 0264-3758. (bi-ann) Carfax Publishing Co., P.O. Box 25, Abingdon, Oxfordshire OX14 3UE, United Kingdom

**Journal of Business Ethics**. ISSN 0167-4544. Kluwer Academic Publishers, P.O. Box 322, 3300 AH Dordrecht, The Netherlands (or P.O.Box 358, Accord Station, Hingham, MA 02018-0358, USA)

**Journal of Chinese Philosophy**. ISSN 0301-8121. (q) Dialogue Publishing Co., P.O. Box 11071, Honolulu, HI 96828, USA

**The Journal of Clinical Ethics**. ISSN 1406-7690. (q) 107 East Church Street, Frederick, MD 21701, USA

**Journal of Consciousness Studies**. ISSN 1355-8250. (bi-m) Imprint Academic c/o Virginia Commonwealth University, PO Box 842025, Richmond, VA 23284-2025, USA

**Journal of Dharma**. ISSN 0253-7222. (q) Center for the Study of World Religions, Dharmaram College, Bangalore 560029, India

**The Journal of Hellenic Studies**. ISSN 0075-4269. (ann) Secretary, The Hellenic Society, 31-34 Gordon Square, London WC1H 0PP, United Kingdom

**Journal of Indian Council of Philosophical Research**. ISSN 0970-7794. (3 times per yr) Indian Council of Philosophical Research, Rajendra Bhavan (4th floor), 210 Deen Dayal Upadhyaya Marg, New Delhi 110002, India

**Journal of Indian Philosophy**. ISSN 0022-1791. Kluwer Academic Publishers, P.O. Box 322, 3300 AH Dordrecht, The Netherlands (or P.O.Box 358, Accord Station, Hingham, MA 02018-0358, USA)

**Journal of Information Ethics**. ISSN 1061-9321. (bi-ann) McFarland and Co., Inc., Publishers, Box 611, Jefferson, NC 28640, USA

**The Journal of Libertarian Studies**. ISSN 0363-2873. (q) Center for Libertarian Studies, P.O. Box 4091, Burlingame, CA 94011, USA

**Journal of Logic, Language and Information**. ISSN 0925-8531. (4 times per yr), P.O. Box 230, Accord, MA 02018-0230, USA

**Journal of Medical Ethics: The Journal of the Institute of Medical Ethics**. ISSN 0306-6800. (q) Subscription Manager, Professional and Scientific Publications (JME), Tavistock House East, Tavistock Square, London WC1H 9JR, United Kingdom (or Professional and Scientific Publications, 1172 Commonwealth Avenue, Boston, MA 02134, USA)

**The Journal of Medical Humanities**. ISSN 1041-3545. (q) Human Sciences Press, 233 Spring Street, New York, NY 10013, USA

**The Journal of Medicine and Philosophy**. ISSN 0360-5310. (6 times per yr) Kluwer Academic Publishers, P.O. Box 322, 3300 AH Dordrecht, The Netherlands (or P.O.Box 358, Accord Station, Hingham, MA 02018-0358, USA)

**The Journal of Mind and Behavior**. ISSN 0271-0137. (q) Circulation Dept., P.O. Box 522, Village Station, New York, NY 10014, USA

**Journal of Moral Education**. ISSN 0305-7240. (3 times per yr) Carfax Publishing Co., P.O. Box 25, Abingdon, Oxfordshire OX14 3UE, United Kingdom

**The Journal of Neoplatonic Studies**. ISSN 1065-5840. (semi-ann) Dr. James Martin, Editor, Department of Philosophy, St. John's University, Jamaica, NY 11439, USA

**The Journal of Non-Classical Logic**. (bi-ann) Centro de Lógica-Unicamp, C.P. 6133, 13.081 Campinas, São Paulo, Brazil

**Journal of Philosophical Logic**. ISSN 0022-3611. Kluwer Academic Publishers, P.O. Box 322, 3300 AH Dordrecht, The Netherlands (or P.O.Box 358, Accord Station, Hingham, MA 02018-0358, USA)

**Journal of Philosophical Research**. ISSN 1053-8364. (ann) Philosophy Documentation Center, Bowling Green State University, Bowling Green, OH 43403-0189, USA

**The Journal of Philosophy**. ISSN 0022-362X. (m) 709 Philosophy Hall, Columbia University, New York, NY 10027, USA

**Journal of Philosophy of Education**. ISSN 0309-8249. (semi-ann) Carfax Publishing Co., P.O. Box 25, Abingdon, Oxford-shire OX14 3UE, United Kingdom

**Journal of Pragmatics**. ISSN 0378-2166. (bi-m) Elsevier Science Publishers, P.O. Box 211, 1000 AE Amsterdam, The Netherlands

**The Journal of Religious Ethics**. ISSN 0384-9694. (bi-ann) Scholars Press, P.O. Box 15288, Atlanta, GA 30333, USA

**Journal of Semantics**. ISSN 0167-5133. (q) Oxford University Press, Pinkhill House, Southfield Road, Eynsham, Oxford OX8 1JJ, United Kingdom

**Journal of Social and Biological Structures** . ISSN 1040-1750. (q) JAI Press, Inc., 55 Old Post Road-No. 2, Greenwich, CT 06836, USA (For the United Kingdom, Europe, Africa, and Asia: 118 Pentonville, Road, London N1 9JN, United Kingdom)

**Journal of Social Philosophy**. ISSN 0047-2786. (3 times per yr) Dr. Peter French, Editor, Trinity University, San Antonio, TX 78212, USA

**The Journal of Speculative Philosophy**. ISSN 0891-625X. (q) Pennsylvania State University Press, Suite C, 820 North University Drive, University Park, PA 16802, USA

**The Journal of Symbolic Logic**. ISSN 0022-4812. Association for Symbolic Logic, Dept. of Mathematics, University of Illinois, 1409 West Green Street, Urbana, IL 61801, USA

**The Journal of the British Society for Phenomenology**. ISSN 007-1773. (3 times per yr) Haigh & Hochland, JBSP Department, Precinct Centre, Manchester M13 9QA, United Kingdom

**Journal of the History of Ideas**. ISSN 0022-5037. (q) Donald R. Kelley, Executive Editor, 442 Rush Rhees Library, University of Rochester, Rochester, NY 14627, USA

**Journal of the History of Philosophy**. ISSN 0022-5053. (q) Business Office, Dept. of Philosophy, Washington University, St. Louis, MO 63130, USA

**Journal of the Philosophy of Sport**. ISSN 0094-8705. (ann) Human Kinetics Publishers, Box 5076, Champaign, IL 61820-9971, USA

**Journal of Theoretical and Philosophical Psychology**. ISSN 1068-8471. (bi-ann) Divisions Service Office, American Psychological Assoc., 750 First Street, NE, Washington, DC 20002-4242, USA

**Journal of Thought**. ISSN 0022-5231. (q) Dr. Robert M. Lang, Editor, College of Education, Leadership, and Educational Policy Studies, Northern Illinois University, Dekalb, IL 60115, USA

**The Journal of Value Inquiry**. ISSN 0022-5363. (q) Kluwer Academic Publishers, P.O. Box 322, 3300 AH Dordrecht, The Netherlands (or P.O.Box 358, Accord Station, Hingham, MA 02018-0358, USA)

**Kant-Studien: Philosophische Zeitschrift der Kant-Gesellschaft**. ISSN 0022-8877. (q) Walter de Gruyter, Genthiner Str. 13, D-10785 Berlin, Germany

**Kennedy Institute of Ethics Journal**. ISSN 1054-6863. (q) The Johns Hopkins University Press, Journals Publishing Division, 701 West 40th Street, Suite 275, Baltimore, MD 21211-2190, USA

**Kennis en Methode: Tijdschrift voor Wetenschapsfilosofie en Wetenschapsonderzoek**. ISSN 0165-1773. (q) Boompers, Postbus 400, 7940 AK Meppel, The Netherlands

**Kinesis: Graduate Journal in Philosophy**. ISSN 0023-1568. (bi-ann) Dept. of Philosophy, Southern Illinois University, Carbondale, IL 62901, USA

**Kriterion: Revista de Filosofia**. (bi-ann) Faculdade de Filosofia e Ciências Humanas, da UFMG, Av Antonio Carlos, C.P. 6627, Belo Horizonte, MG, Brazil

**Kriterion: Zeitschrift für Philosophie**. ISSN 1019-8288 (bi-ann) Institut für Philosophie, Franziskanergasse 1, A-5020 Salzburg, Austria

**Kwartalnik Filozoficzny**. ISSN 1230-4050 (q) Polska Akademia Umiejtnoci, Sawkowska 17, 31-016 Kraków, Poland

**Laval Théologique et Philosophique**. ISSN 0023-9054. (3 times per yr) Service de Revues, Les Presses de l'Université Laval, C.P. 2447, Québec G1K 7R4, Canada

**Law and Philosophy: An International Journal for Jurisprudence and Legal Philosophy**. ISSN 0167-5249. (q) Kluwer Academic Publishers, P.O. Box 322, 3300 AH Dordrecht, The Netherlands (or P.O.Box 358, Accord Station, Hingham, MA 02018-0358, USA)

**Legal Theory**. ISSN 1352-3252. (q) Cambridge University Press, The Edinburgh Building, Shaftesbury Road, Cambridge CB2 2RU, United Kingdom (or 40 West 20th Street, New York, NY 10011-4211, USA)

**Leibniz Society Review**. ISSN 1069-5192. Dr. Glenn A. Hartz, Editor, Dept. of Philosophy, 1680 University Drive, Ohio State University, Mansfield, OH 44906-1599, USA

**Lekton.** ISSN 1180-2308. (q) Presses de l'Université du Québec, C.P. 250 Sillery, Québec G1T 2R1, Canada

**Linguistics and Philosophy: A Journal of Natural Language Syntax, Semantics, Logic, Pragmatics, and Processing**. ISSN 0165-0157. (6 times per yr) Kluwer Academic Publishers, P.O. Box 322, 3300 AH Dordrecht, The Netherlands (or P.O.Box 358, Accord Station, Hingham, MA 02018-0358, USA)

**Listening: Journal of Religion and Culture**. ISSN 0024-4414. (3 times per yr) P.O. Box 1108, Route 53, Romeoville, IL 60441-2298, USA

**Literature and Aesthetics: The Journal of the Sydney Society of Literature and Aesthetics**. ISSN 1036-9368. (ann) Dr. C. A. Runcie, Editor, Dept. of English, A20, University of Sydney, Sydney 2006, Australia

**The Locke Newsletter: An Annual Journal of Locke Research**. ISSN 0307-2606 (ann) Roland Hall, Editor, Summerfields, The Glade, Escrick, York YO4 6JH United Kingdom

**Logique et Analyse**. ISSN 0024-5836. (q) Professor Jean Paul Van Bendegem, Editor, U. G. Rozier 44, B-9000 Gent, Belgium

**Logos: Revista de Filosofía**. ISSN 0185-6375. (3 times per yr) Apartado Postal 18-907, Colonia Tacubaya, Delegación Miguel Hidalgo, C.P. 11800, México, DF, Mexico

**Lua: The Journal of Philosophy and Sociology**. ISSN 0352-4973. (bi-ann) Prof. Bogoljub Šijakovi, Filosofski fakultet, YU-81400 Nikši, Yugoslavia

**Lyceum.** (bi-ann) Saint Anselm College, Box 1698, 87 Saint Anselm Drive, Manchester, NH 03102-1310, USA

**Magyar Filozófiai Szemle**. ISSN 0025-0090. (bi-m) Kultura, P.O. Box 149, H-1389 Budapest 62, Hungary

**Man and Nature/L'homme et la Nature: Yearbook of the Canadian Society for Eighteenth-Century Studies**. (ann) Academic Printing and Publishing, P.O. Box 4834, South Edmonton, Alberta T6E 5G7, Canada

**Man and World: An International Philosophical Review**. ISSN 0025-1534. (q) Robert C. Scharff, Editor, Dept. of Philosophy, Univ. of New Hampshire, Durham, NH 03824-3574, USA

**Manuscrito: Revista Internacional de Filosofia**. ISSN 0100-6045. (bi-ann) Circulation Dept., Centro de Lógica, Unicamp C.P. 6133, 13.081 Campinas, São Paulo, Brazil

**Maritain Studies-Études Maritainiennes**. ISSN 0826-9920 (ann) Canadian Jacques Maritain Assoc., c/o Dept. of Philosophy, 65 University Dr., University of Ottawa, ON K1N 6N5, Canada

**Mathesis**. ISSN 0185-6200 (q) Departamento de Matemáticas, Facultad de Ciencias, Universidad Nacional Autónoma de México, Ciudad Universitaria, 04510 México, D.F., México

**Mediaeval Studies**. ISSN 0076-5872. (ann) Dr. Ron B. Thomson, Director of Publications, Pontifical Institute of Mediaeval Studies, 59 Queen's Park Crescent East, Toronto, Ontario M5S 2C4, Canada

**Medical Humanities Review**. ISSN 0892-2772. (bi-ann) Institute for the Medical Humanities, University of Texas Medical Branch, Galveston, TX 77550, USA

**Metaphilosophy**. ISSN 0026-1068. Blackwell Publishers, 108 Cowley Road, Oxford OX4 1JF, United Kingdom (or 238 Main St., Cambridge, MA 02142, USA)

**Method: Journal of Lonergan Studies**. ISSN 0736-7392. (bi-ann) The Lonergan Institute, Boston College, Chestnut Hill, MA 02167, USA

**Methodology and Science: International Journal for the Empirical Study of the Foundations of Science and their Methodology**. ISSN 0543-6095. (q) Dr. P.H. Esser, Secretary and Editor, Beelslaan 20, 2012 PK Haarlem, The Netherlands

**Midwest Studies in Philosophy**. No ISSN. (ann/mono) Dr. Peter A. French, Editor, Dept. of Philosophy, Trinity University, San Antonio, TX 78212 USA

**Mind: A Quarterly Review of Philosophy**. ISSN 0026-4423. (q) Oxford University Press, Pinkhill House, Southfield Road, Eynsham, Oxford OX8 1JJ, United Kingdom

**Mind & Language**. ISSN 0268-1064. (q) Blackwell Publishers, 108 Cowley Road, Oxford OX4 1JF, United Kingdom (or 238 Main St., Cambridge, MA 02142, USA)

**Minds and Machines: Journal for Artificial Intelligence, Philosophy, and Cognitive Science**. ISSN 0924-6495. (q) Kluwer Academic Publishers, P.O. Box 322, 3300 AH Dordrecht, The Netherlands (or P.O.Box 358, Accord Station, Hingham, MA 02018-0358, USA)

**The Modern Schoolman: A Quarterly Journal of Philosophy**. ISSN 0026-8402. (q) William C. Charron, Editor, Dept. of Philosophy, St. Louis University, St. Louis, MO 63103, USA

**Modern Theology**. ISSN 0266-7177. (q) Blackwell Publishers, 108 Cowley Road, Oxford OX4 1JF, United Kingdom (or 238 Main St., Cambridge, MA 02142, USA)

**The Monist: An International Quarterly Journal of General Philosophic Inquiry**. ISSN 0026-9662. (q) The Hegler Institute, P.O. Box 600, La Salle, IL 61301, USA

**NAO Revista de la Cultura del Mediterráneo**. (3 times per yr) Mansilla 3344, 1⊃ C, 1425 Capital Federal, Argentina

**National Forum: Phi Kappa Phi Journal**. ISSN 0162-1831. (q) Subscription Dept., 129 Quad Center, Auburn University, Auburn University, AL 36849, USA

**Nature, Society, and Thought**. ISSN 0890-6130. (q) University of Minnesota, 116 Church Street, S.E., Minneapolis, MN 55455, USA

**Neue Hefte für Philosophie**. ISSN H085-3917. (irr/ann) Vandenhoeck & Ruprecht, Postfach 3753, D-37027 Göttingen, Germany

**New Vico Studies**. ISSN 0733-9542. (ann) Institute for Vico Studies, 69 Fifth Avenue, New York, NY 10003, USA (or Humanities Press International, 171 First Avenue, Atlantic Highlands, NJ 07716, USA)

**Nietzsche-Studien: Internationales Jahrbuch für die Nietzsche-Forschung**.(ann) Walter de Gruyter, Genthiner Str. 13, D-10785 Berlin, Germany

**Nomos: Yearbook of the American Society for Political and Legal Philosophy**. No ISSN. (ann) Order Dept., New York University Press, 70 Washington Square South, New York, NY 10012, USA

**Notre Dame Journal of Formal Logic**. ISSN 0029-4527. (q) Business Manager, University of Notre Dame, Box 5, Notre Dame, IN 46556, USA

**Notre Dame Journal of Law, Ethics & Public Policy**. (bi-ann) Zigad I. Naccasha, Managing Editor, University of Notre Dame, Notre Dame, IN 46556, USA

**Noûs**. ISSN 0029-4624. (q) Dept. of Philosophy, 126 Sycamore Hall, Indiana University, Bloomington, IN 47405, USA

**Nouvelles de la République des Lettres**. ISSN 0392-2332. (bi-ann) C.C. 1794767/01, Banca Commerciale Italiana, AG3 Naples, Italy

**The Owl of Minerva**. ISSN 0030-7580. (bi-ann) Dept. of Philosophy, Villanova University, Villanova, PA 19085, USA

**Pacific Philosophical Quarterly**. ISSN 0279-0750. (q) Expediters of the Printed Word, 5155 Madison Avenue, New York, NY 10022, USA

**Patristica et Mediaevalia**. ISSN 0235-2280. (ann) Editor, Miembros del Centro de Estudios de Filosofía Medieval, 25 de Mayo 217, 2° Piso, 1002 Buenos Aires, Argentina

**Pensamiento: Revista de Investigación e Información Filosófica**. ISSN 0031-4749. (q) Administración, Pablo Aranda 3, 28006 Madrid, Spain

**Per la Filosofia**. ISSN 0394-4131. (3 times per yr) Editrice Massimo, Viale Bacchiglione, 20A, 20139 Milano, Italy

**The Personalist Forum**. ISSN 0889-065X. Editor, Dept. of Philosophy, Furman University, Greenville, SC 29613, USA

**Philo-Logica: Rassegna di analisi linguistica ed ironia culturale**. No ISSN. (bi-ann) Edizioni Zara, Via Portilia, 6, 43100 Parma, Italy

**Philosopher: Revue de l'enseignment de la philosophie au Québec**. ISSN 0827-1887. (ann) Pierre Cohen-Bacrie, Directeur, Département de Philosophie, Collège Montmorency, 475, Boulevard de l'Avenir, Laval, Québec H7N 5H9, Canada

**Philosophia**. ISSN 0031-8000. (ann) Editorial Office-Distribution, Research Center for Greek Philosophy, Academy of Athens, 14 Anagnostopoulou Street, Athens 106 73, Greece

**Philosophia: Philosophical Quarterly of Israel**. ISSN 0048-3893. (q) Bar-Ilan University, Subscriptions, Dept. of Philosophy, Ramat-Gan 52100, Israel

**Philosophia: Revista de Filosofia**. No ISSN. (bi-ann) Editora Universitária Champagnat, Rua Imaculada Conceição, 1155, Curitiba-Paraná, 80215-901 Brazil

**Philosophia Mathematica**. ISSN 0031-8019. (3 times per yr) Journals Division, University of Toronto Press, 5201 Dufferin Street, Downsville, Ontario M3H 5T8, Canada

**Philosophia Naturalis**. ISSN 0031-8027. (bi-ann) Vittorio Klostermann GmbH, Postfach 90 06 01, Frauenlobstrasse 22, D-60487 Frankfurt/M, Germany

**Philosophia Reformata**. ISSN 0031-8035. (q) Centrum voor Reformatorische Wijsbegeerte, P.O. Box 368, 3500 AJ Utrecht, The Netherlands

**Philosophic Exchange: Annual Proceedings**. ISSN 0193-5046. (ann) Center for Philosophic Exchange, SUNY at Brockport, Brockport, NY 14420, USA

**Philosophica**. ISSN 0379-8402. (bi-ann) Rozier 44, B-9000 Gent, Belgium

**Philosophica**. (q) 38A/10 Belgachia Road, Calcutta 700037, India

**Philosophica: Revista do Departamento de Filosofia da Faculdade de Letras da Universidade de Lisboa**. (q) Leonel Ribeiro dos Santos, Editor, Departamento de Filosofia, Faculdade de Letras da Universidade de Lisboa, Cidade Universitaria, P-1699, Lisboa Codex, Portugal

**Philosophica: Zborník Univerzity Komenského**. (ann) Dr. Miroslav Marcelli, Editor, Department of Philosophy & History of Philosophy, Faculty of Arts, Comenius University, Gondova 8, 81801 Bratislava, Slovakia

**Philosophical Books**. ISSN 0031-8051. (q) Blackwell Publishers, 108 Cowley Road, Oxford OX4 1JF, United Kingdom (or 238 Main St., Cambridge, MA 02142, USA)

**The Philosophical Forum**. ISSN 0031-806X. (q) CUNY, Baruch College, Box 239, 17 Lexington Avenue, New York, NY 10010, USA

**Philosophical Inquiry: An International Philosophical Quarterly**. (q) Prof. D.Z. Andriopoulos, Editor, School of Philosophy, Aristotelian University of Thessaloniki, P.O. Box 84, Thessaloniki, Greece (or P.O. Box 61116, Maroussi, Athens, Greece)

**Philosophical Investigations**. ISSN 0190-0536. (q) Blackwell Publishers, 108 Cowley Road, Oxford OX4 1JF, United Kingdom (or 238 Main St., Cambridge, MA 02142, USA)

**Philosophical Papers**. ISSN 0556-8641. (3 times per yr) Dept. of Philosophy, Rhodes University, P.O. Box 94, Grahamstown 6140, South Africa

**Philosophical Psychology**. ISSN 0951-5089. (3 times per yr) Carfax Publishing Co., P.O. Box 25, Abingdon, Oxfordshire OX14 3UE, United Kingdom

**The Philosophical Quarterly**. ISSN 0031-8094. (q) Blackwell Publishers, 108 Cowley Road, Oxford OX4 1JF, United Kingdom (or 238 Main St., Cambridge, MA 02142, USA)

**Philosophical Review**. (ann) Editor-in-Chief, Dept. of Philosophy, National Taiwan University, Taipei 10764, Taiwan

**The Philosophical Review**. ISSN 0031-8103. (q) 327 Goldwin Smith Hall, Cornell University, Ithaca, NY 14853, USA

**Philosophical Studies: An International Journal for Philosophy in the Analytic Tradition**. ISSN 0031-8116. (12 times per yr) Kluwer Academic Publishers, P.O. Box 322, 3300 AH Dordrecht, The Netherlands (or P.O.Box 358, Accord Station, Hingham, MA 02018-0358, USA)

**Philosophical Studies in Education: Proceedings of the Annual Meeting of the Ohio Valley Philosophy of Education Society**. ISSN 0160-7561. (ann) Terence O'Connor, Indiana State University, Terre Haute, IN 47809, USA

**Philosophical Topics**. ISSN 0276-2080. (bi-ann) Christopher Hill, Editor, Dept. of Philosophy, University of Arkansas, Fayetteville, AR 72701, USA

**Philosophie et Logique**. ISSN 0035-4031. (q) Editura Academiei Republicii Socialiste Romania, Str. Gutenberg 3 bis, Sector 6, Bucaresti, Romania

**Die Philosophin: Forum für feministische Theorie und Philosophie**. ISSN 0936-7586 (bi-ann) Edition Diskord, Dr. G. Kimmerle, Schwärzlocherstr. 104/b, D-72070 Tübingen, Germany

**Philosophique**. ISSN 0980-0891. (ann) Faculté des Lettres et Sciences Humaines, Université de Franche-Comté, 30 rue Megevand, 25000 Besançon Cédex, France

**Philosophiques**. ISSN 0316-2923. (bi-ann) Les Editions Bellarmin, 165 rue Deslauriers, Saint-Laurent, Québec H4N 2S4, Canada

**Philosophische Rundschau**. ISSN 0031-8159. (q) J.C.B. Mohr (Paul Siebeck), Postfach 20 40, D-72010 Tübingen, Germany

**Philosophy: The Journal of the Royal Institute of Philosophy**. ISSN 0031-8191. (q plus 2 supps). Cambridge University Press, The Edinburgh Building, Shaftesbury Road, Cambridge, CB2 2RU, United Kingdom, (or 40 West 20th Street, New York, NY 10011-4211, USA)

**Philosophy and Literature**. ISSN 0190-0013. (semi-ann) The Johns Hopkins University Press, 701 West 40th Street, Suite 275, Baltimore, MD 21211-2190, USA

**Philosophy and Phenomenological Research**. ISSN 0031-8205. (q) Brown University, Box 1947, Providence, RI 02912, USA

**Philosophy and Public Affairs**. ISSN 0048-3915. (q) The Johns Hopkins University Press, 701 West 40th Street, Suite 275, Baltimore, MD 21211-2190, USA

**Philosophy and Rhetoric**. ISSN 0031-8213. (q) Dept. of Philosophy, The Pennsylvania State University, University Park, PA 16802, USA

**Philosophy and Social Action**. ISSN 0377-2772. (q) Business Editor, M-120 Greater Kailash-I, New Delhi 110048, India

**Philosophy and Social Criticism**. ISSN 0191-4537. (q) David M. Rasmussen, Editor, P.O. Box 368, Lawrence, KS 66044, USA

**Philosophy and the History of Science**. ISSN 1022-4874. (bi-ann) Dr. Yu-Houng, Managing Editor, Yuan-Liou Publishing Co., Ltd., 7F-5, 184, Sec. 3, Ding-Chou Road, Taipei, Taiwan

**Philosophy and Theology: Marquette University Quarterly**. ISSN 0-87462-559-9. (q) A. Tallon, Dept. of Philosophy and Theology, Marquette University, Milwaukee, WI 53233, USA

**Philosophy East and West**. ISSN 0031-8221. (q) The University of Hawaii Press, 2840 Kolowalu Street, Honolulu, HI 96822, USA

**Philosophy in Science**. ISSN 0277-2434. (ann) Pachart Publishing House, 1130 San Lucas Circle, Tucson, AZ 85704, USA

**Philosophy in the Contemporary World**. ISSN 1077-1999. (q) Jack Weir, Editor, UPO 662, Morehead State University, Morehead, KY 40351-1689, USA

**Philosophy of Education: Proceedings of the Annual Meeting of the Philosophy of Education Society**. No ISSN (ann) Philosophy of Education Society, Dept. of Teacher Education, San Jose State University, 1 Washington Square, San Jose, CA 95192

**Philosophy of Music Education Review**. ISSN 1063-5734. (bi-ann) Music Education Dept., SY405, School of Music, Indiana University, Bloomington, IN 47405, USA

**Philosophy of Science**. ISSN 0031-8248. (q) Executive Secretary, Philosophy of Science Assoc., Dept. of Philosophy, 114 Morrill Hall, Michigan State University, East Lansing, MI 48824-1036, USA

**Philosophy of the Social Sciences**. ISSN 0048-3931. (q) Sage Publications, 2455 Teller Road, Newbury Park, CA 91320, USA

**Philosophy, Psychiatry, and Psychology**. ISSN 1071-6076. (q) The Johns Hopkins University Press, Journals Publishing Division, P.O. Box 19966, Baltimore, MD 21211, USA

**Philosophy Today**. ISSN 0031-8256. (q) DePaul University, 802 West Belden Avenue, Chicago, IL 60614, USA

**Phoenix: The Journal of the Classical Association of Canada**. ISSN 0031-8299. (q) J. Schutz, Editorial Assistant, Trinity College, Larkin 339, University of Toronto, Toronto, Ontario M5S 1H8, Canada

**Phronesis: A Journal for Ancient Philosophy**. ISSN 0031-8868. (3 times per yr) E.J. Brill, P.O. Box 9000, 2300 PA Leiden, The Netherlands

**Polis**. (bi-ann) P. P. Nicholson, Dept. of Politics, University of York, York YO1 5DD, United Kingdom (or Prof. Kent F. Moors, Dept. of Political Science, Duquesne University, Pittsburgh, PA 15282-0001, USA)

**Political Theory: An International Journal of Political Philosophy**. ISSN 0090-5917. (q) Sage Publications, 2455 Teller Road, Newbury Park, CA 91320, USA

**Pragmatics and Cognition**. ISSN 0929-0907. (bi-ann) John Benjamins Publishing Co., Amsteldijk 44, P.O. Box 75577, 1070 AN Amsterdam, The Netherlands

**Prilozi za Istraivanje Hrvatske Filozofske Baštine**. ISSN 0350-2791 (bi-ann) Ljerka Schiffler-Premec, ed., Institut za Filosofiju, Ul. grada Vukovara 54, 41000 Zagreb, Croatia

**Prima Philosophia**. ISSN 0933-5749. (q) Traude Junghans Verlag, Flat 5, 21 Essex Rd., Dartford/Kent DA1 2AU, United Kingdom

**Proceedings and Addresses of the American Philosophical Association**. ISSN 0065-972X. (7 times per yr) The American Philosophical Assoc., University of Delaware, Newark, DE 19716, USA

**Proceedings of the American Catholic Philosophical Association**. ISSN 0065-7638. (ann) Treasurer, The American Catholic Philosophical Assoc., Catholic University of America, Washington, DC 20064, USA

**Proceedings of the Aristotelian Society**. ISSN 0066-7374. Members: The Aristotelian Society, Dept. of Philosophy, Birkbeck College, Malet Street, London WC1E 7HX, United Kingdom. Non-members: Blackwell Publishers, 108 Cowley Road, Oxford OX4 1JF, United Kingdom (or 238 Main St., Cambridge, MA 02142, USA)

**Proceedings of the Biennial Meetings of the Philosophy of Science Association**. ISSN 0270-8647. (ann) Philosophy of Science Assoc., 18 Morrill Hall, Michigan State University, East Lansing, MI 48824-1036, USA

**Proceedings of the Boston Area Colloquium in Ancient Philosophy**. (ann) Co-publishing Program, University Press of America, 4720 Boston Way, Lanham, MD 20706, USA

**Proceedings of the Heraclitean Society**. (irr) Dept. of Philosophy, Western Michigan University, Kalamazoo, MI 49008, USA

**Proceedings of the South Atlantic Philosophy of Education Society**. (ann) Joseph W. Congleton, School of Education, SAPES, East Carolina University, Greenville, NC 27858, USA

**Process Studies**. ISSN 0360-6503. (q) Center for Process Studies, 1325 North College Avenue, Claremont, CA 91711, USA

**Professional Ethics: A Multidisciplinary Journal**. ISSN 1063-6579. Center for Applied Philosophy, 331 Griffin-Floyd Hall, University of Florida, Gainesville, FL 32611, USA

**Protosoziologie**. ISSN 0940-4147 (bi-ann) Gerhard Preyer, ed., Dept. of Social Sciences, J.W.Goethe University, Stephan-Heise Str. 56, D-60488 Frankfurt/M, Germany

**Public Affairs Quarterly**. ISSN 0887-0373. (q) Philosophy Documentation Center, Bowling Green State University, Bowling Green, OH 43403-0189, USA

**Quadernos de Filosofia i Ciència**. ISSN 0213-5965. (irr) Societat de Filosofia del País Valencià, Facultat de Filosofia i Cièn-cies de l'Educació, Universitat de València, Av. Blasco Ibáñez, 21-46010 València, Spain

**Quest: Philosophical Discussions**. ISSN 1011-226X. (bi-ann) Circulation Manager, P.O. Box 9114, 9703 LC Groningen, The Netherlands

**Radical Philosophy: A Journal of Socialist and Feminist Philosophy**. ISSN 0300-211X. (3 times per yr) Central Books (RP Subscriptions), 99 Wallis Rd., London E9 5LN, United Kingdom

**Ratio: An International Journal of Analytic Philosophy**. ISSN 0034-0066. (3 times per yr) Blackwell Publishers, 108 Cowley Road, Oxford OX4 1JF, United Kingdom (or 238 Main St., Cambridge, MA 02142, USA)

**Ratio Juris: An International Journal of Jurisprudence and Philosophy of Law**. ISSN 0952-1919. (3 times per year) Blackwell Publishers, 108 Cowley Rd., Oxford OX4 1JF, United Kingdom (or 238 Main St., Cambridge, MA 02142 USA)

**Reason Papers: A Journal of Interdisciplinary Normative Studies**. ISSN 0363-1893. (ann) Dept. of Philosophy, Auburn University, Auburn University, AL 36849, USA

**Religious Humanism**. ISSN 0034-4095. (q) Fellowship of Religious Humanists, P.O. Box 278, Yellow Springs, OH 42387, USA

**Religious Studies: An International Journal for the Philosophy of Religion**. ISSN 0034-4125. (q) Cambridge University Press, The Edinburgh Building, Shaftesbury Road, Cambridge, CB2 2RU, United Kingdom (or 40 West 20th Street, New York, NY 10011-4211, USA)

**Reports on Mathematical Logic**. ISSN 0137-2904. (ann) Centrala Handlu Zagranicznego "Ars Polona," ul. Krakowskie Przedmiescie 7, 00-068 Warsaw, Poland

**Reports on Philosophy**. ISSN 0324-8712. Elzbieta Paczkowska-Lagowska, Editor-in-Chief, Instytut Filozofii, ul. Grodzka 52, 31-044 Krakow, Poland

**Research in Phenomenology**. ISSN 0085-5553. (ann) Humanities Press International, Atlantic Highlands, NJ 07716, USA

**Research in Philosophy and Technology**. (ann) JAI Press, Inc., 55 Old Post Road-No. 2, Greenwich, CT 06836, USA

**The Review of Metaphysics**. ISSN 0034-6632. (q) Catholic University of America, Washington, DC 20064, USA

**Revista de Filosofía**. ISSN 0185-3481. (3 times per yr) Universidad Iberoamericana, Prolongación Paseo de la Reforma No. 880, Lomas de Santa Fé, 01210 México, DF, Mexico

**Revista de Filosofía**. No ISSN. (bi-ann) Centro de Estudios Filosóficos, Edificio Viyaluz Piso 8, Apartado 526, Mara-caibo, Venezuela

**Revista de Filosofía: Publicación de la Asociación de Estudios Filosóficos**. ISSN 0326-8160. (bi-ann) Mar-celo Diego Boeri, ADEF C.C. 3758 Correo Central, 1000 Capital Federal, Argentina

**Revista de Filosofía de la Universidad de Costa Rica**. ISSN 0034-8252. (bi-ann) Editor, Universidad de Costa Rica, Apartado 75-2060, San José, Costa Rica

**Revista de Filosofie**. ISSN 0034-8260. (bi-m) Rompresfilatelia, Calea Victoriei 125, 79717 Bucharest, Romania

**Revista Española de Filosofía Medieval**. ISSN 1133-0902. (ann) Servicio de Publicaciones, Edificio de Geológicas, Ciudad Universitaria, 50,009 Zaragoza, Spain

**Revista Latinoamericana de Filosofía**. ISSN 0325-0725. (3 times per yr) Box 1192, Birmingham, AL 35201, USA (or Casilla de Correo 5379, Correo Central, 1000 Buenos Aires, Argentina)

**Revista Portuguesa de Filosofia**. ISSN 0035-0400. (q) Faculdade de Filosofia, UCP, 4719 Braga, Portugal

**Revue de Métaphysique et de Morale**. ISSN 0035-1571. (q) 156 Avenue Parmentier, 75010 Paris, France

**Revue de Théologie et de Philosophie**. ISSN 0035-1784. (q) 7 ch. des Cèdres, CH-1004 Lausanne, Switzerland

**Revue Internationale de Philosophie**. ISSN 0048-8143. (q) Prof. Michael Meyer, Institut de Philosophie (CP/188), Université Libre de Bruxelles, Av. F. D. Roosevelt, 50, B-1050 Brussels, Belgium

**Revue Philosophique de la France et de L'étranger**. ISSN 0035-3833. (q) Redaction de la Revue Philosophique, 12 rue Jean-de-Beauvais, 75005 Paris, France

**Revue Philosophique de Louvain**. ISSN 0035-3841. (q) Editions Peeters, B.P. 41, B-3000 Leuven, Belgium

**Revue Thomiste: Revue Doctrinale de Théologie et de Philosophie**. ISSN 0035-4295. (q) Ecole de Théologie, Avenue Lacordaire, Cedex, 31078 Toulouse, France

**Rivista di Filosofia**. ISSN 0035-6239. (q) Società Editrice Il Mulino, Strada Maggiore 37, 40125 Bologna, Italy

**Rivista di Filosofia Neo-Scolastica**. ISSN 0035-6247. (q) Pubblicazioni dell'Universita Cattolica del Sacro Cuore, Vita e Pensiero, Largo A. Gemelli, 20123 Milan, Italy

**Rivista di Studi Crociani**. ISSN 0035-659X. (q) Presso la Societa di Storia Partia, Piazza Municipio, Maschio Angiolino, 80133 Naples, Italy

**Rivista Internazionale di Filosofia del Diritto**. (q) Casa Editrice Dott. A. Giuffrè, via Busto Arsizio 40, 20151 Milan, Italy

**Russell: The Journal of the Bertrand Russell Archives**. ISSN 0036-0163. (q) McMaster University Library Press, McMaster University, Hamilton, Ontario L8S 4L6, Canada

**Russian Studies in Philosophy: A Journal of Translations**. ISSN 0038-5883. (q) M.E. Sharpe, 80 Business Park Drive, Armonk, NY 10504, USA

**S'vara: A Journal of Philosophy, Law, and Judaism**. ISSN 1044-0011. (bi-ann) Business Manager, AFSHI, 280 Grand Avenue, Englewood, NJ 07631, USA

**Sapientia**. ISSN 0036-4703. (q) Bartolome Mitre 1869, 1039 Buenos Aires, Argentina

**Sapienza**. ISSN 0036-4711. (q) Vicoletto S. Pietro a Maiella, 4-80134 Naples, Italy

**Schopenhauer-Jahrbuch**. ISSN 0080-6935. (ann) Heinz Gerd Ingenkamp, Editor, Albertus-Magnus-Str. 35a, D-53177 Bonn, Germany

**Science and Engineering Ethics**. ISSN 1353-3452. (q) Raymond Spier, Editor, Opragen Publications, P. O. Box 54, Guildford, Surrey GU1 2YF, United Kingdom

**Science, Technology, and Human Values**. ISSN 0162-2439. (q) Sage Publications, 2455 Teller Road, Newbury Park, CA 91320, USA

**Social Epistemology: A Journal of Knowledge, Culture, and Policy**. ISSN 0269-1728. (q) Taylor and Francis Ltd, 4 John St., London WC1N 2ET, United Kingdom (or Taylor & Francis Inc, 242 Cherry St., Philadelphia, PA 19106-1906, USA)

**Social Indicators Research: An International and Interdisciplinary Journal for Quality-of-Life Measurement**. ISSN 0303-8300. Kluwer Academic Publishers, P.O. Box 322, 3300 AH Dordrecht, The Netherlands (or P.O.Box 358, Accord Station, Hingham, MA 02018-0358, USA)

**Social Philosophy and Policy**. ISSN 0265-0525. (bi-ann) Cambridge University Press, The Edinburgh Building, Shaftesbury Road, Cambridge CB2 2RU, United Kingdom (or 40 West 20th Street, New York, NY 10011-4211, USA)

**Social Theory and Practice: An International and Interdisciplinary Journal of Social Philosophy**. ISSN 0037-802X. (3 times per yr) Dept. of Philosophy R-36C, 203 Dodd Hall, The Florida State University, Tallahassee, FL 32306-1054, USA

**Sophia: A Journal for Philosophical Theology and Cross-Cultural Philosophy of Religion**. ISSN 0038-1527. (3 times per yr) School of Humanities, Deakin University, Victoria 3217, Australia

**Sorites: An International Electronic Quarterly of Analytic Philosophy**. ISSN 1135-1349 (q) c/o Prof. Lorenzo Peña, CSIC-Institute of Philosophy, Pinar 25, E-28006 Madrid, Spain

**South African Journal of Philosophy**. ISSN 0258-0136. (q) Bureau for Scientific Publications, P.O. Box 1758, Pretoria 0001, South Africa

**The Southern Journal of Philosophy**. ISSN 0038-4283. (q) Editor, Department of Philosophy, Memphis State University, Memphis, TN 38152, USA

**Southwest Philosophical Studies**. ISSN 0885-9310. (3 times per yr) Jack Weir, Co-Editor, Department of Philosophy, Hardin-Simmons University, Abilene, TX 79698, USA (or Joseph D. Stamey, Co-Editor, Dept. of Philosophy, McMurry University, Abilene, TX 79697, USA)

**Southwest Philosophy Review**. ISSN 0897-2346. (bi-ann) Dept. of Philosophy, University of Central Arkansas, Conway, AR 72302, USA

**Stromata**. ISSN 0049-2353. (q) Universidad del Salvador, C.C. 10, 1663 San Miguel, Argentina

**Studia Leibnitiana: Zeitschrift für Geschichte der Philosophie und der Wissenschaften**. ISSN 0039-3185. (bi-ann) Franz Steiner Verlag Wiesbaden GmbH, Postfach 101526, D-70014 Stuttgart, Germany

**Studia Logica**. ISSN 0039-3215. Kluwer Academic Publishers, P.O. Box 322, 3300 AH Dordrecht, The Netherlands (or P.O.Box 358, Accord Station, Hingham, MA 02018-0358, USA)

**Studia Philosophiae Christianae**. ISSN 0585-5470. (bi-ann) ATK, ul. Dewajtis 5, 01-653 Warsaw, Poland

**Studia Philosophica**. (ann) Helmut Holzhey and Jean-Pierre Leyvraz, Editors, Verlag Paul Haupt, Falkenplatz 11/14, CH-3001 Berne, Switzerland

**Studia Spinozana**. ISSN 0179-3896. (ann) Douglas J. Den Uyl, Bellarmine College, Newburg Road, Louisville, KY 40205, USA

**Studies in East European Thought**. ISSN 0925-9392. Kluwer Academic Publishers, P.O. Box 322, 3300 AH Dordrecht, The Netherlands (or P.O.Box 358, Accord Station, Hingham, MA 02018-0358, USA)

**Studies in History and Philosophy of Modern Physics**. ISSN 1355-2198. Nicholas Jardine, Editor, Elsevier Science Inc, 660 White Plains Road, Tarrytown, NY 10591-5153 USA

**Studi Filosofici: Annali del Dipartimento di Filosofia e Politica, Istituto Universitario Orientale**. No ISSN (ann) Dip. di Filosofia e Politica, Via dei Fiorentini, 10, 80133 Napoli, Italy

**Studies in History and Philosophy of Science**. ISSN 0039-3681. (q) Pergamon Press, Maxwell House, Fairview Park, Elmsford, NY 10523, USA

**Studies in Philosophy and Education**. ISSN 0039-3746. (q) Kluwer Academic Publishers, P.O. Box 322, 3300 AH Dordrecht, The Netherlands (or P.O.Box 358, Accord Station, Hingham, MA 02018-0358, USA)

**Synthese: An International Journal for Epistemology, Methodology, and Philosophy of Science**. ISSN 0039-7857. (12 times per yr) Kluwer Academic Publishers, P.O. Box 322, 3300 AH Dordrecht, The Netherlands (or P.O.Box 358, Accord Station, Hingham, MA 02018-0358, USA)

**Teaching Business Ethics**. ISSN 1382-6891. (q) Kluwer Academic Publishers, P.O. Box 322, 3300 AH Dordrecht, The Netherlands (or P.O.Box 358, Accord Station, Hingham, MA 02018-0358, USA

**Teaching Philosophy**. ISSN 0145-5788. (q) Philosophy Documentation Center, Bowling Green State University, Bowling Green, OH 43403-0189, USA

**Telos: Revista Iberoamericana de Estudios Utilitaristas**. ISSN 1132-0877 (bi-ann) S.I.E.U., Facultad de Filosofía y CC.EE., Campus Sur, E-15706 Santiago de Compostela, Spain

**Teorema**. ISSN 0210-1602. (q) Apdo. 4437, E-30080 Murcia, Spain

**Teoria: Rivista di Filosofia**. (bi-ann) E.T.S., C.C.P. 12157566, Piazza Torricelli 4, 56100 Pisa, Italy

**Thémata: Revista de Filosofía**. ISSN 0210-8365. (ann) Servicio de Publicaciones de la Universidad de Sevilla, C. San Fernando 4, E-41004, Sevilla C, Spain

**Theologie und Philosophie: Vierteljahresschrift**. ISSN 0040-5655. (q) Schriftleitung, Offenbacher Landstrasse 224, D-60599 Frankfurt/M, Germany

**Theoretical Medicine: An International Journal for the Philosophy and Methodology of Medical Research and Practice**. ISSN 0167-9902. (q) Kluwer Academic Publishers, P.O. Box 322, 3300 AH Dordrecht, The Netherlands (or P.O.Box 358, Accord Station, Hingham, MA 02018-0358, USA)

**Theoria**. ISSN 0495-4548. (3 times per yr) Plaza de Pio XII, 1, 6°, 1$^{a}$, Apartado 1.594, 20.080 San Sebastian, Spain

**Theoria: A Swedish Journal of Philosophy**. ISSN 0040-5825. (3 times per yr) Filosofiska Institution, Kungshuset i Lundagard, S-223 50 Lund, Sweden

**Theoria: Casopis Filozofskog Drustva Srbije**. ISSN 0351-2274. (q) Cika Ljubina 18-20, 11000 Beograd, Yugoslavia

**Theory and Decision: An International Journal for Multidisciplinary Advances in Decision Science**. ISSN 0040-5833. (6 times per year) Kluwer Academic Publishers, P.O. Box 322, 3300 AH Dordrecht, The Netherlands (or P.O.Box 358, Accord Station, Hingham, MA 02018-0358, USA)

**Theory, Culture and Society.** ISSN 0263-2764. (q) Sage Publications, LTD, 6 Bonhill Street, London, EC2A 4PU, United Kingdom

**Thinking: The Journal of Philosophy for Children**. ISSN 0190-3330. (q) The Institute for the Advancement of Philosophy for Children, Montclair State College, Upper Montclair, NJ 07043, USA

**The Thomist: A Speculative Quarterly Review**. ISSN 0040-6325. (q) The Thomist Press, 487 Michigan Avenue NE, Washington, DC 20017, USA

**Tijdschrift voor de Studie van de Verlichting en van Het Vrije Denken**. ISSN 0774-1847. (q) Centrum voor de Studie van de Verlichting en van Het Vrije Denken, Vrije Universiteit Brussel, Pleinlaan 2-B416, 1050 Brussels, Belgium

**Tijdschrift voor Filosofie**. ISSN 0040-750X. (q) Kardinaal Mercierplein 2, B-3000 Leuven, Belgium

**Tópicos: Revista de Filosofía**. ISSN 0188-6649. (ann) Dr. Héctor Zagal, Editor, Facultad de Filosofía, Universidad Panamericana, A Rodin #498, Plaza de Mixcoac, 03910 México, DF, Mexico

**Topoi: An International Review of Philosophy**. ISSN 0167-7411. Kluwer Academic Publishers, P.O. Box 322, 3300 AH Dordrecht, The Netherlands (or P.O.Box 358, Accord Station, Hingham, MA 02018-0358, USA)

**Tradition and Discovery: The Polanyi Society Periodical**. ISSN 1057-1027. (irr) Dr. Richard Gelwick, University of New England, Biddeford, ME 04005, USA

**Trans/Form/Ação**. ISSN 0101-3173. (ann) Biblioteca Central da UNESP, Av. Vicente Ferreira, 1278 C.P. 603, 17500 Marilia, SP, Brazil

**Transactions of the Charles S. Peirce Society: A Quarterly Journal in American Philosophy**. ISSN 0009-1774. (q) Editor, Dept. of Philosophy, Baldy Hall, SUNY at Buffalo, Buffalo, NY 14260, USA

**Tulane Studies in Philosophy**. ISSN 0082-6776. (ann) Dept. of Philosophy, Tulane University, New Orleans, LA 70118, USA

**Ultimate Reality and Meaning: Interdisciplinary Studies in the Philosophy of Understanding**. ISSN 0709-549X. (q) University of Toronto Press, 5201 Dufferin Street, Downsview, Ontario M3H 5T8, Canada

**Utilitas: A Journal of Utilitarian Studies**. (bi-ann) Oxford University Press, Pinkhill House, Southfield Road, Eynsham, Oxford OX8 1JJ, United Kingdom

**Vera Lex**. ISSN 0893-4851. (bi-ann) Prof. Virginia Black, Editor, Dept. of Philosophy and Religious Studies, Pace University, Pleasantville, NY 10570, USA

**Vienna Circle Institute Yearbook**. ISSN 0929-6328. (ann) Institut 'Wiener Kreis', Museumstr. 5/2/19, A-1070 Vienna, Austria

# Guidance on the Use of the Subject Index

The Subject Index lists in alphabetical order the significant subject descriptors and proper names that describe the content of the articles and books indexed. Since titles are frequently misleading, the editors read each article and book to determine which subject headings accurately describe it. Each entry under a subject heading includes the complete title of the book or article and the author's name.

Subject entries fall into the following classes:

1) proper names, such as Quine, Kant, and Hegel;
2) nationalities, such as American and German;
3) historical periods, which are: ancient, medieval, renaissance, modern, nineteenth-century, and twentieth-century;
4) major fields of philosophy, which are: aesthetics, axiology, education, epistemology, ethics, history, language, logic, metaphysics, philosophical anthropology, philosophy, political philosophy, religion, science, and social philosophy;
5) subdivisions of the major fields of philosophy, such as: utilitarianism, induction, realism, and nominalism;
6) other specific topics, such as grue, pain, paradox, and Turing-machine;
7) bibliographies, which are listed under "bibliographies," the person or subject, and the appropriate historical period.

The Subject Index is used like the index found in the back of a textbook. Scan the alphabetical listing of significant words until the desired subject is found. If the title confirms your interest, then locate the author's name, which occurs after the title, in the section entitled "Author Index with Abstracts." The title, in addition to suggesting the content of the article or book, indicates the language in which the document is written.

Although every effort is made to standardize subject headings, complete uniformity is impossible. Hence, check for various spellings of subject headings, particularly of proper names. Due consideration should be given to subject headings that sometimes are written with a space, a hyphen, or an umlaut. The following example illustrates some possibilities:

DE MORGAN
DE-MORGAN
DEMORGAN

Not only does the computer treat the above subject headings as different, but it may file other subject headings between them.

Generally, only the last names of famous philosophers are used as subject headings. Last names and first initials usually are used for other philosophers. The following list indicates who of two or more philosophers with the same last name is designated by last name only.

Alexander (Samuel)
Austin (J L)
Bacon (Francis)
Bradley (Francis H)
Brown (Thomas)
Butler (Joseph)
Collins (Anthony)
Darwin (Charles)
Eckhart (Meister)
Edwards (Jonathan)
Green (Thomas H)
Hartmann (Edward von)
Huxley (T H)

James (William)
Jung (Carl G)
Lewis (C I)
Mill (John Stuart)
Moore (G E)
Niebuhr (Reinhold)
Paul (Saint)
Price (Richard)
Russell (Bertrand)
Schiller (Friedrich)
Toynbee (Arnold)
Wolff (Christian)

## ABSOLUTE
The Legacy of Jean Bodin: Absolutism, Populism or Constitutionalism?. Salmon, J H M.
The Problem of Moral Absolutes in the Ethics of Vladimir Solov'ëv. Sergeevich Pugachev, Oleg.
The 'Late Seriousness' of Cora Diamond. Lovibond, Sabina.
Trascendentalità, inferenza e trascendenza: Dopo Kant e Heidegger. Penati, Giancarlo.
True and Ultimate Responsibility. Nathan, Nicholas.
Vom sprachlichen Zugang zum Absoluten. Mittmann, Jörg-Peter.
Zwischen Sein und Setzen: Fichtes Kritik am dreifachen Absoluten der kantischen Philosophie. Bickmann, Claudia.

## ABSOLUTENESS
A Characterization of Martin's Axiom in Terms of Absoluteness. Bagaria, Joan.
Step by Recursive Step: Church's Analysis of Effective Calculability. Sieg, Wilfried.

## ABSOLUTISM
"Between Relativism and Absolutism: The Popperian Ideal of Knowledge" in The Significance of Popper's Thought, Amsterdamski, Stefan (ed). Amsterdamski, Stefan.
Mechanismus und Subjektivität in der Philosophie von Thomas Hobbes. Esfeld, Michael.

## ABSORPTION
The Manufacture of the Positron. Roqué, Xavier.

## ABSTRACT
Astrattezza e concretezza nella filosofia di Giovanni Gentile. Frigerio, Aldo.
Fictional Characters: Dependent or Abstract? A Reply to Reicher's Objections. Thomasson, Amie L.
Framing the Thisness Issue. O'Leary-Hawthorne, John and Cover, J A.
Katz Astray. George, Alexander.
Las parábolas ficinianas del bosque y el jardín en las Stanze per la Giostra de Angelo Poliziano. Manzi, Attilio.

## ABSTRACT IDEA
Berkeley, Lee and Abstract Ideas. Benschop, Hans Peter.
Berkeley: Crítica de las ideas abstractas: La abstracción como simple semántica. Vicente Burgoa, Lorenzo.

## ABSTRACT OBJECT
"Nominalism and the Contingency of Abstract Objects" in Frege: Importance and Legacy, Schirn, Matthias (ed). Hale, Bob and Wright, Crispin.

## ABSTRACTION
"Chi pensa astratto? traduzione e commento di Franca Mastromatteo e Leonardo Paganelli" in Hegel e Aristotele, Ferrarin, A. Hegel, G W F.
"Hypostatic Abstraction in Self-Consciousness" in The Rule of Reason: The Philosophy of Charles Sanders Peirce, Forster, Paul (ed). Short, T L.
"Productive Abstraction for Sets" in Verdad: lógica, representación y mundo, Villegas Forero, L. Kuper, Jan.
Idealisierungen und das Ziel der Physik: Eine Untersuchung zum Realismus, Empirismus und Konstruktivismus in der Wissenschaftstheorie. Hüttemann, Andreas.
Abstration, Inseparability, and Identity. Baxter, Donald L M.

## ABSTRACTIONISM
Las Disputaciones metafísicas de F. Suárez S.J., su inspiración y algunas de sus líneas maestras: En el IV centenario de la primera edición (1597-1997). Burillo, Santiago Fernández.

## ABUSE
"The Use and Abuse of Modernity: Postmodernism and the American Philosophic Tradition" in Philosophy in Experience: American Philosophy in Transition, Hart, Richard (ed). Ryder, John.
A Gift of Fire: Social, Legal, and Ethical Issues in Computing. Baase, Sara.
Children and Bioethics: Uses and Abuses of The Best-Interest Standard: Introduction. Kopelman, Loretta M.
Children's Refusal of Gynecologic Examinations for Suspected Sexual Abuse. Muram, David, Aiken, Margaret M and Strong, Carson.
Ethics Violations: A Survey of Investment Analysts. Veit, E Theodore and Murphy, Michael R.
Plutarch on the Treatment of Animals: The Argument from Marginal Cases. Newmyer, Stephen T.
Sex Education as Moral Education: Teaching for Pleasure, about Fantasy, and against Abuse. Lamb, Sharon.
Sexual Harassment and Negligence. Hajdin, Mane.
The Best-Interests Standard as Threshold, Ideal, and Standard of Reasonableness. Kopelman, Loretta M.
The Ethics of Information Transfer in the Electronic Age: Scholars Unite!. Laidlaw-Johnson, Elizabeth A.

## ACADEMIA
"How Sceptical were the Academic Sceptics?" in Scepticism in the History of Philosophy: A Pan-American Dialogue, Popkin, Richard H (ed). Frede, Dorothea.
"The American University: National Treasure or Endangered Species?" in The American University: National Treasure or Endangered Species?, Ehrenberg, Ronald G (ed). Rhodes, Frank H T.
"The Ideal University and Reality" in The Idea of University, Brzezinski, Jerzy (ed). Gumanski, Leon.

"The Majesty of the University" in The Idea of University, Brzezinski, Jerzy (ed). Twardowski, Kazimierz.
Academic Freedom and Tenure: Ethical Issues. De George, Richard T.
Diversity and Community in the Academy: Affirmative Action in Faculty Appointments. Wolf-Devine, Celia.
Rethinking College Education. Allan, George.
The American University: National Treasure or Endangered Species?. Ehrenberg, Ronald G (ed).
The Idea of University. Brzezinski, Jerzy (ed) and Nowak, Leszek (ed).
A Critique of Academic Nationalism. Macdonald, Amie A.
Academic Corruption. Kekes, John.
Academic Feminism and Applied Ethics: Closing the Gap between Private Scholarship and Public Policy. LeMoncheck, Linda.
Academic Skepticism in Early Modern Philosophy. Maia Neto, José R.
Aesthetics and the Literal Imagination. Bérubé, Michael.
Charting the Currents of the Third Wave. Orr, Catherine M.
Improving Academic Writing. Bennett, Jonathan and Gorovitz, Samuel.
It's not the Principle, It's the Money!: An Economic Revisioning of Publishing Ethics. Hinz, Evelyn J.
Non-Academic Critics of Business Ethics in Canada. Michalos, Alex C.
Of Heapers, Splitters and Academic Woodpiles in the Study of Intense Religious Experiences. Forman, Robert K C.
Perception of What the Ethical Climate Is and What It Should Ɔə: The Role of Gender, Academic Status, and Ethical Education. Luthar, Harsh K, DiBattista, Ron A and Gautschi, Theodore.
Rethinking Philosophy in the Third Wave of Feminism. Golumbia, David.
Speaking for Myself in Philosophy. Duhan Kaplan, Laura.
Surfing the Third Wave: A Dialogue Between Two Third Wave Feminists. Alfonso, Rita and Trigilio, Jo.
Survival Skills and Ethics Training for Graduate Students: A Graduate Student Perspective. Rittenhouse, Cynthia D.
The Impact of Culture on Education. Thomas, Cornell.
The Vocation of Higher Education: Modern and Postmodern Rhetorics in the Israeli Academia on Strike. Gur-Ze'ev, Ilan.
True Colors: The Response of Business Schools to Declining Enrollment. McKendall, Marie A and Lindquist, Stanton C.

## ACADEMIC
Enlarging the Conversation. Herman, Steward W.
It's not the Principle, It's the Money!: An Economic Revisioning of Publishing Ethics. Hinz, Evelyn J.
Policies and Perspectives on Authorship. Rose, Mary and Fischer, Karla.

## ACADEMIC FREEDOM
Academic Freedom and Tenure: Ethical Issues. De George, Richard T.
Bertrand Russell and Academic Freedom. Irvine, A D.

## ACCEPTABILITY
Premise Acceptability, Deontology, Internalism, Justification. Freeman, James B.

## ACCEPTANCE
A Nonmonotonic Modal Formalization of the Logic of Acceptance and Rejection. Gomolinska, Anna.

## ACCIDENT
Handlungstheoretische Aspekte der Fahrlässigkeit. Seebass, Gottfried.
Modern Accident Law Does Not Fit Corrective Justice Theory. Grady, Mark F.
On Substances, Accidents and Universals: In Defence of a Constituent Ontology. Smith, Barry.

## ACCOUNTABILITY
Accountability in a Computerized Society. Nissenbaum, Helen.
Moral Accountancy and Moral Worth. Smilansky, Saul.
Sources of Error and Accountability in Computer Systems: Comments on "Accountability in a Computerized Society". Szolovits, Peter.

## ACCOUNTANT
Auditors' Ability to Discern the Presence of Ethical Problems. Karcher, Julia N.
Factors that Influence the Moral Reasoning Abilities of Accountants: Implications for Universities and the Profession. Eynon, Gail, Thorley Hill, Nancy and Stevens, Kevin T.

## ACCOUNTING
Business Ethics in Theory in Practice: Diagnostic Notes A: A Prescription for Value. Welch, Edward J.
Chief Financial Officers' Perceptions Concerning the IMA's Standards of Ethical Conduct. Moyes, Glen D and Park, Kyungjoo.
Could Auditing Standards Be Based on Society's Values?. Zaid, Omar Abdullah.
Functionalist and Conflict Views of AICPA Code of Conduct: Public Interest vs. Self Interest. Lindblom, Cristi K and Ruland, Robert G.
Helping Professionals in Business Behave Ethically: Why Business Cannot Abdicate Its Responsibility to the Profession. Cooper, Robert W and Frank, Garry L.
Professional Ethics Code Conflict Situations: Ethical and Value Orientation of Collegiate Accounting Students. McCarthy, Irene N.
The Ethics of Creative Accounting. Archer, Simon.
Truth or Consequences: A Study of Critical Issues and Decision Making in Accounting. Gibson, Annetta and Frakes, Albert H.

## ACCURACY
Kitcher's Compromise: A Critical Examination of the Compromise Model of Scientific Closure, and its Implications for the Relationship between History and Philosophy of Science. Shanahan, Timothy.

## ACCURACY
Variation and the Accuracy of Predictions. Kruse, Michael.

## ACHENBACH, G
Philosophical Counselling, Truth and Self-Interpretation. Jopling, David A.

## ACHINSTEIN, P
Waves, Particles, and Explanatory Coherence. Eliasmith, Chris and Thagard, Paul.

## ACKERMAN, B
"Political Dialogue and Political Virtue" in *Political Dialogue: Theories and Practices,* Esquith, Stephen L (ed). Esquith, Stephen L.
Is There a Neutral Justification for Liberalism?. Brighouse, Harry.
Three Paths in Moral Philosophy. Walzer, Michael.

## ACKRILL, J
Incoherence in the Aristotelian Philosophy of Action? (Spanish). Bravo, Francisco.

## ACQUAINTANCE
Sequence of Tense and Temporal De Re. Abusch, Dorit.

## ACQUISITION
Ethics in Government: A Survey of Misuse of Position for Personal Gain and Its Implications for Developing Acquisition Strategy. McCampbell, Atefeh Sadri and Rood, Tina L.
Hospital Mergers and Acquisitions: A New Catalyst for Examining Organizational Ethics. Hofmann, Paul B.
The Logical Problem of Language Acquisition. Cowie, Fiona.

## ACT
*see also* Conduct, Speech Act
"Atto puro e pensiero nell'interpretazione di Hegel" in *Hegel e Aristotele,* Ferrarin, A. Samonà, Leonardo.
Coding Elementary Contributions to Dialogue: Individual Acts versus Dialogical Interaction. Marková, Ivana and Linell, Per.
Intellectus principiorum: De Tomás de Aquino a Leonardo Polo (y "vuelta"). Fernandez Burillo, Santiago.
La precisividad del pensamiento. Esquer Gallardo, Héctor.
Probleme der Zurechnung bei impulsivem Handeln. Silva-Sánchez, Jesús-Maria.
The "But-Everyone-Does-That!" Defense. Husak, Douglas.
The Concept of Act in the Naturalistic Idealism of John William Miller. Tyman, Stephen.
The Intentionality of Mental Reference. Motilal, Shashi.
Visual Metaphors. Jensen, Hans Siggaard.

## ACTING
*see* Doing

## ACTION
"Actions, Causes, and Mental Ascriptions" in *Objections to Physicalism,* Robinson, Howard (ed). Gillett, Grant.
"Cinco tesis sobre la racionalidad de la acción" in *La racionalidad: su poder y sus límites,* Nudler, Oscar (ed). Maliandi, Ricardo.
"Doing as We Ought: Towards a Logic of Simply Dischargeable Obligations" in *Deontic Logic, Agency and Normative Systems,* Brown, Mark A (ed). Brown, Mark A.
"Indirect Action, Influence and Responsibility" in *Deontic Logic, Agency and Normative Systems,* Brown, Mark A (ed). Santos, Filipe and Carmo, José.
"La logica della vita morale in M. Blondel" in *Momenti di Storia della Logica e di Storia della Filosofia,* Guetti, Carla (ed). Rigobello, Armando.
"Per una topologia dell'ego" in *Geofilosofia,* Bonesio, Luisa (ed). Vitiello, Vincenzo.
"Personal Autonomy, Freedom of Action, and Coercion" in *A Question of Values: New Canadian Perspectives in Ethics and Political Philosophy,* Brennan, Samantha (ed). Dimock, Susan.
"Prioridad del acto en la génesis de los hábitos operativos" in *Ensayos Aristotélicos,* Rivera, José Luis (ed). Mier y Terán, Rocío.
"Racionalidad y teoría de la acción: ¿es la teoría evidencial de la decisión una teoría de la racionalidad mínima?" in *La racionalidad: su poder y sus límites,* Nudler, Oscar (ed). Arló Costa, Horacio.
"Reason and Action in Africa" in *Averroës and the Enlightenment,* Wahba, Mourad (ed). Oruka, Odera.
"The Interpretational Paradigm in the Philosophy of the Human Sciences" in *Epistemology and History,* Zeidler-Janiszewska, Anna (ed). Swiderski, Edward.
*Against Liberalism.* Kekes, John.
*Facets of Faith and Science Volume 4: Interpreting God's Action in the World.* Van der Meer, Jitse M (ed).
*Language, Action, and Context: The Early History of Pragmatics in Europe and America, 1780-1930.* Nerlich, Brigitte and Clarke, David D.
*Mechanismus und Subjektivität in der Philosophie von Thomas Hobbes.* Esfeld, Michael.
*Order in the Twilight.* Waldenfels, Bernhard and Parent, David J (trans).
*Practicing Philosophy: Pragmatism and the Philosophical Life.* Shusterman, Richard.
*Promising, Intending, and Moral Autonomy.* Robins, Michael H.
*Rationalität und Theoriebildung: Studien zu Karl R. Poppers Methodologie der Sozialwissenschaften.* Schmid, Michael.
*Society, Economics & Philosophy: Selected Papers.* Allen, R T (ed) and Polanyi, Michael.

*Tempo Linguaggio e Azione: Le Strutture Vichiane della Storia Ideale Eterna.* Botturi, Francesco.
*Temporalità e Comunicazione.* Reda, Clementina Gily.
*The Self After Postmodernity.* Boling, Patricia.
*Things That Happen Because They Should: A Teleological Approach to Action.* Stout, Rowland.
*Was sind Handlungen? Eine philosophische Auseinandersetzung mit dem Naturalismus.* Runggaldier, Edmund.
A Conception of Practical Reasoning. Coombs, Jerrold and Wright, Ian.
A Dialéctica da Acçao em L'Action (1893) de Maurice Blondel. Morujao, Alexandre Fradique.
A Longitudinal Examination of American Business Ethics: Clark's Scales Revisited. Harich, Katrin R and Curren, Mary T.
A Obra como Facto Comunicativo. Rodrigues, Manuel J.
Action Incompleteness. Segerberg, Krister.
Addiction and Self-Control. Mele, Alfred R.
Agent-Neutral Reasons: Are They for Everyone?. Postow, B C.
All Existing is the Action of God: The Philosophical Theology of David Braine. Bradshaw, David.
An Epistemic Dimension of Blameworthiness. Haji, Ishtiyaque.
An Overlooked Motive in Alcibiades' *Symposium* Speech. Scott, Gary Alan and Welton, William A.
Antimodern, Ultramodern, Postmodern: A Plea for the Perennial. Dewan, Lawrence.
Aquinas's Account of Double Effect. Cavanaugh, Thomas A.
Ascriptions of Responsibility. Oshana, Marina A L.
Autonomy and Hierarchical Compatibilism. Jennings, Ian.
Belief, Foreknowledge, and Theological Fatalism. Hughes, Charles T.
Blameworthiness, Character, and Cultural Norms. Haji, Ishtiyaque.
Can There Be a Science of Action? Paul Ricoeur. Van den Hengel, John.
Chief Bumbu en de Verklaring van Menselijk Gedrag. Mackor, Anne Ruth and Peijnenburg, Jeanne.
Choosing the Best: Against Paternalistic Practice Guidelines. Savulescu, Julian.
Communicative Action and Philosophical Foundations: Comments on the Apel-Habermas Debate. Papastephanou, Marianna.
Communicative Action, the Lifeworlds of Learning and the Dialogue that we Aren't. Hogan, Pádraig.
Consistency Among Intentions and the 'Simple View'. Sverdlik, Steven.
Courage Alone. Putnam, Daniel.
Criminal Responsibility. Elliot, Carl.
Das Verstehen singulärer Handlungen: Ein Kommentar zu Davidson und von Wright. Wyller, Truls.
Del acto de ser a la acción moral. Ponferrada, Gustavo Eloy.
Divine Action in a World Chaos: An Evaluation of John Polkinghorne's Model of Special Divine Action. Crain, Steven D.
Doing One's Own Thing: The Genealogy of a Slogan. Weidhorn, Manfred.
Doing Without Concepts: An Interpretation of C.I. Lewis' Action-Oriented Foundationalism. Stufflebeam, Robert.
Donagan on Cases of Necessity. Malone, Michael J.
Explanation, Understanding and Typical Action. Manicas, Peter T.
Externalism and Action-Guiding Epistemic Norms. Jacobson, Stephen.
Getting Started: Beginnings in the Logic of Action. Segerberg, Krister.
Gilles Deleuze and the Redemption from Interest. Hallward, Peter.
How to Do Things with Things: Objects trouvés and Symbolization. Streeck, Jürgen.
Human Nature's Natural Law. Humphrey, Robert L.
Hume's Utilitarian Theory of Right Action. Sobel, Jordan Howard.
Hume—Not a "Humean" about Motivation. Persson, Ingmar.
In Defence of Representations. Jovchelovitch, Sandra.
Incoherence in the Aristotelian Philosophy of Action? (Spanish). Bravo, Francisco.
Indexical Reference and Bodily Causal Diagrams in Intentional Action. Castañeda, Héctor-Neri.
Interpretation as Action: The Risk of Inquiry. Awbrey, Jon and Awbrey, Susan.
Is It Rational To Carry Out Strategic Intentions?. Robins, Michael H.
Just Do It: Deniability and Renegades. Brimlow, Robert W.
Knowledge vs True Belief in the Socratic Psychology of Action. Penner, Terry.
La ética del discurso como ética de la corresponsabilidad por las actividades colectivas. Apel, Karl-Otto.
La fuerza del PC (Principio de Caridad): Circunstancia, habilidad y contenido en la explicación de la acción. Broncano, Fernando.
La persona como fuente de autenticidad. Yepes Stork, Ricardo.
La seriedad de la ética. Del Barco, José Luis.
Liberating Constraints. Haji, Ishtiyaque.
Maxims, "Practical Wisdom," and the Language of Action: Beyond Grand Theory. Nichols, Ray.
Mercy: In Defense of Caprice. Rainbolt, George.
Moral Responsibility and Leeway for Action. Wyma, Keith D.
Moral Responsibility and the Problem of Induced Pro-Attitudes. Haji, Ishtiyaque.
Moral Status and the Impermissibility of Minimizing Violations. Lippert-Rasmussen, Kasper.
No Good Deed Ever Goes Unpunished. Buchanan, James.
Norm and End: A Kantian Theory of Action (in French). Joós, Jean-Ernest.

## AESTHETICS

*Changing Theories of Collegiate Theatrical Curricula 1900-1945.* Berkeley, Anne.

Chaos and Literature. Matheson, Carl and Kirchhoff, Evan.

Characterisation and Interpretation: The Importance of Drama in Plato's *Sophist.* Benitez, Eugenio E.

Characterization in Samuel Beckett's *Not I.* Daisuke, Hirakawa.

Christoph Menke: herméneutique, déconstruction et raison dans le problème de l'expérience esthétique. Ratté, Michel.

Compétence, survenance et émotion esthétique. Poivet, Roger.

Conceptual Frameworks for World Musics in Education. Boyce-Tillman, June.

Conceptualizing Art Criticism for Effective Practice. Geahigan, George.

Concluding Observations. Smith, Ralph A.

Confession of a Weak Anti-Intentionalist: Exposing Myself. Wilson, W Kent.

Country Fashion (in Portuguese). Arantes, Otília Beatriz Fiori and Arantes, Paulo Eduardo.

Crafting Marks into Meanings. Catalano, Joseph S.

Creation and Discovery in Musical Works. Woodruff, David M.

Critical Perspectives on Early Twentieth-Century American Avant-Garde Composers. O'Grady, Terence J.

Cyprian Norwid—The Poet of Truth. Zajaczkowski, Ryszard.

Damned if You Do and Damned if You Don't: Sexual Aesthetics and the Music of Dame Ethel Smyth. Gates, Eugene.

Dance and the Question of Fidelity. Cohen, Selma Jeanne.

Dance Metaphors: A Reply to Julie Van Camp. Whittock, Trevor.

*Das kleine Buch* und das *laute* Weltereignis: Fichtes *Wissenschaftslehre* als Paradigma und Problem der *Romantik.* Schanze, Helmut.

Das Schweben der Einbildungskraft: Eine frühromantische Metapher in Rücksicht auf Fichte. Hühn, Lore.

Defining Art Responsibly. Young, James O.

Der "Neuanfang" in der Ästhetik (J.-F. Lyotard). Seubold, Günter.

Descartes, Error, and the Aesthetic-Totality Solution to the Problem of Evil. Gilbertson, Mark.

Die Philosophie Nishidas als eine "Kunstlehre": Überlegungen zu Nishidas Beziehung zur Kunsttheorie Fiedlers (in Japanese). Tomohiro, Takanashi.

Dogen on *seppo* and *jodo.* Nakajima, Keita.

Dos estudios italianos sobre Vico y la estética. Amoroso, Leonardo.

Dramaturgy of Picture (Essay on Diderot's *The Natural Child*) (in Portuguese). De Matos, Franklin.

Edwin Gordon Responds. Gordon, Edwin.

Een anatomie van de beeldende kunst. Herzog, Katalin.

El cant gregorià, un model de música perfecta. Banyeres Baltasà, Hug.

El desinterés en la actitud estética. García Leal, José.

El Greco's Statements on Michelangelo the Painter. Rodetis, George A.

El sujeto en la estética kantiana (Primera parte). Cañas Quiros, Roberto.

El universo de la precisión: Galileo versus Vico: Del confuso conocimiento de la representación al transmundo antivital de la ciencia. Zacares Pamblanco, Amparo.

Embracing the Subject: Harsa's Play within a Play. Shulman, David.

Empirical Questions Deserve Empirical Answers. Martindale, Colin.

Escaping Reality: Digital Imagery and the Resources of Photography. Savedoff, Barbara E.

Estética y hermenéutica. Gadamer, Hans-Georg.

Esthétique de l'interprétation créatrice—Essai sur l'idée "interprétation" de Gisèle Brelet. Shibaike, Masami.

Ethics and the Philosophy of Music Education. Richmond, John W.

Ethik der Endlichkeit: Zum Verweisungscharakter des Erhabenen bei Kant. Briese, Olaf.

Evaluating Edwin Gordon's Music Learning Theory from a Critical Thinking Perspective. Woodford, Paul G.

Evaluating Music. Levinson, Jerrold.

Everydayness, Aesthetics, Ontology: Notes on the Later Lukács (in Hungarian). Jung, Werner.

Exemplifikatorische Darstellung: Zu den Grundlagen einer kognitiven Ästhetik. Taube, Volkmar.

Existe ou Nao uma Estética no Século XVII?. Soeiro Chaimovich, Felipe.

Explanations of Everyday Life: Georg Lukács and Agnes Heller (in Hungarian). Rózsa, Erzsébet.

Fact, Fiction and Feeling. Hanfling, Oswald.

Faits et interprétations en musicologie. Nattiez, Jean-Jacques.

Fat, Felt and Fascism: The Case of Joseph Beuys. O'Leary, Timothy.

Feeling and Aesthetic Judgment: A Rejoinder to Tom Huhn. Matthews, Patricia M.

Fetishism and the Identity of Art. Farrelly-Jackson, Steven.

Fictional Characters: Dependent or Abstract? A Reply to Reicher's Objections. Thomasson, Amie L.

First Art and Art's Definition. Davies, Stephen.

Form and Theory: Meyer Schapiro's *Theory and Philosophy of Art.* Mattick, Paul.

Francis Sparshott, Poet. Anderson Silber, C and Macpherson, Jay.

Freedom of Expression at the National Endowment for the Arts: An Opportunity for Interdisciplinary Education. Van Camp, Julie.

From *The World is Beautiful* to *The Family of Man*: The Plight of Photography as a Modern Art. Seamon, Roger.

From Aesthetic Education to Environmental Aesthetics. Fischer, Norman.

From Work to Work. Livingston, Paisley.

Frühromantische Subjektkritik. Iber, Christian.

Für einen anderen Umgang mit Nietzsche. Riedel, Manfred.

Gadamer on Art, Morality, and Authority. Buckman, Kenneth L.

Georg Lukács and Lajos Fülep Dante (in Hungarian). Kaposi, Márton.

Georg Lukács's Plans for an Ethics (in Hungarian). Palcsó, Mária.

Georg Lukács—A Spiritual Portrait (in Hungarian). Stern, Laurent.

Gilda de Mello e Souza (in Portuguese). Prado Júnior, Bento.

Gli Affreschi nelle Celle del Dormitorio del Convento di San Marco: Devozione e Figurazione di Fra Angelico (in Japanese). Akari, Kitamura.

Goodman's Rejection of Resemblance. Files, Craig.

Guided Rapid Unconscious Reconfiguration in Poetry and Art. Seamon, Roger.

Harmony in Space: A Perspective on the Work of Rudolf Laban. Brooks, Lynn Matluck.

Harvesting the Cognitive Revolution: Reflections on *The Arts, Education, and Aesthetic Knowing.* Klempay DiBlasio, Margaret.

Hearing Musical Works in their Entirety. McAdoo, Nick.

Hegel and the End of Art. Markus, György.

Hölderlins Trennung von Fichte. Jürgensen, Sven.

Hume's Moral Sublime. Neill, Elizabeth.

Ideas estéticas en Platón. Romero R, María Margarita.

Il singolo kierkegaardiano: una sintesi in divenire. Fazio, Mariano.

In Defense of Hume and the Causal Theory of Taste. Mothersill, Mary.

In Which Henry James Strikes Bedrock. Berry, Ralph M.

Individual Style in Photographic Art. Warburton, Nigel.

Ingres au milieu de l'école davidienne. Shigeki, Abe.

Innovation and Conservatism in Performance Practice. Godlovitch, Stanley.

Instrumentalism and the Interpretation of Narrative. Savile, Anthony.

Interpreting Contextualities. Davies, Stephen.

Interpretive Pluralism and the Ontology of Art. Davies, David.

Introduction. Maynard, Patrick.

Ir à Opera e Gostar de lá Voltar! A Faculdade de Filosofia e as Licenciaturas em Ensino. Nuno Salgado Vaz, Carlos.

Irrationalität und kritisches Bewusstsein. Stamer, Gerhard.

Irrecoverable Intentions and Literary Interpretation. Rosebury, Brian.

Is Edwin Gordon's Learning Theory a Cognitive One?. Stokes, W Ann.

Is Literature Self-Referential?. Miller, Eric.

Is there a Paradox of Suspense? A Reply to Yanal. Gerrig, Richard J.

Joseph Margolis on Interpretation. Casey, Edward S.

Kafka's China and the Parable of Parables. Wood, Michael.

Kairos: Balance ou rasoir? La statue de Lysippe et l'épigramme de Poseidippos. Moutsopoulos, Evanghélos.

Kant sur la musique. Parret, Herman.

Kant without Sade. Sparshott, Francis.

Kant's Pre-Critical Aesthetics: Genesis of the Notions of "Taste" and Beauty (in French). Dumouchel, Daniel.

Kant's Sadism. Bencivenga, Ermanno.

Kierkegaard: Metaphor and the Musical Erotic. Grund, Cynthia M.

Kurosawa's Existential Masterpiece: A Meditation on the Meaning of Life. Gordon, Jeffrey.

L'esthétique et l'artistique. Rochlitz, Rainer.

L'esthétique musicale de Descartes et le cartésianisme. Van Wymeersch, Brigitte.

L'inconscio come finzione linguistica. Ugolini, Consuelo.

La amenaza latente del vagabundo en la literatura política del siglo XVI. Rivera García, Antonio.

La cohérence de la théorie esthétique de Moses Mendelssohn. Dumouchel, Daniel.

La literatura como juego. Palazón M, María Rosa.

La pérdida del carácter transcendental de la belleza en el *De pulchro* de Agostino Nifo. Fernández García, María Socorro.

La philosophie de l'art et les branches scientifiques y afférentes. Andrijauskas, Antanas.

Lamarque and Olsen on Literature and Truth. Rowe, M W.

Landscape and the Metaphysical Imagination. Hepburn, Ronald W.

Langer's Aesthetics of Poetry. Hart, Richard E.

Las parábolas ficinianas del bosque y el jardín en las *Stanze per la Giostra* de Angelo Poliziano. Manzi, Attilio.

Laughter, Freshness, and Titillation. Pfeifer, Karl.

Le concept d'heuristique dans la création de la forme esthétique: mimésis et liberté. Bruneau, Alain-Philippe.

Le sens du poétique: Approche phénoménologique. Roose, Marie-Clotilde.

Leadership as Aesthetic Process. Smith, Ralph A.

Leading Creatively: The Art of Making Sense. Palus, Charles J and Horth, David M.

Lermontov and the Omniscience of Narrators. Goldfarb, David A.

Listening to Music: Performances and Recordings. Gracyk, Theodore A.

Listening, Heeding, and Respecting the Ground at One's Feet: Knowledge and the Arts Across Cultures. O'Loughlin, Marjorie.

Literature and Life. Smith, David, Greco, Michael A and Deleuze, Gilles.

Lo sguardo di Blanchot e la musica di Orfeo: Visione e ascolto nell'ispirazione poetica. Carrera, Alessandro.

Maarten Doormans kwantitatieve argumenten voor vooruitgang in de kunst. Lokhorst, Gert-Jan C.

Maurice Merleau-Ponty and Rudolf Laban—An Interactive Appropriation of Parallels and Resonances. Connolly, Maureen and Lathrop, Anna.

## AESTHETICS

*Sagacious Reasoning: Henry Odera Oruka in Memoriam.* Graness, Anke (ed) and Kresse, Kai (ed).

A Theoretical Basis for Non-Western Art History Instruction. Chanda, Jacqueline.

African Philosophy and the African Crisis. Owolabi, Kolawole Aderemi.

African Philosophy in Comparison with Western Philosophy. Okafor, Fidelis U.

Afrikanische Kunst—Ein Drama kultureller Wiederentdeckung oder eine europäische Tragödie?. Behrens, Roger.

An African Savant: Henry Odera Oruka. Ochieng'-Odhiambo, F.

An Analysis of John Mbiti's Treatment of the Concept of Event in African Ontologies. Johnson, Clarence Sholé.

Black Athena and Africa's Contribution to Global Cultural History. Van Binsbergen, Wim.

Conscience, Morality and Social Acceptability in an African Culture. Ebijuwa, T.

From Savages and Barbarians to Primitives: Africa, Social Typologies, and History in Eighteenth-Century French Philosophy. Jacques, T Carlos.

Idiographic Theorizing and Ideal Types: Max Weber's Methodology of Social Science. Collin, Finn.

In Defense of Afro-Japanese Ethnophilosophy. Okafor, Fidelis U.

Interview with Professor Henry Odera Oruka. Kresse, Kai.

Interview with Professor Peter O. Bodunrin. Ganesh, Anke.

Just-So Stories about "Inner Cognitive Africa": Some Doubts about Sorensen's Evolutionary Epistemology of Thought Experiments. Maffie, James.

Le "Dépassement de la Philosophie": Réflexion sur le statut contemporain de la philosophie. Gueye, Sémou Pathé.

Politics of Discourse on Liberal Economic Reform: The Case of Africa. Jeong, Ho-Won.

Racism, *Black Athena*, and the Historiography of Ancient Philosophy. Flory, Dan.

Some Problems in the Writing of the History of African Philosophy. Ogbogbo, C B N.

The Notion of African Philosophy. Uduigwomen, Andrew F.

The Parochial Universalist Conception of 'Philosophy' and 'African Philosophy'. Ikuenobe, Polycarp.

The Special Political Responsibilities of African Philosophers. Imbo, Samuel Oluoch.

The Supreme God in African (Igbo) Religious Thought. Aja, Egbeke.

Wine-Farming, Heresy Trials and the 'Whole Personality': The Emergence of the Stellenbosch Philosophical Tradition, 1916-40. Nash, Andrew.

## AFRO-AMERICAN

"Afterword" in *The Liberation Debate: Rights at Issue,* Leahy, Michael (ed). Leahy, Michael.

"Black Liberation—Yes!" in *The Liberation Debate: Rights at Issue,* Michael (ed). Boxill, Bernard R.

"Blacks Don't Need Liberating" in *The Liberation Debate: Rights at Issue,* Leahy, Michael (ed). Levin, Michael.

"Cornel West as Pragmatist and Existentialist" in *Existence in Black: An Anthology of Black Existential Philosophy,* Gordon, Lewis R (ed). Johnson, Clarence Sholé.

"Existence, Identity, and Liberation" in *Existence in Black: An Anthology of Black Existential Philosophy,* Gordon, Lewis R (ed). Birt, Robert.

"Fragmentation, Race, and Gender: Building Solidarity in the Postmodern Era" in *Existence in Black: An Anthology of Black Existential Philosophy,* Gordon, Lewis R (ed). Huntington, Patricia J.

"On Violence in the Struggle for Liberation" in *Existence in Black: An Anthology of Black Existential Philosophy,* Gordon, Lewis R (ed). McGary, Howard.

"Return from the United States" in *Existence in Black: An Anthology of Black Existential Philosophy,* Gordon, Lewis R (ed). Sharpley-Whiting, T Denean (ed & trans) and Sartre, Jean-Paul.

"Self-Transformation in American Blacks: The Harlem Renaissance and Black Theology" in *Existence in Black: An Anthology of Black Existential Philosophy,* Gordon, Lewis R (ed). Morrison II, Roy D.

"Toni Morrison at the Movies: Theorizing Race Through *Imitation of Life* (for Barbara Siegel)" in *Existence in Black: An Anthology of Black Existential Philosophy,* Gordon, Lewis R (ed). Schwartz, Gary.

*African-American Perspectives and Philosophical Traditions.* Pittman, John P (ed).

*Existence in Black: An Anthology of Black Existential Philosophy.* Gordon, Lewis R (ed).

*Gender, I-deology Essays on Theory, Fiction and Film.* D'Arcy, Chantal Cornut-G (ed) and García Landa, José Angel (ed).

*Plessy V. Ferguson* in Libertarian Perspective. Tushnet, Mark.

*Powerless Fictions? Ethics, Cultural Critique, and American Fiction in the Age of Postmodernism.* Miguel-Alfonso, Ricardo (ed).

*The Liberation Debate: Rights at Issue.* Leahy, Michael (ed) and Cohn-Sherbok, Dan (ed).

*The Second Wave: A Reader in Feminist Theory.* Nicholson, Linda (ed).

*W.E.B. Du Bois on* Race and Culture. Grosholz, Emily (ed), Bell, Bernard W (ed) and Stewart, James B (ed).

American Political Culture, Prophetic Narration, and Toni Morrison's *Beloved.* Shulman, George.

An African American Looks at Death. Secundy, Marian Gray.

Bioethical Issues Confronting The African American Community. Calloway, Kelvin T.

Enduring Crises and Challenges of African-American Studies. Adeleke, Tunde.

Existential Phenomenology and the Problem of Race: A Critical Assessment of Lewis Gordon's *Bad Faith and Antiblack Racism.* Headley, Clevis R.

How It Feels to Be a Problem: Du Bois, Fanon, and the "Impossible Life" of the Black Intellectual. Posnock, Ross.

How We Got Over: The Moral Teachings of The African-American Church on Business Ethics. Trimiew, Darryl M and Greene, Michael.

Malcolm X and the Enigma of Martin Luther King, Jr.'s Nonviolence. Bove, Laurence.

Reexamining Dr. King and Malcolm X On Violence. Whitlock, Greg.

Religion and the New African American Intellectuals. Allen, Norm R.

Toward an Aesthetic of Black Musical Expression. Duran, Jane and Stewart, Earl.

## AFTERLIFE

*Immortality.* Edwards, Paul (ed).

One Short Sleep Past?. Herbert, Robert T.

## AGAMBEN, G

Homo sacer, di Giorgio Agamben. Grottanelli, Cristiano and Sini, Carlo.

## AGAPE

Aspiring to the Divine: Love and Grace. Mahoney, Timothy A.

## AGE

Allocating Healthcare By QALYs: The Relevance of Age. McKie, John, Kuhse, Helga and Richardson, Jeff.

## AGE OF REASON

*see* Enlightenment

## AGENCY

"Combining Agency and Obligation (Preliminary Version)" in *Deontic Logic, Agency and Normative Systems,* Brown, Mark A (ed). Horty, John F.

"From the Fundamental Legal Conceptions of Hohfeld to Legal Relations: Refining the Enrichment of Solely Deontic Legal Relations" in *Deontic Logic, Agency and Normative Systems,* Brown, Mark A (ed). Allen, Layman E.

"Some Reflections on Deleuze's Spinoza: Composition and Agency" in *Deleuze and Philosophy: The Difference Engineer,* Ansell Pearson, Keith (ed). Armstrong, Aurelia.

"The Logic of Normative Systems" in *Deontic Logic, Agency and Normative Systems,* Brown, Mark A (ed). Johanson, Arnold A.

"Wholeness in Manifoldness: Genealogical Methods and Conditions of Agency in Nietzsche and Foucault" in *Critical Studies: Ethics and the Subject,* Simms, Karl (ed). Phillips, Lisa.

*Deontic Logic, Agency and Normative Systems.* Brown, Mark A (ed) and Carmo, José (ed).

Agency. Simester, A P.

Agency and Obligation. Horty, John F.

Agency and the Imputation of Consequences in Kant's Ethics. Reath, Andrews.

Agent-Neutral Reasons: Are They for Everyone?. Postow, B C.

Eine Explikation des Begriffes der Zurechnung. Meixner, Uwe.

Ethical Community Without Communitarianism. Winfield, Richard Dien.

Getting Started: Beginnings in the Logic of Action. Segerberg, Krister.

Libertarian Choice. Goetz, Stewart.

Norm and End: A Kantian Theory of Action (in French). Joós, Jean-Ernest.

Noumenal Causality Reconsidered: Affection, Agency, and Meaning in Kant. Westphal, Kenneth H.

Rational Self-Interest and Fear of Death: An Argument for an Agency Theory in Hobbes' *Leviathan.* Von Eschenbach, Warren J.

Reason and Agency. Pink, Thomas.

Reification as Dependence of Extrinsic Information. Sensat, Julius.

Robert Adams and the Best Possible World. Thomas, Mark L.

Structure, Culture and Agency: Rejecting the Current Orthodoxy of Organisation Theory. Willmott, Robert.

Taking Hindrance Seriously. Beebee, Helen.

The Modal Logic of Discrepancy. Cross, Charles B.

Two Problems with Knowing the Future. Hunt, David P.

## AGENT

Accepting Agent Centred Norms: A Problem for Non-Cognitivists and a Suggestion for Solving It. Dreier, James.

An Agent Model Integrating Multiple Reasoning Mechanisms. Moulin, Bernard and Boury-Brisset, Anne-Claire.

Approximate Knowledge of Many Agents and Discovery Systems. Zytkow, Jan M.

Ascriptions of Responsibility. Oshana, Marina A L.

Behavioral Expression and Related Concepts. Berckmans, Paul R.

Decidability of *Stit* Theory with a Single Agent and *Refref* Equivalence. Xu, Ming.

Hume—Not a "Humean" about Motivation. Persson, Ingmar.

La seriedad de la ética. Del Barco, José Luis.

Le devenir, le moteur et l'argent dans la philosophie de la nature d'Aristote. Hubert, Bernard.

Reasoning about Action and Change. Prendinger, Helmut and Schurz, Gerhard.

**AGENT**
Reasoning about Information Change. Gerbrandy, Jelle and Groeneveld, Willem.
The Health Care Agent: Selected but Neglected. Lane, Arline and Dubler, Nancy Neveloff.
The Way of the Agent. Belnap, Nuel and Perloff, Michael.
Time and Modality in the Logic of Agency. Chellas, Brian F.

**AGENT INTELLECT**
Quelques réactions thomistes à la critique de l'intellect agent par Durand de Saint-Pourçain. Bonino, Serge-Thomas.

**AGGREGATION**
On the Completeness of First Degree Weakly Aggregative Modal Logics. Apostoli, Peter.

**AGING**
Plato, Prejudice, and the Mature-Age Student in Antiquity. Tarrant, Harold.

**AGNOSTICISM**
Consistency, Paraconsistency and Truth (Logic, the Whole Logic and Nothing but 'the' Logic). Da Costa, Newton C A and Bueno, Otavio.
Some Problems of Approach to Nagarjuna's Philosophy (in Serbo-Croatian). Djordjevic, Dejan.
The Sceptical Life. Weintraub, Ruth.

**AGREEMENT**
Play, Agreement and Consensus. DiTommaso, Tanya.
Political Concertation (Agreement) Among Social Actors: The Challenge of Venezuelan Democracy (Spanish). Bozo de Carmona, Ana Julia.

**AGRICULTURE**
Community Shared Agriculture. Fieldhouse, Paul.
Critics of Pesticides: Whistleblowing or Suppression of Dissent?. Martin, Brian.
Research, Extension, and User Partnerships: Models for Collaboration and Strategies for Change. Lacy, William B.

**AHIMSA**
*Mahatma Ghandi: Selected Political Writings*. Dalton, Dennis (ed.)
Gandhi's Qualified Acceptance of Violence. Richards, Jerald.

**AIDS**
AIDS, Confidentiality, and Ethical Models. Gorbett, Jason.
AIDS, Confidentiality, and Ethical Models: Appendix. Gorbett, Jason.
Ethical Issues in Research on Preventing HIV Infection among Injecting Drug Users. Des Jarlais, Don D, Gaist, Paul A and Friedman, Samuel R.
Ethics and Relationships in Laboratories and Research Communities. Weil, Vivian and Arzbaecher, Robert.
HIV Infection, Risk Taking, and the Duty to Treat. Smolkin, Doran.
Mandatory HIV Testing in Newborns: Not Yet, Maybe Never. Davis, Dena S.
Suicide and Advance Directives: One Doctor's Dilemma. Kane, Gregory C.
The Effect of Ethnicity on ICU Use and DNR Orders in Hospitalized AIDS Patients. Tulsky, James A.

**AIM**
*see also* Purpose
*Rationality* and *Human Dignity*—Confucius, Kant and Scheffler on the Ultimate Aim of Education. Park, Ynhui.

**AINSLIE, G**
What Can't We Do with Economics?: Some Comments on George Ainslie's Picoeconomics. De Sousa, Ronald B.

**AKAIKE, H**
Akaike Information Criterion, Curve-Fitting, and the Philosophical Problem of Simplicity. Kieseppä, I A.

**AKRASIA**
Addiction and Self-Control. Mele, Alfred R.
Aristotelian *Akrasia* and Psychoanalytic Regression. Stocker, Michael.
Aristotle and Others. Sharples, Bob.
Commentary on "Aristotelian *Akrasia* and Psychoanalytic Regression". Sturdee, P G.
Knowledge vs True Belief in the Socratic Psychology of Action. Penner, Terry.
Self-Knowledge, Akrasia, and Self-Criticism. Scott-Kakures, Dion.
Socratic Akratic Action. Mele, Alfred R.
The Nature of Motivation (and Why it Matters Less to Ethics than One Might Think). Noggle, Robert.
The Social and Political Sources of Akrasia. Rorty, Amélie Oksenberg.

**AL-FARABI**
Compassion for Wisdom: The Attitude of Some Medieval Arab Philosophers towards to Codification of Philosophy. Stroumsa, Sarah.

**AL-GHAZALI**
"No Necessary Connection": The Medieval Roots of the Occasionalist Roots of Hume. Nadler, Steven.
Al-Ghazali on Necessary Causality in *The Incoherence of the Philosophers*. Riker, Stephen.

**AL-MUQAMMAS**
Pascal's Wager and Al-Muqammas (in Hebrew). Harvey, Warren Z.

**AL-SHAHRASTANI**
L'apport avicennien à la cosmologie à la lumière de la critique d'al-Shahrastāni. Steigerwald, Diane.

**ALBERT THE GREAT**
Zur Rezeption des Aristotelischen Freundschaftsbegriffs in der Scholastik. McEvoy, James.

**ALBERT, D**
Modal Interpretations, Decoherence and Measurements. Bacciagaluppi, Guido and Hemmo, Meir.
On What Being a World Takes Away. Clifton, Robert.

**ALBERT, H**
Fichtes Wissenschaftslehre vor der aktuellen Diskussion um die Letztbegründung. Gerten, Michael.

**ALBINUS**
Alkinous: Explanation of Plato's Doctrines (in Hungarian). Somos, Róbert.

**ALCIBIADES**
An Overlooked Motive in Alcibiades' *Symposium* Speech. Scott, Gary Alan and Welton, William A.

**ALEXANDER OF APHRODISIAS**
"Ein drittes modallogisches Argument für den Determinismus: Alexander von Aphrodisias" in *Das weite Spektrum der analytischen Philosophie*, Lenzen, Wolfgang. Weidemann, Hermann.
*Alexander of Aphrodisias: On Aristotle's Meteorology 4*. Lewis, Eric (trans).
Alexander of Aphrodisias on Celestial Motions. Bodnár, István M.
Der Alexandrismus an den Universitäten im späten Mittelalter. Pluta, Olaf.

**ALEXANDER OF HALES**
Distinct Ideas and Perfect Solicitude: Alexander of Hales, Richard Rufus, and Odo Rigaldus. Wood, Rega.

**ALEXANDER, H**
"Can Reasons for Rationality be Redeemed?" in *Philosophy of Education (1996)*, Margonis, Frank (ed). Siegel, Harvey.

**ALEXY, R**
The Model of Procedural Ethics: Formalism and Argumentation in Law (Spanish). Carrión Wam, Roque.

**ALGEBRA**
*see also* Boolean Algebra, Post Algebra
"From the Algebra of Relations to the Logic of Quantifiers" in *Studies in the Logic of Charles Sanders Peirce*, Houser, Nathan (ed). Brady, Geraldine.
"Genuine Triads and Teridentity" in *Studies in the Logic of Charles Sanders Peirce*, Houser, Nathan (ed). Brunning, Jacqueline.
"Peirce between Logic and Mathematics" in *Studies in the Logic of Charles Sanders Peirce*, Houser, Nathan (ed). Grattan-Guinness, Ivor.
A Gentzen System for Conditional Logic. Guzmán, Fernando.
A Logic-Based Modelling of Prolog Resulation Sequences Including the Negation as Failure Rule. Jeavons, John S and Crossley, John N.
A Remark on the Maximal Extensions of the Relevant Logic *R*. Swirydowicz, Kazimierz.
A Syntactic Proof of a Conjecture of Andrzej Wronski. Kowalski, Tomasz.
Acerca de las contribuciones actuales de una didáctica de antaño: el caso de la serie de Taylor. Cantoral, Ricardo.
Algebra and Theory of Order-Deterministic Pomsets. Rensink, Arend.
An Algebraic Approach to Logics in Research Work of Helena Rasiowa and Cecylia Rauszer. Jankowski, Andrzej W.
An Elementary Proof of Chang's Completeness Theorem for the Infinite-Valued Calculus of Lukasiewicz. Cignoli, Roberto and Mundici, Daniele.
An Equational Axiomatization of Dynamic Negation and Relational Composition. Hollenberg, Marco.
An Essay on Resolution Logics. Stachniak, Zbigniew.
Automated Theorem Proving for Lukasiewicz Logics. Beavers, Gordon.
Axiomática y álgebra estructural en la obra de David Hilbert. Corry, Leo.
Axiomatization and Completeness of Uncountably Valued Approximation Logic. Rasiowa, Helena.
Brouwer-Zadeh Logic, Decidability and Bimodal Systems. Giuntini, Roberto.
Bruno de Finetti and the Logic of Conditional Events. Milne, Peter.
Canonicity for Intensional Logics without Iterative Axioms. Surendonk, Timothy J.
Characterizing Equivalential and Algebraizable Logics by the Leibniz Operator. Herrmann, Burghard.
Combining Algebraizable Logics. Jánossy, A, Kurucz, A and Eiben, A E.
Conceptions of Space—Time: Problems and Possible Solutions. Monk, Nicholas A M.
Constructive Canonicity in Non-Classical Logics. Ghilardi, Silvio and Meloni, Giancarlo.
Decidable and Undecidable Logics with a Binary Modality. Németi, István, Kurucz, Agnes and Sain, Ildikó (& others).
Decidable Varieties of Hoops. Burris, Stanley and Ferreirim, Isabel M A.
Definability of Directly Indecomposable Congruence Modular Algebras. Vaggione, Diego.
Display Logic and Gaggle Theory. Restall, Greg.
Dissezioni e intersezioni di regioni in A.N. Whitehead. Gerla, Giangiacomo and Tortora, Roberto.
Domain Representability of Metric Spaces. Blanck, Jens.
Duality for Lattice-Ordered Algebras and for Normal Algebraizable Logics. Hartonas, Chrysafis.
Dynamic Bracketing and Discourse Representation. Visser, Albert and Vermeulen, Kees.
Dynamic Interpretations of Constraint-Based Grammar Formalisms. Moss, Lawrence S and Johnson, David E.
Dynamic Relation Logic Is the Logic of DPL-Relations. Visser, Albert.

**AMBIVALENCE**
Reduktion und Ambivalenz: Zur Reflexionsstruktur von E. Lévinas' *Autrement qu'être*. Schällibaum, Urs.

**AMERICAN**
*see also* Latin American
"American Philosophy's Way around Modernism (and Postmodernism)" in *The Recovery of Philosophy in America: Essays in Honor of John Edwin Smith*, Kasulis, Thomas P (ed). Neville, Robert Cummings.
"Classical American Metaphysics: Retrospect and Prospect" in *Philosophy in Experience: American Philosophy in Transition*, Hart, Richard (ed). Corrington, Robert S.
"How Universal is Psychoanalysis? The Self in India, Japan, and the United States" in *Culture and Self*, Allen, Douglas (ed). Roland, Alan.
"No Limits" in *The American University: National Treasure or Endangered Species?*, Ehrenberg, Ronald G (ed). Bowen, William G.
"Philosophy in America: Recovery and Future Development" in *The Recovery of Philosophy in America: Essays in Honor of John Edwin Smith*, Kasulis, Thomas P (ed). Smith, John E.
"Reflections on Philosophic Recovery" in *The Recovery of Philosophy in America: Essays in Honor of John Edwin Smith*, Kasulis, Thomas P (ed). Neville, Robert Cummings.
"Return from the United States" in *Existence in Black: An Anthology of Black Existential Philosophy*, Gordon, Lewis R (ed). Sharpley-Whiting, T Denean (ed & trans) and Sartre, Jean-Paul.
"Speaking of Politics in the United States: Who Talks to Whom, Why, and Why Not" in *Political Dialogue: Theories and Practices*, Esquith, Stephen L (ed). Bennett, Stephen Earl, Fisher, Bonnie and Resnick, David.
"The American University: National Treasure or Endangered Species?" in *The American University: National Treasure or Endangered Species?*, Ehrenberg, Ronald G (ed). Rhodes, Frank H T.
"The Goldilocks Syndrome" in *The Recovery of Philosophy in America: Essays in Honor of John Edwin Smith*, Kasulis, Thomas P (ed). Sherburne, Donald W.
"The Influence of William James on American Culture" in *The Cambridge Companion to William James*, Putnam, Ruth Anna (ed). Posnock, Ross.
"The Spirit of Pragmatism and the Pragmatic Spirit" in *The Recovery of Philosophy in America: Essays in Honor of John Edwin Smith*, Kasulis, Thomas P (ed). Wu, Kuang-Ming.
"The Use and Abuse of Modernity: Postmodernism and the American Philosophic Tradition" in *Philosophy in Experience: American Philosophy in Transition*, Hart, Richard (ed). Ryder, John.
"Theft and Conversion: Two Augustinian Confessions" in *The Recovery of Philosophy in America: Essays in Honor of John Edwin Smith*, Kasulis, Thomas P (ed). Vaught, Carl G.
"Toting Technology: Taking It to the Streets" in *Existence in Black: An Anthology of Black Existential Philosophy*, Gordon, Lewis R (ed). Dixon, Bobby R.
*American Modern: The Path Not Taken*: Aesthetics, Metaphysics, and Intellectual History in Classic American Philosophy. Tejera, Victorino.
*Applied Social Sciences in the Plutocratic Era of the United States: Dialectics of the Concrete*. Schindler, Ronald Jeremiah.
*Basic Rights: Subsistence, Affluence, and U.S. Foreign Policy.* Shue, Henry.
*Freedom's Law: The Moral Reading of the American Constitution.* Dworkin, Ronald.
*Kenneth Macgowan and the Aesthetic Paradigm for the New Stagecraft in America.* Bloom, Thomas Alan.
*Language, Action, and Context: The Early History of Pragmatics in Europe and America, 1780-1930.* Nerlich, Brigitte and Clarke, David D.
*Legal Realism: American and Scandinavian.* Martin, Michael.
*Liberation Theologies, Postmodernity, and the Americas.* Batstone, David, Mendieta, Eduardo and Lorentzen, Lois Ann (& others).
*Philosophy in Experience: American Philosophy in Transition.* Hart, Richard E (ed) and Anderson, Douglas R (ed).
*Powerless Fictions? Ethics, Cultural Critique, and American Fiction in the Age of Postmodernism.* Miguel-Alfonso, Ricardo (ed).
*The American University: National Treasure or Endangered Species?*. Ehrenberg, Ronald G (ed).
*The Origins of Moral Theology in the United States: Three Different Approaches.* Curran, Charles E.
*The Recovery of Philosophy in America: Essays in Honor of John Edwin Smith.* Kasulis, Thomas P (ed) and Neville, Robert Cummings (ed).
*Twentieth-Century Philosophy.* Baird, Forrest E (ed) and Kaufmann, Walter.
A Historical Interpretation of Deceptive Experiments in American Psychology. Herrera, Christopher D.
A Longitudinal Examination of American Business Ethics: Clark's Scales Revisited. Harich, Katrin R and Curren, Mary T.
A Plaything in Their Hands: American Exceptionalism and the Failure of Socialism—A Reassessment. Kieve, Ronald A.
Aboriginal Right: A Conciliatory Concept. Morito, Bruce.
Academic Corruption. Kekes, John.
Alfred North Whitehead's Informal Philosophy of Education. Blasius, Ronald F.
American Ethnophobia, e.g., Irish-American, in Phenomenological Perspective. Embree, Lester.
American Political Culture, Prophetic Narration, and Toni Morrison's *Beloved*. Shulman, George.

An American Naturalist Account of Culture. Baeten, Elizabeth M.
An Ethical Approach to Lobbying Activities of Businesses in the United States. Keffer, Jane M and Hill, Ronald Paul.
An Examination of the Relationship Between Ethical Behavior, Espoused Ethical Values and Financial Performance in the U S Defense Industry: 1988-1992. Mayer-Sommer, Alan P and Roshwalb, Alan.
Baldwin, Cattell and the *Psychological Review*: A Collaboration and Its Discontents. Sokal, Michael M.
Catastrophic Thinking in the Modern World: Russia and America. Shlapentokh, Vladimir.
Centering Culture: Teaching for Critical Sexual Literacy using the Sexual Diversity Wheel. Sears, James T.
Children's Refusal of Gynecologic Examinations for Suspected Sexual Abuse. Muram, David, Aiken, Margaret M and Strong, Carson.
Classical American Pragmatism: The Other Naturalism. Rosenthal, Sandra B.
End-of-Life Care in the Netherlands and the United States: A Comparison of Values, Justifications, and Practices. Quill, Timothy E and Kimsma, Gerrit K.
Epistemic-Virtue Talk: The Reemergence of American Axiology?. Axtell, Guy.
Frederic Henry Hedge, H.A.P. Torrey, and the Early Reception of Leibniz in America. Mulvaney, Robert J.
Gearing Up, Crashing Loud: Should We Punish High-Flyers for Insolvency?. Kilpi, Jukka.
Hans Morgenthau's Realism and American Foreign Policy. Myers, Robert J.
Human Rights Education, Moral Education and Modernisation: The General Relevance of Some Latin American Experiences: A Conversation. Misgeld, Dieter and Magendzo, Abraham.
Instead of Leaders They Have Become Bankers of Men: Gramsci's Alternative to the U.S. Neoinstitutionalists' Theory of Trade-Union Bureaucratization. Devinatz, Victor G.
Japanese Death Factories and the American Cover-Up. Chen, Yuan-Fang.
Just Healthcare beyond Individualism: Challenges for North American Bioethics. Benatar, Solomon R.
Landmarks in Critical Thinking Series: Ennis on the Concept of Critical Thinking. Hoaglund, John.
Market Meditopia: A Glimpse at American Health Care in 2005. Churchill, Larry R.
National Goals for Education and *The Language of Education.* McCree, Herbert L and Bowyer, Carlton H.
Naturalism and Business Ethics: Inevitable Foes or Possible Allies?. Fort, Timothy L.
Politics, Politics, Politics. Garver, Newton.
Regendering the U.S. Abortion Debate. Jaggar, Alison.
Relating the Psychological Literature to the American Psychological Association Ethical Standards. Thompson, Anthony P.
Shifting Perspectives: Filial Morality Revisited. Li, Chenyang.
Standards Versus Struggle: The Failure of Public Housing and the Welfare-State Impulse. Husock, Howard.
Susanne K. Langer and American Philosophic Naturalism in the Twentieth Century. Dryden, Donald.
The American Naturalist Tradition. Hare, Peter H.
The Colonization of Subjectivity: The Privatized Curriculum and the Marketing of American Education in a Postmodern Era. Weil, Danny.
The Economic Attributes of Medical Care: Implications for Rationing Choices in the United States and United Kingdom. Banks, Dwayne A.
The Ethical Neutrality of Prospective Payments: Justice Issues. McDowell, Jean.
The Hermeneutical Turn in American Critical Theory, 1830-1860. Walhout, M D.
The Only Feasible Means: The Pentagon's Ambivalent Relationship with the Nuremberg Code. Moreno, Jonathan D.
The Significance of American Philosophical Naturalism. Romanell, Patrick.
The United States and the Genocide Convention: Leading Advocate and Leading Obstacle. Korey, William.
Universal Values, Behavioral Ethics and Entrepreneurship. Clarke, Ruth and Aram, John.
Untameable Singularity (Some Remarks on *Broken Hegemonies*). Granel, Gérard and Wolfe, Charles T (trans).
What Classical American Philosophers Missed: Jane Addams, Critical Pragmatism, and Cultural Feminism. Mahowald, Mary B.
Wisconsin Healthcare Ethics Committees. Shapiro, Robyn S, Klein, John P and Tym, Kristen A.
Women, the Family, and Society: Discussions in the Feminist Thought of the United States. Iulina, Nina S.
Yuri K. Melvil and American Pragmatism. Ryder, John.

**AMERICAN INDIAN**
*Defending Mother Earth: Native American Perspectives on Environmental Justice.* Weaver, Jace (ed).
*Making Mortal Choices: Three Exercises in Moral Casuistry.* Bedau, Hugo Adam.
Coyote Politics: Trickster Tales and Feminist Futures. Phelan, Shane.

**AMES, R**
Conversing with Straw Men While Ignoring Dictators: A Reply to Roger Ames. Donnelly, Jack.

**AMOR RUIBAL, A**
Vicente Munoz Delgado y Angel Amor Ruibal. Dafonte, César Raña.

## ANABAPTIST
On Being Ethical Without Moral Sadism: Two Readings of Augustine and the Beginnings of the Anabaptist Revolution. Heilke, Thomas.

## ANACHARSIS
*The Cynics: The Cynic Movement in Antiquity and Its Legacy.* Branham, R Bracht (ed) and Goulet-Cazé, Marie-Odile (ed).

## ANALOGY
"Su alcuni elementi del confronto di Otto Hintze con l'*Historismus*" in *Lo Storicismo e la Sua Storia: Temi, Problemi, Prospettive*, Cacciatore, Giuseppe (ed). Di Costanzo, Giuseppe.
A Strategy for the Acquisition of Problem-Solving Expertise in Humans: The Category-as-Analogy Approach. Alma, Carine V.
Analogy and Argument. McKay, Thomas J.
Analogy and Exchangeability in Predictive Inferences. Festa, Roberto.
Modelli filosofici e interpretazione quantistica. Rebaglia, Alberta.
Protesi, ovvero la metamorfosi. Marchis, Vittorio.
Teleology and the Product Analogy. Matthen, Mohan.

## ANALYSIS
*see also* Linguistic Analysis, Logical Analysis, Nonstandard Analysis
*Genese und Analyse.* Petrus, Klaus.
*Premises and Conclusions: Symbolic Logic for Legal Analysis.* Rodes, Robert E and Pospesel, Howard.
A Model-Theoretic Approach to Ordinal Analysis. Avigad, Jeremy and Sommer, Richard.
Analytical Marxism—An Ex-Paradigm? The Odyssey of G.A. Cohen. Roberts, Marcus.
Analyticity, Necessity, and the Epistemology of Semantics. Katz, Jerrold J.
Argument Management, Informal Logic and Critical Thinking. Blair, J Anthony.
Definability in Functional Analysis. Iovino, José.
Economies, Technology, and the Structure of Human Living. Sauer, James B.
Emotion and Feeling. Madell, Geoffrey and Ridley, Aaron.
Finkish Dispositions. Lewis, David.
Hilbert's Formalism and Arithmetization of Mathematics. Webb, Judson C.
Husserl's Phenomenology and Weyl's Predictivism. Da Silva, Jairo José.
Isolation and Unification: The Realist Analysis of Possible Worlds. Bricker, Phillip.
L'analyse cartésienne et la construction de l'ordre des raisons. Timmermans, Benoît.
Material Implication and General Indicative Conditionals. Barker, Stephen.
Metaphysics as the Empirical Study of the Interface between Language and Reality. Place, Ullin T.
Método analítico y transcendentalidad. Blasco, Josep L.
On the Proof-Theoretic Strength of Monotone Induction in Explicit Mathematics. Schlüter, Andreas, Glass, Thomas and Rathjen, Michael.
Systems of Explicit Mathematics with Non-Constructive Mu-Operator and Join. Glass, Thomas and Strahm, Thomas.
The Analysis of Possibility and the Possibility of Analysis. Divers, John.
The Analysis of Rights. Penner, J E.
Trust and the Collection, Selection, Analysis and Interpretation of Data: A Scientist's View. Bird, Stephanie J and Housman, David E.

## ANALYTIC
"Bradley, Russell and Analysis" in *Philosophy after F.H. Bradley*, Bradley, James (ed). Dwyer, Philip.
"Carnap and Wittgenstein's *Tractatus*" in *Early Analytic Philosophy*, Tait, William W (ed). Friedman, Michael.
"Hommage und Einleitung" in *Das weite Spektrum der analytischen Philosophie*, Lenzen, Wolfgang. Lenzen, Wolfgang.
*Analytic Theism, Hartshorne, and the Concept of God.* Dombrowski, Daniel A.
*Contemporary Analytic Philosophy.* Baillie, James.
*Das weite Spektrum der analytischen Philosophie.* Lenzen, Wolfgang.
*Early Analytic Philosophy.* Tait, William W (ed).
*Philosophy's Second Revolution: Early and Recent Analytic Philosophy.* Clarke, D S.
*Rethinking Identity and Metaphysics: On the Foundations of Analytic Philosophy.* Hill, Claire Ortiz.
Analytic Cell Decomposition and the Closure of *p*-ADIC Semianalytic Sets. Liu, Nianzheng.
Analytic Ideals. Solecki, Slawomir.
Analytic Philosophy in Greece. Virvidakis, Stelios.
Analytic Philosophy of Film: History, Issues, Prospects. Gaut, Berys.
Analytic Philosophy: What Is It and Why Should One Engage in It?. Follesdal, Dagfinn.
Analytische Religionsphilosophie: Zwischen Intersubjektivität und Esoterik. Runggaldier, Edmund.
Aspects of Analytic Deduction. Tzouvaras, Athanassios.
Frege on Meaning. Sluga, Hans.
Gottlob Frege and the Analytic-Synthetic Distinction within the framework of the Aristotelian Model of Science. De Jong, Willem R.
Introduction: On the Interface of Analytic and Process Philosophy. Shields, George W.
Kant's Theory of Geometrical Reasoning and the Analytic-Synthetic Distinction: On Hintikka's Interpretation of Kant's Philosophy of Mathematics. De Jong, Willem R.
La ciencia analítica en la primera mitad del siglo XIX: el teorema del valor intermedio. Alarcón, Jesús, Rigo, Mirela and Waldegg, Guillermina.

Meaning and Mattering. O'Brien, Wendell.
Mythology of the Given. Sosa, Ernest.
Razón y Lógica: La Tradición Analítica en Polonia. Kleszcz, Ryszard.
Sao os Problemas Filosóficos Tradicionais Confusoes Linguísticas ou Investigaçoes Legítimas Sobre as Coisas?. Junqueira Smith, Plínio.
The Relative Complexity of Analytic Tableaux and SL-Resolution. Vellino, André.
The Rise of Twentieth Century Analytic Philosophy. Hacker, P M S.
The Underdetermination/Indeterminacy Distinction and the Analytic/Synthetic Distinction. Moore, A W.
Was Russell an Analytical Philosopher?. Monk, Ray.
Why did Language Matter to Analytic Philosophy?. Skorupski, John.
Zum Stellenwert der *Grundlage* aus der Sicht von 1804: Eine Interpretation des Wechsels von analytisch-synthetischer und genetischer Methode in Kapitel 5 der *Grundlage*. Beeler-Port, Josef.

## ANALYTICITY
Analyse logique et analyticité; de Carnap à Gödel. Couture, Jocelyne.
Analyticity Reconsidered. Boghossian, Paul Artin.
Analyticity Regained?. Harman, Gilbert.
Internal Relations and Analyticity: Wittgenstein and Quine. Hymers, Michael.
Zur Analytizität der *Grundlegung*. Schönecker, Dieter.

## ANAPHORA
Believing in Language. Dwyer, Susan and Pietroski, Paul M.
E-Type Pronouns, DRT, Dynamic Semantics and the Quantifier/Variable-Binding Model. Barker, Stephen J.
On the Theory of Anaphor: Dynamic Predicate Logic vs. Game-Theoretical Semantics. Sandu, Gabriel.
Parametrized Sum Individuals for Plural Anaphora. Krifka, Manfred.
Quantifiers, Anaphora, and Intensionality. Dalrymple, Mary, Lamping, John and Pereira, Fernando (& others).
Sequence of Tense and Temporal De Re. Abusch, Dorit.

## ANARCHISM
An Idea of Total Freedom? (in Czech). Tomek, Václav.
Aristotle and the Ancient Roots of Anarchism. Keyt, David.
Moral Constraints and Justice in Distribution (in Czech). Nozick, Robert.

## ANARCHY
The Hermeneutics of Origin: Arché and the Anarchic in John Van Buren's *The Young Heidegger*. Bambach, Charles.

## ANATOMY
"Más allá de "El nacimiento de la clínica": La comprensión de la "Anatomía General" de Bichat desde la *Naturphilosophie* de Schelling" in *El inicio del Idealismo alemán*, Market, Oswaldo. Montiel, Luis.
Una lettera inedita del Carcavi al Magliabechi con un parere sul Redi. Guerrini, Luigi.

## ANCESTOR
Myths as Instructions from Ancestors: The Example of Oedipus. Steadman, Lyle B and Palmer, Craig T.

## ANCIENT
*see also* Greek, Roman
"Freedom of Choice and the Choice of Freedom on the Path to Democracy" in *The Ancients and the Moderns*, Lilly, Reginald (ed). Meier, Christian.
"Impact and Limits of the Idea of Progress in Antiquity" in *The Idea of Progress*, McLaughlin, Peter (ed). Burkert, Walter.
"Kierkegaard's Distinction between Modern and Ancient Scepticism" in *Scepticism in the History of Philosophy: A Pan-American Dialogue*, Popkin, Richard H (ed). Maia Neto, José R.
"Reducing Concern with Self: Parfit and the Ancient Buddhist Schools" in *Culture and Self*, Allen, Douglas (ed). Basu, Ananyo.
"Scepticism and the Limits of Charity" in *Scepticism in the History of Philosophy: A Pan-American Dialogue*, Popkin, Richard H (ed). De Olaso, Ezequiel.
*A History of Philosophy: Volume I.* Hough, Williston S (ed & trans) and Erdmann, Johann Eduard.
*Alexander of Aphrodisias: On Aristotle's Meteorology 4.* Lewis, Eric (trans).
*Ancient Philosophy, 2nd Edition.* Baird, Forrest E (ed) and Kaufmann, Walter.
*Aristotle: Introductory Readings.* Irwin, Terence H (trans) and Fine, Gail (trans).
*Defence of Socrates Euthyphro Crito.* Gallop, David (trans).
*Dialogues with Plato.* Benitez, Eugenio E (ed).
*Encyclopedia of Classical Philosophy.* Devereux, Daniel T (ed) and Mitsis, Phillip T (ed).
*Ensayos Aristotélicos.* Aspe A, Virginia, Llano, Carlos and Mier y Terán, Rocío.
*Parmenides' Lesson.* Sayre, Kenneth M.
*Plato's Parmenides.* Allen, R E (ed & trans).
*Plato's Sophist.* Rojcewicz, Richard (trans) and Schuwer, André (trans).
*Plato: Complete Works.* Cooper, John M (ed) and Hutchinson, D S (ed).
*Protagoras.* Taylor, C C W (trans).
*Simplicius: On Aristotle's Physics 2.* Fleet, Barrie (trans).
*Simplicius: On Aristotle's Physics 5.* Urmson, J O (trans).
*Stoics, Epicureans and Sceptics: An Introduction to Hellenistic Philosophy.* Sharples, R W.
*The Ancients and the Moderns.* Lilly, Reginald (ed).

## ANCIENT

*The Cynics: The Cynic Movement in Antiquity and Its Legacy.* Branham, R Bracht (ed) and Goulet-Cazé, Marie-Odile (ed).

*The Dialogues of Plato: Volume I.* Jowett, Benjamin.

*The Dialogues of Plato: Volume II.* Jowett, Benjamin.

*The Dialogues of Plato: Volume III.* Jowett, Benjamin.

*The Dialogues of Plato: Volume IV.* Jowett, Benjamin.

*The Dialogues of Plato: Volume V.* Jowett, Benjamin.

*The Plato Reader.* Chappell, Tim D J.

*The Question of "Eclecticism": Studies in Later Greek Philosophy.* Dillon, John M (ed) and Long, A A (ed).

*The Truth about Everything.* Stewart, Matthew.

*Thelema*: Hipólito de Roma y la filosofía del siglo II. Forteza Pujol, Bartomeu.

*Themistius: On Aristotle's On the Soul.* Todd, Robert B (trans).

*Tra Esperienza e Ragione: Hegel e il problema dell'inizio della storia della filosofia.* Biscuso, Massimiliano.

A Classicist's Approach to Rhetoric in Plato. Kirby, John T.

Ancient Chinese Aesthetics and its Modernity. Arnheim, Rudolf.

Aristotle and the Ancient Roots of Anarchism. Keyt, David.

Aristotle's Rules of Division in the *Topics*: The Relationship between Genus and Differentia in a Division. Falcon, Andrea.

Between Religion and Philosophy: The Function of Allegory in the Derveni Papyrus. Laks, André.

Bringing Ancient Philosophy of Life: Teaching Aristotelian and Stoic Theories of Responsibility. Sakezles, Priscilla K.

Causality and Demonstration: An Early Scholastic *Posterior Analytics* Commentary. Wood, Rega and Andrews, Robert.

El debate sobre la filosofía de la naturaleza y de la historia de Platón: el IV Symposium Platonicum. Lisi, Francisco L.

El momento *epíkairos* (*Kairós* "espontáneo", *kairós* negativo, *kairós* inducido, contra-kairós). Rossetti, Livio.

How (Not) to Exempt Platonic Forms from *Parmenides'* Third Man. Hunt, David P.

Il desiderio: precedenti storici e concettualizzazione platonica. Malo, Antonio.

Indian Philosophy in the First Millennium AD: Fact and Fiction. Krishna, Daya.

Interview with Martha Nussbaum. Keith, Heather and DeTar, Richard.

Malebranche y el *libertinage érudit*. Leocata, Francisco.

Mind and Madness in Greek Tragedy. Gill, Christopher.

Moses and the Thaumaturges: Philo's *De Vita Mosis* as a Rescue Operation. Remus, Harold.

Oikeiosis: la naturalización de lo moral en el estoicismo antiguo. Velayos Castelo, Carmen.

On the Prelude to the *Timaeus*, and the Atlantis-Story. Tejera, Victorino.

Parmedidean Allusions in *Republic* V. Crystal, Ian.

Plato on Conventionalism. Barney, Rachel.

Plato's First Dialogue. Tomin, Julius.

Racism, *Black Athena*, and the Historiography of Ancient Philosophy. Flory, Dan.

Schema in Plato's Definition of Imitation. Rabel, Robert J.

Socrates versus Plato: The Origins and Development of Socratic Thinking. Ross, George MacDonald.

The Emergence of Concepts of a Sentence in Ancient Greek and in Ancient Chinese Philosophy. Bosely, Richard.

The Impiety of Socrates. Burnyeat, M F.

The Unique Features of Hui Shi's Thought: A Comparative Study between Hui Shi and Other Pre-Qin Philosophers. Xu, Keqian.

Thumos and Thermopylae: Herodotus vii 238. Page, Carl.

Was Socrates Guilty as Charged? *Apology* 24c-28a. Steinberger, Peter J.

Women: The Unrecognized Teachers of the Platonic Socrates. Blair, Elena Duvergès.

## ANDERSON, A

Universal Concerns and Concrete Commitments: In Response to Anderson. Wheeler, David L.

## ANDERSSON, G

Braucht die Wissenschaft methodologische Regeln?. Wettersten, John.

## ANDROCENTRISM

"Androcentrism and Anthropocentrism: Parallels and Politics" in *Ecofeminism: Women, Culture, Nature*, Warren, Karen J (ed). Plumwood, Val.

Mendus on Philosophy and Pervasiveness. Landau, Iddo.

## ANDROGYNY

De Platón a Michael Jackson: Entresijos del imaginario andrógino. Jiménez, Jorge.

Psychological Androgyny: A Concept in Seach of Lesser Substance. Towards the Understanding of the Transformation of a Social Representation. Lorenzi-Cioldi, Fabio.

## ANESTHESIA

Choosing the Best: Against Paternalistic Practice Guidelines. Savulescu, Julian.

Practice Guidelines, Patient Interests, and Risky Procedures. Ross, Isobel A.

The Moral Art of Being a Good Doctor. MacIntosh, David.

## ANGELICO, B

Gli Affreschi nelle Celle del Dormitorio del Convento di San Marco: Devozione e Figurazione di Fra Angelico (in Japanese). Akari, Kitamura.

## ANGER

"Anger" in *On Jean-Luc Nancy: The Sense of Philosophy*, Sheppard, Darren (ed). Lingis, Alphonso.

"Do You Do Well to Be Angry?". Werpehowski, William.

Aristotle on How to Define a Psychological State. Wedin, Michael V.

Blameless, Constructive, and Political Anger. Swaine, Lucas A.

Reasons for Anger: A Response to Narayan and von Hirsch's Provocation Theory. Horder, Jeremy.

What is Involved in Forgiving?. Hughes, Paul M.

## ANIMAL

"Afterword" in *The Liberation Debate: Rights at Issue*, Leahy, Michael (ed). Leahy, Michael.

"In Defence of Speciesism" in *Human Lives: Critical Essays on Consequentialist Bioethics*, Oderberg, David S (ed). Chappell, Tim.

"Rational and Other Animals" in *Verstehen and Humane Understanding*, O'Hear, Anthony (ed). Haldane, John.

"The Moral Uniqueness of the Human Animal" in *Human Lives: Critical Essays on Consequentialist Bioethics*, Oderberg, David S (ed). Scarlett, Brian.

"Women-Animals-Machines: A Grammar for a Wittgensteinian Ecofeminism" in *Ecofeminism: Women, Culture, Nature*, Warren, Karen J (ed). Lee-Lampshire, Wendy.

*Animal Acts: Configuring the Human in Western History.* Ham, Jennifer (ed) and Senior, Matthew (ed).

*Babies and Beasts: The Argument from Marginal Cases.* Dombrowski, Daniel A.

*Brute Science: Dilemmas of Animal Experimentation.* Shanks, Niall and LaFollette, Hugh.

*Mens Sana in Corpore Sano?* Reflexoes sobre o Enigma do Corpo. Simao, Cristiana V.

*Metaphysical Animal: Divine and Human in Man.* Woznicki, Andrew Nicholas.

*The Human Animal: Personal Identity without Psychology.* Olson, Eric T.

*What Is a Person? An Ethical Exploration.* Walters, James W.

A Critical Assessment of Varner's Proposal for Consensus and Convergence in the Biomedical Research Debate. Clune, Alan C.

A Dialogue on Species-Specific Rights: Humans and Animals in Bioethics. Thomasma, David C and Loewy, Erich H.

A Utilitarian Argument for Vegetarianism. Dixon, Nicholas.

Against Strong Speciesism. Graft, Donald.

Animals, Morality and Robert Boyle. MacIntosh, J J.

Autonomy and the Orthodoxy of Human Superiority. Gruzalski, Bart K.

Can Animals Be Evil?: Kekes' Character-Morality, the Hard Reaction to Evil, and Animals. Rosenfeld, Robert.

Contemplating the Interests of Fish: The Angler's Challenge. De Leeuw, A Dionys.

Contracts with Animals: Lucretius, *De Rerum Natura*. Shelton, Jo-Ann.

Contractualism and Animals. Bernstein, Mark.

Deflationary Metaphysics and the Construction of Laboratory Mice. Sismondo, Sergio.

Discourse Ethics and Nature. Krebs, Angelika.

Do Animals Have Rights?. Cohen, Carl.

Donald Davidson, Descartes and How to Deny the Evident. Gosselin, M.

Ecological Motivations of Ethics and the Moral Critique of the Value Orientation of Society (in Czech). Hála, Vlastimil.

En el centro del labertino: la hybris y el Minotauro. Cifuentes Camacho, David.

Environmental Egalitarianism and 'Who do you Save?' Dilemmas. Michael, Mark A.

Ethical Decision Making About Animal Experiments. Orlans, F Barbara.

Ethical Limits to Domestication. Sandoe, Peter, Holtug, Nils and Simonsen, H B.

Ethics Education in Science and Engineering: The Case of Animal Research. Rowan, Andrew N.

Feminism and Utilitarian Arguments for Vegetarianism: A Note on Alex Wellington's "Feminist Positions on Vegetarianism". Dixon, Nicholas.

Feminist Positions on Vegetarianism: Arguments For and Against and Otherwise. Wellington, Alex.

Five Arguments for Vegetarianism. Stephens, William O.

Gender Differences in Attitudes Toward Animal Research. Eldridge, Jennifer J and Gluck, John P.

Harry F. Harlow and Animal Research: Reflection on the Ethical Paradox. Gluck, John P.

Human Beings Are Animals. Lee, Patrick.

Human Versus Nonhuman: Binary Opposition As an Ordering Principle of Western Human Thought. Sheets-Johnstone, Maxine.

Humane Education: A Paradigm for Ethical Problem Solving in Education. Bloom, Joyce.

I Rather Think I Am A Darwinian. Blackburn, Simon.

Legal Rights for Our Fellow Creatures. Favre, David.

Modes de proximités avec l'animal chez Montaigne. Pelosse, Valentin.

On Exploiting Inferiors. Sapontzis, Steve F.

Originary Pain: Animal Life Beyond the Pleasure Principle in Kant's *Anthropology*. Shapiro, Joel.

## AQUINA S

"Being on the Boundary: Aquinas' Metaphor for Subject and Psyche" in *Critical Studies: Ethics and the Subject,* Simms, Karl (ed). Quinn, Patrick.

"Prioridad del acto en la génesis de los hábitos operativos" in *Ensayos Aristotélicos,* Rivera, José Luis (ed). Mier y Terán, Rocío.

1277 Revisited: A New Interpretation of the Doctrinal Investigations of Thomas Aquinas and Giles of Rome. Thijssen, J M M H.

*Ex Possibili et Necessario*: A Re-Examination of Aquinas's Third Way. Kelly, Thomas A F.

*Medieval Philosophy, 2nd Edition.* Baird, Forrest E (ed) and Kaufmann, Walter.

*The Metaphysics of Theism: Aquinas's Natural Theology in Summa contra gentiles* I. Kretzmann, Norman.

*Verbum: Word and Idea in Aquinas Volume 2.* Crowe, Frederick E (ed) and Doran, Robert M (ed).

A Defense of Physicalism. Jensen, Steven J.

Actitudes proposicionales y conocimiento sensible en Tomás de Aquino. Tellkamp, Jörg Alejandro.

Amicitia Politica: Thomas Aquinas on Political Cohesion in Society (in Czech). Molnár, Péter.

Aquinas on Modal Propositions: Introduction, Text, and Translation. O'Grady, Paul.

Aquinas on Passions and Diminished Responsibility. Nisters, Thomas.

Aquinas's Account of Double Effect. Cavanaugh, Thomas A.

Aquinas's Doctrine of Moral Virtue and Its Significance for Theories of Facility. Mirkes, Renée.

Bishop Stephen Tempier and Thomas Aquinas: A Separate Process Against Aquinas?. Wippel, John F.

Bonaventure and the Arguments for the Impossibility of an Infinite Temporal Regression. Davis, Richard.

Cantona and Aquinas on Good and Evil. O'Neill, John.

Ciencia y docencia en Agustín y Tomás de Aquino: (Del maesto agustiniano al maestro tomista). Péréz-Estévez, Antonio.

Civil Disobedience in the Social Theory of Thomas Aquinas. Scholz, Sally J.

Clearing a 'Way' for Aquinas: How the Proof from Motion Concludes to God. Twetten, David B.

Conocimiento del alma después de la muerte: Presentación de la doctrina de Santo Tomás de Aquino expuesta en las *Quaestiones disputatae de veritate q. 19 a. 1. Rodrigo Ewart, Luis.

Del acto de ser a la acción moral. Ponferrada, Gustavo Eloy.

Dio fondamento ultimo della morale e del diritto. Pizzorni, Reginaldo M.

Divinity Must Live Within Herself: Nussbaum and Aquinas on Transcending the Human. McInerny, Daniel.

Duns Scotus on Eternity and Timelessness. Cross, Richard.

Durand et Durandellus sur les rapports de la foi et de la science. Donneaud, Henry.

El aristotelismo y el tomismo frente al egoísmo psicológico. Lukac de Stier, María L.

El concepto de *civitas* en la teoría política de Tomás de Aquino. Lorca, Andrés Martínez.

El deseo natural de ver a Dios en la *Summa contra Gentiles.* Cambiasso, Guillermo Jorge.

El pensamiento práctico: Consideraciones metodológicas a partir de Tomás de Aquino. Massini Correas, Carlos Ignacio.

El titular de la autoridad política en Santo Tomás y Rousseau. Quintas, Avelino M.

Ente ed essenza in un saggio giovanile di Tommaso d'Aquino. Giorgini, Claudio.

Eternal Knowledge of the Temporal in Aquinas. Shanley, Brian J.

Exceptionless Norms in Aristotle?: Thomas Aquinas and Twentieth-Century Interpreters of the *Nicomachean Ethics.* Kaczor, Christopher.

Feminismo y tercer milenio. Balmaseda Cinquina, María F.

Gli oggetti e i metodi delle scienze secondo S. Tommaso. Fiorentino, Fernando.

Heidegger and Aquinas on the Self as Substance. Baur, Michael.

Hervé de Nédellec et les questions ordinaires *De cognitione primi principii.* Conforti, Patrizia.

History of Philosophy: Historical and Rational Reconstruction. Kenny, Anthony.

Human is Generated by Human and Created by God. Farmer, Linda.

Il problema del 'Desiderium naturale videndi Deum' nell'ottica tomista della partecipazione secondo la prospettiva di Cornelio Fabro. Nardone, Marco.

Immortalidad e Intelección según Tomás de Aquino. Téllez Maqueo, David Ezequiel.

Individuation und Prädikation: Ein Überblick aus historisch-systematischer Sicht. Enders, Heinz Werner.

intellectus principiorum: De Tomás de Aquino a Leonardo Polo (y "vuelta"). Fernandez Burillo, Santiago.

Is Aquinas's Proof for the Indestructibility of the Soul Successful?. Cross, Richard.

Jean de Sterngassen et son commentaire des *Sentences.* Senner, Walter.

L'antithomisme de Thierry de Freiberg. Imbach, Ruedi.

L'image d'Albert le Grand et de Thomas d'Aquin chez Dante Alighieri. Ricklin, Thomas.

L'otrepassamento del trascendentale classico quale terza via della metafisica. Cavaciuti, Santino.

La causalidad material de los elementos en la generación de los cuerpos mixtos. Sacchi, Mario Enrique.

La concepción del espacio en la física de Santo Tomás de Aquino. Sacchi, Mario Enrique.

La conception maritainienne de l'intelligence humaine dans antimoderne. Allard, Jean-Louis.

La définition du droit naturel d'Ulpien: sa reprise par Thomas d'Aquin et son actualisation comme critique des droits de l'homme. Ponton, Lionel.

La esencia del hombre como disponer indisponible. Urabayen Pérez, Julia.

La maturità di coscienza alla luce di San Tommaso d'Aquino. Costa, Flavia.

La pérdida del carácter transcendental de la belleza en el *De pulchro* de Agostino Nifo. Fernández García, María Socorro.

La Persona y su naturaleza: Tomás de Aquino y Leonardo Polo. Lombo, José Angel.

Law and Rights in Saint Thomas (Spanish). Beuchot, Mauricio.

Law, Virtue, and Happiness in Aquinas's Moral Theory. Carl, Maria.

Le savoir théologique chez les premiers thomistes. Torrell, Jean-Pierre.

Les *Evidentiae contra Durandum* de Durandellus. Lanczkowski, Miroslaw and Wittwer, Roland.

Matter and the Unity of Being in the Philosophical Theology of Saint Thomas Aquinas. McAleer, Graham.

Neither Enemy nor Friend: Nature as Creation in the Theology of Saint Thomas Aquinas. Pope, Stephen J.

Notule sur le commentaire du *Liber de causis* de Siger de Brabant et ses rapports avec Thomas d'Aquin. Imbach, Ruedi.

Obediential Potency, Human Knowledge, and the Natural Desire for God. Long, Steven A.

Obligaciones humanas Apuntes para la formulación de una idea. Messuti, Ana.

On Ingardenian and Thomistic Conceptions of Being (in Polish). Wojtysiak, Jacek.

Pensiero e realtà nella gnoseologia di S. Tommaso D'Aquino. Ventura, Antonino.

Pressupostos Linguísticos do Conhecimento Ontológico da Identidade em Sao Tomás. Enes, José.

Quelques réactions thomistes à la critique de l'intellect agent par Durand de Saint-Pourçain. Bonino, Serge-Thomas.

Saint Thomas et le mystère de la création: une réponse aux interrogations de l'homme d'aujourd'hui. Philippe, Marie-Dominique.

Saint Thomas et le problème de la possibilité d'un univers créé éternel. De Lassus, Alain-Marie.

Santo Tomás de Aquino y la Medicina. Sacchi, Mario Enrique.

Significación contemporánea de las nociones de experiencia y derecho natural según Santo Tomás de Aquino. Martínez Barrera, Jorge.

St. Thomas and Pre-Conceptual Intellection. Dewan, Lawrence.

St. Thomas Aquinas and the Defense of Mendicant Poverty. Jones, John D.

St. Thomas, Lying and Venial Sin. Dewan, Lawrence.

Sul duplice fine del matrimonio secondo la dottrina tomista. Seidl, Horst.

The Five Ways and the Argument from Composition: A Reply to John Lamont. Côté, Antoine.

The Interdependence of Intellectual and Moral Virtue in Aquinas. Peterson, John.

The Interpretation of Aquinas's *Prima Secundae.* Doig, James C.

The Middle Way: Some Limitations of Human Intellectual Knowledge, According to Thomas Aquinas (in Portuguese). Do Nascimento, Carlos A Ribeiro.

The Order of Charity in Thomas Aquinas. Selner-Wright, Susan C.

The Problem of Language and Mental Representation in Aristotle and St. Thomas. O'Callaghan, John P.

The Real and the Rational: Aquinas's Synthesis. Peterson, John.

The Rectitude of Inclination. Ingham, Nicholas.

The Status of the *Dimensiones Interminatae* in the Thomasian Principle of Individuation. Morris, Nancy A.

The Three Species of Freedom and the Six Species of Will Acts. Pestana, Mark Stephen.

Theistic Arguments and the Crisis of Classical Foundationalism (in Dutch). Van Woudenberg, René.

Thomas Aquinas and the Problem of Nature in Physics II, I. Lang, Helen S.

Thomas de Sutton, ou la liberté controversée. Putallaz, François-Xavier.

Thomasian Natural Law and the Is-Ought Question. Rentto, Juha-Pekka.

Thomism and the Quantum Enigma. Wallace, William A.

Thomistes et antithomistes face à la question de l'infini créé. Solère, Jean-Luc.

Thomistic Natural Philosophy and the Scientific Revolution. Reitan, Eric A.

Transformaçao da Noçao de Beatitude em Descartes. Leopoldo e Silva, Franklin.

Tres tratados "Sobre el maestro": Agustín, Buenaventura, Tomás de Aquino. Perez Ruiz, Francisco.

Two Thomists on the Morality of a Jailbreak. Doyle, John P.

Verbe mental et noétique thomiste dans le *De verbo* d'Hervé de Nédellec. Trottmann, Christian.

What is the Science of the Soul? A Case Study in the Evolution of Late Medieval Natural Philosophy. Zupko, Jack.

Wie einer beschaffen ist, so erscheint ihm das Ziel: Die Rolle des moralischen Habitus bei der Beurteilung des Handlungsziels nach Thomas von Aquin. Darge, Rolf.

# ARISTOTLE

Paul Ricoeur's *Little Ethics* (in Polish). Drwiega, Marek.

Perplexity in Plato, Aristotle, and Tarski. Matthews, Gareth B.

Poiesis and Praxis in Aristotle's *Poetics*. Melissidis, N S.

Political Rights in Aristotle: A Response to Fred Miller, Jr., *Nature, Justice, and Rights in Aristotle's Politics*. Gill, David.

Postille. Del Vecchio, Dante.

Psicología de la libertad política en Aristóteles (comentario de *Política*, I, 4-7 y I, 13). Martínez Barrera, Jorge.

Ragione e retorica: *La mitologia bianca* di Jacques Derrida. Harrison, Bernard.

Reason as the Foundation of *Eudaimonia* in the *Nicomachean Ethics*. Hill, Susan.

Reclaiming Aristotle's *Rhetoric*. Moss, Jean Dietz.

Relational Models for the Modal Syllogistic. Thomason, S K.

Rex Aut Lex. Cohen, Jonathan.

Rights and Responsibilities: Aristotle's Virtues and a Libertarian Dilemma. Cox, L Hughes.

Saying What Aristotle Would Have Said. Tweedale, Martin M.

Self-Consciousness and the Tradition in Aristotle's Psychology. Russon, John Edward.

Self-Knowledge in Aristotle. Lewis, Frank A.

Sensibilidad y espiritualidad según Aristóteles. García Jaramillo, Miguel Alejandro.

Sobre el sentido común y la percepción: Algunas sugerencias acerca de la facultad sensitiva central. Posada, Jorge Mario.

Sujeto, propio y esencia: el fundamento de la distinción aristotélica de modos de predicar. Pérez de Laborda, Miguel.

The Ancient Greek Origins of the Western Debate on Animals. Sorabji, Richard.

The Demonstration by Refutation of the Principle of Non-Contradiction in Aristotle's *Metaphysics*, Book IV. De Praetere, Thomas.

The Doctrine of the Mean. Young, Charles M.

The Limited Unity of Virtue. Badhwar, Neera Kapur.

The Notion of Imagination in the Context of Aristotle's Practical Philosophy (in Serbo-Croatian). Jevremovic, Petar.

The Others In/Of Aristotle's *Poetics*. Fendt, Gene.

The Paradoxes of Thought and Being. Armour, Leslie.

The Problem of Language and Mental Representation in Aristotle and St. Thomas. O'Callaghan, John P.

The Role of Good Upbringing in Aristotle's *Ethics*. Vasiliou, Iakovos.

The Spread of Aristotle's Political Theory in China. Mi, Michael C.

The Structure of Aristotle's Ethical Theory: Is It Teleological or a Virtue Ethics?. Santas, Gerasimos.

The Tension between Aristotle's Theories and Uses of Metaphor. Marcos, Alfredo.

The Unity of the State: Plato, Aristotle and Proclus. Stalley, R F.

Thomas Aquinas and the Problem of Nature in Physics II, I. Lang, Helen S.

Topics and Investigations: Aristotle's *Physics* and *Metaphysics*. Lang, Helen S.

Trascendenza e trascendentalità in Kant. Masi, Giuseppe.

Two Books on the Elements of Physics (or One Movement) by *Proclus of Lykia* (in Hungarian). Geréby, György.

War Aristoteles ein Funktionalist? Überlegungen zum Leib-Seele-Problem. Perler, Dominik.

What is "the Mean Relative to Us" in Aristotle's *Ethics*. Brown, Lesley.

What is Moral Authority?. Louden, Robert B.

Zur Rezeption des Aristotelischen Freundschaftsbegriffs in der Scholastik. McEvoy, James.

# ARITHMETIC

"Der mathematische Hintergrund des Erweiterungsschrittes in Freges "Grundgesetzen der Arithmetik" in *Das weite Spektrum der analytischen Philosophie*, Lenzen, Wolfgang. Thiel, Christian.

"Introduction: Frege on the Foundations of Arithmetic and Geometry" in *Frege: Importance and Legacy*, Schirn, Matthias (ed). Schirn, Matthias.

"Peirce's Axiomatization of Arithmetic" in *Studies in the Logic of Charles Sanders Peirce*, Houser, Nathan (ed). Shields, Paul.

*The Philosophy of Mathematics*. Hart, W D.

A Constructive Game Semantics for the Language of Linear Logic. Japaridze, Giorgi.

A Model-Theoretic Approach to Ordinal Analysis. Avigad, Jeremy and Sommer, Richard.

Classical and Intuitionistic Models of Arithmetic. Wehmeier, Kai F.

Definition in Frege's *Foundations of Arithmetic*. Hunter, David A.

Elementary Realizability. Damnjanovic, Zlatan.

Extensional Realizability. Van Oosten, Jaap.

Finite Sets and Natural Numbers in Intuitionistic TT. Dzierzgowski, Daniel.

Formalizing Forcing Arguments in Subsystems of Second-Order Arithmetic. Avigad, Jeremy.

Fuzzy Logic and Arithmetical Hierarchy, II. Hájek, Petr.

Hilbert and Set Theory. Dreben, Burton and Kanamori, Akihiro.

Immanuel Kants Grundlegung der Arithmetik. Noske, Rainer.

Inconsistent Models of Arithmetic Part I: Finite Models. Priest, Graham.

Induction Rules, Reflection Principles, and Provably Recursive Functions. Beklemishev, Lev D.

Interpolation Theorems, Lower Bounds for Proof Systems, and Independence Results for Bounded Arithmetic. Krajicek, J.

Los fundamentos de la aritmética según Peano. Zubieta R, Francisco.

Minimal Complementation Below Uniform Upper Bounds for the Arithmetical Degrees. Kumabe, Masahiro.

Notes on Polynomially Bounded Arithmetic. Zambella, Domenico.

On Inconsistent Arithmetics: A Reply to Denyer. Priest, Graham.

Reflecting in Epistemic Arithmetic. Horsten, Leon.

Reflexiones en torno al origen de los números aritméticos. Avila del Palacio, Alfonso.

Strong Termination for the Epsilon Substitution Method. Mints, Grigori.

The Logic of Linear Tolerance. Dzhaparidze, Giorgie.

Undecidability and Intuitionistic Incompleteness. McCarty, D C.

# ARITHMETIZATION

Hilbert's Formalism and Arithmetization of Mathematics. Webb, Judson C.

# ARMOUR, L

Making God Go Away and Leave Us Alone. Maxwell, Vance.

# ARMS CONTROL

*Deterrence and the Crisis in Moral Theory: An Analysis of the Moral Literature on the Nuclear Arms Debate*. Palmer-Fernandez, Gabriel.

# ARMSTRONG, D

"A Conceptualist Ontology" in *Dispositions: A Debate*, Armstrong, D M. Place, U T.

"Dispositions as Intentional States" in *Dispositions: A Debate*, Armstrong, D M. Place, U T.

"Final Replies to Place and Armstrong" in *Dispositions: A Debate*, Armstrong, D M. Martin, C B.

"Place's and Armstrong's Views Compared and Contrasted" in *Dispositions: A Debate*, Armstrong, D M. Armstrong, D M.

"Properties and Dispositions" in *Dispositions: A Debate*, Armstrong, D M. Martin, C B.

"Replies to Armstrong and Place" in *Dispositions: A Debate*, Armstrong, D M. Martin, C B.

"Structural Properties: Categorical, Dispositional or Both?" in *Dispositions: A Debate*, Armstrong, D M. Place, U T.

An Argument against Armstrong's Analysis of the Resemblance of Universals. Pautz, Adam.

Armstrong on the Role of Laws in Counterfactual Supporting. Pages, Joan.

Shades of Consciousness. Girle, Roderic A.

# ARNAULD

"Arnauld versus Leibniz and Malebranche on the Limits of Theological Knowledge" in *Scepticism in the History of Philosophy: A Pan-American Dialogue*, Popkin, Richard H (ed). Sleigh, Jr, Robert.

Il Saggio sopra la Filosofia in genere di Lodovico Arnaldi: una traduzione settecentesca inedita del *Discursus praeliminaris* di Christian Wolff. Von Wille, Dagmar.

Leibniz, Middle Knowledge, and the Intricacies of World Design. Knebel, Sven K.

Sleigh's *Leibniz & Arnauld: A Commentary on their Correspondence* (New Haven: Yale University Press). Adams, Robert Merrihew.

# ARNOLD, M

Arnold's Aesthetics and 19th Century Croatian Philosophy of History (in Serbo-Croatian). Posavac, Zlatko.

# ARNSTINE, D

Teaching Democracy Democratically. Worsfold, Victor L.

# ARROW

Decidable and Undecidable Logics with a Binary Modality. Németi, István, Kurucz, Agnes and Sain, Ildikó (& others).

On the Brussels School's Arrow of Time in Quantum Theory. Karakostas, Vassilios.

Taming Logic. Marx, Maarten, Mikulás, Szabolcs and Németi, István.

The Three Arrows of Zeno. Harrison, Craig.

Time's Arrows Today: Recent Physical and Philosophical Work on the Direction of Time. Denbigh, Kenneth G.

# ART

see also Architecture, Ballet, Dance, Drama, Drawing, Painting, Poetry, Sculpture, Work of Art

"*Aesthetic Theory*'s Mimesis of Walter Benjamin" in *The Semblance of Subjectivity*, Huhn, Tom (ed). Nicholsen, Shierry Weber.

"Adorno's Notion of Natural Beauty: A Reconsideration" in *The Semblance of Subjectivity*, Huhn, Tom (ed). Paetzold, Heinz.

"Aesthetic Form Revisited: John Dewey's Metaphysics of Art" in *Philosophy in Experience: American Philosophy in Transition*, Hart, Richard (ed). Marsoobian, Armen T.

"Art is More Powerful Than Knowledge" (in Serbo-Croatian). Salaquarda, Jörg.

"Arte, Vita E Verità In Vladimir Jankélévitch" in *Soggetto E Verità: La questione dell'uomo nella filosofia contemporanea*, Fagiuoli, Ettore. Franzini, Elio.

"August Wilhelm Schlegel y sus lecciones de Jena sobre teoría del arte (1798)" in *El inicio del Idealismo alemán*, Market, Oswaldo. Pinilla Burgos, Ricardo.

"Benjamin, Adorno, Surrealism" in *The Semblance of Subjectivity*, Huhn, Tom (ed). Wolin, Richard.

"Beyond the Death of Art: Community and the Ecology of the Self" in *Philosophy in Experience: American Philosophy in Transition*, Hart, Richard (ed). Alexander, Thomas M.

## ART

"Concept, Image, Name: On Adorno's Utopia of Knowledge" in *The Semblance of Subjectivity*, Huhn, Tom (ed). Tiedemann, Rolf.

"Concerning the Central Idea of Adorno's Philosophy" in *The Semblance of Subjectivity*, Huhn, Tom (ed). Bubner, Rüdiger.

"Deleuze on J. M. W. Turner: Catastrophism in Philosophy?" in *Deleuze and Philosophy: The Difference Engineer*, Ansell Pearson, Keith (ed). Williams, James.

"Dhvani as a Pivot in Sanskrit Literary Aesthetics" in *East and West in Aesthetics*, Marchianò, Grazia (ed). Sukla, Ananta C.

"Form Should Not Be Tautological": Hegel and Adorno on Form (in Japanese). Kin'ya, Nishi.

"How Does a Building Mean?" in *East and West in Aesthetics*, Marchianò, Grazia (ed). Mitias, Michael H.

"Introduction" in *The Semblance of Subjectivity*, Huhn, Tom (ed). Zuidervaart, Lambert.

"La Pittura Come Linguaggio Indiretto Dell'Essere E Prosa Del Mondo" in *Soggetto E Verità: La questione dell'uomo nella filosofia contemporanea*, Fagiuoli, Ettore. Dalla Vigna, Pierre.

"Love's Truths" in *Love Analyzed*, Lamb, Roger E. Marshall, Graeme.

"Mountains of the Mind" in *East and West in Aesthetics*, Marchianò, Grazia (ed). Servomaa, Sonia.

"Philosophy and Art in Munich Around the Turn of the Century" in *In Itinere European Cities and the Birth of Modern Scientific Philosophy*, Poli, Roberto (ed). Schuhmann, Karl.

"Steps to a Comparative Evolutionary Aesthetics (China, India, Tibet and Europe)" in *East and West in Aesthetics*, Marchianò, Grazia (ed). Capriles, Elias.

"Temples of the Body and Temples of the Cosmos: Vision and Visualization in the Vesalian and Copernican Revolutions" in *Picturing Knowledge*, Baigrie, Brian S (ed). Kemp, Martin.

"The 'Transhistoricity' of the Structure of a Work of Art and the Process of Value Transmission in Culture" in *Epistemology and History*, Zeidler-Janiszewska, Anna (ed). Kostyrko, Teresa.

"The Avant-Garde and Contemporary Artistic Consciousness" in *Epistemology and History*, Zeidler-Janiszewska, Anna (ed). Dziamski, Grzegorz.

"The Didactic and the Elegant: Some Thoughts on Scientific and Technological Illustrations in the Middle Ages and Renaissance" in *Picturing Knowledge*, Baigrie, Brian S (ed). Hall, Bert S.

"The Flowers of the *Noh* and the Aesthetics of *Iki*" in *East and West in Aesthetics*, Marchianò, Grazia (ed). Marchianò, Grazia.

"The Night as Category One Angle of Comparative Study in Aesthetics" in *East and West in Aesthetics*, Marchianò, Grazia (ed). Imamichi, Tomonobu.

"The Perception of Science in Modernist and Postmodernist Artistic Practice" in *Epistemology and History*, Zeidler-Janiszewska, Anna (ed). Erjavec, Ales.

"The Problem of the Applicability of Humanistic Interpretation in the Light of Contemporary Artistic Practice" in *Epistemology and History*, Zeidler-Janiszewska, Anna (ed). Zeidler-Janiszewska, Anna.

"The Semantic Transformation of an Axiological Concept" in *East and West in Aesthetics*, Marchianò, Grazia (ed). Hashimoto, Noriko.

"Theses on the 20th Century Crisis of Art and Culture" in *Epistemology and History*, Zeidler-Janiszewska, Anna (ed). Morawski, Stefan.

"Why Rescue Semblance? Metaphysical Experience and the Possibility of Ethics" in *The Semblance of Subjectivity*, Huhn, Tom (ed). Bernstein, J M.

*Aesthetic Theory: Theodore W. Adorno*. Hullot-Kentor, Robert (ed & trans), Adorno, Gretel (ed) and Tiedemann, Rolf (ed).

*After the End of Art: Contemporary Art and the Pale of History*. Danto, Arthur C.

*Art and Its Messages: Meaning, Morality, and Society*. Davies, Stephen (ed).

*Art in the Social Order: The Making of the Modern Conception of Art*. Mortensen, Preben.

*Automatic Woman: The Representation of Woman in Surrealism*. Conley, Katharine.

*Beyond Interpretation: The Meaning of Hermeneutics for Philosophy*. Vattimo, Gianni and Webb, David (trans).

*Carlo Michelstaedter: il coraggio dell'impossibile*. Michelis, Angela.

*Contemporary Art and Its Philosophical Problems*. Stadler, Ingrid.

*Deleuze and Philosophy: The Difference Engineer*. Ansell Pearson, Keith (ed).

*Deshumanización del Arte?: (Arte y Escritura II)*. Molinuevo, José Luis (ed).

*East and West in Aesthetics*. Marchianò, Grazia (ed).

*Emancipation and Illusion: Rationality and Gender in Habermas's Theory of Modernity*. Fleming, Marie.

*Essays on the Nature of Art*. Deutsch, Eliot.

*Food for Thought: Philosophy and Food*. Telfer, Elizabeth.

*From Romanticism to Critical Theory: The Philosophy of German Literary Theory*. Bowie, Andrew.

*George Grant and the Subversion of Modernity: Art, Philosophy, Politics, Religion, and Education*. Davis, Arthur (ed).

*Human, All Too Human, I*. Handwerk, Gary (trans) and Nietzsche, Friedrich.

*Is There Truth in Art?*. Rapaport, Herman.

*Kant's Aesthetic Theory*. Kemal, Salim.

*Kitsch and Art*. Kulka, Tomas.

*Ludwig Wittgenstein: Half-Truths and One-and-a-Half-Truths*. Hintikka, Jaakko.

*Of Art and Wisdom: Plato's Understanding of Techne*. Roochnik, David.

*Phantom Formations: Aesthetic Ideology and the Bildungsroman*. Redfield, Marc.

*Philosophies of Arts: An Essay in Differences*. Kivy, Peter.

*Philosophy and the Arts: Seeing and Believing*. Harrison, Andrew.

*Philosophy Unmasked: A Skeptic's Critique*. Calhoun, Laurie.

*Picturing Knowledge: Historical and Philosophical Problems Concerning the Use of Art in Science*. Baigrie, Brian S (ed).

*Powerless Fictions? Ethics, Cultural Critique, and American Fiction in the Age of Postmodernism*. Miguel-Alfonso, Ricardo (ed).

*Practicing Philosophy: Pragmatism and the Philosophical Life*. Shusterman, Richard.

*Real Beauty*. Zemach, Eddy M.

*Signs of the Time*. Elias, Willem.

*The God Within: Kant, Schelling, and Historicity*. Burbidge, John W (ed) and Fackenheim, Emil L.

*The Lost Steps*. Polizzotti, Mark (trans) and Breton, André.

*The Semblance of Subjectivity*. Huhn, Tom (ed) and Zuidervaart, Lambert (ed).

*The Work of Art: Immanence and Transcendence*. Genette, Gérard and Goshgarian, G M (trans).

A Comprehensivist Theory of Art. Holt, Jason.

A Institucionalizaçao da Arte e o Esvaziamento da *Aisthesis*: Interpretaçao do Ponto de Vista de Mikel Dufrenne. Morais, Carlos Bizarro.

A Lack of Feeling in Kant: Response to Patricia M. Matthews. Huhn, Tom.

A Theory of Oriental Aesthetics: A Prolegomenon. Inada, Kenneth K.

Adorno and Heidegger on Art in the Modern World. Baur, Michael.

Advocacy, Therapy, and Pedagogy. MacKinnon, John E.

Aesthetic Antirealism. Young, James O.

Aesthetic Case Studies and Discipline-Based Art Education. Moore, Ronald.

Aestheticide: Architecture and the Death of Art. Bearn, Gordon C F.

Aestheticism As Seen in British Tiles in the 1870s and 80s (in Japanese). Yoshimura, Noriko.

Aesthetics vs. Ideology: The Case of Canon Formation. Rajagopalan, Kanavillil.

Afrikanische Kunst—Ein Drama kultureller Wiederentdeckung oder eine europäische Tragödie?. Behrens, Roger.

After Aesthetics: Heidegger and Benjamin on Art and Experience. Ziarek, Krzysztof.

An Epistemological Justification for Aesthetic Experience. Bergmann, Sheryle.

Ancient Chinese Aesthetics and its Modernity. Arnheim, Rudolf.

Aneinnander vorbei: Zum Horenstreit zwischen Fichte und Schiller. Wildenburg, Dorothea.

Appreciating Godlovitch. Carlson, Allen.

Architecture: The Confluence of Art, Technology, Politics and Nature. Wood, Robert E.

Arguing over Intentions. Livingston, Paisley.

Art and Aesthetics. Slater, Hartley.

Art and Aesthetics in Scandinavia. Sörbom, Göran.

Art and Anthropology. Sparshott, Francis.

Art and Philosophy in Plato's Dialogues. Irwin, Terence H.

Art as a Form of Negative Dialectics: 'Theory' in Adorno's *Aesthetic Theory*. Melaney, William D.

Art as Aesthetic Statement. Lind, Richard.

Art, Imagination, and the Cultivation of Morals. Kieran, Matthew.

Art, Value, and Philosophy. Levinson, Jerrold.

Art: Function or Procedure—Nature or Culture?. Dickie, George T.

Arte come rappresentazione del mondo. Figal, Günter.

Arte, lenguaje y metafísica en las estéticas de Hegel y Adorno. Gutiérrez, Edgardo.

Arts and Earning a Living. Packer, Arnold H.

Astrattezza e concretezza nella filosofia di Giovanni Gentile. Frigerio, Aldo.

Authentic Photographs. Warburton, Nigel.

Back to Basics: Film/Theory/Aesthetics. Knight, Deborah.

Baten van een formele verheldering. Doorman, Maarten.

Carlson on Appreciation. Godlovitch, Stanley.

Causes and Tastes: A Response. Shiner, Roger A.

Characterisation and Interpretation: The Importance of Drama in Plato's *Sophist*. Benitez, Eugenio E.

Concluding Observations. Smith, Ralph A.

Confession of a Weak Anti-Intentionalist: Exposing Myself. Wilson, W Kent.

Critical Perspectives on Early Twentieth-Century American Avant-Garde Composers. O'Grady, Terence J.

Dance and the Question of Fidelity. Cohen, Selma Jeanne.

Defining Art Responsibly. Young, James O.

Die Philosophie Nishidas als eine "Kunstlehre": Überlegungen zu Nishidas Beziehung zur Kunsttheorie Fiedlers (in Japanese). Tomohiro, Takanashi.

Een anatomie van de beeldende kunst. Herzog, Katalin.

El Greco's Statements on Michelangelo the Painter. Rodetis, George A.

Escaping Reality: Digital Imagery and the Resources of Photography. Savedoff, Barbara E.

Evaluating Music. Levinson, Jerrold.

## ART EDUCATION

Listening, Heeding, and Respecting the Ground at One's Feet: Knowledge and the Arts Across Cultures. O'Loughlin, Marjorie.

Preservice Art Education and Learning in Art Museums. Lauzier Stone, Denise.

The Evolution of Discipline-Based Art Education. Delacruz, Elizabeth Manley and Dunn, Phillip C.

Visual Aesthetic Education: Its Place in General Education. Ahmed, Halim Obeid.

## ART HISTORY

"Art History and Autonomy" in *The Semblance of Subjectivity,* Huhn, Tom (ed). Horowitz, Gregg M.

"Georg Wilhelm Friedrich Hegel and the East" in *East and West in Aesthetics,* Marchianò, Grazia (ed). Dethier, Hubert.

A Theoretical Basis for Non-Western Art History Instruction. Chanda, Jacqueline.

Art as Aesthetic Statement. Lind, Richard.

Fat, Felt and Fascism: The Case of Joseph Beuys. O'Leary, Timothy.

Meyer Shapiro's Essay on Style: Falling into the Void. Wallach, Alan.

Schapiro Style. Holly, Michael Ann.

## ART WORK

*see* Work Of Art

## ARTEAGA, E

Post-reflexiones arteaguianas: análisis de *La Belleza Ideal.* Pator Pérez, Miguel A.

## ARTIFACT

Four-Eighths Hephaistos: Artifacts and Living Things in Aristotle. Koslicki, Kathrin.

From Immanent Natures to Nature as Artifice: The Reinterpretation of Final Causes in Seventeenth-Century Natural Philosophy. Osler, Margaret J.

Philosophy...Artifacts...Friendship—and the History of the Gaze. Illich, Ivan.

The Constructivist's Dilemma. Stecker, Robert A.

## ARTIFICIAL

"Filosofi Artificiali" in *Soggetto E Verità: La questione dell'uomo nella filosofia contemporanea,* Fagiuoli, Ettore. Magnani, Lorenzo.

Darwin and the Inefficacy of Artificial Selection. Richards, Richard A.

## ARTIFICIAL INTELLIGENCE

"Argument Based Reasoning: Some Remarks on the Relation Between Argumentation Theory and Artificial Intelligence" in *Logic and Argumentation,* Van Eemeren, Frans H (ed). Starmans, Richard J C M.

"Die (sei's auch metaphorische) These vom Geist als Computer" in *Das weite Spektrum der analytischen Philosophie,* Lenzen, Wolfgang. Kemmerling, Andreas.

"Practical Reasoning in Oscar" in *AI, Connectionism and Philosophical Psychology, 1995,* Tomberlin, James E (ed). Pollock, John L.

*Mind Design II: Philosophy, Psychology, Artificial Intelligence.* Haugeland, John (ed).

*Philosophical Perspectives, 9, AI, Connectionism and Philosophical Psychology, 1995.* Tomberlin, James E (ed).

Artificial Intelligence Modeling of Spontaneous Self Learning: An Application of Dialectical Philosophy. Stokes, Karina.

Classic Paradoxes in the Context of Non-Monotonic Logic (in Spanish). Beck, Andreas.

Illuminating the Chinese Room. Dartnall, Terry.

Is Default Logic a Reinvention of Inductive-Statistical Reasoning?. Tan, Yao-Hua.

Letter of the Editor: On Knowledge Technology and its Relevance. Vandamme, F.

Reasoning about Change and Persistence: A Solution to the Frame Problem. Pollock, John L.

Rethinking Distributed Representation. Ramsey, William.

Searle's Abstract Argument Against Strong AI. Melnyk, Andrew.

Searle's Chinese Box: Debunking the Chinese Room Argument. Hauser, Larry.

Software Agents and Their Bodies. Kushmerick, Nicholas.

## ARTIST

*Human, All Too Human: A Book of Free Spirits.* Hollingdale, R J (trans) and Nietzsche, Friedrich.

Arguing over Intentions. Livingston, Paisley.

Artistry. Armstrong, John.

Reading Raphael: *The School of Athens* and Its Pre-Text. Most, Glenn W.

What Does Drawing My Hand Have to Do with Leadership? A Look at the Process of Leaders Becoming Artists. De Ciantis, Cheryl.

## ARTISTIC

L'esthétique et l'artistique. Rochlitz, Rainer.

## ARTS

*see also* Fine Art, Visual Art

"Prioridad del acto en la génesis de los hábitos operativos" in *Ensayos Aristotélicos,* Aspe, Virginia. Mier y Terán, Rocío.

Arte e ciência: Acordo e progresso. D'Orey, Carmo.

Freedom of Expression at the National Endowment for the Arts: An Opportunity for Interdisciplinary Education. Van Camp, Julie.

Listening, Heeding, and Respecting the Ground at One's Feet: Knowledge and the Arts Across Cultures. O'Loughlin, Marjorie.

O estatuto das humanidades o regresso às artes. Gonçalves, Joaquim Cerqueira.

Permanence and Renovation in Arts (in Portuguese). Kossovitch, Leon.

Two Concepts of Expression. Robinson, Jenefer.

## ARTWORK

*Artworks: Definition, Meaning, Value.* Stecker, Robert A.

A Comprehensivist Theory of Art. Holt, Jason.

## ASCETICISM

Sobre el concepto de "Racionalidad" en la ética protestante de Max Weber. Berián, Josetxo.

## ASCRIPTION

Self-Ascription, Self-Knowledge, and the Memory Argument. Goldberg, Sanford C.

## ASHBROOK, J

God is Great, God is Good: James Ashbrook's Contribution to Neuroethical Theology. Vaux, Kenneth.

## ASIAN

*see also* Oriental

"Fruchtbarer geistiger Gegensatz Südasien—Europa?" in *Kreativer Friede durch Begegnung der Weltkulturen,* Beck, Heinrich (ed). Beck, Heinrich.

"Social Constructions of Self: Some Asian, Marxist, and Feminist Critiques of Dominant Western Views of Self" in *Culture and Self,* Allen, Douglas (ed). Allen, Douglas.

"Steps to a Comparative Evolutionary Aesthetics (China, India, Tibet and Europe)" in *East and West in Aesthetics,* Marchianò, Grazia (ed). Capriles, Elias.

*Meeting of Minds: Intellectual and Religious Interaction in East Asian Traditions of Thought.* Bloom, Irene (ed) and Fogel, Joshua A (ed).

An East Asian Perspective of Mind-Body. Nagatomo, Shigenori and Leisman, Gerald.

Business Education, Values and Beliefs. Small, Michael W.

Confounding the Paradigm: Asian Americans and Race Preferences. Izumi, Lance T.

Die Wendung nach Asien: Heideggers Ansatz interkultureller Philosophie. Wolz-Gottwald, Eckard.

Ethics in Developing Economies of Asia. Takahashi, Akira.

Ideas of Nature in an Asian Context. Barnhart, Michael G.

The Putative Fascism of the Kyoto School and the Political Correctness of the Modern Academy. Parkes, Graham.

## ASPIRATION

"The Goldilocks Syndrome" in *The Recovery of Philosophy in America: Essays in Honor of John Edwin Smith,* Kasulis, Thomas P (ed). Sherburne, Donald W.

## ASSENT

"*Assent* chez les Platoniciens de Cambridge" in *Mind Senior to the World,* Baldi, Marialuisa. Vienne, Jean-Michel.

## ASSERTIBILITY

Anti-Realist Truth and Concepts of Superassertibility. Edwards, Jim.

## ASSERTION

Is Tennant Selling Truth Short?. Edwards, Jim.

Knowing and Asserting. Williamson, Timothy.

Knowledge, Assertion and Lotteries. DeRose, Keith.

Self-Quotation and Self-Knowledge. Jacobsen, Rockney.

What Assertion Is Not. Stainton, Robert J.

## ASSESSMENT

A Philosophy of Risk Assessment and the Law: A Case Study of the Role of Philosophy in Public Policy. Cranor, Carl F.

## ASSISTED SUICIDE

*Intending Death: The Ethics of Assisted Suicide and Euthanasia.* Beauchamp, Tom L (ed).

A Communitarian Approach to Physician-Assisted Death. Miller, Franklin G.

A Reply to Some Standard Objections to Euthanasia. Shand, John.

Assisted Suicide: Will the Supreme Court Respect the Autonomy Rights of Dying Patients?. Lindsay, Ronald A.

Levinas and the Hippocratic Oath: A Discussion of Physician-Assisted Suicide. Degnin, Francis.

Physician-Assisted Suicide in Psychiatry: Developments in the Netherlands. Gevers, J K M and Legemaate, Johan.

Physician-Assisted Suicide: A Different Approach. Emanuel, Linda L.

Physician-Assisted Suicide: The Role of Mental Health Professionals. Peruzzi, Nico, Canapary, Andrew and Bongar, Bruce.

The Kevorkian Challenge. Picchioni, Anthony.

The Last Chapter of the Book: Who Is the Author? Christian Reflections on Assisted Suicide. Childs, Brian H.

## ASSOCIATION

"The Korporation in Hegel's Interpretation of Civil Society" in *Hegel, History, and Interpretation,* Gallagher, Shaun. Prosch, Michael.

Enforcing Ethical Standards of Professional Associations. Loevinger, Lee.

On the Properties of a Network that Associates Concepts on Basis of Share of Components and Its Relation with the Conceptual Memory of the Right Hemisphere. Van Loocke, Philip.

Predicative Laws of Association in Statistics and Physics. Costantini, D and Garibaldi, U.

## ASSOCIATIONISM

"Bradley's Attack on Associationism" in *Philosophy after F.H. Bradley,* Bradley, James (ed). Ferreira, Phillip.

## BEAUTY

Die Philosophie Nishidas als eine "Kunstlehre": Überlegungen zu Nishidas Beziehung zur Kunsttheorie Fiedlers (in Japanese). Tomohiro, Takanashi.

From *The World is Beautiful* to *The Family of Man*: The Plight of Photography as a Modern Art. Seamon, Roger.

Genealogia di un sentire inorganico: Mario Perniola. Fimiani, Mariapaola.

Ideas estéticas en Platón. Romero R, María Margarita.

Kant's Pre-Critical Aesthetics: Genesis of the Notions of "Taste" and Beauty (in French). Dumouchel, Daniel.

La cohérence de la théorie esthétique de Moses Mendelssohn. Dumouchel, Daniel.

La pérdida del carácter transcendental de la belleza en el *De pulchro* de Agostino Nifo. Fernández García, María Socorro.

Negative Capability Reclaimed: Literature and Philosophy *Contra* Politics. Hassan, Ihab.

Pictures and Beauty. Hopkins, Robert.

Platao, o Amor e a Retórica. Trindade Santos, José.

Post-reflexiones arteaguianas: análisis de *La Belleza Ideal*. Pator Pérez, Miguel A.

Pre-Established Harmony and Other Comic Strategies. Sesonske, Alexander.

Realism and Anti-Realism: A Whiteheadian Response to Richard Rorty Concerning Truth, Propositions, and Practice. Nancarrow, Paul S.

San Agustín: la interioridad bella. Uña Juárez, Agustín.

Schoonheid buiten proportie: Burkes afrekening met een klassiek ideaal. Van Der Schoot, Albert.

Spinoza's Relativistic Aesthetics. Rice, Lee C.

Spirit and Beauty. Lee, Young Sook.

Swift Things Are Beautiful: Contrast in the Natural Aesthetic. Kupfer, Joseph H.

The Concepts of the Sublime and the Beautiful in Kant and Lyotard. Klinger, Cornelia.

The End of Aesthetic Experience. Shusterman, Richard.

The Influence of Chinese Philosophy on the English Style Garden: A Comparative Study of Wörlitz and Koishikawa Korakuen (in Japanese). Seiko, Goto.

The Metaphysics of Poetry: Subverting the "Ancient Quarrel" and Recasting the Problem. Swanger, David.

The Phenomenology of Mathematical Beauty. Rota, Gian-Carlo.

The Reflection of Some Traditional Stoic Ideas in the Thirteenth-Century Scholastic Theories of Beauty. Bychkov, Oleg V.

There Ought to be a Law. Harrell, Jean G.

Thomas Mann e A Montanha Mágica. Joao Correia, Carlos.

Understanding of Beauty and Incarnation in Quest: The Problem of Aesthetics in Plato's *Phaedrus* (in Japanese). Yutaka, Isshiki.

## BECHLER, Z

"Jaako Hintikka Replies" in *Knowledge and Inquiry: Essays on Jaakko Hintikka's Epistemology and Philosophy of Science*, Sintonen, Matti (ed). Hintikka, Jaakko.

## BECK

Kant e Beck face ao problema da "coisa-em-si". Alves, Pedro M S.

## BECKER, O

El finitismo metamatemático de Hilbert y la crítica de Oskar Becker. Roetti, Jorge Alfredo.

Ontologie der Mathematik im Anschluss an Oskar Becker. Poser, Hans.

## BECKETT

*The Temptations of Emile Cioran*. Kluback, William and Finkenthal, Michael.

Characterization in Samuel Beckett's *Not I*. Daisuke, Hirakawa.

## BECOMING

"At the Mountains of Madness: The Demonology of the New Earth and the Politics of Becoming" in *Deleuze and Philosophy: The Difference Engineer*, Ansell Pearson, Keith (ed). Grant, Iain Hamilton.

Being—An Approach to the Beginning of Hegel's *Wissenschaft der Logik* (in German). Von Sivers, Kathrin.

Enigma e relazione: Da Apollo a Edipo. Lo Bue, Elisabetta.

Il singolo kierkegaardiano: una sintesi in divenire. Fazio, Mariano.

L'essere, il nulla e il divenire: Riprendendo le fila di una grande polemica. Turoldo, Fabrizio.

Le devenir, le moteur et l'argent dans la philosophie de la nature d'Aristote. Hubert, Bernard.

Meta(l)morphoses. Braidotti, Rosi.

The Direction of Time. Savitt, Steven F.

## BEERBOHM, M

Contractual Justice: A Modest Defence. Barry, Brian.

## BEGGING THE QUESTION

Sorensen on begging the Question. Yujen Teng, Norman.

The One Fallacy Theory. Powers, Lawrence H.

## BEGINNING

Hegel's Understanding of the Beginning (in Serbo-Croatian). Djuric, Drago.

Nietzsche and the New Beginning (in Serbo-Croatian). Bosto, Sulejman.

Of the *Chora*. Sallis, John.

St. Bonaventure and the Demonstrability of a Temporal Beginning: A Reply to Richard Davis. Baldner, Steven.

## BEHAVIOR

"Law and Order in Psychology" in *AI, Connectionism and Philosophical Psychology, 1995*, Tomberlin, James E (ed). Antony, Louise M.

"Plus Ratio Quam Vis" in *The Idea of University*, Brzezinski, Jerzy (ed). Szaniawski, Klemens.

"The Economic Approach to Homosexuality" in *Sex, Preference, and Family: Essays on Law and Nature*, Nussbaum, Martha C (ed). Posner, Richard A.

*Ethics and Justice in Organisations: A Normative-Empirical Dialogue*. Singer, M.

*Interpreting Minds: The Evolution of a Practice*. Bogdan, Radu J.

*Order in the Twilight*. Waldenfels, Bernhard and Parent, David J (trans).

A Manual on Manners and Courtesies for the Shared Care of Patients. Stoekle, John D, Ronan, Laurence J and Emanuel, Linda L (& others).

A Patterned Process Approach To Brain, Consciousness, and Behavior. Díaz, José-Luis.

Accidental Associations, Local Potency, and a Dilemma for Dretske. Noordhof, Paul.

An Agent Model Integrating Multiple Reasoning Mechanisms. Moulin, Bernard and Boury-Brisset, Anne-Claire.

An Examination of the Relationship Between Ethical Behavior, Espoused Ethical Values and Financial Performance in the U S Defense Industry: 1988-1992. Mayer-Sommer, Alan P and Roshwalb, Alan.

An Historical Preface to Engineering Ethics. Davis, Michael.

An Overlooked Motive in Alcibiades' *Symposium* Speech. Scott, Gary Alan and Welton, William A.

Behavioral Expression and Related Concepts. Berckmans, Paul R.

Behavioral Systems Interpreted as Autonomous Agents and as Coupled Dynamical Systems: A Criticism. Keijzer, Fred A and Bem, Sacha.

Belief and Consciousness. Worley, Sara.

Breaking the Rules When Others Do. Holley, David M.

Can Phronesis Save the Life of Medical Ethics?. Beresford, Eric B.

Cerebral Hemispheres. Davis, Lawrence H.

Commentary on "A Discursive Account of Multiple Personality Disorder". Braude, Stephen E.

Correlation of Gender-Related Values of Independence and Relationship and Leadership Orientation. Butz, Clarence E and Lewis, Phillip V.

Courage Alone. Putnam, Daniel.

Cyberethics and Social Stability. Hauptman, Robert.

Cynthia Macdonald and Graham Macdonald (eds), *Connectionism: Debates on Psychological Explanation, Volume Two*. Mills, Stephen.

Do Explanatory Desire Attributions Generate Opaque Contexts?. Reshotko, Naomi.

Dynamical Systems in Development: Review Essay of Linda V. Smith and Esther Thelen (Eds) *A Dynamics Systems Approach to Development: Applications*. Hooker, Cliff A.

Effectiveness of Research Guidelines in Prevention of Scientific Misconduct. Shore, Eleanor G.

Ethical Attitudes and Behavior of Investment Professionals in the United Kingdom. Baker, H Kent and Veit, E Theodore.

Ethical Behavior in Retail Settings: Is There a Generation Gap?. Strutton, David, Pelton, Lou E and Ferrell, O C.

Ethical Beliefs and Management Behaviour: A Cross-Cultural Comparison. Jackson, Terence and Calafell Artola, Marian.

Ethics and the Internet: Appropriate Behavior in Electronic Communication. Langford, Duncan.

Evaluating Outcomes in Ethics Consultation Research. Fox, Ellen and Arnold, Robert M.

Formal Organizations: A Philosophical Review of Perspectives and Behaviour Dynamics. Johnnie, Palmer B.

Fred Dretske on the Explanatory Role of Semantic Content. Hassrick, Beth.

Genes and Human Behavior: The Emerging Paradigm. Drew, Allan P.

Guidelines for Training in the Ethical Conduct of Scientific Research. Garte, Seymour J.

How Are Scientific Corrections Made?. Kiang, Nelson Yuan-sheng.

In Defense of Shame: Shame in the Context of Guilt and Embarrassment. Sabini, John and Silver, Maury.

Kinesthetic-Visual Matching and the Self-Concept as Explanations of Mirror-Self-Recognition. Mitchell, Robert W.

Language as Emerging from Instinctive Behaviour. Rhees, Rush and Phillips, D E (ed).

Methodological Individualism in Proper Perspective. Jones, Todd.

Modeling Ethical Attitudes and Behaviors under Conditions of Environmental Turbulence: The Case of South Africa. Morris, Michael H, Marks, Amy S and Allen, Jeffrey A.

Moral Climate and the Development of Moral Reasoning: The Effects of Dyadic Discussions between Young Offenders. Taylor, John H and Walker, Lawrence J.

Neighbors in Death. Crowell, Steven Galt.

Overriding the Natural Ought. Sullivan, Philip R.

Parafraud in Biology. Hillman, Harold.

Praktik: Überlegungen zu Fragen der Handlungstheorie. Angstl, Helmut.

Preventing Harm and Promoting Ethical Discourse in the Helping Professions: Conceptual, Research, Analytical, and Action Frameworks. Prilleltensky, Isaac, Rossiter, Amy and Walsh-Bowers, Richard.

Relationship Between Machiavellianism and Type A Personality and Ethical-Orientation. Rayburn, J Michael and Rayburn, L Gayle.

Reply to Kovach. McGrath, Matthew.

Some Remarks on the Concept of Toleration. Garzón Valdés, Ernesto.

Spirituality, Belief, and Action. Reese, Hayne W.

**BELIEF**

The Relevance of Logic to Reasoning and Belief Revision: Harman on 'Change in View'. Knorpp Jr, William Max.

The Transparency of Truth. Kalderon, Mark Eli.

Theological Necessity. Schlesinger, George N.

Tidman On Critical Reflection. Steup, Matthias.

Trust-Relationships and the Moral Case for Religious Belief. Wynn, Mark.

Two Notions of Epistemic Validity: Epistemic Models for Ramsey's Conditionals. Costa, Horacio A and Levi, Isaac.

Two Notions of Warrant and Plantinga's Solution to the Gettier Problem. Greene, Richard and Balmert, N.A..

Understanding, Justification and the A Priori. Hunter, David A.

Virtue as Knowledge: Objections from the Philosophy of Mind. Little, Margaret Olivia.

Warrant and Accidentally True Belief. Plantinga, Alvin.

What do Belief Ascribers Really Mean? A Reply to Stephen Schiffer. Reimer, Marga.

What is Relative Confirmation?. Christensen, David.

What Use Is Empirical Confirmation?. Miller, David.

When to Believe in Miracles. Clarke, Steve.

Why Strong Sociologists Abhor a Vacuum: Shapin and Schaffer on the Boyle/Hobbes Controversy. Norris, Christopher.

**BELL, J**

J. v. Neumanns und J.S. Bells Theorem: Ein Vergleich. Scheibe, Erhard.

Review Essay: Bohmian Mechanics and the Quantum Revolution. Goldstein, Sheldon.

Some Derivations of Bell's Inequality. Hansen, Kaj Borge.

**BELLO**

"Una polemica storiografica nel Cile del XIX secolo: Bello, Lastarria, Chacón" in *Lo Storicismo e la Sua Storia: Temi, Problemi, Prospettive,* Cacciatore, Giuseppe (ed). Scocozza, Antonio.

**BELNAP, N**

What's in a Function?. Antonelli, Gian Aldo.

**BENDER, J**

Causes and Tastes: A Response. Shiner, Roger A.

**BENEFICENCE**

A Relatively Plausible Principle of Beneficence: Reply to Mulgan. Murphy, Liam B.

**BENEFIT**

Choosing the Best: Against Paternalistic Practice Guidelines. Savulescu, Julian.

Ethical Aspects of the University-Industry Interface. Spier, Raymond.

Goals of Ethics Consultation: Toward Clarity, Utility, and Fidelity. Andre, Judith.

Max Weber on Ethics Case Consultation: A Methodological Critique of the Conference on Evaluation of Ethics Consultation. Degnin, Francis.

Practice Guidelines, Patient Interests, and Risky Procedures. Ross, Isobel A.

Reducing Suffering and Ensuring Beneficial Outcomes for Neonates: An Ethical Perspective. Brodeur, Dennis.

Single Payers and Multiple Lists: Must Everyone Get the Same Coverage in a Universal Health Plan?. Veatch, Robert M.

Treating the Patient to Benefit Others. Klepper, Howard.

What is the Good of Health Care?. Harris, John.

Who Benefits? Music Education and the National Standards. Schmidt, Catherine M.

**BENEVOLENCE**

*Against Liberalism.* Kekes, John.

Augustine's Hermeneutics and the Principle of Charity. Glidden, David.

Two Conceptions of Benevolence. Mulgan, Tim.

**BENHABIB, S**

"Ethik und Geschlechterdifferenz" in *Angewandte Ethik: Die Bereichsethiken und ihre theoretische Fundierung,* Nida-Rümelin, Julian (ed). Pauer-Studer, Herlinde.

Asymmetrical Reciprocity: On Moral Respect, Wonder, and Enlarged Thought. Young, Iris Marion.

Debating Critical Theory. Hoy, David Couzens.

Philosophy and Critical Theory: A Reply to Richard Rorty and Seyla Benhabib. McCarthy, Thomas A.

Seyla Benhabib and the Radical Future of the Enlightenment. Nagl-Docekal, Herta.

Situations of the Self: Reflections on Seyla Benhabib's Version of Critical Theory. Forst, Rainer.

The Frankfurt School. Tessin, Timothy.

The Situated but Directionless Self: The Postmetaphysical World of Benhabib's Discourse Ethics. Hepburn, Elizabeth R.

**BENJAMIN, W**

"*Aesthetic Theory*'s Mimesis of Walter Benjamin" in *The Semblance of Subjectivity,* Huhn, Tom (ed). Nicholsen, Shierry Weber.

"Benjamin, Adorno, Surrealism" in *The Semblance of Subjectivity,* Huhn, Tom (ed). Wolin, Richard.

*Konstellation und Existenz.* Goebel, Eckart.

*Walter Benjamin's Passages.* Nicholsen, Shierry Weber (trans) and Missac, Pierre.

*Walter Benjamin: Selected Writings Volume 1 1913-1926.* Bullock, Marcus (ed) and Jennings, Michael W (ed).

After Aesthetics: Heidegger and Benjamin on Art and Experience. Ziarek, Krzysztof.

From City-Dreams to the Dreaming Collective. Miller, Tyrus.

Messianic History in Benjamin and Metz. Ostovich, Steven T.

On Walter Benjamin and Modern Optical Phenomena. Osamu, Maekawa.

The Crisis of Narrative in Contemporary Culture. Kearney, Richard.

Walter Benjamin and Surrealism: The Story of a Revolutionary Spell. Löwy, Michael and Macey, David (trans).

**BENNETT, J**

Opting Out: Bennett on Classifying Conditionals. Cogan, Ross.

**BENTHAM**

*George Bentham: Autobiography 1800-1834.* Filipiuk, Marion (ed).

*Nineteenth-Century Philosophy.* Baird, Forrest E (ed) and Kaufmann, Walter.

*Perfect Equality: John Stuart Mill on Well-Constituted Communities.* Morales, Maria H.

Bentham y los derechos humanos. Montoya, José.

Does Bentham Commit the Naturalistic Fallacy?. Chattopadhyay, Gauriprasad.

Las relaciones entre Jeremías Bentham y S. Bolívar. Schwartz, P and Rodríguez Braun, Carlos.

**BENTLEY, A**

The "Extreme Heresy" of John Dewey and Arthur F. Bentley I: A Star Crossed Collaboration?. Ryan, Frank X.

**BERGER, L**

Commentary on "Non-Cartesian Frameworks". Phillips, James.

**BERGMAN, I**

"Pixels, Decenteredness, Marketization, Totalism, and Ingmar Bergman's Cry for Help" in *Philosophy of Education (1996),* Margonis, Frank (ed). Brosio, Richard A.

**BERGSON**

"Arte, Vita E Verità In Vladimir Jankélévitch" in *Soggetto E Verità: La questione dell'uomo nella filosofia contemporanea,* Fagiuoli, Ettore. Franzini, Elio.

"Il tempo in Bergson e nello spiritualismo francese" in *Il Concetto di Tempo: Atti del XXXII Congresso Nazionale della Società Filosofica Italiana,* Casertano, Giovanni (ed). Rigobello, Armando.

Bergson and the Language of Process. Mullarkey, John C.

Bergson et Nabert, lecteurs de Fichte. Vieillard-Baron, Jean-Louis.

Bergson, Duration and Singularity. Breeur, Roland.

Bergson: The Philosophy of *Durée-Différence.* Mullarkey, John C.

Criacionismo e Evoluçao Criadora: Leonardo Coimbra Perante Henri Bergson. Teixeira, António Braz.

Do Not Listen to What They Say, Look at What They Do. Hobart, Ann and Jankélévitch, Vladimir.

Forget Vitalism: Foucault and *Lebensphilosophie.* Ransom, John S.

Liang Shuming and Henri Bergson on Intuition: Cultural Context and the Evolution of Terms. An, Yanming.

Process: An Answer to Lacey on Bergson. Howe, Lawrence W.

Reality and Appearance in Bergson and Whitehead. Brougham, Richard L.

The Origin of the Concept of Multiplicity in Gilles Deleuze's (in Portuguese). Cardoso Júnior, Hélio Rebello.

Whitehead, Contemporary Metaphysics, and Maritain's Critique of Bergson. Bradley, James.

**BERKELEY**

"Berkeley: Scepticism, Matter and Infinite Divisibility" in *Scepticism in the History of Philosophy: A Pan-American Dialogue,* Popkin, Richard H (ed). Robles, José A.

"How to Write the History of Vision: Understanding the Relationship between Berkeley and Descartes" in *Sites of Vision,* Levin, David Michael (ed). Atherton, Margaret L.

*Nineteenth-Century Philosophy.* Baird, Forrest E (ed) and Kaufmann, Walter.

Abstration, Inseparability, and Identity. Baxter, Donald L M.

Berkeley on the Work of the Six Days. Cates, Lynn D.

Berkeley Revised: On the New Metaphysics for Social Epistemology. 90 Years After "Materialism and Empiriocrticism". Kassavine, Illia.

Berkeley's Argument from Perceptual Relativity. Harris, Stephen.

Berkeley, Lee and Abstract Ideas. Benschop, Hans Peter.

Berkeley: Crítica de las ideas abstractas: La abstracción como simple semántica. Vicente Burgoa, Lorenzo.

Borges and the Refutation of Idealism: A Study of "Tlön, Uqbar, Orbis Tertius". Stewart, Jon.

Kant oder Berkeley? Zum aktuellen Streit um den korrekten Realismus. Lütterfelds, Wilhelm.

Lady Mary Shepherd's Case Against George Berkeley. Atherton, Margaret L.

Must a Classical Theist Be an Immaterialist?. Crain, Steven D.

Quasi-Berkeleyan Idealism as Perspicuous Theism. Everitt, Nicholas.

The Intuitive Basis of Berkeley's Immaterialism. Fogelin, Robert J.

The Theological Orthodoxy of Berkeley's Immaterialism. Spiegel, James S.

**BERLIN, I**

"The Moral Psychology of Nationalism" in *The Morality of Nationalism,* McKim, Robert (ed). Margalit, Avishai.

La *Vía* Vico como pretexto en Isaiah Berlin: contracorriente, antinomismo y pluralismo. Sevilla Fernández, José M.

**BERLIN, I**
The Burdens of Berlin's Modernity. Steinberg, Jonny.
Voces mezcladas: Una reflexión sobre tradición y modernidad. Díaz-Urmeneta Muñoz, Juan Bosco.

**BERLIN, J**
The Future and the History of Ideas. Perkins, Mary Anne.

**BERMUDEZ, J**
Replies. Campbell, John.
The Moral Significance of Primitive Self-Consciousness: A Response to Bermúdez. Gallagher, Shaun.

**BERMUDO, J**
La insoportable liviandad del ser (político). Pastor Pérez, Miguel Antonio.

**BERNAL, M**
Black Athena and Africa's Contribution to Global Cultural History. Van Binsbergen, Wim.
Racism, *Black Athena*, and the Historiography of Ancient Philosophy. Flory, Dan.

**BERNARD OF CHARTRES**
The Function of the *formae nativae* in the Refinement Process of Matter: A Study of Bernard of Chartres's Concept of Matter. Annala, Pauli.

**BERNARD OF CHIARAVALLE**
*Voluntas* nel *De gratia et libero arbitrio* di Bernardo di Chiaravalle. Allegro, Giuseppe.

**BERNAYS, P**
On a Paradox of Hilbert and Bernays. Priest, Graham.

**BERNSTEIN, J**
Romanticism Revisited. Hammer, Espen.

**BERRY, C**
Neoliberalism and the Political Theory of the Market. Gagnier, Regenia.

**BERSANI, L**
Liberté! Egalité! Sexualité!: Theorizing Lesbian and Gay Politics. Kaplan, Morris B.

**BEST**
Must God Create the Best?. Levine, Michael.

**BEST INTEREST**
Parenting and the Best Interests of Minors. Downie, Robin S and Randall, Fiona.
The Best-Interests Standard as Threshold, Ideal, and Standard of Reasonableness. Kopelman, Loretta M.

**BET**
Bruno de Finetti and the Logic of Conditional Events. Milne, Peter.
Risk, Uncertainty and Hidden Information. Morris, Stephen.

**BETANCOURT, R**
Sobre "Filosofía intercultural": Comentario a una obra de R. Fornet Betancourt. Picotti, Dina.

**BETHE, H**
The Analysis of Particle Tracks: A Case for Trust in the Unity of Physics. Falkenburg, Brigitte.

**BEUYS, J**
Fat, Felt and Fascism: The Case of Joseph Beuys. O'Leary, Timothy.

**BEZUIDENHOUT, A**
Pragmatically Determined Aspects of What is Said: A Reply to Bezuidenhout. Grimberg, Mary Lou.

**BHAKTI**
Heidegger, Bhakti, and Vedānta—A Tribute to J.L. Mehta. Dallmayr, Fred R.

**BHARTRHARI**
Cognition, Being, and the Possibility of Expressions: A Bhartrharian Approach. Tiwari, D N.

**BHASKAR, R**
Conflicting Varieties of Realism: Causal Powers and the Problems of Social Structure. Varela, Charles R and Harré, Rom.
Neutrality in the Social Sciences: On Bhaskar's Argument for an Essential Emancipatory Impulse in Social Science. Lacey, Hugh.
'Beyond Determinism'. Spurrett, David.

**BHATIACHARYA, K**
The Concept of Mind in Modern Indian Thought with Special Reference to Sri Aurobindo, Rabindranath and K.C. Bhatiacharyya. Ghosh, Raghunath.

**BIAS**
"Toleration as a Form of Bias" in *Philosophy, Religion, and the Question of Intolerance*, Ambuel, David (ed). Altman, Andrew.
Assessing Conflict of Interest: Sources of Bias. Bird, Stephanie J.
Heuristics and Biases in Evolutionary Biology. Magnus, David.
Market Non-Neutrality: Systematic Bias in Spontaneous Orders. diZerga, Gus.
Understanding Bias in Scientific Practice. Shaffer, Nancy E.

**BIBLE**
*see also* New Testament
Descartes' Secular Paradise: The Discourse on Method as Biblical Criticism. Soffer, Walter.
Dio parla in modo oscuro? Spunti filosofici e teologici sulle oscurità della Bibbia. Vaccaro, Andrea.
G.J. Rheticus on Copernicanism and Bible. Dinis, Alfredo.

Galileo, Science and the Bible. Carroll, William E.
Two Biblical Myths of Creation: An Exploration in Ecological Philosophy. Agera, Cassian R.
Wisdom's Information: Rereading a Biblical Image in the Light of Some Contemporary Science and Speculation. Nancarrow, Paul S.

**BIBLIOGRAPHY**
*50 Years of Events: An Annotated Bibliography 1947 to 1997*. Casati, Roberto and Varzi, Achille C.
*Augusto Ponzio: Bibliografia e Letture Critiche*. Ponzio, Augusto.
*Emmanuel Levinas: A Bibliography*. Nordquist, Joan (ed).
*Encyclopedia of Classical Philosophy*. Devereux, Daniel T (ed) and Mitsis, Phillip T (ed).
*French Feminist Theory (III): Luce Irigaray and Helene Cixous: A Bibliography*. Nordquist, Joan (ed).
*Medieval Thought*. Luscombe, David.
*Mill's On Liberty*. Dworkin, Gerald (ed).
*Rosa Luxemburg and Emma Goldman: A Bibliography*. Nordquist, Joan (ed).
*Social Theory: A Bibliographic Series, No. 42-Martin Heidegger (II): A Bibliography*. Nordquist, Joan.
*Spinoza Bibliography: 1991-1995*. Barbone, Steven (ed) and Rice, Lee (ed).
Bibliografía hispánica de filosofía: Elenco 1997. Santos-Escudero, Ceferino.
Bibliography on Philosophy of Chemistry. Scerri, Eric R.
Guide to the Papers of Michael Polanyi. Cash, John M.
Healthcare Ethics Committees and Ethics Consultants: The State of the Art (Sources/Bibliography). Buehler, David A.
La *Vía* Vico como pretexto en Isaiah Berlin: contracorriente, antimonismo y pluralismo. Sevilla Fernández, José M.
La insoportable liviandad del ser (político). Pastor Pérez, Miguel Antonio.
Recent Acquisitions: Manuscripts, Typescripts and Proofs. Turcon, Sheila.
Recent and Classic References at the Interface of Philosophy, Psychiatry, and Psychology. Sadler, John Z (ed).
Reiner Schürmann's Report of His Visit to Martin Heidegger. Adler, Pierre (trans).
Relación de obras publicadas e inéditos de Leonardo Polo. Pía Tarazona, Salvador and García-Valdecasas, Miguel.
Schleiermacher: edizione critica e bibliografia. Moretto, Giovanni.
The Hume Literature, 1995. Morris, William E.

**BICCHIERI, C**
Inconsistencies in Extensive Games. Dufwenberg, Martin and Lindén, Johan.

**BIESTA, G**
"Narrowing the Gap Between Difference and Identity" in *Philosophy of Education (1996)*, Margonis, Frank (ed). Pignatelli, Frank.

**BIG BANG THEORY**
*Atheistic Humanism*. Flew, Antony.
A Big Bang Cosmological Argument?. Temple, Dennis.
Some Problems Concerning the Big Bang Theory of Creation. Guha, Debashis.
The Origin of the Big Bang Universe in Ultimate Reality with Special Reference to the Cosmology of Stephen Hawking. Sharpe, Kevin.

**BILINGUALISM**
Bilingualism in the Business World in West European Minority Language Regions: Profit or Loss?. Van Langevelde, A. P..

**BILLMAN, D**
Induction, Focused Sampling and the Law of Small Numbers. Pust, Joel.

**BINARY**
"New Light on Peirce's Iconic Notation for the Sixteen Binary Connectives" in *Studies in the Logic of Charles Sanders Peirce*, Houser, Nathan (ed). Clark, Glenn.
"Untapped Potential in Peirce's Iconic Notation for the Sixteen Binary Connectives" in *Studies in the Logic of Charles Sanders Peirce*, Houser, Nathan (ed). Zellweger, Shea.

**BINSWANGER, L**
*Subjectivity and Intersubjectivity in Modern Philosophy and Psychoanalysis*. Frie, Roger.

**BIOCENTRISM**
Rolston, Naturogenic Value and Genuine Biocentrism. Thomas, Emyr Vaughan.

**BIOCHEMISTRY**
"Über die Vernachlässigung der Philosophie der Chemie" in *Philosophie der Chemie: Bestandsaufnahme und Ausblick*, Schummer, Joachim (ed). Van Brakel, Jaap.

**BIODIVERSITY**
Biodiversity as the Source of Biological Resources: A New Look at Biodiversity Values. Wood, Paul M.

**BIOETHICS**
*see also* Medical Ethics
"Bioethics through the Back Door: Phenomenology, Narratives, and Insights into Infertility" in *Philosophical Perspectives on Bioethics*, Sumner, L W (ed). Shanner, Laura.
"Consequentialism in Modern Moral Philosophy and in 'Modern Moral'" in *Human Lives: Critical Essays on Consequentialist Bioethics*, Oderberg, David S (ed). Diamond, Cora.

## BIOETHICS

*Suffering, Ethics, and the Body of Christ: Anointing as a Strategic Alternative Practice.* Lysaught, M Therese.

Suffering, Meaning, and Bioethics. Engelhardt Jr, H Tristram.

The Argument from Potential: A Reappraisal. Reichlin, Massimo.

The Christian Physician in the Non-Christian Institution: Objections of Conscience and Physician Value Neutrality. Peppin, John F.

The European Convention on Bioethics. De Wachter, Maurice A M.

The Heterogeneity of Clinical Ethics: The State of the Field as Reflected in the *Encyclopedia of Bioethics.* Koczwara, Bogda M and Madigan, Timothy J.

The Historical Setting of Latin American Bioethics. Gracia, Diego.

The Importance of Process in Ethical Decision Making. Thornton, Barbara C.

The Moral Art of Being a Good Doctor. MacIntosh, David.

The Reluctant retained Witness: Alleged Sexual Misconduct in the Doctor/Patient Relationship. Yarborough, Mark.

The Role of Minors in Health Care Decision Making: Current Legal Issues. Waxse, David J.

The Teaching of John Paul II on the Christian Meaning of Suffering. Crosby, John F.

Transporting Values by Technology Transfer. De Castro, Leonardo D.

Vulnerable Populations and Morally Tainted Experiments. Luna, Florencia.

What Makes a Good Death?. Callahan, Daniel.

Where Are the Heroes of Bioethics?. Freedman, Benjamin.

Why Bioethics Needs the Philosophy of Medicine: Some Implications of Reflection on Concepts of Health and Disease. Khushf, George.

## BIOGRAPHY

"A Horse Chestnut Is Not a Chestnut Horse": A Refutation of Bray, Davis, MacGregor, and Wollan. Oates, Stephen B.

"A Sin Against Scholarship": Some Examples of Plagiarism in Stephen B. Oates's Biographies of Abraham Lincoln, Martin Luther King, Jr., and William Faulkner. Burlingame, Michael.

"Ludwig Wittgenstein: Life and work an Introduction" in *The Cambridge Companion to Wittgenstein,* Sluga, Hans (ed). Sluga, Hans.

*George Bentham: Autobiography 1800-1834.* Filipiuk, Marion (ed).

*Human, All Too Human, I.* Handwerk, Gary (trans) and Nietzsche, Friedrich.

*Karl R. Popper (1902-1994).* Boladeras Cucurella, Margarita.

A Crying Need for Discourse. Zangrando, Robert L.

An African Savant: Henry Odera Oruka. Ochieng'-Odhiambo, F.

Bertrand Russell's Life in Pictures. Ruja, Harry.

Brief Takes From the Horizon. Marcus, Jacqueline.

Ces *Exercices Spirituels* Que Descartes Aurait Pratiqués. Hermans, Michel and Klein, Michel.

Concerning the Charge of Plagiarism against Stephen B. Oates. Current, Richard N.

Diary: Written by Professor Dr. Gottlob *Frege in the Time from 10 March to 9. April 1924.* Mendelsohn, Richard L (ed & trans), Gabriel, Gottfried (ed) and Kienzler, Wolfgang (ed).

Emmanuel Levinas: Thinker between Jerusalem and Athens. Burggraeve, Roger.

I Never Felt Any Bitterness: Alys Russell's Interpretation of Her Separation from Bertie. Grattan-Guinness, Ivor.

Introduction: On the Interface of Analytic and Process Philosophy. Shields, George W.

Jack London y El Talón de Hierro. Laso Prieto, José Maria.

La Nápoles de Vico. Pinton, Giorgio A.

Panbiographisme chez Sartre. Harvey, Robert.

Poor Bertie. Rée, Jonathan.

Popular Biography, Plagiarism, and Persecution. Jones, Robert E.

Prescott's Conquests: Anthropophagy, Auto-da-Fe and Eternal Return. Pearce, Colin D.

Reading between the Texts: Benjamin Thomas's *Abraham Lincoln* and Stephen Oates's *With Malice Toward None.* Bray, Robert.

Recordando a M. Heidegger. Wagner de Reyna, Alberto.

Russell and His Biographers. Willis, Kirk.

Semblanza de José Echeverría. Badía Cabrera, Miguel A.

Sharing and Stealing: Persistent Ambiguities. Swan, John.

The Early Losev. Gogotishvili, Liudmila Akhilovna.

The Oates Case. Trefousse, Hans L.

The Philosophy of Barrows Dunham: The Progress of an American Radical. Parsons, Howard L.

The Scientific Solitude of Vernadskii. Aksenov, Gennadii Petrovich.

Themes of Ivan Illich: An Intellectual Biography. Inman, Patricia.

Towards a Definition of Plagiarism: The Bray/Oates Controversy Revisited. Kozak, Ellen M.

Traiciones a Luis Vives. Calero, Francisco.

Trayectoria intelectual de Leonardo Polo. Franquet, Maria José.

## BIOLOGY

*see also* Darwinism, Evolution, Life, Vitalism

"Actualidad de la interpretación epigenética del desarrollo de los seres vivos en la filosofía natural de Schelling" in *El inicio del Idealismo alemán,* Market, Oswaldo. Rábano Gutiérrez, Alberto.

"Is Color Psychological or Biological? Or Both?" in *Perception,* Villanueva, Enrique (ed). Sosa, Ernest.

"Progress in Biological Evolution" in *The Idea of Progress,* McLaughlin, Peter (ed). García-Bellido, Antonio.

"The Idea of Progress in Evolutionary Biology: Philosophical Considerations" in *The Idea of Progress,* McLaughlin, Peter (ed). Wolters, Gereon.

"The Structure of Inquiry in Developmental Biology" in *Knowledge and Inquiry: Essays on Jaakko Hintikka's Epistemology and Philosophy of Science,* Sintonen, Matti (ed). Kleiner, Scott A.

"The Topology of Selection: The Limits of Deleuze's Biophilosophy" in *Deleuze and Philosophy: The Difference Engineer,* Ansell Pearson, Keith (ed). Caygill, Howard.

"World 1, World 2 and the Theory of Evolution" in *The Significance of Popper's Thought,* Amsterdamski, Stefan (ed). Watkins, John.

*Analyzing Functions: An Essay on a Fundamental Notion in Biology.* Melander, Peter.

*Body Parts: Property Rights and the Ownership of Human Biological Materials.* Gold, E R.

*From Occam's Razor to the Roots of Consciousness.* Wassermann, Gerhard D.

*Metaphysics and the Origin of Species.* Ghiselin, Michael T.

*The Human Animal: Personal Identity without Psychology.* Olson, Eric T.

*The Invisible World: Early Modern Philosophy and the Invention of the Microscope.* Wilson, Catherine.

A History of the Extraterrestrial Life Debate. Crowe, Michael J.

A Tribute to Donald T. Campbell. Heyes, Cecilia.

Abstraktion und Ideation—Zur Semantik chemischer und biologischer Grundbegriffe. Gutmann, Mathias and Hanekamp, Gerd.

Adaptationism: Hypothesis or Heuristic?. Resnik, David B.

Biodiversity as the Source of Biological Resources: A New Look at Biodiversity Values. Wood, Paul M.

Biological Function, Selection, and Reduction. Manning, Richard N.

Biological Matter and Perceptual Powers in Aristotle's *De Anima.* Scaltsas, Theodore.

Biological Sciences and Ethics: Models of Cooperation. Graber, Glenn C.

Biomathematics: Methods and Limits (in Portuguese). Castilho Piqueira, José Roberto.

Coming in to the Foodshed. Kloppenburg, Jr, Jack, Hendrickson, John and Stevenson, G W.

Commentary on "The Social Responsibilities of Biological Scientists. Salzberg, Aaron A.

Commentary on "The Social Responsibilities of Biological Scientists". Beckwith, Jonathan R and Geller, Lisa N.

Competing Research Programmes on the Origin of Life. Torres, Juan Manuel.

Confessions of a Sentimental Philosopher: Science, Animal Rights, and the Demands of Rational Inquiry. Johnson, David Kenneth.

Confusion in Philosophy: A Comment on Williams (1992). Williams, David M, Scotland, Robert W and Humphries, Christopher J.

Critical Review: Sober's *Philosophy of Biology* and His Philosophy of Biology. Rosenberg, Alex.

Darwin and Dennett: Still Two Mysteries. Cody, Arthur B.

Darwin and the Inefficacy of Artificial Selection. Richards, Richard A.

Darwinism, Process Structuralism, and Natural Kinds. Griffiths, Paul E.

Defending Promiscuous Realism about Natural Kinds. Daly, Chris.

Der Evolutionsbegriff als Mittel zur Synthese: Leistung und Grenzen. Vollmer, Gerhard.

Discovering the Functional Mesh: On the Methods of Evolutionary Psychology. Davies, Paul Sheldon.

Disunity in Psychology and Other Sciences: The Network or the Block Universe?. Viney, Wayne.

Dominance Hierarchies and the Evolution of Human Reasoning. Cummins, Denise Dellarosa.

Economics, Biology, and Naturalism: Three Problems Concerning the Question of Individuality. Khalil, Elias L.

Emotion as an Explanatory Principle in Early Evolutionary Theory. Campbell, Sue.

Empathy, Passion, Imagination: A Medical Triptych. Coulehan, Jack.

Epistemische Leistungen technischer Simulationen. Loeck, Gisela.

Essential Membership. LaPorte, Joseph.

Ethics and the Biology of Reproduction. Harris, David J.

Fitness and Function. Walsh, Denis M.

Fitness Made Physical: The Supervenience of Biological Concepts Revisited. Weber, Marcel.

Gould on Laws in Biological Science. McIntyre, Lee.

Granny Versus Mother Nature—No Contest. Dennett, Daniel C.

Heroic Antireductionism and Genetics: A Tale of One Science. Vance, Russell E.

Human Beings Are Animals. Lee, Patrick.

Human Nature and Biological Nature in Mencius. Bloom, Irene.

I Rather Think I Am A Darwinian. Blackburn, Simon.

Innateness and Canalization. Ariew, André.

Integrating Neuroscience, Psychology, and Evolutionary Biology through a Teleological Conception of Function. Mundale, Jennifer and Bechtel, William.

Kann es eine ontologiefreie evolutionäre Erkenntnistheorie geben?. Diettrich, Olaf.

Maschinentheoretische Grundlagen der organismischen Konstruktionslehre. Gutmann, Wolfgang Friedrich and Weingarten, Michael.

## BIOLOGY

Modelling Reciprocal Altruism. Stephens, Christopher.

Natural Law, Nature, and Biology: A Modern Synthesis. Hartigan, Richard Shelly.

Neither Enemy nor Friend: Nature as Creation in the Theology of Saint Thomas Aquinas. Pope, Stephen J.

Niels Bohrs Argument für die Nichtreduzierbarkeit der Biologie auf die Physik. Hoyningen-Huene, Paul.

Optimalität der Natur?. Zoglauer, Thomas.

Parafraud in Biology. Hillman, Harold.

Promiscuous Realism: Reply to Wilson. Dupré, John.

Random Drift and the Omniscient Viewpoint. Millstein, Roberta L.

Realität, Anpassung und Evolution. Diettrich, Olaf.

Shaping a New Biological Factor, 'The Interferon', in Room 215 of the National Institute for Medical Research, 1956/57. Pieters, Toine.

Some Comments on Rosenberg's Review. Sober, Elliott.

Species, Rules and Meaning: The Politics of Language and the Ends of Definitions in 19th Century Natural History. McOuat, Gordon R.

Teleologie und Teleonomie aus Sicht der philosophischen Qualia-Thematik. Pohlenz, Gerd.

The Beanbag Genetics Controversy: Towards a Synthesis of Opposing Views of Natural Selection. De Winter, Willem.

The Biological Child. MacKellar, Calum.

The Epic of Evolution as a Framework for Human Orientation in Life. Kaufman, Gordon D.

The Historical Turn in the Study of Adaptation. Griffiths, Paul E.

The Ideology and Biology of Gender Difference. Rhode, Deborah L.

The Indeterministic Character of Evolutionary Theory: No "No Hidden Variables Proof" but No Room for Determinism Either. Brandon, Robert N and Carson, Scott.

The Social Responsibilities of Biological Scientists. Reiser, Stanley Joel and Bulger, Ruth Ellen.

The Story of the Mind: Psychological and Biological Explanations of Human Behavior. Schechtman, Marya.

The Tension between Aristotle's Theories and Uses of Metaphor. Marcos, Alfredo.

Theoretical Modeling and Biological Laws. Cooper, Gregory.

Theory, Practice, and Epistemology in the Development of Species Concepts. Magnus, David.

Treating Race as a Social Construction. Lauer, Henle.

What is Scientism?. Stenmark, Mikael.

What Rationality Adds to Animal Morality. Waller, Bruce N.

Who's Afraid of a Non-Metaphorical Evolutionary Epistemology?. Heschl, Adolf.

## BIOMEDICAL RESEARCH

On the Hazards of Whistleblowers and on Some Problems of Young Biomedical Scientists in our Time. Edsall, John T.

## BIOMEDICINE

Der Begriff 'Praktischer Fortschritt' in den biomedizinischen Wissenschaften: Strukturalistischer Ansatz zur Rekonstruktion wissenschaftstheoretischer Begriffe in der Medizin. Eleftheriadis, Anastassia.

Genetics and Biomedicine: The Perils of Popularization. Shanks, Niall.

## BIOTECHNOLOGY

"Natural Integrity and Biotechnology" in *Human Lives: Critical Essays on Consequentialist Bioethics*, Oderberg, David S (ed). Clark, Stephen R L.

Food Biotechnology's Challenge to Cultural Integrity and Individual Consent. Thompson, Paul B.

## BIRDWHISTELL, A

Commentary on the AAS Panel: Shun, Bloom, Cheng, and Birdwhistell. Neville, Robert Cummings.

## BIRTH

*The Perfect Baby: A Pragmatic Approach to Genetics*. McGee, Glenn.

Buddhism as Radical Religion. Seidel, George J.

Preferring not to have been Born. Smilansky, Saul.

The Birth of Difference. Schües, Christina.

The Nature of Transpersonal Experience. Beskova, Irina Aleksandrovna.

## BIRTH CONTROL

*see* Contraception

## BISEXUALITY

In Praise of Unreliability. Heldke, Lisa.

Swear by the Moon. Bedecarré, Corinne.

## BISHOP, J

Deviant Causal Chains and the Irreducibility of Teleological Explanation. Sehon, Scott.

## BLACK, M

Black's "Twin Globe" Counterexample. Ferraiolo, William.

Bundles and Indiscernibility: A Reply to O'Leary-Hawthorne. Vallicella, William F.

Max Black's "Interaction View" of Metaphor. Scherzinger, Martin.

## BLACKETT, P

The Manufacture of the Positron. Roqué, Xavier.

## BLACKS

"Black Feminism: Liberation Limbos and Existence in Gray" in *Existence in Black: An Anthology of Black Existential Philosophy*, Gordon, Lewis R (ed). James, Joy Ann.

"Black Liberation—Yes!" in *The Liberation Debate: Rights at Issue*, Leahy, Michael (ed). Boxill, Bernard R.

"Blacks Don't Need Liberating" in *The Liberation Debate: Rights at Issue*, Leahy, Michael (ed). Levin, Michael.

"Boxill's Reply" in *The Liberation Debate: Rights at Issue*, Leahy, Michael (ed). Boxill, Bernard R.

"Existential Dynamics of Theorizing Black Invisibility" in *Existence in Black: An Anthology of Black Existential Philosophy*, Gordon, Lewis R (ed). Gordon, Lewis R.

"Liberalism and the Politics of Emancipation: The Black Experience" in *Existence in Black: An Anthology of Black Existential Philosophy*, Gordon, Lewis R (ed). Carew, George.

"Nietzsche on Blacks" in *Existence in Black: An Anthology of Black Existential Philosophy*, Gordon, Lewis R (ed). Preston, William A.

"On Disappointment in the Black Context" in *Existence in Black: An Anthology of Black Existential Philosophy*, Gordon, Lewis R (ed). Lawson, Bill E.

"The Concept of Double Vision in Richard Wright's *The Outsider*" in *Existence in Black: An Anthology of Black Existential Philosophy*, Gordon, Lewis R (ed). Hayes III, FLoyd W.

"Toting Technology: Taking It to the Streets" in *Existence in Black: An Anthology of Black Existential Philosophy*, Gordon, Lewis R (ed). Dixon, Bobby R.

*Existence in Black: An Anthology of Black Existential Philosophy*. Gordon, Lewis R (ed).

Rastafarianism and the Reality of Dread"" in *Existence in Black: An Anthology of Black Existential Philosophy*, Gordon, Lewis R (ed). Henry, Paget.

## BLAKE

Ch'an Buddhism and the Prophetic Poems of William Blake. Ferrara, Mark S.

## BLAKEMORE, D

Conventional Implicatures as Tacit Performatives. Rieber, Steven.

## BLAME

Blameless, Constructive, and Political Anger. Swaine, Lucas A.

Direct and Indirect Responsibility: Distributing Blame. Goodnow, Jacqueline J and Warton, Pamela M.

Recklessness. Brady, James B.

## BLAMEWORTHINESS

An Epistemic Dimension of Blameworthiness. Haji, Ishtiyaque.

## BLAMEWORTHY

A Plea for Accuses. Zimmerman, Michael J.

Blameworthiness, Character, and Cultural Norms. Haji, Ishtiyaque.

Utilitarianism for Sinners. Eriksson, Björn.

## BLANCHOT, M

*Is There Truth in Art?*. Rapaport, Herman.

*Maurice Blanchot: The Demand of Writing*. Gill, Carolyn Bailey.

Blanchot/Levinas: Interruption (On the Conflict of Alterities). Bruns, Gerald L.

For the Sake of Truth...The Demand of Discontinuity in Foucault, Blanchot and Levinas. Purcell, Michael.

Lo sguardo di Blanchot e la musica di Orfeo: Visione e ascolto nell'ispirazione poetica. Carrera, Alessandro.

The "Passion for the Outside": Foucault, Blanchot, and Exteriority. Saghafi, Kas.

## BLANSHARD, B

"Brand Blanshard—A 'Student' of Bradley" in *Philosophy after F.H. Bradley*, Bradley, James (ed). Walsh, Michael.

*Philosophy after F.H. Bradley*. Bradley, James (ed).

## BLASIUS, M

Liberté! Egalité! Sexualité!: Theorizing Lesbian and Gay Politics. Kaplan, Morris B.

## BLIND

The Experience of Spatiality for Congenitally Blind People: A Phenomenological-Psychological Study. Karlsson, Gunnar.

## BLINDNESS

Waarom het beoordelen van technologieën voor gehandicapten problematisch is. Blume, Stuart.

## BLISS

Orgasmic Rapture and Divine Ecstasy: The Semantic History of Ānanda. Olivelle, Patrick.

## BLOCH, E

"Between Ernest Renan and Ernst Bloch: Averroës Remembered, Discovered, and Invented. The European Reception Since the Nineteenth Century" in *Averroës and the Enlightenment*, Wahba, Mourad (ed). Wild, Stefan.

"Mannheim e Bloch: storicismo e utopia" in *Lo Storicismo e la Sua Storia: Temi, Problemi, Prospettive*, Cacciatore, Giuseppe (ed). Riccio, Monica.

*Paraísos y Utopías: Una Clave Antropológica*. De la Pienda, Jesús Avelino.

Discutono *Il principio speranza*, di Ernst Bloch. Boella, Laura, Moneti, Maria and Schmidt, Burghart.

Socialist Socrates: Ernst Bloch in the GDR. Ernst, Anna-Sabine and Klinger, Gerwin.

## BLOCK, N

"Layered Perceptual Representation" in *Perception*, Villanueva, Enrique (ed). Lycan, William G.

## BLOCK, N

"Orgasms Again" in *Perception,* Villanueva, Enrique (ed). Tye, Michael.

"Replies to Tomberlin, Tye, Stalnaker and Block" in *Perception,* Villanueva, Enrique (ed). Lycan, William G.

"Ruritania and Ecology" in *Contents,* Villanueva, Enrique (ed). Toribio, Josefa.

## BLONDEL, M

"La logica della vita morale in M. Blondel" in *Momenti di Storia della Logica e di Storia della Filosofia,* Guetti, Carla (ed). Rigobello, Armando.

A Dialéctica da Acçao em L'Action (1893) de Maurice Blondel. Morujao, Alexandre Fradique.

Blondel and Husserl: A Continuation of the Conversation. Hart, James G.

Blondels *Action* von 1893 und Rahners transzendentaler Ansatz im *Grundkurs*—eine unterirdische Wirkungsgeschichte. Knoepffler, Nikolaus.

Maurice Blondel: A Philosopher of Tolerance and Human Dignity. Lasic, Hrvoje.

Un aperçu de la "logique de la vie morale" chez Maurice Blondel. Létourneau, Alain.

## BLOOM, A

"Education's Ills and the Vanity of the Philosopher" in *Philosophy of Education (1996),* Margonis, Frank (ed). Farber, Paul.

"Infinitely Interesting: Bloom, Kierkegaard, and the Educational Quest" in *Philosophy of Education (1996),* Margonis, Frank (ed). Rohrer, Patricia.

## BLOOM, I

Commentary on the AAS Panel: Shun, Bloom, Cheng, and Birdwhistell. Neville, Robert Cummings.

## BLOOMFIELD, L

The Unfinished Chomskyan Revolution. Katz, Jerrold J.

## BLUFF

Business and Game-Playing: The False Analogy. Koehn, Daryl.

## BLUMENBERG, H

*Imaginationssysteme.* Haefliger, Jürg.

Hans Blumenberg: sobre la modernidad, la historia y los límites de la razón. Palti, Elías José.

Keeping One's Distance from the Absolute: Blumenberg's Metaphorology between Pragmatics and Metaphysics (in Dutch). De Ruyter, Geertrui.

Ockham and *Potentia Absoluta.* Finn, Steve.

Secolarizzazione e originalità del moderno: In margine a *La legittimità dell'epoca moderna* di Hans Blumenberg. Carosotti, Gianni.

## BOBBIO, N

On Norberto Bobbio's "Theory of Democracy". Yturbe, Corina.

## BOCHENSKI, J

O. Profesor Józef Maria Bochenski (30. VIII. 1902—8. II. 1995) (in Polish). Strózewski, Wladyslaw.

## BODENHEIMER, E

Bodenheimer's Empirical Theory of Natural Law. Dennehy, Raymond.

## BODHISATTVA

The Bodhisattva Ideal in Theravāda Buddhist Theory and Practice: A Reevaluation of the Bodhisattva-Srāvaka Opposition. Samuels, Jeffrey.

## BODIN, J

Jean Bodin, Scepticism and Absolute Sovereignty. Engster, Dan.

La amenaza latente del vagabundo en la literatura política del siglo XVI. Rivera García, Antonio.

The Concept of Sovereignty in Jean Bodin's *Methodus* (in Spanish). Ribeiro de Barros, Alberto.

The Legacy of Jean Bodin: Absolutism, Populism or Constitutionalism?. Salmon, J H M.

## BODUNRIN, P

Interview with Professor Peter O. Bodunrin. Ganesh, Anke.

## BODY

*see also* Minds

"Blue Prints and Bodies: Paradigms of Desire in Pornography" in *Critical Studies: Ethics and the Subject,* Simms, Karl (ed). Brottman, Mikita.

"Die Logik der Überzeugungen und das Leib-Seele-Problem" in *Das weite Spektrum der analytischen Philosophie,* Lenzen, Wolfgang. Kamlah, Andreas.

"Introduction to Part I" in *Critical Studies: Ethics and the Subject,* Simms, Karl (ed). Simms, Karl.

"Of Property: On 'Captive' Bodies', Hidden 'Flesh', and Colonization" in *Existence in Black: An Anthology of Black Existential Philosophy,* Gordon, Lewis R (ed). Gonzalez, G M James.

"Temples of the Body and Temples of the Cosmos: Vision and Visualization in the Vesalian and Copernican Revolutions" in *Picturing Knowledge,* Baigrie, Brian S (ed). Kemp, Martin.

"Transgressive Bodies: Destruction and Excessive Display of the Human Form in the Horror Film" in *Critical Studies: Ethics and the Subject,* Simms, Karl (ed). Mendik, Xavier.

*Body Parts: Property Rights and the Ownership of Human Biological Materials.* Gold, E R.

*Descartes' Dualism.* Baker, Gordon and Morris, Katherine J.

*Explaining Consciousness—The 'Hard Problem'.* Shear, Jonathan (ed).

*Immortality.* Edwards, Paul (ed).

*Malebranche's Theory of the* Soul: A Cartesian Interpretation. Schmaltz, Tad M.

*Mens Sana in Corpore Sano?* Reflexoes sobre o Enigma do Corpo. Simao, Cristiana V.

*Parapsychology, Philosophy, and Spirituality: A Postmodern Exploration.* Griffin, David Ray.

*Representation and the* Mind-Body Problem *in* Spinoza. Della Rocca, Michael.

*Self and World.* Cassam, Quassim.

*The Gift of Truth: Gathering the Good.* Ross, Stephen David.

*The Self and Its Body in Hegel's Phenomenology of Spirit.* Russon, John Edward.

A Patterned Process Approach To Brain, Consciousness, and Behavior. Díaz, José-Luis.

A Whiteheadian Contribution to the "Mind-body" Relation. Bertocci, Rosemary Juel.

An East Asian Perspective of Mind-Body. Nagatomo, Shigenori and Leisman, Gerald.

Ancora sulla teoria vichiana del linguaggio: In margine ad alcune recenti pubblicazioni. Gensini, Stefano.

Ansätze zur physikalischen Untersuchung des Leib-Seele-Problems. Arendes, Lothar.

Are Leibnizian Monads Spatial?. Cover, J A and Hartz, Glenn A.

Bemerkungen zum Verhältnis zwischen Neurophysiologie und Psychologie. Ros, Arno.

Body-Subjectivity in Psychiatry: The Initial Argument. Mondal, Parthasarathi.

Commentary on "The Ethics of Normalization". Corsale, Massimo.

Cosmological Mysticism: The Imitation of the Heavenly Bodies in Ibn Tufayl's *Hayy ibn Yaqzan.* Brague, Rémi.

Cuypers' Persoonlijke aangelegenheden. Meijsing, Monica.

Das Leib-Seele-Problem in der Psychologie. Goller, Hans.

Denying the Body? Memory and the Dilemmas of History in Descartes. Reiss, Timothy J.

Descartes's Dualism?. Baker, Gordon and Morris, Katherine J.

Domination and Dialogue in Merleau-Ponty's *Phenomenology of Perception.* Sullivan, Shannon.

Dos estudios italianos sobre Vico y la estética. Amoroso, Leonardo.

Eigenschafts-Physikalismus. Beckermann, Ansgar.

Ethical Obligations in the Body Politic: The Case of Normalization Policy for Marginal Populations. D'Oronzio, Joseph C.

Éthique féministe de relation et perspectives sur le corps. Dumais, Monique.

Facing Ourselves: Incorrigibility and the Mind-Body Problem. Warner, Richard.

Fenomenología y corporalidad en le ética de Emmanuel Lévinas: Lectura de *De l'éxistence à l'existant.* Costa, Márcio Luis.

Fleshing Gender, Sexing the Body: Refiguring the Sex/Gender Distinction. Tuana, Nancy.

Foucault's Attack on Sex-Desire. McWhorter, Ladelle.

From Atlas to Adolph: Body Building, Physical Culture, and National Socialism. Pickens, Donald K.

G.W. Leibniz: Consequence de l'Hypothese generalle publiée il y a quelque temps, pour expliquer le Phenomene de l'attachement dans le vuide, ou dans une place dont l'air a esté tiré. Luna Alcoba, Manuel.

Ghost Gestures: Phenomenological Investigations of Bodily Micromovements and Their Intercorporeal Implications. Behnke, Elizabeth A.

Hellenization and Keeping Body and Soul Together. Keizer, H M.

Hobbes's Theory of Causality and Its Aristotelian Background. Leijenhorst, Cees.

Human Beings Are Animals. Lee, Patrick.

Imaginability, Conceivability, Possibility and the Mind-Body Problem. Hill, Christopher S.

Indexical Reference and Bodily Causal Diagrams in Intentional Action. Castañeda, Héctor-Neri.

Introduction: Feminist Approaches to Bioethics. Tong, Rosemarie.

Kim on the Mind—Body Problem. Horgan, Terence.

Kripke's Critique of the Mind-Body Identity Theory (in Serbo-Croatian). Bogdanovski, Masan.

La critica rosminiana alla cosmologia di Aristotele. Messina, Gaetano.

La relazione tra l'uomo e la natura: una prospettiva. Sagnotti, Simona C.

Las verdades del cuerpo cartesiano. Duque, Félix.

Libertad básica. Skutch, Alexander F.

Materiality and Language: Butler's Interrogation of the History of Philosophy. Olkowski, Dorothea.

Materiality in Theodor W. Adorno and Judith Butler. Hull, Carrie L.

Mediations of the Female Imaginary and Symbolic. Campbell, Jan.

Minds and Bodies: Human and Divine. Peterson, Gregory R.

O Modelo Psicofisiológico Cartesiano e o Materialismo das Luzes. Nascimento, Maria das Graças S.

On Swampkinds. Millikan, Ruth Garrett.

One Short Sleep Past?. Herbert, Robert T.

Oneself as Oneself and Not as Another. Johnstone, Albert A.

Panexperientialist Physicalism and the Mind-Body Problem. Griffin, David Ray.

Pedagogy in the Myth of Plato's *Statesman:* Body and Soul in Relation to Philosophy and Politics. Hemmenway, Scott R.

Pirrone e i maestri indiani. De Bernardi, Paolo.

Possibilities in Philosophy of Mind. Taliaferro, Charles.

## BODY
*Searle on Consciousness and Dualism.* Collins, Corbin.
Searle's Regimen for Rediscovering the Mind. Hershfield, Jeffrey.
Self-Observation. Martin, M G F.
Software Agents and Their Bodies. Kushmerick, Nicholas.
St. Thomas Aquinas and the Defense of Mendicant Poverty. Jones, John D.
Suffering, Ethics, and the Body of Christ: Anointing as a Strategic Alternative Practice. Lysaught, M Therese.
Swear by the Moon. Bedecarré, Corrinne.
The Being of Leibnizian Phenomena. Hoffman, Paul.
The Body as an "Object" of Historical Knowledge. Mann, Doug.
The Brain/Body Problem. Schechtman, Marya.
The Condition of Postmodernity and the Discourse of the Body. Kumar Giri, Ananta.
The Curious Tale of Atlas College. Cahn, Steven M.
The Ethics of Normalization. Reinders, Hans S.
The Mind-Body Problem: A Comparative Study. Umapathy, Ranjan.
The Problematic Situation of Post-Humanism and the Task of Recreating a Symphysical Ethos. Acampora, Ralph.
The Regress-Problem: A Reply to Vermazen. Moya, Carlos J.
The Rhetorical Force of Ambiguity: The No-Harm Argument in Medical Ethics (in Dutch). Van der Scheer, Lieke.
Un diálogo con la tradición: Foucault en su contexto. Vega, José Fernádez.
War Aristoteles ein Funktionalist? Überlegungen zum Leib-Seele-Problem. Perler, Dominik.
What-Is? On Mimesis and the Logic of Identity and Difference in Heidegger and the Frankfurt School. Levin, David Michael.
Working within Contradiction: The Possibility of Feminist Cosmetic Surgery. Kirkland, Anna and Tong, Rosemarie.
Yang Chu's Discovery of the Body. Emerson, John.
'Now I Can Go On:' Wittgenstein and Our Embodied Embeddedness in the 'Hurly-Burly' of Life. Shotter, John.

## BOEHM, F
Franz Böhms "Deutsche Philosophie": Über den Versuch einer erkenntnistheoretischen Grundlegung des "Nationalsozialismus". Hailer, Martin.

## BOETHIUS
"L'influenza della logica sulla ricerca storiografica su Hume" in *Momenti di Storia della Logica e di Storia della Filosofia*, Guetti, Carla (ed). Lecaldano, Eugenio.
The Distinction Between Being and Essence According to Boethius, Avicenna, and William of Auvergne. Caster, Kevin J.

## BOEVE, L
Looking for a Truth that Obliges (in Dutch). Jonkers, Peter.
Particularity of Religion and Universality of Reason (in Dutch). Van der Veken, Jan.

## BOGHOSSIAN, P
A Note on Truth, Deflationism and Irrealism. Miraglia, Pierluigi.
Analyticity Regained?. Harman, Gilbert.
Boghossian on Reductive Dispositionalism about Content: The Case Strengthened. Miller, Alexander.
Self-Ascription, Self-Knowledge, and the Memory Argument. Goldberg, Sanford C.
Trascendentalismo, contenido semántico y verdad. Barrio, Eduardo Alejandro.

## BOHM, D
*Unfolding Meaning: A Weekend of Dialogue with David Bohm.* Bohm, David.
Antidote or Theory?. Dickson, Michael.
Descrying the World in the Wave Function. Maudlin, Tim.
Review Essay: Bohmian Mechanics and the Quantum Revolution. Goldstein, Sheldon.
Time, Bohm's Theory, and Quantum Cosmology. Callender, Craig and Weingard, Robert.
Trouble in Paradise? Problems for Bohm's Theory. Callender, Craig and Weingard, Robert.

## BOHR, N
A Schism in Quantum Physics or How Locality May Be Salvaged. Antonopoulos, Constantin.
Bohr on Nonlocality: The Facts and the Fiction. Antonopoulos, Constantin.
Bohr's Theory of the Atom 1913-1923: A Case Study in the Progress of Scientific Research Programmes. Hettema, Hinne.
Innate Ideas, Categories and Objectivity. Antonopoulos, Constantin.
Naturalizing Metaphysics. Saunders, Simon.
Niels Bohrs Argument für die Nichtreduzierbarkeit der Biologie auf die Physik. Hoyningen-Huene, Paul.
Once More: Bohr-Hoffding. Faye, Jan.

## BOLIVAR, S
Bolívar and the Latin American Unity (Spanish). Aparicio de La Hera, Beatriz.
Las relaciones entre Jeremías Bentham y S. Bolívar. Schwartz, P and Rodríguez Braun, Carlos.

## BOLZANO
Proofs and Pictures. Brown, James Robert.

## BONALD, L
La influencia de la Revolución Francesa en el pensamiento de Bonald. Osés Gorráiz, Jesús María.

## BONAVENTURE
Bonaventure and the Arguments for the Impossibility of an Infinite Temporal Regression. Davis, Richard.
Contemplación filosófica y contemplación mística en San Buenaventura. Andereggen, Ignacio E. M.
St. Bonaventure and the Demonstrability of a Temporal Beginning: A Reply to Richard Davis. Baldner, Steven.
St. Bonaventure's Journey into God. Barbone, Steven.
The Spark of Conscience: Bonaventure's View of Conscience and Synderesis. Langston, Douglas.
Tres tratados "Sobre el maestro": Agustín, Buenaventura, Tomás de Aquino. Perez Ruiz, Francisco.
Zur subsistentia absoluta in der Trinitätstheologie. Obenauer, Klaus.

## BONDAGE
"Love and Human Bondage in Maugham, Spinoza, and Freud" in *Love Analyzed*, Lamb, Roger E. Hannan, Barbara.

## BONHOEFFER, D
Oh Our Children! (in Czech). Pokorny, Petr.

## BONKOVSKY, F
Commentary on "Family Dynamics and Children in Medical Research". Robinson, Walter.

## BONS, W
The Frankfurt School. Tessin, Timothy.

## BOOK
Mere Reading. Brann, Eva T H.
Of Bread and Chaff: The Reviewer Re-viewed. Novitz, David.
Some Notes about the Ethics of Editing Book Anthologies. Kostelanetz, Richard.
What Ethics?. Rabben, Linda.

## BOOLEAN
Boolean Operations, Borel Sets, and Hausdorff's Question. Dasgupta, Abhijit.

## BOOLEAN ALGEBRA
A General Approach to the Algebras of Unary Functions in a Boolean Semantics for Natural Language. Nowak, Marek.
Cardinal Functions on Ultraproducts of Boolean Algebras. Peterson, Douglas.
Colouring and Non-Productivity of Aleph$_2$-C.C.. Shelah, Saharon.
Decidability of Finite Boolean Algebras with a Distinguished Subset Closed under Some Operations. Hanusek, Jerzy.
Decidable and Undecidable Logics with a Binary Modality. Németi, István, Kurucz, Agnes and Sain, Ildikó (& others).
Finite Distributive Lattices as Sums of Boolean Algebras. Kotas, Jerzy and Wojtylak, Piotr.
H Rasiowa's and C Rauszer's Contribution to Algebra. Bartol, Wiktor.
Non-Classical Logics in Quantum Mechanics and Physics. Maczynski, M J.
On Boolean Subalgebras of $P(omega_1)/ctble$. Dow, Alan.
On Countably Closed Complete Boolean Algebras. Jech, Thomas and Shelah, Saharon.
On Negatively Restricting Boolean Algebras. Zuber, R.
Probability Logic and Measures on Epimorphic Images of Coproducts of Measurable Spaces. Amer, Mohamed A.
Region-Based Topology. Roeper, Peter.
Undecidability in Diagonalizable Algebras. Shavrukov, V Yu.

## BOOLOS, G
"Reply to Boolos" in *Frege: Importance and Legacy*, Schirn, Matthias (ed). Dummett, Michael.
What is Frege's Relativity Argument?. Yourgrau, Palle.

## BOONIN-VAIL, D
Acts and Outcomes: A Reply to Boonin-Vail. Parfit, Derek.

## BOOTH, W
Neoliberalism and the Political Theory of the Market. Gagnier, Regenia.

## BOREDOM
Tedium Vitae: Or, My Life as a 'Net Serf'. Gehring, Verna V.

## BORGES, J
*Justice.* Westphal, Jonathan (ed).
Borges and the Refutation of Idealism: A Study of "Tlön, Uqbar, Orbis Tertius". Stewart, Jon.

## BORGMANN, A
Highway Bridges and Feasts: Heidegger and Borgmann on How to Affirm Technology. Dreyfus, Hubert L and Spinosa, Charles.

## BOSANQUET
"F.H. Bradley and Bernard Bosanquet" in *Philosophy after F.H. Bradley*, Bradley, James (ed). Sweet, William.
*Idealism and Rights: The Social Ontology of Human Rights in the Political Thought of Bernard Bosanquet.* Sweet, William.

## BOSNIAN
"Nationalism and Modernity" in *The Morality of Nationalism*, McKim, Robert (ed). Taylor, Charles.
"Nationalism in a Comparative Mode: A Response to Charles Taylor" in *The Morality of Nationalism*, McKim, Robert (ed). Feinberg, Walter.
"The Sources of Nationalism: Commentary on Taylor" in *The Morality of Nationalism*, McKim, Robert (ed). Kymlicka, Will.

BOTERO, G

42

SUBJECT INDEX

**BOTERO, G**
Giovanni Botero y la *Razon de Estado*. Sánchez, Antonio.

**BOUND**
Minimal Complementation Below Uniform Upper Bounds for the Arithmetical Degrees. Kumabe, Masahiro.

**BOUNDARY**
"The Takings Clause and the Meanings of Land" in *Philosophy and Geography I: Space, Place, and Environmental Ethics*, Light, Andrew (ed). Trachtenberg, Zev.
Boundaries, Continuity, and Contact. Varzi, Achille C.

**BOUNDED**
Bounded Contraction and Gentzen-style Formulation of Lukasiewicz Logics. Prijatelj, Andreja.
Game-Theoretic Axioms for Local Rationality and Bounded Knowledge. Bicchieri, Cristina and Antonelli, Gian Aldo.
Interpolation Theorems, Lower Bounds for Proof Systems, and Independence Results for Bounded Arithmetic. Krajicek, J.
Notes on Polynomially Bounded Arithmetic. Zambella, Domenico.
Violations of Present-Value Maximization in Income Choice. Gigliotti, Gary and Sopher, Barry.

**BOURDIEU, P**
Bourdieu and Foucault on Power and Modernity. Cronin, Ciaran.
Bourdieu and the Social Conditions of Wittgensteinian Language Games. Gay, William C.
On the Limit of Iconology through the "Mental Habit"—Comparison between E. Panofsky's "Mental Habit" and P. Bourdieu's "Habitus" (in Japanese). Ichijo, Kazuhiko.
Practices and Actions: A Wittgensteinian Critique of Bourdieu and Giddens. Schatzki, Theodore R.

**BOXILL, B**
"Blacks Don't Need Liberating" in *The Liberation Debate: Rights at Issue*, Leahy, Michael (ed). Levin, Michael.

**BOYCOTT**
Should We Boycott Boycotts?. Mills, Claudia.

**BOYD, D**
"But That Is Not What I Mean" Criticizing With Care and Respect" in *Philosophy of Education (1996)*, Margonis, Frank (ed). Applebaum, Barbara.
"Criticizing With Care and With Respect For What We Are All Up Against" in *Philosophy of Education (1996)*, Margonis, Frank (ed). Diller, Ann.

**BOYD, R**
From Moral Realism to Moral Relativism in One Easy Step. Horgan, Terence and Timmons, Mark.

**BOYLE**
"Triangulating Divine Will: Henry More, Robert Boyle, and René Descartes on God's Relationship to the Creation" in *Mind Senior to the World*, Baldi, Marialuisa. Osler, Margaret J.
Animals, Morality and Robert Boyle. MacIntosh, J J.
Why Strong Sociologists Abhor a Vacuum: Shapin and Schaffer on the Boyle/Hobbes Controversy. Norris, Christopher.

**BOYLE, J**
A Response. Walzer, Michael.

**BOYLES, D**
"Sophistry and Wisdom in Plato's *Meno*" in *Philosophy of Education (1996)*, Margonis, Frank (ed). Hall, Terry.

**BRACKETING**
Dynamic Bracketing and Discourse Representation. Visser, Albert and Vermeulen, Kees.

**BRADLEY**
"Bradley and MacIntyre: A Comparison" in *Philosophy after F.H. Bradley*, Bradley, James (ed). MacNiven, Don.
"Bradley and the Canadian Connection" in *Philosophy after F.H. Bradley*, Bradley, James (ed). Trott, Elizabeth.
"Bradley on Truth and Judgement" in *Philosophy after F.H. Bradley*, Bradley, James (ed). Creery, Walter.
"Bradley's Attack on Associationism" in *Philosophy after F.H. Bradley*, Bradley, James (ed). Ferreira, Phillip.
"Bradley's Contribution to the Development of Logic" in *Philosophy after F.H. Bradley*, Bradley, James (ed). Griffin, Nicholas.
"Bradley's Impact on Empiricism" in *Philosophy after F.H. Bradley*, Bradley, James (ed). Wilson, Fred.
"Bradley, Russell and Analysis" in *Philosophy after F.H. Bradley*, Bradley, James (ed). Dwyer, Philip.
"Brand Blanshard—A 'Student' of Bradley" in *Philosophy after F.H. Bradley*, Bradley, James (ed). Walsh, Michael.
"Desire and Desirability: Bradley, Russell and Moore versus Mill" in *Early Analytic Philosophy*, Tait, William W (ed). Gerrard, Steve.
"F.H. Bradley and Bernard Bosanquet" in *Philosophy after F.H. Bradley*, Bradley, James (ed). Sweet, William.
"F.H. Bradley and C.A. Campbell" in *Philosophy after F.H. Bradley*, Bradley, James (ed). Maclachlan, Lorne.
"F.H. Bradley and Later Idealism: From Disarray to Reconstruction" in *Philosophy after F.H. Bradley*, Bradley, James (ed). Armour, Leslie.
"From Presence to Process: Bradley and Whitehead" in *Philosophy after F.H. Bradley*, Bradley, James (ed). Bradley, James.

"Justification and the Foundations of Empirical Knowledge" in *Philosophy after F.H. Bradley*, Bradley, James (ed). Crossley, David J.
"The Autonomy of History: Collingwood's Critique of F.H. Bradley's Copernican Revolution in Historical Knowledge" in *Philosophy after F.H. Bradley*, Bradley, James (ed). Rubinoff, Lionel.
"Unity, Theory and Practice: F.H. Bradley and Pragmatism" in *Philosophy after F.H. Bradley*, Bradley, James (ed). Forster, Paul D.
*Assoluto: Frammenti di misticismo nella filosofia di Francis Herbert Bradley*. Taroni, Paolo.
*Philosophy after F.H. Bradley*. Bradley, James (ed).

**BRADSTREET, A**
The Flesh and the Spirit: Anne Bradstreet and Seventeenth Century Dualism, Materialism, Vitalism and Reformed Theology. Whelan, Timothy.

**BRADWARDINE**
La estructura formal del *De causa Dei* de Thomas Bradwardine. Verdú Berganza, Ignacio.
La tradizione ermetica a Oxford nei secoli XIII e XIV: Ruggero Bacone e Tommaso Bradwardine. Sannino, Antonella.

**BRAHMAN**
A Critique on Brahman-Realization. Prabhakara Rao, M.

**BRAHMANISM**
Pāndava-Purāna of Vādicandra: Text and Translation. Jaini, Padmanabh S.

**BRAIN**
"Mind" as Humanizing the Brain: Toward a Neurotheology of Meaning. Ashbrook, James B.
"Processing of Negative Sentences by Adults with Unilateral Cerebral Lesions" in *Verdad: lógica, representación y mundo*, Villegas Forero, L. Juncos-Rabadán, Onésimo.
*Cervello-Mente: Pensatori del XX secolo*. Gava, Giacomo.
*Das phänomenale Bewusstsein: Eine Verteidigung*. Lanz, Peter.
A Patterned Process Approach To Brain, Consciousness, and Behavior. Díaz, José-Luis.
Brains in Vats Revisited. Leeds, Stephen.
Cerebral Hemispheres. Davis, Lawrence H.
Consciousness and Connectionism—The Problem of Compatability of Type Identity Theory and of Connectionism. Potrc, Matjaz.
Crisis of Brain and Self. Keyes, C Don.
Die vierte bis siebte Kränkung des Menschen—Gehirn, Evolution und Menschenbild. Vollmer, Gerhard.
Enhancing Cognition in the Intellectually Intact. Juengst, Eric T, Whitehouse, Peter J and Mehlman, Maxwell (& others).
Gehirn und Ich: Zwei Hauptakteure des Geistes?. Kaeser, Eduard.
Internal Realism, Metaphysical Realism, and Brains in a Vat. Forrai, Gábor.
Lost the Plot? Reconstructing Dennett's Multiple Drafts Theory of Consciousness. Akins, Kathleen.
Mind Architecture and Brain Architecture. Cela-Conde, Camilo J and Marty, Gisèle.
On the Mechanism of Consciousness. Cotterill, Rodney M J.
On the Use of Visualizations in the Practice of Science. Sargent, Pauline.
On Wittgenstein on Cognitive Science. Proudfoot, Diane.
Problemas del empirismo en la filosofía de la mente. Hierro, José S Pescador.
Syntax in a Dynamic Brain. Garson, James W.
The Brain and the I: Neurodevelopment and Personal Identity. Mahowald, Mary B.
The Brain/Body Problem. Schechtman, Marya.
The Psychology of Harry F. Harlow: A Bridge from Radical to Rational Behaviorism. Rumbaugh, Duane M.
Three Comparative Maps of the Human. Samuelson, Norbert M.
Understanding Metaphors with the Two Hemispheres of the Brain. Frandsen, Nikolaj.
When a Pain Is Not. Hardcastle, Valerie Gray.

**BRAIN DEATH**
*Death, Brain Death and Ethics*. Lamb, David.
Is it Time to Abandon Brain Death?. Truog, Robert D.

**BRAIN, R**
On Helmholtz and 'Bürgerliche Intelligenz': A Response to Robert Brain. Cahan, David.

**BRAINE, D**
All Existing is the Action of God: The Philosophical Theology of David Braine. Bradshaw, David.
David Braine's Project: The Human Person. Burrell, David B.

**BRANCH**
Agency and Obligation. Horty, John F.
Criteria for Admissibility of Inference Rules: Modal and Intermediate Logics with the Branching Property. Rybakov, Vladimir V.
Partially-Ordered (Branching) Generalized Quantifiers: A General Definition. Sher, G Y.
The Way of the Agent. Belnap, Nuel and Perloff, Michael.

**BRANDAO, C**
Filosofia da Educaçao na Experiência Educativa Inter-Cultural de D. Frei Caetano Brandao em Terras de Belém do Pará 1782-1789. Dias, José Ribeiro.

**BRANDOM, R**
"Reply to Gibson, Byrne, and Brandom" in *Perception*, Villanueva, Enrique (ed). McDowell, John.

**BRANDOM, R**
Brandom on Representation and Inference. McDowell, John.
Brandom's *Making It Explicit*: A First Encounter. Rosenberg, Jay F.
Success Again: Replies to Brandom and Godfrey-Smith. Whyte, J T.
What Do You Do When They Call You a 'Relativist'. Rorty, Richard.
Who Makes the Rules Around Here?. Rosen, Gideon.

**BRANDON, R**
Theoretical Modeling and Biological Laws. Cooper, Gregory.

**BRANDT, R**
Brandt on Utilitarianism and the Foundations of Ethics. Carson, Thomas L.

**BRATMAN, M**
Consistency Among Intentions and the 'Simple View'. Sverdlik, Steven.
Rational Cooperation, Intention, and Reconsideration. Mintoff, Joe.

**BRAUDE, S**
Response to the Commentary. Gillett, Grant.

**BRAY, R**
"A Horse Chestnut Is Not a Chestnut Horse": A Refutation of Bray, Davis, MacGregor, and Wollan. Oates, Stephen B.
Towards a Definition of Plagiarism: The Bray/Oates Controversy Revisited. Kozak, Ellen M.

**BRAZILIAN**
*Odisseias do Espírito: Estudos de Filosofia Luso-Brasileira*. Cândido Pimentel, Manuel.
A Educaçao no Imaginário Liberal. Silva Filho, Lauro de Barros.
Country Fashion (in Portuguese). Arantes, Otília Beatriz Fiori and Arantes, Paulo Eduardo.
Gender and Social Awareness: A Story from Buenos Aires. Pac, Andrea.
O "Romantismo", o "Enciclopedismo" e o "Criticismo" Manifestos no Magistério da Filosofia no Ensino Médio em Uberlândia. Pereira da Silva, Sérgio.
Rebecca Reichmann on Womens' Health and Reproductive Rights in Brazil. Heilig, Steve.
Subsídios para uma Análise da Política da Educaçao Escolar Brasileira. Donatoni, Alaíde Rita and Cândida P Coelho, Maria.

**BREAL, M**
De Aristóteles a Bréal: Da *Homonímia* à *Polissemia*. Da Silva, Augusto Soares.

**BRECKMAN, W**
The Birth of Economic Competitiveness: Rejoinder to Breckman and Trägårdh. Greenfeld, Liah.

**BRELET, G**
Esthétique de l'interprétation créatrice—Essai sur l'idée "interprétation" de Gisèle Brelet. Shibaike, Masami.

**BRENTANO**
"The Relational vs. Directional Conception of Intentionality" in *Epistemology and History*, Zeidler-Janiszewska, Anna (ed). Pasniczek, Jacek.
*Husserl's Position in the School of Brentano*. Rollinger, Robin Daryl.
*Intenzioni: D'amore di scienza e d'anarchia*. Donnici, Rocco.
Austrian Philosophy: The Legacy of Franz Brentano. Brandl, Johannes.

**BRETON, A**
*The Lost Steps*. Polizzotti, Mark (trans) and Breton, André.

**BREUILLY, J**
The State of Nationalism. Tilly, Charles.

**BRIBERY**
Don't Change the Subject: Interpreting Public Discourse over Quid Pro Quo. Stark, Andrew.

**BRIDGES, D**
Quantum Mechanical Unbounded Operators and Constructive Mathematics—A Rejoinder to Bridges. Hellman, Geoffrey.

**BRINK, D**
From Moral Realism to Moral Relativism in One Easy Step. Horgan, Terence and Timmons, Mark.
Moral Realism and the Burden of Argument. Yasenchuk, Ken.

**BRINKMAN, B**
The Heythrop Journal (1960-1996): From In-House Review to International Journal. Levi, A H T.
'Outsidelessness' and the 'Beyond' of Signification. Griffith-Dickson, Gwen.

**BRITISH**
see also English
"...Equality from the Masculine Point of View...": The 2nd Earl Russell and Divorce Law Reform in England. Savage, Gail.
"Cambridge and the Austrian Connection" in *In Itinere* European Cities and the Birth of Modern Scientific Philosophy, Poli, Roberto (ed). Dappiano, Luigi.
"James, Aboutness, and his British Critics" in *The Cambridge Companion to William James*, Putnam, Ruth Anna (ed). Sprigge, T L S.
*Hegel, Marx, and the English State*. MacGregor, David.
*The Social Philosophy of Ernest Gellner*. Jarvie, Ian (ed) and Hall, John A (ed).
*The Sovereignty of Reason: The Defense of Rationality in the Early English Enlightenment*. Beiser, Frederick C.
*Twentieth-Century Philosophy*. Baird, Forrest E (ed) and Kaufmann, Walter.
Aestheticism As Seen in British Tiles in the 1870s and 80s (in Japanese). Yoshimura, Noriko.

Alexander Pope and Eighteenth Century Conflicts about Ultimacy. Leigh, David J.
Blurred Boundaries. Morriss, Peter.
Centering Culture: Teaching for Critical Sexual Literacy using the Sexual Diversity Wheel. Sears, James T.
Ethical Attitudes and Behavior of Investment Professionals in the United Kingdom. Baker, H Kent and Veit, E Theodore.
Expressions of Corporate Social Responsibility in U.K. Firms. Robertson, Diana C and Nicholson, Nigel.
How Should Schools Respond to the Plurality of Values in a Multi-Cultural Society?. Burwood, Les R V.
Hume and the 1763 Edition of His *History of England*: His Frame of Mind as a Revisionist. Van Holthoon, Frederic L.
Learning Moral Commitment in Higher Education?. Collier, Gerald.
Linguistic Relativity in French, English, and German Philosophy. Harvey, William.
Muslims and Sex Education. Halstead, J Mark.
Not at Home in Empire. Guha, Ranajit.
Public Preferences for Health Care: Prioritisation in the United Kingdom. Shickle, Darren.
Spenser and the Historical Revolution: *Briton Moniments* and the *Problem of Roman Britain*. Curran Jr, John E.
The Economic Attributes of Medical Care: Implications for Rationing Choices in the United States and United Kingdom. Banks, Dwayne A.
The Eighteenth-Century British Reviews of Hume's Writings. Fieser, James.
The Influence of Chinese Philosophy on the English Style Garden: A Comparative Study of Wörlitz and Koishikawa Korakuen (in Japanese). Seiko. Goto.
The Moral and Spiritual Dimension to Education: Some Reflections on the British Experience. Rossiter, Graham.
Utilitarianism and the Punishment of the Innocent: The Origins of a False Doctrine. Rosen, F.
Who is Authorized to Speak? Katherine Mayo and the Politics of Imperial Feminism in British India. Wilson, Liz.
Wisdom. Dilman, Ilham.

**BROAD**
Descriptive and Revisionary Theories of Events. McHenry, Leemon B.

**BROADIE, S**
Reason as the Foundation of *Eudaimonia* in the *Nicomachean Ethics*. Hill, Susan.

**BROCKMEIER, J**
Commentary on "Autobiography, Narrative, and the Freudian Concept of Life History". Robinson, Daniel N.

**BRODY, H**
Knowledge and Power in the Clinical Setting. McMillan, John and Anderson, Lynley.

**BRONNER, S**
The Frankfurt School. Tessin, Timothy.

**BRONTE, C**
"Versions of the Feminine Subject in Charlotte Brontë's *Villette*" in *Critical Studies: Ethics and the Subject*, Simms, Karl (ed). Watkins, Susan.

**BROOME, J**
The Two Envelope Paradox and Infinite Expectations. Arntzenius, Frank and McCarthy, David.
What's in the Two Envelope Paradox?. Scott, Alexander D and Scott, Michael.

**BROUWER, L**
Introduction to *Life, Art, and Mysticism*. Van Stigt, Walter P.

**BROWN, H**
'Many Minds' Interpretations of Quantum Mechanics: Replies to Replies. Lockwood, Michael.

**BROWN, J**
Externalist Self-Knowledge and the Scope of the A Priori. Miller, Richard W.

**BRUNO**
La actualidad de Giordano Bruno en castellano. Rábade, Ana Isabel.

**BRUNSCHVICG, L**
The Heritage of Léon Brunschvicg (and Commentary by P. Horák) (in Czech). Rivenc, François and Horák, Petr.

**BRZEZINSKI, Z**
Millennium Approaches: Previewing the Twenty-first Century. Miller, Linda B.

**BUBER**
*Nietzsche and Jewish Culture*. Golomb, Jacob (ed).
*The Martin Buber-Carl Rogers Dialogue: A New Transcript with Commentary*. Anderson, Rob and Cissna, Kenneth N.
Born to Affirm the Eternal Recurrence: Nietzsche, Buber, and Springsteen. Cohen, Jonathan.
Education as Encounter: Buber's Pragmatic Ontology. McHenry Jr, Henry D.
The Meaning of History: A Further Contribution to URAM Buber Studies (URAM 17:33-49). Kovacs, George.

**BUCHLER, J**
"Buchler's *The Main of Light*: The Role of Metaphysics in Literary Theory and Interpretation" in *Philosophy in Experience: American Philosophy in Transition*. Hart, Richard E (ed).

**BUSINESS ETHICS**
The New Federalism: Implications for the Legitimacy of Corporate Political Activity. Christensen, Sandra L.
The Why's of Business Revisited. Duska, Ronald F.
Thou Shalt and Shalt Not: An Alternative to the Ten Commandments Approach to Developing a Code of Ethics for Schools of Business. Kleiner, Deborah S and Maury, Mary D.
Truth or Consequences: A Study of Critical Issues and Decision Making in Accounting. Gibson, Annetta and Frakes, Albert H.
Universal Values, Behavioral Ethics and Entrepreneurship. Clarke, Ruth and Aram, John.
Useful Friendships: A Foundation for Business Ethics. Sommers, Mary Catherine.
Using the "Ethical Environment" Paradigm to Teach Business Ethics: The Case of the Maquiladoras. Raisner, Jack A.
What Cognitive Science Tells Us about Ethics and the Teaching of Ethics. Anderson, James A.
Without a Care in the World: The Business Ethics Course and Its Exclusion of a Care Perspective. DeMoss, Michelle A and McCann, Greg K.

**BUTLER**
Butler, Hobbes, and Human Nature. O'Brien, Wendell.
Foucault's Reconfiguration of the Subject: From Nietzsche to Butler, Laclau/Mouffe, and Beyond. Schrift, Alan D.

**BUTLER, J**
Between Emergence and Possibility: Foucault, Derrida, and Judith Butler on Performative Identity. Nealon, Jeffrey T.
Materiality and Language: Butler's Interrogation of the History of Philosophy. Olkowski, Dorothea.
Materiality in Theodor W. Adorno and Judith Butler. Hull, Carrie L.
What is a Woman? Butler and Beauvoir on the Foundations of the Sexual Difference. Heinämaa, Sara.

**BUTTERFIELD, H**
Herbert Butterfield (1900-79) as a Christian Historian of Science. Cabral, Regis.

**BUTTERFIELD, J**
'Many Minds' Interpretations of Quantum Mechanics: Replies to Replies. Lockwood, Michael.

**BUYER**
Identifying Ethical Problems Confronting Small Retail Buyers during the Merchandise Buying Process. Arbuthnot, Jeanette Jaussaud.

**BYRNE, A**
"Reply to Gibson, Byrne, and Brandom" in *Perception,* Villanueva, Enrique (ed). McDowell, John.

**BYRON**
"Lord Byron: To Create, and in Creating Live a Being More Intense" in *Critical Studies: Ethics and the Subject,* Simms, Karl (ed). Rawes, Alan.

**CABANCHIK, S**
Nota sobre la certeza: Una discusión con Samuel Cabanchik. Palavecino, Sergio R.

**CADAVER**
Non-Heart-Beating Cadaver Procurement and the Work of Ethics Committees. Spielman, Bethany and Verhulst, Steve.

**CAICEDO, X**
Logics of Rejection: Two Systems of Natural Deduction. Tamminga, Allard M.

**CALCULATION**
Step by Recursive Step: Church's Analysis of Effective Calculability. Sieg, Wilfried.

**CALCULUS**
see also Lambda Calculus
"Das Kalkül der Moral" in *Ökonomie und Moral: Beiträge zur Theorie ökonomischer Rationalität,* Lohmann, Karl Reinhard (ed). Kirsch, Guy.
*A New Introduction to Modal Logic.* Cresswell, M J and Hughes, G E.
*Lingua Universalis vs. Calculus Ratiocinator: An Ultimate Presupposition of Twentieth-Century Philosophy.* Hintikka, Jaakko.
Cardinalities of Models for Pure Calculi of Names. Pietruszczak, Andrzej.
Le statut de la vérité dans le calcul implicationnel de Russell en 1903. Vernant, Denis.
On the Proof Theory of Coquand's Calculus of Constructions. Seldin, Jonathan P.
Probability as a Guide to Life. Beebee, Helen and Papineau, David.
The Infinitesimals as Useful Fictions for Leibniz: The Controversy in the Paris Academy of Sciences (Spanish). Joven, Fernando.
Zur Begründung des Infinitesimalkalküls durch Leibniz. Krämer, Sybille.

**CALLAHAN, D**
Struggle. Miller, Patrick.

**CALLICLES**
Callicles' Examples of *nomos tes phuseos* in Plato's *Gorgias.* Fussi, Alessandra.

**CALVINISM**
*Knowing Other-Wise: Philosophy at the Threshold of Spirituality.* Olthuis, James H (ed).
Catholics vs. Calvinists on Religious Knowledge. Greco, John.
Covenant and Ethics? Comments from a South African Perspective. Smit, Dirk J.

Jean Calvin et la triste richesse: Du travail, du loisir et du salut de l'âme. Reymond, Bernard.
Mechanistic Individualism Versus Organismic Totalitarianism: Toward a Neo-Calvinist Perspective. Venter, J J.

**CAMERON, E**
Thick Paintings and the Logic of Things: The Non-Ultimate Nature of Particular Works of Art. Risser, Rita.

**CAMPANELLA**
"Una città senza storia: la perfezione immobile e l'utopia di Tommaso Campenella" in *Lo Storicismo e la Sua Storia: Temi, Problemi, Prospettive,* Cacciatore, Giuseppe (ed). Cambi, Maurizio.

**CAMPBELL, C**
"F.H. Bradley and C.A. Campbell" in *Philosophy after F.H. Bradley,* Bradley, James (ed). Maclachlan, Lorne.
*Philosophy after F.H. Bradley.* Bradley, James (ed).

**CAMPBELL, D**
A Tribute to Donald T. Campbell. Heyes, Cecilia.

**CAMPBELL, G**
*Hume on Miracles.* Tweyman, Stanley (ed).

**CAMPBELL, J**
"Comments on John Campbell, 'Molineux's Question'" in *Perception,* Villanueva, Enrique (ed). Loar, Brian.
"Shape Properties and Perception" in *Perception,* Villanueva, Enrique (ed). Ludwig, Kirk A.
Indexing Truths: A Critical Notice of John Campbell's *Past, Space, and Self.* McGilvray, James.
Practical Understanding vs Reflective Understanding. Bermúdez, José Luis.
Sense, Validity and Context. Williamson, Timothy.
Subjects and Objects. Cassam, Quassim.

**CAMPBELL, K**
A Critique of Campbell's Refurbished Nominalism. Moreland, J P.

**CAMPBELL, N**
A Hundred Years of Numbers: An Historical Introduction to Measurement Theory 1887-1990: Part I: The Formation Period: Two Lines of Research: Axiomatics and Real Morphisms, Scales and Invariance. Díez, José A.

**CAMUS**
God Is Love, Therefore There Is Evil. Fendt, Gene.

**CANADIAN**
"Bradley and the Canadian Connection" in *Philosophy after F.H. Bradley,* Bradley, James (ed). Trott, Elizabeth.
"Epistemic Responsibility and the Inuit of Canada's Eastern Arctic: An Ecofeminist Appraisal" in *Ecofeminism: Women, Culture, Nature,* Warren, Karen J (ed). Buege, Douglas J.
*A Question of Values: New Canadian Perspectives in Ethics and Political Philosophy.* Brennan, Samantha (ed), Isaacs, Tracy (ed) and Milde, Michael (ed).
A propos de l'Éducation et de l'Institution scolaire au Québec. Louis, Desmeules and Desjardins, Richard.
Business Ethics and National Identity in Quebec: Distinctiveness and Directions. Pasquero, Jean.
Business Ethics in Canada: A Personal View. Boyd, Colin.
Business Ethics in Canada: Distinctiveness and Directions. Brooks, Leonard J.
Business Ethics in Canada: Integration and Interdisciplinarity. McDonald, Michael.
Cultural Nationalism, Neither Ethnic Nor Civic. Nielsen, Kai.
Dimensions of Citizenship and National Identity in Canada. Carens, Joseph H.
Eliminating the Barriers to Employment Equity in the Canadian Workplace. Falkenberg, L E and Boland, L.
Entrevue avec Monique Séguin. Leroux, François.
Entrevue avec Richard Carpentier. Leroux, François.
État fragile, démocratie précaire: le lieu de l'insouciance. Comeau, Paul-André.
Intersecting Memories: Bearing Witness to the 1989 Massacre of Women in Montreal. Rosenberg, Sharon.
Issues for Business Ethics in the Nineties and Beyond. Michalos, Alex C.
Non-Academic Critics of Business Ethics in Canada. Michalos, Alex C.

**CANCER**
"Decoding" Informed Consent: Insights from Women regarding Breast Cancer Susceptibility Testing. Geller, Gail, Strauss, Misha and Bernhardt, Barbara A (& others).
Ethical Issues in Pediatric Life-Threatening Illness: Dilemmas of Consent, Assent, and Communication. Kunin, Howard.

**CANEY, S**
Contractual Justice: A Modest Defence. Barry, Brian.

**CANNOT**
'Cannot,' 'Not Can' and 'Can Not'. Davson-Galle, Peter.

**CANON**
Canonizing Measures. Gasché, Rodolphe.

**CANONICAL**
Canonical Models for Temporal Deontic Logic. Bailhache, Patrice.
Canonical Seeds and Prikry Trees. Hamkins, Joel David.

## CARING
Shared Decision Making: The Ethics of Caring and Best Respect. Beltran, Joseph E.

## CARLSON, A
Carlson on Appreciation. Godlovitch, Stanley.

## CARLYLE, T
Unamuno traductor de Th. Carlyle. Robles, Laureano.

## CARMAN, T
Heidegger on Presence: A Reply. Olafson, Frederick A.

## CARNAL
"Carnal Knowledge in the *Charmides*" in *Dialogues with Plato*, Benitez, Eugenio (ed). McAvoy, Martin.

## CARNAP
"Carnap and Wittgenstein's *Tractatus*" in *Early Analytic Philosophy*, Tait, William W (ed). Friedman, Michael.
"Carnap's Principle of Tolerance" in *Philosophy, Religion, and the Question of Intolerance*, Ambuel, David (ed). Barker, Stephen F.
"Carnap: From Logical Syntax to Semantics" in *Origins of Logical Empiricism*, Giere, Ronald N (ed). Ricketts, Thomas.
"From Epistemology to the Logic of Science: Carnap's Philosophy of Empirical Knowledge in the 1930s" in *Origins of Logical Empiricism*, Giere, Ronald N (ed). Richardson, Alan W.
"Languages without Logic" in *Origins of Logical Empiricism*, Giere, Ronald N (ed). Creath, Richard.
"Neurath against Method" in *Origins of Logical Empiricism*, Giere, Ronald N (ed). Cartwright, Nancy.
"Overcoming Metaphysics: Carnap and Heidegger" in *Origins of Logical Empiricism*, Giere, Ronald N (ed). Friedman, Michael.
"Relativity, *Eindeutigkeit*, and Monomorphism: Rudolph Carnap and the Development of the Categoricity Concept in Formal Semantics" in *Origins of Logical Empiricism*, Giere, Ronald N (ed). Howard, Don.
"The Carnap-Hintikka Programme in Inductive Logic" in *Knowledge and Inquiry: Essays on Jaakko Hintikka's Epistemology and Philosophy of Science*, Sintonen, Matti (ed). Kuipers, Theo A F.
*Lingua Universalis vs. Calculus Ratiocinator: An Ultimate Presupposition of Twentieth-Century Philosophy.* Hintikka, Jaakko.
Analyse logique et analyticité; de Carnap à Gödel. Couture, Jocelyne.
Anti-Foundationalism and the Vienna Circle's Revolution in Philosophy. Uebel, Thomas E.
Carnap and Quine on Empiricism. Almeder, Robert F.
Conventions in the *Aufbau*. Uebel, Thomas E.
Der Weg weg von der Metaphysik—ein Rundweg?. Schulthess, Peter.
Gödel Meets Carnap: A Prototypical Discourse on Science and Religion. Gierer, Alfred.
Holismo Semántico e Inconmensurabilidad en el Debate Positivismo-Antipositivismo. Gentile, Nélida.
In Defence of Philosophy Against the Endists. Uroh, Chris Okechukwu.
La metalógica en la propuesta de R. Carnap. Padilla-Gálvez, Jesús.

## CARPENTIER, R
Entrevue avec Richard Carpentier. Leroux, François.

## CARR, A
Business and Game-Playing: The False Analogy. Koehn, Daryl.

## CARR, D
"*Akrasia*: Irremediable but not Unapproachable" in *Philosophy of Education (1996)*, Margonis, Frank (ed). Worsfold, Victor L.
Remarks on History and Interpretation: Replies to Casey, Carr, and Rockmore. Margolis, Joseph.

## CARRA, C
Carlo Carrà's Metaphysical Painting—The Works Reproduced in *Valori Plastici* (in Japanese). Demura, Masaya.

## CARRIER, R
Response to Richard Carrier. Reinsmith, William.

## CARRILLO, R
El filósofo Rafael Carrillo. Cataño, Gonzalo.

## CARROLL, L
Contraposition and Lewis Carrol's Barber Shop Paradox. Gillon, Brendan S.

## CARROLL, N
Confession of a Weak Anti-Intentionalist: Exposing Myself. Wilson, W Kent.
Reply to Noël Carroll. Dickie, George T.

## CARRUTHERS, P
Contractualism and Animals. Bernstein, Mark.
Essay: *Human Knowledge and Human Nature: A New Introduction to an Ancient Debate* by Peter Carruthers and *Knowledge and the State of Nature: An Essay in Conceptual Synthesis* by Edward Craig. Feldman, Richard.
Some Nonhuman Animals Can Have Pains in a Morally Relevant Sense. Robinson, William S.

## CARTESIANISM
"De la metafisica a la fisica en el programa cartesiano" in *Memorias Del Seminario En Conmemoración De Los 400 Anos Del Nacimiento De René Descartes*, Albis, Víctor S (ed). Cardona, Carlos Albert.
"Introduction to Part II" in *Critical Studies: Ethics and the Subject*, Simms, Karl (ed). Simms, Karl.
"Non-Cartesian Coordinates in the Contemporary Humanities" in *Epistemology and History*, Zeidler-Janiszewska, Anna (ed). Grzegorczyk, Anna.

"Subjectivity in the Twentieth Century" in *Critical Studies: Ethics and the Subject*, Simms, Karl (ed). Rée, Jonathan.
"World 1, World 2 and the Theory of Evolution" in *The Significance of Popper's Thought*, Amsterdamski, Stefan (ed). Watkins, John.
*Cartesian Nightmare: An Introduction to Transcendental Sophistry.* Redpath, Peter A.
*Descartes' Dualism.* Baker, Gordon and Morris, Katherine J.
*Lo stile de' Geometri*: La filosofia cartesiana nell'opera di Alessandro Pascoli (1669-1757). Guerrini, Luigi.
*Malebranche's Theory of the Soul: A Cartesian Interpretation.* Schmaltz, Tad M.
A proposito di centenari cartesiani. Garin, Eugenio.
A Theological Escape from the Cartesian Circle?. Dalton, Peter.
An Objection to Swinburne's Argument for Dualism. Stump, Eleonore and Kretzmann, Norman.
Cartesian Epistemics and Descartes' *Regulae*. Thomas, Bruce M.
Commentary on "Non-Cartesian Frameworks". Phillips, James.
Descartes e os Jesuítas: Para um estudo da personalidade cartesiana. Dinis, Alfredo.
From Kerlin's Pizzeria to MJK Reynolds: A Socratic and Cartesian Approach to Business Ethics. Kerlin, Michael J.
Genovesi e Cartesio. Marcialis, Maria Teresa.
Il cartesianesimo matematico a Napoli. Gatto, Romano.
L'arrivo del *Discours* e dei *Principia,D* in Italia: prime letture dei testi cartesiani a Napoli. Lojacono, Ettore.
La métaphysique aristotélicienne et son sosie cartésien. Cunningham, Henri-Paul.
La reazione a Cartesio nella Napoli del Seicento: Giovambattista De Benedictis. De Liguori, Girolamo.
Note su traduzioni manoscritte delle opere cartesiane. Guerrini, Luigi.
Note sulle polemiche antifrancesi di Vico. Agrimi, Mario.
Possibilities in Philosophy of Mind. Taliaferro, Charles.
Reply to Stump and Kretzmann. Swinburne, Richard.
Self-Knowledge in Aristotle. Lewis, Frank A.
Sulla presenza di Descartes nella *Galleria di Minerva*. Crasta, Francesca Maria.
The Method of the Geometer: A New Angle on Husserl's Cartesianism. Kasely, Terry S.
Toward a Non-Cartesian Psychotherapeutic Framework: Radical Pragmatism as an Alternative. Berger, Louis S.
Why is the Fifth Cartesian Meditation Necessary?. Haney, Kathleen.

## CARTWRIGHT, N
The Analysis of Particle Tracks: A Case for Trust in the Unity of Physics. Falkenburg, Brigitte.

## CASE STUDY
*Critical Reasoning: A Practical Introduction.* Thomson, Anne.
*Ethics for Professionals in Education: Perspectives for Preparation and Practice.* Strike, Kenneth A (ed) and Ternasky, P Lance (ed).
Aesthetic Case Studies and Discipline-Based Art Education. Moore, Ronald.
An Empirical Study of Moral Reasoning Among Managers in Singapore. Wimalasiri, Jayantha S, Pavri, Francis and Jalil, Abdul A K.
Bad Night in the ER—Patients' Preferences and Reasonable Accommodation: Discussed by Douglas A. Beer, Ruth Macklin, Walter Robinson, and Philip Wang. Beer, Douglas A, Macklin, Ruth and Robinson, Walter (& others).
Bohr's Theory of the Atom 1913-1923: A Case Study in the Progress of Scientific Research Programmes. Hettema, Hinne.
Case Commentary. Flanigan, Rosemary.
Case Studies for Teaching Research Ethics. Elliott, Deni.
Criminal Children. Richards, Norvin.
Ethical Issues and Relationships between House Staff and Attending Physicians: A Case Study. Beckerman, Aaron, Doerfler, Martin and Couch, Elsbeth (& others).
Ethics Consultants and Surrogates: Can We Do Better?. Fletcher, John C.
Evaluation Research and the Future of Ethics Consultation. Fox, Ellen and Tulsky, James A.
Futile Care in Neonatology: An Interim Report from Colorado. Hulac, Peter and Barbour, Elizabeth.
Hope and the Limits of Research: Commentary. Daugherty, Christopher K.
Individual, Family, and Societal Dimensions of Genetic Discrimination: A Case Study Analysis. Geller, Lisa N, Alper, Joseph S and Billings, Paul R (& others).
Mass Extinctions and the Teaching of Philosophy of Science. Boersema, David B.
More is Better. Flanigan, Rosemary.
On Grading Apples and Arguments. Mendenhall, Vance.
Response to Gregory Pence's Case Study in the Teaching of Ethics. Makus, Robert.
Shared Decision Making: The Ethics of Caring and Best Respect. Beltran, Joseph E.
Suicide and Advance Directives: One Doctor's Dilemma. Kane, Gregory C.
The Baby K Case: A Search for the Elusive Standard of Medical Care. Schneiderman, Lawrence J and Manning, Sharyn.
The Case of the Slain President: Teaching Critical Thinking in Context. Walters, Kerry.

## CASE STUDY

*What Are the Goals of Ethics Consultation: A Consensus Statement.* Fletcher, John C and Siegler, Mark.

Where Is Will Rogers When We Need Him Most? Toward a Traditional Morality in Biomedical Ethics. Sample, Tex.

## CASEY, E

Remarks on History and Interpretation: Replies to Casey, Carr, and Rockmore. Margolis, Joseph.

## CASSAM, Q

Replies. Campbell, John.

## CASSIRER

"Cassirers Renaissance-Auffassung" in *Grenzen der kritischen Vernunft*, Schmid, Peter A. Schmidt-Biggemann, Wilhelm.

"Ernst Cassirer e il problema dell'oggettività nelle scienze della cultura" in *Lo Storicismo e la Sua Storia: Temi, Problemi, Prospettive*, Cacciatore, Giuseppe (ed). Martirano, Maurizio.

"L'incontro problematico tra *Historismus* e neo-kantiano" in *Lo Storicismo e la Sua Storia: Temi, Problemi, Prospettive*, Cacciatore, Giuseppe (ed). Bonito Oliva, Rossella.

"Mythos und Moderne in der *Philosophie der symbolischen Formen* Ernst Cassirers" in *Epistemology and History*, Zeidler-Janiszewska, Anna (ed). Paetzold, Heinz.

"Technik und symbolische Form bei Cassirer" in *Grenzen der kritischen Vernunft*, Schmid, Peter A. Robbeck, Johannes.

"Zum Problem der Farbe in Cassirers *Philosophie der symbolischen Formen*" in *Grenzen der kritischen Vernunft*, Schmid, Peter A. Bertolini, Luisa.

*Grenzen der kritischen Vernunft*. Schmid, Peter A and Zurbuchen, Simone.

*The Magic Mirror: Myth's Abiding Power*. Baeten, Elizabeth M.

Ernst Cassirer, Historian of the Will. Wisner, David A.

Gegenstand und Methode in der Geschichte der Mathematik. Otte, Michael.

Renormalized Quantum Field Theory and Cassirer's Epistemological System. Dosch, Hans Günter.

## CASTANEDA, H

Are (Possible) Guises Internally Characterizable?. Voltolini, Alberto.

Raúl Orayen's Views on Philosophy of Logic. Peña, Lorenzo.

The Validity of Indexical Arguments. Elkatip, S H.

## CASUISTRY

"Morally Appreciated Circumstances: A Theoretical Problem for Casuistry" in *Philosophical Perspectives on Bioethics,* Sumner, L W (ed). Jonsen, Albert R.

"The Role of Principles in Practical Ethics" in *Philosophical Perspectives on Bioethics,* Sumner, L W (ed). Beauchamp, Tom L.

*Just and Unjust Wars*: Casuistry and the Boundaries of the Moral World. Boyle, Joseph.

*Making Mortal Choices: Three Exercises in Moral Casuistry*. Bedau, Hugo Adam.

Evading Responsibility: The Ethics of Ingenuity. Katz, Leo.

William James's Ethics and the New Casuistry. Mehl, Peter J.

## CAT-HO, N

H Rasiowa's and C Rauszer's Contribution to Algebra. Bartol, Wiktor.

## CATEGORIAL

Extending Lambek Grammars to Basic Categorial Grammars. Buszkowski, Wojciech.

Fibred Semantics for Feature-Based Grammar Logic. Dörre, Jochen, König, Esther and Gabbay, Dov.

Identification in the Limit of Categorial Grammars. Kanazawa, Makoto.

Multimodal Linguistic Inference. Moortgat, Michael.

Tree Models and (Labeled) Categorial Grammar. Venema, Yde.

## CATEGORICAL

Potential, Propensity, and Categorical Realism. Liu, Chuang.

## CATEGORICAL GRAMMAR

Infinite Set Unification with Application to Categorical Grammar. Marciniec, Jacek.

## CATEGORICAL IMPERATIVE

Desmoralizar la Promesa?. Botero C, Juan J.

Hegel's Critique of Kant's Empiricism and the Categorial Imperative. Sedgwick, Sally.

Justifying Kant's Principles of Justice. Kerstein, Samuel.

Kant and Clint: Dirty Harry Meets the Categorical Imperative. De Bolt, Darian.

Prometer en Falso: La Contradicción Práctica y el Imperativo Categórico. Rosas, Alejandro.

Transcendentalism, Nomicity and Modal Thought. Muresan, Valentin.

What should we Treat as an End in Itself?. Dean, Richard.

Zur Analytizität der *Grundlegung*. Schönecker, Dieter.

## CATEGORICAL LANGUAGES

Higher Order Unification and the Interpretation of Focus. Pulman, Stephen G.

## CATEGORY

"Dispositions as Categorical States" in *Dispositions: A Debate,* Armstrong, D M. Armstrong, D M.

"Genuine Triads and Teridentity" in *Studies in the Logic of Charles Sanders Peirce*, Houser, Nathan (ed). Brunning, Jacqueline.

"Pragmatic Experimentalism and the Derivation of the Categories" in *The Rule of Reason: The Philosophy of Charles Sanders Peirce*, Forster, Paul (ed). Rosenthal, Sandra B.

*Kant's Criticism of Metaphysics*. Walsh, W H.

A Categorical Approach to Higher-Level Introduction and Elimination Rules. Poubel, Hardée Werneck and Pereira, Luiz Carlos P D.

A Objectividade como categoria filosófica: Subsídios para uma caracterizaçao. Barata-Moura, José.

A Strategy for the Acquisition of Problem-Solving Expertise in Humans: The Category-as-Analogy Approach. Alma, Carine V.

Aristotle's Criticism of the Subject Criterion. Yu, Jiyuan.

Capitalizer of Binary Relations and the Fork Operator as Image of a General Disjoint Union-Function of Cartesian Product Functions. Marlangeon, Mauricio Pablo.

Categoricalist versus Dispositionalist Accounts of Properties. Armstrong, David M.

Categorization, Anomalies and the Discovery of Nuclear Fission. Andersen, Hanne.

Combining Algebraizable Logics. Jánossy, A, Kurucz, A and Eiben, A E.

Constructive Canonicity in Non-Classical Logics. Ghilardi, Silvio and Meloni, Giancarlo.

Deductive Completeness. Dosen, Kosta.

Dynamic Bracketing and Discourse Representation. Visser, Albert and Vermeulen, Kees.

Innate Ideas, Categories and Objectivity. Antonopoulos, Constantin.

Kant's Doctrine of Categories: An Attempt at Some Clarification. Gupta, R K.

Kinds and Categories: Proceedings of the Twentieth Annual Greensboro Symposium in Philosophy. Loux, Michael J.

Kripke Models and the (In)equational Logic of the Second-Order Lambda-Calculus. Gallier, Jean.

La filosofía de la matemática de Albert Lautman. Zalamea, Fernando.

Le système stoïcien: monde et langage. Mattéi, Jean-François.

Nietzsche in Dr. Antonio Pérez Estévez's Thought (Spanish). Delgado Ocando, José Manuel.

On the Unification Problem for Cartesian Closed Categories. Narendran, Paliath, Pfenning, Frank and Statman, Richard.

Ontological Categories and Natural Kinds. Lowe, E J.

Perception and Kant's Categories. Greenberg, Robert.

Process and Action: Relevant Theory and Logics. Sylvan, Richard.

Quantified Extensions of Canonical Propositional Intermediate Logics. Ghilardi, Silvio.

Syntactic Characterizations of Closure under Pullbacks and of Locally Polypresentable Categories. Hébert, Michel.

The Category of the State of Things in Husserl's *Logical Investigations* (in Polish). Lukasiewicz, Dariusz.

The Figures of Subjectivity in Éric Weil's *Logique de la philosophie* (in French). Kirscher, Gilbert.

The Finite Model Property for BCI and Related Systems. Buszkowski, Wojciech.

## CATHARSIS

Cartesis en la *Poética* de Aristóteles. Sánchez Palencia, Angel.

## CATHOLIC

A Case for Proposition 209. Bradley, Gerard V.

## CATHOLICISM

"Arnauld versus Leibniz and Malebranche on the Limits of Theological Knowledge" in *Scepticism in the History of Philosophy: A Pan-American Dialogue*, Popkin, Richard H (ed). Sleigh, Jr, Robert.

*A Preserving Grace: Protestants, Catholics, and Natural Law*. Cromartie, Michael (ed).

*Business Ethics in the African Context Today*. Rosemann, Philipp W (ed) and LeJeune, Michel (ed).

*Erasmus of the Low Countries*. Tracy, James D.

Catholic Social Justice and Health Care Entitlement Packages. Boyle, Joseph.

Catholic Social Teaching in an Ara of Economic Globalization: A Resource for Business Ethics. McCann, Dennis P.

Catholics vs. Calvinists on Religious Knowledge. Greco, John.

Desire for Happiness and the Commandments in the First Chapter of *Veritatis Splendor*. Melina, Livio.

Do the Bishops Have It Right On Health Care Reform?. Sulmasy, Daniel P.

Enlarging the Conversation. Herman, Steward W.

Ethical Issues in Managed Care: A Catholic Christian Perspective. Pellegrino, Edmund D.

False and Genuine Knowledge: A Philosophical Look at the Peasant of the Garonne. Killoran, John B.

Fata ducunt. Hinske, Norbert.

Foundational Virtues for Community. Allen, Prudence.

Galileo and the Church: An Untidy Affair. Schoen, Edward L.

Infallibility, Authority and Faith. Haldane, John.

Maritain et le débat postconciliaire: Le paysan de la garonne. Fourcade, Michel.

Natural Law and Business Ethics. Velasquez, Manuel and Brady, Neil.

Roman Catholic Tradition and Ritual and Business Ethics: A Feminist Perspective. Andolsen, Barbara Hilkert.

Sexuality, Masculinity, and Confession. May, Larry and Bohman, James.

Sleigh's *Leibniz & Arnauld: A Commentary on their Correspondence* (New Haven: Yale University Press). Adams, Robert Merrihew.

## CATHOLICISM

Sobre los sentidos objetivo y sujetivo del trabajo según Polo. Pintado, Patricia.

Sozzini's Ghost: Pierre Bayle and Socinian Toleration. Tinsley, Barbara Sher.

The Business Ethics of Evangelicals. Roels, Shirley J.

The Cracow Circle (in Polish). Bochenski, Józef Maria.

The Sirens' Song of the Traditions: A plea for a Universal Ethics (in Dutch). Merks, Karl-Wilhelm.

Truth and History: The Question. Bonsor, Jack.

Understanding Equality in Health Care: A Christian Free-Market Approach. Gronbacher, Gregory M A.

Une relecture du paysan de la garonne. Allard, Jean-Louis.

Was the Peasant of the Garonne a Mistake?. Hudson, Deal.

Weber e lo spirito del capitalismo: Storia di un problema e nuove prospettive. Burgos, Juan Manuel.

## CATTELL, J

Baldwin, Cattell and the *Psychological Review*: A Collaboration and Its Discontents. Sokal, Michael M.

## CAUSAL

A Remark Concerning Prediction and Spacetime Singularities. Hogarth, Mark.

Antidote or Theory?. Dickson, Michael.

Enunciados causales de Burks y contrafácticos substanciales. Vilanova Arias, Javier.

Humphreys's Paradox and the Interpretation of Inverse Conditional Propensities. McCurdy, Christopher S I.

Indexical Reference and Bodily Causal Diagrams in Intentional Action. Castañeda, Héctor-Neri.

On the Logic of Event-Causation: Jaskowski-Style Systems of Causal Logic. Urchs, Max.

## CAUSAL EXPLANATION

Sobre referencia y causalidad. Lo Monaco, Vicenzo P.

## CAUSALITY

"Contraintes socio-culturelles et conversions philosphiques chez Descartes..." in *Memorias Del Seminario En Conmemoración De Los 400 Anos Del Nacimiento De René Descartes*, Albis, Víctor S (ed). Mazhary, Djahanguir R.

"Ontología causal: ¿sucesos o hechos?" in *Verdad: lógica, representación y mundo*, Villegas Forero, L. García Encinas, María José.

"Una crítica de la versión causal del tiempo" in *Verdad: lógica, representación y mundo*, Villegas Forero, L. Alvarez Toledo, Sebastián.

*Was sind Handlungen? Eine philosophische Auseinandersetzung mit dem Naturalismus.* Runggaldier, Edmund.

Ancora su nuvole ed orologi. Messeri, Marco.

Chief Bumbu en de Verklaring van Menselijk Gedrag. Mackor, Anne Ruth and Peijnenburg, Jeanne.

Descartes y Hume: causalidad, temporalidad y existencia de Dios. Badía Cabrera, Miguel A.

Descartes, Davidson and the Causal Impotence of Thought (in Czech). Hríbek, Tomás.

Hume, Bayle e il *principio di causalità*: Parte I. Gilardi, Roberto.

Kausalität und singuläre Referenz: Eine sprachphilosophische Rekonstruktion des empirischen Realismus bei Kant. Wyller, Truls.

La causalidad material de los elementos en la generación de los cuerpos mixtos. Sacchi, Mario Enrique.

La causalità. Salmon, Wesley C.

Metafisica tra scienza e sapienza: Tafsir Lãm 52-58 di Ibn Rusd. Roccaro, Giuseppe.

Metamorfosi della libertà nel *Sistema di Etica* di Fichte. Fonnesu, Luca.

Noumenal Causality Reconsidered: Affection, Agency, and Meaning in Kant. Westphal, Kenneth R.

Past, Present, Future, and Special Relativity. Rakié, Natasa.

Pragmatische Bedingungen des wissenschaftlichen Realismus. Kügler, Peter.

Quasi-Formal Causality, or the Other-in-Me: Rahner and Lévinas. Purcell, Michael.

Sobre referencia y causalidad. Lo Monaco, Vicenzo P.

Totalidad y causalidad en Polo. Haya Segovia, Fernando.

Über den Charakter von Einsteins philosophischem Realismus. Polikarov, Asaria.

Verbe mental et noétique thomiste dans le *De verbo* d'Hervé de Nédellec. Trottmann, Christian.

Vernunft als Epiphänomen der Naturkausalität: Zu Herkunft und Bedeutung des ursprünglichen Determinismus J.G. Fichtes. Wildfeuer, Armin G.

Wie definiert man einen physikalischen Gegenstand?. Rudolph, Enno.

## CAUSATION

"A Conceptualist Ontology" in *Dispositions: A Debate*, Armstrong, D M. Place, U T.

"Actions, Causes, and Mental Ascriptions" in *Objections to Physicalism*, Robinson, Howard (ed). Gillett, Grant.

"Causally Relevant Properties" in *AI, Connectionism and Philosophical Psychology, 1995*, Tomberlin, James E (ed). Braun, David.

"Difficulties with Physicalism, and a Programme for Dualists" in *Objections to Physicalism*, Robinson, Howard (ed). Forrest, Peter.

"Explanation by Intentional, Functional, and Causal Specification" in *Epistemology and History*, Zeidler-Janiszewska, Anna (ed). Kuipers, Theo A F.

"I'm a Mother, I Worry" in *Contents*, Villanueva, Enrique (ed). Antony, Louise M.

"Kim on the Exclusion Problem" in *Contents*, Villanueva, Enrique (ed). Campos, Manuel.

"Mental Causation: A Query for Kim" in *Contents*, Villanueva, Enrique (ed). Tomberlin, James E.

"Mental Causation: What? Me Worry?" in *Contents*, Villanueva, Enrique (ed). Kim, Jaegwon.

"Moral Causation" in *A Question of Values: New Canadian Perspectives in Ethics and Political Philosophy*, Brennan, Samantha (ed). Pietroski, Paul M.

"Reference from the First Person Perspective" in *Contents*, Villanueva, Enrique (ed). Loar, Brian.

"Singling Out Properties" in *AI, Connectionism and Philosophical Psychology, 1995*, Tomberlin, James E (ed). Yablo, Stephen.

*A World of States of Affairs.* Armstrong, D M.

*Causation and Persistence: A Theory of Causation.* Ehring, Douglas.

*Cognition and Commitment in Hume's Philosophy.* Garrett, Don.

*Contents.* Villanueva, Enrique (ed).

*Descartes' Dualism.* Baker, Gordon and Morris, Katherine J.

*Dispositions: A Debate.* Armstrong, D M, Martin, C B and Place, Ullin T.

*Malebranche's Theory of the Soul: A Cartesian Interpretation.* Schmaltz, Tad M.

*Object and Property.* Denkel, Arda.

*Problems of Vision: Rethinking the Causal Theory of Perception.* Vision, Gerald.

*Proclus: Neo-Platonic Philosophy and Science.* Siorvanes, Lucas.

*Simple Mindedness: In Defense of Naive Naturalism in the Philosophy of Mind.* Hornsby, Jennifer.

*The Ontology of Mind: Events, Processes, and States.* Steward, Helen.

*The Possible Universe.* Tallet, J A.

*Things That Happen Because They Should: A Teleological Approach to Action.* Stout, Rowland.

*Time, Tense, and Causation.* Tooley, Michael.

A Conversation with Sylvère Lotringer. Lotringer, Sylvère.

A Counterfactual Analysis of Causation. Ramachandran, Murali.

A Pragmatic Theory of Causal Analysis. Shein, David.

Al-Ghazali on Necessary Causality in *The Incoherence of the Philosophers*. Riker, Stephen.

Biological Function, Selection, and Reduction. Manning, Richard N.

Causality and Demonstration: An Early Scholastic *Posterior Analytics* Commentary. Wood, Rega and Andrews, Robert.

Causation and Intensionality: A Problem for Naturalism. Rheinwald, Rosemarie.

Causes and Tastes: A Response. Shiner, Roger A.

Chances, Individuals and Toxic Torts. Parascandola, Mark.

Completeness and Indeterministic Causation. DeVito, Scott.

Conflicting Varieties of Realism: Causal Powers and the Problems of Social Structure. Varela, Charles R and Harré, Rom.

Counterfactuals and Preemptive Causation. Ganeri, Jonardon, Noordhoof, Paul and Ramachandran, Murali.

Counterfactuals in Pragmatic Perspective. Rescher, Nicholas.

Counterfactuals, Causation, and Overdetermination. Worley, Sara.

Crane on Mental Causation. Child, William.

Descartes on Causation. Flage, Daniel E and Bonnen, Clarence A.

Deviant Causal Chains and the Irreducibility of Teleological Explanation. Sehon, Scott.

Disjunctive Properties and Causal Efficacy. Penczek, Alan.

Does the Problem of Mental Causation Generalize?. Kim, Jaegwon.

Explanation, Understanding and Typical Action. Manicas, Peter T.

Finkish Dispositions. Lewis, David.

Formal Causation and the Explanation of Intentionality in Descartes. Schmitter, Amy M.

Hobbes's Theory of Causality and Its Aristotelian Background. Leijenhorst, Cees.

How Properties Emerge. Humphreys, Paul.

Hume and Causal Power: The Influences of Malebranche and Newton. Bell, Martin.

In Defense of Hume and the Causal Theory of Taste. Mothersill, Mary.

Just So Stories and Inference to the Best Explanation in Evolutionary Psychology. Holcomb III, Harmon R.

Kalam: A Swift Argument from Origins to First Cause?. Taylor, John.

Karl Jaspers: The Person and His Cause, Not the Person or His Cause. Wisser, Richard.

Love's Power and the Causality of Mind: C.S. Peirce on the Place of Mind and Culture in Evolution. Pape, Helmut.

Lynne Rudder Baker, *Explaining Attitudes: A Practical Approach to the Mind*. Hill, Christopher S.

Memory: A Logical Learning Theory Account. Rychlak, Joseph F.

Modal Fatalism. Beedle, Andrew.

Moving Forward on the Problem of Consciousness. Chalmers, David J.

On Shiner's "Hume and the Causal Theory of Taste". Bender, John W.

On the Notion of Cause 'Philosophically Speaking'. Steward, Helen.

On the Relation between Behaviorism and Cognitive Psychology. Moore, Jay.

**52**

## CHANGE

*Springing Forward and Falling Back: Traveling through Time.* Edwards, Anne M.

Suggested Management Responses to Ethical Issue Raised by Technological Change. Cordeiro, William P.

The Changes of Painting Techniques in the Early Tang Wall Paintings of Dunhuang Mogao Grottos; The Relationship between "Pattern" and Pictorial Structure (in Japanese). Yamasaki, Toshiko.

The Concept of Disease: Structure and Change. Thagard, Paul.

The Logic of Belief Persistence. Battigalli, Pierpaolo and Bonanno, Giacomo.

The Regress-Problem: A Reply to Vermazen. Moya, Carlos J.

Transitional Regimes and the Rule of Law. Golding, Martin P.

## CHANNING, W

William Ellery Channing: Philosopher, Critic of Orthodoxy, and Cautious Reformer. Madden, Edward H.

## CHAOS

*Finding Philosophy in Social Science.* Bunge, Mario.

*Streitgespräche und Kontroversen in der Philosophie des 20.Jahrhunderts.* Wuchterl, Kurt.

Chaos and a New Environmental Ethic: The Land Ethic Revisited. Catalano, George D.

Chaos and Control: Reading Plato's *Politicus.* McCabe, Mary Margaret.

Chaos and Literature. Matheson, Carl and Kirchhoff, Evan.

Chaos, Berechnungskomplexität und Physik: Neue Grenzen wissenschaftlicher Erkenntnis?. Leiber, Theodor.

Die Freiheit des Deterministen: Chaos und Neurophilosophie. Walter, Henrik.

Divine Action in a World Chaos: An Evaluation of John Polkinghorne's Model of Special Divine Action. Crain, Steven D.

Hölderlin e o *Retorno Natal.* Beckert, Cristina.

Mother Nature Doesn't Know Her Name: Reflections on a Term. Fell, Gil S.

Some Problems Concerning the Big Bang Theory of Creation. Guha, Debashis.

Speculations on Cosmology & God. State, Stanley.

## CHAPLAIN

Physicians' Collaboration with Chaplains: Difficulties and Benefits. Thiel, Mary Martha and Robinson, Mary Redner.

## CHAPPELL, T

Response to Chappell. Penelhum, Terence.

## CHARACTER

"Cognition, Character, and Culture in Undergraduate Education: Rhetoric and Reality" in *The American University: National Treasure or Endangered Species?,* Ehrenberg, Ronald G (ed). Shapiro, Harold T.

Ascriptions of Responsibility. Oshana, Marina A L.

Blameworthiness, Character, and Cultural Norms. Haji, Ishtiyaque.

Character Education: Reclaiming the Social. Duncan, Barbara J.

Character-Principlism and the Particularity Objection. Blustein, Jeffrey.

Commentary on Charles M. Young's "The Doctrine of the Mean". Blankenship, J David.

Fictional Characters: Dependent or Abstract? A Reply to Reicher's Objections. Thomasson, Amie L.

Hypocrisy and Self-Deception. Statman, Daniel.

Reason's Practical Idea of Perpetual Peace, Human Character, and the Pedagogical Function of the Republican Constitution. Munzel, G Felicitas.

Schicksal und Charakter: Für die Philosophische Praxis ist vieles von Schopenhauer zu lernen: Vortrag auf dem Kolloquium der GPP am 30. Oktober 1994 in Tübingen. Achenbach, Gerd B.

The Doctrine of the Mean. Young, Charles M.

The Virtues of Externalism. Jacobs, Jonathan.

The Youth Charter: Towards the Formation of Adolescent Moral Identity. Damon, William and Gregory, Anne.

What is "the Mean Relative to Us" in Aristotle's *Ethics.* Brown, Lesley.

## CHARACTERIZATION

Some Characterization Theorems for Infinitary Universal Horn Logic without Equality. Dellunde, Pilar and Jansana, Ramon.

## CHARGE

Tibbles the Cat: A Modern *Sophisma.* Burke, Michael B.

## CHARITY

"Scepticism and the Limits of Charity" in *Scepticism in the History of Philosophy: A Pan-American Dialogue,* Popkin, Richard H (ed). De Olaso, Ezequiel.

*Altruism in Later Life.* Midlarsky, Elizabeth and Kahana, Eva.

*Leibniz' Universal Jurisprudence: Justice as the Charity of the Wise.* Riley, Patrick.

Augustine's Hermeneutics and the Principle of Charity. Glidden, David.

Charity, Interpretation, Fallacy. Adler, Jonathan E.

Epistemic Rationality, Epistemic Motivation, and Interpretive Charity. Henderson, David.

Hegel's Logic as a Theory of Meaning. Stekeler-Weithofer, Pirmin.

La fuerza del PC (Principio de Caridad): Circunstancia, habilidad y contenido en la explicación de la acción. Broncano, Fernando.

Les conditions de l'interprétation. Montminy, Martin.

The Order of Charity in Thomas Aquinas. Selner-Wright, Susan C.

## CHARLES, D

On David Charles's Account of Aristotle's Semantics for Simple Names. Butler, Travis.

## CHASTITY

Contraceptive Risk-Taking and Norms of Chastity. Stubblefield, Anna.

## CHATTERBOROUGH, K

Formal Causation and the Explanation of Intentionality in Descartes. Schmitter, Amy M.

## CHATTOM, W

The Nature of the Common Concept in William of Ockham (in Czech). Saxlová, Tereza.

## CHAUVINISM

*Caveat Emptor.* Ethical Chauvinism in the Global Economy. Vega, Gina.

## CHAVEZ, C

César Chávez and La Causa: Toward a Hispanic Christian Social Ethic. Piar, Carlos R.

## CHEATING

Cheating: Limits of Individual Integrity. Johnston, D Kay.

When the Trial *Is* the Punishment: The Ethics of Plagiarism Accusations. Yanikoski, Charles S.

## CHELLAS, B

Getting Started: Beginnings in the Logic of Action. Segerberg, Krister.

## CHEMICALS

Ethical Aspects of the Safety of Medicines and Other Social Chemicals. Parke, Dennis V.

## CHEMISTRY

*see also* Biochemistry

"Chemie und Philosophie: Anmerkungen zur Entwicklung des Gebietes in der Geschichte der DDR" in *Philosophie der Chemie: Bestandsaufnahme und Ausblick,* Schummer, Joachim (ed). Laitko, Hubert.

"Die Chemie als Gegenstand philosophischer Reflexion" in *Philosophie der Chemie: Bestandsaufnahme und Ausblick,* Schummer, Joachim (ed). Psarros, Nikos.

"Die Notwendigkeit einer Philosophie der Chemie" in *Philosophie der Chemie: Bestandsaufnahme und Ausblick,* Schummer, Joachim (ed). Han, Edzard.

"Illustrating Chemistry" in *Picturing Knowledge,* Baigrie, Brian S (ed). Knight, David.

"Poppers Beitrag für eine Philosophie der Chemie" in *Philosophie der Chemie: Bestandsaufnahme und Ausblick,* Schummer, Joachim (ed). Akeroyd, F Michael.

"Reduktion und Erklärung in der Chemie" in *Philosophie der Chemie: Bestandsaufnahme und Ausblick,* Schummer, Joachim (ed). Scerri, Eric R.

"Über die Vernachlässigung der Philosophie der Chemie" in *Philosophie der Chemie: Bestandsaufnahme und Ausblick,* Schummer, Joachim (ed). Van Brakel, Jaap.

"Warum ist die Chemie ein Steifkind der Philosophie?" in *Philosophie der Chemie: Bestandsaufnahme und Ausblick,* Schummer, Joachim (ed). Ruthenberg, Klaus.

"Wem nützt eine Philosophie der Chemie—den Chemikern oder den Philosophen?" in *Philosophie der Chemie: Bestandsaufnahme und Ausblick,* Schummer, Joachim (ed). Eisvogel, Martin.

*Facets of Faith and Science Volume 4: Interpreting God's Action in the World.* Van der Meer, Jitse M (ed).

*Philosophie der Chemie: Bestandsaufnahme und Ausblick.* Schummer, Joachim (ed), Psarros, Nikos (ed) and Ruthenberg, Klaus (ed).

*Real Process: How Logic and Chemistry Combine in Hegel's Philosophy of Nature.* Burbidge, John W.

*Realismus und Chemie: Philosophische Untersuchungen der Wissenschaft von den Stoffen.* Schummer, Joachim.

Abstraktion und Ideation—Zur Semantik chemischer und biologischer Grundbegriffe. Gutmann, Mathias and Hanekamp, Gerd.

Bibliography on Philosophy of Chemistry. Scerri, Eric R.

Chemistry as the Science of the Transformation of Substances. Van Brakel, Jaap.

Molecular Shape, Reduction, Explanation and Approximate Concepts. Ramsey, Jeffry L.

Philosophical Issues in the History of Chemistry. Gavroglu, Kostas.

The Case for the Philosophy of Chemistry. McIntyre, Lee and Scerri, Eric R.

The Peculiar Notion of Exchange Forces—I: Origins in Quantum Mechanics, 1926-1928. Carson, Cathryn.

## CHENG, C

Commentary on the AAS Panel: Shun, Bloom, Cheng, and Birdwhistell. Neville, Robert Cummings.

## CHESTERTON, G

How Chesterton Read History. Clark, Stephen R L.

## CHICANO

Reclaiming the Borderlands: Chicana/o Identity, Difference, and Critical Pedagogy. Elenes, C Alejandra.

## CHIHARA, C

*A Subject with No Object: Strategies for Nominalistic Interpretation of Mathematics.* Burgess, John P and Rosen, Gideon.

On Chihara's 'The Howson-Urbach Proofs of Bayesian Principles'. Howson, Colin.

## CHILD, W
Reply to Child. Crane, Tim.

## CHILDREN
see also Adolescents, Infant

"Causes of Declining Well-Being Among U.S. Children" in *Sex, Preference, and Family: Essays on Law and Nature,* Nussbaum, Martha C (ed). Galston, William A.

"Children's Liberation: A Blueprint for Disaster" in *The Liberation Debate: Rights at Issue,* Leahy, Michael (ed). Purdy, Laura M.

"Harris' Reply" in *The Liberation Debate: Rights at Issue,* Leahy, Michael (ed). Harris, John.

"Liberating Children" in *The Liberation Debate: Rights at Issue,* Leahy, Michael (ed). Harris, John.

"The Just Claims of Dyslexic Children" in *Reproduction, Technology, and Rights: Biomedical Ethics Reviews,* Humber, James M (ed). Hull, Richard T.

*Reasonable Children: Moral Education and Moral Learning.* Pritchard, Michael S.

*Reconstructing Political Theory: Feminist Perspectives.* Shanley, Mary Lyndon (ed) and Narayan, Uma (ed).

*Teaching with Love: A Feminist Approach to Early Childhood Education.* Goldstein, Lisa S.

*The Ethics of Special Education.* Howe, Ken and Miramontes, Ofelia B.

Affect and the Moral-Conventional Distinction. Blair, R J R.

Arguments Against Health Care Autonomy for Minors. Ross, Lainie Friedman.

Aristotle's *Child*: Development Through *Genesis, Oikos*, and *Polis*. McGowan Tress, Daryl.

Aristotle's Criticism of Plato's Communism of Women and Children. Mayhew, Robert.

Audience and Authority: The Story in Front of the Story. Zoloth-Dorfman, Laurie.

Child's Play. Nersessian, Nancy J.

Children and Bioethics: Uses and Abuses of The Best-Interest Standard: Introduction. Kopelman, Loretta M.

Children's Refusal of Gynecologic Examinations for Suspected Sexual Abuse. Muram, David, Aiken, Margaret M and Strong, Carson.

Children, Society, and Health Care Decision Making. Caccamo, James M.

Cochlear Implants and the Claims of Culture? A Response to Lane and Grodin. Davis, Dena S.

Commentary on "Family Dynamics and Children in Medical Research". Robinson, Walter.

Commentary on Alison Gopnik's "The Scientist As Child". Solomon, Miriam.

Criminal Children. Richards, Norvin.

Do Children Understand the Mind by Means of Simulation or a Theory? Evidence from their Understanding of Inference. Ruffman, Ted.

Ecological Validity and 'White Room Effects': The Interaction of Cognitive and Cultural Models in the Pragmatic Analysis of Elicited Narratives from Children. Cicourel, Aaron V.

Educational Reform: A Complex Matter. Reynolds, Sherrie and Martin, Kathleen.

Ethical Issues in Cochlear Implant Surgery: An Exploration into Disease, Disability, and the Best Interests of the Child. Lane, Harlan and Grodin, Michael.

Ethical Issues in Pediatric Life-Threatening Illness: Dilemmas of Consent, Assent, and Communication. Kunin, Howard.

European Children Thinking Together in 100. Heesen, Berrie.

Family Dynamics and Children in Medical Research. Bonkovsky, Frederick O and Gordon, Valery M.

Feminist Epistemology and Philosophy for Children. Field, Terri.

Filial Morality. Archard, David.

Filial Responsibility and the Care of the Aged. Collingridge, Michael and Miller, Seumas.

Gender and Social Awareness: A Story from Buenos Aires. Pac, Andrea.

Genetic Dilemmas and the Child's Right to an Open Future. Davis, Dena S.

Genetic Testing in Children. Clayton, Ellen Wright.

Hearing Children's Voices. Bartholome, William G.

Improving Scientific Reasoning through Philosophy for Children: An Empirical Study. Sprod, Tim.

Landmarks in Critical Thinking Series: John Passmore: On Teaching to be Critical. Splitter, Laurance.

Language in Stories for Boys and Girls. Velasco, Mónica.

Learning Philosophy Collaboratively with a Student. Weiss, Andrea and Katzner, James.

Letting the Deaf Be Deaf: Reconsidering the Use of Cochlear Implants in Prelingually Deaf Children. Crouch, Robert A.

Literary Development as Spiritual Development in the Common School. Newby, Mike.

Lost Times/Recovered Times. Reed, Ronald.

Love and Death in a Pediatric Intensive Care Unit. Miller, Richard B.

Lui's Complaint. Lee, Zosimo E.

Medicating Children: The Case of Ritalin. Perring, Christian.

Minority Minors and Moral Research Medicine. Bonkovsky, Frederick O.

Moral Growth in Children's Literature: A Primer with Examples. Jones, III, Joe Frank.

Parenting and the Best Interests of Minors. Downie, Robin S and Randall, Fiona.

Passing on the Faith: How Mother-Child Communication Influences Transmission of Moral Values. Taris, Toon W and Semin, Gün R.

Patterns of Reasoning Exhibited by Children and Adolescents in Response to Moral Dilemmas Involving Plants, Animals and Ecosystems. Nevers, Patricia, Gebhard, Ulrich and Billmann-Mahecha, Elfriede.

Philosophy and Shifting Morality. Infinito-Allocco, Justen.

Philosophy for Children and the Discipline of Philosophy. Gazzard, Ann.

Philosophy for Children: One Way of Developing Children's Thinking. Green, Lena.

Products of the Will: Robertson's *Children of Choice*. Meilaender, Gilbert.

Re-Thinking Consciousness Raising: Citizenship and the Law and Politics of Adoption. Cornell, Drucilla.

Reasoning and Children: The Wide Glare of the Children's Day. Slade, Christina.

Reply to Commentaries. Gopnik, Alison.

Respecting the Health Care Decision-Making Capacity of Minors. Strong, Carson.

Reviving Ophelia: A Role for Philosophy in Helping Young Women Achieve Selfhood. Turgeon, Wendy C.

Science and Core Knowledge. Carey, Susan and Spelke, Elizabeth.

Science As Child's Play: Tales from the Crib. Fine, Arthur.

Shifting Perspectives: Filial Morality Revisited. Li, Chenyang.

Teaching the Three Rs: Rights, Roles and Responsibilities—A Curriculum for Pediatric Patient Rights. Davis, Kathleen G.

The Biological Child. MacKellar, Calum.

The Educational Contributions of Sir Thomas More. Masterson, David L.

The Impact of Culture on Education. Thomas, Cornell.

The Moral Status of Children: Children's Rights, Parents' Rights, and Family Justice. Brennan, Samantha and Noggle, Robert.

The Scientist as Adult. Giere, Ronald N.

The Scientist as Child. Gopnik, Alison.

Theories in Children and the Rest of Us. Schwitzgebel, Eric.

Tobacco Advertising and Children: The Limits of First Amendment Protection. Wong, Kenman L.

Una aproximación a la ética en el programa Filosofía para Niños de Matthew Lipman. Accorinti, Stella.

Using Moral Dilemmas in Children's Literature as a Vehicle for Moral Education and Teaching Reading Comprehension. Clare, Lindsay, Gallimore, Ronald and Patthey-Chavez, G Genevieve.

Voices in the Classroom: Girls and Philosophy for Children. Mohr-Lane, Jana.

What is a Child?. Friquenon, Marie-Louise.

Why God. Mishra, Amarendra.

Wisdom and Intelligence in Philosophy for Children. Lindop, Clive.

## CHINESE
see also Buddhism, Confucianism, Taoism

"Mountains of the Mind" in *East and West in Aesthetics,* Marchianò, Grazia (ed). Servomaa, Sonia.

"Steps to a Comparative Evolutionary Aesthetics (China, India, Tibet and Europe)" in *East and West in Aesthetics,* Marchianò, Grazia (ed). Capriles, Elias.

"The Chinese "Cyclic" View of History vs. Japanese "Progress" in *The Idea of Progress,* McLaughlin, Peter (ed). Nakayama, Shigeru.

*Meeting of Minds: Intellectual and Religious Interaction in East Asian Traditions of Thought.* Bloom, Irene (ed) and Fogel, Joshua A (ed).

A Chinese Critique on Western Ways of Warfare. Hagen, Kurtis.

A Preliminary Analysis of "National Consciousness". Xiyuan, Xiong.

A Tentative Discussion on the Common Mental Attributes of the Han Nationality. Xiyuan, Xiong.

A Tentative Discussion on the Common Mental Attributes of the Huihui Nationality. Xiyuan, Xiong.

An Inquiry into the Liminology in Language in the *Zhuangzi* and in Chan Buddhism. Wang, Youru.

Ancient Chinese Aesthetics and its Modernity. Arnheim, Rudolf.

Approaches to Conserving Vulnerable Wildlife in China: Does the Colour of Cat Matter—if it Catches Mice?. Harris, Richard B.

Business Ethics and Politics in China. Steidlmeier, Paul.

Conflict and Constellation: The New Trend of Value Development in China. Chen, Xun Wu.

Confucian Value and Democratic Value. Li, Chenyang.

Contemporary Significance of Chinese Buddhist Philosophy. Ichimura, Shohei.

Continuing the Conversation on Chinese Human Rights. Ames, Roger T.

Conversing with Straw Men While Ignoring Dictators: A Reply to Roger Ames. Donnelly, Jack.

Culture, Power and the Social Construction of Morality: Moral Voices of Chinese Students. Chang, Kimberly A.

Han Classicists Writing in Dialogue about their Own Tradition. Nylan, Michael.

Human Nature and Biological Nature in Mencius. Bloom, Irene.

Investigation of Things, Philosophical Counseling, and the Misery of the *Last Man*. Duessel, Reinhard.

La liberté a-t-elle un sens dans la tradition chinoise?. Drivod, Lucien.

Liang Shuming and Henri Bergson on Intuition: Cultural Context and the Evolution of Terms. An, Yanming.

Mencius on *Jen-Hsing*. Shun, Kwong-loi.

National Consciousness and Motherland Consciousness. Xiyuan, Xiong.

## CHINESE

National Consciousness and Nationalism. Xiyuan, Xiong.

On Freedom. Liquin, Deng.

On Human Rights. Sharpe, M E (trans).

On Imagination—A Correspondence with Prof. Zhang Longxi. Yuanhua, Wang.

Philosophical Significance of Gongsun Long: A New Interpretation of Theory of *Zhi* as Meaning and Reference. Cheng, Chung-ying.

Points East and West: Acupuncture and Comparative Philosophy of Science. Allchin, Douglas.

Socialism and National Consciousness. Xiyuan, Xiong.

The Changes of Painting Techniques in the Early Tang Wall Paintings of Dunhuang Mogao Grottos; The Relationship between "Pattern" and Pictorial Structure (in Japanese). Yamasaki, Toshiko.

The Chinese Doctrinal Acceptance of Buddhism. Inada, Kenneth K.

The Chinese Theory of Forms and Names (*xingming zhi xue*) and Its Relation to "Philosophy of Signs". Möller, Hans Georg.

The Common Mental Attributes of the Dai Nationality Explored. Xiyuan, Xiong.

The Emergence of Concepts of a Sentence in Ancient Greek and in Ancient Chinese Philosophy. Bosely, Richard.

The Influence of Chinese Philosophy on the English Style Garden: A Comparative Study of Wörlitz and Koishikawa Korakuen (in Japanese). Seiko, Goto.

The Popularity of Existentialism: Causes and Effects. Feng, Lei.

The Spread of Aristotle's Political Theory in China. Mi, Michael C.

The Transformation of Things: A Reanalysis of Chuang Tzus Butterfly Dream. Gaskins, Robert W.

The Unique Features of Hui Shi's Thought: A Comparative Study between Hui Shi and Other Pre-Qin Philosophers. Xu, Keqian.

The Way of the Lotus: Critical Reflections on the Ethics of the *Saddharmapundarīka* Sūtra. Herman, A L.

Time and Emptiness in the *Chao-Lun*. Berman, Michael.

Yan: A Dimension of Praxis and Its Philosophical Implications (A Chinese Perspective on Language). Zhenbin, Sun.

Yang Chu's Discovery of the Body. Emerson, John.

## CHINESE ROOM

Searle's Chinese Box: Debunking the Chinese Room Argument. Hauser, Larry.

## CHISHOLM, R

"Epistemological Reversals between Chisholm and Lyotard" in *Philosophy of Education (1996)*, Margonis, Frank (ed). Gunzenhauser, Michael G.

Is Nondefectively Justified True Belief Knowledge?. Jacquette, Dale.

Rescuing the Counterfactual Solution to Chisholm's Paradox. Niles, Ian.

Son "Opacos" los Estados Mentales?: Los Criterios de Chisholm. Botero C, Juan J.

## CHODOROW, N

Rethinking Kymlick's Critique of Humanist Liberalism. Greene, Stephen A.

## CHOICE

*see also* Decision

"Freedom of Choice and the Choice of Freedom on the Path to Democracy" in *The Ancients and the Moderns*, Lilly, Reginald (ed). Meier, Christian.

"Moralische Überzeugung und wirtschaftliche Wahl" in *Ökonomie und Moral: Beiträge zur Theorie ökonomischer Rationalität*, Lohmann, Karl Reinhard (ed). Lohmann, Karl Reinhard.

"Union, Autonomy, and Concern" in *Love Analyzed*, Lamb, Roger E. Soble, Alan.

*Making a Necessity of Virtue*. Sherman, Nancy.

*Making Choices: A Recasting of Decision Theory*. Schick, Frederic.

*Making Mortal Choices: Three Exercises in Moral Casuistry*. Bedau, Hugo Adam.

*Metaphilosophy and Free Will*. Double, Richard.

*Rational Choice and Moral Agency*. Schmidtz, David.

*The Significance of Free Will*. Kane, Robert.

Advocating for the Dying: The View of Family and Friends. Moretti, Anna M.

Authentische Entscheidungen und emotive Neurowissenschaft. Walter, Henrik.

Better Communication between Engineers and Managers: Some Ways to Prevent Many Ethically Hard Choices. Davis, Michael.

Choice Functions and the Scopal Semantics of Indefinites. Winter, Yoad.

Choosing the Best: Against Paternalistic Practice Guidelines. Savulescu, Julian.

Commentary on "Better Communication between Engineers and Managers. Loui, Michael.

Commentary on "Better Communication between Engineers and Managers". Pritchard, Michael S.

Davidson's Second Person. Verheggen, Claudine.

Gender Differences in Ethical Frameworks and Evaluation of Others' Choices in Ethical Dilemmas. Schminke, Marshall.

Hare's Reductive Justification of Preference Utilitarianism. Paden, Roger.

Individual Autonomy and Collective Decisionmaking. Goldworth, Amnon.

Joining in Life and Death: On Separating the Lakeberg Twins. Dougherty, Charles J.

Kitcher on Theory Choice. Roorda, Jonathan.

Kitcher's Compromise: A Critical Examination of the Compromise Model of Scientific Closure, and its Implications for the Relationship Between History and Philosophy of Science. Shanahan, Timothy.

La maturità di coscienza alla luce di San Tommaso d'Aquino. Costa, Flavia.

Libertarian Choice. Goetz, Stewart.

On the Limits of Rights. Marmor, Andrei.

Preference for Gradual Resolution of Uncertainty. Ahlbrecht, Martin and Weber, Martin.

Products of the Will: Robertson's *Children of Choice*. Meilaender, Gilbert.

Quantifier Scope: How Labor is Divided between QR and Choice Functions. Reinhart, Tanya.

Reassessing the Reliability of Advance Directives. May, Thomas.

Resolute Choice and Rational Deliberation: A Critique and a Defense. Gauthier, David.

Risk and Diversification in Theory Choice. Rueger, Alexander.

Subjectivism, Utility, and Autonomy. Lottenbach, Hans.

The Individual Rationality of Maintaining a Sense of Justice. Cave, Eric M.

The Moral Art of Being a Good Doctor. MacIntosh, David.

The Task of Group Rationality: The Subjectivist's View—Part I. Sarkar, Husain.

Two Applications of a Theorem of Dvoretsky, Wald, and Wolfovitz to Cake Division. Barbanel, Julius B and Zwicker, William S.

Uniformization, Choice Functions and Well Orders in the Class of Trees. Lifsches, Shmuel and Shelah, Saharon.

Violations of Present-Value Maximization in Income Choice. Gigliotti, Gary and Sopher, Barry.

Why Preference is not Transitive. Gendin, Sidney.

## CHOMSKY, N

"The Grammar of Chomsky is not Mentalist" in *Verdad: lógica, representación y mundo*, Villegas Forero, L. Peris-Viñé, Luis M.

A Critique of the Minimalist Program. Johnson, David E and Lappin, Shalom.

A Note on the Nature of "Water". Abbott, Barbara.

Characterization of the Basic Notions of Chomsky's Grammar (in Spanish). Peris-Viñé, Luis M.

Chomsky tra linguistica e filosofia: A proposito di R. Raggiunti, La "Conoscenza del linguaggio" e il mito della grammatica universale. Costa, Filippo.

Habermas' Pragmatic Universals. Mukherji, Arundhati.

Interactionism and Physicality. Mills, Eugene.

Is Chomsky's Linguistics Non-Empirical?. Kanthamani, A.

Katz Astray. George, Alexander.

The Unfinished Chomskyan Revolution. Katz, Jerrold J.

## CHRIST

Nouvelles réponses à Nunzio Incardona. Tilliette, Xavier.

Tres tratados "Sobre el maestro": Agustín, Buenaventura, Tomás de Aquino. Perez Ruiz, Francisco.

## CHRISTENDOM

Modernity, Postmodernity and Transmodernity: Hope in Search of Time (in Spanish). Mendieta, Eduardo.

## CHRISTENSEN, D

Interlocution, Perception, and Memory. Burge, Tyler.

## CHRISTIAN

"Origène était-il pour Cudworth le modèle du philosophe chrétien?" in *Mind Senior to the World*, Baldi, Marialuisa. Breteau, Jean-Louis.

Suárez y Vico, veinte años después. Badillo O'Farrell, Pablo.

## CHRISTIANITY

*see also* Catholicism, Protestantism

"An Elephant, an Ocean, and the Freedom of Faith" in *Philosophy, Religion, and the Question of Intolerance*, Ambuel, David (ed). Cain, David.

"Beyond Toleration" in *Philosophy, Religion, and the Question of Intolerance*, Ambuel, David (ed). O'Meara, William.

"Das Christentum als Verwirklichung des Religionsbegriffs in Fichtes Spätphilosophie 1813" in *Sein—Reflexion—Freiheit: Aspekte der Philosophie Johann Gottlieb Fichtes*, Asmuth, Christoph (ed). Schmid, Dirk.

"Do You Do Well to Be Angry?". Werpehowski, William.

"Gift of the Egyptians" (On the History of Christian Philosophy) (in Czech). Rugási, Gyula.

"Nel nome di Europa" in *Geofilosofia*, Bonesio, Luisa (ed). Derrida, Jacques.

"On Limits of the Rationalistic Paradigm" in *Epistemology and History*, Zeidler-Janiszewska, Anna (ed). Nowak, Leszek.

*A Comprehensive History of Western Ethics: What Do We Believe?*. Ashby, W Allen (ed) and Ashby, Warren.

*A Preserving Grace: Protestants, Catholics, and Natural Law*. Cromartie, Michael (ed).

*A Watch Over Mortality: The Philosophical Story of Julián Marías*. Raley, Harold.

*Alciphron oder der Kleine Philosoph*. Berkeley, George.

*Auferstehung im Denken: Der Christusimpuls in der "Philosophie der Freiheit" und in der Bewusstseinsgeschichte*. Teichmann, Frank.

*Averroës and the Enlightenment*. Wahba, Mourad (ed) and Abousenna, Mona (ed).

*Business Ethics in the African Context Today*. Rosemann, Philipp W (ed) and LeJeune, Michel (ed).

*Christian Philosophy: Greek, Medieval, Contemporary Reflections*. Sweeney, Leo

**CITIZENSHIP**

Re-Thinking Consciousness Raising: Citizenship and the Law and Politics of Adoption. Cornell, Drucilla.

Rights and Citizenship: The Instrumentality of the Community. Barnes, Mahlon W.

Rights, Citizenship, and the Modern Form of the Social: Dilemmas of Arendtian Republicanism. Cohen, Jean L.

Zelfbeheersing en democratie. Tjong Tjin Tai, Eric.

**CITY**

"L'utopia della nuova città" in *Geofilosofia,* Bonesio, Luisa (ed). Cervellati, Pierluigi.

"Una città senza storia: la perfezione immobile e l'utopia di Tommaso Campenella" in *Lo Storicismo e la Sua Storia: Temi, Problemi, Prospettive,* Cacciatore, Giuseppe (ed). Cambi, Maurizio.

*The Play of the Platonic Dialogues.* Freydberg, Bernard.

Gittà, materia del tempo. Berardi, Roberto.

Una repubblica mondiale come ideale politico. Höffe, Otfried.

**CIVIC**

Civic Education: A New Proposal. Wingo, Ajume H.

Civic Liberalism and Educational Reform. Weinstein, Michael A.

**CIVIC DUTY**

Mandatory Rights and Compulsory Education. Klepper, Howard.

**CIVIC STATE**

Civic Nationalism: Oxymoron?. Xenos, Nicholas.

The Myth of the Civic Nation. Yack, Bernard.

**CIVICS**

From Exasperating Virtues to Civic Virtues. Rorty, Amélie Oksenberg.

On Civic Friendship. Schwarzenbach, Sibyl A.

**CIVIL**

"Sobre Política y Reformismo Cívico: A Partir de Ortega" in *Política y Sociedad en José Ortega y Gasset: En Torno a "Vieja y Nueva Política",* Lopez de la Vieja, Maria Teresa (ed). Rosales, José María.

Avarice and Civil Unity: The Contribution of Sir Thomas Smith. Wood, Neal.

**CIVIL DISOBEDIENCE**

*Feminist Interpretations of Jacques Derrida.* Holland, Nancy J (ed).

*Law and Morality: Readings in Legal Philosophy.* Dyzenhaus, David (ed) and Ripstein, Arthur (ed).

*Mahatma Ghandi: Selected Political Writings.* Dalton, Dennis (ed).

*Morality and the Law.* Baird, Robert M (ed) and Rosenbaum, Stuart E (ed).

Civil Disobedience in the Social Theory of Thomas Aquinas. Scholz, Sally J.

Civil Disobedience: Justice against Legality. Miniotaite, Grazina.

Commentary on "Technology and Civil Disobedience: Why Engineers Have a Special Duty to Obey the Law". Boisjoly, Roger M.

Should We Boycott Boycotts?. Mills, Claudia.

Technology and Civil Disobedience: Why Engineers Have a Special Duty to Obey the Law. Schlossberger, Eugene.

The Morality of Anti-Abortion Civil Disobedience. Dixon, Nicholas.

**CIVIL RIGHT**

Grocio, por derecho. Pastor Pérez, Miguel Antonio.

The Future of Civil Rights: Affirmative Action Redivivus. Erler, Edward J.

The Political Philosophy of Martin Luther King Jr.. Mannath, Joe.

The Rise and Fall of Affirmative Action. Platt, Anthony M.

Theoretical Issues in Social Movements. Michael, S M.

Tradizione romanistica e dommatica moderna. Nardozza, Massimo.

**CIVIL SOCIETY**

"The Korporation in Hegel's Interpretation of Civil Society" in *Hegel, History, and Interpretation,* Gallagher, Shaun. Prosch, Michael.

"The Russian Way" and Civil Society. Vorontsova, L M and Filatov, S B.

*Coming Together/Coming Apart: Religion, Community, and Modernity.* Bounds, Elizabeth M.

Civil Society and Ideology: A Matter of Freedom. Van der Zweerde, Evert.

Civil Society Ethics: An Approach from K-O Apel's Philosophy (in Spanish). Durán Casas, Vicente.

Compassion and Societal Well-Being. Brown, Lee M.

Logics of Power in Marx. Brown, Wendy.

Michael Oakeshott on History, Practice and Political Theory. Smith, Thomas W.

Neo-Functionalist Critical Theory?. Turner, Charles.

P.A. Kropotkin on Legality and Ethics. Slatter, John.

Pandering. Sullivan, Timothy.

Pufendorf, Sociality and the Modern State. Carr, Craig L and Seidler, Michael J.

State Prerogatives, Civil Society, and Liberalization: The Paradoxes of the Late Twentieth Century in the Third World. Monshipouri, Mahmood.

The Contemporary Political Significance of John Locke's Conception of Civil Society. Dunn, John.

The Struggle for the Constitution in Russia and the Triumph of Ethical Individualism. Sakwa, Richard.

Volunteerism and Democracy: A Latin American Perspective. Rich, Paul and De los Reyes, Guillermo.

**CIVIL STATE**

"An Integral Part of his Species...?" in *Jean-Jacques Rousseau and the Sources of the Self,* O'Hagan, Timothy (ed). Dent, Nicholas.

**CIVILIZATION**

"Il compito dello storico nella lezione inaugurale di Richard Henry Tawney (1932)" in *Lo Storicismo e la Sua Storia: Temi, Problemi, Prospettive,* Cacciatore, Giuseppe (ed). Tagliaferri, Teodoro.

"La Verità Come Tragedia: Immaginazione e immagine del Vero: Note sulla "civilizzazione" in *Soggetto E Verità: La questione dell'uomo nella filosofia contemporanea,* Fagiuoli, Ettore. Zanini, Adelino.

"Prospettive di storia universale nell'opera di Spengler" in *Lo Storicismo e la Sua Storia: Temi, Problemi, Prospettive,* Cacciatore, Giuseppe (ed). Conte, Domenico.

*Martin Heidegger und Hans Jonas: Die Metaphysik der Subjektivität und die Krise der technologischen Zivilisation.* Jakob, Eric.

*Social Control Through Law.* Treviño, A Javier (ed) and Pound, Roscoe.

*W.E.B. Du Bois on* Race and Culture. Grosholz, Emily (ed), Bell, Bernard W (ed) and Stewart, James B (ed).

Aussichten der Zivilgesellschaft unter Bedingungen neoliberaler Globalisierungspolitik. Haug, Wolfgang Fritz.

Historiography of Civilizations: A Review. Kaul, R K.

La culture comme force. Yahot, Christophe.

Patologie del sociale: Tradizione e attualità della filosofia sociale. Honneth, Axel.

**CIXOUS, H**

*French Feminist Theory (III): Luce Irigaray and Helene Cixous: A Bibliography.* Nordquist, Joan (ed).

**CLADISTICS**

Confusion in Philosophy: A Comment on Williams (1992). Williams, David M, Scotland, Robert W and Humphries, Christopher J.

**CLARA, A**

La filósofa rancia: un pensamiento ignorado. Crujeiras Lustres, María José.

**CLARK, J**

An Essay in the Applied Philosophy of Political Economy. Iachkina, Galina.

**CLARK, S**

The Value of Truth and the Care of the Soul. Witherall, Arthur.

**CLARKE**

"Samuel Clarke's Four Categories of Deism, Isaac Newton, and the Bible" in *Scepticism in the History of Philosophy: A Pan-American Dialogue,* Popkin, Richard H (ed). Force, James E.

L'apologétique de Samuel Clarke. Sina, Mario.

The Cosmological Argument Without the Principle of Sufficient Reason. Katz, Bernard D and Kremer, Elmar J.

West or Best? Sufficient Reason in the Leibniz-Clarke Correspondence. Grover, Stephen.

**CLARKE, M**

Logic Crystallized. Viney, Donald Wayne.

**CLARKE, N**

Personal Receptivity and Act: A Thomistic Critique. Long, Steven A.

**CLASS**

*see also* Set, Virtual Classes, Working Class

"Peirce and Russell: The History of a Neglected 'Controversy'" in *Studies in the Logic of Charles Sanders Peirce,* Houser, Nathan (ed). Hawkins, Benjamin S.

"Peirce on the Application of Relations to Relations" in *Studies in the Logic of Charles Sanders Peirce,* Houser, Nathan (ed). Burch, Robert W.

*Introduction to Metalogic.* Ruzsa, Imre.

Advice Classes of Parameterized Tractability. Cai, Liming, Chen, Jianer and Downey, Rodney G (& others).

Boolean Pairs Formed by the Delta$^0_n$-Sets. Hermann, E.

Characterizing Classes Defined without Equality. Elgueta, R.

Communication through Interpreters in Health Care: Ethical Dilemmas Arising from Differences in Class, Culture, Language, and Power. Kaufert, Joseph M and Putsch, Robert W.

On Elementary Equivalence for Equality-free Logic. Casanovas, E, Dellunde, Pilar and Jansana, Ramon.

On the Härtig-Style Axiomatization of Unprovable and Satisfiable Formulas of Bernays and Schönfinkel's Classes. Inoué, Takao.

Peirce's Teleological Approach to Natural Classes. Hulswit, Menno.

Pi$^0_1$ Classes and Minimal Degrees. Groszek, Marcia J and Slaman, Theodore A.

Rawls's "The Closed Society Assumption" (in Serbo-Croatian). Strncevic, Ljubica and Gligorov, Vladimir.

Some Applications of Coarse Inner Model Theory. Hjorth, Greg.

Uniformization, Choice Functions and Well Orders in the Class of Trees. Lifsches, Shmuel and Shelah, Saharon.

**CLASS CONSCIOUSNESS**

Chvostism and Dialectics (Introduced and Commentaries by László Illés) (in Hungarian). Lukács, Georg.

Contributions to the Reconstruction of the Later Lukacs's Philosophy (in Hungarian). Himmer, Péter.

Plekhanov, Lenin and Working-Class Consciousness. Mayer, Robert.

**CLASSICAL**

*Figuring the Self: Subject, Absolute, and Others in Classical German Philosophy.* Zöller, Günter (ed) and Klemm, David E (ed).

**CLASSICISM**

A Classicist's Approach to Rhetoric in Plato. Kirby, John T.

On Canova's Marble Sculptures (in Japanese). Tadashi, Kanai.

**CLASSICISM**

Tensor Products and Split-Level Architecture: Foundational Issues in the Classicism-Connectionism Debate. Guarini, Marcello.

**CLASSIFICATION**

Borel Equivalence Relations and Classifications of Countable Models. Hjorth, Greg and Kechris, Alexander S.

Kinds and Categories: Proceedings of the Twentieth Annual Greensboro Symposium in Philosophy. Loux, Michael J.

Naturgemässe Klassifikation und Kontinuität, Wissenschaft und Geschichte: Überlegungen zu Pierre Duhem. Petrus, Klaus.

Realismus in Duhems naturgemässer Klassifikation. Burri, Alex.

**CLASSROOM**

"Moral Dimensions of Classroom Discourse: A Deweyan Perspective" in *Philosophy of Education (1996)*, Margonis, Frank (ed). Rosner, Fay.

"Moral Reflection and Moral Education" in *Philosophy of Education (1996)*, Margonis, Frank (ed). Covaleskie, John F.

*Democratic Discipline: Foundation and Practice.* Hoover, Randy L and Kindsvatter, Richard.

Autonomy and the Very Limited Role of Advocacy in the Classroom. Kupperman, Joel J.

Disciplined Emotions: Philosophies of Educated Feelings. Boler, Megan.

Diversity in the Classroom. Maitzen, Stephen.

Feeling Fraudulent: Some Moral Quandaries of a Feminist Instructor. Overall, Christine.

Lost Times/Recovered Times. Reed, Ronald.

Powerful Pedagogy in the Science-and-Religion Classroom. Grassie, William.

Teaching for Presence in the Democratic Classroom. Richardson, Brenda.

The Arts and Educational Reform: More Critical Thinking in the Classrooms of the Future?. Olson, Ivan.

The Philosophy They Bring to Class: Companion Student Papers in PHL 101. Chiles, Robert E.

The Teaching of Ethics. Doorley, Mark J.

Trust Is Not Enough: Classroom Self-Disclosure and the Loss of Private Lives. Bishop, Nicole.

Voices in the Classroom: Girls and Philosophy for Children. Mohr-Lane, Jana.

**CLAUSE**

Individualism, Individuation and That-Clauses. Rechenauer, Martin.

**CLAUSIUS, R**

Adaptive Logic in Scientific Discovery: The Case of Clausius. Meheus, Joke.

**CLAVIERE, E**

Commerce, Constitutions, and the Manners of a Nation: Etienne Clavière's Revolutionary Political Economy, 1788-93. Whatmore, Richard.

**CLAVIGERO, F**

Los aspectos de ciencia moderna en la filosofía de Clavigero. Navarro, Bernabé.

**CLAYTON, E**

Children and Bioethics: Uses and Abuses of The Best-Interest Standard: Introduction. Kopelman, Loretta M.

**CLEANLINESS**

Sparkle and Shine. Leddy, Thomas.

**CLEANTHES**

Le tableau de Cléanthe. Rossetti, Livio.

**CLEMENCY**

The Quiddity of Mercy—A Response. Pearn, John.

**CLIENT**

Clients or Citizens?. Bender, Thomas.

Identifying the Real EAP Client: Ensuing Ethical Dilemmas. Lee, Sandra S and Schonberg, Sue E.

**CLIFFORD, W**

"James, Clifford, and the Scientific Conscience" in *The Cambridge Companion to William James,* Putnam, Ruth Anna (ed). Hollinger, David A.

**CLIMATE**

*Earthly Goods: Environmental Change and Social Justice.* Hampson, Fen Osler (ed) and Reppy, Judith (ed).

**CLINIC**

Bioethical Analysis of an Integrated Medicine Clinic. Potter, Robert Lyman and Schneider, Jennifer.

**CLINICAL**

About Signs and Symptoms: Can Semiotics Expand the View of Clinical Medicine?. Nessa, John.

Clinical Pragmatism: A Method of Moral Problem Solving. Fins, Joseph J, Bacchetta, Matthew D and Miller, Franklin G.

Community Equipoise and the Architecture of Clinical Research. Karlawish, Jason H T and Lantos, John.

The Promises and Perils of Pragmatism: Commentary on Fins, Bacchetta, and Miller. Tong, Rosemarie.

**CLINICAL ETHICS**

Bad Night in the ER—Patients' Preferences and Reasonable Accommodation: Discussed by Douglas A. Beer, Ruth Macklin, Walter Robinson, and Philip Wang. Beer, Douglas A, Macklin, Ruth and Robinson, Walter (& others).

Clinical Ethics and Ethics Committees. Bartholome, William G.

Clinical Ethics and the Suffering Christian. Wear, Stephen and Phillips, Benjamin.

Concepts in Evaluation Applied to Ethics Consultation Research. Fox, Ellen.

Ethics Expert Testimony: Against the Skeptics. Agich, George J and Spielman, Bethan J.

Evaluating Ethics Consultation: Framing the Questions. Tulsky, James A and Fox, Ellen.

Evaluation Research and the Future of Ethics Consultation. Fox, Ellen and Tulsky, James A.

From Clinical Ethics to Organizational Ethics: The Second Stage of the Evolution of Bioethics. Potter, Robert Lyman.

Learning to "Real/Hear": Narrative Ethics and Ethics Committee Education. Potter, Robert Lyman.

Listening or Telling? Thoughts on Responsibility in Clinical Ethics Consultation. Zaner, Richard M.

Persistent Vegetative State: Clinical and Ethical Issues. Celesia, Gastone G.

Phronesis in Clinical Ethics. McGee, Glenn.

Quality Control for Hospitals' Clinical Ethics Services: Proposed Standards. Leeman, Cavin P, Fletcher, John C and Spencer, Edward M (& others).

Speaking Truth to Employers. Andre, Judith.

The Economics of Clinical Ethics Programs: A Quantitative Justification. Bacchetta, Matthew D and Fins, Joseph J.

The Heterogeneity of Clinical Ethics: The State of the Field as Reflected in the *Encyclopedia of Bioethics.* Koczwara, Bogda M and Madigan, Timothy J.

The Management of Instability and Incompleteness: Clinical Ethics and Abstract Expressionism. McCullough, Laurence B.

The Personal Is the Organizational in the Ethics of Hospital Social Workers. Walsh-Bowers, Richard, Rossiter, Amy and Prilleltensky, Isaac.

The Three Deadly Sins of Ethics Consultation. Howe, Edmund G.

Understanding the Practice of Ethics Consultation: Results of an Ethnographic Multi-Site Study. Kelly, Susan E, Marshall, Patricia A and Sanders, Lee M (& others).

What Are the Goals of Ethics Consultation: A Consensus Statement. Fletcher, John C and Siegler, Mark.

**CLONING**

Heroic Antireductionism and Genetics: A Tale of One Science. Vance, Russell E.

Human Cloning: A Case of No Harm Done?. Roberts, Melinda A.

L'embrione è arrivato tra noi. Viano, Carlo Augusto.

Taboos Without a Clue: Sizing up Religious Objections to Cloning. Lindsay, Ronald A.

**CLOSED**

Higman's Embedding Theorem in a General Setting and its Application to Existentially Closed Algebras. Belegradek, Oleg V.

On Countably Closed Complete Boolean Algebras. Jech, Thomas and Shelah, Saharon.

On the Unification Problem for Cartesian Closed Categories. Narendran, Paliath, Pfenning, Frank and Statman, Richard.

Some Model Theory for Almost Real Closed Fields. Delon, Françoise and Farré, Rafel.

**CLOSURE**

Analytic Cell Decomposition and the Closure of $p$-ADIC Semianalytic Sets. Liu, Nianzheng.

Formal Properties of Natural Language and Linguistic Theories. Culy, C.

Religious 'Doctrines' and the Closure of Minds. Leahy, Michael and Laura, Ronald S.

Syntactic Characterizations of Closure under Pullbacks and of Locally Polypresentable Categories. Hébert, Michel.

The Causal Closure Principle of the Physical Domain and Quantum Mechanics. Mixie, Joseph.

The Lattice of Distributive Closure Operators Over an Algebra. Font, Josep Maria and Verdú, Ventura.

The Price of Universality. Hemaspaandra, Edith.

**COADY, C**

Against Coady on Hume on Testimony. Hríbek, Tomás.

Testimony and Perception. Prijic-Samarzija, Snjezana.

Testimony, Induction and Folk Psychology. Lyons, Jack.

**COBAIN, K**

La question du suicide. Lanteigne, Josette.

**COCCHIARELLA, N**

A Minimal Logical System for Computable Concepts and Effective Knowability. Freund, Max A.

Semantics for Two Second-Order Logical Systems. Freund, Max A.

**CODE OF CONDUCT**

Influencing Ethical Development: Exposing Students to the AICPA Code of Conduct. Green, Sharon and Weber, James.

**CODE OF ETHICS**

A Call for a Statement of Expectations for the Global Information Infrastructure. Connolly, Frank W.

An Historical Preface to Engineering Ethics. Davis, Michael.

Code Types: Functions and Failings and Organizational Diversity. Condren, Conal.

**COMMITTEE**

The Enforcement of Professional Ethics by Scientific Societies. Gardner, William.

UNESCO, Genetics, and Human Rights. Lenoir, Noëlle.

**COMMODIFICATION**

*Contested Commodities.* Radin, Margaret Jane.

**COMMODITY**

Commodity or Public Work? Two Perspectives on Health Care. Hanson, Mark J and Jennings, Bruce.

The Cultural Commodity (in Portuguese). Bolognesi, Mário Fernando.

**COMMON**

*The Commons of the Mind.* Baier, Annette C.

Approximate Common Knowledge and Co-Ordination: Recent Lessons from Game Theory. Morris, Stephen and Shin, Hyun Song.

**COMMON GOOD**

*A Politics of the Common Good.* Riordan, Patrick.

*Universal Justice: A Dialectical Approach.* Anderson, Albert A.

Health Care as a Public Good. Fisk, Milton.

Sul contrattualismo di Hobbes: una recente interpretazione. Longega, Andrea.

**COMMON LAW**

Paul Ramsey and the Common Law Tradition. Tuttle, Robert W.

**COMMON SENSE**

"The Succinct Case for Idealism" in *Objections to Physicalism,* Robinson, Howard (ed). Foster, John.

*Ingegnerie della Conoscenza: Introduzione alla Filosofia Computazionale.* Magnani, Lorenzo.

*Quest for Self-Knowledge: An Essay in Lonergan's Philosophy.* Flanagan, Joseph.

*Vico and Moral Perception.* Black, David W.

Common Sense and a "Wigner-Dirac" Approach to Quantum Mechanics. Forrest, Peter.

Common Sense und Logik in Jan Smedslunds 'Psychologik'. Mock, Verena.

Identity, Quantum Mechanics and Common Sense. Huggett, Nick.

L'etica laica e l'enciclica "Evangelium vitae". Lecaldano, Eugenio.

Sentido común "común" y sentido común "sensato". Una reivindicación de Thomas Reid. Prado, José Hernández.

Sobre el sentido común y la percepción: Algunas sugerencias acerca de la facultad sensitiva central. Posada, Jorge Mario.

**COMMONWEALTH**

Building the Union: The Nature of Sovereignty in the Political Architecture of Europe. Bellamy, Richard and Castiglione, Dario.

Democracy, Subsidiarity, and Citizenship in the 'European Commonwealth'. MacCormick, Neil.

**COMMUNALISM**

"Democracy and Communal Self-Determination" in *The Morality of Nationalism,* McKim, Robert (ed). Copp, David.

**COMMUNICATION**

"Argumentation in the Tradition of Speech Communication Studies" in *Logic and Argumentation,* Van Eemeren, Frans H (ed). Zarefsky, David.

"Embedding Logic in Communication: Lessons from the Logic Classroom" in *Logic and Argumentation,* Van Eemeren, Frans H (ed). Stenning, Keith.

"Essere, Materia, Soggetto, Alterità: Per una critica filosofica della comunicazione mondializzata" in *Soggetto E Verità: La questione dell'uomo nella filosofia contemporanea,* Fagiuoli, Ettore. Ponzio, Augusto.

"How to Avoid Not Speaking: Attestations" in *Knowing Other-Wise: Philosophy at the Threshold of Spirituality,* Olthuis, James H (ed). Smith, James K A.

"Sozialphilosophische Aspekte der Übersetzbarkeit" in *Epistemology and History,* Zeidler-Janiszewska, Anna (ed). Siemek, Marek J.

*Augusto Ponzio: Bibliografia e Letture Critiche.* Ponzio, Augusto.

*Comunicación, Ética Y Política: Habermas Y Sus Críticos.* Boladeras, Margarita.

*Karl-Otto Apel: Selected Essays.* Mendieta, Eduardo (ed).

*Language and Reason: A Study of Habermas's Pragmatics.* Cooke, Maeve.

*On Dialogue.* Nichol, Lee (ed) and Bohm, David.

*Temporalità e Comunicazione.* Reda, Clementina Gily.

*Transgressing Discourses: Communication and the Voice of Other.* Huspek, Michael (ed) and Radford, Gary P (ed).

A Obra como Facto Comunicativo. Rodrigues, Manuel J.

Alle origini dei diritti dell'uomo: i diritti della comunicazione di Francisco de Vitoria. Trujillo Pérez, Isabel.

Better Communication between Engineers and Managers: Some Ways to Prevent Many Ethically Hard Choices. Davis, Michael.

Comment: What We Can Learn from "Better Communication between Engineers and Managers" (M. Davis). Whitbeck, Caroline.

Commentary on "Better Communication between Engineers and Managers. Loui, Michael.

Commentary on "Better Communication between Engineers and Managers". Pritchard, Michael S.

Communication, Criticism, and the Postmodern Consensus: An Unfashionable Interpretation of Michel Foucault. Johnson, James.

Communicative Action and Philosophical Foundations: Comments on the Apel-Habermas Debate. Papastephanou, Marianna.

Communicative Action, the Lifeworlds of Learning and the Dialogue that we Aren't. Hogan, Pádraig.

Conciencia subjetiva y conciencia comunicativa en el discurso ético. Michelini, Dorando J.

Contesting Consensus: Rereading Habermas on the Public Sphere. Markell, Patchen.

Descartes and the Communication of Passions (in Czech). Kambouchner, Denis.

El educador viquiano. Rebollo Espinosa, Maria José.

Environmental Responsibility: Individual Choice, Communication, Institutional Risks (in Czech). Susa, Oleg.

Ethics and the Internet: Appropriate Behavior in Electronic Communication. Langford, Duncan.

Habermas and Apel on Communicative Ethics: Their Difference and the Difference It Makes. Gamwell, Franklin I.

Hannah Arendt: On Power. Penta, Leo J.

Knowledge and Discourse in Gorgias's *On the Non-Existent or On Nature.* Gaines, Robert N.

Landmarks in Critical Thinking Series: Pragmatics and Critical Thinking. Yoos, George.

Malinowksi: La Importancia de la Pragmática y del Bla-bla-bla en la Comunicación. Patiño A, Alejandro.

Marc Augé e l'antropologia dei mondi contemporanei. Soldati, Adriana.

On the Practical Relevance of Habermas's Theory of Communicative Action. Parkin, Andrew C.

Pandering. Sullivan, Timothy.

Principles and Purpose: The Patient Surrogate's Perspective and Role. Koch, Tom.

Social Representations and Mass Communication Research. Rouquette, Michel-Louis.

Sprechakttheoretische Erläuterungen zum Begriff der kommunikativen Rationalität. Habermas, Jürgen.

Symbol and Communication in Politics (Spanish). Fiorino, Víctor R Martín.

Tecnopolitica: Le idee del cyberpunk. Nacci, Michela.

Teoría de la acción y racionalidad en Donald Davidson. Pérez-Wicht, Pablo Quintanilla.

The Communication of *De Re* Thoughts. Bezuidenhout, Anne L.

The Possibility of a Mathematical Sociology of Scientific Communication. Leydesdorff, Loet.

The Situated but Directionless Self: The Postmetaphysical World of Benhabib's Discourse Ethics. Hepburn, Elizabeth R.

The Voice on the Skin: Self-Mutilation and Merleau-Ponty's Theory of Language. McLane, Janice.

Tra materialismo e critica della comunicazione: Paolo Virno. Genovese, Rino.

Una teoría del estado de derecho. De Zan, Julio.

Une éthique est-elle possible en l'absence de croyances dogmatiques?. Boudon, Raymond.

Wilbur Schramm and the Founding of Communication Studies. Glander, Timothy.

**COMMUNISM**

*see also* Historical Materialism, Leninism, Marxism

Aristotle's Criticism of Plato's Communism of Women and Children. Mayhew, Robert.

Complexity and Deliberative Democracy. Femia, Joseph V.

Dal primato della prassi all'anomia: Una interpretazione filosofica della crisi odierna. Cotta, Sergio.

Dr. Pangloss Goes to Market. Schweickart, David.

Hegelianism in Slovenia: A Short Introduction. Vezjak, Boris.

Jan Patocka's World Movement as Ultimate. Tucker, Aviezer.

Lived Thought between Affirmation and Critique: Georg Lukács and Stalinism (in Hungarian). Tietz, Udo.

On Freedom. Liquin, Deng.

Science as a Battlefield: Methodological and Historical Considerations on the Misuse of Science by Totalitarian Regimes of Central Europe. Hajduk, Anton.

The Edge of Crisis/The Crisis of the Edge. Grgas, Stipe.

Through Sin to Salvation (in Hungarian). Bell, Daniel.

Transitional Regimes and the Rule of Law. Golding, Martin P.

**COMMUNITARIANISM**

"Conventions and Conversions, or, Why Is Nationalism Sometimes So Nasty?" in *The Morality of Nationalism,* McKim, Robert (ed). Goodin, Robert E.

"Politische Ethik I: Ethik der politischen Institutionen und der Bürgerschaft" in *Angewandte Ethik: Die Bereichsethiken und ihre theoretische Fundierung,* Nida-Rümelin, Julian (ed). Nida-Rümelin, Julian.

"Rechtsethik" in *Angewandte Ethik: Die Bereichsethiken und ihre theoretische Fundierung,* Nida-Rümelin, Julian (ed). Von der Pfordten, Dietmar.

"Werte und Entscheidungen" in *Werte und Entscheidungen im Management,* Schmidt, Thomas. Schmidt, Thomas.

*Liberalismo y Comunitarismo: Derechos Humanos y Democracia.* Monsalve Solórzano, Alfonso (ed) and Cortés Rodas, Francisco (ed).

A Communitarian Approach to Physician-Assisted Death. Miller, Franklin G.

A Communitarian Critique of Authoritarianism. Bell, Daniel A.

## COMPATIBILISM

Misdirection in the Free Will Problem. Double, Richard.

Strategies for Free Will Compatibilists. O'Leary-Hawthorne, John and Petit, Philip.

## COMPATIBILITY

Divine Foreknowledge and Human Freedom Are Compatible. Warfield, Ted A.

## COMPATRIOT

Special Obligations to Compatriots. Mason, Andrew.

## COMPENSATION

see Income, Wage

## COMPETENCE

Compétence sémantique et psychologie du raisonnement. Dokic, Jérôme.

Competence-Based Education and Training: Progress or Villainy?. Bridges, David.

Fostering Market Competence. Askland, Andrew.

Technological Escalation and the Exploration Model of Natural Science. Rescher, Nicholas.

## COMPETENCY

The Role of Emotions in Decisional Competence, Standards of Competency, and Altruistic Acts. Silverman, Henry.

## COMPETITION

Business Ethics in the African Context Today. Rosemann, Philipp W (ed) and LeJeune, Michel (ed).

Stretched Lines, Averted Leaps, and Excluded Competition: A Theory of Scientific Counterfactuals. Mikkelson, Gregory M.

## COMPLEMENTATION

Minimal Complementation Below Uniform Upper Bounds for the Arithmetical Degrees. Kumabe, Masahiro.

## COMPLETENESS

see also Hallden-Completeness, Incompleteness

"Storia del teorema di completezza" in Momenti di Storia della Logica e di Storia della Filosofia, Guetti, Carla (ed). Lolli, Gabriele.

A Completeness Proof for a Logic with an Alternative Necessity Operator. Demri, Stéphane.

A Constructive Game Semantics for the Language of Linear Logic. Japaridze, Giorgi.

A Logic for Information Systems. Archangelsky, Dmitri A and Taitslin, Mikhail A.

A Logic for Reasoning about Relative Similarity. Konikowska, Beata.

A New Theory of Content II: Model Theory and Some Alternative. Gemes, Ken.

A Note on the Completeness of Kozen's Axiomatisation of the Propositional mu-Calculus. Walukiewicz, Igor.

A Revolution in the Foundations of Mathematics?. Hintikka, Jaakko.

A Uniform Tableau Method for Intuitionistic Modal Logics I. Amati, Giambattista and Pirri, Fiora.

An Elementary Proof of Chang's Completeness Theorem for the Infinite-Valued Calculus of Lukasiewicz. Cignoli, Roberto and Mundici, Daniele.

An Extension of the Formulas-as-Types Paradigm. Lambek, J.

Axiomatising First-Order Temporal Logic: Until and Since over Linear Time. Reynolds, Mark.

Axiomatization and Completeness of Uncountably Valued Approximation Logic. Rasiowa, Helena.

Bounded Contraction and Gentzen-style Formulation of Lukasiewicz Logics. Prijatelj, Andreja.

Cauchy Completeness in Elementary Logic. Cifuentes, J C, Sette, A M and Mundici, Daniele.

Classical and Intuitionistic Models of Arithmetic. Wehmeier, Kai F.

Completeness and Decidability of Tense Logics Closely Related to Logics Above K4. Wolter, Frank.

Completeness and Incompleteness for Plausibility Logic. Schlechta, Karl.

Completeness of Global Intuitionistic Set Theory. Titani, Satoko.

Completeness Results for Linear Logic on Petri Nets. Engberg, Uffe.

Completeness Theorem for Dummett's L C Quantified and Some of Its Extensions. Corsi, Giovanna.

Cut-Free Sequent Calculi for Some Tense Logics. Kashima, Ryo.

Deductive Completeness. Dosen, Kosta.

Extensions of Modal Logic S5 Preserving NP-Completeness. Demri, Stéphane.

From Completeness to Archimedean Completeness: An Essay in the Foundations of Euclidean Geometry. Ehrlich, Philip.

Generalized Quantification as Substructural Logic. Alechina, Natasha and Van Lambalgen, Michiel.

Husserl and Hilbert on Completeness: A Neglected Chapter in Early Twentieth Century Foundations of Mathematics. Majer, Ulrich.

Kripke Completeness of Some Intermediate Predicate Logics with the Axiom of Constant Domain and a Variant of Canonical Formulas. Shimura, Tatsuya.

Kripke Models and the (In)equational Logic of the Second-Order Lambda-Calculus. Gallier, Jean.

Logic in Russell's Principles of Mathematics. Landini, Gregory.

Logics of Rejection: Two Systems of Natural Deduction. Tamminga, Allard M.

Object Theory Foundations for Intensional Logic. Jacquette, Dale.

On Countably Closed Complete Boolean Algebras. Jech, Thomas and Shelah, Saharon.

On the Completeness of First Degree Weakly Aggregative Modal Logics. Apostoli, Peter.

Refutation Systems in Modal Logic. Goranko, Valentin.

Some Aspects of Refutation Rules. Skura, Tomasz.

T x W Completeness. Von Kutschera, Franz.

The Completeness of the Factor Semantics for Lukasiewicz's Infinite-Valued Logics. Vasyukov, Vladimir L.

The Structure of Lattices of Subframe Logics. Wolter, Frank.

Une Preuve Formelle et Intuitionniste du Théorème de Complétude de la Logique Classique. Krivine, Jean-Louis.

## COMPLEX

Complex Predicates and Conversion Principles. Swoyer, Chris.

Towards a Rough Mereology-Based Logic for Approximate Solution. Komorowski, Jan, Polkowski, Lech T and Skowron, Andrzej.

## COMPLEXITY

see also Computational Complexity

A Theory of Complexes. Greenberg, William J.

Chaos, Berechnungskomplexität und Physik: Neue Grenzen wissenschaftlicher Erkenntnis?. Leiber, Theodor.

Infinite Versions of Some Problems from Finite Complexity Theory. Hirst, Jeffry L and Lempp, Steffen.

New Blades for Occam's Razor. Lauth, Bernhard.

Organized Complexity in Human Affairs: The Tobacco Industry. Bella, David A.

Simplified Lower Bounds for Propositional Proofs. Urquhart, Alasdair and Fu, Xudong.

Sparse Parameterized Problems. Cesati, Marco.

The Combinatorics of the Splitting Theorem. Kontostathis, Kyriakos.

The Paradox of Identity. Greenberg, William J.

The Trouble with Truth-Makers. Cox, Damian.

## COMPOSITION

Coincidence and Principles of Composition. Levey, Samuel.

Composition and Coincidence. Olson, Eric T.

Creation and Discovery in Musical Works. Woodruff, David M.

Is Compositionality Compatible with Holism?. Pagin, Peter.

Two Spurious Varieties of Compositionality. García-Carpintero, Manuel.

## COMPREHENSION

Intersubjetividad como intramundanidad: Hacia una ética del tercero incluido. Cristin, Renato.

Superamento della complessità attraverso la capacità di apprendimento del diritto: L'adeguamento del diritto alle condizioni del Postmoderno. Ladeur, Karl-Heinz.

## COMPROMISE

Kitcher's Compromise: A Critical Examination of the Compromise Model of Scientific Closure, and its Implications for the Relationship Between History and Philosophy of Science. Shanahan, Timothy.

## COMPUTABILITY

Computability and Recursion. Soare, Robert I.

Polynomial Time Operations in Explicit Mathematics. Strahm, Thomas.

The Undecidability of the Spatialized Prisoner's Dilemma. Grim, Patrick.

## COMPUTABLE

A Minimal Logical System for Computable Concepts and Effective Knowability. Freund, Max A.

Notes on Polynomially Bounded Arithmetic. Zambella, Domenico.

## COMPUTATION

"Content, Computation and Externalism" in Contents, Villanueva, Enrique (ed). Peacocke, Christopher.

"Understanding Understanding: Syntactic Semantics and Computational Cognition" in AI, Connectionism and Philosophical Psychology, 1995, Tomberlin, James E (ed). Rapaport, William J.

Computation, Dynamics, and Cognition. Giunti, Marco.

A Furry Tile about Mental Representation. Brown, Deborah J.

Content, Computation, and Individualism in Vision Theory. Butler, Keith.

Does a Rock Implement Every Finite-State Automation?. Chalmers, David J.

How We Get There From Here: Dissolution of the Binding Problem. Hardcastle, Valerie Gray.

Individualism and Marr's Computational Theory of Vision. Butler, Keith.

On Alan Turing's Anticipation of Connectionism. Copeland, B Jack and Proudfoot, Diane.

Software Agents and Their Bodies. Kushmerick, Nicholas.

The Skeptic and the Hoverfly (A Teleo-Computational View of Rule-Following). Miscevic, Nenad.

Thinking Machines: Some Fundamental Confusions. Kearns, John T.

What is Computation?. Copeland, B Jack.

## COMPUTATIONAL

"Towards a Computational Treatment of Deontic Defeasibility" in Deontic Logic, Agency and Normative Systems, Brown, Mark A (ed). Artosi, Alberto, Governatori, Guido and Sartor, Giovanni.

A Clearer Vision. Shapiro, Lawrence A.

On the Very Idea of a Theory of Meaning for a Natural Language. Fischer, Eugen.

## COMPUTATIONAL COMPLEXITY

Advice Classes of Parameterized Tractability. Cai, Liming, Chen, Jianer and Downey, Rodney G (& others).

Extensions of Modal Logic S5 Preserving NP-Completeness. Demri, Stéphane.

Laplace's Demon Consults an Oracle: The Computational Complexity of Prediction. Pitowsky, Itamar.

Linear Logic Proof Games and Optimization. Lincoln, Patrick D, Mitchell, John C and Scedrov, Andre.

On the Complexity of Propositional Quantification in Intuitionistic Logic. Kremer, Philip.

The Price of Universality. Hemaspaandra, Edith.

The Relative Complexity of Analytic Tableaux and SL-Resolution. Vellino, André.

## COMPUTATIONAL MODEL

"Filosofi Artificiali" in *Soggetto E Verità: La questione dell'uomo nella filosofia contemporanea,* Fagiuoli, Ettore. Magnani, Lorenzo.

## COMPUTER

*see also* Machine

"Die (sei's auch metaphorische) These vom Geist als Computer" in *Das weite Spektrum der analytischen Philosophie,* Lenzen, Wolfgang. Kemmerling, Andreas.

"¿Siguen las pruebas realizadas por ordenador algún patrón de verdad matemática?" in *Verdad: lógica, representación y mundo,* Villegas Forero, L. Beltrán Orenes, Pilar.

*A Gift of Fire: Social, Legal, and Ethical Issues in Computing.* Baase, Sara.

*CyberSpace Virtual Reality: Fortschritt und Gefahr einer innovativen Technologie.* Wedde, Horst F (ed).

*Ingegneria della Conoscenza: Introduzione alla Filosofia Computazionale.* Magnani, Lorenzo.

*Life as Narcissism: A Unified Theory of Life.* Tabrizi, Firooz N.

*Mind Design II: Philosophy, Psychology, Artificial Intelligence.* Haugeland, John (ed).

Accountability in a Computerized Society. Nissenbaum, Helen.

An Exploration into Teaching with Computers. Kowalski, Ludwik.

Approximate Knowledge of Many Agents and Discovery Systems. Zytkow, Jan M.

Chaos, Berechnungskomplexität und Physik: Neue Grenzen wissenschaftlicher Erkenntnis?. Leiber, Theodor.

Computers, Information and Ethics: A Review of Issues and Literature. Mitcham, Carl.

Computers, Radiation, and Ethics. Schenkman, Bo.

Cyborg Identities and the Relational Web: Recasting 'Narrative Identity' in Moral and Political Theory. Brothers, Robyn F.

Die vierte bis siebte Kränkung des Menschen—Gehirn, Evolution und Menschenbild. Vollmer, Gerhard.

Ethical Issues in a Study of Internet Use: Uncertainty, Responsibility, and the Spirit of Research Relationships. Bier, Melinda C, Sherblom, Stephen A and Gallo, Michael A.

Ethics and the Internet: Appropriate Behavior in Electronic Communication. Langford, Duncan.

Helena Rasiowa and Cecylia Rauszer Research on Logical Foundations of Computer Science. Pawlak, Zdzislaw and Skowron, Andrzej.

Informática na Educaçao: Perspectivas. Miranda Carrao, Eduardo Vitor.

Introduction and Overview: Global Information Ethics. Bynum, Terrell Ward.

Letter of the Editor: On Knowledge Technology and its Relevance. Vandamme, F.

On Alan Turing's Anticipation of Connectionism. Copeland, B Jack and Proudfoot, Diane.

Philosophical Counseling: A Computer-Assisted, Logic-Based Approach. Cohen, Elliot D.

Privacy and the Computer: Why we need Privacy in the Information Society. Introna, Lucas D.

Prove-Once More and Again. Hersh, Reuben.

Situational Determinants of Software Piracy: An Equity Theory Perspective. Glass, Richard S and Wood, Wallace A.

Sources of Error and Accountability in Computer Systems: Comments on "Accountability in a Computerized Society". Szolovits, Peter.

Tecnopolitica: Le idee del cyberpunk. Nacci, Michela.

The Art of Interaction: Interactivity, Performativity, and Computers. Saltz, David Z.

The Computer Revolution and the Problem of Global Ethics. Gorniak-Kocikowska, Krystyna.

The Vitality of Digital Creation. Binkley, Timothy.

Unique Ethical Problems in Information Technology. Maner, Walter.

Using Computer-Assisted Instruction and Developmental Theory to Improve Argumentative Writing. Irwin, Ronald R.

## COMPUTER ETHICS

Business Ethics and Computer Ethics: The View from Poland. Sojka, Jacek.

Computer Ethics and Moral Methodology. Van den Hoven, Jeroen.

Geography and Computer Ethics: An Eastern European Perspective. Kocikowski, Andrzej.

International Federation for Information Processing's Framework for Computer Ethics. Berleur, Jacques.

Symposium on Computer Ethics. Ward Bynum, Terrell.

## COMPUTER SCIENCE

Integrating the Ethical and Social Context of Computing into the Computer Science Curriculum. Huff, Chuck, Anderson, Ronald E and Little, Joyce Currie (& others).

Special Selection in Logic in Computer Science. Vardi, Moshe Y.

## COMTE

A Comparative Study between Comte's and Mill's View on Women. Lang'at, Wilson K A.

## CONANT, J

A Funny Thing Happened to Me on the Way to Salvation: Climacus as Humorist in Kierkegaard's *Concluding Unscientific Postscript.* Lippitt, John.

## CONATION

Transcendental Truth in Vico. Wilson, Gerald.

## CONCEIVABILITY

Hume on Conceivability and Inconceivability. Lightner, D Tycerium.

Imaginability, Conceivability, Possibility and the Mind-Body Problem. Hill, Christopher S.

## CONCEPT

*see also* Idea, Theoretical Concepts

"Conceptos y concepciones: sobre la posibilidad del cambio conceptual" in *Verdad: lógica, representación y mundo,* Villegas Forero, L. Gomila Benejam, Antoni.

"Il concetto di tempo" in *Il Concetto di Tempo: Atti del XXXII Congresso Nazionale della Società Filosofica Italiana,* Casertano, Giovanni (ed). Scarcella, Attilio.

"On What It Is Like To Grasp a Concept" in *Contents,* Villanueva, Enrique (ed). Levine, Joseph.

*Disputazioni Metafisiche I-III.* Suárez, Francisco and Esposito, Costantino (ed & trans).

A Minimal Logical System for Computable Concepts and Effective Knowability. Freund, Max A.

Conceptual Realism as a Theory of Logical Form. Cocchiarella, Nino B.

Doing Without Concepts: An Interpretation of C.I. Lewis' Action-Oriented Foundationalism. Stufflebeam, Robert.

La transformacion de una teoría matemática: el caso de los números poligonales. Radford, Luis.

Locke's Acceptance of Innate Concepts. Wendler, Dave.

Molecular Shape, Reduction, Explanation and Approximate Concepts. Ramsey, Jeffry L.

On (Virtuous?) Circles of Concepts in Goodman—and Quine. Read, Rupert.

On Historicity of History and Stupidity of Concepts: Nietzsche's Nihilism (in Polish). Michalski, Krzysztof.

On the Properties of a Network that Associates Concepts on Basis of Share of Components and Its Relation with the Conceptual Memory of the Right Hemisphere. Van Loocke, Philip.

On the Right Idea of a Conceptual Scheme. Case, Jennifer.

Précis of *The Construction of Social Reality.* Searle, John R.

Stich on Intentionality and Rationality. Gibson, Roger.

Syncatégorèmes, concepts, équivocité: Deux questions anonymes, conservées dans le ms. Paris, B.N., lat. 16.401, liées à la sémantique de Pierre d'Ailly (c. 1350-1420). Bakker, Paul J J M.

The Nature of Human Concepts/Evidence from an Unusual Source. Pinker, Steven and Prince, Alan.

The Nature of the Common Concept in William of Ockham (in Czech). Saxlová, Tereza.

The Philosophical and Methodological Thought of N. I. Lobachevsky. Perminov, V Ya.

The Relationship Between Connectionist Models and a Dynamic Data-Oriented Theory of Concept Formation. Bartsch, Renate.

Tractarian Support for a Nonpropositional Paradigm. Bozicevic, Vanda.

## CONCEPTION

"Conceptos y concepciones: sobre la posibilidad del cambio conceptual" in *Verdad: lógica, representación y mundo,* Villegas Forero, L. Gomila Benejam, Antoni.

Kinesthetic-Visual Matching and the Self-Concept as Explanations of Mirror-Self-Recognition. Mitchell, Robert W.

## CONCEPTUALISM

Semantics for Two Second-Order Logical Systems. Freund, Max A.

## CONCERN

Consequentialism, Moralities of Concern, and Selfishness. Honderich, Ted.

Self-Interest and Self-Concern. Darwall, Stephen.

## CONCLUSION

Is the Repugnant Conclusion Repugnant?. Ryberg, Jesper.

On Teaching Premise/Conclusion Distinctions. Fawkes, Don.

The Reliability of Premise and Conclusion Indicators. Smythe, Thomas W.

## CONCORD

*Homonoia* in Aristotle's Ethics and Politics. Klonoski, Richard J.

## CONCORDANCE

*A Concordance to the Critique of Pure Reason.* Reuscher, Jay.

## CONCRETE

Astrattezza e concretezza nella filosofia di Giovanni Gentile. Frigerio, Aldo.

Created Receptivity and the Philosophy of the Concrete. Schmitz, Kenneth L.

Reply. Long, Steven A.

**CONCUPISCENCE**
*Voluntas* nel *De gratia et libero arbitrio* di Bernardo di Chiaravalle. Allegro, Giuseppe.

**CONDENSED**
A Simplified Form of Condensed Detachment. Bunder, M W.

**CONDILLAC**
Lamarck's Method (in Portuguese). De Andrade Martins, Roberto and Pareira Martins, Lilian Al-Chueyr.

**CONDITION**
*see also* Truth Condition
Counterfactuals, Causation, and Overdetermination. Worley, Sara.
On Making and Keeping Promises. Fox, Richard M.
On the Significance of Conditional Probabilities. Sobel, Jordan Howard.
Probability as a Guide to Life. Beebee, Helen and Papineau, David.
Problems in developing a Practical Theory of Moral Responsibility. Anderson, Susan Leigh.
Truth Conditions of Tensed Sentence Types. Paul, L A.
Two Types of Circularity. Humberstone, I Lloyd.

**CONDITIONAL**
*see also* Implication
"Lógica condicional con múltiples operadores" in *Verdad: lógica, representación y mundo*, Villegas Forero, L. Vilanova Arias, Javier.
"Peirce and Philo" in *Studies in the Logic of Charles Sanders Peirce*, Houser, Nathan (ed). Zeman, Jay.
"Ruritania and Ecology" in *Contents*, Villanueva, Enrique (ed). Toribio, Josefa.
A Gentzen System for Conditional Logic. Guzmán, Fernando.
Absolute and Conditional Rights. Dowling, Keith.
An Indefinability Argument for Conditional Obligation. Innala, Heikki-Pekka.
Armstrong on the Role of Laws in Counterfactual Supporting. Pages, Joan.
Bayesian Rules of Updating. Howson, Colin.
Bruno de Finetti and the Logic of Conditional Events. Milne, Peter.
Can Edgington Gibbard Counterfactuals?. Morton, Adam.
Circumstances and the Truth of Words: A Reply to Travis. Simmons, Howard.
Cognitive Homelessness. Williamson, Timothy.
Coincidence under a Sortal. Oderberg, David S.
Conditional Probability and Conditional Beliefs. Lowe, E J.
Conditionals, Imaging, and Subjunctive Probability. Lepage, François.
Counterfactuals and Updates as Inverse Modalities. Ryan, Mark and Schobbens, Pierre-Yves.
Denied Conditionals Are Not Negated Conditionals. Fulda, Joseph S.
Dispositional Properties (Czech). Vlasáková, Marta.
Evidence for the Innateness of Deontic Reasoning. Cummins, Denise Dellarosa.
Fainthearted Conditionals. Morreau, Michael.
Finkish Dispositions. Lewis, David.
Humphreys's Paradox and the Interpretation of Inverse Conditional Propensities. McCurdy, Christopher S I.
Inductive Confirmation, Counterfactual Conditionals, and Laws of Nature. Lange, Marc.
Introduction. Müller, Benito.
La cuestión de lo Incondicionado: Dialéctica y revelación de lo sagrado en Paul Tillich. Pastor, Félix-Alejandro.
Logic Crystallized. Viney, Donald Wayne.
Lowe on Conditional Probability. Edgington, Dorothy.
Material Implication and General Indicative Conditionals. Barker, Stephen.
On S. Fuhrmann, André and Mares, Edwin D.
On the Semantics of Comparative Conditionals. Beck, Sigrid.
Opting Out: Bennett on Classifying Conditionals. Cogan, Ross.
Parsing If-Sentences and the Conditions of Sentencehood. Barker, Stephen J.
Quick Triviality Proofs for Probabilities of Conditionals. Milne, Peter.
Reply to Simmons. Travis, Charles.
Revision Algebra Semantics for Conditional Logic. Pais, John.
The Conditional Quality of Gandhi's Love. Harris, Ian M.
The Ramsey Test and Conditional Semantics. Döring, Frank.
Thomas' Second Way: A Defense by Modal Scientific Reasoning. Trundle, Jr, Robert C.
Truth, Objectivity, Counterfactuals and Gibbard. Edgington, Dorothy.
Two Notions of Epistemic Validity: Epistemic Models for Ramsey's Conditionals. Costa, Horacio A and Levi, Isaac.
What's an Approximate Conditional?. De Soto, A R and Trillas, Enric.

**CONDITIONING**
Cultural Conditioning: The Dark Underside of Multiculturalism (Part Two: A Way Out). Reinsmith, William.

**CONDORCET**
Secularization and Tolerance. Spini, Giorgio.

**CONDUCT**
*see also* Act
*Ethics for Professionals in Education: Perspectives for Preparation and Practice.* Strike, Kenneth A (ed) and Ternasky, P Lance (ed).
Ah! My Foolish Heart: A Reply to Alan Soble's "Antioch's 'Sexual Offense Policy': A Philosophical Exploration". Kittay, Eva Felder.

An Empirical Examination of the Multi-Dimensionality of Ethical Climate in Organizations. Wimbush, James C, Shepard, Jon M and Markham, Steven E.
Aristotle on Variation and Indefiniteness in Ethics and Its Subject Matter. Anagnostopoulos, Georgios.
Code Types: Functions and Failings and Organizational Diversity. Condren, Conal.
Functionalist and Conflict Views of AICPA Code of Conduct: Public Interest vs. Self Interest. Lindblom, Cristi K and Ruland, Robert G.
Guidelines for Training in the Ethical Conduct of Scientific Research. Garte, Seymour J.
In Defense of Israel Scheffler's Conception of Moral Education. Coombs, Jerrold.
Jon Elster y el pensamiento del límite. Ambrosini, Cristina.
La conducta humana y la naturaleza. Roig, Arturo Andres.
Managers' Perception of Proper Ethical Conduct: The Effect of Sex, Age, and Level and Education. Deshpande, Satish P.
On the Acceptability of Biopharmaceuticals. Spier, Raymond.
Relato Verbal e Julgamento da Professora sobre o Rendimento do aluno: Relaçao com os Comportamentos Observados em Sala de Aula. Maimoni, Eulália Henrique.
The Effect of Published Reports of Unethical Conduct on Stock Prices. Rao, Spuma M and Hamilton III, J Brooke.
The Semantics of Symbolic Speech. Berckmans, Paul R.

**CONFERENCE**
A "Third Wave" Manifesto: Keynotes of the Sonoma Conference. Paul, Richard.

**CONFESSION**
Confession of Sin: A Catharsis!. Kakade, R M.
Fateful Rendezvous: The Young Althusser. Elliott, Gregory.
Sexuality, Masculinity, and Confession. May, Larry and Bohman, James.

**CONFIDENCE**
Selbstbewusstsein: ein Problem der Philosophie nach Kant. Stolzenberg, Jürgen.

**CONFIDENTIALITY**
"A Deontic Logic for Reasoning about Confidentiality" in *Deontic Logic, Agency and Normative Systems*, Brown, Mark A (ed). Cuppens, Frédéric and Demolombe, Robert.
AIDS, Confidentiality, and Ethical Models. Gorbett, Jason.
AIDS, Confidentiality, and Ethical Models: Appendix. Gorbett, Jason.
Personal Privacy and Confidentiality in an Electronic Environment. Schick, Ida Critelli.
Professional Ethics of Psychologists and Physicians: Morality, Confidentiality, and Sexuality in Israel. Shimshon Rubin, Simon and Dror, Omer.

**CONFIRMABILILTY**
Laws of Nature, Cosmic Coincidences and Scientific Realism. Lange, Marc.

**CONFIRMATION**
*see also* Verification
Confirmation and the Indispensability of Mathematics to Science. Vineberg, Susan.
Confirmation Holism and Semantic Holism. Harrell, Mack.
Confirmation, Explanation, and Logical Strength. Nelson, David E.
Confirming Universal Generalizations. Zabell, S L.
Discussion: Thoughts on Maher's Predictivism. Barnes, Eric.
Inductive Confirmation, Counterfactual Conditionals, and Laws of Nature. Lange, Marc.
Metaconfirmation. Zwirn, Denis and Zwirn, Hervé P.
Resolving Hempel's Raven Paradox. Leavitt, Fred.
Social Predictivism. Barnes, Eric.
Wayne, Horwich, and Evidential Diversity. Fitelson, Branden.
What is Relative Confirmation?. Christensen, David.
What Use Is Empirical Confirmation?. Miller, David.

**CONFLICT**
"Nations, Identity, and Conflict" in *The Morality of Nationalism*, McKim, Robert (ed). Glover, Jonathan.
"Semantic Intuitions: Conflict Resolution in the Formal Sciences" in *Logic and Argumentation*, Van Eemeren, Frans H (ed). Woods, John.
"Teaching Environmental Ethics as a Method of Conflict Management" in *Environmental Pragmatism*, Light, Andrew (ed). Varner, Gary E, Gilbertz, Susan J and Peterson, Tarla Rai.
*Kreativer Friede durch Begegnung der Weltkulturen.* Beck, Heinrich (ed) and Schmirber, Gisela (ed).
*The Dissonance of Democracy: Listening, Conflict, and Citizenship.* Bickford, Susan.
*The Morality of Nationalism.* McKim, Robert (ed) and McMahan, Jeff (ed).
A Reply to McDonald: A Defense in Favor of Requirement Conflicts. McKenna, Michael S.
Are Ethical Conflicts Irreconcilable?. Cooke, Maeve.
Are Science and Religion in Conflict?. Watts, Fraser N.
Conflict and Co-Ordination in the Aftermath of Oracular Statements. Thalos, Mariam.
Conflict and Constellation: The New Trend of Value Development in China. Chen, Xun Wu.

## CONFLICT

Conflicts of Interest, Conflicting Interests, and Interesting Conflicts, Part 3. Vinicky, Janicemarie K, Orlowski, James P and Shevlin Edwards, Sue.

Die Bewältigung von Technikkonflikten: Theoretische Möglichkeit und praktische Relevanz einer Ethik der Technik in der Moderne. Grunwald, Armin.

Do Complex Moral Reasoners Experience Greater Ethical Work Conflict?. Mason, E Sharon and Mudrack, Peter E.

Galileo and the Church: An Untidy Affair. Schoen, Edward L.

Identifying the Real EAP Client: Ensuing Ethical Dilemmas. Lee, Sandra S and Schonberg, Sue E.

Identity Politics as a Transposition of Fraser's Needs Politics. Tittle, Peg.

Irreconcilable Conflicts in Bioethics. Winslade, William J.

Jean Piaget: razón y conflicto. Sansubrino, Rosana.

La noción de inconmensurabilidad y la realidad de los otros o el derecho a la diferencia. López Gil, Marta.

Libertad básica. Skutch, Alexander F.

Managers' Perception of Proper Ethical Conduct: The Effect of Sex, Age, and Level and Education. Deshpande, Satish P.

Prematernal Duty and the Resolution of Conflict. Yeast, John D.

Professional Ethics Code Conflict Situations: Ethical and Value Orientation of Collegiate Accounting Students. McCarthy, Irene N.

Taking Coercion Seriously. Mansbridge, Jane.

The Consensual Basis of Conflictual Power: A Critical Response to "Using Power, Fighting Power" by Jane Mansbridge. Haugaard, Mark.

The Ethical and Economic Implications of Smoking in Enclosed Public Facilities: A Resolution of Conflicting Rights. Ostapski, S Andrew, Plumly, L Wayne and Love, Jim L.

The Negotiation of Equivalence. Arditi, Benjamin.

## CONFLICT OF INTEREST

Assessing Conflict of Interest: Sources of Bias. Bird, Stephanie J.

Competing Interests: The Need to Control Conflict of Interests in Biomedical Research. Steiner, Daniel.

Conflicts of Interest and Conflicts of Commitment. Werhane, Patricia and Doering, Jeffrey.

Conflicts of Interest, Conflicting Interests, and Interesting Conflicts, Part 3. Vinicky, Janicemarie K, Orlowski, James P and Shevlin Edwards, Sue.

## CONFUCIANISM

"Classical Confucian and Contemporary Feminist Perspectives on the Self: Some Parallels and their Implications" in Culture and Self, Allen, Douglas (ed). Rosemont, Henry.

Enlightenment East and West. Angel, Leonard.

Meeting of Minds: Intellectual and Religious Interaction in East Asian Traditions of Thought. Bloom, Irene (ed) and Fogel, Joshua A (ed).

Mein Geist ist das Universum: Ontologische und erkenntnistheoretische Aspekte in der Lehre des Lu Jiuyuan (1139-1193). Ommerborn, Wolfgang.

Confucian Value and Democratic Value. Li, Chenyang.

From Self-Cultivation to Philosophical Counseling: An Introduction. Cheng, Chung-ying.

Han Classicists Writing in Dialogue about their Own Tradition. Nylan, Michael.

La liberté a-t-elle un sens dans la tradition chinoise?. Drivod, Lucien.

On a Comprehensive Theory of Xing (Naturality) in Song-Ming Neo-Confucian Philosophy: A Critical and Integrative Development. Cheng, Chung-ying.

Self-Construction and Identity: The Confucian Self in Relation to Some Western Perceptions. Yao, Xinzhong.

The Conception of Ming in Early Confucian Thought. Slingerland, Ted.

## CONFUCIUS

Rationality and Human Dignity—Confucius, Kant and Scheffler on the Ultimate Aim of Education. Park, Ynhui.

Self-Construction and Identity: The Confucian Self in Relation to Some Western Perceptions. Yao, Xinzhong.

## CONGRUENCE

An Update on "Might". Van der Does, Jaap, Groeneveld, Willem and Veltman, Frank.

Definability of Directly Indecomposable Congruence Modular Algebras. Vaggione, Diego.

P1 Algebras. Lewin, Renato A, Mikenberg, Irene F and Schwarze, Maria G.

## CONJECTURE

Conjecture. Mazur, B.

## CONJUNCTION

Contraposition and Lewis Carrol's Barber Shop Paradox. Gillon, Brendan S.

Lipton on Compatible Contrasts. Carroll, John W.

What Are the Fuzzy Conjunctions and Disjunctions? (in Spanish). Alsina, Claudi.

## CONNECTION

Connection Structures: Grzegorczyk's and Whitehead's Definitions of Point. Biacino, Loredana and Gerla, Giangiacomo.

Dissezioni e intersezioni di regioni in A.N. Whitehead. Gerla, Giangiacomo and Tortora, Roberto.

On Non-Verbal Representation. Brook, Donald.

## CONNECTIONISM

"Connectionism and the Commitments of Folk Psychology" in AI, Connectionism and Philosophical Psychology, 1995, Tomberlin, James E (ed). Horgan, Terence and Tienson, John.

"Connectionism and the Rationale Constraint on Cognitive Explanation" in AI, Connectionism and Philosophical Psychology, 1995, Tomberlin, James E (ed). Cummins, Robert.

Connectionism and Eliminativism: Reply to Stephen Mills in Vol. 5, No. 1. Macdonald, Cynthia.

Mind Design II: Philosophy, Psychology, Artificial Intelligence. Haugeland, John (ed).

Philosophical Perspectives, 9, AI, Connectionism and Philosophical Psychology, 1995. Tomberlin, James E (ed).

Connectionism and the Philosophical Foundations of Cognitive Science. Horgan, Terence.

Consciousness and Connectionism—The Problem of Compatability of Type Identity Theory and of Connectionism. Potrc, Matjaz.

Cynthia Macdonald and Graham Macdonald (eds), Connectionism: Debates on Psychological Explanation, Volume Two. Mills, Stephen.

Directions in Connectionist Research: Tractable Computations without Syntactically Structured Representations. Waskan, Jonathan and Bechtel, William.

Do Connectionist Representations Earn Their Explanatory Keep?. Ramsey, William.

Ethical Connectionism. Gibbs, Paul J.

Exhibiting versus Explaining Systematicity: A Reply to Hadley and Hayward. Aizawa, Kenneth.

Finding the Right Level for Connectionist Representations (A Critical Note on Ramsey's Paper). Markic, Olga.

La estructura de las representaciones mentales: una perspectiva integradora. Liz, Manuel.

Language of Thought: The Connectionist Contribution. Aydede, Murat.

Modelos cognoscitivos para la filosofía contemporánea de la mente. Rodríguez Rodríguez, Rodolfo J.

On Alan Turing's Anticipation of Connectionism. Copeland, B Jack and Proudfoot, Diane.

PDP Networks can Provide Models that are not Mere Implementations of Classical Theories. Dawson, Michael R W, Medler, David A and Berkeley, Istvan S N.

Quantification without Variables in Connectionism. Barnden, John A and Srinivas, Kankanahalli.

Strong Semantic Systematicity from Hebbian Connectionist Learning. Hadley, Robert F and Hayward, Michael B.

The Relationship Between Connectionist Models and a Dynamic Data-Oriented Theory of Concept Formation. Bartsch, Renate.

## CONNECTIVE

"New Light on Peirce's Iconic Notation for the Sixteen Binary Connectives" in Studies in the Logic of Charles Sanders Peirce, Houser, Nathan (ed). Clark, Glenn.

"Untapped Potential in Peirce's Iconic Notation for the Sixteen Binary Connectives" in Studies in the Logic of Charles Sanders Peirce, Houser, Nathan (ed). Zellweger, Shea.

Logical Operations. McGee, Vann.

On the Logic of Event-Causation: Jaskowski-Style Systems of Causal Logic. Urchs, Max.

Singulary Extensional Connectives: A Closer Look. Humberstone, I Lloyd.

The k-Variable Property is Stronger than H-Dimension k. Simon, András and Hodkinson, Ian.

## CONQUEST

Prescott's Conquests: Anthropophagy, Auto-da-Fe and Eternal Return. Pearce, Colin D.

## CONRAD OF MEGENBERG

Conrad of Megenberg: The Parisian Years. Courtenay, William J.

## CONSCIENCE

La Laïcité. Haarscher, Guy.

Scienza e filosofia della coscienza. Gava, Giacomo.

Conciencia subjetiva y conciencia comunicativa en el discurso ético. Michelini, Dorando J.

Coscienza morale e realtà secondo J.G. Fichte. Schrader, Wolfgang H.

Il concetto di coscienza nella fenomenologia di E. Husserl e di E. Stein. Schulz, Peter.

Kant, Smith and Locke: The Locksmith's Mending of Tradition: A Reaction to Mr. Fleischacker's Thesis. Perreijn, Willem.

La maturità di coscienza alla luce di San Tommaso d'Aquino. Costa, Flavia.

Le stoïcisme ou la conscience de Rome. Jerphagnon, Lucien.

The Conscience Principle. Murphy, Mark C.

The Inalienable Right of Conscience: A Madisonian Argument. McConnell, Terrance C.

The Progression and Regression of Slave Morality in Nietzsche's Genealogy: The Moralization of Bad Conscience and Indebtedness. Lindstedt, David.

The Spark of Conscience: Bonaventure's View of Conscience and Synderesis. Langston, Douglas.

## CONSCIENTIOUSNESS

Formal Ethics. Gensler, Harry J.

## CONSCIOUSNESS

see also Awareness, Class Consciousness, Self-Consciousness, Unconsciousness

"Consciousness As a Pragmatist Views It" in The Cambridge Companion to William James, Putnam, Ruth Anna (ed). Flanagan, Owen.

## CONSCIOUSNESS

*"Consciousness as Internal Monitoring, I"* in *AI, Connectionism and Philosophical Psychology, 1995,* Tomberlin, James E (ed). Lycan, William G.

"Consciousness Evaded: Comments on Dennett" in *AI, Connectionism and Philosophical Psychology, 1995,* Tomberlin, James E (ed). McGinn, Colin.

"How Should We Understand the Relation between Intentionality and Phenomenal Consciousness?" in *AI, Connectionism and Philosophical Psychology, 1995,* Tomberlin, James E (ed). Van Gulick, Robert.

"L'Uno e i molti: Sulla logica hegeliana dell'Essere per sé" in *Hegel e Aristotele,* Ferrarin, A. Movia, Giancarlo.

"Moore's Paradox and Consciousness" in *AI, Connectionism and Philosophical Psychology, 1995,* Tomberlin, James E (ed). Rosenthal, David M.

"On the Reading of Riddles: Rethinking Du Boisian 'Double Consciousness'" in *Existence in Black: An Anthology of Black Existential Philosophy,* Gordon, Lewis R (ed). Allen Jr, Ernest.

"The Avant-Garde and Contemporary Artistic Consciousness" in *Epistemology and History,* Zeidler-Janiszewska, Anna (ed). Dziamski, Grzegorz.

*Consciousness and Self-Consciousness: A Defense of the Higher-Order Thought Theory of Consciousness.* Gennaro, Rocco J.

*Das phänomenale Bewusstsein: Eine Verteidigung.* Lanz, Peter.

*Descartes' Dualism.* Baker, Gordon and Morris, Katherine J.

*Descriptive Psychology.* Müller, Benito (ed & trans) and Brentano, Franz.

*Explaining Consciousness—The 'Hard Problem'.* Shear, Jonathan (ed).

*From Occam's Razor to the Roots of Consciousness.* Wassermann, Gerhard D.

*Head and Heart: Affection, Cognition, Volition as Triune Consciousness.* Tallon, Andrew.

*Hegel e Aristotele.* Movia, Giancarlo (ed).

*Heidegger's Hidden Sources: East Asian Influences on His Work.* Parkes, Graham (trans) and May, Reinhard.

*Malebranche's Theory of the Soul: A Cartesian Interpretation.* Schmaltz, Tad M.

*Paul Ricoeur: A Key to Husserl's Ideas I.* Vandevelde, Pol (ed & trans), Spurlock, Jacqueline Bouchard (trans) and Harris, Bond (trans).

*Self-Trust: A Study of Reason, Knowledge and Autonomy.* Lehrer, Keith.

*Ten Problems of Consciousness: A Representational Theory of the Phenomenal Mind.* Tye, Michael.

*The Character of Mind: An Introduction to the Philosophy of Mind.* McGinn, Colin.

A Patterned Process Approach To Brain, Consciousness, and Behavior. Díaz, José-Luis.

A Preliminary Analysis of "National Consciousness". Xiyuan, Xiong.

An East Asian Perspective of Mind-Body. Nagatomo, Shigenori and Leisman, Gerald.

An Integral Theory of Consciousness. Wilber, Ken.

Ansätze zur physikalischen Untersuchung des Leib-Seele-Problems. Arendes, Lothar.

Are Plants Conscious?. Nagel, Alexandra H M.

Are Qualia Just Representations? A Critical Notice of Michael Tye's *Ten Problems of Consciousness.* Levine, Joseph.

Awareness, Mental Phenomena and Consciousness: A Synthesis of Dennett and Rosenthal. Rockwell, Teed.

Belief and Consciousness. Worley, Sara.

Bewusstsein, Erfahrung und Unterschneidensleistung. Moltchanov, Viktor I.

Blondel and Husserl: A Continuation of the Conversation. Hart, James G.

Buddhist Meditation and the Consciousness of Time. Novak, Philip.

Can One be Cognitively Conscious of God?. Baxter, Anthony.

Can People Think?. De Bruijn, N G.

Cerebral Hemispheres. Davis, Lawrence H.

Commentary on "Searle and the 'Deep Unconscious'". Lloyd, Dan.

Conciencia subjetiva y conciencia comunicativa en el discurso ético. Michelini, Dorando J.

Conocimiento del alma después de la muerte: Presentación de la doctrina de Santo Tomás de Aquino expuesta en las *Quaestiones disputatae de veritate q. 19 a. 1.* Rodrigo Ewart, Luis.

Consapevolezza etica ed esperienza della virtù. Marra, Bruno.

Consciousness and Connectionism—The Problem of Compatability of Type Identity Theory and of Connectionism. Potrc, Matjaz.

Consciousness and Self-Awareness—Part I: Consciousness$_1$, Consciousness$_2$, and Consciousness$_3$. Natsoulas, Thomas.

Consciousness and Self-Awareness—Part II: Consciousness$_4$, Consciousness$_5$, and Consciousness$_6$. Natsoulas, Thomas.

Consciousness Disputed. Levin, Janet.

Critical Notice of Fred Dretske *Naturalizing the Mind.* Seager, William.

Dennett on Qualia and Consciousness: A Critique. Johnsen, Bredo.

Emotion and the Function of Consciousness. DeLancey, Craig.

Empathy before and after Husserl. Sawicki, Marianne.

Ensayo de síntesis acerca de la distinción especulativo-práctico y su estructuración metodolón metodológica. Massini Correas, Carlos Ignacio.

Ethical Connectionism. Gibbs, Paul J.

Facing Ourselves: Incorrigibility and the Mind-Body Problem. Warner, Richard.

Functionalism's Response to the Problem of Absent Qualia: More Discussion of Zombies. Hardcastle, Valerie Gray.

Happiness Doesn't Come in Bottles: Neuroscientists Learn That Joy Comes Through Dancing, Not Drugs. Freeman, Walter J.

Heidegger and Derrida: On Play and Difference. Dastur, Françoise.

Hermenéutica y metafísica en la *Scienza Nuova.* Damiani, Alberto M.

How We Get There From Here: Dissolution of the Binding Problem. Hardcastle, Valerie Gray.

I = Awareness. Diekman, Arthur J.

If the Eye Were an Animal...: The Problem of Representation in Understanding, Meaning and Intelligence. Horner, John M.

Immanence: A Life.... Deleuze, Gilles and Millett, Nick.

Intentions, Self-Monitoring and Abnormal Experiences. Morris, R C.

Josiah Royce's Reading of Plato's *Theaetetus.* Glidden, David K.

La conscience n'est pas suject: pour un matérialisme authentique. Kail, Michel.

La paradoja de la unidad originaria de la conciencia en la intuición pura y de la multiplicidad a priori de la sensibilidad. López Fernández, Alvaro.

Logics of Power in Marx. Brown, Wendy.

Lost the Plot? Reconstructing Dennett's Multiple Drafts Theory of Consciousness. Akins, Kathleen.

Memory, Forgetfulness, and History. Ricoeur, Paul.

Meta(l)morphoses. Braidotti, Rosi.

Metaphysical Models of the Mind in Aristotle. Scaltsas, Theodore.

Moving Forward on the Problem of Consciousness. Chalmers, David J.

Mutual Enlightenment: Recent Phenomenology in Cognitive Science. Gallagher, Shaun.

National Consciousness and Motherland Consciousness. Xiyuan, Xiong.

National Consciousness and Nationalism. Xiyuan, Xiong.

Neurophenomenology: A Methodological Remedy for the Hard Problem. Varela, Francisco J.

Offene Intersubjektivität—nach Johann Gottlieb Fichte. Schmidig, Dominik.

On the Mechanism of Consciousness. Cotterill, Rodney M J.

One World, But a Big One. Midgley, Mary.

Ontología y conocimiento en M. Merleau-Ponty. Arce Carrascoso, José Luis.

Perceptual Content and the Subpersonal. Gunther, York.

Phenomenology of Spirit and Logic (in French). Lécrivain, André.

Phenomenon and Sensation: A Reflection on Husserl's Concept of *Sinngebung.* Dodd, James.

Physicalism and Classical Theism. Forrest, Peter.

Physics, Machines, and the Hard Problem. Bilodeau, Douglas J.

Postmodern Personhood: A Matter of Consciousness. Rich, Ben A.

Précis of *Past*, Space and Self. Campbell, John.

Putting the Puzzle Together: Part I: Towards a General Theory of the Neural Correlates of Consciousness. Newman, James.

Representation and Resemblance: A Review Essay of Richard A. Watson's *Representational Ideas: From Plato to Patricia Churchland.* Meyering, Theo C.

Sartre, Emotions, and Wallowing. Weberman, David.

Searle and the "Deep Unconscious". Gillett, Eric.

Searle on Consciousness and Dualism. Collins, Corbin.

Self-Creating Selves: Sartre and Foucault. Morris, Phyllis Sutton.

Shades of Consciousness. Girle, Roderic A.

Should We Expect To Feel As If We Understand Consciousness?. Price, Mark C.

Socialism and National Consciousness. Xiyuan, Xiong.

Some Like it Hot: Consciousness and Higher-Order Thoughts. Byrne, Alex.

Some Nonhuman Animals Can Have Pains in a Morally Relevant Sense. Robinson, William S.

State Consciousness Revisited. Jacob, Pierre.

Structure, Strategy and Self in the Fabrication of Conscious Experience. Claxton, Guy.

Subjects and Objects. Cassam, Quassim.

Superveniencia y determinación del contenido amplio. García-Carpintero, Manuel.

The Case for Intrinsic Theory: I. An Introduction. Natsoulas, Thomas.

The Case for Intrinsic Theory: II. An Examination of a Conception of Consciousness$_4$ as Intrinsic, Necessary, and Concomitant. Natsoulas, Thomas.

The Definition of Man Needs. Gairola, M P.

The Elements of Consciousness and their Neurodynamical Correlates. MacLennan, Bruce.

The Function of Consciousness. Tye, Michael.

The Hard Problem: A Quantum Approach. Stapp, Henry P.

The Hornswoggle Problem. Smith Churchland, Patricia.

The Invention of History and the Reinvention of Memory. Motzkin, Gabriel.

The Modern Religion?. Greenfeld, Liah.

The Negative Dialectic of Modernity and the Speculative Resolution of the Contradiction of Modern Moral Consciousness (in Spanish). Lutz Müller, Marcos.

The Notion of Imagination in the Context of Aristotle's Practical Philosophy (in Serbo-Croatian). Jevremovic, Petar.

The Presence of Environmental Objects to Perceptual Consciousness: Consideration of the Problem with Special Reference to Husserl's Phenomenological Account. Natsoulas, Thomas.

## CONSISTENCY

On Inconsistent Arithmetics: A Reply to Denyer. Priest, Graham.
On the Significance of Conditional Probabilities. Sobel, Jordan Howard.
The Epistemic Virtues of Consistency. Ryan, Sharon.
The Sure Thing Principle and the Value of Information. Schlee, Edward E.

## CONSONANCE

A Micro-Phenomenology of Consonance and Dissonance. Lind, Richard.

## CONSTANCY

Commitment and the Bond of Love. Van Hooft, Stan.

## CONSTANT, B

"Brevi note su liberalismo e storia in Constant e Tocqueville" in *Lo Storicismo e la Sua Storia: Temi, Problemi, Prospettive,* Cacciatore, Giuseppe (ed). Mazziotti, Stelio.

## CONSTITUTION

"Homosexuality and the Constitution" in *Sex, Preference, and Family: Essays on Law and Nature,* Nussbaum, Martha C (ed). Sunstein, Cass R.
*Classics of Modern Political Theory: Machiavelli to Mill.* Cahn, Steven M.
*Democracy's Place.* Shapiro, Ian.
*Freedom's Law: The Moral Reading of the American Constitution.* Dworkin, Ronald.
*Radical Critiques of the Law.* Griffin, Stephen M (ed) and Moffat, Robert C L (ed).
Adam Smith's Influence on James Madison. Ross, Thomas.
Beyond Realism and Idealism Husserl's Late Concept of Constitution. Zahavi, Dan.
Constitutional Patriotism. Ingram, Attracta.
Identidad, Constitución y Superveniencia. Bordes Solanas, Montserrat.
Individuelle Zurechnung im demokratischen Verfassungsstaat. Günther, Klaus.
Jean Bodin, Scepticism and Absolute Sovereignty. Engster, Dan.
Must Constitutional Democracy Be "Responsive"?. Michelman, Frank I.
Originalism, Moralism and the Public Opinion State of Mitchell Franklin. Lawler, James.
Permissions, Principles and Rights: A Paper on Statements Expressing Constitutional Liberties. Atienza, Manuel and Ruiz Manero, Juan.
The Legacy of Jean Bodin: Absolutism, Populism or Constitutionalism?. Salmon, J H M.
The Struggle for the Constitution in Russia and the Triumph of Ethical Individualism. Sakwa, Richard.
Thinking Critical History: Young Hegel and the German Constitution (in French). Leydet, Dominique.

## CONSTITUTIONALISM

Constitutionalism—Medieval and Modern: Against Neo-Figgisite Orthodoxy (Again). Nederman, Cary J.

## CONSTRAINT

A Rational Reconstruction of the Domain of Feature Structures. Moshier, M Andrew.
Applying Allen's Constraint Propagation Algorithm for Non-Linear Time. Hajnicz, Elzbieta.
Dynamic Interpretations of Constraint-Based Grammar Formalisms. Moss, Lawrence S and Johnson, David E.
Liberating Constraints. Haji, Ishtiyaque.
Moral Constraints and Justice in Distribution (in Czech). Nozick, Robert.
Supervaluations and the Propositional Attitude Constraint. Burgess, J A.
The Constraint Rule of the Maximum Entropy Principle. Uffink, Jos.

## CONSTRUCTIBILITY

A Very Weak Square Principle. Foreman, Matthew and Magidor, Menachem.

## CONSTRUCTION

A Model-Theoretic Interpretation of Science. Ruttkamp, Emma.
On the Proof Theory of Coquand's Calculus of Constructions. Seldin, Jonathan P.
Shaping a New Biological Factor, 'The Interferon', in Room 215 of the National Institute for Medical Research, 1956/57. Pieters, Toine.

## CONSTRUCTIONISM

Bridging Social Constructionism and Cognitive Constructivism: A Psychology of Human Possibility and Constraint. Martin, Jack and Sugarman, Jeff.
Complex Kinds. Hirsch, Eli.
Queries about Social Representation and Construction. Wagner, Wolfgang.

## CONSTRUCTIVE

A Constructive Valuation Semantics for Classical Logic. Barbanera, Franco and Berardi, Stefano.
A Sheaf-Theoretic Foundation for Nonstandard Analysis. Palmgren, Erik.
In Defense of a Constructive, Information-Based Approach to Decision Theory. Yilmaz, M R.
On Maximal Intermediate Predicate Constructive Logics. Avelone, Alessandro, Fiorentini, Camillo and Mantovani, Paolo (& others).

## CONSTRUCTIVISM

*Idealisierungen und das Ziel der Physik: Eine Untersuchung zum Realismus, Empirismus und Konstruktivismus in der Wissenschaftstheorie.* Hüttemann, Andreas.
*Moral Discourse and Practice: Some Philosophical Approaches.* Darwall, Stephen (ed), Gibbard, Allan (ed) and Railton, Peter (ed).
*The Principles of Mathematics Revisited.* Hintikka, Jaakko.

*Vom Begründen zum Handeln: Aufsätze zur angewandten Ethik.* Ott, Konrad.
Anti-Foundationalism and the Vienna Circle's Revolution in Philosophy. Uebel, Thomas E.
Constructive Canonicity in Non-Classical Logics. Ghilardi, Silvio and Meloni, Giancarlo.
Implicit Epistemic Aspects of Constructive Logic. Sundholm, Göran.
Intention, Rule Following and the Strategic Role of Wright's Order of Determination Test. Thornton, Tim.
Legal Theory and Value Judgments. Villa, Vittorio.
Protowissenschaft und Rekonstruktion. Hartmann, Dirk.
Quantum Mechanical Unbounded Operators and Constructive Mathematics—A Rejoinder to Bridges. Hellman, Geoffrey.
Rational Reconstruction: Preconditions and Limits. Iliescu, Adrian-Paul.
Response to Thomas McCarthy: The Political Alliance between Ethical Feminism and Rawls's Kantian Constructivism. Cornell, Drucilla.
Science Studies and Language Suppression—A Critique of Bruno Latour's *We Have Never Been Modern.* Cohen, Sande.
Splendours and Miseries of the Science Wars. Jardine, Nick and Frasca-Spada, Marina.
The Conservative Constructivist. Bloor, David.
The Constructivist's Dilemma. Stecker, Robert A.
The Legacy of Lakatos: Reconceptualising the Philosophy of Mathematics. Ernest, Paul.

## CONSULTANT

Ethics Consultants and Surrogates: Can We Do Better?. Fletcher, John C.
Liability of Ethics Consultants: A Case Analysis. DuVal, Gordon.
Relationships between Primary Care Physicians and Consultants in Managed Care. Brett, Allan S.
The Quality of Primary Care/Consultant Relationships in Managed Care: Have We Gone Forward or Backward?. Povar, Gail J.

## CONSULTATION

Concepts in Evaluation Applied to Ethics Consultation Research. Fox, Ellen.
Consultectonics: Ethics Committee Case Consultation as Mediation. Reynolds, Don F.
Evaluating Ethics Consultation: Framing the Questions. Tulsky, James A and Fox, Ellen.
Evaluating Outcomes in Ethics Consultation Research. Fox, Ellen and Arnold, Robert M.
Evaluation Research and the Future of Ethics Consultation. Fox, Ellen and Tulsky, James A.
Goals of Ethics Consultation: Toward Clarity, Utility, and Fidelity. Andre, Judith.
Introduction: Feminist Approaches to Bioethics. Tong, Rosemarie.
Max Weber on Ethics Case Consultation: A Methodological Critique of the Conference on Evaluation of Ethics Consultation. Degnin, Francis.
Obstacles and Opportunities in the Design of Ethics Consultation Evaluation. Tulsky, James A and Stocking, Carol B.
The Three Deadly Sins of Ethics Consultation. Howe, Edmund G.
Understanding the Practice of Ethics Consultation: Results of an Ethnographic Multi-Site Study. Kelly, Susan E, Marshall, Patricia A and Sanders, Lee M (& others).
What Are the Goals of Ethics Consultation: A Consensus Statement. Fletcher, John C and Siegler, Mark.

## CONSUMER

Community Shared Agriculture. Fieldhouse, Paul.
Identifying Ethical Problems Confronting Small Retail Buyers during the Merchandise Buying Process. Arbuthnot, Jeanette Jaussaud.

## CONSUMERISM

*Cultural History and Postmodernity: Disciplinary Readings and Challenges.* Poster, Mark.
Can Designing and Selling Low-Quality Products Be Ethical?. Bakker II, Willem and Loui, Michael.
Liberalism and Consumerism. Paden, Roger.
The Contradictions of Free Market Doctrine: Is There a Solution?. McMurtry, John.
What's Wrong with Consumer Capitalism? *The Joyless Economy* after Twenty Years. Schor, Juliet.

## CONSUMPTION

"Moralischer Konsum: Über das Verhältnis von Rationalität, Präferenzen und Personen" in *Ökonomie und Moral: Beiträge zur Theorie ökonomischer Rationalität,* Lohmann, Karl Reinhard (ed). Priddat, Birger P.
Beyond Satisfaction: Desire, Consumption, and the Future of Socialism. Meister, Robert.
Consuming Because Others Consume. Lichtenberg, Judith.

## CONTACT

Boundaries, Continuity, and Contact. Varzi, Achille C.

## CONTE, A

Deontics between Semantics and Ontology. Alarcón Cabrera, Carlos.

## CONTEMPLATION

*Gesamtausgabe II. Abteilung: Vorlesungen (Band 27: Einleitung in die Philosophie).* Heidegger, Martin.
*Life Contemplative, Life Practical: An Essay on Fatalism.* Eilstein, Helena.
Contemplación filosófica y contemplación mística en San Buenaventura. Andereggen, Ignacio E M.

**CONTEMPLATION**

Gli Affreschi nelle Celle del Dormitorio del Convento di San Marco: Devozione e Figurazione di Fra Angelico (in Japanese). Akari, Kitamura.

Moral Virtue and Contemplation: A Note on the Unity of Moral Life. Gallagher, David M.

**CONTEMPORARY**

see also Twentieth

"The Meaning of the Hermeneutic Tradition in Contemporary Philosophy" in *Verstehen and Humane Understanding,* O'Hear, Anthony (ed). Bowie, Andrew.

*After the End of Art: Contemporary Art and the Pale of History.* Danto, Arthur C.

*Contemporary Art and Its Philosophical Problems.* Stadler, Ingrid.

*Debating the State of Philosophy: Habermas, Rorty, and Kolakowski.* Niznik, Jozef (ed) and Sanders, John T (ed).

*Soggetto E Verità: La questione dell'uomo nella filosofia contemporanea.* Fagiuoli, Ettore and Fortunato, Marco.

*The Ancients and the Moderns.* Lilly, Reginald (ed).

*The Truth about Everything.* Stewart, Matthew.

A imagem de Ludwig Feuerbach na literatura mais recente (1988-1993). Veríssimo Serrao, Adriana.

Le "Dépassement de la Philosophie": Réflexion sur le statut contemporain de la philosophie. Gueye, Sémou Pathé.

The New View of Plato. Krämer, Hans Joachim.

**CONTENT**

"A Note on Boghossian's Master Argument" in *Contents,* Villanueva, Enrique (ed). Gibson, Roger.

"Can We Knock Off the Shackles of Syntax?" in *Contents,* Villanueva, Enrique (ed). Andler, Daniel.

"Conceptual Structure and the Individuation of Content" in *AI, Connectionism and Philosophical Psychology, 1995,* Tomberlin, James E (ed). Pereboom, Derk.

"Connectionism and the Rationale Constraint on Cognitive Explanation" in *AI, Connectionism and Philosophical Psychology, 1995,* Tomberlin, James E (ed). Cummins, Robert.

"Content, Computation and Externalism" in *Contents,* Villanueva, Enrique (ed). Peacocke, Christopher.

"Moving Minds: Situating Content in the Service of Real-Time Success" in *AI, Connectionism and Philosophical Psychology, 1995,* Tomberlin, James E (ed). Clark, Andy.

"Précis of *Mind and World*" in *Perception,* Villanueva, Enrique (ed). McDowell, John.

"The Disciplinary Conception of Truth" in *Verdad: lógica, representación y mundo,* Villegas Forero, L. Luntley, Michael.

"Understanding Understanding: Syntactic Semantics and Computational Cognition" in *AI, Connectionism and Philosophical Psychology, 1995,* Tomberlin, James E (ed). Rapaport, William J.

*Contents.* Villanueva, Enrique (ed).

*Descriptive Psychology.* Müller, Benito (ed & trans) and Brentano, Franz.

*Finding Philosophy in Social Science.* Bunge, Mario.

*Locke's Philosophy: Content and Context.* Rogers, G A J (ed).

*Representation and the* Mind-Body Problem *in* Spinoza. Della Rocca, Michael.

A Clearer Vision. Shapiro, Lawrence A.

A New Theory of Content II: Model Theory and Some Alternative. Gemes, Ken.

A Note on Truth, Deflationism and Irrealism. Miraglia, Pierluigi.

An Epistemological Justification for Aesthetic Experience. Bergmann, Sheryle.

Another Look at Color. McGinn, Colin.

Belief Content and Compositionality. Kimbrough, Scott.

Belief in the *Tractatus.* Blum, Alex.

Boghossian on Reductive Dispositionalism about Content: The Case Strengthened. Miller, Alexander.

Content and Criticism: The Aims of Schooling. Hare, William.

Content, Computation, and Individualism in Vision Theory. Butler, Keith.

De *A* et *B*, de leur indépendance logique, et de ce qu'ils n'ont aucun contenu factuel commun. Roeper, Peter and Leblanc, Hughes.

Discussion: [Explanation] Is Explanation Better. Hardcastle, Valerie Gray.

Domain of Discourse. Gauker, Christopher.

Doubtful Intuitions. Papineau, David.

Externalism and Knowledge of Content. Gibbons, John.

Externalism and Memory. Brueckner, Anthony.

Externalist Self-Knowledge and the Scope of the A Priori. Miller, Richard W.

Foundations of Perceptual Knowledge. Brewer, Bill.

Fred Dretske on the Explanatory Role of Semantic Content. Hassrick, Beth.

From *intellectus verus/falsus* to the *dictum propositionis*: The Semantics of Peter Abelard and his Circle. King, Peter, Jacobi, Klaus and Strub, Christian.

Grundlagen Paragraph 64. Hale, Bob.

How Can a Metaphor Be Genuinely Illuminating?. Rasmussen, Stig Alstrup.

Illuminating the Chinese Room. Dartnall, Terry.

Individualism, Individuation and That-Clauses. Rechenauer, Martin.

Is There a Problem about Intentionality?. Beckermann, Ansgar.

Mental Content and External Representations. Houghton, David.

Must Conceptually Informed Perceptual Experience Involve Non-Conceptual Content?. Sedivy, Sonia.

On the Content of Natural Kind Concepts. Kistler, Max.

Perceptual Content and the Subpersonal. Gunther, York.

Sense, Reference and Selective Attention. Campbell, John and Martin, M G F.

Simulation and Cognitive Penetrability. Heal, Jane.

Skewered on the Unicorn's Horn. Nelson, Craig E.

Sticking Up for Oedipus: Fodor on Intentional Generalizations and Broad Content. Arjo, Dennis.

Teleological Semantics. Rowlands, Mark.

The Aesthetics of a *Tabula Rasa*: Western Art Music's Avant-Garde from 1949-1953. Toop, Richard.

The Function of Consciousness. Tye, Michael.

The Irrelevance of Meaning. Gylfason, Thorsteinn.

Weak Deflationism. McGrath, Matthew.

What the Externalist Can Know A Priori. Boghossian, Paul Artin.

**CONTENTMENT**

Happiness, Tranquility, and Philosophy. Griswold, Jr, Charles L.

**CONTEXT**

"Context, Continuity, and Fairness" in *The Morality of Nationalism,* McKim, Robert (ed). Ripstein, Arthur.

*Language, Action, and Context: The Early History of Pragmatics in Europe and America, 1780-1930.* Nerlich, Brigitte and Clarke, David D.

*Locke's Philosophy: Content and Context.* Rogers, G A J (ed).

A Context-Sensitive Liar. Juhl, Cory F.

Contextos, Creencías y Anáforas. Ezcurdia, Maite.

Cultural Context and Moral Responsibility. Isaacs, Tracy.

Frege's Context Principle. Bar-Elli, Gilead.

Historical Contingency. Ben-Menahem, Yemima.

Metaphor, Interpretation, and Contextualization. Entzenberg, Claes.

On Understanding: Standing Under Wittgenstein. Goswami, Chinmoy.

Product-Free Lambek Calculus and Context-Free Grammars. Pentus, Mati.

Sense, Validity and Context. Williamson, Timothy.

Sequence of Tense and Temporal De Re. Abusch, Dorit.

Talk about Fiction. Predelli, Stefano.

The Context Principle in Frege's *Grundgesetze* (in Spanish). Schirn, Matthias.

The Importance of Context: The Ethical Work Climate Construct and Models of Ethical Decision Making—An Agenda for Research. Wyld, David and Jones, Coy A.

Universal Instantiation: A Study of the Role of Context in Logic. Gauker, Christopher.

What What It's Like Isn't Like. Stoljar, Daniel.

**CONTEXTUALISM**

"Moral Philosophy and Bioethics: Contextualism versus the Paradigm Theory" in *Philosophical Perspectives on Bioethics,* Sumner, L W (ed). Winkler, Earl.

"Universalismo vs. contextualismo: (Un intento de aproximación desde la pragmática del lenguaje)" in *Liberalismo y Comunitarismo: Derechos Humanos y Democracia,* Monsalve Solórzano, Alfonso (ed). Gallego Vásquez, Frederico.

Convergence and Contextualism: Some Clarifications and a Reply to Steverson. Norton, Bryan G.

Meanings and Psychology: A Response to Mark Richard. Devitt, Michael.

Old Fashioned Normativity: Just What the Doctor Ordered. Leeser, Jaimie M.

What Does Commonsense Psychology Tell Us about Meaning?. Richard, Mark.

**CONTEXTUALITY**

"Contextuality, Reflexivity, Iteration, Logic" in *AI, Connectionism and Philosophical Psychology, 1995,* Tomberlin, James E (ed). Crimmins, Mark.

Interpreting Contextualities. Davies, Stephen.

**CONTINENTAL**

*Twentieth-Century Philosophy.* Baird, Forrest E (ed) and Kaufmann, Walter.

Analytic Philosophy in Greece. Virvidakis, Stelios.

Analytic Philosophy: What Is It and Why Should One Engage in It?. Follesdal, Dagfinn.

**CONTINGENCY**

Continuity, Contingency, and Time: The Divergent Intuitions of Whitehead and Pragmatism. Rosenthal, Sandra B.

Historical Contingency. Ben-Menahem, Yemima.

I percorsi del soggetto moderno. Barcellona, Pietro.

La contingence dans la mécanique hégélienne. Février, Nicolas.

La metafisica dell'ermetismo. Montini, Pierino.

Meteore. Serres, Michel.

The Normativity of Meaning. Gampel, Eric H.

**CONTINGENT**

Darwin: Evolution and Contingency (in Spanish). Rodriguez Camarero, Luis.

**CONTINUITY**

Boundaries, Continuity, and Contact. Varzi, Achille C.

El problema del continuo en la escolástica española: Francisco de Oviedo (1602-1651). Luna Alcoba, Manuel.

Four-dimensionalist Remarks: A Defence of Temporal Parts (Spanish). Bordes Solanas, Montserrat.

## CONTINUITY

G.W. Leibniz: *Geschichte des Kontinuumproblems*. Luna Alcoba, Manuel.

G.W. Leibniz: Consequence de l'Hypothese generalle publiée il y a quelque temps, pour expliquer le Phenomene de l'attachement dans le vuide, ou dans une place dont l'air a esté tiré. Luna Alcoba, Manuel.

Identidad y Continuidad Causal: Una Crítica a la Teoría de la Continuidad Causal de Shoemaker. Bordes Solanas, Montserrat.

Leibniz's Theory of Variation in 1676: An Interpretation of the Dialogue Pacidius *Pacidius Philalethi* through the *Characteristica geometrica*) (Spanish). Alcantara, Jean-Pascal.

Lokale Quantenfeldtheorie und Kontinuumslimes. Müller, Volkhard F.

Naturgemässe Klassifikation und Kontinuität, Wissenschaft und Geschichte: Überlegungen zu Pierre Duhem. Petrus, Klaus.

Peirce on Continuity and Laws of Nature. Sfendoni-Mentzou, Demetra.

Sartre and the Self: Discontinuity or Continuity?. Goldthorpe, Rhiannon.

Ser, verdad y lenguaje: la continuidad filosófica de la obra de Tugendhat. Bonet Sánchez, José V.

The Leibniz Continuity Condition, Inconsistency and Quantum Dynamics. Mortensen, Chris.

Two Books on the Elements of Physics (or One Movement) by *Proclus of Lykia (in Hungarian)*. Geréby, György.

Was I Ever A Fetus?. Olson, Eric T.

## CONTINUOUS

A Definable Continuous Rank for Nonmultidimensional Superstable Theories. Chowdhury, Ambar, Loveys, James and Tanovic, Predrag.

## CONTINUUM

"Sul problema della considerazione matematica dell'infinito e del continuo in Aristotele e Hegel" in *Hegel e Aristotele*, Ferrarin, A. Moretto, Antonio.

Hipotesis del continuo, definibilidad y funciones recursivas: historia de un desencuentro (1925-1955). Zalamea, Fernando.

Husserl's Phenomenology and Weyl's Predictivism. Da Silva, Jairo José.

Para una ontología del continuo. Pérez Herranz, Fernando-M.

The Three Arrows of Zeno. Harrison, Craig.

## CONTINUUM HYPOTHESIS

Hilbert and Set Theory. Dreben, Burton and Kanamori, Akihiro.

## CONTRACEPTION

Contraceptive Risk-Taking and Norms of Chastity. Stubblefield, Anna.

## CONTRACT

*see also* Social Contract

*Le contrat dans les pays anglo-saxons: théories et pratiques*. Breteau, Jean-Louis.

A "Meeting of the Minds": The Greater Illusion. Damren, Samuel C.

Autonomy and Authority in Kant's *Rechtslehre*. Dodson, Kevin E.

Contract or Coincidence: George Herbert Mead and Adam Smith on Self and Society. Costelloe, Timothy M.

Contracts with Animals: Lucretius, *De Rerum Natura*. Shelton, Jo-Ann.

Drug Testing and Privacy: Why Contract Arguments Do Not Work. Carson, A Scott.

Esquema para Reexaminar la Filosofía Política de Kant. Astorga, Omar.

Stakeholder Theory and A Principle of Fairness. Phillips, Robert A.

The Currency of Covenant. Mount, Jr, Eric.

Violence and Authority in Kant. Protevi, John.

## CONTRACTARIANISM

Gibt es eine universelle Moral?. Leist, Anton.

Grounding Hypernorms: Towards a Contractarian Theory of Business Ethics. Rowan, John R.

## CONTRACTION

A Consistent Theory of Attributes in a Logic without Contraction. White, Richard B.

Bounded Contraction and Gentzen-style Formulation of Lukasiewicz Logics. Prijatelj, Andreja.

Contraction-Elimination for Implicational Logics. Kashima, Ryo.

Lambek Calculus with Restricted Contraction and Expansion. Prijateljz, Andreja.

Partial Monotonicity and a New Version of the Ramsey Test. Pais, John and Jackson, Peter.

Simple Gentzenizations for the Normal Formulae of Contraction-less Logics. Brady, Ross T.

## CONTRACTUALISM

"Theoretische und angewandte Ethik: Paradigmen, Begründungen, Bereiche" in *Angewandte Ethik: Die Bereichsethiken und ihre theoretische Fundierung*, Nida-Rümelin, Julian (ed). Nida-Rümelin, Julian.

*Moral Discourse and Practice: Some Philosophical Approaches*. Darwall, Stephen (ed), Gibbard, Allan (ed) and Railton, Peter (ed).

Contractual Justice: A Modest Defence. Barry, Brian.

Contractualism and Animals. Bernstein, Mark.

La justice peut-elle naître du contrat social?. Poltier, Hugues.

Sul contrattualismo di Hobbes: una recente interpretazione. Longega, Andrea.

What's 'Wrong' in Contractualism?. Matravers, Matt.

Worlds Apart? Habermas and Levinas. Vetlesen, Arne J.

## CONTRADICTION

"Frege über Widerspruchsfreiheit und die Schöpfung mathematischer Gegenstände" in *Das weite Spektrum der analytischen Philosophie*, Lenzen, Wolfgang. Schirn, Matthias.

"La Libertà Della Contraddizione" in *Soggetto E Verità: La questione dell'uomo nella filosofia contemporanea*, Fagiuoli, Ettore. Màdera, Romano.

"Reply to Boolos" in *Frege: Importance and Legacy*, Schirn, Matthias (ed). Dummett, Michael.

"Whence the Contradiction?" in *Frege: Importance and Legacy*, Schirn, Matthias (ed). Boolos, George.

A Dilemma for Priest's Dialethism?. Everett, Anthony.

Absolutheit und Widerspruch in der *Grundlage der gesamten Wissenschaftslehre*. Duso, Giuseppe.

Being—An Approach to the Beginning of Hegel's *Wissenschaft der Logik* (in German). Von Sivers, Kathrin.

Cuando las contradictorias son verdaderas. Villalba de Tablón, Marisa.

Deontica in Rose Rand. Lorini, Giuseppe.

Graham Priest's "Dialectheism"—Is It Altogether True?. Peña, Lorenzo.

La negación de los juicios estrictamente particulares en la tetravalencia. Öffenberger, Niels and Bustos López, Javier.

Peirce's "Entanglement" with the Principles of Excluded Middle and Contradiction. Lane, Robert.

Replica a Emanuele Severino. Crescini, Angelo.

Zur Rehabilitation des Unbewussten. Neubauer, Patrick.

## CONTRAST

Lipton on Compatible Contrasts. Carroll, John W.

## CONTROL

*Social Control Through Law*. Treviño, A Javier (ed) and Pound, Roscoe.

Chaos and Control: Reading Plato's *Politicus*. McCabe, Mary Margaret.

Corporate Ethics Initiatives as Social Control. Laufer, William S and Robertson, Diana C.

Epistemology of Technology Assessment: Collingridge, Forecasting Methodologies, and Technological Control. Pinnick, Cassandra L.

Ethics as a Control System Component. Spier, Raymond.

Executive Perceptions of Superior and Subordinate Information Control: Practice Versus Ethics. Dulek, Ronald E, Motes, William H and Hilton, Chadwick B.

Privacy and Control. Davison, Scott A.

Strength of Motivation and Being in Control. Mele, Alfred R.

The Myth of the Control of Suffering. Sobel, Reuven.

Why Simple Foreknowledge Offers No More Providential Control than the Openness of God. Sanders, John.

## CONVENIENCE

Trading Lives for Convenience: It's Not Just for Consequentialists. Norcross, Alastair.

## CONVENTION

"Conventions and Conversions, or, Why Is Nationalism Sometimes So Nasty?" in *The Morality of Nationalism*, McKim, Robert (ed). Goodin, Robert E.

Can We Ascribe to Past Thinkers Concepts they had No Linguistic Means to Express?. Prudovsky, Gad.

Domande e risposte sul problema della giustizia. Bagolini, Luigi.

Raison et Convention, ou la Raison Politique chez Hobbes. Boss, Gilbert.

The European Convention on Bioethics. De Wachter, Maurice A M.

## CONVENTIONALISM

Plato on Conventionalism. Barney, Rachel.

## CONVERGENCE

Infinitary Logics and Very Sparse Random Graphs. Lynch, James F.

## CONVERSATION

Abusing Use. Glock, H J.

Enlarging the Conversation. Herman, Steward W.

Foundational Standards and Conversational Style: The Humean Essay as an Issue of Philosophical Genre. Engström, Timothy H.

Non-Axiomatizability of Grice's Implicature. Tokarz, Marek.

Thinking in Community. Lipman, Matthew.

## CONVERSE

Eliminating "Converse" from Converse PDL. De Giacomo, Giuseppe.

The Converse Principal Type-Scheme Theorem in Lambda Calculus. Hirokawa, Sachio.

## CONVERSION

Complex Predicates and Conversion Principles. Swoyer, Chris.

Lonergan on Newman's Conversion. Egan, Philip A.

Moral Conversion and Problems in Proportionalism. Beards, Andrew.

## CONVEX

T-Convexity and Tame Extensions II. Van den Dries, Lou.

## CONVICTION

El rol de la convicción en la sabiduría práctica de Paul Ricoeur. Beguè, Marie-France.

Es Posible una Ética de las Emociones?. Marinabarreto, Luz.

## CONZE, E

The Way of the Lotus: Critical Reflections on the Ethics of the *Saddharmapundar* ika Sūtra. Herman, A L.

## COOPERATION

A Relatively Plausible Principle of Beneficence: Reply to Mulgan. Murphy, Liam B.

Biological Sciences and Ethics: Models of Cooperation. Graber, Glenn C.

Cooperation and Equality: A Reply to Pojman. Norman, Richard.

En torno a la sociabilidad humana en el pensamiento de Leonardo Polo. Naval, Concepción.

## COOPERATION

Guarantees. Schmidtz, David.

Rational Cooperation and Collective Goals. Tuomela, Raimo.

Rational Cooperation, Intention, and Reconsideration. Mintoff, Joe.

Signaling Cooperation: Prisoner's Dilemmas and Psychological Dispositions in Hobbes's State of Nature. Paden, Roger.

## COORDINATION

Approximate Common Knowledge and Co-Ordination: Recent Lessons from Game Theory. Morris, Stephen and Shin, Hyun Song.

Joint Beliefs in Conflictual Coordination Games. Vanderschraaf, Peter and Richards, Diana.

Payoff Dominance and the Stackelberg Heuristic. Colman, Andrew M and Bacharach, Michael.

Synchrony Lost, Synchrony Regained: The Achievement of Musical Co-ordination. Weeks, Peter.

## COOTER, R

The Lie Detector, *Wonder Woman* and Liberty: The Life and Work of William Moulton Marston. Bunn, Geoffrey C.

## COPERNICUS

"Temples of the Body and Temples of the Cosmos: Vision and Visualization in the Vesalian and Copernican Revolutions" in *Picturing Knowledge,* Baigrie, Brian S (ed). Kemp, Martin.

Die Kopernikanische und die semiotische Wende der Philosophie. Zeidler, Kurt W.

G.J. Rheticus on Copernicanism and Bible. Dinis, Alfredo.

Lecture Delivered During the Ceremony of Granting the Title of Doctor Honoris Causa of the Jagiellonian University (in Polish). Bochenski, Józef Maria.

## COPI, I

The Five Forms of the Ad Hominem Fallacy. Engel, S Morris.

## COPP, D

The Importance of the Proportionality Condition to the Doctrine of Double Effect: A Response to Fischer, Ravizza, and Copp. Woodward, P A.

## COPY

Permitting, Forcing, and Copying of a given Recursive Relation. Cholak, P, Knight, J F and Ash, C J.

Possible Degrees in Recursive Copies II. Knight, J F and Ash, C J.

Quasi-Simple Relations in Copies of a given Recursive Structure. Knight, J F, Remmel, J B and Ash, C J.

## COPYING

Plagiarism and the Art of Copying. Wollan, Jr, Laurin A.

When the Trial *Is* the Punishment: The Ethics of Plagiarism Accusations. Yanikoski, Charles S.

## COQUAND, T

On the Proof Theory of Coquand's Calculus of Constructions. Seldin, Jonathan P.

## CORNELL, D

The Philosophy of the Limit and its Other. McCarthy, Thomas A.

## COROLLARY

"Peirce's Theoremic/Corollarial Distinction and the Interconnections between Mathematics and Logic" in *Studies in the Logic of Charles Sanders Peirce,* Houser, Nathan (ed). Levy, Stephen H.

## CORPORATION

"Statt einer Einleitung: Essay über Unternehmensphilosophie—und darüber, was sie nicht ist" in *Werte und Entscheidungen im Management,* Schmidt, Thomas. Briddat, Birger P.

*Business Ethics in the African Context Today.* Rosemann, Philipp W (ed) and LeJeune, Michel (ed).

A Better Statutory Approach to Whistle-Blowing. Morehead Dworkin, Terry and Near, Janet P.

An Ethical Approach to Lobbying Activities of Businesses in the United States. Keffer, Jane M and Hill, Ronald Paul.

Corporate Ethics Codes: A Practical Application of Liability Prevention. Blodgett, Mark S and Carlson, Patricia J.

Corporate Ethics Initiatives as Social Control. Laufer, William S and Robertson, Diana C.

Corporate Social Performance, Stakeholder Orientation, and Organizational Moral Development. Logsdon, Jeanne M and Yuthas, Kristi.

Criteria for Evaluating the Legitimacy of Corporate Social Responsibility. Pava, Moses L and Krausz, Joshua.

Ethical Dilemmas of Doing Business in Post-Soviet Ukraine. Fuxman, Leonora.

Ethical Standards for Business Lobbying: Some Practical Suggestions. Hamilton III, J Brooke and Hoch, David.

Expressions of Corporate Social Responsibility in U.K. Firms. Robertson, Diana C and Nicholson, Nigel.

Gearing Up, Crashing Loud: Should We Punish High-Flyers for Insolvency?. Kilpi, Jukka.

Global Ethics: An Integrative Framework for MNEs. Desai, Ashay B and Rittenburg, Terri.

Globalizing Corporate Ethics Programs: Perils and Prospects. Jackson, Kevin T.

In Search of a Common Ethical Ground: Corporate Environmental Responsibility from the Perspective of Christian Environmental Stewardship. Enderle, Georges.

Just Do It: Deniability and Renegades. Brimlow, Robert W.

Moralische Beobachtung, interner Realismus und Korporatismus. Graeser, Andreas.

Naturalism and Business Ethics: Inevitable Foes or Possible Allies?. Fort, Timothy L.

Opening the Black Box: Corporate Codes of Ethics in Their Organizational Context. Cassell, Cathy, Johnson, Phil and Smith, Ken.

Peter French, Corporate Ethics and The Wizard of Oz. Kerlin, Michael J.

Private Parts: A Global Analysis of Privacy Protection Schemes and a Proposed Innovation for their Comparative Evaluation. Pincus, Laura and Johns, Roger.

Regulating Virtue: Formulating, Engendering and Enforcing Corporate Ethical Codes. Brien, Andrew.

Reinforcing Ethical Decision Making Through Corporate Culture. Chen, Al Y S, Sawyers, Roby B and Williams, Paul F.

Soul As in Ethic. Gini, Al.

Technology in Opposition Power—Must (Czech). Lenk, Hans and Maring, Matthias.

The Ethical Management Practices of Australian Firms. Batten, Jonathan, Hettihewa, Samanthala and Mellor, Robert.

The Ethics of Investing: A Reply to William Irvine. Larmer, Robert.

The Influence of Corporate Culture on Managerial Ethical Judgments. Vitell, Scott J and Nwachukwu, Saviour L S.

The Morality of Human Gene Patents. Resnik, David B.

The New Federalism: Implications for the Legitimacy of Corporate Political Activity. Christensen, Sandra L.

The Proactive Corporation: Its Nature and Causes. Shepard, Jon M, Betz, Michael and O'Connell, Lenahan.

Unbundling the Moral Dispute About Unbundling in South Africa. Rossouw, Gedeon J.

Women on Corporate Boards of Directors: A Needed Resource. Burke, Ronald A.

## CORPOREALITY

Incarnato comparire: Corpo e politica nelle proposte di Adriana Cavarero. Famiani, Mariapaola.

## CORPOREITY

"La corporeità del tempo: Ancora su Ensidemo e il suo eraclitismo" in *Il Concetto di Tempo: Atti del XXXII Congresso Nazionale della Società Filosofica Italiana,* Casertano, Giovanni (ed). Spinelli, Emidio.

## CORRADO, M

Preventive Detention, Corrado, and Me. Davis, Michael.

Reply to Corrado. Davis, Michael.

## CORRECTION

Commentary on: "How Are Scientific Corrections Made?". Guertin, Robert P.

How Are Scientific Corrections Made?. Kiang, Nelson Yuan-sheng.

## CORRESPONDENCE

Consideraçoes sobre o Problema da Verdade em Espinosa. Gleizer, Marcos André.

Correspondence on the Cheap. Alward, Peter.

Counterfactuals and Updates as Inverse Modalities. Ryan, Mark and Schobbens, Pierre-Yves.

Gainsborough's Wit. Asfour, Amal and Williamson, Paul.

Hybrid Languages. Blackburn, Patrick and Seligman, Jerry.

Nota sobre los conceptos de verdad en una interpretación y verdad como correspondencia. Garrido Garrido, Julián.

On Imagination—A Correspondence with Prof. Zhang Longxi. Yuanhua, Wang.

Reiner Schürmann's Report of His Visit to Martin Heidegger. Adler, Pierre (trans).

Sleigh's *Leibniz & Arnauld: A Commentary on their Correspondence* (New Haven: Yale University Press). Adams, Robert Merrihew.

Sobre la interpretación deflacionaria de la teoría de Tarski. Orlando, Eleonora.

Teoría de la verdad: sobre ciencia y verdad. Pérez de Laborda, Alfonso.

The Correspondence Theory of Truth. New, Kostja.

Une Correspondance entre Anneaux Partiels et Groupes. Simonetta, Patrick.

## CORRIGIBILITY

see Incorrigibility

## CORRUPTION

"Positività Della Corruzione: Per una fenomenologia della mutazione" in *Soggetto E Verità: La questione dell'uomo nella filosofia contemporanea,* Fagiuoli, Ettore. Fadini, Ubaldo.

Academic Corruption. Kekes, John.

The Revolutionary Humanism of Jayaprakash Narayan. Manimala, Varghes.

## CORSINO, B

Responding to JCAHO Standards: Everybody's Business. Fletcher, John C.

## CORTAZAR, J

Qué se sentiría ser Charlie Parker? (What is it like to be a bird?). Vargas Calvo, Jorge A.

## COSMIC

Laws of Nature, Cosmic Coincidences and Scientific Realism. Lange, Marc.

## CRICHTON, M

Can a Woman Harass a Man?: Toward a Cultural Understanding of Bodies and Power. Bordo, Susan.

## CRIME

*Radical Critiques of the Law.* Griffin, Stephen M (ed) and Moffat, Robert C L (ed).

Actio illicita in causa und Zurechnung zum Vorverhalten bei Provokation von Rechtfertigungsgründen. Lúzon, Diego-Manuel.

Actio libera in causa: Ordentliche oder ausserordentliche Zurechnung?. Joshi Jubert, Ujala.

Battered Women Who Kill: Victims and Agents of Violence. Hartline, Sharon E.

Business Entities and the State: Who Should Provide Security from Crime?. Scheid, Don E.

Crime, Property, and Justice: The Ethics of Civil Forfeiture. Rainbolt, George and Reif, Alison F.

Criminal Children. Richards, Norvin.

Das Opferverhalten als Schlüssel zum System der Sachentziehungsdelikte. Hruschka, Joachim.

Don't Change the Subject: Interpreting Public Discourse over Quid Pro Quo. Stark, Andrew.

George Sher's Theory of Deserved Punishment, and the Victimized Wrongdoer. Kershnar, Stephen.

Hobbes and Criminal Procedure, Torture and Pre-Trial Detention. Cattaneo, Mario A.

How Much Punishment Does a Bad Samaritan Deserve?. Davis, Michael.

Improving our Practice of Sentencing. Baker, Brenda M.

International Criminal Adjudication and the Right to Punish. Blake, Michael.

Preventive Detention, Corrado, and Me. Davis, Michael.

Punishment and Race. Pittman, John P.

Punishment, Quarantine, and Preventive Detention. Corrado, Michael.

Reply to Corrado. Davis, Michael.

Republican Theory and Criminal Punishment. Pettit, Philip.

Response to Michael Davis. Corrado, Michael.

Tackling Crime by Other Means. Luke, Andrew.

The "But-Everyone-Does-That!" Defense. Husak, Douglas.

Thinking about Private Prisons. Lippke, Richard L.

Wesentliche und unwesentliche Abweichungen zurechnungsrelevanter Urteile des Täters von denen des Richters. Joerden, Jan C.

Zur Rechtfertigung von Pflicht- und Obliegenheitsverletzungen im Strafrecht. Kindhäuser, Urs.

## CRIMINAL JUSTICE

Form and Substance in Criminal Justice Scholarship: H. Richard Uviller, *Virtual Justice*. Dripps, Donald A.

Hobbes and Criminal Procedure, Torture and Pre-Trial Detention. Cattaneo, Mario A.

## CRIMINAL LAWS

Action Theory and Criminal Law. Dolinko, David.

Dangerous Games and the Criminal Law. Yeager, Daniel B.

The Sanctions of the Criminal Law. Clark, Michael.

## CRISIS

"Is the Present Crisis a Specifically Modern Phenomenon?" in *The Ancients and the Moderns,* Lilly, Reginald (ed). Ricoeur, Paul.

"Remarks on the History of the Concept of Crisis" in *The Ancients and the Moderns,* Lilly, Reginald (ed). Koselleck, Reinhart.

"The Present Crisis of the Universities" in *The Idea of University,* Brzezinski, Jerzy (ed). Bauman, Zygmunt.

*Martin Heidegger und Hans Jonas: Die Metaphysik der Subjektivität und die Krise der technologischen Zivilisation.* Jakob, Eric.

Another View on the Crisis in Marxism. Gamberg, Herb.

Enduring Crises and Challenges of African-American Studies. Adeleke, Tunde.

La ética y la crisis del deporte. Csepregi, Gabor.

La Filosofía como cuarta destreza cultural para la realización humana de la vida. Martens, Ekkehard.

Proactive Crisis Management and Ethical Discourse: Dow Chemical's Issues Management Bulletins 1979-1990. Kernisky, Debra A.

The Edge of Crisis/The Crisis of the Edge. Grgas, Stipe.

The Measureless of Crisis (in Spanish). Grespan, Jorge.

This Project is Mad: Descartes, Derrida, and the Notion of Philosophical Crisis. Steiner, Gary.

Vico y la retórica que no cesa. Marín-Casanova, José Antonio.

## CRITCHLEY, S

"Remarks on Deconstruction and Pragmatism" in *Deconstruction and Pragmatism,* Mouffe, Chantal (ed). Derrida, Jacques.

"Response to Simon Critchley" in *Deconstruction and Pragmatism,* Mouffe, Chantal (ed). Rorty, Richard.

## CRITERIA

Nonparametric Statistics in Multicriteria Analysis. Scarelli, Antonino and Venzi, Lorenzo.

## CRITICAL

Critical Reflection: An Alleged Epistemic Duty. Tidman, Paul.

Tidman On Critical Reflection. Steup, Matthias.

## CRITICAL RATIONALISM

*Grenzen der kritischen Vernunft.* Schmid, Peter A and Zurbuchen, Simone.

Braucht die Wissenschaft methodologische Regeln?. Wettersten, John.

## CRITICAL REALISM

"Gedanken vor einem Jubiläum" in *Grenzen der kritischen Vernunft,* Schmid, Peter A. Fontius, Martin.

## CRITICAL THEORY

"Concerning the Central Idea of Adorno's Philosophy" in *The Semblance of Subjectivity,* Huhn, Tom (ed). Bubner, Rüdiger.

"Hegel, Foucault, and Critical Hermeneutics" in *Hegel, History, and Interpretation,* Gallagher, Shaun. Gallagher, Shaun.

"Mimesis and Mimetology: Adorno and Lacoue-Labarthe" in *The Semblance of Subjectivity,* Huhn, Tom (ed). Jay, Martin.

"Mundo administrado" o "Colonización del mundo de la vida": La depotenciación de la Teoría crítica de la sociedad en J. Habermas. Gómez Ibáñez, Vicente.

*Critical Studies: Language and the Subject.* Simms, Karl (ed).

*From Romanticism to Critical Theory: The Philosophy of German Literary Theory.* Bowie, Andrew.

*Kant, Critique and Politics.* Hutchings, Kimberly.

*Las Caras del Leviatán: Una Lectura Política de la Teoría Crítica.* Colom González, Francisco.

*The Language of Criticism: Linguistic Models and Literary Theory.* Henkel, Jacqueline M.

A Concepçao de Filosofia em Adorno. Cordeiro Silva, Rafael.

Beyond Enlightenment? After the Subject of Foucault, Who Comes?. Venn, Couze.

Chaos and Literature. Matheson, Carl and Kirchhoff, Evan.

Conceptualizing Art Criticism for Effective Practice. Geahigan, George.

Critical Theory between Modernity and Postmodernity. Fleming, Marie.

Debating Critical Theory. Hoy, David Couzens.

Kritische Theorie als Erfahrungswissenschaft: Lagebericht anlässlich einiger Neuerscheinungen. Behrens, Roger.

Meta(l)morphoses. Braidotti, Rosi.

Neo-Functionalist Critical Theory?. Turner, Charles.

On the Practical Relevance of Habermas's Theory of Communicative Action. Parkin, Andrew C.

Philosophy and Critical Theory: A Reply to Richard Rorty and Seyla Benhabib. McCarthy, Thomas A.

Romanticism Revisited. Hammer, Espen.

Situations of the Self: Reflections on Seyla Benhabib's Version of Critical Theory. Forst, Rainer.

Socrates, Friendship, and the Community of Inquiry. Glaser, Jen.

The "Political" Dimension of Italian Critico-Problematic Historicism (in Serbo-Croatian). Cacciatore, Giuseppe.

The Ambiguity of 'Rationality'. Rorty, Richard.

The Hermeneutical Turn in American Critical Theory, 1830-1860. Walhout, M D.

The Local, the Contextual and/or Critical. Benhabib, Seyla.

Thinking in Community. Lipman, Matthew.

## CRITICAL THINKING

"Can Reasons for Rationality be Redeemed?" in *Philosophy of Education (1996),* Margonis, Frank (ed). Siegel, Harvey.

"Critical Thinking" as a Teaching Methodology: A Questionable Idea at the Wrong Time. Kuczewski, Mark.

"Decentering and Reasoning" in *Philosophy of Education (1996),* Margonis, Frank (ed). Weinstein, Mark.

"Democracy and the Foundations of Morality" in *Philosophy of Education (1996),* Margonis, Frank (ed). Curren, Randall R.

"Democracy, Education and the Critical Citizen" in *Philosophy of Education (1996),* Margonis, Frank (ed). Puolimatka, Tapio.

"Habermas and Critical Thinking" in *Philosophy of Education (1996),* Margonis, Frank (ed). Endres, Ben.

"Rationality and Redemption: Ideology, Indoctrination, and Learning Communities" in *Philosophy of Education (1996),* Margonis, Frank (ed). Alexander, H A.

*Critical Reasoning: A Practical Introduction.* Thomson, Anne.

*Philosophy of Education (1996).* Margonis, Frank (ed), Boler, Megan (ed) and Callan, Eamonn (ed).

*Thinking from A to Z.* Warburton, Nigel.

A "Third Wave" Manifesto: Keynotes of the Sonoma Conference. Paul, Richard.

A Brief Response to Jack Russell Weinstein. Reinsmith, William.

A Conception of Practical Reasoning. Coombs, Jerrold and Wright, Ian.

A Strategy for the Acquisition of Problem-Solving Expertise in Humans: The Category-as-Analogy Approach. Alma, Carine V.

An Instructional Model for Critical Thinking. Leshowitz, Barry and Yoshikawa, Elaine.

Analogy and Argument. McKay, Thomas J.

Are Appeals to the Emotions Necessarily Fallacious?. Hinman, Lawrence M.

Argument Management, Informal Logic and Critical Thinking. Blair, J Anthony.

Caring as Thinking. Lipman, Matthew.

Cognitive Reengineering: A Process for Cultivating Critical Thinking Skills in RNs. Young, Michele M.

Combining Critical Thinking and Written Composition: The Whole Is Greater Than The Sum Of The Parts. Hatcher, Donald L.

Confessions of a Sentimental Philosopher: Science, Animal Rights, and the Demands of Rational Inquiry. Johnson, David Kenneth.

## CULTURE

Modern/Postmodern: Off the Beaten Path of Antimodernism. Kramer, Eric Mark.

*Nature and Society: Anthropological Perspectives.* Descola, Philippe (ed) and Pálsson, Gísli (ed).

*Nietzsche and Jewish Culture.* Golomb, Jacob (ed).

*Nietzsche and the Modern Crisis of the Humanities.* Levine, Peter.

*Philosophy of Education (1996).* Margonis, Frank (ed), Boler, Megan (ed) and Callan, Eamonn (ed).

*Reclaiming Truth: Contribution to a Critique of Cultural Relativism.* Norris, Christopher.

*Rousseau and the Politics of Ambiguity: Self, Culture, and Society.* Morgenstern, Mira.

*Saber, Sentir, Pensar: La cultura en la frontera de dos siglos.* Nieto Blanco, Carlos (ed).

*Sociedades sin Estado: El Pensamiento de los Otros.* Lorite Mena, José.

*The Indian Renouncer and Postmodern Poison: A Cross-Cultural Encounter.* Olson, Carl.

*The Magic Mirror: Myth's Abiding Power.* Baeten, Elizabeth M.

*The Second Wave: A Reader in Feminist Theory.* Nicholson, Linda (ed).

*W.E.B. Du Bois on Race and Culture.* Grosholz, Emily (ed), Bell, Bernard W (ed) and Stewart, James B (ed).

A Tentative Discussion on the Common Mental Attributes of the Han Nationality. Xiyuan, Xiong.

Afrikanische Kunst—Ein Drama kultureller Wiederentdeckung oder eine europäische Tragödie?. Behrens, Roger.

Alexander Pope and Eighteenth Century Conflicts about Ultimacy. Leigh, David J.

American Political Culture, Prophetic Narration, and Toni Morrison's *Beloved.* Shulman, George.

An American Naturalist Account of Culture. Baeten, Elizabeth M.

Ancora sulla teoria vichiana del linguaggio: In margine ad alcune recenti pubblicazioni. Gensini, Stefano.

Animating Rawls's Original Position. Regan, Thomas J.

Art and Anthropology. Sparshott, Francis.

Art: Function or Procedure—Nature or Culture?. Dickie, George T.

Aspekte internationaler Ethik. Betzler, Monika.

Bach's Butterfly Effect: Culture, Environment and History. Simmons, I G.

Beyond Ontology: Ideation, Phenomenology and the Cross Cultural Study of Emotion. Solomon, Robert C.

Blameworthiness, Character, and Cultural Norms. Haji, Ishtiyaque.

Blurred Boundaries. Morriss, Peter.

Can Religion Survive the Rationalization? Questions at Habermas's Theory of Culture (in Dutch). Jespers, F P M.

Can we Understand Ourselves?. Winch, Peter.

Catholic Social Ethics in a Pluralist Age. Chmielewski, Philip J.

Centering Culture: Teaching for Critical Sexual Literacy using the Sexual Diversity Wheel. Sears, James T.

Citizenship and Culture in Early Modern Europe. Miller, Peter N.

Communication through Interpreters in Health Care: Ethical Dilemmas Arising from Differences in Class, Culture, Language, and Power. Kaufert, Joseph M and Putsch, Robert W.

Conceptual Frameworks for World Musics in Education. Boyce-Tillman, June.

Conscience, Morality and Social Acceptability in an African Culture. Ebijuwa, T.

Conversazione con Cornelio Fabro. Burghi, Giancarlo.

Cor Dippel, denker op de grens van twee werelden. Van Dijk, Paul.

Crisis and Narrativity. Hirschbein, Ron.

Critical Thinking and Command of Language. Johnson, Ralph H.

Cross-cultural Understanding: Its Philosophical and Anthropological Problems. Jamme, Christoph.

Cultura mundial y mundos culturales. Scannone, Juan Carlos.

Cultura y Desarrollo Global. Dallmayr, Fred R.

Cultura y reflexión en torno a Meditaciones del Quijote. Lasaga Medina, José.

Cultural Conditioning: The Dark Underside of Multiculturalism (Part Two: A Way Out). Reinsmith, William.

Cultural Context and Moral Responsibility. Isaacs, Tracy.

Cultural Diversity and the Systems View. Hammond, Debora.

Cultural Diversity in Medicine and Medical Ethics: What Are the Key Questions?. La Puma, John.

Cultural Nationalism, Neither Ethnic Nor Civic. Nielsen, Kai.

Cultural Psychology as Metatheory. Hoshmand, Lisa Tsoi.

Cultural Relativism and Social Criticism from a Taylorian Perspective. Rosa, Hartmut.

Culture, Power and the Social Construction of Morality: Moral Voices of Chinese Students. Chang, Kimberly A.

Dal primato della prassi all'anomia: Una interpretazione filosofica della crisi odierna. Cotta, Sergio.

De la culture aux cultures: Délimitations d'un concept pluri-sémantique. Laberge, Yves.

De oorspronkelijkheid en actuele betekenis van H. van Riessen als filosoof van de techniek: Deel I—De oorspronkelijkheid van zijn werk. Haaksma, Hans W H.

De Platón a Michael Jackson: Entresijos del imaginario andrógino. Jiménez, Jorge.

Desarrollo técnico y evolución histórica: modelos metafísicos y antropológico-culturales. Rodríguez, Amán Rosales.

Descripción del fenómeno religioso en la postmodernidad. Barrera Vélez, Julio César.

Die Wendung nach Asien: Heideggers Ansatz interkultureller Philosophie. Wolz-Gottwald, Eckard.

Dimensions of Citizenship and National Identity in Canada. Carens, Joseph H.

Doing One's Own Thing: The Genealogy of a Slogan. Weidhorn, Manfred.

Economics, Business Principles and Moral Sentiments. Sen, Amartya.

Electric Technology and Poetic Mimesis. McInerny, Daniel.

Environmental Values: A Place-Based Theory. Norton, Bryan G and Hannon, Bruce.

Equality, Autonomy, and Cultural Rights. Levey, Goeffrey Brahm.

Ethical Beliefs and Management Behaviour: A Cross-Cultural Comparison. Jackson, Terence and Calafell Artola, Marian.

Explaining Monoculturalism: Beyond Gellner's Theory of Nationalism. Tambini, Damian.

Fonament de l'axiologia de Plató (La tradició del platonisme a l'escola de Tubinga). Canals Surís, Manuel.

Food Biotechnology's Challenge to Cultural Integrity and Individual Consent. Thompson, Paul B.

Forgiare e dimenticare: i doveri dell'oblio. Lowenthal, David.

From the Mexican Chiapas Crisis: A Different Perspective for Environmental Ethics. Szatzscheider, Teresa Kwiatkowska.

Georg Simmel on Philosophy and Culture: Postscript to a Collection of Essays. Habermas, Jürgen and Deflem, Mathieu (trans).

Gilles Deleuze and the Politics of Time. May, Todd.

Gramsci, teórico de la superestructura. Giglioli, Giovanna.

Hermenêutica da Cultura e Ontologia em Paul Ricoeur. Gama, José.

Histoire de la philosophie et philosophie au tribunal de la vérité. Cunningham, Henri-Paul.

Histories of Cultural Populism. Ryle, Martin.

How Liberal Can Nationalism Be?. Lichtenberg, Judith.

In a Different Voice: Technology, Culture, and Post-Modern Bioethics. McNair, Douglas.

Incommensurable Differences: Cultural Relativism and Antirationalism Concerning Self and Other. Wagner, Joseph.

Information Technology and Technologies of the Self. Capurro, Rafael.

Irigaray Anxiety: Luce Irigaray and Her Ethics for Improper Selves. Deutscher, Penelope.

Irresolvable Disagreement and the Case Against Moral Realism. Bennigson, Thomas.

Italo Mancini lettore di Agostino: Percorso e contenuti di un incontro. Cangiotti, Marco.

Krise der europäischen Kultur—ein Problemerbe der husserlschen Philosophie. Ströker, Elisabeth.

L'astuzia della follia: Un'antologia di Lombroso. Savorelli, Alessandro.

La culture comme force. Yahot, Christophe.

La Filosofía como cuarta destreza cultural para la realización humana de la vida. Martens, Ekkehard.

La filosofia personalista di Dietrich von Hildebrand e la sua opposizione contro il nazionalsocialismo. Seifert, Josef.

La literatura como juego. Palazón M, María Rosa.

La noción de inconmensurabilidad y la realidad de los otros o el derecho a la diferencia. López Gil, Marta.

La persuasión desde las *Institutiones Oratoriae* a la *Scienza Nuova.* Fabiani, Paolo.

La posibilidad de pensar la democracia en Latinoamérica desde la óptica de la ética discursiva. Fernández, Alejandra.

La teoría de la cultura de Leonardo Polo. Murillo, José Ignacio.

Language and Reality, One More Time. Gill, Jerry H.

Liang Shuming and Henri Bergson on Intuition: Cultural Context and the Evolution of Terms. An, Yanming.

Liberalism and Culture. Carnes, Joseph H.

Liberalism and Culture: Will Kymlicka on Multicultural Citizenship (in Dutch). Van de Putte, André and Chaerle, Dries.

Life, Culture and Value: Reflections on Wittgenstein's *Culture and Value.* Pradhan, R C.

Listening, Heeding, and Respecting the Ground at One's Feet: Knowledge and the Arts Across Cultures. O'Loughlin, Marjorie.

Lyotard: Modern Postmodernist?. Hurst, Andrea.

Metafisica e trascendentalità: Confronto con l'epistemologia e l'ermeneutica. Totaro, Francesco.

Modèles historique et modèles culturels. Moutsopoulos, Evanghélos.

Modern Medicine in a Multicultural Setting. Rasinski Gregory, Dorothy.

Moving Literary Theory On. Harris, Wendell V.

Muchas Culturas: Sobre el problema filosófico y práctico de la diversidad cultural. Ramírez, Mario Teodoro.

Music, Imagination, and Play. Reichling, Mary J.

Naturaleza/cultura: Un enfoque estético. Ramírez, Mario Teodoro.

Naturalism and Business Ethics: Inevitable Foes or Possible Allies?. Fort, Timothy L.

Netzverdichtung: Zur Philosophie industriegesellschaftlicher Entwicklungen. Lübbe, Hermann.

On the Crisis of Culture, Its Values and Value Education (in German). Braun, Walter.

## CUT ELIMINATION
Cut-Free Sequent Calculi for Some Tense Logics. Kashima, Ryo.
Dual-Intuitionistic Logic. Urbas, Igor.
Game Logic and Its Applications II. Kaneko, Mamoru and Nagashima, Takashi.
Induction Rules, Reflection Principles, and Provably Recursive Functions. Beklemishev, Lev D.
Interpolants, Cut Elimination and Flow Graphs for the Propositional Calculus. Carbone, A.
Strong Cut-Elimination in Display Logic. Wansing, Heinrich.

## CUYPERS, S
Cuypers' Persoonlijke aangelegenheden. Meijsing, Monica.

## CYBERNETICS
Cyberethics and Social Stability. Hauptman, Robert.
Evolutionary Paradigms of Some New Scientific Disciplines (Two Examples: Cybernetics and Fuzzy Sets Theory) (in Spanish). Termini, Settimo.
Tecnopolitica: Le idee del cyberpunk. Nacci, Michela.

## CYBERSPACE
CyberSpace Virtual Reality: Fortschritt und Gefahr einer innovativen Technologie. Wedde, Horst F (ed).
Filosofia e realtà virtuale. Marturano, Antonio.
Virtual Sexes and Feminist Futures: The Philosophy of 'Cyberfeminism'. Marsden, Jill.

## CYCLICAL
Cyclical Preferences and World Bayesianism. Sobel, Jordan Howard.

## CYLINDRIC ALGEBRA
Step by Step—Building Representations in Algebraic Logic. Hirsch, Robin and Hodkinson, Ian.

## CYNIC
The Cynics: The Cynic Movement in Antiquity and Its Legacy. Branham, R Bracht (ed) and Goulet-Cazé, Marie-Odile (ed).

## CYNICISM
Classical Cynicism: A Critical Study. Navia, Luis E.
La Politeia, entre cynisme et stoïcisme. Dorandi, Tiziano.

## CYPRIAN
Hommage à Anastase Léventis. Vélissaropoulos, D.
La fidélité de Zénon envers Chypre. Gabaude, Jean-Marc.
Les écoles philosophiques d'Athènes et les princes de Chypre. Berti, Enrico.
Survol du Colloque. Lang, André.

## CZECH
"Prague Mosaic: Encounters with Prague Philosophers" in In Itinere European Cities and the Birth of Modern Scientific Philosophy, Poli, Roberto (ed). Sebestik, Jan.
Four Summers: A Czech Kaleidoscope. Page, Benjamin.
An Idea of Total Freedom? (in Czech). Tomek, Václav.
Veritas vincit (in Czech). Skorpíková, Zuzana.

## CZEZOWSKI, T
The Problem of Justification of Abduction in C.S. Peirce in the Light of Tadeusz Czezowski's Views (in Polish). Mirek, Ryszard.

## D'AILLY, P
Syncatégorèmes, concepts, équivocité: Deux questions anonymes, conservées dans le ms. Paris, B.N., lat. 16.401, liées à la sémantique de Pierre d'Ailly (c. 1350-1420). Bakker, Paul J J M.

## D'COSTA, G
The Possibility of Religious Pluralism: A Reply to Gavin D'Costa. Hick, John.

## DADAISM
The Lost Steps. Polizzotti, Mark (trans) and Breton, André.

## DAILY LIFE
Re-Claiming Hestia: Goddess of Everyday Life. Thompson, Patricia J.
The Forms and Functions of Real-Life Moral Decision-Making. Krebs, Dennis L, Denton, Kathy and Wark, Gillian.

## DALGLEISH, T
Felt and Unfelt Emotions: A Rejoinder to Dalgleish. Kupperman, Joel J.

## DALLMAYR, F
The New Hegel. Dallmayr, Fred R, Hardimon, Michael O and Pinkard, Terry.
The Ruptured Idiom: Of Dallmayr, Matilal and Ramanujan's 'Way of Thinking'. Venkat Rao, D.

## DAMASCIUS
Socratic Anti-Empiricism in the Phaedo. Baltzly, Dirk.
The Ontological Relation "One-Many" according to the Neoplatonist Damascius. Térézis, Christos.

## DANCE
see also Ballet
Essays on the Nature of Art. Deutsch, Eliot.
Individuality and Expression: The Aesthetics of the New German Dance, 1908-1936. Howe, Dianne S.
Beauty and the Breast: Dispelling Significations of Feminine Sensuality in the Aesthetics of Dance. Jaeger, Suzanne M.
Dance and the Question of Fidelity. Cohen, Selma Jeanne.
Dance Metaphors: A Reply to Julie Van Camp. Whittock, Trevor.
Harmony in Space: A Perspective on the Work of Rudolf Laban. Brooks, Lynn Matluck.
Maurice Merleau-Ponty and Rudolf Laban—An Interactive Appropriation of Parallels and Resonances. Connolly, Maureen and Lathrop, Anna.
Some Remarks on Sparshott on the Dance. Margolis, Joseph.

## DANCY, J
Against Thin-Property Reductivism: Toleration as Supererogatory. Newey, Glen.
Principle Ethics, Particularism and Another Possibility. Reader, Soran.

## DANGER
A Threat to Disabled Persons? On the Genetics Approach to Developmental Disabilities. Reinders, Hans S.

## DANIELS, N
Three Paths in Moral Philosophy. Walzer, Michael.

## DANTE
L'image d'Albert le Grand et de Thomas d'Aquin chez Dante Alighieri. Ricklin, Thomas.
Well-Being and Despair: Dante's Ugolino. Qizilbash, Mozaffar.

## DANTE, L
Georg Lukács and Lajos Fülep Dante (in Hungarian). Kaposi, Márton.

## DANTO, A
The Nonfixity of the Historical Past. Weberman, David.

## DARBY, H
The Relations between Geography and History Reconsidered. Guelke, Leonard.

## DARWIN
From Soul to Mind: The Emergence of Psychology from Erasmus Darwin to William James. Reed, Edward S.
Back to Darwin and Popper: Criticism, Migration of Piecemeal Conceptual Schemes, and the Growth of Knowledge. De Freitas, Renan Springer.
Darwin and Dennett: Still Two Mysteries. Cody, Arthur B.
Darwin and the Inefficacy of Artificial Selection. Richards, Richard A.
Darwin's Origin and Mill's Subjection. Missimer, Connie.
Darwin: Evolution and Contingency (in Spanish). Rodriguez Camarero, Luis.
Deconstructing Dennett's Darwin. Fodor, Jerry.
In the Beginning, There Was Darwin: Darwin's Dangerous Idea: Evolution and the Meanings of Life. Dennett, Daniel C and Mulhauser, Gregory R.
Taking the 'Error' Out of Ruse's Error Theory. Ryan, James A.

## DARWINISM
Creacionismo y evolucionismo en el siglo XIX: las repercusiones del Darwinismo en la comunidad científica española. Pelayo, Francisco.
Darwinism, Process Structuralism, and Natural Kinds. Griffiths, Paul E.
Die wertlose Natur: Eine Bilanz der Diskussion um eine "Evolutionäre Ethik". Funken, Michael.
Directed Evolution. Van Eyken, Albert.
Granny Versus Mother Nature—No Contest. Dennett, Daniel C.
I Rather Think I Am A Darwinian. Blackburn, Simon.
Modelos cognoscitivos para la filosofía contemporánea de la mente. Rodríguez Rodríguez, Rodolfo J.
Plantinga's Case Against Naturalistic Epistemology. Fales, Evan.
Social Darwinism: The Concept. Crook, Paul.
Stove's Anti-Darwinism. Franklin, James.
The Historical Turn in the Study of Adaptation. Griffiths, Paul E.
Who's Afraid of a Non-Metaphorical Evolutionary Epistemology?. Heschl, Adolf.
Yvon Quiniou, il materialismo e l'impossibile immoralismo di Nietzsche. Franco, Vittoria.

## DAS, R
Philosophy as Critical Reflection: The Philosophy of Rasvihary Das. Sen, Sanat Kumar.
Rasvihary Das on 'Value of Doubt': Some Reflections. Ghosh, Raghunath.

## DASEIN
"La Verità Storica: La comprensione della storia nella riflessione di Martin Heidegger" in Soggetto E Verità: La questione dell'uomo nella filosofia contemporanea, Fagiuoli, Ettore. Cassinari, Flavio.
Gesamtausgabe II. Abteilung: Vorlesungen (Band 27: Einleitung in die Philosophie). Heidegger, Martin.
Heidegger and Being and Time. Mulhall, Stephen.
Egyptian Priests and German Professors: On the Alleged Difficulty of Philosophy. Protevi, John.
Filosofia e Estilo Literário em Heidegger e em Platao: Um Exemplo. Borges-Duarte, Irene.
Hyperbolic Doubt and "Machiavelism": The Modern Foundation of the Subject in Descartes (in French). Richir, Marc.
L'éthique aristotélicienne et le chemin de Heidegger. Kontos, Pavlos.
The Transcendental Circle. Malpas, Jeff.

## DASGUPTA, A
Is Chomsky's Linguistics Non-Empirical?. Kanthamani, A.

## DASTON, L
From Aperspectival Objectivity to Strong Objectivity: The Quest for Moral Objectivity. Tannoch-Bland, Jennifer.

## DATA
"Data and Theory in Aesthetics: Philosophical Understanding and Misunderstanding" in Verstehen and Humane Understanding, O'Hear, Anthony (ed). Hepburn, Ronald W.
"Taking Empirical Data Seriously: An Ecofeminist Philosophical Perspective" in Ecofeminism: Women, Culture, Nature, Warren, Karen J (ed). Warren, Karen J.

# DATA

(Not) Giving Credit Where Credit Is Due: Citation of Data Sets. Sieber, Joan E and Trumbo, Bruce E.

*Problems of Vision: Rethinking the Causal Theory of Perception.* Vision, Gerald.

*Reason, Reality, and Speculative Philosophy.* Singer, Marcus G (ed) and Murphy, Arthur E.

Collecting "Sensitive" Data in Business Ethics Research: A Case for the Unmatched Count Technique (UCT). Dalton, Dan R, Daily, Catherine M and Wimbush, James C.

Commentary on "Good to the Last Drop? Millikan Stories as 'Canned' Pedagogy. Bird, Stephanie J.

Ecological Validity and 'White Room Effects': The Interaction of Cognitive and Cultural Models in the Pragmatic Analysis of Elicited Narratives from Children. Cicourel, Aaron V.

Formal Organizations: A Philosophical Review of Perspectives and Behaviour Dynamics. Johnnie, Palmer B.

Function Identification from Noisy Data with Recursive Error Bounds. Changizi, Mark.

Good to the Last Drop? Millikan Stories as "Canned" Pedagogy. Segerstrale, Ullica.

How Are Scientific Corrections Made?. Kiang, Nelson Yuan-sheng.

Laudan and Leplin on Empirical Equivalence. Okasha, Samir.

Mental Models in Data Interpretation. Chinn, Clark A and Brewer, William F.

Severe Tests, Arguing from Error, and Methodological Underdetermination. Mayo, Deborah G.

Symbolic Praxis. Schürmann, Reiner.

Technological Escalation and the Exploration Model of Natural Science. Rescher, Nicholas.

The Impact of the Lambda Calculus in Logic and Computer Science. Barendregt, Henk.

The Relationship Between Connectionist Models and a Dynamic Data-Oriented Theory of Concept Formation. Bartsch, Renate.

The Role of Data and Theory in Covariation Assessment: Implications for the Theory-Ladenness of Observation. Freedman, Eric G and Smith, Laurence D.

Trust and the Collection, Selection, Analysis and Interpretation of Data: A Scientist's View. Bird, Stephanie J and Housman, David E.

Using a Dialectical Scientific Brief in Peer Review. Stamps III, Arthur E.

# DATE, V

Professor Date's New Light on the Vedanta of Samkara. Sharma, M L.

# DATTAI, D

Prof. D. M. Dattai: As a Process-Philosopher from an Alternative Inter-Cultural Perspective. Sarkar, Anil K.

# DAUGHTER

*Without a Woman to Read: Toward the Daughter in Postmodernism.* Price, Daniel.

# DAVID, M

"A Disquotational Theory of Truth" in *Verdad: lógica, representación y mundo,* Villegas Forero, L. Seymour, Michel.

# DAVIDSON, D

"Las explicacioines homunculares de la irracionalidad" in *La racionalidad: su poder y sus límites,* Nudler, Oscar (ed). Gianella, Alicia E.

"The Broken Bonds with the World" in *Epistemology and History,* Zeidler-Janiszewska, Anna (ed). Ozdowski, Pawel.

*Davidson's Theory of Truth and Its Implications for Rorty's Pragmatism.* Letson, Ben H.

*Practicing Philosophy: Pragmatism and the Philosophical Life.* Shusterman, Richard.

*Wahrheit, Referenz und Realismus: Eine Studie zur Sprachphilosophie und Metaphysik.* Schantz, Richard.

Absent Qualia. Dretske, Fred.

Agency. Simester, A P.

Charity, Interpretation, Fallacy. Adler, Jonathan E.

Countering the Counting Problem: A Reply to Holton. Dodd, Julian.

Cow-Sharks, Magnets, and Swampman. Dennett, Daniel C.

Das Verstehen singulärer Handlungen: Ein Kommentar zu Davidson und von Wright. Wyller, Truls.

Davidson on First-Person Authority. Hacker, P M S.

Davidson's Action Theory and Epiphenomenalism. Cheng, Kam-Yuen.

Davidson's Second Person. Verheggen, Claudine.

Davidson, Interdeterminacy, and Measurement. Davies, David.

Descartes, Davidson and the Causal Impotence of Thought (in Czech). Hríbek, Tomás.

Die Grenzen des Selbstwissens. Bernecker, Sven.

Donald Davidson, Descartes and How to Deny the Evident. Gosselin, M.

Donald Davidson: L'incontro con la filosofia e la definizione del progetto teorico. Lepore, Ernest.

Doubting Castel or the Slough of Despond: Davidson and Schiffer on the Limits of Analysis. Norris, Christopher.

Duplicating Thoughts. Ludwig, Kirk A.

Equal Rights for Swamp-Persons. Antony, Louise M.

How Should We Revise the Paratactic Theory?. Frankish, Keith.

Les conditions de l'interprétation. Montminy, Martin.

Meaning and Triangulation. Talmage, Catherine J L.

Metaphor and Ambiguity. Engstrom, Anders.

On Swampkinds. Millikan, Ruth Garrett.

On the Notion of Cause 'Philosophically Speaking'. Steward, Helen.

Quotation Marks: Demonstratives or Demonstrations?. Reimer, Marga.

Rationality and the Argument for Anomalous Monism. Yalowitz, Steven.

Reason and Agency. Pink, Thomas.

Rorty and Davidson. Sullivan, Arthur.

Strength of Motivation and Being in Control. Mele, Alfred R.

SwampJoe: Mind or Simulation?. Levine, Joe.

Swampman Meets Swampcow. Neander, Karen.

Teoría de la acción y racionalidad en Donald Davidson. Pérez-Wicht, Pablo Quintanilla.

The Normativity of Meaning. Gampel, Eric H.

The Propositional Attitudes. Heil, John.

The Theory of Meaning: An Impasse. Razzaque, Abdur.

The Vagaries of Paraphrase: A Reply to Holton on the Counting Problem. Rumfitt, Ian.

Varieties of Quotation. Cappelen, Herman and Lepore, Ernest.

# DAVIES, M

Navigating the Social World: Simulation Versus Theory. Sterelny, Kim.

# DAVIES, S

Art: Function or Procedure—Nature or Culture?. Dickie, George T.

# DAVIS, A

Educational Assessment: Reply to Andrew Davis. Winch, Christopher and Gingell, John.

# DAVIS, M

Comment: What We Can Learn from "Better Communication between Engineers and Managers" (M. Davis). Whitbeck, Caroline.

Commentary on "Better Communication between Engineers and Managers. Loui, Michael.

Commentary on "Better Communication between Engineers and Managers". Pritchard, Michael S.

Response to Michael Davis. Corrado, Michael.

# DAVIS, R

St. Bonaventure and the Demonstrability of a Temporal Beginning: A Reply to Richard Davis. Baldner, Steven.

# DAWSON, G

Comment on Dawson's 'Exit, Voice and Values in Economic Institutions'. Anderson, Elizabeth.

# DAYAKRISHNA

Approach of Hinduism to Its Scriptures. Nayak, G C.

# DE BEAUVOIR

*Philosophy as Passion: The Thinking of Simone de Beauvoir.* Vintges, Karen.

*The Philosophy of Simone de Beauvoir: Gendered Phenomenologies, Erotic Generosities.* Bergoffen, Debra B.

A Critique of Normative Heterosexuality: Identity, Embodiment, and Sexual Difference in Beauvoir and Irigaray. Schutte, Ofelia.

What is a Woman? Butler and Beauvoir on the Foundations of the Sexual Difference. Heinämaa, Sara.

# DE BENEDICTIS, G

La reazione a Cartesio nella Napoli del Seicento: Giovambattista De Benedictis. De Liguori, Girolamo.

# DE BOER, T

Denken in trouw aan leven en geloof. Van Tongeren, Paul.

# DE FINETTI, B

Bruno de Finetti and the Logic of Conditional Events. Milne, Peter.

De Finetti's Reconstruction of the Bayes-Laplace Paradigm. Regazzini, Eugenio.

Probabilism and Beyond. Galavotti, Maria Carla.

# DE HERRERA, A

Agustin de Herrera, A Treatise on Aleatory Probability *De Necessitate Morali in Genere.* Knebel, Sven K (ed & trans).

# DE LA CRUZ, J

Dos propuestas sobre epistemología y ciencia en el siglo XVII novohispano: Carlos de Sigüenza y Sor Juana Inés de la Cruz. Benítez G, Laura.

# DE MAISTRE, J

Voces mezcladas: Una reflexión sobre tradición y modernidad. Díaz-Urmeneta Muñoz, Juan Bosco.

# DE MAN, P

"A Revolution by Any Other Name" in *Philosophy of Education (1996),* Margonis, Frank (ed). Hutchinson, Jaylynne N.

"A Rhetorical Revolution for Philosophy of Education" in *Philosophy of Education (1996),* Margonis, Frank (ed). Stone, Lynda.

# DE MARBASIO, M

A Fragment of Michael de Marbasio, Summa de modis significandi. Kelly, L G.

# DE MUYNCK, W

Non-Locality: A Defense of Widespread Beliefs. Laudisa, Federico.

Still in Defence: A Short Reply on Non-Locality and Widespread Beliefs. Laudisa, Federico.

# DE RE

Sequence of Tense and Temporal De Re. Abusch, Dorit.

The Elimination of *De Re* Formulas. Kaminski, Michael.

**DE SANCTIS, F**
Grocio, por derecho. Pastor Pérez, Miguel Antonio.
Igualdad no es fraternidad. Pastor Pérez, Miguel Antonio.

**DE SAUSSERE, F**
Sobre algunos rasgos distintos del estructuralismo. Leiser, Eckart.

**DE SOUSA, R**
"Love and Intentionality: Roxane's Choice" in *Love Analyzed*, Lamb, Roger E. Campbell, Sue.

**DE VITORIA, F**
Alle origini dei diritti dell'uomo: i diritti della comunicazione di Francisco de Vitoria. Trujillo Pérez, Isabel.
El contraluz de Vitoria en el Siglo de las Luces. Ocaña García, Marcelino.
The Spanish School of the Sixteenth and Seventeenth Centuries: A Precursor of the Theory of Human Rights. García y García, Antonio.

**DEAF**
Letting the Deaf Be Deaf: Reconsidering the Use of Cochlear Implants in Prelingually Deaf Children. Crouch, Robert A.

**DEAFNESS**
Waarom het beoordelen van technologieën voor gehandicapten problematisch is. Blume, Stuart.

**DEAN, T**
Single-World versus Plural-World Antiessentialism: A Reply to Tim Dean. Dreyfus, Hubert L and Spinosa, Charles.

**DEATH**
see also Dying
"Death and Nothingness in Literature" in *The Ancients and the Moderns*, Lilly, Reginald (ed). Mohr, Heinrich.
"El sentido de la muerte en Fichte" in *El inicio del Idealismo alemán*, Market, Oswaldo. Cruz Cruz, Juan.
"Pro Patria Mori!: Death and the State" in *The Morality of Nationalism*, McKim, Robert (ed). Tamir, Yael.
*Death, Brain Death and Ethics*. Lamb, David.
*Ethical Issues in Death and Dying*. Beauchamp, Tom L (ed) and Veatch, Robert M (ed).
*Filosofia Criacionista da Morte: Meditaçao sobre o Problema da Morte No Pensamento Filosófico de Leonardo Coimbra*. Cândido Pimentel, Manuel.
*Immortality*. Edwards, Paul (ed).
*Intending Death: The Ethics of Assisted Suicide and Euthanasia*. Beauchamp, Tom L (ed).
*Kierkegaard and Nietzsche: Faith and Eternal Acceptance*. Kellenberger, J.
*Leben-und Sterbenkönnen: Gedanken zur Sterbebegleitung und zur Selbstbestimmung der Person*. Wettstein, R Harri.
*Organ Transplants and Ethics*. Lamb, David.
*Prescription: Medicine*. Kevorkian, Jack.
A Good Death—Oxymoron?. McCormick, Richard A.
A Good Death: Improving Care Inch-by-Inch. Ayers, Elise, Harrold, Joan and Lynn, Joanne.
Adieu. Derrida, Jacques.
Advocating for the Dying: The View of Family and Friends. Moretti, Anna M.
Amor e Morte: Meditaçao Antropológica. Pinto, José Rui da Costa.
An African American Looks at Death. Secundy, Marian Gray.
Buddhism as Radical Religion. Seidel, George J.
Conocimiento del alma después de la muerte: Presentación de la doctrina de Santo Tomás de Aquino expuesta en las *Quaestiones disputatae de veritate q. 19 a. 1*. Rodrigo Ewart, Luis.
Death and Philosophy—The Desire for Immortality among the Greeks (in Portuguese). Alves dos Santos, Maria Carolina.
Eugen Finks Phänomenologie des Todes. Schmidt, Gerhart.
Euthanasia. Mitra, Kumar.
Fred Feldman's *Confrontations with the Reaper: A Philosophical Study of the Nature and Value of Death*. Marquis, Don.
Goldilocks and Mrs. Ilych: A Critical Look at the "Philosophy of Hospice". Ackerman, Felicia.
Images of Death and Dying in the Intensive Care Unit. Pascalev, Assya.
Japanese Death Factories and the American Cover-Up. Chen, Yuan-Fang.
Japanese Psychiatrists' Attitudes toward Patients Wishing to Die in the General Hospital: A Cultural Perspective. Berger, Douglas, Takahashi, Yoshitomo and Fukunishi, Isao (& others).
Joy in Dying. Lingis, Alphonso F.
L'uomo superiore dopo la morte di Dio: Appunti di lettura. Campioni, Giuliano.
La muerte, ese escándalo. Pfeiffer, María Luisa.
La pauta del muro: re-convocaciones del pensamiento de José Echeverría. Kerkhoff, Manfred.
Le désir et la mort chez Pascal: Hypothèses pour une lecture. Bove, Laurent.
Love and Death in a Pediatric Intensive Care Unit. Miller, Richard B.
Martin Heidegger fra Misticismo e Nazionalsocialismo. Di Meola, Nestore.
Neighbors in Death. Crowell, Steven Galt.
Nietzsche "On Apostates" and Divine Laughter. Neeley, G Steven.
Nietzsche bei Heidegger und Fink. Ebeling, Hans.
November 4, 1995: Deleuze's Death as an Event. Colombat, André Pierre.
One Short Sleep Past?. Herbert, Robert T.
Para una fenomenología de la muerte. Iribarne, Julia V.

Personal Survival and the Closest-Continuer Theory. Johnson, Jeffery L.
Plato's *Phaedrus*: Philosophy as Dialogue with the Dead. Zwicky, Jan.
Rational Self-Interest and Fear of Death: An Argument for an Agency Theory in Hobbes' *Leviathan*. Von Eschenbach, Warren J.
Reflections on a Good Death: An Interview with Carl E. Flemister. Flemister, Carl E.
Santo Tomás de Aquino y la Medicina. Sacchi, Mario Enrique.
Still Here/Above Ground. Bartholome, William G.
Struggle. Miller, Patrick.
The Death of God and Hegel's System of Philosophy. Anderson, Deland.
The Nature of Transpersonal Experience. Beskova, Irina Aleksandrovna.
Theological Foundations for Death and Dying Issues. Hollinger, Dennis.
Thomas Mann e A Montanha Mágica. Joao Correia, Carlos.
Thoughts about the End-of-Life Decision-Making Process. Terry, Peter B.
Una ética para tiempos de luto. Echeverría, José.
What Kind of Life? What Kind of Death? An Interview with Dr. Henk Prins. Klotzko, Arlene Judith.
What Makes a Good Death?. Callahan, Daniel.
Zur Euthanasie-Diskussion in den USA: Eine kritische Einführung. Holderegger, Adrian.

**DEBATE**
La philosophie est un spectacle qu'on n'applaudit jamais mais qui tient l'affiche éternellement. Senécal, Jacques.

**DEBT**
State-Primacy and Third World Debt. Carter, Alan.
The Nation's Debt and the Birth of the Modern Republic: The French Fiscal Deficit and the Politics of the Revolution of 1789. Sonenscher, Michael.

**DECADENCE**
Hegel and the End of Art. Markus, György.
L'uomo superiore dopo la morte di Dio: Appunti di lettura. Campioni, Giuliano.
Nietzsche on Socrates as a Source of the Metaphysical Error. Harwood, Larry D.

**DECEIT**
Lying, Deceiving, or Falsely Implicating. Adler, Jonathan E.
The Ethics of Creative Accounting. Archer, Simon.

**DECEPTION**
see also Self-Deception
"Not-Being and Linguistic Deception" in *Dialogues with Plato*, Benitez, Eugenio (ed). O'Leary-Hawthorne, Diane.
Défense de la philosophie selon Pierre Abélard (in Serbo-Croatian). Deretic, Milena.
Lying, Deceiving, or Falsely Implicating. Adler, Jonathan E.
Not-Being and Linguistic Deception. O'Leary-Hawthorne, Diane.
Political Lying: A Defense. Newey, Glen.
The Morality of Adultery. Halwani, Raja.
The Rise and Fall of Deception in Social Psychology and Personality Research, 1921 to 1994. Korn, James H, Nicks, Sandra D and Mainieri, Tina.

**DECESION**
"La reflexión de la *proairesis* aristotélica" in *Ensayos Aristotélicos*, Aspe, Virginia. Cifuentes, Carlos Llano.

**DECIDABILITY**
A Constructive Game Semantics for the Language of Linear Logic. Japaridze, Giorgi.
A Finite Lattice without Critical Triple That Cannot Be Embedded into the Enumerable Turing Degrees. Lerman, Manuel and Lempp, Steffen.
All Free Metabelian Groups. Chapuis, Olivier.
Brouwer-Zadeh Logic, Decidability and Bimodal Systems. Giuntini, Roberto.
Completeness and Decidability of Tense Logics Closely Related to Logics Above K4. Wolter, Frank.
Decidability by Filtrations for Graded Normal Logics (Graded Modalities V). Cerrato, Claudio.
Decidability of *Stit* Theory with a Single Agent and *Refref* Equivalence. Xu, Ming.
Decidability of Finite Boolean Algebras with a Distinguished Subset Closed under Some Operations. Hanusek, Jerzy.
Decidability of the Two-Quantifier Theory of the Recursive Enumerable Weak Truth-Table Degrees and Other Distributive Semi-Lattices. Ambos-Spies, Klaus, Fejer, Peter A and Lempp, Steffen (& others).
Decidability Results for Metric and Layered Temporal Logics. Montanari, Angelo and Policriti, Alberto.
Decidable and Undecidable Logics with a Binary Modality. Németi, István, Kurucz, Agnes and Sain, Ildikó (& others).
Decidable Varieties of Hoops. Burris, Stanley and Ferreirim, Isabel M A.
Dual-Intuitionistic Logic. Urbas, Igor.
On a Decidable Generalized Quantifier Logic Corresponding to a Decidable Fragment of First-Order Logic. Alechina, Natasha.
Second Order Propositional Operators Over Cantor Space. Polacik, Tomasz.
Taming Logic. Marx, Maarten, Mikulás, Szabolcs and Németi, István.
The Structure of Lattices of Subframe Logics. Wolter, Frank.
The Theory of Integer Multiplication with Order Restricted to Primes is Decidable. Maurin, Françoise.
Théorie de la valuation. Da Costa, Newton C A and Béziau, Jean-Yves.

## DECISION

"El lugar de la decisión en la acción racional: de la decisión como deseo, cálculo y acto" in *La racionalidad: su poder y sus límites,* Nudler, Oscar (ed). Naishtat, Francisco.

"Vom Versuch angewandter Philosophie: Warum sich Philosophen mit Managern unterhalten" in *Werte und Entscheidungen im Management,* Schmidt, Thomas. Lohmann, Karl R.

"Zur Integration von Werten in Entscheidungen: Entscheidungsorientierung und eine liberale Theorie der Werte" in *Werte und Entscheidungen im Management,* Schmidt, Thomas. Lohmann, Karl R.

*Sexual Harassment: Confrontations and Decisions.* Wall, Edmund (ed).

*Werte und Entscheidungen im Management.* Schmidt, Thomas and Lohmann, Karl R.

A Test of a Person—Issue Contingent Model of Ethical Decision Making in Organizations. Harrington, Susan J.

Adolescent Parents and Medical Decision-Making. De Ville, Kenneth.

Advance Directives Outside the USA: Are They the Best Solution Everywhere?. Sanchez-Gonzalez, Miguel A.

Bargaining and Delay: The Role of External Information. Hyde, Charles E.

Bargaining with Incomplete Information: An Axiomatic Approach. Rosenmüller, Joachim.

Children, Society, and Health Care Decision Making. Caccamo, James M.

Clinical Pragmatism: A Method of Moral Problem Solving. Fins, Joseph J, Bacchetta, Matthew D and Miller, Franklin G.

Complexity of Ethical Decision Making in Psychiatry. Morenz, Barry and Sales, Bruce.

Congestion Models and Weighted Bayesian Potential Games. Faccini, Giovanni, Van Megen, Freek and Borm, Peter (& others).

Decision Theoretic Foundations for Axioms of Rational Preference. Hansson, Sven Ove.

Decision, Deliberation, and Democratic Ethos. Mouffe, Chantal.

Ethical Decision Making in Managed Care Environments. Ross, Judith Wilson.

Ethical Decision Making in Marketing: A Synthesis and Evaluation of Scales Measuring the Various Components of Decision Making in Ethical Situations. Vitell, Scott J and Ho, Foo Nin.

Ethical Decision Making: The Effects of Escalating Commitment. Street, Marc D, Robertson, Chris and Geiger, Scott W.

Exploring the Contextual and Individual Factors on Ethical Decision Making of Salespeople. Verbeke, Willem, Ouwerkerk, Cok and Peelen, Ed.

Forward Induction in Games with an Outside Option. Olcina, Gonzalo.

From "The Ethical Treatment of Patients in a Persistent Vegetative State" To a Philosophical Reflection on Contemporary Medicine. Lamau, M L, Cadore, B and Boitte, P.

Funciones no lineales de Bienestar social: ¿Tienen los economistas del Bienestar una exención especial de la racionalidad bayesiana?. Harsanyi, John C.

Gender Differences in Ethical Frameworks and Evaluation of Others' Choices in Ethical Dilemmas. Schminke, Marshall.

Identifying Ethical Problems Confronting Small Retail Buyers during the Merchandise Buying Process. Arbuthnot, Jeanette Jaussaud.

Il diritto tra decisione ed ordine: Brevi note su *I tre tipi di pensiero giuridico* di Carl Schmitt. Caserta, Marco.

In Defense of a Constructive, Information-Based Approach to Decision Theory. Yilmaz, M R.

Individual Autonomy and Collective Decisionmaking. Goldworth, Amnon.

Jury Wisdom: Norman J. Finkel, *Commonsense Justice: Juror's Notions of the Law.* Levine, James P.

Liberal Rationalism and Medical Decision-Making. Savulescu, Julian.

Managing Business Ethics and Opportunity Costs. Primeaux, Patrick and Stieber, John.

Minors and Health Care Decisions: Broadening the Scope. Frader, Joel.

Observer Judgements about Moral Agents' Ethical Decisions: The Role of Scope of Justice and Moral Intensity. Singer, Ming S and Singer, Alan E.

On Law and Logic. Alchourrón, Carlos E.

Parenting and the Best Interests of Minors. Downie, Robin S and Randall, Fiona.

People with Developmental Disabilities Focusing on Their Own Health Care. St Clair, Becky.

Persistent Vegetative State: Clinical and Ethical Issues. Celesia, Gastone G.

Re-Examining the Influence of Individual Values on Ethical Decision Making. Glover, Saundra H, Bumpus, Minnette A and Logan, John E (& others).

Reinforcing Ethical Decision Making Through Corporate Culture. Chen, Al Y S, Sawyers, Roby B and Williams, Paul F.

Respecting the Health Care Decision-Making Capacity of Minors. Strong, Carson.

Response to "Discounting Life Support in an Infant of a Drug Addicted Mother: Whose Decision Is It?" by Renu Jain and David C. Thomasma (CQ Vol 6, No 1). Oberman, Michelle.

Risk and the Value of Information in Irreversible Decisions. Gersbach, Hans.

Shared Decision Making: The Ethics of Caring and Best Respect. Beltran, Joseph E.

The Best-Interests Standard as Threshold, Ideal, and Standard of Reasonableness. Kopelman, Loretta M.

The Forms and Functions of Real-Life Moral Decision-Making. Krebs, Dennis L, Denton, Kathy and Wark, Gillian.

The Health Care Agent: Selected but Neglected. Lane, Arline and Dubler, Nancy Neveloff.

The Importance of Context: The Ethical Work Climate Construct and Models of Ethical Decision Making—An Agenda for Research. Wyld, David and Jones, Coy A.

The Importance of Process in Ethical Decision Making. Thornton, Barbara C.

The Invalid Advance Directive. Wenger, Neil S and FitzGerald, John.

The Organizational Bases of Ethical Work Climates in Lodging Operations as Perceived by General Managers. Upchurch, Randall S and Ruhland, Sheila K.

The Role of Minors in Health Care Decision Making: Current Legal Issues. Waxse, David J.

The Sure Thing Principle and the Value of Information. Schlee, Edward E.

The Two Envelope Paradox and Infinite Expectations. Arntzenius, Frank and McCarthy, David.

The Two-Envelope Paradox Resolved. McGrew, Timothy J, Shier, David and Silverstein, Harry S.

The Undecidability of the Spatialized Prisoner's Dilemma. Grim, Patrick.

Thoughts about the End-of-Life Decision-Making Process. Terry, Peter B.

Towards an Ethical Dimension of Decision Making in Organizations. Gottlieb, Jonathan Z and Sanzgiri, Jyotsna.

Uncertain Decisions and the Many-Minds Interpretation of Quantum Mechanics. Papineau, David.

Understanding and Structuring Complex Problems Within Organisational Contexts. Ostanello, A.

What's in the Two Envelope Paradox?. Scott, Alexander D and Scott, Michael.

Who Plays What Role in Decisions about Withholding and Withdrawing Life-Sustaining Treatment?. Reckling, JoAnn Bell.

## DECISION MAKING

Pascal's Wager Updated. Shoaf, Richard.

## DECISION PROCEDURE

"A Decision Method for Existential Graphs" in *Studies in the Logic of Charles Sanders Peirce,* Houser, Nathan (ed). Roberts, Don D.

A Decision Procedure for Von Wright's Obs-Calculus. Buekens, Filip.

Automated Theorem Proving for Lukasiewicz Logics. Beavers, Gordon.

Eliminating "Converse" from Converse PDL. De Giacomo, Giuseppe.

On the Decision Problem for Two-Variable First-Order Logic. Grädel, Erich, Kolaitis, Phokion G and Vardi, Moshe Y.

## DECISION THEORY

"Die Newcomb-Paradoxie—und ihre Lösung" in *Das weite Spektrum der analytischen Philosophie,* Lenzen, Wolfgang. Lenzen, Wolfgang.

"Ethik des Risikos" in *Angewandte Ethik: Die Bereichsethiken und ihre theoretische Fundierung,* Nida-Rümelin, Julian (ed). Nida-Rümelin, Julian.

*Making Choices: A Recasting of Decision Theory.* Schick, Frederic.

Correlated Strategies as Institutions. Arce M, Daniel G.

David Hume, David Lewis, and Decision Theory. Byrne, Alex and Hájek, Alan.

De Minimis and Equity in Risk. Mosler, Karl.

Ethics and Performance: A Simulation Analysis of Team Decision Making. Hunt, Tammy G and Jennings, Daniel F.

Interpersonal Dependency of Preferences. Nida-Rümelin, Julian, Schmidt, Thomas and Munk, Axel.

Joint Beliefs in Conflictual Coordination Games. Vanderschraaf, Peter and Richards, Diana.

Risk, Uncertainty and Hidden Information. Morris, Stephen.

Self-Interest, Autonomy, and the Presuppositions of Decision Theory. Thalos, Mariam.

Tempered Regrets Under Total Ignorance. Acker, Mary H.

## DECOHERENCE

Modal Interpretations, Decoherence and Measurements. Bacciagaluppi, Guido and Hemmo, Meir.

## DECOMPOSITION

Analytic Cell Decomposition and the Closure of $p$-ADIC Semianalytic Sets. Liu, Nianzheng.

## DECONSTRUCTION

"Anti-Meaning as Ideology: The Case of Deconstruction" in *Verstehen and Humane Understanding,* O'Hear, Anthony (ed). Grant, Robert.

"Deconstructing the Self on the Wild Side" in *Jean-Jacques Rousseau and the Sources of the Self,* O'Hagan, Timothy (ed). Wokler, Robert.

"Deconstruction and Pragmatism—Is Derrida a Private Ironist or a Public Liberal?" in *Deconstruction and Pragmatism,* Mouffe, Chantal (ed). Critchley, Simon.

"Deconstruction, Pragmatism and the Politics of Democracy" in *Deconstruction and Pragmatism,* Mouffe, Chantal (ed). Mouffe, Chantal.

"Deconstruction, Pragmatism, Hegemony" in *Deconstruction and Pragmatism,* Mouffe, Chantal (ed). Laclau, Ernesto.

"Epistemological Reversals between Chisholm and Lyotard" in *Philosophy of Education (1996),* Margonis, Frank (ed). Gunzenhauser, Michael G.

"Rationalität und Relativismus in den Geisteswissenschaften" in *Grenzen der kritischen Vernunft,* Schmid, Peter A. Haakonssen, Knud.

"Remarks on Deconstruction and Pragmatism" in *Deconstruction and Pragmatism,* Mouffe, Chantal (ed). Rorty, Richard.

## DEONTOLOGICAL

"Ethik des Risikos" in *Angewandte Ethik: Die Bereichsethiken und ihre theoretische Fundierung,* Nida-Rümelin, Julian (ed). Nida-Rümelin, Julian.

"Wert des Lebens" in *Angewandte Ethik: Die Bereichsethiken und ihre theoretische Fundierung,* Nida-Rümelin, Julian (ed). Nida-Rümelin, Julian.

## DEONTOLOGY

Algunos elementos para una deontología periodística. Rodríguez Ramírez, Carlos Alberto.

Consequentialism, Deontological Ethics, and Terrorism (in Serbo-Croatian). Jokic, Aleksandar.

Deontica in Rose Rand. Lorini, Giuseppe.

Die Moral des Rechts: Deontologische und konsequentialistische Argumentationen in Recht und Moral. Neumann, Ulfrid.

I metodi dell'etica di Henry Sidgwick. Lecaldano, Eugenio, Schneewind, J B and Vacatello, Marzio.

Identidade e Deontologia em Educaçao. Da Veiga, Manuel Alte.

L'Éthique et les Stress. Baertschi, Bernard.

The Influence of Deontological and Teleological Considerations and Ethical Climate on Sales Managers' Intentions to Reward or Punish Sales Force Behavior. DeConinck, James B and Lewis, William F.

## DEPENDENCE

Humphreys's Paradox and the Interpretation of Inverse Conditional Propensities. McCurdy, Christopher S I.

Reification as Dependence of Extrinsic Information. Sensat, Julius.

## DEPICTION

Essay: Kendall L. Walton, *Mimesis as Make-Believe.* Howell, Robert.

## DERIVABILITY

Valuational Semantics of Rule Derivability. Humberstone, I Lloyd.

## DERRIDA, J

"Deconstruction and Pragmatism—Is Derrida a Private Ironist or a Public Liberal?" in *Deconstruction and Pragmatism,* Mouffe, Chantal (ed). Critchley, Simon.

"Deconstruction, Pragmatism and the Politics of Democracy" in *Deconstruction and Pragmatism,* Mouffe, Chantal (ed). Mouffe, Chantal.

"Firing the Steel of Hermeneutics: Hegelianized versus Radical Hermeneutics" in *Hegel, History, and Interpretation,* Gallagher, Shaun. Caputo, John D.

"Keeping Foucault and Derrida in Sight: Panopticism and the Politics of Subversion" in *Sites of Vision,* Levin, David Michael (ed). Levin, David Michael.

"Neutrality in Education and Derrida's call for "Double Duty" in *Philosophy of Education (1996),* Margonis, Frank (ed). Egéa-Kuehne, Denise.

"Reclaiming Metaphysics for the Present: Postmodernism, Time, and American Thought" in *Philosophy in Experience: American Philosophy in Transition,* Hart, Richard (ed). Calore, Gary S.

"Remarks on Deconstruction and Pragmatism" in *Deconstruction and Pragmatism,* Mouffe, Chantal (ed). Rorty, Richard.

"Response to Simon Critchley" in *Deconstruction and Pragmatism,* Mouffe, Chantal (ed). Rorty, Richard.

"The Double-Bind of "Double Duty" in *Philosophy of Education (1996),* Margonis, Frank (ed). Davis, Hilary E.

"The Vulnerability of Democracy" in *Philosophy and Democracy in Intercultural Perspective,* Kimmerle, Heinz (ed). Hoogland, Jan.

"Una Disavventura Della Differenza: Heidegger e i "francesi" in *Soggetto E Verità: La questione dell'uomo nella filosofia contemporanea,* Fagiuoli, Ettore. Vaccaro, G Battista.

*Conversations with French Philosophers.* Aylesworth, Gary E (trans) and Rötzer, Florian.

*Das Multiversum der Kulturen.* Kimmerle, Heinz.

*Deconstruction in a Nutshell: A Conversation with Jacques Derrida.* Caputo, John D (ed).

*Feminist Interpretations of Jacques Derrida.* Holland, Nancy J (ed).

*Habermas and the Unfinished Project of Modernity.* Passerin d'Entrèves, Maurizio (ed) and Benhabib, Seyla (ed).

*Maurice Blanchot: The Demand of Writing.* Gill, Carolyn Bailey.

*Proper Names.* Smith, Michael B (trans) and Levinas, Emmanuel.

*The Prayers and Tears of Jacques Derrida Religion without Religion.* Caputo, John D.

A Community without Truth: Derrida and the Impossible Community. Caputo, John D.

A Critique of Pure Meaning: Wittgenstein and Derrida. Sonderegger, Ruth.

Between Emergence and Possibility: Foucault, Derrida, and Judith Butler on Performative Identity. Nealon, Jeffrey T.

Beyond Ironist Theory and Private Fantasy: A Critique of Rorty's Derrida. Ellsworth, Jonathan.

Deconstruction and Marxism: Jacques Derrida's Specters of Marx. Plangesis, Yannis.

Deconstruction and Pragmatism—Is Derrida a Private Ironist or a Public Liberal?. Critchley, Simon.

Deconstruction Deconstructed: The Resurrection of Being. Dunn Koblentz, Evelynn.

Derrida e la rivendicazione dello spirito del marxismo. Iofrida, Manlio.

Derrida's Watch/Foucault's Pendulum. Naas, Michael B.

Discutono *Il principio speranza,* di Ernst Bloch. Boella, Laura, Moneti, Maria and Schmidt, Burghart.

Emergence and Deconstruction (in Czech). Cibulka, Josef.

Fairy Tales for Politics: The Other, Once More. Cladwell, Anne.

Formal Contamination: A Reading of Derrida's Argument. Donkel, Douglas L.

Given Time and the Gift of Life. Protevi, John.

Heidegger and Derrida: On Play and Difference. Dastur, Françoise.

Infinity and the Relation: The Emergence of a Notion of Infinity in Derrida's Reading of Husserl. Maloney, Philip J.

L'état idéal de finitude chez Gadamer. Beaulieu, Alain.

Laughing at Hegel. Westphal, Merold.

Meaning, Truth and Phenomenology. Bevir, Mark.

Meyer Shapiro's Essay on Style: Falling into the Void. Wallach, Alan.

Much Obliged. Wood, David.

Openings: Derrida, *Différance,* and the Production of Justice. Manning, Robert J S.

Otra vuelta de tuerca: A propósito de *Espectros de Marx* de J. Derrida. Sucasas Peón, J Alberto.

Postmodernism: What One Needs to Know. Grassie, William.

Questions of Proximity: "Woman's Place" in Derrida and Irigaray. Armour, Ellen T.

Ragione e retorica: *La mitologia bianca* di Jacques Derrida. Harrison, Bernard.

Remissions on Jacques Derrida's Work (Spanish). Navarro, Rolando.

Rest for the Restless? Karl Rahner, Being, and the Evocation of Transcendence. Sanders, Theresa.

The Bacchanalian Revel: Hegel and Deconstruction. Haas, Andrew.

The Blessed Gods Mourn: What is Living-Dead in the Legacy of Hegel. Cutrofello, Andrew.

The Jewish Question Revisited: Marx, Derrida and Ethnic Nationalism. Hull, Gordon.

The Origins and Crisis of Continental Philosophy. Steinbock, Anthony J.

The Philosophy of the Limit and its Other. McCarthy, Thomas A.

This Project is Mad: Descartes, Derrida, and the Notion of Philosophical Crisis. Steiner, Gary.

Transcendental is the Difference: Derrida's Deconstruction of Husserl's Phenomenology of Language. Vila-Cha, Joao J.

Truth and Thickness. Tietz, John.

## DESCARTES

*see also* Cartesianism

"Analytic Geometry, Experimental Truth and Metaphysics in Descartes" in *Memorias Del Seminario En Conmemoración De Los 400 Anos Del Nacimiento De René Descartes,* Albis, Víctor S (ed). Laserna Pinzón, Mario.

"And so I Err and Sin": Considerations on Error in Descartes (Spanish). Díaz, Jorge Aurelio.

"Conocimiento y libertad" in *Memorias Del Seminario En Conmemoración De Los 400 Anos Del Nacimiento De René Descartes,* Albis, Víctor S (ed). Díaz, Jorge Aurelio.

"Contraintes socio-culturelles et conversions philosphiques chez Descartes..." in *Memorias Del Seminario En Conmemoración De Los 400 Anos Del Nacimiento De René Descartes,* Albis, Víctor S (ed). Mazhary, Djahanguir R.

"De la metafisica a la fisica en el programa cartesiano" in *Memorias Del Seminario En Conmemoración De Los 400 Anos Del Nacimiento De René Descartes,* Albis, Víctor S (ed). Cardona, Carlos Albert.

"Descartes's Scientific Illustrations and 'la grand mécanique de la nature'" in *Picturing Knowledge,* Baigrie, Brian S (ed). Baigrie, Brian S.

"Descartes, investigador matemático afortunado" in *Memorias Del Seminario En Conmemoración De Los 400 Anos Del Nacimiento De René Descartes,* Albis, Víctor S (ed). Campos, Alberto.

"How to Write the History of Vision: Understanding the Relationship between Berkeley and Descartes" in *Sites of Vision,* Levin, David Michael (ed). Atherton, Margaret L.

"La creación de las verdades eternas y la fábula del mundo" in *Memorias Del Seminario En Conmemoración De Los 400 Anos Del Nacimiento De René Descartes,* Albis, Víctor S (ed). Margot, Jean-Paul.

"La dudas de Descartes y el lenguaje privado" in *Memorias Del Seminario En Conmemoración De Los 400 Anos Del Nacimiento De René Descartes,* Albis, Víctor S (ed). Thompson, Garret.

"Mathesis universalis e inteligibilidad en Descartes" in *Memorias Del Seminario En Conmemoración De Los 400 Anos Del Nacimiento De René Descartes,* Albis, Víctor S (ed). Paty, Michel.

"Triangulating Divine Will: Henry More, Robert Boyle, and René Descartes on God's Relationship to the Creation" in *Mind Senior to the World,* Baldi, Marialuisa. Osler, Margaret J.

"¿Qué nos importa Descartes todavía?" in *Memorias Del Seminario En Conmemoración De Los 400 Anos Del Nacimiento De René Descartes,* Albis, Víctor S (ed). Serrano, Gonzalo.

"¿René Descartes, cientifista?" in *Memorias Del Seminario En Conmemoración De Los 400 Anos Del Nacimiento De René Descartes,* Albis, Víctor S (ed). Sierra, Guillermo Restrepo.

*Aprender a filosofar preguntando: con Platón, Epicuro, Descartes.* Echeverría, José.

*Cervello-Mente: Pensatori del XX secolo.* Gava, Giacomo.

*Descartes' Dualism.* Baker, Gordon and Morris, Katherine J.

*Descartes's Legacy: Minds and Meaning in Early Modern Philosophy.* Hausman, David B and Hausman, Alan.

## DESCARTES

*Matemáticas, método y* mathesis universalis *en las* Regulae *de Descartes.* Arenas, Luis.

*Memorias Del Seminario En Conmemoración De Los 400 Años Del Nacimiento De René Descartes.* Albis, Víctor S (ed), Charum, Jorge (ed) and Sánchez, Clara Helena (& others).

*Primeras Interpretaciones del Mundo en la Modernidad: Descartes y Leibniz.* Schneider, Martin.

*Ragione e Scrittura tra Descartes e Spinoza: Saggio sulla Philosophia S. Scripturae Interpres* di Lodewijk Meyer e sulla sua recezione. Bordoli, Roberto.

*Repräsentation bei Descartes.* Perler, Dominik.

*Trayectoria Voluntarista de la Libertad: Escoto, Descartes, Mill.* Alvarez-Valdés, Lourdes Gordillo.

A proposito di centenari cartesiani. Garin, Eugenio.

Abkehr vom Mythos: Descartes in der gegenwärtigen Diskussion. Perler, Dominik.

An Analysis of "Res cogitans". Almeida, Eduardo.

An Aspect of Love: Descartes on Friendship. Morgan, Vance G.

An Essay in Epistemic Kuklophobia: Husserl's Critique of Descartes' Conception of Evidence. Heffernan, George.

Analyse und Kontext des Wachsbeispiels bei Descartes. Petrus, Klaus.

Ancora sulla teoria vichiana del linguaggio: In margine ad alcune recenti pubblicazioni. Gensini, Stefano.

As Metamorfoses da Luz, ou a Retórica da Evidência na Filosofia Cartesiana. Ribeiro dos Santos, Leonel.

Believing That God Exists Because the Bible Says So. Lamont, John.

Brief Takes From the Horizon. Marcus, Jacqueline.

Cartesian Epistemics and Descartes' *Regulae*. Thomas, Bruce M.

Ces *Exercices Spirituels* Que Descartes Aurait Pratiqués. Hermans, Michel and Klein, Michel.

Cogito ergo sum como conculcación al axioma A. Merino, Magdalena.

Cognitive Homelessness. Williamson, Timothy.

Comentario a la *Represión de la metafísica de Renato Descartes, Benito Espinosa y Juan Locke*: Un añadido a la *Ciencia Nueva*. Verene, Donald Phillip.

Cómo resolver la problemática pirrónica: lo que se aprende de Descartes. Sosa, Ernesto.

Conoscenza metafisica dell'esistenza. Possenti, Vittorio.

Consideraçoes sobre o Problema da Verdade em Espinosa. Gleizer, Marcos André.

Constativas kantianas y realizativas cartesianas: el yo pienso como emisión realizativa. López Fernández, Alvaro.

Critical Thinking vs. Pure Thought. Coccia, Orestes.

De la liberté absolute: A propos de la théorie cartésienne de la création des vérités éternelles. Depré, Olivier.

De lo uno a lo otro: conocimiento, razón y subjetividad en Descartes. Arenas, Luis.

Denying the Body? Memory and the Dilemmas of History in Descartes. Reiss, Timothy J.

Descartes and Metaphysical Thought (in Czech). Sobotka, Milan.

Descartes and Other Minds. Avramides, Anita.

Descartes and the Communication of Passions (in Czech). Kambouchner, Denis.

Descartes Desconstruído. Loparic, Zeljko.

Descartes e os Jesuítas: Para um estudo da personalidade cartesiana. Dinis, Alfredo.

Descartes et la mélancholie. Darriulat, Jacques.

Descartes in the Context of Husserl's and Patocka's Phenomenology (in Czech). Major, Ladislav.

Descartes on Causation. Flage, Daniel E and Bonnen, Clarence A.

Descartes on God and the Laws of Logic. Tierno, Joel Thomas.

Descartes on Love and/as Error. Williston, Byron.

Descartes on the Power of "Ideas". Wagner, Stephen I.

Descartes on the Real Existence of Matter. Friedman, Michael.

Descartes según Leibniz. Silva de Choudens, José R.

Descartes y Hume: causalidad, temporalidad y existencia de Dios. Badía Cabrera, Miguel A.

Descartes' Secular Paradise: The Discourse on Method as Biblical Criticism. Soffer, Walter.

Descartes's Demon and the Madness of Don Quixote. Nadler, Steven.

Descartes's Dualism?. Baker, Gordon and Morris, Katherine J.

Descartes's Ontology. Chappell, Vere.

Descartes's Ontology of Thought. Nelson, Alan.

Descartes's Wax and the Typology of Early Modern Philosophy. Glouberman, Mark.

Descartes, Davidson and the Causal Impotence of Thought (in Czech). Hríbek, Tomás.

Descartes, El Argumento del Sueño. Zuluaga, Mauricio.

Descartes, Error, and the Aesthetic-Totality Solution to the Problem of Evil. Gilbertson, Mark.

Descartes: La Libertad de Pensamiento, Fundamento de La Moral Provisional. Madanes, Leiser.

Descartes: un nuevo modo de hacer filosofía. Corazón, Rafael.

Did he Walk with a Mask...? (in Czech). Dokulil, Milos.

Discours et Méthode. Boss, Gilbert.

Donald Davidson, Descartes and How to Deny the Evident. Gosselin, M.

Du bon sens le mieux partagé.... Lories, Danielle.

Dualism Intact. Swinburne, Richard.

E. Husserl and Descartes's Method of Doubt (in Czech). Sousedík, Stanislav.

El cartesianismo de la vida (La influencia de Descartes sobre la filosofía madura de Ortega y Gasset). Csejtei, Dezsö.

El mecanicismo como pardigma "exitoso". Coronado, Luis Guillermo.

Entrevistas: René Descartes, Cuatrocientos años de actualidad. Naishtat, Francisco.

Ergo Cogito. Struyker Boudier, C E M.

Esperienza e ragione nel convenzionalismo geometrico di Henri Poincaré. Fortino, Mirella.

Espinosa e o "Círculo Cartesiano". Gleizer, Marcos André.

Fichte, die sujektive Wende und der kartesianische Traum. Rockmore, Tom.

Formal Causation and the Explanation of Intentionality in Descartes. Schmitter, Amy M.

Foucault: *Da Morte do* Sujeito *Ao Sujeito da* Morte. Pereira Arêdes, José de Almeida.

Freedom, the Self and Epistemic Voluntarism in Descartes. Imlay, Robert A.

Fundamentación de la metafísica y gnoseología del sujeto en Descartes. Mayos, Gonçal.

Gegenstand und Methode in der Geschichte der Mathematik. Otte, Michael.

Genovesi e Cartesio. Marcialis, Maria Teresa.

God's Place in Descartes' Philosophy (in Spanish). Schöndorf, Harald.

Hobbes contra Descartes: A Questao da Substância Imaterial. Rocha, Ethel M.

How to Resolve the Pyrrhonian Problematic: A Lesson from Descartes. Sosa, Ernest.

Husserl's Phenomenology and its Relation to Descartes (in Czech). Bayerová, Marie.

Hyperbolic Doubt and "Machiavelism": The Modern Foundation of the Subject in Descartes (in French). Richir, Marc.

Il cartesianesimo matematico a Napoli. Gatto, Romano.

Individualism and Descartes. Ferraiolo, William.

L'analyse cartésienne et la construction de l'ordre des raisons. Timmermans, Benoît.

L'arrivo del *Discours* e dei *Principia,D in Italia: prime letture dei testi cartesiani a Napoli.* Lojacono, Ettore.

L'esthétique musicale de Descartes et le cartésianisme. Van Wymeersch, Brigitte.

La polémique de Malebranche contre Aristote et la philosophie scolastique. Gilson, Étienne.

La puissance propre de la volonté selon Pascal. Pécharman, Martine.

La teoría de las ideas de Descartes. Gomila Benejam, Antoni.

Las verdades del cuerpo cartesiano. Duque, Félix.

Le cogito ébloui ou la noèse sans noème. Dupuis, Michel.

Leitura Medieval e Moderna de Descartes. Gonçalves, Joaquim Cerqueira.

Lo que debemos considerar como principio del conocimiento para filosofar. Aguilar Espinosa, Gerardo.

Mathesis Universalis cartesiana. Villalobos, José.

Mechanism and Fracture in Cartesian Physics. Wilson, Mark.

Modal Voluntarism in Descartes's Jesuit Predecessors. Coombs, Jeffrey.

Note napoletante alle *Passioni dell'anima*. Serrapica, Salvatore.

Note su traduzioni manoscritte delle opere cartesiane. Guerrini, Luigi.

Note sulle polemiche antifrancesi di Vico. Agrimi, Mario.

O Modelo Psicofisiológico Cartesiano e o Materialismo das Luzes. Nascimento, Maria das Graças S.

On the Moral Philosophy of René Descartes: Or, How Morals are Derived from Method. Bagley, Paul J.

Ontological "Proofs" in Descartes and Sartre: God, the "I," and the Group. McBride, William L.

Passions of the Soul (in Czech). Descartes, René and Benes, Jiri (trans).

Patrizzi and Descartes (in Czech). Floss, Pavel.

Per una storia dei cartesiani in Italia: Avvertenza. Garin, Eugenio.

Philosophy and Egypt. Glouberman, Mark.

Pode o *Cogito* Ser Posto em Questao?. Landim Filho, Raul.

Por qué no Descartes? Tres razones de actualidad. Gómez, Angel Alvarez.

Reductionism and Nominalism in Descartes's Theory of Attributes. Nolan, Lawrence.

Scepticism and Criticism (in Polish). Hanuszewicz, Stanislaw.

Scepticism at the Time of Descartes. Popkin, Richard H.

Skepticism and Pyrotechnics. Kaplan, Mark.

Subjectivity in Descartes and Kant. Schwyzer, Hubert.

Sulla presenza di Descartes nella *Galleria di Minerva*. Crasta, Francesca Maria.

The Ghost in the Machine—Fights—the Last Battle for the Human Soul. Watson, Richard A.

The Ontological Status of Cartesian Natures. Nolan, Lawrence.

Théorie des préjugés selon Descartes et Gadamer. Ipperciel, Donald.

This Project is Mad: Descartes, Derrida, and the Notion of Philosophical Crisis. Steiner, Gary.

Transformaçao da Noçao de Beatitude em Descartes. Leopoldo e Silva, Franklin.

Über das Verhältnis von Algebra und Geometrie in Descartes'"Geometrie". Krämer, Sybille.

**DESCARTES**
Über das Verhältnis von Metaphysik und Physik bei Descartes. Hüttemann, Andreas.
Was Descartes an Individualist? A Critical Discussion of W. Ferraiolo's "Individualism and Descartes". Moya, Carlos J.

**DESCRIPTION**
Commentary on W.V. Quine's "Free Logic, Description, and Virtual Classes". Leblanc, Hughes.
Conceptions of Space—Time: Problems and Possible Solutions. Monk, Nicholas A M.
Contextos, Creencías y Anáforas. Ezcurdia, Maite.
Free Logic, Description, and Virtual Classes. Quine, Willard V.

**DESCRIPTIVE SET THEORY**
Boolean Operations, Borel Sets, and Hausdorff's Question. Dasgupta, Abhijit.
Louveau's Theorem for the Descriptive Set Theory of Internal Sets. Schilling, Kenneth and Zivaljevic, Bosko.
Mouse Sets. Rudominer, Mitch.
Some Applications of Coarse Inner Model Theory. Hjorth, Greg.
Strong Cardinals in the Core Model. Hauser, Kai and Hjorth, Greg.

**DESIGN**
*The Constitution of Good Societies.* Soltan, Karol Edward (ed) and Elkin, Stephen L (ed).

**DESIRE**
"And of That Other and Her Desire: The Embracing Language of Wallace Stevens" in *Critical Studies: Ethics and the Subject,* Simms, Karl (ed). Cleghorn, Angus.
"Blue Prints and Bodies: Paradigms of Desire in Pornography" in *Critical Studies: Ethics and the Subject,* Simms, Karl (ed). Brottman, Mikita.
"Constructing Love, Desire, and Care" in *Sex, Preference, and Family: Essays on Law and Nature,* Nussbaum, Martha C (ed). Nussbaum, Martha C.
"Desire and Desirability: Bradley, Russell and Moore versus Mill" in *Early Analytic Philosophy,* Tait, William W (ed). Gerrard, Steve.
"Is Love an Emotion?" in *Love Analyzed,* Lamb, Roger E. Green, O H.
"Jealousy and Desire" in *Love Analyzed,* Lamb, Roger E. Farrell, Daniel M.
"Love and Autonomy" in *Love Analyzed,* Lamb, Roger E. Lehrer, Keith.
"Love and Solipsism" in *Love Analyzed,* Lamb, Roger E. Langton, Rae.
Feminist Interpretations of Jacques Derrida. Holland, Nancy J (ed).
*Love Analyzed.* Lamb, Roger E.
*Morals Based on Needs.* Öhlsson, Ragnar.
*Mortals and Others: American Essays 1931-1935.* Russell, Bertrand and Ruja, Harry (ed).
*Sex, Love, and Friendship: Studies of the Society for the Philosophy of Sex and Love 1977-1992.* Soble, Alan (ed).
*Welfare, Happiness, and Ethics.* Sumner, L W.
Against Nagel: In Favor of a Compound Human Ergon. Christie, Juliette.
Ai margini del discorso poetico. Dell'Erba, Paola.
Ato e potência: implicaçoes éticas de uma doutrina metafísica. Perine, Marcelo.
Autonomy and Hierarchical Compatibilism. Jennings, Ian.
Beauty and Desire: Frans Hemsterhuis' Aesthetic Experiments. Sonderen, Peter C.
Belief, Desire and Motivation: An Essay in Quasi-Hydraulics. Lenman, James.
Deep Therapy. Clay, Diskin.
Desire for Happiness and the Commandments in the First Chapter of *Veritatis Splendor.* Melina, Livio.
Desires and Human Nature in J.S. Mill. Jenkins, Joyce L.
Eros e nostalgia: Ensaio sobre Freud. Nunes Correia, Carlos Joao.
Foucault's Attack on Sex-Desire. McWhorter, Ladelle.
Glück und Glas... Martha Nussbaum über die Zerbrechlichkeit des Guten im menschlichen Leben. Frede, Dorothea.
Il desiderio: precedenti storici e concettualizzazione platonica. Malo, Antonio.
Il problema del 'Desiderium naturale videndi Deum' nell'ottica tomista della partecipazione secondo la prospettiva di Cornelio Fabro. Nardone, Marco.
Love's Bitter Fruits: Martha C Nussbaum *The Therapy of Desire: Theory and Practice in Hellenistic Ethics.* Osborne, Catherine.
Obediential Potency, Human Knowledge, and the Natural Desire for God. Long, Steven A.
Paedophilia, Sexual Desire and Perversity. Spiecker, Ben and Steutel, Jan.
Plato's *Lysis:* A Socratic Treatise on Desire and Attraction. Reshotko, Naomi.
Powers of Desire: Deleuze and Mores. Schérer, René.
Pragmatism, Thomism, and the Metaphysics of Desire: Two Rival Versions of Liberal Education. Neiman, Alven.
Romantic Love and Sexual Desire. Ben-Ze'ev, Aaron.
Virtue as Knowledge: Objections from the Philosophy of Mind. Little, Margaret Olivia.

**DESMOND, W**
On the Nature of the Absolute: A Response to Desmond. Coolidge Jr, Francis P.

**DESPAIR**
*A Kantian Condemnation of Atheistic Despair: A Declaration of Dependence.* Kielkopf, Charles F.

La fonction libératrice du désespoir chez Eugen Drewermann. Saint-Germain, Christian.

**DESPOTISM**
"Les éléments démocratiques dans des proverbes gikouyou" in *Philosophy and Democracy in Intercultural Perspective,* Kimmerle, Heinz (ed). Wanjohi, Gerald J.

**DESTINY**
*A Western Approach to Reincarnation and Karma: Selected Lectures and Writings by Rudolf Steiner.* Querido, René (ed).
Deification in the *Summa Theologiae:* A Structural Interpretation of the *Prima Pars.* Williams, A N.
Reflections on Russia's Destiny in the Philosophical Work of Russian Romanticism. Abramov, A I.
The Conception of *Ming* in Early Confucian Thought. Slingerland, Ted.

**DETACHMENT**
A Simplified Form of Condensed Detachment. Bunder, M W.

**DETENTION**
Preventive Detention, Corrado, and Me. Davis, Michael.
Punishment, Quarantine, and Preventive Detention. Corrado, Michael.
Reductivism, Retributivism, and the Civil Detention of Dangerous Offenders. Wood, David.
Reply to Corrado. Davis, Michael.
Response to Michael Davis. Corrado, Michael.

**DETERMINACY**
*see* Indeterminacy

**DETERMINATION**
*see also* Self-Determination
Alertness and Determination: A Note on Moral Phenomenology. Wilson, John.
Superveniencia y determinación del contenido amplio. García-Carpintero, Manuel.
Underdetermination in Economics: The Duhem-Quine Thesis. Sawyer, K R, Beed, Clive and Sankey, H.

**DETERMINISM**
*see also* Fatalism, Indeterminism
"Ein drittes modallogisches Argument für den Determinismus: Alexander von Aphrodisias" in *Das weite Spektrum der analytischen Philosophie,* Lenzen, Wolfgang. Weidemann, Hermann.
*Analytical Marxism: A Critique.* Roberts, Marcus.
*Life Contemplative, Life Practical: An Essay on Fatalism.* Eilstein, Helena.
Ancora su nuvole ed orologi. Messeri, Marco.
Authentische Entscheidungen und emotive Neurowissenschaft. Walter, Henrik.
Determinism and Locality in Quantum Systems. Dickson, W Michael.
Die Freiheit des Deterministen: Chaos und Neurophilosophie. Walter, Henrik.
Discutono *Il caso domato,* di Ian Hacking. Dessì, Paola, Sassoli, Bernardo and Sklar, Lawrence.
Freedom without Determinism: Decent Logics of Relevance and Necessity Applied to Problems of Free-Will. Sylvan, Richard.
Honderich on the Consequences of Determinism. Double, Richard.
Il problema del realismo tra meccanica quantistica e relatività speciale. Dorato, Mauro.
Is the See-Battle About to Be Lost? On Aristotle's *De interpretatione,* Ch. 9. A Reconstruction (in Czech). Cziszter, Kálmán.
Karl Popper y la crítica al determinismo. Bonetti, José Andrés.
La contradiction du stoïcisme. Gobry, Ivan.
Laplace's Demon Consults an Oracle: The Computational Complexity of Prediction. Pitowsky, Itamar.
Methods and Systematic Reflections: Unitary States, Free Will and Ultimate Reality. Newberg, Andrew B.
Moral Responsibility and Leeway for Action. Wyma, Keith D.
Rethinking Leibniz. Parkinson, G H R.
Tellurische Teleologie oder Determinismus und Freiheit Carl Ritters natürliches System einer sittlichen Welt. Beck, Günther.
The Bell Inequalities and all that. Bunge, Mario.
The Origin of Stoic Fatalism. Pierris, A L.
Time, Quantum Mechanics, and Tense. Saunders, Simon.
Transition Chances and Causation. Arntzenius, Frank.
Vernunft als Epiphänomen der Naturkausalität: Zu Herkunft und Bedeutung des ursprünglichen Determinismus J.G. Fichtes. Wildfeuer, Armin G.
Zwischen äusserem Zwang und innerer Freiheit. Aschoff, Frank.
'Beyond Determinism'. Spurrett, David.

**DETERMINISTIC**
Algebra and Theory of Order-Deterministic Pomsets. Rensink, Arend.

**DEUTSCH, D**
A New Grandfather Paradox?. Sider, Theodore.
'Many Minds' Interpretations of Quantum Mechanics: Replies to Replies. Lockwood, Michael.

**DEVELOPING COUNTRIES**
Can Foreign Aid Be Used to Promote Good Government in Developing Countries?. Moore, Mick and Robinson, Mark.
Ethics in Developing Economies of Asia. Takahashi, Akira.

**DEVELOPMENT**

*see also* Self-Development

"African Consensus Democracy Revisited" in *Philosophy and Democracy in Intercultural Perspective,* Kimmerle, Heinz (ed). Uyanne, Francis U.

"Ethical Elements in a Democratic State: Tanzania" in *Philosophy and Democracy in Intercultural Perspective,* Kimmerle, Heinz (ed). Kente, Maria G.

"Philosophy in America: Recovery and Future Development" in *The Recovery of Philosophy in America: Essays in Honor of John Edwin Smith,* Kasulis, Thomas P (ed). Smith, John E.

"Sozio-ökonomische Entwicklung unter humanitären Kriterien als Friedens-postulat" in *Kreativer Friede durch Begegnung der Weltkulturen,* Beck, Heinrich (ed). Pichler, Hanns.

"Temporalità e storicità" in *Il Concetto di Tempo: Atti del XXXII Congresso Nazionale della Società Filosofica Italiana,* Casertano, Giovanni (ed). Seidl, Horst.

*Ethics and Economic Progress.* Buchanan, James M.

Against Education. Nordenbo, Sven Erik.

Aristotle's *Child*: Development Through *Genesis, Oikos,* and *Polis.* McGowan Tress, Daryl.

Business Ethics in the Former Soviet Union: A Report. Neimanis, George J.

Child's Play. Nersessian, Nancy J.

Cognitive Moral Development and Attitudes Toward Women Executives. Everett, Linda, Thorne, Debbie and Danehower, Carol.

Concepts of Moral Management and Moral Maximization. Sikula, Sr, Andrew.

Critical Thinking and Foundational Development. Van Haaften, Wouter and Snik, Ger.

Cultura y Desarrollo Global. Dallmayr, Fred R.

Dynamical Systems in Development: Review Essay of Linda V. Smith and Esther Thelen (Eds) *A Dynamics Systems Approach to Development: Applications.* Hooker, Cliff A.

Educational Assessment: Reply to Andrew Davis. Winch, Christopher and Gingell, John.

Educational Psychologists as Trainers for Intellectual Development. Hartman, Hope J.

Función, plan y proyecto. Llano Cifuentes, Carlos.

Influencing Ethical Development: Exposing Students to the AICPA Code of Conduct. Green, Sharon and Weber, James.

Kohlberg's Dormant Ghosts: The Case of Education. Oser, Fritz K.

Literary Development as Spiritual Development in the Common School. Newby, Mike.

Marx on Full and Free Development. Jenkins, Joyce L.

Sustainable Development and the Local Justice Framework. Roe, Emery.

The Dying Vine. Mawby, Ronald.

The Measure of Morality: Rethinking Moral Reasoning. Vine, Ian.

The Perceived Role of Ethics and Social Responsibility: A Scale Development. Singhapakdi, Anusorn, Vitell, Scott J and Rallapalli, Kumar C.

The Scientist as Child. Gopnik, Alison.

Unity and Development: Social Homogeneity, the Totalitarian Imaginary, and the Classical Marxist Tradition. Louw, Stephen.

Using Computer-Assisted Instruction and Developmental Theory to Improve Argumentative Writing. Irwin, Ronald R.

Using Moral Dilemmas in Children's Literature as a Vehicle for Moral Education and Teaching Reading Comprehension. Clare, Lindsay, Gallimore, Ronald and Patthey-Chavez, G Genevieve.

**DEVILLE, K**

Children and Bioethics: Uses and Abuses of The Best-Interest Standard: Introduction. Kopelman, Loretta M.

**DEVITT, M**

What Does Commonsense Psychology Tell Us about Meaning?. Richard, Mark.

**DEWEY**

"Aesthetic Form Revisited: John Dewey's Metaphysics of Art" in *Philosophy in Experience: American Philosophy in Transition,* Hart, Richard (ed). Marsoobian, Armen T.

"Dewey on Virtue" in *Philosophy of Education (1996),* Margonis, Frank (ed). Smith, Timothy H.

"Dewey Without Doing" in *Philosophy of Education (1996),* Margonis, Frank (ed). Arnstine, Donald.

"Dewey's Conception of "Virtue" and its Educational Implications" in *Philosophy of Education (1996),* Margonis, Frank (ed). Rice, Suzanne.

"Dewey's Critique of Democratic Visual Culture and its Political Implications" in *Sites of Vision,* Levin, David Michael (ed). Ezrahi, Yaron.

"Dewey's Idea of Sympathy and the Development of the Ethical Self: A Japanese Perspective" in *Philosophy of Education (1996),* Margonis, Frank (ed). Saito, Naoko.

"John Dewey's Naturalization of William James" in *The Cambridge Companion to William James,* Putnam, Ruth Anna (ed). Gale, Richard M.

"Moral Dimensions of Classroom Discourse: A Deweyan Perspective" in *Philosophy of Education (1996),* Margonis, Frank (ed). Rosner, Fay.

"Moral Reflection and Moral Education" in *Philosophy of Education (1996),* Margonis, Frank (ed). Covaleskie, John F.

"Nature as Culture: John Dewey's Pragmatic Naturalism" in *Environmental Pragmatism,* Light, Andrew (ed). Hickman, Larry A.

"Taking the Risk of Essence: A Deweyan Theory in Some Feminist Conversations" in *Knowing Other-Wise: Philosophy at the Threshold of Spirituality,* Olthuis, James H (ed). Hart, Carroll Guen.

*John Dewey: Scienza, prassi, democrazia.* Alcaro, Mario.

Clinical Pragmatism: A Method of Moral Problem Solving. Fins, Joseph J, Bacchetta, Matthew D and Miller, Franklin G.

Community of Inquiry and Differences of the Heart. Thomas, John C.

Democracy and the Individual: To What Extent is Dewey's Reconstruction Nietzsche's Self-Overcoming?. Sullivan, Shannon.

Dewey and Moore on the Science of Ethics. Welchman, Jennifer.

Dewey's Conception of "Virtue" and its Implications for Moral Education. Rice, Suzanne.

Dewey's Moral Theory: Experience as Method. Pappas, Gregory Fernando.

Dewey, Quine, and Pragmatic Naturalized Epistemology. Capps, John.

John Dewey's Legal Pragmatism. Hill, H Hamner.

La paradoja del Taxidermista: Una ilustración negativa del juicio práctico deweyano. Catalán, Miguel.

Moral Theory and the Reflective Life. Rosenbaum, Stuart E.

Remembering John Dewey and Sidney Hook. Rorty, Richard.

The "Extreme Heresy" of John Dewey and Arthur F. Bentley I: A Star Crossed Collaboration?. Ryan, Frank X.

The Ties of Communication: Dewey on Ideal and Political Democracy. Festenstein, Matthew.

Theory and Practice in the Experience of Art: John Dewey and the Barnes Foundation. Glass, Newman Robert.

Unity and Diversity through Education: A Comparison of the Thought of W.E.B. DuBois and John Dewey. Burks, Ben.

**DHARMA**

Religion and Politics in India: Some Philosophical Perspectives. Perrett, Roy W.

The Spriritual Dimension of Gandhi's Activism. Spretnak, Charlene.

'rnam krtvā ghrtam pibet'—Who Said This?. Bhattacharya, Ramkrishna.

**DHILLON, P**

"Epistemological Reversals between Chisholm and Lyotard" in *Philosophy of Education (1996),* Margonis, Frank (ed). Gunzenhauser, Michael G.

**DIAGONAL**

Combining Temporal Logic Systems. Finger, Marcelo and Gabbay, Dov.

Constructing Cantorian Counterexamples. Boolos, George.

**DIAGONALIZATION**

Undecidability in Diagonalizable Algebras. Shavrukov, V Yu.

**DIAGRAM**

"The Interconnectedness of Peirce's Diagrammatic Thought" in *Studies in the Logic of Charles Sanders Peirce,* Houser, Nathan (ed). Kent, Beverley.

"What is Deduction?" in *Studies in the Logic of Charles Sanders Peirce,* Houser, Nathan (ed). Crombie, E James.

Indexical Reference and Bodily Causal Diagrams in Intentional Action. Castañeda, Héctor-Neri.

Towards a Model Theory of Diagrams. Hammer, Eric and Danner, Norman.

**DIALECTIC**

"Accounting for Transformations in the Dialectical Reconstruction of Argumentative Discourse" in *Logic and Argumentation,* Van Eemeren, Frans H (ed). Van Rees, M Agnès.

"Developments in Argumentation Theory" in *Logic and Argumentation,* Van Eemeren, Frans H (ed). Van Eemeren, Frans H and Grootendorst, Rob.

"Emergence and Embodiment: A Dialectic within Process" in *The Recovery of Philosophy in America: Essays in Honor of John Edwin Smith,* Kasulis, Thomas P (ed). Hocking, Richard.

"Fichte und das Problem der Dialektik" in *Sein—Reflexion—Freiheit: Aspekte der Philosophie Johann Gottlieb Fichtes,* Asmuth, Christoph (ed). Hammacher, Klaus.

"Fichtes frühe Wissenschaftslehre als dialektische Erörterung" in *Sein—Reflexion—Freiheit: Aspekte der Philosophie Johann Gottlieb Fichtes,* Asmuth, Christoph (ed). Krämer, Felix.

"Sophistry, Dialectic, and Teacher Education: A Reinterpretation of Plato's *Meno*" in *Philosophy of Education (1996),* Margonis, Frank (ed). Boyles, Deron R.

*Dialectical Readings: Three Types of Interpretation.* Dunning, Stephen N.

A Concepçao de Filosofia em Adorno. Cordeiro Silva, Rafael.

A Dialéctica da Acçao em L'Action (1893) de Maurice Blondel. Morujao, Alexandre Fradique.

A World of Difference: The Rich State of Argumentation Theory. Van Eemeren, Frans H.

Absolutes Denken: Neuere Interpretationen der Hegelschen Logik. Quante, Michael.

Art as a Form of Negative Dialectics: 'Theory' in Adorno's *Aesthetic Theory.* Melaney, William D.

Chvostism and Dialectics (Introduced and Commentaries by László Illés) (in Hungarian). Lukács, Georg.

Défense de la philosophie selon Pierre Abélard (in Serbo-Croatian). Deretic, Milena.

Dialéctica e História em J.P. Sartre. Reimao, Cassiano.

Dialectics and Rhetoric in Peter Abelard (in Portuguese). Pires Da Silva, Joao Carlos Salles.

Eine auch sich selbst missverstehende Kritik: Über das reflexionsdefizit formaler Explikationen. Wandschneider, Dieter.

Ética y dialéctica: Sócrates, Platón y Aristóteles. Yarza, Ignacio.

Fra filologia e storiografia: progetti di edizioni settecentesche. Generali, Dario.

Gewirth und die Begründung der normativen Ethik. Steigleder, Klaus.

# DIALECTIC
Graham Priest's "Dialectheism"—Is It Altogether True?. Peña, Lorenzo.

L'Esprit absolu de Hegel est-il Dieu?. Beauvais, Chantal.

La dialéctica de lo universal y lo particular y el ideal de la abolición del estado (Segunda parte). Salas, Mario.

La didáctica de la filosofía en Italia. Sánchez Huertas, María José.

La funció crítica de la "inventio" i el "iudicium" en la *Dialèctica de Petrus Ramus*. Grau i Arau, Andrés.

Lässt sich der Begriff der Dialektik klären?. Puntel, Lorenz.

Merleau-Ponty's Phenomenology as a Dialectical Philosophy of Expression. Mancini, Sandro.

Naturaleza/cultura: Un enfoque estético. Ramírez, Mario Teodoro.

Notas sobre modernidade e sujeito na dialética do esclarecimento. Duarte, Rodrigo A P.

Para uma Explicitaçao da Dialética Hegeliana entre o Senhor e o Escravo na Fenomenologia do Espírito. Ferreira Chagas, Eduardo.

Phenomenology of Spirit and Logic (in French). Lécrivain, André.

Ramistische Spuren in Leibniz' Gestaltung der Begriffe ‚dialectica', ‚topica' und ‚ars inveniendi'. Varani, Giovanna.

Reason as Antithesis: Dialectical Theology and the Crisis of Modern Culture. Lazich, Michael C.

Response. Goldstick, Danny.

Some Comments on Dialectical and Logical Contradictions. Marquit, Erwin.

Textuality and Imagination: The Refracted Image of Hegelian Dialectic. Schalow, Frank.

The Heritage of Léon Brunschvicg (and Commentary by P. Horák) (in Czech). Rivenc, François and Horák, Petr.

The Principle of Vulnerability. Johnson, Ralph H.

The Right to Life and the Death Penalty (Spanish). Papacchini, Angelo.

The Tragedy of Lukács and the Problem of Alternatives (in Hungarian). Mészáros, István.

Using Computer-Assisted Instruction and Developmental Theory to Improve Argumentative Writing. Irwin, Ronald R.

# DIALECTICAL
*Applied Social Sciences in the Plutocratic Era of the United States: Dialectics of the Concrete.* Schindler, Ronald Jeremiah.

# DIALECTICAL MATERIALISM
*see also* Historical Materialism

O Materialismo Histórico e Dialético nas Abordagens de Vigotsky e Wallon acerca do Pensamento e da Linguagem. Marques Veríssimo, Mara Rúba Alves.

# DIALOGUE
"Can we Ever Pin One Down to a Formal Fallacy?" in *Logic and Argumentation,* Van Eemeren, Frans H (ed). Krabbe, Erik C W.

"The Straw Man Fallacy" in *Logic and Argumentation,* Van Eemeren, Frans H (ed). Walton, Douglas.

*Dialogues with Plato.* Benitez, Eugenio E (ed).

*On Dialogue.* Nichol, Lee (ed) and Bohm, David.

*The Art of Plato: Ten Essays in Platonic Interpretation.* Rutherford, R B.

*The Dialogues of Plato: Volume I.* Jowett, Benjamin.

*The Dialogues of Plato: Volume II.* Jowett, Benjamin.

*The Dialogues of Plato: Volume III.* Jowett, Benjamin.

*The Dialogues of Plato: Volume IV.* Jowett, Benjamin.

*The Dialogues of Plato: Volume V.* Jowett, Benjamin.

*The Martin Buber-Carl Rogers Dialogue: A New Transcript with Commentary.* Anderson, Rob and Cissna, Kenneth N.

*The Play of the Platonic Dialogues.* Freydberg, Bernard.

Argumentation, Education and Reasoning. Binkley, Robert W.

Concerning Saint Augustine's *De Magistro* (in Portuguese). Abreu, Joao Azevedo.

É legítimo o Uso da Literatura no Processo de Transmissao da Filosofia?. Henriques, Fernanda.

Filosofia e Estilo Literário em Heidegger e em Platao: Um Exemplo. Borges-Duarte, Irene.

Foucault, Ethics and Dialogue. Gardiner, Michael.

Heidegger, escritor de diálogos: ¿Recuperación de una forma literaria de la Filosofía?. Borges-Duarte, Irene.

On the Aims and Effects of Platonic Dialogues. Rist, John M.

Plato's *Phaedrus*: Philosophy as Dialogue with the Dead. Zwicky, Jan.

Plato's First Dialogue. Tomin, Julius.

Structures of Natural Reasoning within Functional Dialogues. Trognon, Alain and Grusenmeyer, Corinne.

Who Speaks? Who Writes? Dialogue and Authorship in the *Phaedrus*. Burke, Seán.

# DIAMOND, C
Metaphysics and Nonsense: On Cora Diamond's *The Realistic Spirit*. Goldfarb, Warren.

The 'Late Seriousness' of Cora Diamond. Lovibond, Sabina.

# DIARY
Diary: Written by Professor Dr. Gottlob *Frege in the Time from 10 March to 9. April 1924*. Mendelsohn, Richard L (ed & trans), Gabriel, Gottfried (ed) and Kienzler, Wolfgang (ed).

# DICARO, A
*Oltre Wittgenstein.* Di Caro, Alessandro.

# DICKIE, G
The Intentional Fallacy: Defending Myself. Carroll, Noël.

# DICTATORSHIP
The 'Volatile' Marxian Concept of the Dictatorship of the Proletariat. Barany, Zoltan.

# DICTIONARY
*Dictionary of Philosophy and Religion: Eastern and Western Thought.* Reese, William L.

# DIDEROT
Dramaturgy of Picture (Essay on Diderot's *The Natural Child*) (in Portuguese). De Matos, Franklin.

The Fool's Truth: Diderot, Goethe, and Hegel. Schmidt, James.

# DIFFERANCE
Formal Contamination: A Reading of Derrida's Argument. Donkel, Douglas L.

Openings: Derrida, *Différance*, and the Production of Justice. Manning, Robert J S.

# DIFFERENCE
"Deconstructing "Difference" and the Difference This Makes to Education" in *Philosophy of Education (1996)*, Margonis, Frank (ed). Burbules, Nicholas C.

"Differences: Indifference or Dialogue" in *Philosophy, Religion, and the Question of Intolerance,* Ambuel, David (ed). Conway, Gertrude D.

"Humpty Dumpty An Ovular Model of Resistance to Modernist Recidivism" in *Philosophy of Education (1996)*, Margonis, Frank (ed). Morgan, Kathryn Pauly.

"Una Disavventura Della Differenza: Heidegger e i "francesi" in *Soggetto E Verità: La questione dell'uomo nella filosofia contemporanea,* Fagiuoli, Ettore. Vaccaro, G Battista.

*Reconsidering Difference.* May, Todd.

*Transgressing Discourses: Communication and the Voice of Other.* Huspek, Michael (ed) and Radford, Gary P (ed).

*W.E.B. Du Bois on* Race and Culture. Grosholz, Emily (ed), Bell, Bernard W (ed) and Stewart, James B (ed).

A Non-Splitting Theorem for d.r.e. Sets. Yi, Xiaoding.

Bergson: The Philosophy of *Durée-Différence*. Mullarkey, John C.

Between Fact and Fiction: Dialogue within Encounters of Difference. Conle, Carola.

Desigualdades de Bienestar y axiomática rawlsiana. Sen, Amartya K.

Difference and Consensus. Luksic, Branimir.

Heidegger and Derrida: On Play and Difference. Dastur, Françoise.

Interrogative Wh-Movement in Slovene and English. Golden, Marija.

Irigaray Anxiety: Luce Irigaray and Her Ethics for Improper Selves. Deutscher, Penelope.

Is There a Natural Sexual Inequality of Intellect? A Reply to Kimura. Foss, Jeffrey E.

L'essere, il nulla e il divenire: Riprendendo le fila di una grande polemica. Turoldo, Fabrizio.

La noción de inconmensurabilidad y la realidad de los otros o el derecho a la diferencia. López Gil, Marta.

Reclaiming the Borderlands: Chicana/o Identity, Difference, and Critical Pedagogy. Elenes, C Alejandra.

Reflections on Cultural Difference and Advance Directives. Michel, Vicki.

The Birth of Difference. Schües, Christina.

The Ideology and Biology of Gender Difference. Rhode, Deborah L.

The Ontological Difference. Nicholson, Graeme.

The Politics of Difference: Statehood and Toleration in a Multicultural World. Walzer, Michael.

What is a Woman? Butler and Beauvoir on the Foundations of the Sexual Difference. Heinämaa, Sara.

Zur Fichte-Darstellung in Hegels *Differenzschrift*. Kiss, Endre.

# DIGITAL
Analog Representation Beyond Mental Imagery. Blachowicz, James.

Escaping Reality: Digital Imagery and the Resources of Photography. Savedoff, Barbara E.

The Vitality of Digital Creation. Binkley, Timothy.

# DIGNITY
*Dignity and Dying: A Christian Appraisal.* Miller, Arlene B (ed), Kilner, John F (ed) and Pellegrino, Edmund D (ed).

La dignidad del hombre y la dignidad de la persona. Forment, Eudaldo.

La dignidad humana desde una perspectiva metafísica. Lobato, Abelardo.

Maurice Blondel: A Philosopher of Tolerance and Human Dignity. Lasic, Hrvoje.

Renaissance and Human Nature: Pico's "Dignity of Man". Dominioni, Stefano.

The Humanism of Sartre: Toward a Psychology of Dignity. Iuculano, John and Burkum, Keith.

# DILEMMA
Hard Cases and Moral Dilemmas. Statman, Daniel.

Publishing Programs and Moral Dilemmas. I Iorowitz, Irving Louis.

Slote on Rational Dilemmas and Rational Supererogation. Mintoff, Joe.

The Mysterious Grand Properties of Forrest. Noordhof, Paul.

The Real Issues Concerning Dirty Hands—A Response to Kai Nielsen. De Wijze, Stephen.

# DILLER, A
"But That Is Not What I Mean" Criticizing With Care and Respect" in *Philosophy of Education (1996)*, Margonis, Frank (ed). Applebaum, Barbara.

Replies. Scheffler, Israel.

## DISTRIBUTION

A Proposal for a New System of Credit Allocation in Science. Resnik, David B.

A Type Free Theory and Collective/Distributive Predication. Kamareddine, Fairouz.

Alfred Schutz on the Social Distribution of Knowledge. Nnoruka, Sylvanos I.

Aristotle and Fair Admissions. Cordero, Ronald A.

Finite Distributive Lattices as Sums of Boolean Algebras. Kotas, Jerzy and Wojtylak, Piotr.

Hayek's Political Philosophy and His Economics. Friedman, Jeffrey.

Journals and Justice. Curzer, Howard J.

Let Them Eat Chances: Probability and Distributive Justice. Wasserman, David.

Redistributive Taxation, Self-Ownership and the Fruit of Labour. Michael, Mark A.

The Lattice of Distributive Closure Operators Over an Algebra. Font, Josep Maria and Verdú, Ventura.

Unbundling the Moral Dispute About Unbundling in South Africa. Rossouw, Gedeon J.

## DISTRIBUTIVE JUSTICE

"Sozio-ökonomische Entwicklung unter humanitären Kriterien als Friedenspostulat" in *Kreativer Friede durch Begegnung der Weltkulturen*, Beck, Heinrich (ed). Pichler, Hanns.

*Theories of Distributive Justice*. Roemer, John E.

Moral Constraints and Justice in Distribution (in Czech). Nozick, Robert.

Persona Moral y Justicia Distributiva. Bertomeu, María Julia and Vidiella, Graciela.

Where the Action Is: On the Site of Distributive Justice. Cohen, G A.

## DISTRIBUTIVITY

Combinatorics and Forcing with Distributive Ideals. Matet, Pierre.

## DIVERSIFICATION

Risk and Diversification in Theory Choice. Rueger, Alexander.

## DIVERSITY

"All in the Family and In All Families: Membership, Loving, and Owing" in *Sex, Preference, and Family: Essays on Law and Nature*, Nussbaum, Martha C (ed). Minow, Martha.

"Differences: Indifference or Dialogue" in *Philosophy, Religion, and the Question of Intolerance*, Ambuel, David (ed). Conway, Gertrude D.

"Disagreement: Appreciating the Dark Side of Tolerance" in *Philosophy, Religion, and the Question of Intolerance*, Ambuel, David (ed). Langerak, Edward.

"Research Universities: Overextended, Underfocused; Overstressed, Underfunded" in *The American University: National Treasure or Endangered Species?*, Ehrenberg, Ronald G (ed). Vest, Charles M.

*A Pluralistic Universe*. Levinson, Henry Samuel and James, William.

*African-American Perspectives and Philosophical Traditions*. Pittman, John P (ed).

*Diversity and Community in the Academy: Affirmative Action in Faculty Appointments*. Wolf-Devine, Celia.

*Ethical Norms, Particular Cases*. Wallace, James D.

*Reasonable Children: Moral Education and Moral Learning*. Pritchard, Michael S.

*Structure and Diversity: Studies in the Phenomenological Philosophy of Max Scheler*. Kelly, Eugene.

Bayesianism and Diverse Evidence: A Reply to Andrew Wayne. Myrvold, Wayne C.

Bayesianism and the Value of Diverse Evidence. Steel, Daniel.

Biodiversity as the Source of Biological Resources: A New Look at Biodiversity Values. Wood, Paul M.

Centering Culture: Teaching for Critical Sexual Literacy using the Sexual Diversity Wheel. Sears, James T.

Che cosa ha veramente detto il Comitato Nazionale per la Bioetica sull'individualità dell'embrione?. Mori, Maurizio.

Code Types: Functions and Failings and Organizational Diversity. Condren, Conal.

Crisis and Narrativity. Hirschbein, Ron.

Cultural Conditioning: The Dark Underside of Multiculturalism (Part Two: A Way Out). Reinsmith, William.

Cultural Diversity and the Systems View. Hammond, Debora.

Cultural Diversity in Medicine and Medical Ethics: What Are the Key Questions?. La Puma, John.

Diversity and Ancient Democracy: A Response to Schwartz. Saxonhouse, Arlene W.

Diversity in the Classroom. Maitzen, Stephen.

Diversity, Values and Social Change: Renegotiating a Consensus on Sex Education. Thomson, Rachel.

Expanding Diversity Education for Preservice Teachers: Teaching about Racial Isolation in Urban Schools. Malone, Patricia.

Freedom and Moral Diversity: The Moral Failures of Health Care in the Welfare State. Engelhardt Jr, H Tristram.

Genes and Human Behavior: The Emerging Paradigm. Drew, Allan P.

Michel Serres (in Hebrew). Wohlman, Avital.

Moral Paralysis and the Ethnocentric Fallacy. Applebaum, Barbara.

Muchas Culturas: Sobre el problema filosófico y práctico de la diversidad cultural. Ramírez, Mario Teodoro.

No Goddess Was Your Mother: Western Philosophy's Abandonment of Its Multicultural Matrix. Schroeder, Steven.

Postmodernity: the End of Modernism or the End of Diversity? (Spanish). Maríñez Navarro, Freddy.

Second Thoughts on Multi-Culturalism. Davis, Michael.

The Great Sphere: Education Against Servility. Callan, Eamonn.

The Heterogeneity of Clinical Ethics: The State of the Field as Reflected in the *Encyclopedia of Bioethics*. Koczwara, Bogda M and Madigan, Timothy J.

The Hobbes Game, Human Diversity, and Learning Styles. Gerwin, Martin E.

The Relationship of Board Member Diversity to Organizational Performance. Siciliano, Julie I.

Unity and Diversity through Education: A Comparison of the Thought of W.E.B. DuBois and John Dewey. Burks, Ben.

Unity, Diversity, and Leftist Support for the Canon. Casement, William.

Wayne, Horwich, and Evidential Diversity. Fitelson, Branden.

## DIVINE

Enigma e relazione: Da Apollo a Edipo. Lo Bue, Elisabetta.

Essere e idea. Tagliavia, Grazia.

How Things Happen: Divine-Natural Law in Spinoza. Mason, Richard.

## DIVINE WILL

"Triangulating Divine Will: Henry More, Robert Boyle, and René Descartes on God's Relationship to the Creation" in *Mind Senior to the World*, Baldi, Marialuisa. Osler, Margaret J.

## DIVINITY

*Exploring Unseen Worlds: William James and the Philosophy of Mysticism*. Barnard, G William.

*Metaphysical Animal: Divine and Human in Man*. Woznicki, Andrew Nicholas.

*The Human Constitution*. Regan, Richard J (trans).

A Divine Intimation: Appreciating Natural Beauty. Kieran, Matthew.

An Interpretation of Plutarch's *Cato the Younger*. Frost, Bryan-Paul.

Barth on the Divine 'Conscription' of Language. Richards, Jay Wesley.

Divine Action in a World Chaos: An Evaluation of John Polkinghorne's Model of Special Divine Action. Crain, Steven D.

Divine Intervention. Fales, Evan.

Divinity Must Live Within Herself: Nussbaum and Aquinas on Transcending the Human. McInerny, Daniel.

Frankfurt Counterexamples: Some Comments on the Widerker-Fischer Debate. Hunt, David P.

La critica rosminiana alla cosmologia di Aristotele. Messina, Gaetano.

La teología epicúrea: la concepción de la divinidad y su incidencia en la vida humana. Méndez Lloret, Isabel.

Liturgy: Divine and Human Service. Purcell, Michael.

Minds and Bodies: Human and Divine. Peterson, Gregory R.

Mysticism and Divine Mutability. Dombrowski, Daniel A.

On the Argument for Divine Timelessness from the Incompleteness of Temporal Life. Craig, William Lane.

Orgasmic Rapture and Divine Ecstasy: The Semantic History of Ānanda. Olivelle, Patrick.

Petrus Hispanus O.P., Auctor Summularum. D'Ors, Angel.

Predicative Interpretations of Spinoza's Divine Extension. Huenemann, Charles.

Privacy and Control. Davison, Scott A.

Response to Howard-Snyder. Schellenberg, J L.

Rolston's Theological Ethic. Benzoni, Francisco.

Simplicity, Personhood, and Divinity. Wynn, Mark.

The Argument from Divine Hiddenness. Howard-Snyder, Daniel.

The Divine Infinity: Can Traditional Theists *Justifiably* Reject Pantheism?. Oakes, Robert.

The Philosophical-Theological Idea of Sophia: The Contemporary Context of Interpretation. Ivanov, A V.

William of Auvergne's Adaptation of IBN Gabirol's Doctrine of the Divine Will. Caster, Kevin J.

## DIVISION

Aristotle's Rules of Division in the *Topics*: The Relationship between Genus and Differentia in a Division. Falcon, Andrea.

Two Applications of a Theorem of Dvoretsky, Wald, and Wolfovitz to Cake Division. Barbanel, Julius B and Zwicker, William S.

## DIVORCE

"...Equality from the Masculine Point of View...": The 2nd Earl Russell and Divorce Law Reform in England. Savage, Gail.

## DIXON, N

Feminist Positions on Vegetarianism: Arguments For and Against and Otherwise. Wellington, Alex.

## DOBZHANSKY, T

Theory, Practice, and Epistemology in the Development of Species Concepts. Magnus, David.

## DOCTRINE

The Chinese Doctrinal Acceptance of Buddhism. Inada, Kenneth K.

Truth and Meaning in George Lindbeck's *The Nature of Doctrine*. Richards, Jay Wesley.

## DOERFFEL, G

Korrespondenten von G.W. Leibniz: Georg Samuel Dörffel, geb. 11 Oktober 1643 in Plauen/Vogtland—gest. 6. August 1688 in Weida. Pfitzner, Elvira.

**DOGEN**
Who is arguing about the Cat? Moral Action and Enlightenment according to Dōgen. Mikkelson. Douglas K.

**DOGEN KIGEN**
Dogen on *seppo* and *jodo*. Nakajima, Keita.
Some Problems in Interpretation: The Early and Late Writings of Dōgen. Putney, David.

**DOGMA**
Il Metodo della Filosofia della Religione di A. Sabatier. Savignano, Armando.

**DOGMATISM**
"Scepticism and the Limits of Charity" in *Scepticism in the History of Philosophy: A Pan-American Dialogue,* Popkin, Richard H (ed). De Olaso, Ezequiel.
*2000 Years of Disbelief: Famous People with the Courage to Doubt.* Haught, James A.

**DOING**
"Doing as We Ought: Towards a Logic of Simply Dischargeable Obligations" in *Deontic Logic, Agency and Normative Systems,* Brown, Mark A (ed). Brown, Mark A.
Doing One's Own Thing: The Genealogy of a Slogan. Weidhorn, Manfred.
How to Do Things with Things: Objects trouvés and Symbolization. Streeck, Jürgen.

**DOLAN, F**
Political Theory of and in America. Isaac, Jeffrey C.

**DOMAIN**
A Rational Reconstruction of the Domain of Feature Structures. Moshier, M Andrew.
Domain Representability of Metric Spaces. Blanck, Jens.
Structured Meanings and Reflexive Domains. Lapierre, Serge.

**DOMESTICATION**
Ethical Limits to Domestication. Sandoe, Peter, Holtug, Nils and Simonsen, H B.

**DOMINANCE**
Evolution and Ultimatum Bargaining. Harms, William.
Nonparametric Statistics in Multicriteria Analysis. Scarelli, Antonino and Venzi, Lorenzo.
Payoff Dominance and the Stackelberg Heuristic. Colman, Andrew M and Bacharach, Michael.

**DOMINATION**
"L'*Account of the Nature and the Extent of the Divine Dominion and Goodnesses* di Samuel Parker: dalla teologia alla filosofia politica" in *Mind Senior to the World,* Baldi, Marialuisa. Lupoli, Agostino.
"Nature's Presence: Reflections on Healing and Domination" in *Philosophy and Geography I: Space, Place, and Environmental Ethics,* Light, Andrew (ed). Katz, Eric.
Carnival and Domination: Pedagogies of Neither Care Nor Justice. Sidorkin, Alexander M.
Loopholes, Gaps, and What is Held Fast: Democratic Epistemology and Claims to Recovered Memories. Potter, Nancy.
Self-Ownership and Equality: Brute Luck, Gifts, Universal Dominance, and Leximin. Vallentyne, Peter.

**DOMINICANS**
El Camino de Santiago y el descubrimiento racional de la naturaleza en los siglos XII y XIII. Ballester, Luis García.

**DONAGAN, A**
Donagan on Cases of Necessity. Malone, Michael J.
Donagan, Abortion, and Civil Rebellion. Tollefsen, Christopher.

**DONALDSON, T**
Grounding Hypernorms: Towards a Contractarian Theory of Business Ethics. Rowan, John R.

**DONNER, W**
Making Sense of Mill. Weinstock, Daniel M.

**DONOR**
*Organ Transplants and Ethics.* Lamb, David.

**DONOSO CORTES, J**
Algo donoso pero no cortés: Una lectura diferencial del bifronte Marqués de Valdegamas a tenor de la modernidad de Vico. Sevilla Fernández, José M.

**DOOMSDAY**
A Shooting-Room View of Doomsday. Eckhardt, William.

**DOORMAN, M**
Maarten Doormans kwantitatieve argumenten voor vooruitgang in de kunst. Lokhorst, Gert-Jan C.

**DOOYEWEERD, H**
"Points of Convergence Between Dooyeweerdian and Feminist Views of the Philosophic Self" in *Knowing Other-Wise: Philosophy at the Threshold of Spirituality,* Olthuis, James H (ed). Wesselius, Janet Catherina.
Schepping, transcendentie, religie. Dengerink, J D.

**DORIA, M**
Il cartesianesimo matematico a Napoli. Gatto, Romano.

**DOSTOEVSKII**
On Studying Dostoevskii. Florovskii, Georgii.

**DOSTOYEVSKY**
Dostoyevsky and the Problem of God. Devi, S Sreekala and Narayanadas, V C.
From Nimrod to the Grand Inquisitor: The Problem of the Demonisation of Freedom in the Work of Dostoevskij. Blumenkrantz, Mikhail.
Georg Lukács and Lajos Fülep Dante (in Hungarian). Kaposi, Márton.
La colpa e il tempo in Fëdor Dostoevskij. Colonnello, Pio.

**DOUBLE EFFECT**
Aquinas's Account of Double Effect. Cavanaugh, Thomas A.
Collateral Violence and the Doctrine of Double Effect. Bica, Camillo C.
The Importance of the Proportionality Condition to the Doctrine of Double Effect: A Response to Fischer, Ravizza, and Copp. Woodward, P A.

**DOUBT**
"La dudas de Descartes y el lenguaje privado" in *Memorias Del Seminario En Conmemoración De Los 400 Anos Del Nacimiento De René Descartes,* Albis, Víctor S (ed). Thompson, Garret.
*2000 Years of Disbelief: Famous People with the Courage to Doubt.* Haught, James A.
*The God of Spinoza.* Mason, Richard.
Comments on Michael Williams' *Unnatural Doubts.* Rorty, Richard.
Critical Thinking vs. Pure Thought (Part One of Two). Coccia, Orestes.
Doubting and Believing: Both are Important for Critical Thinking. Thayer-Bacon, Barbara.
E. Husserl and Descartes's Method of Doubt (in Czech). Sousedík, Stanislav.
Espinosa e o "Círculo Cartesiano". Gleizer, Marcos André.
Hume's Arguments for His Sceptical Doubts. Passell, Dan.
Hyperbolic Doubt and "Machiavelism": The Modern Foundation of the Subject in Descartes (in French). Richir, Marc.
Philosophy as Critical Reflection: The Philosophy of Rasvihary Das. Sen, Sanat Kumar.
Rasvihary Das on 'Value of Doubt': Some Reflections. Ghosh, Raghunath.
Skepticism and Foundationalism: A Reply to Michael Williams. Vogel, Jonathan.
Still Unnatural: A Reply to Vogel and Rorty. Williams, Michael.
The Validity of Indexical Arguments. Elkatip, S H.

**DOUGLAS, M**
Blurred Boundaries. Morriss, Peter.

**DOUGLASS, F**
"The Fight with Covey" in *Existence in Black: An Anthology of Black Existential Philosophy,* Gordon, Lewis R (ed). Boxill, Bernard R.

**DOWNS-LOMBARDI, J**
Some Thoughts on Thinking and Teaching Styles. Schwerin, Alan.

**DOXASTIC LOGIC**
*Formal Ethics.* Gensler, Harry J.

**DOXOGRAPHY**
Fragments from *Timon of Phleius* & Diogenes Laertius on Timon of Phleius (in Hungarian). Steiger, Kornél.
Timon of Phleius and the *Silloi* (in Czech). Steiger, Kornél.

**DRABKIN, D**
Moral Crutches and Nazi Theists: A Defense of and Reservations about Undertaking Theism. Lemos, John.

**DRAFT**
Let Them Eat Chances: Probability and Distributive Justice. Wasserman, David.

**DRAMA**
"*Drama* O Dell'"Espressione A Ogni Costo": L'azione tragica: Nietzsche critico di Wagner" in *Soggetto E Verità: La questione dell'uomo nella filosofia contemporanea,* Fagiuoli, Ettore. Fagiuoli, Ettore.
"Moral Education and Inspiration Through Theatre" in *Philosophy of Education (1996),* Margonis, Frank (ed). Valentine, Timothy S.
"Music and Negative Emotion" in *Music and Meaning,* Robinson, Jenefer (ed). Levinson, Jerrold.
*Kenneth Macgowan and the Aesthetic Paradigm for the New Stagecraft in America.* Bloom, Thomas Alan.
*Nietzsches Werke Kritische Gesamtausgabe: III 5/1.* Groddeck, Wolfram (ed) and Kohlenbach, Michael (ed).
Characterisation and Interpretation: The Importance of Drama in Plato's *Sophist.* Benitez, Eugenio E.
Characterization in Samuel Beckett's *Not I.* Daisuke, Hirakawa.
Embracing the Subject: Harsa's Play within a Play. Shulman, David.
Narrative, Drama, and Emotion in Instrumental Music. Maus, Fred Everett.
Other People's Products: The Value of Performing and Appreciating. Bailin, Sharon.
The Aesthetics of the Marketplace: Women Playwrights, 1770-1850. Newey, Katherine.
Theatre and Moral Education. Levy, Jonathan.
'Between the Brutely Given, and the Brutally, Banally Free': Von Balthasar's Theology of Drama in Dialogue with Hegel. Quash, J B.

**DRANGE, T**
Bolstering the Argument from Non-Belief. Cosculluela, Victor.

**DRATH, W**
Leadership as Aesthetic Process. Smith, Ralph A.

**DRAWING**
"Descartes's Scientific Illustrations and 'la grand mécanique de la nature'" in *Picturing Knowledge,* Baigrie, Brian S (ed). Baigrie, Brian S.

## DREAM

"Il Paiolo Bucato" in *Soggetto E Verità: La questione dell'uomo nella filosofia contemporanea,* Fagiuoli, Ettore. Rovatti, Pier Aldo.

"La dimensione del tempo nella psicanalisi di Freud" in *Il Concetto di Tempo: Atti del XXXII Congresso Nazionale della Società Filosofica Italiana,* Casertano, Giovanni (ed). Tricomi, Flavia.

Critical Notice: Freud, Philosophical and Empirical Issues. Cioffi, Frank.

From City-Dreams to the Dreaming Collective. Miller, Tyrus.

Problems with the Cognitive Psychological Modeling of Dreaming. Blagrove, Mark.

## DREAMING

Aristotle on Dreaming: What Goes On in Sleep When the 'Big Fire' Goes Out. Holowchak, Mark A.

The Concept of Dreaming: On Three Theses by Malcolm. Schroeder, Severin.

## DRETSKE, F

"Comment on Dretske" in *Perception,* Villanueva, Enrique (ed). Horwich, Paul.

"Dretske on Phenomenal Externalism" in *Perception,* Villanueva, Enrique (ed). Biro, John.

"Dretske's Qualia Externalism" in *Perception,* Villanueva, Enrique (ed). Kim, Jaegwon.

Accidental Associations, Local Potency, and a Dilemma for Dretske. Noordhof, Paul.

Critical Notice of Fred Dretske *Naturalizing the Mind.* Seager, William.

Escepticismo, verdad y confiabilidad. Cresto, Eleonora.

Fred Dretske on the Explanatory Role of Semantic Content. Hassrick, Beth.

Rethinking Distributed Representation. Ramsey, William.

State Consciousness Revisited. Jacob, Pierre.

The Prospects for Dretske's Account of the Explanatory Role of Belief. Melnyk, Andrew.

What Does a Pyrrhonist Know?. Fogelin, Robert J.

## DREWERMANN, E

La fonction libératrice du désespoir chez Eugen Drewermann. Saint-Germain, Christian.

## DREYFUS, H

The Machine That Couldn't Think Straight. Dinan, Stephen A.

## DRUG

Conflicts of Interest, Conflicting Interests, and Interesting Conflicts, Part 3. Vinicky, Janicemarie K, Orlowski, James P and Shevlin Edwards, Sue.

Drug Testing and Privacy: Why Contract Arguments Do Not Work. Carson, A Scott.

Enhancing Cognition in the Intellectually Intact. Juengst, Eric T, Whitehouse, Peter J and Mehlman, Maxwell (& others).

Ethical Aspects of the Safety of Medicines and Other Social Chemicals. Parke, Dennis V.

Ethical Considerations in the Testing of Biopharmaceuticals for Adventitious Agents. Woodward, Richard S.

Ethical Issues in Research on Preventing HIV Infection among Injecting Drug Users. Des Jarlais, Don D, Gaist, Paul A and Friedman, Samuel R.

Medicating Children: The Case of Ritalin. Perring, Christian.

Response to "Discounting Life Support in an Infant of a Drug Addicted Mother: Whose Decision Is It?" by Renu Jain and David C. Thomasma (CQ Vol 6, No 1). Oberman, Michelle.

## DRYZEK, J

Complexity and Deliberative Democracy. Femia, Joseph V.

## DUALISM

*see also* Body, Minds

"Akrasia: Irremediable but not Unapproachable" in *Philosophy of Education (1996),* Margonis, Frank (ed). Worsfold, Victor L.

"Difficulties with Physicalism, and a Programme for Dualists" in *Objections to Physicalism,* Robinson, Howard (ed). Forrest, Peter.

"The Freedom of the Playpen" in *Philosophy of Education (1996),* Margonis, Frank (ed). Macmillan, C J B.

"Theoretical and Practical Reasoning: An Intractable Dualism?" in *Philosophy of Education (1996),* Margonis, Frank (ed). McClellan, Jr, James E.

"Varieties of Incotinence: Towards an Aristotelian Approach to Moral Weakness in Moral Education" in *Philosophy of Education (1996),* Margonis, Frank (ed). Carr, David.

*Cartesian Nightmare: An Introduction to Transcendental Sophistry.* Redpath, Peter A.

*Cervello-Mente: Pensatori del XX secolo.* Gava, Giacomo.

*Descartes' Dualism.* Baker, Gordon and Morris, Katherine J.

*Malebranche's Theory of the Soul: A Cartesian Interpretation.* Schmaltz, Tad M.

*Martin Heidegger und Hans Jonas: Die Metaphysik der Subjektivität und die Krise der technologischen Zivilisation.* Jakob, Eric.

*Rational Choice and Moral Agency.* Schmidtz, David.

Abkehr vom Mythos: Descartes in der gegenwärtigen Diskussion. Perler, Dominik.

An Objection to Swinburne's Argument for Dualism. Stump, Eleonore and Kretzmann, Norman.

Cartesian Epistemics and Descartes' *Regulae.* Thomas, Bruce M.

Critical Thinking vs. Pure Thought. Coccia, Orestes.

David Braine's Project: The Human Person. Burrell, David B.

Descartes's Demon and the Madness of Don Quixote. Nadler, Steven.

Descartes's Dualism?. Baker, Gordon and Morris, Katherine J.

Descartes's Wax and the Typology of Early Modern Philosophy. Glouberman, Mark.

Did he Walk with a Mask...? (in Czech). Dokulil, Milos.

Does the Problem of Mental Causation Generalize?. Kim, Jaegwon.

Dualism Intact. Swinburne, Richard.

Eigenschafts-Physikalismus. Beckermann, Ansgar.

Lacuna in Sankara Studies: *A Thousand Teachings* (*Upadesasāhasri*). Tuck, Donald R.

Le mal moral, pierre de touche de l'ontologie: Monisme idéal et dualisme réel du sens de l'être. Lamblin, Robert.

Letters to Elizabeth of Palatinate: (P. Horák: Commentary) (in Czech). Horák, Petr (trans) and Descartes, René.

Libertad básica. Skutch, Alexander F.

Locke, Metaphysical Dualism and Property Dualism. Bermúdez, José Luis.

Mendus on Philosophy and Pervasiveness. Landau, Iddo.

O Modelo Psicofisiológico Cartesiano e o Materialismo das Luzes. Nascimento, Maria das Graças S.

Possibilities in Philosophy of Mind. Taliaferro, Charles.

Reply to Stump and Kretzmann. Swinburne, Richard.

Searle on Consciousness and Dualism. Collins, Corbin.

The Flesh and the Spirit: Anne Bradstreet and Seventeenth Century Dualism, Materialism, Vitalism and Reformed Theology. Whelan, Timothy.

The Ghost in the Machine—Fights—the Last Battle for the Human Soul. Watson, Richard A.

## DUALITY

"Radical Nonduality in Ecofeminist Philosophy" in *Ecofeminism: Women, Culture, Nature,* Warren, Karen J (ed). Spretnak, Charlene.

Duality for Lattice-Ordered Algebras and for Normal Algebraizable Logics. Hartonas, Chrysafis.

## DUBOIS, W

"On the Reading of Riddles: Rethinking Du Boisian 'Double Consciousness'" in *Existence in Black: An Anthology of Black Existential Philosophy,* Gordon, Lewis R (ed). Allen Jr, Ernest.

How It Feels to Be a Problem: Du Bois, Fanon, and the "Impossible Life" of the Black Intellectual. Posnock, Ross.

Unity and Diversity through Education: A Comparison of the Thought of W.E.B. DuBois and John Dewey. Burks, Ben.

## DUCHAMP, M

Defining Art Responsibly. Young, James O.

## DUDMAN, V

Parsing If-Sentences and the Conditions of Sentencehood. Barker, Stephen J.

## DUFF, R

Recklessness. Brady, James B.

Response to the Commentaries. Fields, Lloyd.

## DUFRENNE, M

A Institucionalizaçao da Arte e o Esvaziamento da *Aisthesis*: Interpretaçao do Ponto de Vista de Mikel Dufrenne. Morais, Carlos Bizarro.

Le sens du poétique: Approche phénoménologique. Roose, Marie-Clotilde.

## DUHEM, M

Science: Augustinian or Duhemian?. Plantinga, Alvin.

## DUHEM, P

Duhems Holismus. Flügel, Martin.

Naturgemässe Klassifikation und Kontinuität, Wissenschaft und Geschichte: Überlegungen zu Pierre Duhem. Petrus, Klaus.

Realismus in Duhems naturgemässer Klassifikation. Burri, Alex.

Underdetermination in Economics: The Duhem-Quine Thesis. Sawyer, K R, Beed, Clive and Sankey, H.

## DUMMETT, M

"Singular Terms (1)" in *Frege: Importance and Legacy,* Schirn, Matthias (ed). Hale, Bob.

Anti-Realism, Truth-Value Links and Tensed Truth Predicates. Weiss, Bernhard.

Meaning and Semantic Knowledge. Antony, Louise M and Davies, Martin.

What Assertion Is Not. Stainton, Robert J.

Why did Language Matter to Analytic Philosophy?. Skorupski, John.

## DUNFEE, T

Grounding Hypernorms: Towards a Contractarian Theory of Business Ethics. Rowan, John R.

## DUNHAM, B

The Philosophy of Barrows Dunham: The Progress of an American Radical. Parsons, Howard L.

## DUNN, J

Intrinsic/Extrinsic. Humberstone, I Lloyd.

## DUNS SCOTUS

*Trayectoria Voluntarista de la Libertad: Escoto, Descartes, Mill.* Alvarez-Valdés, Lourdes Gordillo.

Alnwick on the Origin, Nature, and Function of the Formal Distinction. Noone, Timothy B.

Do Princípio de Individuaçao. Ribas Cezar, Cesar (trans) and Scotus, John Duns.

Duns Scotus on Eternity and Timelessness. Cross, Richard.

Imputabilitas als Merkmal des Moralischen: Die Diskussion bei Duns Scotus und Wilhelm von Ockham. Kaufmann, Matthias.

## DYNAMICS

*Computation, Dynamics, and Cognition.* Giunti, Marco.

Classical Particle Dynamics, Indeterminism and a Supertask. Laraudogoitia, Jon Perez.

Dynamical Systems in Development: Review Essay of Linda V. Smith and Esther Thelen (Eds) *A Dynamics Systems Approach to Development: Applications.* Hooker, Cliff A.

Joint Beliefs in Conflictual Coordination Games. Vanderschraaf, Peter and Richards, Diana.

The Leibniz Continuity Condition, Inconsistency and Quantum Dynamics. Mortensen, Chris.

The Structure of Radical Probabilism. Skyrms, Brian.

## DYSLEXIA

"The Just Claims of Dyslexic Children" in *Reproduction, Technology, and Rights: Biomedical Ethics Reviews,* Humber, James M (ed). Hull, Richard T.

## E-MAIL

Ethical and Legal Issues in E-Mail Therapy. Shapiro, Daniel Edward and Schulman, Charles Eric.

## EAGLETON, T

"Forms of Life: Mapping the Rough Ground" in *The Cambridge Companion to Wittgenstein,* Sluga, Hans (ed). Scheman, Naomi.

Foucault's Alimentary Philosophy: Care of the Self and Responsibility for the Other. Boothroyd, David.

## EARMAN, J

Is There a Syntactic Solution to the Hole Problem?. Rynasiewicz, Robert.

## EARNINGS

Myth, Measurement, and the Minimum Wage: Sound and Fury Signifying What?. Whitman, Glen.

## EARTH

*Defending Mother Earth: Native American Perspectives on Environmental Justice.* Weaver, Jace (ed).

*Earth Community: Earth Ethics.* Rasmussen, Larry L.

*Geofilosofia del Paesaggio.* Bonesio, Luisa.

Earthday 25: A Retrospective of Reform Environmental Movements. Devall, Bill.

Genetic Engineering and Environmental Ethics. Dobson, Andrew.

The Living Cosmos: Man Among the Forces of Earth and Heaven. Filatov, Vladimir Petrovich.

Whole Earth Measurements: How Many Phenomenologists Does It Take to Detect a "Greenhouse Effect"?. Ihde, Don.

## EAST EUROPEAN

As Transformaçoes da Tirania. Bignotto, Newton.

Geography and Computer Ethics: An Eastern European Perspective. Kocikowski, Andrzej.

## EASTERN

see also Oriental

*Culture and Self.* Allen, Douglas (ed) and Malhotra, Ashok K.

*Dictionary of Philosophy and Religion: Eastern and Western Thought.* Reese, William L.

*East and West in Aesthetics.* Marchianò, Grazia (ed).

*Meeting of Minds: Intellectual and Religious Interaction in East Asian Traditions of Thought.* Bloom, Irene (ed) and Fogel, Joshua A (ed).

Points East and West: Acupuncture and Comparative Philosophy of Science. Allchin, Douglas.

Scientific Attitudes Towards an Eastern Mystic. Danyluk, Angie.

## EBNER, F

The Word as Ultimate Reality: The Christian Dialogical Personalism of Ferdinand Ebner. Kunszt, György.

## ECHEVERRIA, J

La pauta del muro: re-convocaciones del pensamiento de José Echeverría. Kerkhoff, Manfred.

Semblanza de José Echeverría. Badía Cabrera, Miguel A.

## ECKHART

"Dieses Ich: Meister Eckharts Ich-Konzeption: Ein Beitrag zur 'Aufklärung' im Mittelalter" in *Sein—Reflexion—Freiheit: Aspekte der Philosophie Johann Gottlieb Fichtes,* Asmuth, Christoph (ed). Mojsisch, Burkhard.

Aristotelische Intellekttheorie und die "Sohnesgeburt" bei Meister Eckehart. Helting, Holger.

Eckhart's Anachorism. Bernasconi, Robert.

La creación como encuentro del ser y de la nada en la teología del maestro Eckhart de Hochheim O.P. (1260-1327). Farrelly, Brian J.

Maître Eckhart et le discernement mystique: A propos de la rencontre de Suso avec *la (chose) sauvage sans nom.* Wackernagel, Wolfgang.

## ECLECTICISM

*The Question of "Eclecticism": Studies in Later Greek Philosophy.* Dillon, John M (ed) and Long, A A (ed).

Eclecticism or Skepticism? A Problem of the Early Enlightenment. Mulsow, Martin.

Pragmatismus, Dekonstruktion, ironischer Eklektizismus: Richard Rortys Heidegger-Lektüre. Burkhard, Philipp.

The Notion of African Philosophy. Uduigwomen, Andrew F.

## ECLIPSE

Fuentes para la historia de la astronomia de los siglos XIV y XV. Eclipses y tablas. Lértora Mendoza, Celina A.

## ECO, U

Una lettura possibile: A proposito de "I boschi narrativi" di Umberto Eco. Savorelli, Mirella Brini.

## ECOCENTRISM

Attributing 'Priority' to Habitats. Miller, Chris.

Between Anthropocentrism and Ecocentrism. Boulting, Noel E.

Ecocentrism and Persons. Baxter, Brian H.

Human-Centered or Ecocentric Environmental Ethics?. Howie, John.

## ECOFEMINISM

"Androcentrism and Anthropocentrism: Parallels and Politics" in *Ecofeminism: Women, Culture, Nature,* Warren, Karen J (ed). Plumwood, Val.

"Kant and Ecofeminism" in *Ecofeminism: Women, Culture, Nature,* Warren, Karen J (ed). Wilson, Holyn.

"Radical Nonduality in Ecofeminist Philosophy" in *Ecofeminism: Women, Culture, Nature,* Warren, Karen J (ed). Spretnak, Charlene.

"Taking Empirical Data Seriously: An Ecofeminist Philosophical Perspective" in *Ecofeminism: Women, Culture, Nature,* Warren, Karen J (ed). Warren, Karen J.

"Women-Animals-Machines: A Grammar for a Wittgensteinian Ecofeminism" in *Ecofeminism: Women, Culture, Nature,* Warren, Karen J (ed). Lee-Lampshire, Wendy.

*Ecofeminism: Women, Culture, Nature.* Warren, Karen J (ed) and Erkal, Nisvan (ed).

Ecofeminism and Wilderness. Gaard, Greta.

Ecofeminism: What One Needs to Know. Howell, Nancy R.

Toward a Queer Ecofeminism. Gaard, Greta.

Warren, Plumwood, a Rock and a Snake: Some Doubts about Critical Ecological Feminism. Andrews, John N.

## ECOLOGY

"Before Environmental Ethics" in *Environmental Pragmatism,* Light, Andrew (ed). Weston, Anthony.

"Compatibilism in Political Ecology" in *Environmental Pragmatism,* Light, Andrew (ed). Light, Andrew.

"Counter the Dangers of Education" in *Philosophy of Education (1996),* Margonis, Frank (ed). Huang, Xiaodan.

"Critical Questions in Environmental Philosophy" in *Philosophy and Geography I: Space, Place, and Environmental Ethics,* Light, Andrew (ed). Booth, Annie L.

"Ecology, Modernity, and the Intellectual Legacy of the Frankfurt School" in *Philosophy and Geography I: Space, Place, and Environmental Ethics,* Light, Andrew (ed). Gandy, Matthew.

"Integration or Reduction: Two Approaches to Environmental Values" in *Environmental Pragmatism,* Light, Andrew (ed). Norton, Bryan G.

"Radical Nonduality in Ecofeminist Philosophy" in *Ecofeminism: Women, Culture, Nature,* Warren, Karen J (ed). Spretnak, Charlene.

"Reconceiving the Foundations of Education: An Ecological Model" in *Philosophy of Education (1996),* Margonis, Frank (ed). Morgan, Paul.

"Revaluing Nature" in *Ecofeminism: Women, Culture, Nature,* Warren, Karen J (ed). Gruen, Lori.

"Ruritania and Ecology" in *Contents,* Villanueva, Enrique (ed). Toribio, Josefa.

*Colour Vision: A Study in Cognitive Science and the Philosophy of Perception.* Thompson, Evan.

*Defending Mother Earth: Native American Perspectives on Environmental Justice.* Weaver, Jace (ed).

*Earthly Goods: Environmental Change and Social Justice.* Hampson, Fen Osler (ed) and Reppy, Judith (ed).

*Nature and Society: Anthropological Perspectives.* Descola, Philippe (ed) and Pálsson, Gísli (ed).

*Philosophy and Geography I: Space, Place, and Environmental Ethics.* Light, Andrew (ed) and Smith, Jonathan M (ed).

*Principia Ecologica* Eco-Principles as a Conceptual Framework for a New Ethics in Science and Technology. Moser, Anton.

*Vom Begründen zum Handeln: Aufsätze zur angewandten Ethik.* Ott, Konrad.

A Case Study of Conflicting Interests: Flemish Engineers Involved in Environmental Impact Assessment. Holemans, Dirk.

A Political-Ecology Approach to Wildlife Conservation in Kenya. Akama, John S, Lant, Christopher L and Burnett, G Wesley.

A Virtue Ethics Approach to Aldo Leopold's Land Ethic. Shaw, Bill.

An Ecologically-Informed Ontology for Environmental Ethics. Buege, Douglas J.

Anthropocentrism: A Misunderstood Problem. Hayward, Tim.

Being and Subjectivity (and Commentary V. Hála) (in Czech). Hösle, Vittorio and Hála, Vlastimil.

Bioethics of Fish Production: Energy and the Environment. Pimentel, David, Shanks, Roland E and Rylander, Jason C.

Commentary On: "There is no Such Thing as Environmental Ethics". Chorover, Stephan L, Gruen, Lori and List, Peter.

Convergence and Contextualism: Some Clarifications and a Reply to Steverson. Norton, Bryan G.

Deep Ecology and its Significance for Philosophical Thought (in Czech). Kolársky, Rudolf.

Deep Ecology and the Irrelevance of Morality. Reitan, Eric H.

Desarrollo sostenible y valoración de la vida humana. Vargas, Celso and Alfaro, Mario.

## ECOLOGY

Do Deconstructive Ecology and Sociobiology Undermine Leopold's Land Ethic?. Callicott, J Baird.

Ecofeminism and Wilderness. Gaard, Greta.

Ecological Motivations of Ethics and the Moral Critique of the Value Orientation of Society (in Czech). Hála, Vlastimil.

Environmental Economics, Ecological Economics, and the Concept of Sustainable Development. Munda, Giuseppe.

Environmental Education and Beyond. Bonnett, Michael.

Environmental Ethics and the Critique of Anthropocentrism (Czech). Kolársky, Rudolf.

Environmental Ethics, Anthropocentrism and Rationality (in Czech). Jemelka, Petr.

Environmentalism for Europe—One Model?. De-Shalit, Avner.

Five Arguments for Vegetarianism. Stephens, William O.

Forms of Tolerance as Types of Democracy (in Czech). Znoj, Milan.

From the Mexican Chiapas Crisis: A Different Perspective for Environmental Ethics. Szatzscheider, Teresa Kwiatkowska.

Gilles Deleuze and Naturalism: A Convergence with Ecological Theory and Politics. Hayden, Patrick.

Hegel and Marx on Nature and Ecology. Berthold-Bond, Daniel.

Human-Centered or Ecocentric Environmental Ethics?. Howie, John.

Internationalisierung des Kapitals, Gesamtkapital und nationalstaat. Milios, Jean.

Is Deep Ecology Too Radical?. Aiken, William.

Jharkhand: A Movement from Ethnicity to Empowerment of Autonomy. Vadakumchery, Johnson.

La problemática ética del uso del DBCP en Costa Rica. Giralt-Bermúdez, María de los Angeles.

Natur im westlichen und östlichen Verständnis. Gloy, Karen.

O Futuro Ecológico como Tarefa da Filosofia. Schmied-Kowarzik, Wolfdietrich.

On Warwick Fox's Assessment of Deep Ecology. Glasser, Harold.

Patterns of Reasoning Exhibited by Children and Adolescents in Response to Moral Dilemmas Involving Plants, Animals and Ecosystems. Nevers, Patricia, Gebhard, Ulrich and Billmann-Mahecha, Elfriede.

Phenomenology and Ecology—Support and Interdependence (in Czech). Kohák, Erazim.

Prediction and Rolston's Environmental Ethics: Lessons from the Philosophy of Science. McKinney, William J.

Questione ecologica e nuove identità collettive. Eder, Klaus.

Religion in the Critical Decades. Al Brynaichi, Javan.

The Ecological Ideology and Russia's Future. Gorelov, A A.

The Evolutionary Ontological Foundation of the New Ethics? (in Czech). Smajs, Josef.

The Political Philosophy of the New Indian Renaissance. Sachidanand, Achayra John.

There is No Such Thing as Environmental Ethics. Vesilind, P Aarne.

Thinking Naturally. O'Neill, John.

Two Biblical Myths of Creation: An Exploration in Ecological Philosophy. Agera, Cassian R.

Varieties of Ecological Experience. Kohák, Erazim.

Warren, Plumwood, a Rock and a Snake: Some Doubts about Critical Ecological Feminism. Andrews, John N.

What is Natural?. Abney, Keith.

Why Norton's Approach is Insufficient for Environmental Ethics. Westra, Laura.

## ECONOMICS

"Avalutatività come principio metodico nella logica delle scienze sociali" in Momenti di Storia della Logica e di Storia della Filosofia, Guetti, Carla (ed). Bianco, Franco.

"Das Problem der Steuerhinterziehung: Eine moral ökonomische Analyse" in Ökonomie und Moral: Beiträge zur Theorie ökonomischer Rationalität, Lohmann, Karl Reinhard (ed). Leschke, Martin.

"Gibt es moralische Probleme der Wirtschaft?" in Ökonomie und Moral: Beiträge zur Theorie ökonomischer Rationalität, Lohmann, Karl Reinhard (ed). Wolf, Ursula.

"Il compito dello storico nella lezione inaugurale di Richard Henry Tawney (1932)" in Lo Storicismo e la Sua Storia: Temi, Problemi, Prospettive, Cacciatore, Giuseppe (ed). Tagliaferri, Teodoro.

"Moralische Überzeugung und wirtschaftliche Wahl" in Ökonomie und Moral: Beiträge zur Theorie ökonomischer Rationalität, Lohmann, Karl Reinhard (ed). Lohmann, Karl Reinhard.

"No Limits" in The American University: National Treasure or Endangered Species?, Ehrenberg, Ronald G (ed). Bowen, William G.

"Ökologische Ethik II: Gerechtigkeit, Ökonomie, Politik" in Angewandte Ethik: Die Bereichsethiken und ihre theoretische Fundierung, Nida-Rümelin, Julian (ed). Leist, Anton.

"Ökonomische Optimierung in den Grenzen struktureller Rationalität" in Ökonomie und Moral: Beiträge zur Theorie ökonomischer Rationalität, Lohmann, Karl Reinhard (ed). Nida-Rümelin, Julian.

"The Economic Approach to Homosexuality" in Sex, Preference, and Family: Essays on Law and Nature, Nussbaum, Martha C (ed). Posner, Richard A.

"The Sexual Economist and Legal Regulation of the Sexual Orientations" in Sex, Preference, and Family: Essays on Law and Nature, Nussbaum, Martha C (ed). Halley, Janet E.

"Verdirbt der homo oeconomicus die Moral?" in Ökonomie und Moral: Beiträge zur Theorie ökonomischer Rationalität, Lohmann, Karl Reinhard (ed). Suchanek, Andreas.

"Wirtschaftsethik" in Angewandte Ethik: Die Bereichsethiken und ihre theoretische Fundierung, Nida-Rümelin, Julian (ed). Zimmerli, Walther Christoph and Assländer, Michael.

Beyond Economics: Postmodernity, Globalization and National Sustainability. Sauer-Thompson, Gary and Smith, Joseph Wayne.

Business Ethics in the African Context Today. Rosemann, Philipp W (ed) and LeJeune, Michel (ed).

Darf Pedro sein Land verkaufen? Versuch einer sozialwissenschaftlichen Perspektive in der Ökonomik. Lohmann, Karl R.

Ethics and Economic Progress. Buchanan, James M.

Il Disincanto Della Ragione E L'Assolutezza Del Bonheur Studio Sull'Abate Galiani. Amodio, Paolo.

Nature and Society: Anthropological Perspectives. Descola, Philippe (ed) and Pálsson, Gísli (ed).

Ökonomie und Moral: Beiträge zur Theorie ökonomischer Rationalität. Lohmann, Karl Reinhard (ed) and Priddat, Birger P (ed).

On Economic Inequality. Sen, Amartya.

Society, Economics & Philosophy: Selected Papers. Allen, R T (ed) and Polanyi, Michael.

Theories of Distributive Justice. Roemer, John E.

A Modern Conception of the Human Rights (Spanish). Yadira Martínez, Agustina.

An Essay in the Applied Philosophy of Political Economy. Iachkina, Galina.

An 'Inexact' Philosophy of Economics?. Backhouse, Roger E.

Arts and Earning a Living. Packer, Arnold H.

Capitalism, Coordination, and Keynes: Rejoinder to Horwitz. Hill, Greg.

Comment on Dawson's 'Exit, Voice and Values in Economic Institutions'. Anderson, Elizabeth.

Complexity, Value, and the Psychological Postulates of Economics. Benedikt, Michael.

Die Globalisierungsthese—von der kritischen Analyse zum politischen Opportunismus. Burchardt, Hans-Jürgen.

Dr. Pangloss Goes to Market. Schweickart, David.

Economics as Separate and Inexact. Hausman, Daniel.

Economics, Biology, and Naturalism: Three Problems Concerning the Question of Individuality. Khalil, Elias L.

Economics, Business Principles and Moral Sentiments. Sen, Amartya.

El marxismo analítico. Gallichio, Santiago J.

En torno a la justicia médica. Cortina, Adela.

Enforcing Ethical Standards of Professional Associations. Loevinger, Lee.

Environmental Economics, Ecological Economics, and the Concept of Sustainable Development. Munda, Giuseppe.

Ethics in Developing Economies of Asia. Takahashi, Akira.

Exit, Voice and Values in Economic Institutions. Dawson, Graham.

Expected Utility, Ordering, and Context Freedom. Rawling, Piers.

Financial Interests of Authors in Scientific Journals: A Pilot Study of 14 Publications. Krimsky, Sheldon, Rothenberg, L S and Stott, P.

Funciones no lineales de Bienestar social: ¿Tienen los economistas del Bienestar una exención especial de la racionalidad bayesiana?. Harsanyi, John C.

Glokalisierung oder Was für die einen Globalisierung, ist für die anderen Lokalisierung. Bauman, Zygmunt.

Gramscianismus in der Internationalen Politischen Ökonomie. Bieling, Hans-Jürgen and Deppe, Frank.

Hayek's Attack on Social Justice. Johnston, David.

Hayek's Political Philosophy and His Economics. Friedman, Jeffrey.

Henk van Riessen, pionier van de filosofie van de techniek. Haaksma, Hans W H and Vlot, Ad.

Homo Economicus in the 20th Century: Écriture Masculine and Women's Work. Still, Judith.

Il Tractatus yconomicus di Galvano Fiamma O.P. (1282-dopo il 1344). Fioravanti, Gianfranco.

Internationalisierung des Kapitals, Gesamtkapital und nationalstaat. Milios, Jean.

Introduction: Recent Currents in Marxist Philosophy. Little, Daniel.

Let Them Eat Chances: Probability and Distributive Justice. Wasserman, David.

Neoclassical Economics and the Last Dogma of Positivism: Is the Normative-Positive Distinction Justified?. Keita, L D.

Nonuse Values and the Environment: Economic and Ethical Motivations. Crowards, Tom.

On the Foundations of Nash Equilibrium. Jacobsen, Jans Jorgen.

On the Road Again: Hayek and the Rule of Law. Williams, Juliet.

On the Theoretical Basis of Prediction in Economics. González, Wenceslao J.

Pensar frente al exceso. Innerarity, Daniel.

Perspectivas da Prospectiva: Acerca da Obra de Lúcio Craveiro da Silva. Rocha, Acílio da Silva.

Physicians and Managed Care: Employees or Professionals?. Christensen, Kate T.

Politics of Discourse on Liberal Economic Reform: The Case of Africa. Jeong, Ho-Won.

Provider Disclosure of Financial Incentives in Managed Care: Pros and Cons. McCormack, Robert.

## EDUCATION

"The Goals of Multicultural Education: A Critical Re-Evaluation" in *Philosophy of Education (1996)*, Margonis, Frank (ed). Feinberg, Walter.

"The Master and the Magician" in *Jean-Jacques Rousseau and the Sources of the Self*, O'Hagan, Timothy (ed). Caygill, Howard.

"The Moral Presuppositions of Multicultural Education" in *Philosophy of Education (1996)*, Margonis, Frank (ed). Heslep, Robert D.

"The Paradoxes of Education in Rorty's Liberal Utopia" in *Philosophy of Education (1996)*, Margonis, Frank (ed). Reich, Rob.

"The Politics of the "Good" in *Good Sexuality Education*" in *Philosophy of Education (1996)*, Margonis, Frank (ed). Boyd, Dwight and McKay, Alexander.

"The Relevance of the Anthropocentric-Ecocentric Debate" in *Philosophy of Education (1996)*, Margonis, Frank (ed). Snauwaert, Dale T.

"Theoretical and Practical Reasoning: An Intractable Dualism?" in *Philosophy of Education (1996)*, Margonis, Frank (ed). McClellan, Jr, James E.

"Tolerance and Intolerance Gricean Intention and Doing Right by our Students" in *Philosophy of Education (1996)*, Margonis, Frank (ed). Wagner, Paul A.

"Universities and Democracy" in *The Idea of University*, Brzezinski, Jerzy (ed). Samsonowicz, Henryk.

"Utopia Flawed? A Response to Reich on Rorty" in *Philosophy of Education (1996)*, Margonis, Frank (ed). Pendlebury, Shirley.

"What Are Universities For?" in *The Idea of University*, Brzezinski, Jerzy (ed). Kolakowski, Leszek.

"What Can Be Saved of the Idea of the University?" in *The Idea of University*, Brzezinski, Jerzy (ed). Ziembinski, Zygmunt.

"When You Know It, and I Know It, What is It We Know? Pragmatic Realism and the Epistemologically Absolute" in *Philosophy of Education (1996)*, Margonis, Frank (ed). McCarthy, Christine.

(Re)Inventing Scheffler, or, Defending Objective Educational Research. Phillips, D C.

*"Real World" Ethics: Frameworks for Educators and Human Service Professionals.* Nash, Robert J.

*Academic Freedom and Tenure: Ethical Issues.* De George, Richard T.

*Democratic Discipline: Foundation and Practice.* Hoover, Randy L and Kindsvatter, Richard.

*Diversity and Community in the Academy: Affirmative Action in Faculty Appointments.* Wolf-Devine, Celia.

*Ethics for Professionals in Education: Perspectives for Preparation and Practice.* Strike, Kenneth A (ed) and Ternasky, P Lance (ed).

*Ethics in School Counseling.* Schulte, John M and Cochrane, Donald B.

*George Grant and the Subversion of Modernity: Art, Philosophy, Politics, Religion, and Education.* Davis, Arthur (ed).

*John Locke: Some Thoughts Concerning Education* and *Of the Conduct of the Understanding.* Grant, Ruth W (ed) and Tarcov, Nathan (ed).

*Lecturas de Historia de la Filosofía.* Nieto Blanco, Carlos (ed).

*Life as Narcissism: A Unified Theory of Life.* Tabrizi, Firooz N.

*Mentoring the Mentor: A Critical Dialogue with Paulo Freire.* Torres, Amadeu (ed).

*Nietzsche and the Modern Crisis of the Humanities.* Levine, Peter.

*Philosophy of Education (1996).* Margonis, Frank (ed), Boler, Megan (ed) and Callan, Eamonn (ed).

*Plato's Epistemology: How Hard Is It to Know?.* Laidlaw-Johnson, Elizabeth A.

*Rationality* and *Human Dignity*—Confucius, Kant and Scheffler on the Ultimate Aim of Education. Park, Ynhui.

*Reason and Education: Essays in Honor of Isreal Scheffler.* Siegel, Harvey (ed).

*Reasonable Children: Moral Education and Moral Learning.* Pritchard, Michael S.

*Representation and the Text: Re-Framing the Narrative Voice.* Tierney, William G (ed) and Lincoln, Yvonna S (ed).

*Rethinking College Education.* Allan, George.

*Teaching with Love: A Feminist Approach to Early Childhood Education.* Goldstein, Lisa S.

*The American University: National Treasure or Endangered Species?.* Ehrenberg, Ronald G (ed).

*The Ethics of Special Education.* Howe, Ken and Miramontes, Ofelia B.

*The Idea of University.* Brzezinski, Jerzy (ed) and Nowak, Leszek (ed).

*The Moral Base for Teacher Professionalism.* Sockett, Hugh.

*The Order of Learning: Essays on the Contemporary University.* Altbach, Philip G (ed) and Shils, Edward.

*The Reformation of Society Through Adequate Education.* Provost, C Antonio.

A "Third Wave" Manifesto: Keynotes of the Sonoma Conference. Paul, Richard.

A *Física* Subjacente à "Educaçao Filosófica": Proposta por Martinho de Mendonça de Pina e de Proença. Cunha, Norberto.

A Articulaçao entre Infância, Cidadania e História: Uma Questao para a Pedagogia. Marques Veríssimo, Mara Rúba Alves.

A Business Ethics Experiential Learning Module: The Maryland Business School Experience. Loeb, Stephen E and Ostas, Daniel T.

A Conception of Practical Reasoning. Coombs, Jerrold and Wright, Ian.

A Critique of Academic Nationalism. Macdonald, Amie A.

A Educaçao no Imaginário Liberal. Silva Filho, Lauro de Barros.

A Framework for Teaching Business Ethics. Oddo, Alfonso R.

A Method for Teaching Ethics. Gampel, Eric.

A Organizaçao do Trabalho Escolar e os Especialistas da Educaçao. Pizzi, Laura Cristina V.

A Práxis Freireana na Educaçao. Marinho Sampaio, Tânia Maria.

A propos de l'Éducation et de l'Institution scolaire au Québec. Louis, Desmeules and Desjardins, Richard.

A Psychoanalytic Interpretation of the Effectiveness of Humor for Teaching Philosophy. Gibbs, Paul J.

A Purple Sky: The Challenged Chance for Change. Birkhahn, Talya.

A Questao do Método em História da Educaçao. Fonseca Vieira, Márcia Núbia.

A Questao Freireana da Educaçao como Práxis Político-Filosófica. Marinho Sampaio, Tânia Maria.

A Strategy for the Acquisition of Problem-Solving Expertise in Humans: The Category-as-Analogy Approach. Alma, Carine V.

Accommodating Ideological Pluralism in Sexuality Education. McKay, Alexander.

Acerca de las contribuciones actuales de una didáctica de antaño: el caso de la serie de Taylor. Cantoral, Ricardo.

Advocating Values: Professionalism in Teaching Ethics. Martin, Mike W.

Affirmative Action in Higher Education as Redistribution. Guenin, Louis M.

Against Education. Nordenbo, Sven Erik.

Alertness and Determination: A Note on Moral Phenomenology. Wilson, John.

Alfred North Whitehead's Informal Philosophy of Education. Blasius. Ronald F.

An Exercise in Moral Philosophy: Seeking to Understand "Nobody". King, Jonathan B.

An Expanded Theoretical Discourse on Human Sexuality Education. Anderson, Peter B.

An Exploration into Teaching with Computers. Kowalski, Ludwik.

An Instructional Model for Critical Thinking. Leshowitz, Barry and Yoshikawa, Elaine.

Analogy and Argument. McKay, Thomas J.

Animating Rawls's Original Position. Regan, Thomas J.

Argument is War...and War is Hell: Philosophy, Education, and Metaphors for Argumentation. Cohen, Daniel H.

Argumentation, Education and Reasoning. Binkley, Robert W.

Ayudar a crecer: notas sobre la educación en el pensamiento de Leonardo Polo. González Umeres, Luz.

Bertrand Russell and Academic Freedom. Irvine, A D.

Between Fact and Fiction: Dialogue within Encounters of Difference. Conle, Carola.

Beyond Acceptance and Rejection?. Martin, Dan.

Bilingualism in the Business World in West European Minority Language Regions: Profit or Loss?. Van Langevelde, A. P..

Bringing Ancient Philosophy of Life: Teaching Aristotelian and Stoic Theories of Responsibility. Sakezles, Priscilla K.

Building Theory in Music Education: A Personal Account. LeBlanc, Albert.

Business Education, Values and Beliefs. Small, Michael W.

Caring as Thinking. Lipman, Matthew.

Carnival and Domination: Pedagogies of Neither Care Nor Justice. Sidorkin, Alexander M.

Case Studies for Teaching Research Ethics. Elliott, Deni.

Centering Culture: Teaching for Critical Sexual Literacy using the Sexual Diversity Wheel. Sears, James T.

Character Education: Reclaiming the Social. Duncan, Barbara J.

Cheating: Limits of Individual Integrity. Johnston, D Kay.

Civic Education: A New Proposal. Wingo, Ajume H.

Civic Liberalism and Educational Reform. Weinstein, Michael A.

Cognitive Reengineering: A Process for Cultivating Critical Thinking Skills in RNs. Young, Michele M.

Combining Critical Thinking and Written Composition: The Whole Is Greater Than The Sum Of The Parts. Hatcher, Donald L.

Community of Inquiry and Differences of the Heart. Thomas, John C.

Competence-Based Education and Training: Progress or Villainy?. Bridges, David.

Concepçoes de Mundo Veiculadas no Ensino de História do Curso Ginasial em Minas: 1954-1964. Nunes, Silma do Carmo.

Conceptualizing Art Criticism for Effective Practice. Geahigan, George.

Confessions of a Sentimental Philosopher: Science, Animal Rights, and the Demands of Rational Inquiry. Johnson, David Kenneth.

Confronting the Assumptions That Dominate Education Reform. Robenstine, Clark.

Conrad of Megenberg: The Parisian Years. Courtenay, William J.

Content and Criticism: The Aims of Schooling. Hare, William.

Context, Politics and Moral Education: Comments on the Misgeld/Magendzo Conversation about Human Rights Education. Brabeck, Mary M and Ting, Kathleen.

Counterpoint Thinking: Connecting Learning and Thinking in Schools. Melchior, Timothy.

Critical Comparisons of Thinking Skills Programs: Making Curriculum Decisions. Martin, David S.

Critical Thinking and Command of Language. Johnson, Ralph H.

Critical Thinking and Emotional Intelligence. Elder, Linda.

Critical Thinking and Epistemic Obligations. Hatcher, Donald L.

## EDUCATION

Critical Thinking and Foundational Development. Van Haaften, Wouter and Snik, Ger.

Critical Thinking and Its Courses. Fawkes, Don.

Critical Thinking and the Moral Sentiments: Adam Smith's Moral Psychology and Contemporary Debate in Critical Thinking and Informal Logic. Weinstein, Jack Russell.

Critical Thinking and the State of Education Today. Paul, Richard.

Critical Thinking Education Faces the Challenge of Japan. Davidson, Bruce W.

Critical Thinking in College English Studies. Lazere, Donald.

Critical Thinking Pedagogy: A Possible Solution to the "Transfer-Problem. Avery, Jon.

Critical Thinking: Expanding the Paradigm. Weinstein, Mark.

Cultural Conditioning: The Dark Underside of Multiculturalism (Part Two: A Way Out). Reinsmith, William.

Culture, Power and the Social Construction of Morality: Moral Voices of Chinese Students. Chang, Kimberly A.

Defending Freirean Intervention. Roberts, Peter.

Democracy in Education: Beyond the Conservative or Progressivist Stances. Portelli, John.

Democracy, Meritocracy, and the Cognitive Elite: The Real Thesis of *The Bell Curve*. Kaplan, Laura Duhan and Kaplan, Charles.

Développement Moral et Jugement Moral: Réexamen de la Controverse Kohlberg-Gilligan. Savard, Nathalie.

Dewey's Conception of "Virtue" and its Implications for Moral Education. Rice, Suzanne.

Differences in Moral Reasoning Between College and University Business Majors and Non-Business Majors. Snodgrass, James and Behling, Robert.

Direct and Indirect Responsibility: Distributing Blame. Goodnow, Jacqueline J and Warton, Pamela M.

Disciplined Emotions: Philosophies of Educated Feelings. Boler, Megan.

Diversity in the Classroom. Maitzen, Stephen.

Diversity, Values and Social Change: Renegotiating a Consensus on Sex Education. Thomson, Rachel.

Do Religious Life and Critical Thought Need Each Other? A Reply to Reinsmith. Carrier, Richard.

Does it Make Sense to Teach History Through Thinking Skills?. Van Veuren, Pieter.

Does Religious Faith Mean Uncritical Thought? Exploration of a False Dilemma. Davidson, Bruce.

Educaçao e Movimento Social: a Questao da Qualidade do Ensino na Perspectiva de um Sindicato de Educadores. Pinto Furtado, Joao.

Education and Nationality. White, John.

Education as Encounter: Buber's Pragmatic Ontology. McHenry Jr, Henry D.

Education for Imaginative Knowledge. Nuyen, A T.

Education of Ethics Committees. Thomasma, David C.

Education, Work and Well-Being. White, John.

Educational Assessment: Reply to Andrew Davis. Winch, Christopher and Gingell, John.

Educational Psychologists as Trainers for Intellectual Development. Hartman, Hope J.

Educational Reform: A Complex Matter. Reynolds, Sherrie and Martin, Kathleen.

El Concepto de "Hombre Natural" en Rousseau (Consideraciones Etico-Educativas). Molina, Katiuska.

El Derecho al Sentido en lo Posmoderno. Follari, Roberto A.

El educador viquiano. Rebollo Espinosa, Maria José.

Elecciones epistemológicas y práctica docente. Marincevic, Juan and Becerra Batán, Marcela.

Elementos para a Construçao Teórica da Historicidade das Práticas Educativas Escolares. Pereira da Silva, Marcelo Soares.

En torno a la sociabilidad humana en el pensamiento de Leonardo Polo. Naval, Concepción.

Enduring Crises and Challenges of African-American Studies. Adeleke, Tunde.

Ensino de Ciências e Formaçao Continuada de Professores: Algumas Consideraçao Históricas. Flória Gouveia, Mariley Simoes.

Environmental Education and Beyond. Bonnett, Michael.

Ethics and MIS Education. McGowan, Matthew K and McGowan, Richard J.

Ethics and the Philosophy of Music Education. Richmond, John W

Ethics Outside the Limits of Philosophy: Ethical Inquiry at Metropolitan State University. Salzberger, Ronald Paul.

European Children Thinking Together in 100. Heesen, Berrie.

Evaluating Edwin Gordon's Music Learning Theory from a Critical Thinking Perspective. Woodford, Paul G.

Evaluating Teaching and Students' Learning of Academic Research Ethics. Elliott, Deni.

Expanding Diversity Education for Preservice Teachers: Teaching about Racial Isolation in Urban Schools. Malone, Patricia.

Experience and the Postmodern Spirit. McCarty, Luise Prior.

Fawkes On Indicator Words. Smythe, Thomas W.

Feeling Fraudulent: Some Moral Quandaries of a Feminist Instructor. Overall, Christine.

Feminist Pedagogy Theory: Reflections on Power and Authority. Luke, Carmen.

Filosofia da Educaçao e História da Pedagogia. Casulo, José Carlos.

Filosofia da Educaçao na Experiência Educativa Inter-Cultural de D. Frei Caetano Brandao em Terras de Belém do Pará 1782-1789. Dias, José Ribeiro.

Filosofía de la educación: tareas y desafíos. Cordero C, Gerardo Arturo.

Filosofía española en el bachillerato?. Mora, José Luis.

Finalidad y libertad en educación. Altarejos, Francisco.

Fostering Autonomy. Fowler Morse, Jane.

Fostering Market Competence. Askland, Andrew.

Foucault's Genealogy and Teaching Multiculturalism as a Subversive Activity. Kazmi, Y.

Foucault, Education, the Self and Modernity. Wain, Kenneth.

Gerência da Qualidade Total: Conservaçao ou Superaçao do Processo de Alienaçao. Vieira Silva, Maria.

Giambattista Vico, la Universidad y el saber: el modelo retórico. Patella, Giuseppe.

God and Jacques Maritain's Philosophy of Education: Uninvited Guests at the Postmodern Party. D'Souza, Mario O.

Good Thinking. Lipman, Matthew.

Harvesting the Cognitive Revolution: Reflections on *The Arts, Education, and Aesthetic Knowing*. Klempay DiBlasio, Margaret.

High School Teaching of Bioethics in New Zealand, Australia and Japan. Asada, Yukiko, Tsuzuki, Miho and Akiyama, Shiro.

How Should Schools Respond to the Plurality of Values in a Multi-Cultural Society?. Burwood, Les R V.

Human Rights Education, Moral Education and Modernisation: The General Relevance of Some Latin American Experiences: A Conversation. Misgeld, Dieter and Magendzo, Abraham.

Humane Education: A Paradigm for Ethical Problem Solving in Education. Bloom, Joyce.

Identidade e Deontologia em Educaçao. Da Veiga, Manuel Alte.

Illusory Freedoms: Liberalism, Education and the Market. Jonathan, Ruth.

Improving Academic Writing. Bennett, Jonathan and Gorovitz, Samuel.

Improving Scientific Reasoning through Philosophy for Children: An Empirical Study. Sprod, Tim.

In Defense of Israel Scheffler's Conception of Moral Education. Coombs, Jerrold.

In Defense of Public Reason: On the Nature of Historical Rationality. Ellet Jr, Frederick S and Ericson, David P.

In Praise of Objective-Subjectivity: Teaching the Pursuit of Precision. Diller, Ann.

In Search of Bioethics: A Personal Postscript. Mainetti, Joé Alberto.

Incorporating Critical Thinking in the Curriculum: An Introduction to Some Basic Issues. Ennis, Robert H.

Increasing Effectiveness in Teaching Ethics to Undergraduate Business Students. Lampe, Marc.

Indoctrination and Moral Reasoning: A Comparison between Dutch and East German Students. De Mey, Langha and Schulze, Hans-Joachim.

Informática na Educaçao: Perspectivas. Miranda Carrao, Eduardo Vitor.

Integrity and the Feminist Teacher. O'Dea, Jane.

Interpretation as Action: The Risk of Inquiry. Awbrey, Jon and Awbrey, Susan.

Is Edwin Gordon's Learning Theory a Cognitive One?. Stokes, W Ann.

Is Peer Review Overrated?. Shatz, David.

Is There a "Language of Education?". Oelkers, Jürgen.

Israel Scheffler on Religion, Reason and Education. McLaughlin, Terence H.

Israel Scheffler's "Moral Education and the Democratic Ideal". Siegel, Harvey.

Israel Scheffler's Ethics: Theory and Practice. Worsfold, Victor L.

Kohlberg's Dormant Ghosts: The Case of Education. Oser, Fritz K.

L'ultimo dei porcospini: Intervista biografico-teorica a René Girard. Antonello, Pierpaolo (ed) and De Castro Rocha, Joao Cezar (ed).

La didáctica de la filosofía en Italia. Sánchez Huertas, María José.

La Paideia Durkheimiana: una teoría general de la educación. López de Dicastillo, Luis.

Landmarks in Critical Thinking Series: Ennis on the Concept of Critical Thinking. Hoaglund, John.

Landmarks in Critical Thinking Series: John Passmore: On Teaching to be Critical. Splitter, Laurance.

Landmarks in Critical Thinking Series: Plato's Euthyphro. Spangler, Al.

Language in Stories for Boys and Girls. Velasco, Mónica.

Language: Definition and Metaphor. Barrow, Robin.

Learning Moral Commitment in Higher Education?. Collier, Gerald.

Learning Philosophy Collaboratively with a Student. Weiss, Andrea and Katzner, James.

Literary Development as Spiritual Development in the Common School. Newby, Mike.

Living Educational Theories and Living Contradictions: A Response to Mike Newby. Whitehead, Jack.

Lost Times/Recovered Times. Reed, Ronald.

Lui's Complaint. Lee, Zosimo E.

Lyin' T(*)gers, and "Cares," Oh My: The Case for Feminist Integration of Business Ethics. Rabouin, Michelle.

Managers' Perception of Proper Ethical Conduct: The Effect of Sex, Age, and Level and Education. Deshpande, Satish P.

## EDUCATION

## EDUCATION

The Inseparability of Morality and Well-Being: The Duty/Virtue Debate Revisited. Keefer, Matthew Wilks.

The Measure of Morality: Rethinking Moral Reasoning. Vine, Ian.

The Moral and Spiritual Dimension to Education: Some Reflections on the British Experience. Rossiter, Graham.

The Much-Maligned Cliché Strikes Back. Brown, William R.

The NCTM Standards and the Philosophy of Mathematics. Toumasis, Charalampos.

The Need for Comprehensiveness in Critical Thinking Instruction. Nosich, Gerald.

The Nurturing of a Relational Epistemology. Thayer-Bacon, Barbara J.

The Ombudsman for Research Practice: A Proposal for a New Position and an Invitation to Comment. Fischbach, Ruth L and Gilbert, Diane C.

The Philosophy They Bring to Class: Companion Student Papers in PHL 101. Chiles, Robert E.

The Qualitymongers. Hart, W A.

The Revisionary Visionary: Leadership and the Aesthetics of Adaptability. DeGraff, Jeff and Merritt, Suzanne.

The Summer Philosophy Institute of Colorado: Building Bridges. Figueroa, Robert and Goering, Sara.

The Teaching of Ethics. Dooley, Mark J.

The Value(s) of Sex Education. Reiss, Michael J.

The Virtual Seminar Room: Using a World Wide Web Site in Teaching Ethics. Hinman, Lawrence M.

The Vocation of Higher Education: Modern and Postmodern Rhetorics in the Israeli Academia on Strike. Gur-Ze'ev, Ilan.

The Youth Charter: Towards the Formation of Adolescent Moral Identity. Damon, William and Gregory, Anne.

Thinking Critically About Critical Thinking: An Unskilled Inquiry into Quinn and McPeck. Gardner, Peter and Johnson, Steve.

Thinking Critically About Identities. Webster, Yehudi O.

Those Who Can, Do: A Response to Sidney Gendin's "Am I Wicked?". Warren, Dona.

Thou Shalt and Shalt Not: An Alternative to the Ten Commandments Approach to Developing a Code of Ethics for Schools of Business. Kleiner, Deborah S and Maury, Mary D.

Tocqueville on Democratic Education: The Problem of Public Passivity. Blits, Jan H.

Total Quality Management: A Plan for Optimizing Human Potential?. Wagner, Paul A.

Towards a Whole School or College Policy for a Pre-Philosophical and Higher Order Thinking 'Entitlement' Curriculum. Thornbury, Robert.

True Colors: The Response of Business Schools to Declining Enrollment. McKendall, Marie A and Lindquist, Stanton C.

Trust Is Not Enough: Classroom Self-Disclosure and the Loss of Private Lives. Bishop, Nicole.

Two Significant Problems in Education—the General One and the Particular One (in Serbo-Croatian). Babic, Jovan.

Una aproximación a la ética en el programa Filosofía para Niños de Matthew Lipman. Accorinti, Stella.

Unity and Diversity through Education: A Comparison of the Thought of W.E.B. DuBois and John Dewey. Burks, Ben.

Using Moral Dilemmas in Children's Literature as a Vehicle for Moral Education and Teaching Reading Comprehension. Clare, Lindsay, Gallimore, Ronald and Patthey-Chavez, G Genevieve.

Voices in the Classroom: Girls and Philosophy for Children. Mohr-Lane, Jana.

What Cognitive Science Tells Us about Ethics and the Teaching of Ethics. Anderson, James A.

What is a Child?. Friquenon, Marie-Louise.

What Rough Beast...? Narrative Relationships and Moral Education. Gooderham, David W.

When Manipulation Is Indispensable to Education: The Moral Work of Fiction. Thompson, Audrey.

Whether Logic Should Satisfy the Humanities Requirement. Martin, John N.

Who Benefits? Music Education and the National Standards. Schmidt, Catherine M.

Who's Afraid of Assessment? Remarks on Winch and Gingell's Reply. Davis, Andrew.

Why Should Educators Care about Argumentation?. Siegel, Harvey.

Wilbur Schramm and the Founding of Communication Studies. Glander, Timothy.

Wisdom and Intelligence in Philosophy for Children. Lindop, Clive.

Without a Care in the World: The Business Ethics Course and Its Exclusion of a Care Perspective. DeMoss, Michelle A and McCann, Greg K.

Women, Ethics, and MBAs. MacLellan, Cheryl and Dobson, John.

## EDWARDS

*Jonathan Edwards's Writings*: Text, Context, Interpretation. Stein, Stephen J (ed).

## EDWARDS, P

The Hume-Edwards Objection to the Cosmological Argument. Vallicella, William F.

## EFFECT

"Conceptualism and the Ontological Independence of Cause and Effect" in *Dispositions: A Debate*, Armstrong, D M. Place, U T.

*Dispositions: A Debate*. Armstrong, D M, Martin, C B and Place, Ullin T.

Curie's Principle. Ismael, Jenann.

Taking Hindrance Seriously. Beebee, Helen.

The Five Ways and the Argument from Composition: A Reply to John Lamont. Côté, Antoine.

## EFFECTIVE

A Minimal Logical System for Computable Concepts and Effective Knowability. Freund, Max A.

Formalizing Forcing Arguments in Subsystems of Second-Order Arithmetic. Avigad, Jeremy.

Step by Recursive Step: Church's Analysis of Effective Calculability. Sieg, Wilfried.

What's in a Function?. Antonelli, Gian Aldo.

## EFFECTIVENESS

Logique, effectivité et faisabilité. Dubucs, Jacques.

## EFFICIENCY

The Return of the Group. Sterelny, Kim.

## EGALITARIANISM

"Liberalism, Nationalism, and Egalitarianism" in *The Morality of Nationalism*, McKim, Robert (ed). Scheffler, Samuel.

*Equality: Selected Readings*. Pojman, Louis (ed) and Westmoreland, Robert (ed).

A Question for Egalitarians. Kekes, John.

Between Inconsistent Nominalists and Egalitarian Idealists. Nelson, Ralph C.

Can An Egalitarian Justify Universal Access to Health Care?. Jacobs, Lesley A.

Egalitarian Justice and the Importance of the Free Will Problem. Smilansky, Saul.

Egalitarian Liberalism and the Fact of Pluralism. Lund, William.

Environmental Egalitarianism and 'Who do you Save?' Dilemmas. Michael, Mark A.

Equality in Health Care: Christian Engagement with a Secular Obsession. Engelhardt Jr, H Tristram.

Equality, Priority, and Time. Kappel, Klemens.

Self-Ownership and Equality: Brute Luck, Gifts, Universal Dominance, and Leximin. Vallentyne, Peter.

## EGAN, F

A Clearer Vision. Shapiro, Lawrence A.

## EGEA-KUEHNE, D

"The Double-Bind of "Double Duty" in *Philosophy of Education (1996)*, Margonis, Frank (ed). Davis, Hilary E.

## EGO

*see also* Transcendental Ego

"Per una topologia dell'ego" in *Geofilosofia*, Bonesio, Luisa (ed). Vitiello, Vincenzo.

"Points of Convergence Between Dooyeweerdian and Feminist Views of the Philosophic Self" in *Knowing Other-Wise: Philosophy at the Threshold of Spirituality*, Olthuis, James H (ed). Wesselius, Janet Catherina.

Apperception and Spontaneity. Carl, Wolfgang.

Husserl et le *Ichprinzip*: Le tournant en question. Paquette, Éric.

## EGOCENTRISM

Working Without a Net: A Study of Egocentric Epistemology. David, Marian.

## EGOISM

Accepting Agent Centred Norms: A Problem for Non-Cognitivists and a Suggestion for Solving It. Dreier, James.

Aristotle's Ethical Egoism. Gottlieb, Paula.

Butler, Hobbes, and Human Nature. O'Brien, Wendell.

El aristotelismo y el tomismo frente al egoísmo psicológico. Lukac de Stier, María L.

Il fondamento etico e metafisico del diritto. Bagolini, Luigi.

Rationality and Ethics. French, Peter.

The Wisdom of the Egoist: The Moral and Political Implications of Valuing the Self. Hampton, Jean.

## EGYPTIAN

"Gift of the Egyptians" (On the History of Christian Philosophy) (in Czech). Rugási, Gyula.

Egyptian Priests and German Professors: On the Alleged Difficulty of Philosophy. Protevi, John.

Philosophy and Egypt. Glouberman, Mark.

## EIGHTEENTH CENTURY

*see* Modern

## EINSTEIN

"Einstein *Agonists*: Weyl and Reichenbach on Geometry and the General Theory of Relativity" in *Origins of Logical Empiricism*, Giere, Ronald N (ed). Ryckman, T A.

Classical Physics and Early Quantum Theory: A Legitimate Case of Theoretical Underdetermination. Hudson, Robert G.

Conferencias de Einstein. Jacinto Z, Agustin.

Die Bedeutung des Machschen Prinzips in der Kosmologie. Dambmann, Holger.

Einstein's 1927 Unpublished Hidden-Variable Theory: Its Background Context and Significance. Belousek, Darrin W.

Einsteins Zug und logische Gesetze. Strobach, Niko.

Laws of Nature, Cosmic Coincidences and Scientific Realism. Lange, Marc.

## EINSTEIN

Picturing Einstein's Train of Thought. White, V Alan.

The Definition of Rigidity in the Special Theory of Relativity and the Genesis of the General Theory of Relativity. Maltese, Giulio and Orlando, Lucia.

The Research Program in Natural Philosophy from Gauss and Riemann to Einstein and Whitehead: From the Theory of Invariants to the Idea of a Field Theory of Cognition. Stolz, Joachim.

Über den Charakter von Einsteins philosophischem Realismus. Polikarov, Asaria.

## EL GRECO

El Greco's Statements on Michelangelo the Painter. Rodetis, George A.

## ELDERLY

Can Old-Age Social Insurance Be Justified. Shapiro, Daniel J.

## ELECTIONS

"Speaking of Politics in the United States: Who Talks to Whom, Why, and Why Not" in *Political Dialogue: Theories and Practices,* Esquith, Stephen L (ed). Bennett, Stephen Earl, Fisher, Bonnie and Resnick, David.

Elección pública y Democracia representativa. Carreras, Mercedes.

## ELECTRODYNAMICS

The Peculiar Notion of Exchange Forces—II: From Nuclear Forces to QED, 1929-1950. Carson, Cathryn.

## ELECTRON

Rethinking the 'Discover' of the Electron. Arabatzis, Theodore.

## ELECTRONICS

Fares and Free Riders on the Information Highway. Rosen, C Martin and Carr, Gabrielle M.

Principles and Purpose: The Patient Surrogate's Perspective and Role. Koch, Tom.

The Ethics of Information Transfer in the Electronic Age: Scholars Unite!. Laidlaw-Johnson, Elizabeth A.

## ELEMENT

Hyperalgebraic Primitive Elements for Relational Algebraic and Topological Algebraic Models. Insall, Matt.

La causalidad material de los elementos en la generación de los cuerpos mixtos. Sacchi, Mario Enrique.

Translating the Hypergame Paradox: Remarks on the Set of Founded Elements of a Relation. Bernardi, Claudio and D'Agostino, Giovanna.

## ELEMENTARY

Boolean Pairs Formed by the Delta$^0_n$-Sets. Hermann, E.

Cauchy Completeness in Elementary Logic. Cifuentes, J C, Sette, A M and Mundici, Daniele.

Elementary Realizability. Damnjanovic, Zlatan.

On Elementary Equivalence for Equality-free Logic. Casanovas, E, Dellunde, Pilar and Jansana, Ramon.

Term Rewriting Theory for the Primitive Recursive Functions. Cichon, E A and Weiermann, A.

## ELEPHANTS

When Preservationism Doesn't Preserve. Schmidtz, David.

## ELGIN, C

Elgin on Lewis's Putnam's Paradox. Van Fraassen, Bas C.

Interpretive Pluralism and the Ontology of Art. Davies, David.

## ELIADE, M

*The Magic Mirror: Myth's Abiding Power.* Baeten, Elizabeth M.

## ELIMINATION

Contraction-Elimination for Implicational Logics. Kashima, Ryo.

The Elimination of *De Re* Formulas. Kaminski, Michael.

## ELIMINATIVISM

*Connectionism and Eliminativism: Reply to Stephen Mills in Vol. 5, No. 1.* Macdonald, Cynthia.

Testament of a Recovering Eliminativist. Melnyk, Andrew.

## ELIOT, G

*Phantom Formations: Aesthetic Ideology and the Bildungsroman.* Redfield, Marc.

## ELITISM

"Élites Sin Privilegio" in *Política y Sociedad en José Ortega y Gasset: En Torno a "Vieja y Nueva Política",* Lopez de la Vieja, Maria Teresa (ed). López de la Vieja, Maria Teresa.

Advocacy, Therapy, and Pedagogy. MacKinnon, John E.

Democracy, Meritocracy, and the Cognitive Elite: The Real Thesis of *The Bell Curve*. Kaplan, Laura Duhan and Kaplan, Charles.

## ELLIOT, D

Aesthetic and Praxial Philosophies of Music Education Compared: A Semiotic Consideration. Spychiger, Maria B.

## ELLIOT, R

Genetic Therapy, Person-Regarding Reasons and the Determination of Identity: A Reply to Robert Elliot. Persson, Ingmar.

## ELLIS, G

The Principal Paradox of Time Travel. Riggs, Peter.

## ELLUL, J

Jacques Ellul on the Technical System and the Challenge of Christian Hope. Punzo, Vincent A.

## ELSTER, J

Jon Elster y el pensamiento del límite. Ambrosini, Cristina.

Let Them Eat Chances: Probability and Distributive Justice. Wasserman, David.

Realizability as Constituent Element of the Justificatin Structure of the Public Decision. Cuñarro Conde, Edith Mabel.

Sustainable Development and the Local Justice Framework. Roe, Emery.

## ELUSIVE

Elusive Knowledge. Lewis, David.

## EMANCIPATION

"Liberalism and the Politics of Emancipation: The Black Experience" in *Existence in Black: An Anthology of Black Existential Philosophy.* Gordon, Lewis R (ed). Carew, George.

*Emancipation and Illusion: Rationality and Gender in Habermas's Theory of Modernity.* Fleming, Marie.

Emancipatory Social Science: Habermas on Nietzsche. Kerckhove, Lee.

## EMBEDDING

A Finite Lattice without Critical Triple That Cannot Be Embedded into the Enumerable Turing Degrees. Lerman, Manuel and Lempp, Steffen.

Higman's Embedding Theorem in a General Setting and its Application to Existentially Closed Algebras. Belegradek, Oleg V.

Modal Companions of Intermediate Propositional Logics. Chagrov, Alexander and Zakharyashchev, Michael.

The Self-Embedding Theorem of $WKL_0$ and a Non-Standard Method. Tanaka, Kazuyuki.

## EMBRYO

"Ethical Considerations in the Multiplication of Human Embryos" in *Reproduction, Technology, and Rights: Biomedical Ethics Reviews,* Humber, James M (ed). Ganss Gibson, Kathleen and Massey, Joe B.

Che cosa ha veramente detto il Comitato Nazionale per la Bioetica sull'individualità dell'embrione?. Mori, Maurizio.

Embryo Experimentation, Personhood and Human Rights. Van Niekerk, Anton A and Van Zyl, Liezl.

Ethical Reflections on the Status of the Preimplantation Embryo Leading to the German Embryo Protection Act. Michelmann, H W and Hinney, B.

Experimenting with Embryos: Can Philosophy Help?. Heyd, David.

L'embrione è arrivato tra noi. Viano, Carlo Augusto.

Preimplantation Embryos, Research Ethics, and Public Policy. Tauer, Carol A.

The Argument from Potential: A Reappraisal. Reichlin, Massimo.

## EMBRYOLOGY

*Vom Begründen zum Handeln: Aufsätze zur angewandten Ethik.* Ott, Konrad.

Physiology, Embryology and Psychopathology: A Test Case for Hegelian Thought (in French). Rozenberg, Jacques J.

## EMERGENCE

De structuur van Searles filosofische project. Meijers, Anthonie.

Emergence and Deconstruction (in Czech). Cibulka, Josef.

Explaining Emergence: Towards an Ontology of Levels. Emmeche, Claus, Koppe, Simo and Stjernfelt, Frederik.

How Properties Emerge. Humphreys, Paul.

## EMERGENCY

In Case of Emergency: No Need for Consent. Brody, Baruch A, Katz, Jay and Dula, Annette.

## EMERGENTISM

*Cervello-Mente: Pensatori del XX secolo.* Gava, Giacomo.

## EMERSON

"Peirce and Representative Persons" in *Philosophy in Experience: American Philosophy in Transition,* Hart, Richard (ed). Anderson, Douglas R.

Rolston, Naturogenic Value and Genuine Biocentrism. Thomas, Emyr Vaughan.

## EMIGRATION

Georg Lukács's *Destruction of Reason* and the Political Theories of the Western Emigration: Some Theses (in Hungarian). Söllner, Alfons.

## EMOTION

see also Feeling, Sentiment

"Is Love an Emotion?" in *Love Analyzed,* Lamb, Roger E. Green, O H.

"Music and Negative Emotion" in *Music and Meaning,* Robinson, Jenefer (ed). Levinson, Jerrold.

"Schleiermacher on the Self: Immediate Self-Consciousness as Feeling and as Thinking" in *Figuring the Self: Subject, Absolute, and Others in Classical German Philosophy,* Zöller, Günter (ed). Klemm, David E.

"Why Listen to Sad Music If It Makes One Feel Sad?" in *Music and Meaning,* Robinson, Jenefer (ed). Davies, Stephen.

"'Tempus movet pathos': tratti retorico-poetici del tempo" in *Il Concetto di Tempo: Atti del XXXII Congresso Nazionale della Società Filosofica Italiana,* Casertano, Giovanni (ed). Furnari Luvarà, Giusi.

*Love Analyzed.* Lamb, Roger E.

*Making a Necessity of Virtue.* Sherman, Nancy.

*Music and Meaning.* Robinson, Jenefer (ed).

A Lack of Feeling in Kant: Response to Patricia M. Matthews. Huhn, Tom.

An Anti-Anti-Essentialist View of the Emotions: A Reply to Kupperman. Dalgleish, Tim.

Appraisal Theories of Emotions. Ben-Ze'ev, Aaron.

Aquinas on Passions and Diminished Responsibility. Nisters, Thomas.

Are Appeals to the Emotions Necessarily Fallacious?. Hinman, Lawrence M.

Aristotle on How to Define a Psychological State. Wedin, Michael V.

## EMPIRICISM

The Modularity of Language—Some Empirical Considerations. Grodzinsky, Yosef.

The Needs of Understanding: Kant on Empirical Laws and Regulative Ideals. O'Shea, James R.

Thick Epistemic Access: Distinguishing the Mathematical from the Empirical. Azzouni, Jody.

Unhewn Demonstrations. Collier, Andrew.

Using a Dialectical Scientific Brief in Peer Review. Stamps III, Arthur E.

What is Given? Thought and Event (in French). Benoist, Jocelyn.

What Use Is Empirical Confirmation?. Miller, David.

Whewell on the Ultimate Problem of Philosophy. Morrison, Margaret.

Why It Is Better Never To Come Into Existence. Benatar, David.

Zu Fichtes Kritik an Reinholds *empirischem* Satz des Bewusstseins und ihrer Vorgeschichte. Bondeli, Martin.

## EMPLOYEE

Identifying the Real EAP Client: Ensuing Ethical Dilemmas. Lee, Sandra S and Schonberg, Sue E.

Perceived Seriousness of Business Ethics Issues. Fusilier, Marcelline R, Aby, Carroll D and Worley, Joel K (& others).

The After-Acquired Evidence Defense: The Unethical Repercussions to Employees. Brady, Teresa.

## EMPLOYER

Speaking Truth to Employers. Andre, Judith.

## EMPLOYMENT

Eliminating the Barriers to Employment Equity in the Canadian Workplace. Falkenberg, L E and Boland, L.

Impression Management, Fairness, and the Employment Interview. Rosenfeld, Paul.

Institutionalized Resistance to Organizational Change: Denial, Inaction and Repression. Agócs, Carol.

The Case for Maintaining and Encouraging the Use of Voluntary Affirmative Action in Private Sector Employment. Fick, Barbara J.

## EMPOWERMENT

Jharkhand: A Movement from Ethnicity to Empowerment of Autonomy. Vadakumchery, Johnson.

## EMPTINESS

"Tempo vuoto/tempo proprio" in *Il Concetto di Tempo: Atti del XXXII Congresso Nazionale della Società Filosofica Italiana,* Casertano, Giovanni (ed). Gregorio, Giuliana.

Down the Slope. Karasev, L V.

La muerte, ese escándalo. Pfeiffer, María Luisa.

Time and Emptiness in the *Chao-Lun.* Berman, Michael.

## ENCYCLOPEDIA

*Encyclopedia of Classical Philosophy.* Devereux, Daniel T (ed) and Mitsis, Phillip T (ed).

*The Social Philosophy of Ernest Gellner.* Jarvie, Ian (ed) and Hall, John A (ed).

The *Philosophical Encyclopedia* Is Twenty-Five. Kamenskii, Z A.

The Heterogeneity of Clinical Ethics: The State of the Field as Reflected in the *Encyclopedia of Bioethics.* Koczwara, Bogda M and Madigan, Timothy J.

## END

*see also* Teleology

"*Drama* O Dell'"Espressione A Ogni Costo": L'azione tragica: Nietzsche critico di Wagner" in *Soggetto E Verità: La questione dell'uomo nella filosofia contemporanea,* Fagiuoli, Ettore. Fagiuoli, Ettore.

"De servo arbitrio: La fine della libertà in Martin Heidegger" in *Lo Storicismo e la Sua Storia: Temi, Problemi, Prospettive,* Cacciatore, Giuseppe (ed). Mazzarella, Eugenio.

Diritti umani e dover essere. Troncarelli, Barbara.

The Limited Unity of Virtue. Badhwar, Neera Kapur.

## ENDOSCOPY

The Gastroenterologist and His Endoscope: The Embodiment of Technology and the Necessity for a Medical Ethics. Cooper, M Wayne.

## ENDRES, B

"Decentering and Reasoning" in *Philosophy of Education (1996),* Margonis, Frank (ed). Weinstein, Mark.

## ENERGY

*Vom Begründen zum Handeln: Aufsätze zur angewandten Ethik.* Ott, Konrad.

## ENGELHARDT, T

Los fundamentos de la bioética de H. Tristram Engelhardt. Martínez Barrera, Jorge.

## ENGELS

*Classics of Modern Political Theory: Machiavelli to Mill.* Cahn, Steven M.

*Introduction to Marx and Engels: A Critical Reconstruction.* Schmitt, Richard.

Frederick Engels: Scholar and Revolutionary. Labica, Georges.

The Revolutionary Aesthetics of Frederick Engels. San Juan Jr, E.

Why Did Marx and Engels Concern Themselves with Natural Science?. Griese, Anneliese and Pawelzig, Gerd.

## ENGINEER

Better Communication between Engineers and Managers: Some Ways to Prevent Many Ethically Hard Choices. Davis, Michael.

Commentary on "Better Communication between Engineers and Managers. Loui, Michael.

Commentary on "Better Communication between Engineers and Managers". Pritchard, Michael S.

Commentary on "Technology and Civil Disobedience: Why Engineers Have a Special Duty to Obey the Law". Boisjoly, Roger M.

Technology and Civil Disobedience: Why Engineers Have a Special Duty to Obey the Law. Schlossberger, Eugene.

The Engineer's Moral Right to Reputational Fairness. McGinn, Robert E.

## ENGINEERING

A Case Study of Conflicting Interests: Flemish Engineers Involved in Environmental Impact Assessment. Holemans, Dirk.

An Historical Preface to Engineering Ethics. Davis, Michael.

Cognitive Reengineering: A Process for Cultivating Critical Thinking Skills in RNs. Young, Michele M.

Comment: What We Can Learn from "Better Communication between Engineers and Managers" (M. Davis). Whitbeck, Caroline.

Computer Ethics and Moral Methodology. Van den Hoven, Jeroen.

Promoting Ethical Standards in Science and Engineering. Frankel, Mark S.

Responsible Engineering: *Gilbane Gold* Revisited. Pritchard, Michael S and Holtzapple, Mark.

Symposium on Computer Ethics. Ward Bynum, Terrell.

Teaching Ethics in Science and Engineering: Animals in Research. Jamieson, Dale.

Teaching Ethics to Scientists and Engineers: Moral Agents and Moral Problems. Whitbeck, Caroline.

Technology in Opposition Power—Must (Czech). Lenk, Hans and Maring, Matthias.

What Place does Religion have in the Ethical Thinking of Scientists and Engineers?. Fisher, Ian StJohn.

Why Teach Ethics in Science and Engineering?. Johnson, Deborah G, Hollander, Rachelle D and Beckwith, Jonathan R (& others).

## ENGLISH

*see also* British

*Hegel, Marx, and the English State.* MacGregor, David.

Critical Thinking in College English Studies. Lazere, Donald.

English-Language History and the Creation of Historical Paradigm. Merridale, Catherine.

Interrogative Wh-Movement in Slovene and English. Golden, Marija.

Reason, Rhetoric and the Price of Linguistic Revision. McGrew, Lydia M.

## ENHANCEMENT

Can Enhancement Be Distinguished from Prevention in Genetic Medicine?. Juengst, Eric T.

## ENLIGHTENMENT

"Averroës and Inquiry: The Need for an Enlightened Community" in *Averroës and the Enlightenment,* Wahba, Mourad (ed). Madigan, Timothy J.

"Enlightenment in the Islamic World: Muslims—Victims of Mneumonic Success" in *Averroës and the Enlightenment,* Wahba, Mourad (ed). Irfan, Ghazala.

"Ibn Rushd, European Enlightenment, Africa, and African Philosophy" in *Averroës and the Enlightenment,* Wahba, Mourad (ed). Beyaraza, Ernest K.

"Intellectual Freedom, Rationality, and Enlightenment: The Contributions of Averroës" in *Averroës and the Enlightenment,* Wahba, Mourad (ed). Kurtz, Paul.

"Islam and Enlightenment" in *Averroës and the Enlightenment,* Wahba, Mourad (ed). Howeidy, Yehia.

"Metodo e modelli storiografici nel tardo illuminismo tedesco" in *Lo Storicismo e la Sua Storia: Temi, Problemi, Prospettive,* Cacciatore, Giuseppe (ed). D'Allessandro, Giuseppe.

"Secularization in Turkey" in *Averroës and the Enlightenment,* Wahba, Mourad (ed). Kuçuradi, Ioanna.

"The Averroistic Ethos Beyond the Enlightenment" in *Averroës and the Enlightenment,* Wahba, Mourad (ed). Teffo, Joe.

"The Islamic Perspective on Enlightenment: Principles and Implementation" in *Averroës and the Enlightenment,* Wahba, Mourad (ed). Shahrestani, S M A.

"The Third World and Enlightenment" in *Averroës and the Enlightenment,* Wahba, Mourad (ed). Osman, Mahmoud.

*Averroës and the Enlightenment.* Wahba, Mourad (ed) and Abousenna, Mona (ed).

*Enlightenment East and West.* Angel, Leonard.

*The Sovereignty of Reason: The Defense of Rationality in the Early English Enlightenment.* Beiser, Frederick C.

*Utilitarianism.* Scarre, Geoffrey.

Beyond Enlightenment? After the Subject of Foucault, Who Comes?. Venn, Couze.

Dead or Alive? Reflective Versus Unreflective Traditions. Tate, John W.

Der Klagenfurter Herbert-Kreis zwischen Aufklärung und Romantik. Baum, Wilhelm.

Deutsche Aufklärung und französiche *Lumières.* D'Hondt, Jacques.

Did the Enlightenment Just Happen to Men?. Whyte, Philip.

Dissatisfied Enlightenment: Certain Difficulties Concerning the Public Use of One's Reason. Deligiorgi, Katerina.

Eclecticism or Skepticism? A Problem of the Early Enlightenment. Mulsow, Martin.

## ENLIGHTENMENT

Habermas and Foucault: How to Carry Out the Enlightenment Project. Nielsen, Kai.

Hegel and the Enlightenment: A Study in Ambiguity. Dupré, Louis.

Hegel on Historical Meaning: For Example, The Enlightenment. Pippin, Robert B.

Is Nietzsche a Political Thinker?. Nussbaum, Martha C.

La Ilustración española: Entre el reformismo y la utopía. Fernández Sanz, Amable.

Ningen: Intersubjectivity in the Ethics of Watsuji Tetsuro. McCarthy, Erin.

Plato's Enlightenment: The Good as the Sun. Wheeler III, Samuel C.

Romanticized Enlightenment? Enlightened Romanticism? Universalism and Particularism in Hegel's *Understanding of the Enlightenment*. Pinkard, Terry.

Santayana's Sage: The Disciplines of Aesthetic Enlightenment. Alexander, Thomas M.

Seyla Benhabib and the Radical Future of the Enlightenment. Nagl-Docekal, Herta.

Stain, Disfiguration and Orgy (in Spanish). Cardona Suárez, Luis Fernando.

The Fool's Truth: Diderot, Goethe, and Hegel. Schmidt, James.

The French Revolutionary Roots of Political Modernity in Hegel's Philosophy, or the Enlightenment at Dusk. Wokler, Robert.

Thomas Abbt and the Formation of an Enlightened German "Public". Redekop, Benjamin W.

## ENNIS, R

Landmarks in Critical Thinking Series: Ennis on the Concept of Critical Thinking. Hoaglund, John.

## ENQUIRY

*see* Inquiry

## ENROLLMENT

True Colors: The Response of Business Schools to Declining Enrollment. McKendall, Marie A and Lindquist, Stanton C.

## ENTAILMENT

"Bestätigung und Relevanz" in *Das weite Spektrum der analytischen Philosophie*, Lenzen, Wolfgang. Stelzner, Werner.

"Semantic Considerations on Relevance" in *Das weite Spektrum der analytischen Philosophie*, Lenzen, Wolfgang. Orlowska, Ewa.

Generalising Tautological Entailment. Lavers, Peter.

Polarity Sensitivity as Lexical Semantics. Israel, M.

The Completeness of the Factor Semantics for Lukasiewicz's Infinite-Valued Logics. Vasyukov, Vladimir L.

## ENTHYMEME

Aristoteles über die Rationalität rhetorischer Argumente. Rapp, Christof.

## ENTITLEMENT

Towards a Whole School or College Policy for a Pre-Philosophical and Higher Order Thinking 'Entitlement' Curriculum. Thornbury, Robert.

## ENTITY

*see also* Theoretical Entity

*Entity and Identity and Other Essays*. Strawson, P F.

## ENTRENCHMENT

Belief Change as Change in Epistemic Entrenchment. Nayak, Abhaya C, Nelson, Paul and Polansky, Hanan.

## ENTREPRENEUR

Universal Values, Behavioral Ethics and Entrepreneurship. Clarke, Ruth and Aram, John.

## ENTROPY

Can the Maximum Entropy Principle Be Explained as a Consistency Requirement?. Uffink, Jos.

The Constraint Rule of the Maximum Entropy Principle. Uffink, Jos.

The 'Reality' of the Wave Function: Measurements, Entropy and Quantum Cosmology. Zeh, Heinz-Dieter.

## ENUMERATION

Cupping and Noncupping in the Enumeration Degrees of $\Sigma^0_2$ Sets [1]. Cooper, S Barry, Sorbi, Andrea and Yi, Xiaoding.

Noncappable Enumeration Degrees Below $O'_e$. Cooper, S Barry and Sorbi, Andrea.

The $Pi^0_2$ Enumeration Degrees are not Dense. Calhoun, William C and Slaman, Theodore A.

## ENVIRONMENT

"A Pluralistic, Pragmatic and Evolutionary Approach to Natural Resource Management" in *Environmental Pragmatism*, Light, Andrew (ed). Castle, Emery N.

"Critical Questions in Environmental Philosophy" in *Philosophy and Geography I: Space, Place, and Environmental Ethics*, Light, Andrew (ed). Booth, Annie L.

"Critical Reflections on Biocentric Environmental Ethics: Is It an Alternative to Anthropocentrism?" in *Philosophy and Geography I: Space, Place, and Environmental Ethics*, Light, Andrew (ed). King, Roger.

"Environmental Pragmatism as Philosophy or Metaphilosophy? On Weston-Katz Debate" in *Environmental Pragmatism*, Light, Andrew (ed). Light, Andrew.

"Epistemic Responsibility and the Inuit of Canada's Eastern Arctic: An Ecofeminist Appraisal" in *Ecofeminism: Women, Culture, Nature*, Warren, Karen J (ed). Buege, Douglas J.

"Kant and Ecofeminism" in *Ecofeminism: Women, Culture, Nature*, Warren, Karen J (ed). Wilson, Holyn.

"Laws of Nature vs. Laws of Respect: Non-Violence in Practice in Norway" in *Environmental Pragmatism*, Light, Andrew (ed). Rothenberg, David.

"Mead and Heidegger: Exploring the Ethics and Theory of Space, Place, and Environment" in *Philosophy and Geography I: Space, Place, and Environmental Ethics*, Light, Andrew (ed). Steelwater, Eliza.

"Muslim Contributions to Geography and Environmental Ethics: The Challenges of Comparison and Pluralism" in *Philosophy and Geography I: Space, Place, and Environmental Ethics*, Light, Andrew (ed). Wescoat Jr, James L.

"Nature's Presence: Reflections on Healing and Domination" in *Philosophy and Geography I: Space, Place, and Environmental Ethics*, Light, Andrew (ed). Katz, Eric.

"On the Ethical Determination of Geography: A Kantian Prolegomenon" in *Philosophy and Geography I: Space, Place, and Environmental Ethics*, Light, Andrew (ed). Burch, Robert.

"On the Nature of Environmental Education: Anthropocentrism versus Non-Anthropocentrism: The Irrelevant Debate" in *Philosophy of Education (1996)*, Margonis, Frank (ed). Huey-li, Li.

"Pragmatism and Environmental Thought" in *Environmental Pragmatism*, Light, Andrew (ed). Parker, Kelly A.

"Pragmatism and Policy: The Case of Water" in *Environmental Pragmatism*, Light, Andrew (ed). Thompson, Paul B.

"Self and Community in Environmental Ethics" in *Ecofeminism: Women, Culture, Nature*, Warren, Karen J (ed). Donner, Wendy.

"The Dialectical Social Geography of Elisée Reclus" in *Philosophy and Geography I: Space, Place, and Environmental Ethics*, Light, Andrew (ed). Clark, John.

"The Environmental Value in G.H. Mead's Cosmology" in *Environmental Pragmatism*, Light, Andrew (ed). Santas, Ari.

"The Maintenance of Natural Capital: Motivations and Methods" in *Philosophy and Geography I: Space, Place, and Environmental Ethics*, Light, Andrew (ed). Spash, Clive L and Clayton, M H.

"The Relevance of the Anthropocentric-Ecocentric Debate" in *Philosophy of Education (1996)*, Margonis, Frank (ed). Snauwaert, Dale T.

"The Takings Clause and the Meanings of Land" in *Philosophy and Geography I: Space, Place, and Environmental Ethics*, Light, Andrew (ed). Trachtenberg, Zev.

"Towards a Pragmatic Approach to Definition: 'Wetlands' and the Politics of Meaning" in *Environmental Pragmatism*, Light, Andrew (ed). Schiappa, Edward.

"Unfair to Swamps: A Reply to Katz Unfair to Foundations? A Reply to Weston" in *Environmental Pragmatism*, Light, Andrew (ed). Weston, Anthony and Katz, Eric.

"Wilderness Management" in *Philosophy and Geography I: Space, Place, and Environmental Ethics*, Light, Andrew (ed). Paden, Roger.

*Defending Mother Earth: Native American Perspectives on Environmental Justice*. Weaver, Jace (ed).

*Earth Community: Earth Ethics*. Rasmussen, Larry L.

*Earthly Goods: Environmental Change and Social Justice*. Hampson, Fen Osler (ed) and Reppy, Judith (ed).

*Ecofeminism: Women, Culture, Nature*. Warren, Karen J (ed) and Erkal, Nisvan (ed).

*Environmental Pragmatism*. Light, Andrew (ed) and Katz, Eric (ed).

*Nature as Subject: Human Obligation and Natural Community*. Katz, Eric.

*Philosophy and Geography I: Space, Place, and Environmental Ethics*. Light, Andrew (ed) and Smith, Jonathan M (ed).

*Principia Ecologica* Eco-Principles as a Conceptual Framework for a New Ethics in Science and Technology. Moser, Anton.

*Wrongness, Wisdom, and Wilderness: Toward a Libertarian Theory of Ethics and the Environment*. Scriven, Tal.

A Case Study of Conflicting Interests: Flemish Engineers Involved in Environmental Impact Assessment. Holemans, Dirk.

A Comment on 'Radiation Protection and Moral Theory'. Miller, Chris.

An Ecologically-Informed Ontology for Environmental Ethics. Buege, Douglas J.

Anthropocentrism: A Misunderstood Problem. Hayward, Tim.

Approaches to Conserving Vulnerable Wildlife in China: Does the Colour of Cat Matter—if it Catches Mice?. Harris, Richard B.

Attitudes and Issues Preventing Bans on Toxic Lead Shot and Sinkers in North America and Europe. Thomas, Vernon G.

Bach's Butterfly Effect: Culture, Environment and History. Simmons, I G.

Bioethics of Fish Production: Energy and the Environment. Pimentel, David, Shanks, Roland E and Rylander, Jason C.

Chaos and a New Environmental Ethic: The Land Ethic Revisited. Catalano, George D.

Coming in to the Foodshed. Kloppenburg, Jr, Jack, Hendrickson, John and Stevenson, G W.

Community Food Security and Environmental Justice: Searching for a Common Discourse. Gottlieb, Robert and Fisher, Andrew.

Deep Ecology and the Irrelevance of Morality. Reitan, Eric H.

Definitional and Responsive Environmental Meanings: A Meadian Look at Landscapes and Drought. Weigert, Andrew J.

Democratising Nature? The Political Morality of Wilderness Preservationists. Mason, Michael.

Discourse Ethics and Nature. Krebs, Angelika.

Earthday 25: A Retrospective of Reform Environmental Movements. Devall, Bill.

## EPISTEMOLOGY

*Exploring Unseen Worlds: William James and the Philosophy of Mysticism.* Barnard, G William.
*Foucault's Discipline: The Politics of Subjectivity.* Ransom, John S.
*Frege: Importance and Legacy.* Schirn, Matthias (ed).
*Grenzen der kritischen Vernunft.* Schmid, Peter A and Zurbuchen, Simone.
*Grundlegung eines Neorationalismus: Dekognition und Dissens.* Radermacher, Hans.
*Habermas and the Unfinished Project of Modernity.* Passerin d'Entrèves, Maurizio (ed) and Benhabib, Seyla (ed).
*Hegel, History, and Interpretation.* Gallagher, Shaun.
*Hermeneutics and the Voice of the Other: Re-reading Gadamer's Philosophical Hermeneutics.* Risser, James.
*Husserl's Position in the School of Brentano.* Rollinger, Robin Daryl.
*Imaginationssysteme.* Haefliger, Jürg.
*Ingegnerie della Conoscenza: Introduzione alla Filosofia Computazionale.* Magnani, Lorenzo.
*Intenzioni: D'amore di scienza e d'anarchia.* Donnici, Rocco.
*Introduction to Philosophical Hermeneutics.* Grondin, Jean, Gadamer, Hans-Georg and Weinsheimer, Joel (trans).
*Jean-Jacques Rousseau and the Sources of the Self.* O'Hagan, Timothy (ed).
*John Dewey: Scienza, prassi, democrazia.* Alcaro, Mario.
*John Locke: An Essay Concerning Human Understanding.* Winkler, Kenneth P (ed) and Locke, John.
*Kant und die These vom Paradigmenwechsel: Eine Gegenüberstellung seiner Transzendentalphilosophie mit der Wissenschaftstheorie Thomas S. Kuhns.* Quitterer, Josef.
*Knowledge and Inquiry: Essays on Jaakko Hintikka's Epistemology and Philosophy of Science.* Sintonen, Matti (ed).
*Kritik des Naturalismus.* Keil, Geert.
*La racionalidad: su poder y sus límites.* Nudler, Oscar (ed).
*Language and Reason: A Study of Habermas's Pragmatics.* Cooke, Maeve.
*Language, Action, and Context: The Early History of Pragmatics in Europe and America, 1780-1930.* Nerlich, Brigitte and Clarke, David D.
*Lo stile de' Geometri: La filosofia cartesiana nell'opera di Alessandro Pascoli (1669-1757).* Guerrini, Luigi.
*Locke's Philosophy: Content and Context.* Rogers, G A J (ed).
*Ludwig Wittgenstein: Half-Truths and One-and-a-Half-Truths.* Hintikka, Jaakko.
*Making Choices: A Recasting of Decision Theory.* Schick, Frederic.
*Mapping Reality: An Evolutionary Realist Methodology for the Natural and Social Sciences.* Azevedo, Jane.
*Maurice Blanchot: The Demand of Writing.* Gill, Carolyn Bailey.
*Mein Geist ist das Universum: Ontologische und erkenntnistheoretische Aspekte in der Lehre des Lu Jiuyuan (1139-1193).* Ommerborn, Wolfgang.
*Mind Design II: Philosophy, Psychology, Artificial Intelligence.* Haugeland, John (ed).
*Moral Knowledge?: New Readings in Moral Epistemology.* Sinnott-Armstrong, Walter (ed) and Timmons, Mark (ed).
*New Essays on Human Understanding.* Bennett, Jonathan (trans) and Remnant, Peter (trans).
*Objections to Physicalism.* Robinson, Howard (ed).
*Objectivity: The Obligations of Impersonal Reason.* Rescher, Nicholas.
*Oltre Wittgenstein.* Di Caro, Alessandro.
*On Dialogue.* Nichol, Lee (ed) and Bohm, David.
*On Knowing and the Known: Introductory Readings in Epistemology.* Lucey, Kenneth G (ed).
*Origins of Logical Empiricism.* Giere, Ronald N (ed) and Richardson, Alan W (ed).
*Passion in Theory: Conceptions of Freud and Lacan.* Ferrell, Robyn.
*Peirce, Signs, and Meaning.* Merrell, Floyd.
*Perception.* Villanueva, Enrique (ed).
*Philosophical Perspectives, 9, AI, Connectionism and Philosophical Psychology, 1995.* Tomberlin, James E (ed).
*Philosophy after F.H. Bradley.* Bradley, James (ed).
*Philosophy and the Return to Self-Knowledge.* Verene, Donald Phillip.
*Philosophy's Second Revolution: Early and Recent Analytic Philosophy.* Clarke, D S.
*Plato's Epistemology: How Hard Is It to Know?.* Laidlaw-Johnson, Elizabeth A.
*Practical Reasoning about Final Ends.* Richardson, Henry.
*Pragmatism and Realism.* Westphal, Kenneth R (ed), Will, Frederick L and MacIntyre, Alasdair.
*Pragmatism as a Principle and Method of Right Thinking.* Turrisi, Patricia Ann (ed) and Sanders Peirce, Charles.
*Quest for Self-Knowledge: An Essay in Lonergan's Philosophy.* Flanagan, Joseph.
*Ratio Indifferens* (in Serbo-Croatian). Sakota, Jasna.
*Reason, Reality, and Speculative Philosophy.* Singer, Marcus G (ed) and Murphy, Arthur E.
*Repräsentation bei Descartes.* Perler, Dominik.
*Representation of the World: A Naturalized Semantics.* Melnick, Arthur.
*Rethinking Identity and Metaphysics: On the Foundations of Analytic Philosophy.* Hill, Claire Ortiz.

*Rule-Following and Realism.* Ebbs, Gary.
*Scepticism and the Foundation of Epistemology: A Study in the Metalogical Fallacies.* Floridi, Luciano.
*Scepticism in the History of Philosophy: A Pan-American Dialogue.* Popkin, Richard H (ed).
*Self-Knowledge in the Age of Theory.* Hartle, Ann.
*Self-Trust: A Study of Reason, Knowledge and Autonomy.* Lehrer, Keith.
*Sites of Vision.* Levin, David Michael (ed).
*Socratic Puzzles.* Nozick, Robert.
*Stoics, Epicureans and Sceptics: An Introduction to Hellenistic Philosophy.* Sharples, R W.
*Subjectivity and Intersubjectivity in Modern Philosophy and Psychoanalysis.* Frie, Roger.
*Systematische Wahrheitstheorie: Methodische und wissenschaftstheoretische Überlegungen zur Frage nach dem grundlegenden Einheitsprinzip.* Siebel, Wigand.
*Ten Problems of Consciousness: A Representational Theory of the Phenomenal Mind.* Tye, Michael.
*The Age of Structuralism: From Lévi-Strauss to Foucault.* Kurzweil, Edith.
*The Cambridge Companion to Wittgenstein.* Sluga, Hans (ed) and Stern, David G (ed).
*The Continuity of Wittgenstein's Thought.* Koethe, John.
*The Last Word.* Nagel, Thomas.
*The Metaphysics of Pragmatism.* Hook, Sidney.
*The Sense of Reference: Intentionality in Frege.* Bar-Elli, Gilead.
*The Table of Judgments: Critique of Pure Reason A 67-76; B 92-101.* Watkins, Eric (ed & trans) and Brandt, Reinhard.
*The Two Pragmatisms: From Peirce to Rorty.* Mounce, H O.
*The Zero Fallacy and Other Essays in Neoclassical Philosophy.* Valady, Mohammad (ed) and Hartshorne, Charles.
*Time, Tense, and Causation.* Tooley, Michael.
*Un'Introduzione All'Epistemologia Contemporanea.* Gava, Giacomo (ed).
*Verbum: Word and Idea in Aquinas Volume 2.* Crowe, Frederick E (ed) and Doran, Robert M (ed).
*Verdad: lógica, representación y mundo.* Villegas Forero, L, Martínez Vidal, C and Rivas Monroy, Uxía.
*Verstehen and Humane Understanding.* O'Hear, Anthony (ed).
*Western Philosophy: An Anthology.* Cottingham, John (ed).
*What is Truth?.* Pivcevic, Edo.
*Wittgensteinian Themes: Essays 1978-1989.* Von Wright, Georg Henrik (ed) and Malcolm, Norman.
*A Ciência e a Virtude No Noviciado da Cotovia (1603-1759): Organizaçao do Espaço, Produçao do Discurso e Sistema Epistémico.* Janeira, Ana Luisa.
*A Concepçao de Filosofia em Adorno.* Cordeiro Silva, Rafael.
*A Consistent Relativism.* Hales, Steven D.
*A Conversation with Sylvère Lotringer.* Lotringer, Sylvère.
*A Counterfactual Analysis of Causation.* Ramachandran, Murali.
*A Critical Reconstruction of Paul Tillich's Epistemology.* Grube, Dirk-Martin.
*A Critique of Campbell's Refurbished Nominalism.* Moreland, J P.
*A Critique of Pure Meaning: Wittgenstein and Derrida.* Sonderegger, Ruth.
*A Defence of Van Fraassen's Critique of Abductive Inference: Reply to Psillos.* Ladyman, James, Douven, Igor and Horsten, Leon (& others).
*A Dialogue between L1 and L2: Discussing on Seven Kinds of Privacy.* Lenka, Laxminarayan.
*A Furry Tile about Mental Representation.* Brown, Deborah J.
*A Neo-Kantian Critique of Von Mises's Epistemology.* Barrotta, Pierluigi.
*A New Skeptical Solution.* Gauker, Christopher.
*A Noçao de Sujeito como Aparece nas Meditaçoes Considerada à Luz das Sugestoes Wittgensteinianas a Respeito da Linguagem.* Alvarenga, Ethel.
*A Note on the Nature of "Water".* Abbott, Barbara.
*A Objectividade como categoria filosófica: Subsídios para uma caracterizaçao.* Barata-Moura, José.
*A Paradox for Empiricism (?).* Douven, Igor.
*A Pragmatic Theory of Causal Analysis.* Shein, David.
*A Priori Knowledge.* Inglis, Sam.
*A propósito de la crítica de Feyerabend al racionalismo crítico.* Marqués, Gustavo L.
*A Relaçao entre a Razao e as Paixoes na Antropologia Hobbesiana.* Papterra Limongi, Maria Isabel.
*A Response to John Hick.* Mavrodes, George I.
*A Solipsist in a Real World.* Pihlström, Sami.
*A Taxonomy of Functions.* Walsh, Denis M and Ariew, André.
*A Work on Philosophy.* Shpet, G G.
*Abkehr vom Mythos: Descartes in der gegenwärtigen Diskussion.* Perler, Dominik.
*Absent Qualia.* Dretske, Fred.
*Abstration, Inseparability, and Identity.* Baxter, Donald L M.
*Academic Skepticism in Early Modern Philosophy.* Maia Neto, José R.
*Accidental Associations, Local Potency, and a Dilemma for Dretske.* Noordhof, Paul.
*Acerca de "Una teoría de la textualidad".* Topuzian, Carlos Marcelo.
*Actitudes proposicionales y conocimiento sensible en Tomás de Aquino.* Tellkamp, Jörg Alejandro.
*Acts and Outcomes: A Reply to Boonin-Vail.* Parfit, Derek.
*Actualism and Iterated Modalities.* Jubien, Michael.

## EPISTEMOLOGY

## EPISTEMOLOGY

*Fichtes Erfindung der Wissenschaftslehre.* Tilliette, Xavier.

Fichtes Sprachphilosophie und der Begriff einer Wissenschaftslehre. Surber, Jere Paul.

Fichtes Wissenschaftslehre und die philosophischen Anfänge Heideggers. Denker, Alfred.

Fichtes Wissenschaftslehre vor der aktuellen Diskussion um die Letztbegründung. Gerten, Michael.

Fiction, Modality and Dependent Abstracta. Thomasson, Amie L.

Fidelity to Zeno's Theory. Ioppolo, Anna Maria.

Filosofía de la educación: tareas y desafíos. Cordero C, Gerardo Arturo.

Filosofía Trascendental Mundaneizada. Heymann, Ezra.

Finding the Right Level for Connectionist Representations (A Critical Note on Ramsey's Paper). Markic, Olga.

Finkish Dispositions. Lewis, David.

Fodor's Information Semantics between Naturalism and Mentalism. Meyering, Theo C.

Folk Psychology and the Simulationist Challenge. Levin, Janet.

For a Minimal Theory of Truth. Mercier, Jean L.

Forgiare e dimenticare: i doveri dell'oblio. Lowenthal, David.

Formal Contamination: A Reading of Derrida's Argument. Donkel, Douglas L.

Formal Organizations: A Philosophical Review of Perspectives and Behaviour Dynamics. Johnnie, Palmer B.

Foucault on Power and the Will to Knowledge. Detel, Wolfgang.

Foucault's Analysis of Power's Methodologies. Scott, Gary Alan.

Foucault's Reconfiguration of the Subject: From Nietzsche to Butler, Laclau/Mouffe, and Beyond. Schrift, Alan D.

Foucault: *Da Morte do* Sujeito *Ao Sujeito da* Morte. Pereira Arêdes, José de Almeida.

Foundationalism and Practical Reason. Heath, Joseph.

Foundations of Perceptual Knowledge. Brewer, Bill.

Four Naturalist Accounts of Moral Responsibility. Double, Richard.

Framework of an Intersubjetivist Theory of Meaning. Corredor, Cristina.

Franz Böhms "Deutsche Philosophie": Über den Versuch einer erkenntnistheoretischen Grundlegung des "Nationalsozialismus". Hailer, Martin.

Fred Dretske on the Explanatory Role of Semantic Content. Hassrick, Beth.

Frege on Meaning. Sluga, Hans.

Frege's Context Principle. Bar-Elli, Gilead.

From *intellectus verus/falsus* to the *dictum propositionis*: The Semantics of Peter Abelard and his Circle. King, Peter, Jacobi, Klaus and Strub, Christian.

From Aperspectival Objectivity to Strong Objectivity: The Quest for Moral Objectivity. Tannoch-Bland, Jennifer.

From Work to Work. Livingston, Paisley.

Fuzzy Truth Values (in Spanish). Godo, Lluís.

G. Bachelard y la iconoclastia científica de lo imaginario. González Rodríguez, Antonio M.

Gadamer's Hermeneutic Externalism. Kuenning, Matthew.

Galen Strawson on Mental Reality. Crane, Tim.

Geist oder Gespenst? Fichtes Noumenalismus in der *Wissenschaftslehre nova methodo.* Zöller, Günter.

Genovesi e Cartesio. Marcialis, Maria Teresa.

Getting Around Language. Mason, Richard.

Giambattista Vico y el actual debate sobre la argumentación jurídica. Pérez Luño, Antonio-Enrique.

Gibt es ein subjektives Fundament unseres Wissens?. Grundmann, Thomas.

Gibt es etwas ausser mir selbst? Überlegungen zur semantischen Begründung des Realismus. Moulines, C Ulises.

Giving the Skeptic Her Due?. Hughes, Christopher.

God's Blindspot. Kroon, Frederick W.

Goldman's New Reliabilism. Markie, Peter J.

Granny Versus Mother Nature—No Contest. Dennett, Daniel C.

Gregorio Klimovsky y las desventuras del conocimiento cientíico. Flichman, Eduardo.

Gregory Vlastos: *Socratic Studies.* Nussbaum, Martha C.

Habermas and Foucault: How to Carry Out the Enlightenment Project. Nielsen, Kai.

Hegel und Weber im Vergleich: Die Bahnen der Rationalität. Senigaglia, Cristiana.

Hegel's Nonfoundationalism: A Phenomenological Account of the Structure of Philosophy of Right. Tunick, Mark.

Hegels Theorie des spekulativen Satzes in der Vorrede zur *Phänomenologie des Geistes.* Haucke, Kai.

Heraclitus of Ephesus on Knowledge. Krkac, Kristijan.

Hervé de Nédellec et les questions ordinaires *De cognitione primi principii.* Conforti, Patrizia.

Heterology: A Postmodern Theory of Foundations. Fairlamb, Horace L.

Honderich on the Consequences of Determinism. Double, Richard.

Horizontal Intentionality and Transcendental Intersubjectivity (in Dutch). Zahavi, Dan.

How Can Pictures Be Propositions?. Shier, David.

How Demonstrations Connect with Referential Intentions. Roberts, Lawrence D.

How Innocent is Mereology?. Forrest, Peter.

How not to Defend Constructive Empiricism: A Rejoinder. Psillos, Stathis.

How Reasons Explain Behaviour: Reply to Melnyk and Noordhof. Dretske, Fred.

How to Read Wittgenstein. Cook, John W.

How to Resolve the Pyrrhonian Problematic: A Lesson from Descartes. Sosa, Ernest.

How To Share An Intention. Velleman, J David.

How Well does Direct Reference Semantics Fit with Pragmatics?. Lumsden, David.

Hume's Arguments for His Sceptical Doubts. Passell, Dan.

Hume's Reflective Return to the Vulgar. O'Shea, James R.

Hume's Scepticism with Regard to Reason: A Reconsideration. Dauer, Francis W.

Husserl et le *Ichprinzip:* Le tournant en question. Paquette, Éric.

Husserl's Phenomenology and its Relation to Descartes (in Czech). Bayerová, Marie.

Husserl, Wittgenstein and the Snark: Intentionality and Social Naturalism. Gillett, Grant.

Hypothesis and Realism: A Comment on Sutton. Johnson, David Kenneth.

I Married an Empiricist: A Phenomenologist Examines Philosophical Personae. Duhan Kaplan, Laura.

Idealismo y materialismo: Max Horkheimer y la constitución del conocimiento en la ciencia social. Vergara, Eliseo Cruz.

Ideen von mehr oder weniger Süsse oder Licht: Zur Darstellung von Intensitäten bei Locke. Specht, Rainer.

Identidad y Continuidad Causal: Una Crítica a la Teoría de la Continuidad Causal de Shoemaker. Bordes Solanas, Montserrat.

Identity, Relation R, and What Matters. Baillie, James.

If *p*, Then What? Thinking in Cases. Forrester, John.

Il problema del realismo tra meccanica quantistica e relatività speciale. Dorato, Mauro.

Illuminating the Chinese Room. Dartnall, Terry.

Immanenza y trascendenza en la intencionalidad. Bosch, Magdalena.

In Defence of a Radical Millianism. Nelson, John O.

In Defence of Philosophy Against the Endists. Uroh, Chris Okechukwu.

In Defense of Coherentism. Kvanvig, Jonathan.

In Defense of One Form of Traditional Epistemology. Markie, Peter J.

In Defense of the Contingently Nonconcrete. Linsky, Bernard and Zalta, Edward.

In the Beginning, There Was Darwin: *Darwin's Dangerous Idea: Evolution and the Meanings of Life.* Dennett, Daniel C and Mulhauser, Gregory R.

In What Sense is Kripke's Wittgensteinian Paradox a Scepticism? On the Opposition between its Epistemological and its Metaphysical Aspects. Read, Rupert.

Indexing Truths: A Critical Notice of John Campbell's *Past, Space, and Self.* McGilvray, James.

Individualism and Descartes. Ferraiolo, William.

Individualism and Marr's Computational Theory of Vision. Butler, Keith.

Información y Bases de Datos Situadas. Migura, Fernando.

Innate Ideas, Categories and Objectivity. Antonopoulos, Constantin.

Insularità del vero: Omogeneità ed eterogeneità negli sviluppi dialettici della "Analitica trascendentale". Carugno, Daniela.

Intention, Rule Following and the Strategic Role of Wright's Order of Determination Test. Thornton, Tim.

Intentionalism and Rationality (A Criticism of Stich's Slippery Slope Argument). Smokrovic, Nenad.

Intentionality and One-Sided Relations. Haldane, John.

Intentionality and Scepticism (in Spanish). Sá Pereira, Roberto Horácio.

Intentionality as the Mark of the Dispositional. Place, U T.

Interlocution, Perception, and Memory. Burge, Tyler.

Internal Realism, Metaphysical Realism, and Brains in a Vat. Forrai, Gábor.

Internal Relations and Analyticity: Wittgenstein and Quine. Hymers, Michael.

Internalism and Perceptual Knowledge. Brewer, Bill.

Internalism, Externalism and the No-Defeater Condition. Bergmann, Michael.

Interpreting Peirce's Interpretant: A Response To Lalor, Liszka, and Meyers. Short, T L.

Introducción a la teoría de la verdad de Michel Henry. García-Baró, Miguel.

Is "Self-Knowledge" an Empirical Problem? Renogotiating the Space of Philosophical Explanation. McGeer, Victoria.

Is It Rational To Carry Out Strategic Intentions?. Robins, Michael H.

Is Naturalized Epistemology Experientially Vacuous?. Barnhart, Michael G.

Is Nondefectively Justified True Belief Knowledge?. Jacquette, Dale.

Is Presentness a Property?. Craig, William Lane.

Is Tennant Selling Truth Short?. Edwards, Jim.

Isolation and Unification: The Realist Analysis of Possible Worlds. Bricker, Phillip.

John McDowell's *Mind and World* and Early Romantic Epistemology. Bowie, Andrew.

John Searle's *The Construction of Social Reality.* Ruben, David-Hillel.

Justification of Empirical Belief: Problems with Haack's Foundherentism. Clune, Alan C.

Justified, True Belief: Is it Relevant to Knowledge?. Leeser, Jamie.

Kann es rational sein, eine inkonsistente Theorie zu akzeptieren?. Bartelborth, Thomas.

Kant and Husserl. Mohanty, J N.

Kant e l'epistemologia contemporanea. Castagni, Laura.

## EPISTEMOLOGY

## EPISTEMOLOGY

*Self-Knowledge: Discovery, Resolution, and Undoing.* Moran, Richard.

Self-Quotation and Self-Knowledge. Jacobsen, Rockney.

Self-Reference, Self-Knowledge and the Problem of Misconception. Cassam, Quassim.

Sense, Reference and Selective Attention. Campbell, John and Martin, M G F.

Sense, Validity and Context. Williamson, Timothy.

Sensibilidad y espiritualidad según Aristóteles. García Jaramillo, Miguel Alejandro.

Sentido común "común" y sentido común "sensato". Una reivindicación de Thomas Reid. Prado, José Hernández.

Sex, Fairness, and the Theory of Games. D'Arms, Justin.

Should Anti-Realists Teach Critical Thinking?. Hatcher, Donald L.

Should I Be Grateful to You for Not Harming Me?. Smilansky, Saul.

Should We Abandon Epistemic Justification. Meeker, Kevin.

Simulation and Cognitive Penetrability. Heal, Jane.

Skepticism and Foundationalism: A Reply to Michael Williams. Vogel, Jonathan.

Skepticism and Pyrotechnics. Kaplan, Mark.

So Do We Know or Don't We?. Dretske, Fred.

Sobre la Facticidad de la Memoria. Schumacher, Christian.

Sobre la interpretación deflacionaria de la teoría de Tarski. Orlando, Eleonora.

Social Epistemology and the Ethics of Research. Resnik, David B.

Social Epistemology and the Recovery of the Normative in the Post-Epistemic Era. Fuller, Steve.

Social Externalism and Memory: A Problem?. Ludlow, Peter.

Solipsism and Subjectivity. Moore, A W.

Some Like it Hot: Consciousness and Higher-Order Thoughts. Byrne, Alex.

Some Remarks on Scientific Positivism and Constructivist Epistemology in Science. Vijh, Ashok K.

Some Tendencies in Modern Epistemology (in Polish). Ingarden, Roman and Jadczak, Ryszard.

Sozialstruktur und Sematik: Der wissenssoziologische Ansatz Niklas Luhmanns. Götke, Povl.

Speech-Acts, Kierkegaard, and Postmodern Thought. Martinez, Roy.

Spinoza and Indexicals. Sprigge, T L S.

State Consciousness Revisited. Jacob, Pierre.

Stich on Intentionality and Rationality. Gibson, Roger.

Sticking Up for Oedipus: Fodor on Intentional Generalizations and Broad Content. Arjo, Dennis.

Still Unnatural: A Reply to Vogel and Rorty. Williams, Michael.

Strength of Motivation and Being in Control. Mele, Alfred R.

Stretched Lines, Averted Leaps, and Excluded Competition: A Theory of Scientific Counterfactuals. Mikkelson, Gregory M.

Stroud and Moore on Skepticism. Neta, Ram.

Subjective, Not Objective, Truths. Subramaniam, Sharada.

Subjectivity in Descartes and Kant. Schwyzer, Hubert.

Subjects and Objects. Cassam, Quassim.

Supervenience and Co-Location. Rea, Michael C.

Supposing for the Sake of Argument. Cargile, James.

Supposition and Truth in Ockham's Mental Language. Yrjönsuuri, Mikko.

SwampJoe: Mind or Simulation?. Levine, Joe.

Swampman Meets Swampcow. Neander, Karen.

Symbolic Difference. Schürmann, Reiner.

Symbolic Praxis. Schürmann, Reiner.

Syncatégorèmes, concepts, équivocité: Deux questions anonymes, conservées dans le ms. Paris, B.N., lat. 16.401, liées à la sémantique de Pierre d'Ailly (c. 1350-1420). Bakker, Paul J J M.

Synchronic Self-Control is Always Non-Actional. Kennett, Jeanette and Smith, Michael.

Syntax, Imagery and Naturalization. Duran, Jane.

Synthesising Intersubjectively. Elkatip, S H.

System und Methode—Zur methodologischen Begründung transzendentalen Philosophierens in Fichtes *Begriffsschrift*. Stahl, Jürgen.

Systematicity. Cummins, Robert.

Teleological Semantics. Rowlands, Mark.

Teleology and the Product Analogy. Matthen, Mohan.

Teoría de la verdad: sobre ciencia y verdad. Pérez de Laborda, Alfonso.

Teorías actuales de la verdad. Frápolli, María José and Nicolás, Juan A.

Testament of a Recovering Eliminativist. Melnyk, Andrew.

Testimony and Perception. Prijic-Samarzija, Snjezana.

Testimony, Induction and Folk Psychology. Lyons, Jack.

Testimony, Memory and the Limits of the *A Priori*. Christensen, David and Kornblith, Hilary.

Textuality and Imagination: The Refracted Image of Hegelian Dialectic. Schalow, Frank.

The "Alien Abduction" Phenomenon: Forbidden Knowledge of Hidden Events. Zimmerman, Michael E.

The "Extreme Heresy" of John Dewey and Arthur F. Bentley I: A Star Crossed Collaboration?. Ryan, Frank X.

The "Passion for the Outside": Foucault, Blanchot, and Exteriority. Saghafi, Kas.

The Achievement of Personhood. Goodenough, Jerry.

The Active and the Passive. Raz, Joseph and Ruben, David-Hillel.

The Apriority of the Starting-Point of Kant's Transcendental Epistemology. Politis, Vasilis.

The Body as an "Object" of Historical Knowledge. Mann, Doug.

The Category of the State of Things in Husserl's *Logical Investigations* (in Polish). Lukasiewicz, Dariusz.

The Cognitive Turn in Philosophy (in Czech). Jacob, Pierre.

The Concept of Dreaming: On Three Theses by Malcolm. Schroeder, Severin.

The Constitution of the World of Experience and the Problem of the New (in German). Köveker, Dietmar.

The Context Principle in Frege's *Grundgesetze* (in Spanish). Schirn, Matthias.

The Correspondence Theory of Truth. New, Kostja.

The Delimitation of Argument. Gilbert, Michael A.

The Demarcation of the Metaphorical. Engstrom, Anders.

The Discourse Principle and Those Affected. Skirbekk, Gunnar.

The Dispositional Account of Colour. Pitson, Tony.

The Early Buddhist Theory of Truth: A Contextualist Pragmatic Interpretation. Holder, John J.

The Elements of Consciousness and their Neurodynamical Correlates. MacLennan, Bruce.

The Emancipation of Reason. Paske, Gerald H.

The End of Plasticity. Philipse, Herman.

The Epistemological Argument Against Socialism: A Wittgensteinian Critique of Hayek and Giddens. Pleasants, Nigel.

The Epistemological Challenge of Religious Pluralism. Hick, John.

The Epistemology of Humanism. Mojsisch, Burkhard.

The Epistemology of Possible Worlds: A Guided Tour. O'Leary-Hawthorne, John.

The Experience of Spatiality for Congenitally Blind People: A Phenomenological-Psychological Study. Karlsson, Gunnar.

The Extension of Deconstruction and Commentary (in Czech). Wheeler III, Samuel C and Peregrin, Jaroslav.

The Facts of Causation. Mellor, D H.

The Father of Modern Hermeneutics in a Postmodern Age: A Reinterpretation of Schleiermacher's Hermeneutics. Huang, Yong.

The Figures of Subjectivity in Éric Weil's *Logique de la philosophie* (in French). Kirscher, Gilbert.

The Heritage of Léon Brunschvicg (and Commentary by P. Horák) (in Czech). Rivenc, François and Horák, Petr.

The Hermeneutic Significance of the *Sensus Communis*. Hance, Allen.

The Hermeneutical Turn in American Critical Theory, 1830-1860. Walhout, M D.

The Import of the Puzzle about Belief. Sosa, David.

The Importance of Ideals. Van der Burg, Wibren.

The Impossibility of Interpersonal Utility. Hausman, Daniel.

The Inadequacy of Hume's Psychological Impressions. Bartzeliotis, L.

The Inaugural Address: The Grounding of Reason. Trigg, Roger.

The Individuation of Actions. Mackie, David.

The Internal Connectedness of Philosophy of History and Philosophy of Language in Nietzsche's Early Writings (in Serbo-Croatian). Margreiter, Reinhard.

The Limits of Limit Experience: Bataille and Foucault. Jay, Martin.

The Metaphysical Roots of Philosophical Tolerance and its Substitutes. Brajicic, Rudolf.

The Method of the Geometer: A New Angle on Husserl's Cartesianism. Kasely, Terry S.

The Middle Way: Some Limitations of Human Intellectual Knowledge, According to Thomas Aquinas (in Portuguese). Do Nascimento, Carlos A Ribeiro.

The Modernity Crisis and the Pedagogical Reason (Spanish). Márquez, Alvaro.

The Modularity of Language—Some Empirical Considerations. Grodzinsky, Yosef.

The Nature of Temptation. Nuyen, A T.

The Needs of Understanding: Kant on Empirical Laws and Regulative Ideals. O'Shea, James R.

The Nominalist Argument of the *New Essays*. Bolton, Martha Brandt.

The Normativity of Meaning. Gampel, Eric H.

The Nurturing of a Relational Epistemology. Thayer-Bacon, Barbara J.

The Origin of the Concept of Multiplicity in Gilles Deleuze's (in Portuguese). Cardoso Júnior, Hélio Rebello.

The Perils of Epistemic Reductionism. Horgan, Terence.

The Poverty of Rhetoricism: Popper, Mises and the Riches of Historicism. Keaney, Michael.

The Practice of Philosophy. Nevo, Isaac.

The Problems of "External" Experience in Roman Ingarden's Philosophy: Part I (in Polish). Póltawski, Andrzej.

The Problems of "External" Experience in Roman Ingarden's Philosophy: Part II (in Polish). Póltawski, Andrzej.

The Properties of Mental Causation. Robb, David.

The Prospects for Dretske's Account of the Explanatory Role of Belief. Melnyk, Andrew.

The Psychological Reality of Reasons. Collins, Arthur W.

The Puzzle of Names in Ockham's Theory of Mental Language. Brown, Deborah J.

## EPISTEMOLOGY

## EPISTEMOLOGY

*Zum wirkungsgeschichtlichen Bewusstsein (in Serbo-Croatian).* Jakovljevic, Goran.

Zur Aufgabe transzendentaler Interpretation. Gawlina, Manfred.

'Cannot,' 'Not Can' and 'Can Not'. Davson-Galle, Peter.

'Now I Can Go On:' Wittgenstein and Our Embodied Embeddedness in the 'Hurly-Burly' of Life. Shotter, John.

'Outsidelessness' and the 'Beyond' of Signification. Griffith-Dickson, Gwen.

## EQUAL OPPORTUNITY

Affirmative Action: Retrospect and Prospect. Van Patten, Jim.

Conflicting Accounts of Equal Opportunity. Askland, Andrew.

## EQUALITY

*see also* Egalitarianism, Inequality

"Maternity, Paternity, and Equality" in *Reproduction, Technology, and Rights: Biomedical Ethics Reviews,* Humber, James M (ed). Humber, James M.

"Taylor, Equality, and the Metaphysics of Persons" in *Philosophy of Education (1996),* Margonis, Frank (ed). Strike, Kenneth A.

"Uguaglianza e disuguaglianza: un tema di filosofia della storia" in *Lo Storicismo e la Sua Storia: Temi, Problemi, Prospettive,* Cacciatore, Giuseppe (ed). Gentile, Giulio.

"White Normativity and the Rhetoric of Equal Protection" in *Existence in Black: An Anthology of Black Existential Philosophy,* Gordon, Lewis R (ed). Westley, Robert St. Martin.

*Affirmative Action: Social Justice or Unfair Preference?.* Mosley, Albert G and Capaldi, Nicholas.

*Babies and Beasts: The Argument from Marginal Cases.* Dombrowski, Daniel A.

*Democracy and Disagreement.* Gutmann, Amy and Thompson, Dennis.

*Equality: Selected Readings.* Pojman, Louis (ed) and Westmoreland, Robert (ed).

*From Sex Objects to Sexual Subjects.* Moscovici, Claudia.

*Justice as Fittingness.* Cupit, Geoffrey.

*Justice.* Westphal, Jonathan (ed).

*Mill's On Liberty.* Dworkin, Gerald (ed).

*Perfect Equality: John Stuart Mill on Well-Constituted Communities.* Morales, Maria H.

*Social Cohesion and Legal Coercion: A Critique of Weber, Durkheim, and Marx.* Shaskolsky Sheleff, Leon.

*The Second Wave: A Reader in Feminist Theory.* Nicholson, Linda (ed).

*The Zero Fallacy and Other Essays in Neoclassical Philosophy.* Valady, Mohammad (ed) and Hartshorne, Charles.

A Communion of Saints...Maybe. Bailey Stoneking, Carole.

Affirmative Action: Retrospect and Prospect. Van Patten, Jim.

Associative Obligations, Voluntarism, and Equality. Jeske, Diane.

Basal Inequalities: Reply to Sen. Kane, John.

Characterizing Classes Defined without Equality. Elgueta, R.

Conflicting Accounts of Equal Opportunity. Askland, Andrew.

Cooperation and Equality: A Reply to Pojman. Norman, Richard.

Counselling for Tolerance. Almond, Brenda.

Cow-Sharks, Magnets, and Swampman. Dennett, Daniel C.

Democracy Means Equality. Rancière, Jacques.

Does Democracy Reveal the Voice of the People? Four Takes on Rousseau. Gaus, Gerald.

Dynamic Resemblance: Hegel's Early Theory of Ethical Equality. Gammon, Martin.

Equal Access to Health Care: A Lutheran Lay Person's Expanded Footnote. Delkeskamp-Hayes, Corinna.

Equal Rights for Swamp-Persons. Antony, Louise M.

Equality in Health Care: Christian Engagement with a Secular Obsession. Engelhardt Jr, H Tristram.

Equality, Autonomy, and Cultural Rights. Levey, Goeffrey Brahm.

Equality, Priority, and Time. Kappel, Klemens.

Generality and Equality. Schauer, Frederick.

Is There a Natural Sexual Inequality of Intellect? A Reply to Kimura. Foss, Jeffrey E.

Journals and Justice. Curzer, Howard J.

Justice, Impartiality, and Equality: Why the Concept of Justice Does Not Presume Equality. Kane, John.

La riforma del Welfare e un'idea di equità. Veca, Salvatore.

Liberty—Equality—Fraternity—Justice (in Czech). Münnix, Gabriele.

Multiculturalism and Gender Equity: The U.S. "Difference" Debates Revisited. Adler, Pierre.

On Being Equally Free and Unequally Restricted. Samraj, Tennyson.

On the Proof Theory of Coquand's Calculus of Constructions. Seldin, Jonathan P.

On the Status of Equality. Sen, Amartya K.

Political Equality in Justice as Fairness. Brighouse, Harry.

Punishment in Environmental Protection. Poesche, Jürgen S.

Reformulating Equality of Resources. Arnsperger, Christian.

Self-Ownership and Equality: Brute Luck, Gifts, Universal Dominance, and Leximin. Vallentyne, Peter.

Single Payers and Multiple Lists: Must Everyone Get the Same Coverage in a Universal Health Plan?. Veatch, Robert M.

The Political Philosophy of Martin Luther King Jr.. Mannath, Joe.

Understanding Equality in Health Care: A Christian Free-Market Approach. Gronbacher, Gregory M A.

What's 'Wrong' in Contractualism?. Matravers, Matt.

Women and Society in Russia. Ianovskii, Rudol'f Grigor'evich, Perminova, Alla Ivanovna and Mel'nikova, Tatiana A.

## EQUATION

A Compactness Theorem for Linear Equations. Cowen, Robert and Emerson, William.

An Intensional Epistemic Logic. Jiang, Yue J.

Equational Reasoning in Non-Classical Logics. Frias, Marcelo F and Orlowska, Ewa.

Equational Theories for Inductive Types. Loader, Ralph.

Equivalential and Algebraizable Logics. Herrmann, Burghard.

What's in a Function?. Antonelli, Gian Aldo.

## EQUILIBRIUM

Correlated Strategies as Institutions. Arce M, Daniel G.

Forward Induction in Games with an Outside Option. Olcina, Gonzalo.

Game Logic and its Applications I. Kaneko, Mamoru and Nagashima, Takashi.

Global Population Equilibrium: A Model for the Twenty-First Century. Cavanaugh, Michael.

On the Foundations of Nash Equilibrium. Jacobsen, Jans Jorgen.

Payoff Dominance and the Stackelberg Heuristic. Colman, Andrew M and Bacharach, Michael.

Reciprocal Justification in Science and Moral Theory. Blachowicz, James.

Reflective Equilibrium or Evolving Tradition?. Aronovitch, Hilliard.

Where Did Economics Go Wrong? Modern Economics As a Flight from Reality. Boettke, Peter J.

## EQUIPOISE

Community Equipoise and the Architecture of Clinical Research. Karlawish, Jason H T and Lantos, John.

## EQUITY

*On Economic Inequality.* Sen, Amartya.

Gender Equity, Organizational Transformation and Challenger. Maier, Mark.

Situational Determinants of Software Piracy: An Equity Theory Perspective. Glass, Richard S and Wood, Wallace A.

Some Critical Considerations Regarding the Function of the Equity in the Law. Urdaneta Sandoval, Carlos Alberto.

## EQUIVALENCE

"Peirce's Axiomatization of Arithmetic" in *Studies in the Logic of Charles Sanders Peirce,* Houser, Nathan (ed). Shields, Paul.

Almost Everywhere Equivalence of Logics in Finite Model Theory. Hella, Lauri.

Borel Equivalence Relations and Classifications of Countable Models. Hjorth, Greg and Kechris, Alexander S.

Characterizing Equivalential and Algebraizable Logics by the Leibniz Operator. Herrmann, Burghard.

Decidability of *Stit* Theory with a Single Agent and *Refref* Equivalence. Xu, Ming.

Laudan and Leplin on Empirical Equivalence. Okasha, Samir.

On Elementary Equivalence for Equality-free Logic. Casanovas, E, Dellunde, Pilar and Jansana, Ramon.

Putnam, Equivalence, Realism. Cox, Damian.

Replaceability and Infanticide. Uniacke, Suzanne.

Some Elementary Results in Intuitionistic Model Theory. Veldman, Wim and Waaldijk, Frank.

The Equivalence Myth of Quantum Mechanics—Part I. Muller, F A.

The Negotiation of Equivalence. Arditi, Benjamin.

## EQUIVALENTIAL

Equivalential and Algebraizable Logics. Herrmann, Burghard.

Linear Equivalential Algebras. Slomczynska, Katarzyna.

Quasivarieties of Equivalential Algebras. Idziak, Katarzyna.

## EQUIVOCATION

The One Fallacy Theory. Powers, Lawrence H.

## ERASMUS

*Erasmus of the Low Countries.* Tracy, James D.

## ERGODIC

Ergodic Theorems and the Basis of Science. Petersen, Karl.

## ERIUGENA

A Divina Natureza Segundo Escoto Eriúgena. Blanc, Mafalda de Faria.

## EROS

"The Right Method of Boy-Loving" in *Love Analyzed,* Lamb, Roger E. Brown, Deborah.

*Empire of the Gods: The Liberation of Eros.* Davies, James W.

An Overlooked Motive in Alcibiades' *Symposium* Speech. Scott, Gary Alan and Welton, William A.

Aspiring to the Divine: Love and Grace. Mahoney, Timothy A.

Eros and Philosophy: The "Spherical-Man-Myth" of Aristophanes in Plato's Symposion (in German). Iber, Christian.

Eros e nostalgia: Ensaio sobre Freud. Nunes Correia, Carlos Joao.

Eros without Perversion? (in Dutch). Thoné, Astrid.

I sandali di Ermes e lo spazio di De Kooning: Appunti per una possibile negazione dell'epelysìa di metaphysikà. Incardona, Nunzio.

On the Nature of the Absolute: A Response to Desmond. Coolidge Jr, Francis P.

## EROTETIC LOGIC

The Logic of Questions as a Theory of Erotetic Arguments. Wisniewski, Andrzej.

## EROTICA

O Arco e a Lira—O inaudito na Erótica de Safo. Leite, Lucimara and Davi Maced, Dion.

## EROTICISM

*From Sex Objects to Sexual Subjects.* Moscovici, Claudia.

*The Philosophy of Simone de Beauvoir: Gendered Phenomenologies, Erotic Generosities.* Bergoffen, Debra B.

A experiência erótica em Leonardo Coimbra. Esteves Borges, Paulo Alexandre.

## ERROR

"And so I Err and Sin": Considerations on Error in Descartes (Spanish). Díaz, Jorge Aurelio.

"Las dimensiones de la racionalidad" in *La racionalidad: su poder y sus límites,* Nudler, Oscar (ed). Broncano, Fernando.

*The Taming of the True.* Tennant, Neil.

*Thinking Straight.* Flew, Antony.

*Vagueness.* Williamson, Timothy.

Analyticity Reconsidered. Boghossian, Paul Artin.

Commentary on "Good to the Last Drop? Millikan Stories as 'Canned' Pedagogy. Bird, Stephanie J.

Descartes on Love and/as Error. Williston, Byron.

Descartes, Error, and the Aesthetic-Totality Solution to the Problem of Evil. Gilbertson, Mark.

Epistemologia e psicologia cognitiva: alcune osservazioni sulla teoria dei modelli mentali. Di Serio, Luciana.

Error in persona vel objecto und aberratio ictus. Toepel, Friedrich.

Error, Hallucination and the Concept of 'Ontology' in the Early Work of Heidegger. McManus, Denis.

Function Identification from Noisy Data with Recursive Error Bounds. Changizi, Mark.

Good to the Last Drop? Millikan Stories as "Canned" Pedagogy. Segerstrale, Ullica.

How Are Scientific Corrections Made?. Kiang, Nelson Yuan-sheng.

On Mathematical Error. Sherry, David.

Severe Tests, Arguing from Error, and Methodological Underdetermination. Mayo, Deborah G.

Taking the 'Error' Out of Ruse's Error Theory. Ryan, James A.

The Effectiveness of the Erratum in Avoiding Error Propagation in Physics. Thomsen, Marshall and Resnik, D.

## ERWIN, E

Critical Notice: Freud, Philosophical and Empirical Issues. Cioffi, Frank.

## ESCHATOLOGY

"Tempo storico e futuro escatologico" in *Il Concetto di Tempo: Atti del XXXII Congresso Nazionale della Società Filosofica Italiana,* Casertano, Giovanni (ed). Dall'Asta, Giuseppe.

Messianic History in Benjamin and Metz. Ostovich, Steven T.

One Short Sleep Past?. Herbert, Robert T.

The Essence of Eschatology: A Modal Interpretation. Davenport, John.

## ESOTERISM

Analytische Religionsphilosophie: Zwischen Intersubjektivität und Esoterik. Runggaldier, Edmund.

## ESSAY

Characterization in Samuel Beckett's *Not I.* Daisuke, Hirakawa.

## ESSE

*see* Being

## ESSENCE

*see also* Form

*Art in the Social Order: The Making of the Modern Conception of Art.* Mortensen, Preben.

*Metafisica de la Intencionalidad.* Bosch, Magdalena.

*Paul Ricoeur: A Key to Husserl's Ideas I.* Vandevelde, Pol (ed & trans), Spurlock, Jacqueline Bouchard (trans) and Harris, Bond (trans).

*The Kinds of Things: A Theory of Personal Identity Based on Transcendental Argument.* Doepke, Frederick C.

Aristotele e la fondazione henologica dell'ontologia. Brandner, Rudolf.

Chemistry as the Science of the Transformation of Substances. Van Brakel, Jaap.

Cosmological Mysticism: The Imitation of the Heavenly Bodies in Ibn Tufayl's *Hayy ibn Yaqzan.* Brague, Rémi.

Ente ed essenza in un saggio giovanile di Tommaso d'Aquino. Giorgini, Claudio.

Essere e tempo: Il primordio dell'annientamento. Incardona, Nunzio.

Genus and *to ti en einai* Essence in Aristotle and Socrates. Fritsche, Johannes.

Metafisica tra scienza e sapienza: Tafsir Lām 52-58 di Ibn Rusd. Roccaro, Giuseppe.

Phenomenology of Spirit and Logic (in French). Lécrivain, André.

Sartre and Human Nature. Anderson, Thomas C.

Sujeto, propio y esencia: el fundamento de la distinción aristotélica de modos de predicar. Pérez de Laborda, Miguel.

The Distinction Between Being and Essence According to Boethius, Avicenna, and William of Auvergne. Caster, Kevin J.

The Marxist Theory of Art. Graham, Gordon.

The Ontological Status of Cartesian Natures. Nolan, Lawrence.

## ESSENTIALISM

"Taking the Risk of Essence: A Deweyan Theory in Some Feminist Conversations" in *Knowing Other-Wise: Philosophy at the Threshold of Spirituality,* Olthuis, James H (ed). Hart, Carroll Guen.

*De Re* Language, *De Re* Eliminability, and the Essential Limits of Both. Schwartz, Thomas.

*Un'Introduzione All'Epistemologia Contemporanea.* Gava, Giacomo (ed).

*Waking to Wonder: Wittgenstein's Existential Investigations.* Bearn, Gordon C F.

Actualism or Possibilism?. Tomberlin, James E.

An Anti-Anti-Essentialist View of the Emotions: A Reply to Kupperman. Dalgleish, Tim.

Anti-Essentialism in Practice: Carol Gilligan and Feminist Philosophy. Heyes, Cressida.

Essential Membership. LaPorte, Joseph.

Felt and Unfelt Emotions: A Rejoinder to Dalgleish. Kupperman, Joel J.

Für und Wider den Essentialismus: Zu Rudolf-Peter Häglers *Kritik des neuen Essentialismus.* Liske, Michael-Thomas.

If I Am Only My Genes, What Am I? Genetic Essentialism and a Jewish Response. Wolpe, Paul Root.

La métaphysique du réalisme modal: régression ou enjeu véritable?. Nef, Frédéric.

Modern Essentialism and the Problem of Individuation of Spacetime Points. Bartels, Andreas.

Overriding the Natural Ought. Sullivan, Philip R.

Quantified Modal Logic, Reference and Essentialism. Perrick, M and Swart, H C M.

Rorty and Davidson. Sullivan, Arthur.

Tibbles the Cat: A Modern *Sophisma.* Burke, Michael B.

Two Kinds of Antiessentialism and Their Consequences. Spinosa, Charles and Dreyfus, Hubert L.

## ESTHETICS

*see* Aesthetics

## ETCHEMENDY, J

Logical Consequence: A Defense of Tarski. Ray, Greg.

## ETERNAL

"*Ewiger Friede*: Warum ein Beweismittel in Kants philosophischem Entwurf?" in *Grenzen der kritischen Vernunft,* Schmid, Peter A. Mainberger, Gonsalv K.

"Dobbiamo ancora pensare il tempo come finito?" in *Il Concetto di Tempo: Atti del XXXII Congresso Nazionale della Società Filosofica Italiana,* Casertano, Giovanni (ed). Morselli, Graziella.

"La creación de las verdades eternas y la fábula del mundo" in *Memorias Del Seminario En Conmemoración De Los 400 Años Del Nacimiento De René Descartes,* Albis, Víctor S (ed). Margot, Jean-Paul.

"Tumbling Dice: Gilles Deleuze and the Economy of *Répétition*" in *Deleuze and Philosophy: The Difference Engineer,* Ansell Pearson, Keith (ed). Conway, Daniel W.

*A Treatise Concerning Eternal and Immutable Morality* with *A Treatise of Freewill.* Hutton, Sarah (ed) and Cudworth, Ralph.

*Tempo Linguaggio e Azione: Le Strutture Vichiane della Storia Ideale Eterna.* Botturi, Francesco.

Bowling Alone: On the Saving Power of Kant's Perpetual Peace. Shell, Susan Meld.

Divine Intervention. Fales, Evan.

Eternal Knowledge of the Temporal in Aquinas. Shanley, Brian J.

Eternal Truths in Aristotle's Posterior Analytics, 1, 8. Magee, Joseph M.

Eternal Verities: Timeless Truth, Ahistorical Standards, and the One True Story. Edidin, Aron.

Josiah Royce's Reading of Plato's *Theaetetus.* Glidden, David K.

Moral Politics and the Limits of Justice in *Perpetual Peace.* Clarke, Michael.

Social Contract among Devils. Verweyen, Hansjürgen.

The Cosmic Route to "Eternal Bliss": (K.E. Tsiolkovskii and the Mythology of Technocracy). Gavriushin, Nikolai K.

The Objective Viewpoint: A Nietzschean Account. Appel, Fredrick.

Under the Sign of Failure. Fenves, Peter.

## ETERNAL RECURRENCE

*Nietzsche's Philosophy of the Eternal Recurrence of the Same.* Lomax, J Harvey (trans) and Löwith, Karl.

Born to Affirm the Eternal Recurrence: Nietzsche, Buber, and Springsteen. Cohen, Jonathan.

El *Nacimiento de la Tragedia* como Introducción a la Filosofía Posterior de Nietzsche. Meléndez, Germán.

## ETERNITY

"Il tempo nell'eternità" in *Il Concetto di Tempo: Atti del XXXII Congresso Nazionale della Società Filosofica Italiana,* Casertano, Giovanni (ed). Longo, Rosaria.

"Tempo ed eternità in Enzo Paci" in *Il Concetto di Tempo: Atti del XXXII Congresso Nazionale della Società Filosofica Italiana,* Casertano, Giovanni (ed). Calapso, Renato.

*How to Live Forever: Science Fiction and Philosophy.* Clark, Stephen R L.

De lo eterno a lo infinito: un intento de reconstrución del argumento de Meliso (B2-4 D-K). Bredlow, Luis.

Duns Scotus on Eternity and Timelessness. Cross, Richard.

How To Do Things with Numbers: MacIntosh on the Possible Eternity of the World. Côté, Antoine.

## ETHICS

*A Right to Die?: The Dax Cowart Case.* Covey, Preston K, Cavalier, Robert J and Andersen, David.

*A Spinoza Reader: The Ethics and Other Works.* Curley, Edwin (ed & trans).

*Altruism in Later Life.* Midlarsky, Elizabeth and Kahana, Eva.

*Angewandte Ethik: Die Bereichsethiken und ihre theoretische Fundierung.* Nida-Rümelin, Julian (ed).

*Aristotle: Introductory Readings.* Irwin, Terence H (trans) and Fine, Gail (trans).

*Atheistic Humanism.* Flew, Antony.

*Augustine the Reader: Meditation, Self-Knowledge, and the Ethics of Interpretation.* Stock, Brian.

*Augusto Ponzio: Bibliografia e Letture Critiche.* Ponzio, Augusto.

*Babies and Beasts: The Argument from Marginal Cases.* Dombrowski, Daniel A.

*Being and Other Realities.* Weiss, Paul.

*Belief and Resistance: Dynamics of Contemporary Intellectual Controversy.* Smith, Barbara Herrnstein.

*Beyond Interpretation: The Meaning of Hermeneutics for Philosophy.* Vattimo, Gianni and Webb, David (trans).

*Beyond Neutrality: Perfectionism and Politics.* Sher, George.

*Body Parts: Property Rights and the Ownership of Human Biological Materials.* Gold, E R.

*Brute Science: Dilemmas of Animal Experimentation.* Shanks, Niall and LaFollette, Hugh.

*Business Ethics in the African Context Today.* Rosemann, Philipp W (ed) and LeJeune, Michel (ed).

*Can We Be Good without God?: A Conversation about Truth, Morality, Culture & A Few Other Things That Matter.* Chamberlain, Paul.

*Caring: Gender-Sensitive Ethics.* Bowden, Peta.

*Carlo Michelstaedter: il coraggio dell'impossibile.* Michelis, Angela.

*Caveat Emptor. Ethical Chauvinism in the Global Economy.* Vega, Gina.

*Comunicación, Ética Y Política: Habermas Y Sus Críticos.* Boladeras, Margarita.

*Critical Studies: Ethics and the Subject.* Simms, Karl (ed).

*Death, Brain Death and Ethics.* Lamb, David.

*Defending Mother Earth: Native American Perspectives on Environmental Justice.* Weaver, Jace (ed).

*Deterrence and the Crisis in Moral Theory: An Analysis of the Moral Literature on the Nuclear Arms Debate.* Palmer-Fernandez, Gabriel.

*Dialogues with Plato.* Benitez, Eugenio E (ed).

*Dignity and Dying: A Christian Appraisal.* Miller, Arlene B (ed), Kilner, John F (ed) and Pellegrino, Edmund D (ed).

*Dio e il male.* Possenti, Vittorio.

*Earth Community: Earth Ethics.* Rasmussen, Larry L.

*Earthly Goods: Environmental Change and Social Justice.* Hampson, Fen Osler (ed) and Reppy, Judith (ed).

*El Krausopositivismo de Urbano González Serrano.* García, Antonio Jiménez.

*Ensayos Aristotélicos.* Rivera, José Luis (ed).

*Environmental Pragmatism.* Light, Andrew (ed) and Katz, Eric (ed).

*Ethical Issues in Death and Dying.* Beauchamp, Tom L (ed) and Veatch, Robert M (ed).

*Ethical Norms, Particular Cases.* Wallace, James D.

*Ethics and Economic Progress.* Buchanan, James M.

*Ethics and Justice in Organisations: A Normative-Empirical Dialogue.* Singer, M.

*Ethics for Professionals in Education: Perspectives for Preparation and Practice.* Strike, Kenneth A (ed) and Ternasky, P Lance (ed).

*Ethics in School Counseling.* Schulte, John M and Cochrane, Donald B.

*Ética: Procedimientos Razonables.* López de la Vieja, Maria Teresa.

*Evolutionäre Ethik? Philosophische Programme, Probleme und Perspektiven der Soziobiologie.* Gräfrath, Bernd.

*Exploring Unseen Worlds: William James and the Philosophy of Mysticism.* Barnard, G William.

*Fact, Value, and God.* Holmes, Arthur F.

*Feminist Approaches to Bioethics: Theoretical Reflections and Practical Applications.* Tong, Rosemarie.

*Finding Philosophy in Social Science.* Bunge, Mario.

*Food for Thought: Philosophy and Food.* Telfer, Elizabeth.

*Formal Ethics.* Gensler, Harry J.

*Fruits of Sorrow.* Spelman, Elizabeth V.

*Gassendi's Ethics: Freedom in a Mechanistic Universe.* Sarasohn, Lisa T.

*Geofilosofia.* Bonesio, Luisa (ed), Baldino, Marco (ed) and Resta, Caterina (ed).

*Head and Heart: Affection, Cognition, Volition as Triune Consciousness.* Tallon, Andrew.

*History and Contemporary Issues: Studies in Moral Theology.* Curran, Charles E.

*Homonoia in Aristotle's Ethics and Politics.* Klonoski, Richard J.

*Human Lives: Critical Essays on Consequentialist Bioethics.* Oderberg, David S (ed) and Laing, Jacqueline A (ed).

*Hypocrisy and Integrity: Machiavelli, Rousseau, and the Ethics of Politics.* Grant, Ruth W.

*Impartiality in Context: Grounding Justice in a Pluralist World.* O'Neill, Shane.

*Improving Nature?.* Reiss, Michael J and Straughan, Roger.

*In Pursuit of Privacy: Law, Ethics, and the Rise of Technology.* DeCew, Judith Wagner.

*Intending Death: The Ethics of Assisted Suicide and Euthanasia.* Beauchamp, Tom L (ed).

*Jonathan Edwards's Writings: Text, Context, Interpretation.* Stein, Stephen J (ed).

*Just and Unjust Wars: Casuistry and the Boundaries of the Moral World.* Boyle, Joseph.

*Kant: La paz perpetua, doscientos años después.* Martínez Guzmán, Vicent (ed).

*Karl-Otto Apel: Selected Essays.* Mendieta, Eduardo (ed).

*La filosofía en la encrucijada: Perfiles del pensamiento de José Ferrater Mora.* Nieto Blanco, Carlos.

*La Volontà di Potenza in Nietzsche e la Storia dell'Europa negli Ultimi Tempi.* Manno, Ambrogio Giacomo.

*Law and Morality: Readings in Legal Philosophy.* Dyzenhaus, David (ed) and Ripstein, Arthur (ed).

*Leben-und Sterbenkönnen: Gedanken zur Sterbebegleitung und zur Selbstbestimmung der Person.* Wettstein, R Harri.

*Lectures on Ethics.* Heath, Peter (ed & trans) and Schneewind, J B (ed).

*Legal Realism: American and Scandinavian.* Martin, Michael.

*Levinas: An Introduction.* Davis, Colin.

*Límites de la Argumentación Ética en Aristóteles: Lógos, physis y éthos.* Zagal, Héctor Arreguín and Aguilar-Alvarez, Sergio.

*Love Analyzed.* Lamb, Roger E.

*Mahatma Ghandi: Selected Political Writings.* Dalton, Dennis (ed).

*Making a Necessity of Virtue.* Sherman, Nancy.

*Making Mortal Choices: Three Exercises in Moral Casuistry.* Bedau, Hugo Adam.

*Metaphilosophy and Free Will.* Double, Richard.

*Momenti di Storia della Logica e di Storia della Filosofia.* Guetti, Carla (ed) and Pujia, Roberto (ed).

*Moral Discourse and Practice: Some Philosophical Approaches.* Darwall, Stephen (ed), Gibbard, Allan (ed) and Railton, Peter (ed).

*Moral Issues in Health Care: An Introduction to Medical Ethics.* McConnell, Terrance C.

*Moral Knowledge?: New Readings in Moral Epistemology.* Sinnott-Armstrong, Walter (ed) and Timmons, Mark (ed).

*Moralidad: Ética universalista y sujeto moral.* Guariglia, Osvaldo.

*Morality and the Good Life.* Moser, Paul K (ed) and Carson, Thomas L (ed).

*Morality and the Law.* Baird, Robert M (ed) and Rosenbaum, Stuart E (ed).

*Morals Based on Needs.* Ohlsson, Ragnar.

*Mortals and Others: American Essays 1931-1935.* Russell, Bertrand and Ruja, Harry (ed).

*Nature as Subject: Human Obligation and Natural Community.* Katz, Eric.

*Nietzsche Werke Kritische Gesamtausgabe: III 5/2.* Groddeck, Wolfram (ed) and Kohlenbach, Michael (ed).

*Ökonomie und Moral: Beiträge zur Theorie ökonomischer Rationalität.* Lohmann, Karl Reinhard (ed) and Priddat, Birger P (ed).

*On Heidegger's Nazism and Philosophy.* Rockmore, Tom.

*On the Genealogy of Morals.* Smith, Douglas (trans) and Nietzsche, Friedrich.

*Organ Transplants and Ethics.* Lamb, David.

*Perspectives on Punishment: An Interdisciplinary Exploration.* Andrews, Richard Mowery (ed).

*Philosophical Perspectives on Bioethics.* Sumner, L W (ed) and Boyle, Joseph (ed).

*Philosophy and Geography I: Space, Place, and Environmental Ethics.* Light, Andrew (ed) and Smith, Jonathan M (ed).

*Philosophy and the Return to Self-Knowledge.* Verene, Donald Phillip.

*Philosophy as Passion: The Thinking of Simone de Beauvoir.* Vintges, Karen.

*Philosophy of Sex and Love: A Reader.* Trevas, Robert (ed), Zucker, Arthur (ed) and Borchert, Donald (ed).

*Philosophy, Religion, and the Question of Intolerance.* Ambuel, David (ed) and Razavi, Mehdi Amin (ed).

*Plessy V. Ferguson in Libertarian Perspective.* Tushnet, Mark.

*Practical Induction.* Millgram, Elijah.

*Prescription: Medicine.* Kevorkian, Jack.

*Presupposti filosofici dell'enciclica Veritatis splendor.* Gigante, Mario.

*Principia Ecologica Eco-Principles as a Conceptual Framework for a New Ethics in Science and Technology.* Moser, Anton.

*Promising, Intending, and Moral Autonomy.* Robins, Michael H.

*Radical Critiques of the Law.* Griffin, Stephen M (ed) and Moffat, Robert C L (ed).

*Rational Choice and Moral Agency.* Schmidtz, David.

*Razón, Naturaleza y Libertad: En Torno a La Crítica de la Razón Práctica Kantiana.* Vegas González, Serafín, Klappenbach, Augusto and Núñez Tomás, Paloma.

*Reasonable Children: Moral Education and Moral Learning.* Pritchard, Michael S.

*Reconsidering Difference.* May, Todd.

*Reproduction, Technology, and Rights: Biomedical Ethics Reviews.* Humber, James M (ed) and Almeder, Robert F (ed).

*Sagacious Reasoning: Henry Odera Oruka in Memoriam.* Graness, Anke (ed) and Kresse, Kai (ed).

# ETHICS

*Sartres Ontologie und die Frage einer Ethik: Zur Vereinbarkeit einer normativen Ethik und/oder Metaethik mit der Ontologie von "L'être et le néant"*. Töllner, Uwe.

*Self-Trust: A Study of Reason, Knowledge and Autonomy*. Lehrer, Keith.

*Sex, Preference, and Family: Essays on Law and Nature*. Nussbaum, Martha C (ed) and Estlund, David M (ed).

*Sexual Harassment: Confrontations and Decisions*. Wall, Edmund (ed).

*Socratic Puzzles*. Nozick, Robert.

*Structure and Diversity: Studies in the Phenomenological Philosophy of Max Scheler*. Kelly, Eugene.

*Testing the Medical Covenant: Active Euthanasia and Health Care Reform*. May, William F.

*The Annual of the Society of Christian Ethics with Cumulative Index*. Beckley, Harlan (ed).

*The Art of Plato: Ten Essays in Platonic Interpretation*. Rutherford, R B.

*The Commons of the Mind*. Baier, Annette C.

*The Constitution of Good Societies*. Soltan, Karol Edward (ed) and Elkin, Stephen L (ed).

*The Ethics of Special Education*. Howe, Ken and Miramontes, Ofelia B.

*The Ethics of the Stoic Epictetus: An English Translation*. Stephens, William O (trans) and Bonhöffer, Adolf Friedrich.

*The Gift of Truth: Gathering the Good*. Ross, Stephen David.

*The Insufficiency of Virtue: Macbeth and the Natural Order*. Blits, Jan H.

*The Last Word*. Nagel, Thomas.

*The Metaphysics of Morals*. Gregor, Mary (ed & trans) and Kant, Immanuel.

*The Moral Base for Teacher Professionalism*. Sockett, Hugh.

*The Morality of Nationalism*. McKim, Robert (ed) and McMahan, Jeff (ed).

*The Plato Reader*. Chappell, Tim D J.

*The Religion of Socrates*. McPherran, Mark L.

*The Right to Know and the Right not to Know*. Chadwick, Ruth (ed), Levitt, Mairi (ed) and Shickle, Darren (ed).

*The Significance of Free Will*. Kane, Robert.

*The Significance of Popper's Thought*. Amsterdamski, Stefan (ed).

*The Welfare State*. Paul, Ellen Frankel (ed), Miller, Fred D (ed) and Paul, Jeffrey (ed).

*Thick and Thin: Moral Argument at Home and Abroad*. Walzer, Michael.

*Universal Justice: A Dialectical Approach*. Anderson, Albert A.

*Unpopular Essays*. Russell, Bertrand.

*Utilitarianism*. Scarre, Geoffrey.

*Values and the Social Order*. Radnitzky, Gerard (ed).

*Verstehen and Humane Understanding*. O'Hear, Anthony (ed).

*Vico and Moral Perception*. Black, David W.

*Virtue Ethics*. Slote, Michael (ed) and Crisp, Roger (ed).

*Voluntas* nel *De gratia et libero arbitrio* di Bernardo di Chiaravalle. Allegro, Giuseppe.

*Vom Begründen zum Handeln: Aufsätze zur angewandten Ethik*. Ott, Konrad.

*W.E.B. Du Bois on* Race and Culture. Grosholz, Emily (ed), Bell, Bernard W (ed) and Stewart, James B (ed).

*Watsuji Tetsurō's Rinrigaku*. Carter, Robert E (trans) and Seisaku, Yamamoto (trans).

*Welfare, Happiness, and Ethics*. Sumner, L W.

*Western Philosophy: An Anthology*. Cottingham, John (ed).

*What Is a Person? An Ethical Exploration*. Walters, James W.

*Wrongness, Wisdom, and Wilderness: Toward a Libertarian Theory of Ethics and the Environment*. Scriven, Tal.

A "Meeting of the Minds": The Greater Illusion. Damren, Samuel C.

A Better Statutory Approach to Whistle-Blowing. Morehead Dworkin, Terry and Near, Janet P.

A Call for a Statement of Expectations for the Global Information Infrastructure. Connolly, Frank W.

A Case for Proposition 209. Bradley, Gerard V.

A Case Study of Conflicting Interests: Flemish Engineers Involved in Environmental Impact Assessment. Holemans, Dirk.

A Chinese Critique on Western Ways of Warfare. Hagen, Kurtis.

A Comment on 'Radiation Protection and Moral Theory'. Miller, Chris.

A Communion of Saints...Maybe. Bailey Stoneking, Carole.

A Communitarian Approach to Physician-Assisted Death. Miller, Franklin G.

A Critical Analysis of Hunters' Ethics. Luke, Brian.

A Critical Assessment of Varner's Proposal for Consensus and Convergence in the Biomedical Research Debate. Clune, Alan C.

A Critique and A Retrieval of Management and the Humanities. Gilbert Jr, Daniel R.

A Critique of Pure Politics. Connolly, William E.

A Crying Need for Discourse. Zangrando, Robert L.

A Defence of Mencius' Ethical Naturalism. Ryan, James A.

A Defense of "A Defense of Abortion": On the Responsibility Objection to Thomson's Argument. Boonin-Vail, David.

A Defense of Physicalism. Jensen, Steven J.

A Dialogue Between Virtue Ethics and Care Ethics. Benner, Patricia.

A Dialogue on Species-Specific Rights: Humans and Animals in Bioethics. Thomasma, David C and Loewy, Erich H.

A experiência erótica em Leonardo Coimbra. Esteves Borges, Paulo Alexandre.

A Feminist Standpoint for Genetics. Mahowald, Mary B.

A Framework for Teaching Business Ethics. Oddo, Alfonso R.

A Global Ethic in an Age of Globalization. Küng, Hans.

A Global Perspective of Ethics in Business. Yamaji, Keizo.

A Good Death—Oxymoron?. McCormick, Richard A.

A Good Death: Improving Care Inch-by-Inch. Ayers, Elise, Harrold, Joan and Lynn, Joanne.

A Historical Interpretation of Deceptive Experiments in American Psychology. Herrera, Christopher D.

A Just Share: Justice and Fairness in Resource Allocation. McCarrick, Pat Milmoe and Darragh, Martina.

A Longitudinal Examination of American Business Ethics: Clark's Scales Revisited. Harich, Katrin R and Curren, Mary T.

A Manual on Manners and Courtesies for the Shared Care of Patients. Stoekle, John D, Ronan, Laurence J and Emanuel, Linda L (& others).

A Method for Teaching Ethics. Gampel, Eric.

A Model Policy Addressing Mistreatment of Medical Students. Strong, Carson, Wall, Hershel P and Jameson, Valerie.

A Multi-Stage Game Model of Morals by Agreement. Heath, Joseph.

A Multicultural Examination of Business Ethics Perceptions. Allmon, Dean E, Chen, Henry C K and Pritchett, Thomas K (& others).

A Non-Solution to a Non-Problem: A Comment on Alan Strudler's "Mass Torts and Moral Principles". Kraus, Jody S.

A Noncognitivist Reading of Quine's Ethics. Broach, Ronald J.

A Noncompliant Patient?. Moseley, Kathryn L and Truesdell, Sandra.

A Note on Moore's Organic Unities. Carlson, Erik.

A Note on—Euthanasia and the Contemporary Debate. Barua, Archna.

A Philosophy of Risk Assessment and the Law: A Case Study of the Role of Philosophy in Public Policy. Cranor, Carl F.

A Plea for Accuses. Zimmerman, Michael J.

A Political-Ecology Approach to Wildlife Conservation in Kenya. Akama, John S, Lant, Christopher L and Burnett, G Wesley.

A Practical Advance Directive Survey. McCanna, Tony.

A Pragmatic Approach to Business Ethics. Shaw, Bill.

A Proposal for a New System of Credit Allocation in Science. Resnik, David B.

A propósito de *Giusnaturalismo ed etica moderna*: Notas sobre Grocio y Vico en la Vª Orazione Inaugurale V (1705). Lomonaco, Fabrizio.

A Question for Egalitarians. Kekes, John.

A Reply to Some Standard Objections to Euthanasia. Shand, John.

A Resource-Based-View of the Socially Responsible Firm: Stakeholder Interdependence, Ethical Awareness, and Issue Responsiveness as Strategic Assets. Litz, Reginald A.

A Response. Walzer, Michael.

A Review of the Origins of the State (Spanish). Ramos, Alberto Arvelo.

A Test of a Person—Issue Contingent Model of Ethical Decision Making in Organizations. Harrington, Susan J.

A Threat to Disabled Persons? On the Genetics Approach to Developmental Disabilities. Reinders, Hans S.

A Utilitarian Argument for Vegetarianism. Dixon, Nicholas.

A Virtue Ethics Approach to Aldo Leopold's Land Ethic. Shaw, Bill.

Abendländische Tugendlehre und moderne Moralphilosophie. Wald, Berthold.

Abortion and Degrees of Personhood: Understanding Why the Abortion Problem (and the Animal Rights Problem) are Irresolvable. Li, Hon-Lam.

Abortion, Infanticide, and the Asymmetric Value of Human Life. Reiman, Jeffrey.

Abortion, Value and the Sanctity of Life. Belshaw, Christopher.

Academic Corruption. Kekes, John.

Academic Feminism and Applied Ethics: Closing the Gap between Private Scholarship and Public Policy. LeMoncheck, Linda.

Accepting Agent Centred Norms: A Problem for Non-Cognitivists and a Suggestion for Solving It. Dreier, James.

Accountability in a Computerized Society. Nissenbaum, Helen.

Action Theory and Criminal Law. Dolinko, David.

Adolescent Parents and Medical Decision-Making. De Ville, Kenneth.

Adolfo Ravà: lo Stato come organismo etico. Fracanzani, Marcello.

Advance Directive Timeline and Case Study *Melinda's Story*. Reynolds, Don F, Flanigan, Rosemary and Emmott, Helen.

Advance Directives and Patient Rights: A Joint Commission Perspective. Worth-Staten, Patricia A and Poniatowski, Larry.

Advance Directives Outside the USA: Are They the Best Solution Everywhere?. Sanchez-Gonzalez, Miguel A.

Advocating for the Dying: The View of Family and Friends. Moretti, Anna M.

Advocating Values: Professionalism in Teaching Ethics. Martin, Mike W.

Affect and the Moral-Conventional Distinction. Blair, R J R.

Affirmative Action at the University of California. Lynch, Michael W.

After *Virtù*: Rhetoric, Prudence and Moral Pluralism in Machiavelli. Garver, Eugene.

Against Ethical Criticism. Posner, Richard A.

Against Strong Speciesism. Graft, Donald.

Against the Golden Rule Argument Against Abortion. Boonin-Vail, David.

Against Thin-Property Reductivism: Toleration as Supererogatory. Newey, Glen.

Agency. Simester, A P.

Agency and the Imputation of Consequences in Kant's Ethics. Reath, Andrews.

Agent-Neutral Reasons: Are They for Everyone?. Postow, B C.

## ETHICS

Agustin de Herrera, A Treatise on Aleatory Probability *De Necessitate Morali in Genere*. Knebel, Sven K (ed & trans).

Ah! My Foolish Heart: A Reply to Alan Soble's "Antioch's 'Sexual Offense Policy': A Philosophical Exploration". Kittay, Eva Felder.

AIDS, Confidentiality, and Ethical Models. Gorbett, Jason.

AIDS, Confidentiality, and Ethical Models: Appendix. Gorbett, Jason.

Alasdair MacIntyre: The Epitaph of Modernity. Kitchen, Gary.

Alertness and Determination: A Note on Moral Phenomenology. Wilson, John.

Algunas reflexiones ante el comunitarismo: MacIntyre, Taylor y Walzer. Dussel, Enrique.

Algunos elementos para una deontología periodística. Rodríguez Ramírez, Carlos Alberto.

Alienación y libertad: La ética en la psicoterapia. Rovaletti, María Lucrecia.

Allocating Healthcare By QALYs: The Relevance of Age. McKie, John, Kuhse, Helga and Richardson, Jeff.

Altering Humans—The Case For and Against Human Gene Therapy. Holtug, Nils.

Alternative Dispute Resolution and Research Misconduct. Guenin, Louis M.

Altruism: A Social Science Chameleon. Grant, Colin.

Ambiguous Democracy and the Ethics of Psychoanalysis. Stavrakakis, Yannis.

An African American Looks at Death. Secundy, Marian Gray.

An Argument against Techno-Privacy. Jones, Leslie E.

An Aspect of Love: Descartes on Friendship. Morgan, Vance G.

An East Asian Perspective of Mind-Body. Nagatomo, Shigenori and Leisman, Gerald.

An Ecologically-Informed Ontology for Environmental Ethics. Buege, Douglas J.

An Egg Takes Flight: The Once and Future Life of the National Bioethics Advisory Commission. Capron, Alexander M.

An Empirical Examination of the Multi-Dimensionality of Ethical Climate in Organizations. Wimbush, James C, Shepard, Jon M and Markham, Steven E.

An Empirical Study of Moral Reasoning Among Managers in Singapore. Wimalasiri, Jayantha S, Pavri, Francis and Jalil, Abdul A K.

An Epistemic Dimension of Blameworthiness. Haji, Ishtiyaque.

An Essay on When to Fully Disclose in Sales Relationships: Applying Two Practical Guidelines for Addressing Truth-Telling Problems. Strutton, David, Hamilton III, J Brooke and Lumpkin, James R.

An Ethical Approach to Lobbying Activities of Businesses in the United States. Keffer, Jane M and Hill, Ronald Paul.

An Examination of the Relationship Between Ethical Behavior, Espoused Ethical Values and Financial Performance in the U S Defense Industry: 1988-1992. Mayer-Sommer, Alan P and Roshwalb, Alan.

An Exercise in Moral Philosophy: Seeking to Understand "Nobody". King, Jonathan B.

An Historical Preface to Engineering Ethics. Davis, Michael.

An Inquiry into Ethical Relativism in Hindu Thought. Jhingran, Saral.

An Introduction to Research Ethics. Friedman, Paul J.

An Investigation of the Components of Moral Intensity. Marshall, Bev and Dewe, Philip.

An Objection to Smith's Argument for Internalism. Miller, Alexander.

An Overlooked Motive in Alcibiades' *Symposium* Speech. Scott, Gary Alan and Welton, William A.

An Unconnected Heap of Duties?. McNaughton, David.

An Untitled Lecture on Plato's *Euthyphron*. Bolotin, David (ed), Strauss, Leo and Bruell, Christopher (& other eds).

Anerkennung und moralische Verpflichtung. Honneth, Axel.

Animals, Morality and Robert Boyle. MacIntosh, J J.

Answering the Free-Rider. Allan, Jim.

Anthropo-centrifugal Ethics (in Czech). Kemp, Peter.

Anthropocentrism: A Misunderstood Problem. Hayward, Tim.

Antifoundationalism and the Possibility of a Moral Philosophy of Medicine. Thomasma, David C.

Antimodern, Ultramodern, Postmodern: A Plea for the Perennial. Dewan, Lawrence.

Antioch's "Sexual Offense Policy": A Philosophical Exploration. Soble, Alan.

Applicability and Effectiveness of Legal Norms. Navarro, Pablo E and Moreso, José Juan.

Applying Ethics: Modes, Motives, and Levels of Commitment. Prasad, Rajendra.

Approaches Responsive to Reproductive Technologies: A Need for Critical Assessment and Directions for Further Study. Kondratowicz, Diane M.

Approaches to Conserving Vulnerable Wildlife in China: Does the Colour of Cat Matter—if it Catches Mice?. Harris, Richard B.

Appropriate Guilt: Between Expansion and Limitations (in Dutch). Van den Beld, A.

Aproximaciones a una evaluación de la aplicación de las nuevas tecnologías reproductivas. Digilio, Patricia.

Aquinas on Passions and Diminished Responsibility. Nisters, Thomas.

Aquinas's Account of Double Effect. Cavanaugh, Thomas A.

Are Ethical Conflicts Irreconcilable?. Cooke, Maeve.

Are We Teaching Ethics in Marketing?: A Survey of Students' Attitudes and Perceptions. Shannon, J Richard and Berl, Robert L.

Argumentation, Values, and Ethics. Monsalve, Alfonso.

Arguments Against Health Care Autonomy for Minors. Ross, Lainie Friedman.

Aristotelian *Akrasia* and Psychoanalytic Regression. Stocker, Michael.

Aristotle and the Idea of Competing Forms of Life. Crittenden, P.

Aristotle on Canonical Science and Ethics. Anagnostopoulos, Georgios.

Aristotle on Pleasure and Political Philosophy: A Study in Book VII of the *Nicomachean Ethics*. Guerra, Marc D.

Aristotle on Variation and Indefiniteness in Ethics and Its Subject Matter. Anagnostopoulos, Georgios.

Aristotle's *Nicomachean Ethics* and Shakespeare's *Troilus and Cressida*. Elton, W R.

Aristotle's Ethical Egoism. Gottlieb, Paula.

Aristotle, *hos epi to polu* Relations, and a Demonstrative Science of Ethics. Winter, Michael.

Ascriptions of Responsibility. Oshana, Marina A L.

Ascriptive Supervenience. Carlin, Laurence.

Aspectos políticos del pensamiento de J. Habermas: una lectura crítica. Bonnet, Alberto.

Aspekte internationaler Ethik. Betzler, Monika.

Assessing Conflict of Interest: Sources of Bias. Bird, Stephanie J.

Assessing the Publication Swamp in Literary Studies. Harris, Wendell V.

Assisted Suicide: Will the Supreme Court Respect the Autonomy Rights of Dying Patients?. Lindsay, Ronald A.

Asymmetric Perceptions of Ethical Frameworks of Men and Women in Business and Nonbusiness Settings. Schminke, Marshall and Ambrose, Maureen L.

Asymmetrical Reciprocity: On Moral Respect, Wonder, and Enlarged Thought. Young, Iris Marion.

Ato e potência: implicaçoes éticas de uma doutrina metafísica. Perine, Marcelo.

Attitudes and Issues Preventing Bans on Toxic Lead Shot and Sinkers in North America and Europe. Thomas, Vernon G.

Attributing 'Priority' to Habitats. Miller, Chris.

Audience and Authority: The Story in Front of the Story. Zoloth-Dorfman, Laurie.

Auditors' Ability to Discern the Presence of Ethical Problems. Karcher, Julia N.

Augustine's Hermeneutics and the Principle of Charity. Glidden, David.

Autarcie et logos conciliateur chez Zénon de Cittium. Kélessidou, Anna.

Authenticity As a Normative Category. Ferrara, Alessandro.

Autonomy and Hierarchical Compatibilism. Jennings, Ian.

Autonomy and the Orthodoxy of Human Superiority. Gruzalski, Bart K.

Autonomy and the Very Limited Role of Advocacy in the Classroom. Kupperman, Joel J.

Autonomy, Life as an Intrinsic Value, and the Right to Die in Dignity. Cohen-Almagor, Raphael.

Autor y represión. Gracia, Jorge J E.

Avant-propos. Bühler, Pierre.

Averting Violence: Domestic, Social and Personal. Wood, Forrest.

Axiological Foundations of "Human Dignity" (Spanish). Sánchez, Angel Martín.

Bach's Butterfly Effect: Culture, Environment and History. Simmons, I G.

Bad Night in the ER—Patients' Preferences and Reasonable Accommodation: Discussed by Douglas A. Beer, Ruth Macklin, Walter Robinson, and Philip Wang. Beer, Douglas A, Macklin, Ruth and Robinson, Walter (& others).

Battered Women Who Kill: Victims and Agents of Violence. Hartline, Sharon E.

Beauty and Desire: Frans Hemsterhuis' Aesthetic Experiments. Sonderen, Peter C.

Beauty and Technology as Paradigms for the Moral Life. Brown, Montague.

Beauty and the Attainment of Temperance. Edelman, John T.

Being Human: Issues in Sexuality for People with Developmental Disabilities. Civjan, Sheryl Robinson.

Bemerkungen zur Natur der Angewandten Ethik (in Serbo-Croatian). Jakovljevic, Dragan.

Better Communication between Engineers and Managers: Some Ways to Prevent Many Ethically Hard Choices. Davis, Michael.

Between Anthropocentrism and Ecocentrism. Boulting, Noel E.

Between Apathy and Revolution: Nonviolent Action in Contemporary Mexico. Inda, Caridad.

Between Doctor and Patient. Capron, Alexander M.

Between Ethics and Epistemology: Sartre and Bachelard, Readers of Descartes (Spanish). López, Bernardo Correa.

Between Inconsistent Nominalists and Egalitarian Idealists. Nelson, Ralph C.

Beyond Living Wills. Tonelli, Mark.

Beyond Self and Other. Rogers, Kelly.

Beyond the Sovereignty of Good. Nelson, Ralph C.

Bij de Grenzen van Verplegingswetenschap. Blokhuis, P.

Biodiversity as the Source of Biological Resources: A New Look at Biodiversity Values. Wood, Paul M.

Bioethical Analysis of an Integrated Medicine Clinic. Potter, Robert Lyman and Schneider, Jennifer.

Bioethical Issues Confronting The African American Community. Calloway, Kelvin T.

## ETHICS

Comparing Harms: Headaches and Human Lives. Norcross, Alastair.

Competing Interests: The Need to Control Conflict of Interests in Biomedical Research. Steiner, Daniel.

Complexity of Ethical Decision Making in Psychiatry. Morenz, Barry and Sales, Bruce.

Computer Ethics and Moral Methodology. Van den Hoven, Jeroen.

Computers, Information and Ethics: A Review of Issues and Literature. Mitcham, Carl.

Computers, Radiation, and Ethics. Schenkman, Bo.

Concept of Duty: A Study in Indian and Western Philosophy. Bhandari, D R and Lata.

Concepts in Evaluation Applied to Ethics Consultation Research. Fox, Ellen.

Concepts of Moral Management and Moral Maximization. Sikula, Sr, Andrew.

Concerning Lev Shestov's Conception of Ethics. Van Goubergen, Martine.

Concerning the Charge of Plagiarism against Stephen B. Oates. Current, Richard N.

Conciencia subjetiva y conciencia comunicativa en el discurso ético. Michelini, Dorando J.

Conducting and Reporting Research. Bird, Stephanie J and Housman, David E.

Confessions of an Expert Ethics Witness. Kipnis, Kenneth.

Conflicts of Interest and Conflicts of Commitment. Werhane, Patricia and Doering, Jeffrey.

Conflicts of Interest, Conflicting Interests, and Interesting Conflicts, Part 3. Vinicky, Janicemarie K, Orlowski, James P and Shevlin Edwards, Sue.

Confounding the Paradigm: Asian Americans and Race Preferences. Izumi, Lance T.

Consapevolezza etica ed esperienza della virtù. Marra, Bruno.

Conscious Negligence. Brady, James B.

Consequentialism, Deontological Ethics, and Terrorism (in Serbo-Croatian). Jokic, Aleksandar.

Consequentialism, Moralities of Concern, and Selfishness. Honderich, Ted.

Constructing a Hall of Reflection. Mulhall, Stephen.

Consultectonics: Ethics Committee Case Consultation as Mediation. Reynolds, Don F.

Contemplating the Interests of Fish: The Angler's Challenge. De Leeuw, A Dionys.

Context, Politics and Moral Education: Comments on the Misgeld/ Magendzo Conversation about Human Rights Education. Brabeck, Mary M and Ting, Kathleen.

Contracts with Animals: Lucretius, De Rerum Natura. Shelton, Jo-Ann.

Contractualism and Animals. Bernstein, Mark.

Convergence and Contextualism: Some Clarifications and a Reply to Steverson. Norton, Bryan G.

Corporate Ethics Codes: A Practical Application of Liability Prevention. Blodgett, Mark S and Carlson, Patricia J.

Corporate Ethics Initiatives as Social Control. Laufer, William S and Robertson, Diana C.

Corporate Social Performance, Stakeholder Orientation, and Organizational Moral Development. Logsdon, Jeanne M and Yuthas, Kristi.

Correlation of Gender-Related Values of Independence and Relationship and Leadership Orientation. Butz, Clarence E and Lewis, Phillip V.

Coscienza morale e realtà secondo J.G. Fichte. Schrader, Wolfgang H.

Costumes e Caracteres na "Ética" de Pedro Abelardo. Chaves-Tannús, Marcio.

Could Auditing Standards Be Based on Society's Values?. Zaid, Omar Abdullah.

Counselling for Tolerance. Almond, Brenda.

Courage Alone. Putnam, Daniel.

Covenant and Ethics? Comments from a South African Perspective. Smit, Dirk J.

Crime, Property, and Justice: The Ethics of Civil Forfeiture. Rainbolt, George and Reif, Alison F.

Criminal Children. Richards, Norvin.

Criminal Responsibility. Elliot, Carl.

Criteria for Evaluating the Legitimacy of Corporate Social Responsibility. Pava, Moses L and Krausz, Joshua.

Critical Thinking and Epistemic Obligations. Hatcher, Donald L.

Critical Thinking: Expanding the Paradigm. Weinstein, Mark.

Critics of Pesticides: Whistleblowing or Suppression of Dissent?. Martin, Brian.

Cultural Context and Moral Responsibility. Isaacs, Tracy.

Cultural Diversity in Medicine and Medical Ethics: What Are the Key Questions?. La Puma, John.

Cyberethics and Social Stability. Hauptman, Robert.

Cyborg Identities and the Relational Web: Recasting 'Narrative Identity' in Moral and Political Theory. Brothers, Robyn F.

Damaged Humanity: The Call for a Patient-Centered Medical Ethic in the Managed Care Era. Churchill, Larry R.

Dangerous Games and the Criminal Law. Yeager, Daniel B.

De epistemologie van het buikspreken en de plooibaarheid van het vertoog. Zwart, Hub.

De l'usage social de l'éthique. Mineau, André, Giroux, Guy and Boisvert, Yves.

De la ética del discurso a la moral del respeto universal: una investigación filosófica acerca de la fundamentación de los derechos humanos. Dias, Maria Clara.

De las emociones morales. Hansberg, Olga Elizabeth.

De si es posible afirmar la construcción de una "eticidad" en la filosofía práctica de Kant. Arpini, Adriana.

De sociale functie van ethiek in de onderneming. Jeurissen, Ronald.

Deep Ecology and the Irrelevance of Morality. Reitan, Eric H.

Defining the Medical Sphere. Trappenburg, Margo J.

Degrees of Personhood. Perring, Christian.

Deleuzean Ethics. Goodchild, Philip.

Deliberating about Bioethics. Gutmann, Amy and Thompson, Dennis.

Deliberation and Moral Expertise in Plato's Crito. Benitez, Eugenio E.

Democratising Nature? The Political Morality of Wilderness Preservationists. Mason, Michael.

Der Begriff 'Praktischer Fortschritt' in den biomedizinischen Wissenschaften: Strukturalistischer Ansatz zur Rekonstruktion wissenschaftstheoretischer Begriffe in der Medizin. Eleftheriadis, Anastassia.

Der fragwürdige Primat der praktischen Vernunft in Fichtes Grundlage der gesamten Wissenschaftslehre. Breazeale, Daniel.

Der Wille als Träger des Ethischen—Überlegungen zur Stellung des Willens in der Frühphilosophie Ludwig Wittgensteins. Haag, Johannes.

Desarrollo sostenible y valoración de la vida humana. Vargas, Celso and Alfaro, Mario.

Descartes on Love and/as Error. Williston, Byron.

Descartes, Error, and the Aesthetic-Totality Solution to the Problem of Evil. Gilbertson, Mark.

Descartes: La Libertad de Pensamiento, Fundamento de La Moral Provisional. Madanes, Leiser.

Desconstruir a Lei?. Rogozinski, Jacob.

Desigualdades de Bienestar y axiomática rawlsiana. Sen, Amartya K.

Desire for Happiness and the Commandments in the First Chapter of Veritatis Splendor. Melina, Livio.

Desires and Human Nature in J.S. Mill. Jenkins, Joyce L.

Desmoralizar la Promesa?. Botero C, Juan J.

Developing Habits and Knowing What Habits to Develop: A Look at the Role of Virtue in Ethics. Loewy, Erich H.

Deviant Uses of "Obligation" in Hobbes' Leviathan. Murphy, Mark C.

Dewey and Moore on the Science of Ethics. Welchman, Jennifer.

Dewey's Moral Theory: Experience as Method. Pappas. Gregory Fernando.

Dialéctica e História em J.P. Sartre. Reimao, Cassiano.

Did Paul Condone Suicide? Implications for Assisted Suicide and Active Euthanasia?. O'Mathúna, Dónal P.

Die Bewältigung von Technikkonflikten: Theoretische Möglichkeit und praktische Relevanz einer Ethik der Technik in der Moderne. Grunwald, Armin.

Die komplementäre disparater Ethikbegründungen in der Gegenwart: Über Martin Seels Buch Versuch über die Form des Glücks. Horster, Detlef.

Die Marxismus—Debatte im "Silbernen Zeitalter". Ignatow, Assen.

Die Moral des Rechts: Deontologische und konsequentialistische Argumentationen in Recht und Moral. Neumann, Ulfrid.

Die wertlose Natur: Eine Bilanz der Diskussion um eine "Evolutionäre Ethik". Funken, Michael.

Differences in Moral Reasoning Between College and University Business Majors and Non-Business Majors. Snodgrass, James and Behling, Robert.

Dio fondamento ultimo della morale e del diritto. Pizzorni, Reginaldo M.

Disciplining the Family: The Case of Gender Identity Disorder. Feder, Ellen K.

Discontinuing Life Support in an Infant of a Drug-Addicted Mother: Whose Decision Is It?. Thomasma, David C and Jain, Renu.

Discounting and Restitution. Cowen, Tyler.

Discourse Ethics and Nature. Krebs, Angelika.

Discretionary Power, Lies, and Broken Trust: Justification and Discomfort. Potter, Nancy.

Divorcing Threats and Offers. Altman, Scott.

Do Animals Have Rights?. Cohen, Carl.

Do Complex Moral Reasoners Experience Greater Ethical Work Conflict?. Mason, E Sharon and Mudrack, Peter E.

Do Deconstructive Ecology and Sociobiology Undermine Leopold's Land Ethic?. Callicott, J Baird.

Do Discurso Ontológico ao Discurso Etico: De Atenas A Jerusalém. De Brito, José Henrique.

Do Doctors Undertreat Pain?. Ruddick, William.

Do No Harm. Kotin, Anthony M.

Do Physicians' Own Preferences for Life-Sustaining Treatment Influence Their Perceptions of Patients' Preferences? A Second Look. Schneiderman, Lawrence J, Kaplan, Robert M and Rosenberg, Esther (& others).

Do Possible People have Moral Standing?. Ryberg, Jesper.

Do the Bishops Have It Right On Health Care Reform?. Sulmasy, Daniel P.

Does Bentham Commit the Naturalistic Fallacy?. Chattopadhyay, Gauriprasad.

Domande e risposte sul problema della giustizia. Bagolini, Luigi.

## ETHICS

## ETHICS

Prometer en Falso: La Contradicción Práctica y el Imperativo Categórico. Rosas, Alejandro.

Promoting Ethical Reasoning, Affect and Behaviour Among High School Students: An Evaluation of Three Teaching Strategies. DeHaan, Robert, Hanford, Russell and Kinlaw, Kathleen.

Promoting Ethical Standards in Science and Engineering. Frankel, Mark S.

Proposing 'Project Mankind'. Singh, Amita.

Prospective Autonomy and Critical Interests: A Narrative Defense of the Moral Authority of Advance Directives. Rich, Ben A.

Prospective Payment System and the Traditional Medical Ethics in Hungary. Jenei, Ilona.

Provider Disclosure of Financial Incentives in Managed Care: Pros and Cons. McCormack, Robert.

Provoking Nonepileptic Seizures: The Ethics of Deceptive Diagnostic Testing. Burack, Jeffrey H, Back, Anthony L and Pearlman, Robert A.

Prudence, Folly and Melancholy in the Thought of Thomas Hobbes. Borrelli, Gianfranco.

Psychopathy, Other-Regarding Moral Beliefs, and Responsibility. Fields, Lloyd.

Public Preferences for Health Care: Prioritisation in the United Kingdom. Shickle, Darren.

Publishing Programs and Moral Dilemmas. Horowitz, Irving Louis.

Punishment and Race. Pittman, John P.

Punishment and the Principle of Fair Play. Ellis, Anthony.

Punishment As Just Cause for War. Kemp, Kenneth.

Punishment in Environmental Protection. Poesche, Jürgen S.

Punishment, Quarantine, and Preventive Detention. Corrado, Michael.

Putnam and Cavell on the Ethics of Democracy. Shusterman, Richard.

Quality Control for Hospitals' Clinical Ethics Services: Proposed Standards. Leeman, Cavin P, Fletcher, John C and Spencer, Edward M (& others).

Qué "nos" dice Habermas: Algunas reflexiones desde las coordenadas histórico-sociales latinoamericanas. Arpini, Adriana.

Quelle universalité pour l'éthique dans une sociétépluraliste? Une réflexion théologique. Fuchs, Eric.

Quest and Question: Suffering and Emulation in the LDS Community. Campbell, Courtney S.

Quinn on Punishment and Using Persons as Means. Otsuka, Michael.

Race, the Rule of Law, and *The Merchant of Venice*: From Slavery to Citizenship. Masugi, Ken.

Rational Cooperation and Collective Goals. Tuomela, Raimo.

Rational Cooperation, Intention, and Reconsideration. Mintoff, Joe.

Rational Intentions and the Toxin Puzzle. Mele, Alfred R.

Rational Passions and Intellectual Virtues: A Conceptual Analysis. Steutel, Jan and Spiecker, Ben.

Rationality and Ethics. French, Peter.

Rawls and International Justice. Räikkä, Juha.

Re-Examining the Influence of Individual Values on Ethical Decision Making. Glover, Saundra H, Bumpus, Minnette A and Logan, John E (& others).

Reaching for the "Low Hanging Fruit": The Pressure for Results in Scientific Research—A Graduate Student's Perspective. Browning, Tyson R.

Readdressing Our Moral Relationship to Nonhuman Creatures. Whitehouse, Peter J.

Reading between the Texts: Benjamin Thomas's *Abraham Lincoln* and Stephen Oates's *With Malice Toward None*. Bray, Robert.

Real Values in a Humean Context. Dancy, Jonathan.

Real World Resource Allocation: The Concept of "Good-Enough" Psychotherapy. Sabin, James E and Neu, Carlos.

Realists Without a Cause: Deflationary Theories of Truth and Ethical Realism. Tenenbaum, Sergio.

Realizability as Constituent Element of the Justification Structure of the Public Decision. Cuñarro Conde, Edith Mabel.

Reason as the Foundation of *Eudaimonia* in the *Nicomachean Ethics*. Hill, Susan.

Reason Without Reasons: A Critique of Alan Gewirth's Moral Philosophy. Kramer, Matthew H and Simmonds, Nigel E.

Reason's Different Tastes. Mitchell, Jeff.

Reason, Value and the Muggletonians. Holton, Richard.

Reasonable Impressions in Stoicism. Brennan, Tad.

Reasonable Self-Interest. Hill Jr, Thomas E.

Reasons for Anger: A Response to Narayan and von Hirsch's Provocation Theory. Horder, Jeremy.

Reassessing the Reliability of Advance Directives. May, Thomas.

Rebecca Reichmann on Womens' Health and Reproductive Rights in Brazil. Heilig, Steve.

Recapturing Justice in the Managed Care Era. Moreno, Jonathan D.

Recent and Classic References at the Interface of Philosophy, Psychiatry, and Psychology. Sadler, John Z (ed).

Recent Work on Virtue Epistemology. Axtell, Guy.

Recenti interpretazioni di J.S. Mill. Marchini, Pier Paolo.

Reciprocity as a Justification for Retributivism. Anderson, Jami.

Recklessness. Brady, James B.

Reconciliation Reaffirmed: A Reply to Steverson. Sterba, James P.

Reconciliation: A Political Requirement for Latin America. May, Jr, Roy H.

Reconsidering Zero-Sum Value: It's How You Play the Game. Smith, Tara.

Reconstituting Praxis: Historialization as Re-Enactment. Flynn, Thomas R.

Rediscovering Virtue. Pinckaers, Servais.

Reducing Suffering and Ensuring Beneficial Outcomes for Neonates: An Ethical Perspective. Brodeur, Dennis.

Reductivism, Retributivism, and the Civil Detention of Dangerous Offenders. Wood, David.

Reflections on a Good Death: An Interview with Carl E. Flemister. Flemister, Carl E.

Reflections on Cultural Difference and Advance Directives. Michel, Vicki.

Reflections on My Father's Experience with Doctors during the Shoah (1939-1945). Bursztajn, Harold J.

Reflexiones sobre la no violencia: Variedades, posibilidades y límites. Sobrevilla, David.

Regret, Trust, and Morality (in Serbo-Croatian). Prokopijevic, Miroslav.

Regulating Virtue: Formulating, Engendering and Enforcing Corporate Ethical Codes. Brien, Andrew.

Reinforcing Ethical Decision Making Through Corporate Culture. Chen, Al Y S, Sawyers, Roby B and Williams, Paul F.

Relating the Psychological Literature to the American Psychological Association Ethical Standards. Thompson, Anthony P.

Relationship Between Machiavellianism and Type A Personality and Ethical-Orientation. Rayburn, J Michael and Rayburn, L Gayle.

Relationships between Primary Care Physicians and Consultants in Managed Care. Brett, Allan S.

Relationships, Relationships, Relationships.... Sugarman, Jeremy and Emanuel, Linda L.

Relatives and Relativism. Jeske, Diane and Fumerton, Richard.

Relatividad agencial: Respuesta a Farrell. Spector, Horacio.

Relativism and James's Pragmatic Notion of Truth. Allen, Michael W.

Relevance of Swami Vivekanand's Concept of Evil Today. Sinha, Rani Rupmati.

Religion and Business Ethics: The Lessons from Political Morality. Fort, Timothy L.

Religion and Rehabilitation. Skotnicki, Andrew.

Religion and the Use of Animals in Research: Some First Thoughts. Smith, David H.

Religion Justifying Morality—A Critique. Behera, Satrughna.

Religiosity, Ethical Ideology, and Intentions to Report a Peer's Wrongdoing. Barnett, Tim, Bass, Ken and Brown, Gene.

Religious Studies and Theology, Ethics and Philosophy (in Czech). Kratochvíl, Zdenek.

Religious Tolerance and Freedom in Continental Europe. Ibán, Iván C.

Reparations Reconstructed. Wheeler III, Samuel C.

Replaceability and Infanticide. Uniacke, Suzanne.

Reply to Corrado. Davis, Michael.

Republican Theory and Criminal Punishment. Pettit, Philip.

Research Ethics: International Perspectives. Brody, Baruch A.

Research, Extension, and User Partnerships: Models for Collaboration and Strategies for Change. Lacy, William B.

Researchers as Professionals, Professionals as Researchers: A Context for Laboratory Research Ethics. Elliott, Deni.

Resentment, Revenge, and Punishment: Origins of the Nietzschean Critique. Small, Robin.

Respecting the Health Care Decision-Making Capacity of Minors. Strong, Carson.

Responding to JCAHO Standards: Everybody's Business. Fletcher, John C.

Response to "Discounting Life Support in an Infant of a Drug Addicted Mother: Whose Decision Is It?" by Renu Jain and David C. Thomasma (CQ Vol 6, No 1). Oberman, Michelle.

Response to "Ethical Concerns about Relapse Studies" by Adil E. Shamoo and Timothy J. Keay (CQ Vol 5, No 3). Bergsma, Jurrit.

Response to "Further Exploration of the Relationship between Medical Education and Moral Development" by Donnie J. Self, DeWitt C. Baldwin, Jr., and Frederic D. Wolinsky (CQ Vol 5, No 3). Burack, Jeffrey H.

Response to Gregory Pence's Case Study in the Teaching of Ethics. Makus, Robert.

Response to Lackey on "Conditional Preventive War". Perkins Jr, Ray.

Response to Michael Davis. Corrado, Michael.

Response to Miller's 'Comment'. Sumner, David and Gilmour, Peter.

Response to the Commentaries. Hinshelwood, R D.

Response to Thomas McCarthy: The Political Alliance between Ethical Feminism and Rawls's Kantian Constructivism. Cornell, Drucilla.

Response: Autonomy, Animals, and Conceptions of the Good. Frey, R G.

Response: Language and Thought. Russow, Lilly-Marlene.

Response: What Does Evolutionary Theory Tell Us about the Moral Status of Animals?. Menta, Timothy.

Responsible Engineering: *Gilbane Gold* Revisited. Pritchard, Michael S and Holtzapple, Mark.

Responsible Technoscience: The Haunting Reality of Auschwitz and Hiroshima. Sassower, Raphael.

Ressentiment (in Serbo-Croatian). Joisten, Karen.

Rethinking Wilderness: The Need for a New Idea of Wilderness. Nelson, Michael P.

Retiring the Pacemaker. Reitemeier, Paul J, Derse, Arthur R and Spike, Jeffrey.

Retributivism and Trust. Dimock, Susan.

Richard Price, the Debate on Free Will, and Natural Rights. Molivas, Gregory I.

## ETHICS

When Preservationism Doesn't Preserve. Schmidtz, David.

When Some Careproviders Have More Power than Others. Howe, Edmund G.

When the Trial *Is* the Punishment: The Ethics of Plagiarism Accusations. Yanikoski, Charles S.

Where Are the Heroes of Bioethics?. Freedman, Benjamin.

Where Is Will Rogers When We Need Him Most? Toward a Traditional Morality in Biomedical Ethics. Sample, Tex.

Who Benefits? Why Personal Identity Does Not Matter in a Moral Evaluation of Germ-Line Gene Therapy. Holtug, Nils.

Who is arguing about the Cat? Moral Action and Enlightenment according to Dōgen. Mikkelson, Douglas K.

Who is Rational Economic Man?. Roback Morse, Jennifer.

Who Plays What Role in Decisions about Withholding and Withdrawing Life-Sustaining Treatment?. Reckling, JoAnn Bell.

Who Speaks? Who Writes? Dialogue and Authorship in the *Phaedrus*. Burke, Seán.

Whole Earth Measurements: How Many Phenomenologists Does It Take to Detect a "Greenhouse Effect"?. Ihde, Don.

Why "Do No Harm?". Sharpe, Virginia A.

Why Bioethics Needs the Philosophy of Medicine: Some Implications of Reflection on Concepts of Health and Disease. Khushf, George.

Why Does Removing Machines Count as "Passive" Euthanasia?. Hopkins, Patrick D.

Why Interpret?. Raz, Joseph.

Why It Is Better Never To Come Into Existence. Benatar, David.

Why Modesty Is a Virtue. Schueler, G F.

Why Norton's Approach is Insufficient for Environmental Ethics. Westra, Laura.

Why Positive Law Theory Makes a Big Difference: Editor's Commentary on "Principles of Lon Fuller's Conception of Natural Law". Tokarczyk, Roman A.

Why Teach Ethics in Science and Engineering?. Johnson, Deborah G, Hollander, Rachelle D and Beckwith, Jonathan R (& others).

Wie einer beschaffen ist, so erscheint ihm das Ziel: Die Rolle des moralischen Habitus bei der Beurteilung des Handlungsziels nach Thomas von Aquin. Darge, Rolf.

William James's Ethics and the New Casuistry. Mehl, Peter J.

Wim Klever: Een Dissonant. Akkerman, F.

Wisconsin Healthcare Ethics Committees. Shapiro, Robyn S, Klein, John P and Tym, Kristen A.

Wisdom. Dilman, Ilham.

Without a Care in the World: The Business Ethics Course and Its Exclusion of a Care Perspective. DeMoss, Michelle A and McCann, Greg K.

Wittgenstein and Animal Minds. Lynch, Joseph J.

Women of the Popular Sectors and Ecofeminist Ethics in Latin America (Spanish). Parentelli, Gladys.

Women on Corporate Boards of Directors: A Needed Resource. Burke, Ronald J.

Women, Ethics, and MBAs. MacLellan, Cheryl and Dobson, John.

Working within Contradiction: The Possibility of Feminist Cosmetic Surgery. Kirkland, Anna and Tong, Rosemarie.

Worlds Apart? Habermas and Levinas. Vetlesen, Arne J.

Writing in Blood: On the Prejudices of Genealogy. Conway, Daniel W.

Zur Analytizität der *Grundlegung*. Schönecker, Dieter.

Zur Rezeption des Aristotelischen Freundschaftsbegriffs in der Scholastik. McEvoy, James.

'Ought' and Reasons for Action. Gewirth, Alan.

¿Comparando qué? La "endeblez metodológica" de la ética según W. V. Quine y sus críticos. Rodríguez Alcázar, Javier.

¿Importan los hechos para los juicios morales? Una defensa contra la navaja de Hume basada en la noción de coste de oportunidad. Schwartz, Pedro.

## ETHICS COMMITTEES

Bioethics Committees and JCAHO Patients' Rights Standards: A Question of Balance. Corsino, Bruce V.

Can Ethics Committees Work in Managed Care Plans?. Felder, Michael.

Case Commentary. Flanigan, Rosemary.

Clinical Ethics and Ethics Committees. Bartholome, William G.

Consultectonics: Ethics Committee Case Consultation as Mediation. Reynolds, Don F.

Education of Ethics Committees. Thomasma, David C.

Ethics Committees and Resource Allocation. Lantos, John D.

Ethics without Walls: The Transformation of Ethics Committees in the New Healthcare Environment. Christensen, Kate T and Tucker, Robin.

Futile Care in Neonatology: An Interim Report from Colorado. Hulac, Peter and Barbour, Elizabeth.

Healthcare Ethics Committees and Ethics Consultants: The State of the Art (Sources/Bibliography). Buehler, David A.

Integrated Ethics Programs: A New Mission for Ethics Committees. Christopher, Myra J.

Justice, Society, Physicians and Ethics Committees: Incorporating Ideas of Justice into Patient Care Decisions. Loewy, Erich H.

Learning to "Real/Hear": Narrative Ethics and Ethics Committee Education. Potter, Robert Lyman.

Non-Heart-Beating Cadaver Procurement and the Work of Ethics Committees. Spielman, Bethany and Verhulst, Steve.

Nurses' Perspectives of Hospital Ethics Committees. Stadler, Holly A, Morrissey, John M and Tucker, Joycelyn E.

The Voices of Nurses on Ethics Committees. Rushton, Cindy Hylton.

Wisconsin Healthcare Ethics Committees. Shapiro, Robyn S, Klein, John P and Tym, Kristen A.

## ETHNICITY

*The Tanner Lectures on Human Values, Volume 18, 1997*. Peterson, Grethe B (ed).

A Multicultural Continuum: A Critique of Will Kymlicka's Ethnic-Nation Dichotomy. Young, Iris Marion.

Civic Nationalism: Oxymoron?. Xenos, Nicholas.

Esodo e tribalismo. Baccelli, Luca.

Gender and "Postmodern War". Schott, Robin May.

Jharkhand: A Movement from Ethnicity to Empowerment of Autonomy. Vadakumchery, Johnson.

Reclaiming the Borderlands: Chicana/o Identity, Difference, and Critical Pedagogy. Elenes, C Alejandra.

The Effect of Ethnicity on ICU Use and DNR Orders in Hospitalized AIDS Patients. Tulsky, James A.

The Jewish Question Revisited: Marx, Derrida and Ethnic Nationalism. Hull, Gordon.

The Limits of Loyalty. Graybosch, Anthony J.

Toleration and Recognition. Lukes, Steven.

## ETHNOCENTRISM

Moral Paralysis and the Ethnocentric Fallacy. Applebaum, Barbara.

## ETHNOGRAPHY

*Representation and the Text: Re-Framing the Narrative Voice*. Tierney, William G (ed) and Lincoln, Yvonna S (ed).

Understanding the Practice of Ethics Consultation: Results of an Ethnographic Multi-Site Study. Kelly, Susan E, Marshall, Patricia A and Sanders, Lee M (& others).

## ETHNOLOGY

Cross-cultural Understanding: Its Philosophical and Anthropological Problems. Jamme, Christoph.

## ETHNOMETHODOLOGY

"Universal Reason" as a Local Organizational Method: Announcement of a Study. Liberman, Kenneth.

Synchrony Lost, Synchrony Regained: The Achievement of Musical Co-ordination. Weeks, Peter.

## ETHNOPHILOSOPHY

In Defense of Afro-Japanese Ethnophilosophy. Okafor, Fidelis U.

## ETHNOPHOBIA

American Ethnophobia, e.g., Irish-American, in Phenomenological Perspective. Embree, Lester.

## ETHOLOGY

Deleuzean Ethics. Goodchild, Philip.

Sex, Gender, Sexuality: Can Ethologists Practice Genealogy?. Gatens, Moira.

## EUCHARIST

Bread and Wine. Sallis, John.

## EUCLID

Metaphysics Delta 15 and Pre-Euclidean Mathematics. Pritchard, Paul.

## EUDAIMONISM

Self-Interest: What's In It For Me?. Schmidtz, David.

## EUDORO DE SOUSA

Reflexoes sobre o Mito: Comentários à Mitologia de Eudoro de Sousa. De Soveral, Eduardo Abranches.

## EUDOXUS

La teoria de las proporciones de Eudoxio interpretada por Dedekind. Corry, Leo.

## EUGENICS

Altering Humans—The Case For and Against Human Gene Therapy. Holtug, Nils.

## EUROCENTRISM

"The Philosophical Text in the African Oral Tradition" in *Philosophy and Democracy in Intercultural Perspective*, Kimmerle, Heinz (ed). Kimmerle, Heinz.

*Catalogue des Publications 1977-1995*. Carratelli, Giovanni Pugliese (ed).

Eurocentrism in Philosophy: The Case of Immanuel Kant. Serequeberhan, Tsenay.

## EUROPE

'Europa' en el pensamiento de Jaspers. Franco Barrio, Jaime.

## EUROPEAN

see also East European

"*In Itinere* Pictures from Central-European Philosophy" in *In Itinere European Cities and the Birth of Modern Scientific Philosophy*, Poli, Roberto (ed). Poli, Roberto.

"Alongside the Horizon" in *On Jean-Luc Nancy: The Sense of Philosophy*, Sheppard, Darren (ed). Gasché, Rodolphe.

"El Ortega de 1914" in *Política y Sociedad en José Ortega y Gasset: En Torno a "Vieja y Nueva Política"*, Lopez de la Vieja, Maria Teresa (ed). Aranguren, José Luis L.

"Europa y una federación global: La visión de Kant" in *Kant: La paz perpetua, doscientos años después*, Martínez Guzmán, Vicent (ed). Pogge, Thomas W.

## EUROPEAN

"Fruchtbarer geistiger Gegensatz Südasien—Europa?" in *Kreativer Friede durch Begegnung der Weltkulturen,* Beck, Heinrich (ed). Beck, Heinrich.

"Ibn Rushd, European Enlightenment, Africa, and African Philosophy" in *Averroës and the Enlightenment,* Wahba, Mourad (ed). Beyaraza, Ernest K.

"In Search of a Civil Union: The Political Theme of European Democracy and Its Primordial Foundation in Greek Philosophy" in *The Ancients and the Moderns,* Lilly, Reginald (ed). Riedel, Manfred.

"Nel nome di Europa" in *Geofilosofia,* Bonesio, Luisa (ed). Derrida, Jacques.

"Steps to a Comparative Evolutionary Aesthetics (China, India, Tibet and Europe)" in *East and West in Aesthetics,* Marchianò, Grazia (ed). Capriles, Elias.

"The Present Crisis of the Universities" in *The Idea of University,* Brzezinski, Jerzy (ed). Bauman, Zygmunt.

*In Itinere* European Cities and the Birth of Modern Scientific Philosophy. Poli, Roberto (ed).

*Catalogue des Publications 1977-1995.* Carratelli, Giovanni Pugliese (ed).

*Europa I El Progrés Sostingut.* Vincent, Martínez Guzmán.

*European Existentialism.* Langiulli, Nino (ed).

*La raíz semítica de lo europeo: Islam y judaísmo medievales.* Lomba, Joaquín.

*Language, Action, and Context: The Early History of Pragmatics in Europe and America, 1780-1930.* Nerlich, Brigitte and Clarke, David D.

*Política y Sociedad en José Ortega y Gasset: En Torno a "Vieja y Nueva Política".* Lopez de la Vieja, Maria Teresa (ed).

*Society, Economics & Philosophy: Selected Papers.* Allen, R T (ed) and Polanyi, Michael.

Advance Directives Outside the USA: Are They the Best Solution Everywhere?. Sanchez-Gonzalez, Miguel A.

Afrikanische Kunst—Ein Drama kultureller Wiederentdeckung oder eine europäische Tragödie?. Behrens, Roger.

Attitudes and Issues Preventing Bans on Toxic Lead Shot and Sinkers in North America and Europe. Thomas, Vernon G.

Bach's Butterfly Effect: Culture, Environment and History. Simmons, I G.

Bilingualism in the Business World in West European Minority Language Regions: Profit or Loss?. Van Langevelde, A. P..

Building the Union: The Nature of Sovereignty in the Political Architecture of Europe. Bellamy, Richard and Castiglione, Dario.

Citizenship and Culture in Early Modern Europe. Miller, Peter N.

Competence-Based Education and Training: Progress or Villainy?. Bridges, David.

Constitutional Patriotism. Ingram, Attracta.

Democracy, Subsidiarity, and Citizenship in the 'European Commonwealth'. MacCormick, Neil.

Die Motive der Atmosphäre um 1820 von C.D. Friedrich: im Zusammenhang mit L. Howards Meteorologie. Hitoshi, Egawa.

Environmentalism for Europe—One Model?. De-Shalit, Avner.

Europa y la Teleología de la razón en Edmund Husserl. García Marqués, Alfonso.

Europa—ein utopisches Konstrukt. Pieper, Annemarie.

European Children Thinking Together in 100. Heesen, Berrie.

Fonament de l'axiologia de Plató (La interpretació del platonisme a l'escola de Tubinga). Canals Surís, Manuel.

From Common Roots to a Broader Vision: A Pragmatic Thrust of European Phenomenology. Bourgeois, Patrick L.

Gearing Up, Crashing Loud: Should We Punish High-Flyers for Insolvency?. Kilpi, Jukka.

Jurisprudential Dilemmas of European Law. Van Roermund, Bert.

Kohlberg's Dormant Ghosts: The Case of Education. Oser, Fritz K.

Krise der europäischen Kultur—ein Problemerbe der husserlschen Philosophie. Ströker, Elisabeth.

Nietzsche and Morality. Geuss, Raymond.

Preserving the Identity Crisis: Autonomy, System and Sovereignty in European Law. Richmond, Catherine.

Religious Tolerance and Freedom in Continental Europe. Ibán, Iván C.

Research Ethics: International Perspectives. Brody, Baruch A.

Science as a Battlefield: Methodological and Historical Considerations on the Misuse of Science by Totalitarian Regimes of Central Europe. Hajduk, Anton.

The Common Europe as a Philosophical Question. Funda, Otakar A.

The Convention on Human Rights and Biomedicine of the Council of Europe. Dommel Jr, F William and Alexander, Duane.

The European Convention on Bioethics. De Wachter, Maurice A M.

The Nature of the Reception of European Musical Phenomena as a Paradigm of the Genuineness of Serbian Music—System of Values and Artistic Horizons. Veselinovic-Hofman, Mirjana.

The New Wine and the Old Cask: Tolerance, Religion and the Law in Contemporary Europe. Ferrari, Silvio.

Un-European Desires: Toward a Provincialism without Romanticism. Visker, Rudi.

## EUTHANASIA

see also Active Euthanasia, Passive Euthanasia

"Voluntary Euthanasia and Justice" in *Human Lives: Critical Essays on Consequentialist Bioethics,* Oderberg, David S (ed). Oderberg, David S.

*A Right to Die?: The Dax Cowart Case.* Covey, Preston K, Cavalier, Robert J and Andersen, David.

*Dignity and Dying: A Christian Appraisal.* Miller, Arlene B (ed), Kilner, John F (ed) and Pellegrino, Edmund D (ed).

*Ethical Issues in Death and Dying.* Beauchamp, Tom L (ed) and Veatch, Robert M (ed).

*Intending Death: The Ethics of Assisted Suicide and Euthanasia.* Beauchamp, Tom L (ed).

*Leben-und Sterbenkönnen: Gedanken zur Sterbebegleitung und zur Selbstbestimmung der Person.* Wettstein, R Harri.

*Moral Issues in Health Care: An Introduction to Medical Ethics.* McConnell, Terrance C.

*Streitgespräche und Kontroversen in der Philosophie des 20.Jahrhunderts.* Wuchterl, Kurt.

*Testing the Medical Covenant: Active Euthanasia and Health Care Reform.* May, William F.

A Note on—Euthanasia and the Contemporary Debate. Barua, Archna.

A Reply to Some Standard Objections to Euthanasia. Shand, John.

Assisted Suicide: Will the Supreme Court Respect the Autonomy Rights of Dying Patients?. Lindsay, Ronald A.

Bioetica Laica. Maffettone, Sebastiano.

Did Paul Condone Suicide? Implications for Assisted Suicide and Active Euthanasia?. O'Mathúna, Dónal P.

End-of-Life Care in the Netherlands and the United States: A Comparison of Values, Justifications, and Practices. Quill, Timothy E and Kimsma, Gerrit K.

Euthanasia. Mitra, Kumar.

Euthanasia in The Netherlands. Admiraal, Pieter V.

Euthanasia, Capital Punishment and Mistakes-Are-Fatal Arguments. Blount, Douglas K.

Hard Cases in Hard Places: Singer's Agenda for Applied Ethics. Danielson, Peter A and MacDonald, Chris J.

Levinas and the Hippocratic Oath: A Discussion of Physician-Assisted Suicide. Degnin, Francis.

Moral Taxonomy and Rachels' Thesis. Haslett, D W.

Philosophy of Medical Practice: A Discursive Approach. Van Leeuwen, Evert and Kimsma, Gerrit K.

Physician-Assisted Suicide: The Role of Mental Health Professionals. Peruzzi, Nico, Canapary, Andrew and Bongar, Bruce.

The *Nazi!* Accusation and Current US Proposals. Cavanaugh, Thomas A.

The Kevorkian Challenge. Picchioni, Anthony.

The Last Chapter of the Book: Who Is the Author? Christian Reflections on Assisted Suicide. Childs, Brian H.

The Right to Suicide. Cosculluela, Victor.

What Kind of Life? What Kind of Death? An Interview with Dr. Henk Prins. Klotzko, Arlene Judith.

Zur Euthanasie-Diskussion in den USA: Eine kritische Einführung. Holderegger, Adrian.

## EUTHYPHRO

*Defence of Socrates Euthyphro Crito.* Gallop, David (trans).

## EVALUATION

"Informal Factors in the Formal Evaluation of Arguments" in *Logic and Argumentation,* Van Eemeren, Frans H (ed). Finocchiaro, Maurice A.

A propósito de la crítica de Feyerabend al racionalismo crítico. Marqués, Gustavo L.

Concepts in Evaluation Applied to Ethics Consultation Research. Fox, Ellen.

Evaluation Research and the Future of Ethics Consultation. Fox, Ellen and Tulsky, James A.

Kant's Conception of Merit. Johnson, Robert Neal.

Obstacles and Opportunities in the Design of Ethics Consultation Evaluation. Tulsky, James A and Stocking, Carol B.

Relativism and the Evaluation of Art. Young, James O.

## EVANGELICALISM

La influencia del jusnaturalismo racionalista en la génesis de la moral cristiana pre-evangélica. Llano Alonso, Fernando H.

## EVANS, G

Complex Predicates and Conversion Principles. Swoyer, Chris.

Reply to Noonan on Vague Identity. Lowe, E J.

## EVENT

"Il segno e l'evento" in *Momenti di Storia della Logica e di Storia della Filosofia,* Guetti, Carla (ed). Sini, Carlo.

"Ontología causal: ¿sucesos o hechos?" in *Verdad: lógica, representación y mundo,* Villegas Forero, L. García Encinas, María José.

"Verità Dell'Evento E Ruolo Del Soggetto Nella Conoscenza Storica: Tre paradigmi" in *Soggetto E Verità: La questione dell'uomo nella filosofia contemporanea,* Fagiuoli, Ettore. Borutti, Silvana.

*50 Years of Events: An Annotated Bibliography 1947 to 1997.* Casati, Roberto and Varzi, Achille C.

*Aristotle on Perception.* Everson, Stephen.

*The Ontology of Mind: Events, Processes, and States.* Steward, Helen.

*Time, Tense, and Causation.* Tooley, Michael.

Agustin de Herrera, A Treatise on Aleatory Probability *De Necessitate Morali in Genere.* Knebel, Sven K (ed & trans).

An Analysis of John Mbiti's Treatment of the Concept of Event in African Ontologies. Johnson, Clarence Sholé.

## EVENT

Bruno de Finetti and the Logic of Conditional Events. Milne, Peter.

Concept and Event. Patton, Paul.

Das Verstehen singulärer Handlungen: Ein Kommentar zu Davidson und von Wright. Wyller, Truls.

Davidson's Action Theory and Epiphenomenalism. Cheng, Kam-Yuen.

Descriptive and Revisionary Theories of Events. McHenry, Leemon B.

Disanalogies between Space and Time. Gale, Richard M.

How Properties Emerge. Humphreys, Paul.

Hume's "Of Miracles" (Part One). Adler, Jonathan.

Kant e l'epistemologia contemporanea. Castagni, Laura.

Kim on the Metaphysics of Explanation. Sabatés, Marcelo H.

November 4, 1995: Deleuze's Death as an Event. Colombat, André Pierre.

On Plantinga's Way Out. Brant, Dale Eric.

On the Logic of Event-Causation: Jaskowski-Style Systems of Causal Logic. Urchs, Max.

On the Notion of Cause 'Philosophically Speaking'. Steward, Helen.

Praktik: Überlegungen zu Fragen der Handlungstheorie. Angstl, Helmut.

Redundant Causation, Composite Events and M-sets. Ramachandran, Murali.

The "Alien Abduction" Phenomenon: Forbidden Knowledge of Hidden Events. Zimmerman, Michael E.

The Chance of a Singular Event?. Stevenson, Leslie F.

The Fission of Time: On the Distinction between Intratemporality and the Event of Time in Kant, Heidegger and Foucault. Crocker, Stephen.

What is Given? Thought and Event (in French). Benoist, Jocelyn.

## EVERETT, A

Everett's Trilogy. Priest, Graham.

## EVERETT, H

On Everett's Formulation of Quantum Mechanics. Barrett, Jeffrey A.

What It Feels Like To Be in a Superposition and Why. Lehner, Christoph.

## EVIDENCE

Systematische Wahrheitstheorie: Methodische und wissenschaftstheoretische Überlegungen zur Frage nach dem grundlegenden Einheitsprinzip. Siebel, Wigand.

An Analysis of "Res cogitans". Almeida, Eduardo.

An Essay in Epistemic Kuklophobia: Husserl's Critique of Descartes' Conception of Evidence. Heffernan, George.

Are PSI Effects Natural? A Preliminary Investigation. Mavrodes, George I.

Aristotle on Variation and Indefiniteness in Ethics and Its Subject Matter. Anagnostopoulos, Georgios.

As Metamorfoses da Luz, ou a Retórica da Evidência na Filosofia Cartesiana. Ribeiro dos Santos, Leonel.

Bayesianism and Diverse Evidence: A Reply to Andrew Wayne. Myrvold, Wayne C.

Bayesianism and the Value of Diverse Evidence. Steel, Daniel.

Evidence for the Effectiveness of Peer Review. Fletcher, Robert H and Fletcher, Suzanne W.

Evidencia e investigación: La Epistemología filosófica reivindicada. Frápolli, María José.

Facts of Legal Reasoning. Boukema, H J M.

Ghost Gestures: Phenomenological Investigations of Bodily Micro-movements and Their Intercorporeal Implications. Behnke, Elizabeth A.

Hume, Bayle e il principio di causalità: Parte I. Gilardi, Roberto.

Nada existe donde faltan las palabras: La quidditas retórica de Vico y la metafísica de la evidencia. Marín-Casanova, José Antonio.

On Evidence: A Reply to McGrew. Achinstein, Peter.

Once More: Bohr-Hoffding. Faye, Jan.

Philosophy and the Good Life: Hume's Defence of Probable Reasoning. Owen, David.

Resolving Hempel's Raven Paradox. Leavitt, Fred.

Taking the Universal Viewpoint: A Descriptive Approach. Wood, Robert.

The After-Acquired Evidence Defense: The Unethical Repercussions to Employees. Brady, Teresa.

The Validation of Induction. Pargetter, Robert and Bigelow, John.

Theory-Ladenness of Observation and Evidence. Basu, Prajit K.

Walker on the Voluntariness of Judgment. Stein, Christian.

Wayne, Horwich, and Evidential Diversity. Fitelson, Branden.

What is Testimony?. Graham, Peter J.

Where's the Evidence?. Missimer, Connie.

You Can Always Count on Reliabilism. Levin, Michael.

## EVIDENTIALISM

A Kantian Condemnation of Atheistic Despair: A Declaration of Dependence. Kielkopf, Charles F.

More Evidence Against Anti-Evidentialism. Timmons, Brent D.

Pragmatic Arguments and Belief. Jordan, Jeff.

## EVIL

see also Theodicy

"Positività Della Corruzione: Per una fenomenologia della mutazione" in Soggetto E Verità: La questione dell'uomo nella filosofia contemporanea, Fagiuoli, Ettore. Fadini, Ubaldo.

A Grammar of Fear and Evil: A Husserlian-Wittgensteinian Hermeneutic. McFarlane, Adrian Anthony.

Dio e il male. Possenti, Vittorio.

God. Robinson, Timothy A (ed).

Philosophische Gedichte. Flasch, Thomas (trans) and Campanella, Tommaso.

The God Within: Kant, Schelling, and Historicity. Burbidge, John W (ed) and Fackenheim, Emil L.

As the Waters Cover the Sea: John Wesley on the Problem of Evil. Walls, Jerry L.

Barth on Evil. Wolterstorff, Nicholas.

Becoming an Evil Society: The Self and Strangers. Thomas, Laurence.

Can Animals Be Evil?: Kekes' Character-Morality, the Hard Reaction to Evil, and Animals. Rosenfeld, Robert.

Cantona and Aquinas on Good and Evil. O'Neill, John.

Das philosophieimmanente Theodizeeproblem und seine theologische Radikalisierung. Schmidt, Josef.

Das Problem des Übels in Richard Swinburnes Religionsphilosophie: Über Sinn und Grenzen seines theistischen Antwortversuches auf das Problem des Übels und dessen Bedeutung für die Theologie. Wiertz, Oliver.

Descartes, Error, and the Aesthetic-Totality Solution to the Problem of Evil. Gilbertson, Mark.

Evil and Imputation in Kant's Ethics. Timmons, Mark.

Eyeballing Evil: Some Epistemic Principles. Langtry, Bruce.

Felix peccator? Kants geschichtsphilosophische Genesis-Exegese im Muthmasslichen Anfang der Menschengeschichte und die Theologie der Aufklärungszeit. Sommer, Andreas Urs.

God Is Love, Therefore There Is Evil. Fendt, Gene.

God vs. Less Than the Very Best. Daniels, Charles.

God, Demon, Good, Evil. Daniels, Charles.

Hannah Arendt y la cuestión del mal radical. Serrano de Haro, Agustín.

Hobbes e il cristianesimo dal De Cive al Leviatano. Siena, Roberto Maria.

Kant on God, Evil, and Teleology. Pereboom, Derk.

La moralité et le mal dans les Principes de la Philosophie du Droit de Hegel. Soual, Philippe.

La providencia y el gobierno del mundo. Caturelli, Alberto.

Le mal moral, pierre de touche de l'ontologie: Monisme idéal et dualisme réel du sens de l'être. Lamblin, Robert.

Mal e Intersubjectividade em Gabriel Marcel. Ganho, Maria de Lourdes S.

Moral Bivalence: What does it Mean to Deceive Yourself?. Cowart, Monica R.

Mutmassungen über das unschuldige Leiden. Bonk, Sigmund.

Naturalizing the Problem of Evil. Cheney, Jim.

Nietzsche e il nichilismo contemporaneo. Volpi, Franco.

O'Connor on Gratuitous Natural Evil. Hasker, William.

Relevance of Swami Vivekanand's Concept of Evil Today. Sinha, Rani Rupmani.

Schleiermacher on Evil. Adams, Robert Merrihew.

Secular Perspective of Salvation. Longacre, Jay.

Stain, Disfiguration and Orgy (in Spanish). Cardona Suárez, Luis Fernando.

Teodicea y sentido de la historia: la respuesta de Hegel. Estrada, Juan A.

The Ethics of Investing: A Reply to William Irvine. Larmer, Robert.

The Evils of Chattel Slavery and the Holocaust: An Examination of Laurence Thomas's Vessels of Evil. Harriott, Howard H.

The Problem of Self-Destroying Sin in John Milton's Samson Agonistes. Boyd, Ian T E.

The Sublimity of Evil. Nuyen, A T.

Three Prospects for Theodicy: Some Anti-Leibnizian Approaches. Romerales Espinosa, Enrique.

Writing in Blood: On the Prejudices of Genealogy. Conway, Daniel W.

Yvon Quiniou, il materialismo e l'impossibile immoralismo di Nietzsche. Franco, Vittoria.

## EVOLUTION

see also Darwinism

"Evolución y racionalidad limitada" in La racionalidad: su poder y sus límites, Nudler, Oscar (ed). Gomila Benejam, Antoni.

"Logic, Learning, and Creativity in Evolution" in Studies in the Logic of Charles Sanders Peirce, Houser, Nathan (ed). Burks, Arthur W.

"Progress in Biological Evolution" in The Idea of Progress, McLaughlin, Peter (ed). García-Bellido, Antonio.

"The Idea of Progress in Evolutionary Biology: Philosophical Considerations" in The Idea of Progress, McLaughlin, Peter (ed). Wolters, Gereon.

"Viroid Life: On Machines, Technics and Evolution" in Deleuze and Philosophy: The Difference Engineer, Ansell Pearson, Keith (ed). Ansell Pearson, Keith.

"World 1, World 2 and the Theory of Evolution" in The Significance of Popper's Thought, Amsterdamski, Stefan (ed). Watkins, John.

Charles S. Peirce's Evolutionary Philosophy. Hausman, Carl R.

Evolutionäre Ethik? Philosophische Programme, Probleme und Perspektiven der Soziobiologie. Gräfrath, Bernd.

Interpreting Minds: The Evolution of a Practice. Bogdan, Radu J.

The Significance of Popper's Thought. Amsterdamski, Stefan (ed).

A Tribute to Donald T. Campbell. Heyes, Cecilia.

An Integral Theory of Consciousness. Wilber, Ken.

Cognitive Versatility. Browne, Derek.

Creacionismo y evolucionismo en el siglo XIX: las repercusiones del Darwinismo en la comunidad científica española. Pelayo, Francisco.

Critical Notice of Ron McClamrock Existential Cognition. Ross, Don.

Critical Review: Sober's Philosophy of Biology and His Philosophy of Biology. Rosenberg, Alex.

**FACT**
Personal Identity and the Coherence of *Q*-Memory. Collins, Arthur W.
Reply to Martin. Armstrong, D M.
Sobre el hacer humano: la posibilidad factiva. Franquet, Maria José.
Sobre la Facticidad de la Memoria. Schumacher, Christian.
The Discourse Principle and Those Affected. Skirbekk, Gunnar.
The Facts of Causation. Mellor, D H.
What's a Gradual Ontology? (in Spanish). Vásconez, Marcelo and Peña, Lorenzo.
¿Importan los hechos para los juicios morales? Una defensa contra la navaja de Hume basada en la noción de coste de oportunidad. Schwartz, Pedro.

**FACTICITY**
Hyperbolic Doubt and "Machiavelism": The Modern Foundation of the Subject in Descartes (in French). Richir, Marc.

**FACTOR**
The Completeness of the Factor Semantics for Lukasiewicz's Infinite-Valued Logics. Vasyukov, Vladimir L.

**FACTORY**
Japanese Death Factories and the American Cover-Up. Chen, Yuan-Fang.

**FACULTY**
*Diversity and Community in the Academy: Affirmative Action in Faculty Appointments.* Wolf-Devine, Celia.
The Curious Tale of Atlas College. Cahn, Steven M.
The Morality of Intimate Faculty-Student Relationships. Dixon, Nicholas.
Two Theories of Knowledge: Locke vs. Stoic. Badwal, Bhajan S.

**FAGIN, R**
Thinking about Reasoning about Knowledge. Kyburg Jr, Henry E.

**FAGUET, E**
The Liberal Critic as Ideologue: Emile Faguet and *fin-de-siècle* Reflections on the Eighteenth Century. Dyrkton, Joerge.

**FAILURE**
A Logic-Based Modelling of Prolog Resulation Sequences Including the Negation as Failure Rule. Jeavons, John S and Crossley, John N.

**FAIR**
Two Applications of a Theorem of Dvoretsky, Wald, and Wolfovitz to Cake Division. Barbanel, Julius B and Zwicker, William S.

**FAIRNESS**
"Context, Continuity, and Fairness" in *The Morality of Nationalism,* McKim, Robert (ed). Ripstein, Arthur.
"Faith and Intellectual Fairness" in *Philosophy, Religion, and the Question of Intolerance,* Ambuel, David (ed). Donovan, John.
"Two Concepts of Rawls" in *A Question of Values: New Canadian Perspectives in Ethics and Political Philosophy,* Brennan, Samantha (ed). Wendling, Karen.
*Affirmative Action: Social Justice or Unfair Preference?.* Mosley, Albert G and Capaldi, Nicholas.
*Mill's On Liberty.* Dworkin, Gerald (ed).
A Just Share: Justice and Fairness in Resource Allocation. McCarrick, Pat Milmoe and Darragh, Martina.
Business Ethics in Islamic Context: Perspectives of a Muslim Business Leader. Abeng, Tanri.
Evolution and Ultimatum Bargaining. Harms, William.
Impression Management, Fairness, and the Employment Interview. Rosenfeld, Paul.
Peer Review for Journals: Evidence on Quality Control, Fairness, and Innovation. Armstrong, J Scott.
Rational, Fair, and Reasonable. Wolff, Jonathan.
Rawls's Problem of Stability. Huemer, Michael.
Sex, Fairness, and the Theory of Games. D'Arms, Justin.
Stakeholder Theory and A Principle of Fairness. Phillips, Robert A.
The Engineer's Moral Right to Reputational Fairness. McGinn, Robert E.
The Ethics of Creative Accounting. Archer, Simon.

**FAITH**
*see also* Bad Faith, Belief, Will To Believe
"Assent chez les Platoniciens de Cambridge" in *Mind Senior to the World,* Baldi, Marialuisa. Vienne, Jean-Michel.
"An Elephant, an Ocean, and the Freedom of Faith" in *Philosophy, Religion, and the Question of Intolerance,* Ambuel, David (ed). Cain, David.
"Faith and Intellectual Fairness" in *Philosophy, Religion, and the Question of Intolerance,* Ambuel, David (ed). Donovan, John.
"Introduction" in *Reason, Experience, and God: John E. Smith in Dialogue,* Colapietro, Vincent M. Westphal, Merold.
"Origène était-il pour Cudworth le modèle du philosophe chrétien?" in *Mind Senior to the World,* Baldi, Marialuisa. Breteau, Jean-Louis.
"Race, Life, Death, Identity, Tragedy and Good Faith" in *Existence in Black: An Anthology of Black Existential Philosophy,* Gordon, Lewis R (ed). Zack, Naomi.
"Religious Faith, Intellectual Responsibility, and Romance" in *The Cambridge Companion to William James,* Putnam, Ruth Anna (ed). Rorty, Richard.
*Does God Exist?: A Dialogue.* Moody, Todd C.
*Earth Community: Earth Ethics.* Rasmussen, Larry L.
*Facets of Faith and Science Volume 2: The Role of Beliefs in Mathematics and the Natural Sciences—An Augustinian Perspective.* Van der Meer, Jitse M (ed).

*Facets of Faith and Science Volume 3: The Role of Beliefs in the Natural Sciences.* Van der Meer, Jitse M (ed).
*Facets of Faith and Science Volume 4: Interpreting God's Action in the World.* Van der Meer, Jitse M (ed).
*Glaube und Vernunft im Denken des Nikolaus von Kues: Prolegomena zu einem Umri_ seiner Auffassung.* Hopkins, Jasper.
*Hofmann-Streit: il dibattito sul rapporto tra filosofia e teologia all'Università di Helmstedt.* Antognazza, Maria Rosa.
*Kierkegaard and Nietzsche: Faith and Eternal Acceptance.* Kellenberger, J.
*Reason, Experience, and God: John E. Smith in Dialogue.* Colapietro, Vincent M.
A Good Death—Oxymoron?. McCormick, Richard A.
A Reply to Professor Hick. Van Inwagen, Peter.
A Response to John Hick. Mavrodes, George I.
Ad Hick. Plantinga, Alvin.
Aufhebung des Religiösen durch Versprachlichung? Eine religions-philosophische Untersuchung des Rationalitätskonzeptes von Jürgen Habermas. Kühnlein, Michael.
Blondels *Action* von 1893 und Rahners transzendentaler Ansatz im *Grundkurs*— eine unterirdische Wirkungsgeschichte. Knoepffler, Nikolaus.
Caminhos da Filosofia ou a Razao e o Desejo. De Fraga, Gustavo.
Concerning Lev Shestov's Conception of Ethics. Van Goubergen, Martine.
Critical Notice of J.J. MacIntosh and H.A. Meynell, eds. *Faith, Scepticism and Personal Identity: A Festschrift for Terence Penelhum.* Loptson, Peter J.
Denken in trouw aan leven en geloof. Van Tongeren, Paul.
Die Vernunft innerhalb der Grenzen des Glaubens: Aspekte der anselmischen Methodologie in werkgenetischer Perspektive. Theis, Robert.
Do Religious Life and Critical Thought Need Each Other? A Reply to Reinsmith. Carrier, Richard.
Does Religious Faith Mean Uncritical Thought? Exploration of a False Dilemma. Davidson, Bruce.
Durand et Durandellus sur les rapports de la foi et de la science. Donneaud, Henry.
Faith in God as Ultimate Strength: A Slovak Physician Who Resisted 'Brain Washing'. Sencik, Stefan.
Francis Bacon: The Theological Foundations of *Valerius Terminus.* Milner, Benjamin.
Free Will and the Dispositional Aspect of Faith: A Dilemma for the Incompatibilist. Ciocchi, David M.
From Common Roots to a Broader Vision: A Pragmatic Thrust of European Phenomenology. Bourgeois, Patrick L.
From Nimrod to the Grand Inquisitor: The Problem of the Demonisation of Freedom in the Work of Dostoevskij. Blumenkrantz, Mikhail.
Gilles Deleuze and the Redemption from Interest. Hallward, Peter.
Habermas, Fichte and the Question of Technological Determinism. Jalbert, John E.
Infallibility, Authority and Faith. Haldane, John.
Kierkegaard's "Three Stages": A Pilgrim's Regress?. Aiken, David W.
L'apologétique de Samuel Clarke. Sina, Mario.
La colpa e il tempo in Fëdor Dostoevskij. Colonnello, Pio.
La fiducia come forma di fede: Alcune riflessioni introduttive ad un problema sociologico. Prandini, Riccardo.
La razón de la esperanza y la esperanza de la razón. Corti, Enrique C.
La teologia esistenziale di S. Kierkegaard. Mondin, Battista.
Le savoir théologique chez les premiers thomistes. Torrell, Jean-Pierre.
Les rapports entre raison et foi à la lumière de la métaphore de la vision. Vienne, Jean-Michel.
Newman on Faith and Rationality. Lamont, John R T.
Newton, *El templo de Salomón* (Editorial Debate, Madrid 1996). Huerga Melcón, Pablo.
Passing on the Faith: How Mother-Child Communication Influences Trans-mission of Moral Values. Taris, Toon W and Semin, Gün R.
Perils of Pluralism. Clark, Kelly James.
Philosophia. Peperzak, Adriaan Theodoor.
Postille. Del Vecchio, Dante.
Psychology, Revelation and Interfaith Dialogue. Knight, Christopher.
Rationally Deciding What To Believe. Chappell, Tim.
Recenti interpretazioni di J.S. Mill. Marchini, Pier Paolo.
Response to Chappell. Penelhum, Terence.
Response to Hick. Alston, William P.
Science et foi: pour un nouveau dialogue. Poupard, Cardinal P.
The Art of Christian Atheism: Faith and Philosophy in Early Heidegger. Smith, James K A.
The Epistemological Challenge of Religious Pluralism. Hick, John.
The Harmonizing Influence of God in the Understanding of J.A. Comenius. Petru, Eduard.
The Logic of Leaping: Kierkegaard's Use of Hegelian Sublation. Johnson, Ronald R.
The Offense of Reason and the Passion of Faith: Kierkegaard and Anti-Rationalism. Carr, Karen L.

**FALKENBERG, J**
La réception de la "Monarchie" de Dante ou Les métamorphoses d'une oeuvre philosophique. Cheneval, Francis.

**FALLACY**
*see also* Begging The Question, Intentionalist Fallacy, Naturalistic Fallacy
"Can we Ever Pin One Down to a Formal Fallacy?" in *Logic and Argumen-tation,* Van Eemeren, Frans H (ed). Krabbe, Erik C W.

## FALLACY

"Developments in Argumentation Theory" in *Logic and Argumentation,* Van Eemeren, Frans H (ed). Van Eemeren, Frans H and Grootendorst, Rob.

"Fallacies and Heuristics" in *Logic and Argumentation,* Van Eemeren, Frans H (ed). Jackson, Sally.

"The Straw Man Fallacy" in *Logic and Argumentation,* Van Eemeren, Frans H (ed). Walton, Douglas.

*Logic and Argumentation.* Van Eemeren, Frans H (ed), Van Benthem, Johan (ed) and Grootendorst, Rob (ed).

*Practical Reasoning in Natural Language.* Thomas, Stephen Naylor.

*A World of Difference: The Rich State of Argumentation Theory.* Van Eemeren, Frans H.

Analysis of Argument Strategies of Attack and Cooption: Stock Cases, Formalization, and Argument Reconstruction. Brinton, Alan.

Are Appeals to the Emotions Necessarily Fallacious?. Hinman, Lawrence M.

Confession of a Weak Anti-Intentionalist: Exposing Myself. Wilson, W Kent.

Conflict and Co-Ordination in the Aftermath of Oracular Statements. Thalos, Mariam.

De lo eterno a lo infinito: un intento de reconstrución del argumento de Meliso (B2-4 D-K). Bredlow, Luis.

Defining Pseudo-Science. Hansson, Sven Ove.

Did Jesus Commit a Fallacy?. Hitchcock, David.

Logical Consequence: A Defense of Tarski. Ray, Greg.

Moral Paralysis and the Ethnocentric Fallacy. Applebaum, Barbara.

Reply to Noël Carroll. Dickie, George T.

Sorensen on begging the Question. Yujen Teng, Norman.

Teaching and the Structural Approach to Fallacies. Adler, Jonathan E.

The "Is-Ought" Fallacy and Musicology: The Assumptions of Pedagogy. Davis, James A.

The Five Forms of the Ad Hominem Fallacy. Engel, S Morris.

The Intentional Fallacy: Defending Myself. Carroll, Noël.

The One Fallacy Theory. Powers, Lawrence H.

The Validity Paradox in Modal $S_5$. Jacquette, Dale.

## FALLIBILISM

"The Dynamics Object and the Deliberative Subject" in *The Rule of Reason: The Philosophy of Charles Sanders Peirce,* Forster, Paul (ed). Colapietro, Vincent M.

*Un'Introduzione All'Epistemologia Contemporanea.* Gava, Giacomo (ed).

C.S. Peirce's Theories of Infinitesimals. Herron, Timothy.

Fallibilism, Ambivalence, and Belief. Roorda, Jonathan.

Hypothesis and Realism: A Comment on Sutton. Johnson, David Kenneth.

Locke as a Fallibilist. Odegard, Douglas.

On Mathematical Error. Sherry, David.

The Redemption of Truth: Idealization, Acceptability and Fallibilism in Habermas' Theory of Meaning. Fultner, Barbara.

## FALLIBILITY

El (Supuesto) Trilema del Saber. Hurtado, Guillermo.

Elusive Knowledge. Lewis, David.

Philosophy in the Age of Thresholding. Erickson, Stephen A.

Prove-Once More and Again. Hersh, Reuben.

## FALLS-CORBITT, M

Privacy and Control. Davison, Scott A.

## FALSE

Defining Pseudo-Science. Hansson, Sven Ove.

## FALSEHOOD

A Theory of Truth that Prefers Falsehood. Fitting, Melvin.

Apparence et fausseté: la double nature de l'ordre politique chez Pascal. Spitz, Jean-Fabien.

L'idée d'une doctrine cohérentiste de la justification épistémique. Schulthess, Daniel.

## FALSIFICATION

*The Taming of the True.* Tennant, Neil.

*Thinking Straight.* Flew, Antony.

Bohr's Theory of the Atom 1913-1923: A Case Study in the Progress of Scientific Research Programmes. Hettema, Hinne.

Philosophy of Science: What One Needs to Know. Clayton, Philip.

The Choice between Popper and Kuhn. Notturno, Mark A.

## FALSIFICATIONISM

*Rationalität und Theoriebildung: Studien zu Karl R. Poppers Methodologie der Sozialwissenschaften.* Schmid, Michael.

## FALSITY

*Vagueness.* Williamson, Timothy.

Ahārya Cognition in Navya-Nyāya. Dravid, N S.

Avoidability and Libertarianism: A Response to Fischer. Widerker, David and Katzoff, Charlotte.

Fanciful Fates. Holland, R F.

Infinite Regress Arguments and Infinite Regresses. Black, Oliver.

Not-Being and Linguistic Deception. O'Leary-Hawthorne, Diane.

One False Virtue of Rule Consequentialism, and One New Vice. Mulgan, Tim.

Supposing for the Sake of Argument. Cargile, James.

The Demarcation of the Metaphorical. Engstrom, Anders.

The Logical Structure of Russell's Negative Facts. Patterson, Wayne A.

## FAME

A Má Fama na Filosofia Política: James Harrington e Maquiavel. Bignotto, Newton.

## FAMILY

"All in the Family and In All Families: Membership, Loving, and Owing" in *Sex, Preference, and Family: Essays on Law and Nature,* Nussbaum, Martha C (ed). Minow, Martha.

"Beyond Lesbian and Gay "Families We Choose" in *Sex, Preference, and Family: Essays on Law and Nature,* Nussbaum, Martha C (ed). Eskridge Jr, William.

"Causes of Declining Well-Being Among U.S. Children" in *Sex, Preference, and Family: Essays on Law and Nature,* Nussbaum, Martha C (ed). Galston, William A.

"Justice, Gender, The Family, and The Practice of Political Philosophy" in *A Question of Values: New Canadian Perspectives in Ethics and Political Philosophy,* Brennan, Samantha (ed). Milde, Michael.

"Shaping and Sex: Commentary on Parts I and II" in *Sex, Preference, and Family: Essays on Law and Nature,* Nussbaum, Martha C (ed). Estlund, David M.

"The Social Construction and Reconstruction of Care" in *Sex, Preference, and Family: Essays on Law and Nature,* Nussbaum, Martha C (ed). Moody-Adams, Michele M.

*Coming Together/Coming Apart: Religion, Community, and Modernity.* Bounds, Elizabeth M.

*Reconstructing Political Theory: Feminist Perspectives.* Shanley, Mary Lyndon (ed) and Narayan, Uma (ed).

*Sex, Preference, and Family: Essays on Law and Nature.* Nussbaum, Martha C (ed) and Estlund, David M (ed).

Advocating for the Dying: The View of Family and Friends. Moretti, Anna M.

Ayudar a crecer: notas sobre la educación en el pensamiento de Leonardo Polo. González Umeres, Luz.

Direct and Indirect Responsibility: Distributing Blame. Goodnow, Jacqueline J and Warton, Pamela M.

Disciplining the Family: The Case of Gender Identity Disorder. Feder, Ellen K.

Edmund D. Pellegrino's Philosophy of Family Practice. Brody, Howard.

El trabajo como división de funciones. Rodríguez Sedano, Alfredo.

Family Dynamics and Children in Medical Research. Bonkovsky, Frederick O and Gordon, Valery M.

Family Outlaws. Calhoun, Cheshire.

Family Therapy Process and Outcome Research: Relationship to Treatment Ethics. Wilson, Carol A, Alexander, James F and Turner, Charles W.

Family, State—Individual. Festini, Heda.

Filial Responsibility and the Care of the Aged. Collingridge, Michael and Miller, Seumas.

Holocaust Memories and History. Turner, Charles.

Individual, Family, and Societal Dimensions of Genetic Discrimination: A Case Study Analysis. Geller, Lisa N, Alper, Joseph S and Billings, Paul R (& others).

Legal Ethics in the Practice of Family Law: Playing Chess While Mountain Climbing. Hotel, Carla and Brockman, Joan.

Persistent Vegetative State: Clinical and Ethical Issues. Celesia, Gastone G.

Rethinking Kymlick's Critique of Humanist Liberalism. Greene, Stephen A.

Selbstverwirklichung und Autorität: Philosophische Einwände gegen ein Begriffspaar aus der Debatte um Familie und Jugendgewalt. Thomä, Dieter.

Surrogate Family Values: The Refeminization of Teaching. Thompson, Audrey.

What Makes a Good Death?. Callahan, Daniel.

Women, the Family, and Society: Discussions in the Feminist Thought of the United States. Iulina, Nina S.

## FAMILY VALUES

*Family Values: Subjects Between Nature and Culture.* Oliver, Kelly.

## FANCY

*see* Imagination

## FANON, F

How It Feels to Be a Problem: Du Bois, Fanon, and the "Impossible Life" of the Black Intellectual. Posnock, Ross.

## FANTASY

Beyond Ironist Theory and Private Fantasy: A Critique of Rorty's Derrida. Ellsworth, Jonathan.

Discutono *Il principio speranza,* di Ernst Bloch. Boella, Laura, Moneti, Maria and Schmidt, Burghart.

Imagery and the Coherence of Imagination: A Critique of White. Thomas, Nigel J T.

The Seven Veils of Paranoia, Or, Why Does the Paranoiac Need Two Fathers?. Zizek, Slavoj.

## FARBER, P

Evolutionary Ethics: An Irresistible Temptation: Some Reflections on Paul Farber's *The Temptation of Evolutionary Ethics.* Rottschaefer, William A.

## FAREWELL

Adieu. Derrida, Jacques.

## FARIA, P

Descartes: La Libertad de Pensamiento, Fundamento de La Moral Provisional. Madanes, Leiser.

## FARMING

Ethical Limits to Domestication. Sandoe, Peter, Holtug, Nils and Simonsen, H B.

## FARRELL, M

Relatividad agencial: Respuesta a Farrell. Spector, Horacio.

**FASCISM**
"Fascism as the Looming Shadow of Democracy" in *Philosophy and Democracy in Intercultural Perspective,* Kimmerle, Heinz (ed). Oosterling, Henk A F.
"How Is It, Then, That we Still Remain Barbarians?" Foucault, Schiller, and the Aestheticization of Ethics. Bennett, Jane.
"Verstehen, Holism and Fascism" in *Verstehen and Humane Understanding,* O'Hear, Anthony (ed). Cooper, David E.
*Heidegger's Silence.* Lang, Berel.
*Heidegger, Philosophy, Nazism.* Young, Julian.
*On Heidegger's Nazism and Philosophy.* Rockmore, Tom.
Blindspot of a Liberal: Popper and the Problem of Community. Eidlin, Fred.
Dal primato della prassi all'anomia: Una interpretazione filosofica della crisi odierna. Cotta, Sergio.
Fat, Felt and Fascism: The Case of Joseph Beuys. O'Leary, Timothy.
Foucault, Politics and the Autonomy of the Aesthetic. O'Leary, Timothy.
Friend or Enemy?: Reading Schmitt Politically. Neocleous, Mark.
Kritische Theorie als Erfahrungswissenschaft: Lagebericht anlässlich einiger Neuerscheinungen. Behrens, Roger.
La filosofia della storia di Giovanni Gentile. Garin, Eugenio.
La nuova destra. Revelli, Marco.
On Human Rights. Sharpe, M E (trans).
The Land of the Fearful and the Free. Tamir, Yael.
The Putative Fascism of the Kyoto School and the Political Correctness of the Modern Academy. Parkes, Graham.
The Suppressed Legacy of Nuremberg. Burt, Robert A.
Why Positive Law Theory Makes a Big Difference: Editor's Commentary on "Principles of Lon Fuller's Conception of Natural Law". Tokarczyk, Roman A.

**FASSO, G**
Guida Fassò: Estudios en torno a Giambattista Vico. Llano Alonso, Fernando H.

**FATAL**
Euthanasia, Capital Punishment and Mistakes-Are-Fatal Arguments. Blount, Douglas K.

**FATALISM**
*Life Contemplative, Life Practical: An Essay on Fatalism.* Eilstein, Helena.
Modal Fatalism. Beedle, Andrew.
The Origin of Stoic Fatalism. Pierris, A L.

**FATE**
"M. Heidegger: Modernità, storia e destino dell'Essere" in *Lo Storicismo e la Sua Storia: Temi, Problemi, Prospettive,* Cacciatore, Giuseppe (ed). Viti Cavaliere, Renata.
Fata ducunt. Hinske, Norbert.
Schicksal und Charakter: Für die Philosophische Praxis ist vieles von Schopenhauer zu lernen: Vortrag auf dem Kolloquium der GPP am 30. Oktober 1994 in Tübingen. Achenbach, Gerd B.
Sieben Jenaer Reflexionen Hegels über Homer. Jeck, Udo Reinhold.
The Conception of *Ming* in Early Confucian Thought. Slingerland, Ted.

**FATHER**
"Abortion and Fathers' Rights" in *Reproduction, Technology, and Rights: Biomedical Ethics Reviews,* Humber, James M (ed). Hales, Steven D.
Is God Exclusively a Father?. Isham, George F.
Matar al padre. Galindo Hervás, Alfonso.

**FATIGUE**
El vivir y la fatiga: La fatiga de vivir. Osés Gorráiz, Jesús María.

**FAULKNER**
"A Sin Against Scholarship": Some Examples of Plagiarism in Stephen B. Oates's Biographies of Abraham Lincoln, Martin Luther King, Jr., and William Faulkner. Burlingame, Michael.

**FAURE, E**
"Mountains of the Mind" in *East and West in Aesthetics,* Marchianò, Grazia (ed). Servomaa, Sonia.

**FAWKES, D**
Fawkes On Indicator Words. Smythe, Thomas W.
The Reliability of Premise and Conclusion Indicators. Smythe, Thomas W.

**FEAR**
*see also* Anxiety
*A Grammar of Fear and Evil: A Husserlian-Wittgensteinian Hermeneutic.* McFarlane, Adrian Anthony.
Catastrophic Thinking in the Modern World: Russia and America. Shlapentokh, Vladimir.
Diversity and Ancient Democracy: A Response to Schwartz. Saxonhouse, Arlene W.
Fear of Reproduction and Desire for Replication in *Dracula.* Colatrella, Carol.
No Fear: How a Humanist Faces Science's New Creation. Hull, Richard T.
Practical Reasoning and the Structure of Fear Appeal Arguments. Walton, Douglas N.
Self-Assessing Emotions and Platonic Fear. Tollefsen, Christopher.

**FEASIBILITY**
Logique, effectivité et faisabilité. Dubucs, Jacques.

**FEATURE**
A Rational Reconstruction of the Domain of Feature Structures. Moshier, M Andrew.

Fibred Semantics for Feature-Based Grammar Logic. Dörre, Jochen, König, Esther and Gabbay, Dov.
Syntactic Features and Synonymy Relations: A Unified Treatment of Some Proofs of the Compactness and Interpolation Theorems. Weaver, George E.

**FEDERAL**
The Federal Role in Influencing Research Ethics Education and Standards in Science. Dustira, Alicia K.

**FEDERALISM**
"Europa y una federación global: La visión de Kant" in *Kant: La paz perpetua, doscientos años después,* Martínez Guzmán, Vicent (ed). Pogge, Thomas W.
The New Federalism: Implications for the Legitimacy of Corporate Political Activity. Christensen, Sandra L.

**FEDOROV, N**
The Fedorovian Roots of Stalinism. Shlapentokh, Dmitry.

**FEELING**
*see also* Emotion
"Del Sentire La Verità: Per Leopardi e Michelstaedter" in *Soggetto E Verità: La questione dell'uomo nella filosofia contemporanea,* Fagiuoli, Ettore. Carrera, Alessandro.
"Feeling and Cognition" in *Verstehen and Humane Understanding,* O'Hear, Anthony (ed). Falk, Barrie.
"Schleiermacher on the Self: Immediate Self-Consciousness as Feeling and as Thinking" in *Figuring the Self: Subject, Absolute, and Others in Classical German Philosophy,* Zöller, Günter (ed). Klemm, David E.
*Fruits of Sorrow.* Spelman, Elizabeth V.
*Saber, Sentir, Pensar: La cultura en la frontera de dos siglos.* Nieto Blanco, Carlos (ed).
A Lack of Feeling in Kant: Response to Patricia M. Matthews. Huhn, Tom.
An Anti-Anti-Essentialist View of the Emotions: A Reply to Kupperman. Dalgleish, Tim.
Die Deduktion des Gefühls in der *Grundlage der gesamten Wissenschaftslehre.* López-Domínguez, Virginia.
Emotion and Feeling. Madell, Geoffrey and Ridley, Aaron.
Es Posible una Ética de las Emociones?. Marinabarreto, Luz.
Fact, Fiction and Feeling. Hanfling, Oswald.
Feeling and Coercion: Kant and the Deduction of Right. Kerszberg, Pierre.
Feeling Fine About the Mind. Antony, Louise M.
Gefühl und Realität: Fichtes Auseinandersetzung mit Jacobi in der *Grundlage der Wissenschaft des Praktischen.* Loock, Reinhard.
Heidegger and the Disclosive Character of the Emotions. Weberman, David.
Reflective Solidarity. Dean, Jodi.
Towards a Reapprehension of Causal Efficacy. Earley Sr, Joseph E.

**FEENBERG, A**
The Legislation of Things. Löwy, Ilana.

**FEIGL, H**
*Cervello-Mente: Pensatori del XX secolo.* Gava, Giacomo.

**FEINBERG, J**
Feinberg on the Criterion of Moral Personhood. Hudson, Hud.
Just Desert. Nuyen, A T.

**FELDMAN, F**
Fred Feldman's *Confrontations with the Reaper: A Philosophical Study of the Nature and Value of Death.* Marquis, Don.

**FEMALE**
*see also* Feminism, Woman, Women
En torno a la díada trascendental. Castilla y Cortázar, Blanca.
Mediations of the Female Imaginary and Symbolic. Campbell, Jan.

**FEMININE**
Commentary and Criticism on Scientific Positivism. Gilmer, Penny J.
Homo Economicus in the 20th Century: *Écriture Masculine* and Women's Work. Still, Judith.
The Feminine And The Natural. Duran, Jane.

**FEMININITY**
Beauty and the Breast: Dispelling Significations of Feminine Sensuality in the Aesthetics of Dance. Jaeger, Suzanne M.

**FEMINISM**
*see also* Female, Woman
"A Feminist Reading of Hegel and Kierkegaard" in *Hegel, History, and Interpretation,* Gallagher, Shaun. Armstrong, Susan.
"A Response to Jean Hampton's Feminism" in *The Liberation Debate: Rights at Issue,* Leahy, Michael (ed). Flew, Antony.
"Black Feminism: Liberation Limbos and Existence in Gray" in *Existence in Black: An Anthology of Black Existential Philosophy,* Gordon, Lewis R (ed). James, Joy Ann.
"Blue Prints and Bodies: Paradigms of Desire in Pornography" in *Critical Studies: Ethics and the Subject,* Simms, Karl (ed). Brottman, Mikita.
"Classical Confucian and Contemporary Feminist Perspectives on the Self: Some Parallels and their Implications" in *Culture and Self,* Allen, Douglas (ed). Rosemont, Henry.
"Construction of a Gendered Subject: A Feminist Reading of Adorno's *Aesthetic Theory*" in *The Semblance of Subjectivity,* Huhn, Tom (ed). Wilke, Sabine and Schlipphacke, Heidi.
"Critical Questions in Environmental Philosophy" in *Philosophy and Geography I: Space, Place, and Environmental Ethics,* Light, Andrew (ed). Booth, Annie L.

## FEMINISM

"Ethik und Geschlechterdifferenz" in *Angewandte Ethik: Die Bereichsethiken und ihre theoretische Fundierung,* Nida-Rümelin, Julian (ed). Pauer-Studer, Herlinde.

"Good Bioethics Must Be Feminist Bioethics" in *Philosophical Perspectives on Bioethics,* Sumner, L W (ed). Purdy, Laura M.

"Hampton's Reply" in *The Liberation Debate: Rights at Issue,* Leahy, Michael (ed). Hampton, Jean.

"Points of Convergence Between Dooyeweerdian and Feminist Views of the Philosophic Self" in *Knowing Other-Wise: Philosophy at the Threshold of Spirituality,* Olthuis, James H (ed). Wesselius, Janet Catherina.

"Pornography Left and Right" in *Sex, Preference, and Family: Essays on Law and Nature,* Nussbaum, Martha C (ed). MacKinnon, Catherine A.

"Public Man" and The Critique of Masculinities. Carver, Terrell.

"Reflections of a Sceptical Bioethicist" in *Philosophical Perspectives on Bioethics,* Sumner, L W (ed). Overall, Christine.

"Social Constructions of Self: Some Asian, Marxist, and Feminist Critiques of Dominant Western Views of Self" in *Culture and Self,* Allen, Douglas (ed). Allen, Douglas.

"Taking the Risk of Essence: A Deweyan Theory in Some Feminist Conversations" in *Knowing Other-Wise: Philosophy at the Threshold of Spirituality,* Olthuis, James H (ed). Hart, Carroll Guen.

"The Case for Feminism" in *The Liberation Debate: Rights at Issue,* Leahy, Michael (ed). Hampton, Jean.

"Versions of the Feminine Subject in Charlotte Brontë's *Villette*" in *Critical Studies: Ethics and the Subject,* Simms, Karl (ed). Watkins, Susan.

*Behind Closed Doors*: Analysis of the Feminine Figures in Sartrean Theatre (Spanish). Comesaña-Santalices, Gloria.

*Compelling Knowledge: A Feminist Proposal for an Epistemology of the Cross.* Solberg, Mary M.

*Feminist Approaches to Bioethics: Theoretical Reflections and Practical Applications.* Tong, Rosemarie.

*Feminist Interpretations of Jacques Derrida.* Holland, Nancy J (ed).

*Feminist Interpretations of Michel Foucault.* Hekman, Susan J (ed).

*French Feminist Theory (III): Luce Irigaray and Helene Cixous: A Bibliography.* Nordquist, Joan (ed).

*Freud and the Passions.* O'Neill, John (ed).

*From Sex Objects to Sexual Subjects.* Moscovici, Claudia.

*Hegel and Feminist Social Criticism: Justice, Recognition, and the Feminine.* Gauthier, Jeffrey A.

*Impartiality in Context: Grounding Justice in a Pluralist World.* O'Neill, Shane.

*Questions of Travel: Postmodern Discourses of Displacement.* Kaplan, Caren.

*Radical Critiques of the Law.* Griffin, Stephen M (ed) and Moffat, Robert C L (ed).

*Reconstructing Political Theory: Feminist Perspectives.* Shanley, Mary Lyndon (ed) and Narayan, Uma (ed).

*Rethinking Masculinity: Philosophical Explorations in Light of Feminism.* May, Larry (ed), Strikwerda, Robert (ed) and Hopkins, Patrick D (ed).

*Sexual Harassment: A Debate.* LeMoncheck, Linda and Hajdin, Mane.

*Teaching with Love: A Feminist Approach to Early Childhood Education.* Goldstein, Lisa S.

*The Annual of the Society of Christian Ethics with Cumulative Index.* Beckley, Harlan (ed).

*The Liberation Debate: Rights at Issue.* Leahy, Michael (ed) and Cohn-Sherbok, Dan (ed).

*The Philosophy of Simone de Beauvoir: Gendered Phenomenologies, Erotic Generosities.* Bergoffen, Debra B.

A Feminist Interpretation of Vulnerability. Annaromao, Nancy J.

A Feminist Standpoint for Genetics. Mahowald, Mary B.

A Purple Sky: The Challenged Chance for Change. Birkhahn, Talya.

Academic Feminism and Applied Ethics: Closing the Gap between Private Scholarship and Public Policy. LeMoncheck, Linda.

Against Marriage and Motherhood. Card, Claudia.

Anti-Essentialism in Practice: Carol Gilligan and Feminist Philosophy. Heyes, Cressida.

Approaches Responsive to Reproductive Technologies: A Need for Critical Assessment and Directions for Further Study. Kondratowicz, Diane M.

Charting the Currents of the Third Wave. Orr, Catherine M.

Circulus Vitiosus Deus? The Dialectical Logic of Feminist Standpoint Theory. Conway, Daniel W.

Communication From One Feminist. Machan, Tibor R.

Community of Inquiry and Differences of the Heart. Thomas, John C.

Coyote Politics: Trickster Tales and Feminist Futures. Phelan, Shane.

Das neoliberale Projekt, der männliche Arbeitsbegriff und die fällige Erneuerung des Geschlechtervertrags. Haug, Frigga.

Did the Enlightenment Just Happen to Men?. Whyte, Philip.

Domination and Dialogue in Merleau-Ponty's *Phenomenology of Perception.* Sullivan, Shannon.

Ein Mann sieht vor lauter Welle das Wasser nicht. Overdiek, Anja.

El Nietzsche práctico de Nolte: Nietzsche, profeta trágico de la guerra y organizador político de la aniquilación. Reguera, Isidoro.

En torno a la frase de Nietzsche *La verdad es mujer*. Münnich, Susana.

Éthique féministe de relation et perspectives sur le corps. Dumais, Monique.

Feeling Fine About the Mind. Antony, Louise M.

Feeling Fraudulent: Some Moral Quandaries of a Feminist Instructor. Overall, Christine.

Feminism and Pantheism. Jantzen, Grace M.

Feminism and Utilitarian Arguments for Vegetarianism: A Note on Alex Wellington's "Feminist Positions on Vegetarianism". Dixon, Nicholas.

Feminism, Foucault and Deleuze. Fraser, Mariam.

Feminismo y tercer milenio. Balmaseda Cinquina, María F.

Feminist Epistemology and Philosophy for Children. Field. Terri.

Feminist Epistemology as a Local Epistemology. Longino, Helen E and Lennon, Kathleen.

Feminist Pedagogy Theory: Reflections on Power and Authority. Luke, Carmen.

Feminist Philosophy and the Philosophy of Feminism: Irigaray and the History of Western Metaphysics. Colebrook, Claire.

Feminist Positions on Vegetarianism: Arguments For and Against and Otherwise. Wellington, Alex.

Feminist Revaluation of the Mythical Triad, Lilith, Adam, Eve: A Contribution to Role Model Theory. Wenkart, Henry.

Fetal Relationality in Feminist Philosophy: An Anthropological Critique. Morgan, Lynn M.

Fleshing Gender, Sexing the Body: Refiguring the Sex/Gender Distinction. Tuana, Nancy.

Foucault and the Subject of Feminism. McLaren, Margaret A.

Friendship Across Generations. Nye, Andrea.

From Aperspectival Objectivity to Strong Objectivity: The Quest for Moral Objectivity. Tannoch-Bland, Jennifer.

Good Women and Bad Men: A Bias in Feminist Research. Landau, Iddo.

Grounding Agency in Depth: The Implications of Merleau-Ponty's Thought for the Politics of Feminism. Fielding, Helen.

Ignorance Is No Excuse: Legal Knowledge and Postmodernism. Bennett, Richard.

In Praise of Unreliability. Heldke, Lisa.

Incarnato comparire: Corpo e politica nelle proposte di Adriana Cavarero. Famiani, Mariapaola.

Incommensurable Differences: Cultural Relativism and Antirationalism Concerning Self and Other. Wagner, Joseph.

Integrity and the Feminist Teacher. O'Dea, Jane.

Intersecting Memories: Bearing Witness to the 1989 Massacre of Women in Montreal. Rosenberg, Sharon.

Introduction: Feminist Approaches to Bioethics. Tong, Rosemarie.

Letter-Writing: A Tool in Feminist Inquiry. Sharp, Ann Margaret.

Lost Times/Recovered Times. Reed, Ronald.

Lyin' T(\*)gers, and "Cares," Oh My: The Case for Feminist Integration of Business Ethics. Rabouin, Michelle.

Making Waves and Drawing Lines: The Politics of Defining the Vicissitudes of Feminism. Bailey, Cathryn.

Materiality and Language: Butler's Interrogation of the History of Philosophy. Olkowski, Dorothea.

Mediations of the Female Imaginary and Symbolic. Campbell, Jan.

Moral Reasoning as Perception: A Reading of Carol Gilligan. Kyte, Richard.

Moral Responsibility and Social Change: A New Theory of Self. Ferguson, Ann.

Multiculturalism and Gender Equity: The U.S. "Difference" Debates Revisited. Adler, Pierre.

Nietzsche Reception Today. Johnson, Pauline.

Nomadism with a Difference: Deleuze's Legacy in a Feminist Perspective. Braidotti, Rosi.

Okin on Feminism and Rawls. Sehon, Scott R.

Philosophy, Gender Politics, and In Vitro Fertilization: A Feminist Ethics of Reproductive Healthcare. LeMoncheck, Linda.

Porn Revisited. Mann, Doug.

Postmodernism: What One Needs to Know. Grassie, William.

Questions of Proximity: "Woman's Place" in Derrida and Irigaray. Armour, Ellen T.

Rape Research and Gender Feminism: So Who's Anti-Male?. Davion, Victoria.

Re-Thinking Consciousness Raising: Citizenship and the Law and Politics of Adoption. Cornell, Drucilla.

Regendering the U.S. Abortion Debate. Jaggar, Alison.

Relational Individualism and Feminist Therapy. Radden, Jennifer.

Response to Thomas McCarthy: The Political Alliance between Ethical Feminism and Rawls's Kantian Constructivism. Cornell, Drucilla.

Rethinking Kymlick's Critique of Humanist Liberalism. Greene, Stephen A.

Rethinking Philosophy in the Third Wave of Feminism. Golumbia, David.

Reviving Ophelia: A Role for Philosophy in Helping Young Women Achieve Selfhood. Turgeon, Wendy C.

Richard Rorty and the "Tricoteuses". Amorós, Celia.

Second-Person Scepticism. Feldman, Susan.

So What's the Difference? Feminist Ethics and Feminist Jurisprudence. Davion, Victoria.

Surfing the Third Wave: A Dialogue Between Two Third Wave Feminists. Alfonso, Rita and Trigilio, Jo.

Tecnopolitica: Le idee del cyberpunk. Nacci, Michela.

The Diabolical Strategy of Mimesis: Luce Irigaray's Reading of Maurice Merleau-Ponty. Kozel, Susan.

The Eclipse of Gender: Simone de Beauvoir and the *Différance* of Translation. Alexander, Anna.

**FICHTE**

"Representación de la alteridad y Derecho desde la *aetas kantiana* a Fichte" in *El inicio del Idealismo alemán,* Market, Oswaldo. Oncina Coves, Faustino.

"Sprachursprung und Sprache bei J.G. Fichte" in *Sein—Reflexion—Freiheit: Aspekte der Philosophie Johann Gottlieb Fichtes,* Asmuth, Christoph (ed). Kahnert, Klaus.

"Über die präreflexive Existenz meiner selbst" in *Sein—Reflexion—Freiheit: Aspekte der Philosophie Johann Gottlieb Fichtes,* Asmuth, Christoph (ed). Mittmann, Jörg-Peter.

*Der Deutsche Idealismus (Fichte, Schelling, Hegel) und die philosophische Problemlage der Gegenwart.* Heidegger, Martin.

*El inicio del Idealismo alemán.* Market, Oswaldo and Rivera de Rosales, Jacinto.

*Grundlegung eines Neorationalismus: Dekognition und Dissens.* Radermacher, Hans.

*Sein—Reflexion—Freiheit: Aspekte der Philosophie Johann Gottlieb Fichtes.* Asmuth, Christoph (ed).

Absolutes Wissen und Sein: Zu Fichtes Wissenschaftslehre von 1801/02. Stolzenberg, Jürgen.

Absolutheit und Widerspruch in der *Grundlage der gesamten Wissenschaftslehre.* Duso, Giuseppe.

Aneinander vorbei: Zum Horenstreit zwischen Fichte und Schiller. Wildenburg, Dorothea.

Beobachtungen zur Methodik in Fichtes *Grundlage der gesamten Wissenschaftslehre.* Meckenstock, Günter.

Bergson et Nabert, lecteurs de Fichte. Vieillard-Baron, Jean-Louis.

Coscienza morale e realtà secondo J.G. Fichte. Schrader, Wolfgang H.

Das "Ich" des ersten Grundsatzes der GWL in der Sicht der Wissenschaftslehre von 1804. Girndt, Helmut.

Das *kleine Buch* und das *laute* Weltereignis: Fichtes *Wissenschaftslehre* als Paradigma und Problem der *Romantik.* Schanze, Helmut.

Das Problem der Natur: Nähe und Differenz Fichtes und Schellings. Schmied-Kowarzik, Wolfdietrich.

Das Problem der transzendentalen Freiheit in semantischer Formulierung (Dargestellt an Fichtes Jenaer Wissenschaftslehren). Poreba, Marcin.

Das Schweben der Einbildungskraft: Eine frühromantische Metapher in Rücksicht auf Fichte. Hühn, Lore.

Das Verhältnis des Selbst zu Gott in Fichtes Wissenschaftslehre. Omine, Akira.

Das Wir in der späten Wissenschaftslehre. Richli, Urs.

Dem blinden Trieb ein Auge einsetzen?: Die Verkehrung von Fichtes ursprünglicher Intention in seiner Auseinandersetzung mit Kant. Hutter, Axel.

Der Begriff des Grundes in Fichtes Wissenschaftslehre. Jiménez-Redondo, Manuel.

Der erste Grundsatz und die Bildlehre. Okada, Katsuaki.

Der fragwürdige *Primat der praktischen Vernunft* in Fichtes *Grundlage der gesamten Wissenschaftslehre.* Breazeale, Daniel.

Der Ichbegriff in Fichtes Erörterung der Substantialität. Klotz, Christian.

Der Philosophiebegriff in Fichtes später Wissenschaftslehre. Falk, Hans-Peter.

Die *Grundlage der gesamten Wissenschaftslehre* und das Problem der Sprache bei Fichte. Hoffmann, Thomas Sören.

Die Bedeutung von Fichtes Angewandter Philosophie für die Praktische Philosophie der Gegenwart. Oesterreich, Peter L.

Die Deduktion der Philosophie nach Fichte und Friedrich von Hardenberg. Rühling, Frank.

Die Deduktion des Gefühls in der *Grundlage der gesamten Wissenschaftslehre.* López-Domínguez, Virginia.

Die Differenz zwischen 'Ich bin' und 'Ich bin Ich'. Ryue, Hisang.

Die Duplizität des Absoluten in der Wissenschaftslehre von 1804 (zweiter Vortrag)—Fichtes Auseinandersetzung mit Schellings identitätsphilosophischer Schrift *Darstellung meines Systems* (1801). Danz, Christian.

Die Einbildungskraft und das Schematismusproblem. Köhler, Dietmar.

Die Fichte-Lektüre des jungen Herbart (1796-1798). Langewand, Alfred.

Die Fichte-Rezeption in der südwestdeutschen Schule des Neukantianismus. Heinz, Marion.

Die Funktion praktischer Momente für Grundelemente der theoretischen Vernunft in Fichtes Manuskripten *Eigne Meditationen über Elementar Philosophie* und *Practische Philosophie* (1793/94). Von Manz, Hans Georg.

Die Hegelsche Fichte-Kritik und ihre Berechtigung. Stadler, Christian M.

Die Rezeption der *Wissenschaftslehre* Fichtes in den Versionen der Hegelschen *Wissenschaft der Logik.* De Vos, Lu.

Die Wissenschaftslehre: Die Auseinandersetzung Schleiermachers mit Fichte. Potepa, Maciej.

Eine neue Möglichkeit der Philosophie nach der *Grundlage der gesamten Wissenschaftslehre.* Nagasawa, Kunihiko.

Ethischer Neu-Fichteanismus und Geschichtsphilosophie: Zur soziopolitischen Rezeption Fichtes im 20. Jahrhundert. Villacañas, José L.

Etre et Apparition selon la doctrine de la science de 1812. Vetö, Miklos.

Fichte et Husserl: Une lecture parallèle. Pentzopoulou-Valadas, Thérèse.

Fichte et la question nationale. Maesschalck, Marc.

Fichte und die Metaphysik des deutschen Idealismus. Jiménez-Redondo, Manuel.

Fichte und die psychiatrische Forschung. Hoff, Paul.

Fichte und die Urteilstheorie Heinrich Rickerts. Piché, Claude.

Fichte und Reinhold über die Begrenzung der Philosophie. Von Schönborn, Alexander.

Fichte, die sujektive Wende und der kartesianische Traum. Rockmore, Tom.

Fichte, Kant's Legacy, and the Meaning of Modern Philosophy. Mandt, A J.

Fichte, Novalis, Hölderlin: die Nacht des gegenwärtigen Zeitalters. Janke, Wolfgang.

Fichte, Schlegel, Nietzsche und die Moderne. Stein, Klaus.

Fichtes *geometrische* Semantik. Jergius, Holger.

Fichtes Anstoss: Anmerkungen zu einem Begriff der *Wissenschaftslehre* von 1794. Eidam, Heinz.

Fichtes Entwicklung von der zweiten Auflage der Offenbarungskritik bis zur Rezeption von Schulzes *Aenesidemus.* Lazzari, Alessandro.

Fichtes Erfindung der Wissenschaftslehre. Tilliette, Xavier.

Fichtes Lehre vom Anstoss, Nicht-Ich und Ding an sich in der GWL: Eine kritische Erörterung. Soller, Alois K.

Fichtes Sprachphilosophie und der Begriff einer Wissenschaftslehre. Surber, Jere Paul.

Fichtes Wissenschaftslehre und die philosophischen Anfänge Heideggers. Denker, Alfred.

Fichtes Wissenschaftslehre vor der aktuellen Diskussion um die Letztbegründung. Gerten, Michael.

Friedrich Schlegel's Theory of an Alternating Principle Prior to His Arrival in Jena (6 August 1796). Behler, Ernst.

From Kant to Hegel: Johann Gottlieb Fichte's Theory of Self-Consciousness. Beck, Gunnar.

Frühromantische Subjektkritik. Iber, Christian.

Gedanken zur gegenwärtigen Bedeutung der Fichteschen Wirtschaftsethik. Fukuyoshi, Masao.

Gefühl und Realität: Fichtes Auseinandersetzung mit Jacobi in der *Grundlage der Wissenschaft des Praktischen.* Loock, Reinhard.

Geist oder Gespenst? Fichtes Noumenalismus in der *Wissenschaftslehre nova methodo.* Zöller, Günter.

Habermas, Fichte and the Question of Technological Determinism. Jalbert, John E.

Heideggers Wende zum Deutschen Idealismus. Strube, Claudius.

Hölderlins frühe Fichte-Kritik und ihre Wirkung auf den Gang der Ausarbeitung der Wissenschaftslehre. Waibel, Violetta.

Hölderlins Trennung von Fichte. Jürgensen, Sven.

La prima lettura fichtiana della *Kritik der Urteilskraft* in alcuni studi del nostro secolo. Fabbianelli, Faustino.

Leibniz im Verständnis Fichtes. Lauth, Reinhard.

Man kannte mich, als man mich rufte: Die Berufung des Magister Fichte an die Gesamt-Akademie Jena im Jahre 1794. Vieweg, Klaus.

Metamorfosi della libertà nel *Sistema di Etica* di Fichte. Fonnesu, Luca.

Offene Intersubjektivität—nach Johann Gottlieb Fichte. Schmidig, Dominik.

Parallelen zwischen Maimon und dem frühen Fichte. Krämer, Felix.

Prinzipien und System: Rezeptionsmodelle der Wissenschaftslehre Fichtes 1794. Stamm, Marcelo.

Satz und Grund: Der Anfang der Philosophie bei Fichte mit Bezugnahme auf die Werke BWL und GWL. Rametta, Gaetano.

Schellings Identitätssystem von 1801 und Fichtes Wissenschaftslehre. Hennigfeld, Jochem.

Schellings Metapher *Blitz*—eine Huldigung an die Wissenschaftslehre. Ehrhardt, Walter E.

Selbstbewusstsein: ein Problem der Philosophie nach Kant. Stolzenberg, Jürgen.

Sobre Hölderlin y los comienzos del Idealismo alemán. Serrano Marín, Vicente.

Sprachliche Vermittlung philosophischer Einsichten nach Fichtes Frühphilosophie. Schmidig, Dominik.

Statt Nicht-Ich—Du! Die Umwendung der Fichteschen Wissenschaftslehre ins Dialogische durch Novalis (Friedrich von Hardenberg). Wanning, Berbeli.

System und Methode—Zur methodologischen Begründung transzendentalen Philosophierens in Fichtes *Begriffsschrift.* Stahl, Jürgen.

The Early Fichte as Disciple of Jacobi. Di Giovanni, George.

Transzendentale Lebenslehre: Zur Königsberger Wissenschaftslehre 1807. Ivaldo, Marco.

Vernunft als Epiphänomen der Naturkausalität: Zu Herkunft und Bedeutung des ursprünglichen Determinismus J.G. Fichtes. Wildfeuer, Armin G.

Vom Begriff der Freiheit: Fichtes Leipziger Kant-Studien (1790). Lindner, Konrad.

Vom sprachlichen Zugang zum Absoluten. Mittmann, Jörg-Peter.

Von der Religionsphilosophie zur Wissenschaftslehre: Die Religionsbegründung in Paragraph 2 der zweiten Auflage von Fichtes *Versuch einer Kritik aller Offenbarung.* Wittekind, Folkart.

War Rickert ein Fichteaner? Die Fichteschen Züge des badischen Neukantianismus. Przylebski, Andrzej.

Wechselbestimmung: Zum Verhältnis von Hölderlin, Schiller und Fichte in Jena. Waibel, Violetta.

Wechselgrundsatz: Friedrich Schlegels philosophischer Ausgangspunkt. Frank, Manfred.

Wege zur Wahrheit: Zur Bedeutung von Fichtes wissenschaftlich- und populär-philosophischer Methode. Traub, Hartmut.

Wissen und Tun: Zur Handlungsweise der transzendentalen Subjektivität in der ersten Wissenschaftslehre Fichtes. Siemek, Marek J.

## FICHTE

Zu den kantischen und fichteschen Motiven bei Nicolai Hartmann. Hála, Vlastimil.

Zu Fichtes Kritik an Reinholds *empirischem* Satz des Bewusstseins und ihrer Vorgeschichte. Bondeli, Martin.

Zum Stellenwert der *Grundlage* aus der Sicht von 1804: Eine Interpretation des Wechsels von analytisch-synthetischer und genetischer Methode in Kapitel 5 der *Grundlage*. Beeler-Port, Josef.

Zur Fichte-Darstellung in Hegels *Differenzschrift*. Kiss, Endre.

Zur Geschichte der romantischen Ästhetik: Von Fichtes Transzendental-philosophie zu Schlegels Transzendentalpoesie. Radrizzani, Ives.

Zwischen äusserem Zwang und innerer Freiheit. Aschoff, Frank.

Zwischen Sein und Setzen: Fichtes Kritik am dreifachen Absoluten der kantischen Philosophie. Bickmann, Claudia.

## FICINO

L'espressività del cielo di Marsilio Ficino, lo Zodiaco medievale e Plotino. Vescovini, Graziella Federici.

Marsilius Ficinus: In *Theaetetum* Platonis vel *De scientia* ad Petrum Medicem, patriae patrem: Epitome. Mojsisch, Burkhard.

The Epistemology of Humanism. Mojsisch, Burkhard.

## FICTION

"Lord Byron: To Create, and in Creating Live a Being More Intense" in *Critical Studies: Ethics and the Subject,* Simms, Karl (ed). Rawes, Alan.

"Perictione in Colophon" in *Verstehen and Humane Understanding,* O'Hear, Anthony (ed). Scruton, Roger.

*Art and Its Messages: Meaning, Morality, and Society.* Davies, Stephen (ed).

*Figuras del Logos: Entre la Filosofía y la Literatura.* López de la Vieja, Maria Teresa (ed).

*Gender, I-deology Essays on Theory, Fiction and Film.* D'Arcy, Chantal Cornut-G (ed) and García Landa, José Angel (ed).

*How to Live Forever: Science Fiction and Philosophy.* Clark, Stephen R L.

*Powerless Fictions? Ethics, Cultural Critique, and American Fiction in the Age of Postmodernism.* Miguel-Alfonso, Ricardo (ed).

A Identidade de Vénus ou as Vantagens da Extensionalidade. D'Orey, Carmo.

Between Fact and Fiction: Dialogue within Encounters of Difference. Conle, Carola.

Characterizing Non-Existents. Kroon, Frederick W.

Could There Have Been Unicorns?. Reimer, Marga.

El relato histórico: ¿hipótesis o ficción? Críticas al "narrativismo imposi-cionalista" de Hayden White. Tozzi, María Verónica.

Essay: Kendall L. Walton, *Mimesis as Make-Believe.* Howell, Robert.

Etica, literatura y crítica. Novo, María del Carmen.

Fact, Fiction and Feeling. Hanfling, Oswald.

Facts of Legal Reasoning. Boukema, H J M.

Fiction, Modality and Dependent Abstracta. Thomasson, Amie L.

Fictional Characters: Dependent or Abstract? A Reply to Reicher's Objections. Thomasson, Amie L.

In Which Henry James Strikes Bedrock. Berry, Ralph M.

Photography as Narrative (in Japanese). Kiyokazu, Nishimura.

Reading the Historians' Resistance to Reading: An Essay On Historiographic Schizophrenia. Cohen, Sande.

Rousseau's Adventure with Robinson Crusoe. Flanders, Todd R.

Talk About Fiction. Predelli, Stefano.

The Demise of the Aesthetic in Literary Study. Goodheart, Eugene.

Three Problems for "Strong" Modal Fictionalism. Nolan, Daniel.

When Manipulation Is Indispensable to Education: The Moral Work of Fiction. Thompson, Audrey.

## FICTIONALITY

The Infinitesimals as Useful Fictions for Leibniz: The Controversy in the Paris Academy of Sciences (Spanish). Joven, Fernando.

## FIDELITY

Treue zwischen Faszination und Institution. Demmer, Klaus.

## FIELD

Axiomática y álgebra estructural en la obra de David Hilbert. Corry, Leo.

Geist als Feld—nur eine Metapher?. Pannenberg, Wolfhart.

More on Imaginaries in *p*-ADIC Fields. Scowcroft, Philip.

Some Model Theory for Almost Real Closed Fields. Delon, Françoise and Farré, Rafel.

T-Convexity and Tame Extensions II. Van den Dries, Lou.

Une Correspondance entre Anneaux Partiels et Groupes. Simonetta, Patrick.

## FIELD THEORY

*An Interpretive Introduction to Quantum Field Theory.* Teller, Paul.

Degrees of Freedom and the Interpretation of Quantum Field Theory. Wayne, Andrew.

Lokale Quantenfeldtheorie und Kontinuumslimes. Müller, Volkhard F.

Renormalized Quantum Field Theory and Cassirer's Epistemological System. Dosch, Hans Günter.

## FIELD, H

*A Subject with No Object: Strategies for Nominalistic Interpretation of Mathematics.* Burgess, John P and Rosen, Gideon.

Field on the Notion of Consistency. Akiba, Ken.

Logical Truth in Modal Logic. McKeon, Matthew.

Pythagorean Powers or A Challenge to Platonism. Pigden, Charles R and Cheyne, Colin.

## FIELDING, H

Filosofia o letteratura? Mandeville, Fielding e il contesto settecentesco. Branchi, Andrea.

## FIELDS, L

Blameworthiness, Character, and Cultural Norms. Haji, Ishtiyaque.

Commentary on "Psychopathy, Other-Regarding Moral Beliefs, and Responsibility". Duff, R A.

## FIFTHTEENTH CENTURY

*see* Renaissance

## FIGURATIVE

Mind and Metaphor. Radovan, Mario.

## FIGURE

*A Defense of the Given.* Fales, Evan.

L'arc-en-ciel et les sacrements: de la sémiologie de la *Logique de Port-Royal* à la théorie pascalienne des figures. Shiokawa, Tetsuya.

## FILIPINO

Peace Zones: Exemplars and Potential. Blume, Francine.

## FILM

"Rashomon and the Sharing of Voices Between East and West" in *On Jean-Luc Nancy: The Sense of Philosophy,* Sheppard, Darren (ed). Naas, Michael B.

"Transgressive Bodies: Destruction and Excessive Display of the Human Form in the Horror Film" in *Critical Studies: Ethics and the Subject,* Simms, Karl (ed). Mendik, Xavier.

*Contemporary Art and Its Philosophical Problems.* Stadler, Ingrid.

*Gender, I-deology Essays on Theory, Fiction and Film.* D'Arcy, Chantal Cornut-G (ed) and García Landa, José Angel (ed).

Analytic Philosophy of Film: History, Issues, Prospects. Gaut, Berys.

Back to Basics: Film/Theory/Aesthetics. Knight, Deborah.

Kurosawa's Existential Masterpiece: A Meditation on the Meaning of Life. Gordon, Jeffrey.

Les Technologies de L'images: Nouveaux Instruments du Bio-Pouvoir. Maybon, Marie-Pierre.

Meta(l)morphoses. Braidotti, Rosi.

Reconsidering Buster Keaton's Heroines. Savedoff, Barbara E.

Scetticismo, riconoscimento, riscoperta dell'ordinario: La filosofia di Stanley Cavell. Sparti, Davide and Lecci, Bernardo.

The Case of the Disappearing Enigma. Knight, Deborah and McNight, George.

Wim Wenders and the Everyday Aesthetics of Technology and Space. Light, Andrew.

## FILMER, R

Locke's Criticism on Robert Filmer about the Origin of Private Property. Papy, Jan.

## FILTER

Decidability by Filtrations for Graded Normal Logics (Graded Modalities V). Cerrato, Claudio.

## FINALITY

*Critique and Totality.* Kerszberg, Pierre.

Finalidad y libertad en educación. Altarejos, Francisco.

La finalidad de la naturaleza humana: Alcance y actualidad de la cuestión. Reyes Oribe, Beatriz Eugenia.

The Inhabitants of Other Planets in Bernardin de Saint-Pierre's *Les Harmonies de la nature* (in French). Duflo, Colas.

## FINANCE

Auditors' Ability to Discern the Presence of Ethical Problems. Karcher, Julia N.

Chief Financial Officers' Perceptions Concerning the IMA's Standards of Ethical Conduct. Moyes, Glen D and Park, Kyungjoo.

Codes of Ethics: Investment Company Money Managers Versus other Financial Professionals. Clarke, James, Duska, Ronald and Rongione, Nicholas.

Ethics Violations: A Survey of Investment Analysts. Veit, E Theodore and Murphy, Michael R.

Helping Professionals in Business Behave Ethically: Why Business Cannot Abdicate Its Responsibility to the Profession. Cooper, Robert W and Frank, Garry L.

Professional Ethics Code Conflict Situations: Ethical and Value Orientation of Collegiate Accounting Students. McCarthy, Irene N.

Some Ethical Issues in Computation and Disclosure of Interest Rate and Cost of Credit. Bhandari, Shyam B.

The Ethics of Creative Accounting. Archer, Simon.

## FINE ART

Artistry. Armstrong, John.

## FINE, A

California Unnatural: On Fine's Natural Ontological Attitude. Brandon, Edwin P.

Reply to Commentaries. Gopnik, Alison.

## FINE, G

Propositions or Objects? A Critique of Gail Fine on Knowledge and Belief in *Republic* V. Gonzalez, Francisco J.

## FINITE

*see also* Infinite

"Dobbiamo ancora pensare il tempo come finito?" in *Il Concetto di Tempo: Atti del XXXII Congresso Nazionale della Società Filosofica Italiana,* Casertano, Giovanni (ed). Morselli, Graziella.

**FODOR, J**
Locke's Acceptance of Innate Concepts. Wendler, Dave.
On the Content of Natural Kind Concepts. Kistler, Max.
Regress Arguments against the Language of Thought. Laurence, Stephen and Margolis, Eric.
Sticking Up for Oedipus: Fodor on Intentional Generalizations and Broad Content. Arjo, Dennis.
Systematicity. Cummins, Robert.
Tensor Products and Split-Level Architecture: Foundational Issues in the Classicism-Connectionism Debate. Guarini, Marcello.
The Theory-Observation Distinction. Kukla, André.

**FOGELIN, R**
So Do We Know or Don't We?. Dretske, Fred.
The Relativity of Skepticism. Moser, Paul K.
Unpurged Pyrrhonism. Stroud, Barry.

**FOLEY, R**
Working Without a Net: A Study of Egocentric Epistemology. David, Marian.

**FOLK**
A Poetics of Psychological Explanation. Knight, Deborah.
Connectionism and the Philosophical Foundations of Cognitive Science. Horgan, Terence.
Goldman's New Reliabilism. Markie, Peter J.
One Cheer for Simulation Theory. Sharpe, R A.
The Tapestry of Alternative Healing. Hudson, Robert.

**FOLK PSYCHOLOGY**
"A Note on Boghossian's Master Argument" in *Contents,* Villanueva, Enrique (ed). Gibson, Roger.
"Can There Be a Rationally Compelling Argument for Anti-Realism about Ordinary ('Folk') Psychology?" in *Contents,* Villanueva, Enrique (ed). Wright, Crispin.
"Connectionism and the Commitments of Folk Psychology" in *AI, Connectionism and Philosophical Psychology, 1995,* Tomberlin, James E (ed). Horgan, Terence and Tienson, John.
A Metaphysical Confirmation of "Folk" Psychology. Rankin, Kenneth.
Actitudes proposicionales y conocimiento sensible en Tomás de Aquino. Tellkamp, Jörg Alejandro.
Folk Psychology and the Simulationist Challenge. Levin, Janet.
Natural-Kind Terms and the Status of Folk Psychology. Sehon, Scott.
Testimony, Induction and Folk Psychology. Lyons, Jack.
The Sociophilosophy of Folk Psychology. Kusch, Martin.
What Do Propositions Measure in Folk Psychology?. Weatherall, Peter.

**FOLKLORE**
A Romanian Myth—Life as a Permanent Miracle. Albu, Mihaela.

**FOLLY**
Prudence, Folly and Melancholy in the Thought of Thomas Hobbes. Borrelli, Gianfranco.

**FOOD**
*Food for Thought: Philosophy and Food.* Telfer, Elizabeth.
Coming in to the Foodshed. Kloppenburg, Jr, Jack, Hendrickson, John and Stevenson, G W.
Community Food Security and Environmental Justice: Searching for a Common Discourse. Gottlieb, Robert and Fisher, Andrew.
Community Shared Agriculture. Fieldhouse, Paul.
Food Biotechnology's Challenge to Cultural Integrity and Individual Consent. Thompson, Paul B.
Research, Extension, and User Partnerships: Models for Collaboration and Strategies for Change. Lacy, William B.

**FOOT, P**
Virtues. Tugendhat, Ernst.

**FORBES, D**
Malthus and the Secularization of Political Ideology. Heavner, Eric K.

**FORBES, G**
Reply to Forbes. Saul, Jennifer M.
Why One Shouldn't Make an Example of a Brain in a Vat. Davies, David.

**FORCE**
Force, Power, and Motive. Yarbrough, Stephen R.
The Peculiar Notion of Exchange Forces—I: Origins in Quantum Mechanics, 1926-1928. Carson, Cathryn.
The Peculiar Notion of Exchange Forces—II: From Nuclear Forces to QED, 1929-1950. Carson, Cathryn.

**FORCING**
A Characterization of Martin's Axiom in Terms of Absoluteness. Bagaria, Joan.
A Non-Generic Real Incompatible with 0#. Stanley, M C.
Can a Small Forcing Create Kurepa Trees. Jin, Renling and Shelah, Saharon.
Canonical Seeds and Prikry Trees. Hamkins, Joel David.
Combinatorics and Forcing with Distributive Ideals. Matet, Pierre.
Forcing Isomorphism II. Laskowski, Michael C and Shelah, Saharon.
Formalizing Forcing Arguments in Subsystems of Second-Order Arithmetic. Avigad, Jeremy.
Permitting, Forcing, and Copying of a given Recursive Relation. Cholak, P, Knight, J F and Ash, C J.
Projective Forcing. Bagaria, Joan and Bosch, Roger.
Small Forcings and Cohen Reals. Zapletal, Jindrich.

Strong Cardinals in the Core Model. Hauser, Kai and Hjorth, Greg.

**FORECASTING**
Epistemology of Technology Assessment: Collingridge, Forecasting Methodologies, and Technological Control. Pinnick, Cassandra L.

**FOREIGN POLICY**
*Basic Rights: Subsistence, Affluence, and U.S. Foreign Policy.* Shue, Henry.
Hans Morgenthau's Realism and American Foreign Policy. Myers, Robert J.

**FOREKNOWLEDGE**
Belief, Foreknowledge, and Theological Fatalism. Hughes, Charles T.
Divine Foreknowledge and Human Freedom Are Compatible. Warfield, Ted A.
Frankfurt Counterexamples: Some Comments on the Widerker-Fischer Debate. Hunt, David P.
On Plantinga's Way Out. Brant, Dale Eric.
Two Problems with Knowing the Future. Hunt, David P.
Why Simple Foreknowledge Offers No More Providential Control than the Openness of God. Sanders, John.

**FOREST**
Preserving Old-Growth Forest Ecosystems: Valuation and Policy. Booth, Douglas E.
What is Good Forestry? An Ethical Examination of Forest Policy and Practice in New Brunswick. Williams, Hugh.

**FORFEITURE**
Crime, Property, and Justice: The Ethics of Civil Forfeiture. Rainbolt, George and Reif, Alison F.
The Problem of Forfeiture in the Welfare State. Epstein, Richard A.

**FORGERY**
Two Kinds of Artistic Duplication. Janaway, Christopher.

**FORGETFULNESS**
Memory, Forgetfulness, and History. Ricoeur, Paul.

**FORGIE, W**
Is Theistic Experience Phenomenologically Possible?. Corcorar , Kevin.

**FORGIVENESS**
Tolerance & Forgiveness: Virtues or Vices?. Smith, Tara.
What is Involved in Forgiving?. Hughes, Paul M.

**FORK**
Capitalizer of Binary Relations and the Fork Operator as Image of a General Disjoint Union-Function of Cartesian Product Functions. Marlangeon, Mauricio Pablo.
Equational Reasoning in Non-Classical Logics. Frias, Marcelo F and Orlowska, Ewa.
Is Fork Set-Theoretical?. Veloso, Paulo A S.

**FORM**
*see also* Essence, Idea
"Aesthetic Form Revisited: John Dewey's Metaphysics of Art" in *Philosophy in Experience: American Philosophy in Transition,* Hart, Richard (ed). Marsoobian, Armen T.
"Form Should Not Be Tautological": Hegel and Adorno on Form (in Japanese). Kin'ya, Nishi.
"Le parti, le forme ed i nomi del tempo nel *Timeo* platonico" in *Il Concetto di Tempo: Atti del XXXII Congresso Nazionale della Società Filosofica Italiana,* Casertano, Giovanni (ed). Casertano, Giovanni.
"Self as Matter and Form: Some Reflections on Kant's View of the Soul" in *Figuring the Self: Subject, Absolute, and Others in Classical German Philosophy,* Zöller, Günter (ed). Aquila, Richard E.
"Technik und symbolische Form bei Cassirer" in *Grenzen der kritischen Vernunft,* Schmid, Peter A. Robbeck, Johannes.
"Zum Problem der Farbe in Cassirers *Philosophie der symbolischen Formen*" in *Grenzen der kritischen Vernunft,* Schmid, Peter A. Bertolini, Luisa.
1277 Revisited: A New Interpretation of the Doctrinal Investigations of Thomas Aquinas and Giles of Rome. Thijssen, J M M H.
*Entity and Identity and Other Essays.* Strawson, P F.
*Philosophies of Arts: An Essay in Differences.* Kivy, Peter.
*Remaking the World: Modeling in Human Experience.* King, James R.
An Epistemological Justification for Aesthetic Experience. Bergmann, Sheryle.
Antonio Rosmini: Aristotele Esposto ed Esaminato. Masi, Giuiseppe.
Aristotle and the Idea of Competing Forms of Life. Crittenden, P.
Die Deduktion der Philosophie nach Fichte und Friedrich von Hardenberg. Rühling, Frank.
Die logische und die dialogische Form des Argumentes vom "Dritten Menschen" in Platons "Parmenides". Strobach, Niko.
Die Philosophie Nishidas als eine "Kunstlehre": Überlegungen zu Nishidas Beziehung zur Kunsttheorie Fiedlers (in Japanese). Tomohiro, Takanashi.
Form and Theory: Meyer Schapiro's *Theory and Philosophy of Art.* Mattick, Paul.
Forms of Individuals in Plotinus: A Re-Examination. Kalligas, Paul.
Forms, Individuals, and Individuation: Mary Margaret McCabe's *Plato's Individuals.* Gentzler, Jyl.
How (Not) to Exempt Platonic Forms from *Parmenides'* Third Man. Hunt, David P.
Ideen, Wissen und Wahrheit nach Platon: Neuere Monographien. Hoffmann, Michael and Von Perger, Mischa.
Infinite Regress Arguments and Infinite Regresses. Black, Oliver.

# FORM

Names, Nominata, the Forms and the *Cratylus*. Wolf II, David F.
On Showing in Argumentation. Lueken, Geert-Lueke.
Practical Possibilities. Adams, Ernest W.
Scary Monsters: Hegel and the Nature of the Monstrous. Gunkel, David.
The *Sophist*, 246a-259e: *Ousia* and *to On* in Plato's Ontologies. Simon, Derek.
The Chinese Theory of Forms and Names (*xingming zhi xue*) and Its Relation to "Philosophy of Signs". Möller, Hans Georg.
The Problem of Motion in the *Sophist*. Lentz, William.
The Semantic of Linear Perspective. Turner, Norman.
The Status of the *Dimensiones Interminatae* in the Thomasian Principle of Individuation. Morris, Nancy A.

# FORMAL

"Can we Ever Pin One Down to a Formal Fallacy?" in *Logic and Argumentation,* Van Eemeren, Frans H (ed). Krabbe, Erik C W.
"Informal Factors in the Formal Evaluation of Arguments" in *Logic and Argumentation,* Van Eemeren, Frans H (ed). Finocchiaro, Maurice A.
A Methodology for the Representation of Legal Knowledge: Formal Ontology Applied to Law. Tiscornia, Daniela.
Formal Properties of Natural Language and Linguistic Theories. Culy, C.

# FORMALISM

Dynamic Interpretations of Constraint-Based Grammar Formalisms. Moss, Lawrence S and Johnson, David E.
El discurso matemático: ideograma y lenguaje natural. De Lorenzo, Javier.
Hilbert Vindicated?. Hintikka, Jaakko.
Hilbert's Formalism and Arithmetization of Mathematics. Webb, Judson C.
History and Values. Dorotíková, Sona.
On the Applicability of the Quantum Measurement Formalism. Chang, Hasok.
The Correspondence between Human Intelligibility Physical Intelligibility: The View of Jean Ladrière. Lee, Kam-lun Edwin.
The Model of Procedural Ethics: Formalism and Argumentation in Law (Spanish). Carrión Wam, Roque.
Tradizione romanistica e dommatica moderna. Nardozza, Massimo.
Why John Von Neumann Did Not Like the Hilbert Space Formalism of Quantum Mechanics (and What he Liked Instead). Rédei, Miklós.

# FORMALIZATION

*Formal Ethics.* Gensler, Harry J.
A Modern Elaboration of the Ramified Theory of Types. Laan, Twan and Nederpelt, Rob.
Analysis of Argument Strategies of Attack and Cooption: Stock Cases, Formalization, and Argument Reconstruction. Brinton, Alan.
Aristotle on Reflective Awareness. Lokhorst, Gert-Jan C.
Formalization of Hilbert's Geometry of Incidence and Parallelism. Von Plato, Jan.
Formalizing Forcing Arguments in Subsystems of Second-Order Arithmetic. Avigad, Jeremy.
Step by Recursive Step: Church's Analysis of Effective Calculability. Sieg, Wilfried.
Technical Notes on a Theory of Simplicity. Scott, Brian M.

# FORMATION

"Il tempo come variabile dei processi formativi" in *Il Concetto di Tempo: Atti del XXXII Congresso Nazionale della Società Filosofica Italiana,* Casertano, Giovanni (ed). Cosetino, Antonio.
The Relationship Between Connectionist Models and a Dynamic Data-Oriented Theory of Concept Formation. Bartsch, Renate.

# FORMS

*Parmenides' Lesson.* Sayre, Kenneth M.
Nietzsche in Dr. Antonio Pérez Estévez's Thought (Spanish). Delgado Ocando, José Manuel.
Plato's First Dialogue. Tomin, Julius.

# FORMULA

$y = 2x$ VS. $y = 3x$. Stolboushkin, Alexei and Niwinski, Damian.
An Extension of the Formulas-as-Types Paradigm. Lambek, J.
Fractal Images of Formal Systems. Grim, Patrick and St. Denis, Paul.
On the Härtig-Style Axiomatization of Unprovable and Satisfiable Formulas of Bernays and Schönfinkel's Classes. Inoué, Takao.
Simple Gentzenizations for the Normal Formulae of Contraction-less Logics. Brady, Ross T.
The Elimination of *De Re* Formulas. Kaminski, Michael.

# FORREST, P

A Mereological Look at Motion. Sayan, Erdinc.
The Mysterious Grand Properties of Forrest. Noordhof, Paul.

# FORST, R

Do We Need a Liberal Theory of Minority Rights? Reply to Carens, Young, Parekh and Forst. Kymlicka, Will.
On Reconciliation and Respect, Justice and the Good Life: Response to Herta Nagl-Docekal and Rainer Forst. Benhabib, Seyla.

# FORTUNE

Luck and Good Fortune in the *Eudemian Ethics*. Johnson, Kent.

# FORWARD

Forward Induction in Games with an Outside Option. Olcina, Gonzalo.

# FOUCAULT, M

"Hegel, Foucault, and Critical Hermeneutics" in *Hegel, History, and Interpretation,* Gallagher, Shaun. Gallagher, Shaun.

"How Is It, Then, That we Still Remain Barbarians?" Foucault, Schiller, and the Aestheticization of Ethics. Bennett, Jane.
"Keeping Foucault and Derrida in Sight: Panopticism and the Politics of Subversion" in *Sites of Vision,* Levin, David Michael (ed). Levin, David Michael.
"Two Walks" in *Critical Studies: Ethics and the Subject,* Simms, Karl (ed). Wheeler, Wendy.
"Wholeness in Manifoldness: Genealogical Methods and Conditions of Agency in Nietzsche and Foucault" in *Critical Studies: Ethics and the Subject,* Simms, Karl (ed). Phillips, Lisa.
*Feminist Interpretations of Michel Foucault.* Hekman, Susan J (ed).
*Foucault's Discipline: The Politics of Subjectivity.* Ransom, John S.
*Habermas and the Unfinished Project of Modernity.* Passerin d'Entrèves, Maurizio (ed) and Benhabib, Seyla (ed).
*The Age of Structuralism: From Lévi-Strauss to Foucault.* Kurzweil, Edith.
*Transgressing Discourses: Communication and the Voice of Other.* Huspek, Michael (ed) and Radford, Gary P (ed).
Arqueologia da Gramática Geral: O Estatuto da Linguagem no Saber da idade Clássica. Matos de Noronha, Nelson.
Between Emergence and Possibility: Foucault, Derrida, and Judith Butler on Performative Identity. Nealon, Jeffrey T.
Beyond Enlightenment? After the Subject of Foucault, Who Comes?. Venn, Couze.
Bourdieu and Foucault on Power and Modernity. Cronin, Ciaran.
Communication, Criticism, and the Postmodern Consensus: An Unfashionable Interpretation of Michel Foucault. Johnson, James.
Deleuzean Ethics. Goodchild, Philip.
Derrida's Watch/Foucault's Pendulum. Naas, Michael B.
Descartes et la mélancholie. Darriulat, Jacques.
Dominio de sí, tecnologías del yo y hermenéutica del sujeto. Lanceros, Patxi.
Feminism, Foucault and Deleuze. Fraser, Mariam.
For the Sake of Truth...The Demand of Discontinuity in Foucault, Blanchot and Levinas. Purcell, Michael.
Forget Vitalism: Foucault and *Lebensphilosophie*. Ransom, John S.
Foucauldian Mutations of Language. Switala, Kristin.
Foucault and the Subject of Feminism. McLaren, Margaret A.
Foucault on Power and the Will to Knowledge. Detel, Wolfgang.
Foucault's Alimentary Philosophy: Care of the Self and Responsibility for the Other. Boothroyd, David.
Foucault's Analysis of Power's Methodologies. Scott, Gary Alan.
Foucault's Attack on Sex-Desire. McWhorter, Ladelle.
Foucault's Genealogy and Teaching Multiculturalism as a Subversive Activity. Kazmi, Y.
Foucault's Phallusy: Intimate Friendship as a Fundamental Ethic (Being a Reconstructive Reading of Foucault's *The Care of the Self*). Van Heerden, Adriaan.
Foucault's Reconfiguration of the Subject: From Nietzsche to Butler, Laclau/Mouffe, and Beyond. Schrift, Alan D.
Foucault, Education, the Self and Modernity. Wain, Kenneth.
Foucault, Ethics and Dialogue. Gardiner, Michael.
Foucault, Politics and the Autonomy of the Aesthetic. O'Leary, Timothy.
Foucault: *Da Morte do* Sujeito *Ao Sujeito da* Morte. Pereira Arêdes, José de Almeida.
Habermas and Foucault: How to Carry Out the Enlightenment Project. Nielsen, Kai.
Michel Foucault, lecteur de Platon ou de l'amour du beau garçon a la contemplation du beau en soi. Catonné, Jean-Philipe.
Postmodernism: What One Needs to Know. Grassie, William.
Restructuring of Social and Political Theory in Education: Foucault and a Social Epistemology of School Practices. Popkewitz, Thomas S and Brennan, Marie.
Self-Creating Selves: Sartre and Foucault. Morris, Phyllis Sutton.
The "Passion for the Outside": Foucault, Blanchot, and Exteriority. Saghafi, Kas.
The Ambiguity of 'Rationality'. Rorty, Richard.
The Eclipse of Gender: Simone de Beauvoir and the *Différance* of Translation. Alexander, Anna.
The Fission of Time: On the Distinction between Intratemporality and the Event of Time in Kant, Heidegger and Foucault. Crocker, Stephen.
The Limits of Limit Experience: Bataille and Foucault. Jay, Martin.
The Modernity Crisis and the Pedagogical Reason (Spanish). Márquez, Alvaro.
Transgressive Theorizing: A Report to Deleuze. Boundas, Constantin V.
Un diálogo con la tradición: Foucault en su contexto. Vega, José Fernádez.
Una perspectiva sobre la relación entre historia y violencia. Longhini, Carlos Guillermo.

# FOUNDATION

A Revolution in the Foundations of Mathematics?. Hintikka, Jaakko.
Aristotele e la fondazione henologica dell'ontologia. Brandner, Rudolf.
Axiomática y álgebra estructural en la obra de David Hilbert. Corry, Leo.
Critical Thinking and Foundational Development. Van Haaften, Wouter and Snik, Ger.
Fondazione metafisica e fondazione teoretica. Laganà, Antonino.
Foundational Standards and Conversational Style: The Humean Essay as an Issue of Philosophical Genre. Engström, Timothy H.
From Completeness to Archimedean Completeness: An Essay in the Foundations of Euclidean Geometry. Ehrlich, Philip.

## FOUNDATION

Hilbert Vindicated?. Hintikka, Jaakko.

Husserl and Hilbert on Completeness: A Neglected Chapter in Early Twentieth Century Foundations of Mathematics. Majer, Ulrich.

Il problema del fondamento nella filosofia di Karl Jaspers. Carpentieri, Rosario.

L'interprétation de la position originelle et la question de la fondation. Ouattara, Ibrahim S.

Los fundamentos de la aritmética según Peano. Zubieta R, Francisco.

## FOUNDATIONALISM

Considered Judgment. Elgin, Catherine Z.

Scepticism and the Foundation of Epistemology: A Study in the Metalogical Fallacies. Floridi, Luciano.

A Neo-Kantian Critique of Von Mises's Epistemology. Barrotta, Pierluigi.

Anti-Foundationalism and the Vienna Circle's Revolution in Philosophy. Uebel, Thomas E.

Antifoundationalism and the Possibility of a Moral Philosophy of Medicine. Thomasma, David C.

Classical American Pragmatism: The Other Naturalism. Rosenthal, Sandra B.

Conventions in the Aufbau. Uebel, Thomas E.

Fanciful Fates. Holland, R F.

Foundationalism and Practical Reason. Heath, Joseph.

Gibt es ein subjektives Fundament unseres Wissens?. Grundmann, Thomas.

Hegel's Nonfoundationalism: A Phenomenological Account of the Structure of Philosophy of Right. Tunick, Mark.

Heterology: A Postmodern Theory of Foundations. Fairlamb, Horace L.

How to Resolve the Pyrrhonian Problematic: A Lesson from Descartes. Sosa, Ernest.

Jacques Maritain and the Nature of Religious Belief. Sweet, William.

Naturalism Radicalized. Rodríguez-Alcázar, Javier.

Philosophy within Theology in Light of the Foundationalism Debate. Guarino, Thomas.

Skepticism and Foundationalism: A Reply to Michael Williams. Vogel, Jonathan.

Some Foundational Problems with Informal Logic and Their Solution. Weinstein, Mark.

Still Unnatural: A Reply to Vogel and Rorty. Williams, Michael.

The Essence of Eschatology: A Modal Interpretation. Davenport, John.

Theistic Arguments and the Crisis of Classical Foundationalism (in Dutch). Van Woudenberg, René.

What Makes Language Possible? Ethological Foundationalism in Reid and Wittgenstein. Robinson, Daniel N and Harré, Rom.

Why Classical Foundationalism Cannot Provide a Proper Account of Premise Acceptability. Freeman, James B.

## FOX, E

Goals of Ethics Consultation: Toward Clarity, Utility, and Fidelity. Andre, Judith.

What Are the Goals of Ethics Consultation: A Consensus Statement. Fletcher, John C and Siegler, Mark.

## FOX, W

Deep Ecology and the Irrelevance of Morality. Reitan, Eric H.

On Warwick Fox's Assessment of Deep Ecology. Glasser, Harold.

## FRACASTORO, G

Hobbes and Fracastoro. Leijenhorst, Cees.

## FRACTAL

Fractal Images of Formal Systems. Grim, Patrick and St. Denis, Paul.

## FRAME

Reasoning about Change and Persistence: A Solution to the Frame Problem. Pollock, John L.

The Structure of Lattices of Subframe Logics. Wolter, Frank.

## FRANCISCANS

El Camino de Santiago y el descubrimiento racional de la naturaleza en los siglos XII y XIII. Ballester, Luis García.

## FRANK, S

On a Mistake Made by Russian Philosophy. Tul'Chinskii, G L.

## FRANKEL, M

Ethics, Standards, Diversity: Dimensions of the Social Construction of Responsibility. Mitcham, Carl.

## FRANKENA, W

Learning from Frankena: A Philosophical Remembrance. Darwall, Stephen.

## FRANKFURT SCHOOL

"Ecology, Modernity, and the Intellectual Legacy of the Frankfurt School" in Philosophy and Geography I: Space, Place, and Environmental Ethics, Light, Andrew (ed). Gandy, Matthew.

"The Frankfurt School and Structuralism in Jerzy Kmita's Analysis" in Epistemology and History, Zeidler-Janiszewska, Anna (ed). Witkowski, Lech.

Las Caras del Leviatán: Una Lectura Política de la Teoría Crítica. Colom González, Francisco.

The Actuality of Adorno: Critical Essays on Adorno and the Postmodern. Pensky, Max (ed).

Walter Benjamin: Selected Writings Volume 1 1913-1926. Bullock, Marcus (ed) and Jennings, Michael W (ed).

Georg Simmel on Philosophy and Culture: Postscript to a Collection of Essays. Habermas, Jürgen and Deflem, Mathieu (trans).

The Frankfurt School. Tessin, Timothy.

What-Is? On Mimesis and the Logic of Identity and Difference in Heidegger and the Frankfurt School. Levin, David Michael.

## FRANKFURT, H

Agency. Simester, A P.

Autonomy and Hierarchical Compatibilism. Jennings, Ian.

Frankfurt Counterexamples: Some Comments on the Widerker-Fischer Debate. Hunt, David P.

Freedom of the Heart. Helm, Bennett.

The Active and the Passive. Raz, Joseph and Ruben, David-Hillel.

The Concept of Person (in Spanish). Dias, Maria Clara.

## FRANKLIN, M

Originalism, Moralism and the Public Opinion State of Mitchell Franklin. Lawler, James.

## FRASER, N

Identity Politics as a Transposition of Fraser's Needs Politics. Tittle, Peg.

## FRATERNITY

Liberty—Equality—Fraternity—Justice (in Czech). Münnix, Gabriele.

This Enormous Army: The Mutual Aid Tradition of American Fraternal Societies before the Twentieth Century. Beito, David T.

## FRAUD

(Not) Giving Credit Where Credit Is Due: Citation of Data Sets. Sieber, Joan E and Trumbo, Bruce E.

A So-Called 'Fraud': Moral Modulations in a Literary Scandal. Lynch, Michael.

Can Designing and Selling Low-Quality Products Be Ethical?. Bakker II, Willem and Loui, Michael.

Feeling Fraudulent: Some Moral Quandaries of a Feminist Instructor. Overall, Christine.

Parafraud in Biology. Hillman, Harold.

## FRAZER, J

Winch's Pluralist Tree and the Roots of Relativism. Phillips, Patrick J J.

## FREDERICK, W

Naturalism and Business Ethics: Inevitable Foes or Possible Allies?. Fort, Timothy L.

## FREE

If There is an Exactly Lambda-Free Abelian Group Then There is an Exactly Lambda-Separable One in Lambda. Shelah, Saharon.

On the Possibility of Rational Free Action. Clarke, Randolph.

Product-Free Lambek Calculus and Context-Free Grammars. Pentus, Mati.

## FREE INQUIRY

An Argument About Free Inquiry. Kitcher, Philip.

## FREE LOGIC

Commentary on W.V. Quine's "Free Logic, Description, and Virtual Classes". Leblanc, Hughes.

Free Logic, Description, and Virtual Classes. Quine, Willard V.

Logiques et sémantiques non classiques. Voizard, Alain.

## FREE MARKET

The Contradictions of Free Market Doctrine: Is There a Solution?. McMurtry, John.

## FREE RIDER

Answering the Free-Rider. Allan, Jim.

Fares and Free Riders on the Information Highway. Rosen, C Martin and Carr, Gabrielle M.

## FREE SPEECH

"The Visit and The Video: Publication and the Line Between Sex and Speech" in Sex, Preference, and Family: Essays on Law and Nature, Nussbaum, Martha C (ed). Estlund, David M.

Free Speech. Weissman, David.

The Words We Love to Hate. Stark, Cynthia A.

## FREE WILL

see also Determinism

A Treatise Concerning Eternal and Immutable Morality with A Treatise of Freewill. Hutton, Sarah (ed) and Cudworth, Ralph.

Metaphilosophy and Free Will. Double, Richard.

No Place for Sovereignty: What's Wrong with Freewill Theism. McGregor Wright, R K.

Sartres Ontologie und die Frage einer Ethik: Zur Vereinbarkeit einer normativen Ethik und/oder Metaethik mit der Ontologie von "L'être et le néant". Töllner, Uwe.

The Case for Freewill Theism: A Philosophical Assessment. Basinger, David.

The Significance of Free Will. Kane, Robert.

Ancora su nuvole ed orologi. Messeri, Marco.

Augustine's Transformation of the Free Will Defence. Greer, Rowan A.

Authentische Entscheidungen und emotive Neurowissenschaft. Walter, Henrik.

Egalitarian Justice and the Importance of the Free Will Problem. Smilansky, Saul.

El libre albedrío entre la omnipotencia y el amor Divino: Problemática ética y consecuencias tecnológicas de la cuestión del libre alberdrío en Hobbes y San Agustín. Garrido Maturano, Angel Enrique.

Fichtes Entwicklung von der zweiten Auflage der Offenbarungskritik bis zur Rezeption von Schulzes Aenesidemus. Lazzari, Alessandro.

**FRUTUOSO, G**
O Homem e a História em Gaspar Frutuoso. Da Luz, José Luís Brandao.

**FRYE, M**
Contraceptive Risk-Taking and Norms of Chastity. Stubblefield, Anna.

**FUKUYAMA, F**
"El Liberalismo como destino: A propósito de la obra de Francis Fukuyama" in *Liberalismo y Comunitarismo: Derechos Humanos y Democracia,* Monsalve Solórzano, Alfonso (ed). Salazar P, Freddy.

**FULFILLMENT**
Self-Deception and Wish-Fulfilment. Pataki, Tamas.

**FULLER, L**
Intuition and Natural Law. Walter, Edgar.
Principles of Lon Fuller's Conception of Natural Law. Tokarczyk, Roman A.
Why Positive Law Theory Makes a Big Difference: Editor's Commentary on "Principles of Lon Fuller's Conception of Natural Law". Tokarczyk, Roman A.

**FULLER, P**
Space for the Imagination. Pateman, Trevor.

**FUNCTION**
*see also* Recursive Function
"Functions, Operations, and Sense in Wittgenstein's *Tractatus*" in *Early Analytic Philosophy,* Tait, William W (ed). Hylton, Peter.
*Analyzing Functions: An Essay on a Fundamental Notion in Biology.* Melander, Peter.
*Charles S. Peirce's Evolutionary Philosophy.* Hausman, Carl R.
A Few Special Ordinal Ultrafilters. Laflamme, Claude.
A General Approach to the Algebras of Unary Functions in a Boolean Semantics for Natural Language. Nowak, Marek.
A Taxonomy of Functions. Walsh, Denis M and Ariew, André.
Art: Function or Procedure—Nature or Culture?. Dickie, George T.
Biological Function, Selection, and Reduction. Manning, Richard N.
Capitalizer of Binary Relations and the Fork Operator as Image of a General Disjoint Union-Function of Cartesian Product Functions. Marlangeon, Mauricio Pablo.
Cardinal Functions on Ultraproducts of Boolean Algebras. Peterson, Douglas.
Choice Functions and the Scopal Semantics of Indefinites. Winter, Yoad.
Coherence as an Ideal of Rationality. Zynda, Lyle.
Computability and Recursion. Soare, Robert I.
Consciousness Disputed. Levin, Janet.
Constructing Cantorian Counterexamples. Boolos, George.
Expected Utility without Utility. Castagnoli, E and Calzi, M Li.
Fitness and Function. Walsh, Denis M.
Function Identification from Noisy Data with Recursive Error Bounds. Changizi, Mark.
Hilbert Vindicated?. Hintikka, Jaakko.
Identification in the Limit of Categorial Grammars. Kanazawa, Makoto.
Individualism and Evolutionary Psychology (or: In Defense of "Narrow" Functions). Buller, David J.
L'astuzia della follia: Un'antologia di Lombroso. Savorelli, Alessandro.
Notes on Polynomially Bounded Arithmetic. Zambella, Domenico.
On Negatively Restricting Boolean Algebras. Zuber, R.
On the Semantics of Comparative Conditionals. Beck, Sigrid.
On the Significance of Conditional Probabilities. Sobel, Jordan Howard.
Passing Likeness. Skillen, Tony.
Plantinga on Functions and the Theory of Evolution. Levin, Michael.
Plantinga's Case Against Naturalistic Epistemology. Fales, Evan.
Proxy Functions, Truth and Reference. Nelson, R J.
Quantifier Scope: How Labor is Divided between QR and Choice Functions. Reinhart, Tanya.
Step by Recursive Step: Church's Analysis of Effective Calculability. Sieg, Wilfried.
Strong Polynomial-Time Reducibility. Shinoda, Juichi.
Structures of Natural Reasoning within Functional Dialogues. Trognon, Alain and Grusenmeyer, Corinne.
T-Convexity and Tame Extensions II. Van den Dries, Lou.
The Argument on Identity Statements and the Problem of Referring to Functions in Frege's Philosophy (Spanish). Ramos, Pedro.
The Function of Consciousness. Tye, Michael.
The Generalized Harmonic Mean and a Portfolio Problem with Dependent Assets. Kijima, Masaaki.
The Return of the Group. Sterelny, Kim.
Troubles with Wagner's Reading of Millikan. Millikan, Ruth Garrett.
Undefeated Naturalism. Ross, Glenn.
Uniformization, Choice Functions and Well Orders in the Class of Trees. Lifsches, Shmuel and Shelah, Saharon.

**FUNCTIONAL**
Definability in Functional Analysis. Iovino, José.

**FUNCTIONALISM**
"Weak Materialism" in *Objections to Physicalism,* Robinson, Howard (ed). Nathan, N M L.
*Das phänomenale Bewusstsein: Eine Verteidigung.* Lanz, Peter.
Functionalism's Response to the Problem of Absent Qualia: More Discussion of Zombies. Hardcastle, Valerie Gray.
Making the Change: the Functionalist's Way. Noordhof, Paul.
Neo-Functionalist Critical Theory?. Turner, Charles.

Norman Malcolm, *Wittgensteinian Themes.* Winch, Peter.
Over Functies en Affordances. De Jong, H Looren and Schouten, M K D.
War Aristoteles ein Funktionalist? Überlegungen zum Leib-Seele-Problem. Perler, Dominik.

**FUNCTIONALITY**
*La Logique Combinatoire.* Ginisti, Jean-Pierre.

**FUNDA, O**
Oh Our Children! (in Czech). Pokorny, Petr.

**FUNDAMENTALISM**
"Fundamentalism in India" in *Averroës and the Enlightenment,* Wahba, Mourad (ed). Singh, Ramjee.
Hermeneutics and Democracy. Vattimo, Gianni.
I confini del fondamento. Lipari, Maria Chiara.
Morality Requires God...or Does It?: Bad News for Fundamentalists and Jean-Paul Sartre. Schick, Theodore.
Ser y hermenéutica: El relativismo contemporáneo o el nuevo fundamentalismo laico. Camacho, Ramón Kuri.

**FUNDING**
Freedom of Expression at the National Endowment for the Arts: An Opportunity for Interdisciplinary Education. Van Camp, Julie.

**FUSION**
Strongly Minimal Fusions of Vector Spaces. Holland, Kitty L.

**FUTILITY**
Futile Care in Neonatology: An Interim Report from Colorado. Hulac, Peter and Barbour, Elizabeth.
Futility and the Varieties of Medical Judgment. Sulmasy, Daniel P.

**FUTURE**
"Classical American Metaphysics: Retrospect and Prospect" in *Philosophy in Experience: American Philosophy in Transition,* Hart, Richard (ed). Corrington, Robert S.
"Esistenza e tempo in Heidegger" in *Il Concetto di Tempo: Atti del XXXII Congresso Nazionale della Società Filosofica Italiana,* Casertano, Giovanni (ed). Cesareo, Rosa.
"Living with the Future: Genetic Information and Human Existence" in *The Right to Know and the Right not to Know,* Chadwick, Ruth (ed). Ten Have, Henk.
"Philosophy in America: Recovery and Future Development" in *The Recovery of Philosophy in America: Essays in Honor of John Edwin Smith,* Kasulis, Thomas P (ed). Smith, John E.
"Postmodernity as a Spectre of the Future: The Force of Capital and the Unmasking of Difference" in *Deleuze and Philosophy: The Difference Engineer,* Ansell Pearson, Keith (ed). Purdom, Judy.
"Progress and the Future" in *The Idea of Progress,* McLaughlin, Peter (ed). Rescher, Nicholas.
"Tempo storico e futuro escatologico" in *Il Concetto di Tempo: Atti del XXXII Congresso Nazionale della Società Filosofica Italiana,* Casertano, Giovanni (ed). Dall'Asta, Giuseppe.
"The Future Life" and Averroës's *Long Commentary on the De Anima of Aristotle*" in *Averroës and the Enlightenment,* Wahba, Mourad (ed). Taylor, Richard C.
*Foundations of Futures Studies: Human Science for a New Era.* Bell, Wendell.
*Life as Narcissism: A Unified Theory of Life.* Tabrizi, Firooz N.
A Universidade na Sociedade Actual. Renaud, Michel.
Acts and Outcomes: A Reply to Boonin-Vail. Parfit, Derek.
Against Education. Nordenbo, Sven Erik.
Don't Stop Thinking About Tomorrow: Two Paradoxes About Duties to Future Generations. Boonin-Vail, David.
Feminismo y tercer milenio. Balmaseda Cinquina, María F.
Funzioni e senso del diritto nel moderno: Riconoscimento e ragione sistemica. Romano, Bruno.
Future Issues in Bioethics. Flanigan, Rosemary.
Intensive Care Ethics in Evolution. Hall, Katherine.
Is the See-Battle About to Be Lost? On Aristotle's *De interpretatione*, Ch. 9. A Reconstruction (in Czech). Cziszter, Kálmán.
La filosofia tra presenza e ulteriorità. Pieretti, Antonio.
La prospectiva de los grandes informes y la metodología Delphi. Hernández de Frutos, Teodoro.
Market Meditopia: A Glimpse at American Health Care in 2005. Churchill, Larry R.
Opening the Future: The Paradox of Promising in the Hobbesian Social Contract. Bernasconi, Robert.
Our Future in J. Krishnamurti. Subrata, Roy.
Past, Present, Future, and Special Relativity. Rakié, Natasa.
Save the Males: Backlash in Organizations. Burke, Ronald J and Black, Susan.
Seyla Benhabib and the Radical Future of the Enlightenment. Nagl-Docekal, Herta.
Staring at Our Future. Iserson, Kenneth V.
Taboos Without a Clue: Sizing up Religious Objections to Cloning. Lindsay, Ronald A.
The Ecological Ideology and Russia's Future. Gorelov, A A.
The Future and the History of Ideas. Perkins, Mary Anne.
The Future of Romantic Love. White, Richard J.
The G.I. Bill and U.S. Social Policy, Past and Future. Skocpol, Theda.
The History of the Future of International Relations. Puchala, Donald J.

## GAME THEORY

"Science and Games" in *Knowledge and Inquiry: Essays on Jaakko Hintikka's Epistemology and Philosophy of Science,* Sintonen, Matti (ed). Wolenski, Jan.

"Verdirbt der *homo oeconomicus* die Moral?" in *Ökonomie und Moral: Beiträge zur Theorie ökonomischer Rationalität,* Lohmann, Karl Reinhard (ed). Suchanek, Andreas.

*Wittgensteinian Themes: Essays 1978-1989.* Von Wright, Georg Henrik (ed) and Malcolm, Norman.

Approximate Common Knowledge and Co-Ordination: Recent Lessons from Game Theory. Morris, Stephen and Shin, Hyun Song.

Evolution and Ultimatum Bargaining. Harms, William.

Game Logic and its Applications I. Kaneko, Mamoru and Nagashima, Takashi.

Game-Theoretic Axioms for Local Rationality and Bounded Knowledge. Bicchieri, Cristina and Antonelli, Gian Aldo.

Inconsistencies in Extensive Games. Dufwenberg, Martin and Lindén, Johan.

Joint Beliefs in Conflictual Coordination Games. Vanderschraaf, Peter and Richards, Diana.

Knowledge, Belief and Counterfactual Reasoning in Games. Stalnaker, Robert.

On the Foundations of Nash Equilibrium. Jacobsen, Jans Jorgen.

Pascalian Wagers. Sobel, Jordan Howard.

Sex, Fairness, and the Theory of Games. D'Arms, Justin.

The Individual Rationality of Maintaining a Sense of Justice. Cave, Eric M.

The Undecidability of the Spatialized Prisoner's Dilemma. Grim, Patrick.

## GAME-THEORETICAL SEMANTICS

A Constructive Game Semantics for the Language of Linear Logic. Japaridze, Giorgi.

On the Theory of Anaphor: Dynamic Predicate Logic vs. Game-Theoretical Semantics. Sandu, Gabriel.

## GANDHI

*Mahatma Ghandi: Selected Political Writings.* Dalton, Dennis (ed).

Civil Disobedience: Justice against Legality. Miniotaite, Grazina.

Gandhi on Love: A Reply to Ian M. Harris. Kohl, Marvin.

Gandhi's Qualified Acceptance of Violence. Richards, Jerald.

Gandhian Concept of Planned Society. Sharma, Akshaya Kumar.

Hannah Arendt on Power, Consent, and Coercion: Some Parallels with Gandhi. Presbey, Gail.

The Conditional Quality of Gandhi's Love. Harris, Ian M.

The Special Features of Gandhian Ethics. Radha, S.

The Sprritual Dimension of Gandhi's Activism. Spretnak, Charlene.

Was Gandhi a Feminist?. Fiore, Karen K.

## GANDHIANISM

"Laws of Nature vs. Laws of Respect: Non-Violence in Practice in Norway" in *Environmental Pragmatism,* Light, Andrew (ed). Rothenberg, David.

## GAOS, J

Gaos y la religión. Valdés, Sylvia.

## GARCIA MAYNEZ, E

El concepto de libertad jurídica en la iusfilosofía de Eduardo García Máynez. Aguayo, Enrique I.

## GARCIA MORENTE, M

Noticia sobre la edición de las *Obras Completas* de Manuel García Morente. Palacios, Juan Miguel and Rovira, Rogelio.

## GARDEN

Las parábolas ficinianas del bosque y el jardín en las *Stanze per la Giostra* de Angelo Poliziano. Manzi, Attilio.

Lessons from the Garden: Rousseau's Solitaires and the Limits of Liberalism. Cladis, Mark S.

On the Aesthetic Appreciation of Japanese Gardens. Carlson, Allen.

The Influence of Chinese Philosophy on the English Style Garden: A Comparative Study of Wörlitz and Koishikawa Korakuen (in Japanese). Seiko, Goto.

## GARDENFORS, P

The Ramsey Test and Conditional Semantics. Döring, Frank.

## GARDNER, W

Ethics, Standards, Diversity: Dimensions of the Social Construction of Responsibility. Mitcham, Carl.

## GARFINKEL, H

La fiducia come forma di fede: Alcune riflessioni introduttive ad un problema sociologico. Prandini, Riccardo.

## GARRISON, J

Liberal Indoctrination and the Problem of Community. Harvey, Charles W.

## GARVER, E

Reclaiming Aristotle's *Rhetoric.* Moss, Jean Dietz.

## GARZON VALDES, E

Democracy: A Convergent Value? Comments on Sheldon Leader and Ernesto Garzón Valdés. Passerin d'Entrèves, Maurizio.

Toleration, Liberalism and Democracy: A Comment on Leader and Garzón Valdés. Bellamy, Richard.

## GASSENDI

*Gassendi's Ethics: Freedom in a Mechanistic Universe.* Sarasohn, Lisa T.

## GASTROENTEROLOGY

The Gastroenterologist and His Endoscope: The Embodiment of Technology and the Necessity for a Medical Ethics. Cooper, M Wayne.

## GAUTHIER, C

Developing Habits and Knowing What Habits to Develop: A Look at the Role of Virtue in Ethics. Loewy, Erich H.

## GAUTHIER, D

A Multi-Stage Game Model of Morals by Agreement. Heath, Joseph.

La ética como estrategia de la razón. Gómez, Pedro Francés.

Morality as Private Property: A Critique of David Gauthier (Spanish). Barreto, Luz Marina.

Rational Cooperation, Intention, and Reconsideration. Mintoff, Joe.

Rational Intentions and the Toxin Puzzle. Mele, Alfred R.

Rationality, Dispositions, and the Newcomb Paradox. Barnes, R Eric.

Subjectivism, Utility, and Autonomy. Lottenbach, Hans.

The Limits of Self Interest: An Hegelian Critique of Gauthier's Compliance Problem. Schwartz, David T.

## GAY

Family Outlaws. Calhoun, Cheshire.

## GAY RIGHTS

"Gay Reservations" in *The Liberation Debate: Rights at Issue,* Leahy, Michael (ed). Scruton, Roger.

"Lesbian and Gay Rights: Pro" in *The Liberation Debate: Rights at Issue,* Leahy, Michael (ed). Nussbaum, Martha C.

"Nussbaum's Reply" in *The Liberation Debate: Rights at Issue,* Leahy, Michael (ed). Nussbaum, Martha C.

*The Liberation Debate: Rights at Issue.* Leahy, Michael (ed) and Cohn-Sherbok, Dan (ed).

Against Marriage and Motherhood. Card, Claudia.

## GEACH, P

Mixed Inferences: A Problem for Pluralism about Truth Predicates. Tappolet, Christine.

Non-Cognitivism, Truth and Logic. Wedgwood, Ralph.

## GEARY, P

Medieval Historiography. Birns, Nicholas.

## GELLMAN, J

Pluralism and Justified Religious Belief: A Response to Gellman. Basinger, David.

## GELLNER, E

*The Social Philosophy of Ernest Gellner.* Jarvie, Ian (ed) and Hall, John A (ed).

Explaining Monoculturalism: Beyond Gellner's Theory of Nationalism. Tambini, Damian.

## GELLYNCKLAAN, J

Repliek op G. Vanheeswijck. Tijmes, Pieter.

## GENDER

"Concerning Zelia Gregoriou's "Reading *Phaedrus* like a Girl" in *Philosophy of Education (1996),* Margonis, Frank (ed). Whitlock, Greg.

"Construction of a Gendered Subject: A Feminist Reading of Adorno's *Aesthetic Theory*" in *The Semblance of Subjectivity,* Huhn, Tom (ed). Wilke, Sabine and Schlipphacke, Heidi.

"Fragmentation, Race, and Gender: Building Solidarity in the Postmodern Era" in *Existence in Black: An Anthology of Black Existential Philosophy,* Gordon, Lewis R (ed). Huntington, Patricia J.

"Gender Rites and Rights: The Biopolitics of Beauty and Fertility" in *Philosophical Perspectives on Bioethics,* Sumner, L W (ed). Morgan, Kathryn Pauly.

"Justice, Gender, The Family, and The Practice of Political Philosophy" in *A Question of Values: New Canadian Perspectives in Ethics and Political Philosophy,* Brennan, Samantha (ed). Milde, Michael.

"Pornography Left and Right" in *Sex, Preference, and Family: Essays on Law and Nature,* Nussbaum, Martha C (ed). MacKinnon, Catherine A.

"Sexual Orientation and Gender: Dichotomizing Differences" in *Sex, Preference, and Family: Essays on Law and Nature,* Nussbaum, Martha C (ed). Okin, Susan Moller.

"The Complex Ethics of Separate Schools" in *Philosophy of Education (1996),* Margonis, Frank (ed). McDonough, Kevin.

"The Coupling of Human Souls: Rousseau and the Problem of Gender Relations" in *Political Dialogue: Theories and Practices,* Esquith, Stephen L (ed). Kukla, Rebecca.

"Voluntary Segregation: Gender and Race as Legitimate Grounds for Differential Treatment and Freedom of Association" in *Philosophy of Education (1996),* Margonis, Frank (ed). Smith, Stacy.

*Angewandte Ethik: Die Bereichsethiken und ihre theoretische Fundierung.* Nida-Rümelin, Julian (ed).

*Art and Its Messages: Meaning, Morality, and Society.* Davies, Stephen (ed).

*Caring: Gender-Sensitive Ethics.* Bowden, Peta.

*Contemporary Perspectives on Masculinity: Men, Women, and Politics in Modern Society.* Clatterbaugh, Kenneth.

*Emancipation and Illusion: Rationality and Gender in Habermas's Theory of Modernity.* Fleming, Marie.

*Feminist Approaches to Bioethics: Theoretical Reflections and Practical Applications.* Tong, Rosemarie.

*Feminist Interpretations of Michel Foucault.* Hekman, Susan J (ed).

*From Sex Objects to Sexual Subjects.* Moscovici, Claudia.

*Gender, I-deology Essays on Theory, Fiction and Film.* D'Arcy, Chantal Cornut-G (ed) and García Landa, José Angel (ed).

*Memory, Identity, Community: The Idea of Narrative in the Human Sciences.* Hinchman, Lewis P (ed) and Hichmann, Sandra K (ed).

# GENDER

*Philosophy as Passion: The Thinking of Simone de Beauvoir.* Vintges, Karen.

*Rethinking Masculinity: Philosophical Explorations in Light of Feminism.* May, Larry (ed), Strikwerda, Robert (ed) and Hopkins, Patrick D (ed).

*Sex, Preference, and Family: Essays on Law and Nature.* Nussbaum, Martha C (ed) and Estlund, David M (ed).

*Sexual Harassment: Confrontations and Decisions.* Wall, Edmund (ed).

*The Philosophy of Simone de Beauvoir: Gendered Phenomenologies, Erotic Generosities.* Bergoffen, Debra B.

*The Political Consequences of Thinking: Gender and Judaism in the Work of Hannah Arendt.* Ring, Jennifer.

*The Psychic Life of Power: Theories in Subjection.* Butler, Judith.

*The Second Wave: A Reader in Feminist Theory.* Nicholson, Linda (ed).

A Critique of Normative Heterosexuality: Identity, Embodiment, and Sexual Difference in Beauvoir and Irigaray. Schutte, Ofelia.

A Feminist Standpoint for Genetics. Mahowald, Mary B.

An Empirical Study of Moral Reasoning Among Managers in Singapore. Wimalasiri, Jayantha S, Pavri, Francis and Jalil, Abdul A K.

Community of Inquiry and Differences of the Heart. Thomas, John C.

Correlation of Gender-Related Values of Independence and Relationship and Leadership Orientation. Butz, Clarence E and Lewis, Phillip V.

Das neoliberale Projekt, der männliche Arbeitsbegriff und die fällige Erneuerung des Geschlechtervertrags. Haug, Frigga.

Direct and Indirect Responsibility: Distributing Blame. Goodnow, Jacqueline J and Warton, Pamela M.

Disciplining the Family: The Case of Gender Identity Disorder. Feder, Ellen K.

Fleshing Gender, Sexing the Body: Refiguring the Sex/Gender Distinction. Tuana, Nancy.

Friendship Across Generations. Nye, Andrea.

Gender and "Postmodern War". Schott, Robin May.

Gender and Social Awareness: A Story from Buenos Aires. Pac, Andrea.

Gender Differences in Attitudes Toward Animal Research. Eldridge, Jennifer J and Gluck, John P.

Gender Differences in Ethical Frameworks and Evaluation of Others' Choices in Ethical Dilemmas. Schminke, Marshall.

Gender Equity, Organizational Transformation and Challenger. Maier, Mark.

Gender, Race, and Difference: Individual Consideration versus Group-Based Affirmative Action in Admission to Higher Education. Jaggar, Alison.

Gender-Related Differences in Ethical and Social Values of Business Students: Implications for Management. Smith, Patricia L and Oakley III, Elwood F.

Grounding Agency in Depth: The Implications of Merleau-Ponty's Thought for the Politics of Feminism. Fielding, Helen.

Introduction: Feminist Approaches to Bioethics. Tong, Rosemarie.

Is God Exclusively a Father?. Isham, George F.

Multiculturalism and Gender Equity: The U.S. "Difference" Debates Revisited. Adler, Pierre.

Okin on Feminism and Rawls. Sehon, Scott R.

Perception of What the Ethical Climate Is and What It Should Be: The Role of Gender, Academic Status, and Ethical Education. Luthar, Harsh K, DiBattista, Ron A and Gautschi, Theodore.

Philosophy, Gender Politics, and In Vitro Fertilization: A Feminist Ethics of Reproductive Healthcare. LeMoncheck, Linda.

Projecting Political Correctness: The Divorce of Affect and Signifier. Brennan, Teresa.

Psychological Androgyny: A Concept in Seach of Lesser Substance. Towards the Understanding of the Transformation of a Social Representation. Lorenzi-Cioldi, Fabio.

Questions of Proximity: "Woman's Place" in Derrida and Irigaray. Armour, Ellen T.

Rape Research and Gender Feminism: So Who's Anti-Male?. Davion, Victoria.

Regendering the U.S. Abortion Debate. Jaggar, Alison.

Sex, Gender, Sexuality: Can Ethologists Practice Genealogy?. Gatens, Moira.

She Said/He Said: Ethics Consultation and the Gendered Discourse. Zoloth-Dorfman, Laurie and Rubin, Susan.

The Diabolical Strategy of Mimesis: Luce Irigaray's Reading of Maurice Merleau-Ponty. Kozel, Susan.

The Eclipse of Gender: Simone de Beauvoir and the *Différance* of Translation. Alexander, Anna.

The Ideology and Biology of Gender Difference. Rhode, Deborah L.

Thinking Life as Relation: An Interview with Luce Irigaray. Pluhacek, Stephen and Bostic, Heidi.

Violencia femenina y autorreferencia. Schultz, Margarita.

What is a Woman? Butler and Beauvoir on the Foundations of the Sexual Difference. Heinämaa, Sara.

What's the Difference? Knowledge and Gender in (Post)Modern Philosophy of Religion. Jantzen, Grace M.

# GENDIN, S

Those Who Can, Do: A Response to Sidney Gendin's "Am I Wicked?". Warren, Dona.

# GENE

*Feminist Approaches to Bioethics: Theoretical Reflections and Practical Applications.* Tong, Rosemarie.

*Sex, Love, and Friendship: Studies of the Society for the Philosophy of Sex and Love 1977-1992.* Soble, Alan (ed).

C'è un organismo in questo testo?. Keller, Evelyn Fox.

Discussion: Phylogenetic Species Concept: Pluralism, Monism, and History. Horvath, Christopher D.

Genes and Human Behavior: The Emerging Paradigm. Drew, Allan P.

If I Am Only My Genes, What Am I? Genetic Essentialism and a Jewish Response. Wolpe, Paul Root.

Polanyian Reflections on Embodiment, the Human Genome Initiative and Theological Anthropology. Lewis, Paul.

The Bell Curse. Haslett, D W.

The Morality of Human Gene Patents. Resnik, David B.

The Return of the Group. Sterelny, Kim.

Who Benefits? Why Personal Identity Does Not Matter in a Moral Evaluation of Germ-Line Gene Therapy. Holtug, Nils.

# GENEALOGY

"Two Walks" in *Critical Studies: Ethics and the Subject,* Simms, Karl (ed). Wheeler, Wendy.

"Wholeness in Manifoldness: Genealogical Methods and Conditions of Agency in Nietzsche and Foucault" in *Critical Studies: Ethics and the Subject,* Simms, Karl (ed). Phillips, Lisa.

Emancipatory Social Science: Habermas on Nietzsche. Kerckhove, Lee.

Modernity, Postmodernity and Transmodernity: Hope in Search of Time (in Spanish). Mendieta, Eduardo.

Nietzsche's Dynamite: The Biography of Modern Nihilism. Roodt, Vasti.

Sex, Gender, Sexuality: Can Ethologists Practice Genealogy?. Gatens, Moira.

The Dance of Dependency: A Genealogy of Domestic Violence Discourse. Ferraro, Kathleen J.

The Normative Force of Genealogy in Ethics. Lekan, Todd.

The Progression and Regression of Slave Morality in Nietzsche's *Genealogy:* The Moralization of Bad Conscience and Indebtedness. Lindstedt, David.

Writing in Blood: On the Prejudices of Genealogy. Conway, Daniel W.

# GENERAL RELATIVITY

Conceptions of Space—Time: Problems and Possible Solutions. Monk, Nicholas A M.

Modern Essentialism and the Problem of Individuation of Spacetime Points. Bartels, Andreas.

Resolving Discordant Results: Modern Solar Oblateness Experiments. Richman, Sam.

# GENERAL WELFARE

Can Democracy Promote the General Welfare?. Buchanan, James M.

# GENERAL WILL

De la volonté générale et des lois. Morissette, Yves.

# GENERALIZATION

see also Induction

Confirming Universal Generalizations. Zabell, S L.

Sticking Up for Oedipus: Fodor on Intentional Generalizations and Broad Content. Arjo, Dennis.

# GENERALIZED

Generalized Nonsplitting in the Recursively Enumerable Degrees. Leonhardi, Steven D.

Generalized Quantification as Substructural Logic. Alechina, Natasha and Van Lambalgen, Michiel.

Generalized Rough Sets (Preclusivity Fuzzy-Intuitionistic (BZ) Lattices). Cattaneo, Gianpiero.

Nominal Comparatives and Generalized Quantifiers. Nerbonne, John.

On a Decidable Generalized Quantifier Logic Corresponding to a Decidable Fragment of First-Order Logic. Alechina, Natasha.

Relativized Logspace and Generalized Quantifiers Over Finite Ordered Structures. Gottlob, Georg.

The Hierarchy Theorem for Generalized Quantifiers. Hella, Lauri, Luosto, Kerkko and Väänänen, Jouko.

# GENERATION

Rawl's Just Savings Principle and the Sense of Justice. Paden, Roger.

Reference and Imperfective Paradox. Graves, P R.

# GENERIC

A Non-Generic Real Incompatible with $0^{\#}$. Stanley, M C.

# GENEROSITY

*The Logic of the Gift: Toward an Ethic of Generosity.* Schrift, Alan D (ed).

Du bon sens le mieux partagé.... Lories, Danielle.

# GENESIS

*Genese und Analyse.* Petrus, Klaus.

Origen and Augustin on the *Hexaemeron* (in Czech). Heidl, György.

Origen's First Homily on the Book of Genesis (in Hungarian). Heidl, György.

# GENETIC ENGINEERING

"Genethik" in *Angewandte Ethik: Die Bereichsethiken und ihre theoretische Fundierung,* Nida-Rümelin, Julian (ed). Irrgang, Bernhard.

*Improving Nature?.* Reiss, Michael J and Straughan, Roger.

Genetic Engineering and Environmental Ethics. Dobson, Andrew.

Karl Rahner and Genetic Engineering: The Use of Theological Principles in Moral Analysis. Kelly, David F.

L'embrione è arrivato tra noi. Viano, Carlo Augusto.

# GENETIC EPISTEMOLOGY

Zum Stellenwert der *Grundlage* aus der Sicht von 1804: Eine Interpretation des Wechsels von analytisch-synthetischer und genetischer Methode in Kapitel 5 der *Grundlage.* Beeler-Port, Josef.

## GEOMETRY

Fichtes *geometrische* Semantik. Jergius, Holger.

Formalization of Hilbert's Geometry of Incidence and Parallelism. Von Plato, Jan.

Fractal Images of Formal Systems. Grim, Patrick and St. Denis, Paul.

From Completeness to Archimedean Completeness: An Essay in the Foundations of Euclidean Geometry. Ehrlich, Philip.

G.W. Leibniz: *Geschichte des Kontinuumproblems*. Luna Alcoba, Manuel.

Hilbert and Set Theory. Dreben, Burton and Kanamori, Akihiro.

Hilbert's Formalism and Arithmetization of Mathematics. Webb, Judson C.

Hobbes's Political Geometry. Valentine, Jeremy.

Immanuel Kants Grundlegung der Arithmetik. Noske, Rainer.

Isaac Barrow on the Mathematization of Nature: Theological Voluntarism and the Rise of Geometrical Optics. Malet, Antoni.

Kant's Theory of Geometrical Reasoning and the Analytic-Synthetic Distinction: On Hintikka's Interpretation of Kant's Philosophy of Mathematics. De Jong, Willem R.

Kennzeichnungen der Räume konstanter Krümmung. Süssmann, Georg.

La demostración "more geometrico": notas para la historia de una exploración. Vega, Luis.

Locke's Geometrical Analogy. Stuart, Matthew.

Michel Serres (in Hebrew). Wohlman, Avital.

Protowissenschaft und Rekonstruktion. Hartmann, Dirk.

Strongly Minimal Fusions of Vector Spaces. Holland, Kitty L.

The Method of the Geometer: A New Angle on Husserl's Cartesianism. Kasely, Terry S.

The Philosophical and Methodological Thought of N. I. Lobachevsky. Perminov, V Ya.

The Semantic of Linear Perspective. Turner, Norman.

Über das Verhältnis von Algebra und Geometrie in Descartes'"Geometrie". Krämer, Sybille.

Whewell on the Ultimate Problem of Philosophy. Morrison, Margaret.

## GEORGE, R

Did Jesus Commit a Fallacy?. Hitchcock, David.

## GERARD OF CREMONA

Métodos y cuestiones filosóficas en la Escuela de Traductores de Toledo. Brasa Díaz, Mariano.

## GERGONNE, J

Extended Gergonne Syllogisms. Johnson, Fred.

## GERMAN

"Chemie und Philosophie: Anmerkungen zur Entwicklung des Gebietes in der Geschichte der DDR" in *Philosophie der Chemie: Bestandsaufnahme und Ausblick*, Schummer, Joachim (ed). Laitko, Hubert.

"Constructing Modernism: The Cultural Location of *Aufbau*" in *Origins of Logical Empiricism*, Giere, Ronald N (ed). Galison, Peter.

"Die Theorie der Urteilsformen in der deutschen Schullogik des 19.Jahrhunderts" in *Das weite Spektrum der analytischen Philosophie*, Lenzen, Wolfgang. Stuhlmann-Laeisz, Rainer.

"Gedanken vor einem Jubiläum" in *Grenzen der kritischen Vernunft*, Schmid, Peter A. Fontius, Martin.

"Nineteenth-Century Würzburg: The Development of the Scientific Approach to Philosophy" in *In Itinere* European Cities and the Birth of Modern Scientific Philosophy, Poli, Roberto (ed). Baumgartner, Wilhelm.

"Nueva religión: Un proyecto del Idealismo alemán" in *El inicio del Idealismo alemán*, Market, Oswaldo. Carmo Ferreira, Manuel J do.

"Observaciones críticas al Idealismo alemán en el bicentenario del "Fundamento de toda la Doctrina de la Ciencia" 1794, de J. G. Fichte" in *El inicio del Idealismo alemán*, Market, Oswaldo. Riobó González, Manuel.

"Philosophy and Art in Munich Around the Turn of the Century" in *In Itinere* European Cities and the Birth of Modern Scientific Philosophy, Poli, Roberto (ed). Schuhmann, Karl.

"Seyn" y "Ur-teilung" in *El inicio del Idealismo alemán*, Market, Oswaldo. Martínez Marzoa, Felipe.

"Theories of Questions in German-Speaking Philosophy" in *Knowledge and Inquiry: Essays on Jaakko Hintikka's Epistemology and Philosophy of Science*, Sintonen, Matti (ed). Kusch, Martin.

"Tierethik II: Zu den ethischen Grundlagen des Deutschen Tierschutzgesetzes" in *Angewandte Ethik: Die Bereichsethiken und ihre theoretische Fundierung*, Nida-Rümelin, Julian (ed). Nida-Rümelin, Julian and Von der Pfordten, Dietmar.

*Der Deutsche Idealismus (Fichte, Schelling, Hegel) und die philosophische Problemlage der Gegenwart*. Heidegger, Martin.

*El inicio del Idealismo alemán*. Market, Oswaldo and Rivera de Rosales, Jacinto.

*Figuring the Self: Subject, Absolute, and Others in Classical German Philosophy*. Zöller, Günter (ed) and Klemm, David E (ed).

*From Romanticism to Critical Theory: The Philosophy of German Literary Theory*. Bowie, Andrew.

*Individuality and Expression: The Aesthetics of the New German Dance, 1908-1936*. Howe, Dianne S.

*The Course of Remembrance and Other Essays on Hölderlin*. Henrich, Dieter and Förster, Eckart (ed).

A Note on the Concept of Alienation. Mohanta, Dilip Kumar.

Austrian Philosophy: The Legacy of Franz Brentano. Brandl, Johannes.

Civil Society Ethics: An Approach from K-O Apel's Philosophy (in Spanish). Durán Casas, Vicente.

Deutsche Aufklärung und französiche *Lumières*. D'Hondt, Jacques.

Ethical Reflections on the Status of the Preimplantation Embryo Leading to the German Embryo Protection Act. Michelmann, H W and Hinney, B.

Experience and the Postmodern Spirit. McCarty, Luise Prior.

Fichte und die Metaphysik des deutschen Idealismus. Jimérez-Redondo, Manuel.

Frederick Engels: Scholar and Revolutionary. Labica, Georges.

German Concord, German Discord: Two Concepts of a Nation and the Challenge of Multiculturalism. Thomä, Dieter.

Heideggers Wende zum Deutschen Idealismus. Strube, Claudius.

Horstmann, Siep, and German Idealism. Pippin, Robert B.

Indoctrination and Moral Reasoning: A Comparison between Dutch and East German Students. De Mey, Langha and Schulze, Hans-Joachim.

L'Allemagne, la modernité, la pensée. Bouckaert, Bertrand.

Linguistic Relativity in French, English, and German Philosophy. Harvey, William.

Naturphilosophie zwischen Naturwissenschaft und Philosophie: Neue Sammelbände zur Naturphilosophie des deutschen Idealismus. Ziche, Paul.

Neighbors in Death. Crowell, Steven Galt.

O Mais Antigo Programa de Sistema do Idealismo Alemao. Carmo Ferreira, Manuel J do.

Persona Politica: Unity and Difference in Edith Stein's Political Philosophy. Calcagno, Antonio.

Perspektiven der Welt: Vielfalt und Einheit im Weltbild der Deutschen Romantik. Köchy, Kristian.

Philosophy of Science and the German Idealists. Clayton, Philip.

Recordando a M. Heidegger. Wagner de Reyna, Alberto.

Ricordo e oblio: La Germania dopo le sconfitte nelle due guerre mondiali. Nolte, Ernst.

Should We Pardon Them?. Hobart, Ann and Jankélévitch, Vladimir.

Sobre Hölderlin y los comienzos del Idealismo alemán. Serrano Marín, Vicente.

Socialist Socrates: Ernst Bloch in the GDR. Ernst, Anna-Sabine and Klinger, Gerwin.

The Greens and the Lust for Power. Sternstein, Wolfgang.

The Suppressed Legacy of Nuremberg. Burt, Robert A.

The Vienna Circle and German Speaking Culture Before and After World War II. Linsky, Bernard.

Thomas Abbt and the Formation of an Enlightened German "Public". Redekop, Benjamin W.

Vico en Italia y en Alemania. Sevilla Fernández, José M.

Was heisst es: einen philosophischen Text historisch lesen?. Flasch, Kurt.

## GESTALT

*A Defense of the Given*. Fales, Evan.

## GETTIER, E

Is Nondefectively Justified True Belief Knowledge?. Jacquette, Dale.

Two Notions of Warrant and Plantinga's Solution to the Gettier Problem. Greene, Richard and Balmert, N.A..

Un análisis lógico del problema de Gettier. Díez-Picazo, Gustavo Fernández.

Warrant and Accidentally True Belief. Plantinga, Alvin.

## GEWIRTH, A

Gewirth und die Begründung der normativen Ethik. Steigleder, Klaus.

Reason Without Reasons: A Critique of Alan Gewirth's Moral Philosophy. Kramer, Matthew H and Simmonds, Nigel E.

## GHOSH, R

Melody in Life: Some Reflections. Roy, Subrata.

## GIBBARD, A

"A Mind-Body Problem at the Surface of Objects" in *Perception*, Villanueva, Enrique (ed). Johnston, Mark.

Appropriate Guilt: Between Expansion and Limitations (in Dutch). Van den Beld, A.

Can Edgington Gibbard Counterfactuals?. Morton, Adam.

Non-Cognitivism, Truth and Logic. Wedgwood, Ralph.

Truth, Objectivity, Counterfactuals and Gibbard. Edgington, Dorothy.

## GIBSON, R

"Reply to Gibson, Byrne, and Brandom" in *Perception*, Villanueva, Enrique (ed). McDowell, John.

## GIDDENS, A

Practices and Actions: A Wittgensteinian Critique of Bourdieu and Giddens. Schatzki, Theodore R.

The Epistemological Argument Against Socialism: A Wittgensteinian Critique of Hayek and Giddens. Pleasants, Nigel.

## GIERE, R

Instrumental Rationality and Naturalized Philosophy of Science. Siegel, Harvey.

Reply to Commentaries. Gopnik, Alison.

## GIFT

*The Logic of the Gift: Toward an Ethic of Generosity*. Schrift, Alan D (ed).

Given Time and the Gift of Life. Protevi, John.

## GILES OF ROME

1277 Revisited: A New Interpretation of the Doctrinal Investigations of Thomas Aquinas and Giles of Rome. Thijssen, J M M H.

## GILL, D

A Reply to David Keyt and David Gill. Miller Jr, Fred D.

**GOD**

"John E. Smith and Metaphysics" in *Reason, Experience, and God: John E. Smith in Dialogue*, Colapietro, Vincent M. Neville, Robert Cummings.

"John Howe: dissidente, neoplatonico e antispinozista" in *Mind Senior to the World*, Baldi, Marialuisa. Simonutti, Luisa.

"L'*Account of the Nature and the Extent of the Divine Dominion and Goodnesses* di Samuel Parker: dalla teologia alla filosofia politica" in *Mind Senior to the World*, Baldi, Marialuisa. Lupoli, Agostino.

"L'europeizzazione come problema europeo" in *Geofilosofia*, Bonesio, Luisa (ed). Pöggler, Otto.

"L'Italia in Bayle, Bayle in Italia: una ricerca mancata" in *Pierre Bayle e l'Italia*, Bianchi, Lorenzo. Borghero, Carlo.

"Living Reason: A Critical Exposition of John E. Smith's Re-Envisioning of Human Rationality" in *Reason, Experience, and God: John E. Smith in Dialogue*, Colapietro, Vincent M. Colapietro, Vincent M.

"Metaphysics, Experience, Being, and God: Response to Robert C. Neville" in *Reason, Experience, and God: John E. Smith in Dialogue*, Colapietro, Vincent M. Smith, John E.

"Origenismo e anti-agostinismo in Jean Le Clerc diffusore della cultura inglese" in *Mind Senior to the World*, Baldi, Marialuisa. Sina, Mario.

"Responses" in *Reason, Experience, and God: John E. Smith in Dialogue*, Colapietro, Vincent M. Smith, John E.

"Samuel Clarke's Four Categories of Deism, Isaac Newton, and the Bible" in *Scepticism in the History of Philosophy: A Pan-American Dialogue*, Popkin, Richard H (ed). Force, James E.

"Triangulating Divine Will: Henry More, Robert Boyle, and René Descartes on God's Relationship to the Creation" in *Mind Senior to the World*, Baldi, Marialuisa. Osler, Margaret J.

*A Free Enquiry into the Vulgarly Received Notion of Nature*. Davis, Edward B (ed), Hunter, Michael (ed) and Boyle, Robert.

*Advice to the Serious Seeker: Meditations on the Teaching of Frithjof Schuon*. Cutsinger, James S.

*Alciphron oder der Kleine Philosoph*. Berkeley, George.

*Analytic Theism, Hartshorne, and the Concept of God*. Dombrowski, Daniel A.

*Arguing for Atheism: An Introduction to the Philosophy of Religion*. Le Poidevin, Robin.

*Assoluto: Frammenti di misticismo nella filosofia di Francis Herbert Bradley*. Taroni, Paolo.

*Atheistic Humanism*. Flew, Antony.

*Can We Be Good without God?: A Conversation about Truth, Morality, Culture & A Few Other Things That Matter*. Chamberlain, Paul.

*Compelling Knowledge: A Feminist Proposal for an Epistemology of the Cross*. Solberg, Mary M.

*Democracy and the "Kingdom of God"*. Kainz, Howard.

*Die Leidenschaft der Erkenntnis: Philosophie und ästhetische Lebensgestaltung bei Nietzsche von Morgenröthe bis Also sprach Zarathustra*. Brusotti, Marco.

*Dio e il male*. Possenti, Vittorio.

*Does God Exist?: A Dialogue*. Moody, Todd C.

*Emmanuel Levinas: Basic Philosophical Writings*. Peperzak, Adriaan Theodoor (ed), Critchley, Simon (ed) and Bernasconi, Robert (ed).

*Empire of the Gods: The Liberation of Eros*. Davies, James W.

*Ex Possibili et Necessario: A Re-Examination of Aquinas's Third Way*. Kelly, Thomas A F.

*Exploring Unseen Worlds: William James and the Philosophy of Mysticism*. Barnard, G William.

*Facets of Faith and Science Volume 3: The Role of Beliefs in the Natural Sciences*. Van der Meer, Jitse M (ed).

*Facets of Faith and Science Volume 4: Interpreting God's Action in the World*. Van der Meer, Jitse M (ed).

*Fact, Value, and God*. Holmes, Arthur F.

*God*. Robinson, Timothy A (ed).

*Heaven's Champion: William James's Philosophy of Religion*. Suckiel, Ellen Kappy.

*Hofmann-Streit: il dibattito sul rapporto tra filosofia e teologia all'Università di Helmstedt*. Antognazza, Maria Rosa.

*Hume on Miracles*. Tweyman, Stanley (ed).

*Kierkegaard and Nietzsche: Faith and Eternal Acceptance*. Kellenberger, J.

*La Volontà di Potenza in Nietzsche e la Storia dell'Europa negli Ultimi Tempi*. Manno, Ambrogio Giacomo.

*Meditations on First Philosophy: With Selections from the Objections and Replies*. Cottingham, John and Descartes, René.

*Metaphysical Animal: Divine and Human in Man*. Woznicki, Andrew Nicholas.

*Mind Senior to the World*. Baldi, Marialuisa.

*Nicholas of Cusa: Selected Spiritual Writings*. Bond, H Lawrence (trans).

*Pierre Bayle e l'Italia*. Bianchi, Lorenzo.

*Presupposti filosofici dell'enciclica Veritatis splendor*. Gigante, Mario.

*Primeras Interpretaciones del Mundo en la Modernidad: Descartes y Leibniz*. Schneider, Martin.

*Reason, Experience, and God: John E. Smith in Dialogue*. Colapietro, Vincent M.

*Religion and Science: Historical and Contemporary Issues*. Barbour, Ian G.

*Spinoza and the Ethics*. Lloyd, Genevieve.

*The Annual of the Society of Christian Ethics with Cumulative Index*. Beckley, Harlan (ed).

*The Anselmian Approach to God and Creation*. Rogers, Katherin A.

*The Case for Freewill Theism: A Philosophical Assessment*. Basinger, David.

*The God of Spinoza*. Mason, Richard.

*The God Within: Kant, Schelling, and Historicity*. Burbidge, John W (ed) and Fackenheim, Emil L.

*The Human Constitution*. Regan, Richard J (trans).

*The Living God: Schleiermacher's Theological Appropriation of Spinoza*. Lamm, Julia A.

*The Metaphysics of Theism: Aquinas's Natural Theology in Summa contra gentiles I*. Kretzmann, Norman.

*The Mind of God and the Works of Man*. Craig, Edward.

*The Neoplatonic Metaphysics and Epistemology of Anselm of Canterbury*. Rogers, Katherin A.

*Theories of Cognition in the Later Middle Ages*. Pasnau, Robert.

A Critical Examination of Schleiermacher's Interpretation of Self-Consciousness. Lang'at, Wilson K A.

A Criticism of Leibniz's Views on the Ontological Argument. Silva, José R.

A Divina Natureza Segundo Escoto Eriúgena. Blanc, Mafalda de Faria.

A New Argument against Pascal (in Hebrew). Zemach, Eddy M.

A New Look at the Cosmological Argument. Koons, Robert C.

A Pessoa e o Seu Universo. Neves, Maria do Céu Patrao.

A Reply to Professor Hick. Van Inwagen, Peter.

A Response to John Hick. Mavrodes, George I.

A Theological Escape from the Cartesian Circle?. Dalton, Peter.

Ad Hick. Plantinga, Alvin.

All Existing is the Action of God: The Philosophical Theology of David Braine. Bradshaw, David.

Amor e Morte: Meditaçao Antropológica. Pinto, José Rui da Costa.

An African American Looks at Death. Secundy, Marian Gray.

Analytische Religionsphilosophie: Zwischen Intersubjektivität und Esoterik. Runggaldier, Edmund.

Apparence et fausseté: la double nature de l'ordre politique chez Pascal. Spitz, Jean-Fabien.

As the Waters Cover the Sea: John Wesley on the Problem of Evil. Walls, Jerry L.

Augustinian Wisdom and the Law of the Heart. Littlejohn, Murray.

Axiological Foundations of "Human Dignity" (Spanish). Sánchez, Angel Martín.

Barth on Evil. Wolterstorff, Nicholas.

Barth on the Divine 'Conscription' of Language. Richards, Jay Wesley.

Beauty and Technology as Paradigms for the Moral Life. Brown, Montague.

Belief, Foreknowledge, and Theological Fatalism. Hughes, Charles T.

Believing That God Exists Because the Bible Says So. Lamont, John.

Berkeley on the Work of the Six Days. Cates, Lynn D.

Beyond the Sovereignty of Good. Nelson, Ralph C.

Bishop Stephen Tempier and Thomas Aquinas: A Separate Process Against Aquinas?. Wippel, John F.

Bits of Broken Glass: Zora Neale Hurston's Conception of the Self. Sartwell, Crispin.

Bolstering the Argument from Non-Belief. Cosculluela, Victor.

Brevi Riflessioni Filosofiche sulla Storicità dell'Uomo. Seidl, Horst.

Buddhism as Radical Religion. Seidel, George J.

Can God Change His Mind?. Guleserian, Theodore.

Can One be Cognitively Conscious of God?. Baxter, Anthony.

Catholic Social Ethics in a Pluralist Age. Chmielewski, Philip J.

Christendom en fenomenologie. Bernet, Rudolf.

Clearing a 'Way' for Aquinas: How the Proof from Motion Concludes to God. Twetten, David B.

Concurrentism or Occasionalism?. Vallicella, William.

Confession of Sin: A Catharsis!. Kakade, R M.

Connatural Knowledge. Thomas, James.

Conservatives, Liberals, and the Colonized: Ontological Reflections. Allan, George.

Contingency of Being—Argument for the Existence of God: Attempt at Critical Analysis Part I (in Polish). Zieminski, Ireneusz.

Conversazione con Cornelio Fabro. Burghi, Giancarlo.

Cosmological Mysticism: The Imitation of the Heavenly Bodies in Ibn Tufayl's Hayy ibn Yaqzan. Brague, Rémi.

Criticismo trascendentale, trascendenza, religione. Jacobelli, Angela Maria Isoldi.

Das "Ich" des ersten Grundsatzes der GWL in der Sicht der Wissenschaftslehre von 1804. Girndt, Helmut.

Das philosophieimmanente Theodizeeproblem und seine theologische Radikalisierung. Schmidt, Josef.

Das Problem des Übels in Richard Swinburnes Religionsphilosophie: Über Sinn und Grenzen seines theistischen Antwortversuches auf das Problem des Übels und dessen Bedeutung für die Theologie. Wiertz, Oliver.

Das Verhältnis des Selbst zu Gott in Fichtes Wissenschaftslehre. Omine, Akira.

De la criatura a Dios: La demostración de la existencia de Dios en la primera dimensión del abandono del límite mental. Piá Tarazona, Salvador.

Deification in the Summa Theologiae: A Structural Interpretation of the Prima Pars. Williams, A N.

Descartes on Causation. Flage, Daniel E and Bonnen, Clarence A.

**GOD**

## GOOD

Sources of Virtue: The Market and the Community. Shaw, Bill.

The *Real* Problem of No Best World. Howard-Snyder, Frances and Howard-Snyder, Daniel.

The Aesthetically Good vs. The Morally Good. Davenport, Manuel.

The Five Ways and the Argument from Composition: A Reply to John Lamont. Côté, Antoine.

The Limited Unity of Virtue. Badhwar, Neera Kapur.

The Problem of Moral Absolutes in the Ethics of Vladimir Solov'ëv. Sergeevich Pugachev, Oleg.

The Rejection of Objective Consequentialism. Howard-Snyder, Frances.

The Right and the Good. Thomson, Judith Jarvis.

The Role of Good Upbringing in Aristotle's *Ethics*. Vasiliou, Iakovos.

Universalism and the Greater Good: A Response to Talbott. Knight, Gordon.

Well-Being: On a Fundamental Concept of Practical Philosophy. Seel, Martin.

What Exactly Is the Good of Self-Deception?. Putman, Daniel A.

What Good is Consciousness?. Dretske, Fred.

What is the Good of Health Care?. Harris, John.

What Makes a Good Death?. Callahan, Daniel.

What should we Treat as an End in Itself?. Dean, Richard.

Writing in Blood: On the Prejudices of Genealogy. Conway, Daniel W.

Yvon Quiniou, il materialismo e l'impossibile immoralismo di Nietzsche. Franco, Vittoria.

## GOOD LIFE

*Morality and the Good Life.* Moser, Paul K (ed) and Carson, Thomas L (ed).

La fragilità del bene: Fortuna ed etica nella tragedia e nella filosofia greca di Martha C. Nussbaum. Berti, Enrico, Conant, James and Vegetti, Mario.

Oltre MacIntyre, a Proposito di: Quale Impostazione per la Filosofia Morale?. Crosti, Massimo.

On Reconciliation and Respect, Justice and the Good Life: Response to Herta Nagl-Docekal and Rainer Forst. Benhabib, Seyla.

## GOODMAN, N

"Die Goodman-Paradoxie: ein Invarianz—und Relevanzproblem" in *Das weite Spektrum der analytischen Philosophie,* Lenzen, Wolfgang. Schurz, Gerhard.

Analog Representation Beyond Mental Imagery. Blachowicz, James.

Anything Goes: Goodman on Relevant Kinds. Pierson, Robert.

Exemplifikatorische Darstellung: Zu den Grundlagen einer kognitiven Ästhetik. Taube, Volkmar.

Goodman's Rejection of Resemblance. Files, Craig.

Interpretive Pluralism and the Ontology of Art. Davies, David.

Musical Works, Improvisation, and the Principle of Continuity. Brown, Lee B.

On (Virtuous?) Circles of Concepts in Goodman—and Quine. Read, Rupert.

Realism, Supervenience, and Irresolvable Aesthetic Disputes. Bender, John W.

Reciprocal Justification in Science and Moral Theory. Blachowicz, James.

Reflections on Iconicity, Representation, and Resemblance: Peirce's Theory of Signs, Goodmann on Resemblance, and Modern Philosophies of Language and Mind. Dipert, Randall R.

The Self Well Lost: Psychotherapeutic Interpretation and Nelson Goodman's Irrealism. Mehl, Peter J.

## GOODNESS

"L'*Account of the Nature and the Extent of the Divine Dominion and Goodnesses* di Samuel Parker: dalla teologia alla filosofia politica" in *Mind Senior to the World,* Baldi, Marialuisa. Lupoli, Agostino.

"Nothing and Nothing Else" in *The Ancients and the Moderns,* Lilly, Reginald (ed). Marion, Jean-Luc.

Metaphilosophy and Free Will. Double, Richard.

Glück und Glas... Martha Nussbaum über die Zerbrechlichkeit des Guten im menschlichen Leben. Frede, Dorothea.

Goodness: Aristotle and the Moderns: A Sketch. Santas, Gerasimos.

Grading Worlds. Menssen, Sandra.

Intelligibility and the Ethical. Miller, Jerome A.

Of *Goodness* and *Healthiness*: A Viable Moral Ontology. Bloomfield, Paul.

The Interpretation of Aquinas's *Prima Secundae*. Doig, James C.

## GOODWILL

Piccolo mondo antico: appunti sul problema dell'identificazione del soggetto morale. Pievatolo, Maria Chiara.

Trust as an Affective Attitude. Jones, Karen.

Useful Friendships: A Foundation for Business Ethics. Sommers, Mary Catherine.

## GOPNIK, A

Child's Play. Nersessian, Nancy J.

Commentary on Alison Gopnik's "The Scientist As Child". Solomon, Miriam.

Science and Core Knowledge. Carey, Susan and Spelke, Elizabeth.

Science As Child's Play: Tales from the Crib. Fine, Arthur.

The Scientist as Adult. Giere, Ronald N.

## GORANKO, V

Logics of Rejection: Two Systems of Natural Deduction. Tamminga, Allard M.

## GORDON, E

Evaluating Edwin Gordon's Music Learning Theory from a Critical Thinking Perspective. Woodford, Paul G.

Is Edwin Gordon's Learning Theory a Cognitive One?. Stokes, W Ann.

## GORDON, L

Existential Phenomenology and the Problem of Race: A Critical Assessment of Lewis Gordon's *Bad Faith and Antiblack Racism.* Headley, Clevis R.

## GORDON, V

Commentary on "Family Dynamics and Children in Medical Research". Robinson, Walter.

## GORGIAS

Gorgias, *On Non-Existence*: Sextus Empiricus. *Against the Logicians* 1.65-87, Translated from the Greek Text in Hermann Diels's *Die Fragmente der Vorsokratiker.* McComiskey, Bruce.

Interpreting Gorgias's "Being" in *On Not-Being or On Nature.* Schiappa, Edward.

Knowledge and Discourse in Gorgias's *On the Non-Existent or On Nature.* Gaines, Robert N.

On the Not-Being of Gorgias's *On Not-Being* (ONB). Gagarin, Michael.

The Letter and the Spirit of the Text: Two Translations of Gorgias's *On Non-Being or On Nature* (MXG). Poulakos, John.

Translating Gorgias in [Aristotle] 980a10. Davis, Janet B.

## GOSPEL

*The Christian Case for Virtue Ethics.* Kotva, Joseph J.

Petri Iohannis Olivi Tractatus de Verbo (Peter John Olivi's Tractatus de Verbo). Pasnau, Robert.

## GOTT, J

A Shooting-Room View of Doomsday. Eckhardt, William.

## GOUHIER, H

Étienne Gilson's Early Study of Nicolas Malebranche. Fafara, Richard J.

## GOULD, S

Darwinism, Process Structuralism, and Natural Kinds. Griffiths, Paul E.

Gould on Laws in Biological Science. McIntyre, Lee.

## GOVERNMENT

*see also* Anarchism

*Values and the Social Order.* Radnitzky, Gerard (ed).

Aboriginal Right: A Conciliatory Concept. Morito, Bruce.

Administrative Lies and Philosopher-Kings. Simpson, David.

Business Ethics and Politics in China. Steidlmeier, Paul.

Business Ethics in the Former Soviet Union: A Report. Neimanis, George J.

Can Foreign Aid Be Used to Promote Good Government in Developing Countries?. Moore, Mick and Robinson, Mark.

Coercion: Description or Evaluation?. Greene, Jennifer K.

Elements of Democratic Justice. Shapiro, Ian.

Eliminating the Barriers to Employment Equity in the Canadian Workplace. Falkenberg, L E and Boland, L.

Ethics in Government: A Survey of Misuse of Position for Personal Gain and Its Implications for Developing Acquisition Strategy. McCampbell, Atefeh Sadri and Rood, Tina L.

Freedom of Expression at the National Endowment for the Arts: An Opportunity for Interdisciplinary Education. Van Camp, Julie.

Global Responsibility and Active Ethical Advocacy (No Apology for Academic Activism). Shrader-Frechette, Kristin.

Government, the Press, and the People's Right to Know. Montague, Phillip.

Putting the Technological into Government. Dean, Mitchell.

The Contradictions of Free Market Doctrine: Is There a Solution?. McMurtry, John.

The Federal Role in Influencing Research Ethics Education and Standards in Science. Dustira, Alicia K.

The United States and the Genocide Convention: Leading Advocate and Leading Obstacle. Korey, William.

World Order: Maritain and Now. MacGuigan, Mark R.

## GRACE

"Pierre Bayle nell'*Index librorum prohibitorum*: I decreti di proibizione delle *Nouvelles de la République des Lettres...*" in *Pierre Bayle e l'Italia,* Bianchi, Lorenzo. Canone, Eugenio.

Aspiring to the Divine: Love and Grace. Mahoney, Timothy A.

Flesh, Grace and Spirit: Metempsychosis and Resurrection from Porphyry to Saint Augustine (in French). Dubreucq, Eric.

La cuestión de lo Incondicionado: Dialéctica y revelación de lo sagrado en Paul Tillich. Pastor, Félix-Alejandro.

Quasi-Formal Causality, or the Other-in-Me: Rahner and Lévinas. Purcell, Michael.

Self-Esteem, Moral Luck, and the Meaning of Grace. Fry, Jeffrey P.

Tolerance as Grace and as Right (in Hebrew). Yovel, Yirmiyahu.

## GRACIA, J

Acerca de "Una teoría de la textualidad". Topuzian, Carlos Marcelo.

## GRADING

On Grading Apples and Arguments. Mendenhall, Vance.

## GRADUATE

"Graduate Students: Too Many and Too Narrow?" in *The American University: National Treasure or Endangered Species?,* Ehrenberg, Ronald G (ed). Fox, Marye Anne.

## GRAHAM, A

Kung-sun Lung on the Point of Pointing: The Moral Rhetoric of Names. Lai, Whalen.

Mencius on *Jen-Hsing*. Shun, Kwong-loi.

## GRAMMAR

"Il linguaggio mentale tra logica e grammatica nel medioevo: il contesto di Ockam" in *Momenti di Storia della Logica e di Storia della Filosofia*, Guetti, Carla (ed). Maierù, Alfonso.

"Philosophy as Grammar" in *The Cambridge Companion to Wittgenstein*, Sluga, Hans (ed). Garver, Newton.

"The Grammar of Chomsky is not Mentalist" in *Verdad: lógica, representación y mundo*, Villegas Forero, L. Peris-Viñé, Luis M.

*Critical Studies: Language and the Subject.* Simms, Karl (ed).

*Hermeneutics and the Rhetorical Tradition.* Eden, Kathy.

A Critique of the Minimalist Program. Johnson, David E and Lappin, Shalom.

Arqueologia da Gramática Geral: O Estatuto da Linguagem no Saber da idade Clássica. Matos de Noronha, Nelson.

Characterization of the Basic Notions of Chomsky's Grammar (in Spanish). Peris-Viñé, Luis M.

Chomsky tra linguistica e filosofia: A proposito di R. Raggiunti, La "Conoscenza del linguaggio" e il mito della grammatica universale. Costa, Filippo.

Does the Grammar of Seeing Aspects Imply a Kantian Concept?. Kanthamani, A.

Dynamic Interpretations of Constraint-Based Grammar Formalisms. Moss, Lawrence S and Johnson, David E.

Extending Lambek Grammars to Basic Categorial Grammars. Buszkowski, Wojciech.

Fibred Semantics for Feature-Based Grammar Logic. Dörre, Jochen, König, Esther and Gabbay, Dov.

Higher Order Unification and the Interpretation of Focus. Pulman, Stephen G.

Identification in the Limit of Categorial Grammars. Kanazawa, Makoto.

Images of Identity: In Search of Modes of Presentation. Millikan, Ruth Garrett.

Kein Etwas, aber auch nicht ein Nichts!: Kann die Grammatik tatsächlich täuschen?. Gaskin, Richard.

Melo Bacelar, Filósofo da "Grammatica" na Lexicografia de Setecentos. Torres, Amadeu.

Multimodal Linguistic Inference. Moortgat, Michael.

Note su conoscenza e grammatica. Marletti, Carlo.

Parsing If-Sentences and the Conditions of Sentencehood. Barker, Stephen J.

Product-Free Lambek Calculus and Context-Free Grammars. Pentus, Mati.

Syntactic Codes and Grammar Refinement. Kracht, Marcus.

The Logical Problem of Language Acquisition. Cowie, Fiona.

Theology as Grammar. Brenner, William H.

Tree Models and (Labeled) Categorial Grammar. Venema, Yde.

## GRAMSCI, A

"Una Relación entre Diferentes: Ortega y Gasset y Gramsci" in *Política y Sociedad en José Ortega y Gasset: En Torno a "Vieja y Nueva Política"*, Lopez de la Vieja, Maria Teresa (ed). Calvo Salamanca, Clara.

*Antonio Gramsci Prison Notebooks: Volume II.* Buttigieg, Joseph A (ed & trans).

Gramsci, teórico de la superestructura. Giglioli, Giovanna.

Gramscianismus in der Internationalen Politischen Ökonomie. Bieling, Hans-Jürgen and Deppe, Frank.

Hegemony and the Crisis of Legitimacy in Gramsci. Martin, James.

Instead of Leaders They Have Become Bankers of Men: Gramsci's Alternative to the U.S. Neoinstitutionalists' Theory of Trade-Union Bureaucratization. Devinatz, Victor G.

O Sentido do Trabalho como Principio Educativo na Concepçao Gramsciana. Mazza Farias, Itamar.

## GRANGER, G

The Heritage of Léon Brunschvicg (and Commentary by P. Horák) (in Czech). Rivenc, François and Horák, Petr.

## GRANT, G

*George Grant and the Subversion of Modernity: Art, Philosophy, Politics, Religion, and Education.* Davis, Arthur (ed).

## GRAPH

"A Decision Method for Existential Graphs" in *Studies in the Logic of Charles Sanders Peirce*, Houser, Nathan (ed). Roberts, Don D.

"A Tarski-Style Semantics for Peirce's Beta Graphs" in *The Rule of Reason: The Philosophy of Charles Sanders Peirce*, Forster, Paul (ed). Burch, Robert W.

"Genuine Triads and Teridentity" in *Studies in the Logic of Charles Sanders Peirce*, Houser, Nathan (ed). Brunning, Jacqueline.

"Matching Logical Structure to Linguistic Structure" in *Studies in the Logic of Charles Sanders Peirce*, Houser, Nathan (ed). Sowa, John F.

"Peirce and Philo" in *Studies in the Logic of Charles Sanders Peirce*, Houser, Nathan (ed). Zeman, Jay.

"Peirce and Russell: The History of a Neglected 'Controversy'" in *Studies in the Logic of Charles Sanders Peirce*, Houser, Nathan (ed). Hawkins, Benjamin S.

"The Interconnectedness of Peirce's Diagrammatic Thought" in *Studies in the Logic of Charles Sanders Peirce*, Houser, Nathan (ed). Kent, Beverley.

"The Tinctures and Implicit Quantification over Worlds" in *The Rule of Reason: The Philosophy of Charles Sanders Peirce*, Forster, Paul (ed). Zeman, Jay.

*Studies in the Logic of Charles Sanders Peirce.* Houser, Nathan (ed), Roberts, Don D (ed) and Van Evra, James (ed).

Consequence Operations Based on Hypergraph Satisfiability. Kolany, Adam.

Identities on Cardinals Less Than Aleph$_{omega}$. Gilchrist, M and Shelah, S.

In the random graph G($n$,$p$), $p = n^{-a}$.... Shelah, Saharon.

Infinitary Logics and Very Sparse Random Graphs. Lynch, James F.

Infinite Versions of Some Problems from Finite Complexity Theory. Hirst, Jeffry L and Lempp, Steffen.

Interpolants, Cut Elimination and Flow Graphs for the Propositional Calculus. Carbone, A.

Representation Theorems for Hypergraph Satisfiability. Kolany, Adam.

The Mathematical Structure of the World: The World as Graph. Dipert, Randall R.

## GRAPHIC

The Art of Interaction: Interactivity, Performativity, and Computers. Saltz, David Z.

The Vitality of Digital Creation. Binkley, Timothy.

## GRAVINA, G

"Storicità e mondo umano nell'estetica di Gravina" in *Lo Storicismo e la Sua Storia: Temi, Problemi, Prospettive*, Cacciatore, Giuseppe (ed). Cantillo, Clementina.

*Le Orationes* Di G. Gravina: Scienza, Sapienza e Diritto. Lomonaco, Fabrizio.

## GRAVITATION

Epistemologische Aspekte der neuen Entwicklungen in der Physik. Münster, Gernot.

Resolving Discordant Results: Modern Solar Oblateness Experiments. Richman, Sam.

Trägheit und Massebegriff bei Johannes Kepler. Ihmig, Karl-Norbert.

Was ist Masse? Newtons Begriff der Materiemenge. Steinle, Friedrich.

## GRAVITY

"Gravity" in the Thought of Simone Weil. Pirrucello, Ann.

Der Zeitbegriff in der Quantengravitation. Kiefer, Claus.

Emerging from Imaginary Time. Deltete, Robert J and Guy, Reed A.

Inferences from Phenomena in Gravitational Physics. Harper, William and DiSalle, Robert.

Newton, die Trägheitskraft und die absolute Bewegung. Dellian, Ed.

## GREED

Avarice and Civil Unity: The Contribution of Sir Thomas Smith. Wood, Neal.

## GREEK

see also Ancient, Logos, Mimesis, Nous, Presocratics

"How Sceptical were the Academic Sceptics?" in *Scepticism in the History of Philosophy: A Pan-American Dialogue*, Popkin, Richard H (ed). Frede, Dorothea.

"Immagini della Grecia: Rosenzweig e Burckhardt" in *Lo Storicismo e la Sua Storia: Temi, Problemi, Prospettive*, Cacciatore, Giuseppe (ed). D'Antuono, Emilia.

"In Search of a Civil Union: The Political Theme of European Democracy and Its Primordial Inauguration in Greek Philosophy" in *The Ancients and the Moderns*, Lilly, Reginald (ed). Riedel, Manfred.

"The *Dissoi Logoi* and Early Greek Scepticism" in *Scepticism in the History of Philosophy: A Pan-American Dialogue*, Popkin, Richard H (ed). Robinson, Thomas M.

"The Greek *Polis* and the Creation of Democracy" in *The Ancients and the Moderns*, Lilly, Reginald (ed). Castoriadis, Cornelius.

*Ancient Philosophy, 2nd Edition.* Baird, Forrest E (ed) and Kaufmann, Walter.

*Bios politikos* and *bios theoretikos* in the Phenomenology of Hannah Arendt. Moran, Dermot (trans) and Taminiaux, Jacques.

*Christian Philosophy: Greek, Medieval, Contemporary Reflections.* Sweeney, Leo.

*Classical Cynicism: A Critical Study.* Navia, Luis E.

*Dunamis* and Being: Heidegger on Plato's *Sophist* 247d8-e4. Ellis, John.

*Protagoras.* Taylor, C C W (trans).

*Schelling und Nietzsche: Zur Auslegung der frühen Werke Friedrich Nietzsches.* Wilson, John Elbert.

*The Question of "Eclecticism": Studies in Later Greek Philosophy.* Dillon, John M (ed) and Long, A A (ed).

*The Thinker as Artist: From Homer to Plato & Aristotle.* Anastaplo, George.

A Note on—Euthanasia and the Contemporary Debate. Barua, Archna.

Analytic Philosophy in Greece. Virvidakis, Stelios.

Concepts of Space in Greek Thought. White, Michael J.

Egyptian Priests and German Professors: On the Alleged Difficulty of Philosophy. Protevi, John.

El placer en Grecia y el mundo hebreo. Fallas, Luis A.

Enesidemo: la recuperación de la tradición escéptica griega. Roman, Leslie.

Fragments from *Timon of Phleius* & Diogenes Laertius on Timon of Phleius (in Hungarian). Steiger, Kornél.

Histoire de la philosophie et philosophie au tribunal de la vérité. Cunningham, Henri-Paul.

History of Science and the Historian's Self-Understanding. Prudovsky, Gad.

Hölderlin e o *Retorno Natal*. Beckert, Cristina.

Homer's Theology and the Concept of Tolerance. Bosnjak, Branko.

Il velo e il fiume: Riflessioni sulle metafore dell'oblio. Rigotti, Francesca.

Interview with Martha Nussbaum. Keith, Heather and DeTar, Richard.

## GUPTA, A
What's in a Function?. Antonelli, Gian Aldo.

## GURNEY, E
Hearing Musical Works in their Entirety. McAdoo, Nick.

## GUSTAFSON, J
Ethics, Theism and Metaphysics: An Analysis of the Theocentric Ethics of James Gustafson. Meyer, William J.

## GUTMANN, A
Civic Education: A New Proposal. Wingo, Ajume H.

## GYNECOLOGY
Children's Refusal of Gynecologic Examinations for Suspected Sexual Abuse. Muram, David, Aiken, Margaret M and Strong, Carson.

## HAACK, S
Evidencia e investigación: La Epistemología filosófica reivindicada. Frápolli, María José.
Justification of Empirical Belief: Problems with Haack's Foundherentism. Clune, Alan C.
You Can Always Count on Reliabilism. Levin, Michael.

## HABERMAS, J
"Phronesis and Political Dialogue" in Political Dialogue: Theories and Practices, Esquith, Stephen L (ed). Kingwell, Mark.
"Decentering and Reasoning" in Philosophy of Education (1996), Margonis, Frank (ed). Weinstein, Mark.
"Democracy and Intellectual Mediation: After Liberalism and Socialism" in Political Dialogue: Theories and Practices, Esquith, Stephen L (ed). Peterson, Richard T.
"Habermas and Critical Thinking" in Philosophy of Education (1996), Margonis, Frank (ed). Endres, Ben.
"Mundo administrado" o "Colonización del mundo de la vida": La depotenciación de la Teoría crítica de la sociedad en J. Habermas. Gómez Ibáñez, Vicente.
Comunicación, Ética Y Política: Habermas Y Sus Críticos. Boladeras, Margarita.
Debating the State of Philosophy: Habermas, Rorty, and Kolakowski. Niznik, Jozef (ed) and Sanders, John T (ed).
Emancipation and Illusion: Rationality and Gender in Habermas's Theory of Modernity. Fleming, Marie.
Ética: Procedimientos Razonables. López de la Vieja, Maria Teresa.
From Sex Objects to Sexual Subjects. Moscovici, Claudia.
Habermas and the Unfinished Project of Modernity. Passerin d'Entrèves, Maurizio (ed) and Benhabib, Seyla (ed).
Kant, Critique and Politics. Hutchings, Kimberly.
Language and Reason: A Study of Habermas's Pragmatics. Cooke, Maeve.
Las Caras del Leviatán: Una Lectura Política de la Teoría Crítica. Colom González, Francisco.
Subjectivity and Intersubjectivity in Modern Philosophy and Psychoanalysis. Frie, Roger.
Are Ethical Conflicts Irreconcilable?. Cooke, Maeve.
Aspectos políticos del pensamiento de J. Habermas: una lectura crítica. Bonnet, Alberto.
Aufhebung des Religiösen durch Versprachlichung? Eine religions-philosophische Untersuchung des Rationalitätskonzeptes von Jürgen Habermas. Kühnlein, Michael.
Authenticity and Autonomy: Taylor, Habermas, and the Politics of Recognition. Cooke, Maeve.
Can Religion Survive the Rationalization? Questions at Habermas's Theory of Culture (in Dutch). Jespers, F P M.
Communicative Action and Philosophical Foundations: Comments on the Apel-Habermas Debate. Papastephanou, Marianna.
Consensus and Normative Validity. Grimen, Harald.
Contesting Consensus: Rereading Habermas on the Public Sphere. Markell, Patchen.
Cosmopolitanism and Citizenship: Kant Against Habermas. Mertens, Thomas.
De la ética del discurso a la moral del respeto universal: una investigación filosófica acerca de la fundamentación de los derechos humanos. Dias, Maria Clara.
El vivir y la fatiga: La fatiga de vivir. Osés Gorráiz, Jesús María.
Emancipatory Social Science: Habermas on Nietzsche. Kerckhove, Lee.
For Non-Relative Difference and Non-Coercive Dialogue (in Serbo-Croatian). Saez Rueda, Luis and Milovic, Miroslav (trans).
Habermas and Apel on Communicative Ethics: Their Difference and the Difference It Makes. Gamwell, Franklin I.
Habermas and Foucault: How to Carry Out the Enlightenment Project. Nielsen, Kai.
Habermas and Mead: On Universality and Individuality. Abdoulafia, Mitchell.
Habermas' Diskursethik. Lumer, Christoph.
Habermas' Philosophy of Liberation. Pereppaden, Jose.
Habermas' Pragmatic Universals. Mukherji, Arundhati.
Habermas's Moral Cognitivism. Kitchen, Gary.
Habermas, Fichte and the Question of Technological Determinism. Jalbert, John E.
La Política de la Razón (In)suficiente. Lindahl, Hans.
La Teoría del Derecho y la Democracia en Jürgen Habermas: En torno a Faktizität und Geltung. Mejía Quintana, Oscar.

Liberalism and Deliberative Democracy: Considerations on the Foundations of Liberty and Equality (Spanish). Cortés Rodas, Francisco.
Metaphysics and the Rationalization of Society. Gamwell, Franklin.
On the Practical Relevance of Habermas's Theory of Communicative Action. Parkin, Andrew C.
Phenomenological Ethics and Moral Sentiments (Spanish). Hoyos Vásquez, Guillermo.
Pragmatismus redivivus? Eine Kritik an der Revitalisierung des pragmatistischen Grundgedankens. Römpp, Georg.
Qué "nos" dice Habermas: Algunas reflexiones desde las coordenadas histórico-sociales latinoamericanas. Arpini, Adriana.
Romanticism Revisited. Hammer, Espen.
Solidarietà e democrazia: Osservazioni su antropologia, diritto e legittimità nella teoria giuridica di Habermas. Pinzani, Alessandro.
Sprechakttheoretische Erläuterungen zum Begriff der kommunikativen Rationalität. Habermas, Jürgen.
Superamento della complessità attraverso la capacità di apprendimento del diritto: L'adeguamento del diritto alle condizioni del Postmoderno. Ladeur, Karl-Heinz.
The Ambiguity of 'Rationality'. Rorty, Richard.
The Discourse Principle and Those Affected. Skirbekk, Gunnar.
The Redemption of Truth: Idealization, Acceptability and Fallibilism in Habermas' Theory of Meaning. Fultner, Barbara.
Una teoría del estado de derecho. De Zan, Julio.
Une éthique est-elle possible en l'absence de croyances dogmatiques?. Boudon, Raymond.
Worlds Apart? Habermas and Levinas. Vetlesen, Arne J.

## HABIT
"Prioridad del acto en la génesis de los hábitos operativos" in Ensayos Aristotélicos, Aspe, Virginia. Mier y Terán, Rocío.
"Prioridad del acto en la génesis de los hábitos operativos" in Ensayos Aristotélicos, Rivera, José Luis (ed). Mier y Terán, Rocío.
Developing Habits and Knowing What Habits to Develop: A Look at the Role of Virtue in Ethics. Loewy, Erich H.
El conocimiento de fe en la filosofía de Leonardo Polo. Conesa, Francisco.
El soporte cognoscitivo de la filosofía en la postmodernidad. Vega Rodríguez, Margarita.
La precisividad del pensamiento. Esquer Gallardo, Héctor.
Los hábitos intelectuales según Polo. Sellés, Juan Fernando.
On the Limit of Iconology through the "Mental Habit"—Comparison between E. Panofsky's "Mental Habit" and P. Bourdieu's "Habitus" (in Japanese). Ichijo, Kazuhiko.
Sindéresis y conciencia moral. Molina Pérez, Francisco.
What I Will Do and What I Intend To Do. Scheer, Richard K.
Wie einer beschaffen ist, so erscheint ihm das Ziel: Die Rolle des moralischen Habitus bei der Beurteilung des Handlungsziels nach Thomas von Aquin. Darge, Rolf.

## HABITAT
Attributing 'Priority' to Habitats. Miller, Chris.

## HABITUATION
Intellectualism and Moral Habituation in Plato's Earlier Dialogues. Yong, Patrick.

## HACKING, I
Discutono Il caso domato, di Ian Hacking. Dessì, Paola, Sassoli, Bernardo and Sklar, Lawrence.
Saving our Souls: Hacking's Archaeology and Churchland's Neurology. Taliaferro, Charles.
The Soul of Knowledge. Allen, Barry.

## HADLEY, R
Exhibiting versus Explaining Systematicity: A Reply to Hadley and Hayward. Aizawa, Kenneth.

## HAEGLER, R
Für und Wider den Essentialismus: Zu Rudolf-Peter Häglers Kritik des neuen Essentialismus. Liske, Michael-Thomas.

## HALE, B
Hale on Caesar. Sullivan, Peter and Potter, Michael.

## HALES, S
"Maternity, Paternity, and Equality" in Reproduction, Technology, and Rights: Biomedical Ethics Reviews, Humber, James M (ed). Humber, James M.

## HALL, N
On Lewis's Objective Chance: "Humean Supervenience Debugged". Hoefer, Carl.

## HALL, R
Speech-Acts, Kierkegaard, and Postmodern Thought. Martinez, Roy.
True Theories, False Colors. Clark, Austen.

## HALLDEN-COMPLETENESS
The Interpolation, Halldén-Completeness, Robinson and Beth Properties in Modal Logics. Wójtowicz, Anna.

## HALLUCINATION
Error, Hallucination and the Concept of 'Ontology' in the Early Work of Heidegger. McManus, Denis.
The Theory of Appearing Defended. Langsam, Harold.

## HALPERIN, D
Liberté! Egalité! Sexualité!: Theorizing Lesbian and Gay Politics. Kaplan, Morris B.

## HALPERN, J
Thinking about Reasoning about Knowledge. Kyburg Jr, Henry E.

## HAMILTON, A
Personal Identity and the Coherence of *Q*-Memory. Collins, Arthur W.

## HAMLYN, D
Aristotle on Reflective Awareness. Lokhorst, Gert-Jan C.

## HAMPTON, J
"A Response to Jean Hampton's Feminism" in *The Liberation Debate: Rights at Issue,* Leahy, Michael (ed). Flew, Antony.

## HANDICAPPED
Muss dieses Buch gelesen werden?—Zum Erscheinen der deutschen Ausgabe von Helga Kuhse/Peter Singer: *Should the Baby Live?*. Joerden, Jan C.

Waarom het beoordelen van technologieën voor gehandicapten problematisch is. Blume, Stuart.

## HANDKE, P
Lenguaje significativo y no significativo: *El Kaspar* de Peter Handke. Gutiérrez, Edgardo.

## HANFLING, O
How to Read Wittgenstein. Cook, John W.

## HAPPINESS
*see also* Hedonism, Pleasure

"Il Senso Della Verità: Desolazione matematica e terapia nietzscheana dell'infelicità" in *Soggetto E Verità: La questione dell'uomo nella filosofia contemporanea,* Fagiuoli, Ettore. Fortunato, Marco.

*Il Disincanto Della Ragione E L'Assolutezza Del Bonheur* Studio Sull'Abate Galiani. Amodio, Paolo.

*Mortals and Others: American Essays 1931-1935.* Russell, Bertrand and Ruja, Harry (ed).

*Welfare, Happiness, and Ethics.* Sumner, L W.

Desire for Happiness and the Commandments in the First Chapter of *Veritatis Splendor*. Melina, Livio.

Die komplementäre disparater Ethikbegründungen in der Gegenwart: Über Martin Seels Buch *Versuch über die Form des Glücks*. Horster, Detlef.

Ética y dialéctica: Sócrates, Platón y Aristóteles. Yarza, Ignacio.

Happiness and Meaning: Two Aspects of the Good Life. Wolf, Susan.

Happiness Doesn't Come in Bottles: Neuroscientists Learn That Joy Comes Through Dancing, Not Drugs. Freeman, Walter J.

Happiness, Tranquility, and Philosophy. Griswold, Jr, Charles L.

Identidad Personal, Nacional y Universal. Tugendhat, Ernst.

Il desiderio: precedenti storici e concettualizzazione platonica. Malo, Antonio.

L'ultimo dei porcospini: Intervista biografico-teorica a René Girard. Antonello, Pierpaolo (ed) and De Castro Rocha, Joao Cezar (ed).

La maturità di coscienza alla luce di San Tommaso d'Aquino. Costa, Flavia.

Law, Virtue, and Happiness in Aquinas's Moral Theory. Carl, Maria.

Mill on Virtue as a Part of Happiness. Crisp, Roger.

Perfection, Happiness, and Duties to Self. Jeske, Diane.

Preferences or Happiness? Tibor Scitovsky's Psychology of Human Needs. Friedman, Jeffrey and McCabe, Adam.

Reasonable Impressions in Stoicism. Brennan, Tad.

Self-Interest and Virtue. Badhwar, Neera Kapur.

The Moral Asymmetry of Happiness and Suffering. Mayerfeld, Jamie.

The Rejection of Objective Consequentialism. Howard-Snyder, Frances.

The Relation between Concepts of Quality-of-Life, Health and Happiness. Musschenga, Albert W.

The Russian Idea at the End of the Twentieth Century. Mil'don, Valerii Il'ich.

Virtue, Happiness, and Intelligibility. Lemos, John.

## HARASSMENT
Can a Woman Harass a Man?: Toward a Cultural Understanding of Bodies and Power. Bordo, Susan.

## HARAWAY, D
Virtual Sexes and Feminist Futures: The Philosophy of 'Cyberfeminism'. Marsden, Jill.

What's the Difference? Knowledge and Gender in (Post)Modern Philosophy of Religion. Jantzen, Grace M.

## HARDENBERG, F
Die Deduktion der Philosophie nach Fichte und Friedrich von Hardenberg. Rühling, Frank.

## HARDIMON, M
The New Hegel. Dallmayr, Fred R, Hardimon, Michael O and Pinkard, Terry.

## HARDIN, C
Can Colour Be Reduced to Anything?. Dedrick, Don.

## HARDING, S
From Aperspectival Objectivity to Strong Objectivity: The Quest for Moral Objectivity. Tannoch-Bland, Jennifer.

## HARE, R
"La universalizabilidad monológica: R.M. Hare" in *La racionalidad: su poder y sus límites,* Nudler, Oscar (ed). Guariglia, Osvaldo.

Against the Golden Rule Argument Against Abortion. Boonin-Vail, David.

Do Possible People have Moral Standing?. Ryberg, Jesper.

Gesellschaftsvertrag oder grösster Gesamtnutzen? Die Vertragstheorie von John Rawls und ihre neo-utilitaristischen Kritiker. Rinderle, Peter.

Hare's Reductive Justification of Preference Utilitarianism. Paden, Roger.

## HARE, W
Replies. Scheffler, Israel.

## HARLOW, H
Harry F. Harlow and Animal Research: Reflection on the Ethical Paradox. Gluck, John P.

The Psychology of Harry F. Harlow: A Bridge from Radical to Rational Behaviorism. Rumbaugh, Duane M.

## HARM
*Mill's On Liberty.* Dworkin, Gerald (ed).

*Morality and the Law.* Baird, Robert M (ed) and Rosenbaum, Stuart E (ed).

Comparable Harm and Equal Inherent Value: The Problem of Dog in the Lifeboat. Francione, Gary L.

Comparing Harms: Headaches and Human Lives. Norcross, Alastair.

Free Speech. Weissman, David.

Humor and Harm. Goldstein, Laurence.

Must Constitutional Democracy Be "Responsive"?. Michelman, Frank I.

Preventing Harm and Promoting Ethical Discourse in the Helping Professions: Conceptual, Research, Analytical, and Action Frameworks. Prilleltensky, Isaac, Rossiter, Amy and Walsh-Bowers, Richard.

Rights, Explanation, and Risks. McCarthy, David.

Should I Be Grateful to You for Not Harming Me?. Smilansky, Saul.

The Rhetorical Force of Ambiguity: The No-Harm Argument in Medical Ethics (in Dutch). Van der Scheer, Lieke.

The Trivialization of Ethics or Ethics Programs in the Workplace: A Cautionary Tale. Marks, Joel.

Why "Do No Harm?". Sharpe, Virginia A.

## HARMAN, G
"Colors, Subjective Relations and Qualia" in *Perception,* Villanueva, Enrique (ed). Shoemaker, Sydney.

"Is Color Psychological or Biological? Or Both?" in *Perception,* Villanueva, Enrique (ed). Sosa, Ernest.

"Orgasms Again" in *Perception,* Villanueva, Enrique (ed). Tye, Michael.

The Relevance of Logic to Reasoning and Belief Revision: Harman on 'Change in View'. Knorpp Jr, William Max.

## HARMONICS
The Generalized Harmonic Mean and a Portfolio Problem with Dependent Assets. Kijima, Masaaki.

## HARMONY
Diversitas identitate compensata: Ein Grundtheorem in Leibniz' Denken und seine Voraussetzungen in der frühen Neuzeit. Leinkauf, Thomas.

Harmony in Space: A Perspective on the Work of Rudolf Laban. Brooks, Lynn Matluck.

Leibniz, Middle Knowledge, and the Intricacies of World Design. Knebel, Sven K.

Melody in Life: Some Reflections. Roy, Subrata.

Pre-Established Harmony and Other Comic Strategies. Sesonske, Alexander.

The Harmony of the World and its Greek Connection (in Czech). Krámsky, David.

The Inhabitants of Other Planets in Bernardin de Saint-Pierre's *Les Harmonies de la nature* (in French). Duflo, Colas.

## HARPER, C
Spenser and the Historical Revolution: *Briton Moniments* and the *Problem of Roman Britain.* Curran Jr, John E.

## HARPER, W
Is God Exclusively a Father?. Isham, George F.

## HARRE, R
*Realismus und Chemie: Philosophische Untersuchungen der Wissenschaft von den Stoffen.* Schummer, Joachim.

Commentary on "Pathological Autobiographies". Norrie, Alan.

The Psychological Subject and Harré's Social Psychology: An Analysis of a Constructionist Case. Scott, Campbell L and Stam, Henderikus J.

## HARRINGTON, J
A Má Fama na Filosofia Política: James Harrington e Maquiavel. Bignotto, Newton.

## HARRIS, E
A Theory of Complexes. Greenberg, William J.

## HARRIS, I
Gandhi on Love: A Reply to Ian M. Harris. Kohl, Marvin.

## HARRIS, J
"Children's Liberation: A Blueprint for Disaster" in *The Liberation Debate: Rights at Issue,* Leahy, Michael (ed). Purdy, Laura M.

## HARRIS, S
Japanese Death Factories and the American Cover-Up. Chen, Yuan-Fang.

## HARSA
Embracing the Subject: Harsa's Play within a Play. Shulman, David.

## HARSANYI, J
Desigualdades de Bienestar y axiomática rawlsiana. Sen, Amartya K.

Entrevista al Prof. J. Harsanyi. Barragan, Julia.

Funciones de Bienestar social no lineales: una réplica al profesor Harsanyi. Sen, Amartya K.

Realizability as Constituent Element of the Justification Structure of the Public Decision. Cuñarro Conde, Edith Mabel.

**HART, H**
Force, Power, and Motive. Yarbrough, Stephen R.
H.L.A. Hart's Contribution to Legal Anthropology. Hund, John.
Legal Principles and Legal Theory. R-Toubes Muñiz, Joaquín.
The Legitimacy of Laws: A Puzzle for Hart. Webb, Mark Owen.
The Will Theory of Rights: A Defence. Graham, Paul.

**HARTMAN, K**
Response to Pinkard. Beiser, Frederick C.

**HARTMANN**
Zu den kantischen und fichteschen Motiven bei Nicolai Hartmann. Hála, Vlastimil.

**HARTSHORNE, C**
Analytic Theism, Hartshorne, and the Concept of God. Dombrowski, Daniel A.
Hartshorne on Heidegger. Dombrowski, Daniel A.

**HARVEY, W**
Révolution scientifique et problématique de l'être vivant. Duchesneau, François.

**HASKELL, T**
Neoliberalism and the Political Theory of the Market. Gagnier, Regenia.

**HASLETT, D**
Neoliberalism and the Political Theory of the Market. Gagnier, Regenia.

**HATCHER, D**
Realism and Other Philosophical Mantras. Sutton, Robert C.

**HATE**
Sovereign Performatives in the Contemporary Scene of Utterance. Butler, Judith.
The Words We Love to Hate. Stark, Cynthia A.

**HAUGAARD, M**
Taking Coercion Seriously. Mansbridge, Jane.

**HAUSER, K**
Lenguaje significativo y no significativo: El Kaspar de Peter Handke. Gutiérrez, Edgardo.

**HAUSMAN, D**
Rerum Cognoscere Causas. Hahn, Frank.
The Impossibility of Interpersonal Utility Comparisons: A Critical Note. Weintraub, Ruth.

**HAWKING, S**
Emerging from Imaginary Time. Deltete, Robert J and Guy, Reed A.
The Origin of the Big Bang Universe in Ultimate Reality with Special Reference to the Cosmology of Stephen Hawking. Sharpe, Kevin.
The Principal Paradox of Time Travel. Riggs, Peter.

**HAYEK, F**
"Límites y desventuras de la racionalidad crítica neoliberal" in La racionalidad: su poder y sus límites, Nudler, Oscar (ed). Gómez, Ricardo J.
Hayek's Attack on Social Justice. Johnston, David.
Hayek's Political Philosophy and His Economics. Friedman, Jeffrey.
Market Non-Neutrality: Systematic Bias in Spontaneous Orders. diZerga, Gus.
On the Road Again: Hayek and the Rule of Law. Williams, Juliet.
Social Justice: The Hayekian Challenge. Lukes, Steven.
The Epistemological Argument Against Socialism: A Wittgensteinian Critique of Hayek and Giddens. Pleasants, Nigel.
Was Hayek an Instrumentalist?. Legutko, Ryszard.

**HAYWARD, M**
Exhibiting versus Explaining Systematicity: A Reply to Hadley and Hayward. Aizawa, Kenneth.

**HAZEN, A**
Worlds by Supervenience: Some Further Problems. Grim, Patrick.

**HE**
The Validity of Indexical Arguments. Elkatip, S H.

**HEALING**
Philosophy of Medical Practice: A Discursive Approach. Van Leeuwen, Evert and Kimsma, Gerrit K.
The Tapestry of Alternative Healing. Hudson, Robert.
The Virtues in Psychiatric Practice. Mann, David W.

**HEALTH**
see also Mental Health
"On Not Destroying the Health of One's Patients" in Human Lives: Critical Essays on Consequentialist Bioethics, Oderberg, David S (ed). Simmons, Lance.
"The Idea of Progress in Human Health" in The Idea of Progress, McLaughlin, Peter (ed). Lazar, Philippe.
The Perfect Baby: A Pragmatic Approach to Genetics. McGee, Glenn.
Bioethical Issues Confronting The African American Community. Calloway, Kelvin T.
Health as a Normative Concept: Towards a New Conceptual Framework. Fedoryka, Kateryna.
Hope and the Limits of Research: Commentary. Daugherty, Christopher K.
My Quality is not Low!. McNair, Douglas.
Philosophie und Medizin: Ein Blick in aktuelle Veröffentlichungen. Schramme, Thomas.
Predicting Our Health: Ethical Implications of Neural Networks and Outcome Potential Predictions. Seddon, Andrew M.

Santo Tomás de Aquino y la Medicina. Sacchi, Mario Enrique.
The Relation between Concepts of Quality-of-Life, Health and Happiness. Musschenga, Albert W.
Waste in Medicine. Baumrin, Bernard.
Why Bioethics Needs the Philosophy of Medicine: Some Implications of Reflection on Concepts of Health and Disease. Khushf, George.

**HEALTH CARE**
"In Vitro Fertilization and the Just Use of Health Care Resources" in Reproduction, Technology, and Rights: Biomedical Ethics Reviews, Humber, James M (ed). Weber, Leonard J.
"Moral oder Eigennutz? Eine experimentelle Analyse" in Ökonomie und Moral: Beiträge zur Theorie ökonomischer Rationalität, Lohmann, Karl Reinhard (ed). Frey, Bruno S and Bohnet, Iris.
"Reflections of a Sceptical Bioethicist" in Philosophical Perspectives on Bioethics, Sumner, L W (ed). Overall, Christine.
"Theory versus Practice in Ethics: A Feminist Perspective on Justice in Health Care" in Philosophical Perspectives on Bioethics, Sumner, L W (ed). Sherwin, Susan.
Moral Issues in Health Care: An Introduction to Medical Ethics. McConnell, Terrance C.
Philosophical Perspectives on Bioethics. Sumner, L W (ed) and Boyle, Joseph (ed).
Testing the Medical Covenant: Active Euthanasia and Health Care Reform. May, William F.
The Welfare State. Paul, Ellen Frankel (ed), Miller, Fred D (ed) and Paul, Jeffrey (ed).
A Communion of Saints...Maybe. Bailey Stoneking, Carole.
A Just Share: Justice and Fairness in Resource Allocation. McCarrick, Pat Milmoe and Darragh, Martina.
A Manual on Manners and Courtesies for the Shared Care of Patients. Stoekle, John D, Ronan, Laurence J and Emanuel, Linda L (& others).
Allocating Healthcare By QALYs: The Relevance of Age. McKie, John, Kuhse, Helga and Richardson, Jeff.
Arguments Against Health Care Autonomy for Minors. Ross, Lainie Friedman.
Between Doctor and Patient. Capron, Alexander M.
Bioethics and Law: A Developmental Perspective. Van der Burg, Wibren.
Body-Subjectivity in Psychiatry: The Initial Argument. Mondal, Parthasarathi.
Can An Egalitarian Justify Universal Access to Health Care?. Jacobs, Lesley A.
Can Ethics Committees Work in Managed Care Plans?. Felder, Michael.
Case Commentary. Flanigan, Rosemary.
Catholic Social Justice and Health Care Entitlement Packages. Boyle, Joseph.
Challenges Across the Life Span for Persons with Disabilities. Rinck, Christine and Calkins, Carl F.
Children, Society, and Health Care Decision Making. Caccamo, James M.
Clinical Ethics and Ethics Committees. Bartholome, William G.
Commodity or Public Work? Two Perspectives on Health Care. Hanson, Mark J and Jennings, Bruce.
Communication through Interpreters in Health Care: Ethical Dilemmas Arising from Differences in Class, Culture, Language, and Power. Kaufert, Joseph M and Putsch, Robert W.
Concepts in Evaluation Applied to Ethics Consultation Research. Fox, Ellen.
Consultectonics: Ethics Committee Case Consultation as Mediation. Reynolds, Don F.
Defining the Medical Sphere. Trappenburg, Margo J.
Do No Harm. Kotin, Anthony M.
Do the Bishops Have It Right On Health Care Reform?. Sulmasy, Daniel P.
Engagement and Suffering in Responsible Caregiving: On Overcoming Maleficience in Health Care. Schultz, Dawson S and Carnevale, Franco A.
Equal Access to Health Care: A Lutheran Lay Person's Expanded Footnote. Delkeskamp-Hayes, Corinna.
Equality in Health Care: Christian Engagement with a Secular Obsession. Engelhardt Jr, H Tristram.
Ethical Decision Making in Managed Care Environments. Ross, Judith Wilson.
Ethical Issues in Managed Care: A Catholic Christian Perspective. Pellegrino, Edmund D.
Ethics in the Outpatient Setting: New Challenges and Opportunities. Young, Ernlé W D.
Ethics without Walls: The Transformation of Ethics Committees in the New Healthcare Environment. Christensen, Kate T and Tucker, Robin.
Evaluating Ethics Consultation: Framing the Questions. Tulsky, James A and Fox, Ellen.
Everyday Heroes, Part 2: Should Careproviders Ever Be Quintilian?. Howe, Edmund G.
Freedom and Democracy in Health Care Ethics: Is the Cart Before the Horse?. Meaney, Mark E.
Freedom and Moral Diversity: The Moral Failures of Health Care in the Welfare State. Engelhardt Jr, H Tristram.
From What's Neutral to What's Meaningful: Reflections on a Study of Medical Interpreters. Solomon, Mildred Z.
Genetic Testing in Children. Clayton, Ellen Wright.
Goldilocks and Mrs. Ilych: A Critical Look at the "Philosophy of Hospice". Ackerman, Felicia.

# HEGEL

Laughing at Hegel. Westphal, Merold.

Le mal moral, pierre de touche de l'ontologie: Monisme idéal et dualisme réel du sens de l'être. Lamblin, Robert.

Making God Go Away and Leave Us Alone. Maxwell, Vance.

Man kannte mich, als man mich rufte: Die Berufung des Magister Fichte an die Gesamt-Akademie Jena im Jahre 1794. Vieweg, Klaus.

Mathesis Universalis cartesiana. Villalobos, José.

Modelo y Fenomenología: Nietzsche contra Hegel: El Renacimiento de la Tragedia en el Renacimiento de la Opera. Cohen-Levinas, Danielle.

Naturphilosophie zwischen Naturwissenschaft und Philosophie: Neue Sammelbände zur Naturphilosophie des deutschen Idealismus. Ziche, Paul.

O Mais Antigo Programa de Sistema do Idealismo Alemao. Carmo Ferreira, Manuel J do.

On the Question of *Mimesis* (in Spanish). Knoll, Victor.

Para uma Explicitaçao da Diálética Hegeliana entre o Senhor e o Escravo na Fenomenologia do Espírito. Ferreira Chagas, Eduardo.

Person and Property in Hegel's *Philosophical Principles of Right* (in French). Soual, Philippe.

Persona, propiedad y reconocimiento intersubjetivo: Una interpretación de los fundamentos normativos del estado de derecho hegeliano. Mizrahi, Esteban.

Phenomenology of Spirit and Logic (in French). Lécrivain, André.

Physiology, Embryology and Psychopathology: A Test Case for Hegelian Thought (in French). Rozenberg, Jacques J.

Reflexión y principio de la lógica en Hegel. Ezquerra Gómez, Jesús.

Response to Pinkard. Beiser, Frederick C.

Romanticized Enlightenment? Enlightened Romanticism? Universalism and Particularism in Hegel's *Understanding of the Enlightenment*. Pinkard, Terry.

Scary Monsters: Hegel and the Nature of the Monstrous. Gunkel, David.

Schellings Metapher *Blitz*—eine Huldigung an die Wissenschaftslehre. Ehrhardt, Walter E.

Sieben Jenaer Reflexionen Hegels über Homer. Jeck, Udo Reinhold.

Teodicea y sentido de la historia: la respuesta de Hegel. Estrada, Juan A.

The Absolute and Kierkegaard's Conception of Selfhood. Buterin, Damir.

The Bacchanalian Revel: Hegel and Deconstruction. Haas, Andrew.

The Blessed Gods Mourn: What is Living-Dead in the Legacy of Hegel. Cutrofello, Andrew.

The Death of God and Hegel's System of Philosophy. Anderson, Deland.

The Fool's Truth: Diderot, Goethe, and Hegel. Schmidt, James.

The French Revolutionary Roots of Political Modernity in Hegel's Philosophy, or the Enlightenment at Dusk. Wokler, Robert.

The Hegelian Sign: Sacrificial Economy and Dialectical Relief (in French). Guibal, Francis.

The Historicity of Philosophy: Hegel and Gadamer (in Serbo-Croatian). Deretic, Irina.

The History of Interpretation and the Interpretation of History in the History of Philosophy. Wiehl, Reiner.

The Limits of Self Interest: An Hegelian Critique of Gauthier's Compliance Problem. Schwartz, David T.

The Negative Dialectic of Modernity and the Speculative Resolution of the Contradiction of Modern Moral Consciousness (in Spanish). Lutz Müller, Marcos.

The New Hegel. Dallmayr, Fred R, Hardimon, Michael O and Pinkard, Terry.

The Norm and History. Travar, Dusan.

The Philosophy of Religion in the System of Freedom. Despot, Blanko.

The Spirit in John's Gospel: A Hegelian Perspective. Viviano, Benedict T.

Thinking Critical History: Young Hegel and the German Constitution (in French). Leydet, Dominique.

Un discorso morale sulla guerra. Loretoni, Anna.

Vragen bij Hegels metafysische logica. De Vos, Ludovicus.

What is the Non-Metaphysical Reading of Hegel? A Reply to Frederick Beiser. Pinkard, Terry.

Zeichenmachende Phantasie: Zum systematischen Zusammenhang von Zeichen und Denken bei Hegel. Simon, Josef.

Zur Fichte-Darstellung in Hegels *Differenzschrift*. Kiss, Endre.

Zur Geschichte des ontologischen Gottesbeweises. Kreimendahl, Lothar.

Zur Logik der Moralität: Einige Fragen an A. Requate. De Vos, Lu.

'Between the Brutely Given, and the Brutally, Banally Free': Von Balthasar's Theology of Drama in Dialogue with Hegel. Quash, J B.

# HEGELIANISM

"The End of Metaphysics and the Possibility of Non-Hegelian Speculative Thought" in *Hegel, History, and Interpretation*, Gallagher, Shaun. Dostal, Robert J.

A Note on the Concept of Alienation. Mohanta, Dilip Kumar.

Circulus Vitiosus Deus? The Dialectical Logic of Feminist Standpoint Theory. Conway, Daniel W.

Commentary on "Wilhelm Griesinger". Mishara, Aaron L.

Hegelian Retribution Re-Examined. Fatic, A.

Hegelianism in Slovenia: A Short Introduction. Vezjak, Boris.

Lässt sich der Begriff der Dialektik klären?. Puntel, Lorenz.

McDowell's Hegelianism. Sedgwick, Sally.

Textuality and Imagination: The Refracted Image of Hegelian Dialectic. Schalow, Frank.

The Logic of Leaping: Kierkegaard's Use of Hegelian Sublation. Johnson, Ronald R.

Wilhelm Griesinger: Psychiatry between Philosophy and Praxis. Arens, Katherine.

# HEGEMONY

Hegemony and the Crisis of Legitimacy in Gramsci. Martin, James.

Untameable Singularity (Some Remarks on *Broken Hegemonies*). Granel, Gérard and Wolfe, Charles T (trans).

# HEIDEGGER

"Aristotele tra Hegel e Heidegger: tracce per una ricostruzione" in *Hegel e Aristotele*, Ferrarin, A. Meazza, Carmelino.

"De servo arbitrio: La fine della libertà in Martin Heidegger" in *Lo Storicismo e la Sua Storia: Temi, Problemi, Prospettive*, Cacciatore, Giuseppe (ed). Mazzarella, Eugenio.

"Esistenza e tempo in Heidegger" in *Il Concetto di Tempo: Atti del XXXII Congresso Nazionale della Società Filosofica Italiana*, Casertano, Giovanni (ed). Cesareo, Rosa.

"Firing the Steel of Hermeneutics: Hegelianized versus Radical Hermeneutics" in *Hegel, History, and Interpretation*, Gallagher, Shaun. Caputo, John D.

"Hegel, Heidegger, and Hermeneutical Experience" in *Hegel, History, and Interpretation*, Gallagher, Shaun. Lammi, Walter.

"Heidegger and Wittgenstein on the Subject of Kantian Philosophy" in *Figuring the Self: Subject, Absolute, and Others in Classical German Philosophy*, Zöller, Günter (ed). Stern, David G.

"Husserl e Heidegger: tempo e fenomenologia" in *Il Concetto di Tempo: Atti del XXXII Congresso Nazionale della Società Filosofica Italiana*, Casertano, Giovanni (ed). Sini, Carlo and Cacciatore, Giuseppe.

"Il Luogo Della Filosofia: La paradossalità della *Seinsfrage* nel giovane Heidegger" in *Soggetto E Verità: La questione dell'uomo nella filosofia contemporanea*, Fagiuoli, Ettore. Vicari, Dario.

"Il mito dell'autoctonia del pensiero (Note su Hegel, Fichte, Heidegger)" in *Geofilosofia*, Bonesio, Luisa (ed). Resta, Caterina.

"Il provincialismo filosofico" in *Geofilosofia*, Bonesio, Luisa (ed). Makowski, François.

"L'europeizzazione come probleme europeo" in *Geofilosofia*, Bonesio, Luisa (ed). Pöggler, Otto.

"L'Ombra Della Ragione: Banfi lettore di Klages" in *Soggetto E Verità: La questione dell'uomo nella filosofia contemporanea*, Fagiuoli, Ettore. Bonesio, Luisa.

"La Verità Storica: La comprensione della storia nella riflessione di Martin Heidegger" in *Soggetto E Verità: La questione dell'uomo nella filosofia contemporanea*, Fagiuoli, Ettore. Cassinari, Flavio.

"M. Heidegger: Modernità, storia e destino dell'Essere" in *Lo Storicismo e la Sua Storia: Temi, Problemi, Prospettive*, Cacciatore, Giuseppe (ed). Viti Cavaliere, Renata.

"Mead and Heidegger: Exploring the Ethics and Theory of Space, Place, and Environment" in *Philosophy and Geography I: Space, Place, and Environmental Ethics*, Light, Andrew (ed). Steelwater, Eliza.

"Nothingness and the Professional Thinker: Arendt versus Heidegger" in *The Ancients and the Moderns*, Lilly, Reginald (ed). Taminiaux, Jacques.

"Ontologia Della Mancanza: Heidegger e la questione dell'uomo" in *Soggetto E Verità: La questione dell'uomo nella filosofia contemporanea*, Fagiuoli, Ettore. Feroldi, Luisella.

"Overcoming Metaphysics: Carnap and Heidegger" in *Origins of Logical Empiricism*, Giere, Ronald N (ed). Friedman, Michael.

"Technik und Ethik" in *Angewandte Ethik: Die Bereichsethiken und ihre theoretische Fundierung*, Nida-Rümelin, Julian (ed). Ott, Konrad.

"The Passion of Facticity: Heidegger and the Problem of Love" in *The Ancients and the Moderns*, Lilly, Reginald (ed). Agamben, Giorgio.

"Una Disavventura Della Differenza: Heidegger e i 'francesi'" in *Soggetto E Verità: La questione dell'uomo nella filosofia contemporanea*, Fagiuoli, Ettore. Vaccaro, G Battista.

"Verità Dell'Evento E Ruolo Del Soggetto Nella Conoscenza Storica: Tre paradigmi" in *Soggetto E Verità: La questione dell'uomo nella filosofia contemporanea*, Fagiuoli, Ettore. Borutti, Silvana.

*Being and Time: A Translation of Sein und Zeit*. Stambaugh, Joan and Stambaugh, Joan (trans).

*Das Multiversum der Kulturen*. Kimmerle, Heinz.

*Die Zweideutigkeit des Ursprünglichen bei Martin Heidegger*. Molinuevo, José Luis.

*Dunamis* and Being: Heidegger on Plato's *Sophist* 247d8-e4. Ellis, John.

*Formen des Anti-Platonismus bei Kant, Nietzsche und Heidegger*. Patt, Walter.

*Forms of Transcendence: Heidegger and Medieval Mystical Theology*. Sikka, Sonya.

*Hegel e Aristotele*. Movia, Giancarlo (ed).

*Heidegger and Being and Time*. Mulhall, Stephen.

*Heidegger and French Philosophy*. Rockmore, Tom.

*Heidegger's Hidden Sources: East Asian Influences on His Work*. Parkes, Graham (trans) and May, Reinhard.

*Heidegger's Silence*. Lang, Berel.

*Heidegger, Philosophy, Nazism*. Young, Julian.

*Konstellation und Existenz*. Goebel, Eckart.

*La "segunda mitad" de Ser y Tiempo*. Von Herrmann, Friedrich-Wilhelm and Borges-Duarte, Irene (trans).

*La Ambigüedad de lo Originario en Martin Heidegger*. Molinuevo, José Luis.

*La Volontà di Potenza in Nietzsche e la Storia dell'Europa negli Ultimi Tempi*. Manno, Ambrogio Giacomo.

## HIGHER EDUCATION
*Rethinking College Education*. Allan, George.
*Academic Corruption*. Kekes, John.
Affirmative Action in Higher Education as Redistribution. Guenin, Louis M.
Gender, Race, and Difference: Individual Consideration versus Group-Based Affirmative Action in Admission to Higher Education. Jaggar, Alison.
Service Learning in Business Ethics. Fleckenstein, Marilynn P.
The Vocation of Higher Education: Modern and Postmodern Rhetorics in the Israeli Academia on Strike. Gur-Ze'ev, Ilan.

## HIGHER ORDER LOGICS
Formalizing Forcing Arguments in Subsystems of Second-Order Arithmetic. Avigad, Jeremy.
Higher Order Unification and the Interpretation of Focus. Pulman, Stephen G.
Kripke Models and the (In)equational Logic of the Second-Order Lambda-Calculus. Gallier, Jean.
Lógica y práctica matemática. Nepomuceno Fernández, Angel.
Non-Axiomatizable Second Order Intuitionistic Propositional Logic. Skvortsov, D.
Second Order Propositional Operators Over Cantor Space. Polacik, Tomasz.
Semantics for Two Second-Order Logical Systems. Freund, Max A.

## HILBERT, D
Axiomática y álgebra estructural en la obra de David Hilbert. Corry, Leo.
El finitismo metamatemático de Hilbert y la crítica de Oskar Becker. Roetti, Jorge Alfredo.
Formalization of Hilbert's Geometry of Incidence and Parallelism. Von Plato, Jan.
From Completeness to Archimedean Completeness: An Essay in the Foundations of Euclidean Geometry. Ehrlich, Philip.
Hilbert and Set Theory. Dreben, Burton and Kanamori, Akihiro.
Hilbert and the Emergence of Modern Mathematical Logic. Moore, Gregory H.
Hilbert Vindicated?. Hintikka, Jaakko.
Hilbert's Formalism and Arithmetization of Mathematics. Webb, Judson C.
Hipotesis del continuo, definibilidad y funciones recursivas: historia de un desencuentro (1925-1955). Zalamea, Fernando.
Husserl and Hilbert on Completeness: A Neglected Chapter in Early Twentieth Century Foundations of Mathematics. Majer, Ulrich.
On a Paradox of Hilbert and Bernays. Priest, Graham.

## HILEY, B
Antidote or Theory?. Dickson, Michael.
Review Essay: Bohmian Mechanics and the Quantum Revolution. Goldstein, Sheldon.

## HILL, G
Keynes on Capitalism: Reply to Hill. Horwitz, Steven.

## HILLMAN, J
*The Magic Mirror: Myth's Abiding Power*. Baeten, Elizabeth M.

## HINAYANA
The Bodhisattva Ideal in Theravāda Buddhist Theory and Practice: A Reevaluation of the Bodhisattva-Srāvaka Opposition. Samuels, Jeffrey.

## HINDUISM
see also Karma, Reincarnation, Sankara, Yoga
*The Indian Renouncer and Postmodern Poison: A Cross-Cultural Encounter*. Olson, Carl.
A Critique on Brahman-Realization. Prabhakara Rao, M.
A Defense of Yogācāra Buddhism. Wayman, Alex.
An Inquiry into Ethical Relativism in Hindu Thought. Jhingran, Saral.
Approach of Hinduism to Its Scriptures. Nayak, G C.
Buddhist Meditation and the Consciousness of Time. Novak, Philip.

## HINSHELWOOD, R
Commentary on "Primitive Mental Processes". Thornton, W Laurence.

## HINTIKKA, J
"Caution and Nonmonotonic Inference" in *Knowledge and Inquiry: Essays on Jaakko Hintikka's Epistemology and Philosophy of Science*, Sintonen, Matti (ed). Levi, Isaac.
"Explanation: The Fifth Decade" in *Knowledge and Inquiry: Essays on Jaakko Hintikka's Epistemology and Philosophy of Science*, Sintonen, Matti (ed). Sintonen, Matti.
"He Is No Good for My Work" in *Knowledge and Inquiry: Essays on Jaakko Hintikka's Epistemology and Philosophy of Science*, Sintonen, Matti (ed). Sahlin, Nils-Eric.
"Hintikka on Plenitude in Aristotle" in *Knowledge and Inquiry: Essays on Jaakko Hintikka's Epistemology and Philosophy of Science*, Sintonen, Matti (ed). Bechler, Zev.
"Inductive Logic, Atomism, and Observational Error" in *Knowledge and Inquiry: Essays on Jaakko Hintikka's Epistemology and Philosophy of Science*, Sintonen, Matti (ed). Niiniluoto, Ilkka.
"Natural Kinds of Questions" in *Knowledge and Inquiry: Essays on Jaakko Hintikka's Epistemology and Philosophy of Science*, Sintonen, Matti (ed). Bromberger, Sylvain.
"On the Logical Structure of Learning Models" in *Knowledge and Inquiry: Essays on Jaakko Hintikka's Epistemology and Philosophy of Science*, Sintonen, Matti (ed). Kiikeri, Mika.
"Science and Games" in *Knowledge and Inquiry: Essays on Jaakko Hintikka's Epistemology and Philosophy of Science*, Sintonen, Matti (ed). Wolenski, Jan.
"Scientific Discovery, Induction, and the Multi-Level Character" in *Knowledge and Inquiry: Essays on Jaakko Hintikka's Epistemology and Philosophy of Science*, Sintonen, Matti (ed). Gebhard, George.
"Scientific Explanation and the Interrogative Model of Inquiry" in *Knowledge and Inquiry: Essays on Jaakko Hintikka's Epistemology and Philosophy of Science*, Sintonen, Matti (ed). Weber, Erik.
"Some Foundational Concepts of Erotetic Semantics" in *Knowledge and Inquiry: Essays on Jaakko Hintikka's Epistemology and Philosophy of Science*, Sintonen, Matti (ed). Wisniewski, Andrzej.
"The Carnap-Hintikka Programme in Inductive Logic" in *Knowledge and Inquiry: Essays on Jaakko Hintikka's Epistemology and Philosophy of Science*, Sintonen, Matti (ed). Kuipers, Theo A F.
"The Structure of Inquiry in Developmental Biology" in *Knowledge and Inquiry: Essays on Jaakko Hintikka's Epistemology and Philosophy of Science*, Sintonen, Matti (ed). Kleiner, Scott A.
"Theories of Questions in German-Speaking Philosophy" in *Knowledge and Inquiry: Essays on Jaakko Hintikka's Epistemology and Philosophy of Science*, Sintonen, Matti (ed). Kusch, Martin.
"Theory of Identifiability" in *Knowledge and Inquiry: Essays on Jaakko Hintikka's Epistemology and Philosophy of Science*, Sintonen, Matti (ed). Mutanen, Arto.
*Knowledge and Inquiry: Essays on Jaakko Hintikka's Epistemology and Philosophy of Science*. Sintonen, Matti (ed).
Commentary to J. Hintikka's Lecture. Olivetti, Marco M.
Kant's Theory of Geometrical Reasoning and the Analytic-Synthetic Distinction: On Hintikka's Interpretation of Kant's Philosophy of Mathematics. De Jong, Willem R.

## HINTZE, O
"Su alcuni elementi del confronto di Otto Hintze con l'*Historismus*" in *Lo Storicismo e la Sua Storia: Temi, Problemi, Prospettive*, Cacciatore, Giuseppe (ed). Di Costanzo, Giuseppe.

## HIPPOCRATIC OATH
Justice and the Individual in the Hippocratic Tradition. Zaner, Richard M.

## HIRSCH, E
Actual Intentionalism vs. Hypothetical Intentionalism. Iseminger, Gary.

## HIRSCHMAN, A
My Own Criticism of *The Joyless Economy*. Scitovsky, Tibor.
Virtuous Markets: The Market as School of the Virtues. Maitland, Ian.

## HISPANIC
César Chávez and La Causa: Toward a Hispanic Christian Social Ethic. Piar, Carlos R.

## HISTORICAL MATERIALISM
see also Dialectical Materialism
Georgii Shakhnazarov and the Soviet Critique of Historical Materialism. Sandle, Mark.
Marx, Columbus, and the October Revolution: Historical Materialism and the Analysis of Revolutions. Losurdo, Domenico.
Marx, Ideólogo dos Ideólogos. Pires, Francisco Videira.

## HISTORICISM
"Etica e storia in Schleiermacher" in *Lo Storicismo e la Sua Storia: Temi, Problemi, Prospettive*, Cacciatore, Giuseppe (ed). Moretto, Giovanni.
"L'incontro problematico tra *Historismus* e neo-kantiano" in *Lo Storicismo e la Sua Storia: Temi, Problemi, Prospettive*, Cacciatore, Giuseppe (ed). Bonito Oliva, Rossella.
"La filosofia morale di Ludovico Limentani tra naturalismo e storicismo" in *Lo Storicismo e la Sua Storia: Temi, Problemi, Prospettive*, Cacciatore, Giuseppe (ed). Rossanno, Giovanna.
"La scienza e la vita: Lo storicismo problematico di Giuseppe Capograssi" in *Lo Storicismo e la Sua Storia: Temi, Problemi, Prospettive*, Cacciatore, Giuseppe (ed). Acocella, Giuseppe.
"Lo storicismo critico-problematico e la tradizione della 'filosofia civile' italiana" in *Lo Storicismo e la Sua Storia: Temi, Problemi, Prospettive*, Cacciatore, Giuseppe (ed). Cacciatore, Giuseppe.
"Mannheim e Bloch: storicismo e utopia" in *Lo Storicismo e la Sua Storia: Temi, Problemi, Prospettive*, Cacciatore, Giuseppe (ed). Riccio, Monica.
"Piovani e lo storicismo" in *Lo Storicismo e la Sua Storia: Temi, Problemi, Prospettive*, Cacciatore, Giuseppe (ed). Lissa, Giuseppe.
"Popper on Prophecies and Predictions" in *The Significance of Popper's Thought*, Amsterdamski, Stefan (ed). Wolenski, Jan.
"Religione e storicismo: Paul Yorck von Wartenburg" in *Lo Storicismo e la Sua Storia: Temi, Problemi, Prospettive*, Cacciatore, Giuseppe (ed). Donadio, Francesco.
"Su alcuni elementi del confronto di Otto Hintze con l'*Historismus*" in *Lo Storicismo e la Sua Storia: Temi, Problemi, Prospettive*, Cacciatore, Giuseppe (ed). Di Costanzo, Giuseppe.
"Uguaglianza e disuguaglianza: un tema di filosofia della storia" in *Lo Storicismo e la Sua Storia: Temi, Problemi, Prospettive*, Cacciatore, Giuseppe (ed). Gentile, Giulio.
"Vico, la storia, lo storicismo" in *Lo Storicismo e la Sua Storia: Temi, Problemi, Prospettive*, Cacciatore, Giuseppe (ed). Nuzzo, Enrico.
*Debating the State of Philosophy: Habermas, Rorty, and Kolakowski*. Niznik, Jozef (ed) and Sanders, John T (ed).
*Introduction to Philosophical Hermeneutics*. Grondin, Jean, Gadamer, Hans-Georg and Weinsheimer, Joel (trans).
*Lo Storicismo e la Sua Storia: Temi, Problemi, Prospettive*. Cacciatore, Giuseppe (ed), Cantillo, Giuseppe (ed) and Lissa, Giuseppe (ed).

**HISTORICISM**

*Rationalität und Theoriebildung: Studien zu Karl R. Poppers Methodologie der Sozialwissenschaften.* Schmid, Michael.

*The Fate of Place: A Philosophical History.* Casey, Edward S.

*The God Within: Kant, Schelling, and Historicity.* Burbidge, John W (ed) and Fackenheim, Emil L.

A História da Filosofia na Aprendizagem/Ensino da Filosofia. Gonçalves, Joaquim Cerqueira.

Historicism and Lacanian Theory. Evans, Dylan.

Karl Popper y la crítica al determinismo. Bonetti, José Andrés.

La revisión neohistoricista del significado de la historia de la filosofía. Vegas González, Serafín.

Restauro artístico: fundamentos e implicaçoes hermenêticas. Abdo, Sandra Neves.

Some Comments on Rosenberg's Review. Sober, Elliott.

The "Political" Dimension of Italian Critico-Problematic Historicism (in Serbo-Croatian). Cacciatore, Giuseppe.

The Historicity of Philosophy: Hegel and Gadamer (in Serbo-Croatian). Deretic, Irina.

The Lessons of Theory. Parini, Jay.

The Poverty of Rhetoricism: Popper, Mises and the Riches of Historicism. Keaney, Michael.

The Quixotic Element in *The Open Society.* Munz, Peter.

Tradizione romanistica e dommatica moderna. Nardozza, Massimo.

Vico y Dilthey: La comprensión del mundo histórico. Damiani, Alberto M.

**HISTORICITY**

"Temporalità e storicità" in *Il Concetto di Tempo: Atti del XXXII Congresso Nazionale della Società Filosofica Italiana,* Casertano, Giovanni (ed). Seidl, Horst.

"Tra finitudine e storicità: il tempo nell'esistenzialismo italiano" in *Il Concetto di Tempo: Atti del XXXII Congresso Nazionale della Società Filosofica Italiana,* Casertano, Giovanni (ed). Faraone, Rosa.

Brevi Riflessioni Filosofiche sulla Storicità dell'Uomo. Seidl, Horst.

Elementos para a Construçao Teórica da Historicidade das Práticas Educativas Escolares. Pereira da Silva, Marcelo Soares.

Elementos para uma Fenomenologia Literária do Texto Filosófico. Pimentel, Manuel Cândido.

Lukács: Ontology and Historicity (in Portuguese). Lessa, Sergio.

On Historicity of History and Stupidity of Concepts: Nietzsche's Nihilism (in Polish). Michalski, Krzysztof.

**HISTORIOGRAPHY**

"L'Italia in Bayle, Bayle in Italia: una ricerca mancata" in *Pierre Bayle e l'Italia,* Bianchi, Lorenzo. Borghero, Carlo.

"Vico e Bayle: Ancora una messa a punto" in *Pierre Bayle e l'Italia,* Bianchi, Lorenzo. Nuzzo, Enrico.

*La Historia de la Filosofía como Hermenéutica.* Sánchez Meca, Diego.

*Objectivity and Historical Understanding.* Beards, Andrew.

*Pierre Bayle e l'Italia.* Bianchi, Lorenzo.

A Historiografia Filosófica Portuguesa Perante o Seiscentismo. Calafate, Pedro.

An Illusive Historiography of the View that the World is *Maya:* Professor Daya Krishna on the Historiography of Vedānta. Chandra, Suresh.

Croce e il superuomo: Una variante nell'edizione della "Filosofia della pratica" del 1923. Cingari, Salvatore.

Fra filologia e storiografia: progetti di edizioni settecentesche. Generali, Dario.

História, historiografia e símbolos. De Paula, Joao Antônio.

Historiography of Civilizations: A Review. Kaul, R K.

Italo Mancini lettore di Agostino: Percorso e contenuti di un incontro. Cangiotti, Marco.

Lakatos as Historian of Mathematics. Larvor, Brendan P.

Leo Strauss: lenguaje, tradición e historia (Reflexiones metodológicas sobre el arte de escribir). Blanco Echauri, Jesús.

Medieval Historiography. Birns, Nicholas.

Paramodern Strategies of Philosophical Historiography. Daniel, Stephen H.

Philosophical Autonomy and the Historiography of Medieval Philosophy. Inglis, John.

Racism, *Black Athena,* and the Historiography of Ancient Philosophy. Flory, Dan.

Reading the Historians' Resistance to Reading: An Essay On Historiographic Schizophrenia. Cohen, Sande.

Syncatégorèmes, concepts, équivocité: Deux questions anonymes, conservées dans le ms. Paris, B.N., lat. 16.401, liées à la sémantique de Pierre d'Ailly (c. 1350-1420). Bakker, Paul J J M.

The Writing of History as Remembering the Future (in Serbo-Croatian). Rauscher, Josef.

**HISTORY**

*see also* Natural History

"*In Itinere* Pictures from Central-European Philosophy" in *In Itinere* European Cities and the Birth of Modern Scientific Philosophy, Poli, Roberto (ed). Poli, Roberto.

"*In Itinere*: Vienna 1870-1918" in *In Itinere* European Cities and the Birth of Modern Scientific Philosophy, Poli, Roberto (ed). Libardi, Massimo.

"Alongside the Horizon" in *On Jean-Luc Nancy: The Sense of Philosophy,* Sheppard, Darren (ed). Gasché, Rodolphe.

"Antropologia ed etica in W. Dilthey" in *Lo Storicismo e la Sua Storia: Temi, Problemi, Prospettive,* Cacciatore, Giuseppe (ed). Ciriello, Giovanni.

"Bayle, I'"anima mundi" e Vico" in *Pierre Bayle e l'Italia,* Bianchi, Lorenzo. Costa, Gustavo.

"Before Environmental Ethics" in *Environmental Pragmatism,* Light, Andrew (ed). Weston, Anthony.

"Brevi note su liberalismo e storia in Constant e Tocqueville" in *Lo Storicismo e la Sua Storia: Temi, Problemi, Prospettive,* Cacciatore, Giuseppe (ed). Mazziotti, Stelio.

"Cohen—Denker in dürftiger Zeit? Über Sprache und Stil der Cohenschen Hermeneutik" in *Grenzen der kritischen Vernunft,* Schmid, Peter A. Fiorato, Pierfrancesco.

"Con Aristotele, otre Aristotele: Meyer e l'antropologia" in *Lo Storicismo e la Sua Storia: Temi, Problemi, Prospettive,* Cacciatore, Giuseppe (ed). Silvestre, Maria Luisa.

"Concepts: A Potboiler" in *Contents,* Villanueva, Enrique (ed). Fodor, Jerry.

"Constructing Modernism: The Cultural Location of *Aufbau*" in *Origins of Logical Empiricism,* Giere, Ronald N (ed). Galison, Peter.

"De servo arbitrio: La fine della libertà in Martin Heidegger" in *Lo Storicismo e la Sua Storia: Temi, Problemi, Prospettive,* Cacciatore, Giuseppe (ed). Mazzarella, Eugenio.

"Die Unterstellung von Vernunft in der Geschichte: Vorläufiger kritischer Versuch über einen Aspekt von Kants Geschichtsphilosophie" in *Grenzen der kritischen Vernunft,* Schmid, Peter A. Lüthe, Rudolf.

"El "Proyecto filosófico para la paz perpetua" de Kant como cuasipronóstico de la filosofía de la historia..." in *Kant: La paz perpetua, doscientos años despúes,* Martínez Guzmán, Vicent (ed). Apel, Karl-Otto.

"El Liberalismo como destino: A propósito de la obra de Francis Fukuyama" in *Liberalismo y Comunitarismo: Derechos Humanos y Democracia,* Monsalve Solórzano, Alfonso (ed). Salazar P, Freddy.

"Emergence and Embodiment: A Dialectic within Process" in *The Recovery of Philosophy in America: Essays in Honor of John Edwin Smith,* Kasulis, Thomas P (ed). Hocking, Richard.

"Esistenza, storia e storia della filosofia nel pensiero di Karl Jaspers" in *Lo Storicismo e la Sua Storia: Temi, Problemi, Prospettive,* Cacciatore, Giuseppe (ed). Miano, Francesco.

"Etica e storia in Schleiermacher" in *Lo Storicismo e la Sua Storia: Temi, Problemi, Prospettive,* Cacciatore, Giuseppe (ed). Moretto, Giovanni.

"F.H. Bradley and Later Idealism: From Disarray to Reconstruction" in *Philosophy after F.H. Bradley,* Bradley, James (ed). Armour, Leslie.

"Figure dell'originario nell'ultimo Husserl" in *Lo Storicismo e la Sua Storia: Temi, Problemi, Prospettive,* Cacciatore, Giuseppe (ed). Caianiello, Silvia.

"From *Wissenschaftliche Philosophie* to Philosophy of Science" in *Origins of Logical Empiricism,* Giere, Ronald N (ed). Giere, Ronald N.

"Gothein, Lamprecht e i fondamenti concettuali della *Kulturgeschichte*" in *Lo Storicismo e la Sua Storia: Temi, Problemi, Prospettive,* Cacciatore, Giuseppe (ed). Giugliano, Antonello.

"Herder, Kant e la storia" in *Lo Storicismo e la Sua Storia: Temi, Problemi, Prospettive,* Cacciatore, Giuseppe (ed). Lomonaco, Fabrizio.

"Heritage and Revolution" in *The Ancients and the Moderns,* Lilly, Reginald (ed). Castoriadis, Cornelius.

"Historians Look at Historical Truth" in *Epistemology and History,* Zeidler-Janiszewska, Anna (ed). Topolski, Jerzy.

"Historical Interpretation vs. Adaptive Interpretation of a Legal Text" in *Epistemology and History,* Zeidler-Janiszewska, Anna (ed). Ziembinski, Zygmunt.

"Homo historicus: Verso una trasformazione del paradigma 'classico' dell'antropologia filosofica" in *Lo Storicismo e la Sua Storia: Temi, Problemi, Prospettive,* Cacciatore, Giuseppe (ed). Giammusso, Salvatore.

"How Is It, Then, That we Still Remain Barbarians?" Foucault, Schiller, and the Aestheticization of Ethics. Bennett, Jane.

"How to Write the History of Vision: Understanding the Relationship between Berkeley and Descartes" in *Sites of Vision,* Levin, David Michael (ed). Atherton, Margaret L.

"Il compito dello storico nella lezione inaugurale di Richard Henry Tawney (1932)" in *Lo Storicismo e la Sua Storia: Temi, Problemi, Prospettive,* Cacciatore, Giuseppe (ed). Tagliaferri, Teodoro.

"Immagini della Grecia: Rosenzweig e Burckhardt" in *Lo Storicismo e la Sua Storia: Temi, Problemi, Prospettive,* Cacciatore, Giuseppe (ed). D'Antuono, Emilia.

"Interpretation in History: Collingwood and Historical Understanding" in *Verstehen and Humane Understanding,* O'Hear, Anthony (ed). Gardiner, Patrick.

"Introduction" in *The Semblance of Subjectivity,* Huhn, Tom (ed). Zuidervaart, Lambert.

"Introduction: Origins of Logical Empiricism" in *Origins of Logical Empiricism,* Giere, Ronald N (ed). Richardson, Alan W.

"L'immagine di Goethe e il pensiero storico (per una discussione dell'interpretazione di Meinecke)" in *Lo Storicismo e la Sua Storia: Temi, Problemi, Prospettive,* Cacciatore, Giuseppe (ed). Pica Ciamarra, Leonardo.

"L'indagine storico-universale di Max Weber sul 'razionalismo occidentale' tra lo storicismo e Nietzsche" in *Lo Storicismo e la Sua Storia: Temi, Problemi, Prospettive,* Cacciatore, Giuseppe (ed). Di Marco, Giuseppe Antonio.

"La concezione del tempo storico nello *Historismus*" in *Il Concetto di Tempo: Atti del XXXII Congresso Nazionale della Società Filosofica Italiana,* Casertano, Giovanni (ed). Cantillo, Giuseppe.

## HISTORY

"La recezione di Humboldt in Droysen: elementi per una ricostruzione" in *Lo Storicismo e la Sua Storia: Temi, Problemi, Prospettive,* Cacciatore, Giuseppe (ed). Caianiello, Silvia.

"La Verità Storica: La comprensione della storia nella riflessione di Martin Heidegger" in *Soggetto E Verità: La questione dell'uomo nella filosofia contemporanea,* Fagiuoli, Ettore. Cassinari, Flavio.

"Le relazioni tra Bayle e l'Italia: i corrispondenti italiani di Bayle e le *Nouvelles de la République des Lettres*" in *Pierre Bayle e l'Italia,* Bianchi, Lorenzo. Bianchi, Lorenzo.

"Lvov" in *In Itinere* European Cities and the Birth of Modern Scientific Philosophy, Poli, Roberto (ed). Wolenski, Jan.

"M. Heidegger: Modernità, storia e destino dell'Essere" in *Lo Storicismo e la Sua Storia: Temi, Problemi, Prospettive,* Cacciatore, Giuseppe (ed). Viti Cavaliere, Renata.

"Malebranche e la storia nella *Recherche de la Vérité*" in *Lo Storicismo e la Sua Storia: Temi, Problemi, Prospettive,* Cacciatore, Giuseppe (ed). Stile, Alessandro.

"Metodo e modelli storiografici nel tardo illuminismo tedesco" in *Lo Storicismo e la Sua Storia: Temi, Problemi, Prospettive,* Cacciatore, Giuseppe (ed). D'Allessandro, Giuseppe.

"Morally Appreciated Circumstances: A Theoretical Problem for Casuistry" in *Philosophical Perspectives on Bioethics,* Sumner, L W (ed). Jonsen, Albert R.

"Nineteenth-Century Würzburg: The Development of the Scientific Approach to Philosophy" in *In Itinere* European Cities and the Birth of Modern Scientific Philosophy, Poli, Roberto (ed). Baumgartner, Wilhelm.

"No Necessary Connection": The Medieval Roots of the Occasionalist Roots of Hume. Nadler, Steven.

"Note sulla concezione leibniziana della storia" in *Lo Storicismo e la Sua Storia: Temi, Problemi, Prospettive,* Cacciatore, Giuseppe (ed). Sanna, Manuela.

"Ou, séance, touche de Nancy, ici" in *On Jean-Luc Nancy: The Sense of Philosophy,* Sheppard, Darren (ed). Hamacher, Werner.

"Pensare La Storia: Soggetto e metodo dell'interpretazione" in *Soggetto E Verità: La questione dell'uomo nella filosofia contemporanea,* Fagiuoli, Ettore. D'Allessandro, Paolo.

"Per Una Genealogia Della Coscienza Storica" in *Soggetto E Verità: La questione dell'uomo nella filosofia contemporanea,* Fagiuoli, Ettore. Merlini, Fabio.

"Philo of Larissa and Platonism" in *Scepticism in the History of Philosophy: A Pan-American Dialogue,* Popkin, Richard H (ed). Glidden, David.

"Philosophical Commitments and Scientific Progress" in *The Idea of Progress,* McLaughlin, Peter (ed). Crombie, A C.

"Philosophie der Philosophie: Zur Frage nach dem Philosophiebegriff" in *Grenzen der kritischen Vernunft,* Schmid, Peter A. Schneiders, Werner.

"Philosophy and Art in Munich Around the Turn of the Century" in *In Itinere* European Cities and the Birth of Modern Scientific Philosophy, Poli, Roberto (ed). Schuhmann, Karl.

"Philosophy as Critique and as Vision" in *The Recovery of Philosophy in America: Essays in Honor of John Edwin Smith,* Kasulis, Thomas P (ed). Westphal, Merold.

"Philosophy's Recovery of Its History: A Tribute to John E. Smith" in *The Recovery of Philosophy in America: Essays in Honor of John Edwin Smith,* Kasulis, Thomas P (ed). Lucas Jr, George R.

"Pierre Bayle nell'*Index librorum prohibitorum*: I decreti di proibizione delle *Nouvelles de la République des Lettres...*" in *Pierre Bayle e l'Italia,* Bianchi, Lorenzo. Canone, Eugenio.

"Piovani e lo storicismo" in *Lo Storicismo e la Sua Storia: Temi, Problemi, Prospettive,* Cacciatore, Giuseppe (ed). Lissa, Giuseppe.

"Postnormative Subjectivity" in *The Ancients and the Moderns,* Lilly, Reginald (ed). Mensch, James Richard.

"Progress and Development in Music History" in *The Idea of Progress,* McLaughlin, Peter (ed). Flotzinger, Rudolf.

"Progress: Fact and Fiction" in *The Idea of Progress,* McLaughlin, Peter (ed). Von Wright, Georg Henrik.

"Progresso o sviluppo? Un problema di filosofia della storia nella prospettiva di W. von Humboldt" in *Lo Storicismo e la Sua Storia: Temi, Problemi, Prospettive,* Cacciatore, Giuseppe (ed). Carrano, Antonio.

"Prospettive di storia universale nell'opera di Spengler" in *Lo Storicismo e la Sua Storia: Temi, Problemi, Prospettive,* Cacciatore, Giuseppe (ed). Conte, Domenico.

"Race, Life, Death, Identity, Tragedy and Good Faith" in *Existence in Black: An Anthology of Black Existential Philosophy,* Gordon, Lewis R (ed). Zack, Naomi.

"Racionalidad y *poiesis*: los límites de la praxis histórica" in *La racionalidad: su poder y sus límites,* Nudler, Oscar (ed). Inés Mudrovcic, María.

"Ragione universale, storia universale, religione universale: il Voltaire illusionista dell'abate Galiani" in *Lo Storicismo e la Sua Storia: Temi, Problemi, Prospettive,* Cacciatore, Giuseppe (ed). Amodio, Paolo.

"Recollection, Forgetting, and the Hermeneutics of History: Meditations on a Theme from Hegel" in *Hegel, History, and Interpretation,* Gallagher, Shaun. Lucas Jr, George R.

"Religione e storia in Wilhelm Roscher" in *Lo Storicismo e la Sua Storia: Temi, Problemi, Prospettive,* Cacciatore, Giuseppe (ed). Catarzi, Marcello.

"Remarks on the History of the Concept of Crisis" in *The Ancients and the Moderns,* Lilly, Reginald (ed). Koselleck, Reinhart.

"Science and the Avant-Garde in Early Nineteenth-Century Florence" in *In Itinere* European Cities and the Birth of Modern Scientific Philosophy, Poli, Roberto (ed). Albertazzi, Liliana.

"Self-Transformation in American Blacks: The Harlem Renaissance and Black Theology" in *Existence in Black: An Anthology of Black Existential Philosophy,* Gordon, Lewis R (ed). Morrison II, Roy D.

"Shaping and Sex: Commentary on Parts I and II" in *Sex, Preference, and Family: Essays on Law and Nature,* Nussbaum, Martha C (ed). Estlund, David M.

"Storia e filologia in Niebuhr" in *Lo Storicismo e la Sua Storia: Temi, Problemi, Prospettive,* Cacciatore, Giuseppe (ed). Montepaone, Claudia.

"Storia e tempo storico in Marx" in *Lo Storicismo e la Sua Storia: Temi, Problemi, Prospettive,* Cacciatore, Giuseppe (ed). Cacciatore, Giuseppe.

"Storicità e mondo umano nell'estetica di Gravina" in *Lo Storicismo e la Sua Storia: Temi, Problemi, Prospettive,* Cacciatore, Giuseppe (ed). Cantillo, Clementina.

"Tempo e storia in Ilya Prigogine" in *Il Concetto di Tempo: Atti del XXXII Congresso Nazionale della Società Filosofica Italiana,* Casertano, Giovanni (ed). Gembillo, Giuseppe.

"Tempo storico e futuro escatologico" in *Il Concetto di Tempo: Atti del XXXII Congresso Nazionale della Società Filosofica Italiana,* Casertano, Giovanni (ed). Dall'Asta, Giuseppe.

"The 'Transhistoricity' of the Structure of a Work of Art and the Process of Value Transmission in Culture" in *Epistemology and History,* Zeidler-Janiszewska, Anna (ed). Kostyrko, Teresa.

"The Absent Signifier: Historical Narrative and the Abstract Subject" in *Critical Studies: Ethics and the Subject,* Simms, Karl (ed). Clayton, Leigh.

"The Autonomy of History: Collingwood's Critique of F.H. Bradley's Copernican Revolution in Historical Knowledge" in *Philosophy after F.H. Bradley,* Bradley, James (ed). Rubinoff, Lionel.

"The Chinese "Cyclic" View of History vs. Japanese "Progress" in *The Idea of Progress,* McLaughlin, Peter (ed). Nakayama, Shigeru.

"The Enlightenment Ambition of Epistemic Utopianism: Otto Neurath's Theory of Science in Historical Perspective" in *Origins of Logical Empiricism,* Giere, Ronald N (ed). Uebel, Thomas E.

"The Hermeneutic Dimension of Social Science and Its Normative Foundation" in *Epistemology and History,* Zeidler-Janiszewska, Anna (ed). Apel, Karl-Otto.

"The Third World and Enlightenment" in *Averroës and the Enlightenment,* Wahba, Mourad (ed). Osman, Mahmoud.

"The Use and Abuse of Modernity: Postmodernism and the American Philosophic Tradition" in *Philosophy in Experience: American Philosophy in Transition,* Hart, Richard (ed). Ryder, John.

"Theoretical and Practical Reasoning: An Intractable Dualism?" in *Philosophy of Education (1996),* Margonis, Frank (ed). McClellan, Jr, James E.

"Troeltsch e Kant: 'Apriori' e 'storia' nella filosofia della religione" in *Lo Storicismo e la Sua Storia: Temi, Problemi, Prospettive,* Cacciatore, Giuseppe (ed). Cantillo, Giuseppe.

"Types of Determination vs. The Development of Science in Historical Epistemology" in *Epistemology and History,* Zeidler-Janiszewska, Anna (ed). Such, Jan.

"Uguaglianza e disuguaglianza: un tema di filosofia della storia" in *Lo Storicismo e la Sua Storia: Temi, Problemi, Prospettive,* Cacciatore, Giuseppe (ed). Gentile, Giulio.

"Una città senza storia: la perfezione immobile e l'utopia di Tommaso Campanella" in *Lo Storicismo e la Sua Storia: Temi, Problemi, Prospettive,* Cacciatore, Giuseppe (ed). Cambi, Maurizio.

"Verità Dell'Evento E Ruolo Del Soggetto Nella Conoscenza Storica: Tre paradigmi" in *Soggetto E Verità: La questione dell'uomo nella filosofia contemporanea,* Fagiuoli, Ettore. Borutti, Silvana.

"Via Media: On the Consequences of Historical Epistemology for the Problem of Rationality" in *Epistemology and History,* Zeidler-Janiszewska, Anna (ed). Buchowski, Michal.

"Vico, la storia, lo storicismo" in *Lo Storicismo e la Sua Storia: Temi, Problemi, Prospettive,* Cacciatore, Giuseppe (ed). Nuzzo, Enrico.

"Vieja y Nueva Política: La Circunstancia Histórica" in *Política y Sociedad en José Ortega y Gasset: En Torno a "Vieja y Nueva Política",* Lopez de la Vieja, Maria Teresa (ed). Morales Moya, Antonio.

"Vita e storia nella 'nuova scienza' del *George-Kreis*" in *Lo Storicismo e la Sua Storia: Temi, Problemi, Prospettive,* Cacciatore, Giuseppe (ed). Massimilla, Edoardo.

"Vita, esistenza, storia nella filosofia di J. Ortega y Gasset" in *Lo Storicismo e la Sua Storia: Temi, Problemi, Prospettive,* Cacciatore, Giuseppe (ed). Pucci, Daniela.

"Warsaw: The Rise and Decline of Modern Scientific Philosophy in the Capital City of Poland" in *In Itinere* European Cities and the Birth of Modern Scientific Philosophy, Poli, Roberto (ed). Jadacki, Jacek Juliusz.

"What Can Be Saved of the Idea of the University?" in *The Idea of University,* Brzezinski, Jerzy (ed). Ziembinski, Zygmunt.

"'The First Times' in Rousseau's *Essay on the Origin of Languages*" in *The Ancients and the Moderns,* Lilly, Reginald (ed). Gourevitch, Victor.

"¿Qué nos importa Descartes todavía?" in *Memorias Del Seminario En Conmemoración De Los 400 Anos Del Nacimiento De René Descartes,* Albis, Víctor S (ed). Serrano, Gonzalo.

## HISTORY

## HISTORY

Arnold's Aesthetics and 19th Century Croatian Philosophy of History (in Serbo-Croatian). Posavac, Zlatko.

Art and Aesthetics. Slater, Hartley.

Art as a Form of Negative Dialectics: 'Theory' in Adorno's *Aesthetic Theory*. Melaney, William D.

Austrian Philosophy: The Legacy of Franz Brentano. Brandl, Johannes.

Autobiography, Narrative, and the Freudian Concept of Life History. Brockmeier, Jens.

Avarice and Civil Unity: The Contribution of Sir Thomas Smith. Wood, Neal.

Bach's Butterfly Effect: Culture, Environment and History. Simmons, I G.

Baldwin, Cattell and the *Psychological Review*: A Collaboration and Its Discontents. Sokal, Michael M.

Benedetto Croce e la Storia della Chiesa. Campanelli, Giuseppina.

Beyond Acceptance and Rejection?. Martin, Dan.

Beyond Enlightenment? After the Subject of Foucault, Who Comes?. Venn, Couze.

Brevi Riflessioni Filosofiche sulla Storicità dell'Uomo. Seidl, Horst.

Business Ethics in the Former Soviet Union: A Report. Neimanis, George J.

Can Navya Nyāya Analysis Make a Distinction between Sense and Reference. Krishna, Daya.

Can We Ascribe to Past Thinkers Concepts they had No Linguistic Means to Express?. Prudovsky, Gad.

Carl Schmitt: An Occasional Nationalist?. Müller, Jan.

Categorization, Anomalies and the Discovery of Nuclear Fission. Andersen, Hanne.

Chronique de philosophie arabe et islamique. Urvoy, Dominique.

Citizenship and Culture in Early Modern Europe. Miller, Peter N.

Collingwood's "Lost" Manuscript of *The Principles of History*. Van der Dussen, Jan.

Comment on "Vedānta in the First Millennium AD: Illusion or Reality?". Murty, K Satchidananda.

Commentary. White, Hayden.

Commentary on "Autobiography, Narrative, and the Freudian Concept of Life History". Robinson, Daniel N.

Commerce, Constitutions, and the Manners of a Nation: Etienne Clavière's Revolutionary Political Economy, 1788-93. Whatmore, Richard.

Complexity and Deliberative Democracy. Femia, Joseph V.

Concepçoes de Mundo Veiculadas no Ensino de História do Curso Ginasial em Minas: 1954-1964. Nunes, Silma do Carmo.

Continuities and Discontinuities in the History of *Republic* Interpretation. Press, Gerald A.

Counterfactuals in Pragmatic Perspective. Rescher, Nicholas.

Courts and Conversions: Intellectual Battles and Natural Knowledge in Counter-Reformation Rome. De Renzi, Silvia.

Critical Notice of Philip Kitcher: *The Advancement of Science: Science without Legend, Objectivity without Illusions*. Kitcher, Philip.

Dead or Alive? Reflective Versus Unreflective Traditions. Tate, John W.

Denying the Body? Memory and the Dilemmas of History in Descartes. Reiss, Timothy J.

Derrida's Watch/Foucault's Pendulum. Naas, Michael B.

Descriptive and Revisionary Theories of Events. McHenry, Leemon B.

Dialéctica e História em J.P. Sartre. Reimao, Cassiano.

Diggers, Ranters, and Women Prophets: The Discourse of Madness and the Cartesian *Cogito* in Seventeenth-Century England. Hayes, Tom.

Discussion: Phylogenetic Species Concept: Pluralism, Monism, and History. Horvath, Christopher D.

Dissatisfied Enlightenment: Certain Difficulties Concerning the Public Use of One's Reason. Deligiorgi, Katerina.

Diversity and Ancient Democracy: A Response to Schwartz. Saxonhouse, Arlene W.

Do Practices Explain Anything? Turner's Critique of the Theory of Social Practices. Bohman, James.

Does it Make Sense to Teach History Through Thinking Skills?. Van Veuren, Pieter.

El principio de reconocimiento en la teoría filosófica del derecho político externo de Hegel. Vieweg, Klaus.

El relato histórico: ¿hipótesis o ficción? Críticas al "narrativismo imposicionalista" de Hayden White. Tozzi, María Verónica.

El seminario 'Orotava' de historia de la ciencia. Montesinos, José.

El tiempo histórico en Giambattista Vico. Botturi, Francesco.

Empathy before and after Husserl. Sawicki, Marianne.

English-Language History and the Creation of Historical Paradigm. Merridale, Catherine.

Ernst Cassirer, Historian of the Will. Wisner, David A.

Ethical Community Without Communitarianism. Winfield, Richard Dien.

Evolutionary Materialism. Dawson, Doyne.

Fateful Rendezvous: The Young Althusser. Elliott, Gregory.

Feminist Philosophy and the Philosophy of Feminism: Irigaray and the History of Western Metaphysics. Colebrook, Claire.

Fetal Subjects and Maternal Objects: Reproductive Technology and the New Fetal/Maternal Relation. Squier, Susan.

Ficçao e História na Narrativa Contemporânea. Malard, Letícia.

Filosofia da Educaçao e História da Pedagogia. Casulo, José Carlos.

Filosofía y teología de Gaston Fessard acerca de la actualidad histórica en el período 1936-46. Sols Lucia, José.

Fitness and Function. Walsh, Denis M.

Foucault's Analysis of Power's Methodologies. Scott, Gary Alan.

Foucault's Phallusy: Intimate Friendship as a Fundamental Ethic (Being a Reconstructive Reading of Foucault's *The Care of the Self*). Van Heerden, Adriaan.

Foucault, Ethics and Dialogue. Gardiner, Michael.

Freedom as Universal. Hartshorne, Charles.

From City-Dreams to the Dreaming Collective. Miller, Tyrus.

From Politics to Paralysis: Critical Intellectuals Answer the National Question. Cocks, Joan.

From Savages and Barbarians to Primitives: Africa, Social Typologies, and History in Eighteenth-Century French Philosophy. Jacques, T Carlos.

Fundamental Principles of Marxism's Self-Criticism. Oizerman, Teodor I.

Galileo and the Church: An Untidy Affair. Schoen, Edward L.

Habermas and Foucault: How to Carry Out the Enlightenment Project. Nielsen, Kai.

Hans Blumenberg: sobre la modernidad, la historia y los límites de la razón. Palti, Elías José.

Hayden White: Meaning and Truth in History. Hammond, David M.

Hegel and the End of Art. Markus, György.

Hegel and the Enlightenment: A Study in Ambiguity. Dupré, Louis.

Hegel on Historical Meaning: For Example, The Enlightenment. Pippin, Robert B.

Hegel's Critique of the Triumph of *Verstand* in Modernity. Houlgate, Stephen.

Hegel's Metaphilosophy and Historical Metamorphosis. Ware, Robert B.

Hegelianism in Merleau-Ponty's Philosophy of History. Nagel, Christopher P.

Hegelianism in Slovenia: A Short Introduction. Vezjak, Boris.

Herbert Butterfield (1900-79) as a Christian Historian of Science. Cabral, Regis.

Heterology: A Postmodern Theory of Foundations. Fairlamb, Horace L.

História, historiografia e símbolos. De Paula, Joao Antônio.

Historical Contingency. Ben-Menahem, Yemima.

Historical Narrative, Identity and the Holocaust. Buckler, Steve.

Historical Narratives and the Meaning of Nationalism. Kramer, Lloyd.

Histories of Cultural Populism. Ryle, Martin.

Historiography of Civilizations: A Review. Kaul, R K.

History and Memory. Geremek, Bronislaw.

History and Periodization. Baker, Robert S.

History and the Advent of the Self. Nelson, Ralph C.

History and the History of the Human Sciences: What Voice?. Smith, Roger.

History and Values. Dorotíková, Sona.

History of Philosophy: Historical and Rational Reconstruction. Kenny, Anthony.

History of Self-Interpretation: Jews and the Holocaust. Yovel, Yirmiyahu.

History of the Lie: Prolegomena. Derrida, Jacques and Kamuf, Peggy (trans).

History, Ethics, and Marxism. Cohen, G A.

History, Narrative, and Time. Mandelbrote, Scott.

Holocaust Memories and History. Turner, Charles.

Homo Economicus in the 20th Century: *Écriture Masculine* and Women's Work. Still, Judith.

How Chesterton Read History. Clark, Stephen R L.

Hume and the 1763 Edition of His *History of England*: His Frame of Mind as a Revisionist. Van Holthoon, Frederic L.

Hume in the Prussian Academy: Jean Bernard Mérian's "On the Phenomenalism of David Hume". Laursen, John Christian, Popkin, Richard H and Briscoe, Peter.

I May Be a Bit of a Jew: Trauma in Human Narrative. Zajko, Vanda.

If *p*, Then What? Thinking in Cases. Forrester, John.

In Defense of Public Reason: On the Nature of Historical Rationality. Ellet Jr, Frederick S and Ericson, David P.

In Support of Significant Modernization of Original Mathematical Texts (In Defense of Presentism). Barabashev, A G.

In the Name of Society, or Three Theses on the History of Social Thought. Osborne, Thomas and Rose, Nikolas.

Indian Philosophy in the First Millennium AD: Fact and Fiction. Krishna, Daya.

Interpreting Contextualities. Davies, Stephen.

Introduction: On the Interface of Analytic and Process Philosophy. Shields, George W.

Is Reductionism the Saving Way?. Dokulil, Milos.

Is Udayana a *pracchanna advaitin*?. Krishna, Daya.

José L. Abellán y la *especificidad* de la filosofía española. Jakovleva, L E.

Joseph Margolis on Interpretation. Casey, Edward S.

Krise der europäischen Kultur—ein Problemerbe der husserlschen Philosophie. Ströker, Elisabeth.

L'Allemagne, la modernité, la pensée. Bouckaert, Bertrand.

L'aporia del pensare fra scienza e storia. Tagliavia, Grazia.

L'Heritage Husserlien chez Koyré et Bachelard. Olesen, Soren Gosvig.

La *Vía* Vico como pretexto en Isaiah Berlin: contracorriente, antinomismo y pluralismo. Sevilla Fernández, José M.

La cuestión de la "caída" de los fundamentos y la ética: Hacia una mayor "responsabilidad" como respuesta al presente. Cragnolini, Mónica B.

La filosofia della storia di Giovanni Gentile. Garin, Eugenio.

La filosofía política y los problemas de nuestro tiempo. Rosenfield, Denis.

La filosofía y su historia. García Moriyón, Félix.

## HISTORY

La réception de la "Monarchie" de Dante ou Les métamorphoses d'une oeuvre philosophique. Cheneval, Francis.

La revisión neohistoricista del significado de la historia de la filosofía. Vegas González, Serafín.

Langer's Understanding of Philosophy. Campbell, James.

Laughing at Hegel. Westphal, Merold.

Le thomisme entre système et histoire. Tourpe, Emmanuel.

Lebensgeschichte als Selbstkonstitution bei Husserl. Tengelyi, Lászlo.

Liberalism and Moral Selfhood. Fairfield, Paul.

Limits and Grounds of History: The Nonhistorical. Haar, Michel.

Lo sminuzzamento dello spazio storico. Duque, Félix.

Lockean Political Apocrypha. Milton, J R.

Looking for a Subject: Latvian Memory and Narrative. Skultans, Vieda.

Margolis and the Historical Turn. Rockmore, Tom.

Margolis and the Philosophy of History. Carr, David.

Más allá del bosque (Reflexiones agoralógicas en torno a Vico). López Lloret, Jorge.

Meanings and Contexts: Mr. Skinner's Hobbes and the English Mode of Political Theory. Miller, Ted and Strong, Tracy B.

Medieval Historiography. Birns, Nicholas.

Memory, Forgetfulness, and History. Ricoeur, Paul.

Messianic History in Benjamin and Metz. Ostovich, Steven T.

Methode der Musikgeschichte von Guido Adler. Ito, Hisae.

Michael Oakeshott on History, Practice and Political Theory. Smith, Thomas W.

Michel Serres, Bruno Latour, and the Edges of Historical Periods. Wesling, Donald.

Michelet and Social Romanticism: Religion, Revolution, Nature. Mitzman, Arthur.

Mind and Method in the History of Ideas. Bevir, Mark.

Modèles historique et modèles culturels. Moutsopoulos, Evanghélos.

Monoteísmo, sacrificio, matadero: teodiceas y realidades históricas. Rodríguez-Campoamor, Hernán.

Moral Judgments in History: Hume's Position. Wertz, S K.

Natural Law as Essentially Definitive of Human Nature. Francis, Richard P.

Naturgemässe Klassifikation und Kontinuität, Wissenschaft und Geschichte: Überlegungen zu Pierre Duhem. Petrus, Klaus.

Neoclassical Economics and the Last Dogma of Positivism: Is the Normative-Positive Distinction Justified?. Keita, L D.

Netzverdichtung: Zur Philosophie industriegesellschaftlicher Entwicklungen. Lübbe, Hermann.

Nietzsche as Mashed Romantic. Picart, Caroline Joan S.

Nietzsche on Logic. Hales, Steven D.

Not at Home in Empire. Guha, Ranajit.

Notícia sobre a Pesquisa de Fontes Histórico-educacionais no Triângualo Mineiro e Alto Paranaíba. Souza Araújo, José Carlos, Gonçalves Neto, Wenceslau and Inácio Filho, Geraldo.

Novelty, Severity, and History in the Testing of Hypotheses: The Case of the Top Quark. Staley, Kent W.

O Homem e a História em Gaspar Frutuoso. Da Luz, José Luís Brandao.

O Materialismo Histórico e Dialético nas Abordagens de Vigotsky e Wallon acerca do Pensamento e da Linguagem. Marques Veríssimo, Mara Rúba Alves.

Obscurity as a Linguistic Device: Introductory and Historical Notes. Mehtonen, Päivi.

On Applying Applied Philosophy. Downing, F Gerald.

On Helmholtz and 'Bürgerliche Intelligenz': A Response to Robert Brain. Cahan, David.

On Historicity of History and Stupidity of Concepts: Nietzsche's Nihilism (in Polish). Michalski, Krzysztof.

Origen on Time. Lampert, Jay.

Outside Presence: Realizing the Holocaust in Contemporary French Narratives. Hand, Seán.

Para qué la historia de la filosofía?. Pintor-Ramos, Antonio.

Paradigmas: ¿construcciones históricas?. García Fallas, Jackeline.

Paramodern Strategies of Philosophical Historiography. Daniel, Stephen H.

Patrizzi and Descartes (in Czech). Floss, Pavel.

Per una storia dei cartesiani in Italia: Avvertenza. Garin, Eugenio.

Periodizing Postmodernism?. Carroll, Noël.

Philosophical Autonomy and the Historiography of Medieval Philosophy. Inglis, John.

Philosophical Psychology in Historical Perspective: Review Essay of J.-C. Smith (Ed.), *Historical Foundations of Cognitive Science*. Meyering, Theo C.

Philosophy in a Fragmented World. Noonan, Jeff.

Philosophy in the Age of Thresholding. Erickson, Stephen A.

Philosophy of Science and the German Idealists. Clayton, Philip.

Philosophy...Artifacts...Friendship—and the History of the Gaze. Illich, Ivan.

Pierre Bayle, the Rights of the Conscience, the "Remedy" of Toleration. Mori, Gianluca.

Popper's Plato: An Assessment. Klosko, George.

Prescott's Conquests: Anthropophagy, Auto-da-Fe and Eternal Return. Pearce, Colin D.

Problems of Formalization in Samvāda Sāstra. Shekhawat, Virendra.

Pufendorf, Sociality and the Modern State. Carr, Craig L and Seidler, Michael J.

Putting the Technological into Government. Dean, Mitchell.

R.G. Collingwood's Pragmatist Approach to Metaphysics. Requate, Angela.

Reading the Historians' Resistance to Reading: An Essay On Historiographic Schizophrenia. Cohen, Sande.

Reconstituting Praxis: Historialization as Re-Enactment. Flynn, Thomas R.

Remarks on History and Interpretation: Replies to Casey, Carr, and Rockmore. Margolis, Joseph.

Republican Readings of Montesquieu: *The Spirit of the Laws* in the Dutch Republic. Velema, Wyger R E.

Response to Pinkard. Beiser, Frederick C.

Response to the Commentaries. Brockmeier, Jens.

Rethinking the Social Contract. Sanjeev, M P.

Richard Rorty and the "Tricoteuses". Amorós, Celia.

Romanticized Enlightenment? Enlightened Romanticism? Universalism and Particularism in Hegel's *Understanding of the Enlightenment*. Pinkard, Terry.

Scheffler Revisited on the Role of History and Philosophy of Science in Science Teacher Education. Matthews, Michael R.

Short Account of the Debates in the Higher Seminary of History of Philosophy, Catholic University in Lublin, in the Years 1953/54 to 1955/56 (in Polish). Strózewski, Wladyslaw.

Sick with Passion. Louch, Alfred.

Social Epistemology and the Recovery of the Normative in the Post-Epistemic Era. Fuller, Steve.

Some Problems in the Writing of the History of African Philosophy. Ogbogbo, C B N.

Sozzini's Ghost: Pierre Bayle and Socinian Toleration. Tinsley, Barbara Sher.

Spenser and the Historical Revolution: *Briton Moniments* and the *Problem of Roman Britain*. Curran Jr, John E.

Strange Epoch! From Modernism to Postmodernism (in Hebrew). Mansbach, Abraham.

Suffering Strangers: An Historical, Metaphysical, and Epistemological Non-Ecumenical Interchange. Cherry, Mark J.

Sulla nostalgia: La memoria tormentata. Starobinski, Jean.

Surrogate Family Values: The Refeminization of Teaching. Thompson, Audrey.

Taming the Infinite. Potter, Michael D.

Technology, Appreciation, and the Historical View of Art. Fisher, John Andrew and Potter, Jason.

Teodicea y sentido de la historia: la respuesta de Hegel. Estrada, Juan A.

The "Passion for the Outside": Foucault, Blanchot, and Exteriority. Saghafi, Kas.

The Aesthetics of the Marketplace: Women Playwrights, 1770-1850. Newey, Katherine.

The Blessed Gods Mourn: What is Living-Dead in the Legacy of Hegel. Cutrofello, Andrew.

The Body as an "Object" of Historical Knowledge. Mann, Doug.

The Centrifugal Forces of Latin American Integration. Morales Manzur, Juan Carlos.

The Common Mental Attributes of the Dai Nationality Explored. Xiyuan, Xiong.

The Conservative Constructivist. Bloor, David.

The Constitution of Our World as the History of Arts (in Hungarian). Benseler, Frank.

The Curious Tale of Atlas College. Cahn, Steven M.

The Delayed Birth of Social Experiments. Brown, Robert.

The Eighteenth-Century British Reviews of Hume's Writings. Fieser, James.

The Epic of Evolution as a Framework for Human Orientation in Life. Kaufman, Gordon D.

The Essential Difference between History and Science. Martin, Raymond.

The Ethics of Philosophical Discourse. Lang, Berel.

The Evils of Chattel Slavery and the Holocaust: An Examination of Laurence Thomas's *Vessels of Evil*. Harriott, Howard H.

The Evolution of Discipline-Based Art Education. Delacruz, Elizabeth Manley and Dunn, Phillip C.

The Fact of Politics: History and Teleology in Kant. Krasnoff, Larry.

The Father of Modern Hermeneutics in a Postmodern Age: A Reinterpretation of Schleiermacher's Hermeneutics. Huang, Yong.

The Female Fulcrum: Rousseau and the Birth of Nationalism. Fermon, Nicole.

The Fool's Truth: Diderot, Goethe, and Hegel. Schmidt, James.

The French Revolutionary Roots of Political Modernity in Hegel's Philosophy, or the Enlightenment at Dusk. Wokler, Robert.

The Hermeneutical Turn in American Critical Theory, 1830-1860. Walhout, M D.

The Historical Setting of Latin American Bioethics. Gracia, Diego.

The Historical Turn in the Study of Adaptation. Griffiths, Paul E.

The Historicity of Philosophy: Hegel and Gadamer (in Serbo-Croatian). Deretic, Irina.

The History of Interpretation and the Interpretation of History in the History of Philosophy. Wiehl, Reiner.

The History of the Future of International Relations. Puchala, Donald J.

The Importance of Ideals. Van der Burg, Wibren.

The Internal Connectedness of Philosophy of History and Philosophy of Language in Nietzsche's Early Writings (in Serbo-Croatian). Margreiter, Reinhard.

## HOLOCAUST

Holocaust Memories and History. Turner, Charles.

I May Be a Bit of a Jew: Trauma in Human Narrative. Zajko, Vanda.

On the Alleged Uniqueness and Incomprehensibility of the Holocaust. Owen, B William.

Outside Presence: Realizing the Holocaust in Contemporary French Narratives. Hand, Seán.

Philosophers and the Holocaust: Mediating Public Disputes. Eagan, Jennifer L.

Should We Pardon Them?. Hobart, Ann and Jankélévitch, Vladimir.

The Evils of Chattel Slavery and the Holocaust: An Examination of Laurence Thomas's *Vessels of Evil*. Harriott, Howard H.

Über Heideggers "Schweigen" reden. Alisch, Rainer.

## HOLTON, R

Countering the Counting Problem: A Reply to Holton. Dodd, Julian.

The Vagaries of Paraphrase: A Reply to Holton on the Counting Problem. Rumfitt, Ian.

## HOLY

Lo santo y lo sagrado. Garrido Maturano, Angel Enrique.

## HOLZHEY, H

"Die Aktualität des Neukantianismus: Bemerkungen zu einem unumgänglichen Thema der Neukantianismusforschung" in *Grenzen der kritischen Vernunft*, Schmid, Peter A. Ollig, Hans-Ludwig.

## HOME

"Il mito dell'autoctonia del pensiero (Note su Hegel, Fichte, Heidegger)" in *Geofilosofia*, Bonesio, Luisa (ed). Resta, Caterina.

Fragmented Selves and Loss of Community. McKenna, Erin and Hanks, J Craig.

## HOMELESSNESS

Caring for "Socially Undesirable" Patients. Jecker, Nancy S.

Does Political Theory Matter for Policy Outcomes? The Case of Homeless Policy in the 1980s. Main, Thomas J.

## HOMER

*The Thinker as Artist: From Homer to Plato & Aristotle*. Anastaplo, George.

Homer's Theology and the Concept of Tolerance. Bosnjak, Branko.

Reading Raphael: *The School of Athens* and Its Pre-Text. Most, Glenn W.

Sieben Jenaer Reflexionen Hegels über Homer. Jeck, Udo Reinhold.

## HOMICIDE

Dangerous Games and the Criminal Law. Yeager, Daniel B.

## HOMOLOGY

Remarks on Galois Cohomology and Definability. Pillay, Anand.

## HOMONYM

De Aristóteles a Bréal: Da *Homonímia* à *Polissemia*. Da Silva, Augusto Soares.

## HOMOSEXUALITY

"Homosexuality and the Constitution" in *Sex, Preference, and Family: Essays on Law and Nature*, Nussbaum, Martha C (ed). Sunstein, Cass R.

"The Economic Approach to Homosexuality" in *Sex, Preference, and Family: Essays on Law and Nature*, Nussbaum, Martha C (ed). Posner, Richard A.

*Freud and the Passions*. O'Neill, John (ed).

*Sex, Love, and Friendship: Studies of the Society for the Philosophy of Sex and Love 1977-1992*. Soble, Alan (ed).

An Expanded Theoretical Discourse on Human Sexuality Education. Anderson, Peter B.

Genes and Human Behavior: The Emerging Paradigm. Drew, Allan P.

Homosexuality and the Practices of Marriage. McCarthy Matzko, David.

In Praise of Unreliability. Heldke, Lisa.

Liberté! Egalité! Sexualité!: Theorizing Lesbian and Gay Politics. Kaplan, Morris B.

Michel Foucault, lecteur de Platon ou de l'amour du beau garçon a la contemplation du beau en soi. Catonné, Jean-Philipe.

Teaching about Homosexuality and Heterosexuality. Reiss, Michael J.

Toward a Feminist Revision of Research Protocols on the Etiology of Homosexuality. Turner, Stephanie S.

Toward a Queer Ecofeminism. Gaard, Greta.

## HONDERICH, T

Honderich on the Consequences of Determinism. Double, Richard.

## HONESTY

Honest Research. Hillman, Harold.

Honesty, Individualism, and Pragmatic Business Ethics: Implications for Corporate Hierarchy. Quinn, J Kevin, Reed, J David and Browne, M Neil (& others).

Hume's Difficulty with the Virtue of Honesty. Cohon, Rachel.

## HONIG, B

Friendship Across Generations. Nye, Andrea.

## HONNETH, A

Worlds Apart? Habermas and Levinas. Vetlesen, Arne J.

## HONOR

Honour, Community, and Ethical Inwardness. Cordner, Christopher.

## HOOK, S

Remembering John Dewey and Sidney Hook. Rorty, Richard.

## HOOKS, B

Religion and the New African American Intellectuals. Allen, Norm R.

## HOOKWAY, C

Peirce on Norms, Evolution and Knowledge. Tiercelin, Claudine.

## HOPE

*Jonathan Edwards's Writings*: Text, Context, Interpretation. Stein, Stephen J (ed).

De la paix perpétuelle et de l'espérance comme devoir. Vuillemin, Jules.

Discutono *Il principio speranza*, di Ernst Bloch. Boella, Laura, Moneti, Maria and Schmidt, Burghart.

Hope and the Limits of Research: Commentary. Geller, Gail.

Jacques Ellul on the Technical System and the Challenge of Christian Hope. Punzo, Vincent A.

La paix perpétuelle chez Kant: du devoir à l'espérance. Perron, Louis.

Modernity, Postmodernity and Transmodernity: Hope in Search of Time (in Spanish). Mendieta, Eduardo.

## HORGAN, T

Explaining Supervenience: Moral and Mental. Zagwill, Nick.

Response to Commentators. Wright, Crispin.

Syntax in a Dynamic Brain. Garson, James W.

## HORIZON

"Physical and Cultural Dimensions of Horizon" in *Philosophy of Education (1996)*, Margonis, Frank (ed). Noel, Jana.

"The Glass Bead Game" in *Philosophy of Education (1996)*, Margonis, Frank (ed). Sidorkin, Alexander M.

Horizontal Intentionality and Transcendental Intersubjectivity (in Dutch). Zahavi, Dan.

## HORKHEIMER, M

Idealismo y materialismo: Max Horkheimer y la constitución del conocimiento en la ciencia social. Vergara, Eliseo Cruz.

Notas sobre modernidade e sujeito na dialética do esclarecimento. Duarte, Rodrigo A P.

The Frankfurt School. Tessin, Timothy.

## HORN SENTENCE

"Characterization Theorems for Infinitary Universal Horn Logic" in *Verdad: lógica, representación y mundo*, Villegas Forero, L. Dellunde, Pilar and Jansana, Ramon.

## HORNSBY, J

Responses to Critics of *The Construction of Social Reality*. Searle, John R.

## HORROR

"Transgressive Bodies: Destruction and Excessive Display of the Human Form in the Horror Film" in *Critical Studies: Ethics and the Subject*, Simms, Karl (ed). Mendik, Xavier.

Monsters and the Paradox of Horror. Vorobej, Mark.

## HORSTMANN, R

Horstmann, Siep, and German Idealism. Pippin, Robert B.

## HORTON, J

Contractual Justice: A Modest Defence. Barry, Brian.

## HORVATH, C

Useful Friendships: A Foundation for Business Ethics. Sommers, Mary Catherine.

## HORWICH, P

Response to Commentators. Wright, Crispin.

The Direction of Time. Savitt, Steven F.

Wayne, Horwich, and Evidential Diversity. Fitelson, Branden.

## HORWITZ, S

Capitalism, Coordination, and Keynes: Rejoinder to Horwitz. Hill, Greg.

## HOSPICE

Goldilocks and Mrs. Ilych: A Critical Look at the "Philosophy of Hospice". Ackerman, Felicia.

Still Here/Above Ground. Bartholome, William G.

## HOSPITAL

A Manual on Manners and Courtesies for the Shared Care of Patients. Stoekle, John D, Ronan, Laurence J and Emanuel, Linda L (& others).

Advance Directives and Patient Rights: A Joint Commission Perspective. Worth-Staten, Patricia A and Poniatowski, Larry.

Bad Night in the ER—Patients' Preferences and Reasonable Accommodation: Discussed by Douglas A. Beer, Ruth Macklin, Walter Robinson, and Philip Wang. Beer, Douglas A, Macklin, Ruth and Robinson, Walter (& others).

Bioethics Committees and JCAHO Patients' Rights Standards: A Question of Balance. Corsino, Bruce V.

Ethics in the Outpatient Setting: New Challenges and Opportunities. Young, Ernlé W D.

Hospital Mergers and Acquisitions: A New Catalyst for Examining Organizational Ethics. Hofmann, Paul B.

Images of Death and Dying in the Intensive Care Unit. Pascalev, Assya.

In Case of Emergency: No Need for Consent. Brody, Baruch A, Katz, Jay and Dula, Annette.

Japanese Psychiatrists' Attitudes toward Patients Wishing to Die in the General Hospital: A Cultural Perspective. Berger, Douglas, Takahashi, Yoshitomo and Fukunishi, Isao (& others).

Nurses' Perspectives of Hospital Ethics Committees. Stadler, Holly A, Morrissey, John M and Tucker, Joycelyn E.

Quality Control for Hospitals' Clinical Ethics Services: Proposed Standards. Leeman, Cavin P, Fletcher, John C and Spencer, Edward M (& others).

Responding to JCAHO Standards: Everybody's Business. Fletcher, John C.

**HOSPITAL**
The Effect of Ethnicity on ICU Use and DNR Orders in Hospitalized AIDS Patients. Tulsky, James A.
The Personal Is the Organizational in the Ethics of Hospital Social Workers. Walsh-Bowers, Richard, Rossiter, Amy and Prilleltensky, Isaac.
The Voices of Nurses on Ethics Committees. Rushton, Cindy Hylton.
Wisconsin Healthcare Ethics Committees. Shapiro, Robyn S, Klein, John P and Tym, Kristen A.

**HOURANI, G**
"Free Inquiry and Islamic Philosophy: The Significance of George Hourani" in *Averroës and the Enlightenment*, Wahba, Mourad (ed). Kurtz, Paul.

**HOUSING**
Standards Versus Struggle: The Failure of Public Housing and the Welfare-State Impulse. Husock, Howard.

**HOWARD-SNYDER, D**
Response to Howard-Snyder. Schellenberg, J L.

**HOWE, J**
"John Howe: dissidente, neoplatonico e antispinozista" in *Mind Senior to the World*, Baldi, Marialuisa. Simonutti, Luisa.

**HOY, D**
The Local, the Contextual and/or Critical. Benhabib, Seyla.

**HSIEH HO**
Ancient Chinese Aesthetics and its Modernity. Arnheim, Rudolf.

**HU SHIH**
Contemporary Significance of Chinese Buddhist Philosophy. Ichimura, Shohei.

**HUARTE DE SAN JUAN**
Huarte de San Juan y Spinoza: consideraciones sobre el vulgo y la filosofía natural. Beltrán, Miquel.

**HUDELSON, R**
Response to Richard Hudelson. Louw, Stephen.

**HUDSON, R**
Conventions in the *Aufbau*. Uebel, Thomas E.

**HUEY-LI, L**
"The Relevance of the Anthropocentric-Ecocentric Debate" in *Philosophy of Education (1996)*, Margonis, Frank (ed). Snauwaert, Dale T.

**HUGHES, L**
Air Raid over Harlem: Langston Hughes's Left Nationalist Poetics, 1927-1936. Keita Cha-Jua, Sundiata.

**HUHN, T**
Feeling and Aesthetic Judgment: A Rejoinder to Tom Huhn. Matthews, Patricia M.

**HUI SHI**
The Unique Features of Hui Shi's Thought: A Comparative Study between Hui Shi and Other Pre-Qin Philosophers. Xu, Keqian.

**HUI-NENG**
The Dialectics of Nothingness: A Reexamination of Shen-hsiu and Hui-neng. Laycock, Steven W.

**HUMAN**
see also Man, Person
"Il tempo dell'interrogare e il tempo dell'invocare" in *Il Concetto di Tempo: Atti del XXXII Congresso Nazionale della Società Filosofica Italiana*, Casertano, Giovanni (ed). Cavaciuti, Santino.
"Storicità e mondo umano nell'estetica di Gravina" in *Lo Storicismo e la Sua Storia: Temi, Problemi, Prospettive*, Cacciatore, Giuseppe (ed). Cantillo, Clementina.
"The Moral Uniqueness of the Human Animal" in *Human Lives: Critical Essays on Consequentialist Bioethics*, Oderberg, David S (ed). Scarlett, Brian.
"Visual Representation in Archaeology: Depicting the Missing-Link in Human Origins" in *Picturing Knowledge*, Baigrie, Brian S (ed). Moser, Stephanie.
"Young Human Beings: Metaphysics and Ethics" in *Human Lives: Critical Essays on Consequentialist Bioethics*, Oderberg, David S (ed). Gillett, Grant.
*Babies and Beasts: The Argument from Marginal Cases*. Dombrowski, Daniel A.
*Human, All Too Human: A Book of Free Spirits*. Hollingdale, R J (trans) and Nietzsche, Friedrich.
*Mens Sana in Corpore Sano? Reflexoes sobre o Enigma do Corpo*. Simao, Cristiana V.
*The Human Constitution*. Regan, Richard J (trans).
*The Possibility of Language: A Discussion of the Nature of Language, with Implications for Human and Machine Translation*. Melby, Alan K and Warner, C Terry.
*Twilight of the Idols Or, How to Philosophize with the Hammer*. Polt, Richard (trans) and Nietzsche, Friedrich.
*Vom Willen zur Macht: Anthropologie und Metaphysik der Macht am exemplarischen Fall Friedrich Nietzsches*. Gerhardt, Volker.
A Dialogue on Species-Specific Rights: Humans and Animals in Bioethics. Thomasma, David C and Loewy, Erich H.
Against Nagel: In Favor of a Compound Human Ergon. Christie, Juliette.
Altering Humans—The Case For and Against Human Gene Therapy. Holtug, Nils.

An Expanded Theoretical Discourse on Human Sexuality Education. Anderson, Peter B.
Autonomy and the Orthodoxy of Human Superiority. Gruzalski, Bart K.
Can We Be Justified in Believing that Humans Are Irrational?. Stein, Edward.
Challenge to Natural Law: The Vital Law. Black, Percy.
Chief Bumbu en de Verklaring van Menselijk Gedrag. Mackor, Anne Ruth and Peijnenburg, Jeanne.
El origen de la experiencia humana. Pochelú, Alicia G.
Enigma e relazione: Da Apollo a Edipo. Lo Bue, Elisabetta.
Human Versus Nonhuman: Binary Opposition As an Ordering Principle of Western Human Thought. Sheets-Johnstone, Maxine.
Immanencia y trascendencia en la intencionalidad. Bosch, Magdalena.
La conducta humana y la naturaleza. Roig, Arturo Andres.
La dignidad humana desde una perspectiva metafísica. Lobato, Abelardo.
La redención oscura. Ortiz-Osés, Andrés.
La unidad de la vida humana (Aristóteles y Leonardo Polo). Castillo Córdova, Genara.
Losing Our Minds: Olafson on Human Being. Cooper, David E.
Machine Learning by Imitating Human Learning. Chang, Kuo-Chin, Hong, Tzung-Pei and Tseng, Shian-Shyong.
Minds and Bodies: Human and Divine. Peterson, Gregory R.
Naturaleza humana en la filosofía de M.F. Sciacca y la concepción *light* de G. Vattimo. Darós, W R.
Obligaciones humanas Apuntes para la formulación de una idea. Messuti, Ana.
Preferences or Happiness? Tibor Scitovsky's Psychology of Human Needs. Friedman, Jeffrey and McCabe, Adam.
Principes pragmatistes pour une démarche pédagogique en enseignement moral. Daniel, Marie-France.
Protesi, ovvero la metamorfosi. Marchis, Vittorio.
Response: Autonomy, Animals, and Conceptions of the Good. Frey, R G.
Response: What Does Evolutionary Theory Tell Us about the Moral Status of Animals?. Menta, Timothy.
Sobre el ser y la creación. García González, Juan A.
The Definition of Man Needs. Gairola, M P.
The Nature of Human Concepts/Evidence from an Unusual Source. Pinker, Steven and Prince, Alan.
The Only Feasible Means: The Pentagon's Ambivalent Relationship with the Nuremberg Code. Moreno, Jonathan D.
The Other Human-Subject Experiments. Herrera, Christopher D.
The Psychology of Harry F. Harlow: A Bridge from Radical to Rational Behaviorism. Rumbaugh, Duane M.
The Rights of Humans and Other Animals. Regan, Tom.
Total Quality Management: A Plan for Optimizing Human Potential?. Wagner, Paul A.

**HUMAN BEING**
*Animal Acts: Configuring the Human in Western History*. Ham, Jennifer (ed) and Senior, Matthew (ed).
*Metaphysical Animal: Divine and Human in Man*. Woznicki, Andrew Nicholas.
*Plato on the Human Paradox*. O'Connell, Robert J.
*The Human Animal: Personal Identity without Psychology*. Olson, Eric T.
El trabajo como división de funciones. Rodríguez Sedano, Alfredo.
Human Beings Are Animals. Lee, Patrick.
Humans, Persons and Selves. Brown, Mark T.
Is Every Human Being a Person?. Spaemann, Robert.
Justifying the Perennial Philosophy. Meynell, Hugo.
La esencia del hombre como disponer indisponible. Urabayen Pérez, Julia.
Los hábitos intelectuales según Polo. Sellés, Juan Fernando.
Man: The Perennial Metaphysician. Dewan, Lawrence.
Persona: Intimidad, don y libertad nativa: Hacia una antropología de los transcendentales personales. Yepes, Ricardo.
St. Thomas and Pre-Conceptual Intellection. Dewan, Lawrence.

**HUMAN CONDITION**
Pascal: A Busca do Ponto Fixo e a Prática da Anatomia Moral. Marton, Scarlett.
Science and Human Condition (in Portuguese). Caponi, Sandra N C.

**HUMAN DIGNITY**
Axiological Foundations of "Human Dignity" (Spanish). Sánchez, Angel Martín.

**HUMAN EXISTENCE**
Kierkegaard's Dialectical Image of Human Existence in *The Concluding Unscientific Postscript to the Philosophical Fragments*. Krentz, Arthur A.

**HUMAN GENOME**
Privacy and the Human Genome Project. Wiesenthal, David L and Wiener, Neil I.

**HUMAN GOOD**
*A Politics of the Common Good*. Riordan, Patrick.

**HUMAN LIFE**
Desarrollo sostenible y valoración de la vida humana. Vargas, Celso and Alfaro, Mario.
La teología epicúrea: la concepción de la divinidad y su incidencia en la vida humana. Méndez Lloret, Isabel.

## HUMANISM

No Fear: How a Humanist Faces Science's New Creation. Hull, Richard T.

Oltre l'umanesimo: Alcune considerazioni su tecnica e modernità. Galli, Carlo.

Pascal e as Grandes Questoes do seu Tempo. Maia Neto, José R.

Reflections on the Other (in Hebrew). Brinker, Menahem.

The Caterpillar's Question: Contesting Anti-Humanism's Contestations. Porpora, Douglas V.

The Educational Contributions of Sir Thomas More. Masterson, David L.

The Epistemology of Humanism. Mojsisch, Burkhard.

The Humanism of Sartre: Toward a Psychology of Dignity. Iuculano, John and Burkum, Keith.

The Infomedia Revolution: Opportunities for Global Humanism. Kurtz, Paul.

The Limits of Tolerance. Kurtz, Paul.

The Problematic Situation of Post-Humanism and the Task of Recreating a Symphysical Ethos. Acampora, Ralph.

The Revolutionary Humanism of Jayaprakash Narayan. Manimala, Varghes.

Thinking Naturally. O'Neill, John.

## HUMANITIES

"Non-Cartesian Coordinates in the Contemporary Humanities" in Epistemology and History, Zeidler-Janiszewska, Anna (ed). Grzegorczyk, Anna.

"Prospect for the Humanities" in The American University: National Treasure or Endangered Species?, Ehrenberg, Ronald G (ed). Gray, Hanna H.

Epistemology and History: Humanities as a Philosophical Problem and Jerzy Kmita's Approach to It. Zeidler-Janiszewska, Anna (ed).

Nietzsche and the Modern Crisis of the Humanities. Levine, Peter.

A Critique and A Retrieval of Management and the Humanities. Gilbert Jr, Daniel R.

A So-Called 'Fraud': Moral Modulations in a Literary Scandal. Lynch, Michael.

Assessing the Publication Swamp in Literary Studies. Harris, Wendell V.

Natural Law, Nature, and Biology: A Modern Synthesis. Hartigan, Richard Shelly.

O estatuto das humanidades o regresso às artes. Gonçalves, Joaquim Cerqueira.

Whether Logic Should Satisfy the Humanities Requirement. Martin, John N.

## HUMANITY

"Respect for Humanity" in The Tanner Lectures on Human Values, Volume 18, 1997, Peterson, Grethe B (ed). Hill Jr, Thomas E.

"The Idea of Progress in Human Health" in The Idea of Progress, McLaughlin, Peter (ed). Lazar, Philippe.

"The Root of Humanity: Hegel on Communication and Language" in Figuring the Self: Subject, Absolute, and Others in Classical German Philosophy, Zöller, Günter (ed). Peters, John Durham.

Foundations of Futures Studies: Human Science for a New Era. Bell, Wendell.

Karl-Otto Apel: Selected Essays. Mendieta, Eduardo (ed).

La Scienza Nuova nella Storia del Pensiero Politico. Voegelin, Eric and Zanetti, Gianfrancesco (trans).

The Tanner Lectures on Human Values, Volume 18, 1997. Peterson, Grethe B (ed).

Unpopular Essays. Russell, Bertrand.

Watsuji Tetsurō's Rinrigaku. Carter, Robert E (trans) and Seisaku, Yamamoto (trans).

An Achievement of Humanity. Kaznacheev, Vlail' Petrovich.

Constructing the Law of Peoples. Moellendorf, Darrel.

Damaged Humanity: The Call for a Patient-Centered Medical Ethic in the Managed Care Era. Churchill, Larry R.

De si es posible afirmar la construcción de una "eticidad" en la filosofía práctica de Kant. Arpini, Adriana.

Deification in the Summa Theologiae: A Structural Interpretation of the Prima Pars. Williams, A N.

Economies, Technology, and the Structure of Human Living. Sauer, James B.

From Self-Cultivation to Philosophical Counseling: An Introduction. Cheng, Chung-ying.

La persona y el autodominio moral. Darós, W R.

Liturgy: Divine and Human Service. Purcell, Michael.

Nature, the Genesis of Value, and Human Understanding. Rolston, III, Holmes.

On Rape: A Crime Against Humanity. Calhoun, Laurie.

Our Future in J. Krishnamurti. Subrata, Roy.

Privacy and Control. Davison, Scott A.

The Hobbes Game, Human Diversity, and Learning Styles. Gerwin, Martin E.

The Meaning of Life. Hartshorne, Charles.

Untameable Singularity (Some Remarks on Broken Hegemonies). Granel, Gérard and Wolfe, Charles T (trans).

What should we Treat as an End in Itself?. Dean, Richard.

Winch and Instrumental Pluralism: A Reply to B. D. Lerner. Keita, L D.

## HUMBER, J

"More on Fathers' Rights" in Reproduction, Technology, and Rights: Biomedical Ethics Reviews, Humber, James M (ed). Hales, Steven D.

## HUMBOLDT

"La recezione di Humboldt in Droysen: elementi per una ricostruzione" in Lo Storicismo e la Sua Storia: Temi, Problemi, Prospettive, Cacciatore, Giuseppe (ed). Caianiello, Silvia.

"Progresso o sviluppo? Un problema di filosofia della storia nella prospettiva di W. von Humboldt" in Lo Storicismo e la Sua Storia: Temi, Problemi, Prospettive, Cacciatore, Giuseppe (ed). Carrano, Antonio.

## HUME

"Hume's Scepticism and his Ethical Depreciation of Religion" in Scepticism in the History of Philosophy: A Pan-American Dialogue, Popkin, Richard H (ed). Badía Cabrera, Miguel A.

"Hume's Scepticism: Natural Instincts and Philosophical Reflection" in Scepticism in the History of Philosophy: A Pan-American Dialogue, Popkin, Richard H (ed). Stroud, Barry.

"L'influenza della logica sulla ricerca storiografica su Hume" in Momenti di Storia della Logica e di Storia della Filosofia, Guetti, Carla (ed). Lecaldano, Eugenio.

"No Necessary Connection": The Medieval Roots of the Occasionalist Roots of Hume. Nadler, Steven.

Cognition and Commitment in Hume's Philosophy. Garrett, Don.

Hume on Miracles. Tweyman, Stanley (ed).

Immanuel Kant's Prolegomena to Any Future Metaphysics. Logan, Beryl.

Justice. Westphal, Jonathan (ed).

A New Theory on Philo's Reversal. Stamos, David N.

Abstration, Inseparability, and Identity. Baxter, Donald L M.

Against Coady on Hume on Testimony. Hríbek, Tomás.

Al-Ghazali on Necessary Causality in The Incoherence of the Philosophers. Riker, Stephen.

Answering the Free-Rider. Allan, Jim.

Causes and Tastes: A Response. Shiner, Roger A.

David Hume, David Lewis, and Decision Theory. Byrne, Alex and Hájek, Alan.

Descartes y Hume: causalidad, temporalidad y existencia de Dios. Badía Cabrera, Miguel A.

Foundational Standards and Conversational Style: The Humean Essay as an Issue of Philosophical Genre. Engström, Timothy H.

Hartstocht en rede. Van der Hoeven, J.

Hume and Causal Power: The Influences of Malebranche and Newton. Bell, Martin.

Hume and Nietzsche: Naturalists, Ethicists, Anti-Christians. Beam, Craig.

Hume and the 1763 Edition of His History of England: His Frame of Mind as a Revisionist. Van Holthoon, Frederic L.

Hume and the Bellman, Zerobabel MacGilchrist. Emerson, Roger L.

Hume in the Prussian Academy: Jean Bernard Mérian's "On the Phenomenalism of David Hume". Laursen, John Christian, Popkin, Richard H and Briscoe, Peter.

Hume on Conceivability and Inconceivability. Lightner, D Tycerium.

Hume on Virtues and Rights. Resende Araújo, Cícero Romao.

Hume's "Bellmen's Petition": The Original Text. Stewart, M A.

Hume's "Of Miracles" (Part One). Adler, Jonathan.

Hume's Aesthetic Theism. Immerwahr, John.

Hume's Arguments for His Sceptical Doubts. Passell, Dan.

Hume's Difficulty with the Virtue of Honesty. Cohon, Rachel.

Hume's Dilemma and the Defense of Interreligious Pluralism (in Hebrew_. Sagi, Avi.

Hume's Moral Sublime. Neill, Elizabeth.

Hume's Philosophy of Religion: Part 2. Stewart, M A.

Hume's Psychology of Identity Ascriptions. Roth, Abraham Sesshu.

Hume's Reflective Return to the Vulgar. O'Shea, James R.

Hume's Refutation of the Cosmological Argument. Campbell, Joseph Keim.

Hume's Scepticism with Regard to Reason: A Reconsideration. Dauer, Francis W.

Hume's Touchstone and the Politics of Meaningful Discourse. Backhaus, Wilfried.

Hume's Utilitarian Theory of Right Action. Sobel, Jordan Howard.

Hume, Bayle e il principio di causalità: Parte I. Gilardi, Roberto.

Hume—Not a "Humean" about Motivation. Persson, Ingmar.

Hutcheson on Practical Reason. Darwall, Stephen.

In Defense of Hume and the Causal Theory of Taste. Mothersill, Mary.

Is Hume a Noncognitivist in the Motivation Argument?. Cohon, Rachel.

Kantian Tunes on a Humean Instrument: Why Hume is not Really a Skeptic About Practical Reasoning. Radcliffe, Elizabeth.

Milagres e leis da natureza em Peirche e Hume. Albieri, Sara.

Miracles and the Shroud of Turin. Griffith, Stephen.

Monkish Virtues, Artificial Lives: On Hume's Genealogy of Morals. Lottenbach, Hans.

Moral Judgments in History: Hume's Position. Wertz, S K.

Natural Obligation and Normative Motivation in Hume's Treatise. Magri, Tito.

Naturalism, Normativity, and Scepticism in Hume's Account of Belief. Falkenstein, Lorne.

On Lewis's Objective Chance: "Humean Supervenience Debugged". Hoefer, Carl.

On Shiner's "Hume and the Causal Theory of Taste". Bender, John W.

Perspectivismo Mitigado. Monteiro, Joao Paulo.

Philosophy and the Good Life: Hume's Defence of Probable Reasoning. Owen, David.

Self-Observation. Martin, M G F.

Sympathy and Other Selves. Pitson, Tony.

The Early Fichte as Disciple of Jacobi. Di Giovanni, George.

## IDEALISM

"F.H. Bradley and Later Idealism: From Disarray to Reconstruction" in *Philosophy after F.H. Bradley,* Bradley, James (ed). Armour, Leslie.

"Fichte: Ein streitbarer Philosoph" in *Sein—Reflexion—Freiheit: Aspekte der Philosophie Johann Gottlieb Fichtes,* Asmuth, Christoph (ed). Asmuth, Christoph.

"From Presence to Process: Bradley and Whitehead" in *Philosophy after F.H. Bradley,* Bradley, James (ed). Bradley, James.

"Georg Wilhelm Friedrich Hegel and the East" in *East and West in Aesthetics,* Marchianò, Grazia (ed). Dethier, Hubert.

"Hölderlin y Fichte o el sujeto descarriado en un mundo sin amor" in *El inicio del Idealismo alemán,* Market, Oswaldo. Villacañas Berlanga, José L.

"Nueva religión: Un proyecto del Idealismo alemán" in *El inicio del Idealismo alemán,* Market, Oswaldo. Carmo Ferreira, Manuel J do.

"Observaciones críticas al Idealismo alemán en el bicentenario del "Fundamento de toda la Doctrina de la Ciencia" 1794, de J. G. Fichte" in *El inicio del Idealismo alemán,* Market, Oswaldo. Riobó González, Manuel.

"Perspectivas sobre religión y filosofía en los inicios del Idealismo alemán: Fichte y Schelling antes de 1794" in *El inicio del Idealismo alemán,* Market, Oswaldo. De Torres, María José.

"Semantic Intuitions: Conflict Resolution in the Formal Sciences" in *Logic and Argumentation,* Van Eemeren, Frans H (ed). Woods, John.

"Seyn" y "Ur-teilung" in *El inicio del Idealismo alemán,* Market, Oswaldo. Martínez Marzoa, Felipe.

"The Logical Structure of Idealism: C.S. Peirce's Search for a Logic of Mental Processes" in *The Rule of Reason: The Philosophy of Charles Sanders Peirce,* Forster, Paul (ed). Pape, Helmut.

"The Question of Linguistic Idealism Revisited" in *The Cambridge Companion to Wittgenstein,* Sluga, Hans (ed). Bloor, David.

"The Succinct Case for Idealism" in *Objections to Physicalism,* Robinson, Howard (ed). Foster, John.

"Vico, la storia, lo storicismo" in *Lo Storicismo e la Sua Storia: Temi, Problemi, Prospettive,* Cacciatore, Giuseppe (ed). Nuzzo, Enrico.

"Vita e sistema: Alle origini del pensiero hegeliano a Jena" in *Lo Storicismo e la Sua Storia: Temi, Problemi, Prospettive,* Cacciatore, Giuseppe (ed). Cantillo, Giuseppe.

*A Short History of Modern Philosophy: From Descartes to Wittgenstein.* Scruton, Roger.

*Assoluto: Frammenti di misticismo nella filosofia di Francis Herbert Bradley.* Taroni, Paolo.

*Catalogue des Publications 1977-1995.* Carratelli, Giovanni Pugliese (ed).

*Der Deutsche Idealismus (Fichte, Schelling, Hegel) und die philosophische Problemlage der Gegenwart.* Heidegger, Martin.

*El inicio del Idealismo alemán.* Market, Oswaldo and Rivera de Rosales, Jacinto.

*Idealism and Rights: The Social Ontology of Human Rights in the Political Thought of Bernard Bosanquet.* Sweet, William.

*Idealism as Modernism: Hegelian Variations.* Pippin, Robert B.

*Philosophy after F.H. Bradley.* Bradley, James (ed).

*The Course of Remembrance and Other Essays on Hölderlin.* Henrich, Dieter and Förster, Eckart (ed).

*The Zero Fallacy and Other Essays in Neoclassical Philosophy.* Valady, Mohammad (ed) and Hartshorne, Charles.

Absolutes Denken: Neuere Interpretationen der Hegelschen Logik. Quante, Michael.

Absolutes Wissen und Sein: Zu Fichtes Wissenschaftslehre von 1801/02. Stolzenberg, Jürgen.

Affinity, Idealism, and Naturalism: The Stability of Cinnabar and the Possibility of Experience. Westphal, Kenneth R.

Beobachtungen zur Methodik in Fichtes *Grundlage der gesamten Wissenschaftslehre.* Meckenstock, Günter.

Berkeley, Lee and Abstract Ideas. Benschop, Hans Peter.

Between Inconsistent Nominalists and Egalitarian Idealists. Nelson, Ralph C.

Beyond Realism and Idealism Husserl's Late Concept of Constitution. Zahavi, Dan.

Borges and the Refutation of Idealism: A Study of "Tlön, Uqbar, Orbis Tertius". Stewart, Jon.

Civil Society Ethics: An Approach from K-O Apel's Philosophy (in Spanish). Durán Casas, Vicente.

Conoscenza metafisica dell'esistenza. Possenti, Vittorio.

Conversazione con Cornelio Fabro. Burghi, Giancarlo.

Dal primato della prassi all'anomia: Una interpretazione filosofica della crisi odierna. Cotta, Sergio.

Das *objektive Selbst* (Nagel)—Eine Destruktion oder Rekonstruktion transzendentaler Subjektivität?. Lütterfelds, Wilhelm.

Das Wir in der späten Wissenschaftslehre. Richli, Urs.

Die *Grundlage der gesamten Wissenschaftslehre* und das Problem der Sprache bei Fichte. Hoffmann, Thomas Sören.

Die Bedeutung von Fichtes Angewandter Philosophie für die Praktische Philosophie der Gegenwart. Oesterreich, Peter L.

Die Duplizität des Absoluten in der Wissenschaftslehre von 1804 (zweiter Vortrag)—Fichtes Auseinandersetzung mit Schellings identitäts-philosophischer Schrift *Darstellung meines Systems* (1801). Danz, Christian.

Die Fichte-Lektüre des jungen Herbart (1796-1798). Langewand, Alfred.

Die Hegelsche Fichte-Kritik und ihre Berechtigung. Stadler, Christian M.

Die Rezeption der *Wissenschaftslehre* Fichtes in den Versionen der Hegelschen *Wissenschaft der Logik.* De Vos, Lu.

Do Wittgenstein's Forms of Life Inaugurate a Kantian Project of Transcendental Idealism?. Kanthamani, A.

Eine neue Möglichkeit der Philosophie nach der *Grundlage der gesamten Wissenschaftslehre.* Nagasawa, Kunihiko.

El krausopositivismo psicológico y sociológico en la obra de U. González Serrano. Jiménez García, Antonio.

Empire, Transzendentalismus und Transzendenz: Neue Literatur zu Arthur Schopenhauer. Kossler, Matthias.

Fichte und die Metaphysik des deutschen Idealismus. Jiménez-Redondo, Manuel.

Fichtes Anstoss: Anmerkungen zu einem Begriff der *Wissenschaftslehre* von 1794. Eidam, Heinz.

Fichtes Erfindung der Wissenschaftslehre. Tilliette, Xavier.

Geist oder Gespenst? Fichtes Noumenalismus in der *Wissenschaftslehre nova methodo.* Zöller, Günter.

Gustav Teichmüller filologo e metafisico tra Italia e Germania: I) Teichmüller, Nietzsche e la critica delle 'mitologie scientifiche'. Orsucci, Andrea.

Hegel's Critique of Kant's Empiricism and the Categorial Imperative. Sedgwick, Sally.

Heideggers Wende zum Deutschen Idealismus. Strube, Claudius.

Hermann Graf Keyserlings "Schule der Weisheit". Gahlings, Ute.

Horstmann, Siep, and German Idealism. Pippin, Robert B.

Idealismo y materialismo: Max Horkheimer y la constitución del conocimiento en la ciencia social. Vergara, Eliseo Cruz.

Internal Relations and Analyticity: Wittgenstein and Quine. Hymers, Michael.

Kant oder Berkeley? Zum aktuellen Streit um den korrekten Realismus. Lütterfelds, Wilhelm.

Kant's Refutation of Idealism. Palmer, Daniel E.

La prima lettura fichtiana della *Kritik der Urteilskraft* in alcuni studi del nostro secolo. Fabbianelli, Faustino.

Logics of Power in Marx. Brown, Wendy.

McTaggart's Argument for Idealism. Mander, W J.

Naturphilosophie zwischen Naturwissenschaft und Philosophie: Neue Sammelbände zur Naturphilosophie des deutschen Idealismus. Ziche, Paul.

Not Ideal: Collingwood's Expression Theory. Ridley, Aaron.

Notes on Peirce's Objective Idealism. Sokolowski, William R.

Nyāya: Realist or Idealist?. Bhattacharya, Sibajiban.

O Mais Antigo Programa de Sistema do Idealismo Alemao. Carmo Ferreira, Manuel J do.

Offene Intersubjektivität—nach Johann Gottlieb Fichte. Schmidig, Dominik.

Peirce's Evolutionary Pragmatic Idealism. Burks, Arthur W.

Philosophy of Science and the German Idealists. Clayton, Philip.

Quasi-Berkeleyan Idealism as Perspicuous Theism. Everitt, Nicholas.

Response to Kanthamani's Comment. Pradhan, R C.

Satz und Grund: Der Anfang der Philosophie bei Fichte mit Bezugnahme auf die Werke BWL und GWL. Rametta, Gaetano.

Sobre Hölderlin y los comienzos del Idealismo alemán. Serrano Marín, Vicente.

Sociología y tipología del fenómeno religioso. Piñon G, Francisco.

Sprachliche Vermittlung philosophischer Einsichten nach Fichtes Früh-philosophie. Schmidig, Dominik.

The Concept of Act in the Naturalistic Idealism of John William Miller. Tyman, Stephen.

The Heritage of Léon Brunschvicg (and Commentary by P. Horák) (in Czech). Rivenc, François and Horák, Petr.

Transcendental Constraints and Transcendental Features. Sacks, Mark.

Transzendentale Lebenslehre: Zur Königsberger Wissenschaftslehre 1807. Ivaldo, Marco.

Two Paradoxes in Heidegger. Margolis, Joseph.

Vernunft und das Andere der Vernunft: Eine modelltheoretische Exposition. Gloy, Karen.

Wechselbestimmung: Zum Verhältnis von Hölderlin, Schiller und Fichte in Jena. Waibel, Violetta.

Wege zur Wahrheit: Zur Bedeutung von Fichtes wissenschaftlich- und populär-philosophischer Methode. Traub, Hartmut.

What is Given? Thought and Event (in French). Benoist, Jocelyn.

## IDEALITY

Idealità del segno e intenzione nella filosofia del linguaggio di Edmund Husserl. Costa, Vincenzo.

## IDEALIZATION

*Idealisierungen und das Ziel der Physik: Eine Untersuchung zum Realismus, Empirismus und Konstruktivismus in der Wissen-schaftstheorie.* Hüttemann, Andreas.

Kitcher's Compromise: A Critical Examination of the Compromise Model of Scientific Closure, and its Implications for the Relationship Between History and Philosophy of Science. Shanahan, Timothy.

Pragmatic Idealization and Structuralist Reconstructions of Theories. Haase, Michaela.

## IDEATION

Beyond Ontology: Ideation, Phenomenology and the Cross Cultural Study of Emotion. Solomon, Robert C.

## INDUCTION
The Hole in the Ground of Induction. Maher, Patrick.

The Problem of Justification of Abduction in C.S. Peirce in the Light of Tadeusz Czezowski's Views (in Polish). Mirek, Ryszard.

The Validation of Induction. Pargetter, Robert and Bigelow, John.

## INDUCTIVE LOGIC
Confirming Universal Generalizations. Zabell, S L.

## INDUSTRIALISM
Netzverdichtung: Zur Philosophie industriegesellschaftlicher Entwicklungen. Lübbe, Hermann.

## INDUSTRY
An Examination of the Relationship Between Ethical Behavior, Espoused Ethical Values and Financial Performance in the U S Defense Industry: 1988-1992. Mayer-Sommer, Alan P and Roshwalb, Alan.

Conflicts of Interest, Conflicting Interests, and Interesting Conflicts, Part 3. Vinicky, Janicemarie K, Orlowski, James P and Shevlin Edwards, Sue.

Daughters of a Better Age. Lim, Tock Keng.

Ethical Aspects of the University-Industry Interface. Spier, Raymond.

Ethical Considerations in the Testing of Biopharmaceuticals for Adventitious Agents. Woodward, Richard S.

Organized Complexity in Human Affairs: The Tobacco Industry. Bella, David A.

Reaching for the "Low Hanging Fruit": The Pressure for Results in Scientific Research—A Graduate Student's Perspective. Browning, Tyson R.

## INEQUALITY
On Economic Inequality. Sen, Amartya.

Can We Escape from Bell's Conclusion that Quantum Mechanics Describes a Non-Local Reality?. De Muynck, Willem M.

Health Care, Equality, and Inequality: Christian Perspectives and Moral Disagreements. Wildes, Kevin W.

Kripke Models and the (In)equational Logic of the Second-Order Lambda-Calculus. Gallier, Jean.

Non-Locality: A Defense of Widespread Beliefs. Laudisa, Federico.

Patologie del sociale: Tradizione e attualità della filosofia sociale. Honneth, Axel.

Some Derivations of Bell's Inequality. Hansen, Kaj Borge.

Still in Defence: A Short Reply on Non-Locality and Widespread Beliefs. Laudisa, Federico.

## INEVITABILITY
Bioethics, Expertise, and the Courts: An Overview and an Argument for Inevitability. Morreim, E Haavi.

## INFALLIBILITY
Infallibility, Authority and Faith. Haldane, John.

## INFANT
Organ Transplants and Ethics. Lamb, David.

Discontinuing Life Support in an Infant of a Drug-Addicted Mother: Whose Decision Is It?. Thomasma, David C and Jain, Renu.

High Risk Infants: Thirty Years of Intensive Care. Harris, Cheryl Hall.

Mandatory HIV Testing in Newborns: Not Yet, Maybe Never. Davis, Dena S.

Prematernal Duty and the Resolution of Conflict. Yeast, John D.

The Baby K Case: A Search for the Elusive Standard of Medical Care. Schneiderman, Lawrence J and Manning, Sharyn.

## INFANTICIDE
Abortion, Infanticide, and the Asymmetric Value of Human Life. Reiman, Jeffrey.

Infanticide and the Right to Life. Carter, Alan.

Replaceability and Infanticide. Uniacke, Suzanne.

## INFERENCE
"Argument Based Reasoning: Some Remarks on the Relation Between Argumentation Theory and Artificial Intelligence" in *Logic and Argumentation*, Van Eemeren, Frans H (ed). Starmans, Richard J C M.

"Caution and Nonmonotonic Inference" in *Knowledge and Inquiry: Essays on Jaakko Hintikka's Epistemology and Philosophy of Science*, Sintonen, Matti (ed). Levi, Isaac.

"Illustration and Inference" in *Picturing Knowledge*, Baigrie, Brian S (ed). Brown, James Robert.

"Inference and Logic According to Peirce" in *The Rule of Reason: The Philosophy of Charles Sanders Peirce*, Forster, Paul (ed). Levi, Isaac.

"Logic and Argumentation" in *Logic and Argumentation*, Van Eemeren, Frans H (ed). Van Benthem, Johan.

"Peirce and the Structure of Abductive Inference" in *Studies in the Logic of Charles Sanders Peirce*, Houser, Nathan (ed). Kapitan, Tomis.

"The Relation of Argument to Inference" in *Logic and Argumentation*, Van Eemeren, Frans H (ed). Pinto, Robert C.

*Logic and Argumentation*. Van Eemeren, Frans H (ed), Van Benthem, Johan (ed) and Grootendorst, Rob (ed).

*Studies in the Logic of Charles Sanders Peirce*. Houser, Nathan (ed), Roberts, Don D (ed) and Van Evra, James (ed).

*The Primary Logic: Instruments for a Dialogue between the Two Cultures*. Malatesta, Michele.

A Defence of Van Fraassen's Critique of Abductive Inference: Reply to Psillos. Ladyman, James, Douven, Igor and Horsten, Leon (& others).

Analogy and Exchangeability in Predictive Inferences. Festa, Roberto.

Brandom on Representation and Inference. McDowell, John.

Characterizing Language Identification in Terms of Computable Numberings. Jain, Sanjay and Sharma, Arun.

Cualidades secundarias y autoconocimiento. Vergara, Julia.

Cualidades Secundarias y autoconocimiento. Scotto, Carolina.

Deontica in Rose Rand. Lorini, Giuseppe.

Do Children Understand the Mind by Means of Simulation or a Theory? Evidence from their Understanding of Inference. Ruffman, Ted.

Function Identification from Noisy Data with Recursive Error Bounds. Changizi, Mark.

How not to Defend Constructive Empiricism: A Rejoinder. Psillos, Stathis.

Implicit Epistemic Aspects of Constructive Logic. Sundholm, Göran.

Inference to the Best Explanation. Clayton, Philip.

Inference: Heuristic vs. Naturalistic Model. Mazumdar, Rinita.

Inferences from Phenomena in Gravitational Physics. Harper, William and DiSalle, Robert.

Just So Stories and Inference to the Best Explanation in Evolutionary Psychology. Holcomb III, Harmon R.

Nonmonotonic Reasoning: From Finitary Relations to Infinitary Inference Operations. Freund, Michael and Lehmann, Daniel.

Nonmonotonic Theories and Their Axiomatic Varieties. Stachniak, Zbigniew.

Practical Possibilities. Adams, Ernest W.

Quantification without Variables in Connectionism. Barnden, John A and Srinivas, Kankanahalli.

The Rule of Adjunction and Reasonable Inference. Kyburg, Jr, Henry E.

Trascendentalità, inferenza e trascendenza: Dopo Kant e Heidegger. Penati, Giancarlo.

Underdetermination and Incommensurability in Contemporary Epidemiology. Weed, Douglas L.

## INFERENCE RULE
A Categorical Approach to Higher-Level Introduction and Elimination Rules. Poubel, Hardée Werneck and Pereira, Luiz Carlos P D.

A Reasoning Method for a Paraconsistent Logic. Buchsbaum, Arthur and Pequeno, Tarcisio.

A Simple Irredundance Test for Tautological Sequents. Schröder, Joachim.

A Simplified Form of Condensed Detachment. Bunder, M W.

Admissible Rule for Temporal Logic LinTGrz. Bezgacheva, Julia V.

Comparing Cubes of Typed and Type Assignment Systems. Van Bakel, Steffen, Liquori, Luigi and Ronchi della Rocca, Simona (& others).

Criteria for Admissibility of Inference Rules: Modal and Intermediate Logics with the Branching Property. Rybakov, Vladimir V.

Generalising Tautological Entailment. Lavers, Peter.

Hume's Is-Ought Thesis in Logics with Alethic-Deontic Bridge Principles. Schurz, Gerhard.

Induction Rules, Reflection Principles, and Provably Recursive Functions. Beklemishev, Lev D.

Lambek Calculus with Restricted Contraction and Expansion. Prijateljz, Andreja.

On Minimal Resolution Proof Systems for Resolution Logics. Stachniak, Zbigniew.

On the Rules of Substitution in the First-Order Predicate Logics. Bugajska-Jaszczolt, Beata and Dyrda, Kazimiera.

Some Aspects of Refutation Rules. Skura, Tomasz.

The omega-Rule. Thau, Michael.

Theorie législative de la négation pure. Béziau, Jean-Yves.

Universal Instantiation: A Study of the Role of Context in Logic. Gauker, Christopher.

Valuational Semantics of Rule Derivability. Humberstone, I Lloyd.

## INFERTILITY
"Bioethics through the Back Door: Phenomenology, Narratives, and Insights into Infertility" in *Philosophical Perspectives on Bioethics*, Sumner, L W (ed). Shanner, Laura.

## INFINITARY CONCEPT
Colouring and Non-Productivity of Aleph$_2$-C.C.. Shelah, Saharon.

The omega-Rule. Thau, Michael.

## INFINITARY LOGIC
Canonization for Two Variables and Puzzles on the Square. Otto, Martin.

Cauchy Completeness in Elementary Logic. Cifuentes, J C, Sette, A M and Mundici, Daniele.

Game Logic and its Applications I. Kaneko, Mamoru and Nagashima, Takashi.

Game Logic and Its Applications II. Kaneko, Mamoru and Nagashima, Takashi.

Infinitary Logics and Very Sparse Random Graphs. Lynch, James F.

Some Characterization Theorems for Infinitary Universal Horn Logic without Equality. Dellunde, Pilar and Jansana, Ramon.

The Hierarchy Theorem for Generalized Quantifiers. Hella, Lauri, Luosto, Kerkko and Väänänen, Jouko.

## INFINITE
see also Finite

"Sul problema della considerazione matematica dell'infinito e del continuo in Aristotele e Hegel" in *Hegel e Aristotele*, Ferrarin, A. Moretto, Antonio.

*Varia: Il De Mente Heroica e gli Scritti Latini Minori*. Vico, Giambattista and Visconti, Gian Galeazzo (ed).

Infinite Regress Arguments and Infinite Regresses. Black, Oliver.

Infinite Set Unification with Application to Categorical Grammar. Marciniec, Jacek.

Is the Human Mind a Turing Machine?. King, David.

Nonmonotonic Reasoning: From Finitary Relations to Infinitary Inference Operations. Freund, Michael and Lehmann, Daniel.

## INFINITE

Para una ontología del continuo. Pérez Herranz, Fernando-M.

Poincaré: Mathematics & Logic & Intuition. McLarty, Colin.

The Concept of Act in the Naturalistic Idealism of John William Miller. Tyman, Stephen.

The Two Envelope Paradox and Infinite Expectations. Arntzenius, Frank and McCarthy, David.

Thomistes et antithomistes face à la question de l'infini créé. Solère, Jean-Luc.

## INFINITE REGRESS

Infinite Regresses of Recurring Problems & Responses. Grattón, Claude.

## INFINITESIMAL

C.S. Peirce's Theories of Infinitesimals. Herron, Timothy.

The Infinitesimals as Useful Fictions for Leibniz: The Controversy in the Paris Academy of Sciences (Spanish). Joven, Fernando.

Zur Begründung des Infinitesimalkalküls durch Leibniz. Krämer, Sybille.

## INFINITY

The Fate of Place: A Philosophical History. Casey, Edward S.

Alternative Mathematics and Alternative Theoretical Physics: The Method for Linking Them Together. Drago, Antonino.

Bonaventure and the Arguments for the Impossibility of an Infinite Temporal Regression. Davis, Richard.

Classical Particle Dynamics, Indeterminism and a Supertask. Laraudogoitia, Jon Perez.

De lo eterno a lo infinito: un intento de reconstrución del argumento de Meliso (B2-4 D-K). Bredlow, Luis.

Exposing the Machinery of Infinite Renormalization. Huggett, Nick and Weingard, Robert.

Hölderlins Trennung von Fichte. Jürgensen, Sven.

Infinity and the Relation: The Emergence of a Notion of Infinity in Derrida's Reading of Husserl. Maloney, Philip J.

Kant's Reflections on the Sublime and the Infinite. Roy, Louis.

L'infinité des attributs chez Spinoza. Boss, Gilbert.

Pseudo-Dionysius Areopagiticus and Saint Simon The New Theologian (in Czech). Perczel, István.

Ralph Cudworth (1617-1688) sobre la infinitud de Dios. Robles, José A and Benítez, Laura.

Taming the Infinite. Potter, Michael D.

The Divine Infinity: Can Traditional Theists Justifiably Reject Pantheism?. Oakes, Robert.

## INFLUENCE

"Indirect Action, Influence and Responsibility" in Deontic Logic, Agency and Normative Systems, Brown, Mark A (ed). Santos, Filipe and Carmo, José.

Algo donoso pero no cortés: Una lectura diferencial del bifronte Marqués de Valdegamas a tenor de la modernidad de Vico. Sevilla Fernández, José M.

Conflicts of Interest, Conflicting Interests, and Interesting Conflicts, Part 3. Vinicky, Janicemarie K, Orlowski, James P and Shevlin Edwards, Sue.

## INFORMAL LOGIC

"Accounting for Transformations in the Dialectical Reconstruction of Argumentative Discourse" in Logic and Argumentation, Van Eemeren, Frans H (ed). Van Rees, M Agnès.

"Argument Based Reasoning: Some Remarks on the Relation Between Argumentation Theory and Artificial Intelligence" in Logic and Argumentation, Van Eemeren, Frans H (ed). Starmans, Richard J C M.

"Argumentation in the Tradition of Speech Communication Studies" in Logic and Argumentation, Van Eemeren, Frans H (ed). Zarefsky, David.

"Argumentation Studies and Dual-Process Models of Persuasion" in Logic and Argumentation, Van Eemeren, Frans H (ed). O'Keefe, Daniel J.

"Can we Ever Pin One Down to a Formal Fallacy?" in Logic and Argumentation, Van Eemeren, Frans H (ed). Krabbe, Erik C W.

"Developments in Argumentation Theory" in Logic and Argumentation, Van Eemeren, Frans H (ed). Van Eemeren, Frans H and Grootendorst, Rob.

"Embedding Logic in Communication: Lessons from the Logic Classroom" in Logic and Argumentation, Van Eemeren, Frans H (ed). Stenning, Keith.

"Fallacies and Heuristics" in Logic and Argumentation, Van Eemeren, Frans H (ed). Jackson, Sally.

"Functioning and Teachings of Adaptive Logics" in Logic and Argumentation, Van Eemeren, Frans H (ed). Batens, Diderik.

"Indicators of Independent and Interdependent Arguments: 'Anyway' and 'Even'" in Logic and Argumentation, Van Eemeren, Frans H (ed). Snoeck Henkemans, Francisca.

"Informal Factors in the Formal Evaluation of Arguments" in Logic and Argumentation, Van Eemeren, Frans H (ed). Finocchiaro, Maurice A.

"Logic and Argumentation" in Logic and Argumentation, Van Eemeren, Frans H (ed). Van Benthem, Johan.

"Semantic Intuitions: Conflict Resolution in the Formal Sciences" in Logic and Argumentation, Van Eemeren, Frans H (ed). Woods, John.

"The Relation of Argument to Inference" in Logic and Argumentation, Van Eemeren, Frans H (ed). Pinto, Robert C.

"The Straw Man Fallacy" in Logic and Argumentation, Van Eemeren, Frans H (ed). Walton, Douglas.

Logic and Argumentation. Van Eemeren, Frans H (ed), Van Benthem, Johan (ed) and Grootendorst, Rob (ed).

Practical Reasoning in Natural Language. Thomas, Stephen Naylor.

A World of Difference: The Rich State of Argumentation Theory. Van Eemeren, Frans H.

Analysis of Argument Strategies of Attack and Cooption: Stock Cases, Formalization, and Argument Reconstruction. Brinton, Alan.

Argument is War...and War is Hell: Philosophy, Education, and Metaphors for Argumentation. Cohen, Daniel H.

Argument Management, Informal Logic and Critical Thinking. Blair, J Anthony.

Argumentation, Education and Reasoning. Binkley, Robert W.

Combining Critical Thinking and Written Composition: The Whole Is Greater Than The Sum Of The Parts. Hatcher, Donald L.

Critical Thinking and the Moral Sentiments: Adam Smith's Moral Psychology and Contemporary Debate in Critical Thinking and Informal Logic. Weinstein, Jack Russell.

Did Jesus Commit a Fallacy?. Hitchcock, David.

Emotions and Argumentation. Ben-Ze'ev, Aaron.

Hybrid Arguments. Vorobej, Mark.

Inconsistency, Rationality and Relativism. Pinto, Robert C.

New Methods for Evaluating Arguments. Walton, Douglas.

Premise Acceptability, Deontology, Internalism, Justification. Freeman, James B.

Reflective Reasoning in Groups. Slade, Christina.

Report of a Year Working on Improving Teaching and Learning. Adler, Jonathan.

Some Foundational Problems with Informal Logic and Their Solution. Weinstein, Mark.

Sorensen on begging the Question. Yujen Teng, Norman.

The Abduction of the Atom: An Exercise in Hypothesizing. Novak, Joseph A.

The Case that Alternative Argumentation Drives the Growth of Knowledge—Some Preliminary Evidence. Missimer, Connie.

The One Fallacy Theory. Powers, Lawrence H.

The Principle of Vulnerability. Johnson, Ralph H.

Using Computer-Assisted Instruction and Developmental Theory to Improve Argumentative Writing. Irwin, Ronald R.

Why Should Educators Care about Argumentation?. Siegel, Harvey.

## INFORMATION

"Education in the Mode of Information: Some Philosophical Considerations" in Philosophy of Education (1996), Margonis, Frank (ed). Marshall, James D.

"Pixels, Decenteredness, Marketization, Totalism, and Ingmar Bergman's Cry for Help" in Philosophy of Education (1996), Margonis, Frank (ed). Brosio, Richard A.

"Wissensordnung, Ethik, Wissensethik" in Angewandte Ethik: Die Bereichsethiken und ihre theoretische Fundierung, Nida-Rümelin, Julian (ed). Spinner, Helmut F.

A Call for a Statement of Expectations for the Global Information Infrastructure. Connolly, Frank W.

A Logic for Information Systems. Archangelsky, Dmitri A and Taitslin, Mikhail A.

Akaike Information Criterion, Curve-Fitting, and the Philosophical Problem of Simplicity. Kieseppä, I A.

Bargaining and Delay: The Role of External Information. Hyde, Charles E.

Bargaining with Incomplete Information: An Axiomatic Approach. Rosenmüller, Joachim.

Business Ethics and Computer Ethics: The View from Poland. Sojka, Jacek.

Computers, Information and Ethics: A Review of Issues and Literature. Mitcham, Carl.

Confirmation, Explanation, and Logical Strength. Nelson, David E.

Counting Information: A Note on Physicalized Numbers. Rotman, Brian.

Entidad y origen de la información. Sanvisens Herreros, Alejandro.

Ethics and MIS Education. McGowan, Matthew K and McGowan, Richard J.

Evolutionary Paradigms of Some New Scientific Disciplines (Two Examples: Cybernetics and Fuzzy Sets Theory) (in Spanish). Termini, Settimo.

Executive Perceptions of Superior and Subordinate Information Control: Practice Versus Ethics. Dulek, Ronald E, Motes, William H and Hilton, Chadwick B.

Fares and Free Riders on the Information Highway. Rosen, C Martin and Carr, Gabrielle M.

In Defense of a Constructive, Information-Based Approach to Decision Theory. Yilmaz, M R.

Información y Bases de Datos Situadas. Migura, Fernando.

Informática na Educaçao: Perspectivas. Miranda Carrao, Eduardo Vitor.

Information Technology and Technologies of the Self. Capurro, Rafael.

Integrating the Ethical and Social Context of Computing into the Computer Science Curriculum. Huff, Chuck, Anderson, Ronald E and Little, Joyce Currie (& others).

International Federation for Information Processing's Framework for Computer Ethics. Berleur, Jacques.

Introduction and Overview: Global Information Ethics. Bynum, Terrell Ward.

Jan Hollak over de betekenis van de techniek voor de filosofie. Coolen, Maarten.

Nonparametric Statistics in Multicriteria Analysis. Scarelli, Antonino and Venzi, Lorenzo.

Ontological Aspects of Information Modeling. Ashenhurst, Robert L.

## INSTRUCTION
see also Teaching

Using Computer-Assisted Instruction and Developmental Theory to Improve Argumentative Writing. Irwin, Ronald R.

## INSTRUMENT
Instrument Driven Theory. Tyron, Warren W.

Narrative, Drama, and Emotion in Instrumental Music. Maus, Fred Everett.

## INSTRUMENTAL
Naturalism, Instrumental Rationality, and the Normativity of Epistemology. Siegel, Harvey.

## INSTRUMENTALISM
see also Pragmatism

"Dialogue: An Essay in the Instrumentalist Tradition" in Political Dialogue: Theories and Practices, Esquith, Stephen L (ed). Koch, Donald F.

Ontology, Realism and Instrumentalism: Comments on Lukács's Criticism of Logical Positivism (in Hungarian). Szécsi, Gábor.

Was Hayek an Instrumentalist?. Legutko, Ryszard.

## INSURANCE
Can Old-Age Social Insurance Be Justified. Shapiro, Daniel J.

Helping Professionals in Business Behave Ethically: Why Business Cannot Abdicate Its Responsibility to the Profession. Cooper, Robert W and Frank, Garry L.

Single Payers and Multiple Lists: Must Everyone Get the Same Coverage in a Universal Health Plan?. Veatch, Robert M.

## INTEGER
The Theory of Integer Multiplication with Order Restricted to Primes is Decidable. Maurin, Françoise.

## INTEGRATION
"Integration or Reduction: Two Approaches to Environmental Values" in Environmental Pragmatism, Light, Andrew (ed). Norton, Bryan G.

Social Science Courses as an Integrating Subject. Broz, Frantisek.

The Centrifugal Forces of Latin American Integration. Morales Manzur, Juan Carlos.

## INTEGRITY
"Natural Integrity and Biotechnology" in Human Lives: Critical Essays on Consequentialist Bioethics, Oderberg, David S (ed). Clark, Stephen R L.

"Personal Integrity, Politics, and Moral Imagination" in A Question of Values: New Canadian Perspectives in Ethics and Political Philosophy, Brennan, Samantha (ed). Babbitt, Susan E.

Hypocrisy and Integrity: Machiavelli, Rousseau, and the Ethics of Politics. Grant, Ruth W.

An Introduction to Research Ethics. Friedman, Paul J.

Character-Principlism and the Particularity Objection. Blustein, Jeffrey.

Cheating: Limits of Individual Integrity. Johnston, D Kay.

Confessions of an Expert Ethics Witness. Kipnis, Kenneth.

Effectiveness of Research Guidelines in Prevention of Scientific Misconduct. Shore, Eleanor G.

Honesty, Individualism, and Pragmatic Business Ethics: Implications for Corporate Hierarchy. Quinn, J Kevin, Reed, J David and Browne, M Neil (& others).

Integrity and Disrespect (and J. Velek Commentary) (in Czech). Honneth, Axel and Velek, Josef.

Integrity and the Feminist Teacher. O'Dea, Jane.

Nietzsche on Ressentiment and Valuation. Reginster, Bernard.

Re-Examining the Influence of Individual Values on Ethical Decision Making. Glover, Saundra H, Bumpus, Minnette A and Logan, John E (& others).

The Ethics of Awareness: Inattention and Integrity. Jenni, Kathie.

The Symposium Viewed from the Organizer's Perspective. Gorski, Andrew.

## INTELLECT
see also Agent Intellect, Nous, Reason

Aristotle and Neoplatonism in Late Antiquity: Interpretations of the De Anima. Blumenthal, H J.

Aristotelische Intellekttheorie und die "Sohnesgeburt" bei Meister Eckehart. Helting, Holger.

Intellect, Will, and Freedom: Leibniz and His Precursors. Murray, Michael.

L'antithomisme de Thierry de Freiberg. Imbach, Ruedi.

Pensiero e realtà nella gnoseologia di S. Tommaso D'Aquino. Ventura, Antonino.

Postille. Del Vecchio, Dante.

Sensibilidad y espiritualidad según Aristóteles. García Jaramillo, Miguel Alejandro.

Verbe mental et noétique thomiste dans le De verbo d'Hervé de Nédellec. Trottmann, Christian.

## INTELLECTUAL
American Modern: The Path Not Taken: Aesthetics, Metaphysics, and Intellectual History in Classic American Philosophy. Tejera, Victorino.

Enhancing Cognition in the Intellectually Intact. Juengst, Eric T, Whitehouse, Peter J and Mehlman, Maxwell (& others).

How It Feels to Be a Problem: Du Bois, Fanon, and the "Impossible Life" of the Black Intellectual. Posnock, Ross.

La Ideología del primer franquismo y los intelectuales. Mateo Gambarte, Eduardo.

Private Scholars—Public Intellectuals: Can These Be Separated?. Godway, Eleanor M.

Rational Passions and Intellectual Virtues: A Conceptual Analysis. Steutel, Jan and Spiecker, Ben.

The Interdependence of Intellectual and Moral Virtue in Aquinas. Peterson, John.

The Moral Status of Intellectually Disabled Individuals. Edwards, Steven D.

## INTELLECTUAL PROPERTY
Conducting and Reporting Research. Bird, Stephanie J and Housman, David E.

Ethical Dilemmas in the Use of Information Technology: An Aristotelian Perspective. Myers, Michael D and Miller, Leigh.

## INTELLECTUALISM
"Intellectualism and Moral Habituation in Plato's Earlier Dialogues" in Dialogues with Plato, Benitez, Eugenio (ed). Yong, Patrick.

Intellectualism and Moral Habituation in Plato's Earlier Dialogues. Yong, Patrick.

La re-presentación extrema del estetismo, del intelectualismo y del moralismo en política. Rendón Rojas, Miguel Angel and Okolova, Marina Dimitrieva.

## INTELLIGENCE
The General Unified Theory of Intelligence: Its Central Conceptions and Specific Application to Domains of Cognitive Science. Wagman, Morton.

Critical Thinking and Emotional Intelligence. Elder, Linda.

Discusiones filosóficas en torno a la creatividad. Molina Delgada, Mauricio.

If the Eye Were an Animal...: The Problem of Representation in Understanding, Meaning and Intelligence. Horner, John M.

The Bell Curse. Haslett, D W.

The Education of Natural Intelligence and the Intellectual Virtues: Has Educational Pastiche had the Last Laugh?. D'Souza, Mario O.

Wisdom and Intelligence in Philosophy for Children. Lindop, Clive.

## INTELLIGENCE QUOTIENT
see IQ

## INTELLIGIBILITY
"Mathesis universalis e inteligibilidad en Descartes" in Memorias Del Seminario En Conmemoración De Los 400 Anos Del Nacimiento De René Descartes, Albis, Víctor S (ed). Paty, Michel.

Intelligibility and the Ethical. Miller, Jerome A.

Pramāna Samplava and Pramāna Vyavasthā. Sharma, A D and Shukla, S K.

The Correspondence between Human Intelligibility Physical Intelligibility: The View of Jean Ladrière. Lee, Kam-lun Edwin.

## INTENSION
"Modelos fregeanos intensionales" in Verdad: lógica, representación y mundo, Villegas Forero, L. Nepomuceno Fernández, Angel.

Sequence of Tense and Temporal De Re. Abusch, Dorit.

The Slingshot Argument. Read, Stephen.

## INTENSIONAL LOGIC
Object Theory Foundations for Intensional Logic. Jacquette, Dale.

## INTENSIONALITY
"Intensionale Semantik und physikalische Grössen" in Das weite Spektrum der analytischen Philosophie, Lenzen, Wolfgang. Oberschelp, Arnold.

A Identidade de Vénus ou as Vantagens da Extensionalidade. D'Orey, Carmo.

Quantifiers, Anaphora, and Intensionality. Dalrymple, Mary, Lamping, John and Pereira, Fernando (& others).

## INTENSITY
An Investigation of the Components of Moral Intensity. Marshall, Bev and Dewe, Philip.

Ideen von mehr oder weniger Süsse oder Licht: Zur Darstellung von Intensitäten bei Locke. Specht, Rainer.

## INTENTION
"A Modal Approach to Intentions, Commitments and Obligations: Intention Plus Commitment Yields Obligation" in Deontic Logic, Agency and Normative Systems, Brown, Mark A (ed). Dignum, Frank, Meyer, John-Jules Ch and Wieringa, Roel J (& others).

"Intention, Rule Following and the Strategic Role of Wright's Order of Determination Test" in Verdad: lógica, representación y mundo, Villegas Forero, L. Thornton, Tim.

"Intentions in Medical Ethics" in Human Lives: Critical Essays on Consequentialist Bioethics, Oderberg, David S (ed). Garcia, Jorge L A.

Intenzioni: D'amore di scienza e d'anarchia. Donnici, Rocco.

Promising, Intending, and Moral Autonomy. Robins, Michael H.

Voluntas nel De gratia et libero arbitrio di Bernardo di Chiaravalle. Allegro, Giuseppe.

Was sind Handlungen? Eine philosophische Auseinandersetzung mit dem Naturalismus. Runggaldier, Edmund.

Are Thought Experiments Just What You Thought?. Norton, John D.

Arguing over Intentions. Livingston, Paisley.

Beyond Acceptance and Rejection?. Martin, Dan.

Courage Alone. Putnam, Daniel.

Criminal Responsibility. Elliot, Carl.

Error in persona vel objecto und aberratio ictus. Toepel, Friedrich.

Handlungstheoretische Aspekte der Fahrlässigkeit. Seebass, Gottfried.

How Demonstrations Connect with Referential Intentions. Roberts, Lawrence D.

How To Share An Intention. Velleman, J David.

Idealità del segno e intenzione nella filosofia del linguaggio di Edmund Husserl. Costa, Vincenzo.

## INTERNAL

"Consciousness as Internal Monitoring, I" in *AI, Connectionism and Philosophical Psychology, 1995,* Tomberlin, James E (ed). Lycan, William G.

Louveau's Theorem for the Descriptive Set Theory of Internal Sets. Schilling, Kenneth and Zivaljevic, Bosko.

Mathematics, Model and Zeno's Paradoxes. Alper, Joseph S and Bridger, Mark.

On the Compresence of Tropes. Denkel, Arda.

## INTERNALISM

*Wahrheit, Referenz und Realismus: Eine Studie zur Sprachphilosophie und Metaphysik.* Schantz, Richard.

A Theological Escape from the Cartesian Circle?. Dalton, Peter.

Internal Realism, Metaphysical Realism, and Brains in a Vat. Forrai, Gábor.

Internalism and Perceptual Knowledge. Brewer, Bill.

Internalism, Externalism and the No-Defeater Condition. Bergmann, Michael.

Level Connections in Epistemology. McGrew, Timothy J and McGrew, Lydia M.

Moralische Beobachtung, interner Realismus und Korporatismus. Graeser, Andreas.

Moralischer Internalismus: Motivation durch Wünsche versus Motivation durch Überzeugungen. Wolf, Jean-Claude.

Pragmatism, Internalism and the Authority of Claims. Crawford, Dan D.

Premise Acceptability, Deontology, Internalism, Justification. Freeman, James B.

Sidgwick's False Friends. Shaver, Robert.

## INTERNATIONAL

"Die Weltfriedensregelung als Problem und Aufgabe der internationalen Politik" in *Kreativer Friede durch Begegnung der Weltkulturen,* Beck, Heinrich (ed). Eisenmann, Peter.

Crisis and Narrativity. Hirschbein, Ron.

Cultural Diversity and the Systems View. Hammond, Debora.

Five Views on International Business Ethics: An Introduction. Enderle, Georges.

International Criminal Adjudication and the Right to Punish. Blake, Michael.

International Federation for Information Processing's Framework for Computer Ethics. Berleur, Jacques.

International Regimes, Religious Ethics, and Emergent Probability. George, William P.

Kant, the Republican Peace, and Moral Guidance in International Law. Lynch, Cecelia.

Minority Rights After Helsinki. Korey, William.

Nature Conservation and the Precautionary Principle. Francis, John M.

Post-Cold War Reflections on the Study of International Human Rights. Donnelly, Jack.

Rawls and International Justice. Räikkä, Juha.

Reconstructing Rawls's Law of Peoples. Paden, Roger.

State Prerogatives, Civil Society, and Liberalization: The Paradoxes of the Late Twentieth Century in the Third World. Monshipouri, Mahmood.

The Collective Enforcement of International Norms Through Economic Sanctions. Damrosch, Lori Fisler.

The League of Nations Experiment in International Protection. Jones, Dorothy V.

The Relationship Between Culture and Perception of Ethical Problems in International Marketing. Armstrong, Robert W.

The Seventh Seal: On the Fate of Whitehead's Proposed Rehabilitation. Lucas Jr, George R.

The United States and the Genocide Convention: Leading Advocate and Leading Obstacle. Korey, William.

## INTERNATIONAL LAW

"Las tesis de Hegel sobre la guerra y el derecho internacional" in *Kant: La paz perpetua, doscientos años después,* Martínez Guzmán, Vicent (ed). Mertens, Thomas.

Internationale Konferenz zu Kants Friedensidee und dem heutigen Problem einer internationalen Rechts—und Friedensordnung in Frankfurt am Main. Grün, Klaus-Jürgen.

## INTERNATIONAL RELATION

"Politische Ethik II: Ethik der Internationalen Beziehungen" in *Angewandte Ethik: Die Bereichsethiken und ihre theoretische Fundierung,* Nida-Rümelin, Julian (ed). Chwaszcza, Christine.

*Kreativer Friede durch Begegnung der Weltkulturen.* Beck, Heinrich (ed) and Schmirber, Gisela (ed).

Millennium Approaches: Previewing the Twenty-first Century. Miller, Linda B.

The History of the Future of International Relations. Puchala, Donald J.

## INTERNATIONALISM

"Die Aggressivität der europaäischen Freiheitsphilosophie, expliziert an Hegels Rechtsphilosophie" in *Kreativer Friede durch Begegnung der Weltkulturen,* Beck, Heinrich (ed). Despot, Blazenka.

Aspekte internationaler Ethik. Betzler, Monika.

Das neoliberale Projekt, der männliche Arbeitsbegriff und die fällige Erneuerung des Geschlechtervertrags. Haug, Frigga.

Die Globalisierungsthese—von der kritischen Analyse zum politischen Opportunismus. Burchardt, Hans-Jürgen.

Glokalisierung oder Was für die einen Globalisierung, ist für die anderen Lokalisierung. Bauman, Zygmunt.

Gramscianismus in der Internationalen Politischen Ökonomie. Bieling, Hans-Jürgen and Deppe, Frank.

Internationalisierung des Kapitals, Gesamtkapital und nationalstaat. Milios, Jean.

Supranationale und staatliche Herrschaft: Staatsphilosophische Aspekte einer neuen Form hoheitlicher Verfasstheit. Von Bogdandy, Armin.

Weltkapitalismus oder Nationalstaat—eine falsch gestellte Frage. Hirsch, Joachim.

## INTERNET

Ethical and Legal Issues in E-Mail Therapy. Shapiro, Daniel Edward and Schulman, Charles Eric.

Ethical Dilemmas in the Use of Information Technology: An Aristotelian Perspective. Myers, Michael D and Miller, Leigh.

Ethical Issues in a Study of Internet Use: Uncertainty, Responsibility, and the Spirit of Research Relationships. Bier, Melinda C, Sherblom, Stephen A and Gallo, Michael A.

Ethics and the Internet: Appropriate Behavior in Electronic Communication. Langford, Duncan.

The Virtual Seminar Room: Using a World Wide Web Site in Teaching Ethics. Hinman, Lawrence M.

Virtual Sexes and Feminist Futures: The Philosophy of 'Cyberfeminism'. Marsden, Jill.

## INTERPOLATION

A Note on the Interpolation Property in Tense Logic. Wolter, Frank.

Extending Lambek Grammars to Basic Categorial Grammars. Buszkowski, Wojciech.

Interpolants, Cut Elimination and Flow Graphs for the Propositional Calculus. Carbone, A.

Interpolation Theorems, Lower Bounds for Proof Systems, and Independence Results for Bounded Arithmetic. Krajicek, J.

Syntactic Features and Synonymy Relations: A Unified Treatment of Some Proofs of the Compactness and Interpolation Theorems. Weaver, George E.

The Interpolation, Halldén-Completeness, Robinson and Beth Properties in Modal Logics. Wójtowicz, Anna.

## INTERPRETATION

"A Feminist Reading of Hegel and Kierkegaard" in *Hegel, History, and Interpretation,* Gallagher, Shaun. Armstrong, Susan.

"Charles Peirce and the Origin of Interpretation" in *The Rule of Reason: The Philosophy of Charles Sanders Peirce,* Forster, Paul (ed). Hausman, Carl R.

"Interpretation in History: Collingwood and Historical Understanding" in *Verstehen and Humane Understanding,* O'Hear, Anthony (ed). Gardiner, Patrick.

"Peirce's Sign and the Process of Interpretation" in *Philosophy in Experience: American Philosophy in Transition,* Hart, Richard (ed). Kruse, Felicia E.

"Pensare La Storia: Soggetto e metodo dell'interpretazione" in *Soggetto E Verità: La questione dell'uomo nella filosofia contemporanea,* Fagiuoli, Ettore. D'Alessandro, Paolo.

"Realistischer Realismus als ein methodologischer und pragmatischer Interpretationismus" in *Das weite Spektrum der analytischen Philosophie,* Lenzen, Wolfgang. Lenk, Hans.

"The Hegelian Organon of Interpretation" in *Hegel, History, and Interpretation,* Gallagher, Shaun. Harris, H S.

*Augustine the Reader: Meditation, Self-Knowledge, and the Ethics of Interpretation.* Stock, Brian.

*Beyond Interpretation: The Meaning of Hermeneutics for Philosophy.* Vattimo, Gianni and Webb, David (trans).

*Dialectical Readings: Three Types of Interpretation.* Dunning, Stephen N.

*Genese und Analyse.* Petrus, Klaus.

*Hegel, History, and Interpretation.* Gallagher, Shaun.

*Jonathan Edwards's Writings*: Text, Context, Interpretation. Stein, Stephen J (ed).

*Plato's Parmenides.* Allen, R E (ed & trans).

*Properties.* Mellor, D H (ed) and Oliver, Alex (ed).

*The Rule of Reason: The Philosophy of Charles Sanders Peirce.* Forster, Paul (ed) and Brunning, Jacqueline (ed).

A Defense of Yogācāra Buddhism. Wayman, Alex.

A Uniqueness Theorem for 'No Collapse' Interpretations of Quantum Mechanics. Bub, Jeffrey and Clifton, Rob.

Algo donoso pero no cortés: Una lectura diferencial del bifronte Marqués de Valdegamas a tenor de la modernidad de Vico. Sevilla Fernández, José M.

Antidote or Theory?. Dickson, Michael.

Autor y represión. Gracia, Jorge J E.

Back to a Monstrous Site: Reiner Schürmann's Reading of Heidegger's *Beiträge.* Janicaud, Dominique.

Beyond Ironist Theory and Private Fantasy: A Critique of Rorty's Derrida. Ellsworth, Jonathan.

Chaos and Control: Reading Plato's *Politicus.* McCabe, Mary Margaret.

Charity, Interpretation, Fallacy. Adler, Jonathan E.

Communication, Criticism, and the Postmodern Consensus: An Unfashionable Interpretation of Michel Foucault. Johnson, James.

Comprensió e interpretación de las obras filosóficas. Sánchez Meca, Diego.

Continuities and Discontinuities in the History of *Republic* Interpretation. Press, Gerald A.

## IRONY
Kierkegaard on Tragedy: The Aporias of Interpretation. Jegstrup, Elsebet.

La donna, tra ironia e diritto. Avitabile, Luisa.

Para uma História da Noçao de Ironia: Da Antiguidade Clássica à Escola Clássica Francesa. Gonçalves, Miguel.

The Irony of Ironic Liberalism. Young, Phillips E.

## IRRATIONAL
Can We Be Justified in Believing that Humans Are Irrational?. Stein, Edward.

La teoria de las proporciones de Eudoxio interpretada por Dedekind. Corry, Leo.

## IRRATIONALITY
"Irracionalidad en el externalismo" in *La racionalidad: su poder y sus límites*, Nudler, Oscar (ed.) Sosa, David.

"Las explicacioines homunculares de la irracionalidad" in *La racionalidad: su poder y sus límites*, Nudler, Oscar (ed.) Gianella, Alicia E.

Expressivism and Irrationality. Van Roojen, Mark.

Husserl's Rational "*Liebesgemeinschaft*". Buckley, R Philip.

Irrationalität und kritisches Bewusstsein. Stamer, Gerhard.

On an Argument for Irrationalism. Weir, Alan.

The Rational and the Irrational: A Philosophical Problem (Reading Arthur Schopenhauer). Mudragei, Nellia Stepanovna.

## IRREDUCIBILITY
The Irreducibility of Causation. Swinburne, Richard.

## IRREVERSIBILITY
Risk and the Value of Information in Irreversible Decisions. Gersbach, Hans.

Selbsterschaffung und die Irreversibilität der Zeit bei A.N. Whitehead. Kather, Regine.

Time, Modernity and Time Irreversibility. Palti, Elías José.

## IRVINE, W
The Ethics of Investing: A Reply to William Irvine. Larmer, Robert.

## IS
Hume's Is-Ought Thesis in Logics with Alethic-Deontic Bridge Principles. Schurz, Gerhard.

Thomasian Natural Law and the Is-Ought Question. Rentto, Juha-Pekka.

## ISIDORE OF SEVILLE
A los orígenes del pensamiento medieval español sobre la historia: Prudencio, Orosio, san Isidoro. Rivera de Ventosa, Enrique.

## ISLAM
"Averroës and the West" in *Averroës and the Enlightenment,* Wahba, Mourad (ed.) Leaman, Oliver.

"Enlightenment in the Islamic World: Muslims—Victims of Mneumonic Success" in *Averroës and the Enlightenment,* Wahba, Mourad (ed.) Irfan, Ghazala.

"Free Inquiry and Islamic Philosophy: The Significance of George Hourani" in *Averroës and the Enlightenment,* Wahba, Mourad (ed.) Kurtz, Paul.

"Ibn Rushd in the Islamic Context" in *Averroës and the Enlightenment,* Wahba, Mourad (ed.) Mokdad, Arfa Mensia.

"Islam and Enlightenment" in *Averroës and the Enlightenment,* Wahba, Mourad (ed.) Howeidy, Yehia.

"Metaphysical Roots of Tolerance and Intolerance: An Islamic Interpretation" in *Philosophy, Religion, and the Question of Intolerance,* Ambuel, David (ed.) Nasr, Seyyed Hossein.

"Religious Truth and Philosophical Truth according to Ibn Rushd" in *Averroës and the Enlightenment,* Wahba, Mourad (ed.) El Ghannouchi, A.

"Secularization in Turkey" in *Averroës and the Enlightenment,* Wahba, Mourad (ed.) Kuçuradi, Ioanna.

"The Islamic Perspective on Enlightenment: Principles and Implementation" in *Averroës and the Enlightenment,* Wahba, Mourad (ed.) Shahrestani, S M A.

*Averroës and the Enlightenment.* Wahba, Mourad (ed.) and Abousenna, Mona (ed.).

*La raíz semítica de lo europeo: Islam y judaísmo medievales.* Lomba, Joaquín.

Business Ethics in Islamic Context: Perspectives of a Muslim Business Leader. Abeng, Tanri.

Muslims and Sex Education. Halstead, J Mark.

Some Observations on the Revelation of the Qu'ran. Islam, Kazi Nurul.

Tolerance and Law. Öktem, Niyazi.

Tolerance and Law: From Islamic Culture to Islamist Ideology. Botiveau, Bernard.

## ISLAMIC
"Muslim Contributions to Geography and Environmental Ethics: The Challenges of Comparison and Pluralism" in *Philosophy and Geography I: Space, Place, and Environmental Ethics,* Light, Andrew (ed.) Wescoat Jr, James L.

"Some Fundamental Features of Arabic-Islamic Culture and Its Possible Contribution to World Peace" in *Kreativer Friede durch Begegnung der Weltkulturen,* Beck, Heinrich (ed.) Al-A'ali, Ebtihaj.

Chronique de philosophie arabe et islamique. Urvoy, Dominique.

Interpreting the *Jihad* of Islam: Militarism versus Muslim Pacifism. Churchill, Robert Paul.

## ISMAEL, J
Quantum Mechanics and Frequentism: A Reply to Ismael. Strevens, Michael.

## ISOCRATES
Les écoles philosophiques d'Athènes et les princes de Chypre. Berti, Enrico.

## ISOMORPHISM
Borel Equivalence Relations and Classifications of Countable Models. Hjorth, Greg and Kechris, Alexander S.

Forcing Isomorphism II. Laskowski, Michael C and Shelah, Saharon.

Infinite Versions of Some Problems from Finite Complexity Theory. Hirst, Jeffry L and Lempp, Steffen.

Symmetry as a Method of Proof. Hammer, Eric.

The Lattice of Distributive Closure Operators Over an Algebra. Font, Josep Maria and Verdú, Ventura.

## ISRAELI
*see also* Jewish

Professional Ethics of Psychologists and Physicians: Morality, Confidentiality, and Sexuality in Israel. Shimshon Rubin, Simon and Dror, Omer.

The Vocation of Higher Education: Modern and Postmodern Rhetorics in the Israeli Academia on Strike. Gur-Ze'ev, Ilan.

## ITALIAN
"Gothein, Lamprecht e i fondamenti concettuali della *Kulturgeschichte*" in *Lo Storicismo e la Sua Storia: Temi, Problemi, Prospettive,* Cacciatore, Giuseppe (ed.) Giugliano, Antonello.

"L'Italia in Bayle, Bayle in Italia: una ricerca mancata" in *Pierre Bayle e l'Italia,* Bianchi, Lorenzo. Borghero, Carlo.

"La fortuna del *Dictionnaire* in Italia in una lettera di Antonio Magliabechi" in *Pierre Bayle e l'Italia,* Bianchi, Lorenzo. Totaro, Giuseppina.

"Le relazioni tra Bayle e l'Italia: i corrispondenti italiani di Bayle e le *Nouvelles de la République des Lettres*" in *Pierre Bayle e l'Italia,* Bianchi, Lorenzo. Bianchi, Lorenzo.

"Lo storicismo critico-problematico e la tradizione della 'filosofia civile' italiana" in *Lo Storicismo e la Sua Storia: Temi, Problemi, Prospettive,* Cacciatore, Giuseppe (ed.) Cacciatore, Giuseppe.

"Metodo e modelli storiografici nel tardo illuminismo tedesco" in *Lo Storicismo e la Sua Storia: Temi, Problemi, Prospettive,* Cacciatore, Giuseppe (ed.) D'Allessandro, Giuseppe.

"Science and the Avant-Garde in Early Nineteenth-Century Florence" in *In Itinere European Cities and the Birth of Modern Scientific Philosophy,* Poli, Roberto (ed.) Albertazzi, Liliana.

"The Presence of Phenomenology in Milan Between the Two World Wars" in *In Itinere European Cities and the Birth of Modern Scientific Philosophy,* Poli, Roberto (ed.) Minazzi, Fabio.

*Carlo Michelstaedter: il coraggio dell'impossibile.* Michelis, Angela.

*Philosophische Gedichte.* Flasch, Thomas (trans) and Campanella, Tommaso.

*Pierre Bayle e l'Italia.* Bianchi, Lorenzo.

L'arrivo del *Discours* e dei *Principia,D* in Italia: prime letture dei testi cartesiani a Napoli. Lojacono, Ettore.

La *Scienza Nuova* (1725) en Nápoles: Testimonios e interpretaciones. Ratto, Franco.

La didáctica de la filosofía en Italia. Sánchez Huertas, María José.

La Nápoles de Vico. Pinton, Giorgio A.

La persuasión desde las *Institutiones Oratoriae* a la *Scienza Nuova.* Fabiani, Paolo.

Medieval Historiography. Birns, Nicholas.

Per una storia dei cartesiani in Italia: Avvertenza. Garin, Eugenio.

Rosmini y Vico: la "filosofía italiana". Ottonello, Pier Paolo.

The "Political" Dimension of Italian Critico-Problematic Historicism (in Serbo-Croatian). Cacciatore, Giuseppe.

Un convegno su *I filosofi e la genesi della coscienza culturale della "nuova Italia".* Semino, Ignazio.

Vico en Italia y en Alemania. Sevilla Fernández, José M.

Vico en Sciacca. Ottonello, Pier Paolo.

## ITERATION
Canonicity for Intensional Logics without Iterative Axioms. Surendonk, Timothy J.

How to Win Some Simple Iteration Games. Steel, J R and Andretta, Alessandro.

The Backward Induction Argument for the Finite Iterated Prisoner's Dilemma and the Surprise Exam Paradox. Bovens, Luc.

## IVEKOVIC, R
Some Problems of Approach to Nagarjuna's Philosophy (in Serbo-Croatian). Djordjevic, Dejan.

## JACKENDOFF, R
Models, Truth and Semantics. Abbott, Barbara.

## JACOBI
Gefühl und Realität: Fichtes Auseinandersetzung mit Jacobi in der *Grundlage der Wissenschaft des Praktischen.* Loock, Reinhard.

L'ethos dell'intersoggettività nei romanzi di Friedrich Heinrich Jacobi. Iovino, Serenella.

The Early Fichte as Disciple of Jacobi. Di Giovanni, George.

## JAGGAR, A
Communication From One Feminist. Machan, Tibor R.

## JAIN, R

Response to "Discounting Life Support in an Infant of a Drug Addicted Mother: Whose Decision Is It?" by Renu Jain and David C. Thomasma (CQ Vol 6, No 1). Oberman, Michelle.

## JAINISM

Pāndava-Purāna of Vādicandra: Text and Translation. Jaini, Padmanabh S.

Persons (Real and Alleged) in Enlightenment Traditions: A Partial Look at Jainism and Buddhism. Yandell, Keith.

Postmodernism: What One Needs to Know. Grassie, William.

The Composition of the *Guan Wuliangshoufo-Jing*: Some Buddhist and Jaina Parallels to its Narrative Frame. Silk, Jonathan A.

The Jain Conception of Liberation with Special Reference to the Sutrakrtanga. Lalitha, Ch.

## JAKOBSON, R

*The Language of Criticism: Linguistic Models and Literary Theory.* Henkel, Jacqueline M.

## JAMAICAN

Rastafarianism and the Reality of Dread"" in *Existence in Black: An Anthology of Black Existential Philosophy,* Gordon, Lewis R (ed). Henry, Paget.

## JAMES

"Interpreting the Universe after a Social Analogy: Intimacy, Panpsychism, and a Finite God in a Pluralistic Universe" in *The Cambridge Companion to William James,* Putnam, Ruth Anna (ed). Lamberth, David C.

"James and the Kantian Tradition" in *The Cambridge Companion to William James,* Putnam, Ruth Anna (ed). Carlson, Thomas.

"James's Theory of Truth" in *The Cambridge Companion to William James,* Putnam, Ruth Anna (ed). Putnam, Hilary.

"James, Aboutness, and his British Critics" in *The Cambridge Companion to William James,* Putnam, Ruth Anna (ed). Sprigge, T L S.

"James, Clifford, and the Scientific Conscience" in *The Cambridge Companion to William James,* Putnam, Ruth Anna (ed). Hollinger, David A.

"John Dewey's Naturalization of William James" in *The Cambridge Companion to William James,* Putnam, Ruth Anna (ed). Gale, Richard M.

"Logical Principles and Philosophical Attitudes: Peirce's Response to James's Pragmatism" in *The Cambridge Companion to William James,* Putnam, Ruth Anna (ed). Hookway, Christopher.

"Moral Philosophy and the Development of Morality" in *The Cambridge Companion to William James,* Putnam, Ruth Anna (ed). Bird, Graham H.

"Pragmatism and Introspective Psychology" in *The Cambridge Companion to William James,* Putnam, Ruth Anna (ed). Myers, Gerald E.

"Pragmatism, Politics, and the Corridor" in *The Cambridge Companion to William James,* Putnam, Ruth Anna (ed). Cormier, Harvey J.

"Religious Faith, Intellectual Responsibility, and Romance" in *The Cambridge Companion to William James,* Putnam, Ruth Anna (ed). Rorty, Richard.

"The Breathtaking Intimacy of the Material World: William James's Last Thoughts" in *The Cambridge Companion to William James,* Putnam, Ruth Anna (ed). Wilshire, Bruce.

"The Influence of William James on American Culture" in *The Cambridge Companion to William James,* Putnam, Ruth Anna (ed). Posnock, Ross.

"The James/Royce Dispute and the Development of James's "Solution" in *The Cambridge Companion to William James,* Putnam, Ruth Anna (ed). Conant, James.

"William James on Religious Experience" in *The Cambridge Companion to William James,* Putnam, Ruth Anna (ed). Niebuhr, Richard R.

"'A Shelter of the Mind': Henry, William, and the Domestic Scene" in *The Cambridge Companion to William James,* Putnam, Ruth Anna (ed). Feldman, Jessica R.

*Exploring Unseen Worlds: William James and the Philosophy of Mysticism.* Barnard, G William.

*From Soul to Mind: The Emergence of Psychology from Erasmus Darwin to William James.* Reed, Edward S.

*Heaven's Champion: William James's Philosophy of Religion.* Suckiel, Ellen Kappy.

*The Cambridge Companion to William James.* Putnam, Ruth Anna (ed).

*William James on The Courage to Believe.* O'Connell, Robert J.

Consciousness and Self-Awareness—Part I: Consciousness$_1$, Consciousness$_2$, and Consciousness$_3$. Natsoulas, Thomas.

Emotion as an Explanatory Principle in Early Evolutionary Theory. Campbell, Sue.

Epistemology of Mysticism. Venkatalakshmi, M.

Pascalian Wagers. Sobel, Jordan Howard.

Psychological and Religious Perspectives on Emotion. Watts, Fraser N.

Re-Reading 'The Will to Believe'. Schlecht, Ludwig F.

Relativism and James's Pragmatic Notion of Truth. Allen, Michael W.

The Impact of William James: A Thought Process for Recognizing Truth in an Unprecedented Future. Curry, Lewis A.

The Inadequacy of Wishful Thinking Charges against William James's *The Will to Believe*. Brown, Hunter.

What Wittgenstein Learned from William James. Goodman, Russell B.

William James on Free Will: The French Connection. Viney, Donald Wayne.

William James's Ethics and the New Casuistry. Mehl, Peter J.

William James's Quest to Have It All. Gale, Richard M.

William James's Theory of Freedom. Gale, Richard M.

## JAMES, H

"'A Shelter of the Mind': Henry, William, and the Domestic Scene" in *The Cambridge Companion to William James,* Putnam, Ruth Anna (ed). Feldman, Jessica R.

In Which Henry James Strikes Bedrock. Berry, Ralph M.

## JAMESON, F

Frederic Jameson: ¿El marxismo el el Mäelstrom textualista?. Palti, Elías José.

## JANKELEVITCH, V

"Arte, Vita E Verità In Vladimir Jankélévitch" in *Soggetto E Verità: La questione dell'uomo nella filosofia contemporanea,* Fagiuoli, Ettore. Franzini, Elio.

## JANSENISM

Jansenismo versus Jesuitismo: Niccoló Pagliarini e o Projecto Político Pombalino. De Castro, Zília Osório.

## JAPANESE

*see also* Buddhism, Zen Buddhism

"How Universal is Psychoanalysis? The Self in India, Japan, and the United States" in *Culture and Self,* Allen, Douglas (ed). Roland, Alan.

"Mountains of the Mind" in *East and West in Aesthetics,* Marchianò, Grazia (ed). Servomaa, Sonia.

"The Chinese "Cyclic" View of History vs. Japanese "Progress" in *The Idea of Progress,* McLaughlin, Peter (ed). Nakayama, Shigeru.

"The Flowers of the *Noh* and the Aesthetics of *Iki*" in *East and West in Aesthetics,* Marchianò, Grazia (ed). Marchianò, Grazia.

"The Semantic Transformation of an Axiological Concept" in *East and West in Aesthetics,* Marchianò, Grazia (ed). Hashimoto, Noriko.

"Views of Japanese Selfhood: Japanese and Western Perspectives" in *Culture and Self,* Allen, Douglas (ed). Miller, Mara.

*Heidegger's Hidden Sources: East Asian Influences on His Work.* Parkes, Graham (trans) and May, Reinhard.

*Nature and Society: Anthropological Perspectives.* Descola, Philippe (ed) and Pálsson, Gísli (ed).

*Watsuji Tetsurō*'s Rinrigaku. Carter, Robert E (trans) and Seisaku, Yamamoto (trans).

A Global Perspective of Ethics in Business. Yamaji, Keizo.

A Theory of Oriental Aesthetics: A Prolegomenon. Inada, Kenneth K.

Business Ethics of Korean and Japanese Managers. Lee, Chung-Yeong and Yoshihara, Hideki.

Critical Thinking Education Faces the Challenge of Japan. Davidson, Bruce W.

Die Wendung nach Asien: Heideggers Ansatz interkultureller Philosophie. Wolz-Gottwald, Eckard.

Dogen on *seppo* and *jodo*. Nakajima, Keita.

High School Teaching of Bioethics in New Zealand, Australia and Japan. Asada, Yukiko, Tsuzuki, Miho and Akiyama, Shiro.

In Defense of Afro-Japanese Ethnophilosophy. Okafor, Fidelis U.

Japanese Death Factories and the American Cover-Up. Chen, Yuan-Fang.

Japanese Moralogy as Business Ethics. Taka, Iwao and Dunfee, Thomas W.

Japanese Psychiatrists' Attitudes toward Patients Wishing to Die in the General Hospital: A Cultural Perspective. Berger, Douglas, Takahashi, Yoshitomo and Fukunishi, Isao (& others).

Ningen: Intersubjectivity in the Ethics of Watsuji Tetsuro. McCarthy, Erin.

On the Aesthetic Appreciation of Japanese Gardens. Carlson, Allen.

Research Ethics: International Perspectives. Brody, Baruch A.

Some Problems in Interpretation: The Early and Late Writings of Dōgen. Putney, David.

Two Mencian Political Notions in Tokugawa Japan. Tucker, John Allen.

World, Emptiness, Nothingness: A Phenomenological Approach to the Religious Tradition of Japan. Held, Klaus.

## JASPERS

"Esistenza, storia e storia della filosofia nel pensiero di Karl Jaspers" in *Lo Storicismo e la Sua Storia: Temi, Problemi, Prospettive,* Cacciatore, Giuseppe (ed). Miano, Francesco.

Commentary on "Edmund Husserl's Influence on Karl Jaspers's Phenomenology". Naudin, Jean and Azorin, Jean-Michel.

Edmund Husserl's Influence on Karl Jaspers's Phenomenology. Wiggins, Osborne P and Schwartz, Michael Alan.

Il problema del fondamento nella filosofia di Karl Jaspers. Carpentieri, Rosario.

Jaspers, Heidegger et le Langage. Di Cesare, Donatella.

Karl Jaspers: The Person and His Cause, Not the Person or His Cause. Wisser, Richard.

'Europa' en el pensamiento de Jaspers. Franco Barrio, Jaime.

## JAZZ

*The Tanner Lectures on Human Values, Volume 18, 1997.* Peterson, Grethe B (ed).

Musical Works, Improvisation, and the Principle of Continuity. Brown, Lee B.

## JEALOUSY

"Jealousy and Desire" in *Love Analyzed,* Lamb, Roger E. Farrell, Daniel M.

Why Modesty Is a Virtue. Schueler, G F.

## JEANS, J

Methodology and the Birth of Modern Cosmological Inquiry. Gale, George and Shanks, Niall.

**JEFFERSON**
Spirituality and Community. Johnson, J Prescott.

**JEFFREY'S, H**
Inductive Skepticism and the Probability Calculus I: Popper and Jeffreys on Induction and the Probability of Law-Like Universal Generalizations. Gemes, Ken.

**JEFFREY, R**
Probabilism and Beyond. Galavotti, Maria Carla.

**JESUITS**
A Second Collection: Papers by Bernard J. F. Lonergan, S.J.. Ryan, William F (ed) and Tyrrell, Bernard J (ed).
Descartes e os Jesuítas: Para um estudo da personalidade cartesiana. Dinis, Alfredo.
Evading Responsibility: The Ethics of Ingenuity. Katz, Leo.
Jansenismo versus Jesuitismo: Niccoló Pagliarini e o Projecto Político Pombalino. De Castro, Zília Osório.
Modal Voluntarism in Descartes's Jesuit Predecessors. Coombs, Jeffrey.

**JESUS**
see Christ
Did Jesus Commit a Fallacy?. Hitchcock, David.

**JEWISH**
see also Judaism
"White Normativity and the Rhetoric of Equal Protection" in Existence in Black: An Anthology of Black Existential Philosophy, Gordon, Lewis R (ed). Westley, Robert St. Martin.
Heidegger's Silence. Lang, Berel.
Jewish Philosophers and Jewish Philosophy. Fackenheim, Emil L and Morgan, Michael L (ed).
Jüdischer Nietzscheanismus. Stegmaier, Werner and Krochmalnik, Daniel.
Modern Political Thought: Readings from Machiavelli to Nietzsche. Wootton, David (ed).
Society, Economics & Philosophy: Selected Papers. Allen, R T (ed) and Polanyi, Michael.
Blurred Boundaries. Morriss, Peter.
Do Critics of Heidegger Commit the Ad Hominem Fallacy?. Dombrowski, Daniel A.
Guiding Principles of Jewish Business Ethics. Green, Ronald M.
I May Be a Bit of a Jew: Trauma in Human Narrative. Zajko, Vanda.
If I Am Only My Genes, What Am I? Genetic Essentialism and a Jewish Response. Wolpe, Paul Root.
Looking for a Subject: Latvian Memory and Narrative. Skultans, Vieda.
Neighbors in Death. Crowell, Steven Galt.
On the Alleged Uniqueness and Incomprehensibility of the Holocaust. Owen, B William.
Paying for Medical Care: A Jewish View. Dorff, Elliot N.
Raimundus Lullus and His Ars Magna,D (in Czech). Láng, Benedek.
Reflections on Israel Scheffler's Philosophy of Religion. Laura, Ronald S.
Should We Pardon Them?. Hobart, Ann and Jankélévitch, Vladimir.
The Challenge of Wealth: Jewish Business Ethics. Tamari, Meir.
The King and 'I': Agency and Rationality in Athens and Jerusalem. Glouberman, Mark.
The Land of the Fearful and the Free. Tamir, Yael.

**JIHAD**
Interpreting the Jihad of Islam: Militarism versus Muslim Pacifism. Churchill, Robert Paul.

**JNANAGARBHA**
Jñānagarbha and the "God's-Eye View". Pyysiäinen, Ilkka.

**JOBS**
Ethics, Success, and Job Satisfaction: A Test of Dissonance Theory in India. Visweswaran, Chockalingam and Deshpande, Satish P.

**JOHN PAUL II**
The Teaching of John Paul II on the Christian Meaning of Suffering. Crosby, John F.

**JOHNSON, M**
More Responses to the Missing-Explanation Argument. Miller, Alexander.

**JOHNSTON, D**
Liberalism and Pluralism. Klosko, George.

**JOHNSTON, M**
"Getting Acquainted with Perception" in Perception, Villanueva, Enrique (ed). Sosa, David.
"Visible Properties of Human Interest Only" in Perception, Villanueva, Enrique (ed). Gibbard, Allan.
"Would More Acquaintance with the External World Relieve Epistemic Anxiety?" in Perception, Villanueva, Enrique (ed). Villanueva, Enrique.
Humans, Persons and Selves. Brown, Mark T.

**JOIN**
Combining Temporal Logic Systems. Finger, Marcelo and Gabbay, Dov.
Systems of Explicit Mathematics with Non-Constructive Mu-Operator and Join. Glass, Thomas and Strahm, Thomas.

**JONAS, H**
Martin Heidegger und Hans Jonas: Die Metaphysik der Subjektivität und die Krise der technologischen Zivilisation. Jakob, Eric.
De la liberté absolue: A propos de la théorie cartésienne de la création des vérités éternelles. Depré, Olivier.

Hans Jonas développe-t-il une anthropologie arendtienne?. Frogneux, Nathalie.
Hans Jonas's Mortality and Morality. Bernstein, Richard J.
Two Concepts of the Ethics of Responsibility: H. Jonas and K.-O. Apel (in Czech). Machalová, Tatiana.

**JORGENSEN, E**
"Can the Justification of Music Education be Justified?" in Philosophy of Education (1996), Margonis, Frank (ed). Yob, Iris M.

**JOURNAL**
Journals and Justice. Curzer, Howard J.
Peer Review for Journals: Evidence on Quality Control, Fairness, and Innovation. Armstrong, J Scott.
Philosophical Periodicals in Russia Today (mid-1995). Van der Zweerde, Evert.
Proliferation of Authors on Research Reports in Medicine. Drenth, Joost P H.
Revistas filosóficas em Portugal. Calafate, Pedro.
The Heythrop Journal (1960-1996): From In-House Review to International Journal. Levi, A H T.
The Return of the Political? New French Journals in the History of Political Thought. Jennings, Jeremy.
Using a Dialectical Scientific Brief in Peer Review. Stamps III, Arthur E.

**JOURNALISM**
"El Ortega de 1914" in Política y Sociedad en José Ortega y Gasset: En Torno a "Vieja y Nueva Política", Lopez de la Vieja, Maria Teresa (ed). Aranguren, José Luis L.
"Journalistische Verantwortung: Medienethik als Qualitätsproblem" in Angewandte Ethik: Die Bereichsethiken und ihre theoretische Fundierung, Nida-Rümelin, Julian (ed). Teichert, Will.
Algunos elementos para una deontología periodística. Rodríguez Ramírez, Carlos Alberto.

**JOY**
Happiness Doesn't Come in Bottles: Neuroscientists Learn That Joy Comes Through Dancing, Not Drugs. Freeman, Walter J.
Rationality, Joy and Freedom. Sen, Amartya K.

**JUDAISM**
Jewish Philosophers and Jewish Philosophy. Fackenheim, Emil L and Morgan, Michael L (ed).
La raíz semítica de lo europeo: Islam y judaísmo medievales. Lomba, Joaquín.
Nietzsche and Jewish Culture. Golomb, Jacob (ed).
The Political Consequences of Thinking: Gender and Judaism in the Work of Hannah Arendt. Ring, Jennifer.
The Temptations of Emile Cioran. Kluback, William and Finkenthal, Michael.
Emmanuel Levinas: Thinker between Jerusalem and Athens. Burggraeve, Roger.
Holy Argument: Some Reflections on the Jewish Piety of Argument, Process Theology and the Philosophy of Religion. Tidwell, N L.
Judaism and Philosophy in Levinas. Peperzak, Adriaan Theodoor.
Judaism, Business and Privacy. Dorff, Elliot N.
Otra vuelta de tuerca: A propósito de Espectros de Marx de J. Derrida. Sucasas Peón, J Alberto.
Philosophic Approaches to Sacred Scripture in Judaism. Jospe, Raphael.
Sendas Perdidas de la Razon (Cuando "el sueño de la razón produce monstruos"). Mate, Reyes.
Three Comparative Maps of the Human. Samuelson, Norbert M.
Yeshayahu Leibowitz—A Breakthrough in Jewish Philosophy: Religion Without Metaphysics. Sagi, Avi.

**JUDEO-CHRISTIAN**
Confession of Sin: A Catharsis!. Kakade, R M.
Natural Law, Nature, and Biology: A Modern Synthesis. Hartigan, Richard Shelly.
New Books on Philosophy of Religion. Moser, Paul K.
The Logical Status of Prayer. Schoenig, Richard.
Trinity or Tritheism?. Clark, Kelly James.

**JUDGING**
Judging Our Own Good. Wilkinson, T M.

**JUDGMENT**
"Assent chez les Platoniciens de Cambridge" in Mind Senior to the World, Baldi, Marialuisa. Vienne, Jean-Michel.
"Bradley on Truth and Judgement" in Philosophy after F.H. Bradley, Bradley, James (ed). Creery, Walter.
"Die Theorie der Urteilsformen in der deutschen Schullogik des 19.Jahrhunderts" in Das weite Spektrum der analytischen Philosophie, Lenzen, Wolfgang. Stuhlmann-Laeisz, Rainer.
"Im Wechsel des Urteils und Bildens: Zu Fichte und Hölderlin" in Sein—Reflexion—Freiheit: Aspekte der Philosophie Johann Gottlieb Fichtes, Asmuth, Christoph (ed). Völkel, Frank.
"Moral Causation" in A Question of Values: New Canadian Perspectives in Ethics and Political Philosophy, Brennan, Samantha (ed). Pietroski, Paul M.
Considered Judgment. Elgin, Catherine Z.
Foundations of Futures Studies: Human Science for a New Era. Bell, Wendell.
Kant's Aesthetic Theory. Kemal, Salim.
The Constitution of Good Societies. Soltan, Karol Edward (ed) and Elkin, Stephen L (ed).

## JUSTICE

Restorative Justice and Punishment. Brunk, Conrad G.
Seeking Justice for Priscilla. Lantos, John D.
Sex, Fairness, and the Theory of Games. D'Arms, Justin.
Social Justice: The Hayekian Challenge. Lukes, Steven.
Sustainable Development and the Local Justice Framework. Roe, Emery.
Taking Utilitarianism Seriously. Kelly, P J.
Temporal Horizons of Justice. Ackerman, Bruce.
The Challenge of Wealth: Jewish Business Ethics. Tamari, Meir.
The Condition of Postmodernity and the Discourse of the Body. Kumar Giri, Ananta.
The Ethical Neutrality of Prospective Payments: Justice Issues. McDowell, Jean.
The Ethics of Law or the Right of Women (Spanish). Aponte, Elida.
The Good, the Bad, and the Impartial. Horton, John.
The Individual Rationality of Maintaining a Sense of Justice. Cave, Eric M.
The Libertarianism of Robert Nozick (in Czech). Barsa, Pavel.
The Moral Economy: Keynes's Critique of Capitalist Justice. Hill, Greg.
The Moral Status of Children: Children's Rights, Parents' Rights, and Family Justice. Brennan, Samantha and Noggle, Robert.
The Ought-Is Question: Discovering The Modern in Post-Modernism. Johnson, David Kenneth.
The Problematic Character of Socrates' Defense of Justice in Plato's *Republic*. Jang, In Ha.
The Quiddity of Mercy—A Response. Pearn, John.
Thomson on the Moral Specification of Rights. Prior, William J and Parent, William A.
Tolerance & Forgiveness: Virtues or Vices?. Smith, Tara.
Toward Social Reform: Kant's Penal Theory Reinterpreted. Holtman, Sarah Williams.
Unbundling the Moral Dispute About Unbundling in South Africa. Rossouw, Gedeon J.
Vernunft heute. Welsch, Wolfgang.
Washington, Du Bois and *Plessy V. Ferguson*. Boxill, Bernard R.
Where the Action Is: On the Site of Distributive Justice. Cohen, G A.
Who is Cephalus?. Steinberger, Peter J.

## JUSTIFICATION

"Can the Justification of Music Education be Justified?" in *Philosophy of Education (1996),* Margonis, Frank (ed). Yob, Iris M.
"Justifying Music in General Education: Belief in Search of Reason" in *Philosophy of Education (1996),* Margonis, Frank (ed). Jorgensen, Estelle R.
"The Justification of Toleration" in *Philosophy, Religion, and the Question of Intolerance,* Ambuel, David (ed). Dees, Richard H.
"The Pre-eminence of Autonomy in Bioethics" in *Human Lives: Critical Essays on Consequentialist Bioethics,* Oderberg, David S (ed). Smith, Janet E.
*Academic Freedom and Tenure: Ethical Issues.* De George, Richard T.
*Against Liberalism.* Kekes, John.
A Question for Egalitarians. Kekes, John.
Against Education. Nordenbo, Sven Erik.
Argumentation, Values, and Ethics. Monsalve, Alfonso.
Can An Egalitarian Justify Universal Access to Health Care?. Jacobs, Lesley A.
Can Old-Age Social Insurance Be Justified. Shapiro, Daniel J.
Can One Lie for Moral Reasons? (in Serbo-Croatian). Vukovic, Ivan.
Collateral Violence and the Doctrine of Double Effect. Bica, Camillo C.
Discretionary Power, Lies, and Broken Trust: Justification and Discomfort. Potter, Nancy.
Epistemic Obligation and Rationality Constraints. Katzoff, Charlotte.
Foundationalism and Practical Reason. Heath, Joseph.
How to Resolve the Pyrrhonian Problematic: A Lesson from Descartes. Sosa, Ernest.
In Defense of Coherentism. Kvanvig, Jonathan.
In Defense of One Form of Traditional Epistemology. Markie, Peter J.
Internalism, Externalism and the No-Defeater Condition. Bergmann, Michael.
Just Desert. Nuyen, A T.
Justification of Empirical Belief: Problems with Haack's Foundherentism. Clune, Alan C.
Justified Wrongdoing. Buss, Sarah.
Justified, True Belief: Is it Relevant to Knowledge?. Leeser, Jamie.
Kant Was Not Able to Distinguish True from False Experiences. Lorca, Daniel.
L'idée d'une doctrine cohérentiste de la justification épistémique. Schulthess, Daniel.
Norm-Endorsement Utilitarianism and the Nature of Utility. Baron, Jonathan.
On Making and Keeping Promises. Fox, Richard M.
On Motivation of Judicial Decisions (in Spanish). García Leal, Laura.
On the Impossibility of Epistemology. Ketchum, Richard J.
On Tolerance. Bercic, Boran.
Op zoek naar Mr. Spock: Kort commentaar op Apostel en Walry, 'Minimale rationaliteit van emoties en van overtuigingen'. Pott, Heleen.
Para una Lógica de las Razones Prima Facie. Alchourrón, Carlos E.
Political Justification, Theoretical Complexity, and Democratic Community. Bertram, Christopher.

Précis of *Pyrrhonian Reflections on Knowledge and Justification.* Fogelin, Robert J.
Premise Acceptability, Deontology, Internalism, Justification. Freeman, James B.
Public Justification and the Transparency Argument. Wall, Steven P.
Reciprocal Justification in Science and Moral Theory. Blachowicz, James.
Should We Abandon Epistemic Justification?. Meeker, Kevin.
Some Paradoxes of Whistleblowing. Davis, Michael.
Stufen der Rechtfertigung. Ulfig, Alexander.
The Crisis of Virtue: Arming for the Cultural Wars and Pellegrino at the Limes. Engelhardt Jr, H Tristram.
The Economics of Clinical Ethics Programs: A Quantitative Justification. Bacchetta, Matthew D and Fins, Joseph J.
The Secret History of Public Reason: Hobbes to Rawls. Ivison, Duncan.
The Weakness of Strong Justification. Riggs, Wayne D.
Three Aspects of Rational Explanation. Pettit, Philip.
Tracking Truth and Solving Puzzles. Gjelsvik, Olav.
Understanding, Justification and the A Priori. Hunter, David A.

## JUSTIN MARTYR

"Gift of the Egyptians" (On the History of Christian Philosophy) (in Czech). Rugási, Gyula.

## KABBALA

Raimundus Lullus and His *Ars Magna,D (in Czech). Láng, Benedek.*

## KAFKA

*Nietzsche and Jewish Culture.* Golomb, Jacob (ed).
Kafka's China and the Parable of Parables. Wood, Michael.

## KAGAME, A

African Philosophy in Comparison with Western Philosophy. Okafor, Fidelis U.

## KAGAN, S

Ordinary Morality and the Pursuit of the Good. Childs, Zena.
The "Negative" and "Positive" Arguments of Moral Moderates. Montague, Phillip.

## KAIROS

El momento *epíkairos (Kairós* "espontáneo", *kairós* negativo, *kairós* inducido, contra-kairós). Rossetti, Livio.

## KALAM

In Defense of the *Kalam* Cosmological Argument. Craig, William Lane.

## KALIDASA

Embracing the Subject: Harsa's Play within a Play. Shulman, David.

## KANE, J

On the Status of Equality. Sen, Amartya K.

## KANGER, S

Getting Started: Beginnings in the Logic of Action. Segerberg, Krister.

## KANT

"*Ewiger Friede*: Warum ein Beweismittel in Kants philosophischem Entwurf?" in *Grenzen der kritischen Vernunft,* Schmid, Peter A. Mainberger, Gonsalv K.
"Analytic Geometry, Experimental Truth and Metaphysics in Descartes" in *Memorias Del Seminario En Conmemoración De Los 400 Anos Del Nacimiento De René Descartes,* Albis, Víctor S (ed). Laserna Pinzón, Mario.
"Aportación de la Ética a la Paz Perpetua" in *Kant: La paz perpetua, doscientos años después,* Martínez Guzmán, Vicent (ed). Innerarity, Carmen.
"August Stadler als Kant-Interpret" in *Grenzen der kritischen Vernunft,* Schmid, Peter A. Ferrari, Massimo.
"Del Sentire La Verità: Per Leopardi e Michelstaedter" in *Soggetto E Verità: La questione dell'uomo nella filosofia contemporanea,* Fagiuoli, Ettore. Carrera, Alessandro.
"Deleuze, Kant and Indifference" in *Deleuze and Philosophy: The Difference Engineer,* Ansell Pearson, Keith (ed). Beddoes, Diane.
"Die Unterstellung von Vernunft in der Geschichte: Vorläufiger kritischer Versuch über einen Aspekt von Kants Geschichtsphilosophie" in *Grenzen der kritischen Vernunft,* Schmid, Peter A. Lüthe, Rudolf.
"El "Proyecto filosófico para la paz perpetua" de Kant como cuasipronóstico de la filosofía de la historia..." in *Kant: La paz perpetua, doscientos años después,* Martínez Guzmán, Vicent (ed). Apel, Karl-Otto.
"El descubrimiento de la Doctrina de la Ciencia" in *El inicio del Idealismo alemán,* Market, Oswaldo. Tilliette, Xavier.
"El ideal de la Paz en el Humanismo Ético de Kant" in *Kant: La paz perpetua, doscientos años después,* Martínez Guzmán, Vicent (ed). Conill, Jesús.
"El idealismo transcendental como vía de superación del realismo e idealismo dogmáticos" in *El inicio del Idealismo alemán,* Market, Oswaldo. Medina Medina, Francisco.
"Europa y una federación global: La visión de Kant" in *Kant: La paz perpetua, doscientos años después,* Martínez Guzmán, Vicent (ed). Pogge, Thomas W.
"Friede als Ziel der Geschichte? Drei europäische Positionen: Augustinus-Comenius-Kant" in *Kreativer Friede durch Begegnung der Weltkulturen,* Beck, Heinrich (ed). Voigt, Uwe.
"Gedanken vor einem Jubiläum" in *Grenzen der kritischen Vernunft,* Schmid, Peter A. Fontius, Martin.

**KMITA, J**

"Explaining Social Phenomena" in *Epistemology and History*, Zeidler-Janiszewska, Anna (ed). Mejbaum, Waclaw.

"Explanation by Intentional, Functional, and Causal Specification" in *Epistemology and History*, Zeidler-Janiszewska, Anna (ed). Kuipers, Theo A F.

"Generationszugehörigkeit und Selbsterfahrung von (deutschen) Schriftstellern" in *Epistemology and History*, Zeidler-Janiszewska, Anna (ed). Orlowski, Hubert.

"Historical Interpretation vs. Adaptive Interpretation of a Legal Text" in *Epistemology and History*, Zeidler-Janiszewska, Anna (ed). Ziembinski, Zygmunt.

"Humanistic Interpretation between Hempel and Popper" in *Epistemology and History*, Zeidler-Janiszewska, Anna (ed). Coniglione, Francesco.

"Humanistic Valuation and Some Social Functions of the Humanities" in *Epistemology and History*, Zeidler-Janiszewska, Anna (ed). Kotowa, Barbara.

"Jerzy Kmita's Epistemology" in *Epistemology and History*, Zeidler-Janiszewska, Anna (ed). Czerwinski, Marcin.

"Jerzy Kmita's Social-Regulational Theory of Culture and the Category of Subject" in *Epistemology and History*, Zeidler-Janiszewska, Anna (ed). Zamiara, Krystyna.

"Musical Culture as a Configuration of Subcultures" in *Epistemology and History*, Zeidler-Janiszewska, Anna (ed). Banaszak, Grzegorz.

"Non-Cartesian Coordinates in the Contemporary Humanities" in *Epistemology and History*, Zeidler-Janiszewska, Anna (ed). Grzegorczyk, Anna.

"On Limits of the Rationalistic Paradigm" in *Epistemology and History*, Zeidler-Janiszewska, Anna (ed). Nowak, Leszek.

"Some Issues of Historical Epistemology in the Light of the Structuralist Philosophy of Science" in *Epistemology and History*, Zeidler-Janiszewska, Anna (ed). Zeidler, Pawel.

"The 'Transhistoricity' of the Structure of a Work of Art and the Process of Value Transmission in Culture" in *Epistemology and History*, Zeidler-Janiszewska, Anna (ed). Kostyrko, Teresa.

"The Avant-Garde and Contemporary Artistic Consciousness" in *Epistemology and History*, Zeidler-Janiszewska, Anna (ed). Dziamski, Grzegorz.

"The Broken Bonds with the World" in *Epistemology and History*, Zeidler-Janiszewska, Anna (ed). Ozdowski, Pawel.

"The Decahedron of Education (Components and Aspects): The Need for a Comprehensive Approach" in *Epistemology and History*, Zeidler-Janiszewska, Anna (ed). Kwiecinski, Zbigniew.

"The Frankfurt School and Structuralism in Jerzy Kmita's Analysis" in *Epistemology and History*, Zeidler-Janiszewska, Anna (ed). Witkowski, Lech.

"The Functional Theory of Culture and Sociology" in *Epistemology and History*, Zeidler-Janiszewska, Anna (ed). Ziolkowski, Marek.

"The Interpretational Paradigm in the Philosophy of the Human Sciences" in *Epistemology and History*, Zeidler-Janiszewska, Anna (ed). Swiderski, Edward.

"The Perception of Science in Modernist and Postmodernist Artistic Practice" in *Epistemology and History*, Zeidler-Janiszewska, Anna (ed). Erjavec, Ales.

"The Problem of the Applicability of Humanistic Interpretation in the Light of Contemporary Artistic Practice" in *Epistemology and History*, Zeidler-Janiszewska, Anna (ed). Zeidler-Janiszewska, Anna.

"Theory and Social Practice: One or Two Psychologies?" in *Epistemology and History*, Zeidler-Janiszewska, Anna (ed). Brzezinski, Jerzy.

"Theses on the 20th Century Crisis of Art and Culture" in *Epistemology and History*, Zeidler-Janiszewska, Anna (ed). Morawski, Stefan.

"Three Types of Theories of Religion and Magic" in *Epistemology and History*, Zeidler-Janiszewska, Anna (ed). Jerzak-Gierszewska, Teresa.

"Types of Determination vs. The Development of Science in Historical Epistemology" in *Epistemology and History*, Zeidler-Janiszewska, Anna (ed). Such, Jan.

"Via Media: On the Consequences of Historical Epistemology for the Problem of Rationality" in *Epistemology and History*, Zeidler-Janiszewska, Anna (ed). Buchowski, Michal.

"Who is Afraid of Scientism?" in *Epistemology and History*, Zeidler-aniszewska, Anna (ed). Sójka, Jacek.

*Epistemology and History: Humanities as a Philosophical Problem and Jerzy Kmita's Approach to It.* Zeidler-Janiszewska, Anna (ed).

**KNOWABILITY**

A Minimal Logical System for Computable Concepts and Effective Knowability. Freund, Max A.

**KNOWING**

"Autonomy and a Right not to Know" in *The Right to Know and the Right not to Know*, Chadwick, Ruth (ed). Husted, Jorgen.

"Conceptual Understanding and Knowing *Other*-Wise: Reflections on Rationality and Spirituality..." in *Knowing Other-Wise: Philosophy at the Threshold of Spirituality*, Olthuis, James H (ed). Hart, Hendrik.

"Do 'All Men Desire to Know'? A Right of Society to Choose not to Know About the Genetics of Personality Traits" in *The Right to Know and the Right not to Know*, Chadwick, Ruth (ed). Shickle, Darren.

"Frege on Knowing the Third Realm" in *Frege: Importance and Legacy*, Schirn, Matthias (ed). Burge, Tyler.

"Sociological Perspectives on the Right to Know and the Right not to Know" in *The Right to Know and the Right not to Know*, Chadwick, Ruth (ed). Levitt, Mairi.

"The Philosophy of the Right to Know and the Right not to Know" in *The Right to Know and the Right not to Know*, Chadwick, Ruth (ed). Chadwick, Ruth.

*Knowing Other-Wise: Philosophy at the Threshold of Spirituality.* Olthuis, James H (ed).

*The Right to Know and the Right not to Know.* Chadwick, Ruth (ed), Levitt, Mairi (ed) and Shickle, Darren (ed).

Against Coady on Hume on Testimony. Hríbek, Tomás.

Knowing and Asserting. Williamson, Timothy.

Los hábitos intelectuales según Polo. Sellés, Juan Fernando.

Metacognition and Consciousness: Review Essay of Janet Metcalfe and Arthur P. Shimamura (Eds) *Metacognition: Knowing about Knowing.* Kobes, Bernard W.

Not-Knowing in the Work of Georges Bataille (in Serbo-Croatian). Hewitt, Peter.

Nyāya Realism: Some Reflections. Sharma, Ramesh Kumar.

On What Sort of Speech Act Wittgenstein's *Investigations* Is and Why It Matters. Leiber, Justin.

So Do We Know or Don't We?. Dretske, Fred.

Testimony and Perception. Prijic-Samardzija, Snjezana.

The "Extreme Heresy" of John Dewey and Arthur F. Bentley I: A Star Crossed Collaboration?. Ryan, Frank X.

**KNOWLEDGE**

*see also* Epistemology, Self-Knowledge

"A Deontic Logic for Reasoning about Confidentiality" in *Deontic Logic, Agency and Normative Systems*, Brown, Mark A (ed). Cuppens, Frédéric and Demolombe, Robert.

"Alle Wahrheit ist relativ, alles wissen symbolisch". Frank, Manfred.

"Analytic Geometry, Experimental Truth and Metaphysics in Descartes" in *Memorias Del Seminario En Conmemoración De Los 400 Anos Del Nacimiento De René Descartes*, Albis, Víctor S (ed). Laserna Pinzón, Mario.

"Art History and Autonomy" in *The Semblance of Subjectivity*, Huhn, Tom (ed). Horowitz, Gregg M.

"Art is More Powerful Than Knowledge" (in Serbo-Croatian). Salaquarda, Jörg.

"Believing in Order to Understand" in *Verstehen and Humane Understanding*, O'Hear, Anthony (ed). Barrett, Cyril.

"Between Relativism and Absolutism: The Popperian Ideal of Knowledge" in *The Significance of Popper's Thought*, Amsterdamski, Stefan (ed). Amsterdamski, Stefan.

"But That Is Not What I Mean" Criticizing With Care and Respect" in *Philosophy of Education (1996)*, Margonis, Frank (ed). Applebaum, Barbara.

"Can There be an Epistemology of Moods?" in *Verstehen and Humane Understanding*, O'Hear, Anthony (ed). Mulhall, Stephen.

"Carnal Knowledge in the *Charmides*" in *Dialogues with Plato*, Benitez, Eugenio (ed). McAvoy, Martin.

"Carnal Knowledges: Beyond Rawls and Sandel" in *A Question of Values: New Canadian Perspectives in Ethics and Political Philosophy*, Brennan, Samantha (ed). Mills, Charles W.

"Concept, Image, Name: On Adorno's Utopia of Knowledge" in *The Semblance of Subjectivity*, Huhn, Tom (ed). Tiedemann, Rolf.

"Conceptual Knowledge and Intuitive Experience: Schlick's Dilemma" in *Origins of Logical Empiricism*, Giere, Ronald N (ed). Turner, Joia Lewis.

"Conoscere immediato e conoscere discorsivo in Herbert of Cherbury e in alcuni autori della Scuola di Cambridge" in *Mind Senior to the World*, Baldi, Marialuisa. Bianchi, Massimo Luigi.

"Content Preservation" in *Contents*, Villanueva, Enrique (ed). Burge, Tyler.

"Das Wissen ist an sich die absolute Existenz": Der oberste Grundsatz in Fichtes 4: Vortrag der Wissenschaftslehre: Erlangen im Sommer 1805. Janke, Wolfgang.

"Del Sentire La Verità: Per Leopardi e Michelstaedter" in *Soggetto E Verità: La questione dell'uomo nella filosofia contemporanea*, Fagiuoli, Ettore. Carrera, Alessandro.

"Deleuze Outside/Outside Deleuze: On the Difference Engineer" in *Deleuze and Philosophy: The Difference Engineer*, Ansell Pearson, Keith (ed). Ansell Pearson, Keith.

"Education in the Mode of Information: Some Philosophical Considerations" in *Philosophy of Education (1996)*, Margonis, Frank (ed). Marshall, James D.

"Education, Not Initiation" in *Philosophy of Education (1996)*, Margonis, Frank (ed). Biesta, Gert.

"Epistemological Reversals between Chisholm and Lyotard" in *Philosophy of Education (1996)*, Margonis, Frank (ed). Gunzenhauser, Michael G.

"Frege's 'Epistemology in Disguise" in *Frege: Importance and Legacy*, Schirn, Matthias (ed). Gabriel, Gottfried.

"From Epistemology to the Logic of Science: Carnap's Philosophy of Empirical Knowledge in the 1930s" in *Origins of Logical Empiricism*, Giere, Ronald N (ed). Richardson, Alan W.

"Hume's Scepticism: Natural Instincts and Philosophical Reflection" in *Scepticism in the History of Philosophy: A Pan-American Dialogue*, Popkin, Richard H (ed). Stroud, Barry.

## KNOWLEDGE

## KNOWLEDGE

*Mein Geist ist das Universum*: Ontologische und erkenntnistheoretische Aspekte in der Lehre des Lu Jiuyuan (1139-1193). Ommerborn, Wolfgang.

*Metaphysics and the Origin of Species*. Ghiselin, Michael T.

*Mind Design II: Philosophy, Psychology, Artificial Intelligence*. Haugeland, John (ed).

*Moral Knowledge?: New Readings in Moral Epistemology*. Sinnott-Armstrong, Walter (ed) and Timmons, Mark (ed).

*New Essays on Human Understanding*. Bennett, Jonathan (trans) and Remnant, Peter (trans).

*Objections to Physicalism*. Robinson, Howard (ed).

*Objectivity and Historical Understanding*. Beards, Andrew.

*Objectivity: The Obligations of Impersonal Reason*. Rescher, Nicholas.

*Of Art and Wisdom: Plato's Understanding of Techne*. Roochnik, David.

*On Knowing and the Known: Introductory Readings in Epistemology*. Lucey, Kenneth G (ed).

*Perception*. Villanueva, Enrique (ed).

*Philosophy's Second Revolution: Early and Recent Analytic Philosophy*. Clarke, D S.

*Plato's Epistemology: How Hard Is It to Know?*. Laidlaw-Johnson, Elizabeth A.

*Pragmatism and Realism*. Westphal, Kenneth R (ed), Will, Frederick L and MacIntyre, Alasdair.

*Pragmatism as a Principle and Method of Right Thinking*. Turrisi, Patricia Ann (ed) and Sanders Peirce, Charles.

*Proclus: Neo-Platonic Philosophy and Science*. Siorvanes, Lucas.

*Proper Names*. Smith, Michael B (trans) and Levinas, Emmanuel.

*Properties*. Mellor, D H (ed) and Oliver, Alex (ed).

*Ragione e Scrittura tra Descartes e Spinoza: Saggio sulla Philosophia S. Scripturae Interpres di Lodewijk Meyer e sulla sua recezione*. Bordoli, Roberto.

*Ratio Indifferens* (in Serbo-Croatian). Sakota, Jasna.

*Reason, Reality, and Speculative Philosophy*. Singer, Marcus G (ed) and Murphy, Arthur E.

*Saber, Sentir, Pensar: La cultura en la frontera de dos siglos*. Nieto Blanco, Carlos (ed).

*Scepticism and the Foundation of Epistemology: A Study in the Metalogical Fallacies*. Floridi, Luciano.

*Scepticism in the History of Philosophy: A Pan-American Dialogue*. Popkin, Richard H (ed).

*Self-Trust: A Study of Reason, Knowledge and Autonomy*. Lehrer, Keith.

*Socratic Puzzles*. Nozick, Robert.

*Strong Wits and Spider Webs: A Study in Hobbes's Philosophy of Language*. Soles, Deborah Hansen.

*Systematische Wahrheitstheorie: Methodische und wissenschafts-theoretische Überlegungen zur Frage nach dem grundlegenden Einheitsprinzip*. Siebel, Wigand.

*The Continuity of Wittgenstein's Thought*. Koethe, John.

*The Fate of Place: A Philosophical History*. Casey, Edward S.

*The Idea of University*. Brzezinski, Jerzy (ed) and Nowak, Leszek (ed).

*The Language of Criticism: Linguistic Models and Literary Theory*. Henkel, Jacqueline M.

*The Neoplatonic Metaphysics and Epistemology of Anselm of Canterbury*. Rogers, Katherin A.

*The Play of the Platonic Dialogues*. Freydberg, Bernard.

*The Prayers and Tears of Jacques Derrida Religion without Religion*. Caputo, John D.

*The Recalcitrant Synthetic A Priori*. Zelaniec, Wojciech and Smith, Barry.

*The Semblance of Subjectivity*. Huhn, Tom (ed) and Zuidervaart, Lambert (ed).

*The Taming of the True*. Tennant, Neil.

*Time, Tense, and Causation*. Tooley, Michael.

*Vagueness*. Williamson, Timothy.

*Verstehen and Humane Understanding*. O'Hear, Anthony (ed).

*Western Philosophy: An Anthology*. Cottingham, John (ed).

*Wholeness and the Implicate Order*. Bohm, David.

*Wittgensteinian Themes: Essays 1978-1989*. Von Wright, Georg Henrik (ed) and Malcolm, Norman.

A Completeness Proof for a Logic with an Alternative Necessity Operator. Demri, Stéphane.

A Critique of Pure Meaning: Wittgenstein and Derrida. Sonderegger, Ruth.

A Logic for Information Systems. Archangelsky, Dmitri A and Taitslin, Mikhail A.

A Methodology for the Representation of Legal Knowledge: Formal Ontology Applied to Law. Tiscornia, Daniela.

A Neo-Kantian Critique of Von Mises's Epistemology. Barrotta, Pierluigi.

A Noncompliant Patient?. Moseley, Kathryn L and Truesdell, Sandra.

A Nonmonotonic Modal Formalization of the Logic of Acceptance and Rejection. Gomolinska, Anna.

A Priori Knowledge. Inglis, Sam.

A Psychologically Plausible Logical Model of Conceptualization. Kim, Hong-Gee.

A Taxonomy of Functions. Walsh, Denis M and Ariew, André.

A Work on Philosophy. Shpet, G G.

Academic Skepticism in Early Modern Philosophy. Maia Neto, José R.

Acerca de dos modelos de conocimiento tecnológico. González, María Cristina.

Actitudes proposicionales y conocimiento sensible en Tomás de Aquino. Tellkamp, Jörg Alejandro.

Acts and Outcomes: A Reply to Boonin-Vail. Parfit, Derek.

Advocacy, Therapy, and Pedagogy. MacKinnon, John E.

Against Characterizing Mental States as Propositional Attitudes. Ben-Yami, Hanoch.

Ai margini del discorso poetico. Dell'Erba, Paola.

Alfred North Whitehead's Informal Philosophy of Education. Blasius, Ronald F.

Alfred Schutz on the Social Distribution of Knowledge. Nnoruka, Sylvanos I.

Algunas tesis sobre la tecnología. Herrera J, Rodolfo.

Algunos Problemas de las Ciencias Reconstructivas. Villegas, Luis.

An Analysis of "Res cogitans". Almeida, Eduardo.

An Argument About Free Inquiry. Kitcher, Philip.

An Engaging Practice?. Luntley, Michael.

An Epistemic Dimension of Blameworthiness. Haji, Ishtiyaque.

An Objectivistic Critic of Phenomenological Hermeneutics (in Serbo-Croatian). Milosavljevic, Boris.

Analyticity, Necessity, and the Epistemology of Semantics. Katz, Jerrold J.

Antisoggettivismo e l'autorità della prima persona. Soldati, Gianfranco.

Apperception and Spontaneity. Carl, Wolfgang.

Approximate Common Knowledge and Co-Ordination: Recent Lessons from Game Theory. Morris, Stephen and Shin, Hyun Song.

Approximate Knowledge of Many Agents and Discovery Systems. Zytkow, Jan M.

Are Thought Experiments Just What You Thought?. Norton, John D.

Aristotle on Canonical Science and Ethics. Anagnostopoulos, Georgios.

Aristotle on Variation and Indefiniteness in Ethics and Its Subject Matter. Anagnostopoulos, Georgios.

Arqueologia da Gramática Geral: O Estatuto da Linguagem no Saber da idade Clássica. Matos de Noronha, Nelson.

Artificial Intelligence Modeling of Spontaneous Self Learning: An Application of Dialectical Philosophy. Stokes, Karina.

Astrology: Science, Pseudoscience, Ideology. Pruzhinin, Boris Isaevich.

Back to Darwin and Popper: Criticism, Migration of Piecemeal Conceptual Schemes, and the Growth of Knowledge. De Freitas, Renan Springer.

Behavioral Expression and Related Concepts. Berckmans, Paul R.

Belief and Knowledge. Naik, A D.

California Unnatural: On Fine's Natural Ontological Attitude. Brandon, Edwin P.

Callicles' Examples of *nomos tes phuseos* in Plato's *Gorgias*. Fussi, Alessandra.

Can Navya Nyāya Analysis Make a Distinction between Sense and Reference. Krishna, Daya.

Can There Be a Science of Action? Paul Ricoeur. Van den Hengel, John.

Can There Be Moral Knowledge?. Sweet, William.

Can We Believe What We Do Not Understand?. Récanati, François.

Can we Understand Ourselves?. Winch, Peter.

Canonizing Measures. Gasché, Rodolphe.

Carnap and Quine on Empiricism. Almeder, Robert F.

Cartesian Epistemics and Descartes' *Regulae*. Thomas, Bruce M.

Catholics vs. Calvinists on Religious Knowledge. Greco, John.

Charting the Currents of the Third Wave. Orr, Catherine M.

Classic Paradoxes in the Context of Non-Monotonic Logic (in Spanish). Beck, Andreas.

Cogito ergo sum como conculcación al axioma A. Merino, Magdalena.

Cognition, Being, and the Possibility of Expressions: A Bhartrharian Approach. Tiwari, D N.

Collaborative Knowledge. Thagard, Paul.

Collectives and Intentionality. Hornsby, Jennifer.

Collingwood's "Lost" Manuscript of *The Principles of History*. Van der Dussen, Jan.

Coming to Know Principles in *Posterior Analytics* II 19. Bayer, Greg.

Commentary. White, Hayden.

Commentary on "Loopholes, Gaps, and What is Held Fast". Code, Lorraine.

Compatibilism, Incompatibilism, and the Smart Aleck. Honderich, Ted.

Completeness and Indeterministic Causation. DeVito, Scott.

Conditions on Understanding Language. Lepore, Ernest.

Conflicting Varieties of Realism: Causal Powers and the Problems of Social Structure. Varela, Charles R and Harré, Rom.

Connatural Knowledge. Thomas, James.

Conoscenza metafisica dell'esistenza. Possenti, Vittorio.

Critical Notice of Philip Kitcher: *The Advancement of Science: Science without Legend, Objectivity without Illusions*. Kitcher, Philip.

Critical Thinking and Epistemic Obligations. Hatcher, Donald L.

Critical Thinking vs. Pure Thought (Part One of Two). Coccia, Orestes.

Criticismo trascendentale, trascendenza, religione. Jacobelli, Angela Maria Isoldi.

Cualidades secundarias y autoconocimiento. Vergara, Julia.

Cualidades Secundarias y autoconocimiento. Scotto, Carolina.

Darwin's Origin and Mill's Subjection. Missimer, Connie.

Davidson on First-Person Authority. Hacker, P M S.

Deconstructing Dennett's Darwin. Fodor, Jerry.

Deontic Reasoning, Modules and Innateness: A Second Look. Chater, Nick and Oaksford, Mike.

Derrida's Watch/Foucault's Pendulum. Naas, Michael B.

## KNOWLEDGE

Descartes and Metaphysical Thought (in Czech). Sobotka, Milan.

Descartes and Other Minds. Avramides, Anita.

Descartes, El Argumento del Sueño. Zuluaga, Mauricio.

Dewey, Quine, and Pragmatic Naturalized Epistemology. Capps, John.

Die Funktion praktischer Momente für Grundelemente der theoretischen Vernunft in Fichtes Manuskripten *Eigne Meditationen über Elementar Philosophie* und *Practische Philosophie* (1793/94). Von Manz, Hans Georg.

Do Children Understand the Mind by Means of Simulation or a Theory? Evidence from their Understanding of Inference. Ruffman, Ted.

Do Practices Explain Anything? Turner's Critique of the Theory of Social Practices. Bohman, James.

Does it Make Sense to Teach History Through Thinking Skills?. Van Veuren, Pieter.

Does the Scientific Paper Accurately Mirror the Very Grounds of Scientific Assessment?. Flonta, Mircea.

Doing Without Concepts: An Interpretation of C.I. Lewis' Action-Oriented Foundationalism. Stufflebeam, Robert.

Don't Stop Thinking About Tomorrow: Two Paradoxes About Duties to Future Generations. Boonin-Vail, David.

Doom Soon?. Tännsjö, Torbjörn.

Dos estudios italianos sobre Vico y la estética. Amoroso, Leonardo.

Doubting and Believing: Both are Important for Critical Thinking. Thayer-Bacon, Barbara.

Doubting Castel or the Slough of Despond: Davidson and Schiffer on the Limits of Analysis. Norris, Christopher.

Ecological Validity and 'White Room Effects': The Interaction of Cognitive and Cultural Models in the Pragmatic Analysis of Elicited Narratives from Children. Cicourel, Aaron V.

Economics as Separate and Inexact. Hausman, Daniel.

Education for Imaginative Knowledge. Nuyen, A T.

El conocimiento de fe en la filosofía de Leonardo Polo. Conesa, Francisco.

El soporte cognoscitivo de la filosofía en la postmodernidad. Vega Rodríguez, Margarita.

Elecciones epistemológicas y práctica docente. Marincevic, Juan and Becerra Batán, Marcela.

Elusive Knowledge. Lewis, David.

Emotion and Feeling. Madell, Geoffrey and Ridley, Aaron.

Environmental Education and Beyond. Bonnett, Michael.

Epistemic Obligation and Rationality Constraints. Katzoff, Charlotte.

Epistemology of J. Krishnamurti. Sardesai, Arundhati.

Epistemology of Mysticism. Venkatalakshmi, M.

Epistemology of Sri Aurobindo. Venkatalakshmi, M.

Erkenntnis als Anpassung. Gesang, Bernward.

Ernst Cassirer, Historian of the Will. Wisner, David A.

Error, Hallucination and the Concept of 'Ontology' in the Early Work of Heidegger. McManus, Denis.

Escepticismo, verdad y confiabilidad. Cresto, Eleonora.

Espinosa e o "Círculo Cartesiano". Gleizer, Marcos André.

Essay: *Human Knowledge and Human Nature: A New Introduction to an Ancient Debate* by Peter Carruthers and *Knowledge and the State of Nature: An Essay in Conceptual Synthesis* by Edward Craig. Feldman, Richard.

Evidence and Association: Epistemic Confusion in Toxic Tort Law. Parascandola, Mark.

Extensions of Modal Logic S5 Preserving NP-Completeness. Demri, Stéphane.

Externalism and Knowledge of Content. Gibbons, John.

False and Genuine Knowledge: A Philosophical Look at the Peasant of the Garonne. Killoran, John B.

Fanciful Fates. Holland, R F.

Feeling Fine About the Mind. Antony, Louise M.

Feminist Epistemology and Philosophy for Children. Field, Terri.

Feminist Epistemology as a Local Epistemology. Longino, Helen E and Lennon, Kathleen.

Fenomenología y Epistemología genética: revisión de la crítica de Piaget a la fenomenología y algunas vías de convergencia. Vargas Bejarano, Julio César.

Filosofía Trascendental Mundaneizada. Heymann, Ezra.

First Person Plural Ontology and Praxis. Chitty, Andrew.

Folk Psychology and the Simulationist Challenge. Levin, Janet.

For a Minimal Theory of Truth. Mercier, Jean L.

Forbidding Nasty Knowledge: On the Use of Ill-Gotten Information. Godlovitch, Stanley.

Formal Contamination: A Reading of Derrida's Argument. Donkel, Douglas L.

Formal Organizations: A Philosophical Review of Perspectives and Behaviour Dynamics. Johnnie, Palmer B.

Foucauldian Mutations of Language. Switala, Kristin.

Foucault on Power and the Will to Knowledge. Detel, Wolfgang.

Foundationalism and Practical Reason. Heath, Joseph.

Foundations of Perceptual Knowledge. Brewer, Bill.

Framework of an Intersubjectivist Theory of Meaning. Corredor, Cristina.

Franz Böhms "Deutsche Philosophie": Über den Versuch einer erkenntnis-theoretischen Grundlegung des "Nationalsozialismus". Hailer, Martin.

From Aperspectival Objectivity to Strong Objectivity: The Quest for Moral Objectivity. Tannoch-Bland, Jennifer.

Gadamer's Hermeneutic Externalism. Kuenning, Matthew.

Game Logic and its Applications I. Kaneko, Mamoru and Nagashima, Takashi.

Game Logic and Its Applications II. Kaneko, Mamoru and Nagashima, Takashi.

Game-Theoretic Axioms for Local Rationality and Bounded Knowledge. Bicchieri, Cristina and Antonelli, Gian Aldo.

Gaos y la religión. Valdés, Sylvia.

Getting Around Language. Mason, Richard.

Giambattista Vico, la Universidad y el saber: el modelo retórico. Patella, Giuseppe.

Gibt es ein subjektives Fundament unseres Wissens?. Grundmann, Thomas.

Giving the Skeptic Her Due?. Hughes, Christopher.

Gödel Meets Carnap: A Prototypical Discourse on Science and Religion. Gierer, Alfred.

Goldman's New Reliabilism. Markie, Peter J.

Granny Versus Mother Nature—No Contest. Dennett, Daniel C.

Gregory Vlastos: *Socratic Studies*. Nussbaum, Martha C.

Hans Kronning. Modalité, cognition et polysémie: sémantique du verbe modal devoir. Rossetti, Andrea.

Heraclitus of Ephesus on Knowledge. Krkac, Kristijan.

Hervé de Nédellec et les questions ordinaires *De cognitione primi principii*. Conforti, Patrizia.

Heterology: A Postmodern Theory of Foundations. Fairlamb, Horace L.

How Innocent is Mereology?. Forrest, Peter.

How Postmodern was Neurath's Idea of Unity of Science?. Reisch, George A.

How Scientific is Aristotle's Ethics?. Reeve, C D C.

How to Read Wittgenstein. Cook, John W.

Hume's Arguments for His Sceptical Doubts. Passell, Dan.

I Married an Empiricist: A Phenomenologist Examines Philosophical Personae. Duhan Kaplan, Laura.

I sandali di Ermes e lo spazio di De Kooning: Appunti per una possibile negazione dell'epelysìa di metaphyskà. Incardona, Nunzio.

Idealismo y materialismo: Max Horkheimer y la constitución del conocimiento en la ciencia social. Vergara, Eliseo Cruz.

Ideen, Wissen und Wahrheit nach Platon: Neuere Monographien. Hoffmann, Michael and Von Perger, Mischa.

If the Eye Were an Animal...: The Problem of Representation in Understanding, Meaning and Intelligence. Horner, John M.

Ignorance Is No Excuse: Legal Knowledge and Postmodernism. Bennett, Richard.

Il fondamento etico e metafisico del diritto. Bagolini, Luigi.

Il Saggio sopra la Filosofia in genere di Lodovico Arnaldi: una traduzione settecentesca inedita del *Discursus praeliminaris* di Christian Wolff. Von Wille, Dagmar.

In the Beginning, There Was Darwin: *Darwin's Dangerous Idea: Evolution and the Meanings of Life*. Dennett, Daniel C and Mulhauser, Gregory R.

Inconsistencies in Extensive Games. Dufwenberg, Martin and Lindén, Johan.

Instrument Driven Theory. Tyron, Warren W.

Intellectus principiorum: De Tomás de Aquino a Leonardo Polo (y "vuelta"). Fernandez Burillo, Santiago.

Intelligibility and the Ethical. Miller, Jerome A.

Intentionality and Scepticism (in Spanish). Sá Pereira, Roberto Horácio.

Internal Relations and Analyticity: Wittgenstein and Quine. Hymers, Michael.

Internalism and Perceptual Knowledge. Brewer, Bill.

Introduction to the Publication of G.G. Shpet's "A Work on Philosophy". Kuznetsov, V G.

Is "Self-Knowledge" an Empirical Problem? Renogotiating the Space of Philosophical Explanation. McGeer, Victoria.

Is Chomsky's Linguistics Non-Empirical?. Kanthamani, A.

Is Language an *A Priori* Accessible Platonic Object?. Jutronic-Tihomirovic, Dunja.

Is Nondefectively Justified True Belief Knowledge?. Jacquette, Dale.

Is Presentness a Property?. Craig, William Lane.

John McDowell's *Mind and World* and Early Romantic Epistemology. Bowie, Andrew.

John Searle's *The Construction of Social Reality*. Ruben, David-Hillel.

Justified, True Belief: Is it Relevant to Knowledge?. Leeser, Jamie.

Kann es eine ontologiefreie evolutionäre Erkenntnistheorie geben?. Diettrich, Olaf.

Kant e l'epistemologia contemporanea. Castagni, Laura.

Kant on the Illusion of a Systematic Unity of Knowledge. Grier, Michelle.

Knowing-Attributions as Endorsements. Cameron, J R.

Knowledge and Discourse in Gorgias's *On the Non-Existent or On Nature*. Gaines, Robert N.

Knowledge and Luck. Harper, William.

Knowledge and Power in the Clinical Setting. McMillan, John and Anderson, Lynley.

Knowledge vs True Belief in the Socratic Psychology of Action. Penner, Terry.

Knowledge, Assertion and Lotteries. DeRose, Keith.

Knowledge, Belief and Counterfactual Reasoning in Games. Stalnaker, Robert.

L'atteggiamento metafisico come espressione del trascendentale nella soggettività. Rizzacasa, Aurelio.

# KNOWLEDGE

**KRAUSE, K**
"El problema de la introducción a la filosofía en el pensamiento de K. Chr. Krause en Jena (1797-1804)" in *El inicio del Idealismo alemán,* Market, Oswaldo. Orden Jiménez, Rafael.

**KRAUZ, M**
Historiography of Civilizations: A Review. Kaul, R K.

**KRETZMANN, N**
Reply to Stump and Kretzmann. Swinburne, Richard.

**KRIPKE, S**
"Begründungen a priori—oder: ein frischer Blick auf Dispositionsprädikate" in *Das weite Spektrum der analytischen Philosophie,* Lenzen, Wolfgang. Spohn, Wolfgang.
"Can Peter Be Rational?" in *Contents,* Villanueva, Enrique (ed). Valdivia, Lourdes.
*Rule-Following and Realism.* Ebbs, Gary.
*Wittgensteinian Themes: Essays 1978-1989.* Von Wright, Georg Henrik (ed) and Malcolm, Norman.
A New Skeptical Solution. Gauker, Christopher.
A Theory of Truth that Prefers Falsehood. Fitting, Melvin.
Could There Have Been Unicorns?. Reimer, Marga.
Counterexamples, Idealizations, and Intuitions: A Study in Philosophical Method. Prudovsky, Gad.
Die Rolle der vollständigen Induktion in der Theorie des Wahrheitsbegriffes. Padilla-Gálvez, Jesús.
Für und Wider den Essentialismus: Zu Rudolf-Peter Häglers *Kritik des neuen Essentialismus.* Liske, Michael-Thomas.
Imaginability, Conceivability, Possibility and the Mind-Body Problem. Hill, Christopher S.
In What Sense is Kripke's Wittgensteinian Paradox a Scepticism? On the Opposition between its Epistemological and its Metaphysical Aspects. Read, Rupert.
Kripke's Critique of the Mind-Body Identity Theory (in Serbo-Croatian). Bogdanovski, Masan.
Logical Truth in Modal Logic. McKeon, Matthew.
Marcus, Kripke, and Names. Burgess, John P.
Meaning, Mistake and Miscalculation. Coates, Paul.
On Necessity and Existence. Rosado Haddock, Guillermo E.
Sobre referencia y causalidad. Lo Monaco, Vicenzo P.
Tarskian and Kripkean Truth. Halbach, Volker.
The Ambiguity Thesis Versus Kripke's Defence of Russell. Ramachandran, Murali.
The Community View. Canfield, John V.
The Import of the Puzzle about Belief. Sosa, David.
The Skeptic and the Hoverfly (A Teleo-Computational View of Rule-Following). Miscevic, Nenad.

**KRISHNA**
Comment on "Vedānta in the First Millennium AD: Illusion or Reality?". Murty, K Satchidananda.

**KRISHNA, D**
An Illusive Historiography of the View that the World is *Maya*: Professor Daya Krishna on the Historiography of Vedānta. Chandra, Suresh.
Daya Krishna's Retrospective Delusion. Balasubramanian, R.
Kant's Doctrine of Categories: An Attempt at Some Clarification. Gupta, R K.
Nyāya is Realist par Excellence (A supplementary note). Dravid, N S.
Nyāya Realism: Some Reflections. Sharma, Ramesh Kumar.
Nyāya: Realist or Idealist?. Bhattacharya, Sibajiban.

**KRISHNAMURTI**
*Krishnamurti: Reflections on the Self.* Martin, Raymond (ed) and Krishnamurti, J.
Epistemology of J. Krishnamurti. Sardesai, Arundhati.
Our Future in J. Krishnamurti. Subrata, Roy.

**KRONNING, H**
Hans Kronning. Modalité, cognition et polysémie: sémantique du verbe modal devoir. Rossetti, Andrea.

**KROPOTKIN**
P.A. Kropotkin on Legality and Ethics. Slatter, John.

**KRUEGER, A**
Myth, Measurement, and the Minimum Wage: Sound and Fury Signifying What?. Whitman, Glen.

**KRUEGER, L**
Lorenz Krüger. Scheibe, Erhard.

**KRYLOV, N**
Krylov's Proof that Statistical Mechanics Cannot Be Founded on Classical Mechanics and Interpretation of Classical Statistical Mechanical Probabilities. Rédei, Miklós.

**KUHLMANN, W**
Fichtes Wissenschaftslehre vor der aktuellen Diskussion um die Letztbegründung. Gerten, Michael.

**KUHN, A**
A Resource-Based-View of the Socially Responsible Firm: Stakeholder Interdependence, Ethical Awareness, and Issue Responsiveness as Strategic Assets. Litz, Reginald A.

**KUHN, T**
"Filosofi Artificiali" in *Soggetto E Verità: La questione dell'uomo nella filosofia contemporanea,* Fagiuoli, Ettore. Magnani, Lorenzo.

"Prigogine y Kuhn, dos personajes en la historia externa de la ciencia y la epistemología contemporáneas" in *La racionalidad: su poder y sus límites,* Nudler, Oscar (ed). Flichman, Eduardo Héctor.
"The Declension of Progressivism" in *Epistemology and History,* Zeidler-Janiszewska, Anna (ed). Margolis, Joseph.
*Kant und die These vom Paradigmenwechsel: Eine Gegenüberstellung seiner Transzendentalphilosophie mit der Wissenschaftstheorie Thomas S. Kuhns.* Quitterer, Josef.
Bête Noire of the Science Worshipers. Gross, Paul R.
Beyond Postmodernism: Restoring the Primal Quest for Meaning to Political Inquiry. Herman, Louis G.
Categorization, Anomalies and the Discovery of Nuclear Fission. Andersen, Hanne.
Die neuzeitliche Naturerkenntnis zerstört die Natur: Zu Georg Pichts Theorie der modernen Naturwissenschaften. Hoyningen-Huene, Paul.
Discutono *Il caso domato,* di Ian Hacking. Dessì, Paola, Sassoli, Bernardo and Sklar, Lawrence.
El concepto de "paradigma" en Thomas Kuhn y la filosofía. Salazar, Omar.
El mecanicismo como pardigma "exitoso". Coronado, Luis Guillermo.
El problema de la "Theory Ladenness" de los juicios singulares en la epistemología contemporánea. Zanotti, Gabriel J.
Holismo Semántico e Inconmensurabilidad en el Debate Positivismo-Antipositivismo. Gentile, Nélida.
Inconmensurabilidad: Problemas y Fecundidad de una metáfora. Cupani, Alberto.
Kuhn y la estructura de las evoluciones científicas. Gaeta, Rodolfo.
Kuhn's Mature Philosophy of Science and Cognitive Psychology. Barker, Peter, Andersen, Hanne and Chen, Xiang.
La scienza e la dimenticanza. Rossi, Paolo.
Lorenz Krüger. Scheibe, Erhard.
Ontological Relativity and Meaning-Variance: A Critical-Constructive Review. Norris, Christopher.
Paradigmas: ¿construcciones históricas?. García Fallas, Jackeline.
The Analysis of Particle Tracks: A Case for Trust in the Unity of Physics. Falkenburg, Brigitte.
The Choice between Popper and Kuhn. Notturno, Mark A.
The Conservative Constructivist. Bloor, David.
Thomas Kuhn and the Legacy of Logical Positivism. Notturno, Mark A.
Thomas Kuhn: A Personal Judgement. Fuller, Steve.
Thomas S. Kuhn, een moderne komedie van vergissingen. Derksen, A A.

**KUHSE, H**
"Intentions in Medical Ethics" in *Human Lives: Critical Essays on Consequentialist Bioethics,* Oderberg, David S (ed). Garcia, Jorge L A.
Muss dieses Buch gelesen werden?—Zum Erscheinen der deutschen Ausgabe von Helga Kuhse/Peter Singer: *Should the Baby Live?.* Joerden, Jan C.

**KUNG-SUN LUNG**
Kung-sun Lung on the Point of Pointing: The Moral Rhetoric of Names. Lai, Whalen.

**KUPPERMAN, J**
An Anti-Anti-Essentialist View of the Emotions: A Reply to Kupperman. Dalgleish, Tim.

**KUROSAWA, A**
"Rashomon and the Sharing of Voices Between East and West" in *On Jean-Luc Nancy: The Sense of Philosophy,* Sheppard, Darren (ed). Naas, Michael B.
Kurosawa's Existential Masterpiece: A Meditation on the Meaning of Life. Gordon, Jeffrey.

**KUSCH, M**
*Lingua Universalis vs. Calculus Ratiocinator: An Ultimate Presupposition of Twentieth-Century Philosophy.* Hintikka, Jaakko.

**KUTSCHERA, F**
"Bemerkungen zu den *Grundlagen der Ethik*" in *Das weite Spektrum der analytischen Philosophie,* Lenzen, Wolfgang. Corradini, Antonella.
"Die Logik der Überzeugungen und das Leib-Seele-Problem" in *Das weite Spektrum der analytischen Philosophie,* Lenzen, Wolfgang. Kamlah, Andreas.
"It is NOW" in *Das weite Spektrum der analytischen Philosophie,* Lenzen, Wolfgang. Meixner, Uwe.
"On Certain Extensions of von Kutschera's Preference-Based Dyadic Deontic Logic" in *Das weite Spektrum der analytischen Philosophie,* Lenzen, Wolfgang. Aqvist, Lennart.
"Sind moralische Aussagen objektiv wahr?" in *Das weite Spektrum der analytischen Philosophie,* Lenzen, Wolfgang. Trapp, Rainer.

**KYBURG, H**
Reasoning about Knowledge: A Response by the Authors. Fagin, Ronald, Halpern, Joseph Y and Moses, Yoram (& others).

**KYMLICKA, W**
A Multicultural Continuum: A Critique of Will Kymlicka's Ethnic-Nation Dichotomy. Young, Iris Marion.
Dilemmas of a Multicultural Theory of Citizenship. Parekh, Bhikhu.
Foundations of a Theory of Multicultural Justice. Forst, Rainer.
Liberalism and Culture. Carnes, Joseph H.
Liberalism and Culture: Will Kymlicka on Multicultural Citizenship (in Dutch). Van de Putte, André and Chaerle, Dries.
Rethinking Kymlick's Critique of Humanist Liberalism. Greene, Stephen A.

## LA PALME REYES, M

Has Trinitarianism Been Shown To Be Coherent?. Feser, E.

## LABAN, R

Harmony in Space: A Perspective on the Work of Rudolf Laban. Brooks, Lynn Matluck.

Maurice Merleau-Ponty and Rudolf Laban—An Interactive Appropriation of Parallels and Resonances. Connolly, Maureen and Lathrop, Anna.

## LABELED

Tree Models and (Labeled) Categorial Grammar. Venema, Yde.

## LABOR

*Reflections on Commercial Life: An Anthology of Classic Texts from Plato to the Present.* Murray, Patrick (ed).

El marxismo analítico. Gallichio, Santiago J.

Issues for Business Ethics in the Nineties and Beyond. Michalos, Alex C.

Marx on Full and Free Development. Jenkins, Joyce L.

Phänomenologische Versuche, sich den Grundlagen der gesellschaftlichen Praxis zu nähern. Schmied-Kowarzik, Wolfdietrich.

Redistributive Taxation, Self-Ownership and the Fruit of Labour. Michael, Mark A.

Roman Catholic Tradition and Ritual and Business Ethics: A Feminist Perspective. Andolsen, Barbara Hilkert.

The Ontology of Production in Marx: The Paradox of Labor and the Enigma of *Praxis*. Lachterman, David.

The Revolutionary Aesthetics of Frederick Engels. San Juan Jr, E.

Using the "Ethical Environment" Paradigm to Teach Business Ethics: The Case of the Maquiladoras. Raisner, Jack A.

## LABORATORY

Deflationary Metaphysics and the Construction of Laboratory Mice. Sismondo, Sergio.

Ethics and Relationships in Laboratories and Research Communities. Weil, Vivian and Arzbaecher, Robert.

Researchers as Professionals, Professionals as Researchers: A Context for Laboratory Research Ethics. Elliott, Deni.

## LACAN, J

*Passion in Theory: Conceptions of Freud and Lacan.* Ferrell, Robyn.

*Subjectivity and Intersubjectivity in Modern Philosophy and Psychoanalysis.* Frie, Roger.

Ambiguous Democracy and the Ethics of Psychoanalysis. Stavrakakis, Yannis.

Historicism and Lacanian Theory. Evans, Dylan.

Kant's Sadism. Bencivenga, Ermanno.

Response to Zizek. Whitebook, Joel.

Sobre algunos rasgos distintos del estructuralismo. Leiser, Eckart.

The Seven Veils of Paranoia, Or, Why Does the Paranoiac Need Two Fathers?. Zizek, Slavoj.

## LACEY, A

Process: An Answer to Lacey on Bergson. Howe, Lawrence W.

## LACKEY, D

Response to Lackey on "Conditional Preventive War". Perkins Jr, Ray.

## LACLAU, E

"Remarks on Deconstruction and Pragmatism" in *Deconstruction and Pragmatism,* Mouffe, Chantal (ed). Derrida, Jacques.

"Response to Ernesto Laclau" in *Deconstruction and Pragmatism,* Mouffe, Chantal (ed). Rorty, Richard.

## LACOUE-LABARTHE, P

"Mimesis and Mimetology: Adorno and Lacoue-Labarthe" in *The Semblance of Subjectivity,* Huhn, Tom (ed). Jay, Martin.

## LADRIERE, J

The Correspondence between Human Intelligibility Physical Intelligibility: The View of Jean Ladrière. Lee, Kam-lun Edwin.

## LAHAV, R

Philosophical Counselling, Truth and Self-Interpretation. Jopling, David A.

## LAKATOS, I

"The Declension of Progressivism" in *Epistemology and History,* Zeidler-Janiszewska, Anna (ed). Margolis, Joseph.

Assaying Lakatos's Philosophy of Mathematics. Corfield, David.

Bohr's Theory of the Atom 1913-1923: A Case Study in the Progress of Scientific Research Programmes. Hettema, Hinne.

Inference to the Best Explanation. Clayton, Philip.

Kann es rational sein, eine inkonsistente Theorie zu akzeptieren?. Bartelborth, Thomas.

Lakatos as Historian of Mathematics. Larvor, Brendan P.

The Legacy of Lakatos: Reconceptualising the Philosophy of Mathematics. Ernest, Paul.

## LAKOFF, G

Models, Truth and Semantics. Abbott, Barbara.

## LALOR, B

Interpreting Peirce's Interpretant: A Response To Lalor, Liszka, and Meyers. Short, T L.

## LAMARCK, J

Lamarck's Method (in Portuguese). De Andrade Martins, Roberto and Pareira Martins, Lilian Al-Chueyr.

## LAMARQUE, P

Lamarque and Olsen on Literature and Truth. Rowe, M W.

## LAMBDA CALCULUS

A Modern Elaboration of the Ramified Theory of Types. Laan, Twan and Nederpelt, Rob.

Comparing Cubes of Typed and Type Assignment Systems. Van Bakel, Steffen, Liquori, Luigi and Ronchi della Rocca, Simona (& others).

Equational Theories for Inductive Types. Loader, Ralph.

Kripke Models and the (In)equational Logic of the Second-Order Lambda-Calculus. Gallier, Jean.

Lambek Calculus with Restricted Contraction and Expansion. Prijateljz, Andreja.

On the Proof Theory of Coquand's Calculus of Constructions. Seldin, Jonathan P.

Step by Recursive Step: Church's Analysis of Effective Calculability. Sieg, Wilfried.

The Converse Principal Type-Scheme Theorem in Lambda Calculus. Hirokawa, Sachio.

The Impact of the Lambda Calculus in Logic and Computer Science. Barendregt, Henk.

## LAMBEK CALCULUS

Extending Lambek Grammars to Basic Categorial Grammars. Buszkowski, Wojciech.

Fibred Semantics for Feature-Based Grammar Logic. Dörre, Jochen, König, Esther and Gabbay, Dov.

Multimodal Linguistic Inference. Moortgat, Michael.

Product-Free Lambek Calculus and Context-Free Grammars. Pentus, Mati.

## LAMBEK, J

Deductive Completeness. Dosen, Kosta.

## LAMONT, J

The Five Ways and the Argument from Composition: A Reply to John Lamont. Côté, Antoine.

## LAND

"The Constancy of Leopold's Land Ethic" in *Environmental Pragmatism,* Light, Andrew (ed). Norton, Bryan G.

"The Takings Clause and the Meanings of Land" in *Philosophy and Geography I: Space, Place, and Environmental Ethics,* Light, Andrew (ed). Trachtenberg, Zev.

"Towards a Pragmatic Approach to Definition: 'Wetlands' and the Politics of Meaning" in *Environmental Pragmatism,* Light, Andrew (ed). Schiappa, Edward.

"Volti della Terra" in *Geofilosofia,* Bonesio, Luisa (ed). Bonesio, Luisa.

*Geofilosofia.* Bonesio, Luisa (ed), Baldino, Marco (ed) and Resta, Caterina (ed).

A Virtue Ethics Approach to Aldo Leopold's Land Ethic. Shaw, Bill.

Aboriginal Right: A Conciliatory Concept. Morito, Bruce.

Between Anthropocentrism and Ecocentrism. Boulting, Noel E.

Coming in to the Foodshed. Kloppenburg, Jr, Jack, Hendrickson, John and Stevenson, G W.

Do Deconstructive Ecology and Sociobiology Undermine Leopold's Land Ethic?. Callicott, J Baird.

Kant and the Land Ethic. Welchman, Jennifer.

The Consequentialistic Side of Environmental Ethics. Holbrook, Daniel.

The Emergence of the Land Ethic: Aldo Leopold's Idea of Ultimate Reality and Meaning. Boulting, Noel E.

## LANDAUER, R

Counting Information: A Note on Physicalized Numbers. Rotman, Brian.

## LANDSCAPE

"Are Pictures Really Necessary? The Case of Sewall Wright's 'Adaptive Landscapes'" in *Picturing Knowledge,* Baigrie, Brian S (ed). Ruse, Michael E.

"Il pittoresco e il sublime nella natura e nel paesaggio" in *Geofilosofia,* Bonesio, Luisa (ed). Scaramellini, Guglielmo.

"Volti della Terra" in *Geofilosofia,* Bonesio, Luisa (ed). Bonesio, Luisa.

*Geofilosofia del Paesaggio.* Bonesio, Luisa.

Definitional and Responsive Environmental Meanings: A Meadian Look at Landscapes and Drought. Weigert, Andrew J.

Landscape and the Metaphysical Imagination. Hepburn, Ronald W.

## LANE, H

Cochlear Implants and the Claims of Culture? A Response to Lane and Grodin. Davis, Dena S.

## LANGAN, T

Beyond Postmodernism: Langan's Foundational Ontology. Calcagno, Antonio.

## LANGER, S

Langer's Aesthetics of Poetry. Hart, Richard E.

Langer's Understanding of Philosophy. Campbell, James.

Susanne K. Langer and American Philosophic Naturalism in the Twentieth Century. Dryden, Donald.

Susanne K. Langer's Philosophy of Mind. Liddy, Richard M.

Symposium on Susanne K. Langer: A Foreward. McDermott, John J.

The Cognitive Emotions and Emotional Cognitions. Yob, Iris M.

## LANGEVIN, P

Dialectical Materialism and the Quantum Controversy: The Viewpoints of Fock, Langevin, and Taketani. Freire Jr, Olival.

## LANGFORD, C

Interpreted Logical Forms as Objects of the Attitudes. Dusche, M.

## LANGUAGE

A First-Order Axiomatization of the Theory of Finite Trees. Backofen, Rolf, Rogers, James and Vijay-Shanker, K.

A Furry Tile about Mental Representation. Brown, Deborah J.

A Identidade de Vénus ou as Vantagens da Extensionalidade. D'Orey, Carmo.

A New Skeptical Solution. Gauker, Christopher.

A Note on the Nature of "Water". Abbott, Barbara.

A Obra como Facto Comunicativo. Rodrigues, Manuel J.

A proposito di centenari cartesiani. Garin, Eugenio.

A Semiquotational Solution to Substitution Puzzles. Rieber, Steven.

A Solipsist in a Real World. Pihlström, Sami.

Abschattung. Sommer, Manfred.

Absent Qualia. Dretske, Fred.

Abusing Use. Glock, H J.

Acerca de "Una teoría de la textualidad". Topuzian, Carlos Marcelo.

Adams on Actualism and Presentism. Craig, William Lane.

Aesthetic Antirealism. Young, James O.

Ai margini del discorso poetico. Dell'Erba, Paola.

Algunos Problemas de las Ciencias Reconstructivas. Villegas, Luis.

An Inquiry into the Liminology in Language in the *Zhuangzi* and in Chan Buddhism. Wang, Youru.

An Objection to Smith's Argument for Internalism. Miller, Alexander.

Analytic Philosophy: What Is It and Why Should One Engage in It?. Follesdal, Dagfinn.

Analyticity Reconsidered. Boghossian, Paul Artin.

Analyticity Regained?. Harman, Gilbert.

Ancora sulla teoria vichiana del linguaggio: In margine ad alcune recenti pubblicazioni. Gensini, Stefano.

Anti-Realism, Truth-Value Links and Tensed Truth Predicates. Weiss, Bernhard.

Arqueologia da Gramática Geral: O Estatuto da Linguagem no Saber da idade Clássica. Matos de Noronha, Nelson.

Arte e ciência: Acordo e progresso. D'Orey, Carmo.

Arte, lenguaje y metafísica en las estéticas de Hegel y Adorno. Gutiérrez, Edgardo.

Barth on the Divine 'Conscription' of Language. Richards, Jay Wesley.

Believing in Language. Dwyer, Susan and Pietroski, Paul M.

Bergson and the Language of Process. Mullarkey, John C.

Between Saying and Doing: Peirce's Propositional Space. Thibaud, Pierre.

Bilingualism in the Business World in West European Minority Language Regions: Profit or Loss?. Van Langevelde, A. P..

Blanchot/Levinas: Interruption (On the Conflict of Alterities). Bruns, Gerald L.

Boghossian on Reductive Dispositionalism about Content: The Case Strengthened. Miller, Alexander.

Brandom's *Making It Explicit*: A First Encounter. Rosenberg, Jay F.

Callicles' Examples of *nomos tes phuseos* in Plato's *Gorgias*. Fussi, Alessandra.

Can We Be Justified in Believing that Humans Are Irrational?. Stein, Edward.

Can We Speak of Regional Logics? (in French). Largeault, Jean.

Characterization of the Basic Notions of Chomsky's Grammar (in Spanish). Peris-Viñé, Luis M.

Characterizing Language Identification in Terms of Computable Numberings. Jain, Sanjay and Sharma, Arun.

Chomsky tra linguistica e filosofia: A proposito di R. Raggiunti, La "Conoscenza del linguaggio" e il mito della grammatica universale. Costa, Filippo.

Concept and Event. Patton, Paul.

Concerning Saint Augustine's *De Magistro* (in Portuguese). Abreu, Joao Azevedo.

Conditions on Understanding Language. Lepore, Ernest.

Consideraciones acerca de la idea de retórica en Hans-Georg Gadamer. Escalante, Evodio.

Contemporary Philosophy and the Problem of Truth. Hintikka, Jaakko.

Contemporary Significance of Chinese Buddhist Philosophy. Ichimura, Shohei.

Contextos, Creencías y Anáforas. Ezcurdia, Maite.

Contrariety and "Carving up Reality". Elder, Crawford L.

Could There Have Been Unicorns?. Reimer, Marga.

Cow-Sharks, Magnets, and Swampman. Dennett, Daniel C.

Crafting Marks into Meanings. Catalano, Joseph S.

Critical Thinking and Command of Language. Johnson, Ralph H.

Critical Thinking and Its Courses. Fawkes, Don.

Davidson's Second Person. Verheggen, Claudine.

De Aristóteles a Bréal: Da *Homonímia* à *Polissemia*. Da Silva, Augusto Soares.

De Locke a Grice: los entresijos de la filosofía del lenguaje. García Suárez, Alfonso.

Debiti dello strutturalismo. Peruzzi, Alberto.

Deconstruction Deconstructed: The Resurrection of Being. Dunn Koblentz, Evelynn.

Defending Promiscuous Realism about Natural Kinds. Daly, Chris.

Deleuze's Style. Bogue, Ronald.

Dialectics and Rhetoric in Peter Abelard (in Portuguese). Pires Da Silva, Joao Carlos Salles.

Diary: Written by Professor Dr. Gottlob *Frege in the Time from 10 March to 9. April 1924*. Mendelsohn, Richard L (ed & trans), Gabriel, Gottfried (ed) and Kienzler, Wolfgang (ed).

Die *Grundlage der gesamten Wissenschaftslehre* und das Problem der Sprache bei Fichte. Hoffmann, Thomas Sören.

Die Idee hinter Tarskis Definition von Wahrheit. Greimann, Dirk.

Die impliziten Prämissen in Quines Kritik der semantischen Begriffe. Greimann, Dirk.

Die Kopernikanische und die semiotische Wende der Philosophie. Zeidler, Kurt W.

Die Rolle der vollständigen Induktion in der Theorie des Wahrheits-begriffes. Padilla-Gálvez, Jesús.

Discourse Theory and Human Rights. Alexy, Robert.

Discurso Científico e Poético na Filosofia de Aristóleles. Paisana, Joao.

Do Children Understand the Mind by Means of Simulation or a Theory? Evidence from their Understanding of Inference. Ruffman, Ted.

Do Explanatory Desire Attributions Generate Opaque Contexts?. Reshotko, Naomi.

Domain of Discourse. Gauker, Christopher.

Doubtful Intuitions. Papineau, David.

Duplicating Thoughts. Ludwig, Kirk A.

E possibile decidere argomentativemente il linguaggio in cui argomen-tiamo? La svolta linguistica di K.-O. Apel. Marzocchi, Virginio.

E. Levinas: Da ética à linguagem. Beckert, Cristina.

Ecological Validity and 'White Room Effects': The Interaction of Cognitive and Cultural Models in the Pragmatic Analysis of Elicited Narratives from Children. Cicourel, Aaron V.

El argumento fregeano de las oraciones aseverativas como nombres propios. Ramos, Pedro.

El retorno de la referencia. Navarro Pérez, Jorge.

English-Language History and the Creation of Historical Paradigm. Merridale, Catherine.

Enunciados causales de Burks y contrafácticos substanciales. Vilanova Arias, Javier.

Ersatz Worlds and Ontological Disagreement. Heller, Mark.

Etica della responsabilità e impegno politico in Aranguren. Savignano, Armando.

Euthyphro's Second Chance. Amico, Robert P.

Everett's Trilogy. Priest, Graham.

Explaining Referential/Attributive. Patton, Thomas E.

Expressivism and Irrationality. Van Roojen, Mark.

Extended Gergonne Syllogisms. Johnson, Fred.

Fainthearted Conditionals. Morreau, Michael.

Fawkes On Indicator Words. Smythe, Thomas W.

Fenomenologia del giuramento: un approccio antropologico. Scillitani, Lorenzo.

Fichtes *geometrische* Semantik. Jergius, Holger.

Fichtes Sprachphilosophie und der Begriff einer Wissenschaftslehre. Surber, Jere Paul.

Fiction, Modality and Dependent Abstracta. Thomasson, Amie L.

Force, Power, and Motive. Yarbrough, Stephen R.

Formal Properties of Natural Language and Linguistic Theories. Culy, C.

Forward to Aristotle: The Case for a Hybrid Ontology. Harré, Rom.

Foucauldian Mutations of Language. Switala, Kristin.

Fra filologia e storiografia: progetti di edizioni settecentesche. Generali, Dario.

Frege on Meaning. Sluga, Hans.

Frege über den Sinn des Wortes "Ich". Kemmerling, Andreas.

Frege über indexikalische Ausdrücke. Perry, John.

Frege's Context Principle. Bar-Elli, Gilead.

Fregean Innocence. Pietroski, Paul M.

Fregean Sense and Russellian Propositions. Gaskin, Richard.

From a Semiotic to a Neo-Pragmatic Understanding of Metaphor. Von der Fehr, Drude.

From Name to Metaphor...and Back. Haase, Ullrich M.

Getting Around Language. Mason, Richard.

Goodman's Rejection of Resemblance. Files, Craig.

Habermas' Pragmatic Universals. Mukherji, Arundhati.

Hans Kronning. Modalité, cognition et polysémie: sémantique du verbe modal devoir. Rossetti, Andrea.

Hechos semánticos y presiones fisicalistas. Acero, Juan José.

Hermenéutica metafísica y metafísica hermenéutica. Pompa, Leon.

Historical Contingency. Ben-Menahem, Yemima.

Historical Narratives and the Meaning of Nationalism. Kramer, Lloyd.

Hobbes, Shakespeare and the Temptation to Skepticism. Saracino, Marilena.

How Can a Metaphor Be Genuinely Illuminating?. Rasmussen, Stig Alstrup.

How Can Pictures Be Propositions?. Shier, David.

How Demonstrations Connect with Referential Intentions. Roberts, Lawrence D.

How Much Substitutivity?. Forbes, Graeme.

How Reasons Explain Behaviour: Reply to Melnyk and Noordhof. Dretske, Fred.

Hypercomparatives. Morton, Adam.

Idealità del segno e intenzione nella filosofia del linguaggio di Edmund Husserl. Costa, Vincenzo.

Il patico e il nostro tempo: A proposito di Aldo Masullo. Fimiani, Mariapaola.

Il soggetto e l'etica del discorso. Rovatti, Pier Aldo.

**LANGUAGE GAME**

El desmigajador de la realidad: Wittgenstein y las matemáticas. Espinoza, Miguel.

Ludwig Wittgenstein: Matemáticas y ética. Rivera, Silvia.

Wittgenstein on Certainty. Good, Michael.

**LARGE CARDINALS**

A Very Weak Square Principle. Foreman, Matthew and Magidor, Menachem.

How to Win Some Simple Iteration Games. Steel, J R and Andretta, Alessandro.

Strong Cardinals in the Core Model. Hauser, Kai and Hjorth, Greg.

**LARUELLE, F**

Mystics and Pragmatics in the Non-Philosophy of F. Laruelle: Lessons for Rorty's Metaphilosophizing. Sumares, Manuel.

**LAS CASAS, B**

El Fundamento de los Derechos Humanos en Bartolomé de las Casas. Beuchot, Mauricio.

**LASH, N**

The Nascent Noeticism of Narrative Theology: An Examination of the Relationship between Narrative and Metaphysics in Nicholas Lash. Heide, Gale Z.

**LASK, E**

Die Fichte-Rezeption in der südwestdeutschen Schule des Neukantianismus. Heinz, Marion.

War Rickert ein Fichteaner? Die Fichteschen Züge des badischen Neukantianismus. Przylebski, Andrzej.

**LASTARRIA, J**

"Una polemica storiografica nel Cile del XIX secolo: Bello, Lastarria, Chacón" in *Lo Storicismo e la Sua Storia: Temi, Problemi, Prospettive,* Cacciatore, Giuseppe (ed). Scocozza, Antonio.

**LATIN AMERICAN**

"Die spezifisch mexikanisch-lateinamerikanische Struktur des Geistes und ihr möglicher Beitrag zu weltweiter Freiheit" in *Kreativer Friede durch Begegnung der Weltkulturen,* Beck, Heinrich (ed). Basave Fernández, Augustin.

"The Other Through Dialogue: Latinamerican Contribution to Intercultural Peace" in *Kreativer Friede durch Begegnung der Weltkulturen,* Beck, Heinrich (ed). Pérez-Estévez, Antonio.

"Una polemica storiografica nel Cile del XIX secolo: Bello, Lastarria, Chacón" in *Lo Storicismo e la Sua Storia: Temi, Problemi, Prospettive,* Cacciatore, Giuseppe (ed). Scocozza, Antonio.

*Latin American Philosophy in the Twentieth Century.* Gracia, Jorge J E.

*The Annual of the Society of Christian Ethics with Cumulative Index.* Beckley, Harlan (ed).

*Valores Latinoamericanos y del Caribe: ¿Obstaculos o Ayudas para el Desarrollo?.* Orozco Cantillo, Alvaro J.

Acerca del Pensador Profesional. Schumacher, Christian.

Algunos aportes de Don Leonardo a un país hispanoamericano: Colombia. González Couture, Gustavo.

Bioethical Perspectives from Ibero-America. Drane, James F.

Bioethics in Ibero-America and the Caribbean. Figueroa, Patricio R and Fuenzalida, Hernan.

Bolívar and the Latin American Unity (Spanish). Aparicio de La Hera, Beatriz.

Defending Freirean Intervention. Roberts, Peter.

Double Binds: Latin American Women's Prison Memories. Treacy, Mary Jane.

El libro de filosofía en Costa Rica (1940-1995). Jiménez Matarrita, Alexander.

In Search of Bioethics: A Personal Postscript. Mainetti, Joé Alberto.

La conducta humana y la naturaleza. Roig, Arturo Andres.

La Meteorología de Suárez de Urbina: Filosofía, Filokalia, Cosmología o sólo "Folklórica"?. Muñoz García, Angel.

La posibilidad de pensar la democracia en Latinoamérica desde la óptica de la ética discursiva. Fernández, Alejandra.

Luis E. Nieto Arteta: Crítica del Marxismo y de los Sistemas Filosóficos. Cataño, Gonzalo.

Maniobras doctrinales de un tomista colonial: tiempo y lugar según Suárez de Urbina. Knabenschuh de Porta, Sabine.

Qué "nos" dice Habermas: Algunas reflexiones desde las coordenadas histórico-sociales latinoamericanas. Arpini, Adriana.

Reconciliation: A Political Requirement for Latin America. May, Jr, Roy H.

Rethinking Latinoamericanism: On the (Re)Articulations of the Global and the Local. Poblete, Juan.

The Centrifugal Forces of Latin American Integration. Morales Manzur, Juan Carlos.

The Historical Setting of Latin American Bioethics. Gracia, Diego.

The Infomedia Revolution: Opportunities for Global Humanism. Kurtz, Paul.

Volunteerism and Democracy: A Latin American Perspective. Rich, Paul and De los Reyes, Guillermo.

Women of the Popular Sectors and Ecofeminist Ethics in Latin America (Spanish). Parentelli, Gladys.

**LATOUR, B**

Bête Noire of the Science Worshipers. Gross, Paul R.

Michel Serres, Bruno Latour, and the Edges of Historical Periods. Wesling, Donald.

Science Studies and Language Suppression—A Critique of Bruno Latour's *We Have Never Been Modern.* Cohen, Sande.

**LATTICE**

A Double Deduction System for Quantum Logic Based on Natural Deduction. Delmas-Rigoutsos, Yannis.

A Finite Lattice without Critical Triple That Cannot Be Embedded into the Enumerable Turing Degrees. Lerman, Manuel and Lempp, Steffen.

Brouwer-Zadeh Logic, Decidability and Bimodal Systems. Giuntini, Roberto.

Decidability of the Two-Quantifier Theory of the Recursive Enumerable Weak Truth-Table Degrees and Other Distributive Semi-Lattices. Ambos-Spies, Klaus, Fejer, Peter A and Lempp, Steffen.

Decidable Varieties of Hoops. Burris, Stanley and Ferreirim, Isabel M A.

Duality for Lattice-Ordered Algebras and for Normal Algebraizable Logics. Hartonas, Chrysafis.

Finite Distributive Lattices as Sums of Boolean Algebras. Kotas, Jerzy and Wojtylak, Piotr.

Generalising Tautological Entailment. Lavers, Peter.

Generalized Rough Sets (Preclusivity Fuzzy-Intuitionistic (BZ) Lattices). Cattaneo, Gianpiero.

Linear Equivalential Algebras. Slomczynska, Katarzyna.

P1 Algebras. Lewin, Renato A, Mikenberg, Irene F and Schwarze, Maria G.

Superintuitionistic Comparisons of Classical Modal Logics. Wolter, Frank.

The Bottom of the Lattice of BCK-Varieties. Kowalski, Tomasz.

The Lattice of Distributive Closure Operators Over an Algebra. Font, Josep Maria and Verdú, Ventura.

The Structure of Lattices of Subframe Logics. Wolter, Frank.

What Is the Upper Part of the Lattice of Bimodal Logics?. Wolter, Frank.

**LATVIAN**

Looking for a Subject: Latvian Memory and Narrative. Skultans, Vieda.

**LAUDAN, L**

"The Declension of Progressivism" in *Epistemology and History,* Zeidler-Janiszewska, Anna (ed). Margolis, Joseph.

Antirealist Explanations of the Success of Science. Kukla, André.

Instrumental Rationality and Naturalized Philosophy of Science. Siegel, Harvey.

Laudan and Leplin on Empirical Equivalence. Okasha, Samir.

Risk and Diversification in Theory Choice. Rueger, Alexander.

The Empirical Character of Methodological Rules. Schmaus, Warren.

**LAUDISA, F**

Can We Escape from Bell's Conclusion that Quantum Mechanics Describes a Non-Local Reality?. De Muynck, Willem M.

**LAUGHTER**

Laughter, Freshness, and Titillation. Pfeifer, Karl.

Nietzsche "On Apostates" and Divine Laughter. Neeley, G Steven.

**LAUTMAN, A**

La filosofía de la matemática de Albert Lautman. Zalamea, Fernando.

**LAVELLE, L**

Theory of Participation and Louis Lavelle's Philosophy (in Polish). Kielbasa, Jan.

**LAVINE, S**

Taming the Infinite. Potter, Michael D.

**LAW**

see also International Law, Jurisprudence, Justice, Property, Punishment, Responsibility, Right

"...Equality from the Masculine Point of View...": The 2nd Earl Russell and Divorce Law Reform in England. Savage, Gail.

"Law and Order in Psychology" in *AI, Connectionism and Philosophical Psychology, 1995,* Tomberlin, James E (ed). Antony, Louise M.

"Self-Determination, Secession, and the Rule of Law" in *The Morality of Nationalism,* McKim, Robert (ed). Buchanan, Allen.

"The Philosopher and the Understanding of the Law" in *Averroës and the Enlightenment,* Wahba, Mourad (ed). Gracia, Jorge J E.

"Zum Problem der Rechtsgeltung: Kelsens Lehre von der Grundnorm und das Hypothesis-Theorem Cohens" in *Grenzen der kritischen Vernunft,* Schmid, Peter A. Edel, Geert.

*Formal Ethics.* Gensler, Harry J.

*Freedom's Law: The Moral Reading of the American Constitution.* Dworkin, Ronald.

*Law and Morality: Readings in Legal Philosophy.* Dyzenhaus, David (ed) and Ripstein, Arthur (ed).

*Radical Critiques of the Law.* Griffin, Stephen M (ed) and Moffat, Robert C L (ed).

*Social Control Through Law.* Treviño, A Javier (ed) and Pound, Roscoe.

*Wholeness and the Implicate Order.* Bohm, David.

A "Meeting of the Minds": The Greater Illusion. Damren, Samuel C.

A Call for a Statement of Expectations for the Global Information Infrastructure. Connolly, Frank W.

A Methodology for the Representation of Legal Knowledge: Formal Ontology Applied to Law. Tiscornia, Daniela.

A Philosophy of Risk Assessment and the Law: A Case Study of the Role of Philosophy in Public Policy. Cranor, Carl F.

A propósito de *Giusnaturalismo ed etica moderna*: Notas sobre Grocio y Vico en la Vª Orazione Inaugurale V (1705). Lomonaco, Fabrizio.

Advance Directives and Patient Rights: A Joint Commission Perspective. Worth-Staten, Patricia A and Poniatowski, Larry.

## LAW

Can Locke's Theory of Property Inform the Court on Fifth Amendment "Takings" Law?. Levin-Waldman, Oren M.

Civil Society and Ideology: A Matter of Freedom. Van der Zweerde, Evert.

Conscious Negligence. Brady, James B.

Constructing the Law of Peoples. Moellendorf, Darrel.

Cosmologie et Politique Chez Antiphon: Séance du 20 mai 1995 (Discussion avec: Gilbert Romeyer Dherbey, Bernard Bourgeois, Jean-Louis Bureau, Maurice de Gandillac, Solange Mericer Josa, Anne Souriau). Romeyer Dherbey, Gilbert.

De l'indéconstructible justice. Dufour, Mario.

Desconstruir a Lei?. Rogozinski, Jacob.

Die Moral des Rechts: Deontologische und konsequentialistische Argumentationen in Recht und Moral. Neumann, Ulfrid.

El concepto de libertad jurídica en la iusfilosofía de Eduardo García Máynez. Aguayo, Enrique I.

Evading Responsibility: The Ethics of Ingenuity. Katz, Leo.

Evidence and Association: Epistemic Confusion in Toxic Tort Law. Parascandola, Mark.

Fuzzifying the Natural Law-Legal Positivist Debate. Adams, Edward W and Spaak, Torben.

Inductive Confirmation, Counterfactual Conditionals, and Laws of Nature. Lange, Marc.

Inductive Skepticism and the Probability Calculus I: Popper and Jeffreys on Induction and the Probability of Law-Like Universal Generalizations. Gemes, Ken.

Interpretation and the Law: Averroes's Contribution to the Hermeneutics of Sacred Texts. Gracia, Jorge J E.

John Dewey's Legal Pragmatism. Hill, H Hamner.

Kant on Obligation and Motivation in Law and Ethics. Potter, Nelson.

L'autodétermination des peuples comme principe juridique. Gingras, Denis.

La Teoría del Derecho y la Democracia en Jürgen Habermas: En torno a *Faktizität und Geltung*. Mejía Quintana, Oscar.

Las teoría y su influencia política y socio-jurídica en los problemas de la democracia. Mari, Enrique E.

Law and Rights in Saint Thomas (Spanish). Beuchot, Mauricio.

Law, Virtue, and Happiness in Aquinas's Moral Theory. Carl, Maria.

Legal Ethics in the Practice of Family Law: Playing Chess While Mountain Climbing. Hotel, Carla and Brockman, Joan.

Modern Accident Law Does Not Fit Corrective Justice Theory. Grady, Mark F.

O Direito como conceito limitado da justiça. De Sousa e Brito, José.

On Law and Logic. Alchourrón, Carlos E.

On Motivation of Judicial Decisions (in Spanish). García Leal, Laura.

On the Road Again: Hayek and the Rule of Law. Williams, Juliet.

Predicative Laws of Association in Statistics and Physics. Costantini, D and Garibaldi, U.

Re-Thinking Consciousness Raising: Citizenship and the Law and Politics of Adoption. Cornell, Drucilla.

Rex Aut Lex. Cohen, Jonathan.

Rules, Institutions, Transformations: Considerations on the "Evolution of Law" Paradigm. La Torre, Massimo.

Some Critical Considerations Regarding the Function of the Equity in the Law. Urdaneta Sandoval, Carlos Alberto.

Some Remarks on Carl Schmitt's Notion of "Exception". Dotti, Jorge E.

Suárez y Vico, veinte años después. Badillo O'Farrell, Pablo.

Surrender of Judgment and the Consent Theory of Political Authority. Murphy, Mark C.

The Case for the Philosophy of Chemistry. McIntyre, Lee and Scerri, Eric R.

The Ethics of Law or the Right of Women (Spanish). Aponte, Elida.

The Impact of Ethical Considerations on Present-Day Russian Law. Feldbrugge, F J M.

The Model of Procedural Ethics: Formalism and Argumentation in Law (Spanish). Carrión Wam, Roque.

The New Wine and the Old Cask: Tolerance, Religion and the Law in Contemporary Europe. Ferrari, Silvio.

The Problem of Mass Torts. Strudler, Alan.

The Quiddity of Mercy—A Response. Pearn, John.

The Semantics of Symbolic Speech. Berckmans, Paul R.

The Specificity and Autonomy of Right: Alexandre Kojève's Legal Philosophy. Frost, Bryan-Paul and Howse, Robert.

The Will Theory of Rights: A Defence. Graham, Paul.

Tolerance and Law. Öktem, Niyazi.

Tolerance and Law in Countries with an Established Church. Papastathis, Charalambos.

Tolerance and Law: From Islamic Culture to Islamist Ideology. Botiveau, Bernard.

Tolerance and the Law. Broglio, Francesco Margiotta.

Toleration and Law: Historical Aspects. Imbert, Jean.

Toleration and the Law in the West 1500-1700. Kamen, Henry.

Transitional Regimes and the Rule of Law. Golding, Martin P.

Un *topos* in Hugo Grotius: *Etiamsi daremus non esse deum*. Negro, Paola.

Vico: entre historia y naturaleza. Vitiello, Vincenzo.

Zur Typologie und Deontik von Privatrechtsinstituten. Von Kempski, Jürgen.

## LAWS

*see also* Common Law, Criminal Laws, Natural Law, Penal Law

"All in the Family and In All Families: Membership, Loving, and Owing" in *Sex, Preference, and Family: Essays on Law and Nature*, Nussbaum, Martha C (ed). Minow, Martha.

"Homosexuality and the Constitution" in *Sex, Preference, and Family: Essays on Law and Nature*, Nussbaum, Martha C (ed). Sunstein, Cass R.

*A World of States of Affairs*. Armstrong, D M.

*Democratic Discipline: Foundation and Practice*. Hoover, Randy L and Kindsvatter, Richard.

*Ethical Issues in Death and Dying*. Beauchamp, Tom L (ed) and Veatch, Robert M (ed).

*In Pursuit of Privacy: Law, Ethics, and the Rise of Technology*. DeCew, Judith Wagner.

*Metaphysics and the Origin of Species*. Ghiselin, Michael T.

*Moral Issues in Health Care: An Introduction to Medical Ethics*. McConnell, Terrance C.

*Morality and the Law*. Baird, Robert M (ed) and Rosenbaum, Stuart E (ed).

*Plessy V. Ferguson* in Libertarian Perspective. Tushnet, Mark.

*Punishment as Societal-Defense*. Montague, Phillip.

*Sex, Morality, and the Law*. Gruen, Lori (ed) and Panichas, George E (ed).

*Sexual Harassment: A Debate*. LeMoncheck, Linda and Hajdin, Mane.

*Sexual Harassment: Confrontations and Decisions*. Wall, Edmund (ed).

*The Tanner Lectures on Human Values, Volume 18, 1997*. Peterson, Grethe B (ed).

*Values and the Social Order*. Radnitzky, Gerard (ed).

A Case for Proposition 209. Bradley, Gerard V.

A Non-Solution to a Non-Problem: A Comment on Alan Strudler's "Mass Torts and Moral Principles". Kraus, Jody S.

Actio illicita in causa und Zurechnung zum Vorverhalten bei Provokation von Rechtfertigungsgründen. Lúzon, Diego-Manuel.

Actio libera in causa: Ordentliche oder ausserordentliche Zurechnung?. Joshi Jubert, Ujala.

Affirmative Action at the University of California. Lynch, Michael W.

Agency. Simester, A P.

An Argument against Techno-Privacy. Jones, Leslie E.

An Essay in the Applied Philosophy of Political Economy. Iachkina, Galina.

Applicability and Effectiveness of Legal Norms. Navarro, Pablo E and Moreso, José Juan.

Armstrong on the Role of Laws in Counterfactual Supporting. Pages, Joan.

Bacon, Hobbes and the Aphorisms at Chatsworth House. Pagallo, Ugo.

Bioethics and Law: A Developmental Perspective. Van der Burg, Wibren.

Bioethics in a Legal Forum: Confessions of an "Expert" Witness. Fletcher, John C.

Breaking the Rules When Others Do. Holley, David M.

Challenges Across the Life Span for Persons with Disabilities. Rinck, Christine and Calkins, Carl F.

Chances, Individuals and Toxic Torts. Parascandola, Mark.

Civil Disobedience: Justice against Legality. Miniotaite, Grazina.

Computers, Information and Ethics: A Review of Issues and Literature. Mitcham, Carl.

Confounding the Paradigm: Asian Americans and Race Preferences. Izumi, Lance T.

Criminal Children. Richards, Norvin.

De la toute relativité des lois. Gerbeau, Alexis.

De la volonté générale et des lois. Morissette, Yves.

Descartes on God and the Laws of Logic. Tierno, Joel Thomas.

Dio fondamento ultimo della morale e del diritto. Pizzorni, Reginaldo M.

Divine Inspiration and the Origins of the Laws in Plato's *Laws*. Welton, William A.

Divorcing Threats and Offers. Altman, Scott.

Dynamic Resemblance: Hegel's Early Theory of Ethical Equality. Gammon, Martin.

Ethical and Legal Issues in E-Mail Therapy. Shapiro, Daniel Edward and Schulman, Charles Eric.

Ethical Reflections on the Status of the Preimplantation Embryo Leading to the German Embryo Protection Act. Michelmann, H W and Hinney, B.

Ethics Expert Testimony: Against the Skeptics. Agich, George J and Spielman, Bethan J.

Etica secondo il ruolo: Un'introduzione filosofico-morale. Cosi, Giovanni.

Euthanasia in The Netherlands. Admiraal, Pieter V.

Facts of Legal Reasoning. Boukema, H J M.

Fragments of a Theory of Legal Sources. Guastini, Riccardo.

Gauge Invariance, Cauchy Problem, Indeterminism, and Symmetry Breaking. Liu, Chuang.

Generality and Equality. Schauer, Frederick.

Gould on Laws in Biological Science. McIntyre, Lee.

Hard Cases and Moral Dilemmas. Statman, Daniel.

Healthy Skepticism: The Emperor Has Very Few Clothes. Wildes, Kevin WM.

Hegelian Retribution Re-Examined. Fatic, A.

Hobbes and Criminal Procedure, Torture and Pre-Trial Detention. Cattaneo, Mario A.

How Much Punishment Does a Bad Samaritan Deserve?. Davis, Michael.

Impossible Laws. D'Amico, Robert.

Improving our Practice of Sentencing. Baker, Brenda M.

Is Being a Carrier of a Disability, a Disability?. Perry, Clifton B.

Jurisprudential Dilemmas of European Law. Van Roermund, Bert.

Kant, the Republican Peace, and Moral Guidance in International Law. Lynch, Cecelia.

L'astuzia della follia: Un'antologia di Lombroso. Savorelli, Alessandro.

La justicia en el pensamiento jurídico angloamericano contemporáneo: Acotaciones críticas. Rus Rufino, Salvador.

## LEIBNIZ

Leibniz, el cristianismo europeo y la *Teodicea*. Andreu Rodrigo, Agustín.

Leibniz, Middle Knowledge, and the Intricacies of World Design. Knebel, Sven K.

Leibniz, Resumo de Metafísica. Cardoso, Adelino.

Mathesis Leibniziana. Cardoso, Adelino.

Monad as a Triadic Structure—Leibniz' Contribution to Post-Nihilistic Search for Identity. Schadel, Erwin.

Newton and Leibniz: Rivalry in the Family. Feist, Richard.

Non-Basic Time and Reductive Strategies: Leibniz's Theory of Time. Cover, J A.

Note sulle polemiche antifrancesi di Vico. Agrimi, Mario.

Perspectivity: G. W. Leibniz on the Representation of Ontological Structure. Pape, Helmut.

Pre-Established Harmony and Other Comic Strategies. Sesonske, Alexander.

Présentation du professeur François Duchesneau. Troisfontaines, Claude.

Quelques Réflexions sur la Philosophie de Leibniz (in Serbo-Croatian). Deretic, Milena.

Ramistische Spuren in Leibniz' Gestaltung der Begriffe ‚dialectica', ‚topica' und ‚ars inveniendi'. Varani, Giovanna.

Rethinking Leibniz. Parkinson, G H R.

Sleigh's *Leibniz & Arnauld: A Commentary on their Correspondence* (New Haven: Yale University Press). Adams, Robert Merrihew.

Substances are not Windowless: A Suarézian Critique of Monadism. Kronen, John D.

Sufficient Reason. Walker, Ralph.

The Being of Leibnizian Phenomena. Hoffman, Paul.

The Infinitesimals as Useful Fictions for Leibniz: The Controversy in the Paris Academy of Sciences (Spanish). Joven, Fernando.

The Leibniz Continuity Condition, Inconsistency and Quantum Dynamics. Mortensen, Chris.

The Nominalist Argument of the *New Essays*. Bolton, Martha Brandt.

The Proofs for the Existence of God: Henry of Ghent and Duns Scotus as Precursors of Leibniz. Latzer, Michael.

Unpacking the Monad: Leibniz's Theory of Causality. Clatterbaugh, Kenneth and Bobro, Marc.

West or Best? Sufficient Reason in the Leibniz-Clarke Correspondence. Grover, Stephen.

What Leibniz Thought Perennial. Hunter, Graeme.

Zum Verhältnis von Existenz und Freiheit in Leibniz' Metaphysik. Buchheim, Thomas.

Zur Begründung des Infinitesimalkalküls durch Leibniz. Krämer, Sybille.

## LEIBOWITZ, Y

Yeshayahu Leibowitz—A Breakthrough in Jewish Philosophy: Religion Without Metaphysics. Sagi, Avi.

## LEISURE

Technology and the Decline of Leisure. Anderson, Thomas.

## LENGTH

Predicates, Properties and the Goal of a Theory of Reference. Zalabardo, José L.

## LENIN

Chvostism and Dialectics (Introduced and Commentaries by László Illés) (in Hungarian). Lukács, Georg.

Die Marxismus—Debatte im "Silbernen Zeitalter". Ignatow, Assen.

Is Subjective Materialism Possible? (in German). Delport, Hagen.

Plekhanov, Lenin and Working-Class Consciousness. Mayer, Robert.

The Status of a Classic Text: Lenin's *What Is To Be Done?* After 1902. Mayer, Robert.

## LENINISM

Introduction to the Publication of G.G. Shpet's "A Work on Philosophy". Kuznetsov, V G.

## LEOPARDI, G

Tra stupore e malinconia: Osservazioni sul pensiero di G. Leopardi. Franchi, Alfredo.

## LEOPOLD, A

"The Constancy of Leopold's Land Ethic" in *Environmental Pragmatism*, Light, Andrew (ed). Norton, Bryan G.

A Virtue Ethics Approach to Aldo Leopold's Land Ethic. Shaw, Bill.

Between Anthropocentrism and Ecocentrism. Boulting, Noel E.

Do Deconstructive Ecology and Sociobiology Undermine Leopold's Land Ethic?. Callicott, J Baird.

Kant and the Land Ethic. Welchman, Jennifer.

The Emergence of the Land Ethic: Aldo Leopold's Idea of Ultimate Reality and Meaning. Boulting, Noel E.

## LEPLIN, J

Antirealist Explanations of the Success of Science. Kukla, André.

Laudan and Leplin on Empirical Equivalence. Okasha, Samir.

## LEPORE, E

Confirmation Holism and Semantic Holism. Harrell, Mack.

## LEQUYER, J

Jules Lequyer and the Openness of God. Viney, Donald Wayne.

## LERMONTOV, M

Lermontov and the Omniscience of Narrators. Goldfarb, David A.

## LERNER, B

Winch and Instrumental Pluralism: A Reply to B. D. Lerner. Keita, L D.

Winch's Pluralist Tree and the Roots of Relativism. Phillips, Patrick J J.

## LESBIAN

"Afterword" in *The Liberation Debate: Rights at Issue,* Leahy, Michael (ed). Leahy, Michael.

"Beyond Lesbian and Gay "Families We Choose" in *Sex, Preference, and Family: Essays on Law and Nature,* Nussbaum, Martha C (ed). Eskridge Jr, William.

"Gay Reservations" in *The Liberation Debate: Rights at Issue,* Leahy, Michael (ed). Scruton, Roger.

"Lesbian and Gay Rights: Pro" in *The Liberation Debate: Rights at Issue,* Leahy, Michael (ed). Nussbaum, Martha C.

"Nussbaum's Reply" in *The Liberation Debate: Rights at Issue,* Leahy, Michael (ed). Nussbaum, Martha C.

*Sex, Morality, and the Law.* Gruen, Lori (ed) and Panichas, George E (ed).

Birds Do It. Bees Do It. So Why Not Single Women and Lesbians?. Robinson, Bambi E S.

Family Outlaws. Calhoun, Cheshire.

Liberté! Egalité! Sexualité!: Theorizing Lesbian and Gay Politics. Kaplan, Morris B.

Warning! Contents Under Heterosexual Pressure. O'Connor, Peg.

## LESLIE, J

A Shooting-Room View of Doomsday. Eckhardt, William.

Doom Soon?. Tännsjö, Torbjörn.

## LESNIEWSKI, S

Lesniewski and Generalized Quantifiers. Simons, Peter.

## LESSING

Pictures and Beauty. Hopkins, Robert.

## LETTER

Carta al Padre William Richardson. Borges-Duarte, Irene (trans) and Heidegger, Martin.

Letter-Writing: A Tool in Feminist Inquiry. Sharp, Ann Margaret.

## LEVENTIS, A

Hommage à Anastase Léventis. Vélissaropoulos, D.

## LEVI, I

"Jaako Hintikka Replies" in *Knowledge and Inquiry: Essays on Jaakko Hintikka's Epistemology and Philosophy of Science,* Sintonen, Matti (ed). Hintikka, Jaakko.

## LEVI-STRAUSS, C

"The Sceptical Epistemology on *Triste Tropiques*" in *Scepticism in the History of Philosophy: A Pan-American Dialogue,* Popkin, Richard H (ed). Watson, Richard A.

*The Age of Structuralism: From Lévi-Strauss to Foucault.* Kurzweil, Edith.

Anthropology and the *Sciences Humaines*: The Voice of Lévi-Strauss. Johnson, Christopher.

Sobre algunos rasgos distintos del estructuralismo. Leiser, Eckart.

## LEVIN, M

"Boxill's Reply" in *The Liberation Debate: Rights at Issue,* Leahy, Michael (ed). Boxill, Bernard R.

## LEVINAS, E

"Again Ethics: A Levinasian Reading of Caputo Reading Levinas" in *Knowing Other-Wise: Philosophy at the Threshold of Spirituality,* Olthuis, James H (ed). Dudiak, Jeffrey M.

"Indication and the Awakening of Subjectivity" in *Critical Studies: Ethics and the Subject,* Simms, Karl (ed). Durie, Robin.

"Structures of Violence, Structures of Peace: Levinasian Reflections on Just War and Pacifism" in *Knowing Other-Wise: Philosophy at the Threshold of Spirituality,* Olthuis, James H (ed). Dudiak, Jeffrey M.

"The Ethical Subject: The Philosophy of Emmanuel Levinas" in *Critical Studies: Ethics and the Subject,* Simms, Karl (ed). Woods, Tim.

*Conversations with French Philosophers.* Aylesworth, Gary E (trans) and Rötzer, Florian.

*Emmanuel Levinas: Basic Philosophical Writings.* Peperzak, Adriaan Theodoor (ed), Critchley, Simon (ed) and Bernasconi, Robert (ed).

*Emmanuel Levinas: A Bibliography.* Nordquist, Joan (ed).

*Levinas: An Introduction.* Davis, Colin.

*Proper Names.* Smith, Michael B (trans) and Levinas, Emmanuel.

A intencionalidade na filosofia de Levinas. Macedo Lourenço, Joao.

Adieu. Derrida, Jacques.

Blanchot/Levinas: Interruption (On the Conflict of Alterities). Bruns, Gerald L.

Christendom en fenomenologie. Bernet, Rudolf.

Das Subjekt jenseits seines Grundes—Emmanuel Lévinas' Deduktion des Selbstbewusstseins. Mayer, Michael.

Do Discurso Ontológico ao Discurso Etico: De Atenas A Jerusalém. De Brito, José Henrique.

E. Levinas: Da ética à linguagem. Beckert, Cristina.

Emmanuel Levinas: Thinker between Jerusalem and Athens. Burggraeve, Roger.

Empiricism and Transcendentalism: Franz Rosenzweig and Emmanuel Levinas (in Dutch). Anckaert, Luc.

Eros without Perversion? (in Dutch). Thoné, Astrid.

Fenomenología y corporalidad en le ética de Emmanuel Lévinas: Lectura de *De l'éxistence à l'existant*. Costa, Márcio Luis.

For the Sake of Truth...The Demand of Discontinuity in Foucault, Blanchot and Levinas. Purcell, Michael.

Here I Am! Kierkegaard and Levinas: The Tensions of Responsibility (in French). Janiaud, Joël.

## LIBERATION

"For Animal Rights" in *The Liberation Debate: Rights at Issue*, Leahy, Michael (ed). Linzey, Andrew.

"Gay Reservations" in *The Liberation Debate: Rights at Issue*, Leahy, Michael (ed). Scruton, Roger.

"Hampton's Reply" in *The Liberation Debate: Rights at Issue*, Leahy, Michael (ed). Hampton, Jean.

"Harris' Reply" in *The Liberation Debate: Rights at Issue*, Leahy, Michael (ed). Harris, John.

"Lesbian and Gay Rights: Pro" in *The Liberation Debate: Rights at Issue*, Leahy, Michael (ed). Nussbaum, Martha C.

"Liberating Children" in *The Liberation Debate: Rights at Issue*, Leahy, Michael (ed). Harris, John.

"Linzey's Reply" in *The Liberation Debate: Rights at Issue*, Leahy, Michael (ed). Linzey, Andrew.

"Nussbaum's Reply" in *The Liberation Debate: Rights at Issue*, Leahy, Michael (ed). Nussbaum, Martha C.

"Some Procedural Problems" in *The Liberation Debate: Rights at Issue*, Leahy, Michael (ed). Wilson, John.

"The Case for Feminism" in *The Liberation Debate: Rights at Issue*, Leahy, Michael (ed). Hampton, Jean.

*Diskurs und Befreiung: Studien zur philosophischen Ethik von Karl-Otto Apel und Enrique Dussel*. Schelkshorn, Hans.

*The Liberation Debate: Rights at Issue*. Leahy, Michael (ed) and Cohn-Sherbok, Dan (ed).

Habermas' Philosophy of Liberation. Pereppaden, Jose.

Liberating Experience from the Vice of Structuralism: The Methods of Merleau-Ponty and Nagarjuna. Levin, David Michael.

Medical Ethics in the Developing World: A Liberation Theology Perspective. Fabri Dos Anjos, Marcio.

Philosophy of Liberation According to Buddhism. Tsering, Khenpo Migmar.

Reflections on the Other (in Hebrew). Brinker, Menahem.

Secular Perspective of Salvation. Longacre, Jay.

The Architectonic of the Ethics of Liberation. Dussel, Enrique.

The Ethics of Liberation and the Ethics of Discourse (Spanish). Trías, Susana.

The Jain Conception of Liberation with Special Reference to the Sutrakrtanga. Lalitha, Ch.

## LIBERATION THEOLOGY

Liberation Theology and the Search for Peace in Ireland. Marsden, John.

Theologies of Religion and Theologies of Liberation: A Search for Relationship. Samartha, S J.

## LIBERMAN, A

Matar al padre. Galindo Hervás, Alfonso.

## LIBERTARIANISM

"Theoretische und angewandte Ethik: Paradigmen, Begründungen, Bereiche" in *Angewandte Ethik: Die Bereichsethiken und ihre theoretische Fundierung*, Nida-Rümelin, Julian (ed). Nida-Rümelin, Julian.

*Plessy V. Ferguson* in Libertarian Perspective. Tushnet, Mark.

*Wrongness, Wisdom, and Wilderness: Toward a Libertarian Theory of Ethics and the Environment*. Scriven, Tal.

A Moderate Communitarian Proposal. Etzioni, Amitai.

Avoidability and Libertarianism: A Response to Fischer. Widerker, David and Katzoff, Charlotte.

Between Libertarian Utopia and Political Realism: Godwin and Shelley on Revolution (in Portuguese). Piozzi, Patrizia.

Dr. Pangloss Goes to Market. Schweickart, David.

Libertarian Choice. Goetz, Stewart.

Libertarianism, Self-Ownership, and Motherhood. Jeske, Diane.

Malebranche y el *libertinage érudit*. Leocata, Francisco.

Moral Constraints and Justice in Distribution (in Czech). Nozick, Robert.

Porn Revisited. Mann, Doug.

Poverty, Development, and Sustainability: The Hidden Moral Argument. Weir, Jack.

Rights and Responsibilities: Aristotle's Virtues and a Libertarian Dilemma. Cox, L Hughes.

The Libertarianism of Robert Nozick (in Czech). Barsa, Pavel.

The Seven Pillars of Popper's Social Philosophy. Bunge, Mario.

## LIBERTY

"Conocimiento y libertad" in *Memorias Del Seminario En Conmemoración De Los 400 Anos Del Nacimiento De René Descartes*, Albis, Víctor S (ed). Díaz, Jorge Aurelio.

"La polisemia del concepto de libertad en Fichte" in *El inicio del Idealismo alemán*, Market, Oswaldo. Hammacher, Klaus.

"La reflexión de la *proairesis* aristotélica" in *Ensayos Aristotélicos*, Rivera, José Luis (ed). Llano Cifuentes, Carlos.

"Sexuality and Liberty: Making Room for Nature and Tradition?" in *Sex, Preference, and Family: Essays on Law and Nature*, Nussbaum, Martha C (ed). Macedo, Stephen.

*E.C. Tolman e l'epistemologia del primo novecento*. Donadon, Eleonora.

*Idealism and Rights: The Social Ontology of Human Rights in the Political Thought of Bernard Bosanquet*. Sweet, William.

*Mill's On Liberty*. Dworkin, Gerald (ed).

*Razón, Naturaleza y Libertad: En Torno a La Crítica de la Razón Práctica Kantiana*. Vegas González, Serafín, Klappenbach, Augusto and Núñez Tomás, Paloma.

*Trayectoria Voluntarista de la Libertad: Escoto, Descartes, Mill*. Alvarez-Valdés, Lourdes Gordillo.

*Voluntas* nel *De gratia et libero arbitrio* di Bernardo di Chiaravalle. Allegro, Giuseppe.

Accountability in a Computerized Society. Nissenbaum, Helen.

Alcuni rilievi sul nesso fra verità, libertà e temporalità nella filosofia di F. Nietzsche. Sacchi, Dario.

Attualità di un carteggio del Settecento. Fabris, Matteo.

Between Ethics and Epistemology: Sartre and Bachelard, Readers of Descartes (Spanish). López, Bernardo Correa.

Between Political Loyalty and Religious Liberty: Political Theory and Toleration in Huguenot Thought in the Epoch of Bayle. Simonutti, Luisa.

Brèves réflexions, suite à une relecture du paysan de la garonne, 25 ans après sa parution. Allard, Jean-Louis.

Cousin e l'"istituzionalizzazione' della filosofia. Ragghianti, Renzo.

Da Filosofia como Universalizaçao: Universalidade e Situaçao da Filosofia num Passo Nuclear de *A Razao Experimental* de Leonardo Coimbra. Mesquita, António Pedro.

De la liberté absolute: A propos de la théorie cartésienne de la création des vérités éternelles. Depré, Olivier.

De la volonté générale et des lois. Morissette, Yves.

Diritti umani e dover essere. Troncarelli, Barbara.

Do Not Listen to What They Say, Look at What They Do. Hobart, Ann and Jankélévitch, Vladimir.

El concepto de libertad jurídica en la iusfilosofía de Eduardo García Máynez. Aguayo, Enrique I.

Fenomenología de la verdad en H.U. von Balthasar II. Fares, Diego J.

Filosofia do *Carnival* Surrealista. Martins, J. Cândido.

Finalidad y libertad en educación. Altarejos, Francisco.

Funzioni e senso del diritto nel moderno: Riconoscimento e ragione sistemica. Romano, Bruno.

Gli "ultimi uomini": a proposito di un libro su Max Weber. Salzano, Giorgio.

I percorsi del soggetto moderno. Barcellona, Pietro.

Il singolo kierkegaardiano: una sintesi in divenire. Fazio, Mariano.

Information and Human Liberty. Weinberger, Ota.

Irreconcilable Conflicts in Bioethics. Winslade, William J.

Jesus: Parable or Sacrament of God?. McDermott, John M.

Kant et l'expérience esthétique de la liberté. Dumouchel, Daniel.

L'Etica Politica nell'Attuale Fase Istituzionale. Alfano, Giulio.

La "Freiheitsschrift" del 1809 come momento decisivo tra la filosofia dell'identità e il rilievo dell'esistenza nel pensiero di Schelling. Millucci, Marco.

La demostración de la existencia de Dios a partir de la libertad. Moros Claramunt, Enrique R.

La liberté paradoxale. Bolduc, Sébastien.

La moralité et le mal dans les *Principes de la Philosophie du Droit* de Hegel. Soual, Philippe.

Liberty—Equality—Fraternity—Justice (in Czech). Münnix, Gabriele.

Nationalism in Theory and Reality. Friedman, Jeffrey.

Negative Procreative Liberties and Liberalism. Wolf II, David F.

Obéir aux lois c'est être libre. Dumont-Tremblay, Maxime.

On Tolerance. Primorac, Igor.

Permissions, Principles and Rights: A Paper on Statements Expressing Constitutional Liberties. Atienza, Manuel and Ruiz Manero, Juan.

Spinoza y el Poder Constituyente. Aragüés, Juán Manuel.

Sulla destra e i suoi principi. Veca, Salvatore.

Systemic Historical Criticism of the Concept of Tolerance (Spanish). Gutiérrez, Carlos B.

The Liberty Dimension of Historic and Contemporary Segregation. Nickel, James.

The Right to Life and the Death Penalty (Spanish). Papacchini, Angelo.

Una repubblica mondiale come ideale politico. Höffe, Otfried.

'Europa' en el pensamiento de Jaspers. Franco Barrio, Jaime.

## LIBET, B

Strength of Motivation and Being in Control. Mele, Alfred R.

## LIBRARIES

Journals and Justice. Curzer, Howard J.

Stalin and Marxism: A Research Note. Van Ree, E.

## LIE

Administrative Lies and Philosopher-Kings. Simpson, David.

Can One Lie for Moral Reasons? (in Serbo-Croatian). Vukovic, Ivan.

Discretionary Power, Lies, and Broken Trust: Justification and Discomfort. Potter, Nancy.

Politics: Truth, Freedom, Peace: Lie, Rule, War (in Serbo-Croatian). Baruzzi, Arno.

The Lie Detector, *Wonder Woman* and Liberty: The Life and Work of William Moulton Marston. Bunn, Geoffrey C.

## LIESSE, J

Soul As in Ethic. Gini, Al.

## LIFE

*see also* Sanctity of Life

"Arte, Vita E Verità In Vladimir Jankélévitch" in *Soggetto E Verità: La questione dell'uomo nella filosofia contemporanea*, Fagiuoli, Ettore. Franzini, Elio.

"Aspekte des Lebens: Fichtes Wissenschaftslehre von 1804 und Hegels Phänomenologie des Geistes" in *Sein—Reflexion—Freiheit: Aspekte der Philosophie Johann Gottlieb Fichtes*, Asmuth, Christoph (ed). Sell, Annette.

**LIMITATION**

Hope and the Limits of Research: Commentary. Daugherty, Christopher K.

**LIMITS**

"Nationalism and the Limits of Global Humanism" in *The Morality of Nationalism*, McKim, Robert (ed). Nathanson, Stephen.

*Límites de la Argumentación Ética en Aristóteles: Lógos, physis y éthos.* Zagal, Héctor Arreguín and Aguilar-Alvarez, Sergio.

Jon Elster y el pensamiento del límite. Ambrosini, Cristina.

Limits and Grounds of History: The Nonhistorical. Haar, Michel.

Platonism at the Limit of Metaphysics. Sallis, John.

Problemas Filosóficos y Filosofías del Límite. Nudler, Oscar.

**LINCOLN**

"A Horse Chestnut Is Not a Chestnut Horse": A Refutation of Bray, Davis, MacGregor, and Wollan. Oates, Stephen B.

"A Sin Against Scholarship": Some Examples of Plagiarism in Stephen B. Oates's Biographies of Abraham Lincoln, Martin Luther King, Jr., and William Faulkner. Burlingame, Michael.

A Crying Need for Discourse. Zangrando, Robert L.

Concerning the Charge of Plagiarism against Stephen B. Oates. Current, Richard N.

Plagiarism and the Art of Copying. Wollan, Jr, Laurin A.

Popular Biography, Plagiarism, and Persecution. Jones, Robert E.

Reading between the Texts: Benjamin Thomas's *Abraham Lincoln* and Stephen Oates's *With Malice Toward None*. Bray, Robert.

Sharing and Stealing: Persistent Ambiguities. Swan, John.

The Oates Case. Trefousse, Hans L.

**LINDBECK, G**

Truth and Meaning in George Lindbeck's *The Nature of Doctrine*. Richards, Jay Wesley.

**LINEAR**

$y = 2x$ VS. $y = 3x$. Stolboushkin, Alexei and Niwinski, Damian.

A Compactness Theorem for Linear Equations. Cowen, Robert and Emerson, William.

Linear Equivalential Algebras. Slomczynska, Katarzyna.

The Dense Linear Ordering Principle. Pincus, David.

The Logic of Linear Tolerance. Dzhaparidze, Giorgie.

**LINEAR LOGIC**

A Constructive Game Semantics for the Language of Linear Logic. Japaridze, Giorgi.

An Alternative Linear Semantics for Allowed Logic Programs. Jeavons, John S.

Bounded Contraction and Gentzen-style Formulation of Lukasiewicz Logics. Prijatelj, Andreja.

Completeness Results for Linear Logic on Petri Nets. Engberg, Uffe.

Linear Logic Proof Games and Optimization. Lincoln, Patrick D, Mitchell, John C and Scedrov, Andre.

Quantifiers, Anaphora, and Intensionality. Dalrymple, Mary, Lamping, John and Pereira, Fernando (& others).

**LINEARITY**

The Semantic of Linear Perspective. Turner, Norman.

**LINGUISTIC ANALYSIS**

On the Intentionality of Moods: Phenomenology and Linguistic Analysis. Arregui, Jorge V.

**LINGUISTICS**

"Matching Logical Structure to Linguistic Structure" in *Studies in the Logic of Charles Sanders Peirce*, Houser, Nathan (ed). Sowa, John F.

"Not-Being and Linguistic Deception" in *Dialogues with Plato*, Benitez, Eugenio (ed). O'Leary-Hawthorne, Diane.

"Ortega entre Literatos y Lingüistas" in *Política y Sociedad en José Ortega y Gasset: En Torno a "Vieja y Nueva Política"*, Lopez de la Vieja, Maria Teresa (ed). Pascual, José A.

"The Case for Linguistic Self-Defense" in *The Morality of Nationalism*, McKim, Robert (ed). Fletcher, George P.

"The Question of Linguistic Idealism Revisited" in *The Cambridge Companion to Wittgenstein*, Sluga, Hans (ed). Bloor, David.

*Critical Studies: Language and the Subject*. Simms, Karl (ed).

*Introduction to Philosophical Hermeneutics*. Grondin, Jean, Gadamer, Hans-Georg and Weinsheimer, Joel (trans).

*La conciencia lingüística de la filosofía: Ensayo de una crítica de la razón lingüística*. Nieto Blanco, Carlos.

*Reconsidering Difference*. May, Todd.

*Strong Wits and Spider Webs: A Study in Hobbes's Philosophy of Language*. Soles, Deborah Hansen.

*The Language of Criticism: Linguistic Models and Literary Theory*. Henkel, Jacqueline M.

*The Sense of Reference: Intentionality in Frege*. Bar-Elli, Gilead.

*Ways of Meaning: An Introduction to a Philosophy of Language*. Platts, Mark.

A Critique of the Minimalist Program. Johnson, David E and Lappin, Shalom.

A Rational Reconstruction of the Domain of Feature Structures. Moshier, M Andrew.

A Semiquotational Solution to Substitution Puzzles. Rieber, Steven.

Actualism Again. Hazen, A P.

Algunos Problemas de las Ciencias Reconstructivas. Villegas, Luis.

Believing in Language. Dwyer, Susan and Pietroski, Paul M.

Brandom on Representation and Inference. McDowell, John.

Can We Ascribe to Past Thinkers Concepts they had No Linguistic Means to Express?. Prudovsky, Gad.

Characterization of the Basic Notions of Chomsky's Grammar (in Spanish). Peris-Viñé, Luis M.

Choice Functions and the Scopal Semantics of Indefinites. Winter, Yoad.

Conventional Implicatures as Tacit Performatives. Rieber, Steven.

Conventions, Cognitivism, and Necessity. Shalkowski, Scott A.

Davidson's Second Person. Verheggen, Claudine.

Die *Grundlage der gesamten Wissenschaftslehre* und das Problem der Sprache bei Fichte. Hoffmann, Thomas Sören.

Dynamic Interpretations of Constraint-Based Grammar Formalisms. Moss, Lawrence S and Johnson, David E.

E possibile decidere argomentativamente il linguaggio in cui argomentiamo? La svolta linguistica di K.-O. Apel. Marzocchi, Virginio.

E-Type Pronouns, DRT, Dynamic Semantics and the Quantifier/Variable-Binding Model. Barker, Stephen J.

El retorno de la referencia. Navarro Pérez, Jorge.

Fichtes Sprachphilosophie und der Begriff einer Wissenschaftslehre. Surber, Jere Paul.

Fregean Sense and Russellian Propositions. Gaskin, Richard.

Habermas' Pragmatic Universals. Mukherji, Arundhati.

Higher Order Unification and the Interpretation of Focus. Pulman, Stephen G.

Identification in the Limit of Categorial Grammars. Kanazawa, Makoto.

Individualism and Marr's Computational Theory of Vision. Butler, Keith.

Individuation und Prädikation: Ein Überblick aus historisch-systematischer Sicht. Enders, Heinz Werner.

Interview with Richard Rorty. Kuehn, Glenn, Siliceo-Roman, Laura and Salyards, Jane.

Is Chomsky's Linguistics Non-Empirical?. Kanthamani, A.

La delimitación de la pragmática con respecto a la sociolingüística. De Cózar Escalante, José Manuel.

La revitalización hermenéutico-lingüstica de la memoria en H. G. Gadamer y E. Lledó. Esteban Ortega, Joaquín.

Linguistic Relativity in French, English, and German Philosophy. Harvey, William.

Linguistic Solipsism. Lenka, Laxminarayan.

Linguistics and Politics in the Early 19th Century: James Cowles Prichard's Moral Philology. Augstein, Hannah Franziska.

Meaning and Triangulation. Talmage, Catherine J L.

Models, Truth and Semantics. Abbott, Barbara.

Nominal Comparatives and Generalized Quantifiers. Nerbonne, John.

Not-Being and Linguistic Deception. O'Leary-Hawthorne, Diane.

Obscurity as a Linguistic Device: Introductory and Historical Notes. Mehtonen, Päivi.

On the Autonomy of Linguistic Meaning. Green, Mitchell S.

On the Semantics of Comparative Conditionals. Beck, Sigrid.

On the Theory of Anaphor: Dynamic Predicate Logic vs. Game-Theoretical Semantics. Sandu, Gabriel.

Practices and Actions: A Wittgensteinian Critique of Bourdieu and Giddens. Schatzki, Theodore R.

Pragmatically Determined Aspects of What is Said: A Reply to Bezuidenhout. Grimberg, Mary Lou.

Précis of *Making It Explicit*. Brandom, Robert.

Pressupostos Linguísticos do Conhecimento Ontológico da Identidade em Sao Tomás. Enes, José.

Processes. Stout, Rowland.

Quantifier Scope: How Labor is Divided between QR and Choice Functions. Reinhart, Tanya.

Replies. Brandom, Robert.

Sequence of Tense and Temporal De Re. Abusch, Dorit.

Sobre algunos rasgos distintos del estructuralismo. Leiser, Eckart.

Sprachliche Vermittlung philosophischer Einsichten nach Fichtes Frühphilosophie. Schmidig, Dominik.

Syntactic Codes and Grammar Refinement. Kracht, Marcus.

The Active and the Passive. Raz, Joseph and Ruben, David-Hillel.

The Great Scope Inversion Conspiracy. Büring, Daniel.

The Intentionality of Mental Reference. Motilal, Shashi.

The State of the Art in Speech Act Theory. Weigand, Edda.

Truth and Metaphor in Rorty's Liberalism. Hymers, Michael.

What Assertion Is Not. Stainton, Robert J.

What Do You Do When They Call You a 'Relativist'. Rorty, Richard.

What's Wrong with Metalinguistic Views. Saul, Jennifer M.

**LINSKY, L**

"Wittgenstein on Fixity of Meaning" in *Early Analytic Philosophy*, Tait, William W (ed). Goldfarb, Warren.

*Early Analytic Philosophy*. Tait, William W (ed).

**LINZEY, A**

"Brute Equivocation" in *The Liberation Debate: Rights at Issue*, Leahy, Michael (ed). Leahy, Michael.

**LIPMAN, M**

Una aproximación a la ética en el programa Filosofía para Niños de Matthew Lipman. Accorinti, Stella.

**LIPTON, P**

Inference to the Best Explanation. Clayton, Philip.

Lipton on Compatible Contrasts. Carroll, John W.

## LOGIC

"Box" in Intuitionistic Modal Logic. DeVidi, David and Solomon, Graham.

"Bradley's Contribution to the Development of Logic" in *Philosophy after F.H. Bradley*, Bradley, James (ed). Griffin, Nicholas.

"Caution and Nonmonotonic Inference" in *Knowledge and Inquiry: Essays on Jaakko Hintikka's Epistemology and Philosophy of Science*, Sintonen, Matti (ed). Levi, Isaac.

"Characterization Theorems for Infinitary Universal Horn Logic" in *Verdad: lógica, representación y mundo*, Villegas Forero, L. Dellunde, Pilar and Jansana, Ramon.

"Charles Peirce's Theory of Proper Names" in *Studies in the Logic of Charles Sanders Peirce*, Houser, Nathan (ed). DiLeo, Jeffrey R.

"Conceptual Structure and the Individuation of Content" in *AI, Connectionism and Philosophical Psychology, 1995*, Tomberlin, James E (ed). Pereboom, Derk.

"Contextuality, Reflexivity, Iteration, Logic" in *AI, Connectionism and Philosophical Psychology, 1995*, Tomberlin, James E (ed). Crimmins, Mark.

"Die Theorie der Urteilsformen in der deutschen Schullogik des 19.Jahrhunderts" in *Das weite Spektrum der analytischen Philosophie*, Lenzen, Wolfgang. Stuhlmann-Laeisz, Rainer.

"Doing as We Ought: Towards a Logic of Simply Dischargeable Obligations" in *Deontic Logic, Agency and Normative Systems*, Brown, Mark A (ed). Brown, Mark A.

"Forms of Life: Mapping the Rough Ground" in *The Cambridge Companion to Wittgenstein*, Sluga, Hans (ed). Scheman, Naomi.

"From Epistemology to the Logic of Science: Carnap's Philosophy of Empirical Knowledge in the 1930s" in *Origins of Logical Empiricism*, Giere, Ronald N (ed). Richardson, Alan W.

"From the Fundamental Legal Conceptions of Hohfeld to Legal Relations: Refining the Enrichment of Solely Deontic Legal Relations" in *Deontic Logic, Agency and Normative Systems*, Brown, Mark A (ed). Allen, Layman E.

"Il linguaggio mentale tra logica e grammatica nel medioevo: il contesto di Ockam" in *Momenti di Storia della Logica e di Storia della Filosofia*, Guetti, Carla (ed). Maierù, Alfonso.

"Il segno e l'evento" in *Momenti di Storia della Logica e di Storia della Filosofia*, Guetti, Carla (ed). Sini, Carlo.

"Inductive Logic, Atomism, and Observational Error" in *Knowledge and Inquiry: Essays on Jaakko Hintikka's Epistemology and Philosophy of Science*, Sintonen, Matti (ed). Niiniluoto, Ilkka.

"Inference and Logic According to Peirce" in *The Rule of Reason: The Philosophy of Charles Sanders Peirce*, Forster, Paul (ed). Levi, Isaac.

"L'influenza della logica sulla ricerca storiografica su Hume" in *Momenti di Storia della Logica e di Storia della Filosofia*, Guetti, Carla (ed). Lecaldano, Eugenio.

"L'interpretazione hegeliana della logica di Aristotele" in *Hegel e Aristotele*, Ferrarin, A. Mignucci, Mario.

"Languages without Logic" in *Origins of Logical Empiricism*, Giere, Ronald N (ed). Creath, Richard.

"Logic and Mathematics in Charles Sanders Peirce's "Description of a Notation for the Logic of Relatives"" in *Studies in the Logic of Charles Sanders Peirce*, Houser, Nathan (ed). Van Evra, James.

"Lógica condicional con múltiples operadores" in *Verdad: lógica, representación y mundo*, Villegas Forero, L. Vilanova Arias, Javier.

"Logica e filosofia nel pensiero contemporaneo" in *Momenti di Storia della Logica e di Storia della Filosofia*, Guetti, Carla (ed). Nave, Alberto.

"Logica ed ermeneutica: Una precisazione necessaria nell'interpretazione dei contenuti della conoscenza" in *Momenti di Storia della Logica e di Storia della Filosofia*, Guetti, Carla (ed). Pantaleo, Pasquale.

"Logical Principles and Philosophical Attitudes: Peirce's Response to James's Pragmatism" in *The Cambridge Companion to William James*, Putnam, Ruth Anna (ed). Hookway, Christopher.

"Matching Logical Structure to Linguistic Structure" in *Studies in the Logic of Charles Sanders Peirce*, Houser, Nathan (ed). Sowa, John F.

"Materialism and the Logical Structure of Intentionality" in *Objections to Physicalism*, Robinson, Howard (ed). Bealer, George.

"On Positing Mathematical Objects" in *Frege: Importance and Legacy*, Schirn, Matthias (ed). Resnik, Michael D.

"On the Structure of Frege's System of Logic" in *Frege: Importance and Legacy*, Schirn, Matthias (ed). Thiel, Christian.

"Peirce's Influence on Logic in Poland" in *Studies in the Logic of Charles Sanders Peirce*, Houser, Nathan (ed). Hiz, Henry.

"Peirce's Theoremic/Corollarial Distinction and the Interconnections between Mathematics and Logic" in *Studies in the Logic of Charles Sanders Peirce*, Houser, Nathan (ed). Levy, Stephen H.

"Per una storia delle ricerche sul concetto di dimostrazione logica nel novecento" in *Momenti di Storia della Logica e di Storia della Filosofia*, Guetti, Carla (ed). Abrusci, Michele.

"Pictures, Logic, and the Limits of Sense in Wittgenstein's *Tractatus*" in *The Cambridge Companion to Wittgenstein*, Sluga, Hans (ed). Ricketts, Thomas.

"Plasticidad neuronal, verdad y lógica" in *Verdad: lógica, representación y mundo*, Villegas Forero, L. Garay, Carlos Alberto.

"Propositional Constants in Classical and Linear Logic" in *Verdad: lógica, representación y mundo*, Villegas Forero, L. Piazza, Mario.

"Relations and Quantification in Peirce's Logic, 1870-1885" in *Studies in the Logic of Charles Sanders Peirce*, Houser, Nathan (ed). Merrill, Daniel D.

"Storia del teorema di completezza" in *Momenti di Storia della Logica e di Storia della Filosofia*, Guetti, Carla (ed). Lolli, Gabriele.

"Tarski's Development of Peirce's Logic of Relations" in *Studies in the Logic of Charles Sanders Peirce*, Houser, Nathan (ed). Anellis, Irving H.

"The Carnap-Hintikka Programme in Inductive Logic" in *Knowledge and Inquiry: Essays on Jaakko Hintikka's Epistemology and Philosophy of Science*, Sintonen, Matti (ed). Kuipers, Theo A F.

"The Horizontal" in *Frege: Importance and Legacy*, Schirn, Matthias (ed). Simons, Peter.

"The Politics of Logic" in *Averroës and the Enlightenment*, Wahba, Mourad (ed). Wahba, Mourad.

"Whence the Contradiction?" in *Frege: Importance and Legacy*, Schirn, Matthias (ed). Boolos, George.

*A New Introduction to Modal Logic*. Cresswell, M J and Hughes, G E.

*A Subject with No Object: Strategies for Nominalistic Interpretation of Mathematics*. Burgess, John P and Rosen, Gideon.

*An Essay on the Foundations of Geometry*. Russell, Bertrand.

*An Inquiry into Meaning and Truth: The William James Lectures for 1940 Delivered at Harvard University*. Russell, Bertrand.

*Computation, Dynamics, and Cognition*. Giunti, Marco.

*Critical Reasoning: A Practical Introduction*. Thomson, Anne.

*De Re Language, De Re Eliminability, and the Essential Limits of Both*. Schwartz, Thomas.

*Deontic Logic, Agency and Normative Systems*. Brown, Mark A (ed) and Carmo, José (ed).

*El Krausopositivismo de Urbano González Serrano*. García, Antonio Jiménez.

*Frege: Importance and Legacy*. Schirn, Matthias (ed).

*Genese und Analyse*. Petrus, Klaus.

*Husserl's Position in the School of Brentano*. Rollinger, Robin Daryl.

*Introduction to Metalogic*. Ruzsa, Imre.

*John Dewey: Scienza, prassi, democrazia*. Alcaro, Mario.

*Kant's Criticism of Metaphysics*. Walsh, W H.

*Knowledge and Inquiry: Essays on Jaakko Hintikka's Epistemology and Philosophy of Science*. Sintonen, Matti (ed).

*La Logique Combinatoire*. Ginisti, Jean-Pierre.

*Lingua Universalis vs. Calculus Ratiocinator: An Ultimate Presupposition of Twentieth-Century Philosophy*. Hintikka, Jaakko.

*Logic and Argumentation*. Van Eemeren, Frans H (ed), Van Benthem, Johan (ed) and Grootendorst, Rob (ed).

*Logic and Existence*. Lawlor, Leonard (trans), Sen, Amit (trans) and Hyppolite, Jean.

*Logic with Trees: An Introduction to Symbolic Logic*. Howson, Colin.

*Medieval Thought*. Luscombe, David.

*Meinongian Logic: The Semantics of Existence and Nonexistence*. Jacquette, Dale.

*Momenti di Storia della Logica e di Storia della Filosofia*. Guetti, Carla (ed) and Pujia, Roberto (ed).

*On Economic Inequality*. Sen, Amartya.

*Origins of Logical Empiricism*. Giere, Ronald N (ed) and Richardson, Alan W (ed).

*Philosophy of Mathematics: Structure and Ontology*. Shapiro, Stewart.

*Practical Reasoning in Natural Language*. Thomas, Stephen Naylor.

*Premises and Conclusions: Symbolic Logic for Legal Analysis*. Rodes, Robert E and Pospesel, Howard.

*Readings in the Philosophy of Language*. Ludlow, Peter (ed).

*Real Process: How Logic and Chemistry Combine in Hegel's Philosophy of Nature*. Burbidge, John W.

*Reductio Without Assumptions?*. Hansen, Hans Vilhelm.

*Studies in the Logic of Charles Sanders Peirce*. Houser, Nathan (ed), Roberts, Don D (ed) and Van Evra, James (ed).

*The Cambridge Companion to Wittgenstein*. Sluga, Hans (ed) and Stern, David G (ed).

*The Last Word*. Nagel, Thomas.

*The Philosophy of Mathematics*. Hart, W D.

*The Primary Logic: Instruments for a Dialogue between the Two Cultures*. Malatesta, Michele.

*The Principles of Mathematics Revisited*. Hintikka, Jaakko.

*The Recalcitrant Synthetic A Priori*. Zelaniec, Wojciech and Smith, Barry.

*The Taming of the True*. Tennant, Neil.

*Thinking Straight*. Flew, Antony.

*Vagueness*. Williamson, Timothy.

*Verdad: lógica, representación y mundo*. Villegas Forero, L, Martínez Vidal, C and Rivas Monroy, Uxía.

*Wittgensteinian Themes: Essays 1978-1989*. Von Wright, Georg Henrik (ed) and Malcolm, Norman.

$y = 2x$ VS. $y = 3x$. Stolboushkin, Alexei and Niwinski, Damian.

A Basic System of Congruential-to-Monotone Bimodal Logic and Two of its Extensions. Humberstone, I Lloyd.

A Bayesian Examination of Time-Symmetry in the Process of Measurement. Shimony, Abner.

A Calculus for First Order Discourse Representation Structures. Kamp, Hans and Beyle, Uwe.

A Categorical Approach to Higher-Level Introduction and Elimination Rules. Poubel, Hardée Werneck and Pereira, Luiz Carlos P D.

A Characterization of Martin's Axiom in Terms of Absoluteness. Bagaria, Joan.

## LOGIC

## LOGOS

*Der Satz vom Grund.* Heidegger, Martin.

*Myth and the Limits of Reason.* Stambovsky, Phillip.

An Untitled Lecture on Plato's *Euthyphron.* Bolotin, David (ed), Strauss, Leo and Bruell, Christopher (& other eds).

Aristotle on Perception: The Dual-Logos Theory. Bradshaw, David.

Aristotle on the Nature of *Logos.* Anton, John P.

Autarcie et logos conciliateur chez Zénon de Cittium. Kélessidou, Anna.

Bits of Broken Glass: Zora Neale Hurston's Conception of the Self. Sartwell, Crispin.

Hegel's Critique of Solger: The Problem of Scientific Communication (in French). Reid, Jeffrey.

Heraklit—eine Herausforderung: In freundschaftlichem Gedenken an Eugen Fink. Berlinger, Rudolph.

I sandali di Ermes e lo spazio di De Kooning: Appunti per una possibile negazione dell'epelysìa di metaphysikà. Incardona, Nunzio.

Kinesis versus logos en la filosofía de Leonardo Polo. Aspe A, Virginia.

L'épistémologie génétique dans la philosophie ancienne. Chiesa, Curzio.

Limits and Grounds of History: The Nonhistorical. Haar, Michel.

The Private and Public Logos: Philosophy and the Other in Greek Thought until Socrates (in Hebrew). Scolnicov, Samuel.

The 'Epochality' of Deleuzean Thought. Surin, Ken.

## LOKHORST, G

Baten van een formele verheldering. Doorman, Maarten.

## LONDON, J

Jack London y El Talón de Hierro. Laso Prieto, José Maria.

## LONERGAN, B

*A Second Collection: Papers by Bernard J. F. Lonergan, S.J..* Ryan, William F (ed) and Tyrrell, Bernard J (ed).

*Quest for Self-Knowledge: An Essay in Lonergan's Philosophy.* Flanagan, Joseph.

*The Lonergan Reader.* Morelli, Mark (ed) and Morelli, Elizabeth A (ed).

*Verbum: Word and Idea in Aquinas Volume 2.* Crowe, Frederick E (ed) and Doran, Robert M (ed).

International Regimes, Religious Ethics, and Emergent Probability. George, William P.

Lonergan on Newman's Conversion. Egan, Philip A.

Moral Conversion and Problems in Proportionalism. Beards, Andrew.

## LONG, G

Philosophical Significance of Gongsun Long: A New Interpretation of Theory of *Zhi* as Meaning and Reference. Cheng, Chung-ying.

## LORENZ, K

Entwicklung von Erkenntnissen und Entwicklung von Erkenntnis- fähigkeiten. Ros, Arno.

## LOSEV, A

Aleksei Fedorovich Losev and Orthodoxy. Mokhov, V V.

Losev and Marxism: Lessons of a Life: 1893-1988. Nakhov, Isai.

The Early Losev. Gogotishvili, Liudmila Akhilovna.

The Idea of Total-Unity from Heraclitus to Losev. Khoruzhii, Sergei Sergeevich.

## LOTRINGER, S

A Conversation with Sylvère Lotringer. Lotringer, Sylvère.

## LOTTERY

Expected Utility without Utility. Castagnoli, E and Calzi, M Li.

Knowledge, Assertion and Lotteries. DeRose, Keith.

The Epistemic Virtues of Consistency. Ryan, Sharon.

## LOTTO, L

L'immagine, il sermone, la meditazione: La pratica della orazione nel *Commiato di Cristo dalla Madre* di Lorenzo Lotto. Ciyori, Kitagaki.

## LOTZE, H

"Psyche und Psychologie bei Rudolph Hermann Lotze" in *Grenzen der kritischen Vernunft,* Schmid, Peter A. Orth, Ernst Wolfgang.

## LOUW, S

Is Marxism Totalitarian?. Hudelson, Richard.

## LOVE

*see also* Agape, Eros, Self-Love

"All in the Family and In All Families: Membership, Loving, and Owing" in *Sex, Preference, and Family: Essays on Law and Nature,* Nussbaum, Martha C (ed). Minow, Martha.

"Constructing Love, Desire, and Care" in *Sex, Preference, and Family: Essays on Law and Nature,* Nussbaum, Martha C (ed). Nussbaum, Martha C.

"Crossing the Threshold: Sojourning Together in the Wild Spaces of Love" in *Knowing Other-Wise: Philosophy at the Threshold of Spirituality,* Olthuis, James H (ed). Olthuis, James H.

"Giustizia divina e apocatastasi in John Smith, platonico di Cambridge" in *Mind Senior to the World,* Baldi, Marialuisa. Micheletti, Mario.

"Il provincialismo filosofico" in *Geofilosofia,* Bonesio, Luisa (ed). Makowski, François.

"Is Love an Emotion?" in *Love Analyzed,* Lamb, Roger E. Green, O H.

"Jealousy and Desire" in *Love Analyzed,* Lamb, Roger E. Farrell, Daniel M.

"Love and Autonomy" in *Love Analyzed,* Lamb, Roger E. Lehrer, Keith.

"Love and Human Bondage in Maugham, Spinoza, and Freud" in *Love Analyzed,* Lamb, Roger E. Hannan, Barbara.

"Love and Intentionality: Roxane's Choice" in *Love Analyzed,* Lamb, Roger E. Campbell, Sue.

"Love and Its Place in Moral Discourse" in *Love Analyzed,* Lamb, Roger E. Pettit, Philip.

"Love and Rationality" in *Love Analyzed,* Lamb, Roger E. Lamb, Roger E.

"Love and Solipsism" in *Love Analyzed,* Lamb, Roger E. Langton, Rae.

"Love and the Individual: Romantic Rightness and Platonic Aspiration" in *Love Analyzed,* Lamb, Roger E. Nussbaum, Martha C.

"Love Undigitized" in *Love Analyzed,* Lamb, Roger E. De Sousa, Ronald.

"Love's Truths" in *Love Analyzed,* Lamb, Roger E. Marshall, Graeme.

"The Passion of Facticity: Heidegger and the Problem of Love" in *The Ancients and the Moderns,* Lilly, Reginald (ed). Agamben, Giorgio.

"The Right Method of Boy-Loving" in *Love Analyzed,* Lamb, Roger E. Brown, Deborah.

"Union, Autonomy, and Concern" in *Love Analyzed,* Lamb, Roger E. Soble, Alan.

*Both/And: Reading Kierkegaard from Irony to Edification.* Strawser, Michael.

*Empire of the Gods: The Liberation of Eros.* Davies, James W.

*Head and Heart: Affection, Cognition, Volition as Triune Consciousness.* Tallon, Andrew.

*Intenzioni: D'amore di scienza e d'anarchia.* Donnici, Rocco.

*Love Analyzed.* Lamb, Roger E.

*Philosophische Gedichte.* Flasch, Thomas (trans) and Campanella, Tommaso.

*Philosophy of Sex and Love: A Reader.* Trevas, Robert (ed), Zucker, Arthur (ed) and Borchert, Donald (ed).

*Self-Trust: A Study of Reason, Knowledge and Autonomy.* Lehrer, Keith.

*Sex, Love, and Friendship: Studies of the Society for the Philosophy of Sex and Love 1977-1992.* Soble, Alan (ed).

*Spinoza and the Ethics.* Lloyd, Genevieve.

*Systematische Wahrheitstheorie: Methodische und wissenschafts- theoretische Überlegungen zur Frage nach dem grundlegenden Einheitsprinzip.* Siebel, Wigand.

*Teaching with Love: A Feminist Approach to Early Childhood Education.* Goldstein, Lisa S.

*Wie wächst man in die Anthroposophie hinein?.* Dostal, Jan.

*Wuthering Heights: The Romantic Ascent.* Nussbaum, Martha C.

A experiência erótica em Leonardo Coimbra. Esteves Borges, Paulo Alexandre.

Amor e Morte: Meditaçao Antropológica. Pinto, José Rui da Costa.

An Aspect of Love: Descartes on Friendship. Morgan, Vance G.

Aspiring to the Divine: Love and Grace. Mahoney, Timothy A.

Catholic Social Ethics in a Pluralist Age. Chmielewski, Philip J.

Commitment and the Bond of Love. Van Hooft, Stan.

Descartes on Love and/as Error. Williston, Byron.

El libre albedrío entre la omnipotencia y el amor Divino: Problemática ética y consecuencias tecnológicas de la cuestión del libre alberdrío en Hobbes y San Agustín. Garrido Maturano, Angel Enrique.

Florbela Espanca: Tónica da sua Inspiraçao. Freire, António.

Friendship and Political Philosophy. Schall, James V.

From Logic to Love: The Finnish Tradition in Philosophy. Niiniluoto, Ilkka.

Gandhi on Love: A Reply to Ian M. Harris. Kohl, Marvin.

Glück und Glas... Martha Nussbaum über die Zerbrechlichkeit des Guten im menschlichen Leben. Frede, Dorothea.

God Is Love, Therefore There Is Evil. Fendt, Gene.

Husserl's Rational "*Liebesgemeinschaft*". Buckley, R Philip.

Kung-sun Lung on the Point of Pointing: The Moral Rhetoric of Names. Lai, Whalen.

L'amour selon Pascal. Comte-Sponville, André.

Love and Death in a Pediatric Intensive Care Unit. Miller, Richard B.

Love For God: Is It Obligatory?. Vacek, S.J., Edward C.

Love's Bitter Fruits: Martha C Nussbaum *The Therapy of Desire: Theory and Practice in Hellenistic Ethics.* Osborne, Catherine.

Love's Power and the Causality of Mind: C.S. Peirce on the Place of Mind and Culture in Evolution. Pape, Helmut.

Michel Foucault, lecteur de Platon ou de l'amour du beau garçon a la contemplation du beau en soi. Catonné, Jean-Philipe.

Platao, o Amor e a Retórica. Trindade Santos, José.

Reflexiones sobre la no violencia: Variedades, posibilidades y límites. Sobrevilla, David.

Response to Howard-Snyder. Schellenberg, J L.

Romantic Love and Loving Commitment: Articulating a Modern Ideal. Delaney, Neil.

Romantic Love and Sexual Desire. Ben-Ze'ev, Aaron.

The Argument from Divine Hiddenness. Howard-Snyder, Daniel.

The Conditional Quality of Gandhi's Love. Harris, Ian M.

The Future of Romantic Love. White, Richard J.

The Love of God and Neighbor in Simone Weil's Philosophy. Stephenson, Wendell.

The Words We Love to Hate. Stark, Cynthia A.

What's Love Got to Do with It? The Altruistic Giving of Organs. Spike, Jeffrey.

## LOVIBOND, S

Realism and Resolution: Reply to Warren Goldfarb and Sabina Lovibond. Diamond, Cora.

## LOWE, E

Coinciding Objects: Reply to Lowe and Denkel. Burke, Michael B.

Lowe on Conditional Probability. Edgington, Dorothy.

There Might Be Nothing. Baldwin, Thomas.

**LOWENHEIM-SKOLEM THEOREM**
A Finite Analog to the Löwenheim-Skolem Theorem. Isles, David.

**LOYALTY**
Between Political Loyalty and Religious Liberty: Political Theory and Toleration in Huguenot Thought in the Epoch of Bayle. Simonutti, Luisa.
Identifying the Real EAP Client: Ensuing Ethical Dilemmas. Lee, Sandra S and Schonberg, Sue E.
Josiah Royce's Reading of Plato's *Theaetetus*. Glidden, David K.
Personal Loyalty to Superiors in Public Service. Souryal, Sam S and McKay, Brian W.
Police Loyalties: A Refuge for Scoundrels?. Kleinig, John.
The Limits of Loyalty. Graybosch, Anthony J.

**LU HSIANG-SHAN**
*Mein Geist ist das Universum*: Ontologische und erkenntnistheoretische Aspekte in der Lehre des Lu Jiuyuan (1139-1193). Ommerborn, Wolfgang.

**LU JIUYUAN**
Social Reality and Lu Jiuyuan (1139-1193). Birdwhistell, Anne D.

**LUCK**
Knowledge and Luck. Harper, William.
Luck and Good Fortune in the *Eudemian Ethics*. Johnson, Kent.
Moral Luck and Practical Judgment. Makkuni, Santosh.
Self-Esteem, Moral Luck, and the Meaning of Grace. Fry, Jeffrey P.
Self-Ownership and Equality: Brute Luck, Gifts, Universal Dominance, and Leximin. Vallentyne, Peter.
The Time to Punish and the Problem of Moral Luck. Statman, Daniel.
When is Knowledge a Matter of Luck?. Katzoff, Charlotte.

**LUCRETIUS**
Contracts with Animals: Lucretius, *De Rerum Natura*. Shelton, Jo-Ann.

**LUDWIG, B**
Antwort auf Bernd Ludwig: Will die Natur unwiderstehlich die Republik?. Brandt, Reinhard.

**LUDWIG, G**
How Can Reality Be Proved?. Neumann, Holger.

**LUDWIG, K**
"Shape Properties, Experience of Shape and Shape Concepts" in *Perception*, Villanueva, Enrique (ed). Campbell, John.

**LUHMANN, N**
Funzioni e senso del diritto nel moderno: Riconoscimento e ragione sistemica. Romano, Bruno.
Sozialstruktur und Sematik: Der wissenssoziologische Ansatz Niklas Luhmanns. Götke, Povl.
Trust as Noncognitive Security about Motives. Becker, Lawrence C.

**LUKACS, G**
A Note on Weber and Lukács (in Hungarian). Tarr, Zoltan.
Contributions to the Reconstruction of the Later Lukacs's Philosophy (in Hungarian). Himmer, Péter.
Ethischer Neu-Fichteanismus und Geschichtsphilosophie: Zur sozio-politischen Rezeption Fichtes im 20. Jahrhundert. Villacañas, José L.
Everydayness, Aesthetics, Ontology: Notes on the Later Lukács (in Hungarian). Jung, Werner.
Explanations of Everyday Life: Georg Lukács and Agnes Heller (in Hungarian). Rózsa, Erzsébet.
Georg Lukács and Lajos Fülep Dante (in Hungarian). Kaposi, Márton.
Georg Lukács's *Destruction of Reason* and the Political Theories of the Western Emigration: Some Theses (in Hungarian). Söllner, Alfons.
Georg Lukács's Criticism of Societal Reason—The Crisis of Marxism and Marxist Ontology (in Hungarian). Dannemann, Rüdiger.
Georg Lukács's Plans for an Ethics (in Hungarian). Palcsó, Mária.
Georg Lukács—A Spiritual Portrait (in Hungarian). Stern, Laurent.
Letter to Georg Lukács and Karl Barth (in Hungarian). Iwand, Hans-Joachim.
Lived Thought between Affirmation and Critique: Georg Lukács and Stalinism (in Hungarian). Tietz, Udo.
Lukács: Ontology and Historicity (in Portuguese). Lessa, Sergio.
Nietzsche Reception Today. Johnson, Pauline.
Ontology, Realism and Instrumentalism: Comments on Lukács's Criticism of Logical Positivism (in Hungarian). Szécsi, Gábor.
The Constitution of Our World as the History of Arts (in Hungarian). Benseler, Frank.
The Thought of the Late Lukács (in Hungarian). Tertulian, Nikolae.
The Tragedy of Lukács and the Problem of Alternatives (in Hungarian). Mészáros, István.
Through Sin to Salvation (in Hungarian). Bell, Daniel.
Tragedy as the Form of Existence (in Hungarian). Heller, Agnes.
Utopia or Reconciliation with Reality—Lukács's 1922-23 Literary Essays (in Hungarian). Löwy, Michael.

**LUKASIEWICZ**
Logics of Rejection: Two Systems of Natural Deduction. Tamminga, Allard M.

**LULL**
Las claves hermenéuticas del pensamiento de Ramón Llull. Trías Mercant, Sebastià.
Raimundus Lullus and His *Ars Magna,D* (in Czech). Láng, Benedek.

**LURIA, A**
Sub-Phenomenology. Jopling, David A.

**LUST**
The Greens and the Lust for Power. Sternstein, Wolfgang.

**LUTHER**
*Vom Willen zur Macht: Anthropologie und Metaphysik der Macht am exemplarischen Fall Friedrich Nietzsches*. Gerhardt, Volker.
Business in an Age of Downsizing. Childs, James M.

**LUTHERANISM**
Equal Access to Health Care: A Lutheran Lay Person's Expanded Footnote. Delkeskamp-Hayes, Corinna.

**LUXEMBURG, R**
*Rosa Luxemburg and Emma Goldman: A Bibliography*. Nordquist, Joan (ed).

**LYCAN, W**
"A Mind-Body Problem at the Surface of Objects" in *Perception*, Villanueva, Enrique (ed). Johnston, Mark.
"On a Defense of the Hegemony of Representation" in *Perception*, Villanueva, Enrique (ed). Stalnaker, Robert.
"Perception and Possibilia" in *Perception*, Villanueva, Enrique (ed). Tomberlin, James E.
"Perceptual Experience Is a Many-Layered Thing" in *Perception*, Villanueva, Enrique (ed). Tye, Michael.

**LYING**
History of the Lie: Prolegomena. Derrida, Jacques and Kamuf, Peggy (trans).
Lying, Deceiving, or Falsely Implicating. Adler, Jonathan E.
Political Lying: A Defense. Newey, Glen.
St. Thomas, Lying and Venial Sin. Dewan, Lawrence.

**LYNCH, B**
*Values and the Social Order*. Radnitzky, Gerard (ed).

**LYNCH, J**
Response: Language and Thought. Russow, Lilly-Marlene.

**LYNCH, M**
Relativism and Truth: A Rejoinder to Lynch. Rappaport, Steven.

**LYOTARD, J**
"Epistemological Reversals between Chisholm and Lyotard" in *Philosophy of Education (1996)*, Margonis, Frank (ed). Gunzenhauser, Michael G.
"The Perception of Science in Modernist and Postmodernist Artistic Practice" in *Epistemology and History*, Zeidler-Janiszewska, Anna (ed). Erjavec, Ales.
"Una Disavventura Della Differenza: Heidegger e i "francesi" in *Soggetto E Verità: La questione dell'uomo nella filosofia contemporanea*, Fagiuoli, Ettore. Vaccaro, G Battista.
*Conversations with French Philosophers*. Aylesworth, Gary E (trans) and Rötzer, Florian.
Der "Neuanfang" in der Ästhetik (J.-F. Lyotard). Seubold, Günter.
Lyotard: Modern Postmodernist?. Hurst, Andrea.
Richard Kearney's Hermeneutic Imagination. Stark, Tracey.
The Concepts of the Sublime and the Beautiful in Kant and Lyotard. Klinger, Cornelia.

**MACDONALD, C**
Cynthia Macdonald and Graham Macdonald (eds), *Connectionism: Debates on Psychological Explanation, Volume Two*. Mills, Stephen.

**MACE, C**
Response to the Commentaries. Hinshelwood, R D.

**MACGILCHRIST, Z**
Hume and the Bellman, Zerobabel MacGilchrist. Emerson, Roger L.

**MACGOWAN, K**
*Kenneth Macgowan and the Aesthetic Paradigm for the New Stagecraft in America*. Bloom, Thomas Alan.

**MACH**
Die Bedeutung des Machschen Prinzips in der Kosmologie. Dambmann, Holger.

**MACHIAVELLI**
"Civic Prudence in Machiavelli: Toward the Paradigm Transformation in Philosophy in the Transition to Modernity" in *The Ancients and the Moderns*, Lilly, Reginald (ed). Held, Klaus.
*Classics of Modern Political Theory: Machiavelli to Mill*. Cahn, Steven M.
*Hypocrisy and Integrity: Machiavelli, Rousseau, and the Ethics of Politics*. Grant, Ruth W.
*Machiavelli, Leonardo, and the Science of Power*. Masters, Roger D.
*Modern Political Thought: Readings from Machiavelli to Nietzsche*. Wootton, David (ed).
After *Virtù*: Rhetoric, Prudence and Moral Pluralism in Machiavelli. Garver, Eugene.
La insoportable liviandad del ser (político). Pastor Pérez, Miguel Antonio.
Landmarks in Critical Thinking Series: Machiavelli's *The Prince*. Salmon, Merrilee H.
Machiavelli and Rousseau: The Standpoint of the City and the Authorial Voice in Political Theory. Buckler, Steve.
Maquiavelo y la episteme política. Sevilla Fernández, José M.
No Good Deed Ever Goes Unpunished. Buchanan, James.
The Machiavellian Cosmos. Qviller, Bjorn.

**MACHIAVELLIANISM**
A Má Fama na Filosofia Política: James Harrington e Maquiavel. Bignotto, Newton.
Relationship Between Machiavellianism and Type A Personality and Ethical-Orientation. Rayburn, J Michael and Rayburn, L Gayle.

## MACHINE

see also Technology

"Machinic Thinking" in *Deleuze and Philosophy: The Difference Engineer,* Ansell Pearson, Keith (ed). Welchman, Alistair.

"Viroid Life: On Machines, Technics and Evolution" in *Deleuze and Philosophy: The Difference Engineer,* Ansell Pearson, Keith (ed). Ansell Pearson, Keith.

"Women-Animals-Machines: A Grammar for a Wittgensteinian Ecofeminism" in *Ecofeminism: Women, Culture, Nature,* Warren, Karen J (ed). Lee-Lampshire, Wendy.

*The Possibility of Language: A Discussion of the Nature of Language, with Implications for Human and Machine Translation.* Melby, Alan K and Warner, C Terry.

Asymptotic Probabilities for Second-Order Existential Kahr-Moore-Wang Sentences. Vedo, Anne.

Machine Learning by Imitating Human Learning. Chang, Kuo-Chin, Hong, Tzung-Pei and Tseng, Shian-Shyong.

Maschinen und Kreativität: Metamathematische Argumente für das menschliche Denken. Ebbinghaus, H D.

Physics, Machines, and the Hard Problem. Bilodeau, Douglas J.

The Machine That Couldn't Think Straight. Dinan, Stephen A.

Thinking Machines: Some Fundamental Confusions. Kearns, John T.

Where Do Laws of Nature Come From?. Cartwright, Nancy.

Why Does Removing Machines Count as "Passive" Euthanasia?. Hopkins, Patrick D.

## MACHINERY

Exposing the Machinery of Infinite Renormalization. Huggett, Nick and Weingard, Robert.

## MACINTOSH, J

Critical Notice of J.J. MacIntosh and H.A. Meynell, eds. *Faith, Scepticism and Personal Identity: A Festschrift for Terence Penelhum.* Loptson, Peter J.

How To Do Things with Numbers: MacIntosh on the Possible Eternity of the World. Côté, Antoine.

## MACINTYRE, A

"Bradley and MacIntyre: A Comparison" in *Philosophy after F.H. Bradley,* Bradley, James (ed). MacNiven, Don.

"On Not Destroying the Health of One's Patients" in *Human Lives: Critical Essays on Consequentialist Bioethics,* Oderberg, David S (ed). Simmons, Lance.

Abendländische Tugendlehre und moderne Moralphilosophie. Wald, Berthold.

Alasdair MacIntyre: The Epitaph of Modernity. Kitchen, Gary.

Algunas reflexiones ante el comunitarianismo: MacIntyre, Taylor y Walzer. Dussel, Enrique.

El tema de la virtud: A. Macintyre, lector de Aristóteles. Mas Torres, Salvador.

Interview with Alasdair MacIntyre. Pearson, Thomas D.

Kantian Ethics and a Theory of Justice; Reiman, Kaufman and MacIntyre. O'Reilly-Meacock, Heather.

La revisión neohistoricista del significado de la historia de la filosofía. Vegas González, Serafín.

Management as a Practice: A Response to Alasdair MacIntyre. Brewer, Kathryn Balstad.

Oltre MacIntyre, a Proposito di: Quale Impostazione per la Filosofia Morale?. Crosti, Massimo.

Virtue, Happiness, and Intelligibility. Lemos, John.

## MACKIE, J

Explaining Supervenience: Moral and Mental. Zagwill, Nick.

Infinite Regresses of Recurring Problems & Responses. Gratton, Claude.

Mackie on Kant's Moral Argument. Burgess-Jackson, Keith.

## MACKINNON, C

The Phenomenology of Pornography: *A Comment on Catharine MacKinnon's Only Words.* Willis, Clyde E.

## MACMILLAN, C

Liberal Indoctrination and the Problem of Community. Harvey, Charles W.

## MACNAMARA, J

Has Trinitarianism Been Shown To Be Coherent?. Feser, E.

## MADDY, P

"Physicalism and Mathematics" in *Objections to Physicalism,* Robinson, Howard (ed). Hale, Bob.

El realismo en matemáticas. Alemán, Anastasio.

## MADHYAMIKA

Jñānagarbha and the "God's-Eye View". Pyysiäinen, Ilkka.

The Ruptured Idiom: Of Dallmayr, Matilal and Ramanujan's 'Way of Thinking'. Venkat Rao, D.

## MADISON

Adam Smith's Influence on James Madison. Ross, Thomas.

The Inalienable Right of Conscience: A Madisonian Argument. McConnell, Terrance C.

## MADNESS

*Classical Cynicism: A Critical Study.* Navia, Luis E.

Descartes et la mélancholie. Darriulat, Jacques.

Descartes's Demon and the Madness of Don Quixote. Nadler, Steven.

Diggers, Ranters, and Women Prophets: The Discourse of Madness and the Cartesian *Cogito* in Seventeenth-Century England. Hayes, Tom.

Mind and Madness in Greek Tragedy. Gill, Christopher.

## MAGIC

"Three Types of Theories of Religion and Magic" in *Epistemology and History,* Zeidler-Janiszewska, Anna (ed). Jerzak-Gierszewska, Teresa.

## MAGNITUDE

Bertrand Russell's 1897 Critique of the Traditional Theory of Measurement. Michell, Joel.

## MAHAYANA

Der erste Grundsatz und die Bildlehre. Okada, Katsuaki.

The Bodhisattva Ideal in Theravāda Buddhist Theory and Practice: A Reevaluation of the Bodhisattva-Srāvaka Opposition. Samuels, Jeffrey.

## MAHER, P

Discussion: Thoughts on Maher's Predictivism. Barnes, Eric.

Social Predictivism. Barnes, Eric.

## MAIMON, S

Parallelen zwischen Maimon und dem frühen Fichte. Krämer, Felix.

## MAIMONIDES

Compassion for Wisdom: The Attitude of Some Medieval Arab Philosophers towards to Codification of Philosophy. Stroumsa, Sarah.

From Negation to Silence: Maimonides' Reception in the Latin West (in Hebrew). Schwartz, Yosef.

On the Concept of Awe (Yira) in Maimonides (In Hebrew). Bar-Elli, Gilead.

## MAKKREEL, R

The Hermeneutic Significance of the *Sensus Communis.* Hance, Allen.

## MALCOLM X

Malcolm X and the Enigma of Martin Luther King, Jr.'s Nonviolence. Bove, Laurence.

Reexamining Dr. King and Malcolm X On Violence. Whitlock, Greg.

## MALCOLM, N

Language as Emerging from Instinctive Behaviour. Rhees, Rush and Phillips, D E (ed).

Norman Malcolm, *Wittgensteinian Themes.* Winch, Peter.

Sobre la Facticidad de la Memoria. Schumacher, Christian.

The Concept of Dreaming: On Three Theses by Malcolm. Schroeder, Severin.

## MALE

see also Men

En torno a la díada trascendental. Castilla y Cortázar, Blanca.

Eternal Verities: Timeless Truth, Ahistorical Standards, and the One True Story. Edidin, Aron.

Save the Males: Backlash in Organizations. Burke, Ronald J and Black, Susan.

## MALEBRANCHE

"Arnauld versus Leibniz and Malebranche on the Limits of Theological Knowledge" in *Scepticism in the History of Philosophy: A Pan-American Dialogue,* Popkin, Richard H (ed). Sleigh, Jr, Robert.

"Discourses of Vision in Seventeenth-Century Metaphysics" in *Sites of Vision,* Levin, David Michael (ed). Wilson, Catherine.

"Malebranche e la storia nella *Recherche de la vérité*" in *Lo Storicismo e la Sua Storia: Temi, Problemi, Prospettive,* Cacciatore, Giuseppe (ed). Stile, Alessandro.

*Malebranche's Theory of the Soul: A Cartesian Interpretation.* Schmaltz, Tad M.

Apresentaçao da metafísica de Malebranche. De Faria Blanc, Mafalda.

Étienne Gilson's Early Study of Nicolas Malebranche. Fafara, Richard J.

Hume and Causal Power: The Influences of Malebranche and Newton. Bell, Martin.

La polémique de Malebranche contre Aristote et la philosophie scolastique. Gilson, Étienne.

Malebranche et l'argument ontologique. Lardic, Jean-Marie.

Malebranche on the Soul's Power. Scott, David.

Malebranche y el *libertinage érudit.* Leocata, Francisco.

## MALEFICENCE

Should I Be Grateful to You for Not Harming Me?. Smilansky, Saul.

## MALINOWSKI, B

Malinowksi: La Importancia de la Pragmática y del Bla-bla-bla en la Comunicación. Patiño A, Alejandro.

## MALLIK, B

Basanta Kumar Mallik and the Negative. Walker, Mary M.

## MALLY, E

*Meinongian Logic: The Semantics of Existence and Nonexistence.* Jacquette, Dale.

## MALRAUX

Catastrophic Thinking in the Modern World: Russia and America. Shlapentokh, Vladimir.

## MALTHUS

Malthus and the Secularization of Political Ideology. Heavner, Eric K.

## MAN

see also Human, Individual, Person, Philosophical Anthropology

"El destino religioso del hombre en la filosofía de Fichte" in *El inicio del Idealismo alemán,* Market, Oswaldo. Goddard, Jean-Chr.

"El Liberalismo como destino: A propósito de la obra de Francis Fukuyama" in *Liberalismo y Comunitarismo: Derechos Humanos y Democracia,* Monsalve Solórzano, Alfonso (ed). Salazar P, Freddy.

"Giustizia divina e apocatastasi in John Smith, platonico di Cambridge" in *Mind Senior to the World,* Baldi, Marialuisa. Micheletti, Mario.

## MAN

"Homo historicus: Verso una trasformazione del paradigma 'classico' dell'antropologia filosofica" in *Lo Storicismo e la Sua Storia: Temi, Problemi, Prospettive*, Cacciatore, Giuseppe (ed). Giammusso, Salvatore.

"La Verità Come Tragedia: Immaginazione e immagine del Vero: Note sulla "civilizzazione" in *Soggetto E Verità: La questione dell'uomo nella filosofia contemporanea*, Fagiuoli, Ettore. Zanini, Adelino.

"Ontologia Della Mancanza: Heidegger e la questione dell'uomo" in *Soggetto E Verità: La questione dell'uomo nella filosofia contemporanea*, Fagiuoli, Ettore. Feroldi, Luisella.

"Pensare La Storia: Soggetto e metodo dell'interpretazione" in *Soggetto E Verità: La questione dell'uomo nella filosofia contemporanea*, Fagiuoli, Ettore. D'Alessandro, Paolo.

"Tempo, uomo e memoria nella *Teogonia* di Esiodo" in *Il Concetto di Tempo: Atti del XXXII Congresso Nazionale della Società Filosofica Italiana*, Casertano, Giovanni (ed). Rotondaro, Serafina.

*Augusto Ponzio: Bibliografia e Letture Critiche*. Ponzio, Augusto.

*Contemporary Perspectives on Masculinity: Men, Women, and Politics in Modern Society*. Clatterbaugh, Kenneth.

*L'Homme sans image: Une anthropologie négative*. Minazzoli, Agnès.

*Soggetto E Verità: La questione dell'uomo nella filosofia contemporanea*. Fagiuoli, Ettore and Fortunato, Marco.

*The Mind of God and the Works of Man*. Craig, Edward.

A Parábola Humana (Uma Leitura Metafísica da Fisicidade Humana: Uma Expressao Matemática do Metafísicio do Homem). Coutinho, Jorge.

A Pessoa e o Seu Universo. Neves, Maria do Céu Patrao.

Alcuni rilievi sul nesso fra verità, libertà e temporalità nella filosofia di F. Nietzsche. Sacchi, Dario.

Algumas Notas sobre a Filosofia Política de Hobbes. Queiroz Guimaraes, Alexandre.

Alle origini dei diritti dell'uomo: i diritti della comunicazione di Francisco de Vitoria. Trujillo Pérez, Isabel.

Antropología y alteridad: De la naturaleza humana a la normalidad social. Lorite Mena, José.

Aportaciones de Leonardo Polo para una teoría antropológica del aprendizaje. García Viúdez, Marcos.

Aristotle on the Nature of *Logos*. Anton, John P.

Articulación crítica de ontología y política en B. Spinoza. Fernández G, Eugenio.

Augustinian Wisdom and the Law of the Heart. Littlejohn, Murray.

Brevi Riflessioni Filosofiche sulla Storicità dell'Uomo. Seidl, Horst.

Caminhos da Filosofia ou a Razao e o Desejo. De Fraga, Gustavo.

Che cosa ha veramente detto il Comitato Nazionale per la Bioetica sull'individualità dell'embrione?. Mori, Maurizio.

Crecimiento irrestricto y libertad en el pensamiento de Leonardo Polo. Riaza Molina, Carmen.

Descartes and Other Minds. Avramides, Anita.

El carácter sistémico del liderazgo. Bañares Parera, Leticia.

El Concepto de "Hombre Natural" en Rousseau (Consideraciones Etico-Educativas). Molina, Katiuska.

El habitar y la técnica: Polo en diálogo con Marx. Múgica, Fernando.

El mundo incuestionado (Ortega y Schütz). Hermida, Pablo.

En el centro del labertino: la hybris y el Minotauro. Cifuentes Camacho, David.

En memoria de la memoria de Martin Heidegger. Duque, Félix.

Florbela Espanca: Tónica da sua Inspiraçao. Freire, António.

Il) Teichmüller e gli amici napoletani. Savorelli, Alessandro.

Introducción a la teoría de la verdad de Michel Henry. García-Baró, Miguel.

José Maria da Cunha Seixas, Um Homem e um Filósofo Ignorado. De Brito, Maria Amélia Araújo.

L'astuzia della follia: Un'antologia di Lombroso. Savorelli, Alessandro.

L'Istoria dell'Uomo dipinta ne' linguaggi: Il Vico di Diego Colao Agata. Martone, Arturo.

La dignidad del hombre y la dignidad de la persona. Forment, Eudaldo.

La relazione tra l'uomo e la natura: una prospettiva. Sagnotti, Simona C.

La teologia esistenziale di S. Kierkegaard. Mondin, Battista.

Leibniz, el cristianismo europeo y la *Teodicea*. Andreu Rodrigo, Agustín.

Les Technologies de L'images: Nouveaux Instruments du Bio-Pouvoir. Maybon, Marie-Pierre.

Libertà e verità oggettiva. Givone, Sergio.

Man and a Marxist Approach. Baruah, Girish Chandra.

Modes de proximités avec l'animal chez Montaigne. Pelosse, Valentin.

Nature, Technology and Man in the Works of Dominik Pecka (in Czech). Jemelka, Petr.

Notas sobre el origen del hombre y la técnica. Díaz Caballero, José Ricardo.

Note sulle polemiche antifrancesi di Vico. Agrimi, Mario.

Nuove frontiere della scienza. Manno, Ambrogio Giacomo.

O Futuro Ecológico como Tarefa da Filosofia. Schmied-Kowarzik, Wolfdietrich.

O Homem da Evoluçao Temporal. Alves, Vitorino M de Sousa.

O Homem e a História em Gaspar Frutuoso. Da Luz, José Luís Brandao.

O Objecto de Reflexao da Antropologia Filosófica desde uma Ontologia da Indeterminaçao Humana. Teles, Carlos.

On Aristotle's 'Animal Capable of Reason'. Goodey, C F.

On the Logic of Intentional Help: Some Metaphysical Questions. Chisholm, Roderick M and Zimmerman, Dean W.

Ontología y conocimiento en M. Merleau-Ponty. Arce Carrascoso, José Luis.

Outline for a Theory of Action. Hernáez, Jesús.

Pensiero medievale e modernità. Gregory, Tullio.

Per una teoria del diritto ambientale: considerazioni a partire da un libro recente. Iagulli, Paolo.

Preghiera e Filosofia della Religione. Santi, Giorgio.

The God and a Man-Philosopher: Vocation for Philosophy on the Basis of F.W.I. Schelling's Anthropotheology (in Polish). Kolas, Pawel.

Visiones del mundo: Lógica simbólica. Ortiz-Osés, Andrés.

## MANAGED CARE

Can Ethics Committees Work in Managed Care Plans?. Felder, Michael.

Damaged Humanity: The Call for a Patient-Centered Medical Ethic in the Managed Care Era. Churchill, Larry R.

Ethical Decision Making in Managed Care Environments. Ross, Judith Wilson.

Ethical Issues in Managed Care: A Catholic Christian Perspective. Pellegrino, Edmund D.

Physicians and Managed Care: Employees or Professionals?. Christensen, Kate T.

Provider Disclosure of Financial Incentives in Managed Care: Pros and Cons. McCormack, Robert.

Recapturing Justice in the Managed Care Era. Moreno, Jonathan D.

Relationships between Primary Care Physicians and Consultants in Managed Care. Brett, Allan S.

The Ethics of Referral Kickbacks and Self-Referral and the HMO Physician as Gatekeeper: An Ethical Analysis. Beckwith, Francis J.

The Quality of Primary Care/Consultant Relationships in Managed Care: Have We Gone Forward or Backward?. Povar, Gail J.

## MANAGEMENT

"Vom Versuch angewandter Philosophie: Warum sich Philosophen mit Managern unterhalten" in *Werte und Entscheidungen im Management*, Schmidt, Thomas. Lohmann, Karl R.

"Werte im Management: Eine empirische Untersuchung" in *Werte und Entscheidungen im Management*, Schmidt, Thomas. Wegner, Marion.

*Business Ethics in the African Context Today*. Rosemann, Philipp W (ed) and LeJeune, Michel (ed).

*Werte und Entscheidungen im Management*. Schmidt, Thomas and Lohmann, Karl R.

A Critique and A Retrieval of Management and the Humanities. Gilbert Jr, Daniel R.

An Empirical Study of Moral Reasoning Among Managers in Singapore. Wimalasiri, Jayantha S, Pavri, Francis and Jalil, Abdul A K.

Chief Financial Officers' Perceptions Concerning the IMA's Standards of Ethical Conduct. Moyes, Glen D and Park, Kyungjoo.

Cognitive Moral Development and Attitudes Toward Women Executives. Everett, Linda, Thorne, Debbie and Danehower, Carol.

Comment: What We Can Learn from "Better Communication between Engineers and Managers" (M. Davis). Whitbeck, Caroline.

Crises and Way Outs of the Public Administration Theory. Ochoa Henríquez, Haydée.

Durkheim, Mayo, Morality and Management. Dingley, James C.

Ethical Beliefs and Management Behaviour: A Cross-Cultural Comparison. Jackson, Terence and Calafell Artola, Marian.

Ethics and MIS Education. McGowan, Matthew K and McGowan, Richard J.

Exploring the Contextual and Individual Factors on Ethical Decision Making of Salespeople. Verbeke, Willem, Ouwerkerk, Cok and Peelen, Ed.

Gender-Related Differences in Ethical and Social Values of Business Students: Implications for Management. Smith, Patricia L and Oakley III, Elwood F.

Imagining Unmanaging Health Care. Campo, Rafael.

Impression Management, Fairness, and the Employment Interview. Rosenfeld, Paul.

Management as a Practice: A Response to Alasdair MacIntyre. Brewer, Kathryn Balstad.

Management-Science and Business-Ethics. Singer, Alan E and Singer, Ming S.

Managing Business Ethics and Opportunity Costs. Primeaux, Patrick and Stieber, John.

Proactive Crisis Management and Ethical Discourse: Dow Chemical's Issues Management Bulletins 1979-1990. Kernisky, Debra A.

Reinforcing Ethical Decision Making Through Corporate Culture. Chen, Al Y S, Sawyers, Roby B and Williams, Paul F.

Suggested Management Responses to Ethical Issue Raised by Technological Change. Cordeiro, William P.

The Effect of Published Reports of Unethical Conduct on Stock Prices. Rao, Spuma M and Hamilton III, J Brooke.

The Relationship of Board Member Diversity to Organizational Performance. Siciliano, Julie I.

Total Quality Management: A Plan for Optimizing Human Potential?. Wagner, Paul A.

Valuation as Revelation and Reconciliation. O'Riordan, Tim.

## MANAGER

Better Communication between Engineers and Managers: Some Ways to Prevent Many Ethically Hard Choices. Davis, Michael.

Business Ethics of Korean and Japanese Managers. Lee, Chung-Yeong and Yoshihara, Hideki.

## MANAGER

Codes of Ethics: Investment Company Money Managers Versus other Financial Professionals. Clarke, James, Duska, Ronald and Rongione, Nicholas.

Commentary on "Better Communication between Engineers and Managers. Loui, Michael.

Commentary on "Better Communication between Engineers and Managers". Pritchard, Michael S.

Ethics and Performance: A Simulation Analysis of Team Decision Making. Hunt, Tammy G and Jennings, Daniel F.

Managers' Perception of Proper Ethical Conduct: The Effect of Sex, Age, and Level and Education. Deshpande, Satish P.

Personal Ethics and Business Ethics: The Ethical Attitudes of Owner/Managers of Small Business. Quinn, John J.

The Ethical Management Practices of Australian Firms. Batten, Jonathan, Hettihewa, Samanthala and Mellor, Robert.

The Influence of Corporate Culture on Managerial Ethical Judgments. Vitell, Scott J and Nwachukwu, Saviour L S.

The Influence of Deontological and Teleological Considerations and Ethical Climate on Sales Managers' Intentions to Reward or Punish Sales Force Behavior. DeConinck, James B and Lewis, William F.

The Organizational Bases of Ethical Work Climates in Lodging Operations as Perceived by General Managers. Upchurch, Randall S and Ruhland, Sheila K.

## MANCINI, I

Italo Mancini lettore di Agostino: Percorso e contenuti di un incontro. Cangiotti, Marco.

## MANDEVILLE, B

Filosofia o letteratura? Mandeville, Fielding e il contesto settecentesco. Branchi, Andrea.

## MANIPULATION

"The Concept of Manipulativeness" in *AI, Connectionism and Philosophical Psychology, 1995,* Tomberlin, James E (ed). Ackerman, Felicia.

From Observability to Manipulability: Extending the Inductive Arguments for Realism. Harré, Rom.

## MANKIND

Our Future in J. Krishnamurti. Subrata, Roy.

## MANN, T

Für einen anderen Umgang mit Nietzsche. Riedel, Manfred.

Thomas Mann e A Montanha Mágica. Joao Correia, Carlos.

## MANNHEIM, K

"Mannheim e Bloch: storicismo e utopia" in *Lo Storicismo e la Sua Storia: Temi, Problemi, Prospettive,* Cacciatore, Giuseppe (ed). Riccio, Monica.

Meditated History: An Approach to Karl Mannheim's Sociology of Knowledge through his Analysis of Mentalities (Spanish). Rodríguez Fouz, Marta.

## MANNING, R

Causes and Tastes: A Response. Shiner, Roger A.

## MANSBRIDGE, J

The Consensual Basis of Conflictual Power: A Critical Response to "Using Power, Fighting Power" by Jane Mansbridge. Haugaard, Mark.

## MANU

When Many Met Mahāsammata. Huxley, Andrew.

## MANUEL DE S. LUIS

Frei Manuel de S. Luís Escritor e Orador Açoriano dos Séculos XVII-XVIII (1660-1736). Pimentel, Manuel Cândido.

## MANUFACTURING

How to Do Things with Things: Objects trouvés and Symbolization. Streeck, Jürgen.

## MANUSCRIPT

A Fragment of Michael de Marbasio, Summa de modis significandi. Kelly, L G.

Collingwood's "Lost" Manuscript of *The Principles of History.* Van der Dussen, Jan.

Einstein's 1927 Unpublished Hidden-Variable Theory: Its Background Context and Significance. Belousek, Darrin W.

Lockean Political Apocrypha. Milton, J R.

Recent Acquisitions: Manuscripts, Typescripts and Proofs. Turcon, Sheila.

## MANY

*see also* Pluralism

The Ontological Relation "One-Many" according to the Neoplatonist Damascius. Térézis, Christos.

## MANY-VALUED LOGICS

"Vagueness, Many-Valued Logic, and Probability" in *Das weite Spektrum der analytischen Philosophie,* Lenzen, Wolfgang. Simons, Peter.

A Gentzen System for Conditional Logic. Guzmán, Fernando.

An Elementary Proof of Chang's Completeness Theorem for the Infinite-Valued Calculus of Lukasiewicz. Cignoli, Roberto and Mundici, Daniele.

Automated Theorem Proving for Lukasiewicz Logics. Beavers, Gordon.

Axiomatization and Completeness of Uncountably Valued Approximation Logic. Rasiowa, Helena.

Bounded Contraction and Gentzen-style Formulation of Lukasiewicz Logics. Prijatelj, Andreja.

Bruno de Finetti and the Logic of Conditional Events. Milne, Peter.

Fuzzy Logic and Arithmetical Hierarchy, II. Hájek, Petr.

On Generalizaed I-Algebras and 4-Valued Modal Algebras. Figallo, Aldo V and Landini, Paolo.

On Lukasiewicz-Moisil Algebras of Fuzzy Sets. Rudeanu, Sergiu.

The Completeness of the Factor Semantics for Lukasiewicz's Infinite-Valued Logics. Vasyukov, Vladimir L.

Wajsberg Algebras and Post Algebras. Rodríguez Salas, Antonio Jesús and Torrens, Antoni.

## MAP

Sparshott and the Philosophy of Philosophy. Shiner, Roger A.

## MARCEL

Created Receptivity and the Philosophy of the Concrete. Schmitz, Kenneth L.

Mal e Intersubjectividade em Gabriel Marcel. Ganho, Maria de Lourdes S. Reply. Long, Steven A.

## MARCUS, R

Marcus, Kripke, and Names. Burgess, John P.

## MARCUSE, H

Marcuse: La última utopía. López de Dicastillo, Luis.

## MARGOLIS, J

Joseph Margolis on Interpretation. Casey, Edward S.

Margolis and the Historical Turn. Rockmore, Tom.

Margolis and the Philosophy of History. Carr, David.

## MARIAS, J

*A Watch Over Mortality: The Philosophical Story of Julián Marías.* Raley, Harold.

## MARIN, L

Les *Lectures traversières* de Louis Marin. Cavaillé, Jean-Pierre.

## MARITAIN

Antimodern, Ultramodern, Postmodern: A Plea for the Perennial. Dewan, Lawrence.

Beyond the Sovereignty of Good. Nelson, Ralph C.

Brèves réflexions, suite à une relecture du paysan de la garonne, 25 ans après sa parution. Allard, Jean-Louis.

Connatural Knowledge. Thomas, James.

False and Genuine Knowledge: A Philosophical Look at the Peasant of the Garonne. Killoran, John B.

God and Jacques Maritain's Philosophy of Education: Uninvited Guests at the Postmodern Party. D'Souza, Mario O.

History and the Advent of the Self. Nelson, Ralph C.

Jacques Maritain and the Nature of Religious Belief. Sweet, William.

Justifying the Perennial Philosophy. Meynell, Hugo.

La *philosophia perennis*: De la continuité et du progrès en philosophie. Allard, Jean-Louis.

La conception maritainienne de l'intelligence humaine dans antimoderne. Allard, Jean-Louis.

Le statut de l'éthique aristotélicienne dans la morale 'adéquatement prise' de Jacques Maritain. Ponton, Lionel.

Man: The Perennial Metaphysician. Dewan, Lawrence.

Maritain et le débat postconciliaire: Le paysan de la garonne. Fourcade, Michel.

Maritain's Criticisms of Natural Law Theories. Sweet, William.

Maritain, Gilson, and the Ontology of Knowledge. Armour, Leslie.

Maritain, Post-Modern Epistemologies and the Rationality of Religious Belief. Sweet, William.

Maritain, the Intuition of Being, and the Proper Starting Point for Thomistic Metaphysics. Pugh, Matthew S.

Natural Law and the First Act of Freedom: Maritain Revisited. Dewan, Lawrence.

Self, Deconstruction and Possibility: Maritain's Sixth Way Revisited. Armour, Leslie.

The Aesthetically Good vs. The Morally Good. Davenport, Manuel.

The Inaccessible God. Thomas, James.

Une relecture du paysan de la garonne. Allard, Jean-Louis.

Was the Peasant of the Garonne a Mistake?. Hudson, Deal.

What Leibniz Thought Perennial. Hunter, Graeme.

Whitehead, Contemporary Metaphysics, and Maritain's Critique of Bergson. Bradley, James.

World Order: Maritain and Now. MacGuigan, Mark R.

## MARKET

*Ethics and Economic Progress.* Buchanan, James M.

*The Logic of the Gift: Toward an Ethic of Generosity.* Schrift, Alan D (ed).

Adam Smith's Other Hand: A Capitalist Theory of Exploitation. Fairlamb, Horace L.

Between Immorality and Unfeasibility: The Market Socialist Predicament. Steele, David Ramsay.

Comment on Dawson's 'Exit, Voice and Values in Economic Institutions'. Anderson, Elizabeth.

Discounting and Restitution. Cowen, Tyler.

Exit, Voice and Values in Economic Institutions. Dawson, Graham.

Fostering Market Competence. Askland, Andrew.

Illusory Freedoms: Liberalism, Education and the Market. Jonathan, Ruth.

Is Peer Review Overrated?. Shatz, David.

Keynes on Capitalism: Reply to Hill. Horwitz, Steven.

Los Substratos 'Metafísicos' de la Teoría Demo-Liberal: Prolegómenos. Kohn Wacher, Carlos.

Market Meditopia: A Glimpse at American Health Care in 2005. Churchill, Larry R.

**MARXISM**

Aussichten der Zivilgesellschaft unter Bedingungen neoliberaler Globalisierungspolitik. Haug, Wolfgang Fritz.

Between the Lines. Dix, Douglas Shields.

Circulus Vitiosus Deus? The Dialectical Logic of Feminist Standpoint Theory. Conway, Daniel W.

Containing Indeterminacy: Problems of Representation and Determination in Marx and Althusser. Corlett, William.

Debating Critical Theory. Hoy, David Couzens.

Derrida e la rivendicazione dello spirito del marxismo. Iofrida, Manlio.

Die Kunst der Anspielung: Hans-Georg Gadamers philosophische Interventionen im NS. Orozco, Teresa.

Die Marxismus—Debatte im "Silbernen Zeitalter". Ignatow, Assen.

El Maxismo y el ocaso de la política. Colom González, Francisco.

El Nietzsche práctico de Nolte: Nietzsche, profeta trágico de la guerra y organizador político de la aniquilación. Reguera, Isidoro.

Ethischer Neu-Fichteanismus und Geschichtsphilosophie: Zur sozio-politischen Rezeption Fichtes im 20. Jahrhundert. Villacañas, José L.

Everydayness, Aesthetics, Ontology: Notes on the Later Lukács (in Hungarian). Jung, Werner.

Frederic Jameson: ¿El marxismo el el Mäelstrom textualista?. Palti, Elías José.

Frederick Engels: Scholar and Revolutionary. Labica, Georges.

Fundamental Principles of Marxism's Self-Criticism. Oizerman, Teodor I.

Georg Lukács's *Destruction of Reason* and the Political Theories of the Western Emigration: Some Theses (in Hungarian). Söllner, Alfons.

Georg Lukács's Criticism of Societal Reason—The Crisis of Marxism and Marxist Ontology (in Hungarian). Dannemann, Rüdiger.

Georg Lukács's Plans for an Ethics (in Hungarian). Palcsó, Mária.

Georg Lukács—A Spiritual Portrait (in Hungarian). Stern, Laurent.

Georgii Shakhnazarov and the Soviet Critique of Historical Materialism. Sandle, Mark.

Gramscianismus in der Internationalen Politischen Ökonomie. Bieling, Hans-Jürgen and Deppe, Frank.

Habermas' Philosophy of Liberation. Pereppaden, Jose.

Hegemony and the Crisis of Legitimacy in Gramsci. Martin, James.

Historicism and Lacanian Theory. Evans, Dylan.

History, Ethics, and Marxism. Cohen, G A.

Is Marxism Totalitarian?. Hudelson, Richard.

Is Subjective Materialism Possible? (in German). Delport, Hagen.

Jack London y El Talón de Hierro. Laso Prieto, José Maria.

La dialéctica de lo universal y lo particular y el ideal de la abolición del estado (Segunda parte). Salas, Mario.

La filosofía política y los problemas de nuestro tiempo. Rosenfield, Denis.

Lived Thought between Affirmation and Critique: Georg Lukács and Stalinism (in Hungarian). Tietz, Udo.

Losev and Marxism: Lessons of a Life: 1893-1988. Nakhov, Isai.

Luis E. Nieto Arteta: Crítica del Marxismo y de los Sistemas Filosóficos. Cataño, Gonzalo.

Lukács: Ontology and Historicity (in Portuguese). Lessa, Sergio.

M.N. Roy's Concept of Freedom: A Philosophical Analysis. Amar, Rudra Kant.

Man and Nature: A Marxist Approach. Baruah, Girish Chandra.

Marx, Columbus, and the October Revolution: Historical Materialism and the Analysis of Revolutions. Losurdo, Domenico.

On Freedom. Liquin, Deng.

On Human Rights. Sharpe, M E (trans).

Plekhanov, Lenin and Working-Class Consciousness. Mayer, Robert.

Response to Richard Hudelson. Louw, Stephen.

Should Marxists Care About Alienation?. Brighouse, Harry.

Socialism and National Consciousness. Xiyuan, Xiong.

Stalin and Marxism: A Research Note. Van Ree, E.

State-Primacy and Third World Debt. Carter, Alan.

The Challenge of Explanation. Whitehead, Fred.

The Infomedia Revolution: Opportunities for Global Humanism. Kurtz, Paul.

The Lessons of Theory. Parini, Jay.

The Marxist Theory of Art. Graham, Gordon.

The Revolutionary Aesthetics of Frederick Engels. San Juan Jr, E.

The Role of Marxism and Deconstruction in Demystifying Aesthetics. Pokker, P K.

The Thought of the Late Lukács (in Hungarian). Tertulian, Nikolae.

The Tragedy of Lukács and the Problem of Alternatives (in Hungarian). Mészáros, István.

The 'Volatile' Marxian Concept of the Dictatorship of the Proletariat. Barany, Zoltan.

Unity and Development: Social Homogeneity, the Totalitarian Imaginary, and the Classical Marxist Tradition. Louw, Stephen.

Utopia or Reconciliation with Reality—Lukács's 1922-23 Literary Essays (in Hungarian). Löwy, Michael.

Walter Benjamin and Surrealism: The Story of a Revolutionary Spell. Löwy, Michael and Macey, David (trans).

Weltkapitalismus oder Nationalstaat—eine falsch gestellte Frage. Hirsch, Joachim.

Wither Marxism?. Warnke, Camilla.

**MASCULINITY**

"Public Man" and The Critique of Masculinities. Carver, Terrell.

*Rethinking Masculinity: Philosophical Explorations in Light of Feminism.* May, Larry (ed), Strikwerda, Robert (ed) and Hopkins, Patrick D (ed).

Sexuality, Masculinity, and Confession. May, Larry and Bohman, James.

**MASON, A**

Contractual Justice: A Modest Defence. Barry, Brian.

**MASS**

Contrariety and "Carving up Reality". Elder, Crawford L.

Trägheit und Massebegriff bei Johannes Kepler. Ihmig, Karl-Norbert.

Was ist Masse? Newtons Begriff der Materiemenge. Steinle, Friedrich.

**MASS MEDIA**

"Mass Media and Public Discussion in Bioethics" in *The Right to Know and the Right not to Know,* Chadwick, Ruth (ed). Chadwick, Ruth and Levitt, Mairi.

De Platón a Michael Jackson: Entresijos del imaginario andrógino. Jiménez, Jorge.

Mass Media and Critical Thinking: Reasoning for a Second-Hand World. Dorman, William.

The Ontology of Mass Art. Carroll, Noël.

**MASSEY, G**

"Can we Ever Pin One Down to a Formal Fallacy?" in *Logic and Argumentation,* Van Eemeren, Frans H (ed). Krabbe, Erik C W.

"Informal Factors in the Formal Evaluation of Arguments" in *Logic and Argumentation,* Van Eemeren, Frans H (ed). Finocchiaro, Maurice A.

**MASTERPIECE**

Some Remarks on the Notion of a Masterpiece. Coveos, Costis M.

**MASTURBATION**

Masturbation: A Kantian Condemnation. Kielkopf, Charles F.

**MATERIAL**

Van Inwagen and Gunk: A Response to Sider. Salsbery, Kelly Joseph.

**MATERIAL IMPLICATION**

Contraposition and Lewis Carroll's Barber Shop Paradox. Gillon, Brendan S.

Counterfactuals Revisited. Fulda, Joseph S.

Material Implication and General Indicative Conditionals. Barker, Stephen.

**MATERIAL OBJECT**

All the World's a Stage. Sider, Theodore.

Coincidence and Principles of Composition. Levey, Samuel.

Coincident Objects: Could a 'Stuff Ontology' Help?. Zimmerman, Dean W.

Coinciding Objects: Reply to Lowe and Denkel. Burke, Michael B.

The Theory of Appearing Defended. Langsam, Harold.

There might be Nothing: The Subtraction Argument Improved. Rodriguez-Pereyra, Gonzalo.

**MATERIALISM**

*see also* Atomism, Dialectical Materialism, Historical Materialism, Matter

"Incarnation, Difference, and Identity: Materialism, Self, and the Life of Spirit" in *Philosophy in Experience: American Philosophy in Transition,* Hart, Richard (ed). Wallace, Kathleen.

"Materialism and the Logical Structure of Intentionality" in *Objections to Physicalism,* Robinson, Howard (ed). Bealer, George.

"Materialist Mutations of the *Bilderverbot*" in *Sites of Vision,* Levin, David Michael (ed). Comay, Rebecca.

"Phenomenal Externalism" in *Perception,* Villanueva, Enrique (ed). Dretske, Fred.

"The Anti-Materialist Strategy and the 'Knowledge Argument'" in *Objections to Physicalism,* Robinson, Howard (ed). Robinson, Howard.

"The Breathtaking Intimacy of the Material World: William James's Last Thoughts" in *The Cambridge Companion to William James,* Putnam, Ruth Anna (ed). Wilshire, Bruce.

"Weak Materialism" in *Objections to Physicalism,* Robinson, Howard (ed). Nathan, N M L.

Berkeley Revised: On the New Metaphysics for Social Epistemology. 90 Years After "Materialism and Empiriocrticism". Kassavine, Illia.

Consuming Because Others Consume. Lichtenberg, Judith.

David Braine's Project: The Human Person. Burrell, David B.

Dialectical Materialism and the Quantum Controversy: The Viewpoints of Fock, Langevin, and Taketani. Freire Jr, Olival.

Idealismo y materialismo: Max Horkheimer y la constitución del conocimiento en la ciencia social. Vergara, Eliseo Cruz.

In Defense of Advertising: A Social Perspective. Phillips, Barbara J.

Is Subjective Materialism Possible? (in German). Delport, Hagen.

Justifying the Perennial Philosophy. Meynell, Hugo.

Kim on the Mind—Body Problem. Horgan, Terence.

La conscience n'est pas suject: pour un matérialisme authentique. Kail, Michel.

La filosofía materialista en la época de la Revolución Francesa. José Martínez, Francisco.

Materiality in Theodor W. Adorno and Judith Butler. Hull, Carrie L.

O Modelo Psicofisiológico Cartesiano e o Materialismo das Luzes. Nascimento, Maria das Graças S.

Out-Law Discourse: The Critical Politics of Material Judgment. Sloop, John M and Ono, Kent A.

Response. Goldstick, Danny.

Some Comments on Dialectical and Logical Contradictions. Marquit, Erwin.

The Challenge of Explanation. Whitehead, Fred.

The Cultural Commodity (in Portuguese). Bolognesi, Mário Fernando.

The Flesh and the Spirit: Anne Bradstreet and Seventeenth Century Dualism, Materialism, Vitalism and Reformed Theology. Whelan, Timothy.

The Ghost in the Machine—Fights—the Last Battle for the Human Soul. Watson, Richard A.

## MATERIALISM

Tra materialismo e critica della comunicazione: Paolo Virno. Genovese, Rino.

Translation, Philosophy, Materialism. Venuti, Lawrence.

Variedades de Superveniencia. Perez, Diana Inés.

Witkacy and Eddington—Two Conceptions of Metaphysics (in Polish). Kosciuszko, Krzysztof.

Yuri K. Melvil and American Pragmatism. Ryder, John.

Yvon Quiniou, il materialismo e l'impossibile immoralismo di Nietzsche. Franco, Vittoria.

Zénon, matérialiste et nominaliste?. Brinkman, Klaus.

## MATERNITY

"Maternity, Paternity, and Equality" in *Reproduction, Technology, and Rights: Biomedical Ethics Reviews,* Humber, James M (ed). Humber, James M.

Per la costruzione di un'autorità femminile. Vegetti Finzi, Silvia.

Premat ernal Duty and the Resolution of Conflict. Yeast, John D.

## MATHEMATICS

*see also* Addition, Algebra, Calculus, Geometry, Metamathematics

"A Philosophy of Mathematics between Two Camps" in *The Cambridge Companion to Wittgenstein,* Sluga, Hans (ed). Gerrard, Steve.

"Analytic Geometry, Experimental Truth and Metaphysics in Descartes" in *Memorias Del Seminario En Conmemoración De Los 400 Anos Del Nacimiento De René Descartes,* Albis, Víctor S (ed). Laserna Pinzón, Mario.

"Berkeley: Scepticism, Matter and Infinite Divisibility" in *Scepticism in the History of Philosophy: A Pan-American Dialogue,* Popkin, Richard H (ed). Robles, José A.

"Box" in Intuitionistic Modal Logic. DeVidi, David and Solomon, Graham.

"Der mathematische Hintergrund des Erweiterungsschrittes in Freges "Grundgesetzen der Arithmetik" in *Das weite Spektrum der analytischen Philosophie,* Lenzen, Wolfgang. Thiel, Christian.

"Descartes, investigador matemático afortunado" in *Memorias Del Seminario En Conmemoración De Los 400 Anos Del Nacimiento De René Descartes,* Albis, Víctor S (ed). Campos, Alberto.

"El estatuto epistemológico de las matemáticas en el origen del pensamiento moderno" in *Verdad: lógica, representación y mundo,* Villegas Forero, L. Arbaizar Gil, Benito. ·

"Frege über Widerspruchsfreiheit und die Schöpfung mathematischer Gegenstände" in *Das weite Spektrum der analytischen Philosophie,* Lenzen, Wolfgang. Schirn, Matthias.

"Frege Versus Cantor and Dedekind: On the Concept of Number" in *Early Analytic Philosophy,* Tait, William W (ed). Tait, W W.

"Frege versus Cantor and Dedekind: On the Concept of Number" in *Frege: Importance and Legacy,* Schirn, Matthias (ed). Tait, William W.

"Frege's Influence on Wittgenstein: Reversing Metaphysics via the Context Principle" in *Early Analytic Philosophy,* Tait, William W (ed). Reck, Erich.

"Il Senso Della Verità: Desolazione matematica e terapia nietzscheana dell'infelicità" in *Soggetto E Verità: La questione dell'uomo nella filosofia contemporanea,* Fagiuoli, Ettore. Fortunato, Marco.

"Introduction: Peirce as Logician" in *Studies in the Logic of Charles Sanders Peirce,* Houser, Nathan (ed). Houser, Nathan.

"Mathesis universalis e inteligibilidad en Descartes" in *Memorias Del Seminario En Conmemoración De Los 400 Anos Del Nacimiento De René Descartes,* Albis, Víctor S (ed). Paty, Michel.

"On Positing Mathematical Objects" in *Frege: Importance and Legacy,* Schirn, Matthias (ed). Resnik, Michael D.

"Peirce between Logic and Mathematics" in *Studies in the Logic of Charles Sanders Peirce,* Houser, Nathan (ed). Grattan-Guinness, Ivor.

"Peirce's Pre-Logistic Account of Mathematics" in *Studies in the Logic of Charles Sanders Peirce,* Houser, Nathan (ed). Kerr-Lawson, Angus.

"Peirce's Theoremic/Corollarial Distinction and the Interconnections between Mathematics and Logic" in *Studies in the Logic of Charles Sanders Peirce,* Houser, Nathan (ed). Levy, Stephen H.

"Physicalism and Mathematics" in *Objections to Physicalism,* Robinson, Howard (ed). Hale, Bob.

"Productive Abstraction for Sets" in *Verdad: lógica, representación y mundo,* Villegas Forero, L. Kuper, Jan.

"Sul problema della considerazione matematica dell'infinito e del continuo in Aristotele e Hegel" in *Hegel e Aristotele,* Ferrarin, A. Moretto, Antonio.

"The Philosophy of Mathematics in Early Positivism" in *Origins of Logical Empiricism,* Giere, Ronald N (ed). Goldfarb, Warren.

"The Role of the Matrix Representation in Peirce's Development of the Quantifiers" in *Studies in the Logic of Charles Sanders Peirce,* Houser, Nathan (ed). Iliff, Alan J.

"Wittgenstein's Critique of Philosophy" in *The Cambridge Companion to Wittgenstein,* Sluga, Hans (ed). Fogelin, Robert J.

"Wittgenstein, Mathematics, and Ethics: Resisting the Attractions of Realism" in *The Cambridge Companion to Wittgenstein,* Sluga, Hans (ed). Diamond, Cora.

"¿Qué nos importa Descartes todavía?" in *Memorias Del Seminario En Conmemoración De Los 400 Anos Del Nacimiento De René Descartes,* Albis, Víctor S (ed). Serrano, Gonzalo.

"¿René Descartes, cientifista?" in *Memorias Del Seminario En Conmemoración De Los 400 Anos Del Nacimiento De René Descartes,* Albis, Víctor S (ed). Sierra, Guillermo Restrepo.

"¿Siguen las pruebas realizadas por ordenador algún patrón de verdad matemática?" in *Verdad: lógica, representación y mundo,* Villegas Forero, L. Beltrán Orenes, Pilar.

*A New Introduction to Modal Logic.* Cresswell, M J and Hughes, G E.

*A Subject with No Object: Strategies for Nominalistic Interpretation of Mathematics.* Burgess, John P and Rosen, Gideon.

*An Essay on the Foundations of Geometry.* Russell, Bertrand.

*Computation, Dynamics, and Cognition.* Giunti, Marco.

*Frege: Importance and Legacy.* Schirn, Matthias (ed).

*Immanuel Kant's Prolegomena to Any Future Metaphysics.* Logan, Beryl.

*Logic and Existence.* Lawlor, Leonard (trans), Sen, Amit (trans) and Hyppolite, Jean.

*Ludwig Wittgenstein: Half-Truths and One-and-a-Half-Truths.* Hintikka, Jaakko.

*Matemáticas, método y mathesis universalis en las Regulae de Descartes.* Arenas, Luis.

*Mathematische und naturwissenschaftliche Modelle in der Philosophie Schellings und Hegels.* Ziche, Paul.

*Mentoring the Mentor: A Critical Dialogue with Paulo Freire.* Torres, Amadeu (ed).

*Philosophy of Mathematics: Structure and Ontology.* Shapiro, Stewart.

*Self-Trust: A Study of Reason, Knowledge and Autonomy.* Lehrer, Keith.

*Studies in the Logic of Charles Sanders Peirce.* Houser, Nathan (ed), Roberts, Don D (ed) and Van Evra, James (ed).

*The Philosophy of Mathematics.* Hart, W D.

*The Primary Logic: Instruments for a Dialogue between the Two Cultures.* Malatesta, Michele.

*The Principles of Mathematics Revisited.* Hintikka, Jaakko.

*The Taming of the True.* Tennant, Neil.

*Zur Meta-Theorie der Physik.* Schröter, Joachim.

A Hundred Years of Numbers: An Historical Introduction to Measurement Theory 1887-1990: Part I: The Formation Period: Two Lines of Research: Axiomatics and Real Morphisms, Scales and Invariance. Díez, José A.

A Parábola Humana (Uma Leitura Metafísica da Fisicidade Humana: Uma Expressao Matemática do Metafísicio do Homem). Coutinho, Jorge.

A Revolution in the Foundations of Mathematics?. Hintikka, Jaakko.

A Theory of Truth that Prefers Falsehood. Fitting, Melvin.

Acerca de las contribuciones actuales de una didáctica de antaño: el caso de la serie de Taylor. Cantoral, Ricardo.

Alternative Mathematics and Alternative Theoretical Physics: The Method for Linking Them Together. Drago, Antonino.

An Exploration into Teaching with Computers. Kowalski, Ludwik.

Assaying Lakatos's Philosophy of Mathematics. Corfield, David.

Axiomática y álgebra estructural en la obra de David Hilbert. Corry, Leo.

Bertrand Russell (in Polish). Mann, Golo.

Biomathematics: Methods and Limits (in Portuguese). Castilho Piqueira, José Roberto.

C.S. Peirce's Theories of Infinitesimals. Herron, Timothy.

Confirmation and the Indispensability of Mathematics to Science. Vineberg, Susan.

Conjecture. Mazur, B.

Consideraciones comparativas sobre nuevas investigaciones geométricas. Klein, Felix.

Counting Information: A Note on Physicalized Numbers. Rotman, Brian.

Definition in Frege's Foundations of Arithmetic. Hunter, David A.

Despite Physicists, Proof is Essential in Mathematics. Mac Lane, Saunders.

El De Numeris Datis de Jordanus Nemorarius como sistema matemático de signos. Puig, Luis.

El desmigajador de la realidad: Wittgenstein y las matemáticas. Espinoza, Miguel.

El discurso matemático: ideograma y lenguaje natural. De Lorenzo, Javier.

El finitismo metamatemático de Hilbert y la crítica de Oskar Becker. Roetti, Jorge Alfredo.

El realismo en matemáticas. Alemán, Anastasio.

Etica y matemática en Platón. Lan, Conrado Eggers.

G.W. Leibniz: Geschichte des Kontinuumproblems. Luna Alcoba, Manuel.

Gegenstand und Methode in der Geschichte der Mathematik. Otte, Michael.

Getting in Touch with Numbers: Intuition and Mathematical Platonism. Cheyne, Colin.

God and the New Math. Bigelow, John.

Hilbert Vindicated?. Hintikka, Jaakko.

Hilbert's Formalism and Arithmetization of Mathematics. Webb, Judson C.

Hipotesis del continuo, definibilidad y funciones recursivas: historia de un desencuentro (1925-1955). Zalamea, Fernando.

How Did Russell Write The Principles of Mathematics 1903?. Grattan-Guinness, Ivor.

Husserl and Hilbert on Completeness: A Neglected Chapter in Early Twentieth Century Foundations of Mathematics. Majer, Ulrich.

Il cartesianesimo matematico a Napoli. Gatto, Romano.

Immanuel Kants Grundlegung der Arithmetik. Noske, Rainer.

In Support of Significant Modernization of Original Mathematical Texts (In Defense of Presentism). Barabashev, A G.

Isaac Barrow on the Mathematization of Nature: Theological Voluntarism and the Rise of Geometrical Optics. Malet, Antoni.

Katz Astray. George, Alexander.

Korrespondenten von G.W. Leibniz: Georg Samuel Dörffel, geb. 11 Oktober 1643 in Plauen/Vogtland—gest. 6. August 1688 in Weida. Pfitzner, Elvira.

## MATHEMATICS

La ciencia analítica en la primera mitad del siglo XIX: el teorema del valor intermedio. Alarcón, Jesús, Rigo, Mirela and Waldegg, Guillermina.

La contribución de Christian Wolff (1679-1754) a la popularización de las matemáticas en la primera mitad del siglo XVIII. Nobre, Sergio.

La demostración "more geometrico": notas para la historia de una exploración. Vega, Luis.

La filosofía de la matemática de Albert Lautman. Zalamea, Fernando.

La teoria de las proporciones de Eudoxio interpretada por Dedekind. Corry, Leo.

La transformacion de una teoría matemática: el caso de los números poligonales. Radford, Luis.

Lakatos as Historian of Mathematics. Larvor, Brendan P.

Lequier and the Documents of the Renouvier Library. Clair, André.

Living Together and Living Apart: On the Interactions between Mathematics and Logics from the Franch Revolution to the First World War (Spanish). Grattan-Guinness, Ivor.

Lógica y práctica matemática. Nepomuceno Fernández, Angel.

Lógica, conjuntos y logicismo: desarrollos alemanes de 1870 a 1908. Ferreirós, José.

Los fundamentos de la aritmética según Peano. Zubieta R, Francisco.

Ludwig Wittgenstein: Matemáticas y ética. Rivera, Silvia.

Maschinen und Kreativität: Metamathematische Argumente für das menschliche Denken. Ebbinghaus, H D.

Metaphysics Delta 15 and Pre-Euclidean Mathematics. Pritchard, Paul.

On Mathematical Error. Sherry, David.

On Wittgenstein's Philosophy of Mathematics II. Conant, James.

Ontologie der Mathematik im Anschluss an Oskar Becker. Poser, Hans.

Parts III-IV of *The Principles of Mathematics*. Byrd, Michael.

Philosophy and Mathematics. Powell, Andrew.

Poincaré: Mathematics & Logic & Intuition. McLarty, Colin.

Proof and the Evolution of Mathematics. Jaffe, Arthur.

Prove-Once More and Again. Hersh, Reuben.

Pythagorean Powers or A Challenge to Platonism. Pigden, Charles R and Cheyne, Colin.

Re-Interpeting Frege. Born, Rainer.

Red and Green after All These Years. Zelaniec, Wojciech.

Schoonheid buiten proportie: Burkes afrekening met een klassiek ideaal. Van Der Schoot, Albert.

Silvester Mauro, S.J. (1619-1687) on Four Degrees of Abstraction. Doyle, John P.

Sobre a Ciência e o Magistério Filosófico de Pitágoras. Spinelli, Miguel.

The Epistemic Status of Probabilistic Proof. Fallis, Don.

The Legacy of Lakatos: Reconceptualising the Philosophy of Mathematics. Ernest, Paul.

The Mathematical Structure of the World: The World as Graph. Dipert, Randall R.

The NCTM Standards and the Philosophy of Mathematics. Toumasis, Charalampos.

The Phenomenology of Mathematical Beauty. Rota, Gian-Carlo.

The Phenomenology of Mathematical Proof. Rota, Gian-Carlo.

The Philosophical and Methodological Thought of N. I. Lobachevsky. Perminov, V Ya.

The Popularization of Mathematics or The Pop-Music of the Spheres. Van Bendegem, Jean Paul.

The Possibility of a Mathematical Sociology of Scientific Communication. Leydesdorff, Loet.

The Way of Logic into Mathematics. Peckhaus, Volker.

Thick Epistemic Access: Distinguishing the Mathematical from the Empirical. Azzouni, Jody.

Über das Verhältnis von Algebra und Geometrie in Descartes'"Geometrie". Krämer, Sybille.

Was Russell an Analytical Philosopher?. Monk, Ray.

Who Needs Mereology?. Pollard, Stephen.

Why Mathematical Solutions of Zeno's Paradoxes Miss the Point: Zeno's One and Many Relation and Parmenides' Prohibition. Papa-Grimaldi, Alba.

Y a-t-il de la place pour philosopher sur les mathématiques au collégial?. Daniel, Marie-France, LaFortune, Louise and Pallascio, Richard (& others).

Zur Begründung des Infinitesimalkalküls durch Leibniz. Krämer, Sybille.

## MATILAL, B

The Ruptured Idiom: Of Dallmayr, Matilal and Ramanujan's 'Way of Thinking'. Venkat Rao, D.

## MATRAVERS, M

Contractual Justice: A Modest Defence. Barry, Brian.

## MATRIX

"The Role of the Matrix Representation in Peirce's Development of the Quantifiers" in *Studies in the Logic of Charles Sanders Peirce,* Houser, Nathan (ed). Iliff, Alan J.

A Remark on the Maximal Extensions of the Relevant Logic *R*. Swirydowicz, Kazimierz.

On Minimal Resolution Proof Systems for Resolution Logics. Stachniak, Zbigniew.

On Reduced Matrices. Rautenberg, Wolfgang.

Predicative Laws of Association in Statistics and Physics. Costantini, D and Garibaldi, U.

Singulary Extensional Connectives: A Closer Look. Humberstone, I Lloyd.

The Equivalence Myth of Quantum Mechanics—Part I. Muller, F A.

Theory Matrices (for Modal Logics) Using Alphabetical Monotonicity. Gent, Ian P.

## MATTER

see also Mass, Materialism, Prime Matter, Substance

"Berkeley: Scepticism, Matter and Infinite Divisibility" in *Scepticism in the History of Philosophy: A Pan-American Dialogue,* Popkin, Richard H (ed). Robles, José A.

"Die Chemie als Gegendstand philosophischer Reflexion" in *Philosophie der Chemie: Bestandsaufnahme und Ausblick,* Schummer. Joachim (ed). Psarros, Nikos.

"Essere, Materia, Soggetto, Alterità: Per una critica filosofica della comunicazione mondializzata" in *Soggetto E Verità: La questione dell'uomo nella filosofia contemporanea,* Fagiuoli, Ettore. Ponzio, Augusto.

"Philosophie der Stoffe, Bestandsaufnahme und Ausblicke" in *Philosophie der Chemie: Bestandsaufnahme und Ausblick,* Schummer, Joachim (ed). Schummer, Joachim.

"Self as Matter and Form: Some Reflections on Kant's View of the Soul" in *Figuring the Self: Subject, Absolute, and Others in Classical German Philosophy,* Zöller, Günter (ed). Aquila, Richard E.

*Object and Property.* Denkel, Arda.

*Philosophie der Chemie: Bestandsaufnahme und Ausblick.* Schummer, Joachim (ed), Psarros, Nikos (ed) and Ruthenberg, Klaus (ed).

*Übergang Von Den Metaphysischen Anfangsgründen Der Naturwissenschaft Zur Physik.* Kant, Immanuel.

A Essência da Matéria Prima em Averróis Latino (Com uma Referência a Henrique de Gand). Santiago de Carvalho, Mário A.

Analyse und Kontext des Wachsbeispiels bei Descartes. Petrus, Klaus.

Antonio Rosmini: Aristotele Esposto ed Esaminato. Masi, Giuiseppe.

Biological Matter and Perceptual Powers in Aristotle's *De Anima.* Scaltsas, Theodore.

Descartes on the Real Existence of Matter. Friedman, Michael.

Down the Slope. Karasev, L V.

Gittà, materia del tempo. Berardi, Roberto.

Kantian Matters: The Structure of Permanence. O'Shea, James R.

Le réceptacle platonicien: nature, fonction, contenu. Narbonne, Jean-Marc.

Materie in Raum und Zeit? Philosophische Aspekte der Raum-Zeit-Interpretation der Quantenfeldtheorie. Stöckler, Manfred.

Matter and the Unity of Being in the Philosophical Theology of Saint Thomas Aquinas. McAleer, Graham.

The Function of the *formae nativae* in the Refinement Process of Matter: A Study of Bernard of Chartres's Concept of Matter. Annala, Pauli.

## MATTHEWS, P

A Lack of Feeling in Kant: Response to Patricia M. Matthews. Huhn, Tom.

## MAUDLIN, T

Is There a Syntactic Solution to the Hole Problem?. Rynasiewicz, Robert.

Maudlin and Modal Mystery. Lewis, David.

Modern Essentialism and the Problem of Individuation of Spacetime Points. Bartels, Andreas.

## MAUGHAM, S

"Love and Human Bondage in Maugham, Spinoza, and Freud" in *Love Analyzed,* Lamb, Roger E. Hannan, Barbara.

## MAURO, S

Silvester Mauro, S.J. (1619-1687) on Four Degrees of Abstraction. Doyle, John P.

## MAXIM

Prometer en Falso: La Contradicción Práctica y el Imperativo Categórico. Rosas, Alejandro.

## MAXIMAL

A Remark on the Maximal Extensions of the Relevant Logic *R*. Swirydowicz, Kazimierz.

On Maximal Intermediate Predicate Constructive Logics. Avelone, Alessandro, Fiorentini, Camillo and Mantovani, Paolo (& others).

## MAXIMALITY

*Thick and Thin: Moral Argument at Home and Abroad.* Walzer, Michael.

## MAXIMIZATION

A Multi-Stage Game Model of Morals by Agreement. Heath, Joseph.

Concepts of Moral Management and Moral Maximization. Sikula, Sr, Andrew.

Rationality and Ethics. French, Peter.

Violations of Present-Value Maximization in Income Choice. Gigliotti, Gary and Sopher, Barry.

## MAXWELL, N

On Becoming, Relativity, and Nonseparability. Dorato, Mauro.

## MAYA

An Illusive Historiography of the View that the World is *Maya*: Professor Daya Krishna on the Historiography of Vedānta. Chandra, Suresh.

Does the Grammar of Seeing Aspects Imply a Kantian Concept?. Kanthamani, A.

## MAYAN

Crafting Marks into Meanings. Catalano, Joseph S.

## MAYO, C

"Opening the Closet Door: Sexualities Education and "Active Ignorance" in *Philosophy of Education (1996),* Margonis, Frank (ed). Ford, Maureen.

## MEASURE

Louveau's Theorem for the Descriptive Set Theory of Internal Sets. Schilling, Kenneth and Zivaljevic, Bosko.

New Blades for Occam's Razor. Lauth, Bernhard.

Probability Logic and Measures on Epimorphic Images of Coproducts of Measurable Spaces. Amer, Mohamed A.

Two Applications of a Theorem of Dvoretsky, Wald, and Wolfovitz to Cake Division. Barbanel, Julius B and Zwicker, William S.

## MEASUREMENT

"Eudosso di Cnido e la misura del tempo nell'astrononmia greca" in *Il Concetto di Tempo: Atti del XXXII Congresso Nazionale della Società Filosofica Italiana*, Casertano, Giovanni (ed). Simeoni, Luca.

A Bayesian Examination of Time-Symmetry in the Process of Measurement. Shimony, Abner.

A Hundred Years of Numbers: An Historical Introduction to Measurement Theory 1887-1990: Part I: The Formation Period: Two Lines of Research: Axiomatics and Real Morphisms, Scales and Invariance. Díez, José A.

A Hundred Years of Numbers: An Historical Introduction to Measurement Theory 1887-1990: Part II: Suppes and the Mature Theory: Representation and Uniqueness. Díez, José A.

An Empirical Examination of the Multi-Dimensionality of Ethical Climate in Organizations. Wimbush, James C, Shepard, Jon M and Markham, Steven E.

Analytic Ideals. Solecki, Slawomir.

Bertrand Russell's 1897 Critique of the Traditional Theory of Measurement. Michell, Joel.

Davidson, Interdeterminacy, and Measurement. Davies, David.

Ergodic Theorems and the Basis of Science. Petersen, Karl.

Insolubility of the Quantum Measurement Problem for Unsharp Observables. Busch, Paul and Shimony, Abner.

Lexicographic Additivity for Multi-Attribute Preferences on Finite Sets. Nakamura, Yutaka.

Mathematical Quantum Theory I: Random Ultrafilters as Hidden Variables. Boos, William.

Measurement Units and Theory Construction. Tyron, Warren W.

Modal Interpretations, Decoherence and Measurements. Bacciagaluppi, Guido and Hemmo, Meir.

Myth, Measurement, and the Minimum Wage: Sound and Fury Signifying What?. Whitman, Glen.

On the Applicability of the Quantum Measurement Formalism. Chang, Hasok.

Protowissenschaft und Rekonstruktion. Hartmann, Dirk.

Still in Defence: A Short Reply on Non-Locality and Widespread Beliefs. Laudisa, Federico.

Subjective Decoherence in Quantum Measurements. Breuer, Thomas.

The Measure of Morality: Rethinking Moral Reasoning. Vine, Ian.

The Measureless of Crisis (in Spanish). Grespan, Jorge.

The Properties of Modal Interpretations of Quantum Mechanics. Clifton, Robert.

The Rule of Adjunction and Reasonable Inference. Kyburg, Jr, Henry E.

Van Fraassen on Preparation and Measurement. Ruetsche, Laura.

What It Feels Like To Be in a Superposition and Why. Lehner, Christoph.

Whole Earth Measurements: How Many Phenomenologists Does It Take to Detect a "Greenhouse Effect"?. Ihde, Don.

## MECHANICS

*see also* Quantum Mechanics

An Axiomatic Framework for Classical Particle Mechanics without Force. Schlup Sant'Anna, Adonai.

El mecanicismo como paradigma "exitoso". Coronado, Luis Guillermo.

Irreversibility and Time's Arrow. Landsberg, Peter T.

Krylov's Proof that Statistical Mechanics Cannot Be Founded on Classical Mechanics and Interpretation of Classical Statistical Mechanical Probabilities. Rédei, Miklós.

La contingence dans la mécanique hégélienne. Février, Nicolas.

Time, Quantum Mechanics, and Tense. Saunders, Simon.

## MECHANISM

*Causation and Persistence: A Theory of Causation.* Ehring, Douglas.

*Gassendi's Ethics: Freedom in a Mechanistic Universe.* Sarasohn, Lisa T.

*Il Riduzionismo della Scienza.* Gava, Giacomo.

*Mechanismus und Subjektivität in der Philosophie von Thomas Hobbes.* Esfeld, Michael.

*Real Process: How Logic and Chemistry Combine in Hegel's Philosophy of Nature.* Burbidge, John W.

An Agent Model Integrating Multiple Reasoning Mechanisms. Moulin, Bernard and Boury-Brisset, Anne-Claire.

Epistemische Leistungen technischer Simulationen. Loeck, Gisela.

Individualism and Evolutionary Psychology (or: In Defense of "Narrow" Functions). Buller, David J.

Maschinentheoretische Grundlagen der organismischen Konstruktionslehre. Gutmann, Wolfgang Friedrich and Weingarten, Michael.

Mechanism and Fracture in Cartesian Physics. Wilson, Mark.

Mechanistic Individualism Versus Organismic Totalitarianism: Toward a Neo-Calvinist Perspective. Venter, J J.

Melding the Public and Private Spheres: Taking Commensality Seriously. Hirschman, Albert O.

Note sulle polemiche antifrancesi di Vico. Agrimi, Mario.

On the Mechanism of Consciousness. Cotterill, Rodney M J.

The Mechanist and the Snail. Hitchcock, Christopher Read.

What I Will Do and What I Intend To Do. Scheer, Richard K.

## MEDIA

Algunos elementos para una deontología periodística. Rodríguez Ramírez, Carlos Alberto.

Government, the Press, and the People's Right to Know. Montague, Phillip.

Textual Travel and Translation in an Age of Globalized Media. Rapping, Elayne.

## MEDIATION

Alternative Dispute Resolution and Research Misconduct. Guenin, Louis M.

Consultectonics: Ethics Committee Case Consultation as Mediation. Reynolds, Don F.

Valuation as Revelation and Reconciliation. O'Riordan, Tim.

## MEDICAL ETHICS

*see also* Abortion, Bioethics, Clinical Ethics, Euthanasia

"Genethik" in *Angewandte Ethik: Die Bereichsethiken und ihre theoretische Fundierung*, Nida-Rümelin, Julian (ed). Irrgang, Bernhard.

"Intentions in Medical Ethics" in *Human Lives: Critical Essays on Consequentialist Bioethics*, Oderberg, David S (ed). Garcia, Jorge L A.

"Medizinethik" in *Angewandte Ethik: Die Bereichsethiken und ihre theoretische Fundierung*, Nida-Rümelin, Julian (ed). Schöne-Seifert, Bettina.

*Leben-und Sterbenkönnen: Gedanken zur Sterbebegleitung und zur Selbstbestimmung der Person.* Wettstein, R Harri.

*Moral Issues in Health Care: An Introduction to Medical Ethics.* McConnell, Terrance C.

Anthropo-centrifugal Ethics (in Czech). Kemp, Peter.

Can Ethics Committees Work in Managed Care Plans?. Felder, Michael.

Can Phronesis Save the Life of Medical Ethics?. Beresford, Eric B.

Cultural Diversity in Medicine and Medical Ethics: What Are the Key Questions?. La Puma, John.

Dwingende feiten en hun verborgen moraal: Over doen en laten in de neonatologiepraktijk. Mesman, Jessica.

Eine Skizze zur Grundlegung der Bioethik. Siep, Ludwig.

En torno a la justicia médica. Cortina, Adela.

Ethical Decision Making in Managed Care Environments. Ross, Judith Wilson.

Ethics Consultants and Surrogates: Can We Do Better?. Fletcher, John C.

Evading Responsibility: The Ethics of Ingenuity. Katz, Leo.

Goals of Ethics Consultation: Toward Clarity, Utility, and Fidelity. Andre, Judith.

Healthcare Ethics Committees and Ethics Consultants: The State of the Art (Sources/Bibliography). Buehler, David A.

Integrated Ethics Programs: A New Mission for Ethics Committees. Christopher, Myra J.

Is it Time to Abandon Brain Death?. Truog, Robert D.

Liability of Ethics Consultants: A Case Analysis. DuVal, Gordon.

Life Sciences, Medicine and the Normative Communities: Early Cooperation. Kasher, Asa.

Max Weber on Ethics Case Consultation: A Methodological Critique of the Conference on Evaluation of Ethics Consultation. Degnin, Francis.

Medical Ethics in the Courtroom: A Reappraisal. Sharpe, Virginia A and Pellegrino, Edmund D.

Medical Ethics in the Developing World: A Liberation Theology Perspective. Fabri Dos Anjos, Marcio.

Muss dieses Buch gelesen werden?—Zum Erscheinen der deutschen Ausgabe von Helga Kuhse/Peter Singer: *Should the Baby Live?*. Joerden, Jan C.

Non-Heart-Beating Cadaver Procurement and the Work of Ethics Committees. Spielman, Bethany and Verhulst, Steve.

Nurses' Perspectives of Hospital Ethics Committees. Stadler, Holly A, Morrissey, John M and Tucker, Joycelyn E.

Prospective Payment System and the Traditional Medical Ethics in Hungary. Jenei, Ilona.

Some Reflections on Postgraduate Medical Ethics Education. Levine, Robert J.

Telling Tales Out of School—Portrayals of the Medical Student Experience by Physician-Novelists. Bryant, Daniel C.

The Inadequacy of Role Models for Educating Medical Students in Ethics with Some Reflections on Virtue Theory. Erde, Edmund L.

The Rhetorical Force of Ambiguity: The No-Harm Argument in Medical Ethics (in Dutch). Van der Scheer, Lieke.

The Voices of Nurses on Ethics Committees. Rushton, Cindy Hylton.

Where is Truth? A Commentary from a Medical-Ethical and Personalistic Perspective (in Dutch). Schotsmans, Paul.

Where Is Will Rogers When We Need Him Most? Toward a Traditional Morality in Biomedical Ethics. Sample, Tex.

Zur Euthanasie-Diskussion in den USA: Eine kritische Einführung. Holderegger, Adrian.

## MEDICINE

"Decoding" Informed Consent: Insights from Women regarding Breast Cancer Susceptibility Testing. Geller, Gail, Strauss, Misha and Bernhardt, Barbara A (& others).

"Don't Think Zebras": Uncertainty, Interpretation, and the Place of Paradox in Clinical Education. Hunter, Kathryn.

"Más allá de "El nacimiento de la clínica": La comprensión de la "Anatomía General" de Bichat desde la *Naturphilosophie* de Schelling" in *El inicio del Idealismo alemán*, Market, Oswaldo. Montiel, Luis.

## MEDICINE

Retiring the Pacemaker. Reitemeier, Paul J, Derse, Arthur R and Spike, Jeffrey.

Santo Tomás de Aquino y la Medicina. Sacchi, Mario Enrique.

Scientific Misconduct: Ill-Defined, Redefined. Palca, Joseph.

Sick with Passion. Louch, Alfred.

Staring at Our Future. Iserson, Kenneth V.

Teaching the Virtues: Justifications and Recommendations. Gauthier, Candace Cummins.

The Advisory Committee on Human Radiation Experiments: Reflections on a Presidential Commission. Faden, Ruth.

The Baby K Case: A Search for the Elusive Standard of Medical Care. Schneiderman, Lawrence J and Manning, Sharyn.

The Best-Interests Standard as Threshold, Ideal, and Standard of Reasonableness. Kopelman, Loretta M.

The Biological Child. MacKellar, Calum.

The Blessings of Injustice: Animals and the Right to Accept Medical Treatment. Stell, Lance K.

The Christian Physician in the Non-Christian Institution: Objections of Conscience and Physician Value Neutrality. Peppin, John F.

The Concept of Disease: Structure and Change. Thagard, Paul.

The Convention on Human Rights and Biomedicine of the Council of Europe. Dommel Jr, F William and Alexander, Duane.

The Crisis of Virtue: Arming for the Cultural Wars and Pellegrino at the Limes. Engelhardt Jr, H Tristram.

The Eclipse of the Individual in Policy (Where is the Place for Justice?). Bliton, Mark J and Finder, Stuart G.

The Evolving Health Care Marketplace: How Important is the Patient?. Berkowitz, Eric N.

The Forum. Gluck, John P and Shapiro, Kenneth J.

The Gastroenterologist and His Endoscope: The Embodiment of Technology and the Necessity for a Medical Ethics. Cooper, M Wayne.

The Historical Setting of Latin American Bioethics. Gracia, Diego.

The Inadequacy of Role Models for Educating Medical Students in Ethics with Some Reflections on Virtue Theory. Erde, Edmund L.

The Kevorkian Challenge. Picchioni, Anthony.

The Relation between Concepts of Quality-of-Life, Health and Happiness. Musschenga, Albert W.

The Social Concept of Disease. Räikkä, Juha.

The Three Deadly Sins of Ethics Consultation. Howe, Edmund G.

Theological Foundations for Death and Dying Issues. Hollinger, Dennis.

Theoretical Medicine: A Proposal for Reconceptualizing Medicine as a Science of Actions. Lolas, Fernando.

Transporting Values by Technology Transfer. De Castro, Leonardo D.

Treating the Patient to Benefit Others. Klepper, Howard.

Trust: The Fragile Foundation of Contemporary Biomedical Research. Kass, Nancy E, Sugarman, Jeremy and Faden, Ruth.

Waarom het beoordelen van technologieën voor gehandicapten problematisch is. Blume, Stuart.

Waste in Medicine. Baumrin, Bernard.

Where Are the Heroes of Bioethics?. Freedman, Benjamin.

Why "Do No Harm?". Sharpe, Virginia A.

Why Bioethics Needs the Philosophy of Medicine: Some Implications of Reflection on Concepts of Health and Disease. Khushf, George.

Ziekte leven: Bouwstenen voor een medische sociologie zonder *disease/illness*-onderscheid. Mol, Annemarie and Pols, Jeannette.

## MEDIEVAL

see also Epistemology, Metaphysics, Religion

"A Medieval Model of Subjectivity: Toward a Rediscovery of Fleshliness" in *The Ancients and the Moderns,* Lilly, Reginald (ed). Brague, Rémi.

"Il linguaggio mentale tra logica e grammatica nel medioevo: il contesto di Ockam" in *Momenti di Storia della Logica e di Storia della Filosofia,* Guetti, Carla (ed). Maierù, Alfonso.

"Medieval Scholasticism and Averroism: The Implication of the Writings of Ibn Rushd to Western Science" in *Averroës and the Enlightenment,* Wahba, Mourad (ed). Bullough, Vern L.

"No Necessary Connection": The Medieval Roots of the Occasionalist Roots of Hume. Nadler, Steven.

"Some Traces of the Presence of Scepticism in Medieval Thought" in *Scepticism in the History of Philosophy: A Pan-American Dialogue,* Popkin, Richard H (ed). Beuchot, Mauricio.

'Pseudo-Dionísio Areapagita' ou 'Dionísio Pseudo-Aeropagita'? Uma confusao a respeito de nomes e descriçoes definidas. Perini Santos, Ernesto.

*A History of Philosophy: Volume I.* Hough, Williston S (ed & trans) and Erdmann, Johann Eduard.

*An Introduction to Medieval Philosophy.* Martin, Christopher F J.

*Averroës and the Enlightenment.* Wahba, Mourad (ed) and Abousenna, Mona (ed).

*Christian Philosophy: Greek, Medieval, Contemporary Reflections.* Sweeney, Leo.

*Forms of Transcendence: Heidegger and Medieval Mystical Theology.* Sikka, Sonya.

*La raíz semítica de lo europeo: Islam y judaísmo medievales.* Lomba, Joaquín.

*Medieval Philosophy, 2nd Edition.* Baird, Forrest E (ed) and Kaufmann, Walter.

*Medieval Thought.* Luscombe, David.

*The Truth about Everything.* Stewart, Matthew.

*Theories of Cognition in the Later Middle Ages.* Pasnau, Robert.

*Tolerantia*: A Medieval Concept. Bejczy, István.

A Fragment of Michael de Marbasio, Summa de modis significandi. Kelly, L G.

A los orígenes del pensamiento medieval español sobre la historia: Prudencio, Orosio, san Isidoro. Rivera de Ventosa, Enrique.

Approches du Moyen Age tardif. Bonino, Serge-Thomas.

Aquinas on Modal Propositions: Introduction, Text, and Translation. O'Grady, Paul.

Augustine's Three Visions and Three Heavens in Some Early Medieval Florilegia. Moreira, Isabel.

Burley's So-Called *Tractatus Primus*, with an Edition of the Additional *Quaestio* "Utrum contradictio sit maxima oppositio". De Rijk, L M.

Conrad of Megenberg: The Parisian Years. Courtenay, William J.

Conspecto do Desenvolvimento da Filosofia em Portugal (Séculos XIII-XVI). Santiago de Carvalho, Mário A.

Constitutionalism—Medieval and Modern: Against Neo-Figgisite Orthodoxy (Again). Nederman, Cary J.

El *De Numeris Datis* de Jordanus Nemorarius como sistema matemático de signos. Puig, Luis.

El Camino de Santiago y el descubrimiento racional de la naturaleza en los siglos XII y XIII. Ballester, Luis García.

El Ideario Pirrónico en el Oriente Medieval (Presencia y Divulgación). González Fernández, Martín.

Ente ed essenza in un saggio giovanile di Tommaso d'Aquino. Giorgini, Claudio.

Fuentes para la historia de la astronomia de los siglos XIV y XV. Eclipses y tablas. Lértora Mendoza, Celina A.

How To Do Things with Numbers: MacIntosh on the Possible Eternity of the World. Côté, Antoine.

Italo Mancini lettore di Agostino: Percorso e contenuti di un incontro. Cangiotti, Marco.

La définition du droit naturel d'Ulpien: sa reprise par Thomas d'Aquin et son actualisation comme critique des droits de l'homme. Ponton, Lionel.

La estructura formal del *De causa Dei* de Thomas Bradwardine. Verdú Berganza, Ignacio.

La prima scuola tomistica: Erveo di Nedellec e l'epistemologia teologica. Piccari, Paolo.

La tradizione ermetica a Oxford nei secoli XIII e XIV: Ruggero Bacone e Tommaso Bradwardine. Sannino, Antonella.

Leitura Medieval e Moderna de Descartes. Gonçalves, Joaquim Cerqueira.

Lógica filosófica medieval: San Anselmo y Guillermo de Occam. Trueba Atienza, Carmen.

Medieval Historiography. Birns, Nicholas.

Medieval Technology and the Husserlian Critique of Galilean Science. Casey, Timothy.

Note sur des *Accessus ad Macrobium.* Caiazzo, Irene.

Petrus Hispanus O.P., Auctor Summularum. D'Ors, Angel.

Philosophical Autonomy and the Historiography of Medieval Philosophy. Inglis, John.

Roger Roseth and Medieval Deontic Logic. Knuuttila, Simo and Hallamaa, Olli.

The Meaning of "Aristotelianism" in Medieval Moral and Political Thought. Nederman, Cary J.

The Reflection of Some Traditional Stoic Ideas in the Thirteenth-Century Scholastic Theories of Beauty. Bychkov, Oleg V.

Things in the Mind: Fourteenth-Century Controversies over "Intelligible Species". Perler, Dominik.

Tragedia e cristianesimo: Agostino e il platonismo spezzato. Todisco, Orlando.

Two Errors in the Most Recent Edition of Peter of Spain's *Summulae Logicales*. Skoble, Aeon James.

What is the Science of the Soul? A Case Study in the Evolution of Late Medieval Natural Philosophy. Zupko, Jack.

## MEDITATION

*Advice to the Serious Seeker: Meditations on the Teaching of Frithjof Schuon.* Cutsinger, James S.

*Meditations on First Philosophy: With Selections from the Objections and Replies.* Cottingham, John and Descartes, René.

Buddhist Meditation and the Consciousness of Time. Novak, Philip.

Descartes on the Power of "Ideas". Wagner, Stephen I.

Descartes on the Real Existence of Matter. Friedman, Michael.

Descartes's Ontology. Chappell, Vere.

Gli Affreschi nelle Celle del Dormitorio del Convento di San Marco: Devozione e Figurazione di Fra Angelico (in Japanese). Akari, Kitamura.

Kurosawa's Existential Masterpiece: A Meditation on the Meaning of Life. Gordon, Jeffrey.

L'immagine, il sermone, la meditazione: La pratica della orazione nel *Commiato di Cristo dalla Madre* di Lorenzo Lotto. Ciyori, Kitagaki.

Teaching Business Ethics Through Meditation. La Forge, Paul G.

## MEDITERRANEAN

*In Search of a Better World: Lectures and Essays from Thirty Years.* Popper, Karl and Bennet, Laura J (trans).

## MEHTA, J

Heidegger, Bhakti, and Vedānta—A Tribute to J.L. Mehta. Dallmayr, Fred R.

## MEIER, C

Making Exceptions: Some Remarks on the Concept of Coup d'état and Its History. Bartelson, Jens.

## MEIER, H

Taking Exception to Liberalism: Heinrich Meier's *Carl Schmitt and Leo Strauss: The Hidden Dialogue*. Vatter, Miguel E.

## MEIKLEJOHN, A

Must Constitutional Democracy Be "Responsive"?. Michelman, Frank I.

## MEINECKE, F

"L'immagine di Goethe e il pensiero storico (per una discussione dell'interpretazione di Meinecke)" in *Lo Storicismo e la Sua Storia: Temi, Problemi, Prospettive*, Cacciatore, Giuseppe (ed). Pica Ciamarra, Leonardo.

## MEINONG

"Gegenstandstheoretische Betrachtungen" in *Das weite Spektrum der analytischen Philosophie*, Lenzen, Wolfgang. Haller, Rudolf.

*Meinongian Logic: The Semantics of Existence and Nonexistence*. Jacquette, Dale.

Characterizing Non-Existents. Kroon, Frederick W.

Object Theory Foundations for Intensional Logic. Jacquette, Dale.

The Simplest Meinongian Logic. Pasniczek, Jacek.

## MEIXNER, U

Meixner über Parmenides (Zu Uwe Meixner: Parmenides und die Logik der Existenz) *Grazer Philosophische Studien* 47, (1994). Tegtmeier, Erwin.

## MELANCHOLY

Descartes et la mélancholie. Darriulat, Jacques.

Prudence, Folly and Melancholy in the Thought of Thomas Hobbes. Borrelli, Gianfranco.

Tra stupore e malinconia: Osservazioni sul pensiero di G. Leopardi. Franchi, Alfredo.

## MELE, A

Deviant Causal Chains and the Irreducibility of Teleological Explanation. Sehon, Scott.

## MELISSUS OF SAMOS

De lo eterno a lo infinito: un intento de reconstrución del argumento de Meliso (B2-4 D-K). Bredlow, Luis.

## MELLO E SOUZA, G

Country Fashion (in Portuguese). Arantes, Otília Beatriz Fiori and Arantes, Paulo Eduardo.

Gilda de Mello e Souza (in Portuguese). Prado Júnior, Bento.

## MELLOR, D

Taking Hindrance Seriously. Beebee, Helen.

The Facts of Causation. Mellor, D H.

The New B-Theory's *Tu Quoque* Argument. Craig, William Lane.

Truth Conditions of Tensed Sentence Types. Paul, L A.

## MELNYK, A

How Reasons Explain Behaviour: Reply to Melnyk and Noordhof. Dretske, Fred.

## MELODY

Melody in Life: Some Reflections. Roy, Subrata.

## MELVIL, Y

Yuri K. Melvil and American Pragmatism. Ryder, John.

## MEMBERSHIP

Essential Membership. LaPorte, Joseph.

## MEMORY

"Marcel Proust e i 'miracoli' della memoria involontaria" in *Il Concetto di Tempo: Atti del XXXII Congresso Nazionale della Società Filosofica Italiana*, Casertano, Giovanni (ed). Perna Marano, Enrica.

"Tempo, uomo e memoria nella *Teogonia* di Esiodo" in *Il Concetto di Tempo: Atti del XXXII Congresso Nazionale della Società Filosofica Italiana*, Casertano, Giovanni (ed). Rotondaro, Serafina.

*Memory, Identity, Community: The Idea of Narrative in the Human Sciences*. Hinchman, Lewis P (ed) and Hichmann, Sandra K (ed).

*On Dialogue*. Nichol, Lee (ed) and Bohm, David.

*The Shape of the Past*. Graham, Gordon.

About Ends: On the Way in Which the End is Different from an Ending. Steedman, Carolyn.

Beside us, in Memory. Olkowski, Dorothea.

Can People Think?. De Bruijn, N G.

Commentary. White, Hayden.

Commentary on "Loopholes, Gaps, and What is Held Fast". Code, Lorraine.

Debbo io ricordare? L'arte e la negazione della memoria. Fisch, Harold.

Denying the Body? Memory and the Dilemmas of History in Descartes. Reiss, Timothy J.

Due corsi della vita: la memoria e l'oblio. Wollheim, Richard.

Externalism and Memory. Brueckner, Anthony.

Forgiare e dimenticare: i doveri dell'oblio. Lowenthal, David.

History and Memory. Geremek, Bronislaw.

Holocaust Memories and History. Turner, Charles.

Il delirio della memoria e la memoria come delirio. Ballerini, Arnaldo.

Il velo e il fiume: Riflessioni sulle metafore dell'oblio. Rigotti, Francesca.

Interlocution, Perception, and Memory. Burge, Tyler.

La percezione è il "bordo d'attacco" della memoria?. Dennett, Daniel C.

Loopholes, Gaps, and What is Held Fast: Democratic Epistemology and Claims to Recovered Memories. Potter, Nancy.

Memory and Intuition: A Focal Debate in Fourteenth Century Cognitive Psychology. Adams, Marilyn McCord and Wolter, Allan B.

Memory, Forgetfulness, and History. Ricoeur, Paul.

Memory: A Logical Learning Theory Account. Rychlak, Joseph F.

Mourning, Memory, and Identity: A Comparative Study of the Constitution of the Self in Grief. Olberding, Amy.

On Originating and Presenting Another Time. Scott, Charles E.

On the Properties of a Network that Associates Concepts on Basis of Share of Components and Its Relation with the Conceptual Memory of the Right Hemisphere. Van Loocke, Philip.

Per una ontologia del ricordare. Papi, Fulvio.

Personal Identity and the Coherence of *Q*-Memory. Collins, Arthur W.

Ricordo e oblio: La Germania dopo le sconfitte nelle due guerre mondiali. Nolte, Ernst.

Self-Ascription, Self-Knowledge, and the Memory Argument. Goldberg, Sanford C.

Sobre la Facticidad de la Memoria. Schumacher, Christian.

Social Externalism and Memory: A Problem?. Ludlow, Peter.

Sulla nostalgia: La memoria tormentata. Starobinski, Jean.

Testimony, Memory and the Limits of the *A Priori*. Christensen, David and Kornblith, Hilary.

The Ends of Pedagogy: From the Dialectic of Memory to the Deconstruction of the Institution. Trifonas, Peter.

The Invention of History and the Reinvention of Memory. Motzkin, Gabriel.

The Soul of Knowledge. Allen, Barry.

The Writing of History as Remembering the Future (in Serbo-Croatian). Rauscher, Josef.

Theorie als Gedächtniskunst. Soentgen, Jens.

What Matters About Memory. Cherry, Christopher.

## MEN

*see also* Male

Asymmetric Perceptions of Ethical Frameworks of Men and Women in Business and Nonbusiness Settings. Schminke, Marshall and Ambrose, Maureen L.

Did the Enlightenment Just Happen to Men?. Whyte, Philip.

Ein Mann sieht vor lauter Welle das Wasser nicht. Overdiek, Anja.

Ethical Differences Between Men and Women in The Sales Profession. Dawson, Leslie M.

Good Women and Bad Men: A Bias in Feminist Research. Landau, Iddo.

The Dance of Dependency: A Genealogy of Domestic Violence Discourse. Ferraro, Kathleen J.

## MENCIUS

A Defence of Mencius' Ethical Naturalism. Ryan, James A.

Human Nature and Biological Nature in Mencius. Bloom, Irene.

Mencius on *Jen-Hsing*. Shun, Kwong-loi.

On a Comprehensive Theory of *Xing* (Naturality) in Song-Ming Neo-Confucian Philosophy: A Critical and Integrative Development. Cheng, Chung-ying.

On Avoiding Domination in Philosophical Counseling. Kerr, Donna H and Buchmann, Margret.

Two Mencian Political Notions in Tokugawa Japan. Tucker, John Allen.

## MENDELSSOHN

La cohérence de la théorie esthétique de Moses Mendelssohn. Dumouchel, Daniel.

## MENDUS, S

Mendus on Philosophy and Pervasiveness. Landau, Iddo.

## MENGER, A

*An Essay on Rights* by Hillel Steiner. Wolff, Jonathan.

## MENGER, C

Universals and the *Methodenstreit*: a Re-examination of Carl Menger's Conception of Economics as an Exact Science. Mäki, Uskali.

## MENGER, K

Menger's Trace in Fuzzy Logic. Trillas, Enric.

## MENTAL

"Actions, Causes, and Mental Ascriptions" in *Objections to Physicalism*, Robinson, Howard (ed). Gillett, Grant.

"I'm a Mother, I Worry" in *Contents*, Villanueva, Enrique (ed). Antony, Louise M.

"Kim on the Exclusion Problem" in *Contents*, Villanueva, Enrique (ed). Campos, Manuel.

"Mental Causation: A Query for Kim" in *Contents*, Villanueva, Enrique (ed). Tomberlin, James E.

"Mental Causation: What? Me Worry?" in *Contents*, Villanueva, Enrique (ed). Kim, Jaegwon.

"Mental Paint and Mental Latex" in *Perception*, Villanueva, Enrique (ed). Block, Ned.

"The Grammar of Chomsky is not Mentalist" in *Verdad: lógica, representación y mundo*, Villegas Forero, L. Peris-Viñé, Luis M.

*Unfolding Meaning: A Weekend of Dialogue with David Bohm*. Bohm, David.

A Furry Tile about Mental Representation. Brown, Deborah J.

A Tentative Discussion on the Common Mental Attributes of the Han Nationality. Xiyuan, Xiong.

Accidental Associations, Local Potency, and a Dilemma for Dretske. Noordhof, Paul.

Analog Representation Beyond Mental Imagery. Blachowicz, James.

Analyzing Mental Demonstratives. Jarrett, Greg.

Aristotle on How to Define a Psychological State. Wedin, Michael V.

Awareness, Mental Phenomena and Consciousness: A Synthesis of Dennett and Rosenthal. Rockwell, Teed.

## METAPHYSICS

Against Nagel: In Favor of a Compound Human Ergon. Christie, Juliette.

Agency and Obligation. Horty, John F.

Ahārya Cognition in Navya-Nyāya. Dravid, N S.

Al-Ghazali on Necessary Causality in *The Incoherence of the Philosophers*. Riker, Stephen.

Alcuni rilievi sul nesso fra verità, libertà e temporalità nella filosofia di F. Nietzsche. Sacchi, Dario.

Alkinous: Explanation of Plato's Doctrines (in Hungarian). Somos, Róbert.

All the World's a Stage. Sider, Theodore.

American Ethnophobia, e.g., Irish-American, in Phenomenological Perspective. Embree, Lester.

Amor e Morte: Meditaçao Antropológica. Pinto, José Rui da Costa.

An Analysis of John Mbiti's Treatment of the Concept of Event in African Ontologies. Johnson, Clarence Sholé.

An Illusive Historiography of the View that the World is *Maya*: Professor Daya Krishna on the Historiography of Vedānta. Chandra, Suresh.

An Objection to Swinburne's Argument for Dualism. Stump, Eleonore and Kretzmann, Norman.

Analyse und Kontext des Wachsbeispiels bei Descartes. Petrus, Klaus.

Ancora su nuvole ed orologi. Messeri, Marco.

Ansätze zur physikalischen Untersuchung des Leib-Seele-Problems. Arendes, Lothar.

Anti-Realist Truth and Concepts of Superassertibility. Edwards, Jim.

Antonio Rosmini: Aristotele Esposto ed Esaminato. Masi, Giuiseppe.

Antropología y alteridad: De la naturaleza humana a la normalidad social. Lorite Mena, José.

Anything Goes: Goodman on Relevant Kinds. Pierson, Robert.

Aporías sobre el universo y su temporalidad a la luz de la filosofía de Leonardo Polo. Sanguineti, Juan José.

Aportaciones de Leonardo Polo para una teoría antropológica del aprendizaje. García Viúdez, Marcos.

Appraisal Theories of Emotions. Ben-Ze'ev, Aaron.

Approches du Moyen Age tardif. Bonino, Serge-Thomas.

Apresentaçao da metafísica de Malebranche. De Faria Blanc, Mafalda.

Are (Possible) Guises Internally Characterizable?. Voltolini, Alberto.

Are Possible, Non Actual Objects Real?. Marcus, Ruth Barcan.

Are PSI Effects Natural? A Preliminary Investigation. Mavroves, George I.

Are Qualia Just Representations? A Critical Notice of Michael Tye's *Ten Problems of Consciousness*. Levine, Joseph.

Aristotele e la fondazione henologica dell'ontologia. Brandner, Rudolf.

Aristóteles: Sobre las Ideas. Ariza, Sergio (trans), Gerena, Luis Alonso and Aristotle.

Aristotle *Metaphysics* H6: A Dialectic with Platonism. Harte, Verity.

Aristotle and Dedekind (in Czech). Geréby, György.

Aristotle and Others. Sharples, Bob.

Aristotle and the Question of Being as Being: Reflections on S. Rosen's *The Question of Being* (in French). Narbonne, Jean-Marc.

Aristotle on How to Define a Psychological State. Wedin, Michael V.

Aristotle on Reflective Awareness. Lokhorst, Gert-Jan C.

Aristotle on the Nature of *Logos*. Anton, John P.

Aristotle's *Child*: Development Through *Genesis, Oikos*, and *Polis*. McGowan Tress, Daryl.

Aristotle's Discussion of Time: an Overview. Bolotin, David.

Aristotle's Razor. Drozdek, Adam.

Arte, lenguaje y metafísica en las estéticas de Hegel y Adorno. Gutiérrez, Edgardo.

Articulación crítica de ontología y política en B. Spinoza. Fernández G, Eugenio.

Aspectos gnoseológicos de la noción de mundo. Padial Benticuaga, Juan José.

Astrology: Science, Pseudoscience, Ideology. Pruzhinin, Boris Isaevich.

Augustinus und die Entstehung des philosophischen Willensbegriffs. Horn, Christoph.

Authentic Existence and the Political World. Held, Klaus.

Authentische Entscheidungen und emotive Neurowissenschaft. Walter, Henrik.

Back to a Monstrous Site: Reiner Schürmann's Reading of Heidegger's *Beiträge*. Janicaud, Dominique.

Back to the Things Themselves: Introduction. Steinbock, Anthony J.

Basanta Kumar Mallik and the Negative. Walker, Mary M.

Being—An Approach to the Beginning of Hegel's *Wissenschaft der Logik* (in German). Von Sivers, Kathrin.

Believing Sentences. Vision, Gerald.

Bergson and the Language of Process. Mullarkey, John C.

Bergson et Nabert, lecteurs de Fichte. Vieillard-Baron, Jean-Louis.

Bergson, Duration and Singularity. Breeur, Roland.

Berkeley Revised: On the New Metaphysics for Social Epistemology. 90 Years After "Materialism and Empiriocrticism". Kassavine, Illia.

Bertrand Russell (in Polish). Mann, Golo.

Beside us, in Memory. Olkowski, Dorothea.

Between the Subject and Sociology: Alfred Schutz's Phenomenology of the Life-World. Costelloe, Timothy M.

Between Transcendental and Transcendental: The Missing Link?. Doyle, John P.

Bewusstes Leben und Metaphysik: Gespräch mit Dieter Henrich. Schefczyk, Michael and Murmann, Sven.

Beyond Postmodernism: Langan's Foundational Ontology. Calcagno, Antonio.

Beyond Realism and Idealism Husserl's Late Concept of Constitution. Zahavi, Dan.

Bioethics, Metaphysical Involvements, and Biomedical Practice. Fan, Ruiping.

Biological Matter and Perceptual Powers in Aristotle's *De Anima*. Scaltsas, Theodore.

Bits of Broken Glass: Zora Neale Hurston's Conception of the Self. Sartwell, Crispin.

Blanchot/Levinas: Interruption (On the Conflict of Alterities). Bruns, Gerald L.

Body-Subjectivity in Psychiatry: The Initial Argument. Mondal, Parthasarathi.

Borges and the Refutation of Idealism: A Study of "Tlön, Uqbar, Orbis Tertius". Stewart, Jon.

Boris Uexkülls Aufzeichnungen Zum Subjektiven Geist—Eine Vorlesungsnachschrift?. Kreysing, Helmuth.

Born to Affirm the Eternal Recurrence: Nietzsche, Buber, and Springsteen. Cohen, Jonathan.

Boundaries, Continuity, and Contact. Varzi, Achille C.

Buddhist Conception of Reality. Tola, Fernando and Dragonetti, Carmen.

Buddhist Critique of Relation with Special Reference to *Samavᵃya*. Bhatt, S R.

Buddhist Meditation and the Consciousness of Time. Novak, Philip.

Bundles and Indiscernibility: A Reply to O'Leary-Hawthorne. Vallicella, William F.

Burley's So-Called *Tractatus Primus*, with an Edition of the Additional *Quaestio* "Utrum contradictio sit maxima oppositio". De Rijk, L. M.

Caminhos da Filosofia ou a Razao e o Desejo. De Fraga, Gustavo.

Carlo Carrà's Metaphysical Painting—The Works Reproduced in *Valori Plastici* (in Japanese). Demura, Masaya.

Categoricalist versus Dispositionalist Accounts of Properties. Armstrong. David M.

Causality and Demonstration: An Early Scholastic *Posterior Analytics* Commentary. Wood, Rega and Andrews, Robert.

Causation and Intensionality: A Problem for Naturalism. Rheinwald, Rosemarie.

Characterizing Non-Existents. Kroon, Frederick W.

Chief Bumbu en de Verklaring van Menselijk Gedrag. Mackor, Anne Ruth and Peijnenburg, Jeanne.

Ciencia y docencia en Agustín y Tomás de Aquino: (Del maesto agustiniano al maestro tomista). Pérez-Estévez, Antonio.

Coincidence and Principles of Composition. Levey, Samuel.

Coincident Objects: Could a 'Stuff Ontology' Help?. Zimmerman, Dean W.

Coinciding Objects: Reply to Lowe and Denkel. Burke, Michael B.

Come pensare diversamente l'identico: incontrovertibilità dell'essere e irreversibilità del tempo. Penati, Giancarlo.

Comentario a la *Reprensión de la metafísica de Renato Descartes, Benito Espinosa y Juan Locke*: Un añadido a la *Ciencia Nueva*. Verene, Donald Phillip.

Commentary on the AAS Panel: Shun, Bloom, Cheng, and Birdwhistell. Neville, Robert Cummings.

Commitment and the Bond of Love. Van Hooft, Stan.

Cómo he de criticar a Zubiri o "Much Ado about Nothing": Contrarréplica heterodoxa a Rafael Martínez Castro. Wessell, Leonard P.

Complex Predicates and Conversion Principles. Swoyer, Chris.

Concepts of Space in Greek Thought. White, Michael J.

Connatural Knowledge. Thomas, James.

Conocimiento del alma después de la muerte: Presentación de la doctrina de Santo Tomás de Aquino expuesta en las *Quaestiones disputatae de veritate q. 19 a. 1. Rodrigo Ewart, Luis*.

Conoscenza metafisica dell'esistenza. Possenti, Vittorio.

Consciousness and Connectionism—The Problem of Compatability of Type Identity Theory and of Connectionism. Potrc, Matjaz.

Consciousness and Self-Awareness—Part I: $Consciousness_1$, $Consciousness_2$, and $Consciousness_3$. Natsoulas, Thomas.

Consciousness and Self-Awareness—Part II: $Consciousness_4$, $Consciousness_5$, and $Consciousness_6$. Natsoulas, Thomas.

Constructing a Hall of Reflection. Mulhall, Stephen.

Continuity, Contingency, and Time: The Divergent Intuitions of Whitehead and Pragmatism. Rosenthal, Sandra B.

Contrariety and "Carving up Reality". Elder, Crawford L.

Corporeal Substances and True Unities. Baxter, Donald L M.

Counterfactuals and Preemptive Causation. Ganeri, Jonardon, Noordhoof, Paul and Ramachandran, Murali.

Crane on Mental Causation. Child, William.

Crecimiento irrestricto y libertad en el pensamiento de Leonardo Polo. Riaza Molina, Carmen.

Criacionismo e Evoluçao Criadora: Leonardo Coimbra Perante Henri Bergson. Teixeira, António Braz.

Critical Notice of Fred Dretske *Naturalizing the Mind*. Seager, William.

Critical Notice of J. Gracia's *Individuation and Identity in Early Modern Philosophy*. Kronen, John D.

Critical Notice of J.J. MacIntosh and H.A. Meynell, eds. *Faith, Scepticism and Personal Identity: A Festschrift for Terence Penelhum*. Loptson, Peter J.

## METAPHYSICS

## METAPHYSICS

I rapporti tra scienza e metafisica. Marsonet, Michele.

I sandali di Ermes e lo spazio di De Kooning: Appunti per una possibile negazione dell'epelysìa di metaphysikà. Incardona, Nunzio.

Ideen, Wissen und Wahrheit nach Platon: Neuere Monographien. Hoffmann, Michael and Von Perger, Mischa.

Identidad personal, acontecimiento, alteridad desde Paul Ricoeur. Fornari, Aníbal.

Identidad Personal, Nacional y Universal. Tugendhat, Ernst.

Identidad, Constitución y Superveniencia. Bordes Solanas, Montserrat.

Il) Teichmüller e gli amici napoletani. Savorelli, Alessandro.

Il concetto di coscienza nella fenomenologia di E. Husserl e di E. Stein. Schulz, Peter.

Il delirio della memoria e la memoria come delirio. Ballerini, Arnaldo.

Il fondamento etico e metafisico del diritto. Bagolini, Luigi.

Il Platone insegnato da Hegel: Alcune considerazioni sul quaderno di Griesheim (Wintersemester 1825-1826). Bozzetti, Mauro.

Il problema del fondamento nella filosofia di Karl Jaspers. Carpentieri, Rosario.

Il trascendentale contenuto metafisico della realtà. Crescini, Angelo.

Imagery and the Coherence of Imagination: A Critique of White. Thomas, Nigel J T.

Imaginability, Conceivability, Possibility and the Mind-Body Problem. Hill, Christopher S.

Immanence and Light: Spinoza, Vermeer and Rembrandt (in Portuguese). Chauí, Marilena.

Immanence: A Life.... Deleuze, Gilles and Millett, Nick.

Immortalidad e Intelección según Tomás de Aquino. Téllez Maqueo, David Ezequiel.

Immortality of the Soul in Plato's Thought: The Phaedo Arguments and their Context. Thero, Daniel P.

In What Sense is Kripke's Wittgensteinian Paradox a Scepticism? On the Opposition between its Epistemological and its Metaphysical Aspects. Read, Rupert.

Incoherence in the Aristotelian Philosophy of Action? (Spanish). Bravo, Francisco.

Individualism, Individuation and That-Clauses. Rechenauer, Martin.

Inductive Confirmation, Counterfactual Conditionals, and Laws of Nature. Lange, Marc.

Infinity and the Relation: The Emergence of a Notion of Infinity in Derrida's Reading of Husserl. Maloney, Philip J.

Ingarden on Time: Part I (in Polish). Blaszczyk, Piotr.

Instinct of Nature: Natural Law, Synderesis, and the Moral Sense. Greene, Robert A.

Intellect, Will, and Freedom: Leibniz and His Precursors. Murray, Michael.

Intellectus principiorum: De Tomás de Aquino a Leonardo Polo (y "vuelta"). Fernandez Burillo, Santiago.

Interactionism and Physicality. Mills, Eugene.

Interpreting Gorgias's "Being" in On Not-Being or On Nature. Schiappa, Edward.

Intrinsic/Extrinsic. Humberstone, I Lloyd.

Introduction. Cometti, Jean-Pierre.

Introduction to Life, Art, and Mysticism. Van Stigt, Walter P.

Introspection and its Objects. Arnold, Denis G.

Intuition and Immediacy in Kant's Critique of Pure Reason. Kelley, Andrew.

Intuitive and Reflective Beliefs. Sperber, Dan.

Investigation of Things, Philosophical Counseling, and the Misery of the Last Man. Duessel, Reinhard.

Is Aquinas's Proof for the Indestructibility of the Soul Successful?. Cross, Richard.

Is Naturalized Epistemology Experientially Vacuous?. Barnhart, Michael G.

Is Subjective Materialism Possible? (in German). Delport, Hagen.

Is the Human Mind a Turing Machine?. King, David.

Is the See-Battle About to Be Lost? On Aristotle's De interpretatione, Ch. 9. A Reconstruction (in Czech). Cziszter, Kálmán.

Is There a Problem about Intentionality?. Beckermann, Ansgar.

Isaac Barrow on the Mathematization of Nature: Theological Voluntarism and the Rise of Geometrical Optics. Malet, Antoni.

It is What You Think: Intentional Potency and Anti-Individualism. Lalor, Brendan J.

Jenseits von Moderne und Postmoderne: Whiteheads Metaphysik und ihre Anwendungen in der theoretischen und praktischen Philosophie der Gegenwart. Hampe, Michael.

John Locke on Passion, Will and Belief. Losonsky, Michael.

Josiah Royce's Reading of Plato's Theaetetus. Glidden, David K.

Justifying the Perennial Philosophy. Meynell, Hugo.

Kant and the Imposition of Time and Space. Waxman, Wayne.

Kant e Beck face ao problema da "coisa-em-si". Alves, Pedro M S.

Kant oder Berkeley? Zum aktuellen Streit um den korrekten Realismus. Lütterfelds, Wilhelm.

Kant on Existence as a Property of Individuals. Djukic, George.

Kant Was Not Able to Distinguish True from False Experiences. Lorca, Daniel.

Kant y Husserl: El Problema de la Subjetividad. Montero Moliner, Fernando.

Kant's Doctrine of Categories: An Attempt at Some Clarification. Gupta, R K.

Kant's Refutation of Idealism. Palmer, Daniel E.

Kant, Frege, and the Ontological Proof (in Hebrew). Steinitz, Yuval.

Kantian Matters: The Structure of Permanence. O'Shea, James R.

Kants Schlussstein: Wie die Teleologie die Einheit der Vernunft stiftet. Freudiger, Jürg.

Karl Jaspers: The Person and His Cause, Not the Person or His Cause. Wisser, Richard.

Kausalität und singuläre Referenz: Eine sprachphilosophische Rekonstruktion des empirischen Realismus bei Kant. Wyller, Truls.

Keeping One's Distance from the Absolute: Blumenberg's Metaphorology between Pragmatics and Metaphysics (in Dutch). De Ruyter, Geertrui.

Kierkegaard on the Madness of Reason. Maybee, Julie E.

Kierkegaard on Tragedy: The Aporias of Interpretation. Jegstrup, Elsebet.

Kierkegaard's Dialectical Image of Human Existence in The Concluding Unscientific Postscript to the Philosophical Fragments. Krentz, Arthur A.

Kim on the Metaphysics of Explanation. Sabatés, Marcelo H.

Kim on the Mind—Body Problem. Horgan, Terence.

Kinesis versus logos en la filosofía de Leonardo Polo. Aspe A, Virginia.

Kripke's Critique of the Mind-Body Identity Theory (in Serbo-Croatian). Bogdanovski, Masan.

Kurosawa's Existential Masterpiece: A Meditation on the Meaning of Life. Gordon, Jeffrey.

L'antithomisme de Thierry de Freiberg. Imbach, Ruedi.

L'aporia del pensare fra scienza e storia. Tagliavia, Grazia.

L'apport avicennien à la cosmologie à la lumière de la critique d'al-Shahrastānī. Steigerwald, Diane.

L'arrivo del Discours e dei Principia,D in Italia: prime letture dei testi cartesiani a Napoli. Lojacono, Ettore.

L'astuzia della follia: Un'antologia di Lombroso. Savorelli, Alessandro.

L'atteggiamento metafisico come espressione del trascendentale nella soggettività. Rizzacasa, Aurelio.

L'Aurora degli Idoli: Una breva ricerca del senso dell'essere oltre Heidegger. Turchi, Athos.

L'esperienza del pensare: Indagine su un paradosso. Treppiedi, Anna Maria.

L'espressività del cielo di Marsilio Ficino, lo Zodiaco medievale e Plotino. Vescovini, Graziella Federici.

L'Esprit absolu de Hegel est-il Dieu?. Beauvais, Chantal.

L'essere, il nulla e il divenire: Riprendendo le fila di una grande polemica. Turoldo, Fabrizio.

L'infinité des attributs chez Spinoza. Boss, Gilbert.

L'otrepassamento del trascendentale classico quale terza via della metafisica. Cavaciuti, Santino.

L'uomo superiore dopo la morte di Dio: Appunti di lettura. Campioni, Giuliano.

La "Freiheitsschrift" del 1809 come momento·decisivo tra la filosofia dell'identità e il rilievo dell'esistenza nel pensiero di Schelling. Millucci, Marco.

La causalidad material de los elementos en la generación de los cuerpos mixtos. Sacchi, Mario Enrique.

La concepción del espacio en la física de Santo Tomás de Aquino. Sacchi, Mario Enrique.

La concepción wittgensteiniana de los objetos en el Tractatus. García Berger, Mario.

La conception maritainienne de l'intelligence humaine dans antimoderne. Allard, Jean-Louis.

La conscience n'est pas suject: pour un matérialisme authentique. Kail, Michel.

La contingence dans la mécanique hégélienne. Février, Nicolas.

La contradiction du stoïcisme. Gobry, Ivan.

La creación de la nada: ¿apoteosis de la producción o misterio revelado?. Rivera, José A.

La criatura es hecha como comienzo o principio. Pérez Guerrero, Fco Javier.

La demostración de la existencia de Dios a partir de la libertad. Moros Claramunt, Enrique R.

La Dialectique Ascendante du Banquet de Platon. Liberman, Gauthier.

La dignidad del hombre y la dignidad de la persona. Forment, Eudaldo.

La dignidad humana desde una perspectiva metafísica. Lobato, Abelardo.

La esencia del hombre como disponer indisponible. Urabayen Pérez, Julia.

La fable du psychologisme de Fries. Bonnet, Christian.

La fenomenología en Zubiri. Conill, Jesús.

La fidélité de Zénon envers Chypre. Gabaude, Jean-Marc.

La filosofia tra presenza e ulteriorità. Pieretti, Antonio.

La finalidad de la naturaleza humana: Alcance y actualidad de la cuestión. Reyes Oribe, Beatriz Eugenia.

La generación absoluta, según la exposición aquiniana de Aristóteles. Velázquez Fernández, Héctor.

La lógica de la identidad en G. Frege. Sánchez Sánchez, Juana.

La metafisica dell'ermetismo. Montini, Pierino.

La métaphysique aristolélicienne et son sosie cartésien. Cunningham, Henri-Paul.

La métaphysique du réalisme modal: régression ou enjeu véritable?. Nef, Frédéric.

La Meteorología de Suárez de Urbina: Filosofía, Filokalia, Cosmología o sólo "Folklórica"?. Muñoz García, Angel.

La necesidad como totalidad de la posibilidad en Leibniz. Socorro Fernández, María.

## METAPHYSICS

Naturalism and Self-Defeat: Plantinga's Version. Nathan, N M L.

Naturalizing Metaphysics. Saunders, Simon.

Nature and Human Nature in an Existential Perspective. Jackson, Arthur F.

Naturphilosophie zwischen Naturwissenschaft und Philosophie: Neue Sammelbände zur Naturphilosophie des deutschen Idealismus. Ziche, Paul.

Neighbors in Death. Crowell, Steven Galt.

Nietzsche "On Apostates" and Divine Laughter. Neeley, G Steven.

Nietzsche as a Theological Resource. Westphal, Merold.

Nietzsche bei Heidegger und Fink. Ebeling, Hans.

Nietzsche e il nichilismo contemporaneo. Volpi, Franco.

Nietzsche in Dr. Antonio Pérez Estévez's Thought (Spanish). Delgado Ocando, José Manuel.

Nietzsche on Socrates as a Source of the Metaphysical Error. Harwood, Larry D.

Nietzsche's Kinesthetics (in Serbo-Croatian). Grätzel, Stephan.

Nihilism and Beatitude. Birault, Henri.

Nihilismo y metáfora: La fábula imaginera en Vico y Nietzsche. Marín-Casanova, José Antonio.

Nirodha, Yoga Praxis and the Transformation of the Mind. Whicher, Ian.

Noetic Philosophizing: Rhetoric's Displacement of Metaphysics *Alcestis* and *Don Quixote*. Baer, Eugen.

Non-Basic Time and Reductive Strategies: Leibniz's Theory of Time. Cover, J A.

Nonreductive Naturalism. Silvers, Stuart.

Norm and End: A Kantian Theory of Action (in French). Joós, Jean-Ernest.

Norman Malcolm, *Wittgensteinian Themes*. Winch, Peter.

Nota sobre el no reduccionismo y la realizabilidad variable. Rabossi, Eduardo.

Notas sobre el origen del hombre y la técnica. Díaz Caballero, José Ricardo.

Note sulle polemiche antifrancesi di Vico. Agrimi, Mario.

Notes on Peirce's Objective Idealism. Sokolowski, William R.

Notule sur le commentaire du *Liber de causis* de Siger de Brabant et ses rapports avec Thomas d'Aquin. Imbach, Ruedi.

Noumenal Causality Reconsidered: Affection, Agency, and Meaning in Kant. Westphal, Kenneth R.

Nyāya is Realist par Excellence (A supplementary note). Dravid, N S.

Nyāya Realism: Some Reflections. Sharma, Ramesh Kumar.

Nyāya: Realist or Idealist?. Bhattacharya, Sibajiban.

O argumento ontológico em Platao: (I) O problema da imortalidade. Mesquita, António Pedro.

O argumento ontológico em Platao: (II) A imortalidade do problema. Mesquita, António Pedro.

O Conimbricense Manuel Góis e a Eternidade do Mundo. Martins, António Manuel.

O Homem da Evoluçao Temporal. Alves, Vitorino M de Sousa.

O Mais Antigo Programa de Sistema do Idealismo Alemao. Carmo Ferreira, Manuel J do.

O Modelo Psicofisiológico Cartesiano e o Materialismo das Luzes. Nascimento, Maria das Graças S.

O positivismo científico de Anteno de Quental. Brito, Maria Amélia.

O tema da existência na *Nova Dilucidatio* de Kant. Viegas, Pedro.

Of Existence and Serenity: An Essay in Nonconceptual Awareness. Onigbinde, Akinyemi.

Of the *Chora*. Sallis, John.

On a Comprehensive Theory of *Xing* (Naturality) in Song-Ming Neo-Confucian Philosophy: A Critical and Integrative Development. Cheng, Chung-ying.

On Alan Turing's Anticipation of Connectionism. Copeland, B Jack and Proudfoot, Diane.

On Aristotle's 'Animal Capable of Reason'. Goodey, C F.

On Being Equally Free and Unequally Restricted. Samraj, Tennyson.

On Imagination—A Correspondence with Prof. Zhang Longxi. Yuanhua, Wang.

On Ingardenian and Thomistic Conceptions of Being (in Polish). Wojtysiak, Jacek.

On Originating and Presenting Another Time. Scott, Charles E.

On Speaking: A Phenomenological Recovering of a Forgotten Sense. Anton, Corey.

On Studying Dostoevskii. Florovskii, Georgii.

On Substances, Accidents and Universals: In Defence of a Constituent Ontology. Smith, Barry.

On the Applicability of the Quantum Measurement Formalism. Chang, Hasok.

On the Impossibility of David Lewis' Modal Realism. Maudlin, Tim.

On the Intentionality of Moods: Phenomenology and Linguistic Analysis. Arregui, Jorge V.

On the Main Articles in this Issue. Horák, Petr.

On the Nature of the Absolute: A Response to Desmond. Coolidge Jr, Francis P.

On the Necessary Existence of Numbers. Tennant, Neil.

On the Not-Being of Gorgias's *On Not-Being* (ONB). Gagarin, Michael.

On the Notion of Cause 'Philosophically Speaking'. Steward, Helen.

On the Ontological Determination of the States of Affairs (in German). Hüntelmann, Rafael.

On the Possibility of Rational Free Action. Clarke, Randolph.

On the Possibility of Self-Transcendence: Philosophical Counseling, Zen, and the Psychological Perspective. Blass, Rachel B.

Oneself as Oneself and Not as Another. Johnstone, Albert A.

Ontología y conocimiento en M. Merleau-Ponty. Arce Carrascoso, José Luis.

Ontological "Proofs" in Descartes and Sartre: God, the "I," and the Group. McBride, William L.

Ontological Constraints and Understanding Quantum Phenomena. Folse, Henry J.

Ontology and Axiology. Hatzimoysis, Anthony.

Ontology and Ethics in Sartre's *Being and Nothingness*: On the Conditions of the Possibility of Bad Faith. Zheng, Yiwei.

Opening Words. Niiniluoto, Ilkka.

Orgasmic Rapture and Divine Ecstasy: The Semantic History of Ānanda. Olivelle, Patrick.

Orientierung über Orientierung: Zur Medialität der Kultur als Welt des Menschen. Orth, Ernst Wolfgang.

Otherness in J.P. Sartre's *Being and Nothingness* (Spanish). Iglesias, Mercedes.

Outline for a Theory of Action. Hernáez, Jesús.

Over Functies en Affordances. De Jong, H Looren and Schouten, M K D.

Panexperientialist Physicalism and the Mind-Body Problem. Griffin, David Ray.

Panpsychism and the Early History of Prehension. Ford, Lewis S.

Para uma Explicitaçao da Dialética Hegeliana entre o Senhor e o Escravo na Fenomenologia do Espírito. Ferreira Chagas, Eduardo.

Para una fenomenología de la muerte. Iribarne, Julia V.

Para una ontología del continuo. Pérez Herranz, Fernando-M.

Paralelismos entre el "Sofista" de Platón y el libro *Gamma* de la "Metafísica" de Aristóteles?. Königshausen, Johann-Heinrich.

Parmenides and the Battle of Stalingrad. Heller, Agnes.

Pascal croyait-il en la loi naturelle?. Vianty, Bernard.

Pascal e as Grandes Questoes do seu Tempo. Maia Neto, José R.

Pascal: A Busca do Ponto Fixo e a Prática da Anatomia Moral. Marton, Scarlett.

Passions of the Soul (in Czech). Descartes, René and Benes, Jiri (trans).

Patocka's Phenomenology of Meaning and Heidegger. Major, Ladislav.

Patricia Kitcher and "Kant's Real Self". Brown, David S.

Paul Virilio and the Articulation of Post-Reality. Hanes, Marc.

Paul Weiss's Methods(s) and System(s). Kennedy, Kevin E.

Pedagogy in the Myth of Plato's *Statesman*: Body and Soul in Relation to Philosophy and Politics. Hemmenway, Scott R.

Peirce on Norms, Evolution and Knowledge. Tiercelin, Claudine.

Peirce's Evolutionary Pragmatic Idealism. Burks, Arthur W.

Pensiero medievale e modernità. Gregory, Tullio.

Per una ontologia del ricordare. Papi, Fulvio.

Per una storia dei cartesiani in Italia: Avvertenza. Garin, Eugenio.

Perennidad y prosecución de la filosofía en el pensamiento de Leonardo Polo. Flamarique, Lourdes.

Persona: Intimidad, don y libertad nativa: Hacia una antropología de los transcendentales personales. Yepes, Ricardo.

Personal Receptivity and Act: A Thomistic Critique. Long, Steven A.

Perspectivismo Mitigado. Monteiro, Joao Paulo.

Pessimism, Nihilism, and the Nietzschean Response. Shah, Sankiv.

Phenomenological Personalism: Edith Stein and Karol Wojtyla (in Polish). Póltawski, Andrzej.

Phenomenology, Dialectic, and Time in Levinas's *Time and the Other*. Miller, Hugh.

Phenomenon and Sensation: A Reflection on Husserl's Concept of *Sinngebung*. Dodd, James.

Philosophical Counseling and Taoism: Wisdom and Lived Philosophical Understanding. Lahav, Ran.

Philosophical Counseling and the *I Ching*. Fleming, Jess.

Physicalism and Mental Causes: Contra Papineau. Moser, Paul K.

Plantinga's Case Against Naturalistic Epistemology. Fales, Evan.

Platao Revisitado: Ética e Metafísica nas Origens Platônicas. De Lima Vaz, H C.

Platao, Heraclito e a estrutura metafórica do real. Trindade Santos, José.

Plato's *Phaedrus*: Philosophy as Dialogue with the Dead. Zwicky, Jan.

Platonism at the Limit of Metaphysics. Sallis, John.

Pluralist Metaphysics. Daly, Chris.

Ponto de Partida da Ontologia: O Primeiro Princípio "O Ente é". Alves, Angelo.

Por qué no Descartes? Tres razones de actualidad. Gómez, Angel Alvarez.

Possibilities in Philosophy of Mind. Taliaferro, Charles.

Power and the Constitution of Sartre's Identity. Seitz, Brian.

Praktik: Überlegungen zu Fragen der Handlungstheorie. Angstl, Helmut.

Précis of *Past*, Space and Self. Campbell, John.

Predicative Interpretations of Spinoza's Divine Extension. Huenemann, Charles.

Preferring not to have been Born. Smilansky, Saul.

Presence and Post-Modernism. Mensch, James Richard.

Pressupostos Linguísticos do Conhecimento Ontológico da Identidade em Sao Tomás. Enes, José.

Primacía y dependencia metafísicas: consideraciones acerca de las ontologías de tropos. Bordes Solanas, M.

## METAPHYSICS

Problems of Existence—Recapitulation (in Polish). Hartman, Jan.

Process: An Answer to Lacey on Bergson. Howe, Lawrence W.

Prof. Shimony on "The Transient Now". Eilstein, Helena.

Professor Date's New Light on the Vedanta of Samkara. Sharma, M L.

Prolegómenos a uma ontologia da acçao. Barata-Moura, José.

Promiscuous Realism: Reply to Wilson. Dupré, John.

Putting the Puzzle Together: Part I: Towards a General Theory of the Neural Correlates of Consciousness. Newman, James.

Pythagorean Powers or A Challenge to Platonism. Pigden, Charles R and Cheyne, Colin.

Qualia und Physikalismus. Schröder, Jürgen.

Quantum Objects are Vague Objects. French, Steven and Krause, Décio.

Quasi-Formal Causality, or the Other-in-Me: Rahner and Lévinas. Purcell, Michael.

Quasi-Logicism (in Hebrew). Buzaglo, Meir.

Qué se sentiría ser Charlie Parker? (What is it like to be a bird?). Vargas Calvo, Jorge A.

Quelques réactions thomistes à la critique de l'intellect agent par Durand de Saint-Pourçain. Bonino, Serge-Thomas.

Quelques Réflexions sur la Philosophie de Leibniz (in Serbo-Croatian). Deretic, Milena.

R.G. Collingwood's Pragmatist Approach to Metaphysics. Requate, Angela.

Ragione e retorica: La mitologia bianca di Jacques Derrida. Harrison, Bernard.

Ralph Cudworth (1617-1688) sobre la infinitud de Dios. Robles, José A and Benítez, Laura.

Rational Self-Interest and Fear of Death: An Argument for an Agency Theory in Hobbes' Leviathan. Von Eschenbach, Warren J.

Rationality and Trustworthiness. Lehrer, Keith.

Realism and Resolution: Reply to Warren Goldfarb and Sabina Lovibond. Diamond, Cora.

Realism and Spacetime: Of Arguments Against Metaphysical Realism and Manifold Realism. Liu, Chuang.

Reality and Appearance in Bergson and Whitehead. Brougham, Richard L.

Reductionism and Nominalism in Descartes's Theory of Attributes. Nolan, Lawrence.

Reduktion und Ambivalenz: Zur Reflexionsstruktur von E. Lévinas' Autrement qu'être. Schällibaum, Urs.

Reflections on Iconicity, Representation, and Resemblance: Peirce's Theory of Signs, Goodman on Resemblance, and Modern Philosophies of Language and Mind. Dipert, Randall R.

Reflections on the Other (in Hebrew). Brinker, Menahem.

Reflexión y principio de la lógica en Hegel. Ezquerra Gómez, Jesús.

Reflexiones en torno a ser y tiempo de Martín Heidegger. Montero Anzola, Jaime.

Regress Arguments against the Language of Thought. Laurence, Stephen and Margolis, Eric.

Reiner Schürmann's Report of His Visit to Martin Heidegger. Adler, Pierre (trans).

Relativism and Truth: A Rejoinder to Lynch. Rappaport, Steven.

Relativism and Truth: A Reply to Steven Rappaport. Lynch, Michael P.

Relectura heideggeriana de Kant: el tiempo como horizonte ontológico y posibilidad de la metafísica. Hayling Fonseca, Annie.

Remarks on Disembodied Existence. Pecnjak, Davor.

Renaissance and Human Nature: Pico's "Dignity of Man". Dominioni, Stefano.

Replica a Emanuele Severino. Crescini, Angelo.

Replies. Campbell, John.

Reply to Child. Crane, Tim.

Reply to Noonan on Vague Identity. Lowe, E J.

Reply to Stump and Kretzmann. Swinburne, Richard.

Resolute Choice and Rational Deliberation: A Critique and a Defense. Gauthier, David.

Response to Kanthamani's Comment. Pradhan, R C.

Response to Pinkard. Beiser, Frederick C.

Rest for the Restless? Karl Rahner, Being, and the Evocation of Transcendence. Sanders, Theresa.

Retelling the Representational Story: An Anti-Representationalist's Agenda. Dartnall, Terry.

Ricoeur and Merleau-Ponty on Narrative Identity. Muldoon, Mark S.

Rorty's History of Philosophy as Story of Progress. Easton, Patricia.

Rosmini y Vico: la "filosofía italiana". Ottonello, Pier Paolo.

Russian Sophiology and Anthroposophy. Bonetskaia, N K.

Santayana's Sage: The Disciplines of Aesthetic Enlightenment. Alexander, Thomas M.

Santo Tomás de Aquino y la Medicina. Sacchi, Mario Enrique.

Sartre and Human Nature. Anderson, Thomas C.

Sartre and Ricoeur on Imagination. Busch, Thomas.

Sartre and the Self: Discontinuity or Continuity?. Goldthorpe, Rhiannon.

Sartre, Emotions, and Wallowing. Weberman, David.

Saving our Souls: Hacking's Archaeology and Churchland's Neurology. Taliaferro, Charles.

Saying What Aristotle Would Have Said. Tweedale, Martin M.

Scary Monsters: Hegel and the Nature of the Monstrous. Gunkel, David.

Scepticisme et Usage du Monde. Vincent, Hubert.

Schicksal und Charakter: Für die Philosophische Praxis ist vieles von Schopenhauer zu lernen: Vortrag auf dem Kolloquium der GPP am 30. Oktober 1994 in Tübingen. Achenbach, Gerd B.

Schleiermacher's Idea of Hermeneutics and the Feeling of Absolute Dependence. Vedder, Ben.

Scott-Kakures on Believing at Will. Radcliffe, Dana.

Searle on Consciousness and Dualism. Collins, Corbin.

Searle's Abstract Argument Against Strong AI. Melnyk, Andrew.

Searle's Regimen for Rediscovering the Mind. Hershfield, Jeffrey.

Selbstbewusstsein in der Spätantike: Neuere Untersuchungen zu Plotins Schrift V 3 [49]. Horn, Christoph.

Selbstbewusstsein: ein Problem der Philosophie nach Kant. Stolzenberg, Jürgen.

Self and Will. Nathan, N M L.

Self, Community, and Time: A Shared Sociality. Rosenthal, Sandra B.

Self, Deconstruction and Possibility: Maritain's Sixth Way Revisited. Armour, Leslie.

Self-Ascription, Self-Knowledge, and the Memory Argument. Goldberg, Sanford C.

Self-Construction and Identity: The Confucian Self in Relation to Some Western Perceptions. Yao, Xinzhong.

Self-Creating Selves: Sartre and Foucault. Morris, Phyllis Sutton.

Self-Knowledge and Embedded Operators. Williamson, Timothy.

Self-Observation. Martin, M G F.

Sendas Perdidas de la Razon (Cuando "el sueño de la razón produce monstruos"). Mate, Reyes.

Sensibility and Understanding. Millar, Alan.

Ser y hermenéutica: El relativismo contemporáneo o el nuevo funda-mentalismo laico. Camacho, Ramón Kuri.

Ser y no ser en el Sofista de Platón. Echauri, Raúl.

Shades of Consciousness. Girle, Roderic A.

Short Account of the Debates in the Higher Seminary of History of Philosophy, Catholic University in Lublin, in the Years 1953/54 to 1955/56 (in Polish). Strózewski, Wladyslaw.

Significación contemporánea de las nociones de experiencia y derecho natural según Santo Tomás de Aquino. Martínez Barrera, Jorge.

Silence Revisited: Taking the Sight Out of Auditory Qualities. Muldoon, Mark S.

Silvester Mauro, S.J. (1619-1687) on Four Degrees of Abstraction. Doyle, John P.

Simplicity and Why the Universe Exists. Smith, Quentin.

Sobre el concepto trascendental de Dios en Kant. Romerales Espinosa, Enrique.

Sobre el hacer humano: la posibilidad factiva. Franquet, Maria José.

Sobre el sentido común y la percepción: Algunas sugerencias acerca de la facultad sensitiva central. Posada, Jorge Mario.

Sobre el ser y la creación. García González, Juan A.

Sobre Hölderlin y los comienzos del Idealismo alemán. Serrano Marín, Vicente.

Sobre la idealidad de los significados en la filosofía de Husserl. Castilla Lázaro, Ramón.

Sobre una versión del nominalismo de semejanzas. Rodriguez Pereyra, Gonzalo.

Social Reality and Lu Jiuyuan (1139-1193). Birdwhistell, Anne D.

Socrates' Soul and Our Own. Jackson, Michael.

Socratic Anti-Empiricism in the Phaedo. Baltzly, Dirk.

Solipsism and First Person/Third Person Asymmetries. Child, William.

Solipsism and Self-Reference. O'Brien, Lucy F.

Solipsism and Subjectivity. Bell, David.

Solo un dios puede salvarnos todavía. Sanabria, José Rubén.

Some Like it Hot: Consciousness and Higher-Order Thoughts. Byrne, Alex.

Some Problems Concerning the Big Bang Theory of Creation. Guha, Debashis.

Some Problems of Approach to Nagarjuna's Philosophy (in Serbo-Croatian). Djordjevic, Dejan.

Souffrance et temps: Esquisse phénoménologique. Porée, Jérôme.

Space and Sociality. Malpas, Jeff.

Spinoza à la Mode: A Defence of Spinozistic Anti-Pluralism. Glouberman, Mark.

Spinoza's Demonstration of Monism: A New Line of Defense. Kulstad, Mark A.

Spinozistic Delusions (in Dutch). Steenbakkers, Piet.

Spirituality, Belief, and Action. Reese, Hayne W.

Strategies for Free Will Compatibilists. O'Leary-Hawthorne, John and Petit, Philip.

Substances are not Windowless: A Suarézian Critique of Monadism. Kronen, John D.

Sufficient Reason. Walker, Ralph.

Sufrimiento y humildad ontológica: Kant y Schopenhauer. Torralba Roselló, Francisco.

Sul duplice fine del matrimonio secondo la dottrina tomista. Seidl, Horst.

Superveniencia y determinación del contenido amplio. García-Carpintero, Manuel.

Susanne K. Langer and American Philosophic Naturalism in the Twentieth Century. Dryden, Donald.

Susanne K. Langer's Philosophy of Mind. Liddy, Richard M.

Sym-Phenomenologizing: Talking Shop. Casey, Edward S.

## METAPHYSICS

The Spinoza-Intoxicated Man: Deleuze on Expression. Piercey, Robert.
The Status of the *Dimensiones Interminatae* in the Thomasian Principle of Individuation. Morris, Nancy A.
The Structure of Time in Autobiographical Memory. Campbell, John.
The Sublime and Human Existence. Hurst, Andrea.
The Sublime and the Other. White, Richard J.
The Temporal Nature of Thought and Concepts of Life (Czech). Pstruzina, Karel.
The Theory of Appearing Defended. Langsam, Harold.
The Three Arrows of Zeno. Harrison, Craig.
The Transcendental Circle. Malpas, Jeff.
The Transformation of Things: A Reanalysis of Chuang Tzus Butterfly Dream. Gaskins, Robert W.
The Trick of Singularity. Millett, Nick.
The Unbearable Vagueness of Being. Levi, Don S.
The Validity of Indexical Arguments. Elkatip, S H.
The Will as the Genuine Postscript of Modern Thought: At the Crossroads of an Anomaly. Schalow, Frank.
The Worldhood of the the *Kosmos* in Heidegger's Reading of Heraclitus. De Oliveira, Nythamar Fernandes.
The 'Epochality' of Deleuzean Thought. Surin, Ken.
The 'I' and Personal Identity in Russell's Logical Atomism (in Dutch). Cuypers, Stefaan E.
The 'Late Seriousness' of Cora Diamond. Lovibond, Sabina.
Theory of Participation and Louis Lavelle's Philosophy (in Polish). Kielbasa, Jan.
There Might Be Nothing. Baldwin, Thomas.
There might be Nothing: The Subtraction Argument Improved. Rodriguez-Pereyra, Gonzalo.
Things in the Mind: Fourteenth-Century Controversies over "Intelligible Species". Perler, Dominik.
Thinking and Action in Hannah Arendt (in Portuguese). Simoes Francisco, Maria de Fátima.
Thisness and Time Travel. Adams, Robert Merrihew.
Thomas Aquinas and the Problem of Nature in Physics II, I. Lang, Helen S.
Thomas de Sutton, ou la liberté controversée. Putallaz, François-Xavier.
Thomas' Second Way: A Defense by Modal Scientific Reasoning. Trundle, Jr, Robert C.
Three Aspects of Rational Explanation. Pettit, Philip.
Three Prospects for Theodicy: Some Anti-Leibnizian Approaches. Romerales Espinosa, Enrique.
Time and Emptiness in the *Chao-Lun*. Berman, Michael.
Time and the Static Image. Le Poidevin, Robin.
Time of the Concept, Time of the Ritual (in Dutch). Cortois, Paul.
Time, Tense and Topology. Le Poidevin, Robin.
Timelessness and Creation. Craig, William Lane.
Timon of Phleius and the *Silloi* (in Czech). Steiger, Kornél.
Toch Geen Representaties? Een Reacties op J. Sleutels' Zonnebrandon-tologie. Buekens, F.
Topics and Investigations: Aristotle's *Physics* and *Metaphysics*. Lang, Helen S.
Totalidad y causalidad en Polo. Haya Segovia, Fernando.
Tractarian Support for a Nonpropositional Paradigm. Bozicevic, Vanda.
Transcendental Constraints and Transcendental Features. Sacks, Mark.
Transcendentalism and Speculative Realism in Whitehead. Bradley, James.
Transcendentalism, Nomicity and Modal Thought. Muresan, Valentin.
Translating Gorgias in [Aristotle] 980a10. Davis, Janet B.
Transzendentale Lebenslehre: Zur Königsberger Wissenschaftslehre 1807. Ivaldo, Marco.
Trascendentalità della metafisica. Laganà, Antonio.
Trascendentalità, inferenza e trascendenza: Dopo Kant e Heidegger. Penati, Giancarlo.
Trascendenza e trascendentalità in Kant. Masi, Giuseppe.
Troubles with Wagner's Reading of Millikan. Millikan, Ruth Garrett.
Truth and Success: Searle's Attack on Minimalism. Clark, Michael.
Two Books on the Elements of Physics (or One Movement) by *Proclus of Lykia (in Hungarian)*. Geréby, György.
Two Paradoxes in Heidegger. Margolis, Joseph.
Über das Verhältnis von Metaphysik und Physik bei Descartes. Hüttemann, Andreas.
Über die Intentionalität von Emotionen. Dorschel, Andreas.
Ulteriorità del pensare. Masi, Giuseppe.
Un *topos* in Hugo Grotius: *Etiamsi daremus non esse deum*. Negro, Paola.
Un aperçu de la "logique de la vie morale" chez Maurice Blondel. Létourneau, Alain.
Un convegno su *I filosofi e la genesi della coscienza culturale della "nuova Italia"*. Semino, Ignazio.
Una lettura possibile: A proposito de "I boschi narrativi" di Umberto Eco. Savorelli, Mirella Brini.
Unconfigured Tractarian Objects. Page, James.
Under the Sign of Failure. Fenves, Peter.
Understanding the Representational Mind: A Phenomenological Perspective. Marbach, Eduard.
Unpacking the Monad: Leibniz's Theory of Causality. Clatterbaugh, Kenneth and Bobro, Marc.
Van Inwagen and Gunk: A Response to Sider. Salsbery, Kelly Joseph.

Variedades de Superveniencia. Perez, Diana Inés.
Vasubandhu's Philosophical Critique of the Vātsiputrīyas' Theory of Person (I). Duerlinger, James.
Vernunft als Epiphänomen der Naturkausalität: Zu Herkunft und Bedeutung des ursprünglichen Determinismus J.G. Fichtes. Wildfeuer, Armin G.
Vico en Sciacca. Ottonello, Pier Paolo.
Vico lector de Espinosa (Sobre la reprensión de la *Etica*, II, 7 en la *Scienza Nuova*, 1744, 238). Remaud, Oliver.
Visiones del mundo: Lógica simbólica. Ortiz-Osés, Andrés.
Vom Begriff der Freiheit: Fichtes Leipziger Kant-Studien (1790). Lindner, Konrad.
Vom sprachlichen Zugang zum Absoluten. Mittmann, Jörg-Peter.
Vragen bij Hegels metafysische logica. De Vos, Ludovicus.
War Aristoteles ein Funktionalist? Überlegungen zum Leib-Seele-Problem. Perler, Dominik.
Was I Ever A Fetus?. Olson, Eric T.
Weakness of Will. Buss, Sarah.
Wechselgrundsatz: Friedrich Schlegels philosophischer Ausgangspunkt. Frank, Manfred.
West or Best? Sufficient Reason in the Leibniz-Clarke Correspondence. Grover, Stephen.
What Does Commonsense Psychology Tell Us about Meaning?. Richard, Mark.
What Does It All Come To? A Response to Reviews of *The Young Heidegger*. Van Buren, John.
What does McGinn Think we cannot Know?. Garvey, James.
What Good is Consciousness?. Dretske, Fred.
What is Computation?. Copeland, B Jack.
What is Metaphysics?. Dewan, Lawrence.
What is the Science of the Soul? A Case Study in the Evolution of Late Medieval Natural Philosophy. Zupko, Jack.
What Is the Status of Jiva (Individualised Soul) in the Samkarite Advaita Vedanta?. Dasgupta, Sanghamitra.
What Leibniz Thought Perennial. Hunter, Graeme.
What There Is, How Things Are. Ossorio, Peter G.
What What It's Like Isn't Like. Stoljar, Daniel.
What-Is? On Mimesis and the Logic of Identity and Difference in Heidegger and the Frankfurt School. Levin, David Michael.
Whitehead's Panpsychism as the Subjectivity of Prehension. McHenry, Leemon B.
Whitehead, Contemporary Metaphysics, and Maritain's Critique of Bergson. Bradley, James.
Why has the Question of the Meaning of Life Arisen in the Last Two and a Half Centuries?. Landau, Iddo.
Why is the Fifth Cartesian Meditation Necessary?. Haney, Kathleen.
Why One Shouldn't Make an Example of a Brain in a Vat. Davies, David.
Why Possible Worlds Aren't. Felt, James W.
Why We should Lose Our Natural Ontological Attitudes. Kovach, Adam.
William James on Free Will: The French Connection. Viney, Donald Wayne.
William James's Theory of Freedom. Gale, Richard M.
William of Ockham's Distinction between "Real" Efficient Causes and Strictly *Sine Qua Non* Causes. Goddu, André.
Witkacy and Eddington—Two Conceptions of Metaphysics (in Polish). Kosciuszko, Krzysztof.
Wittgenstein and the Doctrine of Kinaesthesis. Candlish, Stewart.
Wittgenstein, Heidegger and Humility. Cooper, David E.
Wittgenstein, Tolstoy and the Meaning of Life. Thompson, Caleb.
Yang Chu's Discovery of the Body. Emerson, John.
Yeshayahu Leibowitz—A Breakthrough in Jewish Philosophy: Religion Without Metaphysics. Sagi, Avi.
Yolton and Rorty on the Veil of Ideas in Locke. Dlugos, Peter.
Yvon Quiniou, il materialismo e l'impossibile immoralismo di Nietzsche. Franco, Vittoria.
Zeitalter der hermeneutischen Vernunft. Demmerling, Christoph.
Zénon, matérialiste et nominaliste?. Brinkman, Klaus.
Zu den kantischen und fichteschen Motiven bei Nicolai Hartmann. Hála, Vlastimil.
Zum Verhältnis von Existenz und Freiheit in Leibniz' Metaphysik. Buchheim, Thomas.
Zur Fichte-Darstellung in Hegels *Differenzschrift*. Kiss, Endre.
Zur Komplementarität von Freiheit und Notwendigkeit des menschlichen Handelns. Hoche, Hans-Ulrich.
Zur Lage der Philosophischen Praxis. Zdrenka, Michael.
Zur Rehabilitation des Unbewussten. Neubauer, Patrick.
Zwischen äusserem Zwang und innerer Freiheit. Aschoff, Frank.
Zwischen Sein und Setzen: Fichtes Kritik am dreifachen Absoluten der kantischen Philosophie. Bickmann, Claudia.
'Gloria' e 'Essere': Heidegger nel pensiero di hans urs von Balthasar. Rossi, Osvaldo.
'rnam krtvā ghrtam pibet'—Who Said This?. Bhattacharya, Ramkrishna.

## METATHEORY

*Finding Philosophy in Social Science*. Bunge, Mario.
*Zur Meta-Theorie der Physik*. Schröter, Joachim.
Cultural Psychology as Metatheory. Hoshmand, Lisa Tsoi.
Truth and Metatheory in Frege. Stanley, Jason.

## METCALFE, J

Metacognition and Consciousness: Review Essay of Janet Metcalfe and Arthur P. Shimamura (Eds) *Metacognition: Knowing about Knowing*. Kobes, Bernard W.

**METEMPSYCHOSIS**

Flesh, Grace and Spirit: Metempsychosis and Resurrection from Porphyry to Saint Augustine (in French). Dubreucq, Eric.

**METEOROLOGY**

*Alexander of Aphrodisias: On Aristotle's Meteorology 4.* Lewis, Eric (trans).

Die Motive der Atmosphäre um 1820 von C.D. Friedrich: im Zusammenhang mit L. Howards Meteorologie. Hitoshi, Egawa.

**METHOD**

*see also* Scientific Method, Socratic Method

"Conocimiento y libertad" in *Memorias Del Seminario En Conmemoración De Los 400 Anos Del Nacimiento De René Descartes*, Albis, Víctor S (ed). Díaz, Jorge Aurelio.

"Il segno e l'evento" in *Momenti di Storia della Logica e di Storia della Filosofia*, Guetti, Carla (ed). Sini, Carlo.

"Los momentos metodológicos en Aristóteles" in *Ensayos Aristotélicos*, Rivera, José Luis (ed). Morán y Castellanos, Jorge.

"Methods of Bioethics: Some Defective Proposals" in *Philosophical Perspectives on Bioethics*, Sumner, L W (ed). Hare, R M.

"Metodo e modelli storiografici nel tardo illuminismo tedesco" in *Lo Storicismo e la Sua Storia: Temi, Problemi, Prospettive*, Cacciatore, Giuseppe (ed). D'Alessandro, Giuseppe.

"Piovani e lo storicismo" in *Lo Storicismo e la Sua Storia: Temi, Problemi, Prospettive*, Cacciatore, Giuseppe (ed). Lissa, Giuseppe.

"Una Relación entre Diferentes: Ortega y Gasset y Gramsci" in *Política y Sociedad en José Ortega y Gasset: En Torno a "Vieja y Nueva Política"*, Lopez de la Vieja, Maria Teresa (ed). Calvo Salamanca, Clara.

*Aprender a filosofar preguntando: con Platón, Epicuro, Descartes.* Echeverría, José.

*La metáfora moderna del pensamiento.* Lorite-Mena, José.

*Lo stile de' Geometri:* La filosofia cartesiana nell'opera di Alessandro Pascoli (1669-1757). Guerrini, Luigi.

*Lo Storicismo e la Sua Storia: Temi, Problemi, Prospettive.* Cacciatore, Giuseppe (ed), Cantillo, Giuseppe (ed) and Lissa, Giuseppe (ed).

*Matemáticas, método y* mathesis universalis *en las* Regulae *de Descartes.* Arenas, Luis.

A Questao do Método em História da Educaçao. Fonseca Vieira, Márcia Núbia.

Beobachtungen zur Methodik in Fichtes *Grundlage der gesamten Wissenschaftslehre.* Meckenstock, Günter.

Biomathematics: Methods and Limits (in Portuguese). Castilho Piqueira, José Roberto.

Descartes según Leibniz. Silva de Choudens, José R.

Discours et Méthode. Boss, Gilbert.

Fawkes On Indicator Words. Smythe, Thomas W.

Giving the Skeptic Her Due?. Hughes, Christopher.

Gli oggetti e i metodi delle scienze secondo S. Tommaso. Fiorentino, Fernando.

I metodi dell'etica di Henry Sidgwick. Lecaldano, Eugenio, Schneewind, J B and Vacatello, Marzio.

Il Metodo della Filosofia della Religione di A. Sabatier. Savignano, Armando.

Kant und die Methode der Philosophie Zur Kant-Interpretation Massimo Barales. La Rocca, Claudio.

L'analyse cartésienne et la construction de l'ordre des raisons. Timmermans, Benoît.

L'arrivo del *Discours* e dei *Principia,D in Italia: prime letture dei testi cartesiani a Napoli. Lojacono, Ettore.

La *méthode* de Lipman: un outil dangereux de propagande auprès des enfants? Une réplique à Pierre Desjardins. Laberge, Jean.

La estructura formal del *De causa Dei* de Thomas Bradwardine. Verdú Berganza, Ignacio.

Metafisica e "transcendentali". Moscato, Alberto.

Método analítico y transcendentalidad. Blasco, Josep L.

No al Método Unico. Gutiérrez, Carlos B.

O "Romantismo", o "Enciclopedismo" e o "Criticismo" Manifestos no Magistério da Filosofia no Ensino Médio em Uberlândia. Pereira da Silva, Sérgio.

On Chihara's 'The Howson-Urbach Proofs of Bayesian Principles'. Howson, Colin.

On Schneewind and Kant's Method in Ethics (in Spanish). Ameriks, Karl.

On the Moral Philosophy of René Descartes: Or, How Morals are Derived from Method. Bagley, Paul J.

Philosophy, Solipsism and Thought. Mounce, H O.

Recalling the Hermeneutic Circle. Schmidt, Lawrence K.

Some Thoughts on Thinking and Teaching Styles. Schwerin, Alan.

Symmetry as a Method of Proof. Hammer, Eric.

System und Methode—Zur methodologischen Begründung transzendentalen Philosophierens in Fichtes *Begriffsschrift*. Stahl, Jürgen.

Teaching Styles that Encourage (and Discourage) Thinking Skills. Downs-Lombardi, Judy.

Um Problema no Ensino de Ciências: organizaçao conceitual do conteúdo ou estudo dos fenômenos. Pacheco, Décio.

**METHODOLOGICAL INDIVIDUALISM**

*Rationalität und Theoriebildung: Studien zu Karl R. Poppers Methodologie der Sozialwissenschaften.* Schmid, Michael.

**METHODOLOGY**

"Concepts: A Potboiler" in *Contents*, Villanueva, Enrique (ed). Fodor, Jerry.

"Critical Thinking" as a Teaching Methodology: A Questionable Idea at the Wrong Time. Kuczewski, Mark.

"Explaining Social Phenomena" in *Epistemology and History*, Zeidler-Janiszewska, Anna (ed). Mejbaum, Waclaw.

"Fodor's Concepts" in *Contents*, Villanueva, Enrique (ed). Higginbotham, James.

"Historians Look at Historical Truth" in *Epistemology and History*, Zeidler-Janiszewska, Anna (ed). Topolski, Jerzy.

"La dudas de Descartes y el lenguaje privado" in *Memorias Del Seminario En Conmemoración De Los 400 Anos Del Nacimiento De René Descartes*, Albis, Víctor S (ed). Thompson, Garret.

"Neurath against Method" in *Origins of Logical Empiricism*, Giere, Ronald N (ed). Cartwright, Nancy.

"Towards Cultural Relativism 'With a Small R'" in *Epistemology and History*, Zeidler-Janiszewska, Anna (ed). Kmita, Jerzy.

*Epistemology and History: Humanities as a Philosophical Problem and Jerzy Kmita's Approach to It.* Zeidler-Janiszewska, Anna (ed).

*Ethics for Professionals in Education: Perspectives for Preparation and Practice.* Strike, Kenneth A (ed) and Ternasky, P Lance (ed).

*Husserl's Position in the School of Brentano.* Rollinger, Robin Daryl.

*La Historia de la Filosofía como Hermenéutica.* Sánchez Meca, Diego.

*Mapping Reality: An Evolutionary Realist Methodology for the Natural and Social Sciences.* Azevedo, Jane.

*Mentoring the Mentor: A Critical Dialogue with Paulo Freire.* Torres, Amadeu (ed).

*Representation and the Text: Re-Framing the Narrative Voice.* Tierney, William G (ed) and Lincoln, Yvonna S (ed).

*Rule-Following and Realism.* Ebbs, Gary.

*Scientific Method: An Historical and Philosophical Introduction.* Gower, Barry S.

*Socratic Puzzles.* Nozick, Robert.

*The Fate of Place: A Philosophical History.* Casey, Edward S.

*The Significance of Popper's Thought.* Amsterdamski, Stefan (ed).

*Wittgenstein and the Philosophical Investigations.* McGinn, Marie.

A Longitudinal Examination of American Business Ethics: Clark's Scales Revisited. Harich, Katrin R and Curren, Mary T.

A Methodology for the Representation of Legal Knowledge: Formal Ontology Applied to Law. Tiscornia, Daniela.

A Pragmatic Theory of Causal Analysis. Shein, David.

Abstraktion und Ideation—Zur Semantik chemischer und biologischer Grundbegriffe. Gutmann, Mathias and Hanekamp, Gerd.

Advances in Peer Review Research: an Introduction. Stamps III, Arthur E.

Animating Rawls's Original Position. Regan, Thomas J.

Anti-Foundationalism and the Vienna Circle's Revolution in Philosophy. Uebel, Thomas E.

Antinomies of Practice and Research of Group Psychotherapy (in Serbo-Croatian). Opalic, Petar.

Aristotle's Rules of Division in the *Topics*: The Relationship between Genus and Differentia in a Division. Falcon, Andrea.

Braucht die Wissenschaft methodologische Regeln?. Wettersten, John.

Case Commentary. Flanigan, Rosemary.

Collingwood's "Lost" Manuscript of *The Principles of History*. Van der Dussen, Jan.

Computer Ethics and Moral Methodology. Van den Hoven, Jeroen.

Conflicts of Interest and Conflicts of Commitment. Werhane, Patricia and Doering, Jeffrey.

Counterexamples, Idealizations, and Intuitions: A Study in Philosophical Method. Prudovsky, Gad.

Critical Thinking Education Faces the Challenge of Japan. Davidson, Bruce W.

Critical Thinking Pedagogy: A Possible Solution to the "Transfer-Problem. Avery, Jon.

Critical Thinking, Critical Reasoning, and Methodological Reflection. Finocchiaro, Maurice A.

Descartes' Secular Paradise: The Discourse on Method as Biblical Criticism. Soffer, Walter.

Dialogic or Dialogistic? Dialogicity or Dialogism? A Word of Warning against Rigor Metodologiae. Itkonen, Matti.

El método de la filosofía en la filosofía moderna. Gómez Pardo, Rafael.

Ensayo de síntesis acerca de la distinción especulativo-práctico y su estructuración metodolón metodológica. Massini Correas, Carlos Ignacio.

Foucault's Analysis of Power's Methodologies. Scott, Gary Alan.

Genovesi e Cartesio. Marcialis, Maria Teresa.

Giambattista Vico y el actual debate sobre la argumentación jurídica. Pérez Luño, Antonio-Enrique.

Hannah Arendt on Hobbes. Bazzicalupo, Laura.

Hayden White: Meaning and Truth in History. Hammond, David M.

History and Periodization. Baker, Robert S.

History, Narrative, and Time. Mandelbrote, Scott.

If *p*, Then What? Thinking in Cases. Forrester, John.

Karl Popper's Political Philosophy of Social Science. Stokes, Geoff.

La méthodologie de la science constitutionnelle de la liberté. Sabete, Wagdi.

Lässt sich der Begriff der Dialektik klären?. Puntel, Lorenz.

Landmarks in Critical Thinking Series: Plato's Euthyphro. Spangler, Al.

Leo Strauss: lenguaje, tradición e historia (Reflexiones metodológicas sobre el arte de escribir). Blanco Echauri, Jesús.

Living in a Wittgensteinian World: Beyond Theory to a Poetics of Practices. Shotter, John.

## METHODOLOGY

Max Weber: Sugerencias para una "reconstrucción". Crespo, Ricardo F.
Method, Morality and the Impossibility of Legal Positivism. Toddington, Stuart.
Methodological Individualism in Proper Perspective. Jones, Todd.
Methodology and the Birth of Modern Cosmological Inquiry. Gale, George and Shanks, Niall.
Milgram, Method and Morality. Pigden, Charles R and Gillet, Grant R.
Mind and Method in the History of Ideas. Bevir, Mark.
Neurophenomenology: A Methodological Remedy for the Hard Problem. Varela, Francisco J.
New Blades for Occam's Razor. Lauth, Bernhard.
New Methods for Evaluating Arguments. Walton, Douglas.
Novelty, Severity, and History in the Testing of Hypotheses: The Case of the Top Quark. Staley, Kent W.
On the Main Articles in this Issue. Horák, Petr.
On the Question of Method in Philosophical Research. Reichling, Mary J.
On the Theoretical Basis of Prediction in Economics. González, Wenceslao J.
Opening Words. Niiniluoto, Ilkka.
Orientational Pluralism in Religion. Heim, S Mark.
Paramodern Strategies of Philosophical Historiography. Daniel, Stephen H.
Paul Weiss's Methods(s) and System(s). Kennedy, Kevin E.
Periodizing Postmodernism?. Carroll, Noël.
Psychische Vertrautheit und epistemische Selbstzuschreibung (in Serbo-Croatian). Frank, Manfred and Gordic, Aleksandar (trans).
Questioning and Thinking. Fasko, Jr, Daniel.
Reconstituting Praxis: Historialization as Re-Enactment. Flynn, Thomas R.
Sartre and Ricoeur on Imagination. Busch, Thomas.
Scientific Study of Religions: Some Methodological Reflections. Pathil, Kuncheria.
Severe Tests, Arguing from Error, and Methodological Underdetermination. Mayo, Deborah G.
Skepticism and Pyrotechnics. Kaplan, Mark.
Socrates versus Plato: The Origins and Development of Socratic Thinking. Ross, George MacDonald.
Some Problems in the Writing of the History of African Philosophy. Ogbogbo, C B N.
Some Remarks on Scientific Positivism and Constructivist Epistemology in Science. Vijh, Ashok K.
Symbols and the Nature of Teaching. Götz, Ignacio L.
Teaching Democracy Democratically. Worsfold, Victor L.
Ted Schoen on "The Methodological Isolation of Religious Belief". Ferré, Frederick.
The Blessed Gods Mourn: What is Living-Dead in the Legacy of Hegel. Cutrofello, Andrew.
The Contradictions of Free Market Doctrine: Is There a Solution?. McMurtry, John.
The Diatopical Hermeneutics: R. Panikkar's Response to the Scientific Study of Religions. Savari Raj, L Anthony.
The Empirical Character of Methodological Rules. Schmaus, Warren.
The Legacy of Lakatos: Reconceptualising the Philosophy of Mathematics. Ernest, Paul.
The Philosophical and Methodological Thought of N. I. Lobachevsky. Perminov, V Ya.
The Principles and Practices of Peer Review. Kostoff, Ronald N.
The Significance of R.G. Collingwood's *Principles of History*. Boucher, David.
The Soul of Knowledge. Allen, Barry.
Two Significant Problems in Education—the General One and the Particular One (in Serbo-Croatian). Babic, Jovan.
Understanding Bias in Scientific Practice. Shaffer, Nancy E.
¿Comparando qué? La "endeblez metodológica" de la ética según W. V. Quine y sus críticos. Rodríguez Alcázar, Javier.

## METRICS

A Hundred Years of Numbers: An Historical Introduction to Measurement Theory 1887-1990: Part II: Suppes and the Mature Theory: Representation and Uniqueness. Díez, José A.
Decidability Results for Metric and Layered Temporal Logics. Montanari, Angelo and Policriti, Alberto.
Domain Representability of Metric Spaces. Blanck, Jens.
Use and Misuse of Metrics in Research Evaluation. Kostoff, Ronald N.

## METZ, J

Messianic History in Benjamin and Metz. Ostovich, Steven T.

## MEXICAN

"Die spezifisch mexikanisch-lateinamerikanische Struktur des Geistes und ihr möglicher Beitrag zu weltweiter Freiheit" in *Kreativer Friede durch Begegnung der Weltkulturen*, Beck, Heinrich (ed). Basave Fernández, Augustin.
Between Apathy and Revolution: Nonviolent Action in Contemporary Mexico. Inda, Caridad.
From the Mexican Chiapas Crisis: A Different Perspective for Environmental Ethics. Szatzscheider, Teresa Kwiatkowska.
Importancia de la filosofía novohispana para el hispanismo filosófico. Beuchot, Mauricio.

## MEYER, E

"Con Aristotele, otre Aristotele: Meyer e l'antropologia" in *Lo Storicismo e la Sua Storia: Temi, Problemi, Prospettive*, Cacciatore, Giuseppe (ed). Silvestre, Maria Luisa.

## MEYERS, R

Interpreting Peirce's Interpretant: A Response To Lalor, Liszka, and Meyers. Short, T L.

## MEYNELL, H

Critical Notice of J.J. MacIntosh and H.A. Meynell, eds. *Faith, Scepticism and Personal Identity: A Festschrift for Terence Penelhum*. Loptson, Peter J.

## MICHALOS, A

A Pragmatic Approach to Business Ethics. Shaw, Bill.

## MICHELANGELO

El Greco's Statements on Michelangelo the Painter. Rodetis, George A.

## MICHELET, J

Michelet and Social Romanticism: Religion, Revolution, Nature. Mitzman, Arthur.

## MICHELSTAEDTER, C

"Del Sentire La Verità: Per Leopardi e Michelstaedter" in *Soggetto E Verità: La questione dell'uomo nella filosofia contemporanea*, Fagiuoli, Ettore. Carrera, Alessandro.
*Carlo Michelstaedter: il coraggio dell'impossibile*. Michelis, Angela.

## MICHNIK, A

Explorations in Morality and Nonviolence: Martin Luther King, Jr. and Adam Michnik. Baxter, Liliane Kshensky.

## MICROSCOPE

*The Invisible World: Early Modern Philosophy and the Invention of the Microscope*. Wilson, Catherine.

## MIGHT

An Update on "Might". Van der Does, Jaap, Groeneveld, Willem and Veltman, Frank.
Hierocracy either Sacradness of Authority (Spanish). Sánchez, Angel Martín.

## MILGRAM, S

Milgram, Method and Morality. Pigden, Charles R and Gillet, Grant R.

## MILITARY

Interpreting the *Jihad* of Islam: Militarism versus Muslim Pacifism. Churchill, Robert Paul.
Proposing 'Project Mankind'. Singh, Amita.
Rape as a Weapon of War. Card, Claudia.
The Laws of War and Women's Human Rights. Philipose, Liz.
War Is Not Just an Event: Reflections on the Significance of Everyday Violence. Cuomo, Chris J.

## MILL

"Consequentialism in Modern Moral Philosophy and in 'Modern Moral" in *Human Lives: Critical Essays on Consequentialist Bioethics*, Oderberg, David S (ed). Diamond, Cora.
"Desire and Desirability: Bradley, Russell and Moore versus Mill" in *Early Analytic Philosophy*, Tait, William W (ed). Gerrard, Steve.
"Religious Faith, Intellectual Responsibility, and Romance" in *The Cambridge Companion to William James*, Putnam, Ruth Anna (ed). Rorty, Richard.
*Classics of Modern Political Theory: Machiavelli to Mill*. Cahn, Steven M.
*Mill's On Liberty*. Dworkin, Gerald (ed).
*Perfect Equality: John Stuart Mill on Well-Constituted Communities*. Morales, Maria H.
*Trayectoria Voluntarista de la Libertad: Escoto, Descartes, Mill*. Alvarez-Valdés, Lourdes Gordillo.
A Comparative Study between Comte's and Mill's View on Women. Lang'at, Wilson K A.
Darwin's Origin and Mill's Subjection. Missimer, Connie.
Desires and Human Nature in J.S. Mill. Jenkins, Joyce L.
Esperando a Mill. Guisán Seijas, Esperanza.
Is Peer Review Overrated?. Shatz, David.
La recepción del Utilitarismo en el mundo hispánico: El caso de Ortega y Gasset. López Frías, Francisco.
Le projet fondationnel de Frege: De la nature du concept de nombre à la question de la preuve des lois de l'arithmétique. Djibo, Mamadou.
Making Sense of Mill. Weinstock, Daniel M.
Mill on Virtue as a Part of Happiness. Crisp, Roger.
Moral Synonymy: John Stuart Mill and the Ethics of Style. Burnstone, Dan.
On the Notion of Cause 'Philosophically Speaking'. Steward, Helen.
Philosophy in the Age of Thresholding. Erickson, Stephen A.
Recenti interpretazioni di J.S. Mill. Marchini, Pier Paolo.
Stuart Mill. Pardo Bazán, Emilia.
Why Tolerate? Reflections on the Millian Truth Principle. Cohen-Almagor, Raphael.

## MILLER, A

The Argument for Internalism: Reply to Miller. Smith, Michael.

## MILLER, C

Response to Miller's 'Comment'. Sumner, David and Gilmour, Peter.

## MILLER, D

Complexity and Deliberative Democracy. Femia, Joseph V.
Deduction, Induction and Probabilistic Support. Cussens, James.

## MILLER, F

Fred Miller on Aristotle's Political Naturalism. Keyt, David.
Political Rights in Aristotle: A Response to Fred Miller, Jr., *Nature, Justice, and Rights in Aristotle's Politics*. Gill, David.
The Promises and Perils of Pragmatism: Commentary on Fins, Bacchetta, and Miller. Tong, Rosemarie.

**MILLER, J**
The Concept of Act in the Naturalistic Idealism of John William Miller. Tyman, Stephen.

**MILLER, S**
Mathematics, Model and Zeno's Paradoxes. Alper, Joseph S and Bridger, Mark.

**MILLIANISM**
In Defence of a Radical Millianism. Nelson, John O.

**MILLIKAN, R**
Externalismo semántico y determinación del contenido: el enfoque teleológico de R. Millikan. Gomila Benejam, Antoni.
Individualism and Evolutionary Psychology (or: In Defense of "Narrow" Functions). Buller, David J.
Teleology and the Product Analogy. Matthen, Mohan.

**MILLS, S**
*Connectionism and Eliminativism: Reply to Stephen Mills in Vol. 5, No. 1.* Macdonald, Cynthia.

**MILNE, E**
Methodology and the Birth of Modern Cosmological Inquiry. Gale, George and Shanks, Niall.

**MILTON**
The Problem of Self-Destroying Sin in John Milton's *Samson Agonistes.* Boyd, Ian T E.

**MIMESIS**
"*Aesthetic Theory*'s Mimesis of Walter Benjamin" in *The Semblance of Subjectivity,* Huhn, Tom (ed). Nicholsen, Shierry Weber.
"Mimesis and Mimetology: Adorno and Lacoue-Labarthe" in *The Semblance of Subjectivity,* Huhn, Tom (ed). Jay, Martin.
"Sacrifice Revisited" in *On Jean-Luc Nancy: The Sense of Philosophy,* Sheppard, Darren (ed). De Beistegui, Miguel.
Essay: Kendall L. Walton, *Mimesis as Make-Believe.* Howell, Robert.
Ideas estéticas en Platón. Romero R, María Margarita.
Le concept d'heuristique dans la création de la forme esthétique: mimésis et liberté. Bruneau, Alain-Philippe.
Making Things with Words: Plato on Mimesis in *Republic.* Lycos, Kimon.
On the Question of *Mimesis* (in Spanish). Knoll, Victor.

**MIND**
*see also* Nous, Panpsychism, Soul, Spirit
"Analytic Geometry, Experimental Truth and Metaphysics in Descartes" in *Memorias Del Seminario En Conmemoración De Los 400 Anos Del Nacimiento De René Descartes,* Albis, Víctor S (ed). Laserna Pinzón, Mario.
"Basic Minds" in *AI, Connectionism and Philosophical Psychology, 1995,* Tomberlin, James E (ed). Sterelny, Kim.
"Connectionism and the Rationale Constraint on Cognitive Explanation" in *AI, Connectionism and Philosophical Psychology, 1995,* Tomberlin, James E (ed). Cummins, Robert.
"Consciousness as Internal Monitoring, I" in *AI, Connectionism and Philosophical Psychology, 1995,* Tomberlin, James E (ed). Lycan, William G.
"Consciousness Evaded: Comments on Dennett" in *AI, Connectionism and Philosophical Psychology, 1995,* Tomberlin, James E (ed). McGinn, Colin.
"Die (sei's auch metaphorische) These vom Geist als Computer" in *Das weite Spektrum der analytischen Philosophie,* Lenzen, Wolfgang. Kemmerling, Andreas.
"Die Logik der Überzeugungen und das Leib-Seele-Problem" in *Das weite Spektrum der analytischen Philosophie,* Lenzen, Wolfgang. Kamlah, Andreas.
"Feeling and Cognition" in *Verstehen and Humane Understanding,* O'Hear, Anthony (ed). Falk, Barrie.
"Hannah Arendt: The Activity of the Spectator" in *Sites of Vision,* Levin, David Michael (ed). Birmingham, Peg.
"How Should We Understand the Relation between Intentionality and Phenomenal Consciousness?" in *AI, Connectionism and Philosophical Psychology, 1995,* Tomberlin, James E (ed). Van Gulick, Robert.
"McDowell's Direct Realism and Platonic Naturalism" in *Perception,* Villanueva, Enrique (ed). Gibson, Roger.
"Mind" as Humanizing the Brain: Toward a Neurotheology of Meaning. Ashbrook, James B.
"Mind, Meaning, and Practice" in *The Cambridge Companion to Wittgenstein,* Sluga, Hans (ed). Stroud, Barry.
"Moore's Paradox and Consciousness" in *AI, Connectionism and Philosophical Psychology, 1995,* Tomberlin, James E (ed). Rosenthal, David M.
"Moving Minds: Situating Content in the Service of Real-Time Success" in *AI, Connectionism and Philosophical Psychology, 1995,* Tomberlin, James E (ed). Clark, Andy.
"Peirce and Representative Persons" in *Philosophy in Experience: American Philosophy in Transition,* Hart, Richard (ed). Anderson, Douglas R.
"Perception and Rational Constraint: McDowell's *Mind and World*" in *Perception,* Villanueva, Enrique (ed). Brandom, Robert.
"Practical Reasoning in Oscar" in *AI, Connectionism and Philosophical Psychology, 1995,* Tomberlin, James E (ed). Pollock, John L.
"Précis of *Mind and World*" in *Perception,* Villanueva, Enrique (ed). McDowell, John.

"Qualia and Color Concepts" in *Perception,* Villanueva, Enrique (ed). Harman, Gilbert.
"Reply to Gibson, Byrne, and Brandom" in *Perception,* Villanueva, Enrique (ed). McDowell, John.
"Spin Control: Comment on John McDowell's *Mind and World*" in *Perception,* Villanueva, Enrique (ed). Byrne, Alex.
"Tierethik I: Zu den philosophischen und ethischen Grundlagen des Tierschutzes" in *Angewandte Ethik: Die Bereichsethiken und ihre theoretische Fundierung,* Nida-Rümelin, Julian (ed). Nida-Rümelin, Julian.
"Understanding Understanding: Syntactic Semantics and Computational Cognition" in *AI, Connectionism and Philosophical Psychology, 1995,* Tomberlin, James E (ed). Rapaport, William J.
"Whose House is That? Wittgenstein on the Self" in *The Cambridge Companion to Wittgenstein,* Sluga, Hans (ed). Sluga, Hans.
"'A Shelter of the Mind': Henry, William, and the Domestic Scene" in *The Cambridge Companion to William James,* Putnam, Ruth Anna (ed). Feldman, Jessica R.
A Theory of Language and Mind. Bencivenga, Ermanno.
Auferstehung im Denken: Der Christusimpuls in der "Philosophie der Freiheit" und in der Bewusstseinsgeschichte. Teichmann, Frank.
Cervello-Mente: Pensatori del XX secolo. Gava, Giacomo.
Das phänomenale Bewusstsein: Eine Verteidigung. Lanz, Peter.
Descartes' Dualism. Baker, Gordon and Morris, Katherine J.
Descartes' Legacy: Minds and Meaning in Early Modern Philosophy. Hausman, David B and Hausman, Alan.
Descriptive Psychology. Müller, Benito (ed & trans) and Brentano, Franz.
Die Sprache des Geistes: Vergleich einer repräsentationalistischen und einer syntaktischen Theorie des Geistes. Saporiti, Katia.
Empiricism and the Philosophy of Mind. Sellars, Wilfrid.
Explaining Consciousness—The 'Hard Problem'. Shear, Jonathan (ed).
From Occam's Razor to the Roots of Consciousness. Wassermann, Gerhard D.
From Soul to Mind: The Emergence of Psychology from Erasmus Darwin to William James. Reed, Edward S.
Meeting of Minds: Intellectual and Religious Interaction in East Asian Traditions of Thought. Bloom, Irene (ed) and Fogel, Joshua A (ed).
Mind Design II: Philosophy, Psychology, Artificial Intelligence. Haugeland, John (ed).
Philosophical Perspectives, 9, AI, Connectionism and Philosophical Psychology, 1995. Tomberlin, James E (ed).
Primeras Interpretaciones del Mundo en la Modernidad: Descartes y Leibniz. Schneider, Martin.
Repräsentation bei Descartes. Perler, Dominik.
Representation and the Mind-Body Problem in Spinoza. Della Rocca, Michael.
Simple Mindedness: In Defense of Naive Naturalism in the Philosophy of Mind. Hornsby, Jennifer.
Spinoza and the Ethics. Lloyd, Genevieve.
Ten Problems of Consciousness: A Representational Theory of the Phenomenal Mind. Tye, Michael.
The Character of Mind: An Introduction to the Philosophy of Mind. McGinn, Colin.
The Commons of the Mind. Baier, Annette C.
The Meaning of Mind: Language, Morality, and Neuroscience. Szasz, Thomas.
The Mind of God and the Works of Man. Craig, Edward.
The Ontology of Mind: Events, Processes, and States. Steward, Helen.
The Rule of Reason: The Philosophy of Charles Sanders Peirce. Forster, Paul (ed) and Brunning, Jacqueline (ed).
A Patterned Process Approach To Brain, Consciousness, and Behavior. Díaz, José-Luis.
A Whiteheadian Contribution to the "Mind-body" Relation. Bertocci, Rosemary Juel.
An East Asian Perspective of Mind-Body. Nagatomo, Shigenori and Leisman, Gerald.
Ansätze zur physikalischen Untersuchung des Leib-Seele-Problems. Arendes, Lothar.
Antisoggettivismo e l'autorità della prima persona. Soldati, Gianfranco.
Appraisal Theories of Emotions. Ben-Ze'ev, Aaron.
Behavioral Systems Interpreted as Autonomous Agents and as Coupled Dynamical Systems: A Criticism. Keijzer, Fred A and Bem, Sacha.
Bemerkungen zum Verhältnis zwischen Neurophysiologie und Psychologie. Ros, Arno.
C.S. Peirce's Theories of Infinitesimals. Herron, Timothy.
Can God Change His Mind?. Gulesarian, Theodore.
Causation and Intensionality: A Problem for Naturalism. Rheinwald, Rosemarie.
Cognition Poised at the Edge of Chaos: A Complex Alternative to a Symbolic Mind. Garson, James W.
Counting Information: A Note on Physicalized Numbers. Rotman, Brian.
Crane on Mental Causation. Child, William.
Critical Notice of Fred Dretske Naturalizing the Mind. Seager, William.
Critical Notice of John McDowell Mind and World. Pietroski, Paul M.
Critical Thinking and Emotional Intelligence. Elder, Linda.
Cuypers' Persoonlijke aangelegenheden. Meijsing, Monica.
Das Leib-Seele-Problem in der Psychologie. Goller, Hans.

## MIND

Wittgenstein and Animal Minds. Lynch, Joseph J.

Yolton and Rorty on the Veil of Ideas in Locke. Dlugos, Peter.

'Many Minds' Interpretations of Quantum Mechanics: Replies to Replies. Lockwood, Michael.

## MINDS

see also Other Minds

Interpreting Minds: The Evolution of a Practice. Bogdan, Radu J.

## MING

The Conception of *Ming* in Early Confucian Thought. Slingerland, Ted.

## MINIMAL

Minimal Temporal Epistemic Logic. Engelfriet, Joeri.

On Aleph$_1$ Many Minimal Models. Hjorth, Greg.

Pi$^0_1$ Classes and Minimal Degrees. Groszek, Marcia J and Slaman, Theodore A.

Strongly Minimal Fusions of Vector Spaces. Holland, Kitty L.

## MINIMALISM

A Critique of the Minimalist Program. Johnson, David E and Lappin, Shalom.

Correspondence on the Cheap. Alward, Peter.

Minimalism and Truth. O'Leary-Hawthorne, John and Oppy, Graham.

Truth and Success: Searle's Attack on Minimalism. Clark, Michael.

## MINIMAX

Correlated Strategies as Institutions. Arce M, Daniel G.

Tempered Regrets Under Total Ignorance. Acker, Mary H.

## MINIMIZING

"How to Combine Ordering and Minimizing in a Deontic Logic Based on Preferences" in *Deontic Logic, Agency and Normative Systems,* Brown, Mark A (ed). Tan, Yao-Hua and Van der Torre, Leendert W N.

## MINOR

Arguments Against Health Care Autonomy for Minors. Ross, Lainie Friedman.

Minors and Health Care Decisions: Broadening the Scope. Frader, Joel.

Respecting the Health Care Decision-Making Capacity of Minors. Strong, Carson.

The Role of Minors in Health Care Decision Making: Current Legal Issues. Waxse, David J.

## MINORITY

Affirmative Action: Retrospect and Prospect. Van Patten, Jim.

Conflicting Accounts of Equal Opportunity. Askland, Andrew.

Liberalism and Culture. Carnes, Joseph H.

Liberalism and Culture: Will Kymlicka on Multicultural Citizenship (in Dutch). Van de Putte, André and Chaerle, Dries.

Minority Maneuvers and Unsettled Negotiations. Bhabha, Homi.

Minority Minors and Moral Research Medicine. Bonkovsky, Frederick O.

Minority Populations and Advance Directives: Insights from a Focus Group Methodology. Fischbach, Ruth L, Hauser, Joshua M and Kleefield, Sharon F (& others).

The Culture of Polemic: Misrecognizing Recognition. Düttmann, Alexander García and Walker, Nicholas (trans).

The State of Nationalism. Tilly, Charles.

Tobacco Targeting: The Ethical Complexity of Marketing to Minorities. Sautter, Elise Truly and Oretskin, Nancy A.

## MIRACLE

*Does God Exist?: A Dialogue.* Moody, Todd C.

*Hume on Miracles.* Tweyman, Stanley (ed).

Al-Ghazali on Necessary Causality in *The Incoherence of the Philosophers.* Riker, Stephen.

Are PSI Effects Natural? A Preliminary Investigation. Mavrodes, George I.

Hume's "Of Miracles" (Part One). Adler, Jonathan.

Milagres e leis da natureza em Peirche e Hume. Albieri, Sara.

Miracles and the Shroud of Turin. Griffith, Stephen.

When to Believe in Miracles. Clarke, Steve.

Wissenschaftstheorie oder Ästhetik der Wunder?. Gräfrath, Bernd.

## MIRROR

L'utilisation philosophique de la métaphore en Grèce et en Chine: Vers une métaphorologie comparée. Reding, Jean-Paul.

## MISCONDUCT

(Not) Giving Credit Where Credit Is Due: Citation of Data Sets. Sieber, Joan E and Trumbo, Bruce E.

Alternative Dispute Resolution and Research Misconduct. Guenin, Louis M.

Effectiveness of Research Guidelines in Prevention of Scientific Misconduct. Shore, Eleanor G.

Ethical Issues in Biomedical Research: Perceptions and Practices of Postdoctoral Research Fellows Responding to a Survey. Eastwood, Susan, Derish, Pamela and Leash, Evangeline (& others).

Honest Research. Hillman, Harold.

Scientific Misconduct: Ill-Defined, Redefined. Palca, Joseph.

Scientific Reasoning and Due Process. Guenin, Louis M and Davis, Bernard D.

Teaching Science at the University Level: What About the Ethics?. Gilmer, Penny J.

The Reluctant retained Witness: Alleged Sexual Misconduct in the Doctor/Patient Relationship. Yarborough, Mark.

Truth and Trustworthiness in Research. Whitbeck, Caroline.

## MISES, L

The Epistemological Argument Against Socialism: A Wittgensteinian Critique of Hayek and Giddens. Pleasants, Nigel.

## MISOGYNY

Wittgenstein's Women: The Philosophical Significance of Wittgenstein's Misogyny. Szabados, Béla.

## MITCHELL, O

"From the Algebra of Relations to the Logic of Quantifiers" in *Studies in the Logic of Charles Sanders Peirce,* Houser, Nathan (ed). Brady, Geraldine.

## MODAL

Logical Consequence: A Defense of Tarski. Ray, Greg.

Maudlin and Modal Mystery. Lewis, David.

Modal Interpretations, Decoherence and Measurements. Bacciagaluppi, Guido and Hemmo, Meir.

On the Impossibility of David Lewis' Modal Realism. Maudlin, Tim.

The Modal Unity of Anselm's *Proslogion.* Mar, Gary.

The Properties of Modal Interpretations of Quantum Mechanics. Clifton, Robert.

Unique Transition Probabilities in the Modal Interpretation. Vermaas, Pieter E.

## MODAL LOGIC

"Box" in Intuitionistic Modal Logic. DeVidi, David and Solomon, Graham.

"Ein drittes modallogisches Argument für den Determinismus: Alexander von Aphrodisias" in *Das weite Spektrum der analytischen Philosophie,* Lenzen, Wolfgang. Weidemann, Hermann.

"It is NOW" in *Das weite Spektrum der analytischen Philosophie,* Lenzen, Wolfgang. Meixner, Uwe.

"Multimodal Logics and Epistemic Attitudes" in *Verdad: lógica, representación y mundo,* Villegas Forero, L. Alonso González, Enrique.

"On Certain Extensions of von Kutschera's Preference-Based Dyadic Deontic Logic" in *Das weite Spektrum der analytischen Philosophie,* Lenzen, Wolfgang. Aqvist, Lennart.

"The Place of C.S. Peirce in the History of Logical Theory" in *The Rule of Reason: The Philosophy of Charles Sanders Peirce,* Forster, Paul (ed). Hintikka, Jaakko.

"The Tinctures and Implicit Quantification over Worlds" in *The Rule of Reason: The Philosophy of Charles Sanders Peirce,* Forster, Paul (ed). Zeman, Jay.

"Towards a Computational Treatment of Deontic Defeasibility" in *Deontic Logic, Agency and Normative Systems,* Brown, Mark A (ed). Artosi, Alberto, Governatori, Guido and Sartor, Giovanni.

*A New Introduction to Modal Logic.* Cresswell, M J and Hughes, G E.

*A Subject with No Object: Strategies for Nominalistic Interpretation of Mathematics.* Burgess, John P and Rosen, Gideon.

*De Re* Language, *De Re* Eliminability, and the Essential Limits of Both. Schwartz, Thomas.

*Logic with Trees: An Introduction to Symbolic Logic.* Howson, Colin.

*The Rule of Reason: The Philosophy of Charles Sanders Peirce.* Forster, Paul (ed) and Brunning, Jacqueline (ed).

A Basic System of Congruential-to-Monotone Bimodal Logic and Two of its Extensions. Humberstone, I Lloyd.

A Class of Modal Logics with a Finite Model Property with Respect to the Set of Possible-Formulae. Demri, Stéphane and Orlowska, Ewa.

A Completeness Proof for a Logic with an Alternative Necessity Operator. Demri, Stéphane.

A Counterexample in Tense Logic. Wolter, Frank.

A Logic for Information Systems. Archangelsky, Dmitri A and Taitslin, Mikhail A.

A Logic for Reasoning about Relative Similarity. Konikowska, Beata.

A New Argument from Actualism to Serious Actualism. Bergmann, Michael.

A Nonmonotonic Modal Formalization of the Logic of Acceptance and Rejection. Gomolinska, Anna.

A Note on the Completeness of Kozen's Axiomatisation of the Propositional mu-Calculus. Walukiewicz, Igor.

A Note on the Interpolation Property in Tense Logic. Wolter, Frank.

A Uniform Tableau Method for Intuitionistic Modal Logics I. Amati, Giambattista and Pirri, Fiora.

Admissible Rule for Temporal Logic LinTGrz. Bezgacheva, Julia V.

An Equational Axiomatization of Dynamic Negation and Relational Composition. Hollenberg, Marco.

Axiomatising First-Order Temporal Logic: Until and Since over Linear Time. Reynolds, Mark.

Bisimulations for Temporal Logic. Kurtonina, Natasha and De Rijke, Maarten.

Brouwer-Zadeh Logic, Decidability and Bimodal Systems. Giuntini, Roberto.

Canonicity for Intensional Logics without Iterative Axioms. Surendonk, Timothy J.

Completeness and Decidability of Tense Logics Closely Related to Logics Above K4. Wolter, Frank.

Constructive Canonicity in Non-Classical Logics. Ghilardi, Silvio and Meloni, Giancarlo.

Counterfactuals and Updates as Inverse Modalities. Ryan, Mark and Schobbens, Pierre-Yves.

Counterpart Theory as a Semantics for Modal Logic. Woollaston, Lin.

Criteria for Admissibility of Inference Rules: Modal and Intermediate Logics with the Branching Property. Rybakov, Vladimir V.

# MODAL LOGIC

## MODAL REALISM

## MODAL THEORY

# MODALITY

# MODE

# MODEL

# MODEL

A Non-Generic Real Incompatible with 0#. Stanley, M C.

A Psychologically Plausible Logical Model of Conceptualization. Kim, Hong-Gee.

A Sheaf-Theoretic Foundation for Nonstandard Analysis. Palmgren, Erik.

A Study of Intermediate Propositional Logics on the Third Slice. Hosoi, Tsutomu and Masuda, Isao.

A Test of a Person—Issue Contingent Model of Ethical Decision Making in Organizations. Harrington, Susan J.

A Type Free Theory and Collective/Distributive Predication. Kamareddine, Fairouz.

A Very Weak Square Principle. Foreman, Matthew and Magidor, Menachem.

Admissible Rule for Temporal Logic LinTGrz. Bezgacheva, Julia V.

AIDS, Confidentiality, and Ethical Models. Gorbett, Jason.

AIDS, Confidentiality, and Ethical Models: Appendix. Gorbett, Jason.

An Agent Model Integrating Multiple Reasoning Mechanisms. Moulin, Bernard and Boury-Brisset, Anne-Claire.

An Instructional Model for Critical Thinking. Leshowitz, Barry and Yoshikawa, Elaine.

Analogy and Argument. McKay, Thomas J.

Asymptotic Probabilities for Second-Order Existential Kahr-Moore-Wang Sentences. Vedo, Anne.

Belief Change as Change in Epistemic Entrenchment. Nayak, Abhaya C, Nelson, Paul and Polansky, Hanan.

Beyond Self and Other. Rogers, Kelly.

Bisimulations for Temporal Logic. Kurtonina, Natasha and De Rijke, Maarten.

Borel Equivalence Relations and Classifications of Countable Models. Hjorth, Greg and Kechris, Alexander S.

Bounded Contraction and Gentzen-style Formulation of Lukasiewicz Logics. Prijatelj, Andreja.

Can a Small Forcing Create Kurepa Trees. Jin, Renling and Shelah, Saharon.

Canonical Models for Temporal Deontic Logic. Bailhache, Patrice.

Cardinalities of Models for Pure Calculi of Names. Pietruszczak, Andrzej.

Classical and Intuitionistic Models of Arithmetic. Wehmeier, Kai F.

Classical Particle Dynamics, Indeterminism and a Supertask. Laraudogoitia, Jon Perez.

Clinical Ethics and Ethics Committees. Bartholome, William G.

Combining Temporal Logic Systems. Finger, Marcelo and Gabbay, Dov.

Commentary on "A Model Policy Addressing Mistreatment of Students". Kornfeld, Donald S.

Completeness and Incompleteness for Plausibility Logic. Schlechta, Karl.

Complex Kinds. Hirsch, Eli.

Congestion Models and Weighted Bayesian Potential Games. Faccini, Giovanni, Van Megen, Freek and Borm, Peter (& others).

Countable Model of Trivial Theories Which Admit Finite Coding. Loveys, James and Tanovic, Predrag.

Criteria for Admissibility of Inference Rules: Modal and Intermediate Logics with the Branching Property. Rybakov, Vladimir V.

Decidability of *Stit* Theory with a Single Agent and *Refref* Equivalence. Xu, Ming.

Desires and Human Nature in J.S. Mill. Jenkins, Joyce L.

Determinism and Locality in Quantum Systems. Dickson, W Michael.

Discount-Neutral Utility Models for Denumerable Time Streams. Fishburn, Peter C and Edwards, Ward.

Duality for Lattice-Ordered Algebras and for Normal Algebraizable Logics. Hartonas, Chrysafis.

Dynamic Relation Logic Is the Logic of DPL-Relations. Visser, Albert.

El cant gregorià, un model de música perfecta. Banyeres Baltasà, Hug.

Environmentalism for Europe—One Model?. De-Shalit, Avner.

Epistemic Aspects of Identity (in Serbo-Croatian). Andjelkovic, Miroslava.

Epistemologia e psicologia cognitiva: alcune osservazioni sulla teoria dei modelli mentali. Di Serio, Luciana.

Equational Theories for Inductive Types. Loader, Ralph.

Ergodic Theorems and the Basis of Science. Petersen, Karl.

Ethical Decision Making in Marketing: A Synthesis and Evaluation of Scales Measuring the Various Components of Decision Making in Ethical Situations. Vitell, Scott J and Ho, Foo Nin.

Ethical Decision Making: The Effects of Escalating Commitment. Street, Marc D, Robertson, Chris and Geiger, Scott W.

Evolution and Ultimatum Bargaining. Harms, William.

Facts, Semantics and Intuitionism. Akama, Seiki.

Feminist Revaluation of the Mythical Triad, Lilith, Adam, Eve: A Contribution to Role Model Theory. Wenkart, Henry.

Finding the Right Level for Connectionist Representations (A Critical Note on Ramsey's Paper). Markic, Olga.

Forcing Isomorphism II. Laskowski, Michael C and Shelah, Saharon.

Foundationalism and Practical Reason. Heath, Joseph.

Freedom and Democracy in Health Care Ethics: Is the Cart Before the Horse?. Meaney, Mark E.

From Completeness to Archimedean Completeness: An Essay in the Foundations of Euclidean Geometry. Ehrlich, Philip.

Gender Differences in Ethical Frameworks and Evaluation of Others' Choices in Ethical Dilemmas. Schminke, Marshall.

Generalized Quantification as Substructural Logic. Alechina, Natasha and Van Lambalgen, Michiel.

Global Population Equilibrium: A Model for the Twenty-First Century. Cavanaugh, Michael.

Hybrid Languages. Blackburn, Patrick and Seligman, Jerry.

Identities on Cardinals Less Than Aleph$_{omega}$. Gilchrist, M and Shelah, S.

In Defense of a Constructive, Information-Based Approach to Decision Theory. Yilmaz, M R.

Inconsistent Models of Arithmetic Part I: Finite Models. Priest, Graham.

Indiscernible Sequences for Extenders, and the Singular Cardinal Hypothesis. Gitik, Moti and Mitchell, William J.

Inference: Heuristic vs. Naturalistic Model. Mazumdar, Rinita.

Informed Consent as a Parent Involvement Model in the NICU. Luckner, Kleia R and Weinfeld, Irwin J.

Kant's Theory of Geometrical Reasoning and the Analytic-Synthetic Distinction: On Hintikka's Interpretation of Kant's Philosophy of Mathematics. De Jong, Willem R.

Kinesthetic-Visual Matching and the Self-Concept as Explanations of Mirror-Self-Recognition. Mitchell, Robert W.

Kitcher on Theory Choice. Roorda, Jonathan.

Kitcher's Compromise: A Critical Examination of the Compromise Model of Scientific Closure, and its Implications for the Relationship Between History and Philosophy of Science. Shanahan, Timothy.

Kripke Bundle Semantics and C-set Semantics. Isoda, Eiko.

Kripke Completeness of Some Intermediate Predicate Logics with the Axiom of Constant Domain and a Variant of Canonical Formulas. Shimura, Tatsuya.

Kripke Models and the (In)equational Logic of the Second-Order Lambda-Calculus. Gallier, Jean.

Landmarks in Critical Thinking Series: Plato's "Meno": A Model for Critical Thinkers. Hatcher, Donald L.

Logic Crystallized. Viney, Donald Wayne.

Logical Consequence: A Defense of Tarski. Ray, Greg.

Lost the Plot? Reconstructing Dennett's Multiple Drafts Theory of Consciousness. Akins, Kathleen.

Mathematics, Model and Zeno's Paradoxes. Alper, Joseph S and Bridger, Mark.

Mental Models in Data Interpretation. Chinn, Clark A and Brewer, William F.

Metaphysical Models of the Mind in Aristotle. Scaltsas, Theodore.

Modal Interpretations, Decoherence and Measurements. Bacciagaluppi, Guido and Hemmo, Meir.

Modal Logic over Finite Structures. Rosen, Eric.

Modèles historique et modèles culturels. Moutsopoulos, Evanghélos.

Modeling Ethical Attitudes and Behaviors under Conditions of Environmental Turbulence: The Case of South Africa. Morris, Michael H, Marks, Amy S and Allen, Jeffrey A.

Models, Truth and Semantics. Abbott, Barbara.

More on Imaginaries in *p*-ADIC Fields. Scowcroft, Philip.

Mostly Meyer Modal Models. Mares, Edwin D.

Nonmonotonic Reasoning: From Finitary Relations to Infinitary Inference Operations. Freund, Michael and Lehmann, Daniel.

Nonparametric Statistics in Multicriteria Analysis. Scarelli, Antonino and Venzi, Lorenzo.

Notes on Polynomially Bounded Arithmetic. Zambella, Domenico.

On Aleph$_1$ Many Minimal Models. Hjorth, Greg.

On the Notion of Second-Order Exchangeability. Wedlin, Attilio.

On the Subjectivity of Welfare. Sobel, David.

On the Use of Visualizations in the Practice of Science. Sargent, Pauline.

Ontological Aspects of Information Modeling. Ashenhurst, Robert L.

Paraconsistent Default Logic. Van den Akker, Johan and Tan, Yao Hua.

Parallel Action: Concurrent Dynamic Logic with Independent Modalities. Goldblatt, Robert.

Parametrized Sum Individuals for Plural Anaphora. Krifka, Manfred.

PDP Networks can Provide Models that are not Mere Implementations of Classical Theories. Dawson, Michael R W, Medler, David A and Berkeley, Istvan S N.

Perceptions of Ethics Across Situations: A View Through Three Different Lenses. Carlson, Dawn S and Kacmar, K Michele.

Perceptual Content and the Subpersonal. Gunther, York.

Philosophy of Science: What One Needs to Know. Clayton, Philip.

Political Concertation (Agreement) Among Social Actors: The Challenge of Venezuelan Democracy (Spanish). Bozo de Carmona, Ana Julia.

Pragmatics and the Processing of Metaphors: Category Dissimilarity in Topic and Vehicle Asymmetry. Katz, Albert N.

Preference for Gradual Resolution of Uncertainty. Ahlbrecht, Martin and Weber, Martin.

Problems with the Cognitive Psychological Modeling of Dreaming. Blagrove, Mark.

Quantum Dynamical Reduction and Reality: Replacing Probability Densities with Densities in Real Space. Ghirardi, Giancarlo.

Reasoning about Action and Change. Prendinger, Helmut and Schurz, Gerhard.

Reflecting in Epistemic Arithmetic. Horsten, Leon.

Relational Models for the Modal Syllogistic. Thomason, S K.

Research, Extension, and User Partnerships: Models for Collaboration and Strategies for Change. Lacy, William B.

Revision Algebra Semantics for Conditional Logic. Pais, John.

Semantics for Relevance Logic with Identity. Mares, Edwin D.

Sequential Asymmetric Auctions with Endogenous Participation. Menezes, Flavio M and Monteiro, Paulo K.

**MODERN**

Originality and Its Origin in Modern Aesthetics (in Japanese). Otabe, Tanehisa.

Plato's First Dialogue. Tomin, Julius.

Ralph Cudworth (1617-1688) sobre la infinitud de Dios. Robles, José A and Benítez, Laura.

Romantic Love and Loving Commitment: Articulating a Modern Ideal. Delaney, Neil.

Science Studies and Language Suppression—A Critique of Bruno Latour's We Have Never Been Modern. Cohen, Sande.

Scotists vs. Thomists: What Seventeenth-Century Scholastic Psychology was About. Knebel, Sven K.

Suárez y Vico, veinte años después. Badillo O'Farrell, Pablo.

Sulla nostalgia: La memoria tormentata. Starobinski, Jean.

The Infinitesimals as Useful Fictions for Leibniz: The Controversy in the Paris Academy of Sciences (Spanish). Joven, Fernando.

The Liberal Critic as Ideologue: Emile Faguet and fin-de-siècle Reflections on the Eighteenth Century. Dyrkton, Joerge.

The Spanish School of the Sixteenth and Seventeenth Centuries: A Precursor of the Theory of Human Rights. García y García, Antonio.

**MODERN ART**

Bemerkungen zur musikalischen Künstlerästhetik des 20.Jahrhunderts. Von Thülen, Bodil.

Der "Neuanfang" in der Ästhetik (J.-F. Lyotard). Seubold, Günter.

From The World is Beautiful to The Family of Man: The Plight of Photography as a Modern Art. Seamon, Roger.

**MODERNISM**

"American Philosophy's Way around Modernism (and Postmodernism)" in The Recovery of Philosophy in America: Essays in Honor of John Edwin Smith, Kasulis, Thomas P (ed). Neville, Robert Cummings.

"Constructing Modernism: The Cultural Location of Aufbau" in Origins of Logical Empiricism, Giere, Ronald N (ed). Galison, Peter.

"Modernism, Postmodernism, and the Pragmatic Recovery of an Educational Canon" in The Recovery of Philosophy in America: Essays in Honor of John Edwin Smith, Kasulis, Thomas P (ed). Allan, George.

Modern/Postmodern: Off the Beaten Path of Antimodernism. Kramer, Eric Mark.

The Lost Steps. Polizzotti, Mark (trans) and Breton, André.

Jenseits von Moderne und Postmoderne: Whiteheads Metaphysik und ihre Anwendungen in der theoretischen und praktischen Philosophie der Gegenwart. Hampe, Michael.

Lyotard: Modern Postmodernist?. Hurst, Andrea.

Strange Epoch! From Modernism to Postmodernism (in Hebrew). Mansbach, Abraham.

**MODERNITY**

"Civic Prudence in Machiavelli: Toward the Paradigm Transformation in Philosophy in the Transition to Modernity" in The Ancients and the Moderns, Lilly, Reginald (ed). Held, Klaus.

"Ecology, Modernity, and the Intellectual Legacy of the Frankfurt School" in Philosophy and Geography I: Space, Place, and Environmental Ethics, Light, Andrew (ed). Gandy, Matthew.

"Élites Sin Privilegio" in Política y Sociedad en José Ortega y Gasset: En Torno a "Vieja y Nueva Política", Lopez de la Vieja, Maria Teresa (ed). López de la Vieja, Maria Teresa.

"M. Heidegger: Modernità, storia e destino dell'Essere" in Lo Storicismo e la Sua Storia: Temi, Problemi, Prospettive, Cacciatore, Giuseppe (ed). Viti Cavaliere, Renata.

"Nationalism and Modernity" in The Morality of Nationalism, McKim, Robert (ed). Taylor, Charles.

"Nationalism in a Comparative Mode: A Response to Charles Taylor" in The Morality of Nationalism, McKim, Robert (ed). Feinberg, Walter.

"Nietzsche on Blacks" in Existence in Black: An Anthology of Black Existential Philosophy, Gordon, Lewis R (ed). Preston, William A.

"Postnormative Subjectivity" in The Ancients and the Moderns, Lilly, Reginald (ed). Mensch, James Richard.

"Radicalizing Liberalism and Modernity" in Philosophy, Religion, and the Question of Intolerance, Ambuel, David (ed). Ruf, Henry L.

"Sobre Política y Reformismo Cívico: A Partir de Ortega" in Política y Sociedad en José Ortega y Gasset: En Torno a "Vieja y Nueva Política", Lopez de la Vieja, Maria Teresa (ed). Rosales, José María.

"The Sources of Nationalism: Commentary on Taylor" in The Morality of Nationalism, McKim, Robert (ed). Kymlicka, Will.

African-American Perspectives and Philosophical Traditions. Pittman, John P (ed).

Coming Together/Coming Apart: Religion, Community, and Modernity. Bounds, Elizabeth M.

Emancipation and Illusion: Rationality and Gender in Habermas's Theory of Modernity. Fleming, Marie.

George Grant and the Subversion of Modernity: Art, Philosophy, Politics, Religion, and Education. Davis, Arthur (ed).

Habermas and the Unfinished Project of Modernity. Passerin d'Entrèves, Maurizio (ed) and Benhabib, Seyla (ed).

Idealism as Modernism: Hegelian Variations. Pippin, Robert B.

La Scienza Nuova nella Storia del Pensiero Politico. Voegelin, Eric and Zanetti, Gianfrancesco (trans).

Política y Sociedad en José Ortega y Gasset: En Torno a "Vieja y Nueva Política". Lopez de la Vieja, Maria Teresa (ed).

Primeras Interpretaciones del Mundo en la Modernidad: Descartes y Leibniz. Schneider, Martin.

Seditions: Heidegger and the Limit of Modernity. Boeder, Heribert and Brainard, Marcus (ed & trans).

The Actuality of Adorno: Critical Essays on Adorno and the Postmodern. Pensky, Max (ed).

A proposito di centenari cartesiani. Garin, Eugenio.

Alasdair MacIntyre: The Epitaph of Modernity. Kitchen, Gary.

Algo donoso pero no cortés: Una lectura diferencial del bifronte Marqués de Valdegamas a tenor de la modernidad de Vico. Sevilla Fernández, José M.

Ancient Chinese Aesthetics and its Modernity. Arnheim, Rudolf.

Beyond Enlightenment? After the Subject of Foucault, Who Comes?. Venn, Couze.

Bourdieu and Foucault on Power and Modernity. Cronin, Ciaran.

Charles Taylor e le due facce dell'individualismo. Cremaschi, Sergio.

Crisis de la modernidad en el pensamiento español: desde el Barroco y en la europeización del siglo XX. Jiménez Moreno, Luis.

Critical Theory between Modernity and Postmodernity. Fleming, Marie.

De l'usage social de l'éthique. Mineau, André, Giroux, Guy and Boisvert, Yves.

Descripción del fenómeno religioso en la postmodernidad. Barrera Vélez, Julio César.

El límite de la modernidad y el "Legado" de Heidegger. Boeder, Heriberto.

Fateful Rendezvous: The Young Althusser. Elliott, Gregory.

Foucault, Education, the Self and Modernity. Wain, Kenneth.

Funzioni e senso del diritto nel moderno: Riconoscimento e ragione sistemica. Romano, Bruno.

Hans Blumenberg: sobre la modernidad, la historia y los límites de la razón. Palti, Elías José.

Hegel's Critique of the Triumph of Verstand in Modernity. Houlgate, Stephen.

Heidegger y la modernidad. Colomer, Eusebi.

Hobbes's Political Geometry. Valentine, Jeremy.

I percorsi del soggetto moderno. Barcellona, Pietro.

Italo Mancini lettore di Agostino: Percorso e contenuti di un incontro. Cangiotti, Marco.

L'Allemagne, la modernité, la pensée. Bouckaert, Bertrand.

L'arrivo del Discours e dei Principia,D in Italia: prime letture dei testi cartesiani a Napoli. Lojacono, Ettore.

La Modernidad cansada (o ¿para qué aún filosofía). Lanceros, Patxi.

La nuova destra. Revelli, Marco.

La philosophie morale depuis la mort de Dieu. Couture, Jocelyne.

Locke, "The Father of Modernity"?: A Discussion of Wolterstorff's John Locke and the Ethics of Belief. Schouls, Peter A.

Modernità e morte dell'arte: Büchner e Celan. Samonà, Leonardo.

Notas sobre modernidade e sujeito na dialética do esclarecimento. Duarte, Rodrigo A P.

Oltre l'umanesimo: Alcune considerazioni su tecnica e modernità. Galli, Carlo.

Opening the Future: The Paradox of Promising in the Hobbesian Social Contract. Bernasconi, Robert.

Pensiero medievale e modernità. Gregory, Tullio.

Richard Kearney's Hermeneutic Imagination. Stark, Tracey.

Science, Religion, and Modernity: Values and Lifestyles of University Professors. Houtman, Dick.

Secolarizzazione e originalità del moderno: In margine a La legittimità dell'epoca moderna di Hans Blumenberg. Carosotti, Gianni.

Stain, Disfiguration and Orgy (in Spanish). Cardona Suárez, Luis Fernando.

The Abdication of Philosophy: On the Modernity of the Relation between Philosophy and Politics in Kant. Gerhardt, Volker.

The Burdens of Berlin's Modernity. Steinberg, Jonny.

The French Revolutionary Roots of Political Modernity in Hegel's Philosophy, or the Enlightenment at Dusk. Wokler, Robert.

The Modernity Crisis and the Pedagogical Reason (Spanish). Márquez, Alvaro.

The Negative Dialectic of Modernity and the Speculative Resolution of the Contradiction of Modern Moral Consciousness (in Spanish). Lutz Müller, Marcos.

The New Hegel. Dallmayr, Fred R, Hardimon, Michael O and Pinkard, Terry.

The Ought-Is Question: Discovering The Modern in Post-Modernism. Johnson, David Kenneth.

Time, Modernity and Time Irreversibility. Palti, Elías José.

Transgressive Theorizing: A Report to Deleuze. Boundas, Constantin V.

Vico en Sciacca. Ottonello, Pier Paolo.

Vico y la retórica que no cesa. Marín-Casanova, José Antonio.

Voces mezcladas: Una reflexión sobre tradición y modernidad. Díaz-Urmeneta Muñoz, Juan Bosco.

**MODERNIZATION**

"Against Culture and the Aliens of Modernization" in Philosophy and Democracy in Intercultural Perspective, Kimmerle, Heinz (ed). Neugebauer, Christian.

In Support of Significant Modernization of Original Mathematical Texts (In Defense of Presentism). Barabashev, A G.

**MODESTY**

Comments on the Paradox of Modesty (in Hebrew). Kosman, Admiel.

Why Modesty Is a Virtue. Schueler, G F.

## MODULAR

Definability of Directly Indecomposable Congruence Modular Algebras. Vaggione, Diego.

## MOGAO, D

The Changes of Painting Techniques in the Early Tang Wall Paintings of Dunhuang Mogao Grottos; The Relationship between "Pattern" and Pictorial Structure (in Japanese). Yamasaki, Toshiko.

## MOHAMMEDANISM

see Islam

## MOHANTY, J

On Talk of Modes of Thought. Ramakrishnan, Lakshmi.

## MOLECULAR

Molecular Shape, Reduction, Explanation and Approximate Concepts. Ramsey, Jeffry L.

## MOLECULAR BIOLOGY

Heroic Antireductionism and Genetics: A Tale of One Science. Vance, Russell E.

## MOLECULE

The Peculiar Notion of Exchange Forces—I: Origins in Quantum Mechanics, 1926-1928. Carson, Cathryn.

## MOLINISM

Explanatory Priority: Transitive and Unequivocal, A Reply to William Craig. Hasker, William.

## MOLTMANN, J

Paraísos y Utopías: Una Clave Antropológica. De la Pienda, Jesús Avelino.

## MONAD

"Die Stufen zum Vernunftvermögen: Richard Hönigswalds Begriff der monas als Gegenstand erkenntniskritischer Reflexion" in Grenzen der kritischen Vernunft, Schmid, Peter A. Merz-Benz, Peter-Ulrich.

Filosofia e realtà virtuale. Marturano, Antonio.

Monad as a Triadic Structure—Leibniz' Contribution to Post-Nihilistic Search for Identity. Schadel, Erwin.

Substances are not Windowless: A Suarézian Critique of Monadism. Kronen, John D.

## MONADIC

The Order Types of Termination Orderings on Monadic Terms, Strings and Multisets. Martin, Ursula and Scott, Elizabeth.

Unary Quantifiers on Finite Models. Väänänen, Jouko.

## MONADOLOGY

Leibniz im Verständnis Fichtes. Lauth, Reinhard.

## MONADS

Are Leibnizian Monads Spatial?. Cover, J A and Hartz, Glenn A.

Corporeal Substances and True Unities. Baxter, Donald L M.

Unpacking the Monad: Leibniz's Theory of Causality. Clatterbaugh, Kenneth and Bobro, Marc.

## MONARCHY

Attualità di un carteggio del Settecento. Fabris, Matteo.

La réception de la "Monarchie" de Dante ou Les métamorphoses d'une oeuvre philosophique. Cheneval, Francis.

## MONASTIC

The Suppression of Nuns and the Ritual Murder of their Special Dead in Two Buddhist Monastic Texts. Schopen, Gregory.

## MONEY

Money and the Medical Profession. May, William F.

Solidarietà e democrazia: Osservazioni su antropologia, diritto e legittimità nella teoria giuridica di Habermas. Pinzani, Alessandro.

## MONISM

A Proof of One Substance Monism. Naik, A D.

Discussion: Phylogenetic Species Concept: Pluralism, Monism, and History. Horvath, Christopher D.

Ein Pluralismus von prima-facie Pflichten als Alternative zu monistischen Theorien der Ethik. Wolf, Jean-Claude.

Gustav Teichmüller filologo e metafisico tra Italia e Germania: I) Teichmüller, Nietzsche e la critica delle 'mitologie scientifiche'. Orsucci, Andrea.

How Physicalists Can Avoid Reductionism. Kirk, Robert.

Lacuna in Sankara Studies: A Thousand Teachings (Upadesasāhasrī). Tuck, Donald R.

Le mal moral, pierre de touche de l'ontologie: Monisme idéal et dualisme réel du sens de l'être. Lamblin, Robert.

Monismo metodológico y metafísico en Spinoza: la mente como idea del cuerpo. Martínez Velasco, Jesús.

Nonaggregatability, Inclusiveness, and the Theory of Focal Value: Nichomachean Ethics 1.7.1097b16-20. Lawrence, Gavin.

Rationality and the Argument for Anomalous Monism. Yalowitz, Steven.

Spinoza à la Mode: A Defence of Spinozistic Anti-Pluralism. Glouberman, Mark.

Spinoza's Demonstration of Monism: A New Line of Defense. Kulstad, Mark A.

The Advaita View of the Self. Bhattacharya, A N.

## MONOTHEISM

Monoteísmo, sacrificio, matadero: teodiceas y realidades históricas. Rodríguez-Campoamor, Hernán.

## MONOTONE

On the Proof-Theoretic Strength of Monotone Induction in Explicit Mathematics. Schlüter, Andreas, Glass, Thomas and Rathjen, Michael.

## MONOTONIC

Structuring Methods for Nonmonotonic Knowledge Bases. Antoniou, Grigoris.

## MONOTONICITY

Partial Monotonicity and a New Version of the Ramsey Test. Pais, John and Jackson, Peter.

Theory Matrices (for Modal Logics) Using Alphabetical Monotonicity. Gent, Ian P.

## MONSTERS

Animal Acts: Configuring the Human in Western History. Ham, Jennifer (ed) and Senior, Matthew (ed).

Scary Monsters: Hegel and the Nature of the Monstrous. Gunkel, David.

## MONTAIGNE

Modes de proximités avec l'animal chez Montaigne. Pelosse, Valentin.

Notas sobre a Presença de Sêneca nos Essais de Montaigne. Alves Eva, Luiz Antonio.

## MONTESQUIEU

Rousseau, La Politica e la Storia: Tra Montesquieu e Robespierre. Burgio, Alberto.

Republican Readings of Montesquieu: The Spirit of the Laws in the Dutch Republic. Velema, Wyger R E.

## MONTINARI, M

"La volontéde puissance" n'existe pas: A proposito dell'edizione francese di alcuni saggi di Mazzino Montinari. Viola, Salvatore.

## MOOD

"Can There be an Epistemology of Moods?" in Verstehen and Humane Understanding, O'Hear, Anthony (ed). Mulhall, Stephen.

On the Intentionality of Moods: Phenomenology and Linguistic Analysis. Arregui, Jorge V.

## MOODY, E

What is the Science of the Soul? A Case Study in the Evolution of Late Medieval Natural Philosophy. Zupko, Jack.

## MOOR, J

The Computer Revolution and the Problem of Global Ethics. Gorniak-Kocikowska, Krystyna.

## MOORE

"Desire and Desirability: Bradley, Russell and Moore versus Mill" in Early Analytic Philosophy, Tait, William W (ed). Gerrard, Steve.

"Moore's Paradox and Consciousness" in AI, Connectionism and Philosophical Psychology, 1995, Tomberlin, James E (ed). Rosenthal, David M.

"Telic Higher-Order Thoughts and Moore's Paradox" in AI, Connectionism and Philosophical Psychology, 1995, Tomberlin, James E (ed). Kobes, Bernard W.

A Note on Moore's Organic Unities. Carlson, Erik.

Dewey and Moore on the Science of Ethics. Welchman, Jennifer.

Does Bentham Commit the Naturalistic Fallacy?. Chattopadhyay, Gauriprasad.

Intrinsic/Extrinsic. Humberstone, I Lloyd.

Reflective Knowledge in the Best Circles. Sosa, Ernest.

Stroud and Moore on Skepticism. Neta, Ram.

The Right and the Good. Thomson, Judith Jarvis.

Verità e prescrizione in etica. Vacatello, Marzio.

## MOORE, M

Action Theory and Criminal Law. Dolinko, David.

## MOORE, R

Concluding Observations. Smith, Ralph A.

## MORAL

"La Paz en Kant: Ética y Política" in Kant: La paz perpetua, doscientos años después, Martínez Guzmán, Vicent (ed). Cortina, Adela.

"Moral Philosophy and the Development of Morality" in The Cambridge Companion to William James, Putnam, Ruth Anna (ed). Bird, Graham H.

"Objektivität und Moral" in Das weite Spektrum der analytischen Philosophie, Lenzen, Wolfgang. Nida-Rümelin, Julian.

Ley moral, Ley positiva. Griffin, James.

On the Moral Philosophy of René Descartes: Or, How Morals are Derived from Method. Bagley, Paul J.

Phenomenology as Fundamental Moral Philosophy by Stephen Strasser (in Polish). Póltawski, Andrzej.

The Interdependence of Intellectual and Moral Virtue in Aquinas. Peterson, John.

## MORAL AGENT

Rational Choice and Moral Agency. Schmidtz, David.

Moral Deliberations, Nonmoral Ends, and the Virtuous Agent. Isaacs, Tracy L and Jeske, Diane.

Piccolo mondo antico: appunti sul problema dell'identificazione del soggetto morale. Pievatolo, Maria Chiara.

## MORAL DEVELOPMENT

Corporate Social Performance, Stakeholder Orientation, and Organizational Moral Development. Logsdon, Jeanne M and Yuthas, Kristi.

Développement Moral et Jugement Moral: Réexamen de la Controverse Kohlberg-Gilligan. Savard, Nathalie.

Ethical Work Climate as a Factor in the Development of Person-Organization Fit. Sims, Randi L and Keon, Thomas L.

Factors that Influence the Moral Reasoning Abilities of Accountants: Implications for Universities and the Profession. Eynon, Gail, Thorley Hill, Nancy and Stevens, Kevin T.

## MORAL DEVELOPMENT

Moral Development: Whose Ethics in the Teaching of Religious Education?. Bolton, Andrew.

Re-Examining the Influence of Individual Values on Ethical Decision Making. Glover, Saundra H, Bumpus, Minnette A and Logan, John E (& others).

Response to "Further Exploration of the Relationship between Medical Education and Moral Development" by Donnie J. Self, DeWitt C. Baldwin, Jr., and Frederic D. Wolinsky (CQ Vol 5, No 3). Burack, Jeffrey H.

## MORAL EDUCATION

"*Akrasia*: Irremediable but not Unapproachable" in *Philosophy of Education (1996)*, Margonis, Frank (ed). Worsfold, Victor L.

"Are You a Good Witch or a Bad Witch? And Other Questions the Jesuits Left for Me" in *Philosophy of Education (1996)*, Margonis, Frank (ed). Alston, Kal.

"Good Sex as the Aim of Sexual Education" in *Philosophy of Education (1996)*, Margonis, Frank (ed). Steutel, Jan and Spiecker, Ben.

"Moral Education and Inspiration Through Theatre" in *Philosophy of Education (1996)*, Margonis, Frank (ed). Valentine, Timothy S.

"Moral Reflection and Moral Education" in *Philosophy of Education (1996)*, Margonis, Frank (ed). Covaleskie, John F.

"The Politics of the "Good" in *Good Sexuality Education*" in *Philosophy of Education (1996)*, Margonis, Frank (ed). Boyd, Dwight and McKay, Alexander.

"Varieties of Incotinence: Towards an Aristotelian Approach to Moral Weakness in Moral Education" in *Philosophy of Education (1996)*, Margonis, Frank (ed). Carr, David.

*Philosophy of Education (1996)*. Margonis, Frank (ed), Boler, Megan (ed) and Callan, Eamonn (ed).

*Reasonable Children: Moral Education and Moral Learning*. Pritchard, Michael S.

Affect and the Moral-Conventional Distinction. Blair, R J R.

Character Education: Reclaiming the Social. Duncan, Barbara J.

Context, Politics and Moral Education: Comments on the Misgeld/Magendzo Conversation about Human Rights Education. Brabeck, Mary M and Ting, Kathleen.

Dewey's Conception of "Virtue" and its Implications for Moral Education. Rice, Suzanne.

Ethics Education in Science and Engineering: The Case of Animal Research. Rowan, Andrew N.

Fostering Autonomy. Fowler Morse, Jane.

Human Rights Education, Moral Education and Modernisation: The General Relevance of Some Latin American Experiences: A Conversation. Misgeld, Dieter and Magendzo, Abraham.

In Defense of Israel Scheffler's Conception of Moral Education. Coombs, Jerrold.

Integrating the Ethical and Social Context of Computing into the Computer Science Curriculum. Huff, Chuck, Anderson, Ronald E and Little, Joyce Currie (& others).

Israel Scheffler's "Moral Education and the Democratic Ideal". Siegel, Harvey.

Learning Moral Commitment in Higher Education?. Collier, Gerald.

Moral Climate and the Development of Moral Reasoning: The Effects of Dyadic Discussions between Young Offenders. Taylor, John H and Walker, Lawrence J.

Moral Development: Whose Ethics in the Teaching of Religious Education?. Bolton, Andrew.

Moral Education and the Democratic Ideal. Scheffler, Israel.

Passing on the Faith: How Mother-Child Communication Influences Transmission of Moral Values. Taris, Toon W and Semin, Gün R.

Patterns of Reasoning Exhibited by Children and Adolescents in Response to Moral Dilemmas Involving Plants, Animals and Ecosystems. Nevers, Patricia, Gebhard, Ulrich and Billmann-Mahecha, Elfriede.

Philosophy for Children: One Way of Developing Children's Thinking. Green, Lena.

Promoting Ethical Reasoning, Affect and Behaviour Among High School Students: An Evaluation of Three Teaching Strategies. DeHaan, Robert, Hanford, Russell and Kinlaw, Kathleen.

Sex Education as Moral Education: Teaching for Pleasure, about Fantasy, and against Abuse. Lamb, Sharon.

The Care of the Self: Poststructuralist Questions About Moral Education and Gender. Golden, Jill.

The Education of Natural Intelligence and the Intellectual Virtues: Has Educational Pastiche had the Last Laugh?. D'Souza, Mario O.

The Forms and Functions of Real-Life Moral Decision-Making. Krebs, Dennis L, Denton, Kathy and Wark, Gillian.

The Moral and Spiritual Dimension to Education: Some Reflections on the British Experience. Rossiter, Graham.

Theatre and Moral Education. Levy, Jonathan.

What Rough Beast...? Narrative Relationships and Moral Education. Gooderham, David W.

Why Teach Ethics in Science and Engineering?. Johnson, Deborah G, Hollander, Rachelle D and Beckwith, Jonathan R (& others).

## MORAL KNOWLEDGE

The Conscience Principle. Murphy, Mark C.

## MORAL PHILOSOPHY

Antifoundationalism and the Possibility of a Moral Philosophy of Medicine. Thomasma, David C.

Reason Without Reasons: A Critique of Alan Gewirth's Moral Philosophy. Kramer, Matthew H and Simmonds, Nigel E.

The Limits of Self Interest: An Hegelian Critique of Gauthier's Compliance Problem. Schwartz, David T.

## MORAL REASONING

Indoctrination and Moral Reasoning: A Comparison between Dutch and East German Students. De Mey, Langha and Schulze, Hans-Joachim.

Taking Ethics Seriously: Virtue, Validity, and the Art of Moral Reasoning. Hughes, Paul.

The Measure of Morality: Rethinking Moral Reasoning. Vine, Ian.

## MORAL SENTIMENT

Economics, Business Principles and Moral Sentiments. Sen, Amartya.

Phenomenological Ethics and Moral Sentiments (Spanish). Hoyos Vásquez, Guillermo.

Verantwortung und moralische Gefühle. Flury, Andreas.

## MORAL THEORY

"Is Anything Absolutely Wrong?" in *Human Lives: Critical Essays on Consequentialist Bioethics*, Oderberg, David S (ed). Denyer, Nicholas.

"Love and Its Place in Moral Discourse" in *Love Analyzed*, Lamb, Roger E. Pettit, Philip.

"Moral Dimensions of Classroom Discourse: A Deweyan Perspective" in *Philosophy of Education (1996)*, Margonis, Frank (ed). Rosner, Fay.

*"Real World" Ethics: Frameworks for Educators and Human Service Professionals*. Nash, Robert J.

*A Practical Companion to Ethics*. Weston, Anthony.

*A Preserving Grace: Protestants, Catholics, and Natural Law*. Cromartie, Michael (ed).

*Animal Acts: Configuring the Human in Western History*. Ham, Jennifer (ed) and Senior, Matthew (ed).

*Babies and Beasts: The Argument from Marginal Cases*. Dombrowski, Daniel A.

*History and Contemporary Issues: Studies in Moral Theology*. Curran, Charles E.

*Jonathan Edwards's Writings: Text, Context, Interpretation*. Stein, Stephen J (ed).

*Law and Morality: Readings in Legal Philosophy*. Dyzenhaus, David (ed) and Ripstein, Arthur (ed).

*Making a Necessity of Virtue*. Sherman, Nancy.

*Pragmatism and Realism*. Westphal, Kenneth R (ed), Will. Frederick L and MacIntyre, Alasdair.

*Virtue Ethics*. Slote, Michael (ed) and Crisp, Roger (ed).

A Comment on 'Radiation Protection and Moral Theory'. Miller, Chris.

A Question for Egalitarians. Kekes, John.

Against Strong Speciesism. Graft, Donald.

An Exercise in Moral Philosophy: Seeking to Understand "Nobody". King, Jonathan B.

Communicative Action, the Lifeworlds of Learning and the Dialogue that we Aren't. Hogan, Pádraig.

Cultural Context and Moral Responsibility. Isaacs, Tracy.

Culture, Power and the Social Construction of Morality: Moral Voices of Chinese Students. Chang, Kimberly A.

Dewey's Moral Theory: Experience as Method. Pappas, Gregory Fernando.

Epicurean Moral Theory. Rosenbaum, Stephen E.

Finding an Appropriate Ethic in a World of Moral Acquaintances. Loewy, Erich H.

Forbidding Nasty Knowledge: On the Use of Ill-Gotten Information. Godlovitch, Stanley.

Genetic Therapy: Mapping the Ethical Challanges. Gorovitz, Samuel.

Infinite Value and Finitely Additive Value Theory. Vallentyne, Peter and Kagan, Shelly.

Intrinsic Value, Moral Standing, and Species. O'Neil, Rick.

Irresolvable Disagreement and the Case Against Moral Realism. Bennigson, Thomas.

Japanese Moralogy as Business Ethics. Taka, Iwao and Dunfee, Thomas W.

Kohlberg's Dormant Ghosts: The Case of Education. Oser, Fritz K.

Learning from Frankena: A Philosophical Remembrance. Darwall, Stephen.

Misdirection in the Free Will Problem. Double, Richard.

Moral Crutches and Nazi Theists: A Defense of and Reservations about Undertaking Theism. Lemos, John.

Moral Leadership: An Overview. Gini, Al.

Moral Politics and the Limits of Justice in *Perpetual Peace*. Clarke, Michael.

Moral Reasoning as Perception: A Reading of Carol Gilligan. Kyte, Richard.

Moral Rules. Shafer-Landau, Russ.

Moral Theory and the Reflective Life. Rosenbaum, Stuart E.

Problems in developing a Practical Theory of Moral Responsibility. Anderson, Susan Leigh.

Reasonable Self-Interest. Hill Jr, Thomas E.

Smith's Moral Problem. Darwall, Stephen.

Temporal Horizons of Justice. Ackerman, Bruce.

The Aesthetically Good vs. The Morally Good. Davenport, Manuel.

The Intended/Foreseen Distinction's Ethical Relevance. Cavanaugh, Thomas A.

The Loss of Practical Reason and Some Consequences for the Idea of Postmodernism. Painter, Mark.

## MORAL THEORY

The Moral Significance of Primitive Self-Consciousness: A Response to Bermúdez. Gallagher, Shaun.

The Need for Plans, Projects and Reasoning about Ends: Kant and Williams. Kemal, Salim.

The Real Issues Concerning Dirty Hands—A Response to Kai Nielsen. De Wijze, Stephen.

The Right and the Good. Thomson, Judith Jarvis.

The Structure of Residual Obligations. Brummer, James J.

When Manipulation Is Indispensable to Education: The Moral Work of Fiction. Thompson, Audrey.

Wisdom. Dilman, Ilham.

## MORALISM

La re-presentación extrema del estetismo, del intelectualismo y del moralismo en política. Rendón Rojas, Miguel Angel and Okolova, Marina Dimitrieva.

Originalism, Moralism and the Public Opinion State of Mitchell Franklin. Lawler, James.

## MORALITY

"Anmerkungen zu Funktion und Stellenwert des Eigeninteresses" in Ökonomie und Moral: Beiträge zur Theorie ökonomischer Rationalität, Lohmann, Karl Reinhard (ed). Chwaszcza, Christine.

"Beyond Moral Stories" in Philosophy of Education (1996), Margonis, Frank (ed). Sichel, Betty A.

"Comunidad y Moralidad" in Liberalismo y Comunitarismo: Derechos Humanos y Democracia, Monsalve Solórzano, Alfonso (ed). Fisk, Milton.

"Concerning Moral Toleration" in Philosophy, Religion, and the Question of Intolerance, Ambuel, David (ed). Jordan, Jeff.

"Das Kalkül der Moral" in Ökonomie und Moral: Beiträge zur Theorie ökonomischer Rationalität, Lohmann, Karl Reinhard (ed). Kirsch, Guy.

"Das Problem der Steuerhinterziehung: Eine moral ökonomische Analyse" in Ökonomie und Moral: Beiträge zur Theorie ökonomischer Rationalität, Lohmann, Karl Reinhard (ed). Leschke, Martin.

"Deliberation and Moral Expertise in Plato's Crito" in Dialogues with Plato, Benitez, Eugenio (ed). Benitez, Eugenio E.

"Democracy in an Ethical Community" in Philosophy and Democracy in Intercultural Perspective, Kimmerle, Heinz (ed). Louw, Tobias J G.

"Do You Do Well to Be Angry?". Werpehowski, William.

"Élites Sin Privilegio" in Política y Sociedad en José Ortega y Gasset: En Torno a "Vieja y Nueva Política", Lopez de la Vieja, Maria Teresa (ed). López de la Vieja, Maria Teresa.

"Gibt es moralische Probleme der Wirtschaft?" in Ökonomie und Moral: Beiträge zur Theorie ökonomischer Rationalität, Lohmann, Karl Reinhard (ed). Wolf, Ursula.

"Intellectualism and Moral Habituation in Plato's Earlier Dialogues" in Dialogues with Plato, Benitez, Eugenio (ed). Yong, Patrick.

"La logica della vita morale in M. Blondel" in Momenti di Storia della Logica e di Storia della Filosofia, Guetti, Carla (ed). Rigobello, Armando.

"Moral Causation" in A Question of Values: New Canadian Perspectives in Ethics and Political Philosophy, Brennan, Samantha (ed). Pietroski, Paul M.

"Moral oder Eigennutz? Eine experimentelle Analyse" in Ökonomie und Moral: Beiträge zur Theorie ökonomischer Rationalität, Lohmann, Karl Reinhard (ed). Frey, Bruno S and Bohnet, Iris.

"Moral Rights and Moral Math: Three Arguments against Aggregation" in A Question of Values: New Canadian Perspectives in Ethics and Political Philosophy, Brennan, Samantha (ed). Brennan, Samantha.

"Moral Stories: How Much Can We Learn from Them and Is It Enough?" in Philosophy of Education (1996), Margonis, Frank (ed). Katz, Michael S.

"Moralische Überzeugung und wirtschaftliche Wahl" in Ökonomie und Moral: Beiträge zur Theorie ökonomischer Rationalität, Lohmann, Karl Reinhard (ed). Lohmann, Karl Reinhard.

"Morality and Obligation" in Reason, Experience, and God: John E. Smith in Dialogue, Colapietro, Vincent M. Roth, Robert J.

"Morality, Religion, and the Force of Obligation: Response to Robert J. Roth, S.J." in Reason, Experience, and God: John E. Smith in Dialogue, Colapietro, Vincent M. Smith, John E.

"Morally Appreciated Circumstances: A Theoretical Problem for Casuistry" in Philosophical Perspectives on Bioethics, Sumner, L W (ed). Jonsen, Albert R.

"Natural Law, Morality, and Sexual Complementarity" in Sex, Preference, and Family: Essays on Law and Nature, Nussbaum, Martha C (ed). Weithman, Paul J.

"Originality: Moral Good, Private Vice, or Self-Enchantment" in Jean-Jacques Rousseau and the Sources of the Self, O'Hagan, Timothy (ed). Mason, John Hope.

"Personal Integrity, Politics, and Moral Imagination" in A Question of Values: New Canadian Perspectives in Ethics and Political Philosophy, Brennan, Samantha (ed). Babbitt, Susan E.

"Prelude to a Liberal Morality of Nationalism" in A Question of Values: New Canadian Perspectives in Ethics and Political Philosophy, Brennan, Samantha (ed). Norman, Wayne.

"Professional Morality: Can an Examined Life Be Lived?" in Philosophical Perspectives on Bioethics, Sumner, L W (ed). Callahan, Daniel.

"Sind moralische Aussagen objektiv wahr?" in Das weite Spektrum der analytischen Philosophie, Lenzen, Wolfgang. Trapp, Rainer.

"The Conflict of Morality with Basic Life Instincts" (in Serbo-Croatian). Wischke, Mirko.

"Verdirbt der homo oeconomicus die Moral?" in Ökonomie und Moral: Beiträge zur Theorie ökonomischer Rationalität, Lohmann, Karl Reinhard (ed). Suchanek, Andreas.

A Treatise Concerning Eternal and Immutable Morality with A Treatise of Freewill. Hutton, Sarah (ed) and Cudworth, Ralph.

Art and Its Messages: Meaning, Morality, and Society. Davies, Stephen (ed).

Can We Be Good without God?: A Conversation about Truth, Morality, Culture & A Few Other Things That Matter. Chamberlain, Paul.

El Krausopositivismo de Urbano González Serrano. García, Antonio Jiménez.

Kant: La paz perpetua, doscientos años después. Martínez Guzmán, Vicent (ed).

Metaphilosophy and Free Will. Double, Richard.

Momenti di Storia della Logica e di Storia della Filosofia. Guetti, Carla (ed) and Pujia, Roberto (ed).

Moral Discourse and Practice: Some Philosophical Approaches. Darwall, Stephen (ed), Gibbard, Allan (ed) and Railton, Peter (ed).

Moral Knowledge?: New Readings in Moral Epistemology. Sinnott-Armstrong, Walter (ed) and Timmons, Mark (ed).

Moralidad: Ética universalista y sujeto moral. Guariglia, Osvaldo.

Morality and the Good Life. Moser, Paul K (ed) and Carson, Thomas L (ed).

Morality and the Law. Baird, Robert M (ed) and Rosenbaum, Stuart E (ed).

Morals Based on Needs. Ohlsson, Ragnar.

Ökonomie und Moral: Beiträge zur Theorie ökonomischer Rationalität. Lohmann, Karl Reinhard (ed) and Priddat, Birger P (ed).

On the Genealogy of Morals. Smith, Douglas (trans) and Nietzsche, Friedrich.

Promising, Intending, and Moral Autonomy. Robins, Michael H.

Social Cohesion and Legal Coercion: A Critique of Weber, Durkheim, and Marx. Shaskolsky Sheleff, Leon.

The Constitution of Good Societies. Soltan, Karol Edward (ed) and Elkin, Stephen L (ed).

The Meaning of Mind: Language, Morality, and Neuroscience. Szasz, Thomas.

The Metaphysics of Morals. Gregor, Mary (ed & trans) and Kant, Immanuel.

The Morality of Nationalism. McKim, Robert (ed) and McMahan, Jeff (ed).

The Origins of Moral Theology in the United States: Three Different Approaches. Curran, Charles E.

Thick and Thin: Moral Argument at Home and Abroad. Walzer, Michael.

Values and the Social Order. Radnitzky, Gerard (ed).

Vico and Moral Perception. Black, David W.

A Case for Proposition 209. Bradley, Gerard V.

A Critique of Pure Politics. Connolly, William E.

A Plea for Accuses. Zimmerman, Michael J.

A So-Called 'Fraud': Moral Modulations in a Literary Scandal. Lynch, Michael.

After Virtù: Rhetoric, Prudence and Moral Pluralism in Machiavelli. Garver, Eugene.

Alertness and Determination: A Note on Moral Phenomenology. Wilson, John.

An Inquiry into Ethical Relativism in Hindu Thought. Jhingran, Saral.

An Investigation of the Components of Moral Intensity. Marshall, Bev and Dewe, Philip.

An Objection to Smith's Argument for Internalism. Miller, Alexander.

Anerkennung und moralische Verpflichtung. Honneth, Axel.

Animals, Morality and Robert Boyle. MacIntosh, J J.

Appropriate Guilt: Between Expansion and Limitations (in Dutch). Van den Beld, A.

Aquinas's Doctrine of Moral Virtue and Its Significance for Theories of Facility. Mirkes, Renée.

Art, Imagination, and the Cultivation of Morals. Kieran, Matthew.

Axiological Foundations of "Human Dignity" (Spanish). Sánchez, Angel Martín.

Bemerkungen zur Natur der Angewandten Ethik (in Serbo-Croatian). Jakovljevic, Dragan.

Beyond Self and Other. Rogers, Kelly.

Can One Lie for Moral Reasons? (in Serbo-Croatian). Vukovic, Ivan.

Can There Be Moral Knowledge?. Sweet, William.

Character-Principlism and the Particularity Objection. Blustein, Jeffrey.

Cognitive and Moral Obstacles to Imputation. Murphy, Jeffrie G.

Cognitive Moral Development and Attitudes Toward Women Executives. Everett, Linda, Thorne, Debbie and Danehower, Carol.

Comments on the Paradox of Modesty (in Hebrew). Kosman, Admiel.

Computer Ethics and Moral Methodology. Van den Hoven, Jeroen.

Conceptions of Persons. Frohock, Fred M.

Concepts of Moral Management and Moral Maximization. Sikula, Sr, Andrew.

Conscience, Morality and Social Acceptability in an African Culture. Ebijuwa, T.

Consequentialism, Moralities of Concern, and Selfishness. Honderich, Ted.

Constructing a Hall of Reflection. Mulhall, Stephen.

Coscienza morale e realtà secondo J.G. Fichte. Schrader, Wolfgang H.

Critical Thinking and the Moral Sentiments: Adam Smith's Moral Psychology and Contemporary Debate in Critical Thinking and Informal Logic. Weinstein, Jack Russell.

De si es posible afirmar la construcción de una "eticidad" en la filosofía práctica de Kant. Arpini, Adriana.

## MORALITY

The Problem of Moral Absolutes in the Ethics of Vladimir Solov'ëv. Sergeevich Pugachev, Oleg.

The Special Features of Gandhian Ethics. Radha, S.

The Time to Punish and the Problem of Moral Luck. Statman, Daniel.

Three Paths in Moral Philosophy. Walzer, Michael.

Towards an Ethical Dimension of Decision Making in Organizations. Gottlieb, Jonathan Z and Sanzgiri, Jyotsna.

Trading Lives for Convenience: It's Not Just for Consequentialists. Norcross, Alastair.

Two Thomists on the Morality of a Jailbreak. Doyle, John P.

UN Responses in the Former Yugoslavia: Moral and Operational Choices. Weiss, Thomas G.

Using Moral Dilemmas in Children's Literature as a Vehicle for Moral Education and Teaching Reading Comprehension. Clare, Lindsay, Gallimore, Ronald and Patthey-Chavez, G Genevieve.

Utilitarianism for Sinners. Eriksson, Björn.

Vulnerable Populations and Morally Tainted Experiments. Luna, Florencia.

Well-Being and Despair: Dante's Ugolino. Qizilbash, Mozaffar.

Well-Being: On a Fundamental Concept of Practical Philosophy. Seel, Martin.

What is Conservatism?. Kekes, John.

What is Moral Authority?. Louden, Robert B.

What Makes Something Practically Worth Thinking About. Passell, Dan.

What Rationality Adds to Animal Morality. Waller, Bruce N.

Who is arguing about the Cat? Moral Action and Enlightenment according to Dōgen. Mikkelson, Douglas K.

Zur Logik der Moralität: Einige Fragen an A. Requate. De Vos, Lu.

'Ought' and Reasons for Action. Gewirth, Alan.

## MORALIZING

Moral Rhetoric in the Face of Strategic Weakness: Emperimental Clues for an Ancient Puzzle. Varoufakis, Yanis.

## MORE, H

"Henry More and Anne Conway on Preexistence and Universal Salvation" in *Mind Senior to the World,* Baldi, Marialuisa. Hutton, Sarah.

"Triangulating Divine Will: Henry More, Robert Boyle, and René Descartes on God's Relationship to the Creation" in *Mind Senior to the World,* Baldi, Marialuisa. Osler, Margaret J.

The Metaphysical Systems of Henry More and Isaac Newton. Jacob, Alexander.

## MORE, T

Integrity and the Feminist Teacher. O'Dea, Jane.

The Educational Contributions of Sir Thomas More. Masterson, David L.

## MOREIRAS, A

Rethinking Latinoamericanism: On the (Re)Articulations of the Global and the Local. Poblette, Juan.

## MORGAN, P

"Counter the Dangers of Education" in *Philosophy of Education (1996),* Margonis, Frank (ed). Huang, Xiaodan.

## MORMONISM

Quest and Question: Suffering and Emulation in the LDS Community. Campbell, Courtney S.

## MORRISON, T

"Toni Morrison at the Movies: Theorizing Race Through *Imitation of Life* (for Barbara Siegel)" in *Existence in Black: An Anthology of Black Existential Philosophy,* Gordon, Lewis R (ed). Schwartz, Gary.

American Political Culture, Prophetic Narration, and Toni Morrison's *Beloved.* Shulman, George.

## MORTALITY

*A Watch Over Mortality: The Philosophical Story of Julián Marías.* Raley, Harold.

Eugen Finks Phänomenologie des Todes. Schmidt, Gerhart.

Hans Jonas's *Mortality and Morality.* Bernstein, Richard J.

## MORTON, A

Truth, Objectivity, Counterfactuals and Gibbard. Edgington, Dorothy.

## MORUZZI, N

Political Toleration or Politics or Recognition: The Headscarves Affair Revisited. Köker, Levent.

## MOSER, P

What Does a Pyrrhonist Know?. Fogelin, Robert J.

## MOSES

Moses and the Thaumaturges: Philo's *De Vita Mosis* as a Rescue Operation. Remus, Harold.

## MOSES, Y

Thinking about Reasoning about Knowledge. Kyburg Jr, Henry E.

## MOTHER

*Teaching with Love: A Feminist Approach to Early Childhood Education.* Goldstein, Lisa S.

*Without a Woman to Read: Toward the Daughter in Postmodernism.* Price, Daniel.

Discontinuing Life Support in an Infant of a Drug-Addicted Mother: Whose Decision Is It?. Thomasma, David C and Jain, Renu.

Passing on the Faith: How Mother-Child Communication Influences Transmission of Moral Values. Taris, Toon W and Semin, Gün R.

Response to "Discounting Life Support in an Infant of a Drug Addicted Mother: Whose Decision Is It?" by Renu Jain and David C. Thomasma (CQ Vol 6, No 1). Oberman, Michelle.

## MOTHERHOOD

*Privacy: And the Politics of Intimate Life.* Boling, Patricia.

Against Marriage and Motherhood. Card, Claudia.

Fetal Motherhood: Toward a Compulsion to Generate Lives?. Bonnicksen, Andrea L.

Libertarianism, Self-Ownership, and Motherhood. Jeske, Diane.

## MOTHERING

"The Consequences of Single Motherhood" in *Sex, Preference, and Family: Essays on Law and Nature,* Nussbaum, Martha C (ed). McLanahan, Sara.

*Caring: Gender-Sensitive Ethics.* Bowden, Peta.

Feminist Critiques of New Fertility Technologies: Implications for Social Policy. Donchin, Anne.

Fetal Subjects and Maternal Objects: Reproductive Technology and the New Fetal/Maternal Relation. Squier, Susan.

## MOTHERSILL, M

Causes and Tastes: A Response. Shiner, Roger A.

## MOTION

"Hintikka on Plenitude in Aristotle" in *Knowledge and Inquiry: Essays on Jaakko Hintikka's Epistemology and Philosophy of Science,* Sintonen, Matti (ed). Bechler, Zev.

"La corporeità del tempo: Ancora su Ensidemo e il suo eraclitismo" in *Il Concetto di Tempo: Atti del XXXII Congresso Nazionale della Società Filosofica Italiana,* Casertano, Giovanni (ed). Spinelli, Emidio.

"Note sul tempo e sul moto attraverso la storia della fisica e le critiche" in *Il Concetto di Tempo: Atti del XXXII Congresso Nazionale della Società Filosofica Italiana,* Casertano, Giovanni (ed). Gianetto, Enrico.

*Malebranche's Theory of the* Soul: A Cartesian Interpretation. Schmaltz, Tad M.

A Mereological Look at Motion. Sayan, Erdinc.

Alexander of Aphrodisias on Celestial Motions. Bodnár, István M.

Clearing a 'Way' for Aquinas: How the Proof from Motion Concludes to God. Twetten, David B.

Eine aristotelische Logik der Intervalle, die Cantorsche Logik der Punkte und die physikalischen und kinematischen Prädikate. Arsenijevic, Milos.

Freedom as Motion: Thomas Hobbes and the Images of Liberalism. Feldman, Leslie D.

Mathematics, Model and Zeno's Paradoxes. Alper, Joseph S and Bridger, Mark.

Newton, die Trägheitskraft und die absolute Bewegung. Dellian, Ed.

Ontología del Movimiento en la Cosmología Venezolana del Siglo XVIII. Knabenschuh de Porta, Sabine.

The Problem of Motion in the *Sophist.* Lentz, William.

The Three Arrows of Zeno. Harrison, Craig.

## MOTIVATION

Applying Ethics: Modes, Motives, and Levels of Commitment. Prasad, Rajendra.

Emotion and the Function of Consciousness. DeLancey, Craig.

Epistemic Rationality, Epistemic Motivation, and Interpretive Charity. Henderson, David.

From Duty, Moral Worth, Good Will. Curzer, Howard J.

Hume—Not a "Humean" about Motivation. Persson, Ingmar.

Is Hume a Noncognitivist in the Motivation Argument?. Cohon, Rachel.

Judging Our Own Good. Wilkinson, T M.

Kant on Obligation and Motivation in Law and Ethics. Potter, Nelson.

Moralischer Internalismus: Motivation durch Wünsche versus Motivation durch Überzeugungen. Wolf, Jean-Claude.

Nonuse Values and the Environment: Economic and Ethical Motivations. Crowards, Tom.

On Motivation of Judicial Decisions (in Spanish). García Leal, Laura.

Reasons and Motivation. Parfit, Derek and Broome, John.

Smith on Moral Fetishism. Lillehammer, Hallvard.

Strength of Motivation and Being in Control. Mele, Alfred R.

The Nature of Motivation (and Why it Matters Less to Ethics than One Might Think). Noggle, Robert.

The Why's of Business Revisited. Duska, Ronald F.

Voting and Motivation. Graham, Keith.

## MOTIVE

Trust as Noncognitive Security about Motives. Becker, Lawrence C.

## MOTT, N

The Analysis of Particle Tracks: A Case for Trust in the Unity of Physics. Falkenburg, Brigitte.

## MOTT, P

Rescuing the Counterfactual Solution to Chisholm's Paradox. Niles, Ian.

## MOULINES, C

"Sobre objetividad y verdad en algunos escritos de Frege" in *Verdad: lógica, representación y mundo,* Villegas Forero, L. Corredor, Cristina.

## MOUNTAINS

*Geofilosofia del Paesaggio.* Bonesio, Luisa.

## MOUROUX, J

The Problem of Person and Jean Mouroux. McDermott, John M and Comandini, Glenn J.

## MOUTSOPOULOS, E

L'oeuvre musicale d'Evanghelos Moutsopoulos. Gabaude, Jean-Marc.

## MOVEMENT

Earthday 25: A Retrospective of Reform Environmental Movements. Devall, Bill.

## MOVEMENT

El problema del continuo en la escolástica española: Francisco de Oviedo (1602-1651). Luna Alcoba, Manuel.

Ghost Gestures: Phenomenological Investigations of Bodily Micromovements and Their Intercorporeal Implications. Behnke, Elizabeth A.

Maurice Merleau-Ponty and Rudolf Laban—An Interactive Appropriation of Parallels and Resonances. Connolly, Maureen and Lathrop, Anna.

Springing Forward and Falling Back: Traveling through Time. Edwards, Anne M.

Theoretical Issues in Social Movements. Michael, S M.

## MOVIE

*see* Film

## MUENSTER, G

Bemerkung zu: "Epistemologische Aspekte der neuen Entwicklungen in der Physik" von G. Münster. Mielke, Eckehard W.

## MUGUERZA, J

La Resolución del Perplejo. Gutiérrez, Edgardo.

## MULGAN, T

A Relatively Plausible Principle of Beneficence: Reply to Mulgan. Murphy, Liam B.

## MULTICULTURALISM

"Liberalismo y Multiculturalidad" in *Liberalismo y Comunitarismo: Derechos Humanos y Democracia,* Monsalve Solórzano, Alfonso (ed). Gutiérrez, Carlos B.

"Multiculturalism and a Politics of Persistence" in *Philosophy of Education (1996),* Margonis, Frank (ed). Houston, Barbara.

"The Goals of Multicultural Education: A Critical Re-Evaluation" in *Philosophy of Education (1996),* Margonis, Frank (ed). Feinberg, Walter.

"The Moral Presuppositions of Multicultural Education" in *Philosophy of Education (1996),* Margonis, Frank (ed). Heslep, Robert D.

"The Politics of Difference: Statehood and Toleration in a Multicultural World" in *The Morality of Nationalism,* McKim, Robert (ed). Walzer, Michael.

"Tolerance and Intolerance Gricean Intention and Doing Right by our Students" in *Philosophy of Education (1996),* Margonis, Frank (ed). Wagner, Paul A.

A Multicultural Continuum: A Critique of Will Kymlicka's Ethnic-Nation Dichotomy. Young, Iris Marion.

A Multicultural Examination of Business Ethics Perceptions. Allmon, Dean E, Chen, Henry C K and Pritchett, Thomas K (& others).

Cultural Conditioning: The Dark Underside of Multiculturalism (Part Two: A Way Out). Reinsmith, William.

Dilemmas of a Multicultural Theory of Citizenship. Parekh, Bhikhu.

Diversity in the Classroom. Maitzen, Stephen.

Do We Need a Liberal Theory of Minority Rights? Reply to Carens, Young, Parekh and Forst. Kymlicka, Will.

Foucault's Genealogy and Teaching Multiculturalism as a Subversive Activity. Kazmi, Y.

Foundations of a Theory of Multicultural Justice. Forst, Rainer.

German Concord, German Discord: Two Concepts of a Nation and the Challenge of Multiculturalism. Thomä, Dieter.

How Should Schools Respond to the Plurality of Values in a Multi-Cultural Society?. Burwood, Les R V.

Liberalism and Culture. Carnes, Joseph H.

Modern Medicine in a Multicultural Setting. Rasinski Gregory, Dorothy.

Moral Paralysis and the Ethnocentric Fallacy. Applebaum, Barbara.

Multiculturalism and Gender Equity: The U.S. "Difference" Debates Revisited. Adler, Pierre.

Multiculturalism: An Unhappy Marriage of Multicultural Education and Postmodernism. Webster, Yehudi O.

No Goddess Was Your Mother: Western Philosophy's Abandonment of Its Multicultural Matrix. Schroeder, Steven.

Plurality of the Good? The Problem of Affirmative Tolerance in a Multicultural Society from an Ethical Point of View. Apel, Karl-Otto.

Second Thoughts on Multi-Culturalism. Davis, Michael.

The Limits of Tolerance. Kurtz, Paul.

The Multiculturalism of Fear. Levy, Jacob T.

The Politics of Difference: Statehood and Toleration in a Multicultural World. Walzer, Michael.

## MULTINATIONAL

Global Ethics: An Integrative Framework for MNEs. Desai, Ashay B and Rittenburg, Terri.

## MULTIPLICATION

The Theory of Integer Multiplication with Order Restricted to Primes is Decidable. Maurin, Françoise.

Une Correspondance entre Anneaux Partiels et Groupes. Simonetta, Patrick.

## MULTIPLICITY

The Origin of the Concept of Multiplicity in Gilles Deleuze's (in Portuguese). Cardoso Júnior, Hélio Rebello.

## MULTISET

The Order Types of Termination Orderings on Monadic Terms, Strings and Multisets. Martin, Ursula and Scott, Elizabeth.

## MUNOZ DELGADO, V

Lógica, ciencia y filosofía en Vicente Munoz Delgado (1922-1995). Fuertes Herreros, José Luis.

Vicente Munoz Delgado y Angel Amor Ruibal. Dafonte, César Raña.

## MURDER

A Critical Analysis of Hunters' Ethics. Luke, Brian.

Battered Women Who Kill: Victims and Agents of Violence. Hartline, Sharon E.

Le meurtre de soi. Dugré, François.

Reasons for Anger: A Response to Narayan and von Hirsch's Provocation Theory. Horder, Jeremy.

The Suppression of Nuns and the Ritual Murder of their Special Dead in Two Buddhist Monastic Texts. Schopen, Gregory.

## MURDOCH, I

*The Annual of the Society of Christian Ethics with Cumulative Index.* Beckley, Harlan (ed).

Constructing a Hall of Reflection. Mulhall, Stephen.

Imagining the Good: Iris Murdoch's Godless Theology. Antonaccio, Maria.

## MURRAY, C

The Bell Curse. Haslett, D W.

## MUSEUM

*After the End of Art: Contemporary Art and the Pale of History.* Danto, Arthur C.

Preservice Art Education and Learning in Art Museums. Lauzier Stone, Denise.

## MUSIC

*see also* Jazz, Rock Music

"Introduction: New Ways of Thinking about Musical Meaning" in *Music and Meaning,* Robinson, Jenefer (ed). Robinson, Jenefer.

"Justifying Music in General Education: Belief in Search of Reason" in *Philosophy of Education (1996),* Margonis, Frank (ed). Jorgensen, Estelle R.

"Language and the Interpretation of Music" in *Music and Meaning,* Robinson, Jenefer (ed). Cahn, Steven M.

"Listening with Imagination: Is Music Representational?" in *Music and Meaning,* Robinson, Jenefer (ed). Walton, Kendall.

"Music and Negative Emotion" in *Music and Meaning,* Robinson, Jenefer (ed). Levinson, Jerrold.

"Musical Culture as a Configuration of Subcultures" in *Epistemology and History,* Zeidler-Janiszewska, Anna (ed). Banaszak, Grzegorz.

"Musical Idiosyncrasy and Perspectival Listening" in *Music and Meaning,* Robinson, Jenefer (ed). Higgins, Kathleen Marie.

"Progress and Development in Music History" in *The Idea of Progress,* McLaughlin, Peter (ed). Flotzinger, Rudolf.

"The Philosophy of Dissonance: Adorno and Schoenberg" in *The Semblance of Subjectivity,* Huhn, Tom (ed). Hullot-Kentor, Robert.

"Why Listen to Sad Music If It Makes One Feel Sad?" in *Music and Meaning,* Robinson, Jenefer (ed). Davies, Stephen.

*Art and Its Messages: Meaning, Morality, and Society.* Davies, Stephen (ed).

*Essays on the Nature of Art.* Deutsch, Eliot.

*Making a Necessity of Virtue.* Sherman, Nancy.

*Music and Meaning.* Robinson, Jenefer (ed).

*Nietzsches Werke Kritische Gesamtausgabe: III 5/2.* Groddeck, Wolfram (ed) and Kohlenbach, Michael (ed).

*Philosophies of Arts: An Essay in Differences.* Kivy, Peter.

*The Tanner Lectures on Human Values, Volume 18, 1997.* Peterson, Grethe B (ed).

A Micro-Phenomenology of Consonance and Dissonance. Lind, Richard.

Aestheticide: Architecture and the Death of Art. Bearn, Gordon C F.

Art, Value, and Philosophy. Levinson, Jerrold.

Bemerkungen zur musikalischen Künstlerästhetik des 20.Jahrhunderts. Von Thülen, Bodil.

Born to Affirm the Eternal Recurrence: Nietzsche, Buber, and Springsteen. Cohen, Jonathan.

Brahms-Bruckner: deux univers en dissonance. Moutsopoulos, Evanghélos.

Conceptual Frameworks for World Musics in Education. Boyce-Tillman, June.

Creation and Discovery in Musical Works. Woodruff, David M.

Critical Perspectives on Early Twentieth-Century American Avant-Garde Composers. O'Grady, Terence J.

Damned if You Do and Damned if You Don't: Sexual Aesthetics and the Music of Dame Ethel Smyth. Gates, Eugene.

El canto gregorià, un model de música perfecta. Banyeres Baltasà, Hug.

Esthétique de l'interprétation créatrice—Essai sur l'idée "interprétation" de Gisèle Brelet. Shibaike, Masami.

Evaluating Edwin Gordon's Music Learning Theory from a Critical Thinking Perspective. Woodford, Paul G.

Evaluating Music. Levinson, Jerrold.

Hearing Musical Works in their Entirety. McAdoo, Nick.

Innovation and Conservatism in Performance Practice. Godlovitch, Stanley.

Ir à Opera e Gostar de lá Voltar! A Faculdade de Filosofia e as Licenciaturas em Ensino. Nuno Salgado Vaz, Carlos.

Is Edwin Gordon's Learning Theory a Cognitive One?. Stokes, W Ann.

Kant sur la musique. Parret, Herman.

Kierkegaard: Metaphor and the Musical Erotic. Grund, Cynthia M.

Kritische Theorie als Erfahrungswissenschaft: Lagebericht anlässlich einiger Neuerscheinungen. Behrens, Roger.

L'esthétique musicale de Descartes et le cartésianisme. Van Wymeersch, Brigitte.

## MUSIC

L'oeuvre musicale d'Evanghelos Moutsopoulos. Gabaude, Jean-Marc.
Listening to Music: Performances and Recordings. Gracyk, Theodore A.
Listening, Heeding, and Respecting the Ground at One's Feet: Knowledge and the Arts Across Cultures. O'Loughlin, Marjorie.
Meaning and the Art-Status of 'Music Alone'. McFee, Graham.
Melody in Life: Some Reflections. Roy, Subrata.
Methode der Musikgeschichte von Guido Adler. Ito, Hisae.
Modelo y Fenomenología: Nietzsche contra Hegel: El Renacimiento de la Tragedia en el Renacimiento de la Opera. Cohen-Levinas, Danielle.
Music, Imagination, and Play. Reichling, Mary J.
Musical Works, Improvisation, and the Principle of Continuity. Brown, Lee B.
Musicalisation of Metaphor and Metaphoricalness in Music. Klempe, Hroar.
Musik und Sprache beim Frühen Nietzsche (in Japanese). Toshiyuki, Matsuzaki.
Narrative, Drama, and Emotion in Instrumental Music. Maus, Fred Everett.
O retorno ao mito, Nietzsche, a música e a tragédia. Ribeiro dos Santos, Leonel.
On Scores and Works of Music: Interpretation and Identity. Edlund, Bengt.
On the Question of Method in Philosophical Research. Reichling, Mary J.
Rock Aesthetics and Musics of the World. Regev, Motti.
Romanticizing Rock Music. Gracyk, Theodore A.
Singing and Speaking. Sparshott, Francis.
So, You Want to Sing with *The Beatles*? Too Late!. Davies, Stephen.
Sonate, que te fais-je? Toward a Theory of Interpretation. Edlund, Bengt.
Synchrony Lost, Synchrony Regained: The Achievement of Musical Co-ordination. Weeks, Peter.
Text and Music Revisited. Fornäs, Johan.
The Aesthetically Good vs. The Morally Good. Davenport, Manuel.
The Aesthetics of a *Tabula Rasa*: Western Art Music's Avant-Garde from 1949-1953. Toop, Richard.
The Aesthetics of Silence in Live Musical Performance. Judkins, Jennifer.
The Harmony of the World and its Greek Connection (in Czech). Krámsky, David.
The Issue of Music in Schools: An *Unfinished Symphony*?. Carlin, Joi L.
The Nature of the Reception of European Musical Phenomena as a Paradigm of the Genuineness of Serbian Music—System of Values and Artistic Horizons. Veselinovic-Hofman, Mirjana.
Toward an Aesthetic of Black Musical Expression. Duran, Jane and Stewart, Earl.
Value Monism, Value Pluralism, and Music Education: Sparshott as Fox. Alperson, Philip.
Virtuosity as a Performance Concept: A Philosophical Analysis. Howard, Vernon A.
Wittgenstein's Musical Understanding. Worth, Sarah E.

## MUSIC EDUCATION

"Can the Justification of Music Education be Justified?" in *Philosophy of Education (1996)*, Margonis, Frank (ed). Yob, Iris M.
Aesthetic and Praxial Philosophies of Music Education Compared: A Semiotic Consideration. Spychiger, Maria B.
Building Theory in Music Education: A Personal Account. LeBlanc, Albert.
Conceptual Frameworks for World Musics in Education. Boyce-Tillman, June.
Edwin Gordon Responds. Gordon, Edwin.
Ethics and the Philosophy of Music Education. Richmond, John W.
The "Is-Ought" Fallacy and Musicology: The Assumptions of Pedagogy. Davis, James A.
The Issue of Music in Schools: An *Unfinished Symphony*?. Carlin, Joi L.
Value Monism, Value Pluralism, and Music Education: Sparshott as Fox. Alperson, Philip.
Who Benefits from the National Standards: A Response to Catherine M. Schmidt's "Who Benefits? Music Education and the National Standards.". Lehman, Paul R.
Who Benefits? Music Education and the National Standards. Schmidt, Catherine M.

## MUSICOLOGY

Faits et interprétations en musicologie. Nattiez, Jean-Jacques.
Text and Music Revisited. Fornäs, Johan.
The "Is-Ought" Fallacy and Musicology: The Assumptions of Pedagogy. Davis, James A.

## MUSIL, R

*Konstellation und Existenz.* Goebel, Eckart.
Las teoría y su influencia política y socio-jurídica en los problemas de la democracia. Mari, Enrique E.

## MUSLIM

*see also* Islam
"Enlightenment in the Islamic World: Muslims—Victims of Mneumonic Success" in *Averroës and the Enlightenment*, Wahba, Mourad (ed). Irfan, Ghazala.
Business Ethics in Islamic Context: Perspectives of a Muslim Business Leader. Abeng, Tanri.
Muslims and Sex Education. Halstead, J Mark.

## MUST

"Must I Do What I Ought? (Or Will the Least I Can Do Do?)" in *Deontic Logic, Agency and Normative Systems*, Brown, Mark A (ed). McNamara, Paul.

## MYSTERY

*"La volontéde puissance" n'existe pas*: A proposito dell'edizione francese di alcuni saggi di Mazzino Montinari. Viola, Salvatore.
Fred Feldman's *Confrontations with the Reaper: A Philosophical Study of the Nature and Value of Death*. Marquis, Don.
God and Cosmos: Can the "Mystery of Mysteries" be Solved?. Oakes, Robert.
La creación de la nada: ¿apoteosis de la producción o misterio revelado?. Rivera, José A.
La muerte, ese escándalo. Pfeiffer, María Luisa.
The Mysterious Grand Properties of Forrest. Noordhof, Paul.

## MYSTIC

Mystics and Pragmatics in the Non-Philosophy of F. Laruelle: Lessons for Rorty's Metaphilosophizing. Sumares, Manuel.

## MYSTICAL EXPERIENCE

Pursuing Peirce. Brent, Joseph.

## MYSTICISM

*Assoluto: Frammenti di misticismo nella filosofia di Francis Herbert Bradley.* Taroni, Paolo.
*Enlightenment East and West.* Angel, Leonard.
*Exploring Unseen Worlds: William James and the Philosophy of Mysticism.* Barnard, G William.
*Forms of Transcendence: Heidegger and Medieval Mystical Theology.* Sikka, Sonya.
Contemplación filosófica y contemplación mística en San Buenaventura. Andereggen, Ignacio E M.
Eckhart's Anachorism. Bernasconi, Robert.
Epistemology of Mysticism. Venkatalakshmi, M.
Frei Manuel de S. Luís Escritor e Orador Açoriano dos Séculos XVII-XVIII (1660-1736). Pimentel, Manuel Cândido.
Jñãnagarbha and the "God's-Eye View". Pyysiäinen, Ilkka.
La religion de Pascal. Wetzel, Marc.
Life, Art, and Mysticism. Van Stigt, Walter P.
Maître Eckhart et le discernement mystique: A propos de la rencontre de Suso avec *la (chose) sauvage sans nom*. Wackernagel, Wolfgang.
Martin Heidegger fra Misticismo e Nazionalsocialismo. Di Meola, Nestore.
Mysticism and Divine Mutability. Dombrowski, Daniel A.
Mysticism and Social Action: The Mystic's Calling, Development and Social Activity. Woods, Richard.
Mythical Perspective and Philosophical Speculation in Late Greek Philosophy (in Czech). Mogyoródi, Emese.
Scientific Attitudes Towards an Eastern Mystic. Danyluk, Angie.
The Role of Marxism and Deconstruction in Demystifying Aesthetics. Pokker, P K.
Wechselgrundsatz: Friedrich Schlegels philosophischer Ausgangspunkt. Frank, Manfred.

## MYTH

"Mythos und Moderne in der *Philosophie der symbolischen Formen* Ernst Cassirers" in *Epistemology and History*, Zeidler-Janiszewska, Anna (ed). Paetzold, Heinz.
"Progress in Philosophy" in *The Idea of Progress*, McLaughlin, Peter (ed). Prawitz, Dag.
*African Philosophy: Myth and Reality.* Hountondji, Paulin J and Evans, Henri (trans).
*European Existentialism.* Langiulli, Nino (ed).
*Kenneth Burke and the Scapegoat Process.* Carter, C Allen.
*Lex Regia.* Lomonaco, Fabrizio.
*Myth and the Limits of Reason.* Stambovsky, Phillip.
*The Magic Mirror: Myth's Abiding Power.* Baeten, Elizabeth M.
Animal symbolicum?. Loewenstein, Bedrich.
I sandali di Ermes e lo spazio di De Kooning: Appunti per una possibile negazione dell'epelysìa di metaphysikà. Incardona, Nunzio.
La psychanalyse: mythe et théorie. Laplanche, Jean.
La questione del mito. Genovese, Rino.
Lo sguardo di Blanchot e la musica di Orfeo: Visione e ascolto nell'ispirazione poetica. Carrera, Alessandro.
Myth, Measurement, and the Minimum Wage: Sound and Fury Signifying What?. Whitman, Glen.
Myths as Instructions from Ancestors: The Example of Oedipus. Steadman, Lyle B and Palmer, Craig T.
Myths of Sexuality Education. Morris, Ronald.
Nouveautés Schellingiennes. Tilliette, Xavier.
O retorno ao mito, Nietzsche, a música e a tragédia. Ribeiro dos Santos, Leonel.
Protesi, ovvero la metamorfosi. Marchis, Vittorio.
Re-Claiming Hestia: Goddess of Everyday Life. Thompson, Patricia J.
Reflexoes sobre o Mito: Comentários à Mitologia de Eudoro de Sousa. De Soveral, Eduardo Abranches.
Religión entre Ilustración y Romanticismo. Ortiz-Osés, Andrés.
The Myths of Learning Disabilities: The Social Construction of a Disorder. Zuriff, G E.
The Post-Canonica! Adventures of Mahāsammata. Collins, Steven and Huxley, Andrew.
Two Biblical Myths of Creation: An Exploration in Ecological Philosophy. Agera, Cassian R.
Vico e la Poesia. Placella, Vincenzo.
Vittorio Imbriani e il *Kant poeta*. Petrone, Giuseppe Landolfi.

## NATURE

Rolston, Naturogenic Value and Genuine Biocentrism. Thomas, Emyr Vaughan.

Scary Monsters: Hegel and the Nature of the Monstrous. Gunkel, David.

Sensibility and Understanding. Millar, Alan.

Sulla presenza di Descartes nella *Galleria di Minerva*. Crasta, Francesca Maria.

Sur l'origine de l'éthique de Zénon de Cittium. Seidl, Horst.

Swift Things Are Beautiful: Contrast in the Natural Aesthetic. Kupfer, Joseph H.

The Hole in the Ground of Induction. Maher, Patrick.

The Inhabitants of Other Planets in Bernardin de Saint-Pierre's *Les Harmonies de la nature* (in French). Duflo, Colas.

The Nature of Transpersonal Experience. Beskova, Irina Aleksandrovna.

The Parochial Universalist Conception of 'Philosophy' and 'African Philosophy'. Ikuenobe, Polycarp.

The Philosophical Challenge of Technology. Mitcham, Carl.

Thinking Naturally. O'Neill, John.

Thomas Aquinas and the Problem of Nature in Physics II, I. Lang, Helen S.

Translating Gorgias in [Aristotle] 980a10. Davis, Janet B.

Truth and Meaning in George Lindbeck's *The Nature of Doctrine*. Richards, Jay Wesley.

Twistors and Self-Reference: On the Generic Non-Linearity of Nature. Zimmermann, Rainer E.

Unpacking the Monad: Leibniz's Theory of Causality. Clatterbaugh, Kenneth and Bobro, Marc.

Was kann heute unter Naturphilosophie verstehen?. Stöckler, Manfred.

Where Do Laws of Nature Come From?. Cartwright, Nancy.

Will die Natur unwiderstehlich die Republik? Einige Reflexionen anlässlich einer rätselhaften Textpassage in Kants Friedensschrift. Ludwig, Bernd.

## NAUDE, G

*Rinascimento e Libertinismo: Studi su Gabriel Naudé.* Bianchi, Lorenzo.

## NAZISM

*Animal Acts: Configuring the Human in Western History.* Ham, Jennifer (ed) and Senior, Matthew (ed).

*Heidegger, Philosophy, Nazism.* Young, Julian.

*Nietzsche and Jewish Culture.* Golomb, Jacob (ed).

*On Heidegger's Nazism and Philosophy.* Rockmore, Tom.

*The Political Consequences of Thinking: Gender and Judaism in the Work of Hannah Arendt.* Ring, Jennifer.

Die Kunst der Anspielung: Hans-Georg Gadamers philosophische Interventionen im NS. Orozco, Teresa.

Forbidding Nasty Knowledge: On the Use of Ill-Gotten Information. Godlovitch, Stanley.

Franz Böhms "Deutsche Philosophie": Über den Versuch einer erkenntnistheoretischen Grundlegung des "Nationalsozialismus". Hailer, Martin.

From Atlas to Adolph: Body Building, Physical Culture, and National Socialism. Pickens, Donald K.

Heideggers "Schweigen" Technik, Nazi-Medizin und Wissenschaftskultur. Cox, Philip N.

Moral Crutches and Nazi Theists: A Defense of and Reservations about Undertaking Theism. Lemos, John.

Reflections on My Father's Experience with Doctors during the Shoah (1939-1945). Bursztajn, Harold J.

The *Nazi*! Accusation and Current US Proposals. Cavanaugh, Thomas A.

The Land of the Fearful and the Free. Tamir, Yael.

Transitional Regimes and the Rule of Law. Golding, Martin P.

Über Heideggers "Schweigen" reden. Alisch, Rainer.

Untameable Singularity (Some Remarks on *Broken Hegemonies*). Granel, Gérard and Wolfe, Charles T (trans).

## NEALE, S

Contextos, Creencías y Anáforas. Ezcurdia, Maite.

The Philosophical Insignificance of Gödel's Slingshot. Oppy, Graham.

## NECESSARY

"Box" in Intuitionistic Modal Logic. DeVidi, David and Solomon, Graham.

## NECESSARY BEING

Contingency of Being—Argument for the Existence of God: Attempt at Critical Analysis Part I (in Polish). Zieminski, Ireneusz.

## NECESSITY

"Again Ethics: A Levinasian Reading of Caputo Reading Levinas" in *Knowing Other-Wise: Philosophy at the Threshold of Spirituality,* Olthuis, James H (ed). Dudiak, Jeffrey M.

"Necessity and Normativity" in *The Cambridge Companion to Wittgenstein,* Sluga, Hans (ed). Glock, Hans-Johann.

"The Logical Foundations of Peirce's Indeterminism" in *The Rule of Reason: The Philosophy of Charles Sanders Peirce,* Forster, Paul (ed). Forster, Paul.

"The Personality of Researchers and the Necessity of Schools in Science" in *The Idea of University,* Brzezinski, Jerzy (ed). Nowak, Leszek.

*Arguing for Atheism: An Introduction to the Philosophy of Religion.* Le Poidevin, Robin.

*Pierre Bayle e l'Italia.* Bianchi, Lorenzo.

A Completeness Proof for a Logic with an Alternative Necessity Operator. Demri, Stéphane.

Agustin de Herrera, A Treatise on Aleatory Probability *De Necessitate Morali in Genere.* Knebel, Sven K (ed & trans).

Conventions, Cognitivism, and Necessity. Shalkowski, Scott A.

Darwin: Evolution and Contingency (in Spanish). Rodriguez Camarero, Luis.

Dem blinden Trieb ein Auge einsetzen?: Die Verkehrung von Fichtes ursprünglicher Intention in seiner Auseinandersetzung mit Kant. Hutter, Axel.

Donagan on Cases of Necessity. Malone, Michael J.

Essere e tempo: Il primordio dell'annientamento. Incardona, Nunzio.

Kant and Wittgenstein: Philosophy, Necessity and Representation. Glock, Hans-Johann.

La necesidad como totalidad de la posibilidad en Leibniz. Socorro Fernández, Maria.

Modal Bloopers: Why Believable Impossibilities are Necessary. Sorensen, Roy A.

Moralität und Nützlichkeit. Enskat, Rainer.

Necessity, Apriority, and Logical Structure. Weitzman, Leora.

Notes on Peirce's Objective Idealism. Sokolowski, William R.

On Necessity and Existence. Rosado Haddock, Guillermo E.

Rights, Necessity, and Tort Liability. Devlin, Kai.

Theological Necessity. Schlesinger, George N.

Thomas' Second Way: A Defense by Modal Scientific Reasoning. Trundle, Jr, Robert C.

Transcendentalism, Nomicity and Modal Thought. Muresan, Valentin.

Vom Begriff der Freiheit: Fichtes Leipziger Kant-Studien (1790). Lindner, Konrad.

Zur Komplementarität von Freiheit und Notwendigkeit des menschlichen Handelns. Hoche, Hans-Ulrich.

## NEDELLEC, E

La prima scuola tomistica: Erveo di Nedellec e l'epistemologia teologica. Piccari, Paolo.

## NEED

*Morals Based on Needs.* Ohlsson, Ragnar.

*On Economic Inequality.* Sen, Amartya.

Preferences or Happiness? Tibor Scitovsky's Psychology of Human Needs. Friedman, Jeffrey and McCabe, Adam.

The Definition of Man Needs. Gairola, M P.

Two Concepts of the Ethics of Responsibility: H. Jonas and K.-O. Apel (in Czech). Machalová, Tatiana.

What Can't We Do with Economics?: Some Comments on George Ainslie's Picoeconomics. De Sousa, Ronald B.

## NEGATION

*Logic and Existence.* Lawlor, Leonard (trans), Sen, Amit (trans) and Hyppolite, Jean.

*The Primary Logic: Instruments for a Dialogue between the Two Cultures.* Malatesta, Michele.

*The Principles of Mathematics Revisited.* Hintikka, Jaakko.

A Logic-Based Modelling of Prolog Resulation Sequences Including the Negation as Failure Rule. Jeavons, John S and Crossley, John N.

An Equational Axiomatization of Dynamic Negation and Relational Composition. Hollenberg, Marco.

Considerations on the Plurality of the "Nothing-Speech" (in German). Sonderegger, Erwin.

Debbo io ricordare? L'arte e la negazione della memoria. Fisch, Harold.

Denied Conditionals Are Not Negated Conditionals. Fulda, Joseph S.

From Negation to Silence: Maimonides' Reception in the Latin West (in Hebrew). Schwartz, Yosef.

Kant's Doctrine of Categories: An Attempt at Some Clarification. Gupta, R K.

La negación de los juicios estrictamente particulares en la tetravalencia. Öffenberger, Niels and Bustos López, Javier.

Le désir et la mort chez Pascal: Hypothèses pour une lecture. Bove, Laurent.

Peirce's "Entanglement" with the Principles of Excluded Middle and Contradiction. Lane, Robert.

Some Problems of Approach to Nagarjuna's Philosophy (in Serbo-Croatian). Djordjevic, Dejan.

Theorie législative de la négation pure. Béziau, Jean-Yves.

## NEGATIVE

"Processing of Negative Sentences by Adults with Unilateral Cerebral Lesions" in *Verdad: lógica, representación y mundo,* Villegas Forero, L. Juncos-Rabadán, Onésimo.

Basanta Kumar Mallik and the Negative. Walker, Mary M.

Extended Gergonne Syllogisms. Johnson, Fred.

Negative Capability Reclaimed: Literature and Philosophy *Contra* Politics. Hassan, Ihab.

The Logical Structure of Russell's Negative Facts. Patterson, Wayne A.

## NEGLIGENCE

Conscious Negligence. Brady, James B.

Handlungstheoretische Aspekte der Fahrlässigkeit. Seebass, Gottfried.

## NEGOTIATION

The Negotiation of Equivalence. Arditi, Benjamin.

## NEGRO

see Blacks

## NEHAMAS, A

Nehamas' *Life as Literature*: A Case for the Defence. Godden, David M.

## NEIGHBOR

Good Neighbors Make Good Fences: Frost's "Mending Wall". Trachtenberg, Zev.

The Love of God and Neighbor in Simone Weil's Philosophy. Stephenson, Wendell.

**NELSON, M**
Infinite Utility: Insisting on Strong Monotonicity. Lauwers, Luc.

**NEMORARIUS, J**
El *De Numeris Datis* de Jordanus Nemorarius como sistema matemático de signos. Puig, Luis.

**NEO-KANTIANISM**
"Cassirers Renaissance-Auffassung" in *Grenzen der kritischen Vernunft,* Schmid, Peter A. Schmidt-Biggemann, Wilhelm.
"Die Aktualität des Neukantianismus: Bemerkungen zu einem unumgänglichen Thema der Neukantianismusforschung" in *Grenzen der kritischen Vernunft,* Schmid, Peter A. Ollig, Hans-Ludwig.
"L'incontro problematico tra *Historismus* e neo-kantiano" in *Lo Storicismo e la Sua Storia: Temi, Problemi, Prospettive,* Cacciatore, Giuseppe (ed). Bonito Oliva, Rossella.
*Grenzen der kritischen Vernunft.* Schmid, Peter A and Zurbuchen, Simone.
Die Fichte-Rezeption in der südwestdeutschen Schule des Neukantianismus. Heinz, Marion.
War Rickert ein Fichteaner? Die Fichteschen Züge des badischen Neukantianismus. Przylebski, Andrzej.

**NEO-PLATONISM**
*Aristotle and Neoplatonism in Late Antiquity: Interpretations of the De Anima.* Blumenthal, H J.
*Christian Philosophy: Greek, Medieval, Contemporary Reflections.* Sweeney, Leo.
*La Scienza Nuova* nella Storia del Pensiero Politico. Voegelin, Eric and Zanetti, Gianfrancesco (trans).
*Proclus: Neo-Platonic Philosophy and Science.* Siorvanes, Lucas.
*The Neoplatonic Metaphysics and Epistemology of Anselm of Canterbury.* Rogers, Katherin A.
A Neoplatonist's Pantheism. Leslie, John.
Characterisation and Interpretation: The Importance of Drama in Plato's *Sophist.* Benitez, Eugenio E.
Origen on Time. Lampert, Jay.
Pseudo-Dionysius Areopagiticus and Saint Simon The New Theologian (in Czech). Perczel, István.
The Ontological Relation "One-Many" according to the Neoplatonist Damascius. Térézis, Christos.

**NEONATE**
Dwingende feiten en hun verborgen moraal: Over doen en laten in de neonatologiepraktijk. Mesman, Jessica.
Futile Care in Neonatology: An Interim Report from Colorado. Hulac, Peter and Barbour, Elizabeth.
Informed Consent as a Parent Involvement Model in the NICU. Luckner, Kleia R and Weinfeld, Irwin J.
Reducing Suffering and Ensuring Beneficial Outcomes for Neonates: An Ethical Perspective. Brodeur, Dennis.

**NEOPOSITIVISM**
*Un'Introduzione All'Epistemologia Contemporanea.* Gava, Giacomo (ed).
I rapporti tra scienza e metafisica. Marsonet, Michele.

**NEOREALISM**
Panlogismo, Pantagrismo, e o *Saber Mais* do Romance—Uma Leitura de *Mudança* de Vergílio Ferreira. Mourao, Luís.

**NET**
Completeness Results for Linear Logic on Petri Nets. Engberg, Uffe.

**NETWORK**
Disunity in Psychology and Other Sciences: The Network or the Block Universe?. Viney, Wayne.
PDP Networks can Provide Models that are not Mere Implementations of Classical Theories. Dawson, Michael R W, Medler, David A and Berkeley, Istvan S N.
Rethinking Distributed Representation. Ramsey, William.

**NEUMANN, J**
J. v. Neumanns und J.S. Bells Theorem: Ein Vergleich. Scheibe, Erhard.
Theodore Karman, Paul Wigner, John Neumann, Leo Szilard, Edward Teller and Their Ideas of Ultimate Reality and Meaning. Horvath, Tibor.

**NEURAL**
A Rippling Relatableness in Reality. Ashbrook, James B.
Neural Fetal Tissue Transplants: Old and New Issues. Nora, Lois Margaret and Mahowald, Mary B.
Structure, Strategy and Self in the Fabrication of Conscious Experience. Claxton, Guy.
Sub-Phenomenology. Jopling, David A.
The Brain and the I: Neurodevelopment and Personal Identity. Mahowald, Mary B.

**NEURAL NETWORK**
Predicting Our Health: Ethical Implications of Neural Networks and Outcome Potential Predictions. Seddon, Andrew M.

**NEURATH, O**
"Neurath against Method" in *Origins of Logical Empiricism,* Giere, Ronald N (ed). Cartwright, Nancy.
"The Enlightenment Ambition of Epistemic Utopianism: Otto Neurath's Theory of Science in Historical Perspective" in *Origins of Logical Empiricism,* Giere, Ronald N (ed). Uebel, Thomas E.
Anti-Foundationalism and the Vienna Circle's Revolution in Philosophy. Uebel, Thomas E.

How Postmodern was Neurath's Idea of Unity of Science?. Reisch, George A.

**NEUROLOGY**
An Integral Theory of Consciousness. Wilber, Ken.
Modelos cognoscitivos para la filosofía contemporánea de la mente. Rodríguez Rodríguez, Rodolfo J.
On the Mechanism of Consciousness. Cotterill, Rodney M J.
The Ghost in the Machine—Fights—the Last Battle for the Human Soul. Watson, Richard A.

**NEUROPHYSIOLOGY**
Die vierte bis siebte Kränkung des Menschen—Gehirn, Evolution und Menschenbild. Vollmer, Gerhard.

**NEUROSCIENCE**
"Mind" as Humanizing the Brain: Toward a Neurotheology of Meaning. Ashbrook, James B.
*Explaining Consciousness—The 'Hard Problem'.* Shear, Jonathan (ed).
*Scienza e filosofia della coscienza.* Gava, Giacomo.
*The Meaning of Mind: Language, Morality, and Neuroscience.* Szasz, Thomas.
Crisis of Brain and Self. Keyes, C Don.
Happiness Doesn't Come in Bottles: Neuroscientists Learn That Joy Comes Through Dancing, Not Drugs. Freeman, Walter J.
Honderich on the Consequences of Determinism. Double, Richard.
How We Get There From Here: Dissolution of the Binding Problem. Hardcastle, Valerie Gray.
Integrating Neuroscience, Psychology, and Evolutionary Biology through a Teleological Conception of Function. Mundale, Jennifer and Bechtel, William.
Moving Forward on the Problem of Consciousness. Chalmers, David J.
On the Use of Visualizations in the Practice of Science. Sargent, Pauline.

**NEUTRALITY**
"Neutrality in Education and Derrida's call for "Double Duty" in *Philosophy of Education (1996),* Margonis, Frank (ed). Egéa-Kuehne, Denise.
"The Double-Bind of "Double Duty" in *Philosophy of Education (1996),* Margonis, Frank (ed). Davis, Hilary E.
*Beyond Neutrality: Perfectionism and Politics.* Sher, George.
Defending Freirean Intervention. Roberts, Peter.
Impartiality and Liberal Neutrality. Caney, Simon.
Market Non-Neutrality: Systematic Bias in Spontaneous Orders. diZerga, Gus.
Myths of Paulo Freire. Weiler, Kathleen.
Polanyi on Liberal Neutrality. Goodman, C P.
Value Neutrality and Ideological Commitment in Political Philosophy. Sidorsky, David.

**NEVILLE, R**
"Metaphysics, Experience, Being, and God: Response to Robert C. Neville" in *Reason, Experience, and God: John E. Smith in Dialogue,* Colapietro, Vincent M. Smith, John E.

**NEW TESTAMENT**
Interiority and Epiphany: A Reading in New Testament Ethics. Williams, Rowan D.

**NEW ZEALAND**
High School Teaching of Bioethics in New Zealand, Australia and Japan. Asada, Yukiko, Tsuzuki, Miho and Akiyama, Shiro.

**NEW, C**
The Time to Punish and the Problem of Moral Luck. Statman, Daniel.

**NEWBERG, A**
Methods and Systematic Reflections: Unitary States, Free Will and Ultimate Reality. Newberg, Andrew B.

**NEWBY, M**
Living Educational Theories and Living Contradictions: A Response to Mike Newby. Whitehead, Jack.

**NEWMAN, H**
La fonction argumentative dans les discours théologiques: L'exemple de la *Grammaire de l'assentiment* de Neuman. Viau, Marcel.

**NEWMAN, J**
Lonergan on Newman's Conversion. Egan, Philip A.
Newman on Faith and Rationality. Lamont, John R T.

**NEWS**
"Journalistische Verantwortung: Medienethik als Qualitätsproblem" in *Angewandte Ethik: Die Bereichsethiken und ihre theoretische Fundierung,* Nida-Rümelin, Julian (ed). Teichert, Will.

**NEWTON**
"Il tempo come percezione: gli empiristi inglesi" in *Il Concetto di Tempo: Atti del XXXII Congresso Nazionale della Società Filosofica Italiana,* Casertano, Giovanni (ed). Bellini, Ornella.
"Il tempo in Newton e in Leibniz" in *Il Concetto di Tempo: Atti del XXXII Congresso Nazionale della Società Filosofica Italiana,* Casertano, Giovanni (ed). Rossi, Paolo.
"Samuel Clarke's Four Categories of Deism, Isaac Newton, and the Bible" in *Scepticism in the History of Philosophy: A Pan-American Dialogue,* Popkin, Richard H (ed). Force, James E.
Em que Sentido Newton pode Dizer *Hypotheses Non Fingo*?. Oliveira Barra, Eduardo Salles De.
Hume and Causal Power: The Influences of Malebranche and Newton. Bell, Martin.

## NOMINALISM

The Nominalist Argument of the *New Essays*. Bolton, Martha Brandt.
The Real and the Rational: Aquinas's Synthesis. Peterson, John.
Zénon, matérialiste et nominaliste?. Brinkman, Klaus.

## NON-EUCLIDEAN

Les géométries non euclidiennes, le problème philosophique de l'espace et la conception transcendantale; Helmholtz et Kant, les néo-kantiens, Einstein, Poincaré et Mach. Boi, Luciano.

## NONBEING

La generación absoluta, según la exposición aquiniana de Aristóteles. Velázquez Fernández, Héctor.
Not-Being and Linguistic Deception. O'Leary-Hawthorne, Diane.

## NONCOGNITIVISM

A Noncognitivist Reading of Quine's Ethics. Broach, Ronald J.
Is Hume a Noncognitivist in the Motivation Argument?. Cohon, Rachel.
Non-Cognitivism, Truth and Logic. Wedgwood, Ralph.

## NONCOMPLIANCE

A Noncompliant Patient?. Moseley, Kathryn L and Truesdell, Sandra.
Care, Support, and Concern for Noncompliant Patients. Muskin, Philip R.

## NONCONTRADICTION

Einsteins Zug und logische Gesetze. Strobach, Niko.
The Demonstration by Refutation of the Principle of Non-Contradiction in Aristotle's *Metaphysics*, Book IV. De Praetere, Thomas.

## NONLINEAR

Applying Allen's Constraint Propagation Algorithm for Non-Linear Time. Hajnicz, Elzbieta.
Some Considerations on Non-Linear Time Intervals. Hajnicz, Elzbieta.

## NONMONOTONIC

"A Nonmonotonic Approach to Tychist Logic" in *Studies in the Logic of Charles Sanders Peirce,* Houser, Nathan (ed). Maróstica, Ana H.
A Nonmonotonic Modal Formalization of the Logic of Acceptance and Rejection. Gomolinska, Anna.
Completeness and Incompleteness for Plausibility Logic. Schlechta, Karl.
Minimal Temporal Epistemic Logic. Engelfriet, Joeri.
Nonmonotonic Reasoning: From Finitary Relations to Infinitary Inference Operations. Freund, Michael and Lehmann, Daniel.
Nonmonotonic Theories and Their Axiomatic Varieties. Stachniak, Zbigniew.
Paraconsistent Default Logic. Van den Akker, Johan and Tan, Yao Hua.
Reasoning about Action and Change. Prendinger, Helmut and Schurz, Gerhard.
Some Syntactic Approaches to the Handling of Inconsistent Knowledge Bases: A Comparative Study. Benferhat, Salem, Dubois, Didier and Prade, Henri.

## NONSTANDARD ANALYSIS

A Sheaf-Theoretic Foundation for Nonstandard Analysis. Palmgren, Erik.
Mathematics, Model and Zeno's Paradoxes. Alper, Joseph S and Bridger, Mark.
The Three Arrows of Zeno. Harrison, Craig.

## NONSTANDARD MODELS

A Recursive Nonstandard Model of Normal Open Induction. Berarducci, Alessandro and Otero, Margarita.
Hyperalgebraic Primitive Elements for Relational Algebraic and Topological Algebraic Models. Insall, Matt.
The Self-Embedding Theorem of $WKL_0$ and a Non-Standard Method. Tanaka, Kazuyuki.

## NONVIOLENCE

"Laws of Nature vs. Laws of Respect: Non-Violence in Practice in Norway" in *Environmental Pragmatism,* Light, Andrew (ed). Rothenberg, David.
*Mahatma Ghandi: Selected Political Writings.* Dalton, Dennis (ed).
Between Apathy and Revolution: Nonviolent Action in Contemporary Mexico. Inda, Caridad.
Civil Disobedience: Justice against Legality. Miniotaite, Grazina.
Explorations in Morality and Nonviolence: Martin Luther King, Jr. and Adam Michnik. Baxter, Liliane Kshensky.
Gandhi on Love: A Reply to Ian M. Harris. Kohl, Marvin.
Gandhian Concept of Planned Society. Sharma, Akshaya Kumar.
Hannah Arendt on Power, Consent, and Coercion: Some Parallels with Gandhi. Presbey, Gail.
Malcolm X and the Enigma of Martin Luther King, Jr.'s Nonviolence. Bove, Laurence.
Nonviolence as a Way of Life: Issues of Justice. Fogliatti, Karen.
Reflexiones sobre la no violencia: Variedades, posibilidades y límites. Sobrevilla, David.
The Ethics of Community: The Ethical and Metaphysical Presuppositions of AVP. Reitan, Eric.
The Special Features of Gandhian Ethics. Radha, S.

## NOONAN, H

Reply to Noonan on Vague Identity. Lowe, E J.

## NOORDHOF, P

How Reasons Explain Behaviour: Reply to Melnyk and Noordhof. Dretske, Fred.

## NORIEGA, S

De viajes y naufragios: Sobre el Libro de Santiago González Noriega *El Viaje a Siracusa: Ensayos de Filosofía y Teoría Social* Balsa de la Medusa 1994. Villacañas Berlanga, José Luis.

## NORM

"The Logic of Normative Systems" in *Deontic Logic, Agency and Normative Systems,* Brown, Mark A (ed). Johanson, Arnold A.
*Ethical Norms, Particular Cases.* Wallace, James D.
A Decision Procedure for Von Wright's Obs-Calculus. Buekens, Filip.
Accepting Agent Centred Norms: A Problem for Non-Cognitivists and a Suggestion for Solving It. Dreier, James.
Applicability and Effectiveness of Legal Norms. Navarro, Pablo E and Moreso, José Juan.
Blameworthiness, Character, and Cultural Norms. Haji, Ishtiyaque.
Consensus and Normative Validity. Grimen, Harald.
Contraceptive Risk-Taking and Norms of Chastity. Stubblefield, Anna.
Du phénomène de la valeur au discours de la norme. Lacoste, Jean-Yves.
Exceptionless Norms in Aristotle?: Thomas Aquinas and Twentieth-Century Interpreters of the *Nicomachean Ethics.* Kaczor, Christopher.
Externalism and Action-Guiding Epistemic Norms. Jacobson, Stephen.
I metodi dell'etica di Henry Sidgwick. Lecaldano, Eugenio, Schneewind, J B and Vacatello, Marzio.
Il diritto tra decisione ed ordine: Brevi note su *I tre tipi di pensiero giuridico* di Carl Schmitt. Caserta, Marco.
Ley moral, Ley positiva. Griffin, James.
Normes logiques et évolution. Engel, Pascal.
Norms for Patents Concerning Human and Other Life Forms. Guenin, Louis M.
On Showing in Argumentation. Lueken, Geert-Lueke.
Overruling Rules?. Yovel, Jonathan.
Peirce on Norms, Evolution and Knowledge. Tiercelin, Claudine.
Situationist Deontic Logic. Hansson, Sven Ove.
Social Epistemology and the Recovery of the Normative in the Post-Epistemic Era. Fuller, Steve.
Some Remarks on the Concept of Toleration. Garzón Valdés, Ernesto.
The Collective Enforcement of International Norms Through Economic Sanctions. Damrosch, Lori Fisler.
The Discourse Principle and Those Affected. Skirbekk, Gunnar.
The Dynamics of Legal Positivism: Some Remarks on Shiner's *Norm and Nature.* Navarro, Pablo E and Moreso, José Juan.
The Norm and History. Travar, Dusan.
Verso una concezione unitaria della norma fondamentale. Falcón y Tella, María José.

## NORMAL

A Recursive Nonstandard Model of Normal Open Induction. Berarducci, Alessandro and Otero, Margarita.
Antropología y alteridad: De la naturaleza humana a la normalidad social. Lorite Mena, José.
Cut-Free Tableau Calculi For Some Propositional Normal Modal Logics. Amerbauer, Martin.
Jónsson's Lemma for Regular and Nilpotent Shifts of Pseudovarieties. Chajda, Ivan and Graczynska, Ewa.
Normal Bimodal Logics of Ability and Action. Brown, Mark A.
Simple Gentzenizations for the Normal Formulae of Contraction-less Logics. Brady, Ross T.

## NORMALITY

"Deconstructing "Difference" and the Difference This Makes to Education" in *Philosophy of Education (1996),* Margonis, Frank (ed). Burbules, Nicholas C.
"Humpty Dumpty An Ovular Model of Resistance to Modernist Recidivism" in *Philosophy of Education (1996),* Margonis, Frank (ed). Morgan, Kathryn Pauly.

## NORMALIZATION

Commentary on "The Ethics of Normalization". Corsale, Massimo.
Ethical Obligations in the Body Politic: The Case of Normalization Policy for Marginal Populations. D'Oronzio, Joseph C.
Exposing the Machinery of Infinite Renormalization. Huggett, Nick and Weingard, Robert.
On the Proof Theory of Coquand's Calculus of Constructions. Seldin, Jonathan P.
The Ethics of Normalization. Reinders, Hans S.

## NORMAN, R

Education, Work and Well-Being. White, John.

## NORMATIVE

"Objetividad normativa" in *La racionalidad: su poder y sus límites,* Nudler, Oscar (ed). Sosa, Ernest.
"The Logic of Normative Systems" in *Deontic Logic, Agency and Normative Systems,* Brown, Mark A (ed). Johanson, Arnold A.
*Deontic Logic, Agency and Normative Systems.* Brown, Mark A (ed) and Carmo, José (ed).
Authenticity As a Normative Category. Ferrara, Alessandro.
Coercion: Description or Evaluation?. Greene, Jennifer K.
Health as a Normative Concept: Towards a New Conceptual Framework. Fedoryka, Kateryna.
Moral Accountancy and Moral Worth. Smilansky, Saul.
Natural Obligation and Normative Motivation in Hume's *Treatise.* Magri, Tito.
Naturalized Epistemology and the Is/Ought Gap. Rodríguez-Alcázar, Javier.
Non-Cognitivism, Truth and Logic. Wedgwood, Ralph.

## NORMATIVE

Objetividad Normativa. Sosa, Ernesto.

Old Fashioned Normativity: Just What the Doctor Ordered. Leeser, Jaimie M.

Practical Reasoning and the Structure of Fear Appeal Arguments. Walton, Douglas N.

Some Skeptical Reflectiones on Renewed Ethics (Spanish). Sasso, Javier.

There is No Such Thing as Environmental Ethics. Vesilind, P Aarne.

Troubles for Michael Smith's Metaethical Rationalism. Horgan, Terence and Timmons, Mark.

## NORMATIVE ETHICS

*Sartres Ontologie und die Frage einer Ethik: Zur Vereinbarkeit einer normativen Ethik und/oder Metaethik mit der Ontologie von "L'être et le néant"*. Töllner, Uwe.

Bemerkungen zur Natur der Angewandten Ethik (in Serbo-Croatian). Jakovljevic, Dragan.

Gewirth und die Begründung der normativen Ethik. Steigleder, Klaus.

Healthy Skepticism: The Emperor Has Very Few Clothes. Wildes, Kevin WM.

Un siglo de oro para la Etica. Guisán Seijas, Esperanza.

## NORMATIVITY

"Necessity and Normativity" in *The Cambridge Companion to Wittgenstein,* Sluga, Hans (ed). Glock, Hans-Johann.

Meaning, Mistake and Miscalculation. Coates, Paul.

Naturalism, Instrumental Rationality, and the Normativity of Epistemology. Siegel, Harvey.

Noch einmal: Rationalität und Normativität. Wüstehube, Axel.

Normativité et vérification immanentes des valeurs chez Max Scheler. Porée, Jérôme.

The Normativity of Meaning. Gampel, Eric H.

## NORRIE, A

Response to the Commentaries. Harré, Rom.

## NORTH AMERICAN

Attitudes and Issues Preventing Bans on Toxic Lead Shot and Sinkers in North America and Europe. Thomas, Vernon G.

## NORTON, B

Why Norton's Approach is Insufficient for Environmental Ethics. Westra, Laura.

## NORTON, J

Is There a Syntactic Solution to the Hole Problem?. Rynasiewicz, Robert.

## NORWEGIAN

"Laws of Nature vs. Laws of Respect: Non-Violence in Practice in Norway" in *Environmental Pragmatism,* Light, Andrew (ed). Rothenberg, David.

## NORWID, C

Cyprian Norwid—The Poet of Truth. Zajaczkowski, Ryszard.

## NOSOLOGY

Commentary on "Epistemic Value Commitments". Luntley, Michael.

Epistemic Value Commitments in the Debate Over Categorical vs. Dimensional Personality Diagnosis. Sadler, John Z.

## NOSTALGIA

Sulla nostalgia: La memoria tormentata. Starobinski, Jean.

## NOTATION

"Logic and Mathematics in Charles Sanders Peirce's "Description of a Notation for the Logic of Relatives" in *Studies in the Logic of Charles Sanders Peirce,* Houser, Nathan (ed). Van Evra, James.

"New Light on Peirce's Iconic Notation for the Sixteen Binary Connectives" in *Studies in the Logic of Charles Sanders Peirce,* Houser, Nathan (ed). Clark, Glenn.

"Untapped Potential in Peirce's Iconic Notation for the Sixteen Binary Connectives" in *Studies in the Logic of Charles Sanders Peirce,* Houser, Nathan (ed). Zellweger, Shea.

## NOTHING

"Das absolute Nichts als selbstloses Selbst; Nishitanis Erläuterungen der zen-buddhistischen Wirklichkeitsauffassung" in *Kreativer Friede durch Begegnung der Weltkulturen,* Beck, Heinrich (ed). Schadel, Erwin.

Considerations on the Plurality of the "Nothing-Speech" (in German). Sonderegger, Erwin.

Il problema del fondamento nella filosofia di Karl Jaspers. Carpentieri, Rosario.

L'essere, il nulla e il divenire: Riprendendo le fila di una grande polemica. Turoldo, Fabrizio.

La "Freiheitsschrift" del 1809 come momento decisivo tra la filosofia dell'identità e il rilievo dell'esistenza nel pensiero di Schelling. Millucci, Marco.

Reflexión y principio de la lógica en Hegel. Ezquerra Gómez, Jesús.

Replica a Emanuele Severino. Crescini, Angelo.

There might be Nothing: The Subtraction Argument Improved. Rodriguez-Pereyra, Gonzalo.

## NOTHINGNESS

"Death and Nothingness in Literature" in *The Ancients and the Moderns,* Lilly, Reginald (ed). Mohr, Heinrich.

"Nothing and Nothing Else" in *The Ancients and the Moderns,* Lilly, Reginald (ed). Marion, Jean-Luc.

"Nothingness and the Professional Thinker: Arendt versus Heidegger" in *The Ancients and the Moderns,* Lilly, Reginald (ed). Taminiaux, Jacques.

*Heidegger's Hidden Sources: East Asian Influences on His Work.* Parkes, Graham (trans) and May, Reinhard.

La creación de la nada: ¿apoteosis de la producción o misterio revelado?. Rivera, José A.

Metafisica e silenzio. Caramuta, Ersilia.

Sartre's Early Theory of Language. Anderson, Kenneth L.

The Dialectics of Nothingness: A Reexamination of Shen-hsiu and Hui-neng. Laycock, Steven W.

World, Emptiness, Nothingness: A Phenomenological Approach to the Religious Tradition of Japan. Held, Klaus.

## NOUMENA

*see also* Thing In Itself

Trascendenza e trascendentalità in Kant. Masi, Giuseppe.

## NOUMENALISM

Geist oder Gespenst? Fichtes Noumenalismus in der *Wissenschaftslehre nova methodo.* Zöller, Günter.

## NOUS

Coming to Know Principles in *Posterior Analytics* II 19. Bayer, Greg.

## NOVAK, J

Teaching Democracy Democratically. Worsfold, Victor L.

## NOVALIS

"Romantic Conceptions of the Self in Hölderlin and Novalis" in *Figuring the Self: Subject, Absolute, and Others in Classical German Philosophy,* Zöller, Günter (ed). Kneller, Jane E.

Das *kleine Buch* und das *laute Weltereignis:* Fichtes *Wissenschaftslehre* als Paradigma und Problem der *Romantik.* Schanze, Helmut.

Fichte, Novalis, Hölderlin: die Nacht des gegenwärtigen Zeitalters. Janke, Wolfgang.

Frühromantische Subjektkritik. Iber, Christian.

Statt Nicht-Ich—Du! Die Umwendung der Fichteschen Wissenschaftslehre ins Dialogische durch Novalis (Friedrich von Hardenberg). Wanning, Berbeli.

The *Poet's* Figure in Friedrich von Hardenburg (Novalis) and Gaston Bachelard: Some Considerations (in Portuguese). De Oliveira, Maria Elisa.

## NOVEL

Filosofia o letteratura? Mandeville, Fielding e il contesto settecentesco. Branchi, Andrea.

Lost Times/Recovered Times. Reed, Ronald.

Mere Reading. Brann, Eva T H.

The Demise of the Aesthetic in Literary Study. Goodheart, Eugene.

The Writer and Society: An Interpretation of *Nausea.* McGinn, Marie.

Thomas Mann e A Montanha Mágica. Joao Correia, Carlos.

## NOVELTY

Novelty, Severity, and History in the Testing of Hypotheses: The Case of the Top Quark. Staley, Kent W.

## NOVICIADO DA COTOVIA

A Ciência e a Virtude No Noviciado da Cotovia (1603-1759): Organizaçao do Espaço, Produçao do Discurso e Sistema Epistémico. Janeira, Ana Luisa.

## NOW

"Il tempo nell'eternità" in *Il Concetto di Tempo: Atti del XXXII Congresso Nazionale della Società Filosofica Italiana,* Casertano, Giovanni (ed). Longo, Rosaria.

Prof. Shimony on "The Transient Now". Eilstein, Helena.

Thisness and Time Travel. Adams, Robert Merrihew.

## NOWAK, L

"Historical Interpretation vs. Adaptive Interpretation of a Legal Text" in *Epistemology and History,* Zeidler-Janiszewska, Anna (ed). Ziembinski, Zygmunt.

"The Interpretational Paradigm in the Philosophy of the Human Sciences" in *Epistemology and History,* Zeidler-Janiszewska, Anna (ed). Swiderski, Edward.

## NOZICK, R

"Die Newcomb-Paradoxie—und ihre Lösung" in *Das weite Spektrum der analytischen Philosophie,* Lenzen, Wolfgang. Lenzen, Wolfgang.

Defining the Medical Sphere. Trappenburg, Margo J.

Giving the Skeptic Her Due?. Hughes, Christopher.

Libertarianism, Self-Ownership, and Motherhood. Jeske, Diane.

Moral Status and the Impermissibility of Minimizing Violations. Lippert-Rasmussen, Kasper.

Nozick's Socrates. Fine, Gail.

Redistributive Taxation, Self-Ownership and the Fruit of Labour. Michael, Mark A.

The Libertarianism of Robert Nozick (in Czech). Barsa, Pavel.

## NUCLEAR

The Chaos-Cosmos Transformation Cycle with Special Reference to the Chernobyl Disaster: Toward the Ultimate Reality and Meaning of the Ukraine. Milov, Yury P, Girnyk, Andryi and Salamatov, Vladimir.

The Peculiar Notion of Exchange Forces—II: From Nuclear Forces to QED, 1929-1950. Carson, Cathryn.

## NUCLEAR FISSION

Categorization, Anomalies and the Discovery of Nuclear Fission. Andersen, Hanne.

## NUCLEAR WEAPON

*Deterrence and the Crisis in Moral Theory: An Analysis of the Moral Literature on the Nuclear Arms Debate.* Palmer-Fernández, Gabriel.

## ONTOLOGY

## ONTOLOGY

Substances are not Windowless: A Suarézian Critique of Monadism. Kronen, John D.

Sufrimiento y humildad ontológica: Kant y Schopenhauer. Torralba Roselló, Francisco.

Temporal Parts, Temporal Portions, and Temporal Slices: An Exercise in Naive Mereology. Sanford, David H.

Temporalidad y trascendencia: La concepción heideggeriana de la trascendencia intencional en *Sein und Zeit*. Vigo, Alejandro G.

The *Sophist*, 246a-259e: *Ousia* and *to On* in Plato's Ontologies. Simon, Derek.

The Evolutionary Ontological Foundation of the New Ethics? (in Czech). Smajs, Josef.

The Myth of Substance and the Fallacy of Misplaced Concreteness. Seibt, Johanna.

The Ontological Difference. Nicholson, Graeme.

The Ontological Interpretation of the Wave Function of the Universe. Smith, Quentin.

The Ontological Status of Cartesian Natures. Nolan, Lawrence.

The Ontological Status of Ideation: A Continuing Issue. Smith, Charles W.

The Ontological Status of Sensible Qualities for Democritus and Epicurus. O'Keefe, Timothy.

The Promise of Process Philosophy. Rescher, Nicholas.

The Simplest Meinongian Logic. Pasniczek, Jacek.

The Spinoza-Intoxicated Man: Deleuze on Expression. Piercey, Robert.

The Thought of the Late Lukács (in Hungarian). Tertulian, Nikolae.

The 'Umbau'—From Constitution Theory to Constructional Ontology. Seibt, Johanna.

Thinking Critical History: Young Hegel and the German Constitution (in French). Leydet, Dominique.

Weak Ontology and Liberal Political Reflection. White, Stephen K.

What There Is, How Things Are. Ossorio, Peter G.

Where Do Laws of Nature Come From?. Cartwright, Nancy.

Why We should Lose Our Natural Ontological Attitudes. Kovach, Adam.

William James's Quest to Have It All. Gale, Richard M.

Zu den kantischen und fichteschen Motiven bei Nicolai Hartmann. Hála, Vlastimil.

'Gloria' e 'Essere': Heidegger nel pensiero di hans urs von Balthasar. Rossi, Osvaldo.

## OPEN

A Recursive Nonstandard Model of Normal Open Induction. Berarducci, Alessandro and Otero, Margarita.

## OPENNESS

"Geometrie dell'Aperto" in *Geofilosofia*, Bonesio, Luisa (ed). Marcenaro, Alessandro.

Jules Lequyer and the Openness of God. Viney, Donald Wayne.

Social Foundations of Openness. Hall, John A.

The Morality of Scientific Openness. Munthe, Christian and Welin, Stellan.

The Quixotic Element in *The Open Society*. Munz, Peter.

Why Simple Foreknowledge Offers No More Providential Control than the Openness of God. Sanders, John.

## OPERA

Ir à Opera e Gostar de lá Voltar! A Faculdade de Filosofia e as Licenciaturas em Ensino. Nuno Salgado Vaz, Carlos.

Modelo y Fenomenología: Nietzsche contra Hegel: El Renacimiento de la Tragedia en el Renacimiento de la Opera. Cohen-Levinas, Danielle.

Trustworthiness. Hardin, Russell.

## OPERATION

A Class of Modal Logics with a Finite Model Property with Respect to the Set of Possible-Formulae. Demri, Stéphane and Orlowska, Ewa.

A Completeness Proof for a Logic with an Alternative Necessity Operator. Demri, Stéphane.

Boolean Operations, Borel Sets, and Hausdorff's Question. Dasgupta, Abhijit.

Characterizing Equivalential and Algebraizable Logics by the Leibniz Operator. Herrmann, Burghard.

Consequence Operations Based on Hypergraph Satisfiability. Kolany, Adam.

Logical Operations. McGee, Vann.

Nonmonotonic Reasoning: From Finitary Relations to Infinitary Inference Operations. Freund, Michael and Lehmann, Daniel.

Polynomial Time Operations in Explicit Mathematics. Strahm, Thomas.

Strong Versus Weak Quantum Consequence Operations. Malinowski, Jacek.

## OPERATIONALISM

*Un'Introduzione All'Epistemologia Contemporanea*. Gava, Giacomo (ed).

Erkenntnistheoretische und ontologische Probleme der theoretischen Begriffe. Buzzoni, Marco.

## OPERATOR

"Peirce's Reduction Thesis" in *Studies in the Logic of Charles Sanders Peirce*, Houser, Nathan (ed). Burch, Robert W.

A Categorical Approach to Higher-Level Introduction and Elimination Rules. Poubel, Hardée Werneck and Pereira, Luiz Carlos P D.

Action Incompleteness. Segerberg, Krister.

Capitalizer of Binary Relations and the Fork Operator as Image of a General Disjoint Union-Function of Cartesian Product Functions. Marlangeon, Mauricio Pablo.

Decidability of Finite Boolean Algebras with a Distinguished Subset Closed under Some Operations. Hanusek, Jerzy.

Decidable and Undecidable Logics with a Binary Modality. Németi, István, Kurucz, Agnes and Sain, Ildikó (& others).

Naive Realism about Operators. Daumer, Martin, Dürr, Detlef and Goldstein, Sheldon (& others).

Quantum Mechanical Unbounded Operators and Constructive Mathematics— A Rejoinder to Bridges. Hellman, Geoffrey.

Second Order Propositional Operators Over Cantor Space. Polacik, Tomasz.

Self-Knowledge and Embedded Operators. Williamson, Timothy.

Sigma$_2$ Induction and Infinite Injury Priority Arguments: Part II: Tame Sigma$_2$ Coding and the Jump Operator. Chong, C T and Yang, Yue.

Systems of Explicit Mathematics with Non-Constructive Mu-Operator and Join. Glass, Thomas and Strahm, Thomas.

Taming Logic. Marx, Maarten, Mikulás, Szabolcs and Németi, István.

The Great Scope Inversion Conspiracy. Büring, Daniel.

The Lattice of Distributive Closure Operators Over an Algebra. Font, Josep Maria and Verdú, Ventura.

## OPINION

Il fondamento etico e metafisico del diritto. Bagolini, Luigi.

## OPPOSITION

Boundaries, Continuity, and Contact. Varzi, Achille C.

## OPPRESSION

"On Violence in the Struggle for Liberation" in *Existence in Black: An Anthology of Black Existential Philosophy*, Gordon, Lewis R (ed). McGary, Howard.

*The Second Wave: A Reader in Feminist Theory*. Nicholson, Linda (ed).

Crítica del llamado de Heidelberg. Lecourt, Dominique.

## OPPY, G

In Defense of the *Kalam* Cosmological Argument. Craig, William Lane.

Slingshots and Boomerangs. Neale, Stephen and Dever, Josh.

## OPTICAL

On Walter Benjamin and Modern Optical Phenomena. Osamu, Maekawa.

## OPTIMALITY

"Ökonomische Optimierung in den Grenzen struktureller Rationalität" in *Ökonomie und Moral: Beiträge zur Theorie ökonomischer Rationalität*, Lohmann, Karl Reinhard (ed). Nida-Rümelin, Julian.

La justice peut-elle naître du contrat social?. Poltier, Hugues.

Optimalität der Natur?. Zoglauer, Thomas.

## OPTIMISM

"Progress and the Future" in *The Idea of Progress*, McLaughlin, Peter (ed). Rescher, Nicholas.

Leibniz on Possible Worlds. Rescher, Nicholas.

Tragedia e cristianesimo: Agostino e il platonismo spezzato. Todisco, Orlando.

Trust as an Affective Attitude. Jones, Karen.

## OPTIMIZATION

Linear Logic Proof Games and Optimization. Lincoln, Patrick D, Mitchell, John C and Scedrov, Andre.

## OPTION

Forward Induction in Games with an Outside Option. Olcina, Gonzalo.

Pascalian Wagers. Sobel, Jordan Howard.

## OR

*see* Disjunction

## ORAL TRADITION

"The Philosophical Text in the African Oral Tradition" in *Philosophy and Democracy in Intercultural Perspective,* Kimmerle, Heinz (ed). Kimmerle, Heinz.

## ORAYEN, R

Raúl Orayen's Views on Philosophy of Logic. Peña, Lorenzo.

## ORDER

*see also* Social Order

"Law and Order in Psychology" in *AI, Connectionism and Philosophical Psychology, 1995*, Tomberlin, James E (ed). Antony, Louise M.

"Practical Reasoning in Oscar" in *AI, Connectionism and Philosophical Psychology, 1995*, Tomberlin, James E (ed). Pollock, John L.

"Wissensordnung, Ethik, Wissensethik" in *Angewandte Ethik: Die Bereichsethiken und ihre theoretische Fundierung*, Nida-Rümelin, Julian (ed). Spinner, Helmut F.

*Law and Morality: Readings in Legal Philosophy*. Dyzenhaus, David (ed) and Ripstein, Arthur (ed).

*Order in the Twilight*. Waldenfels, Bernhard and Parent, David J (trans).

*The Insufficiency of Virtue: Macbeth and the Natural Order*. Blits, Jan H.

*The Play of the Platonic Dialogues*. Freydberg, Bernard.

*Unfolding Meaning: A Weekend of Dialogue with David Bohm*. Bohm, David.

*Values and the Social Order*. Radnitzky, Gerard (ed).

*Wholeness and the Implicate Order*. Bohm, David.

Algebra and Theory of Order-Deterministic Pomsets. Rensink, Arend.

Habermas, Fichte and the Question of Technological Determinism. Jalbert, John E.

Hegelian Retribution Re-Examined. Fatic, A.

Il diritto tra decisione ed ordine: Brevi note su *I tre tipi di pensiero giuridico* di Carl Schmitt. Caserta, Marco.

**ORIGIN**

"Jacob Burckhardt and Max Weber: Two Conceptions of the Origin of the Modern World" in *The Ancients and the Moderns,* Lilly, Reginald (ed). Hardtwig, Wolfgang.

*Die Zweideutigkeit des Ursprünglichen bei Martin Heidegger.* Molinuevo, José Luis.

*La Ambigüedad de lo Originario en Martin Heidegger.* Molinuevo, José Luis.

*Metaphysics and the Origin of Species.* Ghiselin, Michael T.

Bioethics: A New Interdisciplinary Paradigm in the Relations Between Science and Ethics. Bernard, Brigitte.

Competing Research Programmes on the Origin of Life. Torres, Juan Manuel.

Reflexiones en torno al origen de los números aritméticos. Avila del Palacio, Alfonso.

The Hermeneutics of Origin: Arché and the Anarchic in John Van Buren's *The Young Heidegger.* Bambach, Charles.

The Loss of Origin and Heidegger's Question of *Unheimlichkeit.* Ciaramelli, Fabio.

The Processual Origins of Social Representations. Puddifoot, John E.

**ORIGINAL SIN**

Felix peccator? Kants geschichtsphilosophische Genesis-Exegese im *Muthmasslichen Anfang der Menschengeschichte* und die Theologie der Aufklärungszeit. Sommer, Andreas Urs.

**ORIGINALITY**

Originality and Its Origin in Modern Aesthetics (in Japanese). Otabe, Tanehisa.

**OROSIUS**

A los orígenes del pensamiento medieval español sobre la historia: Prudencio, Orosio, san Isidoro. Rivera de Ventosa, Enrique.

**OROZ RETA, J**

Un polifacético de la cultura: José Oroz Reta. Galindo Rodrigo, J A.

**ORPHISM**

Between Religion and Philosophy: Allegorical Interpretation in Derveni Papyrus (in Czech). Laks, André.

**ORTEGA**

"El Ortega de 1914" in *Política y Sociedad en José Ortega y Gasset: En Torno a "Vieja y Nueva Política",* Lopez de la Vieja, Maria Teresa (ed). Aranguren, José Luis L.

"Élites Sin Privilegio" in *Política y Sociedad en José Ortega y Gasset: En Torno a "Vieja y Nueva Política",* Lopez de la Vieja, Maria Teresa (ed). López de la Vieja, Maria Teresa.

"Experimentos de Nueva España" in *Política y Sociedad en José Ortega y Gasset: En Torno a "Vieja y Nueva Política",* Lopez de la Vieja, Maria Teresa (ed). Cerezo, Pedro.

"La Autodisolución de la Vieja Política en Ortega" in *Política y Sociedad en José Ortega y Gasset: En Torno a "Vieja y Nueva Política",* Lopez de la Vieja, Maria Teresa (ed), Carvajal Cordón, Julián.

"La Crisis del Socialism Ético en Ortega" in *Política y Sociedad en José Ortega y Gasset: En Torno a "Vieja y Nueva Política",* Lopez de la Vieja, Maria Teresa (ed). Molinuevo, José Luis.

"Ortega entre Literatos y Lingüistas" in *Política y Sociedad en José Ortega y Gasset: En Torno a "Vieja y Nueva Política",* Lopez de la Vieja, Maria Teresa (ed). Pascual, José A.

"Política y Filosofía en Ortega: Teoría Orteguiana de la Modernidad" in *Política y Sociedad en José Ortega y Gasset: En Torno a "Vieja y Nueva Política",* Lopez de la Vieja, Maria Teresa (ed). Flórez Miguel, Cirilo.

"Sobre Política y Reformismo Cívico: A Partir de Ortega" in *Política y Sociedad en José Ortega y Gasset: En Torno a "Vieja y Nueva Política",* Lopez de la Vieja, Maria Teresa (ed). Rosales, José María.

"Una Relación entre Diferentes: Ortega y Gasset y Gramsci" in *Política y Sociedad en José Ortega y Gasset: En Torno a "Vieja y Nueva Política",* Lopez de la Vieja, Maria Teresa (ed). Calvo Salamanca, Clara.

"Vieja y Nueva Política y el Semanario *España* en el Nacimiento" in *Política y Sociedad en José Ortega y Gasset: En Torno a "Vieja y Nueva Política",* Lopez de la Vieja, Maria Teresa (ed). Menéndez Alzamora, Manuel.

"Vieja y Nueva Política: La Circunstancia Histórica" in *Política y Sociedad en José Ortega y Gasset: En Torno a "Vieja y Nueva Política",* Lopez de la Vieja, Maria Teresa (ed). Morales Moya, Antonio.

"Vita, esistenza, storia nella filosofia di J. Ortega y Gasset" in *Lo Storicismo e la Sua Storia: Temi, Problemi, Prospettive,* Cacciatore, Giuseppe (ed). Pucci, Daniela.

*Política y Sociedad en José Ortega y Gasset: En Torno a "Vieja y Nueva Política".* Lopez de la Vieja, Maria Teresa (ed).

Crisis de la modernidad en el pensamiento español: desde el Barroco y en la europeización del siglo XX. Jiménez Moreno, Luis.

Cultura y reflexión en torno a Meditaciones del Quijote. Lasaga Medina, José.

Dieu en vu chez Ortega et María Zambrano. Duque, Félix.

El cartesianismo de la vida (La influencia de Descartes sobre la filosofía madura de Ortega y Gasset). Csejtei, Dezsö.

El mundo incuestionado (Ortega y Schütz). Hermida, Pablo.

La recepción del Utilitarismo en el mundo hispánico: El caso de Ortega y Gasset. López Frías, Francisco.

Ortega's (Implicit) Critique of Natural Law. Donoso, Antón.

**ORTHODOXY**

Aleksei Fedorovich Losev and Orthodoxy. Mokhov, V V.

William Ellery Channing: Philosopher, Critic of Orthodoxy, and Cautious Reformer. Madden, Edward H.

**ORTON, R**

"Can Hypocrites Be Good Teachers?" in *Philosophy of Education (1996),* Margonis, Frank (ed). Suttle, Bruce B.

**ORUKA, H**

*Sagacious Reasoning: Henry Odera Oruka in Memoriam.* Graness, Anke (ed) and Kresse, Kai (ed).

An African Savant: Henry Odera Oruka. Ochieng'-Odhiambo, F.

Interview with Professor Henry Odera Oruka. Kresse, Kai.

**OTHER**

"Conceptual Understanding and Knowing *Other*-Wise: Reflections on Rationality and Spirituality..." in *Knowing Other-Wise: Philosophy at the Threshold of Spirituality,* Olthuis, James H (ed). Hart, Hendrik.

"The Subject of the Other: Ordinary Language and Its Enigmatic Ground" in *Critical Studies: Ethics and the Subject,* Simms, Karl (ed). Phillips, J W P.

*Sociedades sin Estado: El Pensamiento de los Otros.* Lorite Mena, José.

*Transgressing Discourses: Communication and the Voice of Other.* Huspek, Michael (ed) and Radford, Gary P (ed).

Beyond Self and Other. Rogers, Kelly.

Foucault's Alimentary Philosophy: Care of the Self and Responsibility for the Other. Boothroyd, David.

Incommensurable Differences: Cultural Relativism and Antirationalism Concerning Self and Other. Wagner, Joseph.

Intersubjetividad como intramundanidad: Hacia una ética del tercero incluido. Cristin, Renato.

La metafísica dell'ermetismo. Montini, Pierino.

La noción de inconmensurabilidad y la realidad de los otros o el derecho a la diferencia. López Gil, Marta.

La redención oscura. Ortiz-Osés, Andrés.

Minority Maneuvers and Unsettled Negotiations. Bhabha, Homi.

Oneself as Oneself and Not as Another. Johnstone, Albert A.

Phenomenology, Dialectic, and Time in Levinas's *Time and the Other.* Miller, Hugh.

Reflections on the Other (in Hebrew). Brinker, Menahem.

Single-World versus Plural-World Antiessentialism: A Reply to Tim Dean. Dreyfus, Hubert L and Spinosa, Charles.

The Gestation of the Other in Phenomenology. Oliver, Kelly.

The Mine and That of Others (and M. Petrícek Commentary) (in Czech). Waldenfels, Bernhard and Petrícek Jr, Miroslav.

The Sublime and the Other. White, Richard J.

Treating the Patient to Benefit Others. Klepper, Howard.

Two Kinds of Other and Their Consequences. Dean, Tim.

**OTHER MINDS**

Descartes and Other Minds. Avramides, Anita.

**OTHERNESS**

*Augusto Ponzio: Bibliografia e Letture Critiche.* Ponzio, Augusto.

Deleuze and the Prepersonal. Colwell, C.

Marc Augé e l'antropologia dei mondi contemporanei. Soldati, Adriana.

Otherness in J.P. Sartre's *Being and Nothingness* (Spanish). Iglesias, Mercedes.

**OUGHT**

"Must I Do What I Ought? (Or Will the Least I Can Do Do?)" in *Deontic Logic, Agency and Normative Systems,* Brown, Mark A (ed). McNamara, Paul.

Agency and Obligation. Horty, John F.

Hume's Is-Ought Thesis in Logics with Alethic-Deontic Bridge Principles. Schurz, Gerhard.

Thomasian Natural Law and the Is-Ought Question. Rentto, Juha-Pekka.

'Ought' and Extensionality. Goble, Lou.

**OUTCOME**

Acts and Outcomes: A Reply to Boonin-Vail. Parfit, Derek.

**OUTPATIENT**

Ethics in the Outpatient Setting: New Challenges and Opportunities. Young, Ernlé W D.

**OUTSIDE**

Forward Induction in Games with an Outside Option. Olcina, Gonzalo.

**OVIEDUS, F**

El problema del continuo en la escolástica española: Francisco de Oviedo (1602-1651). Luna Alcoba, Manuel.

**OWNERS**

Personal Ethics and Business Ethics: The Ethical Attitudes of Owner/Managers of Small Business. Quinn, John J.

**OWNERSHIP**

Libertarianism, Self-Ownership, and Motherhood. Jeske, Diane.

Redistributive Taxation, Self-Ownership and the Fruit of Labour. Michael, Mark A.

St. Thomas Aquinas and the Defense of Mendicant Poverty. Jones, John D.

Strategies for Free Will Compatibilists. O'Leary-Hawthorne, John and Petit, Philip.

The Reasonableness of John Locke's Majority: Property Rights, Consent, and Resistance in the *Second Treatise.* Stevens, Jacqueline.

**OZONE**

Strategies of Environmental Organisations in the Netherlands regarding the Ozone Depletion Problem. Pleune, Ruud.

## PACI, E
"Tempo ed eternità in Enzo Paci" in *Il Concetto di Tempo: Atti del XXXII Congresso Nazionale della Società Filosofica Italiana,* Casertano, Giovanni (ed). Calapso, Renato.

## PACIFISM
"Structures of Violence, Structures of Peace: Levinasian Reflections on Just War and Pacifism" in *Knowing Other-Wise: Philosophy at the Threshold of Spirituality,* Olthuis, James H (ed). Dudiak, Jeffrey M.

Interpreting the *Jihad* of Islam: Militarism versus Muslim Pacifism. Churchill, Robert Paul.

La dottrina del "justum bellum" nell'etica militare di Michael Walzer. Zolo, Danilo.

Pugnacity and Pacifism. Garver, Newton.

The Ethics of Community: The Ethical and Metaphysical Presuppositions of AVP. Reitan, Eric.

Un discorso morale sulla guerra. Loretoni, Anna.

Une guerre juste est-elle possible?. Loetscher, Catherine.

War-Pacifism. Cochran, David Carroll.

## PADEL, R
Mind and Madness in Greek Tragedy. Gill, Christopher.

## PAGAN
Sozzini's Ghost: Pierre Bayle and Socinian Toleration. Tinsley, Barbara Sher.

## PAGLIARINI, N
Jansenismo versus Jesuitismo: Niccoló Pagliarini e o Projecto Político Pombalino. De Castro, Zília Osório.

## PAIN
"A Representational Theory of Pains and Their Phenomenal Character" in *AI, Connectionism and Philosophical Psychology, 1995,* Tomberlin, James E (ed). Tye, Michael.

*Leben-und Sterbenkönnen: Gedanken zur Sterbebegleitung und zur Selbstbestimmung der Person.* Wettstein, R Harri.

A Dialogue between L1 and L2: Discussing on Seven Kinds of Privacy. Lenka, Laxminarayan.

Do Doctors Undertreat Pain?. Ruddick, William.

Some Nonhuman Animals Can Have Pains in a Morally Relevant Sense. Robinson, William S.

The Agony of Pain. Blum, Alex.

The Analogical Argument for Animal Pain. Perrett, Roy W.

The Myth of the Control of Suffering. Sobel, Reuven.

When a Pain Is Not. Hardcastle, Valerie Gray.

## PAINTING
"Deleuze on J. M. W. Turner: Catastrophism in Philosophy?" in *Deleuze and Philosophy: The Difference Engineer,* Ansell Pearson, Keith (ed). Williams, James.

*After the End of Art: Contemporary Art and the Pale of History.* Danto, Arthur C.

*Contemporary Art and Its Philosophical Problems.* Stadler, Ingrid.

*Ludwig Wittgenstein: Half-Truths and One-and-a-Half-Truths.* Hintikka, Jaakko.

*Phantom Formations: Aesthetic Ideology and the Bildungsroman.* Redfield, Marc.

*The Lost Steps.* Polizzotti, Mark (trans) and Breton, André.

Aesthetic Value: Beauty, Ugliness and Incoherence. Kieran, Matthew.

Ancient Chinese Aesthetics and its Modernity. Arnheim, Rudolf.

Artistry. Armstrong, John.

Carlo Carra's Metaphysical Painting—The Works Reproduced in *Valori Plastici* (in Japanese). Demura, Masaya.

Country Fashion (in Portuguese). Arantes, Otília Beatriz Fiori and Arantes, Paulo Eduardo.

Critical Perspectives on Early Twentieth-Century American Avant-Garde Composers. O'Grady, Terence J.

Der "Neuanfang" in der Ästhetik (J.-F. Lyotard). Seubold, Günter.

Dramaturgy of Picture (Essay on Diderot's *The Natural Child*) (in Portuguese). De Matos, Franklin.

El Greco's Statements on Michelangelo the Painter. Rodetis, George A.

Gilda de Mello e Souza (in Portuguese). Prado Júnior, Bento.

Meyer Shapiro's Essay on Style: Falling into the Void. Wallach, Alan.

Permanence and Renovation in Arts (in Portuguese). Kossovitch, Leon.

Pictures and Beauty. Hopkins, Robert.

Plotinus and his Portrait. Stern-Gillet, Suzanne.

Reading Raphael: *The School of Athens* and Its Pre-Text. Most, Glenn W.

Some Remarks on the Notion of a Masterpiece. Coveos, Costis M.

The Aesthetic Face of Leadership. Howard, V A.

The Changes of Painting Techniques in the Early Tang Wall Paintings of Dunhuang Mogao Grottos; The Relationship between "Pattern" and Pictorial Structure (in Japanese). Yamasaki, Toshiko.

Thick Paintings and the Logic of Things: The Non-Ultimate Nature of Particular Works of Art. Risser, Rita.

## PAIR
Boolean Pairs Formed by the Delta$^0_n$-Sets. Hermann, E.

## PAIS
Conspecto do Desenvolvimento da Filosofía em Portugal (Séculos XIII-XVI). Santiago de Carvalho, Mário A.

## PALAVECINO, S
Réplica a la discusión sobre el revés de la filosofía, lenguaje y escepticismo. Cabanchik, Samuel Manuel.

## PALUS, C
Leadership as Aesthetic Process. Smith, Ralph A.

## PANIKKAR, R
The Diatopical Hermeneutics: R. Panikkar's Response to the Scientific Study of Religions. Savari Raj, L Anthony.

## PANNEERSELVAM, S
Does the Grammar of Seeing Aspects Imply a Kantian Concept?. Kanthamani, A.

## PANOFSKY, E
On the Limit of Iconology through the "Mental Habit"—Comparison between E. Panofsky's "Mental Habit" and P. Bourdieu's "Habitus" (in Japanese). Ichijo, Kazuhiko.

## PANPSYCHISM
Panpsychism and the Early History of Prehension. Ford, Lewis S.

Whitehead's Panpsychism as the Subjectivity of Prehension. McHenry, Leemon B.

## PANTHEISM
A Neoplatonist's Pantheism. Leslie, John.

Feminism and Pantheism. Jantzen, Grace M.

Pantheism. Sprigge, T L S.

Pantheism and Science. Forrest, Peter.

Pantheism vs. Theism: A Re-Appraisal. Ford, Lewis S.

Pantheism, Quantification and Mereology. Oppy, Graham.

Platonic Polypsychic Pantheism. Lenzi, Mary.

The Divine Infinity: Can Traditional Theists *Justifiably* Reject Pantheism?. Oakes, Robert.

## PAP, A
Red and Green after All These Years. Zelaniec, Wojciech.

## PAPINEAU, D
"La mosca salió volando de la botella: éxito y correspondencia en una teoría de la verdad" in *Verdad: lógica, representación y mundo,* Villegas Forero, L. Broncano, Fernando.

Physicalism and Mental Causes: Contra Papineau. Moser, Paul K.

## PARABLE
Kafka's China and the Parable of Parables. Wood, Michael.

## PARACONSISTENCY
Consistency, Paraconsistency and Truth (Logic, the Whole Logic and Nothing but 'the' Logic). Da Costa, Newton C A and Bueno, Otavio.

## PARACONSISTENT LOGICS
"Functioning and Teachings of Adaptive Logics" in *Logic and Argumentation,* Van Eemeren, Frans H (ed). Batens, Diderik.

A Dilemma for Priest's Dialethism?. Everett, Anthony.

A Naive Variety of Logical Consequence. Alonso González, Enrique.

A Reasoning Method for a Paraconsistent Logic. Buchsbaum, Arthur and Pequeno, Tarcisio.

Adaptive Logic in Scientific Discovery: The Case of Clausius. Meheus, Joke.

G. H. Von Wright's Truth-Logics as Paraconsistent Logics. Halonen, Ilpo.

Graham Priest's "Dialectheism"—Is It Altogether True?. Peña, Lorenzo.

Inconsistent Models of Arithmetic Part I: Finite Models. Priest, Graham.

On the Logic of Event-Causation: Jaskowski-Style Systems of Causal Logic. Urchs, Max.

P1 Algebras. Lewin, Renato A, Mikenberg, Irene F and Schwarze, Maria G.

Paraconsistent Default Logic. Van den Akker, Johan and Tan, Yao Hua.

Proof-Theoretical Considerations about the Logic of Epistemic Inconsistency. Pequeno, Tarcisio and Castro Martins, Ana Teresa.

Théorie de la valuation. Da Costa, Newton C A and Béziau, Jean-Yves.

## PARADIGM
"Liberalismo y Legitimidad: Consideraciones sobre los límites del Paradigma Liberal" in *Liberalismo y Comunitarismo: Derechos Humanos y Democracia,* Monsalve Solórzano, Alfonso (ed). Cortés Rodas, Francisco.

"Paradigm Evolution in Political Philosophy: Aristotle and Hobbes" in *The Ancients and the Moderns,* Lilly, Reginald (ed). Riedel, Manfred.

*Kant und die These vom Paradigmenwechsel: Eine Gegenüberstellung seiner Transzendentalphilosophie mit der Wissenschaftstheorie Thomas S. Kuhns.* Quitterer, Josef.

El concepto de "paradigma" en Thomas Kuhn y la filosofía. Salazar, Omar.

El mecanicismo como pardigma "exitoso". Coronado, Luis Guillermo.

On Wittgenstein on Cognitive Science. Proudfoot, Diane.

Paradigmas: ¿construcciones históricas?. García Fallas, Jackeline.

Sobre una versión del nominalismo de semejanzas. Rodriguez Pereyra, Gonzalo.

## PARADISE
*Paraísos y Utopías: Una Clave Antropológica.* De la Pienda, Jesús Avelino.

## PARADOX
"Die Lügner-Antinomie: eine pragmatische Lösung" in *Das weite Spektrum der analytischen Philosophie,* Lenzen, Wolfgang. Von Savigny, Eike.

"Die Newcomb-Paradoxie—und ihre Lösung" in *Das weite Spektrum der analytischen Philosophie,* Lenzen, Wolfgang. Lenzen, Wolfgang.

"Epistemic Theories of Truth: The Justifiability Paradox Investigated" in *Verdad: lógica, representación y mundo,* Villegas Forero, L. Müller, Vincent C and Stein, Christian.

"Moore's Paradox and Consciousness" in *AI, Connectionism and Philosophical Psychology, 1995,* Tomberlin, James E (ed). Rosenthal, David M.

## PATIENCE
Practicing Patience: How Christians Should Be Sick. Hauerwas, Stanley and Pinches, Charles.

## PATIENT
"On Not Destroying the Health of One's Patients" in *Human Lives: Critical Essays on Consequentialist Bioethics,* Oderberg, David S (ed). Simmons, Lance.

A Manual on Manners and Courtesies for the Shared Care of Patients. Stoekle, John D, Ronan, Laurence J and Emanuel, Linda L (& others).

A Noncompliant Patient?. Moseley, Kathryn L and Truesdell, Sandra.

A Practical Advance Directive Survey. McCanna, Tony.

Advance Directives and Patient Rights: A Joint Commission Perspective. Worth-Staten, Patricia A and Poniatowski, Larry.

Advance Directives Outside the USA: Are They the Best Solution Everywhere?. Sanchez-Gonzalez, Miguel A.

Bad Night in the ER—Patients' Preferences and Reasonable Accommodation: Discussed by Douglas A. Beer, Ruth Macklin, Walter Robinson, and Philip Wang. Beer, Douglas A, Macklin, Ruth and Robinson, Walter (& others).

Between Doctor and Patient. Capron, Alexander M.

Bioethics Committees and JCAHO Patients' Rights Standards: A Question of Balance. Corsino, Bruce V.

Care, Support, and Concern for Noncompliant Patients. Muskin, Philip R.

Choosing the Best: Against Paternalistic Practice Guidelines. Savulescu, Julian.

Damaged Humanity: The Call for a Patient-Centered Medical Ethic in the Managed Care Era. Churchill, Larry R.

Discretionary Power, Lies, and Broken Trust: Justification and Discomfort. Potter, Nancy.

Do Physicians' Own Preferences for Life-Sustaining Treatment Influence Their Perceptions of Patients' Preferences? A Second Look. Schneiderman, Lawrence J, Kaplan, Robert M and Rosenberg, Esther (& others).

Education of Ethics Committees. Thomasma, David C.

Ethical Issues in Alternative Medicine. Edelberg, David.

Ethics at the Interface: Conventional Western and Complementary Medical Systems. Brody, Howard, Rygwelski, Janis and Fetters, Michael D.

Ethics in the Outpatient Setting: New Challenges and Opportunities. Young, Ernlé W D.

Ethics without Walls: The Transformation of Ethics Committees in the New Healthcare Environment. Christensen, Kate T and Tucker, Robin.

Evaluating Outcomes in Ethics Consultation Research. Fox, Ellen and Arnold, Robert M.

Everyday Heroes in Ethics: Part I. Howe, Edmund G.

From "The Ethical Treatment of Patients in a Persistent Vegetative State" To a Philosophical Reflection on Contemporary Medicine. Lamau, M L, Cadore, B and Boitte, P.

Goldilocks and Mrs. Ilych: A Critical Look at the "Philosophy of Hospice". Ackerman, Felicia.

In Case of Emergency: No Need for Consent. Brody, Baruch A, Katz, Jay and Dula, Annette.

Irreconcilable Conflicts in Bioethics. Winslade, William J.

Japanese Psychiatrists' Attitudes toward Patients Wishing to Die in the General Hospital: A Cultural Perspective. Berger, Douglas, Takahashi, Yoshitomo and Fukunishi, Isao (& others).

Justice, Society, Physicians and Ethics Committees: Incorporating Ideas of Justice into Patient Care Decisions. Loewy, Erich H.

Patient Rights and Organization Ethics: The Joint Commission Perspective. Schyve, Paul M.

Patient Self-Determination and Complementary Therapies. Burkhardt, Margaret A and Nathaniel, Alvita K.

Persistent Vegetative State: A Presumption to Treat. Cattorini, Paolo and Reichlin, Massimo.

Personal Privacy and Confidentiality in an Electronic Environment. Schick, Ida Critelli.

Philosophical Counseling and the *I Ching*. Fleming, Jess.

Practice Guidelines, Patient Interests, and Risky Procedures. Ross, Isobel A.

Principles and Purpose: The Patient Surrogate's Perspective and Role. Koch, Tom.

Reassessing the Reliability of Advance Directives. May, Thomas.

Relationships, Relationships, Relationships.... Sugarman, Jeremy and Emanuel, Linda L.

Retiring the Pacemaker. Reitemeier, Paul J, Derse, Arthur R and Spike, Jeffrey.

Stability of Treatment Preferences: Although Most Preferences Do Not Change, Most People Change Some of Their Preferences. Singer, Peter A, Kohut, Nitsa and Sam, Mehran (& others).

Still Here/Above Ground. Bartholome, William G.

Struggle. Miller, Patrick.

The Effect of Ethnicity on ICU Use and DNR Orders in Hospitalized AIDS Patients. Tulsky, James A.

The Evolving Health Care Marketplace: How Important is the Patient?. Berkowitz, Eric N.

The Moral Art of Being a Good Doctor. MacIntosh, David.

The Moral Status of Intellectually Disabled Individuals. Edwards, Steven D.

The Reluctant retained Witness: Alleged Sexual Misconduct in the Doctor/Patient Relationship. Yarborough, Mark.

The Suppressed Legacy of Nuremberg. Burt, Robert A.

Treating the Patient to Benefit Others. Klepper, Howard.

When Some Careproviders Have More Power than Others. Howe, Edmund G.

Who Plays What Role in Decisions about Withholding and Withdrawing Life-Sustaining Treatment?. Reckling, JoAnn Bell.

## PATIENT RIGHTS
"Medizinethik" in *Angewandte Ethik: Die Bereichsethiken und ihre theoretische Fundierung,* Nida-Rümelin, Julian (ed). Schöne-Seifert, Bettina.

## PATOCKA, J
Descartes in the Context of Husserl's and Patocka's Phenomenology (in Czech). Major, Ladislav.

Jan Patocka's World Movement as Ultimate. Tucker, Aviezer.

Patocka's Phenomenology of Meaning and Heidegger. Major, Ladislav.

## PATRIARCHY
*Feminist Approaches to Bioethics: Theoretical Reflections and Practical Applications.* Tong, Rosemarie.

*Rethinking Masculinity: Philosophical Explorations in Light of Feminism.* May, Larry (ed), Strikwerda, Robert (ed) and Hopkins, Patrick D (ed).

A Feminist Interpretation of Vulnerability. Annaromao, Nancy J.

Eternal Verities: Timeless Truth, Ahistorical Standards, and the One True Story. Edidin, Aron.

Is God Exclusively a Father?. Isham, George F.

The Dance of Dependency: A Genealogy of Domestic Violence Discourse. Ferraro, Kathleen J.

## PATRIOTISM
Carl Schmitt: An Occasional Nationalist?. Müller, Jan.

Constitutional Patriotism. Ingram, Attracta.

National Consciousness and Motherland Consciousness. Xiyuan, Xiong.

National Consciousness and Nationalism. Xiyuan, Xiong.

Patriotic Gore, Again. McCabe, David.

Should Nationalists be Communitarians?. Archard, David.

Thoreauvian Patriotism as an Environmental Virtue. Cafaro, Philip.

## PATRIZZI, F
Patrizzi and Descartes (in Czech). Floss, Pavel.

## PATTERN
A Patterned Process Approach To Brain, Consciousness, and Behavior. Díaz, José-Luis.

## PATZIG, G
Moralität und Nützlichkeit. Enskat, Rainer.

## PAWLAK, Z
Generalized Rough Sets (Preclusivity Fuzzy-Intuitionistic (BZ) Lattices). Cattaneo, Gianpiero.

## PAY
*see* Income, Wage

## PAYOFF
Payoff Dominance and the Stackelberg Heuristic. Colman, Andrew M and Bacharach, Michael.

## PEACE
"*Ewiger Friede*: Warum ein Beweismittel in Kants philosophischem Entwurf?" in *Grenzen der kritischen Vernunft,* Schmid, Peter A. Mainberger, Gonsalv K.

"Aportación de la Ética a la Paz Perpetua" in *Kant: La paz perpetua, doscientos años después,* Martínez Guzmán, Vicent (ed). Innerarity, Carmen.

"El ideal de la Paz en el Humanismo Ético de Kant" in *Kant: La paz perpetua, doscientos años después,* Martínez Guzmán, Vicent (ed). Conill, Jesús.

"Europa y una federación global: La visión de Kant" in *Kant: La paz perpetua, doscientos años después,* Martínez Guzmán, Vicent (ed). Pogge, Thomas W.

"Hobbes on Peace and Truth" in *Scepticism in the History of Philosophy: A Pan-American Dialogue,* Popkin, Richard H (ed). Madanes, Leiser.

"Interkulturelle Identität bzw. Variabilität und ihr möglicher Beitrag zum Frieden" in *Kreativer Friede durch Begegnung der Weltkulturen,* Beck, Heinrich (ed). Wallner, Fritz G.

"La Paz en Kant: Ética y Política" in *Kant: La paz perpetua, doscientos años después,* Martínez Guzmán, Vicent (ed). Cortina, Adela.

"Las tesis de Hegel sobre la guerra y el derecho internacional" in *Kant: La paz perpetua, doscientos años después,* Martínez Guzmán, Vicent (ed). Mertens, Thomas.

"Politische Ethik II: Ethik der Internationalen Beziehungen" in *Angewandte Ethik: Die Bereichsethiken und ihre theoretische Fundierung,* Nida-Rümelin, Julian (ed). Chwaszcza, Christine.

"Possibilities and Limitations of Indian Culture Concerning the Foundation of Peace" in *Kreativer Friede durch Begegnung der Weltkulturen,* Beck, Heinrich (ed). Chauhan, Brij Rai.

"Reconstruir la paz doscientos años después: Una Filosofía Transkantiana para la Paz" in *Kant: La paz perpetua, doscientos años después,* Martínez Guzmán, Vicent (ed). Martínez Guzmán, Vicent.

"Religión y paz en Kant" in *Kant: La paz perpetua, doscientos años después,* Martínez Guzmán, Vicent (ed). Cabedo, Salvador.

"República y Democrácia en la Paz Perpetua: Un comentario desde la Teoría Democrática" in *Kant: La paz perpetua, doscientos años después,* Martínez Guzmán, Vicent (ed). García Marzá, V Domingo.

## PEACE

"Some Fundamental Features of Arabic-Islamic Culture and Its Possible Contribution to World Peace" in *Kreativer Friede durch Begegnung der Weltkulturen,* Beck, Heinrich (ed). Al-A'ali, Ebtihaj.

"Specific African Thought Structures and Their Possible Contribution to World Peace" in *Kreativer Friede durch Begegnung der Weltkulturen,* Beck, Heinrich (ed). Ramose, Mogobe B.

"Spezifisch indischer Beitrag zur Interkulturalität und Interreligiosität als ein möglicher Weg zum Weltfrieden" in *Kreativer Friede durch Begegnung der Weltkulturen,* Beck, Heinrich (ed). Mall, Ram Adhar.

"The Other Through Dialogue: Latinamerican Contribution to Intercultural Peace" in *Kreativer Friede durch Begegnung der Weltkulturen,* Beck, Heinrich (ed). Pérez-Estévez, Antonio.

"The Relation to Nature, Time and Individuality as the Foundation of the African Concept of Harmony and Peace" in *Kreativer Friede durch Begegnung der Weltkulturen,* Beck, Heinrich (ed). Oniang'o, Clement M P.

"Weltfriede als dynamische Einheit kultureller Gegensätze" in *Kreativer Friede durch Begegnung der Weltkulturen,* Beck, Heinrich (ed). Beck, Heinrich.

*Emmanuel Levinas: Basic Philosophical Writings.* Peperzak, Adriaan Theodoor (ed), Critchley, Simon (ed) and Bernasconi, Robert (ed).

*Kant: La paz perpetua, doscientos años después.* Martínez Guzmán, Vicent (ed).

*Kreativer Friede durch Begegnung der Weltkulturen.* Beck, Heinrich (ed) and Schmirber, Gisela (ed).

Bowling Alone: On the Saving Power of Kant's Perpetual Peace. Shell, Susan Meld.

De la paix perpétuelle et de l'espérance comme devoir. Vuillemin, Jules.

Dinamic Peace in the Encounter of Vital Cultures (Spanish). Borges-Duarte, Irene.

Internationale Konferenz zu Kants Friedensidee und dem heutigen Problem einer internationalen Rechts—und Friedensordnung in Frankfurt am Main. Grün, Klaus-Jürgen.

Kant, the Republican Peace, and Moral Guidance in International Law. Lynch, Cecelia.

La dottrina del "justum bellum" nell'etica militare di Michael Walzer. Zolo, Danilo.

La paix perpétuelle chez Kant: du devoir à l'espérance. Perron, Louis.

Las ideas de 'ciudadanía universal' y 'paz perpetua' en la *Metafísica de la costumbres* de Kant. Piulats Riu, Octavi.

Liberation Theology and the Search for Peace in Ireland. Marsden, John.

Moral Politics and the Limits of Justice in *Perpetual Peace.* Clarke, Michael.

O Estatuto da Paz na Teoria Política Hobbesiana. Pavan Baptista, Ligia.

Peace Zones: Exemplars and Potential. Blume, Francine.

Politics: Truth, Freedom, Peace: Lie, Rule, War (in Serbo-Croatian). Baruzzi, Arno.

Reason's Practical Idea of Perpetual Peace, Human Character, and the Pedagogical Function of the Republican Constitution. Munzel, G Felicitas.

Reconstructing Rawls's Law of Peoples. Paden, Roger.

Social Contract among Devils. Verweyen, Hansjürgen.

The Promise of Peace? Hume and Smith on the Effects of Commerce on War and Peace. Manzer, Robert A.

Under the Sign of Failure. Fenves, Peter.

War and Peace in Levinas (in Hebrew). Meir, Ephraim.

War as a Phenomenon and as a Practice (in Serbo-Croatian). Babic, Jovan.

Will die Natur unwiderstehlich die Republik? Einige Reflexionen anlässlich einer rätselhaften Textpassage in Kants Friedensschrift. Ludwig, Bernd.

## PEACOCKE, C

"Can We Knock Off the Shackles of Syntax?" in *Contents,* Villanueva, Enrique (ed). Andler, Daniel.

Deviant Causal Chains and the Irreducibility of Teleological Explanation. Sehon, Scott.

Must Conceptually Informed Perceptual Experience Involve Non-Conceptual Content?. Sedivy, Sonia.

## PEANO

Los fundamentos de la aritmética según Peano. Zubieta R, Francisco.

Nominal Definitions and Logical Consequence in the Peano School. Rodríguez-Consuegra, Francisco.

## PEANO ARITHMETIC

On the Relationship between $ATR_0$ and *ID-hat-sub-less than-omega.* Avigad, Jeremy.

Some Theories with Positive Induction of Ordinal Strength *psi omega 0.* Gerhard, Jäger and Strahm, Thomas.

The Self-Embedding Theorem of $WKL_0$ and a Non-Standard Method. Tanaka, Kazuyuki.

## PEARS, D

Solipsism and First Person/Third Person Asymmetries. Child, William.

## PEARSON, A

Replies. Scheffler, Israel.

## PEARSON, K

Philosophy, Solipsism and Thought. Mounce, H O.

## PECKA, D

Nature, Technology and Man in the Works of Dominik Pecka (in Czech). Jemelka, Petr.

## PEDAGOGY

*Mentoring the Mentor: A Critical Dialogue with Paulo Freire.* Torres, Amadeu (ed).

A *Física* Subjacente à "Educaçao Filosófica": Proposta por Martinho de Mendonça de Pina e de Proença. Cunha, Norberto.

A Articulaçao entre Infância, Cidadania e História: Uma Questao para a Pedagogia. Marques Veríssimo, Mara Rúba Alves.

Against Education. Nordenbo, Sven Erik.

Building Theory in Music Education: A Personal Account. LeBlanc, Albert.

Carnival and Domination: Pedagogies of Neither Care Nor Justice. Sidorkin, Alexander M.

Diversity in the Classroom. Maitzen, Stephen.

É legítimo o Uso da Literatura no Processo de Transmissao da Filosofia?. Henriques, Fernanda.

El educador viquiano. Rebollo Espinosa, Maria José.

Feminist Pedagogy Theory: Reflections on Power and Authority. Luke, Carmen.

Filosofia da Educaçao e História da Pedagogia. Casulo, José Carlos.

Increasing Effectiveness in Teaching Ethics to Undergraduate Business Students. Lampe, Marc.

Is There a "Language of Education?". Oelkers, Jürgen.

Lyin' T(*)gers, and "Cares," Oh My: The Case for Feminist Integration of Business Ethics. Rabouin, Michelle.

Myths of Paulo Freire. Weiler, Kathleen.

Nietzsche in Dr. Antonio Pérez Estévez's Thought (Spanish). Delgado Ocando, José Manuel.

Powerful Pedagogy in the Science-and-Religion Classroom. Grassie, William.

Principes pragmatistes pour une démarche pédagogique en enseignement moral. Daniel, Marie-France.

Recent Curriculum Theory: Proposals for Understanding, Critical Praxis, Inquiry, and Expansion of Conversation. Thomas, Thomas P and Schubert, William H.

Reclaiming the Borderlands: Chicana/o Identity, Difference, and Critical Pedagogy. Elenes, C Alejandra.

Religious Pedagogy from Tender to Twilight Years: Parenting, Mentoring, and Pioneering Discoveries by Religious Masters as Viewed from within Polanyi's Sociology and Epistemology of Science. Milavec, Aaron.

The "Is-Ought" Fallacy and Musicology: The Assumptions of Pedagogy. Davis, James A.

The Ends of Pedagogy: From the Dialectic of Memory to the Deconstruction of the Institution. Trifonas, Peter.

The Modernity Crisis and the Pedagogical Reason (Spanish). Márquez, Alvaro.

The NCTM Standards and the Philosophy of Mathematics. Toumasis, Charalampos.

Who's Afraid of Assessment? Remarks on Winch and Gingell's Reply. Davis, Andrew.

## PEDIATRICS

Ethical Issues in Pediatric Life-Threatening Illness: Dilemmas of Consent, Assent, and Communication. Kunin, Howard.

Teaching the Three Rs: Rights, Roles and Responsibilities—A Curriculum for Pediatric Patient Rights. Davis, Kathleen G.

## PEDOPHILIA

Paedophilia, Sexual Desire and Perversity. Spiecker, Ben and Steutel, Jan.

## PEER REVIEW

Advances in Peer Review Research: an Introduction. Stamps III, Arthur E.

Assessing Conflict of Interest: Sources of Bias. Bird, Stephanie J.

Evidence for the Effectiveness of Peer Review. Fletcher, Robert H and Fletcher, Suzanne W.

Financial Interests of Authors in Scientific Journals: A Pilot Study of 14 Publications. Krimsky, Sheldon, Rothenberg, L S and Stott, P.

Is Peer Review Overrated?. Shatz, David.

Peer Review for Journals: Evidence on Quality Control, Fairness, and Innovation. Armstrong, J Scott.

Peer Review: Selecting the Best Science. Baldwin, Wendy and Seto, Belinda.

Referees, Editors, and Publication Practices: Improving the Reliability and Usefulness of the Peer Review System. Cicchetti, Domenic V.

Reflections on Peer Review Practices in Committees Selecting Laureates for Prestigious Awards and Prizes: Some Relevant and Irrelevant Criteria. Vijh, Ashok K.

The Morality of Scientific Openness. Munthe, Christian and Welin, Stellan.

The Principles and Practices of Peer Review. Kostoff, Ronald N.

Using a Dialectical Scientific Brief in Peer Review. Stamps III, Arthur E.

## PEERS

Virtuous Peers in Work Organizations. Moberg, Dennis.

## PEIRCE

"A Decision Method for Existential Graphs" in *Studies in the Logic of Charles Sanders Peirce,* Houser, Nathan (ed). Roberts, Don D.

"A Nonmonotonic Approach to Tychist Logic" in *Studies in the Logic of Charles Sanders Peirce,* Houser, Nathan (ed). Maróstica, Ana H.

"A Political Dimension of Fixing Belief" in *The Rule of Reason: The Philosophy of Charles Sanders Peirce,* Forster, Paul (ed). Anderson, Douglas R.

"A Tarski-Style Semantics for Peirce's Beta Graphs" in *The Rule of Reason: The Philosophy of Charles Sanders Peirce,* Forster, Paul (ed). Burch, Robert W.

**PENDULUM**

Lebenswelt Structures of Galilean Physics: The Case of Galileo's Pendulum. Bjelic, Dusan I.

**PENELHUM, T**

Critical Notice of J.J. MacIntosh and H.A. Meynell, eds. *Faith, Scepticism and Personal Identity: A Festschrift for Terence Penelhum.* Loptson, Peter J.

Rationally Deciding What To Believe. Chappell, Tim.

**PENROSE, R**

Twistors and Self-Reference: On the Generic Non-Linearity of Nature. Zimmermann, Rainer E.

**PEOPLE**

Constructing the Law of Peoples. Moellendorf, Darrel.

Government, the Press, and the People's Right to Know. Montague, Phillip.

Why It Is Better Never To Come Into Existence. Benatar, David.

**PERCEPTION**

*see also* Apperception. Illusion, Sense Data

"Aristotle and Specular Regimes: The Theater of Philosophical Discourse" in *Sites of Vision,* Levin, David Michael (ed). Porter, James I.

"Charles Peirce and the Origin of Interpretation" in *The Rule of Reason: The Philosophy of Charles Sanders Peirce,* Forster, Paul (ed). Hausman, Carl R.

"Colors, Subjective Relations and Qualia" in *Perception,* Villanueva, Enrique (ed). Shoemaker, Sydney.

"Explaining Objective Color in Terms of Subjective Experience" in *Perception,* Villanueva, Enrique (ed). Harman, Gilbert.

"Getting Acquainted with Perception" in *Perception,* Villanueva, Enrique (ed). Sosa, David.

"Il tempo come percezione: gli empiristi inglesi" in *Il Concetto di Tempo: Atti del XXXII Congresso Nazionale della Società Filosofica Italiana,* Casertano, Giovanni (ed). Bellini, Ornella.

"Is Color Psychological or Biological? Or Both?" in *Perception,* Villanueva, Enrique (ed). Sosa, Ernest.

"Is the External World Invisible?" in *Perception,* Villanueva, Enrique (ed). Johnston, Mark.

"Layered Perceptual Representation" in *Perception,* Villanueva, Enrique (ed). Lycan, William G.

"Mental Paint and Mental Latex" in *Perception,* Villanueva, Enrique (ed). Block, Ned.

"Musical Idiosyncrasy and Perspectival Listening" in *Music and Meaning,* Robinson, Jenefer (ed). Higgins, Kathleen Marie.

"On a Defense of the Hegemony of Representation" in *Perception,* Villanueva, Enrique (ed). Stalnaker, Robert.

"Orgasms Again" in *Perception,* Villanueva, Enrique (ed). Tye, Michael.

"Perception and Possibilia" in *Perception,* Villanueva, Enrique (ed). Tomberlin, James E.

"Perception and Rational Constraint: McDowell's *Mind and World*" in *Perception,* Villanueva, Enrique (ed). Brandom, Robert.

"Perceptual Experience Is a Many-Layered Thing" in *Perception,* Villanueva, Enrique (ed). Tye, Michael.

"Précis of *Mind and World*" in *Perception,* Villanueva, Enrique (ed). McDowell, John.

"Qualia and Color Concepts" in *Perception,* Villanueva, Enrique (ed). Harman, Gilbert.

"Replies to Tomberlin, Tye, Stalnaker and Block" in *Perception,* Villanueva, Enrique (ed). Lycan, William G.

"Shape Properties and Perception" in *Perception,* Villanueva, Enrique (ed). Ludwig, Kirk A.

"Visible Properties of Human Interest Only" in *Perception,* Villanueva, Enrique (ed). Gibbard, Allan.

"Would More Acquaintance with the External World Relieve Epistemic Anxiety?" in *Perception,* Villanueva, Enrique (ed). Villanueva, Enrique.

*Aristotle and Neoplatonism in Late Antiquity: Interpretations of the De Anima.* Blumenthal, H J.

*Aristotle on Perception.* Everson, Stephen.

*Being and Other Realities.* Weiss, Paul.

*Colour Vision: A Study in Cognitive Science and the Philosophy of Perception.* Thompson, Evan.

*Immanuel Kant: Principios Formales del Mundo Sensible y del Inteligible (Disertación de 1770).* Gómez Caffarena, José (ed), Ceñal Lorente, Ramón (trans) and Kant, Immanuel.

*Malebranche's Theory of the Soul: A Cartesian Interpretation.* Schmaltz, Tad M.

*Mechanismus und Subjektivität in der Philosophie von Thomas Hobbes.* Esfeld, Michael.

*Perception.* Villanueva, Enrique (ed).

*Problems of Vision: Rethinking the Causal Theory of Perception.* Vision, Gerald.

*The Philosophy of Mathematics.* Hart, W D.

*Vico and Moral Perception.* Black, David W.

A Multicultural Examination of Business Ethics Perceptions. Allmon, Dean E, Chen, Henry C K and Pritchett, Thomas K (& others).

Admiration: A New Obstacle. Nathan, N M L.

Against Coady on Hume on Testimony. Hríbek, Tomás.

Another Look at Color. McGinn, Colin.

Aristotle on Perception: The Dual-Logos Theory. Bradshaw, David.

Asymmetric Perceptions of Ethical Frameworks of Men and Women in Business and Nonbusiness Settings. Schminke, Marshall and Ambrose, Maureen L.

Bergson: The Philosophy of *Durée-Différence.* Mullarkey, John C.

Berkeley's Argument from Perceptual Relativity. Harris, Stephen.

Chief Financial Officers' Perceptions Concerning the IMA's Standards of Ethical Conduct. Moyes, Glen D and Park, Kyungjoo.

Cualidades secundarias y autoconocimiento. Stigol, Nora.

Descartes's Ontology of Thought. Nelson, Alan.

Domination and Dialogue in Merleau-Ponty's *Phenomenology of Perception.* Sullivan, Shannon.

Eindigen met een nieuw begin: Zien en denken in de laatste geschriften van M. Merleau-Ponty. Kwant, Remigius C.

El origen de la experiencia humana. Pochelú, Alicia G.

Formal Causation and the Explanation of Intentionality in Descartes. Schmitter, Amy M.

Foundations of Perceptual Knowledge. Brewer, Bill.

From Exasperating Virtues to Civic Virtues. Rorty, Amélie Oksenberg.

Hearing Musical Works in their Entirety. McAdoo, Nick.

Heraclitus of Ephesus on Knowledge. Krkac, Kristijan.

How We Get There From Here: Dissolution of the Binding Problem. Hardcastle, Valerie Gray.

Interlocution, Perception, and Memory. Burge, Tyler.

Internalism and Perceptual Knowledge. Brewer, Bill.

Introspection and its Objects. Arnold, Denis G.

La percezione è il "bordo d'attacco" della memoria?. Dennett, Daniel C.

La reversibilidad de silencio y lenguaje según Merleau-Ponty. Ralón de Walton, Graciela.

Lady Mary Shepherd's Case Against George Berkeley. Atherton, Margaret L.

Marsilius Ficinus: In *Theaetetum* Platonis vel *De scientia* ad Petrum Medicem, patriae patrem: Epitome. Mojsisch, Burkhard.

O Nilismo de Merleau-Ponty. Clemente, Isabel.

On What Being a World Takes Away. Clifton, Robert.

Percepción, particulares y predicados. Mulligan, Kevin.

Perception and Kant's Categories. Greenberg, Robert.

Perception of What the Ethical Climate Is and What It Should Be: The Role of Gender, Academic Status, and Ethical Education. Luthar, Harsh K, DiBattista, Ron A and Gautschi, Theodore.

Perceptions of Ethics Across Situations: A View Through Three Different Lenses. Carlson, Dawn S and Kacmar, K Michele.

Self-Construction and Identity: The Confucian Self in Relation to Some Western Perceptions. Yao, Xinzhong.

Shades of Consciousness. Girle, Roderic A.

Silence Revisited: Taking the Sight Out of Auditory Qualities. Muldoon, Mark S.

Sobre el sentido común y la percepción: Algunas sugerencias acerca de la facultad sensitiva central. Posada, Jorge Mario.

Testimony and Perception. Prijic-Samarzija, Snjezana.

The Buddhist Conditional in Set-Theoretic Terms. Galloway, Brian.

The Dispositional Account of Colour. Pitson, Tony.

The Evolution of Color Vision without Color. Hall, Richard J.

The Inadequacy of Hume's Psychological Impressions. Bartzeliotis, L.

The Presence of Environmental Objects to Perceptual Consciousness: Consideration of the Problem with Special Reference to Husserl's Phenomenological Account. Natsoulas, Thomas.

The Relationship Between Culture and Perception of Ethical Problems in International Marketing. Armstrong, Robert W.

The Role of Imagination in Perception. Pendlebury, Michael.

Wahrnehmung und Mentale Repräsentation. Pauen, Michael.

**PEREDA, C**

El (Supuesto) Trilema del Saber. Hurtado, Guillermo.

**PERENNIAL PHILOSOPHY**

Antimodern, Ultramodern, Postmodern: A Plea for the Perennial. Dewan, Lawrence.

Beyond the Sovereignty of Good. Nelson, Ralph C.

Justifying the Perennial Philosophy. Meynell, Hugo.

La *philosophia perennis*: De la continuité et du progrès en philosophie. Allard, Jean-Louis.

Man: The Perennial Metaphysician. Dewan, Lawrence.

Self, Deconstruction and Possibility: Maritain's Sixth Way Revisited. Armour, Leslie.

The Idea of a Perennial Philosophy. Armour, Leslie.

The Inaccessible God. Thomas, James.

What Leibniz Thought Perennial. Hunter, Graeme.

**PEREZ ESTEVEZ, A**

Nietzsche in Dr. Antonio Pérez Estévez's Thought (Spanish). Delgado Ocando, José Manuel.

**PERFECT**

El cant gregorià, un model de música perfecta. Banyeres Baltasà, Hug.

**PERFECTION**

*Analytic Theism, Hartshorne, and the Concept of God.* Dombrowski, Daniel A.

*Beyond Neutrality: Perfectionism and Politics.* Sher, George.

La cohérence de la théorie esthétique de Moses Mendelssohn. Dumouchel, Daniel.

Perfection, Happiness, and Duties to Self. Jeske, Diane.

The Coherence of Omniscience: A Defense. Abbruzzese, John E.

**PERFORMANCE**

"Opening the Closet Door: Sexualities Education and "Active Ignorance" in *Philosophy of Education (1996),* Margonis, Frank (ed). Ford, Maureen.

"Performance Anxiety: Sexuality and School Controversy" in *Philosophy of Education (1996),* Margonis, Frank (ed). Mayo, Cris.

## PHILOSOPHER

*Jewish Philosophers and Jewish Philosophy.* Fackenheim, Emil L and Morgan, Michael L (ed).
*Latin American Philosophy in the Twentieth Century.* Gracia, Jorge J E.
*My Philosophical Development.* Russell, Bertrand.
A Tribute to Donald T. Campbell. Heyes, Cecilia.
Adieu. Derrida, Jacques.
Bertrand Russell's Life in Pictures. Ruja, Harry.
Interview with A. J. Ayer. Price, Thomas, Russell, Robert and Kennett, Stephen.
Interview with Alasdair MacIntyre. Pearson, Thomas D.
Interview with Herman J. Saatkamp, Jr.. Detar, Richard.
Interview with Richard Rorty. Kuehn, Glenn, Siliceo-Roman, Laura and Salyards, Jane.
Philosophers as Experts: A Response to Pfeifer. Klein, E R.
Populismus in der Philosophie: Nicholas Reschers wissenschaftlicher Relativismus. Niemann, Hans-Joachim.
Professor Prasad on Working Out a Lead from Swami Vivekananda: Some Reflections. Ghosh, Ranjan K.
William Durant the Younger and Conciliar Theory. Fasolt, Constantin.
Y a-t-il de la place pour philosopher sur les mathématiques au collégial?. Daniel, Marie-France, LaFortune, Louise and Pallascio, Richard (& others).

## PHILOSOPHER-KING

Administrative Lies and Philosopher-Kings. Simpson, David.

## PHILOSOPHICAL ANTHROPOLOGY

"Homo historicus: Verso una trasformazione del paradigma 'classico' dell'antropologia filosofica" in *Lo Storicismo e la Sua Storia: Temi, Problemi, Prospettive,* Cacciatore, Giuseppe (ed). Giammusso, Salvatore.
*Das Multiversum der Kulturen.* Kimmerle, Heinz.
*Kreativer Friede durch Begegnung der Weltkulturen.* Beck, Heinrich (ed) and Schmirber, Gisela (ed).
*Wie wächst man in die Anthroposophie hinein?.* Dostal, Jan.
Animal symbolicum?. Loewenstein, Bedrich.
Brevi Riflessioni Filosofiche sulla Storicità dell'Uomo. Seidl, Horst.
Enigma e relazione: Da Apollo a Edipo. Lo Bue, Elisabetta.
Genealogia di un sentire inorganico: Mario Perniola. Fimiani, Mariapaola.
La persona como fuente de autenticidad. Yepes Stork, Ricardo.
La relazione tra l'uomo e la natura: una prospettiva. Sagnotti, Simona C.
Marc Augé e l'antropologia dei mondi contemporanei. Soldati, Adriana.
Oltre l'umanesimo: Alcune considerazioni su tecnica e modernità. Galli, Carlo.
On the Meaning of an Intercultural Philosophy (With Reply from H. Kimmerle). Hoogland, Jan.
Philosophie als kreatives Interpretieren. Lenk, Hans.
Self-Enlargement or Purification? On the Meaning of the Fragmentary Subject in René Girard's Early Writings (in Dutch). Vanheeswijck, Guido.
The Common Europe as a Philosophical Question. Funda, Otakar A.
Un'introduzione all'antropologia giuridica. Scillitani, Lorenzo.

## PHILOSOPHIZING

El Ejercicio de la Filosofía. Ramos Arenas, Jaime.
El grito de Libertad del Pensamiento. Rosas, Alejandro.

## PHILOSOPHY

see also Metaphilosophy, Natural Philosophy, Perennial Philosophy, Process Philosophy
"*In Itinere* Pictures from Central-European Philosophy" in *In Itinere* European Cities and the Birth of Modern Scientific Philosophy, Poli, Roberto (ed). Poli, Roberto.
"*In Itinere*: Vienna 1870-1918" in *In Itinere* European Cities and the Birth of Modern Scientific Philosophy, Poli, Roberto (ed). Libardi, Massimo.
"All Philosophy as *Religionsphilosophy*" in *The Recovery of Philosophy in America: Essays in Honor of John Edwin Smith,* Kasulis, Thomas P (ed). Harris, Errol E.
"American Philosophy's Way around Modernism (and Postmodernism)" in *The Recovery of Philosophy in America: Essays in Honor of John Edwin Smith,* Kasulis, Thomas P (ed). Neville, Robert Cummings.
"Averroës on the Harmony of Philosophy and Religion" in *Averroës and the Enlightenment,* Wahba, Mourad (ed). Druart, Therese-Anne.
"Between Ernest Renan and Ernst Bloch: Averroës Remembered, Discovered, and Invented. The European Reception Since the Nineteenth Century" in *Averroës and the Enlightenment,* Wahba, Mourad (ed). Wild, Stefan.
"Bradley and the Canadian Connection" in *Philosophy after F.H. Bradley,* Bradley, James (ed). Trott, Elizabeth.
"Brand Blanshard—A 'Student' of Bradley" in *Philosophy after F.H. Bradley,* Bradley, James (ed). Walsh, Michael.
"Cambridge and the Austrian Connection" in *In Itinere* European Cities and the Birth of Modern Scientific Philosophy, Poli, Roberto (ed). Dappiano, Luigi.
"Chemie und Philosophie: Anmerkungen zur Entwicklung des Gebietes in der Geschichte der DDR" in *Philosophie der Chemie: Bestandsaufnahme und Ausblick,* Schummer, Joachim (ed). Laitko, Hubert.
"David Savan: In Memoriam" in *The Rule of Reason: The Philosophy of Charles Sanders Peirce,* Forster, Paul (ed). Normore, Calvin G.
"Deleuze Outside/Outside Deleuze: On the Difference Engineer" in *Deleuze and Philosophy: The Difference Engineer,* Ansell Pearson, Keith (ed). Ansell Pearson, Keith.

"Die Chemie als Gegenstand philosophischer Reflexion" in *Philosophie der Chemie: Bestandsaufnahme und Ausblick,* Schummer, Joachim (ed). Psarros, Nikos.
"Die Notwendigkeit einer Philosophie der Chemie" in *Philosophie der Chemie: Bestandsaufnahme und Ausblick,* Schummer, Joachim (ed). Han, Edzard.
"El problema de la introducción a la filosofía en el pensamiento de K. Chr. Krause en Jena (1797-1804)" in *El inicio del Idealismo alemán,* Market, Oswaldo. Orden Jiménez, Rafael.
"Esistenza, storia e storia della filosofia nel pensiero di Karl Jaspers" in *Lo Storicismo e la Sua Storia: Temi, Problemi, Prospettive,* Cacciatore, Giuseppe (ed). Miano, Francesco.
"Filosofi Artificiali" in *Soggetto E Verità: La questione dell'uomo nella filosofia contemporanea,* Fagiuoli, Ettore. Magnani, Lorenzo.
"Forms of Political Thinking and the Persistence of Practical Philosophy" in *Political Dialogue: Theories and Practices,* Esquith, Stephen L (ed). Simpson, Evan.
"Free Inquiry and Islamic Philosophy: The Significance of George Hourani" in *Averroës and the Enlightenment,* Wahba, Mourad (ed). Kurtz, Paul.
"Il Luogo Della Filosofia: La paradossalità della *Seinsfrage* nel giovane Heidegger" in *Soggetto E Verità: La questione dell'uomo nella filosofia contemporanea,* Fagiuoli, Ettore. Vicari, Dario.
"James and the Kantian Tradition" in *The Cambridge Companion to William James,* Putnam, Ruth Anna (ed). Carlson, Thomas.
"Le relazioni tra Bayle e l'Italia: i corrispondenti italiani di Bayle e le *Nouvelles de la République des Lettres*" in *Pierre Bayle e l'Italia,* Bianchi, Lorenzo. Bianchi, Lorenzo.
"Logica e filosofia nel pensiero contemporaneo" in *Momenti di Storia della Logica e di Storia della Filosofia,* Guetti, Carla (ed). Nave, Alberto.
"Lvov" in *In Itinere* European Cities and the Birth of Modern Scientific Philosophy, Poli, Roberto (ed). Wolenski, Jan.
"Moral Philosophy and the Development of Morality" in *The Cambridge Companion to William James,* Putnam, Ruth Anna (ed). Bird, Graham H.
"Nineteenth-Century Würzburg: The Development of the Scientific Approach to Philosophy" in *In Itinere* European Cities and the Birth of Modern Scientific Philosophy, Poli, Roberto (ed). Baumgartner, Wilhelm.
"No Necessary Connection": The Medieval Roots of the Occasionalist Roots of Hume. Nadler, Steven.
"Perspectivas sobre religión y filosofía en los inicios del Idealismo alemán: Fichte y Schelling antes de 1794" in *El inicio del Idealismo alemán,* Market, Oswaldo. De Torres, María José.
"Philosophie der Philosophie: Zur Frage nach dem Philosophiebegriff" in *Grenzen der kritischen Vernunft,* Schmid, Peter A. Schneiders, Werner.
"Philosophy and Art in Munich Around the Turn of the Century" in *In Itinere* European Cities and the Birth of Modern Scientific Philosophy, Poli, Roberto (ed). Schuhmann, Karl.
"Philosophy as Critique and as Vision" in *The Recovery of Philosophy in America: Essays in Honor of John Edwin Smith,* Kasulis, Thomas P (ed). Westphal, Merold.
"Philosophy as Grammar" in *The Cambridge Companion to Wittgenstein,* Sluga, Hans (ed). Garver, Newton.
"Philosophy in America: Recovery and Future Development" in *The Recovery of Philosophy in America: Essays in Honor of John Edwin Smith,* Kasulis, Thomas P (ed). Smith, John E.
"Philosophy's Recovery of Its History: A Tribute to John E. Smith" in *The Recovery of Philosophy in America: Essays in Honor of John Edwin Smith,* Kasulis, Thomas P (ed). Lucas Jr, George R.
"Phrase VII" in *On Jean-Luc Nancy: The Sense of Philosophy,* Sheppard, Darren (ed). Lacoue-Labarthe, Philippe.
"Poppers Beitrag für eine Philosophie der Chemie" in *Philosophie der Chemie: Bestandsaufnahme und Ausblick,* Schummer, Joachim (ed). Akeroyd, F Michael.
"Prague Mosaic: Encounters with Prague Philosophers" in *In Itinere* European Cities and the Birth of Modern Scientific Philosophy, Poli, Roberto (ed). Sebestik, Jan.
"Progress in Philosophy" in *The Idea of Progress,* McLaughlin, Peter (ed). Prawitz, Dag.
"Reflections on Philosophic Recovery" in *The Recovery of Philosophy in America: Essays in Honor of John Edwin Smith,* Kasulis, Thomas P (ed). Neville, Robert Cummings.
"Science and the Avant-Garde in Early Nineteenth-Century Florence" in *In Itinere* European Cities and the Birth of Modern Scientific Philosophy, Poli, Roberto (ed). Albertazzi, Liliana.
"The Availability of Wittgenstein's Philosophy" in *The Cambridge Companion to Wittgenstein,* Sluga, Hans (ed). Stern, David G.
"The Broken Bonds with the World" in *Epistemology and History,* Zeidler-Janiszewska, Anna (ed). Ozdowski, Pawel.
"The Goldilocks Syndrome" in *The Recovery of Philosophy in America: Essays in Honor of John Edwin Smith,* Kasulis, Thomas P (ed). Sherburne, Donald W.
"The Philosopher and the Understanding of the Law" in *Averroës and the Enlightenment,* Wahba, Mourad (ed). Gracia, Jorge J E.
"The Philosophy of the Right to Know and the Right not to Know" in *The Right to Know and the Right not to Know,* Chadwick, Ruth (ed). Chadwick, Ruth.
"The Shared World—Philosophy, Violence, Freedom" in *On Jean-Luc Nancy: The Sense of Philosophy,* Sheppard, Darren (ed). Caygill, Howard.

## PHILOSOPHY

"Theft and Conversion: Two Augustinian Confessions" in *The Recovery of Philosophy in America: Essays in Honor of John Edwin Smith*, Kasulis, Thomas P (ed). Vaught, Carl G.

"Warsaw: The Rise and Decline of Modern Scientific Philosophy in the Capital City of Poland" in *In Itinere* European Cities and the Birth of Modern Scientific Philosophy, Poli, Roberto (ed). Jadacki, Jacek Juliusz.

"Warum ist die Chemie ein Steifkind der Philosophie?" in *Philosophie der Chemie: Bestandsaufnahme und Ausblick*, Schummer, Joachim (ed). Ruthenberg, Klaus.

"Weiterführendes Forschungsprojekt für philosophisch-interdisziplinäre und interkuturelle Zusammenarbeit" in *Kreativer Friede durch Begegnung der Weltkulturen*, Beck, Heinrich (ed). Beck, Heinrich.

"Wem nützt eine Philosophie der Chemie—den Chemikern oder den Philosophen?" in *Philosophie der Chemie: Bestandsaufnahme und Ausblick*, Schummer, Joachim (ed). Eisvogel, Martin.

"Wittgenstein's Critique of Philosophy" in *The Cambridge Companion to Wittgenstein*, Sluga, Hans (ed). Fogelin, Robert J.

"*La volontéde puissance*" n'existe pas: A proposito dell'edizione francese di alcuni saggi di Mazzino Montinari. Viola, Salvatore.

*In Itinere* European Cities and the Birth of Modern Scientific Philosophy. Poli, Roberto (ed).

*A Concordance to the Critique of Pure Reason*. Reuscher, Jay.

*A History of Philosophy: Volume I*. Hough, Williston S (ed & trans) and Erdmann, Johann Eduard.

*A History of Philosophy: Volume II*. Hough, Williston S (ed & trans) and Erdmann, Johann Eduard.

*A History of Philosophy: Volume III*. Hough, Williston S (ed & trans) and Erdmann, Johann Eduard.

*A Short History of Modern Philosophy: From Descartes to Wittgenstein*. Scruton, Roger.

*A Spinoza Reader: The Ethics and Other Works*. Curley, Edwin (ed & trans).

*African Philosophy: Myth and Reality*. Hountondji, Paulin J and Evans, Henri (trans).

*African-American Perspectives and Philosophical Traditions*. Pittman, John P (ed).

*American Modern: The Path Not Taken*: Aesthetics, Metaphysics, and Intellectual History in Classic American Philosophy. Tejera, Victorino.

*An Introduction to Medieval Philosophy*. Martin, Christopher F J.

*An Introduction to the Thought of Karl Popper*. Corvi, Roberta and Camiller, Patrick (trans).

*Antonio Gramsci Prison Notebooks: Volume II*. Buttigieg, Joseph A (ed & trans).

*Aprender a filosofar preguntando: con Platón, Epicuro, Descartes*. Echeverría, José.

*Both/And: Reading Kierkegaard from Irony to Edification*. Strawser, Michael.

*Catalogue des Publications 1977-1995*. Carratelli, Giovanni Pugliese (ed).

*Charles S. Peirce's Evolutionary Philosophy*. Hausman, Carl R.

*Conversations with French Philosophers*. Aylesworth, Gary E (trans) and Rötzer, Florian.

*Culture and Self*. Allen, Douglas (ed) and Malhotra, Ashok K.

*Das weite Spektrum der analytischen Philosophie*. Lenzen, Wolfgang.

*Debating the State of Philosophy: Habermas, Rorty, and Kolakowski*. Niznik, Jozef (ed) and Sanders, John T (ed).

*Deconstruction in a Nutshell: A Conversation with Jacques Derrida*. Caputo, John D (ed).

*Deleuze and Philosophy: The Difference Engineer*. Ansell Pearson, Keith (ed).

*Dictionary of Philosophy and Religion: Eastern and Western Thought*. Reese, William L.

*Emmanuel Levinas: Basic Philosophical Writings*. Peperzak, Adriaan Theodoor (ed), Critchley, Simon (ed) and Bernasconi, Robert (ed).

*Encyclopedia of Classical Philosophy*. Devereux, Daniel T (ed) and Mitsis, Phillip T (ed).

*Ensayos Aristotélicos*. Rivera, José Luis (ed).

*Figuras del Logos: Entre la Filosofía y la Literatura*. López de la Vieja, Maria Teresa (ed).

*Filosofia Criacionista da Morte: Meditaçao sobre o Problema da Morte No Pensamento Filosófico de Leonardo Coimbra*. Cândido Pimentel, Manuel.

*Food for Thought: Philosophy and Food*. Telfer, Elizabeth.

*Four Summers: A Czech Kaleidoscope*. Page, Benjamin.

*From Physics to Metaphysics*. Redhead, Michael.

*From Plato to Nietzsche, 2nd Edition*. Baird, Forrest E (ed) and Kaufmann, Walter.

*From Soul to Mind: The Emergence of Psychology from Erasmus Darwin to William James*. Reed, Edward S.

*George Bentham: Autobiography 1800-1834*. Filipiuk, Marion (ed).

*George Grant and the Subversion of Modernity: Art, Philosophy, Politics, Religion, and Education*. Davis, Arthur (ed).

*Gesamtausgabe II. Abteilung: Vorlesungen (Band 27: Einleitung in die Philosophie)*. Heidegger, Martin.

*Habermas and the Unfinished Project of Modernity*. Passerin d'Entrèves, Maurizio (ed) and Benhabib, Seyla (ed).

*Hannah Arendt and the Limits of Philosophy: With a New Preface*. Disch, Lisa J.

*Heidegger, Philosophy, Nazism*. Young, Julian.

*History as the Story of Freedom: Philosophy in Intercultural Context*. Butler, Clark.

*Hofmann-Streit*: il dibattito sul rapporto tra filosofia e teologia all'Università di Helmstedt. Antognazza, Maria Rosa.

*How to Live Forever: Science Fiction and Philosophy*. Clark, Stephen R L.

*Human, All Too Human, I*. Handwerk, Gary (trans) and Nietzsche, Friedrich.

*Human, All Too Human: A Book of Free Spirits*. Hollingdale, R J (trans) and Nietzsche, Friedrich.

*Il Disincanto Della Ragione E L'Assolutezza Del Bonheur* Studio Sull'Abate Galiani. Amodio, Paolo.

*Jewish Philosophers and Jewish Philosophy*. Fackenheim, Emil L and Morgan, Michael L (ed).

*Karl R. Popper (1902-1994)*. Boladeras Cucurella, Margarita.

*Karl-Otto Apel: Selected Essays*. Mendieta, Eduardo (ed).

*Kenneth Burke and the Scapegoat Process*. Carter, C Allen.

*Knowledge, Belief, and Witchcraft: Analytic Experiments in African Philosophy*. Hallen, Barry and Olubi Sodipo, J.

*La Historia de la Filosofía como Hermenéutica*. Sánchez Meca, Diego.

*Latin American Philosophy in the Twentieth Century*. Gracia, Jorge J E.

*Lecturas de Historia de la Filosofía*. Nieto Blanco, Carlos (ed).

*Leibniz' Universal Jurisprudence: Justice as the Charity of the Wise*. Riley, Patrick.

*Léopold Sédar Senghor: From Politics to Poetry*. Kluback, William.

*Levinas: An Introduction*. Davis, Colin.

*Life as Narcissism: A Unified Theory of Life*. Tabrizi, Firooz N.

*Max Scheler: A Concise Introduction into the World of a Great Thinker*. Frings, Manfred S.

*Medieval Thought*. Luscombe, David.

*Memorias Del Seminario En Conmemoración De Los 400 Anos Del Nacimiento De René Descartes*. Albis, Víctor S (ed), Charum, Jorge (ed) and Sánchez, Clara Helena (& others).

*Mortals and Others: American Essays 1931-1935*. Russell, Bertrand and Ruja, Harry (ed).

*My Philosophical Development*. Russell, Bertrand.

*Nietzsche and the Promise of Philosophy*. Klein, Wayne.

*Odisseias do Espírito: Estudos de Filosofia Luso-Brasileira*. Cândido Pimentel, Manuel.

*Of Art and Wisdom: Plato's Understanding of Techne*. Roochnik, David.

*On Heidegger's Nazism and Philosophy*. Rockmore, Tom.

*On Jean-Luc Nancy: The Sense of Philosophy*. Sheppard, Darren (ed), Sparks, Simon (ed) and Thomas, Colin (ed).

*Organicism: Origin and Development*. Bahm, Archie J.

*Parapsychology, Philosophy, and Spirituality: A Postmodern Exploration*. Griffin, David Ray.

*Philosophie der Chemie: Bestandsaufnahme und Ausblick*. Schummer, Joachim (ed), Psarros, Nikos (ed) and Ruthenberg, Klaus (ed).

*Philosophische Gedichte*. Flasch, Thomas (trans) and Campanella, Tommaso.

*Philosophy after F.H. Bradley*. Bradley, James (ed).

*Philosophy as Passion: The Thinking of Simone de Beauvoir*. Vintges, Karen.

*Philosophy History Sophistry*. Rohatyn, Dennis.

*Philosophy in Experience: American Philosophy in Transition*. Hart, Richard E (ed) and Anderson, Douglas R (ed).

*Philosophy in Literature*. Rickman, H P.

*Philosophy of Sex and Love: A Reader*. Trevas, Robert (ed), Zucker, Arthur (ed) and Borchert, Donald (ed).

*Philosophy Unmasked: A Skeptic's Critique*. Calhoun, Laurie.

*Philosophy, Religion, and the Question of Intolerance*. Ambuel, David (ed) and Razavi, Mehdi Amin (ed).

*Plato: Complete Works*. Cooper, John M (ed) and Hutchinson, D S (ed).

*Postcolonial African Philosophy: A Critical Reader*. Chukwudi Eze, Emmanuel (ed).

*Practicing Philosophy: Pragmatism and the Philosophical Life*. Shusterman, Richard.

*Premises: Essays on Philosophy and Literature from Kant to Celan*. Hamacher, Werner and Fenves, Peter (trans).

*Proper Names*. Smith, Michael B (trans) and Levinas, Emmanuel.

*Ragione e Scrittura tra Descartes e Spinoza: Saggio sulla Philosophia S. Scripturae Interpres di Lodewijk Meyer e sulla sua recezione*. Bordoli, Roberto.

*Rethinking the Rhetorical Tradition: From Plato to Postmodernism*. Kastely, James L.

*Saber, Sentir, Pensar: La cultura en la frontera de dos siglos*. Nieto Blanco, Carlos (ed).

*Sagacious Reasoning: Henry Odera Oruka in Memoriam*. Graness, Anke (ed) and Kresse, Kai (ed).

*Simplicius: On Aristotle's Physics 2*. Fleet, Barrie (trans).

*Sites of Vision*. Levin, David Michael (ed).

*Society, Economics & Philosophy: Selected Papers*. Allen, R T (ed) and Polanyi, Michael.

*The Art of Plato: Ten Essays in Platonic Interpretation*. Rutherford, R B.

*The Cambridge Companion to William James*. Putnam, Ruth Anna (ed).

*The Cambridge Companion to Wittgenstein*. Sluga, Hans (ed) and Stern, David G (ed).

*The Case for Freewill Theism: A Philosophical Assessment*. Basinger, David.

## PHILOSOPHY

## PHILOSOPHY

## PHILOSOPHY

Philosophy as Experience, as Elucidation and as Profession: An Attempt to Reconstruct Early Wittgenstein's Philosophy. Linhe, Han.

Philosophy for Children and the Discipline of Philosophy. Gazzard, Ann.

Philosophy for Children: One Way of Developing Children's Thinking. Green, Lena.

Philosophy in a Fragmented World. Noonan, Jeff.

Philosophy in an Age of Overinformation, or: What We Ought to Ignore in Order to Know What Really Matters. Hösle, Vittorio.

Philosophy Outside the Academy: The Role of Philosophy in People-Oriented Professions and the Prospects for Philosophical Counseling. Pfeifer, Karl.

Philosophy within Theology in Light of the Foundationalism Debate. Guarino, Thomas.

Philosophy...Artifacts...Friendship—and the History of the Gaze. Illich, Ivan.

Plato's *Phaedrus*: Philosophy as Dialogue with the Dead. Zwicky, Jan.

Poor Bertie. Rée, Jonathan.

Practical Philosophy and the Human Sciences Today (in Serbo-Croatian). Pazanin, Ante.

Présentation du professeur François Duchesneau. Troisfontaines, Claude.

Problemas Filosóficos y Filosofías del Límite. Nudler, Oscar.

Problemas o Preguntas?. Gutiérrez, Carlos B.

Problems of Formalization in Samvāda Sāstra. Shekhawat, Virendra.

Prof. D. M. Dattai: As a Process-Philosopher from an Alternative Inter-Cultural Perspective. Sarkar, Anil K.

Professor Prasad on Working Out a Lead from Swami Vivekananda: Some Reflections. Ghosh, Ranjan K.

Psychological Courage. Putman, Daniel.

Questionnaire on Deleuze. Alliez, Éric.

Raison et Convention, ou la Raison Politique chez Hobbes. Boss, Gilbert.

Readings of Barthes V. Hidden Philosophy? (in Portuguese). Soto, L G.

Realism and Anti-Realism: A Whiteheadian Response to Richard Rorty Concerning Truth, Propositions, and Practice. Nancarrow, Paul S.

Recent and Classic References at the Interface of Philosophy, Psychiatry, and Psychology. Sadler, John Z (ed).

Recordando a M. Heidegger. Wagner de Reyna, Alberto.

Religious Studies and Theology, Ethics and Philosophy (in Czech). Kratochvil, Zdenek.

Rereading Hannah Arendt's Kant Lectures. Beiner, Ronald.

Resistances: Meyer Schapiro's *Theory and Philosophy of Art*. Schwabsky, Barry.

Rethinking Leibniz. Parkinson, G H R.

Rethinking Philosophy in the Third Wave of Feminism. Golumbia, David.

Revistas filosóficas em Portugal. Calafate, Pedro.

Reviving Ophelia: A Role for Philosophy in Helping Young Women Achieve Selfhood. Turgeon, Wendy C.

Russell and His Biographers. Willis, Kirk.

Sao os Problemas Filosóficos Tradicionais Confusoes Lingüísticas ou Investigaçoes Legítimas Sobre as Coisas?. Junqueira Smith, Plínio.

Schicksal und Charakter: Für die Philosophische Praxis ist vieles von Schopenhauer zu lernen: Vortrag auf dem Kolloquium der GPP am 30. Oktober 1994 in Tübingen. Achenbach, Gerd B.

Secolarizzazione e originalità del moderno: In margine a *La legittimità dell'epoca moderna* di Hans Blumenberg. Carosotti, Gianni.

Short Account of the Debates in the Higher Seminary of History of Philosophy, Catholic University in Lublin, in the Years 1953/54 to 1955/56 (in Polish). Strózewski, Wladyslaw.

Silvester Mauro, S.J. (1619-1687) on Four Degrees of Abstraction. Doyle, John P.

Sobre a Ciência e o Magistério Filosófico de Pitágoras. Spinelli, Miguel.

Some Problems in the Writing of the History of African Philosophy. Ogbogbo, C B N.

Spinoza en discusión. Fernández G, Eugenio.

Spinoza y el Poder Constituyente. Aragüés, Juán Manuel.

Stigmata: Job the Dog. Cixous, Hélène.

Surfing the Third Wave: A Dialogue Between Two Third Wave Feminists. Alfonso, Rita and Trigilio, Jo.

Tedium Vitae: Or, My Life as a 'Net Serf'. Gehring, Verna V.

Tempo e pensiero topologico tra scienza e filosofia. Polizzi, Gaspare.

The *Philosophical Encyclopedia* Is Twenty-Five. Kamenskii, Z A.

The Abdication of Philosophy: On the Modernity of the Relation between Philosophy and Politics in Kant. Gerhardt, Volker.

The Bacchanalian Revel: Hegel and Deconstruction. Haas, Andrew.

The Blessed Gods Mourn: What is Living-Dead in the Legacy of Hegel. Cutrofello, Andrew.

The Cognitive Turn in Philosophy (in Czech). Jacob, Pierre.

The Common Europe as a Philosophical Question. Funda, Otakar A.

The Early Losev. Gogotishvili, Liudmila Akhilovna.

The Eighteenth-Century British Reviews of Hume's Writings. Fieser, James.

The Ethics of Philosophical Discourse. Lang, Berel.

The Five Communities. Kennedy, David.

The Frankfurt School. Tessin, Timothy.

The Future and the History of Ideas. Perkins, Mary Anne.

The God and a Man-Philosopher: Vocation for Philosophy on the Basis of F.W.I. Schelling's Anthropotheology (in Polish). Kolas, Pawel.

The Historicity of Philosophy: Hegel and Gadamer (in Serbo-Croatian). Deretic, Irina.

The History of Interpretation and the Interpretation of History in the History of Philosophy. Wiehl, Reiner.

The Hornswoggle Problem. Smith Churchland, Patricia.

The Hume Literature, 1995. Morris, William E.

The Idea of the University and the Role of Philosophy. Hufnagel, Erwin.

The Internal Connectedness of Philosophy of History and Philosophy of Language in Nietzsche's Early Writings (in Serbo-Croatian). Margreiter, Reinhard.

The King and 'I': Agency and Rationality in Athens and Jerusalem. Glouberman, Mark.

The Metaphysical Roots of Philosophical Tolerance and its Substitutes. Brajicic, Rudolf.

The Metaphysics of Poetry: Subverting the "Ancient Quarrel" and Recasting the Problem. Swanger, David.

The New Translation of *Sein und Zeit*: A Grammatological Lexicographer's Commentary. Kisiel, Theodore J.

The New View of Plato. Krämer, Hans Joachim.

The Notion of African Philosophy. Uduigwomen, Andrew F.

The Origins and Crisis of Continental Philosophy. Steinbock, Anthony J.

The Parochial Universalist Conception of 'Philosophy' and 'African Philosophy'. Ikuenobe, Polycarp.

The Philosophy of Barrows Dunham: The Progress of an American Radical. Parsons, Howard L.

The Philosophy of Medium-Grade Art. Ridley, Aaron.

The Philosophy of Religion in the System of Freedom. Despot, Blanko.

The Philosophy They Bring to Class: Companion Student Papers in PHL 101. Chiles, Robert E.

The Rational and the Irrational: A Philosophical Problem (Reading Arthur Schopenhauer). Mudragei, Nellia Stepanovna.

The Russian Idea at the End of the Twentieth Century. Mil'don, Valerii Il'ich.

The Seventh Seal: On the Fate of Whitehead's Proposed Rehabilitation. Lucas Jr, George R.

The Spread of Aristotle's Political Theory in China. Mi, Michael C.

The State of the Question in the Study of Plato. Press, Gerald A.

The Summer Philosophy Institute of Colorado: Building Bridges. Figueroa, Robert and Goering, Sara.

The 'Person' in Philosophical Counselling vs. Psychotherapy and the Possibility of Interchange between the Fields. Blass, Rachel B.

Theology and Philosophy (in Serbo-Croatian). Zurovac, Mirko.

Thinking Life as Relation: An Interview with Luce Irigaray. Pluhacek, Stephen and Bostic, Heidi.

This Project is Mad: Descartes, Derrida, and the Notion of Philosophical Crisis. Steiner, Gary.

Tra stupore e malinconia: Osservazioni sul pensiero di G. Leopardi. Franchi, Alfredo.

Trabajo Filosófico y Comunidad Filosófica. Parra, Lisímaco.

Traiciones a Luis Vives. Calero, Francisco.

Translation, Philosophy, Materialism. Venuti, Lawrence.

Überlegungen zur Anwendungsdimension der Philosophie. Krämer, Hans.

Una aproximación a la ética en el programa Filosofía para Niños de Matthew Lipman. Accorinti, Stella.

Una Crítica "Romántica" al Romanticismo. Díaz, Jorge Aurelio.

Una lettera inedita del Carcavi al Magliabechi con un parere sul Redi. Guerrini, Luigi.

Veritas vincit (in Czech). Skorpíková, Zuzana.

Vicente Munoz Delgado y Angel Amor Ruibal. Dafonte, César Raña.

Vico en Italia y en Alemania. Sevilla Fernández, José M.

Vico político antimoderno? (Breves observaciones sobre la reciente interpretación de Mark Lilla). Ratto, Franco.

Vico: entre historia y naturaleza. Vitiello, Vincenzo.

We Pragmatists...; Peirce and Rorty in Conversation. Haack, Susan.

What Exactly Is the Good of Self-Deception?. Putman, Daniel A.

What is Natural?. Abney, Keith.

What is Philosophical in Philosophical Counselling?. Lahav, Ran.

William Durant the Younger and Conciliar Theory. Fasolt, Constantin.

Wine-Farming, Heresy Trials and the 'Whole Personality': The Emergence of the Stellenbosch Philosophical Tradition, 1916-40. Nash, Andrew.

Y a-t-il de la place pour philosopher sur les mathématiques au collégial?. Daniel, Marie-France, LaFortune, Louise and Pallascio, Richard (& others).

Zur Lage der Philosophischen Praxis. Zdrenka, Michael.

'Ideia Poética' e 'Ideaia Filosófica': Sobre a Relaçao entre Poesia e Filosofia na Obra de Antero de Quental. Ribeiro dos Santos, Leonel.

¿La filosofía como amor del saber o saber efectivo?. Schumacher, Bernard.

## PHILOSOPHY OF EDUCATION
*see* Education

## PHILOSOPHY OF HISTORY
*see* History

## PHILOSOPHY OF LANGUAGE
*see* Language

## PHILOSOPHY OF LAW
*see* Law

## PHILOSOPHY OF MIND
*see* Mind

## PHILOSOPHY OF RELIGION
*see* Religion

## PHILOSOPHY OF SCIENCE
*see* Science

## PHOTOGRAPHY
Antero: As Imagens: Contexto Estético e Antropológico. Lambert, Maria de Fátima.

Authentic Photographs. Warburton, Nigel.

Escaping Reality: Digital Imagery and the Resources of Photography. Savedoff, Barbara E.

From *The World is Beautiful* to *The Family of Man*: The Plight of Photography as a Modern Art. Seamon, Roger.

Individual Style in Photographic Art. Warburton, Nigel.

Photography as Narrative (in Japanese). Kiyokazu, Nishimura.

Sujet(s) à interprétation(s): sur la relative transparence d'une photographie positiviste. Lauzon, Jean.

## PHRONESIS
"Don't Think Zebras": Uncertainty, Interpretation, and the Place of Paradox in Clinical Education. Hunter, Kathryn.

"Phronesis": Um Conceito Inoportuno?. Perine, Marcelo.

Can Phronesis Save the Life of Medical Ethics?. Beresford, Eric B.

Engagement and Suffering in Responsible Caregiving: On Overcoming Maleficience in Health Care. Schultz, Dawson S and Carnevale, Franco A.

L'éthique aristotélicienne et le chemin de Heidegger. Kontos, Pavlos.

Phronesis in Clinical Ethics. McGee, Glenn.

The Architectonic of the Ethics of Liberation. Dussel, Enrique.

## PHYLOGENY
Discussion: Phylogenetic Species Concept: Pluralism, Monism, and History. Horvath, Christopher D.

## PHYSICAL
Fitness Made Physical: The Supervenience of Biological Concepts Revisited. Weber, Marcel.

From Atlas to Adolph: Body Building, Physical Culture, and National Socialism. Pickens, Donald K.

Krylov's Proof that Statistical Mechanics Cannot Be Founded on Classical Mechanics and Interpretation of Classical Statistical Mechanical Probabilities. Rédei, Miklós.

The Architecture of Representation. Grush, Rick.

## PHYSICAL OBJECT
Wie definiert man einen physikalischen Gegenstand?. Rudolph, Enno.

## PHYSICAL REALITY
The Incompleteness of Quantum Mechanics as a Description of Physical Reality. Unnerstall, Thomas.

## PHYSICALISM
"Actions, Causes, and Mental Ascriptions" in *Objections to Physicalism,* Robinson, Howard (ed). Gillett, Grant.

"Difficulties with Physicalism, and a Programme for Dualists" in *Objections to Physicalism,* Robinson, Howard (ed). Forrest, Peter.

"Non-Reductive Physicalism?" in *Objections to Physicalism,* Robinson, Howard (ed). Smith, A D.

"Physicalism and Mathematics" in *Objections to Physicalism,* Robinson, Howard (ed). Hale, Bob.

"The Grain Problem" in *Objections to Physicalism,* Robinson, Howard (ed). Lockwood, Michael.

"Transcendental Arguments against Physicalism" in *Objections to Physicalism,* Robinson, Howard (ed). Walker, Ralph.

"Truth, Physicalism, and Ultimate Theory" in *Objections to Physicalism,* Robinson, Howard (ed). Wagner, Steven J.

*Objections to Physicalism.* Robinson, Howard (ed).

*Was sind Handlungen? Eine philosophische Auseinandersetzung mit dem Naturalismus.* Runggaldier, Edmund.

*What Is a Person? An Ethical Exploration.* Walters, James W.

*Zur Meta-Theorie der Physik.* Schröter, Joachim.

A Defense of Physicalism. Jensen, Steven J.

Ansätze zur physikalischen Untersuchung des Leib-Seele-Problems. Arendes, Lothar.

Does the Problem of Mental Causation Generalize?. Kim, Jaegwon.

Eigenschafts-Physikalismus. Beckermann, Ansgar.

Gehirn und Ich: Zwei Hauptakteure des Geistes?. Kaeser, Eduard.

Hechos semánticos y presiones fisicalistas. Acero, Juan José.

How Physicalists Can Avoid Reductionism. Kirk, Robert.

Interactionism and Physicality. Mills, Eugene.

Nonreductive Naturalism. Silvers, Stuart.

On the Metaphysical Utility of Claims of Global Supervenience. Melnyk, Andrew.

Panexperientialist Physicalism and the Mind-Body Problem. Griffin, David Ray.

Physicalism and Classical Theism. Forrest, Peter.

Physicalism and Mental Causes: Contra Papineau. Moser, Paul K.

Qualia und Physikalismus. Schröder, Jürgen.

Science and Moral Skepticism in Hobbes. Black, Sam.

Towards a Reapprehension of Causal Efficacy. Earley Sr, Joseph E.

Über das Verhältnis von Metaphysik und Physik bei Descartes. Hüttemann, Andreas.

Who Needs Mereology?. Pollard, Stephen.

'Beyond Determinism'. Spurrett, David.

## PHYSICIAN
A Communitarian Approach to Physician-Assisted Death. Miller, Franklin G.

Between Doctor and Patient. Capron, Alexander M.

Conflicts of Interest, Conflicting Interests, and Interesting Conflicts, Part 3. Vinicky, Janicemarie K, Orlowski, James P and Shevlin Edwards, Sue.

Do Physicians' Own Preferences for Life-Sustaining Treatment Influence Their Perceptions of Patients' Preferences? A Second Look. Schneiderman, Lawrence J, Kaplan, Robert M and Rosenberg, Esther (& others).

Ethical Issues and Relationships between House Staff and Attending Physicians: A Case Study. Beckerman, Aaron, Doerfler, Martin and Couch, Elsbeth (& others).

Justice, Society, Physicians and Ethics Committees: Incorporating Ideas of Justice into Patient Care Decisions. Loewy, Erich H.

Levinas and the Hippocratic Oath: A Discussion of Physician-Assisted Suicide. Degnin, Francis.

Physician-Assisted Suicide in Psychiatry: Developments in the Netherlands. Gevers, J K M and Legemaate, Johan.

Physician-Assisted Suicide: A Different Approach. Emanuel, Linda L.

Physician-Assisted Suicide: The Role of Mental Health Professionals. Peruzzi, Nico, Canapary, Andrew and Bongar, Bruce.

Physicians and Managed Care: Employees or Professionals?. Christensen, Kate T.

Physicians' Collaboration with Chaplains: Difficulties and Benefits. Thiel, Mary Martha and Robinson, Mary Redner.

PremAternal Duty and the Resolution of Conflict. Yeast, John D.

Professional Ethics of Psychologists and Physicians: Morality, Confidentiality, and Sexuality in Israel. Shimshon Rubin, Simon and Dror, Omer.

Reflections on My Father's Experience with Doctors during the Shoah (1939-1945). Bursztajn, Harold J.

Relationships between Primary Care Physicians and Consultants in Managed Care. Brett, Allan S.

Relationships, Relationships, Relationships.... Sugarman, Jeremy and Emanuel, Linda L.

Response to "Ethical Concerns about Relapse Studies" by Adil E. Shamoo and Timothy J. Keay (CQ Vol 5, No 3). Bergsma, Jurrit.

Retiring the Pacemaker. Reitemeier, Paul J, Derse, Arthur R and Spike, Jeffrey.

Suicide and Advance Directives: One Doctor's Dilemma. Kane, Gregory C.

The Christian Physician in the Non-Christian Institution: Objections of Conscience and Physician Value Neutrality. Peppin, John F.

The Ethics of Referral Kickbacks and Self-Referral and the HMO Physician as Gatekeeper: An Ethical Analysis. Beckwith, Francis J.

The Quality of Primary Care/Consultant Relationships in Managed Care: Have We Gone Forward or Backward?. Povar, Gail J.

The Reluctant retained Witness: Alleged Sexual Misconduct in the Doctor/Patient Relationship. Yarborough, Mark.

The Virtues in Psychiatric Practice. Mann, David W.

## PHYSICS
*see also* Quantum Physics

"A Free Man's Worship," 1902 (El culto del hombre libre) El problema de la existencia humana en su relación con el destino y los ideales éticos. Sancho García, Isabel.

"Arthur Stanley Eddington e la 'scoperta' della freccia del tempo" in *Il Concetto di Tempo: Atti del XXXII Congresso Nazionale della Società Filosofica Italiana,* Casertano, Giovanni (ed). Giordano, Giuseppe.

"De la metafisica a la fisica en el programa cartesiano" in *Memorias Del Seminario En Conmemoración De Los 400 Anos Del Nacimiento De René Descartes,* Albis, Víctor S (ed). Cardona, Carlos Albert.

"Il tempo nella fisica moderna" in *Il Concetto di Tempo: Atti del XXXII Congresso Nazionale della Società Filosofica Italiana,* Casertano, Giovanni (ed). Bernardini, Carlo.

*A Novel Defense of Scientific Realism.* Leplin, Jarrett.

*Explaining Consciousness—The 'Hard Problem'.* Shear, Jonathan (ed).

*From Physics to Metaphysics.* Redhead, Michael.

*Idealisierungen und das Ziel der Physik: Eine Untersuchung zum Realismus, Empirismus und Konstruktivismus in der Wissenschafts-theorie.* Hüttemann, Andreas.

*In Search of a Better World: Lectures and Essays from Thirty Years.* Popper, Karl and Bennet, Laura J (trans).

*Lo stile de' Geometri*: La filosofia cartesiana nell'opera di Alessandro Pascoli (1669-1757). Guerrini, Luigi.

*Simplicius: On Aristotle's Physics 2.* Fleet, Barrie (trans).

*Simplicius: On Aristotle's Physics 5.* Urmson, J O (trans).

*Übergang Von Den Metaphysischen Anfangsgründen Der Naturwissenschaft Zur Physik.* Kant, Immanuel.

*Wholeness and the Implicate Order.* Bohm, David.

*Zur Meta-Theorie der Physik.* Schröter, Joachim.

A Origem do Conceito do *Impetus.* Rodrigues Évora, Fátima Regina.

A Remark Concerning Prediction and Spacetime Singularities. Hogarth, Mark.

Alternative Mathematics and Alternative Theoretical Physics: The Method for Linking Them Together. Drago, Antonino.

An Axiomatic Framework for Classical Particle Mechanics without Force. Schlup Sant'Anna, Adonai.

Antidote or Theory?. Dickson, Michael.

Aristotle's Razor. Drozdek, Adam.

Bemerkung zu: "Epistemologische Aspekte der neuen Entwicklungen in der Physik" von G. Münster. Mielke, Eckehard W.

Bemerkungen über die gegenwärtige Arbeit im Bereich der Naturphilosophie an der FEST und über die *Philosophy-and-Physics-Workshops.* Stamatescu, Ion-Olimpiu.

**PLACE**

Maniobras doctrinales de un tomista colonial: tiempo y lugar según Suárez de Urbina. Knabenschuh de Porta, Sabine.

Más allá del bosque (Reflexiones agoralógicas en torno a Vico). López Lloret, Jorge.

**PLACE, U**

"Conceptualism and the Ontological Independence of Cause and Effect" in *Dispositions: A Debate,* Armstrong, D M. Place, U T.

"Final Replies to Place and Armstrong" in *Dispositions: A Debate,* Armstrong, D M. Martin, C B.

"Place's and Armstrong's Views Compared and Contrasted" in *Dispositions: A Debate,* Armstrong, D M. Armstrong, D M.

"Properties and Dispositions" in *Dispositions: A Debate,* Armstrong, D M. Martin, C B.

"Replies to Armstrong and Place" in *Dispositions: A Debate,* Armstrong, D M. Martin, C B.

"Reply to Martin" in *Dispositions: A Debate,* Armstrong, D M. Armstrong, D M.

Consciousness and Connectionism—The Problem of Compatability of Type Identity Theory and of Connectionism. Potrc, Matjaz.

**PLAGIARISM**

"A Horse Chestnut Is Not a Chestnut Horse": A Refutation of Bray, Davis, MacGregor, and Wollan. Oates, Stephen B.

"A Sin Against Scholarship": Some Examples of Plagiarism in Stephen B. Oates's Biographies of Abraham Lincoln, Martin Luther King, Jr., and William Faulkner. Burlingame, Michael.

A Crying Need for Discourse. Zangrando, Robert L.

Concerning the Charge of Plagiarism against Stephen B. Oates. Current, Richard N.

Plagiarism and Reviewer/Editor Responsibility. Riggan, William.

Plagiarism and the Art of Copying. Wollan, Jr, Laurin A.

Popular Biography, Plagiarism, and Persecution. Jones, Robert E.

Sharing and Stealing: Persistent Ambiguities. Swan, John.

The Oates Case. Trefousse, Hans L.

Towards a Definition of Plagiarism: The Bray/Oates Controversy Revisited. Kozak, Ellen M.

When the Trial *Is* the Punishment: The Ethics of Plagiarism Accusations. Yanikoski, Charles S.

**PLANCK, M**

Classical Physics and Early Quantum Theory: A Legitimate Case of Theoretical Underdetermination. Hudson, Robert G.

**PLANET**

Alexander of Aphrodisias on Celestial Motions. Bodnár, István M.

**PLANNING**

Función, plan y proyecto. Llano Cifuentes, Carlos.

On the Theoretical Basis of Prediction in Economics. González, Wenceslao J.

The Invalid Advance Directive. Wenger, Neil S and FitzGerald, John.

**PLANT**

Are Plants Conscious?. Nagel, Alexandra H M.

**PLANTINGA, A**

God and the Best. Langtry, Bruce.

In Defense of Coherentism. Kvanvig, Jonathan.

More Evidence Against Anti-Evidentialism. Timmons, Brent D.

Naturalism and Self-Defeat: Plantinga's Version. Nathan, N M L.

On Plantinga's Way Out. Brant, Dale Eric.

Plantinga on Functions and the Theory of Evolution. Levin, Michael.

Plantinga's Case Against Naturalistic Epistemology. Fales, Evan.

Two Notions of Warrant and Plantinga's Solution to the Gettier Problem. Greene, Richard and Balmert, N.A..

Undefeated Naturalism. Ross, Glenn.

**PLATO**

"Carnal Knowledge in the *Charmides*" in *Dialogues with Plato,* Benitez, Eugenio (ed). McAvoy, Martin.

"Deliberation and Moral Expertise in Plato's *Crito*" in *Dialogues with Plato,* Benitez, Eugenio (ed). Benitez, Eugenio E.

"Glaucons Herausforderung: Was ist Motiv und Lohn der Tugend?" in *Das weite Spektrum der analytischen Philosophie,* Lenzen, Wolfgang. Hegselmann, Rainer.

"Il concetto di tempo nel mondo antico fino a Platone" in *Il Concetto di Tempo: Atti del XXXII Congresso Nazionale della Società Filosofica Italiana,* Casertano, Giovanni (ed). Giannantoni, Gabriele.

"Il provincialismo filosofico" in *Geofilosofia,* Bonesio, Luisa (ed). Makowski, François.

"Intellectualism and Moral Habituation in Plato's Earlier Dialogues" in *Dialogues with Plato,* Benitez, Eugenio (ed). Yong, Patrick.

"La causa della conoscenza: discorso logico ed esigenza etica nel *Fedone* platonico" in *Momenti di Storia della Logica e di Storia della Filosofia,* Guetti, Carla (ed). Casertano, Giovanni.

"Le parti, le forme ed i nomi del tempo nel *Timeo* platonico" in *Il Concetto di Tempo: Atti del XXXII Congresso Nazionale della Società Filosofica Italiana,* Casertano, Giovanni (ed). Casertano, Giovanni.

"Mrs. Bates in Plato's Cave" in *Critical Studies: Ethics and the Subject,* Simms, Karl (ed). Brottman, David.

"Not-Being and Linguistic Deception" in *Dialogues with Plato,* Benitez, Eugenio (ed). O'Leary-Hawthorne, Diane.

"Plato's *Philebus*: The Numbering of a Unity" in *Dialogues with Plato,* Benitez, Eugenio (ed). Barker, Andrew.

"Plato, Prejudice, and the Mature-Age Student in Antiquity" in *Dialogues with Plato,* Benitez, Eugenio (ed). Tarrant, Harold.

"Socratic Anti-Empiricism in the *Phaedo*" in *Dialogues with Plato,* Benitez, Eugenio (ed). Baltzly, Dirk.

"Sophistry and Wisdom in Plato's *Meno*" in *Philosophy of Education (1996),* Margonis, Frank (ed). Hall, Terry.

"Sophistry, Dialectic, and Teacher Education: A Reinterpretation of Plato's *Meno*" in *Philosophy of Education (1996),* Margonis, Frank (ed). Boyles, Deron R.

"What in Plato's *Crito* is Benefited by Justice and Harmed by Injustice?" in *Dialogues with Plato,* Benitez, Eugenio (ed). Blyth, Dougal.

"Zu einer Interpretation von Platons Dialog "Parmenides" in *Das weite Spektrum der analytischen Philosophie,* Lenzen, Wolfgang. Stekeler-Weithofer, Pirmin.

*Aprender a filosofar preguntando: con Platón, Epicuro, Descartes.* Echeverría, José.

*Defence of Socrates Euthyphro Crito.* Gallop, David (trans).

*Dialogues with Plato.* Benitez, Eugenio E (ed).

*Dunamis* and Being: Heidegger on Plato's *Sophist* 247d8-e4. Ellis, John.

*Il Concetto di Tempo: Atti del XXXII Congresso Nazionale della Società Filosofica Italiana.* Casertano, Giovanni (ed).

*Of Art and Wisdom: Plato's Understanding of Techne.* Roochnik, David.

*Plato on the Human Paradox.* O'Connell, Robert J.

*Plato's Parmenides.* Allen, R E (ed & trans).

*Plato's Sophist.* Rojcewicz, Richard (trans) and Schuwer, André (trans).

*Plato's Epistemology: How Hard Is It to Know?.* Laidlaw-Johnson, Elizabeth A.

*Plato: Complete Works.* Cooper, John M (ed) and Hutchinson, D S (ed).

*Rethinking the Rhetorical Tradition: From Plato to Postmodernism.* Kastely, James L.

*The Art of Plato: Ten Essays in Platonic Interpretation.* Rutherford, R B.

*The Dialogues of Plato: Volume I.* Jowett, Benjamin.

*The Dialogues of Plato: Volume II.* Jowett, Benjamin.

*The Dialogues of Plato: Volume III.* Jowett, Benjamin.

*The Dialogues of Plato: Volume IV.* Jowett, Benjamin.

*The Dialogues of Plato: Volume V.* Jowett, Benjamin.

*The Plato Reader.* Chappell, Tim D J.

*The Play of the Platonic Dialogues.* Freydberg, Bernard.

*The Thinker as Artist: From Homer to Plato & Aristotle.* Anastaplo, George.

*Varia: Il De Mente Heroica e gli Scritti Latini Minori.* Vico, Giambattista and Visconti, Gian Galeazzo (ed).

*Vom Willen zur Macht: Anthropologie und Metaphysik der Macht am exemplarischen Fall Friedrich Nietzsches.* Gerhardt, Volker.

A Bastard Kind of Reasoning: The Argument from the Sciences and the Introduction of the Receptacle in Plato's *Timaeus*. Reshotko, Naomi.

A Classicist's Approach to Rhetoric in Plato. Kirby, John T.

A New Theory on Philo's Reversal. Stamos, David N.

Alkinous: Explanation of Plato's Doctrines (in Hungarian). Somos, Róbert.

An Overlooked Motive in Alcibiades' *Symposium* Speech. Scott, Gary Alan and Welton, William A.

An Untitled Lecture on Plato's *Euthyphron*. Bolotin, David (ed), Strauss, Leo and Bruell, Christopher (& other eds).

Antonio Rosmini: Aristotele Esposto ed Esaminato. Masi, Giuseppe.

Aristóteles e a teoria da reminiscência. Figueiredo, Maria José.

Aristotle *Metaphysics* H6: A Dialectic with Platonism. Harte, Verity.

Aristotle's Criticism of Plato's Communism of Women and Children. Mayhew, Robert.

Art and Philosophy in Plato's Dialogues. Irwin, Terence H.

As Transformaçoes da Tirania. Bignotto, Newton.

Aspiring to the Divine: Love and Grace. Mahoney, Timothy A.

Astronomy and Observation in Plato's *Republic*. Gregory, Andrew.

Augustinus und die Entstehung des philosophischen Willensbegriffs. Horn, Christoph.

Callicles' Examples of *nomos tes phuseos* in Plato's *Gorgias*. Fussi, Alessandra.

Carnal Knowledge in the *Charmides*. McAvoy, Martin.

Chaos and Control: Reading Plato's *Politicus*. McCabe, Mary Margaret.

Characterisation and Interpretation: The Importance of Drama in Plato's *Sophist*. Benitez, Eugenio E.

Considerations on the Plurality of the "Nothing-Speech" (in German). Sonderegger, Erwin.

Continuities and Discontinuities in the History of *Republic* Interpretation. Press, Gerald A.

Deliberation and Moral Expertise in Plato's *Crito*. Benitez, Eugenio E.

Die Idee der Einheit in Platons Timaios. Krämer, Hans.

Die Kunst der Anspielung: Hans-Georg Gadamers philosophische Interventionen im NS. Orozco, Teresa.

Die logische und die dialogische Form des Argumentes vom "Dritten Menschen" in Platons "Parmenides". Strobach, Niko.

Divine Inspiration and the Origins of the Laws in Plato's *Laws*. Welton, William A.

El debate sobre la filosofía de la naturaleza y de la historia de Platón: el IV Symposium Platonicum. Lisi. Francisco L.

Enigma e relazione: Da Apollo a Edipo. Lo Bue, Elisabetta.

**PLURALISM**
Value Monism, Value Pluralism, and Music Education: Sparshott as Fox. Alperson, Philip.
Vico y la retórica que no cesa. Marín-Casanova, José Antonio.
Virtue Ethics and the Problem of Indirection: A Pluralistic Value-Centred Approach. Swanton, Christine.
What's 'Wrong' in Contractualism?. Matravers, Matt.
Why Possible Worlds Aren't. Felt, James W.
Winch's Pluralist Tree and the Roots of Relativism. Phillips, Patrick J J.

**PLURALITY**
"Acerca del igual derecho a ser diferente" in *Liberalismo y Comunitarismo: Derechos Humanos y Democracia,* Monsalve Solórzano, Alfonso (ed). Cepeda, Margarita.
Can We Speak of Regional Logics? (in French). Largeault, Jean.

**PLUTARCH**
An Interpretation of Plutarch's *Cato the Younger.* Frost, Bryan-Paul.
Il problema della trascendenza nell'ontologia di Plutarco. Ferrari, Franco.
Pirrone e i maestri indiani. De Bernardi, Paolo.
Plutarch on the Treatment of Animals: The Argument from Marginal Cases. Newmyer, Stephen T.

**POCOCK, J**
Mind and Method in the History of Ideas. Bevir, Mark.
Varieties of Political Thought. Hampsher-Monk, Iain.

**POEGGELER, O**
Zeitalter der hermeneutischen Vernunft. Demmerling, Christoph.

**POETICS**
Discurso Científico e Poético na Filosofia de Aristóleles. Paisana, Joao.
Living in a Wittgensteinian World: Beyond Theory to a Poetics of Practices. Shotter, John.
Richard Kearney's Hermeneutic Imagination. Stark, Tracey.

**POETRY**
"Lost Horizons and Uncommon Grounds: For a Poetics of Finitude in the Work of Jean-Luc Nancy" in *On Jean-Luc Nancy: The Sense of Philosophy,* Sheppard, Darren (ed). Van den Abbeele, Georges.
"Mountains of the Mind" in *East and West in Aesthetics,* Marchianò, Grazia (ed). Servomaa, Sonia.
*From Romanticism to Critical Theory: The Philosophy of German Literary Theory.* Bowie, Andrew.
*Kenneth Burke and the Scapegoat Process.* Carter, C Allen.
*L'Edizione Critica Di Vico: Bilanci E Prospettive.* Cacciatore, Giuseppe and Stile, Alessandro.
*Léopold Sédar Senghor: From Politics to Poetry.* Kluback, William.
*Philosophische Gedichte.* Flasch, Thomas (trans) and Campanella, Tommaso.
*Philosophy in Literature.* Rickman, H P.
Actual Intentionalism vs. Hypothetical Intentionalism. Iseminger, Gary.
Ai margini del discorso poetico. Dell'Erba, Paola.
Air Raid over Harlem: Langston Hughes's Left Nationalist Poetics, 1927-1936. Keita Cha-Jua, Sundiata.
Art, Value, and Philosophy. Levinson, Jerrold.
Bemerkung zu: "Epistemologische Aspekte der neuen Entwicklungen in der Physik" von G. Münster. Mielke, Eckehard W.
Cartesis en la *Poética* de Artistóteles. Sánchez Palencia, Angel.
Ch'an Buddhism and the Prophetic Poems of William Blake. Ferrara, Mark S.
Cyprian Norwid—The Poet of Truth. Zajaczkowski, Ryszard.
Dialectic and the "Two Forces of One Power": Reading Coleridge, Polanyi, and Bakhtin in a New Key. Hocks, Elaine.
Do Not Listen to What They Say, Look at What They Do. Hobart, Ann and Jankélévitch, Vladimir.
Dos estudios italianos sobre Vico y la estética. Amoroso, Leonardo.
Dramaturgy of Picture (Essay on Diderot's *The Natural Child*) (in Portuguese). De Matos, Franklin.
En memoria de la memoria de Martin Heidegger. Duque, Félix.
Feminist Revaluation of the Mythical Triad, Lilith, Adam, Eve: A Contribution to Role Model Theory. Wenkart, Henry.
Florbela Espanca: Tónica da sua Inspiraçao. Freire, António.
Francis Sparshott, Poet. Anderson Silber, C and Macpherson, Jay.
Guided Rapid Unconscious Reconfiguration in Poetry and Art. Seamon, Roger.
Hölderlin e o *Retorno Natal.* Beckert, Cristina.
Hölderlin, le poète des dieux nouveaux: *Germanie* et *Le Rhin.* Giroux, Laurent.
Hölderlins Trennung von Fichte. Jürgensen, Sven.
Langer's Aesthetics of Poetry. Hart, Richard E.
Le sens du poétique: Approche phénoménologique. Roose, Marie-Clotilde.
Lo sguardo di Blanchot e la musica di Orfeo: Visione e ascolto nell'ispirazione poetica. Carrera, Alessandro.
Modèles historique et modèles culturels. Moutsopoulos, Evanghélos.
No Goddess Was Your Mother: Western Philosophy's Abandonment of Its Multicultural Matrix. Schroeder, Steven.
O Arco e a Lira—O inaudito na Erótica de Safo. Leite, Lucimara and Davi Maced, Dion.
O Outro Literário: a Filosofia da Literatura em Levinas. Beckert, Cristina.
Poiesis and Praxis in Aristotle's *Poetics.* Melissidis, N S.

The *Poet's* Figure in Friedrich von Hardenburg (Novalis) and Gaston Bachelard: Some Considerations (in Portuguese). De Oliveira, Maria Elisa.
The Demise of the Aesthetic in Literary Study. Goodheart, Eugene.
The Metaphysics of Poetry: Subverting the "Ancient Quarrel" and Recasting the Problem. Swanger, David.
The Others In/Of Aristotle's *Poetics.* Fendt, Gene.
The Universality of Poetry. Vitsaxis, V.
Through Phenomenology to Sublime Poetry: Martin Heidegger on the Decisive Relation between Truth and Art. Anderson, Travis T.
Tra stupore e malinconia: Osservazioni sul pensiero di G. Leopardi. Franchi, Alfredo.
Un poeta "doctísimo de las antigüedades heroicas" El rol de Virgilio en el pensamiento de G.B. Vico. Battistini, Andrea.
Vico e la Poesia. Placella, Vincenzo.
Vittorio Imbriani e il *Kant poeta.* Petrone, Giuseppe Landolfi.
Zur Geschichte der romantischen Ästhetik: Von Fichtes Transzendentalphilosophie zu Schlegels Transzendentalpoesie. Radrizzani, Ives.
'Ideia Poética' e 'Ideaia Filosófica': Sobre a Relaçao entre Poesia e Filosofia na Obra de Antero de Quental. Ribeiro dos Santos, Leonel.

**POGORZELSKI, W**
On the Rules of Substitution in the First-Order Predicate Logics. Bugajska-Jaszczolt, Beata and Dyrda, Kazimiera.

**POIESIS**
Une philosophie de la "dynamique créative". Tavares de Miranda, Maria Do Carmo.

**POINCARE**
Esperienza e ragione nel convenzionalismo geometrico di Henri Poincaré. Fortino, Mirella.
Poincaré: Mathematics & Logic & Intuition. McLarty, Colin.

**POINT**
Connection Structures: Grzegorczyk's and Whitehead's Definitions of Point. Biacino, Loredana and Gerla, Giangiacomo.
Eine aristotelische Logik der Intervalle, die Cantorsche Logik der Punkte und die physikalischen und kinematischen Prädikate. Arsenijevic, Milos.
Modern Essentialism and the Problem of Individuation of Spacetime Points. Bartels, Andreas.
On a Paradox of Hilbert and Bernays. Priest, Graham.
Region-Based Topology. Roeper, Peter.

**POJMAN, L**
Cooperation and Equality: A Reply to Pojman. Norman, Richard.

**POLAND**
Cecylia Rauszer. Rasiowa, Helena.
Helena Rasiowa and Cecylia Rauszer: Two Generations in Logic. Bartol, Wiktor and Rauszer, Cecylia.

**POLANYI, M**
Criticism, Contact with Reality and Truth. Sanders, Andy F.
Dialectic and the "Two Forces of One Power": Reading Coleridge, Polanyi, and Bakhtin in a New Key. Hocks, Elaine.
Epistemological Congruence between Scientific and Theological Logics in Polanyi's Thinking about Ultimate Reality and Meaning. Gaál, Botond.
Guide to the Papers of Michael Polanyi. Cash, John M.
Polanyi on Liberal Neutrality. Goodman, C P.
Polanyian Reflections on Embodiment, the Human Genome Initiative and Theological Anthropology. Lewis, Paul.
Religious Pedagogy from Tender to Twilight Years: Parenting, Mentoring, and Pioneering Discoveries by Religious Masters as Viewed from within Polanyi's Sociology and Epistemology of Science. Milavec, Aaron.
Sanders' Analytic Rebuttal to Polanyi's Critics, with Some Musings on Polanyi's Idea of Truth. Cannon, Dale.

**POLARITY**
Polarity Sensitivity as Lexical Semantics. Israel, M.

**POLICE**
Police Loyalties: A Refuge for Scoundrels?. Kleinig, John.

**POLICY**
see also Public Policy
"Integration or Reduction: Two Approaches to Environmental Values" in *Environmental Pragmatism,* Light, Andrew (ed). Norton, Bryan G.
"Pragmatism and Policy: The Case of Water" in *Environmental Pragmatism,* Light, Andrew (ed). Thompson, Paul B.
*Earthly Goods: Environmental Change and Social Justice.* Hampson, Fen Osler (ed) and Reppy, Judith (ed).
A Model Policy Addressing Mistreatment of Medical Students. Strong, Carson, Wall, Hershel P and Jameson, Valerie.
A Philosophical Analysis of the Regional Policy of Russia. Orudzhev, Z M.
Ah! My Foolish Heart: A Reply to Alan Soble's "Antioch's 'Sexual Offense Policy': A Philosophical Exploration". Kittay, Eva Felder.
Antioch's "Sexual Offense Policy": A Philosophical Exploration. Soble, Alan.
Coercion: Description or Evaluation?. Greene, Jennifer K.
Commentary on "A Model Policy Addressing Mistreatment of Students". Kornfeld, Donald S.
Community Food Security and Environmental Justice: Searching for a Common Discourse. Gottlieb, Robert and Fisher, Andrew.

## POLICY

Confronting the Assumptions That Dominate Education Reform. Robenstine, Clark.

Does Political Theory Matter for Policy Outcomes? The Case of Homeless Policy in the 1980s. Main, Thomas J.

Educational Reform: A Complex Matter. Reynolds, Sherrie and Martin, Kathleen.

Ethical Obligations in the Body Politic: The Case of Normalization Policy for Marginal Populations. D'Oronzio, Joseph C.

On the Hazards of Whistleblowers and on Some Problems of Young Biomedical Scientists in our Time. Edsall, John T.

Permissions, Principles and Rights: A Paper on Statements Expressing Constitutional Liberties. Atienza, Manuel and Ruiz Manero, Juan.

Policies and Perspectives on Authorship. Rose, Mary and Fischer, Karla.

Preserving Old-Growth Forest Ecosystems: Valuation and Policy. Booth, Douglas E.

Seeking Justice for Priscilla. Lantos, John D.

The Curious Tale of Atlas College. Cahn, Steven M.

Towards a Whole School or College Policy for a Pre-Philosophical and Higher Order Thinking 'Entitlement' Curriculum. Thornbury, Robert.

UN Responses in the Former Yugoslavia: Moral and Operational Choices. Weiss, Thomas G.

## POLISH

"Lvov" in *In Itinere* European Cities and the Birth of Modern Scientific Philosophy, Poli, Roberto (ed). Wolenski, Jan.

"Peirce's Influence on Logic in Poland" in *Studies in the Logic of Charles Sanders Peirce*, Houser, Nathan (ed). Hiz, Henry.

"Warsaw: The Rise and Decline of Modern Scientific Philosophy in the Capital City of Poland" in *In Itinere* European Cities and the Birth of Modern Scientific Philosophy, Poli, Roberto (ed). Jadacki, Jacek Juliusz.

Business Ethics and Computer Ethics: The View from Poland. Sojka, Jacek.

Cyprian Norwid—The Poet of Truth. Zajaczkowski, Ryszard.

Poles and the Göttingen Phenomenological Movement (in Polish). Glombik, Czeslaw.

Razón y Lógica: La Tradición Analítica en Polonia. Kleszcz, Ryszard.

Short Account of the Debates in the Higher Seminary of History of Philosophy, Catholic University in Lublin, in the Years 1953/54 to 1955/56 (in Polish). Strózewski, Wladyslaw.

Some Tendencies in Modern Epistemology (in Polish). Ingarden, Roman and Jadczak, Ryszard.

## POLITEO, J

Family, State—Individual. Festini, Heda.

## POLITICAL

Systemic Historical Criticism of the Concept of Tolerance (Spanish). Gutiérrez, Carlos B.

The Limits of Loyalty. Graybosch, Anthony J.

## POLITICAL CORRECTNESS

The Putative Fascism of the Kyoto School and the Political Correctness of the Modern Academy. Parkes, Graham.

## POLITICAL PHIL

see also Anarchism, Authority, Communism, Conservatism, Democracy, Ethics, Fascism, Freedom, Liberalism, Nationalism, Philosopher-King, Right, Social Contract, Social Phil, Society, State, Utopia

"*Recta ratio* y arbitrariedad en la filosofía política de Hobbes" in *La racionalidad: su poder y sus límites*, Nudler, Oscar (ed). Madanes, Leiser.

"A Political Dimension of Fixing Belief" in *The Rule of Reason: The Philosophy of Charles Sanders Peirce*, Forster, Paul (ed). Anderson, Douglas R.

"El Ortega de 1914" in *Política y Sociedad en José Ortega y Gasset: En Torno a "Vieja y Nueva Política"*, Lopez de la Vieja, Maria Teresa (ed). Aranguren, José Luis L.

"How Is It, Then, That we Still Remain Barbarians?" Foucault, Schiller, and the Aestheticization of Ethics. Bennett, Jane.

"Justice, Gender, The Family, and The Practice of Political Philosophy" in *A Question of Values: New Canadian Perspectives in Ethics and Political Philosophy*, Brennan, Samantha (ed). Milde, Michael.

"La Autodisolución de la Vieja Política en Ortega" in *Política y Sociedad en José Ortega y Gasset: En Torno a "Vieja y Nueva Política"*, Lopez de la Vieja, Maria Teresa (ed). Carvajal Cordón, Julián.

"La Paz en Kant: Ética y Política" in *Kant: La paz perpetua, doscientos años después*, Martínez Guzmán, Vicent (ed). Cortina, Adela.

"Paradigm Evolution in Political Philosophy: Aristotle and Hobbes" in *The Ancients and the Moderns*, Lilly, Reginald (ed). Riedel, Manfred.

"Política y Filosofía en Ortega: Teoría Orteguiana de la Modernidad" in *Política y Sociedad en José Ortega y Gasset: En Torno a "Vieja y Nueva Política"*, Lopez de la Vieja, Maria Teresa (ed). Flórez Miguel, Cirilo.

"Postnormative Subjectivity" in *The Ancients and the Moderns*, Lilly, Reginald (ed). Mensch, James Richard.

"Reconstruir la paz doscientos años después: Una Filosofía Transkantiana para la Paz" in *Kant: La paz perpetua, doscientos años después*, Martínez Guzmán, Vicent (ed). Martínez Guzmán, Vicent.

"República y Democrácia en la Paz Perpetua: Un comentario desde la Teoría Democrática" in *Kant: La paz perpetua, doscientos años después*, Martínez Guzmán, Vicent (ed). García Marzá, V Domingo.

"Sobre Política y Reformismo Cívico: A Partir de Ortega" in *Política y Sociedad en José Ortega y Gasset: En Torno a "Vieja y Nueva Política"*, Lopez de la Vieja, Maria Teresa (ed). Rosales, José María.

"The Russian Way" and Civil Society. Vorontsova, L M and Filatov, S B.

"Una Relación entre Diferentes: Ortega y Gasset y Gramsci" in *Política y Sociedad en José Ortega y Gasset: En Torno a "Vieja y Nueva Política"*, Lopez de la Vieja, Maria Teresa (ed). Calvo Salamanca, Clara.

"Vieja y Nueva Política y el Semanario *España* en el Nacimiento" in *Política y Sociedad en José Ortega y Gasset: En Torno a "Vieja y Nueva Política"*, Lopez de la Vieja, Maria Teresa (ed). Menéndez Alzamora, Manuel.

*A Question of Values: New Canadian Perspectives in Ethics and Political Philosophy*. Brennan, Samantha (ed), Isaacs, Tracy (ed) and Milde, Michael (ed).

*African-American Perspectives and Philosophical Traditions*. Pittman, John P (ed).

*An Essay on Rights* by Hillel Steiner. Wolff, Jonathan.

*Analytical Marxism: A Critique*. Roberts, Marcus.

*Angewandte Ethik: Die Bereichsethiken und ihre theoretische Fundierung*. Nida-Rümelin, Julian (ed).

*Classics of Modern Political Theory: Machiavelli to Mill*. Cahn, Steven M.

*Conservatism*. Muller, Jerry Z (ed).

*Democracy's Place*. Shapiro, Ian.

*Introduction to Marx and Engels: A Critical Reconstruction*. Schmitt, Richard.

*La Scienza Nuova* nella Storia del Pensiero Politico. Voegelin, Eric and Zanetti, Gianfrancesco (trans).

*Las Caras del Leviatán: Una Lectura Política de la Teoría Crítica*. Colom González, Francisco.

*Le contrat dans les pays anglo-saxons: théories et pratiques*. Breteau, Jean-Louis.

*Liberalismo y Comunitarismo: Derechos Humanos y Democracia*. Monsalve Solórzano, Alfonso (ed) and Cortés Rodas, Francisco (ed).

*Mechanismus und Subjektivität in der Philosophie von Thomas Hobbes*. Esfeld, Michael.

*Modern Political Thought: Readings from Machiavelli to Nietzsche*. Wootton, David (ed).

*Nietzsche Werke Kritische Gesamtausgabe: III 5/2*. Groddeck, Wolfram (ed) and Kohlenbach, Michael (ed).

*Philosophische Gedichte*. Flasch, Thomas (trans) and Campanella, Tommaso.

*Philosophy and Democracy in Intercultural Perspective*. Kimmerle, Heinz (ed) and Wimmer, Franz M (ed).

*Política y Sociedad en José Ortega y Gasset: En Torno a "Vieja y Nueva Política"*. Lopez de la Vieja, Maria Teresa (ed).

*Political Dialogue: Theories and Practices*. Esquith, Stephen L (ed).

*Political Philosophy*. Hampton, Jean.

*Republican Paradoxes and Liberal Anxieties*. Terchek, Ronald J.

*Rousseau, La Politica e la Storia: Tra Montesquieu e Robespierre*. Burgio, Alberto.

*Rulers and Ruled: An Introduction to Classical Political Theory from Plato to the Federalists*. Zeitlin, Irving M.

*The Ancients and the Moderns*. Lilly, Reginald (ed).

*The Dissonance of Democracy: Listening, Conflict, and Citizenship*. Bickford, Susan.

A Communitarian Critique of Authoritarianism. Bell, Daniel A.

A Má Fama na Filosofia Política: James Harrington e Maquiavel. Bignotto, Newton.

A Moderate Communitarian Proposal. Etzioni, Amitai.

A Noçao do "Estado" em Santo Agostinho. De Brito, António José.

A Plaything in Their Hands: American Exceptionalism and the Failure of Socialism—A Reassessment. Kieve, Ronald A.

A Plebe e o Vulgo no *Tractatus Politicus*. Chauí, Marilena.

A Pluralist Look at Liberalism, Nationalism, and Democracy: Comments on Shapiro and Tamir. Rosenfeld, Michel.

A Reply to David Keyt and David Gill. Miller Jr, Fred D.

A Review of the Origins of the State (Spanish). Ramos, Alberto Arvelo.

A Sketch of Nietzschean Theory of "Superman" (in Polish). Kusak, Leszek.

Actio illicita in causa und Zurechnung zum Vorverhalten bei Provokation von Rechtfertigungsgründen. Lúzon, Diego-Manuel.

Actio libera in causa: Ordentliche oder ausserordentliche Zurechnung?. Joshi Jubert, Ujala.

Administrative Lies and Philosopher-Kings. Simpson, David.

Adolfo Ravà: lo Stato come organismo etico. Fracanzani, Marcello.

Against Deliberation. Sanders, Lynn M.

Algumas Notas sobre a Filosofia Política de Hobbes. Queiroz Guimaraes, Alexandre.

All Human Rights for All: Zur Unteilbarkeit der Menschenrechte. Witschen, Dieter.

Alle origini dei diritti dell'uomo: i diritti della comunicazione di Francisco de Vitoria. Trujillo Pérez, Isabel.

Amicitia Politica: Thomas Aquinas on Political Cohesion in Society (in Czech). Molnár, Péter.

An Idea of Total Freedom? (in Czech). Tomek, Václav.

An Interpretation of Plutarch's *Cato the Younger*. Frost, Bryan-Paul.

Antwort auf Bernd Ludwig: Will die Natur unwiderstehlich die Republik?. Brandt, Reinhard.

## POLITICAL PHIL

Apparence et fausseté: la double nature de l'ordre politique chez Pascal. Spitz, Jean-Fabien.

Aristotle on Pleasure and Political Philosophy: A Study in Book VII of the *Nicomachean Ethics*. Guerra, Marc D.

Aristotle on Reason and its Limits. Smith, Gregory Bruce.

As Transformaçoes da Tirania. Bignotto, Newton.

Aspetti del dibattito italiano sulla cittadinanza. Henry, Barbara.

At the Core of Hobbes' Thought. Sorgi, Giuseppe.

Attualità di un carteggio del Settecento. Fabris, Matteo.

Aussichten der Zivilgesellschaft unter Bedingungen neoliberaler Globalisierungspolitik. Haug, Wolfgang Fritz.

Authenticity and Autonomy: Taylor, Habermas, and the Politics of Recognition. Cooke, Maeve.

Autonomy and Republicanism: Immanuel Kant's Philosophy of Freedom. Bielefeldt, Heiner.

Bacon, Hobbes and the Aphorisms at Chatsworth House. Pagallo, Ugo.

Bertrand Russell (in Polish). Mann, Golo.

Between Libertarian Utopia and Political Realism: Godwin and Shelley on Revolution (in Portuguese). Piozzi, Patrizia.

Beyond Satisfaction: Desire, Consumption, and the Future of Socialism. Meister, Robert.

Bolívar and the Latin American Unity (Spanish). Aparicio de La Hera, Beatriz.

Building the Union: The Nature of Sovereignty in the Political Architecture of Europe. Bellamy, Richard and Castiglione, Dario.

Capitalism, Coordination, and Keynes: Rejoinder to Horwitz. Hill, Greg.

Carl Schmitt und die Philosophie. Kiel, Albrecht.

Chaos and Control: Reading Plato's *Politicus*. McCabe, Mary Margaret.

Christianity, Commerce and the Canon: Josiah Tucker and Richard Woodward on Political Economy. Young, B W.

Chvostism and Dialectics (Introduced and Commentaries by László Illés) (in Hungarian). Lukács, Georg.

Civic Nationalism: Oxymoron?. Xenos, Nicholas.

Clients or Citizens?. Bender, Thomas.

Complexity and Deliberative Democracy. Femia, Joseph V.

Constitutionalism—Medieval and Modern: Against Neo-Figgisite Orthodoxy (Again). Nederman, Cary J.

Containing Indeterminacy: Problems of Representation and Determination in Marx and Althusser. Corlett, William.

Continuing the Conversation on Chinese Human Rights. Ames, Roger T.

Contributions to the Reconstruction of the Later Lukacs's Philosophy (in Hungarian). Himmer, Péter.

Conversing with Straw Men While Ignoring Dictators: A Reply to Roger Ames. Donnelly, Jack.

Cosmologie et Politique Chez Antiphon: Séance du 20 mai 1995 (Discussion avec: Gilbert Romeyer Dherbey, Bernard Bourgeois, Jean-Louis Bureau, Maurice de Gandillac, Solange Mericer Josa, Anne Souriau). Romeyer Dherbey, Gilbert.

Crises and Way Outs of the Public Administration Theory. Ochoa Henríquez, Haydée.

Crítica a la constitución de una sociedad política como Estado de Derecho (homenaje a Carlos Baliñas). Bueno, Gustavo.

Cultura y reflexión en torno a Meditaciones del Quijote. Lasaga Medina, José.

Dall'*albero del sovrano* all'*ulivo*: Simboli e metafore arboree nella politica lontana e vicina. Rigotti, Francesca.

Das neoliberale Projekt, der männliche Arbeitsbegriff und die fällige Erneuerung des Geschlechtervertrags. Haug, Frigga.

Das Opferverhalten als Schlüssel zum System der Sachentziehungsdelikte. Hruschka, Joachim.

De la paix perpétuelle et de l'espérance comme devoir. Vuillemin, Jules.

Deconstruction and Marxism: Jacques Derrida's Specters of Marx. Plangesis, Yannis.

Democracy as Procedure and Democracy as Regime. Castoriadis, Cornelius.

Democracy, Subsidiarity, and Citizenship in the 'European Commonwealth'. MacCormick, Neil.

Der Kommunitarismus als Alternative? Nachbemerkungen zur Kritik am moralisch-politischen Liberalismus. Höffe, Otfried.

Die Globalisierungsthese—von der kritischen Analyse zum politischen Opportunismus. Burchardt, Hans-Jürgen.

Die Kunst der Anspielung: Hans-Georg Gadamers philosophische Interventionen im NS. Orozco, Teresa.

Die Zurechnung im Strafrecht eines entwickelten sozialen und demokratischen Rechtsstaates. Mir Puig, Santiago.

Difference and Consensus. Luksic, Branimir.

Diritti umani e dover essere. Troncarelli, Barbara.

Diversity and Ancient Democracy: A Response to Schwartz. Saxonhouse, Arlene W.

Divine Inspiration and the Origins of the Laws in Plato's *Laws*. Welton, William A.

Does Democracy Reveal the Voice of the People? Four Takes on Rousseau. Gaus, Gerald.

Dr. Pangloss Goes to Market. Schweickart, David.

El concepto de *civitas* en la teoría política de Tomás de Aquino. Lorca, Andrés Martínez.

El concepto de libertad jurídica en la iusfilosofía de Eduardo García Máynez. Aguayo, Enrique I.

El Maxismo y el ocaso de la política. Colom González, Francisco.

El titular de la autoridad política en Santo Tomás y Rousseau. Quintas, Avelino M.

Elección pública y Democracia representativa. Carreras, Mercedes.

Elements of Democratic Justice. Shapiro, Ian.

Equality, Autonomy, and Cultural Rights. Levey, Goeffrey Brahm.

Esquema para Reexaminar la Filosofía Política de Kant. Astorga, Omar.

Estado, soberanía y democracia. Velásquez Delgado, Jorge.

État fragile, démocratie précaire: le lieu de l'insouciance. Comeau, Paul-André.

Ethischer Neu-Fichteanismus und Geschichtsphilosophie: Zur soziopolitischen Rezeption Fichtes im 20. Jahrhundert. Villacañas, José L.

Extracto de "Libraos de Ultramaria". Bentham, Jeremy.

Facts of Legal Reasoning. Boukema, H J M.

Family, State—Individual. Festini, Heda.

Fichte et la question nationale. Maesschalck, Marc.

Filosofía e politica. Badiou, Alain.

Finks politisches Vermächtnis Fortrag Freiburg Dez. 95. Biemel, Walter.

Foucault, Politics and the Autonomy of the Aesthetic. O'Leary, Timothy.

Fred Miller on Aristotle's Political Naturalism. Keyt, David.

Friendship and Political Philosophy. Schall, James V.

Giovanni Botero y la *Razon de Estado*. Sánchez, Antonio.

Glokalisierung oder Was für die einen Globalisierung, ist für die anderen Lokalisierung. Bauman, Zygmunt.

Gramscianismus in der Internationalen Politischen Ökonomie. Bieling, Hans-Jürgen and Deppe, Frank.

Group Aspirations and Democratic Politics. Shapiro, Ian.

Handlungstheoretische Aspekte der Fahrlässigkeit. Seebass, Gottfried.

Hannah Arendt on Hobbes. Bazzicalupo, Laura.

Hannah Arendt y la cuestión del mal radical. Serrano de Haro, Agustín.

Hans Jonas développe-t-il une anthropologie arendtienne?. Frogneux, Nathalie.

Hans Morgenthau's Realism and American Foreign Policy. Myers, Robert J.

Hayek's Political Philosophy and His Economics. Friedman, Jeffrey.

Hegel y la Participación Política. Cordua, Carla.

Hegemony and the Crisis of Legitimacy in Gramsci. Martin, James.

Heidegger at the Turn of the Century (in Serbo-Croatian). Pejovic, Danilo.

Heideggers "Schweigen" Technik, Nazi-Medizin und Wissenschaftskultur. Cox, Philip N.

History, Ethics, and Marxism. Cohen, G A.

Homer's Theology and the Concept of Tolerance. Bosnjak, Branko.

Homo sacer, di Giorgio Agamben. Grottanelli, Cristiano and Sini, Carlo.

Ideología y comunicación (Yugoslavia como problema). Milovic, Miroslav.

Igualdad no es fraternidad. Pastor Pérez, Miguel Antonio.

Il *Tractatus yconomicus* di Galvano Fiamma O.P. (1282-dopo il 1344). Fioravanti, Gianfranco.

Il gioco degli specchi. Nacci, Michela.

Il re nudo: L'immaginario del potere in Simone Weil. Tommasi, Wanda.

Im Anfang liegt alles beschlossen: Hannah Arendts politisches Denken im Schatten eines Heideggerschen problems. Grossmann, Andreas.

Incarnato comparire: Corpo e politica nelle proposte di Adriana Cavarero. Famiani, Mariapaola.

Individuelle Zurechnung im demokratischen Verfassungsstaat. Günther, Klaus.

Internationale Konferenz zu Kants Friedensidee und dem heutigen Problem einer internationalen Rechts—und Friedensordnung in Frankfurt am Main. Grün, Klaus-Jürgen.

Internationalisierung des Kapitals, Gesamtkapital und nationalstaat. Milios, Jean.

Is Marxism Totalitarian?. Hudelson, Richard.

Jean Bodin, Scepticism and Absolute Sovereignty. Engster, Dan.

Justice éthique et politique chez le jeune Aristote: la *Peri Dikaiosunes*. Rodrigo, Pierre.

Kants kritisches Staatsrecht. Herb, Karlfriedrich and Ludwig, Bernd.

Karl Popper's Political Philosophy of Social Science. Stokes, Geoff.

Keynes on Capitalism: Reply to Hill. Horwitz, Steven.

Kritische Theorie als Erfahrungswissenschaft: Lagebericht anlässlich einiger Neuerscheinungen. Behrens, Roger.

L'autodétermination des peuples comme principe juridique. Gingras, Denis.

L'esclusione dalla cittadinanza: Un casa limite: barbari e selvaggi. Taranto, Domenico.

L'Etica Politica nell'Attuale Fase Istituzionale. Alfano, Giulio.

L'interprétation de la position originelle et la question de la fondation. Ouattara, Ibrahim S.

La *méthode* de Lipman: un outil dangereux de propagande auprès des enfants? Une réplique à Pierre Desjardins. Laberge, Jean.

La *Politeia* tra cinismo et stoïcisme. Dorandi, Tiziano.

La dialéctica de lo universal y lo particular y el ideal de la abolición del estado (Segunda parte). Salas, Mario.

La filosofía materialista en la época de la Revolución Francesa. José Martínez, Francisco.

La filosofia personalista di Dietrich von Hildebrand e la sua opposizione contro il nazionalsocialismo. Seifert, Josef.

La filosofía política en el final de siglo. Montoya Saenz, José.

## POLITICS

Computers, Information and Ethics: A Review of Issues and Literature. Mitcham, Carl.

Context, Politics and Moral Education: Comments on the Misgeld/Magendzo Conversation about Human Rights Education. Brabeck, Mary M and Ting, Kathleen.

Continuing the Conversation on Chinese Human Rights. Ames, Roger T.

Cousin e l''istituzionalizzazione' della filosofia. Ragghianti, Renzo.

Coyote Politics: Trickster Tales and Feminist Futures. Phelan, Shane.

Crisis and Narrativity. Hirschbein, Ron.

Debating Critical Theory. Hoy, David Couzens.

Derrida e la rivendicazione dello spirito del marxismo. Iofrida, Manlio.

Do Critics of Heidegger Commit the *Ad Hominem* Fallacy?. Dombrowski, Daniel A.

Does a Real Albert Nolan Need Don Cupitt? A Response to Ronald Nicolson. Egan, Anthony.

Education and Nationality. White, John.

El Derecho al Sentido en lo Posmoderno. Follari, Roberto A.

El Maxismo y el ocaso de la política. Colom González, Francisco.

El nuevo Rawls. Rosenkrantz, Carlos F.

El principio de reconocimiento en la teoría filosófica del derecho político externo de Hegel. Vieweg, Klaus.

Essentially Contested Concepts. Gallie, W B.

Establishing Liability in War. Bica, Camillo C.

Ethical Obligations in the Body Politic: The Case of Normalization Policy for Marginal Populations. D'Oronzio, Joseph C.

Ethics and the Political Activity of Business: Reviewing the Agenda. Weber, Leonard J.

Etica della responsabilità e impegno politico in Aranguren. Savignano, Armando.

Fairy Tales for Politics: The Other, Once More. Cladwell, Anne.

Filosofia e politica. Badiou, Alain.

Foucault, Politics and the Autonomy of the Aesthetic. O'Leary, Timothy.

Fred Miller on Aristotle's Political Naturalism. Keyt, David.

Frederick Engels: Scholar and Revolutionary. Labica, Georges.

Friend or Enemy?: Reading Schmitt Politically. Neocleous, Mark.

From City-Dreams to the Dreaming Collective. Miller, Tyrus.

From Politics to Paralysis: Critical Intellectuals Answer the National Question. Cocks, Joan.

Gilles Deleuze and Naturalism: A Convergence with Ecological Theory and Politics. Hayden, Patrick.

Gilles Deleuze and the Politics of Time. May, Todd.

Grounding Agency in Depth: The Implications of Merleau-Ponty's Thought for the Politics of Feminism. Fielding, Helen.

Growing Up with *Just and Unjust Wars: An Appreciation. Smith, Michael Joseph.*

Hegel y la Participación Política. Cordua, Carla.

Hermeneutics and Democracy. Vattimo, Gianni.

History and Memory. Geremek, Bronislaw.

Hobbes et la mort du Léviathan: opinion, sédition et dissolution. Malherbe, Michel.

Hobbes on "Bodies Politic". Sorgi, Giuseppe.

Hobbes's Political Geometry. Valentine, Jeremy.

Horstmann, Siep, and German Idealism. Pippin, Robert B.

Hume's Touchstone and the Politics of Meaningful Discourse. Backhaus, Wilfried.

Identity Politics and the Welfare State. Wolfe, Alan and Klausen, Jytte.

Identity Politics as a Transposition of Fraser's Needs Politics. Tittle, Peg.

Im Anfang liegt alles beschlossen: Hannah Arendts politisches Denken im Schatten eines Heideggerschen problems. Grossmann, Andreas.

Impartiality and Liberal Neutrality. Caney, Simon.

In Praise of Unreliability. Heldke, Lisa.

Information and Human Liberty. Weinberger, Ota.

Interview with Alasdair MacIntyre. Pearson, Thomas D.

Interview with Herman J. Saatkamp, Jr.. Detar, Richard.

Is Nietzsche a Political Thinker?. Nussbaum, Martha C.

Jansenismo versus Jesuitismo: Niccoló Pagliarini e o Projecto Político Pombalino. De Castro, Zília Osório.

Jury Wisdom: Norman J. Finkel, *Commonsense Justice: Juror's Notions of the Law*. Levine, James P.

Justiça e *Sentido da Terra*. Soromenho-Marques, José Viriato.

Justice éthique et politique chez le jeune Aristote: la *Peri Dikaiosunes*. Rodrigo, Pierre.

Justice, Impartiality, and Equality: Why the Concept of Justice Does Not Presume Equality. Kane, John.

L'esclusione dalla cittadinanza: Un casa limite: barbari e selvaggi. Taranto, Domenico.

La fiducia come forma di fede: Alcune riflessioni introduttive ad un problema sociologico. Prandini, Riccardo.

La insoportable liviandad del ser (político). Pastor Pérez, Miguel Antonio.

La place du politique dans le système stoïcien. Lang, André.

La Política de la Razón (In)suficiente. Lindahl, Hans.

Las ideas de 'ciudadanía universal' y 'paz perpetua' en la *Metafísica de la costumbres* de Kant. Piulats Riu, Octavi.

Las teoría y su influencia política y socio-jurídica en los problemas de la democracia. Mari, Enrique E.

Liberalism, Nationalism, and the Right to Secede. Moellendorf, Darrel.

Liberté! Egalité! Sexualité!: Theorizing Lesbian and Gay Politics. Kaplan, Morris B.

Linguistics and Politics in the Early 19th Century: James Cowles Prichard's Moral Philology. Augstein, Hannah Franziska.

Lockean Political Apocrypha. Milton, J R.

Making Exceptions: Some Remarks on the Concept of Coup d'état and Its History. Bartelson, Jens.

Making Waves and Drawing Lines: The Politics of Defining the Vicissitudes of Feminism. Bailey, Cathryn.

Malthus and the Secularization of Political Ideology. Heavner, Eric K.

Maquiavelo y la episteme política. Sevilla Fernández, José M.

Maritain et le débat postconciliaire: Le paysan de la garonne. Fourcade, Michel.

Marx's Inverted World. Sensat, Julius.

Marx's Political Universalism. Van der Linden, Harry.

Minority Rights After Helsinki. Korey, William.

Multiculturalism: An Unhappy Marriage of Multicultural Education and Postmodernism. Webster, Yehudi O.

Mutual Respect and Neutral Justification. Bird, Colin.

Nationalism in Theory and Reality. Friedman, Jeffrey.

Negative Capability Reclaimed: Literature and Philosophy *Contra* Politics. Hassan, Ihab.

Nietzsche's Impatience: The Spiritual Necessities of Nietzsche's Politics. Heilke, Thomas.

Noncombatant Immunity in Michael Walzer's *Just and Unjust Wars*. Koontz, Theodore J.

Nonviolence as a Way of Life: Issues of Justice. Fogliatti, Karen.

O Estatuto da Paz na Teoria Política Hobbesiana. Pavan Baptista, Ligia.

On Freedom. Liquin, Deng.

On the Limits of Rights. Marmor, Andrei.

On the Road Again: Hayek and the Rule of Law. Williams, Juliet.

On the Status of Equality. Sen, Amartya K.

Ontologie, philosophie et politique: la critique de la tradition épistémologique chez Charles Taylor. Nootens, Geneviève.

Organizations, Ethics, and Health Care: Building an Ethics Infrastructure for a New Era. Renz, David O and Eddy, William B.

Parmenides and the Battle of Stalingrad. Heller, Agnes.

Peace Zones: Exemplars and Potential. Blume, Francine.

Pedagogy in the Myth of Plato's *Statesman*: Body and Soul in Relation to Philosophy and Politics. Hemmenway, Scott R.

Persona Politica: Unity and Difference in Edith Stein's Political Philosophy. Calcagno, Antonio.

Philosophical Periodicals in Russia Today (mid-1995). Van der Zweerde, Evert.

Philosophical Reasoning in Ethics and the Use of the History of Philosophy. Talaska, Richard A.

Pierre Bayle, the Rights of the Conscience, the "Remedy" of Toleration. Mori, Gianluca.

Plato's Practical Political-Rhetorical Project: The Example of the *Republic*. Mahoney, Timothy A.

Política Educacional Rural. Leite, Sérgio Celani.

Political Equality in Justice as Fairness. Brighouse, Harry.

Political Justification, Theoretical Complexity, and Democratic Community. Bertram, Christopher.

Political Leadership and the Problem of "Dirty Hands". Garrett, Stephen A.

Political Lying: A Defense. Newey, Glen.

Political Rights in Aristotle: A Response to Fred Miller, Jr., *Nature, Justice, and Rights in Aristotle's Politics*. Gill, David.

Political Toleration or Politics or Recognition: The Headscarves Affair Revisited. Köker, Levent.

Politics and Coercion. Goerner, E A and Thompson, Walter J.

Politics of Discourse on Liberal Economic Reform: The Case of Africa. Jeong, Ho-Won.

Politics, Politics, Politics. Garver, Newton.

Politics: Truth, Freedom, Peace: Lie, Rule, War (in Serbo-Croatian). Baruzzi, Arno.

Politiek van de technologie. Harbers, Hans.

Politisering van de technologische cultuur. Bijker, Wiebe E.

Poor Bertie. Rée, Jonathan.

Prescott's Conquests: Anthropophagy, Auto-da-Fe and Eternal Return. Pearce, Colin D.

Prof. D. M. Dattai: As a Process-Philosopher from an Alternative Inter-Cultural Perspective. Sarkar, Anil K.

Projecting Political Correctness: The Divorce of Affect and Signifier. Brennan, Teresa.

Rawls's "The Closed Society Assumption" (in Serbo-Croatian). Strncevic, Ljubica and Gligorov, Vladimir.

Realizability as Constituent Element of the Justification Structure of the Public Decision. Cuñarro Conde, Edith Mabel.

Reason, Rhetoric and the Price of Linguistic Revision. McGrew, Lydia M.

Reconciliation: A Political Requirement for Latin America. May, Jr, Roy H.

Regendering the U.S. Abortion Debate. Jaggar, Alison.

Religion and Business Ethics: The Lessons from Political Morality. Fort, Timothy L.

Religion and Politics in India: Some Philosophical Perspectives. Perrett, Roy W.

## PORTUGUESE

A Historiografia Filosófica Portuguesa Perante o Seiscentismo. Calafate, Pedro.

A imagem de Ludwig Feuerbach na literatura mais recente (1988-1993). Veríssimo Serrao, Adriana.

A primeira síntese global do pensamento saudoso de Teixeira de Pascoaes. Alves, Angelo.

Conspecto do Desenvolvimento da Filosofía em Portugal (Séculos XIII-XVI). Santiago de Carvalho, Mário A.

Filosofia do *Carnival* Surrealista. Martins, J. Cândido.

Florbela Espanca: Tónica da sua Inspiraçao. Freire, António.

Irreversibility and Time's Arrow. Landsberg, Peter T.

Perspectivas da Prospectiva: Acerca da Obra de Lúcio Craveiro da Silva. Rocha, Acílio da Silva.

Revistas filosóficas em Portugal. Calafate, Pedro.

Vicente Munoz Delgado y Angel Amor Ruibal. Dafonte, César Raña.

'Ideia Poética' e 'Ideaia Filosófica': Sobre a Relaçao entre Poesia e Filosofia na Obra de Antero de Quental. Ribeiro dos Santos, Leonel.

## POSITIVE

Positive Tolerance: An Ethical Oxymoron. Zolo, Danilo.

## POSITIVISM

*see also* Logical Positivism

"The Philosophy of Mathematics in Early Positivism" in *Origins of Logical Empiricism*, Giere, Ronald N (ed). Goldfarb, Warren.

*El Krausopositivismo de Urbano González Serrano*. García, Antonio Jiménez.

*Rationalität und Theoriebildung: Studien zu Karl R. Poppers Methodologie der Sozialwissenschaften*. Schmid, Michael.

*Streitgespräche und Kontroversen in der Philosophie des 20.Jahrhunderts*. Wuchterl, Kurt.

Bête Noire of the Science Worshipers. Gross, Paul R.

Commentary and Criticism on Scientific Positivism. Gilmer, Penny J.

El krausopositivismo psicológico y sociológico en la obra de U. González Serrano. Jiménez Garcia, Antonio.

Fuzzifying the Natural Law-Legal Positivist Debate. Adams, Edward W and Spaak, Torben.

Gibt es etwas ausser mir selbst? Überlegungen zur semantischen Begründun des Realismus. Moulines, C Ulises.

II) Teichmüller e gli amici napoletani. Savorelli, Alessandro.

Inconsistencies and Beyond: A Logical-Philosophical Discussion. Batens, Diderik.

La méthodologie de la science constitutionnelle de la liberté. Sabete, Wagdi.

Method, Morality and the Impossibility of Legal Positivism. Toddington, Stuart.

Neoclassical Economics and the Last Dogma of Positivism: Is the Normative-Positive Distinction Justified?. Keita, L D.

O positivismo científico de Anteno de Quental. Brito, Maria Amélia.

Obligaciones humanas Apuntes para la formulación de una idea. Messuti, Ana.

Scienza Nuova y *The New Science of Politics*: Proyección del pensamiento viquiano en la obra de Eric Voeglin. Badillo O'Farrell, Pablo.

Some Remarks on Scientific Positivism and Constructivist Epistemology in Science. Vijh, Ashok K.

Speaking for Myself in Philosophy. Duhan Kaplan, Laura.

The Dynamics of Legal Positivism: Some Remarks on Shiner's *Norm and Nature*. Navarro, Pablo E and Moreso, José Juan.

The Legitimacy of Laws: A Puzzle for Hart. Webb, Mark Owen.

The Role of Data and Theory in Covariation Assessment: Implications for the Theory-Ladenness of Observation. Freedman, Eric G and Smith, Laurence D.

Tradizione romanistica e dommatica moderna. Nardozza, Massimo.

## POSITRON

The Manufacture of the Positron. Roqué, Xavier.

## POSNER, R

"The Sexual Economist and Legal Regulation of the Sexual Orientations" in *Sex, Preference, and Family: Essays on Law and Nature*, Nussbaum, Martha C (ed). Halley, Janet E.

## POSSIBILISM

Actualism and Iterated Modalities. Jubien, Michael.

Actualism or Possibilism?. Tomberlin, James E.

In Defense of the Contingently Nonconcrete. Linsky, Bernard and Zalta, Edward.

## POSSIBILITY

"The Argument from Possibility" in *Scepticism in the History of Philosophy: A Pan-American Dialogue*, Popkin, Richard H (ed). Stroll, Avrum.

*The Possibility of Language: A Discussion of the Nature of Language, with Implications for Human and Machine Translation*. Melby, Alan K and Warner, C Terry.

*The Possible Universe*. Tallet, J A.

Are (Possible) Guises Internally Characterizable?. Voltolini, Alberto.

Essere e idea. Tagliavia, Grazia.

Fuzzy Truth Values (in Spanish). Godo, Lluís.

Imaginability, Conceivability, Possibility and the Mind-Body Problem. Hill, Christopher S.

La métaphysique du réalisme modal: régression ou enjeu véritable?. Nef, Frédéric.

La necesidad como totalidad de la posibilidad en Leibniz. Socorro Fernández, Maria.

Möglichkeits- und Unmöglichkeitsbedingungen des religiösen Diskurses. Bremer, Manuel.

Para una fenomenología de la muerte. Iribarne, Julia V.

Practical Possibilities. Adams, Ernest W.

Sobre el hacer humano: la posibilidad factiva. Franquet, Maria José.

The Analysis of Possibility and the Possibility of Analysis. Divers, John.

Three Problems for "Strong" Modal Fictionalism. Nolan, Daniel.

## POSSIBLE

Possible Degrees in Recursive Copies II. Knight, J F and Ash, C J.

What Makes Language Possible? Ethological Foundationalism in Reid and Wittgenstein. Robinson, Daniel N and Harré, Rom.

## POSSIBLE ENTITY

Are Possible, Non Actual Objects Real?. Marcus, Ruth Barcan.

## POSSIBLE PERSON

Do Possible People have Moral Standing?. Ryberg, Jesper.

## POSSIBLE WORLD

Counterfactuals and Preemptive Causation. Ganeri, Jonardon, Noordhoof, Paul and Ramachandran, Murali.

Counterfactuals Revisited. Fulda, Joseph S.

Ersatz Worlds and Ontological Disagreement. Heller, Mark.

La métaphysique du réalisme modal: régression ou enjeu véritable?. Nef, Frédéric.

Leibniz on Possible Worlds. Rescher, Nicholas.

Maudlin and Modal Mystery. Lewis, David.

On the Impossibility of David Lewis' Modal Realism. Maudlin, Tim.

Temporalized Deontic Worlds with Individuals. Bailhache, Patrice.

The Epistemology of Possible Worlds: A Guided Tour. O'Leary-Hawthorne, John.

There Might Be Nothing. Baldwin, Thomas.

Why Possible Worlds Aren't. Felt, James W.

## POST ALGEBRA

H Rasiowa's and C Rauszer's Contribution to Algebra. Bartol, Wiktor.

On Lukasiewicz-Moisil Algebras of Fuzzy Sets. Rudeanu, Sergiu.

Post Algebras in Helena Rasiowa's Explorations. Traczyk, Tadeusz.

Wajsberg Algebras and Post Algebras. Rodríguez Salas, Antonio Jesús and Torrens, Antoni.

## POSTCOLONIALISM

"Between Postcoloniality and Postcolonialism" in *Philosophy and Democracy in Intercultural Perspective*, Kimmerle, Heinz (ed). Kluyskens, Jups.

"The Need for Conceptual Decolonization in African Philosophy" in *Philosophy and Democracy in Intercultural Perspective*, Kimmerle, Heinz (ed). Wiredu, Kwasi.

*Beyond Orientalism: Essays on Cross-Cultural Encounter*. Dallmayr, Fred R.

*Cultural Universals and Particulars: An African Perspective*. Wiredu, Kwasi.

*Philosophy and Democracy in Intercultural Perspective*. Kimmerle, Heinz (ed) and Wimmer, Franz M (ed).

## POSTMODERNISM

"American Philosophy's Way around Modernism (and Postmodernism)" in *The Recovery of Philosophy in America: Essays in Honor of John Edwin Smith*, Kasulis, Thomas P (ed). Neville, Robert Cummings.

"Between Modernism and Postmodernism: Jerzy Kmita's Epistemology" in *Epistemology and History*, Zeidler-Janiszewska, Anna (ed). Szahaj, Andrzej.

"Face-to-Face: Ethical Asymmetry or the Symmetry of Mutuality?" in *Knowing Other-Wise: Philosophy at the Threshold of Spirituality*, Olthuis, James H (ed). Olthuis, James H.

"Fragmentation, Race, and Gender: Building Solidarity in the Postmodern Era" in *Existence in Black: An Anthology of Black Existential Philosophy*, Gordon, Lewis R (ed). Huntington, Patricia J.

"Modernism, Postmodernism, and the Pragmatic Recovery of an Educational Canon" in *The Recovery of Philosophy in America: Essays in Honor of John Edwin Smith*, Kasulis, Thomas P (ed). Allan, George.

"Of Fractious Traditions and Family Resemblances in Philosophy of Education" in *Philosophy of Education (1996)*, Margonis, Frank (ed). Dhillon, Pradeep A.

"Postmodernity as a Spectre of the Future: The Force of Capital and the Unmasking of Difference" in *Deleuze and Philosophy: The Difference Engineer*, Ansell Pearson, Keith (ed). Purdom, Judy.

"Reclaiming Metaphysics for the Present: Postmodernism, Time, and American Thought" in *Philosophy in Experience: American Philosophy in Transition*, Hart, Richard (ed). Calore, Gary S.

"The Use and Abuse of Modernity: Postmodernism and the American Philosophic Tradition" in *Philosophy in Experience: American Philosophy in Transition*, Hart, Richard (ed). Ryder, John.

*Beyond Economics: Postmodernity, Globalization and National Sustainability*. Sauer-Thompson, Gary and Smith, Joseph Wayne.

*Cultural History and Postmodernity: Disciplinary Readings and Challenges*. Poster, Mark.

*Habermas and the Unfinished Project of Modernity*. Passerin d'Entrèves, Maurizio (ed) and Benhabib, Seyla (ed).

**POTT, H**
Een Reactie op Heleen Pott. Walry, Jenny.

**POTTER, V**
"Experience and Its Religious Dimension: Response to Vincent G. Potter" in *Reason, Experience, and God: John E. Smith in Dialogue*, Colapietro, Vincent M. Smith, John E.

**POULIMATKA, T**
"Democracy and the Foundations of Morality" in *Philosophy of Education (1996)*, Margonis, Frank (ed). Curren, Randall R.

**POVERTY**
Citizenship and Social Policy: T.H. Marshall and Poverty. Mead, Lawrence M.
Fostering Market Competence. Askland, Andrew.
Glokalisierung oder Was für die einen Globalisierung, ist für die anderen Lokalisierung. Bauman, Zygmunt.
Poverty, Development, and Sustainability: The Hidden Moral Argument. Weir, Jack.
St. Thomas Aquinas and the Defense of Mendicant Poverty. Jones, John D.

**POWER**
"Art is More Powerful Than Knowledge" (in Serbo-Croatian). Salaquarda, Jörg.
"Crossing the Threshold: Sojourning Together in the Wild Spaces of Love" in *Knowing Other-Wise: Philosophy at the Threshold of Spirituality*, Olthuis, James H (ed). Olthuis, James H.
"Dialogue: An Essay in the Instrumentalist Tradition" in *Political Dialogue: Theories and Practices*, Esquith, Stephen L (ed). Koch, Donald F.
"Do You Do Well to Be Angry?". Werpehowski, William.
"Interruptions of Necessity: Being Between Meaning and Power in Jean-Luc Nancy" in *On Jean-Luc Nancy: The Sense of Philosophy*, Sheppard, Darren (ed). Librett, Jeffrey S.
"Participation, Power, and Democracy" in *Political Dialogue: Theories and Practices*, Esquith, Stephen L (ed). Read, James H.
*Contested Commodities*. Radin, Margaret Jane.
*Democratic Discipline: Foundation and Practice*. Hoover, Randy L and Kindsvatter, Richard.
*Die Leidenschaft der Erkenntnis: Philosophie und ästhetische Lebensgestaltung bei Nietzsche von Morgenröthe bis Also sprach Zarathustra*. Brusotti, Marco.
*Feminist Interpretations of Michel Foucault*. Hekman, Susan J (ed).
*Foucault's Discipline: The Politics of Subjectivity*. Ransom, John S.
*Habermas and the Unfinished Project of Modernity*. Passerin d'Entrèves, Maurizio (ed) and Benhabib, Seyla (ed).
*Machiavelli, Leonardo, and the Science of Power*. Masters, Roger D.
*Powerless Fictions? Ethics, Cultural Critique, and American Fiction in the Age of Postmodernism*. Miguel-Alfonso, Ricardo (ed).
*Proclus: Neo-Platonic Philosophy and Science*. Siorvanes, Lucas.
*Reconstructing Political Theory: Feminist Perspectives*. Shanley, Mary Lyndon (ed) and Narayan, Uma (ed).
*Rulers and Ruled: An Introduction to Classical Political Theory from Plato to the Federalists*. Zeitlin, Irving M.
*The Magic Mirror: Myth's Abiding Power*. Baeten, Elizabeth M.
*The Psychic Life of Power: Theories in Subjection*. Butler, Judith.
A Feminist Interpretation of Vulnerability. Annaromao, Nancy J.
Biological Matter and Perceptual Powers in Aristotle's *De Anima*. Scaltsas, Theodore.
Bourdieu and Foucault on Power and Modernity. Cronin, Ciaran.
Commentary on "Loopholes, Gaps, and What is Held Fast". Code, Lorraine.
Communication through Interpreters in Health Care: Ethical Dilemmas Arising from Differences in Class, Culture, Language, and Power. Kaufert, Joseph M and Putsch, Robert W.
Confessionals, Testimonials: Women's Speech in/and Contexts of Violence. Supriya, K E.
Crítica a la constitución de una sociedad política como Estado de Derecho (homenje a Carlos Baliñas). Bueno, Gustavo.
Culture, Power and the Social Construction of Morality: Moral Voices of Chinese Students. Chang, Kimberly A.
Democracy as Procedure and Democracy as Regime. Castoriadis, Cornelius.
Descartes on the Power of "Ideas". Wagner, Stephen I.
Dialectic and the "Two Forces of One Power": Reading Coleridge, Polanyi, and Bakhtin in a New Key. Hocks, Elaine.
Disciplining the Family: The Case of Gender Identity Disorder. Feder, Ellen K.
Discretionary Power, Lies, and Broken Trust: Justification and Discomfort. Potter, Nancy.
Feminist Pedagogy Theory: Reflections on Power and Authority. Luke, Carmen.
Force, Power, and Motive. Yarbrough, Stephen R.
Forget Vitalism: Foucault and *Lebensphilosophie*. Ransom, John S.
Foucault and the Subject of Feminism. McLaren, Margaret A.
Foucault on Power and the Will to Knowledge. Detel, Wolfgang.
Foucault's Analysis of Power's Methodologies. Scott, Gary Alan.
Foucault's Genealogy and Teaching Multiculturalism as a Subversive Activity. Kazmi, Yedullah.
From Absurdity to Decision: The Challenge of Responsibility in a Technological Society. Wennemann, Daryl J.

Hannah Arendt on Power, Consent, and Coercion: Some Parallels with Gandhi. Presbey, Gail.
Hannah Arendt: On Power. Penta, Leo J.
Hegemony and the Crisis of Legitimacy in Gramsci. Martin, James.
Homo sacer, di Giorgio Agamben. Grottanelli, Cristiano and Sini, Carlo.
Il re nudo: L'immaginario del potere in Simone Weil. Tommasi, Wanda.
Is There a Basic Ontology for the Physical Sciences?. Harré, Rom.
Knowledge and Power in the Clinical Setting. McMillan, John and Anderson, Lynley.
La filosofía política y los problemas de nuestro tiempo. Rosenfield, Denis.
La puissance propre de la volonté selon Pascal. Pécharman, Martine.
Logics of Power in Marx. Brown, Wendy.
Loopholes, Gaps, and What is Held Fast: Democratic Epistemology and Claims to Recovered Memories. Potter, Nancy.
Love's Power and the Causality of Mind: C.S. Peirce on the Place of Mind and Culture in Evolution. Pape, Helmut.
Malebranche on the Soul's Power. Scott, David.
Modal Voluntarism in Descartes's Jesuit Predecessors. Coombs, Jeffrey.
Ockham and *Potentia Absoluta*. Finn, Steve.
On Helmholtz and 'Bürgerliche Intelligenz': A Response to Robert Brain. Cahan, David.
Poder político e liberdade. Pereira Borges, J F.
Power and the Constitution of Sartre's Identity. Seitz, Brian.
Powers of Desire: Deleuze and Mores. Schérer, René.
Putting the Technological into Government. Dean, Mitchell.
Rethinking Philosophy in the Third Wave of Feminism. Golumbia, David.
Solidarietà e democrazia: Osservazioni su antropologia, diritto e legittimità nella teoria giuridica di Habermas. Pinzani, Alessandro.
Swear by the Moon. Bedecarré, Corinne.
Taking Coercion Seriously. Mansbridge, Jane.
The Concept of Sovereignty in Jean Bodin's *Methodus* (in Spanish). Ribeiro de Barros, Alberto.
The Conditional Quality of Gandhi's Love. Harris, Ian M.
The Consensual Basis of Conflictual Power: A Critical Response to "Using Power, Fighting Power" by Jane Mansbridge. Haugaard, Mark.
The Fedorovian Roots of Stalinism. Shlapentokh, Dmitry.
The Greens and the Lust for Power. Sternstein, Wolfgang.
The Problem of Power in the Feminist Theory (Spanish). Coddetta, Carolina.
The Question of God in an Age of Science: Constructions of Reality and Ultimate Reality in Theology and Science. Case-Winters, Anna.
Un diálogo con la tradición: Foucault en su contexto. Vega, José Fernádez.
Una perspectiva sobre la relación entre historia y violencia. Longhini, Carlos Guillermo.
Universalism and the Greater Good: A Response to Talbott. Knight, Gordon.
What Ethics?. Rabben, Linda.
When Some Careproviders Have More Power than Others. Howe, Edmund G.
Women of the Popular Sectors and Ecofeminist Ethics in Latin America (Spanish). Parentelli, Gladys.

**POWER OF ATTORNEY**
One Woman's Journey. Walsh, Marcia K.

**PRACTICAL**
*Practical Reasoning in Natural Language*. Thomas, Stephen Naylor.
Ethik und die Grenzen der Philosophie. Thomä, Dieter.
Jenseits von Moderne und Postmoderne: Whiteheads Metaphysik und ihre Anwendungen in der theoretischen und praktischen Philosophie der Gegenwart. Hampe, Michael.
La prima lettura fichtiana della *Kritik der Urteilskraft* in alcuni studi del nostro secolo. Fabbianelli, Faustino.
Practical Philosophy and the Human Sciences Today (in Serbo-Croatian). Pazanin, Ante.
Seven Principles for Better Practical Ethics. Scholz, Sally J and Groarke, Leo.

**PRACTICAL REASON**
"Anmerkungen zu Funktion und Stellenwert des Eigeninteresses" in *Ökonomie und Moral: Beiträge zur Theorie ökonomischer Rationalität*, Lohmann, Karl Reinhard (ed). Chwaszcza, Christine.
*Practical Reasoning about Final Ends*. Richardson, Henry.
A Conception of Practical Reasoning. Coombs, Jerrold and Wright, Ian.
Deliberative Coherence. Millgram, Elijah and Thagard, Paul.
Der fragwürdige *Primat der praktischen Vernunft* in Fichtes *Grundlage der gesamten Wissenschaftslehre*. Breazeale, Daniel.
El pensamiento práctico: Consideraciones metodológicas a partir de Tomás de Aquino. Massini Correas, Carlos Ignacio.
El tema de la virtud: A. Macintyre, lector de Aristóteles. Mas Torres, Salvador.
Elección pública y Democracia representativa. Carreras, Mercedes.
Foundationalism and Practical Reason. Heath, Joseph.
Indexical Reference and Bodily Causal Diagrams in Intentional Action. Castañeda, Héctor-Neri.
Kantian Tunes on a Humean Instrument: Why Hume is not *Really* a Skeptic About Practical Reasoning. Radcliffe, Elizabeth.
L'idée de loi naturelle dans le contexte actuel de la raison pratique. Perron, Louis.

## PRACTICAL REASON

Moralischer Internalismus: Motivation durch Wünsche versus Motivation durch Überzeugungen. Wolf, Jean-Claude.

Practical Reason and the Ontology of Statutes. Walt, Steven.

The Loss of Practical Reason and Some Consequences for the Idea of Postmodernism. Painter, Mark.

## PRACTICAL WISDOM

"Phronesis": Um Conceito Inoportuno?. Perine, Marcelo.

Aristotle on Reason and its Limits. Smith, Gregory Bruce.

El rol de la convicción en la sabiduría práctica de Paul Ricoeur. Beguè, Marie-France.

Kant's Conception of Practical Wisdom. Engstrom, Stephen.

## PRACTICE

"Theory versus Practice in Ethics: A Feminist Perspective on Justice in Health Care" in *Philosophical Perspectives on Bioethics,* Sumner, L W (ed). Sherwin, Susan.

"Wide Reflective Equilibrium in Practice" in *Philosophical Perspectives on Bioethics,* Sumner, L W (ed). Daniels, Norman.

*Catalogue des Publications 1977-1995.* Carratelli, Giovanni Pugliese (ed).

*Le contrat dans les pays anglo-saxons: théories et pratiques.* Breteau, Jean-Louis.

*Practicing Philosophy: Pragmatism and the Philosophical Life.* Shusterman, Richard.

Bioethics, Metaphysical Involvements, and Biomedical Practice. Fan, Ruiping.

Conceptualizing Art Criticism for Effective Practice. Geahigan, George.

Croce e il superuomo: Una variante nell'edizione della "Filosofia della pratica" del 1923. Cingari, Salvatore.

Do Practices Explain Anything? Turner's Critique of the Theory of Social Practices. Bohman, James.

Edmund D. Pellegrino's Philosophy of Family Practice. Brody, Howard.

Ensayo de síntesis acerca de la distinción especulativo-práctico y su estructuración metodolón metodológica. Massini Correas, Carlos Ignacio.

Francis Sparshott, Poet. Anderson Silber, C and Macpherson, Jay.

Knowing-Attributions as Endorsements. Cameron, J R.

Lógica y práctica matemática. Nepomuceno Fernández, Angel.

Love's Bitter Fruits: Martha C Nussbaum *The Therapy of Desire: Theory and Practice in Hellenistic Ethics.* Osborne, Catherine.

Management as a Practice: A Response to Alasdair MacIntyre. Brewer, Kathryn Balstad.

Michael Oakeshott on History, Practice and Political Theory. Smith, Thomas W.

Overcoming the Theory/Practice Opposition in Business Ethics. Fairfield, Paul.

Perhaps We All Be Heroes. Reitemeier, Paul J.

Teoresi e prassi nella fondazione della metafisica. Cavaciuti, Santino.

The Social and Sociological Study of Science, and the Convergence Towards the Study of Scientific Practice (in Spanish). Gomez Ferri, Javier.

Theoria and the Priority of the Practical (in Dutch). Sie, Maureen.

Theory and Practice in the Experience of Art: John Dewey and the Barnes Foundation. Glass, Newman Robert.

## PRADHAN, R

Do Wittgenstein's Forms of Life Inaugurate a Kantian Project of Transcendental Idealism?. Kanthamani, A.

Does the Grammar of Seeing Aspects Imply a Kantian Concept?. Kanthamani, A.

## PRAGMATIC

Peirce's Evolutionary Pragmatic Idealism. Burks, Arthur W.

## PRAGMATICISM

"The Interconnectedness of Peirce's Diagrammatic Thought" in *Studies in the Logic of Charles Sanders Peirce,* Houser, Nathan (ed). Kent, Beverley.

Peirce's Evolutionary Pragmatic Idealism. Burks, Arthur W.

## PRAGMATICS

"The Relation of Argument to Inference" in *Logic and Argumentation,* Van Eemeren, Frans H (ed). Pinto, Robert C.

La delimitación de la pragmática con respecto a la sociolingüística. De Cózar Escalante, José Manuel.

Landmarks in Critical Thinking Series: Pragmatics and Critical Thinking. Yoos, George.

Pragmatics and the Processing of Metaphors: Category Dissimilarity in Topic and Vehicle Asymmetry. Katz, Albert N.

Pragmatics, Semantic Underdetermination and the Referential/Attributive Distinction. Bezuidenhout, Anne.

## PRAGMATISM

*see also* Experimentalism, Instrumentalism, Operationalism

"A Pluralistic, Pragmatic and Evolutionary Approach to Natural Resource Management" in *Environmental Pragmatism,* Light, Andrew (ed). Castle, Emery N.

"A Political Dimension of Fixing Belief" in *The Rule of Reason: The Philosophy of Charles Sanders Peirce,* Forster, Paul (ed). Anderson, Douglas R.

"Before Environmental Ethics" in *Environmental Pragmatism,* Light, Andrew (ed). Weston, Anthony.

"Beyond Intrinsic Value: Pragmatism in Environmental Ethics" in *Environmental Pragmatism,* Light, Andrew (ed). Weston, Anthony.

"Classical Pragmatism and Pragmatism's Proof" in *The Rule of Reason: The Philosophy of Charles Sanders Peirce,* Forster, Paul (ed). Robin, Richard S.

"Compatibilism in Political Ecology" in *Environmental Pragmatism,* Light, Andrew (ed). Light, Andrew.

"Consciousness As a Pragmatist Views It" in *The Cambridge Companion to William James,* Putnam, Ruth Anna (ed). Flanagan, Owen.

"Cornel West as Pragmatist and Existentialist" in *Existence in Black: An Anthology of Black Existential Philosophy,* Gordon, Lewis R (ed). Johnson, Clarence Sholé.

"Deconstruction and Pragmatism—Is Derrida a Private Ironist or a Public Liberal?" in *Deconstruction and Pragmatism,* Mouffe, Chantal (ed). Critchley, Simon.

"Deconstruction, Pragmatism and the Politics of Democracy" in *Deconstruction and Pragmatism,* Mouffe, Chantal (ed). Mouffe, Chantal.

"Deconstruction, Pragmatism, Hegemony" in *Deconstruction and Pragmatism,* Mouffe, Chantal (ed). Laclau, Ernesto.

"Die Lügner-Antinomie: eine pragmatische Lösung" in *Das weite Spektrum der analytischen Philosophie,* Lenzen, Wolfgang. Von Savigny, Eike.

"El "Proyecto filosófico para la paz perpetua" de Kant como cuasipronóstico de la filosofía de la historia..." in *Kant: La paz perpetua, doscientos años después,* Martínez Guzmán, Vicent (ed). Apel, Karl-Otto.

"Environmental Pragmatism as Philosophy or Metaphilosophy? On Weston-Katz Debate" in *Environmental Pragmatism,* Light, Andrew (ed). Light, Andrew.

"How Pragmatism *Is* and Environmental Ethic" in *Environmental Pragmatism,* Light, Andrew (ed). Rosenthal, Sandra B.

"James Hayden Tufts on the Social Mission of the University" in *Philosophy in Experience: American Philosophy in Transition,* Hart, Richard (ed). Campbell, James.

"James's Theory of Truth" in *The Cambridge Companion to William James,* Putnam, Ruth Anna (ed). Putnam, Hilary.

"Logical Principles and Philosophical Attitudes: Peirce's Response to James's Pragmatism" in *The Cambridge Companion to William James,* Putnam, Ruth Anna (ed). Hookway, Christopher.

"Nature as Culture: John Dewey's Pragmatic Naturalism" in *Environmental Pragmatism,* Light, Andrew (ed). Hickman, Larry A.

"No More Method! A (Polemical) Response to Audrey Thompson" in *Philosophy of Education (1996),* Margonis, Frank (ed). Neiman, Alven.

"Political Pragmatism and Educational Inquiry" in *Philosophy of Education (1996),* Margonis, Frank (ed). Thompson, Audrey.

"Pragmatic Experimentalism and the Derivation of the Categories" in *The Rule of Reason: The Philosophy of Charles Sanders Peirce,* Forster, Paul (ed). Rosenthal, Sandra B.

"Pragmatism and Environmental Thought" in *Environmental Pragmatism,* Light, Andrew (ed). Parker, Kelly A.

"Pragmatism and Introspective Psychology" in *The Cambridge Companion to William James,* Putnam, Ruth Anna (ed). Myers, Gerald E.

"Pragmatism and Policy: The Case of Water" in *Environmental Pragmatism,* Light, Andrew (ed). Thompson, Paul B.

"Pragmatism, Politics, and the Corridor" in *The Cambridge Companion to William James,* Putnam, Ruth Anna (ed). Cormier, Harvey J.

"Pragmatist Holism as an Expression of Another 'Disenchantment of the World'" in *Epistemology and History,* Zeidler-Janiszewska, Anna (ed). Palubicka, Anna.

"Realistischer Realismus als ein methodologischer und pragmatischer Interpretationismus" in *Das weite Spektrum der analytischen Philosophie,* Lenzen, Wolfgang. Lenk, Hans.

"Really Living in Space-Time" in *Philosophy of Education (1996),* Margonis, Frank (ed). Cunningham, Craig A.

"Remarks on Deconstruction and Pragmatism" in *Deconstruction and Pragmatism,* Mouffe, Chantal (ed). Rorty, Richard.

"Searching for Intrinsic Value: Pragmatism and Despair in Environmental Ethics" in *Environmental Pragmatism,* Light, Andrew (ed). Katz, Eric.

"The Spirit of Pragmatism and the Pragmatic Spirit" in *The Recovery of Philosophy in America: Essays in Honor of John Edwin Smith,* Kasulis, Thomas P (ed). Wu, Kuang-Ming.

"Tradition: First Steps Toward a Pragmaticistic Clarification" in *Philosophy in Experience: American Philosophy in Transition,* Hart, Richard (ed). Colapietro, Vincent M.

"Un escenario pragmático para la verdad en la ciencia" in *Verdad: lógica, representación y mundo,* Villegas Forero, L. Bengoetxea, Juan B, Eizagirre, Xabier and Ibarra, Andoni.

"Unity, Theory and Practice: F.H. Bradley and Pragmatism" in *Philosophy after F.H. Bradley,* Bradley, James (ed). Forster, Paul D.

"When You Know It, and I Know It, What is It We Know? Pragmatic Realism and the Epistemologically Absolute" in *Philosophy of Education (1996),* Margonis, Frank (ed). McCarthy, Christine.

*Davidson's Theory of Truth and Its Implications for Rorty's Pragmatism.* Letson, Ben H.

*Deconstruction and Pragmatism.* Mouffe, Chantal (ed).

*Environmental Pragmatism.* Light, Andrew (ed) and Katz, Eric (ed).

*Language, Action, and Context: The Early History of Pragmatics in Europe and America, 1780-1930.* Nerlich, Brigitte and Clarke, David D.

*Practicing Philosophy: Pragmatism and the Philosophical Life.* Shusterman, Richard.

**PRAGMATISM**

*Pragmatism and Realism.* Westphal, Kenneth R (ed), Will, Frederick L and MacIntyre, Alasdair.

*Pragmatism as a Principle and Method of Right Thinking.* Turrisi, Patricia Ann (ed) and Sanders Peirce, Charles.

*The Cambridge Companion to William James.* Putnam, Ruth Anna (ed).

*The Metaphysics of Pragmatism.* Hook, Sidney.

*The Recovery of Philosophy in America: Essays in Honor of John Edwin Smith.* Kasulis, Thomas P (ed) and Neville, Robert Cummings (ed).

*The Rule of Reason: The Philosophy of Charles Sanders Peirce.* Forster, Paul (ed) and Brunning, Jacqueline (ed).

*The Two Pragmatisms: From Peirce to Rorty.* Mounce, H O.

*Un'Introduzione All'Epistemologia Contemporanea.* Gava, Giacomo (ed).

A Conversation with Sylvère Lotringer. Lotringer, Sylvère.

A Pragmatic Approach to Business Ethics. Shaw, Bill.

A Pragmatic Theory of Causal Analysis. Shein, David.

A Pragmatist in Paris: Fréderic Rauh's "Task of Dissolution". Horner, Richard.

Classical American Pragmatism: The Other Naturalism. Rosenthal, Sandra B.

Clinical Pragmatism: A Method of Moral Problem Solving. Fins, Joseph J, Bacchetta, Matthew D and Miller, Franklin G.

Commentary on "Non-Cartesian Frameworks". Harré, Rom.

Continuity, Contingency, and Time: The Divergent Intuitions of Whitehead and Pragmatism. Rosenthal, Sandra B.

Counterfactuals in Pragmatic Perspective. Rescher, Nicholas.

Deconstruction and Pragmatism—Is Derrida a Private Ironist or a Public Liberal?. Critchley, Simon.

Dewey, Quine, and Pragmatic Naturalized Epistemology. Capps, John.

Education as Encounter: Buber's Pragmatic Ontology. McHenry Jr, Henry D.

From Common Roots to a Broader Vision: A Pragmatic Thrust of European Phenomenology. Bourgeois, Patrick L.

Habermas' Pragmatic Universals. Mukherji, Arundhati.

How to Give Analytical Rigour to 'Soupy' Metaphysics. Robinson, Howard.

Israel Scheffler's Ethics: Theory and Practice. Worsfold, Victor L.

John Dewey's Legal Pragmatism. Hill, H Hamner.

Keeping One's Distance from the Absolute: Blumenberg's Metaphorology between Pragmatics and Metaphysics (in Dutch). De Ruyter, Geertrui.

La paradoja del Taxidermista: Una ilustración negativa del juicio práctico deweyano. Catalán, Miguel.

Los Filósofos y la Pregunta por la Existencia de los Problemas filosóficos. Naishtat, Francisco Samuel.

Malinowksi: La Importancia de la Pragmática y del Bla-bla-bla en la Comunicación. Patiño A, Alejandro.

Mystics and Pragmatics in the Non-Philosophy of F. Laruelle: Lessons for Rorty's Metaphilosophizing. Sumares, Manuel.

Noch einmal: Rationalität und Normativität. Wüstehube, Axel.

Pragmatic Arguments and Belief. Jordan, Jeff.

Pragmatic Idealization and Structuralist Reconstructions of Theories. Haase, Michaela.

Pragmatics and Singular Reference. Bezuidenhout, Anne.

Pragmatische Bedingungen des wissenschaftlichen Realismus. Kügler, Peter.

Pragmatism, Internalism and the Authority of Claims. Crawford, Dan D.

Pragmatism, Thomism, and the Metaphysics of Desire: Two Rival Versions of Liberal Education. Neiman, Alven.

Pragmatismo e interaccionismo simbólico. Uriz Pemán, María Jesús.

Pragmatismus redivivus? Eine Kritik an der Revitalisierung des pragmatistischen Grundgedankens. Römpp, Georg.

Pragmatismus, Dekonstruktion, ironischer Eklektizismus: Richard Rortys Heidegger-Lektüre. Burkhard, Philipp.

Pursuing Peirce. Brent, Joseph.

R.G. Collingwood's Pragmatist Approach to Metaphysics. Requate, Angela.

Remembering John Dewey and Sidney Hook. Rorty, Richard.

Review Essay. Short, T L.

Richard Rorty and the Problem of Cruelty. Haliburton, Rachel.

Sprechakttheoretische Erläuterungen zum Begriff der kommunikativen Rationalität. Habermas, Jürgen.

Strategies of Representation: Autobiographical Metissage and Critical Pragmatism. Zuss, Mark.

The "Extreme Heresy" of John Dewey and Arthur F. Bentley I: A Star Crossed Collaboration?. Ryan, Frank X.

The Early Buddhist Theory of Truth: A Contextualist Pragmatic Interpretation. Holder, John J.

The Practice of Philosophy. Nevo, Isaac.

The Promises and Perils of Pragmatism: Commentary on Fins, Bacchetta, and Miller. Tong, Rosemarie.

The Significance of American Philosophical Naturalism. Romanell, Patrick.

The Social and Sociological Study of Science, and the Convergence Towards the Study of Scientific Practice (in Spanish). Gomez Ferri, Javier.

The Structure of Peirce's Realism. Sokolowski, William R.

The Three Meanings of Truth in Religion. Mercier, Sean L.

Toward a Non-Cartesian Psychotherapeutic Framework: Radical Pragmatism as an Alternative. Berger, Louis S.

Truth vs Rorty. Steinhoff, Uwe.

We Pragmatists...; Peirce and Rorty in Conversation. Haack, Susan.

Yuri K. Melvil and American Pragmatism. Ryder, John.

**PRAMANA**

Pramāṇa Samplava and Pramāṇa Vyavasthā. Sharma, A D and Shukla, S K.

**PRASAD, R**

Professor Prasad on Working Out a Lead from Swami Vivekananda: Some Reflections. Ghosh, Ranjan K.

**PRATT, M**

Rethinking Latinoamericanism: On the (Re)Articulations of the Global and the Local. Poblette, Juan.

**PRATT, V**

Getting Started: Beginnings in the Logic of Action. Segerberg, Krister.

**PRAXIS**

"Racionalidad y *poiesis*: los límites de la praxis histórica" in *La racionalidad: su poder y sus límites,* Nudler, Oscar (ed). Inés Mudrovcic, María.

"Una Relación entre Diferentes: Ortega y Gasset y Gramsci" in *Política y Sociedad en José Ortega y Gasset: En Torno a "Vieja y Nueva Política",* Lopez de la Vieja, Maria Teresa (ed). Calvo Salamanca, Clara.

*Kant: La paz perpetua, doscientos años después.* Martínez Guzmán, Vicent (ed).

A Práxis Freireana na Educaçao. Marinho Sampaio, Tânia Maria.

A Questao Freireana da Educaçao como Práxis Político-Filosófica. Marinho Sampaio, Tânia Maria.

Algunas tesis sobre la tecnología. Herrera J, Rodolfo.

El rol de la convicción en la sabiduría práctica de Paul Ricoeur. Beguè, Marie-France.

Incoherence in the Aristotelian Philosophy of Action? (Spanish). Bravo, Francisco.

Jack London y El Talón de Hierro. Laso Prieto, José Maria.

Jon Elster y el pensamiento del límite. Ambrosini, Cristina.

Kinesis versus logos en la filosofía de Leonardo Polo. Aspe A, Virginia.

Ludwig Wittgenstein: Matemáticas y ética. Rivera, Silvia.

Meta-Technics, Anthropocentrism and Evolution. Vallota, Alfredo D.

Observations on the So-Called Practical Syllogism (Spanish). Bertók, Rozsa and Öffenberger, Niels.

Phänomenologische Versuche, sich den Grundlagen der gesellschaftlichen Praxis zu nähern. Schmied-Kowarzik, Wolfdietrich.

Poiesis and Praxis in Aristotle's *Poetics*. Melissidis, N S.

Prolegómenos a uma ontologia da acçao. Barata-Moura, José.

Reconstituting Praxis: Historialization as Re-Enactment. Flynn, Thomas R.

Teorías actuales de la verdad. Frápolli, María José and Nicolás, Juan A.

The Ontology of Production in Marx: The Paradox of Labor and the Enigma of *Praxis*. Lachterman, David.

Zur Lage der Philosophischen Praxis. Zdrenka, Michael.

**PRAYER**

Philosophy...Artifacts...Friendship—and the History of the Gaze. Illich, Ivan.

Preghiera e Filosofia della Religione. Santi, Giorgio.

The Logical Status of Prayer. Schoenig, Richard.

**PREDICATE**

"Nonextensionality" in *Das weite Spektrum der analytischen Philosophie,* Lenzen, Wolfgang. Lambert, Karel.

"Properties and Dispositions" in *Dispositions: A Debate,* Armstrong, D M. Martin, C B.

Anti-Realism, Truth-Value Links and Tensed Truth Predicates. Weiss, Bernhard.

Complex Predicates and Conversion Principles. Swoyer, Chris.

Grados, franjas y líneas de demarcación. Peña, Lorenzo.

Is There a Problem about Intentionality?. Beckermann, Ansgar.

Mixed Inferences: A Problem for Pluralism about Truth Predicates. Tappolet, Christine.

Percepción, particulares y predicados. Mulligan, Kevin.

Predicates, Properties and the Goal of a Theory of Reference. Zalabardo, José L.

Quantum Objects are Vague Objects. French, Steven and Krause, Décio.

Sujeto, propio y esencia: el fundamento de la distinción aristotélica de modos de predicar. Pérez de Laborda, Miguel.

Vague Predicates and Language Games. Parikh, Rohit.

**PREDICATE LOGIC**

"From the Algebra of Relations to the Logic of Quantifiers" in *Studies in the Logic of Charles Sanders Peirce,* Houser, Nathan (ed). Brady, Geraldine.

*Introduction to Metalogic.* Ruzsa, Imre.

*Logic with Trees: An Introduction to Symbolic Logic.* Howson, Colin.

$y = 2x$ VS. $y = 3x$. Stolboushkin, Alexei and Niwinski, Damian.

A Calculus for First Order Discourse Representation Structures. Kamp, Hans and Beyle, Uwe.

A Constructive Valuation Semantics for Classical Logic. Barbanera, Franco and Berardi, Stefano.

A Finite Analog to the Löwenheim-Skolem Theorem. Isles, David.

A First-Order Axiomatization of the Theory of Finite Trees. Backofen, Rolf, Rogers, James and Vijay-Shanker, K.

An Equational Axiomatization of Dynamic Negation and Relational Composition. Hollenberg, Marco.

# PREDICATE LOGIC

Axiomatising First-Order Temporal Logic: Until and Since over Linear Time. Reynolds, Mark.

Axiomatization of the Logic Determined by the System of Natural Numbers with Identity. Bugajska-Jaszczolt, Beata and Prucnal, Tadeusz.

Characterizing Classes Defined without Equality. Elgueta, R.

Completeness Theorem for Dummett's L C Quantified and Some of Its Extensions. Corsi, Giovanna.

Dynamic Relation Logic Is the Logic of DPL-Relations. Visser, Albert.

Framework for the Transfer of Proofs, Lemmas and Strategies from Classical to Non-Classical Logics. Caferra, Ricardo, Demri, Stéphane and Herment, Michel.

Game Logic and Its Applications II. Kaneko, Mamoru and Nagashima, Takashi.

Hilbert Vindicated?. Hintikka, Jaakko.

Hybrid Languages. Blackburn, Patrick and Seligman, Jerry.

Kripke Completeness of Some Intermediate Predicate Logics with the Axiom of Constant Domain and a Variant of Canonical Formulas. Shimura, Tatsuya.

On a Decidable Generalized Quantifier Logic Corresponding to a Decidable Fragment of First-Order Logic. Alechina, Natasha.

On Elementary Equivalence for Equality-free Logic. Casanovas, E, Dellunde, Pilar and Jansana, Ramon.

On Maximal Intermediate Predicate Constructive Logics. Avelone, Alessandro, Fiorentini, Camillo and Mantovani, Paolo (& others).

On the Decision Problem for Two-Variable First-Order Logic. Grädel, Erich, Kolaitis, Phokion G and Vardi, Moshe Y.

On the Härtig-Style Axiomatization of Unprovable and Satisfiable Formulas of Bernays and Schönfinkel's Classes. Inoué, Takao.

On the Rules of Substitution in the First-Order Predicate Logics. Bugajska-Jaszczolt, Beata and Dyrda, Kazimiera.

On the Theory of Anaphor: Dynamic Predicate Logic vs. Game-Theoretical Semantics. Sandu, Gabriel.

Quantified Deontic Logic with Definite Descriptions. Goble, Lou.

Quantified Extensions of Canonical Propositional Intermediate Logics. Ghilardi, Silvio.

Quantified Modal Logic, Reference and Essentialism. Perrick, M and Swart, H C M.

Relational and Partial Variable Sets and Basic Predicate Logic. Ghilardi, Silvio and Meloni, Giancarlo.

Schrödinger Logics. Da Costa, Newton C A and Krause, Décio.

Some Results on the Kripke Sheaf Semantics for Super-Intuitionistic Predicate Logics. Suzuki, Nobu-Yuki.

The $k$-Variable Property is Stronger than H-Dimension $k$. Simon, András and Hodkinson, Ian.

The Interpolation, Halldén-Completeness, Robinson and Beth Properties in Modal Logics. Wójtowicz, Anna.

The omega-Rule. Thau, Michael.

The Simplest Meinongian Logic. Pasniczek, Jacek.

Une Preuve Formelle et Intuitionniste du Théorème de Complétude de la Logique Classique. Krivine, Jean-Louis.

# PREDICATION

A Type Free Theory and Collective/Distributive Predication. Kamareddine, Fairouz.

Eine auch sich selbst missverstehende Kritik: Über das reflexionsdefizit formaler Explikationen. Wandschneider, Dieter.

Individuation und Prädikation: Ein Überblick aus historisch-systematischer Sicht. Enders, Heinz Werner.

Sujeto, propio y esencia: el fundamento de la distinción aristotélica de modos de predicar. Pérez de Laborda, Miguel.

# PREDICATIVE

Husserl's Phenomenology and Weyl's Predictivism. Da Silva, Jairo José.

On the Relationship between $ATR_0$ and ID-hat-sub-less than-omega. Avigad, Jeremy.

Systems of Explicit Mathematics with Non-Constructive Mu-Operator and Join. Glass, Thomas and Strahm, Thomas.

# PREDICTION

"Popper on Prophecies and Predictions" in The Significance of Popper's Thought, Amsterdamski, Stefan (ed). Wolenski, Jan.

A Remark Concerning Prediction and Spacetime Singularities. Hogarth, Mark.

Instrument Driven Theory. Tyron, Warren W.

La prospectiva de los grandes informes y la metodología Delphi. Hernández de Frutos, Teodoro.

Laplace's Demon Consults an Oracle: The Computational Complexity of Prediction. Pitowsky, Itamar.

On the Theoretical Basis of Prediction in Economics. González, Wenceslao J.

Social Predictivism. Barnes, Eric.

Variation and the Accuracy of Predictions. Kruse, Michael.

# PREDICTIVE

Analogy and Exchangeability in Predictive Inferences. Festa, Roberto.

Discussion: Thoughts on Maher's Predictivism. Barnes, Eric.

Predicative Laws of Association in Statistics and Physics. Costantini, D and Garibaldi, U.

# PREEMPTION

Counterfactuals and Preemptive Causation. Ganeri, Jonardon, Noordhoof, Paul and Ramachandran, Murali.

# PREEXISTENCE

"Henry More and Anne Conway on Preexistence and Universal Salvation" in Mind Senior to the World, Baldi, Marialuisa. Hutton, Sarah.

# PREFERENCE

"How to Combine Ordering and Minimizing in a Deontic Logic Based on Preferences" in Deontic Logic, Agency and Normative Systems, Brown, Mark A (ed). Tan, Yao-Hua and Van der Torre, Leendert W N.

"Moralischer Konsum: Über das Verhältnis von Rationalität, Präferenzen und Personen" in Ökonomie und Moral: Beiträge zur Theorie ökono-mischer Rationalität, Lohmann, Karl Reinhard (ed). Priddat, Birger P.

"Sexual Orientation and Gender: Dichotomizing Differences" in Sex, Preference, and Family: Essays on Law and Nature, Nussbaum, Martha C (ed). Okin, Susan Moller.

"Shaping and Sex: Commentary on Parts I and II" in Sex, Preference, and Family: Essays on Law and Nature, Nussbaum. Martha C (ed). Estlund, David M.

Sex, Preference, and Family: Essays on Law and Nature. Nussbaum, Martha C (ed) and Estlund, David M (ed).

Agency and Obligation. Horty, John F.

Completeness and Incompleteness for Plausibility Logic. Schlechta, Karl.

Confounding the Paradigm: Asian Americans and Race Preferences. Izumi, Lance T.

Cyclical Preferences and World Bayesianism. Sobel, Jordan Howard.

Decision Theoretic Foundations for Axioms of Rational Preference. Hansson, Sven Ove.

Discount-Neutral Utility Models for Denumerable Time Streams. Fishburn, Peter C and Edwards, Ward.

Do Physicians' Own Preferences for Life-Sustaining Treatment Influence Their Perceptions of Patients' Preferences? A Second Look. Schneiderman, Lawrence J, Kaplan, Robert M and Rosenberg, Esther (& others).

Hare's Reductive Justification of Preference Utilitarianism. Paden, Roger.

How To Share An Intention. Velleman, J David.

In Defense of a Constructive, Information-Based Approach to Decision Theory. Yilmaz, M R.

Interpersonal Dependency of Preferences. Nida-Rümelin, Julian, Schmidt, Thomas and Munk, Axel.

Lexicographic Additivity for Multi-Attribute Preferences on Finite Sets. Nakamura, Yutaka.

Preference for Gradual Resolution of Uncertainty. Ahlbrecht, Martin and Weber, Martin.

Preferring not to have been Born. Smilansky, Saul.

Public Preferences for Health Care: Prioritisation in the United Kingdom. Shickle, Darren.

Rationality, Dispositions, and the Newcomb Paradox. Barnes, R Eric.

Resolute Choice and Rational Deliberation: A Critique and a Defense. Gauthier, David.

Situationist Deontic Logic. Hansson, Sven Ove.

Stability of Treatment Preferences: Although Most Preferences Do Not Change, Most People Change Some of Their Preferences. Singer, Peter A, Kohut, Nitsa and Sam, Mehran (& others).

Stochastic Evolution of Rationality. Falmagne, Jean-Claude and Doignon, Jean-Paul.

The Abolition of Public Racial Preference—An Invitation to Private Racial Sensitivity. Kmiec, Douglas W.

The Life and Death of Racial Preferences. Fullinwider, Robert K.

The Logic of Permission and Obligation in the Framework of ALX.3: How to avoid the Paradoxes of Deontic Logics. Huang, Zhisheng and Masuch, Michael.

Value Based On Preferences: On Two Interpretations of Preference Utilitarianism. Rabinowicz, Wlodzimierz and Österberg, Jan.

Why Preference is not Transitive. Gendin, Sidney.

# PREJUDICE

"Plato, Prejudice, and the Mature-Age Student in Antiquity" in Dialogues with Plato, Benitez, Eugenio (ed). Tarrant, Harold.

"Toleration as a Form of Bias" in Philosophy, Religion, and the Question of Intolerance, Ambuel, David (ed). Altman, Andrew.

Moral Prejudices: Essays on Ethics. Held, Virginia.

Philosophy and Shifting Morality. Infinito-Allocco, Justen.

Plato, Prejudice, and the Mature-Age Student in Antiquity. Tarrant, Harold.

Progressive and Regressive Uses of Reasonable Distrust. Hedman, Carl.

Reconsidering Buster Keaton's Heroines. Savedoff, Barbara E.

Théorie des préjugés selon Descartes et Gadamer. Ipperciel, Donald.

Violencia femenina y autorreferencia. Schultz, Margarita.

# PREMISE

On Teaching Premise/Conclusion Distinctions. Fawkes, Don.

Premise Acceptability, Deontology, Internalism, Justification. Freeman, James B.

The Reliability of Premise and Conclusion Indicators. Smythe, Thomas W.

# PRESCOTT, W

Prescott's Conquests: Anthropophagy, Auto-da-Fe and Eternal Return. Pearce, Colin D.

## PSYCHIATRY

Physician-Assisted Suicide in Psychiatry: Developments in the Netherlands. Gevers, J K M and Legemaate, Johan.

Psychiatry and Capitalism. U'Ren, Richard.

Psychische Vertrautheit und epistemische Selbstzuschreibung (in Serbo-Croatian). Frank, Manfred and Gordic, Aleksandar (trans).

Recent and Classic References at the Interface of Philosophy, Psychiatry, and Psychology. Sadler, John Z (ed).

Response to "Ethical Concerns about Relapse Studies" by Adil E. Shamoo and Timothy J. Keay (CQ Vol 5, No 3). Bergsma, Jurrit.

The Virtues in Psychiatric Practice. Mann, David W.

Wilhelm Griesinger: Psychiatry between Philosophy and Praxis. Arens, Katherine.

## PSYCHIC

*The Psychic Life of Power: Theories in Subjection.* Butler, Judith.

## PSYCHOANALYSIS

"How Universal is Psychoanalysis? The Self in India, Japan, and the United States" in *Culture and Self,* Allen, Douglas (ed). Roland, Alan.

"Introduction to Part II" in *Critical Studies: Ethics and the Subject,* Simms, Karl (ed). Simms, Karl.

"Looking Up the Adolescent in Freud's Index" in *Critical Studies: Ethics and the Subject,* Simms, Karl (ed). Croft, Jo.

"Technologies of the Self" in *Critical Studies: Ethics and the Subject,* Simms, Karl (ed). Ball, Elaine.

*Freud and the Passions.* O'Neill, John (ed).

*Passion in Theory: Conceptions of Freud and Lacan.* Ferrell, Robyn.

*Subjectivity and Intersubjectivity in Modern Philosophy and Psycho-analysis.* Frie, Roger.

*Wittgenstein Reads Freud: The Myth of the Unconscious.* Bouveresse, Jacques, Cosman, Carol (trans) and Descombes, Vincent.

A Psychoanalytic Interpretation of the Effectiveness of Humor for Teaching Philosophy. Gibbs, Paul J.

Ambiguous Democracy and the Ethics of Psychoanalysis. Stavrakakis, Yannis.

Commentary on "Non-Cartesian Frameworks". Phillips, James.

Critical Notice: Freud, Philosophical and Empirical Issues. Cioffi, Frank.

Ethical Connectionism. Gibbs, Paul J.

Freud's 'Tally' Argument, Placebo Control Treatments, and the Evaluation of Psychotherapy. Greenwood, John D.

Hegel on the Unconscious Abyss: Implications for Psychoanalysis. Mills, Jon.

Historicism and Lacanian Theory. Evans, Dylan.

If *p*, Then What? Thinking in Cases. Forrester, John.

Kant's Sadism. Bencivenga, Ermanno.

La psychanalyse: mythe et théorie. Laplanche, Jean.

Paul Ricoeur et la question de la preuve en psychanalyse. Kaboré, Boniface.

Philosophical Counselling: Bridging the Narrative Rift. Zoë, K A.

Primitive Mental Processes: Psychoanalysis and the Ethics of Integration. Hinshelwood, R D.

Psychoanalysis as Anti-Hermeneutics. Laplanche, Jean and Thurston, Luke (trans).

Psychoanalysis: Past, Present, and Future. Erwin, Edward.

Sobre algunos rasgos distintos del estructuralismo. Leiser, Eckart.

Space for the Imagination. Pateman, Trevor.

Zur Rehabilitation des Unbewussten. Neubauer, Patrick.

## PSYCHOGENESIS

Psychogenesis and the History of Science: Piaget and the Problem of Scientific Change. Messerly, John G.

## PSYCHOLOGISM

"Frege's Anti-Psychologism" in *Frege: Importance and Legacy,* Schirn, Matthias (ed). Picardi, Eva.

Compétence sémantique et psychologie du raisonnement. Dokic, Jérôme.

Frege's Context Principle. Bar-Elli, Gilead.

Illuminating the Chinese Room. Dartnall, Terry.

L'explication psychologique de la logique est-elle circulaire?. Freuler, Léo.

La fable du psychologisme de Fries. Bonnet, Christian.

Référence directe et psychologisme. Corazza, Eros.

Resisting the Step Toward Naturalism. Bezuidenhout, Anne.

Sigwart, Husserl and Frege on Truth and Logic, or Is Psychologism Still a Threat?. Picardi, Eva.

Wittgenstein et la fin du psychologisme. Chiesa, Curzio.

## PSYCHOLOGIST

Educational Psychologists as Trainers for Intellectual Development. Hartman, Hope J.

Nonsexual Relationships between Psychotherapists and Their Former Clients: Obligations of Psychologists. Pipes, Randolph B.

Professional Ethics of Psychologists and Physicians: Morality, Confidentiality, and Sexuality in Israel. Shimshon Rubin, Simon and Dror, Omer.

## PSYCHOLOGY

*see also* Behaviorism, Psychiatry, Psychoanalysis, Social Psychology

"Consciousness As a Pragmatist Views It" in *The Cambridge Companion to William James,* Putnam, Ruth Anna (ed). Flanagan, Owen.

"Ethical Problems of Research Work of Psychologists" in *The Idea of University,* Brzezinski, Jerzy (ed). Brzezinski, Jerzy.

"La dimensione del tempo nella psicanalisi di Freud" in *Il Concetto di Tempo: Atti del XXXII Congresso Nazionale della Società Filosofica Italiana,* Casertano, Giovanni (ed). Tricomi, Flavia.

"Law and Order in Psychology" in *AI, Connectionism and Philosophical Psychology, 1995,* Tomberlin, James E (ed). Antony, Louise M.

"Objekt und Methode: Das Problem der Psychologie in Natorps Philosophie" in *Grenzen der kritischen Vernunft,* Schmid, Peter A. Gigliotti, Gianna.

"Pragmatism and Introspective Psychology" in *The Cambridge Companion to William James,* Putnam, Ruth Anna (ed). Myers, Gerald E.

"Psyche und Psychologie bei Rudolph Hermann Lotze" in *Grenzen der kritischen Vernunft,* Schmid, Peter A. Orth, Ernst Wolfgang.

"Science and Psychology" in *Verstehen and Humane Understanding,* O'Hear, Anthony (ed). Dilman, Ilham.

"The Concept of Manipulativeness" in *AI, Connectionism and Philosophical Psychology, 1995,* Tomberlin, James E (ed). Ackerman, Felicia.

"The Moral Psychology of Nationalism" in *The Morality of Nationalism,* McKim, Robert (ed). Margalit, Avishai.

"Theory and Social Practice: One or Two Psychologies?" in *Epistemology and History,* Zeidler-Janiszewska, Anna (ed). Brzezinski, Jerzy.

"Two Notions of Implicit Rules" in *AI, Connectionism and Philosophical Psychology, 1995,* Tomberlin, James E (ed). Davies, Martin.

*A Defense of the Given.* Fales, Evan.

*Cognition and Commitment in Hume's Philosophy.* Garrett, Don.

*Connectionism and Eliminativism: Reply to Stephen Mills in Vol. 5, No. 1.* Macdonald, Cynthia.

*Descriptive Psychology.* Müller, Benito (ed & trans) and Brentano, Franz.

*El Krausopositivismo de Urbano González Serrano.* García, Antonio Jiménez.

*From Soul to Mind: The Emergence of Psychology from Erasmus Darwin to William James.* Reed, Edward S.

*Interpreting Minds: The Evolution of a Practice.* Bogdan, Radu J.

*Kritik des Naturalismus.* Keil, Geert.

*Mind Design II: Philosophy, Psychology, Artificial Intelligence.* Haugeland, John (ed).

*Philosophical Perspectives, 9, AI, Connectionism and Philosophical Psychology, 1995.* Tomberlin, James E (ed).

*Scienza e filosofia della coscienza.* Gava, Giacomo.

*The Human Animal: Personal Identity without Psychology.* Olson, Eric T.

*The Two Pragmatisms: From Peirce to Rorty.* Mounce, H O.

*Thomas Hobbes.* Taylor, A E.

A Discursive Account of Multiple Personality Disorder. Gillett, Grant.

A Historical Interpretation of Deceptive Experiments in American Psychology. Herrera, Christopher D.

A Poetics of Psychological Explanation. Knight, Deborah.

A Psychologically Plausible Logical Model of Conceptualization. Kim, Hong-Gee.

An Anti-Anti-Essentialist View of the Emotions: A Reply to Kupperman. Dalgleish, Tim.

Appraisal Theories of Emotions. Ben-Ze'ev, Aaron.

Aristotelian *Akrasia* and Psychoanalytic Regression. Stocker, Michael.

Aristotle on How to Define a Psychological State. Wedin, Michael V.

Autobiography, Narrative, and the Freudian Concept of Life History. Brockmeier, Jens.

Baldwin, Cattell and the *Psychological Review*: A Collaboration and Its Discontents. Sokal, Michael M.

Behavioral Systems Interpreted as Autonomous Agents and as Coupled Dynamical Systems: A Criticism. Keijzer, Fred A and Bem, Sacha.

Bemerkungen zum Verhältnis zwischen Neurophysiologie und Psycho-logie. Ros, Arno.

Boris Uexkülls Aufzeichnungen Zum Subjektiven Geist—Eine Vorlesungs-nachschrift?. Kreysing, Helmuth.

Bridging Social Constructionism and Cognitive Constructivism: A Psychology of Human Possibility and Constraint. Martin, Jack and Sugarman, Jeff.

Cognition Poised at the Edge of Chaos: A Complex Alternative to a Symbolic Mind. Garson, James W.

Cognitive Versatility. Browne, Derek.

Commentary on "Aristotelian *Akrasia* and Psychoanalytic Regression". Sturdee, P G.

Commentary on "Autobiography, Narrative, and the Freudian Concept of Life History". Robinson, Daniel N.

Commentary on "Loopholes, Gaps, and What is Held Fast". Code, Lorraine.

Commentary on "Primitive Mental Processes". Thornton, W Laurence.

Commentary on "Psychological Courage". Moore, Andrew.

Commentary on "Sanity and Irresponsibility". Fields, Lloyd.

Commentary on "Searle and the 'Deep Unconscious'". Lloyd, Dan.

Commentary on "Wilhelm Griesinger". Mishara, Aaron L.

Common Sense und Logik in Jan Smedslunds 'Psychologik'. Mock, Verena.

Complexity, Value, and the Psychological Postulates of Economics. Benedikt, Michael.

Connectionism and the Philosophical Foundations of Cognitive Science. Horgan, Terence.

Consciousness and Self-Awareness—Part I: $Consciousness_1$, $Consciousness_2$, and $Consciousness_3$. Natsoulas, Thomas.

## PUNISHMENT

Punishment in Environmental Protection. Poesche, Jürgen S.
Punishment, Quarantine, and Preventive Detention. Corrado, Michael.
Quinn on Punishment and Using Persons as Means. Otsuka, Michael.
Reasons for Anger: A Response to Narayan and von Hirsch's Provocation Theory. Horder, Jeremy.
Reciprocity as a Justification for Retributivism. Anderson, Jami.
Religion and Rehabilitation. Skotnicki, Andrew.
Reply to Corrado. Davis, Michael.
Republican Theory and Criminal Punishment. Pettit, Philip.
Resentment, Revenge, and Punishment: Origins of the Nietzschean Critique. Small, Robin.
Response to Michael Davis. Corrado, Michael.
Restorative Justice and Punishment. Brunk, Conrad G.
Retributivism and Trust. Dimock, Susan.
Tackling Crime by Other Means. Luke, Andrew.
The Sanctions of the Criminal Law. Clark, Michael.
The Time to Punish and the Problem of Moral Luck. Statman, Daniel.
Thinking about Private Prisons. Lippke, Richard L.
Utilitarianism and the Punishment of the Innocent: The Origins of a False Doctrine. Rosen, F.
Was Socrates Guilty as Charged? *Apology* 24c-28a. Steinberger, Peter J.

## PUOLIMATKA, T

Teaching Democracy Democratically. Worsfold, Victor L.

## PUPIL

*see* Student

## PURANA

Pāndava-Purāna of Vādicandra: Text and Translation. Jaini, Padmanabh S.

## PURDY, L

"Harris' Reply" in *The Liberation Debate: Rights at Issue,* Leahy, Michael (ed). Harris, John.

## PURE EGO

*see* Transcendental Ego

## PURE REASON

Critical Thinking vs. Pure Thought. Coccia, Orestes.

## PURIFICATION

Self-Enlargement or Purification? On the Meaning of the Fragmentary Subject in René Girard's Early Writings (in Dutch). Vanheeswijck, Guido.

## PURPOSE

*see also* Aim
"What Are Universities For?" in *The Idea of University,* Brzezinski, Jerzy (ed). Kolakowski, Leszek.
*Arguing for Atheism: An Introduction to the Philosophy of Religion.* Le Poidevin, Robin.
*E.C. Tolman e l'epistemologia del primo novecento.* Donadon, Eleonora.
*The Idea of University.* Brzezinski, Jerzy (ed) and Nowak, Leszek (ed).
What Can't We Do with Economics?: Some Comments on George Ainslie's Picoeconomics. De Sousa, Ronald B.

## PUTNAM, D

Commentary on "Psychological Courage". Moore, Andrew.
Honour, Community, and Ethical Inwardness. Cordner, Christopher.

## PUTNAM, H

"Ruritania Revisited" in *Contents,* Villanueva, Enrique (ed). Block, Ned.
"The Broken Bonds with the World" in *Epistemology and History,* Zeidler-Janiszewska, Anna (ed). Ozdowski, Pawel.
A Note on the Nature of "Water". Abbott, Barbara.
Brains in Vats Revisited. Leeds, Stephen.
Der Weg weg von der Metaphysik—ein Rundweg?. Schulthess, Peter.
Does a Rock Implement Every Finite-State Automation?. Chalmers, David J.
Elgin on Lewis's Putnam's Paradox. Van Fraassen, Bas C.
Entrevistas: René Descartes, Cuatrocientos años de actualidad. Naishtat, Francisco.
Internal Realism, Rationality and Dynamic Semantics. Naumann, Ralf.
Jñānagarbha and the "God's-Eye View". Pyysiäinen, Ilkka.
La inefabilidad de la semántica y el realismo interno. Cabanchik, Samuel Manuel.
Models, Truth and Semantics. Abbott, Barbara.
On the Right Idea of a Conceptual Scheme. Case, Jennifer.
Pragmatische Bedingungen des wissenschaftlichen Realismus. Kügler, Peter.
Putnam and Cavell on the Ethics of Democracy. Shusterman, Richard.
Putnam on Reference and Constructible Sets. Levin, Michael.
Putnam's Born-Again Realism. Sommers, Fred.
Putnam's Dewey Lectures. García-Carpintero, Manuel.
Putnam, Equivalence, Realism. Cox, Damian.
Realism and Spacetime: Of Arguments Against Metaphysical Realism and Manifold Realism. Liu, Chuang.
Red and Green after All These Years. Zelaniec, Wojciech.
The Inaugural Address: The Grounding of Reason. Trigg, Roger.
The Practice of Philosophy. Nevo, Isaac.
Truth and Thickness. Tietz, John.
Truth in Pure Semantics: A Reply to Putnam. Moreno, Luis Fernández.
Why One Shouldn't Make an Example of a Brain in a Vat. Davies, David.

## PUZZLE

"Frege on Knowing the Third Realm" in *Frege: Importance and Legacy,* Schirn, Matthias (ed). Burge, Tyler.
*Socratic Puzzles.* Nozick, Robert.
A New Skeptical Solution. Gauker, Christopher.
A Semiquotational Solution to Substitution Puzzles. Rieber, Steven.
Dion's Foot. Olson, Eric T.
Distinct Indiscernibles and the Bundle Theory. Zimmerman, Dean W.
Infinite Value and Finitely Additive Value Theory. Vallentyne, Peter and Kagan, Shelly.
Isolation and Unification: The Realist Analysis of Possible Worlds. Bricker, Phillip.
Modelling Reciprocal Altruism. Stephens, Christopher.
Moral Status and the Impermissibility of Minimizing Violations. Lippert-Rasmussen, Kasper.
On Art and Intention. Farrelly-Jackson, Steven.
On the Paradox of the Question. Sider, Theodore.
Reply to Forbes. Saul, Jennifer M.
Same-Kind Coincidence and the Ship of Theseus. Hughes, Christopher.
Self-Respect and the Stefford Wives. McKinnon, Catriona.
Slingshots and Boomerangs. Neale, Stephen and Dever, Josh.
Substitution and Simple Sentences. Saul, Jennifer M.
Supervenience and Co-Location. Rea, Michael C.
Synchronic Self-Control is Always Non-Actional. Kennett, Jeanette and Smith, Michael.
The Epistemology of Possible Worlds: A Guided Tour. O'Leary-Hawthorne, John.
The Import of the Puzzle about Belief. Sosa, David.
The Paradox of the Question. Markosian, Ned.
The Philosophical Insignificance of Gödel's Slingshot. Oppy, Graham.
The Regress-Problem: A Reply to Vermazen. Moya, Carlos J.
The Skeptic and the Hoverfly (A Teleo-Computational View of Rule-Following). Miscevic, Nenad.
Tibbles the Cat: A Modern *Sophisma.* Burke, Michael B.
Tracking Truth and Solving Puzzles. Gjelsvik, Olav.
Underestimating Self-Control: Kennett and Smith on Frog and Toad. Mele, Alfred R.
What's Wrong with Metalinguistic Views. Saul, Jennifer M.

## PYLYSHYN, Z

Tensor Products and Split-Level Architecture: Foundational Issues in the Classicism-Connectionism Debate. Guarini, Marcello.

## PYRRHO

Was Pyrrho a Pyrrhonist? (in Hungarian). Brunschwig, Jacques.

## PYRRHONISM

Cómo resolver la problemática pirrónica: lo que se aprende de Descartes. Sosa, Ernesto.
El Ideario Pirrónico en el Oriente Medieval (Presencia y Divulgación). González Fernández, Martín.
Há Problemas Filosóficos? Uma Avaliaçao da Resposta do Pirronismo. Margutti Pinto, Paolo Roberto.
O Ceticismo Pirrônico e os Problemas Filosóficos. Porchat Pereira, Oswaldo.
Précis of *Pyrrhonian Reflections on Knowledge and Justification.* Fogelin, Robert J.
The Relativity of Skepticism. Moser, Paul K.
Unpurged Pyrrhonism. Stroud, Barry.
Was Pyrrho a Pyrrhonist? (in Hungarian). Brunschwig, Jacques.
What Does a Pyrrhonist Know?. Fogelin, Robert J.

## PYTHAGORAS

Sobre a Ciência e o Magistério Filosófico de Pitágoras. Spinelli, Miguel.

## QUAKERS

The Ethics of Community: The Ethical and Metaphysical Presuppositions of AVP. Reitan, Eric.

## QUALIA

"Colors, Subjective Relations and Qualia" in *Perception,* Villanueva, Enrique (ed). Shoemaker, Sydney.
"Comment on Dretske" in *Perception,* Villanueva, Enrique (ed). Horwich, Paul.
"Dretske on Phenomenal Externalism" in *Perception,* Villanueva, Enrique (ed). Biro, John.
"Dretske's Qualia Externalism" in *Perception,* Villanueva, Enrique (ed). Kim, Jaegwon.
"Phenomenal Externalism" in *Perception,* Villanueva, Enrique (ed). Dretske, Fred.
"Qualia and Color Concepts" in *Perception,* Villanueva, Enrique (ed). Harman, Gilbert.
"Reply to Commentators" in *Perception,* Villanueva, Enrique (ed). Dretske, Fred.
*Perception.* Villanueva, Enrique (ed).
Absent Qualia. Dretske, Fred.
Analyzing Mental Demonstratives. Jarrett, Greg.
Are Qualia Just Representations? A Critical Notice of Michael Tye's *Ten Problems of Consciousness.* Levine, Joseph.
Dennett on Qualia and Consciousness: A Critique. Johnsen, Bredo.
Functionalism's Response to the Problem of Absent Qualia: More Discussion of Zombies. Hardcastle, Valerie Gray.

**RAHNER, K**
Quasi-Formal Causality, or the Other-in-Me: Rahner and Lévinas. Purcell, Michael.
Rest for the Restless? Karl Rahner, Being, and the Evocation of Transcendence. Sanders, Theresa.
The Metaphysics of Symbol in Thomism: *Aeterni Patris* to Rahner. Fields, Stephen.

**RAMAKRISHNA**
Scientific Attitudes Towards an Eastern Mystic. Danyluk, Angie.

**RAMANUJAN, A**
The Ruptured Idiom: Of Dallmayr, Matilal and Ramanujan's 'Way of Thinking'. Venkat Rao, D.

**RAMIFIED**
A Modern Elaboration of the Ramified Theory of Types. Laan, Twan and Nederpelt, Rob.

**RAMSEY TEST**
Partial Monotonicity and a New Version of the Ramsey Test. Pais, John and Jackson, Peter.
The Ramsey Test and Conditional Semantics. Döring, Frank.

**RAMSEY, F**
"He Is No Good for My Work" in *Knowledge and Inquiry: Essays on Jaakko Hintikka's Epistemology and Philosophy of Science,* Sintonen, Matti (ed). Sahlin, Nils-Eric.
"Jaako Hintikka Replies" in *Knowledge and Inquiry: Essays on Jaakko Hintikka's Epistemology and Philosophy of Science,* Sintonen, Matti (ed). Hintikka, Jaakko.

**RAMSEY, P**
*The Annual of the Society of Christian Ethics with Cumulative Index.* Beckley, Harlan (ed).
Paul Ramsey and the Common Law Tradition. Tuttle, Robert W.
Probabilism and Beyond. Galavotti, Maria Carla.

**RAMSEY, W**
Finding the Right Level for Connectionist Representations (A Critical Note on Ramsey's Paper). Markic, Olga.

**RAMUS, P**
La funció crítica de la "inventio" i el "iudicium" en la *Dialèctica de Petrus Ramus.* Grau i Arau, Andrés.
Ramistische Spuren in Leibniz' Gestaltung der Begriffe ,dialectica', ,topica' und ,ars inveniendi'. Varani, Giovanna.

**RANCIERE, J**
Democracy Means Equality. Rancière, Jacques.

**RAND, R**
Deontica in Rose Rand. Lorini, Giuseppe.

**RANDALL, J**
An American Naturalist Account of Culture. Baeten, Elizabeth M.

**RANDOM**
In the random graph $G(n,p)$, $p = n^{-a}$.... Shelah, Saharon.
Infinitary Logics and Very Sparse Random Graphs. Lynch, James F.
Mathematical Quantum Theory I: Random Ultrafilters as Hidden Variables. Boos, William.

**RANDOMNESS**
The Rule of Adjunction and Reasonable Inference. Kyburg, Jr, Henry E.

**RANK**
A Definable Continuous Rank for Nonmultidimensional Superstable Theories. Chowdhury, Ambar, Loveys, James and Tanovic, Predrag.
The Morley Rank of a Banach Space. Iovino, José.

**RANKING**
Nonparametric Statistics in Multicriteria Analysis. Scarelli, Antonino and Venzi, Lorenzo.

**RAPE**
Antioch's "Sexual Offense Policy": A Philosophical Exploration. Soble, Alan.
Deconstructive Strategies and the Movement Against Sexual Violence. Heberle, Renee.
On Rape: A Crime Against Humanity. Calhoun, Laurie.
Rape as a Weapon of War. Card, Claudia.
Rape Research and Gender Feminism: So Who's Anti-Male?. Davion, Victoria.

**RAPHAEL**
Reading Raphael: *The School of Athens* and Its Pre-Text. Most, Glenn W.

**RAPPAPORT, S**
Relativism and Truth: A Reply to Steven Rappaport. Lynch, Michael P.

**RASIOWA, H**
An Algebraic Approach to Logics in Research Work of Helena Rasiowa and Cecylia Rauszer. Jankowski, Andrzej W.
H Rasiowa's and C Rauszer's Contribution to Algebra. Bartol, Wiktor.
Helena Rasiowa and Cecylia Rauszer Research on Logical Foundations of Computer Science. Pawlak, Zdzislaw and Skowron, Andrzej.
Helena Rasiowa and Cecylia Rauszer: Two Generations in Logic. Bartol, Wiktor and Rauszer, Cecylia.
Post Algebras in Helena Rasiowa's Explorations. Traczyk, Tadeusz.
Proof-Theoretical Investigations of Helena Rasiowa. Orlowska, Ewa.

**RASTAFARIANISM**
Rastafarianism and the Reality of Dread"" in *Existence in Black: An Anthology of Black Existential Philosophy,* Gordon, Lewis R (ed). Henry, Paget.

**RATIO**
Aristotle on Perception: The Dual-Logos Theory. Bradshaw, David.
Metaphysics Delta 15 and Pre-Euclidean Mathematics. Pritchard, Paul.

**RATIONAL**
Decision Theoretic Foundations for Axioms of Rational Preference. Hansson, Sven Ove.
On the Possibility of Rational Free Action. Clarke, Randolph.
Reflexiones sobre la no violencia: Variedades, posibilidades y límites. Sobrevilla, David.
Resolute Choice and Rational Deliberation: A Critique and a Defense. Gauthier, David.

**RATIONALISM**
see also Reason
"L'*Account of the Nature and the Extent of the Divine Dominion and Goodnesses* di Samuel Parker: dalla teologia alla filosofia politica" in *Mind Senior to the World,* Baldi, Marialuisa. Lupoli, Agostino.
"L'indagine storico-universale di Max Weber sul 'razionalismo occidentale' tra lo storicismo e Nietzsche" in *Lo Storicismo e la Sua Storia: Temi, Problemi, Prospettive,* Cacciatore, Giuseppe (ed). Di Marco, Giuseppe Antonio.
"L'Ombra Della Ragione: Banfi lettore di Klages" in *Soggetto E Verità: La questione dell'uomo nella filosofia contemporanea,* Fagiuoli, Ettore. Bonesio, Luisa.
"Note sulla concezione leibniziana della storia" in *Lo Storicismo e la Sua Storia: Temi, Problemi, Prospettive,* Cacciatore, Giuseppe (ed). Sanna, Manuela.
*A Short History of Modern Philosophy: From Descartes to Wittgenstein.* Scruton, Roger.
*Grundlegung eines Neorationalismus: Dekognition und Dissens.* Radermacher, Hans.
*Modern Philosophy, 2nd Edition.* Baird, Forrest E (ed) and Kaufmann, Walter.
*Un'Introduzione All'Epistemologia Contemporanea.* Gava, Giacomo (ed).
A propósito de la crítica de Feyerabend al racionalismo crítico. Marqués, Gustavo L.
Crítica del llamado de Heidelberg. Lecourt, Dominique.
Descartes and Metaphysical Thought (in Czech). Sobotka, Milan.
Did he Walk with a Mask...? (in Czech). Dokulil, Milos.
El método de la filosofía en la filosofía moderna. Gómez Pardo, Rafael.
Fichtes Wissenschaftslehre vor der aktuellen Diskussion um die Letztbegründung. Gerten, Michael.
L'épistémologie génétique dans la philosophie ancienne. Chiesa, Curzio.
La *méthode* de Lipman: un outil dangereux de propaganda auprès des enfants? Une réplique à Pierre Desjardins. Laberge, Jean.
Moralischer Internalismus: Motivation durch Wünsche versus Motivation durch Überzeugungen. Wolf, Jean-Claude.
O tema da existência na *Nova Dilucidatio* de Kant. Viegas, Pedro.
On the Moral Philosophy of René Descartes: Or, How Morals are Derived from Method. Bagley, Paul J.
Preghiera e Filosofia della Religione. Santi, Giorgio.
Scienza Nuova y *The New Science of Politics*: Proyección del pensamiento viquiano en la obra de Eric Voeglin. Badillo O'Farrell, Pablo.
Sociología y tipología del fenómeno religioso. Piñon G, Francisco.
Whewell on the Ultimate Problem of Philosophy. Morrison, Margaret.

**RATIONALIST**
Critical Notice of J. Gracia's *Individuation and Identity in Early Modern Philosophy.* Kronen, John D.

**RATIONALITY**
see also Irrationality
"A Note on Boghossian's Master Argument" in *Contents,* Villanueva, Enrique (ed). Gibson, Roger.
"Autoconocimiento, racionalidad y contenido mental" in *La racionalidad: su poder y sus límites,* Nudler, Oscar (ed). Sabatés, Marcelo H.
"Can Peter Be Rational?" in *Contents,* Villanueva, Enrique (ed). Valdivia, Lourdes.
"Can There Be a Rationally Compelling Argument for Anti-Realism about Ordinary ('Folk') Psychology?" in *Contents,* Villanueva, Enrique (ed). Wright, Crispin.
"Cinco tesis sobre la racionalidad de la acción" in *La racionalidad: su poder y sus límites,* Nudler, Oscar (ed). Maliandi, Ricardo.
"Das Kalkül der Moral" in *Ökonomie und Moral: Beiträge zur Theorie ökonomischer Rationalität,* Lohmann, Karl Reinhard (ed). Kirsch, Guy.
"Die Newcomb-Paradoxie—und ihre Lösung" in *Das weite Spektrum der analytischen Philosophie,* Lenzen, Wolfgang. Lenzen, Wolfgang.
"Evolución y racionalidad limitada" in *La racionalidad: su poder y sus límites,* Nudler, Oscar (ed). Gomila Benejam, Antoni.
"La racionalidad y las tres fuerzas del universo epistémico" in *La racionalidad: su poder y sus límites,* Nudler, Oscar (ed). Broncano, Fernando.
"Las dimensiones de la racionalidad" in *La racionalidad: su poder y sus límites,* Nudler, Oscar (ed). Broncano, Fernando.
"Las variedades del escepticismo" in *La racionalidad: su poder y sus límites,* Nudler, Oscar (ed). Liz, Manuel.

## RATIONALITY

## RATIONALITY

Rhetoric's Revenge: The Prospect of a Critical Legal Rhetoric. Hasian, Jr, Marouf and Croasmun, Earl.

Slote on Rational Dilemmas and Rational Supererogation. Mintoff, Joe.

Sprechakttheoretische Erläuterungen zum Begriff der kommunikativen Rationalität. Habermas, Jürgen.

Stich on Intentionality and Rationality. Gibson, Roger.

Stochastic Evolution of Rationality. Falmagne, Jean-Claude and Doignon, Jean-Paul.

Stufen der Rechtfertigung. Ulfig, Alexander.

Teoría de la acción y racionalidad en Donald Davidson. Pérez-Wicht, Pablo Quintanilla.

The Ambiguity of 'Rationality'. Rorty, Richard.

The Individual Rationality of Maintaining a Sense of Justice. Cave, Eric M.

The King and 'I': Agency and Rationality in Athens and Jerusalem. Glouberman, Mark.

The Political Turning Point (in Spanish). Camps, Victoria.

The Rational and the Irrational: A Philosophical Problem (Reading Arthur Schopenhauer). Mudragei, Nellia Stepanovna.

The Sceptical *Epokhé* and its Presuppositions (in Spanish). Bolzani Filho, Roberto.

The Sociophilosophy of Folk Psychology. Kusch, Martin.

The Task of Group Rationality: The Subjectivist's View—Part I. Sarkar, Husain.

The Task of Group Rationality: The Subjectivist's View—Part II. Sarkar, Husain.

The Unity of Scientific Knowledge in the Framework of a Typological Approach of Theories. Parvu, Ilie.

Three Aspects of Rational Explanation. Pettit, Philip.

Troubles for Michael Smith's Metaethical Rationalism. Horgan, Terence and Timmons, Mark.

Une éthique est-elle possible en l'absence de croyances dogmatiques?. Boudon, Raymond.

Vernunft heute. Welsch, Wolfgang.

Vernunftmetaphorik und Rationalitätstheorie. Früchtl, Josef.

Violations of Present-Value Maximization in Income Choice. Gigliotti, Gary and Sopher, Barry.

Weakness of Will. Buss, Sarah.

What Rationality Adds to Animal Morality. Waller, Bruce N.

When to Believe in Miracles. Clarke, Steve.

Who is Rational Economic Man?. Roback Morse, Jennifer.

Why Should Educators Care about Argumentation?. Siegel, Harvey.

## RATIONALIZATION

Can Religion Survive the Rationalization? Questions at Habermas's Theory of Culture (in Dutch). Jespers, F P M.

## RATIONING

The Economic Attributes of Medical Care: Implications for Rationing Choices in the United States and United Kingdom. Banks, Dwayne A.

## RAUH, F

A Pragmatist in Paris: Fréderic Rauh's "Task of Dissolution". Horner, Richard.

## RAULET, G

*Conversations with French Philosophers.* Aylesworth, Gary E (trans) and Rötzer, Florian.

## RAUSZER, C

An Algebraic Approach to Logics in Research Work of Helena Rasiowa and Cecylia Rauszer. Jankowski, Andrzej W.

Cecylia Rauszer. Rasiowa, Helena.

H Rasiowa's and C Rauszer's Contribution to Algebra. Bartol, Wiktor.

Helena Rasiowa and Cecylia Rauszer Research on Logical Foundations of Computer Science. Pawlak, Zdzislaw and Skowron, Andrzej.

Helena Rasiowa and Cecylia Rauszer: Two Generations in Logic. Bartol, Wiktor and Rauszer, Cecylia.

## RAVA, A

Adolfo Ravà: lo Stato come organismo etico. Fracanzani, Marcello.

## RAVAISSON

Théorie de la sensibilité dans le spritualisme français (in Japanese). Uemura, Hiroshi.

## RAVIZZA, M

Sensitivity and Responsibility for Consequences. Glannon, Walter.

The Importance of the Proportionality Condition to the Doctrine of Double Effect: A Response to Fischer, Ravizza, and Copp. Woodward, P A.

## RAWLS, J

"Acerca del igual derecho a ser diferente" in *Liberalismo y Comunitarismo: Derechos Humanos y Democracia,* Monsalve Solórzano, Alfonso (ed). Cepeda, Margarita.

"Carnal Knowledges: Beyond Rawls and Sandel" in *A Question of Values: New Canadian Perspectives in Ethics and Political Philosophy,* Brennan, Samantha (ed). Mills, Charles W.

"La idea del Consenso en Rawls: Una exposición crítica" in *Liberalismo y Comunitarismo: Derechos Humanos y Democracia,* Monsalve Solórzano, Alfonso (ed). Monsalve Solórzano, Alfonso.

"Political Dialogue and Political Virtue" in *Political Dialogue: Theories and Practices,* Esquith, Stephen L (ed). Esquith, Stephen L.

"Two Concepts of Rawls" in *A Question of Values: New Canadian Perspectives in Ethics and Political Philosophy,* Brennan, Samantha (ed). Wendling, Karen.

A Critique of Rawls's Hermeneutics as Translation. Josefson, Jim and Bach, Jonathan.

Animating Rawls's Original Position. Regan, Thomas J.

Constructing the Law of Peoples. Moellendorf, Darrel.

Contractual Justice: A Modest Defence. Barry, Brian.

Contractualism and Animals. Bernstein, Mark.

Defining the Medical Sphere. Trappenburg, Margo J.

Desigualdades de Bienestar y axiomática rawlsiana. Sen, Amartya K.

Droits naturels et devoir naturel chez Rawls. Sosoé, Varus Atadi.

El nuevo Rawls. Rosenkrantz, Carlos F.

Gesellschaftsvertrag oder grösster Gesamtnutzen? Die Vertragstheorie von John Rawls und ihre neo-utilitaristischen Kritiker. Rinderle, Peter.

L'interprétation de la position originelle et la question de la fondation. Ouattara, Ibrahim S.

Liberalism and Deliberative Democracy: Considerations on the Foundations of Liberty and Equality (Spanish). Cortés Rodas, Francisco.

Okin on Feminism and Rawls. Sehon, Scott R.

On Equal Rights to Be Different: A Communitarian Criticism of Rawls' Liberalism (Spanish). Cepeda, Margarita.

On Reasonableness. Moore, Margaret.

Persona Moral y Justicia Distributiva. Bertomeu, María Julia and Vidiella, Graciela.

Political Equality in Justice as Fairness. Brighouse, Harry.

Promising, Consent, and Citizenship. Mulhall, Stephen.

Public Justification and the Transparency Argument. Wall, Steven P.

Rawl's Just Savings Principle and the Sense of Justice. Paden, Roger.

Rawls and International Justice. Räikkä, Juha.

Rawls's "The Closed Society Assumption" (in Serbo-Croatian). Strncevic, Ljubica and Gligorov, Vladimir.

Rawls's Problem of Stability. Huemer, Michael.

Reciprocal Justification in Science and Moral Theory. Blachowicz, James.

Reconstructing Rawls's Law of Peoples. Paden, Roger.

Reflective Equilibrium or Evolving Tradition?. Aronovitch, Hilliard.

Response to Thomas McCarthy: The Political Alliance between Ethical Feminism and Rawls's Kantian Constructivism. Cornell, Drucilla.

Some Skeptical Reflections on Renewed Ethics (Spanish). Sasso, Javier.

The Libertarianism of Robert Nozick (in Czech). Barsa, Pavel.

The Political Turning Point (in Spanish). Camps, Victoria.

The Secret History of Public Reason: Hobbes to Rawls. Ivison, Duncan.

Why Rational Argument Needs Defending. Rowland, Robert C.

## RAZ, J

On Raz and the Obligation to Obey the Law. May, Thomas.

The Analysis of Rights. Penner, J E.

## RAZZAQUE, A

Linguistic Solipsism. Lenka, Laxminarayan.

## READ, S

The Validity Paradox in Modal $S_5$. Jacquette, Dale.

## READING

"Concerning Zelia Gregoriou's "Reading *Phaedrus* like a Girl" in *Philosophy of Education (1996),* Margonis, Frank (ed). Whitlock, Greg.

"Reading *Phaedrus* Like a Girl Misfires and Rhizomes in Reading Performances" in *Philosophy of Education (1996),* Margonis, Frank (ed). Gregoriou, Zelia.

Back to a Monstrous Site: Reiner Schürmann's Reading of Heidegger's *Beiträge.* Janicaud, Dominique.

How to Read Heidegger. Schürmann, Reiner.

Mere Reading. Brann, Eva T H.

Reading for Ethos: Literary Study and Moral Thought. Hogan, Patrick Colm.

The Ethics of Reading: A Traveler's Guide. Rorty, Amélie Oksenberg.

The Place of Nietzsche in Reiner Schürmann's Thought and in His Reading of Heidegger. Haar, Michel.

## REAL

A Non-Generic Real Incompatible with $0^{\#}$. Stanley, M C.

La ontología spinociana de las modalidades entitativas. Moya Bedoya, Juan Diego.

$Pi^0_1$ Classes and Minimal Degrees. Groszek, Marcia J and Slaman, Theodore A.

Quantum Dynamical Reduction and Reality: Replacing Probability Densities with Densities in Real Space. Ghirardi, Giancarlo.

Small Forcings and Cohen Reals. Zapletal, Jindrich.

Some Model Theory for Almost Real Closed Fields. Delon, Françoise and Farré, Rafel.

## REALE, G

The New View of Plato. Krämer, Hans Joachim.

## REALISM

*see also* Critical Realism, Surrealism

"Can There Be a Rationally Compelling Argument for Anti-Realism about Ordinary ('Folk') Psychology?" in *Contents,* Villanueva, Enrique (ed). Wright, Crispin.

"Inducción pesimista y verdad" in *Verdad: lógica, representación y mundo,* Villegas Forero, L. Iranzo, Valeriano.

"Realism: Neural Networks and Representation" in *Verdad: lógica, representación y mundo,* Villegas Forero, L. Carreras, Alberto.

"Realistischer Realismus als ein methodologischer und pragmatischer Interpretationismus" in *Das weite Spektrum der analytischen Philosophie,* Lenzen, Wolfgang. Lenk, Hans.

## REASON

*The Inaugural Address: The Grounding of Reason. Trigg, Roger.*

The Intended/Foreseen Distinction's Ethical Relevance. Cavanaugh, Thomas A.

The Limits of Comparison: Kant and Sartre on the Fundamental Project. Lieberman, Marcel.

The Modernity Crisis and the Pedagogical Reason (Spanish). Márquez, Alvaro.

The Need for Plans, Projects and Reasoning about Ends: Kant and Williams. Kemal, Salim.

The Needs of Understanding: Kant on Empirical Laws and Regulative Ideals. O'Shea, James R.

The Offense of Reason and the Passion of Faith: Kierkegaard and Anti-Rationalism. Carr, Karen L.

The Problem of Salvation in Kant's *Religion within the Limits of Reason Alone.* Michalson, Gordon E.

The Propositional Attitudes. Heil, John.

The Prospects for an Evolutionary Psychology: Human Language and Human Reasoning. Richardson, Robert C.

The Real Marketplace of Ideas. Weissberg, Robert.

The Relevance of Logic to Reasoning and Belief Revision: Harman on 'Change in View'. Knorpp Jr, William Max.

The Ring of Gyges: Overridingness and the Unity of Reason. Copp, David.

The Secret History of Public Reason: Hobbes to Rawls. Ivison, Duncan.

The Why's of Business Revisited. Duska, Ronald F.

Thinking about Reasoning about Knowledge. Kyburg Jr, Henry E.

Trolley, Transplant and Consent. Dimas, Panagiotis.

Troubles for Michael Smith's Metaethical Rationalism. Horgan, Terence and Timmons, Mark.

Ulteriorità del pensare. Masi, Giuseppe.

Unamuno e l'esistenzialismo "cristiano". Colonnello, Pio.

Under the Sign of Failure. Fenves, Peter.

Values, Reasons and Perspectives. Thomas, Alan.

Vernunft heute. Welsch, Wolfgang.

Vernunft und das Andere der Vernunft: Eine modelltheoretische Exposition. Gloy, Karen.

Vernunftmetaphorik und Rationalitätstheorie. Früchtl, Josef.

Vichiana. Amoroso, Leonardo.

Vico y la retórica que no cesa. Marín-Casanova, José Antonio.

What Makes Something Practically Worth Thinking About. Passell, Dan.

What's Wrong with Relativism: Why Postmodernism's Most Radical Doctrine is Dead in the Water. Vaughn, Lewis.

When Is An Excuse A Reason?. Mendenhall, Vance.

When Several Bayesians Agree That There Will Be No Reasoning to a Foregone Conclusion. Seidenfeld, Teddy, Kadane, Joseph B and Schervish, Mark J.

Why Interpret?. Raz, Joseph.

Why Rational Argument Needs Defending. Rowland, Robert C.

Zeitalter der hermeneutischen Vernunft. Demmerling, Christoph.

Zur Aufgabe transzendentaler Interpretation. Gawlina, Manfred.

'Ought' and Reasons for Action. Gewirth, Alan.

## REASONABLENESS

On Reasonableness. Moore, Margaret.

Rational, Fair, and Reasonable. Wolff, Jonathan.

Reasonable Impressions in Stoicism. Brennan, Tad.

## REASONING

*see also* Deduction, Induction, Moral Reasoning, Thinking

"Argument Based Reasoning: Some Remarks on the Relation Between Argumentation Theory and Artificial Intelligence" in *Logic and Argumentation,* Van Eemeren, Frans H (ed). Starmans, Richard J C M.

"Defeasible Reasoning with Legal Rules" in *Deontic Logic, Agency and Normative Systems,* Brown, Mark A (ed). Royakkers, Lambèr and Dignum, Frank.

"Logic and Argumentation" in *Logic and Argumentation,* Van Eemeren, Frans H (ed). Van Benthem, Johan.

*Logic and Argumentation.* Van Eemeren, Frans H (ed), Van Benthem, Johan (ed) and Grootendorst, Rob (ed).

*Practical Reasoning in Natural Language.* Thomas, Stephen Naylor.

A Logic for Reasoning about Relative Similarity. Konikowska, Beata.

Argumentation, Education and Reasoning. Binkley, Robert W.

Critical Thinking, Critical Reasoning, and Methodological Reflection. Finocchiaro, Maurice A.

Equational Reasoning in Non-Classical Logics. Frias, Marcelo F and Orlowska, Ewa.

Improving Scientific Reasoning through Philosophy for Children: An Empirical Study. Sprod, Tim.

Is Default Logic a Reinvention of Inductive-Statistical Reasoning?. Tan, Yao-Hua.

Kant's Theory of Geometrical Reasoning and the Analytic-Synthetic Distinction: On Hintikka's Interpretation of Kant's Philosophy of Mathematics. De Jong, Willem R.

Moral Climate and the Development of Moral Reasoning: The Effects of Dyadic Discussions between Young Offenders. Taylor, John H and Walker, Lawrence J.

New Trends and Open Problems in Fuzzy Logic and Approximate Reasoning. Prade, Henri and Dubois, Didier.

Nonmonotonic Reasoning: From Finitary Relations to Infinitary Inference Operations. Freund, Michael and Lehmann, Daniel.

Philosophical Reasoning in Ethics and the Use of the History of Philosophy. Talaska, Richard A.

Promoting Ethical Reasoning, Affect and Behaviour Among High School Students: An Evaluation of Three Teaching Strategies. DeHaan, Robert, Hanford, Russell and Kinlaw, Kathleen.

Reasoning and Children: The Wide Glare of the Children's Day. Slade, Christina.

Reasoning with Imperatives Using Classical Logic. Fulda, Joseph S.

Reflective Reasoning in Groups. Slade, Christina.

Some Syntactic Approaches to the Handling of Inconsistent Knowledge Bases: A Comparative Study. Benferhat, Salem, Dubois, Didier and Prade, Henri.

Thomas' Second Way: A Defense by Modal Scientific Reasoning. Trundle, Jr, Robert C.

Towards a Rough Mereology-Based Logic for Approximate Solution. Komorowski, Jan, Polkowski, Lech T and Skowron, Andrzej.

What's an Approximate Conditional?. De Soto, A R and Trillas, Enric.

## REASONS

*see also* Sufficient Reason

Een Reactie op Heleen Pott. Walry, Jenny.

Op zoek naar Mr. Spock: Kort commentaar op Apostel en Walry, 'Minimale rationaliteit van emoties en van overtuigingen'. Pott, Heleen.

Para una Lógica de las Razones Prima Facie. Alchourrón, Carlos E.

The Psychological Reality of Reasons. Collins, Arthur W.

## REBELLION

Donagan, Abortion, and Civil Rebellion. Tollefsen, Christopher.

Esquema para Reexaminar la Filosofía Política de Kant. Astorga, Omar.

## REBIRTH

*see also* Reincarnation

Persons (Real and Alleged) in Enlightenment Traditions: A Partial Look at Jainism and Buddhism. Yandell, Keith.

## RECEPTACLE

Le réceptacle platonicien: nature, fonction, contenu. Narbonne, Jean-Marc.

## RECIPROCAL

Reciprocal Justification in Science and Moral Theory. Blachowicz, James.

## RECIPROCITY

El educador viquiano. Rebollo Espinosa, Maria José.

## RECLUS, E

"The Dialectical Social Geography of Elisée Reclus" in *Philosophy and Geography I: Space, Place, and Environmental Ethics,* Light, Andrew (ed). Clark, John.

## RECOGNITION

Anerkennung und moralische Verpflichtung. Honneth, Axel.

Authenticity and Autonomy: Taylor, Habermas, and the Politics of Recognition. Cooke, Maeve.

Kinesthetic-Visual Matching and the Self-Concept as Explanations of Mirror-Self-Recognition. Mitchell, Robert W.

Political Toleration or Politics or Recognition: The Headscarves Affair Revisited. Köker, Levent.

The Right to Life and the Death Penalty (Spanish). Papacchini, Angelo.

## RECONCILIATION

Progress in Reconciliation: Evidence from the Right and the Left. Sterba, James P.

Tolerance and War: The Real Meaning of an Irreconcilability. Gianformaggio, Letizia.

## RECONSTRUCTION

"Storia e filologia in Niebuhr" in *Lo Storicismo e la Sua Storia: Temi, Problemi, Prospettive,* Cacciatore, Giuseppe (ed). Montepaone, Claudia.

Characterization of the Basic Notions of Chomsky's Grammar (in Spanish). Peris-Viñé, Luis M.

Rational Reconstruction: Preconditions and Limits. Iliescu, Adrian-Paul.

## RECONSTRUCTIVISM

Algunos Problemas de las Ciencias Reconstructivas. Villegas, Luis.

## RECORDING

Innovation and Conservatism in Performance Practice. Godlovitch, Stanley.

Listening to Music: Performances and Recordings. Gracyk, Theodore A.

So, You Want to Sing with *The Beatles*? Too Late!. Davies, Stephen.

## RECOVERY

"Philosophy in America: Recovery and Future Development" in *The Recovery of Philosophy in America: Essays in Honor of John Edwin Smith,* Kasulis, Thomas P (ed). Smith, John E.

## RECURSION

Computability and Recursion. Soare, Robert I.

## RECURSION THEORY

Boolean Pairs Formed by the $\Delta^0_n$-Sets. Hermann, E.

On a Paradox of Hilbert and Bernays. Priest, Graham.

Possible Degrees in Recursive Copies II. Knight, J F and Ash, C J.

Sigma$_2$ Induction and Infinite Injury Priority Arguments: Part II: Tame Sigma$_2$ Coding and the Jump Operator. Chong, C T and Yang, Yue.

The Combinatorics of the Splitting Theorem. Kontostathis, Kyriakos.

## RECURSIVE FUNCTION

Characterizing Language Identification in Terms of Computable Numberings. Jain, Sanjay and Sharma, Arun.

Elementary Realizability. Damnjanovic, Zlatan.

Hipotesis del continuo, definibilidad y funciones recursivas: historia de un desencuentro (1925-1955). Zalamea, Fernando.

Induction Rules, Reflection Principles, and Provably Recursive Functions. Beklemishev, Lev D.

Term Rewriting Theory for the Primitive Recursive Functions. Cichon, E A and Weiermann, A.

Translating the Hypergame Paradox: Remarks on the Set of Founded Elements of a Relation. Bernardi, Claudio and D'Agostino, Giovanna.

What's in a Function?. Antonelli, Gian Aldo.

## RECURSIVELY ENUMERABLE SETS

A Finite Lattice without Critical Triple That Cannot Be Embedded into the Enumerable Turing Degrees. Lerman, Manuel and Lempp, Steffen.

A Non-Splitting Theorem for d.r.e. Sets. Yi, Xiaoding.

Automorphisms in the *PTIME*-Turing Degrees of Recursive Sets. Haught, Christine Ann and Slaman, Theodore A.

Decidability of the Two-Quantifier Theory of the Recursive Enumerable Weak Truth-Table Degrees and Other Distributive Semi-Lattices. Ambos-Spies, Klaus, Fejer, Peter A and Lempp, Steffen (& others).

Definability in the Recursively Enumerable Degrees. Nies, André, Shore, Richard A and Slaman, Theodore A.

Generalized Nonsplitting in the Recursively Enumerable Degrees. Leonhardi, Steven D.

Noncappable Enumeration Degrees Below O'ₑ. Cooper, S Barry and Sorbi, Andrea.

Permitting, Forcing, and Copying of a given Recursive Relation. Cholak, P, Knight, J F and Ash, C J.

Quasi-Simple Relations in Copies of a given Recursive Structure. Knight, J F, Remmel, J B and Ash, C J.

The Pi⁰₂ Enumeration Degrees are not Dense. Calhoun, William C and Slaman, Theodore A.

## RECURSIVENESS

A Recursive Nonstandard Model of Normal Open Induction. Berarducci, Alessandro and Otero, Margarita.

## REDEMPTION

Creación y salvación, o Naturaleza y redención. Anoz, José (trans) and Bonafede, Giulio.

Gilles Deleuze and the Redemption from Interest. Hallward, Peter.

Jesus: Parable or Sacrament of God?. McDermott, John M.

## REDISTRIBUTION

Affirmative Action in Higher Education as Redistribution. Guenin, Louis M.

## REDUCED

On Reduced Matrices. Rautenberg, Wolfgang.

## REDUCIBILITY

Noncappable Enumeration Degrees Below O'ₑ. Cooper, S Barry and Sorbi, Andrea.

Strong Polynomial-Time Reducibility. Shinoda, Juichi.

## REDUCTIO AD ABSURDUM

*Reductio* Without Assumptions?. Hansen, Hans Vilhelm.

## REDUCTION

"Genuine Triads and Teridentity" in *Studies in the Logic of Charles Sanders Peirce*, Houser, Nathan (ed). Brunning, Jacqueline.

"Peirce on the Application of Relations to Relations" in *Studies in the Logic of Charles Sanders Peirce*, Houser, Nathan (ed). Burch, Robert W.

"Peirce's Reduction Thesis" in *Studies in the Logic of Charles Sanders Peirce*, Houser, Nathan (ed). Burch, Robert W.

"Reduktion und Erklärung in der Chemie" in *Philosophie der Chemie: Bestandsaufnahme und Ausblick,* Schummer, Joachim (ed). Scerri, Eric R.

"Warum ist die Chemie ein Steifkind der Philosophie?" in *Philosophie der Chemie: Bestandsaufnahme und Ausblick,* Schummer, Joachim (ed). Ruthenberg, Klaus.

*Philosophie der Chemie: Bestandsaufnahme und Ausblick.* Schummer, Joachim (ed), Psarros, Nikos (ed) and Ruthenberg, Klaus (ed).

Chemistry as the Science of the Transformation of Substances. Van Brakel, Jaap.

Extending Lambek Grammars to Basic Categorial Grammars. Buszkowski, Wojciech.

Logic in Russell's *Principles of Mathematics*. Landini, Gregory.

Lorenz Krüger. Scheibe, Erhard.

Molecular Shape, Reduction, Explanation and Approximate Concepts. Ramsey, Jeffry L.

Niels Bohrs Argument für die Nichtreduzierbarkeit der Biologie auf die Physik. Hoyningen-Huene, Paul.

Quantum Dynamical Reduction and Reality: Replacing Probability Densities with Densities in Real Space. Ghirardi, Giancarlo.

Reduktion und Ambivalenz: Zur Reflexionsstruktur von E. Lévinas' *Autrement qu'être*. Schällibaum, Urs.

Teleology and the Product Analogy. Matthen, Mohan.

The Mysterious Grand Properties of Forrest. Noordhof, Paul.

What Multiple Realizability Does Not Show. Francescotti, Robert M.

## REDUCTIONISM

"The Grain Problem" in *Objections to Physicalism*, Robinson, Howard (ed). Lockwood, Michael.

*Il Riduzionismo della Scienza*. Gava, Giacomo.

Are Science and Religion in Conflict?. Watts, Fraser N.

Bemerkungen zum Verhältnis zwischen Neurophysiologie und Psychologie. Ros, Arno.

Eigenschafts-Physikalismus. Beckermann, Ansgar.

Explaining Emergence: Towards an Ontology of Levels. Emmeche, Claus, Koppe, Simo and Stjernfelt, Frederik.

How Physicalists Can Avoid Reductionism. Kirk, Robert.

Is Reductionism the Saving Way?. Dokulil, Milos.

Nonreductive Naturalism. Silvers, Stuart.

Nota sobre el no reduccionismo y la realizabilidad variable. Rabossi, Eduardo.

Philosophical Issues in the History of Chemistry. Gavroglu, Kostas.

Praktische Kohärenz. Nida-Rümelin, Julian.

Reductionism and Nominalism in Descartes's Theory of Attributes. Nolan, Lawrence.

The Case for the Philosophy of Chemistry. McIntyre, Lee and Scerri, Eric R.

The Perils of Epistemic Reductionism. Horgan, Terence.

The Unity of Science without Reductionism. Lucas, John R.

## REDUCTIVISM

"Non-Reductive Physicalism?" in *Objections to Physicalism,* Robinson, Howard (ed). Smith, A D.

Against Thin-Property Reductivism: Toleration as Supererogatory. Newey, Glen.

Non-Basic Time and Reductive Strategies: Leibniz's Theory of Time. Cover, J A.

## REEVE, C

Aristotle, *hos epi to polu* Relations, and a Demonstrative Science of Ethics. Winter, Michael.

## REFERENCE

*see also* Self-Reference

"Disquotation and Cause in the Theory of Reference" in *Contents,* Villanueva, Enrique (ed). Horwich, Paul.

"Doubts about Fregean Reference" in *Contents,* Villanueva, Enrique (ed). García-Carpintero, Manuel.

"Frege's Treatment of Indirect Reference" in *Frege: Importance and Legacy,* Schirn, Matthias (ed). Mendelsohn, Richard L.

"More on Fregean Reference" in *Contents,* Villanueva, Enrique (ed). Sosa, Ernest.

"Reference from a Perspective *versus* Reference" in *Contents,* Villanueva, Enrique (ed). Sosa, David.

"Reference from the First Person Perspective" in *Contents,* Villanueva, Enrique (ed). Loar, Brian.

"Rigidity and Genuine Reference" in *Verdad: lógica, representación y mundo,* Villegas Forero, L. Martí, Genoveva.

*The Sense of Reference: Intentionality in Frege*. Bar-Elli, Gilead.

*Wahrheit, Referenz und Realismus: Eine Studie zur Sprachphilosophie und Metaphysik*. Schantz, Richard.

Can Navya Nyāya Analysis Make a Distinction between Sense and Reference. Krishna, Daya.

Direct Reference for the Narrow Minded. Shier, David.

El retorno de la referencia. Navarro Pérez, Jorge.

Explaining Referential/Attributive. Patton, Thomas E.

Frege über indexikalische Ausdrücke. Perry, John.

Gale on Reference and Religious Experience. Jeffrey, Andrew V.

How Demonstrations Connect with Referential Intentions. Roberts, Lawrence D.

How Well does Direct Reference Semantics Fit with Pragmatics?. Lumsden, David.

Indexical Reference and Bodily Causal Diagrams in Intentional Action. Castañeda, Héctor-Neri.

Indexicals and Descriptions. García-Murga, Fernando.

Intentionality as the Mark of the Dispositional. Place, U T.

Kausalität und singuläre Referenz: Eine sprachphilosophische Rekonstruktion des empirischen Realismus bei Kant. Wyller, Truls.

Nominal Comparatives and Generalized Quantifiers. Nerbonne, John.

On Talk of Modes of Thought. Ramakrishnan, Lakshmi.

Pragmatically Determined Aspects of What is Said: A Reply to Bezuidenhout. Grimberg, Mary Lou.

Pragmatics, Semantic Underdetermination and the Referential/Attributive Distinction. Bezuidenhout, Anne.

Predicates, Properties and the Goal of a Theory of Reference. Zalabardo, José L.

Proxy Functions, Truth and Reference. Nelson, R J.

Putnam on Reference and Constructible Sets. Levin, Michael.

Quantified Modal Logic, Reference and Essentialism. Perrick, M and Swart, H C M.

Recent and Classic References at the Interface of Philosophy, Psychiatry, and Psychology. Sadler, John Z (ed).

Reference and Imperfective Paradox. Graves, P R.

Référence directe et psychologisme. Corazza, Eros.

Reference, Truth and Realism. Hochberg, Herbert.

Sense, Reference and Selective Attention. Campbell, John and Martin, M G F.

Sense, Validity and Context. Williamson, Timothy.

Sobre referencia y causalidad. Lo Monaco, Vicenzo P.

Structured Propositions and Sentence Structure. King, Jeffrey C.

## RELIGION

## RELIGION

A Funny Thing Happened to Me on the Way to Salvation: Climacus as Humorist in Kierkegaard's *Concluding Unscientific Postscript*. Lippitt, John.

A History of the Extraterrestrial Life Debate. Crowe, Michael J.

A marca do vazio: Reflexoes sobre a subjetividade em Blaise Pascal. De Souza Birchal, Telma.

A Neoplatonist's Pantheism. Leslie, John.

A New Argument against Pascal (in Hebrew). Zemach, Eddy M.

A Reply to Professor Hick. Van Inwagen, Peter.

A Response to John Hick. Mavrodes, George I.

A Rippling Relatableness in Reality. Ashbrook, James B.

A Theological Escape from the Cartesian Circle?. Dalton, Peter.

Ad Hick. Plantinga, Alvin.

Against a Straussian Interpretation of Marsilius of Padua's Poverty Thesis. Kaye, Sharon.

Agustin de Herrera, A Treatise on Aleatory Probability *De Necessitate Morali in Genere*. Knebel, Sven K (ed & trans).

Aleksei Fedorovich Losev and Orthodoxy. Mokhov, V V.

All Existing is the Action of God: The Philosophical Theology of David Braine. Bradshaw, David.

Alnwick on the Origin, Nature, and Function of the Formal Distinction. Noone, Timothy B.

Ambiguity and Bad Faith. Morris, Katherine J.

Analytische Religionsphilosophie: Zwischen Intersubjektivität und Esoterik. Runggaldier, Edmund.

Animal symbolicum?. Loewenstein, Bedrich.

Approach of Hinduism to Its Scriptures. Nayak, G C.

Aquinas's Doctrine of Moral Virtue and Its Significance for Theories of Facility. Mirkes, Renée.

Architecture: The Confluence of Art, Technology, Politics and Nature. Wood, Robert E.

Are Science and Religion in Conflict?. Watts, Fraser N.

Arianisme mitigé ou apologétique nouvelle?. Lagrée, Jacqueline.

Aristotelische Intellekttheorie und die "Sohnesgeburt" bei Meister Eckehart. Helting, Holger.

As the Waters Cover the Sea: John Wesley on the Problem of Evil. Walls, Jerry L.

Aspiring to the Divine: Love and Grace. Mahoney, Timothy A.

Aufhebung des Religiösen durch Versprachlichung? Eine religionsphilosophische Untersuchung des Rationalitätskonzeptes von Jürgen Habermas. Kühnlein, Michael.

Augustine's Three Visions and Three Heavens in Some Early Medieval Florilegia. Moreira, Isabel.

Augustine's Transformation of the Free Will Defence. Greer, Rowan A.

Augustinian Wisdom and the Law of the Heart. Littlejohn, Murray.

Barth on Evil. Wolterstorff, Nicholas.

Barth on the Divine 'Conscription' of Language. Richards, Jay Wesley.

Beauty and Technology as Paradigms for the Moral Life. Brown, Montague.

Beauty, Providence and the Biophilia Hypothesis. Wynn, Mark.

Belief, Foreknowledge, and Theological Fatalism. Hughes, Charles T.

Believing That God Exists Because the Bible Says So. Lamont, John.

Believing the Word: A Proposal about Knowing Other Persons. Cary, Phillip.

Benedetto Croce e la Storia della Chiesa. Campanelli, Giuseppina.

Berkeley on the Work of the Six Days. Cates, Lynn D.

Between Political Loyalty and Religious Liberty: Political Theory and Toleration in Huguenot Thought in the Epoch of Bayle. Simonutti, Luisa.

Between Religion and Philosophy: Allegorical Interpretation in Derveni Papyrus (in Czech). Laks, André.

Between Religion and Philosophy: The Function of Allegory in the Derveni Papyrus. Laks, André.

Beyond Acceptance and Rejection?. Martin, Dan.

Beyond the Sovereignty of Good. Nelson, Ralph C.

Bioethical Perspectives from Ibero-America. Drane, James F.

Bioethics: A New Interdisciplinary Paradigm in the Relations Between Science and Ethics. Bernard, Brigitte.

Bioetica Laica. Maffettone, Sebastiano.

Bishop Stephen Tempier and Thomas Aquinas: A Separate Process Against Aquinas?. Wippel, John F.

Blondel and Husserl: A Continuation of the Conversation. Hart, James G.

Blondels *Action* von 1893 und Rahners transzendentaler Ansatz im *Grundkurs*—eine unterirdische Wirkungsgeschichte. Knoepffler, Nikolaus.

Bolstering the Argument from Non-Belief. Cosculluela, Victor.

Bonaventure and the Arguments for the Impossibility of an Infinite Temporal Regression. Davis, Richard.

Bread and Wine. Sallis, John.

Buddhism as Radical Religion. Seidel, George J.

Business Ethics in Theory and Practice: Diagnostic Notes B: A Prescription for Profit Maximization. Primeaux, Patrick.

Can God Change His Mind?. Guleserian, Theodore.

Can One be Cognitively Conscious of God?. Baxter, Anthony.

Can Religion Survive the Rationalization? Questions at Habermas's Theory of Culture (in Dutch). Jespers, F P M.

Catholics vs. Calvinists on Religious Knowledge. Greco, John.

César Chávez and La Causa: Toward a Hispanic Christian Social Ethic. Piar, Carlos R.

Christendom en fenomenologie. Bernet, Rudolf.

Christian Identity and Augustine's *Confessions*. Thompson, Christopher J.

Civil Disobedience in the Social Theory of Thomas Aquinas. Scholz, Sally J.

Clearing a 'Way' for Aquinas: How the Proof from Motion Concludes to God. Twetten, David B.

Compassion in Mahayana Buddhism. Da Silva, José Antunes.

Concerning Lev Shestov's Conception of Ethics. Van Goubergen, Martine.

Concurrentism or Occasionalism?. Vallicella, William.

Confession of Sin: A Catharsis!. Kakade, R M.

Contingency of Being—Argument for the Existence of God: Attempt at Critical Analysis Part I (in Polish). Zieminski, Ireneusz.

Conversazione con Cornelio Fabro. Burghi, Giancarlo.

Cosmological Mysticism: The Imitation of the Heavenly Bodies in Ibn Tufayl's *Hayy ibn Yaqzan*. Brague, Rémi.

Creación y salvación, o Naturaleza y redención. Anoz, José (trans) and Bonafede, Giulio.

Created Receptivity and the Philosophy of the Concrete. Schmitz, Kenneth L.

Crisis of Brain and Self. Keyes, C Don.

Critical Notice of J.J. MacIntosh and H.A. Meynell, eds. *Faith, Scepticism and Personal Identity: A Festschrift for Terence Penelhum*. Loptson, Peter J.

Criticism of Religion in Sweden. Hiorth, Finngeir.

Criticismo trascendentale, trascendenza, religione. Jacobelli, Angela Maria Isoldi.

Das philosophieimmanente Theodizeeproblem und seine theologische Radikalisierung. Schmidt, Josef.

Das Problem des Übels in Richard Swinburnes Religionsphilosophie: Über Sinn und Grenzen seines theistischen Antwortversuches auf das Problem des Übels und dessen Bedeutung für die Theologie. Wiertz, Oliver.

De romaneske waarheid bij René Girard. Vanheeswijck, Guido.

De viajes y naufragios: Sobre el Libro de Santiago González Noriega *El Viaje a Siracusa: Ensayos de Filosofia y Teoría Social* Balsa de la Medusa 1994. Villacañas Berlanga, José Luis.

Deification in the *Summa Theologiae*: A Structural Interpretation of the *Prima Pars*. Williams, A N.

Denken in trouw aan leven en geloof. Van Tongeren, Paul.

Descartes' Secular Paradise: The Discourse on Method as Biblical Criticism. Soffer, Walter.

Descripción del fenómeno religioso en la postmodernidad. Barrera Vélez, Julio César.

Desire for Happiness and the Commandments in the First Chapter of *Veritatis Splendor*. Melina, Livio.

Die Vernunft innerhalb der Grenzen des Glaubens: Aspekte der anselmischen Methodologie in werkgenetischer Perspektive. Theis, Robert.

Die 'dunklen Jahre' von Hegels Entwicklung als Aufgabe der Hegelforschung. De Angelis, Marco.

Dieu en vu chez Ortega et María Zambrano. Duque, Félix.

Difference and Consensus. Luksic, Branimir.

Dio parla in modo oscuro? Spunti filosofici e teologici sulle oscurità della Bibbia. Vaccaro, Andrea.

Distinct Ideas and Perfect Solicitude: Alexander of Hales, Richard Rufus, and Odo Rigaldus. Wood, Rega.

Divine Action in a World Chaos: An Evaluation of John Polkinghorne's Model of Special Divine Action. Crain, Steven D.

Divine Intervention. Fales, Evan.

Divine Timelessness and Necessary Existence. Craig, William Lane.

Divinity Must Live Within Herself: Nussbaum and Aquinas on Transcending the Human. McInerny, Daniel.

Do Religious Life and Critical Thought Need Each Other? A Reply to Reinsmith. Carrier, Richard.

Does Religious Faith Mean Uncritical Thought? Exploration of a False Dilemma. Davidson, Bruce.

Dostoyevsky and the Problem of God. Devi, S Sreekala and Narayanadas, V C.

Dualism Intact. Swinburne, Richard.

Duns Scotus on Eternity and Timelessness. Cross, Richard.

Durand et Durandellus sur les rapports de la foi et de la science. Donneaud, Henry.

Ecofeminism: What One Needs to Know. Howell, Nancy R.

El conocimiento de fe en la filosofía de Leonardo Polo. Conesa, Francisco.

El deseo natural de ver a Dios en la *Summa contra Gentiles*. Cambiasso, Guillermo Jorge.

El recurso a la providencia (Un comentario a *Vico: A Study of the New Science* de Leon Pompa). Bocardo Crespo, Enrique.

En quel sens l'*Unique fondement possible d'une démonstration de l'existence de Dieu* de Kant est-il *unique* fondement *possible*?. Theis, Robert.

Epistemological Congruence between Scientific and Theological Logics in Polanyi's Thinking about Ultimate Reality and Meaning. Gaál, Botond.

Ernst Troeltsch: aboutissement ou dépassement du néo-protestantisme?. Gisel, Pierre.

Essentially Contested Concepts. Gallie, W B.

Eternal Knowledge of the Temporal in Aquinas. Shanley, Brian J.

Ethical Considerations in Vedanta—A Scientific Approach. Nayak, G C.

Ethics, Theism and Metaphysics: An Analysis of the Theocentric Ethics of James Gustafson. Meyer, William J.

## RELIGION

## RELIGION

The Order of Charity in Thomas Aquinas. Selner-Wright, Susan C.

The Philosophical Challenge of Technology. Mitcham, Carl.

The Philosophical-Theological Idea of Sophia: The Contemporary Context of Interpretation. Ivanov, A V.

The Philosophy of Barrows Dunham: The Progress of an American Radical. Parsons, Howard L.

The Philosophy of Religion in the System of Freedom. Despot, Blanko.

The Political Philosophy of the New Indian Renaissance. Sachidanand, Achayra John.

The Possibility of Religious Pluralism: A Reply to Gavin D'Costa. Hick, John.

The Post-Canonical Adventures of Mahāsammata. Collins, Steven and Huxley, Andrew.

The Problem of Salvation in Kant's *Religion within the Limits of Reason Alone*. Michalson, Gordon E.

The Problem of Self-Destroying Sin in John Milton's *Samson Agonistes*. Boyd, Ian T E.

The Proofs for the Existence of God: Henry of Ghent and Duns Scotus as Precursors of Leibniz. Latzer, Michael.

The Question of God in an Age of Science: Constructions of Reality and Ultimate Reality in Theology and Science. Case-Winters, Anna.

The Re-Discovery of Ludwig Feuerbach. Harvey, Van A.

The Real and the Rational: Aquinas's Synthesis. Peterson, John.

The Rectitude of Inclination. Ingham, Nicholas.

The Self and the Person as Treated in Some Buddhist Texts [1]. Ishigami-Iagolnitzer, Mitchiko.

The Sirens' Song of the Traditions: A plea for a Universal Ethics (in Dutch). Merks, Karl-Wilhelm.

The Spark of Conscience: Bonaventure's View of Conscience and Synderesis. Langston, Douglas.

The Spirit in John's Gospel: A Hegelian Perspective. Viviano, Benedict T.

The Sublime in Kierkegaard. Milbank, John.

The Sublimity of Evil. Nuyen, A T.

The Suppression of Nuns and the Ritual Murder of their Special Dead in Two Buddhist Monastic Texts. Schopen, Gregory.

The Supreme God in African (Igbo) Religious Thought. Aja, Egbeke.

The Theological Orthodoxy of Berkeley's Immaterialism. Spiegel, James S.

The Three Meanings of Truth in Religion. Mercier, Sean L.

The Three Species of Freedom and the Six Species of Will Acts. Pestana, Mark Stephen.

The Value of Truth and the Care of the Soul. Witherall, Arthur.

The Way, the Truth and the Life: Religious Tradition and Truth in the Postmodern Context... (in Dutch). Boeve, Lieven.

The Word as Ultimate Reality: The Christian Dialogical Personalism of Ferdinand Ebner. Kunszt, György.

Theistic Arguments and the Crisis of Classical Foundationalism (in Dutch). Van Woudenberg, René.

Theological Necessity. Schlesinger, George N.

Theologies of Religion and Theologies of Liberation: A Search for Relationship. Samartha, S J.

Theology and Philosophy (in Serbo-Croatian). Zurovac, Mirko.

Theology and Tense. Chisholm, Roderick M and Zimmerman, Dean W.

Theology as Grammar. Brenner, William H.

Theoretical Virtues and Theological Construction. Shalkowski, Scott A.

Thomism and the Quantum Enigma. Wallace, William A.

Thomistes et antithomistes face à la question de l'infini créé. Solère, Jean-Luc.

Three Comparative Maps of the Human. Samuelson, Norbert M.

Three Types of Critical Thinking about Religion: A Response to William Reinsmith. Weinstein, Jack Russell.

Tolerance and Law in Countries with an Established Church. Papastathis, Charalambos.

Tolerance as Grace and as Right (in Hebrew). Yovel, Yirmiyahu.

Transcendance et manifestation: La place de Dieu dans la philosophie d'Emmanuel Lévinas. Bernier, Jean-François.

Transformaçao da Noçao de Beatitude em Descartes. Leopoldo e Silva, Franklin.

Tres tratados "Sobre el maestro": Agustín, Buenaventura, Tomás de Aquino. Perez Ruiz, Francisco.

Treue zwischen Faszination und Institution. Demmer, Klaus.

Trinity or Tritheism?. Clark, Kelly James.

Trust-Relationships and the Moral Case for Religious Belief. Wynn, Mark.

Truth and History: The Question. Bonsor, Jack.

Truth and Meaning in George Lindbeck's *The Nature of Doctrine*. Richards, Jay Wesley.

Tun und Unterlassen: Ein Beitrag von Dieter Birnbacher zu einem bedeutenden Problem ethischer Handlungstheorie. Zimmermann-Acklin, Markus.

Two Biblical Myths of Creation: An Exploration in Ecological Philosophy. Agera, Cassian R.

Ultimate Reality and Meaning as Portrayed in the Religious Symbolism of Aron Tamási. Muray, Leslie A.

Unamuno e l'esistenzialismo "cristiano". Colonnello, Pio.

Une relecture du paysan de la garonne. Allard, Jean-Louis.

Universal Concerns and Concrete Commitments: In Response to Anderson. Wheeler, David L.

Universalism and the Greater Good: A Response to Talbott. Knight, Gordon.

Van God los? Actuele godsdienstfilosofie in Nederland. Struyker Boudier, C E M.

Von der Religionsphilosophie zur Wissenschaftslehre: Die Religionsbegründung in Paragraph 2 der zweiten Auflage von Fichtes *Versuch einer Kritik aller Offenbarung*. Wittekind, Folkart.

What is Scientism?. Stenmark, Mikael.

What Is the Status of Jiva (Individualised Soul) in the Samkarite Advaita Vedanta?. Dasgupta, Sanghamitra.

What Place does Religion have in the Ethical Thinking of Scientists and Engineers?. Fisher, Ian StJohn.

What's the Difference? Knowledge and Gender in (Post)Modern Philosophy of Religion. Jantzen, Grace M.

When Many Met Mahāsammata. Huxley, Andrew.

Where to Look for Truth: Focusing on the Symposium's Highlights. Vanheeswijck, Guido.

Why God. Mishra, Amarendra.

Why Simple Foreknowledge Offers No More Providential Control than the Openness of God. Sanders, John.

Why Trusting God Differs from All Other Forms of Trust. Sarot, Marcel.

William Alston, *Perceiving God: The Epistemology of Religious Experience*. Steup, Matthias.

William Durant the Younger and Conciliar Theory. Fasolt, Constantin.

William Ellery Channing: Philosopher, Critic of Orthodoxy, and Cautious Reformer. Madden, Edward H.

William James's Theory of Freedom. Gale, Richard M.

William of Auvergne's Adaptation of IBN Gabirol's Doctrine of the Divine Will. Caster, Kevin J.

William of Ockham's Distinction between "Real" Efficient Causes and Strictly *Sine Qua Non* Causes. Goddu, André.

Wisdom's Information: Rereading a Biblical Image in the Light of Some Contemporary Science and Speculation. Nancarrow, Paul S.

Wissenschaftstheorie oder Ästhetik der Wunder?. Gräfrath, Bernd.

World, Emptiness, Nothingness: A Phenomenological Approach to the Religious Tradition of Japan. Held, Klaus.

Yeshayahu Leibowitz—A Breakthrough in Jewish Philosophy: Religion Without Metaphysics. Sagi, Avi.

Yogic Revolution and Tokens of Conservatism in Vyāsa-Yoga. Grinshpon, Yohanan.

Zu den Anfängen des Deismus. Frank, Günter.

Zur Geschichte des ontologischen Gottesbeweises. Kreimendahl, Lothar.

Zur subsistentia absoluta in der Trinitätstheologie. Obenauer, Klaus.

'Between the Brutely Given, and the Brutally, Banally Free' Von Balthasar's Theology of Drama in Dialogue with Hegel. Quash, J B.

'Outsidelessness' and the 'Beyond' of Signification. Griffith-Dickson, Gwen.

## RELIGIOUS EXPERIENCE

"John E. Smith and the Recovery of Religious Experience" in *Reason, Experience, and God: John E. Smith in Dialogue*, Colapietro, Vincent M. Potter, Vincent G.

"William James on Religious Experience" in *The Cambridge Companion to William James*, Putnam, Ruth Anna (ed). Niebuhr, Richard R.

Gale on Reference and Religious Experience. Jeffrey, Andrew V.

La filosofía y el fenómeno religioso. Sierra-Gutiérrez, Francisco (trans) and Lonergan, Bernard J F.

William Alston, *Perceiving God: The Epistemology of Religious Experience*. Steup, Matthias.

## REMEMBERING

Per una ontologia del ricordare. Papi, Fulvio.

## REMINISCENCE

Aristóteles e a teoria da reminiscência. Figueiredo, Maria José.

## RENAISSANCE

"Cassirers Renaissance-Auffassung" in *Grenzen der kritischen Vernunft*, Schmid, Peter A. Schmidt-Biggemann, Wilhelm.

"The Didactic and the Elegant: Some Thoughts on Scientific and Technological Illustrations in the Middle Ages and Renaissance" in *Picturing Knowledge*, Baigrie, Brian S (ed). Hall, Bert S.

*Disputazioni Metafisiche I-III*. Suárez, Francisco and Esposito, Costantino (ed & trans).

*Lex Regia*. Lomonaco, Fabrizio.

Aristóteles en la España del siglo XVI. Antecedentes, alcance y matices de su influencia. Bravo García, Antonio.

Aristóteles en el Renacimiento. Bertelloni, Francisco.

Aspectos generales del pensamiento en el siglo XIV. Verdú Berganza, Ignacio.

Schapiro Style. Holly, Michael Ann.

## RENAN, E

"Between Ernest Renan and Ernst Bloch: Averroës Remembered, Discovered, and Invented. The European Reception Since the Nineteenth Century" in *Averroës and the Enlightenment*, Wahba, Mourad (ed). Wild, Stefan.

## RENOUVIER

William James on Free Will: The French Connection. Viney, Donald Wayne.

## RENUNCIATION

*The Indian Renouncer and Postmodern Poison: A Cross-Cultural Encounter*. Olson, Carl.

## REPRESENTATION

Toch Geen Representaties? Een Reacties op J. Sleutels' Zonnebrandontologie. Buekens, F.

Towards an Epistemology of Social Representations. Marková, Ivana.

## REPRESENTATION

Tractarian Support for a Nonpropositional Paradigm. Bozicevic, Vanda.

Understanding the Representational Mind: A Phenomenological Perspective. Marbach, Eduard.

Wahrnehmung und Mentale Repräsentation. Pauen, Michael.

Weak Deflationism. McGrath, Matthew.

## REPRESENTATIONALISM

Die Sprache des Geistes: Vergleich einer repräsentationalistischen und einer syntaktischen Theorie des Geistes. Saporiti, Katia.

Ten Problems of Consciousness: A Representational Theory of the Phenomenal Mind. Tye, Michael.

La teoría de las ideas de Descartes. Gomila Benejam, Antoni.

Rorty and Davidson. Sullivan, Arthur.

## REPRESSION

Autor y represión. Gracia, Jorge J E.

El disciplinamiento social como factor del desarrollo histórico: Una visión heterodoxa desde el tercer mundo (Primera parte). Mansilla, H C Felipe.

## REPRODUCTION

"Ethical Considerations in the Multiplication of Human Embryos" in Reproduction, Technology, and Rights: Biomedical Ethics Reviews, Humber, James M (ed). Ganss Gibson, Kathleen and Massey, Joe B.

"Moral Philosophy and Public Policy: The Case of New Reproductive Technologies" in Philosophical Perspectives on Bioethics, Sumner, L W (ed). Kymlicka, Will.

"The Morality of Selective Termination" in Reproduction, Technology, and Rights: Biomedical Ethics Reviews, Humber, James M (ed). Glannon, Walter.

Reproduction, Technology, and Rights: Biomedical Ethics Reviews. Humber, James M (ed) and Almeder, Robert F (ed).

The Perfect Baby: A Pragmatic Approach to Genetics. McGee, Glenn.

Approaches Responsive to Reproductive Technologies: A Need for Critical Assessment and Directions for Further Study. Kondratowicz, Diane M.

Aproximaciones a una evaluación de la aplicación de las nuevas tecnologías reproductivas. Digilio, Patricia.

Ethical Reflections on the Status of the Preimplantation Embryo Leading to the German Embryo Protection Act. Michelmann, H W and Hinney, B.

Ethics and the Biology of Reproduction. Harris, David J.

Fear of Reproduction and Desire for Replication in Dracula. Colatrella, Carol.

Feminist Critiques of New Fertility Technologies: Implications for Social Policy. Donchin, Anne.

Fetal Motherhood: Toward a Compulsion to Generate Lives?. Bonnicksen, Andrea L.

Fetal Subjects and Maternal Objects: Reproductive Technology and the New Fetal/Maternal Relation. Squier, Susan.

Human Cloning: A Case of No Harm Done?. Roberts, Melinda A.

Philosophy, Gender Politics, and In Vitro Fertilization: A Feminist Ethics of Reproductive Healthcare. LeMoncheck, Linda.

Products of the Will: Robertson's Children of Choice. Meilaender, Gilbert.

Rebecca Reichmann on Womens' Health and Reproductive Rights in Brazil. Heilig, Steve.

What Can Progress in Reproductive Technology Mean for Women?. Purdy, Laura M.

## REPUBLIC

Hobbes et la mort du Léviathan: opinion, sédition et dissolution. Malherbe, Michel.

Una repubblica mondiale come ideale politico. Höffe, Otfried.

## REPUBLICANISM

Republican Paradoxes and Liberal Anxieties. Terchek, Ronald J.

Antwort auf Bernd Ludwig: Will die Natur unwiderstehlich die Republik?. Brandt, Reinhard.

Are Ethical Conflicts Irreconcilable?. Cooke, Maeve.

Autonomy and Republicanism: Immanuel Kant's Philosophy of Freedom. Bielefeldt, Heiner.

Reason's Practical Idea of Perpetual Peace, Human Character, and the Pedagogical Function of the Republican Constitution. Munzel, G Felicitas.

Republican Theory and Criminal Punishment. Pettit, Philip.

Rights, Citizenship, and the Modern Form of the Social: Dilemmas of Arendtian Republicanism. Cohen, Jean L.

Will die Natur unwiderstehlich die Republik? Einige Reflexionen anlässlich einer rätselhaften Textpassage in Kants Friedensschrift. Ludwig, Bernd.

## REQUIREMENT

A Reply to McDonald: A Defense in Favor of Requirement Conflicts. McKenna, Michael S.

## RESCHER, N

Noch einmal: Rationalität und Normativität. Wüstehube, Axel.

Populismus in der Philosophie: Nicholas Reschers wissenschaftlicher Relativismus. Niemann, Hans-Joachim.

## RESEARCH

"Dal gruppo di ricerca al laboratorio didattico disciplinare" in Momenti di Storia della Logica e di Storia della Filosofia, Guetti, Carla (ed). Ferrari, Franco.

"Ethical Problems of Research Work of Psychologists" in The Idea of University, Brzezinski, Jerzy (ed). Brzezinski, Jerzy.

"Graduate Students: Too Many and Too Narrow?" in The American University: National Treasure or Endangered Species?, Ehrenberg, Ronald G (ed). Fox, Marye Anne.

"Research Universities: Overextended, Underfocused; Overstressed, Underfunded" in The American University: National Treasure or Endangered Species?, Ehrenberg, Ronald G (ed). Vest, Charles M.

"The Personality of Researchers and the Necessity of Schools in Science" in The Idea of University, Brzezinski, Jerzy (ed). Nowak, Leszek.

(Re)Inventing Scheffler, or, Defending Objective Educational Research. Phillips, D C.

Brute Science: Dilemmas of Animal Experimentation. Shanks, Niall and LaFollette, Hugh.

Death, Brain Death and Ethics. Lamb, David.

Feminist Approaches to Bioethics: Theoretical Reflections and Practical Applications. Tong, Rosemarie.

Improving Nature?. Reiss, Michael J and Straughan, Roger.

Metaphysics and the Origin of Species. Ghiselin, Michael T.

Representation and the Text: Re-Framing the Narrative Voice. Tierney, William G (ed) and Lincoln, Yvonna S (ed).

Scientific Method: An Historical and Philosophical Introduction. Gower, Barry S.

A Critical Assessment of Varner's Proposal for Consensus and Convergence in the Biomedical Research Debate. Clune, Alan C.

A Dialogue on Species-Specific Rights: Humans and Animals in Bioethics. Thomasma, David C and Loewy, Erich H.

A Proposal for a New System of Credit Allocation in Science. Resnik, David B.

Advances in Peer Review Research: an Introduction. Stamps III, Arthur E.

Alternative Dispute Resolution and Research Misconduct. Guenin, Louis M.

An Egg Takes Flight: The Once and Future Life of the National Bioethics Advisory Commission. Capron, Alexander M.

An Introduction to Research Ethics. Friedman, Paul J.

An Investigation of the Components of Moral Intensity. Marshall, Bev and Dewe, Philip.

Antinomies of Practice and Research of Group Psychotherapy (in Serbo-Croatian). Opalic, Petar.

Bohr's Theory of the Atom 1913-1923: A Case Study in the Progress of Scientific Research Programmes. Hettema, Hinne.

Case Studies for Teaching Research Ethics. Elliott, Deni.

Collecting "Sensitive" Data in Business Ethics Research: A Case for the Unmatched Count Technique (UCT). Dalton, Dan R, Daily, Catherine M and Wimbush, James C.

Community Equipoise and the Architecture of Clinical Research. Karlawish, Jason H T and Lantos, John.

Competing Interests: The Need to Control Conflict of Interests in Biomedical Research. Steiner, Daniel.

Conducting and Reporting Research. Bird, Stephanie J and Housman, David E.

Conflicts of Interest and Conflicts of Commitment. Werhane, Patricia and Doering, Jeffrey.

Does the Scientific Paper Accurately Mirror the Very Grounds of Scientific Assessment?. Flonta, Mircea.

Effectiveness of Research Guidelines in Prevention of Scientific Misconduct. Shore, Eleanor G.

Embryo Experimentation, Personhood and Human Rights. Van Niekerk, Anton A and Van Zyl, Liezl.

Ethical and Legal Risks Associated with Archival Research. Taube, Daniel O and Burkhardt, Susan.

Ethical Aspects of the Safety of Medicines and Other Social Chemicals. Parke, Dennis V.

Ethical Considerations in the Testing of Biopharmaceuticals for Adventitious Agents. Woodward, Richard S.

Ethical Decision Making About Animal Experiments. Orlans, F Barbara.

Ethical Decision Making in Marketing: A Synthesis and Evaluation of Scales Measuring the Various Components of Decision Making in Ethical Situations. Vitell, Scott J and Ho, Foo Nin.

Ethical Issues in a Study of Internet Use: Uncertainty, Responsibility, and the Spirit of Research Relationships. Bier, Melinda C, Sherblom, Stephen A and Gallo, Michael A.

Ethical Issues in Biomedical Research: Perceptions and Practices of Postdoctoral Research Fellows Responding to a Survey. Eastwood, Susan, Derish, Pamela and Leash, Evangeline (& others).

Ethical Issues in Research on Preventing HIV Infection among Injecting Drug Users. Des Jarlais, Don D, Gaist, Paul A and Friedman, Samuel R.

Ethics and Relationships in Laboratories and Research Communities. Weil, Vivian and Arzbaecher, Robert.

Ethics as a Control System Component. Spier, Raymond.

Ethics Education in Science and Engineering: The Case of Animal Research. Rowan, Andrew N.

Evaluating Outcomes in Ethics Consultation Research. Fox, Ellen and Arnold, Robert M.

Evaluating Teaching and Students' Learning of Academic Research Ethics. Elliott, Deni.

Evaluation Research and the Future of Ethics Consultation. Fox, Ellen and Tulsky, James A.

## RESOURCE

A Just Share: Justice and Fairness in Resource Allocation. McCarrick, Pat Milmoe and Darragh, Martina.

## RESOURCE

Allocating Healthcare By QALYs: The Relevance of Age. McKie, John, Kuhse, Helga and Richardson, Jeff.

Ethics Committees and Resource Allocation. Lantos, John D.

Reconsidering Zero-Sum Value: It's How You Play the Game. Smith, Tara.

Reformulating Equality of Resources. Arnsperger, Christian.

## RESPECT

*see also* Self-Respect

"National Identity and Respect among Nations" in *The Morality of Nationalism,* McKim, Robert (ed). McKim, Robert.

"Respect for Humanity" in *The Tanner Lectures on Human Values, Volume 18, 1997,* Peterson, Grethe B (ed). Hill Jr, Thomas E.

*Rational Choice and Moral Agency.* Schmidtz, David.

*Utilitarianism.* Scarre, Geoffrey.

Asymmetrical Reciprocity: On Moral Respect, Wonder, and Enlarged Thought. Young, Iris Marion.

Integrity and Disrespect (and J. Velek Commentary) (in Czech). Honneth, Axel and Velek, Josef.

Mutual Respect and Neutral Justification. Bird, Colin.

## RESPONSE

Reasoning about Knowledge: A Response by the Authors. Fagin, Ronald, Halpern, Joseph Y and Moses, Yoram (& others).

## RESPONSIBILITY

"Epistemic Responsibility and the Inuit of Canada's Eastern Arctic: An Ecofeminist Appraisal" in *Ecofeminism: Women, Culture, Nature,* Warren, Karen J (ed). Buege, Douglas J.

"Indirect Action, Influence and Responsibility" in *Deontic Logic, Agency and Normative Systems,* Brown, Mark A (ed). Santos, Filipe and Carmo, José.

"Journalistische Verantwortung: Medienethik als Qualitätsproblem" in *Angewandte Ethik: Die Bereichsethiken und ihre theoretische Fundierung,* Nida-Rümelin, Julian (ed). Teichert, Will.

"Wissenschaftsethik" in *Angewandte Ethik: Die Bereichsethiken und ihre theoretische Fundierung,* Nida-Rümelin, Julian (ed). Nida-Rümelin, Julian.

*Alciphron oder der Kleine Philosoph.* Berkeley, George.

*Justice as Fittingness.* Cupit, Geoffrey.

*Martin Heidegger und Hans Jonas: Die Metaphysik der Subjektivität und die Krise der technologischen Zivilisation.* Jakob, Eric.

*Rational Choice and Moral Agency.* Schmidtz, David.

*The Significance of Free Will.* Kane, Robert.

A Resource-Based-View of the Socially Responsible Firm: Stakeholder Interdependence, Ethical Awareness, and Issue Responsiveness as Strategic Assets. Litz, Reginald A.

Aquinas on Passions and Diminished Responsibility. Nisters, Thomas.

Ascriptions of Responsibility. Oshana, Marina A L.

Bringing Ancient Philosophy of Life: Teaching Aristotelian and Stoic Theories of Responsibility. Sakezles, Priscilla K.

Catholic Social Ethics in a Pluralist Age. Chmielewski, Philip J.

Cognitive and Moral Obstacles to Imputation. Murphy, Jeffrie G.

Commentary on "Psychopathy, Other-Regarding Moral Beliefs, and Responsibility". Radden, Jennifer.

Commentary on "Sanity and Irresponsibility". Fields, Lloyd.

Commentary on "The Social Responsibilities of Biological Scientists. Salzberg, Aaron A.

Commentary on "The Social Responsibilities of Biological Scientists". Beckwith, Jonathan R and Geller, Lisa N.

Criminal Responsibility. Elliot, Carl.

Criteria for Evaluating the Legitimacy of Corporate Social Responsibility. Pava, Moses L and Krausz, Joshua.

Cultural Context and Moral Responsibility. Isaacs, Tracy.

Deviant Uses of "Obligation" in Hobbes' *Leviathan.* Murphy, Mark C.

Die Zurechnung im Strafrecht eines entwickelten sozialen und demokratischen Rechtsstaates. Mir Puig, Santiago.

Direct and Indirect Responsibility: Distributing Blame. Goodnow, Jacqueline J and Warton, Pamela M.

Eine Explikation des Begriffes der Zurechnung. Meixner, Uwe.

Emotions and Morality. Ben-Ze'ev, Aaron.

Environmental Responsibility: Individual Choice, Communication, Institutional Risks (in Czech). Susa, Oleg.

Error in persona vel objecto und aberratio ictus. Toepel, Friedrich.

Ethical Issues in a Study of Internet Use: Uncertainty, Responsibility, and the Spirit of Research Relationships. Bier, Melinda C, Sherblom, Stephen A and Gallo, Michael A.

Ethics and Relationships in Laboratories and Research Communities. Weil, Vivian and Arzbaecher, Robert.

Ethics, Standards, Diversity: Dimensions of the Social Construction of Responsibility. Mitcham, Carl.

Evading Responsibility: The Ethics of Ingenuity. Katz, Leo.

Expressions of Corporate Social Responsibility in U.K. Firms. Robertson, Diana C and Nicholson, Nigel.

Filial Responsibility and the Care of the Aged. Collingridge, Michael and Miller, Seumas.

Fischer on Moral Responsibility. Van Inwagen, Peter.

Foucault's Alimentary Philosophy: Care of the Self and Responsibility for the Other. Boothroyd, David.

Four Naturalist Accounts of Moral Responsibility. Double, Richard.

Geographies of Responsibility. Walker, Margaret.

Global Responsibility and Active Ethical Advocacy (No Apology for Academic Activism). Shrader-Frechette, Kristin.

Helping Professionals in Business Behave Ethically: Why Business Cannot Abdicate Its Responsibility to the Profession. Cooper, Robert W and Frank, Garry L.

Here I Am! Kierkegaard and Levinas: The Tensions of Responsibility (in French). Janiaud, Joël.

In Search of a Common Ethical Ground: Corporate Environmental Responsibility from the Perspective of Christian Environmental Stewardship. Enderle, Georges.

Individual Scapetribing and Responsibility Ascriptions. Bailey, Jeffrey.

Individuals Bear Responsibility. Potter, Van Rensselaer.

Individuelle Zurechnung im demokratischen Verfassungsstaat. Günther, Klaus.

Just Do It: Deniability and Renegades. Brimlow, Robert W.

Kant on Responsibility for Consequences. Hill Jr, Thomas E.

La crisi del sapere moderno. Alheit, Peter.

La cuestión de la "caída" de los fundamentos y la ética: Hacia una mayor "responsabilidad" como respuesta al presente. Cragnolini, Mónica B.

La ética de los negocios. Ramírez B, Edgar Roy.

La ética del discurso como ética de la corresponsabilidad por las actividades colectivas. Apel, Karl-Otto.

Listening or Telling? Thoughts on Responsibility in Clinical Ethics Consultation. Zaner, Richard M.

Moral Prejudices: Essays on Ethics. Held, Virginia.

Moral Responsibility and Ignorance. Zimmerman, Michael J.

Moral Responsibility and Leeway for Action. Wyma, Keith D.

Moral Responsibility and the Problem of Induced Pro-Attitudes. Haji, Ishtiyaque.

On Disassociating Oneself from Collective Responsibility. Räikkä, Juha.

On the Acceptability of Biopharmaceuticals. Spier, Raymond.

On the Main Articles in this Issue. Horák, Petr.

On the Problem of Collective Guilt (In Czech). Sousedík, Stanislav.

Opening Words. Niiniluoto, Ilkka.

Personal Ideals in Professional Ethics. Martin, Mike W.

Plagiarism and Reviewer/Editor Responsibility. Riggan, William.

Praktik: Überlegungen zu Fragen der Handlungstheorie. Angstl, Helmut.

Presidential Address: Bioethics and Social Responsibility. Wikler, Daniel.

Problems in developing a Practical Theory of Moral Responsibility. Anderson, Susan Leigh.

Procreation and Parental Responsibility. Blustein, Jeffrey.

Psychopathy, Other-Regarding Moral Beliefs, and Responsibility. Fields, Lloyd.

Rationality and Responsibility in Heidegger's and Husserl's View of Technology. Buckley, R Philip.

Reaching for the "Low Hanging Fruit": The Pressure for Results in Scientific Research—A Graduate Student's Perspective. Browning, Tyson R.

Realizability as Constituent Element of the Justification Structure of the Public Decision. Cuñarro Conde, Edith Mabel.

Researchers as Professionals, Professionals as Researchers: A Context for Laboratory Research Ethics. Elliott, Deni.

Response to the Commentaries. Fields, Lloyd.

Responsibility and Social Traps. Lenk, Hans and Maring, Matthias.

Responsible Technoscience: The Haunting Reality of Auschwitz and Hiroshima. Sassower, Raphael.

Rights and Responsibilities: Aristotle's Virtues and a Libertarian Dilemma. Cox, L Hughes.

Sanity and Irresponsibility. Wilson, Paul Eddy.

Sensitivity and Responsibility for Consequences. Glannon, Walter.

Sexuality, Politics and "Taking Responsibilty": On a Continuum. Eberhard, Julaine.

Sources of Error and Accountability in Computer Systems: Comments on "Accountability in a Computerized Society". Szolovits, Peter.

Strategies for Free Will Compatibilists. O'Leary-Hawthorne, John and Petit, Philip.

Sujeito e ética. Herrero, F Javier.

Teaching the Three Rs: Rights, Roles and Responsibilities—A Curriculum for Pediatric Patient Rights. Davis, Kathleen G.

Technology in Opposition Power—Must (Czech). Lenk, Hans and Maring, Matthias.

The Institutional Context for Research. Berger, Edward M and Gert, Bernard.

The Perceived Role of Ethics and Social Responsibility: A Scale Development. Singhapakdi, Anusorn, Vitell, Scott J and Rallapalli, Kumar C.

The Proactive Corporation: Its Nature and Causes. Shepard, Jon M, Betz, Michael and O'Connell, Lenahan.

The Social Responsibilities of Biological Scientists. Reiser, Stanley Joel and Bulger, Ruth Ellen.

The Special Political Responsibilities of African Philosophers. Imbo, Samuel Oluoch.

The Teaching of Ethics. Doorley, Mark J.

## ROMAN

*Ancient Philosophy, 2nd Edition*. Baird, Forrest E (ed) and Kaufmann, Walter.

*Thelema*: Hipólito de Roma y la filosofía del siglo II. Forteza Pujol, Bartomeu.

An Interpretation of Plutarch's *Cato the Younger*. Frost, Bryan-Paul.

Courts and Conversions: Intellectual Battles and Natural Knowledge in Counter-Reformation Rome. De Renzi, Silvia.

Le stoïcisme ou la conscience de Rome. Jerphagnon, Lucien.

Spenser and the Historical Revolution: *Briton Moniments* and the *Problem of Roman Britain*. Curran Jr, John E.

## ROMAN CATHOLICISM

*see* Catholicism

## ROMANCE

Panlogismo, Pantagrismo, e o *Saber Mais* do Romance—Uma Leitura de *Mudança* de Vergílio Ferreira. Mourao, Luís.

Romantic Love and Sexual Desire. Ben-Ze'ev, Aaron.

The Future of Romantic Love. White, Richard J.

## ROMANIAN

A Romanian Myth—Life as a Permanent Miracle. Albu, Mihaela.

## ROMANTICISM

"Alle Wahrheit ist relativ, alles wissen symbolisch". Frank, Manfred.

"Romantic Conceptions of the Self in Hölderlin and Novalis" in *Figuring the Self: Subject, Absolute, and Others in Classical German Philosophy*, Zöller, Günter (ed). Kneller, Jane E.

*A Comprehensive History of Western Ethics: What Do We Believe?*. Ashby, W Allen (ed) and Ashby, Warren.

*From Romanticism to Critical Theory: The Philosophy of German Literary Theory*. Bowie, Andrew.

*Wuthering Heights*: The Romantic Ascent. Nussbaum, Martha C.

Acerca del Pensador Profesional de Schumacher. Meléndez, Germán.

Brahms-Bruckner: deux univers en dissonance. Moutsopoulos, Evanghélos.

Das *kleine Buch* und das *laute* Weltereignis: Fichtes *Wissenschaftslehre* als Paradigma und Problem der *Romantik*. Schanze, Helmut.

Das Schweben der Einbildungskraft: Eine frühromantische Metapher in Rücksicht auf Fichte. Hühn, Lore.

Der Klagenfurter Herbert-Kreis zwischen Aufklärung und Romantik. Baum, Wilhelm.

Filosofia o letteratura? Mandeville, Fielding e il contesto settecentesco. Branchi, Andrea.

Frühromantische Subjektkritik. Iber, Christian.

Hegel's Critique of Solger: The Problem of Scientific Communication (in French). Reid, Jeffrey.

John McDowell's *Mind and World* and Early Romantic Epistemology. Bowie, Andrew.

L'esthétique et l'artistique. Rochlitz, Rainer.

L'ethos dell'intersoggettività nei romanzi di Friedrich Heinrich Jacobi. Iovino, Serenella.

L'ultimo dei porcospini: Intervista biografico-teorica a René Girard. Antonello, Pierpaolo (ed) and De Castro Rocha, Joao Cezar (ed).

Les fondements philosophiques du premier romantisme allemand. Frank, Manfred.

Michelet and Social Romanticism: Religion, Revolution, Nature. Mitzman, Arthur.

Nietzsche as Mashed Romantic. Picart, Caroline Joan S.

Perspektiven der Welt: Vielfalt und Einheit im Weltbild der Deutschen Romantik. Köchy, Kristian.

Reflections on Russia's Destiny in the Philosophical Work of Russian Romanticism. Abramov, A I.

Religión entre Ilustración y Romanticismo. Ortiz-Osés, Andrés.

Romantic Love and Loving Commitment: Articulating a Modern Ideal. Delaney, Neil.

Romanticism Revisited. Hammer, Espen.

Romanticized Enlightenment? Enlightened Romanticism? Universalism and Particularism in Hegel's *Understanding of the Enlightenment*. Pinkard, Terry.

Romanticizing Rock Music. Gracyk, Theodore A.

Sociología y tipología del fenómeno religioso. Piñon G, Francisco.

Un-European Desires: Toward a Provincialism without Romanticism. Visker, Rudi.

Una Crítica "Romántica" al Romanticismo. Díaz, Jorge Aurelio.

## RORTY, R

"Deconstruction, Pragmatism and the Politics of Democracy" in *Deconstruction and Pragmatism*, Mouffe, Chantal (ed). Mouffe, Chantal.

"Pragmatist Holism as an Expression of Another 'Disenchantment of the World'" in *Epistemology and History*, Zeidler-Janiszewska, Anna (ed). Palubicka, Anna.

"Remarks on Deconstruction and Pragmatism" in *Deconstruction and Pragmatism*, Mouffe, Chantal (ed). Derrida, Jacques.

"Singular Interruptions: Rortian Liberalism and the Ethics of Deconstruction" in *Knowing Other-Wise: Philosophy at the Threshold of Spirituality*, Olthuis, James H (ed). Kuipers, Ronald A.

"The Paradoxes of Education in Rorty's Liberal Utopia" in *Philosophy of Education (1996)*, Margonis, Frank (ed). Reich, Rob.

"The Perception of Science in Modernist and Postmodernist Artistic Practice" in *Epistemology and History*, Zeidler-Janiszewska, Anna (ed). Erjavec, Ales.

"Utopia Flawed? A Response to Reich on Rorty" in *Philosophy of Education (1996)*, Margonis, Frank (ed). Pendlebury, Shirley.

*Cervello-Mente: Pensatori del XX secolo*. Gava, Giacomo.

*Davidson's Theory of Truth and Its Implications for Rorty's Pragmatism*. Letson, Ben H.

*Debating the State of Philosophy: Habermas, Rorty, and Kolakowski*. Niznik, Jozef (ed) and Sanders, John T (ed).

*The Two Pragmatisms: From Peirce to Rorty*. Mounce, H O.

Bête Noire of the Science Worshipers. Gross, Paul R.

Beyond Ironist Theory and Private Fantasy: A Critique of Rorty's Derrida. Ellsworth, Jonathan.

Debating Critical Theory. Hoy, David Couzens.

Deconstruction and Pragmatism—Is Derrida a Private Ironist or a Public Liberal?. Critchley, Simon.

Interview with Richard Rorty. Kuehn, Glenn, Siliceo-Roman, Laura and Salyards, Jane.

Kant e l'epistemologia contemporanea. Castagni, Laura.

La revisión neohistoricista del significado de la historia de la filosofía. Vegas González, Serafín.

Mystics and Pragmatics in the Non-Philosophy of F. Laruelle: Lessons for Rorty's Metaphilosophizing. Sumares, Manuel.

Ontology according to Van Fraassen: Some Problems with Constructive Empiricism. Norris, Christopher.

Philosophy and Critical Theory: A Reply to Richard Rorty and Seyla Benhabib. McCarthy, Thomas A.

Pragmatismus, Dekonstruktion, ironischer Eklektizismus: Richard Rortys Heidegger-Lektüre. Burkhard, Philipp.

Realism and Anti-Realism: A Whiteheadian Response to Richard Rorty Concerning Truth, Propositions, and Practice. Nancarrow, Paul S.

Replies. Brandom, Robert.

Richard Rorty and the "Tricoteuses". Amorós, Celia.

Richard Rorty and the Problem of Cruelty. Haliburton, Rachel.

Rorty and Davidson. Sullivan, Arthur.

Rorty's History of Philosophy as Story of Progress. Easton, Patricia.

Rorty, Ironist Theory, and Socio-Political Control. Depp, Dane.

Self-Enlargement or Purification? On the Meaning of the Fragmentary Subject in René Girard's Early Writings (in Dutch). Vanheeswijck, Guido.

Still Unnatural: A Reply to Vogel and Rorty. Williams, Michael.

The Irony of Ironic Liberalism. Young, Phillips E.

Theoria and the Priority of the Practical (in Dutch). Sie, Maureen.

Truth and Metaphor in Rorty's Liberalism. Hymers, Michael.

Truth vs Rorty. Steinhoff, Uwe.

We Pragmatists...; Peirce and Rorty in Conversation. Haack, Susan.

## ROSALES, A

Filosofía Trascendental Mundaneizada. Heymann, Ezra.

## ROSAS, A

Poder Pensar y "Poder Querer": Acerca de Moral y Prudencia en Kant. Parra, Lisímaco.

## ROSATI, C

Sidgwick's False Friends. Shaver, Robert.

## ROSCHER, W

"Religione e storia in Wilhelm Roscher" in *Lo Storicismo e la Sua Storia: Temi, Problemi, Prospettive*, Cacciatore, Giuseppe (ed). Catarzi, Marcello.

## ROSEN, G

Replies. Brandom, Robert.

## ROSENBERG, A

Fitness Made Physical: The Supervenience of Biological Concepts Revisited. Weber, Marcel.

Random Drift and the Omniscient Viewpoint. Millstein, Roberta L.

Some Comments on Rosenberg's Review. Sober, Elliott.

Theoretical Modeling and Biological Laws. Cooper, Gregory.

## ROSENBERG, J

Replies. Brandom, Robert.

## ROSENZWEIG, F

"Immagini della Grecia: Rosenzweig e Burckhardt" in *Lo Storicismo e la Sua Storia: Temi, Problemi, Prospettive*, Cacciatore, Giuseppe (ed). D'Antuono, Emilia.

"L'europeizzazione come probleme europeo" in *Geofilosofia*, Bonesio, Luisa (ed). Pöggler, Otto.

*Jüdischer Nietzscheanismus*. Stegmaier, Werner and Krochmalnik, Daniel.

Empiricism and Transcendentalism: Franz Rosenzweig and Emmanuel Levinas (in Dutch). Anckaert, Luc.

## ROSETH, R

Roger Roseth and Medieval Deontic Logic. Knuuttila, Simo and Hallamaa, Olli.

## ROSMINI, A

Antonio Rosmini: Aristotele Esposto ed Esaminato. Masi, Giuiseppe.

Essere e idea. Tagliavia, Grazia.

La critica rosminiana alla cosmologia di Aristotele. Messina, Gaetano.

Rosmini y Vico: la "filosofía italiana". Ottonello, Pier Paolo.

## SCHELLING

"Más allá de "El nacimiento de la clínica": La comprensión de la "Anatomía General" de Bichat desde la *Naturphilosophie* de Schelling" in *El inicio del Idealismo alemán,* Market, Oswaldo. Montiel, Luis.

"Ontología y filosofía transcendental en el primer Schelling" in *El inicio del Idealismo alemán,* Market, Oswaldo. Serrano, Vicente.

"Perspectivas sobre religión y filosofía en los inicios del Idealismo alemán: Fichte y Schelling antes de 1794" in *El inicio del Idealismo alemán,* Market, Oswaldo. De Torres, María José.

*Der Deutsche Idealismus (Fichte, Schelling, Hegel) und die philosophische Problemlage der Gegenwart.* Heidegger, Martin.

*Die Begründung einer Naturphilosophie bei Kant, Schelling, Fries und Hegel.* Bonsiepen, Wolfgang.

*El inicio del Idealismo alemán.* Market, Oswaldo and Rivera de Rosales, Jacinto.

*Mathematische und naturwissenschaftliche Modelle in der Philosophie Schellings und Hegels.* Ziche, Paul.

*Schelling und Nietzsche: Zur Auslegung der frühen Werke Friedrich Nietzsches.* Wilson, John Elbert.

*The God Within: Kant, Schelling, and Historicity.* Burbidge, John W (ed) and Fackenheim, Emil L.

Aestheticide: Architecture and the Death of Art. Bearn, Gordon C F.

Das Problem der Natur: Nähe und Differenz Fichtes und Schellings. Schmied-Kowarzik, Wolfdietrich.

Die Duplizität des Absoluten in der Wissenschaftslehre von 1804 (zweiter Vortrag)—Fichtes Auseinandersetzung mit Schellings identitätsphilosophischer Schrift *Darstellung meines Systems* (1801). Danz, Christian.

Die Fichte-Lektüre des jungen Herbart (1796-1798). Langewand, Alfred.

La "Freiheitsschrift" del 1809 come momento decisivo tra la filosofia dell'identità e il rilievo dell'esistenza nel pensiero di Schelling. Millucci, Marco.

Las Agendas de Schelling. Galcerán Huguet, Montserrat.

Man kannte mich, als man mich rufte: Die Berufung des Magister Fichte an die Gesamt-Akademie Jena im Jahre 1794. Vieweg, Klaus.

Nouveautés Schellingiennes. Tilliette, Xavier.

Nouvelles réponses à Nunzio Incardona. Tilliette, Xavier.

O Mais Antigo Programa de Sistema do Idealismo Alemao. Carmo Ferreira, Manuel J do.

Originality and Its Origin in Modern Aesthetics (in Japanese). Otabe, Tanehisa.

Schellings Identitätssystem von 1801 und Fichtes Wissenschaftslehre. Hennigfeld, Jochem.

Schellings Metapher *Blitz*—eine Huldigung an die Wissenschaftslehre. Ehrhardt, Walter E.

The God and a Man-Philosopher: Vocation for Philosophy on the Basis of F.W.I. Schelling's Anthropotheology (in Polish). Kolas, Pawel.

Transzendentale Lebenslehre: Zur Königsberger Wissenschaftslehre 1807. Ivaldo, Marco.

## SCHEMAN, N

Reply to Louise Antony. Scheman, Naomi.

## SCHEMATISM

Die Einbildungskraft und das Schematismusproblem. Köhler, Dietmar.

## SCHEME

On the Right Idea of a Conceptual Scheme. Case, Jennifer.

The Converse Principal Type-Scheme Theorem in Lambda Calculus. Hirokawa, Sachio.

## SCHIFFER, S

Conditions on Understanding Language. Lepore, Ernest.

Doubting Castel or the Slough of Despond: Davidson and Schiffer on the Limits of Analysis. Norris, Christopher.

What do Belief Ascribers Really Mean? A Reply to Stephen Schiffer. Reimer, Marga.

## SCHILLER

"How Is It, Then, That we Still Remain Barbarians?" Foucault, Schiller, and the Aestheticization of Ethics. Bennett, Jane.

Aneinnander vorbei: Zum Horenstreit zwischen Fichte und Schiller. Wildenburg, Dorothea.

From Aesthetic Education to Environmental Aesthetics. Fischer, Norman.

Hegels Manuskripte aus der Berner Zeit: Kant—Rousseau—Herder—Schiller. Sobotka, Milan.

Wechselbestimmung: Zum Verhältnis von Hölderlin, Schiller und Fichte in Jena. Waibel, Violetta.

## SCHLEGEL

"August Wilhelm Schlegel y sus lecciones de Jena sobre teoría del arte (1798)" in *El inicio del Idealismo alemán,* Market, Oswaldo. Pinilla Burgos, Ricardo.

Das *kleine Buch* und das *laute* Weltereignis: Fichtes *Wissenschaftslehre* als Paradigma und Problem der *Romantik*. Schanze, Helmut.

Das Schweben der Einbildungskraft: Eine frühromantische Metapher in Rücksicht auf Fichte. Hühn, Lore.

Fichte, Schlegel, Nietzsche und die Moderne. Stein, Klaus.

Friedrich Schlegel's Theory of an Alternating Principle Prior to His Arrival in Jena (6 August 1796). Behler, Ernst.

Frühromantische Subjektkritik. Iber, Christian.

Wechselgrundsatz: Friedrich Schlegels philosophischer Ausgangspunkt. Frank, Manfred.

Zur Geschichte der romantischen Ästhetik: Von Fichtes Transzendental-philosophie zu Schlegels Transzendentalpoesie. Radrizzani, Ives.

## SCHLEIERMACHER

"Appropriating Selfhood: Schleiermacher and Hegel on Subjectivity as Mediated Activity" in *Figuring the Self: Subject, Absolute, and Others in Classical German Philosophy,* Zöller, Günter (ed). Hoover, Jeffrey L.

"Autocoscienza e rivelazione: Solger e Schleiermacher di fronte alla storia" in *Lo Storicismo e la Sua Storia: Temi, Problemi, Prospettive,* Cacciatore, Giuseppe (ed). Pinto, Valeria.

"El mundo como imagen: Acerca de Fichte y Schleiermacher" in *El inicio del Idealismo alemán,* Market, Oswaldo. Flamarique, Lourdes.

"Etica e storia in Schleiermacher" in *Lo Storicismo e la Sua Storia: Temi, Problemi, Prospettive,* Cacciatore, Giuseppe (ed). Moretto, Giovanni.

"Schleiermacher on the Self: Immediate Self-Consciousness as Feeling and as Thinking" in *Figuring the Self: Subject, Absolute, and Others in Classical German Philosophy,* Zöller, Günter (ed). Klemm, David E.

"Three Major Originators of the Concept of *Verstehen*: Vico, Herder, Schleiermacher" in *Verstehen and Humane Understanding,* O'Hear, Anthony (ed). Hausheer, Roger.

*The Living God: Schleiermacher's Theological Appropriation of Spinoza.* Lamm, Julia A.

A Critical Examination of Schleiermacher's Interpretation of Self-Consciousness. Lang'at, Wilson K A.

Die Wissenschaftslehre: Die Auseinandersetzung Schleiermachers mit Fichte. Potepa, Maciej.

Schleiermacher on Evil. Adams, Robert Merrihew.

Schleiermacher's Idea of Hermeneutics and the Feeling of Absolute Dependence. Vedder, Ben.

Schleiermacher: edizione critica e bibliografia. Moretto, Giovanni.

The Father of Modern Hermeneutics in a Postmodern Age: A Reinterpretation of Schleiermacher's Hermeneutics. Huang, Yong.

Un problème d'appropriation: Schleiermacher entre Gadamer et Todorov. Fitch, Brian T.

## SCHLESINGER, G

A Purported Theorem of Epistemic Logic. Blum, Alex.

## SCHLICK

"Conceptual Knowledge and Intuitive Experience: Schlick's Dilemma" in *Origins of Logical Empiricism,* Giere, Ronald N (ed). Turner, Joia Lewis.

Anti-Foundationalism and the Vienna Circle's Revolution in Philosophy. Uebel, Thomas E.

Schlick, Altruism and Psychological Hedonism. Ablondi, Fred.

## SCHLOSSBERGER, E

Commentary on "Technology and Civil Disobedience: Why Engineers Have a Special Duty to Obey the Law". Boisjoly, Roger M.

## SCHMIDT, C

Who Benefits from the National Standards: A Response to Catherine M. Schmidt's "Who Benefits? Music Education and the National Standards.". Lehman, Paul R.

## SCHMITT, C

Aristóteles en el Renacimiento. Bertelloni, Francisco.

Carl Schmitt und die Philosophie. Kiel, Albrecht.

Carl Schmitt: An Occasional Nationalist?. Müller, Jan.

Friend or Enemy?: Reading Schmitt Politically. Neocleous, Mark.

From Immanent Natures to Nature as Artifice: The Reinterpretation of Final Causes in Seventeenth-Century Natural Philosophy. Osler, Margaret J.

Some Remarks on Carl Schmitt's Notion of "Exception". Dotti, Jorge E.

Taking Exception to Liberalism: Heinrich Meier's *Carl Schmitt and Leo Strauss: The Hidden Dialogue*. Vatter, Miguel E.

## SCHMITZ, K

Reply. Long, Steven A.

## SCHNAEDELBACH, H

Noch einmal: Rationalität und Normativität. Wüstehube, Axel.

Stufen der Rechtfertigung. Ulfig, Alexander.

## SCHNEEWIND, J

On Schneewind and Kant's Method in Ethics (in Spanish). Ameriks, Karl.

## SCHOCHET, G

Varieties of Political Thought. Hampsher-Monk, Iain.

## SCHOEMAN, F

Intimacy and Parental Authority in the Philosophy of Ferdinand Schoeman. Klepper, Howard.

Moral Responsibility and the Problem of Induced Pro-Attitudes. Haji, Ishtiyaque.

## SCHOEN, T

Ted Schoen on "The Methodological Isolation of Religious Belief". Ferré, Frederick.

## SCHOENBERG, A

"The Philosophy of Dissonance: Adorno and Schoenberg" in *The Semblance of Subjectivity,* Huhn, Tom (ed). Hullot-Kentor, Robert.

Bemerkungen zur musikalischen Künstlerästhetik des 20.Jahrhunderts. Von Thülen, Bodil.

## SCHOLARSHIP

"The Commonwealth of Scholars and New Conceptions of Truth" in *The Idea of University,* Brzezinski, Jerzy (ed). Topolski, Jerzy.

Academic Feminism and Applied Ethics: Closing the Gap between Private Scholarship and Public Policy. LeMoncheck, Linda.

## SCHOLARSHIP

Charting the Currents of the Third Wave. Orr, Catherine M.

Form and Substance in Criminal Justice Scholarship: H. Richard Uviller, *Virtual Justice*. Dripps, Donald A.

Of Heapers, Splitters and Academic Woodpiles in the Study of Intense Religious Experiences. Forman, Robert K C.

Private Scholars—Public Intellectuals: Can These Be Separated?. Godway, Eleanor M.

Strobos—On Issues of Origins, Development and Phenomenology in Some Areas of Science and Scholarship. Rif, Alan.

Who Speaks and Who Replies in Human Science Scholarship?. Gergen, Kenneth.

## SCHOLASTICISM

*see also* Thomism

Between Transcendental and Transcendental: The Missing Link?. Doyle, John P.

Lógica filosófica medieval: San Anselmo y Guillermo de Occam. Trueba Atienza, Carmen.

## SCHOOL

*see also* High School

"Opening the Closet Door: Sexualities Education and "Active Ignorance" in *Philosophy of Education (1996)*, Margonis, Frank (ed). Ford, Maureen.

"Performance Anxiety: Sexuality and School Controversy" in *Philosophy of Education (1996)*, Margonis, Frank (ed). Mayo, Cris.

*Ethics for Professionals in Education: Perspectives for Preparation and Practice*. Strike, Kenneth A (ed) and Ternasky, P Lance (ed).

*Ethics in School Counseling*. Schulte, John M and Cochrane, Donald B.

A Organizaçao do Trabalho Escolar e os Especialistas da Educaçao. Pizzi, Laura Cristina V.

Accommodating Ideological Pluralism in Sexuality Education. McKay, Alexander.

Character Education: Reclaiming the Social. Duncan, Barbara J.

Cheating: Limits of Individual Integrity. Johnston, D Kay.

Confronting the Assumptions That Dominate Education Reform. Robenstine, Clark.

Content and Criticism: The Aims of Schooling. Hare, William.

Counterpoint Thinking: Connecting Learning and Thinking in Schools. Melchior, Timothy.

Daughters of a Better Age. Lim, Tock Keng.

Differences in Moral Reasoning Between College and University Business Majors and Non-Business Majors. Snodgrass, James and Behling, Robert.

Diversity, Values and Social Change: Renegotiating a Consensus on Sex Education. Thomson, Rachel.

Educational Reform: A Complex Matter. Reynolds, Sherrie and Martin, Kathleen.

European Children Thinking Together in 100. Heesen, Berrie.

Fostering Market Competence. Askland, Andrew.

Generality and Equality. Schauer, Frederick.

How Should Schools Respond to the Plurality of Values in a Multi-Cultural Society?. Burwood, Les R V.

Literary Development as Spiritual Development in the Common School. Newby, Mike.

Mass Media and Critical Thinking: Reasoning for a Second-Hand World. Dorman, William.

On the Education of Generalists: Religion, Public Schools, and Teacher Education. Summers, Landon.

Restructuring of Social and Political Theory in Education: Foucault and a Social Epistemology of School Practices. Popkewitz, Thomas S and Brennan, Marie.

Sex Education as Moral Education: Teaching for Pleasure, about Fantasy, and against Abuse. Lamb, Sharon.

Subsídios para uma Análise da Política da Educaçao Escolar Brasileira. Donatoni, Alaíde Rita and Cândida P Coelho, Maria.

The Great Sphere: Education Against Servility. Callan, Eamonn.

The Issue of Music in Schools: An *Unfinished Symphony*?. Carlin, Joi L.

The Need for Comprehensiveness in Critical Thinking Instruction. Nosich, Gerald.

The Qualitymongers. Hart, W A.

The Value(s) of Sex Education. Reiss, Michael J.

To Be or Not to Be: Charles Taylor and the Politics of Recognition. Nicholson, Linda.

Towards a Whole School or College Policy for a Pre-Philosophical and Higher Order Thinking 'Entitlement' Curriculum. Thornbury, Robert.

Virtuous Markets: The Market as School of the Virtues. Maitland, Ian.

Voices in the Classroom: Girls and Philosophy for Children. Mohr-Lane, Jana.

## SCHOPENHAUER

*Ästhetische Autonomie als Abnormalität: Kritische Analysen zu Schopenhauers Ästhetik im Horizont seiner Willensmetaphysik*. Neymeyr, Barbara.

*Nietzsche Werke Kritische Gesamtausgabe: III 5/1*. Groddeck, Wolfram (ed) and Kohlenbach, Michael (ed).

*Schopenhauer's Early Fourfold Root*. White, F C.

*Vom Willen zur Macht: Anthropologie und Metaphysik der Macht am exemplarischen Fall Friedrich Nietzsches*. Gerhardt, Volker.

Antero: As Imagens: Contexto Estético e Antropológico. Lambert, Maria de Fátima.

Empire, Transzendentalismus und Transzendenz: Neue Literatur zu Arthur Schopenhauer. Kossler, Matthias.

Schicksal und Charakter: Für die Philosophische Praxis ist vieles von Schopenhauer zu lernen: Vortrag auf dem Kolloquium der GPP am 30. Oktober 1994 in Tübingen. Achenbach, Gerd B.

Sufrimiento y humildad ontológica: Kant y Schopenhauer. Torralba Roselló, Francisco.

The Rational and the Irrational: A Philosophical Problem (Reading Arthur Schopenhauer). Mudragei, Nellia Stepanovna.

## SCHOR, J

My Own Criticism of *The Joyless Economy*. Scitovsky, Tibor.

## SCHRAMM, W

Wilbur Schramm and the Founding of Communication Studies. Glander, Timothy.

## SCHRODINGER, E

The Equivalence Myth of Quantum Mechanics—Part I. Muller, F A.

## SCHULZE, G

Zu Fichtes Kritik an Reinholds *empirischem* Satz des Bewusstseins und ihrer Vorgeschichte. Bondeli, Martin.

## SCHUON, F

*Advice to the Serious Seeker: Meditations on the Teaching of Frithjof Schuon*. Cutsinger, James S.

## SCHURMANN, R

Back to a Monstrous Site: Reiner Schürmann's Reading of Heidegger's *Beiträge*. Janicaud, Dominique.

Platonism at the Limit of Metaphysics. Sallis, John.

Reiner Schürmann's Report of His Visit to Martin Heidegger. Adler, Pierre (trans).

The Intellectual Background of Reiner Schürmann's Heidegger Interpretation. Hösle, Vittorio.

The Place of Nietzsche in Reiner Schürmann's Thought and in His Reading of Heidegger. Haar, Michel.

## SCHUTZ, A

Alfred Schutz on the Social Distribution of Knowledge. Nnoruka, Sylvanos I.

Between the Subject and Sociology: Alfred Schutz's Phenomenology of the Life-World. Costelloe, Timothy M.

El mundo incuestionado (Ortega y Schütz). Hermida, Pablo.

La fiducia come forma di fede: Alcune riflessioni introduttive ad un problema sociologico. Prandini, Riccardo.

## SCHWARTZ, J

Diversity and Ancient Democracy: A Response to Schwartz. Saxonhouse, Arlene W.

## SCHWARTZ, M

Commentary on "Edmund Husserl's Influence on Karl Jaspers's Phenomenology". Naudin, Jean and Azorin, Jean-Michel.

## SCHWOERER, L

Varieties of Political Thought. Hampsher-Monk, Iain.

## SCIACCA, M

Naturaleza humana en la filosofía de M.F. Sciacca y la concepción *light* de G. Vattimo. Darós, W R.

Vico en Sciacca. Ottonello, Pier Paolo.

## SCIENCE

*see also* Anthropology, Archeology, Biology, Chemistry, Economics, Human Sciences, Life Science, Matter, Medicine, Natural Sciences, Physics, Political Science, Quantum Mechanics, Relativity, Scientific Method, Social Sciences, Sociology, Space, Time, Unified Science

"*In Itinere*: Vienna 1870-1918" in *In Itinere* European Cities and the Birth of Modern Scientific Philosophy, Poli, Roberto (ed). Libardi, Massimo.

"An Ideal of Intuitionistic Kind Representing the Organisation of a Physical or Mathematical Theory" in *Verdad: lógica, representación y mundo*, Villegas Forero, L. Drago, Antonino.

"Are Pictures Really Necessary? The Case of Sewall Wright's 'Adaptive Landscapes'" in *Picturing Knowledge*, Baigrie, Brian S (ed). Ruse, Michael E.

"Avalutatività come principio metodico nella logica delle scienze sociali" in *Momenti di Storia della Logica e di Storia della Filosofia*, Guetti, Carla (ed). Bianco, Franco.

"Cambridge and the Austrian Connection" in *In Itinere* European Cities and the Birth of Modern Scientific Philosophy, Poli, Roberto (ed). Dappiano, Luigi.

"Contagium Vivum Philosophia: Schizophrenic Philosophy, Viral Empiricism and Deleuze" in *Deleuze and Philosophy: The Difference Engineer*, Ansell Pearson, Keith (ed). O'Toole, Robert.

"Dal gruppo di ricerca al laboratorio didattico disciplinare" in *Momenti di Storia della Logica e di Storia della Filosofia*, Guetti, Carla (ed). Ferrari, Franco.

"De la metafisica a la fisica en el programa cartesiano" in *Memorias Del Seminario En Conmemoración De Los 400 Anos Del Nacimiento De René Descartes*, Albis, Víctor S (ed). Cardona, Carlos Albert.

"Descartes's Scientific Illustrations and 'la grand mécanique de la nature'" in *Picturing Knowledge*, Baigrie, Brian S (ed). Baigrie, Brian S.

"El descubrimiento de la Doctrina de la Ciencia" in *El inicio del Idealismo alemán*, Market, Oswaldo. Tilliette, Xavier.

## SCIENCE

"El progreso cognoscitivo en la primera Doctrina de la Ciencia de Fichte" in *El inicio del Idealismo alemán*, Market, Oswaldo. Lauth, Reinhard.

"Ernst Cassirer e il problema dell'oggettività nelle scienze della cultura" in *Lo Storicismo e la Sua Storia: Temi, Problemi, Prospettive*, Cacciatore, Giuseppe (ed). Martirano, Maurizio.

"From *Wissenschaftliche Philosophie* to Philosophy of Science" in *Origins of Logical Empiricism*, Giere, Ronald N (ed). Giere, Ronald N.

"From Epistemology to the Logic of Science: Carnap's Philosophy of Empirical Knowledge in the 1930s" in *Origins of Logical Empiricism*, Giere, Ronald N (ed). Richardson, Alan W.

"Gravity" in the Thought of Simone Weil. Pirrucello, Ann.

"Illustration and Inference" in *Picturing Knowledge*, Baigrie, Brian S (ed). Brown, James Robert.

"Introduction: Origins of Logical Empiricism" in *Origins of Logical Empiricism*, Giere, Ronald N (ed). Richardson, Alan W.

"James, Clifford, and the Scientific Conscience" in *The Cambridge Companion to William James*, Putnam, Ruth Anna (ed). Hollinger, David A.

"Karl Popper—The Thinker and the Man" in *The Significance of Popper's Thought*, Amsterdamski, Stefan (ed). Gellner, Ernest.

"L'Italia in Bayle, Bayle in Italia: una ricerca mancata" in *Pierre Bayle e l'Italia*, Bianchi, Lorenzo. Borghero, Carlo.

"La démocratie et les tâches bio-éthiques de l'état" in *Philosophy and Democracy in Intercultural Perspective*, Kimmerle, Heinz (ed). Diallo, Saliou.

"La scienza e la vita: Lo storicismo problematico di Giuseppe Capograssi" in *Lo Storicismo e la Sua Storia: Temi, Problemi, Prospettive*, Cacciatore, Giuseppe (ed). Acocella, Giuseppe.

"Le relazioni tra Bayle e l'Italia: i corrispondenti italiani di Bayle e le *Nouvelles de la République des Lettres*" in *Pierre Bayle e l'Italia*, Bianchi, Lorenzo. Bianchi, Lorenzo.

"Límites y desventuras de la racionalidad crítica neoliberal" in *La racionalidad: su poder y sus límites*, Nudler, Oscar (ed). Gómez, Ricardo J.

"Lvov" in *In Itinere European Cities and the Birth of Modern Scientific Philosophy*, Poli, Roberto (ed). Wolenski, Jan.

"Machinic Thinking" in *Deleuze and Philosophy: The Difference Engineer*, Ansell Pearson, Keith (ed). Welchman, Alistair.

"Medieval Scholasticism and Averroism: The Implication of the Writings of Ibn Rushd to Western Science" in *Averroës and the Enlightenment*, Wahba, Mourad (ed). Bullough, Vern L.

"Mind" as Humanizing the Brain: Toward a Neurotheology of Meaning. Ashbrook, James B.

"Natural Kinds of Questions" in *Knowledge and Inquiry: Essays on Jaakko Hintikka's Epistemology and Philosophy of Science*, Sintonen, Matti (ed). Bromberger, Sylvain.

"Nineteenth-Century Würzburg: The Development of the Scientific Approach to Philosophy" in *In Itinere European Cities and the Birth of Modern Scientific Philosophy*, Poli, Roberto (ed). Baumgartner, Wilhelm.

"On Freedom of Science" in *The Idea of University*, Brzezinski, Jerzy (ed). Ajdukiewicz, Kazimierz.

"Philosophical Commitments and Scientific Progress" in *The Idea of Progress*, McLaughlin, Peter (ed). Crombie, A C.

"Prague Mosaic: Encounters with Prague Philosophers" in *In Itinere European Cities and the Birth of Modern Scientific Philosophy*, Poli, Roberto (ed). Sebestik, Jan.

"Prigogine y Kuhn, dos personajes en la historia externa de la ciencia y la epistemología contemporáneas" in *La racionalidad: su poder y sus límites*, Nudler, Oscar (ed). Flichman, Eduardo Héctor.

"Prospect for Science and Technology" in *The American University: National Treasure or Endangered Species?*, Ehrenberg, Ronald G (ed). Lane, Neal.

"Prospect for the Social Sciences in the Land Grand University" in *The American University: National Treasure or Endangered Species?*, Ehrenberg, Ronald G (ed). Bronfenbrenner, Urie.

"Representations of the Natural System in the Nineteenth Century" in *Picturing Knowledge*, Baigrie, Brian S (ed). O'Hara, Robert J.

"Science and Games" in *Knowledge and Inquiry: Essays on Jaakko Hintikka's Epistemology and Philosophy of Science*, Sintonen, Matti (ed). Wolenski, Jan.

"Science and Psychology" in *Verstehen and Humane Understanding*, O'Hear, Anthony (ed). Dilman, Ilham.

"Science and the Avant-Garde in Early Nineteenth-Century Florence" in *In Itinere European Cities and the Birth of Modern Scientific Philosophy*, Poli, Roberto (ed). Albertazzi, Liliana.

"Science, Teaching, and Values" in *The Idea of University*, Brzezinski, Jerzy (ed). Koj, Leon.

"Scientific Discovery, Induction, and the Multi-Level Character" in *Knowledge and Inquiry: Essays on Jaakko Hintikka's Epistemology and Philosophy of Science*, Sintonen, Matti (ed). Gebhard, George.

"Scientific Explanation and the Interrogative Model of Inquiry" in *Knowledge and Inquiry: Essays on Jaakko Hintikka's Epistemology and Philosophy of Science*, Sintonen, Matti (ed). Weber, Erik.

"The Didactic and the Elegant: Some Thoughts on Scientific and Technological Illustrations in the Middle Ages and Renaissance" in *Picturing Knowledge*, Baigrie, Brian S (ed). Hall, Bert S.

"The Enlightenment Ambition of Epistemic Utopianism: Otto Neurath's Theory of Science in Historical Perspective" in *Origins of Logical Empiricism*, Giere, Ronald N (ed). Uebel, Thomas E.

"The Ethics of Scientific Criticism" in *The Idea of University*, Brzezinski, Jerzy (ed). Szaniawksi, Klemens.

"The Idea of Progress in Evolutionary Biology: Philosophical Considerations" in *The Idea of Progress*, McLaughlin, Peter (ed). Wolters, Gereon.

"The Personality of Researchers and the Necessity of Schools in Science" in *The Idea of University*, Brzezinski, Jerzy (ed). Nowak, Leszek.

"The Presence of Phenomenology in Milan Between the Two World Wars" in *In Itinere European Cities and the Birth of Modern Scientific Philosophy*, Poli, Roberto (ed). Minazzi, Fabio.

"The Structure of Inquiry in Developmental Biology" in *Knowledge and Inquiry: Essays on Jaakko Hintikka's Epistemology and Philosophy of Science*, Sintonen, Matti (ed). Kleiner, Scott A.

"The Topology of Selection: The Limits of Deleuze's Biophilosophy" in *Deleuze and Philosophy: The Difference Engineer*, Ansell Pearson, Keith (ed). Caygill, Howard.

"Theory and Social Practice: One or Two Psychologies?" in *Epistemology and History*, Zeidler-Janiszewska, Anna (ed). Brzezinski, Jerzy.

"Theory of Identifiability" in *Knowledge and Inquiry: Essays on Jaakko Hintikka's Epistemology and Philosophy of Science*, Sintonen, Matti (ed). Mutanen, Arto.

"Towards an Epistemology of Scientific Illustration" in *Picturing Knowledge*, Baigrie, Brian S (ed). Topper, David.

"Towards Honest Public Relations of Science" in *The Significance of Popper's Thought*, Amsterdamski, Stefan (ed). Agassi, Joseph.

"Tradition in Science" in *The Idea of University*, Brzezinski, Jerzy (ed). Gockowski, Janusz.

"Types of Determination vs. The Development of Science in Historical Epistemology" in *Epistemology and History*, Zeidler-Janiszewska, Anna (ed). Such, Jan.

"Un escenario pragmático para la verdad en la ciencia" in *Verdad: lógica, representación y mundo*, Villegas Forero, L. Bengoetxea, Juan B, Eizagirre, Xabier and Ibarra, Andoni.

"Vico e Bayle: Ancora una messa a punto" in *Pierre Bayle e l'Italia*, Bianchi, Lorenzo. Nuzzo, Enrico.

"Viroid Life: On Machines, Technics and Evolution" in *Deleuze and Philosophy: The Difference Engineer*, Ansell Pearson, Keith (ed). Ansell Pearson, Keith.

"Visual Models and Scientific Judgment" in *Picturing Knowledge*, Baigrie, Brian S (ed). Giere, Ronald N.

"Warsaw: The Rise and Decline of Modern Scientific Philosophy in the Capital City of Poland" in *In Itinere European Cities and the Birth of Modern Scientific Philosophy*, Poli, Roberto (ed). Jadacki, Jacek Juliusz.

"Wissenschaftsethik" in *Angewandte Ethik: Die Bereichsethiken und ihre theoretische Fundierung*, Nida-Rümelin, Julian (ed). Nida-Rümelin, Julian.

"¿Qué nos importa Descartes todavía?" in *Memorias Del Seminario En Conmemoración De Los 400 Anos Del Nacimiento De René Descartes*, Albis, Víctor S (ed). Serrano, Gonzalo.

(Not) Giving Credit Where Credit Is Due: Citation of Data Sets. Sieber, Joan E and Trumbo, Bruce E.

(Re)Inventing Scheffler, or, Defending Objective Educational Research. Phillips, D C.

*In Itinere European Cities and the Birth of Modern Scientific Philosophy.* Poli, Roberto (ed).

*A Novel Defense of Scientific Realism.* Leplin, Jarrett.

*A Passage to the Hermeneutic Philosophy of Science.* Ginev, Dimitri.

*An Interpretive Introduction to Quantum Field Theory.* Teller, Paul.

*An Introduction to the Thought of Karl Popper.* Corvi, Roberta and Camiller, Patrick (trans).

*Analyzing Functions: An Essay on a Fundamental Notion in Biology.* Melander, Peter.

*Aristotle on Perception.* Everson, Stephen.

*Belief and Resistance: Dynamics of Contemporary Intellectual Controversy.* Smith, Barbara Herrnstein.

*Beyond Interpretation: The Meaning of Hermeneutics for Philosophy.* Vattimo, Gianni and Webb, David (trans).

*Critical Reflections on the Paranormal.* Stoeber, Michael (ed) and Meynell, Hugo (ed).

*CyberSpace Virtual Reality: Fortschritt und Gefahr einer innovativen Technologie.* Wedde, Horst F (ed).

*Descriptive Psychology.* Müller, Benito (ed & trans) and Brentano, Franz.

*Dialectical Readings: Three Types of Interpretation.* Dunning, Stephen N.

*E.C. Tolman e l'epistemologia del primo novecento.* Donadon, Eleonora.

*Europa I El Progrés Sostingut.* Vincent, Martínez Guzmán.

*Explaining Consciousness—The 'Hard Problem'.* Shear, Jonathan (ed).

*Facets of Faith and Science Volume 1: Historiography and Modes of Interaction.* Van der Meer, Jitse M (ed).

*Facets of Faith and Science Volume 2: The Role of Beliefs in Mathematics and the Natural Sciences—An Augustinian Perspective.* Van der Meer, Jitse M (ed).

*Facets of Faith and Science Volume 3: The Role of Beliefs in the Natural Sciences.* Van der Meer, Jitse M (ed).

## SCIENCE

Facets of Faith and Science Volume 4: Interpreting God's Action in the World. Van der Meer, Jitse M (ed).

*Freud and the Passions.* O'Neill, John (ed).

*From Occam's Razor to the Roots of Consciousness.* Wassermann, Gerhard D.

*From Physics to Metaphysics.* Redhead, Michael.

*Gesamtausgabe II. Abteilung: Vorlesungen (Band 27: Einleitung in die Philosophie).* Heidegger, Martin.

*Idealisierungen und das Ziel der Physik: Eine Untersuchung zum Realismus, Empirismus und Konstruktivismus in der Wissenschafts-theorie.* Hüttemann, Andreas.

*Il Riduzionismo della Scienza.* Gava, Giacomo.

*Improving Nature?.* Reiss, Michael J and Straughan, Roger.

*In Search of a Better World: Lectures and Essays from Thirty Years.* Popper, Karl and Bennet, Laura J (trans).

*Intenzioni: D'amore di scienza e d'anarchia.* Donnici, Rocco.

*Interpreting Minds: The Evolution of a Practice.* Bogdan, Radu J.

*John Dewey: Scienza, prassi, democrazia.* Alcaro, Mario.

*Karl-Otto Apel: Selected Essays.* Mendieta, Eduardo (ed).

*Knowledge and Inquiry: Essays on Jaakko Hintikka's Epistemology and Philosophy of Science.* Sintonen, Matti (ed).

*L'Edizione Critica Di Vico: Bilanci E Prospettive.* Cacciatore, Giuseppe and Stile, Alessandro.

*Le Orationes Di G. Gravina: Scienza, Sapienza e Diritto.* Lomonaco, Fabrizio.

*Machiavelli, Leonardo, and the Science of Power.* Masters, Roger D.

*Mathematische und naturwissenschaftliche Modelle in der Philosophie Schellings und Hegels.* Ziche, Paul.

*Medieval Thought.* Luscombe, David.

*Memorias Del Seminario En Conmemoración De Los 400 Anos Del Nacimiento De René Descartes.* Albis, Víctor S (ed), Charum, Jorge (ed) and Sánchez, Clara Helena (& others).

*Metaphysics and the Origin of Species.* Ghiselin, Michael T.

*Mind Design II: Philosophy, Psychology, Artificial Intelligence.* Haugeland, John (ed).

*Momenti di Storia della Logica e di Storia della Filosofia.* Guetti, Carla (ed) and Pujia, Roberto (ed).

*Mortals and Others: American Essays 1931-1935.* Russell, Bertrand and Ruja, Harry (ed).

*Origins of Logical Empiricism.* Giere, Ronald N (ed) and Richardson, Alan W (ed).

*Philosophical Perspectives, 9, AI, Connectionism and Philosophical Psychology, 1995.* Tomberlin, James E (ed).

*Philosophie der Chemie: Bestandsaufnahme und Ausblick.* Schummer, Joachim, Psarros, Nikos (ed) and Ruthenberg, Klaus (ed).

*Picturing Knowledge: Historical and Philosophical Problems Concerning the Use of Art in Science.* Baigrie, Brian S (ed).

*Pierre Bayle e l'Italia.* Bianchi, Lorenzo.

*Postcolonial African Philosophy: A Critical Reader.* Chukwudi Eze, Emmanuel (ed).

*Principia Ecologica Eco-Principles as a Conceptual Framework for a New Ethics in Science and Technology.* Moser, Anton.

*Proclus: Neo-Platonic Philosophy and Science.* Siorvanes, Lucas.

*Real Process: How Logic and Chemistry Combine in Hegel's Philosophy of Nature.* Burbidge, John W.

*Realismus und Chemie: Philosophische Untersuchungen der Wissen-schaft von den Stoffen.* Schummer, Joachim.

*Religion and Science: Historical and Contemporary Issues.* Barbour, Ian G.

*Scientific Method: An Historical and Philosophical Introduction.* Gower, Barry S.

*Society, Economics & Philosophy: Selected Papers.* Allen, R T (ed) and Polanyi, Michael.

*The General Unified Theory of Intelligence: Its Central Conceptions and Specific Application to Domains of Cognitive Science.* Wagman, Morton.

*The Human Animal: Personal Identity without Psychology.* Olson, Eric T.

*The Idea of Progress.* McLaughlin, Peter (ed), Burgen, Arnold (ed) and Mittelstrass, Jürgen (ed).

*The Invisible World: Early Modern Philosophy and the Invention of the Microscope.* Wilson, Catherine.

*The Last Word.* Nagel, Thomas.

*The Lonergan Reader.* Morelli, Mark (ed) and Morelli, Elizabeth A (ed).

*The Meaning of Mind: Language, Morality, and Neuroscience.* Szasz, Thomas.

*The Perfect Baby: A Pragmatic Approach to Genetics.* McGee, Glenn.

*The Right to Know and the Right not to Know.* Chadwick, Ruth (ed), Levitt, Mairi (ed) and Shickle, Darren (ed).

*The Significance of Popper's Thought.* Amsterdamski, Stefan (ed).

*Thomas Hobbes.* Martinich, A P.

*Un'Introduzione All'Epistemologia Contemporanea.* Gava, Giacomo (ed).

*Unfolding Meaning: A Weekend of Dialogue with David Bohm.* Bohm, David.

*Western Philosophy: An Anthology.* Cottingham, John (ed).

*Wholeness and the Implicate Order.* Bohm, David.

*Zur Meta-Theorie der Physik.* Schröter, Joachim.

A Bastard Kind of Reasoning: The Argument from the Sciences and the Introduction of the Receptacle in Plato's *Timaeus.* Reshotko, Naomi.

A Ciência e a Virtude No Noviciado da Cotovia (1603-1759): Organização do Espaço, Produçao do Discurso e Sistema Epistémico. Janeira, Ana Luisa.

A Clearer Vision. Shapiro, Lawrence A.

A Discursive Account of Multiple Personality Disorder. Gillett, Grant.

A Historical Interpretation of Deceptive Experiments in American Psychology. Herrera, Christopher D.

A History of the Extraterrestrial Life Debate. Crowe, Michael J.

A Mereological Look at Motion. Sayan, Erdinc.

A Model-Theoretic Interpretation of Science. Ruttkamp, Emma.

A New Grandfather Paradox?. Sider, Theodore.

A Origem do Conceito do *Impetus.* Rodrigues Évora, Fátima Regina.

A Patterned Process Approach To Brain, Consciousness, and Behavior. Díaz, José-Luis.

A Poetics of Psychological Explanation. Knight, Deborah.

A Proposal for a New System of Credit Allocation in Science. Resnik, David B.

A Psychologically Plausible Logical Model of Conceptualization. Kim, Hong-Gee.

A Refutation of Pure Conjecture. Cleveland, Timothy.

A Remark Concerning Prediction and Spacetime Singularities. Hogarth, Mark.

A Schism in Quantum Physics or How Locality May Be Salvaged. Antonopoulos, Constantin.

A So-Called 'Fraud': Moral Modulations in a Literary Scandal. Lynch, Michael.

A Taxonomy of Functions. Walsh, Denis M and Ariew, André.

A Uniqueness Theorem for 'No Collapse' Interpretations of Quantum Mechanics. Bub, Jeffrey and Clifton, Rob.

About Signs and Symptoms: Can Semiotics Expand the View of Clinical Medicine?. Nessa, John.

Abstraktion und Ideation—Zur Semantik chemischer und biologischer Grundbegriffe. Gutmann, Mathias and Hanekamp, Gerd.

Acerca de dos modelos de conocimiento tecnológico. González, María Cristina.

Adaptationism: Hypothesis or Heuristic?. Resnik, David B.

Advances in Peer Review Research: an Introduction. Stamps III, Arthur E.

Akaike Information Criterion, Curve-Fitting, and the Philosophical Problem of Simplicity. Kieseppä, I A.

Alexander of Aphrodisias on Celestial Motions. Bodnár, István M.

Algunas tesis sobre la tecnología. Herrera J, Rodolfo.

Algunos Problemas de las Ciencias Reconstructivas. Villegas, Luis.

Alternative Mathematics and Alternative Theoretical Physics: The Method for Linking Them Together. Drago, Antonino.

An Anti-Anti-Essentialist View of the Emotions: A Reply to Kupperman. Dalgleish, Tim.

An Argument About Free Inquiry. Kitcher, Philip.

An Axiomatic Framework for Classical Particle Mechanics without Force. Schlup Sant'Anna, Adonai.

An Integral Theory of Consciousness. Wilber, Ken.

An Introduction to Research Ethics. Friedman, Paul J.

Antidote or Theory?. Dickson, Michael.

Antinomies of Practice and Research of Group Psychotherapy (in Serbo-Croatian). Opalic, Petar.

Antirealist Explanations of the Success of Science. Kukla, André.

Are Plants Conscious?. Nagel, Alexandra H M.

Are Science and Religion in Conflict?. Watts, Fraser N.

Are Thought Experiments Just What You Thought?. Norton, John D.

Aristóleles en la España del siglo XVI. Antecedentes, alcance y matices de su influencia. Bravo García, Antonio.

Aristotelian *Akrasia* and Psychoanalytic Regression. Stocker, Michael.

Aristotle and the Idea of Competing Forms of Life. Crittenden, P.

Aristotle on Canonical Science and Ethics. Anagnostopoulos, Georgios.

Aristotle, *hos epi to polu* Relations, and a Demonstrative Science of Ethics. Winter, Michael.

Armstrong on the Role of Laws in Counterfactual Supporting. Pages, Joan.

Arte e ciência: Acordo e progresso. D'Orey, Carmo.

Assessing Conflict of Interest: Sources of Bias. Bird, Stephanie J.

Astrology: Science, Pseudoscience, Ideology. Pruzhinin, Boris Isaevich.

Astronomy and Observation in Plato's *Republic.* Gregory, Andrew.

Awareness, Mental Phenomena and Consciousness: A Synthesis of Dennett and Rosenthal. Rockwell, Teed.

Back to Darwin and Popper: Criticism, Migration of Piecemeal Conceptual Schemes, and the Growth of Knowledge. De Freitas, Renan Springer.

Baldwin, Cattell and the *Psychological Review*: A Collaboration and Its Discontents. Sokal, Michael M.

Bayesianism and Diverse Evidence: A Reply to Andrew Wayne. Myrvold, Wayne C.

Bayesianism and the Value of Diverse Evidence. Steel, Daniel.

Behavioral Systems Interpreted as Autonomous Agents and as Coupled Dynamical Systems: A Criticism. Keijzer, Fred A and Bem, Sacha.

Belief and Consciousness. Worley, Sara.

Bemerkung zu: "Epistemologische Aspekte der neuen Entwicklungen in der Physik" von G. Münster. Mielke, Eckehard W.

Bemerkungen über die gegenwärtige Arbeit im Bereich der Naturphilosophie an der FEST und über die *Philosophy-and-Physics-Workshops.* Stamatescu, Ion-Olimpiu.

## SCIENCE

## SCIENCE

Objektive Beschreibung und Messprozess in der Quantenmechanik. Neumann, Holger.

On Becoming, Relativity, and Nonseparability. Dorato, Mauro.

On Chihara's 'The Howson-Urbach Proofs of Bayesian Principles'. Howson, Colin.

On Everett's Formulation of Quantum Mechanics. Barrett, Jeffrey A.

On Helmholtz and 'Bürgerliche Intelligenz': A Response to Robert Brain. Cahan, David.

On Mathematical Error. Sherry, David.

On the Acceptability of Biopharmaceuticals. Spier, Raymond.

On the Assessment of Genetic Technology: Reaching Ethical Judgments in the Light of Modern Technology. Sinemus, Kristina, Platzer, Katrin and Bender, Wolfgang.

On the Brussels School's Arrow of Time in Quantum Theory. Karakostas, Vassilios.

On the Hazards of Whistleblowers and on Some Problems of Young Biomedical Scientists in our Time. Edsall, John T.

On the Mechanism of Consciousness. Cotterill, Rodney M J.

On the Possible Non-Existence of Emotions: The Passions. Sabini, John and Silver, Maury.

On the Relation between Behaviorism and Cognitive Psychology. Moore, Jay.

On the Use of Visualizations in the Practice of Science. Sargent, Pauline.

On What Being a World Takes Away. Clifton, Robert.

On Wittgenstein on Cognitive Science. Proudfoot, Diane.

Once More: Bohr-Hoffding. Faye, Jan.

One World, But a Big One. Midgley, Mary.

Ontic Realism and Scientific Explanation. Bradie, Michael.

Ontological Categories and Natural Kinds. Lowe, E J.

Ontological Constraints and Understanding Quantum Phenomena. Folse, Henry J.

Ontological Relativity and Meaning-Variance: A Critical-Constructive Review. Norris, Christopher.

Open Realism. d'Espagnat, Bernard.

Optimalität der Natur?. Zoglauer, Thomas.

Oracles, Aesthetics, and Bayesian Consensus. Barrett, Jeffrey A.

Overzicht van de filosofie van de techniek in Nederland tijdens het interbellum. Haaksma, Hans W H.

Panexperientialist Physicalism and the Mind-Body Problem. Griffin, David Ray.

Pantheism and Science. Forrest, Peter.

Paradigmas: ¿construcciones históricas?. García Fallas, Jackeline.

Parafraud in Biology. Hillman, Harold.

Past, Present, Future, and Special Relativity. Rakié, Natasa.

Pathological Autobiographies. Harré, Rom.

Paul Ricoeur et la question de la preuve en psychanalyse. Kaboré, Boniface.

PDP Networks can Provide Models that are not Mere Implementations of Classical Theories. Dawson, Michael R W, Medler, David A and Berkeley, Istvan S N.

Peer Review for Journals: Evidence on Quality Control, Fairness, and Innovation. Armstrong, J Scott.

Peer Review: Selecting the Best Science. Baldwin, Wendy and Seto, Belinda.

Peirce on Continuity and Laws of Nature. Sfendoni-Mentzou, Demetra.

Peirce's Teleological Approach to Natural Classes. Hulswit, Menno.

Perspektiven der Welt: Vielfalt und Einheit im Weltbild der Deutschen Romantik. Köchy, Kristian.

Philosophical Issues in the History of Chemistry. Gavroglu, Kostas.

Philosophical Psychology in Historical Perspective: Review Essay of J.-C. Smith (Ed.), *Historical Foundations of Cognitive Science*. Meyering, Theo C.

Philosophie als Existenzwissenschaft: Empirismuskritik und Wissenschaftsklassifikation bei Soren Kierkegaard. Schulz, Heiko.

Philosophie und Medizin: Ein Blick in aktuelle Veröffentlichungen. Schramme, Thomas.

Philosophy as an Exact Science (in Czech). Seifert, Josef.

Philosophy in an Age of Overinformation, or: What We Ought to Ignore in Order to Know What Really Matters. Hösle, Vittorio.

Philosophy of Science and the German Idealists. Clayton, Philip.

Philosophy of Science: What One Needs to Know. Clayton, Philip.

Philosophy, Solipsism and Thought. Mounce, H O.

Physics, Machines, and the Hard Problem. Bilodeau, Douglas J.

Physiology, Embryology and Psychopathology: A Test Case for Hegelian Thought (in French). Rozenberg, Jacques J.

Picturing Einstein's Train of Thought. White, V Alan.

Plantinga on Functions and the Theory of Evolution. Levin, Michael.

Points East and West: Acupuncture and Comparative Philosophy of Science. Allchin, Douglas.

Polanyian Reflections on Embodiment, the Human Genome Initiative and Theological Anthropology. Lewis, Paul.

Popularization and Pseudo-Science. Cornelis, Gustaaf C.

Populismus in der Philosophie: Nicholas Reschers wissenschaftlicher Relativismus. Niemann, Hans-Joachim.

Possible Worlds in the Modal Interpretation. Hemmo, Meir.

Postmodernism: What One Needs to Know. Grassie, William.

Potential, Propensity, and Categorical Realism. Liu, Chuang.

Powerful Pedagogy in the Science-and-Religion Classroom. Grassie, William.

Practical Philosophy and the Human Sciences Today (in Serbo-Croatian). Pazanin, Ante.

Pragmatic Idealization and Structuralist Reconstructions of Theories. Haase, Michaela.

Pragmatische Bedingungen des wissenschaftlichen Realismus. Kügler, Peter.

Predicative Laws of Association in Statistics and Physics. Costantini, D and Garibaldi, U.

Prediction and Rolston's Environmental Ethics: Lessons from the Philosophy of Science. McKinney, William J.

Proliferation of Authors on Research Reports in Medicine. Drenth, Joost P H.

Promoting Ethical Standards in Science and Engineering. Frankel, Mark S.

Protowissenschaft und Rekonstruktion. Hartmann, Dirk.

Psychoanalysis: Past, Present, and Future. Erwin, Edward.

Psychogenesis and the History of Science: Piaget and the Problem of Scientific Change. Messerly, John G.

Psychological Courage. Putman, Daniel.

Psychological Realism, Morality, and Chimpanzees. Harnden-Warwick, David.

Psychological Research as the Formulation, Demonstration, and Critique of Psychological Theories. Martin, Jack.

Putting the Puzzle Together: Part I: Towards a General Theory of the Neural Correlates of Consciousness. Newman, James.

Quantum Dynamical Reduction and Reality: Replacing Probability Densities with Densities in Real Space. Ghirardi, Giancarlo.

Quantum Mechanics and Frequentism: A Reply to Ismael. Strevens, Michael.

Quantum Paradoxes and Physical Reality. Selleri, Franco.

Random Drift and the Omniscient Viewpoint. Millstein, Roberta L.

Reaching for the "Low Hanging Fruit": The Pressure for Results in Scientific Research—A Graduate Student's Perspective. Browning, Tyson R.

Realismus in Duhems naturgemässer Klassifikation. Burri, Alex.

Reasoning about Change and Persistence: A Solution to the Frame Problem. Pollock, John L.

Recent Bulgarian Studies in the Fields of Psychology, Parapsychology & Yoga. Atreya, Prakash.

Referees, Editors, and Publication Practices: Improving the Reliability and Usefulness of the Peer Review System. Cicchetti, Domenic V.

Reflections on Peer Review Practices in Committees Selecting Laureates for Prestigious Awards and Prizes: Some Relevant and Irrelevant Criteria. Vijh, Ashok K.

Reply to Commentaries. Gopnik, Alison.

Representation and Resemblance: A Review Essay of Richard A. Watson's *Representational Ideas: From Plato to Patricia Churchland*. Meyering, Theo C.

Representation from Bottom and Top. Shapiro, Lawrence A.

Rerum Cognoscere Causas. Hahn, Frank.

Research Monographs on the History of Science. Shekhawat, Virendra.

Resolving Discordant Results: Modern Solar Oblateness Experiments. Richman, Sam.

Resolving Hempel's Raven Paradox. Leavitt, Fred.

Response to the Commentaries. Harré, Rom.

Response to the Commentary. Gillett, Grant.

Responsible Technoscience: The Haunting Reality of Auschwitz and Hiroshima. Sassower, Raphael.

Rethinking the 'Discover' of the Electron. Arabatzis, Theodore.

Review Essay: Bohmian Mechanics and the Quantum Revolution. Goldstein, Sheldon.

Révolution scientifique et problématique de l'être vivant. Duchesneau, François.

Scheffler Revisited on the Role of History and Philosophy of Science in Science Teacher Education. Matthews, Michael R.

Science and Core Knowledge. Carey, Susan and Spelke, Elizabeth.

Science and Human Condition (in Portuguese). Caponi, Sandra N C.

Science as a Battlefield: Methodological and Historical Considerations on the Misuse of Science by Totalitarian Regimes of Central Europe. Hajduk, Anton.

Science As Child's Play: Tales from the Crib. Fine, Arthur.

Science et foi: pour un nouveau dialogue. Poupard, Cardinal P.

Science Studies and Language Suppression—A Critique of Bruno Latour's *We Have Never Been Modern*. Cohen, Sande.

Science, Morality and Religion: An Essay. Postgate, John.

Science, Religion, and Modernity: Values and Lifestyles of University Professors. Houtman, Dick.

Science, Religious Language, and Analogy. Porter, Andrew P.

Science, Social Theory, and Science Criticism. Restivo, Sal and Bauchspies, Wenda K.

Science: Augustinian or Duhemian?. Plantinga, Alvin.

Scientific Attitudes Towards an Eastern Mystic. Danyluk, Angie.

Scientific Misconduct: Ill-Defined, Redefined. Palca, Joseph.

Scientific Realism and the 'Pessimistic Induction'. Psillos, Stathis.

Scientific Reasoning and Due Process. Guenin, Louis M and Davis, Bernard D.

## SCIENCE

The Return of the Group. Sterelny, Kim.

The Role of Data and Theory in Covariation Assessment: Implications for the Theory-Ladenness of Observation. Freedman, Eric G and Smith, Laurence D.

The Scientific Solitude of Vernadskii. Aksenov, Gennadii Petrovich.

The Scientist as Adult. Giere, Ronald N.

The Scientist as Child. Gopnik, Alison.

The Sciousness Hypothesis: Part I. Natsoulas, Thomas.

The Social and Sociological Study of Science, and the Convergence Towards the Study of Scientific Practice (in Spanish). Gomez Ferri, Javier.

The Social Concept of Disease. Räikkä, Juha.

The Story of the Mind: Psychological and Biological Explanations of Human Behavior. Schechtman, Marya.

The Symposium Viewed from the Organizer's Perspective. Gorski, Andrew.

The Task of Group Rationality: The Subjectivist's View—Part I. Sarkar, Husain.

The Task of Group Rationality: The Subjectivist's View—Part II. Sarkar, Husain.

The Unity of Science without Reductionism. Lucas, John R.

The Unity of Scientific Knowledge in the Framework of a Typological Approach of Theories. Parvu, Ilie.

The Weakest Local Realism Is still Incompatible with Quantum Theory. Selleri, Franco.

The 'Reality' of the Wave Function: Measurements, Entropy and Quantum Cosmology. Zeh, Heinz-Dieter.

The 'Umbau'—From Constitution Theory to Constructional Ontology. Seibt, Johanna.

Theodore Karman, Paul Wigner, John Neumann, Leo Szilard, Edward Teller and Their Ideas of Ultimate Reality and Meaning. Horvath, Tibor.

Theoretical Medicine: A Proposal for Reconceptualizing Medicine as a Science of Actions. Lolas, Fernando.

Theoretical Modeling and Biological Laws. Cooper, Gregory.

Theorie als Gedächtniskunst. Soentgen, Jens.

Theory, Practice, and Epistemology in the Development of Species Concepts. Magnus, David.

There Is No Hard Problem of Consciousness. O'Hara, Kieron and Scutt, Tom.

There is No Such Thing as Environmental Ethics. Vesilind, P Aarne.

Thinking Machines: Some Fundamental Confusions. Kearns, John T.

Thomas Kuhn and the Legacy of Logical Positivism. Notturno, Mark A.

Thomas Kuhn: A Personal Judgement. Fuller, Steve.

Thomas S. Kuhn, een moderne komedie van vergissingen. Derksen, A A.

Thomism and the Quantum Enigma. Wallace, William A.

Thomistic Natural Philosophy and the Scientific Revolution. Reitan, Eric A.

Three Comparative Maps of the Human. Samuelson, Norbert M.

Time's Arrows Today: Recent Physical and Philosophical Work on the Direction of Time. Denbigh, Kenneth G.

Time, Bohm's Theory, and Quantum Cosmology. Callender, Craig and Weingard, Robert.

Time, Quantum Mechanics, and Tense. Saunders, Simon.

Toward a Feminist Revision of Research Protocols on the Etiology of Homosexuality. Turner, Stephanie S.

Toward a Non-Cartesian Psychotherapeutic Framework: Radical Pragmatism as an Alternative. Berger, Louis S.

Towards a Reapprehension of Causal Efficacy. Earley Sr, Joseph E.

Trägheit und Massebegriff bei Johannes Kepler. Ihmig, Karl-Norbert.

Transition Chances and Causation. Arntzenius, Frank.

Trouble in Paradise? Problems for Bohm's Theory. Callender, Craig and Weingard, Robert.

True Theories, False Colors. Clark, Austen.

Trust and the Collection, Selection, Analysis and Interpretation of Data: A Scientist's View. Bird, Stephanie J and Housman, David E.

Truth and Trustworthiness in Research. Whitbeck, Caroline.

Truth, Verisimilitude, and Natural Kinds. Aronson, Jerrold L.

Turning 'The Hard Problem' Upside Down & Sideways. Hut, Piet and Shepard, Roger N.

Twistors and Self-Reference: On the Generic Non-Linearity of Nature. Zimmermann, Rainer E.

Two Skepticism and Skeptic Challenge in Philip Kitcher's The Advancement of Science. Attala Pochón, Daniel.

Über das Verhältnis von Algebra und Geometrie in Descartes'"Geometrie". Krämer, Sybille.

Über den Charakter von Einsteins philosophischem Realismus. Polikarov, Asaria.

Ulteriorità del pensare. Masi, Giuseppe.

Um Problema no Ensino de Ciências: organizaçao conceitual do conteúdo ou estudo dos fenômenos. Pacheco, Décio.

Una lettera inedita del Carcavi al Magliabechi con un parere sul Redi. Guerrini, Luigi.

Uncertain Decisions and the Many-Minds Interpretation of Quantum Mechanics. Papineau, David.

Understanding Bias in Scientific Practice. Shaffer, Nancy E.

Understanding Subjectivity: Global Workspace Theory and the Resurrection of the Observing Self. Baars, Bernard J.

Understanding the Representational Mind: A Phenomenological Perspective. Marbach, Eduard.

Unique Transition Probabilities in the Modal Interpretation. Vermaas, Pieter E.

Unity of Science and Culture. Prigogine, Ilya and Cornelis, Gustaaf C.

Universals and the Methodenstreit: a Re-examination of Carl Menger's Conception of Economics as an Exact Science. Mäki, Uskali.

Universell und unvollständig: Theorien über alles?. Breuer, Thomas.

Using a Dialectical Scientific Brief in Peer Review. Stamps III, Arthur E.

Van Fraassen on Preparation and Measurement. Ruetsche, Laura.

Van woorden en wekkers: Temporele ordening op een leefgroep voor autistische jongeren. Hendriks, Ruud.

Waarom het beoordelen van technologieën voor gehandicapten problematisch is. Blume, Stuart.

Was ist Masse? Newtons Begriff der Materiemenge. Steinle, Friedrich.

Was kann heute unter Naturphilosophie verstehen?. Stöckler, Manfred.

Was macht eine Erkenntnistheorie naturalistisch?. Koppelberg, Dirk.

Waves, Particles, and Explanatory Coherence. Eliasmith, Chris and Thagard, Paul.

Wayne, Horwich, and Evidential Diversity. Fitelson, Branden.

What Do Propositions Measure in Folk Psychology?. Weatherall, Peter.

What is Natural?. Abney, Keith.

What is Scientism?. Stenmark, Mikael.

What is the Thematic Structure of Science? (Czech). Tondl, Ladislav.

What It Feels Like To Be in a Superposition and Why. Lehner, Christoph.

What Multiple Realizability Does Not Show. Francescotti, Robert M.

What Society Will Expect from the Future Research Community. Jamieson, Dale.

When a Pain Is Not. Hardcastle, Valerie Gray.

When Several Bayesians Agree That There Will Be No Reasoning to a Foregone Conclusion. Seidenfeld, Teddy, Kadane, Joseph B and Schervish, Mark J.

Where Do Laws of Nature Come From?. Cartwright, Nancy.

Who Needs Reality?. Stamatescu, Ion-Olimpiu.

Who's Afraid of a Non-Metaphorical Evolutionary Epistemology?. Heschl, Adolf.

Why General Relativity Does Need an Interpretation. Belot, Gordon.

Why John Von Neumann Did Not Like the Hilbert Space Formalism of Quantum Mechanics (and What he Liked Instead). Rédei, Miklós.

Why Not Science Critics?. Ihde, Don.

Why Teach Ethics in Science and Engineering?. Johnson, Deborah G, Hollander, Rachelle D and Beckwith, Jonathan R (& others).

Wie definiert man einen physikalischen Gegenstand?. Rudolph, Enno.

Wie kommt es zum Quantum?. Wheeler, John Archibald.

Wilhelm Griesinger: Psychiatry between Philosophy and Praxis. Arens, Katherine.

Wisdom's Information: Rereading a Biblical Image in the Light of Some Contemporary Science and Speculation. Nancarrow, Paul S.

Ziekte leven: Bouwstenen voor een medische sociologie zonder disease/illness-onderscheid. Mol, Annemarie and Pols, Jeannette.

Zur Begründung des Infinitesimalkalküls durch Leibniz. Krämer, Sybille.

'Beyond Determinism'. Spurrett, David.

'Europa' en el pensamiento de Jaspers. Franco Barrio, Jaime.

'Many Minds' Interpretations of Quantum Mechanics: Replies to Replies. Lockwood, Michael.

¿Comparando qué? La "endeblez metodológica" de la ética según W. V. Quine y sus críticos. Rodríguez Alcázar, Javier.

## SCIENCE FICTION

How to Live Forever: Science Fiction and Philosophy. Clark, Stephen R L.

## SCIENTIFIC

Adaptive Logic in Scientific Discovery: The Case of Clausius. Meheus, Joke.

Laws of Nature, Cosmic Coincidences and Scientific Realism. Lange, Marc.

Thomas' Second Way: A Defense by Modal Scientific Reasoning. Trundle, Jr, Robert C.

## SCIENTIFIC METHOD

Lamarck's Method (in Portuguese). De Andrade Martins, Roberto and Pareira Martins, Lilian Al-Chueyr.

## SCIENTIFIC REVOLUTION

"Temples of the Body and Temples of the Cosmos: Vision and Visualization in the Vesalian and Copernican Revolutions" in Picturing Knowledge, Baigrie, Brian S (ed). Kemp, Martin.

Natural Law and the Scientific Revolution. Koenig, Bernie.

Thomas S. Kuhn, een moderne komedie van vergissingen. Derksen, A A.

Thomistic Natural Philosophy and the Scientific Revolution. Reitan, Eric A.

## SCIENTISM

"Who is Afraid of Scientism?" in Epistemology and History, Zeidler-Janiszewska, Anna (ed). Sójka, Jacek.

Against Naturalizing Rationality. Moser, Paul K and Yandell, David.

Between Scientism and Conversationalism. Haack, Susan.

Commentary and Criticism on Scientific Positivism. Gilmer, Penny J.

On the Poverty of Scientism, or: The Ineluctable Roughness of Rationality. Code, Murray.

Scientism, Deconstruction, Atheism. Meynell, Hugo.

What is Scientism?. Stenmark, Mikael.

## SCIENTIST

"¿René Descartes, cientifista?" in Memorias Del Seminario En Conmemoración De Los 400 Anos Del Nacimiento De René Descartes, Albis, Víctor S (ed). Sierra, Guillermo Restrepo.

Child's Play. Nersessian, Nancy J.

## SELECTION

Biological Function, Selection, and Reduction. Manning, Richard N.

Journals and Justice. Curzer, Howard J.

Reflections on Peer Review Practices in Committees Selecting Laureates for Prestigious Awards and Prizes: Some Relevant and Irrelevant Criteria. Vijh, Ashok K.

The Import of Skinner's Three-Term Contingency. Moxley, Roy A.

The Return of the Group. Sterelny, Kim.

## SELF

see also Ego, Personal Identity

"Absolute Subject and Absolute Subjectivity in Hegel" in Figuring the Self: Subject, Absolute, and Others in Classical German Philosophy, Zöller, Günter (ed). Jaeschke, Walter.

"An Eye for an I: Fichte's Transcendental Experiment" in Figuring the Self: Subject, Absolute, and Others in Classical German Philosophy, Zöller, Günter (ed). Zöller, Günter.

"And of That Other and Her Desire: The Embracing Language of Wallace Stevens" in Critical Studies: Ethics and the Subject, Simms, Karl (ed). Cleghorn, Angus.

"Appropriating Selfhood: Schleiermacher and Hegel on Subjectivity as Mediated Activity" in Figuring the Self: Subject, Absolute, and Others in Classical German Philosophy, Zöller, Günter (ed). Hoover, Jeffrey L.

"Beyond the Death of Art: Community and the Ecology of the Self" in Philosophy in Experience: American Philosophy in Transition, Hart, Richard (ed). Alexander, Thomas M.

"Buddhi-Taoist and Western Metaphysics of the Self" in Culture and Self, Allen, Douglas (ed). Inada, Kenneth K.

"Classical Confucian and Contemporary Feminist Perspectives on the Self: Some Parallels and their Implications" in Culture and Self, Allen, Douglas (ed). Rosemont, Henry.

"Deconstructing the Self on the Wild Side" in Jean-Jacques Rousseau and the Sources of the Self, O'Hagan, Timothy (ed). Wokler, Robert.

"Dewey Without Doing" in Philosophy of Education (1996), Margonis, Frank (ed). Arnstine, Donald.

"Dewey's Idea of Sympathy and the Development of the Ethical Self: A Japanese Perspective" in Philosophy of Education (1996), Margonis, Frank (ed). Saito, Naoko.

"Ethics, Relativism, and the Self" in Culture and Self, Allen, Douglas (ed). Bockover, Mary I.

"Heidegger and Wittgenstein on the Subject of Kantian Philosophy" in Figuring the Self: Subject, Absolute, and Others in Classical German Philosophy, Zöller, Günter (ed). Stern, David G.

"Hypostatic Abstraction in Self-Consciousness" in The Rule of Reason: The Philosophy of Charles Sanders Peirce, Forster, Paul (ed). Short, T L.

"Incarnation, Difference, and Identity: Materialism, Self, and the Life of Spirit" in Philosophy in Experience: American Philosophy in Transition, Hart, Richard (ed). Wallace, Kathleen.

"Introduction to Part I" in Critical Studies: Ethics and the Subject, Simms, Karl (ed). Simms, Karl.

"John E. Smith and the Heart of Experience" in The Recovery of Philosophy in America: Essays in Honor of John Edwin Smith, Kasulis, Thomas P (ed). Anderson, Douglas R.

"Kant and the Self: A Retrospective" in Figuring the Self: Subject, Absolute, and Others in Classical German Philosophy, Zöller, Günter (ed). Ameriks, Karl.

"Making Jean-Jacques" in Jean-Jacques Rousseau and the Sources of the Self, O'Hagan, Timothy (ed). Gauthier, David.

"Mrs. Bates in Plato's Cave" in Critical Studies: Ethics and the Subject, Simms, Karl (ed). Brottman, David.

"On Disappointment in the Black Context" in Existence in Black: An Anthology of Black Existential Philosophy, Gordon, Lewis R (ed). Lawson, Bill E.

"Originality: Moral Good, Private Vice, or Self-Enchantment" in Jean-Jacques Rousseau and the Sources of the Self, O'Hagan, Timothy (ed). Mason, John Hope.

"Realizing Nature in the Self: Schelling on Art and Intellectual Intuition" in Figuring the Self: Subject, Absolute, and Others in Classical German Philosophy, Zöller, Günter (ed). Velkley, Richard L.

"Reducing Concern with Self: Parfit and the Ancient Buddhist Schools" in Culture and Self, Allen, Douglas (ed). Basu, Ananyo.

"Romantic Conceptions of the Self in Hölderlin and Novalis" in Figuring the Self: Subject, Absolute, and Others in Classical German Philosophy, Zöller, Günter (ed). Kneller, Jane E.

"Sartre and Samkhya-Yoga on Self" in Culture and Self, Allen, Douglas (ed). Malhotra, Ashok K.

"Self and Community in Environmental Ethics" in Ecofeminism: Women, Culture, Nature, Warren, Karen J (ed). Donner, Wendy.

"Self as Matter and Form: Some Reflections on Kant's View of the Soul" in Figuring the Self: Subject, Absolute, and Others in Classical German Philosophy, Zöller, Günter (ed). Aquila, Richard E.

"Social Constructions of Self: Some Asian, Marxist, and Feminist Critiques of Dominant Western Views of Self" in Culture and Self, Allen, Douglas (ed). Allen, Douglas.

"Subject and Citizen: Hobbes and Rousseau on Sovereignty and the self" in Jean-Jacques Rousseau and the Sources of the Self, O'Hagan, Timothy (ed). Trachtenberg, Zev.

"Subjectivity and Individuality: Survey of a Problem" in Figuring the Self: Subject, Absolute, and Others in Classical German Philosophy, Zöller, Günter (ed). Frank, Manfred.

"Technologies of the Self" in Critical Studies: Ethics and the Subject, Simms, Karl (ed). Ball, Elaine.

"The Subject of the Other: Ordinary Language and Its Enigmatic Ground" in Critical Studies: Ethics and the Subject, Simms, Karl (ed). Phillips, J W P.

"Views of Japanese Selfhood: Japanese and Western Perspectives" in Culture and Self, Allen, Douglas (ed). Miller, Mara.

"Whose House is That? Wittgenstein on the Self" in The Cambridge Companion to Wittgenstein, Sluga, Hans (ed). Sluga, Hans.

A Free Enquiry into the Vulgarly Received Notion of Nature. Davis, Edward B (ed), Hunter, Michael (ed) and Boyle, Robert.

A Theory of Language and Mind. Bencivenga, Ermanno.

Becoming a Self: A Reading of Kierkegaard's Concluding Unscientific Postscript. Westphal, Merold.

Being and Time: A Translation of Sein und Zeit. Stambaugh, Joan and Stambaugh, Joan (trans).

Coming Together/Coming Apart: Religion, Community, and Modernity. Bounds, Elizabeth M.

Critical Studies: Ethics and the Subject. Simms, Karl (ed).

Culture and Self. Allen, Douglas (ed) and Malhotra, Ashok K.

European Existentialism. Langiulli, Nino (ed).

Existence, Thought, Style: Perspectives of a Primary Relation: Portrayed through the Work of Soren Kierkegaard. King, G Heath and Kircher, Timothy (ed).

Figuring the Self: Subject, Absolute, and Others in Classical German Philosophy. Zöller, Günter (ed) and Klemm, David E (ed).

Forms of Transcendence: Heidegger and Medieval Mystical Theology. Sikka, Sonya.

Human, All Too Human, I. Handwerk, Gary (trans) and Nietzsche, Friedrich.

Jean-Jacques Rousseau and the Sources of the Self. O'Hagan, Timothy (ed).

Kant and the Problem of Metaphysics. Taft, Richard (trans) and Heidegger, Martin.

Krishnamurti: Reflections on the Self. Martin, Raymond (ed) and Krishnamurti, J.

Max Scheler: A Concise Introduction into the World of a Great Thinker. Frings, Manfred S.

Memory, Identity, Community: The Idea of Narrative in the Human Sciences. Hinchman, Lewis P (ed) and Hichmann, Sandra K (ed).

My Philosophical Development. Russell, Bertrand.

Nietzsche's Philosophy of the Eternal Recurrence of the Same. Lomax, J Harvey (trans) and Löwith, Karl.

Philosophy History Sophistry. Rohatyn, Dennis.

Representation and the Mind-Body Problem in Spinoza. Della Rocca, Michael.

Republican Paradoxes and Liberal Anxieties. Terchek, Ronald J.

Rousseau and the Politics of Ambiguity: Self, Culture, and Society. Morgenstern, Mira.

Self and World. Cassam, Quassim.

Self-Trust: A Study of Reason, Knowledge and Autonomy. Lehrer, Keith.

The Cambridge Edition of the Works of Immanuel Kant: Lectures on Metaphysics. Ameriks, Karl (ed & trans), Naragon, Steve (ed & trans) and Kant, Immanuel.

The Constitution of Selves. Schechtman, Marya.

The Self After Postmodernity. Boling, Patricia.

The Self and Its Body in Hegel's Phenomenology of Spirit. Russon, John Edward.

The Solitary Self: Jean-Jacques Rousseau in Exile and Adversity. Cranston, Maurice.

Transgressing Discourses: Communication and the Voice of Other. Huspek, Michael (ed) and Radford, Gary P (ed).

William James On The Courage to Believe. O'Connell, Robert J.

Without a Woman to Read: Toward the Daughter in Postmodernism. Price, Daniel.

A Critical Analysis of John Locke's Criterion of Personal Identity. Chakraborty, Alpana.

A marca do vazio: Reflexoes sobre a subjetividade em Blaise Pascal. De Souza Birchal, Telma.

A Noçao de Sujeito como Aparece nas Meditaçoes Considerada à Luz das Sugestoes Wittgensteinianas a Respeito da Linguagem. Alvarenga, Ethel.

Abkehr vom Mythos: Descartes in der gegenwärtigen Diskussion. Perler, Dominik.

Adams on Actualism and Presentism. Craig, William Lane.

Antisoggettivismo e l'autorità della prima persona. Soldati, Gianfranco.

Artificial Intelligence Modeling of Spontaneous Self Learning: An Application of Dialectical Philosophy. Stokes, Karina.

Becoming an Evil Society: The Self and Strangers. Thomas, Laurence.

Beyond Postmodernism: Langan's Foundational Ontology. Calcagno, Antonio.

Beyond Self and Other. Rogers, Kelly.

Bits of Broken Glass: Zora Neale Hurston's Conception of the Self. Sartwell, Crispin.

Born to Affirm the Eternal Recurrence: Nietzsche, Buber, and Springsteen. Cohen, Jonathan.

**SELF-SUFFICIENCY**
Autarcie et logos conciliateur chez Zénon de Cittium. Kélessidou, Anna.
Gedanken zur gegenwärtigen Bedeutung der Fichteschen Wirtschaftsethik. Fukuyoshi, Masao.

**SELFHOOD**
Reviving Ophelia: A Role for Philosophy in Helping Young Women Achieve Selfhood. Turgeon, Wendy C.
The Absolute and Kierkegaard's Conception of Selfhood. Buterin, Damir.

**SELFISHNESS**
Consequentialism, Moralities of Concern, and Selfishness. Honderich, Ted.

**SELLARS, W**
Descrying the World in the Wave Function. Maudlin, Tim.

**SEMANTICS**
see also Linguistics, Meaning
"A Tarski-Style Semantics for Peirce's Beta Graphs" in *The Rule of Reason: The Philosophy of Charles Sanders Peirce*, Forster, Paul (ed). Burch, Robert W.
"Can Peter Be Rational?" in *Contents*, Villanueva, Enrique (ed). Valdivia, Lourdes.
"Can Semantic Properties Be Non-Causal?" in *Contents*, Villanueva, Enrique (ed). Jacob, Pierre.
"Can We Knock Off the Shackles of Syntax?" in *Contents*, Villanueva, Enrique (ed). Andler, Daniel.
"Carnap: From Logical Syntax to Semantics" in *Origins of Logical Empiricism*, Giere, Ronald N (ed). Ricketts, Thomas.
"Functioning and Teachings of Adaptive Logics" in *Logic and Argumentation*, Van Eemeren, Frans H (ed). Batens, Diderik.
"How to Combine Ordering and Minimizing in a Deontic Logic Based on Preferences" in *Deontic Logic, Agency and Normative Systems*, Brown, Mark A (ed). Tan, Yao-Hua and Van der Torre, Leendert W N.
"Intensionale Semantik und physikalische Grössen" in *Das weite Spektrum der analytischen Philosophie*, Lenzen, Wolfgang. Oberschelp, Arnold.
"Model Theory in the Analysis of Natural Language" in *Verdad: lógica, representación y mundo*, Villegas Forero, L. Zimmermann, Thomas Ede.
"Must I Do What I Ought? (Or Will the Least I Can Do Do?)" in *Deontic Logic, Agency and Normative Systems*, Brown, Mark A (ed). McNamara, Paul.
"On Sosa's 'Fregean Reference Defended'" in *Contents*, Villanueva, Enrique (ed). Lycan, William G.
"Per una storia delle ricerche sul concetto di dimostrazione logica nel novecento" in *Momenti di Storia della Logica e di Storia della Filosofia*, Guetti, Carla (ed). Abrusci, Michele.
"Propositional Attitudes and Compositional Semantics" in *AI, Connectionism and Philosophical Psychology, 1995*, Tomberlin, James E (ed). Boër, Steven E.
"Reference from the First Person Perspective" in *Contents*, Villanueva, Enrique (ed). Loar, Brian.
"Relativity, *Eindeutigkeit*, and Monomorphism: Rudolph Carnap and the Development of the Categoricity Concept in Formal Semantics" in *Origins of Logical Empiricism*, Giere, Ronald N (ed). Howard, Don.
"Semantic Considerations on Relevance" in *Das weite Spektrum der analytischen Philosophie*, Lenzen, Wolfgang. Orlowska, Ewa.
"Semantic Intuitions: Conflict Resolution in the Formal Sciences" in *Logic and Argumentation*, Van Eemeren, Frans H (ed). Woods, John.
"Significado y denotación en J.A. Fodor" in *Verdad: lógica, representación y mundo*, Villegas Forero, L. Blanco Salgueiro, Antonio.
"Some Foundational Concepts of Erotetic Semantics" in *Knowledge and Inquiry: Essays on Jaakko Hintikka's Epistemology and Philosophy of Science*, Sintonen, Matti (ed). Wisniewski, Andrzej.
"Teoría de situaciones: Semántica de tipos para un lenguaje formal con concepto de verdad" in *Verdad: lógica, representación y mundo*, Villegas Forero, L. Beck, Andreas.
"The Logic of Normative Systems" in *Deontic Logic, Agency and Normative Systems*, Brown, Mark A (ed). Johanson, Arnold A.
"The Semantic Transformation of an Axiological Concept" in *East and West in Aesthetics*, Marchianò, Grazia (ed). Hashimoto, Noriko.
"Theories of Questions in German-Speaking Philosophy" in *Knowledge and Inquiry: Essays on Jaakko Hintikka's Epistemology and Philosophy of Science*, Sintonen, Matti (ed). Kusch, Martin.
*Meinongian Logic: The Semantics of Existence and Nonexistence*. Jacquette, Dale.
*Readings in the Philosophy of Language*. Ludlow, Peter (ed).
*Representation of the World: A Naturalized Semantics*. Melnick, Arthur.
*The Continuity of Wittgenstein's Thought*. Koethe, John.
*Vagueness*. Williamson, Timothy.
*Ways of Meaning: An Introduction to a Philosophy of Language*. Platts, Mark.
*Zur Meta-Theorie der Physik*. Schröter, Joachim.
A Basic System of Congruential-to-Monotone Bimodal Logic and Two of its Extensions. Humberstone, I Lloyd.
A Class of Modal Logics with a Finite Model Property with Respect to the Set of Possible-Formulae. Demri, Stéphane and Orlowska, Ewa.
A Constructive Valuation Semantics for Classical Logic. Barbanera, Franco and Berardi, Stefano.
A Context-Sensitive Liar. Juhl, Cory F.
A Counterexample in Tense Logic. Wolter, Frank.
A Decision Procedure for Von Wright's Obs-Calculus. Buekens, Filip.
A General Approach to the Algebras of Unary Functions in a Boolean Semantics for Natural Language. Nowak, Marek.

A Logic for Information Systems. Archangelsky, Dmitri A and Taitslin, Mikhail A.
A Logic-Based Modelling of Prolog Resulation Sequences Including the Negation as Failure Rule. Jcavons, John S and Crossley, John N.
A Minimal Logical System for Computable Concepts and Effective Knowability. Freund, Max A.
A Naive Variety of Logical Consequence. Alonso González, Enrique.
A New Argument from Actualism to Serious Actualism. Bergmann, Michael.
A New Theory of Content II: Model Theory and Some Alternative. Gemes, Ken.
A Nonmonotonic Modal Formalization of the Logic of Acceptance and Rejection. Gomolinska, Anna.
A Note on the Nature of "Water". Abbott, Barbara.
A Note on Truth, Deflationism and Irrealism. Miraglia, Pierluigi.
A Type Free Theory and Collective/Distributive Predication. Kamareddine, Fairouz.
A Uniform Tableau Method for Intuitionistic Modal Logics I. Amati, Giambattista and Pirri, Fiora.
Abstraktion und Ideation—Zur Semantik chemischer und biologischer Grundbegriffe. Gutmann, Mathias and Hanekamp, Gerd.
Action Incompleteness. Segerberg, Krister.
An Alternative Linear Semantics for Allowed Logic Programs. Jeavons, John S.
An Axiomatization for Until and Since over the Reals without the IRR Rule. Reynolds, Mark.
An Essay on Resolution Logics. Stachniak, Zbigniew.
An Intensional Epistemic Logic. Jiang, Yue J.
Analyticity, Necessity, and the Epistemology of Semantics. Katz, Jerrold J.
Arte e ciência: Acordo e progresso. D'Orey, Carmo.
Axiomatising First-Order Temporal Logic: Until and Since over Linear Time. Reynolds, Mark.
Axiomatization and Completeness of Uncountably Valued Approximation Logic. Rasiowa, Helena.
Belief Content and Compositionality. Kimbrough, Scott.
Believing in Language. Dwyer, Susan and Pietroski, Paul M.
Bisimulations for Temporal Logic. Kurtonina, Natasha and De Rijke, Maarten.
Brandom's *Making It Explicit*: A First Encounter. Rosenberg, Jay F.
Brouwer-Zadeh Logic, Decidability and Bimodal Systems. Giuntini, Roberto.
Canonical Models for Temporal Deontic Logic. Bailhache, Patrice.
Choice Functions and the Scopal Semantics of Indefinites. Winter, Yoad.
Combining Temporal Logic Systems. Finger, Marcelo and Gabbay, Dov.
Comment construit-on une explication déductive-nomologique?. Weber, Erik.
Comments on Peter Roeper's "The Link between Probability Functions and Logical Consequence". Van Fraassen, Bas C.
Completeness and Decidability of Tense Logics Closely Related to Logics Above K4. Wolter, Frank.
Completeness and Incompleteness for Plausibility Logic. Schlechta, Karl.
Completeness Results for Linear Logic on Petri Nets. Engberg, Uffe.
Completeness Theorem for Dummett's L C Quantified and Some of Its Extensions. Corsi, Giovanna.
Conditions on Understanding Language. Lepore, Ernest.
Confirmation Holism and Semantic Holism. Harrell, Mack.
Counterexamples, Idealizations, and Intuitions: A Study in Philosophical Method. Prudovsky, Gad.
Counterfactuals and Updates as Inverse Modalities. Ryan, Mark and Schobbens, Pierre-Yves.
Counterfactuals with True Components. Penczek, Alan.
Counterpart Theory as a Semantics for Modal Logic. Woollaston, Lin.
Criteria for Admissibility of Inference Rules: Modal and Intermediate Logics with the Branching Property. Rybakov, Vladimir V.
Cut-Free Sequent Calculi for Some Tense Logics. Kashima, Ryo.
Das Problem der transzendentalen Freiheit in semantischer Formulierung (Dargestellt an Fichtes Jenaer Wissenschaftslehren). Poreba, Marcin.
De Aristóteles a Bréal: Da *Homonímia* à *Polissemia*. Da Silva, Augusto Soares.
Decidability by Filtrations for Graded Normal Logics (Graded Modalities V). Cerrato, Claudio.
Decidability of *Stit* Theory with a Single Agent and *Refref* Equivalence. Xu, Ming.
Decidability Results for Metric and Layered Temporal Logics. Montanari, Angelo and Policriti, Alberto.
Deontics between Semantics and Ontology. Alarcón Cabrera, Carlos.
Die Idee hinter Tarskis Definition von Wahrheit. Greimann, Dirk.
Die impliziten Prämissen in Quines Kritik der semantischen Begriffe. Greimann, Dirk.
Die Rolle der vollständigen Induktion in der Theorie des Wahrheitsbegriffes. Padilla-Gálvez, Jesús.
Display Logic and Gaggle Theory. Restall, Greg.
Duality for Lattice-Ordered Algebras and for Normal Algebraizable Logics. Hartonas, Chrysafis.
El argumento fregeano de las oraciones aseverativas como nombres propios. Ramos, Pedro.
Equivalential and Algebraizable Logics. Herrmann, Burghard.
Everett's Trilogy. Priest, Graham.

## SEMANTICS

Facts, Semantics and Intuitionism. Akama, Seiki.

Fibred Semantics and the Weaving of Logics Part 1: Modal and Intuitionistic Logics. Gabbay, D M.

Fibred Semantics for Feature-Based Grammar Logic. Dörre, Jochen, König, Esther and Gabbay, Dov.

Fichtes *geometrische* Semantik. Jergius, Holger.

Fodor's Information Semantics between Naturalism and Mentalism. Meyering, Theo C.

Fred Dretske on the Explanatory Role of Semantic Content. Hassrick, Beth.

From *intellectus verus/falsus* to the *dictum propositionis*: The Semantics of Peter Abelard and his Circle. King, Peter, Jacobi, Klaus and Strub, Christian.

Gibt es etwas ausser mir selbst? Überlegungen zur semantischen Begründung des Realismus. Moulines, C Ulises.

Hans Kronning. Modalité, cognition et polysémie: sémantique du verbe modal devoir. Rossetti, Andrea.

Hechos semánticos y presiones fisicalistas. Acero, Juan José.

Hegel's Logic as a Theory of Meaning. Stekeler-Weithofer, Pirmin.

How Much Substitutivity?. Forbes, Graeme.

How Well does Direct Reference Semantics Fit with Pragmatics?. Lumsden, David.

Hybrid Languages. Blackburn, Patrick and Seligman, Jerry.

Hypercomparatives. Morton, Adam.

Identity in Modal Logic Theorem Proving. Pelletier, Francis J.

Internal Realism, Rationality and Dynamic Semantics. Naumann, Ralf.

Is Compositionality Compatible with Holism?. Pagin, Peter.

Is There a Problem about Intentionality?. Beckermann, Ansgar.

Kein Etwas, aber auch nicht ein Nichts!: Kann die Grammatik tatsächlich täuschen?. Gaskin, Richard.

Kripke Bundle Semantics and C-set Semantics. Isoda, Eiko.

Kripke Completeness of Some Intermediate Predicate Logics with the Axiom of Constant Domain and a Variant of Canonical Formulas. Shimura, Tatsuya.

La inefabilidad de la semántica y el realismo interno. Cabanchik, Samuel Manuel.

La théorie intuitionniste des types: sémantique des preuves et théorie des constructions. Bourdeau, Michel.

Logiques et sémantiques non classiques. Voizard, Alain.

Meaning and Semantic Knowledge. Antony, Louise M and Davies, Martin.

Meanings and Psychology: A Response to Mark Richard. Devitt, Michael.

Modal Companions of Intermediate Propositional Logics. Chagrov, Alexander and Zakharyashchev, Michael.

Modal Logic over Finite Structures. Rosen, Eric.

Models, Truth and Semantics. Abbott, Barbara.

Mostly Meyer Modal Models. Mares, Edwin D.

Nominal Comparatives and Generalized Quantifiers. Nerbonne, John.

Nonmonotonic Theories and Their Axiomatic Varieties. Stachniak, Zbigniew.

Normal Bimodal Logics of Ability and Action. Brown, Mark A.

Object Theory Foundations for Intensional Logic. Jacquette, Dale.

On David Charles's Account of Aristotle's Semantics for Simple Names. Butler, Travis.

On Maximal Intermediate Predicate Constructive Logics. Avelone, Alessandro, Fiorentini, Camillo and Mantovani, Paolo (& others).

On Negatively Restricting Boolean Algebras. Zuber, R.

On S. Fuhrmann, André and Mares, Edwin D.

On the Completeness of First Degree Weakly Aggregative Modal Logics. Apostoli, Peter.

On the Link Between Frege's Platonic-Realist Semantics and His Doctrine of Private Senses. Ellenbogen, Sara.

On the Logic of Event-Causation: Jaskowski-Style Systems of Causal Logic. Urchs, Max.

On the Semantics of Comparative Conditionals. Beck, Sigrid.

On the Very Idea of a Theory of Meaning for a Natural Language. Fischer, Eugen.

Orgasmic Rapture and Divine Ecstasy: The Semantic History of Ānanda. Olivelle, Patrick.

Overruling Rules?. Yovel, Jonathan.

Parallel Action: Concurrent Dynamic Logic with Independent Modalities. Goldblatt, Robert.

Partial Monotonicity and a New Version of the Ramsey Test. Pais, John and Jackson, Peter.

Partially-Ordered (Branching) Generalized Quantifiers: A General Definition. Sher, G Y.

Polarity Sensitivity as Lexical Semantics. Israel, M.

Posits and Positing. Wilburn, Ron.

Pragmatics and Singular Reference. Bezuidenhout, Anne.

Pragmatics, Semantic Underdetermination and the Referential/Attributive Distinction. Bezuidenhout, Anne.

Property Identity and 'Intrinsic' Designation. Goldstick, Danny.

Putnam, Equivalence, Realism. Cox, Damian.

Quantified Deontic Logic with Definite Descriptions. Goble, Lou.

Quantified Extensions of Canonical Propositional Intermediate Logics. Ghilardi, Silvio.

Reasoning about Action and Change. Prendinger, Helmut and Schurz, Gerhard.

Refutation Systems in Modal Logic. Goranko, Valentin.

Relevant Logic and the Theory of Information. Mares, Edwin D.

Revision Algebra Semantics for Conditional Logic. Pais, John.

Salmon Trapping. Yagisawa, Takashi.

Schrödinger Logics. Da Costa, Newton C A and Krause, Décio.

Semantics for Relevance Logic with Identity. Mares, Edwin D.

Semantics for Two Second-Order Logical Systems. Freund, Max A.

Sémantique pour la Logique Déontique. Sart, Frédéric.

Similarity as an Intertheory Relation. Gorham, Geoffrey.

Sobre la interpretación deflacionaria de la teoría de Tarski. Orlando, Eleonora.

Sobre referencia y causalidad. Lo Monaco, Vicenzo P.

Some Considerations on Non-Linear Time Intervals. Hajnicz, Elzbieta.

Some Results on the Kripke Sheaf Semantics for Super-Intuitionistic Predicate Logics. Suzuki, Nobu-Yuki.

Sozialstruktur und Sematik: Der wissenssoziologische Ansatz Niklas Luhmanns. Götke, Povl.

Strong Semantic Systematicity from Hebbian Connectionist Learning. Hadley, Robert F and Hayward, Michael B.

Strong Versus Weak Quantum Consequence Operations. Malinowski, Jacek.

Structured Meanings and Reflexive Domains. Lapierre, Serge.

Success Again: Replies to Brandom and Godfrey-Smith. Whyte, J T.

Superintuitionistic Comparisons of Classical Modal Logics. Wolter, Frank.

Supervaluations and the Propositional Attitude Constraint. Burgess, J A.

Suppositio and Significatio in Ockham's *Summa Logicae* (in Portuguese). Perini Santos, Ernesto.

Swampman Meets Swampcow. Neander, Karen.

T x W Completeness. Von Kutschera, Franz.

Talk About Fiction. Predelli, Stefano.

Taming Logic. Marx, Maarten, Mikulás, Szabolcs and Németi, István.

Teleological Semantics. Rowlands, Mark.

Temporalized Deontic Worlds with Individuals. Bailhache, Patrice.

The Ambiguity Thesis Versus Kripke's Defence of Russell. Ramachandran, Murali.

The Completeness of the Factor Semantics for Lukasiewicz's Infinite-Valued Logics. Vasyukov, Vladimir L.

The Elimination of *De Re* Formulas. Kaminski, Michael.

The Finite Model Property for BCK and BCIW. Meyer, Robert K and Ono, Hiroakira.

The Link between Probability Functions and Logical Consequence. Roeper, Peter.

The Logic of Belief Persistence. Battigalli, Pierpaolo and Bonanno, Giacomo.

The Logic of Peirce Algebras. De Rijke, Maarten.

The Logic of Permission and Obligation in the Framework of ALX.3: How to avoid the Paradoxes of Deontic Logics. Huang, Zhisheng and Masuch, Michael.

The Meaning of "Mental Meaning" (in Spanish). Blanco Salgueiro, Antonio.

The Modal Logic of Discrepancy. Cross, Charles B.

The Price of Universality. Hemaspaandra, Edith.

The Problem of Transworld Identity. Gundersen, Lars.

The Ramsey Test and Conditional Semantics. Döring, Frank.

The Semantic of Linear Perspective. Turner, Norman.

The Semantics of Fictional Names. Adams, Frederick, Fuller, Gary and Stecker, Robert.

The Slingshot Argument. Read, Stephen.

The Structure of Lattices of Subframe Logics. Wolter, Frank.

The Way of the Agent. Belnap, Nuel and Perloff, Michael.

Théorie de la valuation. Da Costa, Newton C A and Béziau, Jean-Yves.

Time and Modality in the Logic of Agency. Chellas, Brian F.

Tree Models and (Labeled) Categorial Grammar. Venema, Yde.

Troubles with Wagner's Reading of Millikan. Millikan, Ruth Garrett.

Truth and Metatheory in Frege. Stanley, Jason.

Truth in Pure Semantics: A Reply to Putnam. Moreno, Luis Fernández.

Two Kinds of Antiessentialism and Their Consequences. Spinosa, Charles and Dreyfus, Hubert L.

Undecidability and Intuitionistic Incompleteness. McCarty, D C.

Vague Predicates and Language Games. Parikh, Rohit.

Valuational Semantics of Rule Derivability. Humberstone, I Lloyd.

Varieties of Quotation. Cappelen, Herman and Lepore, Ernest.

What Cannot Be Evaluated Cannot Be Evaluated, and it Cannot Be Supervalued Either. Fodor, Jerry A and Lepore, Ernest.

What do Belief Ascribers Really Mean? A Reply to Stephen Schiffer. Reimer, Marga.

What Do You Do When They Call You a 'Relativist'. Rorty, Richard.

What is Semantics? A Brief Note on a Huge Question. Da Costa, Newton C A, Bueno, Otávio and Béziau, Jean-Yves.

What Is the Upper Part of the Lattice of Bimodal Logics?. Wolter, Frank.

Who Makes the Rules Around Here?. Rosen, Gideon.

'Ought' and Extensionality. Goble, Lou.

## SEMETIC

La raíz semítica de lo europeo: Islam y judaísmo medievales. Lomba, Joaquín.

## SEMINAR

El seminario 'Orotava' de historia de la ciencia. Montesinos, José.

## SEMIOLOGY

L'arc-en-ciel et les sacrements: de la sémiologie de la *Logique de Port-Royal* à la théorie pascalienne des figures. Shiokawa, Tetsuya.

## SEMIOTICS

*see also* Sign

"Peirce and Russell: The History of a Neglected 'Controversy'" in *Studies in the Logic of Charles Sanders Peirce,* Houser, Nathan (ed). Hawkins, Benjamin S.

"Peirce's Sign and the Process of Interpretation" in *Philosophy in Experience: American Philosophy in Transition,* Hart, Richard (ed). Kruse, Felicia E.

"The Dynamical Object and the Deliberative Subject" in *The Rule of Reason: The Philosophy of Charles Sanders Peirce,* Forster, Paul (ed). Colapietro, Vincent M.

*Augusto Ponzio: Bibliografia e Letture Critiche.* Ponzio, Augusto.

*Language, Action, and Context: The Early History of Pragmatics in Europe and America, 1780-1930.* Nerlich, Brigitte and Clarke, David D.

*Literature, Criticism, and the Theory of Signs.* Tejera, Victorino.

*Peirce, Signs, and Meaning.* Merrell, Floyd.

*Signs of the Time.* Elias, Willem.

About Signs and Symptoms: Can Semiotics Expand the View of Clinical Medicine?. Nessa, John.

Aesthetic and Praxial Philosophies of Music Education Compared: A Semiotic Consideration. Spychiger, Maria B.

Die Kopernikanische und die semiotische Wende der Philosophie. Zeidler, Kurt W.

From a Semiotic to a Neo-Pragmatic Understanding of Metaphor. Von der Fehr, Drude.

Interpreting Peirce's Interpretant: A Response To Lalor, Liszka, and Meyers. Short, T L.

Metaphor—A Semiotic Perspective. Larsen, Svend Erik.

Paramodern Strategies of Philosophical Historiography. Daniel, Stephen H.

The Angel in the Machine. Schachter, Jean-Pierre.

The Chinese Theory of Forms and Names (*xingming zhi xue*) and Its Relation to "Philosophy of Signs". Möller, Hans Georg.

The Transposition of the Linguistic Sign in Peirce's Contributions to *The Nation.* Deledalle-Rhodes, Janice.

## SEN, A

Basal Inequalities: Reply to Sen. Kane, John.

Funciones de Bienestar social no lineales: una réplica al profesor Sen. Harsanyi, John C.

My Own Criticism of *The Joyless Economy.* Scitovsky, Tibor.

Welfarism in Moral Theory. Moore, Andrew and Crisp, Roger.

## SENECA

La place du politique dans le système stoïcien. Lang, André.

Le stoïcisme ou la conscience de Rome. Jerphagnon, Lucien.

Notas sobre a Presença de Sêneca nos *Essais* de Montaigne. Alves Eva, Luiz Antonio.

## SENG-CHAO

Time and Emptiness in the *Chao-Lun.* Berman, Michael.

## SENGHOR, L

*Léopold Sédar Senghor: From Politics to Poetry.* Kluback, William.

## SENOR, T

New Books on Philosophy of Religion. Moser, Paul K.

## SENSATION

*see also* Emotion, Feeling, Perception

"Pictures, Logic, and the Limits of Sense in Wittgenstein's *Tractatus*" in *The Cambridge Companion to Wittgenstein,* Sluga, Hans (ed). Ricketts, Thomas.

*Critique of Pure Reason: Unified Edition (With All Variants from the 1781 and 1787 Editions).* Pluhar, Werner S (trans) and Kant, Immanuel.

*Immanuel Kant: Principios Formales del Mundo Sensible y del Inteligible (Disertación de 1770).* Gómez Caffarena, José (ed), Ceñal Lorente, Ramón (trans) and Kant, Immanuel.

Genealogia di un sentire inorganico: Mario Perniola. Fimiani, Mariapaola.

Introspection and its Objects. Arnold, Denis G.

Kant's Empiricism. Falkenstein, Lorne.

Mythology of the Given. Sosa, Ernest.

Phenomenon and Sensation: A Reflection on Husserl's Concept of *Sinngebung.* Dodd, James.

Reason's Different Tastes. Mitchell, Jeff.

Wittgenstein and the Doctrine of Kinaesthesis. Candlish, Stewart.

## SENSE

*Problems of Vision: Rethinking the Causal Theory of Perception.* Vision, Gerald.

Can Navya Nyāya Analysis Make a Distinction between Sense and Reference. Krishna, Daya.

Frege über indexikalische Ausdrücke. Perry, John.

It's Not What You Say, It's *That* You Say It: Speech, Performance, and Sense in Austin and Deleuze. Thomas, Douglas E.

Leading Creatively: The Art of Making Sense. Palus, Charles J and Horth, David M.

On the Link Between Frege's Platonic-Realist Semantics and His Doctrine of Private Senses. Ellenbogen, Sara.

Remissions on Jacques Derrida's Work (Spanish). Navarro, Rolando.

Sense, Reference and Selective Attention. Campbell, John and Martin, M G F.

The Argument on Identity Statements and the Problem of Referring to Functions in Frege's Philosophy (Spanish). Ramos, Pedro.

The Dispositional Account of Colour. Pitson, Tony.

What Does Commonsense Psychology Tell Us about Meaning?. Richard, Mark.

## SENSE DATA

Donald Davidson: L'incontro con la filosofia e la definizione del progetto teorico. Lepore, Ernest.

## SENSES

"Comments on John Campbell, 'Molineux's Question'" in *Perception,* Villanueva, Enrique (ed). Loar, Brian.

"Molineux's Question" in *Perception,* Villanueva, Enrique (ed). Campbell, John.

## SENSIBILITY

Kant's Pre-Critical Aesthetics: Genesis of the Notions of "Taste" and Beauty (in French). Dumouchel, Daniel.

La paradoja de la unidad originaria de la conciencia en la intuición pura y de la multiplicidad a priori de la sensibilidad. López Fernández, Alvaro.

Sensibilidad y espiritualidad según Aristóteles. García Jaramillo, Miguel Alejandro.

Sensibility and Understanding. Millar, Alan.

Théorie de la sensibilité dans le spritualisme français (in Japanese). Uemura, Hiroshi.

## SENSIBLE

Actitudes proposicionales y conocimiento sensible en Tomás de Aquino. Tellkamp, Jörg Alejandro.

## SENSITIVE

A Context-Sensitive Liar. Juhl, Cory F.

## SENSITIVITY

Polarity Sensitivity as Lexical Semantics. Israel, M.

The Abolition of Public Racial Preference—An Invitation to Private Racial Sensitivity. Kmiec, Douglas W.

## SENSUALITY

Beauty and the Breast: Dispelling Significations of Feminine Sensuality in the Aesthetics of Dance. Jaeger, Suzanne M.

## SENTENCE

*see also* Proposition, Statement

"Processing of Negative Sentences by Adults with Unila'eral Cerebral Lesions" in *Verdad: lógica, representación y mundo,* Villegas Forero, L. Juncos-Rabadán, Onésimo.

"Representación de la relación de afianzamiento epistémico en *Prolog*" in *Verdad: lógica, representación y mundo,* Villegas Forero, L. Ubeda Rives, José Pedro and Lorente Tallada, Juan Manuel.

*Readings in the Philosophy of Language.* Ludlow, Peter (ed).

*Ways of Meaning: An Introduction to a Philosophy of Language.* Platts, Mark.

Asymptotic Probabilities for Second-Order Existential Kahr-Moore-Wang Sentences. Vedo, Anne.

Believing Sentences. Vision, Gerald.

E-Type Pronouns, DRT, Dynamic Semantics and the Quantifier/ Variable-Binding Model. Barker, Stephen J.

El argumento fregeano de las oraciones aseverativas como nombres propios. Ramos, Pedro.

Fainthearted Conditionals. Morreau, Michael.

Fregean Innocence. Pietroski, Paul M.

How Should We Revise the Paratactic Theory?. Frankish, Keith.

Indirect Speech, Parataxis and the Nature of Things Said. Dodd, Julian.

Katz Astray. George, Alexander.

Melo Bacelar, Filósofo da "Grammatica" na Lexicografia de Setecentos. Torres, Amadeu.

Mental Sentences According to Burley and to the Early Ockham. Karger, Elizabeth.

Parsing If-Sentences and the Conditions of Sentencehood. Barker, Stephen J.

Property Identity and 'Intrinsic' Designation. Goldstick, Danny.

Reference and Imperfective Paradox. Graves, P R.

Reply to Forbes. Saul, Jennifer M.

Sentence Meaning, Intentionalism, and the Literary Text: An Interface. Ghosh, Ranjan K.

Some 15th and Early 16th Century Logicians on the Quantification of Categorical Sentences. Karger, Elizabeth.

Structured Propositions and Sentence Structure. King, Jeffrey C.

Substitution and Simple Sentences. Saul, Jennifer M.

Talk About Fiction. Predelli, Stefano.

The Context Principle in Frege's *Grundgesetze* (in Spanish). Schirn, Matthias.

The Emergence of Concepts of a Sentence in Ancient Greek and in Ancient Chinese Philosophy. Bosely, Richard.

The State of the Art in Speech Act Theory. Weigand, Edda.

The Unfinished Chomskyan Revolution. Katz, Jerrold J.

Truth Conditions of Tensed Sentence Types. Paul, L A.

What Cannot Be Evaluated Cannot Be Evaluated, and it Cannot Be Supervalued Either. Fodor, Jerry A and Lepore, Ernest.

## SENTENCING

Improving our Practice of Sentencing. Baker, Brenda M.

Reductivism, Retributivism, and the Civil Detention of Dangerous Offenders. Wood, David.

## SEX

Sex, Gender, Sexuality: Can Ethologists Practice Genealogy?. Gatens, Moira.

Sexual Perversion. Primoratz, Igor.

The Ethics of Genetic Research on Sexual Orientation. Schüklenk, Udo, Stein, Edward and Kerin, Jacinta (& others).

The Ideology and Biology of Gender Difference. Rhode, Deborah L.

The Morality of Intimate Faculty-Student Relationships. Dixon, Nicholas.

The Reluctant retained Witness: Alleged Sexual Misconduct in the Doctor/Patient Relationship. Yarborough, Mark.

To Be or Not to Be: Charles Taylor and the Politics of Recognition. Nicholson, Linda.

Virtual Sexes and Feminist Futures: The Philosophy of 'Cyberfeminism'. Marsden, Jill.

## SEX EDUCATION

"Good Sex as the Aim of Sexual Education" in *Philosophy of Education (1996)*, Margonis, Frank (ed). Steutel, Jan and Spiecker, Ben.

"The Politics of the "Good" in *Good Sexuality Education" in Philosophy of Education (1996)*, Margonis, Frank (ed). Boyd, Dwight and McKay, Alexander.

Accommodating Ideological Pluralism in Sexuality Education. McKay, Alexander.

Centering Culture: Teaching for Critical Sexual Literacy using the Sexual Diversity Wheel. Sears, James T.

Diversity, Values and Social Change: Renegotiating a Consensus on Sex Education. Thomson, Rachel.

Muslims and Sex Education. Halstead, J Mark.

Myths of Sexuality Education. Morris, Ronald.

Sex Education as Moral Education: Teaching for Pleasure, about Fantasy, and against Abuse. Lamb, Sharon.

Teaching about Homosexuality and Heterosexuality. Reiss, Michael J.

The Value(s) of Sex Education. Reiss, Michael J.

## SEXISM

*Behind Closed Doors*: Analysis of the Feminine Figures in Sartrean Theatre (Spanish). Comesaña-Santalices, Gloria.

Current Conceptions of Racism: A Critical Examination of Some Recent Social Philosophy. Garcia, Jorge L A.

Feeling Fraudulent: Some Moral Quandaries of a Feminist Instructor. Overall, Christine.

Humor and Harm. Goldstein, Laurence.

What Can Progress in Reproductive Technology Mean for Women?. Purdy, Laura M.

## SEXTUS EMPIRICUS

"The *Dissoi Logoi* and Early Greek Scepticism" in *Scepticism in the History of Philosophy: A Pan-American Dialogue*, Popkin, Richard H (ed). Robinson, Thomas M.

Gorgias, *On Non-Existence*: Sextus Empiricus, *Against the Logicians* 1.65-87, Translated from the Greek Text in Hermann Diels's *Die Fragmente der Vorsokratiker*. McComiskey, Bruce.

Knowledge and Discourse in Gorgias's *On the Non-Existent or On Nature*. Gaines, Robert N.

The Sceptical *Epokhé* and its Presuppositions (in Spanish). Bolzani Filho, Roberto.

## SEXUAL HARASSMENT

*Sexual Harassment: A Debate*. LeMoncheck, Linda and Hajdin, Mane.

*Sexual Harassment: Confrontations and Decisions*. Wall, Edmund (ed).

On the Persistence of Sexual Harassment in the Workplace. Baugh, S Gayle.

Sexual Harassment and Negligence. Hajdin, Mane.

Sexual Harassment and the University. Holmes, Robert L.

Sexual Harassment: A Matter of Individual Ethics, Legal Definitions, or Organizational Policy?. Keyton, Joann and Rhodes, Steven C.

## SEXUALITY

"Constructing Love, Desire, and Care" in *Sex, Preference, and Family: Essays on Law and Nature*, Nussbaum, Martha C (ed). Nussbaum, Martha C.

"Democratic Sex: Reynolds v. U.S., Sexual Relations, and Community" in *Sex, Preference, and Family: Essays on Law and Nature*, Nussbaum, Martha C (ed). Rosenblum, Nancy L.

"Love Undigitized" in *Love Analyzed*, Lamb, Roger E. De Sousa, Ronald.

"Natural Law, Morality, and Sexual Complementarity" in *Sex, Preference, and Family: Essays on Law and Nature*, Nussbaum, Martha C (ed). Weithman, Paul J.

"Opening the Closet Door: Sexualities Education and "Active Ignorance" in *Philosophy of Education (1996)*, Margonis, Frank (ed). Ford, Maureen.

"Performance Anxiety: Sexuality and School Controversy" in *Philosophy of Education (1996)*, Margonis, Frank (ed). Mayo, Cris.

"Sexuality and Liberty: Making Room for Nature and Tradition?" in *Sex, Preference, and Family: Essays on Law and Nature*, Nussbaum, Martha C (ed). Macedo, Stephen.

"The Sexual Economist and Legal Regulation of the Sexual Orientations" in *Sex, Preference, and Family: Essays on Law and Nature*, Nussbaum, Martha C (ed). Halley, Janet E.

*Freud and the Passions*. O'Neill, John (ed).

*The Concept of Woman*. Allen, Prudence.

*The Reformation of Society Through Adequate Education*. Provost, C Antonio.

A Critique of Normative Heterosexuality: Identity, Embodiment, and Sexual Difference in Beauvoir and Irigaray. Schutte, Ofelia.

A Defense of Physicalism. Jensen, Steven J.

Accommodating Ideological Pluralism in Sexuality Education. McKay, Alexander.

Ah! My Foolish Heart: A Reply to Alan Soble's "Antioch's 'Sexual Offense Policy': A Philosophical Exploration". Kittay, Eva Felder.

An Expanded Theoretical Discourse on Human Sexuality Education. Anderson, Peter B.

Antioch's "Sexual Offense Policy": A Philosophical Exploration. Soble, Alan.

Battered Women Who Kill: Victims and Agents of Violence. Hartline, Sharon E.

Being Human: Issues in Sexuality for People with Developmental Disabilities. Civjan, Sheryl Robinson.

Contraceptive Risk-Taking and Norms of Chastity. Stubblefield, Anna.

Damned if You Do and Damned if You Don't: Sexual Aesthetics and the Music of Dame Ethel Smyth. Gates, Eugene.

Deconstructive Strategies and the Movement Against Sexual Violence. Heberle, Renee.

Dominio de sí, tecnologías del yo y hermenéutica del sujeto. Lanceros, Patxi.

Double Binds: Latin American Women's Prison Memories. Treacy, Mary Jane.

Foucault's Phallusy: Intimate Friendship as a Fundamental Ethic (Being a Reconstructive Reading of Foucault's *The Care of the Self*). Van Heerden, Adriaan.

Grounding Agency in Depth: The Implications of Merleau-Ponty's Thought for the Politics of Feminism. Fielding, Helen.

In Praise of Unreliability. Heldke, Lisa.

Irigaray Anxiety: Luce Irigaray and Her Ethics for Improper Selves. Deutscher, Penelope.

Is There a Natural Sexual Inequality of Intellect? A Reply to Kimura. Foss, Jeffrey E.

Natural Law: Alive and Kicking? A Look at the Constitutional Morality of Sexual Privacy in Ireland. O'Connell, Rory.

Nonsexual Relationships between Psychotherapists and Their Former Clients: Obligations of Psychologists. Pipes, Randolph B.

Professional Ethics of Psychologists and Physicians: Morality, Confidentiality, and Sexuality in Israel. Shimshon Rubin, Simon and Dror, Omer.

Sex, Gender, Sexuality: Can Ethologists Practice Genealogy?. Gatens, Moira.

Sexual Activity, Consent, Mistaken Belief, and *Mens Rea*. Tittle, Peg.

Sexuality, Masculinity, and Confession. May, Larry and Bohman, James.

Sexuality, Politics and "Taking Responsibilty": On a Continuum. Eberhard, Julaine.

Swear by the Moon. Bedecarré, Corrinne.

The Diabolical Strategy of Mimesis: Luce Irigaray's Reading of Maurice Merleau-Ponty. Kozel, Susan.

Toward a Feminist Revision of Research Protocols on the Etiology of Homosexuality. Turner, Stephanie S.

Warning! Contents Under Heterosexual Pressure. O'Connor, Peg.

## SHADOW

Abschattung. Sommer, Manfred.

## SHAFTESBURY

Arianisme mitigé ou apologétique nouvelle?. Lagrée, Jacqueline.

Shaftesbury: esquisse d'un manifeste théiste dans l'*Enquête*. Brugère, Fabienne.

## SHAKESPEARE

*The Insufficiency of Virtue: Macbeth* and the Natural Order. Blits, Jan H.

Aristotle's *Nicomachean Ethics* and Shakespeare's *Troilus and Cressida*. Elton, W R.

De romaneske waarheid bij René Girard. Vanheeswijck, Guido.

Debbo io ricordare? L'arte e la negazione della memoria. Fisch, Harold.

Hobbes, Shakespeare and the Temptation to Skepticism. Saracino, Marilena.

La amenaza latente del vagabundo en la literatura política del siglo XVI. Rivera García, Antonio.

Philosophy and Egypt. Glouberman, Mark.

## SHAKHNAZAROV, G

Georgii Shakhnazarov and the Soviet Critique of Historical Materialism. Sandle, Mark.

## SHAME

In Defense of Shame: Shame in the Context of Guilt and Embarrassment. Sabini, John and Silver, Maury.

## SHAMOO, A

Response to "Ethical Concerns about Relapse Studies" by Adil E. Shamoo and Timothy J. Keay (CQ Vol 5, No 3). Bergsma, Jurrit.

## SHAPE

"Molineux's Question" in *Perception*, Villanueva, Enrique (ed). Campbell, John.

Molecular Shape, Reduction, Explanation and Approximate Concepts. Ramsey, Jeffry L.

**SHAPIN, S**

Why Strong Sociologists Abhor a Vacuum: Shapin and Schaffer on the Boyle/Hobbes Controversy. Norris, Christopher.

**SHAREHOLDER**

The Effect of Published Reports of Unethical Conduct on Stock Prices. Rao, Spuma M and Hamilton III, J Brooke.

**SHARING**

"Rashomon and the Sharing of Voices Between East and West" in *On Jean-Luc Nancy: The Sense of Philosophy,* Sheppard, Darren (ed). Naas, Michael B.

*On Jean-Luc Nancy: The Sense of Philosophy.* Sheppard, Darren (ed), Sparks, Simon (ed) and Thomas, Colin (ed).

**SHEAF**

A Sheaf-Theoretic Foundation for Nonstandard Analysis. Palmgren, Erik.

Relational and Partial Variable Sets and Basic Predicate Logic. Ghilardi, Silvio and Meloni, Giancarlo.

Some Results on the Kripke Sheaf Semantics for Super-Intuitionistic Predicate Logics. Suzuki, Nobu-Yuki.

**SHEETS-JOHNSTONE, M**

Response: What Does Evolutionary Theory Tell Us about the Moral Status of Animals?. Menta, Timothy.

**SHELLEY, P**

Between Libertarian Utopia and Political Realism: Godwin and Shelley on Revolution (in Portuguese). Piozzi, Patrizia.

**SHEN-HSIU**

The Dialectics of Nothingness: A Reexamination of Shen-hsiu and Hui-neng. Laycock, Steven W.

**SHEPHERD, M**

Lady Mary Shepherd's Case Against George Berkeley. Atherton, Margaret L.

**SHER, G**

George Sher's Theory of Deserved Punishment, and the Victimized Wrongdoer. Kershnar, Stephen.

**SHESTOV, L**

Concerning Lev Shestov's Conception of Ethics. Van Goubergen, Martine.

**SHIMAMURA, A**

Metacognition and Consciousness: Review Essay of Janet Metcalfe and Arthur P. Shimamura (Eds) *Metacognition: Knowing about Knowing.* Kobes, Bernard W.

**SHIMONY, A**

Prof. Shimony on "The Transient Now". Eilstein, Helena.

Search for a Naturalistic World View by Abner Shimony, Volume I. Redhead, Michael.

**SHIN, S**

Towards a Model Theory of Diagrams. Hammer, Eric and Danner, Norman.

**SHINER, R**

In Defense of Hume and the Causal Theory of Taste. Mothersill, Mary.

On Shiner's "Hume and the Causal Theory of Taste". Bender, John W.

The Dynamics of Legal Positivism: Some Remarks on Shiner's *Norm and Nature.* Navarro, Pablo E and Moreso, José Juan.

**SHKLAR, J**

The Land of the Fearful and the Free. Tamir, Yael.

The Multiculturalism of Fear. Levy, Jacob T.

**SHOEMAKER, S**

Identidad y Continuidad Causal: Una Crítica a la Teoría de la Continuidad Causal de Shoemaker. Bordes Solanas, Montserrat.

**SHPET, G**

Gustav Shpet and Phenomenology in an Orthodox Key. Cassedy, Steven.

Introduction to the Publication of G.G. Shpet's "A Work on Philosophy". Kuznetsov, V G.

**SHUMING, L**

Liang Shuming and Henri Bergson on Intuition: Cultural Context and the Evolution of Terms. An, Yanming.

**SHUN, K**

Commentary on the AAS Panel: Shun, Bloom, Cheng, and Birdwhistell. Neville, Robert Cummings.

**SICHEL, B**

"Moral Stories: How Much Can We Learn from Them and Is It Enough?" in *Philosophy of Education (1996),* Margonis, Frank (ed). Katz, Michael S.

**SICKNESS**

Practicing Patience: How Christians Should Be Sick. Hauerwas, Stanley and Pinches, Charles.

**SIDER, T**

Van Inwagen and Gunk: A Response to Sider. Salsbery, Kelly Joseph.

**SIDGWICK**

I metodi dell'etica di Henry Sidgwick. Lecaldano, Eugenio, Schneewind, J B and Vacatello, Marzio.

Self-Interest and Self-Concern. Darwall, Stephen.

Sidgwick's False Friends. Shaver, Robert.

**SIDNEY, P**

Sir Philip Sidney's Dilemma: On the Ethical Function of Narrative Art. Jacobson, Daniel.

**SIEGEL, H**

"Rationality and Redemption: Ideology, Indoctrination, and Learning Communities" in *Philosophy of Education (1996),* Margonis, Frank (ed). Alexander, H A.

Liberal Indoctrination and the Problem of Community. Harvey, Charles W.

The Ought-Is Question: Discovering The Modern in Post-Modernism. Johnson, David Kenneth.

**SIEP, L**

Horstmann, Siep, and German Idealism. Pippin, Robert B.

**SIERPINSKI, W**

Hipotesis del continuo, definibilidad y funciones recursivas: historia de un desencuentro (1925-1955). Zalamea, Fernando.

**SIGER OF BRABANT**

Notule sur le commentaire du *Liber de causis* de Siger de Brabant et ses rapports avec Thomas d'Aquin. Imbach, Ruedi.

**SIGHT**

"Keeping Foucault and Derrida in Sight: Panopticism and the Politics of Subversion" in *Sites of Vision,* Levin, David Michael (ed). Levin, David Michael.

The Experience of Spatiality for Congenitally Blind People: A Phenomenological-Psychological Study. Karlsson, Gunnar.

**SIGN**

*see also* Symbol

"El signo y el sentido de la realidad" in *Verdad: lógica, representación y mundo,* Villegas Forero, L. Rivas Monroy, Uxía.

"Il segno e l'evento" in *Momenti di Storia della Logica e di Storia della Filosofia,* Guetti, Carla (ed). Sini, Carlo.

"Peirce's Sign and the Process of Interpretation" in *Philosophy in Experience: American Philosophy in Transition,* Hart, Richard (ed). Kruse, Felicia E.

*Between the Absolute and the Arbitrary.* Elgin, Catherine Z.

*Literature, Criticism, and the Theory of Signs.* Tejera, Victorino.

*Peirce, Signs, and Meaning.* Merrell, Floyd.

*The Two Pragmatisms: From Peirce to Rorty.* Mounce, H O.

Beside us, in Memory. Olkowski, Dorothea.

Bread and Wine. Sallis, John.

Coding Elementary Contributions to Dialogue: Individual Acts versus Dialogical Interaction. Marková, Ivana and Linell, Per.

Concept and Event. Patton, Paul.

Crafting Marks into Meanings. Catalano, Joseph S.

From a Semiotic to a Neo-Pragmatic Understanding of Metaphor. Von der Fehr, Drude.

I confini del fondamento. Lipari, Maria Chiara.

Idealità del segno e intenzione nella filosofia del linguaggio di Edmund Husserl. Costa, Vincenzo.

Interpretation as Action: The Risk of Inquiry. Awbrey, Jon and Awbrey, Susan.

Interpreting Peirce's Interpretant: A Response To Lalor, Liszka, and Meyers. Short, T L.

Metaphor—A Semiotic Perspective. Larsen, Svend Erik.

Reconstructing Deconstruction for a Prospective Realism. Olshewsky, Thomas M.

Reflections on Iconicity, Representation, and Resemblance: Peirce's Theory of Signs, Goodmann on Resemblance, and Modern Philosophies of Language and Mind. Dipert, Randall R.

Symbols, Icons and Stupas. Perrett, Roy W.

The Case of the Disappearing Enigma. Knight, Deborah and McNight, George.

The Chinese Theory of Forms and Names (*xingming zhi xue*) and Its Relation to "Philosophy of Signs". Möller, Hans Georg.

The Hegelian Sign: Sacrificial Economy and Dialectical Relief (in French). Guibal, Francis.

The Meaning of "Mental Meaning" (in Spanish). Blanco Salgueiro, Antonio.

The Transposition of the Linguistic Sign in Peirce's Contributions to *The Nation.* Deledalle-Rhodes, Janice.

Zeichenmachende Phantasie: Zum systematischen Zusammenhang von Zeichen und Denken bei Hegel. Simon, Josef.

**SIGNIFICANCE**

A Naive Variety of Logical Consequence. Alonso González, Enrique.

Lenguaje significativo y no significativo: *El Kaspar* de Peter Handke. Gutiérrez, Edgardo.

The Intended/Foreseen Distinction's Ethical Relevance. Cavanaugh, Thomas A.

The Moral Significance of Primitive Self-Consciousness: A Response to Bermúdez. Gallagher, Shaun.

**SIGNIFICATION**

"Fitting versus Tracking: Wittgenstein on Representation" in *The Cambridge Companion to Wittgenstein,* Sluga, Hans (ed). Summerfield, Donna M.

"How Does a Building Mean?" in *East and West in Aesthetics,* Marchianò, Grazia (ed). Mitias, Michael H.

"The Absent Signifier: Historical Narrative and the Abstract Subject" in *Critical Studies: Ethics and the Subject,* Simms, Karl (ed). Clayton, Leigh.

Interprétation, signification et "usage" chez Wittgenstein. Sauvé, Denis.

On the Properties of Discourse: A Translation of *Tractatus de Proprietatibus Sermonum* (Author Anonymous). Barney, Stephen (trans), Lewis, Wendy (trans) and Normore, Calvin G (& other trans).

## SKLAR, L
*Il Riduzionismo della Scienza*. Gava, Giacomo.

## SKYRMS, B
Analogy and Exchangeability in Predictive Inferences. Festa, Roberto.
Sex, Fairness, and the Theory of Games. D'Arms, Justin.

## SLAVERY
"The Fight with Covey" in *Existence in Black: An Anthology of Black Existential Philosophy*, Gordon, Lewis R (ed). Boxill, Bernard R.
*Fruits of Sorrow*. Spelman, Elizabeth V.
Aristotle and the Ancient Roots of Anarchism. Keyt, David.
Gesellschaftsvertrag oder grösster Gesamtnutzen? Die Vertragstheorie von John Rawls und ihre neo-utilitaristischen Kritiker. Rinderle, Peter.
Natural Subordination, Aristotle On. Levin, Michael.
Psicología de la libertad política en Aristóteles (comentario de *Política*, I, 4-7 y I, 13). Martínez Barrera, Jorge.
Race, the Rule of Law, and *The Merchant of Venice*: From Slavery to Citizenship. Masugi, Ken.
The Arc of the Moral Universe. Cohen, Joshua.
The Evils of Chattel Slavery and the Holocaust: An Examination of Laurence Thomas's *Vessels of Evil*. Harriott, Howard H.

## SLAVIC
Transformations of the Slavophile Idea in the Twentieth Century. Khoruzhii, Sergei Sergeevich.

## SLEEP
Aristotle on Dreaming: What Goes On in Sleep When the 'Big Fire' Goes Out. Holowchak, Mark A.

## SLEIGH, R
Sleigh's *Leibniz & Arnauld: A Commentary on their Correspondence* (New Haven: Yale University Press). Adams, Robert Merrihew.

## SLEUTEL, J
Toch Geen Representaties? Een Reacties op J. Sleutels' Zonnebrand-ontologie. Buekens, F.

## SLICES
A Study of Intermediate Propositional Logics on the Third Slice. Hosoi, Tsutomu and Masuda, Isao.
The Simple Substitution Property of the Intermediate Propositional Logics on Finite Slices. Sasaki, Katsumi.

## SLOTE, M
Slote on Rational Dilemmas and Rational Supererogation. Mintoff, Joe.

## SLOVAKIAN
Faith in God as Ultimate Strength: A Slovak Physician Who Resisted 'Brain Washing'. Sencik, Stefan.

## SLOVENE
Interrogative Wh-Movement in Slovene and English. Golden, Marija.

## SLOVENIAN
Hegelianism in Slovenia: A Short Introduction. Vezjak, Boris.

## SMART, J
*Cervello-Mente: Pensatori del XX secolo*. Gava, Giacomo.

## SMEDSLUND, J
Common Sense und Logik in Jan Smedslunds 'Psychologik'. Mock, Verena.

## SMITH
*Modern Political Thought: Readings from Machiavelli to Nietzsche*. Wootton, David (ed).
Adam Smith's Influence on James Madison. Ross, Thomas.
Adam Smith's Other Hand: A Capitalist Theory of Exploitation. Fairlamb, Horace L.
Contract or Coincidence: George Herbert Mead and Adam Smith on Self and Society. Costelloe, Timothy M.
Critical Thinking and the Moral Sentiments: Adam Smith's Moral Psychology and Contemporary Debate in Critical Thinking and Informal Logic. Weinstein, Jack Russell.
Kant, Smith and Locke: The Locksmith's Mending of Tradition: A Reaction to Mr. Fleischacker's Thesis. Perreijn, Willem.
Modi del dire, intenzioni ed immagini per la *Theory of Moral Sentiments* di Adam Smith. Zanini, Adelino.
The Intuitive Basis of Berkeley's Immaterialism. Fogelin, Robert J.
The Promise of Peace? Hume and Smith on the Effects of Commerce on War and Peace. Manzer, Robert A.
The Why's of Business Revisited. Duska, Ronald F.
Values Behind the Market: Kant's Response to the *Wealth of Nations*. Fleischacker, Samuel.
Virtues. Tugendhat, Ernst.

## SMITH, B
Austrian Philosophy: The Legacy of Franz Brentano. Brandl, Johannes.

## SMITH, J
"American Philosophy's Way around Modernism (and Postmodernism)" in *The Recovery of Philosophy in America: Essays in Honor of John Edwin Smith*, Kasulis, Thomas P (ed). Neville, Robert Cummings.
"Giustizia divina e apocatastasi in John Smith, platonico di Cambridge" in *Mind Senior to the World*, Baldi, Marialuisa. Micheletti, Mario.
"Intimations of Religious Experience and Interreligious Truth" in *The Recovery of Philosophy in America: Essays in Honor of John Edwin Smith*, Kasulis, Thomas P (ed). Kasulis, Thomas P.

"John E. Smith and Metaphysics" in *Reason, Experience, and God: John E. Smith in Dialogue*, Colapietro, Vincent M. Neville, Robert Cummings.
"John E. Smith and the Heart of Experience" in *The Recovery of Philosophy in America: Essays in Honor of John Edwin Smith*, Kasulis, Thomas P (ed). Anderson, Douglas R.
"John E. Smith and the Recovery of Religious Experience" in *Reason, Experience, and God: John E. Smith in Dialogue*, Colapietro, Vincent M. Potter, Vincent G.
"Living Reason: A Critical Exposition of John E. Smith's Re-Envisioning of Human Rationality" in *Reason, Experience, and God: John E. Smith in Dialogue*, Colapietro, Vincent M. Colapietro, Vincent M.
"Modernism, Postmodernism, and the Pragmatic Recovery of an Educational Canon" in *The Recovery of Philosophy in America: Essays in Honor of John Edwin Smith*, Kasulis, Thomas P (ed). Allan, George.
"Philosophy's Recovery of Its History: A Tribute to John E. Smith" in *The Recovery of Philosophy in America: Essays in Honor of John Edwin Smith*, Kasulis, Thomas P (ed). Lucas Jr, George R.
"Reflections on Philosophic Recovery" in *The Recovery of Philosophy in America: Essays in Honor of John Edwin Smith*, Kasulis, Thomas P (ed). Neville, Robert Cummings.
"The Goldilocks Syndrome" in *The Recovery of Philosophy in America: Essays in Honor of John Edwin Smith*, Kasulis, Thomas P (ed). Sherburne, Donald W.
"The Spirit of Pragmatism and the Pragmatic Spirit" in *The Recovery of Philosophy in America: Essays in Honor of John Edwin Smith*, Kasulis, Thomas P (ed). Wu, Kuang-Ming.
"Whitehead's Distinctive Features" in *The Recovery of Philosophy in America: Essays in Honor of John Edwin Smith*, Kasulis, Thomas P (ed). Ford, Lewis S.
*Reason, Experience, and God: John E. Smith in Dialogue*. Colapietro, Vincent M.
*The Recovery of Philosophy in America: Essays in Honor of John Edwin Smith*. Kasulis, Thomas P (ed) and Neville, Robert Cummings (ed).
Philosophical Psychology in Historical Perspective: Review Essay of J.-C. Smith (Ed.), *Historical Foundations of Cognitive Science*. Meyering, Theo C.

## SMITH, L
Dynamical Systems in Development: Review Essay of Linda V. Smith and Esther Thelen (Eds) *A Dynamics Systems Approach to Development: Applications*. Hooker, Cliff A.

## SMITH, M
A Response. Walzer, Michael.
An Objection to Smith's Argument for Internalism. Miller, Alexander.
Is the Moral Problem Solved?. Swanton, Christine.
Real Values in a Humean Context. Dancy, Jonathan.
Reason, Value and the Muggletonians. Holton, Richard.
Reasons and Advice for the Practically Rational. Johnson, Robert Neal.
Smith on Moral Fetishism. Lillehammer, Hallvard.
Smith's Moral Problem. Darwall, Stephen.
Synchronic Self-Control is Always Non-Actional. Kennett, Jeanette and Smith, Michael.
Troubles for Michael Smith's Metaethical Rationalism. Horgan, Terence and Timmons, Mark.
Underestimating Self-Control: Kennett and Smith on Frog and Toad. Mele, Alfred R.

## SMITH, Q
Emerging from Imaginary Time. Deltete, Robert J and Guy, Reed A.
McTaggart's Paradox and Smith's Tensed Theory of Time. Oaklander, L Nathan.
Truth Conditions of Tensed Sentence Types. Paul, L A.

## SMITH, S
"The Complex Ethics of Separate Schools" in *Philosophy of Education (1996)*, Margonis, Frank (ed). McDonough, Kevin.

## SMITH, T
Avarice and Civil Unity: The Contribution of Sir Thomas Smith. Wood, Neal.

## SMITH, W
Thomism and the Quantum Enigma. Wallace, William A.

## SMOKING
The Ethical and Economic Implications of Smoking in Enclosed Public Facilities: A Resolution of Conflicting Rights. Ostapski, S Andrew, Plumly, L Wayne and Love, Jim L.

## SMYTH, E
Damned if You Do and Damned if You Don't: Sexual Aesthetics and the Music of Dame Ethel Smyth. Gates, Eugene.

## SNEED, J
"Some Issues of Historical Epistemology in the Light of the Structuralist Philosophy of Science" in *Epistemology and History*, Zeidler-Janiszewska, Anna (ed). Zeidler, Pawel.

## SNIK, G
Replies. Scheffler, Israel.

## SOBEL, D
Sidgwick's False Friends. Shaver, Robert.

## SOBER, E
Accidental Associations, Local Potency, and a Dilemma for Dretske. Noordhof, Paul.

## SOBER, E

Adaptationism: Hypothesis or Heuristic?. Resnik, David B.

Critical Review: Sober's *Philosophy of Biology* and His Philosophy of Biology. Rosenberg, Alex.

Fitness Made Physical: The Supervenience of Biological Concepts Revisited. Weber, Marcel.

## SOBLE, A

Ah! My Foolish Heart: A Reply to Alan Soble's "Antioch's 'Sexual Offense Policy': A Philosophical Exploration". Kittay, Eva Felder.

Commitment and the Bond of Love. Van Hooft, Stan.

## SOBRINHO, J

Conspecto do Desenvolvimento da Filosofía em Portugal (Séculos XIII-XVI). Santiago de Carvalho, Mário A.

## SOCIABILITY

En torno a la sociabilidad humana en el pensamiento de Leonardo Polo. Naval, Concepción.

## SOCIAL

"Explaining Social Phenomena" in *Epistemology and History*, Zeidler-Janiszewska, Anna (ed). Mejbaum, Waclaw.

"Jerzy Kmita's Social-Regulational Theory of Culture and the Category of Subject" in *Epistemology and History*, Zeidler-Janiszewska, Anna (ed). Zamiara, Krystyna.

"The Decahedron of Education (Components and Aspects): The Need for a Comprehensive Approach" in *Epistemology and History*, Zeidler-Janiszewska, Anna (ed). Kwiecinski, Zbigniew.

"Theory and Social Practice: One or Two Psychologies?" in *Epistemology and History*, Zeidler-Janiszewska, Anna (ed). Brzezinski, Jerzy.

Averting Violence: Domestic, Social and Personal. Wood, Forrest.

Bridging Social Constructionism and Cognitive Constructivism: A Psychology of Human Possibility and Constraint. Martin, Jack and Sugarman, Jeff.

Character Education: Reclaiming the Social. Duncan, Barbara J.

Collectives and Intentionality. Hornsby, Jennifer.

Commentary on "The Social Responsibilities of Biological Scientists. Salzberg, Aaron A.

Commentary on "The Social Responsibilities of Biological Scientists". Beckwith, Jonathan R and Geller, Lisa N.

Husserl, Wittgenstein and the Snark: Intentionality and Social Naturalism. Gillett, Grant.

John Searle's *The Construction of Social Reality*. Ruben, David-Hillel.

Ley moral, Ley positiva. Griffin, James.

Meaning and Triangulation. Talmage, Catherine J L.

Précis of *The Construction of Social Reality*. Searle, John R.

Responses to Critics of *The Construction of Social Reality*. Searle, John R.

Social Epistemology and the Ethics of Research. Resnik, David B.

Social Predictivism. Barnes, Eric.

The Legacy of Lakatos: Reconceptualising the Philosophy of Mathematics. Ernest, Paul.

The Social and Political Sources of Akrasia. Rorty, Amélie Oksenberg.

The Social Responsibilities of Biological Scientists. Reiser, Stanley Joel and Bulger, Ruth Ellen.

## SOCIAL CHANGE

Algunos aportes de Don Leonardo a un país hispanoamericano: Colombia. González Couture, Gustavo.

Dinamic Peace in the Encounter of Vital Cultures (Spanish). Borges-Duarte, Irene.

Moral Responsibility and Social Change: A New Theory of Self. Ferguson, Ann.

Postmodernity: the End of Modernism or the End of Diversity? (Spanish). Maríñez Navarro, Freddy.

## SOCIAL CONTRACT

"An Integral Part of his Species...?" in *Jean-Jacques Rousseau and the Sources of the Self*, O'Hagan, Timothy (ed). Dent, Nicholas.

"Deconstructing the Self on the Wild Side" in *Jean-Jacques Rousseau and the Sources of the Self*, O'Hagan, Timothy (ed). Wokler, Robert.

"The Master and the Magician" in *Jean-Jacques Rousseau and the Sources of the Self*, O'Hagan, Timothy (ed). Caygill, Howard.

*Political Philosophy*. Hampton, Jean.

*Rousseau and Geneva: From the First Discourse to the Social Contract, 1749-1762*. Rosenblatt, Helena.

Gesellschaftsvertrag oder grösster Gesamtnutzen? Die Vertragstheorie von John Rawls und ihre neo-utilitaristischen Kritiker. Rinderle, Peter.

Kants kritisches Staatsrecht. Herb, Karlfriedrich and Ludwig, Bernd.

La justice peut-elle naître du contrat social?. Poltier, Hugues.

Le statut du contrat social chez Rousseau selon Yves Vargas: Une lecture critique. Etane, Yombo.

Opening the Future: The Paradox of Promising in the Hobbesian Social Contract. Bernasconi, Robert.

Rethinking the Social Contract. Sanjeev, M P.

Rousseau: le contrat social en question. Etane, Yomba.

Social Contract among Devils. Verweyen, Hansjürgen.

## SOCIAL CONTROL

De l'usage social de l'éthique. Mineau, André, Giroux, Guy and Boisvert, Yves.

## SOCIAL INSTITUTION

The Sociophilosophy of Folk Psychology. Kusch, Martin.

## SOCIAL ORDER

Fra filologia e storiografia: progetti di edizioni settecentesche. Generali, Dario.

Symbol and Communication in Politics (Spanish). Fiorino, Víctor R Martín.

## SOCIAL PHIL

*see also* Anarchism, Authority, Communism, Conservatism, Equality, Ethics, Freedom, General Will, Political Phil, Progress, Punishment, Society, Toleration, Utopia

"...Equality from the Masculine Point of View...": The 2nd Earl Russell and Divorce Law Reform in England. Savage, Gail.

"Afterword" in *The Liberation Debate: Rights at Issue*, Leahy, Michael (ed). Leahy, Michael.

"Community, Identity, and Difference: Pragmatic Social Thought in Transition" in *Philosophy in Experience: American Philosophy in Transition*, Hart, Richard (ed). Stuhr, John J.

"Mundo administrado" o "Colonización del mundo de la vida": La depotenciación de la Teoría crítica de la sociedad en J. Habermas. Gómez Ibáñez, Vicente.

"Public Man" and The Critique of Masculinities. Carver, Terrell.

"Respect for Humanity" in *The Tanner Lectures on Human Values, Volume 18, 1997*, Peterson, Grethe B (ed). Hill Jr, Thomas E.

"Sozialphilosophische Aspekte der Übersetzbarkeit" in *Epistemology and History*, Zeidler-Janiszewska, Anna (ed). Siemek, Marek J.

*Affirmative Action: Social Justice or Unfair Preference?*. Mosley, Albert G and Capaldi, Nicholas.

*Against Liberalism*. Kekes, John.

*Animal Acts: Configuring the Human in Western History*. Ham, Jennifer (ed) and Senior, Matthew (ed).

*Antonio Gramsci Prison Notebooks: Volume II*. Buttigieg, Joseph A (ed & trans).

*Applied Social Sciences in the Plutocratic Era of the United States: Dialectics of the Concrete*. Schindler, Ronald Jeremiah.

*Atheistic Humanism*. Flew, Antony.

*Basic Rights: Subsistence, Affluence, and U.S. Foreign Policy*. Shue, Henry.

*Behind Closed Doors: Analysis of the Feminine Figures in Sartrean Theatre* (Spanish). Comesaña-Santalices, Gloria.

*Belief and Resistance: Dynamics of Contemporary Intellectual Controversy*. Smith, Barbara Herrnstein.

*Beyond Economics: Postmodernity, Globalization and National Sustainability*. Sauer-Thompson, Gary and Smith, Joseph Wayne.

*Beyond Orientalism: Essays on Cross-Cultural Encounter*. Dallmayr, Fred R.

*Bios politikos* and *bios theoretikos* in the Phenomenology of Hannah Arendt. Moran, Dermot (trans) and Taminiaux, Jacques.

*Coming Together/Coming Apart: Religion, Community, and Modernity*. Bounds, Elizabeth M.

*Contemporary Perspectives on Masculinity: Men, Women, and Politics in Modern Society*. Clatterbaugh, Kenneth.

*Contested Commodities*. Radin, Margaret Jane.

*Cultural History and Postmodernity: Disciplinary Readings and Challenges*. Poster, Mark.

*Cultural Universals and Particulars: An African Perspective*. Wiredu, Kwasi.

*Darf Pedro sein Land verkaufen? Versuch einer sozialwissenschaftlichen Perspektive in der Ökonomik*. Lohmann, Karl R.

*Democracy and Disagreement*. Gutmann, Amy and Thompson, Dennis.

*Dialogues with Plato*. Benitez, Eugenio E (ed).

*Diskurs und Befreiung: Studien zur philosophischen Ethik von Karl-Otto Apel und Enrique Dussel*. Schelkshorn, Hans.

*Ecofeminism: Women, Culture, Nature*. Warren, Karen J (ed) and Erkal, Nisvan (ed).

*Emancipation and Illusion: Rationality and Gender in Habermas's Theory of Modernity*. Fleming, Marie.

*Emmanuel Levinas: Basic Philosophical Writings*. Peperzak, Adriaan Theodoor (ed), Critchley, Simon (ed) and Bernasconi, Robert (ed).

*Equality: Selected Readings*. Pojman, Louis (ed) and Westmoreland, Robert (ed).

*Existence in Black: An Anthology of Black Existential Philosophy*. Gordon, Lewis R (ed).

*Family Values: Subjects Between Nature and Culture*. Oliver, Kelly.

*Feminist Interpretations of Jacques Derrida*. Holland, Nancy J (ed).

*Feminist Interpretations of Michel Foucault*. Hekman, Susan J (ed).

*Finding Philosophy in Social Science*. Bunge, Mario.

*Foundations of Futures Studies: Human Science for a New Era*. Bell, Wendell.

*Four Summers: A Czech Kaleidoscope*. Page, Benjamin.

*Freedom's Law: The Moral Reading of the American Constitution*. Dworkin, Ronald.

*French Feminist Theory (III): Luce Irigaray and Helene Cixous: A Bibliography*. Nordquist, Joan (ed).

*Freud and the Passions*. O'Neill, John (ed).

*From Sex Objects to Sexual Subjects*. Moscovici, Claudia.

*George Grant and the Subversion of Modernity: Art, Philosophy, Politics, Religion, and Education*. Davis, Arthur (ed).

*Hegel and Feminist Social Criticism: Justice, Recognition, and the Feminine*. Gauthier, Jeffrey A.

*Hegel, Marx, and the English State*. MacGregor, David.

## SOCIAL PHIL

Another View on the Crisis in Marxism. Gamberg, Herb.

Anthropology and the *Sciences Humaines*: The Voice of Lévi-Strauss. Johnson, Christopher.

Aproximaciones a una evaluación de la aplicación de las nuevas tecnologías reproductivas. Digilio, Patricia.

Are Human Rights Self-Contradictory?: Critical Remarks on a Hypothesis by Hannah Arendt. Brunkhorst, Hauke.

Aristotle and Fair Admissions. Cordero, Ronald A.

Aristotle and the Ancient Roots of Anarchism. Keyt, David.

Aristotle's Criticism of Plato's Communism of Women and Children. Mayhew, Robert.

Associative Obligations, Voluntarism, and Equality. Jeske, Diane.

Asymmetrical Reciprocity: On Moral Respect, Wonder, and Enlarged Thought. Young, Iris Marion.

Autobiography, Narrative, and the Freudian Concept of Life History. Brockmeier, Jens.

Autonomía y Comunidad: Sobre el debate entre comunitaristas y liberales. López Castellón, Enrique.

Autonomy and Authority in Kant's *Rechtslehre*. Dodson, Kevin E.

Avoidability and Libertarianism: A Response to Fischer. Widerker, David and Katzoff, Charlotte.

Basal Inequalities: Reply to Sen. Kane, John.

Becoming an Evil Society: The Self and Strangers. Thomas, Laurence.

Being and Subjectivity (and Commentary V. Hála) (in Czech). Hösle, Vittorio and Hála, Vlastimil.

Bentham y los derechos humanos. Montoya, José.

Bertrand Russell and Academic Freedom. Irvine, A D.

Between Immorality and Unfeasibility: The Market Socialist Predicament. Steele, David Ramsay.

Between Political Loyalty and Religious Liberty: Political Theory and Toleration in Huguenot Thought in the Epoch of Bayle. Simonutti, Luisa.

Beyond Enlightenment? After the Subject of Foucault, Who Comes?. Venn, Couze.

Beyond Ontology: Ideation, Phenomenology and the Cross Cultural Study of Emotion. Solomon, Robert C.

Black Athena and Africa's Contribution to Global Cultural History. Van Binsbergen, Wim.

Blameless, Constructive, and Political Anger. Swaine, Lucas A.

Blameworthiness, Character, and Cultural Norms. Haji, Ishtiyaque.

Blindspot of a Liberal: Popper and the Problem of Community. Eidlin, Fred.

Blurred Boundaries. Morriss, Peter.

Bourdieu and Foucault on Power and Modernity. Cronin, Ciaran.

Bourdieu and the Social Conditions of Wittgensteinian Language Games. Gay, William C.

Bowling Alone: On the Saving Power of Kant's Perpetual Peace. Shell, Susan Meld.

Business Entities and the State: Who Should Provide Security from Crime?. Scheid, Don E.

Can a Woman Harass a Man?: Toward a Cultural Understanding of Bodies and Power. Bordo, Susan.

Can Democracy Promote the General Welfare?. Buchanan, James M.

Can Old-Age Social Insurance Be Justified. Shapiro, Daniel J.

Catastrophic Thinking in the Modern World: Russia and America. Shlapentokh, Vladimir.

Charles Taylor e le due facce dell'individualismo. Cremaschi, Sergio.

Circulus Vitiosus Deus? The Dialectical Logic of Feminist Standpoint Theory. Conway, Daniel W.

Citizenship and Culture in Early Modern Europe. Miller, Peter N.

Citizenship and Social Policy: T.H. Marshall and Poverty. Mead, Lawrence M.

Civil Society and Ideology: A Matter of Freedom. Van der Zweerde, Evert.

Coercion: Description or Evaluation?. Greene, Jennifer K.

Comment on Dawson's 'Exit, Voice and Values in Economic Institutions'. Anderson, Elizabeth.

Commentary. White, Hayden.

Commentary on "Autobiography, Narrative, and the Freudian Concept of Life History". Robinson, Daniel N.

Communication From One Feminist. Machan, Tibor R.

Communication, Criticism, and the Postmodern Consensus: An Unfashionable Interpretation of Michel Foucault. Johnson, James.

Communicative Action and Philosophical Foundations: Comments on the Apel-Habermas Debate. Papastephanou, Marianna.

Compassion and Societal Well-Being. Brown, Lee M.

Complexity, Value, and the Psychological Postulates of Economics. Benedikt, Michael.

Conceptions of Persons. Frohock, Fred M.

Confessionals, Testimonials: Women's Speech in/and Contexts of Violence. Supriya, K E.

Conflict and Constellation: The New Trend of Value Development in China. Chen, Xun Wu.

Conflicting Accounts of Equal Opportunity. Askland, Andrew.

Conflicting Varieties of Realism: Causal Powers and the Problems of Social Structure. Varela, Charles R and Harré, Rom.

Confucian Value and Democratic Value. Li, Chenyang.

Conquista y conciencia en el Leviatán. Galimidi, José Luis.

Conscience, Morality and Social Acceptability in an African Culture. Ebijuwa, T.

Conservatives, Liberals, and the Colonized: Ontological Reflections. Allan, George.

Constitutional Patriotism. Ingram, Attracta.

Constructing the Law of Peoples. Moellendorf, Darrel.

Consuming Because Others Consume. Lichtenberg, Judith.

Contemporary Pluralism and Toleration. Galeotti, Anna Elisabetta.

Contesting Consensus: Rereading Habermas on the Public Sphere. Markell, Patchen.

Contraceptive Risk-Taking and Norms of Chastity. Stubblefield, Anna.

Contract or Coincidence: George Herbert Mead and Adam Smith on Self and Society. Costelloe, Timothy M.

Contractual Justice: A Modest Defence. Barry, Brian.

Cooperation and Equality: A Reply to Pojman. Norman, Richard.

Cor Dippel, denker op de grens van twee werelden. Van Dijk, Paul.

Cosmopolitanism and Citizenship: Kant Against Habermas. Mertens, Thomas.

Cosmopolitanism and the Experience of Nationality. Rée, Jonathan.

Coyote Politics: Trickster Tales and Feminist Futures. Phelan, Shane.

Cracking The Division Bell: A Philosophic Attack On *The Bell Curve*. LaBossiere, Michael C.

Crisis and Narrativity. Hirschbein, Ron.

Crítica del llamado de Heidelberg. Lecourt, Dominique.

Cross-cultural Understanding: Its Philosophical and Anthropological Problems. Jamme, Christoph.

Cultura mundial y mundos culturales. Scannone, Juan Carlos.

Cultura y Desarrollo Global. Dallmayr, Fred R.

Cultura y reflexión en torno a Meditaciones del Quijote. Lasaga Medina, José.

Cultural Diversity and the Systems View. Hammond, Debora.

Cultural Nationalism, Neither Ethnic Nor Civic. Nielsen, Kai.

Cultural Relativism and Social Criticism from a Taylorian Perspective. Rosa, Hartmut.

Current Conceptions of Racism: A Critical Examination of Some Recent Social Philosophy. Garcia, Jorge L A.

Cyborg Identities and the Relational Web: Recasting 'Narrative Identity' in Moral and Political Theory. Brothers, Robyn F.

Dal primato della prassi all'anomia: Una interpretazione filosofica della crisi odierna. Cotta, Sergio.

Daughters of a Better Age. Lim, Tock Keng.

De l'indéconstructible justice. Dufour, Mario.

De l'usage social de l'éthique. Mineau, André, Giroux, Guy and Boisvert, Yves.

De la toute relativité des lois. Gerbeau, Alexis.

De la volonté générale et des lois. Morissette, Yves.

De oorspronkelijkheid en actuele betekenis van H. van Riessen als filosoof van de techniek: Deel I—De oorspronkelijkheid van zijn werk. Haaksma, Hans W H.

De Platón a Michael Jackson: Entresijos del imaginario andrógino. Jiménez, Jorge.

De viajes y naufragios: Sobre el Libro de Santiago González Noriega *El Viaje a Siracusa: Ensayos de Filosofía y Teoría Social* Balsa de la Medusa 1994. Villacañas Berlanga, José Luis.

Dead or Alive? Reflective Versus Unreflective Traditions. Tate, John W.

Debating Critical Theory. Hoy, David Couzens.

Decision, Deliberation, and Democratic Ethos. Mouffe, Chantal.

Deconstruction and Pragmatism—Is Derrida a Private Ironist or a Public Liberal?. Critchley, Simon.

Deconstruction and Rationality: A Response to Rowland, or Postmodernism 101. Thomas, Douglas E.

Deconstructive Strategies and the Movement Against Sexual Violence. Heberle, Renee.

Deep Ecology and its Significance for Philosophical Thought (in Czech). Kolársky, Rudolf.

Definitional and Responsive Environmental Meanings: A Meadian Look at Landscapes and Drought. Weigert, Andrew J.

Democracy and the Individual: To What Extent is Dewey's Reconstruction Nietzsche's Self-Overcoming?. Sullivan, Shannon.

Democracy Means Equality. Rancière, Jacques.

Democracy: A Convergent Value? Comments on Sheldon Leader and Ernesto Garzón Valdés. Passerin d'Entrèves, Maurizio.

Derrida e la rivendicazione dello spirito del marxismo. Iofrida, Manlio.

Desarrollo técnico y evolución histórica: modelos metafísicos y antropológico-culturales. Rodríguez, Amán Rosales.

Deutsche Aufklärung und französiche *Lumières*. D'Hondt, Jacques.

Dialogical Realities: The Ordinary, the Everyday, and Other Strange New Worlds. Shotter, John.

Did the Enlightenment Just Happen to Men?. Whyte, Philip.

Die Bedeutung von Fichtes Angewandter Philosophie für die Praktische Philosophie der Gegenwart. Oesterreich, Peter L.

Die neuzeitliche Naturerkenntnis zerstört die Natur: Zu Georg Pichts Theorie der modernen Naturwissenschaften. Hoyningen-Huene, Paul.

Die Wendung nach Asien: Heideggers Ansatz interkultureller Philosophie. Wolz-Gottwald, Eckard.

Dilemmas of a Multicultural Theory of Citizenship. Parekh, Bhikhu.

Dimensions of Citizenship and National Identity in Canada. Carens, Joseph H.

Dinamic Peace in the Encounter of Vital Cultures (Spanish). Borges-Duarte, Irene.

**SOCIAL PHIL**

Hobbes et la mort du Léviathan: opinion, sédition et dissolution. Malherbe, Michel.

Hobbes on "Bodies Politic". Sorgi, Giuseppe.

Hobbes's Political Geometry. Valentine, Jeremy.

Holocaust Memories and History. Turner, Charles.

Hommage à Anastase Léventis. Vélissaropoulos, D.

Homo Economicus in the 20th Century: *Écriture Masculine* and Women's Work. Still, Judith.

How It Feels to be a Problem: Du Bois, Fanon, and the "Impossible Life" of the Black Intellectual. Posnock, Ross.

How Liberal Can Nationalism Be?. Lichtenberg, Judith.

How to Do Things with Things: Objects trouvés and Symbolization. Streeck, Jürgen.

Human Rights and Legal Pluralism in Venezuela: An Approximation to the Native Inhabitants Rights (Spanish). Colmenares Olivar, Ricardo.

Humans, Persons and Selves. Brown, Mark T.

Hume's Touchstone and the Politics of Meaningful Discourse. Backhaus, Wilfried.

Husserl's Rational "*Liebesgemeinschaft*". Buckley, R Philip.

Husserl, Weber, Freud, and the Method of the Human Sciences. McIntosh, Donald.

I May Be a Bit of a Jew: Trauma in Human Narrative. Zajko, Vanda.

I percorsi del soggetto moderno. Barcellona, Pietro.

I rischi di una società dei "giusti". Lami, Gian Franco.

Identity Politics and the Welfare State. Wolfe, Alan and Klausen, Jytte.

Identity Politics as a Transposition of Fraser's Needs Politics. Tittle, Peg.

Idiographic Theorizing and Ideal Types: Max Weber's Methodology of Social Science. Collin, Finn.

Il patico e il nostro tempo: A proposito di Aldo Masullo. Fimiani, Mariapaola.

Impartiality and Liberal Neutrality. Caney, Simon.

Impossible Laws. D'Amico, Robert.

In Defence of Representations. Jovchelovitch, Sandra.

In Defense of Shame: Shame in the Context of Guilt and Embarrassment. Sabini, John and Silver, Maury.

In Praise of Unreliability. Heldke, Lisa.

In the Name of Society, or Three Theses on the History of Social Thought. Osborne, Thomas and Rose, Nikolas.

Incommensurable Differences: Cultural Relativism and Antirationalism Concerning Self and Other. Wagner, Joseph.

Information and Human Liberty. Weinberger, Ota.

Instead of Leaders They Have Become Bankers of Men: Gramsci's Alternative to the U.S. Neoinstitutionalists' Theory of Trade-Union Bureaucratization. Devinatz, Victor G.

Integrity and Disrespect (and J. Velek Commentary) (in Czech). Honneth, Axel and Velek, Josef.

Interpretation, Dialogue, and Friendship: On the Remainder of Community. Watson, Stephen H.

Intersecting Memories: Bearing Witness to the 1989 Massacre of Women in Montreal. Rosenberg, Sharon.

Interview with Herman J. Saatkamp, Jr.. Detar, Richard.

Intimacy and Parental Authority in the Philosophy of Ferdinand Schoeman. Klepper, Howard.

Introduction. Kelly, P J.

Introduction: National Identity as a Philosophical Problem. Dahbour, Omar.

Introduction: Recent Currents in Marxist Philosophy. Little, Daniel.

Is Nietzsche a Political Thinker?. Nussbaum, Martha C.

Is There a Natural Sexual Inequality of Intellect? A Reply to Kimura. Foss, Jeffrey E.

Is There a Neutral Justification for Liberalism?. Brighouse, Harry.

Jan Patocka's World Movement as Ultimate. Tucker, Aviezer.

Jharkhand: A Movement from Ethnicity to Empowerment of Autonomy. Vadakumchery, Johnson.

Justiça e *Sentido da Terra*. Soromenho-Marques, José Viriato.

Justice, Care, and Questionable Dichotomies. Rumsey, Jean P.

Justice, Contestability, and Conceptions of the Good. Mason, Andrew.

Justice, Impartiality, and Equality: Why the Concept of Justice Does Not Presume Equality. Kane, John.

Justifying Kant's Principles of Justice. Kerstein, Samuel.

Kantian Ethics and Global Justice. Tan, Kok-Chor.

Karl Popper in Exile: The Viennese Progressive Imagination and the Making of *The Open Society*. Hacohen, Malachi Haim.

Karl Popper y la crítica al determinismo. Bonetti, José Andrés.

L'allegoria sociale. Chiodi, Giulio M.

L'engagement dans le *Journale de guerre I* de Jean-Paul Sartre. Idt, Geneviève.

La crisi del sapere moderno. Alheit, Peter.

La culture comme force. Yahot, Christophe.

La fiducia come forma di fede: Alcune riflessioni introduttive ad un problema sociologico. Prandini, Riccardo.

La Filosofía como cuarta destreza cultural para la realización humana de la vida. Martens, Ekkehard.

La función del legislador en Giambattista Vico. Pompa, Leon.

La Ideología del primer franquismo y los intelectuales. Mateo Gambarte, Eduardo.

La influencia de la Revolución Francesa en el pensamiento de Bonald. Osés Gorráiz, Jesús María.

La justicia en el pensamiento jurídico angloamericano contemporáneo: Acotaciones críticas. Rus Rufino, Salvador.

La liberté paradoxale. Bolduc, Sébastien.

La mediatizzazione del soggetto. Fadini, Ubaldo.

La Modernidad cansada (o ¿para qué aún filosofía). Lanceros, Patxi.

La prospectiva de los grandes informes y la metodología Delphi. Hernández de Frutos, Teodoro.

La science n'est pas toujours neutre: biodiversité, commercialisation et génétique humaine. Gendron, Pierre.

La structure ontique de la communauté d'après Edith Stein. Beauvais, Chantal.

La teoría de la cultura de Leonardo Polo. Murillo, José Ignacio.

La Teoría del Derecho y la Democracia en Jürgen Habermas: En torno a *Faktizität und Geltung*. Mejía Quintana, Oscar.

La tesis heideggeriana acerca de la técnica. Borges-Duarte, Irene.

Language and Authenticity. Marková, Ivana.

Le cosmopolitisme kantien. Lema-Hincapié, Andrés.

Le contrat du contrat social chez Rousseau selon Yves Vargas: Une lecture critique. Etane, Yombo.

Les Technologies de L'images: Nouveaux Instruments du Bio-Pouvoir. Maybon, Marie-Pierre.

Lessons from the Garden: Rousseau's Solitaires and the Limits of Liberalism. Cladis, Mark S.

Liberalism and Consumerism. Paden, Roger.

Liberalism and Culture. Carnes, Joseph H.

Liberalism and Moral Selfhood. Fairfield, Paul.

Liberalism and Pluralism. Klosko, George.

Liberalism, Nationalism, and the Right to Secede. Moellendorf, Darrel.

Liberation Theology and the Search for Peace in Ireland. Marsden, John.

Libertarianism, Self-Ownership, and Motherhood. Jeske, Diane.

Liberté! Egalité! Sexualité!: Theorizing Lesbian and Gay Politics. Kaplan, Morris B.

Life, Culture and Value: Reflections on Wittgenstein's *Culture and Value*. Pradhan, R C.

Living in a Wittgensteinian World: Beyond Theory to a Poetics of Practices. Shotter, John.

Looking for a Subject: Latvian Memory and Narrative. Skultans, Vieda.

Losing Our Minds: Olafson on Human Being. Cooper, David E.

Luis E. Nieto Arteta: Crítica del Marxismo y de los Sistemas Filosóficos. Cataño, Gonzalo.

Lyotard: Modern Postmodernist?. Hurst, Andrea.

Machiavelli and Rousseau: The Standpoint of the City and the Authorial Voice in Political Theory. Buckler, Steve.

Malthus and the Secularization of Political Ideology. Heavner, Eric K.

Marcuse: La última utopía. López de Dicastillo, Luis.

Market Non-Neutrality: Systematic Bias in Spontaneous Orders. diZerga, Gus.

Marx and the Spiritual Dimension. Brien, Kevin M.

Marx on Full and Free Development. Jenkins, Joyce L.

Marx's Inverted World. Sensat, Julius.

Matar al padre. Galindo Hervás, Alfonso.

Materiality and Language: Butler's Interrogation of the History of Philosophy. Olkowski, Dorothea.

Materiality in Theodor W. Adorno and Judith Butler. Hull, Carrie L.

Mechanistic Individualism Versus Organismic Totalitarianism: Toward a Neo-Calvinist Perspective. Venter, J J.

Mediations of the Female Imaginary and Symbolic. Campbell, Jan.

Melding the Public and Private Spheres: Taking Commensality Seriously. Hirschman, Albert O.

Memory, Forgetfulness, and History. Ricoeur, Paul.

Menschen ernähren oder Natur erhalten?. Rolston, III, Holmes.

Merleau-Ponty and the Liberal/Communitarian Debate. Low, Douglas.

Michael Oakeshott on History, Practice and Political Theory. Smith, Thomas W.

Minority Maneuvers and Unsettled Negotiations. Bhabha, Homi.

Modernity, Postmodernity and Transmodernity: Hope in Search of Time (in Spanish). Mendieta, Eduardo.

Monde reçu et monde à construire: l'*oikéiosis* stoïcienne et la *philia* d'Épicure. Duvernoy, Jean-François.

Moral Politics and the Limits of Justice in *Perpetual Peace*. Clarke, Michael.

Moral Reasoning as Perception: A Reading of Carol Gilligan. Kyte, Richard.

Moral Responsibility and Social Change: A New Theory of Self. Ferguson, Ann.

Muchas Culturas: Sobre el problema filosófico y práctico de la diversidad cultural. Ramírez, Mario Teodoro.

Multiculturalism and Gender Equity: The U.S. "Difference" Debates Revisited. Adler, Pierre.

My Own Criticism of *The Joyless Economy*. Scitovsky, Tibor.

Mysticism and Social Action: The Mystic's Calling, Development and Social Activity. Woods, Richard.

Myth, Measurement, and the Minimum Wage: Sound and Fury Signifying What?. Whitman, Glen.

Nation-States and States of Mind: Nationalism as Psychology. Tyrrell, Martin.

National Consciousness and Motherland Consciousness. Xiyuan, Xiong.

National Consciousness and Nationalism. Xiyuan, Xiong.

Nationality: Some Replies. Miller, David.

## SOCIAL PHIL

## SOCIAL SCIENCES

Altruism: A Social Science Chameleon. Grant, Colin.

Business Ethics in Canada: Integration and Interdisciplinarity. McDonald, Michael.

El krausopositivismo psicológico y sociológico en la obra de U. González Serrano. Jiménez García, Antonio.

Emancipatory Social Science: Habermas on Nietzsche. Kerckhove, Lee.

Evolutionary Materialism. Dawson, Doyne.

Friendship and Political Philosophy. Schall, James V.

Idiographic Theorizing and Ideal Types: Max Weber's Methodology of Social Science. Collin, Finn.

Karl Popper's Political Philosophy of Social Science. Stokes, Geoff.

Language and Authenticity. Marková, Ivana.

Max Weber: Sugerencias para una "reconstrucción". Crespo, Ricardo F.

Neutrality in the Social Sciences: On Bhaskar's Argument for an Essential Emancipatory Impulse in Social Science. Lacey, Hugh.

Social Darwinism: The Concept. Crook, Paul.

Social Science Courses as an Integrating Subject. Broz, Frantisek.

The Discovery of Situated Worlds: Analytic Commitments, or Moral Orders?. Macbeth, Douglas.

The Ontological Status of Ideation: A Continuing Issue. Smith, Charles W.

The Significance of the Skin as a Natural Boundary in the Sub-Division of Psychology. Farr, Robert M.

Thomas S. Kuhn, een moderne komedie van vergissingen. Derksen, A A.

Winch's Pluralist Tree and the Roots of Relativism. Phillips, Patrick J J.

## SOCIAL SECURITY

Privatization of Social Security: The Transition Issue. Ferrara, Peter J.

## SOCIAL STRUCTURE

Sozialstruktur und Sematik: Der wissenssoziologische Ansatz Niklas Luhmanns. Götke, Povl.

## SOCIAL STUDIES

"Avalutatività come principio metodico nella logica delle scienze sociali" in Momenti di Storia della Logica e di Storia della Filosofia, Guetti, Carla (ed). Bianco, Franco.

## SOCIAL THEORY

"Capitalism and Schizophrenia: Wildstyle in Full Effect" in Deleuze and Philosophy: The Difference Engineer, Ansell Pearson, Keith (ed). Mackay, Robin.

"Tönnies versus Weber: El debate Comunitarista desde la teoría social" in Liberalismo y Comunitarismo: Derechos Humanos y Democracia, Monsalve Solórzano, Alfonso (ed). Villacañas Berlanga, José L.

Deleuze and Philosophy: The Difference Engineer. Ansell Pearson, Keith (ed).

Hegel and Feminist Social Criticism: Justice, Recognition, and the Feminine. Gauthier, Jeffrey A.

Hegel, History, and Interpretation. Gallagher, Shaun.

Love Analyzed. Lamb, Roger E.

Sexual Harassment: Confrontations and Decisions. Wall, Edmund (ed).

Social Theory: A Bibliographic Series, No. 42-Martin Heidegger (II): A Bibliography. Nordquist, Joan.

Society, Economics & Philosophy: Selected Papers. Allen, R T (ed) and Polanyi, Michael.

Blameless, Constructive, and Political Anger. Swaine, Lucas A.

Civil Disobedience in the Social Theory of Thomas Aquinas. Scholz, Sally J.

De viajes y naufragios: Sobre el Libro de Santiago González Noriega El Viaje a Siracusa: Ensayos de Filosofia y Teoría Social Balsa de la Medusa 1994. Villacañas Berlanga, José Luis.

Dialogical Realities: The Ordinary, the Everyday, and Other Strange New Worlds. Shotter, John.

Do Practices Explain Anything? Turner's Critique of the Theory of Social Practices. Bohman, James.

Impossible Laws. D'Amico, Robert.

In the Name of Society, or Three Theses on the History of Social Thought. Osborne, Thomas and Rose, Nikolas.

Medical Practice and Social Authority. Pippin, Robert B.

Nothing is Concealed: De-centring Tacit Knowledge and Rules from Social Theory. Pleasants, Nigel.

Restructuring of Social and Political Theory in Education: Foucault and a Social Epistemology of School Practices. Popkewitz, Thomas S and Brennan, Marie.

Social Ethics?. Lemert, Charles.

Technology and the Crisis of Contemporary Culture. Borgmann, Albert.

The Condition of Postmodernity and the Discourse of the Body. Kumar Giri, Ananta.

The Legislation of Things. Löwy, Ilana.

The Relevance of Race in Adoption Law and Social Practice. Simon, Rita J and Altstein, Howard.

What There Is, How Things Are. Ossorio, Peter G.

Why Preference is not Transitive. Gendin, Sidney.

## SOCIAL WORK

The Personal Is the Organizational in the Ethics of Hospital Social Workers. Walsh-Bowers, Richard, Rossiter, Amy and Prilleltensky, Isaac.

## SOCIALISM

"Democracy and Intellectual Mediation: After Liberalism and Socialism" in Political Dialogue: Theories and Practices, Esquith, Stephen L (ed). Peterson, Richard T.

"La Crisis del Socialism Ético en Ortega" in Política y Sociedad en José Ortega y Gasset: En Torno a "Vieja y Nueva Política", Lopez de la Vieja, Maria Teresa (ed). Molinuevo, José Luis.

"Política y Filosofía en Ortega: Teoría Orteguiana de la Modernidad" in Política y Sociedad en José Ortega y Gasset: En Torno a "Vieja y Nueva Política", Lopez de la Vieja, Maria Teresa (ed). Flórez Miguel, Cirilo.

"Una Relación entre Diferentes: Ortega y Gasset y Gramsci" in Política y Sociedad en José Ortega y Gasset: En Torno a "Vieja y Nueva Política", Lopez de la Vieja, Maria Teresa (ed). Calvo Salamanca, Clara.

An Essay on Rights by Hillel Steiner. Wolff, Jonathan.

Analytical Marxism: A Critique. Roberts, Marcus.

On Heidegger's Nazism and Philosophy. Rockmore, Tom.

Political Dialogue: Theories and Practices. Esquith, Stephen L (ed).

A Plaything in Their Hands: American Exceptionalism and the Failure of Socialism—A Reassessment. Kieve, Ronald A.

A Preliminary Analysis of "National Consciousness". Xiyuan, Xiong.

Analytical Marxism—An Ex-Paradigm? The Odyssey of G.A. Cohen. Roberts, Marcus.

Between Immorality and Unfeasibility: The Market Socialist Predicament. Steele, David Ramsay.

Beyond Satisfaction: Desire, Consumption, and the Future of Socialism. Meister, Robert.

Die Marxismus—Debatte im "Silbernen Zeitalter". Ignatow, Assen.

Dr. Pangloss Goes to Market. Schweickart, David.

El Maxismo y el ocaso de la política. Colom González, Francisco.

From Atlas to Adolph: Body Building, Physical Culture, and National Socialism. Pickens, Donald K.

Internationale Konferenz zu Kants Friedensidee und dem heutigen Problem einer internationalen Rechts—und Friedensordnung in Frankfurt am Main. Grün, Klaus-Jürgen.

La filosofía política en el final de siglo. Montoya Saenz, José.

Netzverdichtung: Zur Philosophie industriegesellschaftlicher Entwick-lungen. Lübbe, Hermann.

On a Mistake Made by Russian Philosophy. Tul'Chinskii, G L.

Sartre e o pensamento de Marx. Paisana, Joao.

Socialism and National Consciousness. Xiyuan, Xiong.

Socialist Socrates: Ernst Bloch in the GDR. Ernst, Anna-Sabine and Klinger, Gerwin.

The Art of Allusion: Hans-Georg Gadamer's Philosophical Interventions under National Socialism. Orozco, Teresa.

The Ecological Ideology and Russia's Future. Gorelov, A A.

The Epistemological Argument Against Socialism: A Wittgensteinian Critique of Hayek and Giddens. Pleasants, Nigel.

The Status of a Classic Text: Lenin's What Is To Be Done? After 1902. Mayer, Robert.

The Tragedy of Lukács and the Problem of Alternatives (in Hungarian). Mészáros, István.

Who Won the Socialist Calculation Debate?. O'Neill, John.

## SOCIALITY

Monde reçu et monde à construire: l'oikéiosis stoïcienne et la philia d'Épicure. Duvernoy, Jean-François.

Space and Sociality. Malpas, Jeff.

## SOCIETY

see also Civil Society

"A New Agenda for Society" in The Liberation Debate: Rights at Issue, Leahy, Michael (ed). Cohn-Sherbok, Dan.

"Amour-propre" in Jean-Jacques Rousseau and the Sources of the Self, O'Hagan, Timothy (ed). O'Hagan, Timothy.

"An 'Inoperative' Global Community? Reflections on Nancy" in On Jean-Luc Nancy: The Sense of Philosophy, Sheppard, Darren (ed). Dallmayr, Fred R.

"Beginning Again: Teaching, Natality and Social Transformation" in Philosophy of Education (1996), Margonis, Frank (ed). Levinson, Natasha.

"Cohn-Sherbok's Reply" in The Liberation Debate: Rights at Issue, Leahy, Michael (ed). Cohn-Sherbok, Dan.

"Hegel and the Social Function of Reason" in Hegel, History, and Interpretation, Gallagher, Shaun. Rockmore, Tom.

"Kant, Adorno, and the Social Opacity of the Aesthetic" in The Semblance of Subjectivity, Huhn, Tom (ed). Huhn, Tom.

"L'utopia della nuova città" in Geofilosofia, Bonesio, Luisa (ed). Cervellati, Pierluigi.

"Materialist Mutations of the Bilderverbot" in Sites of Vision, Levin, David Michael (ed). Comay, Rebecca.

"Mundo administrado" o "Colonización del mundo de la vida": La depotenciación de la Teoría crítica de la sociedad en J. Habermas. Gómez Ibáñez, Vicente.

"On Disappointment in the Black Context" in Existence in Black: An Anthology of Black Existential Philosophy, Gordon, Lewis R (ed). Lawson, Bill E.

"Political Progress: Reality or Illusion?" in The Idea of Progress, McLaughlin, Peter (ed). Blondel, Jean.

"Public Moral Discourse" in Philosophical Perspectives on Bioethics, Sumner, L W (ed). Brock, Dan W.

"Some Procedural Problems" in The Liberation Debate: Rights at Issue, Leahy, Michael (ed). Wilson, John.

## SOCIETY

*"Teaching In/For the Enunciative Present" in Philosophy of Education (1996),* Margonis, Frank (ed). Kohli, Wendy.

*"The Social Construction and Reconstruction of Care" in Sex, Preference, and Family: Essays on Law and Nature,* Nussbaum, Martha C (ed). Moody-Adams, Michele M.

*"Three Types of Theories of Religion and Magic" in Epistemology and History,* Zeidler-Janiszewska, Anna (ed). Jerzak-Gierszewska, Teresa.

*"Toleration as a Form of Bias" in Philosophy, Religion, and the Question of Intolerance,* Ambuel, David (ed). Altman, Andrew.

*"What in Plato's Crito is Benefited by Justice and Harmed by Injustice?" in Dialogues with Plato,* Benitez, Eugenio (ed). Blyth, Dougal.

*A History of Philosophy: Volume II.* Hough, Williston S (ed & trans) and Erdmann, Johann Eduard.

*Aesthetic Theory: Theodore W. Adorno.* Hullot-Kentor, Robert (ed & trans), Adorno, Gretel (ed) and Tiedemann, Rolf (ed).

*African-American Perspectives and Philosophical Traditions.* Pittman, John P (ed).

*An Introduction to the Thought of Karl Popper.* Corvi, Roberta and Camiller, Patrick (trans).

*Art and Its Messages: Meaning, Morality, and Society.* Davies, Stephen (ed).

*Art in the Social Order: The Making of the Modern Conception of Art.* Mortensen, Preben.

*Earthly Goods: Environmental Change and Social Justice.* Hampson, Fen Osler (ed) and Reppy, Judith (ed).

*Family Values: Subjects Between Nature and Culture.* Oliver, Kelly.

*Feminist Approaches to Bioethics: Theoretical Reflections and Practical Applications.* Tong, Rosemarie.

*In Search of a Better World: Lectures and Essays from Thirty Years.* Popper, Karl and Bennet, Laura J (trans).

*Introduction to Marx and Engels: A Critical Reconstruction.* Schmitt, Richard.

*La Laïcité.* Haarscher, Guy.

*Léopold Sédar Senghor: From Politics to Poetry.* Kluback, William.

*Living in a Technological Culture: Human Tools and Human Values.* Tiles, Mary and Oberdiek, Hans.

*Machiavelli, Leonardo, and the Science of Power.* Masters, Roger D.

*Making a Necessity of Virtue.* Sherman, Nancy.

*Morality and the Law.* Baird, Robert M (ed) and Rosenbaum, Stuart E (ed).

*Mortals and Others: American Essays 1931-1935.* Russell, Bertrand and Ruja, Harry (ed).

*Nature and Society: Anthropological Perspectives.* Descola, Philippe (ed) and Pálsson, Gísli (ed).

*Postcolonial African Philosophy: A Critical Reader.* Chukwudi Eze, Emmanuel (ed).

*Principles of Social Reconstruction.* Russell, Bertrand and Rempel, Richard A.

*Punishment as Societal-Defense.* Montague, Phillip.

*Rational Choice and Moral Agency.* Schmidtz, David.

*Rousseau and the Politics of Ambiguity: Self, Culture, and Society.* Morgenstern, Mira.

*Sex, Preference, and Family: Essays on Law and Nature.* Nussbaum, Martha C (ed) and Estlund, David M (ed).

*Sexual Harassment: Confrontations and Decisions.* Wall, Edmund (ed).

*Social Control Through Law.* Treviño, A Javier (ed) and Pound, Roscoe.

*Sociedades sin Estado: El Pensamiento de los Otros.* Lorite Mena, José.

*The Annual of the Society of Christian Ethics with Cumulative Index.* Beckley, Harlan (ed).

*The Constitution of Good Societies.* Soltan, Karol Edward (ed) and Elkin, Stephen L (ed).

*The Cynics: The Cynic Movement in Antiquity and Its Legacy.* Branham, R Bracht (ed) and Goulet-Cazé, Marie-Odile (ed).

*The Logic of the Gift: Toward an Ethic of Generosity.* Schrift, Alan D (ed).

*The Lost Steps.* Polizzotti, Mark (trans) and Breton, André.

*The Reformation of Society Through Adequate Education.* Provost, C Antonio.

*The Textual Society.* Taborsky, Edwina.

*The Zero Fallacy and Other Essays in Neoclassical Philosophy.* Valady, Mohammad (ed) and Hartshorne, Charles.

*Values and the Social Order.* Radnitzky, Gerard (ed).

A Community without Truth: Derrida and the Impossible Community. Caputo, John D.

A Conception of Justice. Yearwood, Stephen.

A Moderate Communitarian Proposal. Etzioni, Amitai.

A Relatively Plausible Principle of Beneficence: Reply to Mulgan. Murphy, Liam B.

A Resource-Based-View of the Socially Responsible Firm: Stakeholder Interdependence, Ethical Awareness, and Issue Responsiveness as Strategic Assets. Litz, Reginald A.

A Universidade na Sociedade Actual. Renaud, Michel.

Accountability in a Computerized Society. Nissenbaum, Helen.

African Philosophy and the African Crisis. Owolabi, Kolawole Aderemi.

Alfred Schutz on the Social Distribution of Knowledge. Nnoruka, Sylvanos I.

Alle origini dei diritti dell'uomo: i diritti della comunicazione di Francisco de Vitoria. Trujillo Pérez, Isabel.

Another View on the Crisis in Marxism. Gamberg, Herb.

Are Ethical Conflicts Irreconcilable?. Cooke, Maeve.

Aristotle on Canonical Science and Ethics. Anagnostopoulos, Georgios.

Aristotle's *Child*: Development Through *Genesis, Oikos,* and *Polis.* McGowan Tress, Daryl.

Becoming an Evil Society: The Self and Strangers. Thomas, Laurence.

Being Human: Issues in Sexuality for People with Developmental Disabilities. Civjan, Sheryl Robinson.

Beside us, in Memory. Olkowski, Dorothea.

Beyond Living Wills. Tonelli, Mark.

Business Ethics in Canada: A Personal View. Boyd, Colin.

Business Ethics in Canada: Distinctiveness and Directions. Brooks, Leonard J.

Caring for "Socially Undesirable" Patients. Jecker, Nancy S.

Catastrophic Thinking in the Modern World: Russia and America. Shlapentokh, Vladimir.

Children, Society, and Health Care Decision Making. Caccamo, James M.

Christian Identity and Augustine's *Confessions.* Thompson, Christopher J.

Concept of Duty: A Study in Indian and Western Philosophy. Bhandari, D R and Lata.

Conflicting Varieties of Realism: Causal Powers and the Problems of Social Structure. Varela, Charles R and Harré, Rom.

Contract or Coincidence: George Herbert Mead and Adam Smith on Self and Society. Costelloe, Timothy M.

Corporate Ethics Initiatives as Social Control. Laufer, William S and Robertson, Diana C.

Corporate Social Performance, Stakeholder Orientation, and Organizational Moral Development. Logsdon, Jeanne M and Yuthas, Kristi.

Could Auditing Standards Be Based on Society's Values?. Zaid, Omar Abdullah.

Criteria for Evaluating the Legitimacy of Corporate Social Responsibility. Pava, Moses L and Krausz, Joshua.

Crítica a la constitución de una sociedad política como Estado de Derecho (homenje a Carlos Baliñas). Bueno, Gustavo.

Crítica del llamado de Heidelberg. Lecourt, Dominique.

Davidson's Second Person. Verheggen, Claudine.

De Minimis and Equity in Risk. Mosler, Karl.

Dinamic Peace in the Encounter of Vital Cultures (Spanish). Borges-Duarte, Irene.

Discutono *Il principio speranza*, di Ernst Bloch. Boella, Laura, Moneti, Maria and Schmidt, Burghart.

Domande e risposte sul problema della giustizia. Bagolini, Luigi.

Dominance Hierarchies and the Evolution of Human Reasoning. Cummins, Denise Dellarosa.

Don't Stop Thinking About Tomorrow: Two Paradoxes About Duties to Future Generations. Boonin-Vail, David.

El disciplinamiento social como factor del desarrollo histórico: Una visión heterodoxa desde el tercer mundo (Primera parte). Mansilla, H C Felipe.

El marxismo analítico. Gallichio, Santiago J.

Essentially Contested Concepts. Gallie, W B.

Etica della responsabilità e impegno politico in Aranguren. Savignano, Armando.

Evolutionary Materialism. Dawson, Doyne.

Fateful Rendezvous: The Young Althusser. Elliott, Gregory.

Fenomenologia del giuramento: un approccio antropologico. Scillitani, Lorenzo.

Foucault's Alimentary Philosophy: Care of the Self and Responsibility for the Other. Boothroyd, David.

Friendship and Political Philosophy. Schall, James V.

From Absurdity to Decision: The Challenge of Responsibility in a Technological Society. Wennemann, Daryl J.

Función, plan y proyecto. Llano Cifuentes, Carlos.

Gandhian Concept of Planned Society. Sharma, Akshaya Kumar.

Gli "ultimi uomini": a proposito di un libro su Max Weber. Salzano, Giorgio.

Grading Worlds. Menssen, Sandra.

Gramsci, teórico de la superestructura. Giglioli, Giovanna.

Group Rights and Social Ontology. Gould, Carol C.

Guarantees. Schmidtz, David.

Habermas and Apel on Communicative Ethics: Their Difference and the Difference It Makes. Gamwell, Franklin I.

Hegelian Retribution Re-Examined. Fatic, A.

Holiness, Virtue, and Social Justice: Contrasting Understandings of the Moral Life. Engelhardt Jr, H Tristram.

I rischi di una società dei "giusti". Lami, Gian Franco.

Identity Politics as a Transposition of Fraser's Needs Politics. Tittle, Peg.

In Defence of Representations. Jovchelovitch, Sandra.

In Defense of Advertising: A Social Perspective. Phillips, Barbara J.

In the Name of Society, or Three Theses on the History of Social Thought. Osborne, Thomas and Rose, Nikolas.

Information and Human Liberty. Weinberger, Ota.

Is Marxism Totalitarian?. Hudelson, Richard.

Is Science Socially Constructed—And Can It Still Inform Public Policy. Jasanoff, Sheila.

Justice, Society, Physicians and Ethics Committees: Incorporating Ideas of Justice into Patient Care Decisions. Loewy, Erich H.

Karl Popper y la crítica al determinismo. Bonetti, José Andrés.

L'allegoria sociale. Chiodi, Giulio M.

La ética de la ciencia y la ciencia de la ética. Badía Cabrera, Miguel A.

## SOCIETY

La méthodologie de la science constitutionnelle de la liberté. Sabete, Wagdi.

La Nápoles de Vico. Pinton, Giorgio A.

La posibilidad de pensar la democracia en Latinoamérica desde la óptica de la ética discursiva. Fernández, Alejandra.

La problemática ética del uso del DBCP en Costa Rica. Giralt-Bermúdez, María de los Angeles.

La questione del mito. Genovese, Rino.

Le "Dépassement de la Philosophie": Réflexion sur le statut contemporain de la philosophie. Gueye, Sémou Pathé.

Le cosmopolitisme kantien. Lema-Hincapié, Andrés.

Living in a Wittgensteinian World: Beyond Theory to a Poetics of Practices. Shotter, John.

Locke on Toleration: The Transformation of Constraint. Creppell, Ingrid.

Man and Nature: A Marxist Approach. Baruah, Girish Chandra.

Marx's Concept of Alienation. Schmitt, Richard.

Maxims, "Practical Wisdom," and the Language of Action: Beyond Grand Theory. Nichols, Ray.

Mechanistic Individualism Versus Organismic Totalitarianism: Toward a Neo-Calvinist Perspective. Venter, J J.

Metaphysics and the Rationalization of Society. Gamwell, Franklin.

Moral Responsibility and Social Change: A New Theory of Self. Ferguson, Ann.

Moral Rules. Shafer-Landau, Russ.

My Own Criticism of *The Joyless Economy*. Scitovsky, Tibor.

My Quality is not Low!. McNair, Douglas.

Mysticism and Social Action: The Mystic's Calling, Development and Social Activity. Woods, Richard.

Naturaleza humana en la filosofía de M.F. Sciacca y la concepción *light* de G. Vattimo. Darós, W R.

Nature's Experiments, Society's Closures. Leiber, Justin.

Navigating the Social World: Simulation Versus Theory. Sterelny, Kim.

Nietzsche's Dynamite: The Biography of Modern Nihilism. Roodt, Vasti.

Nihilism and the Continuing Crisis of Reason. Moser, Edward.

Non-Academic Critics of Business Ethics in Canada. Michalos, Alex C.

On Community. Noddings, Nel.

On Kant's *Rechtslehre*. Flikschuh, Katrin.

On Rape: A Crime Against Humanity. Calhoun, Laurie.

One World, But a Big One. Midgley, Mary.

Paradigmas: ¿construcciones históricas?. García Fallas, Jackeline.

Phase II of Bioethics: The Turn to the Social Nature of Individuals. Glaser, John W.

Plato and K.R. Popper: Toward a Critique of Plato's Political Philosophy. Eidlin, Fred (trans) and Giannaras, Anastasios.

Platón: justicia y pluralismo. Bubner, Rüdiger.

Polanyi on Liberal Neutrality. Goodman, C P.

Politics and Coercion. Goerner, E A and Thompson, Walter J.

Politics, Politics, Politics. Garver, Newton.

Presidential Address: Bioethics and Social Responsibility. Wikler, Daniel.

Progressive and Regressive Uses of Reasonable Distrust. Hedman, Carl.

Psychological Androgyny: A Concept in Seach of Lesser Substance. Towards the Understanding of the Transformation of a Social Representation. Lorenzi-Cioldi, Fabio.

Qual è la destra che manca in Italia: Per un discorso realistico sul conservatorismo e le istituzioni. Cofrancesco, Dino.

Queries about Social Representation and Construction. Wagner, Wolfgang.

Rawls's "The Closed Society Assumption" (in Serbo-Croatian). Strncevic, Ljubica and Gligorov, Vladimir.

Relevance of Swami Vivekanand's Concept of Evil Today. Sinha, Rani Rupmati.

Religion and Politics in India: Some Philosophical Perspectives. Perrett, Roy W.

Religion in the Critical Decades. Al Brynaichi, Javan.

Responsibility and Social Traps. Lenk, Hans and Maring, Matthias.

Responsible Technoscience: The Haunting Reality of Auschwitz and Hiroshima. Sassower, Raphael.

Rorty, Ironist Theory, and Socio-Political Control. Depp, Dane.

Saint Anselm: An Ethics of *Caritas* for a Relativist Age. McAleer, Graham.

Searle on Social Institutions. Tuomela, Raimo.

Social Darwinism: The Concept. Crook, Paul.

Social Epistemology and the Recovery of the Normative in the Post-Epistemic Era. Fuller, Steve.

Social Ethics Under the Sign of the Cross. Hollenbach, S.J., David.

Social Foundations of Openness. Hall, John A.

Social Justice: The Hayekian Challenge. Lukes, Steven.

Social Reality and Lu Jiuyuan (1139-1193). Birdwhistell, Anne D.

Social Representations and Mass Communication Research. Rouquette, Michel-Louis.

Some Problems in the Writing of the History of African Philosophy. Ogbogbo, C B N.

Superamento della complessità attraverso la capacità di apprendimento del diritto: L'adeguamento del diritto alle condizioni del Postmoderno. Ladeur, Karl-Heinz.

Technology and the Decline of Leisure. Anderson, Thomas.

The Christian Roots of a Free Society. Minogue, Kenneth.

The Conservatism of Konstantin Leont'ev in Present-Day Russia. Poliakov, L V.

The Double Face of the Political and the Social: Hannah Arendt and America's Racial Divisions. Bernasconi, Robert.

The Education of Natural Intelligence and the Intellectual Virtues: Has Educational Pastiche had the Last Laugh?. D'Souza, Mario O.

The Impact of Culture on Education. Thomas, Cornell.

The Impact of Ethical Considerations on Present-Day Russian Law. Feldbrugge, F J M.

The Marxist Theory of Art. Graham, Gordon.

The Model of Procedural Ethics: Formalism and Argumentation in Law (Spanish). Carrión Wam, Roque.

The Myths of Learning Disabilities: The Social Construction of a Disorder. Zuriff, G E.

The Perceived Role of Ethics and Social Responsibility: A Scale Development. Singhapakdi, Anusorn, Vitell, Scott J and Rallapalli, Kumar C.

The Political Turning Point (in Spanish). Camps, Victoria.

The Proactive Corporation: Its Nature and Causes. Shepard, Jon M, Betz, Michael and O'Connell, Lenahan.

The Problematic Character of Socrates' Defense of Justice in Plato's *Republic*. Jang, In Ha.

The Processual Origins of Social Representations. Puddifoot, John E.

The Propagation of Social Representations. Lahlou, Saadi.

The Quixotic Element in *The Open Society*. Munz, Peter.

The Russian Idea at the End of the Twentieth Century. Mil'don, Valerii Il'ich.

The Shock of the New: A Psycho-Dynamic Extension of Social Representational Theory. Joffe, Hélène.

The Social Concept of Disease. Räikkä, Juha.

The Special Features of Gandhian Ethics. Radha, S.

The Writer and Society: An Interpretation of *Nausea*. McGinn, Marie.

Themes of Ivan Illich: An Intellectual Biography. Inman, Patricia.

This Enormous Army: The Mutual Aid Tradition of American Fraternal Societies before the Twentieth Century. Beito, David T.

Towards an Epistemology of Social Representations. Marková, Ivana.

Transgressing the Boundaries: An Afterword. Sokal, Alan D.

Treating Race as a Social Construction. Lauer, Henle.

Two Significant Problems in Education—the General One and the Particular One (in Serbo-Croatian). Babic, Jovan.

Un modelo de Filosofía Social y Política: la Filosofía de la Filantropía. Uriz Pemán, María Jesús.

Unity and Development: Social Homogeneity, the Totalitarian Imaginary, and the Classical Marxist Tradition. Louw, Stephen.

Weber e lo spirito del capitalismo: Storia di un problema e nuove prospettive. Burgos, Juan Manuel.

Well-Being: On a Fundamental Concept of Practical Philosophy. Seel, Martin.

What is Conservatism?. Kekes, John.

What Rough Beast?. Weber, Eugen.

What Should We Expect From More Democracy? Radically Democratic Responses to Politics. Warren, Mark E.

What Society Will Expect from the Future Research Community. Jamieson, Dale.

What's Wrong with Consumer Capitalism? *The Joyless Economy* after Twenty Years. Schor, Juliet.

Why Did Marx and Engels Concern Themselves with Natural Science?. Griese, Anneliese and Pawelzig, Gerd.

Why God. Mishra, Amarendra.

William James's Ethics and the New Casuistry. Mehl, Peter J.

Women and Society in Russia. Ianovskii, Rudol'f Grigor'evich, Perminova, Alla Ivanovna and Mel'nikova, Tatiana A.

Women, the Family, and Society: Discussions in the Feminist Thought of the United States. Iulina, Nina S.

Working within Contradiction: The Possibility of Feminist Cosmetic Surgery. Kirkland, Anna and Tong, Rosemarie.

## SOCINIAN

Sozzini's Ghost: Pierre Bayle and Socinian Toleration. Tinsley, Barbara Sher.

## SOCIOBIOLOGY

*Evolutionäre Ethik? Philosophische Programme, Probleme und Perspektiven der Soziobiologie*. Gräfrath, Bernd.

Do Deconstructive Ecology and Sociobiology Undermine Leopold's Land Ethic?. Callicott, J Baird.

How a Kantian Can Accept Evolutionary Metaethics. Rauscher, Frederick.

Sociobiology and Evil: Ultimate Reality and Meaning Through Biology. Sharpe, Kevin.

Was kann heute unter Naturphilosophie verstehen?. Stöckler, Manfred.

What Rationality Adds to Animal Morality. Waller, Bruce N.

## SOCIOLOGY

"Sociological Perspectives on the Right to Know and the Right not to Know" in *The Right to Know and the Right not to Know*, Chadwick, Ruth (ed). Levitt, Mairi.

"The Functional Theory of Culture and Sociology" in *Epistemology and History*, Zeidler-Janiszewska, Anna (ed). Ziolkowski, Marek.

"Towards Honest Public Relations of Science" in *The Significance of Popper's Thought*, Amsterdamski, Stefan (ed). Agassi, Joseph.

*Objectivity: The Obligations of Impersonal Reason*. Rescher, Nicholas.

A Comparative Study between Comte's and Mill's View on Women. Lang'at, Wilson K A.

## SOCIOLOGY

A Note on Weber and Lukács (in Hungarian). Tarr, Zoltan.
An Inquiry into Ethical Relativism in Hindu Thought. Jhingran, Saral.
Animal symbolicum?. Loewenstein, Bedrich.
Bourdieu and the Social Conditions of Wittgensteinian Language Games. Gay, William C.
Gli "ultimi uomini": a proposito di un libro su Max Weber. Salzano, Giorgio.
La "Revue de métaphysique et de morale" e la guerra: Lettere inedite di Durkheim. De Paola, Gregorio.
La Paideia Durkheimiana: una teoría general de la educación. López de Dicastillo, Luis.
Max Weber: Sugerencias para una "reconstrucción". Crespo, Ricardo F.
Medical Practice and Social Authority. Pippin, Robert B.
On the Ontological Status of Ideas. Bhaskar, Roy.
Phänomenologische Versuche, sich den Grundlagen der gesellschaftlichen Praxis zu nähern. Schmied-Kowarzik, Wolfdietrich.
Relativismo filosófico contemporáneo: tres enfoques complementarios para dilucidar la génesis de un problema. Sola Gutiérrez, Luis.
Science Studies and Language Suppression—A Critique of Bruno Latour's We Have Never Been Modern. Cohen, Sande.
Science, Social Theory, and Science Criticism. Restivo, Sal and Bauchspies, Wenda K.
Sociología y tipología del fenómeno religioso. Piñon G, Francisco.
Splendours and Miseries of the Science Wars. Jardine, Nick and Frasca-Spada, Marina.
The Possibility of a Mathematical Sociology of Scientific Communication. Leydesdorff, Loet.
Theorie als Gedächtniskunst. Soentgen, Jens.
Why Not Science Critics?. Ihde, Don.
Why Strong Sociologists Abhor a Vacuum: Shapin and Schaffer on the Boyle/Hobbes Controversy. Norris, Christopher.
Ziekte leven: Bouwstenen voor een medische sociologie zonder disease/illness-onderscheid. Mol, Annemarie and Pols, Jeannette.
Zur Phänomenologie der Technikentwicklung. Kühn, Rolf.

## SOCIOLOGY OF KNOWLEDGE

Meditated History: An Approach to Karl Mannheim's Sociology of Knowledge through his Analysis of Mentalities (Spanish). Rodríguez Fouz, Marta.
The Social and Sociological Study of Science, and the Convergence Towards the Study of Scientific Practice (in Spanish). Gomez Ferri, Javier.

## SOCRATES

"La argumentación aristotélica contra el socratismo" in Ensayos Aristotélicos, Rivera, José Luis (ed). Zagal, Héctor Arreguín.
"La parole à la poule" in Philosophy and Democracy in Intercultural Perspective, Kimmerle, Heinz (ed). De Schipper, Elisabeth H.
"Plato, Prejudice, and the Mature-Age Student in Antiquity" in Dialogues with Plato, Benitez, Eugenio (ed). Tarrant, Harold.
"Socratic Anti-Empiricism in the Phaedo" in Dialogues with Plato, Benitez, Eugenio (ed). Baltzly, Dirk.
Classical Cynicism: A Critical Study. Navia, Luis E.
Defence of Socrates Euthyphro Crito. Gallop, David (trans).
Of Art and Wisdom: Plato's Understanding of Techne. Roochnik, David.
Schelling und Nietzsche: Zur Auslegung der frühen Werke Friedrich Nietzsches. Wilson, John Elbert.
Socrates's Discursive Democracy: Logos and Ergon in Platonic Political Philosophy. Mara, Gerald M.
Socratic Puzzles. Nozick, Robert.
The Art of Plato: Ten Essays in Platonic Interpretation. Rutherford, R B.
The Religion of Socrates. McPherran, Mark L.
Aristotle on Reason and its Limits. Smith, Gregory Bruce.
Art and Philosophy in Plato's Dialogues. Irwin, Terence H.
Brief Takes From the Horizon. Marcus, Jacqueline.
Caminhos da Filosofia ou a Razao e o Desejo. De Fraga, Gustavo.
Carnal Knowledge in the Charmides. McAvoy, Martin.
Ética y dialéctica: Sócrates, Platón y Aristóteles. Yarza, Ignacio.
Euthyphro's Second Chance. Amico, Robert P.
Genus and to ti en einai Essence in Aristotle and Socrates. Fritsche, Johannes.
Integrity and the Feminist Teacher. O'Dea, Jane.
Knowledge vs True Belief in the Socratic Psychology of Action. Penner, Terry.
Maître Eckhart et le discernement mystique: A propos de la rencontre de Suso avec la (chose) sauvage sans nom. Wackernagel, Wolfgang.
Nietzsche on Socrates as a Source of the Metaphysical Error. Harwood, Larry D.
Nozick's Socrates. Fine, Gail.
Of Dialogues and Seeds. Seeskin, Kenneth.
On Goods Wrongly Used: Axiological Antinomy in Plato's Euthydemus (in Polish). Galewic, Wlodzimierz.
Para uma História da Noçao de Ironia: Da Antiguidade Clássica à Escola Clássica Francesa. Gonçalves, Miguel.
Parmedidean Allusions in Republic V. Crystal, Ian.
Plato, Prejudice, and the Mature-Age Student in Antiquity. Tarrant, Harold.
Problemas Filosóficos y Filosofías del Límite. Nudler, Oscar.
Socialist Socrates: Ernst Bloch in the GDR. Ernst, Anna-Sabine and Klinger, Gerwin.

Socrates versus Plato: The Origins and Development of Socratic Thinking. Ross, George MacDonald.
Socrates' Soul and Our Own. Jackson, Michael.
Socrates, Friendship, and the Community of Inquiry. Glaser, Jen.
Socratic Akratic Action. Mele, Alfred R.
Socratic Anti-Empiricism in the Phaedo. Baltzly, Dirk.
The Definition of Man Needs. Gairola, M P.
The Impiety of Socrates. Burnyeat, M F.
The Problematic Character of Socrates' Defense of Justice in Plato's Republic. Jang, In Ha.
Was Socrates Guilty as Charged? Apology 24c-28a. Steinberger, Peter J.
Who is Cephalus?. Steinberger, Peter J.
Women: The Unrecognized Teachers of the Platonic Socrates. Blair, Elena Duvergès.

## SOCRATIC METHOD

From Kerlin's Pizzeria to MJK Reynolds: A Socratic and Cartesian Approach to Business Ethics. Kerlin, Michael J.
Gregory Vlastos: Socratic Studies. Nussbaum, Martha C.
Questioning and Thinking. Fasko, Jr, Daniel.

## SOFT

Swift Things Are Beautiful: Contrast in the Natural Aesthetic. Kupfer, Joseph H.

## SOFTWARE

Geography and Computer Ethics: An Eastern European Perspective. Kocikowski, Andrzej.
Situational Determinants of Software Piracy: An Equity Theory Perspective. Glass, Richard S and Wood, Wallace A.
Software Agents and Their Bodies. Kushmerick, Nicholas.

## SOKAL, A

A So-Called 'Fraud': Moral Modulations in a Literary Scandal. Lynch, Michael.
Splendours and Miseries of the Science Wars. Jardine, Nick and Frasca-Spada, Marina.

## SOLAR

Resolving Discordant Results: Modern Solar Oblateness Experiments. Richman, Sam.

## SOLDIER

Rape as a Weapon of War. Card, Claudia.

## SOLGER, K

"Autocoscienza e rivelazione: Solger e Schleiermacher di fronte alla storia" in Lo Storicismo e la Sua Storia: Temi, Problemi, Prospettive, Cacciatore, Giuseppe (ed). Pinto, Valeria.

## SOLIDARITY

Freedom and Solidarity in Sartre and Simon. Pappin III, Joseph.
Medical Ethics in the Developing World: A Liberation Theology Perspective. Fabri Dos Anjos, Marcio.
Reflective Solidarity. Dean, Jodi.
Rorty, Ironist Theory, and Socio-Political Control. Depp, Dane.
Solidarietà e democrazia: Osservazioni su antropologia, diritto e legittimità nella teoria giuridica di Habermas. Pinzani, Alessandro.

## SOLIPSISM

"Love and Solipsism" in Love Analyzed, Lamb, Roger E. Langton, Rae.
A Solipsist in a Real World. Pihlström, Sami.
Anti-Foundationalism and the Vienna Circle's Revolution in Philosophy. Uebel, Thomas E.
Berkeley Revised: On the New Metaphysics for Social Epistemology. 90 Years After "Materialism and Empiriocrticism". Kassavine, Illia.
Die Grenzen des Selbstwissens. Bernecker, Sven.
Identidad personal, acontecimiento, alteridad desde Paul Ricoeur. Fornari, Aníbal.
Linguistic Solipsism. Lenka, Laxminarayan.
Philosophy, Solipsism and Thought. Mounce, H O.
Solipsism and First Person/Third Person Asymmetries. Child, William.
Solipsism and Self-Reference. O'Brien, Lucy F.
Solipsism and Subjectivity. Moore, A W.
The Originality of Wittgenstein's Investigation of Solipsism. Pears, David.
The 'Truth' in Solipsism, and Wittgenstein's Rejection of the A Priori. Sullivan, Peter M.
Why is the Fifth Cartesian Meditation Necessary?. Haney, Kathleen.

## SOLITARY

The Solitary Self: Jean-Jacques Rousseau in Exile and Adversity. Cranston, Maurice.

## SOLITUDE

Geofilosofia del Paesaggio. Bonesio, Luisa.

## SOLOMON, R

On Emotion and Rationality: A Response to Barrett. Steutel, Jan.

## SOLOV'EV, V

The Problem of Moral Absolutes in the Ethics of Vladimir Solov'ëv. Sergeevich Pugachev, Oleg.

## SOMALIAN

Can We Think Systematically About Ethics and Statecraft?. Welch, David A.

## SOMMERS, C

Rape Research and Gender Feminism: So Who's Anti-Male?. Davion, Victoria.

## SPIRITUALITY

The Living Cosmos: Man Among the Forces of Earth and Heaven. Filatov, Vladimir Petrovich.

The Moral and Spiritual Dimension to Education: Some Reflections on the British Experience. Rossiter, Graham.

The Reflection of Some Traditional Stoic Ideas in the Thirteenth-Century Scholastic Theories of Beauty. Bychkov, Oleg V.

The Spriritual Dimension of Gandhi's Activism. Spretnak, Charlene.

## SPLITTING

A Non-Splitting Theorem for d.r.e. Sets. Yi, Xiaoding.

Generalized Nonsplitting in the Recursively Enumerable Degrees. Leonhardi, Steven D.

Splitting Number at Uncountable Cardinals. Zapletal, Jindrich.

Superintuitionistic Comparisons of Classical Modal Logics. Wolter, Frank.

The Combinatorics of the Splitting Theorem. Kontostathis, Kyriakos.

## SPONTANEITY

Metamorfosi della libertà nel *Sistema di Etica* di Fichte. Fonnesu, Luca.

## SPORT

A Critical Analysis of Hunters' Ethics. Luke, Brian.

La ética y la crisis del deporte. Csepregi, Gabor.

## SPRINGSTEEN, B

Born to Affirm the Eternal Recurrence: Nietzsche, Buber, and Springsteen. Cohen, Jonathan.

## SQUARE

A Very Weak Square Principle. Foreman, Matthew and Magidor, Menachem.

## STABILITY

A Definable Continuous Rank for Nonmultidimensional Superstable Theories. Chowdhury, Ambar, Loveys, James and Tanovic, Predrag.

Stability of Treatment Preferences: Although Most Preferences Do Not Change, Most People Change Some of Their Preferences. Singer, Peter A, Kohut, Nitsa and Sam, Mehran (& others).

Stable Structures with Few Substructures. Laskowski, Michael C and Mayer, Laura L.

The Morley Rank of a Banach Space. Iovino, José.

## STADLER, A

"August Stadler als Kant-Interpret" in *Grenzen der kritischen Vernunft,* Schmid, Peter A. Ferrari, Massimo.

## STAFFORD, B

"Towards an Epistemology of Scientific Illustration" in *Picturing Knowledge,* Baigrie, Brian S (ed). Topper, David.

## STAGE

*Kenneth Macgowan and the Aesthetic Paradigm for the New Stagecraft in America.* Bloom, Thomas Alan.

All the World's a Stage. Sider, Theodore.

Kierkegaard's "Three Stages": A Pilgrim's Regress?. Aiken, David W.

## STAHL, G

Leibniz et Stahl: divergences sur le concept d'organisme. Duchesneau, François.

## STAKEHOLDER

Stakeholder Theory and A Principle of Fairness. Phillips, Robert A.

## STALIN

Lived Thought between Affirmation and Critique: Georg Lukács and Stalinism (in Hungarian). Tietz, Udo.

## STALINISM

Deconstruction and Marxism: Jacques Derrida's Specters of Marx. Plangesis, Yannis.

Stalin and Marxism: A Research Note. Van Ree, E.

The Fedorovian Roots of Stalinism. Shlapentokh, Dmitry.

## STALNAKER, R

"Replies to Tomberlin, Tye, Stalnaker and Block" in *Perception,* Villanueva, Enrique (ed). Lycan, William G.

Conditionals, Imaging, and Subjunctive Probability. Lepage, François.

The Ramsey Test and Conditional Semantics. Döring, Frank.

Universal Instantiation: A Study of the Role of Context in Logic. Gauker, Christopher.

## STAMBAUGH, J

Let a Hundred Translations Bloom! A Modest Proposal about *Being and Time.* Sheehan, Thomas.

The New Translation of *Sein und Zeit:* A Grammatological Lexicographer's Commentary. Kisiel, Theodore J.

## STANDARD

Bioethics Committees and JCAHO Patients' Rights Standards: A Question of Balance. Corsino, Bruce V.

Responding to JCAHO Standards: Everybody's Business. Fletcher, John C.

Who Benefits? Music Education and the National Standards. Schmidt, Catherine M.

## STANDARDS

"The Goldilocks Syndrome" in *The Recovery of Philosophy in America: Essays in Honor of John Edwin Smith,* Kasulis, Thomas P (ed). Sherburne, Donald W.

*Rethinking College Education.* Allan, George.

Confronting the Assumptions That Dominate Education Reform. Robenstine, Clark.

Enforcing Ethical Standards of Professional Associations. Loevinger, Lee.

Ethical Standards for Business Lobbying: Some Practical Suggestions. Hamilton III, J Brooke and Hoch, David.

Promoting Ethical Standards in Science and Engineering. Frankel, Mark S.

Quality Control for Hospitals' Clinical Ethics Services: Proposed Standards. Leeman, Cavin P, Fletcher, John C and Spencer, Edward M (& others).

The NCTM Standards and the Philosophy of Mathematics. Toumasis, Charalampos.

The Qualitymongers. Hart, W A.

Who Benefits from the National Standards: A Response to Catherine M. Schmidt's "Who Benefits? Music Education and the National Standards.". Lehman, Paul R.

## STANLEY, J

"...Equality from the Masculine Point of View...": The 2nd Earl Russell and Divorce Law Reform in England. Savage, Gail.

## STASZEK, W

Logics of Rejection: Two Systems of Natural Deduction. Tamminga, Allard M.

## STATE

*see also* Mental States, Welfare State

"Palimpsest: Towards a Minor Literature in Monstrosity" in *Deleuze and Philosophy: The Difference Engineer,* Ansell Pearson, Keith (ed). Sawhney, Deepak Narang.

"Pro Patria Mori!: Death and the State" in *The Morality of Nationalism,* McKim, Robert (ed). Tamir, Yael.

"The Politics of Difference: Statehood and Toleration in a Multicultural World" in *The Morality of Nationalism,* McKim, Robert (ed). Walzer, Michael.

*Hegel, Marx, and the English State.* MacGregor, David.

*Las Caras del Leviatán: Una Lectura Política de la Teoría Crítica.* Colom González, Francisco.

*Lex Regia.* Lomonaco, Fabrizio.

*Rulers and Ruled: An Introduction to Classical Political Theory from Plato to the Federalists.* Zeitlin, Irving M.

*Sociedades sin Estado: El Pensamiento de los Otros.* Lorite Mena, José.

*Thomas Hobbes.* Taylor, A E.

A Noçao do "Estado" em Santo Agostinho. De Brito, António José.

A Organizaçao do Trabalho Escolar e os Especialistas da Educaçao. Pizzi, Laura Cristina V.

A propos de l'Éducation et de l'Institution scolaire au Québec. Louis, Desmeules and Desjardins, Richard.

A Review of the Origins of the State (Spanish). Ramos, Alberto Arvelo.

Adolfo Ravà: lo Stato come organismo etico. Fracanzani, Marcello.

Against a Straussian Interpretation of Marsilius of Padua's Poverty Thesis. Kaye, Sharon.

Against Marriage and Motherhood. Card, Claudia.

Benedetto Croce e la Storia della Chiesa. Campanelli, Giuseppina.

Business Entities and the State: Who Should Provide Security from Crime?. Scheid, Don E.

Cousin e l'"istituzionalizzazione' della filosofia. Ragghianti, Renzo.

Crítica a la constitución de una sociedad política como Estado de Derecho (homenje a Carlos Baliñas). Bueno, Gustavo.

Does a Rock Implement Every Finite-State Automation?. Chalmers, David J.

El concepto de *civitas* en la teoría política de Tomás de Aquino. Lorca, Andrés Martínez.

El Maxismo y el ocaso de la política. Colom González, Francisco.

El principio de reconocimiento en la teoría filosófica del derecho político externo de Hegel. Vieweg, Klaus.

Estado, soberanía y democracia. Velásquez Delgado, Jorge.

État fragile, démocratie précaire: le lieu de l'insouciance. Comeau, Paul-André.

Family, State—Individual. Festini, Heda.

Filosofia e politica. Badiou, Alain.

Giovanni Botero y la *Razon de Estado.* Sánchez, Antonio.

Hobbes on "Bodies Politic". Sorgi, Giuseppe.

Ideología y comunicación (Yugoslavia como problema). Milovic, Miroslav.

Igualidad no es fraternidad. Pastor Pérez, Miguel Antonio.

Il gioco degli specchi. Nacci, Michela.

Kants kritisches Staatsrecht. Herb, Karlfriedrich and Ludwig, Bernd.

L'esclusione dalla cittadinanza: Un casa limite: barbari e selvaggi. Taranto, Domenico.

La dialéctica de lo universal y lo particular y el ideal de la abolición del estado (Segunda parte). Salas, Mario.

La filosofia personalista di Dietrich von Hildebrand e la sua opposizione contro il nazionalsocialismo. Seifert, Josef.

La riforma del Welfare e un'idea di equità. Veca, Salvatore.

Making Exceptions: Some Remarks on the Concept of Coup d'état and Its History. Bartelson, Jens.

Nation-States and States of Mind: Nationalism as Psychology. Tyrrell, Martin.

O Estatuto da Paz na Teoria Política Hobbesiana. Pavan Baptista, Ligia.

Per una teoria del diritto ambientale: considerazioni a partire da un libro recente. Iagulli, Paolo.

Prospective Payment System and the Traditional Medical Ethics in Hungary. Jenei, Ilona.

Pufendorf, Sociality and the Modern State. Carr, Craig. L and Seidler, Michael J.

**STOICISM**

Fidelity to Zeno's Theory. Ioppolo, Anna Maria.

La *Politeia*, entre cynisme et stoïcisme. Dorandi, Tiziano.

La conducta humana y la naturaleza. Roig, Arturo Andres.

La contradiction du stoïcisme. Gobry, Ivan.

La fidélité de Zénon envers Chypre. Gabaude, Jean-Marc.

La place du politique dans le système stoïcien. Lang, André.

Le stoïcisme ou la conscience de Rome. Jerphagnon, Lucien.

Le système stoïcien: monde et langage. Mattéi, Jean-François.

Le tableau de Cléanthe. Rossetti, Livio.

Les écoles philosophiques d'Athènes et les princes de Chypre. Berti, Enrico.

Monde reçu et monde à construire: l'*oikéiosis* stoïcienne et la *philia* d'Épicure. Duvernoy, Jean-François.

Notas sobre a Presença de Sêneca nos *Essais* de Montaigne. Alves Eva, Luiz Antonio.

Oikeiosis: la naturalización de lo moral en el estoicismo antiguo. Velayos Castelo, Carmen.

Philosophia. Peperzak, Adriaan Theodoor.

Reasonable Impressions in Stoicism. Brennan, Tad.

Sur l'origine de l'éthique de Zénon de Cittium. Seidl, Horst.

Survol du Colloque. Lang, André.

The Origin of Stoic Fatalism. Pierris, A L.

The Reflection of Some Traditional Stoic Ideas in the Thirteenth-Century Scholastic Theories of Beauty. Bychkov, Oleg V.

Two Theories of Knowledge: Locke vs. Stoic. Badwal, Bhajan S.

Zénon et la statue (fr. 246 Arnim). Brancacci, Aldo.

Zénon, matérialiste et nominaliste?. Brinkman, Klaus.

**STOICS**

"Peirce and Philo" in *Studies in the Logic of Charles Sanders Peirce*, Houser, Nathan (ed). Zeman, Jay.

**STOKER, B**

Fear of Reproduction and Desire for Replication in *Dracula*. Colatrella, Carol.

**STOKES, A**

Edwin Gordon Responds. Gordon, Edwin.

**STONE, I**

"Socratic Intolerance and Aristotelian Toleration" in *Philosophy, Religion, and the Question of Intolerance,* Ambuel, David (ed). Barker, Evelyn M.

**STONE, L**

"A Revolution by Any Other Name" in *Philosophy of Education (1996)*, Margonis, Frank (ed). Hutchinson, Jaylynne N.

**STONE, T**

Navigating the Social World: Simulation Versus Theory. Sterelny, Kim.

**STORY**

"Beyond Moral Stories" in *Philosophy of Education (1996)*, Margonis, Frank (ed). Sichel, Betty A.

"Moral Stories: How Much Can We Learn from Them and Is It Enough?" in *Philosophy of Education (1996)*, Margonis, Frank (ed). Katz, Michael S.

"Perictione in Colophon" in *Verstehen and Humane Understanding*, O'Hear, Anthony (ed). Scruton, Roger.

Coyote Politics: Trickster Tales and Feminist Futures. Phelan, Shane.

El relato histórico: ¿hipótesis o ficción? Críticas al "narrativismo imposicionalista" de Hayden White. Tozzi, María Verónica.

Fairy Tales for Politics: The Other, Once More. Cladwell, Anne.

Language in Stories for Boys and Girls. Velasco, Mónica.

Protesi, ovvero la metamorfosi. Marchis, Vittorio.

Retelling the Representational Story: An Anti-Representationalist's Agenda. Dartnall, Terry.

Symbols and the Nature of Teaching. Götz, Ignacio L.

**STORY TELLING**

Philosophical Counselling: Bridging the Narrative Rift. Zoë, K A.

**STOVE, D**

I Rather Think I Am A Darwinian. Blackburn, Simon.

Stove's Anti-Darwinism. Franklin, James.

**STRASSER, S**

Phenomenology as Fundamental Moral Philosophy by Stephen Strasser (in Polish). Póltawski, Andrzej.

**STRATEGY**

An Ethical Approach to Lobbying Activities of Businesses in the United States. Keffer, Jane M and Hill, Ronald Paul.

Combinatorics and Forcing with Distributive Ideals. Matet, Pierre.

Ethics, Discovery, and Strategy. Foss, Nicolai J.

Is It Rational To Carry Out Strategic Intentions?. Robins, Michael H.

Moral Rhetoric in the Face of Strategic Weakness: Experimental Clues for an Ancient Puzzle. Varoufakis, Yanis.

Non-Basic Time and Reductive Strategies: Leibniz's Theory of Time. Cover, J A.

On the Significance of Conditional Probabilities. Sobel, Jordan Howard.

Sequential Asymmetric Auctions with Endogenous Participation. Menezes, Flavio M and Monteiro, Paulo K.

**STRAUSS, L**

La culture comme force. Yahot, Christophe.

Leo Strauss: lenguaje, tradición e historia (Reflexiones metodológicas sobre el arte de escribir). Blanco Echauri, Jesús.

Taking Exception to Liberalism: Heinrich Meier's *Carl Schmitt and Leo Strauss: The Hidden Dialogue*. Vatter, Miguel E.

**STRAWSON**

Ancora su nuvole ed orologi. Messeri, Marco.

Images of Identity: In Search of Modes of Presentation. Millikan, Ruth Garrett.

Las dos estrategias anti-escépticas de Strawson. Frangiotti, Marco Antonio.

Phenomenological Ethics and Moral Sentiments (Spanish). Hoyos Vásquez, Guillermo.

The Concept of Person (in Spanish). Dias, Maria Clara.

**STRAWSON, G**

Galen Strawson on Mental Reality. Crane, Tim.

On the Possibility of Rational Free Action. Clarke, Randolph.

True and Ultimate Responsibility. Nathan, Nicholas.

**STREAM**

Discount-Neutral Utility Models for Denumerable Time Streams. Fishburn, Peter C and Edwards, Ward.

**STRENGTH**

Confirmation, Explanation, and Logical Strength. Nelson, David E.

**STRESS**

L'Éthique et les Stress. Baertschi, Bernard.

**STRIKE, K**

In Defense of Public Reason: On the Nature of Historical Rationality. Ellet Jr, Frederick S and Ericson, David P.

**STRONG**

Indiscernible Sequences for Extenders, and the Singular Cardinal Hypothesis. Gitik, Moti and Mitchell, William J.

Searle's Abstract Argument Against Strong AI. Melnyk, Andrew.

Strong Cut-Elimination in Display Logic. Wansing, Heinrich.

Strong Termination for the Epsilon Substitution Method. Mints, Grigori.

Strong Versus Weak Quantum Consequence Operations. Malinowski, Jacek.

The Order Types of Termination Orderings on Monadic Terms, Strings and Multisets. Martin, Ursula and Scott, Elizabeth.

**STROUD, B**

Stroud and Moore on Skepticism. Neta, Ram.

What Does a Pyrrhonist Know?. Fogelin, Robert J.

**STRUCTURALISM**

"Deleuze and Structuralism: Towards a Geometry of Sufficient Reason" in *Deleuze and Philosophy: The Difference Engineer,* Ansell Pearson, Keith (ed). Clark, Tim.

"Some Issues of Historical Epistemology in the Light of the Structuralist Philosophy of Science" in *Epistemology and History,* Zeidler-Janiszewska, Anna (ed). Zeidler, Pawel.

"The Frankfurt School and Structuralism in Jerzy Kmita's Analysis" in *Epistemology and History,* Zeidler-Janiszewska, Anna (ed). Witkowski, Lech.

"Una Disavventura Della Differenza: Heidegger e i "francesi" in *Soggetto E Verità: La questione dell'uomo nella filosofia contemporanea,* Fagiuoli, Ettore. Vaccaro, G Battista.

*Philosophy of Mathematics: Structure and Ontology.* Shapiro, Stewart.

*Signs of the Time.* Elias, Willem.

*The Age of Structuralism: From Lévi-Strauss to Foucault.* Kurzweil, Edith.

*The Philosophy of Mathematics.* Hart, W D.

Anthropology and the *Sciences Humaines*: The Voice of Lévi-Strauss. Johnson, Christopher.

Debiti dello strutturalismo. Peruzzi, Alberto.

Lambek Calculus with Restricted Contraction and Expansion. Prijateljz, Andreja.

Las ideas básicas del estructuralismo metacientífico. Moulines, Carlos Ulises.

Liberating Experience from the Vice of Structuralism: The Methods of Merleau-Ponty and Nagarjuna. Levin, David Michael.

Pragmatic Idealization and Structuralist Reconstructions of Theories. Haase, Michaela.

Sobre algunos rasgos distintos del estructuralismo. Leiser, Eckart.

Structural Approach in Physics (in Spanish). Moulines, C Ulises.

The Equivalence Myth of Quantum Mechanics—Part I. Muller, F A.

The Unity of Scientific Knowledge in the Framework of a Typological Approach of Theories. Parvu, Ilie.

**STRUCTURE**

*see also* Social Structure

"Conceptual Structure and the Individuation of Content" in *AI, Connectionism and Philosophical Psychology, 1995,* Tomberlin, James E (ed). Pereboom, Derk.

"Matching Logical Structure to Linguistic Structure" in *Studies in the Logic of Charles Sanders Peirce,* Houser, Nathan (ed). Sowa, John F.

"Structural Properties: Categorical, Dispositional or Both?" in *Dispositions: A Debate,* Armstrong, D M. Place, U T.

"Tempo vuoto/tempo proprio" in *Il Concetto di Tempo: Atti del XXXII Congresso Nazionale della Società Filosofica Italiana,* Casertano, Giovanni (ed). Gregorio, Giuliana.

*Remaking the World: Modeling in Human Experience.* King, James R.

## SUBJECTIVITY

Contesting Consensus: Rereading Habermas on the Public Sphere. Markell, Patchen.

Coscienza morale e realtà secondo J.G. Fichte. Schrader, Wolfgang H.

Das *objektive Selbst* (Nagel)—Eine Destruktion oder Rekonstruktion transzendentaler Subjektivität?. Lütterfelds, Wilhelm.

De lo uno a lo otro: conocimiento, razón y subjetividad en Descartes. Arenas, Luis.

Dialogic or Dialogistic? Dialogicity or Dialogism? A Word of Warning against Rigor Metodologiae. Itkonen, Matti.

Die Beziehung zwischen der *Jenaer Metaphysik* von 1804/05 und der *Phänomenologie des Geistes*. Stewart, Jon.

Die Differenz zwischen 'Ich bin' und 'Ich bin Ich'. Ryue, Hisang.

Elementos' para uma Fenomenologia Literária do Texto Filosófico. Pimentel, Manuel Cândido.

Epistemic Aspects of Identity (in Serbo-Croatian). Andjelkovic, Miroslava.

Fichte, die sujektive Wende und der kartesianische Traum. Rockmore, Tom.

Forms of Tolerance as Types of Democracy (in Czech). Znoj, Milan.

Framework of an Intersubjetivist Theory of Meaning. Corredor, Cristina.

Gibt es ein subjektives Fundament unseres Wissens?. Grundmann, Thomas.

In Praise of Objective-Subjectivity: Teaching the Pursuit of Precision. Diller, Ann.

Is Subjective Materialism Possible? (in German). Delport, Hagen.

Kant y Husserl: El Problema de la Subjetividad. Montero Moliner, Fernando.

Kant's Pre-Critical Aesthetics: Genesis of the Notions of "Taste" and Beauty (in French). Dumouchel, Daniel.

L'atteggiamento metafisico come espressione del trascendentale nella soggettività. Rizzacasa, Aurelio.

La mediatizzazione del soggetto. Fadini, Ubaldo.

Levinas, Substitution, and Transcendental Subjectivity. Maloney, Philip J.

O Nilismo de Merleau-Ponty. Clemente, Isabel.

On Subjectivity and Intersubjectivity. Rieman, Fred.

On the Subjectivity of Welfare. Sobel, David.

Pensiero medievale e modernità. Gregory, Tullio.

Religious Life and Critical Thought: Do They Need Each Other?. Reinsmith, William.

Should We Expect To Feel As If We Understand Consciousness?. Price, Mark C.

Solipsism and Subjectivity. Moore, A W.

Space and Sociality. Malpas, Jeff.

Subjective, Not Objective, Truths. Subramaniam, Sharada.

Subjectivism, Utility, and Autonomy. Lottenbach, Hans.

Subjectivity and Illusion (in Dutch). Van Nierop, Maarten.

Subjectivity in Descartes and Kant. Schwyzer, Hubert.

The Colonization of Subjectivity: The Privatized Curriculum and the Marketing of American Education in a Postmodern Era. Weil, Danny.

The Essential Difference between History and Science. Martin, Raymond.

The Figures of Subjectivity in Éric Weil's *Logique de la philosophie* (in French). Kirscher, Gilbert.

The Logic of Autonomy and the Logic of Authenticity: A Two-Tiered Conception of Moral Subjectivity. Thiebaut, Carlos.

The Reflecting Symmetry of Subjective and Extra-Subjective Processes (and To Theme... M. Vlasáková) (in Czech). Lhoták, Kamil and Vlasáková, Marta.

Theory-Ladenness of Observation and Evidence. Basu, Prajit K.

Understanding Subjectivity: Global Workspace Theory and the Resurrection of the Observing Self. Baars, Bernard J.

Weak Ontology and Liberal Political Reflection. White, Stephen K.

Whitehead's Panpsychism as the Subjectivity of Prehension. McHenry, Leemon B.

Wissen und Tun: Zur Handlungsweise der transzendentalen Subjektivität in der ersten Wissenschaftslehre Fichtes. Siemek, Marek J.

Zum wirkungsgeschichtlichen Bewusstsein (in Serbo-Croatian). Jakovljevic, Goran.

Zur Logik der Moralität: Einige Fragen an A. Requate. De Vos, Lu.

## SUBJUNCTIVE

Conditionals, Imaging, and Subjunctive Probability. Lepage, François.

Introduction. Müller, Benito.

## SUBLIMATION

*The Reformation of Society Through Adequate Education*. Provost, C Antonio.

La literatura como juego. Palazón M, María Rosa.

## SUBLIME

"Il pittoresco e il sublime nella natura e nel paesaggio" in *Geofilosofia*, Bonesio, Luisa (ed). Scaramellini, Guglielmo.

*Waking to Wonder: Wittgenstein's Existential Investigations*. Bearn, Gordon C F.

Ethik der Endlichkeit: Zum Verweisungscharakter des Erhabenen bei Kant. Briese, Olaf.

Feeling and Aesthetic Judgment: A Rejoinder to Tom Huhn. Matthews, Patricia M.

Hume's Moral Sublime. Neill, Elizabeth.

Hyperbolic Doubt and "Machiavelism": The Modern Foundation of the Subject in Descartes (in French). Richir, Marc.

Kant's Reflections on the Sublime and the Infinite. Roy, Louis.

Landscape and the Metaphysical Imagination. Hepburn, Ronald W.

The Concepts of the Sublime and the Beautiful in Kant and Lyotard. Klinger, Cornelia.

The Sublime and Human Existence. Hurst, Andrea.

The Sublime and the Other. White, Richard J.

The Sublime in Kierkegaard. Milbank, John.

The Sublime, Unpresentability and Postmodern Cultural Complexity. Olivier, Bert.

The Sublimity of Evil. Nuyen, A T.

Through Phenomenology to Sublime Poetry: Martin Heidegger on the Decisive Relation between Truth and Art. Anderson, Travis T.

## SUBORDINATION

Natural Subordination, Aristotle On. Levin, Michael.

## SUBSISTENCE

*Basic Rights: Subsistence, Affluence, and U.S. Foreign Policy.* Shue, Henry.

## SUBSTANCE

see also Attribute, Immaterial Substance, Matter

"Berkeley: Scepticism, Matter and Infinite Divisibility" in *Scepticism in the History of Philosophy: A Pan-American Dialogue,* Popkin, Richard H (ed). Robles, José A.

"Il Luogo Della Filosofia: La paradossalità della *Seinsfrage* nel giovane Heidegger" in *Soggetto E Verità: La questione dell'uomo nella filosofia contemporanea*, Fagiuoli, Ettore. Vicari, Dario.

1277 Revisited: A New Interpretation of the Doctrinal Investigations of Thomas Aquinas and Giles of Rome. Thijssen, J M M H.

*Descartes's Legacy: Minds and Meaning in Early Modern Philosophy.* Hausman, David B and Hausman, Alan.

*Entity and Identity and Other Essays.* Strawson, P F.

*Representation of the World: A Naturalized Semantics.* Melnick, Arthur.

*Substance: Its Nature and Existence.* Hoffman, Joshua and Rosenkrantz, Gary S.

A Idéia de Parte da Natureza em Espinosa. Chauí, Marilena.

A Proof of One Substance Monism. Naik, A D.

Analyse und Kontext des Wachsbeispiels bei Descartes. Petrus, Klaus.

Aristotle *Metaphysics* H6: A Dialectic with Platonism. Harte, Verity.

Chemistry as the Science of the Transformation of Substances. Van Brakel, Jaap.

Contrariety and "Carving up Reality". Elder, Crawford L.

Corporeal Substances and True Unities. Baxter, Donald L M.

Der Ichbegriff in Fichtes Erörterung der Substantialität. Klotz, Christian.

Descartes según Leibniz. Silva de Choudens, José R.

Ente ed essenza in un saggio giovanile di Tommaso d'Aquino. Giorgini, Claudio.

Form and Substance in Criminal Justice Scholarship: H. Richard Uviller, *Virtual Justice*. Dripps, Donald A.

Heidegger and Aquinas on the Self as Substance. Baur, Michael.

Immanence and Light: Spinoza, Vermeer and Rembrandt (in Portuguese). Chauí, Marilena.

Interactionism and Physicality. Mills, Eugene.

Is Aquinas's Proof for the Indestructibility of the Soul Successful?. Cross, Richard.

Kantian Matters: The Structure of Permanence. O'Shea, James R.

L'infinité des attributs chez Spinoza. Boss, Gilbert.

La generación absoluta, según la exposición aquiniana de Aristóteles. Velázquez Fernández, Héctor.

McTaggart's Argument for Idealism. Mander, W J.

Metafisica tra scienza e sapienza: Tafsir Lām 52-58 di Ibn Rusd. Roccaro, Giuseppe.

On Substances, Accidents and Universals: In Defence of a Constituent Ontology. Smith, Barry.

Ontological Categories and Natural Kinds. Lowe, E J.

Per una storia dei cartesiani in Italia: Avvertenza. Garin, Eugenio.

Property Identity and 'Intrinsic' Designation. Goldstick, Danny.

Reductionism and Nominalism in Descartes's Theory of Attributes. Nolan, Lawrence.

Reply to Martin. Armstrong, D M.

Secolarizzazione e originalità del moderno: In margine a *La legittimità dell'epoca moderna* di Hans Blumenberg. Carosotti, Gianni.

Spinoza à la Mode: A Defence of Spinozistic Anti-Pluralism. Glouberman, Mark.

Substances are not Windowless: A Suarézian Critique of Monadism. Kronen, John D.

The Buddhist Conditional in Set-Theoretic Terms. Galloway, Brian.

The Function of the *formae nativae* in the Refinement Process of Matter: A Study of Bernard of Chartres's Concept of Matter. Annala, Pauli.

The Myth of Substance and the Fallacy of Misplaced Concreteness. Seibt, Johanna.

The Paradox of Identity. Greenberg, William J.

The Spinoza-Intoxicated Man: Deleuze on Expression. Piercey, Robert.

Unconfigured Tractarian Objects. Page, James.

Wie definiert man einen physikalischen Gegenstand?. Rudolph, Enno.

## SUBSTITUTION

A Modern Elaboration of the Ramified Theory of Types. Laan, Twan and Nederpelt, Rob.

A Semiquotational Solution to Substitution Puzzles. Rieber, Steven.

How Much Substitutivity?. Forbes, Graeme.

## SYMBOLISM

Il Metodo della Filosofia della Religione di A. Sabatier. Savignano, Armando.

Mediations of the Female Imaginary and Symbolic. Campbell, Jan.

Symbolic Difference. Schürmann, Reiner.

Symbolic Praxis. Schürmann, Reiner.

The Semantics of Symbolic Speech. Berckmans, Paul R.

Ultimate Reality and Meaning as Portrayed in the Religious Symbolism of Aron Tamási. Muray, Leslie A.

## SYMMETRY

A Bayesian Examination of Time-Symmetry in the Process of Measurement. Shimony, Abner.

Curie's Principle. Ismael, Jenann.

De *A* et *B*, de leur indépendance logique, et de ce qu'ils n'ont aucun contenu factuel commun. Roeper, Peter and Leblanc, Hughes.

Gauge Invariance, Cauchy Problem, Indeterminism, and Symmetry Breaking. Liu, Chuang.

Symmetry as a Method of Proof. Hammer, Eric.

The Reflecting Symmetry of Subjective and Extra-Subjective Processes (and To Theme... M. Vlasáková) (in Czech). Lhoták, Kamil and Vlasáková, Marta.

## SYMPATHY

Kant, Smith and Locke: The Locksmith's Mending of Tradition: A Reaction to Mr. Fleischacker's Thesis. Perreijn, Willem.

Sympathy and Other Selves. Pitson, Tony.

## SYMPOSIUM

The Symposium Viewed from the Organizer's Perspective. Gorski, Andrew.

## SYMPTOMS

About Signs and Symptoms: Can Semiotics Expand the View of Clinical Medicine?. Nessa, John.

## SYNONYMY

Die impliziten Prämissen in Quines Kritik der semantischen Begriffe. Greimann, Dirk.

Syntactic Features and Synonymy Relations: A Unified Treatment of Some Proofs of the Compactness and Interpolation Theorems. Weaver, George E.

## SYNTACTIC

Syntactic Codes and Grammar Refinement. Kracht, Marcus.

Syntactic Features and Synonymy Relations: A Unified Treatment of Some Proofs of the Compactness and Interpolation Theorems. Weaver, George E.

## SYNTAX

"Can We Knock Off the Shackles of Syntax?" in *Contents,* Villanueva, Enrique (ed). Andler, Daniel.

"Carnap: From Logical Syntax to Semantics" in *Origins of Logical Empiricism,* Giere, Ronald N (ed). Ricketts, Thomas.

*Die Sprache des Geistes: Vergleich einer repräsentationalistischen und einer syntaktischen Theorie des Geistes.* Saporiti, Katia.

A Critique of the Minimalist Program. Johnson, David E and Lappin, Shalom.

A First-Order Axiomatization of the Theory of Finite Trees. Backofen, Rolf, Rogers, James and Vijay-Shanker, K.

El argumento fregeano de las oraciones aseverativas como nombres propios. Ramos, Pedro.

Interrogative Wh-Movement in Slovene and English. Golden, Marija.

Language of Thought: The Connectionist Contribution. Aydede, Murat.

Structured Propositions and Sentence Structure. King, Jeffrey C.

Syntax in a Dynamic Brain. Garson, James W.

Syntax, Imagery and Naturalization. Duran, Jane.

Towards a Model Theory of Diagrams. Hammer, Eric and Danner, Norman.

## SYNTHESIS

Der Evolutionsbegriff als Mittel zur Synthese: Leistung und Grenzen. Vollmer, Gerhard.

The Hegelian Sign: Sacrificial Economy and Dialectical Relief (in French). Guibal, Francis.

## SYNTHETIC

Gottlob Frege and the Analytic-Synthetic Distinction within the framework of the Aristotelian Model of Science. De Jong, Willem R.

Kant's Theory of Geometrical Reasoning and the Analytic-Synthetic Distinction: On Hintikka's Interpretation of Kant's Philosophy of Mathematics. De Jong, Willem R.

The Underdetermination/Indeterminacy Distinction and the Analytic/Synthetic Distinction. Moore, A W.

Zum Stellenwert der *Grundlage* aus der Sicht von 1804: Eine Interpretation des Wechsels von analytisch-synthetischer und genetischer Methode in Kapitel 5 der *Grundlage*. Beeler-Port, Josef.

Zur Analytizität der *Grundlegung*. Schönecker, Dieter.

## SYNTHETIC A PRIORI

Kant e l'epistemologia contemporanea. Castagni, Laura.

## SYSTEM

"On the Structure of Frege's System of Logic" in *Frege: Importance and Legacy,* Schirn, Matthias (ed). Thiel, Christian.

"The Logic of Normative Systems" in *Deontic Logic, Agency and Normative Systems,* Brown, Mark A (ed). Johanson, Arnold A.

"Vita e sistema: Alle origini del pensiero hegeliano a Jena" in *Lo Storicismo e la Sua Storia: Temi, Problemi, Prospettive,* Cacciatore, Giuseppe (ed). Cantillo, Giuseppe.

*Deontic Logic, Agency and Normative Systems.* Brown, Mark A (ed) and Carmo, José (ed).

*Tra Esperienza e Ragione: Hegel e il problema dell'inizio della storia della filosofia.* Biscuso, Massimiliano.

A Logic for Information Systems. Archangelsky, Dmitri A and Taitslin, Mikhail A.

Approximate Knowledge of Many Agents and Discovery Systems. Zytkow, Jan M.

Classic Paradoxes in the Context of Non-Monotonic Logic (in Spanish). Beck, Andreas.

Cultural Diversity and the Systems View. Hammond, Debora.

Ethics as a Control System Component. Spier, Raymond.

Le thomisme entre système et histoire. Tourpe, Emmanuel.

Luis E. Nieto Arteta: Crítica del Marxismo y de los Sistemas Filosóficos. Cataño, Gonzalo.

Prinzipien und System: Rezeptionsmodelle der Wissenschaftslehre Fichtes 1794. Stamm, Marcelo.

System und Methode—Zur methodologischen Begründung transzendentalen Philosophierens in Fichtes *Begriffsschrift*. Stahl, Jürgen.

The Possibility of a Mathematical Sociology of Scientific Communication. Leydesdorff, Loet.

## SYSTEMATICITY

Systematicity. Cummins, Robert.

## SYSTEMS THEORY

De sociale functie van ethiek in de onderneming. Jeurissen, Ronald.

## SZILARD, L

Theodore Karman, Paul Wigner, John Neumann, Leo Szilard, Edward Teller and Their Ideas of Ultimate Reality and Meaning. Horvath, Tibor.

## TABLE

Fuentes para la historia de la astronomia de los siglos XIV y XV. Eclipses y tablas. Lértora Mendoza, Celina A.

## TABLEAU PROOF

A Note on the Completeness of Kozen's Axiomatisation of the Propositional mu-Calculus. Walukiewicz, Igor.

A Reasoning Method for a Paraconsistent Logic. Buchsbaum, Arthur and Pequeno, Tarcisio.

A Uniform Tableau Method for Intuitionistic Modal Logics I. Amati, Giambattista and Pirri, Fiora.

Cut-Free Tableau Calculi For Some Propositional Normal Modal Logics. Amerbauer, Martin.

The Relative Complexity of Analytic Tableaux and SL-Resolution. Vellino, André.

Theory Matrices (for Modal Logics) Using Alphabetical Monotonicity. Gent, Ian P.

## TABOO

Blurred Boundaries. Morriss, Peter.

## TACIT

Conventional Implicatures as Tacit Performatives. Rieber, Steven.

## TAGORE, R

The Concept of Mind in Modern Indian Thought with Special Reference to Sri Aurobindo, Rabindranath and K.C. Bhatiacharyya. Ghosh, Raghunath.

## TAKETANI, M

Dialectical Materialism and the Quantum Controversy: The Viewpoints of Fock, Langevin, and Taketani. Freire Jr, Olival.

## TALBOTT, T

Universalism and the Greater Good: A Response to Talbott. Knight, Gordon.

## TALLON, A

On the Intentionality of Moods: Phenomenology and Linguistic Analysis. Arregui, Jorge V.

## TAMASI, A

Ultimate Reality and Meaning as Portrayed in the Religious Symbolism of Aron Tamási. Muray, Leslie A.

## TAOISM

"Buddhi-Taoist and Western Metaphysics of the Self" in *Culture and Self,* Allen, Douglas (ed). Inada, Kenneth K.

*Meeting of Minds: Intellectual and Religious Interaction in East Asian Traditions of Thought.* Bloom, Irene (ed) and Fogel, Joshua A (ed).

Is Deep Ecology Too Radical?. Aiken, William.

La liberté a-t-elle un sens dans la tradition chinoise?. Drivod, Lucien.

Philosophical Counseling and Taoism: Wisdom and Lived Philosophical Understanding. Lahav, Ran.

Philosophical Significance of Gongsun Long: A New Interpretation of Theory of *Zhi* as Meaning and Reference. Cheng, Chung-ying.

Taoism and Jung: Synchronicity and the Self. Coward, Harold.

The Chinese Doctrinal Acceptance of Buddhism. Inada, Kenneth K.

## TARSKI

"Tarski's Development of Peirce's Logic of Relations" in *Studies in the Logic of Charles Sanders Peirce,* Houser, Nathan (ed). Anellis, Irving H.

Die Idee hinter Tarskis Definition von Wahrheit. Greimann, Dirk.

Logical Consequence Revisited. Sagüillo, José M.

Logical Consequence: A Defense of Tarski. Ray, Greg.

Perplexity in Plato, Aristotle, and Tarski. Matthews, Gareth B.

Que és la Verdad?. Barrio, Eduardo Alejandro.

## TEACHING

High School Teaching of Bioethics in New Zealand, Australia and Japan. Asada, Yukiko, Tsuzuki, Miho and Akiyama, Shiro.

Improving Academic Writing. Bennett, Jonathan and Gorovitz, Samuel.

In Praise of Objective-Subjectivity: Teaching the Pursuit of Precision. Diller, Ann.

Incorporating Critical Thinking in the Curriculum: An Introduction to Some Basic Issues. Ennis, Robert H.

Increasing Effectiveness in Teaching Ethics to Undergraduate Business Students. Lampe, Marc.

Interpretation as Action: The Risk of Inquiry. Awbrey, Jon and Awbrey, Susan.

Israel Scheffler on Religion, Reason and Education. McLaughlin, Terence H.

Kohlberg's Dormant Ghosts: The Case of Education. Oser, Fritz K.

Landmarks in Critical Thinking Series: Ennis on the Concept of Critical Thinking. Hoaglund, John.

Landmarks in Critical Thinking Series: John Passmore: On Teaching to be Critical. Splitter, Laurance.

Language: Definition and Metaphor. Barrow, Robin.

Learning Philosophy Collaboratively with a Student. Weiss, Andrea and Katzner, James.

Living Educational Theories and Living Contradictions: A Response to Mike Newby. Whitehead, Jack.

Lui's Complaint. Lee, Zosimo E.

Mass Extinctions and the Teaching of Philosophy of Science. Boersema, David B.

My Profession and Its Duties. Sher, George.

O "Romantismo", o "Enciclopedismo" e o "Criticismo" Manifestos no Magistério da Filosofia no Ensino Médio em Uberlândia. Pereira da Silva, Sérgio.

On Teaching Premise/Conclusion Distinctions. Fawkes, Don.

On the Theme of "Teaching for Higher Order Thinking Skills". Splitter, Laurance J.

Philosophical Counseling: A Computer-Assisted, Logic-Based Approach. Cohen, Elliot D.

Philosophy and Critical Thinking. Verharen, Charles.

Philosophy Class as Commercial. Wenz, Peter S.

Philosophy for Children and the Discipline of Philosophy. Gazzard, Ann.

Philosophy for Children: One Way of Developing Children's Thinking. Green, Lena.

Powerful Pedagogy in the Science-and-Religion Classroom. Grassie, William.

Principes pragmatistes pour une démarche pédagogique en enseignement moral. Daniel, Marie-France.

Reason in Teaching: Scheffler's Philosophy of Education "A Maximum of Vision and a Minimum of Mystery". Hare, William.

Replies. Scheffler, Israel.

Report of a Year Working on Improving Teaching and Learning. Adler, Jonathan.

Response to Gregory Pence's Case Study in the Teaching of Ethics. Makus, Robert.

Responsible Engineering: *Gilbane Gold* Revisited. Pritchard, Michael S and Holtzapple, Mark.

Scheffler Revisited on the Role of History and Philosophy of Science in Science Teacher Education. Matthews, Michael R.

Seven Principles for Better Practical Ethics. Scholz, Sally J and Groarke, Leo.

Should Anti-Realists Teach Critical Thinking?. Hatcher, Donald L.

Skewered on the Unicorn's Horn. Nelson, Craig E.

Some Reflections on Postgraduate Medical Ethics Education. Levine, Robert J.

Some Thoughts on Thinking and Teaching Styles. Schwerin, Alan.

Surrogate Family Values: The Refeminization of Teaching. Thompson, Audrey.

Symbols and the Nature of Teaching. Götz, Ignacio L.

Taking Ethics Seriously: Virtue, Validity, and the Art of Moral Reasoning. Hughes, Paul.

Teaching and Learning Research Ethics. Bird, Stephanie J and Swazey, Judith P.

Teaching and the Structural Approach to Fallacies. Adler, Jonathan E.

Teaching Business Ethics Through Literature. Shepard, Jon M, Goldsby, Michael G and Gerde, Virginia W.

Teaching Business Ethics Through Meditation. La Forge, Paul G.

Teaching Business Ethics: The Role of Ethics in Business and in Business Education. Cragg, Wesley.

Teaching Democracy Democratically. Worsfold, Victor L.

Teaching Ethics to Scientists and Engineers: Moral Agents and Moral Problems. Whitbeck, Caroline.

Teaching for Presence in the Democratic Classroom. Richardson, Brenda.

Teaching Science at the University Level: What About the Ethics?. Gilmer, Penny J.

Teaching Styles that Encourage (and Discourage) Thinking Skills. Downs-Lombardi, Judy.

Teaching the Three Rs: Rights, Roles and Responsibilities—A Curriculum for Pediatric Patient Rights. Davis, Kathleen G.

Teaching the Virtues: Justifications and Recommendations. Gauthier, Candace Cummins.

Teaching, Reason and Risk. Pearson, Allen T.

The Best Teacher I Ever Had Was... J. Coert Rylaarsdam. Michalos, Alex C.

The Case of the Slain President: Teaching Critical Thinking in Context. Walters, Kerry.

The Concept of Indoctrination. Puolimatka, Tapio.

The NCTM Standards and the Philosophy of Mathematics. Toumasis, Charalampos.

The Need for Comprehensiveness in Critical Thinking Instruction. Nosich, Gerald.

The New View of Plato. Krämer, Hans Joachim.

The Nurturing of a Relational Epistemology. Thayer-Bacon, Barbara J.

The Philosophy They Bring to Class: Companion Student Papers in PHL 101. Chiles, Robert E.

The Summer Philosophy Institute of Colorado: Building Bridges. Figueroa, Robert and Goering, Sara.

The Teaching of Ethics. Doorley, Mark J.

The Virtual Seminar Room: Using a World Wide Web Site in Teaching Ethics. Hinman, Lawrence M.

Thinking Critically About Critical Thinking: An Unskilled Inquiry into Quinn and McPeck. Gardner, Peter and Johnson, Steve.

Those Who Can, Do: A Response to Sidney Gendin's "Am I Wicked?". Warren, Dona.

Thou Shalt and Shalt Not: An Alternative to the Ten Commandments Approach to Developing a Code of Ethics for Schools of Business. Kleiner, Deborah S and Maury, Mary D.

Trust Is Not Enough: Classroom Self-Disclosure and the Loss of Private Lives. Bishop, Nicole.

Um Problema no Ensino de Ciências: organizaçao conceitual do conteúdo ou estudo dos fenômenos. Pacheco, Décio.

Using Moral Dilemmas in Children's Literature as a Vehicle for Moral Education and Teaching Reading Comprehension. Clare, Lindsay, Gallimore, Ronald and Patthey-Chavez, G Genevieve.

Using the "Ethical Environment" Paradigm to Teach Business Ethics: The Case of the Maquiladoras. Raisner, Jack A.

What Cognitive Science Tells Us about Ethics and the Teaching of Ethics. Anderson, James A.

Who's Afraid of Assessment? Remarks on Winch and Gingell's Reply. Davis, Andrew.

Why Teach Ethics in Science and Engineering?. Johnson, Deborah G, Hollander, Rachelle D and Beckwith, Jonathan R (& others).

Women: The Unrecognized Teachers of the Platonic Socrates. Blair, Elena Duvergès.

## TECHNIQUE

Incoherence in the Aristotelian Philosophy of Action? (Spanish). Bravo, Francisco.

Une philosophie de la "dynamique créative". Tavares de Miranda, Maria Do Carmo.

## TECHNOCRACY

Hacia una filosofía de la tecnología. Camacho, Luis.

The Cosmic Route to "Eternal Bliss": (K.E. Tsiolkovskii and the Mythology of Technocracy). Gavriushin, Nikolai K.

## TECHNOLOGY

*see also* Machine

"Constructing Modernism: The Cultural Location of *Aufbau*" in *Origins of Logical Empiricism,* Giere, Ronald N (ed). Galison, Peter.

"Moral Philosophy and Public Policy: The Case of New Reproductive Technologies" in *Philosophical Perspectives on Bioethics,* Sumner, L W (ed). Kymlicka, Will.

"Prospect for Science and Technology" in *The American University: National Treasure or Endangered Species?,* Ehrenberg, Ronald G (ed). Lane, Neal.

"Technik und Ethik" in *Angewandte Ethik: Die Bereichsethiken und ihre theoretische Fundierung,* Nida-Rümelin, Julian (ed). Ott, Konrad.

"Technik und symbolische Form bei Cassirer" in *Grenzen der kritischen Vernunft,* Schmid, Peter A. Robbeck, Johannes.

"Technologies of the Self" in *Critical Studies: Ethics and the Subject,* Simms, Karl (ed). Ball, Elaine.

"The Didactic and the Elegant: Some Thoughts on Scientific and Technological Illustrations in the Middle Ages and Renaissance" in *Picturing Knowledge,* Baigrie, Brian S (ed). Hall, Bert S.

"Toting Technology: Taking It to the Streets" in *Existence in Black: An Anthology of Black Existential Philosophy,* Gordon, Lewis R (ed). Dixon, Bobby R.

"Verdad y tecnología" in *Verdad: lógica, representación y mundo,* Villegas Forero, L. Vega Encabo, Jesús.

*A Gift of Fire: Social, Legal, and Ethical Issues in Computing.* Baase, Sara.

*Analytical Marxism: A Critique.* Roberts, Marcus.

*CyberSpace Virtual Reality: Fortschritt und Gefahr einer innovativen Technologie.* Wedde, Horst F (ed).

*Feminist Approaches to Bioethics: Theoretical Reflections and Practical Applications.* Tong, Rosemarie.

*In Pursuit of Privacy: Law, Ethics, and the Rise of Technology.* DeCew, Judith Wagner.

*Living in a Technological Culture: Human Tools and Human Values.* Tiles, Mary and Oberdiek, Hans.

*Martin Heidegger und Hans Jonas: Die Metaphysik der Subjektivität und die Krise der technologischen Zivilisation.* Jakob, Eric.

## TECHNOLOGY

*Nature and Society: Anthropological Perspectives.* Descola, Philippe (ed) and Pálsson, Gísli (ed).

*On Dialogue.* Nichol, Lee (ed) and Bohm, David.

*Philosophy and the Return to Self-Knowledge.* Verene, Donald Phillip.

*Principia Ecologica* Eco-Principles as a Conceptual Framework for a New Ethics in Science and Technology. Moser, Anton.

*Reproduction, Technology, and Rights: Biomedical Ethics Reviews.* Humber, James M (ed) and Almeder, Robert F (ed).

*Temporalità e Comunicazione.* Reda, Clementina Gily.

*The Perfect Baby: A Pragmatic Approach to Genetics.* McGee, Glenn.

Acerca de dos modelos de conocimiento tecnológico. González, María Cristina.

Algunas tesis sobre la tecnología. Herrera J, Rodolfo.

An Argument against Techno-Privacy. Jones, Leslie E.

An Historical Preface to Engineering Ethics. Davis, Michael.

Approaches Responsive to Reproductive Technologies: A Need for Critical Assessment and Directions for Further Study. Kondratowicz, Diane M.

Aproximaciones a una evaluación de la aplicación de las nuevas tecnologías reproductivas. Digilio, Patricia.

Architecture: The Confluence of Art, Technology, Politics and Nature. Wood, Robert E.

Aspetti del dibattito italiano sulla cittadinanza. Henry, Barbara.

Beauty and Technology as Paradigms for the Moral Life. Brown, Montague.

Bête Noire of the Science Worshipers. Gross, Paul R.

Bij de Grenzen van Verplegingswetenschap. Blokhuis, P.

Body-Subjectivity in Psychiatry: The Initial Argument. Mondal, Parthasarathi.

Commentary on "Technology and Civil Disobedience: Why Engineers Have a Special Duty to Obey the Law". Boisjoly, Roger M.

Cor Dippel, denker op de grens van twee werelden. Van Dijk, Paul.

Cultural Diversity and the Systems View. Hammond, Debora.

Cyberethics and Social Stability. Hauptman, Robert.

Dal primato della prassi all'anomia: Una interpretazione filosofica della crisi odierna. Cotta, Sergio.

De oorspronkelijkheid en actuele betekenis van H. van Riessen als filosoof van de techniek: Deel I—De oorspronkelijkheid van zijn werk. Haaksma, Hans W H.

Desarrollo técnico y evolución histórica: modelos metafísicos y antropológico-culturales. Rodríguez, Amán Rosales.

Die Bewältigung von Technikkonflikten: Theoretische Möglichkeit und praktische Relevanz einer Ethik der Technik in der Moderne. Grunwald, Armin.

Economies, Technology, and the Structure of Human Living. Sauer, James B.

El habitar y la técnica: Polo en diálogo con Marx. Múgica, Fernando.

El libre albedrío entre la omnipotencia y el amor Divino: Problemática ética y consecuencias tecnológicas de la cuestión del libre alberdrío en Hobbes y San Agustín. Garrido Maturano, Angel Enrique.

Electric Technology and Poetic Mimesis. McInerny, Daniel.

Epistemology of Technology Assessment: Collingridge, Forecasting Methodologies, and Technological Control. Pinnick, Cassandra L.

Ethical Dilemmas in the Use of Information Technology: An Aristotelian Perspective. Myers, Michael D and Miller, Leigh.

Ethics Education in Science and Engineering: The Case of Animal Research. Rowan, Andrew N.

Fertility Technologies and Trans-Kin Altruism. Murphy, George L.

Fetal Subjects and Maternal Objects: Reproductive Technology and the New Fetal/Maternal Relation. Squier, Susan.

Filosofia e realtà virtuale. Marturano, Antonio.

From Absurdity to Decision: The Challenge of Responsibility in a Technological Society. Wennemann, Daryl J.

Ha ancora senso una domanda metafisica su Dio?. Romera, Luis.

Habermas, Fichte and the Question of Technological Determinism. Jalbert, John E.

Hacia una filosofía de la tecnología. Camacho, Luis.

Heidegger y el problema de la técnica. Boburg, Felipe.

Heidegger's Concept of the Technological 'Gestell' under Discussion. Coolsaet, Willy.

Heideggers "Schweigen" Technik, Nazi-Medizin und Wissenschaftskultur. Cox, Philip N.

Henk van Riessen, pionier van de filosofie van de techniek. Haaksma, Hans W H and Vlot, Ad.

High Risk Infants: Thirty Years of Intensive Care. Harris, Cheryl Hall.

Highway Bridges and Feasts: Heidegger and Borgmann on How to Affirm Technology. Dreyfus, Hubert L and Spinosa, Charles.

Human Cloning: A Case of No Harm Done?. Roberts, Melinda A.

In a Different Voice: Technology, Culture, and Post-Modern Bioethics. McNair, Douglas.

Information Technology and Technologies of the Self. Capurro, Rafael.

Introduction. Maynard, Patrick.

Jacques Ellul on the Technical System and the Challenge of Christian Hope. Punzo, Vincent A.

Jan Hollak over de betekenis van de techniek voor de filosofie. Coolen, Maarten.

La ética y la crisis del deporte. Csepregi, Gabor.

La instrumentalización del tiempo. Burrieza, Alfredo and Diéguez, Antonio.

La tesis heideggeriana acerca de la técnica. Borges-Duarte, Irene.

Les Technologies de L'images: Nouveaux Instruments du Bio-Pouvoir. Maybon, Marie-Pierre.

Letter of the Editor: On Knowledge Technology and its Relevance. Vandamme, F.

Marc Augé e l'antropologia dei mondi contemporanei. Soldati, Adriana.

Medieval Technology and the Husserlian Critique of Galilean Science. Casey, Timothy.

Natur im westlichen und östlichen Verständnis. Gloy, Karen.

Nature Conservation and the Precautionary Principle. Francis, John M.

Nature, Technology and Man in the Works of Dominik Pecka (in Czech). Jemelka, Petr.

Notas sobre el origen del hombre y la técnica. Díaz Caballero, José Ricardo.

Oltre l'umanesimo: Alcune considerazioni su tecnica e modernità. Galli, Carlo.

On the Assessment of Genetic Technology: Reaching Ethical Judgments in the Light of Modern Technology. Sinemus, Kristina, Platzer, Katrin and Bender, Wolfgang.

Ontological Aspects of Information Modeling. Ashenhurst, Robert L.

Optimalität der Natur?. Zoglauer, Thomas.

Overzicht van de filosofie van de techniek in Nederland tijdens het interbellum. Haaksma, Hans W H.

Paul Virilio and the Articulation of Post-Reality. Hanes, Marc.

Philosophy of Medical Practice: A Discursive Approach. Van Leeuwen, Evert and Kimsma, Gerrit K.

Planetary Politics and the Essence of Technology: A Heideggerian Analysis. Swazo, Norman K.

Politiek van de technologie. Harbers, Hans.

Politisering van de technologische cultuur. Bijker, Wiebe E.

Predicting Our Health: Ethical Implications of Neural Networks and Outcome Potential Predictions. Seddon, Andrew M.

Privacy Versus Accessibility: The Impact of Situationally Conditioned Belief. Lally, Laura.

Privacy, autonomia e regole. Neri, Demetrio.

Private Parts: A Global Analysis of Privacy Protection Schemes and a Proposed Innovation for their Comparative Evaluation. Pincus, Laura and Johns, Roger.

Putting the Technological into Government. Dean, Mitchell.

Rationality and Responsibility in Heidegger's and Husserl's View of Technology. Buckley, R Philip.

Research Monographs on the History of Science. Shekhawat, Virendra.

Responsibility and Social Traps. Lenk, Hans and Maring, Matthias.

Responsible Technoscience: The Haunting Reality of Auschwitz and Hiroshima. Sassower, Raphael.

Retiring the Pacemaker. Reitemeier, Paul J, Derse, Arthur R and Spike, Jeffrey.

Science, Morality and Religion: An Essay. Postgate, John.

So, You Want to Sing with *The Beatles*? Too Late!. Davies, Stephen.

Suggested Management Responses to Ethical Issue Raised by Technological Change. Cordeiro, William P.

Technological Escalation and the Exploration Model of Natural Science. Rescher, Nicholas.

Technology and Civil Disobedience: Why Engineers Have a Special Duty to Obey the Law. Schlossberger, Eugene.

Technology and the Crisis of Contemporary Culture. Borgmann, Albert.

Technology and the Decline of Leisure. Anderson, Thomas.

Technology in Opposition Power—Must (Czech). Lenk, Hans and Maring, Matthias.

Technology, Appreciation, and the Historical View of Art. Fisher, John Andrew and Potter, Jason.

Technology, Workplace Privacy and Personhood. Brown, William S.

Tecnopolitica: Le idee del cyberpunk. Nacci, Michela.

The Art of Interaction: Interactivity, Performativity, and Computers. Saltz, David Z.

The Biological Child. MacKellar, Calum.

The Ethics of Information Transfer in the Electronic Age: Scholars Unite!. Laidlaw-Johnson, Elizabeth A.

The Gastroenterologist and His Endoscope: The Embodiment of Technology and the Necessity for a Medical Ethics. Cooper, M Wayne.

The Legislation of Things. Löwy, Ilana.

The Machine That Couldn't Think Straight. Dinan, Stephen A.

The Morality of Human Gene Patents. Resnik, David B.

The Ontology of Mass Art. Carroll, Noël.

The Philosophical Challenge of Technology. Mitcham, Carl.

Thinking Non-Interpretively: Heidegger on Technology and Heraclitus. Scott, Charles E.

Transporting Values by Technology Transfer. De Castro, Leonardo D.

Über Heideggers "Schweigen" reden. Alisch, Rainer.

Unique Ethical Problems in Information Technology. Maner, Walter.

Vico e la Poesia. Placella, Vincenzo.

Waarom het beoordelen van technologieën voor gehandicapten problematisch is. Blume, Stuart.

What Can Progress in Reproductive Technology Mean for Women?. Purdy, Laura M.

Wilbur Schramm and the Founding of Communication Studies. Glander, Timothy.

## TECHNOLOGY
Wim Wenders and the Everyday Aesthetics of Technology and Space. Light, Andrew.
Winch and Instrumental Pluralism: A Reply to B. D. Lerner. Keita, L D.
Zur Phänomenologie der Technikentwicklung. Kühn, Rolf.

## TECHNOSCIENCE
Why Not Science Critics?. Ihde, Don.

## TEICHGRAEBER, R
Neoliberalism and the Political Theory of the Market. Gagnier, Regenia.

## TEICHMÜLLER, G
Gustav Teichmüller filologo e metafisico tra Italia e Germania: I) Teichmüller, Nietzsche e la critica delle 'mitologie scientifiche'. Orsucci, Andrea.
II) Teichmüller e gli amici napoletani. Savorelli, Alessandro.

## TELEOLOGY
"Herder, Kant e la storia" in Lo Storicismo e la Sua Storia: Temi, Problemi, Prospettive, Cacciatore, Giuseppe (ed). Lomonaco, Fabrizio.
"Kants Empiriologie: Naturteleologie als Wissenschaftstheorie" in Grenzen der kritischen Vernunft, Schmid, Peter A. Flach, Werner.
Analyzing Functions: An Essay on a Fundamental Notion in Biology. Melander, Peter.
Martin Heidegger und Hans Jonas: Die Metaphysik der Subjektivität und die Krise der technologischen Zivilisation. Jakob, Eric.
Ragione e Scrittura tra Descartes e Spinoza: Saggio sulla Philosophia S. Scripturae Interpres di Lodewijk Meyer e sulla sua recezione. Bordoli, Roberto.
The Christian Case for Virtue Ethics. Kotva, Joseph J.
Things That Happen Because They Should: A Teleological Approach to Action. Stout, Rowland.
Belief, Desire and Motivation: An Essay in Quasi-Hydraulics. Lenman, James.
Blondel and Husserl: A Continuation of the Conversation. Hart, James G.
Darwin: Evolution and Contingency (in Spanish). Rodriguez Camarero, Luis.
Deviant Causal Chains and the Irreducibility of Teleological Explanation. Sehon, Scott.
Europa y la Teleología de la razón en Edmund Husserl. García Marqués, Alfonso.
Il problema della trascendenza nell'ontologia di Plutarco. Ferrari, Franco.
Integrating Neuroscience, Psychology, and Evolutionary Biology through a Teleological Conception of Function. Mundale, Jennifer and Bechtel, William.
Kant on God, Evil, and Teleology. Pereboom, Derk.
Kant's Integration of Morality and Anthropology. Wilson, Holly L.
Kants Schlussstein: Wie die Teleologie die Einheit der Vernunft stiftet. Freudiger, Jürg.
Leibniz and the Two Clocks. Scott, David.
Over Functies en Affordances. De Jong, H Looren and Schouten, M K D.
Peirce's Teleological Approach to Natural Classes. Hulswit, Menno.
Problems of Existence—Recapitulation (in Polish). Hartman, Jan.
Teleological Semantics. Rowlands, Mark.
Teleologie und Teleonomie aus Sicht der philosophischen Qualia-Thematik. Pohlenz, Gerd.
Teleology and the Product Analogy. Matthen, Mohan.
Tellurische Teleologie oder Determinismus und Freiheit Carl Ritters natürliches System einer sittlichen Welt. Beck, Günther.
The Fact of Politics: History and Teleology in Kant. Krasnoff, Larry.
The Influence of Deontological and Teleological Considerations and Ethical Climate on Sales Managers' Intentions to Reward or Punish Sales Force Behavior. DeConinck, James B and Lewis, William F.
The Origins and Crisis of Continental Philosophy. Steinbock, Anthony J.
The Structure of Aristotle's Ethical Theory: Is It Teleological or a Virtue Ethics?. Santas, Gerasimos.
Troubles with Wagner's Reading of Millikan. Millikan, Ruth Garrett.
Vichiana. Amoroso, Leonardo.

## TELEPHONE
The Phenomenology of Telephone Space. Backhaus, Gary.

## TELLER, E
Theodore Karman, Paul Wigner, John Neumann, Leo Szilard, Edward Teller and Their Ideas of Ultimate Reality and Meaning. Horvath, Tibor.

## TEMKIN, L
Equality, Priority, and Time. Kappel, Klemens.

## TEMPERANCE
Beauty and the Attainment of Temperance. Edelman, John T.
Carnal Knowledge in the Charmides. McAvoy, Martin.

## TEMPIER, S
Bishop Stephen Tempier and Thomas Aquinas: A Separate Process Against Aquinas?. Wippel, John F.

## TEMPORAL
All the World's a Stage. Sider, Theodore.
Sequence of Tense and Temporal De Re. Abusch, Dorit.
What's the Fuzzy Temporary Reasoning? (in Spanish). Marín, R and Taboada, M.

## TEMPORAL LOGIC
"It is NOW" in Das weite Spektrum der analytischen Philosophie, Lenzen, Wolfgang. Meixner, Uwe.

Admissible Rule for Temporal Logic LinTGrz. Bezgacheva, Julia V.
Bisimulations for Temporal Logic. Kurtonina, Natasha and De Rijke, Maarten.
The k-Variable Property is Stronger than H-Dimension k. Simon, András and Hodkinson, Ian.

## TEMPORALITY
"Kant e la temporalità" in Il Concetto di Tempo: Atti del XXXII Congresso Nazionale della Società Filosofica Italiana, Casertano, Giovanni (ed). Salvucci, Pasquale.
"Tempo vissuto e temporalità originaria in M. Merleau-Ponty" in Il Concetto di Tempo: Atti del XXXII Congresso Nazionale della Società Filosofica Italiana, Casertano, Giovanni (ed). Calabrò, Daniela.
"Temporalità e storicità" in Il Concetto di Tempo: Atti del XXXII Congresso Nazionale della Società Filosofica Italiana, Casertano, Giovanni (ed). Seidl, Horst.
Time, Tense, and Causation. Tooley, Michael.
Alcuni rilievi sul nesso fra verità, libertà e temporalità nella filosofia di F. Nietzsche. Sacchi, Dario.
Bonaventure and the Arguments for the Impossibility of an Infinite Temporal Regression. Davis, Richard.
Can God Change His Mind?. Gulesarian, Theodore.
Descartes y Hume: causalidad, temporalidad y existencia de Dios. Badía Cabrera, Miguel A.
Eternal Knowledge of the Temporal in Aquinas. Shanley, Brian J.
Four-dimensionalist Remarks: A Defence of Temporal Parts (Spanish). Bordes Solanas, Montserrat.
Fregean Sense and Russellian Propositions. Gaskin, Richard.
On the Argument for Divine Timelessness from the Incompleteness of Temporal Life. Craig, William Lane.
Persistence and Presentism. Zimmerman, Dean W.
Souffrance et temps: Esquisse phénoménologique. Porée, Jérôme.
St. Bonaventure and the Demonstrability of a Temporal Beginning: A Reply to Richard Davis. Baldner, Steven.
Temporal Horizons of Justice. Ackerman, Bruce.
Temporalidad y trascendencia: La concepción heideggeriana de la trascendencia intencional en Sein und Zeit. Vigo, Alejandro G.
The Nominalist Argument of the New Essays. Bolton, Martha Brandt.

## TEMPTATION
The Nature of Temptation. Nuyen, A T.

## TENNANT, F
Beauty, Providence and the Biophilia Hypothesis. Wynn, Mark.

## TENNANT, N
Is Tennant Selling Truth Short?. Edwards, Jim.

## TENSE
Time, Tense, and Causation. Tooley, Michael.
McTaggart's Paradox and Smith's Tensed Theory of Time. Oaklander, L Nathan.
Sequence of Tense and Temporal De Re. Abusch, Dorit.
The New B-Theory's Tu Quoque Argument. Craig, William Lane.
Theology and Tense. Chisholm, Roderick M and Zimmerman, Dean W.
Time, Quantum Mechanics, and Tense. Saunders, Simon.
Time, Tense and Topology. Le Poidevin, Robin.
Truth Conditions of Tensed Sentence Types. Paul, L A.

## TENSE LOGIC
A Counterexample in Tense Logic. Wolter, Frank.
A Note on the Interpolation Property in Tense Logic. Wolter, Frank.
An Axiomatization for Until and Since over the Reals without the IRR Rule. Reynolds, Mark.
Applying Allen's Constraint Propagation Algorithm for Non-Linear Time. Hajnicz, Elzbieta.
Axiomatising First-Order Temporal Logic: Until and Since over Linear Time. Reynolds, Mark.
Canonical Models for Temporal Deontic Logic. Bailhache, Patrice.
Combining Temporal Logic Systems. Finger, Marcelo and Gabbay, Dov.
Completeness and Decidability of Tense Logics Closely Related to Logics Above K4. Wolter, Frank.
Cut-Free Sequent Calculi for Some Tense Logics. Kashima, Ryo.
Decidability Results for Metric and Layered Temporal Logics. Montanari, Angelo and Policriti, Alberto.
Minimal Temporal Epistemic Logic. Engelfriet, Joeri.
Some Considerations on Non-Linear Time Intervals. Hajnicz, Elzbieta.
T x W Completeness. Von Kutschera, Franz.
Temporalized Deontic Worlds with Individuals. Bailhache, Patrice.
The Structure of Lattices of Subframe Logics. Wolter, Frank.

## TENURE
Academic Freedom and Tenure: Ethical Issues. De George, Richard T.

## TERM
see also Singular Term, Theoretical Term
On a Property of BCK-Identities. Nagayama, Misao.
On the Canonicity of Sahlqvist Identities. Jónsson, Bjarni.
On the Proof Theory of Coquand's Calculus of Constructions. Seldin, Jonathan P.
Term Rewriting Theory for the Primitive Recursive Functions. Cichon, E A and Weiermann, A.
The Converse Principal Type-Scheme Theorem in Lambda Calculus. Hirokawa, Sachio.

**THEODICY**

"Die kritische Vernunft in der Theodizee von Leibniz" in *Grenzen der kritischen Vernunft*, Schmid, Peter A. Poma, Andrea.

*No Place for Sovereignty: What's Wrong with Freewill Theism*. McGregor Wright, R K.

Das philosophieimmanente Theodizeeproblem und seine theologische Radikalisierung. Schmidt, Josef.

God vs. Less Than the Very Best. Daniels, Charles.

Sociobiology and Evil: Ultimate Reality and Meaning Through Biology. Sharpe, Kevin.

Teodicea y sentido de la historia: la respuesta de Hegel. Estrada, Juan A.

Three Prospects for Theodicy: Some Anti-Leibnizian Approaches. Romerales Espinosa, Enrique.

**THEOGONY**

Between Religion and Philosophy: Allegorical Interpretation in Derveni Papyrus (in Czech). Laks, André.

**THEOLOGY**

*see also* God, Miracle, Natural Theology

"A New Agenda for Society" in *The Liberation Debate: Rights at Issue*, Leahy, Michael (ed). Cohn-Sherbok, Dan.

"All Philosophy as *Religionsphilosophy*" in *The Recovery of Philosophy in America: Essays in Honor of John Edwin Smith*, Kasulis, Thomas P (ed). Harris, Errol E.

"Beyond Toleration" in *Philosophy, Religion, and the Question of Intolerance*, Ambuel, David (ed). O'Meara, William.

"Cohn-Sherbok's Reply" in *The Liberation Debate: Rights at Issue*, Leahy, Michael (ed). Cohn-Sherbok, Dan.

"Le relazioni tra Bayle e l'Italia: i corrispondenti italiani di Bayle e le *Nouvelles de la République des Lettres*" in *Pierre Bayle e l'Italia*, Bianchi, Lorenzo. Bianchi, Lorenzo.

"Prague Mosaic: Encounters with Prague Philosophers" in *In Itinere European Cities and the Birth of Modern Scientific Philosophy*, Poli, Roberto (ed). Sebestik, Jan.

"Religión y teología en el origen del pensamiento filosófico de Fichte" in *El inicio del Idealismo alemán*, Market, Oswaldo. Artola, José María.

"Self-Transformation in American Blacks: The Harlem Renaissance and Black Theology" in *Existence in Black: An Anthology of Black Existential Philosophy*, Gordon, Lewis R (ed). Morrison II, Roy D.

"Some Procedural Problems" in *The Liberation Debate: Rights at Issue*, Leahy, Michael (ed). Wilson, John.

*A Second Collection: Papers by Bernard J. F. Lonergan, S.J.*. Ryan, William F (ed) and Tyrrell, Bernard J (ed).

*History and Contemporary Issues: Studies in Moral Theology*. Curran, Charles E.

*Hofmann-Streit: il dibattito sul rapporto tra filosofia e teologia all'Università di Helmstedt*. Antognazza, Maria Rosa.

*Immanuel Kant's Prolegomena to Any Future Metaphysics*. Logan, Beryl.

*Liberation Theologies, Postmodernity, and the Americas*. Batstone, David, Mendieta, Eduardo and Lorentzen, Lois Ann (& others).

*Religion and Science: Historical and Contemporary Issues*. Barbour, Ian G.

*Teología de la fe: Una aproximación al misterio de la fe cristiana*. Odero, José Miguel.

*The Annual of the Society of Christian Ethics with Cumulative Index*. Beckley, Harlan (ed).

*The Living God: Schleiermacher's Theological Appropriation of Spinoza*. Lamm, Julia A.

*The Origins of Moral Theology in the United States: Three Different Approaches*. Curran, Charles E.

*Verbum: Word and Idea in Aquinas Volume 2*. Crowe, Frederick E (ed) and Doran, Robert M (ed).

A Critical Reconstruction of Paul Tillich's Epistemology. Grube, Dirk-Martin.

A History of the Extraterrestrial Life Debate. Crowe, Michael J.

A marca do vazio: Reflexoes sobre a subjetividade em Blaise Pascal. De Souza Birchal, Telma.

A Rippling Relatableness in Reality. Ashbrook, James B.

A Theological Escape from the Cartesian Circle?. Dalton, Peter.

A Whiteheadian Contribution to the "Mind-body" Relation. Bertocci, Rosemary Juel.

All Existing is the Action of God: The Philosophical Theology of David Braine. Bradshaw, David.

Are Science and Religion in Conflict?. Watts, Fraser N.

Arianisme mitigé ou apologétique nouvelle?. Lagrée, Jacqueline.

Aspectos generales del pensamiento en el siglo XIV. Verdú Berganza, Ignacio.

Avant-propos. Bühler, Pierre.

Averroes, filósofo y teólogo. Maiza Ozcoidi, Idoia.

Barth on Evil. Wolterstorff, Nicholas.

Believing the Word: A Proposal about Knowing Other Persons. Cary, Phillip.

Business in an Age of Downsizing. Childs, James M.

César Chávez and La Causa: Toward a Hispanic Christian Social Ethic. Piar, Carlos R.

Christian Identity and Augustine's *Confessions*. Thompson, Christopher J.

De la métaphysique à la phénoménologie: une "relève"?. Gabellieri, Emmanuel.

Deification in the *Summa Theologiae*: A Structural Interpretation of the *Prima Pars*. Williams, A N.

Descartes' Secular Paradise: The Discourse on Method as Biblical Criticism. Soffer, Walter.

Die Vernunft innerhalb der Grenzen des Glaubens: Aspekte der anselmischen Methodologie in werkgenetischer Perspektive. Theis, Robert.

Dio parla in modo oscuro? Spunti filosofici e teologici sulle oscurità della Bibbia. Vaccaro, Andrea.

Distinct Ideas and Perfect Solicitude: Alexander of Hales, Richard Rufus, and Odo Rigaldus. Wood, Rega.

Edmund D. Pellegrino on the Future of Bioethics. Thomasma, David C.

En quel sens l'*Unique fondement possible d'une démonstration de l'existence de Dieu* de Kant est-il *unique* fondement *possible*?. Theis, Robert.

Ernst Troeltsch: aboutissement ou dépassement du néo-protestantisme?. Gisel, Pierre.

Éthique féministe de relation et perspectives sur le corps. Dumais, Monique.

Évolution et Création: La Théorie de L'évolution: Ses Rapports avec la Philosophie de la Nature et la Théologie de la Création. Maldamé, Jean-Michel.

Felix peccator? Kants geschichtsphilosophische Genesis-Exegese im *Muthmasslichen Anfang der Menschengeschichte* und die Theologie der Aufklärungszeit. Sommer, Andreas Urs.

Filosofía y teología de Gaston Fessard acerca de la actualidad histórica en el período 1936-46. Sols Lucia, José.

Francis Bacon: The Theological Foundations of *Valerius Terminus*. Milner, Benjamin.

Frei Manuel de S. Luís Escritor e Orador Açoriano dos Séculos XVII-XVIII (1660-1736). Pimentel, Manuel Cândido.

God is Great, God is Good: James Ashbrook's Contribution to Neuroethical Theology. Vaux, Kenneth.

Gödel Meets Carnap: A Prototypical Discourse on Science and Religion. Gierer, Alfred.

Hervé de Nédellec et les questions ordinaires *De cognitione primi principii*. Conforti, Patrizia.

Homer's Theology and the Concept of Tolerance. Bosnjak, Branko.

Il *Tractatus yconomicus* di Galvano Fiamma O.P. (1282-dopo il 1344). Fioravanti, Gianfranco.

Imagining the Good: Iris Murdoch's Godless Theology. Antonaccio, Maria.

In Defense of the *Kalam* Cosmological Argument. Craig, William Lane.

Introduction. Herman, Steward W and Gross Schaefer, Arthur.

Isaac Barrow on the Mathematization of Nature: Theological Voluntarism and the Rise of Geometrical Optics. Malet, Antoni.

Jean de Sterngassen et son commentaire des *Sentences*. Senner, Walter.

Jules Lequyer and the Openness of God. Viney, Donald Wayne.

Karl Rahner and Genetic Engineering: The Use of Theological Principles in Moral Analysis. Kelly, David F.

L'apologétique de Samuel Clarke. Sina, Mario.

L'incomplétude, logique du religieux?. Debray, Régis.

La creación como encuentro del ser y de la nada en la teología del maestro Eckhart de Hochheim O.P. (1260-1327). Farrelly, Brian J.

La critique des preuves de l'existence de Dieu et la valeur du discours apologétique. Bouchilloux, Hélène.

La fonction argumentative dans les discours théologiques: L'exemple de la *Grammaire de l'assentiment* de Neuman. Viau, Marcel.

La pervivencia del corpus teológico ciceroniano en España. Escobar Chico, Angel.

La philosophie comme *ancilla theologiae* chez Stillingfleet. Hutton, Sarah.

La polémique de Malebranche contre Aristote et la philosophie scolastique. Gilson, Étienne.

La prima scuola tomistica: Erveo di Nedellec e l'epistemologia teologica. Piccari, Paolo.

La reazione a Cartesio nella Napoli del Seicento: Giovambattista De Benedictis. De Liguori, Girolamo.

La teología epicúrea: la concepción de la divinidad y su incidencia en la vida humana. Méndez Lloret, Isabel.

La teologia esistenziale di S. Kierkegaard. Mondin, Battista.

Le savoir théologique chez les premiers thomistes. Torrell, Jean-Pierre.

Les *Evidentiae contra Durandum* de Durandellus. Lanczkowski, Miroslaw and Wittwer, Roland.

Les rapports entre raison et foi à la lumière de la métaphore de la vision. Vienne, Jean-Michel.

Medical Ethics in the Developing World: A Liberation Theology Perspective. Fabri Dos Anjos, Marcio.

Modalidades aristotélicas de san Agustín. Trundle, Robert.

Moral Conversion and Problems in Proportionalism. Beards, Andrew.

Nietzsche as a Theological Resource. Westphal, Merold.

Nouvelles réponses à Nunzio Incardona. Tilliette, Xavier.

Nuove frontiere della scienza. Manno, Ambrogio Giacomo.

Ockham and *Potentia Absoluta*. Finn, Steve.

On Studying Dostoevskii. Florovskii, Georgii.

On the Argument for Divine Timelessness from the Incompleteness of Temporal Life. Craig, William Lane.

Orgasmic Rapture and Divine Ecstasy: The Semantic History of Ānanda. Olivelle, Patrick.

**THOMPSON, J**

On the Value of Natural Relations. Cox, Damian.

The Revisionary Visionary: Leadership and the Aesthetics of Adaptability. DeGraff, Jeff and Merritt, Suzanne.

Trolley, Transplant and Consent. Dimas, Panagiotis.

**THOMSON, J**

"Acts and Value" in *A Question of Values: New Canadian Perspectives in Ethics and Political Philosophy,* Brennan, Samantha (ed). Isaacs, Tracy and Milde, Michael (ed).

A Defense of "A Defense of Abortion": On the Responsibility Objection to Thomson's Argument. Boonin-Vail, David.

Thomson on the Moral Specification of Rights. Prior, William J and Parent, William A.

**THOMSON, R**

The Value(s) of Sex Education. Reiss, Michael J.

**THOREAU**

Scetticismo, riconoscimento, riscoperta dell'ordinario: La filosofia di Stanley Cavell. Sparti, Davide and Lecci, Bernardo.

The Inalienable Right of Conscience: A Madisonian Argument. McConnell, Terrance C.

Thoreauvian Patriotism as an Environmental Virtue. Cafaro, Philip.

**THORNTON, L**

Response to the Commentaries. Hinshelwood, R D.

**THOUGHT**

"A Not 'Merely Empirical' Argument for a Language of Thought" in *AI, Connectionism and Philosophical Psychology, 1995,* Tomberlin, James E (ed). Rey, Georges.

"Atto puro e pensiero nell'interpretazione di Hegel" in *Hegel e Aristotele,* Ferrarin, A. Samonà, Leonardo.

"Chi pensa astratto? traduzione e commento di Franca Mastromatteo e Leonardo Paganelli" in *Hegel e Aristotele,* Ferrarin, A. Hegel, G W F.

"Il Soggetto E La Verità" in *Soggetto E Verità: La questione dell'uomo nella filosofia contemporanea,* Fagiuoli, Ettore. Sini, Carlo.

"Plato's *Philebus*: The Numbering of a Unity" in *Dialogues with Plato,* Benitez, Eugenio (ed). Barker, Andrew.

*Hegel e Aristotele.* Movia, Giancarlo (ed).

*La metáfora moderna del pensamiento.* Lorite-Mena, José.

*Practical Induction.* Millgram, Elijah.

*Pragmatism as a Principle and Method of Right Thinking.* Turrisi, Patricia Ann (ed) and Sanders Peirce, Charles.

*Saber, Sentir, Pensar: La cultura en la frontera de dos siglos.* Nieto Blanco, Carlos (ed).

*The Political Consequences of Thinking: Gender and Judaism in the Work of Hannah Arendt.* Ring, Jennifer.

A Critical Analysis of John Locke's Criterion of Personal Identity. Chakraborty, Alpana.

A los orígenes del pensamiento medieval español sobre la historia: Prudencio, Orosio, san Isidoro. Rivera de Ventosa, Enrique.

Are Thought Experiments Just What You Thought?. Norton, John D.

Can People Think?. De Bruijn, N G.

Critical Thinking and Command of Language. Johnson, Ralph H.

Descartes's Ontology of Thought. Nelson, Alan.

Donald Davidson, Descartes and How to Deny the Evident. Gosselin, M.

El grito de Libertad del Pensamiento. Rosas, Alejandro.

Epistemology of J. Krishnamurti. Sardesai, Arundhati.

Il *cogito* ferito e l'ontologia problematica dell'ultimo Ricoeur. Jervolino, D.

L'aporia del pensare fra scienza e storia. Tagliavia, Grazia.

L'esperienza del pensare: Indagine su un paradosso. Treppiedi, Anna Maria.

L'utilisation philosophique de la métaphore en Grèce et en Chine: Vers une métaphorologie comparée. Reding, Jean-Paul.

La filosofia tra presenza e ulteriorità. Pieretti, Antonio.

Las claves hermenéuticas del pensamiento de Ramón Llull. Trías Mercant, Sebastià.

Maschinen und Kreativität: Metamathematische Argumente für das menschliche Denken. Ebbinghaus, H D.

Meditated History: An Approach to Karl Mannheim's Sociology of Knowledge through his Analysis of Mentalities (Spanish). Rodríguez Fouz, Marta.

Merleau-Ponty's Phenomenology as a Dialectical Philosophy of Expression. Mancini, Sandro.

On Talk of Modes of Thought. Ramakrishnan, Lakshmi.

Parsing If-Sentences and the Conditions of Sentencehood. Barker, Stephen J.

Pensiero e realtà nella gnoseologia di S. Tommaso D'Aquino. Ventura, Antonino.

Pensiero medievale e modernità. Gregory, Tullio.

Regress Arguments against the Language of Thought. Laurence, Stephen and Margolis, Eric.

Symbols and Thought. Schwartz, Robert.

Syntax in a Dynamic Brain. Garson, James W.

Teoresi e prassi nella fondazione della metafisica. Cavaciuti, Santino.

The Birth of Difference. Schües, Christina.

The Cognitive Turn in Philosophy (in Czech). Jacob, Pierre.

The Communication of *De Re* Thoughts. Bezuidenhout, Anne L.

The Machine That Couldn't Think Straight. Dinan, Stephen A.

The Paradoxes of Thought and Being. Armour, Leslie.

The Temporal Nature of Thought and Concepts of Life (Czech). Pstruzina, Karel.

Toch Geen Representaties? Een Reacties op J. Sleutels' Zonnebrand-ontologie. Buekens, F.

Two Spurious Varieties of Compositionality. García-Carpintero, Manuel.

Ulteriorità del pensare. Masi, Giuseppe.

What Makes Something Practically Worth Thinking About. Passell, Dan.

When is Thought Political?. Griffin, Miriam.

Wittgenstein et la fin du psychologisme. Chiesa, Curzio.

Zeichenmachende Phantasie: Zum systematischen Zusammenhang von Zeichen und Denken bei Hegel. Simon, Josef.

**THREAT**

Divorcing Threats and Offers. Altman, Scott.

**TIBETAN**

"Steps to a Comparative Evolutionary Aesthetics (China, India, Tibet and Europe)" in *East and West in Aesthetics,* Marchianò, Grazia (ed). Capriles, Elias.

"Universal Reason" as a Local Organizational Method: Announcement of a Study. Liberman, Kenneth.

Beyond Acceptance and Rejection?. Martin, Dan.

**TIDMAN, P**

Tidman On Critical Reflection. Steup, Matthias.

**TIENSON, J**

Syntax in a Dynamic Brain. Garson, James W.

**TILE**

Aestheticism As Seen in British Tiles in the 1870s and 80s (in Japanese). Yoshimura, Noriko.

**TILES, M**

The Legislation of Things. Löwy, Ilana.

**TILLICH**

A Critical Reconstruction of Paul Tillich's Epistemology. Grube, Dirk-Martin.

From Nimrod to the Grand Inquisitor: The Problem of the Demonisation of Freedom in the Work of Dostoevskij. Blumenkrantz, Mikhail.

God, Revelation, and Religious Truth: Some Themes and Problems in the Theology of Paul Tillich. Coburn, Robert C.

La cuestión de lo Incondicionado: Dialéctica y revelación de lo sagrado en Paul Tillich. Pastor, Félix-Alejandro.

**TIME**

*see also* Duration

"Arthur Stanley Eddington e la 'scoperta' della freccia del tempo" in *Il Concetto di Tempo: Atti del XXXII Congresso Nazionale della Società Filosofica Italiana,* Casertano, Giovanni (ed). Giordano, Giuseppe.

"Dobbiamo ancora pensare il tempo come finito?" in *Il Concetto di Tempo: Atti del XXXII Congresso Nazionale della Società Filosofica Italiana,* Casertano, Giovanni (ed). Morselli, Graziella.

"En arche: una confutazione cristiana della dottrina aristotelica del tempo" in *Il Concetto di Tempo: Atti del XXXII Congresso Nazionale della Società Filosofica Italiana,* Casertano, Giovanni (ed). Crepaldi, Maria Grazia.

"Esistenza e tempo in Heidegger" in *Il Concetto di Tempo: Atti del XXXII Congresso Nazionale della Società Filosofica Italiana,* Casertano, Giovanni (ed). Cesareo, Rosa.

"Eudosso di Cnido e la misura del tempo nell'astrononmia greca" in *Il Concetto di Tempo: Atti del XXXII Congresso Nazionale della Società Filosofica Italiana,* Casertano, Giovanni (ed). Simeoni, Luca.

"Husserl e Heidegger: tempo e fenomenologia" in *Il Concetto di Tempo: Atti del XXXII Congresso Nazionale della Società Filosofica Italiana,* Casertano, Giovanni (ed). Sini, Carlo and Cacciatore, Giuseppe.

"Il concetto di tempo nel mondo antico fino a Platone" in *Il Concetto di Tempo: Atti del XXXII Congresso Nazionale della Società Filosofica Italiana,* Casertano, Giovanni (ed). Giannantoni, Gabriele.

"Il concetto di tempo" in *Il Concetto di Tempo: Atti del XXXII Congresso Nazionale della Società Filosofica Italiana,* Casertano, Giovanni (ed). Scarcella, Attilio.

"Il tempo come percezione: gli empiristi inglesi" in *Il Concetto di Tempo: Atti del XXXII Congresso Nazionale della Società Filosofica Italiana,* Casertano, Giovanni (ed). Bellini, Ornella.

"Il tempo come variabile dei processi formativi" in *Il Concetto di Tempo: Atti del XXXII Congresso Nazionale della Società Filosofica Italiana,* Casertano, Giovanni (ed). Cosetino, Antonio.

"Il tempo dell'interrogare e il tempo dell'invocare" in *Il Concetto di Tempo: Atti del XXXII Congresso Nazionale della Società Filosofica Italiana,* Casertano, Giovanni (ed). Cavaciuti, Santino.

"Il tempo e l'etica" in *Il Concetto di Tempo: Atti del XXXII Congresso Nazionale della Società Filosofica Italiana,* Casertano, Giovanni (ed). Masullo, Aldo.

"Il tempo in Aristotele" in *Il Concetto di Tempo: Atti del XXXII Congresso Nazionale della Società Filosofica Italiana,* Casertano, Giovanni (ed). Berti, Enrico.

"Il tempo in Bergson e nello spiritualismo francese" in *Il Concetto di Tempo: Atti del XXXII Congresso Nazionale della Società Filosofica Italiana,* Casertano, Giovanni (ed). Rigobello, Armando.

"Il tempo in Newton e in Leibniz" in *Il Concetto di Tempo: Atti del XXXII Congresso Nazionale della Società Filosofica Italiana,* Casertano, Giovanni (ed). Rossi, Paolo.

**TOLERANCE**
Tolerance and the Law. Broglio, Francesco Margiotta.
Tolerance and War: The Real Meaning of an Irreconcilability. Gianformaggio, Letizia.
Tolerance as Grace and as Right (in Hebrew). Yovel, Yirmiyahu.
Tolerance of the Intolerant?. Haarscher, Guy.
Tolerancia y escepticismo: el caso de J. Locke. Herráiz Martínez, Pedro José.
Toleration and Law: Historical Aspects. Imbert, Jean.
Toleration and Recognition. Lukes, Steven.
Toleration and the Law in the West 1500-1700. Kamen, Henry.
Toleration without Liberal Foundations. Leader, Sheldon.
Toleration, Liberalism and Democracy: A Comment on Leader and Garzón Valdés. Bellamy, Richard.
Why Tolerate? Reflections on the Millian Truth Principle. Cohen-Almagor, Raphael.

**TOLERATION**
Between Political Loyalty and Religious Liberty: Political Theory and Toleration in Huguenot Thought in the Epoch of Bayle. Simonutti, Luisa.

**TOLMAN, E**
*E.C. Tolman e l'epistemologia del primo novecento.* Donadon, Eleonora.

**TOLSTOY**
The Aesthetically Good vs. The Morally Good. Davenport, Manuel.
Wittgenstein, Tolstoy and the Meaning of Life. Thompson, Caleb.

**TOMBERLIN, J**
"Replies to Tomberlin, Tye, Stalnaker and Block" in *Perception,* Villanueva, Enrique (ed). Lycan, William G.
In Defense of the Contingently Nonconcrete. Linsky, Bernard and Zalta, Edward.

**TONNIES, F**
"Tönnies versus Weber: El debate Comunitarista desde la teoría social" in *Liberalismo y Comunitarismo: Derechos Humanos y Democracia,* Monsalve Solórzano, Alfonso (ed). Villacañas Berlanga, José L.

**TOOLEY, M**
Infanticide and the Right to Life. Carter, Alan.

**TOPOGRAPHY**
Tempo e pensiero topologico tra scienza e filosofia. Polizzi, Gaspare.

**TOPOI**
Extensional Realizability. Van Oosten, Jaap.
Intuitionistic Sets and Ordinals. Taylor, Paul.

**TOPOLOGY**
"Geometrie dell'Aperto" in *Geofilosofia,* Bonesio, Luisa (ed). Marcenaro, Alessandro.
Another Use of Set Theory. Dehornoy, Patrick.
Boundaries, Continuity, and Contact. Varzi, Achille C.
Cauchy Completeness in Elementary Logic. Cifuentes, J C, Sette, A M and Mundici, Daniele.
Colouring and Non-Productivity of Aleph$_2$-C.C.. Shelah, Saharon.
Definability in Functional Analysis. Iovino, José.
Hyperalgebraic Primitive Elements for Relational Algebraic and Topological Algebraic Models. Insall, Matt.
Region-Based Topology. Roeper, Peter.
Second Order Propositional Operators Over Cantor Space. Polacik, Tomasz.

**TOPUZIAN, C**
Respuesta a C.M. Topuzian. Gracia, Jorge J E.

**TORAH**
Guiding Principles of Jewish Business Ethics. Green, Ronald M.

**TORREY, H**
Frederic Henry Hedge, H.A.P. Torrey, and the Early Reception of Leibniz in America. Mulvaney, Robert J.

**TORT**
A Non-Solution to a Non-Problem: A Comment on Alan Strudler's "Mass Torts and Moral Principles". Kraus, Jody S.
Chances, Individuals and Toxic Torts. Parascandola, Mark.
Evidence and Association: Epistemic Confusion in Toxic Tort Law. Parascandola, Mark.
The Problem of Mass Torts. Strudler, Alan.

**TORT LAW**
Rights, Necessity, and Tort Liability. Devlin, Kai.

**TORTURE**
Hobbes and Criminal Procedure, Torture and Pre-Trial Detention. Cattaneo, Mario A.
The Logic of Torture: A Critical Examination. Tindale, Christopher W.

**TOTALITARIANISM**
*Politics and Truth: Political Theory and the Postmodernist Challenge.* Man Ling Lee, Theresa.
Are Human Rights Self-Contradictory?: Critical Remarks on a Hypothesis by Hannah Arendt. Brunkhorst, Hauke.
Hannah Arendt y la cuestión del mal radical. Serrano de Haro, Agustín.
Il re nudo: L'immaginario del potere in Simone Weil. Tommasi, Wanda.
Is Marxism Totalitarian?. Hudelson, Richard.
La re-presentación extrema del estetismo, del intelectualismo y del moralismo en política. Rendón Rojas, Miguel Angel and Okolova, Marina Dimitrieva.

Mechanistic Individualism Versus Organismic Totalitarianism: Toward a Neo-Calvinist Perspective. Venter, J J.
Parsing "A Right to Have Rights". Michelman, Frank I.
Popper's Plato: An Assessment. Klosko, George.
Response to Richard Hudelson. Louw, Stephen.
Science as a Battlefield: Methodological and Historical Considerations on the Misuse of Science by Totalitarian Regimes of Central Europe. Hajduk, Anton.
Trust and Totalitarianism: Some Suggestive Examples. Govier, Trudy.
Unity and Development: Social Homogeneity, the Totalitarian Imaginary, and the Classical Marxist Tradition. Louw, Stephen.

**TOTALITY**
*Critique and Totality.* Kerszberg, Pierre.
*The Possible Universe.* Tallet, J A.
Feminism and Pantheism. Jantzen, Grace M.
L'essere, il nulla e il divenire: Riprendendo le fila di una grande polemica. Turoldo, Fabrizio.
Los límites éticos del "ser-en-el-mundo". Garrido Maturano, Angel Enrique.
The Idea of Total-Unity from Heraclitus to Losev. Khoruzhii, Sergei Sergeevich.
Totalidad y causalidad en Polo. Haya Segovia, Fernando.
Vernunft heute. Welsch, Wolfgang.

**TOULMIN, S**
"Logic and Argumentation" in *Logic and Argumentation,* Van Eemeren, Frans H (ed). Van Benthem, Johan.
Can Phronesis Save the Life of Medical Ethics?. Beresford, Eric B.
Some Foundational Problems with Informal Logic and Their Solution. Weinstein, Mark.

**TOXIC**
Attitudes and Issues Preventing Bans on Toxic Lead Shot and Sinkers in North America and Europe. Thomas, Vernon G.

**TRACE**
Après l'herméneutique: Analyse et interprétation des traces et des oeuvres. Molino, Jean.

**TRADE**
Instead of Leaders They Have Become Bankers of Men: Gramsci's Alternative to the U.S. Neoinstitutionalists' Theory of Trade-Union Bureaucratization. Devinatz, Victor G.

**TRADITION**
"Éléments démocratiques dans les sagesses du Sénégal" in *Philosophy and Democracy in Intercultural Perspective,* Kimmerle, Heinz (ed). Diallo, Massaër.
"Nietzsche and Nishitani on Nihilism and Tradition" in *Culture and Self,* Allen, Douglas (ed). Parkes, Graham.
"Paradojas recurrentes de la argumentación comunitarista" in *Liberalismo y Comunitarismo: Derechos Humanos y Democracia,* Monsalve Solórzano, Alfonso (ed). Giusti, Miguel.
"Plus Ratio Quam Vis" in *The Idea of University,* Brzezinski, Jerzy (ed). Szaniawski, Klemens.
"Sexuality and Liberty: Making Room for Nature and Tradition?" in *Sex, Preference, and Family: Essays on Law and Nature,* Nussbaum, Martha C (ed). Macedo, Stephen.
"Tradition in Science" in *The Idea of University,* Brzezinski, Jerzy (ed). Gockowski, Janusz.
"Tradition: First Steps Toward a Pragmaticistic Clarification" in *Philosophy in Experience: American Philosophy in Transition,* Hart, Richard (ed). Colapietro, Vincent M.
*African-American Perspectives and Philosophical Traditions.* Pittman, John P (ed).
*Meeting of Minds: Intellectual and Religious Interaction in East Asian Traditions of Thought.* Bloom, Irene (ed) and Fogel, Joshua A (ed).
*The Actuality of Adorno: Critical Essays on Adorno and the Postmodern.* Pensky, Max (ed).
Aleksei Fedorovich Losev and Orthodoxy. Mokhov, V V.
Dead or Alive? Reflective Versus Unreflective Traditions. Tate, John W.
Do Practices Explain Anything? Turner's Critique of the Theory of Social Practices. Bohman, James.
Electric Technology and Poetic Mimesis. McInerny, Daniel.
Epicurean Moral Theory. Rosenbaum, Stephen E.
Han Classicists Writing in Dialogue about their Own Tradition. Nylan, Michael.
Myths as Instructions from Ancestors: The Example of Oedipus. Steadman, Lyle B and Palmer, Craig T.
Reflective Equilibrium or Evolving Tradition?. Aronovitch, Hilliard.
Roman Catholic Tradition and Ritual and Business Ethics: A Feminist Perspective. Andolsen, Barbara Hilkert.
The Sirens' Song of the Traditions: A plea for a Universal Ethics (in Dutch). Merks, Karl-Wilhelm.
Voces mezcladas: Una reflexión sobre tradición y modernidad. Díaz-Urmeneta Muñoz, Juan Bosco.

**TRADITIONALISM**
La nuova destra. Revelli, Marco.

**TRAGARDH, L**
The Birth of Economic Competitiveness: Rejoinder to Breckman and Trägårdh. Greenfeld, Liah.

## TRANSCENDENTAL

Selbstbewusstsein in der Spätantike: Neuere Untersuchungen zu Plotins Schrift V 3 [49]. Horn, Christoph.

Sobre el concepto trascendental de Dios en Kant. Romerales Espinosa, Enrique.

System und Methode—Zur methodologischen Begründung transzendentalen Philosophierens in Fichtes *Begriffsschrift*. Stahl, Jürgen.

The Constitution of the World of Experience and the Problem of the New (in German). Köveker, Dietmar.

Transcendental is the Difference: Derrida's Deconstruction of Husserl's Phenomenology of Language. Vila-Cha, Joao J.

Transzendentale Lebenslehre: Zur Königsberger Wissenschaftslehre 1807. Ivaldo, Marco.

Trascendentalità della metafisica. Laganà, Antonio.

Wissen und Tun: Zur Handlungsweise der transzendentalen Subjektivität in der ersten Wissenschaftslehre Fichtes. Siemek, Marek J.

Zur Aufgabe transzendentaler Interpretation. Gawlina, Manfred.

Zur Geschichte der romantischen Ästhetik: Von Fichtes Transzendentalphilosophie zu Schlegels Transzendentalpoesie. Radrizzani, Ives.

## TRANSCENDENTAL EGO

Das *objektive Selbst* (Nagel)—Eine Destruktion oder Rekonstruktion transzendentaler Subjektivität?. Lütterfelds, Wilhelm.

## TRANSCENDENTALISM

*De la razón pura a la razón interesada*. Arce Carrascoso, José Luis.

Criticismo trascendentale, trascendenza, religione. Jacobelli, Angela Maria Isoldi.

El Naturalismo Trascendental del Ultimo Wittgenstein. Krebs, Víctor J.

Empire, Transzendentalismus und Transzendenz: Neue Literatur zu Arthur Schopenhauer. Kossler, Matthias.

Empiricism and Transcendentalism: Franz Rosenzweig and Emmanuel Levinas (in Dutch). Anckaert, Luc.

La pérdida del carácter transcendental de la belleza en el *De pulchro* de Agostino Nifo. Fernández García, María Socorro.

Transcendentalism, Nomicity and Modal Thought. Muresan, Valentin.

Trascendentalismo, contenido semántico y verdad. Barrio, Eduardo Alejandro.

## TRANSCENDENTALS

Metafisica e "transcendentali". Moscato, Alberto.

## TRANSFER

Framework for the Transfer of Proofs, Lemmas and Strategies from Classical to Non-Classical Logics. Caferra, Ricardo, Demri, Stéphane and Herment, Michel.

Transporting Values by Technology Transfer. De Castro, Leonardo D.

## TRANSFORMATION

"Beginning Again: Teaching, Natality and Social Transformation" in *Philosophy of Education (1996)*, Margonis, Frank (ed). Levinson, Natasha.

"Self-Transformation in American Blacks: The Harlem Renaissance and Black Theology" in *Existence in Black: An Anthology of Black Existential Philosophy*, Gordon, Lewis R (ed). Morrison II, Roy D.

"Teaching In/For the Enunciative Present" in *Philosophy of Education (1996)*, Margonis, Frank (ed). Kohli, Wendy.

Chemistry as the Science of the Transformation of Substances. Van Brakel, Jaap.

Evolutionary Materialism. Dawson, Doyne.

Gender Equity, Organizational Transformation and Challenger. Maier, Mark.

La transformacion de una teoría matemática: el caso de los números poligonales. Radford, Luis.

Nirodha, Yoga Praxis and the Transformation of the Mind. Whicher, Ian.

## TRANSGRESSION

"Transgressive Bodies: Destruction and Excessive Display of the Human Form in the Horror Film" in *Critical Studies: Ethics and the Subject*, Simms, Karl (ed). Mendik, Xavier.

*Transgressing Discourses: Communication and the Voice of Other*. Huspek, Michael (ed) and Radford, Gary P (ed).

Nietzsche as Self-Made Man. Nehamas, Alexander.

Transgressing the Boundaries: An Afterword. Sokal, Alan D.

## TRANSITION

Unique Transition Probabilities in the Modal Interpretation. Vermaas, Pieter E.

## TRANSITIVITY

A intencionalidade na filosofia de Levinas. Macedo Lourenço, Joao.

The Price of Universality. Hemaspaandra, Edith.

## TRANSLATION

"Return from the United States" in *Existence in Black: An Anthology of Black Existential Philosophy*, Gordon, Lewis R (ed). Sharpley-Whiting, T Denean (ed & trans) and Sartre, Jean-Paul.

*Alexander of Aphrodisias: On Aristotle's Meteorology 4*. Lewis, Eric (trans).

*Proper Names*. Smith, Michael B (trans) and Levinas, Emmanuel.

*The Possibility of Language: A Discussion of the Nature of Language, with Implications for Human and Machine Translation*. Melby, Alan K and Warner, C Terry.

A Critique of Rawls's Hermeneutics as Translation. Josefson, Jim and Bach, Jonathan.

Aquinas on Modal Propositions: Introduction, Text, and Translation. O'Grady, Paul.

Die impliziten Prämissen in Quines Kritik der semantischen Begriffe. Greimann, Dirk.

Framework for the Transfer of Proofs, Lemmas and Strategies from Classical to Non-Classical Logics. Caferra, Ricardo, Demri, Stéphane and Herment, Michel.

Hume in the Prussian Academy: Jean Bernard Mérian's "On the Phenomenalism of David Hume". Laursen, John Christian, Popkin, Richard H and Briscoe, Peter.

Let a Hundred Translations Bloom! A Modest Proposal about *Being and Time*. Sheehan, Thomas.

Man as Wolf (Once More). Hauksson, Thorleifur.

Metaphor and Conceptual Change. Rantala, Veikko.

Métodos y cuestiones filosóficas en la Escuela de Traductores de Toledo. Brasa Díaz, Mariano.

Note su traduzioni manoscritte delle opere cartesiane. Guerrini, Luigi.

On the Not-Being of Gorgias's *On Not-Being* (ONB). Gagarin, Michael.

The Eclipse of Gender: Simone de Beauvoir and the *Différance* of Translation. Alexander, Anna.

The Letter and the Spirit of the Text: Two Translations of Gorgias's *On Non-Being or On Nature* (MXG). Poulakos, John.

Translating Gorgias in [Aristotle] 980a10. Davis, Janet B.

Translation, Philosophy, Materialism. Venuti, Lawrence.

Unamuno traductor de Th. Carlyle. Robles, Laureano.

## TRANSMISSION

"Education, Not Initiation" in *Philosophy of Education (1996)*, Margonis, Frank (ed). Biesta, Gert.

"Narrowing the Gap Between Difference and Identity" in *Philosophy of Education (1996)*, Margonis, Frank (ed). Pignatelli, Frank.

## TRANSPARENCY

Sujet(s) à interprétation(s): sur la relative transparence d'une photographie positiviste. Lauzon, Jean.

The Transparency of Truth. Kalderon, Mark Eli.

## TRANSPLANT

Neural Fetal Tissue Transplants: Old and New Issues. Nora, Lois Margaret and Mahowald, Mary B.

What's Love Got to Do with It? The Altruistic Giving of Organs. Spike, Jeffrey.

## TRAVEL

*Questions of Travel: Postmodern Discourses of Displacement*. Kaplan, Caren.

Springing Forward and Falling Back: Traveling through Time. Edwards, Anne M.

Textual Travel and Translation in an Age of Globalized Media. Rapping, Elayne.

The Ethics of Reading: A Traveler's Guide. Rorty, Amélie Oksenberg.

The Principal Paradox of Time Travel. Riggs, Peter.

## TRAVIS, C

Circumstances and the Truth of Words: A Reply to Travis. Simmons, Howard.

## TREATMENT

A Noncompliant Patient?. Moseley, Kathryn L and Truesdell, Sandra.

Do Doctors Undertreat Pain?. Ruddick, William.

Ethical Issues in Alternative Medicine. Edelberg, David.

Ethics at the Interface: Conventional Western and Complementary Medical Systems. Brody, Howard, Rygwelski, Janis and Fetters, Michael D.

Family Therapy Process and Outcome Research: Relationship to Treatment Ethics. Wilson, Carol A, Alexander, James F and Turner, Charles W.

HIV Infection, Risk Taking, and the Duty to Treat. Smolkin, Doran.

Intentions, Self-Monitoring and Abnormal Experiences. Morris, R C.

More is Better. Flanigan, Rosemary.

Ought we to Sentence People to Psychiatric Treatment?. Tännsjö, Torbjörn.

Persistent Vegetative State: A Presumption to Treat. Cattorini, Paolo and Reichlin, Massimo.

Reassessing the Reliability of Advance Directives. May, Thomas.

Reducing Suffering and Ensuring Beneficial Outcomes for Neonates: An Ethical Perspective. Brodeur, Dennis.

Stability of Treatment Preferences: Although Most Preferences Do Not Change, Most People Change Some of Their Preferences. Singer, Peter A, Kohut, Nitsa and Sam, Mehran (& others).

Treating the Patient to Benefit Others. Klepper, Howard.

## TREE

*Logic with Trees: An Introduction to Symbolic Logic*. Howson, Colin.

$y = 2x$ VS. $y = 3x$. Stolboushkin, Alexei and Niwinski, Damian.

A First-Order Axiomatization of the Theory of Finite Trees. Backofen, Rolf, Rogers, James and Vijay-Shanker, K.

Are Plants Conscious?. Nagel, Alexandra H M.

Can a Small Forcing Create Kurepa Trees. Jin, Renling and Shelah, Saharon.

Canonical Seeds and Prikry Trees. Hamkins, Joel David.

How to Win Some Simple Iteration Games. Steel, J R and Andretta, Alessandro.

On Boolean Subalgebras of $P(omega_1)/ctble$. Dow, Alan.

$Pi^0_1$ Classes and Minimal Degrees. Groszek, Marcia J and Slaman, Theodore A.

Projective Forcing. Bagaria, Joan and Bosch, Roger.

## TREE

Tree Models and (Labeled) Categorial Grammar. Venema, Yde.
Uniformization, Choice Functions and Well Orders in the Class of Trees. Lifsches, Shmuel and Shelah, Saharon.

## TRIAD

Monad as a Triadic Structure—Leibniz' Contribution to Post-Nihilistic Search for Identity. Schadel, Erwin.

## TRIAL

Rights Theories and Public Trial. Jaconelli, Joseph.
Wine-Farming, Heresy Trials and the 'Whole Personality': The Emergence of the Stellenbosch Philosophical Tradition, 1916-40. Nash, Andrew.

## TRIBALISM

Esodo e tribalismo. Baccelli, Luca.

## TRINITY

Has Trinitarianism Been Shown To Be Coherent?. Feser, E.
Self-Complaceny and Self-Probation in the Argument of St. Anselme's *Proslogion* (in French). Galonnier, Alain.
The Function of Repetition in Scholastic Theology of the Trinity. Robb, Fiona.
Trinity or Tritheism?. Clark, Kelly James.
Zu den Anfängen des Deismus. Frank, Günter.
Zur subsistentia absoluta in der Trinitätstheologie. Obenauer, Klaus.

## TRIVIALITY

Countable Model of Trivial Theories Which Admit Finite Coding. Loveys, James and Tanovic, Predrag.
Quick Triviality Proofs for Probabilities of Conditionals. Milne, Peter.

## TROELTSCH, E

"Troeltsch e Kant: 'Apriori' e 'storia' nella filosofia della religione" in *Lo Storicismo e la Sua Storia: Temi, Problemi, Prospettive*, Cacciatore, Giuseppe (ed). Cantillo, Giuseppe.
Ernst Troeltsch: aboutissement ou dépassement du néo-protestantisme?. Gisel, Pierre.

## TROPE

On the Compresence of Tropes. Denkel, Arda.
Primacía y dependencia metafísicas: consideraciones acerca de las ontologías de tropos. Bordes Solanas, M.

## TRUE

"Wissen und wahre Meinung" in *Das weite Spektrum der analytischen Philosophie*, Lenzen, Wolfgang. Beckermann, Ansgar.

## TRUST

*Self-Trust: A Study of Reason, Knowledge and Autonomy*. Lehrer, Keith.
Discretionary Power, Lies, and Broken Trust: Justification and Discomfort. Potter, Nancy.
La fiducia come forma di fede: Alcune riflessioni introduttive ad un problema sociologico. Prandini, Riccardo.
Mutual Respect and Neutral Justification. Bird, Colin.
On the Hazards of Whistleblowers and on Some Problems of Young Biomedical Scientists in our Time. Edsall, John T.
Progressive and Regressive Uses of Reasonable Distrust. Hedman, Carl.
Regret, Trust, and Morality (in Serbo-Croatian). Prokopijevic, Miroslav.
Retributivism and Trust. Dimock, Susan.
The Morality of Adultery. Halwani, Raja.
Trust and the Collection, Selection, Analysis and Interpretation of Data: A Scientist's View. Bird, Stephanie J and Housman, David E.
Trust and Totalitarianism: Some Suggestive Examples. Govier, Trudy.
Trust as an Affective Attitude. Jones, Karen.
Trust as Noncognitive Security about Motives. Becker, Lawrence C.
Trust Is Not Enough: Classroom Self-Disclosure and the Loss of Private Lives. Bishop, Nicole.
Trust-Relationships and the Moral Case for Religious Belief. Wynn, Mark.
Trust: The Fragile Foundation of Contemporary Biomedical Research. Kass, Nancy E, Sugarman, Jeremy and Faden, Ruth.
Trustworthiness. Hardin, Russell.
Truth and Trustworthiness in Research. Whitbeck, Caroline.
Why Trusting God Differs from All Other Forms of Trust. Sarot, Marcel.

## TRUTH

"A Disquotational Theory of Truth" in *Verdad: lógica, representación y mundo*, Villegas Forero, L. Seymour, Michel.
"Alle Wahrheit ist relativ, alles wissen symbolisch". Frank, Manfred.
"Arte, Vita E Verità In Vladimir Jankélévitch" in *Soggetto E Verità: La questione dell'uomo nella filosofia contemporanea*, Fagiuoli, Ettore. Franzini, Elio.
"Bradley on Truth and Judgement" in *Philosophy after F.H. Bradley*, Bradley, James (ed). Creery, Walter.
"Conoscere immediato e conoscere discorsivo in Herbert of Cherbury e in alcuni autori della Scuola di Cambridge" in *Mind Senior to the World*, Baldi, Marialuisa. Bianchi, Massimo Luigi.
"Del Sentire La Verità: Per Leopardi e Michelstaedter" in *Soggetto E Verità: La questione dell'uomo nella filosofia contemporanea*, Fagiuoli, Ettore. Carrera, Alessandro.
"Deleuze Outside/Outside Deleuze: On the Difference Engineer" in *Deleuze and Philosophy: The Difference Engineer*, Ansell Pearson, Keith (ed). Ansell Pearson, Keith.
"Desire and Desirability: Bradley, Russell and Moore versus Mill" in *Early Analytic Philosophy*, Tait, William W (ed). Gerrard, Steve.

"El ideal de la Paz en el Humanismo Ético de Kant" in *Kant: La paz perpetua, doscientos años después*, Martínez Guzmán, Vicent (ed). Conill, Jesús.
"Epistemic Theories of Truth: The Justifiability Paradox Investigated" in *Verdad: lógica, representación y mundo*, Villegas Forero, L. Müller, Vincent C and Stein, Christian.
"Fregean Theories of Truth and Meaning" in *Frege: Importance and Legacy*, Schirn, Matthias (ed). Parsons, Terence.
"Historians Look at Historical Truth" in *Epistemology and History*, Zeidler-Janiszewska, Anna (ed). Topolski, Jerzy.
"Hobbes on Peace and Truth" in *Scepticism in the History of Philosophy: A Pan-American Dialogue*, Popkin, Richard H (ed). Madanes, Leiser.
"Il Paiolo Bucato" in *Soggetto E Verità: La questione dell'uomo nella filosofia contemporanea*, Fagiuoli, Ettore. Rovatti, Pier Aldo.
"Il Senso Della Verità: Desolazione matematica e terapia nietzscheana dell'infelicità" in *Soggetto E Verità: La questione dell'uomo nella filosofia contemporanea*, Fagiuoli, Ettore. Fortunato, Marco.
"Il Soggetto E La Verità" in *Soggetto E Verità: La questione dell'uomo nella filosofia contemporanea*, Fagiuoli, Ettore. Sini, Carlo.
"Incorrigibility" in *Objections to Physicalism*, Robinson, Howard (ed). Warner, Richard.
"Inducción pesimista y verdad" in *Verdad: lógica, representación y mundo*, Villegas Forero, L. Iranzo, Valeriano.
"James's Theory of Truth" in *The Cambridge Companion to William James*, Putnam, Ruth Anna (ed). Putnam, Hilary.
"La creación de las verdades eternas y la fábula del mundo" in *Memorias Del Seminario En Conmemoración De Los 400 Años Del Nacimiento De René Descartes*, Albis, Víctor S (ed). Margot, Jean-Paul.
"La mosca salió volando de la botella: éxito y correspondencia en una teoría de la verdad" in *Verdad: lógica, representación y mundo*, Villegas Forero, L. Broncano, Fernando.
"La Pittura Come Linguaggio Indiretto Dell'Essere E Prosa Del Mondo" in *Soggetto E Verità: La questione dell'uomo nella filosofia contemporanea*, Fagiuoli, Ettore. Dalla Vigna, Pierre.
"La Teoría Constructivista de la Verdad" in *Verdad: lógica, representación y mundo*, Villegas Forero, L. Velarde Lombraña, J.
"La Verità Come Tragedia: Immaginazione e immagine del Vero: Note sulla "civilizzazione" in *Soggetto E Verità: La questione dell'uomo nella filosofia contemporanea*, Fagiuoli, Ettore. Zanini, Adelino.
"La Verità Storica: La comprensione della storia nella riflessione di Martin Heidegger" in *Soggetto E Verità: La questione dell'uomo nella filosofia contemporanea*, Fagiuoli, Ettore. Cassinari, Flavio.
"Love's Truths" in *Love Analyzed*, Lamb, Roger E. Marshall, Graeme.
"Malebranche e la storia nella *Recherche de la Vérité*" in *Lo Storicismo e la Sua Storia: Temi, Problemi, Prospettive*, Cacciatore, Giuseppe (ed). Stile, Alessandro.
"Multimodal Logics and Epistemic Attitudes" in *Verdad: lógica, representación y mundo*, Villegas Forero, L. Alonso González, Enrique.
"Neurophenomenalism and the Theories of Truth" in *Verdad: lógica, representación y mundo*, Villegas Forero, L. Zamora Bonilla, Jesús P.
"Nonextensionality" in *Das weite Spektrum der analytischen Philosophie*, Lenzen, Wolfgang. Lambert, Karel.
"Ontologia Della Mancanza: Heidegger e la questione dell'uomo" in *Soggetto E Verità: La questione dell'uomo nella filosofia contemporanea*, Fagiuoli, Ettore. Feroldi, Luisella.
"Peirce and Scepticism" in *Scepticism in the History of Philosophy: A Pan-American Dialogue*, Popkin, Richard H (ed). Herrera Ibáñez, Alejandro.
"Perspectives and Horizons: Husserl on Seeing the Truth" in *Sites of Vision*, Levin, David Michael (ed). Rawlinson, Mary C.
"Plasticidad neuronal, verdad y lógica" in *Verdad: lógica, representación y mundo*, Villegas Forero, L. Garay, Carlos Alberto.
"Religious Truth and Philosophical Truth according to Ibn Rushd" in *Averroès and the Enlightenment*, Wahba, Mourad (ed). El Ghannouchi, A.
"Sobre objetividad y verdad en algunos escritos de Frege" in *Verdad: lógica, representación y mundo*, Villegas Forero, L. Corredor, Cristina.
"Sozialphilosophische Aspekte der Übersetzbarkeit" in *Epistemology and History*, Zeidler-Janiszewska, Anna (ed). Siemek, Marek J.
"Teoría de situaciones: Semántica de tipos para un lenguaje formal con concepto de verdad" in *Verdad: lógica, representación y mundo*, Villegas Forero, L. Beck, Andreas.
"The Broken Bonds with the World" in *Epistemology and History*, Zeidler-Janiszewska, Anna (ed). Ozdowski, Pawel.
"The Commonwealth of Scholars and New Conceptions of Truth" in *The Idea of University*, Brzezinski, Jerzy (ed). Topolski, Jerzy.
"The Disciplinary Conception of Truth" in *Verdad: lógica, representación y mundo*, Villegas Forero, L. Luntley, Michael.
"Truth, Physicalism, and Ultimate Theory" in *Objections to Physicalism*, Robinson, Howard (ed). Wagner, Steven J.
"Un escenario pragmático para la verdad en la ciencia" in *Verdad: lógica, representación y mundo*, Villegas Forero, L. Bengoetxea, Juan B, Eizagirre, Xabier and Ibarra, Andoni.
"Universal Reason" as a Local Organizational Method: Announcement of a Study. Liberman, Kenneth.
"Variations in the Notion of "Truth" in *K. R. Popper's Philosophy*" in *Verdad: lógica, representación y mundo*, Villegas Forero, L. Martínez-Solano, José Francisco.

## TRUTH

The Transparency of Truth. Kalderon, Mark Eli.

The Trouble with Truth-Makers. Cox, Damian.

The Truths of Logic. Hammer, Eric M.

The Value of Truth and the Care of the Soul. Witherall, Arthur.

The Way, the Truth and the Life: Religious Tradition and Truth in the Postmodern Context... (in Dutch). Boeve, Lieven.

The Weakness of Strong Justification. Riggs, Wayne D.

The 'Truth' in Solipsism, and Wittgenstein's Rejection of the A Priori. Sullivan, Peter M.

Three Problems for the Singularity Theory of Truth. Hardy, James.

Through Phenomenology to Sublime Poetry: Martin Heidegger on the Decisive Relation between Truth and Art. Anderson, Travis T.

Timothy Williamson *Vagueness*. Simons, Peter.

Tracking Truth and Solving Puzzles. Gjelsvik, Olav.

Transcendental Truth in Vico. Wilson, Gerald.

Trascendentalismo, contenido semántico y verdad. Barrio, Eduardo Alejandro.

True and Ultimate Responsibility. Nathan, Nicholas.

True Theories, False Colors. Clark, Austen.

Truth and Community. Volf, Miroslav.

Truth and History: The Question. Bonsor, Jack.

Truth and Idiomatic Truth in Santayana. Kerr-Lawson, Angus.

Truth and Logic of Text: An Outline of the Metatext Theory of Truth (in Polish). Gawronski, Alfred.

Truth and Meaning in George Lindbeck's *The Nature of Doctrine*. Richards, Jay Wesley.

Truth and Metaphor in Rorty's Liberalism. Hymers, Michael.

Truth and Metatheory in Frege. Stanley, Jason.

Truth and Success: Searle's Attack on Minimalism. Clark, Michael.

Truth and Thickness. Tietz, John.

Truth Conditions of Tensed Sentence Types. Paul, L A.

Truth in Pure Semantics: A Reply to Putnam. Moreno, Luis Fernández.

Truth or Consequences: A Study of Critical Issues and Decision Making in Accounting. Gibson, Annetta and Frakes, Albert H.

Truth vs Rorty. Steinhoff, Uwe.

Truth Without People?. Glock, Hans-Johann.

Truth, Verisimilitude, and Natural Kinds. Aronson, Jerrold L.

Truth: The Identity Theory. Hornsby, Jennifer.

Una polémica entre historiadores de la filosofía. Badaloni, Nicola.

Unreflective Realism. Williamson, Timothy.

Verdad del desvelamiento y verdad del testimonio. Levinas, Emmanuel and Nicolás, Juan A (trans).

Verità e prescrizione in etica. Vacatello, Marzio.

Veritas vincit (in Czech). Skorpíková, Zuzana.

Weak Deflationism. McGrath, Matthew.

Wege zur Wahrheit: Zur Bedeutung von Fichtes wissenschaftlich- und populär-philosophischer Methode. Traub, Hartmut.

What Cannot Be Evaluated Cannot Be Evaluated, and it Cannot Be Supervalued Either. Fodor, Jerry A and Lepore, Ernest.

What is Relative Confirmation?. Christensen, David.

What's a Gradual Ontology? (in Spanish). Vásconez, Marcelo and Peña, Lorenzo.

What's an Approximate Conditional?. De Soto, A R and Trillas, Enric.

What's in a Function?. Antonelli, Gian Aldo.

What's the Fuzzy Temporary Reasoning? (in Spanish). Marín, R and Taboada, M.

Where is Truth? A Commentary from a Medical-Ethical and Personalistic Perspective (in Dutch). Schotsmans, Paul.

Where to Look for Truth: Focusing on the Symposium's Highlights. Vanheeswijck, Guido.

Why Preference is not Transitive. Gendin, Sidney.

Why Tolerate? Reflections on the Millian Truth Principle. Cohen-Almagor, Raphael.

Why We should Lose Our Natural Ontological Attitudes. Kovach, Adam.

Wright's Argument from Neutrality. Kölbel, Max.

## TRUTH CONDITION

A Note on Truth, Deflationism and Irrealism. Miraglia, Pierluigi.

## TRUTH TABLE

Decidability of the Two-Quantifier Theory of the Recursive Enumerable Weak Truth-Table Degrees and Other Distributive Semi-Lattices. Ambos-Spies, Klaus, Fejer, Peter A and Lempp, Steffen (& others).

## TRUTH TELLING

An Essay on When to Fully Disclose in Sales Relationships: Applying Two Practical Guidelines for Addressing Truth-Telling Problems. Strutton, David, Hamilton III, J Brooke and Lumpkin, James R.

## TRUTH VALUE

"Truth-Values and Courses-of-Value in Frege's *Grundgesetze*" in *Early Analytic Philosophy*, Tait, William W (ed). Ricketts, Thomas.

Counterfactuals with True Components. Penczek, Alan.

Fuzzy Truth Values (in Spanish). Godo, Lluís.

La negación de los juicios estrictamente particulares en la tetravalencia. Öffenberger, Niels and Bustos López, Javier.

## TSIOLKOVSKII, K

The Cosmic Route to "Eternal Bliss": (K.E. Tsiolkovskii and the Mythology of Technocracy). Gavriushin, Nikolai K.

## TSOHATZIDIS, S

The State of the Art in Speech Act Theory. Weigand, Edda.

## TUCKER, J

Christianity, Commerce and the Canon: Josiah Tucker and Richard Woodward on Political Economy. Young, B W.

The Influence of Utilitarianism on Natural Rights Doctrines. Molivas, Gregory I.

## TUFAYL

Cosmological Mysticism: The Imitation of the Heavenly Bodies in Ibn Tufayl's *Hayy ibn Yaqzan*. Brague, Rémi.

## TUFTS, J

"James Hayden Tufts on the Social Mission of the University" in *Philosophy in Experience: American Philosophy in Transition*, Hart, Richard (ed). Campbell, James.

## TUGENDHAT, E

Bedeutungen und Gegenständlichkeiten: Zu Tugendhats sprachanalytischer Kritik von Husserls früher Phänomenologie. Soldati, Gianfranco.

Gibt es eine universelle Moral?. Leist, Anton.

Moral und Gemeinschaft: Eine Kritik an Tugendhat. Krebs, Angelika.

Phenomenological Ethics and Moral Sentiments (Spanish). Hoyos Vásquez, Guillermo.

Ser, verdad y lenguaje: la continuidad filosófica de la obra de Tugendhat. Bonet Sánchez, José V.

## TULSKY, J

Goals of Ethics Consultation: Toward Clarity, Utility, and Fidelity. Andre, Judith.

## TUOMELA, R

Responses to Critics of *The Construction of Social Reality*. Searle, John R.

## TURING MACHINES

Is the Human Mind a Turing Machine?. King, David.

Self-Knowledge and Embedded Operators. Williamson, Timothy.

## TURING, A

Computability and Recursion. Soare, Robert I.

On Alan Turing's Anticipation of Connectionism. Copeland, B Jack and Proudfoot, Diane.

Thinking Machines: Some Fundamental Confusions. Kearns, John T.

What is Computation?. Copeland, B Jack.

## TURKISH

"Secularization in Turkey" in *Averroës and the Enlightenment*, Wahba, Mourad (ed). Kuçuradi, Ioanna.

## TURNER, J

"Deleuze on J. M. W. Turner: Catastrophism in Philosophy?" in *Deleuze and Philosophy: The Difference Engineer*, Ansell Pearson, Keith (ed). Williams, James.

## TURNER, S

Do Practices Explain Anything? Turner's Critique of the Theory of Social Practices. Bohman, James.

## TWAIN, M

The Morality of Huck Finn. Freedman, Carol.

## TWARDOWSKI, K

"Reflections on the University" in *The Idea of University*, Brzezinski, Jerzy (ed). Brzezinski, Jerzy.

"The Commonwealth of Scholars and New Conceptions of Truth" in *The Idea of University*, Brzezinski, Jerzy (ed). Topolski, Jerzy.

## TWENTIETH

*see also* Contemporary

"David Savan: In Memoriam" in *The Rule of Reason: The Philosophy of Charles Sanders Peirce*, Forster, Paul (ed). Normore, Calvin G.

"Vieja y Nueva Política y el Semanario *España* en el Nacimiento" in *Política y Sociedad en José Ortega y Gasset: En Torno a "Vieja y Nueva Política"*, Lopez de la Vieja, Maria Teresa (ed). Menéndez Alzamora, Manuel.

*50 Years of Events: An Annotated Bibliography 1947 to 1997*. Casati, Roberto and Varzi, Achille C.

*Das weite Spektrum der analytischen Philosophie*. Lenzen, Wolfgang.

*Emmanuel Levinas: A Bibliography*. Nordquist, Joan (ed).

*Latin American Philosophy in the Twentieth Century*. Gracia, Jorge J E.

*Rosa Luxemburg and Emma Goldman: A Bibliography*. Nordquist, Joan (ed).

*Social Theory: A Bibliographic Series, No. 42-Martin Heidegger (II): A Bibliography*. Nordquist, Joan.

*Soggetto E Verità: La questione dell'uomo nella filosofia contemporanea*. Fagiuoli, Ettore and Fortunato, Marco.

*Streitgespräche und Kontroversen in der Philosophie des 20.Jahrhunderts*. Wuchterl, Kurt.

*Twentieth-Century Philosophy*. Baird, Forrest E (ed) and Kaufmann, Walter.

Axiomática y álgebra estructural en la obra de David Hilbert. Corry, Leo.

Bertrand Russell's Life in Pictures. Ruja, Harry.

Bibliografía hispánica de filosofía: Elenco 1997. Santos-Escudero, Ceferino.

Carta al Padre William Richardson. Borges-Duarte, Irene (trans) and Heidegger, Martin.

Cecylia Rauszer. Rasiowa, Helena.

Crisis de la modernidad en el pensamiento español: desde el Barroco y en la europeización del siglo XX. Jiménez Moreno, Luis.

## UNITY

La unidad de la vida humana (Aristóteles y Leonardo Polo). Castillo Córdova, Genara.

La unidad del conocimiento: desde la *especulación* a la ciencia. (Introducción a la *Dendrognoseología*). Tagliacozzo, Giorgio.

Matter and the Unity of Being in the Philosophical Theology of Saint Thomas Aquinas. McAleer, Graham.

On Preserving the Unity of the Moral Virtues in the *Nichomachean Ethics*. Clifton, Michael H.

Selbstbewusstsein in der Spätantike: Neuere Untersuchungen zu Plotins Schrift V 3 [49]. Horn, Christoph.

Skepticism and the Question of Community. Burke, Patrick.

The Idea of Total-Unity from Heraclitus to Losev. Khoruzhii, Sergei Sergeevich.

The Limited Unity of Virtue. Badhwar, Neera Kapur.

The Myriad Faces of Personal Survival. Nelson, John O.

The Ring of Gyges: Overridingness and the Unity of Reason. Copp, David.

The Unity of the State: Plato, Aristotle and Proclus. Stalley, R F.

Unity and Development: Social Homogeneity, the Totalitarian Imaginary, and the Classical Marxist Tradition. Louw, Stephen.

Unity and Diversity through Education: A Comparison of the Thought of W.E.B. DuBois and John Dewey. Burks, Ben.

Unity, Diversity, and Leftist Support for the Canon. Casement, William.

William James's Quest to Have It All. Gale, Richard M.

## UNIVERSAL

"L'indagine storico-universale di Max Weber sul 'razionalismo occidentale' tra lo storicismo e Nietzsche" in *Lo Storicismo e la Sua Storia: Temi, Problemi, Prospettive,* Cacciatore, Giuseppe (ed). Di Marco, Giuseppe Antonio.

"L'ombra dei lumi: Il problema della storia universale in Francia tra Settecento e Ottocento" in *Lo Storicismo e la Sua Storia: Temi, Problemi, Prospettive,* Cacciatore, Giuseppe (ed). Imbruglia, Girolamo.

"Prospettive di storia universale nell'opera di Spengler" in *Lo Storicismo e la Sua Storia: Temi, Problemi, Prospettive,* Cacciatore, Giuseppe (ed). Conte, Domenico.

"Ragione universale, storia universale, religione universale: il Voltaire illusionista dell'abate Galiani" in *Lo Storicismo e la Sua Storia: Temi, Problemi, Prospettive,* Cacciatore, Giuseppe (ed). Amodio, Paolo.

*Cultural Universals and Particulars: An African Perspective.* Wiredu, Kwasi.

*Formal Ethics.* Gensler, Harry J.

*Leibniz' Universal Jurisprudence: Justice as the Charity of the Wise.* Riley, Patrick.

*Properties.* Mellor, D H (ed) and Oliver, Alex (ed).

*Universal Justice: A Dialectical Approach.* Anderson, Albert A.

Ahnlichkeit. Spaemann, Robert.

An Argument against Armstrong's Analysis of the Resemblance of Universals. Pautz, Adam.

Armstrong on the Role of Laws in Counterfactual Supporting. Pages, Joan.

Between Inconsistent Nominalists and Egalitarian Idealists. Nelson, Ralph C.

Bundles and Indiscernibility: A Reply to O'Leary-Hawthorne. Vallicella, William F.

Confirming Universal Generalizations. Zabell, S L.

Freedom as Universal. Hartshorne, Charles.

Gibt es eine universelle Moral?. Leist, Anton.

Habermas' Pragmatic Universals. Mukherji, Arundhati.

Identidad Personal, Nacional y Universal. Tugendhat, Ernst.

Kung-sun Lung on the Point of Pointing: The Moral Rhetoric of Names. Lai, Whalen.

La dialéctica de lo universal y lo particular y el ideal de la abolición del estado (Segunda parte). Salas, Mario.

On Substances, Accidents and Universals: In Defence of a Constituent Ontology. Smith, Barry.

Sartre and Human Nature. Anderson, Thomas C.

Some Characterization Theorems for Infinitary Universal Horn Logic without Equality. Dellunde, Pilar and Jansana, Ramon.

The Nature of the Common Concept in William of Ockham (in Czech). Saxlová, Tereza.

The Negotiation of Equivalence. Arditi, Benjamin.

The Price of Universality. Hemaspaandra, Edith.

Universal Instantiation: A Study of the Role of Context in Logic. Gauker, Christopher.

Universal Rights and Explicit Principles (in Dutch). Burms, Arnold.

Universal Values, Behavioral Ethics and Entrepreneurship. Clarke, Ruth and Aram, John.

Universals and the *Methodenstreit*: a Re-examination of Carl Menger's Conception of Economics as an Exact Science. Mäki, Uskali.

## UNIVERSALISM

"The Justification of National Partiality" in *The Morality of Nationalism,* McKim, Robert (ed). Hurka, Thomas.

"Universalismo vs. contextualismo: (Un intento de aproximación desde la pragmática del lenguaje)" in *Liberalismo y Comunitarismo: Derechos Humanos y Democracia,* Monsalve Solórzano, Alfonso (ed). Gallego Vásquez, Frederico.

Authenticity As a Normative Category. Ferrara, Alessandro.

Habermas and Apel on Communicative Ethics: Their Difference and the Difference It Makes. Gamwell, Franklin I.

Habermas and Mead: On Universality and Individuality. Abdoulafia, Mitchell.

History of Philosophy, Personal or Impersonal? Reflections on Etienne Gilson. Dewan, Lawrence.

How Innocent is Mereology?. Forrest, Peter.

Marx's Political Universalism. Van der Linden, Harry.

On the Meaning of an Intercultural Philosophy (With Reply from H. Kimmerle). Hoogland, Jan.

On Values: Universal or Relative?. Aarnio, Aulis.

Recalling the Hermeneutic Circle. Schmidt, Lawrence K.

Romanticized Enlightenment? Enlightened Romanticism? Universalism and Particularism in Hegel's *Understanding of the Enlightenment.* Pinkard, Terry.

Taking the Universal Viewpoint: A Descriptive Approach. Wood, Robert.

The Facts of Causation. Mellor, D H.

The Local, the Contextual and/or Critical. Benhabib, Seyla.

The Notion of African Philosophy. Uduigwomen, Andrew F.

The Parochial Universalist Conception of 'Philosophy' and 'African Philosophy'. Ikuenobe, Polycarp.

Universalism and the Greater Good: A Response to Talbott. Knight, Gordon.

Well-Being: On a Fundamental Concept of Practical Philosophy. Seel, Martin.

## UNIVERSALITY

Particularity of Religion and Universality of Reason (in Dutch). Van der Veken, Jan.

Quelle universalité pour l'éthique dans une sociétépluraliste? Une réflexion théologique. Fuchs, Eric.

The Sirens' Song of the Traditions: A plea for a Universal Ethics (in Dutch). Merks, Karl-Wilhelm.

The Universality of Poetry. Vitsaxis, V.

Where to Look for Truth: Focusing on the Symposium's Highlights. Vanheeswijck, Guido.

## UNIVERSALIZABILITY

"La universalizabilidad monológica: R.M. Hare" in *La racionalidad: su poder y sus límites,* Nudler, Oscar (ed). Guariglia, Osvaldo.

Accepting Agent Centred Norms: A Problem for Non-Cognitivists and a Suggestion for Solving It. Dreier, James.

Civil Society Ethics: An Approach from K-O Apel's Philosophy (in Spanish). Durán Casas, Vicente.

## UNIVERSALIZATION

*Moralidad: Ética universalista y sujeto moral.* Guariglia, Osvaldo.

Da Filosofia como Universalizaçao: Universalidade e Situaçao da Filosofia num Passo Nuclear de *A Razao Experimental* de Leonardo Coimbra. Mesquita, António Pedro.

Habermas' Diskursethik. Lumer, Christoph.

Sartre e o pensamento de Marx. Paisana, Joao.

Universalización Moral y Prudencia en Kant. Rosas, Alejandro.

## UNIVERSE

"Interpreting the Universe after a Social Analogy: Intimacy, Panpsychism, and a Finite God in a Pluralistic Universe" in *The Cambridge Companion to William James,* Putnam, Ruth Anna (ed). Lamberth, David C.

"Philosophie der Stoffe, Bestandsaufnahme und Ausblicke" in *Philosophie der Chemie: Bestandsaufnahme und Ausblick,* Schummer, Joachim (ed). Schummer, Joachim.

"Time in the Universe" in *The Idea of Progress,* McLaughlin, Peter (ed). Barrow, John D.

*A Pluralistic Universe.* Levinson, Henry Samuel and James, William.

*The Possible Universe.* Tallet, J A.

Aporías sobre el universo y su temporalidad a la luz de la filosofía de Leonardo Polo. Sanguineti, Juan José.

Aportaciones de Leonardo Polo para una teoría antropológica del aprendizaje. García Viúdez, Marcos.

Four-Eighths Hephaistos: Artifacts and Living Things in Aristotle. Koslicki, Kathrin.

Irreversibility and Time's Arrow. Landsberg, Peter T.

L'Aurora degli Idoli: Una breva ricerca del senso dell'essere oltre Heidegger. Turchi, Athos.

Lady Mary Shepherd's Case Against George Berkeley. Atherton, Margaret L.

Leibniz, el cristianismo europeo y la *Teodicea.* Andreu Rodrigo, Agustín.

Mother Nature Doesn't Know Her Name: Reflections on a Term. Fell, Gil S.

Naturalizing Metaphysics. Saunders, Simon.

Nuove frontiere della scienza. Manno, Ambrogio Giacomo.

Saint Thomas et le problème de la possibilité d'un univers créé éternel. De Lassus, Alain-Marie.

Simplicity and Why the Universe Exists. Smith, Quentin.

Sobre el ser y la creación. García González, Juan A.

The Hume-Edwards Objection to the Cosmological Argument. Vallicella, William F.

The Ontological Interpretation of the Wave Function of the Universe. Smith, Quentin.

The Origin of the Big Bang Universe in Ultimate Reality with Special Reference to the Cosmology of Stephen Hawking. Sharpe, Kevin.

Thomism and the Quantum Enigma. Wallace, William A.

**UNIVERSITY**

*see also* College

"Cognition, Character, and Culture in Undergraduate Education: Rhetoric and Reality" in *The American University: National Treasure or Endangered Species?*, Ehrenberg, Ronald G (ed). Shapiro, Harold T.

"Graduate Students: Too Many and Too Narrow?" in *The American University: National Treasure or Endangered Species?*, Ehrenberg, Ronald G (ed). Fox, Marye Anne.

"Is a 'Creative Man of Knowledge' Needed in University Teaching" in *The Idea of University*, Brzezinski, Jerzy (ed). Kmita, Jerzy.

"James Hayden Tufts on the Social Mission of the University" in *Philosophy in Experience: American Philosophy in Transition*, Hart, Richard (ed). Campbell, James.

"No Limits" in *The American University: National Treasure or Endangered Species?*, Ehrenberg, Ronald G (ed). Bowen, William G.

"On Freedom of Science" in *The Idea of University*, Brzezinski, Jerzy (ed). Ajdukiewicz, Kazimierz.

"Plus Ratio Quam Vis" in *The Idea of University*, Brzezinski, Jerzy (ed). Szaniawski, Klemens.

"Prospect for Science and Technology" in *The American University: National Treasure or Endangered Species?*, Ehrenberg, Ronald G (ed). Lane, Neal.

"Prospect for the Humanities" in *The American University: National Treasure or Endangered Species?*, Ehrenberg, Ronald G (ed). Gray, Hanna H.

"Prospect for the Social Sciences in the Land Grant University" in *The American University: National Treasure or Endangered Species?*, Ehrenberg, Ronald G (ed). Bronfenbrenner, Urie.

"Reflections on the University" in *The Idea of University*, Brzezinski, Jerzy (ed). Brzezinski, Jerzy.

"Research Universities: Overextended, Underfocused; Overstressed, Underfunded" in *The American University: National Treasure or Endangered Species?*, Ehrenberg, Ronald G (ed). Vest, Charles M.

"The American University: National Treasure or Endangered Species?" in *The American University: National Treasure or Endangered Species?*, Ehrenberg, Ronald G (ed). Rhodes, Frank H T.

"The Commonwealth of Scholars and New Conceptions of Truth" in *The Idea of University*, Brzezinski, Jerzy (ed). Topolski, Jerzy.

"The Ideal University and Reality" in *The Idea of University*, Brzezinski, Jerzy (ed). Gumanski, Leon.

"The Majesty of the University" in *The Idea of University*, Brzezinski, Jerzy (ed). Twardowski, Kazimierz.

"The Present Crisis of the Universities" in *The Idea of University*, Brzezinski, Jerzy (ed). Bauman, Zygmunt.

"Tradition in Science" in *The Idea of University*, Brzezinski, Jerzy (ed). Gockowski, Janusz.

"Universities and Democracy" in *The Idea of University*, Brzezinski, Jerzy (ed). Samsonowicz, Henryk.

"What Are Universities For?" in *The Idea of University*, Brzezinski, Jerzy (ed). Kolakowski, Leszek.

"What Can Be Saved of the Idea of the University?" in *The Idea of University*, Brzezinski, Jerzy (ed). Ziembinski, Zygmunt.

*Rethinking College Education.* Allan, George.

*The American University: National Treasure or Endangered Species?.* Ehrenberg, Ronald G (ed).

*The Idea of University.* Brzezinski, Jerzy (ed) and Nowak, Leszek (ed).

*The Order of Learning: Essays on the Contemporary University.* Altbach, Philip G (ed) and Shils, Edward.

A Business Ethics Experiential Learning Module: The Maryland Business School Experience. Loeb, Stephen E and Ostas, Daniel T.

A Universidade na Sociedade Actual. Renaud, Michel.

Affirmative Action at the University of California. Lynch, Michael W.

Antioch's "Sexual Offense Policy": A Philosophical Exploration. Soble, Alan.

Differences in Moral Reasoning Between College and University Business Majors and Non-Business Majors. Snodgrass, James and Behling, Robert.

Ethical Aspects of the University-Industry Interface. Spier, Raymond.

Factors that Influence the Moral Reasoning Abilities of Accountants: Implications for Universities and the Profession. Eynon, Gail, Thorley Hill, Nancy and Stevens, Kevin T.

Giambattista Vico, la Universidad y el saber: el modelo retórico. Patella, Giuseppe.

Perception of What the Ethical Climate Is and What It Should Be: The Role of Gender, Academic Status, and Ethical Education. Luthar, Harsh K, DiBattista, Ron A and Gautschi, Theodore.

Philosophy as a Vocation: Heidegger and University Reform in the Early Interwar Years. Crowell, Steven Galt.

Postmodernism and University (Spanish). Delgado Ocando, José Manuel.

Professing Education in a Postmodern Age. Carr, Wilfred.

Racism, Human Rights, and Universities. Sankowski, Edward.

Sexual Harassment and the University. Holmes, Robert L.

Teaching Science at the University Level: What About the Ethics?. Gilmer, Penny J.

The Best Teacher I Ever Had Was... J. Coert Rylaarsdam. Michalos, Alex C.

The Idea of the University and the Role of Philosophy. Hufnagel, Erwin.

True Colors: The Response of Business Schools to Declining Enrollment. McKendall, Marie A and Lindquist, Stanton C.

Women, Ethics, and MBAs. MacLellan, Cheryl and Dobson, John.

**UNKNOWN**

L'inconscio come finzione linguistica. Ugolini, Consuelo.

**UNPROVABILITY**

On Countably Closed Complete Boolean Algebras. Jech, Thomas and Shelah, Saharon.

**UNREALITY**

McTaggart's Paradox and Smith's Tensed Theory of Time. Oaklander, L Nathan.

**UNTIL**

An Axiomatization for Until and Since over the Reals without the IRR Rule. Reynolds, Mark.

Axiomatising First-Order Temporal Logic: Until and Since over Linear Time. Reynolds, Mark.

**UPANISHAD**

Indian Philosophy in the First Millennium AD: Fact and Fiction. Krishna, Daya.

The Ātmahano Janāh of the Isāvāsya Upanisad. Jayashanmukham, N.

**UPANISHADS**

A Critique on Brahman-Realization. Prabhakara Rao, M.

Comment on "Vedānta in the First Millennium AD: Illusion or Reality?". Murty, K Satchidananda.

Professor Date's New Light on the Vedanta of Samkara. Sharma, M L.

The Advaita View of the Self. Bhattacharya, A N.

**UPBRINGING**

The Role of Good Upbringing in Aristotle's *Ethics*. Vasiliou, Iakovos.

**UPDATE**

Counterfactuals and Updates as Inverse Modalities. Ryan, Mark and Schobbens, Pierre-Yves.

On the Significance of Conditional Probabilities. Sobel, Jordan Howard.

**UPDATING**

Bayesian Rules of Updating. Howson, Colin.

**URBACH, P**

L'anticipazione nella scienza baconiana. Sciaccaluga, Nicoletta.

**URBAN**

Expanding Diversity Education for Preservice Teachers: Teaching about Racial Isolation in Urban Schools. Malone, Patricia.

Más allá del bosque (Reflexiones agorológicas en torno a Vico). López Lloret, Jorge.

**URMSON, J**

On Grading Apples and Arguments. Mendenhall, Vance.

**USE**

Abusing Use. Glock, H J.

What is Philosophical in Philosophical Counselling?. Lahav, Ran.

**UTILITARIANISM**

*see also* Rule Utilitarianism

"Theoretische und angewandte Ethik: Paradigmen, Begründungen, Bereiche" in *Angewandte Ethik: Die Bereichsethiken und ihre theoretische Fundierung*, Nida-Rümelin, Julian (ed). Nida-Rümelin, Julian.

*Democracy and Disagreement.* Gutmann, Amy and Thompson, Dennis.

*Il Disincanto Della Ragione E L'Assolutezza Del Bonheur* Studio Sull'Abate Galiani. Amodio, Paolo.

*On Economic Inequality.* Sen, Amartya.

*Utilitarianism.* Scarre, Geoffrey.

A Utilitarian Argument for Vegetarianism. Dixon, Nicholas.

Against Thin-Property Reductivism: Toleration as Supererogatory. Newey, Glen.

Brandt on Utilitarianism and the Foundations of Ethics. Carson, Thomas L.

Cantona and Aquinas on Good and Evil. O'Neill, John.

Contractual Justice: A Modest Defence. Barry, Brian.

Errors In Moral Reasoning. Grcic, Joseph.

Esperando a Mill. Guisán Seijas, Esperanza.

Feminist Positions on Vegetarianism: Arguments For and Against and Otherwise. Wellington, Alex.

Fred Feldman's *Confrontations with the Reaper: A Philosophical Study of the Nature and Value of Death*. Marquis, Don.

Future Issues in Bioethics. Flanigan, Rosemary.

Gesellschaftsvertrag oder grösster Gesamtnutzen? Die Vertragstheorie von John Rawls und ihre neo-utilitaristischen Kritiker. Rinderle, Peter.

Gibt es eine universelle Moral?. Leist, Anton.

Grounding Hypernorms: Towards a Contractarian Theory of Business Ethics. Rowan, John R.

Hare's Reductive Justification of Preference Utilitarianism. Paden, Roger.

Hume's Utilitarian Theory of Right Action. Sobel, Jordan Howard.

I metodi dell'etica di Henry Sidgwick. Lecaldano, Eugenio, Schneewind, J B and Vacatello, Marzio.

Ilustración y Utilitarismo en Iberoamérica. Rodríguez Braun, Carlos.

Introduction. Kelly, P J.

Is the Repugnant Conclusion Repugnant?. Ryberg, Jesper.

L'Éthique et les Stress. Baertschi, Bernard.

La recepción del Utilitarismo en el mundo hispánico: El caso de Ortega y Gasset. López Frías, Francisco.

Las relaciones entre Jeremías Bentham y S. Bolívar. Schwartz, P and Rodríguez Braun, Carlos.

Making Sense of Mill. Weinstock, Daniel M.

Meaning and Morality. Wolf, Susan.

## VALUE

"Werte im Management: Eine empirische Untersuchung" in *Werte und Entscheidungen im Management*, Schmidt, Thomas. Wegner, Marion.

"Zur Integration von Werten in Entscheidungen: Entscheidungsorientierung und eine liberale Theorie der Werte" in *Werte und Entscheidungen im Management*, Schmidt, Thomas. Lohmann, Karl R.

*"La volontéde puissance" n'existe pas*: A proposito dell'edizione francese di alcuni saggi di Mazzino Montinari. Viola, Salvatore.

*A Practical Companion to Ethics*. Weston, Anthony.

*A Question of Values: New Canadian Perspectives in Ethics and Political Philosophy*. Brennan, Samantha (ed), Isaacs, Tracy (ed) and Milde, Michael (ed).

*Artworks: Definition, Meaning, Value*. Stecker, Robert A.

*Fact, Value, and God*. Holmes, Arthur F.

*Human Lives: Critical Essays on Consequentialist Bioethics*. Oderberg, David S (ed) and Laing, Jacqueline A (ed).

*La Volontà di Potenza in Nietzsche e la Storia dell'Europa negli Ultimi Tempi*. Manno, Ambrogio Giacomo.

*Living in a Technological Culture: Human Tools and Human Values*. Tiles, Mary and Oberdiek, Hans.

*Sartre Ontologie und die Frage einer Ethik: Zur Vereinbarkeit einer normativen Ethik und/oder Metaethik mit der Ontologie von "L'être et le néant"*. Töllner, Uwe.

*Valores Latinoamericanos y del Caribe: ¿Obstaculos o Ayudas para el Desarrollo?*. Orozco Cantillo, Alvaro J.

*Values and the Social Order*. Radnitzky, Gerard (ed).

*Werte und Entscheidungen im Management*. Schmidt, Thomas and Lohmann, Karl R.

A Note on Moore's Organic Unities. Carlson, Erik.

Abortion, Infanticide, and the Asymmetric Value of Human Life. Reiman, Jeffrey.

Advocating Values: Professionalism in Teaching Ethics. Martin, Mike W.

Aesthetic Antirealism. Young, James O.

Against Ethical Criticism. Posner, Richard A.

Argumentation, Values, and Ethics. Monsalve, Alfonso.

Art, Value, and Philosophy. Levinson, Jerrold.

Autonomy, Life as an Intrinsic Value, and the Right to Die in Dignity. Cohen-Almagor, Raphael.

Business Education, Values and Beliefs. Small, Michael W.

Comparable Harm and Equal Inherent Value: The Problem of Dog in the Lifeboat. Francione, Gary L.

Complexity of Ethical Decision Making in Psychiatry. Morenz, Barry and Sales, Bruce.

Complexity, Value, and the Psychological Postulates of Economics. Benedikt, Michael.

Conflict and Constellation: The New Trend of Value Development in China. Chen, Xun Wu.

Confucian Value and Democratic Value. Li, Chenyang.

Could Auditing Standards Be Based on Society's Values?. Zaid, Omar Abdullah.

Counterfactuals, Causation, and Overdetermination. Worley, Sara.

Degrees of Personhood. Perring, Christian.

Die wertlose Natur: Eine Bilanz der Diskussion um eine "Evolutionäre Ethik". Funken, Michael.

Discutono *Oltre l'interpretazione*, di Gianni Vattimo. Ferraris, Maurizio and Carchia, Gianni.

Diversity, Values and Social Change: Renegotiating a Consensus on Sex Education. Thomson, Rachel.

Du phénomène de la valeur au discours de la norme. Lacoste, Jean-Yves.

El decisionismo valorativo: Entre las instancias últimas y la racionalidad crítica. Flax, Javier.

Environmental Egalitarianism and 'Who do you Save?' Dilemmas. Michael, Mark A.

Environmental Values: A Place-Based Theory. Norton, Bryan G and Hannon, Bruce.

Esperando a Mill. Guisán Seijas, Esperanza.

Family Outlaws. Calhoun, Cheshire.

Fetishism and the Identity of Art. Farrelly-Jackson, Steven.

Gutsein. Stemmer, Peter.

Health as a Normative Concept: Towards a New Conceptual Framework. Fedoryka, Kateryna.

History and Values. Dorotíková, Sona.

How Should Schools Respond to the Plurality of Values in a Multi-Cultural Society?. Burwood, Les R V.

How to Combat Nihilism: Reflections on Nietzsche's Critique of Morality. Langsam, Harold.

I confini del fondamento. Lipari, Maria Chiara.

Il fondamento etico e metafisico del diritto. Bagolini, Luigi.

Incommensurability and Vagueness. Leeds, Stephen.

Intrinsic Value and Moral Obligation. Audi, Robert.

Intuitions and the Value of a Person. Haldane, John.

L'uomo superiore dopo la morte di Dio: Appunti di lettura. Campioni, Giuliano.

La Filosofía como cuarta destreza cultural para la realización humana de la vida. Martens, Ekkehard.

La paradoja del Taxidermista: Una ilustración negativa del juicio práctico deweyano. Catalán, Miguel.

Legal Ethics in the Practice of Family Law: Playing Chess While Mountain Climbing. Hotel, Carla and Brockman, Joan.

Making Sense of Moral Realism. Norman, Richard.

Nietzsche and the Value of Truth. Mangiafico, James.

Nonaggregatability, Inclusiveness, and the Theory of Focal Value: *Nichomachean Ethics* 1.7.1097b16-20. Lawrence, Gavin.

Nonuse Values and the Environment: Economic and Ethical Motivations. Crowards, Tom.

Normativité et vérification immanentes des valeurs chez Max Scheler. Porée, Jérôme.

Obligaciones humanas Apuntes para la formulación de una idea. Messuti, Ana.

On the Crisis of Culture, Its Values and Value Education (in German). Braun, Walter.

On the Intrinsic Value of Pleasures. Feldman, Fred.

On Values: Universal or Relative?. Aarnio, Aulis.

Plural Values and Environmental Valuation. Beckerman, Wilfred and Pasek, Joanna.

Pluralism, Liberalism, and the Role of Overriding Values. Lawrence, Matthew.

Powers of Desire: Deleuze and Mores. Schérer, René.

Qual è la destra che manca in Italia: Per un discorso realistico sul conservatorismo e le istituzioni. Cofrancesco, Dino.

Rasvihary Das on 'Value of Doubt': Some Reflections. Ghosh, Raghunath.

Re-Examining the Influence of Individual Values on Ethical Decision Making. Glover, Saundra H, Bumpus, Minnette A and Logan, John E (& others).

Reconsidering Zero-Sum Value: It's How You Play the Game. Smith, Tara.

Reflective Solidarity. Dean, Jodi.

Ressentiment et valeurs morales: Max Scheler, critique de Nietzsche. Glauser, Richard.

Risk and the Value of Information in Irreversible Decisions. Gersbach, Hans.

Rolston, Naturogenic Value and Genuine Biocentrism. Thomas, Emyr Vaughan.

Sexual Activity, Consent, Mistaken Belief, and *Mens Rea*. Tittle, Peg.

Spinoza's Relativistic Aesthetics. Rice, Lee C.

Surrogate Family Values: The Refeminization of Teaching. Thompson, Audrey.

The Intrinsic Value of Non-Basic States of Affairs. Carlson, Erik.

The Structure of Radical Probabilism. Skyrms, Brian.

The Sure Thing Principle and the Value of Information. Schlee, Edward E.

The Value of Truth and the Care of the Soul. Witherall, Arthur.

The Values of Life. Den Hartogh, Govert.

Two Conceptions of Artistic Value. Stecker, Robert A.

Universal Values, Behavioral Ethics and Entrepreneurship. Clarke, Ruth and Aram, John.

Value Monism, Value Pluralism, and Music Education: Sparshott as Fox. Alperson, Philip.

Values Behind the Market: Kant's Response to the *Wealth of Nations*. Fleischacker, Samuel.

Values, Reasons and Perspectives. Thomas, Alan.

Violations of Present-Value Maximization in Income Choice. Gigliotti, Gary and Sopher, Barry.

What Cannot Be Evaluated Cannot Be Evaluated, and it Cannot Be Supervalued Either. Fodor, Jerry A and Lepore, Ernest.

¿Es el "trilema de Fishkin" un verdadero trilema?. Rivera López, Eduardo.

¿Importan los hechos para los juicios morales? Una defensa contra la navaja de Hume basada en la noción de coste de oportunidad. Schwartz, Pedro.

## VALUE FREE

"Avalutatività come principio metodico nella logica delle scienze sociali" in *Momenti di Storia della Logica e di Storia della Filosofia*, Guetti, Carla (ed). Bianco, Franco.

*Streitgespräche und Kontroversen in der Philosophie des 20.Jahrhunderts*. Wuchterl, Kurt.

## VALUE THEORY

Ecocentrism and Persons. Baxter, Brian H.

Facts About Natural Values. Elliot, Robert.

Infinite Value and Finitely Additive Value Theory. Vallentyne, Peter and Kagan, Shelly.

The Personal Lives of Strong Evaluators: Identity, Pluralism, and Ontology in Charles Taylor's Value Theory. Anderson, Joel.

## VAN BUREN, J

The Hermeneutics of Origin: Arché and the Anarchic in John Van Buren's *The Young Heidegger*. Bambach, Charles.

## VAN CAMP, J

Dance Metaphors: A Reply to Julie Van Camp. Whittock, Trevor.

## VAN CLEVE, J

Response to Commentators. Wright, Crispin.

## VAN DER WAALS, J

Philosophical Issues in the History of Chemistry. Gavroglu, Kostas.

## VAN FRAASSEN, B

A Paradox for Empiricism (?). Douven, Igor.

Confirmation, Explanation, and Logical Strength. Nelson, David E.

Facts, Semantics and Intuitionism. Akama, Seiki.

## VIRTUE

The Interdependence of Intellectual and Moral Virtue in Aquinas. Peterson, John.

The Limited Unity of Virtue. Badhwar, Neera Kapur.

The Management of Instability and Incompleteness: Clinical Ethics and Abstract Expressionism. McCullough, Laurence B.

The Nature of Ethical Theorizing in the Eudemian Ethics. Moravcsik, Julius M.

The Relation between Life, Conatus and Virtue in Spinoza's Philosophy. Zac, Sylvain.

The Virtue in Self-Interest. Slote, Michael.

The Virtue of the Free Spirit (in Serbo-Croatian). Gerhardt, Volker.

The Virtues in Psychiatric Practice. Mann, David W.

The Virtues of Externalism. Jacobs, Jonathan.

The Wisdom of the Egoist: The Moral and Political Implications of Valuing the Self. Hampton, Jean.

Theoretical Virtues and Theological Construction. Shalkowski, Scott A.

Thoreauvian Patriotism as an Environmental Virtue. Cafaro, Philip.

Those Who Can, Do: A Response to Sidney Gendin's "Am I Wicked?". Warren, Dona.

Tolerance & Forgiveness: Virtues or Vices?. Smith, Tara.

Two Problems with Knowing the Future. Hunt, David P.

Un siglo de oro para la Etica. Guisán Seijas, Esperanza.

Varieties of Virtue Ethics. Oakley, Justin.

Virtue as Knowledge: Objections from the Philosophy of Mind. Little, Margaret Olivia.

Virtue, Happiness, and Intelligibility. Lemos, John.

Virtues. Tugendhat, Ernst.

Virtues, Opportunities, and the Right To Do Wrong. Cohen, Andrew I.

Virtuous Markets: The Market as School of the Virtues. Maitland, Ian.

Virtuous Peers in Work Organizations. Moberg, Dennis.

Why Modesty Is a Virtue. Schueler, G F.

Wie einer beschaffen ist, so erscheint ihm das Ziel: Die Rolle des moralischen Habitus bei der Beurteilung des Handlungsziels nach Thomas von Aquin. Darge, Rolf.

## VIRTUE ETHICS

"Theoretische und angewandte Ethik: Paradigmen, Begründungen, Bereiche" in Angewandte Ethik: Die Bereichsethiken und ihre theoretische Fundierung, Nida-Rümelin, Julian (ed). Nida-Rümelin, Julian.

The Christian Case for Virtue Ethics. Kotva, Joseph J.

A Dialogue Between Virtue Ethics and Care Ethics. Benner, Patricia.

A Virtue Ethics Approach to Aldo Leopold's Land Ethic. Shaw, Bill.

Engagement and Suffering in Responsible Caregiving: On Overcoming Maleficience in Health Care. Schultz, Dawson S and Carnevale, Franco A.

The Intellectual Bias of Virtue Ethics. Putman, Daniel A.

The Structure of Aristotle's Ethical Theory: Is It Teleological or a Virtue Ethics?. Santas, Gerasimos.

Virtue Ethics and the Problem of Indirection: A Pluralistic Value-Centred Approach. Swanton, Christine.

When Preservationism Doesn't Preserve. Schmidtz, David.

## VIRTUOSITY

Virtuosity as a Performance Concept: A Philosophical Analysis. Howard, Vernon A.

## VISION

see also Seeing

"A Mind-Body Problem at the Surface of Objects" in Perception, Villanueva, Enrique (ed). Johnston, Mark.

"Discourses of Vision in Seventeenth-Century Metaphysics" in Sites of Vision, Levin, David Michael (ed). Wilson, Catherine.

"Ducks and Rabbits: Visuality in Wittgenstein" in Sites of Vision, Levin, David Michael (ed). Earle, William James.

"Hannah Arendt: The Activity of the Spectator" in Sites of Vision, Levin, David Michael (ed). Birmingham, Peg.

"How to Write the History of Vision: Understanding the Relationship between Berkeley and Descartes" in Sites of Vision, Levin, David Michael (ed). Atherton, Margaret L.

"Keeping Foucault and Derrida in Sight: Panopticism and the Politics of Subversion" in Sites of Vision, Levin, David Michael (ed). Levin, David Michael.

"Materialist Mutations of the Bilderverbot" in Sites of Vision, Levin, David Michael (ed). Comay, Rebecca.

"Molineux's Question" in Perception, Villanueva, Enrique (ed). Campbell, John.

"Philosophy as Critique and as Vision" in The Recovery of Philosophy in America: Essays in Honor of John Edwin Smith, Kasulis, Thomas P (ed). Westphal, Merold.

"Shape Properties and Perception" in Perception, Villanueva, Enrique (ed). Ludwig, Kirk A.

"Sighting the Spirit: The Rhetorical Visions of Geist in Hegel's Encyclopedia" in Sites of Vision, Levin, David Michael (ed). Smith, John H.

Colour Vision: A Study in Cognitive Science and the Philosophy of Perception. Thompson, Evan.

Problems of Vision: Rethinking the Causal Theory of Perception. Vision, Gerald.

Sites of Vision. Levin, David Michael (ed).

A Clearer Vision. Shapiro, Lawrence A.

Augustine's Three Visions and Three Heavens in Some Early Medieval Florilegia. Moreira, Isabel.

Can Colour Be Reduced to Anything?. Dedrick, Don.

Content, Computation, and Individualism in Vision Theory. Butler, Keith.

From Common Roots to a Broader Vision: A Pragmatic Thrust of European Phenomenology. Bourgeois, Patrick L.

Il problema del 'Desiderium naturale videndi Deum' nell'ottica tomista della partecipazione secondo la prospettiva di Cornelio Fabro. Nardone, Marco.

Individualism and Marr's Computational Theory of Vision. Butler, Keith.

La mediatizzazione del soggetto. Fadini, Ubaldo.

Language and Reality, One More Time. Gill, Jerry H.

Les rapports entre raison et foi à la lumière de la métaphore de la vision. Vienne, Jean-Michel.

Silence Revisited: Taking the Sight Out of Auditory Qualities. Muldoon, Mark S.

The Dispositional Account of Colour. Pitson, Tony.

The Evolution of Color Vision without Color. Hall, Richard J.

Theory-Ladenness of Observation and Evidence. Basu, Prajit K.

True Theories, False Colors. Clark, Austen.

## VISUAL

"Descartes's Scientific Illustrations and 'la grand mécanique de la nature'" in Picturing Knowledge, Baigrie, Brian S (ed). Baigrie, Brian S.

"Dewey's Critique of Democratic Visual Culture and its Political Implications" in Sites of Vision, Levin, David Michael (ed). Ezrahi, Yaron.

"Difference and the Ruin of Representation in Gilles Deleuze" in Sites of Vision, Levin, David Michael (ed). Olkowski, Dorothea.

"Embodying the Eye of Humanism: Giambattista Vico and the Eye of Ingenium" in Sites of Vision, Levin, David Michael (ed). Luft, Sandra Rudnick.

"For Now We See Through a Glass Darkly": The Systematics of Hegel's Visual Imagery" in Sites of Vision, Levin, David Michael (ed). Russon, John.

"From Acoustics to Optics: The Rise of the Metaphysical and Demise of the Melodic in Aristotle's Poetics" in Sites of Vision, Levin, David Michael (ed). Smith, P Christopher.

"Illustrating Chemistry" in Picturing Knowledge, Baigrie, Brian S (ed). Knight, David.

"Visual Models and Scientific Judgment" in Picturing Knowledge, Baigrie, Brian S (ed). Giere, Ronald N.

"Visual Representation in Archaeology: Depicting the Missing-Link in Human Origins" in Picturing Knowledge, Baigrie, Brian S (ed). Moser, Stephanie.

Philosophy and the Arts: Seeing and Believing. Harrison, Andrew.

Picturing Knowledge: Historical and Philosophical Problems Concerning the Use of Art in Science. Baigrie, Brian S (ed).

Ten Problems of Consciousness: A Representational Theory of the Phenomenal Mind. Tye, Michael.

Individual Style in Photographic Art. Warburton, Nigel.

On Non-Verbal Representation. Brook, Donald.

On the Use of Visualizations in the Practice of Science. Sargent, Pauline.

On Walter Benjamin and Modern Optical Phenomena. Osamu, Maekawa.

Photography as Narrative (in Japanese). Kiyokazu, Nishimura.

Sparkle and Shine. Leddy, Thomas.

Visual Aesthetic Education: Its Place in General Education. Ahmed, Halim Obeid.

Visual Metaphors. Jensen, Hans Siggaard.

## VISUAL ART

Showing Pictures: Aesthetics and the Art Gallery. Feagin, Susan L and Subler, Craig A.

## VITAL

Challenge to Natural Law: The Vital Law. Black, Percy.

## VITALISM

Explaining Emergence: Towards an Ontology of Levels. Emmeche, Claus, Koppe, Simo and Stjernfelt, Frederik.

Forget Vitalism: Foucault and Lebensphilosophie. Ransom, John S.

Gaos y la religión. Valdés, Sylvia.

The Flesh and the Spirit: Anne Bradstreet and Seventeenth Century Dualism, Materialism, Vitalism and Reformed Theology. Whelan, Timothy.

## VITALITY

C'è un organismo in questo testo?. Keller, Evelyn Fox.

## VIVEKANANDA

Professor Prasad on Working Out a Lead from Swami Vivekananda: Some Reflections. Ghosh, Ranjan K.

Relevance of Swami Vivekanand's Concept of Evil Today. Sinha, Rani Rupmati.

## VIVES, J

La amenaza latente del vagabundo en la literatura política del siglo XVI. Rivera García, Antonio.

## VIVES, L

Traiciones a Luis Vives. Calero, Francisco.

## VIVISECTION

Brute Science: Dilemmas of Animal Experimentation. Shanks, Niall and LaFollette, Hugh.

**WAR**

War Is Not Just an Event: Reflections on the Significance of Everyday Violence. Cuomo, Chris J.

War-Pacifism. Cochran, David Carroll.

**WARBURG, A**

Toward Art beyond the Modern World: Aby Warburg and the Comparative Study of Art. Kato, Tetsuhiro.

**WARBURTON, W**

*Hume on Miracles.* Tweyman, Stanley (ed).

**WARFARE**

A Chinese Critique on Western Ways of Warfare. Hagen, Kurtis.

**WARRANT**

Internalism, Externalism and the No-Defeater Condition. Bergmann, Michael.

More On Warrant's Entailing Truth. Merricks, Trenton.

Plantinga's Case Against Naturalistic Epistemology. Fales, Evan.

Premise Acceptability, Deontology, Internalism, Justification. Freeman, James B.

**WARREN, K**

Warren, Plumwood, a Rock and a Snake: Some Doubts about Critical Ecological Feminism. Andrews, John N.

**WASHINGTON, B**

How We Got Over: The Moral Teachings of The African-American Church on Business Ethics. Trimiew, Darryl M and Greene, Michael.

**WASHINGTON, C**

Quotation Marks: Demonstratives or Demonstrations?. Reimer, Marga.

**WASTE**

Waste in Medicine. Baumrin, Bernard.

**WATER**

*Real Process: How Logic and Chemistry Combine in Hegel's Philosophy of Nature.* Burbidge, John W.

**WATKINS, J**

"Racionalidad práctica e inducción: la propuesta neopopperiana de John Watkins" in *La racionalidad: su poder y sus límites,* Nudler, Oscar (ed). Comesaña, Manuel.

**WATSON, R**

Representation and Resemblance: A Review Essay of Richard A. Watson's *Representational Ideas: From Plato to Patricia Churchland.* Meyering, Theo C.

**WAVE**

The Equivalence Myth of Quantum Mechanics—Part I. Muller, F A.

The 'Reality' of the Wave Function: Measurements, Entropy and Quantum Cosmology. Zeh, Heinz-Dieter.

Waves, Particles, and Explanatory Coherence. Eliasmith, Chris and Thagard, Paul.

**WAVE THEORY**

The Ontological Interpretation of the Wave Function of the Universe. Smith, Quentin.

Trouble in Paradise? Problems for Bohm's Theory. Callender, Craig and Weingard, Robert.

**WAYNE, A**

Bayesianism and Diverse Evidence: A Reply to Andrew Wayne. Myrvold, Wayne C.

Bayesianism and the Value of Diverse Evidence. Steel, Daniel.

Wayne, Horwich, and Evidential Diversity. Fitelson, Branden.

**WEAK**

A Very Weak Square Principle. Foreman, Matthew and Magidor, Menachem.

On the Completeness of First Degree Weakly Aggregative Modal Logics. Apostoli, Peter.

Strong Versus Weak Quantum Consequence Operations. Malinowski, Jacek.

**WEAKNESS**

Weakness of Will. Buss, Sarah.

**WEALTH**

The Challenge of Wealth: Jewish Business Ethics. Tamari, Meir.

**WEBER, M**

"Jacob Burckhardt and Max Weber: Two Conceptions of the Origin of the Modern World" in *The Ancients and the Moderns,* Lilly, Reginald (ed). Hardtwig, Wolfgang.

"L'indagine storico-universale di Max Weber sul 'razionalismo occidentale' tra lo storicismo e Nietzsche" in *Lo Storicismo e la Sua Storia: Temi, Problemi, Prospettive,* Cacciatore, Giuseppe (ed). Di Marco, Giuseppe Antonio.

"Tönnies versus Weber: El debate Comunitarista desde la teoría social" in *Liberalismo y Comunitarismo: Derechos Humanos y Democracia,* Monsalve Solórzano, Alfonso (ed). Villacañas Berlanga, José L.

"Weber's Ideal Types as Models in the Social Sciences" in *Verstehen and Humane Understanding,* O'Hear, Anthony (ed). Weinert, Friedel.

*Social Cohesion and Legal Coercion: A Critique of Weber, Durkheim, and Marx.* Shaskolsky Sheleff, Leon.

A Note on Weber and Lukács (in Hungarian). Tarr, Zoltan.

El decisionismo valorativo: Entre las instancias últimas y la racionalidad crítica. Flax, Javier.

Gli "ultimi uomini": a proposito di un libro su Max Weber. Salzano, Giorgio.

Hegel und Weber im Vergleich: Die Bahnen der Rationalität. Senigaglia, Cristiana.

Husserl, Weber, Freud, and the Method of the Human Sciences. McIntosh, Donald.

Idiographic Theorizing and Ideal Types: Max Weber's Methodology of Social Science. Collin, Finn.

La crisi del sapere moderno. Alheit, Peter.

Max Weber on Ethics Case Consultation: A Methodological Critique of the Conference on Evaluation of Ethics Consultation. Degnin, Francis.

Max Weber: Sugerencias para una "reconstrucción". Crespo, Ricardo F.

Sorpresa e giustificazione: Una discussione dell'esempio weberiano della madre intemperante. Paracchini, Franco.

The Concept of a National Community. Gilbert, Paul.

The Norm and History. Travar, Dusan.

Weber e lo spirito del capitalismo: Storia di un problema e nuove prospettive. Burgos, Juan Manuel.

**WEBERN, A**

*Is There Truth in Art?.* Rapaport, Herman.

**WEIL, E**

The Figures of Subjectivity in Éric Weil's *Logique de la philosophie* (in French). Kirscher, Gilbert.

**WEIL, S**

"Gravity" in the Thought of Simone Weil. Pirrucello, Ann.

Il re nudo: L'immaginario del potere in Simone Weil. Tommasi, Wanda.

The Love of God and Neighbor in Simone Weil's Philosophy. Stephenson, Wendell.

**WEININGER, O**

Wittgenstein's Women: The Philosophical Significance of Wittgenstein's Misogyny. Szabados, Béla.

**WEINSTEIN, J**

A Brief Response to Jack Russell Weinstein. Reinsmith, William.

**WEINSTEIN, M**

The Ought-Is Question: Discovering The Modern in Post-Modernism. Johnson, David Kenneth.

**WEINTRAUB, R**

The Impossibility of Interpersonal Utility. Hausman, Daniel.

**WEISS, P**

Paul Weiss's Methods(s) and System(s). Kennedy, Kevin E.

**WELFARE**

"The Moral Uniqueness of the Human Animal" in *Human Lives: Critical Essays on Consequentialist Bioethics,* Oderberg, David S (ed). Scarlett, Brian.

*Darf Pedro sein Land verkaufen? Versuch einer sozialwissenschaftlichen Perspektive in der Ökonomik.* Lohmann, Karl R.

*Democracy and Disagreement.* Gutmann, Amy and Thompson, Dennis.

*Equality: Selected Readings.* Pojman, Louis (ed) and Westmoreland, Robert (ed).

*On Economic Inequality.* Sen, Amartya.

*The Logic of the Gift: Toward an Ethic of Generosity.* Schrift, Alan D (ed).

*Theories of Distributive Justice.* Roemer, John E.

*Welfare, Happiness, and Ethics.* Sumner, L W.

Can Old-Age Social Insurance Be Justified. Shapiro, Daniel J.

Clients or Citizens?. Bender, Thomas.

De Minimis and Equity in Risk. Mosler, Karl.

Ethical Limits to Domestication. Sandoe, Peter, Holtug, Nils and Simonsen, H B.

Freedom and Moral Diversity: The Moral Failures of Health Care in the Welfare State. Engelhardt Jr, H Tristram.

Gandhian Concept of Planned Society. Sharma, Akshaya Kumar.

Identity Politics as a Transposition of Fraser's Needs Politics. Tittle, Peg.

La riforma del Welfare e un'idea di equità. Veca, Salvatore.

Limousine Liberals, Welfare Conservatives: On Belief, Interest, and Inconsistency in Democratic Discourse. Stark, Andrew.

On the Subjectivity of Welfare. Sobel, David.

Privatization of Social Security: The Transition Issue. Ferrara, Peter J.

Progress in Reconciliation: Evidence from the Right and the Left. Sterba, James P.

Special Obligations to Compatriots. Mason, Andrew.

Standards Versus Struggle: The Failure of Public Housing and the Welfare-State Impulse. Husock, Howard.

The Forum. Gluck, John P and Shapiro, Kenneth J.

The Moral Status of Animal Training. Dixon, Beth A.

Two Conceptions of Welfare: Voluntarism and Incorporationism. Davies, Stephen.

Welfare-State Retrenchment: Playing the National Card. Borchert, Jens.

Welfarism in Moral Theory. Moore, Andrew and Crisp, Roger.

**WELFARE STATE**

*The Welfare State.* Paul, Ellen Frankel (ed), Miller, Fred D (ed) and Paul, Jeffrey (ed).

Aspectos políticos del pensamiento de J. Habermas: una lectura crítica. Bonnet, Alberto.

Identity Politics and the Welfare State. Wolfe, Alan and Klausen, Jytte.

The Problem of Forfeiture in the Welfare State. Epstein, Richard A.

## WITTGENSTEIN

Der Wille als Träger des Ethischen—Überlegungen zur Stellung des Willens in der Frühphilosophie Ludwig Wittgensteins. Haag, Johannes.

Do Wittgenstein's Forms of Life Inaugurate a Kantian Project of Transcendental Idealism?. Kanthamani, A.

Does the Grammar of Seeing Aspects Imply a Kantian Concept?. Kanthamani, A.

El desmigajador de la realidad: Wittgenstein y las matemáticas. Espinoza, Miguel.

El Naturalismo Trascendental del Ultimo Wittgenstein. Krebs, Víctor J.

Forward to Aristotle: The Case for a Hybrid Ontology. Harré, Rom.

Hay Problemas Filosóficos? Reflexiones Metafilosóficas Sobre Algunas Ideas Wittgensteineanas. Scotto, Carolina.

Hegel's Logic as a Theory of Meaning. Stekeler-Weithofer, Pirmin.

Hertzian Objects in Wittgenstein's *Tractatus*. Grasshoff, Gerd.

How Can Pictures Be Propositions?. Shier, David.

How to Read Wittgenstein. Cook, John W.

Husserl, Wittgenstein and the Snark: Intentionality and Social Naturalism. Gillett, Grant.

Internal Relations and Analyticity: Wittgenstein and Quine. Hymers, Michael.

Interprétation, signification et "usage" chez Wittgenstein. Sauvé, Denis.

Kant and Wittgenstein: Philosophy, Necessity and Representation. Glock, Hans-Johann.

Kein Etwas, aber auch nicht ein Nichts!: Kann die Grammatik tatsächlich täuschen?. Gaskin, Richard.

L'inconscio come finzione linguistica. Ugolini, Consuelo.

La concepción de "leyes de la naturaleza" en el *Tractatus* de Ludwig Wittgenstein. Balderas Rosas, Gloria del Carmen.

La concepción wittgensteiniana de los objetos en el *Tractatus*. García Berger, Mario.

Language and Problems of Knowledge. Chomsky, Noam.

Life, Culture and Value: Reflections on Wittgenstein's *Culture and Value*. Pradhan, R C.

Living in a Wittgensteinian World: Beyond Theory to a Poetics of Practices. Shotter, John.

Ludwig Wittgenstein: Matemáticas y ética. Rivera, Silvia.

Norman Malcolm, *Wittgensteinian Themes*. Winch, Peter.

Omtrent de kloof, rondom de rite. Cortois, Paul.

On Understanding: Standing Under Wittgenstein. Goswami, Chinmoy.

On What Sort of Speech Act Wittgenstein's *Investigations* Is and Why It Matters. Leiber, Justin.

On Wittgenstein on Cognitive Science. Proudfoot, Diane.

On Wittgenstein's Philosophy of Mathematics II. Conant, James.

Paul Virilio and the Articulation of Post-Reality. Hanes, Marc.

Philosophical Investigations, Section 1—Setting the Stage. Raatzsch, Richard.

Philosophy as Experience, as Elucidation and as Profession: An Attempt to Reconstruct Early Wittgenstein's Philosophy. Linhe, Han.

Practices and Actions: A Wittgensteinian Critique of Bourdieu and Giddens. Schatzki, Theodore R.

Problemas Filosóficos y Filosofías del Límite. Nudler, Oscar.

Rational Reconstruction: Preconditions and Limits. Iliescu, Adrian-Paul.

Response to Kanthamani's Comment. Pradhan, R C.

Response: Language and Thought. Russow, Lilly-Marlene.

Scetticismo, riconoscimento, riscoperta dell'ordinario: La filosofia di Stanley Cavell. Sparti, Davide and Lecci, Bernardo.

Solipsism and First Person/Third Person Asymmetries. Child, William.

Solipsism and Self-Reference. O'Brien, Lucy F.

Solipsism and Subjectivity. Bell, David.

The Community View. Canfield, John V.

The Epistemological Argument Against Socialism: A Wittgensteinian Critique of Hayek and Giddens. Pleasants, Nigel.

The General Form of a Proposition in an Especially Perspicuous Language. Daniels, Charles.

The Originality of Wittgenstein's Investigation of Solipsism. Pears, David.

The Skeptic and the Hoverfly (A Teleo-Computational View of Rule-Following). Miscevic, Nenad.

The 'Truth' in Solipsism, and Wittgenstein's Rejection of the A Priori. Sullivan, Peter M.

Theology as Grammar. Brenner, William H.

Theories of Understanding and Hermeneutical Problematic in Contemporary Anglo-American Philosophy (Czech). Hroch, Jaroslav.

Tractarian Support for a Nonpropositional Paradigm. Bozicevic, Vanda.

Transcendental Constraints and Transcendental Features. Sacks, Mark.

Truth and Thickness. Tietz, John.

Unconfigured Tractarian Objects. Page, James.

Wahrnehmung und Mentale Repräsentation. Pauen, Michael.

What Happens When Wittgenstein Asks "What Happens When...?". Gendlin, E T.

What Makes Language Possible? Ethological Foundationalism in Reid and Wittgenstein. Robinson, Daniel N and Harré, Rom.

What Wittgenstein Learned from William James. Goodman, Russell B.

Winch and Instrumental Pluralism: A Reply to B. D. Lerner. Keita, L D.

Wissenschaftstheorie oder Ästhetik der Wunder?. Gräfrath, Bernd.

Wittgenstein and Animal Minds. Lynch, Joseph J.

Wittgenstein and the Doctrine of Kinaesthesis. Candlish, Stewart.

Wittgenstein et la fin du psychologisme. Chiesa, Curzio.

Wittgenstein et son oeuvre posthume. Marion, Mathieu.

Wittgenstein on Certainty. Good, Michael.

Wittgenstein's Musical Understanding. Worth, Sarah E.

Wittgenstein's Women: The Philosophical Significance of Wittgenstein's Misogyny. Szabados, Béla.

Wittgenstein, Heidegger and Humility. Cooper, David E.

Wittgenstein, Tolstoy and the Meaning of Life. Thompson, Caleb.

Wittgensteins Begriff der "Aesthetischen Erklärung" als Paradigma für die Philosophie. Schönbaumsfeld, Genia.

'Now I Can Go On:' Wittgenstein and Our Embodied Embeddedness in the 'Hurly-Burly' of Life. Shotter, John.

## WOJTYLA, K

Phenomenological Personalism: Edith Stein and Karol Wojtyla (in Polish). Póltawski, Andrzej.

## WOLD, W

L'ethos dell'intersoggettività nei romanzi di Friedrich Heinrich Jacobi. Iovino, Serenella.

## WOLF, K

Medieval Historiography. Birns, Nicholas.

## WOLF, S

Liberating Constraints. Haji, Ishtiyaque.

Sanity and Irresponsibility. Wilson, Paul Eddy.

## WOLFF

Il Saggio sopra la Filosofia in genere di Lodovico Arnaldi: una traduzione settecentesca inedita del *Discursus praeliminaris* di Christian Wolff. Von Wille, Dagmar.

La contribución de Christian Wolff (1679-1754) a la popularización de las matemáticas en la primera mitad del siglo XVIII. Nobre, Sergio.

## WOLFF, J

Contractual Justice: A Modest Defence. Barry, Brian.

Voting and Motivation. Graham, Keith.

## WOLIN, S

Beyond Postmodernism: Restoring the Primal Quest for Meaning to Political Inquiry. Herman, Louis G.

## WOLINSKY, F

Response to "Further Exploration of the Relationship between Medical Education and Moral Development" by Donnie J. Self, DeWitt C. Baldwin, Jr., and Frederic D. Wolinsky (CQ Vol 5, No 3). Burack, Jeffrey H.

## WOLLAN, L

"A Horse Chestnut Is Not a Chestnut Horse": A Refutation of Bray, Davis, MacGregor, and Wollan. Oates, Stephen B.

## WOLLHEIM, R

Een anatomie van de beeldende kunst. Herzog, Katalin.

## WOLTERSTORFF, N

Locke, "The Father of Modernity"?: A Discussion of Wolterstorff's *John Locke and the Ethics of Belief*. Schouls, Peter A.

## WOMAN

see also Female, Feminism, Women

Aspekte internationaler Ethik. Betzler, Monika.

Did the Enlightenment Just Happen to Men?. Whyte, Philip.

La donna, tra ironia e diritto. Avitabile, Luisa.

Putative Self-Defense and Rules of Imputation In Defense of the Battered Woman. Byrd, B Sharon.

Questions of Proximity: "Woman's Place" in Derrida and Irigaray. Armour, Ellen T.

Violencia femenina y autorreferencia. Schultz, Margarita.

What is a Woman? Butler and Beauvoir on the Foundations of the Sexual Difference. Heinämaa, Sara.

## WOMEN

"A Response to Jean Hampton's Feminism" in *The Liberation Debate: Rights at Issue*, Leahy, Michael (ed). Flew, Antony.

"Afterword" in *The Liberation Debate: Rights at Issue*, Leahy, Michael (ed). Leahy, Michael.

"Decoding" Informed Consent: Insights from Women regarding Breast Cancer Susceptibility Testing. Geller, Gail, Strauss, Misha and Bernhardt, Barbara A (& others).

"Hampton's Reply" in *The Liberation Debate: Rights at Issue*, Leahy, Michael (ed). Hampton, Jean.

"Love Undigitized" in *Love Analyzed*, Lamb, Roger E. De Sousa, Ronald.

"On a Woman's Obligation to Have an Abortion" in *Reproduction, Technology, and Rights: Biomedical Ethics Reviews*, Humber, James M (ed). Robinson, Bambi E S.

"Technologies of the Self" in *Critical Studies: Ethics and the Subject*, Simms, Karl (ed). Ball, Elaine.

"The Case for Feminism" in *The Liberation Debate: Rights at Issue*, Leahy, Michael (ed). Hampton, Jean.

"The Consequences of Single Motherhood" in *Sex, Preference, and Family: Essays on Law and Nature*, Nussbaum, Martha C (ed). McLanahan, Sara.

"Women-Animals-Machines: A Grammar for a Wittgensteinian Ecofeminism" in *Ecofeminism: Women, Culture, Nature*, Warren, Karen J (ed). Lee-Lampshire, Wendy.

*Automatic Woman: The Representation of Woman in Surrealism*. Conley, Katharine.

**WOODWARD, R**

Christianity, Commerce and the Canon: Josiah Tucker and Richard Woodward on Political Economy. Young, B W.

**WORD**

"La parole à la poule" in *Philosophy and Democracy in Intercultural Perspective,* Kimmerle, Heinz (ed). De Schipper, Elisabeth H.

"Parole et démocratie" in *Philosophy and Democracy in Intercultural Perspective,* Kimmerle, Heinz (ed). Konaté, Yacouba.

*New Essays on Human Understanding.* Bennett, Jonathan (trans) and Remnant, Peter (trans).

*Verbum: Word and Idea in Aquinas Volume 2.* Crowe, Frederick E (ed) and Doran, Robert M (ed).

Abusing Use. Glock, H J.

Ai margini del discorso poetico. Dell'Erba, Paola.

Believing the Word: A Proposal about Knowing Other Persons. Cary, Phillip.

Concept and Event. Patton, Paul.

Fawkes On Indicator Words. Smythe, Thomas W.

La recuperación de la palabra: Perspectivas hermenéuticas sobre la cuestión del lenguaje. Revilla, Carmen.

Lenguaje significativo y no significativo: *El Kaspar* de Peter Handke. Gutiérrez, Edgardo.

Making Things with Words: Plato on Mimesis in *Republic.* Lycos, Kimon.

Man as Wolf (Once More). Hauksson, Thorleifur.

Nada existe donde faltan las palabras: la *quidditas* retórica de Vico y la metafísica de la evidencia. Marín-Casanova, José Antonio.

On the Properties of Discourse: A Translation of *Tractatus de Proprietatibus Sermonum* (Author Anonymous). Barney, Stephen (trans), Lewis, Wendy (trans) and Normore, Calvin G (& other trans).

Protesi, ovvero la metamorfosi. Marchis, Vittorio.

The Practice of Philosophy. Nevo, Isaac.

The Word as Ultimate Reality: The Christian Dialogical Personalism of Ferdinand Ebner. Kunszt, György.

**WORK**

*On Economic Inequality.* Sen, Amartya.

Do Complex Moral Reasoners Experience Greater Ethical Work Conflict?. Mason, E Sharon and Mudrack, Peter E.

Education, Work and Well-Being. White, John.

El concepto de 'trabajo' en Hegel. León, Virgilio C.

El trabajo como división de funciones. Rodríguez Sedano, Alfredo.

Ethical Work Climate as a Factor in the Development of Person-Organization Fit. Sims, Randi L and Keon, Thomas L.

Trabajo Filosófico y Comunidad Filosófica. Parra, Lisímaco.

Virtuous Peers in Work Organizations. Moberg, Dennis.

**WORK OF ART**

*Mens Sana in Corpore Sano?* Reflexoes sobre o Enigma do Corpo. Simao, Cristiana V.

A Obra como Facto Comunicativo. Rodrigues, Manuel J.

**WORKER**

Myth, Measurement, and the Minimum Wage: Sound and Fury Signifying What?. Whitman, Glen.

The Complexly Constructed Citizen-Worker: Her/His Centrality to the Struggle for Radical Democratic Politics and Education. Brosio, Richard A.

**WORKING CLASS**

Jack London y El Talón de Hierro. Laso Prieto, José Maria.

**WORKPLACE**

Drug Testing and Privacy: Why Contract Arguments Do Not Work. Carson, A Scott.

Eliminating the Barriers to Employment Equity in the Canadian Workplace. Falkenberg, L E and Boland, L.

Liberal and Communitarian Defenses of Workplace Privacy. Manning, Rita C.

On the Persistence of Sexual Harassment in the Workplace. Baugh, S Gayle.

Technology, Workplace Privacy and Personhood. Brown, William S.

The Trivialization of Ethics or Ethics Programs in the Workplace: A Cautionary Tale. Marks, Joel.

**WORKS**

Comprensión e interpretación de las obras filosóficas. Sánchez Meca, Diego.

El contraluz de Vitoria en el Siglo de las Luces. Ocaña García, Marcelino.

Hegel em Berlim—Discurso Inaugural. De Sousa, Maria Carmelita H.

How Did Russell Write *The Principles of Mathematics* 1903?. Grattan-Guinness, Ivor.

La estructura formal del *De causa Dei* de Thomas Bradwardine. Verdú Berganza, Ignacio.

Les *Lectures traversières* de Louis Marin. Cavaillé, Jean-Pierre.

Note su traduzioni manoscritte delle opere cartesiane. Guerrini, Luigi.

Noticia sobre la edición de las *Obras Completas* de Manuel García Morente. Palacios, Juan Miguel and Rovira, Rogelio.

Sobre los sentidos objetivo y sujetivo del trabajo según Polo. Pintado, Patricia.

Vida y concepción del Mundo: Un texto olvidado de Karl Ernst von Baer (1860). Market, Oswaldo.

Wittgenstein et son oeuvre posthume. Marion, Mathieu.

**WORKSHOP**

Sym-Phenomenologizing: Talking Shop. Casey, Edward S.

**WORLD**

*see also* External World, Possible World

"A Mind-Body Problem at the Surface of Objects" in *Perception,* Villanueva, Enrique (ed). Johnston, Mark.

"Bayle, l'"anima mundi" e Vico" in *Pierre Bayle e l'Italia,* Bianchi, Lorenzo. Costa, Gustavo.

"El mundo como imagen: Acerca de Fichte y Schleiermacher" in *El inicio del Idealismo alemán,* Market, Oswaldo. Flamarique, Lourdes.

"Getting Acquainted with Perception" in *Perception,* Villanueva, Enrique (ed). Sosa, David.

"Is the External World Invisible?" in *Perception,* Villanueva, Enrique (ed). Johnston, Mark.

"L'europeizzazione come problema europeo" in *Geofilosofia,* Bonesio, Luisa (ed). Pöggler, Otto.

"McDowell's Direct Realism and Platonic Naturalism" in *Perception,* Villanueva, Enrique (ed). Gibson, Roger.

"Perception and Rational Constraint: McDowell's *Mind and World*" in *Perception,* Villanueva, Enrique (ed). Brandom, Robert.

"Précis of *Mind and World*" in *Perception,* Villanueva, Enrique (ed). McDowell, John.

"Reply to Gibson, Byrne, and Brandom" in *Perception,* Villanueva, Enrique (ed). McDowell, John.

"Representación, realidad y mundo en el Tractatus de Wittgenstein" in *Verdad: lógica, representación y mundo,* Villegas Forero, L. Bonnín Aguiló, Francisco.

"Spin Control: Comment on John McDowell's *Mind and World*" in *Perception,* Villanueva, Enrique (ed). Byrne, Alex.

"Storicità e mondo umano nell'estetica di Gravina" in *Lo Storicismo e la Sua Storia: Temi, Problemi, Prospettive,* Cacciatore, Giuseppe (ed). Cantillo, Clementina.

"Visible Properties of Human Interest Only" in *Perception,* Villanueva, Enrique (ed). Gibbard, Allan.

"Would More Acquaintance with the External World Relieve Epistemic Anxiety?" in *Perception,* Villanueva, Enrique (ed). Villanueva, Enrique.

*A Passion for Wisdom: A Very Brief History of Philosophy.* Solomon, Robert C and Higgins, Kathleen Marie.

*A World of States of Affairs.* Armstrong, D M.

*East and West in Aesthetics.* Marchianò, Grazia (ed).

*Enlightenment East and West.* Angel, Leonard.

*Erasmus of the Low Countries.* Tracy, James D.

*Explaining Consciousness—The 'Hard Problem'.* Shear, Jonathan (ed).

*Exploring Unseen Worlds: William James and the Philosophy of Mysticism.* Barnard, G William.

*Filosofia Criacionista da Morte: Meditaçao sobre o Problema da Morte No Pensamento Filosófico de Leonardo Coimbra.* Cândido Pimentel, Manuel.

*Hannah Arendt and the Limits of Philosophy: With a New Preface.* Disch, Lisa J.

*Immanuel Kant: Principios Formales del Mundo Sensible y del Inteligible (Disertación de 1770).* Gómez Caffarena, José (ed), Ceñal Lorente, Ramón (trans) and Kant, Immanuel.

*Liberation Theologies, Postmodernity, and the Americas.* Batstone, David, Mendieta, Eduardo and Lorentzen, Lois Ann (& others).

*Meeting of Minds: Intellectual and Religious Interaction in East Asian Traditions of Thought.* Bloom, Irene (ed) and Fogel, Joshua A (ed).

*Moral Issues in Health Care: An Introduction to Medical Ethics.* McConnell, Terrance C.

*On Jean-Luc Nancy: The Sense of Philosophy.* Sheppard, Darren (ed), Sparks, Simon (ed) and Thomas, Colin (ed).

*Primeras Interpretaciones del Mundo en la Modernidad: Descartes y Leibniz.* Schneider, Martin.

*Remaking the World: Modeling in Human Experience.* King, James R.

*Self and World.* Cassam, Quassim.

*Thick and Thin: Moral Argument at Home and Abroad.* Walzer, Michael.

*A Solipsist in a Real World.* Pihlström, Sami.

Alcuni rilievi sul nesso fra verità, libertà e temporalità nella filosofia di F. Nietzsche. Sacchi, Dario.

Aristotle's Razor. Drozdek, Adam.

Arte come rappresentazione del mondo. Figal, Günter.

Aspectos gnoseológicos de la noción de mundo. Padial Benticuaga, Juan José.

Authentic Existence and the Political World. Held, Klaus.

Beauty, Providence and the Biophilia Hypothesis. Wynn, Mark.

Between the Subject and Sociology: Alfred Schutz's Phenomenology of the Life-World. Costelloe, Timothy M.

Can We Think Systematically About Ethics and Statecraft?. Welch, David A.

Concepçoes de Mundo Veiculadas no Ensino de História do Curso Ginasial em Minas: 1954-1964. Nunes, Silma do Carmo.

Conceptual Frameworks for World Musics in Education. Boyce-Tillman, June.

Critical Notice of John McDowell *Mind and World.* Pietroski, Paul M.

Cyclical Preferences and World Bayesianism. Sobel, Jordan Howard.

Descartes, El Argumento del Sueño. Zuluaga, Mauricio.

Dialogical Realities: The Ordinary, the Everyday, and Other Strange New Worlds. Shotter, John.

Discurso Científico e Poético na Filosofia de Aristóteles. Paisana, Joao.

El mundo incuestionado (Ortega y Schütz). Hermida, Pablo.

## Guidance on the Use of the Author Index With Abstracts

Each entry in this section begins with the author's name and contains the complete title of the article or book, other bibliographic information, and an abstract if available. The list is arranged in alphabetical order with the author's last name first. Articles by multiple authors are listed under each author's name. Names preceded by the articles De, La, Le, etc. or the prepositions Da, De, Van, Von, etc. are treated as if the article or preposition were a part of the last name.

The vast majority of abstracts are provided by the authors of the articles and books; where an abstract does not appear, it was not received from the author prior to the publication of this edition. The staff of the *Index* prepares some abstracts. These abstracts are followed by "(edited)".

In order to locate all the articles and books written by a given author, various spellings of the author's name should be checked. This publication uses the form of the author's name given in the articles and books. Because some authors have changed the form of their name that they attach to articles and because some editors took liberties with the proper name submitted, variations of an author's name may occur in this index. Particular care should be given to names that have a space, a dash, or an apostrophe in their surnames. Because the computer sorts on each character, the names of other authors may be "filed" between different spellings of a given author's name.

**Aarnio, Aulis**. On Values: Universal or Relative?. *Ratio Juris*, 9(4), 321-330, D 96.

Any value statement belongs to a certain value code shared, to a certain degree, by a number of people. Is the value code itself relative or not? To solve this problem, one must assume that universal value statements and principles always have a *prima-facie* character. *Prima-facie* value propositions not only *claim* universality but can also be understood as *universally valid* in the following sense. First, their validity does not depend on an individual's free preferences. Second, although they are culture-bound, there is something all cultures must have in common. But such *prima-facie* propositions do not logically imply a moral judgment in any particular case. They are merely a starting point of an evaluation procedure, i.e., of weighing and balancing, nothing more. On the other hand, the *final* (contextual, all things considered) evaluations are necessarily relative to a certain culture and, indeed, to individual preferences. When claiming universality of values, people see the first side of the problem. When endorsing relativism, they see only the second side.

**Abbott, Barbara**. A Note on the Nature of "Water". *Mind*, 106(422), 311-319, Ap 97.

Noting that tea and Sprite are not called "water" despite being thought to have roughly the same proportion of $H_2O$ as tap water, Chomsky (1995) challenges essentialist/externalist semantics for "water." I reply to this challenge. The fact that tea is mostly water *in virtue of being* mostly $H_2O$ argues that "water" and "$H_2O$" denote the same thing. Artifactual substances consisting largely or entirely of water but possessing other properties are called by different names for Gricean reasons. Ordinary vagueness accounts for the application of "water" to substances with impurities.

**Abbott, Barbara**. Models, Truth and Semantics. *Ling Phil*, 20(2), 117-138, Ap 97.

This paper exposes weaknesses in arguments given by Lakoff and Jackendoff against model-theoretic semantics, truth conditional semantics and realism. Lakoff's argument, which is an adaptation of Putnam's "model-theoretic argument", is shown to be invalid as well as misguided as an attack on model-theoretic semantics. Jackendoff's arguments are also invalid. One argues from the nonrepresentational nature of phonology, syntax and music to the nonrepresentationality of semantics; another rests on the requirement of conceptualizing what we think about; and the third argues that since we can sometimes refer to mind dependent entities, we can only refer to such entities.

**Abbruzzese, John E**. The Coherence of Omniscience: A Defense. *Int J Phil Relig*, 41(1), 25-34, F 97.

In this essay I consider three recent arguments by Patrick Grim to demonstrate the incoherence of the concept of divine omniscience: the arguments from the essential indexical, from the paradox of the liar, and from Cantor's theorem. After rejecting each of these arguments and proposing resolutions to the problems they raise, I then present a simple analysis of omniscience that avoids these and similar problems and, I suggest, coherently circumscribes the concept.

**Abdo, Sandra Neves**. Restauro artístico: fundamentos e implicaçoes hermenêticas. *Kriterion*, 37(94), 36-54, Jl-D 96.

This article examines the problem of artistic restoration and its hermeneutic implications from the point of view of Luigi Pareyson's "theory of formativity." The article contains three parts: I) Pareyson's hermeneutics; II) theory of formativity; III) the problem of restoration in face of the theory of formativity.

**Abdoulafia, Mitchell**. Habermas and Mead: On Universality and Individuality. *Constellations*, 2(1), 94-113, Ap 95.

**Abeng, Tanri**. Business Ethics in Islamic Context: Perspectives of a Muslim Business Leader. *Bus Ethics Quart*, 7(3), 47-54, Jl 97.

The role of the business leader is key to develop the culture of an enterprise. To exemplify its importance in the national and global context, the Muslim author from Indonesia points with admiration to Konosuke Matsushita, founder of Matsushita Electric Corporation, who already in the 1930s set up the seven ethical principles for healthy business growth, which also are commended by the Islamic imperative.(edited)

**Abiteboul, Olivier**. Pour une rhétorique philosophique. *Philosopher*, 19, 61-71, 1996.

**Ablondi, Fred**. Schlick, Altruism and Psychological Hedonism. *Indian Phil Quart*, 23(3-4), 417-427, Jl-O 96.

I begin this article with a brief summary of Moritz Schlick's *Problems of Ethics*, focusing on 1) what he believes the true task of ethics to be and 2) what he claims is the motivation for our decision-making. The second part of the article is a critical examination of some of the theoretical questions which arise from his theory. As a response to these questions, I suggest a sympathetic projection theory at work in his social psychology.

**Abney, Keith**. What is Natural?. *Cont Phil*, 18(4 & 5), 23-29, Jl-Ag/S-O 96.

The term 'natural' in the sciences supposedly functions as a means of demarcating a particular type of science from the other sciences; it also often embodies an implicit ideal for the sciences, manifest in the greater respect usually shown to the 'natural' sciences as opposed to the 'social' ones. I believe that this usage results in multiple confusions and mistakes and advocates a terminological change with philosophical consequences: to divide the sciences by their causal-explanatory structure and in particular their ability to abstract from human agency or not. Hence, I demarcate the sciences into the "nonteleological" or teleological", rather than 'natural' or 'social'. In addition, I argue that this new classification clarifies the need for the teleological sciences to engage in areas of inquiry usually considered remote from science in order to be successful—specifically, ethical inquiry. I then examine ecology as an example of a teleological science which depends on ethical inquiry in order to be successful.

**Abousenna, Mona**. "Ibn Rushd, Founder of Hermeneutics" in *Averroës and the Enlightenment*, Wahba, Mourad (ed), 105-112. Amherst, Prometheus, 1996.

**Abousenna, Mona** (ed) and Wahba, Mourad (ed). *Averroës and the Enlightenment*. Amherst, Prometheus, 1996.

**Abramov, A I**. Reflections on Russia's Destiny in the Philosophical Work of Russian Romanticism. *Russian Stud Phil*, 35(3), 6-18, Wint 96-97.

**Abreu, Joao Azevedo**. Concerning Saint Augustine's *De Magistro* (in Portuguese). *Trans/Form/Acao*, 19, 211-219, 1996.

This paper is divided in two parts. At first, we show the different roles played by quotations all through Saint Augustine's *De Magistro*. We compare then the structure in which the text is established to the theory that is developed over there. From such a comparison, we can see that in the mentioned text a theory of language isn't philosophically fundamental and that a dialogue isn't the best way to reach the truth.

**Abrusci, Michele**. "Per una storia delle ricerche sul concetto di dimostrazione logica nel novecento" in *Momenti di Storia della Logica e di Storia della Filosofia*, Guetti, Carla (ed), 165-185. Roma, Aracne Editrice, 1996.

**Abusch, Dorit**. Sequence of Tense and Temporal De Re. *Ling Phil*, 20(1), 1-50, F 97.

**Aby, Carroll D** and Fusilier, Marcelline R and Worley, Joel K (& others). Perceived Seriousness of Business Ethics Issues. *Bus Prof Ethics J*, 15(1), 67-78, Spr 96.

Respondents from over 900 businesses rated the seriousness of twenty major ethical issues. As representatives for their organizations, they also identified the issues that were most resolved and those that were least resolved. Workplace safety and employee theft had the two highest average ratings of seriousness. The issue most frequently rated as a) least resolved was theft, and b) most resolved was workplace safety. Results are discussed in the context of previous literature.

**Acampora, Ralph**. The Problematic Situation of Post-Humanism and the Task of Recreating a Symphysical Ethos. *Between Species*, 11(1-2), 25-32, Wint-Spr 95.

To transcend homocentrist ideology, interspecies ethics needs to let go of mentalistic personification as a moral anchor. This residual anthropocentrism can be replaced with a phenomenological and hermeneutic attunement to animate bodies as such. Moving thus to zoomorphize humans alongside other animals, the model of projectively imaginative empathy is abandoned in favor of a 'somatology' of bioethical experience. A 'symphysical' ethos may be re-established through such an approach; this implies sensitivity to the moral phenomena of corporal conviviality (e.g., vulnerability as a living body's inherent openness to damage and death).

**Accorinti, Stella**. Una aproximación a la ética en el programa Filosofía para Niños de Matthew Lipman. *Cuad Etica*, 17-18, 9-17, 1994.

The ethic is the principal fountain of reflection in the child philosophy. The children are specially fascinated with the general question about a "good life". The practice of the child philosophy tries to stimulate this question and to answer it impartially. This paper is the presentation of the program of the child philosophy in Argentine.

**Acero, Juan José**. Hechos semánticos y presiones fisicalistas. *Rev Filosof (Spain)*, 9(16), 9-40, 1996.

In this article I deal with Stephen Schiffer's argument for the No Theory Theory of Meaning, as put forward in *Remnants of Meaning*, aiming at showing two things. First, that there is a close affinity between Schiffer's argument and a strong tradition of semantic nihilism going back up to the positivist eclosion of contemporary philosophy. As then, Schiffer's argument heavily depends on the idea that semantic facts properly arise within translation relationships, the reason for that ultimately being his confessed physicalism. Second, it is argued that given his physicalism and his nominalism, Schiffer cannot defend that there are semantic facts.

**Achenbach, Gerd B**. Schicksal und Charakter: Für die Philosophische Praxis ist vieles von Schopenhauer zu lernen: Vortrag auf dem Kolloquium der GPP am 30. Oktober 1994 in Tübingen. *Z Phil Praxis*, 13-18, 1995.

**Achinstein, Peter**. On Evidence: A Reply to McGrew. *Analysis*, 57(1), 81-83, Ja 97.

**Acker, Mary H**. Tempered Regrets Under Total Ignorance. *Theor Decis*, 42(3), 207-213, My 97.

Several decision rules, including the minimax regret rule, have been posited to suggest optimizing strategies for an individual when neither objective nor subjective probabilities can be associated to the various states of the world. These all share the shortcoming of focusing only on extreme outcomes. This paper suggests an alternative approach of 'tempered regrets' which may more closely replicate the decision process of individuals in those situations in which avoiding the worst outcome tempers the loss from not achieving the best outcome. The assumption of total ignorance of the probabilities associated with the various states is maintained. Applications and illustrations from standard neoclassical theory are discussed.

**Ackerman, Bruce**. Temporal Horizons of Justice. *J Phil*, 94(6), 299-317, Je 97.

**Ackerman, Felicia**. "The Concept of Manipulativeness" in *AI, Connectionism and Philosophical Psychology, 1995*, Tomberlin, James E (ed), 335-340. Atascadero, Ridgeview, 1995.

**Ackerman, Felicia**. Goldilocks and Mrs. Ilych: A Critical Look at the "Philosophy of Hospice". *Cambridge Quart Healthcare Ethics*, 6(3), 314-324, Sum 97.

This paper focuses on analyzing and criticizing the principles of hospice care. It argues that many of these principles are conceptually confused and/or rest on a highly questionable ideology, which many terminally ill people can (and do) reasonably reject. The argument has major implications for health care policy, as it militates against any public policy that would favor hospice care over other types of care for the dying.

**Acocella, Giuseppe**. "La scienza e la vita: Lo storicismo problematico di Giuseppe Capograssi" in *Lo Storicismo e la Sua Storia: Temi, Problemi, Prospettive*, Cacciatore, Giuseppe (ed), 540-556. Milano, Guerini, 1997.

**Adams, Edward W** and Spaak, Torben. Fuzzifying the Natural Law-Legal Positivist Debate. *Vera Lex*, 14(1-2), 1-7, 1994.

**Adams, Ernest W**. Practical Possibilities. *Pac Phil Quart*, 78(2), 113-127, Je 97.

That inferences of the form "If M than S and possibly M, therefore, possibly S" are invalid in possible worlds modal logics can be viewed as another fallacy of material implication. However, this paper argues that properly analyzing this and related inferences requires treating the possibility involved as a *practical modality* Specifically, ordinary language propositions of the form "It is possible that M" must be understood to mean that there is a nonnegligible probability of M being the case. But this entails reexamining the very idea of logical validity.

**Adams, Frederick** and Fuller, Gary and Stecker, Robert. The Semantics of Fictional Names. *Pac Phil Quart*, 78(2), 128-148, Je 97.

In this paper we defend a direct reference theory of names. We maintain that the meaning of a name is its bearer. In the case of vacuous names, there is no bearer and they have no meaning. We develop a unified theory of names such that one theory applies to names whether they occur within or outside fiction. Hence, we apply our theory to sentences containing names within fiction, sentences about fiction or sentences making comparisons across fictions. We then defend our theory against objections and compare our view to the views of Currie, Walton and others.

**Adams, Marilyn McCord** and Wolter, Allan B. Memory and Intuition: A Focal Debate in Fourteenth Century Cognitive Psychology. *Fran Stud*, 53, 175-230, 1993.

**Adams, Robert Merrihew**. Schleiermacher on Evil. *Faith Phil*, 13(4), 563-583, O 96.

Schleiermacher's theology of absolute dependence implies that absolutely everything, including evil, including even sin, is grounded in the divine causality. In addition to God's general, creative causality, however, he thinks that Christian consciousness reveals a special, teleologically ordered divine causality which is at work in redemption but not in evil. He identifies good and evil, respectively, with what furthers and what obstructs the development of the religious consciousness in human beings. Mere pains and natural ills are not truly evil, in his view, apart from a connection with some obstruction of the God-consciousness. These themes are explored in the present essay.

**Adams, Robert Merrihew**. Sleigh's *Leibniz & Arnauld: A Commentary on their Correspondence* (New Haven: Yale University Press). *Nous*, 31(2), 266-277, Je 97.

**Adams, Robert Merrihew**. Thisness and Time Travel. *Philosophia (Israel)*, 25(1-4), 407-415, Ap 97.

**Adeleke, Tunde**. Enduring Crises and Challenges of African-American Studies. *J Thought*, 32(3), 65-96, Fall 97.

The paper critiques three interrelated problems and challenges confronting the field of African-American Studies—intellectual validity, identity and Pan-Africanism. First, the intellectuality of the discipline remains contentious due to failure on the part of many practitioners in the field to prioritize objectivity and clearly distinguish between scholarship and the demands of the black struggle. Second, there is a tendency to ghettoize the field as "for blacks only." Third, Afrocentricity, a philosophical paradigm of the discipline, advances a romanticized and Pan-African view of black diaspora culture and historical experience, while neglecting the cultural complexity and transforming character of that experience.

**Adler, Jonathan**. Hume's "Of Miracles" (Part One). *Inquiry (USA)*, 14(2), 1-10, Wint 94.

Introductory remarks on Hume's "On Miracles" Part I, interwoven with the text.

**Adler, Jonathan**. Report of a Year Working on Improving Teaching and Learning. *Inquiry (USA)*, 16(3), 35-41, Spr 97.

The article has practical and informal recommendations for improvement in reasoning and critical thinking within a liberal-arts curriculum.

**Adler, Jonathan E**. Charity, Interpretation, Fallacy. *Phil Rhet*, 29(4), 329-343, 1996.

Principles of charity imply that if one attributes manifestly illogical reasoning, then one's attribution is dubious, if not false. Consequently, these principles have been appealed to in theoretical argument, but especially in reflection on practices, to yield the conclusion that attributions of fallacy are (almost) never justified. Three initially plausible lines of thought starting from a strong principle of charity and ending with the absurd conclusion are proposed and criticized.

**Adler, Jonathan E**. Lying, Deceiving, or Falsely Implicating. *J Phil*, 94(9), 435-452, S 97.

Is there a moral distinction favoring deliberately asserting what one believes true, inviting the drawing of a conclusion that one believes false (communicative deception) over asserting what one believes false (lying)? There are systematic ethical differences between lying and deceiving that support, though not

uniformly, an affirmative answer. Two attempts to defend the distinction specific to communication are criticized. But the distinction is then defended by focusing on "implicatures" as facilitating tactfulness and economy. For those purposes, a lessened demand of truthfulness for implicatures than assertion is necessary, though when exploited, the asymmetry favoring deception is easily overridden.

**Adler, Jonathan E**. Teaching and the Structural Approach to Fallacies. *Inquiry (USA)*, 15(4), 94-106, Sum 96.

A traditional view of fallacies is that fallacies are defects in structure or form. Recently, an opposing view has become dominant. It claims that fallacies are merely types of argument, instances of which will or will not be fallacious depending upon context. I argue in favor of the traditional, structural view as preferable for teaching. (In a complementary article (Fallacies not fallacious: Not", I argue for the preferability of the structural view in the study of reasoning and as an account of our critical practices.)

**Adler, Pierre**. Multiculturalism and Gender Equity: The U.S. "Difference" Debates Revisited. *Constellations*, 3(1), 61-72, Ap 96.

**Adler, Pierre** (trans). Reiner Schürmann's Report of His Visit to Martin Heidegger. *Grad Fac Phil J*, 19/20(2/1), 67-72, 1997.

**Admiraal, Pieter V**. Euthanasia in The Netherlands. *Free Inq*, 17(1), 5-8, Wint 96/97.

**Adorno, Gretel** (ed) and Hullot-Kentor, Robert (ed & trans) and Tiedemann, Rolf (ed). *Aesthetic Theory: Theodore W. Adorno*. Minneapolis, Univ of Minn Pr, 1997.

The culmination of a lifetime of aesthetic investigation, *Aesthetic Theory* is Adorno's major work, a defense of modernism that is paradoxical in its defense of illusion. In it, Adorno takes up the problem of art in a day when "it goes without saying that nothing concerning art goes without saying." In the course of Adorno's discussion, he revisits such concepts as the sublime, the ugly, and the beautiful, demonstrating that concepts such as these are reservoirs of human experience. These experiences ultimately underlie aesthetics, for in Adorno's formulation "art is the sedimented history of human misery."(publisher,edited)

**Adshead, Gwen**. Commentary on "Pathological Autobiographies". *Phil Psychiat Psych*, 4(2), 111-113, Je 97.

**Adshead, Gwen**. Commentary on "Psychopathy, Other-Regarding Moral Beliefs, and Responsibility". *Phil Psychiat Psych*, 3(4), 279-281, D 96.

In this commentary, I address two points raised by Fields: the origin of other-regarding beliefs, and the management of psychopaths, if they are not criminally responsible (as Fields suggests). I argue that the capacity to form affective bonds is necessary in order to hold other-regarding beliefs and that a psychological developmental perspective may be helpful in understanding the moral understanding of the psychopath. In response to Fields's view that psychopaths should receive "treatment," I suggest that most forensic psychiatrists do not agree.

**Agamben, Giorgio**. "The Passion of Facticity: Heidegger and the Problem of Love" in *The Ancients and the Moderns*, Lilly, Reginald (ed), 211-229. Bloomington, Indiana Univ Pr, 1996.

**Agassi, Joseph**. "Towards Honest Public Relations of Science" in *The Significance of Popper's Thought*, Amsterdamski, Stefan (ed), 39-57. Amsterdam, Rodopi, 1996.

The public relations of science are a complex affair, run by all sorts of popularizers of science, including academic philosophers and historians and sociologists of science. They usually exaggerate claims for science allegedly for the sake of improving its public image for the common good. They oppose the more balanced views of science as self-correcting; Popper's view of science, which is very balanced and commonsensical, is thus rejected out of hand, as their conduct clashes with his refusal to endorse any authority, including scientific authority; they are unfriendly to his suggestion to replace all authority with moral and scientific autonomy.

**Agera, Cassian R**. Two Biblical Myths of Creation: An Exploration in Ecological Philosophy. *J Indian Counc Phil Res*, 13(3), 111-125, My-Ag 96.

**Agich, George J** and Spielman, Bethan J. Ethics Expert Testimony: Against the Skeptics. *J Med Phil*, 22(4), 381-403, Ag 97.

There is great skepticism about the admittance of expert normative ethics testimony into evidence. However, a practical analysis of the way ethics testimony has been used in courts of law reveals that the skeptical position is itself based on assumptions that are controversial. We argue for an alternative way to understand such expert testimony. This alternative understanding is based on the practice of clinical ethics.

**Agócs, Carol**. Institutionalized Resistance to Organizational Change: Denial, Inaction and Repression. *J Bus Ethics*, 16(9), 917-931, Je 97.

Focusing on institutionalized resistance from the standpoint of the advocate of fundamental change, this discussion proposes a typology consisting of a sequence of forms of active resistance to change, from denial through inaction to repression. The typology is illustrated by referring to responses of organizational decision makers to the efforts of employment equity change agents to address issues of systemic discrimination in the work place. The purpose of the typology is to assist change advocates, such as equality seekers, to name, analyze and think strategically about the institutionalized resistance they encounter and about effective responses to the resistance.(edited)

**Agrimi, Mario**. Note sulle polemiche antifrancesi di Vico. *Stud Filosofici*, 243-269, 1995.

**Aguayo, Enrique I**. El concepto de libertad jurídica en la iusfilosofía de Eduardo García Máynez. *Analogia*, 10(2), 175-199, 1996.

Tema original en la iusfilosofía del Doctor Eduardo García Máynez es la *libertad jurídica*. La importancia del tema radica en dos cosas: a) pone de relieve el hecho de que una persona puede o no practicar sus derechos subjetivos; b) la ley (al menos en México) protege el ejercicio de la libertad jurídica aun en el caso de que alguien quisiera renunciar a la práctica legítima de determinados derechos en un momento específico. Esta libertad sólo se ejerce en el caso de derechos, nunca de deberes.

**Aguilar Espinosa, Gerardo**. Lo que debemos considerar como principio del conocimiento para filosofar. *Analogia*, 10(2), 201-212, 1996.

**Aguilar-Alvarez, Sergio** and Zagal, Héctor Arreguín. *Límites de la Argumentación Ética en Aristóteles: Lógos, physis y éthos*. Mexico, Pub Cruz O, 1996.

Un texto documentado y bien escrito. Héctor Zagal y Sergio Aguilar-Alvarez dedican su atención al engranaje entre argumentación y ética. Los autores son honestos y abren su libro con una declaración de principios que es una declaración de modestia: "*Nuestro interés no es sistemático sino histórico*" nos dicen. Y tienen razón: el libro que vamos a leer consiste básicamente en una interpretación de algunos textos de Aristóteles. Sin embargo, ellos no poseen toda la razón en el siguiente sentido: en filosofía ninguna investigación histórica puede escapar de tener, en alguna medida, una dimensión sistemática. De lo contrario, nos encontraríamos ante una labor de anticuarios y no ante un repensar filosófico. Felizmente, como veremos, las repercusiones sistemáticas de este estudio son bien visibles.(publisher, edited)

**Ahlbrecht, Martin** and Weber, Martin. Preference for Gradual Resolution of Uncertainty. *Theor Decis*, 43(2), 167-185, S 97.

Analyzes of preference for the timing of uncertainty resolution usually assumes all uncertainty to resolve in one point in time. More realistically, uncertainty should be modelled to resolve gradually over time. Kreps and Porteus (1978) have introduced an axiomatically based model of time preference which can explain preferences for gradual uncertainty resolution. This paper presents an experimental test of the Kreps-Porteus model. We derive implications of the model relating preferences for gradual and one-time resolving lotteries. Our data do not support the Kreps-Porteus model but show that some of the behaviour observed may be explained by similarity heuristics.

**Ahmed, Halim Obeid**. Visual Aesthetic Education: Its Place in General Education. *J Aes Educ*, 27(2), 1-13, Sum 93.

**Aiken, David W**. Kierkegaard's "Three Stages": A Pilgrim's Regress?. *Faith Phil*, 13(3), 352-367, Jl 96.

The purpose of this paper is to explore an hypothesis rather than draw any unassailable conclusions. I argue that there is a fundamental tension between the sub-Christian account of the "Three Stages" presented in the earlier pseudonymous writings and the explicitly Christian account presented in the anti-Climacean and later acknowledged writings. The earlier version is that of a progress from spiritless "immediacy" toward more complete integrations of the self, culminating in authentic religious faith; while the later is that of a regress from lesser to even greater forms of spiritual peril, culminating in a disordered religiosity that vainly seeks to overthrow the established ecclesiastical order. Tracing the conflict between these two perspectives also enhances our understanding of the purpose underlying Kierkegaard's project by suggesting the possibility that the authorship constitutes a literary confession of Kierkegaard's own spiritual regress.

**Aiken, Margaret M** and Muram, David and Strong, Carson. Children's Refusal of Gynecologic Examinations for Suspected Sexual Abuse. *J Clin Ethics*, 8(2), 158-164, Sum 97.

Cases are presented in which children refuse gynecologic examinations following suspected sexual abuse. Topics discussed include background concerning child sexual abuse, the purpose of the medical examination, and psychosocial aspects of such examinations. A framework for dealing with such refusals is presented that identifies relevant ethical values, distinguishes categories of decision-making capacity in children, and provides an interpretation of the principle of patient advocacy. Using this framework, the authors argue for proposed resolutions of the cases presented.

**Aiken, William**. Is Deep Ecology Too Radical?. *Phil Cont World*, 1(4), 1-5, Wint 94.

The theory of Deep Ecology is characterized as having two essential features: the belief that nature is inherently valuable and the belief that one's self is truly realized by identification with nature. Four common but different meanings of the term "radical" are presented. Whether the theory of Deep Ecology is "too radical" depends upon which of these meanings one is using.

**Aizawa, Kenneth**. Exhibiting versus Explaining Systematicity: A Reply to Hadley and Hayward. *Mind Mach*, 7(1), 39-55, F 97.

Fodor and Pylyshyn, (1988), argued that connectionist models do not provide an explanation of the systematicity of thought. Unfortunately, many of the connectionist attempts seem not to have fully appreciated an important feature of the challenge. It is not enough to show that a connectionist model can exhibit systematicity; one must show how connectionism explains systematicity. Another way to put the point is that it is not enough for connectionist models to save the phenomena; they must save the phenomena *in the right way*. Hadley and Hayward's (1997) connectionist network provides an excellent opportunity to emphasize this point.

**Aja, Egbeke**. The Supreme God in African (Igbo) Religious Thought. *Phil Cont World*, 3(4), 1-7, Wint 96.

From African ontology, religious experiences, myths of creation and language, I argue that even though Africans (Igbo) conceive of supreme deities, none of the adjudged supreme deities is identifiable with the Supreme God propagated by Christian missionaries and theologians. To translate, therefore, the names of African deities, such as *Chukwu* or *Chineke*, to mean the God preached by Christians is to yoke to the Igbo religious thought the concept of "creation out of nothing," which is alien to traditional African cosmology. Such a translation will not only distort the architecture of traditional African religion, it will impose on the Igbo the recognition of a deity that would be beyond the reach of their standard reciprocity arrangements with their Gods. Moreover, throughout Igboland, no shrines are dedicated to the worship of an unknown God identifiable with that propagated by Christians.

**Ajdukiewicz, Kazimierz**. "On Freedom of Science" in *The Idea of University*, Brzezinski, Jerzy (ed), 57-75. Amsterdam, Rodopi, 1997.

**Akama, John S** and Lant, Christopher L and Burnett, G Wesley. A Political-Ecology Approach to Wildlife Conservation in Kenya. *Environ Values*, 5(4), 335-347, N 96.

This essay uses a political-ecological framework in the analysis of the social factors of wildlife conservation in Kenya. It postulates that the overriding socio-economic issue impacting wildlife conservation in Kenya is underdevelopment. The problem of underdevelopment is manifested in forms of increasing levels of poverty, famine and malnutrition. The long term survival of Kenya's wildlife depends on social and ecological solutions to the problems of underdevelopment.(edited)

**Akama, Seiki**. Facts, Semantics and Intuitionism. *Log Anal*, 37(147-8), 227-238, S-D 94.

We outline an intuitive semantics for intuitionism in the light of van Fraassen's theory of facts. We regard an intuitionistic proof as the content of a positive fact. We establish an adequacy result for the given semantics. The connection with Kripke semantics is also investigated.

**Akari, Kitamura**. Gli Affreschi nelle Celle del Dormitorio del Convento di San Marco: Devozione e Figurazione di Fra Angelico (in Japanese). *Bigaku*, 47(1), 37-48, Sum 96.

Fra Angelico, attivo già nel 1417 come pittore Guido di Pietro, entrò poco più tardi nel convento di San Domenico. Fu chiamato Fra Giovanni, ma le sue mani e i suoi occhi erano quelli del pittore; che tentava di creare consapevolmente delle immagini autenticamente devozionali per la vita dei frati Osservanti domenicani, nelle celle del dormitorio del nuovo convento di San Marco a Firenze, essendo perfettamente a conoscenza della sua costruzione e di ogni sua funzione.(edited)

**Akeroyd, F Michael**. "Poppers Beitrag für eine Philosophie der Chemie" in *Philosophie der Chemie: Bestandsaufnahme und Ausblick*, Schummer, Joachim (ed), 67-76. Wurzburg, Koenigshausen, 1996.

This article examines various episodes from the history of chemistry and biochemistry 1810-1990 and concludes that there is considerable support for the falsificationist and antireductionist stance of Karl Popper. Episodes considered include Davy's work on chlorine, Dalton's discovery of the *Law of Multiple Proportions*, Dumas's work on tri-chlor acetic acid, Hopkin's work on artificial diets, Liebig's protein theory of muscular work, Bohr's Quantum Theory and its relationship with the periodic table.

**Akiba, Ken**. Field on the Notion of Consistency. *Notre Dame J Form Log*, 37(4), 625-630, Fall 96.

Field's claim that we have a notion of consistency which is neither model-theoretic nor proof-theoretic but primitive, is examined and criticized. His argument is compared to similar examinations by Kreisel and Etchemendy, and Etchemendy's distinction between interpretational and representational semantics is employed to reveal the flaw in Field's argument.

**Akins, Kathleen**. Lost the Plot? Reconstructing Dennett's Multiple Drafts Theory of Consciousness. *Mind Lang*, 11(1), 1-43, Mr 96.

In *Consciousness Explained*, Daniel Dennett presents the Multiple Drafts Theory of consciousness, a very brief, largely empirical theory of brain function. From these premises, he draws a number of quite radical conclusions—for example, the conclusion that conscious events have no determinate time of occurrence. The problem, as many readers have pointed out, is that there is little discernible route from the empirical premises to the philosophical conclusions. In this article, I try to reconstruct Dennett's argument, providing both the philosophical views behind the empirical premises, and the hidden empirical arguments behind the derivation of the philosophical conclusions.

**Akiyama, Shiro** and Tsuzuki, Miho and Asada, Yukiko. High School Teaching of Bioethics in New Zealand, Australia and Japan. *J Moral Educ*, 25(4), 401-420, D 96.

This paper compares knowledge and teaching of 15 selected topics related to bioethics and biotechnology, with particular focus on the teaching of social, ethical and environmental issues of *in vitro* fertilization, prenatal diagnosis, biotechnology, nuclear power, pesticides and genetic engineering. The survey found that these issues were, generally, covered more in biology classes than in social science classes; and that there were differences in coverage among the three countries, with most coverage in Australia and least in Japan. Open questions looked at images of bioethics, and the reasons why about 90% of teachers thought bioethics was needed in education. Open questions on teaching materials, current and desired are also discussed. The data suggest a need for the development of more and higher quality materials, for the moral education that is conducted, especially in biology and social studies classes.(edited)

**Akkerman, F**. Wim Klever: Een Dissonant. *Alg Ned Tijdschr Wijs*, 88(3), 234-236, Jl 96.

**Aksenov, Gennadii Petrovich**. The Scientific Solitude of Vernadskii. *Russian Stud Phil*, 34(1), 14-35, Sum 95.

**Al Brynaichi, Javan**. Religion in the Critical Decades. *J Dharma*, 21(2), 131-140, Ap-Je 96.

**Al-A'ali, Ebtihaj**. "Some Fundamental Features of Arabic-Islamic Culture and Its Possible Contribution to World Peace" in *Kreativer Friede durch Begegnung der Weltkulturen,* Beck, Heinrich (ed), 253-259. New York, Lang, 1995.

This paper comprises four major sections. The first section elaborates on the Islamic principle of Oneness through "Tawhid," i.e., the belief in one supreme Lord of the universe and the recognition of the unity of God "Allah." The second section explains impacts of Oneness on Islamic philosophy concerning ontology, epistemology and assumptions in relation to human nature. The third section investigates Islam's contribution to liberation of individuals. This liberation leads to peace. The final section presents a summary of the major arguments discussed in this paper.(edited)

**Alarcón, Jesús** and Rigo, Mirela and Waldegg, Guillermina. La ciencia analítica en la primera mitad del siglo XIX: el teorema del valor intermedio. *Mathesis*, 10(1), 93-113, F 94.

During the first half of the nineteenth century, the theories that presumed to be scientific described themselves as 'analytic'. From Lagrange's *Méchanique analytique* to Bolzano's *Purely analytic proof* of the intermediate value theorem, the high level of abstraction and generality reached by a theory was based on the 'analytic methods' used. However, the word 'analytic' did not have the same meaning for all the scientists of this period and remarkable differences can be detected in the assumptions underlying analytic methods in each author. In this article different approaches to the intermediate value theorem are analyzed, revealing the various conceptions of what being an 'analytic' theory entails.

**Alarcón Cabrera, Carlos**. Deontics between Semantics and Ontology. *Sorites*, 18-34, My 96.

As an adjective, the term "Deontic" is traditionally used in the sense of "directive", "normative", "prescriptive", "concerning ought". As a noun, "Deontics" is later introduced by Amedeo G. Conte, referring to the analysis of the theoretical and philosophical foundations of deontic logic. Within the wide field of Contian deontics, I am dealing here with five questions: a) the distinction between "categorical constitutivity" and "hypothetical constitutivity"; b) the typology of the concept of validity; c) the problem of the pragmatic ambivalence of deontic utterances; d) the conception of repeal as an act of rejection; e) the reinterpretation of the "I sought question".

**Albertazzi, Liliana**. "Science and the Avant-Garde in Early Nineteenth-Century Florence" in *In Itinere* European Cities and the Birth of Modern Scientific Philosophy, Poli, Roberto (ed), 177-211. Amsterdam, Rodopi, 1997.

The essay sheds light on cultural life in early nineteenth-century Florence, where philosophy, science and literature were closely interwoven. Idealism and descriptive psychology, futurism, magic and logical pragmatism and experimental analysis in psychological laboratories were all involved in a struggle between two connected but opposite visions of the world: a battle conducted by means of two irreducible languages, a spare, analytic essential language pitted against free verse, free words, pamphlets and manifestoes, fought in the cafés, in the journals and in the university lectures as well. A place were even internationalism and nationalism became a flag for the two intellectual factions.

**Albieri, Sara**. Milagres e leis da natureza em Peirche e Hume. *Rev Latin de Filosof*, 22(2), 207-222, 1996.

This article aims at arguing that Peirce's criticism towards Hume's argument on miracles, rather than pinpointing the antagonism, shows the compatibility of their conceptions of Laws of Nature.

**Albis, Víctor S** (ed) and Charum, Jorge (ed) and Sánchez, Clara Helena (& others). *Memorias Del Seminario En Conmemoración De Los 400 Anos Del Nacimiento De René Descartes*. Sankt Augustin, Academia, 1997.

Con este Seminario en commemoración de los 400 años del nacimiento de René Descartes promovido y organizado conjuntamente por la *Academia Colombiana de Ciencias* y la *Universidad Nacional de Colombia*, se busca relevar la obra de uno de los más grandes creadores del pensamiento científico moderno. (edited)

**Albu, Mihaela**. A Romanian Myth—Life as a Permanent Miracle. *Ultim Real Mean*, 20(2 & 3), 157-164, Je-S 97.

Romanian culture can reveal themes of unsuspected depth with a unique style. Romanian mythology is original and profound because of its peculiar way of perceiving reality and the human destiny in the world. The frequency of the myth of death indicates that the Romanians are dominated by a desire for spiritual eternity. Life means to us a permanent exercise to learn how to die. To have the awareness of death and to know the limits of human existence are the two prerequisites which lead us to change from simple beings into philosophers. In this way we can find our immortality. (edited)

**Alcantara, Jean-Pascal**. Leibniz's Theory of Variation in 1676: An Interpretation of the Dialogue Pacidius *Pacidius Philalethi* through the *Characteristica geometrica*) (Spanish). *Theoria (Spain)*, 12(29), 225-255, My 97.

We know that Leibniz intended to bring new foundations to the Euclidean geometry and he has according to this view formulate a *Characteristica geometrica* which announces few general concepts of set theory. Particularly he tried to formalize his conception of continuity. Before the main interest of the *Pacidius Philalethi* (1676) is here: showing us that Leibniz when he chooses an intensional conception of continuity he chooses in the same time the dual image from which he can deduce the qualitative variation. We reckon again these conception at the grounds of his later philosophy of nature. But now we have to follow Leibniz demonstrating how universal and infinite variations flow from its topological conditions.

**Alcaro, Mario**. *John Dewey: Scienza, prassi, democrazia*. Bari, Laterza, 1997.

In this book the scrupulous analysis of Dewey's theory of scientific inquiry and participatory democracy goes together with the comparison between the instrumentalism and the thesis of Reichenbach, Russell, Popper, Peirce, James, Bridgman, Heisenberg, Rorty.

**Alchourrón, Carlos E**. On Law and Logic. *Ratio Juris*, 9(4), 331-348, D 96.

The main purpose of this paper is to explore the role played by logic in the legal domain. In the tradition conception which underlies the movement of codification, judges are able to find in the legal system (the Master System) a unique answer for every legal problem. This entails its completeness, consistency and the possibility of deriving from it the contents of all judicial decisions. Although the ideal model of this conception is supported by important theoretical and political ideals, it has significant shortcomings. The elements of normative systems (Master Systems) are "norms" and not mere "norm-functions." A "norm" is the meaning attributed to normative linguistic expressions. The set of all normative expressions, such as statutes, codes, etc. forms what is called the Master Book. One of the main problems for the ideal model is the identification of a normative system behind the Master Book. Interpretive arguments are the tools designed to solve these problems. Although the requirements of the model are not totally fulfilled in actual practice, it remains as an effective ideal rational goal behind legal activities linked to adjudication and most theoretical approaches to law.

**Alchourrón, Carlos E**. Para una Lógica de las Razones Prima Facie. *Analisis Filosof*, 16(2), 113-124, N 96.

Standardly, the usual approach to rationality is based on the notion of 'being a reason for'. Honouring the traditional distinction between practical and theoretical philosophy, reasons are classified as a) justificative and b) explicative. In both cases, a reason-statement has the form '(A R B)'. For reasons of type a), 'A' is a factual statement and 'B' is a statement which describes an action of the agent. The reason-statement has a prescriptive sense because 'A is a reason for doing B' means 'A is a reason (why) an agent ought to do B'. So, it is advisable to schematize that kind of statements as '(A R OB)', where 'OB' is a deontic statement prescribing (for the agent) the duty to do B. Reasons of type b) have a descriptive sense and do not require the above-mentioned constraint. (edited)

**Alcoff, Linda Martín**. Philosophy and Racial Identity. *Phil Today*, 41(1-4), 67-76, Spr 97.

Both semantic realists such as Anthony Appiah and poststructuralists who attack identity politics deny that race has explanatory value or epistemological relevance. In this paper, I develop a philosophical conception of racial identity that addresses the concerns about simplistic homogenization and essentialism. What is unique about racialized categories of identity as opposed to ethnic and cultural difference is that race involves a visual registry marked on the body through the interplay of perceptual practices and bodily appearances. This visual registry works within philosophy to distribute epistemic credibility. I develop an argument for the salience of race to philosophy through the work of Lewis Gordon and Charles Mills, and Paul Gilroy.

**Alcolea-Banegas, Jesús**. "Proof as a Way to Increase Understanding" in *Verdad: lógica, representación y mundo,* Villegas Forero, L, 243-251. Santiago de Compostela, Univ Santiago Comp, 1996.

Starting from the opinions of some mathematicians about the problem of understanding, the goal of this paper is to present three dimensions of understanding, to analyse the role of proof and to make some comments about them.

**Alechina, Natasha**. On a Decidable Generalized Quantifier Logic Corresponding to a Decidable Fragment of First-Order Logic. *J Log Lang Info*, 4(3), 177-189, 1995.

The logic of Q without ordinary quantifiers corresponds, therefore, to the fragment of first-order logic which contains only specially restricted quantification. We prove that it is decidable using the method of analytic tableaux. Related results were obtained by Andréka and Németi (1994) using the methods of algebraic logic. (edited)

**Alechina, Natasha** and Van Lambalgen, Michiel. Generalized Quantification as Substructural Logic. *J Sym Log*, 61(3), 1006-1044, S 96.

We show how sequent calculi for some generalized quantifiers can be obtained by generalizing the Herbrand approach to ordinary first order proof theory. Typical of the Herbrand approach, as compared to plain sequent calculus, is increased control over relations of dependence between variables. In the case of generalized quantifiers, explicit attention to relations of dependence becomes indispensable for setting up proof systems. It is shown that this can be done by turning variables into structured objects, governed by various types of structural rules. These structured variables are interpreted semantically by means of a dependence relation. This relation is an analogue of the accessibility relation in modal logic. We then isolate a class of axioms for generalized quantifiers which correspond to first-order conditions on the dependence relation.

**Alemán, Anastasio**. El realismo en matemáticas. *Mathesis*, 11(1), 37-53, F 95.

We are dealing in this article with the examination of two of the fundamental arguments offered by Penelope Maddy in support of a particular conception of realism in mathematics. The first one takes as a basis the thesis that an elemental set is a nonabstract entity perceived by human beings. The second one resorts to the well-known argumentation based on the premise that mathematics is essential to sciences like physics which deal with the real. I will maintain that none of both arguments reaches its goal. The first one because is supported by a highly questionable thesis and because, even supposing such thesis to be true, the existence of sets independent from the mind would not be derived from this. The second one because is tacitly appealing to an unacceptable assumption, that is to say, that confirmations of the physical theory are confirmations of the mathematics used for it.

**Alexander, Anna**. The Eclipse of Gender: Simone de Beauvoir and the *Différance* of Translation. *Phil Today*, 41(1-4), 112-120, Spr 97.

**Alexander, Duane** and Dommel Jr, F William. The Convention on Human Rights and Biomedicine of the Council of Europe. *Kennedy Inst Ethics J*, 7(3), 259-276, S 97.

The Convention on Human Rights and Biomedicine developed by the Council of Europe, now undergoing ratification, is the first international treaty focused on bioethics. This article describes the background of the Convention's development and its general provisions and provides a comparison of its requirements with those of federal regulations governing research with human subjects. Although most provisions are comparable, there are significant differences in scope and applicability, for example, in the areas of compensation for injury, research participation by persons with limited capacity to consent, assisted reproduction, organ transplantation and research in emergency situations. The Convention represents a milestone in international bioethics and protection of human rights that will probably be referred to with increasing frequency.

**Alexander, H A**. "Rationality and Redemption: Ideology, Indoctrination, and Learning Communities" in *Philosophy of Education (1996)*, Margonis, Frank (ed), 65-73. Urbana, Phil Education Soc, 1997.

In this paper, I argue that in *Educating Reason* and other essays Harvey Siegel fails to adequately respond to what he calls the ideology and indoctrination objections to his "reasons conception" of critical thinking. He does, however, offer a compelling case for the role of reason in education to those who already value rationality. This is because dogmatic versions of critical rationality and ideological determinism are incommensurable, while more pragmatic versions of these doctrines are not. To make the case for critical rationality in education from a pragmatic perspective, however, it is necessary to begin with a conception of the good life. Thus, moral and political philosophy turns out to be more fundamental than epistemology for educational thought.

**Alexander, James F** and Wilson, Carol A and Turner, Charles W. Family Therapy Process and Outcome Research: Relationship to Treatment Ethics. *Ethics Behavior*, 6(4), 345-352, 1996.

We know from the research literature that psychotherapy is effective, but we also know that hundreds of diverse therapies are being practiced that have not been subjected to scientific scrutiny; thus, in some circumstances iatrogenic effects do occur. Therefore, it is crucial that we recognize and implement therapeutic interventions that are evidence-based rather than succumb to ethical dilemma, frustration and complacency. Recommendations for family therapists are discussed, including the need to a) keep abreast of research findings, b) translate research findings and developments as they apply to clinical practice, c) prioritize techniques and intervention models and b) reexamine funding priorities and research foci.

**Alexander, Thomas M**. "Beyond the Death of Art: Community and the Ecology of the Self" in *Philosophy in Experience: American Philosophy in Transition*, Hart, Richard (ed), 175-194. New York, Fordham Univ Pr, 1997.

His essay analyzes some twentieth century aesthetic theories regarding the relationships between out and reality and individuality and community. After looking at Lyotard, Adorno, Benjamin and Ortega. I propose that Dewey's view of a community that requires creative individuality. His also reflects his view of nature as requiring creative individuality. His view is essentially "ecological."

**Alexander, Thomas M**. Santayana's Sage: The Disciplines of Aesthetic Enlightenment. *Trans Peirce Soc*, 33(2), 328-357, Spr 97.

This article proposes that Santayana's writings, especially those after 1912, be read as texts written for the realization of the life of spirit rather than as purely academic practices. I discern four major "moments" in their texts for achieving the ideal of the Santayana "sage." Together, these moments achieve a spiritual liberation through the aesthetic mode of apprehension.

**Alexandra, Andrew** and Miller, Seumas. Needs, Moral Self-Consciousness, and Professional Roles. *Prof Ethics*, 5(1-2), 43-61, Spr-Sum 96.

We aim to give a unified account of the concept of a professional role, claiming that the *telos* definitive of this role is the satisfaction of certain kinds of fundamental needs. Having explicated the concept of a fundamental need, we explore the implications of this claim, including the obligation of professionals to develop a high degree of moral self-consciousness, and to organize in distinctive occupational groupings in ways that facilitate the achievement of their *telos*.

**Alexy, Robert**. Discourse Theory and Human Rights. *Ratio Juris*, 9(3), 209-235, S 96.

The author's thesis is that human rights can be substantiated on the basis of discourse theory. The argument has two steps. The first step is the justification of the rules of discourse. The second step consists in the foundation of human rights.

**Alfano, Giulio**. L'Etica Politica nell'Attuale Fase Istituzionale. *Aquinas*, 39(3), 585-595, S-D 96.

**Alfaro, Mario** and Vargas, Celso. Desarrollo sostenible y valoración de la vida humana. *Rev Filosof (Costa Rica)*, 34(83-84), 385-394, D 96.

In this paper we sketch an ethical approach called planetary ethics. Two fundamental values characterize the approach: the planet as the supporter of life and the life as a planetary value. Our approach is a nonanthropocentric one and it is compatible with the general guidelines of the United Nations

Programme 21. An ethical system should incorporate the current knowledge on the human being, particularly that derived from biological sciences, including, of course, ecology. Concerning this requirement the paper draws some of the conclusions and remarks from the philosopher Gehlen as an important stage toward the conceptualization of the "essence" of human being and its place in the cosmos. After that, we sketch a general goal-oriented ethical model aim at allowing the discussion of general and specific questions, and implications of this planetary ethics. (edited)

**Alfonso, Rita** and Trigilio, Jo. Surfing the Third Wave: A Dialogue Between Two Third Wave Feminists. *Hypatia*, 12(3), 7-16, Sum 97.

As third wave feminist philosophers attending graduate schools in different parts of the country, we decided to use our e-mail discussion as the format for presenting our thinking on the subject of third wave feminism. Our dialogue takes us through the subjects of postmodernism, the relationship between theory and practice, the generation gap, and the power relations associated with feminist philosophy as an established part of the academy.

**Alheit, Peter**. La crisi del sapere moderno. *Iride*, 9(18), 329-337, Ag 96.

Nel corso della modernità è divenuto sempre più chiaro che una scienza pura e neutrale rispetto agli interessi non esiste. Le tesi di M. Weber sulla avalutatività della scienza e sul positivismo metodologico appaiono pertanto superate. Per evitare di cadere in uno scientismo irresponsabile, secondo Alheit è indispensabile che entri a far parte della scienza la responsabilità per le consequenze del lavoro scientifico.

**Alisch, Rainer**. Über Heideggers "Schweigen" reden. *Das Argument*, 209(2-3), 303-309, Mr-Je 95.

Three groups of texts dealing with Heidegger's "silence" in regard to the Holocaust are introduced; primary emphasis is given to texts (by Derrida, Lyotard, Schirmacher, a.o.) in which speaker about silence becomes a speaking about "unthought" aspects of Nazism. The article discusses the political implications of this sort of speaking about Heidegger's silence.

**Allan, George**. "Modernism, Postmodernism, and the Pragmatic Recovery of an Educational Canon" in *The Recovery of Philosophy in America: Essays in Honor of John Edwin Smith*, Kasulis, Thomas P (ed), 93-114. Albany, SUNY Pr, 1997.

Advocates (modernists) of canonical education insist learning certain ideas/texts is essential for society to perpetuate its fundamental hierarchy of values. Critics (postmodernists) reject all canons, arguing no values are fundamental and hierarchies stultifying. The pragmatic ontology of William James reconciles ("marries") these contrasting temperaments. Canons are framing devices (Goffman) crucial for orienting members of society to its fundamental beliefs/values. But no particular frame is essential, none transcendent. New beliefs/values need constantly to arise as creative responses to changing experiences. These responses stand outside the canon as threatening alternatives, but their function is to transform not to destroy the value hierarchies.

**Allan, George**. Conservatives, Liberals, and the Colonized: Ontological Reflections. *Process Stud*, 23(3-4), 256-281, Fall-Wint 94.

For political conservatism, societal integrity depends on a shared tradition of beliefs and practices everyone agrees are fundamentally important. I argue instead for political liberalism, claiming that societal unity is best achieved by affirming beliefs and practices in which rules nurturing differences regarding importance are what is most important. I use Whitehead's models of an "actual occasion" and a "structured society" to deploy a theory of "pluralistic hierarchy" as the ontological framework for this analysis. The dilemma for Cameroonians, wanting both to affirm and deny the African and European traditions that shape them individually and collectively, provides a running illustration.

**Allan, George**. *Rethinking College Education*. Lawrence, Univ Pr Kansas, 1997.

Allan argues that the current goal-directedness of America's colleges and universities has undermined the very nature of higher education. He shows that while colleges historically may have been based on a religious sense of mission or on the Enlightenment's commitment to rational inquiry, today's universities have become resource centers providing educational products to a diverse customer base of student consumers. In its commitment to marketing what students want to buy with their tuition dollars, this model of higher education not only neglects the broadening and deepening of minds, it encourages students to recognize the validity of numerous points of view without ever learning to articulate or interact meaningfully with them. (publisher, edited)

**Allan, Jim**. Answering the Free-Rider. *Auslegung*, 21(2), 99-106, Sum 96.

This article considers whether it is possible to answer the free-rider from the perspective of the moral sceptic like David Hume and John Mackie. The author considers these philosophers' arguments but finds them ultimately unconvincing. Nevertheless, the author argues that the moral sceptic can still condemn the free-rider, even if she cannot answer him or convince him to change.

**Allard, Jean-Louis**. Brèves réflexions, suite à une relecture du paysan de la garonne, 25 ans après sa parution. *Maritain Stud*, 8, 61-69, 1992.

**Allard, Jean-Louis**. La *philosophia perennis*: De la continuité et du progrès en philosophie. *Maritain Stud*, 10, 5-10, 1994.

**Allard, Jean-Louis**. La conception maritainienne de l'intelligence humaine dans antimoderne. *Maritain Stud*, 9, 83-95, 1993.

**Allard, Jean-Louis**. Une relecture du paysan de la garonne. *Maritain Stud*, 8, 101-103, 1992.

**Allchin, Douglas**. Points East and West: Acupuncture and Comparative Philosophy of Science. *Proc Phil Sci Ass*, 3(Suppl), S107-S115, 1996.

Acupuncture, the traditional Chinese practice of needling to alleviate pain, offers a striking case where scientific accounts in two cultures, East and West, diverge sharply. Yet the Chinese comfortably embrace the apparent ontological incommensurability. Their pragmatic posture resonates with the New Experimentalism in the West—but with some provocative differences. The development of acupuncture in China (and not in the West) further suggests general research strategies in the context of discovery. My analysis also exemplifies how one might fruitfully pursue a comparative philosophy of science that explores how other cultures investigate and validate their conclusions about the natural world.

**Allegro, Giuseppe**. Voluntas nel De gratia et libero arbitrio di Bernardo di Chiaravalle. G Metaf, 19(1), 49-55, Ja-Ap 97.

**Allen, Barry**. The Soul of Knowledge. Hist Theor, 36(1), 63-82, 1997.

A critical study of Ian Hacking, Rewriting the Soul (1995). Special attention is paid to his idea of the indeterminacy of the past; the truth-value of claims concerning alleged recovered memories; the concept of human kinds and their supposed difference from natural kinds; and Hacking's Foucault-inspired conception of knowledge.

**Allen, Douglas**. "Social Constructions of Self: Some Asian, Marxist, and Feminist Critiques of Dominant Western Views of Self" in Culture and Self, Allen, Douglas (ed), 3-26. Boulder, Westview Pr, 1997.

After formulating a modern, post-Cartesian view of self as the autonomous individual, Allen presents four alternative concepts: Hindu karma yoga of Bhagavad-Gita, Buddha's teaching of anatta (no-self), Marx's analysis of historical constitution of modern capitalist self and de Beauvoir's feminist approach to masculinist formulations of self. These four approaches are related by bringing out differences as well as ways that they may be complementary and integrated in more comprehensive formulations. Finally, Allen maintains the need to relate to other concepts of self, created by other cultures, as catalysts to our own creative process of self-development.

**Allen, Douglas** (ed) and Malhotra, Ashok K. Culture and Self. Boulder, Westview Pr, 1997.

Traditional scholars of philosophy and religion, both East and West, often place a major emphasis on analyzing the nature of "the self." In recent decades, there has been a renewed interest in analyzing self, but most scholars have not claimed knowledge of an ahistorical, objective, essential self free from all cultural determinants. The contributors of this volume recognize the need to contextualize specific views of self and to analyze such views in terms of the dynamic, dialectical relations between self and culture. An unusual feature of this book is that all of the chapters not only focus on traditions and individuals, East and West, but include as primary emphases comparative philosophy, religion and culture, reinforcing individual and cultural creativity. Each chapter brings specific Eastern and Western perspectives into a dynamic, comparative relation. This comparative orientation emphasizes our growing sense of interrelatedness and interdependency. (publisher)

**Allen, Jeffrey A** and Marks, Amy S and Morris, Michael H. Modeling Ethical Attitudes and Behaviors under Conditions of Environmental Turbulence: The Case of South Africa. J Bus Ethics, 15(10), 1119-1130, O 96.

This study explores the impact of environmental turbulence on relationships between personal and organizational characteristics, personal values, ethical perceptions, and behavioral intentions. A causal model is tested using data obtained from a national sample of marketing research professionals in South Africa. The findings suggest turbulent conditions lead professionals to report stronger values and ethical norms, but less ethical behavioral intentions. Implications are drawn for organizations confronting growing turbulence in their external environments. A number of suggestions are made for ongoing research.

**Allen, Layman E**. "From the Fundamental Legal Conceptions of Hohfeld to Legal Relations: Refining the Enrichment of Solely Deontic Legal Relations" in Deontic Logic, Agency and Normative Systems, Brown, Mark A (ed), 1-26. New York, Springer-Verlag, 1996.

This paper is a refinement of the author's earlier efforts to modify, extend and enrich Hohfeld's fundamental legal conceptions into a more general notion of Legal Relations (defined concepts are expressed in all capital letters.) In particular, the agency concept of Done-By is being brought into closer conformity with Belnap's emerging stit logic, with the modifications of deontic logic accompanying such changes. The S4-D2 action modal logic considered here is intended to be a part of the A-Hohfeld logic in which Legal Relations are defined and from which a representation language called the A-Hohfeld language is derived. The A-Hohfeld language is being used as a representation language for constructing Mint (Multiple INTerpretation) interpretation-assistance systems for helping lawyers to detect alternative structural interpretations of sets of legal rules. (edited)

**Allen, Michael W**. Relativism and James's Pragmatic Notion of Truth. SW Phil Rev, 13(1), 103-111, Ja 97.

**Allen, Norm R**. Religion and the New African American Intellectuals. Nature Soc Thought, 9(2), 159-187, 1996.

Contemporary African-American intellectuals are taking a prominent place in debates on a range of social and moral issues. Cornel West attempts a fusion of progressive politics with Christian values, while Stephen Carter links these values with more middle-of-the-road views. But critical thinking makes for an unstable fusion with religious beliefs, and hence, the present situation for African-American intellectuals is fraught with tensions and contradictory cross currents, at the same time as they support progressive politics in general.

**Allen, Prudence**. The Concept of Woman. Grand Rapids, Eerdmans, 1997.

This book is the second edition of a pioneering systematic study of the concept of woman in relation to man in over seventy philosophers from ancient and

medieval traditions. It uncovers four general categories of questions asked by philosophers for two thousand years—the categories of opposites, generation, wisdom, and virtue. The book also reveals the basic lines of three central theories of sex identity: sex unity, sex polarity and sex complementarity. And it considers various forms of sex neutrality as they emerged in Western philosophy. (publisher, edited)

**Allen, R E** (ed & trans). Plato's Parmenides. New Haven, Yale Univ Pr, 1997.

In this book, R.E. Allen provides a superb translation of the Parmenides along with a structural analysis that proceeds on the assumption that formal elements, logical and dramatic, are important to its interpretation and that the argument of the Parmenides is aporetic, a statement of metaphysical perplexities. Allen's original translation and commentary on the Parmenides were published in 1983 to great acclaim and have now been revised by the author. (publisher)

**Allen, R T** (ed) and Polanyi, Michael. Society, Economics & Philosophy: Selected Papers. New Brunswick, Transaction Pub, 1997.

Society, Economics, and Philosophy represents the full range of Polanyi's interests outside of his scientific work: economics, politics, society, philosophy of science, religion and positivist obstacles to it, and art. Polanyi's principal ideas are contained in three essays: on the scientific revolution, the creative imagination and the mind-body relation. Precisely because of Polanyi's work in the physical sciences, his writings have a unique dimension not found in the writings of other advocates of the market and too infrequently found even in the work of philosophers of science. (publisher,edited)

**Allen, Sister Prudence**. Foundational Virtues for Community. Maritain Stud, 12, 133-148, 1996.

**Allen Jr, Ernest**. "On the Reading of Riddles: Rethinking Du Boisian 'Double Consciousness'" in Existence in Black: An Anthology of Black Existential Philosophy, Gordon, Lewis R (ed), 49-68. New York, Routledge, 1997.

**Alliez, Éric**. Questionnaire on Deleuze. Theor Cult Soc, 14(2), 81-87, My 97.

**Allmon, Dean E** and Chen, Henry C K and Pritchett, Thomas K (& others). A Multicultural Examination of Business Ethics Perceptions. J Bus Ethics, 16(2), 183-188, F 97.

This study provides an evaluation of ethical business perception of business students from three countries: Australia, Taiwan and the United States. Although statistically significant differences do exist there is significant agreement with the way students perceive ethical/unethical practices in business. The findings of this paper indicate a universality of business ethical perceptions.

**Alma, Carine V**. A Strategy for the Acquisition of Problem-Solving Expertise in Humans: The Category-as-Analogy Approach. Inquiry (USA), 14(2), 17-28, Wint 94.

The development of expertise in a given domain involves three fundamental processes: 1) the ability to de-construct and reconstruct categories, 2) the ability to form analogical connections between concepts derived from such categories, and 3) the ability to use analogical connection information in asymmetrical and symmetrical mapping formation. First and foremost, problem-solving expertise is predicated on the categorization of critical concepts derived from the initial problem domain. The manner of categorization constrains the search for relevant, parallel information, information that is potentially useful in solution generation.

**Almeder, Robert F**. Carnap and Quine on Empiricism. Hist Phil Quart, 14(3), 349-364, Jl 97.

In this paper I discuss the naturalism of Carnap and Quine. I examine Quine's naturalized epistemology and argue that Carnap's naturalism is considerably more attractive.

**Almeder, Robert F** (ed) and Humber, James M (ed). Reproduction, Technology, and Rights: Biomedical Ethics Reviews. Clifton, Humana Pr, 1996.

In this book philosophers and ethicists debate the central moral issues and problems raised by the revolution in reproductive technology. Leading issues discussed include the ethics of paternal obligations to children, the place of in vitro fertilization in the allocation of health care resources, and the ethical implications of such new technologies as blastomere separation and cloning. Also considered are how parents and society should respond to knowledge gained from prenatal testing and whether or not the right to abort should relieve men of the duty to support unwanted children. (publisher, edited)

**Almeida, Eduardo**. An Analysis of "Res cogitans". Theoria (Spain), 12(29), 281-292, My 97.

The treatment Descartes does of 'I think-I exist' far from any inference, shows the conditioning which is proper of a "res cogitans" thought: my 'attendance to' as the originary conditioning of the strength of reality which I am. Thus, the knowledge I have of myself as thought is prejudicative; it needs no affirmation but it expresses prevolitionally the 'to be-being', or act, that I am as thought and which does not extend to my body.

**Almond, Brenda**. Counselling for Tolerance. J Applied Phil, 14(1), 19-30, 1997.

Tolerance is not neutrality, nor should tolerance in counselling be equated with a spiritual and emotional vacuum. Tolerance applies to style rather than substance and a counsellor needs a conception of the ideal—broadly speaking, a moral position. Originally proclaimed against religious and political tyranny, the political ideal of tolerance has in the twentieth century become confused with permissiveness and is thus sometimes charged with generating many of the ills of modern society, including crime and family breakdown. Counselling has become the universal remedy, replacing punishment and compulsion. (edited)

**Almond, Brenda**. Seeking Wisdom. *Philosophy*, 72(281), 417-433, Jl 97.

Moral philosophers today often offer ethical expertise in place of moral wisdom. This contrasts with the more integrated approach of ancient philosophy. Much contemporary philosophy also rejects the stabilizing constraints of reason and rationality which are basic to wisdom. Wisdom, however, is a richer concept than these, involving feeling as well as intellectual judgement. It is needed for decision-making at both the personal and the public level. But on many public issues commonsense often offers more moral wisdom than the ethical expert and there is a fund of spontaneous or intuitive response to draw on for guidance.

**Alonso González, Enrique**. "Multimodal Logics and Epistemic Attitudes" in *Verdad: lógica, representación y mundo*, Villegas Forero, L, 145-155. Santiago de Compostela, Univ Santiago Comp, 1996.

The most active research program about the dynamics of epistemic states is the AGM model-Alchourrón, Gärdenfors, Makinson. Nevertheless, the AGM model leaves out of its scope the way a community of rational agents share beliefs and experiments changes concerning to their internal relations. First, we introduce a set of epistemic states which take into account the rational agent which adopts a sentence *B* as a belief and the beliefs adopted by the community related to that rational agent. Then we define a bimodal logic which translates the main features of the problem and yield a system which allows us to calculate some conflictive situations states in terms of anomalies referred to beliefs. We finish introducing a tense bimodal logic which analyzes the solutions we can offer for conflictive beliefs configurations along the pattern supplied by some initial conditions.

**Alonso González, Enrique**. A Naive Variety of Logical Consequence. *Sorites*, 12-26, N 95.

The semantic analysis of logical consequence must obey a set of requisites which nowadays have acquired a dogmatic status. This situation prevents the development of other varieties of this fundamental relation. In this issue we try to define what we call a naive variety of logical consequence. The main feature of this relation is the way it depends on formulas in premises and conclusion: every sentence must contribute to the acceptability of an argument in a 'significative' way. This circumstance can be of some interest for research programs demanding a logical apparatus sensitive to application context. We think of the logic LP developed by G. Priest—Priest [1979]—in relation to Gödel incompleteness theorems as a test for our points of view.

**Alper, Joseph S** and Bridger, Mark. Mathematics, Model and Zeno's Paradoxes. *Synthese*, 110(1), 143-166, Ja 97.

A version of nonstandard analysis, *internal set theory*, has been used to provide a resolution of Zeno's paradoxes of motion. This resolution is inadequate because the application of internal set theory to the paradoxes requires a model of the world that is not in accordance with either experience or intuition. A model of standard mathematics in which the ordinary real numbers are defined in terms of rational intervals does provide a formalism for understanding the paradoxes. This model suggests that in discussing motion, only intervals, rather than instants, of time are meaningful. The approach presented here reconciles resolutions of the paradoxes based on considering a finite number of acts with those based on analysis of the full infinite set Zeno seems to require. The paper concludes with a brief discussion of the classical and quantum mechanics of performing an infinite number of acts in a finite time.

**Alper, Joseph S** and Geller, Lisa N and Billings, Paul R (& others). Individual, Family, and Societal Dimensions of Genetic Discrimination: A Case Study Analysis. *Sci Eng Ethics*, 2(1), 71-88, J 96.

As the development and use of genetic tests have increased, so have concerns regarding the uses of genetic information. Genetic discrimination, the differential treatment of individuals based on real or perceived differences in their genomes, is a recently described form of discrimination. The range and significance of experiences associated with this form of discrimination are not yet well-known and are investigated in this study. Individuals at-risk to develop a genetic condition and parents of children with specific genetic conditions were surveyed by questionnaire for reports of genetic discrimination. A total of 27,790 questionnaires were sent out by mail. Of 917 responses received, 206 were followed up with telephone interviews. The responses were analyzed regarding circumstances of the alleged discrimination, the institutions involved, issues relating to the redress of grievances and strategies to avoid discrimination. (edited)

**Alperson, Philip**. Value Monism, Value Pluralism, and Music Education: Sparshott as Fox. *J Aes Educ*, 31(2), 19-30, Sum 97.

**Alsina, Claudi**. What Are the Fuzzy Conjunctions and Disjunctions? (in Spanish). *Agora (Spain)*, 15(2), 63-70, 1996.

In this paper we present an intuitive approach to conjunctions and disjunctions used in fuzzy logic and we focus our presentation on the mathematical models related to these operations as well as to their interpretations.

**Alston, Kal**. "Are You a Good Witch or a Bad Witch? And Other Questions the Jesuits Left for Me" in *Philosophy of Education (1996)*, Margonis, Frank (ed), 451-454. Urbana, Phil Education Soc, 1997.

This essay responds to Valentine's contention that moral education has been undertaken through theater by Jesuits. My contribution is to suggest that the performative requirements of theater participation may have a more substantial impact on moral education than spectatorship of narratives of good and evil.

**Alston, William P**. Response to Hick. *Faith Phil*, 14(3), 287-288, Jl 97.

This is a response to Hick's comments on my approach to the problem of religious diversity in *Perceiving God*. Before unearthing the bones I have to pick with him, let me fully acknowledge that I have not provided a fully satisfactory solution to the problem. At most I have done the best that can be done given the

constraints within which I was working. But this best, I such it be, is not as bad as Hick makes it appear. To show this I need to make several corrections in Hick's depiction of the situation.

**Alston, William P**. Swinburne and Christian Theology. *Int J Phil Relig*, 41(1), 35-57, F 97.

This is a review article on Swinburne's *The Christian God*. Apart from summarizing the book, the article is largely concerned with complexities in Swinburne's distinction between what he calls "ontological necessity" and "metaphysical necessity," and with his contention that all three persons of the Trinity enjoy metaphysical necessity. Considerable modifications are required in Swinburne's account of these modes of necessity in order to make that contention coherent. Swinburne is commended for his attempt to show that "divinity inevitably *tripersonalizes*," but questions are raised concerning whether his view of the Trinity is a form of *tritheism*.

**Altarejos, Francisco**. Finalidad y libertad en educación. *Anu Filosof*, 29(2), 333-345, 1996.

The division between theory and practice is one of the consequences of Rousseau's heritage. In educational knowledge, it falls into the notion of finality, which is conceived mentally from the perspective of the result's principle. Thus, the opposition is reduplicated, confronting finality and freedom. Dilemma can be surpassed with a Polo's freedom enlargement in his transcendental anthropology, setting up as well the possibility of human unrestricted improvement.

**Altbach, Philip G** (ed) and Shils, Edward. *The Order of Learning: Essays on the Contemporary University*. New Brunswick, Transaction Pub, 1997.

The book considers the problems facing higher education by focusing on some of the main underlying factors: the relationship of higher education to government, academic freedom, the responsibilities of the academic profession, among others. Edward Shils believes that higher education has a central role in modern society and that the distractions of the recent past, including undue pressures from government, the fads of some students and faculty, and increasing involvement of the postsecondary education with day-to-day questions, have damaged higher education by deflecting it from its essential commitment to teaching, learning, and research. (publisher, edited)

**Altman, Andrew**. "Toleration as a Form of Bias" in *Philosophy, Religion, and the Question of Intolerance*, Ambuel, David (ed), 230-245. Albany, SUNY Pr, 1997.

**Altman, Scott**. Divorcing Threats and Offers. *Law Phil*, 15(3), 209-226, 96.

Spouses sometimes negotiate divorce settlements by proposing to litigate custody unless given financial concessions. Supported by theories that rely exclusively on rights, courts often uphold these settlements saying things like "[s]imply insisting upon...what one believes to be his legal rights is not coercive." I suggest a means of distinguishing (divorcing) threats from offers that explains why it is sometimes coercive to insist on one's rights in negotiations. The argument relies on counterfactual baselines to define both coercion and exploitation.

**Altstein, Howard** and Simon, Rita J. The Relevance of Race in Adoption Law and Social Practice. *Notre Dame J Law Ethics*, 11(1), 171-195, 1997.

In summarizing the major research that has been conducted on transracial adoptees and their families, the authors emphasize that all of the empirical studies support transracial adoption. The studies show that transracial adoption serves the children's best interests. Simon & Altstein's twenty-year study of primarily black children who were adopted by white families and their recent study of adult Korean children who were adopted by white families show that the transracial adoptees grow up aware of their racial identity, committed to their adoptive families and sensitive to their community. The findings strongly support the 1996 federal statute that prohibits race to be used as a factor to delay or deny adoption.

**Alvarenga, Ethel**. A Noçao de Sujeito como Aparece nas *Meditaçoes* Considerada à Luz das Sugestoes Wittgensteinianas a Respeito da Linguagem. *Discurso*, 24, 47-55, 1994.

O objetivo deste texto é apresentar duas possíveis interpretaçoes relativas ao que é revelado pelo argumento do *cogito* apresentado nas *Meditaçoes* de Descartes, mostrando que, se aceitarmos a tese wittgensteiniana relativa ao sentido das expressoes lingüísticas, entao será necessário concluir que ambas as interpretaçoes envolvem pelo menos uma dificuldade cuja soluçao nao é possível de ser dada no interior de uma filosofia da consciência.

**Alvarez Toledo, Sebastián**. "Una crítica de la versión causal del tiempo" in *Verdad: lógica, representación y mundo*, Villegas Forero, L, 443-453. Santiago de Compostela, Univ Santiago Comp, 1996.

The basic features of the causal theory of time (propounded by Reichenbach, Grünbaum, van Fraassen and others) are examined and two main objections are pointed up: 1) This theory makes use of an odd concept of causality and 2) does not avoid circularity on defining temporal relations, because the meaning of the primitive concepts that it uses in these definitions ("causal continuity", "causal connectibility") refers to the notion of time.

**Alvarez-Valdés, Lourdes Gordillo**. *Trayectoria Voluntarista de la Libertad: Escoto, Descartes, Mill*. Valencia, Nau Llibres, 1996.

The subject exposed in this book is a historical trajectory of liberty considering the primacy of the will over intellect finding result in a conception of voluntary liberty. The initiator of this way of thinking about liberty was Joan Duns Scoto which thinking was consolidated in Descartes arriving at the modern conception of liberty in J. Stuart Mill. The thinking trajectory of a power will, empty of rationality, culminates in a liberty understanding only of psychological dimension and becoming to impulsion or desire. The liberty, which power lies on the will, implies some speculatives and practical consequences. Practical problems show a new way of understanding our personal and educational world. (edited)

**Alves, Angelo**. A primeira síntese global do pensamento saudoso de Teixeira de Pascoaes. *Rev Port Filosof*, 53(1), 88-94, Ja-Mr 97.

The article critically analyzes the essay to a doctoral degree entitled "O Pensamento de Teixeira de Pascoaes," neoromantic and Portuguese "poet-philosopher" (1877-1952). The essay presents truly a globality of "poeta do Marao's" thought in his poetical-metaphysics, philosophical-religious and prophetical-messianic dimensions, establishing his first synthesis with the "saudade" (nostalgy) as hermeneutical key. The article ends up with some different perspectives of interpretation and development: more attention is paid to the author's speculative writings, especially to the implied ontology there and to the "saudosismo"; as well as to the importance to the modern gnosticism as a hermeneutical principle of his philosophical-religious thought. (edited)

**Alves, Angelo**. Ponto de Partida da Ontologia: O Primeiro Princípio "O Ente é". *Rev Port Filosof*, 52(1-4), 27-53, Ja-D 96.

The point of departure of ontology must be the most easier principle, universal and evident: "the being is". The logical-linguistic analysis of its terms and semantic value take to a different meaning from the usual concepts "the being, the essence and to be". In this first principle you will find three valences: the being is, really, truly and absolutely. They draw distinctions to the classic principles that are related to the being and not to the pure to be, and for this reason, derivatives. It concludes by discerning the principle of the absolute identity to the principle of the relative identity based on the "ontological difference".

**Alves, Pedro M S**. Kant e Beck face ao problema da "coisa-em-si". *Philosophica (Portugal)*, 53-81, 1993.

In dieser Arbeit werden die Thesen S.J. Becks über den kantischen Begriff von *Ding-an-sich* geprüft. Es sollen weder die zwei Doktrinen verglichen werden, noch die Punkte, in denen sie übereinstimmen, noch die Punkte, in denen sie sich voneinander entfernen. Basis-Voraussetzung ist mehr die Idee, dass es *eine* kantische Lehre des *Ding-an-sich* nicht gibt, sondern, dass es vielfältige divergente Tendenzen gibt in der Art, wie Kant das Problem bearbeitet. Die Auffassung Becks wird als ein Dialog mit denjenigen divergenten Tendenzen dargestellt, die in Kants Gedanken koexistieren, und dadurch eine Reflexion, die an die eigene innere Entwicklung der kritischen Philosophie gebunden ist. (edited)

**Alves, Vitorino M de Sousa**. O Homem da Evoluçao Temporal. *Rev Port Filosof*, 52(1-4), 55-85, Ja-D 96.

**Alves dos Santos, Maria Carolina**.Death and Philosophy—The Desire for Immortality among the Greeks (in Portuguese). *Trans/Form/Acao*, 19, 185-193, 1996.

This paper focuses on the intimate associations between the exhaustive attempt, undertaken by the Greek spirit, to build on solid ground their colossal foundations of a science of first principles and that which one may suppose to be its secret and ultimate motivation, namely, the aspiration after eternity, the most universal and genuine desire present in every human being, not to be obliterated by time.

**Alves Eva, Luiz Antonio**. Notas sobre a Presença de Sêneca nos *Essais* de Montaigne. *Educ Filosof*, 9(17), 39-52, Ja-Je 95.

Discutimos, brevemente, algumas questoes relativas à influência de Sêneca nos *Essais* de Montaigne, posteriormente ao contato do autor com a filosofia cética, particularmente considerando a presença de um movimento anti-dogmático que guarda certas analogias nos dois autores.

**Alward, Peter**. Correspondence on the Cheap. *Pac Phil Quart*, 77(3), 163-178, S 96.

In this paper, I distinguish between correspondence and deflationary conceptions of truth in terms of the modal status they attribute to the relation between a sentence and its truth conditions. And I distinguish between robust and minimalist correspondence conceptions on the basis of whether they provide a reductive analysis of the relation between a sentence and its truth conditions. I argue, *contra* deflationism, that a correspondence conception of truth is required in explanations of success by appealing to counterfactuals that such explanations must support. But I argue, *contra* Field, that nothing stronger than a minimalist correspondence conception is required.

**Amar, Rudra Kant**. M.N. Roy's Concept of Freedom: A Philosophical Analysis. *Darshana Int*, 35(3/139), 63-66, Jl 95.

**Amati, Giambattista** and Pirri, Fiora. A Uniform Tableau Method for Intuitionistic Modal Logics I. *Stud Log*, 53(1), 29-60, F 94.

We present tableau systems and sequent calculi for the intuitionistic analogues *IK, ID, IT, IKB, IKDB, IB, IK4, IKD4, IS4, IKB4, IK5, IKD5, IK45, IKD45* and *IS5* of the normal classical modal logics. We provide soundness and completeness theorems with respect to the models of intuitionistic logic enriched by a modal accessibility relation, as proposed by G. Fischer Servi. We then show the disjunction property for *IK, ID, IT, IKB, IKDB, IB, IK4, IKD4, IS4, IKB4, IK5, IK45* and *IS5*. We also investigate the relationship of these logics with some other intuitionistic modal logics proposed in the literature.

**Amato Mangiameli, Agata C**. Identità religiosa e cittadinanza Guerrieri di Dio o di Cesare?. *Riv Int Filosof Diritto*, 74(4), 181-196, Ap-Je 97.

**Ambos-Spies, Klaus** and Fejer, Peter A and Lempp, Steffen (& others). Decidability of the Two-Quantifier Theory of the Recursive Enumerable Weak Truth-Table Degrees and Other Distributive Semi-Lattices. *J Sym Log*, 61(3), 880-905, S 96.

We formulate general criteria that allow one to conclude that a distributive upper semilattice has a decidable two-quantifier theory. These criteria are applied not only to the weak truth-table degrees of the recursively enumerable sets but also to various substructures of the polynomial many-one (*pm*) degrees of the recursive sets. These applications to the *pm* degrees require no new complexity-theoretic results. The fact that the *pm*-degrees of the recursive sets have a decidable two-quantifier theory answers a question raised by Shore and Slaman. (edited)

**Ambrose, Maureen L** and Schminke, Marshall. Asymmetric Perceptions of Ethical Frameworks of Men and Women in Business and Nonbusiness Settings. *J Bus Ethics*, 16(7), 719-729, My 97.

This paper examines the relationship between individuals' gender and their ethical decision models. The study seeks to identify asymmetries in men's and women's approaches to ethical decision making and differences in their perceptions of how same-sex and other-sex managers would likely act in business and nonbusiness situations that present an ethical dilemma. Results indicate that the models employed by men and women differ in both business and nonbusiness settings, that both sexes report changing models when leaving business settings, and that women were better predictors of both sex's likely ethical models.

**Ambrosini, Cristina**. Jon Elster y el pensamiento del límite. *Cuad Etica*, 21-22, 167-176, 1996.

**Ambuel, David** (ed) and Razavi, Mehdi Amin (ed). *Philosophy, Religion, and the Question of Intolerance*. Albany, SUNY Pr, 1997.

The book begins with essays by three distinguished scholars, Robert Cummings Neville, J.B. Schneewind, and John McCumber. They assess the origins of intolerance, the genesis of our concept of toleration, and the outlook for the practice of tolerance in contemporary society. Beyond the opening essays, the collection is divided into three sections. The first concentrates on the relationship of religious faith and practice to toleration and inquires how religion might either impede or promote toleration. The second section deals primarily with questions regarding tolerance in the face of modern political realities. The final section discusses ethics, namely the philosophical analysis and definition of toleration as a virtue. (publisher, edited)

**Amer, Mohamed A**. Probability Logic and Measures on Epimorphic Images of Coproducts of Measurable Spaces. *Rep Math Log*, 28, 29-52, 1994.

A morphism between measurable space is defined to be a function under which the inverse image of every measurable set is measurable. With this definition, measurable space and morphisms form a category in which every nonempty family has a coproduct. These results are applied to probability logic, to reformulate Los representation theorem and to fill in the gaps in the attempts to prove it. Moreover, the reformulated theorem is generalized to countable first order languages augmented by arbitrary sets of new individual constants. (edited)

**Amerbauer, Martin**. Cut-Free Tableau Calculi For Some Propositional Normal Modal Logics. *Stud Log*, 57(2-3), 359-372, O 96.

We give sound and complete tableau and sequent calculi for the propositional normal modal logics S4.04, K4B and G0. In addition we show that G0 is not compact (and therefore not canonical), and we proof with the tableau-method that G0 is characterized by the class of all finite, (transitive) trees of degenerate or simple cluster of worlds; therefore G0 is decidable and also characterized by the class of frames of G0. (edited)

**Ameriks, Karl**. "Kant and the Self: A Retrospective" in *Figuring the Self: Subject, Absolute, and Others in Classical German Philosophy*, Zöller, Günter (ed), 55-72. Albany, SUNY Pr, 1997.

In this paper I review recent approaches to Kant's notion of apperception. After distinguishing rationalist and empiricist interpretations, I then focus on the more Cartesian and Fichtean rather than Leibnizian strand within the rationalist school. After summarizing Kant's own treatment of apperception, I defend it against objections raised recently from a Fichtean perspective by Dieter Henrich and especially Frederick Neuhouser. In particular, I argue against Fichtean claims that apperception shows the self is "absolutely self-positing" in a theoretical sense because it supposedly reveals a basic "nonrepresentational self-awareness" or a kind of "self-constituting existence."

**Ameriks, Karl**. On Schneewind and Kant's Method in Ethics (in Spanish). *Ideas Valores*, 29-53, D 96.

Contemporary work on Kantian ethics often ascribes to him a "constructivist" rather than a realist methodology. In this paper I focus on J.B. Schneewind's impressive historical work to the effect that such a reading fits in nicely with stressing several significant similarities between Kant and modern British moralists who employed a kind of "skeptical method" in ethics. After displaying the merits of this interpretation, I argue that there are nonetheless significant and defensible differences between Kant himself and his British predecessors and constructivist successors.

**Ameriks, Karl** (ed & trans) and Naragon, Steve (ed & trans) and Kant, Immanuel. *The Cambridge Edition of the Works of Immanuel Kant: Lectures on Metaphysics*. New York, Cambridge Univ Pr, 1997.

This volume contains the first translation into English of notes from Kant's lectures on metaphysics. These lectures, dating from the 1760s to the 1790s, touch on all the major topics and phases of Kant's philosophy. Most of these notes appeared only recently in the German Academy's edition; this translation offers many corrections of that edition. (publisher, edited)

**Ames, Roger T**. Continuing the Conversation on Chinese Human Rights. *Ethics Int Affairs*, 11, 177-205, 1997.

In recent years China has entered the international human rights debate, consistently making the case for cultural diversity in the formulation of human rights policy. Ames follows this argument of cultural relativism, emphasizing China's cultural differences and critiquing the concept of universal human rights, particularly as presented by Jack Donnelly in his book *Universal Human Rights*. Discussing the history of universal human rights and Confucian values, Ames asserts that a growing dialogue between China and the United States would benefit China in terms of political and individual rights and benefit the United States in terms of a greater sense of civic virtue.

**Amico, Robert P**. Euthyphro's Second Chance. *Phil Inq*, 18(3-4), 36-44, Sum-Fall 96.

There has been a good deal of controversy about Socrates' argument in the *Euthyphro* at 10a-11b, and I would like to add my insights to that discussion. In so doing I shall argue that Socrates' argument is flawed and that *Euthyphro* need never have acceded to its logical force, for it has none that bears on *Euthyphro*'s definition of piety. I give *Euthyphro* a second chance by reconstructing the dialogue the way I think it should have gone. Had *Euthryphro* been consistent during his dialectic exchange with Socrates, he would never have been numbed by that "torpedo fish."

**Amodio, Paolo**. "Ragione universale, storia universale, religione universale: il Voltaire illusionista dell'abate Galiani" in *Lo Storicismo e la Sua Storia: Temi, Problemi, Prospettive,* Cacciatore, Giuseppe (ed), 80-88. Milano, Guerini, 1997.

**Amodio, Paolo**. *Il Disincanto Della Ragione E L'Assolutezza Del Bonheur* Studio Sull'Abate Galiani. Napoli, Guida, 1997.

**Amorós, Celia**. Richard Rorty and the "Tricoteuses". *Constellations*, 3(3), 364-376, Ja 97.

Women, as oppressed people, can not invent a language absolutely new and different as Richard Rorty suggests in "Feminism and pragmatism". Historically, they *resignify* the language of their oppressor. The language in which women formulated their vindications during the French Revolution is a paradigmatic example of this process of resignification, one that brings out the possibilities for emancipation contained in the polemical abstractions used in the language of the Enlightenment. Other ways to resignify language, namely the case of Stoicism, prove significantly different: stoic resignifications do not produce any emancipatory effects, they produce a mistified discourse instead.

**Amoroso, Leonardo**. Dos estudios italianos sobre Vico y la estética. *Cuad Vico*, 7/8, 399-405, 1997.

**Amoroso, Leonardo**. Vichiana. *Teoria*, 16(1), 101-118, 1996.

This review discusses 5 Italian books about Vico, by Andrea Battistini, Paolo Cristofolini, Cecilia Castellani, Giuseppe Patella and Stefano Velotti, all published in 1995.

**Amsterdamski, Stefan**. "Between Relativism and Absolutism: The Popperian Ideal of Knowledge" in *The Significance of Popper's Thought,* Amsterdamski, Stefan (ed), 59-71. Amsterdam, Rodopi, 1996.

The paper discusses three problems concerning the Popperian philosophy of science: 1) Is it possible not to be a relativist when it is claimed that all facts are interpretations of empirical data on the grounds of some background knowledge? 2) Why did Popper in his *Epistemology without a Knowing Subject* advance the conception of the logic of scientific discovery as a mechanism of evolution of world three and abandon his previous interpretation of it as a reconstruction of actual thought processes? 3) Was Popper right in believing that the biological (Darwinian) interpretation of the evolution of knowledge protects epistemology against relativism and is in conformity with Tarski's theory of truth? In the conclusion of his paper the author claims that the interpretation of the evolution of scientific knowledge can avoid neither biological nor historical relativism.

**Amsterdamski, Stefan** (ed). *The Significance of Popper's Thought*. Amsterdam, Rodopi, 1996.

**An, Yanming**. Liang Shuming and Henri Bergson on Intuition: Cultural Context and the Evolution of Terms. *Phil East West*, 47(3), 337-362, Jl 97.

Liang Shuming once applied the concept of intuition to characterize Chinese culture as a whole. Later, he not only replaced the theoretical position of intuition with the concept of reason, but discarded the term for intuition itself. This essay will answer three questions related to this academic riddle. 1) What does intuition mean to both Bergson and Liang? 2) What does the Chinese cultural heritage contribute to the formation of Liang's intuition? 3) What is the relationship between Liang's intuition and reason?

**Anagnostopoulos, Georgios**. Aristotle on Canonical Science and Ethics. *Phil Inq*, 18(1-2), 61-76, Wint-Spr 96.

This paper examines the relation between Aristotle's conception of a canonical science and ethics by considering whether or not ethics meets one of his conditions for being a canonical science—namely, that a discipline marks off a specific domain as its subject matter. It argues against the views that, according to Aristotle, ethics lacks the required type of subject matter because i) it is about concepts, or ii) it is about opinions, since its method is dialectical. It shows that for Aristotle ethics is about human actions or activities, passions, and goals; it is about things that can constitute an underlying subject, and thus it meets the first and most basic requirement a discipline must meet in order to be an Aristotelian science.

**Anagnostopoulos, Georgios**. Aristotle on Variation and Indefiniteness in Ethics and Its Subject Matter. *Topoi*, 15(1), 107-127, Mr 96.

This paper examines the nature and consequences of two types of inexactness Aristotle attributes to ethics: variation and indefiniteness. It shows that he attributes these features to both the elements of the discipline of ethics—e.g., concepts, definitions, propositions—as well as the things the discipline is about—e.g., dispositions, virtues, vices. This explains why he thinks these features cannot be eliminated from ethics. It further argues that Aristotle's claim that ethics suffers from the above kinds of inexactness constitutes a powerful

attack on the type of strict Socratic/Platonic metaphysical essentialism that he also at times criticizes. However, weakening the strict essentialism that is presupposed by the Socratic/Platonic as well as Aristotelian conceptions of science raises problems about the place of ethics among the sciences.

**Anastaplo, George**. *The Thinker as Artist: From Homer to Plato & Aristotle*. Athens, Ohio Univ Pr, 1997.

The book mines the great books to help us discover who we are and what we should be. In their great books, ancient authors talk among themselves across the centuries. Anastaplo makes the conversation audible for readers as he explores how one might read and enjoy such books, which illustrate the thinking done by classical authors ranging from Homer and Sappho to Plato and Aristotle. Anastaplo discusses what he himself has noticed *text by text* as he examines issues relating to chance, art, nature, and divinity. (publisher, edited)

**Anckaert, Luc**. Empiricism and Transcendentalism: Franz Rosenzweig and Emmanuel Levinas (in Dutch). *Bijdragen*, 57(4), 430-451, 1996.

Levinas's thinking is centered on the relation with the *infinite*. This relation is paradoxical. To be possible, the experience of a separated subject is postulated as a transcendental presupposition. But this separation is at the same time unthinkable without the Infinite. In his main work, *The Star of Redemption*, Franz Rosenzweig stimulates the thinking of this relation. The renewal of Levinas's thinking of the paradox is made possible by phenomenology (Husserl's *Cartesianische Meditationen*). But the confrontation with Husserl indicates the limit of Levinas's thinking: the asymmetrical relation with the Infinite is unthinkable without the acceptance of some kind of symmetry.

**Andereggen, Ignacio E M**. Contemplación filosófica y contemplación mística en San Buenaventura. *Sapientia*, 51(200), 485-503, 1996.

**Andersen, David** and Cavalier, Robert J and Covey, Preston K. *A Right to Die?: The Dax Cowart Case*. New York, Routledge, 1996.

As *A Right to Die?* leads users logically through all the aspects of the case, prompting decisions about the patient's future at various stages, and asking for justification, it fosters philosophical exploration of the ethics surrounding the right to die. The CD-ROM presents the story in an accessible way through film footage, stills, and audio testimony of those involved. Supporting this powerful, sometimes disturbing evidence is a wealth of material to help students and educators in medicine, nursing, ethics, or philosophy develop and endorse the arguments both for and against the right to die. This accurately models the real world condition of having to make difficult choices, perhaps without being fully aware of the consequences. (publisher, edited)

**Andersen, Hanne**. Categorization, Anomalies and the Discovery of Nuclear Fission. *Stud Hist Phil Mod Physics*, 27B(4), 463-492, D 96.

In this paper Kuhn's latest attempt to state a principle for distinguishing revolutionary developments will be reviewed and it will be argued that certain developments entailing only partial replacements of the paradigm can be called revolutionary. The discovery of fission will serve as case study to illustrate this idea. (edited)

**Andersen, Hanne** and Barker, Peter and Chen, Xiang. Kuhn's Mature Philosophy of Science and Cognitive Psychology. *Phil Psych*, 9(3), 347-363, S 96.

Drawing on the results of modern psychology and cognitive science we suggest that the traditional theory of concepts is no longer tenable and that the alternative account proposed by Kuhn may now be seen to have independent empirical support quite apart from its success as part of an account of scientific change. We suggest that these mechanisms can also be understood as special cases of general cognitive structures revealed by cognitive science. Against this background, incommensurability is not an insurmountable obstacle to accepting Kuhn's position, as many philosophers of science still believe. Rather it becomes a natural consequence of cognitive structures that appear in all human beings.

**Anderson, Albert A**. *Universal Justice: A Dialectical Approach*. Amsterdam, Rodopi, 1997.

This book is concerned with *how* to think about justice rather than *what* to think about justice. Its dialectical approach to justice offers a postmodern philosophy which is universal without being absolutist. This stands as an alternative to claims of certainty about justice and to the denials of such certainty in the modern era. The Athenian Socrates is the primary symbol in the book, whose goal is to develop a dialectical philosophy applicable to life and open to all. (publisher, edited)

**Anderson, Deland**. The Death of God and Hegel's System of Philosophy. *Sophia (Australia)*, 35(1), 35-61, Mr-Ap 96.

**Anderson, Douglas R**. "A Political Dimension of Fixing Belief" in *The Rule of Reason: The Philosophy of Charles Sanders Peirce,* Forster, Paul (ed), 223-240. Toronto, Univ of Toronto Pr, 1997.

This paper examines Peirce's various descriptions of "belief" in order to get at the political "traditionalism" that seems to pervade his work. Within this traditionalism, Peirce suggests a continuity between theory and practice that establishes the grounds within which experimental thinking occurs. Thus, Peirce's pragmaticism resists the open experimentalisms of James and Dewey, and maintains that the value of experiment requires an attention to the traditions out of which new ideas grow.

**Anderson, Douglas R**. "John E. Smith and the Heart of Experience" in *The Recovery of Philosophy in America: Essays in Honor of John Edwin Smith,* Kasulis, Thomas P (ed), 115-130. Albany, SUNY Pr, 1997.

This essay assesses John E. Smith's conception of the self in light of the American philosophical tradition. It shows how Smith responds to Dewey's marginalization of direct concern for the status of the self. The aim is to show the usefulness of Smith's conception of the self as a center of purpose for pragmatic conceptions of self-realization.

**Anderson, Douglas R**. "Peirce and Representative Persons" in *Philosophy in Experience: American Philosophy in Transition,* Hart, Richard (ed), 77-88. New York, Fordham Univ Pr, 1997.

This essay examines Peirce's conception of self-realization in term of his own categorization of persons as artists, persons of action, and persons of thought. The examination develops in conjunction with Peirce's insistence that there remained an element of transcendentalism in his own thinking. Thus, Emerson's conception of "representative men" is brought to bear as a way of developing Peirce's initial description of self-realization.

**Anderson, Douglas R** (ed) and Hart, Richard E (ed). *Philosophy in Experience: American Philosophy in Transition.* New York, Fordham Univ Pr, 1997.

This collection of essays aims to mark a place for American philosophy as it moves into the twenty-first century. Taking their cue from the work of Peirce, James, Santayana, Dewey, Mead, Buchler and others, the contributors assess and employ philosophy as an activity taking place within experience and culture. Within this broad background of the American tradition, the essays reveal a variety of approaches to the transition in which American philosophy is presently engaged. Some of the pieces argue from a historical dialogue with the tradition, some are more polemically involved with American philosophy's current status among the contemporary philosophical "schools" and others seek to reveal the possibilities for the future of American philosophy. In thus addressing past, present and future, the pieces, taken together, outline a trajectory for American philosophy that reinvests it from a new angle of vision. (publisher)

**Anderson, Elizabeth**. Comment on Dawson's 'Exit, Voice and Values in Economic Institutions'. *Econ Phil*, 13(1), 101-105, Ap 97.

Graham Dawson provides a novel moral defense of market provision by stressing the value of the interpersonal relationships of customer markets. I argue that his distinction between auction and customer markets cannot bear the moral weight he places on it, nor does it undercut my arguments for ethical limitations on the market.

**Anderson, James A**. What Cognitive Science Tells Us about Ethics and the Teaching of Ethics. *J Bus Ethics*, 16(3), 279-291, F 97.

A relatively new and exciting area of collaboration has begun between philosophy of mind and ethics. This paper attempts to explore aspects of this collaboration and how they bear upon traditional ethics. It is the author's contention that much of Western moral philosophy has been guided by largely unrecognized assumptions regarding reason, knowledge and conceptualization, and that when examined against empirical research in cognitive science, these assumptions turn out to be false—or at the very least, unrealistic for creatures with our cognitive structures. The fundamental tension between the Western idea of morality (as basically rule-following) and the way in which people actually confront and experience moral dilemmas is a result of our failure to take the insights of cognitive psychology seriously. This failure has had a dramatic impact on not only how we teach ethics, but how we attempt to live out lives.

**Anderson, Jami**. Reciprocity as a Justification for Retributivism. *Crim Just Ethics*, 16(1), 13-25, Win-Spr 97.

Philosophers have allied retributivism with social contract theory in order to argue that retributive punishment because fairness requires it. This move invites the criticism that our society is ordered by unfair political and social institutions, thus justifying punishment by appealing to fairness is unacceptable. I show that recent attempts to meet this criticism fail because they conflate notions of abstract fairness with concrete fairness. Once this distinction is made, we can see that reciprocity retributivism will require the punishment of even those criminals who experience profound social injustices. And for that reason, it is an unacceptable theory of retributivist punishment.

**Anderson, Joel**. The Personal Lives of Strong Evaluators: Identity, Pluralism, and Ontology in Charles Taylor's Value Theory. *Constellations*, 3(1), 17-38, Ap 96.

This article addresses a tension in Charles Taylor's work between his endorsement of pluralism and his opposition to subjectivism about value. Taylor views "strong evaluation" as based on standards of worth, the objectivity of which he explains in terms of a non-Platonic ontology of value. But he also recognizes what I call "the individuating role of personal commitments," the idea that who I am is a matter of some projects having special value *for me*. I argue that Taylor's strategies for resolving this tension—narrativity and "personal resonance"—are unsuccessful, largely owing to the ontological character of his value theory.

**Anderson, Kenneth L**. Sartre's Early Theory of Language. *Amer Cath Phil Quart*, 70(4), 485-505, Autumn 96.

I derive a coherent theory of language from *Being and Nothingness* which, I demonstrate, plays a crucial role in the ontology of being-for-others, although Sartre does not recognize its importance. Sartre's theory combines the Hegelian concepts of concrete reality and abstract truth and the Saussurean division of language into *langage, langue,* and *parole*. The concrete reality of language appears on the level of *parole*, the spoken word, and this is the *only possible* point of contact between two freedoms. But, given the ontology of *Being and Nothingness*, this possibility is not realized in this early work.

**Anderson, Lynley** and McMillan, John. Knowledge and Power in the Clinical Setting. *Bioethics*, 11(3-4), 265-270, Jl 97.

In this paper we consider the three categories offered by Howard Brody for understanding power in medicine. In his book, *The Healer's Power* Brody

separates out power in medicine into the categories of Aesculapian, social, and charismatic power. We examine these three categories and then apply them to a case. In this case set in an obstetric ward, a junior member of the medical staff makes a clinical decision about a patient. This clinical decision is overruled by a senior medical staff member who then carries out his plan with disastrous consequences for the woman and her baby. This case challenges the three categories of power offered by Brody and highlights the need for a further category of hierarchical power to be added to Brody's framework. We conclude by suggesting that there is a need to recognize the discrepancy in power not only between physician and patient but also between senior and junior staff in a clinical setting.

**Anderson, Peter B**. An Expanded Theoretical Discourse on Human Sexuality Education. *J Thought*, 31(4), 83-89, Wint 96.

This paper discusses three basic ideas that are related to defining sexuality and sexuality education: first, the physical universe cannot be adequately explained; second, in the absence of these explanations humans create meaning through interaction with each other; third, in any professional discourse a level of clarity and simplicity is desirable, both for professionals and for the public they wish to impact. Quantum mechanics, relativity theory, the three laws of robotics, symbolic interactionism and social construction are among the theories used to dramatize these ideas.

**Anderson, Rob** and Cissna, Kenneth N. *The Martin Buber-Carl Rogers Dialogue: A New Transcript with Commentary*. Albany, SUNY Pr, 1997.

The authors highlight hundreds of errors, major and minor, in previously distributed and published transcripts—beginning with the typescript circulated by Rogers himself. They also show how an accurate text enhances our understanding of the relationship between Buber's philosophy and Rogers's client- and person-centered approach to interpersonal relations. Anderson and Cissna discuss the central issues of the conservation, including the limits of mutuality, approaches to "self," alternative models of human nature, confirmation of others, and the nature of dialogic relation itself. Although Buber and Rogers conversed nearly forty years ago, their topics clearly resonate with contemporary debates about postmodernism, forms of otherness, cultural studies, and the possibilities for a dialogic public sphere. (publisher, edited)

**Anderson, Ronald E** and Huff, Chuck and Little, Joyce Currie (& others). Integrating the Ethical and Social Context of Computing into the Computer Science Curriculum. *Sci Eng Ethics*, 2(2), 211-224, A 96.

This paper describes the major components of ImpactCS, a program to develop strategies and curriculum materials for integrating social and ethical considerations into the computer science curriculum. It presents, in particular, the content recommendations of a subcommittee of ImpactCS; and it illustrates the interdisciplinary nature of the field, drawing upon concepts from computer science, sociology, philosophy, psychology, history and economics.

**Anderson, Susan Leigh**. Problems in developing a Practical Theory of Moral Responsibility. *J Value Inq*, 30(3), 415-425, S 96.

Two prerequisites for saying that a person can be held morally responsible for an action are that: 1) the action be, in a significant sense, the self's action and 2) it be done freely. There appears to be a tension between the requirements. The more clearly the self is seen to be the cause of its actions, the less room there seems to be for freedom. And can we make sense of (1) at all or know whether (2) is satisfied so that we can *apply* the concept? These and other problems concerning moral responsibility are considered.

**Anderson, Thomas**. Technology and the Decline of Leisure. *Amer Cath Phil Quart*, 70(Supp), 1-15, 1996.

Although prophets of the Industrial Revolution predicted that increased technological progress would result in decreased labor and increased leisure, Americans today, in the most technologized society in the world, work an average of one month more a year than in 1970. This paper argues that technology, or, better, the way we interact with technology has much to do with the fact that: 1) we have less *free* time, i.e., time away from our jobs; 2) our jobs themselves are more stressful, and 3) we have less genuine leisure even in the scarce free time we do have. It concludes by suggesting ways we can begin to restore the importance of a "leisure ethic" and dethrone our culture's technologically stimulated "work ethics."

**Anderson, Thomas C**. Sartre and Human Nature. *Amer Cath Phil Quart*, 70(4), 585-595, Autumn 96.

Sartre denied a nature common to all human beings. Yet he insisted that a "universal human condition" and that "existential" and "ontological structures" were common. This paper asks: 1) What does Sartre reject in denying human nature? 2) What is the ontological status of the structures he posits as common to humans? To the first, I argue that Sartre denies that humans share a particular, fixed set of features and rejects a timeless, a historical universal nature (both Platonic and Aristotelian). To answer the second, I investigate his "dialectical nominalism" and his "singular universal." I argue he is not a radical nominalist and conclude by noting the ethical ramifications of his position.

**Anderson, Travis T**. Through Phenomenology to Sublime Poetry: Martin Heidegger on the Decisive Relation between Truth and Art. *Res Phenomenol*, 26, 198-229, 1996.

**Anderson Silber, C** and Macpherson, Jay. Francis Sparshott, Poet. *J Aes Educ*, 31(2), 31-36, Sum 97.

Sparshott is rare in being an aesthetician who seriously practices an art. A two-page introduction to three of his poems (previously unpublished) characterizes his poetry and invites its reading.

**Andjelkovic, Miroslava**. Epistemic Aspects of Identity (in Serbo-Croatian). *Theoria (Yugoslavia)*, 38(4), 49-69, D 95.

In this paper a model according to which a cognizer, on the basis of his/her discriminative abilities, concludes that given objects are identical, is presented.

Its logical characteristics and interpretative capacities have been explored by Timothy Williamson in his book *Identity and Discrimination*. In the book a criterion of identity is given on two levels: intentional and nonintentional. On the nonintentional level we discriminate between objects themselves, while on the intentional level objects are discriminated under their presentations. A presentation of an object needs to satisfy the following two conditions. The epistemic condition says that a presentation is a way in which the object is given in cognizer's experience. The logical one says that a presentation is an argument of the function which maps each presentation to the object it presents. Timothy Williamson uses this model to show that the relation of nonintentional indiscriminability is the equivalence relation. By applying the model to the problem of phenomenal characters he defends the claim that phenomenal characters are subjective qualities.

**Andler, Daniel**. "Can We Knock Off the Shackles of Syntax?" in *Contents*, Villanueva, Enrique (ed), 265-270. Atascadero, Ridgeview, 1995.

**Andolsen, Barbara Hilkert**. Roman Catholic Tradition and Ritual and Business Ethics: A Feminist Perspective. *Bus Ethics Quart*, 7(2), 71-82, Mr 97.

Clerical workers are an important segment of the work force. Catholic social teachings and eucharistic practice shed useful moral light on the increase in contingent work arrangements among clerical workers. The venerable concept of "the universal destination of the goods of creation" and a newer understanding of technology as "a shared workbench" illuminate the importance of good jobs for clerical workers. However, in order to apply Catholic social teachings to issues concerning clerical work as women's work, sexist elements in traditional Catholic social teachings must be critically assessed. (edited)

**Andre, Judith**. Goals of Ethics Consultation: Toward Clarity, Utility, and Fidelity. *J Clin Ethics*, 8(2), 193-198, Sum 97.

This paper is a response to a formulation of the goals of ethics consultation drawn up by a consensus panel in 1996. I offer a version (coincidentally created at the same time the expert panel was meeting) developed at a community hospital. This version is clearer; it is more useful across time and across institutions, because its brevity allows for varying interpretations; and it is more faithful to the embodied nature of ethics consultation, which is more than moral reasoning.

**Andre, Judith**. Speaking Truth to Employers. *J Clin Ethics*, 8(2), 199-203, Sum 97.

Benjamin Freedman asked, "Where are the Heroes of Bioethics?" I reply with some historical examples—Henry Beecher, William Bartholome, Norman Fost—but turn quickly to the deeper questions. Bioethics poses special challenges to integrity, as well as special safeguards. The deepest challenge may be the temptation to modify what one says for the sake of the work itself: an ethicist is usually an invited guest and the invitation can be rescinded. The central moral question is this: When should we raise questions and not just answer them?

**Andretta, Alessandro** and Steel, J R. How to Win Some Simple Iteration Games. *Annals Pure Applied Log*, 83(2), 103-164, Ja 97.

**Andreu Rodrigo, Agustín**. Leibniz, el cristianismo europeo y la *Teodicea*. *Daimon Rev Filosof*, 10, 37-46, Ja-Je 95.

Leibniz would have preferred to write his *Theodicy* on the basis of his "new system": the Monadology. The *Theodicy* would have been an essay giving information about the sufficient reason of this Universe and particularly of the Beings endowed with monadological rationality. Thus, the *Theodicy* would become 'Anthropodicy'. Such a *Theodicy* is germane to John's Christianity, to the simple rule of practical love. Classical or conventional *Theodicy* (praedestination, prescience, eschatology...) should be "trans-created". Lessing put forward this Leibnizian operation of "trans-creating" the conventional eschatological dogmas. The great trends of scepticism and antireligious criticism, however, (Bayle, Toland, etc.), compelled Leibniz to collect his occasional and scattered writings and publish them, as he tells us in the Foreword to his *Theodicy*.

**Andrews, John N**. Warren, Plumwood, a Rock and a Snake: Some Doubts about Critical Ecological Feminism. *J Applied Phil*, 13(2), 141-155, 1996.

In this paper I expound and criticise the arguments of two leading exponents of critical ecological feminism. According to critical ecological feminism responsibility for the oppressions of the natural world and the oppressions of racism and sexism can be traced to a logic of domination that is based on suspect value dualities and presupposes an unacceptable 'moral extensionism' (the view that moral status depends on membership of a specified class). I argue firstly that critical ecological feminism's critique of value dualism presupposes the truth of the thesis that humans and nonhumans are morally equal, a thesis for which it offers no persuasive arguments (indeed critical ecological feminism advocates a kind of virtue ethic which is itself incompatible with such supposed equality). Secondly, I maintain that moral extensionism, contrary to the claims of critical ecological feminism, can support a genuine respect for the natural world. Finally I suggest that the arguments for one version of critical ecological feminism, in order to be made convincing, themselves require the truth of moral extensionism.

**Andrews, Richard Mowery** (ed). *Perspectives on Punishment: An Interdisciplinary Exploration*. New York, Lang, 1997.

Punishment seems to be one of the most venerable and universal of moral impulses and social practices. It is central to law and jurisprudence, but it also exists beyond law: within the self; in relationships between individuals; inside families and communities. No single discipline circumscribes the subject of punishment, although it belongs to the matter of most disciplines in the humanities and social sciences. This collection of essays by jurists, philosophers, historians, a literary scholar and a psychoanalyst explores elemental questions of punishment: cultural and psychological roots; justifications and their validity; legal formulations and enactments; crises in contemporary practice. (publisher)

**Andrews, Robert** and Wood, Rega. Causality and Demonstration: An Early Scholastic *Posterior Analytics* Commentary. *Monist*, 79(3), 325-356, Jl 96.

We introduce an early Western medieval posterior analytics commentary, written by Richard Rufus of Cornwall (d. c.1260), as well as an unfamiliar concept of cause: demonstrational cause. Demonstrational cause must be distinguished from metaphysical (explanatory), epistemological (evidentiary), and logical (validating) cause. Demonstrational cause is a concept employed by many medievals; Thomas Aquinas, for example, as well as Richard Rufus, presumes we understand it. So if we want to work with medieval philosophy, whose study is often rewarding precisely because of the extent to which it challenges current assumptions, we must try to comprehend a usage seldom considered today. A statement of the reasons for attributing this posterior analytics commentary to Richard Rufus and an excerpt from it completes our introduction to a puzzling concept in a newly discovered work.

**Andrijauskas, Antanas**. La philosophie de l'art et les branches scientifiques y afférentes. *Diotima*, 25, 148-152, 1997.

**Anellis, Irving H**. "Tarski's Development of Peirce's Logic of Relations" in *Studies in the Logic of Charles Sanders Peirce*, Houser, Nathan (ed), 271-303. Bloomington, Indiana Univ Pr, 1997.

**Angel, Leonard**. *Enlightenment East and West*. Albany, SUNY Pr, 1994.

This book shows that mysticism is incomplete without scientific rationalism, and that our current social and political projects cannot be completed without assimilating the values and practices of mysticism. It discusses cross-cultural ethics, mysticism and value theory, mysticism and metaphysics, mysticism and the theory of knowledge, ethics and religion, parapsychology, patriarchy, and social and political history. (publisher, edited)

**Angstl, Helmut**. Praktik: Überlegungen zu Fragen der Handlungstheorie. *Conceptus*, 29(74), 87-102, 1996.

This article deals with important concepts of the theory of action, starting from the concept of event. Wishing to consider also the indeterministic point of view a sort of modal language is adopted, containing time-independent modalities. In this language a concept of causality is formulated. Then "behavior" is introduced as a class of certain events thus used for defining "bringing about." Up to this point everything remains in the physical world. The inclusion of psychological entities seems to be indispensable, however. The expressions "aim," "willingness," "realizing of aims" as well as "consciousness of freedom" are discussed. This is followed by a section on responsibility. Finally, the concept of "action" is dealt with, which—because of its ambiguity—does not seem to be suitable for being used as a basic one.

**Ankersmit, Frank**. "In Search of the Political Object: Stoic and Aesthetic Political Philosophy" in *The Ancients and the Moderns*, Lilly, Reginald (ed), 267-294. Bloomington, Indiana Univ Pr, 1996.

**Annala, Pauli**. The Function of the *formae nativae* in the Refinement Process of Matter: A Study of Bernard of Chartres's Concept of Matter. *Vivarium*, 35(1), 1-20, Mr 97.

Ever since the appearance of T. Gregory's book on the Chartrian School (Florence 1955) Bernard of Chartres's notion of the *forma nativa* has been in the focus of the research of the 12th century philosophy. The notion was a real contribution to the 12th century philosophy of nature, and it is for this reason that so much attention has been paid to showing the genetic roots of the concept. The main intention of this study is not to take a stand on the *opinio communis*, which says that Bernard developed the notion of the *forma nativa* by reading closely Calcidius's commentary and Boethius's treatise *De Trinitate*. Instead of this, the study wants to show to what extent the notion of the *forma nativa* emerged directly from Bernard's effort to understand Plato himself. When we analyze carefully the Timaean passage 50c 2-5 and Bernard's gloss on it (8: 191-202) we can come to a conclusion that it is not necessary to presume that Bernard needed any support from the part of Calcidius and Boethius to expound his innovative idea of the *forma nativa*.

**Annaromao, Nancy J**. A Feminist Interpretation of Vulnerability. *Phil Cont World*, 3(1), 1-7, Spr 96.

Under patriarchy, the rationally autonomous agent engages in contractual relations in a marketplace society. The contractual model reinforces a negative conception of the vulnerable as weak and as susceptible to injury and exploitation. Recent feminist writing has a positive notion of vulnerability that is in conflict with contractualism. Positive notions of vulnerability, the paper argues, are found in Virginia Held's conception of mothering, Nel Noddings's analysis of teaching and Annette Baier's development of trust as essential for social relationships.

**Annas, Julia**. "Scepticism About Value" in *Scepticism in the History of Philosophy: A Pan-American Dialogue*, Popkin, Richard H (ed), 205-218. Dordrecht, Kluwer, 1996.

The article discusses the various arguments and strategies to be found in ancient sceptical discussions of values comparing them with modern sceptical arguments.

**Anoz, José** (trans) and Bonafede, Giulio. Creación y salvación, o Naturaleza y redención. *Augustinus*, 42(164-5), 69-121, Ja-Je 97.

In the light of Augustine's thinking, the article focuses on the relation between the biblical and, about all, Christian interpretations of the reality, which are called creation, and salvation and investigations show that nature and redemption are harmoniously close. For its analysis of Augustine's theological methodology, it is especially interesting the closing balance of the Augustinian soteriology: the Augustinian speculation has a rational value, also valid for those who do not give their support to his faith. Augustine's answers to so hard questions are not always binding for all his readers, but they encourage still fresh approaches to them and new responses. (edited)

**Ansell Pearson, Keith**. "Deleuze Outside/Outside Deleuze: On the Difference Engineer" in *Deleuze and Philosophy: The Difference Engineer*, Ansell Pearson, Keith (ed), 1-22. New York, Routledge, 1997.

**Ansell Pearson, Keith**. "Viroid Life: On Machines, Technics and Evolution" in *Deleuze and Philosophy: The Difference Engineer*, Ansell Pearson, Keith (ed), 180-210. New York, Routledge, 1997.

**Ansell Pearson, Keith** (ed). *Deleuze and Philosophy: The Difference Engineer*. New York, Routledge, 1997.

This searching new collection considers Deleuze's relation to the philosophical tradition and beyond to the future of philosophy, science and technology. In addition to considering Deleuze's imaginative readings of classic figures such as Spinoza and Kant, the essays also point to the meaning of Deleuze on 'monstrous' and machines thinking, on philosophy and engineering, on philosophy and biology, on modern painting and literature. (publisher, edited)

**Antognazza, Maria Rosa**. *Hofmann-Streit*: il dibattito sul rapporto tra filosofia e teologia all'Università di Helmstedt. *Riv Filosof Neo-Scolas*, 88(3), 390-420, Jl-S 96.

**Anton, Corey**. On Speaking: A Phenomenological Recovering of a Forgotten Sense. *Phil Rhet*, 30(2), 176-189, 1997.

This essay draws upon Drew Leder's *The Absent Body* to argue that speaking is one of the body's natural sensori-motor powers; as a natural part of the lived-body's being-in-the-world, speech operates by way of prereflective intentionalities which maintain prethematized comprehensions. Explicating Leder's critical insights of the lived-body to illustrate many structural similarities between the senses and speaking, the essay issues a warrant for radically rethinking speech's organic being. Additionally, this radical reconsideration of speaking provides challenges into several current assumptions within introductory communication theory and postmodern philosophies of reference.

**Anton, John P**. Aristotle on the Nature of *Logos*. *Phil Inq*, 18(1-2), 1-30, Wint-Spr 96.

After attending to the difficulties due to the complexity of the uses of *logos* and to the fact that Aristotle left no special treatise on the subject, this article attempts to reconstruct the basis for his theory of *logos*. By connecting the two definitions of *anthropos* as a logical and political animal while arguing against interpretations that reduce *logos* to language, the paper defends the possibility of detecting in the *De anima* the location of *logos* in the faculty of judgment. The argument is made that this faculty in turn actualizes and supports the operations of discourse, demonstration, definition, and communication.

**Antonaccio, Maria**. Imagining the Good: Iris Murdoch's Godless Theology. *Annu Soc Christ Ethics*, 223-242, 1996.

This paper attempts to present a coherent account of Iris Murdoch's moral philosophy as a "theology without God." Although she rejects theism, Murdoch does not thereby reject the idea of a moral absolute or the idea of the individual as moral agent. Rather, she defends a transcendental argument based on a reading of the ontological proof which establishes an inextricable relation between selfhood and the idea of the Good. The paper demonstrates the significance of this argument for Murdoch's "Godless theology" and for contemporary moral inquiry by moving between elements of her position and her readings of Kant and Plato.

**Antonelli, Gian Aldo**. What's in a Function?. *Synthese*, 107(2), 167-204, My 96.

In this paper we argue that Revision Rules, introduced by Anil Gupta and Nuel Belnap as a tool for the analysis of the concept of truth, also provide a useful tool for defining computable functions. This also makes good on Gupta's and Belnap's claim that Revision Rules provide a general theory of definition, a claim for which they supply only the example of truth. In particular we show how Revision Rules arise naturally from relaxing and generalizing a classical construction due to Kleene and indicate how they can be employed to reconstruct the class of the general recursive functions. We also point at how Revision Rules can be employed to access nonminimal fixed points of partially defined computing procedures.

**Antonelli, Gian Aldo** and Bicchieri, Cristina. Game-Theoretic Axioms for Local Rationality and Bounded Knowledge. *J Log Lang Info*, 4(2), 145-167, 1995.

We present an axiomatic approach for a class of finite, extensive form games of perfect information that makes use of notions like "rationality at a node" and "knowledge at a node." We distinguish between the game theorist's and the players' own "theory of the game." The latter is a theory that is sufficient for each player to infer a certain sequence of moves, whereas the former is intended as a justification of such a sequence of moves. While in general the game theorist's theory of the game is not and need not be axiomatized, the players' theory must be an axiomatic one, since we model players as analogous to automatic theorem provers that play the game by inferring (or computing) a sequence of moves. We provide the player with an axiomatic theory sufficient to infer a solution for the game (in our case, the backwards induction equilibrium), and prove its consistency. We then inquire what happens when the theory of the game is augmented with information that a move outside the inferred solution has occurred. (edited)

**Antonello, Pierpaolo** (ed) and De Castro Rocha, Joao Cezar (ed). L'ultimo dei porcospini: Intervista biografico-teorica a René Girard. *Iride*, 9(19), 573-620, S-D 96.

**Antoniou, Grigoris**. Structuring Methods for Nonmonotonic Knowledge Bases. *Commun Cog—AI*, 13(1), 13-30, 1996.

The paper investigates some ways in which nonmonotonic knowledge bases can be split into smaller units. This can increase comprehensibility, maintenance, and processing efficiency of systems.

**Antonopoulos, Constantin**. A Schism in Quantum Physics or How Locality May Be Salvaged. *Phil Natur*, 34(1), 33-69, 1997.

It is being constantly affirmed that quantum mechanics (QM) is a physical theory strictly entailing nonlocality. I have been of the contrary opinion myself, as I'm sure Bohr himself also was. For his own wholeness is other then nonlocal and strictly confined to atomic objects and measuring *instruments*. One far too proximal to satisfy nonlocal standards and more than sufficiently proximal to satisfy local ones. Besides, what seems to be the truth in this connection is that *deterministic* QM implies nonlocality. Not that just any kind of QM whatsoever does. (edited)

**Antonopoulos, Constantin**. Bohr on Nonlocality: The Facts and the Fiction. *Phil Natur*, 33(2), 205-241, 1996.

The paper examines Heidegger's confrontation with Nietzsche in his lectures of W3 1936/37 and SS 1937. In the paper is explained why Heidegger has said to his friends that "Nietzsche's philosophy has destroyed" him.

**Antonopoulos, Constantin**. Innate Ideas, Categories and Objectivity. *Phil Natur*, 26(2), 159-191, 1989.

Bohr, if an innatist too, is the ideal sort of innatist for finally driving the point home as to why, innate ideas are still a very great distance afar from functioning as Kantian categories. Bohr is the innatist who has witnessed the *failure* of his forms of perception. Could this happen to a proper Kantian category? I reply in the negative, as I also do regarding the affinity of Bohr to Kant, arguing instead that though of merely innate ideas it can be said that they may be *found* 'a priori' in the intellect, it cannot also be said that they are *valie a priori* for all possible experience. I then contend that a mere innatist and a fortiori a Bohrian type of innatist, namely one who is conscious of the failure of his innate concepts due to their *mis-match* with reality, cannot ever amount to the status of an *idealist*, who latter is known to have postulated an a priori *agreement* between concepts and reality. The former doctrine states an *anthropological fact*, the latter an *ontology*. (edited)

**Antony, Louise M**. "I'm a Mother, I Worry" in *Contents*, Villanueva, Enrique (ed), 160-166. Atascadero, Ridgeview, 1995.

I support Jaegwon Kim's contention that the problem of mental causation is neither an artifact of philosophical confusion, nor the result of misplaced philosophical priorities. I disagree with his conclusion that there is no viable solution to the problem other than strong reductionism. I argue that we can make sense of and have grounds for holding a nonreductive materialist position if we can demonstrate the existence of contingent but reliable regularities that crucially involve mental properties.

**Antony, Louise M**. "Law and Order in Psychology" in *AI, Connectionism and Philosophical Psychology, 1995*, Tomberlin, James E (ed), 429-446. Atascadero, Ridgeview, 1995.

Some philosophers argue that there must be laws in psychology, while others argue that there can't be laws in psychology. I uphold the first claim, arguing that undeniable facts about our abilities to predict and explain human action demonstrate the existence of nomic (that is, nonaccidental empirical) regularities at the intentional level, and I criticize arguments to the contrary by Davidson and Schiffer.

**Antony, Louise M**. Equal Rights for Swamp-Persons. *Mind Lang*, 11(1), 70-75, Mr 96.

I challenge the widely-held view that Davidson's "swampman" is incapable of contentful thought because it lacks an appropriate history. I argue that it is synchronic nomic relationships that confer intentional content on a being's internal states.

**Antony, Louise M**. Feeling Fine About the Mind. *Phil Phenomenol Res*, 57(2), 381-387, Je 97.

The article presents a critique of John Searle's attack on computationalist theories of mind in his recent book, *The Rediscovery of the Mind*. Searle is guilty of caricaturing his opponents and of ignoring their arguments. Moreover, his own positive theory of mind, which he claims "takes account of" subjectivity, turns out to offer no discernible advantages over the views he rejects.

**Antony, Louise M** and Davies, Martin. Meaning and Semantic Knowledge. *Aris Soc*, Supp(71), 177-209, 1997.

**Anzenbacher, Arno**. The Ethics of Peter Singer (in Serbo-Croatian). *Filozof Istraz*, 15(4), 823-843, 1995.

Der Verfasser dieses Artikels stellt in kritischer Absicht das ethische Konzept Peter Singers dar, das in dessen Hauptwerk *Practical Ethics* präsentiert ist. Er bestimmt Singers ethische Position als eine Position angewandter Ethik, die sich mit praktisch-relevanten Fragen befasst, genauer: als modifizierte utilitaristische Position. Diese gründet sich auf den Utilitarismus, unterscheidet sich jedoch von ihm auf, nach Meinung des Autors, entscheidende, aber auch umstrittene Weise durch eine Position, die hier als *Aktualismus* bestimmt wird. Während der klassische Utilitarismus auf dem Konsequenzenprinzip, dem Utilitätsprinzip sowie auf dem Hedonismusund dem Sozialprinzip (mit der Forderung nach grösstmöglicher Nutzensumme bzw. grösstmöglichem Durchschnittsnutzen) beruht, ergänzt Singer den klassischen Utilitarismus durch das Gerechtigkeitsprinzip, das Prinzip der *gleichen Erwägung von Interessen* aller Betroffenen. Eine Konsequenz dieser Denkweise ist die Position Singers, der zufolge wir bei unserem Handeln *moralische Pflichten* gegenüber jenen Menschen haben, die besagtes Handeln betrifft. Diese Pflichten bestehen in der Erwägung von Interessen und Präferenzen. (edited)

**Aparicio de La Hera, Beatriz**. Bolívar and the Latin American Unity (Spanish). *Fronesis*, 2(2), 51-58, D 95.

There is an official truth around the heroes of the independence process which presents them as half-gods far from any criticism. However, their ideas are neither analyzed nor discussed, whereas many teachings for the new generations are made concrete. Simón Bolívar is an example of that condition. Bolívar's doctrine must help to guide the states and their institutions in Latin America since it is based on unity, freedom and justice. *El Libertador* strove to establish Hispano-Americanism, but Monroeism and Pan-Americanism were imposed, dividing the old Spanish America into several countries which faced each other.

**Apel, Karl-Otto**. "El "Proyecto filosófico para la paz perpetua" de Kant como cuasipronóstico de la filosofía de la historia..." in *Kant: La paz perpetua, doscientos años después*, Martínez Guzmán, Vicent (ed), 7-33. Valencia, Nau Llibres, 1997.

**Apel, Karl-Otto**. "The Hermeneutic Dimension of Social Science and Its Normative Foundation" in *Epistemology and History*, Zeidler-Janiszewska, Anna (ed), 11-34. Amsterdam, Rodopi, 1996.

The author discusses two main issues. First, the hermeneutic dimension of social science and the controversies connected with such a view (e.g., explanation vs. understanding). Secondly, the author claims that such a hermeneutic dimension of social science stands in need of a normative foundation (in view of the methodological controversy between the Frankfurt School of Popper's adherents).

**Apel, Karl-Otto**. La ética del discurso como ética de la corresponsabilidad por las actividades colectivas. *Cuad Etica*, 19-20, 9-30, 1995.

This paper criticizes contemporary research about "applied ethics"—especially "scientific ethics"—, based on the analysis of the concept of "responsibility". This concept is insufficient if referred to a singular person. Traditional ethics, on their own, are not able to find the concept of responsibility, not the concept of justice as equity. The condition of applicability of such *ethics* is a *telos* of the political realm, and it is here where correspondivity resides.

**Apel, Karl-Otto**. Plurality of the Good? The Problem of Affirmative Tolerance in a Multicultural Society from an Ethical Point of View. *Ratio Juris*, 10(2), 199-212, Je 97.

Starting from the problem of tolerance in a multicultural society, the author undermines the limits of a classical-liberal foundation (negative tolerance) and suggests the need for a new meaning: a positive concern of tolerance implying appreciation of a variety of social cultures and value traditions. On an ethical level, positive tolerance can be grounded in the *discourse theory, developing the classical Kantian deontological ethics in a transcendental-pragmatic and in a transcendental-hermeneutic sense. In this way, discourse ethics can answer two questions posed by tolerance in a multicultural society: the duty to support all in the pursuit of their ideals and realize positive tolerance as well as its restrictions.*

**Aponte, Elida**. The Ethics of Law or the Right of Women (Spanish). *Fronesis*, 3(1), 11-29, Ap 96.

In the presence of the universalistic moral philosophies various feminist theories from different fields of the social studies have stated that said philosophies, the majority of which are legalistic, center ethics in the idea of justice. The pretended universality is nothing but a mishidden androcentrism and instead, the theories based on the ethics of care show that women have a tendency to develop a moral philosophy and an idea of justice different from that elaborated by men. Yet, a right of women which deconstructs and reelaborates law from a nondiscriminatory perspective is proposed.

**Apostoli, Peter**. On the Completeness of First Degree Weakly Aggregative Modal Logics. *J Phil Log*, 26(2), 169-180, Ap 97.

This paper extends David Lewis's result that all first degree modal logics are complete to weakly aggregative modal logic by providing a filtration-theoretic version of the canonical model construction of Apostoli and Brown. The completeness and decidability of all first-degree weakly aggregative modal logics is obtained, with Lewis's result for Kripkean logics recovered in the case k = 1.

**Appel, Fredrick**. The Objective Viewpoint: A Nietzschean Account. *Hist Phil Quart*, 13(4), 483-500, O 96.

**Applebaum, Barbara**. "But That Is Not What I Mean" Criticizing With Care and Respect" in *Philosophy of Education (1996)*, Margonis, Frank (ed), 77-85. Urbana, Phil Education Soc, 1997.

Educators who value both serious inquiry and nurturance must reexamine the meaning and role of educational criticism. Diller (1993) and Boyd (1993) make important educational contributions with their notion of caring criticism, however, their suggestions are restrictive. Another interpretation of caring is discussed and its relationship to respect for persons elucidated. Criticizing with care and respect, it is argued, does justice to the values of serious inquiry and nurturance and can be used in all educational settings even those in which a "Community of Inquiry and Support" is not feasible and where knowing the psychological make-up of all one's students is not practical. Furthermore, criticizing with care and respect is necessary for certain aspects of antiracist education.

**Applebaum, Barbara**. Moral Paralysis and the Ethnocentric Fallacy. *J Moral Educ*, 25(2), 185-199, Je 96.

One of the greatest achievements ensuing from contemporary commitments to multiculturalism has been a greater awareness of the indignity of ethnocentrism. However, an inadequate understanding of how to avoid ethnocentrism may lead to moral paralysis. In this paper, it is argued that extolling the voices of others does not necessarily imply denigrating our own and that respecting diversity is the only genuine antidote for ethnocentrism.

**Aquila, Richard E**. "Self as Matter and Form: Some Reflections on Kant's View of the Soul" in *Figuring the Self: Subject, Absolute, and Others in Classical German Philosophy*, Zöller, Günter (ed), 31-54. Albany, SUNY Pr, 1997.

Cognitive synthesis is effected from within a presupposed holistic structure incorporating a manifold of parts of one's internal state into a single potential cognition ("manifold of inner sense" in one sense of the term). Insofar as cognitively unifying acts apprehend perceptible "projections" of their own unifying structure, this constitutes the "I of inner sense," or "soul," as a real being at least indirectly given through inner sense. All acts of thought "inhere" in this being as its "states." Unlike the purely formal "I" of apperception, this can satisfy the (practical) demand for a phenomenally real being of which we are required to believe that, regarded in itself, it is the underlying ground of its own acts.

**Aqvist, Lennart**. "On Certain Extensions of von Kutschera's Preference-Based Dyadic Deontic Logic" in *Das weite Spektrum der analytischen Philosophie*, Lenzen, Wolfgang, 8-23. Hawthorne, de Gruyter, 1997.

The paper deals with two sorts of extensions of von Kutschera's preference-based logic of *conditional* obligation/permission, viz. i) an infinite hierarchy $Gm$, with $m$ any positive integer, of dyadic deontic systems having so-called *systematic frame constants* in their primitive logical vocabulary, intended to represent various *levels of perfection*; and ii) a single system $G$ which forms a kind of "core" system in relation to the $Gm$. The main result established in the paper is then to the effect that the logic $G$ is the *intersection* of all the logics $Gm$. Our proof utilizes certain interesting connections between the logic of conditional obligation and the logic of preference, which are emphasized in earlier work of von Kutschera and myself.

**Arabatzis, Theodore**. Rethinking the 'Discover' of the Electron. *Stud Hist Phil Mod Physics*, 27B(4), 405-435, D 96.

This paper attempts to reconceptualize the "discovery" of the electron. It starts with a classification and critique of several approaches to the discovery of unobservable entities. It proposes an historicist approach to discoveries of this kind, according to which an unobservable entity has been discovered only when consensus has been reached, within the relevant scientific community, with respect to its reality. The remainder of the paper is a historical reconstruction, in the light of the methodological issues that were previously raised, of the processes which led to the acceptance of the electron as an element of the ontology of physics.

**Aragüés, Juán Manuel**. Spinoza y el Poder Constituyente. *Philosophica (Portugal)*, 79-94, 1996.

Le projet de Spinoza d'une philosophie de la joie se développe dès une position hipersubjectiviste, presque hobbesienne, laquelle aboutirait à une contraposition entre les subjectivités, vers une autre position dont les traits collectifs sont remarquables. Cette dernière ouvre la porte à une théorie démocratique radicale, munie de tout un batiment épistémologique et ontologique. On peut trouver, dans notre siècle, une autre philosophie, celle de J.-P. Sartre, qui a parcouru un chemin très prochain et qui présente des problèmes politiques parallèles à ceux de la théorie spinozienne, en concret en ce qui concerne la question de la liberté. Le présent article veut penser les limites de la conception spinozienne et sartrienne de la liberté et la dimension politique de la question.

**Aram, John** and Clarke, Ruth. Universal Values, Behavioral Ethics and Entrepreneurship. *J Bus Ethics*, 16(5), 561-572, Ap 97.

This is a comparison of graduate students' attitudes in Spain and the United States on the issue of universal versus relativist ethics. The findings show agreement on fundamental universal values across cultures but differences in responses to behavioral ethics within the context of entrepreneurial dilemmas.

**Aranguren, José Luis L**. "El Ortega de 1914" in *Política y Sociedad en José Ortega y Gasset: En Torno a "Vieja y Nueva Política"*, Lopez de la Vieja, Maria Teresa (ed), 19-21. Barcelona, Anthropos, 1997.

**Arantes, Otília Beatriz Fiori** and Arantes, Paulo Eduardo. Country Fashion (in Portuguese). *Discurso*, 26, 33-68, 1996.

If there is such thing as the Formation of Brazilian Painting, the authors claim that a clue can be given by Gilda de Mello e Souza's solution to the problem of representation of "Brazilian man" in Almeida Júnior's regionalist pictures.

**Arantes, Paulo Eduardo** and Arantes, Otília Beatriz Fiori. Country Fashion (in Portuguese). *Discurso*, 26, 33-68, 1996.

If there is such thing as the Formation of Brazilian Painting, the authors claim that a clue can be given by Gilda de Mello e Souza's solution to the problem of representation of "Brazilian man" in Almeida Júnior's regionalist pictures.

**Arantes, Urias**. Os direitos do homem e a questao social. *Kriterion*, 34(88), 70-86, Ag-D 93.

This article deals with the problem of human rights and its relation with social rights in the works of Claude Lefort.

**Arbaizar Gil, Benito**. "El estatuto epistemológico de las matemáticas en el origen del pensamiento moderno" in *Verdad: lógica, representación y mundo*, Villegas Forero, L, 233-242. Santiago de Compostela, Univ Santiago Comp, 1996.

This study reflects on the transformation in the way of understanding the role of mathematics that took place in the origin of modern thought. It deals with the philosophical roots of new science (the opposite scientific projects defended by the Platonic and the Aristotelic ones) and it underlines the importance of the epistemological background to understand the victory of the mathematical paradigm.

**Arbuthnot, Jeanette Jaussaud**. Identifying Ethical Problems Confronting Small Retail Buyers during the Merchandise Buying Process. *J Bus Ethics*, 16(7), 745-755, My 97.

This research was designed to develop an inventory of vendor-related problems experienced by buyers for small retail apparel stores during the merchandise buying process, determine how frequently each difficulty occurs and identify the experiences perceived to be unethical. Among the 22 vendor-related difficulties examined minimum order requirements, six month advance purchase, incomplete orders, late shipments and shipping overcharges were identified most frequently. Analysis of results suggested that one factor, misleading vendor practices and eight background variables (annual sales, price line, full and part-time employees, retail and buying experience and shopping large or small markets) were associated with unethical experiences. Ethically troublesome experiences mentioned most frequently were padded orders, selling competitor same merchandise, withholding return authorization and credit, shipping overcharges and dealing with vendor's factor.

**Arce Carrascoso, José Luis**. *De la razón pura a la razón interesada*. Barcelona, Univ Barcelona, 1996.

*De la razón pura a la razón interesada* es un trabajo de carácter histórico-sistemático en el que se intenta reivindicar la actualidad e importancia de la filosofía trascendental. Repara en los hitos y problemas más esenciales de esta corriente crítica hasta llegar a sus últimas configuraciones en el campo de la reflexión contemporánea y en las nuevas teorías de la racionalidad que se siguen proponiendo más allá de postulados estrictamente idealistas. Es un viaje por el camino recorrido por la filosofía trascendental, poniendo de relieve la pervivencia de conceptos tales como "sujeto", "crítica" o "reflexión". El núcleo fundamental del libro está en el estudio de la situación terminal a la que llega el planteamiento fenomenológico husserliano y en el hallazgo de nuevos ámbitos de trascendentalidad. De este modo, puede advertirse como la vieja filosofía del sujeto-conciencia llega a trasformarse y girar, para dar cabida en sí, a nuevos temas, -la corporeidad, la intersubjetividad, el lenguaje-, que tradicionalmente habían sido silenciados o minusvalorados. (publisher)

**Arce Carrascoso, José Luis**. Ontología y conocimiento en M. Merleau-Ponty. *Convivium*, 9, 92-116, 1996.

This paper presents a reappraisal of the philosophy of Merleau-Ponty through an analysis of its basic structure, which shapes, both temporally and systematically, the fundamental, joint involvement of the metaphysical and ontological aspect on the one hand and the epistemological and critical on the other, at the heart of which appears the anthropological philosophy of "ambiguity". Underpinning this approach is the binomial analysis of the "human conduct-human existence" of the man-world as a unitary phenomenon, which leads to a mapping out of an integrated monism under the hypothesis of an incomplete systesis that is both fluid and ambiguous.

**Arce M, Daniel G**. Correlated Strategies as Institutions. *Theor Decis*, 42(3), 271-285, My 97.

Two institutions that are often implicit or overlooked in noncooperative games are the assumption of Nash behavior to solve a game and the ability to correlate strategies. We consider two behavioral paradoxes, one in which maximin behavior rules out all Nash equilibria ('chicken') and another in which minimax supergame behavior leads to an 'inefficient' outcome in comparison to the unique stage game equilibrium (asymmetric 'deadlock'). Nash outcomes are achieved in both paradoxes by allowing for correlated strategies, even when individual behavior remains minimax or maximin. However, the interpretation of correlation as a public institution differs for each case.

**Archangelsky, Dmitri A** and Taitslin, Mikhail A. A Logic for Information Systems. *Stud Log*, 58(1), 3-16, 1997.

A conception of an information system has been introduced by Pawlak. The study has been continued in works of Pawlak and Orlowska and in works of Vakarelov. They had proposed some basic relations and had constructed a formal system of a modal logic that describes the relations and some of their Boolean combinations. Our work is devoted to a generalization of this approach. A class of relation systems and a complete calculus construction method for these systems are proposed. As a corollary of our main result, our paper contains a solution of a Vakarelov's problem: how to construct a formal system that describes all the Boolean combinations of the basic relations.

**Archard, David**. Filial Morality. *Pac Phil Quart*, 77(3), 179-192, S 96.

Filial regard is the special consideration that children, even as adults, show their parents and filial morality the demonstration that such a regard is demanded of them. The three main accounts of filial morality, based upon ideas of gratitude, role obligations and friendship, are shown to be unsatisfactory. The article explores the idea, found in traditional Chinese thinking, that filial regard is the 'root' of goodness and suggests that the Chinese model has been viewed unsympathetically due to an understanding both of the family's role in moral education and of the nature of modern morality.

**Archard, David**. Should Nationalists be Communitarians?. *J Applied Phil*, 13(2), 215-220, 1996.

John O'Neill argues in a recent article, "Should Communitarians be Nationalists?" that communitarians are wrong to be committed to the defence of ties of nationhood, both because the nation-state's rise is associated with the disappearance of the ties of community and because the nation is an illusory community. I argue that the evidence that communitarianism is committed as charged to the defence of nationality is unconvincing. Further, the familiar accusation that the nation is a false or unreal community is neither perspicuous nor obviously true. It is important to evaluate the significance and worth of the nation as a community independently of the nationalist prescription that the nation and the state should coincide. The important question is not whether the political community should be a nation, but what sort of community the nation should be.

**Archer, Simon**. The Ethics of Creative Accounting. *Sci Eng Ethics*, 2(1), 55-70, J 96.

Creative accounting, which generally involved the preparation of financial statements with the intention of misleading readers of those statements, is prima facie a form of lying, as defined by Bok. This paper starts by defining and illustrating creative accounting. It examines and rejects the arguments for considering creative accounting, in spite of its deceptive intent, as not being a form of lying. It then examines the ethical issues raised by creative accounting, in the light of the literature on the ethics of lying. This literature includes the evaluation of various excuses and justifications for lying and these are examined here in relation to creative accounting. It is concluded that even in circumstances in which creative accounting would arguably serve a worthy purpose, that purpose would be at least as well served by honest communication.

**Arditi, Benjamin**. The Negotiation of Equivalence. *Phil Soc Crit*, 23(3), 55-76, My 97.

The paper deals with the status of referents for claims among conflicting claimants when multiplicity is a fact and there is no room for a substantive notion of community. It develops a notion of contingent and 'impure' universal as it arises in the negotiation of equivalence in scenarios of conflict between claimants. My argument is that measures of equivalence cannot conform to the caricature of absolute, all-encompassing referents intent on subjugating difference in the name of sameness; that a reflection about decisions and the validity of claims—i.e., concerning singularity—cannot be reduced to a simple application of the rule; and that decisions are lodged in the undecidable terrain between norms and their redescription, which means that the status of universals is an effect of continual political battles.

**Arenas, Luis**. *Matemáticas, método y* mathesis universalis *en las* Regulae *de Descartes*. *Rev Filosof (Spain)*, 8(15), 37-61, 1996.

**Arenas, Luis**. De lo uno a lo otro: conocimiento, razón y subjetividad en Descartes. *An Seminar Hist Filosof*, 13, 97-124, 1996.

In Descartes's philosophy the notion of identity is a guide-idea which is extended to many aspects of his thought, namely his theory of knowledge, theory of science, ontology or theology. Knowing for Descartes is to reconstruct identities partially faded away in the phenomena. Furthermore, the second purpose of the paper is to suggest that the notion of subjectivity and its identity is the result of different and even contradictory discourses. The ambiguity and paradox in Cartesian notion of "subject" come from the heterogeneity of those plural contexts from which it is generated.

**Arendes, Lothar**. Ansätze zur physikalischen Untersuchung des Leib-Seele-Problems. *Phil Natur*, 33(1), 55-81, 1996.

On the basis of the physical theories of quantum mechanics, theory of relativity, and thermodynamics, proposals for the experimental and theoretical investigation of the mind-body problem are made. The mind-body problem consists of the problem of cognition and of the problem of consciousness. It is proposed that visual consciousness is a physical field by analogy with the metric field of general theory of relativity. The unconscious cognitions should be investigated by models of neural networks, but additionally, some processes could take place in the quantum vacuum.

**Arens, Katherine**. Wilhelm Griesinger: Psychiatry between Philosophy and Praxis. *Phil Psychiat Psych*, 3(3), 147-163, S 96.

This essay discusses Wilhelm Griesinger's seminal work on mental illness, *Mental Pathology and Therapeutics* (1867, trans. 1882), in the context of transcendental idealism, as an outgrowth of the work of Kant, Herbart and Hegel. Griesinger drew on an adaptation of Hegel's dialectical model of history and science to offer both a new way to interpret mental illness as a product of an individual's long-term interactions with both nature and culture and a new norm for therapeutic practice based on the patient's role in his community and history. *Mental Pathology and Therapeutics* rests on Griesinger's adaption of the Hegelian dialectic to the context of pragmatic science, first by adopting its model of the mind, then by describing the etiology of mental disease and a taxonomy of its forms. Griesinger's work thus stands in a largely unacknowledged tradition alive as late as Sigmund Freud and Jacques Lacan.

**Ariew, André**. Innateness and Canalization. *Proc Phil Sci Ass*, 3(Suppl), S19-S29, 1996.

Cognitive scientists often employ the notion of innateness without defining it. The issue is, how is innateness defined in biology? Some critics contend that innateness is not a legitimate concept in biology. In this paper I will argue that it is. However, neither the concept of high heritability nor the concept of flat norm of reaction (two popular accounts in the biology literature) define innateness. An adequate account is found in developmental biology. I propose that innateness is best defined in terms of C.H. Waddington's concept of canalization.

**Ariew, André** and Walsh, Denis M. A Taxonomy of Functions. *Can J Phil*, 26(4), 493-514, D 96.

We discuss the way in which a new theory of biological functions, the relational theory, illuminates the relationship between disparate conceptions of function: propensity, aetiological and causal role. According to the relational theory, evolutionary functions (including propensity and aetiological functions) are a type of causal role function—the typical causal contribution of a trait type to average individual fitness. We present a taxonomy showing the relationship between causal role, aetiological and propensity functions and discuss the distinctive explanatory roles played by each.

**Aristotle** and Gerena, Luis Alonso and Ariza, Sergio (trans). Aristóteles: Sobre las Ideas. *Ideas Valores*, 94-103, D 96.

This translation assembles a group of remaining fragments from a presumed youthful work of Aristotle called *On Ideas*. Aristotle there critically discusses several arguments that prove the existence of ideas. His criticism consists essentially of the following: 1) the arguments do not really prove the existence of ideas; 2) they prove a larger population of ideas than the Platonists are willing to admit; 3) they result in logical absurdities like the one known as the *third man*; 4) they eliminate the principles that ground the theory of ideas.

**Ariza, Sergio** (trans) and Gerena, Luis Alonso and Aristotle. Aristóteles: Sobre las Ideas. *Ideas Valores*, 94-103, D 96.

This translation assembles a group of remaining fragments from a presumed youthful work of Aristotle called *On Ideas*. Aristotle there critically discusses several arguments that prove the existence of ideas. His criticism consists essentially of the following: 1) the arguments do not really prove the existence of ideas; 2) they prove a larger population of ideas than the Platonists are willing to admit; 3) they result in logical absurdities like the one known as the *third man*; 4) they eliminate the principles that ground the theory of ideas.

**Arjo, Dennis**. Sticking Up for Oedipus: Fodor on Intentional Generalizations and Broad Content. *Mind Lang*, 11(3), 231-245, S 96.

In *The Elm and the Expert*, Jerry Fodor tries to reconcile three philosophical positions he is presently committed to: a computational theory of mind, intentional realism and a denotational theory of meaning. One problem he faces is this: a denotational semantics, according to which the meaning of a singular term like a name is exhausted by its referent, seems to rule out there being true intentional generalizations, or generalizations which advert to the contents of a subject's mental states. That there are such true generalizations is a major element in Fodor's intentional realism. Accordingly, Fodor is forced to find a way of dissolving this apparent incompatibility. This paper looks at his attempts to do so and concludes that they fail.

**Arló Costa, Horacio**. "Racionalidad y teoría de la acción: ¿es la teoría evidencial de la decisión una teoría de la racionalidad mínima?" in *La racionalidad: su poder y sus límites,* Nudler, Oscar (ed), 295-327. Barcelona, Ed Paidos, 1996.

The article considers two versions of anti-Humeanism on which desires, although contingent, are said to be necessarily aligned with suitable beliefs, namely beliefs about what would be good. These two versions of the *desire as belief thesis* are shown to be incompatible with the hard core of rational choice theory. Savage's theory of elicitation of desires and beliefs is often seen as the culmination of attempts to purge utility theory of all psychological elements. Nevertheless, the class between DAB and Savage's theory can be seen as providing arguments in favor of a view according to which substantive motivational constraints remain.

**Armour, Ellen T**. Questions of Proximity: "Woman's Place" in Derrida and Irigaray. *Hypatia*, 12(1), 63-78, Wint 97.

This article reconsiders the issue of Luce Irigaray's proximity to Jacques Derrida on the question of woman. I use Derrida's reading of Nietzsche in *Spurs: Nietzsche's Styles* (1979) and Irigaray's reading of Heidegger in *L'Oubli de l'air* (1983) to argue that reading them as supplements to one another is more accurate and more productive for feminism than separating one from the other. I conclude by laying out the benefits for feminism that such a reading would offer.

**Armour, Leslie**. "F.H. Bradley and Later Idealism: From Disarray to Reconstruction" in *Philosophy after F.H. Bradley,* Bradley, James (ed), 1-29. Bristol, Thoemmes, 1996.

Idealism faded in the period after World War I. Most of its major British and American figures were dead by the mid-twenties. New thinkers—R. G. Collingwood and G. R. G. Mure among them—emerged but changing sociopolitical conditions and the failure of the movement to develop adequate logical theories created problems. Recently there has been a resurgence and Timothy Sprigge, Nicholas Rescher, Michael Foster and Errol Harris have produced a variety of idealist theories and the experience of this century seems to suggest the viability of yet another variety of idealism.

**Armour, Leslie**. Maritain, Gilson, and the Ontology of Knowledge. *Maritain Stud*, 11, 202-219, 1995.

**Armour, Leslie**. Self, Deconstruction and Possibility: Maritain's Sixth Way Revisited. *Maritain Stud*, 10, 79-108, 1994.

**Armour, Leslie**. The Idea of a Perennial Philosophy. *Maritain Stud*, 10, 57-78, 1994.

**Armour, Leslie**. The Paradoxes of Thought and Being. *Maritain Stud*, 9, 29-58, 1993.

**Armstrong, Aurelia**. "Some Reflections on Deleuze's Spinoza: Composition and Agency" in *Deleuze and Philosophy: The Difference Engineer,* Ansell Pearson, Keith (ed), 44-57. New York, Routledge, 1997.

**Armstrong, D M**. "Dispositions as Categorical States" in *Dispositions: A Debate,* Armstrong, D M, 15-18. New York, Routledge, 1996.

In this preliminary statement of position in the book, *Dispositions: A Debate*, it is argued that the truthmakers for true dispositional properties are purely categorical properties of the disposed object plus the relevant laws of nature. The latter are contingent connections holding between categorical properties.

**Armstrong, D M**. "Place's and Armstrong's Views Compared and Contrasted" in *Dispositions: A Debate,* Armstrong, D M, 33-48. New York, Routledge, 1996.

In this second contribution to the book, *Dispositions: A Debate*, I begin with points of ontology where Place and I agree: that there are particulars, properties and relations, and situations (states of affairs). Place holds that properties and relations are particulars. I argue that they are universals. Place holds that there are both categorical and irreducibly dispositional properties. I argue that all properties are categorical, and rely on my account of laws of nature as relations between universals to supply truthmakers for dispositional truths.

**Armstrong, D M**. "Reply to Martin" in *Dispositions: A Debate,* Armstrong, D M, 88-104. New York, Routledge, 1996.

In this third contribution to the book, *Dispositions: A Debate*, I argue against C.B. Martin's view that every property of particulars has a dispositional or power 'side' as well as a categorical side. A certain merely possible case on which Martin (and Michael Tooley) place considerable reliance is critically discussed, as is the notion of a dispositional 'side' to properties. Finally, an attempt is made to answer Martin's criticism of my account of resemblance, counterfactuals, the manifestation of dispositions and induction.

**Armstrong, D M**. "Second Reply to Martin" in *Dispositions: A Debate,* Armstrong, D M, 147-152. New York, Routledge, 1996.

In this fourth contribution to the book, *Dispositions: A Debate*, the argument with C.B. Martin continues. Issues about universals, laws of nature as connections between universals, functional laws, and various other matters brought up by Martin, are briefly discussed.

**Armstrong, D M**. *A World of States of Affairs*. New York, Cambridge Univ Pr, 1997.

In this study David Armstrong offers a comprehensive system of analytical metaphysics that synthesizes but also develops his thinking over the last twenty years. Armstrong's analysis, which acknowledges the 'logical atomism' of Russell and Wittgenstein, makes facts (or states of affairs, as the author calls them) the fundamental constituents of the world, examining properties, relations, numbers, classes, possibility and necessity, dispositions, causes and laws. All these, it is argued, find their place and can be understood inside a scheme of states of affairs. This is a comprehensive and rigorously this-worldly account of the most general features of reality, argued from a distinctive philosophical perspective, and it will appeal to a wide readership in analytical philosophy.

**Armstrong, D M**. Reply to Martin. *Austl J Phil*, 75(2), 214-217, Je 97.

Totality states of affairs (Russell's 'general facts') are defended against Martin's criticisms. Although higher-order, they are not 'abstract in Quine's sense. If space-time is the whole of being, and if it can be seen as a vast conjunction of states of affairs, then the state of affairs that this is the totality of lower-order states of affairs is not additional to, but completes, space-times. If totality states of affairs are admitted, then there seems no need for any further negative states of affairs additional to totality states of affairs.

**Armstrong, D M** and Martin, C B and Place, Ullin T. *Dispositions: A Debate*. New York, Routledge, 1996.

In this book, first Place and Armstrong debate the ontological nature of dispositions, each setting out their view, and each in a second contribution criticizing the other and expanding their own view. In the second part of the book the debate becomes three-cornered, with three contributions from Martin, and two each from Armstrong and Place. An introduction by Tim Crane summarizes and surveys the debate.

**Armstrong, David M**. Categoricalist versus Dispositionalist Accounts of Properties. *Acta Analytica*, 7-19, 1996.

Should properties be thought of as having a "categorical" nature or should they be thought of as having a "dispositional" nature? The author presents arguments for and against dispositionalism and discusses a middle way between dispositionalism and categoricalism. He defends the position according to which all true properties are nondispositional, they do not have a nature that is exhausted by their possible manifestations. The difficulties for dispositionalism are more serious disadvantage than any facing categoricalism.

**Armstrong, J Scott**. Peer Review for Journals: Evidence on Quality Control, Fairness, and Innovation. *Sci Eng Ethics*, 3(1), 63-84, Ja 97.

This paper reviews the published empirical evidence concerning journal peer review consisting of 68 papers, all but three published since 1975. Peer review improves quality, but its use to screen papers has met with limited success. Current procedures to assure quality and fairness seem to discourage scientific advancement, especially important innovations, because findings that conflict with current beliefs are often judged to have defects. Editors can use procedures to encourage the publication of papers with innovative findings such as invited papers, early-acceptance procedures, author nominations of reviewers, structured rating sheets, open peer review, results-blind review, and in particular, electronic publication. Some journals are currently using these procedures. The basic principle behind the proposals is to change the decision from whether to publish a paper to how to publish it.

**Armstrong, John**. Artistry. *Brit J Aes*, 36(4), 381-388, O 96.

**Armstrong, Robert W**. The Relationship Between Culture and Perception of Ethical Problems in International Marketing. *J Bus Ethics*, 15(11), 1199-1208, N 96.

This research study sought to identify whether there is a relationship between ethical perceptions and culture. An examination of the cultural variables suggests that there is a relationship between two of Hofstede's cultural dimensions (i.e., Uncertainty Avoidance and Individualism) and ethical perceptions. This finding supports the hypothetical linkage between the cultural environment and the perceived ethical problem variables posited in Hunt and Vitell's *General Theory of Marketing Ethics* (1986).

**Armstrong, Susan**. "A Feminist Reading of Hegel and Kierkegaard" in *Hegel, History, and Interpretation,* Gallagher, Shaun, 227-241. Albany, SUNY Pr, 1997.

**Arnheim, Rudolf**. Ancient Chinese Aesthetics and its Modernity. *Brit J Aes*, 37(2), 155-157, Ap 97.

In the fifth century, the Chinese portrait painter Hsieh-Ho formulated six principles that have remained a strong influence on Chinese aesthetics and practice through the ages. The first and most important refers to the breath of life and the resonance of the spirit. It refers to the spirituality of meaning in pictorial shapes.

**Arnold, Denis G**. Introspection and its Objects. *J Phil Res*, 22, 87-94, Ap 97.

Three distinct objections to the traditions account of introspection are considered and rejected. It is argued that critics of the traditional account of introspection fail to adequately distinguish potential objects of introspection. Further, it is argued that at least two cognitive states are properly understood as objects of introspection. The conclusions reached suggest that there are sufficient reasons to reconsider their merits of the traditional account of introspection. (edited)

**Arnold, Robert M** and Fox, Ellen. Evaluating Outcomes in Ethics Consultation Research. *J Clin Ethics*, 7(2), 127-138, Sum 96.

**Arnsperger, Christian**. Reformulating Equality of Resources. *Econ Phil*, 13(1), 61-77, Ap 97.

This essay revisits the link between Ronald Dworkin's criterion of equality of resources and the notion of an envy-free allocation. The central claim is that, contrary to what Dworkin himself does, it is illegitimate to interpret equality of resources in terms of existing results in the envy-freeness literature. These results use the agents' "direct preferences for consumption," whereas Dworkin's analysis can make sense only if one uses a concept of "induced preferences for resources." Two criteria of envy-freeness based on induced preferences are studied, and considerable doubt is shed on the technical feasibility of Dworkin's own project.

**Arnstine, Donald**. "Dewey Without Doing" in *Philosophy of Education (1996)*, Margonis, Frank (ed), 397-399. Urbana, Phil Education Soc, 1997.

**Arntzenius, Frank**. Transition Chances and Causation. *Pac Phil Quart*, 78(2), 149-168, Je 97.

The general claims of this paper are as follows. As a result of chaotic dynamics we can usually not know what the *deterministic* causes of events are. There will, however, be invariant forwards transition chances from earlier types of events, which we typically call the causes, to later types of events, which we typically call the effects. There will be no invariant backwards transition chances between these types of events. This asymmetry has the same origin and explanation as the arrow of time of thermodynamics.

**Arntzenius, Frank** and McCarthy, David. The Two Envelope Paradox and Infinite Expectations. *Analysis*, 57(1), 42-50, Ja 97.

We argue that the two envelope paradox can be dissolved by looking closely at the connection between conditional and unconditional expectation and by being careful when summing an infinite series of positive and negative terms. We argue that it is not another St. Petersburg paradox and that one does not need to ban talk of infinite expectation values in order to dissolve it. We end by posing a new puzzle.

**Aronovitch, Hilliard**. Reflective Equilibrium or Evolving Tradition?. *Inquiry*, 39(3-4), 399-419, D 96.

This paper presents criticisms of the method for moral and political philosophy known as 'reflective equilibrium' (RE), or in its fuller form 'side reflective equilibrium' (WRE). This negative purpose has an ulterior positive aim: to set off, by favourable contrast, an alternative approach based on analogical argument as an instrument of an evolving (liberal) tradition. WRE derives from John Rawls but has been broadly endorsed. Though a metatheory, it involves a certain way of construing liberalism. This essay's target is in key part that construal. It seeks an approach to moral-political philosophy and to liberalism in particular, that is at once rationally grounded and contextually oriented and provides for explanation as well as justification. WRE fails on all counts, plus others. Section I presents WRE and suggests the alternative. Section II presents the critique of WRE, partly drawing on established criticisms and partly presenting new ones. Section III opposes the application suggested for WRE by (surprisingly) a critic of Rawls, M Sandel. The preferability of the analogical alternative is demonstrated throughout.

**Aronson, Jerrold L**. Dispositions as the Foundation for Feynman's Formulation of Quantum Mechanics. *Dialectica*, 51(1), 35-64, 1997.

This paper has two objectives. The major objective is to explore in what way Feynman's formulation of quantum mechanics can be used to explain the mysterious born interpretation, viz., to explain why the relative probability of finding a particle at a particular location equals the square of the wave function rather than the wave function itself. The other objective is to show how Rom Harre's ontology of properties, dispositions and affordances nicely dovetails with Feynman's formulation, given that suitable adjustments are made.

**Aronson, Jerrold L**. Truth, Verisimilitude, and Natural Kinds. *Phil Papers*, 26(1), 71-104, Ap 97.

For decades, adherents of convergent realism have tried to come up with a semantics of verisimilitude or approximate truth and it's safe to say that they have failed. It is my contention that a major source of their failure is that truth—as characterized by the correspondence theory—is a basic primitive in these theories of verisimilitude. It will be argued that instead of characterizing verisimilitude by counting up true propositions, truth should be made a limiting case of verisimilitude. Doing so, however, requires introducing a new primitive for approximate truth: orderings of natural kinds. The result is a theory of truth which is basically nonpropositional and not based on correspondence. Ironically, this theory is more in keeping with J.L. Austin's version of the correspondence theory of truth.

**Arpini, Adriana**. De si es posible afirmar la construcción de una "eticidad" en la filosofía práctica de Kant. *Cuad Etica*, 17-18, 19-43, 1994.

We try a reflection concerning the matter of the subjective and objective moral as it springs from modern thinking, particularly from the Kantian's ethical proposal. As it has been illustrated, Kant took to the last consequences a

thought rooted in his own situation. The depth and richness of such thought offers us the possibility of giving a new meaning to its contents from the perspective of our social and historical circumstances. In this sense, the category of *humanity* is an *a priori* regulator of people's behavior and it gives us a criterion from where to advance in the configuration of a new possible objective moral.

**Arpini, Adriana**. Qué "nos" dice Habermas: Algunas reflexiones desde las coordenadas histórico-sociales latinoamericanas. *Cuad Etica*, 15-16, 9-22, 1993.

We consider Habermas's suggestion to mark three theoretical and methodological aspects. They can be critical included in a reflection whose roots are in our "life world". The aspects are: (1) the exchange of the subjectivity's paradigm for the interaction; (2) the mediator function of interests; (3) the construction of the conditions of the emancipatoring self-reflection. We consider it as a problem the ideal community of communication's suppositions and those of the vital context; the interests' mediation and its relation with the necessities; the subject's possibility of interact under equal conditions to form the general consent; and the perception of the conflict.

**Arregui, Jorge V**. On the Intentionality of Moods: Phenomenology and Linguistic Analysis. *Amer Cath Phil Quart*, 70(3), 397-411, Sum 96.

Both the analytical and the phenomenological traditions have underlined the intentionality of feelings. Nevertheless, some important representative members of both philosophical approaches have restricted their claim to emotions maintaining that moods are preintentional or lack an object. The paper discusses Kenny's position within linguistic analysis, whereas chooses the thought of Strasser as representative of phenomenology. Against both of them and following an Aristotelian-Thomistic inspiration, it claims that moods, as well as emotions, are defined by their object and that mood is an evaluation of the world as a whole. Finally, another criterion is offered for distinguishing between moods and emotions.

**Arsenijevic, Milos**. Eine aristotelische Logik der Intervalle, die Cantorsche Logik der Punkte und die physikalischen und kinematischen Prädikate. *Phil Natur*, 29(2), 161-209, 1992.

For each point-based (interval-based) system there is an interval-based (point-based) system such that under two suitably chosen sets of (noninverse) translation rules the set of all the formulae of the former system is mapped into a set of formulae of the latter and *vice versa* where theorems and only theorems, are always translated into theorems. The point-based and interval-based approaches cease to be trivially different only when one-place predicate letters, denoting nonrelational physical properties, are introduced. Various systems obtainable in such a way are sketched and compared in view of their plausibility for describing the physical world.

**Artola, José María**. "Religión y teología en el origen del pensamiento filosófico de Fichte" in *El inicio del Idealismo alemán*, Market, Oswaldo, 181-194. Madrid, Ed Complutense, 1996.

This contribution to the Symposium is a comparative study on two works by Fichte concerning his philosophy of religion. The first part expounds on certain aspects of the "Anweisung zum seligen Leben", as the most characteristic expression of Fichte's philosophy, where one observes the connections between the WL of 1804 and the gospel of St. John. The second part studies the preceding concepts of the "Aphorismen über Religion und Deismus" of 1790 which shows the opposition of deist philosophy to the religious experience preserved in the New Testament. The opposition between heart and speculation is a nuance in which one perceives the difficulty Fichte has in limiting himself to the deistic pretensions.

**Artosi, Alberto** and Governatori, Guido and Sartor, Giovanni. "Towards a Computational Treatment of Deontic Defeasibility" in *Deontic Logic, Agency and Normative Systems*, Brown, Mark A (ed), 27-46. New York, Springer-Verlag, 1996.

In this paper we describe an algorithmic framework for a multimodal logic arising from the combination of the system of modal (epistemic) logic devised by Meyer and van der Hoek for dealing with nonmonotonic reasoning with a deontic logic of the Jones and Pörn-type. The idea behind this (somewhat eclectic) formal set-up is to have a modal framework expressive enough to model certain kinds of deontic defeasibility, in particular by taking into account preferences on norms. The appropriate inference mechanism is provided by a tableau-like modal theorem proving system which supports a proof method closely related to the semantics of modal operators. We argue that this system is particularly well-suited for mechanizing nonmonotonic forms of inference in a monotonic multimodal setting.

**Arzbaecher, Robert** and Weil, Vivian. Ethics and Relationships in Laboratories and Research Communities. *Prof Ethics*, 4(3-4), 83-125, Spr-Sum 95.

Scientific research is a highly decentralized enterprise. Research groups and laboratories are characterized by extreme disparities of power and they require cooperation and collaboration in a very competitive environment. Opportunities for unfair treatment, even exploitation, of the less powerful and for unchecked competition threaten the trust and responsible conduct on which the scientific enterprise relies. Seven vignettes of situations in research groups highlight important conflicts that arise. Commentary on the vignettes identifies issues of professional ethics and morality in those situations and explores defensible ways for the agents to deal with their situations and policies for their groups to adopt.

**Asada, Yukiko** and Tsuzuki, Miho and Akiyama, Shiro. High School Teaching of Bioethics in New Zealand, Australia and Japan. *J Moral Educ*, 25(4), 401-420, D 96.

This paper compares knowledge and teaching of 15 selected topics related to bioethics and biotechnology, with particular focus on the teaching of social, ethical and environmental issues of *in vitro* fertilization, prenatal diagnosis, biotechnology, nuclear power, pesticides and genetic engineering. The survey found that these issues were, generally, covered more in biology classes than in social science classes; and that there were differences in coverage among the three countries, with most coverage in Australia and least in Japan. Open questions looked at images of bioethics, and the reasons why about 90% of teachers thought bioethics was needed in education. Open questions on teaching materials, current and desired are also discussed. The data suggest a need for the development of more and higher quality materials, for the moral education that is conducted, especially in biology and social studies classes. (edited)

**Aschoff, Frank**. Zwischen äusserem Zwang und innerer Freiheit. *Fichte-Studien*, 9, 27-45, 1997.

**Asfour, Amal** and Williamson, Paul. Gainsborough's Wit. *J Hist Ideas*, 58(3), 479-501, Jl 97.

**Ash, C J** and Knight, J F. Possible Degrees in Recursive Copies II. *Annals Pure Applied Log*, 87(2), 151-165, 15 S 97.

We extend results of Harizanov and Barker. For a relation *R* on a recursive structure *A*, we give conditions guaranteeing that the image of *R* in a recursive copy of *A* can be made to have arbitrary Sigma$^{o}_{x}$ degree over Delta $^{o}_{x}$. We give stronger conditions under which the image of *R* can be made Sigma$^{o}_{x}$ degree as well. The degrees over Delta$^{o}_{x}$ can be replaced by certain more general classes. We also generalize the Friedberg-Muchnik Theorem, giving conditions on a pair of relations *R* and *S* under which the images of *R* and *S* can be made Sigma$^{o}_{x}$ and independent over Delta$^{o}_{x}$ in a recursive copy of *A*.

**Ash, C J** and Knight, J F and Cholak, P. Permitting, Forcing, and Copying of a given Recursive Relation. *Annals Pure Applied Log*, 86(3), 219-236, Jl 97.

**Ash, C J** and Remmel, J B and Knight, J F. Quasi-Simple Relations in Copies of a given Recursive Structure. *Annals Pure Applied Log*, 86(3), 203-218, Jl 97.

**Ashbrook, James B**. "Mind" as Humanizing the Brain: Toward a Neurotheology of Meaning. *Zygon*, 32(3), 301-320, S 97.

The concept "mind" refers to the human and human-like features of the brain. A historical review of thinking about the mind contextualizes humanity's search to understand itself by sketching biblical and philosophical perspectives. Drawing on a holistic paradigm, several features are discernible: empathic rationality, imaginative intentionality, meaningful memory and adaptability. These reflect the evolutionary development of uncommitted cortex that contributes to the brain's explosive capacity for order, complexity and novelty. The basic issue continues, namely, how are the distributed modules of information-processing integrated into the meaning-making reality of human beings?(edited)

**Ashbrook, James B**. A Rippling Relatableness in Reality. *Zygon*, 31(3), 469-482, S 96.

I describe my development as a thinker from that of simple pragmatism to applied theory. My style is that of discerning a rippling relatedness in the various dimensions of reality. I respond to five specific themes raised by colleagues: what it means to be human; the relation of whole to parts; the various methodological melodies; a relational view of reality; and ethical imperatives in the descriptive indicatives.

**Ashby, W Allen** (ed) and Ashby, Warren. *A Comprehensive History of Western Ethics: What Do We Believe?*. Amherst, Prometheus, 1997.

It is possible to explore the view that each of the major ethicists has made a significant contribution to moral truth, and that the history of ethics is the history not only of individuals quarreling endlessly over problems that cannot be solved, but also of the discovery and expansion of ethical truths, truths that are often difficult to discern and decipher. It is possible and perhaps valuable to believe that each of these individuals was right in some of the most important areas they affirmed, but often wrong in matters of secondary importance or in what they denied. It is possible to imagine that each of them adds a significant element to our understanding of what ethics is about and what the content of ethics is. Consequently, if we are to develop an adequate personal ethic for ourselves, we need to be aware of their views and their points of viewing, building facets of their perspectives and positions into a consistent, comprehensive ethic of our own. If we can do all this, then it may not be such a bad party after all. (publisher, edited)

**Ashby, Warren** and Ashby, W Allen (ed). *A Comprehensive History of Western Ethics: What Do We Believe?*. Amherst, Prometheus, 1997.

It is possible to explore the view that each of the major ethicists has made a significant contribution to moral truth, and that the history of ethics is the history not only of individuals quarreling endlessly over problems that cannot be solved, but also of the discovery and expansion of ethical truths, truths that are often difficult to discern and decipher. It is possible and perhaps valuable to believe that each of these individuals was right in some of the most important areas they affirmed, but often wrong in matters of secondary importance or in what they denied. It is possible to imagine that each of them adds a significant element to our understanding of what ethics is about and what the content of ethics is. Consequently, if we are to develop an adequate personal ethic for ourselves, we need to be aware of their views and their points of viewing, building facets of their perspectives and positions into a consistent, comprehensive ethic of our own. If we can do all this, then it may not be such a bad party after all. (publisher, edited)

**Ashenhurst, Robert L**. Ontological Aspects of Information Modeling. *Mind Mach*, 6(3), 287-394, O 96.

Information modelling (also known as conceptual modelling or semantic data modelling) may be characterized as the formulation of a model in which information aspects of objective and subjective reality are presented ("the application"), independent of data sets and processes by which they may be realized ("the system"). A methodology for information modelling should incorporate a number of concepts which have appeared in the literature, but should also be formulated in terms of constructs which are understandable to and expressible by the system user as well as the system developer. This is particularly desirable in connection with certain "intimate" relationships, such as being the same as or being a part of. The conceptual basis for such a methodology, as conventionally approached, seems flavored with notions arising in the systems arena to an inappropriate degree. To counter this tendency it is useful to turn to a discipline not hitherto much involved in technology, namely analytic philosophy.

**Askland, Andrew**. Conflicting Accounts of Equal Opportunity. *Int J Applied Phil*, 10(2), 35-44, Wint-Spr 96.

**Askland, Andrew**. Fostering Market Competence. *J Thought*, 32(1), 87-98, Spr 97.

**Asmuth, Christoph**. "Die Lehre vom Bild in der Wissenstheorie Johann Gottlieb Fichtes" in *Sein—Reflexion—Freiheit: Aspekte der Philosophie Johann Gottlieb Fichtes,* Asmuth, Christoph (ed), 269-299. Amsterdam, Gruner, 1997.

The concept of the image is an essential cultural development of the West. Since Plato, it has played a significant role in philosophy. This essay is concerned with one particular expression of the concept of the image: that of knowledge as an image of the absolute. It sets forth the positions of Plotinus, Augustine, Thomas Aquinas and Meister Eckhart before finally investigating of the concept of the image in Fichte's Wissenschaftslehre 1804, 2. Vortrag.

**Asmuth, Christoph**. "Fichte: Ein streitbarer Philosoph" in *Sein—Reflexion—Freiheit: Aspekte der Philosophie Johann Gottlieb Fichtes,* Asmuth, Christoph (ed), 5-32. Amsterdam, Gruner, 1997.

Fichte's biography was constantly troubled by conflict. Particularly noteworthy are the Atheismusstreit and Fichte's confrontations with his most philosophically competent contemporaries: Kant, Jacobi, Reinhold and, finally, Schelling, whom Fichte long considered his student. This essay portrays these conflicts and provides an introduction to Fichte's philosophy of the I.

**Asmuth, Christoph** (ed). *Sein—Reflexion—Freiheit: Aspekte der Philosophie Johann Gottlieb Fichtes.* Amsterdam, Gruner, 1997.

The essays collected in this volume display the many facets of Fichte's philosophy. After a biographical introduction, the first group takes up Fichte's relation to Schelling, Hegel and Hölderlin, focusing on the concepts of freedom and life. The next group addresses the early Wissenschaftslehre along with the philosophy of nature, language and religion. Other essays set Fichte's thought in the history of philosophy, explicating, for example, Meister Eckhart's antecedent theory of the I; or show the relation of Fichte's theory of the imagistic character of subjectivity to the neo-Platonism of Plotinus and Augustine or to Thomas Aquinas and Eckhart.

**Aspe A, Virginia**. "Algunas precisiones en torno al concepto de *ousia*" in *Ensayos Aristotélicos,* Aspe, Virginia, 1-28. Mexico, Univ Panamericana, 1996.

Edith Stein thinks that the main sense of *ousia* in Aristotle's *Metaphysics* refers to "*sensible substance*". On the contrary, Aspe tries to prove that the first sense of *ousia* is *separated substance.* The mistake of Stein's interpretation is due to an improper understanding of the Greek work *khôriston* in her analysis. (publisher)

**Aspe A, Virginia**. Kinesis versus logos en la filosofía de Leonardo Polo. *Anu Filosof*, 29(2), 359-371, 1996.

'Kinesis versus logos' is in Leonardo Polo's philosophy. Kinesis and praxis are analogous concepts in Aristotle. Although Leonardo Polo's philosophy is right in pointing the differences between these concepts, the article demonstrates that beyond their opposition these terms refer to an analogous *pros en: energeia.* The author explains Leonardo Polo's necessity to point the difference and Aristotle's concern for pointing their similarity.

**Aspe A, Virginia** and Llano, Carlos and Mier y Terán, Rocío. *Ensayos Aristotélicos.* Mexico, Univ Panamericana, 1996.

**Assländer, Michael** and Zimmerli, Walther Christoph. "Wirtschaftsethik" in *Angewandte Ethik: Die Bereichsethiken und ihre theoretische Fundierung,* Nida- Rümelin, Julian (ed), 290-344. Stuttgart, Alfred Kröner, 1996.

**Astorga, Omar**. Esquema para Reexaminar la Filosofía Política de Kant. *Rev Filosof (Venezuela)*, 23(1), 21-29, 1996.

Kant's political philosophy is examined in relation to Hobbes's influence. First, the claim is made that the formalist view of the concept of *ius strictum* is otherwise grounded on the principle of "unsociable sociality." Secondly, Kant's suggestive remarks in his *Critique of Pure Reason* are reappreciated when he compares departure from the state of nature, as quoted from Hobbes, with the tasks set forth by the *Critique.* The concept of the state of nature is also examined as to its identification with the state of war. Then the concept of *contractus originarius* is examined as a hypothetical idea which cannot give rise to rebellion. Finally, the claim is made that juridical justification of the *state* in Kant shifts grounds from an originally formalist position to political conservatism.

**Atherton, Margaret L**. "How to Write the History of Vision: Understanding the Relationship between Berkeley and Descartes" in *Sites of Vision,* Levin, David Michael (ed), 139-165. Cambridge, MIT Pr, 1997.

**Atherton, Margaret L**. Lady Mary Shepherd's Case Against George Berkeley. *Brit J Hist Phil*, 4(2), 347-366, S 96.

**Atienza, Manuel** and Ruiz Manero, Juan. Permissions, Principles and Rights: A Paper on Statements Expressing Constitutional Liberties. *Ratio Juris*, 9(3), 236-247, S 96.

In the first part of the paper the authors analyze how the distinction between mandatory rules, principles in the strict sense and policies can be understood in structural terms and in terms of reasons for action. In the second part, they attempt to clarify which kind of legal provisions embrace constitutional statements recognizing liberty rights are.

**Atreya, Prakash**. Recent Bulgarian Studies in the Fields of Psychology, Parapsychology & Yoga. *Darshana Int*, 36(4/144), 1-3, O 96.

**Attala Pochón, Daniel**. Two Skepticism and Skeptic Challenge in Philip Kitcher's *The Advancement of Science*. *Theoria (Spain)*, 12(29), 317-335, My 97.

The purpose of this article is to carry out an analysis of the epistemologic standpoint on a recent book by Philip Kitcher (*The Advancement of Science*) by discussing the sceptic ideas which are dealt with there. We can discriminate between two kinds of scepticism appearing on Kitcher's book: a weak and a radical one. Then we work towards a definition of the kind of realism held by this author and, finally, we try to show that such a viewpoint as Kitcher's is possible to hold provided that we do not take the radical scepticism into account for that question. Kitcher only objects by means of the weak scepticism. And it is precisely because of that restriction that he is capable of not giving a definition of a crucial alternative: strong realism or realism in "Kantian spirit".

**Attfield, Robin**. Natur erhalten oder Menschen ernähren?. *Conceptus*, 29(74), 27-45, 1996.

To Rolston's case for holding that letting people starve to save nature is sometimes right, I reply that authentic development seldom conflicts with preservation and that the argument from net primary product leads to a miscarriage. Where sustainable development is possible it should be adopted. Important as population policies are, representing population growth as a cancer is incoherent. Neo-Malthusian policies often ignore conflicting evidence. Policies are needed which promote participatory development and preservation. (edited)

**Audi, Robert**. Intrinsic Value and Moral Obligation. *S J Phil*, 35(2), 135-154, Sum 97.

**Augstein, Hannah Franziska**. Linguistics and Politics in the Early 19th Century: James Cowles Prichard's Moral Philology. *Hist Euro Ideas*, 23(1), 1-18, Ja 97.

The Bristol doctor and ethnologist James Cowles Prichard (1786-1848) had the life-long preoccupation to prove monogenism, i.e., the Scriptural tenet that all human tribes were descended from a common stock. In this quest he followed the developments in fields such as anatomy, physiology, mythology and philology. Prichard was one of the first British scientists to adopt historical comparative linguistics which were being developed by German scholars such as Franz Bopp, Jacob Grimm and Wilhelm von Humboldt. But while these authors formulated their methods against the backdrop of notions of "Volk" and nation, Prichard used their linguistics to refute rising racial theories and to bolster the historical truth of Genesis.

**Avelone, Alessandro** and Fiorentini, Camillo and Mantovani, Paolo (& others). On Maximal Intermediate Predicate Constructive Logics. *Stud Log*, 57(2-3), 373-408, O 96.

We extend to the predicate frame a previous characterization of the maximal intermediate propositional constructive logics. This provides a technique to get maximal intermediate predicate constructive logics starting from suitable sets of classically valid predicate formulae we call maximal nonstandard predicate constructive logics. As an example of this technique, we exhibit two maximal intermediate predicate constructive logics, yet leaving open the problem of stating whether the two logics are distinct. Further properties of these logics will be also investigated.

**Avery, Jon**. Critical Thinking Pedagogy: A Possible Solution to the "Transfer-Problem. *Inquiry (USA)*, 14(1), 49-57, Fall 94.

**Avigad, Jeremy**. Formalizing Forcing Arguments in Subsystems of Second- Order Arithmetic. *Annals Pure Applied Log*, 82(2), 165-191, D 96.

We show that certain model-theoretic forcing arguments involving subsystems of second-order arithmetic can be formalized in the base theory, thereby converting them to effective proof-theoretic arguments. We use this method to sharpen the conservation theorems of Harrington and Brown-Simpson, giving an effective proof that $WKL_{+0}$ is conservative over $RCA_0$ with no significant increase in the lengths of proofs.

**Avigad, Jeremy**. On the Relationship between $ATR_0$ and *ID-hat-sub-less than-omega*. *J Sym Log*, 61(3), 768-779, S 96.

We show that the theory $ATR_0$ is equivalent to a second-order generalization of the theory $ID\text{-}hat_{omega}$. As a result $ATR_0$ is conservative over $ID\text{-}had_{omega}$ for arithmetic sentences, though proofs in $ATR_0$ can be much shorter than their $ID\text{-}hat_{omega}$ counterparts.

**Avigad, Jeremy** and Sommer, Richard. A Model-Theoretic Approach to Ordinal Analysis. *Bull Sym Log*, 3(1), 17-52, Mr 97.

We describe a model-theoretic approach to ordinal analysis via the finite combinatorial notion of an alpha-large set of natural numbers. In contrast to syntactic approaches that use cut elimination, this approach involves constructing finite sets of numbers with combinatorial properties that, in nonstandard instances, give rise to models of the theory being analyzed. This method is applied to obtain ordinal analyses of a number of interesting subsystems of first- and second-order arithmetic.

**Avila del Palacio, Alfonso**. Reflexiones en torno al origen de los números aritméticos. *Analogia*, 11(1), 87-107, Ja-Je 97.

The question is how the arithmetic numbers arise? The answer that this work suggests is: (a) in the beginning the people made identical marks on certain suitable surfaces to count objects; (b) later, they isolated the marks of the countable objects; (c) when the marks were isolated, they were like objects

which could be counted and so a group of similar objects arose: the numbers; (d) since the beginning the numbers were worked like special objects: it was similar but different than others objects like units, pairs and so on; (e) those special objects, called numbers, were formed with the repetition of only one of them called *one*; (f) in actual terms we can say that the numbers were worked like abstract individuals. (edited)

**Avitabile, Luisa**. La donna, tra ironia e diritto. *Riv Int Filosof Diritto*, 73(3), 555-564, Jl-S 96.

**Avramides, Anita**. Descartes and Other Minds. *Teorema*, 16(1), 27-46, 1996.

Descartes's distinction between material and thinking substance gives rise to a question both about our knowledge of the external world and about our knowledge of another mind. Descartes says surprisingly little about this second question. In the Second Meditation he writes of our (single) judgement that the figures outside his window are men and not automatic machines. It is argued in this paper that to think of judgement as operating in this way is to overlook the fact that, given the Cartesian metaphysics, our judgement here is susceptible of double error. I may be in error that the figure before me is a human being; and I may be in error that the figure before me has a mind. It is suggested that one reason for Descartes overlooking the possibility of this double error is his assumption that, of corporeal beings, all and only human animals have minds. It is also argued that the suggestion that Descartes overlooks the possibility of a double error here is supported by his proposal, in *Discourse V*, of a "test of a real man": the other's use of language.

**Awbrey, Jon** and Awbrey, Susan. Interpretation as Action: The Risk of Inquiry. *Inquiry (USA)*, 15(1), 40-52, Fall 95.

**Awbrey, Susan** and Awbrey, Jon. Interpretation as Action: The Risk of Inquiry. *Inquiry (USA)*, 15(1), 40-52, Fall 95.

**Axtell, Guy**. Epistemic-Virtue Talk: The Reemergence of American Axiology?. *J Speculative Phil*, 10(3), 172-198, 1996.

A growing number of virtue theorists view a unified, virtue-theoretical account of ethical and epistemic normativity as a viable and worthwhile goal. This article explores the *metaphilosophical* shift that such an account presupposes. In addition to possible theoretic advantages, the appeal of such a shift can be understood *historically*, I argue, in terms of the fortunes of the concepts of "value" and "valuation" in the twentieth century—and more specifically, the against-the-stream effort of certain Continental and American philosophers, including R.B. Perry and John Dewey, to develop and win support for a "general theory of value" (Axtell 1996).

**Axtell, Guy**. Recent Work on Virtue Epistemology. *Amer Phil Quart*, 34(1), 1-26, Ja 97.

This article traces a growing interest among epistemologists in the intellectuals of epistemic virtues. These are cognitive dispositions exercised in the formation of beliefs. Attempts to give intellectual virtues a central normative and/or explanatory role in epistemology occur together with renewed interest in the ethics/epistemology analogy, and in the role of intellectual virtue in Aristotle's epistemology. The central distinction drawn here is between two opposed forms of virtue epistemology, *virtue reliabilism* and *virtue responsibilism*. The article develops the shared and distinctive claims made by contemporary proponents of each form, in their respective treatments of knowledge and justification.

**Aydede, Murat**. Language of Thought: The Connectionist Contribution. *Mind Mach*, 7(1), 57-101, F 97.

In this paper, I offer an analysis of what it is to physically satisfy/realize a formal system. In this context, I examine the minimal truth-conditions of LOT Hypothesis. From my analysis it will follow that concatenative realization of formal systems is irrelevant to LOTH since the very notion of LOT is indifferent to such an implementation level issue as concatenation. I will conclude that to the extent to which they can explain the law-like cognitive regularities, a certain class of connectionist models proposed as radical alternatives to the classical LOT paradigm will in fact turn out to be LOT models, even though new and potentially very exciting ones. (edited)

**Ayers, Elise** and Harrold, Joan and Lynn, Joanne. A Good Death: Improving Care Inch-by-Inch. *Bioethics Forum*, 13(1), 38-40, Spr 97.

As people live longer with chronic diseases before dying, it is increasingly important to define a "good death." This may include freedom from pain, preservation of dignity and family and spiritual reconciliation—goals our health care system rarely recognizes. To ensure a good death, we must measure and improve the quality of end of life care. Ten domains for measurement have been identified: symptom relief; support of function and autonomy; advance care planning; use of aggressive care and appropriate site of death; patient and family satisfaction; global quality of life; family burden; survival time; provider continuity and skill; and bereavement.

**Aylesworth, Gary E** (trans) and Rötzer, Florian. *Conversations with French Philosophers*. Atlantic Highlands, Humanities Pr, 1995.

This volume consists of interviews with eight contemporary French philosophers. The main issue of discussion is how contemporary French philosophy is received in Germany, particularly by thinkers such as Jürgen Habermas, who tend to characterize the French as "irrationalists." The charge of irrationalism is provoked by two aspects of contemporary French thought: its preoccupation with the texts of Nietzsche and Heidegger (both of whom are tainted by an association with National Socialism), and the tendency to "aestheticize" philosophy by dissolving discursive identities into radical pluralities. The charge against the French is answered directly by the theorists interviewed here. They point out that the nonrational is not necessarily "irrational," and that the nonrational is discovered when reason seeks its own grounds or limits. The emergence of the nonrational in philosophy is thus a consequence of reason itself, whose destiny, as Kant says, is to find limit and definition in its other. (publisher)

AUTHOR INDEX 503 Backofen, Rolf

**Azevedo, Jane**. *Mapping Reality: An Evolutionary Realist Methodology for the Natural and Social Sciences*. Albany, SUNY Pr, 1997.

This timely book offers a way out of the current realist/relativist impasse. Azevedo uses the insights of evolutionary epistemology to develop a naturalist realist methodology of science, the "mapping model of knowledge," and applies it to solving the conceptual, practical, and ethical problems faced by sociology as a discipline. The model is developed from the practice of the natural sciences and comes with an easily applied and powerful heuristic based on mapping, filling the gap left by the downfall of positivist and empiricist methodologie. It shows the inescapably social nature of science, but argues that scientific theories can in fact be validated in perspective-neutral ways—not despite the social and interest-driven nature of science, but because of it. (edited)

**Azorin, Jean-Michel** and Naudin, Jean. Commentary on "Edmund Husserl's Influence on Karl Jaspers's Phenomenology". *Phil Psychiat Psych*, 4(1), 37-39, Mr 97.

**Azzouni, Jody**. Thick Epistemic Access: Distinguishing the Mathematical from the Empirical. *J Phil*, 94(9), 472-484, S 97.

An analysis of the significant epistemic properties of observation are given; it is then shown that these very same epistemic properties hold of certain instrumental interventions with what are often described as "theoretical" entities (such as subatomic particles). The suggestion is made that any epistemic means of access to something (called "thick epistemic access") is criterial for ontological commitment; this is a way of undercutting the Quine-Putnam indispensability thesis. A contrast is explored between the way that existential commitments to mathematical objects arise (through the need for facility in manipulating theories) and the way that such commitments arise when access to them is thick. The point is to show that the distinction being drawn is a robust one. The paper concludes pessimistically, however, with the suggestion that any attempt to turn an epistemic distinction into a ontological one is bound to beg the question against competitors.

**Baars, Bernard J**. Understanding Subjectivity: Global Workspace Theory and the Resurrection of the Observing Self. *J Consciousness Stud*, 3(3), 211-216, 1996.

Why is the problem of subjectivity so hard, as David Chalmers claims? This essay suggests that it becomes hard when we adopt an implausible, perfectionistic standard. In the last two decades the standard has come to be 'observer empathy'—the ability to know what it's like to be a bat or another human. That makes understanding consciousness difficult indeed. Far more practical criteria are used every day in medicine and scientific studies of consciousness and indeed traditional philosophy from Kant to James took a much more relaxed view of subjectivity. Once we adopt these more workable standards, subjectivity is suddenly revealed to involve a familiar concept, namely 'the self as observer' of conscious experiences. Contrary to some, this sense of self is conceptually coherent and well-supported by hard evidence. For example, the 'left-hemisphere interpreter' in split-brain patients behaves as one such self. Given a modest and practical approach, we can expect to make progress toward understanding subjectivity.

**Baase, Sara**. *A Gift of Fire: Social, Legal, and Ethical Issues in Computing*. Englewood Cliffs, Prentice Hall, 1997.

*A Gift of Fire* provides in-depth coverage of the challenge and implications of computer technology, including important issues such as the impact of computers on privacy, censorship of the Internet, government policy on encryption, protection of intellectual property in cyberspace, hacking and computer crime, risks from failures of computer systems and ethical dilemmas faced by computer professionals and computer users. (publisher)

**Babbitt, Susan E**. "Personal Integrity, Politics, and Moral Imagination" in *A Question of Values: New Canadian Perspectives in Ethics and Political Philosophy*, Brennan, Samantha (ed), 107-131. Amsterdam, Rodopi, 1997.

**Babic, Jovan**. Two Significant Problems in Education—the General One and the Particular One (in Serbo-Croatian). *Theoria (Yugoslavia)*, 38(4), 127-142, D 95.

**Babic, Jovan**. War as a Phenomenon and as a Practice (in Serbo-Croatian). *Theoria (Yugoslavia)*, 38(2), 7-33, Je 95.

Preparations for war make a part of every state's description. They are a sign that a state has a serious intention to defend itself. This intention is, however, the source of state's entitlement to enact laws. This entails the odd conclusion that a possibility of war is a presumption of validity of laws. But, on the other side, war is a partial suspension of laws. This complicated relation proceeds from the concept of freedom. For this reason war is not only a (social) action, but it is also a phenomenon, an occurrence. Inside the war we have various forms of moral restrictions which are analyzed by means of various ethical theories. The elimination of the causes of war turns out to be the main moral objective. However, different actions in different situations may both be morally right.

**Baccelli, Luca**. Esodo e tribalismo. *Iride*, 8(15), 440-450, Ag 95.

Nelle sue analisi dell'identità collettiva americana e della cittadinanza moderna, nelle sue prese di posizione sul dibattito tra *liberals e communitarians*, nella sua teoria della giustizia, Walzer delinea una nozione complessa, pluralistica e problematica di appartenenza. Ma queste caratteristiche sembrano venir meno negli interventi di Walzer sul risorgere del nazionalismo e dell'etnicismo, su quella che il filosofo americano chiama la "rinascita della tribù". Si tratta invece, secondo Baccelli, di elaborare una concezione "politica" della cittadinanza che tenga conto del carattere "artificiale" dell'appartenenza nazionale e della valenza transculturale dei diritti civili e politici.

**Bacchetta, Matthew D** and Fins, Joseph J. The Economics of Clinical Ethics Programs: A Quantitative Justification. *Cambridge Quart Healthcare Ethics*, 6(4), 451-460, Fall 97.

**Bacchetta, Matthew D** and Fins, Joseph J and Miller, Franklin G. Clinical Pragmatism: A Method of Moral Problem Solving. *Kennedy Inst Ethics J*, 7(2), 129-145, Je 97.

This paper presents a method of moral problem solving in clinical practice that is inspired by the philosophy of John Dewey. This method, called "clinical pragmatism," integrates clinical and ethical decision making. Clinical pragmatism focuses on the interpersonal processes of assessment and consensus formation as well as the ethical analysis of relevant moral considerations. The steps in this method are delineated and then illustrated through a detailed case study. The implications of clinical pragmatism for the use of principles in moral problem solving are discussed.

**Bacciagaluppi, Guido** and Hemmo, Meir. Modal Interpretations, Decoherence and Measurements. *Stud Hist Phil Mod Physics*, 27B(3), 239-277, S 96.

We address Albert and Loewer's criticism of nonideal measurements in the modal interpretation, by examining the implications of the theory of decoherence for the modal interpretation. In the models originally considered by Albert and Loewer, the inclusion of decoherence provides an answer to their criticism. New problems seem to arise in different models and in situations more general than measurements.

**Bach, Jonathan** and Josefson, Jim. A Critique of Rawls's Hermeneutics as Translation. *Phil Soc Crit*, 23(1), 99-124, 1997.

This paper seeks to demonstrate that hermeneutics is a powerful conceptual tool for exploring the current trend towards theorizing justice as a conversation. Specifically we explore the work of John Rawls in order to describe the particular variety of hermeneutics at work in both 'political liberalism' and 'justice as fairness' and to critique this hermeneutics from the perspective of the ontological hermeneutics of Hans-Georg Gadamer. Using the critique of Quinean pragmatism found in Joseph Rouse's epistemology, we draw a parallel between the 'hermeneutics as translation' in Quine and Rawls's public reason. This parallel, we argue, helps us better understand the features and the limitations of political liberalism, especially when Rawls's hermeneutics is contrasted with the possibility of a theory of justice inspired by Gadamer.

**Bacharach, Michael** and Colman, Andrew M. Payoff Dominance and the Stackelberg Heuristic. *Theor Decis*, 43(1), 1-19, Jl 97.

Payoff dominance, a criterion for choosing between equilibrium points in games, is intuitively compelling, especially in matching games and other games of common interests, but it has not been justified from standard game-theoretic rationality assumptions. A psychological explanation of it is offered in terms of a form of reasoning that we call the Stackelberg heuristic in which players assume that their strategic thinking will be anticipated by their coplayer(s). (edited)

**Back, Anthony L** and Burack, Jeffrey H and Pearlman, Robert A. Provoking Nonepileptic Seizures: The Ethics of Deceptive Diagnostic Testing. *Hastings Center Rep*, 27(4), 24-33, Jl-Ag 97.

The use of deception in medical care is highly suspect in this country. Yet there is one condition in which deception is often used as a diagnostic tool. Nonepileptic seizures, a psychiatric condition in which emotional or psychological conflicts manifest themselves unconsciously through bodily symptoms, are currently diagnosed by a procedure called "provocative saline infusion." The test is fundamentally deceptive, but without such deception the test might be useless.

**Backhaus, Gary**. The Phenomenology of Telephone Space. *Human Stud*, 20(2), 203-220, Ap 97.

The temporally immediate transcendence of space through the use of the telephone creates a bilocalized space of interaction. Unique structures of spatial experience are constituted through the intending of spatial sectors in telephonic conversation. In the first section of this paper, six eidetic variations are presented that establish the various ways in which environmental sectors are intended through the intersubjective space of the telephonic medium. The telos of these descriptions is to characterize changes in social praxis that have been made available with the inclusion in the life-world of the telephone as a typical tool. In the second section, a constitutive analysis is undertaken in order to investigate how empty intentions are brought to fulfillment in the telephonic conversational thematizations of environmental sectors. (edited)

**Backhaus, Wilfried**. Hume's Touchstone and the Politics of Meaningful Discourse. *Dialogue (Canada)*, 35(4), 651-676, Fall 96.

**Backhouse, Roger E**. An 'Inexact' Philosophy of Economics?. *Econ Phil*, 13(1), 25-37, Ap 97.

Daniel M. Hausman, in *The Inexact and Separate Science of Economics* (1992) criticized contemporary economics on the grounds that the drive to make economics a separate science was hindering progress. In this article it is argued that, though Hausman has provided a brilliant characterization of equilibrium theory (neoclassical microeconomics), it is only a partial picture of the discipline of economics. There is much empirical work in economics that is not dominated by equilibrium theory, and which he does not consider. This is significant because it seriously weakens the force of his normative conclusions.

**Backofen, Rolf** and Rogers, James and Vijay-Shanker, K. A First-Order Axiomatization of the Theory of Finite Trees. *J Log Lang Info*, 4(1), 5-39, 1995.

We provide first-order axioms for the theories of finite trees with bounded branching and finite trees with arbitrary (finite) branching. The signature is chosen to express, in a natural way, those properties of trees most relevant to linguistic theories. These axioms provide a foundation for results in linguistics that are based on reasoning formally about such properties. We include some observations on the expressive power of these theories relative to traditional language complexity classes.

**Badaloni, Nicola**. Una polémica entre historiadores de la filosofía. *Cuad Vico*, 7/8, 23-47, 1997.

This essay is intended to be an answer of the author regarding the controversy that has been conducted in many places between him and Paolo Rossi during the last ten years. Each objection of his opponent has been explained, analyzed and answered. The main polemical point is Vico, but the argument goes beyond this particular topic and becomes a general debate concerning the very role of the historian of philosophy.

**Badhwar, Neera Kapur**. Self-Interest and Virtue. *Soc Phil Pol*, 14(1), 226-263, Wint 97.

I defend a neo-Aristotelian conception of virtue as a cognitive and emotional disposition to act in ways conducive to human well-being and argue that 1) virtue is essential to practical efficacy (the successful exercise of our fundamental human capacities), 2) efficacy is essential to happiness, hence 3) virtue is essential to happiness. More precisely, virtue is a necessary constitutive condition of an agent's happiness. For virtue empowers us by freeing us of skewed perceptions and irrational emotions and putting us in touch with various aspects of reality. However, virtue is not sufficient for happiness—some good fortune is also requires.

**Badhwar, Neera Kapur**. The Limited Unity of Virtue. *Nous*, 30(3), 306-329, S 96.

According to Aristotle, one moral virtue entails all the others. This unity of virtue (UV) doctrine has important implications for moral understanding, evaluation, and education. I reject UV—as also the commonly advanced alternatives that the virtues are disunited or, even, mutually incompatible—and argue that the major virtues are disunited across different domains but united within domains (the limited unity of virtue of LUV). A domain is an area of practical concern that *can* be psychologically compartmentalized from other areas of concern and that is *important* enough to justify the ascription of virtue. LUV fits what we know of human psychology and character better than the unity, disunity, or incompatibility theses.

**Badía Cabrera, Miguel A**. "Hume's Scepticism and his Ethical Depreciation of Religion" in *Scepticism in the History of Philosophy: A Pan-American Dialogue*, Popkin, Richard H (ed), 99-114. Dordrecht, Kluwer, 1996.

Hume's thesis in *The Natural History of Religion*, that religion invariably exerts a negative influence on morality, is analyzed in the light of important doctrines of his theoretical and moral theory. This somber assessment is not an inevitable conclusion of Hume's scepticism, but stems from a narrowly utilitarian account of the origin and permanent nature of religious beliefs that appears to be at odds with basic principles of his own moral theory. On the whole, Hume's purely egotistical conception of religion prevented him from adequately recognizing that sympathy is as prominent a phenomenon in religion as self-interest undoubtedly is.

**Badía Cabrera, Miguel A**. Descartes y Hume: causalidad, temporalidad y existencia de Dios. *Dialogos*, 32(69), 203-224, Ja 97.

The influence of Descartes on Hume's thought is widely taken to be essentially negative. This paper attempts to show that Hume's philosophical debt to Descartes is more significant and positive than most commentators have traditionally recognized. Thus Hume will employ a Cartesian conception of temporal duration as composed of discreet moments—which is a foundation of the causal proofs for God's existence that Descartes formulates in the *Third Meditation*—in order to question, in Book I of the *Treatise*, the metaphysical foundations of the general principle of causality, whose validity appears to be presupposed by the Cartesian proofs.

**Badía Cabrera, Miguel A**. La ética de la ciencia y la ciencia de la ética. *Dialogos*, 32(70), 109-122, Jl 97.

This is an inquiry on the roots of the unity of ethics and science: First, both activities stem from the same mental faculties. Second, scientific research in general would not be possible if it were not subject to moral standards. Third, science as a form of human existence that one can choose among several others and not so much as a system of theoretical assertions about some sector of reality, can justify itself only in the light of final ends to which it aspires and values which are embedded in it as an activity that are of an ethical character.

**Badía Cabrera, Miguel A**. Semblanza de José Echeverría. *Dialogos*, 32(69), 11-15, Ja 97.

This is a biographical sketch of one of the most distinguished figures of contemporary Latin American philosophy, the Chilean philosopher and jurist José Echeverría, who recently died. It gives a brief overview of his main theoretical works, in areas as diverse as metaphysics, ethics, aesthetics, philosophy of law, of literature, and education. In particular, it emphasizes Echeverría's crucial contribution to the foundation and development of a rigorous program of philosophical studies at the University of Puerto Rico.

**Badillo O'Farrell, Pablo**. Scienza Nuova y *The New Science of Politics*: Proyección del pensamiento viquiano en la obra de Eric Voeglin. *Cuad Vico*, 7/8, 49-58, 1997.

Not withstanding the scattered explicit references to Vico in Voegelin's work, the paper intends to show the incidence of the Vichian thought onto the *The New Science of Politics'* author. The two both contend against strong tendencies of secularism: the first stands against Cartesian rationalism, the latter against positivism.

**Badillo O'Farrell, Pablo**. Suárez y Vico, veinte años después. *Cuad Vico*, 7/8, 239-252, 1997.

Though the perspective purported in the 1977 paper on Suarez's influence on the Vichian thought is still assumed to the extent concerning legal matters; we come now to claim the Neapolitan's work both as the topic-rhetorical method's

great rediscoverer and the last representative of the Roman tradition in the XVIII Century.

**Badiou, Alain**. Filosofia e politica. *Iride*, 8(15), 332-338, Ag 95.

Se possa esistere una politica giusta è la domanda che il filosofo pone alla politica. Nel mondo attuale, caotico e confuso, la filosofia chiama "giustizia" ciò che coglie l'ordine soggettivo di una massima alla cui luce emerge l'inconsistenza statale e sociale di ogni politica egualitaria.

**Badwal, Bhajan S**. Two Theories of Knowledge: Locke vs. Stoic. *Darshana Int*, 36(1/141), 11-17, Ja 96.

**Baer, Eugen**. Noetic Philosophizing: Rhetoric's Displacement of Metaphysics *Alcestis* and *Don Quixote*. *Phil Rhet*, 30(2), 105-149, 1997.

**Baertschi, Bernard**. Ethique et anthropologie: A propos du livre de John Hare, *The Moral Gap*. *Rev Theol Phil*, 128(4), 367-376, 1996.

John Hare's latest book is concerned with the gap between moral demands and our ability to fulfill them. The author is certainly interested in closing the gap because it is a dangerous source of motivation loss for ethical life. His theory is that the Christian conception of humankind and morality permits this. While the author fully accepts that other solutions are possible, we attempt to show that the very wording of his statement on the existence of the gap is heavily weighted with a Christian perception. An anthropology and an ethics of a different inspiration would therefore see the moral situation of humanking quite differently.

**Baertschi, Bernard**. L'Éthique et les Stress. *Rev Theol Phil*, 128(3), 229-252, 1996.

The two great ethical traditions, Kantianism and utilitarianism have at least one common feature: for both, when we take a decision or evaluate behaviour, it is necessary and sufficient to invoke a single general principle—the categorical imperative or the maximization of utility—, valid for any situation. For us, this view is too schematic and idealizing, because there are situations which change the ethical position of the agent. The situation of stress, such as when the agent or his kin are in direct danger, shows this, as we can see in cases of population pressure.

**Baeten, Elizabeth M**. An American Naturalist Account of Culture. *Metaphilosophy*, 27(4), 408-425, O 96.

The basic tenets of "classical" naturalism (exemplified in the work of Mead, Buchler and Randall, among others) are delineated and distinguished from other versions of naturalism. Classical naturalism is also distinguished from reductive materialism and idealism. Nature is asserted to be indefinitely plural and not amenable to monistic or dualistic categorial schemes; that is, the principle of "ontological parity" is maintained. The method of inquiry of naturalism is outlined, along with the notion of truth as perspectivally objective. The metaphysical hypotheses are then used to examine culture. Culture is found to be the specific environment of human being, arising out of, but irreducible to, other natural processes. Culture is described as the cumulative gestures of the human social organism as it discovers and creates itself in mutual constitution with other natural processes and products.

**Baeten, Elizabeth M**. *The Magic Mirror: Myth's Abiding Power*. Albany, SUNY Pr, 1996.

In this book, Elizabeth M. Baeten analyzes the theories of myth propounded by Cassirer, Barthes, Eliade, and Hillman and juxtaposes the insights of these very different perspectives to form a coherent account of myth. She then shows that these theories perform the same function the authors ascribe to myth itself. Moreover, not only do the theories of myth function mythically; the myth embedded in each theory is the same: the *telos* of human existence is absolute freedom, an unbounded power to constitute the subjective and objective features of existence. The correlate of this myth of absolute creative freedom, Baeten argues, is that the truly human must transcend natural determinations. Baeten understands this to be a dangerous myth and offers an alternative original account of myth-making as an essential strand of cultural production demarcating the human process within the setting of broader natural processes. (publisher, edited)

**Bagaria, Joan**. A Characterization of Martin's Axiom in Terms of Absoluteness. *J Sym Log*, 62(2), 366-372, Je 97.

Martin's axiom is equivalent to the statement that the universe is absolute under ccc forcing extensions for Sigma$_1$ sentences with a subset of *kappa*, *kappa* less than $2^{akph \, 0}$, as a parameter.

**Bagaria, Joan** and Bosch, Roger. Projective Forcing. *Annals Pure Applied Log*, 86(3), 237-266, Jl 97.

We study the projective posits and their properties as forcing notions. We also define Martin's axiom restricted to projective sets, *MA(proj)* and show that this axiom is weaker than full Martin's axiom.... (edited)

**Bagley, Paul J**. On the Moral Philosophy of René Descartes: Or, How Morals are Derived from Method. *Tijdschr Filosof*, 58(4), 673-696, D 96.

Treatments of the moral doctrine of René Descartes found in the Cartesian scholarship do not typically regard the Cartesian philosophy as being devoted to moral instruction. In this essay, it is argued that the moral philosophy of Descartes involves the connection of the method enunciated in the *Discourse on the Method* with the "morale par provision" articulated in that work. The affinity between morals and method is found in the fact that moral dispositions are to be adapted to the progress achieved in scientific technology. Accordingly, it is the advance of science that determines the good of man. And it is concluded that the Cartesian moral teaching amounts to this: That which man can do is good or moral to do.

**Bagolini, Luigi**. Domande e risposte sul problema della giustizia. *Riv Int Filosof Diritto*, 73(3), 405-415, Jl-S 96.

**Bagolini, Luigi**. Il fondamento etico e metafisico del diritto. *Riv Int Filosof Diritto*, 74(1), 126-128, Ja-Mr 97.

AUTHOR INDEX 505 Baird, Forrest E

**Bahm, Archie J**. *Organicism: Origin and Development.* Albuquerque, World Books, 1996.

In the fall of 1925 Archie Bahm went off to Taylor University, intending to prepare himself for the Christian ministry. However, during the first semester he was converted from Christian fundamentalism, to use his own words, and abandoned his preministerial plans, "to pursue my quest as a truth seeker." That quest for truth absorbed him for the rest of his long life, and resulted in a rich and distinguished career as a university professor and philosopher. This book ends in a call for the formation of an institute for *world philosophy*, where scholars could refine existing concepts of philosophy. (publisher, edited)

**Baier, Annette C**. *The Commons of the Mind.* Chicago, Open Court, 1997.

A powerful tradition in philosophy, of which Descartes is an influential proponent, holds that mind is something possessed by each individual human, independently of membership in a culture and society. But there is a dissenting tradition, which takes mental activities and states to be essentially social. In these "Carus Lectures," Annette Baier looks at the relation between individual and shared reasoning, intending and moral reflection. In each case she emphasizes the interdependence of minds and the role of social practices in setting the norms governing these activities. Professor Baier defends the view that our reasoning and our intention-information require a commons of the mind—a background of shared reasonings, intentions, and actions. However, she concludes that moral reflection, as a social capacity, is still in its infancy, and that a commons of the mind is by no means assured with regard to morality. (publisher)

**Baigrie, Brian S**. "Descartes's Scientific Illustrations and 'la grand mécanique de la nature'" in *Picturing Knowledge,* Baigrie, Brian S (ed), 86-134. Toronto, Univ of Toronto Pr, 1996.

**Baigrie, Brian S** (ed). *Picturing Knowledge: Historical and Philosophical Problems Concerning the Use of Art in Science.* Toronto, Univ of Toronto Pr, 1996.

The contributors to this volume examine the historical and philosophical issues concerning the role that scientific illustration plays in the creation of scientific knowledge. They regard both text and picture as resources that scientists employ in their practical activities, their value as scientific resources deriving from their ability to convey information.

**Bailey, Cathryn**. Making Waves and Drawing Lines: The Politics of Defining the Vicissitudes of Feminism. *Hypatia,* 12(3), 17-28, Sum 97.

If there actually is a third wave of feminism, it is too close to the second wave for its definition to be clear and uncontroversial, a fact which emphasizes the political nature of declaring the existence of this third wave. Through an examination of some third wave literature, a case is made for emphasizing the continuity of the second and third waves without blurring the differences between older and younger feminists.

**Bailey, Jeffrey**. Individual Scapetribing and Responsibility Ascriptions. *J Bus Ethics,* 16(1), 47-53, Ja 97.

Individual scapetribing is identified as pointing the finger of blame at organizations (or groups, institutions and systems) as a means of excusing or inaccurately ascribing responsibility for one's own actions and their consequences. This type of behavior is shown to be related to corporate scape-goating as described by Wilson (1993). The paper addresses responsibility ascriptions and the importance of corporate responsibility as a significantly influential multiperson system.

**Bailey Stoneking, Carole**. A Communion of Saints...Maybe. *Christian Bioethics,* 2(3), 346-354, 1996.

Descriptively many Protestant perspectives on access to health care share much in common with secular accounts...perhaps too much. A normative account of a Protestant perspective on access to health care must be perceptively qualified by the Christ story. A genuinely theocratic approach may not lead one to the conclusion that the faith commits us to the notion of equality; rather the faith commits us to the notion of *care. What counts as care* may not be the same in every instance (if this is indeed what equality means; in ordinary use, equality is tantamount to sameness). The Christ story reminds us who we are, beloved, sinful, redeemed. Acting out this story is to accept, to give and to receive reconciliation. For many Christians this will mean that we are called to deny ourselves "equal" access to the system (as if equality actually existed!)

**Bailhache, Patrice**. Canonical Models for Temporal Deontic Logic. *Log Anal,* 38(149), 3-21, Mr 95.

The system I called R5-D5 merges alethic, deontic and temporal modalities. Its soundness and completeness were proved, in 1983, with respect to a branching structure. Unfortunately the proof was very complicated, extending the method that [Hughes & Cresswell 1968] have used for various modal systems (T, S4, S5,...). Meanwhile the method of canonical models has been generalized to modal logics and, although not trivially easy, it is now possible to give a new proof based on this method.

**Bailhache, Patrice**. Temporalized Deontic Worlds with Individuals. *Log Anal,* 38(149), 23-42, Mr 95.

Deontic logic handles not only deontic modalities, but also alethic and temporal ones. In addition, individuals like *authorities* and *addresses* play an important role. R5-D5 is a system mixing alethic, deontic and temporal modalities, whose adequation (i.e., soundness plus completeness) has been proved in the previous paper. Similarly for KDUX, a system with sets of authorities (without a proof of completeness). The present article is an attempt to construct a general system combining R5-D5 and KDUX. Adequation, although probable, is only surmised here, for the sake of brevity. In addition, the obtained structure is briefly compared with that which results in a slightly different approach of time, due to [Aqvist and Hoepelman 1981].

**Bailin, Sharon**. Other People's Products: The Value of Performing and Appreciating. *J Aes Educ,* 27(2), 59-69, Sum 93.

**Baillie, James**. *Contemporary Analytic Philosophy.* Upper Saddle River, Prentice Hall, 1997.

This anthology includes some of the most influential readings in 20th century analytic philosophy. Authors are Frege, Russell, Wittgenstein, Ayer, Schlick, Carnap, Moore, Ryle, Grice, Austin, Sellars, Quine, Tarski, Davidson, Krupke, Putnam. Each selection is given a detailed introduction, including biographical details, summary of the argument, criticism and recommendations for further reading.

**Baillie, James**. Identity, Relation R, and What Matters. *Pac Phil Quart,* 77(4), 263-267, D 96.

This paper offers a challenge to Derek Parfit's thesis that one ought to have no preference between these two otherwise identical situations: I) I continue to go on living as before and 2) I do not survive, but am replaced by a duplicate, psychologically continuous to my present self (i.e., an R-related duplicate). I point out that virtually all psychologically normal persons regard some in*animate* objects as being 'irreplaceable' (such that no copy could adequately substitute). I then propose that in every such case, this judgment is based on the subject's regarding some *person* as likewise irreplaceable. It would follow that any such subject would have to reject Parfit's thesis.

**Baird, Forrest E** (ed) and Kaufmann, Walter. *Ancient Philosophy, 2nd Edition.* Upper Saddle River, Prentice Hall, 1997.

An anthology of ancient philosophy including extensive selections from the pre-Socratics, the writings of the most important Greek philosophers (including almost 400 pages from Plato and Aristotle); along with shorter selections from the Hellenistic and Roman philosophers Epicurus, Zeno of Citium, Cleanthes, Epictetus, Lucretius, Marcus Aurelius, Pyrrho and Sextus Empiricus, and Plotinus. In choosing texts for this volume I have tried wherever possible to follow three principles: 1) to use complete works or, where more appropriate, complete sections of works 2) in clear translations 3) of texts central to the thinker's philosophy or widely accepted as part of the "canon."

**Baird, Forrest E** (ed) and Kaufmann, Walter. *From Plato to Nietzsche, 2nd Edition.* Upper Saddle River, Prentice Hall, 1997.

An anthology of Western philosophy including extensive selections from ancient Greek philosophy (Plato, Aristotle), Hellenistic philosophy (Epicurus, Epictetus, Plotinus), medieval philosophy (Augustine, Thomas Aquinas, William of Ockham, and numerous others), modern philosophy (Bacon, Descartes, Hobbes, Spinoza, Locke, Leibniz, Berkeley, Hume, Kant), and nineteenth-century philosophy (Hegel, Mill, Kierkegaard, Marx, and Nietzsche). In choosing texts for this volume I have tried wherever possible to follow three principles: 1) to use complete works or, where more appropriate, complete sections of works, 2) in clear translations, 3) of texts central to the thinker's philosophy or widely accepted as part of the "canon."

**Baird, Forrest E** (ed) and Kaufmann, Walter. *Medieval Philosophy, 2nd Edition.* Upper Saddle River, Prentice Hall, 1997.

An anthology of Medieval philosophy including extensive selections from Augustine, Thomas Aquinas, and William of Ockham, along with representative texts from Boethius, Eriugena, Anselm (and Guanilo), Abelard, Hildegard of Bingen, John of Salisbury, Avicenna, Averroes, Maimonides, Grosseteste, Roger Bacon, Bonaventure, Duns Scotus, Eckhart, Catherine of Siena, Nicholas Cusanas, and Pico and others. In choosing texts for this volume I have tried wherever possible to follow three principles: 1) to use complete works or, where more appropriate, complete sections of works 2) in clear translations 3) of texts central to the thinker's philosophy or widely accepted as part of the "canon."

**Baird, Forrest E** (ed) and Kaufmann, Walter. *Modern Philosophy, 2nd Edition.* Upper Saddle River, Prentice Hall, 1997.

An anthology of modern philosophy including extensive selections from the "British Empiricists" (Francis Bacon, Thomas Hobbes, John Locke, George Berkeley, David Hume, Thomas Reid, and Mary Wollstonecraft) and the "Continental Rationalists" (Rene Descartes, Baruch Spinoza, and Gottfried Leibniz), together with almost 160 pages from the great synthesizer, Immanuel Kant. In choosing texts for this volume I have tried wherever possible to follow three principles: 1) to use complete works or, where more appropriate, complete sections of works, 2) in clear translations, 3) of texts central to the thinker's philosophy or widely accepted as part of the "canon."

**Baird, Forrest E** (ed) and Kaufmann, Walter. *Nineteenth-Century Philosophy.* Upper Saddle River, Prentice Hall, 1997.

An anthology of both Continental and Anglo-American philosophy in the nineteenth century. Continental thinkers include Fichte, Hegel, Schopenhauer, Comte, Kierkegaard, Marx and Nietzsche. Anglo-American philosophers include Bentham, Mill, Peirce, James, and Dewey. In choosing texts for this volume I have tried wherever possible to follow three principles: 1) to use complete works or, where more appropriate, complete sections of works, 2) in clear translations, and 3) of texts central to the thinker's philosophy or widely accepted as part of the "canon."

**Baird, Forrest E** (ed) and Kaufmann, Walter. *Twentieth-Century Philosophy.* Upper Saddle River, Prentice Hall, 1997.

An anthology of both continental and Anglo-American philosophy in the twentieth century. Continental thinkers include Husserl, Heidegger, Gadamer, Sartre, de Beauvoir, Merleau-Ponty, Foucault, Derrida, Irigaray, and Habermas. Anglo-American philosophers include Dewey, Whitehead, DuBois, Russell, Moore, Wittgenstein, Carnap, Quine, Austin, Davidson, Rorty, Putnam, and Taylor. In choosing texts for this volume I have tried to follow three principles: 1) use complete works or, where more appropriate, complete sections of works, 2) in clear translations, 3) of texts central to the thinker's philosophy or widely accepted as part of the "canon" (though some recent philosophy criticizes the very notion of a canon).

**Baird, Robert M** (ed) and Rosenbaum, Stuart E (ed). *Morality and the Law*. Amherst, Prometheus, 1993.

Law and morality spring from the same source: a fundamental social need for order and security. But what are we to do when the dictates of conscience conflict with the statute books? Which should be obeyed? Should the morality of some be visited upon all by giving it the force of law? Are there moral principles that go beyond legal jurisdiction to justify acts of civil disobedience? These and other important questions are addressed in this fascinating collection of essays by some of the most astute minds in law and philosophy: Hugo A. Bedau, Charles L. Black, Jr., Patrick Devlin, Joel Feinberg, Erich Fromm, H.L.A. Hart, Leon Jaworski, John Rawls, Peter Singer and Rudolph Weingartner. (publisher)

**Baker, Brenda M**. Improving our Practice of Sentencing. *Utilitas*, 9(1), 99-114, Mr 97.

Restorative justice should have greater weight as a criterion in criminal justice sentencing practice. It permits a realistic recognition of the kinds of harm and damage caused by offences and encourages individualized noncustodial sentencing options as ways of addressing these harms. Noncustodial sentences have proven more effective than incarceration in securing social reconciliation and preventing recidivism and they avoid the serious social and personal costs of imprisonment. This paper argues in support of restorative justice as a guiding idea in sentencing. As part of this defence, it considers whether the use of the idea of restorative justice will conflate criminal law with civil law or displace the authority of the criminal courts and whether the sentences it recommends are best thought of as punishments or alternatives to punishment.

**Baker, Gordon** and Morris, Katherine J. *Descartes' Dualism*. New York, Routledge, 1996.

The position of Cartesian dualism has come to be accepted as a view of the mind as an inner world of private 'objects' and of the body as an insentient machine; according to the authors, Descartes did not subscribe to this doctrine. Indeed, he could not have done since, Baker and Morris argue, such a view is inconsistent with the logical, scientific, theological and metaphysical frameworks of his thinking. The book has two central aims: the first is to argue for a radically different interpretation of Descartes's doctrine. The second aim is to clarify the philosophical interest of looking at Descartes's actual concept of a person. This is meant to shake complacency about the presuppositions underlying current investigations in areas as diverse as logic, cognitive science and animal rights. (publisher, edited)

**Baker, Gordon** and Morris, Katherine J. Descartes's Dualism?. *Phil Books*, 38(3), 157-169, Jl 97.

Nadler gives an informative, lucid and balanced account of our book, and raises some challenging objections. However, he focuses exclusively on our 'first-order' aim of presenting an alternative to the standard Anglo-American interpretation of Descartes's dualism, at the expense of our 'second-order' aim of showing the *philosophical* interest of such historical explorations. His principal criticisms centre on our account of mind-body interaction; these rest, we argue, on the challengeable axiom that for Descartes, 'the mind alone is active'; on misunderstandings of Descartes's notions of intelligibility and resemblance; and on misrepresentations of the background of scholastic doctrines of causation.

**Baker, H Kent** and Veit, E Theodore. Ethical Attitudes and Behavior of Investment Professionals in the United Kingdom. *Prof Ethics*, 5(1-2), 87-117, Spr-Sum 96.

**Baker, Robert S**. History and Periodization. *Clio*, 26(2), 135-141, Wint 97.

**Bakker, Paul J J M**. Syncatégorèmes, concepts, équivocité: Deux questions anonymes, conservées dans le ms. Paris, B.N., lat. 16.401, liées à la sémantique de Pierre d'Ailly (c. 1350-1420). *Vivarium*, 34(1), 76-131, My 96.

This article offers an analysis and an edition of two anonymous semantical questions. Both questions are concerned with problems relating to mental language. The first question investigates the nature of the mental correlate of vocal or written syncategorematic terms. The second question examines the possibility of equivocal concepts. The article shows that both texts originate from a semantical tradition of which William of Ockham, John Buridan, Albert of Saxony, Marsilius of Inghen and Peter of Ailly were the main representatives. More specifically, the doctrine of both questions appears to be closely related to Peter of Ailly's compendium *Conceptus*.

**Bakker II, Willem** and Loui, Michael. Can Designing and Selling Low-Quality Products Be Ethical?. *Sci Eng Ethics*, 3(2), 153-170, Ap 97.

Whereas previous studies have criticized low-quality products for inadequate safety, this paper considers only safe products and it examines the ethics of designing and selling low-quality products. Product quality is defined as suitability to a general purpose. The duty that companies owe to consumers is summarized in the Consumer-Oriented Process principle: "to place an increase in the consumer's quality of life as the primary goal for producing products." This principle is applied in analyzing the primary ethical justifications for low-quality products: availability and applicability. Finally, a low-quality product should be designed afresh, not by altering an existing high-quality product.

**Balasubramanian, R**. Daya Krishna's Retrospective Delusion. *J Indian Counc Phil Res*, 14(1), 137-156, S-D 96.

**Balderas Rosas, Gloria del Carmen**. La concepción de "leyes de la naturaleza" en el *Tractatus* de Ludwig Wittgenstein. *Analogia*, 10(2), 259-265, 1996.

**Baldi, Marialuisa**. "Confutazione e conferma: l'origenismo nella traduzione latina del *True Intellectual System* (1733)" in *Mind Senior to the World*, Baldi, Marialuisa, 163-204. Milano, FrancoAngeli, 1996.

**Baldi, Marialuisa**. *Mind Senior to the World*. Milano, FrancoAngeli, 1996.

Nella seconda metà del Seicento, in un ambiente dominato dagli sviluppi del cartesianesimo e di lì a poco destinato a essere pervaso dall'empirismo lockiano, la Scuola di Cambridge rilegge l'eredità platonica per trovarvi argomenti a sostegno di una concezione sincretistica della ragione che ricerca la conciliazione tra la fede cristiana e le tradizioni filosofiche. A partire da una soluzione del problema della grazia intesa a salvaguardare la libertà in polemica con le soluzioni calvinista e puritana, l'antiagostinismo è la discriminante che identifica la forma specifica del platonismo inglese e la direzione della sua apologetica.

**Baldino, Marco** (ed) and Bonesio, Luisa (ed) and Resta, Caterina (ed). *Geofilosofia*. Sondrio, Lyasis, 1996.

Primo tentativo italiano organico e ad ampio raggio, il volume *Geofilosofia* fornisce un'idea efficace del dialogo che si può intessere, da molteplici punti di osservazione, a partire dalla prospettiva geofilosofica: gli autori (Jacques Derrida, Jean-Luc Nancy, Otto Pöggeler, François Makowski, Vincenzo Vitiello, Pierluigi Cervellati, Guglielmo Scaramellini, Caterina Resta, Luisa Bonesio, Alessandro Marcenaro) si interrogano sul senso e le possibilità attuali dell'abitare sulla terra: riflessione sul senso del luogo, dell'identità, del paesaggio, dell'urbanistica, dell'Europa a venire; ma anche la rivendicazione dell'appartenenza, delle identità locali, il mondialismo, l'omologazione delle dimensioni culturali nella tecnoeconomia, la progettazione degli spazi tra salvaguardia e sfrenata urbanizzazione, le dimensioni di frontiera, l'emergenza ecologica, e il paesaggio, considerato come il risultato di una cooperazione complessa fra cultura e fisionomia naturale.

**Baldner, Steven**. St. Bonaventure and the Demonstrability of a Temporal Beginning: A Reply to Richard Davis. *Amer Cath Phil Quart*, 71(2), 225-236, Spr 97.

I argue, against Richard Davis, Amer Cath Phil Quart, 70 (3), 361-380, that there is not sufficient evidence to warrant the claim that Bonaventure regarded the temporal beginning of the world as philosophically demonstrable. Aristotle erred, according to Bonaventure, not because he failed to see that the temporal beginning is demonstrable, but because he lacked Christian revelation. Further, Bonaventure's argument from the immortality of the human soul appears not to be a demonstration of the temporal beginning.

**Baldwin, Thomas**. There Might Be Nothing. *Analysis*, 56(4), 231-238, O 96.

Is it a necessary truth that there is something or other? In recent papers van Inwagen and Lowe argue that it is impossible, or vanishingly improbable, for there to be nothing at all. I defend the contrary nihilist hypothesis by a subtraction argument and use the resulting position to criticize the arguments of van Inwagen and Lowe

**Baldwin, Wendy** and Seto, Belinda. Peer Review: Selecting the Best Science. *Sci Eng Ethics*, 3(1), 11-17, Ja 97.

The major challenge facing today's biomedical researchers is the increasing competition for available funds. The competitive review process, through which the National Institutes of Health (NIH) awards grants, is built upon review by a committee of expert scientists. The NIH is firmly committed to ensuring that its peer review system is fair and objective.

**Balibrea Cárceles, Miguel Angel**. La crítica de Polo al argumento anselmiano. *Anu Filosof*, 29(2), 373-380, 1996.

This work is an introduction on Polo's criticism of Saint Anselm's argument, showing that this argument is inefficient with respect to Polo's comprehension of the intellect and Polo's study of the existence.

**Ball, Elaine**. "Technologies of the Self" in *Critical Studies: Ethics and the Subject*, Simms, Karl (ed), 139-145. Amsterdam, Rodopi, 1997.

**Ballerini, Arnaldo**. Il delirio della memoria e la memoria come delirio. *Iride*, 8(14), 46-58, Ap 95.

**Ballester, Luis García**. El Camino de Santiago y el descubrimiento racional de la naturaleza en los siglos XII y XIII. *El Basilisco*, 22, 33-42, Jl-D 96.

**Balmaseda Cinquina, María F**. Feminismo y tercer milenio. *Sapientia*, 51(200), 335-346, 1996.

**Balmert, N.A.** and Greene, Richard. Two Notions of Warrant and Plantinga's Solution to the Gettier Problem. *Analysis*, 57(2), 132-139, Ap 97.

In this paper we offer a critique of Plantinga's solution to the Gettier problem. Specifically, we argue that Plantinga's account of warrant contains an internal inconsistency. He offers a definition of warrant which precludes the possibility of false warranted beliefs (a consequence that Plantinga appears not to countenance) and he offers an account of the necessary and sufficient conditions for warrant which allows for false warranted beliefs. The latter account, we argue, actually gives rise to Gettier problems. We conclude the paper by arguing that the two accounts are not easily reconciled.

**Baltzly, Dirk**. "Socratic Anti-Empiricism in the *Phaedo*" in *Dialogues with Plato*, Benitez, Eugenio (ed), 121-142. Edmonton, Academic, 1996.

In the *Phaedo*, Socrates endorses the view that the senses are not a means whereby we may come to gain knowledge. It is a measure of the success of empiricism that modern commentators take a very different approach to *Phaedo* 65a9-67b3 than their neo-Platonist forebearers did. I argue that if they made too much of Socrates' antiempiricism, we make too little of it. Careful examination of the presuppositions of Socratic questioning reveals some principled reasons which lead to the view endorsed in the *Phaedo*. Socrates' antiempiricism in this dialogue is not simply a gratuitous epistemological reflection of the dialogue's otherworldly, ascetic outlook.

**Baltzly, Dirk**. Socratic Anti-Empiricism in the *Phaedo*. *Apeiron*, 29(4), 121-142, D 96.

Socrates' claims about the role of sense perception in attaining knowledge (*Phaedo* 65a-66e) are neither an ascetic's denigration of the flesh nor an early statement of the *Republic*'s Two Worlds thesis about knowledge and opinion. The position that Socrates takes is best understood as the claim that an understanding of 'that on account of which' something appears F is utterly irrelevant to an understanding of 'that on account of which' it is F. Such a position on the *aitiai* of being and appearing is prefigured in *Hippias Major* 294d7-e5 and is simply a result of taking seriously certain constraints on answers to Socratic questions.

**Bambach, Charles**. The Hermeneutics of Origin: Arché and the Anarchic in John Van Buren's *The Young Heidegger*. *Phil Today*, 41(2), 313-324, Sum 97.

**Bañares Parera, Leticia**. El carácter sistémico del liderazgo. *Anu Filosof*, 29(2), 381-385, 1996.

Man is a dynamic being, a free system. Free systems are interactive systems. Every organization is a cooperative system. In organizations the relation between manager and inferiors is an open system: management and obedience are alternative activities. Leadership is a cooperative system.

**Banaszak, Grzegorz**. "Musical Culture as a Configuration of Subcultures" in *Epistemology and History*, Zeidler-Janiszewska, Anna (ed), 517-529. Amsterdam, Rodopi, 1996.

The article is devoted to a theoretical interpretation of musical practice. It situates music in the sphere of cultural phenomena, indicating the dependence of creative acts and musical perception on the consciousness base which is identified with musical culture. Analyses relating to this culture and also to its bonds with musical practice, are based on foundations and notions taken from J Kmita's theory of culture.

**Bandyopadhyay, Prasanta S** and Boik, Robert J and Basu, Prasun. The Curve Fitting Problem: A Bayesian Approach. *Proc Phil Sci Ass*, 3(Suppl), S264-S272, 1996.

**Banks, Dwayne A**. The Economic Attributes of Medical Care: Implications for Rationing Choices in the United States and United Kingdom. *Cambridge Quart Healthcare Ethics*, 5(4), 546-558, Fall 96.

**Banyeres Baltasà, Hug**. El cant gregorià, un model de música perfecta. *Convivium*, 9, 5-22, 1996.

**Bar-Elli, Gilead**. Frege's Context Principle. *Philosophia (Israel)*, 25(1-4), 99-129, Ap 97.

A distinction is drawn between the "essential interpretation" and the "identifying interpretation" of the principle. The former deals with the question of what the very ascription of meaning amounts to; the latter, with how the meaning of an expression is determined and identified. In the light of this the relationships of the principle with the compositionality thesis and with the sense/reference distinction are discussed.

**Bar-Elli, Gilead**. Logical Structure and Intentionality: Frege and Russell on Definite Descriptions (in Hebrew). *Iyyun*, 46, 167-192, Ap 97.

Differences between Russell's and Frege's theories are rooted in differences concerning meaning and the relations of logical structure and what a proposition is about. Frege's principle, that a proposition is only about what is explicitly mentioned in it, expresses his "local" conception—that the reference of a term and what a proposition is about are determined locally by its sense. Russell rejected this and offered an alternative—that what a proposition is about is determined by its logical structure and need not be among its constituents. Russell thus maintains the "object-directedness" of descriptive propositions in a non-Fregean way.

**Bar-Elli, Gilead**. On the Concept of Awe (Yira) in Maimonides (In Hebrew). *Iyyun*, 45, 381-388, O 96.

**Bar-Elli, Gilead**. *The Sense of Reference: Intentionality in Frege*. Hawthorne, de Gruyter, 1996.

**Barabashev, A G**. In Support of Significant Modernization of Original Mathematical Texts (In Defense of Presentism). *Phil Math*, 5, 21-41, F 97.

At their extremes, the modernization of ancient mathematical texts (absolute presentism) leaves nothing of the source and the refusal to modernize (absolute antiquarism) changes nothing. The extremes exist only as tendencies. This paper attempts to justify the admissibility of broad modernization of mathematical sources (presentism) in the context of a sociocultural (nonfundamentalist) philosophy of mathematics.

**Barany, Zoltan**. The 'Volatile' Marxian Concept of the Dictatorship of the Proletariat. *Stud East Euro Thought*, 49(1), 1-21, Mr 97.

The thesis of this paper is that even some of the most fundamental concepts of Marxism have been used and abused to fit their advocates' purposes. More specifically, the interpretation of the concept of the "dictatorship of the proletariat" has been subject to a dual development. First, the dictatorship of the proletariat has come to denote an increasingly violent regime. Second, the term has been used to refer to a rule exercised by an ever smaller segment of society. This paper seeks to analyze and elucidate this much disputed and frequently misunderstood Marxist concept. (edited)

**Barata-Moura, José**. A Objectividade como categoria filosófica: Subsídios para uma caracterizaçao. *Philosophica (Portugal)*, 13-30, 1993.

In Frage steht der Versuch einer Annäherung an die *Objektivität* als philosophische Kategorie. Hermeneutisch setzt eine unmittelbar vorhandene These

verschiedene problematische Sinneskonstituierende Horizonte voraus. *Objektivität* ist Bedeutungsträger innerhalb mancher semantischen Felder, nämlich der Zweckbestimmtheit, der Entfernung von Subjektives, der Erkenntnistheorie und Epistemologie, der Ontologie. Erkenntnis und Praxis haben zwar Bedingungen; ontologisch verstanden als *Materialität*, besitzt die *Objektivität* keine transmaterielle Möglichkeits-bedingungen, vielmehr ist sie selbst Bedingung.

**Barata-Moura, José**. Prolegómenos a uma ontologia da acçao. *Philosophica (Portugal)*, 51-70, 1994.

Dans cet essai—*Prolégomènes à une ontologie de l'action*—on part de l'inventaire des différents horizons de thématisation du problème de l'action depuis la pensée des Grecs jusqu'aux philosophies contemporaines de l'action et de la *praxis*, ayant pour but, dans un second moment, de tracer les possibles voies pour la constitution d'une ontologie de l'action comme actionalité inscrite au coeur même de l'être, en tant qu'expression, médiation et transformation des figures où se déploie son historicité.

**Barbanel, Julius B** and Zwicker, William S. Two Applications of a Theorem of Dvoretsky, Wald, and Wolfovitz to Cake Division. *Theor Decis*, 43(2), 203-207, S 97.

In this note, we show that a partition of a cake is Pareto optimal if and only if it maximizes some convex combination of the measures used by those who receive the resulting pieces of cake. Also, given any sequence of positive real numbers that sum to one (which may be thought of as representing the players' relative entitlements), we show that there exists a partition in which each player receives either more than, less then, or exactly his or her entitlement (according to his or her measure), in any desired combination, provided that the measures are not all equal.

**Barbanera, Franco** and Berardi, Stefano. A Constructive Valuation Semantics for Classical Logic. *Notre Dame J Form Log*, 37(3), 462-482, Sum 96.

This paper presents a constructive interpretation for the proofs in classical logic of $\mathrm{Sigma}^0_1$-sentences and for a witness extraction procedure based on Prawitz's reduction rules.

**Barbero Santos, Marino**. "Concepto de la pena en el primer Fichte" in *El inicio del Idealismo alemán*, Market, Oswaldo, 159-165. Madrid, Ed Complutense, 1996.

Mientras que la monarquía absoluta consideraba el Derecho penal como un medio para producir terror y asegurar su poder, la Ilustración basó el derecho en la razón, como medio de construcción de la sociedad. Kant es quien más radicalmente se separa del derecho penal anterior, del Estado policial y autoritario, proclamando la igualdad de todos ante la ley; la pena no tiene su fundamento en la moralización o en la ejemplaridad, sino en el deber que se ha infligido. Fichte considera el contrato social como el único marco del derecho y del Estado, en cuanto recíproca garantía del derecho de todos frente a todos. Para él, la mejora civil (no la moral) es el fin de la pena, mientras que la muerte no es una pena, sino una medida de seguridad, un mal, pero necesario frente a los incorregibles. Fichte defiende un humanismo liberal, y en el ámbito penal sostiene un sistema coherente: idealismo en lo teórico y realismo en lo práctico.

**Barbone, Steven**. St. Bonaventure's Journey into God. *Franciscanum*, 37(112), 57-65, Ja-Ap 96.

I argue that St. Bonaventure's *Itinerarium mentis in Deum*, while being a mystical writing, does shed not a little light on the philosopher/theologian's general epistemology and account of illumination. The major analysis centers on Bonaventure's use of the participles *in* ("into") and *ad* ("to/toward") and his use of the accusative case (*in Deum*) rather than the ablative case (*in Deo*) in this and other works. The analysis may have theological importance, but its value lies in its epistemological implications.

**Barbone, Steven** (ed) and Rice, Lee (ed). *Spinoza Bibliography: 1991-1995*. Milwaukee, No Amer Spinoza Soc, 1997.

The 681 references comprising this bibliography were extracted from a larger bibliographical data base which we have maintained for several years: here you find the complete listings of the data base for works published between 1991 and 1995 (inclusive). Following our extraction of the data, we made every effort to verify doubtful entries and to impute incomplete ones. In only a few cases, because of the tendency of European bibliographers to exclude publisher informations from listings, have we been unsuccessful. (edited)

**Barbour, Elizabeth** and Hulac, Peter. Futile Care in Neonatology: An Interim Report from Colorado. *Bioethics Forum*, 11(1), 42-48, Spr 95.

A group of Colorado citizens, parents and health care professionals has begun work on the problem of aggressive medical treatment in cases when such care appears futile or inappropriate. The group is part of a larger project called GUIDe (Guidelines for Intensive Care in Denver). The committee has studied lethal medical conditions, the role of a consultation structure, care of very premature infants and developed some guidelines about newborns with life-threatening conditions.

**Barbour, Ian G**. *Religion and Science: Historical and Contemporary Issues*. San Francisco, Harper San Fran, 1997.

*Religion and Science: Historical and Contemporary Issues* is a contemporary discussion of the many issues surrounding our understanding of God, religious truth and experience in our scientific age. This is a significantly expanded and freshly revised version of *Religion in an Age of Science*. (publisher, edited)

**Barcellona, Pietro**. I percorsi del soggetto moderno. *Iride*, 9(18), 377-393, Ag 96.

Di fronte al sistema, nell'accezione luhmaniana, con la sua configurazione di significati che sembra cancellare anche la terminologia delle tradizionali teorie giuridiche e politiche centrate sulla nozione di potere legittimo, di proprietà, di soggetto (protagonista), i soggetti empirici si trovano immersi in una contingenza fluttuante (ri-presentata dalle filosofie postmoderne) che deve essere analizzata criticamente per ritrovare in essa, in questo esito della modernità, delle ragioni concrete per la rivitalizzazione del legame sociale.

**Barendregt, Henk**. The Impact of the Lambda Calculus in Logic and Computer Science. *Bull Sym Log*, 3(2), 181-215, Je 97.

One of the most important contributions of A. Church to logic is his invention of the lambda calculus. We present the genesis of this theory and its two major areas of application: the representation of computations and the resulting functional programming languages on the one hand and the representation of reasoning and the resulting systems of computer mathematics on the other hand.

**Barker, Andrew**. "Plato's *Philebus*: The Numbering of a Unity" in *Dialogues with Plato*, Benitez, Eugenio (ed), 143-164. Edmonton, Academic, 1996.

**Barker, Evelyn M**. "Socratic Intolerance and Aristotelian Toleration" in *Philosophy, Religion, and the Question of Intolerance*, Ambuel, David (ed), 246-255. Albany, SUNY Pr, 1997.

I challenge I.F. Stone's contention that the Athenian democratic state's execution of Socrates was an aberration provoked by Socrates' own philosophical intolerance, because he could have evaded conviction by appealing to an Athenian democratic "principle of free speech." From Aristotle's conception of "unanimity" in "political friendship," I then develop a justification for toleration consonant with ancient philosophic intolerance and applicable to our own democratic community.

**Barker, Peter** and Andersen, Hanne and Chen, Xiang. Kuhn's Mature Philosophy of Science and Cognitive Psychology. *Phil Psych*, 9(3), 347-363, S 96.

Drawing on the results of modern psychology and cognitive science we suggest that the traditional theory of concepts is no longer tenable and that the alternative account proposed by Kuhn may now be seen to have independent empirical support quite apart from its success as part of an account of scientific change. We suggest that these mechanisms can also be understood as special cases of general cognitive structures revealed by cognitive science. Against this background, incommensurability is not an insurmountable obstacle to accepting Kuhn's position, as many philosophers of science still believe. Rather it becomes a natural consequence of cognitive structures that appear in all human beings.

**Barker, Stephen**. Material Implication and General Indicative Conditionals. *Phil Quart*, 47(187), 195-211, Ap 97.

I present arguments for a pure material implication analysis of singular indicative conditionals. 1) I argue, assuming the correctness of current accounts of generality in English, that consideration of the logical and pragmatic properties of general indicative conditionals, sentences like "*If a boy owns a donkey, he beats it*" or "*Any girl, if she gets a chance, bungee jumps*", shows that singular indicative conditionals must be treated as pure material implications. 2) I argue that the objections raised by writers such as Jackson and Edgington against a pure material implication analysis can be dealt with by a sophisticated theory of pragmatics.

**Barker, Stephen F**. "Carnap's Principle of Tolerance" in *Philosophy, Religion, and the Question of Intolerance*, Ambuel, David (ed), 256-268. Albany, SUNY Pr, 1997.

**Barker, Stephen J**. E-Type Pronouns, DRT, Dynamic Semantics and the Quantifier/Variable-Binding Model. *Ling Phil*, 20(2), 195-228, Ap 97.

I argue that three approaches to donkey pronouns—E-type theories, Discourse Representation Theory (DRT) and Dynamic semantics—all fail to account for a range of intra—and inter-sentential anaphoric relations possible in English. I argue, furthermore, that all fail to do so in ways which are ultimately traceable to a common and fundamental assumption, viz., that pronouns and generality in English are, at base, to be analysed in terms of a semantic apparatus of quantifiers and binding relations on variables. It is speculated that other approaches adopting a quantifier/variable-binding model of anaphora and generality are likely to encounter the same problems.

**Barker, Stephen J**. Parsing If-Sentences and the Conditions of Sentencehood. *Analysis*, 56(4), 210-218, O 96.

V.H. Dudman has argued for an account of *if*-sentence grammar radically at variance with tradition. Dudman's critics have addressed his taxonomical thesis, which is the corollary of his grammatical analysis, urging that it is disconfirmed by certain semantic and syntactic observations. But they have not addressed Dudman's arguments for the grammatical analysis itself. I show that the latter are flawed; they assume an unmaintainable thesis regarding the conditions under which a grammatical constituent expresses a thought. I argue pace Dudman that a mood analysis is needed to explain *if*-sentence grammar and then reconsider the issue of taxonomy.

**Barnard, G William**. *Exploring Unseen Worlds: William James and the Philosophy of Mysticism*. Albany, SUNY Pr, 1997.

*Exploring Unseen Worlds* is a critically sophisticated, yet gripping immersion into the inner worlds of one of America's foremost thinkers. It demonstrates convincingly the extent to which James's psychological and philosophical perspectives continue to be a rich resource for those specifically interested in the study of mysticism. The book focuses on James's enduring fascination with mysticism and not only unearths James's lesser-known works on mysticism, but also probes into the tacit mystical dimensions of James's personal life and uncovers the mystical implications of his decades-long interest in psychical research. (publisher)

**Barnden, John A** and Srinivas, Kankanahalli. Quantification without Variables in Connectionism. *Mind Mach*, 6(2), 173-201, My 96.

Connectionist attention to variables has been too restricted in two ways. First, it has not exploited certain ways of doing without variables in the *symbolic* arena.

One variable-avoidance method, that of logical combinators, is particularly well established there. Secondly, the attention has been largely restricted to variables in long-term rules embodied in connection weight patterns. However, *short-lived* bodies of information, such as sentence interpretations or inference products, may involve quantification. Therefore, short-lived activation patterns may need to achieve the effect of variables. The paper is mainly a theoretical analysis of some benefits and drawbacks of using logical combinators to avoid variables in short-lived connectionist encodings without loss of expressive power. The paper also includes a brief survey of some possible methods for avoiding variables other than by using combinators.

**Barnes, Eric**. Discussion: Thoughts on Maher's Predictivism. *Phil Sci*, 63(3), 401-410, S 96.

Predictivism asserts that where evidence E confirms theory T, E provides stronger support for T when E is predicted on the basis of T and then confirmed than when E is known before T's construction and 'used', in some sense, in the construction of T. Among the most interesting attempts to argue that predictivism is a true thesis (under certain conditions) is that of Patrick Maher (1988, 1990, 1993). The purpose of this paper is to investigate the nature of predictivism using Maher's analysis as a starting point. I briefly summarize Maher's primary argument and expand upon it; I explore related issues pertaining to the causal structure of empirical domains and the logic of discovery.

**Barnes, Eric**. Social Predictivism. *Erkenntnis*, 45(1), 69-89, Jl 96.

Predictivism holds that, where evidence E confirms theory T, E confirms T more strongly when E is predicted on the basis of T and subsequently confirmed than when E is known in advance of T's formulation and 'used', in some sense, in the formulation of T. Predictivism has lately enjoyed some strong supporting arguments from Maher (1988, 1990, 1993) and Kahn, Landsberg, and Stockman (1992). The existence of a scientist who predicted T prior to the establishment that E is true has epistemic import for T only in connection with information regarding the social milieu in which the T-predictor is located and information regarding how the T-predictor was located. The aim of this paper is to show that predictivism is ultimately a social phenomenon that requires a social level of analysis, a thesis I deem 'social predictivism'. (edited)

**Barnes, Mahlon W**. Rights and Citizenship: The Instrumentality of the Community. *Cont Phil*, 18(2-3), 23-27, Mr-Ap/My-Je 96.

This paper discusses the use of concepts of nature in the current controversy between liberals and communitarians. Liberals make extensive use of "natural rights," while communitarians depend on "human nature" and natural tendencies (Aristotelian *teloi*). I argue that neither side can make good on its claims that our relation to one another is regulated by something natural, since neither can reasonably support its use of the natural. I further argue that if these claims are abandoned and our communities are recognized to be instruments, we can preserve the positive aspects of both positions and eliminate the conflict. Natural rights become conditions of the operation of the community; while human nature is replaced with observations about actual human conduct, such as our need for organized communities.

**Barnes, R Eric**. Rationality, Dispositions, and the Newcomb Paradox. *Phil Stud*, 88(1), 1-28, O 97.

In this essay I have argued that generation sentences constitute a class of sentences that are true even though they contain irreferential denoting expressions. Therefore, it seems implausible to suppose that a theory of truth of English sentences can be constructed incorporating the Russellian dictum that atomic sentences with irreferential denoting expressions must be false. I have argued that the Wittgensteinian cluster theories fare no better in interpreting these sentences and Kripke's causal-historical theory of reference also fails. Exploring the generation sentences' truth-conditions also casts serious doubt on Kripke's account of reference across possible worlds. Making sense of generation sentences seems to require a counterpart theory of transworld reference. In this important class of sentences, meaningful discourse cannot be restricted to what is, rather, *pace* Parmenides, we must make sense of talk about what is not.

**Barnett, Tim** and Bass, Ken and Brown, Gene. Religiosity, Ethical Ideology, and Intentions to Report a Peer's Wrongdoing. *J Bus Ethics*, 15(11), 1161-1174, N 96.

Peer reporting is a specific form of whistleblowing in which an individual discloses the wrongdoing of a peer. Previous studies have examined situational variables thought to influence a person's decision to report the wrongdoing of a peer. The present study looked at peer reporting from the individual level. Five hypotheses were developed concerning the relationships between 1) religiosity and ethical ideology, 2) ethical ideology and ethical judgments about peer reporting, and 3) ethical judgments and intentions to report peer wrongdoing. Subjects read a vignette concerning academic cheating, and were asked to respond to a questionnaire concerning the vignette. Data were analyzed using structural equation methodology. Results indicated that religiosity was positively associated with an ethical ideology of nonrelativism. Individuals whose ethical ideologies could be described as idealistic and nonrelativistic were more likely to state that reporting a peer's cheating was ethical. In turn, individuals who believed reporting a peer's cheating was ethical were more likely to say that they would report a peer's cheating.

**Barney, Rachel**. Plato on Conventionalism. *Phronesis*, 42(2), 143-162, 1997.

Hermogenes' 'conventionalist' account of the correctness of names of Plato's *Cratylus* is often seen as incoherent or subjectivist. The paper argues that in fact it represents a commonsensical defense of the 'conservative' thesis that all actual or positive names are correct. For Plato, this uncritical acceptance of the given must be rejected before a serious inquiry into the norms governing

AUTHOR INDEX 509 Barsa, Pavel

naming can get underway. Two implications are noted. First, the *Cratylus* turns out to be closely related to Plato's other critical investigations of social and political institutions. Second, the ambiguous conclusion of the *Cratylus* cannot be meant to rehabilitate conventionalism.

**Barney, Stephen** (trans) and Lewis, Wendy (trans) and Normore, Calvin G (& other trans). On the Properties of Discourse: A Translation of *Tractatus de Proprietatibus Sermonium* (Author Anonymous). *Topoi*, 16(1), 77-93, Mr 97.

This is a translation of part of an anonymous early thirteenth tract on medieval semantics. The author discusses signification, supposition and appellation, including the division of supposition into determinate, distributive and merely confused. Causes of confusion are covered; sophisms are solved by applying the theory. Also covered: ampliation of terms by tenses and modalities.

**Barnhart, Michael G**. Ideas of Nature in an Asian Context. *Phil East West*, 47(3), 417-432, Jl 97.

In his article "Can the East Help the West to Value Nature?" Holmes Rolston, III, wrote that Eastern religious insights would need considerable reformulation in order for us to answer affirmatively the question posed in his title. The present article, while arguing that such an assessment is unduly harsh, goes on to evaluate critically the various Asian ideas of nature, arguing that their ethical consequences are no worse that those of the postmodern concept of nature endorsed by Rolston, Callicott and others.

**Barnhart, Michael G**. Is Naturalized Epistemology Experientially Vacuous?. *Phil Cont World*, 3(2), 1-5, Sum 96.

By naturalized epistemology, I mean those views expressed by Nozick and Margolis among others who favor an evolutionary account of human rationality as an adaptive mechanism which is unlikely to provide the means for its own legitimation and, therefore, unlikely to produce a single set of rules of norms which are certifiably rational. Analyzing the likely relativism that stems from such a view, namely that there could be divergent standards of rationality under different historical or environmental conditions, I conclude that evolutionary epistemologies are unable to account for rationality as an experienced capacity on the part of human beings. After giving a few examples of what seem to me to be cases where we do experience a form of reason that appears antinomian, I challenge a naturalized view of mind to embrace and provide some sort of explanatory account of this kind of mental elasticity that it both seems to make room for and is certainly not unfamiliar to other philosophical perspectives such as that of Zen Buddhism.

**Baron, Jonathan**. Norm-Endorsement Utilitarianism and the Nature of Utility. *Econ Phil*, 12(1), 165-182, Ap 96.

I suggest an approach to the justification of normative moral principles, leading to utilitarianism. It asks what moral norms we would endorse if we had no prior moral commitments. We would endorse norms that lead to the satisfaction of all our nonmoral goals. This approach implies a view of utility as consisting of those goals that we would want satisfied. This view has implications for several issues about the nature of utility: erroneous subgoals; the distinction between goals and preferences; future and past goals; goals for unknown outcomes; the rationality of new goals; and the goals of future people.

**Barragan, Julia**. Entrevista al Prof. J. Harsanyi. *Telos (Spain)*, 5(1), 115-121, Je 96.

**Barrera Vélez, Julio César**. Descripción del fenómeno religioso en la postmodernidad. *Franciscanum*, 37(112), 47-56, Ja-Ap 96.

**Barreto, Luz Marina**. Morality as Private Property: A Critique of David Gauthier (Spanish). *Rev Filosof (Venezuela)*, Supp(2-3), 155-171, 1996.

This essay is a criticism of David Gauthier's book *Morals by Agreement*. In the first part it examines the idea through which perfectly competitive markets bring about just exchanges between negotiators and thus a perfectly equitable and moral transaction. In the second part it analyzes David Gauthier's basis for morality as far as it aspires to pursue and establish in a reflexive and rational manner the moral conditions for a just exchange between cooperative agents.

**Barrett, Cyril**. "Believing in Order to Understand" in *Verstehen and Humane Understanding*, O'Hear, Anthony (ed), 223-233. New York, Cambridge Univ Pr, 1996.

**Barrett, Jeffrey A**. On Everett's Formulation of Quantum Mechanics. *Monist*, 80(1), 70-96, Ja 97.

Everett wanted a formulation of quantum mechanics that i) took the linear dynamics to be a complete and accurate description of the time-evolution of all physical systems and ii) logically entailed the same subjective appearances predicted by the standard formulation of quantum mechanics. In this paper, I consider two very different readings of Everett: the bare reading and the splitting-worlds reading. What distinguishes these is their interpretation of the wave function and how one accounts for the experiences of observers. The difficulty in interpreting Everett, however, is illustrated by the fact that neither reading is entirely compatible with his own description of his project. (edited)

**Barrett, Jeffrey A**. Oracles, Aesthetics, and Bayesian Consensus. *Proc Phil Sci Ass*, 3(Suppl), S273-S280, 1996.

In order for Bayesian inquiry to count as objective one might argue that it must lead to a consensus of opinion among those who use it and share evidence, but presumably this is not enough. It has been proposed (by John Earman) that one should also require that the consensus be reached from very different initial opinions by conditioning only on basis experimental evidence, evidence free from subjective, social, or psychological influence. I argue here, however, that this notion of objectivity in Bayesian inquiry is too narrow: scientists in fact condition on the opinions or other scientists and aesthetic criteria, this is often what explains the rapid development of consensus and there is at least in principle nothing irrational in this practice.

**Barrio, Eduardo Alejandro**. Que és la Verdad?. *Cad Hist Filosof Cie*, 6(Spec), 13-37, Ja-D 96.

In this article, I argue that the question on the relationship between language and the world is a genuine philosophical question. Nevertheless, such a question has no answer for me: after a detailed discussion on the conditions of an answer to this question, I observe that there is nothing to answer to. It is not possible to give an explanation of the relationship between language and the world because there is nothing to explain. Accordingly, I sustain the idea that truth is a linguistical device: to say that a sentence is true is the same as to say the sentence. This is all that is supposed by the Tarskian definition of truth. I discuss two objections to my position: I) the idea that the Tarskian definition of truth reconstructs the correspondentialist conception of truth and II) the idea that viewing truth as no more than a linguistical device lacks philosophical importance.

**Barrio, Eduardo Alejandro**. Trascendentalismo, contenido semántico y verdad. *Analisis Filosof*, 16(1), 43-66, My 96.

In his article "The Status of Content", Boghossian defends what has been called "transcendentalism about content". According to him, the thesis that there is nothing in the world that corresponds to our thoughts "is not merely implausible but incoherent". In other words, he thinks that the thesis in question is not simply false on empirical basis but rather self-refuting or pragmatically incoherent. My purpose in this article is to show that Boghossian's argument for his point of view is not valid. My main thesis is that there is no contradiction in applying the notion of truth to both semantical and psychological sentences and, at the same time, holding that there are neither semantic nor mental contents.

**Barris, Jeremy**. The Foundation in Truth of Rhetoric and Formal Logic. *Phil Rhet*, 29(4), 314-328, 1996.

Arguments in the rhetorical literature against the sufficiency of formal logic show the need for a foundation of both the rhetorically oriented disciples and formal logic in truth. As the rhetorical disciplines have argued, formal logic cannot offer this foundation. But the rhetorical disciplines also cannot provide it: they are structurally too much like formal logic to achieve their distinctive aims. The combined rhetorical and logical nature of this foundation, as conceptual truth, is sketched. Implications are drawn for the foundational importance of ornamental rhetoric, and for the study and teaching of rhetoric as aimed, precisely, not as persuasion.

**Barro, Senén** and Bugarin, Alberto J. Which Are Some of the Applications of Fuzzy Logic? (in Spanish). *Theoria (Spain)*, 11(27), 149-161, S 96.

This paper discusses about the field of fuzzy logic applications, but not from the point of view of its importance or commenting their main features and how they are formally supported by fuzzy logic. Very good and abundant checking of this style (Zadeh, Yager 1992) exist in the field, and so we decided to present some reflections trying to answer very general questions about this issue. Answering, for example, to the question about possible future applications of fuzzy logic is, no doubts, a very risky task. We look forward to be forgiven if our approach proves not to be very successful.

**Barrotta, Pierluigi**. A Neo-Kantian Critique of Von Mises's Epistemology. *Econ Phil*, 12(1), 51-66, Ap 96.

Contrary to Mises's epistemology, in this paper it is shown that a) the category of action does not provide the starting point of an entirely deductive economic science, but the subject-matter or experience to which economic theories (a posteriori introduced and thus in need of empirical justification) refer and b) Mises's deductive procedure of testing does not clearly distinguish proper deduction from meaning analysis. As it is argued, this critique can be labeled as neo-Kantian and, therefore, is very different from the traditional neopositivistic arguments against Mises's epistemology.

**Barrow, John D**. "Time in the Universe" in *The Idea of Progress*, McLaughlin, Peter (ed), 155-174. Hawthorne, de Gruyter, 1997.

The nature of time is discussed in Newtonian, relativistic, and quantum physics. Special attention is given to the 'block of space-time' picture employed by modern cosmologists and the "problem of time" in quantum cosmology. A simple explanation is given of the place of time in certain conceptions of quantum cosmology and of the Euclidean space-time "no boundary" condition of Hartle and Hawking. The implications of these ideas for the issue of whether the universe had a temporal origin are examined.

**Barrow, Robin**. Language: Definition and Metaphor. *Stud Phil Educ*, 16(1-2), 113-124, Ja-Ap 97.

This paper argues that there is an urgent need for philosophers to convince educationalists of the practical value and the necessity of the philosophical task, particularly analysis. The nature of philosophical analysis is outlined in terms of the criteria of clarity, coherence, completeness and compatibility, which, it is argued, in turn lead to a degree of commonality. The tendency to substitute metaphor or analogy for analysis in argument is then considered, with illustrative reference to the idea of teaching as a craft. In the final section, it is suggested that resort to analogy is merely one example of a more general tendency to distance ourselves from the task of coming to grips with what is actually our field of interest, namely education.

**Barry, Brian**. Contractual Justice: A Modest Defence. *Utilitas*, 8(3), 357-380, N 96.

**Barsa, Pavel**. The Libertarianism of Robert Nozick (in Czech). *Filosof Cas*, 44(6), 990-1002, 1996.

The article presents an outline of basic ideas of Nozick's *Anarchy, State, and Utopia*. Its purpose is to provide an introduction to an extract from this book published in the same issue of the Czech *Journal of Philosophy*. *First*, Nozick's individualistic libertarianism of natural rights is distinguished both from

European anarchistic tradition and from other forms of libertarianism. *Second*, the crucial notion of 'moral constraints' is explained and put in the context of a broader tradition of deontologic morality. *Then*, Nozick's 'entitlement theory' of justice together with his critique of Rawls's conception are exposed. *Finally*, the attention is drawn to the contradiction between Nozick's endorsement of deontologic reasoning and his claim that the *state* constructed according to his premises would be 'a framework for utopia'.

**Bartelborth, Thomas**. Kann es rational sein, eine inkonsistente Theorie zu akzeptieren?. *Phil Natur*, 26(1), 91-120, 1989.

Imre Lakatos argued that it is sometimes rational to endorse theories even though one knows them to be inconsistent. His chief witness for this claim was the initially successful development of Bohr's model of the atom. Though in conflict with electrodynamics, the model employed some of the laws of electrostatics. Notwithstanding the discrepancy of the model some laws from are used in the model. The paper presents a logical reconstruction of Bohr's theory (in the structuralist framework) that shows how Bohr managed to avoid an *inner inconsistency* in his theory. Thus, Lakatos looses his major witness for rational inconsistency.

**Bartels, Andreas**. Modern Essentialism and the Problem of Individuation of Spacetime Points. *Erkenntnis*, 45(1), 25-43, Jl 96.

In this paper "Modern Essentialism" is used to solve a problem of individuation of spacetime points in 'general relativity' that has been raised by a *New Leibnizian Argument* against spacetime substantivatism, elaborated by Earman and Norton. An earlier essentialistic solution, proposed by Maudlin, is criticized as being against both the spirit of metrical essentialism and the fundamental principles of "general relativity". I argue for a modified essentialistic account of spacetime points that avoids those obstacles.

**Bartelson, Jens**. Making Exceptions: Some Remarks on the Concept of Coup d'état and Its History. *Polit Theory*, 25(3), 323-346, Je 97.

Commonly regarded as philosophically innocent, the concept of *coup d'état* invariably presupposes some interpretation of the relationship between the regular and the exceptional within political theory and practice. This article analyzes this relationship historically, arguing that the changing historical interpretations of this concept indicate major shifts in the dominant understandings of political authority and legitimacy from the Renaissance onwards. The article concludes by spelling out the implications for our modern democratic political practice in terms of how it handles the relationship between the regular and the exceptional.

**Bartholome, William G**. Clinical Ethics and Ethics Committees. *Bioethics Forum*, 10(4), 5-11, Fall 94.

Traditionally the field of bioethics has been a paternalistic one, dominated by physicians who made all decisions about patients in clinical settings. The advent of the patients' rights movement, the focus on informed consent and the emergence of a radically different ethic for nonphysician health care providers have all contributed to the collapse of this system. It is being replaced by a rapidly evolving system of shared decision making, embodied in health care ethics committees that educate, help develop policy and help resolve ethical problems arising in the care of patients.

**Bartholome, William G**. Hearing Children's Voices. *Bioethics Forum*, 11(4), 3-6, Wint 95.

The *Guidelines* document published in this issue of *Bioethics Forum* is both unique in its approach and ahead of its time. It moves all parties involved in the direction of viewing children as persons whose wishes in matters of health care should be heard and taken seriously.

**Bartholome, William G**. Still Here/Above Ground. *Bioethics Forum*, 13(1), 31-37, Spr 97.

**Bartol, Wiktor**. H Rasiowa's and C Rauszer's Contribution to Algebra. *Bull Sec Log*, 25(3/4), 166-173, O-D 96.

Even if for H. Rasiowa and C. Rauszer the main area of research was mathematical logic, they have left a considerable algebraic output. The paper reviews the most significant contributions. The first part is an overview of algebraic structures associated in Rasiowa's works with various logics. They range from the simplest implicative algebras to topological Boolean algebras with lattices with different complement operations in between. The hierarchy of these structures is made clear and some relations between them are made explicit. In the second part the semi-Post algebras of Rasiowa and Cat-Ho and the semi-Boolean algebras of Rauszer are presented and briefly discussed.

**Bartol, Wiktor** and Rauszer, Cecylia. Helena Rasiowa and Cecylia Rauszer: Two Generations in Logic. *Bull Sec Log*, 25(3/4), 120-125, O-D 96.

**Bartsch, Renate**. The Relationship Between Connectionist Models and a Dynamic Data-Oriented Theory of Concept Formation. *Synthese*, 108(3), 421-454, S 96.

In this paper I shall compare two models of concept formation, both inspired by basic convictions of philosophical empiricism. The first, the connectionist model, will be exemplified by Kohonen maps and the second will be my own dynamic theory of concept formation. Both can be understood in probabilistic terms, both use a notion of convergence or stabilization in modelling how concepts are built up. Both admit destabilization of concepts and conceptual change. Both do not use a notion of representation in some pregiven language, such as a language of thought or some logical language. Representation in a formal language only plays a role on the metalevel, namely within the theory about concept formation.

**Bartzeliotis, L**. The Inadequacy of Hume's Psychological Impressions. *Phil Inq*, 18(3-4), 83-90, Sum-Fall 96.

The inadequacy of Hume's psychologically associated perceptual atoms are seen in his "half-hearted" or "mitigated" skepticism he was led in his effort to

arrive: I) at the relations of ideas, and II) at the status of matter of fact. A simple comparison of his effort with the corresponding efforts of the Skeptic School and of the philosophy of organism shows that it falls short of both of them by being contradictory and circular.

**Barua, Archna**. A Note on—Euthanasia and the Contemporary Debate. *Indian Phil Quart*, 23(3-4), 467-472, Jl-O 96.

The supporters of euthanasia remained loyal to the sanctity of life principle, at the same time defending 'mercy killing' in an abnormal life situation. Similar approach was made by some heterodox and orthodox traditions of India. The Jains reconciled ahimsa principle with religious self willed death, it was an attempt to harness violent death with conscious and sane attitude to it. The Brahmins took help of multiple ethics to accommodate heroic self-willed death and gave it religious sanction. Buddhism's pragmatic approach to the problems of life kept room for exceptional life situations which could be approached differently. The contemporary Indian scholars would prefer to be guided by experts in the medical profession to redefine the boundaries between genuine euthanasia and other types of self-willed deaths, including religious one.

**Baruah, Girish Chandra**. Man and Nature: A Marxist Approach. *Darshana Int*, 36(4/144), 34-41, O 96.

Man is very intimately related to nature, because he has not been created by God, but evolved from nature. Man is not foreign to nature, but an element within it. Man is a creative being; and by dint of his intellectual power he has been able to dominate nature. He lives on nature and harnesses it for his well being. But in doing so he should be responsible, so that natural objects may be sensibly exploited. Man should regard nature as his mother and treat her with love and care. If he behaves recklessly in dealing with nature he will have to pay the price and face extinction in the long run.

**Baruzzi, Arno**. Politics: Truth, Freedom, Peace: Lie, Rule, War (in Serbo-Croatian). *Filozof Istraz*, 15(4), 813-822, 1995.

Von der Jasperschen Auffassung ausgehend, dass Frieden nur durch Freiheit und Freiheit nur durch Wahrheit möglich ist, überprüft der Autor kritisch die Möglichkeiten und Bedingungen der Gültigkeit dieser zentralen Begriffe, indem er ihnen das Oppositionsgefüge der Begriffe: Lüge, Herrschaft, Krieg entgegenstellt. Dabei erklärt der Autor die Mehrdeutigkeit der Hauptbegriffe Freiheit und Wahrheit in verschiedenen soziopolitischen Realitäten und philosophisch-politischen Auffassungen. Er geht deswegen zur Analyse und Interpretation einiger Grundbegriffe der Platonischen philosophisch-politischen Lehre über: Begriff der *Polis* (als einer Lebensordnung und Lebensform), der Philosophie (die durch ihre Beziehung zur Wahrheit als Voraussetzung für ein gutes und freies Leben gilt), der Wahrheit (als des wahren Wissens, der wahren Tugend und der wahren Erziehung in der *Polis*) sowie der *Psyche* (welcher Begriff als politeia en auto interpretiert wird). (edited)

**Barwick, Daniel**. Overpopulation and Prediction: Ethics, Humans, and Nature. *Cont Phil*, 18(2-3), 2-9, Mr-Ap/My-Je 96.

In this paper, I will address first the circumstances that have led to the predictions of overcrowding and associated problems and then respond to Jan Narveson's article "Is There Really a Risk of Overpopulation?", which I believe is fairly representative of the current literature that opposes measures to reduce population growth. I will argue against Narveson, by claiming that 1) his claim that resources are for all intents and purposes infinite stems from an inadequate understanding of our ability to use resources; 2) his confidence in technology cannot be justified, because we cannot draw adequate parallels between the population expansions we face now and those we have faced in the past; and 3) his view that the world can support many more people, while true to some extent, rests on a questionable ethical foundation and does not follow for the general health of the earth's ecosystem, ultimately harming humans.

**Basave Fernández, Augustin**. "Die spezifisch mexikanisch-lateinamerikanische Struktur des Geistes und ihr möglicher Beitrag zu weltweiter Freiheit" in *Kreativer Friede durch Begegnung der Weltkulturen*, Beck, Heinrich (ed), 317-334. New York, Lang, 1995.

**Basinger, David**. Pluralism and Justified Religious Belief: A Response to Gellman. *Faith Phil*, 13(2), 260-265, Ap 96.

I have argued previously (in this journal) that the reality of pervasive religious pluralism obligates a believer to attempt to establish her perspective as the correct one. In a recent response, Jerome Gellman maintains that the believer who affirms a 'religious epistemology' is under no such obligation in that she need not subject her religious beliefs to any 'rule of rationality'. In this paper I contend that there do exist some rules of rationality (some epistemic obligations) that must be acknowledged—and satisfied—with all epistemic systems (including all religious epistemic systems) and that for this reason Gellman's critique of my position fails.

**Basinger, David**. *The Case for Freewill Theism: A Philosophical Assessment*. Downers Grove, InterVarsity Pr, 1996.

Taking up such practical but profound questions, a co-author of the much-discussed *The Openness of God* here offers a probing philosophical examination of freewill theism. This controversial view argues that the God of Christianity desires "responsive relationship" with his creatures. It rejects process theology, but calls for a reassessment of such classical doctrines as God's immutability, impassibility and foreknowledge. David Basinger here especially considers divine omniscience, theodicy and petitionary prayer in freewill perspective. His careful and precise argument contributes to a growing and important discussion within orthodox Christian circles. (publisher)

**Bass, Ken** and Barnett, Tim and Brown, Gene. Religiosity, Ethical Ideology, and Intentions to Report a Peer's Wrongdoing. *J Bus Ethics*, 15(11), 1161-1174, N 96.

Peer reporting is a specific form of whistleblowing in which an individual discloses the wrongdoing of a peer. Previous studies have examined situational variables thought to influence a person's decision to report the wrongdoing of a peer. The present study looked at peer reporting from the individual level. Five hypotheses were developed concerning the relationships between 1) religiosity and ethical ideology, 2) ethical ideology and ethical judgments about peer reporting, and 3) ethical judgments and intentions to report peer wrongdoing. Subjects read a vignette concerning academic cheating, and were asked to respond to a questionnaire concerning the vignette. Data were analyzed using structural equation methodology. Results indicated that religiosity was positively associated with an ethical ideology of nonrelativism. Individuals whose ethical ideologies could be described as idealistic and nonrelativistic were more likely to state that reporting a peer's cheating was ethical. In turn, individuals who believed reporting a peer's cheating was ethical were more likely to say that they would report a peer's cheating.

**Basu, Ananyo**. "Reducing Concern with Self: Parfit and the Ancient Buddhist Schools" in *Culture and Self*, Allen, Douglas (ed), 97-109. Boulder, Westview Pr, 1997.

This article compares Derek Parfit's reductionist view of self with various Buddhist perspectives on self. It begins by examining Parfit's views on self and personal identity and evaluates his responses to his critics. David Bastow's attempt to expand Parfitian reduction along Buddhist lines is shown to be wanting in some regards. A survey of Buddhist schools reveals that there is no perfect fit between Parfit's view of self and Buddhist views on it. In conclusion, reliance on the Madhyamika school is advocated to provide a reliable reductionist, anti-essentialist approach to self. This school provides the best guide for future work.

**Basu, Prajit K**. Theory-Ladenness of Observation and Evidence. *J Indian Counc Phil Res*, 13(3), 87-102, My-Ag 96.

This paper attempts to show that the epistemic situation involving rational theory resolution requires introducing a notion of evidence or evidential bearing of observation. The strength of the voluntary reversal of perception of argument and of its subsequent support to the penetrability of the visual system argument are dependent upon this notion of evidence, or evidential bearing of observation. These arguments, it is argued, do establish theory-ladenness of observation. Hence, the thesis that rational theory resolution is possible by appealing to a pool of observation which is trivially theory-laden, but theory-neutral for competing theories is undermined.

**Basu, Prasun** and Boik, Robert J and Bandyopadhyay, Prasanta S. The Curve Fitting Problem: A Bayesian Approach. *Proc Phil Sci Ass*, 3(Suppl), S264-S272, 1996.

**Batens, Diderik**. "Functioning and Teachings of Adaptive Logics" in *Logic and Argumentation*, Van Eemeren, Frans H (ed), 241-254. Amsterdam, North-Holland, 1994.

This paper concerns some formal systems, viz. adaptive logics, that display a specific flexibility in the meanings of logical terms. Both the flexibility that occurs within the systems and the question as to how we may arrive at such systems is discussed. Both, it is argued, are relevant to bridging the gap between logic and argumentation.

**Batens, Diderik**. Inconsistencies and Beyond: A Logical-Philosophical Discussion. *Rev Int Phil*, 51(200), 259-273, Je 97.

The paper starts off by epistemological arguments for the need of paraconsistent logics. Next it is argued that some contexts require that allow other abnormalities, next to or instead of inconsistencies. The feasibility of such moves is defended in terms of a contextual epistemology. Finally, adaptive logics are defended as means to interpret theories 'as normally as possible', even if they contain some abnormalities.

**Batstone, David** and Mendieta, Eduardo and Lorentzen, Lois Ann (& others). *Liberation Theologies, Postmodernity, and the Americas*. New York, Routledge, 1997.

Over the last thirty years, liberation theology has irrevocably altered religious thinking and practice throughout the Americas. Liberation theology rises up at the margins of social power. Drawing its energies from the black community in the United States, grassroots religious communities in Latin America and feminist circles in North Atlantic countries, theologies of liberation have emerged as a resource and inspiration for people seeking social and political freedom. (publisher, edited)

**Batten, Jonathan** and Hettihewa, Samanthala and Mellor, Robert. The Ethical Management Practices of Australian Firms. *J Bus Ethics*, 16(12-13), 1261-1271, S 97.

This paper addresses a number of important issues regarding the ethical practices and recent behaviour of large Australian firms in nine industries. These issues include whether firms have a written code of ethics, whether firms have a forum for the discussion of ethics, whether managers consider that their firm's activities have an environmental impact and whether there are any statistical relationships between the size, industry class, ownership, international involvement and location of the firm and its ethical management practices. These questions are examined by using data collected from a sample of 136 large firms operating in Australia.

**Battigalli, Pierpaolo** and Bonanno, Giacomo. The Logic of Belief Persistence. *Econ Phil*, 13(1), 39-59, Ap 97.

The interaction between knowledge and belief in a temporal context is analyzed. An axiomatic formulation and semantic characterization of the principle of belief persistence corresponding to the standard conditionalization rule are provided. The principle states that an individual who receives new information consistent with her previous belief set, accommodates this information in the new belief set maintaining her previous beliefs and adding only those beliefs that can be deduced from the previous belief set and the new information. Given standard assumptions about knowledge and belief, it is shown that the principle of persistence of beliefs is characterized by the following axiom schema: the individual believes $o$ at date $t$ if and only if she believes at date $t$ that she will believe $o$ at date $t+1$.

**Battistini, Andrea**. Un poeta "doctísimo de las antigüedades heroicas" El rol de Virgilio en el pensamiento de G.B. Vico. *Cuad Vico*, 5/6, 11-25, 1995/96.

Darkened by Homer, Virgil received no attention at all by Vichian scholars. On the contrary, his *Aeneid* is important for Vico because it showed for him that poetry can exist also in the age of reason, where Virgil lived. So in the *New Science* his epic is said to be both living "in the most civilized times," and having "profound knowledge of heroic antiquities." Before dealing with the *New Science*, this essay analyses what Vico thought of Virgil in his different works: in his poems, in his lessons on rhetoric, *Inaugural Orations*, *De antiquissima*, *Universal Law*, autobiography.

**Bauchspies, Wenda K** and Restivo, Sal. Science, Social Theory, and Science Criticism. *Commun Cog*, 29(2), 249-272, 1996.

The popularization and public understanding of science must necessarily now deal with cultural and social studies of science and not simply 'science' in its traditional sense (that is, as a label for the methods, findings, and authority of the physical and natural sciences). At the same time, theories and criticisms of science must be alert to the implications of postmodernist and multicultural dimensions of science in/and society. This paper, then, is a contribution to the dialogue between science studies and science that we believe should inform discourse on the popularization and public understanding of science. (edited)

**Baugh, S Gayle**. On the Persistence of Sexual Harassment in the Workplace. *J Bus Ethics*, 16(9), 899-908, Je 97.

The persistence of sexual harassment in the workplace, despite the general abhorrence for the behavior and programs designed to eradicate it, is puzzling. This paper proposes that gender differences in perceptions of sexual harassment and power differentials in the workplace which permit men to legitimize and institutionalize their perspective are implicated. These two phenomena combine to result in blaming the victim of sexual harassment for her own plight. Shifting attention to the target of sexual harassment facilitates the persistence of sexual harassment because the institutionalized responses to the problem remain unquestioned.

**Baum, Wilhelm**. Der Klagenfurter Herbert-Kreis zwischen Aufklärung und Romantik. *Rev Int Phil*, 50(197), 483-514, 1996.

**Bauman, Zygmunt**. "The Present Crisis of the Universities" in *The Idea of University*, Brzezinski, Jerzy (ed), 47-54. Amsterdam, Rodopi, 1997.

**Bauman, Zygmunt**. Glokalisierung oder Was für die einen Globalisierung, ist für die anderen Lokalisierung. *Das Argument*, 217(5-6), 653-664, 1996.

Today, after an era in which the struggle between the two power blocs determined the meaning of every event, impoverishment (localization) and increasing wealth (globalization) are two sides of the same coin. Although no one wants to control the world anymore, globalization is still a "global effect", redistributing rights and privileges. While an ever larger number of people permanently drops out of the social process of production and reproduction, a smaller group experiences an increasing freedom of action and accumulation of wealth.

**Baumgartner, Wilhelm**. "Nineteenth-Century Würzburg: The Development of the Scientific Approach to Philosophy" in *In Itinere European Cities and the Birth of Modern Scientific Philosophy*, Poli, Roberto (ed), 79-98. Amsterdam, Rodopi, 1997.

**Baumrin, Bernard**. Waste in Medicine. *J Soc Phil*, 27(3), 5-13, Wint 96.

**Baur, Michael**. Adorno and Heidegger on Art in the Modern World. *Phil Today*, 40(3), 357-366, Fall 96.

First, this article considers some similarities between Adorno and Heidegger concerning the role of art in the modern world. Next, the article outlines some crucial differences; for example, Adorno regards all thought (including that which gives rise to art) as intrinsically dominative, while Heidegger holds that even dominative, objectifying thought presupposes a kind of thought that is not dominative or objectifying. An articulation of these differences helps to illuminate the ways in which the ideas of both Adorno and Heidegger are limited (though in different ways). Finally, the article suggests that these limitations are overcome in the thought of Hegel.

**Baur, Michael**. Heidegger and Aquinas on the Self as Substance. *Amer Cath Phil Quart*, 70(3), 317-337, Sum 96.

This article first examines Heidegger's understanding of Dasein in terms of care and temporality, and his corresponding critique of the metaphysics of presence, especially as this critique applies to one's understanding of the human knower. The article then seeks to determine whether Aquinas's thought concerning the human knower falls prey to the Heideggerian critique. Finally, the article suggests that the Thomist and the Heideggerian both have something to learn from one another.

**Baxter, Anthony**. Can One be Cognitively Conscious of God?. *Heythrop J*, 38(1), 15-34, Ja 97.

How do humans attain knowledge or revelation of God? Analysis is familiar in terms of hypothesis, necessity, authority and commitment. Yet anyway, can there be cognitive experience of God/grace: received widely, not just by a few? An a-conceptual lucidity picture critically fails. But why rule out by definition the very possibility of cognitive awareness of God? We should favour an account of people's epistemic situation respecting God called the "consciousness portrayal". Alertness to nonreligious talk aids finding the religious phrasing meaningful. Cognition is not just a function of calculative reasoning. Broad epistemological views, often linked with 'rationality', are at issue.

**Baxter, Brian H**. Ecocentrism and Persons. *Environ Values*, 5(3), 205-219, Ag 96.

Ecocentrism has to establish an intrinsic connection between its basic value postulate of the noninstrumental value of the nonhuman world and a conception of human flourishing, on pain of failure to motivate acceptance of its social and political prescriptions. This paper explores some ideas recently canvassed by ecocentrists such as Robyn Eckersley, designed to establish this connection—transpersonal ecology, autopoietic value theory and ecofeminism—and finds them open to objection. An alternative approach is developed which concentrates on the connection between nonhuman nature and personhood, via the phenomenon of culture. Persons are conceived of as essentially culture creators, and the fact of their embodiment in ecosystems is argued to be essential to their activities as culture creators. (edited)

**Baxter, Donald L M**. Abstration, Inseparability, and Identity. *Phil Phenomenol Res*, 57(2), 307-330, Je 97.

Berkeley and Hume object to Locke's account of abstraction. Abstraction is separating in the mind what cannot be separated in reality. Their objection is that if *a* is inseparable in reality from *b*, then the idea of *a* is inseparable from the idea of *b*. The former inseparability is the reason for the latter. In most interpretations, however, commentators leave the former unexplained in explaining the latter. This article assumes that Berkeley and Hume present a unified from against Locke. Hume supplements Berkeley's argument just where there are gaps. In particular, Hume makes explicit something Berkeley leaves implicit: The argument against Locke depends on the principle that things are inseparable if and only if they are identical. Abstraction is thinking of one of an inseparable pair while not thinking of the other. But doing so entails thinking of something while not thinking of it. This is the fundamental objection.

**Baxter, Donald L M**. Corporeal Substances and True Unities. *Stud Leibniz*, 27(2), 157-184, 1995.

In the Arnauld correspondence, Leibniz contends that each corporeal substance has a substantial form, because only true unities can be real. I show how this argument precludes Broad's Aristotelian interpretation of corporeal substances as composite unities, and mandates Russell's interpretation that each corporeal substance is a single monad. Next I argue that the textual evidence that corporeal substances have parts, must be interpreted using various special senses of 'part'. Last I suggest that when Leibniz says matter is a phenomenon, he means that it is falsely but usefully supposed real. Making that supposition yields an Aristotelian view of corporeal substance.

**Baxter, Liliane Kshensky**. Explorations in Morality and Nonviolence: Martin Luther King, Jr. and Adam Michnik. *Acorn*, 7(2), 5-17, Fall-Wint 92-93.

**Bayer, Greg**. Coming to Know Principles in *Posterior Analytics* II 19. *Apeiron*, 30(2), 109-142, Je 97.

This paper is a brief commentary on the tortuous last chapter of the *Posterior Analytics*, which purports to show how we come to know the explanatory principles (primarily definitions) of the sciences. I argue that Aristotle's account amounts to this: Universal concomitances (e.g., that all humans are two-footed, civilizable, etc.) discovered through *epagôgê*, "induction," in perceived particulars give rise in *nous* to *problêmata*, scientific "problems," always conceived of in a universal way (Why do all humans have two feet? etc.), which are "solved" by discovering the explanatory principles accounting for these concomitances. And it is *nous* that determines these principles, in a dialectical process that goes beyond *epagôgê*.

**Bayerová, Marie**. Husserl's Phenomenology and its Relation to Descartes (in Czech). *Filosof Cas*, 44(5), 811-832, 1996.

The influence of Descartes on Husserl's phenomenology stretches back to the first appearance of phenomenological thought as transcendental philosophy, but became clear only in the later stage of Husserl's work where it acquired its special value as the historicising aspect of philosophical thought. The logic of the development of phenomenology up to this final phase with respect to Descartes, can be seen primarily in following three main points. The first, in the very start of the shaping of phenomenology's theoretical-understanding role and methods in close connection with Descartes's ideas on doubt in Husserl's *Idea of Phenomenology*. The second, in the legacy of Husserl's work *Ideas* I which is an application of Cartesian thought, being at the same time a scheme of questions inspired by Descartes and successfully superimposed upon it. The third, in Husserl's attempt at a systematic introduction to phenomenology in his *Cartesian meditations*. (edited)

**Bazzicalupo, Laura**. Hannah Arendt on Hobbes. *Hobbes Stud*, 9, 51-54, 1996.

Arendt's interpretation of Hobbes is an external and critical approach: so there are some reductionisms. Hobbes is an example of the nullification of politics typical in Western history—the withdrawal from the contingent nature of action. The artificial genesis of State is an example of eidetic and theoretical coercion of Plato's praxis, to eliminate the risk and to reduce the politics to the modality of cause-effect. What is lost is reality. The Leviathan, born out of an artifice to attain order, includes in his internal logic, the dissolving, the insecurity, a vacillating structure, in a paradoxical heterogenesis of the ends.

**Beabout, Gregory R**. *Freedom and Its Muses: Kierkegaard on Anxiety and Dispair*. Milwaukee, Marquette Univ Pr, 1996.

For Kierkegaard scholars the book provides detailed and careful accounts of his key concept of anxiety and despair, comments on much of the existing secondary literature on these topics, provides many helpful etymological insights and even contains a perceptive and generously noted use of my own Indices. It also does nice things like distinguishing between the "lower pseudonymous works," the "upbuilding works," and the "higher pseudonymous works." It shows why Sartre is no match for Kierkegaard, why and how Alasdair MacIntyre has misrepresented him so badly and why finally Freud has nothing to say about human freedom. (edited)

**Bealer, George**. "Materialism and the Logical Structure of Intentionality" in *Objections to Physicalism*, Robinson, Howard (ed), 101-126. New York, Clarendon/Oxford Pr, 1996.

**Beam, Craig**. Hume and Nietzsche: Naturalists, Ethicists, Anti-Christians. *Hume Stud*, 22(2), 299-324, N 96.

Hume and Nietzsche have more in common than anyone has yet acknowledged. Both philosophize in a way that is naturalistic, antimetaphysical and focused upon human nature. Both mount radical moral critiques of Christianity, which they regard as a blight on human flourishing. The bases of these critiques are quite similar. Hume upholds pride and greatness of mind in a way that virtually calls out for a Nietzschean theory of value inversion. And when it comes to pity and benevolence, their views are not that far apart, for both want to strip virtue of its "dismal dress."

**Beards, Andrew**. Moral Conversion and Problems in Proportionalism. *Gregorianum*, 78(2), 329-357, 1997.

Cet article examine certains des éléments fondamentaux de la pensée de Bernard Lonergan sur l'éthique. Il y est proposé que le traitement des préceptes transcendentaux et des valeurs dans *Method* suggère une continuité avec sa position antérieure dans *Insight*. Cette continuité est exposée par l'examen de la manière dans laquelle Lonergan dérive les 'devoirs' des préceptes transcendentaux de 'l'être' de la structure de la connaissance. Cet approche, dessinée à grands traits, est appliquée à une analyse de l'éthique proportionnaliste. On suggère en outre qu'une telle éthique se révèle incohérente.

**Beards, Andrew**. *Objectivity and Historical Understanding*. Brookfield, Avebury, 1997.

This work is both an introduction to the philosophy of Bernard Lonergan and an essay in the application of his approach in the areas of contemporary epistemology and philosophy of historiography. In the first part of the work, Beards expounds and defends Lonergan's position on cognitional structure and epistemology, comparing and contrasting it with the work of such philosophers as Hintikka, Mackie, Davidson, Rorty, Nielsen and Wittgenstein. Beards goes on in the second part of the book to consider the way Lonergan builds upon his work in epistemology to outline an approach to problems concerning objectivity in historical knowledge. Beards argues that Lonergan's analyses throw considerable light on such controversial issues as the criteria of selection used by historian and the role of value-judgments.

**Bearn, Gordon C F**. Aestheticide: Architecture and the Death of Art. *J Aes Educ*, 31(1), 87-94, Spr 97.

**Bearn, Gordon C F**. *Waking to Wonder: Wittgenstein's Existential Investigations*. Albany, SUNY Pr, 1997.

The central claim of this book is that, early and late, Wittgenstein modelled his approach to existential meaning on his account of linguistic meaning. A reading of Nietzsche's *The Birth of Tragedy* sets up Bearn's reading of the existential point of Wittgenstein's *Tractatus*. Bearn argues that both books try to resolve our anxiety about the meaning of life by appeal to the deep, unutterable essence of the world. Bearn argues that as Wittgenstein's and Nietzsche's thought matured, they both separately came to believe that the answer to our existential anxiety does not lie beneath the surfaces of our lives, but in our acceptance—Nietzsche's "Yes"—of the groundless details of those surfaces themselves: the wonder of the ordinary. (publisher)

**Beauchamp, Tom L**. "The Role of Principles in Practical Ethics" in *Philosophical Perspectives on Bioethics*, Sumner, L W (ed), 79-95. Toronto, Univ of Toronto Pr, 1996.

**Beauchamp, Tom L** (ed). *Intending Death: The Ethics of Assisted Suicide and Euthanasia*. Englewood Cliffs, Prentice Hall, 1996.

Among the most controversial ethical and social issues of our times, assisted suicide and euthanasia have been propelled to the forefront of public awareness. This timely volume contains previously unpublished works that were developed before and after a three-day conference sponsored by selected faculty from the Kennedy Institute of Ethics at Georgetown University and the Schools of Medicine and Public Health at The Johns Hopkins University. The essays explore issues that law and public policy often choose to avoid or confront only indirectly. While they concentrate on a wide range of issues, the most important running topic is intentionally causing death by either an active or passive means. Essays are grouped as follows: 1) Philosophical Perspectives, 2) Clinical Perspectives and 3) Political, Legal, and Economic Perspectives. (publisher)

**Beauchamp, Tom L**. Opposing Views on Animal Experimentation: Do Animals Have Rights?. *Ethics Behavior*, 7(2), 113-121, 1997.

Animals have moral standing; that is, they have properties (including the ability to feel pain) that qualify them for the protections of morality. It follows from this that humans have moral obligations toward animals and because rights are logically correlative to obligations, animals have rights.

**Beauchamp, Tom L** (ed) and Veatch, Robert M (ed). *Ethical Issues in Death and Dying*. Englewood Cliffs, Prentice Hall, 1996.

Since the first edition of *Ethical Issues in Death and Dying* was published in 1978, enormous changes have transpired in the field of biomedical ethics. To give readers a more complete picture of historical developments and current thought, the *Second Edition* has thoroughly revised its coverage of: The Emergence of a Brain-Oriented Definition, Truthtelling with Dying Patients, Suicide, Physician-Assisted Suicide and Euthanasia, Forgoing Treatment and Causing Death, Decisions to Forgo Treatment Involving (once) Competent Patients, Decisions to Forgo Treatment Involving Never-Competent Patients,

AUTHOR INDEX 513 Beck, Heinrich


Futile Treatment and Terminal Care, Social Reasons for Limiting Terminal Care. (publisher)

**Beaulieu, Alain**. L'état idéal de finitude chez Gadamer. *Horiz Phil*, 7(2), 75-90, Spr 97.

The general purpose of the work is to show how the ideal state of finitude at work in Gadamer's philosophical hermeneutic represents a step back in comparison with the philosophy of some other postmodern thinkers. To reach that goal we would first like to show that the ideal circulation of the sense, as theorized by Gadamer in the three parts of *Truth and Method*. We would then like to demonstrate how Gadamer in the first part of *Truth and Method* takes the opposite view of Kant's reflective judgment theory for which only particularities are given without universal laws. Finally we rapidly give some indications of how Heidegger's conception of truth as glade, liberty as opening and Derrida's deconstruction project take the opposite of Gadamer's hermeneutic in assuming this new nonideal state of finitude. (edited)

**Beauvais, Chantal**. L'Esprit absolu de Hegel est-il Dieu?. *De Phil*, 10, 1-20, 1993.

How are we to interpret Hegel's use of religious imagery and Christian theological terms to characterize *absolute spirit*? Two possible approaches to this question are considered, that of P.J. Labarrière, who sees the absolute spirit of Hegel's dialectic as having a purely logical burden, with none of the resonances that "absolute spirit" would have in the Christian onto-theological tradition, and that of Quentin Laurer, who sees Hegel insisting on the continuity between religion and philosophy. The author attempts to clarify the controversy by way of an original reflection on the relations between faith and knowledge.

**Beauvais, Chantal**. La structure ontique de la communauté d'après Edith Stein. *Maritain Stud*, 12, 150-168, 1996.

The author's goal is to present a general analysis of Stein's phenomenological ontology of the community which forms the content of her work entitled: *Beitrage zur philosophischen Begrundung der Psychologie und der Geisteswissenschaften*. Stein's analysis is in turned used as a starting point for a reflection on the bases of ethics for ethical behaviour is ontically rooted in the human being in so far as she is a "living-with-other-beings" being.

**Beavers, Gordon**. Automated Theorem Proving for Lukasiewicz Logics. *Stud Log*, 52(2), 183-196, My 93.

**Becerra Batán, Marcela** and Marincevic, Juan. Elecciones epistemológicas y práctica docente. *Rev Latin de Filosof*, 22(2), 367-374, 1996.

This work purports to give an account of a teaching experience regarding problems of scientific knowledge, which has taken place at the School of Humanistic Sciences of the State University in San Luis. The starting point of this experience was determined by certain positions suggested hypothetically. To begin with, we believe that the "transmission" of knowledge is determined by the epistemological elections. We regard knowledge as a construction and we conceive scientific knowledge as processes historically and culturally situated. The teaching practice consistent with this choice, will permit the reconstruction of relations with the knowledge and with the pupils, active subjects in the process of appropriation and recreation of knowledge.

**Bechler, Zev**. "Hintikka on Plenitude in Aristotle" in *Knowledge and Inquiry: Essays on Jaakko Hintikka's Epistemology and Philosophy of Science*, Sintonen, Matti (ed), 5-18. Amsterdam, Rodopi, 1997.

Jaakko Hintikka was the first to present a detailed argument for the claim that Aristotle subscribed to the so-called *principle of plenitude* according to which all possibilities are eventually actualized. This paper argues that Aristotle's "actualism," the view that only actualities are real, determined his peculiar type of logical determinism as well as his doctrine of plenitude. The paper also argues, in part contrary to what Hintikka seems to have thought, that Aristotle's definition of *kinesis* does not provide an escape from the *principle of plenitude* or from his form of logical determinism. It is also suggested that, as a result, potentialities in Aristotle's scheme cannot have an explanatory role.

**Bechtel, William** and Mundale, Jennifer. Integrating Neuroscience, Psychology, and Evolutionary Biology through a Teleological Conception of Function. *Mind Mach*, 6(4), 481-505, N 96.

The idea of integrating evolutionary biology and psychology has great promise, but one that will be compromised if psychological functions are conceived too abstractly and neuroscience is not allowed to play a constructive role. We argue that the proper integration of neuroscience, psychology, and evolutionary biology requires a teleological as opposed to merely componential analysis of function. A teleological analysis is required in neuroscience itself; we point to traditional and current research methods in neuroscience, which make critical use of distinctly teleological functional considerations in brain cartography. Only by invoking teleological criteria can researchers distinguish the fruitful ways of identifying brain components from the myriad of possible ways. (edited)

**Bechtel, William** and Waskan, Jonathan. Directions in Connectionist Research: Tractable Computations without Syntactically Structured Representations. *Metaphilosophy*, 28(1-2), 31-62, Ja-Ap 97.

Should connectionists abandon the quest for tractably computable cognitive transition functions while retaining syntactically structured mental representations? We argue, in opposition to Horgan, that it should not. We argue that the case against tractably computable functions, based upon the claimed isotropic and Quinean character of cognition, fails since cognition is not as isotropic and Quinean as Fodor and Horgan contend. As to syntactically structured representations, we argue that they are unneeded for most cognitive tasks organisms confront and that when they are needed, they may be provided by external representational media such as natural language. (edited)

**Beck, Andreas**. "Teoría de situaciones: Semántica de tipos para un lenguaje formal con concepto de verdad" in *Verdad: lógica, representación y mundo*, Villegas Forero, L, 157-176. Santiago de Compostela, Univ Santiago Comp, 1996.

When creating a formal language, where it is possible to make statements not only about objects but also about the very language it is necessary to include the *concept of truth* as a relation symbol in the alphabet of syntax. This has turned out to be highly problematical, because so-called *Liar sentences* lead to paradoxes. The outcome is a semantic, where Liar sentences do not lead to paradoxes and the expressive incompleteness of the earlier approaches is eliminated. (edited)

**Beck, Andreas**. Classic Paradoxes in the Context of Non-Monotonic Logic (in Spanish). *Agora (Spain)*, 15(2), 145-152, 1996.

**Beck, Günther**. Tellurische Teleologie oder Determinismus und Freiheit Carl Ritters natürliches System einer sittlichen Welt. *Phil Natur*, 29(2), 210-228, 1992.

Ritters "tellurische Teleologie" kennzeichnet die Auffassung, dass die "wahre" Bestimmung des Menschen und die "äusseren" Verhältnisse auf der Erde von Anfang an in Einklang stehen. Von einer auf platten Geodeterminismus gegründeten Apologetik des Bestehenden hält er sich durchaus fern, wenn er seinen Standpunkt darlegt, dass das Menschengeschlecht geistig-ethischen und nicht—wie die Erdnatur—physisch-kosmischen Gesetzen folge. Die Freiheit des Menschen, das ethische Moment in der Welt, besteht nach Ritter darin, in der Anschauung von einem übergeordneten Mass und Gesetz den eigentümlich vorgegebenen Entwicklungsgang der Völker mit Bewusstsein zu vollziehen. Der Schluss, dass eine so verstandene "Freiheit" dem Menschen konkrete Tugenden abverlangen muss, ist als wesentlicher Ertrag seines "natürlichen Systems einer sittlichen Welt" anzusehen.

**Beck, Gunnar**. From Kant to Hegel: Johann Gottlieb Fichte's Theory of Self-Consciousness. *Hist Euro Ideas*, 22(4), 275-294, Jl 96.

This article emphasizes Fichte's role as a central figure in the period of transition from Kantian moral universalism to Hegelian ontological collectivism and *Sittlichkeitsethik*. Echoing Rousseau's insights into the sociological determinants of human consciousness and drawing on Herder's more comprehensive theory of the linguistic and cultural conditions of all human thought, Fichte, in his writings from 1796 onward, develops a radical reformulation and extension of Kant's theory of reason and self-consciousness. Fichte's theory of the origins and nature of consciousness and knowledge, it is concluded, anticipates Hegel's replacement of the Kantian individual self by the collective *We* as the fount of all rational understanding and moral judgement in the human subject.

**Beck, Heinrich**. "Fruchtbarer geistiger Gegensatz Südasien—Europa?" in *Kreativer Friede durch Begegnung der Weltkulturen*, Beck, Heinrich (ed), 357-365. New York, Lang, 1995.

As another appendix to the volume: "Creative Peace through Encounter of World Cultures" is presented here a report on a journey through India and Nepal. This report can be considered as an example for a vivid illustration of the theoretical perspectives of the mentioned investigation project.

**Beck, Heinrich**. "Weiterführendes Forschungsprojekt für philosophisch-interdisziplinäre und interkuturelle Zusammenarbeit" in *Kreativer Friede durch Begegnung der Weltkulturen*, Beck, Heinrich (ed), 349-356. New York, Lang, 1995.

As an appendix to the volume: "Creative Peace through Encounter of World Cultures" is given here the outline of a corresponding proposal for a project of further studies and philosophical-interdisciplinary cooperation. The outline is meant as an additional incentive, but also, above all, as an invitation; its disposition is: 1) The reason of this project, 2) The scientific structure of the project (its aim and its areas for concretizing); 3) Basic methodological guidelines.

**Beck, Heinrich**. "Weltfriede als dynamische Einheit kultureller Gegensätze" in *Kreativer Friede durch Begegnung der Weltkulturen*, Beck, Heinrich (ed), 17-69. New York, Lang, 1995.

This essay represents an introductory explanation to the volume "Creative Peace through Encounter of World Cultures" (containing 15 other special contributions to this topic). The working hypothesis is that mankind's 'act of being' can be considered as a dialectic-triadic process which unfolds itself 1) primarily resting in itself 2) opening itself, venturing forth and expressing itself, 3) returning into itself, rejoining (fulfilling or completing) itself. This hypothesis first a) is elaborated further in a special respect to the theory of culture, as presented by *Jean Gebser*. This theory subdivides the history of human consciousness in epochs, virtually forming the '*temporal framing*' of mankind's culture. Then, in a second step, b) an onto-anthropologically relevant structuralism of current cultures is elaborated. Thus the '*spatial framing*' of the current cultural fabric of mankind is outlined, which, just like the temporal structure, is based on the dialectic or onto-triadic principle (as expression of the motional and actual character of being). This draft, specified by singular world cultures (the European, Asiatic, African, and (Latin-)American) and their interrelationship, is meant as an impulse for corresponding philosophical and empirical investigations.

**Beck, Heinrich** (ed) and Schmirber, Gisela (ed). *Kreativer Friede durch Begegnung der Weltkulturen*. New York, Lang, 1995.

Diese Veröffentlichung entstand aus einem gleichnamigen Projekt am Lehrstuhl für Philosophie I der Universität Bamberg in Zusammenarbeit mit der Hanns-Seidel-Stiftung. Ziel des Projektes ist es, mit den Mitteln philosophischer Reflexion die für die heutigen Kulturen prägenden geistig-religiösen Ursprünge zu erhellen. Der daraus entspringende Prozess der Selbst- und Fremdwahrnehmung intendiert wechselseitige Anerkennung und innovative interkulturelle Kooperation als Grundlage eines menschlich kreativen Friedens.

Der Band lässt Repräsentanten verschiedener Fachgebiete und Weltreligionen zur Sprache kommen. Eine "philosophische Exposition" (H. Beck) legt dar, welchen Stellenwert die Abhandlungen "zur allgemeinen Problematik von Kulturbegegnung und Weltfrieden" sowie die Beiträge aus spezifischen Kulturbereichen (Europa—Afrika—Asien—(Latein-)Amerika) im "Dialog der Weltkulturen" besitzen.

**Beck, Sigrid**. On the Semantics of Comparative Conditionals. *Ling Phil*, 20(3), 229-271, Je 97.

**Becker, Lawrence C**. Trust as Noncognitive Security about Motives. *Ethics*, 107(1), 43-61, O 96.

My project in this article is to sharpen the distinction between cognitive and noncognitive accounts of trust and to argue for the importance for political philosophy of pursuing an inquiry into the more neglected of the two areas, the noncognitive one. In particular, I will argue for the importance of what I will call a sense of security about other people's benevolence, conscientiousness and reciprocity. Apart from the rather obvious case to be made for its being a crucial element in the formation, stability and productivity of both individuals and large-scale social organizations, such security raises intriguing empirical and theoretical problems often obscured in discussions of other forms of trust. (edited)

**Beckerman, Aaron** and Doerfler, Martin and Couch, Elsbeth (& others). Ethical Issues and Relationships between House Staff and Attending Physicians: A Case Study. *J Clin Ethics*, 8(1), 34-38, Spr 97.

The purpose of the work was to examine a series of ethical issues between attendings and house staff. In the space between dying and death, conflicts emerge between the interests of education and care of the patient, patients' care decision making which are more a function of authority than medical knowledge, and extending the do no (psychological) harm principle to house staff.

**Beckerman, Wilfred** and Pasek, Joanna. Plural Values and Environmental Valuation. *Environ Values*, 6(1), 65-86, F 97.

The paper discusses some of the criticisms of contingent valuation (CV) and allied techniques for estimating the intensity of peoples' preferences for the environment. The weakness of orthodox utilitarian assumptions in economics concerning the commensurability of all items entering into peoples' choices is discussed. The concept of commensurability is explored as is the problem of rational choice between incommensurate alternatives. While the frequent claim that the environment has some unique moral intrinsic value is unsustainable, its preservation often raises ethical and other motivations that are not commensurate with the values that people place on ordinary marketable goods. Nevertheless, CV is also claimed to have some advantages and it is concluded that little progress will be made in this area until both sides in the debate recognize what is valid in their opponents' arguments.

**Beckermann, Ansgar**. "Wissen und wahre Meinung" in *Das weite Spektrum der analytischen Philosophie*, Lenzen, Wolfgang, 24-43. Hawthorne, do Gruyter, 1997.

Following von Kutschera and Sartwell it is argued that the concept of knowledge, understood as justified true belief, is a hybrid concept any systematically oriented theory of knowledge should better eschew. Our epistemic endeavors simply aim at true belief. Hence, we would be entirely satisfied if only we could be rather sure that our beliefs were true. Justification comes into play just because this type of assurance is so hard to get. We ask whether a belief is justified when we are not sure whether it is true and only because we regard justification to be evidence for truth. If a belief is justified then it is at least probable that it is also true. Thus, justification is only a means which enables us to ascertain that we have attained our epistemic goal, viz. truth. The roles truth and justification play in our epistemic life hence are so different that there is no point in coupling these two aspects into one mongrel concept.

**Beckermann, Ansgar**. Eigenschafts-Physikalismus. *Z Phil Forsch*, 50(1/2), 3-25, Ja-Je 96.

There are five main answers to the question how mental properties may relate to physical properties: 1) Mental terms are definable in physical terms (*Semantic Physicalism*); 2) mental properties are identical with physical properties (*Identity Theory*); 3) mental properties are realized by physical properties (*Realization Theory*); 4) mental properties have a physical basis (*Supervenience Theory*); 5) mental properties do not even have a physical basis (*Property Dualism*). Drawing on ideas from C.D. Broad, a precise account that characterizes *realization* as a relation between property-types is developed. Furthermore, it is argued that i) only the first three relations can sustain acceptable forms of physicalism and that ii) *Realization Theory*, understood as suggested, offers the most attractive stance to take for a property-physicalist.

**Beckermann, Ansgar**. Is There a Problem about Intentionality?. *Erkenntnis*, 45(1), 1-23, Jl 96.

It is argued that the problem of intentionality is a pseudoproblem. Intentional states only *appear* to possess a mysterious feature which could render their naturalization problematic. This appearance ensues from the fact that we ascribe intentional states by predicates which contain 'that'-clauses. We do not use intentional vocabulary in ascribing certain mental states because these states have the property of having a semantic content. To the contrary, it is only because and insofar as we ascribe mental states by means of intentional predicates that these very states can, in a sense, be said to have a 'semantic content'. (edited)

**Beckert, Cristina**. E. Levinas: Da ética à linguagem. *Philosophica (Portugal)*, 115-134, 1993.

Dans cet étude bibliographique sur Levinas c'est notre intention de distinguer deux problèmes nucléaires qui ont guidés les interprétations de la philosophie

levinasienne jusqu'à nos jours: le primat de l'étique en face des présuppositions théoriques de la phénoménologie et la question du langage comme créateur de sens au-delà de l'être. Finalement nous présentons l'évolution des études sur Levinas au Portugal, de 1980 jusqu'à 1992.

**Beckert, Cristina**. Hölderlin e o *Retorno Natal*. *Philosophica (Portugal)*, 37-50, 1994.

This article seeks to analyse Hölderlin's concept of *Homeland Return*, both on his fragments about greek tragedy and on his poems. The author sustains that the Greeks have a natural drive for chaos and absence of form, while in modern culture the opposite is true. That is the reason why each try to assume its contrary. In many of Hölderlin's poems we can also find the urge to return to a lost homeland, even facing the "absence of God".

**Beckert, Cristina**. O Outro Literário: a Filosofia da Literatura em Levinas. *Philosophica (Portugal)*, 133-143, 1997.

This paper tries to show how E. Levinas thinks of literature as an expression of the *other*. After having criticized the nature of modern art in general as purely ontological and neutral, he intends to recover the ethical transcendence of the *other* present in the poetic word. To accomplish this task he searches for inspiration in the works of Proust, Leiris, and, most of all, in Blanchot's notion of an "endless writing".

**Beckley, Harlan** (ed). *The Annual of the Society of Christian Ethics with Cumulative Index*. Washington, Georgetown Univ Pr, 1996.

**Beckwith, Francis J**. The Ethics of Referral Kickbacks and Self-Referral and the HMO Physician as Gatekeeper: An Ethical Analysis. *J Soc Phil*, 27(3), 41-48, Wint 96.

The America Medical Association for quite some time now has on ethical grounds forbidden physicians to receive remuneration in exchange for a referral to another physician or health care professional. The reason for this is quite obvious: referral kickbacks create a conflict of interest. That is, if a physician receives a fee for referring a patient to a specific individual, this may compromise the physician's primary concern for her patient's welfare. I argue in this paper that the very thing that makes referral kickbacks unethical in the above two cases is what makes the role of the Health Maintenance Organization (HMO) physician as gatekeeper unethical. Although many medical ethicists have argued that the HMO gatekeeper role is unethical, no one, as far as I know, has argued that it is morally indistinguishable from referral kickbacks and self-referral. Of course, if one does not believe that referral kickbacks and self-referral are unethical, then one would have no problem with HMO physician as gatekeeper. However, if one is convinced that referral kickbacks and self-referral are unethical, then I believe that one is forced to conclude that HMO physician as gatekeeper is unethical as well.

**Beckwith, Jonathan R** and Geller, Lisa N. Commentary on "The Social Responsibilities of Biological Scientists". *Sci Eng Ethics*, 3(2), 145-148, Ap 97.

This paper outlines some recent examples of social responsibility of biologists. These range from actions taken to halt the development of biological warfare weapons to criticisms of genetic arguments that support racial discrimination. It contrasts these examples with the general reluctance of most biologists to involve themselves in dealing with the social consequences of their research. Reasons ranging from lack of awareness of issues to an atmosphere in science that discourages social responsibility are discussed. The most crucial missing element in fostering social responsibility is a scientific education that integrates the study of the social impact of science with the science itself.

**Beckwith, Jonathan R** (& others) and Hollander, Rachelle D and Johnson, Deborah G. Why Teach Ethics in Science and Engineering?. *Sci Eng Ethics*, 1(1), 83-87, J 95.

**Bedau, Hugo Adam**. *Making Mortal Choices: Three Exercises in Moral Casuistry*. New York, Oxford Univ Pr, 1997.

This book is devoted to displaying casuistic decision-making in cases where if anybody is to survive, then not all can survive. Chapter 1 examines the 1841 case of U.S. v. Holmes, where surviving crew in an overcrowded lifeboat sacrificed some of the passengers so that they and others might survive. Chapter 2 examines the famous hypothetical invented by Lon Fuller, the case of the speluncean explorers trapped in a landslide whose survival depends on a lethal lottery. Chapter 3 examines the hypothetical case of Jim and the Indians in the jungle invented by Bernard Williams, where Jim must choose between killing one Indian hostage to save the rest and killing none—only to have soldiers kill all the hostages. An appendix discusses the nature and history of casuistic reasoning in Western moral thinking.

**Beddoes, Diane**. "Deleuze, Kant and Indifference" in *Deleuze and Philosophy: The Difference Engineer*, Ansell Pearson, Keith (ed), 25-43. New York, Routledge, 1997.

Deleuze approaches Kant as an abstract engineering problem and looks for elements indifferent to the rule of the general. This approach illustrates the Deleuzian concepts of caution and antimemory. Without memory, history is neither a source of profit, guilt nor guidance, but n abstract assemblage; rather than the subject appearing to be the source of organization it is the residual effect of machinic processes. With the subject so conceived Deleuze can differentiate between caution and care. These concepts are further developed through examples drawn from feminism (Sandy Stone), biology (Dorion Sagan) and the work of Georg Kampis on component systems.

**Bedecarré, Corrinne**. Swear by the Moon. *Hypatia*, 12(3), 189-197, Sum 97.

In this article I discuss the argument/criticism/concerns of bisexuality that arise from within progressive communities which already accept gay and lesbian rights. Issues discussed include trust, heterosexuality and the body, the power dynamics of patriarchal oppression and subjective verification. The moon is evoked as a material metaphor for phases and changes, I argue that conditions of the world preclude political attachment to an excessively fixed standard of many things, including sexual orientation.

**Beebee, Helen**. Taking Hindrance Seriously. *Phil Stud*, 88(1), 59-79, O 97.

**Beebee, Helen** and Papineau, David. Probability as a Guide to Life. *J Phil*, 94(5), 217-243, My 97.

The article is concerned with the objective constraints on rational agents' degrees of belief. Views which regard single-case chances as the primary providers of objective constraints cannot accommodate agents whose information does not determine single-case chances. The authors argue that the degree of belief in an outcome should correspond instead to its objective probability relative to those relevant features of the world which the agent knows about. This avoids the central problem facing the single-case view, but nonetheless preserves the intuition that agents should set their degrees of belief equal to single-case chances when they are in a position to do so.

**Beed, Clive** and Sawyer, K R and Sankey, H. Underdetermination in Economics: The Duhem-Quine Thesis. *Econ Phil*, 13(1), 1-23, Ap 97.

**Beedle, Andrew**. Modal Fatalism. *Phil Quart*, 46(185), 488-495, O 96.

This essay argues that David Lewis's modal realism implies that fatalism is true. A reexamination of Lewis's response to Robert Adams's claim that modal realism should make us indifferent to moral decisions leads to the conclusion that, since the totality of worlds is 'fixed' under modal realism, the character of each world is fixed. Given Lewis's view on causation, it becomes clear that the fixedness of individual worlds implies fatalism and not simply determinism.

**Beeler-Port, Josef**. Zum Stellenwert der *Grundlage* aus der Sicht von 1804: Eine Interpretation des Wechsels von analytisch-synthetischer und genetischer Methode in Kapitel 5 der *Grundlage*. *Fichte-Studien*, 10, 335-350, 1997.

**Beer, Douglas A** and Macklin, Ruth and Robinson, Walter (& others). Bad Night in the ER—Patients' Preferences and Reasonable Accommodation: Discussed by Douglas A. Beer, Ruth Macklin, Walter Robinson, and Philip Wang. *Ethics Behavior*, 6(4), 371-383, 1996.

**Beguè, Marie-France**. El rol de la convicción en la sabiduría práctica de Paul Ricoeur. *Cuad Etica*, 17-18, 45-56, 1994.

This paper emphasizes the "practical wisdom as conviction" that is a basic category from the author. This practical wisdom must cross the conflicts in order to surmount them. The example here exposes Ricoeur's discussion about the conviction as fidelity to the another. (edited)

**Behera, Satrughna**. Religion Justifying Morality—A Critique. *Darshana Int*, 36(3/143), 36-42, Ap 96.

**Behler, Ernst**. Friedrich Schlegel's Theory of an Alternating Principle Prior to His Arrival in Jena (6 August 1796). *Rev Int Phil*, 50(197), 383-402, 1996.

**Behling, Robert** and Snodgrass, James. Differences in Moral Reasoning Between College and University Business Majors and Non-Business Majors. *Bus Prof Ethics J*, 15(1), 79-84, Spr 96.

**Behnke, Elizabeth A**. Ghost Gestures: Phenomenological Investigations of Bodily Micromovements and Their Intercorporeal Implications. *Human Stud*, 20(2), 181-201, Ap 97.

This paper thematizes the operative kinaesthetic style of world-experiencing life by turning to the ongoing "how" of our habitual bodily comportment: to our deeply sedimented way(s) of "making a body"; to schematic inner vectors or tendencies toward movement that persist as bodily "ghost gestures" even if one is not making the larger, visible gestures they imply; and to "inadvertent isometrics," i.e., persisting patterns of "trying," "bracing," "freezing," etc. All such micromovements witness to our sociality insofar as they are not only socially shaped, but perpetuate certain styles of intercorporeal interaction and sustain certain modes of responsivity. "Reactivating the sediment"—retrieving the tacit "choreography" of everyday life from its anonymity and sensing our ongoing ways of living out the legacy of our "communal body"—not only allows one's individual bodily style to shift, but can open new possibilities for healthy interkinaesthetic comportment. Such work can thus contribute to an "embodied ethics" in both theory and practice.

**Behrens, Roger**. Afrikanische Kunst—Ein Drama kultureller Wiederentdeckung oder eine europäische Tragödie?. *Prima Philosophia*, 10(3), 379-386, 1997.

**Behrens, Roger**. Kritische Theorie als Erfahrungswissenschaft: Lagebericht anlässlich einiger Neuerscheinungen. *Prima Philosophia*, 9(4), 447-455, 1996.

This article starts with an overview of recent publications in critical theory. The high number of these issues seems to prove a growing interest in the traditions of social critique and social philosophy. Particular attention is given to Theodor W. Adorno, mainly on the basis of the edition of his posthumous writings in thirty volumes. The sociology of critical theory, the now published correspondence and the aesthetical perspective on critical theory surround a specific topic in the contemporary interest: to reconstruct and focus critical theory as a kind of science of experience (*Erfahrungswissenschaft*).

**Beiner, Ronald**. Rereading Hannah Arendt's Kant Lectures. *Phil Soc Crit*, 23(1), 21-32, 1997.

This paper offers a restatement of the basic project of Hannah Arendt's *Lectures on Kant's Political Philosophy*, tries to trace its theoretical motivation and presents some criticisms of Arendt's interpretation of Kant's *Critique of Judgment*. Arendt's political philosophy as a whole is an attempt to ground the idea of human dignity on the publicly displayed 'words and deeds' that

constitute the realm of human affairs. This project involves a philosophical response both to Plato's impugning of the dignity of the polis and to Hegel's founding of modern historicism. The Kant *Lectures* bring this philosophical project to its completion because the enactment of public deeds presupposes a company of judging spectators who draw meaning from the spectacle by judging and appreciating what is enacted. But this conception, precisely because it relates so deeply to Arendt's own theoretical impulse, leads to a sometimes one sided and misleading reading of Kant.

**Beiser, Frederick C**. Response to Pinkard. *Bull Hegel Soc Gt Brit*, 34, 21-26, Autumn-Wint 96.

**Beiser, Frederick C**. *The Sovereignty of Reason: The Defense of Rationality in the Early English Enlightenment*. Princeton, Princeton Univ Pr, 1996.

*The Sovereignty of Reason* is a survey of the rule of faith controversy in seventeenth-century England. It examines the arguments by which reason eventually became the sovereign standard of truth in religion and politics, and how it triumphed over its rivals: Scripture, inspiration, and apostolic tradition. (publisher, edited)

**Beito, David T**. This Enormous Army: The Mutual Aid Tradition of American Fraternal Societies before the Twentieth Century. *Soc Phil Pol*, 14(2), 20-38, Sum 97.

**Bejczy, István**. *Tolerantia*: A Medieval Concept. *J Hist Ideas*, 58(3), 365-384, Jl 97.

As a political concept *tolerantia* originated in medieval scholarship. Canon lawyers coined the concept in the 12th and 13th centuries as a principle of noninterference with evil practices in order to prevent still greater evils. Humanists like Erasmus did not develop the concept further and even tended to limit its sphere of application. They introduced, however, the notion of *concordia*, recognizing the pluriform character of truth but offering no possibility to come to terms with the untrue. The modern confusion between *tolerantia* and *concordia* might be a heritage of enlightened philosophy.

**Beklemishev, Lev D**. Induction Rules, Reflection Principles, and Provably Recursive Functions. *Annals Pure Applied Log*, 85(3), 193-242, My 97.

We show that fragments of arithmetic axiomatized by various forms of induction *rules* admit a precise axiomatization in terms of reflection principles as well. Thus, the closure of $EA$ under the induction rule for $Sigma_n$ (or $II_{n+0}$ formulas is equivalent to $Omega$ times iterated $Sigma_n$ reflection principle. Moreover, for $k$ less then $Omega$, $k$ times iterated $Sigma_n$ reflection principle over $EA$ precisely corresponds to the extension of $EA$ by *less than or equal to k* nested applications of $Sigma_n$ induction rule. (edited)

**Belegradek, Oleg V**. Higman's Embedding Theorem in a General Setting and its Application to Existentially Closed Algebras. *Notre Dame J Form Log*, 37(4), 613-624, Fall 96.

For a quasi variety of algebras K, the Higman Theorem is said to be true if every recursively presented K-algebra is embeddable into a finitely presented K-algebra; the Generalized Higman Theorem is said to be true if any K-algebra which is recursively presented over its finitely generated subalgebra is embeddable into a K-algebra which is finitely presented over this subalgebra. We suggest certain general conditions on K under which 1) the Higman Theorem implies the Generalized Higman Theorem; 2) a finitely generated K-algebra A is embeddable into every existentially closed K-algebra containing a finitely generated K-algebra B if and only if the word problem for A is Q-reducible to the word problem for B. The quasi varieties of groups, torsion-free groups and semigroups satisfy these conditions.

**Bell, Bernard W** (ed) and Grosholz, Emily (ed) and Stewart, James B (ed). *W.E.B. Du Bois on Race and Culture*. New York, Routledge, 1996.

W.E.B. Du Bois was one of the most profound and influential African-American intellectuals of the twentieth century. This volume addresses the complexities of Du Bois's legacy, showing how his work gets to the heart of today's theorizing about the color line. (publisher, edited)

**Bell, Daniel**. Through Sin to Salvation (in Hungarian). *Magyar Filozof Szemle*, 4-5-6, 558-573, 1996.

**Bell, Daniel A**. A Communitarian Critique of Authoritarianism. *Polit Theory*, 25(1), 6-32, F 97.

This article is written in the form of an imaginary dialogue between Singaporean elder statesman Lee Kuan Yew and an American democrat named Demo. Demo argues that democratic political practices can contribute to strengthening ties to the national political community in Singapore and that increased public spiritedness can benefit the country. In contrast to the abstract and unhistorical universalism, which often disables Western democrats, Demo draws upon particular features of the Singaporean context to make his points.

**Bell, David**. Solipsism and Subjectivity. *Euro J Phil*, 4(2), 155-174, Ag 96.

**Bell, Martin**. Hume and Causal Power: The Influences of Malebranche and Newton. *Brit J Hist Phil*, 5(1), 67-86, Mr 97.

**Bell, Wendell**. *Foundations of Futures Studies: Human Science for a New Era*. New Brunswick, Transaction Pub, 1997.

In volume 2 of *Foundations of Futures Studies*, Wendell Bell goes beyond possible and probable futures to the study of *preferable* futures. He shows that a concern with ethics, morality, and human values follows directly from the futurist purposes of discovering or inventing, examining, and proposing desirable futures. He examines moral judgments as an inescapable aspect of all decision making and conscious human action, even in the everyday lives of ordinary people. Thus, he argues that moral analysis ought to become a part of all the human sciences. (publisher,edited)

**Bella, David A**. Organized Complexity in Human Affairs: The Tobacco Industry. *J Bus Ethics*, 16(10), 977-999, Jl 97.

Leaked documents and public testimony point to widespread distortion of information within the tobacco industry. The model developed herein described such behaviors as emergent outcomes not reducible to or sufficiently explained by individual fraud and deliberate deceit. Critics of the tobacco industry often fail to appreciate the role of self-organization in complex systems. They presume rational design. Consequently, they imply more intentional deceit, deliberate planning and conspiracy than needed to explain the distortions that actually occurred. (edited)

**Bellamy, Richard**. Toleration, Liberalism and Democracy: A Comment on Leader and Garzón Valdés. *Ratio Juris*, 10(2), 177-186, Je 97.

Leader and Garzón Valdés are correct to link toleration to democracy rather than liberalism. However, it is the democratic character of society and the process of democratic decision making that give rise to a genuine practice of tolerance, not an abstract and regulative ideal of democracy, such as they appeal to. Whereas the latter approach collapses into the standard liberal accounts of toleration both rightly find wanting, the former fits with a republican notion of deliberative democracy. This perspective corresponds to the circumstances of toleration and promotes tolerance as a virtue that is intrinsic both to the nature of democratic debate and to the securing of uncoerced agreement amongst people possessing different beliefs and values. As such, it proves more compatible with pluralism, and hence with toleration, than liberalism.

**Bellamy, Richard** and Castiglione, Dario. Building the Union: The Nature of Sovereignty in the Political Architecture of Europe. *Law Phil*, 16(4), 421-445, Jl 97.

The debate on the nature of the European Union has become a test case of the kind of political and institutional arrangements appropriate in an age of globalization. This paper explores three views of the EU. The two main positions that have hitherto confronted each other appeal to either cosmopolitan or communitarian values. Advocates of the former argue for some form of federal structure in Europe and are convinced that the sovereignty of the nation state belongs to the past. Proponents of the latter make a case on both sociopolitical and normative grounds for a Europe of nations. However a third position, favoured by the authors, is gaining ground. This view combines cosmopolitan and communitarian conceptions. It emphasizes the mixed nature of the European polity and conceives the constitutionalization process as open-ended. (edited)

**Bellini, Ornella**. "Il tempo come percezione: gli empiristi inglesi" in *Il Concetto di Tempo: Atti del XXXII Congresso Nazionale della Società Filosofica Italiana*, Casertano, Giovanni (ed), 183-189. Napoli, Loffredo, 1997.

**Belnap, Nuel** and Perloff, Michael. The Way of the Agent. *Stud Log*, 51(3-4), 463-484, 1992.

The conditional, *if an agent did something, then the agent could have done otherwise*, is analyzed using *stit* theory, which is a logic of "seeing to it that" based on agents making choices in the context of branching time. The truth of the conditional is found to be a subtle matter that depends on how it is interpreted (e.g., on what "otherwise" refers to and on the difference between "could" and "might") and also on whether or not there are "busy choosers" that can make infinitely many choices in a finite span of time.

**Belot, Gordon**. Why General Relativity *Does* Need an Interpretation. *Proc Phil Sci Ass*, 3(Suppl), S80-S88, 1996.

There is a widespread impression that General Relativity, unlike Quantum Mechanics, is in no need of an interpretation. I present two reasons for thinking that this is a mistake. The first is the familiar hole argument. I argue that certain skeptical responses to this argument are too hasty in dismissing it as being irrelevant to the interpretative enterprise. My second reason is that interpretative questions about General Relativity are central to the search for a quantum theory of gravity. I illustrate this claim by examining the interpretative consequences of a particular technical move in canonical quantum gravity.

**Belousek, Darrin W**. Einstein's 1927 Unpublished Hidden-Variable Theory: Its Background Context and Significance. *Stud Hist Phil Mod Physics*, 27B(4), 437-461, D 96.

This paper considers an unpublished manuscript written by Albert Einstein in 1927 that contains an unsuccessful attempt to provide a deterministic hidden-variable completion of quantum mechanics. After laying out the formal scheme of the manuscript and developing its interpretation, its background, context and significance are discussed, particularly in regard to the impact of the failure of the scheme on Einstein's ensuing thoughts concerning the possibility for a complete quantum mechanics.

**Belshaw, Christopher**. Abortion, Value and the Sanctity of Life. *Bioethics*, 11(2), 130-150, Ap 97.

In *Life's Dominion* Dworkin argues that the debate about abortion is habitually misconstrued. Substantial areas of agreement are overlooked, while areas of disagreement are, mistakenly, seen as central. If we uncover a truer picture, then hope of a certain accord may no longer seem vain. I dispute many of these claims. (edited)

**Beltran, Joseph E**. Shared Decision Making: The Ethics of Caring and Best Respect. *Bioethics Forum*, 12(3), 17-25, Fall 96.

Making decisions regarding life-sustaining treatments for patients who are severely disabled involves some of the most difficult clinical dilemmas in bioethics. This paper focuses on two aspects of this kind of decision making: accurately determining a mentally disabled patient's decision-making capacity; and making treatment decisions for patients who have never had or who do not currently have decision-making capacity and who have no available surrogate.

The author examines legislative and community-based solutions and discusses future issues facing developmentally disabled persons, including the need for a legally recognized advance directive and the ramifications of physician-assisted death for this population.

**Beltrán, Miquel**. Huarte de San Juan y Spinoza: consideraciones sobre el vulgo y la filosofía natural. *Pensamiento*, 205(53), 53-64, Ja-Ap 97.

**Beltrán Orenes, Pilar**. "¿Siguen las pruebas realizadas por ordenador algún patrón de verdad matemática?" in *Verdad: lógica, representación y mundo*, Villegas Forero, L, 253-261. Santiago de Compostela, Univ Santiago Comp, 1996.

At the end of the 50s, a new problem arises in the field of mathematics. The use of computers as productive tools makes it possible to prove some new theorems. This fact has set forth the question of the accuracy of the results achieved in such a way. However, the problem about tests compiled by computers can be clarified, from our point of view, by including these kinds of tests into the so-called, by Lakatos, "informal proofs".

**Bem, Sacha** and Keijzer, Fred A. Behavioral Systems Interpreted as Autonomous Agents and as Coupled Dynamical Systems: A Criticism. *Phil Psych*, 9(3), 323-346, S 96.

We will discuss two contexts in which the behavioural systems idea is being developed. Autonomous Agents Research is the enterprise of building behaviour-based robots. Dynamical Systems Theory provides a mathematical framework well suited for describing the interactions between complex systems. We will conclude that both enterprises provide important contributions to the behavioural systems idea. But neither turns it into a full conceptual alternative which will initiate a major paradigm switch in cognitive science. The concept will need a lot of fleshing out before it can assume that role. (edited)

**Ben-Menahem, Yemima**. Historical Contingency. *Ratio*, 10(2), 99-107, S 97.

The paper provides a new characterization of the concepts of necessity and contingency as they should be used in the historical context. The idea is that contingency (necessity) increases in direct (reverse) proportion to sensitivity to initial conditions. The merits of this suggestion are that it avoids the conflation of causality and necessity (or contingency and chance), that it enables the bracketing of the problem of free will while maintaining the concept of human action making a difference, that it sanctions tendencies without recourse to teleology and that it recasts the controversy between historicists and antihistoricists in less dogmatic language.

**Ben-Yami, Hanoch**. Against Characterizing Mental States as Propositional Attitudes. *Phil Quart*, 47(186), 84-89, Ja 97.

Many mental states are not ascribable by means of sentences that justify characterizing them as propositional attitudes. Moreover, the mental states that are ascribable by appropriate sentences do not form any natural subset of mental states. A reason for the characterization relying on beliefs etc. about nonexisting things is also rejected. Lastly, some sentences ascribing abilities and dispositions have the same grammatical form as some sentences that ascribe mental states, so that the attempt to paraphrase the latter would obscure the conceptual relations between the two. It follows that mental states are not relations to propositions.

**Ben-Ze'ev, Aaron**. Appraisal Theories of Emotions. *J Phil Res*, 22, 129-143, Ap 97.

Today appraisal theories are the foremost approach to emotions in philosophy and psychology. The general assumption underlying these theories is that evaluations (appraisals) are the most crucial factor in emotions. This assumption may imply that: a) evaluative patterns distinguish one emotion from another; b) evaluative patterns distinguish emotions from nonemotions; c) emotional evaluations of the eliciting event determine emotional intensity. These claims are not necessarily related. Accepting one of them does not necessarily imply acceptance of the others. I believe that whereas (b) is false, (a) and (c) are basically true.

**Ben-Ze'ev, Aaron**. Emotions and Argumentation. *Inform Log*, 17(2), 189-200, Spr 95.

The relationship between emotions and argumentation is not always clear. I attempt to clarify this issue by referring to three basic questions: 1) Do emotions constitute a certain kind of argumentation?; 2) Do emotions constitute rational argumentation?; 3) Do emotions constitute efficient argumentation? I will claim that there are many circumstances in which the answer to these questions is positive. After describing such circumstances, the educational implications of the connection between emotions and argumentation will be indicated.

**Ben-Ze'ev, Aaron**. Emotions and Morality. *J Value Inq*, 31(2), 195-212, Je 97.

The role of emotions in the moral domain is controversial. Two central features of emotions are particularly problematic in this regard: 1) the nondeliberate nature of emotions, and 2) the partial nature of emotions. The nondeliberate nature has been claimed to contradict the possibility of moral responsibility, and the partial nature of emotions has been perceived to be incompatible with the impartial nature of morality. Although admitting the presence of these features, I claim that emotions are very important in morality. I argue that we have some responsibility over our emotions and emotions have both instrumental and intrinsic moral value.

**Ben-Ze'ev, Aaron**. Romantic Love and Sexual Desire. *Philosophia (Israel)*, 25(1-4), 3-32, Ap 97.

Romantic love and sexual desire are central emotions in our life. Some identify the two emotions and some consider them to be completely different. This paper analyzes the basic characteristics of each emotion and describes the connection between them. It deals with issues such as the basic evaluative patterns and typical object of each emotion, are these emotions blind? Can these emotions be directed at several people at the same time? and the factors responsible for increasing the intensity of these emotions.

**Benatar, David**. Why It Is Better Never To Come Into Existence. *Amer Phil Quart*, 34(3), 345-355, Jl 97.

This article argues against a common assumption in the literature about future possible possible—the assumption that being brought into existence (with decent life prospects) is a benefit. In arguing for the view that it is better never to come into being, the paper points to a crucial difference between harms and benefits such that existence has no real advantages over nonexistence, whereas the disadvantages of existence are real. The paper considers and rejects various objections to this view. It concludes by considering the implications of the preceding arguments, including the question of whether having children is immoral.

**Benatar, Solomon R**. Just Healthcare beyond Individualism: Challenges for North American Bioethics. *Cambridge Quart Healthcare Ethics*, 6(4), 397-415, Fall 97.

The focused attention of ethicists on physician/patient interactions in an increasingly complex medical environment has eclipsed considerations of social justice, population health and broader conceptions of human rights. The economic, scientific and moral power of North America and an overemphasis on self-interest, challenges bioethicists to be introspective, to broaden the scope of bioethics beyond the "medical industrial complex" and to face issues of local and global importance to human rights, health care and medical practice. (edited)

**Bencivenga, Ermanno**. *A Theory of Language and Mind*. Berkeley, Univ of Calif Pr, 1997.

In this book, Bencivenga offers a stylistically and conceptually exciting investigation of the nature of language, mind, and personhood and the many ways the three connect. Bencivenga contests the basic assumptions of analytic (and also, to an extent, postmodern) approaches to these topics. His exploration leads through fascinating discussions of education, courage, pain, time and history, selfhood, subjectivity and objectivity, reality, facts, the empirical, power and transgression, silence, privacy and publicity, and play—all themes that are shown to be integral to our thinking about language. (publisher, edited)

**Bencivenga, Ermanno**. Kant's Sadism. *Phil Lit*, 20(1), 39-46, Ap 96.

Jacques Lacan claimed that Sade's *Philosophy in the Boudoir* represents the (Hegelian) truth of Kant's second *Critique*. But this provocative statement was given by Lacan no rigourous or systematic defense. This paper provides such a defense.

**Bender, John W**. On Shiner's "Hume and the Causal Theory of Taste". *J Aes Art Crit*, 55(3), 317-320, Sum 97.

Roger Shiner has recently argued against the causal theory of taste on the grounds that causal theorists, Hume prominently, fail to appreciate the contrast between judgments of taste and properly aesthetic judgments. In reply we argue that the contrast Shiner relies upon, between aesthetic and gustatory judgment, is illusory.

**Bender, John W**. Realism, Supervenience, and Irresolvable Aesthetic Disputes. *J Aes Art Crit*, 54(4), 371-381, Fall 96.

**Bender, Thomas**. Clients or Citizens?. *Crit Rev*, 10(1), 123-134, Wint 96.

John McKnight's *The Careless Society* tellingly exposes the way the professionalized welfare state creates dependency. But McKnight is too quick to condemn this result as the product of professional self-interest, and to posit as the alternative a selfless, republican model of community. He overlooks the more realistic possibility that the pursuit of their interests by social groups empowered to take care of themselves would better serve those interests and would simultaneously create a feeling of interdependence and civic involvement.

**Bender, Wolfgang** and Platzer, Katrin and Sinemus, Kristina. On the Assessment of Genetic Technology: Reaching Ethical Judgments in the Light of Modern Technology. *Sci Eng Ethics*, 1(1), 21-32, J 95.

The "Model for Reaching Ethical Judgments in the Context of Modern Technologies—the Case of Genetic Technology," which is presented here, has arisen from the project "Ethical Criteria Bearing Upon Decisions Taken in the Field of Biotechnology." This project has been pursued since 1991 in the Zentrum für interdisziplinäre Technikforschung (ZIT) of the Technical University of Darmstadt, with the purpose of examining decision-making in selected activities involving the production of transgenic plants that have a useful application. The model is the basis of an outline for interviews to investigate how far decisions concerning the development of such plants with genetic techniques take ethical criteria into account. It was necessary to design this new model because other models for reaching judgments of this kind were not conceptually suited for concrete application. This model represents a problem related approach and combines methodological with substantive typology. In this it differs from comparable models for reaching ethical judgments.

**Benedikt, Michael**. Complexity, Value, and the Psychological Postulates of Economics. *Crit Rev*, 10(4), 551-594, Fall 96.

Does the contemporary built environment—the ensemble of our humanly created surroundings—make us happy? This question prompts a consideration of the psychological dimensions of economic value, and of Tibor Scitovsky's revisions of standard economic theory. With Scitovsky as a starting point, a model of value based on modern complexity theory and a Maslow-like rendition of human needs can account for some of the more important exceptions to the law of diminishing marginal utility, including those that may undermine the built environment in a market economy.

**Benes, Jiri** (trans) and Descartes, René. Passions of the Soul (in Czech). *Filosof Cas*, 44(5), 713-716, 1996.

**Benferhat, Salem** and Dubois, Didier and Prade, Henri. Some Syntactic Approaches to the Handling of Inconsistent Knowledge Bases: A Comparative Study. *Stud Log*, 58(1), 17-45, 1997.

This paper presents and discusses several methods for reasoning from inconsistent knowledge bases. A so-called argued consequence relation, taking into account the existence of consistent arguments in favor of a conclusion and the absence of consistent arguments in favor of its contrary, is particularly investigated. Flat knowledge bases, i.e., without any priority between their elements, are studied under different inconsistency-tolerant consequence relations, namely the so-called argumentative, free, universal, existential, cardinality-based, and paraconsistent consequence relations. The syntax-sensitivity of these consequence relations is studied. A companion paper is devoted to the case where priorities exist between the pieces of information in the knowledge base.

**Bengoetxea, Juan B** and Eizagirre, Xabier and Ibarra, Andoni. "Un escenario pragmático para la verdad en la ciencia" in *Verdad: lógica, representación y mundo*, Villegas Forero, L, 455-465. Santiago de Compostela, Univ Santiago Comp, 1996.

According to Cartwright fundamental laws do not tell the truth, do not describe objects in reality, but they have superior explanatory power. Others have argued that the notion of truth is unsubstantial for providing an adequate analysis of science, and instead of it they plea for the introduction of other epistemic values. We think that using an adequate notion of truth allows us to make sense of intuitions of scientists; truth is taken by them as something worth pursuing. Accordingly, we propose a pragmatic account of truth able to understand the specific aspect of scientific practice, i.e., the activity of idealizations and approximations. (edited)

**Benhabib, Seyla**. On Reconciliation and Respect, Justice and the Good Life: Response to Herta Nagl-Docekal and Rainer Forst. *Phil Soc Crit*, 23(5), 97-114, S 97.

**Benhabib, Seyla**. The Local, the Contextual and/or Critical. *Constellations*, 3(1), 83-94, Ap 96.

**Benhabib, Seyla** (ed) and Passerin d'Entrèves, Maurizio (ed). *Habermas and the Unfinished Project of Modernity*. Cambridge, MIT Pr, 1997.

This collection of ten essays offers the first systematic assessment of *The Philosophical Discourse of Modernity*, Jürgen Habermas's masterful defense of the rational potential of the modern age. An opening essay by Maurizio Passerin d'Entrèves orients the debate between Habermas and the postmodernists by identifying two different senses of responsibility. Habermas's own essay discusses the themes of his book in the context of a critical engagement with neoconservative cultural and political trends. The main body of essays is divided into two sections—*Critical Rejoinders* and *Thematic Reformulations*. These essays offer an important set of perspectives on Habermas's position by philosophers, social scientists, intellectual historians, and literary critics. (publisher, edited)

**Benitez, Eugenio E**. "Deliberation and Moral Expertise in Plato's *Crito*" in *Dialogues with Plato*, Benitez, Eugenio (ed), 21-47. Edmonton, Academic, 1996.

It has been said that Plato's criterion of correct choice in practical matters is *a priori* and otherworldly. I argue that this is not the case for at least one Platonic dialogue, the *Crito*, which presents a significant humanist and empirical model for deliberation. In the *Crito* Plato depicts Socrates as his criterion of correct choice and moreover, he depicts Socrates as a thoroughly human being who lacks moral expertise. Plato does, however, think that good deliberation requires the ideal of an absolute standard, the moral expert. I argue that the *Crito* carefully observes a distinction between the expert and Socrates and that it provides no account or model of the way that an expert would deliberate. If the *Crito* presents a model of deliberation that is nonscientific, then the question about the function of moral expertise for Plato is not yet settled.

**Benitez, Eugenio E**. Characterisation and Interpretation: The Importance of Drama in Plato's *Sophist*. *Lit Aes*, 6, 27-39, O 96.

I argue that the dramatic form of the *Sophist* does not just complement, but qualifies and reshapes the philosophy of that dialogue. Examination of the characters of Theodorus, Theaetetus, Socrates and the Eleatic Stranger shows that the Eleatic Stranger is not Plato's mouthpiece, but is apparently the object: sophist. If the Eleatic Stranger is not Plato's mouthpiece, then most modern interpretation of the dialogue are mistaken and misguided.

**Benitez, Eugenio E**. Deliberation and Moral Expertise in Plato's *Crito*. *Apeiron*, 29(4), 21-47, D 96.

It has been said that Plato's criterion of correct choice in practical matters is *a priori* and otherworldly. I argue that this is not the case for at least one Platonic dialogue, the *Crito*, which presents a significant humanist and empirical model for deliberation. In the *Crito* Plato depicts Socrates as his criterion of correct choice and moreover he depicts Socrates as a thoroughly human being who lacks moral expertise. Plato does, however, think that good deliberation requires the ideal of an absolute standard, the moral expert. I argue that the *Crito* carefully observes a distinction between the expert and Socrates and that it provides no account or model of the way that an expert would deliberate. If the *Crito* presents a model of deliberation that is nonscientific, then the question about the function of moral expertise for Plato is not yet settled.

**Benitez, Eugenio E** (ed). *Dialogues with Plato*. Edmonton, Academic, 1996.

These original essays about Plato interrogate Plato's dialogues understood as processes of moral habituation. The essays discuss issues of moral expertise, moral training, and the transcendental good, as expounded by Plato. Dialogues considered include *Crito*, *Charmides*, *Phaedo*, Philebus, *Republic* and *Sophist*. (publisher)

**Benítez, Laura** and Robles, José A. Ralph Cudworth (1617-1688) sobre la infinitud de Dios. *Mathesis*, 10(2), 129-152, My 94.

In this paper we put forth and discuss Cudworth's arguments for God's immensity (both temporal and spatial), which he presents in his thick book *The True Intellectual System of the Universe* [Cudworth 1678]. Cudworth, unlike his colleague Henry More (both from the Cambridge neo-Platonists group) argues for an infinite but unextended God. Cudworth in his discussion, makes clear that he follows the Aristotelian proposal with respect to the empirical infinite: if there is anything like that, it can only be a potential infinite; the only actual infinity is that of the divinity and it is not empirical. On the other hand, God's eternity is not a never ending temporal *process* and God's ubiquity is not in need of His being infinitely extended.

**Benítez G, Laura**. Dos propuestas sobre epistemología y ciencia en el siglo XVII novohispano: Carlos de Sigüenza y Sor Juana Inés de la Cruz. *Dialogo Filosof*, 12(3), 367-384, S-D 96.

Don Carlos de Sigüenza y Sor Juana Inés de la Cruz no sólo se encuentran en la encrucijada del paso de la edad media a la moderna, y del viejo al nuevo mundo, sino de la vieja a la nueva vía de reflexión y de la vieja a la nueva ciencia. Es lo que se intenta mostrar en éstas páginas.

**Benner, Patricia**. A Dialogue Between Virtue Ethics and Care Ethics. *Theor Med*, 18(1-2), 47-61, Mr-Je 97.

A dialogue between virtue and care ethics is formed as a step towards meeting Pellegrino's challenge to create a more comprehensive moral philosophy. It is also a dialogue between nursing and medicine since each practice draws on the Greek *virtue tradition* and the Judeo-Christian tradition of care differently. In the Greek *virtue tradition*, the point of scrutiny lies in the inner character of the actor, whereas in the Judeo-Christian tradition the focus is relational, i.e., how virtues are lived out in specific relationships, particularly unequal relationships where vulnerability of one of the members is an issue. In a care ethic relational qualities such as attunement rather than inner qualities are the point of scrutiny. A dialogue between these two traditions makes it possible to consider the relational virtues and skills of openness and responsiveness that are required for a respectful meeting of the other.

**Bennet, Laura J** (trans) and Popper, Karl. *In Search of a Better World: Lectures and Essays from Thirty Years*. New York, Routledge, 1996.

'I wish to begin by saying that I regard scientific knowledge as the most important kind of knowledge we have, though I am far from regarding it as the only one', writes Sir Karl Popper in the opening essay of this book. His subjects range from the beginnings of scientific speculation in classical Greece to the destructive effects of twentieth-century totalitarianism, from major figures of the Enlightenment such as Voltaire and Kant to the role of science and self-criticism in the arts. The essays offer striking new insights; including insights into the mind of their author, a fighter for freedom and one of the most forthright critics of Marxism and all totalitarian ideologies. (publisher,edited)

**Bennett, Jane**. "How Is It, Then, That we Still Remain Barbarians?" Foucault, Schiller, and the Aestheticization of Ethics. *Polit Theory*, 24(4), 653-672, N 96.

In this essay, I explore the relationship between aesthetics and ethics by examining the charge of "aestheticization" as it has been leveled against Foucault by Terry Eagleton, Christopher Norris, Richard Wolin and Alex Callinicos. I do so in some small part to defined Foucault's later writings, but more importantly to make a case for the indispensability of aesthetic matters to ethical practices. I use Friedrich Schiller and Foucault together to argue that while certain forms of the aesthetic do pose ethical dangers, the very possibility of *enacting* worthy ethical ideals depends upon cultivation of an aesthetic sensibility.

**Bennett, Jonathan** and Gorovitz, Samuel. Improving Academic Writing. *Teach Phil*, 20(2), 105-120, Je 97.

**Bennett, Jonathan** (trans) and Remnant, Peter (trans). *New Essays on Human Understanding*. New York, Cambridge Univ Pr, 1996.

In the *New Essays on Human Understanding*, Leibniz argues chapter by chapter with John Locke's *Essay Concerning Human Understanding*, challenging his views about knowledge, personal identity, God, morality, mind and matter, nature versus nurture, logic and language, and a host of other topics. The work is a series of sharp, deep discussions by one great philosopher of the work of another. Leibniz's references to his contemporaries and his discussions of the ideas and institutions of the age make this a fascinating and valuable document in the history of ideas. (publisher,edited)

**Bennett, Richard**. Ignorance Is No Excuse: Legal Knowledge and Postmodernism. *Int Stud Phil*, 29(1), 1-8, 1997.

**Bennett, Stephen Earl** and Fisher, Bonnie and Resnick, David. "Speaking of Politics in the United States: Who Talks to Whom, Why, and Why Not" in *Political Dialogue: Theories and Practices*, Esquith, Stephen L (ed), 263-293. Amsterdam, Rodopi, 1996.

Although normative political theorists have argued that citizens talking with other citizens about public affairs is essential in a democracy, empirically oriented political scientists have tended to ignore political discussions. This paper reviews what normative theories have said about political conversations and then draws on National Election Studies and Social Surveys to plumb the extent and breadth of political conversations in the United States. The paper also explores who talks about public affairs, with whom they speak and why some people discuss politics while others do not.

**Bennigson, Thomas**. Irresolvable Disagreement and the Case Against Moral Realism. *S J Phil*, 34(4), 411-437, Wint 96.

**Benoist, Jocelyn**. What is Given? Thought and Event (in French). *Arch Phil*, 59(4), 629-657, O-D 96.

What is given? The author deals with the difficulties encountered today by the idea of the "given." He tries to show how the idea of "given" that constitutes the core of both empiricism and phenomenology necessarily retains validity and philosophical relevance. However, the "given" should not anymore be confused with matter waiting to be framed by form, as idealism conceived it. The "given" is not a content, and all the mistakes about it come from this conception idealism always attributed to, and maybe succeeded in imposing, on empiricism. A linguistic and phenomenological analysis shows that speaking of "given" or of "giveness" of things really means the same as speaking of their happening. Moreover it can be upheld that if all things are "given," there are actually no "things" at all in the world, but only "events." The world itself happens through events, events which are irreducible to it (each event marking the self-insufficiency of world). To decline these occurrences in a natural history of world and consciousness could yet be a task for thought.

**Benschop, Hans Peter**. Berkeley, Lee and Abstract Ideas. *Brit J Hist Phil*, 5(1), 55-66, Mr 97.

**Benseler, Frank**. The Constitution of Our World as the History of Arts (in Hungarian). *Magyar Filozof Szemle*, 4-5-6, 385-394, 1996.

Gehen wir auf die ganze Gestalt Lukács zu, nicht noch, oder schon auf Einzelheiten ein, so werden alle, die ihn kannten oder sich intensiv mit seinen Äusserungen und Wirkungen beschäftigt haben, bestätigen: Man konnte niemals mit Gewissheit sagen, ob er an dem arbeitete, was wir wissenschaftliche Wahrheit nennen, nicht einmal, ob er in Teilen seiner Werke, was immer sie betrafen, recht oder auch nur teilweise recht hatte. (edited)

**Bentham, Jeremy**. Extracto de "Libraos de Ultramaria". *Telos (Spain)*, 1(3), 11-43, O 92.

**Benzoni, Francisco**. Rolston's Theological Ethic. *Environ Ethics*, 18(4), 339-352, Winter 96.

The centerpiece of Holmes Rolston, III's environmental ethic is his objective value theory. It is ultimately grounded not in the Cartesian duality between subject and object, but in the divine. It is not his value theory, but rather his anthropology that is the weak link in an ethic in which he attempts to weave together the natural, human and divine spheres. With a richer, more fully developed theological anthropology, Rolston could more deeply penetrate and critique those aspects of the present ways of being-in-the-world that are environmentally destructive.

**Berardi, Roberto**. Gittà, materia del tempo. *Iride*, 8(15), 394-408, Ag 95.

La relazione tra società e spazio è particolarmente pregnante nel caso delle città e delle culture cittadine. Lo spazio civile, secondo R. Berardi, è la predisposizione necessaria perché il tempo della storia si incarni nella città; e il tempo della storia è lo spazio di esistenza, costruzione e trasformazione delle società umane.

**Berardi, Stefano** and Barbanera, Franco. A Constructive Valuation Semantics for Classical Logic. *Notre Dame J Form Log*, 37(3), 462-482, Sum 96.

This paper presents a constructive interpretation for the proofs in classical logic of $\Sigma^0_1$-sentences and for a witness extraction procedure based on Prawitz's reduction rules.

**Berarducci, Alessandro** and Otero, Margarita. A Recursive Nonstandard Model of Normal Open Induction. *J Sym Log*, 61(4), 1228-1241, D 96.

Models of normal open induction are those normal discretely ordered rings whose nonnegative part satisfy Peano's axioms for open formulas in the language of ordered semirings. (Where normal means integrally closed in its fraction field.) In 1964 Shepherdson gave a recursive nonstandard model of open induction. His model is not normal and does not have any infinite prime elements. In this paper we present a recursive nonstandard model of normal open induction with an unbounded set of infinite prime elements.

**Bercic, Boran**. On Tolerance. *Acta Analytica*, 153-174, 1995.

This paper has two main parts. In the first part the author expounds two formulations of the alleged tolerance paradox. After analysis he concludes that there is nothing paradoxical in the concept of tolerance. The author also argues that there is no such thing as a "principle of tolerance." The second part of the paper discusses three general strategies for justifying tolerance: relativistic, sceptic and fallibilistic. It is argued, that these strategies are either necessarily untenable or useless.

**Berckmans, Paul R**. Behavioral Expression and Related Concepts. *Behavior Phil*, 24(2), 85-98, Fall 96.

**Berckmans, Paul R**. The Semantics of Symbolic Speech. *Law Phil*, 16(2), 145-176, 97.

More than half a century ago, the Supreme Court held that the free speech protection of the First Amendment is not limited to verbal communication, but also applies to such expressive conduct as saluting a flag or burning a flag. Even though the Supreme Court has decided a number of important cases involving expressive conduct, the Court has never announced any standards for distinguishing such conduct from conduct without communicative value. The aim of this paper is to examine which conceptions of nonverbal expression underlie judicial decisions on expressive conduct and to offer an account of expressive conduct grounded in contemporary semantic theory. The central hypothesis of this paper is that significance of expressive conduct can be explained by principles that explain important features of linguistic meaning. (edited)

**Beresford, Eric B**. Can Phronesis Save the Life of Medical Ethics?. *Theor Med*, 17(3), 209-224, S 96.

There has been a growing interest in casuistry since the ground breaking work of Jonsen and Toulmin. Casuistry, in their view, offers the possibility of securing the moral agreement that policy makers desire but which has proved elusive to theory driven approaches to ethics. However, their account of casuistry is dependent upon the exercise of *phronesis*. As recent discussions of *phronesis* make clear, this requires attention not only to the particulars of the case, but also to the substantive goods at stake in the case. Without agreement on these goods attention to cases is unlikely to secure the productive consensus that Jonson and Toulmin seek.

**Berger, Douglas** and Takahashi, Yoshitomo and Fukunishi, Isao (& others). Japanese Psychiatrists' Attitudes toward Patients Wishing to Die in the General Hospital: A Cultural Perspective. *Cambridge Quart Healthcare Ethics*, 6(4), 470-479, Fall 97.

**Berger, Edward M** and Gert, Bernard. The Institutional Context for Research. *Prof Ethics*, 4(3-4), 17-46, Spr-Sum 95.

**Berger, Louis S**. Toward a Non-Cartesian Psychotherapeutic Framework: Radical Pragmatism as an Alternative. *Phil Psychiat Psych*, 3(3), 169-184, S 96.

Postmodern criticism has identified important impoverishments that necessarily follow from the use of Cartesian frameworks. This criticism is reviewed and its implications for psychotherapy are explored in a psychoanalytic context. The ubiquitous presence of Cartesianism (equivalently, representationism) in psychoanalytic frameworks—even in some that are considered postmodern—is demonstrated and criticized. The postmodern convergence on *praxis* as a desirable alternative to Cartesianism is reported and its relevance for psychoanalysis is considered. The severe conceptual difficulties entailed in formulating such an alternative are discussed, as are those difficulties that would be encountered were psychoanalysis to attempt the shift from explanatory mental science to praxis. The principal psychoanalytic problematics explored are: the paradoxical relationships between theory and therapeutic technique; the therapeutic action; and validation of clinical practices. Initial, nontraditional suggestions for addressing these problems are offered.

**Bergmann, Michael**. A New Argument from Actualism to Serious Actualism. *Nous*, 30(3), 356-359, S 96.

Philosophers such as Kit Fine, Mark Hinchcliff and John Pollock deny that actualism—the view that necessarily everything that there is exists—entails serious actualism—the view that necessarily no object has a property in a world in which it does not exist. I argue, first, that such a denial commits one to the thesis that transworld property exemplification (TPE) is possible. TPE occurs when a property is exemplified in a world W, not by an object in W, but by an object that is in another world W*. Then I argue that TPE is not possible.

**Bergmann, Michael**. Internalism, Externalism and the No-Defeater Condition. *Synthese*, 110(3), 399-417, Mr 97.

Despite various attempts to rectify matters, the internalism-externalism (I-E) debate in epistemology remains mired in serious confusion. I present a new account of this debate, one which fits well with entrenched views on the I-E distinction and illuminates the fundamental disagreements at the heart of the debate. Roughly speaking, the I-E debate is over whether or not certain of the necessary conditions of positive epistemic status are internal. But what is the sense of 'internal' here? And of *which* conditions of *which* positive epistemic status are we speaking? I argue that an adequate answer to these questions requires reference to what I call the no-defeater condition which is satisfied by a subject's belief B just in case she does not believe that B is defeated. I close by stating succinctly the main positions taken in the I-E debate, identifying the basic points of disagreement and suggesting fruitful courses for future discussion.

**Bergmann, Sheryle**. An Epistemological Justification for Aesthetic Experience. *J Aes Educ*, 27(2), 107-112, Sum 93.

In this article, I argue that the strongest justification for the inclusion of the arts in the educational curriculum lies in their potential to foster a rich understanding of the human experience. This proposition necessitates a response to the criticism that I am viewing participation in the arts as instrumentally as opposed to intrinsically valuable. Also, the possibility of attaining understanding presupposes that aesthetic activity has a certain degree of objectivity. I examine the sort of "objective" reasoning involved in appreciating and creating works of art.

**Bergoffen, Debra B**. *The Philosophy of Simone de Beauvoir: Gendered Phenomenologies, Erotic Generosities*. Albany, SUNY Pr, 1997.

This book reads Beauvoir as a philosopher engaged in a three way conversation with Sartre and Merleau-Ponty. Like Sartre and Merleau-Ponty, Beauvoir took up the legacies of the modern and phenomenological philosophical traditions. Unlike them, however, she attended to the phenomenological implications of the sexed body, pursued the idea of ambiguity and developed the philosophical category of the erotic. Her work mirrors her idea of ambiguity. It speaks in two voices; an existential voice that advocates an ethic of liberation and another voice that speaks of the other, generosity, the gift and the ethical possibilities of the erotic event.

**Bergsma, Jurrit**. Response to "Ethical Concerns about Relapse Studies" by Adil E. Shamoo and Timothy J. Keay (CQ Vol 5, No 3). *Cambridge Quart Healthcare Ethics*, 6(2), 233-234, Spr 97.

**Berián, Josetxo**. Sobre el concepto de "Racionalidad" en la ética protestante de Max Weber. *Euridice*, 9-24, 1992.

The main goal of this paper is to analyze the "elective affinity" which exists between several religious ideals (the ascetic Protestantism) and the economic ethos of the capitalism, in order to shape the specific process of the Western rationalization. At the same time, I take into consideration the uncoupled instrumental rationality from the religious symbolic universe (the utilitarianism).

**Berkeley, Anne**. Changing Theories of Collegiate Theatrical Curricula 1900-1945. *J Aes Educ*, 31(3), 77-90, Fall 97.

**Berkeley, George**. *Alciphron oder der Kleine Philosoph*. Hamburg, Meiner, 1996.

**Berkeley, Istvan S N** and Medler, David A and Dawson, Michael R W. PDP Networks can Provide Models that are not Mere Implementations of Classical Theories. *Phil Psych*, 10(1), 25-40, Mr 97.

There is a widespread belief that connectionist networks are dramatically different from classical or symbolic models. However, connectionists rarely test this belief by interpreting the internal structure of their nets. A new approach to interpreting networks was recently introduced by Berkeley et al. (1995). The current paper examines two implications of applying this method: 1) that the internal structure of a connectionist network can have a very classical appearance, and 2) that this interpretation can provide a cognitive theory that cannot be dismissed as a mere implementation.

**Berkowitz, Eric N**. The Evolving Health Care Marketplace: How Important is the Patient?. *Bioethics Forum*, 12(2), 40-44, Sum 96.

The health care marketplace is evolving from a fee-for-service to a managed care environment. As this change occurs, a major concern has been whether the needs of the individual patient will be lost in a setting of large health care providers contracting with large health care buyers. In this paper, the fee-for-service and managed care setting are examined in terms of the implications of whether being market or customer responsive is necessary. As the environment shifts, the underlying change is a move from indemnity plans of individual buyers to the concentration of purchases among a few buying entities. This restructuring may well lead to health care organizations having to be market responsive for the first time.

**Berl, Robert L** and Shannon, J Richard. Are We Teaching Ethics in Marketing?: A Survey of Students' Attitudes and Perceptions. *J Bus Ethics*, 16(10), 1059-1075, Jl 97.

This is a descriptive study which examined the attitudes and perceptions of 273 business students at eight universities across the U.S. towards ethics education. The results indicate that students perceive that the level of discussion of ethics and ethical issues ranges from less than adequate in some marketing courses to adequate in others. Sales/sales management courses received the highest ratings for coverage of ethical issues, while transportation/logistics courses scored the lowest. The study also finds that students believe, quite strongly, that the discussion of ethics and ethical issues is worthwhile and important. (edited)

**Berleur, Jacques**. International Federation for Information Processing's Framework for Computer Ethics. *Sci Eng Ethics*, 2(2), 155-165, A 96.

This paper reviews codes of ethics and codes of conduct from different countries. The differences and similarities between code content and between attitudes are considered. Distinction is drawn between a code of ethics and a code of conduct. Recommendations are made for establishing a common framework for IFIP (International Federation for Information Processing) Member or Affiliate Societies.

**Berlinger, Rudolph**. Heraklit—eine Herausforderung: In freundschaftlichem Gedenken an Eugen Fink. *Perspekt Phil*, 22, 11-28, 1996.

**Berman, Michael**. Time and Emptiness in the *Chao-Lun*. *J Chin Phil*, 24(1), 43-58, Mr 97.

By concentrating on the first chapter of Seng Chao's treatise, I explicate his argument regarding time in light of the second chapter's discussion of the key Buddhist doctrine of *sunyata* (emptiness). After a discussion of the limits of language, the tetralemmical structure of Seng Chao's argument is examined from within the perspective of the enlightened Sage and the common one of those still subject to *duhkha* (suffering). This examination then focuses on the temporal relations of causality, with an additional comparison to Hume's treatment thereof. The conclusion illustrates the tight relations between language, causality, time and emptiness that hold for this Buddha-Taoist monk.

**Bermúdez, José Luis**. Locke, Metaphysical Dualism and Property Dualism. *Brit J Hist Phil*, 4(2), 223, S 96.

Most commentators maintain that Locke is a traditional metaphysical dualist. A close reading of II XXIII (the chapter on complex ideas of substances) shows, however, that although Locke is quite clearly a property dualism, he is nonetheless best seen as agnostic about questions of substance dualism. Moreover, this is the only position that is consistent with his well-known scepticism about the possibility of gaining knowledge of real essences.

**Bermúdez, José Luis**. Practical Understanding vs Reflective Understanding. *Phil Phenomenol Res*, 57(3), 635-641, S 97.

This contribution to a book symposium on John Campbell's *Past, Space and Self* examines the dualism between two different ways of understanding the world developed in the book. One such mode, the causally indexical mode, is practical and engaged. The other, the causally nonindexical mode, is disengaged and reflective. The tenability of this dualism is explored with reference to theories of nonconceptual content, of the conditions upon content ascription and of tacit knowledge.

**Bernard, Brigitte**. Bioethics: A New Interdisciplinary Paradigm in the Relations Between Science and Ethics. *Fronesis*, 2(2), 23-34, D 95.

Starting from the dualisms ethics/science and ought/is, we attempt to define ethics with regard to morality and law. We then explain the qualitative step between ethics and bioethics through which the traditional concept of medical ethics of religious origin has been overcome by the new biological, genetical and medical investigations. Bioethics implies the responsibility of contemporaneous people towards the next generations in transmitting to them an integral genetical heritage in which human, social, political and economical relations acknowledges its true meaning to Montaigne's saying according to which "every people condensates in his being, the whole human condition."(edited)

**Bernardi, Claudio** and D'Agostino, Giovanna. Translating the Hypergame Paradox: Remarks on the Set of Founded Elements of a Relation. *J Phil Log*, 25(5), 545-557, O 96.

In Zwicker (1987) the hypergame paradox is introduced and studied. In this paper we continue this investigation, comparing the hypergame argument with the diagonal one, in order to find a proof schema. In particular, in Theorems 9 and 10 we discuss the complexity of the set of founded elements in a recursively enumerable relation on the set $N$ of natural numbers, in the framework of reduction between relations. We also find an application in the theory of diagonalizable algebras and construct an undecidable formula.

**Bernardini, Carlo.** "Il tempo nella fisica moderna" in *Il Concetto di Tempo: Atti del XXXII Congresso Nazionale della Società Filosofica Italiana*, Casertano, Giovanni (ed), 129-137. Napoli, Loffredo, 1997.

**Bernasconi, Robert.** Eckhart's Anachorism. *Grad Fac Phil J*, 19/20(2/1), 81-90, 1997.

In his early study of Eckhart, Reiner Schürmann advocated understanding union with God as an habitual consciousness rather than an occasional ecstatic state. Schürmann buttressed this "this-worldly" interpretation with an account of the temporality of detachment. The present study complements it with an account of the spatiality of detachment, an anachorism in which one is free of place but not outside of space, as in the figure of the desert. Bernard McGinn's criticism of Schürmann is addressed and the relevance of Schürmann's discussion to Derrida's *On the Name* noted.

**Bernasconi, Robert.** Opening the Future: The Paradox of Promising in the Hobbesian Social Contract. *Phil Today*, 41(1-4), 77-86, Spr 97.

This paper develops a reading of Hobbes that highlights the paradox of a promise that would take one into society, when it is only within society that the conditions for securing promises are met. This interpretation of the social contract, although unpopular today, was accepted by Shaftesbury, Leibniz, Pufendorf, Hume and T. H. Green. However, unlike them, I do not dismiss the paradox but use it to illuminate the interdependence of the individual and society. A brief concluding section applies these considerations to contemporary American individualism with some reference to Derrida.

**Bernasconi, Robert.** The Double Face of the Political and the Social: Hannah Arendt and America's Racial Divisions. *Res Phenomenol*, 26, 3-24, 1996.

Arendt's distinction between the social and the political arises from her privileging of the Greek experience of politics, but an examination of its role in her account of African-American issues leads one to question it. Her notorious remarks in "Reflections on Little Rock" and "Civil Disobedience" reveal her failure to appreciate the social character of anti-Black racism. In *The Origins of Totalitarianism* she privileged the experience of statelessness over slavery. In *On Revolution* she praised the American Revolution for its neglect of social issues in spite of the context of slavery. Both texts show how easily the Greek framework accommodates slavery.

**Bernasconi, Robert** (ed) and Critchley, Simon (ed) and Peperzak, Adriaan Theodoor (ed). *Emmanuel Levinas: Basic Philosophical Writings*. Bloomington, Indiana Univ Pr, 1996.

This anthology of Levinas's key philosophical texts over a period of more than forty years provides an ideal introduction to his thought and offers insights into his most innovative ideas. Five of the ten essays included here appear in English for the first time. An introduction by Adriaan Peperzak outlines Levinas's philosophical development and the basic themes of his writings. Each essay is accompanied by a brief introduction and notes. (publisher,edited)

**Bernecker, Sven.** Die Grenzen des Selbstwissens. *Z Phil Forsch*, 51(2), 216-231, Ap-Je 97.

It is argued that the doctrine of privileged self-knowledge compatible with psychosemantic externalism about mental content is considerably weaker than the Cartesian doctrine of privileged self-knowledge. Firstly, although externalism is compatible with privileged access to one's particular thought contents (P vs. Q), it is consistent with us lacking privileged access to the modes (e.g., believing doubting) in which our thought contents are realized. Secondly, externalism is inconsistent with privileged access to the fact that one's so-called thoughts really are thoughts, rather than purely physical events with no content at all.

**Bernet, Rudolf.** Christendom en fenomenologie. *Tijdschr Filosof*, 58(4), 735-749, D 96.

**Bernhardt, Barbara A** (& others) and Strauss, Misha and Geller, Gail. "Decoding" Informed Consent: Insights from Women regarding Breast Cancer Susceptibility Testing. *Hastings Center Rep*, 27(2), 28-33, Mr-Ap 97.

Cancer susceptibility testing is likely to become routine in medical practice, despite many limitations and unanswered questions. These uncertainties greatly complicate the process of informed consent, creating an excellent opportunity to reconsider exactly how it should be conducted.

**Bernier, Jean-François.** Transcendance et manifestation: La place de Dieu dans la philosophie d'Emmanuel Lévinas. *Rev Phil Louvain*, 94(4), 599-624, N 96.

The fact that the philosophy of Levinas is defined by the initial will to posit the primacy of the ethical order means that the metaphysics that goes with it cannot grant itself the possibility of recognizing in God the fundamental object of its

discourse. But if the metaphysical intention is, then, resolutely turned towards others, Levinas nonetheless gives something to think of God and his work accordingly does not fail to introduce a difficulty related precisely to the establishment of a theological space. The author sets out here to examine the singular system of transcendence which the text of Levinas establishes, in order to see how a certain concept of the divine arises from it, an assuredly original concept that must develop within works in which the absolute founding value granted to the manifestation of one's neighbour is never contested. (edited)

**Bernstein, J M.** "Why Rescue Semblance? Metaphysical Experience and the Possibility of Ethics" in *The Semblance of Subjectivity*, Huhn, Tom (ed), 177-212. Cambridge, MIT Pr, 1997.

**Bernstein, Mark.** Contractualism and Animals. *Phil Stud*, 86(1), 49-72, Ap 97.

Traditionally, contractualism has been unfriendly to nonhuman animals. I argue that, this history not withstanding, this ethical theory has the resources to include nonhuman animals as direct moral objects, i.e., as individuals who deserve moral consideration in virtue of their nonrelational properties. Moreover, the failure of contractualism to take advantage of these resources, results in a very debilitated theory.

**Bernstein, Richard J.** Hans Jonas's *Mortality and Morality*. *Grad Fac Phil J*, 19/20(2/1), 315-321, 1997.

**Berry, Ralph M.** In Which Henry James Strikes Bedrock. *Phil Lit*, 21(1), 61-76, Ap 97.

The essay seeks to understand how the artistic necessities of modernism arise. It begins with a Wittgensteinian analysis of a paragraph in "The Art of Fiction" where James disagrees with Walter Besant over the use of the word "story." By examining James's criticism of Eliot's *Middlemarch* and Maupassant's *Une vie*, it explains why Besant and James no longer know what a story is (what "story" means) and what James (or any novelist) must do to find out.

**Bertelloni, Francisco.** Aristóteles en el Renacimiento. *Rev Latin de Filosof*, 22(2), 331-347, 1996.

Apropos of the recent publication of the book *New Perspectives on Renaissance*, edited by John Henry and Sarah Hutton in memory of Charles B. Schmitt (London 1990), this paper deals with Schmitt's contribution to our knowledge of the evolution of the Aristotelian philosophy after the Middle Ages. In the first part the author points out similarities and differences between the views of Charles Lohr and Charles Schmitt about the reception of Aristotelianism in the Renaissance. In the second part he compares these views with others' views (Cassirer, Kristeller). Thirdly, the author analyzes the papers of the volume. (edited)

**Berthold-Bond, Daniel.** Hegel and Marx on Nature and Ecology. *J Phil Res*, 22, 145-179, Ap 97.

The essay compares Hegel and Marx (and Engels) in terms of their basic conceptions of nature, their critiques of Romantic nature-worship, their notions of how a meaningful unity with nature requires the act of socially transforming nature, their respective calls for a new science of nature and their attitudes towards technology. I argue that we can uncover a largely shared humanistic orientation toward nature and I situate this view within contemporary debates about the anthropocentric or nonanthropocentric foundation of ecological thinking. (edited)

**Berti, Enrico.** "Il tempo in Aristotele" in *Il Concetto di Tempo: Atti del XXXII Congresso Nazionale della Società Filosofica Italiana*, Casertano, Giovanni (ed), 25-36. Napoli, Loffredo, 1997.

Analysis of Aristotle's treatise on time (*Phys*. IV, 10-14), in order to show that for the Greek philosopher the time has a relational character, that it is related not only to the spatial movement, but also to the succession of the psychical states, and that it has an irreversible direction. For these reasons the Aristotelian physics has been appreciated by contemporary science (e.g., by I. Prigogine) more than the Newtonian physics. The *extatic* character of time, i.e., its power of putting things out of themselves, of destroying them, affirmed by Aristotle, gives the Aristotelian conception of time an existential meaning, which makes it similar to the Heidegger's one.

**Berti, Enrico.** "La logica dell'argomentazione filosofica tra Aristotele e Ryle" in *Momenti di Storia della Logica e di Storia della Filosofia*, Guetti, Carla (ed), 59-68. Roma, Aracne Editrice, 1996.

In his paper on *Philosophical Arguments* (1945) G. Ryle considers as the only philosophical argumentation the *reductio ad impossibile* of the "strong" type, i.e., the argumentation which deduces a contradiction from the adversary's thesis. This does not correspond to the *reductio ad impossibile* described by Aristotle in his *Analytics*, but corresponds rather to the procedures which Aristotle suggests in his *Sophistical Refutations*, in order to unmask the tricks made by the Sophists and caused by errors or ambiguities of the language. In this way the analytical philosophy of Ryle renews the dialectic of Aristotle.

**Berti, Enrico.** Les écoles philosophiques d'Athènes et les princes de Chypre. *Diotima*, 25, 15-20, 1997.

Du récit de Stobée, *Ecl*. IV,32,21, il résulte qu'Aristote avait adressé son *Protreptique* à Thémison, roi des Chypriotes, en soutenant que personne n'avait plus d'avantages que lui pour faire de la philosophie. Tandis qu'Isocrate s'adressait au princes de Chypre pour leur enseigner à gouverner, Aristote s'adresse à eux, au nom de l'Académie, pour les exhorter à faire de la philosophie. Du même texte il résulte aussi une troisième position, celle de l'école cynico-stoïcienne, pour laquelle la politique est parfaitement inutile, voir même dangereuse, à l'exercice de la philosophie.

**Berti, Enrico** and Conant, James and Vegetti, Mario. La fragilità del bene: Fortuna ed etica nella tragedia e nella filosofia greca di Martha C. Nussbaum. *Iride*, 10(20), 157-176, Ap 97.

For E. Berti the Aristotelian defended by Martha Nussbaum in her book *The Fragility of Goodness* is not conservative, because it conceives the human good as practicable in a society of "free and equal" citizens and because it proposes as method of philosophy the rational argumentation from the ways of thinking and speaking shared by the whole linguistic community (the *endoxa*). The only reserve advanced by the author to Nussbaum's thesis concerns the lack, in her book, of a clear distinction between the *endoxa* and the *phainomena*, which for Aristotle are all sort of opinions. J. Conant and M. Vegetti discuss other aspects of the book.

**Bertocci, Rosemary Juel**. A Whiteheadian Contribution to the "Mind-body" Relation. *Cont Phil*, 18(1), 20-23, Ja-F 96.

This essay demonstrates that Alfred N. Whitehead's explanation of the "mind-body" relation not only complements but also deepens the descriptions of this relation put forth by Thomas Aquinas and Karl Rahner, S.J. It shows that Whitehead agrees with Aquinas and Rahner that the mind and body are one in self-constitution, in a coordinated interrelation and interdependency, while adding a new understanding of the physical side of self-constitution, emphasizing the chronological priority of the body.

**Bertók, Rozsa** and Öffenberger, Niels. Observations on the So-Called Practical Syllogism (Spanish). *Rev Filosof (Venezuela)*, 24(2), 47-52, Jl-D 96.

On analysis of the idea of practical syllogism as it is suggested by the Aristotelian texts on ethics, a comparison is made between this kind of syllogism and strictly formulated theoretical syllogisms. The research is mainly centered on the background of imprudent action. It is stated that a practical syllogism presents the peculiarity of permitting contradictory conclusions, but that the derivability of false conclusions from true premises is only an apparent one.

**Bertolini, Luisa**. "Zum Problem der Farbe in Cassirers *Philosophie der symbolischen Formen*" in *Grenzen der kritischen Vernunft*, Schmid, Peter A, 213-223. Basel, Schwabe Verlag, 1997.

**Bertomeu, María Julia** and Vidiella, Graciela. Persona Moral y Justicia Distributiva. *Agora (Spain)*, 14(2), 81-97, 1995.

**Bertram, Christopher**. Political Justification, Theoretical Complexity, and Democratic Community. *Ethics*, 107(4), 563-583, Jl 97.

Given the division of labour and normal variations in human cognitive capacity, there is a tension between the liberal principle of legitimacy, stating that the social order should be justifiable before the tribunal of each person's reason and the complexity of much modern political philosophy. It is argued that the importance of a shared culture of justification places limits on the complexity of arguments that may be advanced in good faith in a democratic community.

**Bérubé, Michael**. Aesthetics and the Literal Imagination. *Clio*, 25(4), 439-453, Sum 96.

**Beskova, Irina Aleksandrovna**. The Nature of Transpersonal Experience. *Russian Stud Phil*, 34(1), 63-77, Sum 95.

The purpose of the work is to analyse how rational understanding of such irrational phenomena as human death, transmigration of souls, regression into deeply archaic layers of experience are possible. On the basis of sociobiology, epistemology, anthropology is shown that the aggregation of two factors—the specific nature of relic perception of the world and the possibility of passing on its basic structures to each subsequent generation through a mechanism for handing down vitally significant cultural information—enables to explain how a person can "recollect" something that happened before his birth.

**Betz, Michael** and Shepard, Jon M and O'Connell, Lenahan. The Proactive Corporation: Its Nature and Causes. *J Bus Ethics*, 16(10), 1001-1010, Jl 97.

We argue that the stakeholder perspective on corporate social responsibility is in the process of being enlarged. Due to the process of institutional isomorphism, corporations are increasingly adopting organizational features designed to promote proactivity over mere reactivity in their stakeholder relationships. We identify two sources of pressure promoting the emergence of the proactive corporation—stakeholder activism and the recognition of the social embeddedness of the economy. The final section describes four organizational design dimensions being installed by the more proactive corporations today—cooperation, participation, negotiation, and direct anticipation.

**Betzler, Monika**. Aspekte internationaler Ethik. *Phil Rundsch*, 44(1), 20-32, Mr 97.

**Beuchot, Mauricio**. "Some Traces of the Presence of Scepticism in Medieval Thought" in *Scepticism in the History of Philosophy: A Pan-American Dialogue*, Popkin, Richard H (ed), 37-43. Dordrecht, Kluwer, 1996.

**Beuchot, Mauricio**. El Fundamento de los Derechos Humanos en Bartolomé de las Casas. *Rev Port Filosof*, 52(1-4), 87-95, Ja-D 96.

**Beuchot, Mauricio**. Importancia de la filosofía novohispana para el hispanismo filosófico. *Dialogo Filosof*, 12(3), 399-408, S-D 96.

La filosofía de Nueva España, vista desde diferentes ángulos, es interesante para el hispanismo filosófico, pues es una parte suya que tiende puentes entre España y América. Hay filosofía hecha en la península que repercute en México y a la inversa. Por eso su investigación puede contribuir a una mejor comprensión de la cultura de España y de México.

**Beuchot, Mauricio**. Law and Rights in Saint Thomas (Spanish). *Rev Filosof (Venezuela)*, 24(2), 109-127, Jl-D 96.

A detailed exposition—concept, classes and fundamentals—of the *Thomistic Theory of Law (I-II, 90-92) and Rights (II-II, 57)* is offered in order to open the discussion as to whether both are identified or not—or perhaps with morality—included in this discussion of the *rights of people*.

**Bevir, Mark**. Meaning, Truth and Phenomenology. *Teorema*, 16(2), 61-76, 1997.

This essay approaches Derrida through a consideration of his writings on Saussure and Husserl. Derrida is right to insist, following Saussure, on a

relational theory on meaning: words do not have a one to one correspondence with their referents. However, he is wrong to insist on a purely differential theory of meaning: words can refer to reality within the context of a body of knowledge. Similarly, Derrida is right to reject Husserl's idea of presence: no truths are simply given to consciousness. However, he is wrong to reject the very idea of objective knowledge: we can defend a notion of objective knowledge couched in terms of a comparison of rival bodies of theories. This paper concludes by considering the implications of the preceding arguments for the enterprise of phenomenology.

**Bevir, Mark**. Mind and Method in the History of Ideas. *Hist Theor*, 36(2), 167-189, My 97.

J.G.A. Pocock and Quentin Skinner have led a recent onslaught on the alleged "myth of coherence" in the history of ideas. But their criticisms depend on mistaken views of the nature of mind: respectively, a form of social constructionism, and a focus on illocutionary intentions at the expense of beliefs. An investigation of the coherence constraints that do operate on our ascriptions of belief shows historians should adopt a presumption of coherence, concern themselves with coherence, and proceed to reconstruct sets of beliefs as coherent wholes. The history of ideas merges history with aspects of philosophy, where philosophy is understood as the study of the grammar of our concepts.

**Beyaraza, Ernest K**. "Ibn Rushd, European Enlightenment, Africa, and African Philosophy" in *Averroës and the Enlightenment*, Wahba, Mourad (ed), 133-153. Amherst, Prometheus, 1996.

**Beyle, Uwe** and Kamp, Hans. A Calculus for First Order Discourse Representation Structures. *J Log Lang Info*, 5(3-4), 297-348, O 96.

This paper presents a sound and complete proof systems for the first order fragment of Discourse Representation Theory. Since the inferences that human language users draw from the verbal input they receive for the most transcend the capacities of such a system, it can be no more than a basis on which more powerful systems, which are capable of producing those inferences, may then be built. Nevertheless, even within the general setting of first order logic the structure of the "formulas" of DRS-languages, i.e., of the Discourse Representation Structures suggest for the components of such a system inference rules that differ somewhat from those usually found in proof systems for the first order predicate calculus and which are, we believe, more in keeping with inference patterns that are actually employed in common sense reasoning. (edited)

**Bezgacheva, Julia V**. Admissible Rule for Temporal Logic LinTGrz. *Bull Sec Log*, 26(2), 60-66, Je 97.

In this article the connections between the interpolation, Halldén-completeness, Robinson and Beth properties for sentential and corresponding first-order logics are considered. In particular it will be shown that Gabbay's corollary (formulated in *Craig's interpolation theorem for modal logic, Lecture Notes in Mathematics 255*, (1972) about the interpolation property, in certain first-order and modal logics is false.

**Béziau, Jean-Yves**. Theorie législative de la négation pure. *Log Anal*, 37(147-8), 209-225, S-D 94.

Negation is studied alone, independently of other connectives. The background framework is the concept of logical law. Two groups of laws are presented; members of the latter are weaker versions of members of the former. Then we show that if we take for the structure of the language, not an absolute free algebra as usual, but a symmetric domain, the disparity between weak and strong laws disappears and intuitionistic negation collapses into classical negation.

**Béziau, Jean-Yves** and Bueno, Otávio and Da Costa, Newton C A. What is Semantics? A Brief Note on a Huge Question. *Sorites*, 43-47, N 95.

After mentioning the cogent connection between pure semantics and the particular set theoretical framework in which it is formulated, some issues regarding the conceptual status of semantics itself, as well as its relationship to logic, are concisely raised.

**Béziau, Jean-Yves** and Da Costa, Newton C A. Théorie de la valuation. *Log Anal*, 37(146), 95-117, Je 94.

On montre que les logiques vérifiant les lois d'identité et de coupure infinies (logiques normales) ont une sémantique bivalente adéquate constituée par les fonctions caractéristiques des théories closes (sémantique de l'évaluation). Si de plus ces logiques sont compactes alors on peut prendre la sémantique bivalente constituée par les fonctions caractéristiques des théories saturées (sémantique de la valuation). Cette sémantique est minimale et donc comme toute théorie maximale est saturée, la sémantique constituée par les fonctions caractéristiques des théories maximales s'avère caduque si elle se différencie de la précédente. (edited)

**Bezuidenhout, Anne**. Pragmatics and Singular Reference. *Mind Lang*, 11(2), 133-159, Je 96.

I present arguments in favour of the view that the propositions expressed by utterances containing singularly referring terms have modes of presentation of the objects referred to by those terms as constituents. I rely on recent work by Sperber and Wilson, Recanati and other pragmatists and claim that a Fregean account of singular reference is supported by this work. This is in opposition to Recanati himself, who in his book *Direct Reference* has argued for a view which is closer to that of some neo-Russellians. In particular, I argue contra Recanati for the truth-conditional *relevance* of the modes of presentation associated with demonstratives and other referential terms. That is, I argue that these modes of presentation must be seen as part of the truth-conditional content of utterance-tokens containing such terms.

Bezuidenhout, Anne 522 AUTHOR INDEX

**Bezuidenhout, Anne**. Pragmatics, Semantic Underdetermination and the Referential/Attributive Distinction. *Mind*, 106(423), 375-409, Jl 97.

It has long been recognized that there are referential uses of definite descriptions. It is not as widely recognized that there are attributive uses of indexicals and other such paradigmatically singular terms. I offer an account of the referential/attributive distinction which is intended to give a unified treatment of both sorts of cases. I argue that the best way to account for the referential/attributive distinction is to treat it as semantically underdetermined which sort of proposition is expressed in a context. In certain contexts the proposition expressed will be a descriptive one and in others it will be an object-dependent one. (edited)

**Bezuidenhout, Anne**. Resisting the Step Toward Naturalism. *Phil Phenomenol Res*, 56(4), 743-770, D 96.

Some epistemologists believe that epistemology is a branch of empirical psychology. Others, while not willing to equate epistemology with (any part of) psychology, believe nevertheless that there is an intimate connection between the two. This naturalistic attitude is bolstered by a belief in psychologism, which is defined as the view that epistemic properties of beliefs depend on properties of the psychological processes responsible for those beliefs. Several arguments meant to establish a link between psychologism and naturalism are discussed and shown wanting. Finally, an alternative framework for epistemological investigation is sketched, which endorses psychologism, but is nonnaturalist, in that it relies on the use of a priori methods.

**Bezuidenhout, Anne**. The Truth-Conditional Relevance of *De Re* Modes of Presentation: A Reply to Grimberg. *Mind Lang*, 11(4), 427-432, D 96.

Grimberg identifies four arguments which she alleges are used in my paper 'Pragmatics and Singular Reference' (Bezuidenhout, 1996a) in order to establish the truth-conditional relevance of *de re* modes of presentation. In fact, only one of these, properly understood, is an argument which I would endorse. However, I do plead guilty to having used examples with features which misleadingly suggest that I endorse these various arguments. It is an easy matter to construct examples free from these defects, which is what I attempt to do.

**Bezuidenhout, Anne L**. The Communication of *De Re* Thoughts. *Nous*, 31(2), 197-225, Je 97.

Perry argues that we need singular propositions to get at what we seek to preserve when we communicate with those in different contexts. I argue that the contents of *de re* thoughts have modes of presentation as constituents. When a speaker communicates such a thought, her mental context is necessarily different from the listener's. Following Perry it may seem that the content of the *utterance* the speaker uses to communicate her thought must be a singular proposition. I argue instead that the contents assigned to the utterance by the speaker and listener need only be appropriately similar. Moreover, communicators must be sensitive to such similarities. The worry that they are not is addressed.

**Bhabha, Homi**. Minority Maneuvers and Unsettled Negotiations. *Crit Inquiry*, 23(3), 431-459, Spr 97.

**Bhandari, D R** and Lata. Concept of Duty: A Study in Indian and Western Philosophy. *Darshana Int*, 36(1/141), 44-47, Ja 96.

The notion duty is essentially implied in every ethical theory. A duty means what we ought to perform as 'moral beings'. From Plato to Kant, Moore, Bradley etc. there have been very serious discussions regarding the concept of duty. It has individual as well as social aspect. In ancient Indian philosophical, social and ethical sphere it is said that whole universe is founded on moral law called Rita or Dharma or Duty. Human duties as laid down by the Bhagwad Gita are determined by a man's reaction to the outer World. A man is warned to persue his own Dharma or Duty. Here we find a striking similarity between these ideas of Gita and that of Plato's ideas regarding the concept of Duty.

**Bhandari, Shyam B**. Some Ethical Issues in Computation and Disclosure of Interest Rate and Cost of Credit. *J Bus Ethics*, 16(5), 531-535, Ap 97.

Although the mathematics of interest is very precise, the practice of charging computing and disclosing interest or cost of credit is full of variations and therefore, often questionable on ethical grounds. The purpose of this paper is to examine some of the prevalent practices which are incorrect, illogical, unfair or deceptive. Both utilitarian and formalist schools of ethical theory would find these practices to be inappropriate. The paper will specifically look at unfair practices in the areas of estimation of intrayear rates, use of 360 days in a year, the "rule of 78th", interest rate ('APR') advertising and computation of unpaid balance by credit card issuers to figure interest costs. The author recommends that the Truth in Lending Code of the Federal Reserve should require the disclosure of the effective APR; the use of 360 days in a year methods and the "Rule of 78ths" should be immediately discontinued. (edited)

**Bhaskar, Roy**. On the Ontological Status of Ideas. *J Theor Soc Behav*, 27(2-3), 139-147, Je-S 97.

Four recent turns (realist, processual, holistic and reflexive) in social thought are discussed and related to the four dimensional schema of dialectical realism the author has recently outlined. It is shown how ontology matters and indeed is not only necessary but inevitable, The nature of the reality of ideas (of different types) is demonstrated and the most prevalent mistakes in the metatheory of ideas and ideation analyzed. The significance of categorical realism and the character of those specific types if ideas known as 'ideologies' are then discussed. Finally some good and bad dialectical connections of ideas and related phenomena are sketched.

**Bhatt, S R**. Buddhist Critique of Relation with Special Reference to *Samavāya*. *J Indian Counc Phil Res*, 13(3), 103-110, My-Ag 96.

**Bhattacharya, A N**. The Advaita View of the Self. *Darshana Int*, 35(3/139), 73-75, Jl 95.

**Bhattacharya, Chandidas**. Linguistic Solipsism. *Indian Phil Quart*, 23(3-4), 473, Jl-O 96.

This has a reference to the article "Linguistic Solipsism: A Defense" by Md. Abdur Razzaque (*IPQ*, July, 1995). According to the author this article is an example of what confusion discrete quotation from *Philosophical Investigations* can lead to. The quotation of only the last two lines from the section 243 of P.I. can easily deceive one into thinking that Wittgenstein is in favor of a kind of solipsistic language. There cannot be anything further from the truth.

**Bhattacharya, Ramkrishna**. 'rnam krtva ghrtam pibet'—Who Said This?. *J Indian Counc Phil Res*, 14(1), 170-174, S-D 96.

**Bhattacharya, Sibajiban**. Nyaya: Realist or Idealist?. *J Indian Counc Phil Res*, 14(1), 164, S-D 96.

**Biacino, Loredana** and Gerla, Giangiacomo. Connection Structures: Grzegorczyk's and Whitehead's Definitions of Point. *Notre Dame J Form Log*, 37(3), 431-439, Sum 96.

Whitehead, in his famous book *Process and Reality*, proposed a definition of point assuming the concepts of "region" and "connection relation" as primitive. Several years after and independently Grzegorczyk, in a brief but very interesting paper, proposed another definition of point in a system in which the inclusion relation and the relation of being separated were assumed as primitive. In this paper we compare their definitions and we show that, under rather natural assumptions, they coincide.

**Bianchi, Lorenzo**. "Le relazioni tra Bayle e l'Italia: i corrispondenti italiani di Bayle e le *Nouvelles de la République des Lettres*" in *Pierre Bayle e l'Italia*, Bianchi, Lorenzo, 35-106. Napoli, Liguori Ed, 1996.

The study analyses: a) Bayle's Italian correspondents; b) the Italians books reviewed in the "Nouvelles de la République des Lettres", the literary journal directed by Bayle from Mars 1684 to February 1687. Bayle's has only three Italian correspondents, G. Arconati-Lamberti, G. Leti and A. Magliabechi, the Medici's librarian. The "Appendix" publishes the correspondence between Arconati-Lamberti and Bayle (1 letter) and between Bayle and Magliabechi (7 letters). The "NRL" reviewed few "Italian books" (books by Italian authors in Latin, in Italian or translated in other languages and books published in Italy). We found 11 "articles" reviewed among 376 and a bibliographic list of 22 new Italian books among 321. Bayle is particularly interested in historical and religious themes but he discusses only books published outside Italy.

**Bianchi, Lorenzo**. *Pierre Bayle e l'Italia*. Napoli, Liguori Ed, 1996.

Sono trascorsi molti anni da quando nel 1959 Eugenio Garin richiamava l'attenzione sulle relazioni tra Pierre Bayle e l'Italia, invitando a studiare, da un lato, gli autori italiani discussi o affrontati da Bayle e, dall'altro, a ripercorrere le repliche e le polemiche suscitate dal pensiero bayliano in Italia. Questo volume—che raccoglie gli atti di un seminario di studio tenutosi a Napoli nell'aprile 1993—ritorna sulla questione, tuttora aperta, dei rapporti tra il *filosofo di Rotterdam* e la nostra penisola. Si riaffronta così il tema, ormai classico e centrale, dei nessi tra Bayle e Vico, ma si ricostruisce nel contempo la presenza di Bayle in momenti e ambienti diversi della cultura filosofica del Settecento italiano, considerando inoltre la presenza di opere e di testi italiani in una rivista di respiro europeo quale le *Nouvelles de la République des Lettres*. (publisher, edited)

**Bianchi, Lorenzo**. *Rinascimento e Libertinismo: Studi su Gabriel Naudé*. Naples, Bibliopolis, 1996.

Il volume riconsidera la figura di G. Naudé (1600-1653) mettendo in evidenza il suo rapporto privilegiato—rispetto ad altri autori del "libertinage érudit"—con la cultura italiana del Rinascimento e sottolineando la singolare attività di mediazione che egli compie tra tradizione rinascimentale italiana e primo Illuminismo francese. Medico e filosofo, bibliotecario e editore di testi—di Rorario come di Nifo, Cardano o Campanella—Naudé opera da vero e proprio organizzatore culturale ma elabora anche un'autonoma filosofia "libertina" di stampo eclettico-naturalistico, dove lo scetticismo di origine francese (Montaigne e Charron) si unisce ad Aristotele e alla filosofia italiana della natura. (publisher, edited)

**Bianchi, Massimo Luigi**. "Conoscere immediato e conoscere discorsivo in Herbert of Cherbury e in alcuni autori della Scuola di Cambridge" in *Mind Senior to the World*, Baldi, Marialuisa, 11-33. Milano, FrancoAngeli, 1996.

**Bianco, Franco**. "Avalutatività come principio metodico nella logica delle scienze sociali" in *Momenti di Storia della Logica e di Storia della Filosofia*, Guetti, Carla (ed), 147-163. Roma, Aracne Editrice, 1996.

**Bica, Camillo C**. Collateral Violence and the Doctrine of Double Effect. *Pub Affairs Quart*, 11(1), 87-92, Ja 97.

In this essay, I argue, from a rights-based perspective, that in situations I term "collateral violence," i.e., instances in which an innocent bystander will be killed as a secondary, unintended, though foreseen effect of an act of self-preservation, one must, under pain of moral condemnation and sanctions, opt for a defensive response other than deadly force even if the alternative is riskier or less effective. Consequently, the Doctrine of Double Effect neither justifies collateral violence nor absolves the agent of moral responsibility for his act.

**Bica, Camillo C**. Establishing Liability in War. *Pub Affairs Quart*, 11(3), 217-227, Jl 97.

While it is never in doubt that there are innocents in war, the guidelines established for identifying these individuals are vague. In this essay, I will argue that only those who *actively and directly* engage in the conflict may be categorized as combatants and only unjustifiable combatants, i.e., those combatants who wage a war of aggression, are liable to be targeted, injured and killed. All others, whether they are members of the aggressor nation's military, political elite, munitions workers, etc., are noncombatants, and in compliance with the *jus in bello* criterion of discrimination, must be afforded immunity during war.

**Bicchieri, Cristina** and Antonelli, Gian Aldo. Game-Theoretic Axioms for Local Rationality and Bounded Knowledge. *J Log Lang Info*, 4(2), 145-167, 1995.

We present an axiomatic approach for a class of finite, extensive form games of perfect information that makes use of notions like "rationality at a node" and "knowledge at a node." We distinguish between the game theorist's and the players' own "theory of the game." The latter is a theory that is sufficient for each player to infer a certain sequence of moves, whereas the former is intended as a justification of such a sequence of moves. While in general the game theorist's theory of the game is not and need not be axiomatized, the players' theory must be an axiomatic one, since we model players as analogous to automatic theorem provers that play the game by inferring (or computing) a sequence of moves. We provide the player with an axiomatic theory sufficient to infer a solution for the game (in our case, the backwards induction equilibrium), and prove its consistency. We then inquire what happens when the theory of the game is augmented with information that a move outside the inferred solution has occurred. (edited)

**Bicchieri, Cristina** and Schulte, Oliver. Common Reasoning about Admissibility. *Erkenntnis*, 45(2 & 3), 299-325, Nov 96.

We analyze common reasoning about admissibility in the strategic and extensive form of a game. We define a notion of sequential proper admissibility in the extensive form and show that, in finite extensive games with perfect recall, the strategies that are consistent with common reasoning about sequential proper admissibility in the extensive form are exactly those that are consistent with common reasoning about admissibility in the strategic form representation of the game. Thus in such games the solution given by common reasoning about admissibility does not depend on how the strategic situation is represented. We further explore the links between iterated admissibility and backward and forward induction.

**Bickford, Susan**. *The Dissonance of Democracy: Listening, Conflict, and Citizenship*. Ithaca, Cornell Univ Pr, 1996.

Bickford's analysis draws on the work of Aristotle and of Hannah Arendt to establish the conflictual and contentious character of politics. To analyze the social forces that deflect attention from particular voices, Bickford mobilizes contemporary feminist theory, including Gloria Anzaldúa's work on the connection between identity and politics. She develops a conception of citizen interaction characterized by adversarial communication in a context of inequality. Such a conception posits public identity—and hence public listening—as active and creative, and grounded in particular social and political contexts. (publisher,edited)

**Bickmann, Claudia**. Zwischen Sein und Setzen: Fichtes Kritik am dreifachen Absoluten der kantischen Philosophie. *Fichte-Studien*, 9, 144-161, 1997.

The article elaborates the differences between Kant's and Fichte's attempt to find a secure ground for their philosophical systems. First, we follow the development of Fichte's grounding principles from the "absolute I" (1794) to his later versions of his system (1801; 1804; 1806) within the horizon of the Platonic-neo-Platonic philosophy. Second, in order to judge the validity of Fichte's critique of the "incoherence" of the Kantian system (1804) we confront Kant's transcendental (regressive analytical) method with the synthetic progressive approach of the generative (deductive) method of Fichte's "Doctrine of Science." Third, we rehabilitate the Kantian approach with regard to his "Ethikotheology."

**Bielawka, Maria**. Two Faces of Consciousness in Roman Ingarden's Philosophy (in Polish). *Kwartalnik Filozof*, 23(1), 129-136, 1995.

Consciousness is understood by Ingarden as the "stream," the "flow" of various conscious experiences (first of all of cognitive acts, acts of pure thinking, of will, of imagination etc.). But the role of consciousness is presented in two opposing manners. In his ontological investigations, Ingarden considers consciousness as a very important but only heteronomous, theoretically separated core of psyche. The whole psyche seems to be a fundamental part of man, it is the reality within which we can actualize our deepest nature. This solution implies the acceptance of a psychological idea of consciousness. On the other hand, in Ingarden's epistemological works there occurs a radically antipsychological concept of consciousness. Consciousness turns out to be individual, immediately experienced, unquestionable entity. Human body, psyche and other transcendent objects manifest themselves in this central, essential sphere of man—they are not real things but objects for consciousness, now recognized as constituted by it.

**Bielefeldt, Heiner**. Autonomy and Republicanism: Immanuel Kant's Philosophy of Freedom. *Polit Theory*, 25(4), 524-558, Ag 97.

Dealing with Kant's practical philosophy can enhance the awareness of the genuinely ethical and political aims of modern liberalism. The idea of moral autonomy does not indicate a loss of ethical substance in modern society, as conservative and communitarian critics Kantian liberalism have alleged. On the contrary: by clarifying philosophically the autonomy of the moral agent of Kant point to the transcendental source of all moral and ethical claims: the unalienable dignity of every human being. Respect for human dignity finds its political and legal expression in an order of rights in which free and equal citizens cooperate politically on the basis of mutual recognition.

**Bieling, Hans-Jürgen** and Deppe, Frank. Gramscianismus in der Internationalen Politischen Ökonomie. *Das Argument*, 217(5-6), 729-740, 1996.

Since the early eighties, several authors have tried to use Gramsci's political theory, especially the concept of hegemony, to analyze the current upheavals of global capitalism. For them, the alliance of transnational capital and liberal economic politics is based on changed structures of accumulation, not least on neoliberalism's ability to organize social potentials for consensus. But it is unclear whether neoliberal hegemony is the expression of a new transnational "historic bloc" or whether its character is to be understood, less comprehensively, as a political project.

**Biemel, Walter**. Finks politisches Vermächtnis Fortrag Freiburg Dez. 95. *Perspekt Phil*, 22, 77-104, 1996.

**Bier, Melinda C** and Sherblom, Stephen A and Gallo, Michael A. Ethical Issues in a Study of Internet Use: Uncertainty, Responsibility, and the Spirit of Research Relationships. *Ethics Behavior*, 6(2), 141-151, 1996.

In this article we explore ethical issues arising in a study of home Internet use by low-income families. We consider questions of our responsibility as educational researchers and discuss the ethical implications of some unanticipated consequences of our study. We illustrate ways in which the principles of research ethics for use of human subjects can be ambiguous and possibly inadequate for anticipating potential harm in educational research. In this exploratory research of personal communication technologies, participants experienced changes that were personal and relational. These unanticipated changes in their way of being complicated our research relationships, testing the boundaries of our commitment to the principle of trustworthiness and forcing us to re-evaluate our responsibilities.

**Biesta, Gert**. "Education, Not Initiation" in *Philosophy of Education (1996)*, Margonis, Frank (ed), 90-98. Urbana, Phil Education Soc, 1997.

Is education meant to initiate the child into a common world? Does social interaction require a common ground and is it the task of education to bring about this common ground? In this article it is argued that this is not the case. The main argument—which draws upon Dewey and Mead with respect to education and upon Arendt and Derrida with respect to human interaction—is that *difference* and not *identity* is central to the pedagogical continuation of culture and to human interaction more generally. As an alternative to education as initiation a *performative* conception of education is developed.

**Bigelow, John**. God and the New Math. *Phil Stud*, 84(2-3), 127-154, D 96.

The message I take from twentieth century mathematics is this. There are bigger and bigger things, each encompassing things smaller than itself: but no matter how big these get, there is always something beyond. There is no one big thing of which everything that exists is a part. What is at stake is a last-ditch, pantheistic refuge of Monotheism. When all other gods have fallen away, you cannot console yourself with the certainty that at least there exists the world as a whole and it is both unique and supremely worship-worthy.

**Bigelow, John** and Pargetter, Robert. The Validation of Induction. *Austl J Phil*, 75(1), 62-76, Mr 97.

**Bignotto, Newton**. A Má Fama na Filosofia Política: James Harrington e Maquiavel. *Discurso*, 24, 173-191, 1994.

Neste artigo procuramos analisar o sentido da idéia de "má fama" na filosofia política, através do estudo da recepçao da obra de Maquiavel no século XVII, particularmente nos trabalhos de James Harrington.

**Bignotto, Newton**. As Transformaçoes da Tirania. *Kriterion*, 34(87), 56-69, Ja-Jl 93.

Considering the recent events in East Europe, we try to demonstrate how the study of classical political philosophy, Plato and Aristotle, can help us to think about the transformations of the extreme regimes.

**Bijker, Wiebe E**. Politisering van de technologische cultuur. *Kennis Methode*, 20(3), 294-307, 1996.

**Billings, Paul R** (& others) and Alper, Joseph S and Geller, Lisa N. Individual, Family, and Societal Dimensions of Genetic Discrimination: A Case Study Analysis. *Sci Eng Ethics*, 2(1), 71-88, J 96.

As the development and use of genetic tests have increased, so have concerns regarding the uses of genetic information. Genetic discrimination, the differential treatment of individuals based on real or perceived differences in their genomes, is a recently described form of discrimination. The range and significance of experiences associated with this form of discrimination are not yet well-known and are investigated in this study. Individuals at-risk to develop a genetic condition and parents of children with specific genetic conditions were surveyed by questionnaire for reports of genetic discrimination. A total of 27,790 questionnaires were sent out by mail. Of 917 responses received, 206 were followed up with telephone interviews. The responses were analyzed regarding circumstances of the alleged discrimination, the institutions involved, issues relating to the redress of grievances and strategies to avoid discrimination. (edited)

**Billmann-Mahecha, Elfriede** and Gebhard, Ulrich and Nevers, Patricia. Patterns of Reasoning Exhibited by Children and Adolescents in Response to Moral Dilemmas Involving Plants, Animals and Ecosystems. *J Moral Educ*, 26(2), 169-186, Je 97.

Traditional moral philosophy, developmental psychology and moral education have generally been concerned with relationships between human beings. However, moral philosophy has gradually expanded to include plants, animals and ecosystems as legitimate moral objects and aesthetics has rediscovered nature as an object of consideration. Thus it seems appropriate to begin to include this sphere in moral education and corresponding research as well. In this paper we wish to report on an investigation we have begun using children's philosophy as a hermeneutic tool to assess the morally relevant values and attitudes that children and adolescents hold with respect to nature and the patterns of reasoning with which they are expressed. In the first part of our presentation we will outline current positions in environmental ethics and aesthetics which provide a theoretical framework for such an investigation and the problems they present. Subsequently, the difficulties involved with applying contemporary theories of moral development to the problem at hand will be discussed. Finally, we will describe the project we have begun and summarize preliminary results derived from different age groups.

**Bilodeau, Douglas J**. Physics, Machines, and the Hard Problem. *J Consciousness Stud*, 3(5-6), 386-401, 1996.

The 'hard problem' of the origin of phenomenal consciousness in a physical universe is aggravated by a simplistic and uncritical concept of the physical realm which still predominates in much discussion of the subject. David Chalmers is correct in claiming that phenomenal experience is logically independent of a physical description of the world, but his proposal for a 'natural supervenience' of experience on a physical substrate is misguided. His statements about machine consciousness and the role of information are especially compromised. A careful analysis of physical concepts indicates that the hard problem as originally proposed is insoluble but also fortunately based on misconceptions. Modern physics suggests a more sophisticates and richer ontology which will be essential for a deeper understanding of our rapidly growing knowledge of psychology and neuroscience.

**Binkley, Robert W**. Argumentation, Education and Reasoning. *Inform Log*, 17(2), 127-143, Spr 95.

To find the place of argumentation (argumentation theory) in education one must sort out its relationship to logic. The key point is that the two stand in different relations to reasoning. Logic is the normative study of reasoning and provides the standards for correct reasoning. Argumentation studies the activity of arguing and is related to reasoning only in that arguing involves the attempt to get an audience to reason in a certain way; correctness is not essential. (edited)

**Binkley, Timothy**. The Vitality of Digital Creation. *J Aes Art Crit*, 55(2), 107-116, Spring 97.

Since numbers and pictures are diametric opposites, digital images are at first glance improbable players in the drama of culture. An image is a visible *percept* concretely embodied in a physical object. A number is an invisible *concept* abstractly designated by formal symbols. Despite this apparent contrariety, computers have rapidly infiltrated everyday communications where they routinely ingest, digest and regurgitate vast amounts of digital imagery, along with many other types of information including text, sound and numerical data. For better and for worse, the changes being wrought by our increasing involvement with computers promise to be far-reaching. We are not creating simply a revolution in art, but are overhauling the foundations of culture. (edited)

**Birault, Henri**. Nihilism and Beatitude. *Epoche*, 1(1), 65-76, 1993.

**Bird, Alexander**. The Logic in Logicism. *Dialogue (Canada)*, 36(2), 341-360, Spr 97.

Le logicisme de Frege engage à deux thèses: 1) les vérités de l'arithmétique sont *ipso facto* vérités de logique; 2) les nombres naturels sont des objets. Dans cet article je pose la question: quelle conception de la logique est-elle requise pour étayer ces thèses? Je soutiens qu'il existe une conception appropriée et naturelle de la logique, en vertu de laquelle le principe de Hume est une vérité logique. Le principe de Hume, qui dit que le nombre de *F*s est le nombre de *G*s ssi les concepts *F* et *G* sont équinumériques, est la pièce maîtresse de l'argumentation néologiciste en faveur de 1) et 2). Je défends cette position contre deux objections: a) le principe de Hume ne peut pas à la fois être d'ordre logique, comme le requiert 1), et avoir la portée ontologique requise par 2); et b) l'usage logiciste du principe de Hume à l'appui de 2) se ramène à une preuve ontologique d'un genre plus large, qui est non valide.

**Bird, Colin**. Mutual Respect and Neutral Justification. *Ethics*, 107(1), 62-96, O 96.

**Bird, Graham H**. "Moral Philosophy and the Development of Morality" in *The Cambridge Companion to William James,* Putnam, Ruth Anna (ed), 260-281. New York, Cambridge Univ Pr, 1997.

The paper explores William James's account of morality in his "The Moral Philosopher and the Moral Life." There James either qualifies or rejects utilitarianism, and scepticism in moral philosophy. He concedes a residual subjectivity in moral judgment but it is not one which casts doubt on moral properties themselves. Rather he seeks, through a conceptual experiment, to provide a metaphysical account of the nature of moral properties which accommodates a degree of subjectivity and of realism and naturalism. The conceptual experiment progressively introduces moral features into an imagined possible world in order to demonstrate their provenance. James's discussion of the experiment is considered and contrasted with recent accounts, due to Bennett and Johnston, of certain properties, including moral properties, as mind- or response-dependent. The concluding claim is that James's discussion of the material bases for moral properties both needs and complements some formal account.

**Bird, Stephanie J**. Assessing Conflict of Interest: Sources of Bias. *Sci Eng Ethics*, 2(4), 386-388, O 96.

**Bird, Stephanie J**. Commentary on "Good to the Last Drop? Millikan Stories as 'Canned' Pedagogy. *Sci Eng Ethics*, 1(3), 215-216, Jl 95.

**Bird, Stephanie J** and Housman, David E. Conducting and Reporting Research. *Prof Ethics*, 4(3-4), 127-154, Spr-Sum 95.

**Bird, Stephanie J** and Housman, David E. Trust and the Collection, Selection, Analysis and Interpretation of Data: A Scientist's View. *Sci Eng Ethics*, 1(4), 371-382, O 95.

Trust is a critical component of research: trust in the work of coworkers and colleagues within the scientific community; trust in the work of research scientists by the nonresearch community. A wide range of factors, including internally and externally generated pressures and practical and personal limitations, affect the research process. The extent to which these factors are understood and appreciated influence the development of trust in scientific research findings.

**Bird, Stephanie J** and Swazey, Judith P. Teaching and Learning Research Ethics. *Prof Ethics*, 4(3-4), 155-178, Spr-Sum 95.

**Birdwhistell, Anne D**. Social Reality and Lu Jiuyuan (1139-1193). *Phil East West*, 47(1), 47-65, Ja 97.

A theoretical reconstruction of Lu Jiuyuan's view of the nature of human beings and their world is offered. Rejecting the widespread effort to distinguish among such concepts as *xing* ("human nature"), *xin* ("heartmind"), and *li* ("pattern"), Lu regarded all such concepts as ultimately having the same referent, namely the inherent capability of humans and all things to produce and maintain order and, consequently, existence. Most often using the terms *li* and *xin*, Lu regarded *li* as the patterns of all activities, events, and things of human society and the world. Real in the sense of belonging to actual human experience, these patterns enabled the world to exist to the fullest. *Li* or these patterns were opposed to disorder (*luan*), and thus *li* is called a concept of the "social real."

**Birkhahn, Talya**. A Purple Sky: The Challenged Chance for Change. *Thinking*, 13(1), 37-41, 1997.

This article deals with the relationship between feminism and 'Philosophy for Children' (Lipman). The writer shares her experience of growing up as a woman in Israel and analyzing reality there. There is an effort to move from reality to vision using feminism to shed light on *philosophy for children*. Within the article there is an interplay between philosophy and poetry, logic and feeling.

**Birmingham, Peg**. "Hannah Arendt: The Activity of the Spectator" in *Sites of Vision,* Levin, David Michael (ed), 379-396. Cambridge, MIT Pr, 1997.

**Birns, Nicholas**. Medieval Historiography. *Clio*, 26(2), 229-242, Wint 97.

**Biro, John**. "Dretske on Phenomenal Externalism" in *Perception,* Villanueva, Enrique (ed), 171-178. Atascadero, Ridgeview, 1996.

**Biro, John**. "Testimony and *A Priori* Knowledge" in *Contents,* Villanueva, Enrique (ed), 301-310. Atascadero, Ridgeview, 1995.

**Birt, Robert**. "Existence, Identity, and Liberation" in *Existence in Black: An Anthology of Black Existential Philosophy,* Gordon, Lewis R (ed), 205-213. New York, Routledge, 1997.

Philosophically inspired by Sartre and Fanon, this essay is an existential analysis of the problems of human identity under conditions of social oppression. It argues that struggles for human liberation are struggles for a liberated identity. It focuses on the situation of black peoples and emphasizes the importance of striving for a creative identity free of rigid racial essentialisms and self-depreciation. As freedom is the being of human reality, and we have no predetermined nature, we humans can create autonomous identities. Amidst oppression and alienation, this creation is an act of resistance. Our "spiritual striving" is for a human identity.

**Biscuso, Massimiliano**. *Tra Esperienza e Ragione: Hegel e il problema dell'inizio della storia della filosofia.* Milano, Guerini, 1997.

Il problema dell'inizio della storia della filosofia è un *topos* classico della storiografia filosofica: ne va della concezione stessa della filosofia, della sua partizione storica, della sua unità e continuità, del rapporto tra filosofia e cultura, tra filosofia e società. Per Hegel—come in questo volume viene attentamente documentato, anche alla luce della pubblicazione dei manoscritti e degli appunti delle lezioni berlinesi—, il rapporto con l'inizio della filosofia implica, in primo luogo, il problema dell'origine del pensiero concettuale dal pensiero sensibile e rappresentativo. Da questo "osservatorio privilegiato" Massimiliano Biscuso analizza altre questioni essenziali per la comprensione del pensiero hegeliano, sia interne al suo sistema—quali il rapporto tra filosofia della storia e storia della filosofia, fra spirito finito (soggettivo e oggettivo) e spirito assoluto—sia più universali, come la relazione fra pretesa di verità della filosofia e sua condizionatezza storica. E in quest'ultimo punto, più che nella interpretazione della filosofia greca arcaica (pur difficilmente eguagliabile) che risiede l'attualità di Hegel, quella *miniera di suggerimenti* che tanti stimoli può ancora dare alla ricerca filosofica contemporanea. (publisher)

**Bishop, Nicole**. Trust Is Not Enough: Classroom Self-Disclosure and the Loss of Private Lives. *J Phil Educ*, 30(3), 429-439, N 96.

The paper presents and critiques some important philosophical and educational arguments that are used to support the practice of personal self-disclosure in the classroom, both in group settings and in the form of autobiographical journals. It argues that there are important reasons for valuing privacy even when self-disclosures occur in an environment of perfect trust and caring; that to understand the importance of privacy primarily in terms of trust, or the absence of trust, is to risk overlooking the less apparent, yet more subtle, threats which 'sympathy' and 'caring' can pose to self-disclosures.

**Bjelic, Dusan I**. Lebenswelt Structures of Galilean Physics: The Case of Galileo's Pendulum. *Human Stud*, 19(4), 409-432, O 96.

The aim of this paper is to give a self-reflective account of the building of Galileo's pendulum in order to discover what were the practical contingencies of building and using the pendulum for demonstrating the law of isochronism. In doing this, the unique Lebenswelt structures of "Galilean physics" are explicated through the ethnomethodological concepts developed by Harold Garfinkel. The presupposition is that the practical logic of "Galilean physics" is embedded in the instruments themselves. In building the pendulum and recovering its original use, "Galilean physics" becomes for ethnomethodologists a first-hand practical discovery. This is not a reconstruction of the mind of the historical Galileo but, rather, an explication of Galileo's practical perspective on the instrument as an intersubjective and

AUTHOR INDEX 525 Blanco Echauri, Jesús

interchangeable standpoint available for ethnomethodological analysis. This enables us to study historical facts from the standpoint of the practical logic of the original practice with a pedagogical eye for the instructive reproducibility of science.

**Blachowicz, James**. Analog Representation Beyond Mental Imagery. *J Phil*, 94(2), 55-84, F 97.

Stephen Kosslyn has recently declared the debate on mental imagery to be over, and with it, the debate on the difference between analog and digital forms of mental representation. The object of this paper is to divide these two debates by criticizing the "sense" interpretation of the analog (on which Kosslyn and others have relied) and defending the "model" interpretation, which would permit nonpropositional (analog) mental states to exist in abstract thought (in abstract analogies, for example) without any contribution from sensory (spatial) imagery.

**Blachowicz, James**. Reciprocal Justification in Science and Moral Theory. *Synthese*, 110(3), 447-468, Mr 97.

In this paper, I analyze the particular conception of reciprocal justification proposed by Nelson Goodman and incorporated by John Rawls into what he called "reflective equilibrium." I propose a way of avoiding the twin dangers which threaten to push this idea to either of two extremes: the reliance on epistemically privileged observation reports (or moral judgments in Rawls's version), which tends to disrupt the balance struck between the two sides of the equilibrium and to re-establish foundationalism; and the denial of any privileged status to such reports (or judgments), which makes the equilibrium into a theoretical monolith.

**Black, David W**. *Vico and Moral Perception*. New York, Lang, 1997.

*Vico and Moral Perception* maintains that Vico's *New Science* offers an idiosyncratic theory of ethics that rejects the modernist notion of "principle" but which at the same time promotes a "historical absolutism" that postmodern thought denies. Vico's account of civic metaphor not only responds effectively to questions of moral agency but provides a unique cultural and rhetorical framework for studying the *contexts of attention*, the entry points of conscience, that anchor moral perception. In this respect, Vico not only provides a metaphysic of culture but offers singular instruction in the art of wise living. (publisher)

**Black, Oliver**. Infinite Regress Arguments and Infinite Regresses. *Acta Analytica*, 95-124, 1996.

This paper explains what an infinite regress argument is. Part 1 contains some examples of infinite regress arguments. Part 2 presents a schema for all such arguments and defines an infinite regress argument as one that approximates to the schema. Part 3 tests the schema on the examples. Part 4 contrasts my account of infinite regress arguments with that given by Passmore and shows that Passmore's theory succumbs to objections. Part 5 distinguishes an infinite regress argument from an infinite regress and defines an infinite regress. Part 6 explains the dyslogistic force of "infinite regress".

**Black, Percy**. Challenge to Natural Law: The Vital Law. *Vera Lex*, 14(1-2), 48-50, 1994.

"Natural law" refers to universal moral principles (such as justice, freedom, benevolence) derived from a common source: the unvarying concerns and feelings shared by human beings across cultures and experience. The principles are themselves subject to modification and expansion as thinkers, using primarily practical reason as a guide, seek refined insight into the evolving human condition. These principles provide the independent basis for appraising whether laws of governments fit the laws of the human condition. Despite the compelling acceptability of the principles, they face resistance by many thinkers, in part because the descriptor "natural" in "natural law" does not discriminate between the dastardly and the benevolent in human actions. This article proposes a shift to "vital law" as a less obstructive term because it unambiguously reflects the life-enhancing properties of the principles.

**Black, Sam**. Science and Moral Skepticism in Hobbes. *Can J Phil*, 27(2), 173-207, Je 97.

**Black, Susan** and Burke, Ronald J. Save the Males: Backlash in Organizations. *J Bus Ethics*, 16(9), 933-942, Je 97.

This paper reviews the literature on male backlash in organizations, proposing a research agenda. It defines backlash, examines its causes and manifestations, who is likely to exhibit it and offers suggestions for addressing backlash. Backlash may be on the increase in organizations and society at large. Current efforts to weaken or remove the legislative support for employment equity initiatives are one sign of this.

**Blackburn, Patrick** and Seligman, Jerry. Hybrid Languages. *J Log Lang Info*, 4(3), 251-272, 1995.

Hybrid languages have both modal and first-order characteristics: a Kripke semantics and explicit variable binding apparatus. This paper motivates the development of hybrid languages, sketches their history and examines the expressive power of three hybrid binders. We show that all three binders give rise to languages strictly weaker than the corresponding first-order language, that full first-order expressivity can be gained by adding the universal modality and that all three binders can force the existence of infinite models and have undecidable satisfiability problems.

**Blackburn, Simon**. I Rather Think I Am A Darwinian. *Philosophy*, 71(278), 605-616, O 96.

This paper answers an attack on Darwin's theory of natural selection published in *Philosophy* in 1994. I argue that Stove failed to separate key doctrines of evolutionary biology from crude misinterpretations that are often found. As a result his critique fails to touch the core doctrines.

**Blagrove, Mark**. Problems with the Cognitive Psychological Modeling of Dreaming. *J Mind Behav*, 17(2), 99-134, Spr 96.

It is frequently assumed that dreaming can be likened to such waking cognitive activities as imagination, analogical reasoning and creativity and that these models can then be used to explain instances of problem solving during dreams. This paper emphasizes instead the lack of reflexivity and intentionality within dreams, which undermines their characterization as analogs of the waking world and opposes claims that dreams can complement and aid waking world problem solving. The importance of reflexivity in imagination, in analogical reasoning and in creativity means that dreaming, being usually single-minded, cannot be subsumed into these categories. Freud's hypothesis that dreams result from the translation of latent thoughts into manifest content is taken to support this idea of cognitive deficiency during dreaming. Dream content, however, can still represent and reflect the dreamer's waking concerns.

**Blair, Elena Duvergès**. Women: The Unrecognized Teachers of the Platonic Socrates. *Ancient Phil*, 16(2), 333-351, Fall 96.

Plato's works show particular women relating to Socrates. An examination of each case reveals a pattern: their contributions are pedagogical, mystical or prophetical, and Socrates accepts them unconditionally. This remarkable consistency is traced to Plato's dramatic needs portraying Socrates. While the Platonic Socrates never learns from men, he frequently learns from women. Plato may be documenting Socrates' influence on the discussion about women, and his recognition of their intellectual capacity. By showing him receptive to women's prophetic and mystical pronouncements Plato portrays Socrates' mystical traits. The finding provides a glimpse into the creative process of Plato's mind.

**Blair, J Anthony**. Argument Management, Informal Logic and Critical Thinking. *Inquiry (USA)*, 15(4), 80-93, Sum 96.

The paper aims to locate argument management, informal logic and critical thinking in relation to each other. "Argument management" is the term introduced to denote the practical activity of interpretation, reconstruction, evaluation and construction of arguments and argumentation, in light of all the pertinent theories (linguistic, rhetorical, semantic, pragmatic, logical). Conceptions of informal logic and critical thinking are introduced and defended, according to which informal logic is one aspect of the theory and practice of argument management and argument management is one of the components of critical thinking.

**Blair, R J R**. Affect and the Moral-Conventional Distinction. *J Moral Educ*, 26(2), 187-196, Je 97.

The effect of inducing negative positive or neutral affect on the recall of moral and conventional transgressions and positive moral and conventional acts was examined. It was found that inducing negative affect was associated with higher recall of moral transgressions while inducing positive affect was associated with higher recall of positive moral acts. Affect induction condition did not have a significant effect on the recall of the conventional transgressions or positive acts. The results are interpreted within the *violence inhibition mechanism* model of moral development (Blair, 1995) and by reference to a new, hypothesized system, the *smiling reward response*.

**Blake, Michael**. International Criminal Adjudication and the Right to Punish. *Pub Affairs Quart*, 11(2), 203-215, Ap 97.

Political philosophy has generally been more concerned with the question of how to justify the practice of punishment than with the related question of who may legitimately inflict such punishment. In this paper, I attempt to answer the latter question by developing a theory of the conditions under which an agent may legitimately inflict legal punishment. An agent, I argue, may only inflict legal punishment if that punishment is part of a package designed to protect potential victims from the occurrence of harm. Since the UN response in the former Yugoslavia did not rise to an appropriate level of such protection, I argue, the UN does not have the right to inflict legal punishment and the international criminal tribunal it has set up is, therefore, a morally illegitimate institution.

**Blanc, Mafalda de Faria**. A Divina Natureza Segundo Escoto Eriúgena. *Rev Port Filosof*, 52(1-4), 97-109, Ja-D 96.

**Blanck, Jens**. Domain Representability of Metric Spaces. *Annals Pure Applied Log*, 83(3), 225-247, F 97.

We show that metric spaces and continuous functions between them are domain representable using the category of Scott-Ershov domains. A notion of effectivity for metric spaces is thereby inherited from effective domain theory. It is shown that a separable metric space with an effective metric can be represented by an effective domain. For a class of spaces, including the Euclidean spaces, the usual notions of effectivity are obtained. The Banach fixed point theorem is a consequence of the least fixed point theorem for domains. A notion of semieffective domains is introduced and used to give a new proof of Ceitin's theorem.

**Blanco Echauri, Jesús**. Leo Strauss: lenguaje, tradición e historia (Reflexiones metodológicas sobre el arte de escribir). *Agora (Spain)*, 15(1), 89-108, 1996.

This work is not a revision of the Straussian contribution to the history of political philosophy. It aims to explore the general principles of methodological character that inspire and explain his work in historiography. Unlike other contemporary historians who have successfully carried out their job and thought about their methodological basis at the same time, Strauss lacks texts about the rules of research upon which rests his vast historical-philosophical production. There exists, however, an important exception, *Persecution and Art of Writing*, in which he states the possibility that some authors in the past had adapted their technique of writing to the demands of persecution, presenting their opinions on all the crucial matters of the moment to be read only between the lines. The consideration of this thesis, which would explain the birth of a particular kind of literature, if it were confirmed, would allow its author not only to undertake the search of texts unfairly forgotten but also to return the meaning of some great works, which could be then interpreted from new parameters of reading. The examination of the theoretical relevance of this hermeneutic proposal, both prolific and problematic, constitutes the main purpose of these pages.

**Blanco Salgueiro, Antonio**. "Significado y denotación en J.A. Fodor" in *Verdad: lógica, representación y mundo*, Villegas Forero, L, 275-288. Santiago de Compostela, Univ Santiago Comp, 1996.

In this work I'll try to defend that, despite the fact that Fodor claims in his last writings that the only pertinent semantic notion is *denotation*, this doesn't fit well with his actual practice, where he handles various semantic notions with differentiated explanatory roles. Moreover, we'll see that the last Fodor's two main projects, that of naturalizing semantics and that of providing an adequate semantic notion for psychological explanation, run the risk of going in quite different directions: the most important semantic notion for a psychosemantic project is not the one naturalized by Fodor.

**Blanco Salgueiro, Antonio**. The Meaning of "Mental Meaning" (in Spanish). *Agora (Spain)*, 15(2), 165-172, 1996.

**Blankenship, J David**. Commentary on Charles M. Young's "The Doctrine of the Mean". *Topoi*, 15(1), 101-106, Mr 96.

I accept much of Young's excellent interpretation, but propose some qualifications or additions: that 'location' (virtue as a mean state) is 'causally' dependent upon 'intermediacy' (its hitting the intermediate in emotion and action); that there may be a sense in which location is independent of intermediacy; that intermediacy is about particular passions and actions as well as patterns of them, depending upon the senses in which passions and actions are 'appropriate'; that 'contrariety' is a truth about reality as well as appearance. I disagree with the attribution of contrariety to Plato and claim he anticipated the doctrine of the mean.

**Blasco, Josep L**. Método analítico y transcendentalidad. *Rev Filosof (Spain)*, 9(16), 41-56, 1996.

The aim of the paper is to oppose epistemological descriptivism to normativism: Descriptivism can be logico-syntactic or naturalistic. Normativism is transcendental. The attitude of analytical philosophy towards the task of epistemology, both in the logical and in the conceptual analysis: the failure in analysing the epistemological status of the "verificationist" norm as well as the norm of "the meaning is the use". Quine's naturalistic project does not solve the problem either: the holistic thesis is not naturalized, it is not part of any scientific corpus. Epistemological normativity requires appealing to a 'transcendental' notion which belongs to the activity of the regulative reason.

**Blasius, Ronald F**. Alfred North Whitehead's Informal Philosophy of Education. *Stud Phil Educ*, 16(3), 303-315, Jl 97.

The objective of this article is to show that Whitehead had a very important philosophy of education both on the formal and informal level. The consistency found is well worth noting. I researched many of Whitehead's major works for his formal views and Lucian Price's *Dialogues of Alfred North Whitehead*. In my opinion Price's book is the best available for the purpose of getting Whitehead's candid informal view of education. Whitehead's philosophy of education is sweeping in scope. In his philosophy we find the importance of experience, imagination, speculation, generalization, factual knowledge, specialization, relevance, intuition, novelty, curiosity, theory, practice, pleasure, harmony, freedom, discipline, technical and liberal education and unification. He, in fact, unifies all these seemingly different areas into a coherent philosophy of education. (edited)

**Blass, Rachel B**. On the Possibility of Self-Transcendence: Philosophical Counseling, Zen, and the Psychological Perspective. *J Chin Phil*, 23(3), 277-297, S 96.

This paper distinguishes between two conceptions of philosophical counseling. The one focuses on the clarification of the individuals psychological and philosophical self and the other on the transcendence of that self. A comparison of the latter conception with the self-transcendence that takes place through Zen Buddhism contributes to the examination of the question of whether philosophical counseling can indeed overcome potential psychological obstacles to attaining a transcendent aim. Possible influences of the integration of psychological intervention into the philosophical search for transcendence are also discussed.

**Blass, Rachel B**. The 'Person' in Philosophical Counselling vs. Psychotherapy and the Possibility of Interchange between the Fields. *J Applied Phil*, 13(3), 279-296, 1996.

This paper suggests that a basic distinction between philosophical counselling and psychotherapy is to be found in the conception of 'the person' that is inherent in each of the fields. Understanding this distinction allows not only for a more profound recognition of what is unique to philosophical counselling but also for a better view of possibilities of interchange between the fields.

**Blaszczyk, Piotr**. Ingarden on Time: Part I (in Polish). *Kwartalnik Filozof*, 24(3), 33-61, 1996.

**Blaszczyk, Piotr**. Ingarden on Time: Part II (in Polish). *Kwartalnik Filozof*, 24(4), 125-151, 1996.

**Blau, Jong** and Blau, Ulrich. Epistemische Paradoxien, Teil 2. *Dialectica*, 50(3), 167-182, 1996.

Vagheit (Kontinuität) und Selbstreferenz (Reflexivität) sind die offensichtlichen Ursachen aller logico-philosophischen Paradoxien. Beide Ursachen sind nur ein Stück weit formal zugänglich und führen uns über das Rätsel der mentalen Repräsentation/Partizipation/Produktion zuletzt zur unbegreiflichen Subjekt/Objekt-Trennung. Die epistemischen Paradoxien vom *Henker*-Typ sind ein Labyrinth von Vagheit und Selbstreferenz. In Teil I analysierten wir eine zeitlose Variante von Hollis (1984), in Teil II betrachten wir zwei klassische *Henker*-Varianten.

**Blau, Ulrich** and Blau, Jong. Epistemische Paradoxien, Teil 2. *Dialectica*, 50(3), 167-182, 1996.

Vagheit (Kontinuität) und Selbstreferenz (Reflexivität) sind die offensichtlichen Ursachen aller logico-philosophischen Paradoxien. Beide Ursachen sind nur ein Stück weit formal zugänglich und führen uns über das Rätsel der mentalen Repräsentation/Partizipation/Produktion zuletzt zur unbegreiflichen Subjekt/Objekt-Trennung. Die epistemischen Paradoxien vom *Henker*-Typ sind ein Labyrinth von Vagheit und Selbstreferenz. In Teil I analysieren wir eine zeitlose Variante von Hollis (1984), in Teil II betrachten wir zwei klassische *Henker*-Varianten.

**Bliese, John R E**. Traditionalist Conservatism and Environmental Ethics. *Environ Ethics*, 19(2), 135-151, Sum 97.

Environmentalism is usually thought to be a liberal political position, but the two primary schools of thought within the conservative intellectual movement support environmentalism as well. The free market perspective has received considerable attention for its potential contributions to environmental protection, but the traditionalist perspective has not. In this essay, I consider several important principles of traditionalist conservatism. The traditionalists are not materialists and are highly critical of our consumer culture. They reject ideology and stress piety toward nature, the intergenerational character of society and prudence in political and social action. These basic principles are a solid foundation for environmentalism.

**Bliton, Mark J** and Finder, Stuart G. The Eclipse of the Individual in Policy (Where is the Place for Justice?). *Cambridge Quart Healthcare Ethics*, 5(4), 519-532, Fall 96.

**Blits, Jan H**. The Insufficiency of Virtue: Macbeth and the Natural Order. Lanham, Rowman & Littlefield, 1996.

The first ever scene-by-scene philosophical study of any Shakespeare play, this book demonstrates why Shakespeare's poetic writings still arouse and sustain serious inquiry and reflection. Using a combination of philosophical rigor, political insight, and textual thoroughness, Jan H. Blits delineates the competing forms of virtue with *Macbeth*—the courageous public virtue of warriors like Macbeth and the internal Christian virtue evoked by Duncan. He describes the trust that leading characters in the play place in the power of virtue to rule the world and he explores the fundamental tension within the natural order between virtue and life. This new interpretation of *Macbeth* explains crucial paradoxes overlooked by previous scholars and it will serve as a model for future scholarship in the field. (publisher)

**Blits, Jan H**. Tocqueville on Democratic Education: The Problem of Public Passivity. *Educ Theor*, 47(1), 15-30, Wint 97.

This article examines the necessity for and the proper content of democratic education, according to Tocqueville's *Democracy in America*. It explores Tocqueville's analysis of the twin dangers of democratic self-tyranny—the drift to bureaucratic self-tyranny on the one hand and the pressure of intellectual self-tyranny on the other—and discusses the solution that Tocqueville finds in democratic participation as democratic education.

**Block, Ned**. "Mental Paint and Mental Latex" in *Perception*, Villanueva, Enrique (ed), 19-49. Atascadero, Ridgeview, 1996.

This article argues for the view that the representational content of an experiential state does not exhaust its experiential character. (edited)

**Block, Ned**. "Ruritania Revisited" in *Contents*, Villanueva, Enrique (ed), 171-187. Atascadero, Ridgeview, 1995.

This paper argues for the view that any *substantial* in difference in beliefs paradigmatically expressed with the word W, whether between two people or between one person at two times, requires a difference in the meaning or content of W.

**Blodgett, Mark S** and Carlson, Patricia J. Corporate Ethics Codes: A Practical Application of Liability Prevention. *J Bus Ethics*, 16(12-13), 1363-1369, S 97.

With the great increase in litigation, insurance costs and consumer prices, both managers and businesses should take a proactive position in avoiding liability. Legal liability may attach when a duty has been breached; many actions falling into this category are also considered unethical. Since much of business liability is caused by a breach of a duty by a business to either an individual, another business, or to society, this article asserts that the practice of liability prevention is a practical business application of ethics. (edited)

**Blokhuis, P**. Bij de Grenzen van Verplegingswetenschap. *Phil Reform*, 61(2), 160-174, 1996.

**Blondel, Jean**. "Political Progress: Reality or Illusion?" in *The Idea of Progress*, McLaughlin, Peter (ed), 77-101. Hawthorne, de Gruyter, 1997.

**Bloom, Irene**. Human Nature and Biological Nature in Mencius. *Phil East West*, 47(1), 21-32, Ja 97.

*Ren-xing* can be aptly translated as "human nature," representing as it does the Mencian conviction of and sympathy for a common humanity. The enterprise of comparative philosophy is furthered by drawing attention to the large and important conceptual sphere within which Mencius was working, to his concern for the most fundamental realities of human life, and to his translatability across time and cultures.

**Bloom, Irene** (ed) and Fogel, Joshua A (ed). *Meeting of Minds: Intellectual and Religious Interaction in East Asian Traditions of Thought*. New York, Columbia Univ Pr, 1997.

In *Meeting of Minds*, eleven prominent scholars explore intellectual and religious interactions among diverse traditions of the East Asian world. The authors consider central issues including concepts of religious authority, perceptions of the relation between knowledge and action, the sense of "the sacred" within the realm of ordinary human existence, and the concern with historical experience and practicality as criteria for evaluating ideas and beliefs. (publisher,edited)

**Bloom, Joyce**. Humane Education: A Paradigm for Ethical Problem Solving in Education. *Between Species*, 11(3-4), 144-146, Sum-Fall 95.

What is right? What is wrong? In modern education it is often impossible to achieve single answers to this very difficult question, particularly in the current climate of increasing societal metamorphosis. The purpose of this article is to propose humane education as a paradigm for ethical problem solving in education, the body of knowledge about kindness to animals, from both curriculum and administrative perspective. The paradigm is four-dimensional and may be conceptualized as follows: 1) Problem to be solved, 2) Critical factors which affect the problem and its solution(s), 3) Ethical System—Humane Education, and 4) Time.

**Bloom, Thomas Alan**. Kenneth Macgowan and the Aesthetic Paradigm for the New Stagecraft in America. New York, Lang, 1996.

The American theatrical critic Kenneth Macgowan fashioned an aesthetic defense for a new visual style of scenic design that began to appear on the American stage during the second decade of the twentieth century. Macgowan's defense for this new visual style, which he labeled the "new stagecraft," was modelled after the British art critic Clive Bell's aesthetic theory of "significant form" in art. Bell's formal theory of art, which favored formal abstraction over visual representation, provided Macgowan with an attractive premise upon which he could formulate his own theory of the simplified or abstracted new stagecraft style. Shaping his theory of the new stagecraft from an aesthetic theory devised for the static two-dimensioned space of the painting, Macgowan sought to apply the visual aesthetic of significant form to the four-dimensioned theatrical process. The contradictions caused by the application of Bell's theory to the dynamics of scenic design reanimated the dispute between the pre-eminence of form or content, picture or word in the theater. (publisher)

**Bloomfield, Paul**. Of Goodness and Healthiness: A Viable Moral Ontology. Phil Stud, 87(3), 309-332, S 97.

A moral ontology is introduced that ascribes the same ontological status to moral goodness as is commonly ascribed to physical healthiness; this is strictly analogous to the claim that colors and sounds are ascribed the same ontic status (as secondary qualities). The strategy employed is as follows: Crispin Wright's test for realism (wide cosmological role, cognitive command and the Euthyphro contrast) as discussed in his Truth and Objectivity, are surveyed. It is shown how healthiness passes these tests. It is then shown how goodness can pass these tests, if its ontology is understood as suggested.

**Bloor, David**. "The Question of Linguistic Idealism Revisited" in The Cambridge Companion to Wittgenstein, Sluga, Hans (ed), 354-382. Needham Heights, Cambridge, 1996.

Anscombe said the later work of Wittgenstein contained a strong element of what she called "linguistic idealism". This doctrine says that some realities are created through our references to them, e.g., a coin is only a coin, as distinct from a metal disc, because its users think of it as a coin. The present article supports and illustrates Anscombe's claim in connection with Wittgenstein's basic metaphor of language as a species of "game" and his idea that rule-following is an institution. Anscombe's category of linguistic idealism is reidentified in terms of Wittgenstein's emphasis on the social.

**Bloor, David**. The Conservative Constructivist. Hist Human Sci, 10(1), 123-125, F 97.

This brief appreciation of the work of the late Thomas Kuhn is designed to bring out the respects in which he deserves to be known as a social constructivist—but a form of constructivist who diverges from many of the stereotypes that accompany the (usually critical and dismissive) uses of this label.

**Blount, Douglas K**. Euthanasia, Capital Punishment and Mistakes-Are-Fatal Arguments. Pub Affairs Quart, 10(4), 279-290, O 96.

Consider arguments against liberal euthanasia laws grounded on the fact that mistakes made in euthanasia programs are likely to result in the deaths of innocent persons. Such arguments present difficulties for supporters of capital punishment who find them compelling. For, of course, parallel arguments are available to opponents of capital punishment. And, if such arguments count against euthanasia, it's difficult to see why they don't count against capital punishment. I argue that such arguments do count against euthanasia but not capital punishment. In so doing, I argue that there's an important evidentiary difference between euthanasia candidates and capital punishment candidates.

**Blum, Alex**. A Purported Theorem of Epistemic Logic. Teorema, 16(1), 105-106, 1996.

George Schlesinger contends that he found a genuine epistemic principle. I show that this is not so.

**Blum, Alex**. Belief in the Tractatus. Grazer Phil Stud, 51, 259-260, 1996.

An attempt is made to explain how Wittgenstein meets two challenges posed by belief, the apparent need of: (I) a composite soul; and (II) nontruth functional mode of composition.

**Blum, Alex**. Elementary Logic and Modal Logic. Iyyun, 46, 47-49, Ja 97.

I argue that treating predicate letters as schemata renders modal quantification theory incoherent.

**Blum, Alex**. The Agony of Pain. Phil Inq, 18(3-4), 117-120, Sum-Fall 96.

Pain, it is argued, is emotion at a place.

**Blume, Francine**. Peace Zones: Exemplars and Potential. Acorn, 8(1), 5-13, Spr-Sum 93.

**Blume, Stuart**. Waarom het beoordelen van technologieën voor gehandicapten problematisch is. Kennis Methode, 20(4), 362-376, 1996.

**Blumenkrantz, Mikhail**. From Nimrod to the Grand Inquisitor: The Problem of the Demonisation of Freedom in the Work of Dostoevskij. Stud East Euro Thought, 48(2-4), 231-254, S 96.

The article is an abridged version of a chapter in the book Introduction into Philosophy of Substitution, Moscow, "Vest-Vimo", 1994. The path of spiritual substitutions which appear in the process of secularization of culture, is

researched on the basis of broad historical material. The author analyzes the mechanism of such substitutions and their effect on mass consciousness. The aim of the work is to research certain aspects of crisis in the contemporary culture. The basis of these aspects is formed by a number of fatal spiritual reductions. In this context the article talks about the phenomenon of the demonization of freedom as one of the manifestations of such crisis, which in particular reveals itself in the problem of the contemporary terrorism. The spiritual roots of this occurrence are found as a result of the analysis of the inner life of a character in Dostoevsky's novel Demons, Nikolay Stavrogin. Freedom turned with its reverse, demoniacal side, is a key to the solution of this character's mystery. As a result of the research the author comes to the conclusion that freedom, taken as the Absolute, inevitably destroys any form in which its primary aim is self-realization. In the end the path of the demonization of freedom leads to the suicide of freedom.

**Blumenthal, H J**. Aristotle and Neoplatonism in Late Antiquity: Interpretations of the De Anima. Ithaca, Cornell Univ Pr, 1996.

This book focuses on the commentators' exposition of Aristotle's treatise De anima (On the Soul), because it is relatively well documented and because the concept of the soul was so important in all neo-Platonic systems. Blumenthal explains how the neo-Platonizing of Aristotle's thought, as well as the widespread use of the commentator's works, influenced the understanding of Aristotle in both the Islamic and Judeo-Christian traditions. (publisher,edited)

**Blustein, Jeffrey**. Character-Principlism and the Particularity Objection. Metaphilosophy, 28(1-2), 135-155, Ja-Ap 97.

This paper is a response to particularist critics of the normative force of moral principles. The particularist critique, as I understand it, is a rejection not only of principle-based accounts of moral deliberation and justification, but also of accounts of character in which principles play a central role. I focus on the latter challenge and counter it with a view I call character-principlism. (edited)

**Blustein, Jeffrey**. Procreation and Parental Responsibility. J Soc Phil, 28(2), 79-86, Fall 97.

**Blyth, Dougal**. "What in Plato's Crito is Benefited by Justice and Harmed by Injustice?" in Dialogues with Plato, Benitez, Eugenio (ed), 1-19. Edmonton, Academic, 1996.

I argue that between the Socratic protreptic in the first half of the Crito and the speech of the Laws there is a conceptual discontinuity regarding the nature of agreements, justice, the soul, and human goods. This is explained by the replacement of a philosophical conception of these terms with a political one, required because Crito twice reneges on his agreement that justice excludes ill-treating enemies even in return, showing he is capable only of popular morality. Despite his philosophical incompetence he is led by Socrates' philosophical rhetoric to recognize in Law a stable moral authority beyond unenlightened self-interest.

**Boada, Ignasi**. "El concepto schellingiano del Yo absoluto y los inicios del Idealismo alemán" in El inicio del Idealismo alemán, Market, Oswaldo, 307-313. Madrid, Ed Complutense, 1996.

Para el Schelling de 1795 el carácter infinito de la identidad o interioridad del ser y el pensamiento se expresa como incondicionalidad. El problema que queda abierto con ello, y que va a dinamizar la filosofía de la generación del joven Schelling, es el de la relación entre el ser y el aparecer, así como el de la relación entre el pensamiento y la palabra.

**Bobro, Marc** and Clatterbaugh, Kenneth. Unpacking the Monad: Leibniz's Theory of Causality. Monist, 79(3), 408-425, Jl 96.

Apart from God, what causes the change in the perceptions of monads? The literature contains three interpretations that have been advanced to explain this change: the conceptual unfolding view locates the source of change in the monad's individual concept; the efficacious perception view says that the cause of each perception is to be found in previous perceptions; and, the monadic agency view claims that perceptual changes are caused by the monad's primitive active force. This paper defends the third account, for only it adequately grounds Leibniz's distinctions between reasons and causes, natural and miraculous perceptions, and real and apparent causality.

**Boburg, Felipe**. Heidegger y el problema de la técnica. Rev Filosof (Mexico), 29(87), 373-389, S-D 96.

**Bocardo Crespo, Enrique**. El recurso a la providencia (Un comentario a Vico: A Study of the New Science de Leon Pompa). Cuad Vico, 5/6, 293-312, 1995/96.

The paper deals with Vico's theory of providence. In the first section the difficulties involved with the transcendental interpretation is purported in connection with the main thesis contained in New Science. The second part is entirely devoted to present a consistent account of Professor Pompa's view of Vico's theory, and finally some objections to the immanent interpretation are put forward tentatively to understand the notion of transcendental providence as a second order explanation.

**Bochenski, Józef Maria**. Lecture Delivered During the Ceremony of Granting the Title of Doctor Honoris Causa of the Jagiellonian University (in Polish). Kwartalnik Filozof, 23(1), 15-21, 1995.

**Bochenski, Józef Maria**. The Cracow Circle (in Polish). Kwartalnik Filozof, 23(1), 23-31, 1995.

**Bockover, Mary I**. "Ethics, Relativism, and the Self" in Culture and Self, Allen, Douglas (ed), 43-61. Boulder, Westview Pr, 1997.

**Bodnár, István M**. Alexander of Aphrodisias on Celestial Motions. Phronesis, 42(2), 190-205, 1997.

**Boeder, Heribert** and Brainard, Marcus (ed & trans). Seditions: Heidegger and the Limit of Modernity. Albany, SUNY Pr, 1997.

This is the first book-length work by Heribert Boeder to appear in English. The essays brought together here, several of which are to be found only in this volume, bear witness to a new perspective on metaphysics, modernity and so-called postmodernity. The "seditiousness" of Boeder's undertaking lies in his twofold intention: to explicate what has been thought in metaphysics, modernity and postmodernity as self-contained, rational *totalities*—as history, world and speech, respectively—and by means of those explications to recover dwelling as it has been made visible in the "configurations of wisdom" (for example, in Homer, Paul and Hölderlin). He approaches each of these totalities by way of Heidegger's thought, which marks the limit of modernity and as such is pivotal to Boeder's enterprise. (publisher, edited)

**Boeder, Heriberto**. El límite de la modernidad y el "Legado" de Heidegger. *Rev Filosof (Mexico)*, 29(87), 454-487, S-D 96.

**Boele van Hensbroek, Pieter**. "On Culturalism" in *Philosophy and Democracy in Intercultural Perspective,* Kimmerle, Heinz (ed), 85-93. Amsterdam, Rodopi, 1997.

It is popular today, to conceptualize global differences in terms of 'cultures'. A discourse, however, can be the vehicle of a racist ideology, as is shown in extreme right-wing European politics. This paper claims to identify an analytical instrument to demarcate three types of discourse on culture: firstly, one that can act as a race-discourse; secondly, one that hypostatizes culture within suggesting racist conclusions, and thirdly, a dynamic and open discourse on culture. The demarcating criterion is a combination of 1) an essentialist conception of cultures, and 2) the idea the people 'belong' in a culture.

**Boella, Laura** and Moneti, Maria and Schmidt, Burghart. Discutono *Il principio speranza*, di Ernst Bloch. *Iride*, 8(15), 466-482, Ag 95.

Il ritardo della traduzione italiana del capolavora di E. Bloch, pubblicato in Germania alla fine degli anni cinquanta, probabilmente "offre oggi i vantaggi della maturazione tardiva o persino dell'inattualità permanente che tutti i grandi testi filosofici posseggono" (R. Bodei, *Introduzione*). I tre interventi che seguono rilevano e discutono aspetti essenziali del libro. L. Boella instaura un parallelo tra i "fantasmi" di Derrida e l'utopia di Bloch al fine di rilevare la stringente attualità della questione del presente in entrambi i pensatori; M. Moneti si sofferma su alcune nozioni centrali del *Principio speranza* sottolineandone una "certa debolezza teorica"; B. Schmidt, Presidente della *Ernst Bloch-Gesellschaft* a Ludwigshafen, approfondisce il nesso rintracciabile in Bloch tra ontologia e teoria critica della società.

**Boër, Steven E**. "Propositional Attitudes and Compositional Semantics" in *AI, Connectionism and Philosophical Psychology, 1995,* Tomberlin, James E (ed), 341-380. Atascadero, Ridgeview, 1995.

In recent years a number of philosophers have argued that the presence of propositional attitude constructions in natural languages makes it impossible to provide correct compositional truth theories for them. This paper aims to refute these truth-theoretic skeptics by constructing an artificial language analogous to English in the allegedly problematic respects and showing how, along broadly Fregean lines, this language may be provided with a sense-reference semantics that issues in the desired truth theory. This semantics is then shown to resolve standard puzzles about attitude ascriptions and to be immune to the objections raised by Stephen Schiffer against "sense" theories.

**Boersema, David B**. Mass Extinctions and the Teaching of Philosophy of Science. *Teach Phil*, 19(3), 263-274, S 96.

In this paper I discuss the teaching of philosophy of science in the context of a three-pronged approach: 1) science as doctrine (or content), 2) science as process (or method) and 3) science as social institution (or values). I suggest that this approach is more informative and fruitful for students than traditional approaches to the teaching of philosophy of science, which often focuses on a series of philosophical topics (e.g., confirmation, explanation, realism). In addition, I argue for the fecundity of using a particular case study, viz., the ongoing debates about mass extinction of life on the earth.

**Boettke, Peter J**. Where Did Economics Go Wrong? Modern Economics As a Flight from Reality. *Crit Rev*, 11(1), 11-64, Wint 97.

F.A. Hayek's realistic economic theory has been replaced by the formalistic use of equilibrium models that bear little resemblance to reality. These models are as serviceable to the right as to the left: they allow the economist either to condemn capitalism for failing to measure up to the model of perfect competition, or to praise capitalism as a utopia of perfect knowledge and rational expectations. Hayek, by contrast, used equilibrium to show that while capitalism is not perfect, it contains error-correcting institutions that bring it closer to perfection than is intuitively apparent.

**Boeve, Lieven**. The Way, the Truth and the Life: Religious Tradition and Truth in the Postmodern Context... (in Dutch). *Bijdragen*, 58(2), 164-188, 1997.

In our postmodern times, the question 'where is truth' and surely 'truth with regard to religion' (wherein truth and salvation are implicated with each other) appears to be answered especially with the reply 'in particular traditions'. The combination 'truth, particular tradition and salvation', however, still leaves a number of avenues open. (edited)

**Bogdan, Radu J**. *Interpreting Minds: The Evolution of a Practice*. Cambridge, MIT Pr, 1997.

Bogdan sets out to establish a new evolutionary and practical view of interpretation. According to Bogdan, the ability to interpret others' mental states has evolved under communal, political and epistemic pressures to enable us to cope with the impact of other organisms on our own goals in the competition to survive. Interpretation evolved among primates by natural and then cultural selection. As an adaptation, it is a competence in the form of a battery of practical skills that serve the interpreter's interests in social interactions. (publisher, edited)

**Bogdanovski, Masan**. Kripke's Critique of the Mind-Body Identity Theory (in Serbo-Croatian). *Theoria (Yugoslavia)*, 39(1), 23-36, Mr 96.

It is argued in this article that Kripke's criticism of the mind-body identity theory, although bearing indisputable strength against type identity theories, offers no adequate grounds for refuting the token identity. Functionalist responses are carefully examined and elucidated in the light of Nagel's distinction between the perceptive and sympathetic imagination. Moreover, the first-person and third-person perspective distinction significantly clears up some interesting aspects of this dispute.

**Boghossian, Paul Artin**. Analyticity Reconsidered. *Nous*, 30(3), 360-391, S 96.

I distinguish between an epistemic notion of analyticity (knowledge alone of truth as derived from knowledge of meaning) and a metaphysical notion (truth as derived from meaning alone). And I argue that the analytic explanation of the possibility of a priori knowledge depends only on the epistemic notion, a notion that I defend, in contrast with its metaphysical counterpart.

**Boghossian, Paul Artin**. What the Externalist Can Know A Priori. *Proc Aris Soc*, 97, 161-175, 1997.

This paper argues that Twin Earth-motivated externalist conceptions of mental content are incompatible with traditional accounts of first-person privileged access to contents on the grounds that the combination yields absurd results—for example, that we could know that water exists a priori.

**Bogue, Ronald**. Deleuze's Style. *Man World*, 29(3), 251-268, Jl 96.

How might one describe the style of the French philosopher Gilles Deleuze, or rather, the "Deleuze effect" that plays through his work? Deleuze's style is dry, like a cracker without butter. His pages are like leaking eggs, closed in on themselves yet running in all directions. His books are tripartite, like Spinoza's *Ethics*, rivers of definitions, volcanic chains of fiery aphorisms, aerial lightning flashes of intuition. Deleuze stutters in his own language and makes thought stutter, in paradox, in differential repetition, and in the precepts and affects at the limit of the ineffable *Outside*.

**Bohm, David**. *Unfolding Meaning: A Weekend of Dialogue with David Bohm*. New York, Routledge, 1995.

David Bohm was one of the greatest physicists and foremost thinkers of the twentieth century. He argues that our fragmented, mechanistic notion of order permeates not only modern science and technology today, but also has profound implications for our general attitude to life. Another mode of thinking could bring about a different, more harmonious, reality with implications for individuals, groups and even nations. (publisher, edited)

**Bohm, David**. *Wholeness and the Implicate Order*. New York, Routledge, 1995.

In his classic work, *Wholeness and the Implicate Order*, David Bohm develops a theory of quantum physics which treats the totality of existence, including matter and consciousness, as an unbroken whole. David Bohm presents a rational and scientific theory which explains cosmology and the nature of reality; written clearly and without the use of technical jargon, it is essential reading for those interested in physics, philosophy, psychology and the connection between consciousness and matter. (publisher)

**Bohm, David** and Nichol, Lee (ed). *On Dialogue*. New York, Routledge, 1996.

The question of how we communicate is at the heart of *On Dialogue*. This revised and expanded edition is the most comprehensive documentation to date of best-selling author David Bohm's dialogical world view. While the exercise of dialogue is as old as civilization itself, in recent times a profusion of practices, techniques and definitions has arisen around the term 'dialogue'. None of these approaches can claim to be the correct view, but it is possible to distinguish between them and to clarify the intention of each. To this end, the current edition of *On Dialogue* illuminates the underlying meaning, purpose and uniqueness of David Bohm's work in this field. (publisher)

**Bohman, James**. Do Practices Explain Anything? Turner's Critique of the Theory of Social Practices. *Hist Theor*, 36(1), 93-107, 1997.

Almost all social theories are dependent on the guiding idea of "social practices" or on related concepts such as "rules," "implicit knowledge," and the like. If the concept of practices is epistemologically incoherent and empirically vacuous, then little of value remains of disciplines such as cultural anthropology and interpretive history. This essay defends the explanatory import of social practices from Stephen Turner's powerful critical challenge. While Turner's arguments are successful against certain Durkheimian and Heideggerian excesses, an epistemologically responsible theory of practices escapes his criticisms and solves the "transmission problem." In particular, pragmatist accounts of social norms based on shared practical knowledge (such as those offered by Brandom and Habermas) show how practices really do explain.

**Bohman, James** and May, Larry. Sexuality, Masculinity, and Confession. *Hypatia*, 12(1), 138-154, Wint 97.

The practice of confessing one's sexual sins has historically provided boys and men with mixed messages. Engaging in coercive sex is publicly condemned; yet it is treated as not significantly different from other transgressions that can be easily forgiven. We compare Catholic confessional practices to these of psychoanalytically oriented male writers on masculinity. We argue that the latter is no more justifiable than the former and propose a progressive confessional mode for discussing male sexuality.

**Bohnet, Iris** and Frey, Bruno S. "Moral oder Eigennutz? Eine experimentelle Analyse" in *Ökonomie und Moral: Beiträge zur Theorie ökonomischer Rationalität,* Lohmann, Karl Reinhard (ed), 135-155. München, Oldenbourg, 1997.

**Boi, Luciano**. Les géométries non euclidiennes, le problème philosophique de l'espace et la conception transcendantale; Helmholtz et Kant, les néo-kantiens, Einstein, Poincaré et Mach. *Kantstudien*, 87(3), 257-289, 1996.

**Boik, Robert J** and Bandyopadhyay, Prasanta S and Basu, Prasun. The Curve Fitting Problem: A Bayesian Approach. *Proc Phil Sci Ass*, 3(Suppl), S264-S272, 1996.

AUTHOR INDEX 529 Bondeli, Martin

**Boisjoly, Roger M**. Commentary on "Technology and Civil Disobedience: Why Engineers Have a Special Duty to Obey the Law". *Sci Eng Ethics*, 1(2), 169-171, A 95.

The purpose of the commentary is to expose the serious differences between actions by engineers desired in theory by nonengineers versus what is actually required by practicing engineers in promoting the design of safe products. All engineers, whether licensed or not, have the primary duty to protect the Health, Safety and Welfare of public consumers of products, independent of any law and/or any product design specifications considered by the engineer to be deficient for its intended use, even if directed by the employing organization to use such substandard specifications.

**Boisvert, Yves** and Giroux, Guy and Mineau, André. De l'usage social de l'éthique. *Philosopher*, 19, 9-22, 1996.

Lorsqu'un tel phénomène se produit, il est la résultante de l'usage social que l'on fait de l'éthique à l'intérieur de ces appareils. Il repose sur l'introduction de *codes de conduite* dont l'ultime finalité en est une de contrôle social. Il s'ensuit que la demande d'éthique que nous connaissons aujourd'hui est susceptible de provoquer un effet pervers important. "Ce serait le cas dès lors qu'elle serait interprétée comme un appel en faveur d'un contrôle à exercer sur la société et sur les individus qui la composent, plutôt que de représenter un contrôle de la société par elle-même, d'abord au niveau des individus, puis au niveau de leurs unités d'appartenance, communautaires ou organisationnelles". (edited)

**Boitte, P** and Cadore, B and Lamau, M L. From "The Ethical Treatment of Patients in a Persistent Vegetative State" To a Philosophical Reflection on Contemporary Medicine. *Theor Med*, 18(3), 237-262, S 97.

The reflections put forward in this text concern the clinical and practical difficulties posed by the existence of patients in PVS and the essential ethical issues raised, combining these ethical questions with practical and theoretical experience. Section 1 presents the methodology of the ethical reflection as we see it. Section 2 describes the clinical condition of patients in PVS. Section 3 develops the ethical difficulties relative to PVS from the French point of view. Section 4 illustrates the relevance of debating the ethical significance of such problematic situations, whilst defending a practical position based on a philosophical conviction. Section 5 points out the limits of ethical reflection in a biomedical context, and calls for reflection closer to the source of the problems described. (edited)

**Boladeras, Margarita**. *Comunicación, Ética Y Política: Habermas Y Sus Críticos*. Madrid, Tecnos, 1996.

Jürgen Habermas destaca de manera muy especial en el panorama de la filosofía y la sociología de nuestro siglo, e incluso sus críticos reconocen la magnitud de su obra. En su *Teoría de la acción comunicativa* ha llevado a cabo un análisis y diagnóstico de nuestro tiempo a partir de una concepción basada en la intersubjetividad dialógica; en sus libros posteriores ha desarrollado una ética discursiva y una filosofía del Derecho. El presente trabajo quiere facilitar el acceso a su extensa y compleja producción filosófica. para ello ofrece, en primer lugar, una aproximación a su biografía intelectual y a su talante filosófico; en segundo, una explicación de las cuestiones fundamentales de la *Teoría de la acción comunicativa* y de sus libros más recientes; seguidamente, exposición de las críticas que le han hecho Wellmer, Apel, Tugendhat, Giddens, Hans Albert, Rorty, etc.; y, por último, la posición crítica de la autora. (publisher, edited)

**Boladeras Cucurella, Margarita**. *Karl R. Popper (1902-1994)*. Madrid, Ed Orto, 1997.

**Boland, L** and Falkenberg, L E. Eliminating the Barriers to Employment Equity in the Canadian Workplace. *J Bus Ethics*, 16(9), 963-975, Je 97.

Have employment equity programs achieved the goal of equity for women in the workplace? We argue that they have not because gender stereotypes still persist. In fact, they may have created resentment and antagonism towards successful women and employment equity initiatives. Arguments are developed for the Canadian government to create a self-regulating system, in which the government plays a role of educator as opposed to monitor.

**Bolduc, Sébastien**. La liberté paradoxale. *Philosopher*, 18, 75-83, 1995.

This work tries to explain Jean Jacques Rousseau's thought when he says "obeing to laws is being free". The analysis of his documents help to understand his definition of freedom for humans who live in society. This text also tries to demonstrate that the Rousseau's theory is not applicable in our modern societies because it is utopian, it is difficult to put into effect and it can be totalitarian. Lastly, the Emmanuel Kant's thought gives some alternatives to compensate the lacks of Rousseau's theory.

**Boler, Megan**. Disciplined Emotions: Philosophies of Educated Feelings. *Educ Theor*, 47(2), 203-227, Spr 97.

**Boler, Megan** (ed) and Margonis, Frank (ed) and Callan, Eamonn (ed). *Philosophy of Education (1996)*. Urbana, Phil Education Soc, 1997.

**Boling, Patricia**. *Privacy: And the Politics of Intimate Life*. Ithaca, Cornell Univ Pr, 1996.

Evenly divided between theoretical and issue-oriented discussion, this book makes clear the practical stakes in both the distinction and the connection between private and public. Boling considers how to translate private experience into public claims with regard to such contentious issues as shared parenting, abortion funding, fetal abuse, sodomy laws, and parental consent for minors seeking abortions. She also analyzes the application of privacy in landmark legal cases including *Roe v. Wade*, *Bowers v. Hardwick*, and *Planned Parenthood v. Casey*. (publisher,edited)

**Boling, Patricia**. *The Self After Postmodernity*. New Haven, Yale Univ Pr, 1997.

Sketching a new portrait of the human self in this thought-provoking book, leading American philosopher Calvin O. Schrag challenges bleak deconstructionist and postmodernist views of the self as something ceaselessly changing, without origin or purpose. Discussing the self in new vocabulary, he depicts an action-oriented self defined by the ways in which it communicates. In his discussion, Schrag responds critically to both modernists and postmodernists, avoiding what he calls the modernists' overdetermination of unity and identity and the postmodernists' self-enervating pluralism. (publisher, edited)

**Bolognesi, Mário Fernando**. The Cultural Commodity (in Portuguese). *Trans/Form/Acao*, 19, 75-86, 1996.

Adorno and Horkheimer adopted the notion of the fetishism of commodities for the analysis of art and culture. Material, physical goods are not identical to symbolic ones. In spite of being a predominant cultural industry it cannot be taken as the prototype of all analyses of culture. One cannot reduce all cultural productives of the period of market economy to market products. The plurality of artistic and cultural practices present in countries like Brazil, does make questionable the indiscriminate use of the Frankfurtian framework.

**Bolotin, David**. Aristotle's Discussion of Time: an Overview. *Ancient Phil*, 17(2), 47-62, Spr 97.

**Bolotin, David** (ed) and Strauss, Leo and Bruell, Christopher (& other eds). An Untitled Lecture on Plato's *Euthyphron*. *Interpretation*, 24(1), 3-23, Fall 96.

**Bolton, Andrew**. Moral Development: Whose Ethics in the Teaching of Religious Education?. *J Moral Educ*, 26(2), 197-210, Je 97.

Will British education in general and religious education specifically, foster a nationalistic or global ethic in the coming millennium? Since the 1988 Education Reform Act, the British state has centralised its control over what is taught through the national curriculum. The Chief Executive of the government's School Curriculum and Assessment Authority has been consistently articulating the importance of national consciousness and identity. These developments suggest a worrying trend towards a more nationalistic ethic. Religious education, by contrast, is now mandatory multi-faith, part of the basic school curriculum and remains locally controlled. While the historic and present importance of Christianity in the United Kingdom is acknowledged, it is a secularised nonconformity rather than establishment Christianity that is used by the author to develop a child-centred, nonauthoritarian and communitarian model for fostering moral development through the teaching of multi-faith religious education in state schools.

**Bolton, Martha Brandt**. The Nominalist Argument of the *New Essays*. *Leibniz Soc Rev*, 6, 1-24, D 96.

*New Essays* argues all entities that are uniform, homogeneous, or exactly alike are abstractions that nature precludes; therefore, there are no atoms, vacuum, space, time, *tabula rasa*, inactive faculties, other mainstays of Locke's ontology. These are Platonist abstractions indispensable to science and the reasons for things in God's understanding. They are not Aristotelian abstractions mentally extracted from experience of nature. Some implications are discussed. It is argued that Leibniz took the existence of perceiving, unextended, strictly nonspatio-temporal substances to be logically sufficient for all things in nature with spatio-temporal position (extension). An account of the dependence relation of the latter on the former is offered.

**Bolzani Filho, Roberto**. The Sceptical *Epokhé* and its Presuppositions (in Spanish). *Discurso*, 27, 37-60, 1996.

This text intends to show that sceptical discourse, specially Pyrrhonian sceptical discourse, when is read from the point of view of its "logic time", reveals difficulties which resembles to those we can find in dogmatic philosophies. For this aim, some passages of Sextus Empiricus, Oswaldo Porchat and the concept of suspension of judgement (*epokhé*) are analysed.

**Bonafede, Giulio** and Anoz, José (trans). Creación y salvación, o Naturaleza y redención. *Augustinus*, 42(164-5), 69-121, Ja-Je 97.

In the light of Augustine's thinking, the article focuses on the relation between the biblical and, about all, Christian interpretations of the reality, which are called creation, and salvation and investigations show that nature and redemption are harmoniously close. For its analysis of Augustine's theological methodology, it is especially interesting the closing balance of the Augustinian soteriology: the Augustinian speculation has a rational value, also valid for those who do not give their support to his faith. Augustine's answers to so hard questions are not always binding for all his readers, but they encourage still fresh approaches to them and new responses. (edited)

**Bonanno, Giacomo** and Battigalli, Pierpaolo. The Logic of Belief Persistence. *Econ Phil*, 13(1), 39-59, Ap 97.

The interaction between knowledge and belief in a temporal context is analyzed. An axiomatic formulation and semantic characterization of the principle of belief persistence corresponding to the standard conditionalization rule are provided. The principle states that an individual who receives new information consistent with her previous belief set, accommodates this information in the new belief set maintaining her previous beliefs and adding only those beliefs that can be deduced from the previous belief set and the new information. Given standard assumptions about knowledge and belief, it is shown that the principle of persistence of beliefs is characterized by the following axiom schema: the individual believes $o$ at date $t$ if and only if she believes at date $t$ that she will believe $o$ at date $t$+1.

**Bond, H Lawrence** (trans). *Nicholas of Cusa: Selected Spiritual Writings*. Mahwah, Paulist Pr, 1997.

**Bondeli, Martin**. Zu Fichtes Kritik an Reinholds *empirischem* Satz des Bewusstseins und ihrer Vorgeschichte. *Fichte-Studien*, 9, 199-213, 1997.

Since his review of the *Aenesidemus* Fichte has claimed that Reinhold's first principle of the "elementary philosophy," the principle of consciousness, is not a priori but empirical. For that reason this principle cannot be the first principle of all philosophy. This article shows that Fichte's assertion cannot be maintained, if 'empirical principle' is to mean 'synthetic proposition'. Only on condition that Fichte equates 'empirical' with 'leave freedom out of account' is it to be defended.

**Bonesio, Luisa**. "L'Ombra Della Ragione: Banfi lettore di Klages" in *Soggetto E Verità: La questione dell'uomo nella filosofia contemporanea,* Fagiuoli, Ettore, 163-175. 20136 Milano, Mimesis, 1996.

Il saggio esamina la strategia di denegazione e di assimilazione del pensiero del filosofo italiano Antonio Banfi negli anni '30-50, nei confronti delle filosofie di derivazione nietzschiana, e in particolare quella di L Klages, interpretate come sintomi della crisi della cultura e dei valori, e definite genericamente come "irrazionalismo". Il concetto banfiano di ragione, derivato dall'illuminismo e dal marxismo, non può accettare forme di pensiero diverse dall'ottimismo progressista, razionalistico e dialettico. In tal modo, la ricchezza delle aperture dei pensatori non-dialettici (Nietzsche, Spengler, Klages, Jünger, ecc.) viene connotata in modo sommario e senza adeguate analisi come "pessimismo", "cattivo gusto", "regressione", "romanticismo". Le filosofie che Banfi definisce "irrazionalistiche" sono da lui caratterizzate mediante il rovesciamento negativo della sua idea di ragione, anziché essere riconosciute come differenti forme di pensiero nella loro autonoma dignità teoretica.

**Bonesio, Luisa**. "Volti della Terra" in *Geofilosofia,* Bonesio, Luisa (ed), 101-117. Sondrio, Lyasis, 1996.

Lo scritto sostiene che, di fronte alla cancellazione della pluralità dei luoghi della terra prodotta dall'omologazione della tecnica e dell'economia, occorre cercare strumenti di comprensione per un paesaggio non inteso come panorama e oggetto estetico, ma come luogo dell'identità culturale e simbolica di una comunità. Da questo punto di vista, allora, più che di territori indifferenti e inscrivibili in qualsiasi pianificazione, si dovrà parlare di "Volti" della terra, ossia di luoghi dotati di specifica e inconfondibile espressività e identità simbolica, la cui polifonia è indispensabile alla ricchezza, unitaria e plurale, della vita dell'uomo e della natura.

**Bonesio, Luisa**. *Geofilosofia del Paesaggio.* Milano, Mimesis, 1997.

Il problema dei luoghi plurali della terra, a confronto con la crescente omologazione della tecnica planetaria, è stato argomento di riflessione per tutto il pensiero filosofico che va da Nietzsche a Heidegger, a Jünger. Si tratta di interrogarsi sulla possibilità di aprire, nella deterritorializzazione contemporanea, un discorso *geosimbolico* che, ricomponendo in prospettiva inedita estetica, geografia e filosofia, pensi il paesaggio non tanto come una collezione ideale di scorci o il distillato della bellezza naturale, ma come il palinsesto sedimentato e complesso della nostra identità culturale, il luogo del nostro abitare sulla terra nell'epoca difficile e contraddittoria del nichilismo. (publisher)

**Bonesio, Luisa** (ed) and Baldino, Marco (ed) and Resta, Caterina (ed). *Geofilosofia.* Sondrio, Lyasis, 1996.

Primo tentativo italiano organico e ad ampio raggio, il volume *Geofilosofia* fornisce un'idea efficace del dialogo che si può intessere, da molteplici punti di osservazione, a partire dalla prospettiva geofilosofica: gli autori (Jacques Derrida, Jean-Luc Nancy, Otto Pöggeler, François Makowski, Vincenzo Vitiello, Pierluigi Cervellati, Guglielmo Scaramellini, Caterina Resta, Luisa Bonesio, Alessandro Marcenaro) si interrogano sul senso e le possibilità attuali dell'abitare sulla terra: riflessione sul senso del luogo, dell'identità, del paesaggio, dell'urbanistica, dell'Europa a venire; ma anche la rivendicazione dell'appartenenza, delle identità locali, il mondialismo, l'omologazione delle dimensioni culturali nella tecnoeconomia, la progettazione degli spazi tra salvaguardia e sfrenata urbanizzazione, le dimensioni di frontiera, l'emergenza ecologica, e il paesaggio, considerato come il risultato di una cooperazione complessa fra cultura e fisionomia naturale.

**Bonet Sánchez, José V**. Ser, verdad y lenguaje: la continuidad filosófica de la obra de Tugendhat. *Rev Filosof (Spain),* 8(15), 17-35, 1996.

**Bonetskaia, N K**. Russian Sophiology and Anthroposophy. *Russian Stud Phil,* 35(3), 36-64, Wint 96-97.

**Bonetti, José Andrés**. Karl Popper y la crítica al determinismo. *Rev Filosof (Venezuela),* 23(1), 115-123, 1996.

In this article we want to present the most important thesis of Popper about the determinism-antideterminism debate. They are presented, mainly, in his book *The Open Universe,* which pretends to be a global argument in favour of the indeterminism. The title has an evident connection with another work of Popper, devoted to study the social sciences titled *The Open Society and Its Enemies* (1962), in which and together with *The Poverty of Historicism* (1961), he extends the qualifier of "determinism" to key thinkers such as Hegel and Marx. The objective of this work is to criticize this Popperian thesis, showing with concrete notes of the authors mentioned above, how unfounded they are.

**Bongar, Bruce** and Canapary, Andrew and Peruzzi, Nico. Physician-Assisted Suicide: The Role of Mental Health Professionals. *Ethics Behavior,* 6(4), 353-366, 1996.

A review of the literature was conducted to better understand the (potential) role of mental health professionals in physician-assisted suicide. Numerous studies indicate that depression is one of the most commonly encountered psychiatric illnesses in primary care settings. Yet, depression consistently goes undetected and undiagnosed by nonpsychiatrically trained primary care physicians. Noting the well-studied link between depression and suicide, it is necessary to question giving sole responsibility of assisting patients in making end-of-life treatment decisions to these physicians. Unfortunately, the use of mental health consultation by these physicians is not a common occurrence. Greater involvement of mental health professionals in this emerging and debated area is advocated. (edited)

**Bonhöffer, Adolf Friedrich** and Stephens, William O (trans). *The Ethics of the Stoic Epictetus: An English Translation.* New York, Lang, 1996.

This work remains the most systematic and detailed study of Epictetus's ethics. The basis, content, and acquisition of virtue are methodically described, while important related points in Stoic ethics are discussed in an extensive appendix. Epictetus is compared throughout with the other late Stoics (Seneca, Marcus Aurelius), Cicero, the early Stoics (Zeno, Cleanthes, Chrysippus), and Christian moral thought. This approach shows that Stoic ethics continues to have great practical and pedagogical value. (publisher,edited)

**Bonino, Serge-Thomas**. Approches du Moyen Age tardif. *Rev Thomiste,* 96(3), 479-508, Jl-S 96.

**Bonino, Serge-Thomas**. Quelques réactions thomistes à la critique de l'intellect agent par Durand de Saint-Pourçain. *Rev Thomiste,* 97(1), 99-128, Ja-Mr 97.

**Bonito Oliva, Rossella**. "L'incontro problematico tra *Historismus* e neo-kantiano" in *Lo Storicismo e la Sua Storia: Temi, Problemi, Prospettive,* Cacciatore, Giuseppe (ed), 299-312. Milano, Guerini, 1997.

**Bonk, Sigmund**. Mutmassungen über das unschuldige Leiden. *Theol Phil,* 71(3), 419-480, 1996.

The suffering of the innocent clearly is a stumbling block for traditional theism. Which way could a theist go to surpass the problem?—It is shown that any denying of the fact ("there is no suffering of the innocent") is impossible and the "boiling down" of theism to pantheism (or atheism) is morally dissatisfying: We simply should not be cynical unbelievers in the idea of justice ("there is no justice, neither in this world nor in another") and we are logically allowed to believe that an omniscient, almighty and allgood being can give satisfaction and consolation to all those who guiltless suffered.

**Bonkovsky, Frederick O**. Minority Minors and Moral Research Medicine. *Cambridge Quart Healthcare Ethics,* 6(1), 39-47, Winter 97.

**Bonkovsky, Frederick O** and Gordon, Valery M. Family Dynamics and Children in Medical Research. *J Clin Ethics,* 7(4), 349-354, Wint 96.

**Bonnen, Clarence A** and Flage, Daniel E. Descartes on Causation. *Rev Metaph,* 50(4), 841-872, Je 97.

In his replies of Arnauld, Descartes indicates that God's self-causation can be understood as formal causality. The authors argue that it is reasonable to formal causality pervades Descartes's metaphysics. After showing that Descartes's remarks on formal causality are consistent with the position expressed by Aristotle and Suarez, it is shown that Cartesian natural laws are ontologically and epistemically indistinguishable from eternal truths and it is, therefore, reasonable to construe them as formal causes. Such a position makes intelligible Descartes's remarks on the union of mind and body.

**Bonnet, Alberto**. Aspectos políticos del pensamiento de J. Habermas: una lectura crítica. *Cuad Etica,* 15-16, 121-145, 1993.

In this article, the author makes a critical lecture of the political aspects of Habermas's thought, as it is developed until the early '70s. There is a close report between Habermas's political thought and the force (in the postwar advanced capitalist societies) of the *welfare state.* This critical lecture, beside presenting an approach to the internal problems of Habermas's thought, tries to confront it with the welfare state's.

**Bonnet, Christian**. La fable du psychologisme de Fries. *Rev Phil Fr,* 2, 147-159, Ap-Je 97.

**Bonnett, Michael**. Environmental Education and Beyond. *J Phil Educ,* 31(2), 249-266, Jl 97.

The effect of human activity on the environment is rightly a matter of continuing concern both in general and for education in particular. The nature and place of environmental education is here examined in the light of current debates on what constitutes a proper relationship with nature and the qualities of knowledge appropriate to understanding our environmental situation. It is argued that issues are raised which are fundamental not simply to environmental education, but to the character of education as a whole.

**Bonnicksen, Andrea L**. Fetal Motherhood: Toward a Compulsion to Generate Lives?. *Cambridge Quart Healthcare Ethics,* 6(1), 19-30, Winter 97.

Some researchers have proposed using aborted fetuses as sources for eggs in assisted conception programs where donor eggs are used. The article identifies and explores five concerns raised by this still hypothetical prospect: degree of need, psychological impact on offspring, societal values, health of offspring and difficulties in obtaining informed consent. It concludes that the first three are more compelling than the last two. It also concludes that fetal egg use should be evaluated not only as a discrete technique but as a matter that warns of a disturbing ethos toward generating lives in assisted conception.

**Bonnín Aguiló, Francisco**. "Representación, realidad y mundo en el Tractatus de Wittgenstein" in *Verdad: lógica, representación y mundo,* Villegas Forero, L, 377-388. Santiago de Compostela, Univ Santiago Comp, 1996.

This paper speaks about the realistic conception of Wittgenstein's *Tractatus* and afterwards about the meaning of the words *reality, world* and *total reality* as a reference of the language. It explains the statements of Prof. Ule (Univ. of Ljubljana) and Prof. Varga von Kibéd (Univ. of München) who defend that the meaning of *world* and *total reality* is the totality of states of affairs which are actually given and *reality* is the totality of states of affairs which are actually given (positive facts) and also those which are not actually given (negative facts). So *reality* would be more extensive than the *world* and *total reality.* The author disagrees with their position and states that these three terms seem to have in

AUTHOR INDEX 531 Bordoli, Roberto

the *Tractatus* a similar sense and reference and also that they may refer to both: empiric reality (positive facts) and the whole of positive and negative facts.

**Bonsiepen, Wolfgang**. *Die Begründung einer Naturphilosophie bei Kant, Schelling, Fries und Hegel*. Frankfurt/M, Klostermann, 1997.

Kuno Fischer grenzt diese Kant-Rezeption von der durch J.F. Fries begründeten ab. Fries arbeitete auf der Grundlage seiner anthropologischen Vernunftkritik eine mathematische Naturphilosophie aus, die als Alternative zur spekulativen Naturphilosophie Schellings und Hegels verstanden werden muss. Fries' Naturphilosophie steht nicht nur in einer grösseren Nähe zu den Ergebnissen der zeitgenössischen Naturwissenschaft, sondern zeichnet sich auch durch eine Methodenreflexion aus, die schon bei Kant vorliegende Fehler vermeidet. Sie wird damit für heutige wissenschaftstheoretische Fragen relivant. (publisher, edited)

**Bonsor, Jack**. Truth and History: The Question. *Phil Theol*, 9(1-2), 49-56, 1995.

This essay argues for postmodern, nonmetaphysical, nonfoundational perspectives within Roman Catholic theological discourse. It was originally presented, along with the following article by Thomas Guarino, to the "Theology in the Seminary Context" seminar at the *Catholic Theological Society of America* convention in June, 1995.

**Boolos, George**. "Whence the Contradiction?" in *Frege: Importance and Legacy*, Schirn, Matthias (ed), 234-252. Hawthorne, de Gruyter, 1996.

**Boolos, George**. Constructing Cantorian Counterexamples. *J Phil Log*, 26(3), 237-239, Je 97.

Cantor's diagonal argument provides an indirect proof that there is no one-one function from the power set of a set *A* into *A*. This paper provides a somewhat more constructive proof of Cantor's theorem, showing how, given a function *f* from the power set of *A* into *A*, one can explicitly define a counterexample to the thesis that *f* is one-one.

**Boonin-Vail, David**. A Defense of "A Defense of Abortion": On the Responsibility Objection to Thomson's Argument. *Ethics*, 107(2), 286-313, Ja 97.

The most common objection to the argument in Judith Jarvis Thomson's "A Defense of Abortion" maintains that the argument only succeeds, if it succeeds at all, in cases involving rape. I distinguish between two versions of this objection, one based on the claim that in nonrape cases the woman has tacitly consented to allow the fetus to make use of her body, the other based on the claim that in nonrape cases the woman is responsible for the fact that the fetus stands in need of her assistance. I argue that both objections fail.

**Boonin-Vail, David**. Against the Golden Rule Argument Against Abortion. *J Applied Phil*, 14(2), 187-197, 1997.

R. M. Hare and Harry F. Gensler have each argued that abortion can be shown to be immoral by appealing to a version of the golden rule. I argue that both versions of the golden rule argument against abortion should be rejected: each rests on a version of the golden rule which is objectionable on independent grounds, each is unable to support its conclusion when the rule is satisfactorily modified and each is unable to avoid the implication that contraception is as wrong as abortion and for the same reason. In addition, some further problems particular to each position are identified.

**Boonin-Vail, David**. Don't Stop Thinking About Tomorrow: Two Paradoxes About Duties to Future Generations. *Phil Pub Affairs*, 25(4), 267-307, Fall 96.

In this paper I do four things. First, I present Derek Parfit's Mere Addition Paradox. Second, I reject two arguments for the claim that the paradox is morally trivial. Third, I reject two arguments against one of the paradox's premises. Finally, I identify a variation on the paradox. I argue that it is this variant which poses the serious challenge to our moral convictions which initially seems to be embodied in Parfit's paradox and argue that this second paradox can be resolved. Parfit's paradox may thus remain unresolved without creating the important moral difficulty it initially appeared to create.

**Boos, William**. Mathematical Quantum Theory I: Random Ultrafilters as Hidden Variables. *Synthese*, 107(1), 83-143, Ap 96.

The basic purpose of this essay, the first of an intended pair, is to interpret standard von Neumann *quantum theory* in a framework of iterated measure algebraic 'truth' for mathematical (and thus mathematical-physical) assertions—a framework, that is, in which the 'truth-values' for such assertions are elements of iterated Boolean measure-algebras A. The essay itself employs constructions of Takeuti's Boolean-valued analysis (whose origins lay in work of Scott, Solovay, Krauss and others) to provide a metamathematical interpretation of ideas sometimes considered disparate, 'heuristic', or simply ill-defined: the '*collapse of the wave function*', for example; Everett's *many worlds*'-construal of quantum measurement; and a 'natural' product space of contextual (nonlocal) '*hidden variables*'. (edited)

**Booth, Annie L**. "Critical Questions in Environmental Philosophy" in *Philosophy and Geography I: Space, Place, and Environmental Ethics*, Light, Andrew (ed), 255-273. Lanham, Rowman & Littlefield, 1997.

This article examines some of the key problems developing in three related branches of the environmental ethics tree: bioregionalism, deep ecology and ecofeminism. I do not intend to discredit environmental ethics as a solution. Instead, by illuminating problems in these theories/practices, I hope to suggest what opportunities which might make environmental ethics more relevant and usable to policy makers and resource managers as well as ethicists. In addition, both ecology and bioregionalism have used indigenous ethics in formulating theory as examples of appropriate relationships between humans and the environment, that employment itself requires critical examination.

**Booth, Douglas E**. Preserving Old-Growth Forest Ecosystems: Valuation and Policy. *Environ Values*, 6(1), 31-48, F 97.

If valuation processes are dualistic in the sense that ethical values are given priority over instrumental values, and if old-growth forests are considered to be valuable in their own right, then the cost-benefits approach to valuing old growth is inappropriate. If this is the case, then ethical standards must be used to determine whether preservation is the correct policy when human material needs and ecosystem preservation are in conflict. Such a standard is suggested and evaluated in the context of the policy debate over the preservation of spotted owl habitat in the Pacific Northwest region of the U.S.

**Boothroyd, David**. Foucault's Alimentary Philosophy: Care of the Self and Responsibility for the Other. *Man World*, 29(4), 361-386, O 96.

This article examines the concept of the "ethical subject" understood in terms of "care of the self", in the later Foucault. It uses the ideas of Deleuze and Levinas to critique both critical and postmodernist appraisals of the ethico-political subject in Foucault and proposes an alternative *alimentary* model. It examines the role of the work of art in the earlier works recasting the discussion of the ethico-political in relation to the later notion of the "aesthetics of existence", arguing that the charge of egocentrism levelled at Foucault's ethical subject cannot find its target in the notion of "care of the self".

**Borchert, Donald** (ed) and Zucker, Arthur (ed) and Trevas, Robert (ed). *Philosophy of Sex and Love: A Reader*. Englewood Cliffs, Prentice Hall, 1997.

The human experience of sex and love has direct impact on our social well-being. By studying sexual philosophy, we allow ourselves, through exposure to a variety of alternative belief systems, to consider new possibilities and options as well as to develop a deeper understanding of the philosophy we already possess. This is the underlying principle behind the readings presented in the book. (publisher,edited)

**Borchert, Jens**. Welfare-State Retrenchment: Playing the National Card. *Crit Rev*, 10(1), 63-94, Wint 96.

An analysis of welfare-state restructuring under conservative governments during the 1980s undermines the notion that the nation-state is being rendered obsolete by economic globalization. The nation-state is still the principal site of political conflict. Yet this conflict has to be analyzed in light of global economic and cultural pressures, conservative attempts to restructure the welfare state were parallel events within a larger transition in the world economy, but they had decisively distinct national trajectories.

**Bordes Solanas, M**. Primacía y dependencia metafísicas: consideraciones acerca de las ontologías de tropos. *Analisis Filosof*, 16(2), 135-156, N 96.

In this paper I will consider some questions concerning trope ontologies. I will examine first what I call the subordination argument, which I think is implicitly held by any traditional Aristotelian ontologist and rejects tropes. I will show that this argument, if valid, leans on the controversial notion of metaphysical dependence, which in fact does not allow us to conclude anything against the ontological primacy of tropes. Finally, I will describe the ability of a monist trope ontology to answer or at least mitigate some classical criticism against it (like those presented by Russell's regress argument and Goodman's imperfect community argument) and its instrumental power to analyse some classical problems of epistemology, causality theories and even aesthetics.

**Bordes Solanas, Montserrat**. Four-dimensionalist Remarks: A Defence of Temporal Parts (Spanish). *Theoria (Spain)*, 12(29), 343-377, My 97.

In this paper some answers to certain arguments against temporal parts are presented. The first part explores the very notion of temporal part and tries to describe the main tenets that friends of temporal parts hold. The second one develops some criticisms that friends of continuants have expoused against those entities and argues that most of these criticisms mischaracterize the problems at issue. The discussion focuses on J.J. Thomson's, P. Geach's, D. Mellor's and S. Haslanger's arguments about the impossibility of processualism to escape from some problematic commitments like instantaneous parts, *ex nihilo* existences, time-space analogies and Humean causes. Nevertheless, I will try to show that some of this consequences do not follow and that some other are seen not to be as threatening as they might first have appeared.

**Bordes Solanas, Montserrat**. Identidad y Continuidad Causal: Una Crítica a la Teoría de la Continuidad Causal de Shoemaker. *Agora (Spain)*, 14(2), 113-122, 1995.

**Bordes Solanas, Montserrat**. Identidad, Constitución y Superveniencia. *Critica*, 28(83), 41-73, Ag 96.

This paper is concerned with the notions of constitution and identity. It has a threefold purpose. First, to examine and evaluate the two main position (CII, CNI) that in recent discussion are supposed to be the answers to the puzzles raised on this topic. I will try to show its commitments with certain views on the modal and temporal character of the identity relation. Second, to show that the classical position (CNI) suggest some criticisms because of its acceptance of an anti-occamist coincidence principle that contravenes a reasonable principle of supervenience. Finally, I want to stress the capacity of the rival theory of dealing with those problems.

**Bordo, Susan**. Can a Woman Harass a Man?: Toward a Cultural Understanding of Bodies and Power. *Phil Today*, 41(1-4), 51-66, Spr 97.

**Bordoli, Roberto**. *Ragione e Scrittura tra Descartes e Spinoza: Saggio sulla Philosophia S. Scripturae Interpres* di Lodewijk Meyer e sulla sua recezione. Milano, FrancoAngeli, 1997.

Lodewijk Meyer (1629-1681), medico e filosofo di Amsterdam, cartesiano secondo i teologi, ateo secondo i cartesiani, "libertijn" per tutti, è l'autore di un saggio sulla filosofia interprete della Scrittura pubblicato quattro anni prima del

*Trattato Teologico-Politico* di Spinoza, suo amico e corrispondente. Contro questo testo, che sarà una fonte di Spinoza, insorgono i principali rappresentanti delle numerose tendenze filsofiche, teologiche e religiose nederlandesi. Ne nasce un dibattito ricco da cui risulta il ruolo giocato dai cartesiani di diverso orientamento nella loro irriducibile opposizione a Meyer. (publisher, edited)

**Borges-Duarte, Irene**. Dinamic Peace in the Encounter of Vital Cultures (Spanish). *Rev Filosof (Venezuela)*, 24(2), 131-145, Jl-D 96.

Peace can't be understood as a static situation, but as an order, a *dynamic peace*. The actions of every element must be organized in order to establish justice and peace. Peace can be understood as a *concert*, a symphony or a heavenly order among human beings. It requires cultural clarification —*heliomaquia*—as peace is not only absence of war, but has to be built in collective human life, without renouncing in this union the particularity of individual life patterns.

**Borges-Duarte, Irene**. Filosofia e Estilo Literário em Heidegger e em Platao: Um Exemplo. *Philosophica (Portugal)*, 33-57, 1997.

Die Frage nach dem inneren Bezug zwischen den philosophischen Gehalt eines Gedankens und die Form oder Stil, wodurch er zum Ausdruck gebracht wird, wird hier mit der Hilfe eines Beispiels thematisiert: Heideggers unzeitgemässe Einübung des platonischen Dialog-Stils (bei der *Feldwog-Gespräche*). Auch wenn eine äussere Explikation dafür gefunden werden kann, nur ein im Innerste des heideggerschen Denkens gewürzeltes Motiv kann ein solchen Gebrauch verständlich machen: der Versuch mit dem in der metaphysischen Tradition ungedachten Seyn gestimmt zu bleiben, ihm sein neuen "grossen Stil" zu verschaffen.

**Borges-Duarte, Irene**. Heidegger, escritor de diálogos: ¿Recuperación de una forma literaria de la Filosofía?. *An Seminar Hist Filosof*, 13, 75-93, 1996.

Dass Heidegger 1944/45 drei Schriften im alten Stil des Dialogs verfasst hat, bringt uns in Verlegenheit. Warum hat er diesen seit langem ungeübten literatur-philosophischen Stil ausgewählt? Dies versuchen wir, dadurch zu verstehen, dass es sich dabei nicht so sehr darum handelt, den existenzial-dialogischen Sprachfundamente des Daseins Ausdruck zu geben, sondern vielmehr darum, dass sich dabei der Urdialog des Menschen und des Seyns ereignet. Solche unzeitgemässe Einübung des Dialogs wird uns aber erst als eine Wiederholung des platonischen Initiationswegs zugänglich, der nicht eine Lehre sondern eher eine ontologische Bereitschaft—bei Heidegger die Gelassenheit—zu schaffen sucht.

**Borges-Duarte, Irene**. La tesis heideggeriana acerca de la técnica. *An Seminar Hist Filosof*, 10, 121-156, 1993.

Heideggers These über die Technik drückt sich terminologisch aus durch das Wort *Ge-stell*. Bei der Erörterung dieses Leitworts und durch die Vergleichung von Textstellen aus verschiedenen Epochen stellt sich bei dem oft amphibologischen Gedankengang Heideggers fest, dass damit eine dreifache Bestimmung gemeint wird, die zum Teil die schematische Artikulierung des modernen Weltentwurfs betrifft, zum anderen aber auch das Gestalten einer Gestalt und somit das Aufblitzenlassen des Ereignisses selbst. Im *Ge-stell* spricht also zugleich der griechische Sinn von *Morphe* und das Wesen des modernen vorstellenden Denkens, der ursprüngliche und der nachträgliche Sinn von *Thesis*.

**Borges-Duarte, Irene** (trans) and Heidegger, Martin. Carta al Padre William Richardson. *An Seminar Hist Filosof*, 13, 11-18, 1996.

**Borges-Duarte, Irene** (trans) and Von Herrmann, Friedrich-Wilhelm. La *"segunda mitad" de Ser y Tiempo*. Madrid, Ed Trotta, 1997.

Este libro constituye una aportación decisiva a la comprensión del proyecto heideggeriano que, bajo el título de *Ser y Tiempo. Primera Parte*, apareció sólo parcialmente desarrollado en la publicación de 1927. Partiendo de la anotación en la que Heidegger caracteriza el contenido de su curso de Marburgo de 1927 (*Los problemas fundamentales de la Fenomenología*) como una reelaboración de la temática de *Tiempo y ser*, con la que debía haberse iniciado la *segunda mitad* de *Ser y Tiempo*, el autor ofrece una interpretación fenomenológica de aquel proyector global, a la vez que una introducción a la lectura del texto del citado curso, con cuya publicación en 1975 se dio inicio a la de la *Edición integral*. (publisher, edited)

**Borghero, Carlo**. "L'Italia in Bayle, Bayle in Italia: una ricerca mancata" in *Pierre Bayle e l'Italia,* Bianchi, Lorenzo, 3-33. Napoli, Liguori Ed, 1996.

**Borgmann, Albert**. Technology and the Crisis of Contemporary Culture. *Amer Cath Phil Quart*, 70(Supp), 33-44, 1996.

**Borm, Peter** (& others) and Van Megen, Freek and Faccini, Giovanni. Congestion Models and Weighted Bayesian Potential Games. *Theor Decis*, 42(2), 193-206, Ja 97.

Games associated with congestion situations à la Rosenthal (1973) have pure Nash equilibria. This result implicitly relies on the existence of a potential function. In this paper we provide a characterization of potential games in terms of coordination games and dummy games. Second, we extend Rosenthal's congestion model to an incomplete information setting and show that the related Bayesian games are potential games and therefore, have pure Bayesian equilibria.

**Born, Rainer**. Re-Interpeting Frege. *Conceptus*, 28(73), 185-253, 1995.

The aim of the paper is to put Frege into context, i.e., to explicate his historical roots in Kant's philosophy of mathematics and to do justice to the everlasting scientific significance of Frege's work. This means that one has to study very carefully Frege's early mathematical work and expose the implicit philosophical concerns, especially in *Begriffsschrift* part III, concerning the logical properties of a so-called "series" (of objects) in mathematics. Altogether, this approach

should lead to a better understanding of the origins and aims of analytical philosophy as well as highlight what classical and modern philosophy still have in common. (publisher,edited)

**Borrelli, Gianfranco**. Prudence, Folly and Melancholy in the Thought of Thomas Hobbes. *Hobbes Stud*, 9, 88-97, 1996.

Hobbes's aim is to demonstrate the failure of political action founded on prudence, which cannot produce obedience in the individuals oppressed by the melancholic syndrome. The mental dejection surely hinders the development of man's desire/appetitus, since he who remains anchored to the actuation of the *private Spirit* acts in such a way as to separate the private good from the common one. *Private Spirit, Inspiration, Conspiracy*: a chain of individual, private practices and beliefs intervenes on the public level of the organisation of civil life with effects that can be lacerating for the political unity of the State.

**Borutti, Silvana**. "Verità Dell'Evento E Ruolo Del Soggetto Nella Conoscenza Storica: Tre paradigmi" in *Soggetto E Verità: La questione dell'uomo nella filosofia contemporanea*, Fagiuoli, Ettore, 235-256. 20136 Milano, Mimesis, 1996.

This paper raises some theoretical and epistemological problems concerning historical knowledge. Three paradigms of individual events in history are analysed. Firstly, "nomologic" paradigm, which applies in history the concept of event of natural sciences, is discussed. Secondly, Windelband's opposition between "nomothetic" and "idiographic" sciences is reconstructed. Finally, the author traces the outline of an alternative paradigm, based not on a formalistic idea of form as a law, but on a holistic idea of form as a "composition" and as a "discourse". To develop this paradigm, reference is made to Aristotle's *Poetica* and to the models of comprehension of events in Ricoeur, Danto and Benjamin.

**Bosch, Magdalena**. Immanencia y trascendencia en la intencionalidad. *Acta Phil*, 6(1), 101-116, 1997.

Intentionality is a complex term. I refer to it maining the presence of things in us, when we know and want them. It's a focus to see the immanence and the transcendence of intentionality. The things we know or want have some immanence in their *being*. And have some relative transcendence that is the reference of their *being* to us. In a similar way, we have some immanence of these things because they remain in someway into us. And, simultaneously, we have some transcendence when we go out of us in order to know or want them. These principles are here analyzed from a metaphysical point of view.

**Bosch, Magdalena**. Metafisica de la Intencionalidad. Barcelona, PPU, 1997.

Intentionality has been studied by different philosophical traditions. Each one has emphasized one of the several aspects of this concept. In this work, I try to analyze intentionality by itself. Only in this way is it possible to see the two sides of it. Not only knowledge, neither morality alone, but the two ways in that things can be present in us. If this is achieved we can see then the most important concepts that are related to intentionality: its being, its essence, its immanence and transcendence, its degrees—human degree specially—, its principle, its human executor and its unity in love and freedom.

**Bosch, Roger** and Bagaria, Joan. Projective Forcing. *Annals Pure Applied Log*, 86(3), 237-266, Jl 97.

We study the projective posits and their properties as forcing notions. We also define Martin's axiom restricted to projective sets, *MA(proj)* and show that this axiom is weaker than full Martin's axiom.... (edited)

**Boschi, D** and De Martini, F and Di Giuseppe, G. Test of the Violation of Local Realism in Quantum Mechanics with No Use of Bell's Inequalities. *Erkenntnis*, 45(2 & 3), 367-377, Nov 96.

A novel and versatile polarization-entanglement scheme is adopted to investigate the violation of the EPR local realism for a nonmaximally entangled two-photon system according to the recent "nonlocality proof" by Lucien Hardy. In this context the adoption of a sophisticated detection method allows direct determination of any "element of physical reality" (viz, determined "*with probability equal to unity*" in the words of Einstein, Podolsky and Rosen) for the pair system within complete measurements that are largely *insensitive* to the detector quantum-efficiencies and noise.

**Bosely, Richard**. The Emergence of Concepts of a Sentence in Ancient Greek and in Ancient Chinese Philosophy. *J Chin Phil*, 24(2), 209-229, Je 97.

**Bosnjak, Branko**. Homer's Theology and the Concept of Tolerance. *Filozof Istraz*, 16(3), 601-610, 1996.

La sagesse poétique d'Homère parle de maints faits et événements qui arrivent dans la vie et qui engagent aussi bien les dieux que les hommes. Ensemble, ils évoluent sur la grande scène du monde. Ici, un thème particulier est celui de la grande guerre de Troie. Une immense armée y est engagée, les dieux, eux non plus ne songent toujours rester à l'écart des événements qui se succèdent. (edited)

**Boss, Gilbert**. Discours et Méthode. *Arch Phil*, 59(3), 441-454, Jl-S 96.

A study of the beginning of Descartes's *Discours de la Méthode* allows one to position of the problem of the relation between discourse and method in philosophy. The reflection concerns the following eight themes: 1) the equality of common sense in all people and stupidity, 2) the function of Cartesian irony, 3) the subjective perspective on judgment, 4) the critique of the point of view of technical philosophy, 5) the necessity of a discourse on the method of the discourse on method, 6) the specific difficulty of the discourse on method, 7) the condition of philosophical discourse, 8) the fortune of reason and the narrative style.

**Boss, Gilbert**. L'infinité des attributs chez Spinoza. *Rev Phil Fr*, 4, 487-502, O-D 96.

AUTHOR INDEX 533 Bouveresse, Jacques

**Boss, Gilbert**. Raison et Convention, ou la Raison Politique chez Hobbes. *Hobbes Stud*, 9, 55-70, 1996.

**Bostic, Heidi** and Pluhacek, Stephen. Thinking Life as Relation: An Interview with Luce Irigaray. *Man World*, 29(4), 343-360, O 96.

This interview, conducted in Paris during the Spring of 1996, draws upon Luce Irigaray's recent work, including *I love to you, Je, tu, nous* and *Thinking the Difference*, as well as her 1995-96 seminar on "The question of the other" at the Ecole des Hautes Etudes en Sciences Sociales in Paris. The interview treats questions of nature vs. culture, sexual difference and relational identity.

**Bosto, Sulejman**. Nietzsche and the New Beginning (in Serbo-Croatian). *Filozof Istraz*, 15(4), 775-788, 1995.

In seinem Beitrag versucht der Autor einige Momente von Nietzsches Enttäuschung über die Metaphysik hervorzuheben und den Inhalt seiner "Destruktion" sowie das Pathos des "neuen Anfangs" zu untersuchen, der nicht als blosse Restitution vorsokratischer Paradigmen zu verstehen ist. Der positive Inhalt dieser "Entzauberung" metaphysischer Wahrheit als metaphysischer "Lüge" stellt bei Nietzsche einen eindringlichen Apell dar. Die neue Öffnung der Welt zielt bei Nietzsche auf ein Jenseits der Gleichgültigkeit von Erkenntnis, Moral und Bildung. Dem Neubeginn geht daher eine dramatische Nietzscheanische Enttäuschun, Angst und Ekstase, aber auch Ekel vor der metaphysisch entleerten Welt voraus. (edited)

**Botero, J J**. Defensa del Pluralismo. *Ideas Valores*, 37-52, Ag 97.

**Botero C, Juan J**. Desmoralizar la Promesa?. *Ideas Valores*, 79-85, Ap 97.

**Botero C, Juan J**. Son "Opacos" los Estados Mentales?: Los Criterios de Chisholm. *Ideas Valores*, 3-26, D 96.

In this paper I give an account of Chisholm's criteria for intentionality and of the ensuing discussion held in the 60s around this issue. I try also to bring to light the reasons that would possibly explain the confusion common in those years between intentionality, the Brentanian distinctive feature of the "psychic," and intensionality, a syntactic feature of some linguistic expressions. This mistake has to do with the fact that some intensional contexts, viz. propositional attitudes, are reports of mental intentional states, as has been established by Searle. A complete explanation of this fact should go beyond this paper into a discussion of some contemporary thesis about mental cognitive states, namely Fodor's theory of the *Language of Thought*.

**Botiveau, Bernard**. Tolerance and Law: From Islamic Culture to Islamist Ideology. *Ratio Juris*, 10(1), 61-74, Mr 97.

Tolerance implies both renunciation and negotiation, concepts that assume truth as relative. The rationality of religious faith does not acknowledge the existence of a shared truth, but history reminds us that religions could be directed through their social representatives to engage in social realities. This had been the case with Islam, despite the existence of strong structuring of knowledge and the Ulemas who play a vital role in its control and reproduction.

**Botturi, Francesco**. El tiempo histórico en Giambattista Vico. *Cuad Vico*, 5/6, 27-49, 1995/96.

This paper emphasizes the importance of the notion of time in Vico's thought. It attempts to place it right in the core of his thought and make it clearer through a structural analysis which intends to raise step-by-step the constructive and systematic function in Vico's discursive logic. In so doing, it proposes to distinguish on the basis of the beginning of anthropological time between both a time in the narration, the sharp witted time related with the everlasting truth, which becomes intelligible solely in terms of the *verum ipsum factum*'s thesis, and the historic time, that of *providence*, regarded as metaphysical mediation.

**Botturi, Francesco**. *Tempo Linguaggio e Azione: Le Strutture Vichiane della Storia Ideale Eterna*. Napoli, Guida, 1996.

In un'indagine intesa a illuminare le strutture speculative del pensiero vichiano, Botturi prende in esame gli assi portanti dell'edificio vichiano, identificati nell' "umanesimo linguistico", nella riattivazione originale della tradizione speculativa neoplatonica mediata dalla recezione del postcartesianesimo male-branchiano-occasionalistico e l'ermeneutica romanistica, intrecciata con la problematica moderna del "diritto naturale". A partire dal-l'identificazione dell'agire storico vichiano con un'azione linguistica, viene mostrata la funzione essenziale del linguaggio come chiave ermeneutica dell'antropologia, dalla quale discende la rivalutazione vichiana del valore speculativo del poetico e la valorizzazione della dimensione pragmatica della parola. (edited)

**Boucher, David**. The Significance of R.G. Collingwood's *Principles of History*. *J Hist Ideas*, 58(2), 309-330, Ap 97.

The paper begins by addressing the question why Malcolm Knox explicitly disregarded Collingwood's authorization to publish *The Principles of History*. It is suggested that Knox's suppression of the manuscript has contributed to much of the confusion which surrounds the interpretation of Collingwood's ideas. It is argued that *The Principles of History* show more clearly than his published work how integral *The Principles of Art* and *An Essay on Metaphysics* was to his philosophy of history. Finally, the most significant omission in the manuscript is the issue of re-enactment. It is contended that in the light of Collingwood's new emphasis upon emotions as part of the subject matter of history he needed a new theory of re-enactment. He never developed this himself, but the basis of a new theory can be gleaned from the pages of *The Principles of Art*.

**Bouchilloux, Hélène**. La critique des preuves de l'existence de Dieu et la valeur du discours apologétique. *Rev Int Phil*, 51(199), 5-29, 1997.

Pascal substitue aux preuves de l'existence de Dieu des preuves de la vérité du christianisme. Les premières ne s'adressent qu'à l'esprit en dissimulant que l'idée de Dieu dont elles procèdent a son origine dans le coeur corrompu. En ne convainquant pas de ce qu'elles démontrent, les secondes manifestent la corruption du coeur et la nécessitéde l'accoutumance à défaut de la foi.

**Bouckaert, Bertrand**. L'Allemagne, la modernité, la pensée. *Rev Phil Louvain*, 94(2), 330-337, My 96.

This paper asked: "what is the very signification of German history for modernity and to what extend does the falling down of modern thinking coincide with the growing up of postmodernity?" The conclusions reached are that the speculative style of classical German thinking is related to his growing away from the field of interaction (not in university's but in monastery's). Modernity may be interpreted as an effort to think interaction speculatively. The failure of this effort suggests two answers the postmodern skepticism and the searching for a more interactive thinking.

**Boudon, Raymond**. Une éthique est-elle possible en l'absence de croyances dogmatiques?. *Protosoz*, 8/9, 237-259, 1996.

A cognitive theory of axiological rationality is developed here starting from the basic point that normative statements and axiological beliefs should be analyzed as grounded on reasons with a trans-subjective validity, as positive statements are. This theory is checked in a tentative fashion against some examples of axiological beliefs from ordinary experience and against a few pieces of data drawn from experimental social psychology. (edited)

**Boukema, H J M**. Facts of Legal Reasoning. *Riv Int Filosof Diritto*, 74(1), 3-14, Ja-Mr 97.

**Boulting, Noel E**. Between Anthropocentrism and Ecocentrism. *Phil Cont World*, 2(4), 1-8, Wint 95.

Three ways of relating the structures of human existence to the world are offered by ecological holism moral extensionism and biotic communitarianism. Leopold's attempt to reconcile these three is examined in the light of Peirce's categories, in order to ascertain how far Leopold's final position is anthropocentric, ecocentric, neither, or both.

**Boulting, Noel E**. The Emergence of the Land Ethic: Aldo Leopold's Idea of Ultimate Reality and Meaning. *Ultim Real Mean*, 19(3), 168-188, S 96.

In the development of his *land ethic*, Leopold passed through three intellectual stages once his narrower utilitarian concerns were superseded. His final position can only be understood not literally as a passage from *ecological holism*, through *moral extensionism* to *biotic communitarianism* but rather, as a form of Peircian reasoning where these three positions can be interpreted in terms of Peirce's three categories to be used as fibres in forming a cable of argument to overcome the weaknesses of each.

**Boundas, Constantin V**. Transgressive Theorizing: A Report to Deleuze. *Man World*, 29(3), 327-341, Jl 96.

Deleuze was not fond of transgression. This essay, however, attempts to show that between theories of management and theories of transcendence, there is a third possibility—transgressive theorizing. This kind of theorizing lets itself be guided by regulative ideas in search of concepts that would be adequate to them, counteractualizes the given for the sake of the event and the emergence of the new, witnesses the lines of flight of minor languages, nomadic sciences and arts, and charts revolutions without model summoning up a new race and a new earth.

**Bounds, Elizabeth M**. *Coming Together/Coming Apart: Religion, Community, and Modernity*. New York, Routledge, 1997.

While the idea of "community" is increasingly vital to our individual and social well-being, our ordinary communal relations are being eroded by increased mobility, lost traditions and the growing pluralism of society. Examining this renewed desire for community, *Coming Together/Coming Apart* locates the current problems in modern capitalism. Out of a common matrix of a lifeworld in crisis, contemporary religious, social and feminist discussions compose an ideological struggle over the reformation of society. Bounds analyzes a broad range of theorists from Daniel Bell and Stanley Hauerwas to Sharon Welch and Cornel West. In comparing their arguments about community, she illustrates critical assumptions about the roles of morality and religion including the values of difference, the diversity of traditions and the nature of moral connection. (publisher)

**Bourdeau, Michel**. La théorie intuitionniste des types: sémantique des preuves et théorie des constructions. *Dialogue (Canada)*, 36(2), 323-339, Spr 97.

Martin-Löf's constructive theory introduces, beside proof processes—the Brouwerian mental construction—proof objects that could become the subject matter of a new kind of proof theory. In contradistinction to the classical approach, the proposition can then be defined as the set of its proofs. The lower level type theory is, therefore, a set theory, where the operators Sigma and Pi generalize the Cartesian product and the functional space to families of sets. (edited)

**Bourgeois, Patrick L**. From Common Roots to a Broader Vision: A Pragmatic Thrust of European Phenomenology. *Amer Cath Phil Quart*, 70(3), 381-396, Sum 96.

**Boury-Brisset, Anne-Claire** and Moulin, Bernard. An Agent Model Integrating Multiple Reasoning Mechanisms. *Commun Cog—AI*, 13(1), 57-91, 1996.

In this paper we study various reasoning mechanisms that affect the way that a software agent makes decisions in a multiagent environment: hypothetical reasoning, generation of hypothesis and deduction of knowledge in hypothetical worlds: evolution of the content of hypothetical worlds in order to choose among them a solution that conforms to the agent's preferences; management of deontic modalities in relation to hypothetical reasoning; reasoning on other agents and belief revision.

**Bouveresse, Jacques** and Cosman, Carol (trans) and Descombes, Vincent. *Wittgenstein Reads Freud: The Myth of the Unconscious*. Princeton, Princeton Univ Pr, 1995.

Wittgenstein, who himself had delivered a devastating critique of traditional philosophy, sympathetically pondered Freud's claim to have produced a scientific theory in proposing a new model of the human psyche. What Wittgenstein recognized—and what Bouveresse so eloquently stresses for today's reader—is that psychoanalysis does not aim to produce a change limited to the intellect but rather seeks to provoke an authentic change of human attitudes. (publisher, edited)

**Bove, Laurence**. Malcolm X and the Enigma of Martin Luther King, Jr.'s Nonviolence. *Acorn*, 7(2), 18-23, Fall-Wint 92-93.

**Bove, Laurent**. Le désir et la mort chez Pascal: Hypothèses pour une lecture. *Rev Int Phil*, 51(199), 31-57, 1997.

**Bovens, Luc**. The Backward Induction Argument for the Finite Iterated Prisoner's Dilemma and the Surprise Exam Paradox. *Analysis*, 57(3), 179-186, Jl 97.

It has often been suggested that the Backward Induction Argument (BIA) for the Finite Iterated Prisoner's Dilemma (FIPD) is an instance of the Surprise Exam Paradox (SEP). I argue (I) that both arguments do depend on a common axiomatic structure; (II) that there is a difference between both arguments such that a very plausible solution to the SEP cannot be carried over to the BIA for the FIPD in case the players' pregame beliefs are characterized in a way that does not permit belief revision on Bayesian grounds; (III) that a comparison to the SEP is instructive in that it helps us understand why we are apprehensive about the conclusion of the BIA for *real-life* FIPDs.

**Boverman, Maxwell** and Fletcher, John C. Heroes, Martyrs, and Other Choices. *J Clin Ethics*, 7(4), 301-305, Wint 96.

**Bowden, Peta**. *Caring: Gender-Sensitive Ethics*. New York, Routledge, 1997.

In *Caring*, Peta Bowden extends and challenges recent debates on feminist ethics. She takes issue with accounts of the ethics of care that focus on alleged basic principles of caring rather than analysing caring in practice. Caring, Bowden argues, must be understood by 'working through examples'. Following this approach, Bowden explores four main caring practices: mothering, friendship, nursing and citizenship. Her analysis of the differences and similarities in these practices—their varying degrees of intimacy and reciprocity, formality and informality, vulnerability and choice—reveals the practical complexity of the ethics of care. (publisher)

**Bowen, William G**. "No Limits" in *The American University: National Treasure or Endangered Species?*, Ehrenberg, Ronald G (ed), 18-42. Ithaca, Cornell Univ Pr, 1997.

**Bowie, Andrew**. "The Meaning of the Hermeneutic Tradition in Contemporary Philosophy" in *Verstehen and Humane Understanding*, O'Hear, Anthony (ed), 121-144. New York, Cambridge Univ Pr, 1996.

**Bowie, Andrew**. *From Romanticism to Critical Theory: The Philosophy of German Literary Theory*. New York, Routledge, 1997.

*From Romanticism to Critical Theory* explores the philosophical origins of literary theory via the tradition of German philosophy that began with the Romantic reactions to Kant. It traces the continuation of the Romantic tradition of Novalis, Friedrich Schlegel and Schleiermacher, in Heidegger's approaches to art and truth and in the Critical Theory of Benjamin and Adorno. Andrew Bowie argues, against many current assumptions, that the key aspect of literary theory is not the demonstration of how meaning can be deconstructed, but rather the revelation of how questions of language and literature change modern philosophical conceptions of truth. He shows how the dialogue between literary theory, hermeneutics and analytical philosophy can profit from a reexamination of the understanding of language, truth and literature in modern German philosophy. (publisher)

**Bowie, Andrew**. John McDowell's *Mind and World* and Early Romantic Epistemology. *Rev Int Phil*, 50(197), 515-554, 1996.

**Bowie, Norman**. The Role of Philosophy in Public Policy—A Philosopher in a Business School. *Phil Stud*, 85(2-3), 119-133, Mr 97.

Traditional business ethicists apply ethical theory to ethical issues in business. But we can do more. I point out how ethics can contribute to profits, how ethical notions can function as data, and how an ethical concept can function as an explanatory variable.

**Bowyer, Carlton H** and McCree, Herbert L. National Goals for Education and *The Language of Education*. *Stud Phil Educ*, 16(1-2), 139-148, Ja-Ap 97.

Schools have always been under pressure to change or reform. Recent public criticism of schools provoked an attempt to address weaknesses in American education. Goals 2000 is a legislative effort that would reform schools using national goals for education. Selected goals are highlighted and *The Language of Education* provides a structure to develop understanding of the goals. We contend that Scheffler's method for examining the discussion on education and policies developed from it is valid in the contemporary context. The analysis possible using *The Language of Education* would bring a missing sense of order to educational policy development and possibly give voice to those often disenfranchised by the process.

**Boxill, Bernard R**. "Black Liberation—Yes!" in *The Liberation Debate: Rights at Issue*, Leahy, Michael (ed), 51-64. New York, Routledge, 1996.

**Boxill, Bernard R**. "Boxill's Reply" in *The Liberation Debate: Rights at Issue*, Leahy, Michael (ed), 82-84. New York, Routledge, 1996.

**Boxill, Bernard R**. "The Fight with Covey" in *Existence in Black: An Anthology of Black Existential Philosophy*, Gordon, Lewis R (ed), 273-290. New York, Routledge, 1997.

**Boxill, Bernard R**. Washington, Du Bois and *Plessy V. Ferguson*. *Law Phil*, 16(3), 299-330, My 97.

**Boyce-Tillman, June**. Conceptual Frameworks for World Musics in Education. *Phil Music Educ Rev*, 5(1), 3-13, Spr 97.

**Boyd, Colin**. Business Ethics in Canada: A Personal View. *J Bus Ethics*, 16(6), 605-609, Ap 97.

In this address given at the 1995 Annual Meeting of the Society for Business Ethics, the author identifies two major distinguishing ethical characteristics of the Canadian business environment. First, the degree to which harvesting in the Canadian natural environment produces a concentration of extreme criticism, e.g., of the culling of seals, the trapping of fur-bearing animals, and the harvesting of wood via clear-cut logging techniques. Second, he identifies the core values of civility and tolerance in the Canadian workplace as a particular national phenomenon.

**Boyd, Dwight** and McKay, Alexander. "The Politics of the "Good" in *Good Sexuality Education*" in *Philosophy of Education (1996)*, Margonis, Frank (ed), 408-411. Urbana, Phil Education Soc, 1997.

**Boyd, Ian T E**. The Problem of Self-Destroying Sin in John Milton's *Samson Agonistes*. *Faith Phil*, 13(4), 487-507, O 96.

In this paper, I argue that John Milton, in his tragedy *Samson Agonistes*, raises and offers a solution to a version of the problem of evil raised by Marilyn McCord Adams. Sections I and II are devoted to the presentation of Adams's version of the problem and its place in the current discussion of the problem of evil. In section III, I present Milton's version of the problem as it is raised in *Samson Agonistes*. The solution Milton offers to this problem is taken up in section IV and examined in section V. Last, in section VI, I explore briefly the existential aspect of Milton's solution.

**Boyer, Joy T** and Thomson, Elizabeth J and Meslin, Eric M. The Ethical, Legal, and Social Implications Research Program at the National Human Genome Research Institute. *Kennedy Inst Ethics J*, 7(3), 291-298, S 97.

**Boyle, Joseph**. *Just and Unjust Wars*: Casuistry and the Boundaries of the Moral World. *Ethics Int Affairs*, 11, 83-98, 1997.

Walzer's *Just and Unjust Wars* utilizes a moral doctrine known as casuistry which applies existing moral norms to practical cases while putting aside the actual origins of morality. Boyle contrasts Walzer's casuistry to other methods of moral judgment including consequentialism, institutionalism and deontology. He discusses deontology, which derives precepts from moral principles, particularly with reference to Alan Donagan's *The Theory of Morality*, which appeared the same year as *Just and Unjust Wars*. He cites casuistry as a highly practical method, but cautions that it is an insufficient guide in extreme situations for which there are no existing moral norms. Boyle points out that in cases where casuistry fails Walzer he turns to consequentialism, which bases moral decisions upon the likelihood that the benefit of an action will outweigh the harm. Boyle argues that such utilitarianism weakens the authority of the moral world by allowing exceptions to moral principles in times of emergency. He concludes that the method of rationalistic deontology provided by Donagan is preferable to Walzer's casuistry.

**Boyle, Joseph**. Catholic Social Justice and Health Care Entitlement Packages. *Christian Bioethics*, 2(3), 280-292, 1996.

This paper explores the implications of Roman Catholic teachings on social justice and rights to health care. It argues that contemporary societies, such as those in North America and Western Europe, have an obligation to provide health care to their citizens as a matter of right. Moral considerations provide a basis for evaluating concerns about the role of equality when determining health care entitlements and giving some precision to the widespread belief that the right to health care requires equal entitlement to health care benefits.

**Boyle, Joseph** (ed) and Sumner, L W (ed). *Philosophical Perspectives on Bioethics*. Toronto, Univ of Toronto Pr, 1996.

How should we attempt to resolve concrete bioethical problems? How are we to understand the role of bioethics in the health care system, government, and academe? This collection of original essays raises these and other questions about the nature of bioethics as a discipline. The contributors to the volume discuss various approaches to bioethical thinking and the political and institutional context of bioethics, addressing underlying concerns about the purposes of its practice. Included are extended analyses of such important issues as the conduct of clinical trials, euthanasia, justice in health care, the care of children, cosmetic surgery, and reproductive technologies.

**Boyle, Robert** and Hunter, Michael (ed) and Davis, Edward B (ed). *A Free Enquiry into the Vulgarly Received Notion of Nature*. New York, Cambridge Univ Pr, 1996.

In this book, published in 1686, the scientist Robert Boyle (1627-91) attacked prevailing notions of the natural world which depicted 'Nature' as a wise, benevolent and purposeful being. Boyle, one of the leading mechanical philosophers of his day, believed that the world was best understood as a vast, impersonal machine, fashioned by an infinite, personal God. In this cogent treatise, he drew on his scientific findings, his knowledge of contemporary medicine and his deep reflection on theological and philosophical issues, arguing that it was inappropriate both theologically and scientifically to speak of Nature as if it had a mind of its own: instead, the only true efficient causes of things were the properties and powers given to matter by God. As such, *A Free Enquiry into the Vaguely Received Notion of Nature* represents one of the subtlest statements concerning the philosophical issues raised by the mechanical philosophy to emerge from the period of the scientific revolution. (publisher, edited)

**Boyles, Deron R**. "Sophistry, Dialectic, and Teacher Education: A Reinterpretation of Plato's *Meno*" in *Philosophy of Education (1996)*, Margonis, Frank (ed), 102-109. Urbana, Phil Education Soc, 1997.

This essay argues for a rereading of *Meno* and attempts two specific goals: 1) reviving Plato's indictment of sophistry as an important and timely way to investigate what it means to achieve a deeper sensibility of teaching and learning; and 2) demonstrating that the Socrates/slave-boy "dialectic" is actually a display of sophistry, for sophists, to demonstrate the flaws of sophistry. By offering such an interpretation as 2) an argument is made against sophistry and for authentic dialectic (vs. Socratic dialectic) in contemporary schools. To have authentic dialectic in American schools, teacher-education programs should engage teachers and prospective teachers in the kind of dialectic for which this essay argues.

**Bozicevic, Vanda**. Tractarian Support for a Nonpropositional Paradigm. *Acta Analytica*, 191-207, 1995.

Wittgenstein's *Tractatus*, and particularly his views on 'logical space' and 'formal concepts' are relevant for the contemporary debate on types of mental representation. This paper focuses on the central example—the formal concept of colour and discusses it within the framework of contrasting propositional and nonpropositional representations (along the lines proposed by Peter Gärdenfors). The formal concept may be interpreted as a pattern in a conceptual space with enough quality dimensions (adequate "mathematical multiplicity") to enable the representation of the internal structure of objects within the concept. The nonpropositional model represents the densely graded nature of for example colour properties by the continuous character of the relevant quality-dimension, while Wittgenstein (in "Some Remarks on Logical Form") in vain tries to accommodate these formal properties with his atomistic doctrine. It is argued that Wittgenstein's intuitions regarding the "formal concept" (Formalbegriff) of colour correspond better to the nonpropositional paradigm of representation than his original atomistic and propositional one, which he tried to impose on them.

**Bozo de Carmona, Ana Julia**. Political Concertation (Agreement) Among Social Actors: The Challenge of Venezuelan Democracy (Spanish). *Fronesis*, 3(1), 71-96, Ap 96.

The Venezuelan political system was set up on a framework of constitutive agreements among the 1958 main political actors. Such agreements placed the government among the important actors and based political practice on the negotiation of the leading groups. In the Venezuelan political system, political concentration excludes social actors. Democracy is weak and committed to hegemonic political actors. A transformation of democracy is necessary as an alternative in order to move forward in the solution of the political crisis. Legitimization of the political system, understood as the political participation of the emerging social actors, comes out as a nonviolent possibility of democracy transformation.

**Bozzetti, Mauro**. Il Platone insegnato da Hegel: Alcune considerazioni sul quaderno di Griesheim (Wintersemester 1825-1826). *Riv Filosof Neo-Scolas*, 88(2), 310-324, Ap-Je 96.

**Brabeck, Mary M** and Ting, Kathleen. Context, Politics and Moral Education: Comments on the Misgeld?Magendzo Conversation about Human Rights Education. *J Moral Educ*, 26(2), 147-149, Je 97.

We comment on Misgeld's and Magendzo's call for a political analysis of moral education, in which governmental, economic and social control goals are critically examined. We suggest character education programs overlook the necessity of engagement in historical analysis and critique of unjust systems and fail to recognize that politics are inevitable and inextricably involved in moral education. As a corrective to Kohlbergian theory, moral educators ought to stay close to the experience of people, so as not to get lost in immobilizing intellectual abstraction. Human rights education offers a corrective to both moral education and character education programs.

**Braddon-Mitchell, David** and Nola, Robert. Ramsification and Glymour's Counterexample. *Analysis*, 57(3), 167-169, Jl 97.

**Bradie, Michael**. Ontic Realism and Scientific Explanation. *Proc Phil Sci Ass*, 3(Suppl), S315-S321, 1996.

Wesley Salmon defends an ontic realism that distinguishes explanatory from descriptive knowledge. Explanatory knowledge makes appeals to (unobservable) theoretical acausal mechanisms. Salmon presents an argument designed both to legitimize attributing truth values to theoretical claims and to justify treating theoretical claims as descriptions. The argument succeeds but only at the price of calling the distinction between explanation and description into question. Even if Salmon's attempts to distinguish causal mechanisms from other mechanisms are successful, the assumed centrality of the appeal to such mechanisms in providing scientific explanations is left open by Salmon's account.

**Bradley, Gerard V**. A Case for Proposition 209. *Notre Dame J Law Ethics*, 11(1), 97-119, 1997.

**Bradley, James**. "From Presence to Process: Bradley and Whitehead" in *Philosophy after F.H. Bradley*, Bradley, James (ed), 147-168. Bristol, Thoemmes, 1996.

The nature of F.H. Bradley's theory of feeling as a theory of being, of contradiction, and as a transcendental principle is analyzed. Whitehead takes up Bradley's theory of feeling and his transcendentalism but rejects his view of reality as completely and timelessly present. Taking the step which Bradley's work invites, Whitehead analyzes the real in terms of difference and without reference to any principle of cause or production.

**Bradley, James** (ed). *Philosophy after F.H. Bradley*. Bristol, Thoemmes, 1996.

**Bradley, James**. Transcendentalism and Speculative Realism in Whitehead. *Process Stud*, 23(3-4), 155-191, Fall-Wint 94.

In order to maintain the irreducibility of the thought-existence distinction and the possibility of the rational analysis of self-actualization, Whitehead's speculative event-theory offers a new kind of transcendental philosophy: all the categories of this speculative scheme are transcendental conditions of a special

type—they are transcendental conditions of self-actualization. The question of how Whitehead's transcendental theory is related to his speculative realism is discussed by way of his use and critique of the propositional function to elaborate a theory of speculative construction. Various obstacles to a transcendental reading of Whitehead are considered, as well as the significance of his analysis of existence.

**Bradley, James**. Whitehead, Contemporary Metaphysics, and Maritain's Critique of Bergson. *Maritain Stud*, 9, 113-134, 1993.

**Bradshaw, David**. All Existing is the Action of God: The Philosophical Theology of David Braine. *Thomist*, 60(3), 379-416, Jl 96.

**Bradshaw, David**. Aristotle on Perception: The Dual-Logos Theory. *Apeiron*, 30(2), 143-161, Je 97.

Recent interpretations of Aristotle's theory of perception fall into two camps: those holding that in the act of perception the sense organ literally takes on the quality perceived (Ross, Hamlyn, Sorabji, Cohen) and those holding that it undergoes no physical change at all (Burnyeat, Scaltsas). I argue for a third alternative, the "dual-logos theory." It posits two *logoi* in the sense organ. One is fixed and gives the organ its power to perceive; the other fluctuates to match the *logos* of the perceived quality.

**Brady, Geraldine**. "From the Algebra of Relations to the Logic of Quantifiers" in *Studies in the Logic of Charles Sanders Peirce*, Houser, Nathan (ed), 173-192. Bloomington, Indiana Univ Pr, 1997.

**Brady, James B**. Conscious Negligence. *Amer Phil Quart*, 33(3), 325-335, Jl 96.

The border between recklessness and negligence is a disputed one. Does recklessness require awareness of risk? Does negligence imply unawareness of risk or can there be conscious negligence? The predominant view is that negligence does imply unawareness of risk. This article explores several theories that argue, on descriptive or normative grounds, that there can be conscious negligence. The article draws the distinction between recklessness and negligence, and shows why recklessness, which may differ in degree, is more culpable than negligence. Finally, the article argues that there are borderline cases that are not easily classified as either recklessness or negligence.

**Brady, James B**. Recklessness. *Law Phil*, 15(2), 183-200, 96.

This article argues against the view that there can be 'inadvertent' recklessness. Various accounts of recklessness in terms of awareness of risk and indifference to risk are examined. The argument is that the conceptual requirement of awareness in recklessness point to a normative distinction between recklessness and negligence. The element of awareness is necessary for the 'positive' indifference displayed by recklessness and this indifference is more culpable than the lack of care displayed by negligence.

**Brady, Neil** and Velasquez, Manuel. Natural Law and Business Ethics. *Bus Ethics Quart*, 7(2), 83-107, Mr 97.

We describe the Catholic natural law tradition by examining its origins in the medieval penitentials, the papal decretals, the writings of Thomas Aquinas and seventeenth century casuistry. Catholic natural law emerges as a flexible ethic that conceives of human nature as rational and as oriented to certain basic goods that ought to be pursued and whose pursuit is made possible by the virtues. We then identify four approaches to natural law that have evolved within the United States during the twentieth century, including the traditionalist, proportionalist, right reason and historicist approaches. (edited)

**Brady, Ross T**. Simple Gentzenizations for the Normal Formulae of Contraction-less Logics. *J Sym Log*, 61(4), 1321-1346, D 96.

We develop an innovative method, which makes essential use of a restriction to normality, to establish two simple Gentzenizations for the normal formulae of the logic B and then extend the method to other sentential contraction-less logics. To obtain the first of these Gentzenizations, for the logics B and DW, we remove two branching rules, together with a structural connective, to simplify the elimination of the inversion rules and 't'. We then eliminate two further rules, thus reducing the Gentzen system to one containing only negation and entailment and reduce the remaining types of structures to four simple finite types.

**Brady, Teresa**. The After-Acquired Evidence Defense: The Unethical Repercussions to Employees. *Bus Prof Ethics J*, 15(1), 53-65, Spr 96.

The after-acquired evidence defense is used in employment law cases to shield employers from liability when they fire an employee for a discriminatory reason in violation of law. The defense is available when evidence is uncovered during pretrial litigation that the employee committed misconduct that, if known by the employer, would have resulted in termination. The 1995 Supreme Court precedent setting case, *McKennon v. Nashville Banner Publishing Company*, defined the recovery to the employee as back pay from the date of the discriminatory discharge, to the date that the wrongdoing was discovered. Ethical issues affecting employees include encouraging "witch hunts" by employers to uncover employee wrongdoing.

**Brague, Rémi**. "A Medieval Model of Subjectivity: Toward a Rediscovery of Fleshliness" in *The Ancients and the Moderns*, Lilly, Reginald (ed), 230-247. Bloomington, Indiana Univ Pr, 1996.

The concept of flesh played a central part in the Medieval experience of subjectivity, commonly overlooked in the issue *ancients* vs. *moderns*: as an anthropological criterion to distinguish man as fleshly from the angels as bodiless minds, as a sensory paradigm for self-awareness in the sense of touch, as a moral incentive to humility as the basic virtue. Modern thought could benefit from a rediscovery of man's fleshly dimension: in anthropology, it enables us not to reduce humanity to rationality, in hermeneutics, it underlines the social dimension of understanding, in ethics, it could help us to cope with postsecularization.

**Brague, Rémi**. Cosmological Mysticism: The Imitation of the Heavenly Bodies in Ibn Tufayl's *Hayy ibn Yaqzan*. *Grad Fac Phil J*, 19/20(2/1), 91-102, 1997.

In Ibn Tufayl's (d. 1185) *Hayy ibn Yaqzan*, the hero is supposed to discover by its unaided reason the highest metaphysical truths. The last step but one in his ascension consists in imitating the heavenly bodies and their orderly revolutions, thereby preparing himself to assimilate himself to God. The idea has Greek roots in Plato, but Ibn Tufayl sets it into a broader pattern, in which this imitation parallels practices required by Islamic religious law, and supplements pure assimilation to God with a "political" dimension. (*Grad Fac Phil J*, 19/20 (2/1), 91-102, 1997)

**Braidotti, Rosi**. Meta(l)morphoses. *Theor Cult Soc*, 14(2), 67-80, My 97.

**Braidotti, Rosi**. Nomadism with a Difference: Deleuze's Legacy in a Feminist Perspective. *Man World*, 29(3), 305-314, Jl 96.

This article, written for a special issue dedicated to Deleuze soon after his death, assesses the state of the debate between feminist philosophy and Deleuze's thought. It emphasizes especially the theories of becoming, the nomadology and the issue of affectivity and desire. Special attention is devoted to the question of the becoming-woman in Deleuze's scheme of thought: this notion is first assessed conceptually, then an overview is provided of the feminist discussions of it. Finally a balanced conclusion is proposed, in which a positive evaluation is given of Deleuze's philosophy of desire and becoming and of its contribution to feminist debates about how to rethink the subject.

**Brainard, Marcus** (ed & trans) and Boeder, Heribert. *Seditions: Heidegger and the Limit of Modernity*. Albany, SUNY Pr, 1997.

This is the first book-length work by Heribert Boeder to appear in English. The essays brought together here, several of which are to be found only in this volume, bear witness to a new perspective on metaphysics, modernity and so-called postmodernity. The "seditiousness" of Boeder's undertaking lies in his twofold intention: to explicate what has been thought in metaphysics, modernity and postmodernity as self-contained, rational *totalities*—as history, world and speech, respectively—and by means of those explications to recover dwelling as it has been made visible in the "configurations of wisdom" (for example, in Homer, Paul and Hölderlin). He approaches each of these totalities by way of Heidegger's thought, which marks the limit of modernity and as such is pivotal to Boeder's enterprise. (publisher, edited)

**Brajicic, Rudolf**. The Metaphysical Roots of Philosophical Tolerance and its Substitutes. *Filozof Istraz*, 16(3), 579-585, 1996.

Mit die Toleranz ersetzenden Formen negiert man keineswegs den Geist der Toleranz, sondern die Richtigkeit der jeweiligen Verkörperung dieses Geistes. Dazu gehören: Pantheon, Synkretismus verschiedener Kulte und Religionen, New Age, philosophischer synkretistischer Eklektizismus, Wahrheit-srelativismus, Strukturalismus, Kantismus, Neopositivismus. Zur Eindämmung des philosophischen Pluralismus empfiehlt sich die Methode des Versuchs in Analogie zum Experiment in den exakten Wissenschaften: eine These muss zunächst a priori bewiesen, dann erfahrungsmässig geprüft werden, damit die Gegenthese verworfen werden kann. (edited)

**Brancacci, Aldo**. Zénon et la statue (fr. 246 Arnim). *Diotima*, 25, 110-117, 1997.

**Branchi, Andrea**. Filosofia o letteratura? Mandeville, Fielding e il contesto settecentesco. *Iride*, 9(18), 431-441, Ag 96.

L'articolo prende in considerazione l'ipotesi che l'analisi della vita passionale e morale degli uomini sviluppata dagli "scienziati della natura umana" abbia segnato in modo decisivo le forme della narrativa inglese del Settecento. Sottolineando la necessità di forzare categorie mutuate dalla critica contemporanea, attraverso l'analisi di alcuni lavori del "filosofo" Bernard Mandeville e del "romanziere" Henry Fielding, viene messo in luce come i tratti distintivi del *novel* come nuovo genere—la verosimiglianza dei caratteri e la dominanza del tema morale—emergano da un dibattito sulla natura umana che coinvolge la cultura inglese della prima metà del Settecento nel suo complesso.

**Brandl, Johannes**. Austrian Philosophy: The Legacy of Franz Brentano. *Phil Phenomenol Res*, 57(3), 697-702, S 97.

This review essay critically examines the claim made by Barry Smith in his book on *The Legacy of Franz Brentano* (Open Court 1994), namely that there is a specific unity in Austrian philosophy which connects the members of the Brentano-School with other Austrian philosophers, especially with the logical empiricist. It is argued that this claim can neither be supported by the rising political liberalism in Austria at the time, nor by generalizing the Aristotelianism characteristic of Brentano, nor by tracing back the antimetaphysical attitude characteristic of the Vienna Circle. Despite its questionable historic perspective, however, Smith's book can be recommended as a competent introduction to the philosophy of Brentano and his followers, notably Anton Marty, Alexius Meinong, Kasimir Twardowski, Tadeusz Kotarbinski and Christian Ehrenfels.

**Brandner, Rudolf**. Aristotele e la fondazione henologica dell'ontologia. *Riv Filosof Neo-Scolas*, 88(2), 183-204, Ap-Je 96.

**Brandom, Robert**. "Perception and Rational Constraint: McDowell's *Mind and World*" in *Perception*, Villanueva, Enrique (ed), 241-259. Atascadero, Ridgeview, 1996.

The paper argues that McDowell's well-motivated requirement that a theory of perception explain how perceptible facts can *rationally* and not merely *causally* constrain the perceiver's judgments does not, as he thinks it does, require the postulation of conceptually articulated but prejudgmental perceptual experiences. A latent commitment to individualism blinds McDowell to the significance of rational assessments and criticisms of the warrant for perceptual judgments in light of the facts that are available from a third-person perspective.

**Brandom, Robert**. Précis of *Making It Explicit*. *Phil Phenomenol Res*, 57(1), 153-156, Mr 97.

The book is an attempt to explain the *meanings* of linguistic expressions in terms of their *use*. The explanatory strategy is to begin with an account of social practices, to identify the particular structure they must exhibit in order to qualify as specifically *linguistic* practices, and then to consider what different sorts of semantic contents those practices can confer on states, performances, and expressions caught up in them in suitable ways. The result is a kind of conceptual role semantics that is at once firmly rooted in actual practices of producing and consuming speech acts, and sufficiently finely articulated to make clear how those practices are capable of conferring a rich variety of kinds of content.

**Brandom, Robert**. Replies. *Phil Phenomenol Res*, 57(1), 189-204, Mr 97.

Four replies to comments on *Making It Explicit*. The reply to John McDowell concerns the semantic privileging of inference over representation. The reply to Gideon Rosen concerns the role of discursive norms, specifically the relations between normative statuses and normative attitudes. The reply to Richard Rorty concerns relativism and the identification of facts with true claims (in the sense of what is claimed or claimable, rather than on claimings). The reply to Jay Rosenberg concerns objectivity and the differences between various sorts of facts (for instance, between natural facts and normative facts).

**Brandon, Edwin P**. California Unnatural: On Fine's Natural Ontological Attitude. *Phil Quart*, 47(187), 232-235, Ap 97.

Abela accepts Fine's account of realism and instrumentalism, but thinks we can reject the natural ontological attitude by distinguishing the theoretical attempt to make sense of scientific practice from choosing the attitude we bring to science itself. But Abela's attitudes are vulnerable to Fine's criticisms of the philosophical positions. However, if we take attitude as contrastive and as full-blooded enough to lead to different behavior we see a gap in Fine's position. He cannot tell us why it is science he trusts. When we look more widely, the philosophical positions might be seen as ways of justifying that trust.

**Brandon, Robert N** and Carson, Scott. The Indeterministic Character of Evolutionary Theory: No "No Hidden Variables Proof" but No Room for Determinism Either. *Phil Sci*, 63(3), 315-337, S 96.

In this paper we first briefly review Bell's (1964, 1966) Theorem to see how it invalidates any deterministic "hidden variable" account of the apparent indeterminacy of quantum mechanics (QM). Then we show that quantum uncertainty, at the level of DNA mutations, can "percolate" up to have major populational effects. Interesting as this point may be it does not show any autonomous indeterminism of the evolutionary process. In the next two sections we investigate drift and natural selection as the locus of autonomous biological indeterminacy. Here we conclude that the population-level indeterminacy of natural selection and drift are ultimately based on the assumption of a fundamental indeterminacy at the level of the lives and deaths of individual organisms. The following section examines this assumption and defends it from the determinists' attack. Then we show that, even if one rejects the assumption, there is still an important reason why one might think evolutionary theory (ET) is autonomously indeterministic. In the concluding section we contrast the arguments we have mounted against a deterministic hidden variable account of ET with the proof of the impossibility of such an account of QM.

**Brandt, Reinhard**. Antwort auf Bernd Ludwig: Will die Natur unwiderstehlich die Republik?. *Kantstudien*, 88(2), 229-237, 1997.

What are Kant's views on how a republican constitution could be established given that the subjects of such a constitution are "devils", i.e., agents who are not morally but only egoistically motivated? According to Ludwig, Kant thinks that the task is fulfilled, not *through* the devils, but *for* them: in *Perpetual Peace*, Kant shows how a moral politician can realize his aim to establish a republic for them. Against this interpretation, it is argued that Kant explicitly brings into play a stoic-deistic conception of nature: there are mechanisms in nature governing the conduct of devils and which ultimately force the devils to establish a republican constitution even if they themselves are not morally motivated.

**Brandt, Reinhard** and Watkins, Eric (ed & trans). *The Table of Judgments: Critique of Pure Reason A 67-76; B 92-101*. Atascadero, Ridgeview, 1995.

The "transcendental table of all moments of thought in judgments" (A73), generally called simply the "table of judgments," is located at the beginning of the Transcendental Logic and provides a systematic outline of the rest of the *Critique of Pure Reason's* philosophical development. According to Kant, the concepts of the understanding or categories can be derived from the table of judgments. In turn, the categories provide the plan for the Principles of Pure Understanding. The ideas of reason in the second part of the Transcendental Logic, that is, in the Dialectic, are both situated in the systematic plan justified by the table of judgments and grounded in the table of judgments. Our investigation will show that the Doctrine of Method, which follows upon the doctrines of the *concepts* of the understanding, *principles*, and *inferences*, will find its place in the table of judgments as well; it corresponds to the fourth heading, that of modality. (publisher, edited)

**Branham, R Bracht** (ed) and Goulet-Cazé, Marie-Odile (ed). *The Cynics: The Cynic Movement in Antiquity and Its Legacy*. Berkeley, Univ of Calif Pr, 1996.

This collection of essays—the first of its kind in English—brings together the work of an international group of scholars examining the entire tradition associated with the ancient Cynics. The essays give a history of the movement as well as a state-of-the-art account of the literary, philosophical and cultural significance of Cynicism from antiquity to the present. (publisher)

**Brann, Eva T H**. Mere Reading. *Phil Lit*, 20(2), 383-397, O 96.

"Mere Reading" declares for a straightforward, immediate approach to texts and gives thirteen precepts useful to reading in this unsophisticated and untheoretical way. Among them are: eschewing the pronoun "we" in making epochal assertions; surrendering the notion that critics are superior to authors; doubting the hypothesis that literature is like a natural kind; readmitting the author as standing behind the work; instilling both reverence and discrimination in students; writing the plainest possible, nontheoretical prose when interpreting works; refraining from standing between students and books by doing "backgrounding;" and above all, recovering faith in the representative imagination.

**Brant, Dale Eric**. On Plantinga's Way Out. *Faith Phil*, 14(3), 334-352, Jl 97.

The foreknowledge problem involves two assumptions. First, that "God once believed that an event would occur now" is about the past. Second, that it is equivalent to "God once existed and the event is occurring now." These, Plantinga argues, are incompatible. But *he* (implicitly) makes assumptions. First, that equivalent propositions are *both* about a given time, so is (neither is) its negation. Third, that if two propositions are (are not) about a given time, so is (neither is) their conjunction. *These*, though plausible, are incompatible.

**Brasa Díaz, Mariano**. Métodos y cuestiones filosóficas en la Escuela de Traductores de Toledo. *Rev Espan Filosof Med*, 4, 35-49, 1997.

In this paper, after a preliminary section on twelfth-century Spain, I will present medieval Renaissance Toledo where—in the School of Translators—the great translators did their work and out of which most of the philosophical works by Arab authors, translated to Latin, emerged. I will also talk about other roads, other regions and other translators. Finally, I will consider the Alfonsian translations and I will conclude with two appendices showing the works translated by Ibn Daound-Gundisalvo and by Gerardo de Cremona.

**Braude, Stephen E**. Commentary on "A Discursive Account of Multiple Personality Disorder". *Phil Psychiat Psych*, 4(3), 223-226, S 97.

**Braun, David**. "Causally Relevant Properties" in *AI, Connectionism and Philosophical Psychology, 1995*, Tomberlin, James E (ed), 447-475. Atascadero, Ridgeview, 1995.

A causally relevant property is (roughly) a property of a cause "in virtue of which" it causes its effect. This paper presents and criticizes a well-known counterfactual analysis of causally relevant properties. It then presents a new analysis, one that appeals to the essential properties and natural properties of the cause. Finally, it applies this new analysis to certain cases of mental causation and concludes that the content properties of beliefs can be causally relevant to behavior.

**Braun, Walter**. On the Crisis of Culture, Its Values and Value Education (in German). *Prima Philosophia*, 10(3), 359-378, 1997.

The concept of culture had its beginning with Kant and meant metaphysics, religion and consciousness, but not pluralism. By de Montaigne and Herder, e.g., and in the so-called philosophy of life the term of culture was changing. The concepts of values and goods are linked with it both in modern times. Scheler and N. Hartmann developed two theories of the values and its adherence to the concept of culture; it leads to the formal objectivism of values, but they hollow it out. In the science of education, the term value was started independently and leads to a deeper subjectivism, particularly in Götter, Kerschensteiner and Meister.

**Bravo, Francisco**. Incoherence in the Aristotelian Philosophy of Action? (Spanish). *Rev Filosof (Venezuela)*, Supp(2-3), 87-101, 1996.

In this paper a critical revision is made of the Aristotelian contraposition of the concepts of action and production. The author studies the proposals of H.G. Gadamer, J.L. Ackrill, Hanna Arendt and others, who have treated these concepts and have tried to resolve the initial contraposition as proposed by Aristotle.

**Bravo García, Antonio**. Aristóleles en la España del siglo XVI. Antecedentes, alcance y matices de su influencia. *Rev Espan Filosof Med*, 4, 203-249, 1997.

The aim of this paper is to explain, on the basis of some significant testimonies, the way in which Aristotelianism penetrates in Spain and how this penetration of the new Aristotelian thought in the European countries reveals a permanent conflict between the Middle Ages and the Renaissance, particularly in Spain, where the discovery and the use of the ancient authorities very often constitutes an important theoretical problem. The author shows some of these difficulties with examples from many fields (philosophy, science, literature).

**Bray, Robert**. Reading between the Texts: Benjamin Thomas's *Abraham Lincoln* and Stephen Oates's *With Malice Toward None*. *J Infor Ethics*, 3(1), 8-24, Spr 94.

**Breazeale, Daniel**. Der fragwürdige *Primat der praktischen Vernunft* in Fichtes *Grundlage der gesamten Wissenschaftslehre*. *Fichte-Studien*, 10, 253-271, 1997.

**Breckman, Warren** and Trägårdh, Lars. Nationalism, Individualism, and Capitalism: Reply to Greenfield. *Crit Rev*, 10(3), 389-407, Sum 96.

Reversing the arguments of Anderson, Gellner, and Hobsbawm, Liah Greenfield contends that it is nationalism that produces economic development. Specifically, she claims that nationalism inspired three seminal economic thinkers: Marx, List, and Smith. However, Greenfield's ideological preferences lead her to a problematic conception of individualism as nationalism, as well as to flawed treatments of Smith, List, and Marx. Nationalism is better understood as an attempt to address the deepening conflict between the imperative of community and the secular trends of the marketplace, which challenge national sovereignty and democracy.

**Bredlow, Luis**. De lo eterno a lo infinito: un intento de reconstrución del argumento de Meliso (B2-4 D-K). *Convivium*, 10, 1-16, 1997.

The author attempts to offer a logically consistent and historically plausible reconstruction of Melissus's proof of the infinity of what is (Mel. B 2-4 D-K), traditionally considered a textbook case of fallacy. Melissus's true demonstration of infinity is the one mentioned bay Aristotle in *De gen. et corr.* I 8, 325 a 13 (= Mel. B 4 a Reale), while B 2, where this proof has habitually been searched for, contains only a previous statement (first phrase) of the two arguments to follow and the development of the first one; the latter one, about spatial infinity, was developed in the second part of the fragment, which has been lost except the first phrase (B 3). The reinterpretation of the first part as a proof of infinity is due to Aristotle, who succeeded at masterfully exploiting the formal defects of the argument in order to charge his adversary's most important thesis with a logically inconsistent demonstration never used as such by Melissus himself.

**Breeur, Roland**. Bergson, Duration and Singularity. *Tijdschr Filosof*, 58(3), 439-460, S 96.

This article first attempts to reframe Bergson's elaboration (in *Time and Free Will*) of time as duration within his general critique of Kant. It argues that the key to Bergson's revision of the Kantian image of time is Kant's schematism, and more precisely the scheme of the category of magnitude (*Grösse*). Instead of being a determination of time, as Kant thought, the scheme of magnitude (the number) is a determination of space. Thus, what Kant thought to be time and the form of the inner sensibility is in fact space. Bergson will then develop the more basic image of the *Innerlichkeit* as duration. The second and last part of the article describes his image of duration in relation to the problem of identity and singularity, contrasting his view with that of Marcel Proust.

**Bremer, Manuel**. Möglichkeits- und Unmöglichkeitsbedingungen des religiösen Diskurses. *Frei Z Phil Theol*, 44(1-2), 44-67, 1997.

**Brennan, Marie** and Popkewitz, Thomas S. Restructuring of Social and Political Theory in Education: Foucault and a Social Epistemology of School Practices. *Educ Theor*, 47(3), 287-313, Sum 97.

**Brennan, Samantha**. "Moral Rights and Moral Math: Three Arguments against Aggregation" in *A Question of Values: New Canadian Perspectives in Ethics and Political Philosophy*, Brennan, Samantha (ed), 29-38. Amsterdam, Rodopi, 1997.

Do the numbers count? Sceptical worries about aggregation are usually raised in the context of moral obligation. But this is not the only place such worries arise. This paper examines arguments against aggregation as they affect the conditions that justify infringing moral rights. I examine three arguments: Judith Thomson's appeal to the special nature of rights; Robert Nozick's "separateness of persons" argument; and John Taurek's value scepticism. I argue that all three arguments fail and that we must look elsewhere for the source of our intuitions about the impermissibility of infringing rights on the basis of group benefits.

**Brennan, Samantha** (ed) and Isaacs, Tracy (ed) and Milde, Michael (ed). *A Question of Values: New Canadian Perspectives in Ethics and Political Philosophy.* Amsterdam, Rodopi, 1994.

This book reflects a cross-section of the issues concerning values that are of contemporary philosophical interest in Canada and the United States. In the three parts of the book, ten philosophers bring fresh perspectives to bear upon questions of metaethics, freedom and autonomy and political philosophy. The studies concentrate upon acts, values and human lives; moral character, moral behavior and moral imagination; the limits of liberalism and communitarianism; social contract and institutions; and the morality of nationalism. (publisher)

**Brennan, Samantha** and Noggle, Robert. The Moral Status of Children: Children's Rights, Parents' Rights, and Family Justice. *Soc Theor Pract*, 23(1), 1-26, Spr 97.

This paper aims to provide a philosophical foundation for thinking about the moral status of children. Three plausible constraints on moral theorizing about children are put forward: The Equal Consideration Thesis, the Unequal Treatment Thesis and the Limited Parental Rights Thesis. While these claims underlie much common sense thinking about the moral status and treatment of children, the claims also appear to be inconsistent. A right-based theory of the moral status of children is proposed which both meets the three constraints and resolves their internal conflicts. A final section examines the policy implications of the proposed account.

**Brennan, Tad**. Reasonable Impressions in Stoicism. *Phronesis*, 41(3), 318-334, 1996.

**Brennan, Teresa**. Projecting Political Correctness: The Divorce of Affect and Signifier. *S J Phil*, 34(Supp), 99-108, 1996.

This article explores the way in which postmodernism's emphasis on the uncoupling of signifier and referent has a parallel in the practice of the *new right*. The argument is that this parallel is a historical consequence of a form of objectification that detaches signifiers not from referents as such, but from the emotional meaning they have accrued. Accordingly, despite its questions about postmodernism, the argument runs contra traditional emancipatory theories: the advent of modernity is not progress.

**Brenner, William H**. Theology as Grammar. *S J Phil*, 34(4), 439-454, Wint 96.

Theology is commonly viewed as para-cosmological speculation. My paper is a development and defense of a contrary view, one suggested by the parenthetical remark in *Philosophical Investigation*, sec. 373: "Theology as Grammar." It features a Wittgensteinian interpretation of "religious language" and of the ontological argument.

**Brent, Joseph**. Pursuing Peirce. *Synthese*, 106(3), 301-322, Mr 96.

Charles S Peirce, polymath, philosopher, logician, lived a life of often wild extremes and when he died in 1914, had earned a vile reputation as a

Brentano, Franz 538 AUTHOR INDEX

debauched genius. Yet he created a unified, profound and brilliant work, both published and unpublished, a fact difficult to explain. In my 1993 biography, I proposed three hypotheses to account for his "Jekyll-Hyde" character: his obsession with the puzzle of meaning, two neurological pathologies, trigeminal neuralgia and left-handedness and the powerful influence of his father. After publication, further research has led me to propose two additional hypotheses to explain his extraordinary life: manic-depressive illness and mystical experience, the last greatly influencing the development of his doctrine of semeiotic, of which his logic of science is a part.

**Brentano, Franz** and Müller, Benito (ed & trans). *Descriptive Psychology.* New York, Routledge, 1995.

The book contains a first English translation of a lecture series given by Brentano at the University of Vienna between 1887 and 1891. In these lectures, Brentano presents the mature culmination of the ideas he initially published in his psychology from an Empirical Standpoint (1874). The topics dealt with are: Psychognosy and Genetic Psychology; Elements of Consciousness; The Correct Method of the Psychognost; The Components of Human Consciousness; The Components of Human Consciousness; Psychical Acts; The General Character of Sensations; Inner Perception; Descriptive Psychology or Descriptive Phenomenology; On the Content of Experiences; Psychognostic Sketch; Perceiving, Apperceiving, Clearly Apperceiving, Compounded Apperceiving, Transcendentally Apperceiving.

**Breteau, Jean-Louis**. "Origène était-il pour Cudworth le modèle du philosophe chrétien?" in *Mind Senior to the World,* Baldi, Marialuisa, 127-147. Milano, FrancoAngeli, 1996.

**Breteau, Jean-Louis**. *Le contrat dans les pays anglo-saxons: théories et pratiques.* 31000 Toulouse, Pr Univ Mirail, 1995.

L'ouvrage s'attache d'abord à dégager l'originalité de la notion de contrat dans le droit anglais ou américain. Il retrace ensuite l'émergence du concept de *contrat social*, coeur de la philosophie politique depuis Hobbes jusqu'à Paine. Il tente enfin, après avoir fait le point sur l'évolution récente de la philosophie de Rawls, théoricien moderne du contrat, d'explorer les pratiques contractuelles contemporaines dans des domaines variés: expérience constitutionnelle nord-américaine, discours politique des années soixante-dix et législation déléguée au Royaume-Uni ou relecture du *contrat social* par les sociologues d'aujourd'hui. (publisher, edited)

**Breton, André** and Polizzotti, Mark (trans). *The Lost Steps.* Lincoln, Univ of Nebraska Pr, 1996.

*The Lost Steps* (*Les Pas perdus*) is André Breton's first collection of critical and polemical essays. Composed between 1917 and 1923, these pieces trace his evolution during the years when he was emerging as a central figure in French (and European) intellectual life. They chronicle his tumultuous passage through the Dada movement, proclaim his explosive views on Modernism and its heroes, and herald the emergence of Surrealism itself. Along the way, we are given Breton's serious commentaries on his Modernist predecessors, Guillaume Apollinaire and Alfred Jarry, followed by his not-so-serious Dada manifestoes. (publisher,edited)

**Brett, Allan S**. Relationships between Primary Care Physicians and Consultants in Managed Care. *J Clin Ethics*, 8(1), 60-65, Spr 97.

**Breuer, Thomas**. Subjective Decoherence in Quantum Measurements. *Synthese*, 107(1), 1-17, Ap 96.

General results about restrictions on measurements from inside are applied to quantum mechanics. They imply subjective decoherence: For an apparatus it is not possible to determine whether the joint system consisting of itself and the observed system is in a statistical state with or without interference terms: it is possible that the apparatus systematically mistakes the real pure state of the joint system for the decohered state. We discuss the relevance of subjective decoherence for quantum measurements and for the problem of Wigner's friend.

**Breuer, Thomas**. Universell und unvollständig: Theorien über alles?. *Phil Natur*, 34(1), 1-20, 1997.

Sind universell gültige Theorien angesichts von Gödels Unvollständigkeitssatz möglich? Das ist die Hauptfrage dieser Arbeit. Die Antwort ist ungefähr: Der Unvollständigkeitssatz macht universell gültige Theorien nicht unmöglich; aber Probleme der Selbstreferenz schränken die Nützlichkeit solcher Theorien ein—falls es sie überhaupt gibt und falls wir sie zufällig finden. Es wird immer Fragen geben, die auch eine universell gültige physikalische Theorie nicht beantworten kann.

**Brewer, Bill**. Foundations of Perceptual Knowledge. *Amer Phil Quart*, 34(1), 41-55, Ja 97.

The article elucidates the sense in which perception constitutes a basic source of knowledge. Experience displays things as spatially related to the perceiver, in such a way that his grasp of where they are is given in terms of his understanding of the systematic dependence of their perceptibility upon their location. In arriving at empirical beliefs on its basis, therefore, he knows how he is right: in virtue of the spatial relations things bear to him, which enable his perception of them. This proposal is developed in detail, compared and contrasted with classical foundationalism, and defended against two important objections.

**Brewer, Bill**. Internalism and Perceptual Knowledge. *Euro J Phil*, 4(3), 259-275, D 96.

*Internalism* insists that perceptual knowledge requires a person's knowledge of how he is right about the world on the basis of perception. *Reflective internalism* claims that this condition is met by his independent knowledge of the general reliability of perception as a source of belief. I argue against influential foundationalist and coherentist versions of reflective internalism, and develop and defend a *nonreflective* internalism, according to which, in presenting the world as determinately located around him in the special way in which this is done in experience, perception itself presents things as epistemically accessible to the subject in that very experience.

**Brewer, Kathryn Balstad**. Management as a Practice: A Response to Alasdair MacIntyre. *J Bus Ethics*, 16(8), 825-833, Je 97.

The article is a critical response to the condemnation of the manager contained in Alasdair MacIntyre's book *After Virtue* (1984). First, MacIntyre's view of the manager is inconsistent with his position on the nature of human interaction. He presents the manager as a unified and unidimensional construct and places managerial intention and action within a single locale, thus contradicting his position on the lack of predictability in human behavior. Second, MacIntyre's theory of practice is applied to managerial work by contrasting it to medicine, a work category that is defined as a practice in *After Virtue.*

**Brewer, William F** and Chinn, Clark A. Mental Models in Data Interpretation. *Proc Phil Sci Ass*, 3(Suppl), S211-S219, 1996.

This paper presents a cognitive account of the process of evaluating scientific data. Our account assumes that when individuals evaluate data, they construct a mental model of a data-interpretation package, in which the data and theoretical interpretations of the data are integrated. We propose that individuals attempt to discount data by seeking alternative explanations for events within the mental model; data-interpretation packages are accepted when the individual cannot find alternative accounts for these events. Our analysis indicates that there are many levels at which data-interpretation packages can be accepted or denied.

**Bricker, Phillip**. Isolation and Unification: The Realist Analysis of Possible Worlds. *Phil Stud*, 84(2-3), 225-238, D 96.

If realism about possible worlds is to succeed in eliminating primitive modality, it must provide an *analysis* of possible world: nonmodal criteria for demarcating one world from another. This David Lewis has done. Lewis holds, roughly, that worlds are maximal unified regions of logical space. So far, so good. But what Lewis means by 'unification' is too narrow, I think, in two different ways. First, for Lewis, all worlds are (almost) *globally* unified: at any world, (almost) every part is directly linked to (almost) every other part. I hold instead that some worlds are *locally* unified: at some worlds, parts are directly linked only to "neighboring" parts. Second, for Lewis, each world is (analogically) *spatiotemporally* unified; every world is *spatiotemporally* isolated from every other. I hold instead: a world may be unified by nonspatiotemporal relations; every world is *absolutely* isolated from every other. If I am right, Lewis's conception of logical space is impoverished: perfectly respectable worlds are missing.

**Briddat, Birger P**. "Statt einer Einleitung: Essay über Unternehmens-philosophie—und darüber, was sie nicht ist" in *Werte und Entschei-dungen im Management,* Schmidt, Thomas, 11-18. Marburg, Metropolis, 1996.

**Bridger, Mark** and Alper, Joseph S. Mathematics, Model and Zeno's Paradoxes. *Synthese*, 110(1), 143-166, Ja 97.

A version of nonstandard analysis, *internal set theory*, has been used to provide a resolution of Zeno's paradoxes of motion. This resolution is inadequate because the application of internal set theory to the paradoxes requires a model of the world that is not in accordance with either experience or intuition. A model of standard mathematics in which the ordinary real numbers are defined in terms of rational intervals does provide a formalism for understanding the paradoxes. This model suggests that in discussing motion, only intervals, rather than instants, of time are meaningful. The approach presented here reconciles resolutions of the paradoxes based on considering a finite number of acts with those based on analysis of the full infinite set Zeno seems to require. The paper concludes with a brief discussion of the classical and quantum mechanics of performing an infinite number of acts in a finite time.

**Bridges, David**. Competence-Based Education and Training: Progress or Villainy?. *J Phil Educ*, 30(3), 361-376, N 96.

This paper notes the critical response that the 'competence movement' has received from writers in philosophy of education and argues for a more positive assessment of what it offers in relation to: I) the place of practical competence in a liberal education, II) the meritocratic principles underlying the competence movement, III) the 'transparency' of expectations in assessment and even IV) the element of practical competence in moral performance. It emphasises, however, that not all versions of 'competence' can be defended in these terms and that this requires a more generic and cognitively laden concept of personal and professional competence.

**Brien, Andrew**. Regulating Virtue: Formulating, Engendering and Enforcing Corporate Ethical Codes. *Bus Prof Ethics J*, 15(1), 21-52, Spr 96.

**Brien, Kevin M**. Marx and the Spiritual Dimension. *Topoi*, 15(2), 211-223, S 96.

Making a distinction between "spiritual forces" and the "religious form" these forces take on in most historical circumstances, this article argues for a positive conception of spirituality that is fully in harmony with Marx's philosophical perspective. Extending an analysis of Marx's dialectical method of explanation developed in an earlier work, the author shows how an understanding of the spiritual dimension can be situated in Marx's materialist world view; and that this dimension must be seen as being historically variable. The author explains how an unalienated mode of spirituality is possible; and shows how such a mode resonates with certain Buddhist conceptions of spirituality.

**Briese, Olaf**. Ethik der Endlichkeit: Zum Verweisungscharakter des Erhabenen bei Kant. *Kantstudien*, 87(3), 325-347, 1996.

This article investigates Kant's theory of the "sublime". It points out, that Kant's theory, which describes the intensive aesthetic feelings called forth by outstanding natural or artificial phenomena, like earthquakes, tempests or pyramids, is also extended to include a theory of death. Death, the ultimate and outstanding border of life, can also inspire this feeling of the sublime. But Kant, who prefers theories of immortality to theories of final death, manages to avoid this conclusion in his tree "critics". It was let to his disciples to develop the theory of sublime death.

**Brighouse, Harry**. Is There a Neutral Justification for Liberalism?. *Pac Phil Quart*, 77(3), 193-215, S 96.

Neutralist defenses of liberalism fail because they cannot account for essential features of an acceptable liberal theory: a firm guarantee for a sphere of individual liberty, an account of our interest in being able to revise our moral commitments, a wide range of applicability, and the possibility of legitimate government in the face of rejection by unreasonable citizens. A liberalism based on the value of autonomy can address the problems which motivate neutralists, while succeeding in providing for the essential features just mentioned.

**Brighouse, Harry**. Political Equality in Justice as Fairness. *Phil Stud*, 86(2), 155-184, My 97.

In *A Theory of Justice* Rawls treats the fair value of the political liberties as instrumental for justice; in *Political Liberalism*, without explanation, he includes it in the principles of justice, even though his argument for it, is still that it is functional for justice conceived independently. I explain why the fair value of the political liberties is best understood as equality of resources for political purposes, and give a Rawlsian argument for considering this partly constitutive of justice. I briefly explain that the new integration of the fair value of the political liberties into the conception of justice makes Rawls's theory more egalitarian than his egalitarian critics appear to think.

**Brighouse, Harry**. Should Marxists Care About Alienation?. *Topoi*, 15(2), 149-162, S 96.

The traditional Marxian concern with alienation violates a liberal concern with neutrality and thus presents a barrier to developing a Marxian political morality which is also liberal. I argue that the rational kernel to a Marxian concern with alienation—a concern with personal autonomy and with the transparency of social processes—is already contained within standard liberal views and that what remains should be rejected.

**Brimlow, Robert W**. Just Do It: Deniability and Renegades. *J Bus Ethics*, 16(1), 1-5, Ja 97.

When a "corporation" engages in unethical activity it is frequently difficult to determine whether the responsibility for such an action properly lies with management or should rather be ascribed to the employee engaged in the activity. In this paper I argue that managers ought to be held responsible for the moral environment in which employees work and that this be achieved through the implementation of a morals audit which focuses on the process of achieving objectives rather than on results.

**Brink, David O**. Self-Love and Altruism. *Soc Phil Pol*, 14(1), 122-157, Wint 97.

The metaphysical egoist aims to reconcile the demands of other-regarding morality and self-interest by arguing that people's interests are metaphysically and not just strategically, interdependent. This view models interpersonal relations and concern on intra-personal relations and concern and thereby extends the boundaries of self-love to include the good of others. Metaphysical egoism draws on strands in Greek eudaimonism and British idealism and develops them by appeal to plausible claims about persons and their persistence. After explaining metaphysical egoism, foundational worries about the value, character, scope and weight of metaphysical egoist concern are explored and assessed.

**Brinker, Menahem**. Reflections on the Other (in Hebrew). *Iyyun*, 45, 480-481, O 96.

**Brinkman, Klaus**. Zénon, matérialiste et nominaliste?. *Diotima*, 25, 48-55, 1997.

The article questions the standard perception of Stoic philosophy as materialist and nominalist in nature. Rather than being materialistic, Stoic ontology represents a consistent hylemorphism in which nothing exists without matter and which is intended to circumvent and the matter-form dualism in Aristotle's metaphysics and to avoid Aristotle's epistemological problem of the unknowability of matter. Similarly, Stoic semantics is not entirely nominalistic. Although Stoic universals (*ennoemata, ennoiai*) are *post rem*, unlike word or sentence meanings (*lekta*) they are nonmental noematic or conceptual structures.

**Brinton, Alan**. Analysis of Argument Strategies of Attack and Cooption: Stock Cases, Formalization, and Argument Reconstruction. *Inform Log*, 17(2), 249-258, Spr 95.

Three common strategies used by informal logicians are considered: 1) the appeal to standard cases, 2) the attempt to partially formalize so-called "informal fallacies," and 3) restatement of arguments in such a way as to make their logical character more perspicuous. All three strategies are found to be useful. Attention is drawn to several advantages of a "stock case" approach, a minimalist approach to formalization is recommended and doubts are raised about the applicability, from a logical point of view, of a principle of charitable construal in the reconstruction of arguments.

**Briscoe, Peter** and Popkin, Richard H and Laursen, John Christian. Hume in the Prussian Academy: Jean Bernard Mérian's "On the Phenomenalism of David Hume". *Hume Stud*, 23(1), 153-191, Ap 97.

This article contains a transcription and translation of an important eighteenth-century interpretation of Hume's phenomenalism. A substantial introduction reviews interest in Hume at the Prussian Academy, Jean Bernard Mérian's engagement with skepticism and questions of the self and personal identity and analyzes Mérian's conclusions. Notes draw attention to Mérian's critique of Kant and to some of the later influence of Mérian on Victor Cousin and Maine de Biran.

**Brito, Maria Amélia**. O positivismo científico de Anteno de Quental. *Rev Port Filosof*, 53(1), 39-62, Ja-Mr 97.

After a brief mention of the imported character of Portuguese positivism, we aim to show that, in his eclecticism, Antero de Quental is a positivist in science—although he never clearly criticized the specific thesis of positivism—while at the same time he was antipositivist in philosophy, strongly supporting metaphysics. Throughout his work both his appreciation of positivistic science and his defense of science against religion remain clear.

**Broach, Ronald J**. A Noncognitivist Reading of Quine's Ethics. *Dialectica*, 51(2), 119-134, 1997.

Until recently it has been tacitly assumed that Quine is a cognitivist about ethical sentences, that ethical sentences have cognitive meaning. I argue that for broad systematic reasons Quine must be read as a noncognitivist concerning ethical sentences. Because Quine himself has written as if he were a cognitivist, he has a number of claims about ethics which turn out to conflict with the noncognitivist reading of his position, and I make explicit the conflicts engendered by three particular claims. I tentatively explore a pair of strategies for eliminating the conflicts or reducing their effects. In the end these strategies do not appear promising, and Quinean ethics, on this noncognitivist reading of Quine, ends up somewhat the worse for wear.

**Brock, Dan W**. "Public Moral Discourse" in *Philosophical Perspectives on Bioethics*, Sumner, L W (ed), 271-296. Toronto, Univ of Toronto Pr, 1996.

**Brock, Jarrett**. "The Development of Peirce's Theories of Proper Names" in *Studies in the Logic of Charles Sanders Peirce*, Houser, Nathan (ed), 560-573. Bloomington, Indiana Univ Pr, 1997.

**Brockelman, Paul**. The Miracle of Being: Cosmology and the Experience of God. *Human Stud*, 20(2), 287-301, Ap 97.

**Brockman, Joan** and Hotel, Carla. Legal Ethics in the Practice of Family Law: Playing Chess While Mountain Climbing. *J Bus Ethics*, 16(8), 809-816, Je 97.

Current literature suggests that the adversarial legal system may undergo some changes or may even be transformed by a recent influx of women lawyers into the profession. Such research indicates that women may approach ethical problems differently than men. This paper examines the responses of family law lawyers in Vancouver, British Columbia and the surrounding lower mainland to a hypothetical case which requires an assessment of professional responsibilities in light of potential conflicts in personal moral values.

**Brockmeier, Jens**. Autobiography, Narrative, and the Freudian Concept of Life History. *Phil Psychiat Psych*, 4(3), 175-199, S 97.

This article suggests a narrative reading of the Freudian conception of life history. Its point of departure is the recent discussion on the relationship between autobiography, narrative discourse and the self. In this discussion a new interpretive approach to psychological, philosophical and psychiatric issues of life history has emerged, highlighting the cultural (particularly, narrative and discursive) construction of what we take to be our "lives." This approach will be outlined, specifically in its variant as "psychoanalytic narratology."(edited)

**Brockmeier, Jens**. Response to the Commentaries. *Phil Psychiat Psych*, 4(3), 209-211, S 97.

**Brodeur, Dennis**. Reducing Suffering and Ensuring Beneficial Outcomes for Neonates: An Ethical Perspective. *Bioethics Forum*, 11(1), 17-22, Spr 95.

Although health treatment regulations exist for protecting infants from unnecessary suffering, the ethical dilemmas created by some births have not been successfully resolved. A reconfiguring of neonatal medicine, with more carefully designed studies, greater uniformity about treatment and greater attention to the impact of treatment outcomes may be the solution.

**Brody, Baruch A**. Research Ethics: International Perspectives. *Cambridge Quart Healthcare Ethics*, 6(4), 376-384, Fall 97.

This article compares the treatment of three major ethical issues in research (research on competent adults, research on animals, research on preimplantation zygotes) in the various codes of research ethics throughout the world. It shows substantial agreement on the first set of issues, some disagreement on the second set of issues, and major disagreement on the third set of issues. It concludes with the suggestion that the results support the idea expressed by many cultural anthropologists that ethical disagreement is hardest to reach when there is disagreement about the moral status of the entities involved.

**Brody, Baruch A** and Katz, Jay and Dula, Annette. In Case of Emergency: No Need for Consent. *Hastings Center Rep*, 27(1), 7-12, Ja-F 97.

This article offers a philosophical analysis of the FDA's recent regulations on emergency room research. It argues that these regulations are based upon an appropriate ethical balancing of competing legitimate values. It also argues that two important problems (use of placebo controls and definition of when informal convent is impractical) have not been adequately addressed in these regulations.

**Brody, Howard**. Edmund D. Pellegrino's Philosophy of Family Practice. *Theor Med*, 18(1-2), 7-20, Mr-Je 97.

Family medicine has grown as a specialty from its early days of general practice. It was established as a Board Certified specialty in 1969. This growth and maturation can be traced in the philosophy of family medicine as articulated by

Edmund D. Pellegrino, M.D. Long before it was popular to do so, Pellegrino supported the development of family medicine. In this essay I examine the development of Pellegrino's philosophical thought about family practice and contrast it to other thinkers like Ian McWhinney, Kerr White, Walter Spitzer, Donald Ransom and Hebert Vandervoort. The arguments focus on whether the goals of family medicine and family practice (possibly two distinct entities) can be articulated, especially considering the definitional problems of "family" and "community." I conclude by echoing Pellegrino's hope that family medicine can contribute a fresh alternative to isolated, individualistic and technological thinking in medicine.

**Brody, Howard** and Rygwelski, Janis and Fetters, Michael D. Ethics at the Interface: Conventional Western and Complementary Medical Systems. *Bioethics Forum*, 12(4), 15-23, Wint 96.

Both conventional and complementary medicines have a duty to treat patients ethically. Problems arise in each system's relationships with the other. Recognizing one's assumptions, often unaddressed, and agreeing on common goals will go far to remove suspicion when the two schools meet in the treatment of the same patient.

**Broglio, Francesco Margiotta**. Tolerance and the Law. *Ratio Juris*, 10(2), 252-265, Je 97.

Analyzing the legal dimension of tolerance in the field of international law (especially in international U.N. declarations and covenants on human rights), the author emphasizes how the principle or tolerance implies not merely a legal system "agnostic" to religious truth but also the development of minorities and the principle of nondiscrimination in a democratic system. Nondiscrimination appears to be particularly important in the face of the current phenomena of religious extremism and intolerance; development of a multicultural society is recognized in the U.N. Declaration against Intolerance and Discrimination of 1981.

**Bromberger, Sylvain**. "Natural Kinds of Questions" in *Knowledge and Inquiry: Essays on Jaakko Hintikka's Epistemology and Philosophy of Science*, Sintonen, Matti (ed), 149-163. Amsterdam, Rodopi, 1997.

Science would be impossible without the notion of natural kinds. But that notion is replete with difficulties that have long been the subject of intense philosophic inquiry. In this paper the author begins by reviewing some of these difficulties. He then proposes an analysis of is own based on two tenets. The first tenet is that belief in the kinds needed for science consists of a range of presumptions whose more complex ones entail (but are not entailed by) simpler ones. The second tenet is that natural kinds are characterizable in terms of certain questions pertaining to their members.

**Broncano, Fernando**. "La mosca salió volando de la botella: éxito y correspondencia en una teoría de la verdad" in *Verdad: lógica, representación y mundo*, Villegas Forero, L, 11-21. Santiago de Compostela, Univ Santiago Comp, 1996.

We examine the teleological theory of truth proposed by David Papineau in his *Philosophical naturalism* raising some doubts about his definition of truth conditions. According to Papineau, a redundantist construal of truth conditions is compatible with a substantive view on truth. This point is criticized and a broader concept of truth conditions is proposed. The paper follows a naturalistic conception of semantic concepts that claims to truth have an explanatory role in some epistemological and semantic contexts.

**Broncano, Fernando**. "Las dimensiones de la racionalidad" in *La racionalidad: su poder y sus límites*, Nudler, Oscar (ed), 29-64. Barcelona, Ed Paidos, 1996.

**Broncano, Fernando**. La fuerza del PC (Principio de Caridad): Circunstancia, habilidad y contenido en la explicación de la acción. *Analisis Filosof*, 15(1-2), 73-106, My-N 95.

In this paper, a naturalistic version of the Charity Principle as an *a priori* constraint in the interpretation of actions is proposed. Given its normative and *a priori* character, the classical CP from Quine, Davidson and Dennett, meet some difficulties to be considered as an empirical constraint. We argue that some troubles could be removed if we change the underlying notion of content ascribed to intentional actions. We present, in the first time, the situated character of actions, that involves an analog to the mode-of-presentation problem of indexicals. The necessary relation to a context drives us to the controversy about externalism and internalism. Our proposal is that a nonconceptual dimension of content grounded on the skills of agent is a necessary condition to ascribe content to the intentional action. From this view, we propose to consider the Charity Principle as an historical constraint on the evolution of some classes of cognitive systems. (edited)

**Bronfenbrenner, Urie**. "Prospect for the Social Sciences in the Land Grant University" in *The American University: National Treasure or Endangered Species?*, Ehrenberg, Ronald G (ed), 141-160. Ithaca, Cornell Univ Pr, 1997.

**Brook, Donald**. On Non-Verbal Representation. *Brit J Aes*, 37(3), 232-245, Jl 97.

The serious challenge for a theory of representation is not to explain fiction. Neither is it to elucidate the ontology of represented objects. These are problems for a theory of language. The challenge for representational theory is to explain how language, and with it the powerful device of the represented object, emerged out of a prelinguistic world containing only representation-users, representations and represented subjects. That the emergence of language took place somehow on the back of representational practices exploiting no more than the inability of creatures to discriminate in some respects between representation and the subjects for which they could be influentially substituted, seems probable to the point of certainty.

**Brooks, Leonard J**. Business Ethics in Canada: Distinctiveness and Directions. *J Bus Ethics*, 16(6), 591-604, Ap 97.

This article examines the pressures and players that have shaped business ethics in Canadian corporations, and reports on the status of Canadian corporate social performance in 1995. Business in Canada has not been subject, up to 1996, to a powerful national institutional framework such as the U.S. Securities and Exchange Commission and the *Foreign Corrupt Practices Act*. Consequently, business ethics in Canada have developed primarily in response to broader sociopolitical and socioeconomic factors than in the U.S., and will probably continue to do so. (edited)

**Brooks, Lynn Matluck**. Harmony in Space: A Perspective on the Work of Rudolf Laban. *J Aes Educ*, 27(2), 29-41, Sum 93.

Rudolf Laban (1879-1958) succeeded in creating a systematic way of looking at the body as it moves through space, giving to dance/movement studies a common vocabulary, a structure for analysis, a shorthand for notation and a base from which to expand and develop further. Laban's work has been extended by later researchers into applications in choreography, dance education, general education, directing, actor training, folk dance, child development, worker efficiency, management training, dance/movement therapy, physical therapy, kinesiology, nonverbal communication, ethnology and fitness. Yet the many strands of Laban's thought all converged on the subject of space harmony, the cradle of his theory.

**Broome, John** and Parfit, Derek. Reasons and Motivation. *Aris Soc*, Supp(71), 98-146, 1997.

**Brosio, Richard A**. "Pixels, Decenteredness, Marketization, Totalism, and Ingmar Bergman's Cry for Help" in *Philosophy of Education (1996)*, Margonis, Frank (ed), 277-280. Urbana, Phil Education Soc, 1997.

Rampan "how-to-ism" is the bane of all too many teacher education programs; moreover, this uncritical instrumentalism is useful to capitalism's reproductive use of the schools. It is argued further that the concentration on information rather than knowledge during these postmodernist and late capitalism times is useful to the putatively sovereign consumer who is convinced that market choices are fair substitutes for bona fide, democratic, citizenship participation. This sovereign consumer presently extends her/his choices into the virtual reality of cyberspace. The author asks that we consider the powerful capitalist imperative when evaluating educational methodology and the contemporary electronic communication revolution.

**Brosio, Richard A**. The Complexly Constructed Citizen-Worker: Her/His Centrality to the Struggle for Radical Democratic Politics and Education. *J Thought*, 32(3), 9-26, Fall 97.

This work seeks to explain how ascribed (although resisted) identities such as race, gender, and sexual orientation interact with the categories of citizen and worker. Furthermore, an analysis is offered with regard to the need for inclusive, radical democratic coalitions in order to liberate people from class, race, gender and sexual injustices. These inclusive coalitions must be comprised of the wonderful diversity that characterizes humankind; however, the axis around which to organize effectively is anchored by citizen—one's relationships to government and civil society—as well as worker, including nonpaid labor.

**Brothers, Robyn F**. Cyborg Identities and the Relational Web: Recasting 'Narrative Identity' in Moral and Political Theory. *Metaphilosophy*, 28(3), 249-258, Jl 97.

Current debates surrounding liberalism and communitarianism, modernity and postmodernity, ethical theory and narrative ethics fail to account for shifting foundations of personal identity in an increasingly computer-mediated era of human communication. This paper aims to examine some of the conceptual assumptions about identity and community which are being radically undermined by rapidly evolving information networks and are therefore in need of redefinition. Additionally, I argue for an expansion of the literary imagination to include virtual, coauthored fiction sites where exploration of personal identity will bear upon future ethical and political decision making.

**Brottman, David**. "Mrs. Bates in Plato's Cave" in *Critical Studies: Ethics and the Subject*, Simms, Karl (ed), 173-188. Amsterdam, Rodopi, 1997.

**Brottman, Mikita**. "Blue Prints and Bodies: Paradigms of Desire in Pornography" in *Critical Studies: Ethics and the Subject*, Simms, Karl (ed), 203-216. Amsterdam, Rodopi, 1997.

**Brougham, Richard L**. Reality and Appearance in Bergson and Whitehead. *Process Stud*, 24, 39-43, 1995.

Bergson's continuist, change-as-one-unit process philosophy is at odds with his discernment of a basic rift between the living organism and its environment. This is contrasted with Whitehead's attempt at a balance between the individuality and the "relativity of existence." The divergent usages of the term "simplification" by the two philosophers are pivotal to their respective ontological stances. For Bergson, simplification is a mere pragmatic coping device, a tool of the phenomenal realm. For Whitehead, past established facts are "reality." But this reality is contrasted with the simplifying adjusting of the established by the emerging present. This process of emerging is "appearance" for Whitehead. Appearance (simplification) is at the heart of Whitehead's *ultimate principle, creativity*. For him, it is the motor of time and change. For Bergson, simplification is at the periphery of "being," relatively inconsequential.

**Brown, David S**. Patricia Kitcher and "Kant's Real Self". *SW Phil Rev*, 13(1), 163-174, Ja 97.

**Brown, Deborah**. "The Right Method of Boy-Loving" in *Love Analyzed*, Lamb, Roger E, 49-63. Boulder, Westview Pr, 1997.

AUTHOR INDEX 541 Brown, William S

**Brown, Deborah J**. A Furry Tile about Mental Representation. *Phil Quart*, 46(185), 448-466, O 96.

It was just a humble doormat but it had saved many a sole and the odd carpet to boot and it could see no good metaphysical reason why it too shouldn't count as an intentional system. The creatures (and one rather noisy artifact) from the forest floor argue long into the night about whether causal and teleological theories of mental representation succeed in their aim to give a naturalistic account of the semantics of natural kind concepts. They conclude that these accounts do not offer an analysis of the determinate meaning of natural kind concepts and suggest an alternative approach which does not fall prey to the "disjunction problem".

**Brown, Deborah J**. The Puzzle of Names in Ockham's Theory of Mental Language. *Rev Metaph*, 50(1), 79-99, S 96.

There is a tension within Ockham's theory of mental language between its claim to being a semantics for conventional languages and its claim to being a model of concept acquisition and thought. In particular, the commitment to a redundancy-free mental language which serves to explain important semantic relations such as synonymy and ambiguity conflicts, *prima facie*, with the possibility of opaque belief contexts. I argue that it is preferable to treat the theory of mental language as an idealized theory of cognitive competence than to forfeit, as Jerry Fodor does, the commitment to conceptual parsimony.

**Brown, Gene** and Bass, Ken and Barnett, Tim. Religiosity, Ethical Ideology, and Intentions to Report a Peer's Wrongdoing. *J Bus Ethics*, 15(11), 1161-1174, N 96.

Peer reporting is a specific form of whistleblowing in which an individual discloses the wrongdoing of a peer. Previous studies have examined situational variables thought to influence a person's decision to report the wrongdoing of a peer. The present study looked at peer reporting from the individual level. Five hypotheses were developed concerning the relationships between 1) religiosity and ethical ideology, 2) ethical ideology and ethical judgments about peer reporting, and 3) ethical judgments and intentions to report peer wrongdoing. Subjects read a vignette concerning academic cheating, and were asked to respond to a questionnaire concerning the vignette. Data were analyzed using structural equation methodology. Results indicated that religiosity was positively associated with an ethical ideology of nonrelativism. Individuals whose ethical ideologies could be described as idealistic and nonrelativistic were more likely to state that reporting a peer's cheating was ethical. In turn, individuals who believed reporting a peer's cheating was ethical were more likely to say that they would report a peer's cheating.

**Brown, Hunter**. The Inadequacy of Wishful Thinking Charges against William James's *The Will to Believe*. *Trans Peirce Soc*, 33(2), 488-519, Spr 97.

The purpose of this essay is to show that common charges against *The Will to Believe* for having endorsed wishful thinking are not sustainable. Such charges rely upon an indefensible isolation of *The Will to Believe* from the broad terms of reference to James's epistemology as a whole. Within such broader terms of reference, subjective states do not enjoy the degree of autonomy imputed to them by James's critics. Such states, rather, are framed in and limited in their influence by their interrelations with many other elements which together make up the complex unity of immediate experience.

**Brown, James Robert**. "Illustration and Inference" in *Picturing Knowledge*, Baigrie, Brian S (ed), 250-268. Toronto, Univ of Toronto Pr, 1996.

A number of striking examples of pictures are presented. These are taken from a variety of situations, some from mathematics, some from physics, some from thought experiments. In each of these we seem able to pass from a single, special case to a very general conclusion. How is such an inference possible? An account (drawn from Bogen and Woodward) of the data-phenomena distinction is made and used in conjunction with so-called natural kind inference. It is a highly Platonistic account of how (some) pictures work.

**Brown, James Robert**. Proofs and Pictures. *Brit J Phil Sci*, 48(2), 161-180, Je 97.

Everyone appreciates a clever mathematical picture, but the prevailing attitude is one of scepticism: diagrams, illustrations and pictures prove nothing; they are psychologically important and heuristically useful, but only a traditional verbal/symbolic proof provides genuine evidence for a purported theorem. Like some other recent writers (Barwise and Etchemendy [1991]; Shin [1994]; and Giaquinto [1994]), I take a different view and argue, from historical considerations and some striking examples, for a positive evidential role for pictures in mathematics.

**Brown, Lee B**. Musical Works, Improvisation, and the Principle of Continuity. *J Aes Art Crit*, 54(4), 353-369, Fall 96.

**Brown, Lee M**. Compassion and Societal Well-Being. *Pac Phil Quart*, 77(3), 216-224, S 96.

Although there are compelling reasons for believing otherwise, compassion cannot provide a basis for grounding a viable theory of civil and political society. Firstly, it is often irrational or personally irresponsible to be compassionate. Secondly, relations based on compassion do not require characteristics that are essential for a viable civil and political society. Thirdly, the unpredictable consequences of compassion are such that compassion alone is not sufficient for grounding a viable civil and political society. Finally, obligating people to be compassionate is antithetical to what is required for being compassionate.

**Brown, Lesley**. What is "the Mean Relative to Us" in Aristotle's *Ethics*. *Phronesis*, 42(1), 77-93, 1997.

When Aristotle says (NE2.6, EE2.3) moral virtue involves a 'mean relative to us', he is not making it relative to us as different moral agents, as generally believed. Rather, the 'mean relative to us' is a norm grounded in human nature, needs and purposes; it is relative to us as human beings, not individual possessors of virtue. I correct a misunderstanding of the famous Milo illustration: Aristotle's point is not that good action varies with different agents, any more than that appropriate diets vary with the trainer. He would not allow that virtue is relative to one's moral progress or emotional constitution.

**Brown, Mark A**. "Doing as We Ought: Towards a Logic of Simply Dischargeable Obligations" in *Deontic Logic, Agency and Normative Systems*, Brown, Mark A (ed), 47-65. New York, Springer-Verlag, 1996.

This paper investigates diachronic deontic logic, based on models with forward-branching time. Using such models, supplemented by a choice function to model human agency, and an obligation function to introduce normative features, it is possible to develop a rich language with tense logic, since and until operators, and operators expressing action, ability, and obligation. It then becomes possible to model, not only the interrelationships among our obligations, but also their interrelationships with the actions which give rise to them, the actions which fulfill them, and the abilities these actions require.

**Brown, Mark A**. Normal Bimodal Logics of Ability and Action. *Stud Log*, 51(3-4), 519-532, 1992.

A number of extensions of the basic system K/K are constructed, first by strengthening the two normal sublogics independently and then by linking the two sublogics via axiom schemata involving both operators. The result is a series of increasingly strong systems which more and more adequately fulfill our expectations for a satisfactory logic of action and ability. (edited)

**Brown, Mark A** (ed) and Carmo, José (ed). *Deontic Logic, Agency and Normative Systems*. New York, Springer-Verlag, 1996.

This volume presents a variety of papers bearing on the relation between deontic logics, logics of action, and normative systems, i.e., systems of or about interacting agents (computers, human beings, corporations, etc.) whose behavior is subject to ideal constraints that may not always be fulfilled in practice. The papers range from theoretical studies of the logical and conceptual tools needed, to studies of various applications. The set of papers collected in this book should be of interest to investigators working in a variety of fields from philosophy, logic and legal theory to artificial intelligence, computer and management sciences, since it covers topics ranging from theoretical research on foundational issues in deontic and action logics, defeasible reasoning, decision theory, ethical theory, and legal theory, to research on a variety of issues relevant to applications connected with expert systems in the law, document specification, automation of defeasible reasoning, specification of responsibilities and powers in organizations, normative systems specification, confidentiality in database systems, and a host of other applications. (publisher, edited)

**Brown, Mark T**. Humans, Persons and Selves. *SW Phil Rev*, 13(1), 187-195, Ja 97.

**Brown, Montague**. Beauty and Technology as Paradigms for the Moral Life. *Amer Cath Phil Quart*, 70(Supp), 193-207, 1996.

While modern thinking holds that living a morally upright life may be good for others or likely to bring a net balance of pleasure over pain, the ancient-medieval tradition held that such a life is not only in accordance with duty but delightful. The difference is traceable, in part, to a paradigm shift from the ideal of beauty to that of technology. The paper considers each paradigm in its historical setting and then reflects on the influence of the technological paradigm on contemporary ethics. My thesis is that we have lost more than gained, morally speaking, in this shift of paradigms.

**Brown, Robert**. The Delayed Birth of Social Experiments. *Hist Human Sci*, 10(2), 1-21, My 97.

In the 19th century it was widely believed that scientific experiments on social issues were not and never would be, feasible. Not only was social behaviour unpredictable in principle, but subjecting people to experimentation would be immoral. Although Comte, J.S. Mill, C.G. Lewis and Herbert Spencer all argued to this conclusion, they also believed that natural innovations in society provided an adequate substitute for planned experiments. The question to be examined here is how such beliefs came to be held and why they were never tested.

**Brown, Wendy**. Logics of Power in Marx. *Topoi*, 15(2), 225-234, S 96.

This essay examines the trajectories and the fissures in Marx's several logics of power to argue that Marx's materialism is less obdurate and certainly less empirical, than is often thought.

**Brown, William R**. The Much-Maligned Cliché Strikes Back. *Inquiry (USA)*, 14(1), 89-93, Fall 94.

I challenge two claims in Morton Rich's *Inquiry* column (February/March 1994): 1) Clichés "anesthetiz[e] the reader, who then stops thinking" 2) "Clichés reveal a lazy and unoriginal mind...." Rich's example of bad writing was impoverished, not by the presence of clichés, but by the absence of features I enumerate in a cliché-ridden passage from Frederick Douglass. Clichés are features of language rather than discourse and polishing them out will not make us critical thinkers any more than avoiding sexist language can make us nonsexists. We should present language to student writers as a treasure house, not a prison house.

**Brown, William S**. Technology, Workplace Privacy and Personhood. *J Bus Ethics*, 15(11), 1237-1248, N 96.

This paper traces the intellectual development of the workplace privacy construct in the course of American thinking. The role of technological development in this process is examined, particularly in regard to the information gathering/dissemination dilemmas faced by employers and employees alike. The paper concludes with some preliminary considerations toward a theory of workplace privacy.

**Browne, Derek**. Cognitive Versatility. *Mind Mach*, 6(4), 507-523, N 96.

Jerry Fodor divides the mind into peripheral, domain-specific modules and a domain-general faculty of central cognition. John Tooby and Lisa Cosmides argue instead that the mind is modular all the way through; cognition consists of a multitude of domain-specific processes. But human thought has a flexible, innovative character that contrasts with the inflexible, stereotyped performances of modular systems. My goal is to discover how minds that are constructed on modular principles might come to exhibit cognitive versatility. (edited)

**Browne, M Neil** (& others) and Reed, J David and Quinn, J Kevin. Honesty, Individualism, and Pragmatic Business Ethics: Implications for Corporate Hierarchy. *J Bus Ethics*, 16(12-13), 1419-1430, S 97.

The boundaries of honesty are the focal point of this exploration of the individualistic origins of modernist ethics and the consequent need for a more pragmatic approach to business ethics. The tendency of modernist ethics to see honesty as an individual responsibility is described as a contextually naive approach, one that fails to account for the interactive effect between individual choices and corporate norms. By reviewing the empirical accounts of managerial struggles with ethical dilemmas, the article arrives at the contextual preconditions for encouraging the development of reflective moral agents in modern corporations.

**Browning, Tyson R**. Reaching for the "Low Hanging Fruit": The Pressure for Results in Scientific Research—A Graduate Student's Perspective. *Sci Eng Ethics*, 1(4), 417-426, O 95.

The pressure for results applied by some research funders concerns some academicians. Sometimes, for example, a sponsor requests preliminary data that the researcher is not ready to release. This paper presents three interviews—two with researchers and one with a representative from industry—dealing with these issues and makes recommendations on the basis of those interviews. It also looks briefly at the different norms that exist in industry and academia for research and communication and the tensions these can cause for a scientist working simultaneously in both realms.

**Broz, Frantisek**. Social Science Courses as an Integrating Subject. *Filosof Cas*, 44(3), 463-480, 1996.

This article has come into existence as an experiment to find a content for a voluntary subject called Social Science Courses. The author presents a possible content for the courses which is composed from the texts chosen in different journals. These texts point to some problems which should be discussed in these courses, for example position of man in the world, relation between man and nature, love, violence, hope, toleration etc. There are presented different methods how to work with texts—lecture, commentary reading, discussion. This texts are based on author's experience as a secondary school teacher.

**Bruce, Nigel**. The Immortal David Hume (1711-1776). *Free Inq*, 17(1), 38-40, Wint 96/97.

**Brueckner, Anthony**. Externalism and Memory. *Pac Phil Quart*, 78(1), 1-12, Mr 97.

Paul Boghossian has put forward an influential argument against Tyler Burge's account of basic self-knowledge. The argument focuses on the relation between externalism about mental content and memory. In this paper, I attempt to analyze and answer Boghossian's argument.

**Bruell, Christopher** (& other eds) and Strauss, Leo and Bolotin, David (ed). An Untitled Lecture on Plato's *Euthyphron*. *Interpretation*, 24(1), 3-23, Fall 96.

**Brugère, Fabienne**. Shaftesbury: esquisse d'un manifeste théiste dans l'*Enquête*. *Rev Phil Fr*, 1, 9-19, Ja-Mr 97.

**Brummer, James J**. The Structure of Residual Obligations. *J Soc Phil*, 27(3), 164-180, Wint 96.

The purpose of the article is to examine and begin to systematize a seldom analyzed concept in the literature of ethical theory. Basic to the notion of a residual obligation is the idea that the claims of an initial (or prima facie) obligation are not eliminated if the obligation is overruled. These claims give rise to new obligations that are tied to the original overruled obligation. For example, if a pressing emergency prevents me from showing up for an appointment on time, I have an obligation I did not originally have, a residual obligation, to call to let the other party know that I shall not make it as scheduled. The article discusses thirteen possible types of residual obligation and begins the process of putting these in a more systematic order, showing the role they play in normative ethics.

**Bruneau, Alain-Philippe**. Le concept d'heuristique dans la création de la forme esthétique: mimésis et liberté. *De Phil*, 12, 195-208, 1995-1996.

**Brunk, Conrad G**. Restorative Justice and Punishment. *Dialogue (Canada)*, 35(3), 593-598, Sum 96.

**Brunkhorst, Hauke**. Are Human Rights Self-Contradictory?: Critical Remarks on a Hypothesis by Hannah Arendt. *Constellations*, 3(2), 190-199, O 96.

**Brunning, Jacqueline**. "Genuine Triads and Teridentity" in *Studies in the Logic of Charles Sanders Peirce*, Houser, Nathan (ed), 252-263. Bloomington, Indiana Univ Pr, 1997.

**Brunning, Jacqueline** (ed) and Forster, Paul (ed). *The Rule of Reason: The Philosophy of Charles Sanders Peirce*. Toronto, Univ of Toronto Pr, 1997.

Since the publication of his collected papers began, in 1931, interest in Peirce has grown dramatically. His writings have found audiences in logic,

epistemology, metaphysics, philosophy of science, semiotics, computer science, literary criticism, and film studies. While Peirce scholarship has advanced considerably since its earliest days, many controversies of interpretation persist and several of the more obscure aspects of Peirce's work remain poorly understood. This volume presents a broad selection of work devoted to outstanding issues and difficulties in Peirce's philosophy. Some essays clarify aspects of Peirce's philosophy, some defend its contemporary significance, and some do both. (publisher)

**Bruns, Gerald L**. Blanchot/Levinas: Interruption (On the Conflict of Alterities). *Res Phenomenol*, 26, 132-154, 1996.

**Brunschwig, Jacques**. Was Pyrrho a Pyrrhonist? (in Hungarian). *Magyar Filozof Szemle*, 1-2, 413-424, 1997.

There is more difference than usually acknowledged between Pyrrho's philosophical attitude and the neo-Pyrrhonian scepticism developed much later by Aenesidemus and sextus Empiricus. Pyrrho seems to have been primarily an indifferentist in ethical matters. The crucial epistemological twist might have been brought about by his most famous disciple, Timon. A close analysis of the key evidence (Aristocles in Eusebius, *Praeparatio Evangelica* XIV.18.1-5) allows to dissociate their respective roles. The themes and arguments of this short paper are more fully developed by the author in his *Papers in Hellenistic Philosophy*, Cambridge University Press, 1994, pp. 190-211.

**Brusotti, Marco**. *Die Leidenschaft der Erkenntnis: Philosophie und ästhetische Lebensgestaltung bei Nietzsche von Morgenröthe bis Also sprach Zarathustra*. Hawthorne, de Gruyter, 1997.

**Bruzina, Ronald**. Die Auseinandersetzung Fink—Heidegger: Das Denken des letzten Ursprungs. *Perspekt Phil*, 22, 29-57, 1996.

**Bryant, Daniel C**. Telling Tales Out of School—Portrayals of the Medical Student Experience by Physician-Novelists. *J Med Human*, 17(4), 237-254, Wint 96.

Changes in medical and medical ethics education are being considered with little attention to the experience of the medical students involved. This study attempts to characterize and highlight certain aspects of that experience from a literary perspective. After a brief review of the history of traditional academic studies in the field, eight novels, written by physician-writers and featuring medical student protagonists, are analyzed. Several common themes of the student experience are identified in the novels, and are contrasted with themes found in the medical literature. A plea is made to acknowledge literary as well as scientific interpretations of the medical student experience when considering changes in medical education.

**Brzezinski, Jerzy**. "Ethical Problems of Research Work of Psychologists" in *The Idea of University*, Brzezinski, Jerzy (ed), 139-158. Amsterdam, Rodopi, 1997.

**Brzezinski, Jerzy**. "Reflections on the University" in *The Idea of University*, Brzezinski, Jerzy (ed), 201-221. Amsterdam, Rodopi, 1997.

**Brzezinski, Jerzy**. "Theory and Social Practice: One or Two Psychologies?" in *Epistemology and History*, Zeidler-Janiszowska, Anna (ed), 351-364. Amsterdam, Rodopi, 1996.

Following from Kmita's concept of science and his distinction between two types of practice—that is *social practice* and *research practice*—the author analyses the relationships obtaining between psychology as science (in Kmita's terms) on the one hand and on the other hand, social practice building on the research results obtained by psychologists. The author cites the critique of the methodological model employed by the so-called *practical sciences* and refers it to the common belief entertained by psychologists that there is a need to make a distinction between *two* varieties of psychology—the *academic* variety, enjoying the methodological status of a fundamental science (on the model of physics) and the *applied* variety, awarded the methodological status of a *practical science* (on the model of pedagogy). The author's main argument is that it is only reasonable to speak of *one* psychology with *many* applications. The article is concluded by a presentation of the pattern of information flow between the domains of social practice and research practice.

**Brzezinski, Jerzy** (ed) and Nowak, Leszek (ed). *The Idea of University*. Amsterdam, Rodopi, 1997.

**Bub, Jeffrey** and Clifton, Rob. A Uniqueness Theorem for 'No Collapse' Interpretations of Quantum Mechanics. *Stud Hist Phil Mod Physics*, 27B(2), 181-219, Je 96.

We prove a uniqueness theorem showing that, subject to certain natural constraints, all 'no collapse' interpretations of quantum mechanics can be uniquely characterized and reduced to the choice of a particular preferred observable as determinate (definite, sharp). We show how certain versions of the modal interpretation, Bohm's 'causal' interpretation, Bohr's complementarity interpretation, and the orthodox (Dirac-von Neumann) interpretation without the projection postulate can be recovered from the theorem. Bohr's complementarity and Einstein's realism appear as two quite different proposals for selecting the preferred determinate observable—either settled pragmatically by what we choose to observe, or fixed once and for all, as the Einsteinian realist would require, in which case the preferred observable is a 'beable' in Bell's sense, as in Bohm's interpretation (where the preferred observable is position in configuration space).

**Bubner, Rüdiger**. "Concerning the Central Idea of Adorno's Philosophy" in *The Semblance of Subjectivity*, Huhn, Tom (ed), 147-175. Cambridge, MIT Pr, 1997.

The Marxian *Critique of Ideology* has become self-critical, such that any form of theory in a traditional sense seems no longer trustworthy with regard to truth. Now, art is the only appearance (Schein) that does not deceive. Thus, Adorno tends to transform philosophical reflexion into an aesthetic interaction with works of art.

**AUTHOR INDEX** 543 **Buekens, Filip**

**Bubner, Rüdiger**. "The Modern Dilemma of Political Theory" in *The Ancients and the Moderns,* Lilly, Reginald (ed), 90-100. Bloomington, Indiana Univ Pr, 1996.

**Bubner, Rüdiger**. Platón: justicia y pluralismo. *Cuad Etica*, 19-20, 31-45, 1995.

The familiar view of Plato as an "enemy of open society" is wrong. Plato's *Republic* can be read as a treatise on justice according to the principle, that "everybody should do his own thing". There can be no doubt that this formula underlies the whole of the text, although interpreters seem not prepared to take it seriously. Looking at Plato's proposal for a rational organization of society from this point of view, one should give the *Republic* a voice in the actual debate on liberalism.

**Buchanan, Allen**. "Self-Determination, Secession, and the Rule of Law" in *The Morality of Nationalism,* McKim, Robert (ed), 301-323. New York, Oxford Univ Pr, 1997.

**Buchanan, Allen**. Theories of Secession. *Phil Pub Affairs*, 26(1), 31-61, Wint 97.

**Buchanan, James**. No Good Deed Ever Goes Unpunished. *Cont Phil*, 18(1), 2-7, Ja-F 96.

It is early in the morning and you are on your way to work. Suddenly, the car in front of you bolts across the divider strip, flips over and is quickly engulfed in flames. The driver screams for help even as the flames consume him and without hesitation or regard for personal safety, you pull him free from the flames and call the paramedics. Three weeks later you are being sued by the same motorist you rescued from death. The law suit charges that in aiding a trauma victim you "failed to act efficiently and with proper medical knowledge of traumatic injuries." As a consequence, the plaintiff suffered extreme mental anguish and personal injuries. His attorney is asking for punitive damages in excess of five million dollars. Surprised? Don't be. Welcome to the 90s and the world of Machiavelli where no good deed every goes unpunished.

**Buchanan, James M**. Can Democracy Promote the General Welfare?. *Soc Phil Pol*, 14(2), 165-179, Sum 97.

Outcomes of political process can be classified into two sets—those that are general in application over all citizens and those that are discriminatory. "Democracy," as commonly understood, is not compatible with nondiscriminatory collective action because majority coalitions nationally favor their own numbers. Constitutional constraints are necessary to enforce generality in political treatment. The general welfare state can survive; the discriminatory welfare state cannot.

**Buchanan, James M**. *Ethics and Economic Progress.* Norman, Univ of Oklahoma Pr, 1994.

In *Ethics and Economic Progress*, Nobel Prize-winning economist James M. Buchanan argues that ethical or moral constraints on human behavior exert important economic effects. The work ethic and the saving ethic, for example, may not be fashionable today, but Buchanan asserts that many modern attitudes and habits relate to the decline in productivity growth in the economy. Simply put, the more every member of society works and saves, the better off the entire community will be. In the last chapter, perhaps the most controversial, he suggests that Adam Smith's distinction between productive and nonproductive labor, which has been almost universally dismissed by economists, may indeed have economic relevance. (publisher)

**Buchheim, Thomas**. Zum Verhältnis von Existenz und Freiheit in Leibniz' Metaphysik. *Z Phil Forsch*, 50(3), 386-409, Jl-S 96.

Leibniz must differentiate between "being" and "contingent existence" since he identifies "to be" with "to be possible". Existence needs an additional reason which must not already be included in the identity of the possible, but which nevertheless takes its properties into consideration. This paper argues 1) that the infinite analysis of concepts determines unambiguously the identity of the possible without already including predicates into their subject and thus already implicating the truth of the respective expression; and 2) that although the examination of all things concerning "the good" takes their properties into account accordingly, it gives God no reason to be forced to select one version of reality, so that freedom remains possible.

**Buchmann, Margret** and Kerr, Donna H. On Avoiding Domination in Philosophical Counseling. *J Chin Phil*, 23(3), 341-351, S 96.

**Buchowski, Michal**. "Via Media: On the Consequences of Historical Epistemology for the Problem of Rationality" in *Epistemology and History,* Zeidler-Janiszewska, Anna (ed), 181-196. Amsterdam, Rodopi, 1996.

The problem of the rationality of human actions viewed from the perspective of Jerzy Kmita's historical epistemology is discussed. Several standpoints seeking a *via media* between rationalism and relativism, i.e., those of Jarvie, Horton, Tambiah, Horton and Hanson, are criticized. The assumption of rationality which refers to the consistency of actors' actions with the beliefs shared by them is advanced. It is congruent with the ideas of historical epistemology and leads to a cultural relativization of the notion of rationality. The latter does not contain any universal, e.g., scientifically defined, elements, but is always identified in the context of a given culture.

**Buchsbaum, Arthur** and Pequeno, Tarcisio. A Reasoning Method for a Paraconsistent Logic. *Stud Log*, 52(2), 281-289, My 93.

A proof method for automation of reasoning in a paraconsistent logic, the calculus C1 of da Costa, is presented. The method is analytical, using a specially designed tableau system. Actually two tableau systems were created. A first one, with a small number of rules in order to be mathematically convenient, is used to prove the soundness and the completeness of the method. The other one, which is equivalent to the former, is a system of derived rules designed to enhance computational efficiency. A prototype based on this second system was effectively implemented.

**Buckler, Steve**. Afterword. *Hist Human Sci*, 9(4), 115-121, N 96.

The article follows a previous piece, 'Historical narrative, Identity and the Holocaust', by the same author and takes the form of a reply to critics. A variety of issues are taken up, on the basis of criticisms made, regarding the possibilities of historical representation of the Holocaust. The use of a narrative conception of history is defended as a means of gauging the 'unmasterable' character of the Holocaust from the point of view of historical memory.

**Buckler, Steve**. Historical Narrative, Identity and the Holocaust. *Hist Human Sci*, 9(4), 1-20, N 96.

Difficulties associated with the history of the Holocaust have led to a conviction that the event is 'unmasterable' from a historical point of view. Why the Holocaust should remain resistant to a settled historical discourse is unclear in view of the wealth of research and testimony that is available. The paper is intended as a contribution to the clarification of this issue. Proceeding from a particular controversy, the general requirements of a narrative conception of history are employed as a means of revealing more precisely the character of the problem.

**Buckler, Steve**. Machiavelli and Rousseau: The Standpoint of the City and the Authorial Voice in Political Theory. *Hist Human Sci*, 10(3), 69-86, Ag 97.

A systematic comparison is made between the respective political theories of Machiavelli and Rousseau. Initially, the comparison centres upon key substantive claims made by each theorist with a view to establishing a general, thematic contrast. This is used as a basis for structuring a further comparison between the respective authorial standpoints adopted by Machiavelli and Rousseau. It will be suggested that this comparison establishes, a) that a connection can be made between substantive theory and authorial standpoint and, b) that, in comparison, the authorial standpoint adopted by Machiavelli reflects a fidelity to the political which is absent in Rousseau.

**Buckley, R Philip**. Husserl's Rational "*Liebesgemeinschaft*". *Res Phenomenol*, 26, 116-129, 1996.

The purpose of this paper is to show that the term "community of love" (*Liebesgemeinschaft*) elucidates aspects of Husserl's thought. The first part of this paper arrives at a broader notion of rationality at work in Husserl than the notion which is frequently attributed to him (and just as frequently criticized). On the basis of this expanded notion of rationality, various components of Husserl's theory of community are reconsidered. In a third section, the expanded notion of rationality is utilized to clarify Husserl's critique of calculative rationality. The conclusion is that the sense of noncalculative responsibility which arises out of these considerations is the type of "rational" response at the basis of the community of love.

**Buckley, R Philip**. Rationality and Responsibility in Heidegger's and Husserl's View of Technology. *Amer Cath Phil Quart*, 70(Supp), 121-134, 1996.

The analysis of technology is perhaps the most phenomenological component of Heidegger's later thought. His description of this complex phenomenon called technology, however, produces certain tensions that are frequently resolved through one-sided readings. This presentation aims to preserve the ambiguity of Heidegger's reflections on technology and indicate how they are meant to take us towards a nontechnological thinking by returning to the Husserlian source of much of Heidegger's thought. Following a summary of the salient features of Heidegger's view of technology, the second part of this paper outlines the Husserlian foundation of much of that view. In the concluding part, an attempt is made to develop the sense of rational responsibility for technology which arises out of the juxtaposition of Husserl and Heidegger.

**Buckman, Kenneth L**. Gadamer on Art, Morality, and Authority. *Phil Lit*, 21(1), 144-150, Ap 97.

**Buege, Douglas J**. "Epistemic Responsibility and the Inuit of Canada's Eastern Arctic: An Ecofeminist Appraisal" in *Ecofeminism: Women, Culture, Nature,* Warren, Karen J (ed), 99-111. Bloomington, Indiana Univ Pr, 1997.

**Buege, Douglas J**. An Ecologically-Informed Ontology for Environmental Ethics. *Biol Phil*, 12(1), 1-20, Ja 97.

Since the inception of their subject as a distinct area of study in philosophy, environmental ethicists have quarreled over the choice of entities with which an environmental ethic should be concerned. A dichotomous ontology has arisen with the ethical atomists, e.g., Singer and Taylor, arguing for moral consideration of individual organisms and the holists, e.g., Rolston and Callicott, focusing on moral consideration of systems. This dichotomous view is ecologically misinformed and should be abandoned. In this paper, I argue that the organization of the natural world, as viewed by some ecologists and evolutionary biologists, is structured on various levels that are not reducible to one another. This "hierarchical" view, expressed by Salthe and Eldredge, provides the most complete and accurate ontology for environmental ethics.

**Buehler, David A**. Healthcare Ethics Committees and Ethics Consultants: The State of the Art (Sources/Bibliography). *Cambridge Quart Healthcare Ethics*, 6(3), 302-305, Sum 97.

**Bühler, Pierre**. Avant-propos. *Rev Theol Phil*, 128(4), 321-323, 1996.

**Buekens, F**. Toch Geen Representaties? Een Reacties op J. Sleutels' Zonnebrandontologie. *Alg Ned Tijdschr Wijs*, 88(3), 229-233, Jl 96.

**Buekens, Filip**. A Decision Procedure for Von Wright's Obs-Calculus. *Log Anal*, 38(149), 43-53, Mr 95.

Von Wright (1983) presents an interesting and fruitful integration of action logic into classical deontic logic. The first part of the paper presents a brief overview of von Wright's OBS-calculus and discusses some alternative proposals and amendments to the calculus under scrutiny. The second part of the paper develops a decision procedure for well-formed formulae in the OBS-calculus. I follow Hintikka's approach based on a possible world-semantics for deontic operators.

**Buekens, Filip**. Lynne Rudder Bakers Praktisch Realisme. *Alg Ned Tijdschr Wijs*, 89(3), 240-242, Jl 97.

**Bueno, Gustavo**. Crítica a la constitución de una sociedad política como Estado de Derecho (homenje a Carlos Baliñas). *El Basilisco*, 22, 3-32, Jl-D 96.

**Bueno, Otavio** and Da Costa, Newton C A. Consistency, Para-consistency and Truth (Logic, the Whole Logic and Nothing but 'the' Logic). *Ideas Valores*, 48-60, Ap 96.

After examining some components of a framework articulated in terms of general remarks on logic (in which two inadequate views of it are critically investigated), we present some arguments to the effect that a fallibilist, pluralist, though certainly not relativist, proposal might be interestingly pursued. Based on this proposal, we argue for a comprehensive agnosticism in connection to some issues raised by paraconsistency (in particular with regard to the existence of true contradictions). Such an agnosticism, not being philosophically committed to any particular "interpretative" claims surrounding paraconsistency, seems to be at the moment more adequate than the alternative proposals.

**Bueno, Otávio** and Da Costa, Newton C A and Béziau, Jean-Yves. What is Semantics? A Brief Note on a Huge Question. *Sorites*, 43-47, N 95.

After mentioning the cogent connection between pure semantics and the particular set theoretical framework in which it is formulated, some issues regarding the conceptual status of semantics itself, as well as its relationship to logic, are concisely raised.

**Büring, Daniel**. The Great Scope Inversion Conspiracy. *Ling Phil*, 20(2), 175-194, Ap 97.

The paper deals with disambiguation by intonation. Sentences that contain negation and a quantified noun phrase or a modal, respectively, are often ambiguous, as for example the sentence *all the men didn't go*. Given a special intonational contour, however, only one reading survives. Using examples from German, it is shown how the ambiguity arises and why the pragmatic meaning generally associated with pitch accents prohibits one of the readings by implication. It is thus argued that disambiguation in this case is compositionally achieved by the combination of structural and intonational meaning, which are both modeled using possible world semantics.

**Bugajska-Jaszczolt, Beata** and Dyrda, Kazimiera. On the Rules of Substitution in the First-Order Predicate Logics. *Rep Math Log*, 28, 21-27, 1994.

In this paper we consider two rules of substitution for predicate symbols as introduced by Church [1] and by Pogorzelski, Prucnal [2]. We show that the rules are not equivalent over a standard system of predicate logic.

**Bugajska-Jaszczolt, Beata** and Prucnal, Tadeusz. Axiomatization of the Logic Determined by the System of Natural Numbers with Identity. *Rep Math Log*, 28, 61-71, 1994.

The notion of the first-order predicate logic determined by a relational system was introduced in [3]. In this paper we consider the pure first-order predicate logic determined by the system of natural numbers with identity. We show that this logic is axiomatizable.

**Bugarin, Alberto J** and Barro, Senén. Which Are Some of the Applications of Fuzzy Logic? (in Spanish). *Theoria (Spain)*, 11(27), 149-161, S 96.

This paper discusses about the field of fuzzy logic applications, but not from the point of view of its importance or commenting their main features and how they are formally supported by fuzzy logic. Very good and abundant checking of this style (Zadeh, Yager 1992) exist in the field, and so we decided to present some reflections trying to answer very general questions about this issue. Answering, for example, to the question about possible future applications of fuzzy logic is, no doubts, a very risky task. We look forward to be forgiven if our approach proves not to be very successful.

**Bulger, Ruth Ellen** and Reiser, Stanley Joel. The Social Responsibilities of Biological Scientists. *Sci Eng Ethics*, 3(2), 137-143, Ap 97.

Biological scientists, like scientists in other disciplines, are uncertain about whether or how to use their knowledge and time to provide society with insight and guidance in handling the effects of inventions and discoveries. This article addresses this issue. It presents a typography of structures in which scientists may contribute to social understanding and decisions. It describes the different ways in which these contributions can be made. Finally it develops the ethical arguments that justify the view that biological scientists have social responsibilities.

**Buller, David J**. Individualism and Evolutionary Psychology (or: In Defense of "Narrow" Functions). *Phil Sci*, 64(1), 74-95, Mr 97.

Millikan (1993) and Wilson (1994) argue, for different reasons, that the essential reference to the environment in adaptationist explanations of behavior makes (psychological) individualism inconsistent with evolutionary psychology. I show that their arguments are based on misinterpretations of the role of reference to the environment in such explanations. By exploring these misinterpretations, I develop an account of explanation in evolutionary psychology that is fully consistent with individualism. This does not, however, constitute a full-fledged defense of individualism, since evolutionary psychology is only one explanatory paradigm among many in psychology.

**Bullock, Marcus** (ed) and Jennings, Michael W (ed). *Walter Benjamin: Selected Writings Volume 1 1913-1926*. Cambridge, Harvard Univ Pr, 1997.

Volume I of the *Selected Writings* brings together essays long and short, academic treatises, reviews, fragments, and privately circulated pronouncements. Fully five-sixths of this material has never before been translated into English. The contents begin in 1813, when Benjamin, as an undergraduate in imperial Germany, was president of a radical youth group, and take us through 1926, when he had already begun, with his explorations of the world of mass culture, to emerge as a critical voice in Weimar Germany's most influential journals. The volume includes a number of his most important works, including "Two Poems by Friedrich Hölderlin," "Goethe's Elective Affinities," "The Concept of Criticism in German Romanticism," "The Task of the Translator," and "One-Way Street." He is as compelling and insightful when musing on riddles or children's books as he is when dealing with weightier issues such as the philosophy of language, symbolic logic, or epistemology. We meet Benjamin the youthful idealist, the sober moralist, the political theorist, the experimentalist, the translator, and, above all, the virtual king of criticism, with his magisterial exposition of the basic problems of aesthetics. (publisher,edited)

**Bullough, Vern L**. "Medieval Scholasticism and Averroism: The Implication of the Writings of Ibn Rushd to Western Science" in *Averroës and the Enlightenment*, Wahba, Mourad (ed), 41-51. Amherst, Prometheus, 1996.

**Bumpus, Minnette A** and Glover, Saundra H and Logan, John E (& others). Re-Examining the Influence of Individual Values on Ethical Decision Making. *J Bus Ethics*, 16(12-13), 1319-1329, S 97.

This paper presents the results of five years of research involving three studies. The first two studies investigated the impact of the value honesty/integrity on the ethical decision choice an individual makes, as moderated by the individual personality traits of self-monitoring and private self-consciousness. The third study, which is the focus of this paper, expanded the two earlier studies by varying the level of moral intensity and including the influence of demographic factors and other workplace values; achievement, fairness and concern for others on the ethical decision process. (edited)

**Bunder, M W**. A Simplified Form of Condensed Detachment. *J Log Lang Info*, 4(2), 169-173, 1995.

This paper give a simple, elegant statement of the condensed detachment rule that is independent of most general unifiers and proves that this is equivalent to the longer, more usual formulation.

**Bunge, Mario**. *Finding Philosophy in Social Science*. New Haven, Yale Univ Pr, 1996.

Written by an eminent and original thinker in the philosophy of science, this book takes a fresh, unorthodox look at the key philosophical concepts and assumptions of the social sciences. Mario Bunge contends that social scientists (anthropologists, sociologists, political scientists, economists, and historians) ought not to leave philosophy to philosophers, who have little expertise in or knowledge of the social sciences. Bunge urges social scientists to engage in serious philosophizing and philosophers to participate in social research. The two fields are interrelated, he says, and important advances in each can supply tools for solving problems in the other. (publisher)

**Bunge, Mario**. The Bell Inequalities and all that. *Phil Natur*, 26(1), 121-134, 1989.

The entire family of hidden variables theories, containing inequalities of the Bell type, has recently been refuted experimentally. However, there is confusion as to what exactly this proves. Some claim that realism has been refuted, others that determinism is definitely out and still others that the loser is the conjunction of the EPR criterion of reality and the classical principle of separability or locality. The aim of this papers is to clarify some of the key concepts involved in order to help make a decision among the said alternatives. (edited)

**Bunge, Mario**. The Seven Pillars of Popper's Social Philosophy. *Phil Soc Sci*, 26(4), 528-556, D 96.

The author submits that Popper's social philosophy rests on seven pillars: rationality (both conceptual and practical), individualism (ontological and methodological), libertarianism, the nonexistence of historical laws, negative utilitarianism ("Do no harm"), piecemeal social engineering and a view on social order. The first six pillars are judged to be weak and the seventh broken. In short, it is argued that Popper did not build a comprehensive, profound, or even consistent system of social philosophy on a par with his work in epistemology. Still, he did make some important contributions to the field, such as unveiling the philosophical roots of totalitarianism and defending social engineering against both revolutionists and conservatives.

**Bunn, Geoffrey C**. The Lie Detector, *Wonder Woman* and Liberty: The Life and Work of William Moulton Marston. *Hist Human Sci*, 10(1), 91-119, F 97.

**Burack, Jeffrey H**. Response to "Further Exploration of the Relationship between Medical Education and Moral Development" by Donnie J. Self, DeWitt C. Baldwin, Jr., and Frederic D. Wolinsky (CQ Vol 5, No 3). *Cambridge Quart Healthcare Ethics*, 6(2), 226-232, Spr 97.

This paper is subtitled: "Deriving 'ought' from 'p': methodological and theoretical pitfalls in quantitative ethics." Prescriptive claims based on statistical observations are seductive, but most pass two tests: for the appropriateness of their statistical analyses and for the plausibility of their normative assumptions. The paper by Self *et al* illustrates ways in which research in biomedical ethics can fail these tests, including: confusing failure to find a difference with finding no difference; inadequate statistical power; the interpretation of statistically insignificant results; and distortion by a bounded measurement instrument. Finally, I explore how the authors' controversial theoretical commitments drive interpretation of their data and suggest an alternative multidimensional model of moral development.

**Burack, Jeffrey H** and Back, Anthony L and Pearlman, Robert A. Provoking Nonepileptic Seizures: The Ethics of Deceptive Diagnostic Testing. *Hastings Center Rep*, 27(4), 24-33, Jl-Ag 97.

The use of deception in medical care is highly suspect in this country. Yet there is one condition in which deception is often used as a diagnostic tool. Nonepileptic seizures, a psychiatric condition in which emotional or psychological conflicts manifest themselves unconsciously through bodily symptoms, are currently diagnosed by a procedure called "provocative saline infusion." The test is fundamentally deceptive, but without such deception the test might be useless.

**Burbidge, John W**. *Real Process: How Logic and Chemistry Combine in Hegel's Philosophy of Nature*. Toronto, Univ of Toronto Pr, 1996.

**Burbidge, John W** (ed) and Fackenheim, Emil L. *The God Within: Kant, Schelling, and Historicity*. Toronto, Univ of Toronto Pr, 1996.

**Burbules, Nicholas C**. "Deconstructing "Difference" and the Difference This Makes to Education" in *Philosophy of Education (1996)*, Margonis, Frank (ed), 114-123. Urbana, Phil Education Soc, 1997.

**Burch, Robert**. "On the Ethical Determination of Geography: A Kantian Prolegomenon" in *Philosophy and Geography I: Space, Place, and Environmental Ethics*, Light, Andrew (ed), 15-47. Lanham, Rowman & Littlefield, 1997.

**Burch, Robert W**. "A Tarski-Style Semantics for Peirce's Beta Graphs" in *The Rule of Reason: The Philosophy of Charles Sanders Peirce*, Forster, Paul (ed), 81-95. Toronto, Univ of Toronto Pr, 1997.

**Burch, Robert W**. "Peirce on the Application of Relations to Relations" in *Studies in the Logic of Charles Sanders Peirce*, Houser, Nathan (ed), 206-233. Bloomington, Indiana Univ Pr, 1997.

**Burch, Robert W**. "Peirce's Reduction Thesis" in *Studies in the Logic of Charles Sanders Peirce*, Houser, Nathan (ed), 234-251. Bloomington, Indiana Univ Pr, 1997.

**Burchardt, Hans-Jürgen**. Die Globalisierungsthese—von der kritischen Analyse zum politischen Opportunismus. *Das Argument*, 217(5-6), 741-755, 1996.

The idea of globalization lacks a strong empirical basis; along with the national state's supposed loss of power, it is more a construct of "unbounded" thought than a real development. Its popularity is more the result of political opportunism than of critical analysis.

**Burge, Tyler**. "Content Preservation" in *Contents*, Villanueva, Enrique (ed), 271-300. Atascadero, Ridgeview, 1995.

**Burge, Tyler**. "Frege on Knowing the Third Realm" in *Frege: Importance and Legacy*, Schirn, Matthias (ed), 347-368. Hawthorne, de Gruyter, 1996.

**Burge, Tyler**. Interlocution, Perception, and Memory. *Phil Stud*, 86(1), 21-47, Ap 97.

**Burgen, Arnold** (ed) and McLaughlin, Peter (ed) and Mittelstrass, Jürgen (ed). *The Idea of Progress*. Hawthorne, de Gruyter, 1997.

This volume represents an interdisciplinary attempt to deal with the concept of progress as used in and as viewed by various disciplines, from musicology to physics. Many of the contributions are philosophical or historical analyses of the concept of progress itself. The philosophical essays discuss empirical and valuational aspects as well as the question of whether and how philosophy itself makes progress. Other areas dealt with are progress in time, evolution, politics, health and music.

**Burgess, J A**. Supervaluations and the Propositional Attitude Constraint. *J Phil Log*, 26(1), 103-119, F 97.

For the sentences of languages that contain operators that express the concepts of definiteness and indefiniteness, there is an unavoidable tension between a truth-theoretic semantics that delivers truth conditions for those sentences that capture their propositional contents and *any* model-theoretic semantics that has a story to tell about how indefiniteness in a constituent affects the semantic value of sentences which imbed it. But semantic theories of both kinds play essential roles, so the tension needs to be resolved. I argue that it is the truth theory which correctly characterizes the notion of truth, *per se*. When we take into account the considerations required to bring model theory into harmony with truth theory, those considerations undermine the arguments standardly used to motivate supervaluational model theories designed to validate classical logic. But those considerations also show that celebration would be premature for advocates of the most frequently encountered rival approach—many-valued model theory.

**Burgess, John P**. Marcus, Kripke, and Names. *Phil Stud*, 84(1), 1-47, O 96.

**Burgess, John P** and Rosen, Gideon. *A Subject with No Object: Strategies for Nominalistic Interpretation of Mathematics*. New York, Clarendon/Oxford Pr, 1997.

*A Subject with No Object* cuts through a host of technicalities that have obscured previous discussions of these projects, and presents clear, concise accounts, with minimal prerequisites, of a dozen strategies for nominalistic interpretation of mathematics, thus equipping the reader to evaluate each and to compare different ones. The authors also offer critical discussion, rare in the literature, of the aims and claims of nominalistic interpretation, suggesting that it is significant in a very different way from that usually assumed. (publisher, edited)

**Burgess-Jackson, Keith**. Mackie on Kant's Moral Argument. *Sophia (Australia)*, 35(1), 5-20, Mr-Ap 96.

In *The Miracle of Theism* J.L. Mackie argues that no moral argument for the existence of God, including Immanuel Kant's famous argument, is successful. I argue 1) that Mackie misunderstands and mischaracterizes Kant's argument; 2) that Kant did not take himself to be arguing that God exists, but rather that the

existence of God is presupposed in our moral thinking; 3) that on this construal, Kant's argument will strike many readers—even theists—as unpersuasive; and 4) that if Kant *did* take himself to be arguing for the existence of God, the argument fails—but not, interestingly enough, for the reason Mackie gives.

**Burggraeve, Roger**. Emmanuel Levinas: Thinker between Jerusalem and Athens. *J Soc Phil*, 28(1), 110-126, Spr 97.

**Burghi, Giancarlo**. Conversazione con Cornelio Fabro. *Aquinas*, 39(3), 459-474, S-D 96.

Professor Fabro, Lei è uno dei massimi studiosi del pensiero di Kierkegaard. Eppure la sua lunga e assidua consuetudine con questo autore non le ha consentito—è lei stesso a confessarlo—di svelare il mistero profondo della sua vita, la ragione di quell'oscura malinconia che lo divorava, quel *pungolo della carne* di cui il filosofo danese ripetutamente parla e di cui gli interpreti hanno dato le più diverse interpretazioni. L'*enigma* di Kierkegaard—per usare il titolo di un suo saggio—dopo cinquant'anni di acribia critica e di studio perseverante, le appare, oggi, più decifrabile?

**Burgio, Alberto**. *Rousseau, La Politica e la Storia: Tra Montesquieu e Robespierre*. Milano, Guerini, 1996.

Sottrarre Rousseau alla taccia di "primitivismo", evitando così di ridurre a utopia l'istanza critica del suo pensiero, è l'intento principale di questo libro, nel quale si mette in risalto come lo sguardo di Rousseau sulla realtà del suo tempo sia essenzialmente storico, e come proprio dalla riflessione sull'esperienza storica sorgano i criteri di giudizio che danno forma alla sua teoria politica. D'altra parte il libro non manca di indagare la relazione tra pensiero e contesto storico, dove la storia è *per noi* un essenziale sturmento di interpretazione. (publisher, edited)

**Burgos, Juan Manuel**. Weber e lo spirito del capitalismo: Storia di un problema e nuove prospettive. *Acta Phil*, 5(2), 197-220, 1996.

The impassioned, century-long debate roused by *The Protestant Ethic and the Spirit of Capitalism* has made this work a classic of our time, but it has also made direct access to its content difficult, because of the accumulation of a great number of interpretations and commentaries, at times opposed to one another. This article seeks to help resolve this difficulty, offering a synthetic summary of Weber's theses and guidelines for orienting oneself in the world of the secondary literature on this work. The article also offers some reflections on the significance for this debate of the encyclical *Centesimus Annus* and the thought of Michael Novak.

**Burillo, Santiago Fernández**. Las Disputaciones metafísicas de F. Suárez S.J., su inspiración y algunas de sus líneas maestras: En el IV centenario de la primera edición (1597-1997). *Rev Espan Filosof Med*, 4, 65-86, 1997.

Four centuries after the first edition of *Disputationes Metaphysicae* (1597), that vast work is still the greatest issue from the Spanish philosophy. F. Suárez is the author of one of the most important synthesis of the scholar philosophy. The key of everything he means and also of *Disputations*, can be found in the idea of freedom in causality and action. From this concept, some topics are shown: act and potentiality, cause, creation, etc. We explain Suarez's metaphysics from an existential point of view and refuse the accusation of abstractism.

**Burke, Douglas** and Matsubara, Yo. Ideals and Combinatorial Principles. *J Sym Log*, 62(1), 117-122, Mr 97.

**Burke, Michael B**. Coinciding Objects: Reply to Lowe and Denkel. *Analysis*, 57(1), 11-18, Ja 97.

**Burke, Michael B**. Tibbles the Cat: A Modern *Sophisma*. *Phil Stud*, 84(1), 63-74, O 96.

**Burke, Patrick**. Skepticism and the Question of Community. *Res Phenomenol*, 26, 98-115, 1996.

**Burke, Ronald J**. Women on Corporate Boards of Directors: A Needed Resource. *J Bus Ethics*, 16(9), 909-915, Je 97.

This research reports the results of a study of women serving on boards of directors of Canadian private and public sector organizations. Most were nominated as a result of recommendations from current board members, CEOs, or someone who knew board members or CEOs. Thus personal relationships (the old boys network) as well as track records and appropriate expertise were important factors in board nominations. Women directors thought they had some influence on women's issues with their boards and board companies. (edited)

**Burke, Ronald J** and Black, Susan. Save the Males: Backlash in Organizations. *J Bus Ethics*, 16(9), 933-942, Je 97.

This paper reviews the literature on male backlash in organizations, proposing a research agenda. It defines backlash, examines its causes and manifestations, who is likely to exhibit it and offers suggestions for addressing backlash. Backlash may be on the increase in organizations and society at large. Current efforts to weaken or remove the legislative support for employment equity initiatives are one sign of this.

**Burke, Seán**. Who Speaks? Who Writes? Dialogue and Authorship in the *Phaedrus*. *Hist Human Sci*, 10(3), 40-55, Ag 97.

This paper argues that the concepts of writing and authorship in Plato are associated with monologism and absence rather than presence. The *Phaedrus* objects to writing precisely insofar as it creates that unresponsive figure in the field of discursive which we have subsequently called the 'author'. The dialectical preference for question-and-answer is designed to resist anything resembling an author from entering the field of knowledge; the Socratic method resists monologism on epistemological and ethical grounds. However, the Platonic dialogues are split in their signature between a Socrates who speaks and a Socrates who writes. (edited)

**Burkert, Walter**. "Impact and Limits of the Idea of Progress in Antiquity" in *The Idea of Progress,* McLaughlin, Peter (ed), 19-46. Hawthorne, de Gruyter, 1997.

**Burkhard, Philipp**. Pragmatismus, Dekonstruktion, ironischer Eklektizismus: Richard Rortys Heidegger-Lektüre. *Z Phil Forsch*, 51(2), 268-284, Ap-Je 97.

**Burkhardt, Margaret A** and Nathaniel, Alvita K. Patient Self-Determination and Complementary Therapies. *Bioethics Forum,* 12(4), 24-29, Wint 96.

Many people who seek health care from conventional biomedical health care providers utilize other healing modalities as well, which are often referred to as alternative or complementary therapies. When considering ethical issues regarding complementary therapies, attentiveness to patient self-determination is imperative. Although it is the patient's responsibility to seek information about complementary modalities and to make health choices in this regard, it is prudent for conventional providers to become knowledgeable about other modalities and to provide a nonjudgmental atmosphere in which patients can discuss and explore approaches to addressing their health care needs.

**Burkhardt, Susan** and Taube, Daniel O. Ethical and Legal Risks Associated with Archival Research. *Ethics Behavior,* 7(1), 59-67, 1997.

Mental health facilities and practitioners commonly permit researchers to have direct access to patients' records for the purpose of archival research without the informed consent of patient-participants. Typically these researchers have access to all information in such records as long as they agree to maintain confidentiality and remove any identifying data from subsequent research reports. Changes in the American Psychological Association's Ethical Principles (American Psychological Association, 1992) raise ethical and legal issues that require consideration by practitioners, researchers, and facility Institutional Review Boards. This article addresses these issues and provides recommendations for changes in ethical standards as well as alternative avenues for conducting research using archival mental health records.

**Burks, Arthur W**. "Logic, Learning, and Creativity in Evolution" in *Studies in the Logic of Charles Sanders Peirce,* Houser, Nathan (ed), 497-534. Bloomington, Indiana Univ Pr, 1997.

Peirce's 1890's absolute idealistic teleological (yet pragmatic) theory of cosmic evolution had three components: chance, continuity and goal-directedness. I compare his theory with some computer simulations of evolutionary developments and some computer programs that learn and discover. W. D. Hamilton has explained the advantage of organism diploidy over parasite haploidy by comparing the learning difference of the two rates of reproduction. John Holland has created evolutionary computer programs employing a genetic algorithm and highly parallel learning systems based on instructions called *classifiers* that are analogous to Peirce's practical conditionals and function in an Adam Smith like economy.

**Burks, Arthur W**. Peirce's Evolutionary Pragmatic Idealism. *Synthese,* 106(3), 323-372, Mr 96.

In this paper I synthesize a unified system out of Peirce's life work and name it "Peirce's Evolutionary Pragmatic Idealism". Peirce developed this philosophy in four stages: I) His 1868-69 theory that cognition is a continuous and infinite social semiotic process, in which Man is a sign. II) His *Popular Science Monthly* pragmatism and frequency theory of probabilistic induction. III) His 1891-93 cosmic evolutionism of Tychism, Synechism and Agapism. IV) Prag*maticism*: The doctrine of real potentialities ("would-be's") and Peirce's pragmatic program for developing concrete reasonableness. Peirce's evolutionary conception of the cosmos is pantheistic and he constructed it to reconcile religion with Darwinian evolution.

**Burks, Ben**. Unity and Diversity through Education: A Comparison of the Thought of W.E.B. DuBois and John Dewey. *J Thought,* 32(1), 99-110, Spr 97.

**Burkum, Keith** and Iuculano, John. The Humanism of Sartre: Toward a Psychology of Dignity. *J Theor Phil Psych,* 16(1), 19-29, Spr 96.

This paper is an attempt to make more explicit what we believe is the significance of the concept of dignity for psychology. The paper is grounded in the writings of Husserl and the humanism of Sartre and examines the humanistic position underlying psychology with that of positivism and determinism. Through an examination of Sartre's formulation of the cogito and intersubjectivity, we argue, that humanism more than any other orientation current in psychology is concerned with the human status of the individual and the recognition of dignity as central to that status. We argue that dignity is fundamental to the structure of human existence and is achieved only by holding the other as human in status rather than reduced to the status of an object.

**Burlingame, Michael**. "A Sin Against Scholarship": Some Examples of Plagiarism in Stephen B. Oates's Biographies of Abraham Lincoln, Martin Luther King, Jr., and William Faulkner. *J Infor Ethics,* 3(1), 48-57, Spr 94.

The purpose of this essay is to show how Stephen B. Oates, professor of history at the University of Massachusetts at Amherst, committed plagiarism in his biographies of Abraham Lincoln, Martin Luther King, Jr. and William Faulkner and to reveal how his defenders responded to his literary piracy in public (by dismissing the charges of plagiarism as "totally groundless" and "without foundation") and in private (telling Oates that he had committed a "sin against scholarship.") I also wished to show how timid professional organizations (like the American Historical Association) are in disciplining plagiarists in their ranks.

**Burms, Arnold**. Universal Rights and Explicit Principles (in Dutch). *Bijdragen,* 58(2), 144-152, 1997.

It is argued that the point of the ideal of human rights is to protect individuals against oppressive regimes or cruel traditions. This negative description should not be converted into a positive one: it would be wrong to speak in terms of human rights about whatever people need in order to have meaningful lives. The reason why many philosophers are tempted to make that wrong move is that two kinds of individualism are easily conflated. The thesis that individuals should not be oppressed because of their choices or commitments is translated into the (very different) thesis freedom of individual choice should be maximized. The ideal of individual autonomy which manifests itself in the latter thesis is also at the origin of the belief that our moral intuitions should be justified in terms of the principles we consciously and explicitly endorse. I have argued that this belief has implications which are unacceptable to (practically) anybody.

**Burnett, G Wesley** and Lant, Christopher L and Akama, John S. A Political-Ecology Approach to Wildlife Conservation in Kenya. *Environ Values,* 5(4), 335-347, N 96.

This essay uses a political-ecological framework in the analysis of the social factors of wildlife conservation in Kenya. It postulates that the overriding socio-economic issue impacting wildlife conservation in Kenya is underdevelopment. The problem of underdevelopment is manifested in forms of increasing levels of poverty, famine and malnutrition. The long term survival of Kenya's wildlife depends on social and ecological solutions to the problems of underdevelopment. (edited)

**Burnstone, Dan**. Moral Synonymy: John Stuart Mill and the Ethics of Style. *Phil Lit,* 21(1), 46-60, Ap 97.

**Burnyeat, M F**. The Impiety of Socrates. *Ancient Phil,* 17(2), 1-12, Spr 97.

Plato's *Apology,* being a forensic speech rather than a dialogue, invites the reader to reach a verdict on the charge against Socrates. The verdict argued for here is that Socrates was indeed guilty of not believing in the gods the city believed in. The reader of the *Apology* is confronted with a clash of opposed religions, analogous to that in Salmon Rushdie's *Satanic Verses.*

**Burrell, David B**. David Braine's Project: The Human Person. *Faith Phil,* 13(2), 163-178, AP 96.

The author of *The Reality of Time and the Existence of God* turns his critical conceptual acumen to finding an intellectually viable path between the current polarities of *dualism* and *materialism.* By considering human beings as language-using animals he can critically appraise "representational" views of concept formation, as well as show how current "research programs" which presuppose a "materialist" basis stem from an unwitting adoption of a dualist picture of mind and body. His alternative is rooted in classical thinkers like Aquinas and responsive to the critiques of Wittgenstein, yet constructive in ways in which those critiques failed to be. This essay aims to help readers undertake a taxing inquiry by guiding them through its main theses.

**Burri, Alex**. Realismus in Duhems naturgemässer Klassifikation. *J Gen Phil Sci,* 27(2), 203-213, 1996.

Pierre Duhem is an outstanding exponent of empiricism. According to the empiricist view scientific laws and theories merely describe formal relations between observable phenomena. Duhem's important notion of natural classification is intended to explain the predictive success of science. I shall argue that it can only be interpreted realistically. Besides the success of science, two further arguments are put forward in favor of realism: I) the fact that laws of nature are necessary and II) the extension of observation by using instruments.

**Burrieza, Alfredo** and Diéguez, Antonio. La instrumentalización del tiempo. *Analogia,* 10(2), 113-138, 1996.

In this century we have been witnessing to the development of a functional or instrumental conception of time. According to such conception, time is a tool dependent on the proposed technical and scientific goals. Time is designed to fit the nature of problems which require it. The variety of applications in which time is involved have modified its topology one way or the other. This adaptability of the structure of time has been feasible only when science and technology have paid special attention to it.

**Burris, Stanley** and Ferreirim, Isabel M A. Decidable Varieties of Hoops. *Rep Math Log,* 28, 53-59, 1994.

A description of all varieties of hoops which have a decidable first order theory is given.

**Bursztajn, Harold J**. Reflections on My Father's Experience with Doctors during the Shoah (1939-1945). *J Clin Ethics,* 7(4), 311-314, Wint 96.

The Nazi war of genocide against the Jews and other groups marked for extermination (1939-1945), involved both acts of collaboration and resistance by the medical profession. While the former have been the focus, beginning with the 1946 Nuremberg trials, the latter have been relegated to relative obscurity. The author reports two acts of heroic resistance by Jewish physicians who each saved his father's life. The focus is to remind clinicians that even under the most extreme and life threatening conditions, physicians can behave responsibly toward their patients. This is a useful reminder today when all too often clinical responsibility is avoided by the excuse of "third party" managed care pressures.

**Burt, Robert A**. The Suppressed Legacy of Nuremberg. *Hastings Center Rep,* 26(5), 30-33, S-O 96.

The ideal of patient autonomy was in an important sense irrelevant at the moment it was originally proclaimed.

**Burwood, Les R V**. How Should Schools Respond to the Plurality of Values in a Multi-Cultural Society?. *J Phil Educ,* 30(3), 415-427, N 96.

How should state schools respond to the plurality of values in a multicultural society? The liberal response has been that it is unacceptable to promote only the traditional, mainstream values of dominant groups and impose them on others. During the 1980s this response gradually evolved into an ideology of extreme subjectivism, commonly referred to as cultural relativism. This ideology is rejected and it is argued that the school must make crucial judgments about which values should be promoted, tolerated or condemned.

**Busch, Paul** and Shimony, Abner. Insolubility of the Quantum Measurement Problem for Unsharp Observables. *Stud Hist Phil Mod Physics*, 27B(4), 397-404, D 96.

The quantum mechanical measurement problem is the difficulty of dealing with the indefiniteness of the pointed observable at the conclusion of a measurement process governed by unitary quantum dynamics. There has been hope to solve this problem by eliminating idealizations from the characterization of measurement. We state and prove two 'insolubility theorems' that disappoint this hope. In both the initial state of the apparatus is taken to be mixed rather than pure, and the correlation of the object observable and the pointer observable is allowed to be imperfect. In the *insolubility theorem for sharp observables*, which is only a modest extension of previous results, the object observable is taken to be an arbitrary projection valued measure. (edited)

**Busch, Thomas**. Sartre and Ricoeur on Imagination. *Amer Cath Phil Quart*, 70(4), 507-518, Autumn 96.

**Buss, Sarah**. Justified Wrongdoing. *Nous*, 31(3), 337-369, S 97.

**Buss, Sarah**. Weakness of Will. *Pac Phil Quart*, 78(1), 13-44, Mr 97.

My chief aim is to explain how someone can act freely against her own best judgment. But I also have a second aim: to defend a conception of practical rationality according to which someone cannot do something freely if she believes it would be better to do something else. These aims may appear incompatible. But I argue that practical reason has the capacity of behaving irrationally. Weakness of will is possible because it is possible to conclude that one has sufficient reason to reject the verdicts of one's own reason.

**Bustos López, Javier** and Öffenberger, Niels. La negación de los juicios estrictamente particulares en la tetravalencia. *Rev Filosof (Venezuela)*, 23(1), 67-77, 1996.

In bivalent truth tables we find possible cases, but not conclusive ones; the only possible and conclusive case is the contradiction. In tetravalence, on the other hand, we find three conclusive cases for each relation. This truth table offers certain exceptions when resolving the negation of strictly particular judgements: (a) the negation of the judgement is possible in the qualitative statement itself; (b) the negation of a judgement is also possible in the quantitative statement itself; (c) the negation of a judgement with a truth value Fp is possible in a universal, quantitative judgement; (d) the negation of strictly particular judgements does not admit the possibility of contradictory statements as such; and (e) the tetravalent truth table does not possess universal validity.

**Buszkowski, Wojciech**. Extending Lambek Grammars to Basic Categorial Grammars. *J Log Lang Info*, 5(3-4), 279-295, O 96.

Pentus (1992) proves the equivalence of LCG's and CFG's, and CFG's are equivalent to BCG's by the Gaifman theorem (Bar-Hillel et al., 1960). This paper provides a procedure to extend any LCG to an equivalent BCG by affixing new types to the lexicon; a procedure of that kind was proposed as early, as Cohen (1967), but it was deficient (Buszkowski, 1985). We use a modification of Pentus's proof and a new proof of the Gaifman theorem on the basis of the Lambek calculus.

**Buszkowski, Wojciech**. Representation Theorems for Implication Structures. *Bull Sec Log*, 25(3/4), 152-158, O-D 96.

The paper is concerned with implication structures more general than those related to classical or intuitionistic logic. The structures handled in the paper are residuated semigroups (monoids, groupoids etc.) and their reducts, and they correspond to substructural logics, e.g., BCI, the Lambek calculus, and others. For product-free reducts of these structures one proves representation theorems with respect to powerset residuated algebras by methods similar to standard proofs of, e.g., the Stone representation theorem for Boolean algebras, but structures with products require different techniques of a proof-theoretic style.

**Buszkowski, Wojciech**. The Finite Model Property for BCI and Related Systems. *Stud Log*, 57(2-3), 303-323, O 96.

We prove the finite model property (fmp) for BCI and BCI with additive conjunction, which answers some open questions in Meyer and Ono [11]. We also obtain similar results for some restricted versions of these systems in the style of the Lambek calculus [10, 3]. The key tool is the method of barriers which was earlier introduced by the author to prove fmp for the product-free Lambek calculus [2] and the commutative product-free Lambek calculus [4].

**Buterin, Damion**. Nietzsche: The Philosophical Nihilist and Overcoming Nihilism (in Serbo-Croatian). *Filozof Istraz*, 15(4), 757-773, 1995.

The author in this text examines the primacy of Nietzsche's discovery of nihilism at the centre of our valuations. Nihilism, it is argued, provides Nietzsche with the necessary historical framework within which he is able to conduct his various genealogical investigations. The first part concentrates on the identification of nihilism in three overlapping areas of European culture: metaphysics, science and Christianity. The second part represents an assessment of Nietzsche's confrontation with nihilism as the transvaluation of all values. Of crucial significance to the transvaluation are the concepts of the will to power, the *Übermensch* and the eternal recurrence of the same.

**Buterin, Damir**. The Absolute and Kierkegaard's Conception of Selfhood. *Filozof Istraz*, 16(3), 683-698, 1996.

The author in this text examines Kierkegaard's conception of selfhood in the context of his protest against Hegelian idealism. Kierkegaard opposes Hegel's dialectics by hypothesising the universality of human freedom as the foundation for a proper understanding of the relationship between the self and the Absolute (a relationship that is sustained by faith, not knowledge). In this sense,

Kierkegaard seeks to correct the damage inflicted by metaphysical alienation. The 'problem' of selfhood, viewed from the Kierkegaardian perspective, is based on the articulation of self-defining freedom in relation to God.

**Butler, Clark**. *History as the Story of Freedom: Philosophy in Intercultural Context*. Amsterdam, Rodopi, 1997.

This book advances a rehabilitation of the speculative philosophy of history. It defends the vital quest of humanity for an overarching narrative which will survive rational criticism. It uncovers the world-historical story of freedom. Beginning with the current age of human rights, the book works back through the great role-model civilizations of history. Its striking conclusion is that we can further advance the story of freedom as the story of human rights by de-Westernizing the story. The volume contains critical responses from sixteen scholars who represent several academic specialties and several world cultures. It is complemented by 20 remarkable illustrations drawn from many ages and cultures. (publisher)

**Butler, Judith**. Sovereign Performatives in the Contemporary Scene of Utterance. *Crit Inquiry*, 23(2), 350-377, Wint 97.

**Butler, Judith**. *The Psychic Life of Power: Theories in Subjection*. Stanford, Stanford Univ Pr, 1997.

As a form of power, subjection is paradoxical. To be dominated by a power external to oneself is a familiar and agonizing form power takes. To find, however, that what "one" is, one's very formation as a subject, is dependent upon that very power is quite another. If, following Foucault, we understand power as *forming* the subject as well, it provides the very condition of its existence and the trajectory of its desire. Power is not simply what we depend on for our existence but that which forms reflexivity as well. Drawing upon Hegel, Nietzsche, Freud, Foucault, and Althusser, this challenging and lucid work offers a theory of subject formation that illuminates as ambivalent the psychic effects of social power. (publisher, edited)

**Butler, Keith**. Content, Computation, and Individualism in Vision Theory. *Analysis*, 56(3), 146-154, Jl 96.

**Butler, Keith**. Individualism and Marr's Computational Theory of Vision. *Mind Lang*, 11(4), 313-337, D 96.

A great deal of philosophical work has addressed the question of whether Marr's computational theory of early vision is individualistic. Burge and Davies have argued that, according to Marr's theory, visual states are individuated nonindividualistically. Segal has denied that Marr's theory has these nonindividualistic implications. More recently, Shapiro has argued that the entire debate has been misguided. I argue that Shapiro is mistaken in a fairly deep way, attention to which allows us to raise and clarify several important issues involved in discussions of individualism. Contrary to Burge and Davies and by a route rather different from Segal's, I defend the claim that Marr's theory offers no reason to think that visual states are individuated nonindividualistically.

**Butler, Travis**. On David Charles's Account of Aristotle's Semantics for Simple Names. *Phronesis*, 42(1), 21-31, 1997.

**Butti de Lima, Paulo Francisco**. Nude Discourses, Empty Discourses (in Portuguese). *Trans/Form/Acao*, 19, 177-183, 1996.

In the Socratic-Platonic dialectic, considerations about style and form of discourses have a paradigmatic rule, not only for the critic of sophistry and rhetoric, but also for the characterization of the philosophical discourse. So they allow to establish the place of philosophy in relation to social practices.

**Buttigieg, Joseph A** (ed & trans). *Antonio Gramsci Prison Notebooks: Volume II*. New York, Columbia Univ Pr, 1996.

Antonio Gramsci (1891-1937) is widely recognized as the most original political philosopher in the tradition of Western Marxism. Arrested and imprisoned by the Italian Fascist regime in 1926, he died before fully regaining his freedom. Yet his voluminous notebooks—thousands of pages of brilliant reflections on an extraordinary range of subjects, written within the confines of a tiny prison cell—established an enduring intellectual legacy. (publisher, edited)

**Butz, Clarence E** and Lewis, Phillip V. Correlation of Gender-Related Values of Independence and Relationship and Leadership Orientation. *J Bus Ethics*, 15(11), 1141-1149, N 96.

This study compares the relationship between the moral reasoning modes and leadership orientation of males versus females, and managers versus engineers/scientists. A questionnaire developed by Worthley (1987) was used to measure the degree of each participants' respective independence and justice, and relationships and caring moral reasoning modes. Leadership orientation values and attitudes were measured using the Fiedler and Chemers (1984) Least Preferred Coworker Scale. The results suggest that, although males differ from female in their dominant moral reasoning modes, managers are not distinguishable from the engineers/scientists they manage in terms of their moral reasoning mode or Least Preferred Coworker score.

**Buzaglo, Meir**. Philosophy and Religious Belief: The Soup Fallacy (in Hebrew). *Iyyun*, 45, 413-418, O 96.

**Buzaglo, Meir**. Quasi-Logicism (in Hebrew). *Iyyun*, 46, 115-138, Ap 97.

**Buzzoni, Marco**. Erkenntnistheoretische und ontologische Probleme der theoretischen Begriffe. *J Gen Phil Sci*, 28(1), 19-53, 1997.

I argue for the following theses: 1) All scientific concepts are theory laden in the sense that they allow us to anticipate possible experiences, but they have to be *in principle* fully observable, i.e., integrally convertible into operational-technical applications. 2) The observation/theory distinction can be maintained as a historical one: what is observable depends on the instruments that are available at any stage of the development of science. 3) *In principle* theoretical entities are empirically real in Hacking's sense. However, some aspects of Hacking's realism are to be criticized. Theoretical entities are to be resolved into the totality of the interrelated properties accessible to us by means of theoretical points of view embodied in scientific instruments. (edited)

**Bychkov, Oleg V**. The Reflection of Some Traditional Stoic Ideas in the Thirteenth-Century Scholastic Theories of Beauty. *Vivarium*, 34(2), 141-160, N 96.

The article examines the reflection of three Stoic theories of beauty—transmitted through the texts of Cicero and Augustine—in the 13th-century Latin Scholastic *Summae*. They include a proof of the existence of gods from the beauty of the universe, a parallel between the beauty of the body and the soul and the theory of moral beauty (*honestum, decorum*) as the end in itself which is grounded in the disinterested nature of aesthetic experience. All three theories are reflected in the 13th-century Scholastic treatises (the *Summa Halensis*, Albert the Great, Aquinas, Ulrich of Strassburg) but often misinterpreted and tailored to suit the new Christian agenda.

**Bynum, Terrell Ward**. Introduction and Overview: Global Information Ethics. *Sci Eng Ethics*, 2(2), 131-136, A 96.

This is an introduction to a set of papers on computer ethics from the conference *Ethicomp95*. Taken as a whole, the collection of papers provides arguments and concepts to launch a new development in computer ethics; 'Global Information Ethics'. A rationale for globalization is provided, as well as some early efforts which move in that direction.

**Byrd, B Sharon**. Putative Self-Defense and Rules of Imputation In Defense of the Battered Woman. *Jahr Recht Ethik*, 2, 283-306, 1994.

Der Aufsatz liefert Argumente dafür, dass eine "battered women" für die Tötung ihres schlafenden Ehemannes strafrechtlich nicht zur Verantwortung gezogen werden kann, und zwar insbesondere dann nicht, wenn sie irrig Umstände annimmt, die, wenn sie vorlägen, die Handlung der Frau unter Notwehrgesichtspunkten rechtfertigen würden. Die Unterscheidung zwischen der Zurechnung eines Vorgangs als Handlung und der Zurechnung einer rechtswidrigen Tat zur Schuld wird vorangeschickt (I/II). (edited)

**Byrd, Michael**. Parts III-IV of *The Principles of Mathematics*. *Russell*, 16(2), 145-168, Wint 96-97.

**Byrne, Alex**. "Spin Control: Comment on John McDowell's *Mind and World*" in *Perception*, Villanueva, Enrique (ed), 261-273. Atascadero, Ridgeview, 1996.

How is it that we can have perceptually justified beliefs? In *Mind and World* McDowell argues that two answers—the "Myth of the Given" and a Davidsonian version of coherentism—are inadequate. I argue that McDowell has not given a good reason for rejecting either one.

**Byrne, Alex**. Some Like it Hot: Consciousness and Higher-Order Thoughts. *Phil Stud*, 86(2), 103-129, My 97.

It is argued that two common objections to David Rosenthal's higher-order thought theory of consciousness are inconclusive; that Fred Dretske's recent objection (in "Conscious Experience") to the theory is mistaken; that there are three further objections that are much more serious; and that even if the theory was true, it would not satisfactorily explain phenomenal consciousness.

**Byrne, Alex** and Hájek, Alan. David Hume, David Lewis, and Decision Theory. *Mind*, 106(423), 411-428, Jl 97.

In this paper we investigate whether Lewis's case against "Desire as Belief" (DAB) can be strengthened by examining how it fares under rival versions of decision theory, including other conceptions of rational ways to change one's mind. We prove a stronger version of Lewis's result in "Desire as Belief II." We then argue that the anti-Humean may escape Lewis's argument either by adopting a version of causal decision theory, or by claiming that the refutation only applies to hyper-idealized rational agents, or by denying that the decision-theoretic framework has the expressive capacity to formulate anti-Humeanism. (edited)

**Cabanchik, Samuel Manuel**. La inefabilidad de la semántica y el realismo interno. *Analisis Filosof*, 16(2), 175-187, N 96.

In this paper, I will first develop certain semantic questions underlying the internal realism, specially with respect to the rejection of the idea of independence from reality, in relation to the language. Next, I will point out that Putnam's position in the "Dewey Lectures"—his latest position—intends to recover the notion of independence inherent in common sense, that, as we will try to demonstrate, is consistent with what Hintikka calls "weak thesis of semantic ineffability". Finally, according to this interpretation, Putnam would not reject the idea of independence any longer, but only the idea, which he attributes to the metaphysical realism and not to the natural one that the world is a fixed whole or a super-reality. (edited)

**Cabanchik, Samuel Manuel**. La Naturaleza Problemática de la Filosofía. *Cad Hist Filosof Cie*, 6(Spec), 39-56, Ja-D 96.

In this paper, I will point out that the description of philosophical problems suppose the understanding of the question about philosophical nature as its essential characteristic. Next, I will develop an analysis of such a question, starting from a regard of the peculiar relation established between philosophy and language. Finally, I will propose that the original work of a philosopher is the conceptual creation in order of a more extensive understanding about the way that the concepts reflected in the use of language operate. I will distinguish this synoptic point of view from the traditional point of view of the totality, which is associated with the philosophy.

**Cabanchik, Samuel Manuel**. Réplica a la discusión sobre el revés de la filosofía, lenguaje y escepticismo. *Rev Latin de Filosof*, 22(2), 287-289, 1996.

**Cabedo, Salvador**. "Religión y paz en Kant" in *Kant: La paz perpetua, doscientos años después*, Martínez Guzmán, Vicent (ed), 35-51. Valencia, Nau Llibres, 1997.

**Cabral, Regis**. Herbert Butterfield (1900-79) as a Christian Historian of Science. *Stud Hist Phil Sci*, 27(4), 547-564, D 96.

Why is Butterfield's best-seller *The Origins of Modern Science* (1949) such a powerful big picture, nearly impossible to move away from? Considered in the context of his life, the contrast between his attacks on Whig history and the contents of his best-seller reveals that his big picture of science continues at the centre because of his spiritual beliefs and practices. Butterfield did not make explicit his Christian (Methodist) world view to his history of science readers, although one could infer this from his point that Christianity and the Scientific Revolution were the most significant events in universal history, transcending cultural boundaries. As long as Christian beliefs and practices continue to be at the centre of Western society, so will Butterfield's big picture be at the centre. Western society is a Christian civilization. For Butterfield, the meaning of history is Christianity and *The Origins of Modern Science* is very much a Christian statement of the evolution of knowledge acquisition in Western society. To decentre *The Origins* would require first a decentred view of Christianity.

**Cabral, Roque**. De Kojève a Hegel. *Rev Port Filosof*, 53(1), 85-87, Ja-Mr 97.

**Cabral, Roque**. Lei ou Legislador Natural?. *Rev Port Filosof*, 52(1-4), 179-184, Ja-D 96.

The author tries to show the advantages of speaking of "natural legislator" (the rational human person) instead of "natural law".

**Caccamo, James M**. Children, Society, and Health Care Decision Making. *Bioethics Forum*, 11(4), 32-34, Wint 95.

**Cacciatore, Giuseppe**. "Lo storicismo critico-problematico e la tradizione della 'filosofia civile' italiana" in *Lo Storicismo e la Sua Storia: Temi, Problemi, Prospettive,* Cacciatore, Giuseppe (ed), 582-597. Milano, Guerini, 1997.

The paper shows the weight of the political issue as a basic issue and a unifying element of all the Italian philosophical expressions of historism. Giambattista Vico is considered as one of the first and most important expression of this trend, which is later testified by the political historism of Vincenzo Cuoco as well as the historism of Francesco De Sanctis, whose peculiar form of a "science of the limit" approaches very nearly to the critical-problematic tradition of German historism. The paper discusses the ethical-political pregnancy of this tradition, by delineating its pluralistic, antifinalistic and liberal issues and its renewed expressions in the second half of XX century Italian thought, especially in Pietro Piovani and Fulvio Tessitore.

**Cacciatore, Giuseppe**. "Storia e tempo storico in Marx" in *Lo Storicismo e la Sua Storia: Temi, Problemi, Prospettive,* Cacciatore, Giuseppe (ed), 246-259. Milano, Guerini, 1997.

**Cacciatore, Giuseppe**. The "Political" Dimension of Italian Critico-Problematic Historicism (in Serbo-Croatian). *Filozof Istraz*, 15(4), 875-885, 1995.

Der vorliegende Text befasst sich mit verschiedenen Dimensionen des italienischen Historismus im 19. und im 20. Jahrhundert. Es wird dabei erörtert, dass die historistische Weltanschaunng in Italien in Giambattista Vico ihren Anfang hat, da die Beziehungen zwischen Kritik und Topik, so wie dieser sie vorgeschlagen hatte, auch später im italienischen Historismus des 19. und des 10. Jahrhunderts eine Charakteristik bedeuten. Der Historismus ist keine blosse rhetorische Übung und keine tautologisch maniristische Betrachtung über das historische Wesen des Menschen. In seiner kritisch-problematischen Version ist der Historismus eigentlich eine Grenzwissenschaft, d.h. eine Wissenschaft der Grenzen, die sich sowohl auf das Gebiet der Erkenntnis als auch auf jenes der Ethik und Politik beziehen. (edited)

**Cacciatore, Giuseppe** (ed) and Cantillo, Giuseppe (ed) and Lissa, Giuseppe (ed). *Lo Storicismo e la Sua Storia: Temi, Problemi, Prospettive.* Milano, Guerini, 1997.

Testimonianza dell'affetto dei suoi allievi, questo libro riflette, nell'impostazione e negli esiti, i motivi ispiratori dell'insegnamento e dell'attività scientifica e culturale di Fulvio Tessitore. Gli autori, .uniti da una comunanza di ricerca e di studio, si muovono lungo una pluralità di percorsi tematici che mettono a fuoco le diverse dimensioni teoriche e storiche dello storicismo. Ne emerge una ben determinata visione teoretico-filosofica dello storicismo (lo *storicismo criticoproblematico*, il *nuovo* storicismo) e, insieme, una ricostruzione storiografica della sua genesi e delle connessioni che lo legano ai principali orientamenti filosofici contemporanei. (publisher, edited)

**Cacciatore, Giuseppe** and Sini, Carlo. "Husserl e Heidegger: tempo e fenomenologia" in *Il Concetto di Tempo: Atti del XXXII Congresso Nazionale della Società Filosofica Italiana*, Casertano, Giovanni (ed), 85-90. Napoli, Loffredo, 1997.

**Cacciatore, Giuseppe** and Stile, Alessandro. *L'Edizione Critica Di Vico: Bilanci E Prospettive*. Napoli, Guida, 1997.

**Cadore, B** and Lamau, M L and Boitte, P. From "The Ethical Treatment of Patients in a Persistent Vegetative State" To a Philosophical Reflection on Contemporary Medicine. *Theor Med*, 18(3), 237-262, S 97.

The reflections put forward in this text concern the clinical and practical difficulties posed by the existence of patients in PVS and the essential ethical issues raised, combining these ethical questions with practical and theoretical experience. Section 1 presents the methodology of the ethical reflection as we see it. Section 2 describes the clinical condition of patients in PVS. Section 3 develops the ethical difficulties relative to PVS from the French point of view. Section 4 illustrates the relevance of debating the ethical significance of such problematic situations, whilst defending a practical position based on a philosophical conviction. Section 5 points out the limits of ethical reflection in a biomedical context, and calls for reflection closer to the source of the problems described. (edited)

**Cafaro, Philip**. Thoreauvian Patriotism as an Environmental Virtue. *Phil Cont World*, 2(2), 1-7, Sum 95.

In *Walden* Henry David Thoreau argues for and against patriotism. This paper argues that thoughtful environmentalists should do likewise. It explicates Thoreau's accounts of "settling" and farming as efforts to rethink and deepen his connections to the land. These efforts define a patriotism that is local, thoughtful and moral. Thoreau's economic philosophy can be seen as applied patriotism. Like other virtues such as courage or prudence, patriotism is liable to a skewed development and various kinds of misuse. Yet properly developed it is a part of a good human life. Thoreauvian patriotism provides a strong base from which to oppose militarism and xenophobia, which many intellectuals mistakenly equate with patriotism.

**Caferra, Ricardo** and Demri, Stéphane and Herment, Michel. Framework for the Transfer of Proofs, Lemmas and Strategies from Classical to Non-Classical Logics. *Stud Log*, 52(2), 197-232, My 93.

There exist valuable methods for theorem proving in nonclassical logics based on translation from these logics into first-order classical logic (abbreviated henceforth FOL). The key notion in these approaches is *translation* from a *Source Logic* (henceforth abbreviated SL) to a *Target Logic* (henceforth abbreviated TL). These methods are concerned with the problem of *finding* a proof in TL by translating a formula in SL, but they do not address the very important problem of *presenting proofs* in SL via a backward translation. We propose a framework for presenting proofs in SL based on a partial backward translation of proofs obtained in a familiar TL: Order-Sorted Predicate Logic. (edited)

**Cahan, David**. On Helmholtz and 'Bürgerliche Intelligenz': A Response to Robert Brain. *Stud Hist Phil Sci*, 28(3), 521-532, S 97.

This study criticizes Robert Brain's essay review of a series of books edited by David Cahan and others on the German polymath Hermann von Helmholtz (1821-1898). It shows that Brain committed a number of factual errors in his review that are then used, it is argued, to support a misleading historiographical position concerning Helmholtz's place in 19th-century German life.

**Cahn, Steven M**. "Language and the Interpretation of Music" in *Music and Meaning*, Robinson, Jenefer (ed), 23-56. Ithaca, Cornell Univ Pr, 1997.

**Cahn, Steven M**. *Classics of Modern Political Theory: Machiavelli to Mill*. New York, Oxford Univ Pr, 1997.

*Classics of Modern Political Theory: Machiavelli to Mill* brings together the complete texts or substantial selections from the masterpieces of modern political theory. The most comprehensive collection of its kind, this volume includes well-known works by Hobbes, Locke, Rousseau, Hegel, and Marx, and significant contributions by Spinoza, Montesquieu, Hume, Adam Smith, Kant, Burke, Bentham, and Tocqueville. A distinctive feature is the inclusion of the Declaration of Independence, the United States Constitution, and numerous papers from The Federalist. An extended introduction to each author's writings, provided by a renowned authority on the subject, features biographical data, philosophical commentary, and bibliographical guides. (publisher, edited)

**Cahn, Steven M**. The Curious Tale of Atlas College. *J Soc Phil*, 28(1), 158-160, Spr 97.

I relate the story of a liberal arts college which discriminated on the basis of weight against applicants for faculty positions and was forced subsequently to institute appointment procedures that in order to get beyond weight discrimination required consideration of each applicant's weight. The implications of the story for the affirmative action debate are left for the reader to decide.

**Cai, Liming** and Chen, Jianer and Downey, Rodney G (& others). Advice Classes of Parameterized Tractability. *Annals Pure Applied Log*, 84(1), 119-138, Mr 97.

Many natural computational problems have input consisting of two or more parts, one of which may be considered a *parameter*. For example, there are many problems for which the input consists of a graph and a positive integer. A number of results are presented concerning parameterized problems that can be solved (uniformly with respect to the parameter) in complexity classes below $P$, given a single word of advice for each parameter value. Different ways in which the word of advice can be employed are considered, and it is shown that the class *FPT* of *tractable* parameterized problems (the parameterized analog of $P$) has interesting and natural internal structure.

**Caianiello, Silvia**. "Figure dell'originario nell'ultimo Husserl" in *Lo Storicismo e la Sua Storia: Temi, Problemi, Prospettive,* Cacciatore, Giuseppe (ed), 455-467. Milano, Guerini, 1997.

**Caianiello, Silvia**. "La recezione di Humboldt in Droysen: elementi per una ricostruzione" in *Lo Storicismo e la Sua Storia: Temi, Problemi, Prospettive,* Cacciatore, Giuseppe (ed), 233-245. Milano, Guerini, 1997.

**Caiazzo, Irene**. Note sur des *Accessus ad Macrobium*. *Stud Filosofici*, 7-22, 1995.

**Cain, David**. "An Elephant, an Ocean, and the Freedom of Faith" in *Philosophy, Religion, and the Question of Intolerance,* Ambuel, David (ed), 57-69. Albany, SUNY Pr, 1997.

"*Either* exclusive, intolerant advocacy of one's faith, *or* inclusive intoleration" (at the cost or relativism) is rejected as a false "either/or." "Tolerance" is rejected in favor of "appreciation." The concern is to adumbrate an account of faith as risk in freedom which has force both within and beyond Christianity. "Faithful appreciation" of religious diversity is declared a proper manifestation of the freedom of faith, the freedom which faith demands and grants. Not by backing off from one's faith (aiming for the "ocean") but by digging more deeply into one's faith may resources for openness to otherness be found. The attempt, from one religious perspective or another, to draw an inclusive circle (the great elephant of religious *truth*) is resisted as a temptation.

**Cajthaml, Martin**. Ingardens Theorie der Quasi-Urteile auf dem Hintergrund seiner Gesamtanalyse der Schicht der Bedeutungen und einige kritische Bemerkungen zu dieser Theorie. *Prima Philosophia*, 9(4), 457-468, 1996.

The present paper is devoted to an investigation of so-called quasi-judgments, i.e., those specific meaning units which we find above all in literary works. The Polish phenomenologist, Roman Ingarden, in *The Literary Work of Art* was the first to analyse with great clarity this remarkable type of conceptual units. A presentation is made of the essential parts of Ingarden's analyses while putting them in the context of the whole of his investigations of meanings found in the above-mentioned book. Consequently, a criticism is made of certain of Ingarden's theses, especially the theses that the assertive function of the copula is responsible for the quasi-character of a quasi-judgment and that in a literary work of art no real judgments occur.

**Calabrò, Daniela**. "Tempo vissuto e temporalità originaria in M. Merleau-Ponty" in *Il Concetto di Tempo: Atti del XXXII Congresso Nazionale della Società Filosofica Italiana,* Casertano, Giovanni (ed), 263-271. Napoli, Loffredo, 1997.

**Calafate, Pedro**. A Historiografia Filosófica Portuguesa Perante o Seiscentismo. *Rev Port Filosof*, 52(1-4), 185-196, Ja-D 96.

**Calafate, Pedro**. Revistas filosóficas em Portugal. *Philosophica (Portugal)*, 99-114, 1993.

Il s'agit d'une recension critique des revues philosophiques publiées au Portugal depuis le XVIIIème siècle jusqu'au présent. L'intention principale est celle de mettre à la disposition des étudiants et chercheurs un nombre significatif d'éléments bibliographiques d'indubitable importance, puisqu'on donne non seulement l'indication du titre, mais aussi les principaux colaborateurs, sans oublier les tendances plus marquantes des différentes revues.

**Calafell Artola, Marian** and Jackson, Terence. Ethical Beliefs and Management Behaviour: A Cross-Cultural Comparison. *J Bus Ethics*, 16(11), 1163-1173, Ag 97.

A cross-cultural empirical study is reported in this article which looks at ethical beliefs and behaviours among French and German managers and compares this with previous studies of U.S. and Israeli managers using a similar questionnaire. Significant differences are found by national ownership of the company rather than the country in which it is situated. Significant differences are found, for both individual managers by nationality and for companies by nationality of parents, in the area of 'organizational loyalty'. The attitude towards accepting gifts and favors in exchange for preferential treatment, as a measure of 'societal values', is also found to show significant differences between national groups. However, no significant differences are found for measures for 'group loyalty', 'conflict between organizational and group loyalty' and for 'conflicts between self and group/organization'. (edited)

**Calapso, Renato**. "Tempo ed eternità in Enzo Paci" in *Il Concetto di Tempo: Atti del XXXII Congresso Nazionale della Società Filosofica Italiana,* Casertano, Giovanni (ed), 293-298. Napoli, Loffredo, 1997.

**Calcagno, Antonio**. Beyond Postmodernism: Langan's Foundational Ontology. *Rev Metaph*, 50(4), 817-840, Je 97.

Thomas Langan's latest work, *Being and Truth*, sets as its object of inquiry the possibility of a genuine and meaningful intersubjectivity wherein both self and other come fully to nurture one another. The key to understanding and responding to the possibility of a genuine intersubjective relationship lies within the framework of a serious attempt to comprehend reflectively the constitutive dynamic between being (in the sense of all that is and can be), *esse* (Langan's symbol for the reality of things in themselves) and *Sein* (being interpreted in consciousness). (edited)

**Calcagno, Antonio**. Persona Politica: Unity and Difference in Edith Stein's Political Philosophy. *Int Phil Quart*, 37(2), 203-215, Je 97.

**Calero, Francisco**. Traiciones a Luis Vives. *An Seminar Hist Filosof*, 13, 237-245, 1996.

Some aspects of Luis Vives's life and work, which have been submitted to wrong interpretations are studied in this paper. His Jewish ancestry was not proven until 1964, his painful illness was wrongly interpreted by Dr. Marañón, he became disappointed in his friendship with Erasmus, his pacifist ideas were considered as imperial ones, finally, his texts have been wrongly translated.

**Calhoun, Cheshire**. Family Outlaws. *Phil Stud*, 85(2-3), 181-193, Mr 97.

I argue that lesbian-feminist arguments against marriage and motherhood neglect historical constructions of lesbians and gay men as family outlaws. The 1880-s-1990s image of the mannish lesbian, 1930s-1950s image of the homosexual child molester and 1980s-1990s image of lesbian and gay "pretended family relationships" constructed lesbians and gays as constitutionally unfit for marriage and parenting. By masking heterosexuals' own family-disrupting behavior, these images displaced social anxiety about the heterosexual family's internal collapse onto the spectre of the hostile outsider and served to reserve the private sphere for heterosexuals only.

**Calhoun, Laurie**. On Rape: A Crime Against Humanity. *J Soc Phil*, 28(1), 101-109, Spr 97.

**Calhoun, Laurie**. *Philosophy Unmasked: A Skeptic's Critique*. Lawrence, Univ Pr Kansas, 1997.

**Calhoun, William C** and Slaman, Theodore A. The Pi$^0_2$ Enumeration Degrees are not Dense. *J Sym Log*, 61(4), 1364-1379, D 96.

We show that the II$^0_2$ enumeration degrees are not dense. This answers a question posed by Cooper.

**Calkins, Carl F** and Rinck, Christine. Challenges Across the Life Span for Persons with Disabilities. *Bioethics Forum*, 12(3), 37-46, Fall 96.

Health care issues for persons with developmental disabilities have raised numerous bioethical dilemmas. These controversies bridge the life span from the prenatal period through old age. Some key discussions focus on the impact of genetic testing and amniocentesis on the birth of children with disabilities and the survival of very low birth weight babies. Other issues center on transplants for persons with disabilities, sexuality, and advance directives. With the movement away from institutionalization and toward independence, people with disabilities have more choice in all aspects of their lives. This choice can pose dilemmas for the individual and those who are care providers.

**Callahan, Daniel**. "Professional Morality: Can an Examined Life Be Lived?" in *Philosophical Perspectives on Bioethics*, Sumner, L W (ed), 9-17. Toronto, Univ of Toronto Pr, 1996.

**Callahan, Daniel**. What Makes a Good Death?. *Bioethics Forum*, 13(1), 3-4, Spr 97.

**Callan, Eamonn**. The Great Sphere: Education Against Servility. *J Phil Educ*, 31(2), 221-232, Jl 97.

Educational practices that encourage children to understand ethical diversity commonly conflict with the parental desire to instill unswerving identification with a particular way of life. This paper examines whether the scope of parents' rights to educational choice includes the option of vetoing such practices. Although parents' rights are no less important than the rights of their children, the option of denying children experiences that would expose them to ethical diversity cannot be rightfully claimed by any parent without repudiating the egalitarian basis of rights discourse.

**Callan, Eamonn** (ed) and Boler, Megan (ed) and Margonis, Frank (ed). *Philosophy of Education (1996)*. Urbana, Phil Education Soc, 1997.

**Callender, Craig** and Weingard, Robert. Time, Bohm's Theory, and Quantum Cosmology. *Phil Sci*, 63(3), 470-474, S 96.

The so-called problem of time in canonical quantum gravity follows from the fact that the theory appears to describe a static universe, contrary to what we observe. As we have pointed out, Bohm's interpretation of quantum mechanics offers a neat solution to this problem: one can reintroduce time (and a coherent dynamics) through the Bohm equation of motion. However, a natural question to raise about this solution is how the 'Bohm time' is related to the time appearing in ordinary quantum mechanics. In this paper we explore a plausible way these two times can turn out to be the same.

**Callender, Craig** and Weingard, Robert. Trouble in Paradise? Problems for Bohm's Theory. *Monist*, 80(1), 24-43, Ja 97.

For good reason Bohm's interpretation of quantum mechanics recently has experienced a kind of renaissance. The theory provides us with a consistent, empirically adequate picture of the quantum world. However, it would be naive to think the theory is free of problems. In this essay we present some of the difficulties facing the theory and the prospects there are for solving them. In particular, we look at the problems of 1) its 'spoiled' symmetries, 2) extending it to field theory and quantum gravity, 3) the ontological status of the wavefunction, and 4) the justification of Born's rule.

**Callicott, J Baird**. Do Deconstructive Ecology and Sociobiology Undermine Leopold's Land Ethic?. *Environ Ethics*, 18(4), 353-372, Winter 96.

Recent deconstructive developments in ecology (doubts about the existence of unified communities and ecosystems, the diversity-stability hypothesis and a natural homeostasis or "balance of Nature"; and an emphasis on "chaos," " perturbation," and directionless change in living nature) and the advent of sociobiology (selfish genes) may seem to undermine the scientific foundations of environmental ethics, especially the Leopold land ethic. A reassessment of the Leopold land ethic in light of these developments (and vice versa) indicates that the land ethic is still a viable environmental ethic, if judiciously updated and revised.

**Calloway, Kelvin T**. Bioethical Issues Confronting The African American Community. *Bioethics Forum*, 11(2), 31-34, Sum 95.

The bioethical issues confronting the African American community have evolved out of the historical delivery of health care to the community. By examining these issues, learning from the mistakes of the past and respecting the dignity of every human being, health care professionals strive toward the creation of a level playing field of health for all Americans.

**Calore, Gary S**. "Reclaiming Metaphysics for the Present: Postmodernism, Time, and American Thought" in *Philosophy in Experience: American Philosophy in Transition*, Hart, Richard (ed), 241-258. New York, Fordham Univ Pr, 1997.

**Calvo Salamanca, Clara**. "Una Relación entre Diferentes: Ortega y Gasset y Gramsci" in *Política y Sociedad en José Ortega y Gasset: En Torno a "Vieja y Nueva Política"*, Lopez de la Vieja, Maria Teresa (ed), 211-219. Barcelona, Anthropos, 1997.

**Calzi, M Li** and Castagnoli, E. Expected Utility without Utility. *Theor Decis*, 41(3), 281-301, N 96.

This paper advances an interpretation of Von Neumann-Morgenstern's expected utility model for preferences over lotteries which does not require the notion of a cardinal utility over prizes and can be phrased entirely in the language of probability. According to it, the expected utility of a lottery can be read as the probability that this lottery outperforms another given independent lottery. The implications of this interpretation for some topics and models in decision theory are considered.

**Camacho, Luis**. Hacia una filosofía de la tecnología. *Rev Filosof (Costa Rica)*, 34(83-84), 337-347, D 96.

Two are the main purposes of this paper: (a) To assess in a global fashion what the philosophy of technology has accomplished since its inception and (b) To explore the conditions for a "philosophy of..." Langdon Winner's statement in *The Whale and the Reactor* that the philosophy of technology does not exist is taken as the challenge to be met.

**Camacho, Ramón Kuri**. Ser y hermenéutica: El relativismo contemporáneo o el nuevo fundamentalismo laico. *Analogia*, 10(2), 73-112, 1996.

**Cambi, Maurizio**. "Una città senza storia: la perfezione immobile e l'utopia di Tommaso Campenella" in *Lo Storicismo e la Sua Storia: Temi, Problemi, Prospettive*, Cacciatore, Giuseppe (ed), 15-23. Milano, Guerini, 1997.

**Cambiasso, Guillermo Jorge**. El deseo natural de ver a Dios en la *Summa contra Gentiles*. *Sapientia*, 52(201), 15-31, 1997.

**Cameron, J R**. Knowing-Attributions as Endorsements. *Phil Quart*, 47(186), 19-37, Ja 97.

In saying 'N knows that p', where the supposed knowing is gained through rational reflection (the paradigm for of knowing, conceptually), I endorse N's belief as rationally held and hence correct (the 'RhCB' analysis). We understand this 'hence' not as 'hence, infallibly' but as 'hence in fact'—a reliability reading, not implying infallibility (cf. the use of 'hence' to attribute nondeterministic causation). The false appearance of inconsistency in our taking knowing to require an infallible guarantee of correctness while regularly attributing knowledge where we lack an absolute guarantee arises from misreading of the 'hence' as implying infallibility, partly due to the mistaken assumption that 'know' functions purely descriptively. Though aware that rationality may occasionally fail to ensure correctness, we accept it as sufficing to yield knowledge wherever it does not fail—a consistent noninfallibilist understanding of what knowing requires.

**Camiller, Patrick** (trans) and Corvi, Roberta. *An Introduction to the Thought of Karl Popper*. New York, Routledge, 1997.

This study offers an accessible introduction to the life and work of this extraordinary thinker, including his often-neglected Postscript on scientific method published in three volumes in the 1980s. It charts the development of Popper's philosophy and shows his unfailing political commitment to humanism and enlightenment. At the centre of Popper's thought stands rationality and a strong belief in the power of the human mind to change things for the better. Rationality thus serves as a guide both in his philosophical considerations and for his political views. (publisher)

**Campanella, Tommaso** and Flasch, Thomas (trans). *Philosophische Gedichte*. Frankfurt/M, Klostermann, 1996.

**Campanelli, Giuseppina**. Benedetto Croce e la Storia della Chiesa. *Sapienza*, 49(3), 321-350, 1996.

**Campbell, Courtney S**. Quest and Question: Suffering and Emulation in the LDS Community. *Christian Bioethics*, 2(2), 222-238, Ag 96.

This essay draws on the formative stories of suffering in the Latter-day Saint faith community to affirm that suffering is an invitation to discern the revelation of sacred presence. The meaningfulness of suffering presupposes a narrative context that permits the quest for God to be accompanied by the questioning of God. The narrative ordeal of suffering transforms passion into compassion and outrage into an experience for good. In the midst of suffering, Latter-day Saints are thus called to an ethic of emulation.

**Campbell, James**. "James Hayden Tufts on the Social Mission of the University" in *Philosophy in Experience: American Philosophy in Transition*, Hart, Richard (ed), 91-105. New York, Fordham Univ Pr, 1997.

James Hayden Tufts taught through the full range of educational possibilities—elementary, high school, private college, state university, private research university—and served at all levels of service from temporary instructor to long-time Chair and Dean to Vice-President and Acting President. In the process of his service, he thought and wrote about the nature and role of education in society. This paper explores his analysis of the role that the university should play in the life of the community and the broader society. (publisher)

**Campbell, James**. Langer's Understanding of Philosophy. *Trans Peirce Soc*, 33(1), 133-147, Wint 97.

This paper discusses the neglected American philosopher, Susanne K. Langer (1895-1985). Its function is to examine her conception of philosophical inquiry and her understanding of philosophical progress in hopes of providing a framework for approaching her work.

**Campbell, Jan**. Mediations of the Female Imaginary and Symbolic. *Hist Human Sci*, 10(2), 41-60, My 97.

Many critics view Irigaray's work as an extension or deconstruction of a Lacanian paradigm. Few actually analyse it as a direct challenge to Lacanian concepts of symbolic subjectivity and the consequent, alternative framework this would envisage. This article discusses a possible beyond the phallus, in relation to mediating concepts of the female imaginary and symbolic within her work and an understanding of the female imaginary and symbolic within different feminist interpretations of the maternal imaginary and symbolic, arguing that the imaginary is crucial in delineating a nonseparatist cultural sublimation of female desire. (edited)

**Campbell, John**. "Molineux's Question" in *Perception*, Villanueva, Enrique (ed), 301-318. Atascadero, Ridgeview, 1996.

**Campbell, John**. "Shape Properties, Experience of Shape and Shape Concepts" in *Perception*, Villanueva, Enrique (ed), 351-363. Atascadero, Ridgeview, 1996.

**Campbell, John**. Précis of *Past*, Space and Self. *Phil Phenomenol Res*, 57(3), 633-634, S 97.

**Campbell, John**. Replies. *Phil Phenomenol Res*, 57(3), 655-670, S 97.

**Campbell, John**. The Structure of Time in Autobiographical Memory. *Euro J Phil*, 5(2), 105-117, Ag 97.

**Campbell, John** and Martin, M G F. Sense, Reference and Selective Attention. *Aris Soc*, Supp(71), 55-98, 1997.

**Campbell, Joseph Keim**. Hume's Refutation of the Cosmological Argument. *Int J Phil Relig*, 40(3), 159-173, D 96.

In *Dialogues Concerning Natural Religion, Part IX*, Cleanthes and Philo offer several objections to Demea's version of the cosmological argument. Since recent commentators have been able to adequately respond to each particular objection, it is often assumed that Hume's criticisms, as a whole, are weak. I propose a new interpretation. Underlying Hume's critique is a single argument, taking the form of a complex, constructive dilemma. One, then, cannot merely respond to each particular criticism presented in Part IX since they are much stronger as a unit. In fact, when taken together they yield a conclusive refutation of the cosmological argument.

**Campbell, Sue**. "Love and Intentionality: Roxane's Choice" in *Love Analyzed*, Lamb, Roger E, 225-242. Boulder, Westview Pr, 1997.

**Campbell, Sue**. Emotion as an Explanatory Principle in Early Evolutionary Theory. *Stud Hist Phil Sci*, 28(3), 453-473, S 97.

**Campioni, Giuliano**. L'uomo superiore dopo la morte di Dio: Appunti di lettura. *Teoria*, 16(1), 31-53, 1996.

**Campo, Rafael**. Imagining Unmanaging Health Care. *J Med Human*, 18(2), 85-97, Sum 97.

**Campos, Alberto**. "Descartes, investigador matemático afortunado" in *Memorias Del Seminario En Conmemoración De Los 400 Anos Del Nacimiento De René Descartes*, Albis, Víctor S (ed), 11-24. Sankt Augustin, Academia, 1997.

**Campos, Juan Manuel**. Sobre la lógica modal en Tomás de Mercado (México, s. XVI). *Dialogo Filosof*, 12(3), 356-366, S-D 96.

Objetivo de este artículo es dar una idea de la complejidad de los temas tratados por Tomás de Mercado, dominico del siglo XVI nacido en Sevilla. Se alude a la naturaleza de las proposiciones modales, la relación entre modalidad y temporalidad, las reglas para la equivalencia y oposición entre las proposiciones modales.

**Campos, Manuel**. "Kim on the Exclusion Problem" in *Contents*, Villanueva, Enrique (ed), 167-169. Atascadero, Ridgeview, 1995.

**Camps, Victoria**. The Political Turning Point (in Spanish). *Univ Phil*, 14(27), 11-22, D 96.

In the last years, ethical discourse has entered in public life. It is expected from ethics to bring about the reforms and the new ideas which politics is needed. The author of this article wonders about the role ethics has to play in front of the political shortcomings. Therefore, she goes to Rawls's philosophy and specially to his last book, *Political Liberalism*, where a central place is given to the concept of reasonability as the basis of the political conception of the person. Reasonability means responsibility, an usual concept both in political and moral theories, but nonetheless fundamental in order to put ethics in its right place, as the impulse of good politic.

**Canals Surís, Manuel**. Fonament de l'axiologia de Plató (La interpretació del platonisme a l'escola de Tubinga). *Convivium*, 9, 49-76, 1996.

The central thesis of the article is that the Platonic systematization, such as Leibniz has been requesting, Tubinga's philosophers: G. Reale, Hans Krämer and Konrad Gaiser. The "first academy", "the new Platonism" and Schleiermacher's works, are the "traditional pattern". The, exclusiveness, independence and self-sufficiency are the categories in the Platonic papers. The "new pattern" shows the Platonic testimony in *Fedro 242-278* and *Seventh Letter 340-345* and builds this interpretation into the bilateral complementary written/dialectical dialogue. The "Theory of Principles"—*Unity and Undefined Duality*—is "the most important stage in the Western metaphysics". The main purpose of this paper is showing the Platonic heritage in the European culture; in this *ontological, knowledge* and *ethical-policy* sides.

**Canapary, Andrew** and Peruzzi, Nico and Bongar, Bruce. Physician-Assisted Suicide: The Role of Mental Health Professionals. *Ethics Behavior*, 6(4), 353-366, 1996.

A review of the literature was conducted to better understand the (potential) role of mental health professionals in physician-assisted suicide. Numerous studies indicate that depression is one of the most commonly encountered psychiatric illnesses in primary care settings. Yet, depression consistently goes undetected and undiagnosed by nonpsychiatrically trained primary care physicians. Noting the well-studied link between depression and suicide, it is necessary to question giving sole responsibility of assisting patients in making end-of-life treatment decisions to these physicians. Unfortunately, the use of mental health consultation by these physicians is not a common occurrence. Greater involvement of mental health professionals in this emerging and debated area is advocated. (edited)

**Cañas Quiros, Roberto**. El sujeto en la estética kantiana (Primera parte). *Rev Filosof (Costa Rica)*, 34(83-84), 283-291, D 96.

The first part of this article develops the meaning of "subject" as used in Kantian aesthetics. Then it goes into the faculties of the subject, his power of judgment and the conditions that must obtain for his contemplation of the beautiful.

**Cândida P Coelho, Maria** and Donatoni, Alaíde Rita. Subsídios para uma Análise da Política da Educaçao Escolar Brasileira. *Educ Filosof*, 10(19), 153-161, Ja-Je 96.

This paper aims to give theoretical support to possible discussions concerning Brazilian school education and its different policies. The authors demonstrate that the influence of the state in establishing such policies is a very strong one, especially in cases where the state is outlined under capitalist labor relations that in contemporary capitalism result in deeper inequalities. The relations between education, state and economy run, nevertheless, somewhat dynamically, so that the authors themselves feel encouraged to assert that education, in its political sphere, can build its hegemony in order to overcome the present "state of affairs."(edited)

**Cândido Pimentel, Manuel**. *Filosofia Criacionista da Morte: Meditaçao sobre o Problema da Morte No Pensamento Filosófico de Leonardo Coimbra*. Braga, Ponta Delgada, 1994.

**Cândido Pimentel, Manuel**. *Odisseias do Espírito: Estudos de Filosofia Luso-Brasileira*. Lisboa Codex, Imprensa Nacional, 1997.

O autor estuda na presente obra a filosofia espiritualista do século XIX e da primeira metade do século XX que se desenvolveu em Portugal e no Brasil, na linha representativa que vai de Gonçalves de Magalhães, Amorim Viana, Cunha Seixas, Farias Brito e Sampaio Bruno a Teixeira de Pascoaes e Leonardo Coimbra. Integrando-a no mais vasto contexto da filosofia europeia, investiga ainda a ofensiva antiespiritualista de que são principais representantes Teófilo Braga, em Portugal, e Silvio Romero, no Brasil. (edited)

**Candlish, Stewart**. Wittgenstein and the Doctrine of Kinaesthesis. *Austl J Phil*, 74(4), 581-597, D 96.

This paper is about kinaesthesis—awareness of movement and posture—and Wittgenstein's discussion of it at Philosophical Investigations II, viii. It provides both exposition and background to that discussion, traces its connections with Wittgenstein's persisting philosophical concerns and assesses the significance of it for philosophy and psychology. It shows, using detailed examples, that a long-standing (though now disintegrating) consensus on the topic amongst psychologists owes less to observation than to a priori assumptions shared with philosophers, such as Russell, who have taken for granted that kinaesthesis provides sense-data or sensations enabling the logical construction of the public world. Wittgenstein exposes these assumptions to the awkward epistemic facts of kinaesthesis.

**Caney, Simon**. Impartiality and Liberal Neutrality. *Utilitas*, 8(3), 273-293, N 96.

**Canfield, John V**. The Community View. *Phil Rev*, 105(4), 469-488, O 96.

According to the community view interpretation of Wittgenstein language and rule following are essentially social and thus a lifelong solitaire who speaks or follows rules is conceptually impossible. Some Wittgenstein texts speak for the community view, and some against it. An examination of the presupposed Wittgensteinian notions of essence, possibility, and of the kind of lifelong solitaire in question allows a reconciliation of the seemingly contrary blocks of text. For Wittgenstein language is essentially social and a lifelong solitaire who speaks or follows rules is possible.

**Cangiotti, Marco**. Italo Mancini lettore di Agostino: Percorso e contenuti di un incontro. *Riv Int Filosof Diritto*, 73(4), 734-756, O-D 96.

**Cannon, Dale**. Sanders' Analytic Rebuttal to Polanyi's Critics, with Some Musings on Polanyi's Idea of Truth. *Tradition Discovery*, 23(2), 17-23, 1996-97.

This article reviews *Michael Polanyi's Post-Critical Epistemology* by Andy F. Sanders but goes on to articulate certain crucial aspects of Polanyi's postcritical understanding of truth that seem to be overlooked in Sanders's account and which challenge conventional analyses of truth.

**Canone, Eugenio**. "Pierre Bayle nell'*Index librorum prohibitorum*: I decreti di proibizione delle *Nouvelles de la République des Lettres*..." in *Pierre Bayle e l'Italia*, Bianchi, Lorenzo, 203-220. Napoli, Liguori Ed, 1996.

**Cantillo, Clementina**. "Storicità e mondo umano nell'estetica di Gravina" in *Lo Storicismo e la Sua Storia: Temi, Problemi, Prospettive*, Cacciatore, Giuseppe (ed), 69-79. Milano, Guerini, 1997.

**Cantillo, Giuseppe**. "La concezione del tempo storico nello *Historismus*" in *Il Concetto di Tempo: Atti del XXXII Congresso Nazionale della Società Filosofica Italiana*, Casertano, Giovanni (ed), 91-104. Napoli, Loffredo, 1997.

**Cantillo, Giuseppe**. "Troeltsch e Kant: 'Apriori' e 'storia' nella filosofia della religione" in *Lo Storicismo e la Sua Storia: Temi, Problemi, Prospettive*, Cacciatore, Giuseppe (ed), 334-342. Milano, Guerini, 1997.

**Cantillo, Giuseppe**. "Vita e sistema: Alle origini del pensiero hegeliano a Jena" in *Lo Storicismo e la Sua Storia: Temi, Problemi, Prospettive*, Cacciatore, Giuseppe (ed), 197-212. Milano, Guerini, 1997.

**Cantillo, Giuseppe** (ed) and Cacciatore, Giuseppe (ed) and Lissa, Giuseppe (ed). *Lo Storicismo e la Sua Storia: Temi, Problemi, Prospettive*. Milano, Guerini, 1997.

Testimonianza dell'affetto dei suoi allievi, questo libro riflette, nell'impostazione e negli esiti, i motivi ispiratori dell'insegnamento e dell'attività scientifica e culturale di Fulvio Tessitore. Gli autori, uniti da una comunanza di ricerca e di studio, si muovono lungo una pluralità di percorsi tematici che mettono a fuoco le diverse dimensioni teoriche e storiche dello storicismo. Ne emerge una ben determinata visione teoretico-filosofica dello storicismo (lo *storicismo criticoproblematico*, il *nuovo* storicismo) e, insieme, una ricostruzione storiografica della sua genesi e delle connessioni che lo legano ai principali orientamenti filosofici contemporanei. (publisher, edited)

**Cantoral, Ricardo**. Acerca de las contribuciones actuales de una didáctica de antaño: el caso de la serie de Taylor. *Mathesis*, 11(1), 55-101, F 95.

This paper is the result of a research project in the field of mathematics education. It shows an epistemological view on the diversity of mathematical conceptions that underly to the mathematical notion of analytical function; it also has an insight on the relevance in teaching. The historical view arises from didactical motivations and not from an historian's perspective. It constitutes a search for reasonable answers to questions posed in the educational context; why do we teach what we teach? Our principal sources are historical textbooks and some original mathematical papers.

**Capaldi, Nicholas** and Mosley, Albert G. *Affirmative Action: Social Justice or Unfair Preference?*. Lanham, Rowman & Littlefield, 1996.

In this book, two distinguished philosophers debate one of the most controversial public policy issues of the late twentieth century. Each begins by making a case for or against affirmative action, laying out the major arguments on both sides. Each author then responds to the other's essay. Written in an engaging, accessible style, *Affirmative Action* is an excellent text for junior level philosophy, political theory, public policy and African-American studies courses as well as a guide for professionals navigating this important debate. (publisher, edited)

**Caponi, Sandra N C**. Science and Human Condition (in Portuguese). *Trans/Form/Acao*, 19, 103-114, 1996.

It is proposed in this writing to deal with the theme of the possible links between scientific investigation and ethical reflection. In approaching this question, we propose to backtrack as far as Greek line of thought, and stop at the precise moment when something similar to scientific "truth" first becomes observable, and starts thus to make part of what is "sayable." We are referring to this inaugural instant when historical reflection, medical knowledge, and juridical research have simultaneously appeared. We shall try and demonstrate that, within this context, the concern with truth, far from being alien to ethical reflection, was considered to be the most efficient resource, which could best contribute in the effort to reach a life worth being lived.

**Capozzi, Gino**. La possibilità giuridica. *Riv Int Filosof Diritto*, 73(3), 418-447, Jl-S 96.

The present essay starts from the Aristotelian principles of "need" and "possibility". Its purpose is to show how the "juridical possibility" is not limited to the qualifying scheme of "legal power" but involves a wider formal and informal scheme which includes "licit" and "illicit", "power" and "permissibility", by excluding the "contingency it criticizes". What is the consequence? As to the prescription of the juridical obligation, the subjects can act according to the schemes of "licit" and "illicit", "power" and informat modality so-called "permissibility".

**Cappelen, Herman** and Lepore, Ernest. Varieties of Quotation. *Mind*, 106(423), 429-450, Jl 97.

**Capps, John**. Dewey, Quine, and Pragmatic Naturalized Epistemology. *Trans Peirce Soc*, 32(4), 634-668, Fall 96.

In this article I discuss Dewey's and Quine's attempts to naturalize epistemology. By examining standard objections to Quinean naturalism I arrive at a minimal and pragmatic naturalism—summed up in three theses—that bears a close resemblance to Dewey's theory of inquiry. A Deweyan approach, I contend, avoids the usual objections to naturalized epistemology. I conclude by arguing that such a pragmatic naturalism offers a preferable alternative to other prominent versions of naturalized epistemology.

**Capriles, Elias**. "Steps to a Comparative Evolutionary Aesthetics (China, India, Tibet and Europe)" in *East and West in Aesthetics*, Marchianò, Grazia (ed), 27-51. Pisa, Istituti Editoriali, 1997.

An Aesthetic Theory is outlined, based on the degenerative philosophy of history of Asia, Greece and Rome: primordial art "cleansed the doors of perception" and thus restored recently lost primordial vision, being visionary and more "objective". Then traditional art became even more culturally conditioned and "subjective", until tradition was replaced by fashion and purely "subjective" expression. Chinese, Indian, Tibetan and European examples of "primordial art" are provided: Chinese Taoist and Ch'an painting (compared to Franco-Cantabrian painting): Indian Tantric sculpture (example: Khajuraho): Tibetan mandalas which illustrate the Dzogchen path and *The Divine Comedy* as European equivalent of Tibetan Mandalas.

**Capron, Alexander M**. An Egg Takes Flight: The Once and Future Life of the National Bioethics Advisory Commission. *Kennedy Inst Ethics J*, 7(1), 63-80, Mr 97.

**Capron, Alexander M**. Between Doctor and Patient. *Hastings Center Rep*, 26(5), 23-24, S-O 96.

The rapid evolution of the health care system has altered the relationship between physicians and patients and has lead to some bitter disputes. Managed care firms are now frequently in conflict with health care institutions and professionals, and employers play an increasingly active role in establishing the terms of health care coverage as part of an effort to stunt the growth of this expensive employee benefit. State tort law, which aims to provide patients with redress for harm suffered and to deter future wrongdoing, and state regulation of physicians and insurers have traditionally protected patients' interests in receiving appropriate, high quality care. Certain provisions of the federal Employee Retirement Security Act (ERISA), however, have the effect of tying state regulators' hands and preventing state tort suits against managed care companies leaving injured parties with the right to obtain a wrongly denied benefit but not to recover for the harm occasioned by the denial. Several recent federal cases illustrating this problem are described.

**Capron, Alexander M**. Inside the Beltway Again: A Sheep of a Different Feather. *Kennedy Inst Ethics J*, 7(2), 171-179, Je 97.

The appearance of a sheep named Dolly, the first clone of an adult mammal, dramatically affected the agenda, pace of work and visibility of the National Bioethics Advisory Commission. The Commission's approach to its task and some of the issues it considered in responding to President Clinton's request for review and recommendations within 90 days are described.

**Capurro, Rafael**. Information Technology and Technologies of the Self. *J Infor Ethics*, 5(2), 19-28, Fall 96.

**Caputo, John D**. "Firing the Steel of Hermeneutics: Hegelianized versus Radical Hermeneutics" in *Hegel, History, and Interpretation*, Gallagher, Shaun, 59-70. Albany, SUNY Pr, 1997.

The idea behind "radical hermeneutics" is to adhere rigorously to the terms that were set for hermeneutics in the early Heidegger's "hermeneutics of facticity." That task is accomplished by allowing Derrida's more radical account of judging in the singularity of an undecidable situation to fire the steel of hermeneutics by holding its feet to the fire of facticity. That both steers us away from the more Hegelianized version of hermeneutics found in Gadamer, which treats tradition as a work of reason, and demonstrates the notion of judging in an undecidable situation in deconstruction, which is what a radical hermeneutics is.

**Caputo, John D**. A Community without Truth: Derrida and the Impossible Community. *Res Phenomenol*, 26, 25-37, 1996.

I begin with Derrida's distrust of community, which refers to the common defense we build against the other, the common wall that protects the same from the incoming (*invenire*, invention) of the other, which in that sense, is everything that deconstruction resists. For deconstruction is the affirmation of the other, and so everything that is done in deconstruction takes aim at this wall of defense that community throws up against the other. Then I explore how deconstruction is the recognition or affirmation of "another" community, "an *open* 'quasi-community'."(edited)

**Caputo, John D** (ed). *Deconstruction in a Nutshell: A Conversation with Jacques Derrida*. New York, Fordham Univ Pr, 1997.

Responding to questions put to him at a Roundtable held at Villanova University in 1994, Jacques Derrida leads the reader through an illuminating discussion of the central themes of deconstruction. Speaking in English and extemporaneously, Derrida takes up with unusual clarity and great eloquence such topics as the tradition and the task of philosophy; the Greeks; justice; responsibility; the gift; community; the distinction between the messianic and the concrete Messianisms; and his interpretation of James Joyce. Derrida convincingly refutes the charges of relativism and nihilism that are often leveled at deconstruction by its critics and sets forth the profoundly affirmative and ethico-political thrust of his work. (edited)

**Caputo, John D**. *The Prayers and* Tears of Jacques Derrida *Religion without Religion*. Bloomington, Indiana Univ Pr, 1997.

The book takes its point of departure from Derrida's more recent, sometimes autobiographical writings and closely examines the religious motifs that have emerged in his later works. John D. Caputo's interpretation of Derrida's thinking also makes an original contribution to the question of the relevance of deconstruction for religion. Caputo's Derrida is a man of faith who bridges Jewish and Christian traditions. The deep messianic, apocalyptic, and prophetic tones in Derrida's writings, Caputo's argues, bespeak his broken covenant with Judaism. Through its startling exploration of Derrida's impossible religion, the book sheds light on the implications of deconstruction for an understanding of religion and faith today. (publisher, edited)

**Caramuta, Ersilia**. Metafisica e silenzio. *G Metaf*, 18(1-2), 95-112, Ja-Ag 96.

The wise man expresses a wavering between metaphysics and silence and between the word tired of its inadequacy and silence, the real expression of a man convicted to his own end. Two heroes, Ulysses and Socrates, contrast the hypothesis of wandering thought; they both pretend an "errare" that is only the statement of reason and of the Western dramatic thought that risks of being illusion, because forgetful of having taken a tautology as an absolute truth to which life is to be sacrificed. Every word, tired ad nauseum, prefers silence to the violence of the term. The word is a deceit, a magic illusion. If gazing at things makes us blind, the only shelter are concepts (*Phaedo* 99 d-e). Finally, reason must cling to itself in order not to yield to the mermaids' song (*Odyssey* XII).

**Carbone, A**. Interpolants, Cut Elimination and Flow Graphs for the Propositional Calculus. *Annals Pure Applied Log*, 83(3), 249-299, F 97.

We analyse the structure of propositional proofs in the sequent calculus focusing on the well-known procedures of interpolation and cut elimination. We are motivated in part by the desire to understand why a tautology might be 'hard to prove'. Given a proof we associate to it a logical graph tracing the flow of formulas in it (Buss, 1991). We show some general facts about logical graphs such as acyclicity of cut-free proofs and acyclicity of contraction-free proofs (possibly containing cuts) and we give a proof of a strengthened version of the Craig Interpolation Theorem based on flows of formulas. We show that tautologies having minimal interpolants of *nonlinear* size (i.e., number of symbols) must have proofs with certain precise structural properties. We then show that given a proof Π and a cut-free form Π' associated to it (obtained by a particular cut elimination procedure), certain subgraphs of Π' which are logical graphs (i.e., graphs of proofs) correspond to subgraphs of Π which are logical graphs for the same sequent. this locality property of cut elimination leads to new results on the complexity of interpolants, which *cannot* follow from the known constructions proving the Craig Interpolation Theorem.

**Carchia, Gianni** and Ferraris, Maurizio. Discutono *Oltre l'interpretazione*, di Gianni Vattimo. *Iride*, 8(15), 495-507, Ag 95.

In questo libro Vattimo intende riscattare l'ermeneutica da un'eccessiva fisionomia 'ecumenica', ripropone con alcune significative novità il "pensiero debole" e inaspettatamente "finisce in qualche modo in braccio alla teologia". Del lavoro di Vattimo, G. Carchia sottolinea la difesa dell'originario spirito nichilistico dell'ermeneutica e una interpretazione della secola-rizzazione come una sorta di prolegomeni ad un'ontologia dell'attualità. M. Ferraris si sofferma sul problema del relativismo e delle sue implicazioni ontologiche, rilevando che prendere sul serio, come suggerisce Vattimo, il problema del nichilismo sembra condurci oltre l'ontologia piuttosto che oltre l'interpretazione.

**Card, Claudia**. Against Marriage and Motherhood. *Hypatia*, 11(3), 1-23, Sum 96.

This essay argues that current advocacy of lesbian and gay rights to legal marriage and parenthood insufficiently criticizes both marriage and motherhood as they are currently practiced and structured by Northern legal institutions. Instead we would do better not to let the State define our intimate unions and parenting would be improved if the power presently concentrated in the hands of one or two guardians were diluted and distributed through an appropriately concerned community.

**Card, Claudia**. Rape as a Weapon of War. *Hypatia*, 11(4), 5-18, Fall 96.

This essay examines how rape of women and girls by male soldiers works as a martial weapon. Continuities with other torture and terrorism and with civilian rape are suggested. The inadequacy of past philosophical treatments of the enslavement of war captives is briefly discussed. Social strategies are suggested for responding and a concluding fantasy offered, not entirely social, of a strategy to change the meanings of rape to undermine its use as a martial weapon.

**Cardona, Carlos Albert**. "De la metafisica a la fisica en el programa cartesiano" in *Memorias Del Seminario En Conmemoración De Los 400 Anos Del Nacimiento De René Descartes*, Albis, Víctor S (ed), 25-39. Sankt Augustin, Academia, 1997.

**Cardona Suárez, Luis Fernando**. Stain, Disfiguration and Orgy (in Spanish). *Univ Phil*, 14(27), 87-107, D 96.

These three concepts typify evil's display in modernity. As proposed by enlightenment, the modern project aimed at establishing the full government of reason anchored in the idea of freedom as autonomy or rational self-determination of the will. Notwithstanding the moral optimism that goes along with this project, something, unconceivable to a moralist, has uprosen from its bossom: evil. This essay intends to show how modernity has faced evil's presence in human life, denying its real effective power. This is why this paper means to propose a positive concept of evil which allows us to endure an age ruled by illness, war, unjustice, misery and barbarity.

**Cardoso, Adelino**. Leibniz, Resumo de Metafísica. *Philosophica (Portugal)*, 143-152, 1996.

**Cardoso, Adelino**. Mathesis Leibniziana. *Philosophica (Portugal)*, 51-77, 1996.

Dans cet article, l'auteur éssaie de montrer qu'on trouve chez Leibniz une *mathesis*, c'est-à-dire une conception du savoir et de l'organisation des savoirs, originale, laquelle est entièrement discernable d'autres *mathesis* qui ont été proposées par ses contemporains du XVII^e siècle. Du point de vue thématique, l'auteur croit que cette *mathésis* reçoit son intelligibilité de la relation que Leibniz établit entre la métaphysique et les mathématiques. Sous ce rapport, on constate des vraies transformations dans la pensée de Leibniz, dès le moment où il fait son adhésion au mécanisme (1668) jusqu'à la formulation de sa dernière pensée. Dans cette évolution, la correspondance avec de Volder joue un rôle décisif. (edited)

**Cardoso Júnior, Hélio Rebello**. The Origin of the Concept of Multiplicity in Gilles Deleuze's (in Portuguese). *Trans/Form/Acao*, 19, 151-161, 1996.

Deleuze seeks for his own concept of multiplicity through the issue of multiplicity both in Riemann's physical theory and in Bergson's philosophy. This attempt states for Deleuze's peculiar creation of concepts. In fact, he draws out from Riemannian and Bergsonian concepts of multiplicity new features for the notions of space and time. Hence, he is able to supply his own concept with an ontological spread.

**Carens, Joseph H**. Dimensions of Citizenship and National Identity in Canada. *Phil Forum*, 28(1-2), 111-124, Fall-Wint 97.

**Carew, George**. "Liberalism and the Politics of Emancipation: The Black Experience" in *Existence in Black: An Anthology of Black Existential Philosophy*, Gordon, Lewis R (ed), 225-241. New York, Routledge, 1997.

An African-American philosophy of liberation must come to terms with the context of its theorizing. Liberalism has prestructured the racial discourse in such a way that only certain outcomes are possible. At the heart of the problem is liberalism's inherent difficulty in resolving the tension between liberty and equality. Consequently the injustice produced by uneven social power makes false the hope that skill acquisition would earn blacks social recognition and economic gains. One's social standing as a moral agent ought not to rest on the acquisition of skills, but on the moral and social reciprocity which underpin social relations.

**Carey, Susan** and Spelke, Elizabeth. Science and Core Knowledge. *Phil Sci*, 63(4), 515-533, D 96.

While endorsing Gopnik's proposal that studies of the emergence and modification of scientific theories and studies of cognitive development in children are mutually illuminating, we offer a different picture of the beginning points of cognitive development from Gopnik's picture of "theories all the way down." Human infants are endowed with several distinct core systems of knowledge which are theory-like in some, but not all, important ways. The existence of these core systems of knowledge has implications for the joint research program between philosophers and psychologists that Gopnik advocates and we endorse. A few lessons already gained from this program of research are sketched.

**Cargile, James**. On the Burden of Proof. *Philosophy*, 72(279), 59-83, Ja 97.

**Cargile, James**. Supposing for the Sake of Argument. *Inquiry (USA)*, 15(1), 76-79, Fall 95.

A very common line from elementary texts: "An argument is valid if, supposing the premises to be true, the conclusion must necessarily be true also". Students tend to be confused as to what it is to suppose or assume something for the purpose of evaluating an argument. And yet there is some tendency among philosophers to treat such supposing as important in the evaluation of some arguments. I examine and reject some explanations that have been offered and conclude that the "suppose" location in this context is primarily misleading and eliminable.

**Carl, Maria**. Law, Virtue, and Happiness in Aquinas's Moral Theory. *Thomist*, 61(3), 425-447, Jl 97.

In this paper, I examine Aquinas's understanding of the relationship between the natural law and the intellectual and moral virtues and I demonstrate that law and virtue are neither competing nor unrelated norms standing in need of reconciliation. Rather, Aquinas's conceptions of natural law and virtue are both based on the theory of natural inclinations and more precisely, on the specifically and properly human inclination to reason. Thus, I argue that Aquinas's notions of law and virtue are complementary in the strongest sense; they correspond insofar as they depend on and are expressions of his teleological conception of human nature.

**Carl, Wolfgang**. Apperception and Spontaneity. *Int J Phil Stud*, 5(2), 147-163, Je 97.

The interest contemporary philosophy takes in Kant's notion of apperception is restricted to his criticism of the Cartesian ego and to his refutation of scepticism, but there is a profound lack of concern for the notion itself and for the act of spontaneity in particular which is connected with the use of the word 'I'. Starting from a comparison of Wittgenstein's account of this use with Kant's considerations it is argued that the latter aims at a theory of formal conditions of knowledge which includes the availability of the notion of the I. It is clarified what the determination of apperception as an 'act of spontaneity' amounts to (B: 132). Kant's scattered remarks on the ability of having the representation of the I, of using the word 'I', are considered in order to show that what he called 'the logical I' has something to do with the capacity of performing an act of judgment. It is argued that such an account is not to be found in contemporary discussions of 'essential indexicals', 'first-person view' and mental self-ascriptions.

**Carlin, Joi L**. The Issue of Music in Schools: An *Unfinished Symphony*?. *J Aes Educ*, 31(1), 57-62, Spr 97.

The current position of music education in Canadian public schooling is explored through the metaphor of a musical composition as a work in progress whose outcome is, as yet, undetermined. In the author's view, the status of music in the schools has declined because of the perpetuation of a curriculum which is an institutionalized artifact used for entertainment, public relations or teacher preparation time. Suggestions are given for ways to take music education out of its current fragmentary, disintegrating position and restore its integrity as an artistic expression and a rigorous, meaningful school subject with a sound philosophical base.

**Carlin, Laurence**. Ascriptive Supervenience. *SW Phil Rev*, 13(1), 47-57, Ja 97.

A significant weakness of recent studies of the concept of supervenience is their failure to offer an adequate formulation of that notion. In this paper, I make a start towards remedying the situation. Following James Klagge, I distinguish between two types of supervenience: ascriptive and ontological. I argue that recent formulations of ascriptive supervenience are too weak in that they permit too many judgments to supervene. I then offer a new formulation which overcomes the lately noted defects of formulations offered in recent discussions of supervenience.

**Carlson, Allen**. Appreciating Godlovitch. *J Aes Art Crit*, 55(1), 55-57, Wint 97.

**Carlson, Allen**. On the Aesthetic Appreciation of Japanese Gardens. *Brit J Aes*, 37(1), 47-56, Ja 97.

The objects of aesthetic appreciation range on a spectrum from pure art to pristine nature. At the poles aesthetic experience is typically rich and satisfying. However, toward the middle, where nature and artifice meet and intermingle, appreciation is not always so. We view human intrusions into natural landscapes as eyesores and frequently regard works of environmental art, such as Christo's, with ambivalence. This essay examines the way in which the Japanese garden, one of the classic meetings of art and nature, not only subtlety exemplifies this appreciative problem, but also forcefully and uncompromisingly attempts to solve it.

**Carlson, Dawn S** and Kacmar, K Michele. Perceptions of Ethics Across Situations: A View Through Three Different Lenses. *J Bus Ethics*, 16(2), 147-160, F 97.

This paper examined three approaches for understanding perceptions of ethics: moral philosophies, cognitive moral development and ethical value systems. First, the dimensionality of the moral philosophy approach was examined. Next, an attempt was made to integrate the models. Finally, each of the model's various components were used in a regression equation to isolate the best predictors of ethicality. Results indicated that the moral philosophies can be considered distinct entities, but the common underlying theme between the approaches was not as predicted. Also, individuals used a variety of approaches, not always the same ones, to determine the ethicalness of situations.

**Carlson, Erik**. A Note on Moore's Organic Unities. *J Value Inq*, 31(1), 55-59, Mr 97.

In his *Principia Ethica*, G.E. Moore gives two different definitions of an organic unity. In this note, I argue that neither of his definitions accurately captures the idea he had in mind. Instead, I suggest a third definition which, I believe, better expresses Moore's admittedly somewhat vague notion of organicity. I also try to show that yet another definition, proposed by Peter Vallentyne, is less plausible than my own.

**Carlson, Erik**. The Intrinsic Value of Non-Basic States of Affairs. *Phil Stud*, 85(1), 95-107, Ja 97.

This paper deals with the problem of how to assign intrinsic value to states of affairs that are not 'evaluatively basic', relative to a given theory of the good. After criticizing solutions proposed by Warren Quinn and Edward Oldfield, I state and discuss three alternative solutions of my own. According to the last of these proposals, some states of affairs have 'indeterminate' intrinsic value; they are not good, bad or neutral. Nevertheless, one indeterminate state may be intrinsically better than another. This solution reflects intuitively reasonable judgements about, e.g., certain disjunctive states of affairs.

**Carlson, Patricia J** and Blodgett, Mark S. Corporate Ethics Codes: A Practical Application of Liability Prevention. *J Bus Ethics*, 16(12-13), 1363-1369, S 97.

With the great increase in litigation, insurance costs and consumer prices, both managers and businesses should take a proactive position in avoiding liability. Legal liability may attach when a duty has been breached; many actions falling into this category are also considered unethical. Since much of business liability is caused by a breach of a duty by a business to either an individual, another business, or to society, this article asserts that the practice of liability prevention is a practical business application of ethics. (edited)

**Carlson, Thomas**. "James and the Kantian Tradition" in *The Cambridge Companion to William James*, Putnam, Ruth Anna (ed), 363-383. New York, Cambridge Univ Pr, 1997.

**Carmo, José** (ed) and Brown, Mark A (ed). *Deontic Logic, Agency and Normative Systems*. New York, Springer-Verlag, 1996.

This volume presents a variety of papers bearing on the relation between deontic logics, logics of action, and normative systems, i.e., systems of or about interacting agents (computers, human beings, corporations, etc.) whose behavior is subject to ideal constraints that may not always be fulfilled in practice. The papers range from theoretical studies of the logical and conceptual tools needed, to studies of various applications. The set of papers collected in this book should be of interest to investigators working in a variety of fields from philosophy, logic and legal theory to artificial intelligence, computer and management sciences, since it covers topics ranging from theoretical research on foundational issues in deontic and action logics, defeasible reasoning, decision theory, ethical theory, and legal theory, to research on a variety of issues relevant to applications connected with expert systems in the law, document specification, automation of defeasible reasoning, specification of responsibilities and powers in organizations, normative systems specification, confidentiality in database systems, and a host of other applications. (publisher, edited)

**Carmo, José** and Santos, Filipe. "Indirect Action, Influence and Responsibility" in *Deontic Logic, Agency and Normative Systems*, Brown, Mark A (ed), 194-215. New York, Springer-Verlag, 1996.

The paper focuses on some concepts of agency relevant to the specification and analysis of organizations. It is argued that there is an important distinction to be drawn between a "direct" and an "indirect" agency concept, and that the latter allows an easy and abstract way of expressing the organizational notion of responsibility. An "influence" agency concept is also introduced in order to cope with interactions between different agents. The formal characterization of these concepts is given by means of modal logics, following the same tradition in the logical characterization of act descriptions as employed by Kanger and Pörn.

**Carmo Ferreira, Manuel J do**. "Nueva religión: Un proyecto del Idealismo alemán" in *El inicio del Idealismo alemán*, Market, Oswaldo, 263-277. Madrid, Ed Complutense, 1996.

El proyecto de una nueva religión promueve la articulación de razón, religión e historia, conceptos en los que se concentra el programa del Romanticismo temprano y del Idealismo alemán. Ese proyecto, que tiene su raíz en Lessing y es objeto de una primera fundamentación histórico-transcendental en el *Religionsschrift* de Kant y de Fichte, halla su versión más amplia en la exigencia de una nueva mitología (Fr. Schlegel) y de una revolución del espíritu (Hegel).

**Carmo Ferreira, Manuel J do**. O Mais Antigo Programa de Sistema do Idealismo Alemao. *Philosophica (Portugal)*, 225-237, 1997.

**Carnap, Rudolf**. Metalógica (*Metalogik*). *Mathesis*, 11(2), 137-192, My 95.

**Carnes, Joseph H**. Liberalism and Culture. *Constellations*, 4(1), 35-47, Ap 97.

Will Kymlicka's new book makes important conceptual, methodological and substantive contributions to contemporary discussions of multiculturalism. Nevertheless, Kymlicka's attempt to construct a defense of special rights for minority cultural groups on the basis of his conception of "societal culture" entails implications that are both too radical and too restrictive with regard to the kinds of minority claims they support. In particular, Kymlicka's account undermines the claims of immigrant minorities to the sorts of special rights that Kymlicka thinks they are entitled to demand.

**Carnevale, Franco A** and Schultz, Dawson S. Engagement and Suffering in Responsible Caregiving: On Overcoming Maleficience in Health Care. *Theor Med*, 17(3), 189-207, S 96.

The thesis of this article is that engagement and suffering are essential aspects of responsible caregiving. The sense of medical responsibility engendered by engaged caregiving is referred to herein as 'clinical *phronesis*', i.e., practical wisdom in health care, or, simply, practical health care wisdom. The idea of

clinical phronesis calls to mind a *relational* or *communicative* sense of medical responsibility which can best be understood as a kind of 'virtue ethics', yet one that is informed by the exigencies of moral discourse and dialogue, as well as by the technical rigors of formal reasoning. The ideal of clinical phronesis is not (necessarily) contrary to the more common understandings of medical responsibility as either *beneficence* or *patient autonomy*—except, of course, when these notions are taken in their "disengaged" form (reflecting the malaise of "modern medicine"). (edited)

**Carosotti, Gianni**. Secolarizzazione e originalità del moderno: In margine a *La legittimità dell'epoca moderna* di Hans Blumenberg. *Itinerari Filosof*, 3(5), 50-55, Ja-Ap 93.

**Carpentieri, Rosario**. Il problema del fondamento nella filosofia di Karl Jaspers. *Stud Filosofici*, 173-196, 1995.

The work identifies the question about the foundation as the meeting of the two aspects of Jaspers's philosophy: the *Existenzerhellung* and the *philosophische Logik*. The question of the foundation, which ontology solves by neutralizing nothingness, is raised by Jaspers to an existential dimension, where existence is ever in sight of nothingness. The work shows how the *Existenzerhellung*, through the existential dimension of nothingness, provides an access to the logical and existential proceeding by which each foundation generates at the border of groundlessness, each feeling at home at the border of extraneousness, and the project of the being is grounded in the incessant menace of nothingness.

**Carr, Craig L** and Seidler, Michael J. Pufendorf, Sociality and the Modern State. *Hist Polit Thought*, 17(3), 354-378, Autumn 96.

This essay discusses the nature of Pufendorf's contribution to the history of political ideas. It is argued that his theory of sociality domesticates Hobbesian cynicism, systematizes Grotian visions, and establishes a moral foundation for the legitimacy of the modern state.

**Carr, David**. "Varieties of Incontinence: Towards an Aristotelian Approach to Moral Weakness in Moral Education" in *Philosophy of Education (1996)*, Margonis, Frank (ed), 130-138. Urbana, Phil Education Soc, 1997.

**Carr, David**. Margolis and the Philosophy of History. *Man World*, 30(2), 139-144, Ap 97.

A critical discussion of Joseph Margolis's works on the philosophy of history.

**Carr, Gabrielle M** and Rosen, C Martin. Fares and Free Riders on the Information Highway. *J Bus Ethics*, 16(12-13), 1439-1445, S 97.

Public policy issues around access to networked information are explored and examined. Long viewed as the quintessential public good, information has evolved into a critically important market commodity in little more than a generation. New technologies and a political climate in which the meaning of universal access to information is no longer commonly understood and in which its importance is no longer taken for granted pose significant challenges for American society. Libraries, as information commons, offer the means of meeting those challenges. Historical, economical and professional factors that shape the conflict are described and discussed.

**Carr, Karen L**. The Offense of Reason and the Passion of Faith: Kierkegaard and Anti-Rationalism. *Faith Phil*, 13(2), 236-251, AP 96.

This essay considers and rejects both the irrationalist and the suprarationalist interpretations of Kierkegaard, arguing that a new category—Kierkegaard as "antirationalist"—is needed. The irrationalist reading overemphasizes the subjectivism of Kierkegaard's thought, while the suprarationalist reading underemphasizes the degree of tension between human reason (as corrupted by the will's desire to be autonomous and self-sustaining) and Christian faith. An antirationalist reading, I argue, is both faithful to Kierkegaard's metaphysical and alethiological realism, on the one hand, and his emphasis on the continuing opposition between reason and faith, on the other, as manifested in the ongoing possibility of offense (reason's rejection of the Christian message) in the life of the Christian.

**Carr, Wilfred**. Professing Education in a Postmodern Age. *J Phil Educ*, 31(2), 309-327, Jl 97.

Although this paper is a written version of an inaugural lecture given at the University of Sheffield in December 1995, its central thesis is that, in a postmodern age, the practice of professors of education giving inaugural lectures is incoherent. To advance this thesis in an inaugural lecture entails an obvious contradiction which, it is proposed, can only be resolved by examining the historical origins of the inaugural lecture in the early medieval university. What emerges from this examination is not only that there is a premodern version of the inaugural lecture but that the virtue-based understanding of education which it presupposed can be revised and advanced in the postmodern world.

**Carrano, Antonio**. "Progresso o sviluppo? Un problema di filosofia della storia nella prospettiva di W. von Humboldt" in *Lo Storicismo e la Sua Storia: Temi, Problemi, Prospettive*, Cacciatore, Giuseppe (ed), 159-171. Milano, Guerini, 1997.

**Carratelli, Giovanni Pugliese** (ed). *Catalogue des Publications 1977-1995*. Naples, La Città del Sole, 1995.

**Carrera, Alessandro**. "Del Sentire La Verità: Per Leopardi e Michelstaedter" in *Soggetto E Verità: La questione dell'uomo nella filosofia contemporanea*, Fagiuoli, Ettore, 199-207. 20136 Milano, Mimesis, 1996.

Kant had ruled out the possibility that "feeling" had something to do with the truth. Truth is submitted to judgement and judgement cannot be "felt". Years later, Giacomo Leopardi and Friedrich Nietzsche challenged *de facto* Kant's assumption, reintroducing the issues of feeling (i.e., hermeneutics) within the realm of truth. At the turn of the century the young Italian philosopher Carlo Michelstaedter committed suicide after realizing that truth detached from any hermeneutical frame was an impossible dream.

**Carrera, Alessandro**. Lo sguardo di Blanchot e la musica di Orfeo: Visione e ascolto nell'ispirazione poetica. *Itinerari Filosof*, 3(5), 3-14, Ja-Ap 93.

Maurice Blanchot's assumption that the gaze of Orpheus toward Eurydice is "the beginning of writing" involves a theory of poetical inspiration. Eurydice is the poet's inspiration. As long as Orpheus (the poet) sings, he remains in a nocturnal space, he is not illuminated by the light of Apollo and therefore he does not write. As soon as he turns to Eurydice and he sees her, inspiration (Eurydice) is lost, but writing (the poetical work) is now possible—and impossible at the same time, because it will never compensate for the loss of inspiration. But Blanchot assumes that singing is completely lost in the writing and this is the assumption that the author (with the help of Ovid) challenges.

**Carreras, Alberto**. "Realism: Neural Networks and Representation" in *Verdad: lógica, representación y mundo*, Villegas Forero, L, 289-300. Santiago de Compostela, Univ Santiago Comp, 1996.

This paper is based on various experimental studies carried out within the ambit of the cognitive sciences and sets out to reinforce the realist theory of mental *representation*. As against various doctrines of phenomenological origin, which continue to adopt an ironic attitude towards the existence of a represented *reality*, in this paper I defend its objectivity, that is to say, a correspondence between the representing system and the represented system, specifying the form which this correspondence takes. Further, this realism is extended to the process of *categorization*. (edited)

**Carreras, Mercedes**. Elección pública y Democracia representativa. *Telos (Spain)*, 5(2), 65-85, D 96.

In the first part of this paper I will examine Arrow's Theorem and its implications for parliamentary decision processes. I will also deal with the procedural conception of public interest as a tool for avoiding legislative inconsistencies. After considering the main links and differences between republicanism and public choice, I will conclude by stressing the need of recovering practical reason in order to reach reasonable democratic results.

**Carrier, Richard**. Do Religious Life and Critical Thought Need Each Other? A Reply to Reinsmith. *Inquiry (USA)*, 16(1), 67-75, Fall 96.

**Carrión Wam, Roque**. The Model of Procedural Ethics: Formalism and Argumentation in Law (Spanish). *Rev Filosof (Venezuela)*, Supp(2-3), 121-137, 1996.

The characteristic features of procedural ethics, whose formulation is closely related with the theory of law, is dealt with in the first part of this paper, and then it concentrates on proposals for a theory of legal argumentation (R. Alexy). The last part deals with the principal characteristic of research on the renovation of theoretical perspectives of law and the theory of society. All of this is done with a pragmatic vision which helps to promote the real interest behind the constitution of a just and rationally responsible society.

**Carroll, John W**. Lipton on Compatible Contrasts. *Analysis*, 57(3), 170-178, Jl 97.

The question 'Why did Gulch Dam burst rather than overflow?' is *contrastive*; it mentions both an explanandum fact (the dam's bursting) and its foil (the dam's overflowing). One promising approach to contrastive why-questions is defended against Peter Lipton's counterexamples. The central cases are ones in which the explanandum fact and its foil are compatible.

**Carroll, Noël**. Periodizing Postmodernism?. *Clio*, 26(2), 143-165, Wint 97.

**Carroll, Noël**. The Intentional Fallacy: Defending Myself. *J Aes Art Crit*, 55(3), 305-309, Sum 97.

**Carroll, Noël**. The Ontology of Mass Art. *J Aes Art Crit*, 55(2), 187-199, Spring 97.

**Carroll, William E**. Galileo, Science and the Bible. *Acta Phil*, 6(1), 5-37, 1997.

L'analisi di Galileo sulla relazione tra la scienza e la Bibbia spesso è stata considerata come anticipatrice della moderna comprensione della natura essenzialmente religiosa della Sacra Scrittura, e quindi come un invito all'emancipazione della scienza dall'autorità della Bibbia. Galileo, tuttavia, pensava che la Bibbia contenesse verità scientifiche e che fosse possibile scoprire il vero significato di quei passaggi biblici che riguardano i fenomeni naturali. Galileo e i teologi dell'Inquisizione condividevano gli stessi comuni principi, non solo per ciò che riguarda la nozione aristotelica di dimostrazione scientifica, ma anche per ciò che concerne l'esegesi biblica. Galileo riafferma l'interpretazione tradizionale cattolica della relazione tra la Bibbia e la scienza e, sotto molti aspetti, condivide il modo di intendere questa relazione caratteristica del cattolicesimo della Controriforma.

**Carson, A Scott**. Drug Testing and Privacy: Why Contract Arguments Do Not Work. *Bus Prof Ethics J*, 14(4), 3-22, Wint 95.

**Carson, Cathryn**. The Peculiar Notion of Exchange Forces—I: Origins in Quantum Mechanics, 1926-1928. *Stud Hist Phil Mod Physics*, 27B(1), 23-45, Mr 96.

**Carson, Cathryn**. The Peculiar Notion of Exchange Forces—II: From Nuclear Forces to QED, 1929-1950. *Stud Hist Phil Mod Physics*, 27B(2), 99-131, Je 96.

**Carson, Scott** and Brandon, Robert N. The Indeterministic Character of Evolutionary Theory: No "No Hidden Variables Proof" but No Room for Determinism Either. *Phil Sci*, 63(3), 315-337, S 96.

In this paper we first briefly review Bell's (1964, 1966) Theorem to see how it

invalidates any deterministic "hidden variable" account of the apparent indeterminacy of quantum mechanics (QM). Then we show that quantum uncertainty, at the level of DNA mutations, can "percolate" up to have major populational effects. Interesting as this point may be it does not show any autonomous indeterminism of the evolutionary process. In the next two sections we investigate drift and natural selection as the locus of autonomous biological indeterminacy. Here we conclude that the population-level indeterminacy of natural selection and drift are ultimately based on the assumption of a fundamental indeterminacy at the level of the lives and deaths of individual organisms. The following section examines this assumption and defends it from the determinists' attack. Then we show that, even if one rejects the assumption, there is still an important reason why one might think evolutionary theory (ET) is autonomously indeterministic. In the concluding section we contrast the arguments we have mounted against a deterministic hidden variable account of ET with the proof of the impossibility of such an account of QM.

**Carson, Thomas L**. Brandt on Utilitarianism and the Foundations of Ethics. *Bus Ethics Quart*, 7(1), 87-100, Ja 97.

**Carson, Thomas L** (ed) and Moser, Paul K (ed). *Morality and the Good Life*. New York, Oxford Univ Pr, 1997.

The book is a comprehensive survey of contemporary ethical theory that collects thirty-four selections on morality and the theory of value. Emphasizing value theory, metaethics and normative ethics, it is nontechnical and accessible to a wide range of readers. Selections are organized under six main topics: 1) Concepts of Goodness, 2) What Things are Good? 3) Virtues and Ethics, 4) Realism vs. Anti-Realism, 5) Value and Obligation, and 6) The Value and Meaning of Life. The text includes both a substantial general introduction featuring explanatory summaries of all the selections and an extensive topical bibliography, which enhance the volume's pedagogical and research utility. (publisher, edited)

**Carter, Alan**. Infanticide and the Right to Life. *Ratio*, 10(1), 1-9, Ap 97.

Michael Tooley defends infanticide by analyzing 'A has a right to X' as roughly synonymous with 'If A desires X, then others are under a prima facie obligation to refrain from actions that would deprive him (or her) of it.' An infant who cannot conceive of himself or herself as a continuing subject of experiences cannot desire to continue existing. Hence, on Tooley's analysis, killing the infant is not impermissible, for it does not go against any of the infant's desires. However, Tooley's argument in support of his analysis seems to justify, instead, a slightly more subtle analysis. In short, Tooley's argument in support of his analysis actually implies that infanticide may well be impermissible. (edited)

**Carter, Alan**. State-Primacy and Third World Debt. *Heythrop J*, 38(3), 300-314, Jl 97.

**Carter, C Allen**. *Kenneth Burke and the Scapegoat Process*. Norman, Univ of Oklahoma Pr, 1996.

The writings of twentieth-century thinker Kenneth Burke span seven decades and extend into multiple disciplines. This study by C. Allen Carter examines one particular issue of recurring concern for Burke: the tendency of human beings to seek out scapegoats or victims. By demonstrating the centrality of this theme in the entire range of works by Burke, Carter offers a valuable approach to understanding the philosophy as a whole. (edited)

**Carter, Robert E** (trans) and Seisaku, Yamamoto (trans). *Watsuji Tetsurō's Rinrigaku*. Albany, SUNY Pr, 1996.

Watsuji Tetsurō's *Rinrigaku* (literally, the principles that allow us to live in friendly community) has been regarded as the definitive study of Japanese ethics for half a century. In Japan, ethics is the study of human being or *ningen*. As an ethical being, one negates individuality by abandoning one's independence from others. This selflessness is the true meaning of goodness. (publisher)

**Carter, W R**. Dion's Left Foot (and the Price of Burkean Economy). *Phil Phenomenol Res*, 57(2), 371-379, Je 97.

Two recent papers by Michael Burke bearing upon the persistence of people and commonplace things illustrate the fact that the quest for *synchronic* ontological economy is likely to encourage a disturbing *diachronic* proliferation of entities. This discussion argues that Burke's promise of ontological economy is seriously compromised by the fact that his proposed metaphysic does violence to standard intuitions concerning the persistence of people and commonplace things. In effect, Burke would have us achieve synchronic economy (rejection of coincident entities) by postulating strongly counterintuitive transtemporal claims of numerical diversity. The argument is made that the price of Burkean economy is too high.

**Cartwright, Nancy**. "Neurath against Method" in *Origins of Logical Empiricism*, Giere, Ronald N (ed), 80-90. Minneapolis, Univ of Minnesota Pr, 1996.

The authors draw a connection between logical empiricism, politics and political philosophy in the case of Neurath's use of the notion of conceptual *Ballungen* (congestions) in the protocol-sentence debate in the Vienna Circle. This notion is crucial to Neurath's rejection of a certain ideal of scientific method. They explain this notion in connection with a crucial use of a similar notion in a much earlier debate, which had renewed currency and involved Neurath himself at the time of the debate on protocol sentences. The earlier debate, from the 1890s to the 1910s, was a debate among Marxists on the status of the materialist conception of history and the extent to which it could accommodate the causal role of religious, artistic, philosophical, and other aspects of historical phenomena. According to the authors the notion of complex, or *complexus*, used by Antonio Labriola and Georgy Plekhanov in that discussion formed the basis for Neurath's notion of a *Ballung*.

**Cartwright, Nancy**. Where Do Laws of Nature Come From?. *Dialectica*, 51(1), 65-78, 1997.

The view that laws of nature are basic is rejected. Instead it is argued that capacities are basic and that laws of nature obtain only on account of capacities. Laws of nature, in the regular-association sense of 'law', hold only *ceteris paribus* and only relative to the operation of what the author calls a 'nomological machine'. A nomological machine is a fixed arrangement of components, or factors, with stable capacities that in the right sort of stable environment will, with repeated operation, give rise to the kind of regular behavior that we describe in our scientific laws. Scientific models, which play an important role in the workings of science, from physics to economics, provide precisely the kind of information identified in the characterization of a nomological machine. Examples of physical and socio-economic machines are discussed.

**Carugno, Daniela**. Insularità del vero: Omogeneità ed eterogeneità negli sviluppi dialettici della "Analitica trascendentale". *G Metaf*, 18(3), 369-407, S-D 96.

**Carvajal Cordón, Julián**. "La Autodisolución de la Vieja Política en Ortega" in *Política y Sociedad en José Ortega y Gasset: En Torno a "Vieja y Nueva Política"*, Lopez de la Vieja, Maria Teresa (ed), 195-209. Barcelona, Anthropos, 1997.

**Carvajal Villaplana, Alvaro**. Sobre ética y derechos humanos. *Rev Filosof (Costa Rica)*, 34(83-84), 395-400, D 96.

This article takes off from a controversy sketched by Eduardo Rabossi, who sustains the viewpoint of the nonexistence of an authentic philosophical contention regarding human rights. In his opinion the philosophical foundations of human rights were clearly defined through the recognition of the Universal Declaration of Human Rights as law. It also intends to high light the relevant role that ethics plays in the discussion on human rights.

**Carver, Terrell**. "Public Man" and The Critique of Masculinities. *Polit Theory*, 24(4), 673-686, N 96.

The 'subject' in political theory has been identified by feminists as male and masculine, but by theorists in 'men's studies' and 'sociology of masculinities' as 'not a woman'. This 'abstract individual' has also been identified by feminists as 'degendered' or 'neutered' and even disembodied. This paradox can be understood as a misogynist political strategy, but it also disguises an absence of theorization on male sexuality, reproductive capacities and domestic roles, as well as on varied and oppositional masculinities. Any defensible theorisation of the 'subject' in politics now requires critical attention to the power relations created by dominant masculinities.

**Cary, Phillip**. Believing the Word: A Proposal about Knowing Other Persons. *Faith Phil*, 13(1), 78-90, Ja 96.

Our concept of knowing of other persons ought to include respect for them. Since respect implies considering whether what they say is true, I propose that believing others' words is a necessary condition of knowing them. I explore the contribution such belief makes to knowledge of other persons, as well as some surprising but welcome implications, including theological consequences.

**Casaban, E**. "Verdad e interacción cognitiva" in *Verdad; lógica, representación y mundo*, Villegas Forero, L, 23-31. Santiago de Compostela, Univ Santiago Comp, 1996.

This paper argues about some shortcomings of theories of truth. You have to choose a special subset of natural language or to translate its sentences into a logic language if you want to speak about truth fittingly. Some of these problems are showed. The explanation of cognition from neuroscience doesn't drive toward any theory of truth at all and the use of truth predicates can probably have only a pragmatic value.

**Casanovas, E** and Dellunde, Pilar and Jansana, Ramon. On Elementary Equivalence for Equality-free Logic. *Notre Dame J Form Log*, 37(3), 506-522, Sum 96.

This paper is a contribution to the study of equality-free logic, that is, first-order logic without equality. We mainly devote ourselves to the study of algebraic characterizations of its relation of elementary equivalence by providing some Keisler-Shelah type ultrapower theorems and an Ehrenfeucht-Fraïssé type theorem. We also give characterizations of elementary classes in equality-free logic. As a by-product we characterize the sentences that are logically equivalent to an equality-free one.

**Casas, Jorge Manuel**. Sobre los ecos del silencio en la ética del discurso. *Cuad Etica*, 15-16, 23-47, 1993.

The article makes use of the silence to show a pragmatic failure and a practical one in the discourse's ethic, not only in its transcendental version but also in its universal one. The argument is that such discourse's ethic failures lead to a different destiny from the it looks forward to.

**Casati, Roberto** and Varzi, Achille C. *50 Years of Events: An Annotated Bibliography 1947 to 1997*. Bowling Green, Philosophy Doc Ctr, 1997.

This bibliography is concerned with recent literature on the nature of events and the place they occupy in our conceptual scheme. The subject has received extensive consideration in the philosophical debate over the last few decades, with ramifications reaching far into the domains of allied disciplines such as linguistics and the cognitive sciences. At the same time, the literature is so wide and widely scattered that it has become very difficult to keep track of every line of development. Our hope is that this work will prove useful to overcome that difficulty.

**Case, Jennifer**. On the Right Idea of a Conceptual Scheme. *S J Phil*, 35(1), 1-18, Spr 97.

Hilary Putnam has the right idea of a conceptual scheme. His idea is central to his doctrine of conceptual relativity, which I defend in this paper. My defense entails an explanation of how Putnam's idea of a conceptual scheme escapes condemnation by Donald Davidson's arguments against the very idea of a

conceptual scheme. Reading Davidson's arguments as contravening Putnam's agenda requires overlooking the difference between natural languages and what I call "optional languages". If having a conceptual scheme is to be associated with having a language, I argue, it should be associated with having an optional language.

**Case-Winters, Anna**. The Question of God in an Age of Science: Constructions of Reality and Ultimate Reality in Theology and Science. *Zygon*, 32(3), 351-375, S 97.

This article proposes criteria for assessing models and applies the criteria to one model from each field. The model of understanding evolution as a *struggle for existence* is considered from the field of science and the traditional model for understanding the God-world relation as that of a king's relation to his kingdom is considered from the field of theology. Each of these models is evaluated with respect to its credibility, religious viability and moral adequacy. In each case an alternative analogy is proposed and argued for. (edited)

**Casement, William**. Unity, Diversity, and Leftist Support for the Canon. *J Aes Educ*, 27(3), 35-49, Fall 93.

It is often assumed that postmodernism and left-wing politics are inherently oppositional to the canon. This article demonstrates the assumption is incorrect. Richard Rorty, Elizabeth Fox-Genovese, and Irving Howe are all supporters of the canon. Their views are examined, showing a penchant for unity arising from diversity, but questioning the adequacy of their explanations of it. It is suggested that leftist support for the canon would be strengthened by a stronger identification with foundationalism.

**Caserta, Marco**. Il diritto tra decisione ed ordine: Brevi note su *I tre tipi di pensiero giuridico* di Carl Schmitt. *Riv Int Filosof Diritto*, 73(3), 527-545, Jl-S 96.

**Casertano, Giovanni**. "La causa della conoscenza: discorso logico ed esigenza etica nel *Fedone* platonico" in *Momenti di Storia della Logica e di Storia della Filosofia*, Guetti, Carla (ed), 11-38. Roma, Aracne Editrice, 1996.

This study examines the notion of "cause" in Plato's *Phaedo*, at pages 96a-100a. It makes some peculiarities of the Platonic demonstrative method stand out, stressing some stylistic and conceptual "clues", which in fact make the Platonic statements, apparently dogmatic, problematic. It is thus proved that Plato is fully aware of the fact that the discourse he is building has anyway a quality of likelihood, of probability, i.e., of uncertainty, even though the opposition between true and false, good and evil, has all the characteristics of a "strong" contrast. It follows, in Platonic terms, a peculiar mixture between ethical need and logical discourse, or rather the notion that every logical discourse has an ethical valence.

**Casertano, Giovanni**. "Le parti, le forme ed i nomi del tempo nel *Timeo* platonico" in *Il Concetto di Tempo: Atti del XXXII Congresso Nazionale della Società Filosofica Italiana*, Casertano, Giovanni (ed), 147-150. Napoli, Loffredo, 1997.

The essay examines the mention of time at pages 36e-38c of Plato's *Timaeus*. The Platonic definition of time as "moving image of the eternal" Is examined in the complexity of its relations that link it, on one side, to the presence of Parmenides' perspective, which can be found even in this dialogue; on the other side, to the Platonic considerations on language especially lively in the Athenian's latest dialogues. In this frame the Platonic distinction between the "parts of time" and the "ideas of time" stands particularly out. They signify the dialectic relationship between time and eternity, not only from the linguistic point of view, but also from that of the "thinkability" of time.

**Casertano, Giovanni** (ed). *Il Concetto di Tempo: Atti del XXXII Congresso Nazionale della Società Filosofica Italiana*. Napoli, Loffredo, 1997.

The volume, edited by G.C., includes the Proceedings of the XXXII National Congress of the Italian Philosophical Society, held in Caserta from the 28th of April to the 1st of May 1995. It includes 10 Reports and 28 Papers, the latest divided into a "Historical Section", a "Theoretical Section" and a "Didactic Section". The notion of time is examined from the ancient Greek culture until today, not only in the work of the greatest philosophers (as Plato, Aristotle, Leibniz, Kant, Bergson, Husserl, Heidegger), but even in physics (from Newton to modern Physics), in anthropology (Merleau-Ponty), in literature (Proust), in Freudian psychoanalysis. Some aspect of the "experience" of time and its importance in the formative processes are then examined in the theoretical and didactic sections.

**Casey, Edward S**. Joseph Margolis on Interpretation. *Man World*, 30(2), 127-138, Ap 97.

**Casey, Edward S**. Sym-Phenomenologizing: Talking Shop. *Human Stud*, 20(2), 169-180, Ap 97.

In this essay I discuss the idea of deploying workshops in phenomenology, i.e., teaching the discipline by practicing it. I focus on the model proposed by Herbert Spiegelberg, the first person to give systematic attention to this idea and the first to institutionalize it over a period of several years. Drawing on my experience in several of the workshops he led at Washington University, St. Louis, I detail the method he recommended in preparation for a workshop I then led at the inaugural meeting of "To the Things Themselves" at the University of New Hampshire.

**Casey, Edward S**. *The Fate of Place: A Philosophical History*. Berkeley, Univ of Calif Pr, 1997.

In this study, the author offers a philosophical history of the evolving conceptualizations of place and space in Western thought. Not merely a presentation of the ideas of other philosophers, *The Fate of Place* is acutely sensitive to silences, absences and missed opportunities in the complex history sensitive to silences, absences and missed opportunities in the complex history of philosophical approaches to space and place. A central theme is the increasing neglect of place in favor of space from the seventh century A.D. onward, amounting to the virtual exclusion of place by the end of the eighteenth century. (publisher, edited)

**Casey, Timothy**. Medieval Technology and the Husserlian Critique of Galilean Science. *Amer Cath Phil Quart*, 70(Supp), 219-227, 1996.

**Cash, John M**. Guide to the Papers of Michael Polanyi. *Tradition Discovery*, 23(1), 4-47, 1996-97.

**Cassam, Quassim**. *Self and World*. New York, Clarendon/Oxford Pr, 1997.

I claim that it is a necessary condition of self-consciousness that one is intuitively aware of oneself, *qua* subject, as a physical object. Intuitiveness awareness of oneself as a physical object involves various forms of bodily self-awareness in which one is presented to oneself, *qua* subject, as shaped, solid and located. These forms of bodily self-awareness are required for self-consciousness because they are necessary for consciousness of one's own identity as the subject of different representations and for consciousness of these representations as representations of an objective world. This account of self-consciousness helps to undermine various forms of idealism and reductionism about the self.

**Cassam, Quassim**. Self-Reference, Self-Knowledge and the Problem of Misconception. *Euro J Phil*, 4(3), 276-295, D 96.

It has been argued that the self-ascription of thoughts and experiences requires the ability to distinguish oneself from other things in the world, and hence substantive knowledge of the nature of one's thinking, experiencing self. This view faces the difficulty that even subjects with grossly inaccurate self-conceptions are still capable of self-conscious self-reference. The best response to this problem is to argue that such subjects are able to distinguish themselves from other things in the world, and hence to refer to themselves first-personally, as long as they experience themselves as bounded and located physical objects in a world of such objects. Since experiencing oneself 'qua subject' as corporeal is not the same thing as believing that one's thinking self is corporeal, the falsity of Cartesian dualism would still leave someone with a dualist self-conception with a concrete sense of where she ends and the rest of the world begins.

**Cassam, Quassim**. Subjects and Objects. *Phil Phenomenol Res*, 57(3), 643-648, S 97.

**Cassedy, Steven**. Gustav Shpet and Phenomenology in an Orthodox Key. *Stud East Euro Thought*, 49(2), 81-108, Je 97.

Gustav Gustavovich Shpet (1879-1937) is undoubtedly best known for introducing Husserlian phenomenology to Russia. He applied to aesthetics and the philosophy of language the principles he had discovered in Husserl's *Logical Investigations* and *Ideas I*. But, perhaps without knowing it, he modified the phenomenology he had found in Husserl. His modifications show a thinker who is thoroughly grounded in Russian religious thought of the late nineteenth and early twentieth centuries. The result is a philosophy that combines Husserl's analysis of the structure of consciousness with the fundamental Platonism of Orthodoxy, the doctrine of incarnation and the related notion that matter is to be venerated.

**Cassell, Cathy** and Johnson, Phil and Smith, Ken. Opening the Black Box: Corporate Codes of Ethics in Their Organizational Context. *J Bus Ethics*, 16(10), 1077-1093, Jl 97.

A review of the literature on Corporate Codes of Ethics suggests that while there exists an informative body of literature concerning the prevalence of such codes, their design, implementation and promulgation, it is also evident that there is a relative lack of consideration of their impact upon members' everyday organizational behaviour. By drawing upon organizational sociology and psychology this paper constructs a contextualist and interpretive model which seeks to enable an analysis and evaluation of their effects upon individual, group and organizational behaviour.

**Cassinari, Flavio**. "La Verità Storica: La comprensione della storia nella riflessione di Martin Heidegger" in *Soggetto E Verità: La questione dell'uomo nella filosofia contemporanea*, Fagiuoli, Ettore, 277-296. 20136 Milano, Mimesis, 1996.

The essay points out the link between the notion of understanding (*Verstehen*) and the one of historicity (*Geschichtlichkeit*) in Heidegger's writings of the second half of the twenties. First of all the author considers the object of the historical knowledge, constituted by the "to happen" (*Geschehen*) of the "Being-there" (*Dasein*), then the article shows the impossibility of forming a real philosophy of history, starting from Heidegger's identification of history (*Geschichte*) and to happen (*Geschehen*), and from the Heidegger's notion of repetition (*Wiederholung*) applied to historicity. Finally the essay examines the difficulties arising from Heidegger's dichotomy between history (*Geschichte*) and historiography (*Historie*) in order to work out a theory of historic science.

**Cassini, Alejandro**. Ensayo y error restringido y orientado: Esquema de una lógica del descubrimiento científico. *Analisis Filosof*, 16(1), 67-82, My 96.

This paper outlines a logic of scientific discovery. First, it argues that discovery rules must be general and able to guide the search for novel hypotheses. Then, it criticizes Zahars's deductivist logic of discovery, but accepts his idea of general heuristics principles. It shows that these principles are compatible with a complex version of retroduction. An historical case—the discovery of neutrino—is examined applying this approach. Finally, it concludes that this logic of discovery culminates in a restricted and directed method of trial and error.

**Castagni, Laura**. Kant e l'epistemologia contemporanea. *Iride*, 10(20), 129-134, Ap 97.

**Castagnoli, E** and Calzi, M Li. Expected Utility without Utility. *Theor Decis*, 41(3), 281-301, N 96.

This paper advances an interpretation of Von Neumann-Morgenstern's expected utility model for preferences over lotteries which does not require the notion of a cardinal utility over prizes and can be phrased entirely in the language of probability. According to it, the expected utility of a lottery can be read as the probability that this lottery outperforms another given independent lottery. The implications of this interpretation for some topics and models in decision theory are considered.

**Castañeda, Héctor-Neri**. Indexical Reference and Bodily Causal Diagrams in Intentional Action. *Stud Log*, 51(3-4), 439-462, 1992.

In this paper, completed only months before his death, the author studies a number of concepts of importance for the analysis of intentional action. Four themes in particular are discussed: the intentionality of action, the practical syllogism, what the author terms "the practical causality of practical thinking" and the proximate cause of action.

**Caster, Kevin J**. The Distinction Between Being and Essence According to Boethius, Avicenna, and William of Auvergne. *Mod Sch*, 73(4), 309-332, M 96.

**Caster, Kevin J**. William of Auvergne's Adaptation of IBN Gabirol's Doctrine of the Divine Will. *Mod Sch*, 74(1), 31-42, N 96.

The primary aim of this article is to illustrate the significant influence that Solomon Ibn Gabirol's doctrine of the divine will exercised upon the philosophical thought of William of Auvergne. After discussing each thinker's view of the divine will, I argue that the consequence in William's philosophy of his adaptation of Ibn Gabirol's teaching on the divine will is the radically contingent character of created beings. I also suggest that William's emphasis upon the divine will marks an important point of departure from his fundamentally Avicennian metaphysics.

**Castiglione, Dario** and Bellamy, Richard. Building the Union: The Nature of Sovereignty in the Political Architecture of Europe. *Law Phil*, 16(4), 421-445, Jl 97.

The debate on the nature of the European Union has become a test case of the kind of political and institutional arrangements appropriate in an age of globalization. This paper explores three views of the EU. The two main positions that have hitherto confronted each other appeal to either cosmopolitan or communitarian values. Advocates of the former argue for some form of federal structure in Europe and are convinced that the sovereignty of the nation state belongs to the past. Proponents of the latter make a case on both sociopolitical and normative grounds for a Europe of nations. However a third position, favoured by the authors, is gaining ground. This view combines cosmopolitan and communitarian conceptions. It emphasizes the mixed nature of the European polity and conceives the constitutionalization process as open-ended. (edited)

**Castilho Piqueira, José Roberto**. Biomathematics: Methods and Limits (in Portuguese). *Trans/Form/Acao*, 19, 141-149, 1996.

This article tries to give a general vision of the mathematical methods used to model biological processes. There are two kinds of methods: deterministics using dynamical systems theory and probabilistics, using stochastic differential equations. However, three points can not be neglected for biological processes: complexity, unpredictability and diversity of time scales.

**Castilla Lázaro, Ramón**. Sobre la idealidad de los significados en la filosofía de Husserl. *Dialogos*, 32(69), 97-173, Ja 97.

**Castilla y Cortázar, Blanca**. En torno a la díada trascendental. *Anu Filosof*, 29(2), 397-414, 1996.

In the anthropology, the person has a self-organizing communicative structure, so person cannot be unique, lonely. This has been called by Polo: "Coexistence". It shows that the "Díada" (Duality) is richness, plenitude (fullness). This makes possible to mark the difference between two complementary person's types: the male person and the female person. They could be called: "coexistence-from" and "coexistence-in".

**Castillo Córdova, Genara**. La unidad de la vida humana (Aristóteles y Leonardo Polo). *Anu Filosof*, 29(2), 415-426, 1996.

The unity of human life according to Aristotle is placed in the virtue, which makes possible the integrity of human life. The unity of human life in virtue is at the level of mere actuality, but it is better understood at the level of the personal *esse* (according to L. Polo).

**Castle, Emery N**. "A Pluralistic, Pragmatic and Evolutionary Approach to Natural Resource Management" in *Environmental Pragmatism*, Light, Andrew (ed), 231-250. New York, Routledge, 1996.

The purpose of this work is to provide a useable framework for making contemporary public policy decisions concerning the natural environment. Such a framework should accommodate pluralistic, pragmatic and evolutionary considerations. No single philosophical system is sufficiently broad or flexible to accommodate the diversity of objectives that are legitimate components of public policy. Because pluralism does not forbid inconsistencies, it requires a political system to resolve conflicts. Such a political system provides the necessary pragmatic dimension. Social and natural systems coexist as they move through time; they are unlikely to be either stable or predictable. Environmental policy must be evolutionary in order to adapt and adjust to such change.

**Castoriadis, Cornelius**. "Heritage and Revolution" in *The Ancients and the Moderns*, Lilly, Reginald (ed), 159-169. Bloomington, Indiana Univ Pr, 1996.

**Castoriadis, Cornelius** 558 **AUTHOR INDEX**

The historical singularity of ancient Greece and of the modern Europe (in the large sense) is to have created *politics*, attempting thus to realize autonomous collectivities formed of autonomous individuals. This is our tradition of judging and choosing not about trivia but about the very forms of institution of society, which has to be defended against both conservatism and contemporary nihilism, eclecticism and "postmodernism".

**Castoriadis, Cornelius**. "The Greek *Polis* and the Creation of Democracy" in *The Ancients and the Moderns,* Lilly, Reginald (ed), 29-58. Bloomington, Indiana Univ Pr, 1996.

Current ideas about ancient Greece, as a model or just another society, are criticized and opposed to the understanding of Greece as a *germ* for us. Recent attempts, in the face of the failure of political ideologies, to extract a solution to our political problems from Kant's *Critique of Judgment* are refuted. The main traits of Athenian democracy are discussed in their opposition to the modern practice or "representative democracy" and their roots in the Greek imaginary of *Chaos/Cosmos* pointed out. The fundamental principle of tragedy and democracy as *self-limitation* is analyzed in the light of Sophocles' *Antigone*.

**Castoriadis, Cornelius**. Democracy as Procedure and Democracy as Regime. *Constellations*, 4(1), 1-18, Ap 97.

The text criticizes the recent tendency (I. Berlin, J. Rawls, J. Habermas) to present democracy as simply a series of *procedural* arrangements, shows that it is self-contradictory and argues in favor of a substantive conception of democracy, including the definition of common goals for a democratic polity.

**Castro Martins, Ana Teresa** and Pequeno, Tarcisio. Proof-Theoretical Considerations about the Logic of Epistemic Inconsistency. *Log Anal*, 36(144), 245-260, S-D 93.

The *Logic of Epistemic Inconsistency* (LEI) provides an interesting example of a paraconsistent formal system from the proof theoretical point of view. Although *cut elimination* theorem for its sequent calculus can only be proved with a restriction, this does not damage its main desirable outcomes. Consistency and subformula property, for instance, are preserved. The motivation for LEI designing, its sequent calculus and most remarkable theorems are presented. The sole unremovable cut-proof pattern is analysed.

**Casulo, José Carlos**. Filosofia da Educaçao e História da Pedagogia. *Rev Port Filosof*, 52(1-4), 233-242, Ja-D 96.

This article's purpose is to study the relation between philosophy of education and history of pedagogy. First, a distinction is made between history, history of scientific thought, history of scientific thought on education and history of pedagogy. Afterwards, the relationship between history of philosophy and history of pedagogy is particularly analyzed. Throughout the example of some cases, becomes justified that history of pedagogy can not be completely researched, understood and taught without history of philosophy. The principal conclusion is that history of pedagogy is scientifically attached and is one of the specifics tasks of philosophy of education.

**Catalán, Miguel**. La paradoja del Taxidermista: Una ilustración negativa del juicio práctico deweyano. *Telos (Spain)*, 5(2), 47-63, D 96.

The article, after a brief introduction, begins with a fictitious dialogue that includes the proposed *taxidermist paradox*. This paradox has been conceived with the intention of pointing out the self-annulation in which the naturalistic fallacy falls when we apply to it to criteria of the pragmatist instrumentalism. In a second section, we describe the dicotomy between evaluative and empirical judgments, dicotomy on which the naturalistic fallacy is based and the last section analyzes the *inquiry* category in Dewey. This category allows us to understand his model of transition between facts and values. (edited)

**Catalano, George D**. Chaos and a New Environmental Ethic: The Land Ethic Revisited. *Between Species*, 11(1-2), 64-73, Wint-Spr 95.

**Catalano, Joseph S**. Crafting Marks into Meanings. *Phil Lit*, 20(1), 47-60, Ap 96.

**Cataño, Gonzalo**. El filósofo Rafael Carrillo. *Ideas Valores*, 3-23, Ag 96.

This paper offers a biographical sketch of Rafael Carrillo, the first director of the *Instituto de Filosofia y Letras* of the national University of Colombia. It expounds for the first time the development of his work and the social and historical context that surrounded his educational and organizational achievements. Special care has been taken to consult firsthand sources that may be useful for future investigation on the development of philosophy in Colombia.

**Cataño, Gonzalo**. Luis E. Nieto Arteta: Crítica del Marxismo y de los Sistemas Filosóficos. *Ideas Valores*, 3-17, Ag 97.

This essay is part of a comprehensive study on the life and work of Luis E. Nieto Arteta (1913-1956), that the author is presently developing. It offers a critical account of Nieto's position concerning Marxism and other systematically oriented philosophical traditions and is supported on research of firsthand sources such as letters, press articles, books and intellectual debates in the 1930s. It provides important material for the investigation of philosophical development in Colombia.

**Catarzi, Marcello**. "Religione e storia in Wilhelm Roscher" in *Lo Storicismo e la Sua Storia: Temi, Problemi, Prospettive,* Cacciatore, Giuseppe (ed), 260-273. Milano, Guerini, 1997.

**Cates, Lynn D**. Berkeley on the Work of the Six Days. *Faith Phil*, 14(1), 82-86, Ja 97.

In the *Three Dialogues*, Hylas challenges Philonous to give a plausible account of the mosaic account of creation in subjective idealistic terms. Strangely, when faced with two alternative strategies, Berkeley chooses the less viable option and explicates the mosaic account of creation in terms of *perceptibility.* I shall show that Berkeley's account of creation trivializes the affair, if it does not fail outright.

**Catonné, Jean-Philipe**. Michel Foucault, lecteur de Platon ou de l'amour du beau garçon a la contemplation du beau en soi. *Daimon Rev Filosof*, 12, 13-23, Ja-Je 96.

Michel Foucault, a reader of Plato or from love of beautiful boys to contemplation of beauty itself. Whoever wants to understand Greek pederasty must discard the notion that the Ancients "tolerated homosexuality". The love for boys is an intricate art of loving. Sexual relationship is lawful and keeps being a problem. Plato remains a basic source to think about the way the Greek subject grows up through the experience he has with someone of his own sex. Foucault shows how Plato's philosophy takes root in this relationship between a mature man and a boy, which represents the most valued form of erotic in the Greek world. Platonism takes as a starting point the difficulties that this common erotic arouses to replace it by a new ethics that can be qualified as philosophical erotic.

**Cattaneo, Gianpiero**. Generalized Rough Sets (Preclusivity Fuzzy-Intuitionistic (BZ) Lattices). *Stud Log*, 58(1), 47-77, 1997.

The rough approximation of any fixed subset of the universe is the pair consisting of the best "open" approximation from the bottom and the best "closed" approximation from the top. The properties of this generalized rough approximation mapping are studied in the context of quasi-BZ lattice structures of "closed-open" ordered pairs (the "algebraic logic" of generalized rough set theory), comparing the results with the standard Pawlak approach. A particular weak form of rough representation is also studied. (edited)

**Cattaneo, Mario A**. Hobbes and Criminal Procedure, Torture and Pre-Trial Detention. *Hobbes Stud*, 9, 32-35, 1996.

This article wishes to underline Hobbes's contribution to criminal procedure. From a general point of view, Hobbes settles the principle of a fair trial. He distinguishes between imprisonment as punishment, and imprisonment as custody of the accused before the trial; in the second case the accused ought not to endure any further suffering, above the necessities of custody. In this idea Hobbes is followed by Pufendorf. Hobbes deals also with the subject of torture; although he does not state clearly its injustice and cruelty, Hobbes denies the validity of torture as testimony and proof, because the tortured man who confesses, does it in order to be delivered from pain. A covenant to accuse oneself and not to resist violence, is against the law of nature and, therefore, void.

**Cattorini, Paolo** and Reichlin, Massimo. Persistent Vegetative State: A Presumption to Treat. *Theor Med*, 18(3), 263-281, S 97.

The article briefly analyzes the concept of a person, arguing that personhood does not coincide with the actual enjoyment of certain intellectual capacities, but is coextensive with the embodiment of a human individual. Since in PVS patients we can observe a human individual functioning as a whole, we must conclude that these patients are still human persons, even if in a condition of extreme impairment. It is then argued that some forms of minimal treatment may not be futile for these patients; they may constitute a form of respect for their human dignity and benefit these patients, even if they are not aware of that. The best policy would be to provide, as a general rule, artificial nutrition and hydration to PVS patients: this treatment could be withdrawn, after a period of observation and reflection by the family and proxies, on the basis of the proxies' objection to the continuation or the patient's advance directives specifically referring to this situation. (edited)

**Caturelli, Alberto**. La providencia y el gobierno del mundo. *Sapientia*, 52(201), 175-194, 1997.

**Cavaciuti, Santino**. "Il tempo dell'interrogare e il tempo dell'invocare" in *Il Concetto di Tempo: Atti del XXXII Congresso Nazionale della Società Filosofica Italiana,* Casertano, Giovanni (ed), 301-306. Napoli, Loffredo, 1997.

**Cavaciuti, Santino**. L'otrepassamento del trascendentale classico quale terza via della metafisica. *G Metaf*, 18(1-2), 271-280, Ja-Ag 96.

**Cavaciuti, Santino**. Teoresi e prassi nella fondazione della metafisica. *G Metaf*, 18(1-2), 141-149, Ja-Ag 96.

**Cavaillé, Jean-Pierre**. Les *Lectures traversières* de Louis Marin. *Rev Phil Fr*, 2, 279-284, Ap-Je 96.

Il s'agit d'une analyse de la notion de représentation dans l'ouvrage de Louis Marin lectures traversières.

**Cavalier, Robert J** and Covey, Preston K and Andersen, David. *A Right to Die?: The Dax Cowart Case.* New York, Routledge, 1996.

As *A Right to Die?* leads users logically through all the aspects of the case, prompting decisions about the patient's future at various stages, and asking for justification, it fosters philosophical exploration of the ethics surrounding the right to die. The CD-ROM presents the story in an accessible way through film footage, stills, and audio testimony of those involved. Supporting this powerful, sometimes disturbing evidence is a wealth of material to help students and educators in medicine, nursing, ethics, or philosophy develop and endorse the arguments both for and against the right to die. This accurately models the real world condition of having to make difficult choices, perhaps without being fully aware of the consequences. (publisher, edited)

**Cavanaugh, Michael**. Global Population Equilibrium: A Model for the Twenty-First Century. *Zygon*, 32(2), 163-174, Je 97.

In his prophetic book *Amythia*, Loyal Rue calls for the construction of bold new myths. Responding to his call in light of scientific arguments for global population equilibrium, this article proposes a model that may function as a surrogate form of myth, one that can motivate our age and future ages. Fortunately, the model is not only powerful but achievable, because policy makers have finally begun to realize how thoroughly the human population impacts on other world dynamics. The problem is reviewed, the relevance of scientific and theological studies bearing on it is shown and the new model is described. Above all, an effort is made to show how global equilibrium can support Rue's twin requirements for the myth he commissions: namely, a foundation in plausible descriptions of reality and a compelling normative status.

**Cavanaugh, Thomas A**. Aquinas's Account of Double Effect. *Thomist*, 61(1), 107-121, Ja 97.

Double-effect reasoning (DER) is attributed to Aquinas *tout court*. Aquinas's account, however, differs from contemporary DER insofar as Thomas considers the ethical status of *risking* an assailant's life while contemporary accounts focus on actions causing harm inevitably. Since one cannot claim to risk the inevitable, and since there is a significant difference between risking harm and causing harm inevitably, Thomas's account does not extend to cases of inevitable harm. Thus, the received understanding of Aquinas's account is flawed and leads to untenable attributions of the direction of intention to Aquinas and to misunderstandings of contemporary DER.

**Cavanaugh, Thomas A**. The *Nazi*! Accusation and Current US Proposals. *Bioethics*, 11(3-4), 291-297, Jl 97.

In contemporary ethical discourse generally, and in discussions concerning the legalization of physician-assisted suicide (PAS) and voluntary active euthanasia (VAE) specifically, recourse is sometimes had to the Nazi accusation. Some disputants charge that such practices are or will become equivalent to the Nazi 'euthanasia' program in which over 73,000 handicapped children and adults were killed without consent. This paper reflects on the circumstances that lead to the use of this charge and offers reasons for putting the Nazi charge aside in contemporary discussions of PAS and VAE. (edited)

**Cavanaugh, Thomas A**. The Intended/Foreseen Distinction's Ethical Relevance. *Phil Papers*, 25(3), 179-188, N 96.

It has been argued that double-effect reasoning (DER) rests on a morally insignificant distinction, the intended/foreseen distinction (i/f distinction). Most DER theorists think that the i/f distinction itself has ethical relevance. I argue that the i/f distinction marks ethically significant differences between malicious and nonmalicious actions as well as between benevolent and nonbenevolent actions. Insofar as it marks these ethically important differences, the i/f distinction has ethical relevance. Thus, DER does not rest on a morally insignificant distinction.

**Cave, Eric M**. The Individual Rationality of Maintaining a Sense of Justice. *Theor Decis*, 41(3), 229-256, N 96.

Let us say that an individual possesses a *principled preference* if she prefers satisfying her preferences without violating the principles of justice governing her community to satisfying her preferences by violating these principles. Although living among possessors of principled preferences benefits individuals, maintaining such a preference is individually costly. Further, individuals can benefit from others possessing principled preferences without themselves possessing one. In this paper, I argue that occupying a choice situation which mirrors key aspects of our own situation, maximizing rationality requires individuals to develop and maintain principled preferences. To establish that maintaining a principled preference is individually rational for the occupants of such a choice situation, I define a range of individual strategies for them, model their choice of individual strategies as a game and argue that this game involves an equilibrium in which all of its participants would choose to develop and maintain a principled preference.

**Cavell, Stanley**. "Notes and Afterthoughts on the Opening of Wittgenstein's *Investigations*" in *The Cambridge Companion to Wittgenstein*, Sluga, Hans (ed), 261-295. Needham Heights, Cambridge, 1996.

**Caygill, Howard**. "The Master and the Magician" in *Jean-Jacques Rousseau and the Sources of the Self*, O'Hagan, Timothy (ed), 16-24. Brookfield, Avebury, 1997.

A study of dissemblance is Rousseau's *Emile on Education*.

**Caygill, Howard**. "The Shared World—Philosophy, Violence, Freedom" in *On Jean-Luc Nancy: The Sense of Philosophy,* Sheppard, Darren (ed), 19-31. New York, Routledge, 1997.

**Caygill, Howard**. "The Topology of Selection: The Limits of Deleuze's Biophilosophy" in *Deleuze and Philosophy: The Difference Engineer,* Ansell Pearson, Keith (ed), 149-162. New York, Routledge, 1997.

**Cela-Conde, Camilo J** and Marty, Gisèle. Mind Architecture and Brain Architecture. *Biol Phil*, 12(3), 327-340, Jl 97.

The use of the computer metaphor has led to the proposal of "mind architecture" (Pylyshyn 1984; Newell 1990) as a model of the organization of the mind. The dualist computational model, however, has, since the earliest days of psychological functionalism, required that the concepts "mind architecture" and "brain architecture" be remote from each other. The development of both connectionism and neurocomputational science, has sought to dispense with this dualism and provide general models of consciousness—a "uniform cognitive architecture"—, which is in general reductionist, but which retains the computer metaphor. This paper examines, in the first place, the concepts of mind architecture and brain architecture, in order to evaluate the syntheses which have recently been offered. (edited)

**Celesia, Gastone G**. Persistent Vegetative State: Clinical and Ethical Issues. *Theor Med*, 18(3), 221-236, S 97.

Coma, vegetative state, lock-in syndrome and akinetic mutism are defined. Vegetative state is a state with no evidence of awareness of self or environment and showing cycles of sleep and wakefulness. PVS is an operational definition including time as a variable. PVS is a vegetative state that has endured or continued for at least one month. PVS can be diagnosed with a reasonable

amount of medical certainty; however, the diagnosis of PVS must be kept separate from the outcome. The patient outcome can be predicted based on etiology and age. Using outcome probabilities and etiology as criteria, patients can be subdivided in 5 groups and reasonable management guidelines can be suggested. Three levels of care can be provided to PVS patients: high technology, supportive and compassionate care. Pragmatic options for the various subgroups of patients are suggested. Management decisions will remain difficult for both the family and the health-care team. The role of the physician in these difficult cases is to share the decision making with the family.

**Ceñal Lorente, Ramón** (trans) and Gómez Caffarena, José (ed) and Kant, Immanuel. *Immanuel Kant: Principios Formales del Mundo Sensible y del Inteligible (Disertación de 1770)*. Madrid, CSIC, 1996.

"Principios formales del mundo sensible" (que hacen *un todo* intuitivo de los múltiples datos de percepción sensorial) son el espacio y el tiempo. Para Kant desde 1770 son la estructura constitutiva (*a priori*) de la sensibilidad humana. "Principio formal del mundo inteligible" le parecía en 1770 ser Dios mismo, clave última de los múltiples procesos causales del cosmos. En los años sucesivos se le problematizó el alcance del conocer intelectual humano: las "formas *a priori*" del entendimiento—las categorías—sólo dan conocimiento "esquematizadas", o sea, adaptadas a la percepción sensorial: el "mundo inteligible" es, pues, en primera instancia función del "sensible". Ahora bien, el sujeto y su vivencia moral abren a una afirmación puramente intelectual (*noumenal*) de la libertad y Dios puede ser postulado en "fe racional" como clave última de unidad teleológica: retorna así un "principio formal del mundo inteligible", aunque en figura más modesta. (publisher)

**Cepeda, Margarita**. "Acerca del igual derecho a ser diferente" in *Liberalismo y Comunitarismo: Derechos Humanos y Democracia,* Monsalve Solórzano, Alfonso (ed), 171-185. 36-46003 València, Alfons el Magnànim, 1996.

**Cepeda, Margarita**. On Equal Rights to Be Different: A Communitarian Criticism of Rawls' Liberalism (Spanish). *Rev Filosof (Venezuela)*, Supp(2-3), 201-214, 1996.

This article formulates a criticism of John Rawls's liberalism, in that it is incapable of taking into account plurality even though this is its fundamental purpose. The article affirms the need for a "communitarian correction" of liberalism since the Rawlist society terminates in an explosion of differences in which justice can only be achieved by overcoming the initial premise of the closed society. The paper criticizes the homogenization which results from the liberal position, a fruit of the fixation on the ideal of autonomy, and the subsequent abstraction of contingencies.

**Cerezo, María**. "Tractatus 2.013: La discusión esencialista acerca del espacio lógico vacío" in *Verdad: lógica, representación y mundo,* Villegas Forero, L, 177-192. Santiago de Compostela, Univ Santiago Comp, 1996.

This paper examines the notion of logical space in *Tractatus* 2.013. I offer an interpretation of this paragraph, pointing out that the possibility of thinking of the space as empty means the possibility of thinking that no state of affairs had been the case. In the second part of the article a discussion of some interpretations of this paragraph is given, paying attention to some difficulties encountered by the essentialist approach in *Tractatus* 2.013 with the aim of determining whether these are genuinely the difficulties and whether the modifications which they propose are necessary. I try to show that their mistake is to regard as true the thought of the logical space as empty, because in this case it would not be possible to think.

**Cerezo, Pedro**. "Experimentos de Nueva España" in *Política y Sociedad en José Ortega y Gasset: En Torno a "Vieja y Nueva Política",* Lopez de la Vieja, Maria Teresa (ed), 101-119. Barcelona, Anthropos, 1997.

**Cerrato, Claudio**. Decidability by Filtrations for Graded Normal Logics (Graded Modalities V). *Stud Log*, 53(1), 61-73, F 94.

We prove decidability for all of the main graded normal logics, by a notion of filtration suitably conceived for this environment.

**Cervellati, Pierluigi**. "L'utopia della nuova città" in *Geofilosofia,* Bonesio, Luisa (ed), 119-136. Sondrio, Lyasis, 1996.

From the foundation of the town—according to the rites and the myths handed down by the *Bible*—to the *refoundation* of contemporary urban aggregations. Renewal instead of expansion. The "new" town does not exist. Europe reproduces the American *sub-urbio* model. Single house towns are being built around old historical cities ("housepolis"). The essay contains alternative proposals.

**Cesareo, Rosa**. "Esistenza e tempo in Heidegger" in *Il Concetto di Tempo: Atti del XXXII Congresso Nazionale della Società Filosofica Italiana,* Casertano, Giovanni (ed), 237-242. Napoli, Loffredo, 1997.

**Cesati, Marco**. Sparse Parameterized Problems. *Annals Pure Applied Log*, 82(1), 1-15, N 96.

Sparse languages play an important role in classical structural complexity theory. In this paper we introduce a natural definition of *sparse* problems for parameterized complexity theory. We prove an analog of Mahaney's theorem: there is no sparse parameterized problem which is hard for the $t$th level of the W hierarchy, unless the W hierarchy itself collapses up to level $t$. The main result is proved for the most general form of parametric many: reducibility, where the parameter functions are not assumed to be recursive. This provides one of the few instances in parameterized complexity theory of a full analog of a major classical theorem. The proof involves not only the standard technique of left sets, but also substantial circuit combinatorics to deal with the problem of small weft, and a diagonalization to cope with potentially nonrecursive parallel functions. The latter techniques are potentially of interest for further explorations of parameterized complexity analogs of classical structural results.

**Chabot, Marc**. Nous sommes tous des suicidés. *Horiz Phil*, 7(1), 1-15, Fall 96.

**Chadwick, Ruth**. "The Philosophy of the Right to Know and the Right not to Know" in *The Right to Know and the Right not to Know,* Chadwick, Ruth (ed), 13-22. Brookfield, Avebury, 1997.

Medical ethics has been to a considerable extent concerned with the right of patients to have access to information so that they can make informed decisions: hence the primacy of the principle of autonomy. The possible applications and implications of genetic information, however, have led to a recognition that information may be a burden rather than a help in some cases undermining autonomy. Hence, the argument for a right not to know.

**Chadwick, Ruth** and Levitt, Mairi. "Mass Media and Public Discussion in Bioethics" in *The Right to Know and the Right not to Know,* Chadwick, Ruth (ed), 79-86. Brookfield, Avebury, 1997.

This paper is based on a manual search of coverage of genetic screening in the UK, mainly using the quality press, from 1982 to 1996. New techniques were found to be reported uncritically, not because of journalistic simplifications but because the scientific and medical professions are used as the source of information. Once specific programmes are underway there is a gradual shift to more critical coverage as patients' experiences are incorporated and 'simple tests' turn out to be more complicated in practice than was predicted. It is in the negative coverage that the ethical issues begin to be discussed.

**Chadwick, Ruth** (ed) and Levitt, Mairi (ed) and Shickle, Darren (ed). *The Right to Know and the Right not to Know.* Brookfield, Avebury, 1997.

Developments in genetics raise questions about the ability of traditional principles of biomedical ethics to deal with the complexity of the issues. Of central importance is the debate about the right to know versus the right not to know genetic information. Claims to a right *not* to know challenge the view that access to information is of value in facilitating choice and self-determination. This multidisciplinary collection of essays examines the issues from the perspectives of philosophy, sociology, history, law and public health. The volume goes beyond an examination of individual rights in considering the right of *society* not to know.

**Chaerle, Dries** and Van de Putte, André. Liberalism and Culture: Will Kymlicka on Multicultural Citizenship (in Dutch). *Tijdschr Filosof*, 59(2), 215-252, Je 97.

This study examines Will Kymlicka's liberal defense of minority rights. The starting point of his argument is provided by a particular conception of individual freedom, which stresses the need for a context of choice in which it can be exercised. This context of choice is conceived of as a societal culture, i.e., as "an intergenerational community, more or less institutionally complete, occupying a given territory or homeland, sharing a distinct language and history". As far as societal-cultural membership is constitutive for the freedom and identity of the individuals, it can be considered as a Rawlsian primary good. Confronted with the fact of multinational and polyethnic States, this consideration involves the need for an equal distribution and protection of this good for all (individuals of the) composing national or ethnic minorities. (edited)

**Chagrov, Alexander** and Zakharyashchev, Michael. Modal Companions of Intermediate Propositional Logics. *Stud Log*, 51(1), 49-82, 1992.

This paper is a survey of results concerning embeddings of intuitionistic propositional logic and its extensions into various classical modal systems.

**Chajda, Ivan** and Graczynska, Ewa. Jónsson's Lemma for Regular and Nilpotent Shifts of Pseudovarieties. *Bull Sec Log*, 26(2), 85-93, Je 97.

This is an abstract of the lecture proposed for the 54th Workshop on General Algebra at the University of Klagenfurt, Austria, May 29 - June 1, 1997. We deal with *varieties* and *pseudovarieties* of universal algebras, in the sense of B. Birkhoff and S. Eilenberg, i.e., classes of (finite) algebras closed under the formation of subalgebras, homomorphic images and (finite) direct products. Our aim is to present a variation on Jónsson's Lemma for normal and regular shifts of varieties (pseudovarieties).

**Chakraborty, Alpana**. A Critical Analysis of John Locke's Criterion of Personal Identity. *Indian Phil Quart*, 23(3-4), 349-361, Jl-O 96.

In his "Essay Concerning Human Understanding" Locke endeavors to find out answers to such questions as 'what is person?' and 'what are the criteria of determining personal identity?' Locke identifies 'person' with the self which is consciousness and further states that the criteria of personal identity is dependent on 'remembering' or on the 'same consciousness' or on the 'unity of consciousness'. Determination of 'person' and 'personal identity' is necessary for all the deeds of a person would be accountable on the *Great Day*. Some philosophers reject the thesis by stating that it fails to provide a definition of 'person' and the criteria of determining 'personal identity'. They say that Locke's thesis is full of confusions and is irreparably wrong.

**Chalmers, David J**. Does a Rock Implement Every Finite-State Automation?. *Synthese*, 108(3), 309-333, S 96.

Hilary Putnam has argued that computational functionalism cannot serve as a foundation for the study of the mind, as every ordinary open physical system implements every finite-state automation. I argue that Putnam's argument fails, but that it points out the need for a better understanding of the bridge between the theory of computation and the theory of physical systems: the relation of implementation. It also raises questions about the class of automata that can serve as a basis for understanding the mind. I develop an account of implementation, linked to an appropriate class of automata, such that the requirement that a system implement a given automation places a very strong constraint on the system. This clears the way for computation to play a central role in the analysis of mind.

**Chalmers, David J**. Moving Forward on the Problem of Consciousness. *J Consciousness Stud*, 4(1), 3-46, 1997.

This paper is a response to the twenty-six commentaries on my paper, "Facing Up to the Problem of Consciousness." First, I respond to deflationary critiques, including those that argue that there is no "hard" problem of consciousness or that it can be accommodated within a materialist framework. Second, I respond to nonreductive critiques, including those that argue that the problems of consciousness are harder than I have suggested, or that my framework for addressing them is flawed. Third, I address positive proposals for addressing the problem of consciousness, including those based in neuroscience and cognitive science, phenomenology, physics, and fundamental psychophysical theories.

**Chamberlain, Paul**. *Can We Be Good without God?: A Conversation about Truth, Morality, Culture & A Few Other Things That Matter.* Downers Grove, InterVarsity Pr, 1996.

Our culture is beset by a host of vexing ethical questions. But where do we begin in trying to answer them? Are there any foundational moral principles to guide our discussion? If so, where do they come from? Christians say such principles come from God. But can there be real right and wrong without God? Can we, in fact, be *good* without God? Just such questions are faced by a cast of five, mysteriously invited to the home of a troubled judge. Ted (a Christian) joins Graham (an atheist), Francine (a moral relativist), William (an evolutionist) and Ian (a secular humanist) in a fascinating discussion of right and wrong, truth and conduct in this imaginative drama. Wit and wisdom combine as argument takes center stage and readers are invited to think through these issues for themselves. (publisher)

**Champlin, T S**. "To Mental Illness via a Rhyme for the Eye" in *Verstehen and Humane Understanding,* O'Hear, Anthony (ed), 165-189. New York, Cambridge Univ Pr, 1996.

How are mental and physical illness related? Several answers are examined and rejected, including the suggestion that 'mental illness' is a metaphor. It is argued that mental illness is related to physical illness in the same sort of way that a rhyme for the eye is related to a rhyme for the ear. Rhymes for the eye do not rhyme, i.e., are not rhymes for the ear; and those who are suffering from a mental illness are not ill, i.e., are not physically ill.

**Chanda, Jacqueline**. A Theoretical Basis for Non-Western Art History Instruction. *J Aes Educ*, 27(3), 73-84, Fall 93.

**Chandra, Suresh**. An Illusive Historiography of the View that the World is *Maya*: Professor Daya Krishna on the Historiography of Vedanta. *J Indian Counc Phil Res*, 14(2), 123-133, Ja-Ap 97.

**Chang, Hasok**. On the Applicability of the Quantum Measurement Formalism. *Erkenntnis*, 46(2), 143-163, Mr 97.

Customary discussions of quantum measurements are unrealistic, in the sense that they do not reflect what happens in most actual measurements even under ideal circumstances. Even theories of measurement which discard the projection postulate tend to retain two unrealistic assumptions of the von Neumann theory: that a measurement consists of a single physical interaction, and that the topic of every measurement is information wholly contained in the quantum state of the object of measurement. I suggest that these unrealistic assumptions originate from an overly literal interpretation of the operator formalism of quantum mechanics. I also suggest, following Park, that some issues can be clarified by distinguishing the sense of the term "measurement" occurring in the quantum-mechanical operator formalism, and the sense of "measurement" that refers to actual processes of gaining information about the physical world.

**Chang, Kimberly A**. Culture, Power and the Social Construction of Morality: Moral Voices of Chinese Students. *J Moral Educ*, 25(2), 141-157, Je 96.

This study challenges Carol Gilligan's gendered interpretation of moral voice of examining the ways in which moral problems and responses were socially constructed in the contexts of power relations based not on gender, but culture. (edited)

**Chang, Kuo-Chin** and Hong, Tzung-Pei and Tseng, Shian-Shyong. Machine Learning by Imitating Human Learning. *Mind Mach*, 6(2), 203-228, My 96.

Learning general concepts in imperfect environments is difficult since training instances often include noisy data, inconclusive data, incomplete data, unknown attributes, unknown attribute values and other barriers to effective learning. It is well-known that people can learn effectively in imperfect environments and can manage to process very large amounts of data. Imitating human learning behavior, therefore, provides a useful model for machine learning in real-world applications. This paper proposes a new, more effective way to represent imperfect training instances and rules and based on the new representation, a Human-Like Learning (HULL) algorithm for incrementally learning concepts well in imperfect training environments. Several examples are given to make the algorithm clearer. Finally, experimental results are presented that show the proposed learning algorithm works well in imperfect learning environments

**Changizi, Mark**. Function Identification from Noisy Data with Recursive Error Bounds. *Erkenntnis*, 45(1), 91-102, Jl 96.

New success criteria of inductive inference in computational learning theory are introduced which model learning total (not necessarily recursive) functions with (possibly everywhere) imprecise theories from (possibly always) inaccurate data. It is proved that for any level of error allowable by the new success criteria, there exists a class "theta" of recursive functions such that not all—function is an element of "theta"—are identifiable via the criterion at that level of error. Also,

AUTHOR INDEX 561 Chen, Xiang

necessary and sufficient conditions on the error level are given for when more classes of functions may be identified. (edited)

**Chappell, Tim**. "In Defence of Speciesism" in *Human Lives: Critical Essays on Consequentialist Bioethics,* Oderberg, David S (ed), 96-108. New York, Macmillan, 1997.

The thesis is defended that differences of species can, do and should provide reason to ground major differences in moral significance. Peter Singer's sentence criterion of moral significance is criticized and instead the concept of flourishing is defended. But flourishing is a property of kinds, or species, of thing. Although pain and pleasure are commensurable across individuals, flourishing is not; hence no consequentialist account of flourishing and hence of moral significance, is possible. The unique role of man as regulator of the natural world is defended, as is his consequent right and duty sometimes to discriminate between species, including between man and other animals.

**Chappell, Tim**. Rationally Deciding What To Believe. *Relig Stud*, 33(1), 105-113, Mr 97.

"Rationally Deciding what to Believe" is a critical notice of Terence Penelhum's *Reason and Religious Faith* (Westview Press 1996). It points out that if we see the world as evidentially ambiguous between different religions, then we have to say which religions it is *not* ambiguous between and why not. Penelhum wants to say that the world is ambiguous between e.g., Christianity and Islam, but not between those views and the view that we should worship frogs; why these distinctions? I suggest that Penelhum's answer to this question faces a dilemma, because it rests on a mistaken account of the relation between the will and belief. *Pace* Penelhum, we can choose our beliefs in at least three intellectually respectable ways. It is this possibility and not the presence of ambiguity in the evidence, which makes for the diversity of faiths in the world.

**Chappell, Tim D J**. *The Plato Reader.* Edinburgh, Edinburgh Univ Pr, 1996.

This is the only available single-volume *Plato Reader*—a collection of 46 key readings from the works of Plato in a completely new translation by Dr. Tim Chappell of the University of East Anglia. These are thematically arranged under seven headings: The Death of Socrates; The Search for a Socratic Ethics; Justice and Pleasure; God and the Soul; Knowledge and the Forms; and Plato on Writing Philosophy. All central aspects of philosophy as discussed by Plato are covered and the text is helpfully annotated and cross-referenced, with guides for further reading. (publisher, edited)

**Chappell, Vere**. Descartes's Ontology. *Topoi*, 16(2), 111-127, S 97.

In an often-neglected passage of the *Principles* (Sections 48-70 of Part I), Descartes sketches a comprehensive ontological theory, including features he makes explicit nowhere else in his writings. I first lay out Descartes's theory in some detail, clarifying, interpreting and commenting as I go. I then focus on his conceptualistic account of universals and compare it with the treatment of mathematical objects in the *Fifth Meditation.* I argue that Descartes was not a Platonic realist in the *Meditations,* as Kenny has alleged and that there is no conflict between what he says there and the explicit conceptualism of the *Principles*. In defending my position I criticize claims made by Gewirth and Schmaltz about the status of eternal truths; but I endorse and extend views expressed by Bennett on Descartes's understanding of modality.

**Chapuis, Olivier**. All Free Metabelian Groups. *J Sym Log*, 62(1), 159-174, Mr 97.

**Charum, Jorge** (ed) and Albis, Víctor S (ed) and Sánchez, Clara Helena (& others). *Memorias Del Seminario En Conmemoración De Los 400 Anos Del Nacimiento De René Descartes.* Sankt Augustin, Academia, 1997.

Con este Seminario en commemoración de los 400 años del nacimiento de René Descartes promovido y organizado conjuntamente por la *Academia Colombiana de Ciencias* y la *Universidad Nacional de Colombia*, se busca relevar la obra de uno de los más grandes creadores del pensamiento científico moderno. (edited)

**Chater, Nick** and Oaksford, Mike. Deontic Reasoning, Modules and Innateness: A Second Look. *Mind Lang*, 11(2), 191-202, Je 96.

Cummins (this issue) puts the case for an innate module for deontic reasoning. We argue that this case is not persuasive. First, we claim that Cummins's evolutionary arguments are neutral regarding whether deontic reasoning is learned or innate. Second, we argue that task differences between deontic and indicative reasoning explain many of the phenomena that Cummins takes as evidence for a deontic module. Third, we argue against the suggestion that deontic reasoning is superior to indicative reasoning, either in adults or children. Finally, we reevaluate Cummins's interpretation of differences in children's performance on deontic and indicative versions of Wason's selection task.

**Chattopadhyay, Gauriprasad**. Does Bentham Commit the Naturalistic Fallacy?. *Darshana Int*, 36(4/144), 42-45, O 96.

**Chauhan, Brij Rai**. "Possibilities and Limitations of Indian Culture Concerning the Foundation of Peace" in *Kreativer Friede durch Begegnung der Weltkulturen,* Beck, Heinrich (ed), 277-292. New York, Lang, 1995.

Excessive reliance on magic and religion in the conduct of daily life, organized in small communities and castes, and centuries of foreign rule coupled with a colonial and capitalistic expansion of the European powers have acted as major limiting factors for creative interaction of India with other continents. The struggle for freedom of India in the 19th and 20th centuries accompanied by a renaissance explored rationality within the Indian thought, galvanized people into a mass movement that came to terms with rationality and technological advancements of Europe retaining its traditional spirituality and affinity with nature and is now prepared for entering the creative dialogue.

**Chauí, Marilena**. A Idéia de Parte da Natureza em Espinosa. *Discurso,* 24, 57-127, 1994.

Desde o século XVII, cria-se uma tradiçao interpretativa da obra de Espinosa afirmando a irrealidade dos seres finitos, à maneira dos panteísmos orientais. Tomando as versoes antigas e recentes do suposto orientalismo espinosano, procuramos apontar seus equívocos. Para isto, tomamos as inovaçoes de Espinosa na definiçao das idéias de *substância* e *modo* e o papel central da idéia de *parte de Natureza* para a compreensao dos modos finitos como realidades individuais e suas relaçoes com a substância infinita.

**Chauí, Marilena**. A Plebe e o Vulgo no *Tractatus Politicus. Cad Hist Filosof Cie*, 5(1-2), 15-43, Ja-D 95.

Spinoza criticizes the Dutch republican self-image by criticizing Titus Livius's *topos* on the *plebs* as a threatening animal. Such an analysis implies Spinoza's redefining the political agent and experience as political experience which gives to the *Tractatus Politicus* its originality.

**Chauí, Marilena**. Immanence and Light: Spinoza, Vermeer and Rembrandt (in Portuguese). *Discurso*, 26, 113-130, 1996.

Traditionally, Spinoza's philosophy is interpreted as an acosmism in which the intellectual course of going from God to God, the only reality. We propose to take the Spinozian concept of immanence as the movement by which the infinite knows itself through the finite intellect and the latter realizes itself through divine thought. We consider that an indispensable reference to understanding the refraction of the divine substance in infinite finite intellects and its reflection in them to be Kepler's optics and the Keplerian eye, as practiced in Dutch painting of the seventeenth century.

**Chaves-Tannús, Marcio**. Costumes e Caracteres na "Ética" de Pedro Abelardo. *Educ Filosof*, 10(19), 175-179, Ja-Je 96.

Frente à impossibilidade de transpor, com um único vocábulo, ambos os significados da palavra latina "mores", os tradutores da "Ética" que consultei optaram todos por uma soluçao que, embora adequada à manutençao da coerência interna formal do texto e condizente com uma antiga tradiçao filosófica, é insuficiente para a exata reproduçao do conteúdo original.

**Checkland, David**. Individualism, Subjectivism, Democracy, and "Helping" Professions. *Ethics Behavior,* 6(4), 337-343, 1996.

This article discusses the suggestion, expressed in the three preceding articles in this issue of *Ethics & Behavior,* that ethics as practiced in the helping professions requires greater organizational democratization. The relevance to this proposal of both a cognitive conception of democracy and an account of the nature of values that establishes their objectivity is also discussed.

**Chellas, Brian F**. Time and Modality in the Logic of Agency. *Stud Log,* 51(3-4), 485-517, 1992.

Recent theories of agency (*sees to it that*) of Nuel Belnap and Michael Perloff are examined, particularly in the context of an early proposal of the author.

**Chen, Al Y S** and Sawyers, Roby B and Williams, Paul F. Reinforcing Ethical Decision Making Through Corporate Culture. *J Bus Ethics*, 16(8), 855-865, Je 97.

Behaving ethically depends on the ability to recognize that ethical issues exist, to see from an ethical point of view. This ability to see and respond ethically may be related more to attributes of corporate culture than to attributes of individual employees. Efforts to increase ethical standards and decrease pressure to behave unethically should, therefore, concentrate on the organization and its culture. The purpose of this paper is to discuss how total quality (TQ) techniques can facilitate the development of a cooperative corporate culture that promotes and encourages ethical behavior throughout an organization.

**Chen, Henry C K** and Allmon, Dean E and Pritchett, Thomas K (& others). A Multicultural Examination of Business Ethics Perceptions. *J Bus Ethics*, 16(2), 183-188, F 97.

This study provides an evaluation of ethical business perception of business students from three countries: Australia, Taiwan and the United States. Although statistically significant differences do exist there is significant agreement with the way students perceive ethical/unethical practices in business. The findings of this paper indicate a universality of business ethical perceptions.

**Chen, Jianer** and Cai, Liming and Downey, Rodney G (& others). Advice Classes of Parameterized Tractability. *Annals Pure Applied Log*, 84(1), 119-138, Mr 97.

Many natural computational problems have input consisting of two or more parts, one of which may be considered a *parameter.* For example, there are many problems for which the input consists of a graph and a positive integer. A number of results are presented concerning parameterized problems that can be solved (uniformly with respect to the parameter) in complexity classes below *P,* given a single word of advice for each parameter value. Different ways in which the word of advice can be employed are considered, and it is shown that the class *FPT* of *tractable* parameterized problems (the parameterized analog of *P*) has interesting and natural internal structure.

**Chen, Xiang** and Andersen, Hanne and Barker, Peter. Kuhn's Mature Philosophy of Science and Cognitive Psychology. *Phil Psych*, 9(3), 347-363, S 96.

Drawing on the results of modern psychology and cognitive science we suggest that the traditional theory of concepts is no longer tenable and that the alternative account proposed by Kuhn may now be seen to have independent empirical support quite apart from its success as part of an account of scientific change. We suggest that these mechanisms can also be understood as special cases of general cognitive structures revealed by cognitive science. Against this background, incommensurability is not an insurmountable obstacle to accepting Kuhn's position, as many philosophers of science still believe. Rather it becomes a natural consequence of cognitive structures that appear in all human beings.

**Chen, Xun Wu**. Conflict and Constellation: The New Trend of Value Development in China. *J Value Inq*, 31(1), 97-108, Mr 97.

**Chen, Yuan-Fang**. Japanese Death Factories and the American Cover-Up. *Cambridge Quart Healthcare Ethics*, 6(2), 240-242, Spr 97.

**Cheneval, Francis**. La réception de la "Monarchie" de Dante ou Les métamorphoses d'une oeuvre philosophique. *Vivarium*, 34(2), 254-267, N 96.

The article offers a reflection on the reception of philosophical works. It analyzes very different interpretations of Dante's *Monarchy* by John Falkenberg, Antonio Roselli, Pier Paolo Vergerio and Matthias Flacius Illyricus and thereby illustrates the contextual nature of philosophical works and of there interpretations. Against the hermeneutical position (e.g., Gadamer), a moderate historical objectivism is maintained with regard to the method that enables us to reestablish the contextual facts and to reach an approximate idea of the original intention of the author and of the relevance of the work in its time.

**Cheney, Jim**. Naturalizing the Problem of Evil. *Environ Ethics*, 19(3), 299-313, Fall 97.

I place my analysis and naturalization of the problem of evil in relation to (1) Holmes Rolston's views on disvalues in nature and (2) the challenge posed to theology by environmental philosophy in the work of Frederick Ferré. In the analysis of the problem of evil that follows my discussion of Rolston and Ferré, I first discuss the transformative power for the religious believer of reflection on the problem of evil, using the biblical Job as a case study. I point out difficulties with Job's particular resolution of the problem of evil and suggest that these difficulties can be satisfactorily addressed by naturalizing spirituality.

**Cheng, Chung-ying**. From Self-Cultivation to Philosophical Counseling: An Introduction. *J Chin Phil*, 23(3), 245-257, S 96.

**Cheng, Chung-ying**. On a Comprehensive Theory of *Xing* (Naturality) in Song-Ming Neo-Confucian Philosophy: A Critical and Integrative Development. *Phil East West*, 47(1), 33-46, Ja 97.

The question of *xing* has received much attention in the revival of neo-Confucian philosophy (called Contemporary Neo-Confucianism) in present-day Taiwan, Hong Kong, and China and among scholars of Chinese philosophy in the United States. It also has much to do with a critical consciousness of both the difference and the affinity between the Chinese philosophy of man and morality and the contemporary Western philosophy of human existence and moral virtues. The study of this has great meaning for the development of a global onto-ethics and an onto-ethics of the future of humankind.

**Cheng, Chung-ying**. Philosophical Significance of Gongsun Long: A New Interpretation of Theory of *Zhi* as Meaning and Reference. *J Chin Phil*, 24(2), 139-177, Je 97.

In this article I consider the complete writings of Gongsun Long as included in the present day book named *Gongsun Long*: I make a critical examinations of all Gongsun Long's arguments and come to a new interpretation of his theory of *Zhi* as meaning and reference in light of contemporary philosophy of logic and language. This study goes far beyond any earlier works on Gongsun Long.

**Cheng, Kam-Yuen**. Davidson's Action Theory and Epiphenomenalism. *J Phil Res*, 22, 181-195, Ap 97.

This paper is to examine Davidson's action theory and to contend that his theory treats mental properties as epiphenomenal. In the first half, I explicate Davidson's theory, which includes his anomalous monism and the 'weak' psychophysical supervenience thesis. In the second half, I discuss the charges, made by Ernest Sosa and Lynne Baker, that Davidson's theory treats the mental as epiphenomenal. They both argue that even a property 'strongly' supervenient on physical properties is still causally inert. I argue that even if Davidson succeeds in defending himself from their charges, the mental, on Davidson's account is still causally inert.

**Cherry, Christopher**. What Matters About Memory. *Philosophy*, 71(278), 541-552, O 96.

**Cherry, Mark J**. Bioethics and the Construction of Medical Reality. *J Med Phil*, 21(4), 357-373, Ag 96.

Physicians and patients participate in the creation of medical social reality. Medicine casts patients and physicians into nests of social expectations and treatment goals. I argue that medical judgment is not simply descriptive, or evaluative, but performative. Describing a condition, such as addiction, as a disease for medical treatment, or an activity, such as transplantation, as a licit medical activity advances moral and conceptual judgments that fashion licit and illicit health care practices. A unique set of contentful norms is in principle unavailable. Contentful accounts of these concepts are only found within particular moral communities, wherein particular moral frameworks fashion licit health care, social expectations and the construct of a particular medical reality.

**Cherry, Mark J**. Suffering Strangers: An Historical, Metaphysical, and Epistemological Non-Ecumenical Interchange. *Christian Bioethics*, 2(2), 253-266, Ag 96.

To comprehend pain, disease and suffering as being meaningful—beyond the firing of synapses, the collapse of human abilities, and the mere end of life—requires a context in which to evaluate essential connotations, as well as to place and integrate understandings. If pain and suffering are to have enduring significance, they must be situated within a nest of ontological background assumptions, standards of inquiry, and epistemological foundations. Where secular bioethics fails to give deep meaning of suffering endorsed by the various Christian religions as conceptualized through the different metaphysical, epistemological, and sociological assumptions of each religion.

**Cheyne, Colin**. Getting in Touch with Numbers: Intuition and Mathematical Platonism. *Phil Phenomenol Res*, 57(1), 111-125, Mr 97.

Mathematics is about numbers, sets, functions, etc. and according to one prominent view, these are abstract entities lacking causal powers and spatio-temporal location. If this is so, then it is a puzzle how we come to have knowledge of such remote entities. One suggestion is intuition. But 'intuition' covers a range of notions. This paper identifies and examines those varieties of intuition which are most likely to play a role in the acquisition of our mathematical knowledge, and argues that none of them, singly or in combination, can plausibly account for knowledge of abstract entities.

**Cheyne, Colin** and Pigden, Charles R. Pythagorean Powers or A Challenge to Platonism. *Austl J Phil*, 74(4), 639-645, D 96.

Platonism contends that there are mathematical objects—sets and numbers—which lack locations and causal powers. The chief argument for such objects is that they are indispensable to science. Field replies by trying to construct a 'science without numbers', but so far he has not managed to exercise numbers from relativistic physics. But whether Field's project succeeds or fails, Platonism is in trouble. If Field succeeds, numbers can be dispensed with. If he fails, this shows that numbers play some part in the causal process and hence that they are possessed of causal powers. Platonism loses either way.

**Chiereghin, Franco**. "Essere E Soggettività: Parmenide e Hegel" in *Soggetto E Verità: La questione dell'uomo nella filosofia contemporanea*, Fagiuoli, Ettore, 13-27. 20136 Milano, Mimesis, 1996.

Hegel places at the beginning of his "logik" the absolutely indeterminate being, the conception of which he attributes to Parmenides, to find later the "being" at the apex of the logical process as something that in the meanwhile has become the richest, the most concrete and the most subjective content. The "being" that appears at the apex of Hegel's logic represents the being of the origins much more than it was in Hegel's mind or awareness. Richness, concreteness and subjectivity (not in the "subjectivistic" meaning but meant as the capacity of generating the wholeness of the possible forms) are in fact the features standing out the meaningfulness of the images and the power of thought to be found in Parmenides's word.

**Chiesa, Curzio**. L'épistémologie génétique dans la philosophie ancienne. *Rev Theol Phil*, 129(1), 31-49, 1997.

One of the crucial theses of the theory of empirical knowledge is that concepts have their origin in sensory perception. By examining certain aspects of empiricism in ancient philosophy, particularly in Aristotle and the empirical physicians, this study attempts to show that in these authors, contrary to all appearances, there is no empirical genesis of rational knowledge manifesting itself in experience, as Kant would say, without coming from experience.

**Chiesa, Curzio**. Wittgenstein et la fin du psychologisme. *Rev Phil Fr*, 2, 183-194, Ap-Je 97.

**Child, William**. Crane on Mental Causation. *Proc Aris Soc*, 97, 97-102, 1997.

Tim Crane's argument that psychological constitution theories are unmotivated ("The Mental Causation Debate", *Aristotelian Society Supplementary Volume* 1995) is considered. The argument that the mental must be constituted by the physical, since effects are not overdetermined by their mental and physical causes, is defended against Crane's claim that it cannot coherently be combined with physicalist accounts of the causal relevance of mental properties. Crane's view that mental and physical causes are related nomologically but not by constitution is rejected because, unlike the constitution view, it offers no explanation of why mental and physical properties are related as they are.

**Child, William**. Solipsism and First Person/Third Person Asymmetries. *Euro J Phil*, 4(2), 137-154, Ag 96.

The paper makes two suggestions within a realist reading of the early Wittgenstein's discussion of solipsism. First, it is suggested that we should see the *Tractatus*, like the *Blue Book*, as reflecting on the asymmetry between first-person and third-person points of view; one can be led to make solipsistic claims in trying to articulate what is specially distinctive of one's own first-person viewpoint. Second, a reading is offered of the early Wittgenstein's remarks about ethics, the will and death, elucidating them in terms of the same contrast between first-person and third-person points of view.

**Childs, Brian H**. The Last Chapter of the Book: Who Is the Author? Christian Reflections on Assisted Suicide. *J Med Human*, 18(1), 21-28, Spr 97.

In this paper the author argues that a narrative approach to understanding assisted suicide has been compromised by the notion that all narratives must be both coherent and unified. He asks what we are to do with those narratives that cannot seem to cohere or be other than full of disunity? Is suicide the only way to make meaning out of suffering? He then proposes that the narrative found in the *Gospel of Mark* leads Christians to a life in hope and compassion in spite of apparent incoherence and disunity and threats of abandonment and suffering.

**Childs, James M**. Business in an Age of Downsizing. *Bus Ethics Quart*, 7(2), 123-131, Mr 97.

Fundamental theological and ethical themes of Luther's thought and tradition provide a basis for appreciating both the role of business in God's providential design and the importance of occupation for living out one's Christian vocation. These same insights establish the ethical basis for a critical appraisal of the current practice of downsizing and its negative impact on the quality of individual lives and whole communities. While Lutheran ethics is realistic about the ambiguities of life, it is also an ethic of compassionate love seeking justice in the world of business as in all of life.

**Childs, Zena**. Ordinary Morality and the Pursuit of the Good. *J Value Inq*, 31(2), 213-219, Je 97.

AUTHOR INDEX 563 Christopher, Myra J

Shelly Kagan's arguments against ordinary morality rely upon the view that *ordinary morality* accepts a *pro tanto* reason to promote the good. I argue that ordinary morality does not accept such a reason. This is because in situations where lives are at stake, promotion of the good has no weight whatsoever in the judgements of ordinary morality. If it is correct that ordinary morality does not accept a *pro tanto* reason to promote the good, then ordinary morality is not vulnerable to Kagan's arguments against it.

**Chiles, Robert E**. The Philosophy They Bring to Class: Companion Student Papers in PHL 101. *Teach Phil*, 20(1), 61-69, Mr 97.

This project for beginning students is aimed to introduce them to philosophy by focusing on their own "philosophical" notions. The first week students wrote brief responses to my list of "provocative" statements on major philosophical issues. (e.g., "The freedom to choose is largely an illusion...") Not worrying about being "correct," they were to draw on and identify the sources of the beliefs they brought to class. Small group discussion helped formulate their responses. In a second paper at the end of the term, using what they had learned in class, they wrote critiques of their first paper and its unsophisticated "personal philosophy".

**Chinn, Clark A** and Brewer, William F. Mental Models in Data Interpretation. *Proc Phil Sci Ass*, 3(Suppl), S211-S219, 1996.

This paper presents a cognitive account of the process of evaluating scientific data. Our account assumes that when individuals evaluate data, they construct a mental model of a data-interpretation package, in which the data and theoretical interpretations of the data are integrated. We propose that individuals attempt to discount data by seeking alternative explanations for events within the mental model; data-interpretation packages are accepted when the individual cannot find alternative accounts for these events. Our analysis indicates that there are many levels at which data-interpretation packages can be accepted or denied.

**Chiodi, Giulio M**. L'allegoria sociale. *Iride*, 10(20), 53-67, Ap 97.

**Chisholm, Roderick M** and Zimmerman, Dean W. On the Logic of Intentional Help: Some Metaphysical Questions. *Faith Phil*, 13(3), 402-404, Jl 96.

In this note, we explore certain aspects of "the logic of helping", offer an account of the metaphysics of helping God, and suggest a way in which God's help differs from human help.

**Chisholm, Roderick M** and Zimmerman, Dean W. Theology and Tense. *Nous*, 31(2), 262-265, Je 97.

Should philosophers who "take tense seriously" also "take tenselessness seriously"? Are there truths expressible by tenseless statements that resist all paraphrase into a tensed idiom? Neither the tenselessness of statements made in the "historical present", nor that of the "eternal verities", justifies taking tenselessness seriously. And there is no philosophical motivation for saying that the Deity does not "exist in time", apart from a mistake about the nature of times.

**Chitty, Andrew**. First Person Plural Ontology and Praxis. *Proc Aris Soc*, 97, 81-96, 1997.

The paper asks the 'first person plural ontological question': how should we characterize the basic kind of being to which we human beings (and any beings of other species who may be of the same basic kind) belong? It argues against two ways of rejecting this question, one from a 'scientific naturalist' position and the other from a 'postmodern' one. It then investigates a 'productionist' answer to the question, suggested by the early Marx: this is that we belong to that kind whose members belong to it by virtue of engaging in relations of producing-for and using-the-product-of other members of the same kind. (edited)

**Chmielewski, Philip J**. Catholic Social Ethics in a Pluralist Age. *Gregorianum*, 78(1), 95-137, 1997.

L'article lit la pensée de Mausbach et Nell-Breuning de façon constructive de façon à explorer la base théologique d'une éthique sociale productive. La transcendance divine est continuellement engagée dans l'histoire des hommes; par ailleurs, le développement et l'engagement des hommes dans l'histoire glorifient Dieu. Le discernement des valeurs et la doctrine de la loi naturelle rendent possible l'oeuvre de la justice. L'amour spécifie la justice sociale et libère; il établit ainsi un cadre civique. La révérence vis-à-vis de l'altérité divine fonde la tolérance active qui est l'expression obligée de l'amour en vue de la collaboration qui est nécessaire aujourd'hui. Cette éthique sociale fondée sur des catégories théologiques contribue à la mission chrétienne dans des sociétés complexes et turbulentes. (edited)

**Cholak, P** and Knight, J F and Ash, C J. Permitting, Forcing, and Copying of a given Recursive Relation. *Annals Pure Applied Log*, 86(3), 219-236, Jl 97.

**Chomsky, Noam**. Language and Problems of Knowledge. *Teorema*, 16(2), 5-33, 1997.

Every serious approach to the study of language departs from common sense usage, replacing it by some technical concept. The general practice has been to define "language" as extensional and externalized (E-language). However, such a concept of language and its variants raises numerous problems and it is argued in this paper the E-language is an artifact with no status in a theory of language. A better move would be to consider "language" as intensional and internalized (I-language). Bearing this conception in mind, the approach to the knowledge of language as knowledge of an ability—very common among those philosophers influenced by Wittgenstein—is examined and rejected as a philosopher's pipe dream. (edited)

**Chong, C T** and Yang, Yue. $Sigma_2$ Induction and Infinite Injury Priority Arguments: Part II: Tame $Sigma_2$ Coding and the Jump Operator. *Annals Pure Applied Log*, 87(2), 103-116, 15 S 97.

**Chorover, Stephan L** and Gruen, Lori and List, Peter. Commentary On: "There is no Such Thing as Environmental Ethics". *Sci Eng Ethics*, 2(3), 319-334, Jl 96.

**Chowdhury, Ambar** and Loveys, James and Tanovic, Predrag. A Definable Continuous Rank for Nonmultidimensional Superstable Theories. *J Sym Log*, 61(3), 967-984, S 96.

**Christensen, Carleton B**. Meaning Things and Meaning Others. *Phil Phenomenol Res*, 57(3), 495-522, S 97.

At least phenomenologically the way communicative acts reveal intentions is different from the way noncommunicative acts do this: the former have an "addressed" character which the latter do not. The paper argues that this difference is a real one, reflecting the irreducibly "conventional" character of human communication. It attempts to show this through a critical analysis of the Grician program and its methodologically individualist attempt to explain the "conventional" as derivative from the "nonconventional." It is shown how in order to eliminate certain counterexamples the Gricean analysis of utterer's meaning must be made self-referential. It is then shown how this in turn admits an "ontological difference" which undercuts all methodological individualism: meaning something by an utterance must then have a certain intrinsic, irreducible "conventionality" and "intersubjectivity."(edited)

**Christensen, David**. What is Relative Confirmation?. *Nous*, 31(3), 370-384, S 97.

Logical confirmation theory has centered on analyzing a three-part relation of evidence confirming a hypothesis "relative to" background assumptions. Yet the literature contains little discussion of exactly what confirmation relative to background is supposed to mean. This paper argues that assumptions—usually implicit—about what relative confirmation means have played crucial roles in arguments testing formal confirmation theories against cases. It also shows how the interpretation of relative confirmation that serves best to protect confirmation theories from certain counterexamples also serves to limit the philosophical power and interest of the analyzes it protects.

**Christensen, David** and Kornblith, Hilary. Testimony, Memory and the Limits of the *A Priori*. *Phil Stud*, 86(1), 1-20, Ap 97.

Tyler Burge compares perception's role in testimony-based beliefs to its role in diagram-based mathematical proofs, arguing that testimonial beliefs can be *a priori* warranted. We argue that disanalogies undermine Burge's argument and that perception's role in testimonial beliefs is more closely analogous to its role in clearly *a posteriori* beliefs such as those based on reading clocks. Testimonial beliefs are not *a priori* in any interesting sense. Burge also emphasizes that memory, though only contingently reliable, plays a role in mathematical reasoning. We examine the extent to which human memory's heavy reliance on background beliefs renders memory-based beliefs *a posteriori*.

**Christensen, Kate T**. Physicians and Managed Care: Employees or Professionals?. *Bioethics Forum*, 12(1), 17-20, Spr 96.

There are features of managed care that best promote patient welfare and those that do not. The managed care organization (MCO) that results in the highest quality of patient care allows the physician control over clinical practice and minimizes incentives to withhold care. The nonprofit group practice HMO structure holds the greatest potential for promoting both physician autonomy and benign financial incentives.

**Christensen, Kate T** and Tucker, Robin. Ethics without Walls: The Transformation of Ethics Committees in the New Healthcare Environment. *Cambridge Quart Healthcare Ethics*, 6(3), 299-301, Sum 97.

**Christensen, Sandra L**. The New Federalism: Implications for the Legitimacy of Corporate Political Activity. *Bus Ethics Quart*, 7(3), 81-91, Jl 97.

The new push to move political issue activity from the federal to the state and local levels—a new *New Federalism*—has implications for the ethical and political legitimacy of business political activity. While business political activity at the federal level may be both less costly and less risky than when action shifts to states or localities, at the state or local level it is likely to be more visible, and individual firms may be perceived to have more power. Increased corporate power raises questions about the legitimacy of firm involvement in the political process at the state and local levels. The issue of legitimacy is viewed in the context of the literature on political subcultures being used to study state economic development.

**Christie, Juliette**. Against Nagel: In Favor of a Compound Human Ergon. *Dialogue (PST)*, 38(2-3), 77-81, Ap 96.

I argue that the case Thomas Nagel makes for identifying rationality as the human ergon idion fails. Although Nagel is on the mark in his recognition that the human ergon is simple, he errs in reading Aristotle as providing a case that our ergon idion is both limited and *single*. In fact, the human ergon is complex, though limited. It is Nagel's failure to recognize the intertwined roles of rational desire (which springs from the appetitive part of the soul, not the rational) and rationality—in its theoretical capacity—which precludes him from reaching the conclusion I defend. The fears Nagel identifies (which lead him to argue that the human ergon must be single) are dissolved when we see that in the interactive union of rationality and rational desire the "circle of mutual support" is broken, just as Nagel argues it can only be if the human ergon is rationality alone. The threats of slippery slopes and messiness are similarly avoided. Finally, textual support argues in favor of the position I defend.

**Christopher, Myra J**. Integrated Ethics Programs: A New Mission for Ethics Committees. *Bioethics Forum*, 10(4), 19-21, Fall 94.

Although there is no shortage of ethical conflict in today's health care institutions, ethics committees too often are idle. Integrated Ethics Programs (IEP) is a new, active model for ethics committees that could change that situation. IEPs would covert committee members into ethics faculty whose function would be to disseminate ethics throughout the institution, rather than waiting for ethical problems to come to them.

Chrudzimski, Arkadiusz 564 AUTHOR INDEX

**Chrudzimski, Arkadiusz**. Edmund Husserl's Theory of Intentionality (in Polish). *Kwartalnik Filozof*, 24(3), 89-103, 1996.

**Chukwudi Eze, Emmanuel** (ed). *Postcolonial African Philosophy: A Critical Reader.* Cambridge, Blackwell, 1997.

*Postcolonial African Philosophy* sets out a timely and critical agenda for contemporary African, Afro-Caribbean, and African-American philosophy. With many leading contributors, this collection of newly commissioned work provides key coverage of the postcolonial and the postmodern: the critique of Eurocentrism in philosophy; philosophy in postindependence Africa and postcivil rights black America; multiculturalism; and intercultural dialogue between contemporary African and Western philosophy. In addition, it includes important interventions on contemporary historical, political, and cultural situations of Africa and America at the end of the twentieth century, and philosophy's role in this milieu. (publisher,edited)

**Churchill, Larry R**. Damaged Humanity: The Call for a Patient-Centered Medical Ethic in the Managed Care Era. *Theor Med*, 18(1-2), 113-126, Mr-Je 97.

Edmund Pellegrino claims that medical ethics must be derived from a perception of the patient's "damaged humanity," rather than from the self-imposed duties of professionals. This essay explores the meaning and examines the challenges to this patient-centered ethic. Social scientific and biocthical interpretations of medicine constitute one kind of challenge. A more pervasive challenge is the ascendancy of managed care, and especially investor-owned, for-profit managed care. A list of questions addressed to patients, physicians and organizations is offered as one means of assessing this threat and moving toward morally trustworthy relationships.

**Churchill, Larry R**. Market Meditopia: A Glimpse at American Health Care in 2005. *Hastings Center Rep*, 27(1), 5-6, Ja-F 97.

**Churchill, Robert Paul**. "On the Difference between Non-Moral and Moral Conceptions of Toleration: The Case for Toleration as an Individual..." in *Philosophy, Religion, and the Question of Intolerance,* Ambuel, David (ed), 189-211. Albany, SUNY Pr, 1997.

My objectives in this essay are the following: (1) to clarify and to distinguish among various conceptions of toleration, especially the respective conceptions of toleration as moral indifference, permissiveness, endurance and neutrality; (2) to identify and defend the defining characteristics of a further conception of toleration, namely, toleration as a moral virtue; and (3) to defend toleration as a moral virtue by dissolving the so-called "paradox of toleration," that is, by showing why there is no logical inconsistency between moral disapproval of certain beliefs or behavior and moral approval of, or respect for, the persons whose beliefs or behaviors one disapproves of.

**Churchill, Robert Paul**. Interpreting the *Jihad* of Islam: Militarism versus Muslim Pacifism. *Acorn*, 6(2), 20-28, Fall 91.

This paper explores the potential for pacifism within Islam. It does so in part by showing how three courageous Muslims—Bawa Muhaiyaddeen, Kamil Husain and Mahmoud Mohamed Taha—reinterpreted the sacred texts of Islam so that these texts could be read as supporting peaceful and nonviolent social reform among Muslim peoples. But equally important is an exploration of the characteristics of Islam, such as the militant interpretation of *jihad*, or "holy war," which make Islam problematic as a "carrier" or nurturer of pacifism and nonviolence as a way of life. Reprinted in Laurence F. Bove and Laura Duhan Kaplan (eds.) *from the Eve of the Storm* (Amsterdam, Rodopi, 1996), 191-208.

**Chwaszcza, Christine**. "Anmerkungen zu Funktion und Stellenwert des Eigeninteresses" in *Ökonomie und Moral: Beiträge zur Theorie ökonomischer Rationalität,* Lohmann, Karl Reinhard (ed), 85-100. München, Oldenbourg, 1997.

The notion of 'self-interest' is rather ubiquitous in rational choice oriented philosophy, but usually taken as a pretheoretical, intuitively clear concept. The article tries to open up a critical discussion of 'self-interest' within the paradigm of methodological individualism by examining its explanatory role in theory of action and by criticizing its axiological status in libertarian social philosophy. In discussing the structure and force of "practical reasons," it is argued against an "internalist" conception of human motivation; by criticizing the concept of the 'person,' it is demanded not to restrict the possible contents of self-interest of purely individualistic private goods.

**Chwaszcza, Christine**. "Politische Ethik II: Ethik der Internationalen Beziehungen" in *Angewandte Ethik: Die Bereichsethiken und ihre theoretische Fundierung,* Nida-Rümelin, Julian (ed), 154-198. Stuttgart, Alfred Kröner, 1996.

The article develops a systematic framework of the objects of and approaches to an ethics of international relations: after a rejection of skeptical positions held by realists and communitarians it provides a critical evaluation of the justificationary arguments by Singer, Beitz, Pogge, O'Neill and Rawls. On the basis of this critique it is argued for a two-level normative theory of politics, which differentiates between domestic and global political rights and duties; finally an attempt is made to specify the institutional implications for the establishment of an international peace-order and to sketch the range and the constraints of global distributive justice.

**Ciaramelli, Fabio**. The Loss of Origin and Heidegger's Question of *Unheimlichkeit. Epoche*, 2(1), 13-33, 1994.

Within the self-evidence of our being-at-home in the familiar, arises an essential latency. Heidegger is precisely interested in interrogating this hidden, intimate and secret character of the obviousness of the familiar, which for this reason reveals itself *unheimlich*, uncanny and unfamiliar. But the withdrawing of the familiar, its very uncanniness, is the "umbra" surrounding the givenness of light. It is the *primordial* manifestation of Being. The article tries to show that only through the ontological assumption of *Unheimlichkeit* it is possible to overcome the loss of origin, that is the oblivion of Being.

**Cibulka, Josef**. Emergence and Deconstruction (in Czech). *Filosof Cas*, 45(2), 205-211, 1997.

Hegel saw the process of negation as drawing subjects into itself, thus overcoming their formerly positive nature and leaving them to function in their mutual otherness. Hegel's idea of dialectic disturbance was the inspiration for Gadamer's concept of experience as detypification. Heidegger's ontology of time criticized both the reflective philosophy of consciousness and Husserl's phenomenology as subordinating our receptiveness to the sign of being which is already open to us. Jacques Derrida moved beyond his own semiotic philosophy of pre-Kantian and ahistorical moments. His concept of the generation of meaningful and deeply temporal levels of the process of denomination gives concrete form to Merleau-Ponty's "meaning at the moment of birth".

**Cicchetti, Domenic V**. Referees, Editors, and Publication Practices: Improving the Reliability and Usefulness of the Peer Review System. *Sci Eng Ethics*, 3(1), 51-62, Ja 97.

The documented low levels of reliability of the peer review process present a serious challenge to editors who must often base their publication decisions on conflicting referee recommendations. The purpose of this article is to discuss this process and examine ways to produce a more reliable and useful peer review system.

**Cichon, E A** and Weiermann, A. Term Rewriting Theory for the Primitive Recursive Functions. *Annals Pure Applied Log*, 83(3), 199-223, F 97.

The termination of rewrite systems for parameter recursion, simple nested recursion and unnested multiple recursion is shown by using monotone interpretations both on the ordinals below the first primitive recursively closed ordinal and on the natural numbers. We show that the resulting derivation lengths are primitive recursive. As a corollary we obtain transparent and illuminating proofs of the facts that the schemata of parameter recursion, simple nested recursion and unnested multiple recursion lead from primitive recursive functions to primitive recursive functions.

**Cicourel, Aaron V**. Ecological Validity and 'White Room Effects': The Interaction of Cognitive and Cultural Models in the Pragmatic Analysis of Elicited Narratives from Children. *Prag Cognition*, 4(2), 221-264, 1996.

Controlled elicitation of linguistic and psycholinguistic experimental data facilitate strong inferences about phonological, syntactic, semantic and pragmatic structures and functions, yet neglect the ecological validity of responses. Ecological validity in this paper refers to whether data gathered under controlled conditions are commensurate with routine problem solving and language use in natural settings. All methods produce "white room" effects that compromise data gathering and analysis. Unexamined folk knowledge and experiences also guide the investigator's interpretation of data from field research, laboratories, testing sessions, and target sentences. Story recall data from children in a combined second-third grade classroom and their narrative responses to cartoons without sound are used to illustrate ecological validity issues. The child's spontaneous, imaginative narratives about the story and cartoons resemble adult folk theory, and their semantic content reveal sociocultural knowledge essential for understanding subjects' reasoning and information processing skills.

**Cifuentes, Carlos Llano**. "La reflexión de la *proairesis* aristotélica" in *Ensayos Aristotélicos,* Aspe, Virginia, 29-47. Mexico, Univ Panamericana, 1996.

This paper concerns the problem of attributing choice to a "desiring intelligence" or to an "intelligent will", according to *E.N.* VI 2, 1139b 5, as well as to the role of intelligence and will in free choice. Llano emphasizes the importance of the integral (human) agent, stating the principle that neither intelligence nor will are who properly choose, but the whole individual through these powers. (publisher)

**Cifuentes, J C** and Sette, A M and Mundici, Daniele. Cauchy Completeness in Elementary Logic. *J Sym Log*, 61(4), 1153-1157, D 96.

**Cifuentes Camacho, David**. En el centro del labertino: la hybris y el Minotauro. *Convivium*, 9, 38-48, 1996.

From a double sham was born the Minotaur, a double-shape being: half man and half bull, sacred in Crete and monstrous for the Athenians. But the Minotaur is too the symbol of a double human impulse that tries to transgress the limits: the *hybris* of wanting to be animals and gods at the same time. For the mythic thought, the relationship between the Minotaur and the Labyrinth could mean a way to live the human limits that would fall into oblivion when Theseus, killing the Minotaur, could make the way to a new model of thought that was going to transform the *hybris* in the "first harm that the gods sent to the men".

**Cignoli, Roberto** and Mundici, Daniele. An Elementary Proof of Chang's Completeness Theorem for the Infinite-Valued Calculus of Lukasiewicz. *Stud Log*, 58(1), 79-97, 1997.

The interpretation of propositions in Lukasiewicz's infinite-valued calculus as answers in Ulam's game with lies—the Boolean case corresponding to the traditional *Twenty Questions* game—gives added interest to the completeness theorem. The literature contains several different proofs, but they invariably require technical prerequisites from such areas as model-theory, algebraic geometry, or the theory of ordered groups. The aim of this paper is to provide a self-contained proof, only requiring the rudiments of algebra and convexity in finite-dimensional vector spaces.

**Cingari, Salvatore**. Croce e il superuomo: Una variante nell'edizione della "Filosofia della pratica" del 1923. *Iride*, 8(14), 219-224, Ap 95.

**Ciocchi, David M**. Free Will and the Dispositional Aspect of Faith: A Dilemma for the Incompatibilist. *Dialogos*, 31(68), 127-154, Jl 96.

**Cioffi, Frank**. Critical Notice: Freud, Philosophical and Empirical Issues. *Philosophy*, 72(281), 435-448, Jl 97.

**Ciriello, Giovanni**. "Antropologia ed etica in W. Dilthey" in *Lo Storicismo e la Sua Storia: Temi, Problemi, Prospettive*, Cacciatore, Giuseppe (ed), 274-287. Milano, Guerini, 1997.

**Cissna, Kenneth N** and Anderson, Rob. *The Martin Buber-Carl Rogers Dialogue: A New Transcript with Commentary*. Albany, SUNY Pr, 1997.

The authors highlight hundreds of errors, major and minor, in previously distributed and published transcripts—beginning with the typescript circulated by Rogers himself. They also show how an accurate text enhances our understanding of the relationship between Buber's philosophy and Rogers's client- and person-centered approach to interpersonal relations. Anderson and Cissna discuss the central issues of the conservation, including the limits of mutuality, approaches to "self," alternative models of human nature, confirmation of others, and the nature of dialogic relation itself. Although Buber and Rogers conversed nearly forty years ago, their topics clearly resonate with contemporary debates about postmodernism, forms of otherness, cultural studies, and the possibilities for a dialogic public sphere. (publisher, edited)

**Civjan, Sheryl Robinson**. Being Human: Issues in Sexuality for People with Developmental Disabilities. *Bioethics Forum*, 12(3), 31-36, Fall 96.

Discussion of sexuality issues in the lives of persons with developmental disabilities has been neglected by both the general public and professionals for many years. Despite philosophical shifts that have focused on improved community living and quality of life, most people in the field of developmental disabilities have ignored the central issues of sexuality and sexual expression.

**Cixous, Hélène**. Stigmata: Job the Dog. *Phil Today*, 41(1-4), 12-17, Spr 97.

**Ciyori, Kitagaki**. L'immagine, il sermone, la meditazione: La pratica della orazione nel *Commiato di Cristo dalla Madre* di Lorenzo Lotto. *Bigaku*, 48(1), 25-36, Sum 97.

Una delle questioni più controverse nello studio di Lorenzo Lotto (1480-1557) riguarda l'atteggiamento religioso dell'artista, che lo colloca da una parte in un contesto cattolico, e dall'altra protestante, ponendo in luce il suo carattere inquieto e turbato, il suo difficile rapporto sociale e la crisi della situazione religiosa dell'epoca. Noi intendiamo considerare Lotto, in opposizione a queste discussioni, tenendo presente che questi due contesti religiosi non erano ancora chiari allora. (edited)

**Cladis, Mark S**. Lessons from the Garden: Rousseau's Solitaires and the Limits of Liberalism. *Interpretation*, 24(2), 183-200, Wint 97.

Durkheim, with appropriate equivocation, argued than in Rousseau's view society is neither contrary to nature nor part of it; the seeds of the social life are present in nature, yet remote from it. The ambiguity here is as instructive of a tension found in Rousseau's thought as in Durkheim's. I explore this tension by addressing two questions: What are Rousseau's and Durkheim's views of human nature and how do these views influence their perspectives on what, socially and politically, we can hope for? I give special attention to Durkheim's interpretation of Rousseau's political writings and focus on the light this inquiry casts on their understanding of potential conflict between the individual and society.

**Cladwell, Anne**. Fairy Tales for Politics: The Other, Once More. *Phil Today*, 41(1-4), 40-50, Spr 97.

**Clair, André**. Lequier and the Documents of the Renouvier Library. *Arch Phil*, 60(1), 123-128, Ja-Mr 97.

**Clare, Lindsay** and Gallimore, Ronald and Patthey-Chavez, G Genevieve. Using Moral Dilemmas in Children's Literature as a Vehicle for Moral Education and Teaching Reading Comprehension. *J Moral Educ*, 25(3), 325-341, S 96.

Moral development research has previously demonstrated that more extended discourse is a vital element in effective moral education, although the difficulty of implementing this type of discourse into classroom practice has seldom been discussed. In this study, transcripts of lessons were examined of a teacher systematically assisted to develop a more conversational style. These lessons were taped over the course of the school year at different times, beginning in the fall of the year. In addition, writing samples from children who participated in the lessons were subject to content analysis for themes relating to moral questions. Analysis of the lesson transcripts suggests that young students initiate discussion of values-implications of the texts they read if opportunities for connected discourse are increased. Evidence of the impact of more "conversational" discussions was found in the essays written by students in the class of a teacher using a more conversational style but not in the essays of students who were taught using a conventional format.

**Clark, Andy**. "Moving Minds: Situating Content in the Service of Real-Time Success" in *AI, Connectionism and Philosophical Psychology, 1995*, Tomberlin, James E (ed), 89-104. Atascadero, Ridgeview, 1995.

Recent work in robotics and artificial life is sceptical of the notion of internal representation. I argue that we should not abandon the notion, but recast it in a way which makes real-time control basic. This has consequences both for philosophical treatment of folk psychology and for the explanatory ambitions of cognitive science.

**Clark, Austen**. True Theories, False Colors. *Proc Phil Sci Ass*, 3(Suppl), S143-S150, 1996.

Recent versions of objectivism can reply to the argument from metamers. The deeper rift between subjectivists and objectivists lies in the question of how to explain the structure of qualitative similarities among the colors. Subjectivism grounded in this fashion can answer the circularity objection raised by Dedrick. It endorses skepticism about the claim that there is some one property of objects that it is the function of color vision to detect. Color vision may enable us to detect differences in spectral composition without granting us the capacity to detect identities.

**Clark, Glenn**. "New Light on Peirce's Iconic Notation for the Sixteen Binary Connectives" in *Studies in the Logic of Charles Sanders Peirce*, Houser, Nathan (ed), 304-333. Bloomington, Indiana Univ Pr, 1997.

**Clark, John**. "The Dialectical Social Geography of Elisée Reclus" in *Philosophy and Geography I: Space, Place, and Environmental Ethics*, Light, Andrew (ed), 117-142. Lanham, Rowman & Littlefield, 1997.

Reclus is shown to be not only a pioneering figure in social geography, but also an ecological social theorist who anticipated many themes that have recently become central concerns of ecophilosophy and environmental ethics. The focus of the discussion is on Reclus's holistic, dialectical interpretation of the place of humanity in the natural world.

**Clark, Kelly James**. Perils of Pluralism. *Faith Phil*, 14(3), 303-320, Jl 97.

Two pressures toward religious pluralism are the variety of religious traditions which seem equally successful in the transformation of human lives and that apparently sincere and equally capable truth-seekers reach divergent conclusions about the nature of ultimate reality. I discuss Hick's Kantian explanation of these phenomena. I argue that his account is: neither the only nor the best account; furthermore, that more reasonable accounts allow for the members of competing traditions to affirm the truth of their religious beliefs; and if Hick's explanation were accepted it would undermine the salvific power of the respective religious traditions.

**Clark, Kelly James**. Trinity or Tritheism?. *Relig Stud*, 32(4), 463-476, D 96.

The focus of this paper is the social Trinitarian account in Richard Swinburne's *The Christian God*. After setting out the route Swinburne follows in reaching his conclusions about the Godhead, I endeavour to show two things: I) that his account does not avoid the charge of tritheism and thus is not faithful to key elements in the Christian creeds; II) the philosophical moves behind his conclusions are not compelling if, as we can, we challenge his assumptions about divine necessity. A better account of divine necessity takes us away from Swinburne's version of Trinitarianism/tritheism.

**Clark, Michael**. The Sanctions of the Criminal Law. *Proc Aris Soc*, 97, 25-39, 1997.

On the compromise view, punishment is an intrinsic mischief justifiable only in terms of countervailing beneficial effects; but its imposition is subject to side-constraints which among other things respect the agent's autonomy by proscribing the punishment of innocents. Famously, such consequentialist justification has been condemned for treating the penalized solely as means; more recently, it has been argued that autonomy may be better preserved by violating the side-constraints, that the compromise position is uneconomic, if not inconsistent; and that its side-constraint is appeal to retributive considerations which imply a retributive justification of punishment. Each of these criticisms is met.

**Clark, Michael**. Truth and Success: Searle's Attack on Minimalism. *Analysis*, 57(3), 205-209, Jl 97.

John Searle has recently tried to defend a correspondence theory of truth against minimalism, on the grounds that 'true' describes success in achieving fit for statements. But his defence is vitiated by an act/object confusion: it is the act of asserting that succeeds or fails, but what is asserted that is true or false. What is asserted, the propositional content, is inert, does not aim at anything and so cannot be successful or unsuccessful: nothing Searle says precludes characterizing its truth wholly in terms of the minimalist theory.

**Clark, Philip**. Practical Steps and Reasons for Action. *Can J Phil*, 27(1), 17-45, Mr 97.

Practical reasoning is standardly portrayed either as reasoning about what one wants and how to get it or as reasoning about what one ought to do. The author argues that an accurate understanding of the parallel between practical and theoretical reasoning supports a third and competing view. On that view, the practical analogue of an ordinary inference does not generally take desires as its subject matter and is a step to an action rather than an "ought" conclusion.

**Clark, S H**. "Narrative Identity in Ricoeur's *Oneself as Another*" in *Critical Studies: Ethics and the Subject*, Simms, Karl (ed), 85-95. Amsterdam, Rodopi, 1997.

**Clark, Stephen R L**. "Natural Integrity and Biotechnology" in *Human Lives: Critical Essays on Consequentialist Bioethics*, Oderberg, David S (ed), 58-76. New York, Macmillan, 1997.

Even consequentialists must judge actions by reference to general rules and it is impossible or absurd to devise those rules from a purely neutral standpoint. Once the untenability of rule consequentialism is realized, intrinsic objections to biotechnology can be taken seriously. Certain kinds of biotechnological interference constitute a form of oppression. They also disregard the natural integrity of their victims. We must, in addition, recognize the importance of the concepts of beauty and ugliness to moral thinking, as well as that of the history of a state of affairs and see their bearing on judgments about what is permissible interference with nature. We can then see that much modern biotechnology is gravely at fault.

**Clark, Stephen R L**. How Chesterton Read History. *Inquiry*, 39(3-4), 343-358, D 96.

Chesterton was a serious and even excellent philosopher, whose reputation has suffered because his style was to striking and his conversion to Catholicism so

Clark, Stephen R L 566 AUTHOR INDEX

unpopular with Whiggish Britons. He had many 'politically incorrect' opinions, but those 'faults' were symptoms of a greater virtue, his insistence that 'the whole object of history is to make us realize that humanity can be great and glorious, under conditions quite different and even contrary to our own'. His desire for a united Europe was not for a larger, self-willed state, but for a continent of peasant proprietors, workers owning their own tools, citizens alive to their own local heritage. What he distrusted was the Laodicean mood that best defines modernity, that nothing is worth dying for but life is not worth living. What he consistently opposed was the power of businessmen and aristocrats and their Whiggish supporters' habit of supposing that the actual course of history was inevitable. Speculation about might-have-beens is a way to subvert the oppressive weight of the present. His hope was for a revolution. (edited)

**Clark, Stephen R L**. *How to Live Forever: Science Fiction and Philosophy*. New York, Routledge, 1995.

*How to Live Forever* is a compelling study which introduces students and professional philosophers to the possibilities of using science fiction in their work. It includes extensive suggestions for further reading, both fictional and philosophical. (publisher,edited)

**Clark, Tim**. "Deleuze and Structuralism: Towards a Geometry of Sufficient Reason" in *Deleuze and Philosophy: The Difference Engineer*, Ansell Pearson, Keith (ed), 58-72. New York, Routledge, 1997.

**Clarke, D S**. *Philosophy's Second Revolution: Early and Recent Analytic Philosophy*. Chicago, Open Court, 1997.

D.S. Clarke explains some of the crucial issues raised by the second philosophical revolution, and especially the differences between the early phase of analytic philosophy, covering roughly the first half of the twentieth century, and the new phase which commenced about 1980. Professor Clarke traces the historical background of the analytic movement from its origins, through its development by applications of logic to philosophical problems and by 'ordinary language' philosophers. He then concentrates on the post-1960 phase, with its rejection of earlier views dominated by Wittgenstein's methods. The new phase features the development of a materialist metaphysics, the attempt to assimilate philosophy to the natural sciences, and the attempt to reinstate normative ethics as a guide to conduct. (publisher, edited)

**Clarke, David D** and Nerlich, Brigitte. *Language, Action, and Context: The Early History of Pragmatics in Europe and America, 1780-1930*. Amsterdam, J Benjamins, 1996.

This book explores the often neglected philosophical, psychological and linguistic foundations of modern linguistic pragmatics, which has its deepest roots in ancient rhetoric. The first part of the book describes the emergence of pragmatics in Britain, Germany and France in post-Lockian and post-Kantian philosophies of language. The second part explores pragmatic insights made between 1830 and 1880, when they were relegated to the philosophical and linguistic underground. In a last part the period between 1880 and 1930 is studied, when pragmatic ideas flourished.

**Clarke, James** and Duska, Ronald and Rongione, Nicholas. Codes of Ethics: Investment Company Money Managers Versus other Financial Professionals. *Bus Prof Ethics J*, 14(4), 43-55, Wint 95.

**Clarke, Michael**. Moral Politics and the Limits of Justice in *Perpetual Peace*. *Ideal Stud*, 26(2), 203-209, Wint 96.

**Clarke, Randolph**. On the Possibility of Rational Free Action. *Phil Stud*, 88(1), 37-57, O 97.

Galen Strawson has argued that it is impossible for a human action to be both free and fully rational. This paper examines Strawson's argument and finds it unconvincing. A widely accepted view of causal explanation is drawn upon to argue that nondeterministically caused actions may be fully rational and rationally explicable. The paper provides a sketch of an account of freedom that provides for both fully rational action and greater agent-control than what could be available given determinism.

**Clarke, Ruth** and Aram, John. Universal Values, Behavioral Ethics and Entrepreneurship. *J Bus Ethics*, 16(5), 561-572, Ap 97.

This is a comparison of graduate students' attitudes in Spain and the United States on the issue of universal versus relativist ethics. The findings show agreement on fundamental universal values across cultures but differences in responses to behavioral ethics within the context of entrepreneurial dilemmas.

**Clarke, Steve**. When to Believe in Miracles. *Amer Phil Quart*, 34(1), 95-102, Ja 97.

**Clatterbaugh, Kenneth**. *Contemporary Perspectives on Masculinity: Men, Women, and Politics in Modern Society*. Boulder, Westview Pr, 1997.

This newly updated edition surveys the range of responses to feminism that men have made and puts political theory at the center of men's awareness of their own masculinity. In clear and insightful language, Professor Chatterbaugh surveys not just conservative, liberal, and radical views of masculinity but also the alternatives offered by the men's rights movement, spiritual growth advocates, and black and gay rights activists. Each of these is explored both as a theoretical perspective and as a social movement, and each offers distinctive responses to the questions posed. (publisher,edited)

**Clatterbaugh, Kenneth** and Bobro, Marc. Unpacking the Monad: Leibniz's Theory of Causality. *Monist*, 79(3), 408-425, Jl 96.

Apart from God, what *causes* the change in the perceptions of monads? The literature contains three interpretations that have been advanced to explain this change: the *conceptual unfolding view* locates the source of change in the monad's individual concept; the *efficacious perception view* says that the cause of each perception is to be found in previous perceptions; and, the *monadic agency view* claims that perceptual changes are caused by the monad's primitive active force. This paper defends the third account, for only it adequately grounds Leibniz's distinctions between reasons and causes, natural and miraculous perceptions, and real and apparent causality.

**Claxton, Guy**. Structure, Strategy and Self in the Fabrication of Conscious Experience. *J Consciousness Stud*, 3(2), 98-111, 1996.

Neurophysiological and psychological evidence require us to see perception, the 'fabrication of (conscious) experience', as a process in time. Some of the elapsed time between the onset of stimulation and the appearance of a conscious image is accounted for by considerations of neural hardware. Cognitive science conventionally assumes that these *structural* factors are sufficient to account for the delay. However, I argue in this paper that the human information processing system may interpose an additional *strategic* delay that allows for processes of checking and editing the developing 'sketch' or 'draft', so that elements that might threaten an underlying *self system* can be massaged or deleted. This cognitive model parallels that which is found in the Buddhist *Adhidhamma* and improves upon the traditional, canonical formulation. Mindfulness meditation can be seen as a process of 'attentional retraining', in which the strategic delay is reduced through practice and self-related assumptions, which had previously been dissolved in or presupposed by conscious experience, become crystallized out and capable of being problematized.

**Clay, Diskin**. Deep Therapy. *Phil Lit*, 20(2), 501-505, O 96.

**Clayton, Ellen Wright**. Genetic Testing in Children. *J Med Phil*, 22(3), 233-251, Je 97.

In this article, the author focuses on the allocation of decision-making authority between parents and physicians. She argues that parents should have substantial room to decide whether genetic testing is good for their child and that they may appropriately consider interests in addition to those of their child in making such choices. A physician, however, may refuse to act pursuant to parental views about testing, when in the physician's view, the parents' choice would pose a risk of significant harm to the child. The balance of control between parents and physicians is illustrated by discussion of a series of case vignettes. Refusal to perform requested testing is most often warranted for testing for carrier status and for genetic predisposition to late onset disease. The author concludes her analysis by discussing why it is appropriate to give increasing deference to the views of the child as the child grows older.

**Clayton, Leigh**. "The Absent Signifier: Historical Narrative and the Abstract Subject" in *Critical Studies: Ethics and the Subject*, Simms, Karl (ed), 77-83. Amsterdam, Rodopi, 1997.

**Clayton, M H** and Spash, Clive L. "The Maintenance of Natural Capital: Motivations and Methods" in *Philosophy and Geography I: Space, Place, and Environmental Ethics*, Light, Andrew (ed), 143-173. Lanham, Rowman & Littlefield, 1997.

This paper analyses the reasoning behind defining a class of inputs to production as natural capital as a response to environmental concerns. Two motivations are: ecological criticality and nonhuman intrinsic values. These justifications require the maintenance of resources which are excluded from exploitation, but free market systems cannot achieve this due to a basic assumption of trade-offs derived from utilitarianism and economic value. Three methods for the protection of natural capital are reviewed (compensating projects, cost-benefit analysis, scientifically designated limits) but a more interdisciplinary and inclusive approach is necessary and a type of systems analysis is suggested.

**Clayton, Philip**. Inference to the Best Explanation. *Zygon*, 32(3), 377-391, S 97.

The common role of research programs in science and religion is now widely accepted. The next step in the methodology debate is to specify more concretely the shared standards for adequate explanations. The article presents a detailed account of the method of inference to the best explanation and gives examples of how the method can structure the philosophical and theological interaction with science. The resulting approach dispenses with deductive and inductive proofs of religious propositions and limits itself to initially plausible hypotheses that are to be assessed according to their explanatory power. Only when a domain of data and a particular explanatory task have been specified can any serious claim be made that religious theories are equal or superior to their naturalistic alternatives.

**Clayton, Philip**. Philosophy of Science and the German Idealists. *Hist Phil Quart*, 14(3), 287-304, Jl 97.

The article argues that the links between the logical positivists and classical German philosophy was much more intimate than previous studies have granted: coherence did more work and correspondence less for Carnap than is frequently maintained; Reichenbach was deeply influenced by Kantian questions; even Schlick has his idealist moments. If correct, this portrait reduces the alleged "great divide" between these positivists and post-Kuhnian philosophy of science. The upshot is a view of logical positivism as holding not that all metaphysics is bad but that bad metaphysics is bad—certainly a less radical thesis.

**Clayton, Philip**. Philosophy of Science: What One Needs to Know. *Zygon*, 32(1), 95-104, Mr 97.

This introduction to the philosophy of science offers an overview of the major concepts and developments in contemporary theories of science. Strengths and weaknesses of deductive, inductive and falsificationist models of science are considered. The "Received View" in the theory of science is contrasted with Kuhn's paradigms and Feyerabend's "anything goes," leading to an examination of the merits of a research program-based approach. After touching on the sociology of science, postmodernism and the feminist critique, the article concludes with a summary, in six theses, of the implications for religion/science.

AUTHOR INDEX 567 Coddetta, Carolina

**Cleghorn, Angus**. "And of That Other and Her Desire: The Embracing Language of Wallace Stevens" in *Critical Studies: Ethics and the Subject*, Simms, Karl (ed), 227-235. Amsterdam, Rodopi, 1997.

**Clemente, Isabel**. O Nilismo de Merleau-Ponty. *Philosophica (Portugal)*, 113-122, 1993.

On essaie ici de comprendre la pensée de Merleau-Ponty comme un approfondissement de sa notion première—la perception. Cet approfondissement, dans son exigence de penser la relation du sujet de la perception avec ce qu'il peut percevoir, s'anonçant comme la "réversibilité" du schéma-corporel et des choses, réversibilité qui est elle même l'horizon d'où se détache l'acte perceptif, amène l'auteur a l'anéantissement de la subjectivité. Le sujet radical—le schéma-corporel—est sujet dans un monde, caracterisé lui aussi comme activité de réversibilité. Ainsi, sujet e monde devenus ambigus, la pensée de Merleau-Ponty, qui dit Chair comme le dernier mot, peut bien se dire une pensée niiliste.

**Cleveland, Timothy**. A Refutation of Pure Conjecture. *J Gen Phil Sci*, 28(1), 55-81, 1997.

The present paper explores three interrelated topics in Popper's theory of science: 1) his view of conjecture, 2) the aim of science, and 3) his (never fully articulated) theory of meaning. Central to Popper's theory of science is the notion of conjecture. Popper writes as if scientists faced with a problem proceed to tackle it by conjecture, that is, by guesses uninformed by inferential considerations. This paper develops a contrast between guesses and educated guesses in an attempt to show that there is more to scientific conjecture than conjecture. The suggestion is made that some inductive considerations enter into the process of educated guessing or scientific conjecture in such a way that the 'context of discovery' cannot be sharply separated from the 'context of justification'. This discussion leads to a tension between Popper's negative method of conjecture and his realism. Given Popper's (implicit) theory of meaning it seems Popper's epistemology (the conjecture and refutation method) is incompatible with his metaphysical realism.

**Cleveland, Timothy**. On the Very Idea of Degrees of Truth. *Austl J Phil*, 75(2), 218-221, Je 97.

In his book *Paradoxes*, Mark Sainsbury suggests that degrees of truth can be justified and explained by analogy with degrees of belief. Considerations of vagueness place theoretical limitations on degrees of belief which require degrees of truth. This paper argues that considerations of vagueness and degrees of belief do nothing to illuminate degrees of truth. An account of vagueness need not postulate degrees of truth.

**Clifton, Michael H**. On Preserving the Unity of the Moral Virtues in the *Nichomachean Ethics*. *Kinesis*, 23(2), 16-28, Fall 96.

**Clifton, Rob** and Bub, Jeffrey. A Uniqueness Theorem for 'No Collapse' Interpretations of Quantum Mechanics. *Stud Hist Phil Mod Physics*, 27B(2), 181-219, Je 96.

We prove a uniqueness theorem showing that, subject to certain natural constraints, all 'no collapse' interpretations of quantum mechanics can be uniquely characterized and reduced to the choice of a particular preferred observable as determinate (definite, sharp). We show how certain versions of the modal interpretation, Bohm's 'causal' interpretation, Bohr's complementarity interpretation, and the orthodox (Dirac-von Neumann) interpretation without the projection postulate can be recovered from the theorem. Bohr's complementarity and Einstein's realism appear as two quite different proposals for selecting the preferred determinate observable—either settled pragmatically by what we choose to observe, or fixed once and for all, as the Einsteinian realist would require, in which case the preferred observable is a 'beable' in Bell's sense, as in Bohm's interpretation (where the preferred observable is position in configuration space).

**Clifton, Robert**. On What Being a World Takes Away. *Proc Phil Sci Ass*, 3(Suppl), S151-S159, 1996.

In their article "On What It Takes To Be a World," David Albert and Jeffrey Barrett raise "a rather urgent question about what the proponents of a many-worlds interpretation [of quantum mechanics] can possibly mean by the term 'worlds'" (1995, 35). I argue that their considerations do not translate into an argument against the Many-Worlds conception of a world unless one requires that the dispositions that measurement devices display through the outcomes they record be explainable in terms of facts particular to the worlds in which those devices do their recording. Granting that their conception of a world takes away the possibility of such an explanation, a Many-Worlds proponent can claim that the Universal quantum state, which does not represent a fact about any world in particular, is enough to ground the dispositions of measurement devices.

**Clifton, Robert**. The Properties of Modal Interpretations of Quantum Mechanics. *Brit J Phil Sci*, 47(3), 371-398, S 96.

Orthodox quantum mechanics includes the principle that an observable of a system possesses a well-defined value if and only if the presence of that value in the system is certain to be confirmed on measurement. Modal interpretations reject the controversial 'only if' half of this principle to secure definite outcomes for quantum measurements that leave the apparatus entangled with the object it has measured. However, using a result that turns on the construction of a Kochen-Specker contradiction, I argue that modal interpretations cannot deliver a metaphysically tenable conception of properties in quantum mechanics unless they *also* abandon the less controversial 'if' half of the orthodox principle.

**Clune, Alan C**. A Critical Assessment of Varner's Proposal for Consensus and Convergence in the Biomedical Research Debate. *Between Species*, 12(1-2), 34-39, Wint-Spr 96.

This article is a response to Gary E. Varner's recent attempt to provide a direction for reconciliation between utilitarianism and inherent value views on the subject of biomedical research testing on nonhuman animals. This paper argues that Varner's prospect only fully succeeds on an *improper* construal of Tom Regan's "worse-off" principle. On a *proper* construal of this principle, only a limited version of Varner's prospect succeeds. Moreover, the paper argues that there is a difficulty with Regan's "worse-off" principle which block's even this limited version of Varner's prospect. However, out of these analyses comes a suggestion for a new direction for the possibility of convergence between utilitarianism and inherent value views.

**Clune, Alan C**. Justification of Empirical Belief: Problems with Haack's Foundherentism. *Philosophy*, 72(281), 460-463, Jl 97.

The empirical foundationalist intuition is that a subject's experience alone is what confers justification on a belief. The coherentist intuition is that justification of a belief is solely a matter of how this belief coheres with the subject's other beliefs. In *Evidence and Inquiry* Haack argues for a theory of the justification of empirical beliefs ("Foundherehtism") which includes elements from both empirical foundationalist and coherentist intuitions and is not a form of reliabilism. This paper argues that there are problems with this attempt which imply that Haack's view must collapse into one of the three kinds of views that she wishes to escape: foundationalism, coherentism or reliabilism.

**Coates, Paul**. Meaning, Mistake and Miscalculation. *Mind Mach*, 7(2), 171-197, My 97.

The issue of what distinguishes systems which have original intentionality from those which do not has been brought into sharp focus by Saul Kripke in his discussion of the sceptical paradox he attributes to Wittgenstein. In this paper, I defend a sophisticated version of the dispositionalist account of meaning against the principal objection raised by Kripke in his attack on dispositional views. I argue that the objection put by the sceptic, to the effect that the dispositionalist cannot give a satisfactory account of normativity and mistake, in fact comprises a number of distinct lines of argument, all of which can be satisfactorily answered by the dispositionalist. (edited)

**Coburn, Robert C**. God, Revelation, and Religious Truth: Some Themes and Problems in the Theology of Paul Tillich. *Faith Phil*, 13(1), 3-33, Ja 96.

This paper begins with an explanation of why, despite their obscurity, Tillich's writings have been attractive to a wide audience. I then describe some of the main features of his mature theological position and discuss a number of the central questions and difficulties to which this position gives rise. The discussion focuses on such questions as whether Tillich can justify holding his own "interpretations" of traditional Christian ideas to have a privileged status, whether the deliteralization of traditional Christian language is compatible with the idea that Christianity is a historical religion, how we are to understand Tillich's notion of a symbolic or mythological account's being adequate to revelatory experience, what it is for a "practical interpretation" of revelatory experience to be an adequate expression of such experience, and what is the best way of handling the problems raised by Tillich's claim that there are no literally true statements—or only one literally true statement—about God.

**Cocchiarella, Nino B**. Conceptual Realism as a Theory of Logical Form. *Rev Int Phil*, 51(200), 175-199, Je 97.

**Coccia, Orestes**. Critical Thinking vs. Pure Thought. *Inquiry (USA)*, 15(3), 38-48, Spr 96.

**Coccia, Orestes**. Critical Thinking vs. Pure Thought (Part One of Two). *Inquiry (USA)*, 15(2), 42-58, Wint 95.

**Cochran, David Carroll**. War-Pacifism. *Soc Theor Pract*, 22(2), 161-180, Sum 96.

War-pacifism acknowledges that killing another human being is morally acceptable in certain cases of self-defense. It claims, however, that war is never one of these cases. Rather than objecting to killing per se, it is a form of pacifism that focuses explicitly on the kind of killing found in warfare and on how this killing makes engaging in war morally impermissible. By focusing on the status of individual soldiers in warfare, the article shows that the conditions that justify killing in self-defense cannot apply to the conduct of war.

**Cochrane, Donald B** and Schulte, John M. *Ethics in School Counseling*. New York, Teachers College Pr, 1995.

The authors provide a set of principles that help guide school counselors through the ethical crises they face. Case histories are analyzed to illustrate the many kinds of problems that may arise in the relationships among counselors, students, parents and teachers. Larger issues of ethical reasoning and principles are related and developed and examples of typical dilemmas faced by school counselors are examined. One chapter critiques the professional ethics codes featured in the appendices: the standards of the American Counseling Association and the American School Counselor Association.

**Cocks, Joan**. From Politics to Paralysis: Critical Intellectuals Answer the National Question. *Polit Theory*, 24(3), 518-537, Ag 96.

Nationalism presents perplexities for intellectuals that derive from the tension between the intellectual's critical mentality and political affinities, when those affinities are democratic. Rosa Luxembourg exemplifies the predicament of alienation from the people on the part of the intellectual who criticizes nationalism as mystification and who struggles against it for the sake of the people's real emancipation. The early Tom Nairn, Ernest Gellner, and Benedict Anderson exemplify the predicament of alienation from politics on the part of the intellectual who celebrates the popular resonance of the national myth without believing in that myth, and who hence cannot act either as a nationalist or as an antinationalist.

**Coddetta, Carolina**. The Problem of Power in the Feminist Theory (Spanish). *Fronesis*, 2(2), 59-95, D 95.

Starting from the limited incorporation of women into politics, the work attempts to understand the complex relationship existing between the characteristics of

Code, Lorraine 568 AUTHOR INDEX

the social structure, the historical changes and the aspirations of women with regard to their participation in political power. Fundamental texts are analyzed such as those of Mary Wollstonecraft (*The Vindication of the Rights of Women*, 1792) and Simone de Beauvoir (*The Second Sex*, 1949), which represent periods of crisis values and mark the beginning of new times, although they show as much the slowness of changes in sociocultural patterns as the cyclical recurrency of basic questionings with regard to the social role of women.

**Code, Lorraine**. Commentary on "Loopholes, Gaps, and What is Held Fast". *Phil Psychiat Psych*, 3(4), 255-260, D 96.

**Code, Murray**. On the Poverty of Scientism, or: The Ineluctable Roughness of Rationality. *Metaphilosophy*, 28(1-2), 102-122, Ja-Ap 97.

If there is one rationality there must be a plurality of them. This conclusion follows, I argue, partly from the extreme and ineradicable vagueness of the fundamental concepts that every would-be rational explanation must presuppose. Logicistic/scientistic assaults on this vagueness are doomed to fail partly because they are unable to acknowledge the imaginative dimension of rational thought. Being limited to the play of "outward appearances," scientific investigations are also dependent on "inward imaginings" on their speculative side. The upshot is that schools of philosophy should be characterized by the kind of imaginary they adopt rather than by their logics. In which case, every attempt to get and tell something right about the world is bound to incorporate mythopoeic elements in its explanations.

**Cody, Arthur B**. Darwin and Dennett: Still Two Mysteries. *Inquiry*, 39(3-4), 427-457, D 96.

Daniel Dennett's, *Darwin's Dangerous Idea*, is narrowly reviewed. Attention is concentrated mainly on two issues. The first has to do with a fundamental problem in the Neo-Synthetic theory of evolution having to do with the relationship between genome and organism. Dennett fails to provide an adequate account of it himself or to find anyone else who has succeeded. The second revisits Dennett's long held claim that intention and meaning are made intelligible as evolutionary achievements. Dennett seems not to have seen the dimension of his problem.

**Cofrancesco, Dino**. Qual è la destra che manca in Italia: Per un discorso realistico sul conservatorismo e le istituzioni. *Iride*, 9(18), 346-360, Ag 96.

L'interesse per la destra conservatrice nasce dalla sincera e sofferta conversione della sinistra ai valori della società aperta. Lo stato liberaldemocratico è impensabile senza l'alternarsi al governo—e all'opposizione—di un partito (o di una coalizione) di centro-destra e di un partito (o di una coalizione) di centro-sinistra. Più arguo, invece, è identificare i contenuti etico-politici di una autentica destra liberale senza ripiombare nelle nebbie di un vago discorso storicistico. La soluzione sta, forse, nel vedere il nocciolo duro del conservatorismo nella difesa intransigente del compromesso originario che è alla base di un sistema politico.

**Cogan, Ross**. Opting Out: Bennett on Classifying Conditionals. *Analysis*, 56(3), 142-145, Jl 96.

Jonathan Bennett, in a 1995 paper (*Mind* 104: 331-354) argues for the traditional classification of conditionals into indicative and subjunctive. Central to his paper is the argument that 'indicative' conditionals have the 'confidence property'—they commit their holders to belief in the consequent upon learning the antecedent—whereas 'subjunctive' conditionals allow the holder-scope to abandon belief in the conditional should they learn the antecedent. I show that this is incorrect, thereby leaving the door open to a Dudman-style reclassification of if-sentences.

**Cohen, Andrew I**. Virtues, Opportunities, and the Right To Do Wrong. *J Soc Phil*, 28(2), 43-55, Fall 97.

Rights theorists often defend a right to do wrong by appealing to a commitment to self-definition. I argue that considerations of self-constitution and personal integrity are inconclusive foundations for the right to do wrong. There are instrumentalist appeals to autonomy which argue against a right to do wrong. A fuller statement of what rights are, and what is the nature and role of autonomy, must precede any defense of the right to do wrong.

**Cohen, Carl**. Do Animals Have Rights?. *Ethics Behavior*, 7(2), 91-102, 1997.

A right, unlike an interest, is a valid claim, or potential claim, made by a moral agent, under principles that govern both the claimant and the target of the claim. Animals cannot be the bearers of rights because the concept of rights is essentially human; it is rooted in and has force within a human moral world.

**Cohen, Daniel H**. Argument is War...and War is Hell: Philosophy, Education, and Metaphors for Argumentation. *Inform Log*, 17(2), 177-188, Spr 95.

Our understanding of the concept "argument" is both reflected by and molded by the specific metaphor that argument-is-war, something with winners and losers, offensive and defensive moments, and an essentially adversarial structure. Such arguments may be suitable for teaching *a* philosophy, but not for teaching philosophy. Surely, education and philosophy do not need to be conceived as having an adversarial essence—if indeed they are thought to have any essence at all. Accordingly, philosophy and education need more pragmatic goals that even Peirce's idealized notion of truth as the *end* of inquiry, e.g., the simple *furtherance* of inquiry. For this, new metaphors for framing and understanding the concept of argumentation are needed and some suggestions in that direction will be considered. (edited)

**Cohen, Elliot D**. Philosophical Counseling: A Computer-Assisted, Logic-Based Approach. *Inquiry (USA)*, 15(2), 83-90, Wint 95.

Philosophical counselors are trained practitioners of philosophy who help their clients to "clarify, articulate, explore and comprehend philosophical aspects of their belief systems or "world views" (ASPCP, Standards of Ethical Practice, Preamble). This paper describes a computer-assisted approach to counseling that focuses upon the use of logic and critical thinking to help clients solve their personal problems. It is then argued that philosophical counselors may enhance client autonomy through the use of such a logic-based model.

**Cohen, G A**. History, Ethics, and Marxism. *Iyyun*, 45, 71-83, Jl 96.

The author traces the shift in his own academic work from study of Karl Marx's theory of history to mainstream political philosophy. He also comments on and explains, the neglect of political philosophy proper in the Marxian tradition. That neglect was linked to the existence of a relatively polarised class structure in society, which has gradually disintegrated. Its disintegration means that socialist attention to political philosophy has new become imperative.

**Cohen, G A**. Where the Action Is: On the Site of Distributive Justice. *Phil Pub Affairs*, 26(1), 3-30, Wint 97.

I argue, against John Rawls, that principles of distributive justice apply not only to the basic structure of society, to, that is, its fundamental rules, but also to the choices made by individuals within those rules. Thus, for example, in a society that is just by the standards of the difference principle, not only does government run an economic policy that favours the worst off, but the choices made by talented people with respect to jobs and remuneration reflect an ethos which is informed by that principle: they do not, accordingly, seek to maximize the gains they can get on the market and more social product is therefore available for the less well off. (See my Tanner Lectures on "Incentives, Inequality, and Community" in Volume XIII (1992) of those Lectures).

**Cohen, Jean L**. Rights, Citizenship, and the Modern Form of the Social: Dilemmas of Arendtian Republicanism. *Constellations*, 3(2), 164-189, O 96.

**Cohen, Jonathan**. Born to Affirm the Eternal Recurrence: Nietzsche, Buber, and Springsteen. *Phil Cont World*, 3(3), 1-11, Fall 96.

I argue that the Bruce Springsteen song "Born to Run" needs to be interpreted in light of—and thus gives evidence of a connection between—the philosophies of Friedrich Nietzsche and Martin Buber. Along the way I give an in-depth reading of the Nietzschean doctrines of Eternal Recurrence and Overman as they emerge from *Also Sprach Zarathustra*, as well as a brief overview of Buber's *I and Thou*.

**Cohen, Jonathan**. Rex Aut Lex. *Apeiron*, 29(2), 145-161, Je 96.

On the basic question of ancient political science—whether persons or law should have ultimate sovereignty—Plato and Aristotle differ. Since they share a philosophy of law—emphasizing its generality and rationality—as well as many assumptions about human psychology—namely, ability to attend to particulars and susceptibility to passions—their disagreement can best be explained by reference to their metaphysics. Plato considers law too mundane to map accurately the transcendent form of justice and too rigid to adjust to the fluidity of the material world. Aristotle, lacking these metaphysical commitments, is free to value law's imperviousness to human partiality.

**Cohen, Joshua**. The Arc of the Moral Universe. *Phil Pub Affairs*, 26(2), 91-134, Spr 97.

**Cohen, Sande**. Reading the Historians' Resistance to Reading: An Essay On Historiographic Schizophrenia. *Clio*, 26(1), 1-28, Fall 96.

**Cohen, Sande**. Science Studies and Language Suppression—A Critique of Bruno Latour's *We Have Never Been Modern*. *Stud Hist Phil Sci*, 28(2), 339-361, Je 97.

**Cohen, Selma Jeanne**. Dance and the Question of Fidelity. *J Aes Educ*, 31(2), 51-53, Sum 97.

**Cohen-Almagor, Raphael**. Autonomy, Life as an Intrinsic Value, and the Right to Die in Dignity. *Sci Eng Ethics*, 1(3), 261-272, Jl 95.

This paper examines two models of thinking relating to the issue of the right to die in dignity: one takes into consideration the rights and interests of the individual; the other supposes that human life is inherently valuable. I contend that preference should be given to the first model, and further assert that the second model may be justified in moral terms only as long as it does not resort to paternalism. The view that holds that certain patients are not able to comprehend their own interests in a fully rational manner, and therefore, 'we' know what is good for these patients better than 'they' do, is morally unjustifiable. I proceed by refuting the 'quality of life' argument, asserting that each person is entitled to decide for herself when it is worth living and when it is not. In this connection, a caveat will be made regarding the role of the family.

**Cohen-Almagor, Raphael**. Why Tolerate? Reflections on the Millian Truth Principle. *Philosophia (Israel)*, 25(1-4), 131-152, Ap 97.

The aim of this essay is to explore one of the most important arguments that are made on behalf of tolerance, deriving from the liberalism of Mill. This is the Truth Principle. I examine Mill's classical essay On Liberty and also his early article "Law of Libel and Liberty of the Press", which has not received adequate attention of scholars. I argue (1) that it is difficult to reconcile the arguments expressed by Mill in his earlier article with what he later said in On Liberty; and that (2) the search for truth might generate an atmosphere of intolerance. I maintain that the liberal Kantian directive of respecting others should have precedece over the Truth Principle. I reinforce my criticism of the Truth Principle by pondering some relevant examples, considering the possibilities of postponing and even terminating, the discovery of truth altogether.

**Cohen-Levinas, Danielle**. Modelo y Fenomenología: Nietzsche contra Hegel: El Renacimiento de la Tragedia en el Renacimiento de la Opera. *Ideas Valores*, 69-78, Ap 97.

Nietzsche and Hegel; Nietzsche against Hegel: these two major figures envisage music as the representation of a philosophical ideal. Nietzsche resorts to the Greek tragedy, where he sees the expression of the vital and deep sensibility of artistic creation. Hegel, on the other hand, conceives music as the sensible incarnation of the *idea*. These two opposite conceptions allow to discuss an interpretation of the opera.

**Cohn-Sherbok, Dan**. "A New Agenda for Society" in *The Liberation Debate: Rights at Issue,* Leahy, Michael (ed), 213-226. New York, Routledge, 1996.

This chapter seeks to demonstrate that the insights of liberation theology provide a new framework for restructuring society in such spheres as urban deprivation, women's emancipation, ecology, and socio-economics.

**Cohn-Sherbok, Dan**. "Cohn-Sherbok's Reply" in *The Liberation Debate: Rights at Issue,* Leahy, Michael (ed), 241-243. New York, Routledge, 1996.

This chapter is a defense of the contribution in *The Liberation Debate* concerning the relevance of liberation theology for modern society. It seeks to refute the criticisms made by John Willson in his contribution to the book.

**Cohn-Sherbok, Dan** (ed) and Leahy, Michael (ed). *The Liberation Debate: Rights at Issue.* New York, Routledge, 1996.

Liberation movements of many kinds have exploded onto the contemporary scene, especially in the West. Convinced of their cause they often violently agitate for so-called rights and emancipation. Some regard these rights campaigners as noble; others view with horror their impact upon society. When groups are liberated their ammunition is the rhetoric of 'rights'. This polemical book leaves adversaries to fight it out. It will displease many; particularly on the issues of race and women. Four other topics are fought over, viz. the claims and counterclaims on behalf of gays, children, animals, and the poor. The format consists of original commissions from distinguished experts in the six areas. In each case there is a protagonist, an antagonist, a right to reply, and an element of adjudication in a final overview by the editors.

**Cohon, Rachel**. Hume's Difficulty with the Virtue of Honesty. *Hume Stud*, 23(1), 91-112, Ap 97.

In the *Treaties* Hume makes three incompatible claims: 1) Honesty is a virtue; 2) For every virtue there is in human nature some nonmoral motive; 3) There is no morally approved, virtue-imparting, nonmoral motive of honest action. In this paper I give such an interpretation. The approved motive of honest action is a moral one, a sense of honor developed out of approval of honest action and disapproval of dishonest action. This makes better sense of the text than construing the approved motive of honest actions to be a nonmoral but artificial one, redirected interest. (edited)

**Cohon, Rachel**. Is Hume a Noncognitivist in the Motivation Argument?. *Phil Stud*, 85(2-3), 251-266, Mr 97.

It is fairly usual today to interpret Hume as a noncognitivist or expressivist about moral judgments. One piece of textual evidence is the famous Motivation Argument: (1) Morals...have an influence on the actions and affections; (2) Reason alone...can never have such any influence; (3) It follows, that [morals] cannot be deriv'd from reason.... (T 457) The Motivation Argument certainly seems to be an argument for ethical noncognitivism, especially given Hume's use of the Representation Argument (claiming that passions and actions have no "representative quality") to support its first premise, that "reason is inert." I argue that, nonetheless, a noncognitivist reading is not defensible. I propose a new reading on which the Motivation Argument is not about moral judgments, but about the moral properties themselves (moral good and evil, virtue and vice); and so, of course, not an argument that moral judgments are to be understood noncognitively or expressivitically. The point of the Argument is that the goodness of an action is not its reasonableness, nor is its evil its unreasonableness.

**Colapietro, Vincent M**. "Living Reason: A Critical Exposition of John E. Smith's Re-Envisioning of Human Rationality" in *Reason, Experience, and God: John E. Smith in Dialogue,* Colapietro, Vincent M, 33-69. New York, Fordham Univ Pr, 1997.

This essay identifies and tries to integrate the main strands in John E. Smith's various treatments of "living reason." What emerges is a vision of reason as dialectical, historical, hermeneutical, fallibilistic, contextual, participatory and conciliatory. Moreover, several criticisms are offered of the view of rationality defended by Smith (e.g., the insistence upon a differential principle such as Spirit whereby the totality of things might be interpreted).

**Colapietro, Vincent M**. "The Dynamical Object and the Deliberative Subject" in *The Rule of Reason: The Philosophy of Charles Sanders Peirce,* Forster, Paul (ed), 262-288. Toronto, Univ of Toronto Pr, 1997.

While the notion of dynamical object is an explicit and indeed central one in Peirce's general theory of signs, the notion of deliberative subject (or agent) is largely implicit. This paper not only highlights the Peircean notion of deliberative agency but also connects it with dynamical object and other key notions in Peirce's theory of signs.

**Colapietro, Vincent M**. "Tradition: First Steps Toward a Pragmaticistic Clarification" in *Philosophy in Experience: American Philosophy in Transition,* Hart, Richard (ed), 14-45. New York, Fordham Univ Pr, 1997.

This paper uses Charles Peirce's three grades of clarity (subjective familiarity or "dumb" smarts, abstract definition and pragmatic clarification) as a way of clarifying the concept of tradition. One of its objectives is to show that, despite appearances, Peircean pragmatism ("pragmaticism") has a thick sense of both tradition and historicity.

**Colapietro, Vincent M**. *Reason, Experience, and God: John E. Smith in Dialogue.* New York, Fordham Univ Pr, 1997.

The book provides an important and comprehensive look at the work of John E. Smith by collected essays which each address aspects of his life-long work. A response by John E. Smith himself draws a line of continuity between the pieces. (publisher, edited)

**Colatrella, Carol**. Fear of Reproduction and Desire for Replication in *Dracula. J Med Human*, 17(3), 179-189, Fall 96.

Bram Stoker's novel *Dracula* (1897) explores how dangerous aspects of human biology, especially the erotic and procreative powers of sexuality, struggle against the restraining protective forces of medical and communication technologies. Dracula relies on superhuman seductive abilities to extend his influence and supernatural powers to protect himself, while his opponents rely on both religious and scientific technologies. Stoker's novel outlines a confrontation between the human and the supernatural by encoding forms of human reproduction as superior to Dracula's method of replication. Religious preventives against vampirism and scientific means of coping with its effects, including medical and communication technologies are invoked to guard the reproductive powers of woman.

**Colebrook, Claire**. Feminist Philosophy and the Philosophy of Feminism: Irigaray and the History of Western Metaphysics. *Hypatia*, 12(1), 79-98, Wint 97.

Irigaray demonstrates that metaphysics depends upon the specific negation and exclusion of the female body. Readings of Irigaray's *Speculum of the Other Woman* tend to highlight the status of this excluded materiality: is there an essential female body which precedes negation or is the feminine only an effect of exclusion? I approach Irigaray's work by way of another question: is it possible to move beyond a feminist critique of metaphysics and towards a feminist philosophy?

**Collier, Andrew**. Unhewn Demonstrations. *Rad Phil*, 81, 22-26, Ja-F 97.

This paper is a critical realist account of the abstract science/concrete science distinction and its relevance to environmental issues. It aims to solve the paradox that critical realist philosophy draws its central tenets from arguments about experiment, yet aims mainly to underlabor for the human sciences, in which it argues that experiments are impossible. The solution lies in making clear the difference between abstract sciences and sciences which study concrete particulars, and it draws conclusions for the environmental ethics of applied science: that abstract sciences should not be practically applied directly, but only through their contribution to concrete science.

**Collier, Gerald**. Learning Moral Commitment in Higher Education?. *J Moral Educ*, 26(1), 73-83, Mr 97.

Britain is faced with many intractable problems. These call for detailed analysis, but equally also for examination of the values that inform them and the influences that shape those values. The present paper assumes, first, that the most fundamental of the values to be considered are those—such as integrity—which sustain probity in public life; secondly, that it is important to explore in what ways universities are likely to influence students' moral commitments; thirdly, that moral values are properly regarded as 'valuations', or dispositions to certain kinds of behaviour to which a sense of obligation is attached; and fourthly that, despite the predominantly relativist view of values current in postmodern thinking, it is necessary, if effective action is to be taken in the public domain, to find some "sense of minimum universal values" (Weeks, 1993). The greater part of the paper is taken up with an analysis of four areas of activity through which the staff of an institution are likely to influence their students' moral dispositions and generate commitment.

**Collin, Finn**. Idiographic Theorizing and Ideal Types: Max Weber's Methodology of Social Science. *Dan Yrbk Phil*, 30, 37-67, 1995.

Max Weber held that ideal types make room for autonomous idiographic theorizing in social science, without the need for any nomothetic discipline to supply its conceptual apparatus. Unfortunately, Weber's position is infested with a tension between 1) the claim that the concepts of idiographic science, including the ideal types used, are freely chosen in the light of the investigator's interests, independently of any considerations of general principles and 2) the contention that ideal types have explanatory import. It argued that Weber's notion of an autonomous idiographic science, based on ideal types, will lead either to conventionalism or to a priorism.

**Collingridge, Michael** and Miller, Seumas. Filial Responsibility and the Care of the Aged. *J Applied Phil*, 14(2), 119-128, 1997.

What obligations and responsibilities, if any, do adult children have with respect to their aged parents? This paper briefly considers the sociohistorical and legal bases for filial obligations and suggests there is a mismatch between perceptions in the community over what they see as their obligations, what policy makers would like to impose and how philosophers identify and ground these obligations. Examining four philosophical models of filial obligation, we conclude that no one account provides an adequate justification for the types of responsibility that might be assumed in a family relationship.

**Collins, Arthur W**. Personal Identity and the Coherence of *Q*-Memory. *Phil Quart*, 47(186), 73-80, Ja 97.

Brian Garrett constructs cases satisfying Andy Hamilton's definition of weak q-memory. This does not establish that a peculiar kind of memory is at least conceptually coherent. Any 'apparent memory experiences' that satisfy the definition turn out not to involve remembering anything at all. This conclusion follows if we accept, as both Hamilton and Garrett do, a variety of first-person authority according to which memory judgements may be false, but not on the ground that someone other than the remembering subject had the remembered experience. Garrett's brain-bisection illustration sounds convincing, but only because we retain the idea that the subjects created by implanting a hemisphere each in two different bodies are entitled to say that they remember experiences before the surgery in the ordinary sense. To that extent the illustration presents a case of ordinary memory, not q-memory. (publisher)

**Collins, Arthur W**. The Psychological Reality of Reasons. *Ratio*, 10(2), 108-123, S 97.

Action explanations like 'I am heading to the ferry because the bridge is closed,' are supposed to require restatement: 'I am... because I believe the bridge is closed,' because (I) the objective claim may be false though the intended explanation is correct, and (II) because objective circumstances have to be cognitively mediated if they are to bear on action. This supposition is rejected here. Restatements cannot withdraw the objective claim without withdrawing the explanation. In the context of reason-giving, belief statements do not function as assertions about the inner life. (edited)

**Collins, Corbin**. Searle on Consciousness and Dualism. *Int J Phil Stud*, 5(1), 15-33, Mr 97.

In this article, I examine and criticize John Searle's account of the relation between mind and body. Searle maintains that irreducibility is a 'trivial' result of our 'definitional practices' and is entirely compatible with his theory. I contend that this latter claim is based on an equivocation: Searle's conclusion only seems to follow because he alters and trivializes what philosophers ordinarily mean by 'reduction'. I also maintain that Searle's position *is* reductionist in the ordinary, nontrivial sense. For this reason, his theory fails to accommodate the subjective character of consciousness and fails to solve the traditional mind-body problem. Finally, I briefly discuss Searle's claim that he is not an epiphenomenalist and argue that given the assumptions of his view there is no interesting *causal* role for consciousness in the physical world. (edited)

**Collins, Steven** and Huxley, Andrew. The Post-Canonical Adventures of Mahasammata. *J Indian Phil*, 24(6), 623-648, D 96.

**Colman, Andrew M** and Bacharach, Michael. Payoff Dominance and the Stackelberg Heuristic. *Theor Decis*, 43(1), 1-19, Jl 97.

Payoff dominance, a criterion for choosing between equilibrium points in games, is intuitively compelling, especially in matching games and other games of common interests, but it has not been justified from standard game-theoretic rationality assumptions. A psychological explanation of it is offered in terms of a form of reasoning that we call the Stackelberg heuristic in which players assume that their strategic thinking will be anticipated by their coplayer(s). (edited)

**Colmenares Olivar, Ricardo**. Human Rights and Legal Pluralism in Venezuela: An Approximation to the Native Inhabitants Rights (Spanish). *Fronesis*, 2(2), 35-50, D 95.

During the last years, the cultural diversity in Venezuela has been showing through a group of legal norms which express in its content, the aspirations of the different social groups and especially, those of the native inhabitants. That is why, the *underlying legal pluralism* that has operated within the formal justice system constitutes an alternate and efficient mechanism to guarantee the proper and vital rights of the Venezuelan native inhabitants.

**Colom González, Francisco**. El Maxismo y el ocaso de la política. *Euridice*, 25-46, 1992.

Marxism has often been accused of lacking a consistent theory of politics. Its historical role as a social movement with a revolutionary strategy and the weight of "labor" as an ontological category are the main reasons for that deficiency. From this point of view, politics and State are both considered as a by-product of class domination doomed to fade away in a socialist society. Such an "extinctionist" bias neglected the problem of preserving individual rights versus the State and the means for democratic control of power. The risks of authoritarianism in socialist regimes were in this way increased.

**Colom González, Francisco**. *Las Caras del Leviatán: Una Lectura Política de la Teoría Crítica*. Barcelona, Anthropos, 1992.

Este estudio pretende señalar la entidad y originalidad de esa "otra" Teoría Crítica relativamente desconocida: la configurada por el análisis político y jurídico de la moderna sociedad burguesa. De forma individual y en su respectivo ámbito de competencia, la obra de estos autores ha reflejado las transformaciones históricas sufridas por el Estado capitalista a lo largo del presente siglo, el sucesivo desvelamiento de las caras del moderno Leviatán: la crisis del Estado liberal de derecho en el periodo entreguerras, el terrible fondo de irracionalidad manifiesto en el Behemoth nacionalsocialista y los ambivalentes rendimientos ofrecidos por nuestro debilitado "Estado de bienestar". (publisher, edited)

**Colombat, André Pierre**. November 4, 1995: Deleuze's Death as an Event. *Man World*, 29(3), 235-249, Jl 96.

**Colomer, Eusebi**. Heidegger y la modernidad. *Rev Filosof (Mexico)*, 29(87), 337-372, S-D 96.

**Colonnello, Pio**. La colpa e il tempo in Fëdor Dostoevskij. *Sapienza*, 49(3), 271-297, 1996.

**Colonnello, Pio**. Unamuno e l'esistenzialismo "cristiano". *Sapienza*, 49(4), 449-453, 1996.

*Pio Colonnello discusses the topics presented by Armando Savignano in his book (Radici del pensiero spagnolo del Novecento, Napoli 1995). If for Ortega philosophy is meditatio vitae, for Unamuno it is above all meditatio mortis, focusing on the tragic sentiment of existence. In Unamuno the problem of God is bound up with anxiety about and nostalgia for the eternal. For although he professes no conventional religion, he seeks to outline a philosophy of religion which, while reaching out towards eternity, is grounded in the concrete experience of existence. In this sense one may speak of a "Christian Existentialism" of Unamuno.*

**Colwell, C**. Deleuze and the Prepersonal. *Phil Today*, 41(1-4), 18-23, Spr 97.

While much has been written about the dissolution of the subject, little attention has been paid to what the subject dissolves into. I argue that Deleuze's notion of the prepersonal (along with Foucault's analyses) provides a useful model for this problem. The subject and its correlative structures, the *other* (both human and nonhuman) and community, are analyzed under this model to show that once identity has collapsed the borders that separate and define these structures (which legitimate and marginalize persons) have to be reconceived. I conclude by discussing both the advantages and the dangers of this model for politics.

**Comandini, Glenn J** and McDermott, John M. The Problem of Person and Jean Mouroux. *Sapientia*, 52(201), 75-97, 1997.

In Thomism person denotes "subsistent relation" (Trinity) and "individual subsistence" (Christology), perichoresis and incommunicability, a part and a whole. As freely dominating actions person contrasts with nature, intrinsic principle of motion and free will. Building ascending series of integrating paradoxes upon the form-matter composition, Mouroux identified person with the soul's apex where meet existence-essence, spirit-matter, intellect-will, individual-species, activity-passivity, eternity-time and grace-nature. In love the person is most himself when joined to God and others, called in freedom to become who he is. Unclear are the soul's possession of existence and how Christ's infinite existence actuates a finite nature.

**Comanducci, Paolo**. Some Comments on Toleration. *Ratio Juris*, 10(2), 187-192, Je 97.

**Comay, Rebecca**. "Materialist Mutations of the *Bilderverbot*" in *Sites of Vision*, Levin, David Michael (ed), 337-378. Cambridge, MIT Pr, 1997.

**Comeau, Paul-André**. État fragile, démocratie précaire: le lieu de l'insouciance. *Philosopher*, 18, 9-23, 1995.

**Comesaña, Manuel**. "Racionalidad práctica e inducción: la propuesta neopopperiana de John Watkins" in *La racionalidad: su poder y sus límites*, Nudler, Oscar (ed), 407-424. Barcelona, Ed Paidos, 1996.

A Popperian has no reason to open the faucet when she wants to drink water; to open the faucet is an action grounded on the inductive reliance that the future will be, in certain respects, similar to the past. This is the "pragmatic problem of induction," and John Watkins has dealt with it in at least four occasions, attempting, by a comparison of the strength of forecasts not depending on inductive considerations, to justify the employment of an inductive strategy justifying any inductive principle. We attempt to show that he has had little success.

**Comesaña-Santalices, Gloria**. *Behind Closed Doors*: Analysis of the Feminine Figures in Sartrean Theatre (Spanish). *Rev Filosof (Venezuela)*, 24(2), 53-79, Jl-D 96.

This article forms part of a work in which the feminine figures in Sartrean theater are treated from the feminist and existentialist points of view. The feminine characters in *Behind Closed Doors* are analyzed, focusing on the philosophical categories of Sartrean thought and critically studying through the figures of Ines and Estelle how Sartre, critical philosopher and libertarian, from a feminist point of view, is a promoter of sexism, through the most conventional and retrograde ideas.

**Cometti, Jean-Pierre**. Introduction. *Rev Int Phil*, 50(198), 565-576, 1996.

**Comte-Sponville, André**. L'amour selon Pascal. *Rev Int Phil*, 51(199), 131-160, 1997.

L'amour, chez Pascal, se dit en plusieurs sens, qui s'organisent entre les deux pôles de la concupiscence et de la charité. Le *Discours sur les passions de l'amour*, qui n'est certainement pas de Pascal, ne dit pas l'essentiel, qui se trouve dans les *Pensées*: c'est l'amour qui sauve, et c'est l'amour qui perd. C'est pourqoui l'amour est la question la plus importante, dont toutes les autres dépendent. Il s'agit de s'aimer soi, et de se perdre, ou d'aimer Dieu, qui nous sauve. Le moi n'est haïssable que parce qu'il ne sait pas aimer; l'amour le sauve en l'anéantissant.

**Conant, James**. "The James/Royce Dispute and the Development of James's "Solution" in *The Cambridge Companion to William James*, Putnam, Ruth Anna (ed), 186-213. New York, Cambridge Univ Pr, 1997.

**Conant, James**. On Wittgenstein's Philosophy of Mathematics II. *Proc Aris Soc*, 97, 195-222, 1997.

**Conant, James** and Berti, Enrico and Vegetti, Mario. La fragilità del bene: Fortuna ed etica nella tragedia e nella filosofia greca di Martha C. Nussbaum. *Iride*, 10(20), 157-176, Ap 97.

For E. Berti the Aristotelian defended by Martha Nussbaum in her book *The Fragility of Goodness* is not conservative, because it conceives the human good as practicable in a society of "free and equal" citizens and because it proposes as method of philosophy the rational argumentation from the ways of thinking and speaking shared by the whole linguistic community (the *endoxa*). The only reserve advanced by the author to Nussbaum's thesis concerns the lack, in her book, of a clear distinction between the *endoxa* and the *phainomena*, which for Aristotle are all sort of opinions. J. Conant and M. Vegetti discuss other aspects of the book.

**Condren, Conal**. Code Types: Functions and Failings and Organizational Diversity. *Bus Prof Ethics J*, 14(4), 69-87, Wint 95.

The paper examines the differences between codes of conduct and ethics in terms of characteristic failings. The notion of failing, however, presupposes criteria of success. The different, largely rhetorical functions of code formulations are specified. A model of organizational types is outlined in order to make clear the problems inherent in applying codes appropriate to one form of organization to another. Some attention is given to the linguistic mechanisms used to make codes seem globally applicable.

**Conesa, Francisco**. El conocimiento de fe en la filosofía de Leonardo Polo. *Anu Filosof*, 29(2), 427-439, 1996.

This paper attempts to provide an exposition of the Christian faith as habitual knowledge according to the theory of habits by L. Polo. After the explanation of human person *as a being for God*, the article describes our religious and philosophical knowledge of God. Finally it describes the knowledge achieved through the gift of faith.

**Conforti, Patrizia**. Hervé de Nédellec et les questions ordinaires *De cognitione primi principii. Rev Thomiste*, 97(1), 63-82, Ja-Mr 97.

Saint Thomas n'a pas laissé de traité *De primo principio*. Duns Scot a jugé convenable d'en écrire un. Mais, pour tous les deux, la première question était: *Utrum Deus sit*. Ce n'est pas le cas d'Hervé, car il s'efforce plutôt de produire de longues questions ordinaires *De cognitione primi principii* pour montrer l'efficacité de la raison naturelle et des preuves rationnelles à ce sujet. Son problème est: *Utrum secundum statum viae naturali cognitione Deum esse possit demonstrative probari*, ou: *Utrum Deum esse demonstrative possit probari via causalitatis effectivae*. L'attention va non plus vers l'objet de la démonstration, c'est-à-dire l'existence de Dieu, mais plutôt vers la démonstration elle-même. (edited)

**Coniglione, Francesco**. "Humanistic Interpretation between Hempel and Popper" in *Epistemology and History*, Zeidler-Janiszewska, Anna (ed), 283-301. Amsterdam, Rodopi, 1996.

The theory of rationality (Kmita, Nowak, Swiderski), its assumptions and relation to humanistic interpretation are discussed, followed by comparison between Popper's and Hempel's views on the rationality principle as well as on physical and historical explanations. They are then confronted with W. Dray's concepts. The author presents von Wright's scheme of inference (practical syllogism) pointing out its differences from and analogies with Kmita's scheme. He concludes that Kmita's model is closer to the spirit of the Popper-Hempel conception of scientific explanation than that of von Wright.

**Conill, Jesús**. "El ideal de la Paz en el Humanismo Ético de Kant" in *Kant: La paz perpetua, doscientos años después*, Martínez Guzmán, Vicent (ed), 53-66. Valencia, Nau Llibres, 1997.

**Conill, Jesús**. La fenomenología en Zubiri. *Pensamiento*, 53(206), 177-190, My-Ag 97.

*Recontextualización de la filosofía de Zubiri* en el ámbito fenomenológico de Husserl, Ortega y Heidegger. Zubiri cuenta con la fenomenología como fuente de inspiración para su propia orientación filosófica. Ante todo hay que destacar el *hacia dónde* de la fenomenología, más allá del *de dónde*. En una primera etapa encontramos una fenomenología objetivista, pero pronto se produce una *transformación de la fenomenología* en Zubiri (igual que en Ortega) en dirección *hacia la metafísica*. Ahora bien, una metafísica que ha pasado por el análisis *noológico* de la intelección sentiente, desde donde cabe alumbrar una nueva metafísica *a la altura de los tiempos*.

**Conle, Carola**. Between Fact and Fiction: Dialogue within Encounters of Difference. *Educ Theor*, 47(2), 181-201, Spr 97.

By way of a self-study project, a teacher educator explores facets of her practice that aim to make teaching candidates aware of the need to characterize behavior in an open-ended fashion. She narrates their experiences with a particular exercise that was to develop interpretive competence through narrative modes of experience by creating dialogue that points to the narrative histories of particular actions and episodes and avoids evaluative generalizations. The author also works through some complex connections that tie her work to philosophical traditions and certain 'habits of mind' that seem to have come in their wake.

**Conley, Katharine**. *Automatic Woman: The Representation of Woman in Surrealism*. Lincoln, Univ of Nebraska Pr, 1996.

*Automatic Woman* focuses on the literary representation of woman in the surrealist writing of André Breton, Leonora Carrington and Unica Zürn, and examines how that representation changes when women write. It proposes that surrealism's strong muse-figure anticipated the participation of women. Carrington and Zürn's verbal self-portraits humanize the composite muse-figure that emerges from the writing of Breton and add body to it. Their writing serves as a bridge between surrealist automatic writing and French feminist *écriture féminine*, highlighting points of encounter between the surrealists and more recent avant-garde writers, particularly women.

**Connolly, Frank W**. A Call for a Statement of Expectations for the Global Information Infrastructure. *Sci Eng Ethics*, 2(2), 167-176, A 96.

This paper considers the relationship between ethics, technology and law and the roles and limitations each has in this relationship. It argues that ethics has the key role in establishing a resilient, comprehensive and sensitive information infrastructure. It puts forward a Bill of Rights and Responsibilities for the electronic community.

**Connolly, Maureen** and Lathrop, Anna. Maurice Merleau-Ponty and Rudolf Laban—An Interactive Appropriation of Parallels and Resonances. *Human Stud*, 20(1), 27-45, Ja 97.

In this paper we propose an examination of the shared connections between the French philosopher Maurice Merleau-Ponty and the Austro-Hungarian movement theorist Rudolf Laban. In many ways Merleau-Ponty's philosophy demonstrates a synthesis of the best in existentialism and phenomenology. In like manner, Rudolf Laban was a synthesizer of experiences and theories of movement. We propose to examine the parallels and resonances of their theory with the forum of a hypothetical collegial conversation. (edited)

**Connolly, William E**. A Critique of Pure Politics. *Phil Soc Crit*, 23(5), 1-26, S 97.

This essay examines lines of connection between disgust, the effect of disciplines upon such intensive appraisals, political action and the shape of ethical responsiveness. Philosophies that espouse purity in morality or politics mask these lines of connection; they thereby disparage the significance of techniques of the self to ethical and political life. Immanuel Kant and Hannah Arendt provide the two main figures through whom these themes are explored. Arendt and Kant are brought into relation with each other through the way each comes to terms with disgust and common sense. (edited)

**Conte, Domenico**. "Prospettive di storia universale nell'opera di Spengler" in *Lo Storicismo e la Sua Storia: Temi, Problemi, Prospettive*, Cacciatore, Giuseppe (ed), 418-434. Milano, Guerini, 1997.

**Conway, Daniel W**. "Tumbling Dice: Gilles Deleuze and the Economy of *Répétition*" in *Deleuze and Philosophy: The Difference Engineer*, Ansell Pearson, Keith (ed), 73-90. New York, Routledge, 1997.

The figure of the dice-throw serves, I contend, not only as the master trope of Deleuze's political thinking, but also as a model for his account of the economy of repetition. Most importantly, the figure of the dice-throw provides us with a blueprint for putting Deleuze himself to work, as a desiring-machine in his own right. Here the influence of Nietzsche is doubtly useful to us: We may map outbreaks of Deleuze's own schizophrenia by charting his use and abuse of Nietzsche; we may employ Deleuze's experimentation with Nietzsche as a model for our own experimentation with Deleuze.

**Conway, Daniel W**. Circulus Vitiosus Deus? The Dialectical Logic of Feminist Standpoint Theory. *J Soc Phil*, 28(1), 62-76, Spr 97.

This paper essays a critical appraisal of the logic that underlies feminist standpoint theory. The enduring value of feminist standpoint theory lies not in the Hegelian-Marxist lens through which standpoint theorists characteristically view social relations, but in the epistemic primacy they assign to situated knowledges. The preferred methodology of standpoint theorists, as expressed in the logical apparatus they borrow from Hegel, Marx, and Lukács, is incompatible with their avowed campaign to expose all traces of patriarchy within the practice of epistemology. (edited)

**Conway, Daniel W**. Writing in Blood: On the Prejudices of Genealogy. *Epoche*, 3(1 & 2), 149-181, 1995.

**Conway, Gertrude D**. "Differences: Indifference or Dialogue" in *Philosophy, Religion, and the Question of Intolerance*, Ambuel, David (ed), 157-169. Albany, SUNY Pr, 1997.

Contemporary philosophy and culture are distinguished by the recognition of pluralistic traditions and the privileging of the virtue of tolerance. This paper explores two characterizations and justifications of tolerance. It criticizes Rorty's account for (a) delivering a minimalist list understanding of tolerance bordering on indifference and (b) failing to encourage any engagement of differences. It argues that Gadamer offers a far more positive account which encourages engagement rather than disengagement, dialogue rather than indifference. With such an account, tolerance is transformed from passive acquiescence to pluralism to the judicicous promotion of the mutuality of respect distinctive of rational persons and civil societies at their very best.

**Cook, John W**. How to Read Wittgenstein. *Phil Invest*, 20(3), 224-245, Jl 97.

A defense of the thesis that Wittgenstein, from the *Tractatus* until the end of his life, was a phenomenalist.

**Cooke, Maeve**. Are Ethical Conflicts Irreconcilable?. *Phil Soc Crit*, 23(2), 1-19, Mr 97.

The discussion starts with the fact of ethical disagreement in contemporary liberal democracies. In responding to the question of whether such conflicts are reconcilable, it proposes a normative model of deliberative democracy that seeks to avoid the privatization of ethical concerns. It is argued that many contemporary models of democracy privatize ethical matters either because of a view that ethical conflicts are fundamentally irreconcilable or because of a mistrust of the ideal of rational consensus in the fields of law and politics. Against this, the article contends that most ethical disagreements are reconcilable in principle; it further suggests that mistrust of the ideal of rational consensus in the fields of law and politics is based on misunderstanding. (edited)

**Cooke, Maeve**. Authenticity and Autonomy: Taylor, Habermas, and the Politics of Recognition. *Polit Theory*, 25(2), 258-288, Ap 97.

I discuss Taylor's essay and Habermas's response, focusing initially on Taylor's account of the politics of difference. I see difficulties in Taylor's emphasis on authenticity and a lack of precision concerning what is involved in demanding recognition of specific identity. Here, I outline five distinct ways of understanding this demand. I then consider which of these five interpretations can be accommodated by Habermas's recent theory. I show how Habermas now separates morality from ethics less sharply than before, and argue that his constitutional state is more sensitive to difference than Taylor allows, although it cannot accommodate all forms of difference. However, unlike Taylor who thematizes the moral aspect of liberal political exclusion, Habermas can be criticized for failing to discuss the moral dimensions of inevitable exclusion of difference.

**Cooke, Maeve**. *Language and Reason: A Study of Habermas's Pragmatics*. Cambridge, MIT Pr, 1997.

Readers of Jürgen Habermas's *Theory of Communicative Action* and his later social theory know that the idea of communicative rationality is central to his version of critical theory. *Language and Reason* opens up new territory for social theorists by providing the first general introduction to Habermas's program of formal pragmatics: his reconstruction of the universal principles of possible understanding that, he argues, are already operative in everyday communicative practices. Philosophers of language will discover surprising and fruitful connections between Habermas's account of language and validity (especially his theory of meaning) and their own concerns. (publisher)

**Coolen, Maarten**. Jan Hollak over de betekenis van de techniek voor de filosofie. *Alg Ned Tijdschr Wijs*, 89(1), 44-66, Ja 97.

In his writings on technology, J.H.A. Hollak connects the present stage of technology to the modern self-concept of man as an autonomous subject in a special manner. By interpreting the three stages of technology—hand tool, classical mechanical machine and information-processing machine—within a dialectical framework, he shows how the idea of what technology is about finds its perfect realization in information technology, and how the self-concept of man as an autonomous subject, which reached its full expression in Hegel's philosophy, is externalized in the artifacts of the last stage of technology. What Marx had in mind—the practical realization of Hegel's self-foundation of the human spirit—appears to have come about in information technology, but not in the way Marx had expected. Therefore, this understanding of man cannot be complete. On the basis of this insight in human autonomy, it is the task of man to try to realize a new kind of metaphysical openness, beyond Hegelianism, Marxism and existentialism.

**Coolidge Jr, Francis P**. On the Nature of the Absolute: A Response to Desmond. *SW Phil Rev*, 13(1), 67-74, Ja 97.

I offer a brief and sympathetic synopsis of Desmond's metaphysics with the aim of articulating a kindred, but divergent, account of the *absolute*. Desmond argues that while the human being has both erotic and agapeic capacities, the *absolute* must be solely agapeic, otherwise the integrity of entities as differentiated and "other" than the *absolute* will be compromised. I argue that there must be a sense in which the *absolute* is erotic, otherwise the unity of the *absolute* with the entities it grounds is not adequately explained.

**Coolsaet, Willy**. Heidegger's Concept of the Technological 'Gestell' under Discussion. *Tijdschr Filosof*, 58(3), 461-475, S 96.

*Energeia* is, next to other words such as *aletheia, fusis, objectivity, will to power, Gestell*, one of the fundamental terms through which, according to Heidegger, Western thought expresses Being (to be sure very imperfectly). In our text we make use of Aristotle's concept of *energeia*, implying, according to us, a reversal of the natural relationship of means to ends. We do this to be able to evaluate critically Heidegger's concept of the modern technological *Gestell*. The connecting link in our analysis is the Greek concept of *fusis* and the relation Heidegger introduces between the *fusis* and the Greek doctrine of the four causes. Heidegger seems unwilling to see the overall presence of a reversal of the relation of means to ends. Our interpretation confronts the reader with a choice. The concept of *energeia* leads in two directions. One can assume the means-ends reversal, or one can, as Heidegger does, point to the forgotten Event of Being. But a choice is necessary. Heidegger's point of view seems, moreover, unable to uncover some important relations, such as the analogy we discern between *energeia, fusis*, (modern) natural spontaneity of unhuman nature absorbing man, modern technology, capitalism (producing for the sake of producing)—according to Heidegger all things which are expressions of an overwhelming process of Being.

**Coombs, Jeffrey**. Modal Voluntarism in Descartes's Jesuit Predecessors. *Amer Cath Phil Quart*, 70(Supp), 237-247, 1996.

**Coombs, Jerrold**. In Defense of Israel Scheffler's Conception of Moral Education. *Stud Phil Educ*, 16(1-2), 175-187, Ja-Ap 97.

Israel Scheffler views moral education as having two major objectives; inculcating minimum standards of decent conduct and developing rationality in moral deliberation and judgment. The latter is to be achieved by engaging students in discussions of moral issues in such a way that they come to appreciate and follow standards of rational deliberation and judgment—standards that Scheffler explicates primarily in terms of impartiality. This paper argues that the conception of rational moral deliberation and discussion underlying Scheffler's approach to moral education is inadequate and suggests an alternative conception that gives far more prominence to the problem of interpreting the meaning of substantive moral concepts and determining how they apply to particular cases.

**Coombs, Jerrold** and Wright, Ian. A Conception of Practical Reasoning. *Inquiry (USA)*, 14(2), 48-51, Wint 94.

**Cooper, David E**. "Verstehen, Holism and Fascism" in *Verstehen and Humane Understanding*, O'Hear, Anthony (ed), 95-107. New York, Cambridge Univ Pr, 1996.

**Cooper, David E**. Losing Our Minds: Olafson on Human Being. *Inquiry*, 39(3-4), 479-495, D 96.

**Cooper, David E**. Wittgenstein, Heidegger and Humility. *Philosophy*, 72(279), 105-123, Ja 97.

**Cooper, Gregory**. Theoretical Modeling and Biological Laws. *Proc Phil Sci Ass*, 3(Suppl), S29-S35, 1996.

Recent controversy over the existence of biological laws raises questions about the cognitive aims of theoretical modelling in that science. If there are no laws for successful theoretical models to approximate, then what is it that successful theories do? One response is to regard theoretical models as tools, But this instrumental reading cannot accommodate the explanatory role that theories are supposed to play. Yet accommodating the explanatory function, as articulated by Brandon and Sober for example, seems to involve us once again in a reliance on laws. The paper concludes that we must rethink both the nature of laws *and* theoretical explanation in biology.

**Cooper, John M** (ed) and Hutchinson, D S (ed). *Plato: Complete Works*. Indianapolis, Hackett, 1997.

Outstanding translations by leading contemporary scholars—many commissioned especially for this volume—are presented here in the first single edition to include the entire surviving corpus of works attributed to Plato in antiquity. In his introductory essay, John Cooper explains the presentation of these works, discusses questions concerning the chronology of their composition, comments on the dialogue form in which Plato wrote and offers guidance on approaching the reading and study of Plato's works. Also included are concise introductions by Cooper and Hutchinson to each translation, meticulous annotation designed to serve both scholar and general reader and a comprehensive index. This handsome volume offers fine paper and a high-quality Smyth-sewn cloth binding in a sturdy, elegant edition. (publisher)

**Cooper, M Wayne**. The Gastroenterologist and His Endoscope: The Embodiment of Technology and the Necessity for a Medical Ethics. *Theor Med*, 17(4), 379-398, D 96.

The purpose of this essay is to argue for the necessity of an ethics of the practice of the specialist-technologist in medicine. In the first part I sketch three stages of medical ethics, each with a particular viewpoint regarding the technology of medicine. I focus on Brody's consideration of the "physician's power" as an example of contemporary medical ethics which explicitly excludes the specialist-technologist as a locus of development of medical ethics. Next, the philosophy of Heidegger is examined to suggest an approach to the problem and, finally, some of Levinas's contributions regarding the "other" are introduced to suggest a preliminary approach to a medical ethics of the specialist-technologist.

**Cooper, Robert W** and Frank, Garry L. Helping Professionals in Business Behave Ethically: Why Business Cannot Abdicate Its Responsibility to the Profession. *J Bus Ethics*, 16(12-13), 1459-1466, S 97.

This paper compares the findings of studies of seven groups of professionals in various key segments of the fields of accounting and insurance conducted during 1990 through 1994 in an effort to determine the extent to which they tend to rely on various factors in their business and professional environments for help in behaving ethically in the course of their work. Commonalities among the findings for these rather diverse groups are highlighted and their possible implications for business and the professions are discussed.

**Cooper, S Barry** and Sorbi, Andrea. Noncappable Enumeration Degrees Below $0'_e$. *J Sym Log*, 61(4), 1347-1363, D 96.

We prove that there exists a noncappable enumeration degree strictly below $0'_e$.

**Cooper, S Barry** and Sorbi, Andrea and Yi, Xiaoding. Cupping and Noncupping in the Enumeration Degrees of Sigma$^0_2$ Sets [1]. *Annals Pure Applied Log*, 82(3), 317-342, D 96.

We prove the following three theorems on the enumeration degrees of Sigma$^0_2$ sets. Theorem A: There exists a nonzero noncuppable Sigma$^0_2$ enumeration degree. Theorem B: Every nonzero Delta$^0_2$ enumeration degree is cuppable to $0'_e$ by an incomplete total enumeration degree. Theorem C: There exists a nonzero low Delta$^0_2$ enumeration degree with the anticupping property. (edited)

**Cooper, Wesley**. The Construction of Professional Reality: Implications for Professional Ethics. *Prof Ethics*, 5(1-2), 63-85, Spr-Sum 96.

**Copeland, B Jack**. What is Computation?. *Synthese*, 108(3), 335-359, S 96.

To compute is to execute an algorithm. More precisely, to say that a device or organ computes is to say that there exists a modelling relationship of a certain kind between it and a formal specification of an algorithm and supporting architecture. The key issue is to delimit the phrase 'of a certain kind'. I call this the problem of distinguishing between standard an nonstandard models of computation. The successful drawing of this distinction guards Turing's 1936 analysis of computation against a difficulty that has persistently been raised against it and undercuts various objections that have been made to the computational theory of mind.

**Copeland, B Jack** and Proudfoot, Diane. On Alan Turing's Anticipation of Connectionism. *Synthese*, 108(3), 361-377, S 96.

It is not widely realised that Turing was probably the first person to consider building computing machines out of simple, neuron-like elements connected together into networks in a largely random manner. Turing called his networks 'unorganised machines'. By the application of what he described as 'appropriate interference, mimicking education' an unorganised machine can be trained to perform any task that a Turing machine can carry out, provided the number of 'neurons' is sufficient. Turing proposed simulating both the behavior of the network and the training process by means of a computer program. We outline Turing's connectionist project of 1948.

**Copp, David**. "Democracy and Communal Self-Determination" in *The Morality of Nationalism*, McKim, Robert (ed), 277-300. New York, Oxford Univ Pr, 1997.

Which groups, in which territories, have the right to be or to constitute themselves as states? Which groups have "the right of self-determination"? Under what circumstances is secession justified? I argue that a reasonable answer to the question of why justice requires democracy supports an answer to the question about self-determination. It supports the proposal that, subject to certain qualifications, societies with a territory and with a stable desire for self-government, have the right to constitute themselves as states. I argue that in a world of pluralistic societies, the ideas that "nations" or that "cultural groups" have this right are antidemocratic.

**Copp, David**. The Ring of Gyges: Overridingness and the Unity of Reason. *Soc Phil Pol*, 14(1), 86-106, Wint 97.

Does morality override self-interest? When there is conflict between the overall verdict of morality regarding what we ought to do and the overall verdict of self-interest regarding what we ought to do in our self-interest, which verdict is normatively more important? If morality is overriding, its verdicts must be normatively most important from a *definitive standpoint*, which could not be the standpoint of morality itself. I argue that there is no such definitive standpoint. Hence, neither morality nor self-interest is overriding. In situations where morality and self-interest conflict, there is no truth regarding what we ought *simpliciter* to do.

**Coppinger, Raymond** (& others) and Feinstein, Mark and Warner, Stanley. Global Population Growth and the Demise of Nature. *Environ Values*, 5(4), 285-301, N 96.

We suggest that current trends in population growth are unlikely to abate for three reasons: first, there are intrinsic biological pressures to reproduce regardless of social engineering; second, the character of the domestic alliance makes it a formidable competitor to wildlife; and third, the time-frame before population doubling is, from a biological perspective, virtually instantaneous. This paper draws from a wide body of research in the biological and social sciences. We neither condone nor endorse this picture of inexorable population increase. Rather, we appeal for a change in the nature of the discussion of population among environmentalists, to focus on the question of how best to manage what wildlife will be left on the margins of a domesticated world. (edited)

**Corazón, Rafael**. Descartes: un nuevo modo de hacer filosofía. *Anu Filosof*, 29(2), 441-461, 1996.

The interpretation of Descartes's thinking which is made by professor Polo in *Evidencia y realidad en Descartes* (and, in general, in all his work) is analysed in this article. The key to understanding Descartes is "the voluntary attitude", which lies in placing the attention before the arrival of facts and contents of consciousness. So they can be examined and controlled in order to decide if they are reliable or not. The result is an exaggerated dedication which limits the capacity of intelligence to act according to its nature.

**Corazza, Eros**. Référence directe et psychologisme. *Rev Phil Fr*, 2, 195-204, Ap-Je 97.

**Corcoran, Kevin**. Is Theistic Experience Phenomenologically Possible?. *Relig Stud*, 32(4), 449-461, D 96.

In this paper I examine the phenomenological possibility of peculiarly theistic experience. I present and explicate William Forgie's very powerful arguments against the possibility of such experience and Nelson Pike's recent response to Forgie. I argue that although Pike's refutation of Forgie ultimately miscarries, there are good reasons for rejecting what is the central thesis upon which all of Forgie's arguments rest. After canvassing several of these reasons and recommending an alternative thesis, I conclude that Forgie has not succeeded in establishing the phenomenological impossibility of theistic experience.

**Cordeiro, William P**. Suggested Management Responses to Ethical Issue Raised by Technological Change. *J Bus Ethics*, 16(12-13), 1393-1400, S 97.

The development of technology raises an array of ethical issues related to work. Many of these ethical issues are old issues surfacing under new guises. Technology has not changed the issues, but technology makes the issues' analysis and application more complex. This paper identifies several new ethical issues raised by technological change: computer crime, an over-reliance on computer controlled systems, biotechnical developments, degradation of quality-of-life at work and new categories of work-related injuries. The paper offers a five-step process for the effective management of these ethical issues. (edited)

**Cordeiro Silva, Rafael**. A Concepçao de Filosofia em Adorno. *Educ Filosof*, 9(17), 157-172, Ja-Je 95.

L'article a l'intention d'expliciter la conception de la philosophie chez Adorno et sa critique à la tradition après Hegel. En utilisant deux essais de l'auteur, on veut démontrer comme Adorno s'approprie de la pensée de Hegel dans la construction de la dialectique négative. A la fin, on propose des questions relatives au cadre épistemologique dans lequel Adorno organise ses arguments.

**Cordero, Ronald A**. Aristotle and Fair Admissions. *Pub Affairs Quart*, 11(1), 75-86, Ja 97.

When we give an applicant one of a limited number of places available in a college or university, we are distributing a valuable social good. How can we be fair in this distribution? According to Aristotle, distributions are fair when made in proportion to merit. But what basis of merit is relevant for college admissions? I argue that differential ratings of moral and intellectual qualities are of limited value for determinations of merit in this case and that a fair policy would have to rely heavily on random selection.

**Cordero C, Gerardo Arturo**. Filosofía de la educación: tareas y desafíos. *Rev Filosof (Costa Rica)*, 34(83-84), 275-281, D 96.

This article responds to the following question, What is the role of philosophy of education? The answer is proposed from three complementary areas, namely, the one in charge of the definition of education, the anthropological and axiological point of view and the epistemological approach.

**Cordner, Christopher**. Honour, Community, and Ethical Inwardness. *Philosophy*, 72(281), 401-415, Jl 97.

In an earlier paper, the author argued that there is a dimension of ethical reality, marked by the ideas of inwardness and depth, to which Aristotle's ethics is blind and which has informed a long and powerful Western ethical tradition. Not now focusing on Aristotle, the author tries to develop further this conception of ethical inwardness and depth, and argues that it cannot be acknowledged by any moral philosophical understanding which centralizes what Daniel Putman calls the "communitarian foundation of character". The author also traces some connections of this conception of ethical inwardness with other aspects of ethical understanding.

**Cordua, Carla**. Hegel y la Participación Política. *Ideas Valores*, 19-36, Ap 96.

This paper analyses Hegel's ideas concerning the forms of political participation in the modern state. It submits that a fair account of Hegel's position on democracy should consider aspects of his notion of political freedom, which have been usually neglected because of a few critical remarks of the philosopher. In particular, it should consider Hegel's ideas on 1) modern freedom as *Dabeisein*; 2) modern citizenship as entailing *Befriedigung*. These

two concepts are analyzed in their larger philosophical and political contents and their import for Hegel's thought.

**Corfield, David**. Assaying Lakatos's Philosophy of Mathematics. *Stud Hist Phil Sci*, 28(1), 99-121, Mr 97.

While various of his critics are shown to have been off the mark, two principal theses of Lakatos's philosophy of mathematics are here put to the test in the field of algebraic topology. First, that the *method of proofs and refutations* predominates in the passage from native conjecture to research programme. Second, that axiomatization of a theory marks the end its most dynamic and creative phase. I conclude that axiomatization may act as a spur in the production of a more refined informal thought and that uncertainty in mathematics resides largely in the question of a theory's importance.

**Corlett, William**. Containing Indeterminacy: Problems of Representation and Determination in Marx and Althusser. *Polit Theory*, 24(3), 464-492, Ag 96.

Indeterminacy marks the excess of subject-object dialectics and holds open the possibility of appreciating (subaltern) subjects denied representation in Western Marxism. Using Wittgenstein's examples, I postpone questions of causality and concentrate instead on logical (in)determinacy. Althusser's and Balibar's *Reading Capital* illustrates how a commitment to "structural effectivity" limits an appreciation of logical determinacy in Marx. But Marx's *1857 Introduction* provides evidence of the rule-following one associates with logical forms of life. I also show how to detect indeterminacy in the ruined limits of Marx's writing project on the way to addressing the epistemic violence of silenced subjectivities.

**Cormier, Harvey J**. "Pragmatism, Politics, and the Corridor" in *The Cambridge Companion to William James*, Putnam, Ruth Anna (ed), 343-362. New York, Cambridge Univ Pr, 1997.

**Cornelis, Gustaaf C**. Popularization and Pseudo-Science. *Commun Cog*, 29(2), 273-282, 1996.

This article does not concern the demarcation between science, pseudoscience and nonscience. What it does pertain to is the fact that many attempts to popularize science relate to pseudoscience and nonscience, presenting science in an ambiguous way.

**Cornelis, Gustaaf C** and Prigogine, Ilya. Unity of Science and Culture. *Commun Cog*, 29(2), 239-248, 1996.

**Cornell, Drucilla**. Re-Thinking Consciousness Raising: Citizenship and the Law and Politics of Adoption. *S J Phil*, 34(Supp), 109-127, 1996.

**Cornell, Drucilla**. Response to Thomas McCarthy: The Political Alliance between Ethical Feminism and Rawls's Kantian Constructivism. *Constellations*, 2(2), 189-206, O 95.

**Coronado, Luis Guillermo**. El mecanicismo como paradigma "exitoso". *Rev Filosof (Costa Rica)*, 34(83-84), 349-353, D 96.

**Corradini, Antonella**. "Bemerkungen zu den *Grundlagen der Ethik*" in *Das weite Spektrum der analytischen Philosophie*, Lenzen, Wolfgang, 44-59. Hawthorne, de Gruyter, 1997.

**Corrado, Michael**. Punishment, Quarantine, and Preventive Detention. *Crim Just Ethics*, 15(2), 3-13, Sum-Fall 96.

**Corrado, Michael**. Response to Michael Davis. *Crim Just Ethics*, 15(2), 25-29, Sum-Fall 96.

**Corredor, Cristina**. "Sobre objetividad y verdad en algunos escritos de Frege" in *Verdad: lógica, representación y mundo*, Villegas Forero, L, 33-48. Santiago de Compostela, Univ Santiago Comp, 1996.

Taking a point of departure in Prof. Moulines's study on Frege's notion of truth, an interpretive reading is attempted of Frege's understanding of 'objectivity' and 'truth', and a defense of a certain Kantianism in some of his viewpoints is argued for.

**Corredor, Cristina**. Framework of an Intersubjetivist Theory of Meaning. *Sorites*, 33-60, Je 97.

Here a critical revision is carried out of the intersubjectivist theory of meaning embodied in the formal (Universal) pragmatics developed within the framework of the theory of communicative action (J. Habermas). According to very recent *internal* criticisms, only a version of H. Putnam's theory of direct reference can avoid the kind of meaning holism and linguistic relativism which assails Habermas's foundation of *shared meaning* on the intersubjective validity of a rule. A more detailed analysis of Putnam's views, as well as of the referred criticisms, shows that they in fact represent an unorthodox reading trying to conciliate Putnam's first functionalist theory with his second pragmatical internal realism. Finally, it is concluded that only a *quasi*-Kantian view on the formal-pragmatical presuppositions underlying epistemic language use seems to offer an answer to the core *de iure* question: what makes it possible to justify validity for already constituted meanings in epistemic contexts.

**Corrington, Robert S**. "Classical American Metaphysics: Retrospect and Prospect" in *Philosophy in Experience: American Philosophy in Transition*, Hart, Richard (ed), 260-281. New York, Fordham Univ Pr, 1997.

**Corry, Leo**. Axiomática y álgebra estructural en la obra de David Hilbert. *Mathesis*, 11(4), 291-329, N 95.

The present article discusses David Hilbert's contributions to the theory of algebraic invariants, to the theory of algebraic number fields and to the study of the foundations of geometry. The discussion shows that, although Hilbert advanced many of the central elements that would eventually form the basis of the new, structural approach to algebra, he himself never adopted such an approach, nor suggested that it would be convenient to adopt it in algebraic research.

**Corry, Leo**. La teoria de las proporciones de Eudoxio interpretada por Dedekind. *Mathesis*, 10(1), 1-24, F 94.

The present article presents and discusses the arguments for and against the well-known historical thesis, according to which Eudoxus' theory of proportions fully anticipated modern theories of the irrational numbers, such as Dedekind's or Weierstrass's. Special stress is laid upon Dedekind's theory of cuts and upon Dedekind's own interpretation of the putative connection between his theory and Eudoxus'. This interpretation throws new light upon interesting aspects of the historiographical dispute concerning Eudoxus and Dedekind, and of nineteenth century mathematics as well.

**Corsale, Massimo**. Commentary on "The Ethics of Normalization". *Cambridge Quart Healthcare Ethics*, 6(4), 489-493, Fall 97.

**Corsi, Giovanna**. Completeness Theorem for Dummett's L C Quantified and Some of Its Extensions. *Stud Log*, 51(2), 317-335, 1992.

**Corsino, Bruce V**. Bioethics Committees and JCAHO Patients' Rights Standards: A Question of Balance. *J Clin Ethics*, 7(2), 177-181, Sum 96.

**Cortés Rodas, Francisco**. "Liberalismo y Legitimidad: Consideraciones sobre los límites del Paradigma Liberal" in *Liberalismo y Comunitarismo: Derechos Humanos y Democracia*, Monsalve Solórzano, Alfonso (ed), 187-209. 36-46003 València, Alfons el Magnànim, 1996.

The article points out the limits of the individualistic and humanitarist liberal models in their relation to the issue of the political legitimation of the state. The incoherencies of each model are indicated, using the reconstruction of John Locke's and Robert Nozick's proposals for the first case and John Rawls's proposals for the second. By making the Kantian concept of autonomy explicit, the article tries to establish a new paradigm of legitimation, by including economic and social rights among the fundamental human rights.

**Cortés Rodas, Francisco**. Liberalism and Deliberative Democracy: Considerations on the Foundations of Liberty and Equality (Spanish). *Rev Filosof (Venezuela)*, Supp(2-3), 223-240, 1996.

This paper analyzes the debate on the limitations and possibilities of a democracy based on liberalism. It studies Rawls's proposals of justice as equity and Habermas's ideas about the problematic relationship between liberty and equality, in an attempt to establish a relationship between the discursive principle and the form of rights, in order to establish a mediation between the moral and political principles that Kant and Rawls were unable to achieve.

**Cortés Rodas, Francisco** (ed) and Monsalve Solórzano, Alfonso (ed). *Liberalismo y Comunitarismo: Derechos Humanos y Democracia*. 36-46003 València, Alfons el Magnànim, 1996.

**Corti, Enrique C**. La razón de la esperanza y la esperanza de la razón. *Stromata*, 52(1-2), 3-18, Ja-Je 96.

**Cortina, Adela**. "La Paz en Kant: Ética y Política" in *Kant: La paz perpetua, doscientos años después,* Martínez Guzmán, Vicent (ed), 67-81. Valencia, Nau Llibres, 1997.

**Cortina, Adela**. En torno a la justicia médica. *Cuad Etica*, 19-20, 149-168, 1995.

**Cortois, Paul**. Omtrent de kloof, rondom se rite. *Tijdschr Filosof*, 58(3), 553-566, S 96.

Many attempts have been made to mediate between the sphere of cognition (epistemic meaning) and the sphere of "Bedeutsamkeit" (meaning-as-relevance). Elaborating here on H. De Dijn's "Kan kennis troosten?" (1994), ritual is considered to offer a strong case of resistance against all pre-arranged ("new alliance" or extended Enlightenment) syntheses of the two spheres. The global holism of "one culture" views is displaced by local holisms of mutually communicating yet disparate traditions the interpretation of which is in each case commanded primarily by internal considerations. (In religions, for example, ritualizing and "doctrinal" aspects of meaning cannot be understood except in terms of each other.)

**Cortois, Paul**. Time of the Concept, Time of the Ritual (in Dutch). *Tijdschr Filosof*, 59(1), 28-68, Mr 97.

The arrow of time has been invoked to bridge all gaps between the 'two cultures'. Would time also help to mediate between the sphere of cognition (epistemic meaning) and the sphere of *Bedeutsamkeit* (meaning-as-relevance) when taking ritual to be a strongly idiosyncratic representative of the latter? What is the role of time in the modes of meaning in the realm of scientific concepts in their most rigorous shape (the mathematical) on the one hand, in ritual on the other hand? Taking an external point of view, surprising connections can be laid, especially when focusing on the relations of form and materiality or content in the respective fields. (edited)

**Corvi, Roberta** and Camiller, Patrick (trans). *An Introduction to the Thought of Karl Popper*. New York, Routledge, 1997.

This study offers an accessible introduction to the life and work of this extraordinary thinker, including his often-neglected Postscript on scientific method published in three volumes in the 1980s. It charts the development of Popper's philosophy and shows his unfailing political commitment to humanism and enlightenment. At the centre of Popper's thought stands rationality and a strong belief in the power of the human mind to change things for the better. Rationality thus serves as a guide both in his philosophical considerations and for his political views. (publisher)

**Cosculluela, Victor**. Bolstering the Argument from Non-Belief. *Relig Stud*, 32(4), 507-512, D 96.

This article attempts to strengthen Theodore M. Drange's Argument from Nonbelief for the nonexistence of the evangelical Biblical Christian God. An argument is proposed for the claim that God, if construed as an omniscient,

morally perfect being, does not have conflicting desires of any kind. This argument, combined with Drange's evidence, is used to support the most controversial premise of the Argument from Nonbelief. Biblical evidence is also presented which seems to compel the evangelical Biblical Christian to admit God's omniscience and moral perfection, thus blocking one avenue of retreat.

**Cosculluela, Victor**. The Right to Suicide. *J Value Inq*, 30(3), 431-443, S 96.

This article contends that, because of various individual rights, duties to others are the only considerations that ever make suicide morally wrong. But individual rights sometimes justify suicide despite your duties to others. Individual rights must be weighed against duties to others in order to determine the moral status of particular suicides. Ten objections are answered, most of which come from Margaret Battin. The article also specified some of the rights and circumstances that justify suicide. Two circumstances are explored: personal suffering and degradation.

**Cosetino, Antonio**. "Il tempo come variabile dei processi formativi" in *Il Concetto di Tempo: Atti del XXXII Congresso Nazionale della Società Filosofica Italiana,* Casertano, Giovanni (ed), 365-370. Napoli, Loffredo, 1997.

**Cosi, Giovanni**. Etica secondo il ruolo: Un'introduzione filosofico-morale. *Riv Int Filosof Diritto*, 74(1), 15-79, Ja-Mr 97.

**Cosman, Carol** (trans) and Bouveresse, Jacques and Descombes, Vincent. *Wittgenstein Reads Freud: The Myth of the Unconscious*. Princeton, Princeton Univ Pr, 1995.

Wittgenstein, who himself had delivered a devastating critique of traditional philosophy, sympathetically pondered Freud's claim to have produced a scientific theory in proposing a new model of the human psyche. What Wittgenstein recognized—and what Bouveresse so eloquently stresses for today's reader—is that psychoanalysis does not aim to produce a change limited to the intellect but rather seeks to provoke an authentic change of human attitudes. (publisher, edited)

**Costa, Filippo**. Chomsky tra linguistica e filosofia: A proposito di R. Raggiunti, La "Conoscenza del linguaggio" e il mito della grammatica universale. *G Metaf*, 18(3), 447-464, S-D 96.

**Costa, Flavia**. La maturità di coscienza alla luce di San Tommaso d'Aquino. *Aquinas*, 39(2), 409-430, My-Ag 96.

**Costa, Gustavo**. "Bayle, l'"anima mundi" e Vico" in *Pierre Bayle e l'Italia,* Bianchi, Lorenzo, 107-122. Napoli, Liguori Ed, 1996.

**Costa, Horacio A** and Levi, Isaac. Two Notions of Epistemic Validity: Epistemic Models for Ramsey's Conditionals. *Synthese*, 109(2), 217-262, N 96.

(RT) 'If A, then B' must be accepted with respect to the current epistemic state iff the minimal hypothetical change of it needed to accept A also requires accepting B. In this article we propose a formulation of (RT), which unlike some of its predecessors, is compatible with our best theory of belief revision, the so-called AGM theory (see Gärdenfors 1988), chapters 1-5 for a survey). The new test, which, we claim, encodes some of the crucial insights defended by F.P. Ramsey in (Ramsey 1990), is used to study the conditionals *epistemically validated* by the AGM postulates. Our notion of validity (PV) is compared with the notion of *negative validity* (NV) used by Gärdenfors in (Gärdenfors 1988). It is observed that the notions of PV and NV will in general differ and that when these differences arise it is the notion of PV that is preferable. Finally we compare our formulation of the Ramsey test with a previous formulation offered by Gärdenfors (GRT). We show that any attempt to interpret (GRT) as delivering acceptance conditions for Ramsey's conditionals is doomed to failure.

**Costa, Márcio Luis**. Fenomenología y corporalidad en le ética de Emmanuel Lévinas: Lectura de *De l'éxistence à l'existant*. *Analogia*, 11(1), 19-43, Ja-Je 97.

**Costa, Vincenzo**. Idealità del segno e intenzione nella filosofia del linguaggio di Edmund Husserl. *Riv Filosof Neo-Scolas*, 88(2), 246-286, Ap-Je 96.

**Costantini, D** and Garibaldi, U. Predicative Laws of Association in Statistics and Physics. *Erkenntnis*, 45(2 & 3), 399-422, Nov 96.

In the present paper we face the problem of estimating cell probabilities in the case of a two-dimensional contingency table from a predictive point of view. The solution is given by a double stochastic process. The first subprocess, the unobservable one, is supposed to be exchangeable and invariant. For the second subprocess, the observable one, we suppose it is independent conditional on the first one.

**Costelloe, Timothy M**. Between the Subject and Sociology: Alfred Schutz's Phenomenology of the Life-World. *Human Stud*, 19(3), 247-266, Jl 96.

In his writings Alfred Schutz identifies an artificiality in the concept of "life-world" produced by Edmund Husserl's method of reduction. As an alternative, he proposes to assume intersubjectivity as a given of everyday life. This eradicates Husserl's distinction between "life-world" and "natural attitude." The subsequent phenomenological project appears to center upon sociological descriptions of the "structures of the life-world" rather than on a search for apodictic truth. Schutz, however, actually retains Husserl's emphasis on the subject. A tension then arises between the assumption of intersubjectivity and individual experience. Schutz, it is concluded, initiates a scientistic sociology in which the commonsense structures of the "natural attitude of everyday life" are subverted and replaced by the more rigorous knowledge of the "scientific attitude." Schutz's version of phenomenology is ultimately untrue to the spirit of Husserl's original project; and deploying his work as a clear-cut alternative to scientistic tendencies within sociology is not as straightforward as it might at first seem. (edited)

**Costelloe, Timothy M**. Contract or Coincidence: George Herbert Mead and Adam Smith on Self and Society. *Hist Human Sci*, 10(2), 81-109, My 97.

Although a number of commentators have remarked upon the similarities between aspects of George Herbert Mead's social psychology and Adam Smith's *Theory of Moral Sentiments*, there has been no systematic attempt to document the connection. This article attempts to do precisely that. First, the legitimacy of the connection is established by showing the likelihood that Mead know this particular work by Smith and by bringing together the various treatments of the matter made by commentators. Second, then, the movement of Mead's thought is reconstructed through the terms 'individual' and 'social epistemology'. (edited)

**Côté, Antoine**. How To Do Things with Numbers: MacIntosh on the Possible Eternity of the World. *Amer Cath Phil Quart*, 71(2), 157-169, Spr 97.

**Côté, Antoine**. The Five Ways and the Argument from Composition: A Reply to John Lamont. *Thomist*, 61(1), 123-131, Ja 97.

**Cotta, Sergio**. Dal primato della prassi all'anomia: Una interpretazione filosofica della crisi odierna. *Acta Phil*, 6(1), 39-52, 1997.

Anomia, the loss of the common reference points of one's own identity, is the characteristic of the current crisis which is deeply rooted in certain forms of thought. The philosophical analysis of this article examines the examples provided by the conflicts between fascism and communism, idealism and materialism and liberalism and socialism. In these conflicts, the author observes the affirmation of the primacy of praxis which empties freedom and excludes the possibility of ethical judgment. This is even more evident in the area of the technological revolution. A re-establishment of an adequate relationship between knowledge and action is recommended.

**Cotterill, Rodney M J**. On the Mechanism of Consciousness. *J Consciousness Stud*, 4(3), 231-247, 1997.

The master-module theory of consciousness (Cotterill, 1995; 1996) is considered in the light of experimental evidence that has emerged since the model was first published. It is found that these new results tend to strengthen the original hypothesis. It is also argued that the master module is involved in generation of the schemata previously postulated to be associated with consciousness (Bartlett, 1932). The recent discovery of attention-related activity in the thalamaic intralaminar nuclei is taken to indicate that these structures constitute an important part of the feedback loop which the theory conjectured to mediate thought. The theory is shown to lead to a remarkably simple rationalization of the cerebral cortex, and it offers explanations of attention, binocular rivalry and qualia. It also makes the surprising prediction that Broca's area might not exclusively serve speech.

**Cottin, Jérôme**. Théologie de la Croix et Esthétique Contemporaine. *Rev Theol Phil*, 128(3), 253-272, 1996.

The theology of the cross formulated by Luther and rediscovered in contemporary theology could be understood to condemn all attempts to think faith aesthetically. However, the cross is not fundamentally opposed to beauty but to power. It is possible, therefore, to articulate the cross with aesthetics, especially since contemporary artistic research stands as a radical challenge to human endeavour akin, on the level of meaning, to the paradoxical message of the cross.

**Cottingham, John**. "Medicine, Virtues and Consequences" in *Human Lives: Critical Essays on Consequentialist Bioethics,* Oderberg, David S (ed), 128-143. New York, Macmillan, 1997.

This paper takes issue with the fashionable view that medicine, as an activity of human devising serving human purposes, is just what we make it to be, not what nature decrees it must be. An examination of the Aristotelian notion of *telos* shows that health, as the goal of medicine, depends on naturally given features of the world. It also shows that certain activities, such as killing patients, are conceptually inconsistent with the goal of medicine; and so are certain forms of consequentialist reasoning. An appreciation of the internal properties of the medical profession shows that it is virtue theory, not consequentialism, which can justify them and place them within a broader ethical framework.

**Cottingham, John** (ed). *Western Philosophy: An Anthology*. Cambridge, Blackwell, 1996.

In 100 substantial and carefully chosen extracts, the volume covers all the main branches of philosophy-theory of knowledge and metaphysics, philosophy of mind, religion and science, moral philosophy (theoretical and applied), political theory and aesthetics. Chronologically and thematically arranged, the readings are introduced and linked together by a lucid philosophical commentary which guides the reader through the key arguments. (publisher,edited)

**Cottingham, John** and Descartes, René. *Meditations on First Philosophy: With Selections from the Objections and Replies*. New York, Cambridge Univ Pr, 1996.

The *Mediations*, one of the key texts of Western philosophy, is the most widely studied of all Descartes's writings. This authoritative translation by John Cottingham, taken from the much-acclaimed three-volume Cambridge edition of the *Philosophical Writings of Descartes*, is based upon the best available texts and presents Descartes's central metaphysical writings in clear, readable modern English. As well as the complete text of the *Mediations*, the reader will find a thematic abridgement of the *Objections and Replies* (which were originally published with the *Mediations*) containing Descartes's replies to his critics. These extracts, specially selected for the present volume, indicate the main philosophical difficulties which occurred to Descartes's contemporaries

and show how Descartes developed and clarified his arguments in response. (publisher,edited)

**Couch, Elsbeth** (& others) and Doerfler, Martin and Beckerman, Aaron. Ethical Issues and Relationships between House Staff and Attending Physicians: A Case Study. *J Clin Ethics*, 8(1), 34-38, Spr 97.

The purpose of the work was to examine a series of ethical issues between attendings and house staff. In the space between dying and death, conflicts emerge between the interests of education and care of the patient, patients' care decision making which are more a function of authority than medical knowledge, and extending the do no (psychological) harm principle to house staff.

**Coulehan, Jack**. Empathy, Passion, Imagination: A Medical Triptych. *J Med Human*, 18(2), 99-110, Sum 97.

The autobiographical essay presents some scenes from the author's experience of the relationships among empathy, passion, and imagination as they relate to the practice of medicine. The first section describes the author's search for a creative path in medicine. Through writing poetry he came to understand better the nature of empathy and the potential healing power of patient-physician relationships. There are several interesting similarities between the art of poetry and the art of medicine. Through his passion for poetry, he became a better physician. The second part of the triptych presents a case example of the poetry that can be found in medical practice. The last section evokes the concept of symbolic healing and decries the narrow view that medicine is a purely technical or scientific enterprise.

**Courtenay, William J**. Conrad of Megenberg: The Parisian Years. *Vivarium*, 35(1), 102-124, Mr 97.

**Courtine, Jean-François**. Martin Heidegger's "Logical Investigations." From the Theory of Judgment to the Truth of Being. *Grad Fac Phil J*, 19/20(2/1), 103-127, 1997.

**Courtine, Jean-François**. Martin Heidegger's *Logical Investigations*, from the Theory of Judgement to the Truth of Being (in Spanish). *Discurso*, 27, 7-36, 1996.

This essay attempts to show that in Heidegger's philosophy the question "what is logic?" is closely connected with the *Seinsfrage*. The question of being becomes opaque and unintelligible unless the question of logic is concerned.

**Coutinho, Jorge**. A Parábola Humana (Uma Leitura Metafísica da Fisicidade Humana: Uma Expressao Matemática do Metafísicio do Homem). *Rev Port Filosof*, 52(1-4), 243-251, Ja-D 96.

**Couture, Jocelyne**. Analyse logique et analyticité; de Carnap à Gödel. *Dialectica*, 51(2), 95-117, 1997.

L'objectif principal de cet article est de clarifier le sens et l'extension du concept d'analyticité tel qu'il s'applique aux systèmes formels de la logique. L'enjeu plus général de cette étude est une évaluation méthodologique des approches philosophiques axées sur la reconstruction formelle et l'analyse logique des langues naturelles. Nous avons d'abord soutenu que la reconstruction formelle de l'analyticité élaborée par Rudolf Carnap dans *Meaning and Necessity* met en place des conditions correspondant aux propriétés métalogiques de complétude déductive et de néga-complétude. A la lumière des théorèmes de complétude et d'incomplétude de Kurt Gödel, nous avons ensuite cherché à déterminer dans quelle mesure et dans quelles circonstances ces propriétés pouvaient être réalisées dans des systèmes formels de la logique. (edited)

**Couture, Jocelyne**. La philosophie morale depuis la mort de Dieu. *Dialogue (Canada)*, 36(2), 381-399, Spr 97.

**Covaleskie, John F**. "Moral Reflection and Moral Education" in *Philosophy of Education (1996)*, Margonis, Frank (ed), 386-388. Urbana, Phil Education Soc, 1997.

In this paper I consider the difference between the moral reflection of adults and the moral education of children. I suggest that the purpose of moral education is to teach children the customary morality of their moral community, but to do so in such a way that, as adults, the children are capable of engaging in moral reflection on the norms of that community. This is what Dewey seems to suggest when he refers to the classroom as an apprenticeship in democratic life.

**Coveos, Costis M**. Some Remarks on the Notion of a Masterpiece. *Phil Invest*, 19(4), 308-317, O 96.

'X is a masterpiece' is neither a statement of fact nor an aesthetic judgement. It is not the product of empirical observation, because it is not to be refuted on the basis of divergent empirical evidence. It is not based on criteria either, because what provides the criteria cannot be inferior to what is judged on their basis: It too has to be a masterpiece; and thus we reach an infinite regress. 'X is a masterpiece' is a statement of a rule: It fixes the place of an artwork in an aesthetic system as a *foundation* for—rather than as a *product* of—judgement.

**Cover, J A**. Non-Basic Time and Reductive Strategies: Leibniz's Theory of Time. *Stud Hist Phil Sci*, 28(2), 289-318, Je 97.

Reckoning Leibniz as a kind of "reductionist" about space and time is a commonplace: a) space and time are reduced to relations among things otherwise said to be "in" them; b) space and time, like bodies, are reduced to well-founded phenomena; and c) temporal order is reduced to causal order. My aim is to make more precise Leibniz's view of time by first attending closely to the idea of reduction itself—the source of considerable misunderstanding when applied to historical cases such as Leibniz's—and then giving a historically sensitive and philosophically careful appraisal of claims a)—c).

**Cover, J A** and Hartz, Glenn A. Are Leibnizian Monads Spatial?. *Hist Phil Quart*, 11(3), 295-316, Jl 94.

Leibniz commentators, like Leibniz himself on occasion, tend to be of two minds on the question of whether monads have spatial properties. Our purpose is to evaluate both textual and philosophical lines of thought in support of this "spatiality thesis." In particular, we examine three arguments for the claim that monads have spatial properties in the same, nonderived sense that bodies would otherwise be said to have them; and we examine three arguments for the claim that monads have spatial properties in a derived, nonbasic sense. We show that none of these lines of argument can be sustained.

**Cover, J A** and O'Leary-Hawthorne, John. Framing the Thisness Issue. *Austl J Phil*, 75(1), 102-108, Mr 97.

**Covey, Preston K** and Cavalier, Robert J and Andersen, David. *A Right to Die?: The Dax Cowart Case*. New York, Routledge, 1996.

As *A Right to Die?* leads users logically through all the aspects of the case, prompting decisions about the patient's future at various stages, and asking for justification, it fosters philosophical exploration of the ethics surrounding the right to die. The CD-ROM presents the story in an accessible way through film footage, stills, and audio testimony of those involved. Supporting this powerful, sometimes disturbing evidence is a wealth of material to help students and educators in medicine, nursing, ethics, or philosophy develop and endorse the arguments both for and against the right to die. This accurately models the real world condition of having to make difficult choices, perhaps without being fully aware of the consequences. (publisher, edited)

**Coward, Harold**. Taoism and Jung: Synchronicity and the Self. *Phil East West*, 46(4), 477-495, O 96.

What was the nature and degree of Eastern influence on Carl Jung's complex concept of "the Self?" It is argued that Chinese Taoism rather than Hinduism provided the fundamental formative influence on this central idea, especially as it is expressed through the *I Ching*. This influence came indirectly through the development of Jung's notion of "synchronicity," correlative parallels between the inner and the outer realms of experience.

**Cowart, Monica R**. Moral Bivalence: What does it Mean to Deceive Yourself?. *Cont Phil*, 18(2-3), 10-17, Mr-Ap/My-Je 96.

In "Vessels of Evil," Laurence Thomas remarks that it is almost inconceivable for an individual to be both thoroughly evil and sane. This is because the concept of being 'thoroughly evil' implies that the individual will consistently perform evil acts toward everyone he or she encounters regardless of family ties or other bonds that might exist. Such a person continues to commit evil acts throughout his or her life and there is "no one toward whom the person would not act evilly." Given this description, it is not surprising that very few people can be classified as thoroughly evil. In addition, it is quite unlikely that the few who can are solely responsible for all of the evil found in the world. So, it is still necessary to determine the type of agents who are responsible for committing these other evil acts.

**Cowen, Robert** and Emerson, William. A Compactness Theorem for Linear Equations. *Stud Log*, 57(2-3), 355-357, O 96.

It is proved that a system of linear equations over an arbitrary field has a solution if every finite subsystem has a solution provided that the set of variables can be well ordered.

**Cowen, Tyler**. Discounting and Restitution. *Phil Pub Affairs*, 26(2), 168-185, Spr 97.

How should restitution be made across generations for grievous harms suffered in the distant past? Moral issues arise when we try to translate past economic values into present economic values; specifically, a rate of appropriate compounding must be chosen. I conclude that the market rate of interest and variants thereof, does not provide a correct answer to the problem. Restitution across generations is not fundamentally a matter of translating a resource value from the past into a current valuation, using positive economic analysis. Rather, restitutional policy must make direct value judgments about how much money we wish to transfer today, for what reason and how we weigh the moral importance of present claims, compared to past injustices.

**Cowie, Fiona**. The Logical Problem of Language Acquisition. *Synthese*, 111(1), 17-51, Ap 97.

Arguments from the 'Logical Problem of Language Acquisition' suggest that since linguistic experience provides few negative data that would falsify overgeneralized grammatical hypotheses, innate knowledge of the principles of *universal grammar* must constrain learners' hypothesis formulation. Although this argument indicates a need for domain-specific constraints, it does not support their innateness. Learning from mostly positive data proceeds unproblematically in virtually all domains. Since not every domain can plausibly be accorded its own special faculty, the probative value of the argument in the linguistic case is dubious. In ignoring the holistic and probabilistic nature of theory construction, the argument underestimates the extent to which positive data can supply negative evidence and hence overestimates the intractability of language learning in the absence of a dedicated faculty. While nativism about language remains compelling, the alleged 'Logical Problem' contributes nothing to its plausibility and the emphasis on the problem in the recent acquisition literature has been a mistake.

**Cox, Damian**. On the Value of Natural Relations. *Environ Ethics*, 19(2), 173-183, Sum 97.

In "A Refutation of Environmental Ethics" Janna Thompson argues that by assigning intrinsic value to nonhuman elements of nature either our evaluations become 1) arbitrary and therefore unjustified, or 2) impractical, or 3) justified and practical, but only by reflecting human interest, thus failing to be truly intrinsic to nonhuman nature. There are a number of possible responses to her argument, some of which have been made explicitly in reply to Thompson and others which are implicit in the literature. In this discussion I describe still another response, one which takes Thompson's concerns about value seriously, but does not assign nature intrinsic or nonanthropocentric value. I suggest a relational environmental ethic as the basis for a genuinely ethical stance toward nature in which our relations to nature are a principal object of ethical concern.

**Cox, Damian**. Putnam, Equivalence, Realism. *S J Phil*, 35(2), 155-170, Sum 97.

Putnam presents the argument from conceptual relativity as a refutation metaphysical realism. The refutation fails. The argument fails to demonstrate either the inconsistency, unintelligibility, or falsity of metaphysical realism. It does not successfully refute even the most ambitious metaphysical realist hypothesis: the hypothesis that there is exactly one complete, true, and perfectly natural description of the world. This is not to say that I have shown metaphysical realism to be true, or internal realism to be inconsistent, unintelligible, or false. I have merely argued that one influential attempt refutes metaphysical realism fails.

**Cox, Damian**. The Trouble with Truth-Makers. *Pac Phil Quart*, 78(1), 45-62, Mr 97.

This paper argues that theories of truth which seek to specify the ontological ground of true statements by appealing to an ontology of truth-makers face a severe and possibly insurmountable obstacle in the form of logically complex statements. I argue that there is no apparent way to develop an account of logically complex truth within the confines of a modest and plausible ontology of truth-makers and to this end criticize independent attempts by Armstrong and Pendlebury to develop such an account.

**Cox, L Hughes**. Rights and Responsibilities: Aristotle's Virtues and a Libertarian Dilemma. *Cont Phil*, 18(4 & 5), 37-41, Jl-Ag/S-O 96.

In this essay I will discuss the following dilemma. *The libertarian ideal of political minimalism presupposes a maximum of Aristotle's virtues; the former is inimical to acquisition of the latter*. I plan to use this dilemma to prove that the necessary connection between rights and responsibilities must be much thicker than the one allowed by the political ideal of Libertarian minimalism: the government which governs best governs least. Basically I will show two things. The legal paternalism necessary to acquire the virtues violates a defining characteristic of Libertarian minimalism. The degree to which citizens lack these virtues is the degree to which a polity must move away from Libertarian minimalism and toward the absolute paternalism of Thomas Hobbies. (edited)

**Cox, Philip N**. Heideggers "Schweigen" Technik, Nazi-Medizin und Wissenschaftskultur. *Das Argument*, 209(2-3), 297-302, Mr-Je 95.

In Heidegger's thought there is a contradiction between his life-long scrutinizing of technology and his silence on the Nazi policy of annihilation. The text brings examples of the Nazi technologies of killing which Heidegger refused to analyze and then turns to the question whether Nazi medicine was an aberration. Citing examples from recent US research on the culture of science, Cox shows that silence such as Heidegger's was in no way only symptomatic of dealings with the Nazi past.

**Cragg, Wesley**. Teaching Business Ethics: The Role of Ethics in Business and in Business Education. *J Bus Ethics*, 16(3), 231-245, F 97.

The paper begins with an examination of traditional attitudes towards business ethics. I suggest that these attitudes fail to recognize that a principal function of ethics is to facilitate cooperation. I argue that this focus is unfortunate in as much as it is the second dimension which falls most naturally into the ambit of modern secular educational institutions. It is here that moral education is most obviously unavoidable, and most clearly justifiable in modern secular teaching environments. I conclude by describing the importance of this second dimension for the modern world of business. (edited)

**Cragnolini, Mónica B**. La cuestión de la "caída" de los fundamentos y la ética: Hacia una mayor "responsabilidad" como respuesta al presente. *Cuad Etica*, 17-18, 57-71, 1994.

"Descentered subject", "bursted subject", "fragmented subject", "weakened subject", "individual-dividuum", these are some of the figures which the old Cartesian subject, seems to adopt today. From an ethical point of view, this is a worrying situation. This paper tries to show that the question of responsibility, understood as "response to present", demands a rationality which recognizes its own historical limitations and the death of God, and faces the world of life and its conflicts without trying to dissolve or absolve them. What is required, instead, is to multiply the meanings, so that ethical philosophy does not becomes, again, the funerary monument of disappeared *arkhai*.

**Craig, Edward**. *The Mind of God and the Works of Man*. New York, Clarendon/Oxford Pr, 1996.

Seeking to rediscover the connection between philosophy as studied in universities and those general views of man and reality which are 'philosophy' to the educated layman, Edward Craig here offers a view of philosophy and its history since the early seventeenth century. He presents this period as concerned primarily with just two visions of the essential nature of man. One portrays human beings as made in the image of God, required to resemble him as far as lies in our power; the other sees us as autonomous creators of our own environment and values. The author writes with a broad sweep, yet shows (with particular reference to Hume and Hegel) how textual detail which previous commentators have found opaque becomes transparent when viewed against such a background. In the final chapter he treats passages from recent work in the same way. (publisher, edited)

**Craig, William Lane**. Adams on Actualism and Presentism. *Philosophia (Israel)*, 25(1-4), 401-405, Ap 97.

Robert Adams has defended an argument against the preexistence of singular propositions about oneself on the grounds that it would have been possible for them to have existed even if one had never existed, which is absurd. But the crucial assumption underlying this reasoning, namely, that the only histories of a world which are possible at any time are continuations of that history up to that time, is false, as shown by the illustration of time travel. Furthermore, if Adams were correct, fatalism would follow. The failure of Adam's argument has important implications for the Molinist doctrine of divine middle knowledge.

**Craig, William Lane**. Divine Timelessness and Necessary Existence. *Int Phil Quart*, 37(2), 217-224, Je 97.

Leftow's arguments for the essentiality of timelessness are examined and found wanting. God's existing temporally or a temporally is contingent.

**Craig, William Lane**. In Defense of the *Kalam* Cosmological Argument. *Faith Phil*, 14(2), 236-247, Ap 97.

Graham Oppy's attempt to show that the critiques of the *kalam* cosmological argument offered by Grünbaum, Davies, and Hawking are successful is predicated upon a misunderstanding of the nature of defeaters in rational belief. Neither Grünbaum nor Oppy succeed in showing an incoherence in the Christian doctrine of creation. Oppy's attempts to rehabilitate Davies's critique founders on spurious counterexamples and unsubstantiated claims. Oppy's defense of Hawking's critique fails to allay suspicions about the reality of imaginary time and finally results in the denial of tense and temporal becoming.

**Craig, William Lane**. Is Presentness a Property?. *Amer Phil Quart*, 34(1), 27-40, Ja 97.

In order to discover the ontological status of presentness, a similar inquiry concerning existence is undertaken, which suggests that existence is not a property, but an act. Presentness, then, is a mode of existence, the act of temporal being.

**Craig, William Lane**. On the Argument for Divine Timelessness from the Incompleteness of Temporal Life. *Heythrop J*, 38(2), 165-171, Ap 97.

It has been argued that temporal existence is inherently defective and, therefore, inappropriate for the most perfect being. This argument must be construed experientially, lest it be subverted by a tenseless theory of time. The force of the argument cannot be blunted by the postulation of an everlasting specious present for God. But if God is omniscient, then his experience of temporality is not evidently defective.

**Craig, William Lane**. The New B-Theory's *Tu Quoque* Argument. *Synthese*, 107(2), 249-269, My 96.

The last line of defense of the flagging B-Theory of time is the B-Theorist's *tu quoque* gambit: if temporal tenses are objective features of reality, then so also must be spatial tenses, which no one can countenance. The A-Theorist can defeat this argument by affirming the objective reality of the self and providing a reductive analysis of spatial indexicals in terms of the location of I-now.

**Craig, William Lane**. Timelessness and Creation. *Austl J Phil*, 74(4), 646-656, D 96.

In response to Brian Leftow's claim that a temporal God cannot be the Creator of time and the universe, various alternative conceptions of God's relationship to time, the beginning of time and the beginning of the universe are explored. It is concluded that no good reason has been given to think that a temporal God could not create time and the universe.

**Crain, Steven D**. Divine Action in a World Chaos: An Evaluation of John Polkinghorne's Model of Special Divine Action. *Faith Phil*, 14(1), 41-61, Ja 97.

John Polkinghorne, formerly a physicist and now an Anglican priest and theologian, has made a significant contribution to the current dialogue between Christian theology and the natural sciences. I examine here his reflection on what is commonly called the problem of special divine action in the world. Polkinghorne argues that God acts in the world via a "top-down" or "downward" mode of causation that exploits the indeterministic openness of chaotic systems without requiring that God violate natural laws. In response, I argue: 1) that divine intervention in response to human sin is theologically, as well as scientifically unobjectionable; and 2) that the belief that God is the transcendent creator of the world renders the "causal joint" between God and the world metaphysical in nature, thus obviating the need to uncover a physical feature of the world that God exploits in order to act in the world.

**Crain, Steven D**. Must a Classical Theist Be an Immaterialist?. *Relig Stud*, 33(1), 81-92, Mr 97.

In this paper I examine two arguments, one by R.A. Oakes and the other by P.A. Byrne, that Berkeley's immaterialism is the only metaphysic consistent with classical theism. I show that not only do Oakes and Byrne fail to demonstrate the incompatibility of physical realism with classical theism, but also that their line of argument reveals grave inconsistency between the latter and immaterialism. For as they expound Berkeley's metaphysic, it seems incapable of explicating the metaphysical dependency of finite spirit (mind) on God.

**Crane, Tim**. Galen Strawson on Mental Reality. *Ratio*, 10(1), 82-90, Ap 97.

In *Mental Reality*, Galen Strawson emphasizes the centrality of the notion of consciousness in understanding the mental, while attacking what he calls 'neobehaviourism' and upholding materialism. In this review, Strawson's conception of materialism is questioned and it is argued that his account of the relation between intentionality and consciousness is misconceived.

**Crane, Tim**. Reply to Child. *Proc Aris Soc*, 97, 103-108, 1997.

In "The Mental Causation Debate," I gave an account of why a popular kind of physicalism faces the problem of mental causation and I argued that the way this kind of physicalism responds to the problem undermines the motivation for physicalism in general. In his criticism of this paper, Child challenged this second point and argued in addition that the kind of physicalism in question is preferable to the nonphysicalist alternative I sketched in my paper. In this note, I respond to Child's objections and defend the nonphysicalist alternative.

**Cranor, Carl F**. A Philosophy of Risk Assessment and the Law: A Case Study of the Role of Philosophy in Public Policy. *Phil Stud*, 85(2-3), 135-162, Mr 97.

**Cranston, Maurice**. *The Solitary Self: Jean-Jacques Rousseau in Exile and Adversity*. Chicago, Univ of Chicago Pr, 1997.

In this third and final volume of his masterly biography, Maurice Cranston traces the last tempestuous years of Jean-Jacques Rousseau's life. Professor Cranston died shortly before completing this volume and Sanford Lakoff has written the final chapter using Cranston's notes and the text of a lecture. A monumental achievement, the trilogy provides the definitive account of Rousseau's turbulent life. Marked by Cranston's characteristic elegance, authority and grace, this volume merits the praise lavished on its predecessors, *Jean-Jacques* and *The Noble Savage*. It, too, presents "Rousseau beautifully in the round and leaves him just as extraordinary as ever" (John Weightman, Sunday Independent). (publisher)

**Crasta, Francesca Maria**. Sulla presenza di Descartes nella *Galleria di Minerva*. *G Crit Filosof Ital*, 16(3), 312-329, S-D 96.

**Crawford, Dan D**. Pragmatism, Internalism and the Authority of Claims. *Pac Phil Quart*, 78(1), 63-77, Mr 97.

This paper develops and defends an internalist account of having authority for one's claim. It begins with Robert Brandom's pragmatist account of thinking which locates the root notion of reasoning in a primitive language game of asking for and giving reasons. The idea is that the authority of a claim can be spelled out pragmatically in terms of the social practice of undertaking commitments and attributing entitlements. It is argued that this account fails to acknowledge the role of the subject's grasp of the higher-order concept of *the evidence on which I base my claim*.

**Creath, Richard**. "Languages without Logic" in *Origins of Logical Empiricism*, Giere, Ronald N (ed), 251-265. Minneapolis, Univ of Minnesota Pr, 1996.

**Creery, Walter**. "Bradley on Truth and Judgement" in *Philosophy after F.H. Bradley*, Bradley, James (ed), 231-249. Bristol, Thoemmes, 1996.

**Cremaschi, Sergio**. Charles Taylor e le due facce dell'individualismo. *Iride*, 9(18), 466-472, Ag 96.

Ci si propone di ricostruire la diagnosi dell'individualismo occidentale svolta da Charles Taylor. L'originalità di questa diagnosi sta nell'individuare le cause del "disagio della modernità" nell'incapacità di rendere esplicite le "intuizioni morali" imperniate intorno all'ideale rousseauiano di "autenticità". Gli ostacoli a quest'opera di esplicitazione vengono dalla filosofia morale anglosassone prevalente, che evita ogni discorso esplicito sui beni, e dai neonietzschiani che confondono l'ideale *morale* dell'autenticità con la dottrina *etica* del relativismo.

**Crepaldi, Maria Grazia**. "En arche: una confutazione cristiana della dottrina aristotelica del tempo" in *Il Concetto di Tempo: Atti del XXXII Congresso Nazionale della Società Filosofica Italiana*, Casertano, Giovanni (ed), 173-181. Napoli, Loffredo, 1997.

Nella *Confutatio dogmatum quorundam Aristotelicorum*, opera in lingua greca falsamente attribuita all'apologista Giustino, un anonimo cristiano di età tardoantica difende l'idea di creazione dal nulla confutando la dottrina aristotelica dell'eternità del tempo e del cosmo. In particolare, Pseudo Giustino nega al *chronos* il carattere dell'infinitezza, nella convinzione che solo attribuendo al tempo un inizio e una fine sia possibile salvare l'idea di creazione come dipendenza totale del *mondo* da Dio quale sua causa prima. La *Confutatio* si inserisce così nella tradizione del pensiero cristiano che, fino a Tommaso d'Aquino, non ha posto in discussione che l'atto creatore di Dio si collochi *ab initio temporis* ed ha perciò individuato in Aristotele uno dei bersagli privilegiati della sua polemica.

**Creppell, Ingrid**. Locke on Toleration: The Transformation of Constraint. *Polit Theory*, 24(2), 200-240, My 96.

**Crescini, Angelo**. Il trascendentale contenuto metafisico della realtà. *G Metaf*, 18(1-2), 243-257, Ja-Ag 96.

In this work I demonstrate that the explanation of the experience given by Kant and his explanation of the "transcendental" knowledge, which denies value to the "metaphysical structures", incur into unsurmountable difficulties. These mainly derive because he didn't consider the *concrete metaphysical structure* of the reality: it consists in the *acknowledgement* of the objects, which is identical with the *meaning* of their names. Only the relations of this *concrete metaphysical content* with the *physical* signs through which the object shows itself to the senses are the authentic subject of a "transcendental" knowledge avoiding the difficulties of the Kantian transcendentalism.

**Crescini, Angelo**. Replica a Emanuele Severino. *G Metaf*, 19(1), 137-166, Ja-Ap 97.

1) Puts on the ground of the reality the principle of noncontradiction instead of the principle of identity. That one of noncontradiction only concerns the *speech* upon the reality. 2) He rejects my interpretation of the history of philosophy, particularly of Plato, but he doesn't indicate precisely where it is wrong, what I always do with him. 3) He ignores the radical constitutive indetermination of the human perception and, therefore, of the human knowledge of the reality. Consequently he doesn't distinguish the being from the to be. Therefore, he denies the to become and arrives to a paradoxical conception of the eternity of all the things.

**Crespo, Ricardo F**. Max Weber: Sugerencias para una "reconstrucción". *Topicos*, 23-34, 1996.

Some variations have recently been advanced to the standard interpretation of Max Weber's work. Among these variations there is a nonsociological view of the Weberian corpus. Here I try to show some implications of this new position for the methodology of social sciences and offer a bibliographic overview of the topic. (edited)

**Cresswell, M J** and Hughes, G E. *A New Introduction to Modal Logic*. New York, Routledge, 1996.

The book takes readers from the most basic systems of modal propositional logic right up to systems of modal predicate logic with identity. It covers both technical developments—such as completeness and incompleteness, and finite and infinite models—and their philosophical applications, especially in the area of modal predicate logic. (publisher,edited)

**Cresto, Eleonora**. Algunas estrategias naturalistas contra el escéptico. *Rev Filosof (Argentina)*, 11(1-2), 21-33, N 96.

This paper presents a critical account of some naturalistic strategies against contemporary skepticism. I analyze both a "linguistic" and a "scientific" naturalism. I take the first one to be a position defended by supporters of *Second Wittgenstein's* considerations on meaning and certainty; the second one, on the contrary, is based on Quine's program on naturalized epistemology. I defend two major theses. A) Despite some obvious differences among them, both naturalistic standpoints share the idea that the role of justification in epistemology should be radically redefined. B) Most naturalistic arguments against skepticism can be shown to be circular. Here I argue that circularity should not be so easily admitted. I also suggest that whenever a philosopher proposes an evidently circular argument against skepticism, that means he or she is implicitly engaged with the idea that skepticism is not a genuine philosophical problem at all.

**Cresto, Eleonora**. Escepticismo, verdad y confiabilidad. *Rev Latin de Filosof*, 23(1), 93-125, O 97.

In this paper I suggest an argument against contemporary skepticism within the frame of a reliabilist theory of knowledge. First of all I identify the skeptical statement that should concern any externalist theory, such as reliabilism. This statement says "it is impossible to ensure whether we have knowledge or not," rather than "it is impossible to know." Then I examine, among others, Dretske's attempt to rebut the skeptic in *Knowledge and the Flow of Information* (1981). I argue that, although his proposal is not completely successful, we can profit by some of his ideas. I try to show how they could be re-elaborated so as to admit the adoption of a nonrealist conception of truth for some propositions or beliefs. As a result of this strategy, rational grounds for accepting the existence of reliable belief-forming processes are gained, and so it becomes rational to reject the skeptical statement.

**Crimmins, Mark**. "Contextuality, Reflexivity, Iteration, Logic" in *AI, Connectionism and Philosophical Psychology, 1995,* Tomberlin, James E (ed), 381-399. Atascadero, Ridgeview, 1995.

**Crisp, Roger**. Mill on Virtue as a Part of Happiness. *Brit J Hist Phil*, 4(2), 367-380, S 96.

According to the final stage of Mill's proof of utilitarianism, nothing other than happiness is desirable. Mill considers a possible counterexample, virtue, and claims that it is *part* of happiness. This paper provides an interpretation of that claim. Arguments are offered against Fred Berger's nonhedonistic and pluralistic interpretation of happiness, and against John Skorupski's view that Mill believed that virtue is desired under the idea of it as pleasant. Finally, it is suggested that by 'virtue' Mill must be taken to mean 'the enjoyable experience of being virtuous'.

**Crisp, Roger** and Mooro, Andrew. Welfarism in Moral Theory. *Austl J Phil*, 74(4), 598-613, D 96.

We take welfarism in moral theory to be the claim that the well-being of individuals matters and is the only consideration that fundamentally matters, from a moral point of view. We argue that criticisms of welfarism due to G.E. Moore, Donald Regan, Charles Taylor and Amartya Sen all fail. The final section of our paper is a critical survey of the problems which remain for welfarists in moral theory.

**Crisp, Roger** (ed) and Slote, Michael (ed). *Virtue Ethics*. New York, Oxford Univ Pr, 1997.

This volume brings together much of the strongest and most influential work undertaken in the field of virtue ethics over the last four decades. Divided into four sections, it includes articles critical of other traditions; early attempts to offer a positive vision of virtue ethics; some later criticisms of the revival of virtue ethics; and, finally, some recent, more theoretically ambitious essays in virtue ethics. (publisher)

**Cristin, Renato**. Intersubjetividad como intramundanidad: Hacia una ética del tercero incluido. *Cuad Etica*, 19-20, 47-62, 1995.

This paper proposes: (a) it's impossible to make an intersubjectivity theory, as a theory without a properly ethic context; (b) this intersubjective-ethic has to be followed by the dynamic between the personal consciousness and comprehension of the other; (c) it isn't possible to develop an intersubjective praxis without an ethic respect and an ethic comprehension of natural world as a concrete participant of the dialogue; (e) the terms of this participation, are based on the phenomenological modalities of the relationship with the world. The ethic of third included, is an ethic of "intramundanity" and it is the consequence of a phenomenological interpretation of ethics.

**Cristofolini, Paolo**. Vico penseur de la complexité. *Bull Soc Fr Phil*, 90(2), 43-89, Ap-Je 96.

Any challenge to the interpretation of the historicity of Vico, according to which he held that all history was the work of man, taking place according to a cyclical model, leads to the problem of the model's simplicity. We shall show that only the history of the civil world of nations and not all history, is man's work: the natural history of man in the primitive and savage state is not. On the other hand, the order and plan which appear throughout the history of nations are for Vico carried out under the guidance of providence. The analysis of the axioms relative to history shows that the 'return of human matters' of which Vico speaks does not happen in manner which is cyclical, simple and according to endogenous reasons, but by the interaction of different factors: a complex combination of two models of progression, (linear-ascendant and parabolical), the external action of providence and the intervention of the 'other'.

**Critchley, Simon**. "Deconstruction and Pragmatism—Is Derrida a Private Ironist or a Public Liberal?" in *Deconstruction and Pragmatism,* Mouffe, Chantal (ed), 19-40. New York, Routledge, 1996.

**Critchley, Simon**. Deconstruction and Pragmatism—Is Derrida a Private Ironist or a Public Liberal?. *Euro J Phil*, 2(1), 1-21, Ap 94.

In this paper, I criticize Richard Rorty's interpretation of Jacques Derrida's work, insofar as the former claims that the latter is a private ironist and that deconstruction has no public relevance and, therefore, that questions of ethical and political responsibility cannot be adequately treated from a deconstructive perspective. Against Rorty, I argue that Derridian deconstruction has overriding ethical and political consequences.

**Critchley, Simon** (ed) and Peperzak, Adriaan Theodoor (ed) and Bernasconi, Robert (ed). *Emmanuel Levinas: Basic Philosophical Writings*. Bloomington, Indiana Univ Pr, 1996.

This anthology of Levinas's key philosophical texts over a period of more than forty years provides an ideal introduction to his thought and offers insights into his most innovative ideas. Five of the ten essays included here appear in English for the first time. An introduction by Adriaan Peperzak outlines Levinas's philosophical development and the basic themes of his writings. Each essay is accompanied by a brief introduction and notes. (publisher,edited)

**Crittenden, P**. Aristotle and the Idea of Competing Forms of Life. *Phil Inq*, 18(1-2), 88-100, Wint-Spr 96.

**Croasmun, Earl** and Hasian, Jr, Marouf. Rhetoric's Revenge: The Prospect of a Critical Legal Rhetoric. *Phil Rhet*, 29(4), 384-399, 1996.

**Crocker, Stephen**. The Fission of Time: On the Distinction between Intratemporality and the Event of Time in Kant, Heidegger and Foucault. *Int Stud Phil*, 29(2), 1-22, 1997.

**Croft, Jo**. "Looking Up the Adolescent in Freud's Index" in *Critical Studies: Ethics and the Subject,* Simms, Karl (ed), 147-155. Amsterdam, Rodopi, 1997.

**Cromartie, Michael** (ed). *A Preserving Grace: Protestants, Catholics, and Natural Law.* Grand Rapids, Eerdmans, 1997.

**Crombie, A C**. "Philosophical Commitments and Scientific Progress" in *The Idea of Progress,* McLaughlin, Peter (ed), 47-63. Hawthorne, de Gruyter, 1997.

**Crombie, E James**. "What is Deduction?" in *Studies in the Logic of Charles Sanders Peirce,* Houser, Nathan (ed), 460-476. Bloomington, Indiana Univ Pr, 1997.

**Cronin, Ciaran**. Bourdieu and Foucault on Power and Modernity. *Phil Soc Crit*, 22(6), 55-85, N 96.

Foucault's theory of disciplinary power and Bourdieu's theory of symbolic power are among the most innovative attempts in recent social thought to come to terms with the increasingly elusive character of power in modern society. But Foucault's critique of the subject is so radical that it makes it impossible to identify any determinate social location of the exercise of power or of resistance to its operations. However, Bourdieu's strategic model of social action remains too narrow to allow for the possibility of autonomous agency and an emancipatory political praxis. The theory of symbolic power must be supplemented by a normative conception of practical reason if its emancipatory potential is to be realized. (edited)

**Crook, Paul**. Social Darwinism: The Concept. *Hist Euro Ideas*, 22(4), 261-274, Jl 96.

The paper discerns two definitional traditions within the historical discourse on social Darwinism: a "generalist" one emphasizing the variety of ideological derivatives drawn from a multivalent Darwinism; and a "restrictionist" one that delimits social Darwinism to concepts central to Darwinian biology, such as natural selection or differential reproduction. Concludes that Darwin tended to be more a reform social Darwinist than a capitalistic or militaristic one.

**Crosby, John F**. The Teaching of John Paul II on the Christian Meaning of Suffering. *Christian Bioethics*, 2(2), 154-171, Ag 96.

Taking John Paul II's teaching on the Christian meaning of suffering as my main source for a Catholic perspective on suffering, I show how seriously he takes the reality of suffering and how seriously he takes the question as to the meaning of suffering. I proceed to explore his many-sided teaching on the way in which sin is and is not involved in the meaning of suffering, giving particular attention to his teaching on social dimensions of sin and suffering that are little understood in the individualistic West today. The heart of his teaching on suffering lies in his explication of how it is that we have to be conformed in our suffering to the suffering of Christ so as to share in His resurrection. But it is not the suffering as such but the love that we are called to live when we suffer, that incorporates us into the risen Christ.

**Cross, Charles B**. The Modal Logic of Discrepancy. *J Phil Log*, 26(2), 143-168, Ap 97.

Discrepancies between an agent's goals and beliefs play an important, if implicit, role in determining what a rational agent is motivated to do. This is most obvious in cases where an agent achieves a complex goal incrementally and must deliberate anew as each milestone is reached. In such cases the concept of goal/belief discrepancy defines an appropriate space to which a *degree-of-achievement* yardstick can be applied. This paper presents soundness and completeness results concerning a logic for reasoning about goal/belief discrepancy, and it is suggested that a certain species of goal/belief discrepancy captures the concept of desire.

**Cross, Richard**. Duns Scotus on Eternity and Timelessness. *Faith Phil*, 14(1), 3-25, Ja 97.

Scotus consistently holds that eternity is to be understood as timelessness. In his early *Lectura*, he criticizes Aquinas's account of eternity on the grounds that

1) it entails collapsing past and future into the present, and 2) it entails a B-theory of time, according to which past, present and future are all ontologically on a par with each other. Scotus later comes to accept something like Aquinas's account of God's timelessness and the B-theory of time which it entails. Scotus also offers a refutation of his earlier argument that Aquinas's account of eternity entails collapsing past and future into the present.

**Cross, Richard**. Is Aquinas's Proof for the Indestructibility of the Soul Successful?. *Brit J Hist Phil*, 5(1), 1-20, Mr 97.

According to Aquinas, a subsistent form such as the human soul is identical with its essence. Aquinas believes that this identity entails that there is no natural process by which the soul could be destroyed. I argue that Aquinas's identity claim here is inconsistent with his view that there can be more than one human soul, and hence that he cannot use his identity claim to support an inference to the soul's indestructibility.

**Crossley, David J**. "Justification and the Foundations of Empirical Knowledge" in *Philosophy after F.H. Bradley*, Bradley, James (ed), 307-329. Bristol, Thoemmes, 1996.

Among F. H. Bradley's discussions of immediate experience are some which offer an account of sensory acquaintance: thereby constituting part of a theory of the foundations of empirical knowledge. This paper investigates these with reference to contemporary analyses of foundationalism, arguing that Bradley endorses a kind of noncognitive experience similar to that found in adverbial theories. While this illuminates some of Bradley's views, that immediate sensory experience contains a plurality of features or contents presents a problem since a plurality should always introduce relations and these are, for Bradley, ever the mark of appearance, not reality.

**Crossley, John N** and Jeavons, John S. A Logic-Based Modelling of Prolog Resulation Sequences Including the Negation as Failure Rule. *Log Anal*, 37(147-8), 379-406, S-D 94.

In a previous paper, (Jeavons, J.S. and Crossley, J.N., "A Logic Based Modelling of Prolog Resolution Sequences," *Logique et Analyse*, 137-138: pp. 189-205, 1992) we gave a logic-based model for the procedural aspect of resolution-based logic programming. In this paper we extend the analysis to include the use of the negation as failure rule.

**Crosti, Massimo**. Oltre MacIntyre, a Proposito di: Quale Impostazione per la Filosofia Morale?. *Aquinas*, 39(3), 559-570, S-D 96.

**Crouch, Robert A**. Letting the Deaf Be Deaf: Reconsidering the Use of Cochlear Implants in Prelingually Deaf Children. *Hastings Center Rep*, 27(4), 14-21, Jl-Ag 97.

In theory, cochlear implants hold out the possibility of enabling profoundly prelingually deaf children to hear. For the parents of such children, who are usually hearing, this possibility is a great relief. Yet the decision to have this prosthetic device implanted ought not to be viewed as an easy or obvious one.

**Crowards, Tom**. Nonuse Values and the Environment: Economic and Ethical Motivations. *Environ Values*, 6(2), 143-167, My 97.

Nonuse values are a potentially very important, but controversial, aspect of the economic valuation of the environment. Since no use is envisaged by the individual, a degree of altruism appears to be the driving force behind nonuse values. Whilst much of the controversy has focused upon measurement issues associated with the contingent valuation method, this paper concentrates on the underlying motivations, whether ethical or economic, that form the basis for such values. (edited)

**Crowe, Frederick E** (ed) and Doran, Robert M (ed). *Verbum: Word and Idea in Aquinas Volume 2*. Toronto, Univ of Toronto Pr, 1997.

*Verbum: Word and Idea in Aquinas* is a product of Lonergan's eleven years of study of the thought of Thomas Aquinas. The work is considered by many to be a breakthrough in the history of Lonergan's theology and a foundation upon which his later contributions were constructed. Here he interprets aspects in the writing of Aquinas relevant to Trinitarian theory and, as in most of Lonergan's work, one of the principal aims is to assist the reader in the search to understand the workings of the human mind. (publisher, edited)

**Crowe, Michael J**. A History of the Extraterrestrial Life Debate. *Zygon*, 32(2), 147-162, Je 97.

From antiquity to the present, humans have debated whether intelligent life exists elsewhere in the universe. This presentation will survey this debate, examining the roles played in it by science, religion, philosophy and other areas of human learning. One thesis that will be developed is that whether or not extraterrestrials exist, ideas about them have strongly influenced Western thought.

**Crowell, Steven Galt**. Neighbors in Death. *Phil Today*, 41(1-4), 209-218, Spr 97.

Werner Marx proposes principles for a nonmetaphysical ethics based on a critical appropriation of Heidegger's later thought. He suggests that Heidegger failed to exploit the ethical potential of his idea that human beings, as "mortals," have a motive for ethical behavior toward one another. In this paper I proceed phenomenologically, unpacking the reasons (only partially suggested by Marx himself) why confrontation with one's own death might lead to the specific form of ethical intersubjectivity Marx terms "neighborliness." Specifically, I try to show why kindred forms of the intersubjective bond—e.g., love, friendship—are inappropriate for thinking the nature of the ethical relation in the postmetaphysical age.

**Crowell, Steven Galt**. Philosophy as a Vocation: Heidegger and University Reform in the Early Interwar Years. *Hist Phil Quart*, 14(2), 255-276, Ap 97.

Heidegger's political involvement in the Nazi period is often taken as confirming evidence that he belongs among the "conservative revolutionary" wing of

antimodern thought. This paper tries to complicate this judgment by tracking Heidegger's remarks on the problem of "university reform," much debated during the interwar years. Analyzing the correspondences between Heidegger's Husserl—inspired position between 1919-1927 and Max Weber's in "Science as a Vocation," I show that Heidegger's interest in university reform is essentially an interest in the reform of philosophy and is not motivated by the antimodernism characteristic of conservatives like Rickert. I conclude by reflecting on how Heidegger's handling of the university reform issue in his 1933 Rector's address contrasts with the earlier approach.

**Crujeiras Lustres, María José**. La filósofa rancia: un pensamiento ignorado. *An Seminar Hist Filosof*, 10, 45-55, 1993.

The present article illustrates one chapter of the Spanish reactionary thought arisen as a consequence of the French Revolution and whose objective was to restrain the modern ideas in order to preserve tradition (always identified with the Catholic Church). This article deals mainly with the personality of Agapita Clara, self-named the Stale philosopher in honor of Francisco Alvarado (the Stale Philosopher) and it suggests the hypothesis that the author hidden behind that femenine pseudonym may be Manuel Freyre y Castrillón, a former liberal converted to the ideals of the reaction.

**Cruz Cruz, Juan**. "El sentido de la muerte en Fichte" in *El inicio del Idealismo alemán*, Market, Oswaldo, 195-220. Madrid, Ed Complutense, 1996.

When the author uses the expression "the sense of the death", he refers to the "ontoethics of the death". Using this point of view, he pretends to keep Fichte's intention of going beyond any kind of dogmatism—according with the terminology of his first stage, when Fichte polemises with Spinoza—and any sort of naturalism—in the sense that Fichte gives to this word in his last period, polemising with Schelling. With regard to the use of the word "ontoethics", is grounded in the fact that, according to Fichte, "morality is, in some way, the original stuff of which we are made. Only what is moral and nothing else, is the true being in ourselves". (edited)

**Crystal, Ian**. Parmedidean Allusions in *Republic* V. *Ancient Phil*, 16(2), 351-363, Fall 96.

The final argument of Plato's *Republic* Bk. V has been very controversial. This paper attempts to offer a new interpretation of that argument. In addition to offering an analysis of the text, the paper also draws on Parmenides' *Poem* and attempts to demonstrate how Plato is alluding to it in this final argument. It is argued that he does so because he is employing Parmenidean epistemology as a foil for his own.

**Csejtei, Dezsö**. El cartesianismo de la vida (La influencia de Descartes sobre la filosofía madura de Ortega y Gasset). *Teorema*, 16(1), 87-104, 1996.

Research into the relationship between Descartes and Ortega y Gasset has been somewhat neglected in the literature. It has been frequently stated that Ortega was a strong critic of Cartesianism in general. This essay tries to put more emphasis on the positive side of the connection. It is not by chance that Ortega has frequently called his philosophy the "Cartesianism of Life". The final conclusion of the author is that the mature philosophy of Ortega is a deepening and a critical continuation of Cartesian thinking in many respects.

**Csepregi, Gabor**. La ética y la crisis del deporte. *Cuad Etica*, 15-16, 103-120, 1993.

The purpose of this paper is to make people think about nature and the reach of the present crisis in sports. The quick introduction of certain vital features of this activity lets us identify some of the main aspects of the crisis specially the increasing differentiation, the technification and commercialization of sports practices. In particular, we try to delimit the causes of another significant crisis' aspect: the lack of real ethic concerns about sports. This analysis leads us to suggest educative points of view that may help to wake and develop an ethic engagement in sportsmen.

**Cudworth, Ralph** and Hutton, Sarah (ed). *A Treatise Concerning Eternal and Immutable Morality* with *A Treatise of Freewill*. New York, Cambridge Univ Pr, 1996.

Ralph Cudworth (1617-88) deserves recognition as one of the most important English seventeenth-century philosophers after Hobbes and Locke. In opposition to Hobbes, Cudworth proposes an innatist theory of knowledge which may be contrasted with the empirical position of his younger contemporary Locke, and in moral philosophy he anticipates the ethical rationalists of the eighteenth century. *A Treatise Concerning Eternal and Immutable Morality* is his most important discussion of epistemology and this volume makes it available, together with his shorter *Treatise of Freewill*, in its first modern edition, with a historical introduction, a chronology of his life, and a guide to further reading. (publisher, edited)

**Culy, C**. Formal Properties of Natural Language and Linguistic Theories. *Ling Phil*, 19(6), 599-617, D 96.

**Cummins, Denise Dellarosa**. Dominance Hierarchies and the Evolution of Human Reasoning. *Mind Mach*, 6(4), 463-480, N 96.

Research from ethology and evolutionary biology indicates the following about the evolution of reasoning capacity. First, solving problems of social competition and cooperation have direct impact on survival rates and reproductive success. Second, the social structure that evolved from this pressure is the dominance hierarchy. Third, primates that live in large groups with complex dominance hierarchies also show greater neocortical development, and concomitantly greater cognitive capacity. These facts suggest that the necessity of reasoning effectively about dominance hierarchies left an indelible mark on primate reasoning architectures, including that of humans. (edited)

**Cummins, Denise Dellarosa**. Evidence for the Innateness of Deontic Reasoning. *Mind Lang*, 11(2), 160-190, Je 96.

When reasoning about deontic rules (what one may, should, or should not do in a given set of circumstances), reasoners adopt a violation-detection strategy, a strategy they do not adopt when reasoning about indicative rules (descriptions of purported state of affairs). I argue that this indicative-deontic distinction constitutes a primitive in the cognitive architecture. To support this claim, I show that this distinction emerges early in development, is observed regardless of the cultural background of the reasoner and can be selectively disrupted at the neurological level. I also argue that this distinction emerged as a result of selective pressure favouring the evolution of reasoning strategies that determine survival within dominance hierarchies.

**Cummins, Robert**. "Connectionism and the Rationale Constraint on Cognitive Explanation" in *AI, Connectionism and Philosophical Psychology, 1995*, Tomberlin, James E (ed), 105-125. Atascadero, Ridgeview, 1995.

**Cummins, Robert**. Systematicity. *J Phil*, 93(12), 591-614, D 96.

While the alleged systematicity of thought is problematic because there is no uncontroversial way of specifying the structure of propositions, there are domains that exhibit systematics to which we are sensitive. Since not all of these are isomorphic to each other, it follows that not all of these can be explained by appeal to constituent structure of a single representational scheme. It is certainly possible to account for sensitivity to systematics by appeal to nonstructural encodings of the domain. Although the resulting models will be *ad hoc*, in a certain sense, they are no less likely to be true. (edited)

**Cuñarro Conde, Edith Mabel**. Realizability as Constituent Element of the Justification Structure of the Public Decision. *Fronesis*, 3(1), 125-136, Ap 96.

The models for decision making assumed by Jon Elster in *Justicia Local* and John Harsanyi in *Modelos Teóricos del Juego y la Decisión en la Ética Utilitarista* are compared in this article. The search of the relation existing in both proposals between ethical system and practical order allows us to evaluate its realizability. (edited)

**Cunha, Norberto**. A *Física* Subjacente à "Educação Filosófica": Proposta por Martinho de Mendonça de Pina e de Proença. *Rev Port Filosof*, 52(1-4), 253-280, Ja-D 96.

**Cunningham, Craig A**. "Really Living in Space-Time" in *Philosophy of Education (1996)*, Margonis, Frank (ed), 30-33. Urbana, Phil Education Soc, 1997.

**Cunningham, Henri-Paul**. Histoire de la philosophie et philosophie au tribunal de la vérité. *Maritain Stud*, 11, 32-60, 1995.

**Cunningham, Henri-Paul**. La métaphysique aristolélicienne et son sosie cartésien. *Maritain Stud*, 9, 97-112, 1993.

**Cuomo, Chris J**. War Is Not Just an Event: Reflections on the Significance of Everyday Violence. *Hypatia*, 11(4), 30 45, Fall 96.

Although my position is in basic agreement with the notion that war and militarism are feminist issues, I argue that approaches to the ethics of war and peace which do not consider "peacetime" military violence are inadequate for feminist and environmentalist concerns. Because much of the military violence done to women and ecosystems happens outside the boundaries of declared wars, feminist and environmental philosophers ought to emphasize the significance of everyday military violence.

**Cupani, Alberto**. Inconmensurabilidad: Problemas y Fecundidad de una metáfora. *Manuscrito*, 19(2), 111-143, O 96.

"Incommensurability" is a famous and polemical term in contemporary epistemology and philosophy of science. In this article the evolution of the notion of incommensurability in the thought of Thomas Kuhn is briefly reconstructed. Its metaphorical character is underlined and some misunderstandings are corrected. We also emphasize the fertility of this metaphor through presenting some theoretical developments and by suggesting its utility for understanding nonorthodox points of view in the social sciences.

**Cupit, Geoffrey**. *Justice as Fittingness*. New York, Clarendon/Oxford Pr, 1996.

In *Justice as Fittingness* Geoffrey Cupit puts forward a strikingly original theory of the nature of justice. He maintains that injustice is to be understood as a form of unfitting treatment—typically the treatment of people as less than they are. Justice is therefore closely related to unjustified contempt and disrespect and ultimately to desert. Cupit offers a closely argued discussion of what is at issue when people take differing views on what justice requires. He demonstrates that the language of desert provides a suitable idiom in which to address substantive questions of justice and shows why acting justly may require respect for differing entitlements, contributions and needs. In the course of the book many important issues in moral and political philosophy are illuminated. Cupit offers a fresh account of the nature of the obligation to keep a promise, explains how requests can generate reasons for action and suggests a radically new approach to solving the problem of political obligation. This work will offer fascinating insights to political, moral and legal theorists alike. (publisher)

**Cuppens, Frédéric** and Demolombe, Robert. "A Deontic Logic for Reasoning about Confidentiality" in *Deontic Logic, Agency and Normative Systems*, Brown, Mark A (ed), 66-79. New York, Springer-Verlag, 1996.

This paper presents a deontic logic *epsilon* for reasoning about permission or prohibition to know some parts of the database content in the context of a multilevel confidentiality policy. Finally, it is shown how the logic can be used to express constraints to guarantee the consistency of a policy or to prevent the existence of inference channels. That is, the possibility to infer sentences that are not permitted to know from other sentences that are permitted to know. Both deductive and abductive channels are considered. (edited)

**Curley, Edwin** (ed & trans). *A Spinoza Reader: The Ethics and Other Works*. Princeton, Princeton Univ Pr, 1994.

This anthology of the work of Benedict de Spinoza (1632-1677) presents the text of Spinoza's masterwork, the *Ethics*, in what is now the standard translation by Edwin Curley. Also included are selections from other works by Spinoza, chosen by Curley to make the *Ethics* easier to understand, and a substantial introduction that gives an overview of Spinoza's life and the main themes of his philosophy. *A Spinoza Reader* is a practical tool with which to approach one of the world's greatest but most difficult thinkers, a passionate seeker of the truth who has been viewed by some as an atheist and by others as a religious mystic. (publisher, edited)

**Curran, Charles E**. *History and Contemporary Issues: Studies in Moral Theology*. New York, Continuum, 1996.

The twelve essays corrected in this book attempt to show that what Pope John Paul II describes as a crisis in moral theology actually involves a logical development of the Catholic moral tradition. The first section deals with the history and development of moral theology in general, recent developments in the discipline, medical ethics and the casuistry of the manuals of moral theology. The second section discusses the controverted issues of gay and lesbian rights, academic freedom and identity of Catholic colleges and the two recent papal encyclicals dealing with moral theology.

**Curran, Charles E**. *The Origins of Moral Theology in the United States: Three Different Approaches*. Washington, Georgetown Univ Pr, 1997.

Charles E. Curran presents the first in-depth analysis of the origins of Catholic moral theology in the United States, focusing on three significant figures in the late nineteenth century and demonstrating that methodological pluralism and theological diversity existed in the Church even then. (publisher)

**Curran Jr, John E**. Spenser and the Historical Revolution: *Briton Moniments* and the *Problem of Roman Britain*. Clio, 25(3), 273-292, Spr 96.

The Renaissance discovery of Roman Britain, the process by which the ancient history of the island was gleaned from classical historians, was instrumental in discrediting as serious history the legendary *Historia Regum Britanniae* of Geoffrey of Monmouth. Writing his own Galfridian chronicle, Briton Moniments (*Faerie Queene* II.x), under the influence of this discovery, Spenser's account of the Romano-British period reveals his awareness that tremendous historiographical change was taking place. In his unique treatment of such events as the invasion of Julius Caesar, the Boadicean rebellion, and the Roman withdrawal from Britain, Spenser acknowledges that a new history was emerging to replace the patriotic and glorious Galfridian tradition.

**Curren, Mary T** and Harich, Katrin R. A Longitudinal Examination of American Business Ethics: Clark's Scales Revisited. *Bus Prof Ethics J*, 14(4), 57-68, Wint 95.

**Curren, Randall R**. "Democracy and the Foundations of Morality" in *Philosophy of Education (1996)*, Margonis, Frank (ed), 339-341. Urbana, Phil Education Soc, 1997.

This paper is a response to Tapio Poulimatka's "Democracy, Education and the Critical Citizen." Poulimatka holds that by its very nature democracy requires "critical citizenship," and that "critical citizenship" can be established only through education predicated on moral objectivity and (therefore, he says) moral realism. This response identifies a number of serious deficiencies in Poulimatka's arguments, and in so doing contests the view, which has stood as an article of faith for several decades, that democracy places a greater burden on education than other systems of government do.

**Current, Richard N**. Concerning the Charge of Plagiarism against Stephen B. Oates. *J Infor Ethics*, 3(1), 78-79, Spr 94.

**Currie, Gregory** and Ravenscroft, Ian. Mental Simulation and Motor Imagery. *Phil Sci*, 64(1), 161-180, Mr 97.

Motor imagery typically involves an experience as of moving a body part. Recent studies reveal close parallels between the constraints on motor imagery and those on actual motor performance. How are these parallels to be explained? We advance a simulative theory of motor imagery, modeled on the idea that we predict and explain the decisions of others by simulating their decision-making processes. By proposing that motor imagery is essentially off-line motor action, we explain the tendency of motor imagery to mimic motor performance. We close by arguing that a simulative theory of motor imagery gives (modest) support to and illumination of the simulative theory of decision-prediction.

**Curry, Lewis A**. The Impact of William James: A Thought Process for Recognizing Truth in an Unprecedented Future. *J Thought*, 31(4), 9-16, Wint 96.

**Curzer, Howard J**. From Duty, Moral Worth, Good Will. *Dialogue (Canada)*, 36(2), 287-322, Spr 97.

Je propose, dans cet article, une analyse détaillée des paragraphes 397 à 401 des *Fondements*, réfutant certaines objections traditionnelles à la position de Kant et en soulevant de nouvelles. Je proposerai et défendrai, ce faisant, une interprétation de ce que Kant veut dire par les expressions "par devoir", "valeur morale" et "bonne volonté".

**Curzer, Howard J**. Journals and Justice. *J Infor Ethics*, 5(2), 39-53, Fall 96.

What share of the library journals budget should be spent on journals for each department? I argue that justice requires the library to provide *all* departments with an equal opportunity to carry out their research and teaching missions. Departments have equal opportunities when they have equal percentages of their core journal holdings. Therefore, even though it is inefficient to do so, libraries have a duty to provide equal percentages of core journal holdings to all departments unless departments voluntarily relinquish their claims upon expensive journals.

**Cussens, James**. Deduction, Induction and Probabilistic Support. *Synthese*, 108(1), 1-10, Jl 96.

Elementary results concerning the connections between deductive relations and probabilistic support are given. These are used to show that Popper-Miller's result is a special case of a more general result, and that their result is not "very unexpected" as claimed. According to Popper-Miller, *a* purely inductively supports *b* only if they are "deductively independent"—but this means that *b* can be derived from not -*a*. Hence, it is argued that viewing induction as occurring only in the absence of deductive relations, as Popper-Miller sometimes do, is untenable. Finally, it is shown that Popper-Miller's claim that deductive relations determine probabilistic support is untrue. In general, probabilistic support can vary greatly with fixed deductive relations as determined by the relevant Lindenbaum algebra. (edited)

**Cutrofello, Andrew**. The Blessed Gods Mourn: What is Living-Dead in the Legacy of Hegel. *Owl Minerva*, 28(1), 25-38, Fall 96.

In this essay, I will ask why Hegel in particular should have occasioned philosophical reflection on the concept of a legacy. Section One begins from Lawrence Stepelevich's assessment of how the young Hegelians, especially Max Stirner, saw themselves in relation to the Hegelian legacy. Section Two draws a connection between the way Hegel treats the legacy of the Greek ideal in art and Sigmund Freud's distinction between mourning and melancholia. Section Three suggests a way in which those conclusions might be used to negotiate an impasse in contemporary continental philosophy. (edited)

**Cutsinger, James S**. *Advice to the Serious Seeker: Meditations on the Teaching of Frithjof Schuon*. Albany, SUNY Pr, 1997.

Two books in one, *Advice to the Serious Seeker* is an introduction for scholars to the perennialist school of comparative religious philosophy and at the same time a guidebook for the general reader who is looking for intellectually serious but accessible answers to questions about the spiritual life. (publisher,edited)

**Cuypers, Stefaan E**. The 'I' and Personal Identity in Russell's Logical Atomism (in Dutch). *Bijdragen*, 58(1), 29-55, 1997.

Although the contributions of John Locke's memory-theory and David Hume's bundle-theory to the construction of the contemporary empiricist theory of personal identity are explicitly acknowledged, empiricist philosophers relatively neglect another important source of inspiration in their debate on personal identity in analytical philosophy, namely Bertrand Russell's philosophy of logical atomism. However, Derek Parfit's radically empiricist and impersonal view on personal identity implicitly is a direct heir of Russell's view on personal identity. In this article, then, I try to make explicit the Russellian heritage in the contemporary empiricist theory of personal identity by reconstructing Russell's view on the existence and the nature of the 'I' and the identity of the self. For the purpose of explaining Russell's view that 'I' really is the abbreviation for the description "the subject of the present experience" or "the subject of 'this'," the technical concepts of knowledge by acquaintance and knowledge by description as well as the notion of a proper name in the logical sense are introduced. And, in order to explain Russell's view on self-identity as constituted by the synchronic relation of 'compresence' and the diachronic R-relation of 'copersonality', the technique of logical construction is appealed to.

**Czerwinski, Marcin**. "Jerzy Kmita's Epistemology" in *Epistemology and History*, Zeidler-Janiszewska, Anna (ed), 35-44. Amsterdam, Rodopi, 1996.

Jerzy Kmita's version of Marxism and its relationship to the official Marxism is examined. The peculiarities of his original views are put forward and some of them are critically commented on.

**Cziszter, Kálmán**. Is the See-Battle About to Be Lost? On Aristotle's *De interpretatione*, Ch. 9. A Reconstruction (in Czech). *Magyar Filozof Szemle*, 1-2, 25-44, 1997.

According to the traditional interpretation of *De Interpretatione* ch. 9 (dating back to Boethius, Ammonius et. al., and sustained in our times by Kneal, Frede and Lukasiewicz), Aristotle refutes the fatalist arguments by removing the future-tensed propositions from the scope of the principle of bivalence. I refute this view first of all on textual grounds, by filling the gaps in De Int 9. with arguments taken form the treatment of the principle of bivalence in *Metaphysics Book IV*. My second objection points to the fact that the special ontological status of the future presupposed in this traditional interpretation (which practically equates future events with sheer potentialities) runs counter to Aristotle's concept of time, as presented in the *Physics Book IV*. (edited)

**D'Agostino, Giovanna** and Bernardi, Claudio. Translating the Hypergame Paradox: Remarks on the Set of Founded Elements of a Relation. *J Phil Log*, 25(5), 545-557, O 96.

In Zwicker (1987) the hypergame paradox is introduced and studied. In this paper we continue this investigation, comparing the hypergame argument with the diagonal one, in order to find a proof schema. In particular, in Theorems 9 and 10 we discuss the complexity of the set of founded elements in a recursively enumerable relation on the set *N* of natural numbers, in the framework of reduction between relations. We also find an application in the theory of diagonalizable algebras and construct an undecidable formula.

**D'Alessandro, Paolo**. "Pensare La Storia: Soggetto e metodo dell'interpretazione" in *Soggetto E Verità: La questione dell'uomo nella filosofia contemporanea*, Fagiuoli, Ettore, 257-265. 20136 Milano, Mimesis, 1996.

**D'Allessandro, Giuseppe**. "Metodo e modelli storiografici nel tardo illuminismo tedesco" in *Lo Storicismo e la Sua Storia: Temi, Problemi, Prospettive*, Cacciatore, Giuseppe (ed), 112-127. Milano, Guerini, 1997.

**D'Amico, Robert**. Impossible Laws. *Phil Soc Sci*, 27(3), 309-327, S 97.

John Searle claims that social laws are conceptually impossible. I argue that his claim is, contrary to a first impression, consistent with his biological theory of intentionality and I reject Harold Kincaid's analysis in which the argument's weakness is found in it automatically extending to any special science where phenomena are multiply realized. However, I conclude that Searle's account has the result that either mental causation is epiphenomenal for social phenomena or there are some social laws. Since Searle defends the reality of intentional causation, social laws remain at least conceptually possible on his account.

**D'Antuono, Emilia**. "Immagini della Grecia: Rosenzweig e Burckhardt" in *Lo Storicismo e la Sua Storia: Temi, Problemi, Prospettive*, Cacciatore, Giuseppe (ed), 409-417. Milano, Guerini, 1997.

**D'Arcy, Chantal Cornut-G** (ed) and García Landa, José Angel (ed). *Gender, I-deology Essays on Theory, Fiction and Film*. Amsterdam, Rodopi, 1996.

The essays in this collection address a variety of topics under the general heading of "gender issues"—gender and writing, reading, and representation, sexual options and roles, generic models and stereotypes, sexual ambivalence, or the politics of gender. All the essays examine in one way or another the role of gender and sexuality in fictional texts. The emphasis throughout is on the interface of gender and modernity, as seen through a variety of British and American literary works and films. Most of the contributions assume a feminist perspective on the issues discussed, each adopting a specific critical approach to its subject. (edited)

**D'Arms, Justin**. Sex, Fairness, and the Theory of Games. *J Phil*, 93(12), 615-627, D 96.

This paper explores some problems with a game theoretic approach to the explanation of justice. Brian Skyrms has recently offered an account of the evolution of our concept of justice by modelling the success of various strategies in a Nash bargaining game. His central result is that a tendency to favor equal divisions is adaptive under the parameters of the game. The result depends upon a correlation assumption—that individuals playing the same strategy are more than randomly likely to meet. I argue that the assumption is only justifiable for a range of cases too narrow to generate Skyrms's result. I go on to raise doubts about whether the game, and the strategy of equal division, are helpful models for our notions of justice.

**D'Espagnat, Bernard**. Open Realism. *Phil Natur*, 28(1), 54-69, 1991.

This paper is an analysis of the extent to which the idea of a scientifically describable *mind-independent reality* can be kept when data from contemporary basic physics are taken into consideration. According to the author *mind-independent reality* notion cannot be dispensed with. But we know that no tentative description of it can be reconciled with locality (Bell's theorem). It is suggested that *mind-independent reality* be considered as not knowable as it is, the true subject matter of science being an empirical, *mind-dependent reality*.

**D'Hondt, Jacques**. Deutsche Aufklärung und französische *Lumières*. *Z Phil Forsch*, 51(2), 309-318, Ap-Je 97.

Il y a de grands décalages chronologiques entre les manifestations comparables de l'*Aufklärung* allemande et des *Lumières* françaises. Le Français qui, temporellement, correspond le mieux à Wolff est Marivaux. De fait, malgré d'énormes différences, des rapports significatifs s'établissent entre la pensée de Wolff et ce qu'il y a de proprement philosophique dans celle de Marivaux.

**D'Orey, Carmo**. A Identidade de Vénus ou as Vantagens da Extensionalidade. *Philosophica (Portugal)*, 169-187, 1997.

This paper seeks to show that Goodman's theory allows the explanation of all the subtleties of aesthetics within fully extensional semantics. My strategy is to suggest, following Goodman, that "reference" is wider than is commonly recognized and that many of the functions attributed to intensional notions are functions of different modes of reference. The advantage is double: an elegant solution for ancient logical problems and an advancement of the cognitive conception of art. (edited)

**D'Orey, Carmo**. Arte e ciência: Acordo e progresso. *Philosophica (Portugal)*, 71-84, 1994.

The fact that there is progress and agreement in sciences and not in arts is sometimes adduced as an argument against the cognitive character of art. In this paper this cognitive character is not supported. Its purpose is only to show that this difference, between arts and sciences, in what concerns agreement and progress, is mainly due to the different syntactic and semantic characteristics of the respective systems of symbols and is not to be ascribed to their cognitive potentialities.

**D'Oronzio, Joseph C**. Ethical Obligations in the Body Politic: The Case of Normalization Policy for Marginal Populations. *Cambridge Quart Healthcare Ethics*, 6(4), 480, Fall 97.

**D'Ors, Angel**. Petrus Hispanus O.P., Auctor Summularum. *Vivarium*, 35(1), 21-71, Mr 97.

**D'Souza, Mario O**. God and Jacques Maritain's Philosophy of Education: Uninvited Guests at the Postmodern Party. *Maritain Stud*, 10, 156-168, 1994.

**D'Souza, Mario O**. The Education of Natural Intelligence and the Intellectual Virtues: Has Educational Pastiche had the Last Laugh?. *Maritain Stud*, 11, 234-246, 1995.

**Da Costa, Newton C A** and Béziau, Jean-Yves. Théorie de la valuation. *Log Anal*, 37(146), 95-117, Je 94.

On montre que les logiques vérifiant les lois d'identité et de coupure infinies (logiques normales) ont une sémantique bivalente adéquate constituée par les fonctions caractéristiques des théories closes (sémantique de l'évaluation). Si de plus ces logiques sont compactes alors on peut prendre la sémantique bivalente constituée par les fonctions caractéristiques des théories saturées (sémantique de la valuation). Cette sémantique est minimale et donc comme toute théorie maximale est saturée, la sémantique constituée par les fonctions caractéristiques des théories maximales s'avère caduque si elle se différencie de la précédente. (edited)

**Da Costa, Newton C A** and Bueno, Otavio. Consistency, Para-consistency and Truth (Logic, the Whole Logic and Nothing but 'the' Logic). *Ideas Valores*, 48-60, Ap 96.

After examining some components of a framework articulated in terms of general remarks on logic (in which two inadequate views of it are critically investigated), we present some arguments to the effect that a fallibilist, pluralist, though certainly not relativist, proposal might be interestingly pursued. Based on this proposal, we argue for a comprehensive agnosticism in connection to some issues raised by paraconsistency (in particular with regard to the existence of true contradictions). Such an agnosticism, not being philosophically committed to any particular "interpretative" claims surrounding paraconsistency, seems to be at the moment more adequate than the alternative proposals.

**Da Costa, Newton C A** and Bueno, Otávio and Béziau, Jean-Yves. What is Semantics? A Brief Note on a Huge Question. *Sorites*, 43-47, N 95.

After mentioning the cogent connection between pure semantics and the particular set theoretical framework in which it is formulated, some issues regarding the conceptual status of semantics itself, as well as its relationship to logic, are concisely raised.

**Da Costa, Newton C A** and Krause, Décio. Schrödinger Logics. *Stud Log*, 53(4), 533-550, N 94.

Schrödinger logics are logical systems in which the principle of identity is not true in general. The intuitive motivation for these logics is both Erwin Schrödinger's thesis (which has been advanced by other authors) that identity lacks sense for elementary particles of modern physics, and the way which physicists deal with this concept; normally they understand *identity* as meaning *indistinguishabilty* (agreement with respect to attributes). Observing that these concepts are equivalent in classical logic and mathematics, which underly the usual physical theories, we present a higher-order logical system in which these concepts are systematically separated. A 'classical' semantics for the system is presented and some philosophical related questions are mentioned. (edited)

**Da Luz, José Luís Brandao**. O Homem e a História em Gaspar Frutuoso. *Rev Port Filosof*, 52(1-4), 475-486, Ja-D 96.

The conception of man and the vision of history manifest in the introductory text of Gaspar Frutuoso's *Saudades da Terra* are inspired by the weltanschauung of the *Book of Genesis*. The experience of sin and guilt do not reduce man to a merely temporal dimension, not do they submit him to a naturalist determinism, but confront him with the free assertion of an axiological order, which he can not alter. However, the bond with the unconditional sphere of the transcendence does not pretend to mutilate the comprehension of man or the history of its social components. On the contrary, it responds to the preoccupation of situating those compromises ensuing from man's social insertion and the safeguard of personal dignity in a universe of meaning which, in themselves, they would never possess.

**Da Silva, Augusto Soares**. De Aristóteles a Bréal: Da *Homonímia* à *Polissemia*. *Rev Port Filosof*, 52(1-4), 797-812, Ja-D 96.

We study the history of the concepts and terms *homonymy* (two or more words having the same form) and *polysemy* (a word having several related meanings) from Aristotle to Bréal (a last century philologist) who created the term *polysemy*. Aristotle's thought on "casual" homonymy ('homonymy') and "intentional" homonymy ('polysemy') represents already a synthesis of the modern concepts and of the related problems (delimitation criteria and polysemy's structure) and has inspired his commentators to produce important studies on *aequivocatio/univocatio, significatio/suppositio* and *multiplicitas*. Homonymia is found not only in dialectics, but also in both grammar and rhetoric treatises as a kind of *amphibolia*. The distinction made by the Port-Royal logicians between equivocal and univocal words is in line with the Aristotelian opposition. Both homonymy and polysemy have a long logical-philosophical, rhetorical and grammatical tradition, not of semantic considerations.

**Da Silva, Jairo José**. Husserl's Phenomenology and Weyl's Predictivism. *Synthese*, 110(2), 277-296, F 97.

In this paper I discuss the version of predicative analysis put forward by Hermann Weyl in *Das Kontinuum*. I try to establish how much of the underlying motivation for Weyl's position may be due to his acceptance of phenomenological philosophical perspective. More specifically, I analyze Weyl's philosophical ideas in connection with the work of Husserl, in particular *Logische Untersuchungen* and *Ideen I*. I believe that this interpretation of Weyl can clarify the views on mathematical existence and mathematical intuition which is implicit in *Das Kontinuum*.

**Da Silva, José Antunes**. Compassion in Mahayana Buddhism. *Rev Port Filosof*, 52(1-4), 813-830, Ja-D 96.

**Da Veiga, Manuel Alte**. Identidade e Deontologia em Educaçao. *Rev Port Filosof*, 52(1-4), 953-965, Ja-D 96.

Alte da Veiga argues for an open deontology, rather as an attitude than as a code. Education is a personal project only administratively codified. A deontological code would generate a dangerous situation of indoctrination—the manipulation by the power or by the mediocrity of the community. The identity of teachers and students, is the ever changing result of the dynamic spiral of life-that continuous search for better quality of life, where the acceptance of social and personal error promotes the identity and the deontological attitude. Tolerance, change, conversion, etc. might not be seen as devaluation of the past or of another culture, whose experience only enriches our spiral of life.

**Dafonte, César Raña**. Vicente Munoz Delgado y Angel Amor Ruibal. *Rev Espan Filosof Med*, 4, 175-187, 1997.

With this work, I pretend to introduce the readers to Vicente Muñoz Delgado like a studious proponent and spreader of Angel Amor Ruibal's philosopher. To achieve this objective I am going to take into account the most interesting five writings by the Professor Muñoz which deal with the exceptional philosopher from Santiago de Compostela.

**Dahbour, Omar**. Introduction: National Identity as a Philosophical Problem. *Phil Forum*, 28(1-2), 1-20, Fall-Wint 97.

National identity is considered in relation to concepts such as identity, ideology, rights, citizenship, and community and in the work of thinkers from Rousseau to Walzer. Philosophical debates about national identity are analyzed in terms of the importance of cultural versus political identities, the relation of liberalism to a principle of national self-determination, justifications of the collective rights of nations, the desirability of citizenship criteria based on nationality, and the relation of political community to cultural homogeneity. The importance of philosophical consideration of national identity is found to be its focus on the problem of the nature of community.

**Daily, Catherine M** and Dalton, Dan R and Wimbush, James C. Collecting "Sensitive" Data in Business Ethics Research: A Case for the Unmatched Count Technique (UCT). *J Bus Ethics*, 16(10), 1049-1057, Jl 97.

Some would argue that the more promising areas of business ethics research are "sensitive." In such areas, it would be expected that subjects, if inclined to respond at all, would be guarded in their responses, or respond inaccurately. We provide an introduction to an empirical approach—the unmatched block count (UCT)—for collecting these potentially sensitive data which provides absolute anonymity and confidentiality to subjects and "legal immunity" to the researcher. Interestingly, under UCT protocol researchers could not divulge subjects' responses even if they were inclined to do so. Beyond that, UCTs provide complete disclosure to subjects and there is no deception.

**Daisuke, Hirakawa**. Characterization in Samuel Beckett's *Not I*. *Bigaku*, 48(1), 49-59, Sum 97.

Of Samuel Beckett's later dramatic compositions, *Not I* (1972) is famous for its experimental quality to give sensational shock to the audience and readers. We find in the complete darkness a woman's lips without any other parts of body, called MOUTH, floating on the high level of stage and it speaks incessantly unintelligible fragments of story with slight syntax for fifteen minutes. This essay tries to describe and interpret *Not I* from a point of view that MOUTH is a female dead in Purgatory, which is one of the central types of dramatic characters in Beckett's canon. (edited)

**Dalgleish, Tim**. An Anti-Anti-Essentialist View of the Emotions: A Reply to Kupperman. *Phil Psych*, 10(1), 85-90, Mr 97.

Kupperman (1995) advances an anti-essentialist view of emotions in which he suggests that there can be emotion without feeling or affect, emotion without corresponding motivation, and emotion without an intentional relation to an object such that the emotion is about that object in some way. In this reply to Kupperman's essay, I suggest a number of problems with his rejection of the essentialist position. I argue that in his discussion of feelings Kupperman is crucially not clear about the distinction between the ascription of emotions by others versus the experience of emotions by an individual. Furthermore, I also question his analysis of the role of linguistic empiricism in philosophy and psychology. With respect to Kupperman's analysis of intentionality, I argue that he confuses the ability to readily identify intentional objects with the issue of their actual existence. Finally, I suggest that Kupperman confuses the concepts of action and motivation in his discussion of motivation.

**Dall'Asta, Giuseppe**. "Tempo storico e futuro escatologico" in *Il Concetto di Tempo: Atti del XXXII Congresso Nazionale della Società Filosofica Italiana*, Casertano, Giovanni (ed), 307-315. Napoli, Loffredo, 1997.

**Dalla Vigna, Pierre**. "La Pittura Come Linguaggio Indiretto Dell'Essere E Prosa Del Mondo" in *Soggetto E Verità: La questione dell'uomo nella filosofia contemporanea*, Fagiuoli, Ettore, 137-160. 20136 Milano, Mimesis, 1996.

**Dallmayr, Fred R**. "An 'Inoperative' Global Community? Reflections on Nancy" in *On Jean-Luc Nancy: The Sense of Philosophy*, Sheppard, Darren (ed), 174-196. New York, Routledge, 1997.

**Dallmayr, Fred R**. *Beyond Orientalism: Essays on Cross-Cultural Encounter*. Albany, SUNY Pr, 1996.

After discussing the broad range of possible "modes of cross-cultural encounter" in a historical perspective, the book develops as a preferred option the notion of a deconstructive dialogue or a "hermeneutics of difference" which respects otherness beyond assimilation. This hermeneutics is illustrated in chapters examining several bridge-builders between cultures, primarily the Indian philosophers Radhakrishnan and J.L. Mehta and the Indologist Halbfass. The remaining chapters are devoted to more concrete social-political problems, including issues of modernization, multiculturalism, and the prospects of a globalized democracy which bids farewell to Orientalism and Eurocentrism. (publisher,edited)

**Dallmayr, Fred R**. Cultura y Desarrollo Global. *Topicos*, 9-24, 1996.

This paper argues on behalf of a proper understanding of *culture* (as something like self-formation [*Bildung*]) as a basis for supporting the concept of development, instead of the conception proposed by many economists and social scientists.

**Dallmayr, Fred R**. Heidegger, Bhakti, and Vedanta—A Tribute to J.L. Mehta. *J Indian Counc Phil Res*, 13(2), 117-144, Ja-Ap 96.

**Dallmayr, Fred R**. The Politics of Nonidentity: Adorno, Postmodernism—and Edward Said. *Polit Theory*, 25(1), 33-56, F 97.

Contemporary political theory harbors a strong animus against sameness or identity, which stands accused of promoting "totalizing" if not totalitarian designs. Yet, can identity be simply canceled and can nonidentity itself function as a new kind of identity? The paper initially examines these questions by focusing on Adorno's notion of "nonidentity", on Foucault's emphasis on rupture and discontinuity and on Deleuze's equation of nonidentity with nomadism. All three writers are invoked by Edward Said in his critique of Western cultural and political imperialism. In his own writings, Said sees the task of "secular intellectuals" in their exodus from cultural moorings—which approximates Deleuze's nomadism. The paper asks: can nomadism or the no-man's-land on nonidentity serve as a "space" for public life and political thought?

**Dallmayr, Fred R** and Hardimon, Michael O and Pinkard, Terry. The New Hegel. *Polit Theory*, 25(4), 584-597, Ag 97.

**Dalrymple, Mary** and Lamping, John and Pereira, Fernando (& others). Quantifiers, Anaphora, and Intensionality. *J Log Lang Info*, 6(3), 219-273, Jl 97.

The relationship between Lexical-Functional Grammar (LFG) *functional structures* (f-structures) for sentences and their semantic interpretations can be formalized in *linear logic* in a way that correctly explains the observed interactions between quantifier scope ambiguity, bound anaphora and intensionality. While our approach resembles current categorial approaches in important ways (Moortgat, 1988, 1992a; Carpenter, 1993; Morrill, 1994) it differs from them in allowing the greater compositional flexibility of categorial semantics (van Benthem, 1991) while maintaining a precise connection to syntax. As a result, we are able to provide derivations for certain readings of sentences with intensional verbs and complex direct objects whose derivation in purely categorial accounts of the syntax-semantics interface appears to require otherwise unnecessary semantic decompositions of lexical entries. (publisher, edited)

**Dalton, Dan R** and Daily, Catherine M and Wimbush, James C. Collecting "Sensitive" Data in Business Ethics Research: A Case for the Unmatched Count Technique (UCT). *J Bus Ethics*, 16(10), 1049-1057, Jl 97.

Some would argue that the more promising areas of business ethics research are "sensitive." In such areas, it would be expected that subjects, if inclined to respond at all, would be guarded in their responses, or respond inaccurately. We provide an introduction to an empirical approach—the unmatched block count (UCT)—for collecting these potentially sensitive data which provides absolute anonymity and confidentiality to subjects and "legal immunity" to the researcher. Interestingly, under UCT protocol researchers could not divulge subjects' responses even if they were inclined to do so. Beyond that, UCTs provide complete disclosure to subjects and there is no deception.

**Dalton, Dennis** (ed). *Mahatma Ghandi: Selected Political Writings*. Indianapolis, Hackett, 1996.

The first collection of Gandhi's writings to be based on the complete edition of his works, this new volume presents Gandhi's most important political writings arranged around the two central themes of his political teachings: *satyagraha* (the power of nonviolence) and *swaraj* (freedom). Dennis Dalton's general introduction and headnotes highlight the life of Gandhi, set the readings in historical context, and provide insight into the conceptual framework of Gandhi's political theory. Complete with bibliography, glossary, and index. (publisher)

**Dalton, Peter**. A Theological Escape from the Cartesian Circle?. *Int J Phil Relig*, 42(1), 41-59, Ag 97.

**Daly, Chris**. Defending Promiscuous Realism about Natural Kinds. *Phil Quart*, 46(185), 496-500, O 96.

I defend John Dupre's thesis of "Promiscuous Realism" about natural kinds against two objections by T.E. Wilkerson. First, I show that ordinary language classification is no more (and no less) concerned with practical interests than is scientific classification. Second, I show that the predictions and explanations provided by ordinary language classification are not invariably inferior to those provided by scientific classification.

**Daly, Chris**. Pluralist Metaphysics. *Phil Stud*, 87(2), 185-206, Ag 97.

**Dambmann, Holger**. Die Bedeutung des Machschen Prinzips in der Kosmologie. *Phil Natur*, 27(2), 234-271, 1990.

Mach's principle had been one of the guiding principles in the construction of general relativity by Einstein. Mach's principle dates back to the Newton-Leibniz debate on the absoluteness of space. It is shown that general relativity does not support Mach's ideas on space and inertia, contrary to Einstein's belief. Important versions of Mach's principle are presented (Einstein, Wheeler, Hoenl-Dehnen, Hoyle-Narlikar) and evaluated. Even though none of them is consistent within general relativity, these approaches show there may be a coupling of local properties to cosmological structure. Finally we discuss the relationship of the 'bootstrap principle' and the 'anthropic principle' to Mach's principle.

**Damiani, Alberto M**. Hermenéutica y metafísica en la *Scienza Nuova*. *Cuad Vico*, 5/6, 51-65, 1995/96.

This paper explains the Vichian synthesis of philosophy and philology starting from the metaphysics of mind and Vico's concept of mind. The historical

development of the human nature lies on the bottom of Vico's theory of knowledge. The principle *verum ipsum factum* and the poetic wisdom are examined as the hermeneutics keys of the civil world. The reached conclusion is that the Vico's *Scienza Nuova* has both metaphysical and hermeneutical aspects: metaphysical in that it tries to understand the mental conditions of society; and hermeneutical in that it seeks to apply these conditions to interpret the human history.

**Damiani, Alberto M**. Vico y Dilthey: La comprensión del mundo histórico. *Cuad Vico*, 7/8, 357-375, 1997.

The two lines pursued in this paper are: if there are any parallel theses between the methodological principles of Vico and Dilthey's work; and which direct connection could have existed. The paper starts from the analysis of many different points of view through which this topic has been considered by Vico's scholars. Making clearer the relationship between Vico and Dilthey allows us a better understanding of their philosophical ideas.

**Damico, Alfonso J**. "Reason's Reach: Liberal Tolerance and Political Discourse" in *Political Dialogue: Theories and Practices*, Esquith, Stephen L (ed), 25-44. Amsterdam, Rodopi, 1996.

Building upon Locke's view of toleration, it is possible to elaborate a liberal theory of political dialogue. Tolerance is more than simply a grudging admission that coercion is often ineffective; it is a practice of communication that constrains and disciplines what can be effectively said.

**Damnjanovic, Zlatan**. Elementary Realizability. *J Phil Log*, 26(3), 311-339, Je 97.

A realizability notion that employs only Kalmar elementary functions is defined and relative to it, the soundness of $EA\text{-}(Pi^0{}_1\text{-}IR)$, a fragment of Heyting Arithmetic (HA) with names and axioms for all elementary functions and induction rule restricted to $Pi^0{}_1\text{-}IR$) are precisely the elementary functions. Elementary realizability is proposed as a model of strict arithmetic constructivism, which allows only those constructive procedures for which the amount of computational resources required can be bounded in advance.

**Damon, William** and Gregory, Anne. The Youth Charter: Towards the Formation of Adolescent Moral Identity. *J Moral Educ*, 26(2), 117-130, Je 97.

Studies of adolescent conduct have found that both exemplary and antisocial behaviour can be predicted by the manner in which adolescents integrate moral concerns into their theories and descriptions of self. These findings have led many developmentalists to conclude that moral identity—in contrast to moral judgement or reflection alone—plays a powerful role in mediating social conduct. Moreover, development theory and research have shown that identity formation during adolescence is a process of forging a coherent and systematic sense of self. Despite these well-founded conclusions, many moral education programmes fail to engage a young person's sense of self, focus exclusively on judgement and reflection and make little or no attempt to establish coherence with other formative influences in a young person's life. The authors propose a new method, called "the youth charter", for promoting adolescent self-identification with a coherent set of moral standards.

**Damren, Samuel C**. A "Meeting of the Minds": The Greater Illusion. *Law Phil*, 15(3), 271-291, 96.

**Damrosch, Lori Fisler**. The Collective Enforcement of International Norms Through Economic Sanctions. *Ethics Int Affairs*, 8, 59-75, 1994.

**Dancy, Jonathan**. Real Values in a Humean Context. *Ratio*, 9(2), 171-183, S 96.

**Danehower, Carol** and Thorne, Debbie and Everett, Linda. Cognitive Moral Development and Attitudes Toward Women Executives. *J Bus Ethics*, 15(11), 1227-1235, N 96.

Research has shown that men and women are similar in their capabilities and management competence; however, there appears to be a "glass ceiling" which poses invisible barriers to their promotion to management positions. One explanation for the existence of these barriers lies in stereotyped, biased attitudes toward women in executive positions. This study supports earlier findings that attitudes of men toward women in executive positions are generally negative, while the attitudes of women are generally positive. Additionally, we found that an individual's level of cognitive moral development correlates significantly with attitudes toward women executives. Limitations of the present study and implications for ethics and diversity training in organizations are discussed.

**Daniel, Marie-France**. Principes pragmatistes pour une démarche pédagogique en enseignement moral. *Philosopher*, 18, 127-164, 1995.

Au Québec, depuis les années 1977, la morale est une matière spécifique d'enseignement. La question qui est posée dans cet article est de savoir si l'enseignement moral peut contribuer, de façon significative, à l'éducation morale des jeunes. Nous situant dans une perspective pragmatiste, nous avons, dans un premier temps, défini la morale en tant que concept puis nous avons tenté de cerner sa relation à l'éducation ainsi qu'à l'enseignement. Dans un deuxième temps, nous avons tenté de relever les limites de l'enseignement moral au primaire. Finalement, nous avons proposé quelques éléments d'une pédagogie alternative, basée sur la recherche et la construction du sens en communauté.

**Daniel, Marie-France** and LaFortune, Louise and Pallascio, Richard (& others). Y a-t-il de la place pour philosopher sur les mathématiques au collégial?. *Philosopher*, 18, 107-126, 1995.

Dans cet article, nous explorons l'idée de transférer l'approche de *Philosophie pour enfants* adaptée aux mathématiques à l'enseignement post-secondaire. Dans une expérience où cette approche a été utilisée auprès de jeunes du primaire, les élèves approfondissent grâce aux communautés de recherche, certains concepts utilisés en mathématiques (infini, abstrait, zéro, géométrie, définition, preuve, existence, découverte...). Nous proposons des idées de plans de discussion et d'activités pouvant être transférées à l'enseignement post-secondaire et portant sur: abstrait-concret, figures géométriques, comprendre et connaître. De cette réflexion, nous concluons que différentes disciplines comme les mathématiques auraient avantage à intégrer des éléments d'une approche philosophique et à organiser des communautés de recherche dans leurs cours afin de susciter le processus de réflexion critique des élèves sur les notions enseignées, mais aussi sur leurs apprentissages.

**Daniel, Stephen H**. Paramodern Strategies of Philosophical Historiography. *Epoche*, 1(1), 41-63, 1993.

In postmodern historiography, Berkeley, Vico and Condillac are not representative of "modern" philosophy, and even Descartes and Kant exhibit distinctly unmodern characteristics. Instead of emphasizing Hobbes's rhetoric and the aesthetic nature of Leibniz's metaphysics or Hume's epistemology poststructuralism, deconstruction, and critical theory reveal how so-called modern philosophers are sensitive to their own discursive practices. In terms of postmodern themes, Spinoza's monism becomes Barthes's universal semiotics, Berkeley's immaterialism becomes Quine's or Rorty's semantic realism; and ideas developed by Jonathan Edwards, Diderot, and Rousseau take on new meaning when interpreted by Deleuze, Derrida, and Foucault.

**Daniels, Charles**. God vs. Less Than the Very Best. *Sophia (Australia)*, 35(1), 21-26, Mr-Ap 96.

There is a sense in which 1) there exists a being who is eternally *perfectly well-intentioned* and *perfectly competent* and 2) some possible world is better than the actual one are incompatible. It may be alleged by some, however, that the inconsistency lies in 1) itself: the best possible worlds may all be ones whose perfection is in an essential way the product of a *joint* effort on the parts of the moral agents in them. That is, the perfection of these worlds is held to be beyond the competence of any single individual (God) to bring about. What is best and what is possible for an individual to accomplish are pitted against each other. This is not to say, however, that the story told about the limitations perfection puts on the powers of a creator is one which cries out for belief.

**Daniels, Charles**. God, Demon, Good, Evil. *J Value Inq*, 31(2), 177-181, Je 97.

Theists who argue for the consistency and existence of God have recently been challenged to rebut isometric arguments from evil which proceed to the consistency and existence of the (omniscient, omnipotent, omnimalevolent) demon. By using an argument from Plato, I defeat the challenge.

**Daniels, Charles**. The General Form of a Proposition in an Especially Perspicuous Language. *Log Anal*, 37(147-8), 303-312, S-D 94.

One of Wittgenstein's aims in the *Tractatus* is to describe the general form of a proposition of a perspicuous language. By generalizing one interpretation of the language Wittgenstein himself sketches out in 4.31, 4.4, 4.442, and 5.101, this project is carried to completion for perspicuous languages which (a) make it immediately clear in every case which propositions follow from which, (b) have exactly one name per object, and (c) have exactly one propositional sign per proposition. The form the propositional signs of any such language take is described.

**Daniels, Norman**. "Wide Reflective Equilibrium in Practice" in *Philosophical Perspectives on Bioethics*, Sumner, L W (ed), 96-114. Toronto, Univ of Toronto Pr, 1996.

**Danielson, Peter A** and MacDonald, Chris J. Hard Cases in Hard Places: Singer's Agenda for Applied Ethics. *Dialogue (Canada)*, 35(3), 599-610, Sum 96.

This is a critical notice of the second edition of Singer's deservedly influential book, *Practical Ethics*. First we consider Singer's appeal to a principle of equality as definitive of ethics and subject it to a contractarian criticism. Second, we argue that Singer's discussion of environmental ethics makes clear that he lacks an adequate theory of value. Next, we discuss Singer's involvement in the controversy over euthanasian in the German-speaking countries, and suggest that his analysis is at odds with his earlier discussion of civil disobedience. Finally, we consider Singer's ill-fated attempt to justify the moral life in self-interested terms.

**Dannemann, Rüdiger**. Georg Lukács's Criticism of Societal Reason—The Crisis of Marxism and Marxist Ontology (in Hungarian). *Magyar Filozof Szemle*, 4-5-6, 423-436, 1996.

In den obigen fragmentarischen Bemerkungen möchte ich—sehr thesenhaft—die Folgen der unbezweifelbaren Krise des Marxismus für die Lukács-Rezeption diskutieren. Ich möchte einige Reflexionen vortragen zu dem irritierenden und offenen Problem: Was tun mit Georg Lukács in Zeiten, die definitiv den Tod des Marxismus in einem "Nachruf auf den Marxismus—Leninismus" fixieren? 1) Es wäre töricht, zu leugnen, dass für viele eine Faszination von der Vorstellung ausgeht, die Pfade der überkommenen radikalen Philosophie zu verlassen und sich dem freien Spiel vagbundierenden Philosophierens zu überlassen, dem munteren Taumel der Postmoderne. (edited)

**Danner, Norman** and Hammer, Eric. Towards a Model Theory of Diagrams. *J Phil Log*, 25(5), 463-482, O 96.

A logical system is studied whose well-formed representations consist of diagrams rather than formulas. The system, due to Shin [2,3], is shown to be complete by an argument concerning maximally consistent sets of diagrams. The argument is complicated by the lack of a straight forward counterpart of atomic formulas for diagrams, and by the lack of a counterpart of negation for most diagrams.

**Danto, Arthur C**. *After the End of Art: Contemporary Art and the Pale of History*. Princeton, Princeton Univ Pr, 1997.

Originally delivered as the prestigious Mellon Lectures on the Fine Arts, these writings cover art history, pop art, "people's art," the future role of museums, and the critical contributions of Clement Greenberg—who helped make sense of modernism for viewers over two generations ago through an aesthetics-based criticism. Tracing art history from a mimetic tradition (the idea that art was a progressively more adequate representation of reality) through the modern era of manifestos (when art was defined by the artist's philosophy), Danto shows that it wasn't until the invention of pop art that the historical understanding of the means and ends of art was nullified. Even modernist art, which tried to break with the past by questioning the ways of producing art, hinged on a narrative. (publisher, edited)

**Danyluk, Angie**. Scientific Attitudes Towards an Eastern Mystic. *J Dharma*, 21(2), 170-187, Ap-Je 96.

**Danz, Christian**. "Faktizität und Genesis: Zur subjektivitäts-theoretischen Gundlegung von Religion" in *Sein—Reflexion—Freiheit: Aspekte der Philosophie Johann Gottlieb Fichtes*, Asmuth, Christoph (ed), 253-268. Amsterdam, Gruner, 1997.

The main subject of this article is the conception of religion in Fichte's *Die Anweisung zum seligen Leben* and its interpretation by Friedrich Gogarten (*Fichte als religiöser Denker*). The reconstruction of Fichte's conception of religion is based on the difference between factuality and genesis which is constitutive for his *Wissenschaftslehre* of 1804. The argumentation of the *Wissenschaftslehre* is meant as an explanation of the highest unity as a principle of disjunctive through showing the genetic character of actual entities. Thereby, religion appears as a factual unity, whose genesis must stay hidden for the religious conscience. Gogarten treats the problem of religion independently from the theoretic horizon of the *Wissenschaftslehre*.

**Danz, Christian**. Die Duplizität des Absoluten in der Wissenschaftslehre von 1804 (zweiter Vortrag)—Fichtes Auseinandersetzung mit Schellings identitätsphilosophischer Schrift *Darstellung meines Systems* (1801). *Fichte-Studien*, 12, 335-350, 1997.

**Dappiano, Luigi**. "Cambridge and the Austrian Connection" in *In Itinere European Cities and the Birth of Modern Scientific Philosophy*, Poli, Roberto (ed), 99-124. Amsterdam, Rodopi, 1997.

**Darge, Rolf**. Wie einer beschaffen ist, so erscheint ihm das Ziel: Die Rolle des moralischen Habitus bei der Beurteilung des Handlungsziels nach Thomas von Aquin. *Theol Phil*, 72(1), 53-76, 1997.

Der betrachtete Teil der Konzeption des Thomas von der Funktion des moralischen Habitus im Handlungsaufbau umfasst in seinem Kern die folgenden Gedanken: 1) Der moralische Habitus beeinflusst massgeblich die Handlungsorientierung, indem er das in der Handlungslage gefällte praktische Urteil über das Ziel lenkt. 2) Das praktische Urteil über das Ziel, in dem der moralische Habitus zunächst und in typischer Weise zur Wirkung kommt, hat als Gegenstand das spezielle Handlungsziel, von dem her die Handlung ihre besondere Artgestalt innerhalb des genus moris erhält. 3) Der Einfluss, den der moralische Habitus auf die Einschätzung des speziellen Handlungsziels nimmt, erstreckt sich sowohl auf den Inhalt des Urteils, als auch auf den Modus, in dem der Urteilsakt vollzogen wird: Er betrifft dessen Inhalt, insofern das Urteil unter der Wirkung des Habitus eben das, worauf dieser Habitus als auf sein eigentümliches und nächstes Ziel hingeordnet ist, als das im Tun einfachhin und um seiner selbst willen zu Verfolgende darstellt. (edited)

**Darós, W R**. La persona y el autodominio moral. *Franciscanum*, 37(112), 67-87, Ja-Ap 96.

**Darós, W R**. Naturaleza humana en la filosofía de M.F. Sciacca y la concepción *light* de G. Vattimo. *Analogia*, 10(2), 213-258, 1996.

**Darragh, Martina** and McCarrick, Pat Milmoe. A Just Share: Justice and Fairness in Resource Allocation. *Kennedy Inst Ethics J*, 7(1), 81-102, Mr 97.

Scope Notes provide a current overview to a specific topic in biomedical ethics. This one, number 32 in the series, has a brief two page discussion of the concept of what "fair" or "just", or "fairness" or "justice" could mean in the provision of health care to all who need it. Its' bibliography is divided into seven categories: general works on justice and resource allocation, groups affected by rationing, applied justice, international perspectives, physicians as gatekeepers, organizational statements and references to early works.

**Darriulat, Jacques**. Descartes et la mélancholie. *Rev Phil Fr*, 4, 465-486, O-D 96.

**Dartnall, Terry**. Illuminating the Chinese Room. *Manuscrito*, 19(2), 13-43, O 96.

In this paper I provide a solution to the problem of the Chinese Room. The problem is to determine whether the Chinese Room Argument goes through, and if it does, to explain why symbol handling does not give us cognition. I argue that the real issue is not about symbols, but about the relationship between cognition and content. Artificial intelligence (AI) does not distinguish between these and naively believes that internalising the public symbolisms that express the content of cognition will generate cognition itself. Not only does it do this in practice: the main manifestos of AI explicitly state that the internalized symbolisms are interpreted and contentful. (edited)

**Dartnall, Terry**. Retelling the Representational Story: An Anti-Representationalist's Agenda. *Commun Cog*, 29(3/4), 479-500, 1996.

Classical and connectionist cognitive science hold that representations play a crucial role in cognition and become increasingly important as cognition copes with the absent, the nonexistent, the highly relational and the abstract. I argue that representations wither away in these domains, where the cognitive load is transferred to knowledge about the domain. Such knowledge is not representational. This prompts a retelling of the representational story. I argue that we must have learned to make judgements about the immediate context (which we then learned to use in more complex cases) before we acquired the ability to internalise and deploy representations.

**Darwall, Stephen**. Hutcheson on Practical Reason. *Hume Stud*, 23(1), 73-89, Ap 97.

I describe the various ways in which Hume's critique of practical reason derives from Hutcheson and then consider a tension that arises between Hutcheson's (and Hume's) critique of noninstrumental reasons and his account of calm passions.

**Darwall, Stephen**. Learning from Frankena: A Philosophical Remembrance. *Ethics*, 107(4), 685-705, Jl 97.

A philosophical remembrance of William Frankena that locates his ideas in relation to those of Moore and Sidgwick. I argue that Frankena took Sidgwick's part against Moore in arguing that normativity is the essential core of ethical concepts (necessary to explain the open question), and that this cannot be understood as referring to a simple, intrinsic quality. I also discuss the evolution of Frankena's ideas concerning the relation between normativity and motivation (internalism).

**Darwall, Stephen**. Self-Interest and Self-Concern. *Soc Phil Pol*, 14(1), 158-178, Wint 97.

I consider whether the idea of a person's interest or good might be better understood through that of care or concern for that person for her sake, rather than conversely, as is ordinarily assumed. Contrary to (informed) desire-satisfaction theories of interest, such an account can explain why not everything a person rationally desires is part of her good, since what a person sensibly wants is not necessarily what we (and she) would sensibly want, insofar as we care about her.

**Darwall, Stephen**. Smith's Moral Problem. *Phil Quart*, 46(185), 508-515, O 96.

**Darwall, Stephen** (ed) and Gibbard, Allan (ed) and Railton, Peter (ed). *Moral Discourse and Practice: Some Philosophical Approaches*. New York, Oxford Univ Pr, 1997.

The book is a unique anthology which collects important recent work, much of which is not easily available elsewhere, on core metaethical issues. Naturalist moral realism, once devastated by the charge of "naturalistic fallacy," has been reinvigorated, as have versions of moral realism that insist on the discontinuity between ethics and science. Irrealist, expressivist programs have also developed with great subtlety, encouraging the thought that a noncognitivist account may actually be able to explain ethical judgments' aspirations to objectivity. Neo-Kantian constructivist theories have flourished as well, offering hope that morality can be grounded in a plausible conception of reasonable conduct. (publisher,edited)

**Dascal, Marcelo**. "La balanza de la razón" in *La racionalidad: su poder y sus límites*, Nudler, Oscar (ed), 363-381. Barcelona, Ed Paidos, 1996.

Western conceptions of rationality have been dominated by the image of a balance, according to which rationality rests essentially on our capacity of *weighing* arguments, preferences, decisions, and actions. This paper, taking seriously the role of metaphors in philosophical theorization, examines some of the effects of the balance metaphor upon the conceptualization of rationality in Western thought. Scepticism can be viewed as a concerted attack on the possibility to *calibrate* the Balance of Reason, to ensure its *reliability*, to provide a weighing *procedure* for it and—foremost—to escape the danger that it will be in a permanent state of *equilibrium* which would render it useless. Leibniz, who paid close attention to the image of the balance, devised two different strategies to cope with this criticism. One is his well-known conception of a 'calculative' reason, where a logical calculus decides conclusively in favor of one of the scales of the balance. The other, practically unknown, elaborates a weaker notion of rationality, where computation is replaced by judgment and rational persuasion as a means to *incline without necessitating* the balance. Whereas the former is severely limited in its domains of application, the latter allows to extend significantly the scope of rationality.

**Dasgupta, Abhijit**. Boolean Operations, Borel Sets, and Hausdorff's Question. *J Sym Log*, 61(4), 1287-1304, D 96.

If $T$ has only countably many complete types, yet has a type of infinite multiplicity then there is a c.c.c. forcing notion, there are nonisomorphic models $M_1$ and $M_2$ of $T$ that can be forced isomorphic by a c.c.c. forcing. We give examples showing that the hypothesis on the number of complete types is necessary and what happens if 'c.c.c.' is replaced by other cardinal-preserving adjectives. We also give an example showing that membership in a pseudo-elementary class can be altered by very simple cardinal-preserving forcings. (edited)

**Dasgupta, Sanghamitra**. What Is the Status of Jiva (Individualised Soul) in the Samkarite Advaita Vedanta?. *Darshana Int*, 36(3/143), 64-68, Ap 96.

**Dastur, Françoise**. Heidegger and Derrida: On Play and Difference. *Epoche*, 3(1 & 2), 1-23, 1995.

**Dauer, Francis W**. Hume's Scepticism with Regard to Reason: A Reconsideration. *Hume Stud*, 22(2), 211-229, N 96.

This paper briefly discusses Hume's argument that all knowledge degenerates to probability and is mainly devoted to a reconsideration of his argument that all probability degenerates to nothing. After arguing for the indecisive nature the objections by Fogelin and Hacking (that our credence shouldn't be affected by an assessment of our faculty's fallibility), two interpretations are offered for how our credence may be affected by our fallibility. According to the first, the objections of Imlay and Karlsson seem decisive; but the second interpretation would circumvent those objections. It concludes that we should be less than confident that Hume's arguments have been refuted.

**Daugherty, Christopher K**. Hope and the Limits of Research: Commentary. *Hastings Center Rep*, 26(5), 20, S-O 96.

**Daumer, Martin** and Dürr, Detlef and Goldstein, Sheldon (& others). Naive Realism about Operators. *Erkenntnis*, 45(2 & 3), 379-397, Nov 96.

A source of much difficulty and confusion in the interpretation of quantum mechanics is a "naive realism about operators." By this we refer to various ways of taking too seriously the notion of operator-as-observable and in particular to the all too casual talk about "measuring operators" that occurs when the subject is quantum mechanics. Without a specification of what should be meant by "measuring" a quantum observable, such an expression can have no clear meaning. A definite specification is provided by Bohmian mechanics, a theory that emerges from Schrödinger's equation for a system of particles when we merely insist that "particles" means particles. Bohmian mechanics clarifies the status and the role of operators as observables in quantum mechanics by providing the operational details absent from standard quantum mechanics. It thereby allows us to readily dismiss all the radical claims traditionally enveloping the transition from the classical to the quantum realm—for example, that we must abandon classical logic or classical probability. The moral is rather simple: Beware naive realism, especially about operators!

**Davenport, John**. The Essence of Eschatology: A Modal Interpretation. *Ultim Real Mean*, 19(3), 206-239, S 96.

This paper is a comparative and hermeneutic analysis of what united eschatological beliefs and ideas of the 'end of time' or 'Last Judgment' throughout the history of religion. My approach builds on Kierkegaard's interpretation of the eschatological as a kind of synthetic possibility beyond our rational powers and Hick's notion of 'eschatological verification'. Using scholarship by Eliade and Hick, I argue that eschatology develops out the cosmogonic notion of the sacred, but acquires its soteriological function through combination with noncosmogonic, ethical ideals emerging in the 'axial age'. Eschatology becomes the possibility of a final state (of the individual or cosmos) in which the Good is realized in the Real. I describe four stages in the development of eschatology in this general sense, the ambiguous temporal form of the hereafter between *futurity* and *eternity*, and other essential features of eschatological conceptions that are crucial for understanding the role of this concept in many current debates in the philosophy of religion, the philosophy of history, and existentialism. For example, this hermeneutic explication of the essence of eschatology helps us understand existentialist thinkers such as Buber, Levinas, Heidegger, and Berdayev, and suggests—against Hans Blumberg—that some modernist ideas of progress may result from 'secularization of eschatology'.

**Davenport, Manuel**. The Aesthetically Good vs. The Morally Good. *SW Phil Rev*, 13(1), 205-210, Ja 97.

Plato and Tolstoy claim that works of art which prevent us from knowing what is good by arousing irrational passions are morally bad. Suppose, however, that a woman reads *The Story of O* and is inspired to join a convent. Is the work she read now morally good? Was it now intended to evoke religious feelings? Maritain, by contrast, argued that good religious art has religious content but is morally good only to the extent that it is aesthetically good. Family values, by his standards, would be better served by *The Night Porter* than by *The Brady Bunch*.

**Davi Maced, Dion** and Leite, Lucimara. O Arco e a Lira—O inaudito na Erótica de Safo. *Educ Filosof*, 9(17), 91-111, Ja-Je 95.

**David, Marian**. Working Without a Net: A Study of Egocentric Epistemology. *Phil Phenomenol Res*, 56(4), 943-952, D 96.

This fine book offers a wealth of illuminating and subtle discussions on a wide range of topics unified by the theme of rationality. At its heart lies Foley's proposal of a general framework for the theory of rationality: all rationality judgments are perspective-relative evaluations of how effective a person appears to be in satisfying his goals. Foley's main concern lies with a boldly subjective brand of epistemic rationality: it is egocentrically rational for S to believe p iff, reflecting on her own deepest standards, S would think that believing p furthers her purely epistemic goal of now having an accurate and comprehensive set of beliefs.

**Davidson, Bruce**. Does Religious Faith Mean Uncritical Thought? Exploration of a False Dilemma. *Inquiry (USA)*, 16(1), 55-66, Fall 96.

**Davidson, Bruce W**. Critical Thinking Education Faces the Challenge of Japan. *Inquiry (USA)*, 14(3), 41-53, Spr 95.

Paradoxically, Japan presents both a difficult and a promising setting for the promotion of critical thinking skills. One deep-rooted obstacle consists in antirational ideological traditions and prejudices against logic. Another is the rigidly hierarchical, conformist nature of Japanese society, which does not encourage divergent opinions or their expression. Impediments are also created by the educational system, which is mostly driven by rote-memorization entrance examinations and is rigidly regulated by the educational bureaucracy. On the other hand, the basic rationality of the Japanese, recent educational reforms and the responsiveness of many Japanese to a critical thinking approach give reasons for hope.

**Davidson, Donald**. "¿Puede haber una ciencia de la racionalidad?" in *La racionalidad: su poder y sus límites*, Nudler, Oscar (ed), 273-293. Barcelona, Ed Paidos, 1996.

This article is a Spanish translation of "Could There Be a Science of Rationality?", *International Journal of Philosophical Studies*, 1995, 3, pp. 1-16. It argues that though the concepts of the propositional attitudes cannot be reduced to that of the natural sciences, decision theory, logic, and formal semantics, viewed as empirical theories, have all the marks of serious science.

Davies, David 586 AUTHOR INDEX

**Davies, David**. Davidson, Interdeterminacy, and Measurement. *Acta Analytica*, 37-56, 1995.

The measurement theory of propositional attitude ascription claims that attitudes are ascribed by appeal to the location of psychological state in a measurement space, by analogy with physical measurement. In the paper the theory is criticized and an unappealing trilemma is offered to its upholders.

**Davies, David**. Interpretive Pluralism and the Ontology of Art. *Rev Int Phil*, 50(198), 577-592, 1996.

I critically assess Goodman and Elgin's argument that, to accommodate interpretive pluralism—we must identify literary works with texts ('textualism'). I reject the counter-argument that we can reconcile interpretive pluralism concerning *acceptable* interpretations of works, with interpretive monism concerning *true* interpretations and thus with nontextualism. However the interpetive pluralism to which Goodman and Elgin appeal itself presupposes textualism and thus cannot be assumed in an argument *for* textualism. A resolution of these issues must address more general methodological considerations in the philosophy of art.

**Davies, David**. Why One Shouldn't Make an Example of a Brain in a Vat. *Analysis*, 57(1), 51-59, Ja 97.

**Davies, James W**. *Empire of the Gods: The Liberation of Eros*. New York, Lang, 1997.

*Empires of the Gods* makes a major and original contribution to the literature on love. The history of Eros is its attempted liberation into wholeness and individuality. Its modern expression as a flesh-monism requires expansion to include reason and spirit (including Agape), the classical, to include affect and flesh. The illicit character of the *Romantic Love of the Twelfth Century* (seen as two versions: *utopian* and *historical*) provides a radical key not only to synthesis but also to surmounting oppressive enculturation, particularly in the marriage institution. Relationship is the synthesizing focus of illicit love, philosophical dialogue and psychotherapy.

**Davies, Martin**. "Two Notions of Implicit Rules" in *AI, Connectionism and Philosophical Psychology, 1995,* Tomberlin, James E (ed), 153-183. Atascadero, Ridgeview, 1995.

This paper develops two notions of implicit rules which both allow for the possibility that rules may be embodied in a connectionist network. In Section 1, I review two extreme notions of knowledge of rules. In Section 2, I introduce an intermediate notion which makes use of the idea of a causally systematic process. This is my first notion of implicit rule. In Section 3, I distinguish this from a second notion of implicit rule, which imposes fewer requirements upon the causal processes taking place inside a system. Finally, in Section 4, I use the distinction between the two notions of implicit rule to shed light upon a recent dispute about structure-sensitive processes, between Jerry Fodor, Zenon Pylyshyn and Brian McLaughlin on the one hand and Paul Smolensky on the other.

**Davies, Martin** and Antony, Louise M. Meaning and Semantic Knowledge. *Aris Soc*, Supp(71), 177-209, 1997.

**Davies, Paul Sheldon**. Discovering the Functional Mesh: On the Methods of Evolutionary Psychology. *Mind Mach*, 6(4), 559-585, N 96.

The aim of this paper is to clarify and critically assess the methods of evolutionary psychology, and offer a sketch of an alternative methodology. My thesis is threefold. 1) The methods of inquiry unique to evolutionary psychology rest upon the claim that the discovery of the *adaptive functions* of ancestral psychological capacities leads to the discovery of the *psychological functions* of those ancestral capacities. 2) But this claim is false; in fact, just the opposite is true. We first must discover the psychological functions of our psychological capacities in order to discover their adaptive functions. Hence the methods distinctive of evolutionary psychology are idle in our search for the mechanisms of the mind. 3) There are good reasons for preferring an alternative to the methods of evolutionary psychology, an alternative that aims to discover the functions of our psychological capacities by appeal to the concept of a *whole psychology*.

**Davies, Stephen**. "Why Listen to Sad Music If It Makes One Feel Sad?" in *Music and Meaning,* Robinson, Jenefer (ed), 242-253. Ithaca, Cornell Univ Pr, 1997.

Why do we enjoy and seek out music that makes us feel sad? Traditional replies—that the response lacks life implications, or that we tolerate it for the sake of attendant benefits—are weak. We take pleasure in understanding artworks, even those that engender negative responses. Generally, we accept unpleasant things not only as unavoidable but as intimately associated with activities of great personal importance, such as child-raising. Art is not a training or substitute for life; it is a celebration of the manner in which people engage with each other and the world in giving significance to their existence.

**Davies, Stephen** (ed). *Art and Its Messages: Meaning, Morality, and Society.* University Park, Pennsylvania Univ Pr, 1997.

This volume brings together essays by leading philosophers of art who consider what can be learned from the meaning of art about society, morality and life in general. This subject inevitably leads to discussion of other issues. Is art distinct from life? Is a concern with art's messages consistent with an appropriately aesthetic appreciation of its works? Is there anything distinctive about the manner in which art communicates its messages, or about the messages it conveys? The topic of art's social and moral importance has always been a central one in aesthetics. However, Whereas Plato and Schiller, for instance, viewed art as intimately implicated in a person's moral and social education, modernist theories have argued for art's autonomy and separation from worldly matters. The essays presented here provide a contemporary perspective on this long-standing debate and reveal the recent revitalization of humanist concerns in describing art and its significance. (publisher)

**Davies, Stephen**. First Art and Art's Definition. *S J Phil*, 35(1), 19-34, Spr 97.

Theories offered by James Carney, Noël Carroll, Jerrold Levinson and Robert Stecker hold that something is art if it stands in an appropriate relation to prior artworks. A different story is required about the first artworks, since these had no artistic predecessors. I argue that these theories fail to account adequately for first art. I defend the view that first artworks qualify as such because they are made to have aesthetic properties, ones that concern the whole, that are essential to the ritual or other functions they serve. This explains how we can recognize such pieces as art, despite our cultural and temporal separation from the context in which they were created and used.

**Davies, Stephen**. Interpreting Contextualities. *Phil Lit*, 20(1), 20-38, Ap 96.

One theory of literary interpretation regards the identity and meaning (or meanings) of the work to be fixed at its creation. A second holds that the meaning of the work varies through time. The first view apparently should regard as illegitimate many widely accepted interpretive strategies and styles—such as feminist readings of Shakespeare. The second, by contrast, not only seems to encompass the first but also to accommodate the diversity of interpretive approaches in use. These impressions are misleading, I argue. The first theory might explain the legitimacy of the spread of interpretive styles found in practice. But the difference between the theories is significant, since they differ in their commitments to different ontologies. The issue is whether we are foundationally interested in works as of their authors, or in works *simpliciter*. I favour the former position and see this as supporting the first theory.

**Davies, Stephen**. So, You Want to Sing with *The Beatles*? Too Late!. *J Aes Art Crit*, 55(2), 129-137, Spring 97.

I consider interactive music disks, such as concerto-minus-one recordings and karaoke, asking if one can join with the recorded instrumentalists in playing or singing along. I suggest, that because the recorded performance is completed, one cannot do so, but that such disks serve their purpose in promoting the illusion of joint performance. The latest CD-Rom technology allows for a more complex interaction in that the user can modify the disk's output. The result is a move toward the composition of pieces based on, but distinct from, those that supplied the source material.

**Davies, Stephen**. Two Conceptions of Welfare: Voluntarism and Incorporationism. *Soc Phil Pol*, 14(2), 39-68, Sum 97.

**Davion, Victoria**. Rape Research and Gender Feminism: So Who's Anti-Male?. *Pub Affairs Quart*, 11(3), 229-243, Jl 97.

I examine the view that rape is on a continuum with normal male sexual behavior. In her recent book *Who Stole Feminism*, Christina Hoff Sommers argues that "gender feminists" hold this position, which is inherently antimale. I distinguish between two version of the continuum view. I argue that the version held by many feminists is not antimale and that Sommers herself actually holds it in its antimale version. I include a discussion of Sommers's attack on the MS report on rape in America. I defend this report.

**Davion, Victoria**. So What's the Difference? Feminist Ethics and Feminist Jurisprudence. *J Soc Phil*, 27(3), 101-115, Wint 96.

The difference debate concerns whether women's interests are better promoted by treating men and women equally under law, or by taking certain crucial *differences* between them into account in order to achieve actual equality for women. To answer this, one must have working conceptions of what both women's subordination and emancipation are. The goal of emancipating women will be different depending on what exactly one thinks women's subordination is. I examine this debate, showing how conceptual questions about what equality for women means are central and argue that at least some proposed solutions fail to take these conceptual issues seriously.

**Davis, Andrew**. Who's Afraid of Assessment? Remarks on Winch and Gingell's Reply. *J Phil Educ*, 30(3), 389-400, N 96.

This paper defends my argument that criterion-referenced assessment should not be used to render an education system accountable to the state. Winch and Gingell's reply to my original paper understands me as denying the 'plasticity' of abilities. Considerable space is devoted to further discussion of this issue. 'Plasticity' is not denied, but problems about the 'identity' of capacities, abilities, processes and rules are explored in some depth. Winch and Gingell defend certain kinds of pedagogy such as rote learning and 'teaching to the test'. I remind them that I was not actually discussing pedagogy in the original paper.

**Davis, Arthur** (ed). *George Grant and the Subversion of Modernity: Art, Philosophy, Politics, Religion, and Education.* Toronto, Univ of Toronto Pr, 1996.

This collection begins with a powerful and unusual unpublished writing on Céline by George Grant, follows with ten original essays on Grant's sources and influences in which some of the authors use the unpublished writings of Grant that have been gathered for the forthcoming Collected Works and closes with Grant's letters on the university. The authors discuss the 'unknown Grant,' the thinker behind the public figure. They examine the sources of his subversive critique of modernity including his intense engagement with premodern Christian and Platonic sources (interpreted by Weil and Strauss) and his equally intense engagement with non-Christian and non-Platonic thinkers and artists like Nietzsche, Heidegger and Céline.

**Davis, Bernard D** and Guenin, Louis M. Scientific Reasoning and Due Process. *Sci Eng Ethics*, 2(1), 47-54, J 96.

Recent public hearings on misconduct charges belie the conjecture that due process will preface defeat informed scientific reasoning. One notable case that reviewed an obtuse description of experimental methods displays some of the subtleties of differentiating carelessness from intent to deceive. There the decision of a studious nonscientist panel managed to reach sensible conclusions despite conflicting expert testimony. The significance of such a result may be to suggest that to curtail due process would be both objectionable and unproductive.

**Davis, Colin**. *Levinas: An Introduction*. Notre Dame, Univ Notre Dame Pr, 1996.

Davis traces the development of Levinas's thought over six decades, describing the context in which he worked, and the impact of his writings. He argues that Levinas's remains tied to the ontological tradition with which he wants to break and demonstrates how his later writing tries to overcome this dependency by its increasingly disruptive, sometimes opaque, textual practice. He discusses Levinas's theological writings and his relationship to Judaism, as well as the reception of his work by contemporary thinkers, arguing that the influence of his work has led to a growing interest in ethical issues among poststructuralist and postmodernist thinkers in recent years. (publisher, edited)

**Davis, Dena S**. Cochlear Implants and the Claims of Culture? A Response to Lane and Grodin. *Kennedy Inst Ethics J*, 7(3), 253-258, S 97.

Because I reject the notion that physical characteristics constitute cultural membership, I argue that, even if the claim were persuasive that deafness is a culture rather than a disability, there is no reason to fault hearing parents who choose cochlear implants for their deaf children.

**Davis, Dena S**. Genetic Dilemmas and the Child's Right to an Open Future. *Hastings Center Rep*, 27(2), 7-15, Mr-Ap 97.

Although deeply committed to the model of nondirective counseling, most genetic counselors enter the profession with certain assumptions about health and disability—for example, that it is preferable to be a hearing person than a deaf person. Thus, most genetic counselors are deeply troubled when parents ask for assistance in having a child who shares their disability. This ethical challenge is best understood as a conflict between parental autonomy and the child's future autonomy.

**Davis, Dena S**. Mandatory HIV Testing in Newborns: Not Yet, Maybe Never. *J Clin Ethics*, 7(2), 191-192, Sum 96.

**Davis, Edward B** (ed) and Hunter, Michael (ed) and Boyle, Robert. *A Free Enquiry into the Vulgarly Received Notion of Nature*. New York, Cambridge Univ Pr, 1996.

In this book, published in 1686, the scientist Robert Boyle (1627-91) attacked prevailing notions of the natural world which depicted 'Nature' as a wise, benevolent and purposeful being. Boyle, one of the leading mechanical philosophers of his day, believed that the world was best understood as a vast, impersonal machine, fashioned by an infinite, personal God. In this cogent treatise, he drew on his scientific findings, his knowledge of contemporary medicine and his deep reflection on theological and philosophical issues, arguing that it was inappropriate both theologically and scientifically to speak of Nature as if it had a mind of its own: instead, the only true efficient causes of things were the properties and powers given to matter by God. As such, *A Free Enquiry into the Vaguely Received Notion of Nature* represents one of the subtlest statements concerning the philosophical issues raised by the mechanical philosophy to emerge from the period of the scientific revolution. (publisher, edited)

**Davis, F Daniel**. Phronesis, Clinical Reasoning, and Pellegrino's Philosophy of Medicine. *Theor Med*, 18(1-2), 173-195, Mr-Je 97.

In terms of Aristotle's intellectual virtues, the process of clinical reasoning and the discipline of clinical medicine are often construed as *techne* (art), as *episteme* (science), or as an amalgam or composite of *techne* and *episteme*. Although dimensions of process and discipline are appropriately described in these terms, I argue that *phronesis* (practical reasoning) provides the most compelling paradigm, particularly of the rationality of the physician's knowing and doing in the clinical encounter with the patient. I anchor this argument, moreover, in Pellegrino's philosophy of medicine as a healing relationship, oriented to the end of a right and good healing action for the individual patient.

**Davis, Hilary E**. "The Double-Bind of "Double Duty" in *Philosophy of Education (1996)*, Margonis, Frank (ed), 164-167. Urbana, Phil Education Soc, 1997.

In this response I discuss Denise Egéa-Kuehne's "Neutrality in Education and Derrida's Call for 'Double Duty,'" which argues that genuine learning is dialogical in nature and that so-called 'neutral' approaches to education stagnate the learning process when they exclude controversial material. While I agree with Egéa-Kuehne that such curricular heteroglossia can raise consciousness, I argue that her use of terms life 'intellectual competence' sets a criterion for literacy which perpetuates the dichotomy between reason and emotion, a hierarchy which diminishes differences in situatedness among students. I conclude by suggesting that this problematization heteroglossia is consistent with the 'double duties' of educators outlined by Derrida.

**Davis, Hilary E**. The Temptations and Limitations of a Feminist Deaesthetic. *J Aes Educ*, 27(2), 99-105, Sum 93.

Feminist consciousness involves a "revision" of aesthetic definitions and norms, revealing them to be androcentric if not misogynist. However, neither the rejection of feminist aesthetics nor its replacement with a feminist deaesthetic is satisfactory personally or politically. The abandonment of aesthetics ignores the importance of pleasure to individual response and the ways in which the aesthetic as a social category influences response. And while a deaesthetic is an important critical and deconstructive tool, it is incapable of instigating social change. This paper concludes by suggesting that a possible feminist aesthetic might involve the redefinition and reconstruction of traditional aesthetics.

**Davis, James A**. The "Is-Ought" Fallacy and Musicology: The Assumptions of Pedagogy. *Phil Music Educ Rev*, 5(1), 25-32, Spr 97.

This article argues that musicological pedagogy often attempts to dictate aesthetic taste under the guise of distributing information. To better understand this process, one can view a teacher's classroom presentation as a formal argument; various statements can be linked together to form larger propositions and these propositions are then submitted as the premises of logical arguments to the students. This paper will consider one such case, specifically Hume's 'Is-Ought' fallacy, which argues that it is not possible to logically deduce a normative "ought" from an existent "is". Though originally identified in discussions of ethics, it is likely that a similar logical difficulty can be found acting in aesthetic studies and as a result may underlie a large portion of musicological pedagogy.

**Davis, Janet B**. Translating Gorgias in [Aristotle] 980a10. *Phil Rhet*, 30(1), 31-37, 1997.

**Davis, Kathleen G**. Teaching the Three Rs: Rights, Roles and Responsibilities—A Curriculum for Pediatric Patient Rights. *Bioethics Forum*, 11(4), 27-31, Wint 95.

Education of pediatric patients, health care professionals, and family members is key to ensuring that children have a voice in the decisions that affect their health and their physical and emotional status.

**Davis, Lawrence H**. Cerebral Hemispheres. *Phil Stud*, 87(2), 207-222, Ag 97.

Some say that some commissurotomy patients are two persons in one body. Some say they are never more than one per body. An intermediate position is that each has two "minds" or "consciousnesses," but is only one person. I sketch and defend a version of this intermediate position, interpreting "having two consciousnesses" as "being a union of two conscious beings," neither of which has the explicit self-consciousness needed for personhood. In the process I make and apply various claims about the reference of 'I' in thought and speech.

**Davis, Michael**. An Historical Preface to Engineering Ethics. *Sci Eng Ethics*, 1(1), 33-48, J 95.

This article attempts to distinguish between science and technology, on the one hand, and engineering, on the other, offering a brief introduction to engineering values and engineering ethics. The method is (roughly) a philosophical examination of history. Engineering turns out to be a relatively recent enterprise, barely three hundred years old, to have distinctive commitments both technical and moral, and to have changed a good deal both technically and morally during that period. What motivates the paper is the belief that a too-easy equation of engineering with technology tends to obscure the special contribution of engineers to technology and to their own professional standards and so, to obscure as well both the origin and content of engineering ethics.

**Davis, Michael**. Better Communication between Engineers and Managers: Some Ways to Prevent Many Ethically Hard Choices. *Sci Eng Ethics*, 3(2), 171-212, Ap 97.

This article is concerned with ways better communication between engineers and their managers might help prevent engineers being faced with some of the ethical problems that make up the typical course in engineering ethics. Beginning with observations concerning the *Challenger* disaster, the article moves on to report results of empirical research on the way technical communication breaks down, or doesn't break down, between engineers and managers. The article concludes with nine recommendations for organizational change to help prevent communications breakdown.

**Davis, Michael**. How Much Punishment Does a Bad Samaritan Deserve?. *Law Phil*, 15(2), 93-116, 96.

The now significant literature on bad samaritanism has so far been concerned primarily with whether bad samaritanism should be prohibited by law. The literature, especially the philosophical literature, has been virtually silent on how much bad samaritanism should be punished. That is not because all theories of punishment give the same result. Bad samaritan statutes seem to reveal a fundamental weakness in many theories of punishment, including those purporting to rest on our intuitions about blaming.

**Davis, Michael**. Preventive Detention, Corrado, and Me. *Crim Just Ethics*, 15(2), 13-24, Sum-Fall 96.

This discussion (briefly) clarifies what seem the three chief differences remaining between Corrado's position and mine: 1) Corrado's moral retributivism as against my legal retributivism; 2) Corrado's assumption that individual moral obligations, rather than my assumption that the police power, resting on individual rights, also can justify criminal statutes; and 3) Corrado's assumption that reckless endangerment is an omission, a failing to take precaution, rather than, as I argue, a commission, "living dangerously". These differences are, I think, so fundamental that clarification may be more useful now than any attempt at resolution. They make an informative list: if I am right about any one of them, Corrado's argument either collapses or becomes uninteresting.

**Davis, Michael**. Reply to Corrado. *Crim Just Ethics*, 15(2), 29-33, Sum-Fall 96.

Preventive detention is (primarily) confinement under the criminal law before conviction of a crime in order to prevent the dangerous from committing other crimes. Such confinement can—contrary to Corrado's argument—be justified within a retributive framework respecting the criminal's right to punishment, provided with we understand the dangerousness justifying preventive detention as itself a crime, "reckless endangerment". Since forcing voluntary detention by repeated arrests for reckless endangerment is expensive, (more or less) certain to achieve detention eventually, and already a denial of liberty (more or less) equivalent to preventive detention, the judge might as well refuse the accused bail right off, citing the dangerousness of the accused.

**Davis, Michael**. Second Thoughts on Multi-Culturalism. *Int J Applied Phil*, 11(1), 29-34, Sum-Fall 96.

"Multiculturalism" is an important current in both secondary and higher education, a source of perplexity as well as of outrage and hope. We can distinguish four senses of culture potentially relevant to multiculturalism: culture-as-refinement, culture-as-art, culture-as-traditions-of-making and culture-as-way-of-life. The first two are peripheral to multiculturalism. The third, though potentially important, is generally ignored. The last, though apparently the preferred sense, is hostile to much multiculturalism seeks to achieve. There is no good single alternative to "culture", but multiculturalists should avoid the term.

**Davis, Michael**. Some Paradoxes of Whistleblowing. *Bus Prof Ethics J*, 15(1), 3-19, Spr 96.

The paper first describes the "standard theory of whistle-blowing" (DeGeorge's). The standard theory seeks to justify whistleblowing by its ability to prevent harm. The paper then argues that the standard theory is paradoxical, i.e., that it is inconsistent with what we know about whistle-blowers, for example, that whistle-blowers seldom prevent significant harm. The paper then offers a less paradoxical theory of whistle-blowing, one emphasizing obligations arising from complicity in wrongdoing and tests it using one classic case of whistle-blowing, Roger Boisjoly's testimony before the Presidential Commission investigating the *Challenger* disaster.

**Davis, Richard**. Bonaventure and the Arguments for the Impossibility of an Infinite Temporal Regression. *Amer Cath Phil Quart*, 70(3), 362-380, Sum 96.

**Davison, Scott A**. Privacy and Control. *Faith Phil*, 14(2), 137-151, Ap 97.

In this paper, I explore several privacy issues as they arise with respect to the divine/human relationship. First, in section 1, I discuss the notion of privacy in a general way. Section 2 is devoted to the claim that privacy involves control over information about oneself. In section 3, I summarize the arguments offered recently by Margaret Falls-Corbitt and F. Michael McLain for the conclusion that God respects the privacy of human persons by refraining from knowing certain things about them. Finally, in section 4, I shall criticize Falls-Corbitt and McLain's arguments and make some concluding remarks about God and privacy.

**Davson-Galle, Peter**. 'Cannot,' 'Not Can' and 'Can Not'. *Inquiry (USA)*, 15(2), 91, Wint 95.

In this brief paper the prevalent (and illicit) typographical expansion of 'cannot' into 'can not' and not the more logically correct 'not can' is discussed.

**Dawson, Doyne**. Evolutionary Materialism. *Hist Theor*, 36(1), 83-92, 1997.

**Dawson, Graham**. Exit, Voice and Values in Economic Institutions. *Econ Phil*, 13(1), 87-100, Ap 97.

This paper discusses the values and social relationships associated with auction and customer markets. It concludes that the unmediated exit characteristic of auction markets express impersonal attitudes towards other economic agents, undermining the ethical status of such markets. Economic agents in customer markets still see each other as a means of their own long term self-interest, but are obliged to develop genuinely interpersonal attitudes. The moral argument for the market might be more plausibly based on the scope for reciprocal benefits and obligations in customer markets than on the freedom of autonomous individuals in auction markets.

**Dawson, Leslie M**. Ethical Differences Between Men and Women in The Sales Profession. *J Bus Ethics*, 16(11), 1143-1152, Ag 97.

This research addresses the question of whether men and women in sales differ in their ethical attitudes and decision making. The study asked 209 subjects to respond to 20 ethical scenarios, half of which were "relational" and half "nonrelational." The study concludes (1) that there are significant ethical differences between the sexes in situations that involve relational issues, but not in nonrelational situations and (2) that gender-based ethical differences change with age and years of experience. The implications of these finding for sales organizations are discussed.

**Dawson, Michael R W** and Medler, David A and Berkeley, Istvan S N. PDP Networks can Provide Models that are not Mere Implementations of Classical Theories. *Phil Psych*, 10(1), 25-40, Mr 97.

There is a widespread belief that connectionist networks are dramatically different from classical or symbolic models. However, connectionists rarely test this belief by interpreting the internal structure of their nets. A new approach to interpreting networks was recently introduced by Berkeley et al. (1995). The current paper examines two implications of applying this method: 1) that the internal structure of a connectionist network can have a very classical appearance, and 2) that this interpretation can provide a cognitive theory that cannot be dismissed as a mere implementation.

**De Andrade Martins, Roberto** and Pareira Martins, Lilian Al-Chueyr. Lamarck's Method (in Portuguese). *Trans/Form/Acao*, 19, 115-140, 1996.

This paper studies Lamarck's scientific method both from the point of view of his methodological discourse and according to his scientific *praxis*. Lamarck's methodology is compared to Condillac's as well as to that of the idéologues—a group in which Lamarck is usually included. The analysis of this paper shows that Lamarck's methodological discourse is very similar to Condillac's, but his scientific *praxis* does not follow this view. Instead of following an empiricist approach, Lamarck's work is grounded upon general metaphysical principles concerning nature. Thus, from the idéologues' point of view, Lamarck's work should have been rejected—and that is what really happened—as being a mere metaphysical system (système)—in the pejorative sense employed by Condillac's followers. However, the present work argues that thus is in fact an

important and innovative aspect of Lamarck's work and that it leads to the emergence of modern evolutionism.

**De Angelis, Marco**. Die 'dunklen Jahre' von Hegels Entwicklung als Aufgabe der Hegelforschung. *Jahr Hegelforschung*, 2, 159-163, 1996.

**De Aranguren, Javier**. Caracterización de la voluntad nativa. *Anu Filosof*, 29(2), 347-358, 1996.

This paper makes a phenomenological description about the *native will* (the name that Leonardo Polo uses for the Thomistic *voluntas ut natura*). The author tries to show how this function of the will is the foundation of the greatness of the moral objective. Finally, the native will is a means of developing an optimistic consideration of ethics.

**De Beistegui, Miguel**. "Sacrifice Revisited" in *On Jean-Luc Nancy: The Sense of Philosophy*, Sheppard, Darren (ed), 157-173. New York, Routledge, 1997.

**De Bernardi, Paolo**. Pirrone e i maestri indiani. *Sapienza*, 50(1), 83-102, 1997.

**De Bolt, Darian**. Kant and Clint: Dirty Harry Meets the Categorical Imperative. *SW Phil Rev*, 13(1), 21-28, Ja 97.

The basic thesis of this paper is that Kant's practical theory provides a moral justification for torture. A category of problems, called *Dirty Harry problems* (derived from the 1971 film of the same name), which are specific to law enforcement has been presented as genuine moral dilemmas—moral situations for which there is no satisfactory solution. These problems were initially explored by Carl Klockars in his paper "The Dirty Harry Problem." I argue in this paper that Kant's universal principle of right does provide a way in which some of these problems are amenable to solution.

**De Brito, António José**. A Noçao do "Estado" em Santo Agostinho. *Rev Port Filosof*, 52(1-4), 111-123, Ja-D 96.

**De Brito, José Henrique**. Do Discurso Ontológico ao Discurso Etico: De Atenas A Jerusalém. *Rev Port Filosof*, 52(1-4), 125-145, Ja-D 96.

The finality of this essay is to demonstrate that the Levinasian concept of subjectivity is, in the final analysis, identical in *totality* and *infinity* and *otherwise than being*. In spite of the fact that the first work concedes more to Greek thought than the second's more predominantly Jewish character, it is consistently maintained that subjectivity is passivity and, as such, resists expression in the action-oriented categories of Greek thought. Indeed, the language-categories of the Hebrew Bible prove to be more suitable the passive subjectivity that Levinas always favored.

**De Brito, Maria Amélia Araújo**. José Maria da Cunha Seixas, Um Homem e um Filósofo Ignorado. *Rev Port Filosof*, 52(1-4), 147-178, Ja-D 96.

The intention of this article is to demonstrate that an understanding of the original philosophical thinking of Carlos Seixas (19th Century) constitutes a key to the understanding of Portuguese thought. Pantheistic and spiritualist in character, his philosophical system is based on the fundamental intuition that God is in all: Being, manifestation and harmony are the three laws of the spirit, meaning that the Absolute, its metaphysical and logical reality, is tacitly affirmed whenever factual and valorative judgments are made.

**De Bruijn, N G**. Can People Think?. *J Consciousness Stud*, 3(5-6), 425-447, 1996.

The paper presents a speculative model for associative memory. It has two layers: the lower layer describes memory of a single cell, the upper layer describes how the work is distributed address-free over a large set of cells. Thinking, consciousness and various features of memory are interpreted in terms of the memory model.

**De Castro, Leonardo D**. Transporting Values by Technology Transfer. *Bioethics*, 11(3-4), 193-205, Jl 97.

The introduction of new medical technologies into a developing country is usually greeted with enthusiasm as the possible benefits become an object of great anticipation and provide new hope for therapy or relief. The prompt utilization of new discoveries and inventions by a medical practitioner serves as a positive indicator of high standing in the professional community. But the transfer of medical technology also involves a transfer of concomitant values. There is a danger that, in the process of adopting a particular technology, the user takes for granted the general utility and desirability of the implements and procedures under consideration without recognizing the socio-cultural peculiarities of the adopting country. (edited)

**De Castro, Zília Osório**. Jansenismo versus Jesuitismo: Niccoló Pagliarini e o Projecto Político Pombalino. *Rev Port Filosof*, 52(1-4), 223-232, Ja-D 96.

Being well-known the role played by the Marquês de Pombal in view of the expulsion of the Jesuits from Portugal as well as his major contribution concerning the discredit to the Companhia de Jesus and its future extinction, remained unknown which were the external supports for this action and which was its doctrinal content. The correspondence of Niccoló Pagliarini, famous Roman bookseller at the time in Lisbon, together with Cardeal Bottari, remarkable figure of the Jansenist circle *Archetto*, made possible to find the answers and stop the gap. Niccoló Pagliarini supported in Italy the anti-Jesuit campaign, cooperated with the Portuguese Embassy in Rome, had been persecuted and ended in Portugal where he became quite close to the Marquês de Pombal. By the letters then written we can easily realize the understanding between Pombal and the Jansenists, under the auspices of a common ecclesiastical doctrine.

**De Castro Rocha, Joao Cezar** (ed) and Antonello, Pierpaolo (ed). L'ultimo dei porcospini: Intervista biografico-teorica a René Girard. *Iride*, 9(19), 573-620, S-D 96.

**De Ciantis, Cheryl**. What Does Drawing My Hand Have to Do with Leadership? A Look at the Process of Leaders Becoming Artists. *J Aes Educ*, 30(4), 87-97, Wint 96.

**De Cózar Escalante, José Manuel**. La delimitación de la pragmática con respecto a la sociolingüística. *Daimon Rev Filosof*, 10, 93-101, Ja-Je 95.

The purpose of this paper is to provide a brief account of the domain of linguistic pragmatics with regard to sociolinguistics. It will be argued that, according to the usual definitions of pragmatics, there are no clear boundaries between both disciplines.

**De Faria Blanc, Mafalda**. A Leitura Hegeliana de Espinoza e de Leibniz. *Philosophica (Portugal)*, 95-110, 1996.

La lecture hégélienne des philosophies de Spinoza et de Leibniz est présentée par l'analyse comparative des textes de l'"Anotation" de la *Science de la Logique et des Leçons sur l'Histoire de la Philosophie*. On conclut que les contextes et les dates différentes des deux textes ne changent pas le fond de l'interprétation hégélienne des deux cartésiens, laquelle mesure par rapport à sa propre conception de l'Absolu ces deux philosophies, comprenant leur principe—unilatéral et contradictoire—de la *totalité* (Spinoza) et de l'*individualité* (Leibniz) comme un moment indispensable, mais dépassé, de l'auto-conception de l'Idée.

**De Faria Blanc, Mafalda**. Apresentaçao da metafísica de Malebranche. *Philosophica (Portugal)*, 69-87, 1993.

La philosophie de Malebranche est située par rapport à sa tâche historique: mener à son terme la restauration catholique introduite en France par Descartes pour faire face à la nouvelle "intelligentia" scientifique. L'originalité de l'Oratorien, due à ses sources augustinnienes et dionisiennes, est néanmoins marquée dès les premières oeuvres, éclatant dans la pensée de la maturité par la conception de la métaphysique comme théologie rationelle, construite a partir de la foi et ses dogmes. La rationalité cartésienne est donc reprise, premièrement dans une métaphysique de l'Ordre, deuxièmement dans une philosophie de l'Action, a travers un cheminement de pensée qui se nourri de la conception chrétienne du Dieu-Trinité. Par le relief pris dans les dernières oeuvres par la question de l'action et de son interprétation, la philosophie de Malebranche ouvre la voie à la philosophie de l'Esprit française, annoncée par Ravaisson dans son célèbre "Rapport" et menée de nos jours à son terme par Blondel et Lavelle.

**De Fraga, Gustavo**. Caminhos da Filosofia ou a Razao e o Desejo. *Rev Port Filosof*, 52(1-4), 341-364, Ja-D 96.

**De Freitas, Renan Springer**. Back to Darwin and Popper: Criticism, Migration of Piecemeal Conceptual Schemes, and the Growth of Knowledge. *Phil Soc Sci*, 27(2), 157-179, Je 97.

Popper's thesis that growth of knowledge lies in the emergence of problems out of criticism and takes place in an autonomous world of products of the human mind (his so-called world-3) raises two questions: 1) Why does criticism lead to new problems, and 2) Why can only a limited number of tentative solutions arise at a given time? I propose the following answer: Criticism entails an overlooked evolutionary world-3 mechanism, namely, the migration of piecemeal conceptual schemes from one research tradition to another. Popper by-passed the questions above because he relied very heavily on the selective power of criticism.

**De Garay, Jesús**. El sentido de los trascendentales. *Anu Filosof*, 29(2), 573-586, 1996.

This paper wants to elucidate the meaning of "order of transcendentals". That matter has a preferential place in L. Polo's philosophy. This study is carried out through an analysis of concept of "meaning" and specially "the meaning of being".

**De George, Richard T**. *Academic Freedom and Tenure: Ethical Issues*. Lanham, Rowman & Littlefield, 1997.

Academic freedom and tenure, both cherished institutions of higher education, are currently under attack by many both outside and within the academy. Richard DeGeorge argues that they can be defended on ethical grounds only if they are joined with appropriate accountability, publicly articulated and defended standards, and conscientious enforcement of these standards by academic institutions and the members of the academic community. He discusses the ethical justification of tenure and academic freedom, as well as the ethical issues in their implementation. He argues that academic freedom, which is the basis for tenure, is neither license nor the same as freedom of speech. Properly understood and practiced, both academic freedom and tenure exist not to benefit faculty members or their institutions, but to benefit an open society in which they thrive and of which they are an important part. (publisher, edited)

**De Giacomo, Giuseppe**. Eliminating "Converse" from Converse PDL. *J Log Lang Info*, 5(2), 193-208, 1996.

In this paper we show that it is possible to eliminate the "converse" operator from the propositional dynamic logic CPDL (*Converse PDL*), without compromising the soundness and completeness of inference for it. Specifically we present an encoding of CPDL formulae into PDL that eliminates the converse programs from a CPDL formula, but adds enough information so as not to destroy its original meaning with respect to satisfiability, validity and logical implication. Notably, the resulting PDL formula is polynomially related to the original one. This fact allows one to build inference procedures for CPDL, by encoding CPDL formulae into PDL and then running an inference procedure for PDL.

**De Greiff, Pablo**. "Juicio y castigo, perdón y olvido" in *Liberalismo y Comunitarismo: Derechos Humanos y Democracia*, Monsalve Solórzano, Alfonso (ed), 129-146. 36-46003 València, Alfons el Magnànim, 1996.

**De Jong, H Looren** and Schouten, M K D. Over Functies en Affordances. *Alg Ned Tijdschr Wijs*, 88(3), 216-228, Jl 96.

In this response to Meijering's (1996) article, we examine the concept of functional analysis. We argue that functional analysis should not be understood as resorting only to intrasystemic functions. Rather, an analysis of the functions of a natural (sub)system should take into account the (sub)system's extrasystemic relations with its environment. The relevance of the ecological niche in functional analysis is mirrored in a propensity view of functions. In addition, this view appears to rest comfortably with a view of science as a multitude of mutually constraining levels of analysis. Our approach is exemplified by Gibson's notion of affordances.

**De Jong, Willem R**. Gottlob Frege and the Analytic-Synthetic Distinction within the framework of the Aristotelian Model of Science. *Kantstudien*, 87(3), 290-324, 1996.

It is argued that Frege's research in the methodology of the a priori sciences (arithmetic, geometry and logic) has to be interpreted within the framework of the so-called Aristotelian model of science. A rather precise characterization of this conception of scientific rationality makes it possible to clarify Frege's views concerning the epistemological distinctions analytic-synthetic and a priori-a posteriori. These distinctions not only depend on this model of science but also on a threefold scheme concerning domains or sources of knowledge; i.e., the distinction between logical, intuitive and empirical knowledge.

**De Jong, Willem R**. Kant's Theory of Geometrical Reasoning and the Analytic-Synthetic Distinction: On Hintikka's Interpretation of Kant's Philosophy of Mathematics. *Stud Hist Phil Sci*, 28(1), 141-166, Mr 97.

Kant's distinction between analytic and synthetic method is connected to the so-called Aristotelian model of science and has to be interpreted in a (broad) directional sense. With the distinction between analytic and synthetic judgments the critical Kant did introduced a new way of using the terms 'analytic'-'synthetic', but one that still lies in line with their directional sense. A careful comparison of the conceptions of the critical Kant with ideas of the precritical Kant as expressed in *Über die Deutlichkeit*, leads to the interpretation defended here of Kant's distinction between analytic and synthetic judgments within his philosophy of mathematics.

**De la Pienda, Jesús Avelino**. *Paraísos y Utopías: Una Clave Antropológica*. Oviedo, Ed Paraiso, 1996.

The book describes paradises as a series of myths in which the aspirations of their creators are reflected. It is an analysis of the anthropological bases of man's utopian activity. It describes numerous positive and negative functions which the paradises and utopias perform in the everyday life of people and nations. It offers an anthropological key to interpret their plurality, necessity and longevity on a *utopia scale* capable of legitimizing them all. In this way it lays the foundations of a *new education* for tolerance and intercultural good fellowship. It ends with a critical analysis of E. Bloch's *Das Prinzip Hoffnung* and J. Moltmann's *Theologie der Hoffnung*.

**De Lassus, Alain-Marie**. Saint Thomas et le problème de la possibilité d'un univers créé éternel. *Sapientia*, 52(201), 195-202, 1997.

**De Leeuw, A Dionys**. Contemplating the Interests of Fish: The Angler's Challenge. *Environ Ethics*, 18(4), 373-390, Winter 96.

Hunters are significantly different from anglers in the respect that they show for an animal's interest in avoiding pain and suffering. While hunters make every effort to reduce pain and suffering in their game animals, anglers purposefully inflict these conditions on fish. These similarities and differences have three important consequences: 1) The moral argument justifying the killing of animals for sport in hunting must apply to all of angling as well. 2) Angling, unlike hunting, requires a second justification for the intentional infliction of avoidable pain and suffering in fish. 3) If ethical hunters hold true to their principle of avoiding all suffering in the animals that they pursue, then hunters must reject all sports fishing. (edited)

**De Liguori, Girolamo**. La reazione a Cartesio nella Napoli del Seicento: Giovambattista De Benedictis. *G Crit Filosof Ital*, 16(3), 330-359, S-D 96.

**De Lima Vaz, H C**. Platao Revisitado: Ética e Metafísica nas Origens Platônicas. *Kriterion*, 34(87), 9-30, Ja-Jl 93.

Este texto foi a aula inaugural do curso de Doutorado em Filosofia da Faculdade de Filosofia e Ciências Humanas da UFMG, no dia 18/03/93. O problema estudado é o da profunda unidade entre Ética e Metafísica nas origens do filosofar platônico, levando-se em conta sobretudo os diálogos da juventude e a sua funçao propedêutica com relaçao aos diálogos da maturidade e à teoria dos Princípios, que a crítica recente reconstitui a partir dos fragmentos das doutrinas nao-escritas de Platao. A conclusao situa a natureza ético-metafísica do filosofar platônico em face de algumas tendências da filosofia contemporânea.

**De Lorenzo, Javier**. El discurso matemático: ideograma y lenguaje natural. *Mathesis*, 10(3), 235-254, Ag 94.

The natural Western language is mainly phonological, as opposed to ideogrammatical things. Mathematical way of doing things reverse this relationship and originated in the ideogram, which is not a phoneme transcription but a constructive potentiality. From positions starting from the phonological language, or from the syntactic-formalism ones, the role of the ideogram in the mathematical way of doing things has not been realized and because of that its use is simply called formalism. The purpose of this work is to analyze the specific role of the ideogram in the mathematical way of doing things and to point out some conceptual consequences that deriving from this analysis.

**De los Reyes, Guillermo** and Rich, Paul. Volunteerism and Democracy: A Latin American Perspective. *Cont Phil*, 18(2-3), 59-65, Mr-Ap/My-Je 96.

The myriad number of voluntary organizations in the world are getting scholarly attention with regards to what they contribute to political culture. Nongovernmental associations are increasingly recognized as fundamental to democratization: "In the world of ideas, civil society is hot. It is almost impossible to read an article on foreign or domestic politics without coming across some mention of the concept.... At the heart of the concept of civil society lie 'intermediate institutions', private groups that thrive between the realm of the state and the family."

**De Martini, F** and Di Giuseppe, G and Boschi, D. Test of the Violation of Local Realism in Quantum Mechanics with No Use of Bell's Inequalities. *Erkenntnis*, 45(2 & 3), 367-377, Nov 96.

A novel and versatile polarization-entanglement scheme is adopted to investigate the violation of the EPR local realism for a nonmaximally entangled two-photon system according to the recent "nonlocality proof" by Lucien Hardy. In this context the adoption of a sophisticated detection method allows direct determination of any "element of physical reality" (viz, determined "*with probability equal to unity*" in the words of Einstein, Podolsky and Rosen) for the pair system within complete measurements that are largely *insensitive* to the detector quantum-efficiencies and noise.

**De Matos, Franklin**. Dramaturgy of Picture (Essay on Diderot's *The Natural Child*) (in Portuguese). *Discurso*, 26, 93-112, 1996.

This article analyses the concept of "tableau" in Diderot's theatrical aesthetics. The aim is to show that Diderot approximates theatre to painting in order to investigate the specific qualities of the dramatic genre with respect to the epic genre.

**De Mey, Langha** and Schulze, Hans-Joachim. Indoctrination and Moral Reasoning: A Comparison between Dutch and East German Students. *J Moral Educ*, 25(3), 309-323, S 96.

This contribution presents the results of an empirical study aiming to test Kohlberg's complexity hypothesis. It is assumed that in complex sociopolitical surroundings, individuals are stimulated into higher stages of moral judgments than in a less complicated environment. In order to test the hypothesis we compared the stages of moral judgments of Dutch and former German Democratic Republic (GDR) students belonging to two types of schools. The Dutch (Amsterdam) group was split into VWO (preuniversity) students and MAVO (low general secondary education) students. The East German students attend the "Gymnasium" (preuniversity) and the "Mittelschule" (low general secondary education). The mean age of the Dutch VWO-students was 16.33 and of the MAVO students, 15.39. The mean age of the East German "Gymnasium" students was 16.35 and that of the "Mittelschule" students was 16.00. The individuals of the Dutch and East German groups were asked to rate the moral problems in the Sociomoral Reflection Objective Measure. The scores were subjected to multivariate analyses of variance to detect differences between the groups. The results did not support Kohlberg's complexity hypothesis.

**De Mora Charles, M S**. "Verdad y representación en Leibniz" in *Verdad: lógica, representación y mundo*, Villegas Forero, L, 49-54. Santiago de Compostela, Univ Santiago Comp, 1996.

In this paper I would like to analyse the relation between signs and thought in Leibniz and the distinction between truths of fact and truths of reason. Truths of fact are also grounded on reason, in Leibniz's opinion, as truths of reason themselves. The "new" logic of Alea should be used for the contingent in order to attain the truth, in the same way as we have methods to attain the truth in situations of necessity. I shall use for my paper specially the *Vorausedition der Universität Munster* of Leibniz manuscripts and I will use the references of authors as Marcelo Dascar, Eberhard Knobloch, André Robinet or Georges Kalinowski to Leibniz's logic.

**De Muynck, Willem M**. Can We Escape from Bell's Conclusion that Quantum Mechanics Describes a Non-Local Reality?. *Stud Hist Phil Mod Physics*, 27B(3), 315-330, S 96.

It is argued that for a proper understanding of the question of nonlocality in quantum mechanics and hidden variables theories purporting to reproduce the quantum mechanical measurement results, it is essential to consider stochastic hidden variables theories. Laudisa's (1996) conclusion that in derivations of the Bell inequality an implicit assumption of locality is made, is shown to be a consequence of his restriction to deterministic hidden variables theories. It is also demonstrated how it is possible to draw a clear distinction between contextualism and nonobjectivism, nonobjectivism amounting to the impossibility of reducing an individual quantum mechanical measurement result, either in a deterministic or in a stochastic way, to the hidden variables state the individual object is in independently of measurement. The analogy with thermodynamics is exploited to clarify the issue.

**De Olaso, Ezequiel**. "Scepticism and the Limits of Charity" in *Scepticism in the History of Philosophy: A Pan-American Dialogue*, Popkin, Richard H (ed), 253-266. Dordrecht, Kluwer, 1996.

**De Oliveira, Maria Elisa**. The *Poet's* Figure in Friedrich von Hardenburg (Novalis) and Gaston Bachelard: Some Considerations (in Portuguese). *Trans/Form/Acao*, 19, 47-59, 1996.

Through *fire*—an important element in *Novalis* (XVIII century) and Gaston Bachelard (XX century), we could try an approach between these two authors, separated in time, but close in the aesthetics' imagination value.

**De Oliveira, Nythamar Fernandes**. The Worldhood of the the *Kosmos* in Heidegger's Reading of Heraclitus. *Manuscrito*, 19(2), 201-222, O 96.

This article investigates Heidegger's reading of Heraclitus' conception of *Kosmos*, so as to show how the former's hermeneutical-phenomenological correlation between the worldhood of the world and the mode of being of Dasein qua Being-in-the-World is in full agreement with the latter's articulation of *Phusis* and *Logos* in the so-called "cosmic fragments."

**De Paola, Gregorio**. La "Revue de métaphysique et de morale" e la guerra: Lettere inedite di Durkheim. *G Crit Filosof Ital*, 16(2), 223-265, My-Ag 96.

**De Pasquale, Mario**. "La qualità del tempo nell'insegnamento della filosofia" in *Il Concetto di Tempo: Atti del XXXII Congresso Nazionale della Società Filosofica Italiana*, Casertano, Giovanni (ed), 371-377. Napoli, Loffredo, 1997.

**De Paula, Joao Antônio**. História, historiografia e símbolos. *Kriterion*, 37(94), 64-90, Jl-D 96.

This essay has two main purposes. First, it discusses the emergence of new historiographical tendencies that negate the possibility of encompassing explanations of the historical reality at the same time in which they value/hypertrophy/fetishize certain "fragments" of social life taken as the only legitimate objects of historiography. Against that tendency, this essay attempts to show the important place and the heuristic function of the "fragment" within the movement of totalizing perspectives, such as in Walter Benjamin, for example. Secondly, the essay tries to analytically show the cognitive virtues of the reading of singular objects as indexes of global realities, through the interpretation of a picture by Dürer and of a romance by Thomas Mann.

**De Pierris, Graciela**. "Philosophical Scepticism in Wittgenstein's *On Certainty*" in *Scepticism in the History of Philosophy: A Pan-American Dialogue*, Popkin, Richard H (ed), 181-196. Dordrecht, Kluwer, 1996.

Wittgenstein's criticisms of Moore in *On Certainty* (OC) centers on Moore's misunderstanding of the difference between our ordinary standpoint with respect to the possibility of knowledge and the philosophical skeptical standpoint. OC is mainly devoted to exhibiting this distinction. Thus, OC does not refute philosophical skepticism—nor does it dissolve the philosophical problem of the possibility of knowledge or cure us forever from the philosophical illusion that there is such a problem. This is not to claim that Wittgenstein attempted to legitimize the standpoint external to our whole system of beliefs required for raising the problem of philosophical skepticism. The question of Wittgenstein's intentions on this central point is not settled here. Nevertheless, if it is right to attribute to Wittgenstein the intention of *showing* the impossibility of an external philosophical standpoint, then there appears to be a deep tension in OC. This tension arises from Wittgenstein's seemingly unavoidable use of descriptions of *general* characteristics and presuppositions of our nonphilosophical cognitive practices.

**De Praetere, Thomas**. The Demonstration by Refutation of the Principle of Non-Contradiction in Aristotle's *Metaphysics*, Book IV. *Log Anal*, 36(144), 343-358, S-D 93.

This article is a critique of the demonstration by refutation of the principle of noncontradiction in Aristotle's *Metaphysics*, Book IV. My method will consist in focusing on the dialectical nature of the proof, that means on the situation of dialogue presented by Aristotle as a constitutive element of the proof. Among the eight classical Aristotelian proofs of the impossibility of contradiction developed in Book IV, I have selected the three following: by the necessity of noncontradiction in action, by the necessity of a debate and finally by the necessity of a meaning of words, which is the demonstration by refutation as such. I try to figure out the presuppositions that lie behind those proofs, and simultaneously to show that none of them is absolutely compelling, even if Aristotle succeeds in convincing us of the utility of noncontradiction.

**De Renzi, Silvia**. Courts and Conversions: Intellectual Battles and Natural Knowledge in Counter-Reformation Rome. *Stud Hist Phil Sci*, 27(4), 429-449, D 96.

Military and religious codes, and the harsh conflicts of the Counter Reformation shaped the way in which the members of the Accademia dei Lincei represented their activities on behalf of Galilei and recruited followers to the new philosophy in the first half of the 17th century. This paper analyses the diplomatic channels which especially some German members of the Accademia built and put at the disposal of its intellectual battles. In so doing, it shows that investigations into specific historical factors can fruitfully complement the recent emphasis on courtly etiquette in making sense of intellectual identities, careers and activities in the early modern period.

**De Rijk, L M**. Burley's So-Called *Tractatus Primus*, with an Edition of the Additional *Quaestio* "Utrum contradictio sit maxima oppositio". *Vivarium*, 34(2), 161-191, N 96.

**De Rijke, Maarten**. The Logic of Peirce Algebras. *J Log Lang Info*, 4(3), 227-250, 1995.

Peirce algebras combine sets, relations and various operations linking the two in a unifying setting. This paper offers a modal perspective on Peirce algebras. Using modal logic as a characterization of the full Peirce algebras is given, as well as a finite axiomatization of their equational theory that uses so-called unorthodox derivation rules. In addition, the expressive power of Peirce algebras is analyzed through their connection with first-order logic and the fragment of first-order logic corresponding to Peirce algebras is described in terms of bisimulations.

**De Rijke, Maarten** and Kurtonina, Natasha. Bisimulations for Temporal Logic. *J Log Lang Info*, 6(4), 403-425, O 97.

We define bisimulations for temporal logic with *since* and *until*. This new notion is compared to existing notions of bisimulations and then used to develop the basic model theory of temporal logic with *since* and *until*. Our results concern both invariance and definability. We conclude with a brief discussion of the wider applicability of our ideas.

**De Ruyter, Geertrui**. Keeping One's Distance from the Absolute: Blumenberg's Metaphorology between Pragmatics and Metaphysics (in Dutch). *Tijdschr Filosof*, 58(4), 643-672, D 96.

Although Blumenberg rejects every form of essentialism in his thinking of man and reality, his view on the functioning of metaphors has its foundation in some anthropological and ontological assumptions, with the central notion of man as a "being of lack (*Mängelwesen*) who tries to overcome his unability to adapt to reality, by a rhetorical, i.e., indirect and functional relationship to reality. Blumenberg's metaphorology stands midway between pragmatics and metaphysics. It is more than pragmatics because it also implies a statement on the character of reality. It is less than metaphysics because these statements precisely bring into the open the vanity of conceptual language. Therefore, we propose to characterize Blumenberg's philosophy as a kind of "negative metaphysics". (edited)

**De Schipper, Elisabeth H**. "La parole à la poule" in *Philosophy and Democracy in Intercultural Perspective*, Kimmerle, Heinz (ed), 159-162. Amsterdam, Rodopi, 1997.

**De Soto, A R** and Trillas, Enric. What's an Approximate Conditional?. *Agora (Spain)*, 15(2), 71-81, 1996.

In any logic system, the representation of conditional information is a key element. The main inference rules habitually use propositions with a conditional form, i.e., conditionals, which facilitate an increase of the knowledge by means of making deductions. Fuzzy logic is not an exception, it needs conditionals to model fuzzy conditional statements. In this paper, after a brief discussion about classical conditionals, two forms to define fuzzy conditionals are given. Both of them are two different methods to obtain useful tools to make possible automatic process of approximate reasoning. Appropriate methods for approximate reasoning must necessarily be nonmonotonic because human beings think in a nonmonotonic manner. Several results in this field are also presented.

**De Sousa, Maria Carmelita H**. Hegel em Berlim—Discurso Inaugural. *Rev Port Filosof*, 52(1-4), 831-870, Ja-D 96.

**De Sousa, Ronald**. "Love Undigitized" in *Love Analyzed*, Lamb, Roger E, 189-207. Boulder, Westview Pr, 1997.

While rejecting essentialism about human nature, many remain essentialists about human relationships. I argue that love is routinely corrupted by being "digitalized," i.e., defined as falling into distinct forms, fitting repeatable social roles. A "reformist" view of love will increase the number of categories available. A radical response, exemplified by a certain kind of "queer theory," rejects the project of defining a repertoire of standard emotions. To "undigitize love," I suggest, is to downplay the role of love in social semantics, and restore it to an emotional aesthetics grounded in the unique interactions of individuals.

**De Sousa, Ronald B**. What Can't We Do with Economics?: Some Comments on George Ainslie's Picoeconomics. *J Phil Res*, 22, 197-209, Ap 97.

Ainslie's *Picoeconomics* presents an ingenious theory, based on a remarkably simple basic law about the rate of discounting the value of future prospects, which explains a vast number of psychological phenomena. Hyperbolic discount rates result in changes in the ranking of interests as they get closer in time. Thus quasi-homuncular "interests" situated at different times compete within the person. In this paper I first defend the generality of scope of Ainslie's model, which ranges over several personal and subpersonal levels of psychological analysis. I raise a problem which results from the temporal relativity of assessments of value and affects the possibility of objective values. Finally, I offer one example of a form of time-related irrationality on which Ainslie's scheme does not seem to have a grip, namely one which relates not to a situation's relative position in time, but to its temporal ('progressive' or 'perfect') temporal aspect.

**De Sousa e Brito, José**. O Direito como conceito limitado da justiça. *Telos (Spain)*, 5(2), 9-20, D 96.

1) Modernity (Galileo, Machiavelle, Hume) separated law and justice, by restricting reason to theoretical reason and therefore putting justice outside the sphere of reason. 2) Legal positivists develop the conceptual separation of law and justice. Bentham recovers practical reason (or utility) but distinguishes two kinds of reason (or of principles of utility): the expositive principle applies to law, the deontological principle applies to justice. Kelsen considers that law and justice are two different systems of norms, both outside the scope of reason. 3) Dworkin's theory of principles reintroduces reason in law. But the bounds that the legal sources and the legal procedure impose on reason explain law as restrictive conception of justice and disobedience to law and revolution as possibly rational.

**De Souza Birchal, Telma**. A marca do vazio: Reflexoes sobre a subjetividade em Blaise Pascal. *Kriterion*, 34(88), 50-69, Ag-D 93.

In this paper, we try to elucidate the topic of subjectivity in Pascal, focusing on thought B323. The latter is compared with the philosophies of Augustine, Montaigne and Descartes, who envisage subjectivity respectively as interiority, finiteness and thinking (*cogito*). We show that Pascal, by indicating the limits involved by such ways of thinking, rejects philosophy itself as the site in which the discourse about 'self' occurs; instead, he locates such discourse in the domain of theology.

**De Souza Filho, Danilo M**. "Finding One's Way About: High Windows, Narrow Chimneys, and Open Doors" in *Scepticism in the History of Philosophy: A Pan-American Dialogue*, Popkin, Richard H (ed), 167-179. Dordrecht, Kluwer, 1996.

**De Soveral, Eduardo Abranches**. Reflexoes sobre o Mito: Comentários à Mitologia de Eudoro de Sousa. *Rev Port Filosof*, 52(1-4), 871-888, Ja-D 96.

Eudoro de Sousa considers that the essence of intelligibility which impels science and philosophy, is based on "Leander's myth", i.e., the myth of an "infinitive present" which sustains the primacy of reason, a reason capable of appropriating "all of nature" and "all of sensitivity". However, it is a pseudo myth, as it does not have the structure proper of the authentic myth (which can be defined as having the form of a triangle, with God at its vertex and at the base, face to face, are man and nature. Eudoro also states that both "sensitivity" and "nature" are unlimited. In the authentic myth, sensitivity and creativity allow the passage from the objective to the transobjective, beyond whose horizon the Absolute is apprehended.

**De Torres, María José**. "Perspectivas sobre religión y filosofía en los inicios del Idealismo alemán: Fichte y Schelling antes de 1794" in *El inicio del Idealismo alemán*, Market, Oswaldo, 291-298. Madrid, Ed Complutense, 1996.

Fichte and Schelling began their intellectual way under the influence of the Kantism and its Copernican revolution. The early Fichte is a philosophy of the Enlightenment who wants to put rational limits to all divine revelation, in order to develop a philosophy that has understood completely the Christian faith as the highest manifestation of the universal reason. Schelling, in the other hand, will disapprove the rationalism of Enlightenment and decide to follow a mystic Spinozism, by trying to make the world of religious beliefs the most important complete in fulfillment of human spirit. (edited)

**De Ville, Kenneth**. Adolescent Parents and Medical Decision-Making. *J Med Phil*, 22(3), 253-270, Je 97.

The growing phenomenon of teenage pregnancy introduces the problem of who should serve as surrogate decision makers for the children of adolescent parents. The justifications which sanction society's grant of presumptive decision-making authority for adult parents, and the rationales and empirical evidence supporting a central role for adolescents who wish to make medical decisions regarding their own care, together suggest that older adolescent parents should be viewed as the presumptive decision makers for their children. There is, however, empirical evidence that adolescent parents lack the cognitive abilities of childless adolescents of the same age and that many exhibit lower levels of emotional stability, sensitivity to infant needs, and social adjustment. (edited)

**De Vos, Lu**. Die Rezeption der *Wissenschaftslehre* Fichtes in den Versionen der Hegelschen *Wissenschaft der Logik*. *Fichte-Studien*, 12, 257-271, 1997.

**De Vos, Lu**. Zur Logik der Moralität: Einige Fragen an A. Requate. *Jahr Hegelforschung*, 2, 191-201, 1996.

**De Vos, Ludovicus**. Vragen bij Hegels metafysische logica. *Tijdschr Filosof*, 58(3), 547-552, S 96.

**De Wachter, Maurice A M**. The European Convention on Bioethics. *Hastings Center Rep*, 27(1), 13-23, Ja-F 97.

Nearly fifteen years after the Council of Europe first called for a pan-European convention on issues in bioethics to harmonize disparate national regulations, in November 1996 the council's Committee of Ministers approved the *Convention on Human Rights and Biomedicine* for formal adoption. The draft convention, released in July 1994, provoked strong public, professional and governmental debate among European nations, particularly regarding provisions for biomedical research with subjects unable to give informed consent. If ratified, the "bioethics convention" will become the first such document to have binding force internationally.

**De Wijze, Stephen**. The Real Issues Concerning Dirty Hands—A Response to Kai Nielsen. *S Afr J Phil*, 15(4), 149-152, N 96.

In responding to Kai Nielsen's article "There is no dilemma of dirty hands" (*South African Journal of Philosophy*, 15(1): 1-7), I argue that he misunderstands and misrepresents the problem of dirty hands. Nielsen contends contra Walzer *et al.* that the political problem of dirty hands, understood as a moral dilemma rooted in conceptual confusion, is resolved by choosing, all things considered, the action which brings about the lesser evil. The decision is guided by a weak consequentialism which does not assume any form of utilitarianism. Recapping on some of the main points of my previous article (*South African Journal of Philosophy*, 1994, 13(1): 27-33), I outline why the problem of dirty hands is a much wider and more subtle problem than Nielsen would have us believe. Dirty hands scenarios do not necessarily presuppose moral dilemma situations, nor is there conceptual confusion if one takes into account Stocker's notions of double-counted impossible oughts and nonaction-guiding act evaluations.

**De Winter, Willem**. The Beanbag Genetics Controversy: Towards a Synthesis of Opposing Views of Natural Selection. *Biol Phil*, 12(2), 149-184, Ap 97.

The beanbag genetics controversy can be traced from the dispute between Fisher and Wright, through Mayr's influential promotion of the issue, to the contemporary units of selection debate. It centers on the claim that genic models of natural selection break down in the face of epistatic interactions among genes during phenotypic development. This claim is explored from both a conceptual and a quantitative point of view and is shown to be defective on both counts. (edited)

**De Zan, Julio**. Etica y Capitalismo (Sobre el control social de la racionalidad estratégica). *Cuad Etica*, 15-16, 49-60, 1993.

This rationality is introduced with the process of capitalist modernization. When it goes beyond its restricted working limits it starts to dissolve the communicative ties based on the cultural tradition's belief and values. It also weaken the communicative sources of morality, judicial legitimacy and politic power. Therefore, this instances lose the ability of controlling the social interaction and of restricting the strategic rationality.

**De Zan, Julio**. Una teoría del estado de derecho. *Cuad Etica*, 19-20, 169-180, 1995.

**De-Shalit, Avner**. Environmentalism for Europe—One Model?. *J Applied Phil*, 14(2), 177-186, 1997.

Two models of environmentalism are considered. One—hard line environmentalism—is a theory which unites environmental ethics and political theory; the other—soft environmentalism—is a package of the two as two distinctive levels of moral reasoning. It is argued that hard-line environmentalism is ademocratic, rests on wrong methodological assumptions and is friendly to the environment just so long as being so serves a sought-after 'psychological revolution'. Soft environmentalism is to be preferred also because its idea of democracy must be national and international rather than local. Since in the 'new' Europe people will move very often and will, therefore, fail to develop a sense of 'place' which is local, it may be a waste of time to emphasize 'localism' as part of environmentalism.

**Dean, Burton V** and Van Gigch, John P and Koenigsberg, Ernest. In Search of an Ethical Science: An Interview with C. West Churchman: An 80th Birthday Celebration. *J Bus Ethics*, 16(7), 731-744, My 97.

**Dean, Jodi**. Reflective Solidarity. *Constellations*, 2(1), 114-140, Ap 95.

**Dean, Mitchell**. Putting the Technological into Government. *Hist Human Sci*, 9(3), 47-68, Ag 96.

**Dean, Richard**. What should we Treat as an End in Itself?. *Pac Phil Quart*, 77(4), 268-288, D 96.

One formulation of the *categorical imperative* tells us to treat humanity as an end in itself. It has become common to think that 'humanity' (*die Menschheit*) here refers to some minimal power of rationality that is necessarily possessed by any rational agent, but I argue that this common reading is misguided. Instead, 'humanity' refers to a good will, the will of a being who is committed to moral principles. This good will reading of 'humanity' is not only suggested by passages in which Kant specifically discusses humanity, but also is more consistent with the main ideas of Kant's ethics.

**Dean, Tim**. Two Kinds of Other and Their Consequences. *Crit Inquiry*, 23(4), 910-920, Sum 97.

**Debray, Régis**. L'incomplétude, logique du religieux?. *Bull Soc Fr Phil*, 90(1), 1-35, Ja-Mr 96.

Is it possible to find a logic of so-called religious phenomena in the framework of a topology of stable human groups? Reduced to their most simple form, the latter seem to offer the observer a double characteristic: the establishment surrounding them of a circumscription or enclosure (territorial or immaterial) and also, up-stream or above them, an attachment to an outside point of cohesion, (historical or symbolic) which consists of the 'sacred' of the observed collectivity. It can be supposed that there exists a necessary and rational relationship between these two features, the enclosure and the reference. In a metaphorical echo of Gödel, this constant can be called *the axiom of incompletude*. It is thus that the call of the transcendent, necessary to any body count, proceeds from the most empirical finiteness and not just from a vague feeling of infinity. Examples taken from history and from etymology will illustrate this hypothesis, to be resituated among the various explanations for religious belief.

**DeCew, Judith Wagner**. In Pursuit of Privacy: Law, Ethics, and the Rise of Technology. Ithaca, Cornell Univ Pr, 1997.

In different contexts, privacy has been defined on the basis of information, autonomy, property and intimacy. DeCew's broader claim is that privacy has fundamental value because it allows us to create ourselves as individuals, offering us freedom from judgment, scrutiny and the pressure to conform. Feminist theorists often view privacy as a tool for schielding abuses. DeCew responds to this feminist critique of privacy, as well as the issues of abortion and of gay and lesbian sexuality in the context of specific landmark legal cases. In discussions of Roe v. Wade, Bowers v. Hardwick and the Hart-Devlin debate on decriminalization of homosexuality and prostitution, DeCew applies her broad theory to sexual and reproductive privacy, antisodomy laws and the legislation and enforcement of morals. She concludes with a discussion of the intersection of privacy and public safety concerns, such as drug testing and in light of new communication technologies, such as caller ID. (publisher, edited)

**DeConinck, James B** and Lewis, William F. The Influence of Deontological and Teleological Considerations and Ethical Climate on Sales Managers' Intentions to Reward or Punish Sales Force Behavior. *J Bus Ethics*, 16(5), 497-506, Ap 97.

This study examined how sales managers react to ethical and unethical acts by their salespeople. Deontological considerations and, to a much lesser extent, teleological considerations predicted sales managers' ethical judgments. Sales managers' intentions to reward or discipline ethical or unethical sales force behavior were primarily determined by their ethical judgments. An organization's perceived ethical work climate was not a significant predictor of sales managers' intentions to intervene when ethical and unethical sales force behavior was encountered.

**Dedrick, Don**. Can Colour Be Reduced to Anything?. *Proc Phil Sci Ass*, 3(Suppl), S134-S142, 1996.

C.L. Hardin has argued that the colour opponency of the vision system leads to *chromatic subjectivism*: chromatic sensory states reduce to neurophysiological states. Much of the force of Hardin's argument derives from a critique of *chromatic objectivism*. On this view chromatic sensory states are held to reduce to an external property. While I agree with Hardin's critique of objectivism it is far

from clear that the problems which beset objectivism do not apply to the subjectivist position as well. I develop a critique of subjectivism that parallels Hardin's antiobjectivist argument.

**Dees, Richard H**. "The Justification of Toleration" in *Philosophy, Religion, and the Question of Intolerance*, Ambuel, David (ed), 134-156. Albany, SUNY Pr, 1997.

The classic arguments for toleration found in the works of traditional liberals from John Locke to John Rawls all fail, either because they are based on false premises about what the state can and can not do, or because they beg important questions justification in a pragmatic account of toleration that emphasizes the importance of historical contexts and the dynamics of particular communities of value. If those communities accept toleration provisionally, we find, they change the normative landscape so that they can learn to appreciate toleration for its own sake.

**Deflem, Mathieu** (trans) and Habermas, Jürgen. Georg Simmel on Philosophy and Culture: Postscript to a Collection of Essays. *Crit Inquiry*, 22(3), 403-414, Spr 96.

**Degnin, Francis**. Levinas and the Hippocratic Oath: A Discussion of Physician-Assisted Suicide. *J Med Phil*, 22(2), 99-123, Ap 97.

At least from the standpoint of contemporary cultural and ethical resources, physicians have argued eloquently and exhaustively both for and against physician-assisted suicide. If one avoids the temptation to ruthlessly simplify either position to immorality or error, then a strange dilemma arises. How is it that well educated and intelligent physicians, committed strongly and compassionately to the care of their patients, argue adamantly for opposing positions? Thus rather than simply rehashing old arguments, this essay attempts to rethink the nature of human morality as both a source and a fracturing of human rationality—and with morality, the *question* of human nature in the context of violence, oppression, service and obligation. This interpretation of moral life is laid out roughly along the lines of the Jewish philosopher Emmanuel Levinas and further clarified through a discussion of the Hippocratic Oath. These resources are then brought to bear on the specific arguments and recommendations concerning physician-assisted suicide.

**Degnin, Francis**. Max Weber on Ethics Case Consultation: A Methodological Critique of the Conference on Evaluation of Ethics Consultation. *J Clin Ethics*, 8(2), 181-192, Sum 97.

Using works of Max Weber, this essay argues that while the articles from the *Conference on Evaluation of Ethics Case Consultation* (*Journal of Clinical Ethics*, Summer, 1996) are correct in assessing a need for empirical evaluation, the very process of the conference—by placing a desire for political consensus above the need for conceptual clarity—works against acquiring the conceptual clarity required for empirical evaluation. Not only are the terms cited in the goals statement undefined, they must remain ambiguous in order to sustain the consensus. Moreover, the function of the ethics consultant as an advocate for the marginalized (the gadfly) is also lost.

**DeGraff, Jeff** and Morritt, Suzanne. The Revisionary Visionary: Leadership and the Aesthetics of Adaptability. *J Aes Educ*, 30(4), 69-85, Wint 96.

**DeHaan, Robert** and Hanford, Russell and Kinlaw, Kathleen. Promoting Ethical Reasoning, Affect and Behaviour Among High School Students: An Evaluation of Three Teaching Strategies. *J Moral Educ*, 26(1), 5-20, Mr 97.

Ethics education should aim to promote students' maturity across a broad spectrum of moral functioning, including moral reasoning, moral affect and moral behaviour. To identify the most effective strategy for promoting the comprehensive moral maturity of high school students, we enrolled students in one of four groups: an introductory ethics class, a blended economics-ethics class, a role-model ethics class taught by graduate students and a nonethics comparison class. Pretest and post-test instruments measured the ways students a) reason, b) feel and c) act with regard to ethical-normative issues. The results indicated that the approaches to teaching ethics varied considerably in terms of their ability to promote significant positive changes in students' moral reasoning, empathy and behaviour.

**Dehornoy, Patrick**. Another Use of Set Theory. *Bull Sym Log*, 2(4), 379-391, D 96.

Here, we analyse some recent applications of set theory to topology and argue that set theory is not only the closed domain where mathematics is usually founded, but also a flexible framework where imperfect intuitions can be precisely formalized and technically elaborated before they possibly migrate toward other branches. This apparently new role is mostly reminiscent of the one played by other external fields like theoretical physics and we think that it could contribute to revitalize the interest in set theory in the future.

**Del Barco, José Luis**. La seriedad de la ética. *Anu Filosof*, 29(2), 387-395, 1996.

Ethics is a serious matter as human actions are cybernetics. Actions are not lost nor do they leave the agent unaffected. Every single action returns to the agent in the form of a fine chisel that carves him from inside. The interior quality brought about by our actions is called vice and virtue.

**Del Vecchio, Dante**. Postille. *Sapienza*, 50(1), 109-112, 1997.

**Delacruz, Elizabeth Manley** and Dunn, Phillip C. The Evolution of Discipline-Based Art Education. *J Aes Educ*, 30(3), 67-82, Fall 96.

**DeLancey, Craig**. Emotion and the Function of Consciousness. *J Consciousness Stud*, 3(5-6), 492-499, 1996.

Certain arguments that phenomenal conscious states play no role, or play a role that could be different, depend upon the seeming plausibility of thought experiments such as the inverted spectrum or phenomenal zombie. These thought experiments are always run for perceptual states like colour vision. Run for affective states like emotions, they become absurd, because the prior intention of our concepts of emotional states are that the phenomenal experience is inseparable from their motivational aspects. Our growing scientific understanding of emotion and motivation lends inductive evidence to this view. This points the way towards a positive hypothesis that affective consciousness is type-specific to its function.

**Delaney, Neil**. Romantic Love and Loving Commitment: Articulating a Modern Ideal. *Amer Phil Quart*, 33(4), 339-356, O 96.

**Deledalle-Rhodes, Janice**. The Transposition of the Linguistic Sign in Peirce's Contributions to *The Nation*. *Trans Peirce Soc*, 32(4), 668-682, Fall 96.

**Deleuze, Gilles** and Greco, Michael A and Smith, David. Literature and Life. *Crit Inquiry*, 23(2), 225-230, Wint 97.

**Deleuze, Gilles** and Millett, Nick. Immanence: A Life.... *Theor Cult Soc*, 14(2), 3-7, My 97.

**Delgado Ocando, José Manuel**. Nietzsche in Dr. Antonio Pérez Estévez's Thought (Spanish). *Fronesis*, 2(2), 157-170, D 95.

We synthesize Nietzsche's thinking in the concepts of "cisphilosophical anthropology" which expresses his rejection of metaphysics, itself replaced by what Pérez Estévez calls "Nietzsche's poetical philosophy," that is, "gay science," but its option with regard to the Apollonian kingdom of forms and categories for the Dionysian one in which we find the "happy science," that is to say, a world of creation in freedom, promoting life and power will. The third concept is the one of "cisphilosophical pedagogy," consisting of learning how to read between lines in order to show the Judeo-Christian influence of the hegemonical culture. (edited)

**Delgado Ocando, José Manuel**. Postmodernism and University (Spanish). *Fronesis*, 3(1), 115-123, Ap 96.

In this work is discussed the corporative anachronism of the university and its nexuses with the functions of transmission and production of knowledge. Communicational and economical globalization seem to lead the university to two traumatic dissolutions, i.e., the campus deconcentration and the open recomposition of curriculum, which obliges one to rethink the existence of the institution itself in postmodern terms, that is, with a reconstructive and recontextualizing perspective. (edited)

**Deligiorgi, Katerina**. Dissatisfied Enlightenment: Certain Difficulties Concerning the Public Use of One's Reason. *Bull Hegel Soc Gt Brit*, 35, 39-53, Spr-Sum 97.

Unlike Kant, Hegel is often seen as a critic of the *enlightenment*. Kant's advocacy of the *enlightenment*, however, involves reflection upon the conditions and limits of rational criticism, and this is central also to Hegel's concerns. A product of such reflection is Kant's notion of a public use of reason. This represents a modification of the motto: "think for yourself" which emphasizes the collective and discursive dimensions of the enlightening process that are further developed by Hegel who proposes a different model of public debate. Other authors discussed in the paper are Diderot, Rousseau and Goethe (*Iphengenia in Tauris*).

**Delkeskamp-Hayes, Corinna**. Equal Access to Health Care: A Lutheran Lay Person's Expanded Footnote. *Christian Bioethics*, 2(3), 326-345, 1996.

Can proposing a policy of equal access to health care be justified on Christian grounds? The notion of a "Christian justification" with regard to Christians' political activity is explored in relation to the New Testament texts. The less demanding policy of granting "rights to (basic) health care," the meaning of Jesus' healing activities, early Christian welfare schemes and Christian grounds for the ascription of "rights" are each discussed. As a result, with some stretching of the neighbor-love and missionary imperatives it is proposed that a basic health care policy can be legitimized. With regard to equal access to health care, however, all attempts to derive an equalizing imperative from the spiritual "equality among humans" or by way of the "love your neighbor as yourself" imperative are shown to fail. Particular attention is given to whether "attending to the least of my brothers' needs" obliges Christians to satisfy those needs optimally, as well as to the personal involvement aspect of the love-commandment in its simultaneously spiritual and temporal orientations.

**Dell'Erba, Paola**. Ai margini del discorso poetico. *Stud Filosofici*, 209-240, 1995.

The essay provides a critical perspective on the creativity of language, specifically connected to poetic and psychoanalytic speech, with an attention to its figurative, metaphorical and symbolic value. In the essay's analysis, that moves from a critique of the linguistic tradition according to which language expresses and communicates already-structured identities, language is shown to represent an infinite variety of ways of access to reality for all the individuals involved in the process. Accordingly, the never-finished work on meaning to be discovered in a word turns reality itself into the endless interplay of communicative possibilities and favours proliferation and innovation.

**Della Rocca, Michael**. *Representation and the* Mind-Body Problem *in* Spinoza. New York, Oxford Univ Pr, 1996.

This book offers a powerful new reading of Spinoza's philosophy of mind, the aspect of Spinoza's thought often regarded as the most profound and perplexing. Michael Della Rocca argues that interpreters of Spinoza's philosophy of mind have not paid sufficient attention to his casual barrier between the mental and the physical. The first half of the book shows how this barrier generates Spinoza's strong requirements for having an idea about an object. The second half of the book explains how this causal separation underlies Spinoza's intriguing argument for mind-body identity. Della Rocca

concludes his analysis by solving the famous problem of whether for Spinoza the distinction between attributes is real or somehow merely subjective. (publisher,edited)

**Dellian, Ed**. Newton, die Trägheitskraft und die absolute Bewegung. *Phil Natur*, 26(2), 192-201, 1989.

The paper extends an earlier reconstruction of Sir Isaac Newton's authentic theory of absolute motion to the concept of "materiae vis insita" (force of inertia). It is shown that a necessary but hitherto ignored constant factor of proportionality to connect "force" with "motion" is part of a promising algebraic definition of the "vis insita". Exciting aspects result from the fact that this "Newtonian constant" (as the author has named it) proves dimensionally identical with the constant "vacuum velocity of light" of modern physics.

**Dellunde, Pilar** and Casanovas, E and Jansana, Ramon. On Elementary Equivalence for Equality-free Logic. *Notre Dame J Form Log*, 37(3), 506-522, Sum 96.

This paper is a contribution to the study of equality-free logic, that is, first-order logic without equality. We mainly devote ourselves to the study of algebraic characterizations of its relation of elementary equivalence by providing some Keisler-Shelah type ultrapower theorems and an Ehrenfeucht-Fraïssé type theorem. We also give characterizations of elementary classes in equality-free logic. As a by-product we characterize the sentences that are logically equivalent to an equality-free one.

**Dellunde, Pilar** and Jansana, Ramon. "Characterization Theorems for Infinitary Universal Horn Logic" in *Verdad: lógica, representación y mundo*, Villegas Forero, L, 193-199. Santiago de Compostela, Univ Santiago Comp, 1996.

The purpose of this paper is to characterize the classes of structures axiomatizable by a set of universal Horn sentences and the classes axiomatizable by a set of universal Horn sentences without equality of an arbitrary infinitary language. (edited)

**Dellunde, Pilar** and Jansana, Ramon. Some Characterization Theorems for Infinitary Universal Horn Logic without Equality. *J Sym Log*, 61(4), 1242-1260, D 96.

In the paper we mainly study preservation theorems for the universal strict Horn fragment of the infinitary languages without the equality symbol. We obtain definability, joint consistency and interpolation results for the mentioned fragments. We apply the results to obtain some generalizations of know theorems on the field of abstract algebraic logic.

**Delmas-Rigoutsos, Yannis**. A Double Deduction System for Quantum Logic Based on Natural Deduction. *J Phil Log*, 26(1), 57-67, F 97.

The author presents a deduction system for Quantum Logic. This system is a combination of a natural deduction system and rules based on the relation of compatibility. This relation is the logical correspondent of the commutativity of observables in Quantum Mechanics or perpendicularity in Hilbert spaces. Contrary to the system proposed by Gibbins and Cutland, the natural deduction part of the system is pure: no algebraic artifact is added. The rules of the system are the rules of *classical natural deduction* in which is added a control of contexts using the compatibility relation. The author uses his system to prove the following theorem: If propositions of a quantum logical propositional calculus system are mutually compatible, they form a classical subsystem.

**Delon, Françoise** and Farré, Rafel. Some Model Theory for Almost Real Closed Fields. *J Sym Log*, 61(4), 1121-1152, D 96.

We study the model theory of fields $k$ carrying a Henselian valuation with real closed residue field. We give a criteria for elementary equivalence and elementary inclusion of such fields involving the value group of a not necessarily definable valuation. This allows us to translate theories of such fields to theories of ordered Abelian groups and we study the properties of this translation. We also characterize the first-order definable convex subgroups of a given ordered Abelian group and prove that the definable real valuation rings of $K$ are in correspondence with the definable convex subgroups of the value group of a certain real valuation of $k$.

**Delport, Hagen**. Is Subjective Materialism Possible? (in German). *Prima Philosophia*, 10(3), 263-305, 1997.

This question is the result of a materialistic criticism working with inconsequent basic terms of dialectic materialism. Spirit is called immaterial only by W.I. Lenin in "Materialism and Empiriocriticism." This theorem sprang from the philosophical indifference of J. Dietzgen and the reduction of spirit to physiological phenomena by the "vulgar materialism." But the theoretical reason is Lenin's term of matter, which reduces matter to the outer world. The subjective materialism emphasizes the subject from a materialistic point of view and advocates the priority of subjectivity against the objective background. This does not hold for the ontological and gnosiological aspects but for the ethical one and the course of life.

**Deltete, Robert J** and Guy, Reed A. Emerging from Imaginary Time. *Synthese*, 108(2), 185-203, Ag 96.

Recent models in quantum cosmology make use of the concept of imaginary time. These models all conjecture a join between regions of imaginary time and regions of real time. We examine the model of James Hartle and Stephen Hawking to argue that the various 'no-boundary' attempts to interpret the transition from imaginary to real time in a logically consistent and physically significant way all fail. We believe this conclusion also applies to 'quantum tunneling' models, such as that proposed by Alexander Vilenkin. We conclude, therefore, that the notion of 'emerging from imaginary time' is incoherent. A consequence of this conclusion seems to be that the whole class of cosmological models appealing to imaginary time is thereby refuted.

**Demetriou, Kyriacos**. The Sophists, Democracy, and Modern Interpretation. *Polis*, 14(1-2), 1-29, 1995.

The great sophists of Periclean Athens are widely associated with the democratic tradition. Drawing on the sophists as democrats betrays the impact of the modern notion of liberty as a matter of freedom from interference in the pursuit of one's lawful ends. The sophists are in this work examined within their historical and ideological contexts and it is shown that their advocacy of political individualism eventually turned against the prescriptive basis of Athenian democratic rule and undermined the vital principle of the sovereignty of the demos. In a period of profound political changes, the sophists' teaching rather tended to alienate the aristocratic elite from the social and political framework created by democratic egalitarianism, preparing thereby the transition to the new political ethos of fourth-century Athenian life.

**Demmer, Klaus**. Treue zwischen Faszination und Institution. *Frei Z Phil Theol*, 44(1-2), 18-43, 1997.

**Demmerling, Christoph**. Zeitalter der hermeneutischen Vernunft. *Phil Rundsch*, 43(3), 233-242, S 96.

The article *Hermeneutisches Zeitalter der Vernunft?* contributes to the question of the systematical outlines of a hermeneutical philosophy. Therefore it takes into consideration two recently published books of J. Greisch *Hermeneutik und Metaphysik. Fine Problemgeschichte*. München 1993) and O. Pöggeler *Schritte zu einer hermeneutischen Philosophie*, Freiburg/München 1994). Both authors are criticized because of their exclusively historical orientation. In my view hermeneutics should enter a dialogue with other philosophical traditions as above all analytical philosophy.

**Demolombe, Robert** and Cuppens, Frédéric. "A Deontic Logic for Reasoning about Confidentiality" in *Deontic Logic, Agency and Normative Systems*, Brown, Mark A (ed), 66-79. New York, Springer-Verlag, 1996.

This paper presents a deontic logic *epsilon* for reasoning about permission or prohibition to know some parts of the database content in the context of a multilevel confidentiality policy. Finally, it is shown how the logic can be used to express constraints to guarantee the consistency of a policy or to prevent the existence of inference channels. That is, the possibility to infer sentences that are not permitted to know from other sentences that are permitted to know. Both deductive and abductive channels are considered. (edited)

**DeMoss, Michelle A** and McCann, Greg K. Without a Care in the World: The Business Ethics Course and Its Exclusion of a Care Perspective. *J Bus Ethics*, 16(4), 435-443, Mr 97.

This article analyzes the impact of the rights-oriented business ethics course on student's ethical orientation. This approach, which is predominant in business schools, excludes the care-oriented approach used by a majority of women as well as some men and minorities. The results of this study showed that although students did not shift significantly in their ethical orientation, a majority of the men and an even greater majority of the women were care-oriented before and after a course in business ethics. If business schools are to address society's increasing diversity then the perspective of women and others who are care-oriented must be assimilated into the curriculum. This can only be done by rethinking how the business ethics course (and the entire business curriculum) are taught to include a care-oriented approach.

**Demri, Stéphane**. A Completeness Proof for a Logic with an Alternative Necessity Operator. *Stud Log*, 58(1), 99-112, 1997.

We show the completeness of a Hilbert-style system $L_{Kappa}$ defined by M. Valiev involving the knowledge operator Kappa dedicated to the reasoning with incomplete information. The completeness proof uses a variant of Makinson's canonical model construction. Furthermore, we prove that the theoremhood problem for $L_{Kappa}$ is co-*NP*-complete, using techniques similar to those used to prove that the satisfiability problem for propositional S5 is *NP*-complete.

**Demri, Stéphane**. Extensions of Modal Logic S5 Preserving NP-Completeness. *Bull Sec Log*, 26(2), 73-84, Je 97.

We present a family of multimodal logics having *NP*-complete satisfiability problems and admitting in the language S5-like modal operators, common knowledge and distributed knowledge operators. Our motivation is to find out interaction conditions between the modal operators that affect the computational complexity of the logics.

**Demri, Stéphane** and Caferra, Ricardo and Herment, Michel. Framework for the Transfer of Proofs, Lemmas and Strategies from Classical to Non-Classical Logics. *Stud Log*, 52(2), 197-232, My 93.

There exist valuable methods for theorem proving in nonclassical logics based on translation from these logics into first-order classical logic (abbreviated henceforth FOL). The key notion in these approaches is *translation* from a *Source Logic* (henceforth abbreviated SL) to a *Target Logic* (henceforth abbreviated TL). These methods are concerned with the problem of *finding* a proof in TL by translating a formula in SL, but they do not address the very important problem of *presenting proofs* in SL via a backward translation. We propose a framework for presenting proofs in SL based on a partial backward translation of proofs obtained in a familiar TL: Order-Sorted Predicate Logic. (edited)

**Demri, Stéphane** and Orlowska, Ewa. A Class of Modal Logics with a Finite Model Property with Respect to the Set of Possible-Formulae. *Bull Sec Log*, 26(1), 39-49, Mr 97.

We propose a formalism for presentation and classification of modal logics that admit a possible world semantics. We introduce a broad family of operators acting on binary relations and we show how various classes of accessibility relations from modal frames can be uniformly represented using these operators. Within this framework we define a class of modal logics that possess the finite model property with respect to the set of possible-formulae. (edited)

**Demura, Masaya**. Carlo Carrà's Metaphysical Painting—The Works Reproduced in *Valori Plastici* (in Japanese). *Bigaku*, 47(3), 36-47, Winter 96.

The art magazine *Valori Plastici*, issued from 1918 to 1921, has decisive importance in Italian art between the wars. It stimulated the tendency of "return to order" to appear as *Novecento* movement. Carlo Carrà wrote many articles for the magazine and his metaphysical works were often reproduced in it. His discourse emphasizing the "*Italian principle*" shows some parallelism with M. Sarfatti's. That "*principle*," however, as far as it means the ability of artists who discover the essences of objects and construct them into works, had been manifested in 1916 in his writings about Giotto and Uccello revalued from modern point of view. But in *Valori Plastici* years he tried to justify himself in the name of his race. The word "metaphysical" seems to be a coupler of these attitudes. On the other hand, the fact that his metaphysical works reproduced in *Valori Plastici* were revised possibly not so much later is a proof of his intention to make his own painting in harmony with his discourse since the revision has been done toward some kind of classicism.

**Den Hartogh, Govert**. Ethische theorie en morele ervaring: In discussie met Hub Zwart. *Kennis Methode*, 20(4), 398-409, 1996.

In his book *Weg met de ethiek?* (Away with ethics?) Hub Zwart criticizes the dominant forms of health care ethics for reducing the complexity of moral experience to two principles: a principle of respect for autonomy and a principle of doing good and avoiding harm. His own analyses of some issues point to two additional principles: of respect for life as such and for the human body as such. I argue that these analyses cannot count as an execution of his program of 'taking moral experience more seriously', because these additional principles have the same relation to moral experience as the original ones: they attempt to give the most coherent explanation of our relevant moral intuitions as a whole. Zwart, however, often seems to believe that he can trace his additional principles to experience directly, but this cannot be true on his own account of the status of both principles and experience.

**Den Hartogh, Govert**. The Values of Life. *Bioethics*, 11(1), 43-66, Ja 97.

In *Life's Dominion* Dworkin aims at defusing the controversy about abortion and euthanasia by redefining its terms. Basically it is not a dispute about the right to life, but about its value. Liberals should grant that human life has not only a personal, but also an intrinsic value; conservatives should accept the principle of toleration which requires to let people decide for themselves about matters of intrinsic value. Dworkin fails, however, to distinguish between two kinds of personal value. He also fails to distinguish between two meanings of the concept of 'intrinsic value'. (edited)

**Den Uyl, Douglas J**. Friendship and Transcendence. *Int J Phil Relig*, 41(2), 105-122, Ap 97.

**Denbigh, Kenneth G**. Time's Arrows Today: Recent Physical and Philosophical Work on the Direction of Time. *Stud Hist Phil Mod Physics*, 27B(2), 221-227, Je 96.

**Denecke, Klaus** and Halkowska, Katarzyna. On P-compatible Hybrid Identities and Hyperidentities. *Stud Log*, 53(4), 493-501, N 94.

P-compatible identities are built up from terms with a special structure. We investigate a variety defined by a set of P-compatible hybrid identities and answer the question whether a variety defined by a set of P-compatible hyperidentities can be solid.

**Dengerink, J D**. Schepping, transcendentie, religie. *Phil Reform*, 62(1), 48-74, 1997.

**Denkel, Arda**. *Object and Property*. New York, Cambridge Univ Pr, 1996.

The author develops a unified ontology of objecthood, essences and causation. A principal tenet is that while the basic units of the physical world are substances, particular properties are the analytic ultimates of existence. Although properties must inhere in objects, individual things are nothing more than compresences of properties at particular positions. There exist no mysterious substrata. Principles explaining how properties are held together in compresences are basically the same as those that account for essences and for causal relations. There exist no objective universals. Denkel defends a thoroughgoing particularism and offers purely qualitative accounts of individuation, identity, essences and matter. Throughout, the main alternative positions are surveyed and the relevant historical background is traced. (publisher, edited)

**Denkel, Arda**. On the Compresence of Tropes. *Phil Phenomenol Res*, 57(3), 599-606, S 97.

Once we assume that objects are bundles of tropes, we want to know how that latter cohere. Are they held together by a substratum, are they linked by external relations or do they cling to one another by internal relations? This paper begins by exploring the reasons for eliminating the first two suggestions. Defending that the third option can be made plausible, it advances the following thesis: Maintaining that tropes are held in a compresence by appropriately qualified internal relations avoids the consequence that such properties will be essential to the object. The specific targets of the second part of the paper include, first, a more precise description of the notion of a cohesive internal relation, and second, an explanation of how alteration is possible in an object the particular properties of which hold together by qualified internal relations.

**Denker, Alfred**. "Freiheit ist das höchste Gut des Menschen" in *Sein—Reflexion—Freiheit: Aspekte der Philosophie Johann Gottlieb Fichtes*, Asmuth, Christoph (ed), 35-68. Amsterdam, Gruner, 1997.

In this paper Schelling's reception of Fichte's *Wissenschaftslehre* is discussed within the context of his early writings. Schelling never was a disciple of Fichte in the strict sense of the word. He reinterpreted Fichte's doctrine of the absolute I within the metaphysical framework of his studies of Plato and Kant. Schelling developed his concept of the Absolute as I in opposition to Spinoza's doctrine of absolute substance, and never considered the I to be absolute in Fichte's sense. The philosophical differences between Schelling and Fichte were obvious from the beginning as is shown by their different interpretations of intellectual intuition.

**Denker, Alfred**. Fichtes Wissenschaftslehre und die philosophischen Anfänge Heideggers. *Fichte-Studien*, 13, 35-49, 1997.

In this paper the author shows that Heidegger was not only influenced by Fichte through the neo-Fichteanism of Rickert and Lask, but also through his own reading of Fichte's works. In his 1919 lecture course on the idea of philosophy Heidegger developed his concept of philosophy. From Fichte he took over the notion that philosophy is a pretheoretical science in which the possibility of all other sciences is founded. It is the science of sciences and thus the strictest science. Where Fichte founded this strictest science in practical reason, Heidegger founded it in the facticity of human life.

**Dennehy, Raymond**. Bodenheimer's Empirical Theory of Natural Law. *Vera Lex*, 14(1-2), 18-21, 1994.

Bodenheimer was a prominent figure in the "reemergence of natural law jurisprudence in decisional law." His natural law theory is empirical because it relies on the data of the sciences, natural and social, to support its claims. It is also in the tradition of the moderate realism of classical natural law theorists like Aristotle and Aquinas, both of whom ground their ethical theory in a teleological view of nature. This combination produces a radical incompatibility. Whereas Bodenheimer's realism leads him to advance ethically absolute norms, his empiricism leads him to hold that those norms cannot be true or false.

**Dennett, Daniel C**. Cow-Sharks, Magnets, and Swampman. *Mind Lang*, 11(1), 76-77, Mr 96.

**Dennett, Daniel C**. Granny Versus Mother Nature—No Contest. *Mind Lang*, 11(3), 263-269, S 96.

Fodor's doubts about neo-Darwinism are driven by something other than familiarity with evolutionary biology, so they should be set aside. His claim that a theory of intentionality cannot be constructed on an evolutionary foundation because there is no representation in the process of natural selection reveals that he has been blind to the chief beauty of Darwin's vision: its capacity to explain not just how the living can come, gradually, from the nonliving, but also how meaning can come, by incremental steps, out of the meaningless.

**Dennett, Daniel C**. La percezione è il "bordo d'attacco" della memoria?. *Iride*, 8(14), 59-78, Ap 95.

**Dennett, Daniel C** and Mulhauser, Gregory R. In the Beginning, There Was Darwin: *Darwin's Dangerous Idea: Evolution and the Meanings of Life. Phil Books*, 38(2), 81-92, Ap 97.

**Dent, Nicholas**. "An Integral Part of his Species...?" in *Jean-Jacques Rousseau and the Sources of the Self,* O'Hagan, Timothy (ed), 25-36. Brookfield, Avebury, 1997.

**Denton, Kathy** and Krebs, Dennis L and Wark, Gillian. The Forms and Functions of Real-Life Moral Decision-Making. *J Moral Educ*, 26(2), 131-145, Je 97.

People rarely make the types of moral judgement evoked by Kohlberg's test when they make moral decisions in their everyday lives. The anticipated consequences of real-life moral decisions, to self and to others, may influence moral choices and the structure of moral reasoning. To understand real-life moral judgement we must attend to its functions, which, although they occasionally involve resolving hypothetical moral dilemmas like those on Kohlberg's test, more often involve promoting good social relations, upholding favourable self-concepts and justifying self-interested behaviour. We argue that a functional model of moral judgement and moral behaviour derived from evolutionary theory may supply a better account of real-life morality than the Kohlbergian model.

**Denyer, Nicholas**. "Is Anything Absolutely Wrong?" in *Human Lives: Critical Essays on Consequentialist Bioethics,* Oderberg, David S (ed), 39-57. New York, Macmillan, 1997.

This paper defends absolutism, a view of morality that was once conventional wisdom. The central idea is that certain descriptions are such that any act satisfying any of those descriptions is for that reason wrong, whatever other descriptions it may also satisfy. Some of absolutism's essential features are defended: the causing/allowing to happen distinction; the intention/foresight distinction; and agent-relativity. Direct criticism of consequentialism as a rival to absolutism is then offered, followed by four arguments for the latter.

**Depp, Dane**. Rorty, Ironist Theory, and Socio-Political Control. *Phil Cont World*, 2(1), 1-5, Spr 95.

In *Contingency, Irony, and Solidarity*, Richard Rorty courageously takes a stand against the public dissemination of ironism philosophical theory, such as that produced by Nietzsche, because he sees it as being socially undermining and irreconcilable in theoretical terms with liberal democratic values. And yet, the intellectuals in his ideal society would, privately, share many of the same views from which Rorty would desire that the general public be protected. Thus Rorty would appear to trade tensions between the individual and the state for tensions between the intellectual and the nonintellectual—a dubious improvement. By redescribing both the motives of the typical ironist theorist and his basic view of large-scale, socio-political structure I will try to reinstate the social value of ironist theory. Throughout the paper I will formulate perspectives and raise questions illustrative of such theory and aimed at trying to maintain as full and open a communication as possible between the individual, whether intellectual or not and the socio-political structures within which he finds himself.

**Deppe, Frank** and Bieling, Hans-Jürgen. Gramscianismus in der Internationalen Politischen Ökonomie. *Das Argument*, 217(5-6), 729-740, 1996.

Since the early eighties, several authors have tried to use Gramsci's political theory, especially the concept of hegemony, to analyze the current upheavals of global capitalism. For them, the alliance of transnational capital and liberal economic politics is based on changed structures of accumulation, not least on neoliberalism's ability to organize social potentials for consensus. But it is unclear whether neoliberal hegemony is the expression of a new transnational "historic bloc" or whether its character is to be understood, less comprehensively, as a political project.

**Depraz, Natalie**. Le statut phénoménologique du monde dans la gnose: du dualisme à la non-dualité. *Laval Theol Phil*, 52(3), 625-647, O 96.

How can one rediscover the philosophical rigour of gnosis? On the basis of an inquiry centered on internal differentiations within historical Gnosticism and especially into the polarisation Marcion/Valentine, we try in this article to detect the many influences of Gnosticism on German and French phenomenologies. The question at stake here is: how can a well-conceived, that is to say nondual, gnosis satisfy the strictest phenomenological perspective.

**Depré, Olivier**. De la liberté absolue: A propos de la théorie cartésienne de la création des vérités éternelles. *Rev Phil Louvain*, 94(2), 216-242, My 96.

The Cartesian theory according to which the eternal truths are created is currently attracting considerable interest in the scholarly literature. The present article contributes to this discussion by pursuing a fourfold goal. Firstly, it comments upon the passages in which the doctrine occurs in the Cartesian corpus. Secondly, it examines the doctrine's originality by confronting it with some earlier metaphysical systems in which it may possibly have been prefigured. In the third place, the doctrine is analysed in the light of the critiques to which it has been subjected by Leibniz and Spinoza. Finally, the article considers the present-day interest of Descartes's theory, and this by looking at the implicit critique which one finds in the work of the contemporary philosopher H. Jonas.

**Deretic, Irina**. The Historicity of Philosophy: Hegel and Gadamer (in Serbo-Croatian). *Theoria (Yugoslavia)*, 38(3), 31-45, S 95.

It is in emphasizing the historical dimension of philosophy as essential, that history of philosophy is more philosophical and in a philosophical sense more original than in any other aspect. Gadamer productively adopts Hegel's crucial accounts of the historicity of spirit and philosophy, only to completely depart from him in the end, by radicalizing these accounts. Namely, criticizing the concept of absolute knowledge as an unhistoric substratum of Hegel's philosophy, by which philosophy is closed in the face of its future, Gadamer's hermeneutics implies the openness of philosophical and every other understanding to new future experiences.

**Deretic, Milena**. Défense de la philosophie selon Pierre Abélard (in Serbo-Croatian). *Theoria (Yugoslavia)*, 38(4), 23-27, D 95.

L'auteur se propose de présenter quelques idées recélées dans un écrit bref d'Abélard sur "Invectiva in quemdam ignarum dialectices, qui tamen ejus studium reprehendebat, et omnia ejus dogmata putabat sophismata et deceptiones". Il se trouve que le dessein de philosophie y était de faire ressortir les faiblesses et les causes de la réflexion non-critique, ainsi que d'indiquer les défauts de l'habitude mentale de suivre de près les autorités. En outre, Abélard s'applique de délimiter nettement l'une de l'autre la sophistique et la dialectique. Son dessein pleinement réalisé, cet écrit devient une défense remarquable de la dialectique, voire de la logique et de la philosophie en général. Grâce à la manière dont elle est effectuée, l'apologie de la philosophie selon Abélard ne cesse pas d'être actuelle jusqu'aujourd'hui.

**Deretic, Milena**. Quelques Réflexions sur la Philosophie de Leibniz (in Serbo-Croatian). *Theoria (Yugoslavia)*, 38(3), 79-90, S 95.

Dans une lettre envoyée en 1686 à Landgrave Ernest de Hesse-Rheinfels, accompangnée d'une version abrégée de son *Discourse de métaphysique*, Leibniz s'est attaché d'expliquer à celui-ci quel avantage pourrait-on tirer de la philosophie. A partir de cette lettre ainsi que des questions qui y sont posées, l'auteur de cet article a essayé de réexaminer quelques concepts fondamentaux de la monadologie de Leibniz, se proposant de donner une reponse possible à la question: à quoi bon la métaphysique?, et notamment: à quoi celle-ci peut-elle servir aujourd'hui? La solution en est trouvée dans le pouvoir des connaissances métaphysiques qui éclairent notre esprit, et qui aquiérent par là une certaine puissance rassurante et consolante: c'est ainsi que ces connaissances peuvent, d'une certaine manière, contribuer au bonheur humain.

**Derish, Pamela** and Eastwood, Susan and Leash, Evangeline (& others). Ethical Issues in Biomedical Research: Perceptions and Practices of Postdoctoral Research Fellows Responding to a Survey. *Sci Eng Ethics*, 2(1), 89-114, J 96.

We surveyed 1005 postdoctoral fellows by questionnaire about ethical matters related to biomedical research and publishing; 33% responded. About 18% of respondents said they had taken a course in research ethics and about 31% said they had had a course that devoted some time to research ethics. A substantial majority stated willingness to grant other investigators, except competitors, access to their data before publication and to share research materials. Respondents' opinions about contributions justifying authorship of research papers were mainly consistent but at variance with those of many biomedical journal editors. (edited)

**Derksen, A A**. Thomas S. Kuhn, een moderne komedie van vergissingen. *Alg Ned Tijdschr Wijs*, 89(3), 205-229, Jl 97.

The author distinguishes between the 'real' Kuhn and a much more extreme creature, the pseudo-Kuhn. He observes that Kuhn was rejected by philosophers in the 70s because of their misconception of his views (for which Kuhn's rhetoric was to some extent responsible) and that the praise he received from social scientists was mainly based on the same misconception. Kuhn's problem was that his naturalism was so new that it was difficult to understand in the 60s and that, when the pseudo-Kuhn had been removed from the scene in the 80s and 90s, his naturalism was so familiar that it was hard to see what was new about it.

**DeRose, Keith**. Knowledge, Assertion and Lotteries. *Austl J Phil*, 74(4), 568-579, D 96.

**Derrida, Jacques**. "Nel nome di Europa" in *Geofilosofia,* Bonesio, Luisa (ed), 165-175. Sondrio, Lyasis, 1996.

**Derrida, Jacques**. "Remarks on Deconstruction and Pragmatism" in *Deconstruction and Pragmatism,* Mouffe, Chantal (ed), 77-88. New York, Routledge, 1996.

**Derrida, Jacques**. Adieu. *Phil Today*, 40(3), 334-340, Fall 96.

**Derrida, Jacques** and Kamuf, Peggy (trans). History of the Lie: Prolegomena. *Grad Fac Phil J*, 19/20(2/1), 129-161, 1997.

**Derse, Arthur R** and Reitemeier, Paul J and Spike, Jeffrey. Retiring the Pacemaker. *Hastings Center Rep*, 27(1), 24-26, Ja-F 97.

**Des Jarlais, Don D** and Gaist, Paul A and Friedman, Samuel R. Ethical Issues in Research on Preventing HIV Infection among Injecting Drug Users. *Sci Eng Ethics*, 1(2), 133-144, A 95.

The ethical issues in conducting research on preventing HIV infection are among the most complex of any area of human subjects research. This article is an update of a 1987 article that addressed potential conflicts between research design and ethics with respect to AIDS prevention among injecting drug users. The present article reviews current ethical issues that arise in the design and conduct of HIV/AIDS prevention research focused on injecting drug users.

**Desai, Ashay B** and Rittenburg, Terri. Global Ethics: An Integrative Framework for MNEs. *J Bus Ethics*, 16(8), 791-800, Je 97.

Global ethics has recently emerged as a popular concept among researchers in the field of international management and is of immediate concern among managers of multinational enterprises (MNEs). This paper presents an integrative framework covering a range of factors and issues relevant to multinationals with respect to ethical decision making. The paper provides an overview of the existing literature on the topic, and framework is aimed at providing the managers of multinationals with a basis for relating and synthesizing the perspectives and prescriptions that are available for incorporating ethics into the strategic decision-making process.

**Descartes, René** and Benes, Jiri (trans). Passions of the Soul (in Czech). *Filosof Cas*, 44(5), 713-716, 1996.

**Descartes, René** and Cottingham, John. *Meditations on First Philosophy: With Selections from the Objections and Replies*. New York, Cambridge Univ Pr, 1996.

The *Mediations*, one of the key texts of Western philosophy, is the most widely studied of all Descartes's writings. This authoritative translation by John Cottingham, taken from the much-acclaimed three-volume Cambridge edition of the *Philosophical Writings of Descartes*, is based upon the best available texts and presents Descartes's central metaphysical writings in clear, readable modern English. As well as the complete text of the *Mediations*, the reader will find a thematic abridgement of the *Objections and Replies* (which were originally published with the *Mediations*) containing Descartes's replies to his critics. These extracts, specially selected for the present volume, indicate the main philosophical difficulties which occurred to Descartes's contemporaries and show how Descartes developed and clarified his arguments in response. (publisher,edited)

**Descartes, René** and Horák, Petr (trans). Letters to Elizabeth of Palatinate: (P. Horák: Commentary) (in Czech). *Filosof Cas*, 44(5), 717-730, 1996.

The A. has translated for the first time in to the Czech language four letters by René Descartes to Elisabeth of Palatinate dated by October 6th, 1645, November 3rd 1645, May 1646 and May 1648. The A. has chosen these four letters to illustrate the René Descartes's interest for the moral problems treated by him in his book *Les Passions de l'Ame* (1649).

**Descola, Philippe** (ed) and Pálsson, Gísli (ed). *Nature and Society: Anthropological Perspectives*. New York, Routledge, 1996.

*Nature and Society* looks critically at the nature/society dichotomy and its place in human ecology and social theory. Rethinking the dualism means rethinking ecological anthropology and its notion of the relation between person and environment. *Nature and Society* focuses on the issue of the environment and its relations to humans. By inviting concern for sustainability, ethics, indigenous knowledge, animal rights and social context of science, this book will appeal to students of anthropology, human ecology and sociology. (publisher,edited)

**Descombes, Vincent** and Cosman, Carol (trans) and Bouveresse, Jacques. *Wittgenstein Reads Freud: The Myth of the Unconscious*. Princeton, Princeton Univ Pr, 1995.

Wittgenstein, who himself had delivered a devastating critique of traditional philosophy, sympathetically pondered Freud's claim to have produced a scientific theory in proposing a new model of the human psyche. What Wittgenstein recognized—and what Bouveresse so eloquently stresses for today's reader—is that psychoanalysis does not aim to produce a change limited to the intellect but rather seeks to provoke an authentic change of human attitudes. (publisher, edited)

**Deshpande, Satish P**. Managers' Perception of Proper Ethical Conduct: The Effect of Sex, Age, and Level and Education. *J Bus Ethics*, 16(1), 79-85, Ja 97.

This study examined the impact of sex, age and level of education on the perception of various business practices by managers of a large nonprofit organization. Female managers perceived the acceptance of gifts and favors in exchange for preferential treatment significantly more unethical than male managers. Older managers (40 plus) perceived five practices significantly more unethical than younger managers (giving gifts/favors in exchange for preferential treatment, divulging confidential information, concealing ones error, falsifying reports and calling in sick to take a day off). The practice of padding expense account by over 10% was reported to be significantly more unethical by managers with a graduate degree.

**Deshpande, Satish P** and Viswesvaran, Chockalingam. Ethics, Success, and Job Satisfaction: A Test of Dissonance Theory in India. *J Bus Ethics*, 15(10), 1065-1069, O 96.

A survey of middle level managers in India showed that when respondents perceived that successful managers in their organization behaved unethically their levels of job satisfaction were reduced. Reduction in satisfaction with the facet of supervision was the most pronounced (than with pay or promotion or coworker or work). Results are interpreted within the framework of cognitive dissonance theory. Implications for ethics training programs (behavioral and cognitive) as well as international management are discussed. (edited)

**Desjardins, Richard** and Louis, Desmeules. A propos de l'Éducation et de l'Institution scolaire au Québec. *Philosopher*, 18, 25-36, 1995.

Cet article vise à établir cette distinction, à poser des questions et, ultimement à énoncer des thèses sur l'éducation et l'institution scolaire au Québec. Il s'agit de cerner l'importance des forces économiques qui travaillent le pouvoir de l'État, nous devons aussi reconnaître que l'exercice du pouvoir de l'État s'articule sur d'autres rapports de forces de grande importance, principalement de nature idéologique. Nous croyons que l'institution scolaire, tout comme l'institution des services de santé, subit actuellement les contrecoups d'une réorganisation des économies occidentales capitalistes que les réformes actuelles servent tout à la fois à occulter et à justifier.

**Desmond, William**. "Rethinking the Origin: Nietzsche and Hegel" in *Hegel, History, and Interpretation,* Gallagher, Shaun, 71-94. Albany, SUNY Pr, 1997.

This explores of Hegel's and Nietzsche's sense of origin: one dialectical, the other Dionysian. It examines the metaphysical presuppositions in their concerns with art. Both senses of origin as characterized as erotic origins: in its self-becoming the origin seeks itself, even when it seems to seek what is other. This is criticized in terms of an agapeic sense of origin where a genuine arising of the other as other is made possible. Despite differences, there is a significant proximity of Nietzsche and Hegel. The instability, indeed, incoherence of Nietzsche's monism or will to power is explored—monism despite the fact that will to power is described in terms of difference rather than identity.

**Despot, Blanko**. The Philosophy of Religion in the System of Freedom. *Filozof Istraz*, 16(3), 667-682, 1996.

Philosophie der Religion setzt nicht die Gegebenheit der Religion voraus, sondern begreift die Möglichkeit und die Notwendigkeit des Steins der Religion (Religiosität) als eine Weise des Seins der Freiheit. Die Notwendigkeit der Religiosität liegt in der Freiheit, welche durch das geistige Mensch-Gott-Verhältnis sich selbst in das Reich des Höchsten, des Heiligen und des Besten schlechthin (*to ariston*) erhebt. Dieser Notwendigkeit entspricht die Notwendigkeit der Religionsphilosophie im System der sich durch alle Möglichkeit des Seins im Ganzen in ihrer Wahrheit realisierenden Freiheit. Die Logik als Wissenschaft der Wahrheit (der Freiheit) ist die Formalität und die Transzendentalität des Logischen überwindend-aufhebende spekulative Logik. Im System der Freiheit ist die Philosophie der Religion die "letzte philosophische Wissenschaft", d.h. die Philosophie der Natur, des endlichen und des unmittelbar absoluten Geistes voraussetzende und die Philosophie der Philosophie ermöglichende "Philosophie".

**Despot, Blazenka**. "Die Aggressivität der europaäischen Freiheitsphilosophie, expliziert an Hegels Rechtsphilosophie" in *Kreativer Friede durch Begegnung der Weltkulturen,* Beck, Heinrich (ed), 179-190. New York, Lang, 1995.

**Dessì, Paola** and Sassoli, Bernardo and Sklar, Lawrence. Discutono *Il caso domato,* di Ian Hacking. *Iride*, 8(15), 483-494, Ag 95.

Il libro di I. Hacking ricostruisce nei tratti essenziali il clima intellettuale che nell'Ottocento veda la crisi del "determinismo" e la "rivoluzione probabilistica" e quindi permette l'affermazione di un nuovo "stile di ragionamento" che solleva il "caso" da "superstizione popolare" a evento assoggettabile a legge. P. Dessì discute l'idea dell'Autore che la pratica abbia anticipato la rivoluzione teorica; B. Sassoli si sofferma sull'epistemologia di Hacking e la sua nozione di "stile di ragionamento"; L. Sklar sottolinea il carattere illuminante che possiede la scoperta delle premesse sociali dell'idea di "legge statistica" indispensabile nella ricerca scientifica contemporanea.

**Detar, Richard**. Interview with Herman J. Saatkamp, Jr.. *Kinesis*, 23(1), 26-39, Sum 96.

**DeTar, Richard** and Keith, Heather. Interview with Martha Nussbaum. *Kinesis*, 23(2), 3-15, Fall 96.

This work is one in a series of interviews with philosophers published by *Kinesis*. It is an attempt to detail Martha Nussbaum's views concerning her own work, interpretations of her work, her continuing philosophical interests and goals, and her evaluation of various schools of social and political thought. It also includes autobiographical statements regarding Nussbaum's involvement in philosophy.

**Detel, Wolfgang**. Foucault on Power and the Will to Knowledge. *Euro J Phil*, 4(3), 296-327, D 96.

The two main objectives of the article are, first, to reconstruct, as precisely as possible, the intrinsic relation between power and knowledge, and, second, to work out the definitely positive notion of a nonrepressive power, both of which Foucault envisages in *History of Sexuality* vol. I. The article argues that it is exactly the notion of a nonrepressive power (labeled "regulative power") that can show how knowledge and power are related in the closest possible way. The discussion proceeds on the assumption, first, that Foucault is not a political or social philosopher, but rather a historian of epistemology; second, that his notions of power and discourse can be defined in a nominalistic way; and third, that his alleged neutrality and relativism can be downplayed without weakening the theoretical strength of his analytics of power and his discourse analysis.

**Dethier, Hubert**. "Georg Wilhelm Friedrich Hegel and the East" in *East and West in Aesthetics*, Marchianò, Grazia (ed), 169-195. Pisa, Istituti Editoriali, 1997.

**Deutsch, Eliot**. *Essays on the Nature of Art*. Albany, SUNY Pr, 1996.

In this newest book, the author presents a theory of art which is at once universal in its general conception and historically grounded in its attention to aesthetic practices in diverse cultures. The author argues that especially today art not only enjoys a special kind of autonomy but also has important social and political responsibilities. Deutsch posits that an artwork has as its intentionality the striving to be aesthetically forceful, meaningful, and beautiful, with each of these dimensions culturally situated. Working from traditional imitation and expression theories, he argues that the manner of an artwork's coming into being and one's experience of it constitute an integral whole. (publisher,edited)

**Deutscher, Penelope**. Irigaray Anxiety: Luce Irigaray and Her Ethics for Improper Selves. *Rad Phil*, 80, 6-16, N-D 96.

Irigaray's recent work, such as *I Love To You* (1996), has been criticized as a simplified devolution from earlier work such as *Speculum* (1985). This paper asks to what extent the ethical and political perspective of the later work is present in the earlier work? Irigaray's ethical ideals are nonappropriation and mediation between subjects are interpreted in these three contexts: first, her earlier evocations of undividedness between subjects; second, her own theorization of interconnectedness between sexed subjects; and third, a comparison between cannibal metaphors deployed by Irigaray and Derrida to evoke the inevitability and the impossibility of appropriating the other.

**Devall, Bill**. Earthday 25: A Retrospective of Reform Environmental Movements. *Phil Cont World*, 2(4), 9-15, Wint 95.

Industrial growth and environmental protection have been in perpetual conflict. Reform environmental movements have attempted to address some of the worst abuses of nature by demanding government intervention to restrain pollution. Also, these reform movements have cooperated with corporate elites to obtain some controls on pollution. The 104th Congress attempted to destroy even weak pollution controls. New efforts to mobilize resistance are occurring. The deep, long-range ecology movement inspires resistance by affirming the joy of human participation in nature.

**Dever, Josh** and Neale, Stephen. Slingshots and Boomerangs. *Mind*, 106(421), 144-168, Ja 97.

**Devereux, Daniel T** (ed) and Mitsis, Phillip T (ed). *Encyclopedia of Classical Philosophy*. Westport, Greenwood Pr, 1997.

*The Encyclopedia of Classical Philosophy* is a reference work in the philosophy of Greek and Roman antiquity. As such, its subject matter comprises subjects and figures from the dawn of philosophy in Ionia (on the west coast of modern Turkey) in the sixth century B.C.E. to the decline of the Academy of Athens in the sixth century C.E. (publisher, edited)

**Devi, S Sreekala** and Narayanadas, V C. Dostoyevsky and the Problem of God. *Darshana Int*, 36(2/142), 57-63, Ap 96.

**DeVidi, David** and Solomon, Graham. "Box" in Intuitionistic Modal Logic. *Austl J Phil*, 75(2), 201-213, Je 97.

The box and diamond operators of classical modal logic are interdefinable, but the addition of interdefinable box and diamond to intuitionistic logic leads to intuitionistically implausible theorems, at least when intuitionistic logic and the modal operators are given their usual interpretations. The article discusses interpretations of intuitionistic logic and the modal operators on which the theorems in question are no longer implausible. In particular, the article includes a sketch of an interpretation in which intuitionistic logic is a logic of concepts suited to accounting for borderline cases, and the box operator is taken to be a "precisifier." Applied to a given concept, the box operator yields a concept for which all borderline cases between it and its opposite are resolved.

**Devinatz, Victor G**. Instead of Leaders They Have Become Bankers of Men: Gramsci's Alternative to the U.S. Neoinstitutionalists' Theory of Trade-Union Bureaucratization. *Nature Soc Thought*, 8(4), 381-404, 1995.

This article will compare and contrast the U.S. neoinstitutionalists' theory of trade union bureaucratization with Gramsci's theory, the former theory being implicitly accepted by the mainstream of U.S. industrial relations scholars. The neoinstitutionalist industrial relations scholars have constructed a highly deterministic, unidirectional and linear theory which emphasizes the importance of the internal processes occurring within the union leading to bureaucratization. As an alternative, Gramsci's theory stresses that trade union bureaucratization is the result of a multiplicity of factors which are both internal and external to the union and that bureaucratization arises as a result of the contradictions of capitalist society which pull the unions in a number of conflicting directions. After providing empirical evidence for Gramsci's theory, the implications of the two theories for guiding trade union movement activity in the 1990s are discusses.

**DeVito, Scott**. Completeness and Indeterministic Causation. *Proc Phil Sci Ass*, 3(Suppl), S177-S184, 1996.

In *The Chances of Explanation*, Paul Humphreys presents a metaphysical analysis of causation. In this paper, I argue that this analysis is flawed. Humphreys's model of causality incorporates three completeness requirements. I show that these completeness requirements, when applied in the world, force us to take causally irrelevant factors to be causally relevant. On this basis, I argue that Humphreys's analysis should be rejected.

**Devitt, Michael**. Meanings and Psychology: A Response to Mark Richard. *Nous*, 31(1), 115-131, Mr 97.

In "What Does Commonsense Psychology Tell Us about Meaning," Mark Richard makes four critical points against my views in *Coming to Our Senses*. These criticisms are aimed both at the book's view of the attitude ascriptions and at its "representationalist" view of the meanings ascribed. In response, this paper argues that, with one exception, the criticisms clearly fail. The exception is Richard's defense of "contextualism" (or "the hidden-indexical theory"): the view that attitude ascriptions are radically context-dependent. Even there the paper inclines to the view that the phenomena are best explained pragmatically, in a Gricean way, rather than semantically.

**Devlin, Kai**. Rights, Necessity, and Tort Liability. *J Soc Phil*, 28(2), 87-100, Fall 97.

**Dewan, Lawrence**. Antimodern, Ultramodern, Postmodern: A Plea for the Perennial. *Maritain Stud*, 9, 7-27, 1993.

**Dewan, Lawrence**. History of Philosophy, Personal or Impersonal? Reflections on Etienne Gilson. *Maritain Stud*, 11, 7-31, 1995.

**Dewan, Lawrence**. Man: The Perennial Metaphysician. *Maritain Stud*, 10, 11-33, 1994.

**Dewan, Lawrence**. Natural Law and the First Act of Freedom: Maritain Revisited. *Maritain Stud*, 12, 3-32, 1996.

Thomas Aquinas regularly envisages the young human mind as capable of knowing God in a conscious way and of considering God as a source of law. Cajetan seems less confident that God will be known, preferring to limit the youth to a knowledge of the unqualified good. Maritain thought that it was right to bring God in, but in an implicit way which would be explained in and through the act of the will attaining to love of the unqualified good. I see no reason to disagree with Thomas.

**Dewan, Lawrence**. St. Thomas and Pre-Conceptual Intellection. *Maritain Stud*, 11, 220-233, 1995.

**Dewan, Lawrence**. St. Thomas, Lying and Venial Sin. *Thomist*, 61(2), 279-299, Ap 97.

Kant held that lying even about contingent truths to save a life was gravely wrong. This view affects modern discussions. I recall that for Augustine and Thomas it was a venial sin. I explain what this means, showing that it pertains to revealed religion. I show that, philosophically, Thomas would say that such acts have no moral importance and that the morally important dimension of the situation is the will to save the life.

**Dewan, Lawrence**. What is Metaphysics?. *Maritain Stud*, 9, 145-160, 1993.

**Dewe, Philip** and Marshall, Bev. An Investigation of the Components of Moral Intensity. *J Bus Ethics*, 16(5), 521-530, Ap 97.

While there is a considerable interest in the topic of business ethics, much of the research moves towards measuring components with a view to predicting ethical behavior. To date there has not been a satisfactory definition of business ethics, nor has there been any real attempt to understand the components of a situation that may influence an individual's assessment of that situation as ethical or otherwise. Using Jones's (1991) construct of moral intensity as a basis for investigation, this paper presents some exploratory analysis on the context within which ethical decisions are assessed. The findings reveal that individuals differ in their assessments of the same situation and often use a number of complex reasons to explain whether a situation poses an ethical problem for them. These findings are discussed within a framework of measurement issues and future directions for research.

**Dhillon, Pradeep A**. "Of Fractious Traditions and Family Resemblances in Philosophy of Education" in *Philosophy of Education (1996)*, Margonis, Frank (ed), 142-150. Urbana, Phil Education Soc, 1997.

**Di Caro, Alessandro**. *Oltre Wittgenstein*. Ancona, Transeuropa, 1996.

This book describes the logical itinerary of Ludwig Wittgenstein. It searches to explain the hardest points of *Tractatus* Logico-philosophicus. Wittgenstein's text in fact deals with the philosophy of the logic and deeply criticizes Whitehead, Russell and Frege. This criticism, nevertheless, has not been considered afterwards except by Ramsey. Book besides explains the meaning of language as image, Wittgenstein's heritage in Popper, the meaning of the words "all" and "some", the interpretation of colours. Besides, it explains Wittgenstein's point of view on mathematics and Cantor's problem of continuous.

**Di Cesare, Donatella**. Jaspers, Heidegger et le Langage. *Arch Phil*, 59(3), 381-401, Jl-S 96.

When one seeks to compare Jaspers and Heidegger, the topic of language provides a promising itinerary for exploring the differences between the two philosophers. In fact, one should not neglect the theoretical import that this subject holds for both, although with different emphases. In spite of the common ground they share—both reject analytic philosophy—, Jaspers develops his personal conception of language along a different track than that of Heidegger, an opposition that is sometimes implicit, when it appears for the first time in the essay, "Die Sprache" ("Language") in Von der Wahrheit (On Truth) and sometimes explicit, as one finds in his Philosophische Autobiographie (Philosophical Autobiography), his Notizen zu Martin Heidegger (Notes on Martin Heidegger) and in the recently published Briefwechsel (Heidegger-Jaspers Correspondence).

**Di Costanzo, Giuseppe**. "Su alcuni elementi del confronto di Otto Hintze con l'*Historismus*" in *Lo Storicismo e la Sua Storia: Temi, Problemi, Prospettive,* Cacciatore, Giuseppe (ed), 373-386. Milano, Guerini, 1997.

**Di Giovanni, George**. The Early Fichte as Disciple of Jacobi. *Fichte-Studien*, 9, 257-273, 1997.

The early Jacobi-Fichte relationship is a complex one. Fichte had good reasons to believe that his idealism responded to the demands of Jacobi's personalism. Jacobi, for his part, also had good reasons to believe that the faith Fichte claimed his idealism required had nothing to do with his own religious faith. Both were, however, disingenuous: Fichte, because he should have known that 'common experience' was for him a normative concept; Jacobi, because he had a philosophical theory regarding experience which he could not however press because of consequences he found unacceptable. Ultimately, what the two philosophers had in common was their mistrust of the senses.

**Di Giuseppe, G** and De Martini, F and Boschi, D. Test of the Violation of Local Realism in Quantum Mechanics with No Use of Bell's Inequalities. *Erkenntnis*, 45(2 & 3), 367-377, Nov 96.

A novel and versatile polarization-entanglement scheme is adopted to investigate the violation of the EPR local realism for a nonmaximally entangled two-photon system according to the recent "nonlocality proof" by Lucien Hardy. In this context the adoption of a sophisticated detection method allows direct determination of any "element of physical reality" . (viz, determined "*with probability equal to unity*" in the words of Einstein, Podolsky and Rosen) for the pair system within complete measurements that are largely *insensitive* to the detector quantum-efficiencies and noise.

**Di Marco, Giuseppe Antonio**. "L'indagine storico-universale di Max Weber sul 'razionalismo occidentale' tra lo storicismo e Nietzsche" in *Lo Storicismo e la Sua Storia: Temi, Problemi, Prospettive,* Cacciatore, Giuseppe (ed), 343-354. Milano, Guerini, 1997.

**Di Meola, Nestore**. Martin Heidegger fra Misticismo e Nazional-socialismo. *Aquinas*, 39(3), 571-583, S-D 96.

**Di Serio, Luciana**. Epistemologia e psicologia cognitiva: alcune osservazioni sulla teoria dei modelli mentali. *Epistemologia*, 19(2), 327-346, Jl-D 96.

This work discusses some theoretical incoherences of mental models theory (mmt), a computational theory regarding mental processes. In particular, the definition of the inferential competence and the explanation of the systematic errors in reasoning are considered. In the mmt, the reasoning is not a manipulation of logical forms. It is assumed as semantic and analogical process, conditioned by contents. Nevertheless, in mmt the inferential competence corresponds really to the logical competence. So any evaluation of semantic contents' influence in reasoning fails and the cited assumption runs out. This work points out that this contradiction depends on an erroneous equality... (edited)

**Diaconis, Persi** and Holmes, Susan. Are There Still Things To Do in Bayesian Statistics?. *Erkenntnis*, 45(2 & 3), 145-158, Nov 96.

From the outside, Bayesian statistics may seem like a closed little corner of probability. Once a prior is specified you compute! From the inside the field is filled with problems, conceptual and otherwise. This paper surveys some of what remains to be done and gives examples of the work in progress via a Bayesian peek into Feller Volume I.

**Diallo, Massaër**. "Éléments démocratiques dans les sagesses du Sénégal" in *Philosophy and Democracy in Intercultural Perspective,* Kimmerle, Heinz (ed), 185-195. Amsterdam, Rodopi, 1997.

**Diallo, Saliou**. "La démocratie et les tâches bio-éthiques de l'état" in *Philosophy and Democracy in Intercultural Perspective,* Kimmerle, Heinz (ed), 225-233. Amsterdam, Rodopi, 1997.

**Diamond, Cora**. "Consequentialism in Modern Moral Philosophy and in 'Modern Moral'" in *Human Lives: Critical Essays on Consequentialist Bioethics,* Oderberg, David S (ed), 13-38. New York, Macmillan, 1997.

This paper addresses a major misunderstanding of what consequentialism is, which has given rise to serious misinterpretations of Mill, Ross and Prichard. In order to understand consequentialism, as described by Anscombe in her famous paper, it is necessary to see that even intrinsically wrong (e.g., unjust) acts can be treated as consequences. Ignoring this has meant that Anscombe's original discussion has been bypassed and that moral theorists have failed to see that the English moral philosophers from Sidgwick on do not differ significantly, but all share the consequentialist outlook. A nonconsequentialist interpretation of Mill is sketched and discussed.

**Diamond, Cora**. "Wittgenstein, Mathematics, and Ethics: Resisting the Attractions of Realism" in *The Cambridge Companion to Wittgenstein,* Sluga, Hans (ed), 226-260. Needham Heights, Cambridge, 1996.

**Diamond, Cora**. Realism and Resolution: Reply to Warren Goldfarb and Sabina Lovibond. *J Phil Res*, 22, 75-86, Ap 97.

**Dias, José Ribeiro**. Filosofia da Educaçao na Experiência Educativa Inter-Cultural de D. Frei Caetano Brandao em Terras de Belém do Pará 1782-1789. *Rev Port Filosof*, 52(1-4), 281-297, Ja-D 96.

**Dias, Maria Clara**. De la ética del discurso a la moral del respeto universal: una investigación filosófica acerca de la fundamentación de los derechos humanos. *Ideas Valores*, 42-54, Ag 96.

This article discusses the foundations of human rights and specifically of basic social rights. The first part contains an analysis of Habermas's conception of

basic rights. In *discourse ethic*, basic rights are the conditions which must be fulfilled in order to participate in a discourse on the foundations of legal rights. Basic social rights, on the other hand, express the conditions for the implementation of basic rights. The second part provides an argument for the recognition of basic social rights, inspired on Tugendhat's (1994) *Morals of Universal Respect*, in which basic social rights are a condition for membership in a moral community.

**Dias, Maria Clara**. The Concept of Person (in Spanish). *Discurso*, 27, 181-199, 1996.

My aim in this paper is to explain and qualify the concept of person. To this purpose, I'll consider first of all Strawson's presentation of it as a solution for the traditional body/mind problem. In so far as Strawson's characterization of a person prove to be incomplete, I'll then pursue Frankfurt's suggestion in giving consideration to the "free-will" concept as the decisive criterion of person identification. Agreeing with Frankfurt that only entities to which we ascribe freedom can be describe as persons, it will be my intent nonetheless to show that the crucial aspect that distinguishes personal from nonpersonal entities is, not Frankfurt's concept of free-will, but our understanding of freedom as self-determination.

**Díaz, Jorge Aurelio**. "And so I Err and Sin": Considerations on Error in Descartes (Spanish). *Rev Filosof (Venezuela)*, Supp(2-3), 103-114, 1996.

This paper analyzes the problem of error in the *Fourth Meditation* of Descartes and its incidence on sin. Error is studied in its epistemological, ethical and theological aspects. The author throws light on the subject based on the observations made by Gueroult in relation to Descartes and Spinoza.

**Díaz, Jorge Aurelio**. "Conocimiento y libertad" in *Memorias Del Seminario En Conmemoración De Los 400 Anos Del Nacimiento De René Descartes,* Albis, Víctor S (ed), 41-50. Sankt Augustin, Academia, 1997.

**Díaz, Jorge Aurelio**. Una Crítica "Romántica" al Romanticismo. *Ideas Valores*, 29-36, Ag 97.

**Díaz, José-Luis**. A Patterned Process Approach To Brain, Consciousness, and Behavior. *Phil Psych*, 10(2), 179-195, Je 97.

The architecture of brain, consciousness and behavioral processes is shown to be formally similar in that all three may be conceived and depicted as Petri net patterned processes structured by a series of elements occuring or becoming active in stochastic succession, in parallel, with different rhythms of temporal iteration and with a distinct qualitative manifestation in the spatio-temporal domain. A patterned process theory is derived from the isomorphic features of the models and contrasted with connectionist, dynamic system notions. This empirically derived formulation is considered to be optimally compatible with the dual aspect theory in that the foundation of the diverse aspects would be a highly structured and dynamic process, the psychophysical neutral "ground" of mind and matter posed by dual aspect and neutral monist theories. (edited)

**Díaz Caballero, José Ricardo**. Notas sobre el origen del hombre y la técnica. *G Motaf*, 18(3), 339-340, S-D 96.

**Díaz-Urmeneta Muñoz, Juan Bosco**. Voces mezcladas: Una reflexión sobre tradición y modernidad. *Cuad Vico*, 7/8, 299-322, 1997.

The opposition between two groups of values, as the geopolitical map shows, suggests the limits of both the old imperialism and its opponents: the new nations are so reluctant to the autochtonous administration as to the colonial one that they reclaim managing forms according to their own culture. This fact seems to open the question of tradition, which from the Western point of view requires a critical reflection on the diversity of values and languages. Modernism being challenged, the author follows the example of Geertz as regards those non-Western minorities who adhere the modern values of critical rationality and autonomous ethics. We should listen to the "mixed voices" of traditions and remain on the babel ground, which is unsteady but real, of enlightenment values. The article, which develops some ideas of I. Berlin, attempts an approach to tradition making an analysis of the crucial strategies of De Maistre and Burke.

**DiBattista, Ron A** and Luthar, Harsh K and Gautschi, Theodore. Perception of What the Ethical Climate Is and What It Should Be: The Role of Gender, Academic Status, and Ethical Education. *J Bus Ethics*, 16(2), 205-217, F 97.

This study examined ethical attitudes and perceptions of 691 undergraduate seniors and freshmen in a college of business. Gender was found to be correlated to perceptions of "what the ethical climate should be" with female subjects showing significantly more favorable attitude towards ethical behaviors than males. Further, seniors had a more cynical view of the current ethical climate than freshmen. Freshmen were significantly more likely than seniors to believe that good business ethics is positively related to successful business outcomes. Ethical education was significantly correlated to both perceptions of "current ethical climate" as well as "what the ethical climate should be". Students who had been exposed to ethical issues in a course were more likely to believe both, that ethical behavior is, and should be, positively associated with successful business outcomes.

**Dickie, George T**. Art: Function or Procedure—Nature or Culture?. *J Aes Art Crit*, 55(1), 19-28, Wint 97.

**Dickie, George T**. Reply to Noël Carroll. *J Aes Art Crit*, 55(3), 311-312, Sum 97.

**Dickson, Michael**. Antidote or Theory?. *Stud Hist Phil Mod Physics*, 27B(2), 229-238, Je 96.

Two recent books on Bohm's theory do a nice job of presenting the causal interpretation of quantum mechanics as an antidote to the Copenhagen interpretation. As advocates for, and philosophical investigation of, Bohm's theory, they are useful but nonetheless point the way to the need for a deeper investigation and understanding of Bohm's theory.

AUTHOR INDEX 599 Dillon, John M

**Dickson, Michael**. Logical Foundations for Modal Interpretations of Quantum Mechanics. *Proc Phil Sci Ass*, 3(Suppl), S322-S329, 1996.

Modal interpretations of quantum mechanics suggest an understanding of the logical structure of quantum-mechanical propositions. On this understanding, only a subalgebra of the lattice of propositions contains possibly-true propositions. The rest are necessarily false. The resulting (modal) logical is purely classical, but isomorphic to quantum logic when restricted to possibly-true propositions.

**Dickson, W Michael**. Determinism and Locality in Quantum Systems. *Synthese*, 107(1), 55-82, Ap 96.

Models of the EPR-Bohm experiment usually consider just two times, an initial time and the time of measurement. Within such analyses, it has been argued that 'locality' is equivalent to determinism, given the strict correlations of quantum mechanics. However, an analysis based on such models is only a preliminary to an analysis based on a complete dynamical model. The latter analysis is carried out and it is shown that, given certain definitions of 'locality' and 'determinism' for completely dynamical models, locality implies, but is not implied by, determinism. Further, it is suggested that a local deterministic model has not been ruled out by Bell's theorem. It is suggested that such a model could naturally deny the independence of initial complete states from the settings of the apparatuses (a crucial assumption in the derivation of Bell's inequality).

**Diéguez, Antonio** and Burrieza, Alfredo. La instrumentalización del tiempo. *Analogia*, 10(2), 113-138, 1996.

In this century we have been witnessing to the development of a functional or instrumental conception of time. According to such conception, time is a tool dependent on the proposed technical and scientific goals. Time is designed to fit the nature of problems which require it. The variety of applications in which time is involved have modified its topology one way or the other. This adaptability of the structure of time has been feasible only when science and technology have paid special attention to it.

**Diekman, Arthur J**. I = Awareness. *J Consciousness Stud*, 3(4), 350-356, 1996.

Introspection reveals that the core of subjectivity—the 'I'—is identical to awareness. This 'I' should be differentiated from the various aspects of the physical person and its mental contents which form the 'self'. Most discussions of consciousness confuse the 'I' and the 'self'. In fact, our experience is fundamentally dualistic—not the dualism of mind and matter—but that of the 'I' and that which is observed. The identity of awareness and the 'I' means that we know awareness by being it, thus solving the problem of the infinite regress of observers. It follows that whatever our ontology of awareness may be, it must also be the same for 'I'.

**Dieks, Dennis**. The Quantum Mechanical World Picture and Its Popularization. *Commun Cog*, 29(2), 153-168, 1996.

It is argued that there is no single worldview that is in accordance with quantum mechanics and is accepted by physicists. The task of formulating a consistent quantum mechanical world picture is often considered to be not a proper part of physics. Paradoxically, in daily physical practice (semiconsistent) world pictures do play an important role. It is argued that in this situation it is natural that popularizers focus on outlandish interpretations. The physics community should not reject these out of hand, without giving serious thought to consistent alternatives.

**Diettrich, Olaf**. Kann es eine ontologiefreie evolutionäre Erkenntnistheorie geben?. *Phil Natur*, 34(1), 71-105, 1997.

Most of what nowadays is called evolutionary epistemology tries to explain the phylogenetic acquisition of inborn 'knowledge' and the evolution of the mental instruments concerned—mostly in terms of adaptation to external conditions. These conditions, however, cannot be described but in terms of what is provided by the mental instruments which are said to be brought about just by these conditions themselves. So they cannot be defined in an objective and noncircular way. This problem is approached here by what is called the 'constructivist evolutionary epistemology' (CEE): In analogy to physics where observables are defined as invariants of experimental measurement operators, the CEE considers the perceived patterns and regularities from which we derive the laws of nature to be invariants of inborn cognitive (sensory) operators. (edited)

**Diettrich, Olaf**. Realität, Anpassung und Evolution. *Phil Natur*, 28(2), 147-192, 1991.

A coherent description of cognitive and organic evolution as implicitly suggested by the evolutionary epistemology (EE) requires the application of functional theories and the abandonment of structural theories such as the notion of an ontological reality imposing a teleological horizon on the development of empirical theories contrasting with the nonconvergent character of organic evolution. For this it is shown that the mental category of reality does not need to be explained by an ontological reality. The mental category of reality rather has developed phylogenetically as a tool to establish approved theories definitively. What we call the structure of reality reflects exclusively the boundary conditions arising from man's own mental and physical development. (edited)

**Díez, José A**. A Hundred Years of Numbers: An Historical Introduction to Measurement Theory 1887-1990: Part I: The Formation Period: Two Lines of Research: Axiomatics and Real Morphisms, Scales and Invariance. *Stud Hist Phil Sci*, 28(1), 167-185, Mr 97.

The aim of this paper is to reconstruct the historical evolution of the so-called Measurement Theory (MT). MT has two different periods, the *formation period* and the *mature theory*. The first, formation period corresponds to two complementary research traditions on foundations of measurement: on the one hand, Helmholtz', Campbell's and Hölder's studies on axiomatics and real morphisms; and, on the other, the work undertaken by Stevens and his school on scale types and transformations. This Part I of the paper reconstructs the main traits of these two lines of research. It also contains a conceptual introduction where the use of some notions, specifically those of *measurement* and *metrization*, are clarified.

**Díez, José A**. A Hundred Years of Numbers: An Historical Introduction to Measurement Theory 1887-1990: Part II: Suppes and the Mature Theory: Representation and Uniqueness. *Stud Hist Phil Sci*, 28(2), 237-265, Je 97.

In this Part II, we shall see how this integration is brought about in the foundational work of Suppes, the extensions and modifications which are generated around this work and the mature theory which results from all of this. (edited)

**Díez-Picazo, Gustavo Fernández**. Un análisis lógico del problema de Gettier. *Teorema*, 16(2), 51-59, 1997.

In this paper I draw a distinction between a *special* and a *general* version of the Gettier problem. I argue that the special problem is partially a logical problem, as well as an epistemological one, and I show that it is very easy to solve. This is interesting, since most of the Gettier-style examples that appear in the literature fall under the special problem, and hence as they stand they too are very easy to solve.

**Digilio, Patricia**. Aproximaciones a una evaluación de la aplicación de las nuevas tecnologías reproductivas. *Cuad Etica*, 17-18, 159-167, 1994.

The aim of this article is to reflect on the possible conditions for the application of new reproductive technologies and their ethics and social implications. This paper focuses on the need for a multidisciplinary approach which takes into account that (I) the moral and social implications of these new discoveries in human reproduction fall outside the realm of science and scientific activity; (2) this subject begs for new framework of understanding; (3) the very complexity of these issues creates a challenge for technology assessment.

**Dignum, Frank** and Meyer, John-Jules Ch and Wieringa, Roel J (& others). "A Modal Approach to Intentions, Commitments and Obligations: Intention Plus Commitment Yields Obligation" in *Deontic Logic, Agency and Normative Systems,* Brown, Mark A (ed), 80-97. New York, Springer-Verlag, 1996.

In this paper we introduce some new operators into our framework that make it possible to reason about decisions and commitments to do actions. In our framework, a decision leads to an intention to do an action. The decision in itself does not change the state of the world, but only the relation to possible future worlds. A commitment to actually perform the intended action changes the deontic state of the world such that the intended action becomes obligated. Of course, the obligated action may never actually occur. In our semantic structure, we use static (ought-to-be) and dynamic (ought-to-do) obligation operators. The static operator resembles the classical conception of obligation as truth in ideal worlds, except that it takes the current state as well as the past history of the world into account. This is necessary because it allows us to compare the way a state is actually reached with the way we committed ourselves to reach it. We show that some situations that could formerly not be expressed easily in deontic logic can be described in a natural way using the extended logic described in this paper.

**Dignum, Frank** and Royakkers, Lambèr. "Defeasible Reasoning with Legal Rules" in *Deontic Logic, Agency and Normative Systems,* Brown, Mark A (ed), 174-193. New York, Springer-Verlag, 1996.

The last few years several defeasible deontic reasoning formalisms were developed as a way to solve the problem of deontic inconsistency. However, these formalisms are unable to deal with some very common forms of deontic reasoning, since, e.g., their expressiveness is restricted. In this paper we will establish a priority hierarchy of legal rules to solve the problem of deontic conflicts and we will give a mechanism to reason about nonmonotonicity of legal rules over the priority hierarchy. The theory presented here, based on default logic and a modification and extension of the argumentation framework of Prakken, properly deals with some shortcomings of other defeasible deontic reasoning approaches.

**DiLeo, Jeffrey R**. "Charles Peirce's Theory of Proper Names" in *Studies in the Logic of Charles Sanders Peirce,* Houser, Nathan (ed), 574-594. Bloomington, Indiana Univ Pr, 1997.

**Diller, Ann**. "Criticizing With Care and With Respect For What We Are All Up Against" in *Philosophy of Education (1996),* Margonis, Frank (ed), 86-89. Urbana, Phil Education Soc, 1997.

**Diller, Ann**. In Praise of Objective-Subjectivity: Teaching the Pursuit of Precision. *Stud Phil Educ*, 16(1-2), 73-87, Ja-Ap 97.

Building upon aspects of Israel Scheffler's philosophy, this essay takes up the search for forms of education that will lead to increased participation in "a universal conversation in the making." In particular, it looks at how the rational passions may either enhance or impede the possibility of intelligible discourse between opponents. On the impediment side, the phenomenon of 'communicative isolation' is investigated, along with the nature of arrogant perception and the problematic role played by negative rational passions. The conclusion reached is one that advocates the cultivation of 'objective-subjectivity'—a practice that combines reflexivity and precise self-awareness with the conscious exercise of positive rational passions.

**Dillon, John M** (ed) and Long, A A (ed). *The Question of "Eclecticism": Studies in Later Greek Philosophy.* Berkeley, Univ of Calif Pr, 1996.

This collection of essays is addressed to the growing number of philosophers, classicists, and intellectual historians interested in the development of Greek thought after Aristotle. In nine original studies, the authors explore the meaning and history of "eclecticism" in the context of ancient philosophy. This book casts fresh light on the methodology of such central figures as Cicero, Philo, Plutarch, Sextus, Empiricus, and Ptolemy, and also illuminates many of the conceptual issues discussed most creatively in this period. (publisher, edited)

**Dillon, Robin S**. Self-Respect: Moral, Emotional, Political. *Ethics*, 107(2), 226-249, Ja 97.

Focusing on emotional dimensions of self-respect, which most philosophical accounts underplay or ignore, I argue that self-respect is more complexly structured than previously recognized. In particular, I posit a form of self-respect, which I call "basal self-respect," as the emotional substratum of other forms, shaping their possible enactments in thought, feeling, and action. I also examine gender dimensions of self-respect, exploring roots and possible remedies for damaged self-respect to which women are particularly subject in a sexist society, thus highlighting the intertwining of moral, emotional, and political dimensions of self-respect.

**Dilman, Ilham**. "Science and Psychology" in *Verstehen and Humane Understanding*, O'Hear, Anthony (ed), 145-164. New York, Cambridge Univ Pr, 1996.

Part I of the paper asks: what is knowledge of human beings and how is it acquired? It is concerned to clarify the distinctive features of such knowledge and contrasts them with those of scientific, inductive knowledge. It argues that there are questions amenable to experimental study that fall within the purview of psychology in the broad sense. However, they are concerned with 'the infrastructural conditions' for the exercise of capacities underlying human conduct. As such, their study has little light to throw on individual behavior. Hence, experimental psychology has nothing to contribute to our understanding of human beings as individuals. Part II discusses a few examples to illustrate the disaster which scientific psychology has been in believing that its findings can give us a basis for understanding human conduct.

**Dilman, Ilham**. Wisdom. *Philosophy*, 71(278), 577-590, O 96.

This is the seventh paper in a series of articles on Cambridge philosophers. Section 1 gives a short biography of John Wisdom. Section 2 discusses his contribution in *Other Minds* (1952) to the questions 'how can we know what other people think and feel?' and 'can we be deceived about our own feelings?' and also what he had to say about the nature of philosophy in *Philosophy and Psycho-Analysis* (1953) and in *Paradox and Discovery* (1965). Section 3 discusses his further contribution to these questions in *Proof and Explanation* (1991). Section 4 compares and contrasts wisdom and Wittgenstein.

**Dimas, Panagiotis**. Trolley, Transplant and Consent. *Ratio*, 9(2), 184-190, S 96.

**Dimock, Susan**. "Personal Autonomy, Freedom of Action, and Coercion" in *A Question of Values: New Canadian Perspectives in Ethics and Political Philosophy*, Brennan, Samantha (ed), 65-86. Amsterdam, Rodopi, 1997.

This paper defends three central theses. 1) The recent literature on personal autonomy can perspicuously be classified as defending either internalist or externalist theories of autonomy. 2) All internalist theories of autonomy can recognize only internal threats to personal autonomy, such as weakness of will or compulsion. They cannot recognize strictly external factors as undermining autonomy. Thus they must draw a radical divide between freedom of the will or autonomy, and freedom of action. But this separation thesis is indefensible, since restrictions on freedom of action can surely undermine autonomy. 3) Internalist theories of autonomy cannot provide a plausible account of why coerced actions are nonautonomous.

**Dimock, Susan**. Retributivism and Trust. *Law Phil*, 16(1), 37-62, 97.

In this paper I develop a functionalist theory of law, which is compatible with legal positivism. The purpose of law is to maintain basic trust in society; basic trust is construed objectively and contrasted with subjective trust. I then argue that if the purpose of law is to secure basic trust, legal offenses must be punished. Hence a strong theory of retributivism is defended. The trust-based theory is contrasted with other retributivist theories and some of its implications for sentencing are discussed.

**Dinan, Stephen A**. The Machine That Couldn't Think Straight. *Amer Cath Phil Quart*, 70(Supp), 135-148, 1996.

**Dingley, James C**. Durkheim, Mayo, Morality and Management. *J Bus Ethics*, 16(11), 1117-1129, Ag 97.

One of the most important contributions to management practice and theory (human relations) was built upon a sociological theory that was totally concerned with morality. That sociological theory was borrowed by Mayo without reading the original theory; consequently he missed the real point that the theory made, i.e., a common morality embracing everyone was necessary to maintain order and social cohesion. Such a morality was only possible when we realized our social dimension through continuous contact with each other. Moral man had to be social man; occupational groups were a way of attempting to achieve this. Yet morality is a dimension of group dynamics and management training rarely mentioned, partly through ignorance, partly through a fear of what discussions of morality might lead on to and partly through a structural blindness to nonoperational problems. (edited)

**Dinis, Alfredo**. Descartes e os Jesuítas: Para um estudo da personalidade cartesiana. *Rev Port Filosof*, 53(1), 3-26, Ja-Mr 97.

Descartes's philosophy has often be analized out of context. He then appears like a cold-blooded rationalist, completely void of emotions and responsible for the worst of our modern heritage. However, the study of the emotional relationship between Descartes and his teachers, the Jesuits, based mainly on their correspondence, reveals his emotional character, a man tortured by the desire of truth, of a solidly grounded truth, in a time when cracks in the building of traditional knowledge cracks seemed to appear everywhere. Thus, the rational coolness of Descartes appears as the visible part of the "Cartesian iceberg", whose less visible part was of a deeply emotional nature. On the other hand, taking into account the similarities between the cultural context in which he lived, in a turn of his century, and the present day context of the end of the XXth century, the anxious and troubled personality of Descartes appears as having a particular relevance.

**Dinis, Alfredo**. G.J. Rheticus on Copernicanism and Bible. *Rev Port Filosof*, 52(1-4), 299-314, Ja-D 96.

**Dipert, Randall R**. "Peirce's Philosophical Conception of Sets" in *Studies in the Logic of Charles Sanders Peirce*, Houser, Nathan (ed), 53-76. Bloomington, Indiana Univ Pr, 1997.

**Dipert, Randall R**. Reflections on Iconicity, Representation, and Resemblance: Peirce's Theory of Signs, Goodmann on Resemblance, and Modern Philosophies of Language and Mind. *Synthese*, 106(3), 373-397, Mr 96.

**Dipert, Randall R**. The Mathematical Structure of the World: The World as Graph. *J Phil*, 94(7), 329-358, Jl 97.

Relationalism is the view that some relations (two or more-place predicates) are basic, irreducible features of the world. This essay argues for exclusive relationalism: the view that only relations and in fact only one 2-place, symmetric relation, are adequate for this purpose. It does so by arguing for metaphysical structuralism: that things exist as and can be identified only through their structure. This structure is best described as relational and the world is best portrayed as an asymmetric graph, with all structure being graph-theoretical. It surveys difficulties in existing philosophical logics and set theories, especially difficulties in the concept of an "individual" and the importance of large-scale structural features. The influential arguments of Plato, Aristotle, Leibniz and Castaneda against relationalism are examined and replied to. A detailed considered of this mathematical, but nonlogical, nonatomistic, structure may require radically different concepts for metaphysics than logic since Aristotle has given us.

**Dirlik, Arif**. Three Worlds, or One, or Many? The Reconfiguration of Global Divisions under Contemporary Capitalism. *Nature Soc Thought*, 7(1), 19-42, 1994.

The tripartite division of the world in post-World War II social science has been criticized for its ideological weakness and for ignoring differences across the "three worlds." The fall of socialist states and a new phase within capitalism add plausibility to such criticism. Such criticism, however, may destructure global relations and force analysis toward a relentless empiricism. It also ignores the ways in which the Third World concept empowered oppositional movements to create new political configurations as alternatives both to capitalism and actually existing socialism. What is required now is an account of the restructuring of global relations by a global capitalism and the new forces of opposition it generates. Local movements to contain the ravages of capital, a primary recent form of resistance, have much to learn from indigenous movements that question the very notion of development.

**DiSalle, Robert** and Harper, William. Inferences from Phenomena in Gravitational Physics. *Proc Phil Sci Ass*, 3(Suppl), S46-S54, 1996.

Newton's methodology emphasized propositions "inferred from phenomena." These rest on systematic dependencies that make phenomena measure theoretical parameters. We consider the inferences supporting Newton's inductive argument that gravitation is proportional to inertial mass. We argue that the support provided by these systematic dependencies is much stronger than that provided by bootstrap confirmation; this kind of support thus avoids some of the major objections against bootstrapping. Finally, we examine how contemporary testing equivalence principles exemplifies this Newtonian methodological theme.

**Disch, Lisa J**. *Hannah Arendt and the Limits of Philosophy: With a New Preface*. Ithaca, Cornell Univ Pr, 1994.

In this new interpretation of the political writings of Hannah Arendt, Lisa Jane Disch focuses on an issue that remains central to today's debates in political philosophy and feminist theory: the relationship of experience to critical understanding. Discussing a range of Arendt's work including unpublished writings, Disch explores the function of storytelling as a form of critical theory beyond the limits of philosophy. (publisher, edited)

**DiTommaso, Tanya**. Play, Agreement and Consensus. *Man World*, 29(4), 407-417, O 96.

In this paper I employ the analysis of play to clarify the distinction between an agreement and a consensus and I argue that it is the conditions supplied by the playful process that enable us to partake in the recognition and creation of truth. Gadamer's hermeneutical truth, unlike propositional truth, speaks of the interpretive act whereby meaning is recognized. This interpretive recognition of meaning is described by Gadamer as an occurrence of interpretive play or *genuine* understanding. Regarding Gadamer's conception of truth as modelled on agreement rather than consensus, I demonstrate that it is in the process of play that we achieve the making and maintaining of the conditions that are necessary for agreement and that the nature of understanding is most clearly revealed by viewing it as a playful process.

**Divers, John**. The Analysis of Possibility and the Possibility of Analysis. *Proc Aris Soc*, 97, 141-161, 1997.

Lewis's ambition to provide an analysis or reduction of the modal to the nonmodal has been confronted by paradoxes of analysis, that is, arguments to the effect that the purported analysis cannot simultaneously satisfy all the requirements of successful analysis. Such arguments are suggested by Lycan and by Shalkowski, but each, I argue, trades on an unexplicated notion of noncircularity in analysis or reduction. I attempted to develop an appropriate notion of noncircularity in order to bolster the paradoxes, concluding with some tentative remarks on relevant expressive imitations of genuine modal realist quantification.

**Dix, Douglas Shields**. Between the Lines. *Filosof Cas*, 44(4), 675-689, 1996.

**Dixon, Beth A**. The Moral Status of Animal Training. *Between Species*, 11(1-2), 54-63, Wint-Spr 95.

In this paper I examine whether or not training animals, per se, is morally objectionable. I formulate a "Rights Approach" argument for the conclusion that training an animal violates that animal's right to respectful treatment, and consider some objections to this argument. I conclude that the plausibility of the *rights approach argument* depends on assumptions that are yet unproven about what psychological states humans and animals share.

**Dixon, Bobby R**. "Toting Technology: Taking It to the Streets" in *Existence in Black: An Anthology of Black Existential Philosophy*, Gordon, Lewis R (ed), 135-147. New York, Routledge, 1997.

**Dixon, Nicholas**. A Utilitarian Argument for Vegetarianism. *Between Species*, 11(3-4), 90-97, Sum-Fall 95.

I defend Peter Singer's well-known utilitarian argument for vegetarianism against two types of objection. First, in response to utilitarian defenders of meat eating, I argue that neither R.G. Frey's "concerned individual's tactic" nor the "animal husbandry" argument substantiates their claim that ending meat farming would result in a net decrease in pleasure for humans and nonhumans. Second, while Carl Cohen shows that humans may have *quantitatively* more interests than nonhumans, I argue that he fails to prove a crucial premise of the "human supremacist" justification of meat eating: the greater *qualitative* value of human interests.

**Dixon, Nicholas**. Feminism and Utilitarian Arguments for Vegetarianism: A Note on Alex Wellington's "Feminist Positions on Vegetarianism". *Between Species*, 11(3-4), 105-110, Sum-Fall 95.

Kathryn Paxton George, whom Wellington discusses in her invaluable survey of feminist positions, makes empirical claims that appear to challenge the utilitarian case for vegetarianism. George argues that nutritional and economic factors would make it very difficult for women, poor people and inhabitants of developing countries to convert to vegetarianism. I respond that, even if George's empirical claims are supported by the evidence, they do not undermine the utilitarian argument for vegetarianism. A utilitarian can consistently relativize the duty to refrain from eating meat to those on whom it would not impose an unfair burden.

**Dixon, Nicholas**. The Morality of Anti-Abortion Civil Disobedience. *Pub Affairs Quart*, 11(1), 21-38, Ja 97.

Many arguments that justified the civil disobedience (CD) practiced by the civil rights movement apply equally well to the CD practiced by Operation Rescue and other nonviolent anti-abortion protesters. However, liberals who supported the civil rights movement can still consistently condemn Operation Rescue, because Operation Rescue's protests have far greater general and specific "social costs." In such circumstances, CD is justified only if supported by arguments showing that the contested ruling is very probably unconstitutional or immoral; and given the intractable nature of the constitutional and moral debate over abortion, no such arguments are available.

**Dixon, Nicholas**. The Morality of Intimate Faculty-Student Relationships. *Monist*, 79(4), 519-535, O 96.

Intimate faculty-student relationships are wrong when they involve threats or offers. Even consensual relationships without these improprieties are wrong when they occur between professors and students for whom they have professional responsibility. Inadvertent coercion of students, who may fear retaliation from professors, is a serious risk but is insufficient to justify condemning all such relationships. The reason why these relationships *are* wrong is the conflict of interest that may lead professors to unfairly favor students with whom they are involved. However, consensual intimate relationships are unobjectionable between faculty members and students for whom they have no professional responsibility.

**DiZerga, Gus**. Market Non-Neutrality: Systematic Bias in Spontaneous Orders. *Crit Rev*, 11(1), 121-144, Wint 97.

The market is sometimes thought to be a largely neutral means for coordinating cooperation among strangers under complex conditions because it is, as Hayek noted, a "spontaneous order." But, in fact, the market actively shapes the kinds of values it rewards, as do other spontaneous orders. Recognizing these biases allows us to see how such orders impinge on one another and on other communities basic to human life, sometimes negatively. In this way we may come to acknowledge the inevitability of placing limits on spontaneous orders.

**Djibo, Mamadou**. Le projet fondationnel de Frege: De la nature du concept de nombre à la question de la preuve des lois de l'arithmétique. *De Phil*, 12, 133-154, 1995-1996.

**Djordjevic, Dejan**. Some Problems of Approach to Nagarjuna's Philosophy (in Serbo-Croatian). *Theoria (Yugoslavia)*, 38(1), 41-49, Mr 95.

The article focuses on the interpretation of Nagarjuna's philosophy defended by the famous Yugoslav indologist Rada Ivekovic in her recent works. Special attention has been paid to her belief that *sunya-vada* (Nagarjuna's doctrine) is deprived of metaphysical constructions; in her opinion, Nagarjuna is an agnostic. In order to show that this conviction might be wrong or one-sided, the author exposes some interpretations of nongnosiological aspects of *sunya-vada* which have been adopted by Ivekovic and some other authors. If these interpretations are taken for granted, one can easily arrive at the conclusion that Nagarjuna did establish a metaphysical doctrine.

**Djukic, George**. Kant on Existence as a Property of Individuals. *Hist Phil Quart*, 13(4), 469-481, O 96.

I examine Kant's famous argument in the *Critique of Pure Reason* directed against the thesis that existence is a property of individuals, viz. the argument that being is not a real predicate. Kant's pivotal claim is that a concept must express the whole object in order to be an adequate concept of that object. On my interpretation this means that no object of thought can recognisably (by introspection) represent some real object unless all of that object's properties are represented. I conclude that Kant's argument is inconclusive.

**Djuric, Drago**. Hegel's Understanding of the Beginning (in Serbo-Croatian). *Theoria (Yugoslavia)*, 38(3), 7-22, S 95.

This article deals with the meaning of the term 'understanding' in Hegel's philosophical treatment of the problem of the beginning. According to Hegel, the beginning appears in philosophy always as a result of mediation. The whole mediation is, in fact, the mediation of the beginning. Since in Hegel's philosophy the truth is only the way to truth, the mediation of the beginning is accordingly just the way to the beginning. More precisely, an attempt to understand the beginning is simultaneously a development of the beginning.

**Dlugos, Peter**. Yolton and Rorty on the Veil of Ideas in Locke. *Hist Phil Quart*, 13(3), 317-329, Jl 96.

John Yolton has argued against the received view of Lockean ideas and he has also criticized Richard Rorty for holding Locke largely responsible for the modern epistemological problematic. In this essay it is argued that Locke should not be pardoned for his hand in this problematic, because a) Yolton's alternative "act" interpretation is no more supported by the texts than the standard "object" interpretation, and more importantly, b) the alternate reading does not change the aspect of Lockean ideas that engenders the sceptical problems: their mediating role in perception and cognition.

**Do Nascimento, Carlos A Ribeiro**. The Middle Way: Some Limitations of Human Intellectual Knowledge, According to Thomas Aquinas (in Portuguese). *Trans/Form/Acao*, 19, 205-210, 1996.

This work intends to present the scope and limits of the human intellectual knowledge according to Saint Thomas Aquinas, mainly on the ground of questions 84 and 85 of the first part of his *Theological Summa*.

**Dobson, Andrew**. Genetic Engineering and Environmental Ethics. *Cambridge Quart Healthcare Ethics*, 6(2), 205-221, Spr 97.

**Dobson, John** and MacLellan, Cheryl. Women, Ethics, and MBAs. *J Bus Ethics*, 16(11), 1201-1209, Ag 97.

We argue that the declining female enrollment in graduate business schools is a manifestation of gender bias in business education. The extant conceptual foundation of business education is one which views business activity in terms of a game with fixed and wholly material objectives. This concept betrays an underlying value system that reflects a male orientation. Business education is not merely amoral, therefore, but is gender biased. We suggest that business educators adopt a broadened behavioral rubric. Virtue-ethics theory provides such a rubric.

**Dodd, James**. Phenomenon and Sensation: A Reflection on Husserl's Concept of *Sinngebung*. *Man World*, 29(4), 419-439, O 96.

This essay attempts to understand Husserl's concept of *Sinngebung* ("sense-bestowal"). The proposal is to do so by analyzing the concepts of *phenomenon* and *sensation*. It begins with a comparison of phenomenology to empiricism, the point of connection being the idea of experience as something the meaning of which is always "on the way." It then interprets the concepts of phenomenon and sensation in *Logical Investigations* and *Ideas I* as motivated by this empiricist insight. It ends with the idea of *Sinngebung* as the attempt to articulate the fact that meaning is never something merely "apprehended," but rather entails the movement of "life."

**Dodd, Julian**. Countering the Counting Problem: A Reply to Holton. *Analysis*, 56(4), 239-245, O 96.

**Dodd, Julian**. Indirect Speech, Parataxis and the Nature of Things Said. *J Phil Res*, 22, 211-227, Ap 97.

This paper makes the following recommendation when it comes to the logical form of sentences in indirect speech. Davidson's paratactic account should stand, but with one emendation: the demonstrative 'that' should be taken to refer to the *Fregean thought* expressed by the utterance of the content-sentence, rather than to that utterance itself. The argument for this emendation is that it is the only way of replying to the objections to Davidson's account raised by Schiffer, McFetridge and McDowell. Towards the end of the paper, a view of *Fregean thoughts* as utterance-types is defended; and the recommendation offered in the main body of the paper is distinguished from the similar account offered by Ian Rumfitt.

**Dodson, Kevin E**. Autonomy and Authority in Kant's *Rechtslehre*. *Polit Theory*, 25(1), 93-111, F 97.

In the short essay on theory and practice, Kant declares that the social contract differs from all other types of contracts in that agreement to its is obligatory and may be exacted through the use of force. In this paper, I examine Kant's justification of the moral necessity of civil society. Kant locates the ground of our obligation to enter into a civil union in the necessity of property for action and civil society as the necessary condition of the institution of property. It is my contention that the idea of the social contract is central to this project in that it joins together both moral autonomy and political authority in a conceptual unity that establishes the legitimacy of civil society, or the juridical condition as the collective dimension of autonomy.

**Doepke, Frederick C**. The Kinds of Things: A Theory of Personal Identity Based on Transcendental Argument. Chicago, Open Court, 1996.

What are we? Doepke approaches the riddle of personal identity by way of a general theory of identity and in so doing he challenges the influential Humean view of identity developed in Parfit's *Reasons and Persons*. We normally think of ourselves and the things around us as objects which persist through fairly long stretches of time. Hume, along with Heraclitus and Buddha, denied this degree of permanence. Doepke argues for a view of the self that is more in harmony with both Kant and common sense. With rigorous arguments, *The Kinds of Things* strongly supports the commonsense belief that, in normal human life, persons persist: even changes in our deeply-held affections and ideals do not erode the basis of our identity. (publisher)

**Doerfler, Martin** and Beckerman, Aaron and Couch, Elsbeth (& others). Ethical Issues and Relationships between House Staff and Attending Physicians: A Case Study. *J Clin Ethics*, 8(1), 34-38, Spr 97.

The purpose of the work was to examine a series of ethical issues between attendings and house staff. In the space between dying and death, conflicts emerge between the interests of education and care of the patient, patients' care decision making which are more a function of authority than medical knowledge, and extending the do no (psychological) harm principle to house staff.

**Doering, Jeffrey** and Werhane, Patricia. Conflicts of Interest and Conflicts of Commitment. *Prof Ethics*, 4(3-4), 47-81, Spr-Sum 95.

**Döring, Frank**. The Ramsey Test and Conditional Semantics. *J Phil Log*, 26(4), 359-376, Ag 97.

Proponents of the projection strategy take an epistemic rule for the evaluation of English conditionals, the Ramsey test, as clue to the truth-conditional semantics of conditionals. They also construe English conditionals as stronger than the material conditional. Given plausible assumptions, however, the Ramsey test induces the semantics of the material conditional. The alleged link between Ramsey test and truth conditions stronger than those of the material conditional can be saved by construing conditionals as ternary, rather than binary, propositional functions with a hidden contextual parameter. But such a ternary construal raises problems of its own.

**Dörre, Jochen** and König, Esther and Gabbay, Dov. Fibred Semantics for Feature-Based Grammar Logic. *J Log Lang Info*, 5(3-4), 387-422, O 96.

This paper gives a simple method for providing categorial brands of feature-based unification grammars with a model-theoretic semantics. The key idea is to apply the paradigm of fibred semantics (or layered logics, see Gabbay, 1990) in order to combine the two components of a feature-based grammar logic. We demonstrate the method for the augmentation of Lambek categorial grammar with Kasper/Rounds-style feature logic. These are combined by replacing (or annotating) atomic formulas of the first logic, i.e., the basic syntactic types, by formulas of the second. Modelling such a combined logic is less trivial than one might expect. The direct application of the fibred semantics method where a combined atomic formula like *np (num:sg & pers:3rd)* denotes those strings which have the indicated property and the categorial operators denote the usual left- and right-residuals of these string sets, does not match the intuitive, unification-based proof theory. Unification implements a global bookkeeping with respect to a proof whereas the direct fibring method restricts its view to the atoms of the grammar logic. The solution is to interpret the (embedded) feature terms as global feature constraints while maintaining the same kind of fibred structures. For this adjusted semantics, the anticipated proof system is sound and complete.

**Doig, James C**. The Interpretation of Aquinas's *Prima Secundae*. *Amer Cath Phil Quart*, 71(2), 171-195, Spr 97.

**Doignon, Jean-Paul** and Falmagne, Jean-Claude. Stochastic Evolution of Rationality. *Theor Decis*, 43(2), 107-138, S 97.

Following up on previous results by Falmagne, this paper investigates possible mechanisms explaining how preference relations are created and how they evolve over time. We postulate a preference relation which is initially empty and becomes increasingly intricate under the influence of a random environment delivering discrete tokens of information concerning the alternatives. The framework is that of a class of real-time stochastic processes having interlinked Markov and Poisson components. Asymptotic results are obtained in the form of the limit probabilities of any semiorder. The arguments extend to a much more general situation including interval orders, biorders and partial orders. The results provide (up to a small number of parameters) complete quantitative predictions for panel data of a standard type, in which the same sample of subjects has been asked to compare the alternatives a number of times. (edited)

**Dokic, Jérôme**. Compétence sémantique et psychologie du raisonnement. *Rev Phil Fr*, 2, 171-182, Ap-Je 97.

**Dokulil, Milos**. Did he Walk with a Mask...? (in Czech). *Filosof Cas*, 44(5), 782-810, 1996.

The article evokes the presupposition that Descartes has been appreciated as the founder of the modern rationalism but, at the same time, as a philosopher "with a mask". It reminds his links with the Czech background (Prague, Comenius), but also some of the less registered connections there (contacts with the Princess Elizabeth, but pre-Munich echoes, too). Philosophically, a direct, massive and complex impact of Descartes's thoughts on the Czech world is rather weak, yet the Czech philosophy has been credited with important Cartesian contributions. (edited)

**Dokulil, Milos**. Is Reductionism the Saving Way?. *Filosof Cas*, 44(3), 481-491, 1996.

It is a discussion motivated by A. Tucker's article on the "Normative Philosophy of History," published in the same journal. It invites the treatment of the field of study so neglected in the Czech Republic between 1948-1989. Tucker's statement of a slow decline of the philosophy of history has not been,

notwithstanding, shared. The fruitful criticism of Hempel's contribution of 1942 cannot be overlooked. For all that Tucker's "reductions," not dissimilar to Hempel's and supported by computer literacy, cannot serve as bases for inference schemes in historiography. Tucker's chain of reductions, at last, does not find its operative semantics.

**Dolinko, David**. Action Theory and Criminal Law. *Law Phil*, 15(3), 293-306, 96.

**Dombrowski, Daniel A**. *Analytic Theism, Hartshorne, and the Concept of God*. Albany, SUNY Pr, 1996.

This book initiates a dialogue where one does not exist, and continues a dialogue where one has been tentatively initiated, regarding the concept of God in the neoclassical philosophy of Charles Hartshorne and that found in analytic philosophers who adhere to classical theism. Two distinctive features of the book are a careful examination of Hartshorne's use of position matrices in the philosophy of religion so as to avoid a myopic view of the theoretical options open to us, and an extended treatment of the largely uncritical appropriation by analytic theists of the Aristotelian tradition in theology a tradition that relies on a certain form of Platonism not necessarily held by Plato. (publisher, edited)

**Dombrowski, Daniel A**. *Babies and Beasts: The Argument from Marginal Cases*. Champaign, Univ of Illinois Pr, 1997.

Both its defenders and detractors have described the argument from marginal cases as the most important to date in defense of animal rights. Hotly debated among philosophers for some twenty years, the argument concludes that no morally relevant characteristic distinguishes human beings—including infant, the severely retarded, the comatose, and other "marginal cases"—from any other animals. (publisher, edited)

**Dombrowski, Daniel A**. Do Critics of Heidegger Commit the *Ad Hominem* Fallacy?. *Int J Applied Phil*, 10(2), 71-75, Wint-Spr 96.

I attempt to accomplish two things. First, critics of Heidegger need not commit the *ad hominem* fallacy in that Heidegger's personal character, his political views and his metaphysics are each, singly, deserving of criticism such that one can criticize each one of these without entering into the other two areas. Second, it is Heidegger himself who muddies the waters regarding these three areas.

**Dombrowski, Daniel A**. Hartshorne on Heidegger. *Process Stud*, 25, 19-33, 1996.

**Dombrowski, Daniel A**. Mysticism and Divine Mutability. *Process Stud*, 23(3-4), 149-154, Fall-Wint 94.

I support the case for at least the partial autonomy of mystical experiences against the possible hegemony of the intellect. I attempt to limit this hegemony through a consideration of one particular concept and its "opposite"—divine immutability and divine mutability—as it is found in mystical literature. I will rely heavily and in a positive way on the recent book by Nelson Pike.

**Domingues, Ivan**. O problema da verdade, a questao do sujeito e a serpente de Valéry. *Kriterion*, 34(88), 7-33, Ag-D 93.

In this paper, the problem of truth and the question about the subject along with the history of philosophy is analyzed, in the light of Aristotle's wording of the problem of knowledge, according to which "truth is in the thought, whereas the measure of truth is in the thing."(edited)

**Dominioni, Stefano**. Renaissance and Human Nature: Pico's "Dignity of Man". *Cont Phil*, 18(2-3), 47-51, Mr-Ap/My-Je 96.

Giovanni Pico Della Mirandola's philosophic reputation rests on his famous *Oration on the Dignity of Man*, considered as one of the Renaissance's most authentic manifestos. Pico's doctrine consists in a revolutionary theory of human nature which addresses man's dignity, freedom and creativity in a radically new way. As for other Renaissance thinkers like Machiavelli, with Pico human beings enter into a new realm of individuation, freedom and personal creativity never achieved before. The Renaissance man's most important ability resides in the power of transforming himself, according to his creative functions, desires and aspirations. With Pico, human nature ceases to have a specific and static place in the hierarchically organized cosmic order. Human beings are now able to occupy, according to their will, any level of life.

**Dommel Jr, F William** and Alexander, Duane. The Convention on Human Rights and Biomedicine of the Council of Europe. *Kennedy Inst Ethics J*, 7(3), 259-276, S 97.

The Convention on Human Rights and Biomedicine developed by the Council of Europe, now undergoing ratification, is the first international treaty focused on bioethics. This article describes the background of the Convention's development and its general provisions and provides a comparison of its requirements with those of federal regulations governing research with human subjects. Although most provisions are comparable, there are significant differences in scope and applicability, for example, in the areas of compensation for injury, research participation by persons with limited capacity to consent, assisted reproduction, organ transplantation and research in emergency situations. The Convention represents a milestone in international bioethics and protection of human rights that will probably be referred to with increasing frequency.

**Donadio, Francesco**. "Religione e storicismo: Paul Yorck von Wartenburg" in *Lo Storicismo e la Sua Storia: Temi, Problemi, Prospettive*, Cacciatore, Giuseppe (ed), 288-298. Milano, Guerini, 1997.

**Donadon, Eleonora**. *E.C. Tolman e l'epistemologia del primo novecento*. Roma, Borla, 1997.

E.C. Tolman wants to correct Watson's behaviourism "stimuli-responses" by using the intervening variables (purpose and cognition) as objective, publicly observable behavioural causes. So he explains the "response" as a "performance" of the whole organism engaged in problem-solving. Tolman bases his behaviourism on the "hypothetical constructs" (intervening variables) and proves them by rats' experiments following the trial-and-error method. In psychology, this hypothetical method could refer and anticipate K.R. Popper's conjectures and refutations. In short, Tolman and Popper show the science possibilities and limits and the liberty of the scientist of falsifying the hypothesis and refusing the erroneous ones for the science responsible progress.

**Donatoni, Alaíde Rita** and Cândida P Coelho, Maria. Subsídios para uma Análise da Política da Educaçao Escolar Brasileira. *Educ Filosof*, 10(19), 153-161, Ja-Je 96.

This paper aims to give theoretical support to possible discussions concerning Brazilian school education and its different policies. The authors demonstrate that the influence of the state in establishing such policies is a very strong one, especially in cases where the state is outlined under capitalist labor relations that in contemporary capitalism result in deeper inequalities. The relations between education, state and economy run, nevertheless, somewhat dynamically, so that the authors themselves feel encouraged to assert that education, in its political sphere, can build its hegemony in order to overcome the present "state of affairs."(edited)

**Donchin, Anne**. Feminist Critiques of New Fertility Technologies: Implications for Social Policy. *J Med Phil*, 21(5), 475-498, O 96.

This essay aims to show how feminist theoretical and practical perspectives have enriched and deepened debate about moral and social issues generated by the proliferation and commodification of new reproductive techniques. It evaluates alternative feminist appraisals beginning with the first group to organize a collective response to the medicalization of infertility and explores several weaknesses working within their assessment: objectification of infertile women, naturalizing constructions of motherhood, hostility to technology, and an overly simplistic conception of power relations. Next, it shows how subsequent feminists have reframed the issues to overcome these weaknesses, drawing on themes prominent in recent theoretical debates: the need to reclaim women's agency, to revalue mothering, and to reappraise power relations. Lastly, it weighs the prospects for a collaborative politics that is sensitive to the social marginalization of vulnerable women and suggests practical strategies for responding to mounting pressures to procreate at any price.

**Donkel, Douglas L**. Formal Contamination: A Reading of Derrida's Argument. *Phil Today*, 40(2), 301-309, Sum 96.

This paper examines Derrida's claims regarding the necessity of contamination and the function of *différance* through a phenomenological analysis of the concept of "form." Specifically, it offers a reading of the well-known passage from the essay "Différance" which claims that the "interval that constitutes...must [also] divide" what it would otherwise constitute. Focusing on the question of why the interval *must* so divide, it is shown that contamination is a function of the very structure of form as *transition*, and that *différance* indicates nothing other than the *condition of transition* as such.

**Donneaud, Henry**. Durand et Durandellus sur les rapports de la foi et de la science. *Rev Thomiste*, 97(1), 157-172, Ja-Mr 97.

**Donneaud, Henry**. Note sur le *revelabile* selon Étienne Gilson. *Rev Thomiste*, 96(4), 633-652, O-D 96.

**Donnelly, Jack**. Conversing with Straw Men While Ignoring Dictators: A Reply to Roger Ames. *Ethics Int Affairs*, 11, 207-213, 1997.

In a rebuttal of Ames's critique of his conception of universal human rights, Donnelly asserts that Ames has misrepresented his arguments, creating a straw man from Ames's own preconceived notion of the Western liberal tradition while ignoring the substantive debates. In response to Ames's cultural approach to human rights, Donnelly argues that culture cannot be viewed as static. Structural, political and economic factors have significant effects upon culture and the rights of each citizen. Donnelly concludes that the more significant cause of China's failure to recognize the Universal Declaration of Human Rights is not Confucian culture but rather China's own corrupt and dictatorial regime. For this reason, Donnelly argues that the international community must continue to condemn China's violations of the Universal Declaration of Human Rights.

**Donnelly, Jack**. Post-Cold War Reflections on the Study of International Human Rights. *Ethics Int Affairs*, 8, 97-117, 1994.

**Donner, Wendy**. "Self and Community in Environmental Ethics" in *Ecofeminism: Women, Culture, Nature,* Warren, Karen J (ed), 375-389. Bloomington, Indiana Univ Pr, 1997.

I use as my starting point Val Plumwood's ecofeminist arguments against rationalistic accounts of the self and her defense of the relational self for environmental philosophy. I argue that while some accounts of reason are properly the object of feminist critique, other forms of reason are essential to ecofeminism. I claim that a strongly bounded and distinct self is an important aspect of a plausible ecofeminist ethics. Using some recent case studies of women who are survivors of childhood sexual abuse, I argue that these narratives are moving reminders of the indispensability of reason and autonomy for feminism and ecofeminism.

**Donnici, Rocco**. *Intenzioni: D'amore di scienza e d'anarchia*. Naples, Bibliopolis, 1996.

Up to 1916-1917 Husserl developed, like Brentano, the idea of a scientific ethic and built up a complex logic of emotive-volitive acts (formal practice and formal assiology). Afterwards, both because of the idealistic shift of his phenomenology and the 'revolutionary' theory of epoché and of reduction, he discovered out the ethical-political 'vocation' (à la Fichte) of transcendental subjectivity in the intentionality of 'transcendental instincts'. Such 'instincts' form the fundamental discovery of philosophy or of 'European' humanity. Philosophy, from Husserl's point of view, not only is aspiration or love for truth, but also, as utopias show, desire for a freely self-regulated life and in perspective of a community of subjects capable of living together with no need for an imperialistic apparatus of the *state*. According to the author, Husserl renews, in opposition to postmodernists and followers of Heidegger, the idea of the emancipation of the *whole* of humanity as the 'horizon' or 'telos' of the development of real philosophy and science and not of 'productive forces'.

**Donoso, Antón**. Ortega's (Implicit) Critique of Natural Law. *Vera Lex*, 14(1-2), 32-34, 1994.

Given that Ortega wrote nothing directly on natural law, we must draw our conclusions from his extensive treatment of human life. His ethics of self-determination, or authenticity, emphasizes fidelity to personal vocation within the general vocation we all have to happiness. Ortega tries to steer a path between what he considers ethical and legal absolutism, with its negation of human freedom, and the relativistic attitude that "anything goes." In doing so he implicitly critiques any theory of natural law that posits a fixed human nature as negating human freedom, but not theories of nature law that appeal to a future ideal.

**Donovan, John**. "Faith and Intellectual Fairness" in *Philosophy, Religion, and the Question of Intolerance,* Ambuel, David (ed), 81-93. Albany, SUNY Pr, 1997.

This paper offers a response to the following question: "Is it in the nature of religious belief to be intolerant?" I will argue that Aristotle offers the best approach to such a question: judge things according to the best of their kind, for the best displays a thing's essential possibilities. My conclusion will be that religion at its best is quite capable of fairness. More specifically, I will argue that intellectual fairness, as a virtue intrinsic to healthy religious belief, is best understood as an exercise of Aristotelian *phronesis*. Phronesis, I believe, includes the best elements intended by the contemporary discussion of toleration. I will also show, however, that the philosophy of religion's own origins connect it with certain deep-seated biases that makes it difficult to conceive of intellectual fairness as a virtue intrinsic to healthy religious belief and that predispose us towards notions of toleration that must be imposed on historical faiths from without.

**Doorley, Mark J**. The Teaching of Ethics. *Phil Cont World*, 3(1), 8-13, Spr 96.

The most important philosophy course that contemporary undergraduates may take is ethics. Concerned with how to live a human life, ethics becomes ever more urgent as life unfolds. As the teacher, a philosopher likely wonders about the interaction in the classroom. This paper explores that interaction. Taking a cue from Aristotle, it is argued that the teaching of ethics is an invitation to self-reflection and self-responsibility, more so than a passing on of a set of ethical principles or laws.

**Doorman, Maarten**. Baten van een formele verheldering. *Alg Ned Tijdschr Wijs*, 89(3), 232-233, Jl 97.

**Doran, Robert M** (ed) and Crowe, Frederick E (ed). *Verbum: Word and Idea in Aquinas Volume 2.* Toronto, Univ of Toronto Pr, 1997.

*Verbum: Word and Idea in Aquinas* is a product of Lonergan's eleven years of study of the thought of Thomas Aquinas. The work is considered by many to be a breakthrough in the history of Lonergan's theology and a foundation upon which his later contributions were constructed. Here he interprets aspects in the writing of Aquinas relevant to Trinitarian theory and, as in most of Lonergan's work, one of the principal aims is to assist the reader in the search to understand the workings of the human mind. (publisher, edited)

**Dorandi, Tiziano**. La *Politeia*, entre cynisme et stoïcisme. *Diotima*, 25, 101-109, 1997.

**Dorato, Mauro**. Il problema del realismo tra meccanica quantistica e relatività speciale. *Epistemologia*, 19(1), 113-156, Ja-Je 96.

The conceptual tension between quantum mechanics and special relativity is examined from the point of view of the ontological determinateness of events in Minkowski spacetime. Various possible views of the relationship between time and reality are briefly presented, and it is argued that as a result of well-known experimental tests on the violation of Bell inequality, the metaphysical view attributing the same ontological status to past and future becomes incompatible with modern physics. (edited)

**Dorato, Mauro**. On Becoming, Relativity, and Nonseparability. *Phil Sci*, 63(4), 585-604, D 96.

In a reply to Nicholas Maxwell, Stein has proven that Minkowski space-time can leave room for the kind of indeterminateness required both by certain interpretations of quantum mechanics and by objective becoming. By examining the consequences of outcome dependence in Bell-type experiments for the codeterminateness of spacelike-related events, I argue that the only becoming relation that is compatible with both causal and noncausal readings of the quantum correlations is the universal relation. This result might also undermine interpretations of quantum mechanics requiring nonepistemically indeterminate states before measurement and hyperplane-dependent wave collapse.

**Dorff, Elliot N**. Judaism, Business and Privacy. *Bus Ethics Quart*, 7(2), 31-44, Mr 97.

This article first describes some of the chief contrasts between Judaism and American secularism in their *underlying convictions* about the business environment and the expectations which all involved in business can have of each other—namely, duties vs. rights, communitarianism vs. individualism and ties to God and to the environment based on our inherent status as God's creatures rather than on our pragmatic choice. Conservative Judaism's *methodology* for plumbing the Jewish tradition for guidance is described and contrasted to those of Orthodox and Reform Judaism. (edited)

**Dorff, Elliot N**. Paying for Medical Care: A Jewish View. *Kennedy Inst Ethics J*, 7(1), 15-30, Mr 97.

According to Jewish law, there is a clear obligation to try to heal and this duty devolves upon both the physician and the society. Jewish sources make it clear that health care is not only an individual and familial responsibility, but also a communal one. This social aspect of health care manifests itself in Jewish law in two ways: first, no community is complete until it has the personnel (and, one assumes, the facilities) to provide health care; second, the community must pay for the health care of those who cannot afford it as part of its provision for the poor. The community, in turn, must use its resources wisely, which is the moral basis within the Jewish tradition for some system of managed care. The community must balance its commitment to provide health care with the provision of other services.

**Dorman, William**. Mass Media and Critical Thinking: Reasoning for a Second-Hand World. *Inquiry (USA)*, 16(2), 67-77, Wint 96.

Originally a keynote address at the 16th International Conference on Critical Thinking and Educational Reform (August 1996), this paper moves away from the usual discussion of how media may affect behavior and instead focuses on their effects on thinking. The main thrust is that mass media undermine a fundamental dimension of sound reasoning—our ability to make distinctions. As a result, the overriding logical shortcoming of our time may be the fallacy of lack of proportion. The paper suggests some strategies for teaching about media in the critical thinking classroom.

**Dorner, Samuel**. What is a Right?. *J Value Inq*, 30(3), 427-430, S 96.

A right (not legal but natural) is not a part of the factual universe, physical as well as abstract. It is only a code-word or an abbreviation of a value-judgment such as: "It is just for (such and such living being) to get (such and such benefit)".

**Dorotíková, Sona**. History and Values. *Filosof Cas*, 44(4), 565-588, 1996.

Philosophical reflection on history can have many guises, but in its metaphysical form it virtually always begins with the assumption that history is the sphere of suprapersonal necessity, which is a guarantee of a certain generally valid objective order. In the 19th century the model of laws governing history met with critical opposition from those theories of sociology and the history of philosophy which focused on the subjective motivations of individual behaviour, on the individual nature of history. History, however, has both an objective and a subjective side. There are more problems in the (general) historical process as a whole than just the link between subjective approaches, motivations, value priorities, etc. The two points of view refer to different aspects of history but should not, therefore, be confused or mutually exclusive. (edited)

**Dorschel, Andreas**. The Anthropological Argument in Practical Philosophy and the Logic in Comparison. *De Phil*, 10, 21-42, 1993.

Arnold Gehlen's attempt to give anthropological grounds for morality stems from Kant's idea that being freed from the compulsion of instinct left human beings in need of compensation for the loss of the practical guidance which instinct had hitherto provided. Whereas Kant thought this compensation was to found only in reasoned morality, Gehlen would argue that morality provides recompense by becoming a quasi instinct that functions without reflection and that needs to be bred into human beings. The author maintains that in comparing animals and human beings. Gehlen posits will as a deficient instinct as deficient will; because each side is characterized as the negative of the other, Gehlen's starting point fails to meet the conditions for a valid comparison.

**Dorschel, Andreas**. Über die Intentionalität von Emotionen. *Z Phil Praxis*, 9-12, 1996.

A careful analysis of the intentionality of emotions and the distinction between the cause and the object of an emotion leads to critical conclusions with regard to practices widespread in psychotherapy.

**Dosch, Hans Günter**. Renormalized Quantum Field Theory and Cassirer's Epistemological System. *Phil Natur*, 28(1), 97-114, 1991.

**Dosen, Kosta**. Deductive Completeness. *Bull Sym Log*, 2(3), 243-283, S 96.

This is an exposition of Lambek's strengthening and generalization of the deduction theorem in categories related to intuitionistic propositional logic. Essential notions of category theory are introduced so as to yield a simple reformulation of Lambek's Functional Completeness Theorem, from which its main consequences can be readily drawn. The connections of the theorem with combinatory logic and with modal and substructural logics, are briefly considered at the end.

**Dostal, Jan**. *Wie wächst man in die Anthroposophie hinein?*. Stuttgart, Freies Geistesleben, 1996.

Wer den "Weg Anthroposophie" zu gehen versucht, wird bald auf Erscheinungen stossen, die er nicht anders denn als Gegensätze, ja Widersprüche bezeichnen muss; das gilt sowohl für das Leben als auch beim Studium des Werkes Rudolf Steiners selbst. Es ist das Anliegen Jan Dostals, diese Gegensätzlichkeiten ungeschwächt als Voraussetzung einer wirklichkeitgemässen Erkenntnis bestehen zu lassen. Denn die Anthroposophie will tiefer in die Vielschichtigkeit und Gegensätzlichkeit des Lebens führen und sich nicht in vereinfachenden, abstrakten Theorien und Schemata verlieren. (publisher, edited)

**Dostal, Robert J**. "The End of Metaphysics and the Possibility of Non-Hegelian Speculative Thought" in *Hegel, History, and Interpretation*, Gallagher, Shaun, 33-42. Albany, SUNY Pr, 1997.

Overcoming epistemology and abandoning the question of foundations is not tantamount to overcoming metaphysics. We should disengage the question of metaphysics from the question of foundations. This paper provides an historical introduction to the discussion of the end of metaphysics and considers why the question of metaphysics persists. Kant's transcendental strategy and its development by Husserl and Heidegger are briefly examined. Speculative thought may avoid both scientism and poetism; it is not first but last science. Its end is self-understanding.

**Dotti, Jorge E**. Some Remarks on Carl Schmitt's Notion of "Exception". *Kriterion*, 37(94), 24-35, Jl-D 96.

This article deals mainly with some philosophical connotations of the concept of "exception" in Carl Schmitt, especially with the idea of "finitude" or metaphysical shortcomings of human beings as the basis for every political decision. This leads to the relationship between law and state in the political theology.

**Double, Richard**. Four Naturalist Accounts of Moral Responsibility. *Behavior Phil*, 24(2), 137-143, Fall 96.

In this paper I continue that discussion by considering Kane's, Hocutt's, Waller's and my own strategy for dealing with moral responsibility. I argue that although the accounts of the other three are plausibly naturalistic, the best account is my subjectivist moral nonrealism. (edited)

**Double, Richard**. Honderich on the Consequences of Determinism. *Phil Phenomenol Res*, 56(4), 847-854, D 96.

In *How Free Are You?* Ted Honderich presents his idea of how we should view human freedom and responsibility if we believe that all human actions are determined. In this paper I endorse Honderich's analysis of the attitudinal nature of the free will issue, but argue that on Honderich's conception of attitudes a better conclusion would be that determinism can have no consequences for our attitudes about persons. To show this I develop an analogy between metaethics and normative ethics to show that on the premise that attitudes are neither true nor false, metaphysical claims have no consequences for our lower-level theorizing, whether in normative ethics or in free will.

**Double, Richard**. *Metaphilosophy and Free Will*. New York, Oxford Univ Pr, 1996.

Double begins by elaborating the connection between metaphilosophy and free will. He identifies four distinct metalevel viewpoints that drive different answers to the free will problem: Philosophy as Conversation; Philosophy as Praxis; Philosophy as Underpinnings; and Philosophy as World View Construction. From there, he discusses intermediate-level principles that work in combination with the metaphilosophies, then provides ten applications from recent free will debates that demonstrate how differences in metaphilosophy make the free will problem unsolvable. In the second half of the book Double makes the strongest case he can—consistent with his own metaphilosophical view—for accepting free will subjectivism. (publisher,edited)

**Double, Richard**. Misdirection in the Free Will Problem. *Amer Phil Quart*, 34(3), 357-366, Jl 97.

The key question in the free will debate is: "Under what conditions would our choices be connected to the psychological states that precede them so as to make us morally responsible for the actions those choices produce?" Our verdict will be *metaphysical*, because it needs to specify a connection between our psychological states and our choices: deterministic, indeterministic, or even both. Our answer is also *evaluative*. In saying that a hypothesized connection would or would not be good enough to support moral responsibility, we are making the evaluative claim that some nonmoral, metaphysical fact warrants the application of the moral term "moral responsibility." To answer this question, we need to keep locked onto its metaphysical and evaluative nature and avoid spurious issues. This paper argues that some of the most prominent recent writing on free will, including that of Kane, van Inwagen and Frankfurt, becomes side-tracked from this key issue.

**Dougherty, Charles J**. Joining in Life and Death: On Separating the Lakeberg Twins. *Bioethics Forum*, 11(1), 9-16, Spr 95.

The birth of conjoined twins in 1993 garnered extensive media coverage when the girls were separated, resulting in the death of one twin immediately and the other's nine months later. The cost and experimental nature of the surgery focused attention on ethical issues in neonatalogy and caused society to weigh the fairness of expensive treatments with little probable benefit. By utilizing the principle of double-effect, the author assesses the ethical ramifications of this controversial case.

**Douven, Igor**. A Paradox for Empiricism (?). *Proc Phil Sci Ass*, 3(Suppl), S290-S297, 1996.

According to van Fraassen, constructive empiricism yields a better account of science than does scientific realism. One particularly important advantage van Fraassen claims his position to have over scientific realism is that the former can make sense of science without invoking (what he calls) pre-Kantian metaphysics. In the present paper the consistency of van Fraassen's position is put in doubt. Specifically, it will be argued that van Fraassen faces the paradox that he cannot do with nor without the pre-Kantian metaphysics he abhors.

**Douven, Igor** and Ladyman, James and Horsten, Leon (& others). A Defence of Van Fraassen's Critique of Abductive Inference: Reply to Psillos. *Phil Quart*, 47(188), 305-321, Jl 97.

**Dow, Alan**. On Boolean Subalgebras of *P*(omega$_1$)/ctble. *J Sym Log*, 61(3), 873-879, S 96.

**Dowling, Keith**. Absolute and Conditional Rights. *S Afr J Phil*, 16(1), 1-6, F 97.

Why do some of the rights in the new South African *Constitution* (1996) seem to be absolute whereas others seem to be conditional? In answer to this question, I argue that the idea of human rights may well have its *telos* in an account of our biological and psychological needs. I show that all persons have certain basic biological and psychological needs which must be met if they are to function at all, while there are other things we all need if we are to flourish. I go on to argue that meeting such needs gives a point to most, if not all, of our claims about human rights. Thus we can see why our rights matter to us; judging and acting in accordance with them meets the needs in question. I argue also that it is the difference in our needs,—viz. between the things we need if we are to function at all and the things we need if we are to flourish—which may underlie the distinction we want to make between those rights which are *prima facie* absolute and those which are conditional.

**Downey, Rodney G** (& others) and Chen, Jianer and Cai, Liming. Advice Classes of Parameterized Tractability. *Annals Pure Applied Log*, 84(1), 119-138, Mr 97.

Many natural computational problems have input consisting of two or more parts, one of which may be considered a *parameter*. For example, there are many problems for which the input consists of a graph and a positive integer. A number of results are presented concerning parameterized problems that can be solved (uniformly with respect to the parameter) in complexity classes below *P*, given a single word of advice for each parameter value. Different ways in which the word of advice can be employed are considered, and it is shown that the class *FPT* of *tractable* parameterized problems (the parameterized analog of *P*) has interesting and natural internal structure.

**Downie, Robin S** and Randall, Fiona. Parenting and the Best Interests of Minors. *J Med Phil*, 22(3), 219-231, Je 97.

The treatment decisions of competent adults, especially treatment refusals, are generally respected. In the case of minors something turns on their age, and older minors ought increasingly to make their own decisions. On the other hand, parents decide on behalf of infants and young children. Their right to do so can best be justified in terms of the importance of preserving intimate family relationships, rather than in terms of the child's best interests, although the child's best interests will most often follow from this arrangement. Nevertheless, there are and ought to be legal, ethical, and financial constraints on parental decision making.

**Downing, F Gerald**. On Applying Applied Philosophy. *J Applied Phil*, 13(2), 209-214, 1996.

If 'applied philosophy' is really to be applied it is necessary for its practical implications to be spelled out in some detail: both the specific goals implied if not entailed, and the life-style that would be expected to support such goals. To be specific as this would only be to emulate the ancient Greek philosophers whose influence may still be discerned and is often claimed. Contributions to a recent issue of this journal are taken as a basis for the discussion.

**Downs-Lombardi, Judy**. Teaching Styles that Encourage (and Discourage) Thinking Skills. *Inquiry (USA)*, 15(2), 67-71, Wint 95.

The purpose of this article is to discuss the kinds of teaching styles teachers use to promote or inhibit thinking in their classrooms. Participatory classrooms, in which students receive daily opportunities to address concerns and discuss issues, allow students to reflect on their own thought processes. Classes which are primarily lecture, in which students take copious notes and participate minimally or not at all, discourage exchange of ideas and keep students from practicing higher-order thinking.

**Doyle, John P**. Between Transcendental and Transcendental: The Missing Link?. *Rev Metaph*, 50(4), 783-815, Je 97.

Medieval transcendentals are on the side of things while Kantian transcendentality is on the side of the knower. Is there a link between the two in the seventeenth-century scholastic understanding of "supertranscendentals?" In the century before Kant, scholastic supertranscendental being was primarily identified with extrinsic intelligibility and regarded as a contribution of the knower. It was said to be the same as "the object as such" (*objectum ut tale*). This seems very close to *der Gegenstand überhaupt* which Kant has called a "missing concept" above the dichotomy of the possible and the impossible.

**Doyle, John P**. Silvester Mauro, S.J. (1619-1687) on Four Degrees of Abstraction. *Int Phil Quart*, 36(4), 461-474, D 96.

Mauro says there are four degrees of abstraction. The lowers is *physical*, abstracting from material singulars. The second is *mathematical*, abstracting not just from singulars, but also from sensible and changeable matter as such. A third is *metaphysical*, abstracting from all matter and opening on to real immaterial being. Peculiar to Mauro and marking a departure from orthodox Aristotelianism is the last and highest degree, which is *logical*. At this level, we consider intentional being—which he says is more immaterial than real being, including that studied by metaphysics, in as much as "being known" is identical with being elevated from matter.

**Doyle, John P**. Two Thomists on the Morality of a Jailbreak. *Mod Sch*, 74(2), 95-115, Ja 97.

**Drago, Antonino**. "An Ideal of Intuitionistic Kind Representing the Organisation of a Physical or Mathematical Theory" in *Verdad: lógica, representación y mundo*, Villegas Forero, L, 467-480. Santiago de Compostela, Univ Santiago Comp, 1996.

The original works by the founders of some scientific theories present a collection of double negated statements about crucial ideas. These statements are recognised to belong to an intuitionistic logic rather than the classical one. As a consequence, no more a deductive model of a theory drawn from some principles by the deductive method is possible. An investigation on these scientific theories leads to recognise some common features for characterising a new model of the organisation of a scientific theory.

**Drago, Antonino**. Alternative Mathematics and Alternative Theoretical Physics: The Method for Linking Them Together. *Epistemologia*, 19(1), 33-50, Ja-Je 96.

Qui per matematica alternativa si considera la matematica costruttiva in quanto questa non include l'infinito in atto (ad es. attraverso l'assioma di Zermelo), come invece fa la matematica classica in maniera essenziale. Vengono presi in esame i suoi risultati più importanti per la fisica teorica, cioè le soluzioni delle equazioni differenziali e vengono messi in relazione con l'apparato matematico

delle diverse formulazioni che possono rappresentare le meccanica o la termodinamica. Risulta che sono alternative alle formulazioni dominanti (quella di Newton per la meccanica e quella di Clausius-Kelvin per la termodinamica) le formulazioni di Lazare Carnot, recentemente riscoperta, e la termodinamica di Sadi Carnot. Queste ultime, assieme alla chimica classica, costituiscono la parte più importante della fisica teorica alternativa all'interno della fisica classica. (edited)

**Dragonetti, Carmen** and Tola, Fernando. Buddhist Conception of Reality. *J Indian Counc Phil Res*, 14(1), 35-64, S-D 96.

**Drane, James F**. Bioethical Perspectives from Ibero-America. *J Med Phil*, 21(6), 557-569, D 96.

The modern discipline called bioethics is not much more than thirty years old in the United States. We are much closer to the beginning of the same discipline in Ibero-America. This issue of *The Journal of Medicine and Philosophy* introduces an English-speaking readership to the concerns, emphases and insights of this newer version which has developed in and been conditioned by the particular historical setting, cultural ethos and social reality of the Ibero-America region.

**Dravid, N S**. Ahārya Cognition in Navya-Nyāya. *J Indian Counc Phil Res*, 13(2), 164-168, Ja-Ap 96.

**Dravid, N S**. Nyāya is Realist par Excellence (A supplementary note). *J Indian Counc Phil Res*, 14(1), 164-167, S-D 96.

**Dreben, Burton** and Kanamori, Akihiro. Hilbert and Set Theory. *Synthese*, 110(1), 77-125, Ja 97.

**Dreier, James**. Accepting Agent Centred Norms: A Problem for Non-Cognitivists and a Suggestion for Solving It. *Austl J Phil*, 74(3), 409-422, S 96.

The article presents a problem for noncognitivist metaethical theories and some abortive attempts at solutions, presents a more satisfactory solution and notes some consequences. Noncognitivists need to say what sort of mental state constitutes sincere acceptance of a given normative theory. A natural representation would have the acceptor's preferences map the 'better than' relation induced by the normative theory in question. The problem is that agent centred theories cannot be represented by a single 'better than' relation defined over states of affairs. The solution is to think of properties as the relata of 'better than'.

**Drenth, Joost P H**. Proliferation of Authors on Research Reports in Medicine. *Sci Eng Ethics*, 2(4), 469-480, O 96.

Publication in the biomedical literature is important because it is the major pathway by which new concepts and discoveries are disseminated amongst scientists. In the last 30 years there has been a dramatic increase, not only in the volume of publications but in the number of authors per article as well. This paper summarizes the current literature on authorship and its proliferation in medicine. From the literature it becomes clear that for biomedical articles, the mean number of authors increased from 1.7 in 1960 to 3.1 in 1990, and there are indications that this trend is even greater in clinical medicine such that single authorship almost has disappeared. Formal guidelines of who should be considered an author have been set by the International Committee of Medical Journal Editors. There are studies suggesting that not all authors on multiauthor papers fulfill these criteria. Inappropriate multiple authorship leads to dilution of authorship responsibility and unjustified citation in curriculum vitae. Recommendations regarding the prevention of inappropriate authorship are given in this paper.

**Dretske, Fred**. "Phenomenal Externalism" in *Perception,* Villanueva, Enrique (ed), 143-158. Atascadero, Ridgeview, 1996.

**Dretske, Fred**. "Reply to Commentators" in *Perception,* Villanueva, Enrique (ed), 179-183. Atascadero, Ridgeview, 1996.

**Dretske, Fred**. Absent Qualia. *Mind Lang*, 11(1), 78-85, Mr 96.

**Dretske, Fred**. How Reasons Explain Behaviour: Reply to Melnyk and Noordhof. *Mind Lang*, 11(2), 223-229, Je 96.

Melnyk complains that my account of the way reasons explain behaviour cannot be extended to cover novel behaviours. I admit that I did not extend it, but deny that it is not extendible. This, indeed, is what Chapter 6 of Dretske (1988) was all about. Noordhof finds faults with my account and claims there is another account (partial supervenience) that does a better job. I acknowledge one of the defects—a defect I was aware of when I wrote the book—but deny that the partial supervenience of content on intrinsic properties represents a better theory of the explanatory role of content.

**Dretske, Fred**. So Do We Know or Don't We?. *Phil Phenomenol Res*, 57(2), 407-409, Je 97.

**Dretske, Fred**. What Good is Consciousness?. *Can J Phil*, 27(1), 1-15, Mr 97.

Questions about the good (function, benefits) of consciousness are often muddled by failure to observe three distinctions: 1) the difference between creature consciousness (Tom is conscious of X) and state consciousness (Tom's experience of X is conscious); 2) the difference between objects and acts of awareness (the X of which Tom is aware vs. Tom's awareness of it); and 3) awareness of objects (e.g., turtles) vs. awareness of facts (that they are turtles). Once these distinctions are in place, the good or function of consciousness is obvious.

**Drew, Allan P**. Genes and Human Behavior: The Emerging Paradigm. *Zygon*, 32(1), 41-50, Mr 97.

The physical properties of human beings and other organisms as well as their social behavioral traits are manifestations of both genetic inheritance and environment. Recent behavioral research has indicated that certain characteristics or behaviors—such as schizophrenia, divorce and

Dreyfus, Hubert L 606 AUTHOR INDEX

homosexuality—are highly heritable and are not governed exclusively by social environment. A balanced view of human behavior includes the effects of social learning as well as of genetically determined behavior. A new paradigm promotes enhanced understanding and acceptance of human diversity, be it cultural, racial, or sexual, and has the potential to unite scientists and theologians by creating common grounds of understanding.

**Dreyfus, Hubert L** and Spinosa, Charles. Highway Bridges and Feasts: Heidegger and Borgmann on How to Affirm Technology. *Man World*, 30(2), 159-177, Ap 97.

Borgmann's views seem to clarify and elaborate Heidegger's. Both thinkers understand technology as a way of coping with people and things that reveals them, viz. make them intelligible. Both thinkers also claim that technological coping could devastate not only our environment and communal ties but more importantly the historical, world-opening being that has defined Westerners since the Greeks. Both think that this devastation can be prevented by attending to the practices for coping with simple things like family meals and footbridges. But, contrary to Borgmann, Heidegger claims further that, alongside simple things, we can affirm technological things such as autobahn bridges. For Borgmann, technological coping produces things like central heating that are so dispersed they inhibit skillful interaction with them and, therefore, prevent our being sensitive to ourselves as world-disclosers. For Heidegger, so long as we can still relate to nontechnological things, we can affirm relations with technological things because we can maintain both our technological and the nontechnological *ways of world-disclosing*. So Borgmann sees revealing as primarily directed to things while Heidegger sees it as directed to worlds. If Heidegger is right about us, we have more leeway to save ourselves from technological devastation than Borgmann sees.

**Dreyfus, Hubert L** and Spinosa, Charles. Single-World versus Plural-World Antiessentialism: A Reply to Tim Dean. *Crit Inquiry*, 23(4), 921-932, Sum 97.

**Dreyfus, Hubert L** and Spinosa, Charles. Two Kinds of Antiessentialism and Their Consequences. *Crit Inquiry*, 22(4), 735-763, Sum 96.

**Dripps, Donald A**. Form and Substance in Criminal Justice Scholarship: H. Richard Uviller, *Virtual Justice*. *Crim Just Ethics*, 16(1), 39-48, Win-Spr 97.

**Drivod, Lucien**. La liberté a-t-elle un sens dans la tradition chinoise?. *Philosopher*, 19, 43-57, 1996.

La liberté a-t-elle un sens dans la tradition chinoise? Nous pouvons maintenant répondre de façon positive. Il est vrai que la Chine a toujours vécu sous un régime autoritaire, que la plupart des philosophies chinoises ont prêché la soumission à l'État Mais il reste que, pour parodier une sentence taoïste, là où l'on prêche la soumission, on suscite la possibilité de révolte. Et en effet l'histoire de la Chine n'est pas l'histoire du *Despotisme Oriental*; périodiquement la révolte gronde dans l'Empire du Milieu, les Dynasties tombent; les ministres intègres se lèvent pour rappeler la voie du Ciel aux Souverains despotiques. Le pouvoir n'est pas sans contrepoids et il reste toujours la liberté de l'homme des peuples paysans: l'impôt payé, le paysan ne doit allégeance qu'à la terre, il vaque à ses occupations, sans souci des autres et du politique. C'est la liberté des Taoïstes à laquelle des milliers de poèmes ont rendu hommage; citons Wang Wei: "Drue et dense l'herbe parfumée même en automne verdoie", "Les grands pins si hauts même en été frissonnent", "Boeufs et moutons s'en reviennent par les ruelles du village", "L'enfant au coeur simple ne reconnaît pas la tenue du mandarin".

**Dror, Omer** and Shimshon Rubin, Simon. Professional Ethics of Psychologists and Physicians: Morality, Confidentiality, and Sexuality in Israel. *Ethics Behavior*, 6(3), 213-238, 1996.

Clinical psychologists' and nonpsychiatric physicians' attitudes and behaviors in sexual and confidentiality boundary violations were examined. The 171 participants' responses were analyzed by profession, sex, and status (student, resident, professional) on semantic differential, boundary violation vignettes, and a version of Pope, Tabachnick, and Keith-Spiegel's (1987) ethical scale. Psychologists rated sexual boundary violation as more unethical than did physicians (p001). Rationale (p01) and timing (p0001) influenced ratings. Psychologists reported fewer sexualized behaviors than physicians (p). Professional experience (p01) and sex (p05) were associated with confidence-violating behavior. Overall, 78% of the sample reported attitudes or behaviors associated with boundary violations. The behavior violations were correlated (r=.49). Actual violators rated vignette violators more leniently than did nonviolators (p01).

**Drozdek, Adam**. Aristotle's Razor. *Dialogos*, 32(70), 181-198, Jl 97.

It is argued in this paper that Aristotle conducted his analyses according to the following principle: not only is explanation in terms of the finite always easier and better than in terms of the infinite, but infinity in all respects should be a suspect concept and avoided even at the cost of making explanations more complex. This principle can be called Aristotle's razor to be used to remove infinity from theory and from nature. This razor is a primary principle used by Aristotle in seeing the world as finite and in seeing it through finite means. Aristotle was not altogether consistent in applying this razor, but it was one of the most powerful tools he used in constructing his impressive system, especially in physics. Aristotle's razor is not just a form of the Occam razor, since it specifically singles out infinity as a worse assumption than finitude. In fact, these two razors are orthogonal and can be applied independently.

**Druart, Therese-Anne**. "Averroës on the Harmony of Philosophy and Religion" in *Averroës and the Enlightenment*, Wahba, Mourad (ed), 253-262. Amherst, Prometheus, 1996.

The paper argues that one of the basic issues on which philosophers and religious thinkers differ is the conception of the agent cause. Already Avicenna had carefully defended the view that "the true acting cause is not the observed one". Al-Ghazali, in his *Incoherence of the Philosophers*, attacked Avicenna and claimed that the only true agent cause is God since there is no necessary connection between what is usually believed to be an agent and its effect and, therefore, that miracles are possible. In his rebuttal of the *Incoherence* Averroes simply dodges the philosophical issue to reserve political peace.

**Drwiega, Marek**. Paul Ricoeur's *Little Ethics* (in Polish). *Kwartalnik Filozof*, 24(4), 153-174, 1996.

**Dryden, Donald**. Susanne K. Langer and American Philosophic Naturalism in the Twentieth Century. *Trans Peirce Soc*, 33(1), 161-182, Wint 97.

Susanne Langer's efforts to construct an account of the nature and origins of mind, consciousness, and the uniquely human sphere of culture within the framework of evolutionary biology embodies commitments to the sciences and to antireductionism that have been central to American philosophic naturalism since the time of William James. I argue that the relative neglect of Langer's work is due largely to the originality of her project, which makes sense only when taken in its entirety and interpreted in the light of recent work in philosophy, evolutionary biology, and cognitive science which she anticipated but did not influence.

**Duarte, Rodrigo A P**. Notas sobre modernidade e sujeito na dialética do esclarecimento. *Kriterion*, 34(88), 34-49, Ag-D 93.

This article begins with a characterization of the sui generis concept of modernity proposed by Adorno & Horkheimer and proceeds to point our the various aspects in which the idea of subject appears in connection with that concept. Subsequently, resorting to elements already present in the *Dialectics of Enlightenment*, focus is set on the—generally disregarded—Adornian project of dialectically surpassing that modernity, which underlies his works of maturity—*Negative Dialectics and Aesthetical Theory*.

**Dubler, Nancy Neveloff** and Lane, Arline. The Health Care Agent: Selected but Neglected. *Bioethics Forum*, 13(2), 17-21, Sum 97.

The health care agent or "proxy" whose involvement in medical treatment decision making is triggered by the patient's incapacity, frequently faces a potentially awesome responsibility alone and unprepared. Often neglected or excluded from patient-care planning, the proxy has informational and emotional needs that must be met by the health care team in the very same manner as would those of the patient. By establishing a triad of provider, patient, and proxy early in the patient's care, much of the angst of proxy decision making could be eased.

**Dubois, Didier** and Benferhat, Salem and Prade, Henri. Some Syntactic Approaches to the Handling of Inconsistent Knowledge Bases: A Comparative Study. *Stud Log*, 58(1), 17-45, 1997.

This paper presents and discusses several methods for reasoning from inconsistent knowledge bases. A so-called argued consequence relation, taking into account the existence of consistent arguments in favor of a conclusion and the absence of consistent arguments in favor of its contrary, is particularly investigated. Flat knowledge bases, i.e., without any priority between their elements, are studied under different inconsistency-tolerant consequence relations, namely the so-called argumentative, free, universal, existential, cardinality-based, and paraconsistent consequence relations. The syntax-sensitivity of these consequence relations is studied. A companion paper is devoted to the case where priorities exist between the pieces of information in the knowledge base.

**Dubois, Didier** and Prade, Henri. New Trends and Open Problems in Fuzzy Logic and Approximate Reasoning. *Theoria (Spain)*, 11(27), 109-121, S 96.

This short paper about fuzzy set-based approximate reasoning first emphasizes the three main semantics for fuzzy sets: similarity, preference and uncertainty. The difference between truth-functional many-valued logics of vague or gradual propositions and nonfully compositional calculi such as possibilistic logic (which handles uncertainty) or similarity logics is stressed. Then, potentials of fuzzy set-based reasoning methods are briefly outlined for various kinds of approximate reasoning: deductive reasoning about flexible constraints, reasoning under uncertainty and inconsistency, hypothetical reasoning, exception-tolerant plausible reasoning using generic knowledge, interpolative reasoning, and abductive reasoning (under uncertainty). Open problems are listed in the conclusion.

**Dubreucq, Eric**. Flesh, Grace and Spirit: Metempsychosis and Resurrection from Porphyry to Saint Augustine (in French). *Arch Phil*, 60(1), 25-45, Ja-Mr 97.

To defend the doctrine of the resurrection, Augustine was led to modify his understanding of the self, in opposition to the vision of the ancient philosophers, especially Porphyry. Against the neo-Platonic view that the soul itself was divine while the body was mortal, Augustine saw in the self the possibility, through the graced action of the Holy Spirit on the believer, of unification with and divinization by, God. Theology and soteriology thereby propose a new anthropology.

**Dubucs, Jacques**. Logique, effectivité et faisabilité. *Dialogue (Canada)*, 36(1), 45-68, Wint 97.

This paper can be read as an attempt at providing philosophical foundations to linear logic. The only plausible form of philosophical antirealism deals with practical feasibility rather than with effectivity in principle. The very notion of recognizability is ambiguous and it has to be considered from a stricter perspective than currently done. The intuitionistic assertability conditions are to be reinforced. This change requires a move towards a frame in which the circumstances of the application of a logical rule can be specified. Gentzen's

AUTHOR INDEX 607 Dulek, Ronald E

sequential calculi provide such a frame, when some structural rules have been removed or limited.

**Duchesneau, François**. Leibniz et Stahl: divergences sur le concept d'organisme. *Stud Leibniz*, 27(2), 185-212, 1995.

Both Stahl and Leibniz worked out conceptions of the organism that diverged significantly from the mechanistic models involved in the Cartesian dualism of soul and body. In the polemics which developed in 1709-1710 concerning Stahl's *Theoria medica vera* (1708), Leibniz focused his attacks on what he considered a paralogistic theory of the soul; he wondered in particular how such an abstruse metaphysics could be reconciled with the scientific analysis of vital phenomena. Contrary to Stahl, Leibniz would defend the view that the sufficient reason of organisms at the phenomenal level depends on an integrative combination of specific mechanisms; but the soul conceived as an entelechy needs to be called upon to account for the functional integration of the whole at the substantive level. Thus, the psychic and the somatic would involve a joint rationality unfolding in analogical and expressive relationships. However, both domains would require the use of separate analytic methodologies in any attempt at explaining those relationships.

**Duchesneau, François**. Révolution scientifique et problématique de l'être vivant. *Rev Phil Louvain*, 94(4), 568-597, N 96.

Authoritative assessments of the Scientific Revolution suggest that the question of the living was not central to the new mechanistic natural philosophy which developed in the seventeenth century. But fostering adequate models of the living seemed of foremost importance for modern philosophers who questioned the specificity of organisms in nature and investigates the means of analyzing vital phenomena. The first models that framed up within modern science took their inspiration in neo-Platonist or neo-Aristotelian traditions, while they parted with the Galenist orthodoxy. The author examines herewith the theoretical conceptions Harvey and Van Helmont would subordinate empirical analyses to. In Harvey's case, there is no question of denying the importance of so-called experimental arguments, nor, in Van Helmont's, of challenging the speculative nature of his ontology of psychomorphic vital principles; the aim of the author is rather that of sketching the epistemological profile of those models the protagonists of vital mechanism will have to distance themselves from.

**Dudiak, Jeffrey M**. "Again Ethics: A Levinasian Reading of Caputo Reading Levinas" in *Knowing Other-Wise: Philosophy at the Threshold of Spirituality,* Olthuis, James H (ed), 172-213. New York, Fordham Univ Pr, 1997.

This article engages John Caputo's reading of Levinas in his recent *Against Ethics*. Despite his debt to Levinas, Caputo insists on keeping himself at a certain distance from Levinas "seriousness" and "piety." This essay inhabits the gap opened up by this distancing, challenges Caputo's reading of Levinas and proposes that the gap may be smaller than Caputo contends. While Caputo understands Levinas to be proposing an "ethics" in the traditional, metaphysical sense, a way of thinking that Caputo believes Derrida to have effectively deconstructed, it is argued that Levinas is in fact interested in precisely what Caputo (after Derrida) is concerned about: undeconstructible justice.

**Dudiak, Jeffrey M**. "Structures of Violence, Structures of Peace: Levinasian Reflections on Just War and Pacifism" in *Knowing Other-Wise: Philosophy at the Threshold of Spirituality,* Olthuis, James H (ed), 159-171. New York, Fordham Univ Pr, 1997.

This article is an exposition of Levinas's understanding of necessary yet violent structures, which we cannot live with or without, as this discussion is brought to the traditional just-war/pacifism debate. Each of these traditional positions involves "*un beau risque*" that at once must and cannot be taken. This conceptual paradox, whose terms remain irreducible to the coordinates of a dialectic, forbids the possibility of a definite position on the issue, demanding instead a perpetual and difficult, communal vigilance.

**Duerlinger, James**. Vasubandhu's Philosophical Critique of the Vatsiputriyas' Theory of Person (I). *J Indian Phil*, 25(3), 307-335, Je 97.

**Dürr, Detlef** and Daumer, Martin and Goldstein, Sheldon (& others). Naive Realism about Operators. *Erkenntnis*, 45(2 & 3), 379-397, Nov 96.

A source of much difficulty and confusion in the interpretation of quantum mechanics is a "naive realism about operators." By this we refer to various ways of taking too seriously the notion of operator-as-observable and in particular to the all too casual talk about "measuring operators" that occurs when the subject is quantum mechanics. Without a specification of what should be meant by "measuring" a quantum observable, such an expression can have no clear meaning. A definite specification is provided by Bohmian mechanics, a theory that emerges from Schrödinger's equation for a system of particles when we merely insist that "particles" means particles. Bohmian mechanics clarifies the status and the role of operators as observables in quantum mechanics by providing the operational details absent from standard quantum mechanics. It thereby allows us to readily dismiss all the radical claims traditionally enveloping the transition from the classical to the quantum realm—for example, that we must abandon classical logic or classical probability. The moral is rather simple: Beware naive realism, especially about operators!

**Duessel, Reinhard**. Investigation of Things, Philosophical Counseling, and the Misery of the *Last Man*. *J Chin Phil*, 23(3), 321-339, S 96.

**Düttmann, Alexander García** and Walker, Nicholas (trans). The Culture of Polemic: Misrecognizing Recognition. *Rad Phil*, 81, 27-34, Ja-F 97.

**Duff, R A**. Commentary on "Psychopathy, Other-Regarding Moral Beliefs, and Responsibility". *Phil Psychiat Psych*, 3(4), 283-286, D 96.

I make four criticisms of Fields's account of one type of psychopathy as a responsibility-negating personality disorder which involves an incapacity to form other-regarding moral beliefs. First, his account of what it is to hold moral beliefs (in terms of accepting universal practical principles) actually specifies neither a necessary, nor a sufficient, condition for holding a moral belief. Second, he is too quick to dismiss the suggestion that what psychopaths suffer from is an inability to understand moral concepts and values. Third, he does not show why we should ascribe an incapacity to accept moral beliefs to the psychopaths, rather than a culpable failure to do so. Fourth, he suggests too weak a criterion of criminal liability, as requiring only the capacity to act for prudential reasons.

**Duflo, Colas**. The Inhabitants of Other Planets in Bernardin de Saint-Pierre's *Les Harmonies de la nature* (in French). *Arch Phil*, 60(1), 47-57, Ja-Mr 97.

What good is the fact that each planet offers a marvellous vantage point in regards the universe if there be no observers? For a philosophy which is as integrally finalistic as that of Bernardin de Saint-Pierre, nothing in nature is in vain. Therefore, other planets are inhabited and we can describe them by analogy.

**Dufour, Mario**. De l'indéconstructible justice. *Dialogue (Canada)*, 35(4), 677-701, Fall 96.

This article offers a reading of Derrida's work on law and right and the larger pertinence of these issues to questions about responsibility. Around the main proposition which asserts that there is no present for justice, four points are more developed: the coimplication of force and right in the application and in the creation of law; the relation between undeconstructable justice and deconstructable right; the aporias of justice and of just decision; the critical objections, among those Habermas's ones, which are addressed to Derrida's contribution to contemporary practical philosophy and to the discourse of emancipation. This paper argue that we can not deduce from the impossibility to find a pure rational ground or stable criteria for justice the necessity to see all points of view as equal and that deconstruction give a way to think beyond the traditional opposition between relativism and objectivism.

**Dufwenberg, Martin** and Lindén, Johan. Inconsistencies in Extensive Games. *Erkenntnis*, 45(1), 103-114, Jl 96.

In certain finite extensive games with perfect information, Cristina Bicchieri (1989) derives a logical contradiction from the assumptions that players are rational and that they have common knowledge of the theory of the game. She argues that this may account for play outside the Nash equilibrium. She also claims that no inconsistency arises if the players have the minimal beliefs necessary to perform backward induction. We here show that another contradiction can be derived even with minimal beliefs, so there is no paradox of common knowledge specifically. These inconsistencies do not make play outside Nash equilibrium plausible, but rather indicate that the epistemic specification must incorporate a system for belief revision. Whether rationality is common knowledge is not the issue.

**Dugré, François**. Le meurtre de soi. *Horiz Phil*, 7(1), 25-50, Fall 96.

**Duhan Kaplan, Laura**. I Married an Empiricist: A Phenomenologist Examines Philosophical Personae. *Phil Cont World*, 3(4), 8-13, Wint 96.

I suggest that philosophical writers should connect epistemological theorizing with life experience in order to explore the complex relationship between the two. The relationship of theory of experience does not fit the neat hierarchical model of a small number of general organizing principles giving form to or receiving form from a large mass of facts. Instead, as the narrative of my honeymoon and my life following it suggests, philosophical theories are one of the many genres of stories philosophers tell themselves in the process of creating and recreating personal identities and personae.

**Duhan Kaplan, Laura**. Speaking for Myself in Philosophy. *Phil Cont World*, 1(4), 20-24, Wint 94.

The conventions of positivism, still the standard model for academic discourse, require philosophers to take knowledge out of the context of personal experience. In this essay, I argue that such a decontextualization impoverished the development of moral and epistemological knowledge. I propose to contextualize such knowledge by using the personal essay as a style of philosophical writing. As literary style shapes what can be thought and said, adoption of a different literary style calls for a reinterpretation of philosophy's understanding of the self, the quest for truth and the nature of universality.

**Dula, Annette** and Katz, Jay and Brody, Baruch A. In Case of Emergency: No Need for Consent. *Hastings Center Rep*, 27(1), 7-12, Ja-F 97.

This article offers a philosophical analysis of the FDA's recent regulations on emergency room research. It argues that these regulations are based upon an appropriate ethical balancing of competing legitimate values. It also argues that two important problems (use of placebo controls and definition of when informal convent is impractical) have not been adequately addressed in these regulations.

**Dulek, Ronald E** and Motes, William H and Hilton, Chadwick B. Executive Perceptions of Superior and Subordinate Information Control: Practice Versus Ethics. *J Bus Ethics*, 16(11), 1175-1184, Ag 97.

This study examines executive perceptions of business information control. Specifically, the study explores a) whether executives perceive certain types of information control being practiced within their businesses; and, b) whether the executives regard such practices as ethical. In essence, the study suggests that both superiors and subordinates selectively practice information control. Even more importantly, however, executives see such practices as ethically acceptable on the part of superiors but as ethically questionable on the part of subordinates. A closer look at the responding executives' profile characteristics—age, gender, education and salary—reveals the complexity of these perceptions. Most importantly, gender and age emerge as two prime factors influencing executive perceptions regarding both the practice and the ethics of information control. Suggestions for future research are included at the end of the article.

**Dumais, Monique**. Éthique féministe de relation et perspectives sur le corps. *Laval Theol Phil*, 53(2), 377-384, Je 97.

Ethics of connection or of interrelatedness has been developed by feminist theologians. It allowed me to consider three perspectives concerning the body: firstly to criticize the dichotomy body/spirit and to articulate a dynamic integration of human beings; secondly, to view an ecological planning of the world as God's body; thirdly, to denounce a spiritual tradition focused on domination of cosmos and to propose a theology of world healing.

**Dummett, Michael**. "Reply to Boolos" in *Frege: Importance and Legacy*, Schirn, Matthias (ed), 253-260. Hawthorne, de Gruyter, 1996.

**Dumont-Tremblay, Maxime**. Obéir aux lois c'est être libre. *Philosopher*, 18, 67-74, 1995.

**Dumouchel, Daniel**. Kant et l'expérience esthétique de la liberté. *Dialogue . (Canada)*, 35(3), 571-591, Sum 96.

In his book *Kant and the Experience of Freedom* (1993), Paul Guyer raises anew the complex question of the relation between aesthetics and morals in Kant's thought and has identified usually neglected aspects of Kant's aesthetic. I wish to stress the originality and the importance of this project, while, however, showing its limitations. It will be seen that Guyer's interpretation, despite its undeniable depth, fails to integrate the problem of the "culture of moral sentiment" into the teleological perspective of the *Critique of Judgement*, thereby failing to grasp certain consequences of the evolution of Kant's aesthetic.

**Dumouchel, Daniel**. Kant's Pre-Critical Aesthetics: Genesis of the Notions of "Taste" and Beauty (in French). *Arch Phil*, 60(1), 59-86, Ja-Mr 97.

Kant's commentators have often neglected the formation of his aesthetics (in the sense of a theory of taste and its object, beauty). We therefore want to underline the importance of his precritic thought on aesthetics for the understanding of the first part of his *Critique of Judgment*. Our remarks will concentrate on the crucial period opening in the years 1769-1770, when Kant attempts to lay the philosophical foundation for his notions of taste and beauty on the formal and universal laws of sensibility (Sinnlichkeit).

**Dumouchel, Daniel**. La cohérence de la théorie esthétique de Moses Mendelssohn. *Rev Phil Louvain*, 95(1), 44-75, F 97.

The aim is to stress the philosophical coherency of Moses Mendelssohn's theory of aesthetics by considering the dynamics of the theory's development, thereby discarding the often-repeated charges of psychologism and incoherency. Mendelssohn's thought on aesthetics, which was deeply influenced by English, French and German innovative aesthetic theories, is predicated on the Leibniz-Wolff account of the origins of pleasure and of the unity of subjectivity. The author will show the evolution of Mendelssohn's aesthetics between 1775 and 1785 is mainly the result of his adherence to two procuppositions inherited from Leibniz and Wolff: the unitary theory of the soul and the foundation of pleasure on the perception of a perfection. A comparison between the "aesthetics of perfection" and the paradoxical aesthetic sentiments of the tragic and the "sublime," as well as the application of the rationalist theory of the soul of the new notion of the "autonomy" of the aesthetic sentiment, will show Mendelssohn's late rationalism's surprising adaptability.

**Duncan, Barbara J**. Character Education: Reclaiming the Social. *Educ Theor*, 47(1), 119-130, Wint 97.

**Dunfee, Thomas W** and Taka, Iwao. Japanese Moralogy as Business Ethics. *J Bus Ethics*, 16(5), 507-519, Ap 97.

Moralogy is an indigenous six-decade-old Japanese approach to business ethics which has been particularly influential among middle-sized business. The core themes of moralogy are 1) the inseparability of morality and economic activities, 2) the recognition of a difference between social justice and universal justice, and 3) an emphasis on identification of principles of supreme or universal morality. Moralogy recognizes moral liberty and a principle of "omni-directional fairness"; and may be best described as a virtue-based stakeholder approach to business ethics. It differs in significant ways, however, from Rawls's *theory of justice* and Donaldson and Dunfee's *integrative social contracts theory*.

**Dunn, John**. The Contemporary Political Significance of John Locke's Conception of Civil Society. *Iyyun*, 45, 103-124, Jl 96.

**Dunn, Phillip C** and Delacruz, Elizabeth Manley. The Evolution of Discipline-Based Art Education. *J Aes Educ*, 30(3), 67-82, Fall 96.

**Dunn Koblentz, Evelynn**. Deconstruction Deconstructed: The Resurrection of Being. *Cont Phil*, 18(1), 8-10, Ja-F 96.

From the perspective of a new philosophy of integration, "Deconstruction Deconstructed: The Resurrection of Being" finds that Jacques Derrida's devaluation of traditional Western philosophy is valid, but that his condemnation of metaphysics, per se, is not justified. The article contends that Western philosophy's seminal fault is the anthropocentricity of the paradigm of Being underlying it, logos, which serves as its abstract pseudo-absolute, and that deconstruction has not seen the need to free itself from that invalid traditional paradigm. An integrated scientific and metaphysical approach to Being uncovers it to be an all-encompassing physical process of the *real*, with the metaphysical attribute of *cosmic oneness*; its *absolute*, the *cosmos*, as common to all that exists, can be considered valid.

**Dunning, Stephen N**. *Dialectical Readings: Three Types of Interpretation*. University Park, Pennsylvania Univ Pr, 1997.

In *Dialectical Readings*, Dunning distinguishes three dialectical types of interpretation: Theoretical interpretation assumes binary oppositions,

transactional interpretation seeks reciprocal relations and transformational interpretation discerns paradoxical meanings. This typology enables Dunning to offer new and insightful readings of texts debating a variety of issues: B.F. Skinner, Jacques Ellul and Thomas Kuhn on the implications of science and technology for human values; Claude Lévi-Strauss, Mary Douglas and Joseph Campbell on mythology; Lee Benson, E. H. Carr and Reinhold Niebuhr on history; Roland Barthes, Erich Fromm and Soren Kierkegaard on love; Friedrich Nietzsche, Martin Buber and Paul Tillich on human identity; and Michel Foucault, E.D. Hirsch and Paul Ricoeur on theory and interpretation. *Dialectical Readings* enables readers to recognize the dialectical character of their own understanding as well as that of others on these and a wide variety of other topics.(publisher, edited)

**Dupré, John**. Promiscuous Realism: Reply to Wilson. *Brit J Phil Sci*, 47(3), 441-444, S 96.

This paper presents a brief response to Robert A. Wilson's critical discussion of Promiscuous Realism (1996). I argue that, although convergence on a unique conception of species cannot be ruled out, the evidence against such an outcome is stronger than Wilson allows. In addition, given the failure of biological science to come up with a unique and privileged set of biological kinds, the relevance of the various overlapping kinds of ordinary language to the metaphysics of biological kinds is greater than Wilson admits.

**Dupré, Louis**. Hegel and the Enlightenment: A Study in Ambiguity. *Owl Minerva*, 28(1), 13-24, Fall 96.

In this essay, therefore, I will explore Hegel's treatment of the abyss in mental life and explain how this constitutes a position on the unconscious.(edited)

**Dupuis, Michel**. Le cogito ébloui ou la noèse sans noème. *Rev Phil Louvain*, 94(2), 294-310, My 96.

There is always a subtle link between the thought of Levinas and the great works of classical philosophy. Among the latter, certain texts of Descartes are treated in a very special way of Levinas: they are frequently referred to, also frequently quoted, frequently analysed in detail, and this holds from the start of Levinas's career to his latest publications. At the heart of what the A. recognizes as being a powerful metaphysical inspiration by Descartes that determines the "phenomenology" of Levinas, he attempts to describe here a possible Cartesian and Levinassian vision of the Infinite by dealing with the question of the creation of certain truths, the distinctions of "natural" analogy and of the "ethical" marvel, and finally the topic of the implanting of the idea of the infinite in me and of the overflowing of the cogito. The A. attempts to show that Levinas received from Descartes the inspiration for a phenomenology that is radical in a different way.

**Duque, Félix**. "El corazón del pueblo: La "religión" del Hegel de Berna" in *El inicio del Idealismo alemán*, Market, Oswaldo, 237-262. Madrid, Ed Complutense, 1996.

What firstly seems to be a revenge of Hegel, a former student of the Protestant *Tübinger Stift*, against an ideological manipulation of Kantism, which makes his thought anew acceptable for Christianity, by putting together the spirit of criticism and biblical exegesis, became in 1795 a deep diatribe against the decadent Christianity and, generally speaking, against modern culture. Hegel will struggle against those "horrors of the objective World" with the weapons of the *Empfindung* (a cordial impression of reality through the living folk traditions) and the *Herz* (i.e., the heart, as the sentimental centering of life). He confronts *pleroma* and *fetish*. But this denunciation will prove inane, because this heart, from *his biblical origins*, is already a metaphor derived from monetary circulation. The wound keeps on open.(edited)

**Duque, Félix**. Dieu en vu chez Ortega et María Zambrano. *Frei Z Phil Theol*, 44(1-2), 68-86, 1997.

**Duque, Félix**. En memoria de la memoria de Martin Heidegger. *Rev Filosof (Mexico)*, 29(87), 438-453, S-D 96.

**Duque, Félix**. Las verdades del cuerpo cartesiano. *G Metaf*, 18(3), 303-320, S-D 96.

**Duque, Félix**. Lo sminuzzamento dello spazio storico. *Teoria*, 16(1), 87-92, 1996.

**Duque, Félix**. Martin Heidegger: En los confines de la Metafísica. *An Seminar Hist Filosof*, 13, 19-38, 1996.

The aim of this paper is to offer a thematic re-examination of Heidegger's work focused on the question of being's truth. A truth which is shining in the attitude of the *Dasein zum Tode*, in the work of art as a chiasmatical interference and also in the *World-Cross-Notching* of the *Geviert*, in order to bring out the strong unity of the Heideggerian way of thought, which is far away of the "didactical" and made-up academical divisions, turns and returns, also beyond external interpretations.(edited)

**Duran, Jane**. Syntax, Imagery and Naturalization. *Philosophia (Israel)*, 25(1-4), 373-387, Ap 97.

The imagery debate is analyzed both in terms of its own resolution and insofar as concomitant areas in philosophizing are concerned. The arguments of both the pictorialists and descriptionists are discussed and Tye's work cited. The greater conclusion of the piece is that the naturalization inherent in work that might solve or resolve the imagery problem is naturalization that might prove more than useful in many arenas of contemporary analytic thought. Reference is made both to the PDP theorizing of Rumelhart and McClelland and to the topobiology of Gerald Edelman.

**Duran, Jane**. The Feminine And The Natural. *Int J Applied Phil*, 10(2), 45-50, Wint-Spr 96.

It is sometimes argued that conceptions of the feminine are related to those of the natural. This paper attempts to address that intersection, while establishing the masculinist origins of the hypernormative, admittedly nonnatural, philosophical traditions that have dominated Western thought.

**Duran, Jane** and Stewart, Earl. Toward an Aesthetic of Black Musical Expression. *J Aes Educ*, 31(1), 73-85, Spr 97.

Various types of theories of musical expression, are presented by Kivy and others, are examined with the aim of the development of a Black theory. It is argued that such a theory can be developed, and the resemblance of much Western African music to speech patterns is noted. Several examples of African holdovers in Black American music are presented.

**Durán Casas, Vicente**. Civil Society Ethics: An Approach from K-O Apel's Philosophy (in Spanish). *Univ Phil*, 14(27), 23-62, D 96.

The purpose of this paper is to define, from a philosophical point of view, two concepts that usually appear as alternative when the problems of a violent society are in discussion: civil society and civic ethics. The author's main thesis is that ethics of a civil society must be guided by universalization criteria, inscribing himself in a tradition that goes from German idealism to contemporary German philosophy. From this outlook, denying ethics universalization means to deny the ethics of a civil society. In order to develop this thesis, the author goes through Kohlberg and Piaget's evolutive psychology theories and Apel's discourse ethics and confronts them with the ones Foucault and Lyotard set forth. Finally, he points out how important is the relationship between religion and the ethics of the civil society is.

**Durán Forero, Rosalba**. "El Individualismo Metodológico y perspectivas de un proyecto Democrático" in *Liberalismo y Comunitarismo: Derechos Humanos y Democracia*, Monsalve Solórzano, Alfonso (ed), 315-333. 36-46003 València, Alfons el Magnànim, 1996.

In the search of alternative answers to the request for an agreement between individual rights and freedom, and public, collective interests, a new approach appears supported by theoreticians of public choice elections. *Methodological individualism* is based on a presupposed egotistical, but rational, consideration of external costs, decision-making consequences, and the costs of social interdependence, in order to reach public choice agreements benefiting most or at least the majority. This paper has been written by bearing in mind the need to rationally examine conflict situations, and thereby to build a peace alternative meaning, not the absence of war, but the possibility of negotiation.

**Durie, Robin**. "Indication and the Awakening of Subjectivity" in *Critical Studies: Ethics and the Subject*, Simms, Karl (ed), 43-52. Amsterdam, Rodopi, 1997.

This paper inquires into how Levinas understands the possibility of the transcendent *Other's* having significance for a subject. It is argued that Levinas finds a resource for this possibility in the genetic turn of Husserl's phenomenology generally and in the exemplary phenomenon of indication particularly. In *Experience and Judgement*, Husserl describes indication as an "associative awakening", an "effective affection" to which a subject *submits*. Levinas also accounts for the significance of the *Other* as an affective awakening, but disrupts the straightforwardly Husserlian schema of indication in conceiving the affective awakening as a "trauma" in which the subject is *created*.

**Dusche, M**. Interpreted Logical Forms as Objects of the Attitudes. *J Log Lang Info*, 4(4), 301-315, 1995.

Two arguments favoring propositionalist accounts of attitude sentences are being revisited: the Church-Langford translation argument and Thomason's argument against quotational theories of indirect discourse. None of them proves to be decisive, thus leaving the option of searching for a developed quotational alternative. Such an alternative is found in an interpreted logical form theory of attitude ascription. The theory differentiates elegantly among different attitudes but it fails to account for logical dependencies among them. It is argued, however, that the concept of logical consequence does not well apply to dependencies among belief sentences and that the requirement to account for logical relations among such sentences should be relaxed.

**Duska, Ronald** and Clarke, James and Rongione, Nicholas. Codes of Ethics: Investment Company Money Managers Versus other Financial Professionals. *Bus Prof Ethics J*, 14(4), 43-55, Wint 95.

**Duska, Ronald F**. The Why's of Business Revisited. *J Bus Ethics*, 16(12-13), 1401-1409, S 97.

This paper will attempt to highlight the importance of making the distinction between motive and purpose clearly, show what confusions arise when the distinction is ignored and hint at some of the structural philosophical reasons why the distinction got blurred in the first place. (edited)

**Duso, Giuseppe**. Absolutheit und Widerspruch in der *Grundlage der gesamten Wissenschaftslehre*. *Fichte-Studien*, 10, 285-298, 1997.

**Dussel, Enrique**. Algunas reflexiones ante el comunitarianismo: MacIntyre, Taylor y Walzer. *Stromata*, 52(1-2), 119-140, Ja-Je 96.

**Dussel, Enrique**. The Architectonic of the Ethics of Liberation. *Phil Soc Crit*, 23(3), 1-35, My 97.

This contribution is a critical and constructive engagement with discourse ethics. First, it clarifies why discourse ethics has difficulties with the grounding and application of moral norms. Second, it turns to a positive appropriation of the formal and procedural aspects of discourse ethics. The goal is the elaboration of an ethics that is able to incorporate the material aspects of goods and the formal dimension of ethical validity and consensuability. The essay concludes with six points that need to be considered when formulating a material ethics that is universalizable and, most importantly, that can address the massive poverty and dehumanization of those excluded from the present community of communication. (edited)

**Dustira, Alicia K**. The Federal Role in Influencing Research Ethics Education and Standards in Science. *Prof Ethics*, 5(1-2), 139-156, Spr-Sum 96.

**DuVal, Gordon**. Liability of Ethics Consultants: A Case Analysis. *Cambridge Quart Healthcare Ethics*, 6(3), 269-281, Sum 97.

**Duvernoy, Jean-François**. Monde reçu et monde à construire: l'*oikéiosis* stoïcienne et la *philia* d'Épicure. *Diotima*, 25, 86-89, 1997.

**Dworkin, Gerald** (ed). *Mill's On Liberty*. Lanham, Rowman & Littlefield, 1997.

John Stuart Mill's *On Liberty* (1860) continues to shape modern Western conceptions of individual freedom. Designed with political philosophy and philosophy of law courses in mind, this collection of essays by leading Mill scholars is an ideal introduction to *On Liberty*. Selected for their importance and accessibility, the essays make clear the continued relevance of Mill's work to contemporary struggles to protect individual rights without harming others. The collection is also useful for courses devoted to Mill at either the undergraduate or graduate level.

**Dworkin, Ronald**. *Freedom's Law: The Moral Reading of the American Constitution*. Cambridge, Harvard Univ Pr, 1996.

Ronald Dworkin argues that Americans have been systematically misled about what their Constitution is and how judges interpret it. In spirited and illuminating discussions of both recent constitutional cases and general constitutional principles. Ronald Dworkin argues that a distinctly American version of government based on the moral reading of the Constitution is in fact the best account of what democracy really is. (publisher,edited)

**Dwyer, Philip**. "Bradley, Russell and Analysis" in *Philosophy after F.H. Bradley*, Bradley, James (ed), 331-347. Bristol, Thoemmes, 1996.

There seems to be a widespread impression that when Russell (and Moore) broke from Bradley, they invented, more or less from whole cloth, a new method for philosophy—'analysis'—inaugurating a decisively different sort of philosophy—'analytic philosophy'—from that of Bradley and the idealists and their opponents. The paper demonstrates that Russell's concept of analysis is taken directly from Bradley himself, their differences on the issue revolving mainly around the question of whether analysis necessarily falsifies the analysandum. Long before Russell, Bradley was criticizing 'analysis' in the sense which Russell came to champion, a sense which redeploys, for reasons other than Hume's, the Humean principle that whatever is distinguishable is separable.

**Dwyer, Susan** and Pietroski, Paul M. Believing in Language. *Phil Sci*, 63(3), 338-373, S 96.

We propose that the generalizations of linguistic theory serve to ascribe beliefs to humans. Ordinary speakers would explicitly (and sincerely) deny having these rather esoteric beliefs about language—e.g., the belief that an anaphor must be bound in its governing category. Such ascriptions can also seem problematic in light of certain theoretical considerations having to do with concept possession, revisability, and so on. Nonetheless, we argue that ordinary speakers believe the propositions expressed by certain sentences of linguistic theory, and that linguistics can therefore teach us something about belief as well as language. Rather than insisting that ordinary speakers lack the linguistic beliefs in question, philosophers should try to show how these empirically motivated belief ascriptions can be correct. We argue that Stalnaker's (1984) "pragmatic" account—according to which beliefs are dispositions, and propositions are sets of possible worlds—does just this. Moreover, our construal of explanation in linguistics motivates (and helps provide) responses to two difficulties for the pragmatic account of belief: the phenomenon of opacity, and the so-called problem of deduction.

**Dyrda, Kazimiera** and Bugajska-Jaszczolt, Beata. On the Rules of Substitution in the First-Order Predicate Logics. *Rep Math Log*, 28, 21-27, 1994.

In this paper we consider two rules of substitution for predicate symbols as introduced by Church [1] and by Pogorzelski, Prucnal [2]. We show that the rules are not equivalent over a standard system of predicate logic.

**Dyrkton, Joerge**. The Liberal Critic as Ideologue: Emile Faguet and *fin-de-siècle* Reflections on the Eighteenth Century. *Hist Euro Ideas*, 22(5-6), 321-336, S-N 96.

**Dyzenhaus, David** (ed) and Ripstein, Arthur (ed). *Law and Morality: Readings in Legal Philosophy*. Toronto, Univ of Toronto Pr, 1996.

This anthology fills a longstanding need for a contemporary Canadian textbook in the philosophy of law. It includes articles, readings, and cases in legal philosophy that give students the conceptual tools necessary to consider the general problems of jurisprudence. (publisher, edited)

**Dzhaparidze, Giorgie**. The Logic of Linear Tolerance. *Stud Log*, 51(2), 249-277, 1992.

**Dziamski, Grzegorz**. "The Avant-Garde and Contemporary Artistic Consciousness" in *Epistemology and History*, Zeidler-Janiszewska, Anna (ed), 479-495. Amsterdam, Rodopi, 1996.

In the socio-practical theory of culture art is conceived of as a form of consciousness that regulates artistic practice (J Kmita). The avant-garde is considered as the metaconsciousness of modern art that legitimizes antitraditional artistic practice and looks for a new objective function for art. Several concepts of the avant-garde are discussed (Ortega y Gasset, Greenberg, Adorno, Lukacs), followed by a debate on the relations between the avant-garde and modern art, with references to the theories of Bell, Habermas, Bürger, Ortega y Gasset, Greenberg, Calinescu, Poggioli, Morawski and Kirby. The conflict between aesthetics and the avant-garde interpretation of objective function of art is reviewed.

**Dzierzgowski, Daniel**. Finite Sets and Natural Numbers in Intuitionistic TT. *Notre Dame J Form Log*, 37(4), 585-601, Fall 96.

We show how to interpret Heyting's arithmetic in an intuitionistic version of TT, Russell's Simple Theory of Types. We also exhibit properties of finite sets in this theory and compare them with the corresponding properties of finite sets in this theory and compare them with the corresponding properties in classical TT. Finally, we prove that arithmetic can be interpreted in intuitionistic $TT_3$, the subsystem of intuitionistic TT involving only three types. The definitions of intuitionistic TT and its finite sets and natural numbers are obtained in a straightforward way from the classical definitions. This is very natural and seems to make intuitionistic TT an interesting intuitionistic set theory to study, beside intuitionistic ZF.

**Eagan, Jennifer L**. Philosophers and the Holocaust: Mediating Public Disputes. *Int Stud Phil*, 29(1), 9-17, 1997.

This essay discusses the holocaust and the role of intellectuals in public debate. Through a discussion of Lyotard's and Adorno's works on the Holocaust, I define the Holocaust as both a cultural event which confronts philosophers with the issue of suffering and as an historical idea representing an absolute ethical limit term. Both Lyotard and Adorno are critiquing totalitarianism and its ensuing suffering as they appear not only in fact, but in thought and language. This sort of critique is essential to any ethics. The Holocaust becomes the defining event for postmodern theory. Hence, a postmodern ethics does not try to encapsulate the enormity of the event, nor does it remain indifferent. I argue that what is at stake in the issue of the Holocaust is the future usefulness of philosophy itself.

**Earle, William James**. "Ducks and Rabbits: Visuality in Wittgenstein" in *Sites of Vision*, Levin, David Michael (ed), 293-314. Cambridge, MIT Pr, 1997.

**Earley Sr, Joseph E**. Towards a Reapprehension of Causal Efficacy. *Process Stud*, 24, 34-38, 1995.

Whitehead held that actual entities (occasions) are based on feelings (prehensions) of the antecedent world. He considered both "simple" and "transmuted" (combined) feelings. The notion that some interactions are "simple" was consistent with the dominant thrust of the science of the first third of this century, marked by triumphs of analysis such as identification of neutrons and protons as component of atomic nuclei. The science of the last third of the century is rather different with greater emphasis on synthesis and on complexity. It now seems clear that "simple" feelings are abstractions. All concrete interactions are composite ("transmuted").

**Easton, Patricia**. Rorty's History of Philosophy as Story of Progress. *Maritain Stud*, 11, 85-97, 1995.

**Eastwood, Susan** and Derish, Pamela and Leash, Evangeline (& others). Ethical Issues in Biomedical Research: Perceptions and Practices of Postdoctoral Research Fellows Responding to a Survey. *Sci Eng Ethics*, 2(1), 89-114, J 96.

We surveyed 1005 postdoctoral fellows by questionnaire about ethical matters related to biomedical research and publishing; 33% responded. About 18% of respondents said they had taken a course in research ethics and about 31% said they had had a course that devoted some time to research ethics. A substantial majority stated willingness to grant other investigators, except competitors, access to their data before publication and to share research materials. Respondents' opinions about contributions justifying authorship of research papers were mainly consistent but at variance with those of many biomedical journal editors. (edited)

**Ebbinghaus, H D**. Maschinen und Kreativität: Metamathematische Argumente für das menschliche Denken. *Phil Natur*, 29(1), 1-30, 1992.

The paper shows how results in mathematical logic and theoretical computer science may yield arguments concerning the character of human thinking and the complexity of human creativity. For example, the development of new concepts such as infinity or real number that have evolved in a long creative process may lead to much stronger theories and methods (as demonstrated by arithmetic versus set theory and elementary versus analytical number theory); on the other hand, formal methods cannot avoid to produce trivial results that are hard to prove. The representation is accessible also to philosophers without a background in mathematical logic.

**Ebbs, Gary**. *Rule-Following and Realism*. Cambridge, Harvard Univ Pr, 1997.

This book arrives at a new conception of the proper starting point and task of the philosophy of language. To understand central topics in the philosophy of language and mind, Gary Ebbs contends, we must investigate them from our perspective as participants in shared linguistic practices; but our efforts at adopting this participant perspective are limited by our lingering loyalties to metaphysical realism (the view that we can make objective assertions only if we can grasp metaphysically independent truth conditions) and scientific naturalism (the view that it is only within science that reality can be identified and described). In *Rule-Following and Realism*, Ebbs works to loosen the hold of these views by exposing their roots and developing a different way of looking at our linguistic practices. (publisher, edited)

**Ebeling, Hans**. Nietzsche bei Heidegger und Fink. *Perspekt Phil*, 22, 59-76, 1996.

It is intended to demonstrate and explain why Fink tries to transform Husserl by means of Heidegger and Heidegger by means of Nietzsche. However, Fink—unlike Heidegger—strictly opposing Hitler and Mussolini produces a still more radical kind of nihilism. In a refutation of nihilism it is argued that metaphysics as well as ethics can survive Nietzsche, Heidegger, and Fink.

**Eberhard, Julaine**. Sexuality, Politics and "Taking Responsibilty": On a Continuum. *Conference*, 6(1), 67-88, Sum 95.

**Eberle, Chris**. God's Nature and the Rationality of Religious Belief. *Faith Phil*, 14(2), 152-169, Ap 97.

In this paper, I attempt to provide a rationale for the *ontological principle*. I argue as follows. Any epistemic norm which requires of an agent that she enter into causal relations with an object which she cannot in the 'nature' of the case enter lacks epistemic merit—it violates the ought implies can dictum. Because the epistemic norms properly governing the cognitive activity of a given agent are constrained by the causal relations possible between an agent and an object of belief, and because the causal relations possible between an object of belief and an agent are determined in part by the characteristics of the object of belief, the epistemic norms properly governing the cognitive activity of a given agent are determined in part by the characteristics of the object of belief. That is, the *ontological principle* is true. (edited)

**Ebijuwa, T**. Conscience, Morality and Social Acceptability in an African Culture. *Quest*, 9(2), 86-98, D 96.

Cet article montre que c'est la conscience qui, dans la pensée Yoruba, est la dernière autorité morale. Une conscience bien développée conduit normalement à *iwa rere* ce qui est essentiel pour être accepté dans la société Yoruba. L'article développe ensuite l'idée que la conscience, en tant que "centrale" d'évaluation des jugements moraux, est essentielle dans toute discussion de l'ordre social de quelque société que ce soit, car elle permet la formation de bonnes relations sociales entre les personnes et la promotion de la solidarité dans sa globalité. (edited)

**Eboh, Marie Pauline**. "Is Western Democracy the Answer to the African Problem?" in *Philosophy and Democracy in Intercultural Perspective*, Kimmerle, Heinz (ed), 163-173. Amsterdam, Rodopi, 1997.

**Echauri, Raúl**. Ser y no ser en el *Sofista* de Platón. *Sapientia*, 51(200), 327-334, 1996.

The author attempts to discover the sense of "nonbeing" in Plato's dialogue "The Sophist". There it is admitted that what does not exist, in one sense does in fact exist, since otherwise error and falsehood could not be justified. Thus Plato believes that he is contradicting Parmenides, for whom the nonbeing does not exist. The author, however, demonstrates that the Parmenidian nonbeing is nothingness, whilst the Platonic nonbeing consists of not being this, but that, something different. In brief, he argues that Plato did not attack the Parmenidian thesis, but rather that he proposed a notion of "being" and its correlative of "nonbeing", that are entirely essentialist.

**Echeverría, José**. *Aprender a filosofar preguntando: con Platón, Epicuro, Descartes*. Barcelona, Anthropos, 1997.

José Echeverría propone en este libro un método crítico y dramático de introducción a la filosofía más ágil, ameno y eficaz que los que están en uso. A tal fin, procura que el lector se introduzca en la filosofía no a través de su historia ni de exposiciones, definiciones o explicaciones sobre lo que ella ha sido o es, sino más bien por verse involucrado en una discusión con tres grandes filósofos del pasado: Platón (*Fedón*), Epicuro (*Epístola a Meneceo*) y Descartes (*Meditaciones de Filosofía Primera*), cuyas posiciones son puestas a prueba en el libro a través de diálogos ficticios. (publisher, edited)

**Echeverría, José**. Una ética para tiempos de luto. *Dialogos*, 32(69), 17-61, Ja 97.

**Eckhardt, William**. A Shooting-Room View of Doomsday. *J Phil*, 94(5), 244-259, My 97.

**Eddy, William B** and Renz, David O. Organizations, Ethics, and Health Care: Building an Ethics Infrastructure for a New Era. *Bioethics Forum*, 12(2), 29-39, Sum 96.

The changes occurring in today's health care environment, especially as driven by the emphasis on managed care strategies, focus attention on ethical questions, practices, and implications for all those involved in health care, including health care professionals, patients, administrators, and governing boards. These implications need to be studied and strategies developed to build an ethical infrastructure that will support health care organizations in this changing environment.

**Edel, Geert**. "Zum Problem der Rechtsgeltung: Kelsens Lehre von der Grundnorm und das Hypothesis-Theorem Cohens" in *Grenzen der kritischen Vernunft*, Schmid, Peter A, 178-194. Basel, Schwabe Verlag, 1997.

**Edelberg, David**. Ethical Issues in Alternative Medicine. *Bioethics Forum*, 12(4), 39-42, Wint 96.

**Edelman, John T**. Beauty and the Attainment of Temperance. *Int Phil Quart*, 37(1), 5-12, Mr 97.

This brief paper is a discussion of the Platonic suggestion that the perfection of virtue depends on our apprehension of the *beautiful*. More specifically, the paper is a discussion of the role of beauty in the achievement of temperance and that species of temperance that is chastity. Arguing from a disparity between the "popular" and the "philosophical" conceptions of temperance, the paper suggests that popular temperance is indistinguishable from continence and that the contemplation of beauty provides one means of accomplishing the move from continence to genuine temperance.

**Eden, Kathy**. *Hermeneutics and the Rhetorical Tradition*. New Haven, Yale Univ Pr, 1997.

In this eloquent book, Kathy Eden challenges commonly accepted conceptions about the history of hermeneutics. Contending that the hermeneutical tradition is not a purely modern German specialty, she argues instead that the historical grounding of modern hermeneutics is in the ancient tradition of rhetoric. Eden demonstrates how the early rhetorical model of reading, called *interpretatio scripti* by Cicero and his followers, not only has informed a continuous tradition of interpretation from Republican Rome to Reformation Europe but also has forged such enduring hermeneutical principles as meaning, context and literary economy. (publisher, edited)

AUTHOR INDEX 611 Eiben, A E

**Eder, Klaus**. Questione ecologica e nuove identità collettive. *Iride*, 8(14), 3-27, Ap 95.

**Edgington, Dorothy**. Lowe on Conditional Probability. *Mind*, 105(420), 617-630, O 96.

**Edgington, Dorothy**. Truth, Objectivity, Counterfactuals and Gibbard. *Mind*, 106(421), 107-116, Ja 97.

**Edidin, Aron**. Eternal Verities: Timeless Truth, Ahistorical Standards, and the One True Story. *Amer Phil Quart*, 34(2), 259-271, Ap 97.

**Edlund, Bengt**. On Scores and Works of Music: Interpretation and Identity. *Brit J Aes*, 36(4), 367-380, O 96.

It is argued that Nelson Goodman's ontology of the musical work, based on strict conformance between score and performance, is flawed in important respects and musically counterintuitive. On closer inspection the inscriptions cannot sustain the burden of defining the musical work, nor is it the duty of notation to do so. Musical ontologies of this kind underestimate the vital role of interpretation. Since interpretation is bound to diversify our encounters with musical works, a more fruitful approach to ontology would involve distilling identity, rather than insisting on identification.

**Edlund, Bengt**. Sonate, que te fais-je? Toward a Theory of Interpretation. *J Aes Educ*, 31(1), 23-40, Spr 97.

The limits of interpretative freedom are established by critically examining the "fidelities" generally considered to regulate the musician's work. Five levels of fidelity are distinguished: faithfulness to the notes, to the style, to the text, to the content and to the work. It is argued that properly understood these restrictions allow more initiative than most musicians, prone to declare their loyalty to the composer's intentions, are willing to acknowledge. The scope of interpretative freedom is finally illustrated with reference to the first 8 bars of the slow movement of Beethoven's *Pathétique* Sonata.

**Edsall, John T**. On the Hazards of Whistleblowers and on Some Problems of Young Biomedical Scientists in our Time. *Sci Eng Ethics*, 1(4), 329-340, O 95.

This paper examines two different, but closely related, classes of problems. The first part deals with whistle-blowers, and the difficulties and dangers that they have often faced, although their actions, in the rare cases where they become necessary, are indispensable for the maintenance of honest science. The problems are illustrated by discussion of several specific cases from 1960 to 1990. The second part deals with problems that face many young scientists today, and the stresses to which they are exposed in an increasingly competitive atmosphere. There are powerful pressures for premature publication, and many gifted scientists are driven to spend an inordinate amount of time in writing grant applications that are turned down for lack of funds, while receiving high praise from reviewers. Correction of conditions is an important matter for science policy; it is also important, among other things, to relieve pressures that would tend to encourage deviations from the standards necessary for trustworthy science.

**Edwards, Anne M**. Springing Forward and Falling Back: Traveling through Time. *Cont Phil*, 17(6), 12-24, N-D 95.

In this article, I argue that time travel is both logically and physically possible. After exploring several different concepts of time, I examine the various difficulties with traveling to the past and to the future. I then investigate a number of possible methods of traveling through time, including the time dilation effect of relativity, Wellsian time machines and several recent suggestions from prominent theoretical physicists. I conclude that for time travel to be possible, we must accept a four dimensional block universe concept of time. In addition, the many worlds interpretation of quantum mechanics must be correct. If both of these theories are correct, then time travel is limited only by our level of technology.

**Edwards, Jim**. Anti-Realist Truth and Concepts of Superassertibility. *Synthese*, 109(1), 103-120, O 96.

Crispin Wright offers superassertibility as an antirealist explication of truth. A statement is superassertible, roughly, if there is a state of information available which warrants it and it is warranted by all achievable enlargements of that state of information. However, it is argued, Wright fails to take account of the fact that many of our test procedures are not 'sure fire', even when applied under ideal conditions. An alternative conception of superassertibility is constructed to take this feature into account. However, it is then argued that when this revised concept of superassertibility is taken as the truth predicate of probability statements, statements whose test procedures are paradigmatically not sure fire, then any antirealist theory of the sense of such probability statements cannot be compositional, in Dummett's sense of 'compositional'.

**Edwards, Jim**. Is Tennant Selling Truth Short?. *Analysis*, 57(2), 152-158, Ap 97.

The author argues that Neil Tennant (*Analysis* 55, 1995) has mislocated his disagreement with Crispin Wright (*Truth and Objectivity*: Cambridge, Mass. Harvard University Press, 1992) over how an antirealist should best suppose warranted assertibility and truth to be related. The author argues that in his 1995 article Tennant misread Wright. The author argues that the real difference between Tennant's antirealist and Wright's antirealist emerges in the accounts they each give of what it is for a warrant to be overturned by further evidence.

**Edwards, Paul** (ed). *Immortality*. Amherst, Prometheus, 1997.

This unique anthology presents selections from all the major philosophers who have written on belief in life after death. Traditional Western belief is represented by Tertullian, Aquinas, Butler, Priestley, Geach, and van Inwagen. Reincarnation is defended by Plato, Ducasse, and Johnson. The critics include Lucretius, Hume, Voltaire, Kant, Broad, and Hospers. The evidence from psychical research is evaluated by Paul and Linda Badham and John Beloff. Also included is Ayer's account of his well-known near-death experience. The nature of mind and its relation to the body is discussed by Descartes, J.S. Mill, Elliot, James, and Flew. The philosophical issue of personal identity and its connection with questions of survival is examined by Locke, Hume, Reid, and Parfit. (publisher, edited)

**Edwards, Steven D**. The Moral Status of Intellectually Disabled Individuals. *J Med Phil*, 22(1), 29-42, F 97.

Strong arguments can be given to indicate that the moral status accorded, justly or unjustly, to individuals with intellectual disabilities is less than that accorded to those considered intellectually able. This paper suggests that such a view of the moral status of intellectually disabled individuals derives from individualism. And it is shown that the normative component of individualism further compromises the integrity of intellectually disabled individuals. An alternative view of the self is outlined in which dependence features centrally. It is tentatively suggested that such a view of the self may prove more congenial to enhancing the moral status of individuals with intellectual disabilities. (edited)

**Edwards, Ward** and Fishburn, Peter C. Discount-Neutral Utility Models for Denumerable Time Streams. *Theor Decis*, 43(2), 139-166, S 97.

This paper formulates and axiomatizes utility models for denumerable time streams that make no commitment in regard to discounting future outcomes. The models address decision under certainty and decision under risk. Independence assumptions in both contexts lead to additive or multiplicative utilities over time periods that allow unambiguous comparisons of the relative importance of different periods. The models accommodate all patterns of future valuation. This discount-neutral feature is attained by restricting preference comparisons to outcome streams or probability distributions on outcome streams that differ in at most a finite number of periods.

**Egan, Anthony**. Does a Real Albert Nolan Need Don Cupitt? A Response to Ronald Nicolson. *Heythrop J*, 38(2), 180-190, Ap 97.

**Egan, Philip A**. Lonergan on Newman's Conversion. *Heythrop J*, 37(4), 437-455, O 96.

This paper is in two parts. The first examines the overall influence of John Henry Newman's thought on Bernard Lonergan S.J., with reference to the various stages of Lonergan's intellectual evolution. The second (and shorter) section uses Lonergan's thought to gain a deeper insight into Newman, particularly his conversion and reception into full communion with the Church of Rome. The author argues for a strong linkage of Newman-Lonergan: that anyone with an interest in Newman ought to be interested in Lonergan (and *vice versa*), not least because Lonergan developed many of Newman's seminal ideas.

**Egéa-Kuehne, Denise**. "Neutrality in Education and Derrida's call for "Double Duty" in *Philosophy of Education (1996)*, Margonis, Frank (ed), 154-163. Urbana, Phil Education Soc, 1997.

**Ehrenberg, Ronald G** (ed). *The American University: National Treasure or Endangered Species?*. Ithaca, Cornell Univ Pr, 1997.

Over the past decade, America's research universities have been accused, with increasing frequency and passion, of a wide variety of sins. Universities do not devote enough attention to undergraduate education, the charge goes, or they pursue unnecessary research, or they award doctoral degrees that focus too narrowly and take too long to complete. What have these institutions done to provoke such criticism and why has financial support from both public and private sectors eroded? In this book, a volume published in honor of Frank H. T. Rhodes, President Emeritus of Cornell University, distinguished scholars and administrators address these issues and suggest ways in which research universities can respond to current and future challenges. (publisher, edited)

**Ehrhardt, Walter E**. Schellings Metapher *Blitz*—eine Huldigung an die Wissenschaftslehre. *Fichte-Studien*, 12, 203-210, 1997.

**Ehring, Douglas**. *Causation and Persistence: A Theory of Causation*. New York, Oxford Univ Pr, 1997.

Philosophical tradition dictates that an account of causation should include both a "generalist" component (typically, the instantiation of a law) and a "singularist" component, in the form of certain unremarkable spatial-temporal relations. This pathbreaking book while assuming some generalist component, focuses on the singularist aspect, asserting that causes and effects are tied together by more than spatial-temporal relations. Providing an account of causal influence that stresses the persistence of individual properties or "tropes," Douglas Ehring develops a powerfully original theory of causation, one that outperforms leading theories in explaining preemptive causation and contributes the most sophisticated view yet of causation's singularist component. (publisher, edited)

**Ehrlich, Philip**. From Completeness to Archimedean Completeness: An Essay in the Foundations of Euclidean Geometry. *Synthese*, 110(1), 57-76, Ja 97.

Just as Hilbert's completeness and embedding properties make the system *R* of real numbers a revealing forum for the study of Archimedean ordered fields, the analogous properties of Hahn's number systems provide a similar forum for the analysis of ordered fields more generally. Furthering the analogy, we show that just as Hilbert was able to transfer certain aspects of his completeness and embedding properties for *R* to obtain important insights into the structure and variety of Archimedean Euclidean geometries, the analogous properties for Hahn's number systems are exploited to uncover the spectrum of models of Euclidean geometry more generally.

**Eiben, A E** and Kurucz, A and Jánossy, A. Combining Algebraizable Logics. *Notre Dame J Form Log*, 37(2), 366-380, Spr 96.

The general methodology of "algebraizing" logics is used here for combining different logics. The combination of logics is represented as taking the colimit of the constituent logics in the category of algebaizable logics. The cocompleteness of this category as well as its isomorphism to the corresponding category of certain first-order theories are proved.

**Eidam, Heinz**. Fichtes Anstoss: Anmerkungen zu einem Begriff der *Wissenschaftslehre* von 1794. *Fichte-Studien*, 10, 191-208, 1997.

**Eidlin, Fred**. Blindspot of a Liberal: Popper and the Problem of Community. *Phil Soc Sci*, 27(1), 5-23, Mr 97.

Popper's critique of the philosophical doctrines underlying totalitarian ideology is powerful. Yet, having the regimes of Hitler and Stalin in full view before him, he did not give full and balanced consideration to the range of effects these doctrines can have within actually existing ideologies and regimes. The ideas he correlates with totalitarianism can and do exist in benign forms or tempered by other ideas and by institutions. Moreover, the struggle with totalitarianism is only partly a struggle of philosophical ideas. Political argument and rhetoric appeal to feeling as well as intellect. This tends to be a blindspot of liberalism that often weakens it in the competition with its adversaries.

**Eidlin, Fred** (trans) and Giannaras, Anastasios. Plato and K.R. Popper: Toward a Critique of Plato's Political Philosophy. *Phil Soc Sci*, 26(4), 493-508, D 96.

**Eilstein, Helena**. *Life Contemplative, Life Practical: An Essay on Fatalism*. Amsterdam, Rodopi, 1997.

This is an essay on fatalism. It is also about the relationship between the way of thinking of the "theoretical man" and the "practical man" in us. These are the topics discussed in the main corpus of the essay. It starts with Chapter Two. The first chapter brings a semijoking introduction to that main corpus. It also contains remarks on some "realistic" stories whose heroes face situations which seem to correspond to the Newcomb's problem known in the decision theory. (publisher, edited)

**Eilstein, Helena**. Prof. Shimony on "The Transient Now". *Synthese*, 107(2), 223-247, My 96.

This is a polemic with the paper in Shimony's *Search for Naturalistic World-view*, vol. II. After analysing the conceptual frame adequate for transientism I support Shimony's refutation of McTaggarts "paradox". However, his attempt to prove the self-contradictoriness of eternism is fallacious and so is his attempt to show the compatibility of transientism with Special Relativity. While the dispute cannot be resolved *a priori*, some empirical models of reality make eternism more plausible than transientism and all others are neutral.

**Eisenmann, Peter**. "Die Weltfriedensregelung als Problem und Aufgabe der internationalen Politik" in *Kreativer Friede durch Begegnung der Weltkulturen*, Beck, Heinrich (ed), 85-101. New York, Lang, 1995.

The purpose of the work is to reflect on the fundamental possibilities of a worldwide peace regulation after the ideological East-West conflict. Thereby the structures of the aims, tasks and duties of the United Nations are shown as well as the political methods and instruments that are used in the case of mastering conflicts in the world. The author is working out the idea and the hope as well, that after the structural change in the former socialist community of states a constructive cooperation within the scope of the UN must be possible. On the other side the work characterizes the increasing worldwide interdependencies in international affairs, a fact which requires concrete coordination of political actions, thus considered to be an important factor of security. One of the most important unconventional conclusions is the assertion that without more and more developed means of communication many a conflict menacing world peace would not break out and that there are nowadays a lot of pressure groups interested in a more or less weakening of the strong, aiming at the pauperization of all.

**Eisvogel, Martin**. "Wem nützt eine Philosophie der Chemie—den Chemikern oder den Philosophen?" in *Philosophie der Chemie: Bestandsaufnahme und Ausblick*, Schummer, Joachim (ed), 95-110. Wurzburg, Koenigshausen, 1996.

**Eizagirre, Xabier** and Bengoetxea, Juan B and Ibarra, Andoni. "Un escenario pragmático para la verdad en la ciencia" in *Verdad: lógica, representación y mundo*, Villegas Forero, L, 455-465. Santiago de Compostela, Univ Santiago Comp, 1996.

According to Cartwright fundamental laws do not tell the truth, do not describe objects in reality, but they have superior explanatory power. Others have argued that the notion of truth is unsubstantial for providing an adequate analysis of science, and instead of it they plea for the introduction of other epistemic values. We think that using an adequate notion of truth allows us to make sense of intuitions of scientists; truth is taken by them as something worth pursuing. Accordingly, we propose a pragmatic account of truth able to understand the specific aspect of scientific practice, i.e., the activity of idealizations and approximations. (edited)

**Eklof, Paul C**. Set Theory Generated by Abelian Group Theory. *Bull Sym Log*, 3(1), 1-16, Mr 97.

This survey is intended to introduce to logicians some notions, methods and theorems in set theory which arose—largely through the work of Saharon Shelah—in the course of finding solutions to problems in Abelian group theory, principally the Whitehead problem and the closely related problem of the existence of almost free Abelian groups. While Shelah's first independence result regarding the Whitehead problem used established set-theoretical methods, his later work required new ideas; it is on these that this paper focuses, including the context in which they arose. The ideas include: proper forcing; the weak diamond principle; coloring of ladder systems; the *singular compactness theorem*; and "incompactness" results.

**El Ghannouchi, A**. "Religious Truth and Philosophical Truth according to Ibn Rushd" in *Averroës and the Enlightenment*, Wahba, Mourad (ed), 229. Amherst, Prometheus, 1996.

**Elder, Crawford L**. Contrariety and "Carving up Reality". *Amer Phil Quart*, 33(3), 277-289, Jl 96.

Many philosophers see little need to "carve reality at the joints"; there are innumerable ways one can carve and still end up with slices of reality. Or, without metaphor: predicates which appear disjunctive or "strange" pick out properties as real as those our familiar predicates pick out. For use of such predicates could afford us all the mastery of the world we currently have. This paper argues to the contrary. Familiar predicates work because, as evidence attests, they pick out properties that fall into contrary ranges. The "strange" predicates would not; in consequence, using them would not afford mastery.

**Elder, Linda**. Critical Thinking and Emotional Intelligence. *Inquiry (USA)*, 16(2), 35-49, Wint 96.

**Eldridge, Jennifer J** and Gluck, John P. Gender Differences in Attitudes Toward Animal Research. *Ethics Behavior*, 6(3), 239-256, 1996.

Although gender differences in attitudes toward animal research have been reported in the literature for some time, exploration into the nature of these differences has received less attention. This article examines gender differences in responses to a survey of attitudes toward the use of animals in research. The survey was completed by college students and consisted of items intended to tap different issues related to the animal research debate. Results indicated that women were more likely than men to support tenets of the animal protection movement. Likewise, women were more likely than men to favor increased restrictions on animal use and were more concerned than men about the suffering of research animals. Analysis of item contents suggested that women endorsed items reflecting a general caring for animals, were more willing than men to make personal sacrifices such as giving up meat and medical benefits in an effort to protect animals, and were more likely than men to question the use of animals in research on scientific grounds. Men, on the other hand, tended to emphasize the potential benefits arising from the use of animals in research.

**Eleftheriadis, Anastassia**. Der Begriff 'Praktischer Fortschritt' in den biomedizinischen Wissenschaften: Strukturalistischer Ansatz zur Rekonstruktion wissenschaftstheoretischer Begriffe in der Medizin. *J Gen Phil Sci*, 27(1), 15-27, 1996.

"The Term 'Practical Progress' in Biomedical Sciences: A Structuralist Approach to the Reconstruction of Epistemological Terms in Medicine." An attempt is made to elucidate the structure of the term 'practical progress' and to reconstruct it logically. The importance of discovery and confirmation of new regularities as well as of practical rules arising from them depends on their contribution to the solution of practical problems. The application of this structuralistic definition of 'practical progress' is demonstrated with an example from cardiac surgery concerning the solution of the practical medical problem of myocardial protection during open heart surgery.

**Elenes, C Alejandra**. Reclaiming the Borderlands: Chicana/o Identity, Difference, and Critical Pedagogy. *Educ Theor*, 47(3), 359-375, Sum 97.

C. Alejandra Elenes analyses the influence of *borderlands* theories to critical pedagogy. One of her main arguments is that *borderlands* theories have served, and continues to do so, as a theoretical framework that can advance educational theory by taking into account multiple subjectivity and difference. She first provides a historical background to the development of Chicana/o studies, and its contribution to *borderlands* theories and identities. Then, she analyzes how critical pedagogy has adapted the concept of *borderlands* and the need to retheorize difference. Finally, it elaborates on how *borderlands* theories can be incorporated into educational discourses and pedagogical practice.

**Elgin, Catherine Z**. *Between the Absolute and the Arbitrary*. Ithaca, Cornell Univ Pr, 1997.

In *Between the Absolute and the Arbitrary*, Catherine Z. Elgin maps a constructivist alternative to the standard Anglo-American conception of philosophy's problematic. Under the standard conception, unless answers to philosophical questions are absolute, they are arbitrary. Unless a philosophy is grounded in determinate, agent-neutral facts, it is right only relative to a perspective that cannot in the end be justified. Elgin charts a course between the two poles, showing how fact and value intertwine, where art and science intersect. *Between the Absolute and the Arbitrary* cuts a path through philosophy of science, philosophy of language and philosophy of art, disclosing common problems, resources and solutions. Elgin highlights the ineliminability of values from the realm of facts, the dependence of facts on category schemes and the ways human interests, practices and goals affect the categories we contrive. (publisher)

**Elgin, Catherine Z**. *Considered Judgment*. Princeton, Princeton Univ Pr, 1996.

*Considered Judgment* argues for a reconception of epistemology. After a critique of foundationalist, reliabilist, coherentist, and relativist positions, it advocates taking reflective equilibrium as the standard of rational acceptability and understanding rather than knowledge as epistemology's focus. A system of thought is in reflective equilibrium when its components are reasonable in light of one another and the system as a whole is reasonable in light of our relevant antecedent convictions. Such a reconception yields opportunities for a broader epistemological purview that comprehends the arts and does justice to the sciences. Epistemology is broader and more variegated than is usually recognized.

**Elgueta, R**. Characterizing Classes Defined without Equality. *Stud Log*, 58(3), 357-394, My 97.

In this paper we mainly deal with first-order languages without equality and introduce a weak form of equality predicate, the so-called *Leibniz equality*. This equality is characterized algebraically by means of a natural concept of congruence; in any structure, it turns out to be the maximum congruence of the

AUTHOR INDEX 613 Emanuel, Linda L

structure. We show that first-order logic without equality has two distinct complete semantics (*full semantics* and *reduced semantics*) related by a *reduction operator*. The last and main part of the paper contains a series of Birkhoff-style theorems characterizing certain classes of structures defined without equality, not only full classes but also reduced ones.

**Elias, Willem**. *Signs of the Time*. Amsterdam, Rodopi, 1997.

*Signs of the Time* is an investigation into contemporary art theory and the philosophy of art from 1945 until postmodernism. The author treats important precursors such as Freud and Marx, and contemporary theorists and philosophers such as Gombrich, Lacan, Heidegger, Sartre, Althusser, Marcuse, Gadamer, Derrida, Eco, Barthes, Foucault, Baudrillard, Lyotard. Various texts are discussed, criticized and related to movements in contemporary art and to contemporary artists. The author addresses students in the fields of art history, communications, aesthetics, art education as well as the art lover. Art as a sign of the time reveals the hidden dimensions of the world in which we live. (publisher, edited)

**Eliasmith, Chris** and Thagard, Paul. Waves, Particles, and Explanatory Coherence. *Brit J Phil Sci*, 48(1), 1-19, Mr 97.

This paper discusses the nineteenth-century debate concerning the nature of light. We analyze the debate using a computational theory of coherence that models the acceptance of the wave theory of light and the rejection of the particle theory. We show how our analysis of the controversy avoids Achinstein's criticisms of Whewell's coherentist account, and argue that our interpretation in more computationally tractable and psychologically realistic than Achinstein's probabilistic account.

**Elkatip, S H**. Synthesising Intersubjectively. *Sorites*, 5-14, Je 97.

The question discussed is whether Quine abolishes the analytic synthetic distinction or changes its nature. It is argued that either the point is trivial and the former is not established or the latter holds: Quine challenges the teaching that analytical statements are exchanged intersubjectively whereas some synthetic statements are private.

**Elkatip, S H**. The Validity of Indexical Arguments. *Sorites*, 6-20, N 96.

The paper is concerned with the validity of the first version of indexical arguments as put forth in "'He': A Study in the Logic of Self-Consciousness" in 1966 and is in defence of the view that logical structure of statements containing personal pronouns alone does not account for personal identity. Castañeda's 1966 analysis does not establish that the S-use characterises some usages of the personal pronoun better than the F-use or the E-use. While the major problem with F-use, which involves *de re* belief, is its conflict with the doctrine of propositions as transmitted from Frege, Castañeda's rejection of body or E-use is based on common sense. But, the argument against E-use has no persuasive force against physicalism. It is, also, absurd to maintain that persons could speak an actual language or produce actual sentences the logic of which Castañeda claims to study objectively without bodies.

**Elkin, Stephen L** (ed) and Soltan, Karol Edward (ed). *The Constitution of Good Societies*. University Park, Pennsylvania Univ Pr, 1996.

The first part of the volume considers some of the boundaries of what is humanly possible in politico-economic designs and the role in them of deliberation and the processes of adapting to limits. The second part considers different ways of exercising constitutionalist judgment analyzing a variety of cases, including general visions of the good society. Looking at whole societies and at complexes of institutions, complements and informs the picture of the institutional microscale. Understanding the microscale, on the other hand, often makes the difference between empty slogans and realistic political proposals. (publisher,edited)

**Ellenbogen, Sara**. On the Link Between Frege's Platonic-Realist Semantics and His Doctrine of Private Senses. *Philosophy*, 72(281), 375-382, Jl 97.

John Perry (1977) argues that Frege was led to the doctrine of private senses in spite of his belief in the objectivity of sense through his attempt to solve a problem which demonstratives posed for his theory. This article takes issue with the standard interpretation of the doctrine of private senses. The doctrine did not result from Frege's treatment of demonstratives but instead from his Platonic-realist semantics which led him to construe objectivity without reference to intersubjectivity. It is further argued that although the doctrine of private senses is consistent with Frege's construal of objectivity, it is nevertheless problematic because it cannot account for language acquisition or communication.

**Ellet Jr, Frederick S** and Ericson, David P. In Defense of Public Reason: On the Nature of Historical Rationality. *Educ Theor*, 47(2), 133-161, Spr 97.

**Elliot, Carl**. Criminal Responsibility. *Phil Psychiat Psych*, 3(4), 305-307, D 96.

Mentally disordered persons occasionally do things for which we would ordinarily blame or even punish a nondisordered person. We often do not blame mentally disordered persons for these actions, however, because we regard mental disorders, at least in some circumstances, as an excuse from moral responsibility. For moral philosophy and the law, the challenge is to understand the specific circumstances under which a mental disorder should excuse an offender from responsibility for his or her actions. Because different types of psychopathology influence a person's intentions and character in very different ways, judgments of responsibility crucially depend upon the specific nature of a mental disorder. They also depend on adequate understandings of concepts such as moral understanding, especially in the case of psychopathy, as well as an understanding of the reasons why mental disorders may excuse a person from responsibility.

**Elliot, Robert**. Facts About Natural Values. *Environ Values*, 5(3), 221-234, Ag 96.

Some environmental philosophers believe that the rejection of anthropocentric ethics requires the development and defence of an objectivist metaethical theory according to which values are, in the most literal sense, discovered not conferred. It is argued that nothing of normative or motivational import, however, turns on the metaethical issue. It is also argued that a rejection of normative anthropocentrism is completely consistent with metaethical subjectivism. (edited)

**Elliot, Robert**. Genetic Therapy, Person-Regarding Reasons and the Determination of Identity. *Bioethics*, 11(2), 151-160, Ap 97.

It has been argued, for example by Ingmar Persson, that genetic therapy performed on a conceptus does not alter the identity of the person that develops from it, even if we are essentially persons. If this claim is true then there can be person-regarding reasons for performing genetic therapy on a conceptus. Here it is argued that such person-regarding reasons obtain only if we are essentially persons but essentially animals. This conclusion requires the defeat of the origination theory, which says that personal identity is determined by the identity of the fetus from which one originates. It is argued that the origination theory is false in the special case relevant to performing genetic therapy on a conceptus for person-regarding reasons.

**Elliott, Deni**. Case Studies for Teaching Research Ethics. *Prof Ethics*, 4(3-4), 179-198, Spr-Sum 95.

**Elliott, Deni**. Evaluating Teaching and Students' Learning of Academic Research Ethics. *Sci Eng Ethics*, 2(3), 345-366, Jl 96.

A team of philosophers and scientists at Dartmouth College worked for three years to create, train faculty and pilot test an adequate and exportable class in research methods for graduate students of science and engineering. Developing and testing methods for evaluating students' progress in learning research ethics were part of the project goals. Failure of methods tried in the first year led to the refinement of methods for the second year. These were used successfully in the pilot course and in one university setting external to Dartmouth. The process of development and justification for the final methods are discussed here.

**Elliott, Deni**. Researchers as Professionals, Professionals as Researchers: A Context for Laboratory Research Ethics. *Prof Ethics*, 4(3-4), 5-16, Spr-Sum 95.

**Elliott, Gregory**. Fateful Rendezvous: The Young Althusser. *Rad Phil*, 84, 36-40, Jl-Ag 97.

**Ellis, Anthony**. Morality and Scripture. *Teach Phil*, 19(3), 233-246, S 96.

Teachers of introductory ethics courses usually wish to convince their students that ethics can be reasoned about; many students, however, think that they can derive their morality from the Bible (or some other religious source) in a way that leaves no significant place for moral reasoning. One response to such students is to present them with the 'Euthyprho Dilemma'. I suggest that this is inappropriate and explore an alternative way to convince such students that sensible ethical judgements must be the result of reasoning.

**Ellis, Anthony**. Punishment and the Principle of Fair Play. *Utilitas*, 9(1), 81-97, Mr 97.

What I call the just distribution theory of punishment holds that the justification of punishment is that it rectifies the social distribution of benefits and burdens which has been upset by the offender. I argue that a recent version of this theory is no more viable than earlier versions. Like them, it fails in its avowed intention to deliver fundamental intuitions about crime and punishment. The root problem is its foundation in Hart's *principle of fair play*, a foundation which, I argue, is inappropriate for a theory of punishment.

**Ellis, John**. *Dunamis* and Being: Heidegger on Plato's *Sophist* 247d8-e4. *Epoche*, 3(1 & 2), 43-78, 1995.

**Ellis, Ralph** and Ravita, Tracienne. Scientific Uncertainties, Environmental Policy, and Political Theory. *Phil Forum*, 28(3), 209-231, Spr 97.

Rights-based political theories neglect the problem of environmental destruction by demanding certainties that science cannot provide, resulting in the prevailing attitude that pollution is "innocent until proven guilty." We explore a consequentialist approach, using a *just distribution* principle to balance the competing outcomes of developers' rights, environmental preservation, and public health. Environmentalists fear that a crass consequentialism neglects environmental considerations, especially affecting small numbers; but if just distribution is another valued consequence, 'rights violations' simply become distributively unjust burdens. Because polluting interests can drive the government's interpretation of scientific findings, the solution proposed here also requires campaign finance reform.

**Ellsworth, Jonathan**. Beyond Ironist Theory and Private Fantasy: A Critique of Rorty's Derrida. *Dialogue (PST)*, 39(2-3), 37-48, Ap 97.

I argue that Rorty's label of "ironist theory" insufficiently represents Derrida's early work, for Derrida isn't attempting to break free from the philosophical tradition in the interest of autonomy. The label "private fantasy" belies Derrida's later work by gainsaying its ethico-political resources and utility. Derrida isn't merely striving to see differently from his predecessors, but more justly. Furthermore, I contend that a meticulous depiction of Derrida also reveals a more judicious assessment of both the status and task of philosophy than that which is presented by Rorty.

**Elton, W R**. Aristotle's *Nicomachean Ethics* and Shakespeare's *Troilus and Cressida*. *J Hist Ideas*, 58(2), 331-348, Ap 97.

**Emanuel, Linda L**. Physician-Assisted Suicide: A Different Approach. *Bioethics Forum*, 13(2), 13-16, Sum 97.

Most requests for physician-assisted suicide are not due to present suffering. Steps must be designed to uncover the real roots of the desire so that they can be specifically addressed. Examples of such steps are proposed.

**Emanuel, Linda L** (& others) and Ronan, Laurence J and Stoekle, John D. A Manual on Manners and Courtesies for the Shared Care of Patients. *J Clin Ethics*, 8(1), 22-33, Spr 97.

This paper is written by medical practitioners concerned with diminished *intraprofessional communication* as care becomes more corporate and commercialized while doctor-doctor communications is even more necessary with medicine's expanding specialization for the effective shared care of patients. Several cases and communication failures are illustrated from medical practice: in doctor-doctor, doctor-student, doctor-resident, doctor-nurse, and doctor-institutional relationships. Recommendations on standards of communication are made.

**Emanuel, Linda L** and Sugarman, Jeremy. Relationships, Relationships, Relationships.... *J Clin Ethics*, 8(1), 6-10, Spr 97.

The network of relationships that exist within current medical practice extend well beyond the patient-physician relationship to include such people as healthcare providers, physician assistants, nurses, clergy, insurance representatives, technicians and others. Normative guidelines for these myriad professional roles are needed to enable appropriate responses to ethical difficulties that arise in the care of patients. Nevertheless, such guidelines have not yet been made explicit, and descriptive work related to these relationships, a necessary preliminary step, is just beginning. The authors review several manuscripts that comprise a special journal edition devoted to professional relationships and that provide such descriptions.

**Embree, Lester**. American Ethnophobia, e.g., Irish-American, in Phenomenological Perspective. *Human Stud*, 20(2), 271-286, Ap 97.

**Emerson, John**. Yang Chu's Discovery of the Body. *Phil East West*, 46(4), 533-566, O 96.

Yang Chu is a shadowy figure in classical China brought under philosophical scrutiny. By providing a physical definition of human nature, Yang Chu freed the Chinese elite from the public roles and relationships that defined them, making possible new nonpublic, nonritual forms of individual self-awareness and self-cultivation. The Yangists valorized private and family life at the expense of public, court life.

**Emerson, Roger L**. Hume and the Bellman, Zerobabel MacGilchrist. *Hume Stud*, 23(1), 9-28, Ap 97.

This is the first extensive analysis of Hume's little known broadside. In it he comes as close to openly and explicitly attacking the Bible and Christianity as he does in any other work. The attack in this satirical squib is, of course, indirect but bears upon both the Old and New Testaments. This piece also shows Hume as a social conservative unwilling to raise the stipends of ministers or schoolmasters. Finally, it shows that even though he tried to be Swiftian, satire was not his forte.

**Emerson, William** and Cowen, Robert. A Compactness Theorem for Linear Equations. *Stud Log*, 57(2-3), 355-357, O 96.

It is proved that a system of linear equations over an arbitrary field has a solution if every finite subsystem has a solution provided that the set of variables can be well ordered.

**Emmeche, Claus** and Koppe, Simo and Stjernfelt, Frederik. Explaining Emergence: Towards an Ontology of Levels. *J Gen Phil Sci*, 28(1), 83-119, 1997.

The vitalism/reductionism debate in the life sciences shows that the idea of emergence as something principally unexplainable will often be falsified by the development of science. Nevertheless, the concept of emergence keeps reappearing in various sciences and cannot easily be dispensed with in an evolutionary world-view. We argue that what is needed is an ontological nonreductionist theory of levels of reality which includes a concept of emergence and which can support an evolutionary account of the origin of levels. (edited)

**Emmott, Helen** and Flanigan, Rosemary and Reynolds, Don F. Advance Directive Timeline and Case Study *Melinda's Story*. *Bioethics Forum*, 13(2), 40-43, Sum 97.

**Enderle, Georges**. Five Views on International Business Ethics: An Introduction. *Bus Ethics Quart*, 7(3), 1-4, Jl 97.

**Enderle, Georges**. In Search of a Common Ethical Ground: Corporate Environmental Responsibility from the Perspective of Christian Environmental Stewardship. *J Bus Ethics*, 16(2), 173-181, F 97.

In recent years, corporate environmental policies have become urgently needed, demanded by influential environmentalist groups and launched by an increasing number of companies. Those demands and efforts, however, often lack an ethical underpinning. This paper deals with some basic ethical issues and outlines three perspectives for further investigation: 1) How can we take into account ethical pluralism that characterizes most comtemporary societies?; 2) What is the content of environmental ethics viewed from a Christian perspective, taken as an example of various existent doctrines in the pluralistic world?; and 3) What relevance may this "Christian environmental stewardship" have for the understanding of corporate environmental responsibility?

**Enders, Heinz Werner**. Individuation und Prädikation: Ein Überblick aus historisch-systematischer Sicht. *Acta Analytica*, 91-113, 1995.

How can we bring together medieval semantic systems and the epistemic awareness? What transcription should we use for suppositions, appellations, modi significandi? It is argued that the medieval concepts of individuation and predication aim to put together linguistic objects and the states of affairs they designate.

**Endres, Ben**. "Habermas and Critical Thinking" in *Philosophy of Education (1996)*, Margonis, Frank (ed), 168-177. Urbana, Phil Education Soc, 1997.

**Enes, José**. Pressupostos Linguísticos do Conhecimento Ontológico da Identidade em Sao Tomás. *Rev Port Filosof*, 52(1-4), 315-340, Ja-D 96.

Antero de Quental works—poetry and philosophical essays—were of an extreme importance in the developing of thought, introducing the main currents in aesthetics, philosophy and sociology from Europe—Proudhon, Taine, Hegel, Schopenhauer.... My work is centered on his iconography, as a departure for a brief journey through his ideas about art, creation and beauty and his mystical poetries, acknowledged by his autobiographical beliefs. I tried to capture the aesthetic and anthropological supports, to recognize the main principles behind the images, hidden or revealed by the utopian environment which he conceived and praised. In spite of his despair, disenchantment and obsession on the dead, Antero transposed all by the excellent beauty of the portrait as a revelation of the I.

**Engberg, Uffe**. Completeness Results for Linear Logic on Petri Nets. *Annals Pure Applied Log*, 86(2), 101-135, 16 Je 97.

Completeness is shown for several versions of Girard's linear logic with respect to Petri nets as the class of models. One logic considered is the "circle plus"-free fragment of intuitionistic linear logic without the exponential "!". For this fragment Petri nets form a sound and complete model. (edited)

**Engel, Pascal**. Normes logiques et évolution. *Rev Int Phil*, 51(200), 201-219, Je 97.

**Engel, S Morris**. The Five Forms of the Ad Hominem Fallacy. *Inquiry (USA)*, 14(1), 19-36, Fall 94.

This paper analyses and discusses some of the important and interesting differences between the five standard forms of this personal attack fallacy; it also explores whether there is a possible discoverable order among them. It finds this order in the growing structural complexity discoverable among them.

**Engel, S Morris**. What Is The Fallacy of Hypostatization?. *Inquiry (USA)*, 14(4), 42-51, Sum 95.

The fallacy of hypostatization used to be discussed regularly by informal logicians; indeed it has a long textual history. This paper traces some of this history of the fallacy, explores what might have caused it to disappear from logic texts and why it still deserves our serious attention.

**Engelfriet, Joeri**. Minimal Temporal Epistemic Logic. *Notre Dame J Form Log*, 37(2), 233-259, Spr 96.

In the study of nonmonotonic reasoning the main emphasis has been on static (declarative) aspects. Only recently has there been interest in the dynamic aspects of reasoning processes, particularly in artificial intelligence. We study the dynamics of reasoning processes by using a temporal logic to specify them and to reason about their properties, just as is common in theoretical computer science. This logic is composed of a base temporal epistemic logic with a preference relation on models and an associated nonmonotonic inference relation, in the style of Shoham, to account for the nonmonotonicity. We present an axiomatic proof system for the base logic and study decidability and complexity for both the base logic and the nonmonotonic inference relation based on it. Then we look at an interesting class of formulas, prove a representation result for it and provide a link with the rule of monotonicity.

**Engelhardt Jr, H Tristram**. Equality in Health Care: Christian Engagement with a Secular Obsession. *Christian Bioethics*, 2(3), 355-360, 1996.

A frenetic search for equality lies at the center of much secular and even "Christian" bioethics. In a secular world, if one does not believe in God, if this life is one's whole existence, it would seem that one could not settle for less than equal approbation, especially equality before the risks of suffering and death, which medicine promises to ameliorate. Yet, the concern for equality in health care is puzzling. After a modest level of access to health care there is little difference in average life expectancy. Are concerns for equality in health care even vaguely Christian? The pursuit of Christian perfection has never been correctly equated with state-imposed egalitarianism. Furthermore, an all-encompassing, secular, egalitarian health care system may provide equal access to significantly immoral medical treatments. It contrast to secular thought, the call of Christianity is to holiness, not a call to an egalitarianism that superficially resonates with certain elements of Christian thought.

**Engelhardt Jr, H Tristram**. Freedom and Moral Diversity: The Moral Failures of Health Care in the Welfare State. *Soc Phil Pol*, 14(2), 180-196, Sum 97.

Attempts to enforce welfare entitlements to basic health care packages is morally unjustifiable. Because our disagreements about equality, fairness and justice have depth similar to that of disagreements about particular issues such as contraception and abortion, there is no principled basis for choosing a particular content-full account of morality as canonical. Welfare rights, if established, ought only to be recognized as the creations of limited governmental insurance policies and not as expressions of foundational rights to health care or of moral claims to equality or fairness. Moreover, coercive egalitarianism in health care violates secular rights to purchase better basic as well as luxury care.

**Engelhardt Jr, H Tristram**. Holiness, Virtue, and Social Justice: Contrasting Understandings of the Moral Life. *Christian Bioethics*, 3(1), 3-19, Mr 97.

Being a Christian involves metaphysical, epistemological and social commitments that set Christians a variance with the dominant secular culture. Because Christianity is not syncretical, but proclaims the unique truth of its revelation, Christians will inevitably be placed in some degree of conflict with secular health care institutions. Because being Christian involves a life of holiness, not merely living justly or morally, Christians will also be in conflict with the ethos of many contemporary Christian health care institutions which have abandoned a commitment to Christian spirituality. In this regard, managed care raises the special question of how Christian institutions can act morally under financial constraints and maintain their character while under the control of secular managers. This question itself raises the further question as to why health care institutions need even pose this query when there are Christian physicians and nurses who could work for less, or Christian men and women who could become sisters and brothers and work for nothing. Contemporary challenges to Christians to maintain their integrity in a post-Christian world have much of their force because Christians have failed to maintain traditional Christian spirituality. (edited)

**Engelhardt Jr, H Tristram**. Suffering, Meaning, and Bioethics. *Christian Bioethics*, 2(2), 129-153, Ag 96.

Suffering evokes moral and metaphysical reflection, the bioethics of suffering concerns the proper ethos of living with suffering. Because empirical and philosophical explorations of suffering are imprisoned in the world of immanent experience, they cannot reach to a transcendent meaning. Even if religious and other narratives concerning the meaning of suffering have no transcendent import, they can have aesthetic and moral significance. This understanding of narratives of suffering and of their custodians has substantial ecumenical implications: chaplains can function as general custodians of narratives and sustainers of a generic religious meaning. This understanding is contrary to traditional Christianity. (edited)

**Engelhardt Jr, H Tristram**. The Crisis of Virtue: Arming for the Cultural Wars and Pellegrino at the Limes. *Theor Med*, 18(1-2), 165-172, Mr-Je 97.

Edmund Pellegrino's work has been crucial to the renaissance of interest in the philosophy of medicine and the philosophical grounding of medical ethics that has framed the contemporary field of bioethics in the expectation, of the rational justification of a universal content-full morality. However, this attempt at rational justification has failed, leaving a plurality of bioethics and the inability to secure the canonical account of virtue and character which Pellegrino has sought. This failure is integral to a Western Christian error regarding the nature of virtue.

**Engster, Dan**. Jean Bodin, Scepticism and Absolute Sovereignty. *Hist Polit Thought*, 17(4), 469-499, Winter 96.

In his *Six Books of the Republic*, Jean Bodin broke away from the tradition of medieval constitutionalism and proposed a theory of absolute legislative sovereignty. Scholars have usually explained this philosophical move in terms of the civil strife of late sixteenth century France. This article suggests that it may also be related to the intellectual currents of the period. Throughout his writings, Bodin sought to avoid the relativist conclusions of his sceptical contemporaries. After having initially attempted to find a new universal basis for politics in history, he asserted the idea of absolute sovereignty as the sole foundation of universal right and order.

**Engström, Timothy H**. Foundational Standards and Conversational Style: The Humean Essay as an Issue of Philosophical Genre. *Phil Rhet*, 30(2), 150-175, 1997.

**Engstrom, Anders**. Metaphor and Ambiguity. *Dan Yrbk Phil*, 31, 7-20, 1996.

First, I investigate the view that metaphor can be assigned to determinate metaphorical meaning. This view, I argue, either conflates metaphor with what literal language is designed to do, or results in a postulate of a "special cognitive content" which poses the problem of how metaphor can be connected with literal meaning. Second, I suggest that the signification of metaphor is underdetermined by literal paraphrase. Finally, I show how this leads to the view that metaphor exhibits rampant semantic ambiguity.

**Engstrom, Anders**. The Demarcation of the Metaphorical. *Phil Rhet*, 29(4), 369-383, 1996.

The problem of the demarcation of metaphor is analyzed. It is suggested that those who criticize the delineation of metaphor due to semantic deviance or believed falsity do so primarily by apparent counterexamples. The counterexamples are analyzed and it is shown how these, though not directly identifiable by semantic deviance nor believed falsity, presuppose such conditions as components of a speaker's attitudes when identifying metaphor. It is argued that semantic deviance and believed falsity identify paradigmatic cases of metaphor.

**Engstrom, Stephen**. Kant's Conception of Practical Wisdom. *Kantstudien*, 88(1), 16-43, 1997.

The goal of this essay is to revisit Kant's account of the sublime, from the vantage point of the *Fragestellung* subsequently set up by such thinkers as Schleiermacher, James and Otto. Phenomenologically Kant is close to them, whereas epistemologically he profoundly differs from each of them. Quite central to them is feeling, which seems to give a direct access to the transcendent. In contradistinction to their views, Kant offers us a more sober account of the human mind's openness to the infinite. (edited)

**Ennis, Robert H**. Incorporating Critical Thinking in the Curriculum: An Introduction to Some Basic Issues. *Inquiry (USA)*, 16(3), 1-9, Spr 97.

**Enskat, Rainer**. Moralität und Nützlichkeit. *Phil Rundsch*, 44(2), 152-166, Je 97.

**Entzenberg, Claes**. Metaphor, Interpretation, and Contextualization. *Dan Yrbk Phil*, 31, 21-38, 1996.

This study directs attention to some fundamental aspects of the subject of metaphor. First, it focuses on the effort behind many metalinguistic theories of metaphor to transcend the contextual sense-making activity in an effort to supply a foolproof procedure for identifying metaphors and rule-governed function for calculating it's supposed 'meaning' and 'content'. Second, I try to outline an alternative view on metaphor flexible enough to resist formalization, a

view which emphasizes that metaphor is part of a dynamic, multidimensional process of sense-making and that an illuminating discussion of metaphor must involve describing processes of interpretation and contextualization. By inserting the discussion of metaphor into its proper context of interpretation, tied to different context-specific purposes, we naturally replace the discussion of linguistic 'location' of the metaphorical 'content' with the relational sense-making processes which create the 'content' in a particular act of determination.

**Epstein, Richard A**. The Problem of Forfeiture in the Welfare State. *Soc Phil Pol*, 14(2), 256-284, Sum 97.

**Erde, Edmund L**. The Inadequacy of Role Models for Educating Medical Students in Ethics with Some Reflections on Virtue Theory. *Theor Med*, 18(1-2), 31-45, Mr-Je 97.

Persons concerned with medical education sometimes argued that medical students need no formal education in ethics. They contended that if admissions were restricted to persons of good character and those students were exposed to good role models, the ethics of medicine would take care of itself. However, no one seems to give much philosophic attention to the ideas of *model* or *role model*. In this essay, I undertake such an analysis and add an analysis of *role*. I show the weakness in relying on role models exclusively and draw implications from these for appeals to virtue theory. Furthermore, I indicate some of the problems about how virtue theory is invoked as the ethical theory that would most closely be associated to the role model rhetoric and consider some of the problems with virtue theory. (edited)

**Erdmann, Johann Eduard** and Hough, Williston S (ed & trans). *A History of Philosophy: Volume I*. Bristol, Thoemmes, 1997.

The present translation of Erdmann's *Grundriss der Geschischte der Philosophie* has been made from the third and last edition (Berlin, 1878), and executed by different hands. (publisher, edited)

**Erdmann, Johann Eduard** and Hough, Williston S (ed & trans). *A History of Philosophy: Volume II*. Bristol, Thoemmes, 1997.

**Erdmann, Johann Eduard** and Hough, Williston S (ed & trans). *A History of Philosophy: Volume III*. Bristol, Thoemmes, 1997.

**Erickson, Glenn W** and Fossa, John A. Paradoxes of Salvation. *Dialogos*, 31(68), 165-181, Jl 96.

**Erickson, Stephen A**. Philosophy in the Age of Thresholding. *Int Phil Quart*, 37(3), 263-276, S 97.

Some centuries ago a certain person emerged concerned to maximize worldly opportunities and required a particular set of institutional arrangements (Oakeshott). At the end of this century another sort of person is emerging. Termed "thresholder," this person is concerned to experience and explore ways in which we are not altogether of this world, however, much we are enmeshed in it. "Thresholders" are likely to set the parameters for a new type of philosophizing, both postmetaphysical and oriented away from the analysis of arguments undertaken for their own sake. This reconfiguration requires two activities: disengagement and redirection. How can constructive disengagement be negotiated and achieved?

**Ericson, David P** and Ellet Jr, Frederick S. In Defense of Public Reason: On the Nature of Historical Rationality. *Educ Theor*, 47(2), 133-161, Spr 97.

**Eriksson, Björn**. Utilitarianism for Sinners. *Amer Phil Quart*, 34(2), 213-228, Ap 97.

A theory of degrees of wrongness of actions is defended. The theory is an amendment to classical utilitarianism. It says that the wrongness of any wrong action is a function of how much value was lost by performing the action and how difficult the action was to perform as compared to the other alternatives. This vague idea is given a precise formulation. The theory's relevance for blame- and praiseworthiness is discussed. It is argued that very burdensome actions tend to be wrong to a reduced degree. This provides a kind of answer to the objection that utilitarianism is too burdensome.

**Erjavec, Ales**. "The Perception of Science in Modernist and Postmodernist Artistic Practice" in *Epistemology and History*, Zeidler-Janiszewska, Anna (ed), 469-477. Amsterdam, Rodopi, 1996.

Uses, perceptions and presentations of science in art are discussed. The text focuses on the peculiar change in the relationship between art and science that has occurred in the 20th century. Modernity and the historic artistic avant-garde made use of science. World War II atrocities evoked mistrust of art toward technological developments. Philosophy, however, more than art becomes critical of science (the Frankfurt School). In postmodern art, the role and use of science is limited to use of its technical or technological products (references to the conceptions of Jean-François Lyotard and Richard Rorty).

**Erkal, Nisvan** (ed) and Warren, Karen J (ed). *Ecofeminism: Women, Culture, Nature*. Bloomington, Indiana Univ Pr, 1997.

The strengths and weaknesses of the growing ecofeminist movement are critically assessed by scholars in a variety of academic disciplines and vocations. Writers explore the real-life concerns that have motivated ecofeminism as a grassroots, women-initiated movement around the globe; the appropriateness of ecofeminism to academic and scientific research; and philosophical implications and underpinnings of the movement. (publisher)

**Erler, Edward J**. The Future of Civil Rights: Affirmative Action Redivivus. *Notre Dame J Law Ethics*, 11(1), 15-65, 1997.

The principal contention of this article is that race—and sex—based preferences are destructive of the principle of equal protection understood as the equal protection of equal rights. Beginning with an analysis of the California Civil Rights Initiative, this article traces the origin and transformation of affirmative action from a precept of equal opportunity to one of disparate impact; analyzes the status of civil rights as group rights; discusses the rise and fall and rise of strict scrutiny; chronicles the rise of the new "separate but equal" doctrine; and discusses the role of the judiciary in democratic politics.

**Ernest, Paul**. The Legacy of Lakatos: Reconceptualising the Philosophy of Mathematics. *Phil Math*, 5, 116-134, Je 97.

Kitcher and Aspray distinguish a mainstream tradition in the philosophy of mathematics concerned with foundationalist epistemology and a 'maverick' or naturalistic tradition originating with Lakatos. My claim is that if the consequences of Lakatos's contribution are fully worked out, no less than a radical reconceptualization of the philosophy of mathematics is necessitated, including history, methodology and a fallibilist epistemology as central to the field. In the paper an interpretation of Lakatos's philosophy of mathematics is offered, followed by some critical discussion and an extension to a social constructivist position (which might well have been unacceptable to Lakatos).

**Ernst, Anna-Sabine** and Klinger, Gerwin. Socialist Socrates: Ernst Bloch in the GDR. *Rad Phil*, 84, 6-21, Jl-Ag 97.

**Erwin, Edward**. Psychoanalysis: Past, Present, and Future. *Phil Phenomenol Res*, 57(3), 671-696, S 97.

This article discusses recent philosophic works on psychoanalysis by Patricia Kitcher, Adolf Grünbaum, Donald Levy, and Richard Wollheim. One issue that is addressed concerns the extent to which Freudian hypotheses once received support from discoveries in biology and the social sciences. A second issue concerns the current empirical status of Freud's views. A third issue concerns the future of psychoanalysis if Freudian theory is supplanted by either object relations theory or self psychology.

**Erwin, Edward**. The Evaluation of Psychotherapy: A Reply to Greenwood. *Phil Sci*, 63(4), 642-651, D 96.

John Greenwood (this issue) claims that neglect of an important methodological distinction has contributed directly to the "epistemic impoverishment" of empirical studies of all forms of professional psychotherapy. I challenge this claim, as well as other important claims he makes about the efficacy of psychoanalysis and other forms of psychotherapy.

**Escalante, Evodio**. Consideraciones acerca de la idea de retórica en Hans-Georg Gadamer. *Analogia*, 11(1), 197-207, Ja-Je 97.

**Escalda-Imaz, Gonzalo** and Manyà Serres, Felip and Sobrino, Alejandro. Principles of Logic Programming with Uncertain Information: Description of Some of the Most Relevant Systems (in Spanish). *Theoria (Spain)*, 11(27), 123-148, S 96.

The purpose of this paper is to present the principles of the fuzzy logic programming, exemplifying them by a couple of proposals that we think are representatives of the advances in this field. We include also the description of another systems' programming with uncertain information that are based on other logics of uncertainty which are different from fuzzy logic. This article only presupposes an elementary knowledge of the classical first-order logic.

**Escobar Chico, Angel**. La pervivencia del corpus teológico ciceroniano en España. *Rev Espan Filosof Med*, 4, 189-201, 1997.

The so-called 'theological' works of Cicero (*De natura deorum*, *De divinatione*, *De fato*, and his partial translation of Platonic *Timaeus*) were highly valued from late antiquity on, and had a very rich influence on European medieval literature. However, the transmission of these philosophical dialogues seems to have been very scarce and mainly indirect in Spain until the fourteenth century, only a little more significant in fifteenth and sixteenth century, probably because of the difficulties in adapting the sceptical basis of the Ciceronian thought to the Christian orthodoxy, in spite of the humanistic attempts in this direction.

**Esfeld, Michael**. *Mechanismus und Subjektivität in der Philosophie von Thomas Hobbes*. Stuttgart, Frommann-Holzboog, 1995.

This thesis is a systematic reconstruction of Hobbes's work. It focuses on the relation between his mechanistic ontology and the manifestation of modern subjectivity in his philosophy. Hobbes wants to elaborate a self-conception of man within the new mechanistic paradigm which enables physics to be a successful science of the world. That is why he admits feelings, perceptions, thoughts and intentions as phenomena of self-experience and applies the mechanistic paradigm to them. Paradoxically enough, this very application is shown to make man emerge as a subject in contrast to nature as an object in Hobbes's philosophy. For the first time a theory of a systematic development of this subjectivity from perception to political action is revealed in Hobbes's work. Although the theory of this subjectivity cannot be deduced from the materialistic ontology, the way Hobbes considers this subjectivity depends on this ontology. (edited)

**Eskridge Jr, William**. "Beyond Lesbian and Gay "Families We Choose" in *Sex, Preference, and Family: Essays on Law and Nature*, Nussbaum, Martha C (ed), 277-289. New York, Oxford Univ Pr, 1997.

**Espinoza, Miguel**. El desmigajador de la realidad: Wittgenstein y las matemáticas. *Mathesis*, 10(2), 171-186, My 94.

I have tried to pin down the specificity of Wittgenstein's ideas on mathematics by comparing them to Platonism, intuitionism and conventionalism. Attention is called on the fact that having touched the logical and calculating sides of mathematics, Wittgenstein misses the most interesting part of this science. It is difficult, in those circumstances, to make a real contribution to the true philosophy of mathematics. The most regrettable part of the story is that Wittgenstein's ideas, inadequate to the essence and pertinence of mathematics, follow from some of his central doctrines such as the notion of a language game or form of life, the main causes of the disintegration of mathematical reality. Thus our criticisms can be transmitted by transposition to his general philosophy.

**Esposito, Costantino** (ed & trans) and Suárez, Francisco. *Disputazioni Metafisiche I-III*. Milano, Rusconi, 1996.

Quest'edizione—la prima in italiano—è curata da Costantino Esposito (Università di Bari), che si occupa di storia della metafisica con particolare riferimento a Kant e Heidegger. Dell'immensa mole delle 54 *Disputazioni* vengono tradotte qui le prime tre, per il fatto che esse si presentano, in maniera serrata e compiuta, come una vera e propria "introduzione alla metafisica", un'autentica monografia, in cui è presentata la natura, l'oggetto e il metodo di questa scienza. L'*introduzione* fornisce un primo approccio sintetico all'opera. Negli *apparati* è riportato l'indice completo di tutte le *Disputazioni*; l'indice delle fonti antiche, medioevali e rinascimentali discusse da Suárez; le *parole chiave* del testo e una *bibliografia* comprendente il prospetto degli *Opera omnia* di Suárez, l'elenco delle diverse edizioni delle *Disputazioni* e una raccolta esauriente degli studi sulle *Disputazioni* apparsi nel Novecento. (publisher, edited)

**Esquer Gallardo, Héctor**. La precisividad del pensamiento. *Anu Filosof*, 29(2), 463-480, 1996.

This paper is an investigation into "abandonment of mental limit" in order to distinguish "being" and "thought". The philosophy of Leonardo Polo carries out that distinction with a study on "acts" and "habits" of knowledge. The difference between knowledge and being is exclusively the *mental presence*.

**Esquith, Stephen L**. "Political Dialogue and Political Virtue" in *Political Dialogue: Theories and Practices*, Esquith, Stephen L (ed), 9-22. Amsterdam, Rodopi, 1996.

Bruce Ackerman and now John Rawls have argued that the primary political virtues of liberal democratic citizens are tolerance and conversational restraint. While these virtues are important for a constitutional politics that strives to keep certain divisive moral, religious and philosophical issues of the political agenda, they are not sufficient to see democratic citizens through the political conflicts that they ordinarily confront. Ackerman also has argued that the new democracies of Central and Eastern Europe should seize the current "constitutional moment" by developing these political virtues. I argue, with references to Adam Michnik, that the West has as much to learn from these new democracies about the virtues required for participation in democratic dialogues where power is unequally distributed as they have to gain from liberal constitutional theories of restraint.

**Esquith, Stephen L** (ed). *Political Dialogue: Theories and Practices*. Amsterdam, Rodopi, 1996.

**Esteban Ortega, Joaquín**. La revitalización hermenéutico-lingüística de la memoria en H. G. Gadamer y E. Lledó. *Pensamiento*, 204(52), 403-428, S-D 96.

A lo largo de los siglos el contenido filosófico de la memoria ha sido tratado desde múltiples perspectivas. La actual dimensión hermenéutica del pensamiento, tal y como se especifica en la filosofía de H. G. Gadamer, ha sabido escuchar en la gran tradición platónico-hegeliana la necesidad de reivindicar la dimensión ontológica de la memoria. En el presente estudio, desde las reflexiones de Gadamer, puestas en estrecho diálogo con la proyección que sobre el mismo tema ha venido realizando en nuestro país su discípulo Emilio Lledó, el autor ha pretendido describir un proceso lingüístico y recualificador a través del cual se intenta volver a escuchar la vitalidad originaria de *Mnemosyne*.

**Esteves Borges, Paulo Alexandre**. A experiência erótica em Leonardo Coimbra. *Philosophica (Portugal)*, 19-36, 1994.

Nous essayons de montrer, dans sa constitution généalogique, la formulation de l'expérience érotique en Leonardo Coimbra, laquelle, à partir de l'amour sexuel—et en profitant de sa vertu d'ouverture métaphysique des êtres au Principe même des relations universelle—, se prolonge dans la création des sciences, des arts et de la morale, culminant par se dévoiler comme manifestation—plus qu'analogique—de la transcendance immanente de l'Amour divin. On finit, surtout dans les notes, par suggérer des relations spontanées de cette pensée avec la tradition portugaise médiévale, renaissante et contemporaine avec plusieurs formes de tradition où l'opposition entre Éros et Agapè se dissipe dans l'évidence vécue de l'amour sexuel comme initiation simultanée à la Vérité et à sa dispensation compassionée pour tous les êtres.

**Estlund, David M**. "Shaping and Sex: Commentary on Parts I and II" in *Sex, Preference, and Family: Essays on Law and Nature*, Nussbaum, Martha C (ed), 148-170. New York, Oxford Univ Pr, 1997.

This essay provides brief critical commentary on the essays in Parts I and II of the book of which it is a part. These essays are by Moody-Adams, Nussbaum, Okin, Rosenblum, Macedo, MacKinnon and Estlund.

**Estlund, David M**. "The Visit and The Video: Publication and the Line Between Sex and Speech" in *Sex, Preference, and Family: Essays on Law and Nature*, Nussbaum, Martha C (ed), 126-147. New York, Oxford Univ Pr, 1997.

If a voyeuristic visit to a prostitute is not protected under the First Amendment, then why should a pornographic video produced and used for the same purpose receive such protection? This essay proposes that the video, unlike the visit, ought to receive coverage under the Press Clause of the First Amendment, on the ground that it is a publication. Coverage does not guarantee indefeasible protection, but it distinguishes the video from the visit in a principled way. The more general implications of such a publication criterion are explored, especially for other sexual materials.

**Estlund, David M** (ed) and Nussbaum, Martha C (ed). *Sex, Preference, and Family: Essays on Law and Nature*. New York, Oxford Univ Pr, 1997.

From Dan Quayle's attack on TV's Murphy Brown for giving birth out of wedlock, to the referendum recently passed in Colorado that forbids local communities from enacting nondiscrimination laws for sexual orientation, the public furor over issues of same-sex marriages, gay rights, pornography and single-parent families has erupted with a passion not seen since the 1960s. It is a battle being fought, in large part, over where to draw the line between law and nature, between the political and the personal, the social and the biological. And it is an important struggle to resolve, for as we move into the next century our culture is redefining itself in fundamental ways. How we decide these questions will determine much about the kind of society we and our children will live in. (publisher)

**Estrada, Juan A**. Teodicea y sentido de la historia: la respuesta de Hegel. *Pensamiento*, 204(52), 361-382, S-D 96.

El problema del mal en la historia sigue de actualidad, tanto en cuanto mal moral (la injusticia) como en cuanto mal físico (los sufrimientos). Hegel es el prototipo de la filosofía del progreso y su influencia llega hasta nuestros días. El autor analiza su concepción de la historia como teodicea, las perspectivas desde las que enfoca el problema del mal y la soluciones que propone. Con Hegel la teodicea se convierte en una antropodicea, a costa del individuo que se integra en la suerte colectiva de la humanidad.

**Etane, Yomba**. Rousseau: le contrat social en question. *Philosopher*, 19, 23-42, 1996.

**Etane, Yombo**. Le statut du contrat social chez Rousseau selon Yves Vargas: Une lecture critique. *De Phil*, 11, 1-18, 1994-1995.

**Etzioni, Amitai**. A Moderate Communitarian Proposal. *Polit Theory*, 24(2), 155-171, My 96.

Six fundamental propositions are discussed which together constitute a renewed theoretical understanding of communitarianism. The over-arching purpose is to mediate the conflict ensconced in academic discourse between the values of liberalism (or libertarianism) and the insights of communitarianism. The six propositions concern: 1) the ontological status of the individual in relationship to a social, cultural, or historical context; 2) the premise that the neutral polity of liberal normative theory is not viable; 3) the reciprocal relationship between individual rights and social responsibilities; 4) the commensurability between communitarianism and constitutionally defined limits to majority rule; 5) the need for an independent, moral ground to legitimate a particular community's values; and 6) a communitarian theory of human nature.

**Evans, Dylan**. Historicism and Lacanian Theory. *Rad Phil*, 79, 35-40, S-O 96.

**Evans, Henri** (trans) and Hountondji, Paulin J. *African Philosophy: Myth and Reality*. Bloomington, Indiana Univ Pr, 1996.

In this seminal exploration of the nature and future of African philosophy, Paulin J. Hountondji attacks a myth popularized by ethnophilosophers such as Placide Tempels and Alexis Kagamé that there is an indigenous, collective African philosophy separate and distinct from the Western philosophical tradition. Hountondji contends that ideological manifestations of this view that stress the uniqueness of the African experience are protonationalist reactions against colonialism conducted, paradoxically in the terms of colonialist discourse. Hountondji argues that a genuine African philosophy must assimilate and transcend the theoretical heritage of Western philosophy and must reflect a rigorous process of independent scientific inquiry. This edition is updated with a new preface in which Hountondji responds to his critics and clarifies misunderstandings about the book's conceptual framework. (publisher, edited)

**Everett, Anthony**. A Dilemma for Priest's Dialetheism?. *Austl J Phil*, 74(4), 657-668, D 96.

**Everett, Linda** and Thorne, Debbie and Danehower, Carol. Cognitive Moral Development and Attitudes Toward Women Executives. *J Bus Ethics*, 15(11), 1227-1235, N 96.

Research has shown that men and women are similar in their capabilities and management competence; however, there appears to be a "glass ceiling" which poses invisible barriers to their promotion to management positions. One explanation for the existence of these barriers lies in stereotyped, biased attitudes toward women in executive positions. This study supports earlier findings that attitudes of men toward women in executive positions are generally negative, while the attitudes of women are generally positive. Additionally, we found that an individual's level of cognitive moral development correlates significantly with attitudes toward women executives. Limitations of the present study and implications for ethics and diversity training in organizations are discussed.

**Everitt, Nicholas**. Quasi-Berkeleyan Idealism as Perspicuous Theism. *Faith Phil*, 14(3), 353-377, Jl 97.

In this paper I argue that the kind of idealism defended by Berkeley is a natural and almost unavoidable expression of his theism. Two main arguments are deployed, both starting from a theistic premise and having an idealist conclusion. The first likens the dependence of the physical world in the will of God to the dependence of mental states on a mind. The second likens divine omniscience to the kind of knowledge which it has often been supposed we have of the contents of our own minds. After rebutting objections to these arguments, I conclude that both theists and nonidealists should be surprised and discomforted by my contentions.

**Everson, Stephen**. *Aristotle on Perception*. New York, Clarendon/Oxford Pr, 1997.

Stephen Everson presents a comprehensive new study of Aristotle's account of perception and phantasia. Recent debate about Aristotle's theory of mind has focused on this account, which is Aristotle's most sustained and detailed attempt to describe and explain the behavior of living things. Everson places it in the context of Aristotle's natural science as a whole, showing how he applies the explanatory tools developed in other works to the study of perceptual cognition.

Everson demonstrates that, contrary to the claims of many recent scholars, Aristotle is indeed concerned to explain perceptual activity as the activity of a living body, by reference to material changes in the organs which possess the various perceptual capacities. By emphasizing the unified nature of the perceptual system, Everson is able to explain how Aristotle accounts for our ability to perceive not only such things as colors and sounds but material objects in our environment. (publisher, edited)

**Evlampiev, I I**. The Metaphysical Premises of the Ideology of Liberalism and Its Types. *Russian Stud Phil*, 35(2), 21-31, Fall 96.

**Eynon, Gail** and Thorley Hill, Nancy and Stevens, Kevin T. Factors that Influence the Moral Reasoning Abilities of Accountants: Implications for Universities and the Profession. *J Bus Ethics*, 16(12-13), 1297-1309, S 97.

The need to maintain the public trust in the integrity of the accounting profession has led to increased interest in research that examines the moral reasoning abilities (MRA) of Certified Public Accountants (CPAs). This study examines the MRA of CPAs practicing in small firms or as sole practitioners and the factors that affect MRA throughout their working careers. (edited)

**Ezcurdia, Maite**. Contextos, Creencías y Anáforas. *Critica*, 28(83), 97-129, Ag 96.

The author argues that Stephen Neale's defense of the Russellian theory of definite descriptions a) is incomplete, and b) should be modified. a) It is incomplete because it fails to prove a successful Russellian account of incomplete descriptions especially in the light of Lewis's case "The dog bit the other dog." The author discusses six ways in which Russellians could accommodate such cases, arguing that only one of them will do. b) The theory should be modified with respect to unbound pronouns anaphoric on definite descriptions (and other quantifier phrases) which occur in that-clauses of propositional attitude reports.

**Ezquerra Gómez, Jesús**. Reflexión y principio de la lógica en Hegel. *Daimon Rev Filosof*, 10, 47-56, Ja-Je 95.

The aim of this paper is to show, by the help of Kant's conception of Nothing as *ens rationis*, the reflexive structure of the starting-point of Hegel's logic. That such a structure reveals us, on one hand, the genuine core that organizes and summarizes formally the logical development—the reflexion—and, on the other hand, the ontological impossibility to set abstractly an ultimate immediacy.

**Ezrahi, Yaron**. "Dewey's Critique of Democratic Visual Culture and its Political Implications" in *Sites of Vision*, Levin, David Michael (ed), 315-336. Cambridge, MIT Pr, 1997.

**Fabbianelli, Faustino**. La prima lettura fichtiana della *Kritik der Urteilskraft* in alcuni studi del nostro secolo. *G Crit Filosof Ital*, 16(2), 266-280, My-Ag 96.

**Fabiani, Paolo**. La persuasión desde las *Institutiones Oratoriae* a la *Scienza Nuova*. *Cuad Vico*, 7/8, 59-73, 1997.

In spite of the persistent ambiguity which occurs concerning the relation between rhetoric and philosophy in Vico, this article attempts to explore the continuity rather than the discontinuity between Vico as rhetorician and Vico as philosopher. Such continuity can be found with regard to imagination and persuasion. Both topics are deeply developed in the *Scienza nuova*, where considerations on rhetoric of theoretical import are located, but also and especially in the *Institutiones Oratoriae*.

**Fabri Dos Anjos, Marcio**. Medical Ethics in the Developing World: A Liberation Theology Perspective. *J Med Phil*, 21(6), 629-637, D 96.

Standard medical ethical analyses typically focus on the physician/patient relationship, patient autonomy and the clinical encounter. For Liberation Theology this amounts to neglecting the larger context of social injustice. Medicine is a social institution. Any medical ethics which purports to provide an ethics of medicine and medical practice must necessarily address the larger social issues of class structure, poverty and access to adequate health care. Liberation Theology provides a very specific perspective that draws on the needs of the poverty stricken, assesses the relationship among social classes and focuses on societal conditions. Given such an analysis, medical ethics is reconfigured as concerned not only with clinical encounters but also with background cultural conditions and social justice.

**Fabris, Adriano**. Heidegger, Nietzsche e il problema del senso. *Teoria*, 16(1), 67-85, 1996.

**Fabris, Matteo**. Attualità di un carteggio del Settecento. *G Metaf*, 18(3), 465-472, S-D 96.

**Faccini, Giovanni** and Van Megen, Freek and Borm, Peter (& others). Congestion Models and Weighted Bayesian Potential Games. *Theor Decis*, 42(2), 193-206, Ja 97.

Games associated with congestion situations à la Rosenthal (1973) have pure Nash equilibria. This result implicitly relies on the existence of a potential function. In this paper we provide a characterization of potential games in terms of coordination games and dummy games. Second, we extend Rosenthal's congestion model to an incomplete information setting and show that the related Bayesian games are potential games and therefore, have pure Bayesian equilibria.

**Fackenheim, Emil L** and Burbidge, John W (ed). *The God Within: Kant, Schelling, and Historicity*. Toronto, Univ of Toronto Pr, 1996.

**Fackenheim, Emil L** and Morgan, Michael L (ed). *Jewish Philosophers and Jewish Philosophy*. Bloomington, Indiana Univ Pr, 1996.

If, in content and in method, philosophy and religion conflict, can there be a Jewish philosophy? What makes a Jewish thinker a philosopher? Emil L. Fackenheim confronts these questions in a series of essays on the great Jewish thinkers from Maimonides through Hermann Cohen, Martin Buber, Franz

Rosenzweig, and Leo Strauss. Fackenheim also contemplates the task of Jewish philosophy after the Holocaust. While providing access to key Jewish thinkers of the past, this volume highlights the exciting achievements of one of today's most creative and most important Jewish philosophers. (publisher, edited)

**Faden, Ruth**. The Advisory Committee on Human Radiation Experiments: Reflections on a Presidential Commission. *Hastings Center Rep*, 26(5), 5-10, S-O 96.

Like other appointed commissions, the Advisory Committee on Human Radiation Experiments was formed to carry out specific ethical tasks. Yet this committee also had an "openness" mission, a charge to investigate allegations that the U.S. government secretly exposed Americans to environmental releases of radiation.

**Faden, Ruth** and Sugarman, Jeremy and Kass, Nancy E. Trust: The Fragile Foundation of Contemporary Biomedical Research. *Hastings Center Rep*, 26(5), 25-29, S-O 96.

It is widely assumed that informing prospective subjects about the risks and possible benefits of research not only protects their rights, but empowers them to protect their interests. Yet interviews with patient-subjects suggest this is not always the case. Patient-subjects often trust their physician to guide them through decisions.

**Fadini, Ubaldo**. "Positività Della Corruzione: Per una fenomenologia della mutazione" in *Soggetto E Verità: La questione dell'uomo nella filosofia contemporanea*, Fagiuoli, Ettore, 77-90. 20136 Milano, Mimesis, 1996.

The essay examines the connection between the concept of "corruption" and the one of "mutation". Starting from the reference to philosophical culture of the 18th and 19th century (B De Mandeville, A Smith, K Marx), the author considers some phenomena (such as biotechnological cybernetics) referring to today's relationship between machine and human body. In this way the essay proposes a phenomenology and an anthropology which takes into consideration the contemporary "corporealization of technology" and "technicalisation of corporeity".

**Fadini, Ubaldo**. La mediatizzazione del soggetto. *Iride*, 9(18), 394-403, Ag 96.

Affrontare oggi il tema di una "squalifica" quasi definitiva dell'umano a vantaggio di un condizionamento strumentale della persona vuol dire richiamare le analisi "dromologiche" di Paul Virilio, che appaiono particolarmente significative per una miglior comprensione delle modalità attraverso cui la soggettività viene ad essere prodotta, soprattutto nel momento in cui l'immagine forse più rappresentativa di quest'ultima sembra essere quella dell'ibrido risultante dal complicarsi dell'interfaccia uomo-macchina.

**Fafara, Richard J**. Étienne Gilson's Early Study of Nicolas Malebranche. *Mod Sch*, 74(3), 169-203, Mr 97.

While a student at the Sorbonne, Gilson submitted to Professor Delbos an essay on "Malebranche s Polemic Against Aristotle and Scholastic Philosophy." Delbos questioned Gilson's explanation of Malebranche's vehemence in this polemic. Subsequent study of Descartes and the scholastics led Gilson to appreciate Malebranche's Augustinianism and to interpret Malebranche as a Christian philosopher whose philosophy is inseparable from theology. This interpretation provided Gilson with the authoritative answer to the central question of his earlier essay for Delbos; it also became one of the major contributions to Malebranchian scholarship in this century. A transcription of Gilson's essay is included as an appendix to this article.

**Faggiotto, Pietro**. "Le aporie della concezione kantiana del tempo" in *Il Concetto di Tempo: Atti del XXXII Congresso Nazionale della Società Filosofica Italiana*, Casertano, Giovanni (ed), 191-195. Napoli, Loffredo, 1997.

Il saggio è rivolto ad illustrare le difficoltà che la concezione della soggettività del tempo comporta in tutta la filosofis kantiana, particolarmente sul piano morale. Se il tempo è la forma della realtà fenomenica, tutta la realtà noumenica si colloca fuori del tempo, è sottratta totalmente al divenire, è assolutamente immobile. In questa prospettiva di assoluto immobilismo non c'è alcuna possibilità di progresso autentico, né di regresso sul piano morale (che riguarda appunto il piano nuomenico della vita umana), ma solo una condizione definita una volta per sempre, nel bene o nel male, da un atto di libertà che è fuori del tempo. Analogo immobilismo viene ad investire l'intera storia universale dell'umanità, il cui processo verso lo scopo finale (*Endzweck*), la perfezione morale dell'uomo, diverrebbe impossibile.

**Fagin, Ronald** and Halpern, Joseph Y and Moses, Yoram (& others). Reasoning about Knowledge: A Response by the Authors. *Mind Mach*, 7(1), 113, F 97.

**Fagiuoli, Ettore**. "*Drama O Dell'"Espressione A Ogni Costo*": L'azione tragica: Nietzsche critico di Wagner" in *Soggetto E Verità: La questione dell'uomo nella filosofia contemporanea*, Fagiuoli, Ettore, 209-215. 20136 Milano, Mimesis, 1996.

**Fagiuoli, Ettore** and Fortunato, Marco. *Soggetto E Verità: La questione dell'uomo nella filosofia contemporanea*. 20136 Milano, Mimesis, 1996.

**Fairfield, Paul**. Liberalism and Moral Selfhood. *Phil Today*, 40(3), 341-356, Fall 96.

Whether liberalism may incorporate a strongly situated conception of the self is the main question posed in this paper. That it may, and in so doing counter an important element of the communitarian critique of liberalism, is its central thesis. Drawing primarily upon the work of Paul Ricoeur and John Dewey, I articulate and defend a conception of the self as a narrated and self-narrating agent. Moral selfhood is properly conceived as at once socially constituted and,

in keeping with liberalism, capable of critical distantiation from the traditions and forms of community life within which it stands.

**Fairfield, Paul**. Overcoming the Theory/Practice Opposition in Business Ethics. *Bus Prof Ethics J*, 14(4), 23-42, Wint 95.

Reconceiving the theory/practice relation in business ethics is the principal aim of this paper. Assuming a nonfoundational stance, I argue that the practice of commerce does not stand in need of the kind of "grounding" that ethical theory traditionally seeks to provide and that an immanent mode of reflection is all that is necessary and possible in developing a philosophical critique of business practices. I outline a "practice-immanent" mode of theorizing, one that articulates the principles that phenomenologically are already operative within market practices. It is these principles that furnish a critical perspective for business ethics.

**Fairlamb, Horace L**. Adam Smith's Other Hand: A Capitalist Theory of Exploitation. *Soc Theor Pract*, 22(2), 193-223, Sum 96.

Though Adam Smith believed that the spontaneous forces of the market set prices at the most productive level, he doubted that market forces price wages as fairly as the prices of other commodities. In fact, various observations by Smith suggest that the market tends to undervalue wages almost as naturally as it naturalizes the prices of most commodities under nonmonopolistic conditions. Those observations imply the germ of a capitalist theory of exploitation.

**Fairlamb, Horace L**. Heterology: A Postmodern Theory of Foundations. *Metaphilosophy*, 27(4), 381-398, O 96.

Epistemology has traditionally sought to discover the foundations of knowledge. Recently, antifoundational philosophers have construed epistemology's failure to discover an ultimate ground to indicate the bankruptcy of foundational theory. On closer examination, however, the history of epistemology reveals the aim of foundational theory to be different both from the reductive ideal of its traditional defenders and from the unsystematic relativism that its recent critics offer instead. An alternative history of foundational theory reveals a progress toward multiple necessary foundations which is the task of epistemology to articulate.

**Fairlamb, Horace L**. Nature's Two Ends: The Ambiguity of Progress in Evolution. *S J Phil*, 35(1), 35-55, Spr 97.

**Falcon, Andrea**. Aristotle's Rules of Division in the *Topics*: The Relationship between Genus and Differentia in a Division. *Ancient Phil*, 16(2), 377-387, Fall 96.

By a close examination of *Topics* VI 6, 144b12-30 the author brings out two rules of division. This passage presents evidence for the claim that every differentia is logically dependent on its genus. A full understanding of this could be of some help in order to shed light upon the relationship between genus and differentia in a division. One verb, in Greek *epipherein*, seems to be important to Aristotle's discussion. There appear to be some interesting formal similarities between *Topics* VI 6, 144b12-30 and *Phaedo* 105a1-5. Both Plato and Aristotle use this same relatively unusual verb, namely *epipherein*.

**Falcón y Tella, María José**. Verso una concezione unitaria della norma fondamentale. *Riv Int Filosof Diritto*, 73(3), 450-479, Jl-S 96.

The purpose of this work is to compare Kelsen's doctrine of the "Grundnorm" and Hart's doctrine of the "Rule of Recognition"—analyzing their origin, nature, content, function, etc.—and to try to build a unified theory that would conciliate both. To achieve this, we study the connection between national and international law, analyzing three possibilities: a) the juridical monism, b) the juridical dualism, and c) the juridical pluralism.

**Fales, Evan**. A Defense of the Given. Lanham, Rowman & Littlefield, 1996.

What is the connection between experience and knowledge? Evan Fales defends the contested ideal that sense experience can be used to justify basic beliefs. He explores what it is for a belief to be self-evident and examines implications for his argument of Gestalt psychology and visual phenomena and illusions. Fales diverges from classical foundationalism, however, arguing that basic beliefs are often only probable, rather than infallible. *A Defense of the Given* is an important work not only for epistemologists but for all philosophers interested in how we can justify our beliefs. (publisher, edited)

**Fales, Evan**. Divine Intervention. *Faith Phil*, 14(2), 170-194, Ap 97.

Some philosophers deny than science can investigate the supernatural—specifically, the nature and actions of God. If a divine being is atemporal, then, indeed, this seems plausible—but only, I shall argue, because such a being could not causally interact with anything. Here I discuss in detail two major attempts, those of Stump and Kretzmann, and of Leftow, to make sense of theophysical causation on the supposition that God is eternal. These views are carefully worked out and their failures are instructive for any attempt to reconcile eternality with causal efficacy. I conclude by arguing that if knowledge of God is possible, in virtue of His effects upon the world, then it is science that must play the pre-eminent role in producing that knowledge.

**Fales, Evan**. Plantinga's Case Against Naturalistic Epistemology. *Phil Sci*, 63(3), 432-451, S 96.

In *Warrant and Proper Function*, Alvin Plantinga claims that metaphysical naturalism, when joined to a naturalized epistemology, is self-undermining. Plantinga argues that naturalists are committed to a neo-Darwinian account of our origins, and that the reliability of our cognitive faculties is improbable or unknown relative to that theory. If this is true, then we are in no position to know that, whereas theism, if true, underwrites cognitive reliability. I seek to turn the tables on Plantinga, showing that neo-Darwinism provides strong reasons for expecting general cognitive reliability, whereas the likelihood of that relative to theism is unknowable.

**Falgueras Salinas, Ignacio**. Essbozo de una filosofía trascendental: Introducción. *Anu Filosof*, 29(2), 481-508, 1996.

I mind by transcendental philosophy the pure inquiry of the ultimate realities also called transcendental realities. The whole inquiry is divided in two parts. The first one is dedicated to study the inconditional transcendentals and the second one to study the conditional transcendentals. Both parts are preceded by one introduction, whose content constitutes the present paper.

**Falk, Barrie**. "Feeling and Cognition" in *Verstehen and Humane Understanding*, O'Hear, Anthony (ed), 211-222. New York, Cambridge Univ Pr, 1996.

**Falk, Hans-Peter**. Der Philosophiebegriff in Fichtes später Wissenschaftslehre. *Fichte-Studien*, 12, 365-373, 1997.

**Falkenberg, L E** and Boland, L. Eliminating the Barriers to Employment Equity in the Canadian Workplace. *J Bus Ethics*, 16(9), 963-975, Je 97.

Have employment equity programs achieved the goal of equity for women in the workplace? We argue that they have not because gender stereotypes still persist. In fact, they may have created resentment and antagonism towards successful women and employment equity initiatives. Arguments are developed for the Canadian government to create a self-regulating system, in which the government plays a role of educator as opposed to monitor.

**Falkenburg, Brigitte**. The Analysis of Particle Tracks: A Case for Trust in the Unity of Physics. *Stud Hist Phil Mod Physics*, 27B(3), 337-371, S 96.

With a case study concerning the analysis of particle tracks, I want to show how modelling in physics is based on trust in unity. The paper deals with the calculations of particle tracks made around 1930 by Mott and Bethe and with the way in which Bethe's calculations have been used for decades to measure the particle momentum from individual tracks. The measurement method relies on the assumption that classical mechanics and quantum theory of scattering can be combined consistently into a model of the passage of charged particles through matter which applies to individual tracks. The empirical adequacy of the model is demonstrated by independent tests. I shall argue that the analysis of particle tracks is a case for well-justified trust in a unity of physics which may well be hidden in actual model-building. The measurement method reveals the transcendental status of the idea of unity in physics, while the empirical adequacy of the underlying model indicates that the idea has indeed some counterpart in the contingent structure of the phenomena.

**Falkenstein, Lorne**. Kant's Empiricism. *Rev Metaph*, 50(3), 547-589, Mr 97.

This paper investigates the role played by empirically given data in Kant's accounts of causal reasoning, the systematic unity of laws of nature and realism. Particular attention is devoted to the notion of the exponent of a rule, to Kant's notion of affinity and to the argument of Kant's *Metaphysical Foundations of Natural Science*. It is argued that the limits of a priori knowledge are in fact extremely restricted for Kant.

**Falkenstein, Lorne**. *Kant's Intuitionism: A Commentary on the Transcendental Aesthetic*. Toronto, Univ of Toronto Pr, 1995.

This book presents a paragraph-by-paragraph analysis of all of the major arguments and explanations in the "aesthetic" of Kant's *Critique of Pure Reason*. The first part of the book aims to provide a clear analysis of the meanings of the terms Kant uses to name faculties and types of representation, the second offers a thorough account of the reasoning behind the "metaphysical" and "transcendental" expositions, and the third investigates the basis for Kant's major conclusions about space, time, appearances, things in themselves, and the cognitive constitution of the subject. A major goal of the work is to establish that Kant takes spatiotemporal form to be originally given through the constitution of the subject's receptive faculty, not generated through synthetic procedures of the imagination or understanding.

**Falkenstein, Lorne**. Naturalism, Normativity, and Scepticism in Hume's Account of Belief. *Hume Stud*, 23(1), 29-72, Ap 97.

Hume's scepticism about the ability of demonstrative reasoning to justify many of our most common and important beliefs, such those concerning the connection between causes and effects, does not sit well with his tendency to make normative claims about which beliefs we ought to accept. I argue that Hume's naturalist account of the causes of belief is nonetheless rich enough to provide for normative assessments of belief and even for the modification of beliefs in light of these assessments. I argue, moreover, that far from interfering with his normative claims, Hume's appeals to the force of sceptical arguments are essential premises for this result.

**Fallas, Luis A**. El placer en Grecia y el mundo hebreo. *Rev Filosof (Costa Rica)*, 34(83-84), 247-264, D 96.

We study here the phenomenon of pleasure from the point of view of five Greek positions: Democritean, Cyrenaic, Platonic, Aristotelian and Epicurean. This topic is then confronted with several biblical texts. From both world views, Greek and Hebrew, it is possible to defend hedonism, although the diversity of means in it doesn't seem to allow us to take sides.

**Fallis, Don**. The Epistemic Status of Probabilistic Proof. *J Phil*, 94(4), 165-186, Ap 97.

A deductive argument is considered by mathematicians (and many philosophers) to be the *only* legitimate way to establish that a mathematical claim is true. In this paper, I argue that mathematicians do not have good grounds for their rejection of probabilistic methods as a means of establishing mathematical truths. Specifically, I argue that one particular probabilistic method (which utilizes recent DNA technology) has no *epistemic* drawbacks that are not shared by standard methods of establishing mathematical truths.

**Falmagne, Jean-Claude** and Doignon, Jean-Paul. Stochastic Evolution of Rationality. *Theor Decis*, 43(2), 107-138, S 97.

Following up on previous results by Falmagne, this paper investigates possible mechanisms explaining how preference relations are created and how they

evolve over time. We postulate a preference relation which is initially empty and becomes increasingly intricate under the influence of a random environment delivering discrete tokens of information concerning the alternatives. The framework is that of a class of real-time stochastic processes having interlinked Markov and Poisson components. Asymptomatic results are obtained in the form of the limit probabilities of any semiorder. The arguments extend to a much more general situation including interval orders, biorders and partial orders. The results provide (up to a small number of parameters) complete quantitative predictions for panel data of a standard type, in which the same sample of subjects has been asked to compare the alternatives a number of times. (edited)

**Famiani, Mariapaola**. Incarnato comparire: Corpo e politica nelle proposte di Adriana Cavarero. *Iride*, 9(19), 761-768, S-D 96.

**Fan, Ruiping**. Bioethics, Metaphysical Involvements, and Biomedical Practice. *J Med Phil*, 22(2), 91-98, Ap 97.

There is a tripartite set of relations among bioethics, metaphysics, and biomedical practice. On the one hand, the problems raised by biomedical practice call for bioethical explanations and guidance, which in turn bring respective metaphysical accounts into play. On the other hand, inconsistencies and contradictions contained within bioethical theories stand in need of metaphysical involvements to help resolve them, and this leads to more secure approaches to biomedical reality. Finally, distinct metaphysical positions shape the ways in which bioethical principles are applied in practical biomedical issues. Thus, this essay concludes that there are tight-knit metaphysical involvements in the discipline of bioethics.

**Faraone, Rosa**. "Tra finitudine e storicità: il tempo nell'esistenzialismo italiano" in *Il Concetto di Tempo: Atti del XXXII Congresso Nazionale della Società Filosofica Italiana*, Casertano, Giovanni (ed), 273-284. Napoli, Loffredo, 1997.

**Farber, Paul**. "Education's Ills and the Vanity of the Philosopher" in *Philosophy of Education (1996)*, Margonis, Frank (ed), 378-380. Urbana, Phil Education Soc, 1997.

**Fares, Diego J**. Fenomenología de la verdad en H.U. von Balthasar II. *Stromata*, 52(3-4), 173-219, Ja-Je 96.

**Farmer, Linda**. Human is Generated by Human and Created by God. *Amer Cath Phil Quart*, 70(3), 413-427, Sum 96.

This article argues that Aquinas's embryological analysis of the human being diminishes the strength of his thesis of the unity of the human being. Aquinas's embryological analysis sets forth that the rational soul confers all perfections upon matter only after matter has been appropriately prepared by other forms. However, as the real unity of the human being can, according to Aquinas, only be assured through a unique formal principle, Aquinas's embryological analysis only ensures the real unity of the human being towards the end of embryological development.

**Farr, Robert M**. The Significance of the Skin as a Natural Boundary in the Sub-Division of Psychology. *J Theor Soc Behav*, 27(2-3), 305-323, Je-S 97.

From a phenomenological perspective, skin is an important boundary. My model here is the psychology of interpersonal relations (Heider, 1958). It is the behaviour of "O" that is visible from the perspective of "P," the perceiver. Whether or not one is justified in going beyond the evidence available ("... the behavioural facts") is a matter of some controversy in psychological circles, e.g., between behaviourists (like Skinner) and Gestalt psychologists (like Heider). Here the skin is an important boundary, at least in the visual modality. (edited)

**Farré, Rafel** and Delon, Françoise. Some Model Theory for Almost Real Closed Fields. *J Sym Log*, 61(4), 1121-1152, D 96.

We study the model theory of fields $k$ carrying a Henselian valuation with real closed residue field. We give a criteria for elementary equivalence and elementary inclusion of such fields involving the value group of a not necessarily definable valuation. This allows us to translate theories of such fields to theories of ordered Abelian groups and we study the properties of this translation. We also characterize the first-order definable convex subgroups of a given ordered Abelian group and prove that the definable real valuation rings of $K$ are in correspondence with the definable convex subgroups of the value group of a certain real valuation of $k$.

**Farrell, Daniel M**. "Jealousy and Desire" in *Love Analyzed*, Lamb, Roger E, 165-188. Boulder, Westview Pr, 1997.

The author has argued elsewhere that jealousy necessarily involves a certain general pattern of belief, desire and affect (or "feeling"). This earlier work is rehearsed here, briefly and revised and extended in various ways. The principal focus of the paper, however, is on what, if anything, the fact that jealousy requires a certain kind of desire shows us about the jealous person and in particular, whether any sense can be made of the claim that desires of the relevant sort are in some sense clearly "unhealthy" or otherwise objectionable desires. The author argues that while no convincing case can be made that such desires are *in general* objectionable, there are good reasons for thinking that the desires in certain types of jealousy are prima facie puzzling and are puzzling because of what they suggest about the character of the person who has them. No conclusive case is made for this last suggestion, however, and general and well-known difficulties with supporting such a suggestion are surveyed in the concluding section.

**Farrelly, Brian J**. La creación como encuentro del ser y de la nada en la teología del maestro Eckhart de Hochheim O.P. (1260-1327). *Sapientia*, 52(201), 33-39, 1997.

**Farrelly-Jackson, Steven**. Fetishism and the Identity of Art. *Brit J Aes*, 37(2), 138-154, Ap 97.

This paper takes issue with Eddy Zemach's recent defence of the view that artworks like paintings and sculptures are to be identified as types rather than (as is more usual) particulars. In the process it discusses more generally an overlooked but important feature of art, namely the peculiar way in which works of art emerge from within the lives of artists, and the effect knowledge of this has an aesthetic response. Without questioning Zemach's use of relative identity theory, the paper seeks to establish that when one properly understands the "values and interests" that bear on the identification of paintings, in particular those issuing from this relationship between artwork and artist, these will determine such works as unique particulars, and hence the originals as aesthetically irreplaceable.

**Farrelly-Jackson, Steven**. On Art and Intention. *Heythrop J*, 38(2), 172-179, Ap 97.

This paper discusses a puzzle, first articulated by Richard Wollheim, about the place of intention in art. This puzzle arises when we try to hold jointly three commonly-held claims to do with art and intention: 1) Art is intentional; 2) An artist, in making a work of art, needs to *observe* what he has done in order to *know* what he has done; and 3) A necessary condition of intentional action is that an agent know what he is doing (intentionally) without observation. Wollheim's own solution to this, built around the idea of rule-following, is rejected, and an alternative account, taking its cue from Ryle's distinction between "task" and "achievement" actions, is developed and briefly elaborated.

**Fasko, Jr, Daniel**. Questioning and Thinking. *Inquiry (USA)*, 14(2), 43-47, Wint 94.

Research has been conducted on teachers' questions and their influences on students' thinking. Research suggests that most classroom questions are lower order questions, which require recall of information. The purpose of this paper is to discuss the evidence supporting the use of higher order questions to stimulate thinking. Implications for practice include a) being aware of developmental differences in students when asking questions, b) examining the purpose of one's questions, and c) training in effective questioning. Research is required on the a) effects of abstract questions on students' thinking and b) students' confidence to respond to higher order questions.

**Fasolt, Constantin**. William Durant the Younger and Conciliar Theory. *J Hist Ideas*, 58(3), 385-402, Jl 97.

**Fatic, A**. Hegelian Retribution Re-Examined. *Phil Inq*, 18(3-4), 66-82, Sum-Fall 96.

**Fatic, Aleksandar**. "Retribution in Democracy" in *Political Dialogue: Theories and Practices,* Esquith, Stephen L (ed), 335-355. Amsterdam, Rodopi, 1996.

How should punishment by justified and carried out in emerging democratic societies as well as their established models? I argue that liberal theorists have not been able to reconcile their attraction to retributivist theories of punishment with an otherwise strategic conception of social cooperation and control. As one aspect of a more general functionalist understanding of politics, I advocate a trust-based approach to crime handing. At least in the case of the practice of punishment, democratic politics cannot be morally grounded in a participatory and dialogical way. Democracy, like any other political system, must function to control human nature. A democratic system of crime handling that inculcates trust, not one that Quixotically attempts to separate politics from criminal justice, is most likely to avoid the deliberate infliction of pain. In a society caught in the difficult transition to democracy, punishment should aim at building trust and avoiding the infliction of pain, not at retribution. Dialogues about who is responsible for past crimes inevitably are turned into strategic, self serving contests.

**Faur, José**. Dos estudios sobre Vico y la tradición hebrea. *Cuad Vico*, 7/8, 253, 1997.

In two essays the author studies the affinities between Vico and the Jews: Vico and the Hebrews, when defending their respective traditions against the onslaught of secular rationalism, could appreciate the methods and values that were developed in each other's tradition and could apply them in their own interpretation. The first article shows the case of some leading Sephardic thinkers in the 19th century, who, in their struggle to vindicate their own spiritual tradition, perceived the significance of Vico's contributions as a religious humanist and applied some of his views to meet the challenges of secular rationalism. The second article makes some remarks on Vico and Rabbinic tradition in order to explain how both defend the oneness of the logos against the inaugural split "philosophy/rhetoric" of the West. (edited)

**Favre, David**. Legal Rights for Our Fellow Creatures. *Cont Phil*, 18(4 & 5), 7-10, Jl-Ag/S-O 96.

Under an interests analysis humans have moral obligations to acknowledge the interests of animals. Some of these interest should be recognized as legal rights. With the example of the chimpanzee and by the use of a comparative analysis, it can be shown that such fundamental interests such as freedom from human battery and enslavement should be recognized as a legal right. In reaching this conclusion the paper also seeks to explain what constitutes a legal right.

**Fawkes, Don**. Critical Thinking and Its Courses. *Inquiry (USA)*, 16(1), 78-81, Fall 96.

Fawkes (*Inquiry,* Spring 1996, p74-78) argues that *introducing* students to premise/conclusion distinctions by using rules for "indicator terms" (like "so," "because," "therefore," *etc.*) is confused and a pedagogical mistake. Smythe (*Inquiry,* Autumn 1996, p76-77) responds to Fawkes (Spring 1996). In this paper I reply to Smythe, give further examples, and provide additional rationale for the original thesis.

**Fawkes, Don**. On Teaching Premise/Conclusion Distinctions. *Inquiry (USA)*, 15(3), 74-78, Spr 96.

This paper challenges the notions that rules for indicator words are a reliable way to identify premises and conclusions and that such rules are reliable ways to teach students to identify premises and conclusions. The paper then suggests an alternative approach to teaching, the "direct" approach.

**Faye, Jan**. Once More: Bohr-Hoffding. *Dan Yrbk Phil*, 29, 106-113, 1994.

**Fazio, Mariano**. Il singolo kierkegaardiano: una sintesi in divenire. *Acta Phil*, 5(2), 221-250, 1996.

The thought of Kierkegaard hinges upon what he calls *my category*, the individual. Arising in reaction to the system of idealism, the Kierkegaardian category reproposes a vision of the world, Aristotelian in origin, in which the only existing beings are individuals. As a result of Kierkegaard's exclusively ethical and religious interest, the only real existence, for the Danish thinker, is ethical existence, in which the individual rediscovers himself as a free self, in becoming, founded on the Absolute. Freedom, as the fulcrum of ethical existence, is identified with dependence upon the Absolute. The loss of the self's foundation upon the power that constitutes it—God—leads the individual to despair. The self's self-constitution, upon the Absolute, by way of the ethical choice of oneself, is a free process. In this process the self must leave the immediacy of the aesthetical stage and arrive at the religious stage, which is the domain of faith. The Kierkegaardian individual offers material for reflection to those who wish to found the existential primary of freedom.

**Feagin, Susan L** and Subler, Craig A. Showing Pictures: Aesthetics and the Art Gallery. *J Aes Educ*, 27(3), 63-72, Fall 93.

Students often think that knowledge about technique, artist's intentions, or artistic or cultural context is irrelevant to understanding and appreciating art. Yet, students in an aesthetics class who were required to write a brief essay about an exhibit on campus complained that the gallery did not provide such information—no catalog, brochures, or explanatory wall labels. A newspaper review echoed these frustrations, highlighting questions about the educational functions of galleries, the relevance of artist's intentions to interpretation, how background information enriches one's experience and understanding, yet how viewers' experiences can be channeled by the selective presentation of background information.

**Feder, Ellen K**. Disciplining the Family: The Case of Gender Identity Disorder. *Phil Stud*, 85(2-3), 195-211, Mr 97.

**Fedoryka, Kateryna**. Health as a Normative Concept: Towards a New Conceptual Framework. *J Med Phil*, 22(2), 143-160, Ap 97.

One of the main concerns in defining health is determining its status in relation to value. The main proposals in this direction generally assume a strict dichotomy between descriptive and evaluative dimensions. This essay argues that such a dichotomy leads to a theoretical inconsistency, which becomes evident once a definition of health is practically operative. A new conceptual framework uniting these two moments is proposed as an alternative, capable of preserving the fundamental insights of both descriptive and evaluative accounts of health and of avoiding the theoretical inconsistencies on the level of practical application.

**Feinberg, Walter**. "Nationalism in a Comparative Mode: A Response to Charles Taylor" in *The Morality of Nationalism,* McKim, Robert (ed), 66-73. New York, Oxford Univ Pr, 1997.

I make three points. First is that Charles Taylor is right in viewing dignity as an essential feature of nationalism, but he is wrong in thinking that it can help us understanding contemporary nationalist movements. Second, the concept of dignity as Taylor addresses it provides a psychological spin on the explanation of nationalism, but this spin places two much emphasis on the psychology of elites. Third, different forms of nationalism require different explanations, and dignity relates to these different forms in different ways.

**Feinberg, Walter**. "The Goals of Multicultural Education: A Critical Re-Evaluation" in *Philosophy of Education (1996),* Margonis, Frank (ed), 182-189. Urbana, Phil Education Soc, 1997.

**Feinstein, Mark** and Warner, Stanley and Coppinger, Raymond (& others). Global Population Growth and the Demise of Nature. *Environ Values*, 5(4), 285-301, N 96.

We suggest that current trends in population growth are unlikely to abate for three reasons: first, there are intrinsic biological pressures to reproduce regardless of social engineering; second, the character of the domestic alliance makes it a formidable competitor to wildlife; and third, the time-frame before population doubling is, from a biological perspective, virtually instantaneous. This paper draws from a wide body of research in the biological and social sciences. We neither condone nor endorse this picture of inexorable population increase. Rather, we appeal for a change in the nature of the discussion of population among environmentalists, to focus on the question of how best to manage what wildlife will be left on the margins of a domesticated world. (edited)

**Feist, Richard**. Newton and Leibniz: Rivalry in the Family. *De Phil*, 10, 59-70, 1993.

The debate between Newton and Leibniz as to whether there is absolute motion is distorted when it is interpreted from the perspective of today's science. The author proposes an interpretation of the Newton-Leibniz debate that allows these thinkers to be the children of their own time and that precludes one or the other being crowned the victor by modern developments in space-time theory.

**Fejer, Peter A** and Ambos-Spies, Klaus and Lempp, Steffen (& others). Decidability of the Two-Quantifier Theory of the Recursive Enumerable Weak Truth-Table Degrees and Other Distributive Semi-Lattices. *J Sym Log*, 61(3), 880-905, S 96.

We formulate general criteria that allow one to conclude that a distributive upper semilattice has a decidable two-quantifier theory. These criteria are applied not only to the weak truth-table degrees of the recursively enumerable sets but also to various substructures of the polynomial many-one (*pm*) degrees of the recursive sets. These applications to the *pm* degrees require no new complexity-theoretic results. The fact that the *pm*-degrees of the recursive sets have a decidable two-quantifier theory answers a question raised by Shore and Slaman. (edited)

**Feldbrugge, F J M**. The Impact of Ethical Considerations on Present-Day Russian Law. *Stud East Euro Thought*, 48(2-4), 159-170, S 96.

**Felder, Michael**. Can Ethics Committees Work in Managed Care Plans?. *Bioethics Forum*, 12(1), 10-16, Spr 96.

The evolution of health care financing and delivery has created many ethical challenges. The history of ethics committees in managed care organizations is a short one. The author describes the formation of a committee and includes information on its composition and role within the organization. Perhaps the most challenging and most valuable contribution the committee will make is in reviewing existing policies and formulating new policies which have ethical implications.

**Feldman, Fred**. On the Intrinsic Value of Pleasures. *Ethics*, 107(3), 448-466, Ap 97.

In this article, I first present the Sidgwickian conception of pleasure. I then present the resulting formulation of the hedonic thesis. Next I turn to arguments. I try to reveal the conceptual conflict at the heart of the thesis, so interpreted. In a final section, I sketch a more promising approach. I begin with some thoughts about the nature of pleasure. (edited)

**Feldman, Jessica R**. "'A Shelter of the Mind': Henry, William, and the Domestic Scene" in *The Cambridge Companion to William James*, Putnam, Ruth Anna (ed), 300-321. New York, Cambridge Univ Pr, 1997.

**Feldman, Leslie D**. Freedom as Motion: Thomas Hobbes and the Images of Liberalism. *J Phil Res*, 22, 229-243, Ap 97.

Central to the argument of this article is the sense in which Thomas Hobbes and liberals see freedom as centered around the notion of free movement. Hobbes, in Chapter 21 of *Leviathan*, describes freedom as "the absence of opposition" to motion. This work argues that the Hobbesian view of freedom as motion was taken up by liberalism as its hallmark and flourished most of all in America where emphasis on individualism was greatest. In America, a movement coupled with individualism to create a conception of freedom.

**Feldman, Richard**. Essay: *Human Knowledge and Human Nature: A New Introduction to an Ancient Debate* by Peter Carruthers and *Knowledge and the State of Nature: An Essay in Conceptual Synthesis* by Edward Craig. *Phil Phenomenol Res*, 57(1), 205-221, Mr 97.

**Feldman, Susan**. Second-Person Scepticism. *Phil Quart*, 47(186), 80-84, Ja 97.

In the last decade, some feminist epistemologists have suggested that the global scepticism which results from the Cartesian dream argument is the product of a self-consciously masculine modern era, whose philosophy gave pride of place to the individual cognizer, disconnected from the object of knowledge, from other knowers, indeed from his own body. Lorraine Code claims that under a conception of a cognizer as an essentially social being, Cartesian scepticism would not arise. I argue that this is false: an argument, could arise in an epistemology which recognizes the social nature of human life and knowledge. Against Code, it is not the first-personhood of Cartesianism which generates scepticism. A second-person scepticism could emerge in a socially conscious epistemology.

**Feleppa, Robert**. On the Very Idea of Moral Truth: Contemporary Empiricism and Noncognitivism. *SW Phil Rev*, 13(1), 1-19, Ja 97.

This paper considers the implications of the naturalized epistemologies of W.V. Quine and Donald Davidson for metaethics. It argues that the two positions offer complementary defenses of a sophisticated ethical noncognitivism. As Quine's metaethics rests heavily on the lack of ethical observation sentences and as Davidson's epistemology is highly critical of Quine's general epistemological reliance on observation sentences, the paper attempts to reconcile their differences on this score.

**Fell, Gil S**. Mother Nature Doesn't Know Her Name: Reflections on a Term. *Cont Phil*, 18(1), 11-15, Ja-F 96.

For the sake of clarity, the attempt is made to examine the term "nature" as to its functions, referents, logical connections, relation to cause and effect, and metaphorical employment. Along the way the many often contradictory sense in which the term is employed indicate that the term is systematically ambiguous. Furthermore, taking into account the metaphysical freight that the term has accumulated, it is argued that "nature" is often used to mask and of times to forward a cultural and political agenda. It is pointed out that the term functions neither denotatively nor connotatively, but is essentially a redundancy. Its philosophical utility appears to be limited to seeming as some sort of a linguistic mooring tower.

**Felt, James W**. Why Possible Worlds Aren't. *Rev Metaph*, 50(1), 63-77, S 96.

This is an uncommon argument against the existence of possible worlds as they are usually conceived in contemporary discussion, from the modally real possible worlds of Lewis to the world-story or world-book worlds of Adams and Plantinga. In place of the implicitly Platonic metaphysics underlying such views there is proposed and defended an alternative metaphysical conception of the relation of becoming to being in virtue of which the concept of possible worlds is seen to be a metaphysical mistake as well as unnecessary.

**Femia, Joseph V**. Complexity and Deliberative Democracy. *Inquiry*, 39(3-4), 359-397, D 96.

Communism may be dead, but a quasi-Marxist critique of liberal democracy survives in the writings of a number of thinkers—most notably, David Miller and John Dryzek—who deplore the self-centered apathy of their fellow citizens and defend the radical ideal of deliberative democracy. Inspired mainly by Rousseau and Habermas, this emergent school of thought argues for a more participatory system where the public interest takes precedence over private interest and where rational argument replaces cynical manipulation. The paper questions whether the deliberative model can cope with the incalculable complexity of modern society. Deliberative democracy, it is contended, rests on doubtful metaphysical assumptions, a blinkered approach to empirical evidence and a common misapprehension about the nature of political argument.

**Fendt, Gene**. God Is Love, Therefore There Is Evil. *Phil Theol*, 9(1-2), 3-12, 1995.

This paper attempts to explicate the philosophical and theological premises involved in Fr. Paneloux's second sermon in Camus's *The Plague*. In that sermon Fr. Paneloux says that the suffering of children is our bread of affliction. The article shows where one must start in order to get to that point and what follows from it. Whether or not the argument given should be called a theodicy or a *reductio ad absurdum* of religious belief is an open question for a philosopher, but the argument is shown to cohere with the traditional belief in God's omnipotent goodness.

**Fendt, Gene**. The Others In/Of Aristotle's *Poetics*. *J Phil Res*, 22, 245-260, Ap 97.

This paper aims at interpreting (primarily) the first six chapters of Aristotle's *Poetics* in a way that dissolves many of the scholarly arguments concerning them. It shows that Aristotle frequently identifies the object of his inquiry by opposing it to what is other than it (in several different ways). As a result aporia arise where there is supposed to be illuminating exclusion of one sort or another. Two exemplary cases of this in Chapters 1-6 are Aristotle's account of mimesis as other than enunciative speech (speech that makes truth claims, or representation) and his account of the final cause of tragedy *in itself* as plot, vis-à-vis its final cause as *regards the audience*, which is *katharsis*. Confusions arising from failure to see the otherness of representation and *katharsis* leads to an overly intellectualist understanding of the purpose of tragedy.

**Feng, Lei**. The Popularity of Existentialism: Causes and Effects. *Chin Stud Phil*, 28(1), 50-58, Fall 96.

**Fenves, Peter**. Under the Sign of Failure. *Ideal Stud*, 26(2), 135-151, Wint 96.

**Fenves, Peter** (trans) and Hamacher, Werner. *Premises: Essays on Philosophy and Literature from Kant to Celan*. Cambridge, Harvard Univ Pr, 1996.

In light of the double nature of every premise—that it is promised but never attainable—Hamacher gives us nine decisive themes, topics, and texts of modernity: the hermeneutic circle in Schleiermacher and Heidegger, the structure of ethical commands in Kant, Nietzsche's genealogy of moral terms and his exploration of the aporias of singularity, the irony of reading in de Man, the parabasis of language in Schlegel, Kleist's disruption of narrative representation, the gesture of naming in Benjamin and Kafka, and the incisive caesura that Paul Celan inserts into temporal and linguistic reversals. (edited)

**Ferguson, Ann**. Moral Responsibility and Social Change: A New Theory of Self. *Hypatia*, 12(3), 116-141, Sum 97.

The aim of this essay is to rethink classic issues of freedom and moral responsibility in the context of feminist and antiracist theories of male and white domination. If personal identities are socially constructed by gender, race and ethnicity, class and sexual orientation, how are social change and moral responsibility possible? An aspects theory of selfhood and three reinterpretations of identity politics show how individuals are morally responsible and nonessentialist ways to resist social oppression.

**Fermon, Nicole**. The Female Fulcrum: Rousseau and the Birth of Nationalism. *Phil Forum*, 28(1-2), 21-41, Fall-Wint 97.

**Fernández, Alejandra**. La posibilidad de pensar la democracia en Latinoamérica desde la óptica de la ética discursiva. *Cuad Etica*, 21-22, 9-21, 1996.

Latin America is a morphological, historical and cultural unity. This paper tries to find out if there is a possibility of making that unity effective by means of an ethic of responsibility. This effectiveness should exceed the boundaries of a mere *state of right*. An analysis is made of some of the characteristics of our young democracies, in the light of what a real democracy demands, which is to say, a system which coordinates the reality of things and the concepts used to legitimate its institutions.

**Fernandez Burillo, Santiago**. Intellectus principiorum: De Tomás de Aquino a Leonardo Polo (y "vuelta"). *Anu Filosof*, 29(2), 509-526, 1996.

If a Thomist philosopher wonders how we get the idea of the infinite being, or the act of being implies no limit, he will understand immediately what Polo intends by saying "mental limit" and its abandonment. The principles of such abandonment are habitual and active thinking. That theory of knowledge justifies the fact that we really know that the act (esse) is the fundamental of being (ens) and the judgements and discourses spreading out from the transcendental notion of being.

**Fernández G, Eugenio**. Articulación crítica de ontología y política en B. Spinoza. *Rev Filosof (Spain)*, 8(15), 97-126, 1996.

**Fernández G, Eugenio**. Spinoza en discusión. *An Seminar Hist Filosof*, 10, 225-230, 1993.

**Fernández García, María Socorro**. La pérdida del carácter transcendental de la belleza en el *De pulchro* de Agostino Nifo. *Rev Espan Filosof Med*, 4, 115-122, 1997.

This article studies the transformation of the concept of beauty in Nifo's work. For that purpose the most relevant thesis of his work *De pulchro* are being compared with the most significant writings of the work of Thomás d'Aquino. The results of this study lead us to the following conclusion: In Nifo's work we find the elements related to beauty, that are present in the tradition, but empty of content. As beauty is reduced to the sensitive *ambutis*, it loses its transcendental character.

**Fernandez Moreno, Luis**. An Examination of Frege's Argumentation Against the Definability of Truth (in Spanish). *Theoria (Spain)*, 11(27), 165-176, S 96.

Frege's argumentation against the definability of truth aims to show that a definition of truth is circular or involves us in an infinite regress. In Frege's work two notions of truth can be distinguished: truth expressed by the word "true" and truth conveyed by the assertion. Frege's argumentation does not show that the word "true" is undefinable but, if Frege's view on assertion is accepted, then from his argumentation, suitably reformulated, the undefinability of truth in the second sense can be concluded.

**Fernández Sanz, Amable**. La Ilustración española: Entre el reformismo y la utopía. *An Seminar Hist Filosof*, 10, 57-71, 1993.

Recently, new ways of study about Spanish enlightenment have been opened. The present study tries to obviate the aprioristic assertions or negations and attempts to make a way in a little facet. to analyse some of the basis on which the Spanish enlightenment seats. A change of mentality is produced in Spain, that anchors its roots not only in the European enlightenment, mainly French, but also in Spanish authors as Gracian and the "Novatores". On the other hand, the tempered and reformist character of our enlightenment was not an obstacle either for the utopian ideals to be the vertebral column of the thought of our "Ilustrados", or for some of them to try to shape those ideals on the country's reality.

**Feroldi, Luisella**. "Ontologia Della Mancanza: Heidegger e la questione dell'uomo" in *Soggetto E Verità: La questione dell'uomo nella filosofia contemporanea*, Fagiuoli, Ettore, 91-100. 20136 Milano, Mimesis, 1996.

**Ferraiolo, William**. Black's "Twin Globe" Counterexample. *SW Phil Rev*, 13(1), 59-66, Ja 97.

**Ferraiolo, William**. Individualism and Descartes. *Teorema*, 16(1), 71-86, 1996.

Descartes is generally presumed to have been one of the foremost proponents of the doctrine of individualism of the mental. In this paper, I argue that it may be advisable for Descartes scholars and modern philosophers of mind to be slightly less presumptuous. My claim is that those passages from the Cartesian corpus which are traditionally cited in support of individualism should not be taken as conclusive evidence of Descartes's commitment to that doctrine. The relevant passages are either neutral with respect to the individualism debate or, in some cases, admit of reasonably palatable reinterpretation from an anti-individualistic standpoint. It is, therefore, my contention that we should require more substantial argument and textual analysis than that which is found in the contemporary literature before attributing individualism to Descartes.

**Ferrara, Alessandro**. Authenticity As a Normative Category. *Phil Soc Crit*, 23(3), 77-92, My 97.

**Ferrara, Mark S**. Ch'an Buddhism and the Prophetic Poems of William Blake. *J Chin Phil*, 24(1), 59-73, Mr 97.

This article discusses the fundamental similitude underlying the teaching of the Ch'an School of Buddhism and that of Blake's radical epistemology. In his prophetic poems (*Jerusalem* (1804-1820), *Milton* (1804) and *The Four Zoas* (1797), Blake symbolically works out the salvation of humankind by the restoration of what he calls *the divine vision*. The recovery of this vision is tantamount to Ch'an Buddhism's idea of enlightenment, which can be described as the recovery of the self's native unlimitedness and its expression on the field of perception.

**Ferrara, Peter J**. Privatization of Social Security: The Transition Issue. *Soc Phil Pol*, 14(2), 145-164, Sum 97.

**Ferrari, Franco**. "Dal gruppo di ricerca al laboratorio didattico disciplinare" in *Momenti di Storia della Logica e di Storia della Filosofia*, Guetti, Carla (ed), 255-257. Roma, Aracne Editrice, 1996.

**Ferrari, Franco**. Il problema della trascendenza nell'ontologia di Plutarco. *Riv Filosof Neo-Scolas*, 88(3), 363-389, Jl-S 96.

**Ferrari, Massimo**. "August Stadler als Kant-Interpret" in *Grenzen der kritischen Vernunft*, Schmid, Peter A, 158-177. Basel, Schwabe Verlag, 1997.

This study shows the often neglected importance of August Stadler as Kant's interpreter within the German neo-Kantianism, in the last decades of the XIXth century. His three books on Kant (Kants *Theoleologie*, 1874; *Die GrunsStze der reinen Erkenntnistheorie*, 1876; Kant's *Theorie der Materie*, 1883) represent an original epistemological interpretation of the critical philosophy which is influenced by Friedrich Albert Lange and, moreover, by Hermann Cohen. Stadler's analysis of Kant's teleological judgement, in particular, may be considered the first attempt to show the function played within the Kantian theory of experience by the hypothetical use of reason in connection with the formal finality of the "critic" of judgement.

**Ferrari, Silvio**. The New Wine and the Old Cask: Tolerance, Religion and the Law in Contemporary Europe. *Ratio Juris*, 10(1), 75-89, Mr 97.

The author argues that a correct approach to the question of tolerance cannot ignore the increasing importance of the religious factor on the political, cultural and social scene of the last few years. The common European model of the relationship between the state and religious faiths that may be called the *law* possesses some margins of elasticity. These margins of elasticity may be defined as tolerance. A mechanism of selection allows the law to welcome those new requests for liberty that do not undermine the fundamental features of the model.

**Ferrarin, Alfredo**. "Riproduzione di forme e esibizione di concetti: Immaginazione e pensiero dalla *phantasia* aristotelica alla *Einbildungskraft* in Kant e Hegel" in *Hegel e Aristotele*, Ferrarin, A, 253-293. Cagliari, Edizioni AV, 1997.

**Ferraris, Maurizio** and Carchia, Gianni. Discutono *Oltre l'interpretazione*, di Gianni Vattimo. *Iride*, 8(15), 495-507, Ag 95.

In questo libro Vattimo intende riscattare l'ermeneutica da un'eccessiva fisionomia 'ecumenica', ripropone con alcune significative novità il "pensiero debole" e inaspettatamente "finisce in qualche modo in braccio alla teologia". Del lavoro di Vattimo, G. Carchia sottolinea la difesa dell'originario spirito nichilistico dell'ermeneutica e una interpretazione della secola-rizzazione come una sorta di prolegomeni ad un'ontologia dell'attualità. M. Ferraris si sofferma sul problema del relativismo e delle sue implicazioni ontologiche, rilevando che prendere sul serio, come suggerisce Vattimo, il problema del nichilismo sembra condurci oltre l'ontologia piuttosto che oltre l'interpretazione.

**Ferraro, Kathleen J**. The Dance of Dependency: A Genealogy of Domestic Violence Discourse. *Hypatia*, 11(4), 77-91, Fall 96.

Domestic violence discourse challenges cultural acceptance of male violence against women, yet it is often constituted by gendered, racialized and class-based hierarchies. Transformative efforts have not escaped traces of these hierarchies. Emancipatory ideals guiding 1970s feminist activism have collided with conservative impulses to maintain and strengthen family relationships. Crime control discourse undermines critiques of dominance through its focus on individual men. Domestic violence discourse exemplifies both resistance to and replication of hierarchies of power.

**Ferré, Frederick**. Ted Schoen on "The Methodological Isolation of Religious Belief". *Phil Cont World*, 2(2), 8-10, Sum 95.

In this brief comment on Ted Schoen's paper, I tend to agree more than I disagree. Methodological isolation has been widely and uncritically accepted by thinkers about religion and science, and Schoen's dissipation of the isolationist discourse deserves positive notice. For too long, science has been the bully of the epistemic neighborhood, and religious thinkers have taken refuge in methodological isolation. As Schoen argues, neither religion nor science is isolated; rather, both are interacting in the same comprehensive and value-laden domain, which also includes arts, poetry and metaphysics.

**Ferreira, Phillip**. "Bradley's Attack on Associationism" in *Philosophy after F.H. Bradley*, Bradley, James (ed), 283-306. Bristol, Thoemmes, 1996.

**Ferreira Chagas, Eduardo**. Para uma Explicitação da Dialética Hegeliana entre o Senhor e o Escravo na Fenomenologia do Espírito. *Educ Filosof*, 9(17), 11-15, Ja-Je 95.

**Ferreirim, Isabel M A** and Burris, Stanley. Decidable Varieties of Hoops. *Rep Math Log*, 28, 53-59, 1994.

A description of all varieties of hoops which have a decidable first order theory is given.

**Ferreirós, José**. Lógica, conjuntos y logicismo: desarrollos alemanes de 1870 a 1908. *Mathesis*, 10(3), 255-272, Ag 94.

Departing from an analysis of Dedekind's work on the foundations of mathematics, we offer an interpretation of the origins of the logicist movement and its evolution up to the era of the paradoxes. A brief presentation of Dedekind's view on the foundations of mathematics is followed by a clarification of its historical context, in order to show that his viewpoint was logicist according to then-common conceptions. The latter point is reinforced by considering the reception of Dedekind's work among contemporary mathematical logicians. This, and particularly a comparison between Frege and Dedekind, makes it possible to analyze the prerequisites of nineteenth-century logicism. In this light it is possible, finally, to reconsider the impact of the paradoxes upon traditional conceptions of logic.

**Ferreirós, José**. Notes on Types, Sets and Logicism, 1930-1950. *Theoria (Spain)*, 12(28), 91-124, Ja 97.

The present paper is a contribution to the history of logic and its philosophy toward the mid-20th century. It examines the interplay between logic, type theory and set theory during the 1930s and 40s, before the reign of first-order logic and the closely connected issue of the fate of logicism. After a brief presentation of the emergence of logicism, set theory, and type theory (with particular attention to Carnap and Tarski), Quine's work is our central concern, since he was seemingly the most outstanding logicist around 1940, though he would shortly abandon that viewpoint and promote first-order logic as all of logic. Quine's class-theoretic systems NF and ML and his farewell to logicism, are examined. The last section attempts to summarize the motives why set theory was preferred to other systems and first-order logic won its position as the paradigm logic system after the great War.

**Ferrell, O C** and Pelton, Lou E and Strutton, David. Ethical Behavior in Retail Settings: Is There a Generation Gap?. *J Bus Ethics*, 16(1), 87-105, Ja 97.

A new generation, earmarked the Thirteeners, is an emerging force in the marketplace. The Thirteener cohort group, so designated since they are the thirteenth generation to know the American flag and constitution, encompass over 62 million adult consumers. All the former "Mall Rats" have grown up. The normative structures that these Thirteeners employ in both acquisition and disposition retail settings is empirically assessed in this study through the use of

AUTHOR INDEX 623 Fieser, James

a national sample. The findings suggest that Thirteeners are more likely to attempt to rationalize away unethical retailing consumption behaviors than their parent's generation. The managerial and theoretical implications for the practice of retailing in the 1990s associated with these observations are discussed.

**Ferrell, Robyn**. *Passion in Theory: Conceptions of Freud and Lacan*. New York, Routledge, 1996.

*Passion in Theory* explores the philosophical possibilities of psychoanalysis, focusing on the 'metapsychological' theories of Freud and Lacan. Robyn Ferrell argues that psychoanalysis and the concept of the unconscious in particular, offer philosophy important theoretical opportunities. It is an argument that students, teachers and professionals in psychoanalysis and philosophy cannot afford to ignore. (publisher, edited)

**Ferrini, Cinzia**. "Tra etica e filosofia della natura: il significato della Metafisica aristotelica per il problema delle grandezze del sistema solare nel primo Hegel" in *Hegel e Aristotele,* Ferrarin, A, 135-201. Cagliari, Edizioni AV, 1997.

The standard view places Hegel's early celestial mechanics under the sole influence of the Pythagorean-Platonic tradition and regards his 1801 manipulation of a numerical series determining the distances of the planets from the sun, drawn from the *Timaeus*, as an arbitrary move devoid of any philosophical significance. The purpose of the paper is to find in Hegel's early works traces of a reading of Aristotle's *Metaphysics*. Notions of Aristotelian derivation, which clearly prepare the ethical ground where Hegel roots his *Naturphilosophie*, are also seen to play a decisive role in Hegel's modified use of Plato's mathematics of nature.

**Feser, E**. Has Trinitarianism Been Shown To Be Coherent?. *Faith Phil*, 14(1), 87-97, Ja 97.

Macnamara, La Palme Reyes, and Reyes have recently claimed to have shown decisively that the doctrine of the Trinity is internally consistent. They claim, furthermore, that their account does not commit them to any exotic emendations of standard logical theory. The paper demonstrates that they have established neither of these claims. In particular, it is argued that the set of statements they show to be consistent in fact expresses Sabellianism, not Trinitarianism; and that they can avoid this result only via commitment to the (questionable) doctrine of relative identity.

**Festa, Roberto**. Analogy and Exchangeability in Predictive Inferences. *Erkenntnis*, 45(2 & 3), 229-252, Nov 96.

An important problem in inductive probability theory is the design of exchangeable analogical methods, i.e., of exchangeable inductive methods that take into account certain considerations of analogy by similarity for predictive inferences. Here a precise reformulation of the problem of predictive analogy is given and a new family of exchangeable analogical methods is introduced. Firstly, it is proved that the exchangeable analogical method introduced by Skyrms (1993) does not satisfy the best known general principles of predictive analogy. Secondly, Skyrms's approach—consisting of the usage of particular hyper-Carnapian methods, i.e., mixtures of Carnapian inductive methods—is adopted in the design of a new family of exchangeable analogical methods. Lastly, it is proved that such methods satisfy an interesting general principle of predictive analogy.

**Festenstein, Matthew**. The Ties of Communication: Dewey on Ideal and Political Democracy. *Hist Polit Thought*, 18(1), 104-124, Spr 97.

This paper identifies a split between two conceptions of democracy within the discourse of liberalism, utilitarian and deliberative and explores the case for the deliberative conception through an examination of the writings of John Dewey, a thinker who has recently been often invoked on behalf of the deliberative conception. It is argued that his view is developed in confrontation with two principal rivals: atomistic liberal individualism and a managerial conception of politics. Dewey's communicative ideal of democracy is interpreted as a pivotal component of his general ethical theory of the individual. However, his conception of democracy is divided: the *political* significance to attach to this democratic ideal is unclear and he presents grounds for political democracy which are independent of the ideal and closer to the utilitarian conception. Dewey's thought expresses rather than overcomes the confrontation between the standard liberal and deliberative views of democracy.

**Festini, Heda**. Family, State—Individual. *Filozof Istraz*, 16(3), 653-660, 1996.

Politeo was quite clear: it is not society, or the state, that shapes morality; on the contrary, the influence of the moral world is very great. That is why he held that history is within us, that it is the history of the human mind. When studied, it reveals the general directions of epochs and individuals. Hence his claim that the history of mankind is shaped by the *history of the family* and then the *history of the state*, the central agent being the *individual*, his *free spontaneity* and *human dignity*, rooted in *intersubectivity*. (edited)

**Fetters, Michael D** and Rygwelski, Janis and Brody, Howard. Ethics at the Interface: Conventional Western and Complementary Medical Systems. *Bioethics Forum*, 12(4), 15-23, Wint 96.

Both conventional and complementary medicines have a duty to treat patients ethically. Problems arise in each system's relationships with the other. Recognizing one's assumptions, often unaddressed, and agreeing on common goals will go far to remove suspicion when the two schools meet in the treatment of the same patient.

**Février, Nicolas**. La contingence dans la mécanique hégélienne. *Rev Phil Louvain*, 95(1), 76-102, F 97.

This text deals with the way Hegel thinks the existence of contingent phenomena. It centers particularly on the mechanics of the *Encyclopedia of Philosophical Sciences*. Hegel articulates contingency (which characterizes nature) with blind (or mechanical) necessity and freedom (or conceptual necessity) around the category of exteriority (*Äusserlichkeit*). The hypothesis of D. Wandschneider and V. Hösle agrees with this articulation. It also makes it possible to develop a parallel between the categories of the logic of being and the first forms of nature, leading to an interpretation of contingency as mutual exteriority of the moments of the idea.

**Fick, Barbara J**. The Case for Maintaining and Encouraging the Use of Voluntary Affirmative Action in Private Sector Employment. *Notre Dame J Law Ethics*, 11(1), 159-170, 1997.

**Field, Terri**. Feminist Epistemology and Philosophy for Children. *Thinking*, 13(1), 17-22, 1997.

Using some of the insights from feminist critiques of epistemology and philosophical methods of enquiry, this article undertakes a brief analysis of the *Philosophy for Children* programme. Some advocates of the programme show tendencies towards claims of objectivity, universality and value-neutrality—all of which have been criticised by feminists. I conclude that, whilst some caution is required in making these claims, there are many exciting possibilities that *Philosophy for Children* can offer to those of us interested in different 'ways to know'.

**Fieldhouse, Paul**. Community Shared Agriculture. *Agr Human Values*, 13(3), 43-47, Sum 96.

Community shared agriculture is a concept that brings food producers and consumers together in a relationship that supports values associated with sustainable agriculture, community development, and food security. At the heart of the concept is the notion of sharing. Participants share the real costs of food production through fair prices for the farmer and by assuming part of the risk of poor harvests. They also share the rewards that come through a seasons supply of fresh produce, the development of fellowship, and the knowledge that they are part of an effort to "think globally, act locally."

**Fielding, Helen**. Grounding Agency in Depth: The Implications of Merleau-Ponty's Thought for the Politics of Feminism. *Human Stud*, 19(2), 175-184, Ap 96.

While poststructuralist feminist theorists have clarified our understanding of the gendered subject as produced through a matrix of language, culture and psycho-sexual affects, they have found agency difficult to ground. I argue that this is because in these theories the body has served primarily as an inscribed surface. In response to this surface body, particular to this age, I have turned to Merleau-Ponty's concept of depth which allows us to theorize the agency crucial to feminist politics. While the poststructuralists' rejection of depth is largely due to its roots in Cartesian rationality, depth is much more than this. Rather than allowing for the impossibility of political action, depth means that as bodily moving and acting subjects we are part of Being and thus part of the questions raised in this age, even if it is a mark of this age that this tends to be forgotten.

**Fields, Lloyd**. Commentary on "Sanity and Irresponsibility". *Phil Psychiat Psych*, 3(4), 303-304, D 96.

I make two criticisms of Wilson's proposal to dispense with a loaded axiological criterion of sanity. First, Edwards's axiological criterion of sanity, which Wilson accepts, involves the requirement of impartiality, which at least excludes some standards of right and wrong. Second, value pluralism applies only to morally acceptable forms of life and thus presupposes a standard of right and wrong. I conclude by noting that mental illnesses are not sufficiently characterized by extreme and persistent deviance from practical rationality, as conceived by Edwards and Wilson.

**Fields, Lloyd**. Psychopathy, Other-Regarding Moral Beliefs, and Responsibility. *Phil Psychiat Psych*, 3(4), 261-277, D 96.

In this paper I seek to show that at least one kind of psychopath is incapable of forming other-regarding moral beliefs; hence that they cannot act for other-regarding moral reasons; and hence that they are not appropriate subjects for the assessment of either moral or legal responsibility. Various attempts to characterize psychopaths are considered and rejected, in particular the widely held view that psychopaths are, in general, incapable of understanding moral concepts. The particular disability proposed here, the incapability to form other-regarding moral beliefs, is then derived from an analysis of what is required for someone to be a responsible agent. (edited)

**Fields, Lloyd**. Response to the Commentaries. *Phil Psychiat Psych*, 3(4), 291-292, D 96.

In this response, I address three points raised in the commentaries: the question of whether there is a legitimate formal use of "moral," the claim that a certain sort of affective capacity is required for acquiring the capacity to form other-regarding moral beliefs, and the problem of how to show that psychopaths lack the capacity to form other-regarding moral beliefs. I maintain that there is a use of "moral" according to which moral beliefs need not be rational. Regarding the affective capacity that Adshead identifies, I explain that I had not intended that such a capacity be constitutive of a moral belief, even an other-regarding one. I then try a new approach, in the light of Adshead's commentary, to the third point addressed, according to which the psychopath is unable to form other-regarding moral beliefs because a causally necessary condition for doing so is absent in him.

**Fields, Stephen**. The Metaphysics of Symbol in Thomism: *Aeterni Patris* to Rahner. *Int Phil Quart*, 37(3), 277-290, S 97.

**Fieser, James**. The Eighteenth-Century British Reviews of Hume's Writings. *J Hist Ideas*, 57(4), 645-657, O 96.

This essay takes on two tasks. First it updates the standard list of eighteenth-century British reviews of Hume's writings by providing references to additional reviews which do not appear in the Hume literature. To Jessop's list of eighteen British reviews, thirteen new reviews are listed for first edition publications of Hume's writings and eight new reviews are listed for eighteenth-century abridgments and collections containing Hume's writings. Second, this essay presents a history of the early British review journals and a discussion of the scholarly merits of the Hume reviews.

**Figal, Günter**. Arte come rappresentazione del mondo. *Iride*, 8(15), 339-351, Ag 95.

L'opera d'arte si rivela come lo spazio aperto delle possibili esperienze che si fanno. Sulla base soprattutto delle analisi di Heidegger e di Gadamer—e tenendo presente, su un altro versante, il complesso delle argomentazioni benjaminiane e adorniane—l'opera d'arte, in cui si manifesta il comprendere e l'interpretare dell'artista, viene individuata da Figal come lo spazio di esperienze ulteriori che schiudono il mondo secondo orizzonti diversi.

**Figallo, Aldo V** and Landini, Paolo. On Generalizaed I-Algebras and 4-Valued Modal Algebras. *Rep Math Log*, 29, 3-18, 1995.

In this paper we establish a new characterization of 4-valued modal algebras considered by A. Monteiro. In order to obtain this characterization we introduce a new class of algebras named generalized *l*-algebras. This class contains strictly the class of C-algebras defined by Y. Komori as an algebraic counterpart of the infinite-valued implicative Lukasiewicz propositional calculus. On the other hand, the relationship between *l*-algebras and commutative BACK-algebras, defined by S. Tanaka in 1975, allows us to say that in a certain sense G-algebras are also a generalization of these latter algebras.

**Figueiredo, Maria José**. Aristóteles e a teoria da reminiscência. *Philosophica (Portugal)*, 43-52, 1993.

In the last chapter of the *Posterior Analytics*, Aristotle discusses the methodology of access to the indemonstrable first principles of science. Refusing any solution that seems to him to have anything whatsoever to do with the Platonic reminiscence, Aristotle proposes intuition as one of the methods to the knowledge of first principles, but without explaining what intuition is—and thus compromising his solution and indeed the whole theory of science presented in the *Posterior Analytics*.

**Figueroa, Patricio R** and Fuenzalida, Hernan. Bioethics in Ibero-America and the Caribbean. *J Med Phil*, 21(6), 611-627, D 96.

Bioethics has become a field of new challenges for Ibero-America and the Caribbean. A seeming uniformity in the region hides a rich heterogeneous society. A brief survey of bioethical developments in different Ibero-American countries is provided as well as the bioethical problems and approaches peculiar to the region. Some of the unique features of bioethics in this region, it is suggested, could infuse new life into the U.S. and European bioethics discussion. Finally, a bibliography of Ibero-American bioethics literature is provided for North American and European readers.

**Figueroa, Robert** and Goering, Sara. The Summer Philosophy Institute of Colorado: Building Bridges. *Teach Phil*, 20(2), 155-168, Je 97.

This article explores the creation of the Summer Philosophy Institute of Colorado, a week-long residential program in philosophy for high school students from across Colorado. The program is designed to attract students from diverse backgrounds and to encourage students who are not on the college track to pursue their studies. It relies on the ability of philosophical topics to spark students' natural love of learning and to hone their critical thinking skills. The article offers an overview of the successful summer program's first two years and discusses the introduction of an academic year outreach program.

**Filatov, S B** and Vorontsova, L M. "The Russian Way" and Civil Society. *Russian Stud Phil*, 35(2), 6-20, Fall 96.

**Filatov, Vladimir Petrovich**. The Living Cosmos: Man Among the Forces of Earth and Heaven. *Russian Stud Phil*, 34(1), 48-62, Sum 95.

**Files, Craig**. Goodman's Rejection of Resemblance. *Brit J Aes*, 36(4), 398-412, O 96.

Goodman's rejection of the resemblance theory of representation, on the grounds that resemblance is symmetric while representation is asymmetric, is based on a conflation of two questions: I) what is required for an object to represent and II) what determines representational content. I distinguish the two questions, adopt a triadic rather than dyadic conception of representation and suggest that convention has a role in answering the question of representation. This shows that the symmetric nature of resemblance does not render resemblance unsuitable as an account of pictorial content and that Goodman's conventionalism concerning pictorial content can be resisted.

**Filipiuk, Marion** (ed). *George Bentham: Autobiography 1800-1834*. Toronto, Univ of Toronto Pr, 1997.

The text of the manuscript, preserved in the Archives of the Royal Botanic Gardens, Kew, is published here for the first time with an introduction providing historical context, explanatory notes, and indexes of plant names and of persons and works mentioned. A fascinating story in itself, this autobiography provides a new resource for utilitarian studies and for historians of science. (publisher,edited)

**Fimiani, Mariapaola**. Genealogia di un sentire inorganico: Mario Perniola. *Iride*, 8(15), 451-456, Ag 95.

L'approfondimento delle condizioni e dell'attualità dell'esperienza del sentire costituisce il piano su cui Perniola intende delineare un pensiero post-nichilistico in cui affermare, oltre l'ermeneutica e l'utopismo, una "filosofia del presente". M. Fimiani coglie i passaggi essenziali del ragionamento di Perniola a partire dal suo ultimo libro dedicato al "sentire sessuale".

**Fimiani, Mariapaola**. Il patico e il nostro tempo: A proposito di Aldo Masullo. *Iride*, 9(18), 445-457, Ag 96.

La categoria del patico, affiorata nei linguaggi bio-psicologici e adatta a conquistare, nella ricerca sul trascendentale, la fatticità dell'apriori e il movimento effettivo del soggetto, diviene, per Masullo, ciò che "mette in gioco" il tempo. Tempo è sentire il cambiamento e originario patire. Tempo è quell'affettività radicale che aiuta a pensare, contro l'estraneità e la violenza dei "significati", i "diritti del senso". La scoperta del patico, originario sentire e luogo di solitudine, si fa, nel corso della ricerca, bisogno di accordo col mondo e tensione di cambiamento del presente, del proprio tempo, con una raffinata strumentazione di analisi che si nutre del rischioso ma ricco circolo tra filosofia e saperi positivi.

**Finder, Stuart G** and Bliton, Mark J. The Eclipse of the Individual in Policy (Where is the Place for Justice?). *Cambridge Quart Healthcare Ethics*, 5(4), 519-532, Fall 96.

**Fine, Arthur**. Science As Child's Play: Tales from the Crib. *Phil Sci*, 63(4), 534-537, D 96.

This is a brief critique of Alison Gopnik's use of the "theory-theory" approach to science via the cognitive development of children ("The Scientist as Child", Phil Sci 63: 485-514, 1997). The critical focus is on her employment of evolutionary "just so" stories and her reliance on cognitive individualism.

**Fine, Gail**. Nozick's Socrates. *Phronesis*, 41(3), 233-244, 1996.

**Fine, Gail** (trans) and Irwin, Terence H (trans). *Aristotle: Introductory Readings*. Indianapolis, Hackett, 1996.

Adapted from Irwin and Fine's more comprehensive *Aristotle: Selections* (Hackett, 1995), *Introductory Readings* offers central works of Aristotle in a volume designed especially with the needs of beginning students in mind. The translation renders Aristotle's arguments clearly and accurately, with careful attention to technical terms. Brief clarifying and explanatory notes on selected passages are appended. An extensive Glossary explains some crucial terms and concepts, comments on questions of translation, and provides cross-references. (publisher, edited)

**Finger, Marcelo** and Gabbay, Dov. Combining Temporal Logic Systems. *Notre Dame J Form Log*, 37(2), 204-232, Spr 96.

This paper investigates modular combinations of temporal logic systems. Four combination methods are described and studied with respect to the transfer of logical properties from the component one-dimensional temporal logics to the resulting combined two-dimensional temporal logic. Three basic logical properties are analyzed, namely soundness, completeness and decidability. The *temporalization method* and the *independent combination method* are shown to transfer all three basic logical properties. The method of *full join* of logic systems generates a considerably more expressive language but fails to transfer completeness and decidability in several cases. So a weaker method of *restricted join* is proposed and shown to transfer all three basic logical properties. (edited)

**Finkenthal, Michael** and Kluback, William. *The Temptations of Emile Cioran*. New York, Lang, 1997.

The Romanian-born Emilo Cioran is one of the most important figures of modern French philosophy and literature. Even though most of his French works have been translated into English, this is the first attempt to produce a comprehensive presentation and appraisal of his work to an English-speaking public. Written in the form of a dialogue between two skeptical minds, this book discusses both the prewar Romanian and postwar French works of Cioran. (publisher)

**Finn, Steve**. Ockham and *Potentia Absoluta*. *Conference*, 6(1), 46-58, Sum 95.

**Finocchiaro, Maurice A**. "Informal Factors in the Formal Evaluation of Arguments" in *Logic and Argumentation*, Van Eemeren, Frans H (ed), 143-162. Amsterdam, North-Holland, 1994.

In this paper, it is argued that the Oliver-Massey asymmetry—the asymmetry between showing that a given argument is formally valid and showing that it is formally invalid—does not hold. Both formal validation and invalidation can be justified to a greater or lesser degree. However, both processes are based on formally invalid arguments.

**Finocchiaro, Maurice A**. Critical Thinking, Critical Reasoning, and Methodological Reflection. *Inquiry (USA)*, 15(4), 66-79, Sum 96.

**Fins, Joseph J** and Bacchetta, Matthew D. The Economics of Clinical Ethics Programs: A Quantitative Justification. *Cambridge Quart Healthcare Ethics*, 6(4), 451-460, Fall 97.

**Fins, Joseph J** and Bacchetta, Matthew D and Miller, Franklin G. Clinical Pragmatism: A Method of Moral Problem Solving. *Kennedy Inst Ethics J*, 7(2), 129-145, Je 97.

This paper presents a method of moral problem solving in clinical practice that is inspired by the philosophy of John Dewey. This method, called "clinical pragmatism," integrates clinical and ethical decision making. Clinical pragmatism focuses on the interpersonal processes of assessment and consensus formation as well as the ethical analysis of relevant moral considerations. The steps in this method are delineated and then illustrated through a detailed case study. The implications of clinical pragmatism for the use of principles in moral problem solving are discussed.

**Fiorato, Pierfrancesco**. "Cohen—Denker in dürftiger Zeit? Über Sprache und Stil der Cohenschen Hermeneutik" in *Grenzen der kritischen Vernunft*, Schmid, Peter A, 77-94. Basel, Schwabe Verlag, 1997.

**Fioravanti, Gianfranco**. Il *Tractatus yconomicus* di Galvano Fiamma O.P. (1282-dopo il 1344). *Bochumer Phil Jrbh*, 1, 217-229, 1996.

**Fiore, Karen K**. Was Gandhi a Feminist?. *Acorn*, 8(2), 23-27, Fall 95.

**Fiorentini, Camillo** and Avelone, Alessandro and Mantovani, Paolo (& others). On Maximal Intermediate Predicate Constructive Logics. *Stud Log*, 57(2-3), 373-408, O 96.

**AUTHOR INDEX** 625 **Fisk, Milton**

We extend to the predicate frame a previous characterization of the maximal intermediate propositional constructive logics. This provides a technique to get maximal intermediate predicate constructive logics starting from suitable sets of classically valid predicate formulae we call maximal nonstandard predicate constructive logics. As an example of this technique, we exhibit two maximal intermediate predicate constructive logics, yet leaving open the problem of stating whether the two logics are distinct. Further properties of these logics will be also investigated.

**Fiorentino, Fernando**. Gli oggetti e i metodi delle scienze secondo S. Tommaso. *Sapienza*, 49(3), 245-252, 1996.

**Fiorino, Víctor R Martín**. Symbol and Communication in Politics (Spanish). *Rev Filosof (Venezuela)*, Supp(2-3), 215-222, 1996.

Based on the categories of actuality, feasibility and possibility, all considered as fundamental in political philosophy, this paper addresses the problem of defining a just social order through the full use of the capacity of symbolism. The study of the simultaneous processes of the creation and destruction of symbols, which correspond to the processes of politization and idealization, permits one to affirm the need to reconstruct communication in order to express our vision of a more desirable world, to organize the human experience of living together, and to plot out and decide on political strategies in the confluence between political philosophy, political psychology and the theory of symbols.

**Fisch, Harold**. Debbo io ricordare? L'arte e la negazione della memoria. *Iride*, 8(14), 79-94, Ap 95.

**Fischbach, Ruth L** and Gilbert, Diane C. The Ombudsman for Research Practice: A Proposal for a New Position and an Invitation to Comment. *Sci Eng Ethics*, 1(4), 389-402, O 95.

We propose that institutions consider establishing a position of "Ombudsman for Research Practice." This person would assume several roles: as a *sounding board* to those needing confidential consultation about research issues—basic, applied or clinical; as a *facilitator* for those wishing to pursue a formal grievance process; and as an *educator* to distribute guidelines and standards, to raise the consciousness regarding sloppy or irregular practices in order to prevent misconduct and to promote the responsible conduct of research. While there are compelling features to this position, many complex issues need to be considered and resolved. We invite readers to respond to questions we raise in the text.

**Fischbach, Ruth L** and Hauser, Joshua M and Kleefield, Sharon F (& others). Minority Populations and Advance Directives: Insights from a Focus Group Methodology. *Cambridge Quart Healthcare Ethics*, 6(1), 58-71, Winter 97.

Motivated by the significantly lower prevalence of advance directives among African-American and Hispanic patients at one urban teaching hospital (18% for Caucasians, 4% for African-Americans, and 2% for Hispanics), we used a focus group methodology to examine ways in which diverse populations of patients view the medical, philosophical, and practical issues surrounding advance directives. Our premise was that African-American and Hispanic populations who have higher rates of morbidity and mortality across numerous disease categories, and historically have had limited access to care and opportunities to discuss health concerns, may be more suspicious about the right of autonomy that an advance directive is designed to ensure. Our premise was supported by our data.

**Fischer, Eugen**. On the Very Idea of a Theory of Meaning for a Natural Language. *Synthese*, 111(1), 1-16, Ap 97.

A certain orthodoxy has it that understanding is essentially computational: that information about what a sentence means is something that may be *generated* by means of a *derivational process* from information about the significance of the sentence's constituent parts and of the ways in which they are put together. And that it is, therefore, fruitful to study formal theories acceptable as compositional theories of meaning for natural languages: theories that deliver for each sentence of their object-language a theorem acceptable as statement of its meaning and derivable from axioms characterizing subsentential expressions and operations forming that sentence. This paper is to show that there is something deeply wrong with these ideas, namely that they are based on a certain confusion about ascriptions of semantic knowledge. The paper is to make this point by considering a semantic theorist who has explicit knowledge of a theory of truth for L. (edited)

**Fischer, Francis**. "Jean-Luc Nancy: The Place of a Thinking" in *On Jean-Luc Nancy: The Sense of Philosophy,* Sheppard, Darren (ed), 32-37. New York, Routledge, 1997.

**Fischer, Karla** and Rose, Mary. Policies and Perspectives on Authorship. *Sci Eng Ethics*, 1(4), 361-370, O 95.

Authorship on publications has been described as a "meal ticket" for researchers in academic settings. Given the importance of authorship, inappropriate publication credit is a pertinent ethical issue. This paper presents an overview of authorship problems and policies intended to address them. Previous work has identified three types of inappropriate authorship practices: plagiarism, giving unwarranted credit and failure to give expected credit. Guidelines from universities, journals and professional organizations provide standards about requirements of authors and may describe inappropriate practices; to a lesser extent, they provide guidance for determining authorship order. While policies on authorship may be helpful in some circumstances, they are not panaceas. Formal guidelines may not address serious power imbalances in working relationships and may be difficult to enforce in the face of particular departmental or institutional cultures. In order to develop more effective and useful guidelines, we should gain more knowledge about how students and faculty members perceive policies as well as their understanding of how policies will best benefit collaborators.

**Fischer, Norman**. From Aesthetic Education to Environmental Aesthetics. *Clio*, 25(4), 365-391, Sum 96.

**Fishburn, Peter C** and Edwards, Ward. Discount-Neutral Utility Models for Denumerable Time Streams. *Theor Decis*, 43(2), 139-166, S 97.

This paper formulates and axiomatizes utility models for denumerable time streams that make no commitment in regard to discounting future outcomes. The models address decision under certainty and decision under risk. Independence assumptions in both contexts lead to additive or multiplicative utilities over time periods that allow unambiguous comparisons of the relative importance of different periods. The models accommodate all patterns of future valuation. This discount-neutral feature is attained by restricting preference comparisons to outcome streams or probability distributions on outcome streams that differ in at most a finite number of periods.

**Fisher, Andrew** and Gottlieb, Robert. Community Food Security and Environmental Justice: Searching for a Common Discourse. *Agr Human Values*, 13(3), 23-32, Sum 96.

Community food security and environmental justice are parallel social movements interested in equity and justice and system-wide factors. They share a concern for issues of daily life and the need to establish community empowerment strategies. Both movements have also begun to reshape the discourse of sustainable agriculture, environmentalism and social welfare advocacy. However, community food security and environmental justice remain separate movements, indicating an incomplete process in reshaping agendas and discourse. Joining these movements through a common language of empowerment and systems analysis would strongly enhance the development of a more powerful, integrated approach. That opportunity can be located in the efforts to incorporate community food security and environmental justice approaches in current Farm Bill legislation; in particular, provisions addressing community food production, direct marketing, community development, and community food planning.

**Fisher, Bonnie** and Bennett, Stephen Earl and Resnick, David. "Speaking of Politics in the United States: Who Talks to Whom, Why, and Why Not" in *Political Dialogue: Theories and Practices,* Esquith, Stephen L (ed), 263-293. Amsterdam, Rodopi, 1996.

Although normative political theorists have argued that citizens talking with other citizens about public affairs is essential in a democracy, empirically oriented political scientists have tended to ignore political discussions. This paper reviews what normative theories have said about political conversations and then draws on National Election Studies and Social Surveys to plumb the extent and breadth of political conversations in the United States. The paper also explores who talks about public affairs, with whom they speak and why some people discuss politics while others do not.

**Fisher, Ian StJohn**. What Place does Religion have in the Ethical Thinking of Scientists and Engineers?. *Sci Eng Ethics*, 2(3), 335-344, Jl 96.

Religion, defined as "the idea of a state that transcends ourselves and our world and the working out of the consequences of that idea," may influence the ethical thinking of scientists and engineers in two ways. The first is at the level of the individual and how personal beliefs affect the choice of research, design or development projects, relationships with other researchers and the understanding of the consequences of research on other aspects of life. The second level is that of the social and cultural setting in which scientists and engineers work; how society decides which research to sponsor, how to apply the results of scientific discovery and which technology it chooses to develop and for what purposes. In neither of these areas is religious belief a necessary condition for scientists and engineers to pursue one course of action rather than another. The existence of religious belief within the individual and society is, though, part of the ethical framework in which scientist and engineers work and therefore something to which attention should be paid. Religion provides a particular perspective on what should be. Conversely science and technology provide information on the nature of the person and the universe in which we live, which must be taken into account when theologians and religious moralists apply their ethical norms and principles.

**Fisher, John Andrew** and Potter, Jason. Technology, Appreciation, and the Historical View of Art. *J Aes Art Crit*, 55(2), 169-185, Spring 97.

Appreciative practices pose a difficult problem for historical-contextualist (HC) theorists of art (Danto, Levinson, Davies, etc.). Their theories suggest that historical artworks cannot be appropriately appreciated in contexts divorced from information about the artwork's context of creation, yet modern, technological appreciative practices presuppose the opposite. Either HC theories are wrong, or they must reject the idea that artworks are socially constructed in part by how we appreciate them. We rebut both disjuncts of this dilemma. We defend the role of appreciative practices in determining our common conception of the artwork. We defend HC theories by showing that this common conception contains the historical art object as a regulative idea, even in highly abstracted contexts of appreciation.

**Fisk, Milton**. "Comunidad y Moralidad" in *Liberalismo y Comunitarismo: Derechos Humanos y Democracia,* Monsalve Solórzano, Alfonso (ed), 55-79. 36-46003 València, Alfons el Magnànim, 1996.

Problems with communitarian and liberal views of society and morality have a common root. Neither gives to the diversity among groups in any society the weight it deserves. Communitarians suppose a homogeneity of moral views and of social structures is easily achieved on the basis of an underlying bond. Liberals suppose that no diversity runs deep enough to prevent agreement on a moral and political base sufficient for a stable society. Without relying on unequal power between groups, in order to establish bases for stability, neither view can claim adequacy.

**Fisk, Milton**. Health Care as a Public Good. *J Soc Phil*, 27(3), 14-40, Wint 96.

Conditions are laid down for a system to qualify as a public good. The conditions are that it serve a common good for public rather than private benefit in a publicly accountably way. A principle of collective provision, that is the core of the idea of health insurance, is used to show that a health care system should become a public good. An attempt is then made to show that, as a system that would satisfy the conditions of a public good, a health care system would provide comprehensive care to all comers. This reasoning tends to promote making health care systems national health systems or national health insurance systems.

**Fitch, Brian T**. Un problème d'appropriation: Schleiermacher entre Gadamer et Todorov. *Horiz Phil*, 7(2), 59-74, Spr 97.

**Fitelson, Branden**. Wayne, Horwich, and Evidential Diversity. *Phil Sci*, 63(4), 652-660, D 96.

In a recent article, Wayne (1995) offers a critique of Horwich's (1982) Bayesian explication of the confirmational significance of evidential diversity. Presently, I argue that Wayne's reconstruction of Horwich's account is not faithful to Horwich's original presentation. Because Wayne's reconstruction is uncharitable, his criticisms turn out to be off the mark. I try to provide a more faithful and charitable rendition of Horwich's account. Unfortunately, even this more charitable reconstruction of Horwich's position seems—at best—to provide an incomplete explication of the confirmational significance of evidential diversity.

**Fitting, Melvin**. A Theory of Truth that Prefers Falsehood. *J Phil Log*, 26(5), 477-500, O 97.

We introduce a subclass of Kripke's fixed points in which falsehood is the preferred truth value. In all of these the truthteller evaluates to false, while the liar evaluates to undefined (or overdefined). The mathematical structure of this family of fixed points is investigated and is shown to have many nice features. It is noted that a similar class of fixed points, preferring truth, can also be studied. The notion of intrinsic is shown to relativize to these two subclasses. The mathematical ideas presented here originated in investigations of so-called *stable* models in the semantics of logic programming.

**FitzGerald, John** and Wenger, Neil S. The Invalid Advance Directive. *Bioethics Forum*, 13(2), 32-34, Sum 97.

Advance directives, when they stipulate that specific treatments be withdrawn or withheld, often fail to match the signer's more nuanced situation-based oral instructions. Nevertheless, they remain powerful documents that, when constructed and administered carefully, can direct decision making in end-of-life care.

**Flach, Werner**. "Kants Empiriologie: Naturteleologie als Wissenschaftstheorie" in *Grenzen der kritischen Vernunft*, Schmid, Peter A, 273-289. Basel, Schwabe Verlag, 1997.

**Flage, Daniel E** and Bonnen, Clarence A. Descartes on Causation. *Rev Metaph*, 50(4), 841-872, Je 97.

In his replies of Arnauld, Descartes indicates that God's self-causation can be understood as formal causality. The authors argue that it is reasonable to formal causality pervades Descartes's metaphysics. After showing that Descartes's remarks on formal causality are consistent with the position expressed by Aristotle and Suarez, it is shown that Cartesian natural laws are ontologically and epistemically indistinguishable from eternal truths and it is, therefore, reasonable to construe them as formal causes. Such a position makes intelligible Descartes's remarks on the union of mind and body.

**Flamarique, Lourdes**. "El mundo como imagen: Acerca de Fichte y Schleiermacher" in *El inicio del Idealismo alemán*, Market, Oswaldo, 365-379. Madrid, Ed Complutense, 1996.

Kant's teaching about freedom is contrasted with a vision of the world as wholly in the power of natural necessity, a world of mere phenomena, appearance. The generation which followed Kant saw the whole of the existence of the individual as filled with freedom. Each vital impulse was subject to it. *Die Bestimmung des Menschen* (Fichte) and *Monologen* (Schleiermacher) were published in the same year, 1800. Both works reflect different responses which are both characteristic of Romanticism: they bring into play the phenomenal nature of reality—the will as image—and the difficulties involved in exercising a subjectivity that avoids the danger of turning the consciousness of one's freedom into a mere illusion.

**Flamarique, Lourdes**. Perennidad y prosecución de la filosofía en el pensamiento de Leonardo Polo. *Anu Filosof*, 29(2), 539-552, 1996.

Philosophy is in Polo's view, a living intelligence, an exerted activity. It is always current because it pursuits a knowledge unconcluded by nature. Reason overcomes history if we understand philosophy as a reconsideration of the basic subjects.

**Flanagan, Joseph**. *Quest for Self-Knowledge: An Essay in Lonergan's Philosophy*. Toronto, Univ of Toronto Pr, 1997.

The theme of self-knowledge, introduced by classical philosophers, was taken up and extended by Bernard Lonergan in his major work, *Insight*. In this innovative and complex study, Lonergan worked out a systematic method for understanding the development of self-knowledge. Joseph Flanagan shares with Lonergan the premise that the problem of self-knowledge can be resolved methodically. The purpose of this book is to introduce teachers and students to this difficult subject and to provide readers with a transcultural, normative foundation for a critical evaluation of self-identity and cultural identity. (publisher, edited)

**Flanagan, Owen**. "Consciousness As a Pragmatist Views It" in *The Cambridge Companion to William James*, Putnam, Ruth Anna (ed), 25-48. New York, Cambridge Univ Pr, 1997.

**Flanders, Todd R**. Rousseau's Adventure with Robinson Crusoe. *Interpretation*, 24(3), 319-337, Spr 97.

**Flanigan, Rosemary**. Case Commentary. *Bioethics Forum*, 11(2), 29-30, Sum 95.

Ethical analysis is both a science and an art. As a science, it is not purely theoretical but practical in the sense that one is searching for the right and the good in specific circumstances. As an art, ethical analysis needs to be practiced; it is a skill that can be acquired only by repeatedly performing the unique investigation into the right thing to do. Ethics committees, in particular, practice analysis on mock cases that illustrate different aspects of health care treatment options. Our readers are encouraged to analyze the following case, using the questions as a guide. A commentary on the case appears on page thirty.

**Flanigan, Rosemary**. Future Issues in Bioethics. *Bioethics Forum*, 11(3), 38-41, Fall 95.

In reflecting on the future of bioethics, ethicists need to examine the process of doing ethics as they search for moral truths and right action. As increasingly difficult questions are brought before ethics committees, there is a need for more sophisticated strategies that guarantee depth in ethical analysis.

**Flanigan, Rosemary**. More is Better. *Bioethics Forum*, 11(3), 50-51, Fall 95.

Ethical analysis is not limited to a personal ethic. Because groups and institutions are organized to effect actions that lay beyond the capacities of individuals, there must be an ethic of such entities. Then, too, society at large has its ethic and we are often bound to stretch our moral imagination to encompass a larger picture from what is good for a single person or even an institution.

**Flanigan, Rosemary** and Reynolds, Don F and Emmott, Helen. Advance Directive Timeline and Case Study *Melinda's Story*. *Bioethics Forum*, 13(2), 40-43, Sum 97.

**Flasch, Kurt**. Was heisst es: einen philosophischen Text historisch lesen?. *Bochumer Phil Jrbh*, 1, 1-22, 1996.

In his later thought, Martin Heidegger disclaimed the possibility of a philosophical history of philosophy. In his view, the history of philosophy tends to remain bound to a specific philosophical orientation and offer merely a philosophical position, not philosophy itself, presenting at best nothing more than an assemblage of doctrinal positions. In contrast, Heidegger developed in his early Freiburg lectures of 1919-1923 a historical-phenomenological program of philosophical history directed against the historical school of Dilthey, whose *objekthistorisch* perspective he meant to replace with his own *vollzugshistorisch* method. For Heidegger, there is no perfected subject at the basis of historical investigation, but rather it is the temporality of the observer which makes possible historical knowledge in the first place. Heidegger's later abandonment of this notion is a significant reason for the lack of a philosophical approach to writing the history of philosophy after 1945 in Germany.

**Flasch, Thomas** (trans) and Campanella, Tommaso. *Philosophische Gedichte*. Frankfurt/M, Klostermann, 1996.

**Flax, Javier**. El decisionismo valorativo: Entre las instancias últimas y la racionalidad crítica. *Cuad Etica*, 17-18, 85-109, 1994.

The problem of dualism between facts and values has a main place in Max Weber's methodological concerns, where social sciences are thought to be inhibited to pronounce practical judgements of value. Nevertheless, from a critical rationalist perspective, it is possible to remove the neo-Kantian assumptions which make the values appear as absolute last instances and to regard them as cultural ideals which have been socially constructed. Weber himself offers the elements that enable a scientific and philosophical critic of values and that may establish a communication between facts and decisions, which does not mean to reduce one field to the other.

**Fleckenstein, Marilynn P**. Service Learning in Business Ethics. *J Bus Ethics*, 16(12-13), 1347-1351, S 97.

Those of us engaged in the education of future businesspersons need to ask about the efficacy of our efforts. The business person is, first and foremost, a member of the community, a citizen, attempting to meet the needs of that community by providing goods and services. In this paper, I explore some of the roots of service in higher education and the efficacy of service-learning in business ethics. (edited)

**Fleet, Barrie** (trans). *Simplicius: On Aristotle's Physics 2*. Ithaca, Cornell Univ Pr, 1997.

Book 2 of the *Physics* is arguably the best introduction to Aristotle's ideas. It defines nature and distinguishes natural science from mathematics. Book 2 introduces the seminal idea of four causes, or four modes of explanation. To these riches Simplicius, writing in the sixth century A.D., adds his own considerable contribution. Seeing Aristotle's God as a creator, he discusses how nature relates to soul, adds Stoic and neo-Platonist causes to Aristotle's list of four, and questions the likeness of cause to effect. He discusses missing a great evil or a great good by a hairbreadth and considers whether animals act from reason or natural instinct. He also preserves a Posidonian discussion of mathematical astronomy. (publisher, edited)

**Fleischacker, Samuel**. Values Behind the Market: Kant's Response to the *Wealth of Nations*. *Hist Polit Thought*, 17(3), 379-407, Autumn 96.

One might assume that Smith's *Wealth of Nations* (WN) was discussed in Germany from its publication onwards. This turns out to be wrong: until the late 1790s, WN was practically ignored. Thus it is surprising if, as I argue, Kant was reading Smith in the mid-1780s. Against this historical background I suggest, first, that Kant's speculations on "price" and "dignity" in the *Groundwork* may be intended as a respectful criticism of Smith, and second, that Kant elsewhere

AUTHOR INDEX 627 Flew, Antony

draws on Smith as an ally in his political crusade against "tutelage." Lifting restrictions on the marketplace is one way, for Kant, to discourage childlike passivity in the citizenry.

**Fleming, Jess**. Philosophical Counseling and the *I Ching*. *J Chin Phil*, 23(3), 299-320, S 96.

This paper begins with a brief introduction to "philosophical counseling" ("philosophical practice") as an alternative to psychotherapy and concludes that philosophical counseling is especially useful in assisting troubled clients (facing divorce, unemployment, death, etc.) with "value" problems rather than emotional or cognitive disorders. It is also argued that philosophical counseling could be used in conjunction with psychotherapies (such as psychoanalysis) and as a preventive regiment. Furthermore, it is argued that Asian philosophies (in this case, the *I Ching, Book of Changes*) have much to contribute in theory and practice to this fledgling philosophical movement. The *I Ching*, for example, may be used as both a "diagnostic" and "therapeutic" tool.

**Fleming, Marie**. Critical Theory between Modernity and Postmodernity. *Phil Today*, 41(1-4), 31-39, Spr 97.

This essay introduces the dimension of gender into critical theory's dispute with postmodernism. I begin from Richard Bernstein's and Thomas McCarthy's argument that critical theory's advantage over postmodern theories is constituted by its ability to provide a formal, procedural model for addressing the ethical-political question of "critique in the name of what?" I argue that critical theory cannot deal with this ethical-political question in relation to gender differences and thus also cannot meet the demands of its professed practical intent. I conclude that critical theory needs to rethink its assumptions about modernity, universality, emancipation and rationality.

**Fleming, Marie**. *Emancipation and Illusion: Rationality and Gender in Habermas's Theory of Modernity*. University Park, Pennsylvania Univ Pr, 1997.

In this comprehensive analysis of Jürgen Habermas's philosophy and social theory, Marie Fleming takes strong issue with Habermas over his understanding of rationality and the lifeworld, emancipation, history, and gender. Throughout the book she focuses attention on the various ways in which an idea of emancipation motivates and shapes his universalist theory and how it persists over several major changes in methodology. Her critique of Habermas begins from the view that universalism has to include a vision of gender equality and she asks why Habermas, despite deeply held concerns about equality and inclusiveness, repeatedly and systematically relegates matters of gender to secondary status in his social and moral theory. She extends her critique to a range of issues in his theory of rationality and examines what she views as his very problematical claims about truthfulness, art and bourgeois intimacy. (publisher, edited)

**Flemister, Carl E**. Reflections on a Good Death: An Interview with Carl E. Flemister. *Bioethics Forum*, 13(1), 11-13, Spr 97.

**Fletcher, George P**. "The Case for Linguistic Self-Defense" in *The Morality of Nationalism*, McKim, Robert (ed), 324-339. New York, Oxford Univ Pr, 1997.

Under the metaphor of self-defense, the position that language is a transparent medium of expression which is irrelevant to the habits of thought and the preservation of distinctive cultures is considered and rejected. Each language distinguishes a living culture. Consequently, every group of native speakers has an inherent right to defend its language against influences that threaten to eradicate or displace it: the right of linguistic self-defense. Limited by the bounds of effectiveness, necessity and proportionality, defensive measures might include compulsory instruction of a particular language at school, requiring its use in governmental offices and restricting alternative languages in advertising.

**Fletcher, John C**. Bioethics in a Legal Forum: Confessions of an "Expert" Witness. *J Med Phil*, 22(4), 297-324, Ag 97.

This article reflects on the author's modest experience as an expert witness in two trials: *Osheroff vs. Greenspan* (1983) and *In the Matter of Baby K* (1994). Bioethicists' expertise as scholar-teachers and consultants on particular issues merits qualification by judges as expert witnesses. The article argues that a different kind of expertise—strong moral advocacy—is required to be an effective expert witness. The major lessons of expert witnessing for the author concern the demands and strains on the bioethicist's role as scholar, teacher and consultant. The Baby K case is analyzed in some detail, due to its importance for bioethics, ethics consultation and the testimony of bioethicists on either side of the case. Rules of thumb are offered to guide decisions as to choices regarding expert witnessing, as well as a discussion of the interaction of law and bioethics.

**Fletcher, John C**. Ethics Consultants and Surrogates: Can We Do Better?. *J Clin Ethics*, 8(1), 50-59, Spr 97.

**Fletcher, John C**. Responding to JCAHO Standards: Everybody's Business. *J Clin Ethics*, 7(2), 182-183, Sum 96.

**Fletcher, John C** and Boverman, Maxwell. Heroes, Martyrs, and Other Choices. *J Clin Ethics*, 7(4), 301-305, Wint 96.

**Fletcher, John C** and Leeman, Cavin P and Spencer, Edward M (& others). Quality Control for Hospitals' Clinical Ethics Services: Proposed Standards. *Cambridge Quart Healthcare Ethics*, 6(3), 257-268, Sum 97.

As hospital ethics committees have proliferated, problems in the way in which they operate have become increasingly apparent. In response, the authors propose two sets of standards. Standards for procedure and process are intended to help ensure that clinical ethics services are provided in ways which are fair, open, and procedurally consistent and predictable. Standards for education and training are designed to ensure that the people who provide clinical ethics services have the skills and expertise needed to do so competently, and to engender confidence in them. The standards are discussed, and examples of ways to meet them are offered.

**Fletcher, John C** and Siegler, Mark. What Are the Goals of Ethics Consultation: A Consensus Statement. *J Clin Ethics*, 7(2), 122-126, Sum 96.

This article reports on the outcome of a consensus-development process to frame a statement of the goals of ethics case consultation, (ECC). ECC is a service provided by an individual consultant, team, or committee to address the ethical issues involved in a specific clinical case. The authors coled a Working Group on Goals that convened at the Conference on Evaluation of Ethics Case Consultation in Chicago, Il, September 21-23, 1995. The overall goal of the conference was to explore the feasibility of a controlled study of the efficacy of ECC in several settings. Epidemiological study of evaluation of EEC is not possible without agreement about goals. Previously divided as to the main purpose and goals of ECC, the authors reconciled their differences prior to the meeting and went into the meeting united. Consequently, the Working Group was able to reach consensus on a goals statement of four parts: 1) on the outcome of ECC in maximizing benefit and minimizing harm to patients, families, clinicians and institutions and the process of ECC to foster fair and inclusive decision making, 2) on ECC as a conflict-resolution strategy, 3) on ECC's role in informing institutional efforts at policy development and 4) on the educational role of ECC.

**Fletcher, Robert H** and Fletcher, Suzanne W. Evidence for the Effectiveness of Peer Review. *Sci Eng Ethics*, 3(1), 35-50, Ja 97.

Scientific editors' policies, including peer review, are based mainly on tradition and belief. Do they actually achieve their desired effects, the selection of the best manuscripts and improvement of those published? Editorial decisions have important consequences to investigators, the scientific community, and all who might benefit from correct information or be harmed by misleading research results. These decisions should be judged not just by intentions of reviewers and editors but also by the actual consequences of their actions. A small but growing number of studies has put editorial policies to a strong scientific test. In a randomized, controlled trial, blinding reviewers to author and institution was usually successful and improved the quality of reviews. Two studies have shown that, contrary to conventional wisdom, reviewers early in their careers give better reviews than senior reviewers. Many studies have shown low agreement between reviewers but there is disagreement about whether this represents a failing of peer review or the expected and valuable effect of choosing reviewers with complementary expertise. In a study of whether manuscripts are improved by peer review and editing, articles published in *Annals of Internal Medicine* were improved in 33 of 34 dimensions of reporting quality, but published articles still had room for improvement. Because of the central place of peer review in the scientific community and the resources it requires, more studies are needed to define what it does and does not accomplish.

**Fletcher, Suzanne W** and Fletcher, Robert H. Evidence for the Effectiveness of Peer Review. *Sci Eng Ethics*, 3(1), 35-50, Ja 97.

Scientific editors' policies, including peer review, are based mainly on tradition and belief. Do they actually achieve their desired effects, the selection of the best manuscripts and improvement of those published? Editorial decisions have important consequences to investigators, the scientific community, and all who might benefit from correct information or be harmed by misleading research results. These decisions should be judged not just by intentions of reviewers and editors but also by the actual consequences of their actions. A small but growing number of studies has put editorial policies to a strong scientific test. In a randomized, controlled trial, blinding reviewers to author and institution was usually successful and improved the quality of reviews. Two studies have shown that, contrary to conventional wisdom, reviewers early in their careers give better reviews than senior reviewers. Many studies have shown low agreement between reviewers but there is disagreement about whether this represents a failing of peer review or the expected and valuable effect of choosing reviewers with complementary expertise. In a study of whether manuscripts are improved by peer review and editing, articles published in *Annals of Internal Medicine* were improved in 33 of 34 dimensions of reporting quality, but published articles still had room for improvement. Because of the central place of peer review in the scientific community and the resources it requires, more studies are needed to define what it does and does not accomplish.

**Flew, Antony**. "A Response to Jean Hampton's Feminism" in *The Liberation Debate: Rights at Issue*, Leahy, Michael (ed), 25-40. New York, Routledge, 1996.

Jean Hampton effectively but not explicitly distinguishes two kinds of feminism: classical and neo. Today in the Western democracies the former is scarcely controversial. The present paper is therefore devoted to attacking some presently popular neofeminist contentions—contentions for which she seems to be too sensible to serve as an unreservedly committed advocate. For instance, she has little to say about the vast number of Departments for Womens' Studies. Do any of these require students to come to terms with Goldberg's *Why Men Rule* and Levin's *Feminism and Freedom?* Or are they all institutions for neofeminist indoctrination?

**Flew, Antony**. *Atheistic Humanism*. Amherst, Prometheus, 1993.

This collection of essays addresses the many and diverse aspects of atheistic humanism. Flew begins his comprehensive study with "Fundamentals of Unbelief," in which he argues that there is no good or sufficient natural reason to believe that the universe is created by a conscious, personal, willing and doing Being; In the second part, "Defending Knowledge and Responsibility," Flew disposes of the perennial charge that a naturalistic world outlook presupposes values for which it cannot itself make room. The third section, "*Scientific Socialism?*", consists of three critical analyses of Marxism. Finally, in the fourth part, "Applied Philosophy," Flew looks at three social issues, which have been the subject of much recent debate: the right to die, the definition of mental health and the problem of racism. (publisher, edited)

**Flew, Antony**. *Thinking Straight*. Amherst, Prometheus, 1975.

This book was a primer for people wanting not only to detect and destroy the unsound arguments employed by others but also to think more clearly and more honestly themselves. Its main differences from other works in the same *genre* were two. One is its making numerous references to great philosophers: the hope was to increase recruitment to philosophy courses. The other was to nickname various popular argumentative malpractices: such as *The Subject/Motive Shift*; *The Logically Black is White Slide*; *The But-you-can-understand-why Evasion*; and *The But-they-will-never-agree Diversion*.

**Flichman, Eduardo**. Gregorio Klimovsky y las desventuras del conocimiento cientíico. *Analisis Filosof*, 16(1), 83-92, My 96.

It is a critical study and review of the book *Las desventuras del conocimiento científico* (*The Misfortunes of Scientific Knowledge*), whose author, Gregorio Klimovsky, is one of the most outstanding representatives of the Anglo-Saxon tradition in the philosophy of science of Argentina.

**Flichman, Eduardo Héctor**. "Prigogine y Kuhn, dos personajes en la historia externa de la ciencia y la epistemología contemporáneas" in *La racionalidad: su poder y sus límites*, Nudler, Oscar (ed), 449-457. Barcelona, Ed Paidos, 1996.

Prigogine and Kuhn obtained, with respect to an important part of their intellectual production, a strong acceptance from philosophers and social scientists belonging to some of the so-called "French" philosophical circles and a balancing rebuff from many of the philosophers whose common denominator is their adherence to the "analytical tradition." I believe that in both cases it was the *form* and not the *content* of what was expressed by them, that has seduced the former and repelled the latter. I try to support the idea that both authors defend a rather classic type of rationality.

**Flikschuh, Katrin**. On Kant's *Rechtslehre*. *Euro J Phil*, 5(1), 50-73, Ap 97.

The paper offers a survey of recent work on Immanuel Kant's *Metaphysical Elements of Justice*. The author argues that a distinction should be drawn between the form and the scope of any particular conception of justice. With respect to form, the author further distinguishes between contractarian and obligation-based interpretations of Kant's work; with respect to scope a distinction is made between domestic and global approaches. The author argues that an obligation-based, global reading of Kant's account of justice is more in keeping with Kant's critical philosophy than the domestic focus which dominates contractarian interpretations.

**Flonta, Mircea**. Does the Scientific Paper Accurately Mirror the Very Grounds of Scientific Assessment?. *Theoria (Spain)*, 11(27), 19-31, S 96.

This paper presents a prevalent representation about the objectivity and impartiality of scientific knowledge that emerges from the structure and style of the standard research paper. This representation is critically examined considering some rather untypical scientific papers reporting controversies between researchers in a certain field of experimental science. The role of personal preconceptions and intellectual prejudices in the assessment of scientific theories is emphasized by reference to Einstein's grounds for his general theory of relativity.

**Flórez Miguel, Cirilo**. "Política y Filosofía en Ortega: Teoría Orteguiana de la Modernidad" in *Política y Sociedad en José Ortega y Gasset: En Torno a "Vieja y Nueva Política"*, Lopez de la Vieja, Maria Teresa (ed), 121-139. Barcelona, Anthropos, 1997.

**Flória Gouveia, Mariley Simoes**. Ensino de Ciências e Formaçao Continuada de Professores: Algumas Consideraçao Históricas. *Educ Filosof*, 9(17), 227-257, Ja-Je 95.

A finalidade do estudo é resgatar parte da história (1960-1990) dos cursos de Ciências para professores do 1° grau e entender o papel dos cursos de Ciências no seu contexto histórico. Esta foi a maneira que encontrei para compreender os problemas metodológicos da formaçao continuada no ensino de Ciências. Questionar as estratégias de aperfeiçoamento, usadas no âmbito do ensino de Ciências, via-de-regra desgarradas do cotidiano escolar, é fornecer elementos para que esta importante atividade de formaçao continuada passe a ser pensada de maneira mais abrangente e eficaz.

**Floridi, Luciano**. *Scepticism and the Foundation of Epistemology: A Study in the Metalogical Fallacies*. Leiden, Brill, 1996.

This sceptical challenge—known as the *problem of the criterion*—is one of the major issues in the history of epistemology and this volume provides its first comprehensive study, in a span of time that goes from Sextus Empiricus to Quine. After an essential introduction to the notions of knowledge and of philosophy of knowledge, the book provides a detailed reconstruction of the history of the problem. There follows a conceptual analysis of its logical features, and a comparative examination of a phenomenology of solutions that have been suggested in the course of the history of philosophy in order to overcome it, from Descartes to Popper. In this context, an indirect approach to the problem of the criterion is defended as the most successful strategy against the sceptical challenge. (publisher,edited)

**Florovskii, Georgii**. On Studying Dostoevskii. *Russian Stud Phil*, 35(3), 19-35, Wint 96-97.

**Flory, Dan**. Racism, *Black Athena*, and the Historiography of Ancient Philosophy. *Phil Forum*, 28(3), 183-208, Spr 97.

**Floss, Pavel**. Patrizzi and Descartes (in Czech). *Filosof Cas*, 44(5), 773-781, 1996.

This study forms part of the author's wider research into the historical context of the genesis of Descartes's thought. The work of Patrizzi and Descartes is, at least in part, formed in the same intellectual tradition and this article is concerned with the late renaissance search for method and with the development of the phase of a sensual concept of understanding. There are certain similarities between Patrizzi and Descartes in this phase (the forming of all knowledge according to the "mos geometricus", the understanding of knowledge as an internal intellectual act and the hypostaticmathematical concept of space as an ontological condition for the existence of matter). At the same time, however, certain basic differences can also be distinguished. One of these is Patrizzi's effort to achieve a more scientific understanding of history, which Descartes did not recognize as science. The second difference is the interpretation of human acts of understanding. (edited)

**Flotzinger, Rudolf**. "Progress and Development in Music History" in *The Idea of Progress*, McLaughlin, Peter (ed), 121-138. Hawthorne, de Gruyter, 1997.

In music the idea of progress is strongly linked with organic development. Within the aesthetic discussion the use of the term progress with its valuating implications started only in the 18th century. Nevertheless, up to that time the estimation of something "new" was often articulated, especially at certain turning points in music history.

**Flügel, Martin**. Duhems Holismus. *Phil Natur*, 33(1), 143-167, 1996.

In the actual philosophical discussion Pierre Duhem is normally considered as mere precursor of Quine's. By an analysis of the foundation of Duhem's thesis the article demonstrates that this idea isn't correct. In particular it is shown that Duhem's and Quine's theses rest on different assumptions and that, therefore, Quine's holism isn't simply an extension of Duhem's thesis.

**Flury, Andreas**. Verantwortung und moralische Gefühle. *Frei Z Phil Theol*, 44(1-2), 152-157, 1997.

**Flynn, Thomas R**. Reconstituting Praxis: Historialization as Re-Enactment. *Amer Cath Phil Quart*, 70(4), 597-618, Autumn 96.

Sartre's existentialist philosophy of history turns on our ability to comprehend the historical agent's "historialization" (lived, totalizing experience) of his/her epoch. The approach is existentialist in its focus on our representing the agent's experience of the risk of choice and the pinch of the real. The challenge is to relate history and biography in a manner that respects their mutual illumination without overlooking the specificity of each. History emerges as a poietic undertaking and the historian as dramaturge.

**Fodor, Jerry**. "Concepts: A Potboiler" in *Contents*, Villanueva, Enrique (ed), 1-24. Atascadero, Ridgeview, 1995.

**Fodor, Jerry**. Deconstructing Dennett's Darwin. *Mind Lang*, 11(3), 246-262, S 96.

Daniel Dennett's book, *Darwin's Dangerous Idea*, offers a naturalistic teleology and a theory of the intentionality of the mental. Both are grounded in a neo-Darwinian account of evolutionary adaptation. I argue that Dennett's empirical assumptions about the evolution of psychological phenotypes may well be unwarranted; and that, in any event, the intentionality of minds is quite different from and not reducible to the intensionality of selection.

**Fodor, Jerry A** and Lepore, Ernest. What Cannot Be Evaluated Cannot Be Evaluated, and it Cannot Be Supervalued Either. *J Phil*, 93(10), 516-535, O 96.

Van Fraassen and Fine, among many others, now argue that you can both deny the law of bivalence, thereby doing justice to the intuitions about the present king of France being bald, and hold onto excluded middle, thereby placating the classical logicians. Moreover, it's suggested that the mechanisms that allow you to do this make clear how sentences that lack truth-values can, as it were, be meaningful in virtue of their potential for having them, thereby solving the first problem as well as the second. All this relies essentially on the method of supervaluations. In this paper, we'll argue that there is something fundamentally wrong with using supervaluation techniques either for preserving classical logic or for providing a semantics for linguistic expressions ordinarily thought to produce truth-value gaps. (edited)

**Förster, Eckart** (ed) and Henrich, Dieter. *The Course of Remembrance and Other Essays on Hölderlin*. Stanford, Stanford Univ Pr, 1997.

This volume includes six of Henrich's most important essays on Hölderlin's philosophical significance. Among the topics discussed are Hölderlin's motivation and methodological orientation in his work on German idealism, the intellectual atmosphere of Hölderlin's student years and the philosophical problems that occupied him, Hölderlin's attitude toward any first-principle philosophy and the complex personal and philosophical relationships between Hegel and Hölderlin. The last essay is a long, detailed interpretation of one of Hölderlin's greatest poems, "Remembrance."(publisher,edited)

**Fogel, Joshua A** (ed) and Bloom, Irene (ed). *Meeting of Minds: Intellectual and Religious Interaction in East Asian Traditions of Thought*. New York, Columbia Univ Pr, 1997.

In *Meeting of Minds*, eleven prominent scholars explore intellectual and religious interactions among diverse traditions of the East Asian world. The authors consider central issues including concepts of religious authority, perceptions of the relation between knowledge and action, the sense of "the sacred" within the realm of ordinary human existence, and the concern with historical experience and practicality as criteria for evaluating ideas and beliefs. (publisher,edited)

**Fogelin, Robert J**. "Wittgenstein's Critique of Philosophy" in *The Cambridge Companion to Wittgenstein*, Sluga, Hans (ed), 34-58. Needham Heights, Cambridge, 1996.

**Fogelin, Robert J**. Précis of *Pyrrhonian Reflections on Knowledge and Justification*. *Phil Phenomenol Res*, 57(2), 395-400, Je 97.

**Fogelin, Robert J**. The Intuitive Basis of Berkeley's Immaterialism. *Hist Phil Quart*, 13(3), 331-344, Jl 96.

In the opening sentence of section seven of part one of the *Principles*, Berkeley announces, after roughly a thousand words of prose, that "from what has been said, if follows, there is not any other substance than spirit." I argue that Berkeley does not base this claim on any argument whatsoever—for example, a verifications argument or an argument exploiting the inherent instability of the Lockean position. He based this claim instead on a direct appeal to intuition.

**Fogelin, Robert J**. What Does a Pyrrhonist Know?. *Phil Phenomenol Res*, 57(2), 417-425, Je 97.

**Fogliatti, Karen**. Nonviolence as a Way of Life: Issues of Justice. *Acorn*, 8(1), 14-23, Spr-Sum 93.

**Follari, Roberto A**. El Derecho al Sentido en lo Posmoderno. *Educ Filosof*, 10(19), 45-61, Ja-Je 96.

This article presents problems about the legitimation of schools as an institution in Latin America today. Neoliberal positions have carried this justification only in terms of education to economic patterns; it is a dangerous position, because it makes disappearing education as a human right. So, if education were economically making a deficit, it would be considered useless. Neoliberalism is being abandoned gradually by population; it is not the case of a postmodern condition, which depends on structural factors. This condition has arrived at an inflection point: there is no more celebration today. The problem now is lack of sense. So, a school principally would dedicate its action to make sense to discuss a normative direction of life. (edited)

**Follesdal, Dagfinn**. Analytic Philosophy: What Is It and Why Should One Engage in It?. *Ratio*, 9(3), 193-208, D 96.

**Folse, Henry J**. Ontological Constraints and Understanding Quantum Phenomena. *Dialectica*, 50(2), 121-136, 1996.

The question of whether an "understanding" of quantum phenomena is possible, as raised by Cushing (1991), is considered in terms of a possible revision of basic ontological assumptions which would make rational the pursuit of such an understanding. It is argued that the quantum theory imposes new constraints on ontology which force us to revise classical presuppositions about attributing properties to physical systems, about locality and individuality, and about interaction and space-like separability. Through such ontological revision, it is argued, one may still rationally hope to satisfy the typically realist thirst for an understanding of quantum phenomena.

**Fonnesu, Luca**. Metamorfosi della libertà nel *Sistema di Etica* di Fichte. *G Crit Filosof Ital*, 17(1), 30-46, Ja-Ap 97.

**Fonseca Vieira, Márcia Núbia**. A Questao do Método em História da Educaçao. *Educ Filosof*, 10(19), 97-103, Ja-Je 96.

**Font, Josep Maria** and Verdú, Ventura. The Lattice of Distributive Closure Operators Over an Algebra. *Stud Log*, 52(1), 1-13, F 93.

In our previous paper "Algebraic Logic for Classical Conjunction and Disjunction", we studied some relations between the fragment L of classical logic having just conjunction and disjunction and the variety D of distributive lattices, within the context of algebraic logic. The central tool in that study was a class of closure operators which we called distributive and one of its main results was that for any algebra A of type (2,2) there is an isomorphism between the lattices of all D-congruences of A and of all distributive closure operators over A. In the present paper we study the lattice structure of this last set, give a description of its finite and infinite operations and obtain a topological representation. We also apply the mentioned isomorphism and other results to obtain proofs with a logical flavour for several new or well-known lattice-theoretical properties, like Hashimoto's characterization of distributive lattices and Priestley's topological representation of the congruence lattice of a bounded distributive lattice.

**Fontius, Martin**. "Gedanken vor einem Jubiläum" in *Grenzen der kritischen Vernunft*, Schmid, Peter A, 17-31. Basel, Schwabe Verlag, 1997.

**Forbes, Graeme**. How Much Substitutivity?. *Analysis*, 57(2), 109-113, Ap 97.

This paper is a reply to one by Jennifer Saul in the same issue. Saul argues that we have intuitions of substitution-failure for sentences that do not contain any opacity-inducing contexts; for example, "Lois met Clark before she met Superman". She suggests that there can be no semantic account of substitution-failure for these cases and that the intuitions are to be explained away pragmatically. I offer a semantics that would allow substitution failure in Saul's cases to be a genuine semantic phenomenon.

**Forbes, Graeme**. Substitutivity and the Coherence of Quantifying In. *Phil Rev*, 105(3), 337-372, Jl 96.

In this paper I offer a "hidden indexical" semantics for propositional and objectual attitude ascriptions. The approach takes Quine's example "Giorgione is so-called because of his size" as the paradigm of substitution-failure. The paper offers a theory of why Quine is right that some contexts do not allow quantifying in and wrong that attitude contexts are among them.

**Force, James E**. "Samuel Clarke's Four Categories of Deism, Isaac Newton, and the Bible" in *Scepticism in the History of Philosophy: A Pan-American Dialogue*, Popkin, Richard H (ed), 53-74. Dordrecht, Kluwer, 1996.

**Ford, Lewis S**. "Whitehead's Distinctive Features" in *The Recovery of Philosophy in America: Essays in Honor of John Edwin Smith*, Kasulis, Thomas P (ed), 131-154. Albany, SUNY Pr, 1997.

This brief enumeration of both positive and negative features is prefaced by some explanation of Whitehead's philosophical neglect, occasioned by his twin commitment to theism and to metaphysics. Based squarely on relativity physics, this philosophy of process understood radically as becoming reinterprets subjectivity and objectivity in the temporal categories of present and past. Because of the peculiar way Whitehead wrote *Process and Reality*, retaining everything meant for publication even though he had revised his conceptuality, we are able to determine his philosophical development in greater detail than any other major philosopher. Nevertheless, there are objectionable features: the uncreated eternal objects, the microscopic occasions, the alleged 'pre-Kantianism', and its 'Panpsychism'.

**Ford, Lewis S**. Panpsychism and the Early History of Prehension. *Process Stud*, 24, 15-33, 1995.

Throughout the early part of *Science and the Modern World*, only some events enjoy subjectivity. Prehension as first introduced can be understood strictly in terms of events related by a common eternal object. From the standpoint of one of these events, prehension can be understood in terms of perception only if we substitute a perceiving subject for the event. The revision caused by the epochal theory of time restricts active occasions to the present, yet even so physical occasions may be devoid of subjectivity. Some may find panpsychism in three paragraphs which may be a very late insertion in the chapter on "Abstraction." That value is the intrinsic reality of an event does not entail panpsychism, but merely contrasts with the extrinsic reality evident in scientific materialism. The notion that every actual occasion has a mental occasion is first articulated in the 1926 essay on "Time," but full panpsychism, that every prehension has a subject, first appears in *Process and Reality, Part III*. Prehension in *Science and the Modern World* is an extremely thin and abstract notion which Whitehead was able to develop into the rich notion of *Process and Reality*.

**Ford, Lewis S**. Pantheism vs. Theism: A Re-Appraisal. *Monist*, 80(2), 286-306, Ap 97.

**Ford, Maureen**. "Opening the Closet Door: Sexualities Education and "Active Ignorance"" in *Philosophy of Education (1996)*, Margonis, Frank (ed), 290-293. Urbana, Phil Education Soc, 1997.

**Foreman, Matthew** and Magidor, Menachem. A Very Weak Square Principle. *J Sym Log*, 62(1), 175-196, Mr 97.

**Forman, Robert K C**. Of Heapers, Splitters and Academic Woodpiles in the Study of Intense Religious Experiences. *Sophia (Australia)*, 35(1), 73-100, Mr-Ap 96.

**Forment, Eudaldo**. La dignidad del hombre y la dignidad de la persona. *Sapientia*, 51(200), 405-428, 1996.

**Fornäs, Johan**. Text and Music Revisited. *Theor Cult Soc*, 14(3), 109-123, Ag 97.

The article problematizes theories constructing music and words as opposites. Three crucial distinctions are made. First, between four main symbolic modes resulting from the independent dichotomies of verbality/nonverbality and visuality/aurality: writing, speech, images and music. Second, between texts/musics as sets of genres, words/sounds as elements and textuality/musicality as aspects of communication. Third, between materiality, form, meaning and pragmatics as symbolic levels. Against polarizing semiotic and cultural theories of Langer, Kristeva, Barthes and others, it is argued that words and musics cover a continuum of differences: music is also always 'textual' and texts are 'musical'.

**Fornari, Aníbal**. Identidad personal, acontecimiento, alteridad desde Paul Ricoeur. *Aquinas*, 39(2), 339-365, My-Ag 96.

**Forrai, Gábor**. Internal Realism, Metaphysical Realism, and Brains in a Vat. *Dialectica*, 50(4), 259-274, 1996.

The paper explores the relationship between skepticism on the one hand and the metaphysical realist and the internal realist conceptions of truth on the other. After a brief description of the metaphysical realist and the internal realist positions, it is argued that the former but not the latter is committed to an important sort of skepticism, namely, that we might be wrong about practically everything at the same time. First an abstract argument is presented to this effect, then the issue is further clarified through an analysis of Hilary Putnam's antiskeptical argument about brains in a vat. The analysis shows that the argument can be rejected only from the metaphysical realist standpoint. Since the argument is conclusive from the internal realist point of view, internal realism, in contrast with metaphysical realism, is safe from skepticism.

**Forrest, Peter**. "Difficulties with Physicalism, and a Programme for Dualists" in *Objections to Physicalism*, Robinson, Howard (ed), 251-269. New York, Clarendon/Oxford Pr, 1996.

**Forrest, Peter**. Common Sense and a "Wigner-Dirac" Approach to Quantum Mechanics. *Monist*, 80(1), 131-159, Ja 97.

This paper presents a case for the thesis that quantum mechanics is compatible with common sense. I make this case by exhibiting a Wignerian formulation of quantum mechanics (i.e., the *phase space picture*) and a neo-Dirackian interpretation of quantum mechanics thus formulated. Together these reconcile quantum mechanics with some commonsense theses, which might seem to be violated by quantum mechanics. (edited)

**Forrest, Peter**. How Innocent is Mereology?. *Analysis*, 56(3), 127-131, Jl 96.

Lewis asserts the ontological innocence of mereology. By this he means that "if you are already committed to some things, you incur no further commitment when you affirm the existence of their fusion. The new commitment is redundant, given the old one." In this paper I argue against the innocence of mereology on the grounds that it implies countable fusion, namely, that any countably many regions in space have a fusion which is itself a region. Countable fusion, I shall argue, is incompatible with another thesis that might, for all we know, be true, namely that space is Whiteheadian.

**Forrest, Peter**. Pantheism and Science. *Monist*, 80(2), 307-319, Ap 97.

Does contemporary science tend to favor pantheism over its rivals, namely atheism, polytheism, panentheism and transcendent theism? I argue that the only significant effect of contemporary science is to reduce the probability of polytheism and of some types of pantheism and to correspondingly increase the probability of the type of pantheism in which i) God is identified not with the universe but with the natural order, and ii) God is not personal. Hence any reasons for accepting a personal God are reasons for rejecting pantheism.

**Forrest, Peter**. Physicalism and Classical Theism. *Faith Phil*, 13(2), 179-200, AP 96.

In this paper I compare two versions of noneliminative physicalism (reductive physicalism and supervenience physicalism) with four of the five theses of classical theism: divine noncontingency, divine transcendence, divine simplicity and the aseity thesis. I argue that: 1) Both physicalism (either version) and classical theism require intuition-transcending identifications of some properties or possibilities; 2) Among other identifications, both reductive physicalism and classical theism need to identify psychological with functional properties; 3) Both reductive physicalism and classical theism have a problem with consciousness; 4) Both reductive physicalists and classical theists should distinguish fine and coarse grained theories of properties.

**Forrester, John**. If *p*, Then What? Thinking in Cases. *Hist Human Sci*, 9(3), 1-25, Ag 96.

**Forst, Rainer**. Foundations of a Theory of Multicultural Justice. *Constellations*, 4(1), 63-71, Ap 97.

This paper critically examines the normative basis of Will Kymlicka's theory of multicultural justice. Since any such theory has to be built upon a moral foundation that is reciprocally and generally justifiable to all citizens as members of the political community and as members of diverse cultural groups, it must not be based upon a particular, ethical-liberal notion of personal autonomy and of the good life such as Kymlicka's. Rather, a theory of a just basic structure for a multicultural society requires a more impartial basis, that is, a thinner conception of moral autonomy (including a basic moral "right to justification") combined with a conception of culture as a context of personal identity (and not primarily as a context of individual choice). This combination has advantages both for explaining the value of one's own culture and the moral requirements any cultural group in a multicultural state has to meet. As a consequence, a view of moral toleration emerges with important advantages over Kymlicka's notion of liberal toleration.

**Forst, Rainer**. Situations of the Self: Reflections on Seyla Benhabib's Version of Critical Theory. *Phil Soc Crit*, 23(5), 79-96, S 97.

**Forster, Paul**. "The Logical Foundations of Peirce's Indeterminism" in *The Rule of Reason: The Philosophy of Charles Sanders Peirce*, Forster, Paul (ed), 57-80. Toronto, Univ of Toronto Pr, 1997.

Peirce is often praised for being the first to develop a scientific metaphysics of indeterminism. I argue that Peirce developed the foundations of indeterminism by 1866, 15 to 25 years earlier than previous estimates. This means that indeterminism was not a late development in Peirce's thought but rather one of his earliest discoveries. I show how Peirce derived this view from his early theory of statistical inference. Finally, I argue that the conceptual revolution that Peirce's indeterminism represents was triggered, not by evolutionary theory or by statistical mechanics, as widely assumed, but by his Kantian interpretation of Boole's logic.

**Forster, Paul** (ed) and Brunning, Jacqueline (ed). *The Rule of Reason: The Philosophy of Charles Sanders Peirce*. Toronto, Univ of Toronto Pr, 1997.

Since the publication of his collected papers began, in 1931, interest in Peirce has grown dramatically. His writings have found audiences in logic, epistemology, metaphysics, philosophy of science, semiotics, computer science, literary criticism, and film studies. While Peirce scholarship has advanced considerably since its earliest days, many controversies of interpretation persist and several of the more obscure aspects of Peirce's work remain poorly understood. This volume presents a broad selection of work devoted to outstanding issues and difficulties in Peirce's philosophy. Some essays clarify aspects of Peirce's philosophy, some defend its contemporary significance, and some do both. (publisher)

**Forster, Paul D**. "Unity, Theory and Practice: F.H. Bradley and Pragmatism" in *Philosophy after F.H. Bradley*, Bradley, James (ed), 169-193. Bristol, Thoemmes, 1996.

Bradley and Dewey each seek a conception of the unity of experience that avoids both the reduction of humanity to biology and the ontological separation of the domains of feeling, volition and cognition. Nonetheless their projects are fundamentally opposed. Behind Bradley's charge that Dewey is a crude instrumentalist and Dewey's charge that Bradley is a pernicious intellectualist lies a deep disagreement about how best to reconcile the immanence of experience and the transcendence of normative authority. These intuitions persist in contemporary debates between realists and defenders of the contingency of philosophical authority.

**Fort, Timothy L**. How Relationality Shapes Business and Its Ethics. *J Bus Ethics*, 16(12-13), 1381-1391, S 97.

This paper first argues that relationality based on naturalism is the primary, plausible value for ethics. Second, it adapts a tripartite dialectic from scholars William Frederick and Michael Novak to describe the relational categories with which business must contend. Third, it uses these forces in a way similar to

Porter's competitive forces to offer an analytical language familiar to managers in order to characterize business ethics. (edited)

**Fort, Timothy L**. Naturalism and Business Ethics: Inevitable Foes or Possible Allies?. *Bus Ethics Quart*, 7(3), 145-155, Jl 97.

**Fort, Timothy L**. Religion and Business Ethics: The Lessons from Political Morality. *J Bus Ethics*, 16(3), 263-273, F 97.

The issue of whether religious belief should be an appropriate grounding for business ethics raises issues very similar to those raised in asking whether religious belief should be an appropriate grounding for political morality. In light of that fact that writings in political morality have been a common resource for contemporary business ethics, this paper presents contemporary arguments about the role of religion in political morality while noting the relevance of these debates for business ethics. The paper takes the position that rather than excluding religion from public morality, political morality (and business ethics) ought to take an inclusive, ecumenical approach. To argue this position and to present fully a range of literature normally not studied in business ethics circles, the paper presents and critiques the major contemporary authors in the field of political morality and contrasts them with the inclusionists who seek to keep public grounds open for all moral perspectives.

**Forteza Pujol, Bartomeu**. *Thelema*: Hipólito de Roma y la filosofía del siglo II. *Convivium*, 10, 17-51, 1997.

The comparative analysis of the Greek term *Thelama* (*will*) between the writings of Hyppolitus of Rome (III A.C.), the controverted Christian author and the main philosophical and mystical texts of the II century is a way to consider the doctrine of *creation*, *will* and *liberty*. At that time new philosophical notions appear in relation with the philosophy previous to Christianism and having its origins in the oriental mystic literature.

**Fortino, Mirella**. Esperienza e ragione nel convenzionalismo geometrico di Henri Poincaré. *Epistemologia*, 19(1), 51-83, Ja-Je 96.

Between experience and reason Poincaré's conventionalism—which states the difficult coexistence between logical and psychological reason—establishes a strict link that, although it can be stated that a geometry is neither true not false, does not allow an arbitrary choice between axioms and postulates and a relativization of the concept of geometric truth. (edited)

**Fortunato, Marco**. "Il Senso Della Verità: Desolazione matematica e terapia nietzscheana dell'infelicità" in *Soggetto E Verità: La questione dell'uomo nella filosofia contemporanea*, Fagiuoli, Ettore, 217-231. 20136 Milano, Mimesis, 1996.

**Fortunato, Marco** and Fagiuoli, Ettore. *Soggetto E Verità: La questione dell'uomo nella filosofia contemporanea*. 20136 Milano, Mimesis, 1996.

**Foss, Jeffrey E**. Is There a Natural Sexual Inequality of Intellect? A Reply to Kimura. *Hypatia*, 11(3), 24-46, Sum 96.

The noted psychologist, Doreen Kimura, has argued that we should not expect to find equal numbers of men and women in various professions because there is a natural sexual inequality of intellect. In rebuttal I argue that each of these mutually supporting theses is sufficiently supported by the evidence to be accepted. The social and ethical dimensions of Kimura's work, and of the scientific study of the nature-nurture controversy in general, are briefly discussed.

**Foss, Nicolai J**. Ethics, Discovery, and Strategy. *J Bus Ethics*, 16(11), 1131-1142, Ag 97.

I address the issue of justifiable profits from distinct perspectives in economics, strategy research and ethics. Combining insights from Austrian economics, the resource-based perspective and finders, keepers ethics, I argue that strategy is about the *discovery* of hitherto unexploited possibilities for exchange. To the extent that strategy is about the discovery/creation ex nihilo of products, ways of producing products, etc., the resulting profits are argued to be justifiable from a finders, keepers perspective.

**Fossa, John A** and Erickson, Glenn W. Paradoxes of Salvation. *Dialogos*, 31(68), 165-181, Jl 96.

**Foster, John**. "The Succinct Case for Idealism" in *Objections to Physicalism*, Robinson, Howard (ed), 294-313. New York, Clarendon/Oxford Pr, 1996.

**Fourcade, Michel**. Maritain et le débat postconciliaire: Le paysan de la garonne. *Maritain Stud*, 8, 7-60, 1992.

**Fowler Morse, Jane**. Fostering Autonomy. *Educ Theor*, 47(1), 31-50, Wint 97.

Universally, educational theorists have been interested in how to educate the young in virtue. Nevertheless, there is disagreement over how moral education is to be accomplished. "Fostering Autonomy" reviews the derivation of Kant's categorical imperative and formulates some practical applications to public education, especially at the secondary level. Kant's moral rule, always treat other people as ends in themselves and never as a means to your end, asserts that all people are inherently worthy of respect because they are moral agents free to act on rational principle. Establishing morality by habit, as in Aristotle's rule of moderation, is appropriate for younger children, but Kant's secular, rational ethic provides a way to educate older children so they will make good choices as free and equal citizens in a global, democratic society.

**Fox, Ellen**. Concepts in Evaluation Applied to Ethics Consultation Research. *J Clin Ethics*, 7(2), 116-121, Sum 96.

**Fox, Ellen** and Arnold, Robert M. Evaluating Outcomes in Ethics Consultation Research. *J Clin Ethics*, 7(2), 127-138, Sum 96.

**Fox, Ellen** and Tulsky, James A. Evaluating Ethics Consultation: Framing the Questions. *J Clin Ethics*, 7(2), 109-115, Sum 96.

Case consultation in clinical ethics (ethics consultation) is a rapidly expanding health care service that, proponents argue, can improve patient care by resolving ethical dilemmas, ensuring quality ethical decision-making and mediating value conflicts among patients, families and health care providers. The rapid growth in the practice of ethics consultation has occurred, however, without either consensus about its goals or rigorous evaluation of the effectiveness of various approaches to its delivery. This article reviews the empirical literature in the field and reports on a conference that was held to initiate a process of evaluation for ethics consultation.

**Fox, Ellen** and Tulsky, James A. Evaluation Research and the Future of Ethics Consultation. *J Clin Ethics*, 7(2), 146-149, Sum 96.

**Fox, Marye Anne**. "Graduate Students: Too Many and Too Narrow?" in *The American University: National Treasure or Endangered Species?*, Ehrenberg, Ronald G (ed), 100-114. Ithaca, Cornell Univ Pr, 1997.

The possibility that current practices in graduate education (in which degrees are awarded within a single department) produce too many graduates who are too highly specialized is evaluated.

**Fox, Richard M**. On Making and Keeping Promises. *J Applied Phil*, 13(2), 199-208, 1996.

Do the conditions under which promises are made determine whether they ought to be kept? Philosophers have placed a number of conditions on promising which, they hold, must be met in order to make promise-keeping obligatory. In so doing, they have distinguished valid promises from invalid promises and justified promises from promises that are not justified. Considering such conditions, one by one, we argue that they are mistaken. In the first place, the conditions they lay down are not necessary for either valid or justified promise-making. In the second place, promises need not meet such conditions in order to create moral obligations. In general, such analyses of promising fail because they suffer from a confusion between promise-making and promise-keeping. Philosophers have wrongly supposed that obligations to keep promises are dependent upon, or derivable from, the quality of the promises themselves, at the time they are made, instead of focusing on conditions that must be satisfied at the time when promises are supposed to be kept. It is not the quality of a promise that determines an obligation to keep it but the rightness or wrongness of performing the promised act.

**Fracanzani, Marcello**. Adolfo Ravà: lo Stato come organismo etico. *Riv Int Filosof Diritto*, 73(4), 613-638, O-D 96.

**Frader, Joel**. Minors and Health Care Decisions: Broadening the Scope. *Bioethics Forum*, 11(4), 13-16, Wint 95.

MBC's document on the health care decision making of minors provides health care professionals with guidelines for helping minors participate in their own decision making. What is needed now is to bring these considerations as presented in the document into health care centers outside the hospital walls where children most often encounter the health care system.

**Frakes, Albert H** and Gibson, Annetta. Truth or Consequences: A Study of Critical Issues and Decision Making in Accounting. *J Bus Ethics*, 16(2), 161-171, F 97.

This study applies a theoretical framework, the theory of reasoned action, to the examination of unethical decision making in job-related situations encountered by CPAs. A survey methodology was employed in which respondents were asked to use both self-reported and randomized response techniques for reporting unethical behavior. The results indicate that individuals are unwilling to accurately report either unethical behavior or intention, particularly in situations where there is no question as to the unacceptability of the action or the potential penalty as presented in the AICPA Code of Professional Conduct. Implications for the accounting profession and research are discussed.

**Francescotti, Robert M**. What Multiple Realizability Does Not Show. *J Mind Behav*, 18(1), 13-27, Wint 97.

It is widely held that psychological theories cannot be reduced to those of the natural sciences. Perhaps the most common reason for rejecting psycho-physical reduction is the belief that mental properties are multiply realizable—i.e., that events of different physical types might realize the same mental property. While the multiple realizability argument has had its share of criticism, its major flaw has been overlooked. I aim to show the real reason why the argument fails and why multiple realizability is compatible with even the strongest varieties of reduction.

**Franchi, Alfredo**. Tra stupore e malinconia: Osservazioni sul pensiero di G. Leopardi. *Sapienza*, 50(1), 65-82, 1997.

**Francione, Gary L**. Comparable Harm and Equal Inherent Value: The Problem of Dog in the Lifeboat. *Between Species*, 11(3-4), 81-89, Sum-Fall 95.

**Francis, John M**. Nature Conservation and the Precautionary Principle. *Environ Values*, 5(3), 257-264, Ag 96.

The application of the precautionary principle to an area of environmental protection, such as nature conservation, requires commitment to the idea that full scientific proof of a causal link between a potentially damaging operation and a long term environmental impact is not required. Adoption of the principle in government statements related to sustainable development should therefore be seen in this context. The paper addresses the particular case of marine fish farming in Scotland where the principle was advocated but not upheld in practice. In the light of this experience there is a need for educators and philosophers, ethicists and concerned scientists to ensure that the principle is more widely interpreted and understood.

**Francis, Richard P**. Natural Law as Essentially Definitive of Human Nature. *Vera Lex*, 14(1-2), 65-88, 1994.

The historical philosophy of Cicero first defines the basis of all natural law. This work includes an outline of human nature as depicted in natural law. Natural law comprises the essentials for human conduct. Human experience depends on

natural law and all of the positive law in the courts assumes natural law as the basis for legal determinations. Most of this depends upon the divine law and the Ten Commandments. "Do good and avoid evil," definitive of all human survival, requires the law of reason. "Happiness" is the goal of believers both here and in the hereafter.

**Franco, Vittoria**. Yvon Quiniou, il materialismo e l'impossibile immoralismo di Nietzsche. *Iride*, 8(15), 457-461, Ag 95.

L'Autore preso in considerazione, noto per gli studi sul materialismo e sul darwinismo, collaboratore a "Actuel Marx", ha recentemente proposto un'originale interpretazione "materialista" di Nietzsche in cui si sottolinea l'"impossibile immoralismo" cui approderebbe il filosofo tedesco. Franco rileva gli aspetti suggestivi di questa tesi, ma anche i rischi di una lettura che finisce per semplificare la rete di interessi, di percorsi e di aporie presenti nell'opera di Nietzsche.

**Franco Barrio, Jaime**. 'Europa' en el pensamiento de Jaspers. *Pensamiento*, 205(53), 89-112, Ja-Ap 97.

La reflexión de Jaspers sobre "Europa", que se desarrolla sobre todo a partir de la II Guerra Mundial y como consecuencia de ésta, va estrechamente unida a su reflexión sobre "Alemania". Jaspers presenta a Europa como una entidad cultural peculiar, fundamentada sobre tres principios básicos: la libertad, la historia y la ciencia; y sostiene que, si en el pasado fue grande por su poderío militar y científico-técnico, en la actualidad se ha hecho pequeña, pues los centros de gravedad se han desplazado hacia América y Asia. Por este motivo, y para hacer frente al amenazador peligro de los totalitarismos nacionalsocialista y comunista, Jaspers, aduciendo razones filosóficas e históricas, defiende la tesis de que la meta primordial a conseguir no es la reunificación alemana, sino el restablecimiento de la libertad en la RDA, la consolidación de la democracia en la RFA, y la unión europea, primer paso hacia la unión mundial.

**Frandsen, Nikolaj**. Understanding Metaphors with the Two Hemispheres of the Brain. *Dan Yrbk Phil*, 31, 49-64, 1996.

PET scans of normal volunteers have shown that understanding of metaphors involves not only the language centers of the left hemisphere, but also certain parts of the right hemisphere and investigations of patients with massive damage to one hemisphere have shown that people tend to make a literal interpretation if the right hemisphere is damaged. This article asks what it is that the right hemisphere adds to the interpretation and the answer—based on investigations of a split-brain patient—is that it is better at taking everything into account, including a whole sentence instead of single words, and at seeing visual similarities in images, regardless of what they depict.

**Frangiotti, Marco Antonio**. Las dos estrategias anti-escépticas de Strawson. *Rev Latin de Filosof*, 23(1), 23-34, O 97.

This article aims at showing that Strawson's earlier and later antisceptical attempts do not hold water. His earlier attempt, that ignited the discussions about the adequacy of transcendental arguments against the sceptic, is unworkable because it does not take into consideration the view of the external world upon which the sceptic is based in order to challenge our knowledge claims. Strawson's later attempt that resorts to a Humean-like naturalistic basis is intractable for three reasons: first, because it reproduces the proof structure of transcendental arguments; second, because it requires us to evaluate the cogency of rational proofs; and third, because it matches the sceptic's advice that we should live according to our natural inclinations in order to reach tranquillity.

**Frank, Garry L** and Cooper, Robert W. Helping Professionals in Business Behave Ethically: Why Business Cannot Abdicate Its Responsibility to the Profession. *J Bus Ethics*, 16(12-13), 1459-1466, S 97.

This paper compares the findings of studies of seven groups of professionals in various key segments of the fields of accounting and insurance conducted during 1990 through 1994 in an effort to determine the extent to which they tend to rely on various factors in their business and professional environments for help in behaving ethically in the course of their work. Commonalities among the findings for these rather diverse groups are highlighted and their possible implications for business and the professions are discussed.

**Frank, Günter**. Zu den Anfängen des Deismus. *Theol Phil*, 72(2), 216-230, 1997.

**Frank, Manfred**. "Alle Wahrheit ist relativ, alles wissen symbolisch". *Rev Int Phil*, 50(197), 403-436, 1996.

**Frank, Manfred**. "Subjectivity and Individuality: Survey of a Problem" in *Figuring the Self: Subject, Absolute, and Others in Classical German Philosophy*, Zöller, Günter (ed), 3-30. Albany, SUNY Pr, 1997.

**Frank, Manfred**. Les fondements philosophiques du premier romantisme allemand. *Rev Int Phil*, 50(197), 379-381, 1996.

**Frank, Manfred**. Wechselgrundsatz: Friedrich Schlegels philosophischer Ausgangspunkt. *Z Phil Forsch*, 50(1/2), 26-50, Ja-Je 96.

**Frank, Manfred** and Gordic, Aleksandar (trans). Psychische Vertrautheit und epistemische Selbstzuschreibung (in Serbo-Croatian). *Theoria (Yugoslavia)*, 39(1), 7-22, Mr 96.

Zwei Argumente für eine Sonderstellung des Selbstbewusstseins im Bereich der epistemischen Tatsachen dominieren in der neueren Literatur: Das erste plädiert für die wesentliche Subjektivität selbstbewusster Zustände; das zweite verteidigt die erkenntnistheoretische, ontologische und semantische Priorität epistemischer Selbstzuschreibungen von Eigenschaften vor allen anderen Formen der Bezugnahme und Zuschreibung. Eine kardinale Entdeckung ist, dass dem Wesen von Selbstbewusstsein weder über die Wahrheit von Aussagen noch in einer Ding-Ereignis-Sprache beizukommen ist.

Selbstbewusstsein ist kein Fall von Wahrnehmung, auch und schon gar nicht einer geheimnisvollen 'Inneren'. 'Ich' ist ontologisch und referentiell ausgezeichnet und es besitzt auch erkenntnistheoretische Priorität. Jede mittelbare Bezugnahme auf anderes ist vermittelt durch unmittelbares Selbstbewusstsein.

**Frankel, Mark S**. Promoting Ethical Standards in Science and Engineering. *Prof Ethics*, 5(1-2), 119-123, Spr-Sum 96.

**Frankish, Keith**. How Should We Revise the Paratactic Theory?. *Analysis*, 56(4), 251-263, O 96.

This paper takes another look at Davidson's *paratactic theory* of indirect discourse and evaluates some revisions to it, proposed recently by Ian Rumfitt (*Mind*, 1993). Davidson's original version of the theory—according to which indirect speech reports refer to token utterances—has a problem dealing with ambiguity. Rumfitt suggests that we can solve this problem by supposing that the immediate objects of verbs in indirect speech are token representations of disambiguated LF tree-structures. I argue that this proposal is inadequate and suggest that it is better to think of indirect speech as relating speakers to *utterance types*.

**Franklin, James**. Stove's Anti-Darwinism. *Philosophy*, 72(279), 133-136, Ja 97.

Stove's attack on Darwinism in his *Darwinian Fairytales* and in his "So You Think You Are a Darwinian?", *Philosophy* 69 (1994) is defended against the reply by Simon Blackburn, "I Rather Think I Am a Darwinian," *Philosophy* 71 (1996). Blackburn asserted that Stove had misrepresented Darwinism, and had used irrelevant philosophical instead of relevant arguments against it. It is replied that Stove's essential claim was that Darwinism is overfitted to the data, and so can "explain" anything by a range of unsavory logical stratagems. The truth or otherwise of this is a matter of logic.

**Franklin, Juliah H**. Allegiance and Jurisdiction in Locke's Doctrine of Tacit Consent. *Polit Theory*, 24(3), 407-422, Ag 96.

Obligation by tacit consent in Locke lasts only during residence within a jurisdiction, whereas allegiance expressly undertaken cannot be unilaterally withdrawn. Only the latter makes the individual a member of the political community. Locke's concern was technical not political. He assumed that the territorial jurisdiction of a government could be established only indirectly through the unretractable allegiance of its founders who submitted their persons and properties to its authority. Unretractable allegiance, however, was not required of those coming after who tacitly acknowledged jurisdiction as a condition of their residence. But this ingenious effort to derive public jurisdiction purely from individual consent was unworkable.

**Franquet, Maria José**. Sobre el hacer humano: la posibilidad factiva. *Anu Filosof*, 29(2), 553-571, 1996.

This article about the thought of Leonardo Polo treats of the notion of factive possibility in the consideration of the anthropological radicals which form Western history: the classical radical, the modern radical and the Christian radical.

**Franquet, Maria José**. Trayectoria intelectual de Leonardo Polo. *Anu Filosof*, 29(2), 303-322, 1996.

**Franzini, Elio**. "Arte, Vita E Verità In Vladimir Jankélévitch" in *Soggetto E Verità: La questione dell'uomo nella filosofia contemporanea*, Fagiuoli, Ettore, 177-186. 20136 Milano, Mimesis, 1996.

**Frápolli, María José**. Evidencia e investigación: La Epistemología filosófica reivindicada. *Rev Filosof (Spain)*, 8(15), 209-217, 1996.

This paper is an introduction to the Spanish readers of Susan Haack's epistemological proposal—Foundherentism—as it appears in her book *Evidence and Inquiry: Towards Reconstruction in Epistemology* (Blackwell, 1993). It is also a defense of it. Frápolli stresses the interest of Haack's proposal and comments on some of its most salient characteristics: the metaphor of the *crossword puzzle*, instead of the metaphor of the pyramid, to represent the role that evidence has for the building of knowledge; the complex character of evidence, which comprises internal and external experiences as much as other beliefs; the role of the subject of knowledge in the process of justifying beliefs, the antirelativism of evidence and justification and the acknowledgment that there still are and there will always be genuine philosophical problems in epistemology, which cannot be dealt with by positive sciences.

**Frápolli, María José** and Nicolás, Juan A. Teorías actuales de la verdad. *Dialogo Filosof*, 13(2), 148-178, My-Ag 97.

Se aborda la delimitación de lo que una teoría de la verdad y la clasificación de las principales teorías elaboradas durante el siglo XX. Una teoría de la verdad ha de incluir al menos cuatro apartados: definición del concepto de verdad determinación del criterio de verdad, distinción de los tipos de verdad y fijación del lugar sistemático de la verdad y de la teoría de la verdad en el marco del saber y de la acción. En segundo lugar, se han clasificado las teorías de la verdad en siete grupos: teoría de la correspondencia (semánticas y no semánticas), teorías prooracionales, teorías fenomenológicas, teorías hermenéuticas, teorías coherenciales, teorías pragmáticas y teorías intersubjetivistas de la verdad.

**Frasca-Spada, Marina** and Jardine, Nick. Splendours and Miseries of the Science Wars. *Stud Hist Phil Sci*, 28(2), 219-235, Je 97.

Paul Gross and Norman Levitt's *Higher Superstition* (Baltimore, MD, 1994) and Alan Sokal's spoof 'Transgressing the Boundaries: Toward a Transformation Hermeneutics of Quantum Gravity' (*Social Text*, special 'Science Wars' double issue, 1996) have sparked off extensive and sharp exchanges concerning the credentials of history, philosophy, and social studies of science. Where others have bewailed these 'Science Wars', in this editorial article we celebrate, from a moderate sceptical and pragmatist standpoint, the dialogue with scientists that

they have provoked and the publicity they have given to issues of outstanding concern for the future of our culture.

**Fraser, Mariam**. Feminism, Foucault and Deleuze. *Theor Cult Soc*, 14(2), 23-37, My 97.

Through an analysis of representations of Simone de Beauvoir and of bisexuality, this article explores what Deleuzian thought might offer feminist theorists of identity. In the light of the discursive production of bisexuality—where bisexuality is produced as an identity which does not cohere in the materiality of the self ascribed to be Beauvoir—the author argues that there is a place in feminist theory for analyses which are concerned with *flows* of forces, as well as with those forces which have already been territorialized. Fraser argues that Deleuze, significantly, enables an understanding of desire which is not ultimately arbitrated by subjectivity.

**Frede, Dorothea**. "How Sceptical were the Academic Sceptics?" in *Scepticism in the History of Philosophy: A Pan-American Dialogue*, Popkin, Richard H (ed), 1-25. Dordrecht, Kluwer, 1996.

The essay does not deal with the questions that normally stand in the foreground of the debate on ancient scepticism, such as the criterion of truth in sense-perception or the sceptic's ability to live without opinions. Instead it focuses on the academic sceptic's treatment of higher-order principles, especially of the laws of logic or mathematics. It appears that the sceptics cannot avoid a 'dogmatic' support of the basic principles of reasoning, as soon as they cannot rely 'parasitically' on their dogmatist opponents' commitment to such principles. Cicero in his *Academica* acknowledges this fact, but denies any cognitive impact since in such cases 'reason merely judges about itself'.

**Frede, Dorothea**. Glück und Glas... Martha Nussbaum über die Zerbrechlichkeit des Guten im menschlichen Leben. *Phil Rundsch*, 44(1), 1-19, Mr 97.

This review article pursues the main question of Martha Nussbaum's three major volumes, *The Fragility of Goodness*, *Love's Knowledge*, and *The Therapy of Desire*: How fragile is goodness and how should humans deal with the problem of moral luck? While it must remain controversial whether moral fragility is as central to the main ethical systems in antiquity as Nussbaum contends, the use she makes of classical literature to demonstrate that morality presupposes a proper emotional balance is a valuable complement to current moral thought and its focus on the conditions of happiness, though the question remains who is to serve as arbitrator of the appropriate schooling of the emotions.

**Freedman, Benjamin**. Where Are the Heroes of Bioethics?. *J Clin Ethics*, 7(4), 297-300, Wint 96.

I argue that heroic acts in bioethics are difficult to identify objectively, but Freedman's examples of losing one's employment over a principled stand is too extreme to be a useful standard. On one analysis, the contextual nature of consultation in clinical settings may render all of bioethics "heroic" in a limited sense. Finally, the goals and processes of bioethics are themselves ill defined and persons with empirical experience of heroic acts by bioethicists have never been asked for their evaluative views, but perhaps should be.

**Freedman, Carol**. The Morality of Huck Finn. *Phil Lit*, 21(1), 102-113, Ap 97.

One of the significant features of Barbara Herman's work is her argument that emotions can play a significant role in a Kantian model of impartial moral judgment. By looking at a passage from *Huckleberry Finn*, however, I show how her description of the moral role of emotions ultimately falls short. She fails to do justice to the way in which emotions can provide us with impartial reasons to act.

**Freedman, Eric G** and Smith, Laurence D. The Role of Data and Theory in Covariation Assessment: Implications for the Theory-Ladenness of Observation. *J Mind Behav*, 17(4), 321-344, Autumn 96.

The issue of the theory-ladenness of observation has long troubled philosophers of science, largely because it seems to threaten the objectivity of science. However, the way in which prior beliefs influence the perception of data is in part an empirical issue that can be investigated by cognitive psychology. This point is illustrated through an experimental analogue of scientific data-interpretation tasks in which subjects judging the covariation between personality variables based their judgments on a) pure data, b) their theoretical intuitions about the variables, or c) both data and prior theoretical beliefs. Results showed that the perceived magnitude of correlations was greatest when subjects relied solely on theoretical intuitions; that data-based judgments were drawn in the direction of those prior beliefs; but that exposure to data nonetheless moderated the strength of the prior theories. In addition, prior beliefs were found to influence judgments only after a brief priming interval, suggesting that subjects needed time to retrieve their theoretical intuitions from memory. These results suggest ways to investigate the processes mediating theory-laden observation, and contrary to the fears of positivist philosophers, imply that the theory-ladenness of observation does not entail that theoretical beliefs are immune to data.

**Freeman, James B**. Premise Acceptability, Deontology, Internalism, Justification. *Inform Log*, 17(2), 270-278, Spr 95.

Is our understanding of acceptability as both normative and definable in terms of presumption of warrant philosophically coherent? We shall argue that it *is* a philosophically coherent notion. Presumption of warrant, unlike warrant, is an internalist notion. Our position can be characterized as an externalist internalism. It avoids the charge brought against externalism of allowing one to be justified in accepting some claim even if one has no evidence for it. We meet the classical internalist challenge that acceptance is normatively proper only if one has done one's epistemic duty and thus one is aware of the normative propriety of the acceptance by providing a nondeontological definition of epistemic justification, and arguing that this is still a sufficiently normative notion for acceptability. (edited)

**Freeman, James B**. Why Classical Foundationalism Cannot Provide a Proper Account of Premise Acceptability. *Inquiry (USA)*, 15(4), 17-26, Sum 96.

**Freeman, Walter J**. Happiness Doesn't Come in Bottles: Neuroscientists Learn That Joy Comes Through Dancing, Not Drugs. *J Consciousness Stud*, 4(1), 67-70, 1997.

**Freire, António**. Florbela Espanca: Tónica da sua Inspiraçao. *Rev Port Filosof*, 52(1-4), 365-380, Ja-D 96.

**Freire Jr, Olival**. Dialectical Materialism and the Quantum Controversy: The Viewpoints of Fock, Langevin, and Taketani. *Nature Soc Thought*, 8(3), 309-325, 1995.

A remarkable similarity can be found among the interpretations of quantum physics by Fock (USSR), Langevin (France), and Taketani (Japan). Dogmatic approaches to Marxist philosophy in the 1950s hampered the development of Marxist thought in quantum physics. Nevertheless, Fock, Langevin and Taketani combated this dogmatism and developed interpretations of quantum physics that were both dialectical and materialist.

**French, Peter**. Rationality and Ethics. *Protosoz*, 8/9, 210-222, 1996.

The "Why be moral?" problem has been one of the more persistent problems of ethics. The problem is typically posed as a conflict between what is straightforwardly maximal for a person to do in specific circumstances and what is recommended by the principles or rules of ethics, usually what is communally optimal, in those circumstances. Typically ethicists try to convince us that both collectively and individually we will be better off in the long run if we each adopt cooperative strategies despite the temptations of immediate profit offered by straightforward maximization policies. The policy of straightforward maximization that I defend is more flexible that one of cooperation. I reap the benefits of cooperation when they are to be had and avoids the disasters of cooperation that lurk in every meeting one has with potentially treacherous strangers. (edited)

**French, Steven** and Krause, Décio. Quantum Objects are Vague Objects. *Sorites*, 21-33, Ag 96.

Is there vagueness in the world? This is the central question that we are concerned with. Focusing on identity statements around which much of the recent debate has centred, we argue that 'vague identity' arises in quantum mechanics in one of two ways. First, quantum particles may be described as individuals, with 'entangled' states understood in terms of nonsupervenient relations. In this case, the vagueness is ontic but exists at the level of these relations which act as a kind of 'veil'. Secondly, the particles can be regarded as nonindividuals, where this is understood as a lack of self-identity and given formal expression in terms of quasi-set theory. Here we have ontic vagueness at perhaps the most basic metaphysical level. Our conclusion is that there is genuine vagueness 'in the world' but how it is understood depends on the metaphysical package adopted.

**Freudiger, Jürg**. Kants Schlussstein: Wie die Teleologie die Einheit der Vernunft stiftet. *Kantstudien*, 87(4), 423-435, 1996.

**Freuler, Léo**. L'explication psychologique de la logique est-elle circulaire?. *Rev Phil Fr*, 2, 161-169, Ap-Je 97.

**Freund, Max A**. A Minimal Logical System for Computable Concepts and Effective Knowability. *Log Anal*, 37(147-8), 339-366, S-D 94.

Formalization of logical features of computable concepts and effective knowability given an interpretation of correlates of computable concepts as Turing machines is the main purpose of this work. A justification of such an interpretation is presented. The relative consistency of the epistemic second order logical system resulting from the formalization and the relative consistency of several extensions of such a system (corresponding to philosophically important views of concept-construction) as well as of those of its applied form to the language of arithmetic are proved. The inconsistency or philosophically invalidity of other important extensions is also shown.

**Freund, Max A**. Semantics for Two Second-Order Logical Systems. *Notre Dame J Form Log*, 37(3), 483-505, Sum 96.

We develop a set-theoretic semantics for Cocchiarella's second-order logical system *RRC**. Such a semantics is a modification of the nonstandard sort of second-order semantics described, firstly, by Simms and later extended by Cocchiarella. We formulate a new second-order logical system and prove its relative consistency. Finally, we prove completeness theorems for proper normal extensions of the two systems with respect to certain notions of validity provided by the semantics. (edited)

**Freund, Michael** and Lehmann, Daniel. Nonmonotonic Reasoning: From Finitary Relations to Infinitary Inference Operations. *Stud Log*, 53(2), 161-201, My 94.

A. Tarski [22] proposed the study of infinitary consequence operations as the central topic of mathematical logic. He considered monotonicity to be a property of all such operations. In this paper, we weaken the monotonicity requirement and consider more general operations, inference operations. These operations describe the nonmonotonic logics both humans and machines seem to be using when inferring defeasible information from incomplete knowledge. We single out a number of interesting families of inference operations. This study of infinitary inference operations is inspired by the results of [12] on nonmonotonic inference relations and relies on some of the definitions found there.

**Frey, Bruno S** and Bohnet, Iris. "Moral oder Eigennutz? Eine experimentelle Analyse" in *Ökonomie und Moral: Beiträge zur Theorie ökonomischer Rationalität*, Lohmann, Karl Reinhard (ed), 135-155. München, Oldenbourg, 1997.

**Frey, R G**. Moral Community and Animal Research in Medicine. *Ethics Behavior*, 7(2), 123-136, 1997.

The invocation of moral rights in moral/social debate today is a recipe for deadlock in our consideration of substantive issues. How we treat animals and humans in part should derive from the value of their lives, which is a function of the quality of their lives, which in turn is a function of the richness of their lives. Consistency in argument requires that humans with a low quality of life should be chosen as experimental subjects over animals with a higher quality of life.

**Frey, R G**. Response: Autonomy, Animals, and Conceptions of the Good. *Between Species*, 12(1-2), 8-14, Wint-Spr 96.

**Freydberg, Bernard**. *The Play of the Platonic Dialogues*. New York, Lang, 1997.

Play resides at the heart of the Platonic dialogues, shaping their insights as well as informing their style. *The Play of the Platonic Dialogues* traces the prominent role of play, both as a general philosophical characteristic and as influencing the treatment of key issues. The nature of the forms, of the city, of virtue, of the soul and its immortality—these and others have been shaped by play. This book shows how Platonic playfulness is joined with the deepest seriousness throughout the dialogues. (publisher)

**Frias, Marcelo F** and Orlowska, Ewa. Equational Reasoning in Non-Classical Logics. *Bull Sec Log*, 26(1), 2-11, Mr 97.

In this paper it is shown that a broad class of propositional logics can be interpreted in an equational logic based on fork algebras. This interpretability enables us to develop a fork-algebraic formalization of these logics and, as a consequence, to simulate nonclassical means of reasoning with equational theories of fork algebras. As examples we showed how to reason equationally in modal, relevant, and dynamic logics.

**Frie, Roger**. *Subjectivity and Intersubjectivity in Modern Philosophy and Psychoanalysis*. Lanham, Rowman & Littlefield, 1997.

In this wide-ranging study of subjectivity and intersubjectivity, Roger Frie develops a critical account of recent conceptions of the subject in philosophy and psychoanalytic theory. Using a line of analysis strongly grounded in the European tradition, Frie examines the complex relationship between the theories of subjectivity, intersubjectivity, language and love in the work of a diverse body of philosophers and psychoanalysts. He provides lucid interpretations of the work of Sartre, Binswanger, Lacan, Habermas, Heidegger, Freud and others. Because it integrates perspectives from continental philosophy, analytical philosophy, and psychoanalytical theory, this book will appeal to a wide audience in the areas of philosophy, the history of philosophy, psychoanalysis and social theory. (publisher)

**Friedman, Jeffrey**. Hayek's Political Philosophy and His Economics. *Crit Rev*, 11(1), 1-10, Wint 97.

**Friedman, Jeffrey**. Nationalism in Theory and Reality. *Crit Rev*, 10(2), 155-167, Spr 96.

**Friedman, Jeffrey** and McCabe, Adam. Preferences or Happiness? Tibor Scitovsky's Psychology of Human Needs. *Crit Rev*, 10(4), 471-480, Fall 96.

Tibor Scitovsky's psychological theory holds that human beings have a natural propensity to pursue comfort—the cessation of need and effort—which, he contends, is in its own way as conducive to unhappiness as pain is. This view, supported by a wealth of empirical data, raises troublesome questions for economics as well as for democratic and liberal theory, since it suggests a dichotomy between people's preferences—as expressed in their purchases, their votes and their exercise of autonomy—and their happiness.

**Friedman, Michael**. "Carnap and Wittgenstein's *Tractatus*" in *Early Analytic Philosophy*, Tait, William W (ed), 19-36. Chicago, Open Court, 1997.

**Friedman, Michael**. "Overcoming Metaphysics: Carnap and Heidegger" in *Origins of Logical Empiricism*, Giere, Ronald N (ed), 45-79. Minneapolis, Univ of Minnesota Pr, 1996.

**Friedman, Michael**. Descartes on the Real Existence of Matter. *Topoi*, 16(2), 153-162, S 97.

**Friedman, Michael**. Exorcising the Philosophical Tradition: Comments on John McDowell's *Mind and World*. *Phil Rev*, 105(4), 427-467, O 96.

**Friedman, Paul J**. An Introduction to Research Ethics. *Sci Eng Ethics*, 2(4), 443-456, O 96.

Practical issues throughout scientific research can be found to have an ethical aspect. There is a gray area in which scientific error ("honest error") may be difficult to distinguish from unacceptably poor research practice or an unethical failure to follow scientific norms. Further, there is no clear margin between deceptive practices which are widely accepted and those which must be considered fraudulent. Practical problems arise in matters of data management and presentation, authorship, publication practices, "grantsmanship," and rights of research trainees, as well as the well-recognized areas of human and animal experimentation. Beyond the gray areas, the legal definition of research misconduct is discussed in relation to research fraud, and the latest proposed definition of the Commission on Research Integrity is briefly reviewed. It is noted that the standards of ethical research are changing. Finally, there is a comment on the idea of institutional integrity in research, and the critical role of the mentor in transmitting research standards to the next generation.

**Friedman, Samuel R** and Gaist, Paul A and Des Jarlais, Don D. Ethical Issues in Research on Preventing HIV Infection among Injecting Drug Users. *Sci Eng Ethics*, 1(2), 133-144, A 95.

The ethical issues in conducting research on preventing HIV infection are among the most complex of any area of human subjects research. This article is an update of a 1987 article that addressed potential conflicts between research design and ethics with respect to AIDS prevention among injecting drug users. The present article reviews current ethical issues that arise in the design and conduct of HIV/AIDS prevention research focused on injecting drug users.

**Frigerio, Aldo**. Astrattezza e concretezza nella filosofia di Giovanni Gentile. *Riv Filosof Neo-Scolas*, 88(3), 457-482, Jl-S 96.

**Frings, Manfred S**. *Max Scheler: A Concise Introduction into the World of a Great Thinker*. Milwaukee, Marquette Univ Pr, 1996.

The book aims at giving a microcosm of Scheler's numerous and complex works. It also aims at giving the English speaking reader easy access to central passages scattered throughout the broad range of Scheler's writings by furnishing extensive references to them. This book is a helpful guide to consulting Scheler's original texts, contained in the *German Collected Edition* (*Gesammelte Werke*), on which it is based and of which the author is editor. (publisher,edited)

**Friquenon, Marie-Louise**. What is a Child?. *Thinking*, 13(1), 12-16, 1997.

Two models of childhood have dominated our understanding of the subject, both of them inadequately: The apprentice model of olden times and the noble savage model of modern vintage. The old model results in rushing children toward premature adulthood, while the newer one overrates the intrinsic features of childhood and consequently retards normal development. These two inadequate models should be replaced by an explicitly developmental understanding of childhood that combines the partial insights of both models, viewing childhood as a process of development toward adulthood through rehearsal of adult roles in addition to the enjoyment of the playful and experimental activities distinctive of protected early life. This understanding supports appreciation of the intrinsically valuable qualities of the normal child, while also encouraging an emphasis on education and increasing acceptance of responsibility.

**Fritsche, Johannes**. Genus and *to ti en einai* Essence in Aristotle and Socrates. *Grad Fac Phil J*, 19/20(2/1), 163-202, 1997.

In contrast to common opinion, the expression *to ti en einai* in Aristotle is by no means awkward. Rather, it is just a formalization of everyday questions about causes of events. Plato's and Aristotle's notions of causality and reality revitalize a mythical and everyday understanding of the respective notions, which has been challenged by the natural philosophers and democrats of the fifth century B.C. Aristotle's notion of *ousia*, substance, is modelled after the thinking in terms of lineage and "good blood" for which he has made the strongest possible case in his dialogue *On Noble Birth*.

**Frogneux, Nathalie**. Hans Jonas développe-t-il une anthropologie arendtienne?. *Rev Phil Louvain*, 94(4), 677-686, N 96.

This paper is a critical review of the French translation of some oddly selected portions of Hans Jonas's *Zwischen Nichts und Ewigkeit*. It challenges the position of translator Sylvie Courtine-Denamy in her introductory essay, according to which Jonas investigates the question of Auschwitz in terms of the philosophy of religion, whereas Hannah Arendt addresses it from the angle of political philosophy. Rather it appears that Jonas seeks to think God as a philosophical concept which lies beyond theoretical knowledge and is independent of the religious faith of a people, but remains consistent with contemporary history and science.

**Frohock, Fred M**. Conceptions of Persons. *Soc Theor Pract*, 23(1), 129-158, Spr 97.

Persons in liberal theory are primary variables, moral agents who are competent and, in complex ways, both rational and reasonable. In recent work John Rawls elaborates a critical conception of the person to support a liberal political domain free of substantial metaphysical foundations. But liberal theory requires two metaphysical conceptions of the person. One is property dualism. The other I label practice dualism. I argue that conceptions of the person cannot be developed without an exploration of metaphysics and that a narrative conception of the self may be more useful in political theory, in particular for an adequate theory of public reason.

**Frost, Bryan-Paul**. An Interpretation of Plutarch's *Cato the Younger*. *Hist Polit Thought*, 18(1), 1-23, Spr 97.

In this essay, I argue that Cato the Younger's life can best be understood if we think through what it means *politically* to be an orphan. I claim that an orphan suffers from a fundamental tension, trying simultaneously to be self-sufficient and loved, and that at least in Cato's case, the only apparent resolution of this tension was the pursuit of a rigid and implacable justice. But while Cato's singular pursuit of justice posed grave threats to potential tyrants like Pompey and Caesar, its very rigidity resulted in what might be called the tyranny of law. After discussing why Cato was ultimately unsuccessful in defeating Caesar and how this failure led to his suicide, I conclude the essay with a comparison of Cato to the Greek statesman Phocion the Good, a comparison which suggests that Cato might have misunderstood the character of politics, prudence, and political philosophy.

**Frost, Bryan-Paul** and Howse, Robert. The Specificity and Autonomy of Right: Alexandre Kojève's Legal Philosophy. *Interpretation*, 24(1), 25-65, Fall 96.

The article is a translation of the third chapter of the first section of Alexandre Kojève's *Esquisse d'une phénoménologie du droit (Outline of a Phenomenology of Right)*. We believe that this chapter raises and addresses fundamental questions in legal and political theory; and even though we do not always agree with Kojève's conclusions, we would argue that his bold and often provocative understanding of right and justice, law and politics and religion and morality merits sustained critical scrutiny today. In this brief introduction, we give a short synopsis of Kojève's career; situate the *Esquisse* in his work as a whole; and

provide a short summary of the chapters preceding the translated passage. (edited)

**Früchtl, Josef**. Vernunftmetaphorik und Rationalitätstheorie. *Phil Rundsch*, 43(3), 193-214, S 96.

The article is a detailed review of six books dealing with the topic of reason in (post) modern times. These books are: W. Welsch, *Vernunft* (Frankfurt/Main: Suhrkamp 1995); P. Gehring, *Innen des Aussen - Aussen des Innen* (München: Fink 1994); G. Gamm, *Flucht aus der Kategorie* (Frankfurt/Main) Suhrkamp 1994); C.O. Schrag, *Philosophical Papers* (New York: State University of New York Press 1994); N. Bolz, *Philosophie nach ihrem Ende* (München: Boer 1992); B. Schmidt, *Postmoderne - Strategien des Vergessens* (Frankfurt/Main: Suhrkamp 1994).

**Fry, Jeffrey P**. Self-Esteem, Moral Luck, and the Meaning of Grace. *Cont Phil*, 18(1), 16-19, Ja-F 96.

In recent years moral philosophers have emphasized the role played by luck and contingencies beyond one's control with respect to one's ability to live an exemplary life. Bernard Williams and Thomas Nagel, in particular, have noted that the role of luck extends to the very constitution of the moral agent, thus playing a formative role in the kind of person that one is. In this paper I will look at self-esteem within the context of so-called "moral luck." Specifically, I will attempt to view self-esteem as a function of the "constitutive luck" of the moral agent and, in doing so, to indicate how self-esteem may be viewed as a kind of virtue or excellence. The line of argument leads me, ultimately, however, to forego the notion of luck and to suggest that a notion of grace may be more appropriate in many cases.

**Fu, Xudong** and Urquhart, Alasdair. Simplified Lower Bounds for Propositional Proofs. *Notre Dame J Form Log*, 37(4), 523-544, Fall 96.

This article presents a simplified proof of the result that bounded depth propositional proofs of the pigeonhole principle are exponentially large. The proof uses the new techniques for proving switching lemmas developed by Razborov and Beame. A similar result is also proved for some examples based on graphs.

**Fuchs, Eric**. Quelle universalité pour l'éthique dans une sociétépluraliste? Une réflexion théologique. *Rev Theol Phil*, 128(4), 357-366, 1996.

Ethics today is confronted by a three-sided challenge: pluralism, which questions its universality; the crisis of modernity—a crisis for reason; and the criticism of postmodernity, which exalts the value of differences. This article attempts to show how theological reflection might usefully help to defend ethical universality.

**Fuenzalida, Hernan** and Figueroa, Patricio R. Bioethics in Ibero-America and the Caribbean. *J Med Phil*, 21(6), 611-627, D 96.

Bioethics has become a field of new challenges for Ibero-America and the Caribbean. A booming uniformity in the region hides a rich heterogeneous society. A brief survey of bioethical developments in different Ibero-American countries is provided as well as the bioethical problems and approaches peculiar to the region. Some of the unique features of bioethics in this region, it is suggested, could infuse new life into the U.S. and European bioethics discussion. Finally, a bibliography of Ibero-American bioethics literature is provided for North American and European readers.

**Fuertes Herreros, José Luis**. Lógica, ciencia y filosofía en Vicente Munoz Delgado (1922-1995). *Rev Espan Filosof Med*, 4, 157-173, 1997.

Our aim is to offer an approach to the work of Vicente Muñoz Delgado. The different stages of the production of his work and thought, as well as the nuclei and keystones on which it is structured.

**Fuhrmann, André** and Mares, Edwin D. On S. *Stud Log*, 53(1), 75-91, F 94.

The sentential logic S extends classical logic by an implication-like connective. The logic was first presented by Chellas as the smallest system modelled by constraining the Stalnaker-Lewis semantics for counterfactual conditionals such that the conditional is effectively evaluated as in the ternary relations semantics for relevant logics. The resulting logic occupies a key position among modal and substructural logics. We prove completeness results and study conditions for proceeding from one family of logics to another.

**Fukunishi, Isao** (& others) and Takahashi, Yoshitomo and Berger, Douglas. Japanese Psychiatrists' Attitudes toward Patients Wishing to Die in the General Hospital: A Cultural Perspective. *Cambridge Quart Healthcare Ethics*, 6(4), 470-479, Fall 97.

**Fukuyoshi, Masao**. Gedanken zur gegenwärtigen Bedeutung der Fichteschen Wirtschaftsethik. *Fichte-Studien*, 13, 221-222, 1997.

**Fulda, Joseph S**. Counterfactuals Revisited. *Sorites*, 35-38, My 96.

This paper presents an ontologically leaner, mathematically cleaner and logically keener explication of counterfactuals and possible worlds than the standard Lewis-Stalnaker account.

**Fulda, Joseph S**. Denied Conditionals Are Not Negated Conditionals. *Sorites*, 44-45, Jl 95.

This note addresses the problems that arise from denying conditionals in classical logic and concludes that such problems result from using propositional logic where predicate logic with quantification over cases is indicated.

**Fulda, Joseph S**. Reasoning with Imperatives Using Classical Logic. *Sorites*, 7-11, N 95.

Traditionally, imperatives have been handled with deontic logics, not the logic of propositions which bear truth values. Yet, an imperative is issued by the speaker to cause (stay) actions which change the state of affairs, which is, in turn, with imperatives using classical logic by constructing a one-to-one correspondence between imperatives and a particular class of declaratives.

**Fuller, Gary** and Adams, Frederick and Stecker, Robert. The Semantics of Fictional Names. *Pac Phil Quart*, 78(2), 128-148, Je 97.

In this paper we defend a direct reference theory of names. We maintain that the meaning of a name is its bearer. In the case of vacuous names, there is no bearer and they have no meaning. We develop a unified theory of names such that one theory applies to names whether they occur within or outside fiction. Hence, we apply our theory to sentences containing names within fiction, sentences about fiction or sentences making comparisons across fictions. We then defend our theory against objections and compare our view to the views of Currie, Walton and others.

**Fuller, Steve**. Social Epistemology and the Recovery of the Normative in the Post-Epistemic Era. *J Mind Behav*, 17(2), 83-98, Spr 96.

What marks ours as the "postepistemic era" is that it refuses to confer any special privilege on knowledge production as a social practice: whatever normative strictures apply to social practices in general, they apply specifically to epistemic practices as well. I trace how we have reached this state by distinguishing two conceptions of normativity in the history of epistemology: a top-down approach epitomized by Kant and Bentham and a bottom-up approach associated with the Scottish Enlightenment. The advantage of the latter is that it clearly distinguishes the emergence of norms from the conditions of their maintenance. I then show how more recent evolutionary epistemology has, in a pejorative way, "naturalized" socially constructed norms of cognitive competence, whereas the logical positivists—long the bane of "progressive" epistemologists—recognized the fully artificial character of epistemic norms and hence qualify as the first social epistemologists.

**Fuller, Steve**. Thomas Kuhn: A Personal Judgement. *Hist Human Sci*, 10(1), 129-131, F 97.

Although Thomas Kuhn supposedly instigated the 'historicist' turn in the history and philosophy of science, he had no sense of his own historical situatedness. He never reflected on why his transition from physics to history of science would have been encouraged by Harvard President James Conant, to whom *The Structure of Scientific Revolutions* is dedicated. Conant was worried about a backlash against science in the post-1945 era. Consequently, he wanted people to see science as an exemplary style of reasoning that remains intact across its obvious changes in size and power. Kuhn's model fit the bill, which explains its popularity far beyond the precincts of his own physical sciences.

**Fullinwider, Robert K**. The Life and Death of Racial Preferences. *Phil Stud*, 85(2-3), 163-180, Mr 97.

**Fultner, Barbara**. The Redemption of Truth: Idealization, Acceptability and Fallibilism in Habermas' Theory of Meaning. *Int J Phil Stud*, 4(2), 233-251, S 96.

Jürgen Habermas has proposed a tripartite classification of analytic philosophy of language into formal semantics, intentionalistic semantics, and use-theories of meaning. Here, I focus on the relationship between formal semantics and Habermas's own account of meaning and truth. I argue against his early 'consensus theory of truth', according to which truth is defined as idealized warranted assertibility and explained by the 'discursive redemption' of validity claims. A claim is discursively redeemed if it commands rationally motivated consensus of all discursive partners. I argue that this is not so much a theory of *truth* as of *justification*. (edited)

**Fumerton, Richard** and Jeske, Diane. Relatives and Relativism. *Phil Stud*, 87(2), 143-157, Ag 97.

Many critics would claim that the most compelling objection to consequentialism is the "special obligations" objection, i.e., the claim that consequentialism is unable to accommodate the special obligations that we have to intimates, obligations that play a central role in commonsense morality. Despite the attention that it has received, we do not think that the implications of the objection regarding special obligations have been appreciated. We argue that one must either abandon consequentialism in favor of a deontological view, or, if one retains consequentialism, adopt a radical, relativistic conception of value.

**Funda, Otakar A**. The Common Europe as a Philosophical Question. *Filosof Cas*, 44(4), 589-603, 1996.

The essay looks at the philosophical aspects of Europe. I) For a long period Christianity was the stable base for European culture but today this is no longer the case. What kind of anthropology does this tradition provide; what are the specific elements in the view of the world, life and man in the Christian tradition: seeing the world, life and man in a dimension of thankfulness, grace and hope. II) There are four marks of the postmodern: the rejection of last questions, plurality as a principle, the greater importance of feelings and experiences than precise critical analysis, and an ahistorical stance. III) Some important philosophical components of the common Europe: Plurality means thinking dialogically. History means tradition, education and culture. It is necessary to fall prey neither to the Scylla of absolute ideas, nor the Charybdis of relativism. An attempt to provide and answer: The constructive role of critical and rational thinking, i.e., thinking is relations appropriate to the reality of world, life and man. The common Europe makes the question of a universal base for an ethic necessary, one which has not been developed anthropocentrically but where ecology and nature are also considered. Life is a positive value and does not need to be based on anything else.

**Funken, Michael**. Die wertlose Natur: Eine Bilanz der Diskussion um eine "Evolutionäre Ethik". *Phil Natur*, 33(1), 119-141, 1996.

**Furnari Luvarà, Giusi**. "'Tempus movet pathos': tratti retorico-poetici del tempo" in *Il Concetto di Tempo: Atti del XXXII Congresso Nazionale della Società Filosofica Italiana*, Casertano, Giovanni (ed), 317-326. Napoli, Loffredo, 1997.

**Fusilier, Marcelline R** and Aby, Carroll D and Worley, Joel K (& others). Perceived Seriousness of Business Ethics Issues. *Bus Prof Ethics J*, 15(1), 67-78, Spr 96.

Respondents from over 900 businesses rated the seriousness of twenty major ethical issues. As representatives for their organizations, they also identified the issues that were most resolved and those that were least resolved. Workplace safety and employee theft had the two highest average ratings of seriousness. The issue most frequently rated as a) least resolved was theft, and b) most resolved was workplace safety. Results are discussed in the context of previous literature.

**Fussi, Alessandra**. Callicles' Examples of *nomos tes phuseos* in Plato's *Gorgias*. *Grad Fac Phil J*, 19(1), 119-149, 1996.

**Fuxman, Leonora**. Ethical Dilemmas of Doing Business in Post-Soviet Ukraine. *J Bus Ethics*, 16(12-13), 1273-1282, S 97.

Based on personal experience, interviews and numerous anecdotal evidence documented in the press, this paper analyzes current practices and focuses on future challenges of business development in Ukraine. In particular, the most recent developments in evolution of business relations and ethics are studied. Business ethics practices are viewed within the current political, economic and social context. A unique combination of three factors: old communist mentality, new "mafia-style" capitalism, and Ukrainian nationalism have created a situation where applying internationally accepted ethical concepts may not lead to success. (edited)

**Gaál, Botond**. Epistemological Congruence between Scientific and Theological Logics in Polanyi's Thinking about Ultimate Reality and Meaning. *Ultim Real Mean*, 20(2 & 3), 205-215, Je-S 97.

When Michael Polanyi drew a parallel between the secular way of thinking and Christian belief, both based on experience, he noticed that there were similarities regarding the search for ultimate reality. This ultimate reality served as the basis for everything and the restricted and yet perceptive mind was directed towards it, pointing beyond itself. So, every intellectual or religious act incorporates an internal, personal pole, which is inherently affected by the existence of reality independent of it. Tillich's philosophy, Cantor's mathematical theory of sets and Torrance's theology helps to understand the correlation of these internal and external poles of knowledge.

**Gaard, Greta**. Ecofeminism and Wilderness. *Environ Ethics*, 19(1), 5-24, Spr 97.

I argue that ecofeminism must be concerned with the preservation and expansion of wilderness on the grounds that wilderness is an *Other* to the *Self* of Western culture and the master identity and that ecofeminism is concerned with the liberation of all subordinated *Others*. I suggest replacing the master identity with an ecofeminist ecological self, an identity defined through interdependence with *Others*, and I argue for the necessity of restoring and valuing human relationships with the *Other* of wilderness as integral to the construction and maintenance of an ecofeminist ecological self. I conclude that ecofeminists must be concerned with the redefinition, preservation, and expansion of wilderness.

**Gaard, Greta**. Toward a Queer Ecofeminism. *Hypatia*, 12(1), 114-137, Wint 97.

Although many ecofeminists acknowledge heterosexism as a problem, a systematic exploration of the potential intersections of ecofeminist and queer theories has yet to be made. By interrogating social constructions of the "natural," the various uses of Christianity as a logic of domination and the rhetoric of colonialism, this essay finds those theoretical intersections and argues for the importance of developing a queer ecofeminism.

**Gabaude, Jean-Marc**. L'oeuvre musicale d'Evanghelos Moutsopoulos. *Rev Phil Fr*, 4, 521-525, O-D 96.

E. Moutsopoulos est à la fois philosophe, compositeur et peintre. Vient de sortir un compact-disc de 27 de ses *Lieder*. Il a pratiqué tous les genres musicaux et tous les style et il a finalement préféré un néo-romantisme. Ses *Lieder* ont une ligne mélodique ample et une écriture transparente quoique dense. L'expérience d'artiste créateur a conduit E. Moutsopoulos à élaborer une importante philosophie de l'art et de la distinguer de l'esthétique. Il a notamment instauré une philosophie de la musique.

**Gabaude, Jean-Marc**. La fidélité de Zénon envers Chypre. *Diotima*, 25, 11-14, 1997.

Zénon resta fidèle à Chypre tout en devenant fidèle à Athènes, mais aussi, grâce à la médiation de l'universalisme hellénisé d'Alexandre, à la Cité qu'est l'Univers, Cité du *Logos*, des dieux et des hommes.

**Gabbay, D M**. Fibred Semantics and the Weaving of Logics Part 1: Modal and Intuitionistic Logics. *J Sym Log*, 61(4), 1057-1120, D 96.

This is Part 1 of a paper on fibred semantics and combination of logics. It aims to present a methodology for combining arbitrary logical systems. The methodology is general and is applied to modal and intuitionistic logics as well as to general algebraic logics. We obtain general results on bulk, in the sense that we develop standard combining techniques and refinements which can be applied to any family of initial logics to obtain further combined logics. The main results of this paper is a construction for combining arbitrary, (possibly not normal) modal or intermediate logics, each complete for a class of (not necessarily frame) Kripke models. We show transfer of recursive axiomatizability, decidability and finite model property.

**Gabbay, Dov** and Finger, Marcelo. Combining Temporal Logic Systems. *Notre Dame J Form Log*, 37(2), 204-232, Spr 96.

This paper investigates modular combinations of temporal logic systems. Four combination methods are described and studied with respect to the transfer of logical properties from the component one-dimensional temporal logics to the resulting combined two-dimensional temporal logic. Three basic logical properties are analyzed, namely soundness, completeness and decidability. The *temporalization method* and the *independent combination method* are shown to transfer all three basic logical properties. The method of *full join* of logic systems generates a considerably more expressive language but fails to transfer completeness and decidability in several cases. So a weaker method of *restricted join* is proposed and shown to transfer all three basic logical properties. (edited)

**Gabbay, Dov** and Kempson, Ruth. Language and Proof Theory. *J Log Lang Info*, 5(3-4), 247-251, O 96.

**Gabbay, Dov** and König, Esther and Dörre, Jochen. Fibred Semantics for Feature-Based Grammar Logic. *J Log Lang Info*, 5(3-4), 387-422, O 96.

This paper gives a simple method for providing categorial brands of feature-based unification grammars with a model-theoretic semantics. The key idea is to apply the paradigm of fibred semantics (or layered logics, see Gabbay, 1990) in order to combine the two components of a feature-based grammar logic. We demonstrate the method for the augmentation of Lambek categorial grammar with Kasper/Rounds-style feature logic. These are combined by replacing (or annotating) atomic formulas of the first logic, i.e., the basic syntactic types, by formulas of the second. Modelling such a combined logic is less trivial than one might expect. The direct application of the fibred semantics method where a combined atomic formula like *np (num:sg & pers:3rd)* denotes those strings which have the indicated property and the categorial operators denote the usual left- and right-residuals of these string sets, does not match the intuitive, unification-based proof theory. Unification implements a global bookkeeping with respect to a proof whereas the direct fibring method restricts its view to the atoms of the grammar logic. The solution is to interpret the (embedded) feature terms as global feature constraints while maintaining the same kind of fibred structures. For this adjusted semantics, the anticipated proof system is sound and complete.

**Gabbey, Alan**. The Pandora's Box Model of the History of Philosophy. *Maritain Stud*, 11, 61-74, 1995.

**Gabellieri, Emmanuel**. De la métaphysique à la phénoménologie: une "relève"?. *Rev Phil Louvain*, 94(4), 625-645, N 96.

The polemic approach of D. Janicaud in his work *Le tournant théologique de la phénoménologie française* should not hide from view the reality of the problem it raises. This is the question whether it is the destiny of phenomenology to return to "things in themselve" or else to aim at an "essence of phenomenality" exclusive of the "phenomena" as such. The undertaking of J.L. Marion and of M. Henry shows the radical nature of and the risks involved in an enterprise that seeks to oppose an absolute phenomenality of life to a philosophy of "the world", or the order of a giving "beyond being" to that of "common phenomena". The question is raised here whether, in its desire to be open to the Absolute without the mediation of world, phenomenology can genuinely take over from metaphysics. Should it not rather display again the phenomenological depth and the metaphysical structure of all concrete phenomena of whatever kind?(Trans. by J. Dudley).

**Gabriel, Gottfried**. "Frege's 'Epistemology in Disguise" in *Frege: Importance and Legacy,* Schirn, Matthias (ed), 330-346. Hawthorne, de Gruyter, 1996.

The following article addresses questions concerning the place of epistemology in Frege's philosophy. It first treats Frege's limiting remarks on the traditional modalities of judgment in the "Conceptual Notation". Using a proof-theoretical interpretation or reconstruction, I argue for the claim that there can be no modal logic for Frege, although modal distinctions still have a legitimate place in his epistemology. A central issue is thus the relationship between the concept of necessity (the apodictic) and the epistemological idea of the a priori. It is shown that Frege does not confine the range of apodictic judgments to the a priori. (edited)

**Gabriel, Gottfried** (ed) and Mendelsohn, Richard L (ed & trans) and Kienzler, Wolfgang (ed). Diary: Written by Professor Dr. Gottlob *Frege in the Time from 10 March to 9. April 1924. Inquiry,* 39(3-4), 303-342, D 96.

**Gadamer, Hans-Georg**. Estética y hermenéutica. *Daimon Rev Filosof,* 12, 5-10, Ja-Je 96.

**Gadamer, Hans-Georg** and Grondin, Jean and Weinsheimer, Joel (trans). *Introduction to Philosophical Hermeneutics.* New Haven, Yale Univ Pr, 1994.

In this wide-ranging historical introduction to philosophical hermeneutics, Jean Grondin discusses the major figures from Philo to Habermas, analyzes conflicts between various interpretive schools and provides a persuasive account and a critical appraisal of Gadamer's *Truth and Method.* (publisher)

**Gaeta, Rodolfo**. Kuhn y la estructura de las evoluciones científicas. *Analisis Filosof*, 16(2), 167-174, N 96.

**Gagarin, Michael**. On the Not-Being of Gorgias's *On Not-Being* (ONB). *Phil Rhet*, 30(1), 38-40, 1997.

This paper was a response to several papers at a conference on translating *ONB.* All translation raises questions about the text being translated, especially *ONB*, for which we have no original text, only two later approximations. Thus, we can only reconstruct *ONB* by adducing its pre-Socratic and Sophistic context. *ONB* differs widely from Gorgias's other works in style and form of argument, but shares with them a light-hearted attitude that constantly threatens to undercut the seriousness and meaning of the text. Translation gives us one means to approach this fascinating puzzle.

**Gagnier, Regenia**. Neoliberalism and the Political Theory of the Market. *Polit Theory,* 25(3), 434-454, Je 97.

The article reviews some representative recent works on the political theory of market societies: polemicists for and against markets in analytic philosophy and Marxism; the more neutral classicists, historians, culturalists, and postmodernists; and the pragmatists in law. Beginning with a brief history of the transition from political economy to neoclassical economics, it argues that the dominance of the latter has resulted in economism, universal commodification, and the potential end of political theory in economic reductionism.

**Gagnon, Cielle**. Obéir aux lois c'est être libre. *Philosopher,* 18, 57-65, 1995.

**Gahlings, Ute**. Hermann Graf Keyserlings "Schule der Weisheit". *Prima Philosophia*, 9(4), 419-433, 1996.

Hermann Graf Keyserling, who is generally numbered among the philosophers of life, developed a particular philosophy of culture and sense. After the first world war he saw Europe in a cultural crisis as a result of overrating the intellect. Through his *School of Wisdom*, which he founded in 1920 in Darmstadt, Keyserling intended a cultural renewal with a new synthesis of mind and soul to integrate knowledge into life. The *School of Wisdom* had several spheres of activity: Keyserling organized big conferences under one general theme which had a great public effect, but he also worked with his disciples in an individual way and offered spiritual exercises. In the twenties the *School of Wisdom* was quite famous. In the thirties, when Keyserling was persecuted by the Nazis, the public activities had to be stopped. Keyserling died in 1946, several weeks before the reopening of the *School of Wisdom* in Innsbruck.

**Gaines, Robert N**. Knowledge and Discourse in Gorgias's *On the Non-Existent or On Nature. Phil Rhet*, 30(1), 1-12, 1997.

Gorgias's *On the Non-Existent* has been understood as providing a theory of communication with the central doctrine that, "If anything is comprehensible, it is incommunicable." Following the anonymous *De Melisso, Xenophane, Gorgia* at 980a19-b19, I interpret Gorgias's main claim as, "But if indeed *things* are knowable, how could anyone make *them* known to another?" This interpretation coheres with Gorgias's subsequent argument, where he insists that representations derived from discourse are not identical to perceptions of external existents. Gorgias does not deny the possibility of communication, he denies the ability to create knowledge in another by means of discourse.

**Gairola, M P**. The Definition of Man Needs. *Darshana Int*, 35(3/139), 71-72, Jl 95.

**Gaist, Paul A** and Des Jarlais, Don D and Friedman, Samuel R. Ethical Issues in Research on Preventing HIV Infection among Injecting Drug Users. *Sci Eng Ethics*, 1(2), 133-144, A 95.

The ethical issues in conducting research on preventing HIV infection are among the most complex of any area of human subjects research. This article is an update of a 1987 article that addressed potential conflicts between research design and ethics with respect to AIDS prevention among injecting drug users. The present article reviews current ethical issues that arise in the design and conduct of HIV/AIDS prevention research focused on injecting drug users.

**Galavotti, Maria Carla**. Probabilism and Beyond. *Erkenntnis*, 45(2 & 3), 253-265, Nov 96.

Richard Jeffrey has labeled his philosophy of probability "radical probabilism" and qualified this position as "Bayesian", "nonfoundational" and "antirationalist". This paper explores the roots of radical probabilism, to be traced back to the work of Frank P. Ramsey and Bruno de Finetti.

**Galcerán Huguet, Montserrat**. Las Agendas de Schelling. *An Seminar Hist Filosof*, 13, 165-180, 1996.

Auf Grund eines Kommentars des Schellings Tagebuchs von 1848, vom Prof. H.J. Sandkühler 1990 publiziert, werden die Aussagen von dem deutschen Philosophen zu der achtundvierzigen Revolution ausgesprochen und die Erarbeitung wichtigsten Stellen seiner Philosophie dargestellt. Endlich folgt eine kurze Darstellung der Interpretation der schellingschen Philosophie vom Prof. Sandkühler.

**Gale, George**. Cosmology for Everyone or How Did the Universe Get So Popular?. *Commun Cog*, 29(2), 169-184, 1996.

**Gale, George** and Shanks, Niall. Methodology and the Birth of Modern Cosmological Inquiry. *Stud Hist Phil Mod Physics*, 27B(3), 279-296, S 96.

The central concern of this paper is with the ways in which issues, questions and debates in the domain of the *philosophy of science* can influence the birth and subsequent development of a science. The case study to be discussed is that of modern cosmology. We will argue that the study of events in the early history of modern cosmology affords ample evidence of the many ways in which philosophy of science and science are inextricably intertwined. (edited)

**Gale, Richard M**. "John Dewey's Naturalization of William James" in *The Cambridge Companion to William James,* Putnam, Ruth Anna (ed), 49-68. New York, Cambridge Univ Pr, 1997.

It is argued that Dewey's passionately eloquent exposition and defense of James's philosophy over a period of fifty-one years, stretching from 1897 to 1948, gave a blatantly distorted self-serving account of James's philosophy, the basic aims of which were to "despookify" and depersonalize it so that it would agree with Dewey's naturalism and socialization of all things distinctively human. Only Dewey's attempt to naturalize James is considered.

**Gale, Richard M**. Disanalogies between Space and Time. *Process Stud*, 25, 72-89, 1996.

It is argued that there are deep-seated conceptual disanalogies between space and time; first, with respect to the axiological commitments of agents; and second, concerning our temporal indexical perspectives being objective in ways in which our spatial indexical perspectives are not.

**Gale, Richard M**. William James's Quest to Have It All. *Trans Peirce Soc*, 32(4), 568-596, Fall 96.

By relativizing all reality claims to a person at a time, James allows us, as our interests and purposes change, successively to assert without inconsistency reality claims from these different perspectives or worlds. This universal thesis of ontological relativism clashes with the absolute, nonrelativized reality claims he makes on the basis of mystical experiences. An attempt is made to resolve this deep aporia in James's philosophy.

**Gale, Richard M**. William James's Theory of Freedom. *Mod Sch*, 74(3), 227-247, Mr 97.

This essay has four parts. The first presents James's theory of freedom. The second gives his reasons why it cannot be decided on epistemic grounds that we are or that we are not free in this sense. The third expounds his reasons for thinking that it is morally desirable to believe that we are free. The fourth presents some objections to his theory of freedom and how James could respond to them.

**Galeotti, Anna Elisabetta**. Contemporary Pluralism and Toleration. *Ratio Juris*, 10(2), 223-235, Je 97.

The author outlines a conception of toleration as recognition of differences which she argues to be more adequate than current liberal views in order to face issues arising from contemporary pluralism. The liberal conception of toleration as freedom from government's interference in certain areas is appropriate if pluralism is conceived of as a plurality of conflicting conceptions of the good. By contrast, if pluralism is understood as the plurality of groups and cultures, asymmetrically situated in democratic society, then the issues underlying toleration are seen as the contested claim of minorities for asserting their different identity in the public space. Public toleration of differences is thus viewed as a symbolic public gesture of inclusion of the different identities and their bearers into democratic citizenship on an equal footing as members of minority groups. The argument supporting public toleration is so founded on reason of justice.

**Galewic, Wlodzimierz**. On Goods Wrongly Used: Axiological Antinomy in Plato's *Euthydemus* (in Polish). *Kwartalnik Filozof*, 25(1), 113-127, 1997.

**Galimidi, José Luis**. Conquista y conciencia en el Leviatán. *Rev Latin de Filosof*, 22(2), 265-280, 1996.

In his *Leviathan*, Hobbes has a twofold attitude towards sovereign policies concerning freedom of conscience and expression. This paper holds that, when following an interpretation that points out the importance of the acquisition paradigm, then it is forced to admit Hobbes's theory as an ideologically repressive case.

**Galindo Hervás, Alfonso**. Matar al padre. *Daimon Rev Filosof*, 12, 137-142, Ja-Je 96.

**Galindo Rodrigo, J A**. Un polifacético de la cultura: José Oroz Reta. *Augustinus*, 42(164-5), 7-11, Ja-Je 97.

**Galison, Peter**. "Constructing Modernism: The Cultural Location of *Aufbau*" in *Origins of Logical Empiricism*, Giere, Ronald N (ed), 17-44. Minneapolis, Univ of Minnesota Pr, 1996.

**Gallagher, David M**. Moral Virtue and Contemplation: A Note on the Unity of Moral Life. *Sapientia*, 51(200), 385-392, 1996.

**Gallagher, Shaun**. "Hegel, Foucault, and Critical Hermeneutics" in *Hegel, History, and Interpretation*, Gallagher, Shaun, 145-166. Albany, SUNY Pr, 1997.

In contrast to the main line of critical theory that runs from Kant through Marx and the Frankfurt School of Habermas, I suggest that an alternative conception of critical theory can be traced from the later Hegel to Foucault. The alternative model is more attuned to the real effects of history and less dependent on idealistic utopianism. Contrary to the denial of certain hermeneutical principles found in a critical theory that champions universality and future orientation, the Hegel-Foucault model can be associated with a Gadamerian view that recognizes the force of the past and the particularity of present circumstances.

**Gallagher, Shaun**. *Hegel, History, and Interpretation*. Albany, SUNY Pr, 1997.

*Hegel, History, and Interpretation* is a collection of essays that extend critical discussions of Hegel into contemporary debates about the nature of interpretation and theories of philosophical hermeneutics. Essays by Susan Armstrong, John D. Caputo, William Desmond, Robert J. Dostal, Shaun Gallagher, Philip T. Grier, H.S. Harris, Walter Lammi, George R. Lucas, Jr., Michael Prosch, Tom Rockmore, and P. Christopher Smith explore difficult issues concerning historical interpretation, the nature of hermeneutics at the end of metaphysics, the social and critical function of reason, and the inadequacy of Hegel's interpretation of the experience of otherness. The contributors explore both the themes that form the common ground between Hegelian philosophy and contemporary interpretation theory *and* the mixed reception of Hegel's philosophy into contemporary discussions about history, deconstruction, critical theory, and alterity. (publisher, edited)

**Gallagher, Shaun**. Mutual Enlightenment: Recent Phenomenology in Cognitive Science. *J Consciousness Stud*, 4(3), 195-214, 1997.

This article provides a critical review of recent work at the intersection of phenomenology and cognitive science. What is and what ought to be the relationship between these two approaches to the study of consciousness? This review explores problems involved with expressing subjective experience in an objective fashion, and issues involved in the use of principles of isomorphism to explain how brain and consciousness are interrelated. It suggests that strict lines cannot be drawn between third-person theory and phenomenological description, that the division of labor between phenomenology and cognitive science is not very strict, and that the best model for understanding the relation between these two approaches is one that emphasizes an externalist viewpoint.

**Gallagher, Shaun**. The Moral Significance of Primitive Self-Consciousness: A Response to Bermúdez. *Ethics*, 107(1), 129-140, O 96.

Bermúdez argues against the thesis that there is no morally significant difference between fetus and neonate and contends that the neonate, but not the fetus, has the capacity for primitive self-consciousness. On his view, a morally significant but primitive self-consciousness has three defining features: 1) A primitive body image; 2) A differentiation between self and other; 3) A recognition that the other is of the same sort as oneself. I argue that a primitive self-consciousness can be defined by features 1) and 2) alone and still be morally significant. The question of whether the late-term fetus could have a primitive self-consciousness is addressed.

**Gallego Vásquez, Frederico**. "Universalismo vs. contextualismo: (Un intento de aproximación desde la pragmática del lenguaje)" in *Liberalismo y Comunitarismo: Derechos Humanos y Democracia*, Monsalve Solórzano, Alfonso (ed), 299-313. 36-46003 València, Alfons el Magnànim, 1996.

**Galli, Carlo**. Oltre l'umanesimo: Alcune considerazioni su tecnica e modernità. *Iride*, 9(19), 687-702, S-D 96.

**Gallichio, Santiago J**. El marxismo analítico. *Rev Latin de Filosof*, 23(1), 55-92, O 97.

This paper is divided into two parts. It begins with a survey on the approach of analytical Marxism concerning the implicit ethics of Marx's thinking, the concept of alienation of labour in capitalism, the labor-value theory, and the Marxist central theory of exploitation. Secondly, it is a proposal of how social relationships, of which economic organization of society is a special case, must be understood. They should be considered as depending on the principle of inequality between human beings. Universalist ethics, for which equality is its inevitable principle, must be constrained to judge whether a person, in accepting other people's goals as his own, comprehends the practical consequences of his acceptance or not, and must consider only the latter case as a case of alienation. (edited)

**Gallie, W B**. Essentially Contested Concepts. *Inquiry (USA)*, 14(1), 3-18, Fall 94.

**Gallier, Jean**. Kripke Models and the (In)equational Logic of the Second-Order Lambda-Calculus. *Annals Pure Applied Log*, 84(3), 257-316, Ap 97.

We define a new class of Kripke structures for the second-order lambda-calculus, and investigate the soundness and completeness of some proof systems for proving inequalities (rewrite rules) as well as equations. The Kripke structures under consideration are equipped with preorders that correspond to an abstract form of reduction, and they are not necessarily extensional.... However, we strive for simplicity, and we only use very elementary categorical concepts. Consequently, we believe that the models described in this paper are more palatable than abstract categorical models which require much more sophisticated machinery (and are not models of rewrite rules anyway). We obtain soundness and completeness theorems that generalize some results of Mitchell and Moggi to the second-order lambda-calculus, and to sets of inequalities (rewrite rules). (edited)

**Gallimore, Ronald** and Clare, Lindsay and Patthey-Chavez, G Genevieve. Using Moral Dilemmas in Children's Literature as a Vehicle for Moral Education and Teaching Reading Comprehension. *J Moral Educ*, 25(3), 325-341, S 96.

Moral development research has previously demonstrated that more extended discourse is a vital element in effective moral education, although the difficulty of implementing this type of discourse into classroom practice has seldom been discussed. In this study, transcripts of lessons were examined of a teacher systematically assisted to develop a more conversational style. These lessons were taped over the course of the school year at different times, beginning in the fall of the year. In addition, writing samples from children who participated in the lessons were subject to content analysis for themes relating to moral questions. Analysis of the lesson transcripts suggests that young students initiate discussion of values-implications of the texts they read if opportunities for connected discourse are increased. Evidence of the impact of more "conversational" discussions was found in the essays written by students in the class of a teacher using a more conversational style but not in the essays of students who were taught using a conventional format.

**Gallo, Michael A** and Sherblom, Stephen A and Bier, Melinda C. Ethical Issues in a Study of Internet Use: Uncertainty, Responsibility, and the Spirit of Research Relationships. *Ethics Behavior*, 6(2), 141-151, 1996.

In this article we explore ethical issues arising in a study of home Internet use by low-income families. We consider questions of our responsibility as educational researchers and discuss the ethical implications of some unanticipated consequences of our study. We illustrate ways in which the principles of research ethics for use of human subjects can be ambiguous and possibly inadequate for anticipating potential harm in educational research. In this exploratory research of personal communication technologies, participants experienced changes that were personal and relational. These unanticipated changes in their way of being complicated our research relationships, testing the boundaries of our commitment to the principle of trustworthiness and forcing us to re-evaluate our responsibilities.

**Gallop, David** (trans). *Defence of Socrates Euthyphro Crito*. New York, Oxford Univ Pr, 1997.

**Galloway, Brian**. The Buddhist Conditional in Set-Theoretic Terms. *J Indian Phil*, 24(6), 649-658, D 96.

**Galonnier, Alain**. Self-Complaceny and Self-Probation in the Argument of St. Anselme's *Proslogion* (in French). *Arch Phil*, 59(4), 531-553, O-D 96.

The present study endeavours to establish a new access to the famous *argumentum* of Anselm's *Proslogion*, by stressing the relationship of the structure existing between the connection from unity to trinity as it is perceived in God, and the one from unicity to triplicity as it is expressed by the argument, viz.

unicity in the very elaboration of the statement, which founds its self-sufficiency (its sole being is enough to attain to the proof), and triplicity in its working, which fixes its self-probacy (it proves by activating its proper contents). It then displays how, at the close of this trinitarian dialectic, the thinking creature tests the referring of its interiority to the divine transcendency, which appears at the absolute beginning of the process and through the very experience of its inaccessibility.

**Galston, William A**. "Causes of Declining Well-Being Among U.S. Children" in *Sex, Preference, and Family: Essays on Law and Nature,* Nussbaum, Martha C (ed), 290-305. New York, Oxford Univ Pr, 1997.

**Gama, José**. Hermenêutica da Cultura e Ontologia em Paul Ricoeur. *Rev Port Filosof,* 52(1-4), 381-392, Ja-D 96.

**Gamberg, Herb**. Another View on the Crisis in Marxism. *Nature Soc Thought,* 7(1), 7-18, 1994.

A figure often maligned and neglected in contemporary Marxism is undoubtedly Lenin. It is argued here that this neglect lies at the heart of the crisis in Marxism. The major contribution of Lenin's ideas—their deepening of the activist, antipositivist side of Marxism—is often denied in a plethora of supposedly new syntheses and formulations that recapitulate old errors. What is needed today is a deepening analysis of the dissolution of revolutionary society in *Leninist* terms. Without this analysis, the crisis has little hope of resolution.

**Gammon, Martin**. Dynamic Resemblance: Hegel's Early Theory of Ethical Equality. *Rev Metaph,* 50(2), 315-349, D 96.

**Gampel, Eric**. A Method for Teaching Ethics. *Teach Phil,* 19(4), 371-383, D 96.

This paper explains a five-step procedure that can be used to structure discussions and student work in ethics courses. The procedure begins with creative problem solving and then requires charting the arguments on each side of an issue, diagnosing why people might disagree and justifying one's assessment of the relative merits of the arguments. I recommend the procedure as providing a useful framework for the whirlwind of ethical argument: it is quickly mastered, is appreciated by students and helps students to see the value of more abstract philosophical reflection.

**Gampel, Eric H**. The Normativity of Meaning. *Phil Stud,* 86(3), 221-242, Je 97.

The normative dimension of meaning has been cited by Kripke, Davidson and others in prominent arguments about the nature of language and mind. But these authors have said surprisingly little about the kind of 'normativity' on which their arguments depend. In this paper I develop a precise thesis about the normative character of linguistic meaning. I go on to defend that thesis as both plausible and of philosophical consequence, in that it defines a general constraint on a theory of meaning which many naturalistic theories are unlikely to meet, including most dispositionalist, functionalist and evolutionary accounts.

**Gamwell, Franklin**. Metaphysics and the Rationalization of Society. *Process Stud,* 23(3-4), 219-237, Fall Wint 94.

Alfred North Whitehead outlined a theory of societal rationalization that is summarily similar to the comprehensive project of Jürgen Habermas. But Habermas holds that a critical theory of modern society must be postmetaphysical, and Whitehead insists that it requires the metaphysical backing his later works developed. This paper argues that Habermas's project and, especially, his democratic theory is incoherent in a respect that Whitehead's insistence on metaphysics can be said to predict and suggests that, on Whitehead's account, the rationalization of society requires the rationalization of religion.

**Gamwell, Franklin I**. Habermas and Apel on Communicative Ethics: Their Difference and the Difference It Makes. *Phil Soc Crit,* 23(2), 21-45, Mr 97.

Habermas and Apel commonly defend a form of universal moral theory that is also postmetaphysical. Still, they differ with respect to both the character and the justification of a universal moral principle. Habermas denies and Apel asserts that this principle is a transcendental condition of life practice or human activity as such, and each criticizes the claims of the other. This paper argues that each is correct in his criticism of the other and, therefore, both are wrong. The contention between them cannot be resolved within the postmetaphysical conviction they have in common, and the reasons for this conclusion imply that a universal moral principle cannot be redeemed independently of metaphysics.

**Gandy, Matthew**. "Ecology, Modernity, and the Intellectual Legacy of the Frankfurt School" in *Philosophy and Geography I: Space, Place, and Environmental Ethics,* Light, Andrew (ed), 231-254. Lanham, Rowman & Littlefield, 1997.

This paper argues that ecological problems can best be resolved by an extension of communicative rationality in order to transform relations between society and nature. The attempt to separate ethics and epistemology may lead to specious appeals to nature-based political ideologies. If we reexamine the main tension within environmental ethics between anthropocentric and biocentric conceptions of relations with nature we find that critical theory opens up the possibility of an environmental ethic which remains rooted in social practice yet which enables a critical perspective on technocratic attitudes towards nature through the critique of positivism, scientism and instrumental reason.

**Ganeri, Jonardon** and Noordhoof, Paul and Ramachandran, Murali. Counterfactuals and Preemptive Causation. *Analysis,* 56(4), 219-225, O 96.

**Ganesh, Anke**. Interview with Professor Peter O. Bodunrin. *Quest,* 9(2), 198-210, D 96.

During the process of formation of the postcolonial African philosophy Professor Peter O. Bodunrin became well-known as one of the most distinguished critics

of the so-called ethno-philosophy. He argued against the reconstruction of African philosophy out of folkphilosophy and traditional thinking. Oriented on an Occidental understanding of philosophy he defines philosophy as critical, systematic and analytic reflective thinking and rejects the existence of an African logic or epistemology. Therefore, his opponents accused him to be Westernized and to have lost his African identity. Bodunrin stood during the debate on "What is African philosophy?", which dominated the last 20 years of African philosophy, on the side of famous philosophers like Kwasi Wiredu, Paulin Hountondji and Henry Odera Oruka. (edited)

**Ganho, Maria de Lourdes S**. Mal e Intersubjectividade em Gabriel Marcel. *Rev Port Filosof,* 52(1-4), 393-405, Ja-D 96.

**Ganss Gibson, Kathleen** and Massey, Joe B. "Ethical Considerations in the Multiplication of Human Embryos" in *Reproduction, Technology, and Rights: Biomedical Ethics Reviews,* Humber, James M (ed), 55-71. Clifton, Humana Pr, 1996.

**Ganssle, Gregory E**. The Development of Augustine's View of the Freedom of the Will (386-397). *Mod Sch,* 74(1), 1-18, N 96.

Augustine's view of the freedom of the will underwent significant development during the *first decade* after his conversion to Christianity (386-397). His position developed in three stages. Before his ordination, he held that it is possible for an individual to turn to God or to refuse to turn regardless of divine intervention. During this period, Augustine was an incompatibilist. After his ordination and before his episcopacy, Augustine recognized to a much greater degree the struggle in the human will. During his early years as bishop, Augustine held that it is impossible for an individual to turn to God without divine intervention and it is impossible to refuse to turn, if such intervention is granted. At this point, Augustine adopted a compatibilist position.

**Garaventa, Roberto**. "Noia ed esperienza del tempo" in *Il Concetto di Tempo: Atti del XXXII Congresso Nazionale della Società Filosofica Italiana,* Casertano, Giovanni (ed), 327-338. Napoli, Loffredo, 1997.

**Garay, Carlos Alberto**. "Plasticidad neuronal, verdad y lógica" in *Verdad: lógica, representación y mundo,* Villegas Forero, L, 55-64. Santiago de Compostela, Univ Santiago Comp, 1996.

First, I will show what has to do with a theory of (human) truth in a kind of naturalized epistemology: in a word, it plays a central role defining epistemic value. Truth is what is worthy from the epistemic point of view. Later, a little examination of the main theories of truth (correspondence, coherence, deflationary, semantic and pragmatic) and of what kind of logical problems they attempted to solve. At the end, we will see the inadequacy of a naturalized truth to deal with most of those problems so we must reject the problems or the naturalized truth. (edited)

**Garcia, Jorge L A**. "Intentions in Medical Ethics" in *Human Lives: Critical Essays on Consequentialist Bioethics,* Oderberg, David S (ed), 161-181. New York, Macmillan, 1997.

First, it is argued that there is a genuine psychological difference between intention and foresight. Secondly, it is shown to matter morally whether an agent, including a health-care worker, acted intentionally or merely with knowledge that a result would follow from her action. Thirdly, it is argued that we can have reasonable beliefs about whether an agent acted intentionally. Recent criticisms by Helga Kuhse of the intention/foresight distinction are replied to. Critics who deny its moral relevance are shown to beg the question. Finally, it is shown that intentions are real and profound mental phenomena which fit centrally into a life of planning and execution of projects.

**Garcia, Jorge L A**. Current Conceptions of Racism: A Critical Examination of Some Recent Social Philosophy. *J Soc Phil,* 28(2), 5-42, Fall 97.

**García, Antonio Jiménez**. *El Krausopositivismo de Urbano González Serrano.* Badajoz, Disputación Prov, 1996.

**García Berger, Mario**. La concepción wittgensteiniana de los objetos en el *Tractatus. Analogia,* 11(1), 187-196, Ja-Je 97.

**García de la Mora, José Manuel**. Francisco Suárez: interpretaciones y críticas. *Convivium,* 9, 23-37, 1996.

**García Encinas, María José**. "Ontología causal: ¿sucesos o hechos?" in *Verdad: lógica, representación y mundo,* Villegas Forero, L, 389-399. Santiago de Compostela, Univ Santiago Comp, 1996.

In this paper I am considering the *relata* of causal relations. From the fundamental difference that they make in the logic of causal relations, *events* and *facts* are the main candidates for such a role. While events are usually accepted in this sense, facts are not so easily admitted. Facts and events are both proper causal *relata,* but anyway there seems to be some practical reasons for preferring facts as the best candidates in this old dispute. (edited)

**García Fallas, Jackeline**. Paradigmas: ¿construcciones históricas?. *Rev Filosof (Costa Rica),* 34(83-84), 455-464, D 96.

This paper deals with the concept of paradigm in Kuhn's *The Structure of Scientific Revolutions.* The use of this concept, in the social sciences, is limited to the conformation of epistemological, ontological, heuristical and axiological premises. From this point of view, the historical construction of paradigms is not clear, since it points out their meaning as model or tool, which is the basis of the research and the praxis. Thus, the historical construction of paradigms is analyzed focusing on the legitimation processes of knowledge. These processes define the construction and hegemony of paradigms in relation to their socio-historical contexts.

**García González, Juan A**. Sobre el ser y la creación. *Anu Filosof,* 29(2), 587-614, 1996.

This paper deals with Leonardo Polo's philosophy about the subject of *creation.* The "abandonment of mental limit" permits us to be aware of the real distinction *essentia-esse* (essence-being). That is important in order to think over universe and human being as created.

**García Jaramillo, Miguel Alejandro**. Sensibilidad y espiritualidad según Aristóteles. *Topicos*, 51-76, 1996.

According to Aristotle, the human intellect can be considered as a middle point between material processes and divine nature. This approach requires some review on his theory of sensibility allowing a better understanding of his doctrine of intellect.

**García Landa, José Angel** (ed) and D'Arcy, Chantal Cornut-G (ed). *Gender, I-deology Essays on Theory, Fiction and Film*. Amsterdam, Rodopi, 1996.

The essays in this collection address a variety of topics under the general heading of "gender issues"—gender and writing, reading, and representation, sexual options and roles, generic models and stereotypes, sexual ambivalence, or the politics of gender. All the essays examine in one way or another the role of gender and sexuality in fictional texts. The emphasis throughout is on the interface of gender and modernity, as seen through a variety of British and American literary works and films. Most of the contributions assume a feminist perspective on the issues discussed, each adopting a specific critical approach to its subject. (edited)

**García Leal, José**. El desinterés en la actitud estética. *Dialogo Filosof*, 12(3), 409-420, S-D 96.

This paper deals with the problem of whether there exists an attitude which is specifically aesthetic and with the role that is in it, provided its existence, may play disinterestedness. The discussion is set in the wider context of analysis on the experience we have of works of art. I have tried to show the historical background and also I make some comments on the opposite views defended by J. Stolnitz and G. Dickie. My conclusion is that disinterestedness is an essential component of aesthetic attention. (edited)

**García Leal, Laura**. On Motivation of Judicial Decisions (in Spanish). *Fronesis*, 3(1), 31-48, Ap 96.

Judicial decision must be a motivated one. This motivation can be understood as the justification of the decision, that is to say, a logical justification *sensu largo*, which embraces not only the field of the formal logic but also that of the practical reasonings that implies rules and values belonging to the theory of argumentation. The motivation of the judicial decision understood as a justification, must imply the necessary arguments in order to defend it as just and according to law, beyond its legal basis or the explanation of the decision through psychological or sociological phenomena.

**García Marqués, Alfonso**. Europa y la Teleología de la razón en Edmund Husserl. *Daimon Rev Filosof*, 10, 145-151, Ja-Je 95.

Husserl's concern about vital topics is the answer to the crisis of the Western civilization, which shows itself in the crisis of both science and rational conceptions. Husserl looks for a solution, clarifying the nature of reason and its place as regards to praxis. All this becomes definite, on the one hand, in the criticism of illustrated rationalism and, on the other hand, in the research into the origin of science and philosophy in the Greek world. This origin is the birth of Europe for it supposes the path from a mythical, subjective and particular view of the world to the philosophic conception, that is to say, to the search for an objective truth, based on criticism and as a result, valid for all thinking beings. In this way, humanity—both collectively and individually—reached in Europe its own entelechy, its own human level and became conscious of both its rationality and the rational orientation of work. (edited)

**García Marzá, V Domingo**. "República y Democrácia en la Paz Perpetua: Un comentario desde la Teoría Democrática" in *Kant: La paz perpetua, doscientos años después*, Martínez Guzmán, Vicent (ed), 83-100. Valencia, Nau Llibres, 1997.

**García Morente, Manuel**. La filosofía en España. *Rev Filosof (Spain)*, 8(15), 3-15, 1996.

**García Moriyón, Félix**. La filosofía y su historia. *Dialogo Filosof*, 13(1), 4-32, Ja-Ap.

Por otra parte, se han enriquecido considerablemente los estudios históricos y han ido apareciendo nuevas temáticas como pueden ser la historia de las mentalidades o la historia intelectual, que aportan análisis e información relevantes para la historia de la filosofía clásica. Los nuevos planteamientos en historia del arte o en historia de la ciencia han tenido igualmente un impacto significativo en la historia de la filosofía. Por último, desde la propia historia de la filosofía se ha producido una importante renovación en la manera de enfocar los autores y los problemas, ofreciendo en algunos casos, como la historia de la ideas, planteamientos globales y coherentes alternativos a las clásicas doxografías. Es intención de este artículo ofrecer una visión general de todas esas nuevas aportaciones y enfoques. (edited)

**García Suárez, Alfonso**. De Locke a Grice: los entresijos de la filosofía del lenguaje. *Teorema*, 16(2), 87-95, 1997.

**García Viúdez, Marcos**. Aportaciones de Leonardo Polo para una teoría antropológica del aprendizaje. *Anu Filosof*, 29(2), 627-649, 1996.

Leonardo Polo's transcendental anthropology is based on the absolute distinction between the man's act of being and the universe's act of being; according to it, therefore, we can talk about a new approach dealing with an anthropological theory about learning able to solve the typical paradoxes about the relationship between free learning and human development, inherent in psychological theories and at the same time able to show the ethical dimension always present in learning.

**García y García, Antonio**. The Spanish School of the Sixteenth and Seventeenth Centuries: A Precursor of the Theory of Human Rights. *Ratio Juris*, 10(1), 25-35, Mr 97.

In this paper the author examines certain ideas of the Spanish School of the sixteenth and seventeenth centuries which directly inspired the School of Hugo Grotius in the seventeenth, thus opening the way towards possible declarations of human rights such as that of the United Nations. The line of thought which extends from Francisco de Vitoria (1492/93-1546) to Francisco Suárez (1548-1617) is given the name of the "Spanish natural law and law of nation's School."

**García-Baró, Miguel**. Introducción a la teoría de la verdad de Michel Henry. *Dialogo Filosof*, 13(2), 189-202, My-Ag 97.

Michel Henry, uno de los representantes del Nuevo Pensamiento, que comienza convirtiendo a todo el hombre en pura pregunta que atraviesa las capas endurecidas de la verdad tradicional, está convencido de que la riqueza de la tradición occidental es tan grande que cree que lo esencial de lo que él descubre como lo impensado en Europa se le ha destacado gracias, en buena parte, a la labor magisterial de las figuras más célebres de la propia filosofía europea. Y esto sucede, sobre todo, con Maine de Biran y Descartes. Lo que pretende defender Henry es que la luz del mundo mismo es el verdadero soporte del videre (ver) cuando el hombre se entrega enteramente en sus manos y puensa como si nada más hubiera que su relación al mundo.

**García-Bellido, Antonio**. "Progress in Biological Evolution" in *The Idea of Progress*, McLaughlin, Peter (ed), 175-200. Hawthorne, de Gruyter, 1997.

The observable world contains a variety of microscopic and macroscopic entities that structurally can be ordered in organizational levels. These are discontinuous and capable of performing level specific operations. In this increase of *complexity* higher levels seem to result from subsets of lower nodes. Is in this sense that molecules derive from atoms and these from elementary particles. In the interface between molecules and living cells, particular forms, macromolecules, have taken the role of providing specificity for a multiplicity of chemical interactions. The wealth of the variation is thus the result of a large, but finite, number of combinatorial interactions. The organization level of multicellular organisms is constraint by the finitness of interacting motifs (DNA, RNA sequences and protein) and the inertia to change partners in their interactions. Mutation, giving rise to new associations of these motifs, provides for variation. (edited)

**García-Carpintero, Manuel**. "Doubts about Fregean Reference" in *Contents*, Villanueva, Enrique (ed), 104-112. Atascadero, Ridgeview, 1995.

**García-Carpintero, Manuel**. Putnam's Dewey Lectures. *Theoria (Spain)*, 12(29), 213-223, My 97.

This paper points out several difficulties to understand Putnam's views in his recent "Dewey Lectures", which involve a certain move away from his "internal realism". The main goal is to set into relief tensions in Putnam's thinking probably provoked by his philosophical development. Two such tensions are touched upon. In the first place, Putnam wants to reject an account of phenomenal consciousness (sensory experience in particular) he had subscribed to during his realist times, which he calls "Cartesianism cum Materialism", CM. He puts forward what he takes to be an alternative, apparently based on the traditional Chisholmian "Theory of Appearing". The paper suggest firstly that, in view of the facts to be accounted for, a theory along those lines cannot count as a real alternative to CM. In the second part, the paper develops an analogous tension between the views on truth Putnam seems to be willing to defend in the Dewey Lectures and previous criticisms of the semantic conception of truth by him that he claims still to be willing to subscribe.

**García-Carpintero, Manuel**. Superveniencia y determinación del contenido amplio. *Rev Filosof (Spain)*, 9(16), 57-92, 1996.

**García-Carpintero, Manuel**. Two Spurious Varieties of Compositionality. *Mind Mach*, 6(2), 159-172, My 96.

The paper examines an alleged distinction claimed to exist by Van Gelder between two different, but equally acceptable ways of accounting for the systematicity of cognitive output (two "varieties of compositionality"): "concatenative compositionality" vs. "functional compositionality." The second is supposed to provide an explanation alternative to the Language of Thought Hypothesis. I contend that, if the definition of "concatenative compositionality" is taken in a different way from the official one given by Van Gelder (but one suggested by some of his formulations) then there is indeed a different sort of compositionality; however, the second variety is not an alternative to the language of thought in that case. On the other hand, if the concept of concatenative compositionality is taken in a different way, along the lines of Van Gelder's explicit definition, then there is no reason to think that there is an alternative way of explaining systematicity.

**García-Murga, Fernando**. Indexicals and Descriptions. *Sorites*, 46-56, Jl 95.

Reference is a common feature to indexicals, definite descriptions and, at least some uses of indefinite descriptions. A referential expression triggers a search for a referent, which ranges over the linguistic context, physical environment or encyclopedic knowledge. I argue for a unified theory of reference within which indexicals and definite descriptions refer to salient objects while indefinite descriptions refer to nonsalient objects. The descriptive content attached to each expression provides information making it possible for the addressee to find an object the speaker has referred to. Ostension and other nonlinguistic knowledge helps the addressee's search. Salience, rather than mutual knowledge or givenness, is the crucial aspect the speaker considers when he performs a referential act. Unlike indefinite descriptions, indexicals and definite descriptions presuppose the referent's existence. However, current theories of presupposition-projection maintain inheritance mechanisms which are shown to be inadequate from our present approach.

**García-Valdecasas, Miguel**. La plenitud de identidad real. *Anu Filosof*, 29(2), 615-625, 1996.

The purpose of this paper is to study Leonardo Polo's conception of the *principle of identity*. This identity is also called *origin*; however, an adequate understanding of that expression requires a careful study of the way man comes to be aware of it.

**García-Valdecasas, Miguel** and Pía Tarazona, Salvador. Relación de obras publicadas e inéditos de Leonardo Polo. *Anu Filosof*, 29(2), 323-331, 1996.

**Gardiner, Michael**. Foucault, Ethics and Dialogue. *Hist Human Sci*, 9(3), 27-46, Ag 96.

Although much has been made of the recent "ethical turn" in postmodernist thought, it is argued here that such claims have been more gestural than real. This assertion is substantiated through an examination of the late writings on sexuality and ethics by Michel Foucault. It is claimed that in Foucault's writings, the concrete Other is subordinated to a project of self-actualization that is essentially Nietzschean in inspiration. As such, postmodernism, as exemplified by the work of Foucault, effectively preludes intersubjective recognition and understanding and negates the acceptance of responsibility in and through dialogue. In developing this critique, reference is made to the dialogical thought of the Russian social philosopher Mikhail Bakhtin, which is held to constitute a much more promising alternative to postmodernism vis-à-vis the development of a viable intersubjective ethics.

**Gardiner, Patrick**. "Interpretation in History: Collingwood and Historical Understanding" in *Verstehen and Humane Understanding*, O'Hear, Anthony (ed), 109-119. New York, Cambridge Univ Pr, 1996.

**Gardner, Peter** and Johnson, Steve. Thinking Critically About Critical Thinking: An Unskilled Inquiry into Quinn and McPeck. *J Phil Educ*, 30(3), 441-456, N 96.

Victor Quinn advocates teaching critical thinking as a curriculum subject. He has accused Professor John E. McPeck, a vehement critic of such proposals, not only of being wrong but also of being in need of such a critical thinking course himself. In this paper we examine the five supposed critical thinking weaknesses of which McPeck is accused and consider what Quinn's arguments tell us about critical thinking, its skills, its priorities and its claims to subject status.

**Gardner, William**. The Enforcement of Professional Ethics by Scientific Societies. *Prof Ethics*, 5(1-2), 125-138, Spr-Sum 96.

**Garibaldi, U** and Costantini, D. Predicative Laws of Association in Statistics and Physics. *Erkenntnis*, 45(2 & 3), 399-422, Nov 96.

In the present paper we face the problem of estimating cell probabilities in the case of a two-dimensional contingency table from a predictive point of view. The solution is given by a double stochastic process. The first subprocess, the unobservable one, is supposed to be exchangeable and invariant. For the second subprocess, the observable one, we suppose it is independent conditional on the first one.

**Garin, Eugenio**. A proposito di centenari cartesiani. *G Crit Filosof Ital*, 16(3), 495-499, S-D 96.

**Garin, Eugenio**. La filosofia della storia di Giovanni Gentile. *G Crit Filosof Ital*, 16(2), 174-179, My-Ag 96.

**Garin, Eugenio**. Per una storia dei cartesiani in Italia: Avvertenza. *G Crit Filosof Ital*, 16(3), 307-311, S-D 96.

**Garrett, Don**. *Cognition and Commitment in Hume's Philosophy*. New York, Oxford Univ Pr, 1997.

There exists alongside the celebration of Hume's work for its philosophical brilliance and elegance of style considerable disagreement over the meaning of Hume's most famous doctrines, the precise nature of his philosophical greatness and the value of his contributions for contemporary philosophy. A series of interpretive difficulties has led some to accuse the work of contradiction and disunity. In this vigorous new study, Don Garrett takes up the charges against Hume, demonstrates their weakness and solves a number of well-known interpretive puzzles that have long stood in the way of a complete understanding and accurate assessment of Hume's philosophy. (publisher, edited)

**Garrett, Stephen A**. Political Leadership and the Problem of "Dirty Hands". *Ethics Int Affairs*, 8, 159-175, 1994.

**Garrido Garrido, Julián**. Nota sobre los conceptos de verdad en una interpretación y verdad como correspondencia. *Analisis Filosof*, 16(2), 189-193, N 96.

The concept "truth under an interpretation" simply expresses the formal structure of truth assignations in any type of statement. In the particular case of empirical statements, interpretations consist of sets of material objects whose extent can only be determined by criteria of correspondence with facts. Such correspondence thus constitutes a substantive, nonformal aspect of empirical truth outside the model theory. The existence of other types of truth (logical, by definition, mathematical) also structured by the idea of "truth under an interpretation", but outside the notion of correspondence with facts, reinforces the existence of a line of demarcation between these two categories.

**Garrido Maturano, Angel Enrique**. El libre albedrío entre la omnipotencia y el amor Divino: Problemática ética y consecuencias tecnológicas de la cuestión del libre alberdrío en Hobbes y San Agustín. *Cuad Etica*, 17-18, 111-129, 1994.

This paper makes a comparative analysis of the theological and ethical consequences of Augustinian arguments in favour of freedom as *liberum arbitrium* of the will and the Hobbesian reasons for a strict causal determinism, which results from predestination. After this, a compatibility is sketched between the concepts of omnipotence and omniscience on the one hand and of free will on the other. This compatibility is different from St. Augustine's and while rejecting predestination, it centers on the notions of renunciation and divine love.

**Garrido Maturano, Angel Enrique**. Lo santo y lo sagrado. *Rev Filosof (Mexico)*, 29(87), 390-408, S-D 96.

**Garrido Maturano, Angel Enrique**. Los límites éticos del "ser-en-el-mundo". *Stromata*, 52(1-2), 153-171, Ja-Je 96.

**Garson, James W**. Cognition Poised at the Edge of Chaos: A Complex Alternative to a Symbolic Mind. *Phil Psych*, 9(3), 301-322, S 96.

This paper explores a line of argument against the classical paradigm in cognitive science that is based upon properties of nonlinear dynamical systems, especially in their chaotic and near-chaotic behavior. Systems of this kind are capable of generating information—rich macro behavior that could be useful to cognition. I argue that a brain operating at the edge of chaos could generate high-complexity cognition in this way. If this hypothesis is correct, then the symbolic processing methodology in cognitive science faces serious obstacles. A symbolic description of the mind will be extremely difficult and even if it is achieved to some approximation, there will still be reasons for rejecting the hypothesis that the brain is in fact a symbolic processor.

**Garson, James W**. Syntax in a Dynamic Brain. *Synthese*, 110(3), 343-355, Mr 97.

Proponents of the language of thought (LOT) thesis are realists when it comes to syntactically structured representations and must defend their view against instrumentalists, who would claim that syntactic structures may be useful in *describing* cognition, but have no more causal powers in governing cognition than do the equations of physics in guiding the planets. This paper explores what it will take to provide an argument for LOT that can defend its conclusion from instrumentalism. I illustrate a difficulty in this project by discussing arguments for LOT put forward by Horgan and Tienson. When their evidence is viewed in the light of results in connectionist research, it is hard to see how a realist conception of syntax can be formulated and defended.

**Garte, Seymour J**. Guidelines for Training in the Ethical Conduct of Scientific Research. *Sci Eng Ethics*, 1(1), 59-70, J 95.

Historically, scientists in training have learned the rules of ethical conduct by the example of their advisors and other senior scientists and by practice. This paper is intended to serve as a guide for the beginning scientist to some fundamental principles of scientific research ethics. The paper focuses less on issues of outright dishonesty or fraud, and more on the positive aspects of ethical scientific behavior; in other words, what a scientist should do to maintain a high level of ethical conduct in research. (edited)

**Garver, Eugene**. After *Virtù*: Rhetoric, Prudence and Moral Pluralism in Machiavelli. *Hist Polit Thought*, 17(2), 195-222, Sum 96.

The appearance of Machiavelli's *Prince* and his *Discourses on Livy* is a fundamental event in the history of prudence and the development of pluralism. Machiavelli is a pluralist who does not take the steps, which seem natural and inevitable to us, from pluralism on to liberalism, tolerance, and democracy. He thinks that moderation, so often associated with pluralism and liberalism, is a recipe for disaster. I explore the competitive sides of pluralism and prudence by treating one example of Machiavelli's strategies that allows him to teach prudence without becoming a moderate or a liberal. The imitation of necessity in the *Discourses on Livy* creates a new way of extending the domain of prudence.

**Garver, Newton**. "Philosophy as Grammar" in *The Cambridge Companion to Wittgenstein*, Sluga, Hans (ed), 139-170. Needham Heights, Cambridge, 1996.

Wittgenstein first thought philosophy consists of logic and metaphysics, with logic its basis; he later remarks that grammar tells what kind of object anything is (distinguishing sensations from emotions as well as from material objects). Thus grammar replaces logic as the touchstone of philosophical thought. This essay presents the later view as a generalization of the earlier one; sketches the connection between linguistics and philosophical grammar; reviews the limits this perspective places on philosophy; and argues that the contrast of the certainty (perspicuity) of grammatical propositions with the doubtability-plus-verifiability of scientific propositions fulfills Kant's call for critical philosophy.

**Garver, Newton**. Politics, Politics, Politics. *Int Stud Phil*, 29(1), 19-33, 1997.

Three very different things present themselves under the title "politics." Clarity about their differences can enhance both our understanding of public affairs and the quality of public discourse. One is "zero-sum politics," the partisan activity that begins with the distinction between friends and enemies and culminates in wars or elections. Another is "integrative politics," legislation, administration, and diplomacy that make use of conciliatory negotiation with adversaries. The third, "antipolitics," is civic action aimed at limiting or circumventing the role of the first two. To distinguish the three sorts of activity by sketching their salient differences is the aim of this paper.

**Garver, Newton**. Pugnacity and Pacifism. *Acorn*, 6(2), 7-19, Fall 91.

Pugnacity and pacifism—here understood as opposing propensities toward antagonists: intractable opposition and decisive victory vs. conciliation, negotiation and win-win solutions—have a curious position, with pugnacious behavior admired by those who decry pugnacity and violence and skillful conciliation admired by those who decry pacifism. The paper reviews prominent characteristics of the opposing dispositions, as well as their motivational structures and their respective risks and rewards.

**Garvey, James**. What does McGinn Think we cannot Know?. *Analysis*, 57(3), 196-201, Jl 97.

What is McGinn saying when he claims that we cannot solve the mind-body problem? His text suggests four possibilities and each is given consideration. In the end, there are two principal conclusions. First, by McGinn's understanding of the mind-body problem, he needs to show that we are cognitively closed to how brains generate consciousness, but he argues for something else, that we are cognitively closed to a certain brain property. Second, McGinn is not entitled to the conclusion that we cannot solve the mind-body problem, given any of the four interpretations of what is cognitively closed to us.

**Garzón Valdés, Ernesto**. Some Remarks on the Concept of Toleration. *Ratio Juris*, 10(2), 127-138, Je 97.

The paper contains a conceptual analysis of "act of toleration" and the property of "being tolerant." Being tolerant is understood as a dispositional property of persons manifested in what the author calls the "circumstances of toleration." The main circumstances distinguished are: a tendency to prohibit a certain behavior and the competence to determine the deontic status of the behavior in question. An act of toleration, then, consists in not prohibiting (or cancelling the prohibition of) that behavior. It is argued that this requires the existence of two different normative systems, the "basic system," and the "justifying system."(edited)

**Gasché, Rodolphe**. "Alongside the Horizon" in *On Jean-Luc Nancy: The Sense of Philosophy*, Sheppard, Darren (ed), 140-156. New York, Routledge, 1997.

**Gasché, Rodolphe**. Canonizing Measures. *Grad Fac Phil J*, 19/20(2/1), 203-214, 1997.

**Gaskin, Richard**. Fregean Sense and Russellian Propositions. *Phil Stud*, 86(2), 131-154, My 97.

In Frege's writings the notion of sense plays both a semantic and an epistemological role. In spite of some neo-Fregean enthusiasts, these affiliations cannot be harmonized. For most semantic purposes, we do not need a notion of sense which cuts as finely as is required to solve the epistemological puzzles which Frege discussed. Where we do need to assign a semantic role to sense, this will be registered in an ambiguity between *de re* and *de expressione* contexts introduced by the propositional 'that'.

**Gaskin, Richard**. Kein Etwas, aber auch nicht ein Nichts!: Kann die Grammatik tatsächlich täuschen?. *Grazer Phil Stud*, 51, 85-104, 1996.

Es werden zwei von Wittgenstein entworfene Modelle der Semantik eines Wortes dargelegt und miteinander verglichen: das sog. Muster von, Gegenstand und Bezeichnung' und das Gebrauchsmodell. Im Gegensatz zu der formalistischen Position wird gezeigt, dass das Modell von, Gegenstand und Bezeichnung' für die Semantik unentbehrlich ist. Selbst das Gebrauchsmodell, so unumstritten dieses auch sein mag, vermag das Modell von, Gegenstand und Bezeichunung' nicht abzulösen. Das dargestellte metaphysische Bild wird veranschaulicht, indem einige Bemerkungen Wittgensteins zur Semantik der Empfindungswörter widerlegt werden.

**Gaskins, Robert W**. The Transformation of Things: A Reanalysis of Chuang Tzus Butterfly Dream. *J Chin Phil*, 24(1), 107-122, Mr 97.

Chuang Chou's Butterfly Dream is perhaps the most well-known and widely studied passage in the *Chuang Tzu*. It is also one of the most slippery with regard to its meaning. In this paper, I have proposed that the meaning of this passage can be clarified when the passage is recognized as an embodiment of Chuang Tzu's main theme and the double-bind method of instruction which is found throughout the second chapter of the Chuang Tzu. Understood as such, the passage stands as the quintessential example of this theme and teaching style, pressing the reader to transcend the limits of dualistic thinking and awaken in the fullest sense of the word. (edited)

**Gatens, Moira**. Sex, Gender, Sexuality: Can Ethologists Practice Genealogy?. *S J Phil*, 34(Supp), 1-19, 1996.

This paper argues that the sex/gender distinction has outlived its usefulness. Deleuze's notion of "ethology" offers a more fruitful way of theorizing differences between people because it does not privilege sexual difference over racial, class, or other differences. "Ethology" does not assume that identities are fixed but rather supports a politics of becoming. The paper concludes by suggesting that an ethological approach to political analysis must practice genealogy. Such a practice, in turn, requires a different conception of time than Chronos. Time conceived as Kairos highlights the importance of the art of timing in politics.

**Gates, Eugene**. Damned if You Do and Damned if You Don't: Sexual Aesthetics and the Music of Dame Ethel Smyth. *J Aes Educ*, 31(1), 63-71, Spr 97.

During the last two decades of the nineteenth century, for the first time ever, significant numbers of women entered the traditionally male field of art-music composition. The increasing visibility of women composers was greeted by critics with hostility and alarm. Based on the Rousseauian notion of sexual complementary, they developed the double standard of sexual aesthetics—a system of gendered criteria for the critical evaluation of women's music. This article examines the critical response to the music of Dame Ethel Smyth, and in a brief postscript, the legacy of sexual aesthetics as it exists today.

**Gatto, Romano**. Il cartesianesimo matematico a Napoli. *G Crit Filosof Ital*. 16(3), 360-379, S-D 96.

**Gauker, Christopher**. A New Skeptical Solution. *Acta Analytica*, 113-129, 1995.

Kripke's puzzle about rule-following is a form of the traditional problem of the nature of linguistic meaning. A skeptical solution explains not what meaning is but the role that talk of meaning plays in the linguistic community. Contrary to what some have claimed, the skeptical approach is not self-refuting. However, Kripke's own skeptical solution is inadequate. He has not adequately explained the conditions under which we are justified in attributing meanings or the utility of the practice of attributing meanings. An alternative skeptical solution may be founded on a nonepistemic conception of assertibility. Roughly, a sentence is assertible if it facilitates cooperation. The function of meaning-talk is to resolve certain sorts of conflicts in assertion. Attributions of meaning to persons outside

the community may be a proper expression of a practice whose reason for being lies entirely within the community.

**Gauker, Christopher**. Domain of Discourse. *Mind*, 106(421), 3-32, Ja 97.

The proposition expressed by an utterance of a quantified sentence depends on a domain of discourse somehow determined by the context. How does the context of utterance determine the content of the domain of discourse? Many philosophers would approach this question from the point of view of an *expressive theory of linguistic communication*, according to which the primary function of language is to enable speakers to convey the propositional contents of their thoughts to hearers. This paper argues that from this point of view there is no persuasive treatment of the determinants of the domain of discourse. The argument focuses on an abnormal case in which the domain the speaker has in mind is not evident to the hearer. In this way the question concerning the determinants of the domain of discourse is used to challenge the expressive theory of communication.

**Gauker, Christopher**. Universal Instantiation: A Study of the Role of Context in Logic. *Erkenntnis*, 46(2), 185-214, Mr 97.

The rule of universal instantiation appears to be subject to counterexamples, although the rule of existential generalization is not subject to the same doubts. This paper is a survey of ways of responding to this problem, both conservative and revisionist. The conclusion drawn is that logical validity should be defined in terms of *assertibility in a context* rather than in terms of truth on an interpretation. Contexts are here defined, not in terms of the attitudes of the interlocutors, but in terms of the goals of conversation and assertibility is explained in terms of cooperation.

**Gaull, Marilyn**. From the Cave of Urizen: An Editor Observed. *J Infor Ethics*, 6(1), 59-68, Spr 97.

I was invited to discuss some ethical issues involved in editing "The Wordsworth Circle", a quarterly learned journal devoted to the study of British Romanticism which I founded in 1970. Using a personal history, I described the problems that I encountered as a woman during these transitional years, editing a journal in an academic setting. My particular concern is the appropriation of scholarly publishing for personnel decisions, the exploitation of our peer-review system especially, the terrible and inappropriate burden that has been placed on learned journals and the displacement of our functions as "invisible universities."

**Gaus, Gerald**. Does Democracy Reveal the Voice of the People? Four Takes on Rousseau. *Austl J Phil*, 75(2), 141-162, Je 97.

**Gaut, Berys**. Analytic Philosophy of Film: History, Issues, Prospects. *Phil Books*, 38(3), 145-156, Jl 97.

This paper is a survey of analytic philosophy of film. It provides a brief history of the field, showing how it has been shaped by the pre-existing discipline of film theory. Six issues are then examined in more depth: the question of whether film is in some sense a realist medium; the role of imagination in film viewing; the phenomenology of cinematic space and time; whether there is a language of film; whether films can have a single author; and whether spectators make the meanings of films. The paper concludes with some suggestions about how the philosophy of film might fruitfully develop.

**Gaut, Berys**. Metaphor and the Understanding of Art. *Proc Aris Soc*, 97, 223-241, 1997.

This paper examines the significance of the fact that the descriptions of art works of art by critics are metaphorically laden. It argues that this fact can be adequately accommodated neither by a perceptualist account of metaphorically-ascribed properties (such as Sibley's or Beardsley's), which holds that such properties are simply and literally perceived, nor by an affective theory (such as Scruton's) which holds that such properties are only imagined to be possessed by art works. Instead, a two-level theory of aesthetic experience is defended, based on a distinction between two senses of "seeing-as"; the theory holds that both imagination and perception play an ineliminable role in our understanding of metaphorically-ascribed aesthetic properties. The two-level theory rejects both straightforward realism and straightforward irrealism about such properties.

**Gauthier, Candace Cummins**. Teaching the Virtues: Justifications and Recommendations. *Cambridge Quart Healthcare Ethics*, 6(3), 339-346, Sum 97.

A virtue-based approach to moral decision making in health care delivery is shown to combine the most distinctive features of the ethics of care, casuistry, and narrative ethics. Aristotle and Kant are used to argue that the practical wisdom or practical reason necessary for the exercise of the virtues can be taught. Recommendations are made for the use of medical narrative, modeling, and role playing for the development and exercise of the virtues associated with the delivery of health care and the therapeutic relationship.

**Gauthier, David**. "Making Jean-Jacques" in *Jean-Jacques Rousseau and the Sources of the Self*, O'Hagan, Timothy (ed), 1-15. Brookfield, Avebury, 1997.

**Gauthier, David**. Resolute Choice and Rational Deliberation: A Critique and a Defense. *Nous*, 31(1), 1-25, Mr 97.

I discuss rational deliberation given changing evaluations of outcomes arising from preference shifts, or from perspectival shifts that bring different preferences into play. I use the framework of E.F. McClennen, who has identified four intuitively appealing conditions on deliberation over time, shown that preference shifts make it impossible to satisfy all four, and distinguished three possible consistent modes of choice each satisfying three conditions. I focus on the mode of resolute choice, which subordinates posterior choices to prior choices. I have defended a similar subordination, not primarily for changing

Gauthier, Jeffrey A 642 AUTHOR INDEX

intrapersonal evaluations of outcomes, but for interpersonal cooperation in prisoner's dilemma-like contexts. I now think that McClennen's discussion of the feasibility of resolute choice mistakenly assimilates the intrapersonal to the interpersonal problem. I defend an account of the feasibility of resolute choice that is quite different from the account of rationally feasible planning or intending appropriate to contexts of interpersonal cooperation.

**Gauthier, Jeffrey A**. *Hegel and Feminist Social Criticism: Justice, Recognition, and the Feminine.* Albany, SUNY Pr, 1997.

This book draws mutually enlightening parallels between controversial themes in contemporary feminist thought and Hegel's political philosophy. Jeffrey A. Gauthier argues that feminism can gainfully employ Hegel's historicizing of Kant's ethics of universality, as well as his socializing of Kant's conception of autonomy, in defense of a number of controversial feminist claims. (publisher, edited)

**Gautschi, Theodore** and DiBattista, Ron A and Luthar, Harsh K. Perception of What the Ethical Climate Is and What It Should Be: The Role of Gender, Academic Status, and Ethical Education. *J Bus Ethics*, 16(2), 205-217, F 97.

This study examined ethical attitudes and perceptions of 691 undergraduate seniors and freshmen in a college of business. Gender was found to be correlated to perceptions of "what the ethical climate should be" with female subjects showing significantly more favorable attitude towards ethical behaviors than males. Further, seniors had a more cynical view of the current ethical climate than freshmen. Freshmen were significantly more likely than seniors to believe that good business ethics is positively related to successful business outcomes. Ethical education was significantly correlated to both perceptions of "current ethical climate" as well as "what the ethical climate should be". Students who had been exposed to ethical issues in a course were more likely to believe both, that ethical behavior is, and should be, positively associated with successful business outcomes.

**Gava, Giacomo**. *Cervello-Mente: Pensatori del XX secolo.* Trieste, Editre Edizioni, 1994.

Questo libro presenta le principali dottrine del XX secolo sul problema cervello-mente che si sono sviluppate soprattutto a partire dal mondo anglosassone. Nell'illustrare il pensiero di alcuni tra gli esponenti più rappresentativi, filosofi e neurofisiologi, l'Autore avanza anche alcune tra le più rilevanti critiche sollevate nei loro confronti. Per i suoi contenuti, questo libro si rivolge ad ogni genere di persone interessante al problema ed alle principali ricerche compiute in tale campo. (publisher)

**Gava, Giacomo**. *Il Riduzionismo della Scienza.* Milano, Guerini, 1996.

La questione della validità del riduzionismo, come prospettiva teorica e fondamento della ricerca scientifica, può essere a ragione considerata il punto centrale del dibattito interno agli scienziati e ai filosofi della scienza. Per fare qualche esempio, le leggi della chimica sono riducibili a pure conseguenze delle leggi della fisica? E la psicologia è riducibile nei termini delle neuroscienze? Dalla posizione assunta rispetto a questo importante nodo teorico derivano conseguenze altrettanto importanti non solo nel campo della ricerca pura, ma anche nei differenti ambiti delle scienze umane. Scopo di questo volume è passare in rassegna le concezioni degli autori che, a livello internazionale, hanno riscosso—per l'originalità e la forza delle loro posizioni—i maggiori consensi e critiche, e che continuano a svolgere un ruolo predominante nella discussione, tuttora accesa, su questo tema. La trattazione delle diverse teorie viene svolta all'interno dei rispettivi sistemi epistemologici, sede naturale della loro genesi e portata argomentativa. (publisher, edited)

**Gava, Giacomo**. *Il Riduzionismo della Scienza.* Milano, Guerini, 1996.

The essential purpose of the work is to pave the way for a reductive view of science. In the first six chapters the author summarizes the main conceptions of reductionism and antireductionism put forward by the following thinkers and placed within their respective epistemologies: Hempel C.G., Nagel E., Quine W.V.O., Schaffner K.F., Sklar L., Causey R.L. and Wimsatt W.C. In the last chapter he presents an oversimplified and hierarchical schema of the structural and linguistic levels and of their corresponding scientific disciplines along with their complex relationships. After a criticism of emergentism, holism and the theories of complexity and after having set that every science always looks for more exhaustive theories in order to find the laws of composition and of interaction among the components, the author states that science is guided by three regulative principles: mathematical logic, reductionism and the token identity theory, which is part of reductionism. The book ends with a quite comprehensive bibliography on the above-mentioned authors and topics.

**Gava, Giacomo**. *Scienza e filosofia della coscienza.* Milan, Angeli, 1991.

After a general introduction in which structural and linguistic levels and scientific methods and criteria are touched on, the book presents the thought of some neuroscientists and their predecessors, scholars of animal behavior, experts on artificial intelligence, psychologists and philosophers who have dealt with the problem of consciousness exhaustively. In the conclusion it is shown how a lot of uses of the term "consciousness" are misleading. In order to avoid confusion it is suggested to abolish the word and to substitute it, at all linguistic levels, with more precise expressions. In this way the identity theory, which has a leading role in neuroscience, is laid open to more controls and falsification. Examples of recent research are given to demonstrate that human brain works with different categories from those used in ordinary language. The essay ends with an exhaustive bibliography on the subject-matter.

**Gava, Giacomo** (ed). *Un'Introduzione All'Epistemologia Contemporanea.* Padova, Cleup Ed Padova, 1996.

This is an anthology which provides a concise and clear introduction to contemporary epistemology. The main purpose of the work is to present synthetically, yet exhaustively, the following epistemologies with a relative literature: inductivism, pragmatism, conventionalism, essentialism, instrumentalism, operationism, empiric criticism, neopositivism, fallibilism, post-Popperian epistemology, materialistic rationalism, genetic epistemology, evolutionary epistemology and naturalized epistemology. The book, which includes a general editor's introduction, is accessible to undergraduate students, but also to graduate students and professionals who want a comprehensive survey of the field.

**Gavito, Diana** and Velázquez, Héctor. El hombre como sistema libre, en el pensamiento de Leonardo Polo. *Anu Filosof*, 29(2), 651-663, 1996.

The only valid consideration of human being is what takes the person in his complexity. Human being is an *open system* in his relation with the medium. But, attending his rationality (deepest and most radical dimension), human being is *free system*. So, he is able to assert oneself ends according values.

**Gavriushin, Nikolai K**. The Cosmic Route to "Eternal Bliss": (K.E. Tsiolkovskii and the Mythology of Technocracy). *Russian Stud Phil*, 34(1), 36-47, Sum 95.

**Gavroglu, Kostas**. Philosophical Issues in the History of Chemistry. *Synthese*, 111(3), 283-304, Je 97.

**Gawlina, Manfred**. Zur Aufgabe transzendentaler Interpretation. *Phil Rundsch*, 44(1), 52-63, Mr 97.

**Gawronski, Alfred**. Truth and Logic of Text: An Outline of the Metatext Theory of Truth (in Polish). *Kwartalnik Filozof*, 24(4), 9-47, 1996.

**Gay, William C**. Bourdieu and the Social Conditions of Wittgensteinian Language Games. *Int J Applied Phil*, 11(1), 15-21, Sum-Fall 96.

I use Pierre Bourdieu's sociology to extend Wittgenstein's treatment of language games. Given the social conditions regulating language use, I contend: analysis of language games should not be separated from awareness of social classes and the relative social positions of speakers. Arguing that speaking is inseparable from societal distribution of power, I discuss the symbolic violence of legitimate discourse. Next, I address the linguistic role of educational systems in legitimating inequality. Finally, I treat heretical subversion of legitimate discourse and obstacles which usually neutralize it. I conclude with suggestions for reducing linguistic violence by changing words and rules of language games.

**Gazzard, Ann**. Philosophy for Children and the Discipline of Philosophy. *Thinking*, 12(4), 9-16, 1996.

The purpose of the work is to assess the philosophy for children program in terms of the extent to which it does justice to the discipline of philosophy. To achieve this end, it was necessary to consider that we mean by the term 'philosophy'. Three categories of philosophy are described under which the majority of conceptions of it can be subsumed. The characteristics of each are given and the philosophy for children program is then measured against them. It was concluded that philosophy for children preserves the integrity of the discipline very well.

**Geahigan, George**. Conceptualizing Art Criticism for Effective Practice. *J Aes Educ*, 30(3), 23-42, Fall 96.

During the past three decades, prescriptions for art criticism have been a prominent part of the art education literature. In formulating models of criticism for the schools, educators have traditionally relied upon accounts of criticism in the philosophical literature. This article argues that in doing so, they have conflated two senses of art criticism: critical inquiry (investigations into the meaning and value of works of art) and critical discourse (talk or writing about works of art). The article shows how this confusion occurred and draws out the implications for classroom instruction. It argues that for educational purposes, art criticism is best construed as a form of inquiry rather than as a structured form of classroom discourse.

**Gebhard, George**. "Scientific Discovery, Induction, and the Multi-Level Character" in *Knowledge and Inquiry: Essays on Jaakko Hintikka's Epistemology and Philosophy of Science,* Sintonen, Matti (ed), 261-285. Amsterdam, Rodopi, 1997.

The object of this investigation is the nature of experimental inquiry and its logic, seen from the point of view of Hintikka's interrogative model of inquiry. In this framework scientific inquiry is best seen as a multilevel process in which small operational questions are used to deliver answers to big research questions. (edited)

**Gebhard, Ulrich** and Nevers, Patricia and Billmann-Mahecha, Elfriede. Patterns of Reasoning Exhibited by Children and Adolescents in Response to Moral Dilemmas Involving Plants, Animals and Ecosystems. *J Moral Educ*, 26(2), 169-186, Je 97.

Traditional moral philosophy, developmental psychology and moral education have generally been concerned with relationships between human beings. However, moral philosophy has gradually expanded to include plants, animals and ecosystems as legitimate moral objects and aesthetics has rediscovered nature as an object of consideration. Thus it seems appropriate to begin to include this sphere in moral education and corresponding research as well. In this paper we wish to report on an investigation we have begun using children's philosophy as a hermeneutic tool to assess the morally relevant values and attitudes that children and adolescents hold with respect to nature and the patterns of reasoning with which they are expressed. In the first part of our presentation we will outline current positions in environmental ethics and aesthetics which provide a theoretical framework for such an investigation and the problems they present. Subsequently, the difficulties involved with applying contemporary theories of moral development to the problem at hand will be discussed. Finally, we will describe the project we have begun and summarize preliminary results derived from different age groups.

**AUTHOR INDEX** 643 **Gensler, Harry J**

**Gehring, Verna V**. Tedium Vitae: Or, My Life as a 'Net Serf'. *Ratio*, 10(2), 124-140, S 97.

Boredom, like pain, is a subjective experience, but while the sources of pain can be either internal or external to the subject, the causes of boredom are always external. Understanding boredom as a reaction to external influences requires inquiries into the subjective awareness of boredom and into the social and cultural conditions giving rise to boredom. After briefly investigating these areas, I suggest that in the past boredom was seen as a necessary ingredient to creative inspiration and self-understanding and as a contributor to autonomy in judgment and taste. I argue for a new form of boredom seen only with recent advances in information technology. I conclude with the suggestion that the boredom that accompanies involvement in information technology produces a self-identity crafted by technological intervention and fashion, yields the false autonomy of a manipulated consumer and invites superficial social relations. (edited)

**Geiger, Scott W** and Robertson, Chris and Street, Marc D. Ethical Decision Making: The Effects of Escalating Commitment. *J Bus Ethics*, 16(11), 1153-1161, Ag 97.

In this paper a new variable is introduced into the ethical decision making literature. This variable, exposure to escalation situations, is posited to increase the likelihood that individuals will choose unethical decision alternatives. Further, it is proposed that escalation situations should be included as a variable in Jones's (1991) comprehensive model of ethical decision making. Finally, research propositions are provided based on the relationship between escalating commitment and the ethical decision making process.

**Geller, Gail**. Hope and the Limits of Research: Commentary. *Hastings Center Rep*, 26(5), 21-22, S-O 96.

**Geller, Gail** and Strauss, Misha and Bernhardt, Barbara A (& others). "Decoding" Informed Consent: Insights from Women regarding Breast Cancer Susceptibility Testing. *Hastings Center Rep*, 27(2), 28-33, Mr-Ap 97.

Cancer susceptibility testing is likely to become routine in medical practice, despite many limitations and unanswered questions. These uncertainties greatly complicate the process of informed consent, creating an excellent opportunity to reconsider exactly how it should be conducted.

**Geller, Lisa N** and Alper, Joseph S and Billings, Paul R (& others). Individual, Family, and Societal Dimensions of Genetic Discrimination: A Case Study Analysis. *Sci Eng Ethics*, 2(1), 71-88, J 96.

As the development and use of genetic tests have increased, so have concerns regarding the uses of genetic information. Genetic discrimination, the differential treatment of individuals based on real or perceived differences in their genomes, is a recently described form of discrimination. The range and significance of experiences associated with this form of discrimination are not yet well-known and are investigated in this study. Individuals at-risk to develop a genetic condition and parents of children with specific genetic conditions were surveyed by questionnaire for reports of genetic discrimination. A total of 27,790 questionnaires were sent out by mail. Of 917 responses received, 206 were followed up with telephone interviews. The responses were analyzed regarding circumstances of the alleged discrimination, the institutions involved, issues relating to the redress of grievances and strategies to avoid discrimination. (edited)

**Geller, Lisa N** and Beckwith, Jonathan R. Commentary on "The Social Responsibilities of Biological Scientists". *Sci Eng Ethics*, 3(2), 145-148, Ap 97.

This paper outlines some recent examples of social responsibility of biologists. These range from actions taken to halt the development of biological warfare weapons to criticisms of genetic arguments that support racial discrimination. It contrasts these examples with the general reluctance of most biologists to involve themselves in dealing with the social consequences of their research. Reasons ranging from lack of awareness of issues to an atmosphere in science that discourages social responsibility are discussed. The most crucial missing element in fostering social responsibility is a scientific education that integrates the study of the social impact of science with the science itself.

**Gellner, Ernest**. "Karl Popper—The Thinker and the Man" in *The Significance of Popper's Thought,* Amsterdamski, Stefan (ed), 75-85. Amsterdam, Rodopi, 1996.

**Gembillo, Giuseppe**. "Tempo e storia in Ilya Prigogine" in *Il Concetto di Tempo: Atti del XXXII Congresso Nazionale della Società Filosofica Italiana,* Casertano, Giovanni (ed), 197-207. Napoli, Loffredo, 1997.

**Gemes, Ken**. A New Theory of Content II: Model Theory and Some Alternative. *J Phil Log*, 26(4), 449-476, Ag 97.

This paper develops a semantical model—theoretic account of (logical) content complementing the syntactically specified account of content developed in "A New Theory of Content I," (*JPL* 23: 596-620), 1994. Proofs of completeness are given for both propositional and quantificational languages (without identity). Means for handling a quantificational language with identity are also explored. Finally, this new notion of content is compared, in respect of both logical properties and philosophical applications, to alternative partitions of the standard consequence class relation proposed by Stelzner, Schurz and Weingartner.

**Gemes, Ken**. Inductive Skepticism and the Probability Calculus I: Popper and Jeffreys on Induction and the Probability of Law-Like Universal Generalizations. *Phil Sci*, 64(1), 113-130, Mr 97.

I examine the flaws of two proofs, one an alleged proof of an inductive skeptical conclusion due to Karl Popper; the other an alleged proof of an inductivist thesis due to Harold Jeffreys and John Earman which bears a kind of inverse relation to Popper's proof. Surprisingly, in examining Popper's argument it is shown that certain apparently weak premises, often embraced by both inductivists and deductivists, lend themselves to inductive conclusions. However, it is argued, those premises are still philosophically substantive and not amenable to a purely formal demonstration. The general lesson to be learned here is that inductivism and inductive skepticism are substantive philosophical theses and we should be wary of any alleged merely formal proof of such theses.

**Gendin, Sidney**. Why Preference is not Transitive. *Phil Quart*, 46(185), 482-488, O 96.

Transitivity is *not* the relationship that given xRy and yRz then x *ought* to stand in relation R to z. R is transitive only if it must be true that xRz. "Taller than" is paradigmatically transitive and "prefers" most definitely is not. The author surveys the orthodox reasons for thinking "prefers" and "is indifferent to" are transitive and shows they are defective. The consequences are important for welfare economics and decision theory.

**Gendlin, E T**. What Happens When Wittgenstein Asks "What Happens When...?". *Phil Forum*, 28(3), 268-281, Spr 97.

**Gendron, Pierre**. La science n'est pas toujours neutre: biodiversité, commercialisation et génétique humaine. *Horiz Phil*, 7(1), 85-96, Fall 96.

**Generali, Dario**. Fra filologia e storiografia: progetti di edizioni settecentesche. *Stud Filosofici*, 157-172, 1995.

Arising from the meeting "Incontro sullo studio e l'edizione di testi del Settecento", promoted by Italian Society of eighteenth-century studies in June 1994, it has been possible to illustrate some critical editions of eighteenth-century texts, now in progress. Special attention has been paid to editorial criteria adopted and to discussions on this subject, carried on during the last ten years. Finally, it has been emphasized the avant-garde role brought ahead, today, by critic editorial work and its capability to redesign the thought map of time authors and movements.

**Genette, Gérard** and Goshgarian, G M (trans). *The Work of Art: Immanence and Transcendence.* Ithaca, Cornell Univ Pr, 1997.

According to Gérard Genette, works of art can have two modes of existence: immanence and transcendence. *Immanence* is defined by the type of object the work "consists in"; it can therefore be subdivided into two regimes, here christened, after Nelson Goodman, *autographic* and *allographic*. *Transcendence* is defined by the different ways in which a work exceeds its immanence. Thus a work can consist in several nonidentical objects (works with different "versions"), be incompletely (fragments) or indirectly (copies, reproductions, descriptions) manifested, or operate in different ways, depending on place or period, individuals or circumstances; we never look at the same painting or read the same book twice. It follows that a work cannot be reduced to its object of immanence, because what it is, is inseparable from what is accomplishes. The work of art is always already the work that art does. (publisher, edited)

**Gennaro, Rocco J**. *Consciousness and Self-Consciousness: A Defense of the Higher-Order Thought Theory of Consciousness.* Amsterdam, J Benjamins, 1996.

Following the lead of David Rosenthal, the author argues for the so-called 'higher-order thought theory of consciousness'. This theory holds that what makes a mental state conscious is the presence of a suitable higher-order thought directed at the mental state. In addition, the somewhat controversial claim that consciousness entails self-consciousness" is vigorously defended. The approach is mostly 'analytic' in style and draws on important recent work in cognitive science, perception, artificial intelligence, neuropsychology and psychopathology. However, the book also makes extensive use of numerous Kantian insights in arguing for its main theses and, in turn, sheds historical light on Kant's theory of mind. (edited)

**Genovese, Rino**. La questione del mito. *Iride*, 9(18), 404-413, Ag 96.

Il mito non è alle nostre spalle; il mito è tra noi, dentro la società occidentale moderna, a dispetto di ogni presunta demitizzazione. Non serve rilanciarlo come base di nuove forme di vita di tipo comunitario (la cui rifondazione spetterebbe semmai al rito), né esercitarsi in maniera neoromantica sull'intreccio di ragione e mito, secondo l'impostazione della recente *Mythos-Debatte*. Bisognerebbe piuttosto cercare i motivi della permanenza del mito nella specifica funzione cognitiva propria dell'immagine.

**Genovese, Rino**. Tra materialismo e critica della comunicazione: Paolo Virno. *Iride*, 8(15), 462-465, Ag 95.

Paolo Virno impegna a fondo la tradizione del pensiero critico in un tentativo di rottura, dall'interno, dell'autoreferenzialità del linguaggio verso un'apertura al possibile e al diverso. Una posizione radicale come poche che però stringe la teoria in una nuova alternativa totalizzante.

**Gensini, Stefano**. Ancora sulla teoria vichiana del linguaggio: In margine ad alcune recenti pubblicazioni. *Stud Filosofici*, 271-299, 1995.

This paper reviews books by J. Trabant and M. Danesi on Vico's philosophy of language. Emphasis is cast on the role played by *ingenium* as the cognitive counterpart of linguistic creativity in Vico's work. Accepting Trabant's interpretation of the *Scienza Nuova* in semiotic terms, Gensini adds that the fusion of language and body Vico suggests, shows his indebtedness to an 'Epicurean' framework rooted in the European culture of his times. Gensini further maintains that this has consequences for the contemporary cognitive sciences, insofar as the study of metaphors and metonimies have confirmed that language meanings are embedded into bodily constraints.

**Gensler, Harry J**. *Formal Ethics.* New York, Routledge, 1996.

Gensler shows that the basic principles of ethics are very similar to principles of logic and provide a firm basis for our ethical thinking. Throughout, he uses logic not to blind the reader with science but to make things clear; and he presents his ideas in a way that beginners can understand and will enjoy. While intended primarily for specialists in moral philosophy, the book will also appeal to students of philosophy, ethics and applied logic. Written with exemplary clarity, *Formal Ethics* is that rare thing: a major advance in moral philosophy that is also an ideal introduction to the subject. (publisher)

**Gent, Ian P**. Theory Matrices (for Modal Logics) Using Alphabetical Monotonicity. *Stud Log*, 52(2), 233-257, My 93.

In this paper I give conditions under which a matrix characterization of validity is correct for first order logics where quantifications are restricted by statements from a theory. Unfortunately the usual definition of path closure in a matrix is unsuitable and a less pleasant definition must be used. I derive the matrix theorem from syntactic analysis of a suitable tableau system, but by choosing a tableau system for restricted quantification I generalize Wallen's earlier work on modal logics. The tableau system is only correct if a new condition I call "alphabetical monotonicity" holds. I sketch how the result can be applied to a wide range of logics such as first order variants of many standard modal logics, including nonserial modal logics.

**Gentile, Giulio**. "Uguaglianza e disuguaglianza: un tema di filosofia della storia" in *Lo Storicismo e la Sua Storia: Temi, Problemi, Prospettive*, Cacciatore, Giuseppe (ed), 89-97. Milano, Guerini, 1997.

**Gentile, Nélida**. Holismo Semántico e Inconmensurabilidad en el Debate Positivismo-Antipositivismo. *Critica*, 28(83), 75-96, Ag 96.

According to the widespread interpretation, Kuhn's philosophy of science confronts the core ideas held by logical empiricism, but this standard interpretation is objectionable. This paper attempts to show that two of the main components of Kuhn's doctrine were clearly present in Carnap's development: the incommensurability theory as well as the semantical holism on which that theory is founded—both of them permanently invoked by Kuhn along the road initiated in *The Structure*. There exists, however, some differences between the holistic conception Carnap embraced and that adopted by Kuhn and this paper points out some of them. Finally, we try to evaluate the scope of the ontological commitments met by Carnap and by Kuhn.

**Gentzler, Jyl**. Forms, Individuals, and Individuation: Mary Margaret McCabe's *Plato's Individuals*. *Apeiron*, 29(2), 163-181, Je 96.

**George, Alexander**. Katz Astray. *Mind Lang*, 11(3), 295-305, S 96.

The foundations of linguistics continue to generate philosophical debate. Jerrold Katz claims that the subject matter of linguistics consists of abstract objects and that, as a consequence, the discipline cannot be viewed as part of psychology. I respond by arguing 1) that Katz misinterprets work in the philosophy of mathematics which he believes sheds light on foundational questions in linguistics; 2) that he misunderstands aspects of Noam Chomsky's position, against whose conception of linguistics many of his claims are directed; 3) that Katz fails to dispose of a much more plausible analysis, according to which linguistics remains an empirical inquiry in spite of its abstract subject matter; and finally, 4) that his arguments against what he calls 'generativism', appealing to the existence of an infinitely long grammatical sentence of English, are flawed.

**George, Edwin C**. "Kierkegaard and Tolerance" in *Philosophy, Religion, and the Question of Intolerance*, Ambuel, David (ed), 70-80. Albany, SUNY Pr, 1997.

**George, William P**. International Regimes, Religious Ethics, and Emergent Probability. *Annu Soc Christ Ethics*, 145-170, 1996.

This essay presents the hypothesis that "emergent probability," a scientifically and theologically informed world view developed by philosopher-theologian Bernard Lonergan, can aptly join religious ethics to "regime analysis," a prominent approach to the study of international relations. Regimes, which are institutionalized principles, norms, rules, and decision-making procedures, are reconstrued as the "schemes of recurrence" central to emergent probability. Human agents' intelligent and responsible operations, which exhibit nonsystematic (statistical) characteristics, condition the emergence of new, value-bearing regimes. *The 1982 Law of the Sea* illustrates this hypothesis. Religious ethicists and specialists in international relations and law are invited to test the hypothesis and its several implications.

**Gerbeau, Alexis**. De la toute relativité des lois. *Philosopher*, 18, 85-95, 1995.

**Gerbrandy, Jelle** and Groeneveld, Willem. Reasoning about Information Change. *J Log Lang Info*, 6(2), 147-169, Ap 97.

In this paper we introduce Dynamic Epistemic Logic, which is a logic for reasoning about information change in a multi-agent system. The information structures we use are based on non-well-founded sets and can be conceived as bisimulation classes of Kripke models. On these structures, we define a notion of information change that is inspired by Update Semantics (Veltman, 1996). We give a sound and complete axiomatization of the resulting logic and we discuss applications to the puzzle of the dirty children and to knowledge programs.

**Gerde, Virginia W** and Goldsby, Michael G and Shepard, Jon M. Teaching Business Ethics Through Literature. *Teach Bus Ethics*, 1(1), 33-51, 1997.

America's economic ideology lacks a vocabulary of ethics. If, as we assume, an economic system requires a moral component for long-term survival, students in business schools must be exposed to a vocabulary of ethics that is consistent with the ideology of capitalism. We present a vocabulary of ethics and describe an approach to teaching business ethics based on business-related classic literature and moral philosophy.

**Geréby, György**. Aristotle and Dedekind (in Czech). *Magyar Filozof Szemle*, 1-2, 45-75, 1997.

The paper tries to call attention to a methodologically interesting parallelism and a philosophically significant difference between R. Dedekind's proof (1872) that

there is one and only one real number that produces a "cut" in the body of real numbers and Aristotle's argument for there being one and only one indivisible instant separating the past from the future (*Phys*. 6.3.233b33-234a20). The paper consists of two parts. The first contains a comparison of the two proofs, the second follows the fate of Aristotle's proof in the hands of the commentators. (edited)

**Geréby, György**. Two Books on the Elements of Physics (or One Movement) by *Proclus of Lykia (in Hungarian)*. *Magyar Filozof Szemle*, 1-2, 281-336, 1997.

**Geremek, Bronislaw**. History and Memory. *Iyyun*, 45, 41-53, Jl 96.

**Gerena, Luis Alonso** and Ariza, Sergio (trans) and Aristotle. Aristóteles: Sobre las Ideas. *Ideas Valores*, 94-103, D 96.

This translation assembles a group of remaining fragments from a presumed youthful work of Aristotle called *On Ideas*. Aristotle there critically discusses several arguments that prove the existence of ideas. His criticism consists essentially of the following: 1) the arguments do not really prove the existence of ideas; 2) they prove a larger population of ideas than the Platonists are willing to admit; 3) they result in logical absurdities like the one known as the *third man*; 4) they eliminate the principles that ground the theory of ideas.

**Gergen, Kenneth**. Who Speaks and Who Replies in Human Science Scholarship?. *Hist Human Sci*, 10(3), 151-173, Ag 97.

Intelligibility in the human sciences, as elsewhere, is born of tradition. The present inquiry is into the traditions currently deployed in the human sciences to achieve credibility. In particular, how are we to understand the character of voice in human science writings such that they achieve rhetorical power and how do these writings variously position their readers? Four traditions of voice are identified: the mystical, the prophetic, the mythic and the civil. These modes of annunciation are contrasted with two additional genres of more recent, postmodern vintage: the autobiographical and the fictional. Illustrations are provided from major scientific writings. (edited)

**Gerhard, Jäger** and Strahm, Thomas. Some Theories with Positive Induction of Ordinal Strength *psi omega 0*. *J Sym Log*, 61(3), 818-842, S 96.

This paper deals with i) the theory $ID^{\#}_1$ which results from ID-hat-sub-one by restricting induction on the natural numbers to formulas which are positive in the fixed point constants, ii) the theory BON(mu) plus various forms of positive induction, and iii) a subtheory of Peano arithmetic with ordinals in which induction on the natural numbers is restricted to formulas which are Sigma in the ordinals. We show that these systems have proof-theoretic strength psi-omega-0. (edited)

**Gerhardt, Volker**. The Abdication of Philosophy: On the Modernity of the Relation between Philosophy and Politics in Kant. *Ideal Stud*, 26(2), 175-188, Wint 96.

**Gerhardt, Volker**. The Virtue of the Free Spirit (in Serbo-Croatian). *Filozof Istraz*, 15(4), 739-748, 1995.

Der Autor erinnert zunächst daran, dass die Konzeption des freien Geistes zentral für Nietzsches spätes Denken ist und auch durch seine Kritik an der Freiheit des Willens nichts von ihrer philosophischen Bedeutung verliert. Mit diesem Selbstbegriff aber übernimmt Nietzsche notwendigerweise normative Erwartungen, die sich in den klassischen Tugendkatalog der alteuropäischen Tradition übersetzen lassen. D.h.: Nietzsches "Immoralismus" bedeutet keine Preisgabe aller Tugenden und der Moral als solcher, vielmehr meint sie eine Zurückweisung jener abstrakten, für alle geforderten Tugenden. Auf diese Weise wird deutlich, dass Nietzsche keineswegs bloss als radikaler Kritiker der überlieferten Moral angesehen werden muss, sondern zugleich auch als Vertreter einer exemplarischen Tugendlehre, die keineswegs so weit von Sokrates und Platon, Aristoteles und Kant entfernt ist, wie Nietzsche uns glauben machen will.

**Gerhardt, Volker**. *Vom Willen zur Macht: Anthropologie und Metaphysik der Macht am exemplarischen Fall Friedrich Nietzsches*. Hawthorne, de Gruyter, 1996.

In referring to the traditions of metaphysics and politics, which Nietzsche only fragmentarily considers, it is strongly indicated that the human being lies at the intersection of both perspectives. To that end, Nietzsche's concept of the "will to power" which is of central importance in his late writings will be analyzed. For the first time, this concept is discussed in its genesis, conceptual context and inner logic. It is to be understood as the rhetorical intensification of the two other concepts which are part of it. In addition to this, it comes to the fore that Nietzsche's philosophy is intensely engaged in the project of human self understanding. Thus, in the inner moments of his thoughts, Nietzsche is obliged to Socrates, Plato and Kant—his favored opponents.

**Gerla, Giangiacomo** and Biacino, Loredana. Connection Structures: Grzegorczyk's and Whitehead's Definitions of Point. *Notre Dame J Form Log*, 37(3), 431-439, Sum 96.

Whitehead, in his famous book *Process and Reality*, proposed a definition of point assuming the concepts of "region" and "connection relation" as primitive. Several years after and independently Grzegorczyk, in a brief but very interesting paper, proposed another definition of point in a system in which the inclusion relation and the relation of being separated were assumed as primitive. In this paper we compare their definitions and we show that, under rather natural assumptions, they coincide.

**Gerla, Giangiacomo** and Tortora, Roberto. Dissezioni e intersezioni di regioni in A.N. Whitehead. *Epistemologia*, 19(2), 289-308, Jl-D 96.

Here we take into account two interesting notions in [5], to which Whitehead devoted his Assumptions 13 to 18, namely the notion of *dissection* of a region and that of *intersection* of two regions. We discuss these two concepts in the framework of the general theory of ordered sets and extend the axiom system of [2] to a larger one. In the final section we prove the consistency of the system, constructing a "natural" model for it, which utilizes topological notions of the classical three-dimensional Euclidean space. (edited)

**Gerrard, Steve**. "A Philosophy of Mathematics between Two Camps" in *The Cambridge Companion to Wittgenstein*, Sluga, Hans (ed), 171-197. Needham Heights, Cambridge, 1996.

**Gerrard, Steve**. "Desire and Desirability: Bradley, Russell and Moore versus Mill" in *Early Analytic Philosophy*, Tait, William W (ed), 37-74. Chicago, Open Court, 1997.

**Gerrig, Richard J**. Is there a Paradox of Suspense? A Reply to Yanal. *Brit J Aes*, 37(2), 168-174, Ap 97.

How is it that people can experience suspense when they are already certain of an outcome (as when, for example, they reread a familiar story)? As a solution to this so-called 'paradox of suspense,' Yanal (1996) suggested that people are simply mislabeling other emotions as suspense. This reply argues that Yanal's solution suffers from a lack of evidence. Furthermore, Yanal's solution misunderstands the ordinary operation of memory processes.

**Gersbach, Hans**. Risk and the Value of Information in Irreversible Decisions. *Theor Decis*, 42(1), 37-51, Ja 97.

The analysis of the nexus between the value of information and risk is examined for sequential decision with different degrees of future commitment, as e.g., environmental decisions. We find that in the linear case a riskier environment in general will increase the value of information. This result will be extended in the separable case to decreasing and increasing stochastic returns to scale. An example shows the ambiguity in the general case.

**Gert, Bernard** and Berger, Edward M. The Institutional Context for Research. *Prof Ethics*, 4(3-4), 17-46, Spr-Sum 95.

**Gerten, Michael**. Fichtes Wissenschaftslehre vor der aktuellen Diskussion um die Letztbegründung. *Fichte-Studien*, 13, 173-189, 1997.

**Gerwin, Martin E**. The Hobbes Game, Human Diversity, and Learning Styles. *Teach Phil*, 19(3), 247-258, S 96.

The author presents a modified version of the "Hobbes game" originally developed by John Immerwahr in the 1970s. Pairs of students attempt to earn a credit by playing Prisoner's Dilemma in a setting which simulates a Hobbesian state of nature. A decade's experience shows that different classes of students produce very diverse group histories when playing the game. The near-universal appeal and effectiveness of the game as a teaching device is accounted for by noting that it has features appropriate to all four of the categories of learners distinguished in David Kolb's typology of learning styles.

**Gesang, Bernward**. Erkenntnis als Anpassung. *Phil Natur*, 28(2), 216-230, 1991.

In diesem Aufsatz soll die von E.M. Engels an der Evolutionären Erkenntnistheorie (EE) und dem neodarwinistischen Teil der synthetischen Evolutionstheorie geäusserte Kritik erörtert werden. Das jüngst von der Autorin erschienene Buch "Erkenntnis als Anpassung?" könnte in vieler Hinsicht als grundlegende Kritik an allen bisherigen Modellen der EE gelten. Engels bestreitet eine hochgradige epistemologische Relevanz des Anpassungsbegriffs und damit z.B. auch die Möglichkeit, gewinnbringend vom Anpassungsmechanismus auf Wahrheitsnähe zu schliessen. Ebenso kritisiert sie den hypothetischen Realismus der EE und zahlreiche andere Bereiche dieser Disziplin. Sie betont demgegenüber konstruktivistische Konzepte im Anschluss an Piaget. An dieser Stelle kann ich wohl kaum auf alle relevanten Punkte der Engelsschen Kritik eingehen, jedoch will ich die Kernaspekte andiskutieren. (edited)

**Gessmann, Martin**. Die Entdeckung des frühen Heidegger: Neuere Literatur zur Dezennie von *Sein und Zeit*. *Phil Rundsch*, 43(3), 215-232, S 96.

**Geuss, Raymond**. Nietzsche and Morality. *Euro J Phil*, 5(1), 1-20, Ap 97.

**Gevers, J K M** and Legemaate, Johan. Physician-Assisted Suicide in Psychiatry: Developments in the Netherlands. *Cambridge Quart Healthcare Ethics*, 6(2), 175-188, Spr 97.

**Gewirth, Alan**. 'Ought' and Reasons for Action. *S J Phil*, 35(2), 171-177, Sum 97.

Matthew Kramer and Nigel Simmonds have criticized my argument for the supreme moral principle on the ground that the addresses of its 'ought'-judgment do not have a reason for accepting the judgment. In reply, I show not only that they do have such a reason but also, and especially, that the addressor of the judgment has his own weighty reasons for addressing it to other persons.

**Ghilardi, Silvio**. Quantified Extensions of Canonical Propositional Intermediate Logics. *Stud Log*, 51(2), 195-214, 1992.

The quantified extension of a canonical propositional intermediate logic is complete with respect to the generalization of Kripke semantics taking into consideration set-valued functors defined on a category.

**Ghilardi, Silvio** and Meloni, Giancarlo. Constructive Canonicity in Non-Classical Logics. *Annals Pure Applied Log*, 86(1), 1-32, Je 97.

Sufficient syntactic conditions for canonicity in intermediate and intuitionistic modal logics are given. We present a new technique which does not require semantic first-order reduction and which is constructive in the sense that it works in an intuitionistic metatheory through a model without points which is classically isomorphic to the usual canonical model.

**Ghilardi, Silvio** and Meloni, Giancarlo. Relational and Partial Variable Sets and Basic Predicate Logic. *J Sym Log*, 61(3), 843-872, S 96.

In this paper we study the logic of relational and partial variable sets, seen as a generalization of set-valued presheaves, allowing transition functions to be

arbitrary relations or arbitrary partial functions. We find that such a logic is the usual intuitionistic and cointuitionistic first order logic without Beck and Frobenius conditions relative to quantifiers along arbitrary terms. The important case of partial variable sets is axiomatizable by means of the substitutivity schema for equality. Furthermore, completeness, incompleteness and independence results are obtained for different kinds of Beck and Frobenius conditions.

**Ghirardi, Giancarlo**. Quantum Dynamical Reduction and Reality: Replacing Probability Densities with Densities in Real Space. *Erkenntnis*, 45(2 & 3), 349-365, Nov 96.

Consideration is given to recent attempts to solve the objectification problem of quantum mechanics by considering nonlinear and stochastic modifications of Schrödinger's evolution equation. Such theories agree with all predictions of standard quantum mechanics concerning microsystems but forbid the occurrence of superpositions of macroscopically different states. It is shown that the appropriate interpretation for such theories is obtained by replacing the probability densities of standard quantum mechanics with mass densities in real space. Criteria allowing a precise characterization of the idea of similarity and difference of macroscopic situations are presented and it is shown how they lead to a theoretical picture which is fully compatible with a macrorealistic position about natural phenomena.

**Ghiselin, Michael T**. *Metaphysics and the Origin of Species*. Albany, SUNY Pr, 1997.

In explaining his individuality thesis, Michael T. Ghiselin provides extended discussions of such philosophical topics as definition, the reality of various kinds of groups, and how we classify traits and processes. He develops and applies the implications for general biology and other sciences and makes the case that a better understanding of species and of classification in general puts biologists and paleontologists in a much better position to understand nature in general, and such processes as extinction in particular. (publisher, edited)

**Ghosh, Raghunath**. Rasvihary Das on 'Value of Doubt': Some Reflections. *J Indian Counc Phil Res*, 13(2), 97-105, Ja-Ap 96.

The present paper is an attempt to give a critical and evaluative account of Professor Rasvihary Das on 'value of doubt'. Any doubt regarding some religious activity is sometimes desirable as it prevents even from internal conflict, bloodshed etc. by way of promoting love for humanity, friendliness etc. irrespective of religion. The efficacy of doubt is found when it gives rise to critical-thinking after removing blind faith. Regarding the doubt in the existence of God and other-worldly objects etc. Professor Dasa's arguments are not acceptable to me due to the lack of good argument (*suyukti*) in them. The doubt in these matters, I think, may be dispelled through the employment of good argument.

**Ghosh, Raghunath**. The Concept of Mind in Modern Indian Thought with Special Reference to Sri Aurobindo, Rabindranath and K.C. Bhatiacharyya. *Darshana Int*, 36(3/143), 49-56, Ap 96.

This paper gives a critical account of the concept of mind in modern Indian thought with special reference to Sri Aurobindo, Rabindranath Tagore and Krishna Chandra Bhattacharyya. These three celebrated thinkers have established the inwardness of mind through some reasoning. To Sri Aurobindo human mind is sense-mind which is a link in the evolutionary ladder. To Rabindranath a man may be transformed into Universal Man. K. C. Bhattacharyya has referred to three types of mind-shadow mind, vernacular mind, mind at the stage of Swaraj. All of them have accepted the transformation of mind to its inner world. It can apprehend all i.e., both the whole world (*Visva*) and individuality (*Visesatva*). The search for Universal Man is to be done 'within our mind' but not external nonmental world.

**Ghosh, Ranjan K**. Notes towards Understanding the Art/Life Divide. *J Indian Counc Phil Res*, 13(3), 143-149, My-Ag 96.

The note examines, in the main, Nick McAdoo's argument that since our talk about a work of art comprises words such as 'sad', 'profound', 'graceful', etc. which are used primarily in the context of our daily life there is no special realm of aesthetic purity. Against this contention, it has been argued that notwithstanding the similarity of elements that a work of art may or may not share with life on the basis of which locutions about it may contain words contextually grounded in everyday life the purity of the aesthetic realm remains inviolable. In the end, a few brief remarks on the relationship between art and life have also been made.

**Ghosh, Ranjan K**. Professor Prasad on Working Out a Lead from Swami Vivekananda: Some Reflections. *Indian Phil Quart*, 23(3-4), 476-480, Jl-O 96.

**Ghosh, Ranjan K**. Sentence Meaning, Intentionalism, and the Literary Text: An Interface. *J Indian Counc Phil Res*, 14(2), 57-70, Ja-Ap 97.

The paper focuses on the argument by which John Searle debunks the intentionalist thesis of Knapp and Michaels by insisting on the distinction between sentence meaning and speaker meaning as also the grounds on which the intentionalists in turn maintain their own position and thus reject the notion of sentence meaning. To conclude: (I) the distinction between sentence meaning and speaker meaning may be acceptable if argued only for our everyday language-situations, but (II) Knapp and Michaels seem to be right in rejecting the notion of sentence meaning when what is under consideration is *poetic* language.

**Giammusso, Salvatore**. "Homo historicus: Verso una trasformazione del paradigma 'classico' dell'antropologia filosofica" in *Lo Storicismo e la Sua Storia: Temi, Problemi, Prospettive*, Cacciatore, Giuseppe (ed), 468-485. Milano, Guerini, 1997.

**Gianella, Alicia E**. "Las explicacioines homunculares de la irracionalidad" in *La racionalidad: su poder y sus límites*, Nudler, Oscar (ed), 85-96. Barcelona, Ed Paidos, 1996.

Homuncular explanations have been used for accounting rational and irrational human actions. They postulate agents which subdivide complex structures as persons or social entities. But these kind of explanations have been accused of anthropomorphism and circularity. In this paper the positions of different philosophers as Dennett, Davidson and Glymour are compared. The conclusion is that these kind of explanations could be considered as putting forward a relational estructure, nonanimistic but formal, in which relations take place among parts and wholes, applicable as well to political and social problems as phychological ones.

**Gianetto, Enrico**. "Note sul tempo e sul moto attraverso la storia della fisica e le critiche" in *Il Concetto di Tempo: Atti del XXXII Congresso Nazionale della Società Filosofica Italiana,* Casertano, Giovanni (ed), 209-226. Napoli, Loffredo, 1997.

**Gianformaggio, Letizia**. Tolerance and War: The Real Meaning of an Irreconcilability. *Ratio Juris*, 10(1), 1-8, Mr 97.

Starting from the distinction between concept and conception, the author proposes a pluralistic view of toleration focused on the equality of individuals and cultures on legal-rational control of social relationship. Analyzing the basic marks of toleration (toleration and power, the costs of toleration, toleration and value) the author shows how the option for toleration is a choice for subjecting social relations to reason and rules (law) instead of passions and violence (war).

**Giannantoni, Gabriele**. "Il concetto di tempo nel mondo antico fino a Platone" in *Il Concetto di Tempo: Atti del XXXII Congresso Nazionale della Società Filosofica Italiana,* Casertano, Giovanni (ed), 9-23. Napoli, Loffredo, 1997.

**Giannaras, Anastasios** and Eidlin, Fred (trans). Plato and K.R. Popper: Toward a Critique of Plato's Political Philosophy. *Phil Soc Sci*, 26(4), 493-508, D 96.

**Gibbard, Allan**. "Visible Properties of Human Interest Only" in *Perception,* Villanueva, Enrique (ed), 199-208. Atascadero, Ridgeview, 1996.

In "Is the External World Invisible?" Mark Johnston claims we are unacquainted with colors, in part because color similarity is not essential similarity. Colors, I suggest, are genuine physical properties, but somewhat vague and physically uninteresting. Similarity in color is likewise a physically uninteresting physical metric. Color similarity, then, is not plain similarity, apart from us, among those properties that constitute exact colors; it is visual similarity. To another dictum that Johnston invokes, I offer a counterexample. Nothing in my acquaintance with the yellow of a canary, I conclude, is schematic or bloodless, or grounds for depression.

**Gibbard, Allan** (ed) and Darwall, Stephen (ed) and Railton, Peter (ed). *Moral Discourse and Practice: Some Philosophical Approaches.* New York, Oxford Univ Pr, 1997.

The book is a unique anthology which collects important recent work, much of which is not easily available elsewhere, on core metaethical issues. Naturalist moral realism, once devastated by the charge of "naturalistic fallacy," has been reinvigorated, as have versions of moral realism that insist on the discontinuity between ethics and science. Irrealist, expressivist programs have also developed with great subtlety, encouraging the thought that a noncognitivist account may actually be able to explain ethical judgments' aspirations to objectivity. Neo-Kantian constructivist theories have flourished as well, offering hope that morality can be grounded in a plausible conception of reasonable conduct. (publisher,edited)

**Gibbons, John**. Externalism and Knowledge of Content. *Phil Rev*, 105(3), 287-310, Jl 96.

If the contents of our thoughts are partly determined by facts outside our heads, can we still know those contents directly, without investigating our environment? What if we were surreptitiously switched to Twin-Earth? Would we know the contents of our thoughts under these unusual circumstances? By looking carefully at what determines the content of a second-order thought, a candidate for self-knowledge, the paper argues that we can know the contents of our thoughts directly, even after being switched. Learning about the switch, however, does raise some interesting difficulties.

**Gibbs, Paul J**. A Psychoanalytic Interpretation of the Effectiveness of Humor for Teaching Philosophy. *J Thought*, 32(3), 123-133, Fall 97.

The paper focuses on the difficulties that philosophy professors must confront with regard to teaching disinterested or apathetic students. It is argued that the use of humor is an effective teaching strategy to engage such students. Psychoanalytic insight regarding human motivation, mentality and humor are employed in an attempt to explain why this is the case. The analysis includes the idea that we are pleasure-seekers who are motivated to reduce tension of any kind including that stemming from the constraints of reason. Psychoanalysis views humor as a temporary release from such constraints. Since most students perceive our efforts as strengthening their intellect or rationality, it is argued that occasional use of humor is beneficial as a means of engaging them in philosophy classes. A number of pedagogical implications are drawn from the analysis.

**Gibbs, Paul J**. Ethical Connectionism. *Cont Phil*, 18(4 & 5), 50-57, Jl-Ag/S-O 96.

There is a propensity for humans to harm one another. Nowhere is this illustrated more clearly than through the observation of differing, even if slightly, groups within civilization. The instances of such maltreatment and hatred are numerous, but two of the most prominent cases are differences concerning race and sexual preference.

**Gibson, Annetta** and Frakes, Albert H. Truth or Consequences: A Study of Critical Issues and Decision Making in Accounting. *J Bus Ethics*, 16(2), 161-171, F 97.

This study applies a theoretical framework, the theory of reasoned action, to the examination of unethical decision making in job-related situations encountered by CPAs. A survey methodology was employed in which respondents were asked to use both self-reported and randomized response techniques for reporting unethical behavior. The results indicate that individuals are unwilling to accurately report either unethical behavior or intention, particularly in situations where there is no question as to the unacceptability of the action or the potential penalty as presented in the AICPA Code of Professional Conduct. Implications for the accounting profession and research are discussed.

**Gibson, Roger**. "A Note on Boghossian's Master Argument" in *Contents,* Villanueva, Enrique (ed), 222-226. Atascadero, Ridgeview, 1995.

In his article "The Status of Content," Paul Boghossian articulates what has become known as Boghossian's Master Argument. This argument purports to establish that the application of nonfactualism to content discourse demonstrates the incoherence of nonfactualism. I argue that Boghossian's *master argument fails, essential because it conflates meaning and reference.*

**Gibson, Roger**. "McDowell's Direct Realism and Platonic Naturalism" in *Perception,* Villanueva, Enrique (ed), 275-281. Atascadero, Ridgeview, 1996.

After explaining how in *Mind and World* John McDowell proposes to slip between the horns of a dilemma represented as a choice between a sterile foundationalism and a libertine coherentism, I raise several questions regarding McDowell's proffered direct realism and Platonic naturalism.

**Gibson, Roger**. Stich on Intentionality and Rationality. *Protosoz*, 8/9, 30-38, 1996.

In chapter 2 of *The Fragmentation of Reason*, Stephen Stich argues that certain passages of Quine's *Word and Object* are the source of what he calls the conceptual argument. That argument claims there is a conceptual connection between intentionality and rationality: intentionality requires rationality. Stich rejects the idea that intentionality requires either perfect or fixed bridgehead rationality, but he concedes that it requires minimal rationality. After explaining Stich's position and a criticism of it offered by John Biro and Kirk Ludwig, I sketch an alternative to the conceptual argument. This alternative claims that rationality requires psychological plausibility and/or smoothness of communication, not rationality.

**Giere, Ronald N**. "From *Wissenschaftliche Philosophie* to Philosophy of Science" in *Origins of Logical Empiricism,* Giere, Ronald N (ed), 335-354. Minneapolis, Univ of Minnesota Pr, 1996.

How, between 1930 and 1960, did a dissident European movement advocating the replacement of much established German philosophy by *Wissenschaftliche Philosophie* transform itself into the dominant tradition for philosophy of science in America? In this paper I raise some general issues, pose some specific questions and suggest some hypotheses that might be examined by future historians of this period. My treatment emphasizes context over content. It is suggested, for example, that Reichenbach's insistence on distinguishing discovery from justification was motivated in large part by how badly Einstein and his theories were treated by the Nazis because of his Jewish origins.

**Giere, Ronald N**. "Visual Models and Scientific Judgment" in *Picturing Knowledge,* Baigrie, Brian S (ed), 269-302. Toronto, Univ of Toronto Pr, 1996.

This paper connects several recent themes in the philosophy of science: I) a model-based picture of scientific theories, II) a naturalistic account of epistemic decisions and III) interest in the use of visual images in scientific thinking. The paper assumes a model-based account of scientific theories and uses the fact that it can accommodate visual information to support a particular naturalistic account of crucial decisions. The best conclusion, however, is that these three themes are mutually reinforcing and together support a move away from an exclusive reliance on propositional modes of analysis for understanding modern science.

**Giere, Ronald N**. The Scientist as Adult. *Phil Sci*, 63(4), 538-541, D 96.

This paper is a response to Allison Gopnik's *The Scientist as Child.* I agree that the analogy between conceptual development in science and in individual children has been fruitful for developmental psychology. I question whether it can be as fruitful for understanding the development of modern science. Children born in 1492 were cognitively little different from children born in 1992, but none of the former and some of the latter developed into modern scientists. The difference, I argue, is not to be found in cognitive development but in such things as new instruments, new symbolic notations, printing and experimental methods.

**Giere, Ronald N** (ed) and Richardson, Alan W (ed). *Origins of Logical Empiricism.* Minneapolis, Univ of Minnesota Pr, 1996.

These articles challenge the idea that logical empiricism has its origins in traditional British empiricism, pointing instead to a movement of scientific philosophy that flourished in the German-speaking areas of Europe in the first four decades of the twentieth century. The intellectual refugees from the Third Reich who brought logical empiricism to North America did so in an environment influenced by Einstein's new physics, the ascension of modern logic, the birth of the social sciences as rivals to traditional humanistic philosophy, and other large-scale social, political, and cultural themes. (edited)

**Gierer, Alfred**. Gödel Meets Carnap: A Prototypical Discourse on Science and Religion. *Zygon*, 32(2), 207-217, Je 97.

Modern science, based on the laws of physics, claims validity for all events in space and time. However, it also reveals its own limitations, such as the indeterminacy of quantum physics, the limits of decidability, and, presumably, limits of decodability of the mind-brain relationship. At the philosophical level, these intrinsic limitations allow for different interpretations of the relation between human cognition and the natural order. In particular, modern science may be logically consistent with religious as well as agnostic views of humans and the universe. These points are exemplified through the transcript of a discussion between Kurt Gödel and Rudolf Carnap that took place in 1940. (edited)

**Gigante, Mario**. *Presupposti filosofici dell'enciclica Veritatis splendor.* Rome, Salerno Ed, 1996.

**Giglioli, Giovanna**. Gramsci, teórico de la superestructura. *Rev Filosof (Costa Rica)*, 34(83-84), 237-245, D 96.

After a first essay clarifying the basic concepts of "hegemony" and "historic bloc" in Gramsci political theory, this article considers the topics of ideology and culture. This emphasis on intellectual and cultural influences led Gramsci to develop a consistent superstructure theory.

**Gigliotti, Gary** and Sopher, Barry. Violations of Present-Value Maximization in Income Choice. *Theor Decis*, 43(1), 45-69, Jl 97.

We report results of an experiment testing for present-value maximization in intertemporal income choice. Two-thirds of subjects did not maximize present value. Through a series of experimental manipulations that impose costs on nonpresent value maximizers, we are able to reduce the level of violations substantially. We find, however, that a sizeable proportion of subjects continue to systematically violate present-value principles. Our interpretation is that these subjects either cannot or choose not to distinguish between *income* and *expenditure* in making their choices. Self-management, bounded rationality and sequence preference are suggested as possible explanations for such behavior.

**Gigliotti, Gianna**. "Objekt und Methode: Das Problem der Psychologie in Natorps Philosophie" in *Grenzen der kritischen Vernunft*, Schmid, Peter A, 95-114. Basel, Schwabe Verlag, 1997.

**Gilardi, Roberto**. Hume, Bayle e il *principio di causalità*: Parte I. *Riv Filosof Neo-Scolas*, 88(3), 421-455, Jl-S 96.

The author examines the Section II of Humean *Memoranda* and demonstrates that almost all its entries come from the works of Bayle. Then, he proves that the entries are there neither banal nor a thing of little importance and that they form the outline of a reflection on natural religion, in which Hume was just engaged in 1729, at the time of his *new scene of thought*. With reference to the arguments treated by Bayle, he also begins to prove that it is precisely from them that Hume derived his first intuition of the unnecessary nature of the causality-principle.

**Gilbert, Diane C** and Fischbach, Ruth L. The Ombudsman for Research Practice: A Proposal for a New Position and an Invitation to Comment. *Sci Eng Ethics*, 1(4), 389-402, O 95.

We propose that institutions consider establishing a position of "Ombudsman for Research Practice." This person would assume several roles: as a *sounding board* to those needing confidential consultation about research issues—basic, applied or clinical; as a *facilitator* for those wishing to pursue a formal grievance process; and as an *educator* to distribute guidelines and standards, to raise the consciousness regarding sloppy or irregular practices in order to prevent misconduct and to promote the responsible conduct of research. While there are compelling features to this position, many complex issues need to be considered and resolved. We invite readers to respond to questions we raise in the text.

**Gilbert, Michael A**. The Delimitation of Argument. *Inquiry (USA)*, 15(1), 63-75, Fall 95.

This paper reviews a number of definitions, both technical and commonplace, for the term 'argument'. The definitions are separated into the liberal, conservative and ordinary views. The conservatives stress the ideas of logico-rational acceptance, reasons, and being convinced. The liberals stress the fact of disagreement and de-emphasize the normative process. Finally, the ordinary view holds that argumentation must contain negative conflictual processes. It is claimed that arguments can be divided along two axes: *emotional/clinical* and *dialectical/chaotic. Argumentation theory* must consider all possibilities, and not, as the conservatives claim, only the dialectical, or, as the ordinary view holds, only the emotional. Only the liberal view encompasses all possibilities, and should, therefore, be adopted in *argumentation theory* is to be used to the understanding of marketplace argumentation.

**Gilbert, Paul**. The Concept of a National Community. *Phil Forum*, 28(1-2), 149-166, Fall-Wint 97.

What is a national community? Developing a suggestion of Weber, it is claimed that it is a community of a kind with a right to statehood. But what kind it is held to be differs from one type of nationalism to another. Appropriating some ideas from Hegel, three models of the national community are examined: the family, civil society and the state. Each generates a very different sort of nationalist argument for statehood, though none seems satisfactory. Yet the addition of cultural considerations does not obviously make good their inadequacies.

**Gilbert Jr, Daniel R**. A Critique and A Retrieval of Management and the Humanities. *J Bus Ethics*, 16(1), 23-35, Ja 97.

The use of literature and other sources from the humanities, in management education has become more prominent in recent years. But, there is reason to question the ethical justifications by which the marriage of management and the humanities is customarily defended. This paper is a critique of management and the humanities as it is practiced through the use of literature. By means of a liberal pragmatist kind of criticism and a case analysis about a hypothetical grand theory of management called Theory R, I draw a sharp distinction between a management and the humanities approach that merely confirms conventional truths and a new approach to management and the humanities that enables students to grow as what Henry Giroux calls "critical rather than 'good' citizens." I show how this new approach can enable management educators to retrieve the potential of management and the humanities to contribute to liberal education.

**Gilbertson, Mark**. Descartes, Error, and the Aesthetic-Totality Solution to the Problem of Evil. *SW Phil Rev*, 13(1), 75-82, Ja 97.

Descartes, in *Meditation IV*, argues that his error occurs when his will exceeds his finite intellect. However, questioning the adequacy of this solution, he also includes an "aesthetic-totality" solution, suggesting that the universe as a whole might be more perfect by containing imperfect parts. I argue that this resort can only be compatible with his overall quest for certainty if interpreted historically: error/evil contributes to good by being its occasion or cause, and the totality is understood as the whole over time. However, I also argue that even this is not compatible with Descartes's claim of human freedom.

**Gilbertz, Susan J** and Varner, Gary E and Peterson, Tarla Rai. "Teaching Environmental Ethics as a Method of Conflict Management" in *Environmental Pragmatism,* Light, Andrew (ed), 266-282. New York, Routledge, 1996.

Representatives of diverse interests in regional environmental disputes were brought together for two day workshops on environmental ethics. The workshops introduced participants to concepts and theories commonly discussed in college philosophy courses on the subject and presented them with opportunities to describe themselves and their perceived opponents in those terms. Content analysis of lengthy, unstructured interviews conducted months before and after suggest that such workshops affect participants' ways of framing environmental controversies and encourage related philosophical reflection.

**Gilchrist, M** and Shelah, S. Identities on Cardinals Less Than Aleph$_{\text{omega}}$. *J Sym Log*, 61(3), 780-787, S 96.

**Gill, Carolyn Bailey**. *Maurice Blanchot: The Demand of Writing.* New York, Routledge, 1996.

Maurice Blanchot is one of the key figures of postwar European thought; he has radically transformed our understanding of the relations between philosophy and literature. His strikingly original fiction and his penetrating critical studies of other writers, such as Kafka, Beckett and Mallarmé, have long been recognized as influential. His oeuvre as a whole, with its connections to the thought of Hegel and Heidegger, Derrida, Levinas, Bataille and Foucault, places him at the forefront of contemporary debates on philosophical and literary culture. (publisher)

**Gill, Christopher**. Mind and Madness in Greek Tragedy. *Apeiron*, 29(3), 249-268, S 96.

This is a review article of two books by Ruth Padel, *In and Out of Mind: Greek Images of the Tragic Self* (Princeton, 1992), and *Whom Gods Destroy: Elements of Greek and Tragic Madness* (Princeton, 1995). The article analyses the key themes of these books: human psychological vulnerability to internal and external forces, and the centrality of raving, god-induced madness to Greek tragedy. It argues that Padel's account of both themes needs to be qualified, but that these books express a view about Greek tragic psychology and madness that constitutes an important contribution to current scholarly debate.

**Gill, David**. Political Rights in Aristotle: A Response to Fred Miller, Jr., *Nature, Justice, and Rights in Aristotle's Politics. Ancient Phil*, 16(2), 431-442, Fall 96.

**Gill, Jerry H**. Language and Reality, One More Time. *Phil Today*, 41(2), 255-262, Sum 97.

**Gillet, Grant R** and Pigden, Charles R. Milgram, Method and Morality. *J Applied Phil*, 13(3), 233-250, 1996.

In Milgram's experiments, subjects were induced to inflict what they believed to be electric shocks in obedience to a man in a white coat. This suggests that many can be persuaded to torture and perhaps kill, another person simply on the say-so of an authority figure. But the experiments have been attacked on methodological, moral and methodologico-moral grounds. Patten argues that the subjects probably were not taken in by the charade; Bok argues that lies should not be used in research; and Patten insists that any excuse for Milgram's conduct can be adapted on behalf of his subjects. (Either he was wrong to conduct the experiments or they do not establish the phenomenon of immoral obedience.) We argue that the subjects were indeed taken in, that lies (though usually wrong) were in this case legitimate and that there were excuses available to Milgram which were not available to his subjects. So far from 'disrespecting' his subjects, Milgram enhanced their autonomy as rational agents. We concede, however, that it might be right to prohibit what it was right to do.

**Gillett, Eric**. Searle and the "Deep Unconscious". *Phil Psychiat Psych*, 3(3), 191-200, S 96.

The philosopher, John Searle (1992, 1990), has challenged some of the most basic tenets of cognitive psychology, especially the notion of a "deep unconscious" defined as mental processes that are in principle inaccessible to consciousness. In previous papers I have argued for a broad concept of the unconscious which includes in addition to mental contents accessible to consciousness under appropriate conditions mental processes that can never become conscious under any conditions. The core of my answer to Searle derives from Millikan's (1984) theory of proper functions which provides a definition of intentionality independent of consciousness.

**Gillett, Grant**. "Actions, Causes, and Mental Ascriptions" in *Objections to Physicalism,* Robinson, Howard (ed), 81-101. New York, Clarendon/Oxford Pr, 1996.

**Gillett, Grant**. "Young Human Beings: Metaphysics and Ethics" in *Human Lives: Critical Essays on Consequentialist Bioethics,* Oderberg, David S (ed), 109-127. New York, Macmillan, 1997.

This paper explores the claims and commitments of consequentialism, especially its counterintuitive claim that our beliefs concerning the special regard we should show human infants are mistaken. For instance, preference utilitarianism would countenance heinous behaviour such as child abuse, in certain circumstances. The flaw in consequentialism is located in certain of its commitments, such as Humean reductionism, i.e., the claim that morality is based on the passions rather than the discerning of real factual similarities and differences between cases. Another is methodological individualism, which ignores the relational nature of our attachments to one another. An alternative view is outlined, which places care and nurture at the core of our attitudes to young human lives.

**Gillett, Grant**. A Discursive Account of Multiple Personality Disorder. *Phil Psychiat Psych*, 4(3), 213-222, S 97.

Multiple personality disorder poses a number of problems for philosophers. Ideological battles rage over whether the syndrome is real or an artifact of therapy and of selected therapists. These battles tend to spring from a realist and fairly naive philosophy of mind and depend on an empiricist view of the mind and mental contents. Discursive psychology offers a different way of looking at consciousness and the self in which the narrative role of a subject is an important part of the constitution of the self. The narrative constructed is influenced by cultural and interpersonal contexts and reflects the types of self-conception available from them. In this view there is no simple opposition between the real self and the constructed self and social and personal influences including prevalent conceptions of the mind are in part responsible for both.

**Gillett, Grant**. Husserl, Wittgenstein and the Snark: Intentionality and Social Naturalism. *Phil Phenomenol Res*, 57(2), 331-349, Je 97.

The Snark is an intentional object. I examine the general philosophical characteristics of thoughts of objects from the perspective of Husserl's, hyle, noesis and noema and show how this meets constraints of opacity, normativity and possible existence as generated by a sensitive theory of intentionality. Husserl introduces terms which indicate the normative features of intentional content and attempts to forge a direct relationship between the norms he generates and the actual world object which a thought intends. I then attempt to relate Husserl's account to Fregean insights about the sense and reference of a term. Neither Husserl nor Frege suggests plausible routes to a naturalistic account of intentionality and I turn to Wittgenstein to provide a naturalistic reading of the crucial terms involved in the analysis of intentional content. His account is normative in a way required by both Husserl and Frege and yet manages a kind of Aristotelian naturalism which avoids crude biologism.

**Gillett, Grant**. Response to the Commentary. *Phil Psychiat Psych*, 4(3), 227-229, S 97.

**Gillon, Brendan S**. Contraposition and Lewis Carrol's Barber Shop Paradox. *Dialogue (Canada)*, 36(2), 247-251, Spr 97.

Cet article démontre qu'un exemple cité par Ernest Adams pour montrer que l'implication matérielle n'est pas l'interprétation correcte de la sémantique de la conjonction de subordination si, n'est rien d'autre qu'un corollaire d'une observation déjà faite par Lewis Carroll, il y a cent ans, dans l'exposition de son paradoxe du salon de coiffure.

**Gilmer, Penny J**. Commentary and Criticism on Scientific Positivism. *Sci Eng Ethics*, 1(1), 71-72, J 95.

This is a commentary and criticism of the accompanying paper by Garte, pp. 59-70, who espouses positivism, a system of philosophy which holds that the source of positive knowledge is facts, as elaborated and verified using the methods of empirical sciences. An alternative view, constructivism, is referenced, reminding us all that knowledge is constructed on the basis of our prior knowledge and, therefore, is always inherently uncertain. Using constructivism we can get beyond linear thinking to a fuller science that includes intuitive as well as analytical thinking, facilitated by cooperative group dynamics.

**Gilmer, Penny J**. Teaching Science at the University Level: What About the Ethics?. *Sci Eng Ethics*, 1(2), 173-180, A 95.

Ethics in science is integrated into an interdisciplinary science course called "Science, Technology and Society" (STS). This paper focuses on the section of the course called "Societal Impact on Science and Technology," which includes the topics Misconduct in Science, Scientific Freedom and Responsibility, and the Use of Human Subjects in Research. Students in the course become aware not only of the science itself, but also of the process of sciences, some aspects of the history of science, the social responsibilities of scientists, and the ethical issues of science. Teaching techniques include the instructor sharing experiences as a scientist with the students, sharing books and resources with students, utilizing current courses of information like the weekly "Science Times," inviting guest speakers, and utilizing portfolios to assess student learning.

**Gilmour, Peter** and Sumner, David. Response to Miller's 'Comment'. *Environ Values*, 6(1), 103-104, F 97.

**Gilson, Étienne**. La polémique de Malebranche contre Aristote et la philosophie scolastique. *Mod Sch*, 74(3), 205-218, Mr 97.

**Ginev, Dimitri**. *A Passage to the Hermeneutic Philosophy of Science*. Amsterdam, Rodopi, 1997.

In this book the author has brought together his long-standing interests in theory of scientific rationality and hermeneutic ontology by developing a hermeneutic alternative to analytic (and naturalist) epistemology of science. The "hermeneutic philosophy of science" is less the name of a new field of philosophical than a demand for a "repetition of the basic philosophical questions of science" from hermeneutic point of view. The book addresses chiefly two subjects" 1) The hermeneutic response to the models of rational reconstruction of scientific knowledge; 2) The specificity of hermeneutico-ontological approach to the cognitive pluralism in science. (publisher)

**Ginev, Dimitri**. Entre epistemología y retórica. *Analogia*, 11(1), 3-18, Ja-Je 97.

**Gingell, John** and Winch, Christopher. Educational Assessment: Reply to Andrew Davis. *J Phil Educ*, 30(3), 377-388, N 96.

Assessment is at the heart of teaching as it provides a necessary condition for judging success or failure. It is also necessary to ensure that providers of education are accountable to users and providers of resources. Inferential hazard is an inescapable part of any assessment procedure but cannot be an argument against assessment as such. Rich knowledge may be the aim of education but it does not follow that it is the aim of every stage of education. Teaching to tests is the most natural way of ensuring that teaching matches assessment. Failure to assess places public education in jeopardy.

**Gingras, Denis**. L'autodétermination des peuples comme principe juridique. *Laval Theol Phil*, 53(2), 365-375, Je 97.

The principle of the right of people to dispose of themselves has acquired, since its inscription into the United Nations Charter, which transformed it into a fundamental principle of international law, a juridical dimension which it would be a mistake to belittle by invoking the numerous exceptions that were arbitrarily imposed on it and the absence of a special procedure ensuring its application. The right of people and the rights of man, because they go against established situations, have not yet been systematized, but they retain, thanks to the recognition of their importance by international conscience, their validity and their imperative character.

**Gini, Al**. Moral Leadership: An Overview. *J Bus Ethics*, 16(3), 323-330, F 97.

This paper develops and examines the distinctions between the process of leadership, the person of the leader, and the job of leading. I argue that leadership is a delicate combination of the *process*, the techniques of leadership, the *person*, the specific talents and traits of a/the leader, and the general requirements of the *job* itself. The concept of leadership can and must be distinguishable and definable separately from our understanding of what and who leaders are, although the phenomenon of leadership can only be known and measured in the particular instantiation of a leader doing a job.

**Gini, Al**. Soul As in Ethic. *Bus Ethics Quart*, 7(3), 157-158, Jl 97.

**Ginisti, Jean-Pierre**. *La Logique Combinatoire*. Paris, Pr Univ France, 1997.

This book is an introduction to combinatory logic, a branch of modern logic which eliminates bound variables from formal sciences, tries to replace usual constants by combinators, classified entities into categories. It analyses its formal means (theory of combinators, theory of functionality), its philosophical norms, its applications to standard logics and to human sciences (Louis Frey, Jean-Pierre Desclés) and its history. A chapter is devoted to a deviant form of combinatory logic, the *predicate functor logic* of Quine. The author (Professor in the University of Lyon III) discusses ontological problems which are involved. Bibliography of 89 references.

**Giordano, Giuseppe**. "Arthur Stanley Eddington e la 'scoperta' della freccia del tempo" in *Il Concetto di Tempo: Atti del XXXII Congresso Nazionale della Società Filosofica Italiana,* Casertano, Giovanni (ed), 227-235. Napoli, Loffredo, 1997.

**Giorgini, Claudio**. Ente ed essenza in un saggio giovanile di Tommaso d'Aquino. *Sapienza*, 50(2), 129-146, 1997.

The purpose of the present research is to remark how the +De ente et essentia; work of the young Thomas of Aquinas contains a concise exposition of the Thomist metaphysics. Thomas's work marks the break from the scholastic philosophy of St. Augustin for a new foundation of philosophy. In this work Thomas defines the terms +Essentia; and +Ens;. He underlines how the Essentia accomplishes herself in the composite substances, in the simple substances, in the accidents. He also underlines how the notions of +Essentia; and +Ens; refer themselves to the logical intentions. Moreover Thomas making the real distinction between +Essentia; and +Esse; he characterizes God as the +Ipsum esse subsistens;, the same act of being (Actus essendi).

**Giralt-Bermúdez, María de los Angeles**. La problemática ética del uso del DBCP en Costa Rica. *Rev Filosof (Costa Rica)*, 34(83-84), 415-421, D 96.

In the light of human rights, this paper deals with the ethical repercussions of the use and abuse of dangerous pesticides, especially the right to a healthy and productive life in harmony with the natural and social environment. (edited)

**Girle, Roderic A**. Shades of Consciousness. *Mind Mach*, 6(2), 143-157, My 96.

It has been argued that consciousness might be what differentiates human from machine mentality. What then is consciousness? We discuss consciousness, particularly perception accounts of consciousness. It is argued that perception and consciousness are distinct. Armstrong's (1980) account of consciousness is rejected. It is proposed that perception is a necessary but not sufficient condition for consciousness and that there is a distinction to be drawn between consciousness and self-consciousness. Consciousness is tightly linked to attention and to certain sorts of knowledge. Implications for machine consciousness and machine attention are discussed.

**Girndt, Helmut**. Das "Ich" des ersten Grundsatzes der GWL in der Sicht der Wissenschaftslehre von 1804. *Fichte-Studien*, 10, 319-333, 1997.

**Girnyk, Andryi** and Milov, Yury P and Salamatov, Vladimir. The Chaos-Cosmos Transformation Cycle with Special Reference to the Chernobyl Disaster: Toward the Ultimate Reality and Meaning of the Ukraine. *Ultim Real Mean*, 20(2 & 3), 196-204, Je-S 97.

**Giroux, Guy** and Mineau, André and Boisvert, Yves. De l'usage social de l'éthique. *Philosopher*, 19, 9-22, 1996.

Lorsqu'un tel phénomène se produit, il est la résultante de l'usage social que l'on fait de l'éthique à l'intérieur de ces appareils. Il repose sur l'introduction de

AUTHOR INDEX 649 Glass, Thomas

*codes de conduite* dont l'ultime finalité en est une de contrôle social. Il s'ensuit que la demande d'éthique que nous connaissons aujourd'hui est susceptible de provoquer un effet pervers important. "Ce serait le cas dès lors qu'elle serait interprétée comme un appel en faveur d'un contrôle à exercer sur la société et sur les individus qui la composent, plutôt que de représenter un contrôle de la société par elle-même, d'abord au niveau des individus, puis au niveau de leurs unités d'appartenance, communautaires ou organisationnelles". (edited)

**Giroux, Laurent**. Hölderlin, le poète des dieux nouveaux: *Germanie* et *Le Rhin*. *Laval Theol Phil*, 53(2), 395-402, Je 97.

The question here raised is that of the preponderance bestowed by Heidegger upon Hölderlin in the "historial" destiny of the German people. From the outlook of his concern with *Being*, Heidegger discovers in Hölderlin's poetry a favorable entry into the very realm of *Being*. Is such a reading of the poet in anyway plausible and how can it be understood? What secret aim urges the philosopher in that direction? Could he have seen in the poetical work of Hölderlin—christened by him thinker of Being, herald of the gods to come and poet of poetry—a source of renewal this would make up for the already (in 1934) perceivable risks and hazards of the political future of the 3rd Reich?

**Gisel, Pierre**. Ernst Troeltsch: aboutissement ou dépassement du néo-protestantisme?. *Laval Theol Phil*, 52(3), 719-733, O 96.

Troeltsch assumes the heritage of neo-Protestantism, namely the passage through the Enlightenment and German idealism. He notably inherits the program of Schleiermacher, that is, a new definition of the status of theology and a reformulation of its doctrinal statements. But Troeltsch assumes this heritage by correcting a way of speculative conciliation (stemming from Hegel) as well as a primacy given to the moral (Ritschl). So Troeltsch is the witness of a crisis that at the turn of the century touches modernity which had to confront the plurality of religion and a "malaise of civilization" and he becomes involved in a "metacriticism of the modern critique of religion" that allows a "theory of religion" on the basis of a "method of history of civilization".

**Gitik, Moti** and Mitchell, William J. Indiscernible Sequences for Extenders, and the Singular Cardinal Hypothesis. *Annals Pure Applied Log*, 82(3), 273-316, D 96.

We prove several results giving lower bounds for the large cardinal strength of a failure of the singular cardinal hypothesis. The main result is the following theorem: ...In order to prove these theorems we give a detailed analysis of the sequences of indiscernibles which come from applying the covering lemma to nonoverlapping sequences of extenders. (edited)

**Giugliano, Antonello**. "Gothein, Lamprecht e i fondamenti concettuali della *Kulturgeschichte*" in *Lo Storicismo e la Sua Storia: Temi, Problemi, Prospettive,* Cacciatore, Giuseppe (ed), 313-333. Milano, Guerini, 1997.

**Giunti, Marco**. *Computation, Dynamics, and Cognition*. New York, Oxford Univ Pr, 1997.

Currently there is growing interest in the application of dynamical methods to the study of cognition. *Computation, Dynamics, and Cognition* investigates this convergence from a theoretical and philosophical perspective, generating a provocative new view of the aims and methods of cognitive science. Advancing the dynamical approach as the methodological frame best equipped to guide inquiry in the field's two main research programs—the symbolic and connectionist approaches—Marco Giunti engages a host of questions crucial not only to the science of cognition, but also to computation theory, dynamical systems theory, philosophy of mind, and philosophy of science. (publisher, edited)

**Giuntini, Roberto**. Brouwer-Zadeh Logic, Decidability and Bimodal Systems. *Stud Log*, 51(1), 97-112, 1992.

We prove that Brouwer-Zadeh logic has the finite model property and therefore is decidable. Moreover, we present a bimodal system (BKB) which turns out to be characterized by the class of all Brouwer-Zadeh frames. Finally, we show that Brouwer-Zadeh logic can be translated into BKB.

**Giusti, Miguel**. "Paradojas recurrentes de la argumentación comunitarista" in *Liberalismo y Comunitarismo: Derechos Humanos y Democracia,* Monsalve Solórzano, Alfonso (ed), 99-126. 36-46003 València, Alfons el Magnànim, 1996.

This article is a balance of the communitarian position. Its central thesis is that communitarianism, as a moral conception suffers from a categorical deficiency, which consists in the impossibility to give an adequate treatment to the problems which itself detects or arises. When taken to its furthermost consequences, communitarian argumentation leads to a series of paradoxes which acquire a paradigmatic or topic character. This thesis is developed through the analysis of three central notions of the communitarian conception: the starting point of moral argumentation, the idea of "community" and the idea of tradition. (Translation from the paper "Topische Paradoxien der kommunistaristischen Argumentation," which came out in the *Deutsche Zeitschrift für Philosophie*, 42(1994), pp. 759-781.)

**Givone, Sergio**. Libertà e verità oggettiva. *Iride*, 8(15), 265-273, Ag 95.

L'Autore rileva nell'affermazione della sacralità e inviolabilità della vita la tesi centrale dell'enc. *Evangelium vitae*. Sottolinea inoltre come i presupposti filosofici di questa tesi vadano ritrovati nell'enc. *Veritatis splendor*, dove il concetto di verità oggettiva (e quindi di legge naturale) costituisce il fondamento e insieme il limite della libertà umana. Passa poi a esaminare la prospettiva filosofica di fondo, quale emerge da questi testi di Giovanni Paolo II, mettendola a confronto con alcune delle più significative correnti attuali nell'ambito dell'etica. Se pragmatismo e utilitarismo—questa la conclusione—appaiono risposte piuttosto deboli alla "sfida" che viene mossa alla filosofia contemporanea dai vertici della Chiesa, invece una più radicale problematizzazione è possibile a partire da ermeneutica e pensiero tragico.

**Gjelsvik, Olav**. Tracking Truth and Solving Puzzles. *Inquiry*, 40(2), 209-224, Je 97.

Susan Haack's stated aim in her celebrated *Evidence and Inquiry* is a reconstruction of epistemology. Her most ambitious claim is that she has transcended the dichotomy of foundationalist versus coherentist theories of justification by providing a new position which integrates causal and evidential considerations in novel ways. This critical review article claims that there is doubt about whether this dichotomy can be transcended, and that getting things right in general epistemology hangs on getting right the relationship between theories of belief and theories of justification.

**Glander, Timothy**. Wilbur Schramm and the Founding of Communication Studies. *Educ Theor*, 46(3), 373-391, Sum 96.

This essay reviews the influence of Wilbur Schramm on the founding of communication study as discussed by two recently published books: Everett M. Rogers, *A History of Communication Study: A Biographical Approach* (New York: The Free Press, Macmillan, Inc. 1994) and Christopher Simpson, *Science of Coercion: Communication Research and Psychological Warfare 1945-1960* (New York: Oxford University Press, 1994). By articulating the Cold War context that shaped Schramm's and other key researcher's work, Simpson's book is more historically accurate and important than Rogers's book. Typical of most historical work in this area, Rogers's analysis tends to obfuscate the origins of communication study by refusing to deal with the dominant objectives undergirding communication research at midcentury. The legacy of government sponsored propaganda and psychological warfare research is also discussed, particularly with regard to public perceptions of television and the development of educational broadcasting.

**Glannon, Walter**. "The Morality of Selective Termination" in *Reproduction, Technology, and Rights: Biomedical Ethics Reviews,* Humber, James M (ed), 93-109. Clifton, Humana Pr, 1996.

In reproductive medicine, multiple gestations, caused either by the use of fertility drugs or in vitro fertilization, pose significant risks both to the fetuses and pregnant woman carrying them. This paper argues that medical reasons for selectively terminating some fetuses in bringing one or more to term can be justified on consequentialist moral grounds. Selective termination minimizes overall harm at the same time that it maximizes overall benefit, given the risks in a multiple pregnancy. Moreover, selective termination does not entail any conflict in the maternal-fetal relationship.

**Glannon, Walter**. Sensitivity and Responsibility for Consequences. *Phil Stud*, 87(3), 223-233, S 97.

John Martin Fischer and Mark Ravizza have argued that a person is morally responsible for a consequence just in case it is sensitive to his action. This paper argues that a person may be responsible for a consequence when it is sensitive to his beliefs but not to his action. It is not a physical ability but rather the cognitive ability to foresee the likely outcomes of our actions which ultimately grounds responsibility for consequences.

**Glaser, Jen**. Socrates, Friendship, and the Community of Inquiry. *Inquiry (USA)*, 16(4), 22-46, Sum 97.

**Glaser, John W**. Phase II of Bioethics: The Turn to the Social Nature of Individuals. *Bioethics Forum*, 11(3), 12-22, Fall 95.

Ethics encompasses different spheres of human activity: individual, institutional, and social ethics. The doing of ethics on these different levels points to a need to balance values differently, address new kinds of conflicts, and see consequences which vary widely. The societal impact of physician-assisted suicide serves as an example for analysis.

**Glass, Newman Robert**. Theory and Practice in the Experience of Art: John Dewey and the Barnes Foundation. *J Aes Educ*, 31(3), 91-105, Fall 97.

**Glass, Richard S** and Wood, Wallace A. Situational Determinants of Software Piracy: An Equity Theory Perspective. *J Bus Ethics*, 15(11), 1189-1198, N 96.

Software piracy has become recognized as a major problem for the software industry and for business. One research approach that has provided a theoretical framework for studying software piracy has been to place the illegal copying of software within the domain of ethical decision making and assumes that a person must be able to recognize software piracy as a moral issue. A person who fails to recognize a moral issue will fail to employ moral decision making schemata. There is substantial evidence that many individuals do not perceive software piracy to be an ethical problem. This paper applies social exchange theory, in particular equity theory, to predict the influence of situational factors on subjects' intentions to participate in software piracy. Consistent with the predictions of equity theory this study found that input and outcome situational variables significantly effect a person's intentions to commit software piracy.

**Glass, Thomas** and Schlüter, Andreas and Rathjen, Michael. On the Proof-Theoretic Strength of Monotone Induction in Explicit Mathematics. *Annals Pure Applied Log*, 85(1), 1-46, Ap 97.

We characterize the proof-theoretic strength of systems of explicit mathematics with a general principle (MID) asserting the existence of least fixed points for monotone inductive definitions, in terms of certain systems of analysis and set theory.... In the case of set theory, these are systems containing the Kripke-Platek axioms for a recursively inaccessible universe together with the existence of a stable ordinal. In all cases, the exact strength depends on what forms of induction are admitted in the respective systems. (edited)

**Glass, Thomas** and Strahm, Thomas. Systems of Explicit Mathematics with Non-Constructive Mu-Operator and Join. *Annals Pure Applied Log*, 82(2), 193-219, D 96.

The aim of this article is to give the proof-theoretic analysis of various subsystems of Feferman's theory $T_1$ for explicit mathematics which contain the nonconstructive mu-operator and join. We make use of standard proof-theoretic techniques such as cut-elimination of appropriate semi-formal systems and asymmetrical interpretations in standard structures for explicit mathematics.

**Glasser, Harold**. On Warwick Fox's Assessment of Deep Ecology. *Environ Ethics*, 19(1), 69-85, Spr 97.

I examine Fox's tripartite characterization of deep ecology. His assessment abandons Naess's emphasis upon the pluralism of ultimate norms by distilling what I refer to as the deep ecology approach to "self-realization!" Contrary to Fox, I argue that his *popular sense* is distinctive and his *formal sense* is tenable. Fox's *philosophical sense*, while distinctive, is neither necessary nor sufficient to adequately characterize the deep ecology approach. I contend that the deep ecology approach, as a formal approach to environmental philosophy, is *not* dependent upon and embodies much more than any single ultimate norm. (edited)

**Glauser, Richard**. Ressentiment et valeurs morales: Max Scheler, critique de Nietzsche. *Rev Theol Phil*, 128(3), 209-228, 1996.

Nietzsche's theory of the origin of Christian moral values is based on the psychological phenomenon of ressentiment. Refuting Nietzsche, Scheler asserts a realist theory of axiological hierarchy; but his epistemology of values demands a central role for ressentiment, comparable in importance (but for different reasons) to the role which Nietzsche gives it. This article elucidates Scheler's analysis of ressentiment and its role in his epistemology. Scheler makes important concessions to Nietzsche concerning the necessity of the ressentiment interpretation of certain concrete morals and modern ideologies. These concessions place him on sufficiently similar terrain to explain Nietzsche's erroneous conclusions concerning the real meaning of Christian moral values.

**Gleizer, Marcos André**. Consideraçoes sobre o Problema da Verdade em Espinosa. *Discurso*, 24, 129-145, 1994.

Este artigo examina alguns aspectos do pensamento de Espinosa que tornam que tornam possível o estabelecimento de uma relaçao de complementaridade entre as noçoes de adequaçao e correspondência em sua concepçao da verdade, procurando opor esta relaçao àquela existente entre as noçoes de evidência e verdade na concepçao cartesiana.

**Gleizer, Marcos André**. Espinosa e o "Círculo Cartesiano". *Cad Hist Filosof Cie*, 5(1-2), 45-72, Ja-D 95.

This article intends to examine the solution proposed by Spinoza to the "Cartesian circle" problem. Considering the Spinozistic analysis of the conditions to the authentic doubt, it will be shown how the *verum index sui* philosopher answers the question concerning the self-justification of the rational knowledge objective value.

**Glidden, David**. "Philo of Larissa and Platonism" in *Scepticism in the History of Philosophy: A Pan-American Dialogue*, Popkin, Richard H (ed), 219-234. Dordrecht, Kluwer, 1996.

In the ancient history of philosophy, Platonism proved impervious to scepticism. St. Augustine correctly credited Philo of Larissa with demonstrating this, thereby returning the Academy, such as it was, to Plato's original legacy. Philo of Larissa opened the way toward the revival of Platonism, not by espousing a mitigated form of scepticism, but rather by advancing a form of direct mental recognition, or a form of mental vision which did not require the mediation of sensory appearances. This interpretive speculation is supported by Sextus's discussion of Philo's innovations, at the time of the Sosus affair, when Antiochus broke with Philo.

**Glidden, David**. Augustine's Hermeneutics and the Principle of Charity. *Ancient Phil*, 17(2), 135-157, Spr 97.

Despite Epicurus's great debt to Democritus, he found it necessary to enrich Democritus' ontology in order to avoid the unpalatable skeptical consequences that he thought resulted from Democritus' ontology. The fundamental difference between them was not, as many believe, that Democritus was a reductionist and Epicurus a nonreductionist, but that Democritus believed that only the intrinsic properties of bodies were real, whereas Epicurus was much more permissive in what he was willing to predicate of things. (edited)

**Glidden, David K**. Josiah Royce's Reading of Plato's *Theaetetus*. *Hist Phil Quart*, 13(3), 273-286, Jl 96.

The eristic paradox served as a starting point for Josiah Royce's metaphysical and moral outlook, beginning with *The Religious Aspect of Philosophy* (1885) and continuing to his final *Hope of the Great Community* (1916). In particular, Royce's early reflections on how error proves possible, as the puzzle was specifically presented in Plato's *Theaetetus*, proved foundational for Royce's entire philosophical development. Royce's particular solution to the puzzles of the waxed table and the aviary is suggestive of similar moves in Frege, Wittgenstein, and the neopragmatism of Richard Rorty, not to mention Royce's own theory of community.

**Gligorov, Vladimir** and Strncevic, Ljubica. Rawls's "The Closed Society Assumption" (in Serbo-Croatian). *Theoria (Yugoslavia)*, 38(2), 53-64, Je 95.

The article analyzes "the closed society assumption" that Rawls introduces in his latest book *Political Liberalism*. It is shown that the assumption is i) new (it is stronger than the autarky assumption that is used in *A Theory of Justice*), ii) metaphysical and not political (contrary to Rawls's intentions), iii) contradictory, and iv) not necessary, as it does not have the political consequences.

**Glock, H J**. Abusing Use. *Dialectica*, 50(3), 205-223, 1996.

This paper discusses objections against the idea that the meaning of a word is its use. Sct. 1 accepts Rundle's point that 'meaning' and 'use' are used differently, but insists that this is compatible with holding that use determines meaning, and therefore holds the key to conceptual analysis. Sct. 2-4 rebut three lines of argument which claim that linguistic philosophy goes astray by reading into the meaning of words nonsemantic features of its use: Searle's general speech act fallacy charge, Hacker's use of the Frege-point against Wittgenstein's account of avowals, and Grice's attack on Wittgenstein's discussion of 'trying'. Sct. 5 argues that Grice's doctrine of conversational implicature fails to show that the features he disregards are pragmatic rather than semantic. Sct. 6 ends with some suggestions about how use can be related to meaning without being abused.

**Glock, Hans-Johann**. "Necessity and Normativity" in *The Cambridge Companion to Wittgenstein*, Sluga, Hans (ed), 198-225. Needham Heights, Cambridge, 1996.

The essay tries to shed light on Wittgenstein's account of logical necessity by contrasting it with Quine's. Both reject the positivists' claim that necessary truths are true by virtue of meaning, but while Quine is committed to the idea that necessary truths boil down to well-confirmed empirical truths, Wittgenstein claims that necessary propositions are not descriptions, but have a normative role. I try to show that this position does not fall foul of Quine's attack on the analytic/synthetic distinction, but helps to undermine Quine's 'norm-free' conception of language by establishing that (implicit) linguistic rules are a necessary precondition of meaningful discourse.

**Glock, Hans-Johann**. Kant and Wittgenstein: Philosophy, Necessity and Representation. *Int J Phil Stud*, 5(2), 285-305, Je 97.

Several authors have detected profound analogies between Kant and Wittgenstein. Their claims have been contradicted by scholars, such being the agreed penalty for attributions to authorities. Many of the alleged similarities have either been left unsubstantiated at a detailed exegetical level, or have been confined to highly general points. At the same time, the 'scholarly' backlash has tended to ignore the importance of some of these general points, or has focused on very specific issues or purely terminological matters. To advance the debate, I distinguish four different topics: questions of actual influence; parallels at the methodological level; substantial similarities in philosophical logic; substantial similarities in the philosophy of mind. The article concentrates on the second and third topic. (edited)

**Glock, Hans-Johann**. Truth Without People?. *Philosophy*, 72(279), 85-104, Ja 97.

This paper investigates an anthropocentric conception of truth which makes truth dependent on the activities of people in the following sense: I) the *concept* of truth would not exist without people, II) it is only possible to state what the beavers of truth are in terms that implicitly refer to people, III) truths are identified by grouping actual or potential utterances according to what they say. It argues that this position is not committed to any disreputable antirealisms and that its tenability depends on the question of truth-beaver. Although the nominalist account of truth-beavers fails, Platonism is equally away. What is true or false is what people say or could say.

**Glombik, Czeslaw**. Poles and the Göttingen Phenomenological Movement (in Polish). *Kwartalnik Filozof*, 24(3), 105-132, 1996.

The article attempts to present early contacts of Polish students with Edmund Husserl in times when the phenomenological movement originated in Göttingen. So far Roman Ingarden has been recognized as a Polish follower of Husserl. Also Kazimierz Ajdukiewicz has been associated with the beginnings of the movement. Still, both came to Göttingen after another Polish student from Lvov, Stefan Blachowski (1889-1962). Although Blachowski studied psychology and received Ph. D. under Georg E. Müller, he participated in Husserl's seminars and applied the phenomenological method in his earliest writings. Ingarden is now regarded as a member of Göttingen phenomenological team; the author proposes to treat Ajdukiewicz and Blachowski as sympathizers of the developing phenomenology.

**Glouberman, Mark**. Descartes's Wax and the Typology of Early Modern Philosophy. *Mod Sch*, 74(2), 117-141, Ja 97.

Despite widespread criticism of the 'standard' empiricism/rationalism typology of early modernity, 'empiricism' *can* be given a viable meaning in terms of Locke's theorizing. Locke's actual position is fuzzy because at a crucial ontologico-metaphysical fork he selects the path that he should decline. At the fork stands Descartes's was-experiment. A distinction has to be observed between the experiment's negative side (isolating what is wrong in our sense-based understanding of physical substance) and its positive side (furnishing a proper conception). An empiricist, in the viable sense, is one who accepts only the former. Acceptance of the latter is *definitive of early modern rationalism. Locke's confusion emerges in his elision of the relationality of an ascription and the inessentiality or contingency of the inherence link between the property and that to which it is ascribed.*

**Glouberman, Mark**. Philosophy and Egypt. *Iyyun*, 46, 3-28, Ja 97.

'There are more things in heaven and on earth,' says Hamlet, 'than are dreamt of in our philosophy.' Did not Descartes, the 'father' of the discipline in its modern form, represent his fictional alter ego, the meditator, as conjuring philosophy up while dozing by the hearth, attired in his dressing gown—in that twilit state of consciousness between dreaming and waking? What is the link between philosophy and dreaming? Pace Hamlet, it is argued that epochal philosophizing (as opposed to the menial work of analysis and clarification that philosophers also do) is a controlled kind of dreaming. Descartes's dream-argument and the more general cognitive shake-up of which it is a part, are better read in this way than as straight epistemology.

**Glouberman, Mark**. Spinoza à la Mode: A Defence of Spinozistic Anti-Pluralism. *Austl J Phil*, 75(1), 38-61, Mr 97.

Clues in Spinoza's writings suggest an analysis of the semantics of singular statements on which the everyday distinction between qualities and things is represented as an internal partition of a uniform category of qualities. The result

AUTHOR INDEX 651 Goebel, Eckart

is an ontology free of commonsensical 'things.' The technicalities of the suggested *analysans* are developed in this paper and the result used to defend Spinoza against a criticism of his monism that is often thought to be lethal. Spinoza's practice here, it is also shown, follows a pattern that recurs in 'rationalist' positions. A key objective of the discussion is to illustrate and explain, *ambulando* as it were, the interpretive liabilities of the analytic approach.

**Glouberman, Mark**. The King and 'I': Agency and Rationality in Athens and Jerusalem. *Ratio*, 10(1), 10-34, Ap 97.

Although Western culture draws substantively on Athens *and* Jerusalem, hostility tends to be shown towards Jerusalem from the philosophical wing. I attempt to correct the imbalance. Philosophy, I argue, arose in the Greek context because of a problem of self-confidence. 'Philosophical rationality' cannot therefore be taken as normative for rationality generally. The contrast between the Jerusalemite and the Athenian views of self and of the contrasting estimates and explanations of the efficacy (or inefficacy) of the self's agency is developed through an examination of the main documents of preclassical and classical Greece, and the *Bible*.

**Glover, Jonathan**. "Nations, Identity, and Conflict" in *The Morality of Nationalism,* McKim, Robert (ed), 11-30. New York, Oxford Univ Pr, 1997.

**Glover, Saundra H** and Bumpus, Minnette A and Logan, John E (& others). Re-Examining the Influence of Individual Values on Ethical Decision Making. *J Bus Ethics*, 16(12-13), 1319-1329, S 97.

This paper presents the results of five years of research involving three studies. The first two studies investigated the impact of the value honesty/integrity on the ethical decision choice an individual makes, as moderated by the individual personality traits of self-monitoring and private self-consciousness. The third study, which is the focus of this paper, expanded the two earlier studies by varying the level of moral intensity and including the influence of demographical factors and other workplace values; achievement, fairness and concern for others on the ethical decision process. (edited)

**Gloy, Karen**. Natur im westlichen und östlichen Verständnis. *Frei Z Phil Theol*, 44(1-2), 158-175, 1997.

The article discusses two different and opposite concepts of nature: the Western analytical pattern of natural sciences and the Eastern holistic pattern. The characteristics of the first are: (1) the subject-object-difference, (2) the mechanicism, (3) the experiment, and (4) the master-servant-relation. The characteristics of the second are: (1) unity of all beeing, (2) organicity, (3) the concept of nondoing, and (4) the principle of nonhurting.

**Gloy, Karen**. Vernunft und das Andere der Vernunft: Eine modelltheoretische Exposition. *Z Phil Forsch*, 50(4), 527-562, O-D 96.

**Gluck, John P**. Harry F. Harlow and Animal Research: Reflection on the Ethical Paradox. *Ethics Behavior*, 7(2), 149-161, 1997.

With respect to the ethical debate about the treatment of animals in biomedical and behavioral research, Harry F. Harlow represents a paradox. On the one hand, his work on monkey cognition and social development fostered a view of the animals as having rich subjective lives filled with intention and emotion. On the other, he has been criticized for the conduct of research that seemed to ignore the ethical implications of his own discoveries. The basis of this contradiction is discussed and propositions for current research practice are presented.

**Gluck, John P** and Eldridge, Jennifer J. Gender Differences in Attitudes Toward Animal Research. *Ethics Behavior*, 6(3), 239-256, 1996.

Although gender differences in attitudes toward animal research have been reported in the literature for some time, exploration into the nature of these differences has received less attention. This article examines gender differences in responses to a survey of attitudes toward the use of animals in research. The survey was completed by college students and consisted of items intended to tap different issues related to the animal research debate. Results indicated that women were more likely than men to support tenets of the animal protection movement. Likewise, women were more likely than men to favor increased restrictions on animal use and were more concerned than men about the suffering of research animals. Analysis of item contents suggested that women endorsed items reflecting a general caring for animals, were more willing than men to make personal sacrifices such as giving up meat and medical benefits in an effort to protect animals, and were more likely than men to question the use of animals in research on scientific grounds. Men, on the other hand, tended to emphasize the potential benefits arising from the use of animals in research.

**Gluck, John P** and Shapiro, Kenneth J. The Forum. *Ethics Behavior*, 7(2), 185-192, 1997.

**Goble, Lou**. Quantified Deontic Logic with Definite Descriptions. *Log Anal*, 37(147-8), 239-253, S-D 94.

This paper presents a formal semantics and proves strong consistency and completeness theorems for a system of quantified deontic logic with identity and definite descriptions. Unlike other systems of deontic logic, this system is fully extensional with respect to singular terms allowing unrestricted classical quantifier rules and unrestricted substitution of all coreferring singular terms, including definite descriptions within deontic contexts.

**Goble, Lou**. 'Ought' and Extensionality. *Nous*, 30(3), 330-355, S 96.

This paper argues that, unlike alethic modal and intentional operators, deontic operators are extensional or referentially transparent with respect to singular terms, and that classical rules governing quantification, identity and definite descriptions apply without restriction to statements within quantified deontic logic. Further, it proposes a way to interpret the deontic operators within the framework of first-order quantification theory that satisfies these conditions without sacrificing the operators' deontic character.

**Gobry, Ivan**. La contradiction du stoïcisme. *Diotima*, 25, 56-61, 1997.

**Gockowski, Janusz**. "Tradition in Science" in *The Idea of University,* Brzezinski, Jerzy (ed), 161-178. Amsterdam, Rodopi, 1997.

The author arguing that there is no science without tradition takes up the analysis of the forms of the presence of tradition in science. Tradition in science is understood as multigenerational observation and respect of the patterns of thought and scholarly activity, undertaken because of the axiological option and of the pragmatic reasons. Use of the patterns of thought and scholarly activities is related to multigenerational observation and respect of the problem situation. In science, tradition is multilevel and a change of the problem situation in science is never synonymous with the breaking of the continuity; scientific revolutions are the beginning of new traditions, even though at the same time they relate to some distant precursor. The author argues that the development of the self-knowledge of scientists contribute in a large degree to reaching higher levels of professional awareness. (edited)

**Goddard, Jean-Chr**. "El destino religioso del hombre en la filosofía de Fichte" in *El inicio del Idealismo alemán,* Market, Oswaldo, 221-236. Madrid, Ed Complutense, 1996.

In Abweichung von der Meinung, für die Bestimmung des Menschen eine Wende in religiosen Denken Fichtes seit dem Atheismusstreit darstellt, vertritt der Vortrag die These, dass dieses Werk in derselben Linie mit der Grundlage und sogar mit Fichtes Auffassung vor dieser Schrift steht. Der Vortrag betont die Rolle der Einbildungskraft sowohl als Instrument der Freiheit als auch lebendes Zentrum der religiosen Konzeption Fichtes.

**Godden, David M**. Nehamas' *Life as Literature*: A Case for the Defence. *Kinesis*, 23(2), 29-46, Fall 96.

**Goddu, André**. William of Ockham's Distinction between "Real" Efficient Causes and Strictly *Sine Qua Non* Causes. *Monist*, 79(3), 357-367, Jl 96.

William of Ockham distinguishes between "real" efficient and *sine qua non* causes. A "real" efficient cause requires a potency in the cause for producing the effect. A cause *sine qua non* refers to a necessary condition for an effect to be produced, but it is not a "real" efficient cause, because it is not really productive of an effect. A necessary condition often refers to a hindrance that must be removed before the "real" cause can act effectively. On the sacraments, Ockham concludes that sacraments are *sine qua non* causes and that God is the real efficient cause of grace.

**Godlovitch, Stanley**. Carlson on Appreciation. *J Aes Art Crit*, 55(1), 53-55, Wint 97.

In what does aesthetic appreciation consist? A recent view analyzes appreciation principally along Ziff's epistemic conception as a form of cognition; i.e., 'sizing something up'. This analysis is challenged positively by alternative notions of appreciation arguably more suitable to the aesthetic context, and also negatively by cases where appreciation may be ruined by knowledge of the object. Central to the alternative notions is a sense of appreciation as a form of valuing and of taking pleasure in the good recognized to reside in the object of appreciation.

**Godlovitch, Stanley**. Forbidding Nasty Knowledge: On the Use of Ill-Gotten Information. *J Applied Phil*, 14(1), 1-17, 1997.

I explore a few arguments meant to remove the moral qualms and show them all to be wanting. However, because we in fact regularly and routinely benefit in countless ways from many systematic evils of the distant past without qualms, we seem to be inconsistently selective when it concerns certain evils. This inconsistency can be explained, if not justified, by appeal to a principle of decent delay which allows us after a time to ignore the origins of our present benefits and so make moral fadeout acceptable. This principle itself is grounded in our natural and increasing forgetfulness of events as they recede in time, an adaptive mechanism which allows us both to carry on our lives in relative decency and yet to maintain a fitting sensitivity to newer, closer evils which affect more immediately our relations with others and our sense of moral integrity. (edited)

**Godlovitch, Stanley**. Innovation and Conservatism in Performance Practice. *J Aes Art Crit*, 55(2), 151-168, Spring 97.

**Godo, Lluís**. Fuzzy Truth Values (in Spanish). *Agora (Spain)*, 15(2), 49-62, 1996.

In this paper we focus on the semantical and representational issues of the so-called fuzzy truth-values. One of the distinguishing features of Fuzzy Logic, in contraposition to classical logic, is the use of the whole unit real interval as base set of truth-values. A fuzzy truth-value is nothing but a fuzzy subset of [0, 1], i.e., a fuzzy subset of truth-values. Such fuzzy subsets are used either to truth qualify fuzzy statements, or as a relative measure of the validity of a fuzzy statement with respect to another taken for granted. In this paper we carefully analyze the most relevant semantical aspects of fuzzy truth-values in relation to their role in the modelling of approximate reasoning.

**Godway, Eleanor M**. Private Scholars—Public Intellectuals: Can These Be Separated?. *Int Stud Phil*, 29(1), 35-44, 1997.

**Goebel, Eckart**. *Konstellation und Existenz.* Tubingen, Stauffenburg, 1996.

In *Konstellation und Existenz* werden philosophische und literarische Werke aus der Endphase der Weimarer Republik als Versuche einer Antwort auf "die elementare Lebensverlegenheit" der Epoche interpretiert. Zwei einander entgegengesetzte philosophische Schriften—Heideggers Kantbuch (1929) und Benjamins Trauerspielbuch (1928)—treffen sich, jenseits der Erkenntnistheorie'. Zwei in ihrer Konzeption konträre Prosawerke—Jahnns Perrudja (1929) und Musils Mann ohne Eigenschaften (1930)—sind gleichermassen Antworten auf die "Krisis des Romans". Gemeinsam ist den Autoren der Wille zur Überwindung des "Welt-Bildes" der Neuzeit, in dem das Subjekt als die Bezugsmitte des Seienden angesetzt wird. (publisher, edited)

Goering, Sara 652 AUTHOR INDEX

**Goering, Sara** and Figueroa, Robert. The Summer Philosophy Institute of Colorado: Building Bridges. *Teach Phil*, 20(2), 155-168, Je 97.

This article explores the creation of the Summer Philosophy Institute of Colorado, a week-long residential program in philosophy for high school students from across Colorado. The program is designed to attract students from diverse backgrounds and to encourage students who are not on the college track to pursue their studies. It relies on the ability of philosophical topics to spark students' natural love of learning and to hone their critical thinking skills. The article offers an overview of the successful summer program's first two years and discusses the introduction of an academic year outreach program.

**Goerner, E A** and Thompson, Walter J. Politics and Coercion. *Polit Theory*, 24(4), 620-652, N 96.

We compare communitarian and liberal approaches to coercion by comparing Aquinas's analysis of a hypothetical prelapsarian politics with Rawls's functionally similar, hypothetical, "strict compliance theory". We find 1) that coercion has a far less foundational role in Thomistic politics than in Rawlsian (and most liberal) politics; 2) that this general difference is reversed in a single, but historically crucial area: coercion to eradicate Christian heretics and 3) that this exception has tended to marginalize Thomistic contributions to the current communitarian-liberalism debates because it justifies the religious violence among Christians that historically led to the victory of liberal politics as a reactionary solution to that violence.

**Götke, Povl**. Sozialstruktur und Sematik: Der wissenssoziologische Ansatz Niklas Luhmanns. *Dan Yrbk Phil*, 30, 68-95, 1995.

**Goetz, Stewart**. Libertarian Choice. *Faith Phil*, 14(2), 195-211, Ap 97.

In this paper, I develop a noncausal view of agency. I defend the thesis that choices are uncaused mental actions and maintain, contrary to causal theorists of action, that choices differ intrinsically or inherently from nonactions. I explain how they do by placing them in an ontology favored by causal agency theorists (agent-causationists). This ontology is one of powers and liabilities. After explicating how a choice is an uncaused event, I explain how an adequate account of freedom involves the concept of choosing for a reason. Choosing for a reason is a teleological notion and I set forth what is involved in making a choice for a purpose.

**Götz, Ignacio L**. Symbols and the Nature of Teaching. *Educ Theor*, 47(1), 67-83, Wint 97.

The claim is that the nature of teaching can be captured adequately only in symbolic and narrative terms because the basic ostensive nature of teaching is irreducible to anything else. The argument parallels Paul Ricoeur's contention that there are no nonsymbolic expressions of evil. Similarly, there are no nonsymbolic descriptions of teaching. Teaching activities are first described in symbols, then in narratives and finally in philosophical ways. The argument traces this progress backwards. The conclusion is that teaching actions themselves are symbolic pointings or showings, so that the most adequate thing that can be said about teaching itself is that it is like showing.

**Gogotishvili, Liudmila Akhilovna**. The Early Losev. *Russian Stud Phil*, 35(1), 6-31, Sum 96.

**Gold, E R**. *Body Parts: Property Rights and the Ownership of Human Biological Materials*. Washington, Georgetown Univ Pr, 1996.

In *Body Parts*, E. Richard Gold examines whether the body and materials derived from it—such as human organs and DNA—should be thought of as market commodities and subject to property law. Analyzing a series of court decisions concerning property rights, Gold explores whether the language and assumptions of property law can help society determine who has rights to human biological materials. (publisher,edited)

**Goldberg, Sanford C**. Self-Ascription, Self-Knowledge, and the Memory Argument. *Analysis*, 57(3), 211-219, Jl 97.

Following Burge 1988, many attempts to reconcile externalism with introspective self-knowledge of one's thought attempt to do this by showing that externalism is compatible with true justified self-ascription of the thought. This achieves the reconciliation only on the identification of true justified self-*ascription* with self-*knowledge* of content. I argue that, in the context of the self-knowledge debate, this identification is tendentious. My case consists of revising Boghossian's Memory Argument; I suggest that the argument's appeal to memory is not essential, but instead is to be seen as making a point (which can be made in other ways) that tells against the identification in question. If my reconstruction is cogent, the self-knowledge debate may well hinge on the legitimacy of the identification of self-knowledge with self-ascription, virtually unexamined in the literature.

**Goldblatt, Robert**. Parallel Action: Concurrent Dynamic Logic with Independent Modalities. *Stud Log*, 51(3-4), 551-578, 1992.

In a semantics due to Peleg, each command *alpha* is interpreted as a set of pairs (*s*, *T*), with *T* being the set of states "reachable" from *s* by a single execution of *alpha*, possibly involving several processes acting in parallel. We prove that the logic defined by this modelling is finitely axiomatisable and has the finite model property, hence is decidable. This requires the development a new theory of canonical models and filtrations for "reachability" relations. (edited)

**Golden, Jill**. The Care of the Self: Poststructuralist Questions About Moral Education and Gender. *J Moral Educ*, 25(4), 381-393, D 96.

The relationship between poststructuralist theory and ethics or values in education is a complex and relatively unexplored one, yet in classrooms the ethical implications of theory are lived out daily in the relations between teachers and children. Teachers who are interested in bringing the insights of poststructuralist theory into their work with children still tend to refer back (consciously or otherwise) to the ethics of versions of liberal humanism in making value judgements. The incongruence which results can undermine changes that a teacher wants to bring about. One approach to this dilemma can be through narrative. Narrative, or story, is one of the "technologies of the self" most available to teachers and children for the construction, regulation and care of selves (as knowers, as learners and as moral agents), including the ongoing construction of values associated with feminine and masculine gender identities. Deconstruction of children's classroom and lived narratives can make this process visible. This paper will explore the specific and differing values made visible in one story told by five children.

**Golden, Marija**. Interrogative Wh-Movement in Slovene and English. *Acta Analytica*, 145-187, 1995.

This article is a comparative study of overt interrogative wh-movement in Slovene and English, set within the standard principles-and-parameters theory of language. The focus is on a detailed examination of Slovene, a language not yet included in wh-typologies of (Slavic) languages. The typological variation exhibited by Slovene and English is shown, to a large extent, to involve a systematic correlation of individual properties which follow from the parametrized identification of proper governors for the purposes of the ECP, as well as from the overt syntax of their multiple wh-questions. (edited)

**Goldfarb, David A**. Lermontov and the Omniscience of Narrators. *Phil Lit*, 20(1), 61-73, Ap 96.

**Goldfarb, Warren**. "The Philosophy of Mathematics in Early Positivism" in *Origins of Logical Empiricism*, Giere, Ronald N (ed), 213-230. Minneapolis, Univ of Minnesota Pr, 1996.

**Goldfarb, Warren**. "Wittgenstein on Fixity of Meaning" in *Early Analytic Philosophy*, Tait, William W (ed), 75-89. Chicago, Open Court, 1997.

**Goldfarb, Warren**. Metaphysics and Nonsense: On Cora Diamond's *The Realistic Spirit*. *J Phil Res*, 22, 57-73, Ap 97.

**Golding, Martin P**. Transitional Regimes and the Rule of Law. *Ratio Juris*, 9(4), 387-395, D 96.

This paper seeks to establish a connection between the existence of a legal system and the ideal of the rule of law. Its point of departure is the phenomenon of a transitional regime that is attempting to restore or institute the rule of law. Lon Fuller's formulation of the canons of the rule of law as an internal morality of law is expounded as well as his notion of legal pathology as symptomatic of departure from the canons' requirements. The existence of a legal system, it is argued, it is a matter of degree, covariant with the degree to which the rule of law is realized. Problems inherent to the implementation of the rule of law are examined, such as the effect of the passage of time on reasonable expectations. While legal pathology is always a matter of degree, police states are shown to suffer seriously from it. Among the examples discussed are Nazi Germany and Communist East Germany, although it is granted that there are moral differences between them. Finally, a response is made to some contemporary critiques of the rule of law.

**Goldsby, Michael G** and Shepard, Jon M and Gerde, Virginia W. Teaching Business Ethics Through Literature. *Teach Bus Ethics*, 1(1), 33-51, 1997.

America's economic ideology lacks a vocabulary of ethics. If, as we assume, an economic system requires a moral component for long-term survival, students in business schools must be exposed to a vocabulary of ethics that is consistent with the ideology of capitalism. We present a vocabulary of ethics and describe an approach to teaching business ethics based on business-related classic literature and moral philosophy.

**Goldstein, Laurence**. Humor and Harm. *Sorites*, 27-42, N 95.

For familiar reasons, stereotyping is believed to be irresponsible and offensive. Yet the use of stereotypes in humor is widespread. Particularly offensive are thought to be sexual and racial stereotypes, yet it is just these that figure particularly prominently in jokes. In certain circumstances it is unquestionably wrong to make jokes that employ such stereotypes. Some writers have made the much stronger claim that in all circumstances it is wrong to find such jokes funny; in other words that people who laugh at such jokes betray sexist/racist attitudes. This conclusion seems false. (edited)

**Goldstein, Lisa S**. *Teaching with Love: A Feminist Approach to Early Childhood Education*. New York, Lang, 1997.

Teachers commonly talk about loving their students, yet no effort has been made to explore the powerful educational potential inherent in these loving feelings. *Teaching with Love* breaks new ground by paying careful, scholarly attention to the nature, the scope, the dimensions and the variety of teacherly love. In a highly readable narrative that builds on the feminist notion of an ethic of care and draws from the fields of psychology and women's studies, this book examines and analyzes the experiences of two primary grade teachers as they set about trying to create and enact a vision of early childhood education centered around loving relationships. (publisher)

**Goldstein, Sheldon**. Review Essay: Bohmian Mechanics and the Quantum Revolution. *Synthese*, 107(1), 145-165, Ap 96.

This is a joint review of two important books on the foundations of quantum mechanics: *The Undivided Universe*, by Bohm and Hiley and *Speakable and Unspeakable in Quantum Mechanics*, by Bell. The concern of these books and of this essay, is with Bohmian mechanics, the deterministic reformulation of quantum mechanics proposed by Bohm in 1952, as well as with the nonlocality, implicit in standard quantum theory, that Bohmian mechanics forces upon our attention. The bottom line: If you want to develop an understanding of the genuine innovations of nonrelativistic quantum theory, read Bell's book carefully!

**Goldstein, Sheldon** (& others) and Dürr, Detlef and Daumer, Martin. Naive Realism about Operators. *Erkenntnis*, 45(2 & 3), 379-397, Nov 96.

A source of much difficulty and confusion in the interpretation of quantum mechanics is a "naive realism about operators." By this we refer to various ways of taking too seriously the notion of operator-as-observable and in particular to the all too casual talk about "measuring operators" that occurs when the subject is quantum mechanics. Without a specification of what should be meant by "measuring" a quantum observable, such an expression can have no clear meaning. A definite specification is provided by Bohmian mechanics, a theory that emerges from Schrödinger's equation for a system of particles when we merely insist that "particles" means particles. Bohmian mechanics clarifies the status and the role of operators as observables in quantum mechanics by providing the operational details absent from standard quantum mechanics. It thereby allows us to readily dismiss all the radical claims traditionally enveloping the transition from the classical to the quantum realm—for example, that we must abandon classical logic or classical probability. The moral is rather simple: Beware naive realism, especially about operators!

**Goldstick, Danny**. Property Identity and 'Intrinsic' Designation. *Philosophy*, 72(281), 449-452, Jl 97.

As between two property-designating noun phrases, coreferentiality requires an even tighter synonymity relation than logical equivalence—unless at least one of them designates its referent only extrinsically, rather than intrinsically. To have justified lumping the problem of nonsubstances' identity criteria with the problem of defining intrinsicness is to have achieved something.

**Goldstick, Danny**. Response. *Nature Soc Thought*, 8(2), 160-165, 1995.

Against Erwin Marquit's objection (in the same issue of NST) that Engels (like Hegel) did disagree with the logical Noncontradiction Principle, the author defends his 1995 paper "Marxism on Dialectical and Logical Contradiction" (Australian Journal of Philosophy, 73(1), 102-113).

**Goldthorpe, Rhiannon**. Sartre and the Self: Discontinuity or Continuity?. *Amer Cath Phil Quart*, 70(4), 519-536, Autumn 96.

**Goldworth, Amnon**. Individual Autonomy and Collective Decisionmaking. *Cambridge Quart Healthcare Ethics*, 6(3), 356-357, Sum 97.

**Goller, Hans**. Das Leib-Seele-Problem in der Psychologie. *Theol Phil*, 72(2), 231-246, 1997.

Psychology not only deals with behavior but also with experiences like perception, sensation, feelings, thinking, desires and needs. Scientific and applied psychology as well implicitly raise the question of how inner experience and behavior are connected with each other. How is this connection to be understood? The article stresses the irreducibly subjective character of the mental. This quality raises questions which still remain unresolved. The mind-body problem also touches the way psychology sees itself. The history of psychology can be understood as a struggle over how to do justice both the inner experience and the behavior as well.

**Golomb, Jacob** (ed). *Nietzsche and Jewish Culture*. New York, Routledge, 1997.

This unique collection of essays explores the reciprocal relationship between Nietzsche and Jewish culture. It is organized in two parts: the first examines Nietzsche's attitudes towards Jews and Judaism; the second Nietzsche's reception by Jewish intellectuals as diverse and as famous as Franz Kafka, Martin Buber, Franz Rosenzweig and Sigmund Freud. Each carefully selected essay explores one aspect of Nietzsche's interrelation with Judaism in German-speaking countries, from Heinrich Heine to Nazism. (publisher)

**Golumbia, David**. Rethinking Philosophy in the Third Wave of Feminism. *Hypatia*, 12(3), 100-115, Sum 97.

The influence of feminist theory on philosophy has been less pervasive than it might have been. This is due in part to inherent tensions between feminist critique and the university as an institution, and to philosophy's place in the academy. These tensions, if explored rather than resisted, can result in a revitalized, more explicitly feminist conception of philosophy itself, wherein philosophy is seen as an attempt to rethink the deepest aspects of experience and culture.

**Gómez, Angel Alvarez**. Por qué no Descartes? Tres razones de actualidad. *Agora (Spain)*, 15(1), 109-128, 1996.

It is current relevance that justifies the opinion that Descartes's philosophy is valid because it provides food for thought. The fourth centenary of his birth is an occasion for reflection on this theme. Descartes is relevant for three main reasons. Firstly, because today's cacophony of discordant views and standpoints recalls the similarly radical discord that led him to investigate the foundations of knowledge and to assert the concord of all things with human reason. Secondly, because it was his epistemic inversion of the Aristotelian model of knowledge that made the birth and growth of the new sciences possible. Thirdly, because of the accompanying metaphysical inversion centered on the concepts of freedom and the power of reason, which in a sense defines the sphere of action of modern man and the corresponding perils.

**Gómez, Pedro Francés**. La ética como estrategia de la razón. *Rev Filosof (Spain)*, 8(15), 227-233, 1996.

**Gómez, Ricardo J**. "Límites y desventuras de la racionalidad crítica neoliberal" in *La racionalidad: su poder y sus límites*, Nudler, Oscar (ed), 425-448. Barcelona, Ed Paidos, 1996.

The main purpose is to show that the scientific rationality endorsed by Popper and Hayek has insurmountable limits and generates unavoidable misfortunes. Among them, it is noteworthy to mention its merely formal-instrumental character making it incapable of encompassing practical issues. It has its own shortcomings as it works in the area of the social sciences (like the problems related to the status of the Principle of Rationality and the misunderstandings generated by their views on methodological individualism). Finally, that rationality is the one operating in the neoliberal versions of economics making the scientific character of them a highly debatable issue.

**Gómez, Ricardo J**. Indeterminismo y libertad: físicos cuánticos responden a Popper. *Analisis Filosof*, 16(2), 157-166, N 96.

Popper has claimed that physical indeterminism is a necessary though not a sufficient condition for the possibility of the free will. However, I want to show that I) his arguments for supporting that view are, to say the least, plainly inconclusive and II) outstanding quantum physicists like Bohr, Born and Schrödinger have given different reasons for claiming, contrary to Popper, that physical indeterminism is neither a necessary nor a sufficient condition for the possibility of the free will.

**Gómez Caffarena, José** (ed) and Ceñal Lorente, Ramón (trans) and Kant, Immanuel. *Immanuel Kant: Principios Formales del Mundo Sensible y del Inteligible (Disertación de 1770)*. Madrid, CSIC, 1996.

"Principios formales del mundo sensible" (que hacen *un todo* intuitivo de los múltiples datos de percepción sensorial) son el espacio y el tiempo. Para Kant desde 1770 son la estructura constitutiva (*a priori*) de la sensibilidad humana. "Principio formal del mundo inteligible" le parecía en 1770 ser Dios mismo, clave última de los múltiples procesos causales del cosmos. En los años sucesivos se le problematizó el alcance del conocer intelectual humano: las "formas *a priori*" del entendimiento—las categorías—sólo dan conocimiento "esquematizadas", o sea, adaptadas a la percepción sensorial: el "mundo inteligible" es, pues, en primera instancia función del "sensible". Ahora bien, el sujeto y su vivencia moral abren a una afirmación puramente intelectual (*noumenal*) de la libertad y Dios puede ser postulado en "fe racional" como clave última de unidad teleológica: retorna así un "principio formal del mundo inteligible", aunque en figura más modesta. (publisher)

**Gomez Ferri, Javier**. The Social and Sociological Study of Science, and the Convergence Towards the Study of Scientific Practice (in Spanish). *Theoria (Spain)*, 11(27), 205-225, S 96.

Within the field of science studies, recently a new approach has taken a strong hold—the sociology of scientific knowledge (SSK). Ever since its appearance in the midseventies, within SSK there have been diverse tendencies. Between these and the philosophy of science there has been a perpetual confrontation. Lately, SSK appears to be undergoing a metamorphosis, transforming into a sociology of scientific practice. What is interesting about this case is that both disciplines—philosophy of science and SSK—are finding a common point of confluence, dialogue and study. My aim is to trace the trajectory of SSK and to analyze these points of contact.

**Gómez Ibáñez, Vicente**. "Mundo administrado" o "Colonización del mundo de la vida": La depotenciación de la Teoría crítica de la sociedad en J. Habermas. *Daimon Rev Filosof*, 10, 103-113, Ja-Je 95.

In Beziehung auf Th.W. Adornos Text "Individuum und Organisation" (1953), J. Habermas'Lösung des sogenannten "Verdinglichungsparadoxon" erscheint als eine versöhnende und unkritische Auflösung des Paradoxon, die zu M. Heideggers Kulturkritik nahe ist. Das ist Folge der Abschaffung der Dialecktik in Gesellschaftstheorie.

**Gómez Pardo, Rafael**. El método de la filosofía en la filosofía moderna. *Franciscanum*, 37(111), 395-449, S-D 95.

Modern philosophy from Descartes to Leibniz was built on the model of mathematical science. It makes possible the previous reflections about how low knowledge in mathematics are gotten. This reflection made by Descartes, Hume, Locke, Leibniz, Espinoza and others began to consider that knowledge in mathematics was true and no doubt because of a priori method. Even the empiricist couldn't object to this position and the opposition with the rationalism was more about the source of knowledge than the model of no doubt knowledge. So that, it is possible to say that modern philosophy was born under paradigm of mathematics and that it itself is in some way the *normalization* (Kuhn) of that paradigm. So that, philosophical method turns on the investigation about the faculty that it is able to know a priori. As a result, we can have the following problems: How can human knowledge investigate the human knowledge? How far can we accept this luck of obligation from a method moreover to the "social sciences"? Now a days social sciences does have to mortgage its critical function making an apology to a method that ends on a formal truth, obedient to the demand of scientificity, but unable to discover that other social truths demand the necessity of change. The truth about social sciences does trespass the reflection about the method but about the radicality of its critical function. (edited)

**Gomila Benejam, Antoni**. "Conceptos y concepciones: sobre la posibilidad del cambio conceptual" in *Verdad: lógica, representación y mundo*, Villegas Forero, L, 301-309. Santiago de Compostela, Univ Santiago Comp, 1996.

We are trying to develop an alternative view, one which starts from a certain view of what "having a concept" consists in, and therefore, how some changes in these capacities amount to a conceptual change. "Having a concept," we say, is a capacity to reidentify an individual (or property). This can be done in many different ways: perceptually, descriptively, by criteria, by naming, by ostension,.... None of these ways, though, equals to a definition, to a constitutive component of the concept identity, which is to be conceived in terms of the individual (or property) referred. In fact, some may result in quite different reidentifications, at least in some circumstances. (edited)

**Gomila Benejam, Antoni**. "Evolución y racionalidad limitada" in *La racionalidad: su poder y sus límites*, Nudler, Oscar (ed), 65-83. Barcelona, Ed Paidos, 1996.

Wason's "selection task" and other psychological experiments are purported to show the existence of biases in human reasoning. Against current interpretations, the aim of this paper is to argue that they should be viewed as calling for a rethinking of rationality itself. The logical view of rationality should be substituted for a pragmatic one, which takes into account the fact that human reasoning is the outcome of an evolutionary process. It required an equilibrium between efficiency and reliability which is best reached by context-sensitive mechanisms. From this standpoint, the biases are the consequence of pragmatic ambiguities that mislead those reasoning mechanisms.

**Gomila Benejam, Antoni**. Externalismo semántico y determinación del contenido: el enfoque teleológico de R. Millikan. *Analisis Filosof*, 15(1-2), 107-133, My-N 95.

My goal in this paper is modest. It consists of examining one version of the evolutionary approach to naturalizing intentionality, which is clearly atomistic and externalist, the teleo-functional theory of Ruth Millikan. I want to argue that, even granting her notion of proper function and granting the determinacy of proper functions, her account fails to yield semantic determinacy, despite her claims to the contrary. The reason has to do with her account of representational content in terms of *normal* conditions for proper function: while there is something to the idea of ground normativity in proper functioning, no normativity can be derived from such conditions, even if they are *normal*. I will conclude with a diagnosis of the reasons of failure, a diagnosis that extends, I claim, to all purely externalist approaches. (edited)

**Gomila Benejam, Antoni**. La teoría de las ideas de Descartes. *Teorema*, 16(1), 47-69, 1996.

Against standard readings of Descartes as philosophy of mind's "villain", because of his dualism (Ryle), his subjectivism (followers of the second Wittgenstein), or his individualism (Burge), this paper tries to point out his most valuable legacy, his representationalism, through a reconstruction of his notion of "idea" as a natural sign. To this end, attention is paid not only to the *Meditations*, but also to his scientific works, as they are the key to the rejection of the usual reading of "idea" as an incorporeal image.

**Gomolinska, Anna**. A Nonmonotonic Modal Formalization of the Logic of Acceptance and Rejection. *Stud Log*, 58(1), 113-127, 1997.

The problems we deal with concern reasoning about incomplete knowledge. Knowledge is understood as ability of an ideal rational agent to make decisions about pieces of information. The formalisms we are particularly interested in are Moore's autoepistemic logic (AEL) and its variant, the logic of acceptance and rejection (AEL2). It is well-known that AEL may be seen as the nonmonotonic KD45 modal logic. The aim is to give an appropriate modal formalization for AEL2.

**Gonçalves, Joaquim Cerqueira**. A História da Filosofia na Aprendizagem/Ensino da Filosofia. *Rev Port Filosof*, 52(1-4), 407-415, Ja-D 96.

**Gonçalves, Joaquim Cerqueira**. Leitura Medieval e Moderna de Descartes. *Philosophica (Portugal)*, 5-15, 1996.

On cherche de faire une lecture de la philosophie de Descartes dans l'horizont d'une herméneutique compréhensive, sans rester au niveau extérieur des influences et des conséquences. La lecture médiévale—une des lectures médiévales—de Descartes tendra à voir dans son ouvrage l'expression de la tendance verticale de la raison et la lecture moderne—uno dos lectures modernes—prétère y voir la tendance horizontale.

**Gonçalves, Joaquim Cerqueira**. O estatuto das humanidades o regresso às artes. *Philosophica (Portugal)*, 5-12, 1993.

La tâche d'unification du savoir ne s'arrête jamais. Aujourd'hui telle urgence est plus encore sensible. Pour le faire il faut prendre le savoir au sens large, sans l'identifier avec la science au sens strict. Le savoir est une action de construction du monde. Son niveau le plus radical se trouve peut-être dans l'activité artistique, vue plus du côté de la poétique que du sentiment esthétique. A ce niveau-là art et savoir, théorie et pratique, arts plastiques et Humanités se trouvent.

**Gonçalves, Miguel**. Para uma História da Noçao de Ironia: Da Antiguidade Clássica à Escola Clássica Francesa. *Rev Port Filosof*, 52(1-4), 417-440, Ja-D 96.

Any attempt to integrate the study of irony in actual linguistics can hardly be released from the problem of its own origin either whereas human attitude on from the rhetorical point of view. From the main moments which we distinguish and always close to the importance that manuals assume in their redefinition and commentary we shall entrance the contribution of the antiquity, of Middle Age and of the French classical doctrine. (This article is an abbreviated version of the first chapter of the author's dissertation, *Ironia verbar—contributo para uma análise semântico-pragmática* (Braga, 1993). (edited)

**Gonçalves Neto, Wenceslau** and Souza Araújo, José Carlos and Inácio Filho, Geraldo. Notícia sobre a Pesquisa de Fontes Histórico-educacionais no Triângualo Mineiro e Alto Paranaíba. *Educ Filosof*, 10(19), 115-127, Ja-Je 96.

A group of teachers at the Federal University of Uberlândia made, from 1994 to 1996, a survey and a catalogue of valuable primary and secondary sources for researchers dealing with the history of Brazilian education in the West region of the state of Minas Gerais, called Triângulo Mineiro. The same research program is now being developed in eighteen other regions of Brazil. This activity, included in a group of studies and research entitled *History, Education and Society in Brazil*, aims to, among other goals, give support to the research activities of the postgraduation program in education of the university, that focuses on Brazilian education.

**Gonzalez, Francisco J**. Propositions or Objects? A Critique of Gail Fine on Knowledge and Belief in *Republic* V. *Phronesis*, 41(3), 245-275, 1996.

Gail Fine has maintained that the concluding argument of *Republic* V assigns knowledge and belief, not to different kinds of *objects*, but to different *sets of propositions*. The present paper seeks to show 1) that Fine's interpretation violates her own "dialectical requirement" and cannot yield a plausible reading

of the text and 2) that supposed difficulties in the text are simply the product of an anachronistic distinction between predicative and existential meanings of the word "is." Positively, the paper proposes an interpretation that assigns knowledge and belief to different objects while avoiding the absurdities Fine attributes to a "two-worlds" theory.

**Gonzalez, G M James**. "Of Property: On 'Captive'' Bodies', Hidden 'Flesh', and Colonization" in *Existence in Black: An Anthology of Black Existential Philosophy*, Gordon, Lewis R (ed), 129-133. New York, Routledge, 1997.

**González, Ana Marta**. Persona y naturaleza en la ética de Leonardo Polo. *Anu Filosof*, 29(2), 665-679, 1996.

Polo's anthropology differs both from Aristotelian and modern anthropology in his concept of person. In this paper, I explore the ethical relevance of this concept and its connection with the concept of "human nature", which Polo assumes making a distinction between "essence" and "type". This distinction is important in order to focus the ethical aspect of the relationship between nature and culture correctly.

**González, María Cristina**. Acerca de dos modelos de conocimiento tecnológico. *Analisis Filosof*, 16(1), 7-16, My 96.

M. A. Quintanilla described two different approaches concerning the relationship between science and technics: the intellectualist and the pragmatist. In this paper two different models of knowledge taken for granted by both approaches are identified and developed. Bunge's and Villoro's thesis about science and technics are used for filling out the models. They received critical commentaries which are analyzed. It is suggested that both models are lacking in a theory about representations as a previous step.

**González, Wenceslao J**. On the Theoretical Basis of Prediction in Economics. *J Soc Phil*, 27(3), 201-228, Wint 96.

Economic predictions are necessary (e.g., for planning) and, at the same time, are often unreliable. The problem then is to clarify the basis of prediction in economics. This question is linked to the issue of the subject-matter of this science. From the theoretical point of view, it is a methodological question which depends on semantical and epistemological considerations. The problem of scientific prediction in economics is seen from three different perspectives: the predictivist thesis (Friedman), the quasi-scientific option (Hicks), and the dualist posture (Buchanan). This paper offers an alternative view by first examining the realm and concept of scientific prediction. Later on, the discussion goes on to the role of prediction in economics, to emphasize the existence of quantitative and qualitative predictions. Here, the differences among "foresight", "prediction" and "forecast", which contribute to "planning", are brought out. Finally, the basis for the methodological development of prediction in economics is displayed.

**González Couture, Gustavo**. Algunos aportes de Don Leonardo a un país hispanoamericano: Colombia. *Anu Filosof*, 29(2), 681 693, 1996.

Building on the notions of alternative, the concept of means, lack of productivity in Latin America and the Christian sense of the technical, offered by Professor Polo, a very brief interpretation of social change in Colombian society is attempted.

**González Fernández, Martín**. El Ideario Pirrónico en el Oriente Medieval (Presencia y Divulgación). *Agora (Spain)*, 14(2), 55-77, 1995.

In this article Pyrrhonic skeptical thought's from Hellenistic Age to Renaissance are analysed. The main objective of the same is to prove the importance which had several enclaves and cities from Orient like a privilege way of conservation, penetration and disclosure of this philosophical tendency during the Medieval Age. Consists on two parts: in the first one, after establishing previously some hypothesis of the work and realizing a sequence of conjectures, the real presence of this thought is proved, at last, in Alexandria, Asia Minor (especially in Esmirna) and Constantinople; in the second one, some of the text that allowed their subsequent disclosure at Occident are studied, with an special mention to Philo Judaeus and Photius and with general consideration about this penetration by means of Arab and Jewish ways, holding up especially in the Al-Fârâbî's testimony. (edited)

**González Rodríguez, Antonio M**. G. Bachelard y la iconoclastia científica de lo imaginario. *Pensamiento*, 204(52), 429-440, S-D 96.

**González Umeres, Luz**. Ayudar a crecer: notas sobre la educación en el pensamiento de Leonardo Polo. *Anu Filosof*, 29(2), 695-708, 1996.

Here some reflections from Leonardo Polo about basic questions of educative philosophy are presented: the family, affection, imagination, interest, ethic and the global orientation. He points out the importance of the idea that belongs to the family to obtain the affective stability of the son.

**Good, Michael**. Wittgenstein on Certainty. *Dialogue (PST)*, 38(2-3), 69-76, Ap 96.

In this paper, I elaborate L. Wittgenstein's comments on "certainty." His views are contrasted with G.E. Moore's "common-sense" approach to certainty. Wittgenstein's treatment of certainty is seen as a natural extension of his later method of philosophical, or rather grammatical investigations. I defend the view that, though Wittgenstein's views on certainty might seem to indicate relativism, this is a mistaken reading of his work. Certainty is grounded in forms of life—not in philosophical propositions.

**Goodchild, Philip**. Deleuzean Ethics. *Theor Cult Soc*, 14(2), 39-50, My 97.

This paper contests the view that Gilles Deleuze's thought is unethical. It contends that Deleuze attempted to make thought itself ethical and explores the implicit ethos at work in Deleuze's writing. Deleuze repositions the field of ethics beyond the dichotomies of duty and freedom, or reason and emotion, escaping the ambivalence of the postmodern morality described by Zygmunt Bauman.

AUTHOR INDEX 655 Gorham, Geoffrey

Deleuze's ethics are shown to arise from Spinoza's philosophy of immanence, together with a vitalist conception of temporality. The ethical criteria of immanence are intensity, novelty, joy, affirming all chance and repetition.

**Goodenough, Jerry**. The Achievement of Personhood. *Ratio*, 10(2), 141-156, S 97.

The debate on personal identity tends to conflate or ignore two different usages of the word 'person'. Psychological-continuity proponents concentrate upon its use to refer to human psychology or personality, while animalist critics prefer its use to refer to individual human beings. I argue that this duality undermines any attempt to see 'person' as a genuine sortal term. Instead, adopting suggestions found in Dennett and Sellars, I consider personhood as an ascription rather like an honorific title or achievement-market. (edited)

**Goodenough, Ward H**. Moral Outrage: Territoriality in Human Guise. *Zygon*, 32(1), 5-27, Mr 97.

Moral outrage is a response to the behavior of others, never one's own. It is a response to infringements or transgressions on what people perceive to be the immunities they, or others with whom they identify, can expect on the basis of their rights and privileges and what they understand to be their reasonable expectations regarding the behavior of others. A person's culturally defined social identities and the rights and privileges that go with them in relationships to which those identities can be party make up the contents of that person's social persona and also constitute that person's social territory. (edited)

**Gooderham, David W**. What Rough Beast...? Narrative Relationships and Moral Education. *J Moral Educ*, 26(1), 59-72, Mr 97.

The discussion is concerned with issues arising in the use of fictions written for children in moral education. It focuses on the various ways in which adult narrators address the child readers of such texts and offers a model of the narrative relationships thus established. The analysis of these relationships and consideration of their pedagogical implications is set within a broader discussion of shifts in the contemporary concept of childhood. Drawing initially on current media representations and finally on problematic representations of "beastly" behaviour in children's fictions, attention is directed, beyond pedagogical strategies, to existential questions which new and emerging relationships in children's fiction currently raise for teachers and other adults concerned with moral education.

**Goodey, C F**. On Aristotle's 'Animal Capable of Reason'. *Ancient Phil*, 16(2), 389-403, Fall 96.

Aristotle is said to have asserted in *Categories* and *Topics* that "animal capable of reason" is the essential property of man. Textual analysis of the phrase, and of related passages elsewhere in the corpus, shows that it cannot signify a psychological definition of the species. Rather, it describes a logical relation between "man" and "reason" (or understanding) as classes; this is moreover a weak relation, the claim being merely that the classes are not mutually exclusive. The medieval doctrine "man is a rational animal" can be traced instead to Stoic reductions of Aristotle's phrase.

**Goodheart, Eugene**. The Demise of the Aesthetic in Literary Study. *Phil Lit*, 21(1), 139-143, Ap 97.

Aesthetic judgement is no longer a practice in the profession of literary studies. The current disrepute of aesthetic value has less to do with theoretical disagreement about its constitution than with suspicion about its supposed ideological character. This is an unfortunate situation, because the vitality of a culture (its literature, music and art) depends upon the capacity of readers to discriminate among their experiences. What needs to be recovered is a reading of literature which allows us to listen to its voices, that resists our premature impulse to appropriate it to an ideological agenda.

**Goodin, Robert E**. "Conventions and Conversions, or, Why Is Nationalism Sometimes So Nasty?" in *The Morality of Nationalism*, McKim, Robert (ed), 88-104. New York, Oxford Univ Pr, 1997.

**Goodman, C P**. Polanyi on Liberal Neutrality. *Tradition Discovery*, 23(2), 38-41, 1996-97.

This paper suggests that moral neutrality erodes the liberal practices which sustain a free society. It supports the Polanyian claim that a free society is the political arrangement which is best able to realise universal ideals.

**Goodman, Russell B**. What Wittgenstein Learned from William James. *Hist Phil Quart*, 11(3), 339-354, Jl 94.

**Goodnow, Jacqueline J** and Warton, Pamela M. Direct and Indirect Responsibility: Distributing Blame. *J Moral Educ*, 25(2), 173-184, Je 96.

This paper represents two studies exploring the distribution of blame in situations where one member of a family has asked a brother or sister to do a job normally done by the asker and the sibling fails to do the job. Study 1 samples 14- and 18-year olds. Study 2 samples 19-22-year-olds. The results bring out a) a preference for assigning blame to both parties rather than all to one or the other, b) a bias towards assigning less blame to the asker than to the person who has agreed, c) an effect from circumstances that reflect effort on the part of the asker (blame to the asker is reduced, for instance, if he or she has left a reminder) and d) a difference between the allocations made when subjects are in the role of the person asking against the person who has accepted (least blame to the asker when subjects are in the role of acceptor). Age and gender differences were not significant in either study. The results are discussed in terms of the need for an understanding of the circumstances encouraging the acceptance of indirect or vicarious responsibility.

**Gopnik, Alison**. Reply to Commentaries. *Phil Sci*, 63(4), 552-561, D 96.

**Gopnik, Alison**. The Scientist as Child. *Phil Sci*, 63(4), 485-514, D 96.

This paper argues that there are powerful similarities between cognitive development in children and scientific theory change. These similarities are best explained by postulating an underlying abstract set of rules and representations that underwrite both types of cognitive abilities. In fact, science may be successful largely because it exploits powerful and flexible cognitive devices that were designed by evolution to facilitate learning in young children. Both science and cognitive development involve abstract, coherent systems of entities and rules, theories. In both cases, theories provide predictions, explanations, and interpretations. In both, theories change in characteristic ways in response to counterevidence. These ideas are illustrated by an account of children's developing understanding of the mind.

**Goranko, Valentin**. Refutation Systems in Modal Logic. *Stud Log*, 53(2), 299-324, My 94.

Complete deductive systems are constructed for the nonvalid (refutable) formulae and sequents of some propositional modal logics. Thus, complete syntactic characterizations in the sense of Lukasiewicz are established for these logics and, in particular, purely syntactic decision procedures for them are obtained. The paper also contains some historical remarks and a general discussion on refutation systems.

**Gorbett, Jason**. AIDS, Confidentiality, and Ethical Models. *De Phil*, 10, 71-84, 1993.

What ethical models best provide means of arriving at solutions to problems in biomedical ethics? Using a case study that involves the issue of AIDS and doctor-patient confidentiality, the author argues that models which involve appeals to higher levels of justification are ineffective. A "bottom-up" model that refrains from such appeals is developed and defended.

**Gorbett, Jason**. AIDS, Confidentiality, and Ethical Models: Appendix. *De Phil*, 11, 87-89, 1994-1995.

**Gordic, Aleksandar** (trans) and Frank, Manfred. Psychische Vertrautheit und epistemische Selbstzuschreibung (in Serbo-Croatian). *Theoria (Yugoslavia)*, 39(1), 7-22, Mr 96.

Zwei Argumente für eine Sonderstellung des Selbstbewussteins im Bereich der epistemischen Tatsachen dominieren in der neueren Literatur: Das erste plädiert für die wesentliche Subjektivität selbstbewusster Zustände; das zweite verteidigt die erkenntnistheoretische, ontologische und semantische Priorität epistemischer Selbstzuschreibungen von Eigenschaften vor allen anderen Formen der Bezugnahme und Zuschreibung. Eine kardinale Entdeckung ist, dass dem Wesen von Selbstbewusstsein weder über die Wahrheit von Aussagen noch in einer Ding-Ereignis-Sprache beizukommen ist. Selbstbewusstsein ist kein Fall von Wahrnehmung, auch und schon gar nicht einer geheimnisvollen 'Inneren'. 'Ich' ist ontologisch und referentiell ausgezeichnet und es besitzt auch erkenntnistheoretische Priorität. Jede mittelbare Bezugnahme auf anderes ist vermittelt durch unmittelbares Selbstbewusstsein.

**Gordon, Edwin**. Edwin Gordon Responds. *Phil Music Educ Rev*, 5(1), 57-58, Spr 97.

**Gordon, Jeffrey**. Kurosawa's Existential Masterpiece: A Meditation on the Meaning of Life. *Human Stud*, 20(2), 137-151, Ap 97.

In the first part of the paper, I try to clarify the cluster of moods and questions we refer to generically as the problem of the meaning of life. I propose that the question of meaning emerges when we perform a spontaneous transcendental reduction on the phenomenon 'my life', a reduction that leaves us confronting an unjustified and unjustifiable curiosity. In Part 2, I turn to the film *Ikiru*, Kurosawa's masterpiece of 1952, for an existentialist resolution of the problem.

**Gordon, Lewis R**. "Existential Dynamics of Theorizing Black Invisibility" in *Existence in Black: An Anthology of Black Existential Philosophy*, Gordon, Lewis R (ed), 69-79. New York, Routledge, 1997.

The author argues that black invisibility is a paradoxical "visible" invisibility, where blacks are invisible by virtue of how they are "seen." This seeing is a form of "unseeing" rooted in what he calls "perverted anonymity." He then explores some implications of this invisibility for the problem of studying black people. He argues for a humanistic methodology rooted in existential phenomenological considerations of situated relations of individuals in institutionalized social settings. The result, he concludes, is a method that examines problems faced by people of African descent instead of problematizing people of African descent.

**Gordon, Lewis R** (ed). *Existence in Black: An Anthology of Black Existential Philosophy*. New York, Routledge, 1997.

*Existence in Black* is the first collective statement on the subject of Africana philosophy of existence. Among questions posed and explored in the volume are: What is to be done in a world of near universal sense of superiority to, if not universal hatred of, black folk? What is black suffering? What is the meaning (if any) of black existence? The introduction argues that a response to these questions requires an existential journey through the resources of identity questions in critical race theory and the teleological dimensions of liberation theory. Through an analysis of nearly every dimension of Africana philosophy, the contributors explore some of the central themes of philosophy of existence as posed by the context of what Frantz Fanon has identified as "The Lived-Experience of the Black." The result is effectively the announcement of a new field: Black Existentialism. (publisher)

**Gordon, Valery M** and Bonkovsky, Frederick O. Family Dynamics and Children in Medical Research. *J Clin Ethics*, 7(4), 349-354, Wint 96.

**Gorelov, A A**. The Ecological Ideology and Russia's Future. *Russian Stud Phil*, 35(2), 61-75, Fall 96.

**Gorham, Geoffrey**. Similarity as an Intertheory Relation. *Proc Phil Sci Ass*, 3(Suppl), S220-S229, 1996.

In line with the semantic conception of scientific theories, I develop an account of the intertheory relation of comparative structural similarity. I argue that this relation is useful in explaining the concept of verisimilitude and I support this contention with a concrete historical example. Finally, I defend this relation against the familiar charge that the concept of similarity is insufficiently objective.

**Gorniak-Kocikowska, Krystyna**. The Computer Revolution and the Problem of Global Ethics. *Sci Eng Ethics*, 2(2), 177-190, A 96.

The author agrees with James Moor that computer technology, because it is 'logically malleable', is bringing about a genuine social revolution. Moor compares the computer revolution to the 'industrial revolution' of the late 18th and the 19th centuries; but it is argued here that a better comparison is with the 'printing press revolution' that occurred two centuries before that. Just as the major ethical theories of Bentham and Kant were developed in response to the printing press revolution, so a new ethical theory is likely to emerge from computer ethics in response to the computer revolution. The newly emerging field of information ethics, therefore, is much more important than even its founders and advocates believe.

**Gorovitz, Samuel**. Genetic Therapy: Mapping the Ethical Challanges. *Philosophia (Israel)*, 25(1-4), 83-97, Ap 97.

**Gorovitz, Samuel** and Bennett, Jonathan. Improving Academic Writing. *Teach Phil*, 20(2), 105-120, Je 97.

**Gorski, Andrew**. The Symposium Viewed from the Organizer's Perspective. *Sci Eng Ethics*, 2(4), 441-442, O 96.

**Goshgarian, G M** (trans) and Genette, Gérard. *The Work of Art: Immanence and Transcendence*. Ithaca, Cornell Univ Pr, 1997.

According to Gérard Genette, works of art can have two modes of existence: immanence and transcendence. *Immanence* is defined by the type of object the work "consists in"; it can therefore be subdivided into two regimes, here christened, after Nelson Goodman, *autographic* and *allographic*. *Transcendence* is defined by the different ways in which a work exceeds its immanence. Thus a work can consist in several nonidentical objects (works with different "versions"), be incompletely (fragments) or indirectly (copies, reproductions, descriptions) manifested, or operate in different ways, depending on place or period, individuals or circumstances; we never look at the same painting or read the same book twice. It follows that a work cannot be reduced to its object of immanence, because what it is, is inseparable from what is accomplishes. The work of art is always already the work that art does. (publisher, edited)

**Gosselin, M**. Donald Davidson, Descartes and How to Deny the Evident. *Commun Cog*, 29(2), 285-299, 1996.

In "The Problem of Objectivity" (1995) Donald Davidson denies that animals are capable of thought. He tries to make this position acceptable by excluding from his argumentation intelligence and knowledge, two related concepts, and by reducing thought to propositional thought. Donald Davidson declares that he accepts the results of science, but he does not take them into account. Biologists, ethologists, psychologists and neurobiologists nowadays take thought in higher species for granted. The thesis that animals do not think, which was also held by Descartes, who reduced animals to machines without a soul and yet capable of coping with their environment, is made obsolete by scientific evidence. (edited)

**Goswami, Chinmoy**. On Understanding: Standing Under Wittgenstein. *J Indian Counc Phil Res*, 14(2), 37-55, Ja-Ap 97.

The paper has a twofold purpose. At one level, an attempt is made to understand the writings of Wittgenstein. At another level, an attempt is made to understand the phenomenon called 'understanding'. An analysis is carried out of the related terms like 'misunderstanding', 'nonunderstanding'. These analyzes point to the fact an understanding of understanding, within the Platonic-Cartesian framework, leads to blind alley. Attempt is made to work out a triadic framework to make understanding relational. This calls for something more than mere "rule-following".

**Gottlieb, Jonathan Z** and Sanzgiri, Jyotsna. Towards an Ethical Dimension of Decision Making in Organizations. *J Bus Ethics*, 15(12), 1275-1285, D 96.

There is a growing need to increase our understanding of ethical decision making in U.S. based organizations. The authors examine the complexity of creating uniform ethical standards even when the meaning of ethical behavior is being debated. The nature of these controversies are considered, and three important dimensions for ethical decision making are discussed: leaders with integrity and a strong sense of social responsibility, organization cultures that foster dialogue and dissent, and organizations that are willing to reflect on and learn from their actions. (edited)

**Gottlieb, Paula**. Aristotle's Ethical Egoism. *Pac Phil Quart*, 77(1), 1-18, Mr 96.

Accepting the controversial thesis that Aristotle is an ethical egoist, I argue that Aristotle's brand of ethical egoism is immune to four important objections to such a position. I analyse the causes of the four objections showing a) that Aristotle does not have a conception of happiness which would give rise to the first three, and b) that his account of practical reasoning, of which I provide an original interpretation, can deal with the fourth.

**Gottlieb, Robert** and Fisher, Andrew. Community Food Security and Environmental Justice: Searching for a Common Discourse. *Agr Human Values*, 13(3), 23-32, Sum 96.

Community food security and environmental justice are parallel social movements interested in equity and justice and system-wide factors. They share a concern for issues of daily life and the need to establish community empowerment strategies. Both movements have also begun to reshape the discourse of sustainable agriculture, environmentalism and social welfare advocacy. However, community food security and environmental justice remain

separate movements, indicating an incomplete process in reshaping agendas and discourse. Joining these movements through a common language of empowerment and systems analysis would strongly enhance the development of a more powerful, integrated approach. That opportunity can be located in the efforts to incorporate community food security and environmental justice approaches in current Farm Bill legislation; in particular, provisions addressing community food production, direct marketing, community development, and community food planning.

**Gottlob, Georg**. Relativized Logspace and Generalized Quantifiers Over Finite Ordered Structures. *J Sym Log*, 62(2), 545-574, Je 97.

We here examine the expressive power of first order logic with generalized quantifiers over finite ordered structures. In particular, we address the following problem: Given a family Q of generalized quantifiers expressing a complexity class C, what is the expressive power of first order logic FO(Q) extended by the quantifiers in Q? From previously studied examples, one would expect that FO(Q) captures $L^c$, i.e., logarithmic space relativized to an oracle in C. We show that this is not always true. However, after studying the problem from a general point of view, we derive sufficient conditions on C such that FO(Q) captures $L^c$. These conditions are fulfilled by a large number of relevant complexity classes. (edited)

**Gould, Carol C**. Group Rights and Social Ontology. *Phil Forum*, 28(1-2), 73-86, Fall-Wint 97.

**Goulet-Cazé, Marie-Odile** (ed) and Branham, R Bracht (ed). *The Cynics: The Cynic Movement in Antiquity and Its Legacy*. Berkeley, Univ of Calif Pr, 1996.

This collection of essays—the first of its kind in English—brings together the work of an international group of scholars examining the entire tradition associated with the ancient Cynics. The essays give a history of the movement as well as a state-of-the-art account of the literary, philosophical and cultural significance of Cynicism from antiquity to the present. (publisher)

**Gourevitch, Victor**. "'The First Times' in Rousseau's *Essay on the Origin of Languages*" in *The Ancients and the Moderns*, Lilly, Reginald (ed), 248-266. Bloomington, Indiana Univ Pr, 1996.

**Governatori, Guido** and Artosi, Alberto and Sartor, Giovanni. "Towards a Computational Treatment of Deontic Defeasibility" in *Deontic Logic, Agency and Normative Systems*, Brown, Mark A (ed), 27-46. New York, Springer-Verlag, 1996.

In this paper we describe an algorithmic framework for a multimodal logic arising from the combination of the system of modal (epistemic) logic devised by Meyer and van der Hoek for dealing with nonmonotonic reasoning with a deontic logic of the Jones and Pörn-type. The idea behind this (somewhat eclectic) formal set-up is to have a modal framework expressive enough to model certain kinds of deontic defeasibility, in particular by taking into account preferences on norms. The appropriate inference mechanism is provided by a tableau-like modal theorem proving system which supports a proof method closely related to the semantics of modal operators. We argue that this system is particularly well-suited for mechanizing nonmonotonic forms of inference in a monotonic multimodal setting.

**Govier, Trudy**. Trust and Totalitarianism: Some Suggestive Examples. *J Soc Phil*, 27(3), 149-163, Wint 96.

In this paper, I explore ways in which trust between people is undermined by totalitarian systems. Using information from works by dissidents or expatriates, the cases of East-Central Europe, Iraq, and Chine are briefly explored.

**Gower, Barry S**. *Scientific Method: An Historical and Philosophical Introduction*. New York, Routledge, 1997.

The results, conclusions and claims of natural science are often taken to be reliable because they arise from the use of a distinctive method. Yet today, there is widespread scepticism as to whether we can validly talk of method in modern science. This outstanding new survey explains how this controversy has developed since the seventeenth century and explores its philosophical basis. Questions of scientific method are discussed through key figures such as Galileo, Bacon, Newton, Bayes, Mill, Poincaré, Duhem, Popper, and Carnap. The concluding chapters contain stimulating discussions of attacks on the idea of scientific method by key figures such as Kuhn, Lakatos, and Feyerabend. (publisher,edited)

**Graber, Glenn C**. Biological Sciences and Ethics: Models of Cooperation. *Philosophia (Israel)*, 25(1-4), 71-82, Ap 97.

**Gracia, Diego**. The Historical Setting of Latin American Bioethics. *J Med Phil*, 21(6), 593-609, D 96.

The Latin American society of the last century is divided into two quite different social strata: one bourgeois, which has assimilated the liberal revolution and enjoys a health care quite similar to that available in any other Western country and hence faces the same bioethical problems as any developed Western society; the other a very poor stratum, without any economic or social power and hence unable to exercise its civil rights, such as the rights to life and to humane treatment. In this population sector, which is numerically the larger, the major bioethical problems are those of justice and the distribution of scarce resources. The study of Latin American medical ethics can earn for these subjects, whose deplorable condition has been essentially ignored in the bioethics of the first-world countries, the importance they merit. (edited)

**Gracia, Jorge J E**. "The Philosopher and the Understanding of the Law" in *Averroës and the Enlightenment*, Wahba, Mourad (ed), 243-251. Amherst, Prometheus, 1996.

This paper argues that not only did Averroes not hold that the philosopher is the arbiter of the meaning of the law, as many believe, but that, even if he had, such a view would be contrary to some of the basic principles of his philosophy. The

AUTHOR INDEX 657 Graham, Gordon

philosopher, it argues, does not and cannot know the meaning of the law with the certainty which the philosophical method is supposed to yield. This entails that the common rationalist interpretation of Averroes is mistaken.

**Gracia, Jorge J E**. Autor y represión. *Cuad Etica*, 19-20, 73-86, 1995.

Is the author a repressive agent? The theory of the author's repressive character rests on a mistaken assumption: the belief that limiting the interpretative field of the audience is negative because it restrains the audience's creativity when this attempts to understand a text. The value of creativity in interpretation depends on the purpose of such interpretation. Therefore, the use of the name of the historical author and of what we know or believe to know about him (that is to say, the *pseudo-historical author*) can have repressive or beneficial effects. Both of them must be considered by a theory of textuality.

**Gracia, Jorge J E**. Interpretation and the Law: Averroes's Contribution to the Hermeneutics of Sacred Texts. *Hist Phil Quart*, 14(1), 139-153, Ja 97.

This paper argues that for Averroes there can be no definitive interpretations of sacred texts which are subject to allegorical interpretation by the demonstrative class. This view is akin to those of Foucault and other postmodernists, but unlike them Averroes holds also: 1) the possibility of definitive interpretations of sacred texts whose allegorical interpretation is open to everyone and texts which have only an apparent meaning; 2) that sacred texts have meaning; and 3) the possibility of error in the interpretation of sacred texts.

**Gracia, Jorge J E**. *Latin American Philosophy in the Twentieth Century*. Amherst, Prometheus, 1986.

For more than thirty years the English-speaking world has been without a representative collection of readings by major twentieth-century Latin American philosophers. This important new collection combines the richness, the diversity, and the intensity of fourteen great minds—the result of which is a testament to the philosophical power that is uniquely Latin American. (publisher)

**Gracia, Jorge J E**. Respuesta a C.M. Topuzian. *Rev Latin de Filosof*, 23(1), 137-143, O 97.

This article responds to Topuzian's criticism of my book, *A Theory of Textuality*, (1995). It addresses two objections: The first argues that expected behavior cannot help us escape the hermeneutical circle; the second, that tradition cannot establish with certainty the conditions of expected behavior. To the first, it answers that expected behavior helps us escape the hermeneutical circle if it is appropriately taken as a nonlinguistic effect of the use of language. To the second, it answers that it rests on two mistakes: First, it assumes the certainty involved is apodictic; second, it equates tradition with conscious knowledge of rules.

**Gracia, Jorge J E**. Textual Identity. *Sorites*, 57-75, Jl 95.

What does make texts the same? Three types of sameness are distinguished: achronic, synchronic and diachronic. The latter two involve time and so are more restrictive; thus I concentrate on achronic sameness. After examining various possible views I reach the conclusion that there are three conditions which, taken together, constitute the necessary and sufficient conditions of the achronic sameness of texts and hence explain their identity: sameness of meaning, of syntactical arrangement and of type-sign composition. We can thus understand how different copies of a book are the same text, for they have the same meaning and they are composed of the same type signs arranged in the same way. Thus, in spite of the many differences that characterize them, they are still to be regarded as copies of the same text.

**Gracyk, Theodore A**. Listening to Music: Performances and Recordings. *J Aes Art Crit*, 55(2), 139-150, Spring 97.

This article critically examines the thesis that music should be heard in live performance rather than through the mediation of recordings. It reviews ontological, perceptual, and social defenses of the superiority of live music, and concludes that recorded music does not result in a net aesthetic loss. (edited)

**Gracyk, Theodore A**. Romanticizing Rock Music. *J Aes Educ*, 27(2), 43-58, Sum 93.

Rejects attempts to understand rock music as a manifestation of nineteenth-century ideals associated with Romanticism.

**Graczynska, Ewa** and Chajda, Ivan. Jónsson's Lemma for Regular and Nilpotent Shifts of Pseudovarieties. *Bull Sec Log*, 26(2), 85-93, Je 97.

This is an abstract of the lecture proposed for the 54th Workshop on General Algebra at the University of Klagenfurt, Austria, May 29 - June 1, 1997. We deal with *varieties* and *pseudovarieties* of universal algebras, in the sense of B. Birkhoff and S. Eilenberg, i.e., classes of (finite) algebras closed under the formation of subalgebras, homomorphic images and (finite) direct products. Our aim is to present a variation on Jónsson's Lemma for normal and regular shifts of varieties (pseudovarieties).

**Grady, Mark F**. Modern Accident Law Does Not Fit Corrective Justice Theory. *Jahr Recht Ethik*, 2, 7-35, 1994.

Nach der Theorie der ausgleichenden Gerechtigkeit hat die richterliche Anwendung gesetzlicher Regeln den Zweck, vorangegangenes Unrecht auszugleichen. Die Theorie ist nicht in der Lage, die Behandlung von Fahrlässigkeitstaten in der gerichtlichen Praxis zu erklären. Ernest Weinrib, ein führender Theoretiker der ausgleichenden Gerechtigkeit, behauptet, dass Gerichte, die Fahrlässigkeitsfälle beurteilen, sich ausschliesslich auf die Beziehungen zwischen dem Kläger und dem Beklagten zu konzentrieren haben. Nur auf diese Weise könnten sie der ausgleichenden Gerechtigkeit dienen. (edited)

**Grädel, Erich** and Kolaitis, Phokion G and Vardi, Moshe Y. On the Decision Problem for Two-Variable First-Order Logic. *Bull Sym Log*, 3(1), 53-69, Mr 97.

We identify the computational complexity of the satisfiability problem for $FO^2$, the fragment of first-order logic consisting of all relational first-order sentences with at most two distinct variables. Although this fragment was shown to be decidable a long time ago, the computational complexity of its decision problem has not been pinpointed so far. In 1975 Mortimer proved that $FO^2$ has the *finite-model property*, which means that if an $FO^2$-sentence is satisfiable, then it has a finite model. Moreover, Mortimer showed that every satisfiable $FO^2$-sentence has a model whose size is at most doubly exponential in the size of the sentence. In this paper, we improve Mortimer's bound by one exponential and show that every satisfiable $FO^2$-sentence has a model whose size is at most exponential in the size of the sentence. As a consequence, we establish that the satisfiability problem for $FO^2$ is NEXPTIME-complete.

**Gräfrath, Bernd**. *Evolutionäre Ethik? Philosophische Programme, Probleme und Perspektiven der Soziobiologie*. Hawthorne, de Gruyter, 1997.

The book explores the relevance of sociobiology for philosophical ethics. Sociobiology can explain human behavior and cultural institutions; but ethics is reducible neither to sociobiology nor to game theory. Sociobiological findings are nevertheless helpful, since all acceptable systems of philosophical ethics contain anthropological premises, which can be more or less plausible. For example, a Rawlsian could find sociobiological support for the assumption of an overlapping consensus of basic intuitions. The book contains special analyses of various concepts of progress and anthropocentrism, and considerable attention is paid to the philosophical importance of the works of Stanislaw Lem.

**Gräfrath, Bernd**. Wissenschaftstheorie oder Ästhetik der Wunder?. *Theol Phil*, 72(2), 257-263, 1997.

Christian theology on miracles has to face a philosophical dilemma: it can either try to attack Hume's critique, or it can replace the traditional concept of a miracle as a violation of a law of nature in a Wittgensteinian way by understanding all unusual events as miracles, if they are of religious significance for a particular interpretative community. The first way fails; the second one is incompatible with other parts of traditional dogmatics.

**Graeser, Andreas**. Moralische Beobachtung, interner Realismus und Korporatismus. *Z Phil Forsch*, 50(1/2), 51-64, Ja-Je 96.

This article is an argument to the effect that 1) moral observations are capable of being true or false respectively, 2) that moral facts are part of reality so-called, and 3) that both, moral judgments and principles are subject to revision and, thus, alike theoretical sentences. In particular it is argued that moral judgment, if interpreted as gradings, are cognitive and that what they report may be understood along a realist interpretation. The kind of realism envisaged here resembles a version of internal realism.

**Grätzel, Stephan**. Nietzsche's Kinesthetics (in Serbo-Croatian). *Filozof Istraz*, 15(4), 709-715, 1995.

Nietzsches *physiologischer* Ansatz lässt sich durch sein gesamtes Werk verfolgen. Er ist gegründet auf eine "*Vernunft des Leibes*", die auf die verstehende Wahrnehmung von Bewegungen aufbaut und sie mit der Lebensbewegung überhaupt, dem Willen zur Macht, in Beziehung setzt. Die besondere Weise dieser Kinästhesie besteht darin, dass, vor dem Hintergrund der grundsätzlich steigenden Lebensbewegung, jede individuelle Bewegung eine Gestalt bekommt, die Ausdruck der "plastischen Kraft" dieses Lebewesens ist. In der Angleichung an die Lebensbewegung zeigt sich die Originalität eines Individuums, zugleich kann aber die Stereotypie in den Bewegungen und Handlungen als Dekadenz erkannt werden, weil sie keine Steigerung oder Metamorphose mehr zeigt. Die Gebärden und Handlungen werden somit zu Indizien eines kinästhetischen Urteils, das in Schönheit und Hässlichkeit zugleich den Aufstieg und Niedergang des Lebewesens und der Gattung erkennt.

**Graft, Donald**. Against Strong Speciesism. *J Applied Phil*, 14(2), 107-118, 1997.

Speciesism, difference of treatment based on an appeal to species membership, is often likened to racism and sexism, and condemned on those grounds. Some philosophers, however, reject this argument by analogy and instead forward an argument for speciesism based on a postulated right of species to compete for survival. This paper attacks this strong form of speciesism by showing that the underlying concept of 'species' is incoherent in the context of morality and that strong speciesism has unacceptable corollaries.

**Graham, Gordon**. "Toleration and the Idea of Progress" in *Philosophy, Religion, and the Question of Intolerance*, Ambuel, David (ed), 125-133. Albany, SUNY Pr, 1997.

This essay argues that the acceptance of toleration as a social virtue and the rejection of the idea of moral progress is inconsistent. It defends a view of toleration which makes it better supported by moral objectivism than the cultural relativism with which it is often associated.

**Graham, Gordon**. The Marxist Theory of Art. *Brit J Aes*, 37(2), 109-117, Ap 97.

This paper explores the Marxist theory of art as a sociological alternative to philosophical aesthetics. It argues that the Marxist theory cannot be construed as a theory of art properly so called and that it cannot, in the end, throw any light on the central questions of aesthetics.

**Graham, Gordon**. *The Shape of the Past*. New York, Oxford Univ Pr, 1997.

This pioneering work aims to bring the methods of analytical philosophy to the critical examination of some of these questions. In addition to Hegel and Kant, the discussion ranges over the writings of Augustine, Machiavelli, and Nietzsche. The ideas of historical progress, secularization and the decline of religion, cultural cycles, historical rupture and God in history are all subjected to careful analysis. Gordon Graham argues that, although unfashionable, the claim that history is the story of progress under the guidance of providence is one of the most plausible accounts of the shape of the past. (publisher, edited)

**Graham, Keith**. Voting and Motivation. *Analysis*, 56(3), 184-190, Jl 96.

**Graham, Paul**. The Will Theory of Rights: A Defence. *Law Phil*, 15(3), 257-270, 96.

Hart's will theory of rights has been subjected to at least three significant criticisms. First, it is thought unable to account for the full range of legal rights. Second, it is incoherent, for it values freedom while permitting an agent the option of alienating his or her capacity for choice. Third, any attempt to remedy the first two problems renders the theory reducible to the rival benefit theory. My aim is to address these objections. I argue that will theory has been made vulnerable due to misinterpretation. The theory has been characterized as placing great stress on liberty rights (or claim-protected liberties), whereas it is powers that are central, and hence not choice but control. My argument does, however, depend upon appealing to an extra-legal notion—the hypothetical contract—but I argue that this is consistent with the main aim of a "theory of rights".

**Graham, Peter J**. What is Testimony?. *Phil Quart*, 47(187), 227-232, Ap 97.

C.A.J. Coady, in *Testimony* (Oxford: Clarendon Press, 1922), offers conditions on a statement that P to count as testimony. I argue that his conditions are too strong. Alternative conditions are proposed and defended. Coady was led to strong conditions by investigating testimony as it occurs in legal contexts where special steps are taken to insure that testimony provide the jury or judge with evidence by a competent speaker that is relevant to the disputed question of the guilt or innocence of the defendant.

**Granel, Gérard** and Wolfe, Charles T (trans). Untameable Singularity (Some Remarks on *Broken Hegemonies*). *Grad Fac Phil J*, 19/20(2/1), 215-228, 1997.

**Graness, Anke**. "The Problem of Identity in the African Context" in *Philosophy and Democracy in Intercultural Perspective*, Kimmerle, Heinz (ed), 115-128. Amsterdam, Rodopi, 1997.

The destruction of indigenous economic, political and cultural structures causes a loss of personal identities. Descriptions of the loss of identities after colonization are given by Frantz Fanon, Kwasi Wiredu and Kwame A. Appiah. But also the changes in the former GDR brought for the citizens of this socialist German state not only liberation, but the first-hand experience of the loss of identity. Thus, personal identities seem to be deeply connected with social structures and certain systems of references. The paper describes aspects of personal identities and compares the African and the East-German experience.

**Graness, Anke** (ed) and Kresse, Kai (ed). *Sagacious Reasoning: Henry Odera Oruka in Memoriam*. New York, Lang, 1997.

The tragic death of H. Odera Oruka on December 9th 1995 was a big loss for African philosophy and world philosophy on the whole. This book commemorates the important philosopher by presenting and discussing eminent contributions of his to the African and global philosophical debate, among others his projects of sage philosophy, a philosophy of foreign aid and parental earth ethics.

**Grant, Colin**. Altruism: A Social Science Chameleon. *Zygon*, 32(3), 321-340, S 97.

The self-interest paradigm that has dominated and defined social science is being questioned today in all the social sciences. Frontline research is represented by C. Daniel Batson's experiments, which claim to present empirical evidence of altruism. Impressive though this is against the background of the self-interest paradigm, its ultimate significance might be to illustrate the inadequacy of social science to deal with a transcendent reality like altruism.

**Grant, Iain Hamilton**. "At the Mountains of Madness: The Demonology of the New Earth and the Politics of Becoming" in *Deleuze and Philosophy: The Difference Engineer*, Ansell Pearson, Keith (ed), 93-114. New York, Routledge, 1997.

**Grant, Robert**. "Anti-Meaning as Ideology: The Case of Deconstruction" in *Verstehen and Humane Understanding*, O'Hear, Anthony (ed), 253-285. New York, Cambridge Univ Pr, 1996.

**Grant, Ruth W**. *Hypocrisy and Integrity: Machiavelli, Rousseau, and the Ethics of Politics*. Chicago, Univ of Chicago Pr, 1997.

In her new book, Ruth W. Grant challenges the usual standards for political ethics. Arguing that hypocrisy can be constructive and that strictly principled behavior can be destructive, she explores the full range of ethical choices by brilliantly distinguishing among the varieties of hypocrisy and integrity. Grant focuses primarily on the works of Machiavelli and Rousseau. While Machiavelli is often understood as arguing for the necessity of hypocrisy, Rousseau is portrayed as an antihypocrite who advocates a principled idealism. Grant's reinterpretation of these thinkers, however, allows us to see their considerable common ground. Both understood that political relationships *require* hypocrisy. (publisher, edited)

**Grant, Ruth W** (ed) and Tarcov, Nathan (ed). *John Locke: Some Thoughts Concerning Education* and *Of the Conduct of the Understanding*. Indianapolis, Hackett, 1996.

This volume offers two contemporary works by John Locke, unabridged, in modernized, annotated texts—the only available edition priced for classroom use. Of interest to students and instructors of philosophy, political theory, and education, these important works shed light on conceptions of reason and freedom essential for understanding Locke's philosophy. With renewed interest in the relations between politics and education, Locke's epistemological and educational writings take on added significance. Read alongside Locke's political writings, these works allow the reader to develop a deeper appreciation of the various interconnected concerns at the core of Lockean liberalism. Grant

and Tarcov provide a concise introduction, a note on the texts, and a select bibliography. (publisher)

**Grant II, Don Sherman**. Religion and the Left: The Prospects of a Green Coalition. *Environ Ethics*, 19(2), 115-134, Sum 97.

Religionists and leftists have aligned themselves with several green causes, but have yet to engage each other in a real discussion of environmental issues. In this paper, I try to establish the basis for a dialogue between those segments of the religionist and leftist traditions that appear to have the most promise for forging a united green front. I label these two subgroups constructive postmodern religionists and constructive postmodern leftists. I summarize the key ideas shared by each group, discuss how each can rectify some of the weaknesses of the other and consider some potential philosophical barriers to their union. I conclude by issuing a call for dialogue on the issues presented here.

**Grasshoff, Gerd**. Hertzian Objects in Wittgenstein's *Tractatus*. *Brit J Hist Phil*, 5(1), 87-119, Mr 97.

**Grassie, William**. Postmodernism: What One Needs to Know. *Zygon*, 32(1), 83-94, Mr 97.

This essay is an introduction to postmodernism and deconstruction as they relate to the special challenges of scholarship and teaching in the science and religion multidiscipline.

**Grassie, William**. Powerful Pedagogy in the Science-and-Religion Classroom. *Zygon*, 32(3), 415-421, S 97.

This essay is a discussion of effective teaching in the science-and-religion classroom. I begin by introducing Alfred North Whitehead's three stages of learning—romance, discipline, and generalization—and consider their implications for powerful pedagogy in science and religion. Following Whitehead's three principles, I develop a number of additional heuristics that deal with active, visual, narrative, cooperative and dialogical learning styles. Finally, I present twelve guidelines for how to use e-mail and class-based list serves to achieve some of these outcomes.

**Grattan-Guinness, Ivor**. "Peirce between Logic and Mathematics" in *Studies in the Logic of Charles Sanders Peirce*, Houser, Nathan (ed), 23-42. Bloomington, Indiana Univ Pr, 1997.

The book is the published version of two sessions on logic held at the Peirce sesquicentenary conference at Harvard University in 1989; my paper is the outcome of my role as discussant in the more historically specified one. As such, it is a general review of Peirce's perplexing (perplexed?) views on the relationship between logic and mathematics. Contemptuous of Russell's logicism, he saw each as applied to the other in various ways. In his logic, I stress its *central* background in logic, and its use of part-whole theory, not set theory. I also transcribe a charming letter of introduction of Peirce to De Morgan in 1870 from his father Benjamin.

**Grattan-Guinness, Ivor**. How Did Russell Write *The Principles of Mathematics* 1903?. *Russell*, 16(2), 101-127, Wint 96-97.

Drawing upon the manuscript of the book and other documents, Russell's memory of writing this book is shown to be seriously mistaken. Instead of a "four-month quick write" in the last four months of 1900 after discovering Peano's mathematical logic, he reused only Parts 3-6 of the seven parts at that time from an earlier book draft, and produced the first two only by 1902, when he also had his famous paradox to deal with. Further, he devised his logicist thesis of reducing 'pure' mathematics to logic, during this time—the earlier parts were not written within its conception, although various passages were added in later.

**Grattan-Guinness, Ivor**. I Never Felt Any Bitterness: Alys Russell's Interpretation of Her Separation from Bertie. *Russell*, 16(1), 37-44, Sum 96.

This article contains a transcription of a memorandum written by Russell's first ex-wife near the end of her life in the late 1940s, in which she describes and rewards her own view of their estrangement and eventual separation and divorce. Only one passage has previously been published. While not itself, philosophical at all, the document provides a valuable insight on Russell's life at the time of his peak as a philosopher.

**Grattan-Guinness, Ivor**. Living Together and Living Apart: On the Interactions between Mathematics and Logics from the Franch Revolution to the First World War (Spanish). *Theoria (Spain)*, 12(28), 13-37, Ja 97.

This article contains a broad historical survey of the connections made between branches of mathematics and types of logic during the period 1800-1914. Two principal streams are noted, rather different from each other: algebraic logic, rooted in French Revolutionary *logique* and algebras and culminating via Boole and De Morgan, in the systems of Peirce and Schröder; and mathematical logic, inspired by the mathematical analysis of Cauchy and Weierstrass and culminating, via the initiatives of Peano and the set theory of Cantor, in the work of Russell. Some general conclusions are drawn, with examples given of the state of affairs after 1914.

**Gratton, Claude**. Infinite Regresses of Recurring Problems & Responses. *Log Anal*, 37(147-8), 313-328, S-D 94.

The author examines two infinite regress arguments whose uncommon infinite regresses have been described in terms of recurring problems and solutions; identifies overlooked differences in their regresses that affect the evaluation of such arguments (e.g., some problems recur in different ways and the responses/solutions can have different functions); describes the structure of a typical infinite regress argument, and contrasts it to one of these infinite regresses of recurring problems and responses.

**Grau i Arau, Andrés**. La funció crítica de la "inventio" i el "iudicium" en la *Dialèctica de Petrus Ramus*. *Convivium*, 10, 52-60, 1997.

For Ramus the Dialectic (*ars bene disserendi*) consists of two parts: *inventio* and *iudicium*. The purpose of this partition is double: (1) to distinguish between the fields of argumentation and disposition and (2) to indicate the real subject of *dialectic*. In this paper we intend to show the use of the division in Ramus's criticism to the *Organon* and to the terminist logic.

**Graves, David**. The Institutional Theory of Art: A Survey. *Philosophia (Israel)*, 25(1-4), 51-67, Ap 97.

A brief survey of the institutional theory of art from its inception in the sixties to a new version of the theory, offered by Graves, Kasher and Dickie in 1992. The survey concisely summarizes the main theoretical precepts of each of the three major versions of the institutional theory. The main issues that have been handled over the years are: (a) Describing the institution of the artworld as a complex rule-governed practice, thereby replacing old definitions with constitute rules, (b) Realizing the inflected nature of the rule-systems which constitute the artworld and all its subinstitutions, (c) Suggesting the internal hierarchy of that complex practice.

**Graves, P R**. Reference and Imperfective Paradox. *Phil Stud*, 88(1), 81-101, O 97.

**Gray, Hanna H**. "Prospect for the Humanities" in *The American University: National Treasure or Endangered Species?*, Ehrenberg, Ronald G (ed), 115-127. Ithaca, Cornell Univ Pr, 1997.

**Gray, Wallace**. A Surprising Rediscovery and Partial Review of *The Foundations of Belief* by James Balfour. *Phil Cont World*, 1(4), 6-9, Wint 94.

Well-known as the British politician responsible for the Balfour Declaration during World War I, James Balfour was also a philosopher. Long forgotten, his remarkable book *The Foundations of Belief* (1895) merits contemporary reassessment. Critical of modern compartmentalization, Balfour argues for an integration of religion, philosophy and science—a position now often identified as postmodern. This article presents some of Balfour's contemporary scholarly significance and hints at his usefulness in undergraduate teaching.

**Graybosch, Anthony J**. The Limits of Loyalty. *Acta Analytica*, 115-130, 1995.

The concept of loyalty is analysed on the basis of the political and ethnical situation in former Yugoslavia. Ethnicity is one way to approach the identification of a common culture. Some contemporary analytic philosophers distinguish characteristics which belong to the private and public selves. And so ethnicity, race and religion may be crucial factors of personal identity, but they are irrelevant to the public self, to the self as citizen. It is argued that this is wrong. Political loyalty and personal morality are intimately related, and, consequently, the line between cultural and political loyalties cannot be neatly drawn.

**Grcic, Joseph**. Errors In Moral Reasoning. *Int J Applied Phil*, 10(2), 59-69, Wint-Spr 96.

I argue that the ethics of Aristotle, Kant and Mill would support the claim that the following are errors in reasoning: prejudice, emotionalism, egocentrism, ethnocentrism, specieism, stereotypical thinking, weakness of will, ends/means error, is/ought confused, intuitionism, rationalization scapegoating, judgementalism and appeal to the masses.

**Greco, John**. Catholics vs. Calvinists on Religious Knowledge. *Amer Cath Phil Quart*, 71(1), 13-34, Wint 97.

Plantinga has defended the Calvinist position that religious belief can be properly basic. Zagzebski has responded critically, tracing her virtue theory of knowledge to the Catholic tradition. But the two theories are closer than Zagzebski implies: both are person-based (or virtue-based) and externalist, and Plantinga's view is consistent with social elements stressed by Zagzebski. The real issue is whether knowledge requires praiseworthiness. Zagzebski's neo-Aristotelian approach gives resources for saying that it does. Finally, the consequences for religious knowledge are minimal. Religious belief might still be basic in Plantinga's sense.

**Greco, Michael A** and Smith, David and Deleuze, Gilles. Literature and Life. *Crit Inquiry*, 23(2), 225-230, Wint 97.

**Green, Lena**. Philosophy for Children: One Way of Developing Children's Thinking. *Thinking*, 13(2), 20-22, 1997.

This article was written as an introduction to Lipman's Philosophy for Children program. It describes the materials and the procedures involved and provides a brief overview of the arguments which Lipman and others have offered in support of the value of the program as a means to develop children's thinking abilities and their moral judgement. The discussion raises a concern about the extent to which the program assumes children's mastery of the skills of inquiry and suggests possible problems in different contexts. It concludes, nevertheless, that, with sensitive modification, the program could be of value in South Africa. In this respect the flexibility built in and encouraged by the authors of the program is a distinct advantage.

**Green, Mitchell S**. On the Autonomy of Linguistic Meaning. *Mind*, 106(422), 217-243, Ap 97.

A modified version of Frege's ideal is here propounded according to which an expression is a force indicator just in case it indicates force in any speech act in which it occurs. It is shown that attainment of such an ideal would not have deprived Frege of what he desired of a perspicuous notation. In elaborating this ideal we also espouse an illocutionary conception of validity and argue that the ideal is one to which English conforms: parenthetical speech act verbs in the first person present indicative active are force indicators in the modified sense. But the mere possibility of force indicators in the modified sense is enough to show Davidson's autonomy thesis to be at best a half-truth. (edited)

**Green, O H**. "Is Love an Emotion?" in *Love Analyzed*, Lamb, Roger E, 209-224. Boulder, Westview Pr, 1997.

**Green, Ronald M**. Guiding Principles of Jewish Business Ethics. *Bus Ethics Quart*, 7(2), 21-30, Mr 97.

This discussion develops six of the most important guiding principles of classical Jewish business ethics and illustrates their application to a complex

recent case of product liability. These principles are: 1) the legitimacy of business activity and profit; 2) the divine origin and ordination of wealth (and hence the limits and obligations of human ownership); 3) the pre-eminent position in decision making given to the protection and preservation (sanctity) of human life; 4) the protection of consumers from commercial harm; 5) the avoidance of fraud and misrepresentation in sales transactions; and 6) the moral requirement to go beyond the letter of the law. (edited)

**Green, Ronald M**. NHGRI's Intramural Ethics Experiment. *Kennedy Inst Ethics J*, 7(2), 181-189, Je 97.

**Green, Sharon** and Weber, James. Influencing Ethical Development: Exposing Students to the AICPA Code of Conduct. *J Bus Ethics*, 16(8), 777-790, Je 97.

Although the AICPA code of professional conduct emphasizes the importance of education in ethics, very little is known about how and when the code and the topic of ethics can be presented to enhance the effectiveness of ethics-oriented education. The purpose of this research was to provide preliminary evidence about the ethical development of students prior to, and immediately following, such courses. (edited)

**Greenberg, Robert**. Perception and Kant's Categories. *Hist Phil Quart*, 13(3), 345-361, Jl 96.

**Greenberg, William J**. A Theory of Complexes. *Epistemologia*, 19(1), 85-112, Ja-Je 96.

Nel presente articolo, la teoria classica dell'identità e le tematizzazioni libere da presupposti ontologici di questa relazione, in voga tra i filosofi analitici di orientamento linguistico, sono messe a confronto con una relazione d'identità le cui proprietà classiche, anche se non tutte, sono generate dalla particolarità delle cose su cui variano le variabili individuali. Questa particolarità è assicurata da un'entità che, a differenza dell'unità semplice (non complessa) della logica di Frege-Russell, incorpora il quello ("thatness") e il che cosa ("whatness") essenziali al questo ("thisness") di ogni cosa individuale. Mi riferisco a questa entità come un *complesso*. (edited)

**Greenberg, William J**. The Paradox of Identity. *Epistemologia*, 19(2), 207-225, Jl-D 96.

Diciamo che una semantica è *estensionalista* se afferma che i) il significato di un enunciato è ciò che l'enunciato asserisce e che ii) il significato di un termine singolare è ciò a cui il termine si riferisce. La chiamiamo *classica* se è eretta da un linguaggio del primo ordine in cui le variabili variano sopra, e i termini denotano, oggetti del livello base dell'"ontologia degli individui" (nella terminologia di Van Heijnoort). La chiamiamo inadeguata se non stabilisce che (vero) 'A = B' e 'A = B' separatamente per contenuto cognitivo. (edited)

**Greene, Jennifer K**. Coercion: Description or Evaluation?. *Int J Applied Phil*, 10(2), 7-16, Wint-Spr 96.

I begin by establishing that there are two very different conceptions of the term "coercion" in use, a descriptive sense in which the coercee is not necessarily wronged and a normative one, in which she is. After pointing to the problems which arise as a result of the failure to clearly distinguish between the two, I argue that it is the normative account which is most useful, best accords with ordinary usage, and has the fewest problems with regard to identification. I further conclude that to ignore the problems inherent in the descriptive sense is to render the concept analytically useless.

**Greene, Michael** and Trimiew, Darryl M. How We Got Over: The Moral Teachings of The African-American Church on Business Ethics. *Bus Ethics Quart*, 7(2), 133-147, Mr 97.

An analysis of the business ethics of the African-American church during and after reconstruction reveals that it is a conflicted ethic, oscillating between two poles. The first is the sacralization of the business ethic of Booker T. Washington, in which self-help endeavors which valorize American capitalism but are preferentially oriented to the African-American community are advanced as the best and only options for economic uplift. The second is the "Blackwater" tradition, which rejects any racial discrimination and insists upon social justice. The inability of the Washingtonian business ethic to address the needs of the Black underclass are explored. (edited)

**Greene, Richard** and Balmert, N.A.. Two Notions of Warrant and Plantinga's Solution to the Gettier Problem. *Analysis*, 57(2), 132-139, Ap 97.

In this paper we offer a critique of Plantinga's solution to the Gettier problem. Specifically, we argue that Plantinga's account of warrant contains an internal inconsistency. He offers a definition of warrant which precludes the possibility of false warranted beliefs (a consequence that Plantinga appears not to countenance) and he offers an account of the necessary and sufficient conditions for warrant which allows for false warranted beliefs. The latter account, we argue, actually gives rise to Gettier problems. We conclude the paper by arguing that the two accounts are not easily reconciled.

**Greene, Robert A**. Instinct of Nature: Natural Law, Synderesis, and the Moral Sense. *J Hist Ideas*, 58(2), 173-198, Ap 97.

This essay traces the development of the meaning of instinct of nature in early discussions of the natural law. Ulpian's second-century definition of the law (what nature has taught all animals) is adapted by Isidore of Seville in 625, who paradoxically attributed the law to an instinct of nature, while restricting it to mankind. Bonaventure's relocating of synderesis in man's will and affections made explicit what was latent in Aquinas's thinking and encouraged its association with instinct. Eventually instinct comes to serve as a substitute for the obsolescent synderesis in the early modern writings of Herbert, Hale and Francis Hutcheson.

**Greene, Stephen A**. Rethinking Kymlick's Critique of Humanist Liberalism. *Int J Applied Phil*, 10(2), 51-57, Wint-Spr 96.

**Greenfeld, Liah**. The Birth of Economic Competitiveness: Rejoinder to Breckman and Trägårdh. *Crit Rev*, 10(3), 409-470, Sum 96.

In "The Worth of Nations" I propose that nationalism was a major factor in the emergence of the modern, growth-oriented economy. In response to criticisms, I demonstrate here the nationalistic inspiration of seventeenth-century English—or British—economic tracts. Urging a reconsideration of earlier approaches (such as that of W.W. Rostow) to the problem of why—rather than how—the modern economy emerged, I agree with Max Weber's challenge to the naturalness of our proclivity for constant economic expansion, while departing from his explanation for it.

**Greenfeld, Liah**. The Modern Religion?. *Crit Rev*, 10(2), 169-191, Spr 96.

Nationalism is an essentially secular form of consciousness, one that, indeed, sacralizes the secular. This renders the temptation to treat it as a religion problematic. The framework of individual and collective identities in modern societies, nationalism both obscures the importance of the transcendental concerns that lie at the core of great religions and undermines their authority. Though instrumental in the development of nationalism, religion now exists on its sufferance and serves mainly as a tool for the promotion of nationalist ends, not vice versa.

**Greenwood, John D**. Freud's 'Tally' Argument, Placebo Control Treatments, and the Evaluation of Psychotherapy. *Phil Sci*, 63(4), 605-621, D 96.

Despite the fact that Freud never empirically established that these implications hold, the 'tally argument' does draw attention to a critical distinction that is too often neglected in contemporary empirical studies of psychoanalysis and other forms of psychotherapy: between empirical evaluations of the *efficacy* of psychotherapy and empirical evaluations of *theoretical explanations* of the efficacy of psychotherapy and the different forms of comparative enquiry relevant to each. It is argued that the contemporary neglect of this critical distinction, in conjunction with the common negative conception of placebo control treatments in psychotherapy research, has led to the epistemic impoverishment of experimental studies of the various professional psychotherapies. (edited)

**Greer, Rowan A**. Augustine's Transformation of the Free Will Defence. *Faith Phil*, 13(4), 471-486, O 96.

Augustine's first conversion is to the Christian Platonism of his day, which brought along with it a free-will defence to the problem of evil. Formative as this philosophical influence was, however, Augustine's own experience of sin combines with his sense of God's sovereignty to lead him to modify the views he inherited in significant ways. This transformation is demonstrated by setting Augustine's evolving position against that of Gregory of Nyssa.

**Gregor, Mary** (ed & trans) and Kant, Immanuel. *The Metaphysics of Morals*. New York, Cambridge Univ Pr, 1996.

*The Metaphysics of Morals* is Kant's major work in applied moral philosophy in which he deals with the basic principles of rights and of virtues. It comprises two parts: 'The Doctrine of Right', which deals with the juridical rights which persons have or can acquire, and the 'Doctrine of Virtue', which deals with the virtues they ought to acquire. Mary Gregor's translation, revised publication in Cambridge *Texts in the History of Philosophy*, is the only complete translation of the whole text and includes extensive annotation on Kant's difficult and sometimes unfamiliar vocabulary. A new introduction by Roger Sullivan sets the work within the context of the rest of Kant's moral writings. (publisher, edited)

**Gregorio, Giuliana**. "Tempo vuoto/tempo proprio" in *Il Concetto di Tempo: Atti del XXXII Congresso Nazionale della Società Filosofica Italiana,* Casertano, Giovanni (ed), 253-262. Napoli, Loffredo, 1997.

**Gregoriou, Zelia**. "Reading *Phaedrus* Like a Girl Misfires and Rhizomes in Reading Performances" in *Philosophy of Education (1996),* Margonis, Frank (ed), 203-213. Urbana, Phil Education Soc, 1997.

**Gregory, Andrew**. Astronomy and Observation in Plato's *Republic*. *Stud Hist Phil Sci*, 27(4), 451-471, D 96.

Plato's comments on astronomy and the education of the guardians at *Republic* 528e ff have been hotly disputed, and have provoked much criticism from those who have interpreted them as a rejection or denigration of observational astronomy. Here I argue that the key to interpreting these comments lies in the relationship between the conception of enquiry that is implicit in the epistemological allegories, and the programme for the education of the guardians that Plato subsequently proposes. We have, I suggest, been too eager to stress the similarities here, when recognition of the differences may supply us with the tools required for a better understanding of 528e ff, one that to a large extent disarms the antiempirical critique. (edited)

**Gregory, Anne** and Damon, William. The Youth Charter: Towards the Formation of Adolescent Moral Identity. *J Moral Educ*, 26(2), 117-130, Je 97.

Studies of adolescent conduct have found that both exemplary and antisocial behaviour can be predicted by the manner in which adolescents integrate moral concerns into their theories and descriptions of self. These findings have led many developmentalists to conclude that moral identity—in contrast to moral judgement or reflection alone—plays a powerful role in mediating social conduct. Moreover, development theory and research have shown that identity formation during adolescence is a process of forging a coherent and systematic sense of self. Despite these well-founded conclusions, many moral education programmes fail to engage a young person's sense of self, focus exclusively on judgement and reflection and make little or no attempt to establish coherence with other formative influences in a young person's life. The authors propose a new method, called "the youth charter", for promoting adolescent self-identification with a coherent set of moral standards.

**Gregory, Tullio**. Pensiero medievale e modernità. *G Crit Filosof Ital*, 16(2), 149-173, My-Ag 96.

**Greimann, Dirk**. Die Idee hinter Tarskis Definition von Wahrheit. *J Gen Phil Sci*, 28(1), 121-158, 1997.

*The Idea behind Tarski's Definition of Truth.* In Tarski's presentations of his truth-definition, the steps of the construction are not sufficiently explained. It is not clear, on what general strategy the construction is based, what the fundamental ideas are, how some crucial steps work and especially how the transition from the definition of satisfaction to the definition of truth should be understood. The paper shows that the account given in the model-theoretic literature, which is supported by Tarski's lemmata *A* and *B*, is unsatisfactory, because Tarski's notion of truth can't be interpreted as 'truth independent of the assignment of values to the variables'. Moreover, a satisfactory account of all the crucial steps is given.

**Greimann, Dirk**. Die impliziten Prämissen in Quines Kritik der semantischen Begriffe. *Grazer Phil Stud*, 51, 195-235, 1996.

Quines Kritik an den grundlegenden semantischen Begriffen hat zwei wesentliche Prämissen: erstens dass die Linguistik als wissenschaftliche Disziplin der methodischen Restriktion unterstellt ist, empirisch sinnlose Hypothesen und Begriffe abzulehnen, und zweitens, dass die semantischen Begriffe tatsächlich empirisch sinnlos sind. Um die Überzeugungskraft der Ausführungen Quines untersuchen zu können, werden zunächst die verschiedenen Versionen von seiner Kritik analysiert, klar gegeneinander abgegerenzt und in die Form expliziter Argumentationen gebracht. Prämissen, die in die jeweiligen Versionen implizit eingehen, werden rekonstruiert und darauf hin untersucht, ob sie durch Quines Gesamtsystems gestützt werden, bzw. überhaupt mit ihm verträglich sind. (edited)

**Grespan, Jorge**. The Measureless of Crisis (in Spanish). *Discurso*, 27, 117-138, 1996.

This article proceeds to a reconstitution of central passages of Marx's writings, which explicited the logical-philosophical presuppositions present in the concept of capital as "subject" of its own determination process. The purpose here is to define rigorously crisis as privileged expression of capital's inherent negativity, that gives to it the ability for self-measurement but, on the other side, leads it to a state of measurelessness and devaluation.

**Grgas, Stipe**. The Edge of Crisis/The Crisis of the Edge. *Filozof Istraz*, 16(3), 699-711, 1996.

The supposition on which the author grounds his argument is that the syntagm "Postcommunism and the Crisis of the West" is a performative utterance, stemming out of a recognizable postcommunist setting, which makes claims to be an objective pronouncement on the state of Western civilisation. The steps of his argument can be summed up as follows: he first positions the syntagm in the political relation of the West towards the Balkan war, then refers to the different discourses of the crisis of the West and finally shows the necessity of incorporating the issues of postcommunism within the discourse of postcolonialism. These considerations lead the author to contend that a geopolitical reading of the state of crisis is necessary and to conclude that postcommunism is itself a crisis on the edge which site lends it no warrant to diagnose the crisis of the West.

**Grier, Michelle**. Kant on the Illusion of a Systematic Unity of Knowledge. *Hist Phil Quart*, 14(1), 1-28, Ja 97.

In the Appendix to the Transcendental Dialectic (in the Critique of Pure Reason), Kant attempts to assign a positive function to the principles and ideas of pure reason. In this connection, Kant argues that reason plays an indispensably necessary role in empirical inquiries. In this paper, I argue that Kant's subtle position on the role of reason must be understood in connection with his much neglected doctrine of "transcendental illusion." In line with this, I suggest that the doctrine of transcendental illusion clarified not only a number of prevailing textual ambiguities, but also illuminates Kant's views on the function of ideas in scientific theorizing.

**Grier, Philip T**. "The Speculative Concrete: I. A. Il'in's Interpretation of Hegel" in *Hegel, History, and Interpretation,* Gallagher, Shaun, 169-193. Albany, SUNY Pr, 1997.

**Griese, Anneliese** and Pawelzig, Gerd. Why Did Marx and Engels Concern Themselves with Natural Science?. *Nature Soc Thought*, 8(2), 125-137, 1995.

As work proceeds on the complete original writings of Marx and Engels for the *Marx-Engels Gesamtausgabe (MEGA)*, the extent to which they dealt with the natural sciences is quite striking. Since their interest in the natural sciences was not connected with professional ambitions in these areas, this interest must have been motivated by the connections they saw between developments in the natural sciences and their general sociotheoretical work connected with the working-class movement. Among the principal factors that contributed to their interest in the natural sciences was the need to draw upon the methodology of the natural sciences for the application of dialectical and historical materialism to the social sphere. The often made allegation that Engels's understanding of dialectics, especially in regard to the natural sciences, was incompatible with Marx's is sharply disputed.

**Griffin, David Ray**. Panexperientialist Physicalism and the Mind-Body Problem. *J Consciousness Stud*, 4(3), 248-268, 1997.

The intractable (not merely hard) mind-body problem, which involves accounting for freedom as well as conscious experience, is created by the assumption that the brain is comprised of insentient things. Chalmers is right, accordingly, to suggest that we take experience as fundamental. Given this starting-point, the hard problem is twofold: to see sufficient reason to adopt this long-despised approach, and to develop a plausible theory based on it. We

AUTHOR INDEX 661 Groarke, Leo

have several reasons, I suggest, to reject the notion of 'vacuous actuality' and to adopt, instead, the view that all true individuals have experience and spontaneity. After suggesting criteria for an acceptable theory, chief among which are 'hard-core common-sense notions', I point out why dualism and materialism have been unable to fulfill these criteria. The strength of dualism has been its organizational duality, the strength of materialism its rejection of ontological dualism. I suggest that panexperientialist physicalism, by allowing for 'compound individuals' and thereby a 'nondualistic interactionalism' that combines these strengths, can provide a theory that overcomes the problems of materialist physicalism.

**Griffin, David Ray**. *Parapsychology, Philosophy, and Spirituality: A Postmodern Exploration.* Albany, SUNY Pr, 1997.

After articulating a constructive postmodern philosophy that allows the parapsychological evidence to be taken seriously, Griffin examines this evidence extensively. He identifies four types of repeatable phenomena that suggest the reality of extrasensory perception and psychokinesis. Then, on the basis of a nondualistic distinction between mind and brain, which makes the idea of life after death conceivable, he examines five types of evidence for the reality of life after death: messages from mediums; apparitions; cases of the possession type; cases of the reincarnation type; and out-of-body experiences. His philosophical and empirical examinations of these phenomena suggest they provide support for a postmodern spirituality that overcomes the thinness of modern religion without returning to supernaturalism. (publisher,edited)

**Griffin, James**. Ley moral, Ley positiva. *Telos (Spain)*, 5(2), 21-46, D 96.

What gives moral norms their shape? This is the main object of this paper. After taking into account utilitarianism, deontology and the ethics of virtues, here, the author is suggesting that a) there is no supreme background principle capable of bringing system to ethics, but this does not mean that there are no modest background principles capable of sustaining important criticism of our prevailing ethics; and b) there is no domain of the moral, no field consisting purely of moral considerations and leading to determines conclusions about what to do, but only a wider domain of the social, a kind of thinking in which the considerations are more heterogeneous and more subject to compromise that in the supposed moral kingdom.

**Griffin, Miriam**. When is Thought Political?. *Apeiron*, 29(3), 269-282, S 96.

This is an extended critical notice of *Justice and Generosity*, ed. A. Laks and M. Schofield (CUP, 1995). As well as summarizing and analyzing the essays collected there, the article addresses the general question of the definition of 'political thought' at various times. It concludes that an intellectual explanation for the shift of emphasis often detected, from 'classic' (Aristotelian) concern with the polis to Hellenistic ethical concern with universal humanity, should focus less on the notion of 'shift' and more on the enlargement of the pool of concepts in which political thinking could be done.

**Griffin, Nicholas**. "Bradley's Contribution to the Development of Logic" in *Philosophy after F.H. Bradley*, Bradley, James (ed), 195-230. Bristol, Thoemmes, 1996.

The article explores Bradley's influence on the development of 20th century logic—largely through its influence on Russell, the only modern logician to take Bradley's logic at all seriously. Bradley's influence arises in three ways: 1) his rejection of psychologism; 2) his rejection of the idea that all propositions are of subject-predicate form (in particular his use of conditionals in A-form propositions); and 3), more tentatively, in his criticism of Jevons's equational logic.

**Griffin, Stephen M** (ed) and Moffat, Robert C L (ed). *Radical Critiques of the Law.* Lawrence, Univ Pr Kansas, 1997.

The authors consider whether the critiques advanced in recent legal theory can truly be called radical and what form a radical critique of American law should take. Writing at the cutting edge of the critique of critical legal theory, they offer insights first on critical legal scholarship, then on feminist political and legal theory. A third group of contributions questions the radicalness of these approaches in light of their failure to challenge fundamental aspects of liberalism, while a final section focuses on current issues of legal reform through critical views on criminal punishment, including observations on rape and hate speech. (publisher, edited)

**Griffith, Stephen**. Miracles and the Shroud of Turin. *Faith Phil*, 13(1), 34-49, Ja 96.

Using the scientific investigation of the Shroud of Turin as an extended example, it is argued that miracles are best understood not as violations of natural law, but as scientifically inexplicable events. It is then argued that even though we can imagine circumstances in which science itself might provide us with good grounds for believing that an event is scientifically inexplicable, these grounds would at best provide us with circumstantial evidence that the event was miraculous, and would in any case be inconclusive.

**Griffith-Dickson, Gwen**. 'Outsidelessness' and the 'Beyond' of Signification. *Heythrop J*, 37(3), 258-272, Jl 96.

**Griffiths, Paul E**. Darwinism, Process Structuralism, and Natural Kinds. *Proc Phil Sci Ass*, 3(Suppl), S1-S9, 1996.

Darwinists classify biological traits either by their ancestry (homology) or by their adaptive role. Only the latter can provide traditional natural kinds, but only the former is practicable. Process structuralists exploit this embarrassment to argue for non-Darwinian classifications in terms of underlying developmental mechanisms. This new taxonomy will also explain phylogenetic inertia and developmental constraint. I argue that Darwinian homologies are natural kinds despite having historical essences and being spatio-temporally restricted. Furthermore, process structuralist explanations of biological form require an unwarranted assumption about the space of developmental possibility.

**Griffiths, Paul E**. The Historical Turn in the Study of Adaptation. *Brit J Phil Sci*, 47(4), 511-532, D 96.

A number of philosophers and 'evolutionary psychologists' have argued that attacks on adaptationism in contemporary biology are misguided. These thinkers identify antiadaptationism with advocacy of nonadaptive modes of explanation. They overlook the influence of antiadaptationism in the development of more rigorous forms of adaptive explanation. Many biologists who reject adaptationism do not reject Darwinism. Instead, they have pioneered the contemporary historical turn in the study of adaptation. One real issue which remains unresolved amongst these methodological advances is the nature of 'phylogenetic inertia'. To what extent is an adaptive explanation needed for the persistence of a trait as well as its origin?(edited)

**Grim, Patrick**. The Undecidability of the Spatialized Prisoner's Dilemma. *Theor Decis*, 42(1), 53-80, Ja 97.

In the spatialized *prisoner's dilemma*, players compete against their immediate neighbors and adopt a neighbor's strategy should it prove locally superior. Fields of strategies evolve in the manner of cellular automata. Here it is shown, for finite configurations of *prisoner's dilemma* strategies embedded in a given infinite background, that such questions are formally undecidable: there is no algorithm or effective procedure which, given a specification of a finite configuration, will in all cases tell us whether that configuration will or will not result in progressive conquest by a single strategy when embedded in the given field. (edited)

**Grim, Patrick**. Worlds by Supervenience: Some Further Problems. *Analysis*, 57(2), 146-151, Ap 97.

Allen Hazen has proposed a supervenience approach to possible worlds, designed explicitly to overcome Cantorian difficulties I have emphasized elsewhere for possible worlds as maximal consistent sets of propositions. In this paper I try to emphasize difficulties that remain for Hazen's worlds by supervenience. In a second section I also offer a strengthening of Kaplan-Peacocke argument against a set of *all* possible worlds.

**Grim, Patrick** and St. Denis, Paul. Fractal Images of Formal Systems. *J Phil Log*, 26(2), 181-222, Ap 97.

Here we outline a set of alternative and explicitly visual ways of envisaging and analyzing at least simple formal systems using fractal patterns of infinite depth. Progressively deeper dimensions of such a fractal can be used to map increasingly complex wffs or increasingly complex 'value spaces', with tautologies, contradictions, and various forms of contingency coded in terms of color. This and related approaches, it turns out, offer not only visually immediate and geometrically intriguing representations of formal systems as a whole but also promising formal links 1) between standard systems and classical patterns in fractal geometry, 2) between quite different kinds of value spaces in classical and infinite-valued logics, and 3) between cellular automata and logic. It is hoped that pattern analysis of this kind may open possibilities for a geometrical approach to further questions within logic and metalogic. (edited)

**Grimberg, Mary Lou**. Pragmatically Determined Aspects of What is Said: A Reply to Bezuidenhout. *Mind Lang*, 11(4), 415-426, D 96.

If 'a' and 'b' are (proper) names and if the meaning of a name is exhausted by its referent, how can 'a=a' differ in cognitive value from 'a=b' if 'a=b' is true? This is Frege's famous puzzle and Bezuidenhout reconstructs it using demonstrative NPs in place of names, i.e.,: 'This X is that X.' Her solution is to posit the 'truth-conditional relevance' of the *de re* modes of presentation of such expressions. My major objection is that bezuidenhout's examples are such that the NP to the right of the copula is anaphoric rather than demonstrative and cannot, therefore, support her argument.

**Grimen, Harald**. Consensus and Normative Validity. *Inquiry*, 40(1), 47-61, Mr 97.

A weak and a strong version of discourse theory can be distinguished. In the strong version the only source of normative validity in the nonspecific sense is rational consensus, where all parties concerned accept a norm for the same reasons, which are rationally convincing in the same way for all. In the weak version both rational and overlapping consensus can be sources of validity in the nonspecific sense. It is argued that the weak version is the more adequate, since it can accommodate cases which the strong version cannot, and which it is unreasonable to view as cases of compromise. Discourse theory needs a weaker general discourse principle and a more flexible notion of normative consensus than is found in Habermas's *Between Facts and Norms* (1996).

**Grinshpon, Yohanan**. Yogic Revolution and Tokens of Conservatism in Vyasa-Yoga. *J Indian Phil*, 25(2), 129-138, Ap 97.

**Griswold, Jr, Charles L**. Happiness, Tranquility, and Philosophy. *Crit Rev*, 10(1), 1-32, Wint 96.

Despite the near universal desire for happiness, relatively little philosophy has been done to determine what "happiness" means. In this paper I examine happiness (in the long-term sense) and argue that it is best understood in terms of tranquillity. This is not merely "contentment." Rather, happiness requires reflection—the kind of reflection characteristic of philosophy. Happiness is the product of correctly assessing its conditions and like any assessment, once can be mistaken and thus mistaken about whether one is happy. That is, one needs a correct understanding of happiness in order to be happy.

**Groarke, Leo** and Scholz, Sally J. Seven Principles for Better Practical Ethics. *Teach Phil*, 19(4), 337-355, D 96.

This paper identifies seven problems with traditional approaches to teaching practical (or "applied") ethics. These problems include an over emphasis on theory, intellectualism, formalism, an emphasis on moral disagreement, overspecialization, insularity and negativism. Alternative strategies for ethics courses are suggested, which include: making theory subservient to practice, engaging students in nonintellectual ways, recognizing the limits of formalism, teaching in ways that emphasize agreements, integrating ethics into wider curriculum and public programming, and providing positive examples of moral behavior. These strategies are designed to better assist the student, not only understanding moral theory, but also in being a moral person.

**Grobler, Adam**. "World 3 and the Cunning of Reason" in *The Significance of Popper's Thought,* Amsterdamski, Stefan (ed), 25-35. Amsterdam, Rodopi, 1996.

Karl Popper has been accused (by Feyerabend) of having been implicitly committed in his theory of three worlds to a Hegelian thesis about "the cunning of reason." This is wrong, since the Hegelian Objective Spirit is ontically primary relative to Subjective Spirit and nature, while their Popperian counterparts, Worlds Three, Two and One, are of equal ontological status. The accusation ignores the objective of Popper's theory: to provide a theory of rationality without assuming the (perfect) rationality of the human agent. Thus Popper's theory involves some tacit idealizations. Assuming these idealizations, World Three is expected to evolve in such a way as if the cunning of reason were at work. I suggest that the idealizations in question concern the operation of society (world two-and-a half?).

**Groddeck, Wolfram** (ed) and Kohlenbach, Michael (ed). *Nietzsche Werke Kritische Gesamtausgabe: III 5/1.* Hawthorne, de Gruyter, 1996.

**Groddeck, Wolfram** (ed) and Kohlcnbach, Michael (ed). *Nietzsche Werke Kritische Gesamtausgabe: III 5/2.* Hawthorne, de Gruyter, 1996.

**Grodin, Michael** and Lane, Harlan. Ethical Issues in Cochlear Implant Surgery: An Exploration into Disease, Disability, and the Best Interests of the Child. *Kennedy Inst Ethics J,* 7(3), 231-251, S 97.

This paper examines ethical issues related to medical practices with children and adults who are members of a linguistic and cultural minority known as the *Deaf-World.* Members of that culture characteristically have hearing parents and are treated by hearing professionals whose values, particularly concerning language, speech and hearing, are typically quite different from their own. That disparity has long fueled a debate on several ethical issues, most recently the merits of cochlear implant surgery for *Deaf* children. We explore whether that surgery would be ethical if implants could deliver close to normal hearing for most implanted children, thereby diminishing the ranks of the *Deaf-World.* The ethical implications of eugenic practices with the *Deaf* are explored, as are ethical quandaries in parental surrogacy for *Deaf* children and their parallels in transracial adoption.

**Grodzinsky, Yosef**. The Modularity of Language—Some Empirical Considerations. *Commun Cog,* 29(3/4), 425-444, 1996.

This paper presents several empirical arguments supporting a modular view of language. It begins by formulating certain questions that arise in the context of the modularity of language and proceeds to demonstrate possible answers to each. It provides an example of an argument for a modular view of syntactic knowledge and also gives reasons for believing in the functional and neuro-anatomical distinctness of the syntactic processing device. All these points are supposed to underscore the view that the modularity debate is exclusively empirical.

**Groeneveld, Willem** and Gerbrandy, Jelle. Reasoning about Information Change. *J Log Lang Info,* 6(2), 147-169, Ap 97.

In this paper we introduce Dynamic Epistemic Logic, which is a logic for reasoning about information change in a multi-agent system. The information structures we use are based on non-well-founded sets and can be conceived as bisimulation classes of Kripke models. On these structures, we define a notion of information change that is inspired by Update Semantics (Veltman, 1996). We give a sound and complete axiomatization of the resulting logic and we discuss applications to the puzzle of the dirty children and to knowledge programs.

**Groeneveld, Willem** and Van der Does, Jaap and Veltman, Frank. An Update on "Might". *J Log Lang Info,* 6(4), 361-380, O 97.

This paper is on the update semantics for "might" of Veltman (1996). Three consequence relations are introduced and studied in an abstract setting. Next we present sequent-style systems for each of the consequence relations. We show the logics to be complete and decidable. The paper ends with a syntactic cut elimination result.

**Grohe, Martin**. Arity Hierarchies. *Annals Pure Applied Log,* 82(2), 103-163, D 96.

Many logics considered in finite model theory have a natural notion of an arity. The purpose of this article is to study the hierarchies which are formed by the fragments of such logics whose formulae are of bounded arity. Based on a construction of finite graphs with a certain property of homogeneity, we develop a method that allows us to prove that the arity hierarchies are strict for several logics, including fixed-point logics, transitive closure logic and its deterministic version, variants of the database language Datalog, and extensions of first-order logic by implicit definitions. Furthermore, we show that all our results already hold on the class of finite graphs.

**Gronbacher, Gregory M A**. Understanding Equality in Health Care: A Christian Free-Market Approach. *Christian Bioethics,* 2(3), 293-308, 1996.

This paper examines the arguments presented by the Roman Catholic Bishops in their 1993 Pastoral Resolution, *Comprehensive Health Care Reform: Protecting Human Life, Promoting Human Dignity, Pursuing the Common Good,* concerning health care reform. Focusing on the meaning of equality in health care and traditional Roman Catholic doctrine, it is argued that the Bishops fail to grasp the force of the differences among persons, the value of the market and traditional scholastic arguments concerning obligatory and extraordinary health care. To attempt to equalize the distribution of health care would be ruinous. A more traditional understanding of Christian thought reveals an acceptance of

inequality in health care distribution and a bias against using the secular state to coerce a solution to such concerns for social justice.

**Grondin, Jean** and Gadamer, Hans-Georg and Weinsheimer, Joel (trans). *Introduction to Philosophical Hermeneutics.* New Haven, Yale Univ Pr, 1994.

In this wide-ranging historical introduction to philosophical hermeneutics, Jean Grondin discusses the major figures from Philo to Habermas, analyzes conflicts between various interpretive schools and provides a persuasive account and a critical appraisal of Gadamer's *Truth and Method.* (publisher)

**Grootendorst, Rob** (ed) and Van Benthem, Johan (ed) and Van Eemeren, Frans H (ed). *Logic and Argumentation.* Amsterdam, North-Holland, 1994.

This volume aims at providing some insight into the connections between logic and argumentation. Van Eemeren and Grootendorst survey the state of the art in argumentation theory. Van Bentham describes the interfaces between developments in logic and argumentation theory. Pinto, Batens, and Starmans discuss the links between argumentation and logic, Finocchiaro the Oliver-Massey asymmetry, Jackson, Krabbe and Walton the fallacies. Woods pays attention to paradoxes. Zarefsky distinguishes between four forces that have shaped argumentation studies in the communication discipline. D. O'Keefe discusses interconnections between argumentation studies and persuasion effect research. Linguistic aspects are explored by Stenning, Van Rees, and Snoeck Henkemans.

**Grootendorst, Rob** and Van Eemeren, Frans H. "Developments in Argumentation Theory" in *Logic and Argumentation,* Van Eemeren, Frans H (ed), 9-26. Amsterdam, North-Holland, 1994.

In this paper, a survey is provided of the state of the art in argumentation theory. Some of the most significant approaches of the past two decades are discussed: Informal logic, the formal theory of fallacies, formal dialectics, pragma-dialectics, radical argumentativism, and the modern revival of rhetoric. The survey is based not only on books, but also on papers published in professional journals or included in conference proceedings.

**Grosholz, Emily** (ed) and Bell, Bernard W (ed) and Stewart, James B (ed). *W.E.B. Du Bois on Race and Culture.* New York, Routledge, 1996.

W.E.B. Du Bois was one of the most profound and influential African-American intellectuals of the twentieth century. This volume addresses the complexities of Du Bois's legacy, showing how his work gets to the heart of today's theorizing about the color line. (publisher, edited)

**Gross, Paul R**. Bête Noire of the Science Worshipers. *Hist Human Sci,* 10(1), 125-129, F 97.

**Gross Schaefer, Arthur** and Herman, Steward W. Introduction. *Bus Ethics Quart,* 7(2), 1-3, Mr 97.

**Grossmann, Andreas**. Im Anfang liegt alles beschlossen: Hannah Arendts politisches Denken im Schatten eines Heideggerschen problems. *Man World,* 30(1), 35-47, Ja 97.

The article seeks to understand Hannah Arendt's political thinking by relating it to an issue which is crucial to the thinking of the later Heidegger, i.e., the problem of originality (*Anfänglichkeit*) and history. In opposition to Hegel's thesis of the "end of art," Heidegger envisages in "great art" such as Hölderlin's poetry a new origin of thinking and history. The end of art, which Hegel holds to be necessary, is in Heidegger's view to be overcome precisely because art, for him, entails an origin which is not a "Not yet" of a teleological perfection in Hegel's sense, but a "Not yet" of a future history. However, Heidegger's orientation towards a "pure" origin qua future leads him to poietically escape the realm of the political and the questions of *praxis* and practical rationality. (edited)

**Groszek, Marcia J** and Slaman, Theodore A. Pi$^0_1$ Classes and Minimal Degrees. *Annals Pure Applied Log,* 87(2), 117-144, 15 S 97.

**Grottanelli, Cristiano** and Sini, Carlo. Homo sacer, di Giorgio Agamben. *Iride,* 9(18), 485-494, Ag 96.

In *Homo sacer,* Agamben si interroga sui caratteri essenziali del politico e della democrazia moderni, rivelandone in particolare l'aspetto "biopolitico". Grottanelli si sofferma sull'ambiguità del concetto di sacro e sulla critica dell'ideologia sacrificale proposti da Agamben. Sini approfondisce alcuni concetti centrali delle analisi di Agamben, come quelli connessi al metodo biopolitico del potere, alla nozione di "bando" e di sovranità, per finire con quello di Stato.

**Grover, Stephen**. West or Best? Sufficient Reason in the Leibniz-Clarke Correspondence. *Stud Leibniz,* 28(1), 84-92, 1996.

In der Korrespondenz mit Clarke ist Leibniz' Standardargument gegen die Annahme, dass Raum und Zeit absolut seien, dass Gott sich bei der Wahl des zu erschaffenden Universums gezwungen sähe, gegen das Prinzip des zureichenden Grundes zu verstossen, wenn diese Annahme richtig wäre: Blosse Unterschiede in räumlicher und zeitlicher Hinsicht ergeben keinen Vorteilsunterschied, und da Gott nur aus Vorteilsgründen handelt, sind solche Unterschiede nicht möglich. Leibniz stellt dieses Argument als ausschliesslich abhängig vom Prinzip des zureichenden Grundes dar, eine gängige Interpretation ist aber, dass dies Prinzip determinierte Objekte göttlicher Wahl nur dann ergibt, wenn ein ergänzendes Prinzip von Kontingenz hinzutritt. Diese Auslegung muss falsch sein, wenn Leibniz hier authentisch bleibt, und insofern wäre doch das Prinzip des zureichenden Grundes eher als irgendein Prinzip des Besten Leibniz' Prinzip der Kontingenz.

**Grube, Dirk-Martin**. A Critical Reconstruction of Paul Tillich's Epistemology. *Relig Stud,* 33(1), 67-80, Mr 97.

It is contended that Falk Wagner's famous charge that Tillich just posits the existence of the *unconditional* without further argument overlooks the transcendental character of Tillich's early writings from the 1920s. There the transcendental is utilized for legitimating the transcendent. Tillich's transcendental account resembles the ontological argument in that the question of the transcendent's existence is affirmed via an inquiry into the conceptual implications its concept harbors. In his later writings, Tillich abandons this transcendentalism in favor of his 'critical phenomenology'. The weaknesses of this version of phenomenology are brought out in comparison with Husserlian phenomenology. Finally, a remedy for the weaknesses of Tillich's approach is suggested by drawing on current antifoundationalist thought.

**Gruen, Lori**. "Revaluing Nature" in *Ecofeminism: Women, Culture, Nature,* Warren, Karen J (ed), 356-374. Bloomington, Indiana Univ Pr, 1997.

**Gruen, Lori** and Chorover, Stephan L and List, Peter. Commentary On: "There is no Such Thing as Environmental Ethics". *Sci Eng Ethics*, 2(3), 319-334, Jl 96.

**Gruen, Lori** (ed) and Panichas, George E (ed). *Sex, Morality, and the Law.* New York, Routledge, 1997.

The book combines legal opinions and philosophical analysis to explore the controversial issues surrounding state control of sexual and reproductive behavior. This unique anthology focuses on six topics of enduring moral, social and legal concern: lesbian and gay sex, prostitution, pornography, abortion, sexual harassment and rape. Each section includes introductions by the editors and substantial excerpts from influential court decisions, such as *Bowers v. Hardwock, Roe v. Wade,* and *American Booksellers v. Hudnut,* as well as recent court decisions *Romer v. Evans* and *Casey v. Planned Parenthood.* (publisher)

**Grün, Klaus-Jürgen**. Internationale Konferenz zu Kants Friedensidee und dem heutigen Problem einer internationalen Rechts—und Friedensordnung in Frankfurt am Main. *Kantstudien*, 87(3), 355-359, 1996.

**Grünbaum, Adolf**. Empirical Evaluations of Theoretical Explanations of Psychotherapeutic Efficacy: A Reply to John D. Greenwood. *Phil Sci*, 63(4), 622-641, D 96.

In the present paper, it is argued *contra* Greenwood that: 1) his purportedly "best" reading of Freud's *tally argument* and of its import founders, 2) the distinction that Greenwood bemoans as being neglected by mental health researchers actually is a commonplace in literature on treatment-*process* and therapeutic *outcomes,* 3) Greenwood's defense of Popper's critique of psychoanalysis is an anachronism, and 4) Greenwood's conceptual analysis of placebo controls is nebulous and misconceived. (edited)

**Grund, Cynthia M**. Kierkegaard: Metaphor and the Musical Erotic. *Dan Yrbk Phil*, 31, 65-88, 1996.

**Grundmann, Thomas**. Gibt es ein subjektives Fundament unseres Wissens?. *Z Phil Forsch*, 50(3), 458-472, Jl-S 96.

**Grunwald, Armin**. Die Bewältigung von Technikkonflikten: Theoretische Möglichkeit und praktische Relevanz einer Ethik der Technik in der Moderne. *Z Phil Forsch*, 50(3), 442-457, Jl-S 96.

**Grusenmeyer, Corinne** and Trognon, Alain. Structures of Natural Reasoning within Functional Dialogues. *Prag Cognition*, 4(2), 305-346, 1996.

The aim of this paper is to describe and characterize some structural features of natural reasoning by analyzing a number of conversations held by operators during shift changeovers. During this work phase the operators have to cooperate in order to carry out the same process. This need to cooperate leads to dialogues and joint elaboration of information, especially when involving the reporting of a malfunction. Three dialogues observed at this work phase on two study sites (a paper mill and a nuclear power plant) are analyzed. These analyses show that the step by step follow-up of the operators' collective reasoning is feasible. They highlight that these reasonings are complex experimental and hypothetico-deductive reasonings. They are reasonings for action, that are elaborated as the conversation unfolds and for which the operators do not always have the means of testing their hypotheses.

**Grush, Rick**. The Architecture of Representation. *Phil Psych*, 10(1), 5-23, Mr 97.

In this article I outline, apply, and defend a theory of natural representation. The main consequences of this theory are: i) representational status is a matter of how physical entities are used, and specifically is *not* a matter of causation, nomic relations with the intentional object, or information; ii) there are genuine (brain-)internal representations; iii) such representations are really *representations,* and not just farcical pseudorepresentations, such as attractors, principal components, state-space partitions, or what-have-you; and iv) the theory allows us to sharply distinguish those complex behaviors which are genuinely cognitive from those which are merely cognate and adaptive.

**Gruzalski, Bart K**. Autonomy and the Orthodoxy of Human Superiority. *Between Species*, 12(1-2), 1-18, Wint-Spr 96.

Are the lives of normal adult human beings more valuable than the lives of nonhuman animals because of either the inherent value of autonomy or the instrumental value of autonomy? I argue that (1) the claim (made by Susan Wolf, Willard Gaylin and others) that the lives of the autonomous are inherently more valuable because the autonomous have the ability to be moral is not persuasive; and (2) R.G. Frey's claim that the autonomous experience more satisfaction than those who lack autonomy is unpersuasive. I conclude that we have no reason for thinking that our autonomous lives are more valuable than the lives of nonautonomous nonhuman animals. In "The Instrumental Value of Autonomy," (pp. 14-18) I respond to Frey's criticisms of my argument (in Frey, "Autonomy, Animals and Conceptions of the Good," pp. 8-14). I show that Frey explicitly begs the question about the comparative value of human/nonhuman lives and

that he rests his claim for the value of autonomy on a beguiling but unjustifiable rhetoric reflecting a cultural bias of middle-class luxury and opportunity. The exercise of the capacities Frey groups under the label "autonomy" results in lives less satisfactory than the lives of the nonautonomous. There is no mystery how to begin a grounded comparison of the satisfactoriness of our autonomous lives with the lives of nonautonomous nonhuman animals: we simply compare those moments of our lives when we are exercising autonomy with those moments when we are not.

**Grzegorczyk, Anna**. "Non-Cartesian Coordinates in the Contemporary Humanities" in *Epistemology and History,* Zeidler-Janiszewska, Anna (ed), 75-98. Amsterdam, Rodopi, 1996.

This is an attempt to reconstruct a fragment of A.J. Greimas's semiotic conception of culture concerning the category of truth. Greimas's views are confronted with J. Kmita's conception of the revealed truth of postmodernism in general. Both philosophers, recognizing the philosophical inevitability of postmodernistic views, try to defend the constructivity of modernist assumptions.

**Guariglia, Osvaldo**. "La universalizabilidad monológica: R.M. Hare" in *La racionalidad: su poder y sus límites,* Nudler, Oscar (ed), 471-480. Barcelona, Ed Paidos, 1996.

**Guariglia, Osvaldo**. *Moralidad: Ética universalista y sujeto moral.* Madrid, Fondo de Cultura, 1996.

No es el objetivo del presente libro examinar críticamente las concepciones históricas de la ética como disciplina filosófica o científica, sino establecer una concepción de la ética como una disciplina filosófica autónoma cuya finalidad es, en primer lugar, la reconstrucción metódica de la estructura argumentativa de la moralidad. Pero, ¿qué entiende el autor por "moralidad"? Es, dice, "el ámbito estricto de la obligaciones incondicionales que conforman el marco de la acción social y política". (edited)

**Guarini, Marcello**. Tensor Products and Split-Level Architecture: Foundational Issues in the Classicism-Connectionism Debate. *Proc Phil Sci Ass*, 3(Suppl), S239-S247, 1996.

This paper responds to criticisms levelled by Fodor, Pylyshyn and McLaughlin against connectionism. Specifically, I will rebut the charge that connectionists cannot account for representational systematicity without implementing a classical architecture. This will be accomplished by drawing on Paul Smolensky's Tensor Product model of representation and on his insights about split-level architectures.

**Guarino, Thomas**. Philosophy within Theology in Light of the Foundationalism Debate. *Phil Theol*, 9(1-2), 57-69, 1995.

My paper proceeds in three stages: 1) the traditional relationship between philosophy and theology; 2) how the "foundationalist" issue affects this debate; 3) some final reflections. This essay, along with the previous one by Jack Bonsor, was originally presented to the "Theology in the Seminary Context" seminar at the *Catholic Theological Society of America* convention in June, 1995.

**Guastini, Riccardo**. Fragments of a Theory of Legal Sources. *Ratio Juris*, 9(4), 364-386, D 96.

The author discusses a number of issues in the theory of legal sources. The first topic is whether sources should be conceived of as acts or texts. The alternatives are connected with two competing theories of legal interpretation (viz., the cognitive theory and the sceptical theory), which entail different concepts of legal rules and law-making. The second topic is whether a "formal" or a "material" criterion of recognition of sources should be preferred. The third section is devoted to the analysis of rules of change. Four theories of rules of change are discussed, and five kinds of such rules are distinguished. The fourth section concerns judicial law-making, with special reference to the creation of new legal rules by constitutional courts.

**Guelke, Leonard**. The Relations between Geography and History Reconsidered. *Hist Theor*, 36(2), 216-234, My 97.

The ideas of Sauer, Darby, Clark, and Meinig have had a formative influence on the making of modern Anglo-American historical geography. These scholars emphasized the spatial- and place-focused orientation of geography, contrasting it with history's concern with time, the past, and change. Historical geography was conceived as combining the spatial interests of geography with the temporal interest of history, creating a field concerned with changing spatial patterns and landscapes. This idea of historical geography avoided issues in the philosophy of history by making the historical geographer a kind of spectator to external changes in the ways things were ordered and arranged on the face of the earth. This "natural history" view of historical geography failed to deal with history conceived as an autonomous mode of understanding in which the scholar's task is to understand human activity as an embodiment of thought. Historical geography is more adequately conceived as a Collingwoodian-type historical discipline. (edited)

**Guenin, Louis M**. Affirmative Action in Higher Education as Redistribution. *Pub Affairs Quart*, 11(2), 117-140, Ap 97.

Affirmative action policies admit greater numbers of disadvantaged students than the putative classroom benefits of diversity may justify. In general, quotas may serve, claims Walzer, to effect representation, but admissions are not representative; schemes of weighted qualifications may effectively operate as quotas; recitification founders on subjunctive assertions; and impartial consideration of applicants seems owed. After developing these claims, four arguments are offered that admission is not deserved: 1) even in Nozick's view, talents confer no entitlement to a role or office; 2) by Arrow's theorem (whose independence of irrelevant alternatives is claimed applicable and that Sen's acyclicity result is held not to obviate here), no mapping generating a linear ordering of applicants is possible; 3) admission anticipates future performance;

and 4) following Nagel, desert may be superseded by measures to offset connected injustices in economic rewards. If admission is not deserved, it may be manipulable for collective purposes.

**Guenin, Louis M**. Alternative Dispute Resolution and Research Misconduct. *Cambridge Quart Healthcare Ethics*, 6(1), 72-77, Winter 97.

Should allegations of research misconduct be addressed by alternative dispute resolution ("ADR")? This paper canvasses the suitability, in order of increasing binding effect, of mediation and conciliation, neutral expert fact-finding, minitrial, arbitration and mediation-arbitration. Arbitration and mediation may avail for authorship disputes and for cases of retaliation against witnesses if the panels possess sufficient expertise concerning any relevant technical issues. ADR otherwise appears unsuitable because, notwithstanding the parties' desire for confidentiality or ability to compromise, when research misconduct occurs, there ordinarily obtains a public interest in a reliable, reported determination of what occurred and of what sanctions should be imposed.

**Guenin, Louis M**. Norms for Patents Concerning Human and Other Life Forms. *Theor Med*, 17(3), 279-314, S 96.

The rationale of patents on transgenic organisms leads to the startling notion of the human qua infringement. The moral reasons by which we may tenably reject such notion are not conclusive as to human life forms outside the body. A close look at recombinant DNA experimentation reveals ingenious processes, but not entities that the body lacks. Except for artificial genes, the genes of biotechnology are found on chromosomes, albeit nonconsecutively, and their uninterrupted transcripts appear in messenger RNA. An enhanced form of protection for ingenious processes, the "human methods patent," is proposed and defended as a replacement for product patents. The proposed patent would pertain to biotechnology manufacturing and genetic intervention in somatic and germ cells. A counterpart could govern nonhuman life forms. It is argued that compulsory licensing protections should be a condition of such patent. Contrary to the conservative assumption that statutory sobriquets suffice, the reckoning of what qualifies as a patentable ingenious process will continue to require systemic scientific guidance.

**Guenin, Louis M** and Davis, Bernard D. Scientific Reasoning and Due Process. *Sci Eng Ethics*, 2(1), 47-54, J 96.

Recent public hearings on misconduct charges belie the conjecture that due process will preface defeat informed scientific reasoning. One notable case that reviewed an obtuse description of experimental methods displays some of the subtleties of differentiating carelessness from intent to deceive. There the decision of a studious nonscientist panel managed to reach sensible conclusions despite conflicting expert testimony. The significance of such a result may be to suggest that to curtail due process would be both objectionable and unproductive.

**Günther, Klaus**. Individuelle Zurechnung im demokratischen Verfassungsstaat. *Jahr Recht Ethik*, 2, 143-157, 1994.

In a constitutional democracy, the imputation of a legal violation to an individual must be related to the fact that democratic approval of a norm—under limiting conditions—is coupled with the obligation to follow that norm. The neutrality of modern law toward the quality of motives for following a norm, however, challenges the assumption of such a connection. Individual imputation takes account of this double classification of a person subject to law as citizen and as private autonomous legal subject only if the actor is addressed as citizen in the reasoning given to support the determination of culpability without simultaneously requiring him to actually adopt the perspective of a citizen. (edited)

**Guerra, Marc D**. Aristotle on Pleasure and Political Philosophy: A Study in Book VII of the *Nicomachean Ethics*. *Interpretation*, 24(2), 171-182, Wint 97.

**Guerrini, Luigi**. Lo stile de' Geometri: La filosofia cartesiana nell'opera di Alessandro Pascoli (1669-1757). *G Crit Filosof Ital*, 16(3), 380-394, S-D 96.

**Guerrini, Luigi**. Note su traduzioni manoscritte delle opere cartesiane. *G Crit Filosof Ital*, 16(3), 500-507, S-D 96.

**Guerrini, Luigi**. Una lettera inedita del Carcavi al Magliabechi con un parere sul Redi. *G Crit Filosof Ital*, 16(2), 180-184, My-Ag 96.

**Guertin, Robert P**. Commentary on: "How Are Scientific Corrections Made?". *Sci Eng Ethics*, 1(4), 357-359, O 95.

Written retractions of one's published scientific results are rare. In addition, verification of the work of others is not considered a productive activity: The reward system is based on original results, not on checking the veracity of someone else's: Few animal care and use committees, for example, would allow animals to be sacrificed to duplicate another's data. Modern physics experiments are often so complex that no other group could access the facilities needed to reproduce the results, e.g., the recent discovery of the top quark. A robust skepticism of all results, therefore, is good for the health of the scientific enterprise.

**Guetti, Carla** (ed) and Pujia, Roberto (ed). *Momenti di Storia della Logica e di Storia della Filosofia*. Roma, Aracne Editrice, 1996.

**Gueye, Sémou Pathé**. Le "Dépassement de la Philosophie": Réflexion sur le statut contemporain de la philosophie. *Quest*, 9(2), 44-69, D 96.

We make explicit what we personally regard as the real philosophical status of the debate. Our position is that behind the questioning of the epistemological status of philosophy, which is supposed to be outdated by the progress of the sciences and the way it structures the order of knowledge, what is really questioned is *reason*, but also philosophical discourse as such or, more precisely, philosophical discourse. We are ending with the suggestion that the debate, rather than clarifying the status of contemporary philosophy, opens the

reflection towards an abyss of new and more critical questions. Maybe it is nothing but a new subterfuge by professional philosophy to remain alive and nourish its own servants. (edited)

**Guha, Debashis**. Some Problems Concerning the Big Bang Theory of Creation. *J Indian Counc Phil Res*, 13(2), 31-43, Ja-Ap 96.

The purpose of this paper is to unfold the importance of a heuristic understanding of the Big Bang Theory of creation because the idealistic understanding that stems out of the idealization of the physical theories, facts and findings, fail to socialize science. The heuristic understanding of the Big Bang Theory concentrates on three major problems: the problems of defining 'singularity', the organization and the origin of the nascent states of creation. The conclusion is that the classical definitions of the 'singularity' should be avoided and the possibilities of self organization and material origin of all creation should be considered seriously.

**Guha, Ranajit**. Not at Home in Empire. *Crit Inquiry*, 23(3), 482-493, Spr 97.

**Guibal, Francis**. The Hegelian Sign: Sacrificial Economy and Dialectical Relief (in French). *Arch Phil*, 60(2), 265-297, Ap-Je 97.

From the singular to the universal, from the sensible to the intelligible, the movement, of which the Hegelian sign is at once operator and witness, is always that of sacrificial economy ending in a spiritual synthesis. In this work it is pursued, redrawn and questioned from the point of view of its development in phenomenology of the spirit.

**Guisán Seijas, Esperanza**. Esperando a Mill. *Cuad Etica*, 21-22, 23-44, 1996.

During the first half of this century, it has firmly grown certain kind of skepticism that, founded in Kantism, puts apart facts from values. This movement condemned Mill to ostracism and helped a false perception of utilitarianism. The Millian tradition was accused of lacking, what has precisely been its reason of being: the freedom of the individual, his interests his autonomy, equity and the approach to a more just society. This paper considers the importance of the helpings of a Millian political theory, in the levels of both normative and meta-ethics.

**Guisán Seijas, Esperanza**. Las personas en serio (Los derechos humanos y el Bienestar). *Telos (Spain)*, 5(1), 27-53, Je 96.

Emphasis is placed in the need of *taking persons seriously* instead of only taking their rights seriously. Accordingly human well-being (physical, psychological and moral) is a *trump* against any sort of consideration about alleged rights that could go counter human development and well-being. Instead of current talk about classical rights such as liberty, freedom and dignity, too formal and too abstract, the paper deals with three main rights that prove to be more promising: 1) The right to be considered as a being whose suffering is to be minimized, 2) The right to a free, full, personal development, and 3) The right to receive care and sympathy. (edited)

**Guisán Seijas, Esperanza**. Un siglo de oro para la Etica. *Agora (Spain)*, 15(1), 31-49, 1996.

The twentieth century has been an especially fruitful century for ethical research in general terms, as far as metaethics, normative ethics or applied ethics are concerned. Since 1903 up to the present, the most diverse metaethical theories have been devised which have led to new approaches relative to the foundations of practical reason, a goal especially achieved by Baier. Three different trends can be distinguished in contemporary normative ethics: a) neo-Kantism, b)neoutilitarianism and, c) virtue ethics. Both neo-Kantism and neoutilitarianism shows a clear Kantian influence, already present in G.E. Moore, thus neglecting classical utilitarianism's contributions. Luckily, however, both approaches of some trends of virtue-ethics and some contemporary works on classical utilitarianism, as well as those by Berger and Kelly, rediscover the potentialities of utilitarianism as an ethics for the next century, giving at the same time, due place to the part of emotions and reason in ethics. (edited)

**Guleserian, Theodore**. Can God Change His Mind?. *Faith Phil*, 13(3), 329-351, Jl 96.

A temporal perfect being is best conceived of as having essentially *the power* to change his mind—even from doing a morally right act to doing one that is morally wrong. For, this power allows him to increase his moral worth by *constantly refraining* from changing his intentions to do the right thing. Such a being could not possess the power to form an *unalterable* intention to do the right thing. Could an omnipotent, omniscient being have this power to change his mind and yet know what his future intentions will be? Four arguments that imply a negative answer are considered and rebutted.

**Gumanski, Leon**. "The Ideal University and Reality" in *The Idea of University*, Brzezinski, Jerzy (ed), 35-46. Amsterdam, Rodopi, 1997.

The paper indicates some phenomena that should be eliminated from university life. The postulate of endowing universities with unlimited autonomy is unrealizable and dangerous. The maintenance of a national body controlling universities is necessary. Forms of education and the effectiveness of syllabuses ought to be tested before admission as obligatory. Human weaknesses and mutual relations between faculty members have sometimes a negative influence on research but should be estimated cautiously.

**Gundersen, Lars**. The Problem of Transworld Identity. *Dan Yrbk Phil*, 30, 7-36, 1995.

**Gunkel, David**. Scary Monsters: Hegel and the Nature of the Monstrous. *Int Stud Phil*, 29(2), 23-46, 1997.

This essay, which examines the significance of monstrosity, concerns the reading of a text that not only addresses but gives particular place to monsters, Hegel's *Philosophy of Nature*. The essay begins with a consideration of the dialectical method as presented in the *Logic* and proceeds by tracing two monstrous deformations—exorbitance and wasting. Throughout this reading, the investigation is haunted by a monstrous accomplice, D.A.F. Sade's *The 120 Days of Sodom*. In the end, the essay argues that the monstrosities demonstrated in Hegelian philosophy signify nothing less than deformations of reason in general.

**Gunther, York**. Perceptual Content and the Subpersonal. *Conference*, 6(1), 31-45, Sum 95.

In this paper I criticize Dennett's subpersonal analysis of perceptual content. Attempts like Bilgrami's to supplement the model seem to depend on suspect forms of externalism. In fact any analysis which excludes objects of perception from content is in some way guilty of conflating two senses of 'information' (one syntactic, the other semantic). Once these two senses of 'information' are sharply distinguished, the luster of analyzes like Dennett's is lost and a 'personal approach as McDowell recommends presents itself as the most viable course.

**Gunzenhauser, Michael G**. "Epistemological Reversals between Chisholm and Lyotard" in *Philosophy of Education (1996)*, Margonis, Frank (ed), 151-153. Urbana, Phil Education Soc, 1997.

**Gupta, Omprakash K** and Rominger, Anna S. Blind Man's Bluff: The Ethics of Quantity Surcharges. *J Bus Ethics*, 15(12), 1299-1312, D 96.

Empirical evidence, including a recent field study in Northwest Indiana, indicates that supermarkets and other retail merchants frequently incorporate quantity surcharges in their product pricing strategy. Retailers impose surcharges by charging higher unit prices for products packaged in a larger quantity than smaller quantity of the same goods and brand. The purpose of this article is to examine the business ethics of such pricing strategy in light of empirical findings, existing government regulations, factors that motivate quantity surcharges and prevailing consumer perceptions.

**Gupta, R K**. Kant's Doctrine of Categories: An Attempt at Some Clarification. *J Indian Counc Phil Res*, 14(1), 167-169, S-D 96.

**Gur-Ze'ev, Ilan**. The Vocation of Higher Education: Modern and Postmodern Rhetorics in the Israeli Academia on Strike. *J Thought*, 32(2), 57-74, Sum 97.

**Gutiérrez, Carlos B**. "Liberalismo y Multiculturalidad" in *Liberalismo y Comunitarismo: Derechos Humanos y Democracia*, Monsalve Solórzano, Alfonso (ed), 81-98. 36-46003 València, Alfons el Magnànim, 1996.

**Gutiérrez, Carlos B**. No al Método Unico. *Ideas Valores*, 86-95, Ag 97.

**Gutiérrez, Carlos B**. Problemas o Preguntas?. *Cad Hist Filosof Cie*, 6(Spec), 57-71, Ja-D 96.

Gadamer's critique of the idea of philosophical problems, in particular of its development by the neo-Kantians of Marburg and Heidelberg, are the main topic of this article. Gadamer does not accept that philosophical problems are eternal and a-historical. Rather, he sees them as questions inserted in the dialectical life of experience. A question is raised by a motive and presupposes, in its starting point, the recognition of our ignorance. In the end, some critiques to Gadamer's critique are discussed.

**Gutiérrez, Carlos B**. Systemic Historical Criticism of the Concept of Tolerance (Spanish). *Rev Filosof (Venezuela)*, Supp(2-3), 1-36, 1996.

In this paper the author analyzes the evolution of the concept of *tolerance* from the initial religious reference up to its conception as a pillar of liberal theory, especially in the works of Locke. From this moment on, *tolerance* becomes an aspect of class interest related to the ideas of liberty, property and individual. Afterwards, *tolerance* acquires its significance in its relation with the ideas of pluralism. The authors analyzed are: Spinoza, Locke, Stuart Mill, Leibniz, Marcuse and Mitscherlich.

**Gutiérrez, Edgardo**. Arte, lenguaje y metafísica en las estéticas de Hegel y Adorno. *Dialogos*, 32(70), 199-207, Jl 97.

**Gutiérrez, Edgardo**. La Resolución del Perplejo. *Rev Latin de Filosof*, 23(1), 145-152, O 97.

**Gutiérrez, Edgardo**. Lenguaje significativo y no significativo: *El Kaspar* de Peter Handke. *Rev Latin de Filosof*, 23(1), 153-167, O 97.

The purpose of this article is to point out that *Kaspar* is a theatrical version of a philosophy of language. In this direction the play drama of Peter Handke is related to Wittgenstein's philosophy of language. *Kaspar* is a dramatization of the conflict between the society and the individual through the language. First, the society tries to mold him. However, he finally destroys the learned right language. The schizophrenia of Kaspar is the normal ego explosion. The ego created by society is broken. Nevertheless being crazy does not necessarily imply a breakdown. It might be breakthrough. In *Kaspar* the true insanity is the normal ego who says "I am who I am". Handke's work shows the abyss between Being and Language.

**Gutmann, Amy** and Thompson, Dennis. Deliberating about Bioethics. *Hastings Center Rep*, 27(3), 38-41, My-Je 97.

Bioethics was built on conflicts. Abortion, physician-assisted suicide, patients' demand for autonomy all are staple and contentious issues. What forum best serves such debates? A look at political theories of democracy is helpful: The most promising for bioethics debates are theories that ask citizens and officials to justify any demands for collective action by giving reasons that can be accepted by those who are bound by the action, otherwise known as deliberative democracy.

**Gutmann, Amy** and Thompson, Dennis. *Democracy and Disagreement*. Cambridge, Harvard Univ Pr, 1996.

Gutman and Thompson show how a deliberative democracy can address some of our most difficult controversies—from abortion and affirmative action to health care and welfare—and can allow diverse groups separated by class, race, religion, and gender to reason together. Their work goes beyond that of most political theorists and social scientists by exploring both the principles for reasonable argument and their application to actual cases. Not only do the authors suggest how deliberative democracy can work, they also show why improving our collective capacity for moral argument is better than referring all disagreements to procedural politics or judicial institutions. (edited)

**Gutmann, Mathias** and Hanekamp, Gerd. Abstraktion und Ideation— Zur Semantik chemischer und biologischer Grundbegriffe. *J Gen Phil Sci*, 27(1), 29-53, 1996.

"Abstraction and Ideation—The Semantics of Chemical and Biological Fundamental Concepts." The methods of abstraction and ideation are indispensable tools to introduce new concepts in a scientific terminology. The latter is paradigmatically introduced within the 'protophysical program' whereas abstraction is commonly applied in logics and mathematics. The application within the reconstruction of chemistry and biology causes several problems. Ideation appears to be inadequate whereas the application of abstraction necessitates a critical and minute examination of the corresponding equivalence relations. These problems are solved by the introduction of the method of *materially-synthetic* (material-synthetische) abstraction which is exemplified by the introduction of the concept of 'substance' (Stoff) and the biological concept of 'hereditary factor' (Erbanlage).

**Gutmann, Wolfgang Friedrich** and Weingarten, Michael. Maschinentheoretische Grundlagen der organismischen Konstruktionslehre. *Phil Natur*, 28(2), 231-256, 1991.

**Guy, Reed A** and Deltete, Robert J. Emerging from Imaginary Time. *Synthese*, 108(2), 185-203, Ag 96.

Recent models in quantum cosmology make use of the concept of imaginary time. These models all conjecture a join between regions of imaginary time and regions of real time. We examine the model of James Hartle and Stephen Hawking to argue that the various 'no-boundary' attempts to interpret the transition from imaginary to real time in a logically consistent and physically significant way all fail. We believe this conclusion also applies to 'quantum tunneling' models, such as that proposed by Alexander Vilenkin. We conclude, therefore, that the notion of 'emerging from imaginary time' is incoherent. A consequence of this conclusion seems to be that the whole class of cosmological models appealing to imaginary time is thereby refuted.

**Guzmán, Fernando**. A Gentzen System for Conditional Logic. *Stud Log*, 53(2), 243-257, My 94.

**Gylfason, Thorsteinn**. The Irrelevance of Meaning. *Dan Yrbk Phil*, 31, 89-96, 1996.

**Haack, Susan**. "The First Rule of Reason" in *The Rule of Reason: The Philosophy of Charles Sanders Peirce*, Forster, Paul (ed), 241-261. Toronto, Univ of Toronto Pr, 1997.

What Peirce describes as the first, and in a sense the sole, rule of reason is: in order to learn you must desire to learn, and in so desiring not be satisfied with what you already incline to think. This paper 1) traces the connections of the FRR with the other aspects of Peirce's philosophy into which it ramifies; 2) shows how to reconcile it with the account of the motivation of inquiry in "The Fixation of Belief," with which it appears superficially in conflict; 3) distinguishes stronger and weaker interpretations and argues that, in a weak form, it is true; 4) suggests its relevance to philosophy today.

**Haack, Susan**. Between Scientism and Conversationalism. *Phil Lit*, 20(2), 455-474, O 96.

Disillusionment with the very idea of inquiry underlies Rorty's conception of philosophy as merely "carrying on the conversation" of Western culture. His disillusionment is groundless; and it would undermine literature as well as science. A scientific conception of philosophy, in Peirce's subtle sense, allows a far more plausible account not only of the relation of philosophy to the sciences, but also of its relation to the literature.

**Haack, Susan**. We Pragmatists...; Peirce and Rorty in Conversation. *Agora (Spain)*, 15(1), 53-68, 1996.

A conversation between Peirce and Rorty, composed from their own words, illustrating how different their conceptions are, not only of pragmatism, but of the nature and role of philosophy.

**Haag, Johannes**. Der Wille als Träger des Ethischen—Überlegungen zur Stellung des Willens in der Frühphilosophie Ludwig Wittgensteins. *Acta Analytica*, 131-152, 1995.

In Wittgenstein's *Tractatus logico-philosophicus* the notion of will, described as "the bearer of the ethical," plays a crucial role. Yet, there are very few sentences in the *Tractatus* itself that are concerned with this important concept. Therefore one has to look further back, to the development of Tractarian philosophy of the will in the notebooks of 1916. It will be shown that this development led to a result which didn't change in the finished *Tractatus*. The chief means to obtain this result is Wittgenstein's elaborate notion of the metaphysical subject. In the following discussion of the system of the *Tractatus*, it will be argued that it is possible to embed the notion of will in the *Tractatus* without inconsistencies.

**Haakonssen, Knud**. "Rationalität und Relativismus in den Geisteswissenschaften" in *Grenzen der kritischen Vernunft*, Schmid, Peter A, 43-57. Basel, Schwabe Verlag, 1997.

**Haaksma, Hans W H**. De oorspronkelijkheid en actuele betekenis van H. van Riessen als filosoof van de techniek: Deel I—De oorspronkelijkheid van zijn werk. *Phil Reform*, 62(1), 23-47, 1997.

Van Riessen was the first (Dutch) philosopher to explain modern technology as opposed to traditional craftsmanship as a process of making use of scientific methods, but he rejected the idea of technology being an applied science. To analyze the characteristics of modern technology he first focused on the technical object, then showed the way it is formed, and finally analyzed the designing process needed to control its manufacture. He maintained that the impact of technology on culture could only be studied with this insight into the structure of technology in mind. As an engineer he showed great originality in his philosophical thinking.

**Haaksma, Hans W H**. Overzicht van de filosofie van de techniek in Nederland tijdens het interbellum. *Alg Ned Tijdschr Wijs*, 89(1), 67-85, Ja 97.

According to some *De maat van de techniek* (*The Measure of Technology*), edited by H. Achterhuis, is the first attempt in the Netherlands to bring philosophy to the attention of philosophers and the general public in this country. It is shown that this is not the case. In the period between the two world wars already, many publications in Dutch appeared on this subject. Especially the works of Schermerhorn, Korevaar and Proost demonstrate a remarkable insight of technology. That of Schermerhorn even foreshadows the new turn this subdiscipline of philosophy took during the last fifteen years.

**Haaksma, Hans W H** and Vlot, Ad. Henk van Riessen, pionier van de filosofie van de techniek. *Alg Ned Tijdschr Wijs*, 89(1), 26-43, Ja 97.

Van Riessen applied the philosophy of H. Dooyeweerd and D.T.H. Vollenhoven in an analysis of the structure of technology. This approach enabled him to differentiate between the characteristics of modern technology and those of traditional technology, and to clarify the usually blurred distinctions between technology, economical enterprise and science. According to Van Riessen, any discussion of the cultural impact of technology on society should be based on a philosophical analysis of technology itself. Without such an analysis, technology, is mistaken for an applied science only, and the technological artefact treated as a 'black box' without its own laws and structure.

**Haapala, Arto**. Metaphors for Living—Living Metaphors. *Dan Yrbk Phil*, 31, 97-106, 1996.

**Haar, Michel**. Limits and Grounds of History: The Nonhistorical. *Epoche*, 1(1), 1-11, 1993.

**Haar, Michel**. The Place of Nietzsche in Reiner Schürmann's Thought and in His Reading of Heidegger. *Grad Fac Phil J*, 19/20(2/1), 229-245, 1997.

**Haarscher, Guy**. La Laïcité. Paris, Pr Univ France, 1996.

**Haarscher, Guy**. Tolerance of the Intolerant?. *Ratio Juris*, 10(2), 236-246, Je 97.

In the first part of the essay, the author analyzes the difference and the relation between two different ideas of toleration, the passive and the active meaning. While the former is related to opportunistic and prudential purposes, the second is grounded in an ethical framework and presupposes the individual's freedom of conscience. This second meaning appears to be very important in a multicultural society. On its basis it is possible to develop toleration both as a plurality of contexts of choice and as a priority rule between conscience and culture in Rawlsian terms. In the second part, starting from the case of O. Preminger Institut v. Austria, the author examines the relation between this idea of toleration and freedom of speech.

**Haas, Andrew**. The Bacchanalian Revel: Hegel and Deconstruction. *Man World*, 30(2), 217-226, Ap 97.

This text argues that Hegel's *concept*, insofar as it has already deconstructed all opposed and fixed standpoints, supersedes deconstruction. Reducing the *logic* and *phenomenology* to the same kind of schematic formalism for which Hegel criticized his predecessors (Fichte and Schelling), Derrida misses the ways in which *absolute spirit* shows itself as the "Bacchanalian revel wherein no member is not drunk." Thus, this article defends Hegel against Derrida on Derrida's terms.

**Haase, Michaela**. Pragmatic Idealization and Structuralist Reconstructions of Theories. *J Gen Phil Sci*, 27(2), 215-234, 1996.

The concept of Galilean idealization is based on a pragmatically grounded relation between universes of so-called real and idealized entities. The concept was developed in the course of a critical discussion of different explications of the concept of idealization (e.g., by W. F. Barr, C. G. Hempel and L. Nowak), these being attempts to specify sufficient syntactic and semantic criterions for idealization. But this line of argument shall not be followed here. Instead, first the concept of pragmatic idealization and as its special case the Galilean one, is presented (1) and certain aspects of the application of an idealized theory are discussed (2). Then, working within the Structuralist view of theories, definitions of the idealized variants of the diachronic theory-element and theory-net are presented (3).

**Haase, Ullrich M**. From Name to Metaphor...and Back. *Res Phenomenol*, 26, 230-260, 1996.

This essay investigates the scope and the significance of the question of metaphor. The path it takes leads from an introduction into the problem of metaphor via an investigation into Ricoeur's *La Métaphore Vive*, towards the conclusion that the overcoming of metaphysics has to be achieved by an eradication of metaphor through an attack upon its very condition of possibility: the determination of human being through its transcendence. Consequently, this essay will conclude, with Heidegger, that the notion of the symbolic is insufficient to account for human being and that the concept of metaphor fails to account for human knowledge.

**Habermas, Jürgen**. Sprechakttheoretische Erläuterungen zum Begriff der kommunikativen Rationalität. *Z Phil Forsch*, 50(1/2), 65-91, Ja-Je 96.

**Habermas, Jürgen** and Deflem, Mathieu (trans). Georg Simmel on Philosophy and Culture: Postscript to a Collection of Essays. *Crit Inquiry*, 22(3), 403-414, Spr 96.

**Hacker, P M S**. Davidson on First-Person Authority. *Phil Quart*, 47(188), 285-304, Jl 97.

Davidson's explanation of first-person authority (FPA) in utterances of the form 'I V that *p*' derives FPA from requirements of interpretation. It is committed to the view that utterance-sentences are truth-bearers, that believing is holding true an utterance-sentence and that knowledge of what one means gives one knowledge of what belief one expresses. These claims are faulted. His explanation of FPA by reference to the requirements of interpretability entails that all understanding involves interpretation. This misconceives understanding and speaker's meaning. Davidson accepts that normally when A Vs that *p*, he knows he does. This is challenged. Throughout, Davidson's conception is contrasted with Wittgenstein's.

**Hacker, P M S**. The Rise of Twentieth Century Analytic Philosophy. *Ratio*, 9(3), 243-268, D 96.

The classificatory concept of analytic philosophy cannot fruitfully be given an analytic definition, nor is it a family-resemblance concept. Dummett's contention that it is 'the philosophy of thought' whose main tenet is that an account of thought is to be attained through an account of language is rejected for historical and analytic reasons. Analytic philosophy is most helpfully understood as a historical category earmarking a leading trend in twentieth-century philosophy originating in Cambridge. Its first three phases, viz. Cambridge Platonist pluralism, logical atomism, and logical positivism are adumbrated and their interrelations explained. Wittgenstein is argued to have originated the 'linguistic turn' that characterizes the latter two.

**Hacohen, Malachi Haim**. Karl Popper in Exile: The Viennese Progressive Imagination and the Making of *The Open Society*. *Phil Soc Sci*, 26(4), 452-492, D 96.

This article explores the impact of Popper's exile on the formation of *The Open Society*. It proposes homelessness as a major motif in Popper's life and work. His emigration from clerical-fascist Austria, sojourn in New Zealand during World War II and social isolation in postwar England constituted a permanent exile. In cosmopolitan philosophy, he searched for a new home. His unended quest issued in a liberal cosmopolitan vision of scientific and political communities pursuing truth and reform. The Open Society was their embodiment. As described, it expressed the ideals of fin-de-siècle Viennese progressives. Many progressives were assimilated Jews, whose dilemmas of national identity gave rise to cosmopolitan views that stripped ethnicity and nationality of significance. *The Open Society* was an admirable defense of liberalism against fascism, but it remained a utopian ideal. It could not provide a surrogate community or home where Popper might have reached his destination and rested.

**Hadley, Robert F** and Hayward, Michael B. Strong Semantic Systematicity from Hebbian Connectionist Learning. *Mind Mach*, 7(1), 1-37, F 97.

Herein we describe a network which displays strong semantic systematicity in response to Hebbian connectionist training. During training, two-thirds of all nouns are presented only in a single syntactic position (either as grammatical subject or object). Yet, during testing, the network correctly interprets thousands of sentences containing those nouns in novel positions. In addition, the network generalizes to novel levels of embedding. Successful training requires a corpus of about 1000 sentences and network training is quite rapid. The architecture and learning algorithms are purely connectionist, but 'classical' insights are discernible in one respect, viz. that complex semantic representations spatially contain their semantic constituents. However, in other important respects, the architecture is distinctly nonclassical. (edited)

**Haefliger, Jürg**. *Imaginationssysteme*. New York, Lang, 1996.

**Häyry, Heta**. Bioethics and Political Ideology: The Case of Active Voluntary Euthanasia. *Bioethics*, 11(3-4), 271-276, Jl 97.

In different countries responses to important bioethical issues are different, as exemplified by the attitudes towards the voluntary and active forms of medical euthanasia. But why is this the case? My suggestion is that the roots of the variety are, to a considerable degree, ideological. The most important present-day political ideologies all have their roots in the prevailing doctrines of moral and social philosophy. In the paper these doctrines are outlined and the predicted response towards active voluntary euthanasia within each model is sketched. The conclusion reached is that while it would in some countries be dangerous to allow euthanasia in the prevailing circumstances, the solution is not to hinder the legalization process but to alter the circumstances.

**Hagen, Kurtis**. A Chinese Critique on Western Ways of Warfare. *Asian Phil*, 6(3), 207-217, N 96.

I will argue that there are two pervasive and enduring Western attitudes towards warfare: one involves the romanticism of violent conflict, the other concerns moral justification for it. These stand in sharp contrast to the traditional Chinese attitude as put forward in the Chinese classic treatises on warfare, the *Sun-tzu* and *Sun Pin*. I will reference similar concerns articulated in the Taoist and, to a lesser extent, Confucian classics both to confirm and clarify this position. Using the combination of some of the most important and influential texts with the most relevant to our topic, I will attempt to identify and explicate what I will call "the traditional Chinese attitude toward warfare" as a critique of the two widespread Western attitudes. Finally, I will explore the implications of the West abandoning its romantic and moralistic attitudes.

**Hahn, Frank**. Rerum Cognoscere Causas. *Econ Phil*, 12(1), 183-195, Ap 96.

**Hailer, Martin**. Franz Böhms "Deutsche Philosophie": Über den Versuch einer erkenntnistheoretischen Grundlegung des "Nationalsozialismus". *Das Argument*, 209(2-3), 325-333, Mr-Je 95.

Although Franz Böhm intended to present a philosophical support of nazism, his so-called "Deutsche Philosophie" was rejected by the governmental department (headed by Rosenberg) in charge of ideology. Researching Böhm's

"Deutsche Philosophie" could contribute not only to the reconstruction of national-socialistic epistemology, but also to an understanding of the relationship between Rosenberg and Ernst Krieck.

**Haist, Gordon**. The Texture of Inquiry. *Inquiry (USA)*, 16(4), 47-65, Sum 97.

The dialectical structure of philosophical inquiry calls for an examination of it as a communicative praxis. This essay argues that the hermeneutical space of a community of inquiry enables such an examination and utilizes Freire's intersubjective pedagogy, Lipman's distributive learning and the communicative praxiology of Calvin O. Schraq to rethink the end of philosophy as its completion instead of a silencing of the way of life of dialectical inquiry. Philosophy's praxis rather than its position-takings requires a rediscovery of the other and of the forms of rationality by which the self and other relate in a community of inquiry.

**Hajdin, Mane**. Sexual Harassment and Negligence. *J Soc Phil*, 28(1), 37-53, Spr 97.

This book is a collaborative contribution to contemporary debates on sexual harassment covering a broad range of moral and legal issues central to an informed discussion of the topic. Linda LeMoncheck argues for a feminist perspective on sexual harassment sensitive to gender politics, while Mane Hajdin argues that this perspective on sexual harassment is both morally confusing and legally problematic.

**Hajdin, Mane** and LeMoncheck, Linda. *Sexual Harassment: A Debate*. Lanham, Rowman & Littlefield, 1997.

In this uncompromising yet respectful debate, two philosophers of widely divergent views present clear arguments and then respond directly to each other's reasoning. LeMoncheck argues for a feminist perspective on sexual harassment that is sensitive to the politics of gender. Hajdin contends that this perspective is both morally confusing and legally problematic, and sexual harassment can be better addressed by traditional moral and legal categories. (publisher, edited)

**Hajduk, Anton**. Science as a Battlefield: Methodological and Historical Considerations on the Misuse of Science by Totalitarian Regimes of Central Europe. *Ultim Real Mean*, 20(2 & 3), 216-221, Je-S 97.

**Hájek, Alan**. Mises Redux—Redux: Fifteen Arguments against Finite Frequentism. *Erkenntnis*, 45(2 & 3), 209-227, Nov 96.

According to finite frequentism, the probability of an attribute *A* in a finite reference class *B* is the relative frequency of actual occurrences of *A* within *B*. I present fifteen arguments against this position.

**Hájek, Alan** and Byrne, Alex. David Hume, David Lewis, and Decision Theory. *Mind*, 106(423), 411-428, Jl 97.

In this paper we investigate whether Lewis's case against "Desire as Belief" (DAB) can be strengthened by examining how it fares under rival versions of decision theory, including other conceptions of rational ways to change one's mind. We prove a stronger version of Lewis's result in "Desire as Belief II." We then argue that the anti-Humean may escape Lewis's argument either by adopting a version of causal decision theory, or by claiming that the refutation only applies to hyper-idealized rational agents, or by denying that the decision-theoretic framework has the expressive capacity to formulate anti-Humeanism. (edited)

**Hájek, Alan** and Harper, William. Full Belief and Probability: Comments on Van Fraassen. *Dialogue (Canada)*, 36(1), 91-100, Wint 97.

**Hájek, Petr**. Fuzzy Logic and Arithmetical Hierarchy, II. *Stud Log*, 58(1), 129-141, 1997.

A very simple many-valued predicate calculus is presented; a completeness theorem is proved and the arithmetical complexity of some notions concerning provability is determined.

**Haji, Ishtiyaque**. An Epistemic Dimension of Blameworthiness. *Phil Phenomenol Res*, 57(3), 523-544, S 97.

The author first argues against the view that an agent is morally blameworthy for performing an action only if it is morally wrong for that agent to perform that action. The author then proposes a replacement for this view whose gist is summarized in the principle: an agent S is morally blameworthy for performing action A only if S has the belief that it is wrong for her to do A and this belief plays an appropriate role in S's A-ing. He focuses on explicating the role an agent's belief that a prospective action, A, of hers is wrong must play in the production of her A-ing in order that she be blameworthy for A-ing. Towards this end, the author makes use of cases involving akrasia and self-deception.

**Haji, Ishtiyaque**. Blameworthiness, Character, and Cultural Norms. *J Soc Phil*, 27(3), 116-135, Wint 96.

I first propose and defend an epistemic condition of blameworthiness which says that one is blameworthy for performing an action only if one has the belief that the action is wrong, and this belief plays an appropriate role in its etiology. I then discuss implications of this condition for "intersocietal attributions of blameworthiness": people who are not part of a culture-"outsiders" relative to a culture-often attribute blame to a person within that culture for doing something deemed morally repulsive by outsiders. I argue that the epistemic condition implies that outsiders' attributions of blame are probably frequently erroneous.

**Haji, Ishtiyaque**. Liberating Constraints. *J Phil Res*, 22, 261-287, Ap 97.

Roughly, when an agent performs an action under liberating constraints, the agent could not avoid performing that action, her inability to do otherwise stems from her not being able to will to do otherwise, yet in performing the action, the agent may well regard herself as having acted freely or autonomously, or "in character" (as opposed to "out of character"), or in conformity with her "deep self." As action under liberating constraints issues from one's "deep self," it seems reasonable to suppose, as some have recommended, that whenever a person acts under such constraints, she is morally responsible for her action. I first argue against this recommendation. Then I develop a sketch of an account of control—the sort required for the moral responsibility—which implies that, frequently, those who act under liberating constraints are not morally responsible for their (germane) actions.

**Haji, Ishtiyaque**. Moral Responsibility and the Problem of Induced Pro-Attitudes. *Dialogue (Canada)*, 35(4), 703-720, Fall 96.

The problem of induced proattitudes is this: why is action which ultimately issues from proattitudes such as desires or volitions, induced by techniques such as direct manipulation of the brain, hypnosis, or "value engineering," frequently regarded as action for which its agent cannot be held morally responsible? I start by examining some recently proposed solutions to this problem and indicate their inadequacies. I then advance a solution of my own which is "history sensitive": responsibility for an action depends crucially on how its agent comes to acquire the various elements in its etiology.

**Hajnicz, Elzbieta**. Applying Allen's Constraint Propagation Algorithm for Non-Linear Time. *J Log Lang Info*, 5(2), 157-175, 1996.

The famous Allen's interval relations constraint propagation algorithm was intended for linear time. Its 13 primitive relations define all the possible mutual locations of two intervals on the time-axis. In this paper an application of the algorithm for nonlinear time is suggested. First, a new primitive relation is added. It is called *excludes* since an occurrence of one event in a certain course of events *excludes* an occurrence of the other event in this course. Next, new composition rules for relations between intervals are presented: some of the "old" rules are extended by the relation *excludes* and entirely new ones are formulated for composing the relation *excludes* with the other relations. Four different composition tables are considered. The choice of a composition table depends on whether time is branching or not and whether intervals can contain noncollinear subintervals or not.

**Hajnicz, Elzbieta**. Some Considerations on Non-Linear Time Intervals. *J Log Lang Info*, 4(4), 335-357, 1995.

Most of the descriptions of interval time structures in the first order predicate calculus are based on linear time. However, in the case of intervals, abandoning the condition of *linearity* (e.g., LIN in van Benthem's systems) is not sufficient. In this paper, some properties of nonlinear time structures are discussed. The most important one is the characterization of location of intervals in a fork of branches. This is connected with the fact that an interval can contain noncollinear subintervals. As a result of nonlinearity, some basic properties of interval structures must be formulated in a weaker form. Moreover, time must be filled by intervals to indicate that time cannot pass without events occurring in it. Finally, it is shown that when intervals cannot contain noncollinear subintervals, most of the conditions described in the paper are satisfied.

**Hála, Vlastimil**. Ecological Motivations of Ethics and the Moral Critique of the Value Orientation of Society (in Czech). *Filosof Cas*, 45(3), 393-410, 1997.

In the first part of this study the author focuses on a number of theoretical problems in ecology and especially the relationship between anthropocentrism and biocentrism and the question of the possibility of going further than the intersubjective conception of moral judgement and extend it to nonhuman beings, particularly animals. In this context the author supports the position of "cultivated anthropocentrism" and an extended conception of humanity. In the second part the author reflects on a number of questions of the practical application of ecologically motivated ethics and especially on the significance of the concept of long-term sustainable life. The author is convinced that a change in value orientations is possible not so much in the form of a society-wide process as in the form of struggling for and gaining space for the development of "minority" styles of life that are favourable from the ecological point of view.

**Hála, Vlastimil**. Zu den kantischen und fichteschen Motiven bei Nicolai Hartmann. *Fichte-Studien*, 13, 77-87, 1997.

N. Hartmann estimates the heritage of Kant's and Fichte's philosophy, including ethics, from the systematical point of view. The main topic of Kant's ethics insists in the free—determination of human behaviour by the moral law. From the Hartmann's point of view it would be necessary to keep the frankness of moral decision in the relationship to the moral law, too. With respect to Fichte's concept of ethics, Hartmann emphasizes that the liberty of human moral activity is overshadowed by the unconscious activity of "Ich". In the end, the liberty is sacrificed to the "higher law" in the ontological meaning.

**Hála, Vlastimil** and Hösle, Vittorio. Being and Subjectivity (and Commentary V. Hála) (in Czech). *Filosof Cas*, 45(3), 481-496, 1997.

**Halbach, Volker**. Tarskian and Kripkean Truth. *J Phil Log*, 26(1), 69-80, F 97.

A theory of the transfinite Tarskian hierarchy of languages is outlined and compared to a notion of partial truth by Kripke. It is shown that the hierarchy can be embedded into Kripke's minimal fixed point model. From this results on the expressive power of both approaches are obtained.

**Haldane, John**. "Rational and Other Animals" in *Verstehen and Humane Understanding*, O'Hear, Anthony (ed), 17-28. New York, Cambridge Univ Pr, 1996.

According to a widespread view, there is a distinction to be drawn between explanation (which evokes causal mechanisms and laws of invariable succession) and understanding (which is interpretative and involves ascribing meanings and values). Aversion of this distinction features in the recent work of John McDowell who follows Wilfred Sellars in distinguishing between the 'realm of law' and the 'space of reasons'. The present paper argues that the ways in which this distinction is drawn and applied give rise to various problems concerning nonhuman animals and human evolution. An alternative account of the nature of rational animals is proposed.

**Haldane, John**. Infallibility, Authority and Faith. *Heythrop J*, 38(3), 267-282, Jl 97.

This paper discusses the historical background in 19th century catholicism to the doctrine of infallibility. It relates the idea of papal infallibility in particular to that of religious authority in general and then embarks on a philosophical examination of the idea of inerrant authority. Various semantic and epistemological challenges are considered but it is concluded that the idea is coherent and given certain other theological assumptions actually credible.

**Haldane, John**. Intentionality and One-Sided Relations. *Ratio*, 9(2), 95-114, S 96.

Here a view is explored, which derives from scholastic accounts of intentionality, in particular that presented by John of St Thomas, as this has been elaborated and defended in recent writings by John Deely. While judging it to fail, I suggest that it leads us towards an older tradition according to which the intentionality of thought is constituted by the occurrence of the forms of things in the mind. 'Formally and principally the whole difference between a mind-independent relation and a mind-dependent one comes down to this, that a physical relation has a mind-independent fundament with a coexistent terminus while a mental relation lacks such a foundation.'(edited)

**Haldane, John**. Intuitions and the Value of a Person. *J Applied Phil*, 14(1), 83-86, 1997.

In contemporary moral theory and normative ethics there is frequent recourse to 'intuitions' of value. One current instance of this is the appeal in reproductive and population ethics to the thought that the existence of a human being is not as such good or bad. Here the status and substance of this assumption are challenged. In addition, doubt is cast on the value of appeals to intuition where these are not related to some philosophical account of the grounds of value.

**Hale, Bob**. "Physicalism and Mathematics" in *Objections to Physicalism*, Robinson, Howard (ed), 39-59. New York, Clarendon/Oxford Pr, 1996.

Can a physicalist about mathematics provide a credible account of its epistemology? Penelope Maddy has sought to do so, by appropriating an analogy between mathematics and natural science promoted by Gödel, following a suggestion by Russell. This paper argues that, taken to its logical conclusion, the analogy commits us to the hopelessly implausible idea that ordinary arithmetic statements are experimentally falsifiable; and that Maddy's attempts to evade this implausibility cause the analogy to break down at a crucial point.

**Hale, Bob**. "Singular Terms (1)" in *Frege: Importance and Legacy*, Schirn, Matthias (ed), 438-457. Hawthorne, de Gruyter, 1996.

Frege's analysis of language and ontology call for criteria for identifying singular terms. This paper argues that whilst the inferential tests evolved by Michael Dummett, suitable modified, may provide a satisfactory means of discriminating singular terms within the broader class of grammatically substantial expressions, this is insufficient. An attempt is accordingly made to develop a workable version of an 'Aristotelian' criterion, based on Aristotle's dictum that a substance has no contrary. This criterion cannon—any more than Dummett's inferential tests—serve on its own, but there is a natural way to combine the two that solves the problems of both.

**Hale, Bob**. Grundlagen Paragraph 64. *Proc Aris Soc*, 97, 243-261, 1997.

Frege invites us, in Grundlagen paragraph 64, to view to identity "The direction of line a = the direction of line b" as having the same content as "Lines a and b are parallel", but 'carved up' in a new way. How is this to be understood? This paper argues that interpreting 'content' either as reference or in terms of strongly compositional sense gives rise to serious difficulties and attempts to resolve them by defining a notion of content-identity intermediate in strength between identity of reference and identity of sense.

**Hale, Bob** and Wright, Crispin. "Nominalism and the Contingency of Abstract Objects" in *Frege: Importance and Legacy*, Schirn, Matthias (ed), 174-199. Hawthorne, de Gruyter, 1996.

An apparently serious difficulty for Hartry Field's unorthodox defense of nominalism in mathematics, pressed by both authors in earlier writings, is that it commits Field to an unpalatable contingency thesis: there are in fact no numbers, etc., but there might have been. Field's reply has been that the objection trades on an equivocation over the sense of 'contingent'. This paper attempts to explain why this response is ineffective and to provide a reformulation of the objection which captures its essential core whilst relying principles governing the notion of contingency which should command general assent.

**Hales, Steven D**. "Abortion and Fathers' Rights" in *Reproduction, Technology, and Rights: Biomedical Ethics Reviews*, Humber, James M (ed), 5-26. Clifton, Humana Pr, 1996.

Fathers do not have an absolute obligation to provide for the welfare of their children. If mothers have the right to opt out of future duties towards their children by deciding to have an abortion instead, fathers too should be considered to have the right to avoid similar future duties. I also argue that fathers should be granted a mechanism by which they can exercise such a right. The discussion is initially motivated by showing an apparent inconsistency among three widely accepted principles regarding a woman's right to an abortion, equality, and parental obligations. I argue that by allowing fathers (with certain restrictions) to refuse to support their forthcoming progeny, the inconsistency among the three principles is resolved. I also argue that this is the best resolution, and provide three other independent arguments in favor of a paternal right of refusal.

**Hales, Steven D**. "More on Fathers' Rights" in *Reproduction, Technology, and Rights: Biomedical Ethics Reviews*, Humber, James M (ed), 43-49. Clifton, Humana Pr, 1996.

This paper is a rejoinder to Professor Jim Humber on the issue of fathers' rights. I reaffirm my position that if a woman's right to an abortion is a morally permissible

way of avoiding future duties with respect to parenting, then fathers must have a similar moral right and ought to have a way to exercise this right. I consider and rebut Professor Humber's objections to this view.

**Hales, Steven D**. A Consistent Relativism. *Mind*, 106(421), 33-52, Ja 97.

This paper develops a logic of relativism that 1) illuminates the classic self-refutation charge and shows how to escape it; 2) makes rigorous the ideas of truth as relative and truth as absolute, and shows the relations between them; 3) develops an intensional logic for relativism; 4) provides a framework in which relativists can consistently promote ethical, mathematical, scientific, religious, and political truths (among others) as being relative; 5) argues that the notion of incommensurability is far less troubling than is commonly thought; and 6) argues that the concept of a perspective as needed by the theory is not prey to Davidson's well-known critique of conceptual schemes. The logic of relativism is primarily meant to provide a formal framework in which relativists can consistently develop their theories. (edited)

**Hales, Steven D**. Nietzsche on Logic. *Phil Phenomenol Res*, 56(4), 819-835, D 96.

Nietzsche is infamous for denouncing logic, but despite the importance of logic in contemporary philosophy, there has been very little scholarly attention paid to his criticisms. This paper argues that Nietzsche's antilogic polemics are directed against semantics, which he regards as being committed to a realist metaphysics. It is this metaphysical realism that Nietzsche abhors, not logical syntax or proof theory. Nietzsche is also at pains to critique logicians who naively accept realist semantics. Other interpreters who cast Nietzsche as a logical nihilist are criticized as unjustly neglecting key prologic texts.

**Haliburton, Rachel**. Richard Rorty and the Problem of Cruelty. *Phil Soc Crit*, 23(1), 49-69, 1997.

Truth, the pragmatist claims, is something we make, not something which corresponds to reality. If this view of truth is accepted, Rorty notes, two problems arise: the pragmatist will have little to say to those who abuse others, because he or she will not be able to point to some universal standards that the abusers are violating; and the torturers may be able to quote pragmatic principles in their own defence. Rorty argues that the pragmatist can reduce cruelty by splitting himself or herself into public and private parts. I examine this problem and Rorty's solution. I argue that his solution fails for two reasons: first, keeping our public and private selves apart is unlikely to reduce cruelty; and, second, he cannot maintain the public/private split. Consequently, Rorty is unable to deal with the antipragmatic criticism that his theory of truth could lead to an increase in cruelty.

**Halkowska, Katarzyna** and Denecke, Klaus. On P-compatible Hybrid Identities and Hyperidentities. *Stud Log*, 53(4), 493-501, N 94.

*P*-compatible identities are built up from terms with a special structure. We investigate a variety defined by a set of *P*-compatible hybrid identities and answer the question whether a variety defined by a set of *P*-compatible hyperidentities can be solid.

**Hall, Bert S**. "The Didactic and the Elegant: Some Thoughts on Scientific and Technological Illustrations in the Middle Ages and Renaissance" in *Picturing Knowledge*, Baigrie, Brian S (ed), 3-39. Toronto, Univ of Toronto Pr, 1996.

The cognitive authority of scientific illustrations is analyzed as a historical problem. Against the usual emphasis on Renaissance "naturalistic" illustration, this article argues that didactic illustrations of all sorts depend on a shared code of conventions. Medieval diagrams, for example, are not inferior representations, merely different encodings. Renaissance naturalism destroyed the old codes once shared between artist and viewer, but did not automatically thereby gain authority as a "true" representation in scientific circles. Instead, the article concludes, naturalistic illustrations earned their reputation for "truth-telling" first in printed illustrated books about technology (late 1500s) and only later (early 1600s) in similarly-constructed printed books about science.

**Hall, John A**. Social Foundations of Openness. *Phil Soc Sci*, 27(1), 24-38, Mr 97.

Popper's view of the enemies of the open society is held to rest upon psychologism, a view of the very great dangers of misguided intellectuals and a cyclical view of historical process. While there is something to these claims, they are treated here skeptically. But the purpose of the article is less to attach than to reconstruct. To that end, key elements of a sociology appropriate to an open society are offered.

**Hall, John A** (ed) and Jarvie, Ian (ed). *The Social Philosophy of Ernest Gellner*. Amsterdam, Rodopi, 1996.

A large collection of critical papers about the thought of the late Ernest Gellner, with a lengthy "Reply to Critics" and a definitive bibliography of his writings.

**Hall, Katherine**. Intensive Care Ethics in Evolution. *Bioethics*, 11(3-4), 241-245, Jl 97.

The ethics of treating the seriously and critically ill have not been static throughout the ages. Twentieth-century medicine has inherited from the nineteenth century a science which places an inappropriate weight on diagnosis over prognosis and management, combined with a seventeenth-century duty to prolong life. However, other earlier ethical traditions, both Hippocratic and Christian, respected both the limitations of medicine and emphasized the importance of prognosis. This paper outlines some of the historical precedents for the treatment of the critically ill, and also how the current paradigm limits clinical practice and causes ethical tensions. An understanding that other paradigms have been ethically acceptable in the past allows wider consideration and acceptance of alternatives for the future. However, future alternatives will also have to address the role of technology, given its importance in this area of medicine.

**Hall, Richard J**. The Evolution of Color Vision without Color. *Proc Phil Sci Ass*, 3(Suppl), S125-S133, 1996.

The standard adaptationist explanation of the presence of a sensory mechanism in an organism—that it detects properties useful to the organism—cannot be given for color vision. This is because colors do not exist. After arguing for this latter claim, I consider, but reject, nonadaptationist explanations. I conclude by proposing an explanation of how color vision could have adaptive value even though it does not detect properties in the environment.

**Hall, Terry**. "Sophistry and Wisdom in Plato's *Meno*" in *Philosophy of Education (1996)*, Margonis, Frank (ed), 110-113. Urbana, Phil Education Soc, 1997.

**Hallamaa, Olli** and Knuuttila, Simo. Roger Roseth and Medieval Deontic Logic. *Log Anal*, 38(149), 75-87, Mr 95.

The elements of deontic logic were developed as part of philosophical modal logic in early fourteenth century. Roger Roseth wrote an extensive treatise on the rationality of norms c. 1335. The paper includes an analysis of Roseth's discussions of the types of deontic terms, deontic consequences and conditional norms with an English translation of the main tenets of Roseth's theory.

**Hallen, Barry** and Olubi Sodipo, J. *Knowledge, Belief, and Witchcraft: Analytic Experiments in African Philosophy*. Stanford, Stanford Univ Pr, 1997.

First published in 1986, *Knowledge Belief, and Witchcraft* remains the only analysis of indigenous discourse about an African belief system undertaken from within the framework of Anglo-American analytical philosophy. Taking as its point of departure W.V.O. Quine's thesis about the indeterminacy of translation, the book investigates questions of Yoruba epistemology and of how knowledge is conceived in an oral culture. (publisher, edited)

**Haller, Rudolf**. "Gegenstandstheoretische Betrachtungen" in *Das weite Spektrum der analytischen Philosophie*, Lenzen, Wolfgang, 60-75. Hawthorne, de Gruyter, 1997.

**Halley, Janet E**. "The Sexual Economist and Legal Regulation of the Sexual Orientations" in *Sex, Preference, and Family: Essays on Law and Nature*, Nussbaum, Martha C (ed), 192-207. New York, Oxford Univ Pr, 1997.

**Hallward, Peter**. Gilles Deleuze and the Redemption from Interest. *Rad Phil*, 81, 6-21, Ja-F 97.

**Halonen, Ilpo**. G. H. Von Wright's Truth-Logics as Paraconsistent Logics. *Log Anal*, 36(144), 233-243, S-D 93.

**Halpern, Joseph Y**. Should Knowledge Entail Belief?. *J Phil Log*, 25(5), 483-494, O 96.

The appropriateness of S5 as a logic of knowledge has been attacked at some length in the philosophical literature. Here one particular attack based on the interplay between knowledge and belief is considered: Suppose that knowledge satisfies S5, belief satisfies KD45 and both the *entailment property* (knowledge implies belief) and *positive certainty* (if the agent believes something, she believes she knows it) hold. Then it can be shown that belief reduces to knowledge: it is impossible to have false beliefs. While the entailment property has typically been viewed as perhaps the least controversial of these assumptions, an argument is presented that it can plausibly be viewed as the culprit. More precisely, it is shown that this attack fails if we weaken the entailment property so that it applies only to *objective* (nonmodal) formulas, rather than to arbitrary formulas. Since the standard arguments in favor of the entailment property are typically given only for objective formulas, this observation suggests that care must be taken in applying intuitions that seem reasonable in the case of objective formulas to arbitrary formulas.

**Halpern, Joseph Y** and Fagin, Ronald and Moses, Yoram (& others). Reasoning about Knowledge: A Response by the Authors. *Mind Mach*, 7(1), 113, F 97.

**Halstead, J Mark**. Muslims and Sex Education. *J Moral Educ*, 26(3), 317-330, S 97.

Objections to contemporary practice in sex education are examined in the light of recent calls by Muslim leaders in Britain for Muslim parents to withdraw their children from sex education classes. The dilemma facing liberal policy makers is discussed, as they seek to reconcile the public interest, the wishes of parents with a wide diversity of beliefs and values and the perceived needs of children and the paper concludes with a consideration of how far it is possible to develop an approach to sex education in the common school which is broadly acceptable to all groups, including minorities such as Muslims.

**Halwani, Raja**. The Morality of Adultery. *Dialogue (PST)*, 38(2-3), 43-49, Ap 96.

I argue that, unlike promise-breaking, adultery is not immoral in and of itself. I do so by first replying to certain arguments that attempt to show that adultery is immoral (prima facie). I then provide a model in which committing adultery is not immoral. I discuss the connections between sexual activity and love and the connection between sexually transmitted diseases, especially HIV and AIDS and the morality of adultery.

**Ham, Jennifer** (ed) and Senior, Matthew (ed). *Animal Acts: Configuring the Human in Western History*. New York, Routledge, 1997.

*Animal Acts* records the history of the fluctuating boundary between animals and humans as expressed in literary, philosophical and scientific texts, as well as visual arts and historical practices such as dissections, the hunt, zoo construction and circus acts. Against a general background of the progressive exclusion of animals form human space and consciousness since the Enlightenment, the essays document a persistent return of animality. Essays on Marie de France, Boccaccio, Rabelais, La Fontaine, Schelling, Nietzsche, Flaubert, Kafka, Audubon, E.B. White, Levinas, Derrida, Heidegger, Dian Fossey and Gary Larson trace the lineage of those who have sought to enact the animal—to mime, tame, research, befriend and capture the beast within. (publisher)

**Hamacher, Werner**. "Ou, séance, touche de Nancy, ici" in *On Jean-Luc Nancy: The Sense of Philosophy*, Sheppard, Darren (ed), 38-62. New York, Routledge, 1997.

**Hamacher, Werner** and Fenves, Peter (trans). *Premises: Essays on Philosophy and Literature from Kant to Celan*. Cambridge, Harvard Univ Pr, 1996.

In light of the double nature of every premise—that it is promised but never attainable—Hamacher gives us nine decisive themes, topics, and texts of modernity: the hermeneutic circle in Schleiermacher and Heidegger, the structure of ethical commands in Kant, Nietzsche's genealogy of moral terms and his exploration of the aporias of singularity, the irony of reading in de Man, the parabasis of language in Schlegel, Kleist's disruption of narrative representation, the gesture of naming in Benjamin and Kafka, and the incisive caesura that Paul Celan inserts into temporal and linguistic reversals. (edited)

**Hamilton III, J Brooke** and Hoch, David. Ethical Standards for Business Lobbying: Some Practical Suggestions. *Bus Ethics Quart*, 7(3), 117-129, Jl 97.

Rather than being inherently evil, business lobbying is a socially responsible activity which needs to be restrained by ethical standards. To be effective in a business environment, traditional ethical standards need to be translated into language which business persons can speak comfortably. Economical explanations must also be available to explain why ethical standards are appropriate in business. Eight such standards and their validating arguments are proposed with examples showing their use. (edited)

**Hamilton III, J Brooke** and Rao, Spuma M. The Effect of Published Reports of Unethical Conduct on Stock Prices. *J Bus Ethics*, 15(12), 1321-1330, D 96.

This study adds to the empirical evidence supporting a significant connection between ethics and profitability by examining the connection between published reports of unethical behaviour by publicly traded U.S. and multinational firms and the performance of their stock. Using reports of unethical behaviour published in the Wall Street Journal from 1989 to 1993, the analysis shows that the actual stock performance for those companies was lower than the expected market adjusted returns. Unethical conduct by firms which is discovered and publicized does impact on the shareholders by lowering the value of their stock for an appreciable period of time. Whatever their views on whether ethical behaviour is profitable, managers should be able to see a definite connection between unethical behaviour and the worth of their firm's stock. Stockholders, the press and regulators should find this information important in pressing for greater corporate and managerial accountability.

**Hamilton III, J Brooke** and Strutton, David and Lumpkin, James R. An Essay on When to Fully Disclose in Sales Relationships: Applying Two Practical Guidelines for Addressing Truth-Telling Problems. *J Bus Ethics*, 16(5), 545-560, Ap 97.

Salespeople have a moral obligation to prospect/customer, company and self. As such, they continually encounter truth-telling dilemmas. "Ignorance" and "conflict" often block the path to morally correct sales behaviors. Academics and practitioners agree that adoption of ethical codes is the most effective measure for encouraging ethical sales behaviors. Yet no ethical code has been offered which can be conveniently used to overcome the unique circumstances that contribute to the moral dilemmas often encountered in personal selling. An ethical code is developed that charts ethical paths across a variety of sales settings (addressing "ignorance") while illustrating why the cost associated with acting morally is generally reasonable (addressing "conflict"). (edited)

**Hamkins, Joel David**. Canonical Seeds and Prikry Trees. *J Sym Log*, 62(2), 373-396, Je 97.

Applying the seed concept to Prikry tree forcing $P_{mu}$, I investigate how well $P_{mu}$ preserves the maximality property of ordinary Prikry forcing and prove that $P_{mu}$ Prikry sequences are maximal exactly when $mu$ admits no noncanonical seeds via a finite iteration. In particular, I conclude that if $mu$ is a strongly normal supercompactness measure, then $P_{mu}$ Prikry sequences are maximal, thereby proving, for a large class of measures, a conjecture of W. Hugh Woodin's.

**Hammacher, Klaus**. "Fichte und das Problem der Dialektik" in *Sein—Reflexion—Freiheit: Aspekte der Philosophie Johann Gottlieb Fichtes*, Asmuth, Christoph (ed), 115-141. Amsterdam, Gruner, 1997.

**Hammacher, Klaus**. "La polisemia del concepto de libertad en Fichte" in *El inicio del Idealismo alemán*, Market, Oswaldo, 139-158. Madrid, Ed Compiutense, 1996.

Los diferentes usos que Fichte hace del concepto de libertad pueden retrotraerse a las diversas ideas de libertad de la tradición, como son la libertad de elección y de voluntad, la libertad como autonomía y autodeterminación, la libertad como espontaneidad, la liberación de las pasiones o libertad moral. Que la libertad hace posible y pone su huella en el saber, lo muestra Fichte en las estructuras formales del pensamiento en su *Doctrina de la Ciencia*. Pero cómo ella, en cuante libertad moral, determina la acción en una *constancia* de la voluntad, que sólo puede ser conseguida en la ejercitación, Fichte no puede exponerlo de manera convincente, porque, debido al excesivamente exigente concepto kantiano del deber, que propiamente sólo puede ordenar acciones legales, su mirada se encuentra centrada en la confirmación virtuosa, y una semejante ha de contener la libertad moral.

**Hammer, Eric**. Symmetry as a Method of Proof. *J Phil Log*, 25(5), 523-543, O 96.

This paper is a logical study of valid uses of symmetry in deductive reasoning, of what underlying principles make some appeals to symmetry legitimate but others illegitimate. The issue is first motivated informally. A framework is then given covering a fairly broad range of symmetry arguments and the formulation of symmetry provided is shown to be a valid principle of reasoning, as is a slightly stronger principle of reasoning, one that is shown to be in some sense as strong as possible. The relationship between symmetry and isomorphism is discussed and finally the framework is extended to a more general model-theoretic setting.

**Hammer, Eric** and Danner, Norman. Towards a Model Theory of Diagrams. *J Phil Log*, 25(5), 463-482, O 96.

A logical system is studied whose well-formed representations consist of diagrams rather than formulas. The system, due to Shin [2,3], is shown to be complete by an argument concerning maximally consistent sets of diagrams. The argument is complicated by the lack of a straight forward counterpart of atomic formulas for diagrams, and by the lack of a counterpart of negation for most diagrams.

**Hammer, Eric M**. The Truths of Logic. *Synthese*, 109(1), 27-45, O 96.

Several accounts of logical truth are compared and shown to define distinct concepts. Nevertheless, conditions are given under which they happen to declare exactly the same sentences logically true. These conditions involve the variety of objects in the domain, the richness of the language, and the logical resources available. It is argued that the class of sentences declared logically true by each of the accounts depends on particularities of the actual world.

**Hammer, Espen**. Romanticism Revisited. *Inquiry*, 40(2), 225-242, Je 97.

This paper discusses a book by Jay Bernstein in which it is claimed that Habermas's use of Hegel's doctrine of the dialectic of ethical life is unsuccessful. Even though I sympathize with Bernstein's attempt to soften many of the conceptual dualisms (for example, justice versus the good life) which he believes ultimately are expressive of a disregard on Habermas's part for the moral resources inherent in collective ethical practices, I find a worrisome tendency to collapse these modernist oppositions, and thus towards offering a politics of utopian romanticism entirely at odds with modernity.

**Hammond, David M**. Hayden White: Meaning and Truth in History. *Phil Theol*, 8(4), 291-307, Sum 94.

This essay argues that, although meaning is not already present in the events of the past, neither is it simply imposed on these events by the historian's trope. Lonergan's more adequate construal of historical writing recognizes the dynamism of inquiry which rejects a naive view of facts, yet also argues for the possibility of truthful, albeit always partial representations of events. (edited)

**Hammond, Debora**. Cultural Diversity and the Systems View. *Phil Cont World*, 2(1), 13-18, Spr 95.

While systems concepts had a tremendous impact on social thought in the 1950s and 1960s, they are increasingly under attack in the current postmodern climate with its emphasis on particularity and difference. The idea of the system is associated with technocracy, hierarchical forms of social organization and the suppression of individual difference. However, there is a significant body of work within the systems tradition that fosters an appreciation of diversity through its ecological orientation and supports more participatory forms of social organization based on its understanding of the self-organizing nature of living systems. While the issue of cultural diversity is often addressed in oppositional terms, I suggest that it might be more effectively served through an appreciation of the global interdependence between all peoples and between humans and nature that can only be sustained on a cooperative and participatory basis.

**Hampe, Michael**. Jenseits von Moderne und Postmoderne: Whiteheads Metaphysik und ihre Anwendungen in der theoretischen und praktischen Philosophie der Gegenwart. *Phil Rundsch*, 44(2), 95-112, Je 97.

1) The essay reviews new books on Whitehead by Neville, Hauskeller, Hosinski, Lachmann and others that give an introduction into Whitehead's philosophy or discuss his theoretical or practical philosophy. Neville's approach that Whitehead's metaphysics is neither modern nor postmodern is evaluated as a very useful tool to interpret Whitehead's intentions. Applications of Whitehead's metaphysics to the philosophy of relativity theory and the philosophy of the neuro-sciences are discussed. They are evaluated as too general. Lachmann's book on implications of Whitehead's metaphysics of individuality for ethics is evaluated as a very interesting and fruitful new insight into the practical relevance of Whitehead's metaphysics. 2) The general conclusion is that the research into Whitehead's philosophy has left its infancy stage and is now almost on the level of the Heidegger and Wittgenstein research. It is clear in general that Whitehead is the only twentieth-century philosophy who was able to renew the traditional metaphysical tradition without ignoring the criticism of metaphysics, i.e., without being behind the times of a supposedly postmetaphysical age.

**Hampsher-Monk, Iain**. Varieties of Political Thought. *Brit J Hist Phil*, 4(2), 409-419, S 96.

This review article considers *Varieties of British Political Thought 1500-1800* by J.G.A. Pocock et. al. in both its institutional context—the Folger Library Center for the Study of British Political Thought—and its intellectual context—that is, the 'historical revolution' in political thought, associated with the University of Cambridge, pioneered by Pocock himself, Quentin Skinner and John Dunn. Comparison is invited between this anglophone *oeuvre* and the kind of history of social and political concepts undertaken by Kosseleck et. al. in the *Geschichtliche Grundbegriffe*. The article critically reviews the story of political thought in Britain during the period as the history of the available 'languages of political thought' and their rise, interaction, and decline.

**Hampson, Fen Osler** (ed) and Reppy, Judith (ed). *Earthly Goods: Environmental Change and Social Justice*. Ithaca, Cornell Univ Pr, 1996.

The essays address the role of science in global change and argue that Western science does not provide morally disinterested solutions to environmental problems. They discuss the role of state and substate actors in the international politics of the environment and then use accounts of actual negotiations to argue for the centrality of social justice in reaching desirable and equitable agreements. They conclude that a framework for social justice under conditions of global environmental change must include community values and provide for participatory structures to arbitrate among competing interests. (publisher,edited)

**Hampton, Jean**. "Hampton's Reply" in *The Liberation Debate: Rights at Issue*, Leahy, Michael (ed), 41-44. New York, Routledge, 1996.

**Hampton, Jean**. "The Case for Feminism" in *The Liberation Debate: Rights at Issue*, Leahy, Michael (ed), 3-24. New York, Routledge, 1996.

**Hampton, Jean**. *Political Philosophy*. Boulder, Westview Pr, 1997.

**Hampton, Jean**. The Wisdom of the Egoist: The Moral and Political Implications of Valuing the Self. *Soc Phil Pol*, 14(1), 21-51, Wint 97.

**Han, Edzard**. "Die Notwendigkeit einer Philosophie der Chemie" in *Philosophie der Chemie: Bestandsaufnahme und Ausblick*, Schummer, Joachim (ed), 59-66. Wurzburg, Koenigshausen, 1996.

**Hance, Allen**. The Hermeneutic Significance of the *Sensus Communis*. *Int Phil Quart*, 37(2), 133-148, Je 97.

In Kant's account of the *sensus communis* in the *Critique of Judgment*, Rudolf Makkreel claims to identify transcendental conditions of interpretation which show that we are not only oriented passively *by* traditions—a position he attributes to Gadamer—but also orient ourselves actively and critically *toward* traditions—a position purportedly lacking in Gadamer. This article argues that Makkreel, like Habermas, fails to appreciate sufficiently the *ontological* character of Gadamer's claims about understanding and the *sensus communis*. It concludes that the tasks he assigns to critical hermeneutics are already implicit in Gadamer's conception of hermeneutic understanding.

**Hand, Seán**. Outside Presence: Realizing the Holocaust in Contemporary French Narratives. *Hist Human Sci*, 9(4), 27-43, N 96.

**Hand, Seán**. The Other Voice: Ethics and Expression in Emmanuel Levinas. *Hist Human Sci*, 10(3), 56-68, Ag 97.

Emmanuel Livinas's *Totality and Infinity* (1961) is explicitly concerned with the suppression of the voice of the Other by the synoptic totalizations of the voice of Western philosophy. Levinas contests this emergence of Being and the systems of totality it indicates with the irruption of the face of the other, which signifies through contact and sensibility the presence of infinity within the human situation. Derrida's reading of this fundamental testing of Western ontology rests on the accusation that Western philosophy already has a term for this: empiricism. That is, Derrida exposes an alien voice within Levinas's exposure of the voice alienated from ontological formulations. (edited)

**Handwerk, Gary** (trans) and Nietzsche, Friedrich. *Human, All Too Human, I*. Stanford, Stanford Univ Pr, 1995.

This volume of *Human, All Too Human*, the first of two parts, is the earliest of Nietzsche's works in which his philosophical concerns and methodologies can be glimpsed. In this work Nietzsche began to establish the intellectual difference from his own cultural milieu and time that makes him our contemporary. Published in 1878, it marks both a stylistic and an intellectual shift away from Nietzsche's own youthful affiliation with Romantic excesses of German thought and culture typified by Wagnerian opera. (publisher, edited)

**Hanekamp, Gerd** and Gutmann, Mathias. Abstraktion und Ideation—Zur Semantik chemischer und biologischer Grundbegriffe. *J Gen Phil sincerelyci*, 27(1), 29-53, 1996.

"Abstraction and Ideation—The Semantics of Chemical and Biological Fundamental Concepts." The methods of abstraction and ideation are indispensable tools to introduce new concepts in a scientific terminology. The latter is paradigmatically introduced within the 'protophysical program' whereas abstraction is commonly applied in logics and mathematics. The application within the reconstruction of chemistry and biology causes several problems. Ideation appears to be inadequate whereas the application of abstraction necessitates a critical and minute examination of the corresponding equivalence relations. These problems are solved by the introduction of the method of *materially-synthetic* (material-synthetische) abstraction which is exemplified by the introduction of the concept of 'substance' (Stoff) and the biological concept of 'hereditary factor' (Erbanlage).

**Hanes, Marc**. Paul Virilio and the Articulation of Post-Reality. *Human Stud*, 19(2), 185-197, Ap 96.

This article provides an introductory overview of the theories of Paul Virilio, particularly regarding how technologically-enhanced speed impacts human reality. It positions Virilio as part modernist, part postmodernist and discusses how his ethico-political views color his more aesthetic metaphysics, creating a tension in his final position on the merits of technological speed's blurring of the real and the imaginary. It concludes by contrasting Virilio's position with some comments on aesthetics by Ludwig Wittgenstein.

**Haney, Kathleen**. Why is the Fifth Cartesian Meditation Necessary?. *SW Phil Rev*, 13(1), 197-204, Ja 97.

Although many philosophers assume that empathy explains how we can know others, Husserl disavowed this solution to solipsism. Husserl studied empathy in *Ideas II*. In addition, he directed Edith Stein's summa cum laude dissertation "On the Problem of Empathy". Nevertheless, he revisited the problem of the constitution of the other in the *Cartesian Meditations*. Why was the earlier work on empathy inadequate? In this article, I show that Husserl reopens the question to describe the preconditions for empathy. I conclude that empathy provides knowledge of others, given that I can first recognize that there are others to be known.

**Hanfling, Oswald**. Fact, Fiction and Feeling. *Brit J Aes*, 36(4), 356-366, O 96.

I consider and reject two kinds of solution of the problem of feelings about fictional objects: that the relevant beliefs are not really different as between fiction and fact; and that the relevant feelings are not 'really the same'. The problem should be seen in the context of different phases in acquiring the relevant feeling-concepts and I distinguish three such phases. The first is necessarily 'presentational': the child is presented with suitable objects or pictures and responds with appropriate feelings, without distinguishing fact from fiction. This presentational phase remains part of the concept and our responses to fictional objects should be understood accordingly.

**Hanford, Russell** and DeHaan, Robert and Kinlaw, Kathleen. Promoting Ethical Reasoning, Affect and Behaviour Among High School Students: An Evaluation of Three Teaching Strategies. *J Moral Educ*, 26(1), 5-20, Mr 97.

Ethics education should aim to promote students' maturity across a broad spectrum of moral functioning, including moral reasoning, moral affect and moral behaviour. To identify the most effective strategy for promoting the comprehensive moral maturity of high school students, we enrolled students in one of four groups: an introductory ethics class, a blended economics-ethics class, a role-model ethics class taught by graduate students and a nonethics comparison class. Pretest and post-test instruments measured the ways students a) reason, b) feel and c) act with regard to ethical-normative issues. The results indicated that the approaches to teaching ethics varied considerably in terms of their ability to promote significant positive changes in students' moral reasoning, empathy and behaviour.

**Hanks, Donald**. The Judicial Surcharge: A Violation of Prisoner Rights. *Cont Phil*, 17(6), 8-11, N-D 95.

Frequently we make decisions that bring us under the umbrella of institutional authority. Generally speaking, individuals have a right to institutions which respect the choices they have made; and society has the responsibility for making such institutions available. With regard to criminal behavior in particular, the following right and its corresponding responsibility can be identified. 1) "Right": Prisoners have a right to facilities that respect the choices they have made to engage in criminal acts. 2) "Responsibility": As a society, we have an obligation to provide institutions that do not violate the rights of those persons whose choices have led to their incarceration. (edited)

**Hanks, J Craig** and McKenna, Erin. Fragmented Selves and Loss of Community. *Phil Cont World*, 3(3), 18-23, Fall 96.

In this paper we try to provide the beginning of an analysis of some of the crises of our time. We do so by arguing that a certain account of the individual blocks our ability to think about solutions at the individual and the social levels. As an example we take the industrialization of housework in the United States and its effects on women's identity and on notions of "home." We suggest that the rise of liberal individualism, the industrialization of public and private life and the predomination of capitalism are central to the disintegration of the individual/self and that they limit the possibilities of some to determine the content and direction of self change. We argue that a notion of self as integrated and in process is needed in order to address our rapidly changing world.

**Hannan, Barbara**. "Love and Human Bondage in Maugham, Spinoza, and Freud" in *Love Analyzed*, Lamb, Roger E, 93-106. Boulder, Westview Pr, 1997.

This paper investigates obsessive romantic love. W. Somerset Maugham's novel, *Of Human Bondage*, is utilized for its story of a man who suffers from obsessive love and overcomes the condition. Spinoza's account, in the *Ethics* of "human bondage" or slavery to emotion, is explored, and Maugham's reliance on Spinoza's insights is illustrated. I argue that Spinoza outlines two different ways in which an obsessive emotion may be overcome: 1) a passion (such as obsessive love) is first replaced by another passion (such as suicidal despair) before passion is finally extinguished by a reasoned emotion (such as desire for a stronger character). 2) A reasoned emotion (such as desire for a stronger character) directly overcomes a passion such as obsessive love without the intervention of another passion. I note the similarity between Spinoza's deterministic account of a psychotherapeutic process, and Freud's; I also speculate on why obsessive love, while destructive and painful, is also beguiling and addictive.

**Hannon, Bruce** and Norton, Bryan G. Environmental Values: A Place-Based Theory. *Environ Ethics*, 19(3), 227-245, Fall 97.

Several recent authors have recommended that "sense of place" should become an important concept in our evaluation of environmental policies. In this paper, we explore aspects of this concept, arguing that it may provide the basis for a new, "place-based" approach to environmental values. This approach is based on an empirical hypothesis that place orientation is a feature of all people's experience of their environment. We argue that place orientation requires, in addition to a home perspective, a sense of the space around the home place and that this dual aspect can be modeled using a "hierarchical" methodology. We propose a "triscalar," place-oriented system for the analysis of environmental values, explore the characteristics of place-orientation through several examples and employ these characteristics to distinguish acceptable and unacceptable aspects of the NIMBY (not-in-my-backyard) idea.

**Hansberg, Olga Elizabeth**. De las emociones morales. *Rev Filosof (Spain)*, 9(16), 151-170, 1996.

This paper examines the propositional-attitude structure of a group of emotions which we can consider as "moral emotions", due to their requiring a complex set

of concepts, beliefs and desires related to morality. Among them are indignation (resentment), guilt, remorse and sometimes shame. Each emotion is analysed as well as its relation to the other emotions in this group.

**Hansen, Hans Vilhelm**. *Reductio* Without Assumptions?. *Log Anal*, 37(147-8), 329-337, S-D 94.

A *reductio ad absurdum* proof is one that shows an argument to be valid by showing that the negation of the conclusion is logically inconsistent with its premises. Methods of sentential deduction rely on the use of assumptions to effect such proofs. However, by use of argumental deductions—sequences of arguments rather than sentences—one can carry out a reductio proof without the employment of assumptions.

**Hansen, Hans Vilhelm**. Whately on the *ad Hominem*: A Liberal Exegesis. *Phil Rhet*, 29(4), 400-415, 1996.

This paper freely explores Richard Whately's 'technical' analysis of *ad hominem* arguments and argues that Whately implicitly held that there were nonlogical rules of argumentation which serve to distinguish legitimate from illegitimate uses of *ad hominem* arguments. In conclusion, the paper attempts to understand what Whately meant by '*ad hominem* fallacy'.

**Hansen, Kaj Borge**. Some Derivations of Bell's Inequality. *Dan Yrbk Phil*, 29, 63-105, 1994.

Eight derivations of Bell's inequality are given. First a simple and concrete derivation is given drawing on the full strength of the two hypotheses of locality and hidden variables. Two attempts at deriving Bell's inequality without these are made. They fail, but give valuable insight into the form which nonlocality must take in quantum physics. Arguments are given against this form of nonlocality. Ontological ideas which allow separation, realism and locality in quantum mechanics (QM) are indicated. (edited)

**Hanson, Mark J** and Jennings, Bruce. Commodity or Public Work? Two Perspectives on Health Care. *Bioethics Forum*, 11(3), 3-11, Fall 95.

Much of today's debate over health care reform implicitly views health care services as commodities. This economic point of view obscures morally important features of health care and of the medical profession. By viewing health care service instead as a public work—a civic activity—we recapture its true purposes and are better prepared to debate health policy, health reform and ethical medical practice meaningfully.

**Hansson, Sven Ove**. Decision Theoretic Foundations for Axioms of Rational Preference. *Synthese*, 109(3), 401-412, D 96.

Rationality postulates for preferences are developed from two basic decision theoretic principles, namely: 1) the logic of preference is determined by paradigmatic cases in which preferences are choice-guiding and 2) excessive comparison costs should be avoided. It is shown how the logical requirements on preferences depend on the structure of comparison costs. The preference postulates necessary for choice guidance in a single decision problem are much weaker than completeness and transitivity. Stronger postulates, such as completeness and transitivity, can be derived under the further assumption that the original preference relation should also be capable of guiding choice after any restriction of the original set of alternatives.

**Hansson, Sven Ove**. Defining Pseudo-Science. *Phil Natur*, 33(1), 169-176, 1996.

The etymological definition of pseudo-science as false science does not accord with common usage. Among the nonscientific phenomena falsely claimed to be scientific, only those that belong to a specific nonscientific doctrine are called pseudo-scientific. This "doctrinal" aspect of the concept is problematic. Defenders of (good) science are recommended to be concerned not only with pseudo-scientific practices, but also with the wider category of *unscientific* practices, not all of which are pseudo-scientific.

**Hansson, Sven Ove**. Situationist Deontic Logic. *J Phil Log*, 26(4), 423-448, Ag 97.

Situationist deontic logic is a model of that fraction of normative discourse which refers to only one situation and one set of alternatives. As we can see from a whole series of well-known paradoxes, standard deontic logic (SDL) is seriously mistaken even at the situationist level. In this paper it is shown how a more realistic deontic logic can be based on the assumption that prescriptive predicates satisfy the property of contranegativity. A satisfactory account of situation-specific norms is a necessary prerequisite for a successful treatment of more complex normative structures.

**Hanusek, Jerzy**. Decidability of Finite Boolean Algebras with a Distinguished Subset Closed under Some Operations. *Rep Math Log*, 29, 59-79, 1995.

In 1920 Emil Post classified all possible clones of functions on the set 2 = {0,1}, and gave a set of generating functions for each of them. For a clone $C$ we define a class of structures $B_C$....Let $Th(B_C)$ be the first order theory of $B_C$. In the present paper we show that the theory $Th(B_C)$ is decidable iff a clone $C$ contains the ternary discriminator. (edited)

**Hanuszewicz, Stanislaw**. Scepticism and Criticism (in Polish). *Kwartalnik Filozof*, 24(4), 49-68, 1996.

**Harbers, Hans**. Politiek van de technologie. *Kennis Methode*, 20(3), 308-315, 1996.

**Hardcastle, Valerie Gray**. Discussion: [Explanation] Is Explanation Better. *Phil Sci*, 64(1), 154-160, Mr 97.

Robert Wilson (1994) maintains that many interesting and fundamental aspects of psychology are nonindividualistic because large chunks of psychology depend upon organisms being deeply embedded in some environment. I disagree and present one version of narrow content that allows enough reference to the environment to meet any wide challenge. I argue that most psychologists are already this sort of narrow content theorist and that these narrow content explanations of psychological phenomena meet Wilson's criteria for being a good explanation better than any wide explanation of the same event.

**Hardcastle, Valerie Gray**. Functionalism's Response to the Problem of Absent Qualia: More Discussion of Zombies. *J Consciousness Stud*, 3(4), 357-373, 1996.

It seems that we could be physically the same as we are now, only we would lack conscious awareness. If so, then nothing about our physical world is necessary for qualitative experience. However, a proper analysis of psychological functionalism eliminates this problem concerning the possibility of zombies. 'Friends of absent qualia' rely on an overly simple view of what counts as a functional analysis and of the function/structure distinction. The level of thought is not the only level at which one might perform a functional analysis; all that is required for some description of a state to be functional is that it be defined in terms of its causal relations. Insofar as functionalism is not restricted to a higher level of analysis (hence, any causal interaction could conceivably be found in a functional description), then successful theories of consciousness should include whatever it is that makes those states have a qualitative character.

**Hardcastle, Valerie Gray**. How We Get There From Here: Dissolution of the Binding Problem. *J Mind Behav*, 17(3), 251-266, Sum 96.

On the one hand, we think that our conscious perceptions are tied to some stage of whatever processing stream we have. On the other hand, we think that our conscious experiences have to resemble the computational (or brain) states that instantiate them. However, nothing in our alleged stream resembles our experienced perceptions, hence, a conflict. The question is: How can we go from what we know about neurons, their connections and firing patterns, to explaining what conscious perceptual experiences are like? No intuitive answer seems plausible. Our perceptual experiences are complex and unified; however, brains divide their processing tasks into small chunks and segregate those smaller pieces across the gray matter. In this essay, I conjecture that what corresponds to our visual perceptions are higher order patterns of bifurcation in an attractor phase space. If I am correct, then the problem of the explanatory gap in philosophy, the binding problem in psychology and the problem of perception in neuroscience disappear. If the traditional computational perspective is wrong and sensory processing is not piece-meal, step-wise and segregated, then there is no need for something in the head to tie things together.

**Hardcastle, Valerie Gray**. When a Pain Is Not. *J Phil*, 94(8), 381-406, Ag 97.

I diagnose why we have so little agreement concerning the nature of our pain states. First, there is a basic failure to appreciate the fundamental complexity of our neuronal processing. Second, gate-control theories obscure the fact that we actually have two separate systems involved in our perceptions of pain. One functions as a pain sensory system, quite analogous to our other sensory systems. The other actively inhibits its functioning. Differentiating between the two systems explains most philosophical controversies. My final conclusion is that the sensation of pain is neither a fundamental nor an important component to our pain processing.

**Hardimon, Michael O** and Dallmayr, Fred R and Pinkard, Terry. The New Hegel. *Polit Theory*, 25(4), 584-597, Ag 97.

**Hardin, Russell**. Trustworthiness. *Ethics*, 107(1), 26-42, O 96.

**Hardtwig, Wolfgang**. "Jacob Burckhardt and Max Weber: Two Conceptions of the Origin of the Modern World" in *The Ancients and the Moderns*, Lilly, Reginald (ed), 170-180. Bloomington, Indiana Univ Pr, 1996.

**Hardy, James**. Three Problems for the Singularity Theory of Truth. *J Phil Log*, 26(5), 501-520, O 97.

In this paper I present three problems for Simmons's singularity theory of truth as he presents it in *Universality and the Liar*. I begin with a brief overview of the theory and then present the three problems I see for it. The first problem shows that the singularity theory is in conflict with our ordinary notion of truth. The second problem shows that Simmons's theory is incomplete, in the sense that there are sentences of its object language of which it does not have the resources to evaluate. The third problem suggests that Simmons theory does not, contrary to the claim of the book, allow for semantic universality. I consider Simmons's extension of the singularity theory to accommodate truth-in-a-context and show that it is inconsistent with his basic theory. (edited)

**Hare, Peter H**. The American Naturalist Tradition. *Free Inq*, 16(1), 38-39, Wint 95/96.

From colonial times to the present, American thought can best be understood as the progressive and cumulative development of naturalism. 'Pragmatism' is a helpful way of calling attention to various interconnected features that have supervened on American naturalism in the late 19th and 20th century. We should encourage the most thorough discussion of what appear to be alien types of philosophy in our midst (e.g., analytic philosophy), confident in our belief that the temper of American culture has always been such that immigrant ideas sooner or later enrich American naturalism.

**Hare, R M**. "Methods of Bioethics: Some Defective Proposals" in *Philosophical Perspectives on Bioethics*, Sumner, L W (ed), 18-36. Toronto, Univ of Toronto Pr, 1996.

The right kind of eclecticism in moral philosophy consists in picking out the good points in all theories and discarding the bad, provided that this leaves one with a consistent theory. Four defective theories are considered: situation ethics, caring ethics, virtue ethics and rights-based ethics, and it is shown how to frame a theory which combines their virtues but avoids their defects.

**Hare, William**. Content and Criticism: The Aims of Schooling. *Inquiry (USA)*, 14(3), 13-27, Spr 95.

The view in question is frankly sceptical about what many have claimed to be the school's task of fostering critical thought, autonomy, open-mindedness and similar attributes, urging instead, the acquisition in school of a body of shared information. It is a view, I believe, which until very recently would have been quickly dismissed as traditional and unenlightened. Let us remind ourselves at the outset how the ideals, now apparently being set aside as not belonging to the school's proper mandate, came to capture a central place in statements concerning the aims of schooling in the early part of the twentieth century.

**Hare, William**. Reason in Teaching: Scheffler's Philosophy of Education "A Maximum of Vision and a Minimum of Mystery". *Stud Phil Educ*, 16(1-2), 89-101, Ja-Ap 97.

This discussion concentrates on the distinctive conception of teaching which Scheffler develops, one in which teachers recognize an obligation both to offer reasons for their beliefs and to accept questions and objections raised by their students; and it shows how this conception is rooted in ethical and epistemological considerations. It emerges that Scheffler has anticipated, and answered various arguments currently being raised against an approach to teaching which values critical reflection by students and that he has also succeeded in avoiding the excesses of neutralism and relativism. It is argued too that his work exemplified his own belief in maintaining a linkage between philosophy and practical concerns.

**Harich, Katrin R** and Curren, Mary T. A Longitudinal Examination of American Business Ethics: Clark's Scales Revisited. *Bus Prof Ethics J*, 14(4), 57-68, Wint 95.

**Harman, Gilbert**. "Explaining Objective Color in Terms of Subjective Experience" in *Perception*, Villanueva, Enrique (ed), 1-17. Atascadero, Ridgeview, 1996.

Many salient facts about objective color can be explained only in terms of the biology and psychology of color perception. This might suggest explaining objective color in terms of the subjective reactions of color perceivers, but what reactions? That is, what is it for different people to have relevantly the same reactions. If the relevant reactions are defined as the reactions people have to objective colors, the account verges on emptiness. But if these reactions are defined in certain other ways, we have to take seriously the possibility of unknown inverted spectra. This suggests a definition in terms of biology.

**Harman, Gilbert**. "Qualia and Color Concepts" in *Perception*, Villanueva, Enrique (ed), 75-79. Atascadero, Ridgeview, 1996.

This is a response to commentary by Block, Shoemaker and Sosa on my "Explaining Objective Color in Terms of Subjective Experience." Block's discussion does not provide any reason to think people are ever aware of the mental paint by which their mental representations represent what they represent. Shoemaker and Sosa both need to take more seriously the fact that a general type of experience cannot be isolated simply by saying that it is an experience "like this" or "of the sort I have when I see an apple" because any given experience is of infinitely many types.

**Harman, Gilbert**. Analyticity Regained?. *Nous*, 30(3), 392-400, S 96.

Responding to Boghossian, "Analyticity Reconsidered" (*Nous* 30 (3) 1996): The "radical indeterminacy of meaning" involved in the rejection of the analytic-synthetic distinction is a weaker thesis than Quine's "indeterminacy of radical translation." A conventionalist theory of a priori knowledge escapes Boghossian's objections, but cannot escape Quine's regress argument or the more fundamental objection that intending to use one's terms in such a way that a certain sentence is true cannot guarantee that the sentence really is true. Boghossian's suggestion for meeting the regress argument was anticipated by Quine, who notes correctly that it lacks explanatory force.

**Harms, William**. Evolution and Ultimatum Bargaining. *Theor Decis*, 42(2), 147-175, Ja 97.

Empirical research has discovered that experimental subjects in ultimatum bargaining situations generally fail to play the decision-theoretic optimum strategy and instead play something between that strategy and a fair split. In evolutionary dynamics, fair division and nearly fair division strategies often go to fixation and weakly dominated strategies can do quite well. Computer simulations were done using three different ultimatum bargaining games as determinates of fitness. (edited)

**Harnden-Warwick, David**. Psychological Realism, Morality, and Chimpanzees. *Zygon*, 32(1), 30-40, Mr 97.

The parsimonious consideration of research into food sharing among chimpanzees suggests that the type of social regulation found among our closest genetic relatives can best be understood as a form of morality. Morality is here defined from a naturalistic perspective as a system in which self-aware individuals interact through socially prescribed, psychologically realistic rules of conduct which provide these individuals with an awareness of how one *ought* to behave. The empirical markers of morality within chimpanzee communities and the traditional moral traits to which they correspond are 1) self-awareness/agency; 2) calculated reciprocity/obligation; 3) moralistic aggression/blame; and 4) consolation/empathy.

**Harper, William**. Knowledge and Luck. *S J Phil*, 34(3), 273-283, Fall 96.

Gettier cases highlight the problem that under fallibilist internalist analyses of justification a belief can be justified but true by mere luck. I begin by arguing that fallibilist externalist analyses of epistemic justification are in principle subject to Gettier-type counterexamples and incapable of closing the gap between justification and truth. This suggests that an analysis of knowledge must include a "no-luck" condition, an externalistic requirement of an entirely objective, nonprobabilistic connection between the subject's justification and the truth of the belief in question. This solves Gettier-type problems and leaves room for purely internalist analyses of justification.

**Harper, William** and DiSalle, Robert. Inferences from Phenomena in Gravitational Physics. *Proc Phil Sci Ass*, 3(Suppl), S46-S54, 1996.

Newton's methodology emphasized propositions "inferred from phenomena." These rest on systematic dependencies that make phenomena measure theoretical parameters. We consider the inferences supporting Newton's inductive argument that gravitation is proportional to inertial mass. We argue that the support provided by these systematic dependencies is much stronger than that provided by bootstrap confirmation; this kind of support thus avoids some of the major objections against bootstrapping. Finally, we examine how contemporary testing equivalence principles exemplifies this Newtonian methodological theme.

**Harper, William** and Hájek, Alan. Full Belief and Probability: Comments on Van Fraassen. *Dialogue (Canada)*, 36(1), 91-100, Wint 97.

**Harré, Rom**. Commentary on "Non-Cartesian Frameworks". *Phil Psychiat Psych*, 3(3), 185-186, Is 96.

**Harré, Rom**. Forward to Aristotle: The Case for a Hybrid Ontology. *J Theor Soc Behav*, 27(2-3), 173-191, Je-S 97.

It behooves a science to pay careful attention to its ontological assumptions, especially in cases where they are likely to be complex. Psychology seems to require both material states of humans as organisms and symbolic productions. But we must be careful not to think that the grammars of the latter are some sort of superscience. The duality shows up strongly in the difference between skilled performances and their material enabling conditions. I argues that the dual ontology appears in a science of psychology as a hybrid grammar. If we try to colonize one or the other side of the hybrid by terms from the other, the transplanted terms make no sense in their new surroundings. We find ourselves with a double or hybrid grammar and three main patterns of action to explain, causal, habitual and monitored. By assimilating the latter two under the symbolic ontology apparent problems dissolve. This is illustrated with a sketch of the sources and character of the sense of personal uniqueness.

**Harré, Rom**. From Observability to Manipulability: Extending the Inductive Arguments for Realism. *Synthese*, 108(2), 137-155, Ag 96.

In recent years there have been several attempts to construct inductive arguments for some version of scientific realism. Neither the characteristics of what would count as inductive evidence nor the conclusion to be inferred have been specified in ways that escape sceptical criticism. By introducing the pragmatic criterion of manipulative efficacy for a good theory and by sharpening the specification of the necessary inductive principle, the viability of a mutually supporting pair of argument forms are defended. It is shown that by the use of these forms, taken together, a sequence of inductive arguments could be constructed, given suitable cases histories to serve as evidence. It also shown that the best inductive argument for the most daring realist claim is the weakest when compared with similarly structured arguments for less daring claims.

**Harré, Rom**. Is There a Basic Ontology for the Physical Sciences?. *Dialectica*, 51(1), 17-34, 1997.

Physics has been based on two main ontologies: atoms in space-time or powerful particulars and distributed dispositions. Causal powers are sensitive to apparatus employed. This requires a new concept, 'affordance', from psychology of perception. Using this concept one arrives at a Kantian interpretation of Bohr's philosophy of physics. This scheme also makes 'charge and field' concepts ontologically coherent.

**Harré, Rom**. Pathological Autobiographies. *Phil Psychiat Psych*, 4(2), 99-109, Je 97.

It might seem obvious that an autobiography is a window into its author's soul. But pathological "souls" can find expression either in the unusual content of their stories or in the use of a strange grammar. The study of the expression of self in stories is part of discursive psychology. This development is based on a Vygotskian thesis about the shaping of mind in the learning of linguistic and practical skills in symbiosis with another person and on a Wittgensteinian insight that how we feel and how our thoughts are organized are expressed in characteristic language games. The self-hood of autobiographical telling is expressed predominantly in the uses of first and second person (indexical) pronouns and in the choice of narrative conventions within which to tell the story. (edited)

**Harré, Rom**. Response to the Commentaries. *Phil Psychiat Psych*, 4(2), 119-120, Je 97.

Contrasts like 'true self' and 'false self' and concepts which presuppose that the mental states expressed in discourse are independent of their means of expression, can, at best, be interpreted as referring to linguistic dispositions. Furthermore, the essentially relational character of even such seemingly individual activities as telling an autobiography makes the identification of pathological autobiographies with pathologies of moral character problematic. Only if the positioning of others in the discourse deprives them of personhood is the autobiography morally pathological.

**Harré, Rom** and Robinson, Daniel N. What Makes Language Possible? Ethological Foundationalism in Reid and Wittgenstein. *Rev Metaph*, 50(3), 483-498, Mr 97.

Thomas Reid in the eighteenth century and Wittgenstein in the *Investigations* consider the necessary preconditions for language and arrive, by different paths, at a naturalistic point of origin. Reid's critique of (Lockean) conventionalist explanations of meaning is grounded in the proposition that conventions themselves presuppose the very linguistic resources needed for there to be compacts and convenants. This leads Reid to a theory of natural

language on which artificial languages might then be constructed. Wittgenstein's concept of "natural expressions" are similar and lead to much the same theory. Both accounts successfully avoid the pitfalls of Chomskian "nativistic" theories while, at the same time, preserving the required foundationalism.

**Harré, Rom** and Varela, Charles R. Conflicting Varieties of Realism: Causal Powers and the Problems of Social Structure. *J Theor Soc Behav*, 26(3), 313-325, S 96.

**Harrell, Jean G**. There Ought to be a Law. *J Value Inq*, 31(1), 61-72, Mr 97.

In contrast to the culturally relativistic term "beautiful," the equally common term "profound" points to a lawlike quality in aesthetic judgment. The "profound" is seen to derive from a biological universal, analogous to a logical universal, which is rooted in aspatial hearing prenatally and in semiaspatial vision perinatally. Profound musical and visual art works are thus understood as imitations of universal sensory patterns which override cultural differences and carry with them, often as though dictated by logical law, the rudimentary aesthetic value deriving from the life of which they have been an indelible part. Detailed examples are given.

**Harrell, Mack**. Confirmation Holism and Semantic Holism. *Synthese*, 109(1), 63-101, O 96.

Fodor and Lepore, in their recent book *Holism*, maintain that if an inference from semantic anatomism to semantic holism is allowed, certain fairly deleterious consequences follow. In Section 1 Fodor and Lepore's terminology is construed and amended where necessary with the result that the aforementioned deleterious consequences are neither so apparent nor straightforward as they had suggested. In Section 2 their "Argument A" is considered in some detail. In Section 3 their "argument attributed to Quine" is examined at length and a shorter and more perspicacious argument suggested which avoids their charge that the Quinean argument is guilty of an equivocation on the word 'statement'.

**Harrington, Susan J**. A Test of a Person—Issue Contingent Model of Ethical Decision Making in Organizations. *J Bus Ethics*, 16(4), 363-375, Mr 97.

Despite the existence of a large number of models to explain the ethical decision-making process, rarely have the models been tested. This research validated the use of such models by showing that both issue-contingent variables and individual characteristics affect two commonly-proposed model components: i.e., moral judgment and moral intent. Many ethical decision-making models also argue for the inclusion of individual characteristics in the decision-making process. This study proposed and found that the individual characteristics of rule orientation and denial of responsibility influenced moral judgment and moral intent, respectively. (edited)

**Harriott, Howard H**. The Evils of Chattel Slavery and the Holocaust: An Examination of Laurence Thomas's *Vessels of Evil*. *Int Phil Quart*, 37(3), 329-347, S 97.

**Harris, Bond** (trans) and Spurlock, Jacqueline Bouchard (trans) and Vandevelde, Pol (ed & trans). *Paul Ricoeur: A Key to Husserl's Ideas I*. Milwaukee, Marquette Univ Pr, 1996.

In 1950 Paul Ricoeur translated into French Husserl's major work *Ideen zu einer reinen Phänomenologie und phänomenologischen Philosophie*. In this French translation Ricoeur provided both a lengthy introductory chapter and a large running commentary in the form of notes. These notes were keyed to the beginning of many of Husserl's sections and to important places within the body of the text. The present translation brings at last this famous commentary into English. In undertaking this work the translators have benefited from the encouragement of Professor Ricoeur himself. (publisher, edited)

**Harris, Cheryl Hall**. High Risk Infants: Thirty Years of Intensive Care. *Bioethics Forum*, 11(1), 23-28, Spr 95.

For centuries, infants born prematurely or with a variety of congenital conditions had little hope for survival. The advancement of newborn intensive care during the past thirty years, clinical expertise and technologic advances have changed outcomes and enabled such infants to live. This paper describes these developments in the clinical care of high risk infants and their mothers, along with the ethical considerations and issues that accompany them.

**Harris, David J**. Ethics and the Biology of Reproduction. *Bioethics Forum*, 11(1), 29-34, Spr 95.

In the reproductive cycle, death before birth is the norm rather than the exception. An analysis and better understanding of this cycle adds a new perspective to the ethical dilemmas occurring with increasing frequency in neonatal intensive care units.

**Harris, Errol E**. "All Philosophy as *Religionsphilosophy*" in *The Recovery of Philosophy in America: Essays in Honor of John Edwin Smith*, Kasulis, Thomas P (ed), 201-215. Albany, SUNY Pr, 1997.

**Harris, H S**. "The Hegelian Organon of Interpretation" in *Hegel, History, and Interpretation*, Gallagher, Shaun, 19-31. Albany, SUNY Pr, 1997.

This essay examines the sense in which "Spirit" is the *absolute* (i.e., comprehensive) category for Hegel. He bequeathed to us a concept of the "World Spirit" that is logically *adequate* for the articulation of our experience as a whole. We shall continue to find new perspectives on our past; and to generate new subjective (aesthetic) concepts of life and objective (scientific) concepts of our world. But just as we now understand this logical prophecy, so the future generations that realize it will employ the same *absolute* concept in their retrospective comprehension of us. This is the sense in which Hegel's philosophy is "absolute knowledge".

**Harris, Ian M**. The Conditional Quality of Gandhi's Love. *Acorn*, 7(1), 7-18, Spr-Sum 92.

**Harris, John**. "Harris' Reply" in *The Liberation Debate: Rights at Issue*, Leahy, Michael (ed), 163-165. New York, Routledge, 1996.

**Harris, John**. "Liberating Children" in *The Liberation Debate: Rights at Issue*, Leahy, Michael (ed), 135-146. New York, Routledge, 1996.

**Harris, John**. What is the Good of Health Care?. *Bioethics*, 10(4), 269-291, O 96.

This paper sets out to discuss what precisely is meant by "benefit" when we talk of the requirement that the health care system concern itself with health gain or with maximising beneficial health care. In particular I argue that in discharging the duty to do what is most beneficial we need to choose between rival conceptions of what is meant by beneficial. One is the patient's conception of benefit and the second is the provider's or funder's conception of benefit. I argue that it is the patient's conception of benefit which is paramount and that if this is followed it commits us to a conception of patient care which must be blind to prognosis in so far as prognosis is thought to bear upon issues of prioritisation or resource allocation.

**Harris, Richard B**. Approaches to Conserving Vulnerable Wildlife in China: Does the Colour of Cat Matter—if it Catches Mice?. *Environ Values*, 5(4), 303-334, N 96.

China's environmental problems are well-known, but recently its record in the area of wildlife conservation, particularly with regard to endangered species, has come under scrutiny. Environmental values colour how we in the West view both China's past experience with wildlife and what strategies it should adopt to foster better conservation. Chinese have long taken a utilitarian view of wildlife, valuing species primarily as resources for man's use and only secondarily for other reasons. However, China has not developed institutions capable of sustaining the desired use of wildlife in the face of ever-growing demands. I suggest that Western criticisms of Chinese Utilitarian attitudes are inappropriate, ineffective and possibly counter-productive: deep-seated cultural mores change slowly. (edited)

**Harris, Stephen**. Berkeley's Argument from Perceptual Relativity. *Hist Phil Quart*, 14(1), 99-120, Ja 97.

**Harris, Wendell V**. Assessing the Publication Swamp in Literary Studies. *J Infor Ethics*, 6(1), 47-58, Spr 97.

While the demands for publication in the humanities increases, the process of refereeing submissions is both slowing down and becoming more ideological. This would be an excellent time for press and journal editors publicly to announce 1) that the publication expectations of university humanities departments are unreasonable given the mechanics of selecting, editing, and bringing into print, and 2) that to decrease bias in the selection process and insure the quality of what is published, editorial processes are to be tightened in ways that will in fact further slow acceptances. It is time for deans, chairmen, and personnel committees to recognize and act to ameliorate the present state of affairs.

**Harris, Wendell V**. Moving Literary Theory On. *Phil Lit*, 20(2), 428-435, O 96.

Poststructuralism appears to court, indeed depend upon, self-contradiction. At least twelve poststructuralist principles are egregiously self-cancelling or are contradicted by poststructuralist practices. These include the celebration of the death of New Criticism, the denial of the human subject, the assertion of the irrelevance of authorial intention, and the assertions that all statements about the world must be fictional and that all literary texts are in fact unreadable.

**Harrison, Andrew**. *Philosophy and the Arts: Seeing and Believing*. Bristol, Thoemmes, 1997.

How can pictorial and narrative arts be compared? What in principle can or cannot be communicated in such different media? Why does it seem that, at its best, artistic communication goes beyond the limitations of its own medium—seeming to think and to communicate the uncommunicable? In *Philosophy and the Arts* Andrew Harrison explores these questions. He finds that an understanding of art leads to a richer understanding of what it is to be human. Much of what misleads or baffles us in the arts is what puzzles us about ourselves—the issues raised by art are thus central to philosophy. (publisher)

**Harrison, Bernard**. Ragione e retorica: *La mitologia bianca* di Jacques Derrida. *Iride*, 10(20), 19-49, Ap 97.

**Harrison, Craig**. The Three Arrows of Zeno. *Synthese*, 107(2), 271-292, My 96.

**Harrold, Joan** and Ayers, Elise and Lynn, Joanne. A Good Death: Improving Care Inch-by-Inch. *Bioethics Forum*, 13(1), 38-40, Spr 97.

As people live longer with chronic diseases before dying, it is increasingly important to define a "good death." This may include freedom from pain, preservation of dignity and family and spiritual reconciliation—goals our health care system rarely recognizes. To ensure a good death, we must measure and improve the quality of end of life care. Ten domains for measurement have been identified: symptom relief; support of function and autonomy; advance care planning; use of aggressive care and appropriate site of death; patient and family satisfaction; global quality of life; family burden; survival time; provider continuity and skill; and bereavement.

**Harsanyi, John C**. Funciones de Bienestar social no lineales: una réplica al profesor Sen. *Telos (Spain)*, 5(1), 103-106, Je 96.

**Harsanyi, John C**. Funciones no lineales de Bienestar social: ¿Tienen los economistas del Bienestar una exención especial de la racionalidad bayesiana?. *Telos (Spain)*, 5(1), 55-78, Je 96.

Se argumenta que la teoría de la decisión bayesiana supone una solución a un importante problema filosófico, esto es, el problema de cómo definir el comportamiento racional bajo riesgo e incertidumbre. El autor ha mostrado en

artículos anteriores que si tomamos en serio los postulados bayesianos de racionalidad y adoptamos un punto de vista individualista acerca del bienestar social, entonces nuestra función de bienestar social debe ser una función lineal de las utilidades individuales: de hecho, debe ser su media aritmética. El presente artículo critica la opinión de Diamond y Sen de que uno de los postulados bayesianos (a saber, el principio de lo seguro) no se aplica a las decisiones sociales, por más que pueda aplicarse a decisiones individuales. (edited)

**Hart, Carroll Guen**. "Taking the Risk of Essence: A Deweyan Theory in Some Feminist Conversations" in *Knowing Other-Wise: Philosophy at the Threshold of Spirituality*, Olthuis, James H (ed), 69-101. New York, Fordham Univ Pr, 1997.

**Hart, Hendrik**. "Conceptual Understanding and Knowing *Other*-Wise: Reflections on Rationality and Spirituality..." in *Knowing Other-Wise: Philosophy at the Threshold of Spirituality*, Olthuis, James H (ed), 19-53. New York, Fordham Univ Pr, 1997.

**Hart, James G**. Blondel and Husserl: A Continuation of the Conversation. *Tijdschr Filosof*, 58(3), 490-518, S 96.

The dialogue between Blondel and Husserl carried on by Maréchal and Duméry and other thinkers has been silent for almost fifty years. Yet Husserl's *Nachlass* provides reasons for deepening the dialogue, especially in the area of the basic Blondelian themes: the willing-will and the teleological and religious nature of consciousness. Nevertheless there are intriguing differences in their respective philosophical theologies.

**Hart, Richard E** (ed). "Buchler's *The Main of Light*: The Role of Metaphysics in Literary Theory and Interpretation" in *Philosophy in Experience: American Philosophy in Transition*, 153-172. New York, Fordham Univ Pr, 1997.

This essay employs a reading of Justus Buchler's seminal work on the concept of poetry (*The Main of Light*) so as to explore what role metaphysics plays in aesthetic interpretation and criticism. It argues, along with Buchler, that literary theory cannot be dissociated from metaphysics in that any given theory is grounded in and shaped by pervasive metaphysical constructs. Buchler's unique metaphysics (what has been termed "ordinal naturalism") is explicated and applied to the understanding of poetry and literature generally. The impact of such a metaphysics on the critical/interpretive process (what I call a "democratization") is preliminarily explored.

**Hart, Richard E**. Langer's Aesthetics of Poetry. *Trans Peirce Soc*, 33(1), 183-200, Wint 97.

**Hart, Richard E** (ed) and Anderson, Douglas R (ed). *Philosophy in Experience: American Philosophy in Transition*. New York, Fordham Univ Pr, 1997.

This collection of essays aims to mark a place for American philosophy as it moves into the twenty-first century. Taking their cue from the work of Peirce, James, Santayana, Dewey, Mead, Buchler and others, the contributors assess and employ philosophy as an activity taking place within experience and culture. Within this broad background of the American tradition, the essays reveal a variety of approaches to the transition in which American philosophy is presently engaged. Some of the pieces argue from a historical dialogue with the tradition, some are more polemically involved with American philosophy's current status among the contemporary philosophical "schools" and others seek to reveal the possibilities for the future of American philosophy. In thus addressing past, present and future, the pieces, taken together, outline a trajectory for American philosophy that reinvests it from a new angle of vision. (publisher)

**Hart, W A**. The Qualitymongers. *J Phil Educ*, 31(2), 295-308, Jl 97.

A lot of the talk about education nowadays invokes the notion of 'quality' and it has been suggested that education in schools and universities would benefit from exposure to the kind of quality assurance procedures originally developed by industry to monitor and raise performance. The paper is critical of this suggestion, arguing that the notion of quality which has emerged from industry is a very limited one and that importing the latter into education would change our educational thinking and practice in significant ways for the worse. What we need, instead, is a fuller appreciation of the kind of quality and standards which are proper to education and which depend upon the exercise of personal judgement.

**Hart, W D**. *The Philosophy of Mathematics*. New York, Oxford Univ Pr, 1996.

This volume offers a selection of the most interesting and important work from recent years in the philosophy of mathematics, which has always been closely linked to and has exerted a significant influence upon the main stream of analytical philosophy. The issues discussed are of interest throughout philosophy and no mathematical expertise is required of the reader. (publisher,edited)

**Harte, Verity**. Aristotle *Metaphysics* H6: A Dialectic with Platonism. *Phronesis*, 41(3), 276-304, 1996.

*Metaphysics* H6 asks what makes the object of definition a unity. This paper provides an interpretation of the chapter which demonstrates where and how this question is answered. Aristotle's discussion of the unity of the object of definition is embedded in a dialectic with Platonism and it is this dialectic which explains the structure of the argument of the chapter and the role played within it by the discussion of the unity of a hylomorphic compound.

**Hartigan, Richard Shelly**. Natural Law, Nature, and Biology: A Modern Synthesis. *Vera Lex*, 14(1-2), 35-40, 1994.

The author links the teleological form of natural law both to the *Judaic Decalogue* mandating respect of life, lineage, property, and truth that are compatible with the natural law tradition, and to relevant findings in the science of biology, especially in the study of evolution. No compromise is involved. The natural sciences as we know them do not, Hartigan argues, confirm value relativism—or disconfirm the natural law. Indeed, they contribute to, and forward, an ongoing discussion of morality. Science and morality are partners in the discovery of normative universals. (publisher,edited)

**Hartle, Ann**. *Self-Knowledge in the Age of Theory*. Lanham, Rowman & Littlefield, 1997.

The philosophical ideal of self-knowledge has been all but forgotten in what Walker Percy calls "the age of theory." Hartle attempts to recover that ancient philosophical task and to articulate what that ideal could mean in the context of our historical situation. She considers and rejects claims that we can attain self-knowledge through theory, antitheory, or narrative and she defends philosophy as a humanistic, rather than scientific, endeavor. *Self-Knowledge in the Age of Theory* will be of great interest not only to philosophers but to scholars of literature and other humanities. (publisher)

**Hartline, Sharon E**. Battered Women Who Kill: Victims and Agents of Violence. *J Soc Phil*, 28(2), 56-67, Fall 97.

**Hartman, Hope J**. Educational Psychologists as Trainers for Intellectual Development. *Inquiry (USA)*, 14(2), 29-42, Wint 94.

Educational psychologists have a unique opportunity to contribute to the educational process by becoming more activist and interventionist, training educators to develop intellect. This function can occur through various roles including: school district research specialist, university-school collaboration, independent consultant and summer training courses. This paper describes my experiences training intellect through these roles. Experiences center around a perspective of educational psychologists as contributing more to the educational community than the psychological community. The work evolved from a traditional, linear, prescriptive approach to a social constructivist approach, which is more recursive and interactive.

**Hartman, Jan**. Problems of Existence—Recapitulation (in Polish). *Kwartalnik Filozof*, 25(1), 195-208, 1997.

**Hartmann, Dirk**. Protowissenschaft und Rekonstruktion. *J Gen Phil Sci*, 27(1), 55-69, 1996.

In the article it is shown that the orthodox definition of 'protoscience' is in fact far too narrow. An alternative definition is proposed which on the one hand preserves the classic tasks of protophysics but on the other hand allows for other protosciences as equally useful enterprises. A central concept within the complex topic "protoscience" is the one of 'reconstruction'. It can be shown that there is a certain ambiguity in the use of this critical concept. Therefore the article ends with a reconstruction of the term 'reconstruction'. (edited)

**Hartonas, Chrysafis**. Duality for Lattice-Ordered Algebras and for Normal Algebraizable Logics. *Stud Log*, 58(3), 403-450, My 97.

Part I of this paper is developed in the tradition of Stone-type dualities, where we present a new topological representation for general lattices. In part II, we consider lattice-ordered algebras (lattices with additional operators), extending the Jónsson and Tarski representation results for Boolean algebras with operators. In part III, we discuss applications in logic of the framework developed. Specifically, logics with restricted structural rules give rise to lattices with normal operators (in our sense), such as the full Lambek algebras (*F-L*-algebras) studied by Ono. Our Stone-type representation results can be then used to obtain canonical constructions of Kripke frames for such systems, and to prove a duality of algebraic and Kripke semantics for such logics. (edited)

**Hartshorne, Charles**. Freedom as Universal. *Process Stud*, 25, 1-9, 1996.

**Hartshorne, Charles**. The Meaning of Life. *Process Stud*, 25, 10-18, 1996.

**Hartshorne, Charles** and Valady, Mohammad (ed). *The Zero Fallacy and Other Essays in Neoclassical Philosophy*. Chicago, Open Court, 1997.

This collection of Charles Hartshorne's writings—many never before published—is an indispensible introduction to his rich and indelible contribution to contemporary philosophy. It covers the extraordinary range of Hartshorne's thought, including his reflection on the history of philosophy, philosophical psychology, philosophy of science, epistemology, ethics, aesthetics, literature, ornithology, and, above all, theology and metaphysics. (publisher, edited)

**Hartz, Glenn A** and Cover, J A. Are Leibnizian Monads Spatial?. *Hist Phil Quart*, 11(3), 295-316, Jl 94.

Leibniz commentators, like Leibniz himself on occasion, tend to be of two minds on the question of whether monads have spatial properties. Our purpose is to evaluate both textual and philosophical lines of thought in support of this "spatiality thesis." In particular, we examine three arguments for the claim that monads have spatial properties in the same, nonderived sense that bodies would otherwise be said to have them; and we examine three arguments for the claim that monads have spatial properties in a derived, nonbasic sense. We show that none of these lines of argument can be sustained.

**Harvey, Charles W**. Liberal Indoctrination and the Problem of Community. *Synthese*, 111(1), 115-130, Ap 97.

Responding to claims to the contrary, this essay shows how liberal education, the education of critical exposure, indoctrinates students into a *style* of belief and belief formation. It argues that a common liberal view about what constitutes freedom from indoctrination is precisely the form of indoctrination feared by many conservative communitarians. While I support the style and procedures of liberal education, I argue that we cannot excise all indoctrinating components from it by semantic, logical or epistemic analyses of what "indoctrination" or "education" means.

**Harvey, Robert**. Panbiographisme chez Sartre. *Rev Phil Fr*, 3, 369-382, Jl-S 96.

**Harvey, Van A**. The Re-Discovery of Ludwig Feuerbach. *Free Inq*, 17(1), 45-46, Wint 96/97.

Although relatively unknown today, Feuerbach was one of the most profound critics of religion in the history of Western thought. One of the reasons he is not better known is that his name is so identified with *The Essence of Christianity*. But dissatisfied with this book he turned in his later writings to the view that the gods are born out of desire to transcend the limits of natural necessity and the desire for recognition. Acknowledging the powerful psychological comfort in religious belief, he nevertheless believed, like Nietzsche, that the religious believer pays a high price for this psychological luxury.

**Harvey, Warren Z**. Pascal's Wager and Al-Muqammas (in Hebrew). *Iyyun*, 45, 409-412, O 96.

**Harvey, William**. Linguistic Relativity in French, English, and German Philosophy. *Phil Today*, 40(2), 273-288, Sum 96.

The Sapir-Whorf hypothesis (that grammar influences world view) is employed to explain the differences between German, French and English philosophical traditions. German philosophy's idealist, unitary and systematic tendencies are attributed to German's end-verbs, case system, root morphemes and initial qualifiers. French philosophy's dualism and rationalist analysis are ascribed to that language's more abstract signifiers and its description by progressive discrete divisions. And English philosophy's skeptical materialist empiricism is attributed to English's mixing of French and German syntax and lexicons, and to the higher incidence of passive constructions in English.

**Harwood, Larry D**. Nietzsche on Socrates as a Source of the Metaphysical Error. *Dialogue (PST)*, 38(2-3), 50-55, Ap 96.

Socrates bears an extraordinary share of blame in Nietzsche's criticisms of the failings of philosophers for having created a "true" world out of his pessimism about the real world. For Nietzsche this represents a decadent response to life in comparison to the Greek Tragedians who overcame this world by affirming it. But because most philosophy followed Socrates and not the Tragedians, there has been a colossal effort by subsequent philosophers to uphold the metaphysical error created by Socrates.

**Hashimoto, Noriko**. "The Semantic Transformation of an Axiological Concept" in *East and West in Aesthetics,* Marchianò, Grazia (ed), 87-98. Pisa, Istituti Editoriali, 1997.

**Hasian, Jr, Marouf** and Croasmun, Earl. Rhetoric's Revenge: The Prospect of a Critical Legal Rhetoric. *Phil Rhet*, 29(4), 384-399, 1996.

**Hasker, William**. Explanatory Priority: Transitive and Unequivocal, A Reply to William Craig. *Phil Phenomenol Res*, 57(2), 389-393, Je 97.

According to William Craig, the notion of explanatory priority is the Achilles's heel of Robert Adams's argument against Molinism. Specifically, Craig contends that 1) the notion of explanatory priority is employed equivocally in the argument; 2) Adams is guilty of conflating reasons and causes; and 3) one of the intermediate conclusions of the argument is invalidly inferred, as can be seen by a counterexample. I argue that Craig is mistaken on all counts and that Adams's argument emerges unscathed.

**Hasker, William**. O'Connor on Gratuitous Natural Evil. *Faith Phil*, 14(3), 388-394, Jl 97.

David O'Connor has criticized my arguments for the conclusion that God's existence is compatible with genuinely gratuitous natural evil. In this reply, I show that his own arguments fail to achieve their objective; in addition, I point out several respects in which he has misstated my position.

**Haslett, D W**. Moral Taxonomy and Rachels' Thesis. *Pub Affairs Quart*, 10(4), 291-306, O 96.

James Rachels defends the thesis that, to whatever extent passive euthanasia is morally justified, active euthanasia is also. The cornerstone of his defense is that the bare difference between killing and letting die is not, in itself, morally significant. Through an investigation into moral taxonomy, this paper tries to show that Rachels's defense is flawed, that the bare difference between killing and letting die is indeed morally significant. This paper concludes, however, by arguing that Rachels's thesis nevertheless is correct, but for reasons other than those that Rachels himself gives.

**Haslett, D W**. The Bell Curse. *J Value Inq*, 31(1), 109-125, Mr 97.

The vision of the future that Charles Murray and Richard Herrnstein derive from their examination of human intelligence in their controversial book, the *Bell Curve*, is bleak. The less intelligent, they say, will eventually be forced into a kind of "high-tech and more lavish version of an Indian reservation" with little hope. But, the authors tell us, this dismal scenario can still be avoided and they offer a prescription for how to do so. This article examines their prescription. It is concluded that, although their prescription is misconceived, far beyond parameters of the authors' own ultra-conservative thinking there is indeed hope.

**Hassan, Ihab**. Negative Capability Reclaimed: Literature and Philosophy *Contra* Politics. *Phil Lit*, 20(2), 305-324, O 96.

Stated baldly, the essay argues that the prevalence of politics and the obsession with power skew language, thought, and values in the university. Thus the ancient quarrel between poetry and philosophy, between Homer and Plato now cedes the field to a nastier agon between *both* and politics. The essay touches on texts by diverse writers, including Foucault, D.H. Lawrence, Nietzsche, Emerson, William James, Sontag, and Heaney to reclaim a concept of "negative capability" (Keats), at once spiritual and pragmatic.

**Hassrick, Beth**. Fred Dretske on the Explanatory Role of Semantic Content. *Conference*, 6(1), 59-66, Sum 95.

**Hatcher, Donald L**. Combining Critical Thinking and Written Composition: The Whole Is Greater Than The Sum Of The Parts. *Inquiry (USA)*, 15(2), 20-36, Wint 95.

This paper argues that contrary to skepticism by both philosophy and literature faculty, students become better critical thinkers *and* better writers when instruction in critical thinking is combined with the application of critical thinking skills to writing expository prose. Evidence for this conclusion is provided by data from a five-year study with *pre* and *post* testing with the Test of Standard Written English and the Ennis-Weir Critical Thinking Essay Test. These results were compared with scores of students in the traditional stand-alone critical thinking and composition classes.

**Hatcher, Donald L**. Critical Thinking and Epistemic Obligations. *Inquiry (USA)*, 14(3), 28-40, Spr 95.

While many practical arguments have been given to support teaching critical thinking, this paper argues that we have a moral duty to think critically, that is, to attempt to arrive at judgements only after honestly evaluating the alternatives with respect to available evidence and arguments. Prior to the arguments for this conclusion, the paper criticizes those who claim there are no rational standards to justify our beliefs and those who claim we cannot be held morally responsible for belief formation because we are not in control of our beliefs.

**Hatcher, Donald L**. Landmarks in Critical Thinking Series: Plato's "Meno": A Model for Critical Thinkers. *Inquiry (USA)*, 16(1), 1-8, Fall 96.

This paper argues that of all the Platonic dialogues, the "Memo" is ideal for teaching students ideas fundamental to critical thinking: the importance of clear definition, or giving reasons to support ideas, or analyzing complex problems into simple elements and using a hypothetico-deductive method to test our ideas, e.g., offer a hypothesis and then see what observable consequences should follow. If the consequences do not follow, then the hypothesis should be revised.

**Hatcher, Donald L**. Should Anti-Realists Teach Critical Thinking?. *Inquiry (USA)*, 14(4), 29-35, Sum 95.

This paper argues that the goals of critical thinking are incompatible with the postmodern antirealist views of knowledge. Critical evaluation of beliefs by a community of inquires requires that we at least postulate objective standards of rationality. Pedagogically, asking students to evaluate the rationality of alternatives assumes that some views are closer to the truth than others.

**Hatfield, Gary** (ed & trans) and Kant, Immanuel. *Prolegomena to Any Future Metaphysics*. New York, Cambridge Univ Pr, 1997.

This new translation, the first in nearly fifty years, presents Kant's thought with special attention to the original sentence structure and vocabulary. The volume is intended for student use. It includes selections from the *Critique of Pure Reason*, which fill out some of Kant's arguments and in which Kant introduces some special terminology. Included also are a historical and philosophical introduction, explanatory notes, a chronology, a guide to further reading and a detailed index.

**Hatzimoysis, Anthony**. Ontology and Axiology. *Philosophy*, 72(280), 293-296, Ap 97.

**Haucke, Kai**. Hegels Theorie des spekulativen Satzes in der Vorrede zur *Phänomenologie des Geistes*. *Prima Philosophia*, 10(1), 43-75, 1997.

**Hauerwas, Stanley** and Pinches, Charles. Practicing Patience: How Christians Should Be Sick. *Christian Bioethics*, 2(2), 202-221, Ag 96.

In contemporary society nothing upsets us more than having to wait for our bodies. Our bodies serve us as we direct and when they break down we become angry that they have failed us. Christians, however, are called to be patient people even in illness. Indeed, impatience is a sin. Learning to be patient when sick requires practicing patience while healthy. First, we must learn that our bodies are finite—they will die. Second, we must learn to live with one another in patience as Christians with the love that the presence of others can and does create in us. Third, in life there is time for the acquisition of habits that come from worthy activities that require time and force us to take first one step and then another. In patience one can live with God.

**Haug, Frigga**. Das neoliberale Projekt, der männliche Arbeitsbegriff und die fällige Erneuerung des Geschlechtervertrags. *Das Argument*, 217(5-6), 683-695, 1996.

The ambivalence of the concept of work contributes to the blockages which appear in disputes about the crisis of a society based on work. This concept is fundamentally "masculine" and the absence of resistance to the neoliberal project is tied up with this masculinity. Thus, revision of the gender contract must play a role in the discussion of a new social contract if progressive social transformation is to have a chance in the neoliberal world.

**Haug, Wolfgang Fritz**. Aussichten der Zivilgesellschaft unter Bedingungen neoliberaler Globalisierungspolitik. *Das Argument*, 217(5-6), 665-682, 1996.

Historically, the utopian core of discourses of civil society has been the idea of participatory regulation. Today, deregulation and the dismantling of welfare states are eroding civil society and political culture. Neoliberal globalization strips the idea of civil society of content by economically devaluing national citizenship, thereby endangering liberal democracy, which still has no foothold outside of the nation-state. Neoliberalism has socially devastated Chiapas, Mexico, but new models of participatory politics have also emerged in the Zapatista revolution which has broken with Latin American guerrilla militarism as well as with Bolshevist vanguardism and its centralist and status understanding of power.

**Haugaard, Mark**. The Consensual Basis of Conflictual Power: A Critical Response to "Using Power, Fighting Power" by Jane Mansbridge. *Constellations*, 3(3), 401-406, Ja 97.

In this article it is argued that power takes three forms: consensual, conflictual based upon structural consensus, and conflictual based upon coercion. It is the second category of power (conflictual based upon structural consensus) that is frequently ignored by political theorists including Jane Mansbridge ("Using Power, Fighting Power," *Constellations*, 1994). While it is still the case that

modern states have coercive resources at their disposal, consensually based conflictual power is central to conflict within democratic societies. Usually minorities consent to conflictual outcomes, they are not coerced into them—a fact which has important implications for democratic theory.

**Haugeland, John** (ed). *Mind Design II: Philosophy, Psychology, Artificial Intelligence*. Cambridge, MIT Pr, 1997.

Mind design is the endeavor to understand mind (thinking, intellect) in terms of its design (how it is built, how it works). Unlike traditional empirical psychology, it is more oriented toward the "how" than the "what." An experiment in mind design is more likely to be an attempt to build something and make it work—as in artificial intelligence—than to observe or analyze what already exists. Mind design is psychology by reverse engineering. When *Mind Design* was first published in 1981, it became a classic in the then nascent fields of cognitive science and AI. This second edition retains four landmark essays from the first, adding to them one earlier milestone (Turing's "Computing Machinery and Intelligence") and eleven more recent articles about connectionism, dynamical systems, and symbolic versus nonsymbolic models. The contributors are divided about evenly between philosophers and scientists. Yet all are "philosophical" in that they address fundamental issues and concepts; and all are "scientific" in that they are technically sophisticated and concerned with concrete empirical research. (publisher, edited)

**Haught, Christine Ann** and Slaman, Theodore A. Automorphisms in the *PTIME*-Turing Degrees of Recursive Sets. *Annals Pure Applied Log*, 84(1), 139-152, Mr 97.

**Haught, James A**. *2000 Years of Disbelief: Famous People with the Courage to Doubt*. Amherst, Prometheus, 1996.

*2,000 Years of Disbelief* is a book of quotes that brings together the words of the "greats" of both East and West, from antiquity to the present. Included in this stirring collection are such renowned skeptics as Epicurus, Voltaire, Arthur Schopenhauer, Mark Twain and Bertrand Russell. But also represented are many whose skepticism is not so well-known and who are for this reason regarded by churchmen and others as conventional believers. Notable among these are many U.S. presidents. Thus we learn, for example, that George Washington had no belief in Christianity and that Abraham Lincoln never joined a church. (publisher, edited)

**Hauksson, Thorleifur**. Man as Wolf (Once More). *Dan Yrbk Phil*, 31, 107-110, 1996.

An interesting example of a metaphor of the outlaw as a wolf is to be found in the oldest Icelandic law-collection, parts of which are known to have existed in written form in the beginning of the twelfth century. This, together with related examples, is examined with reference to Max Black's discussion of the wolf-metaphor. The Note is meant as a contribution to the debate of whether metaphors exploit already existing similarities or rather create them.

**Hauptman, Robert**. Cyberethics and Social Stability. *Ethics Behavior*, 6(2), 161-163, 1996.

The computer has had an extraordinary influence on the ways in which human beings do things. Nevertheless, it is not necessary to reorient ethical thinking because traditional systems allow for the new or unusual interactions that may occur in a technological age. That some people contravene what heretofore has been considered acceptable behavior and that others emulate them is no warrant for reconstructing ethical systems. What is required in a networked environment is to shift the emphasis from "netiquette" to ethics and to be wary of the forces that inevitably will appear in order to control the anarchic nature of cyberspace.

**Hauser, Joshua M** and Fischbach, Ruth L and Kleefield, Sharon F (& others). Minority Populations and Advance Directives: Insights from a Focus Group Methodology. *Cambridge Quart Healthcare Ethics*, 6(1), 58-71, Winter 97.

Motivated by the significantly lower prevalence of advance directives among African-American and Hispanic patients at one urban teaching hospital (18% for Caucasians, 4% for African-Americans, and 2% for Hispanics), we used a focus group methodology to examine ways in which diverse populations of patients view the medical, philosophical, and practical issues surrounding advance directives. Our premise was that African-American and Hispanic populations who have higher rates of morbidity and mortality across numerous disease categories, and historically have had limited access to care and opportunities to discuss health concerns, may be more suspicious about the right of autonomy that an advance directive is designed to ensure. Our premise was supported by our data.

**Hauser, Kai** and Hjorth, Greg. Strong Cardinals in the Core Model. *Annals Pure Applied Log*, 83(2), 165-198, Ja 97.

We work with Steel's core model under the assumption that there is no inner class model for a Woodin cardinal. We also show in ZFC that set forcing cannot create class models with a given number of strongs. (edited)

**Hauser, Larry**. Searle's Chinese Box: Debunking the Chinese Room Argument. *Mind Mach*, 7(2), 199-226, My 97.

John Searle's Chinese room argument is perhaps the most influential and widely cited argument against artificial intelligence (AI). Understood as targeting AI proper—claims that computers can *think* or *do think*—Searle's argument, despite its *rhetorical* flash, is *logically* and *scientifically* a dud. Advertised as effective against AI proper, the argument, in its main outlines, is an *ignoratio elenchi*. It musters persuasive force fallaciously by indirection fostered by equivocal deployment of the phrase "strong AI" and reinforced by equivocation on the phrase "'causal powers' (at least) equal to those brains." On a more carefully crafted understanding—understood just to target *metaphysical identification* of thought with computational ("functionalism" or "computationalism") and not AI proper the argument is *still unsound*, though more interestingly so. (edited)

**Hausheer, Roger**. "Three Major Originators of the Concept of *Verstehen*: Vico, Herder, Schleiermacher" in *Verstehen and Humane Understanding*, O'Hear, Anthony (ed), 47-72. New York, Cambridge Univ Pr, 1996.

**Hausman, Alan** and Hausman, David B. *Descartes's Legacy: Minds and Meaning in Early Modern Philosophy*. Toronto, Univ of Toronto Pr, 1997.

We do not present the whole historical Descartes; what we hope to do is present the point of his enterprise—to set out the details of the logic of the problems that must be solved if we are to have knowledge of the world beyond our own ideas. It is for this reason that we believe that certain *current* problems in information theory can be used to elucidate early modern philosophy, and vice versa. Information-theoretic questions, especially as formulated by early functionalist philosophers, have a clarity and precision that, in our opinion, many isomorphic discussions in the history of philosophy have heretofore lacked. If some see, in importing such current terminology, merely a rehash of what has gone on long before, we think it is because the new vocabulary has so swiftly insinuated itself into current thinking. What has not been provided, and what we hope this book does provide, is an essential linkage between the old and the new. (publisher)

**Hausman, Carl R**. "Charles Peirce and the Origin of Interpretation" in *The Rule of Reason: The Philosophy of Charles Sanders Peirce*, Forster, Paul (ed), 185-200. Toronto, Univ of Toronto Pr, 1997.

**Hausman, Carl R**. *Charles S. Peirce's Evolutionary Philosophy*. New York, Cambridge Univ Pr, 1997.

This book is a systematic introduction to the philosophy of Charles S. Peirce. It focuses on four of Peirce's fundamental conceptions: pragmatism and Peirce's development of it into what he called *pragmaticism*; his theory of signs; his phenomenology; and his theory that continuity is of prime importance for philosophy. The author argues that at the center of Peirce's philosophical project is a unique form of metaphysical realism, whereby both continuity and evolutionary change are necessary for our understanding of experience. In his final chapter Professor Hausman applies this version of realism to current controversies between antirealists and anti-idealists. Peirce's views are compared with those of such present-day figures as Davidson, Putnam, and Rorty. The book will be of particular interest to philosophers concerned with classical American philosophy and with the relation of pragmatism to current debates on realism, as well as to linguists working in semiotics.

**Hausman, Daniel**. Economics as Separate and Inexact. *Econ Phil*, 12(1), 207-220, Ap 96.

This essay is a reply to criticisms of *The Inexact and Separate Science of Economics* offered by Frank Hahn and David Miller. In reply to Hahn it argues that it is useful to regard orthodox economics as a separate science and its theories as inexact. Against Miller (and Popper) it argues that confirmation is crucial in science because confirmation provides reason to believe that claims are reliable and in some cases true.

**Hausman, Daniel**. The Impossibility of Interpersonal Utility. *Mind*, 106(421), 99-100, Ja 97.

**Hausman, David B** and Hausman, Alan. *Descartes's Legacy: Minds and Meaning in Early Modern Philosophy*. Toronto, Univ of Toronto Pr, 1997.

We do not present the whole historical Descartes; what we hope to do is present the point of his enterprise—to set out the details of the logic of the problems that must be solved if we are to have knowledge of the world beyond our own ideas. It is for this reason that we believe that certain *current* problems in information theory can be used to elucidate early modern philosophy, and vice versa. Information-theoretic questions, especially as formulated by early functionalist philosophers, have a clarity and precision that, in our opinion, many isomorphic discussions in the history of philosophy have heretofore lacked. If some see, in importing such current terminology, merely a rehash of what has gone on long before, we think it is because the new vocabulary has so swiftly insinuated itself into current thinking. What has not been provided, and what we hope this book does provide, is an essential linkage between the old and the new. (publisher)

**Hawkins, Benjamin S**. "Peirce and Russell: The History of a Neglected 'Controversy'" in *Studies in the Logic of Charles Sanders Peirce*, Houser, Nathan (ed), 111-146. Bloomington, Indiana Univ Pr, 1997.

**Haya Segovia, Fernando**. Totalidad y causalidad en Polo. *Anu Filosof*, 29(2), 709-720, 1996.

L. Polo's doctrine of the first principles is analyzed focusing the study on causality as an indicator of the transcendentality of being and of its real distinction regarding essence. The concept of totality has its origins in the nonrealization of transcendental value of causality.

**Hayden, Patrick**. Gilles Deleuze and Naturalism: A Convergence with Ecological Theory and Politics. *Environ Ethics*, 19(2), 185-204, Sum 97.

Some philosophers in recent discussions concerned with current ecological crises have attempted to address and sometimes to utilize poststructuralist thought. Yet few of their studies have delineated the ecological orientation of a specific poststructuralist. In this paper, I provide a discussion of the naturalistic ontology embraced by the contemporary French philosopher Gilles Deleuze, one of the most significant voices in poststructuralism. I interpret Deleuze as holding an ecologically informed perspective that emphasizes the human place within nature while encouraging awareness of and respect for the differences of interconnected life on the planet. I also suggest that this view may be joined with Deleuze's innovative ethical-political approach, which he refers to as

micropolitics, to create new ways of thinking and feeling that support social and political transformation with respect to the flourishing of ecological diversity. Finally, I briefly show how Deleuze's ecological orientation compares to several versions of ecological theory and politics.

**Hayes, Tom**. Diggers, Ranters, and Women Prophets: The Discourse of Madness and the Cartesian *Cogito* in Seventeenth-Century England. *Clio*, 26(1), 29-50, Fall 96.

**Hayes III, FLoyd W**. "The Concept of Double Vision in Richard Wright's *The Outsider*" in *Existence in Black: An Anthology of Black Existential Philosophy*, Gordon, Lewis R (ed), 173-183. New York, Routledge, 1997.

Focusing on Richard Wright's novel, *The Outsider*, this essay examines the character of black subjective alienation in an American society experiencing change and challenge. Much of the critical discussion of the novel has centered on the existential condition of Kierkegaardian dread as the central organizing concept of the work. Although attentive to this perspective, the present essay slightly, shifts emphasis and investigates Wright's use of the concept of double vision. It will be argued that Wright's complex and fragmented construction of black subjectivity positions him within the historical transition between modernity and postmodernity.

**Hayling Fonseca, Annie**. Relectura heideggeriana de Kant: el tiempo como horizonte ontológico y posibilidad de la metafísica. *Rev Filosof (Costa Rica)*, 34(83-84), 311-322, D 96.

This article restates the role that time plays in the thematic background of *Critique of Pure Reason* from the Heideggerian interpretation of these works as a foundation of ontological knowledge and, therefore, of metaphysics. The fundamental basis of the analysis is time as an ontological horizon and its relationship to transcendental imagination, which is the root of sensibility and understanding, and the possibility of the originating unity of ontological synthesis.

**Haynes, Richard P**. The Muddled Middle: The Search for Ethical Principles to Regulate the Use of Animals in Research. *Between Species*, 12(1-2), 19-33, Wint-Spr 96.

Federally mandated animal care committees (IACUCs), who regulate the use of nonhuman animals in research, should use ethical principles drawn from their analogue, Institutional Review Boards (IRBs), that is required to regulate the use of humans in research. Animal consent can be constructed. Both current bioethicists who propose a "middle position" regarding the use of animals in research and animal liberation theorists like Regan and Singer make the same fatal error in proposing Utopian unsituated ethical theories as models for regulation. These theories can and do function to justify using animals rather than to regulate how and when they can be used.

**Hayward, Michael B** and Hadley, Robert F. Strong Semantic Systematicity from Hebbian Connectionist Learning. *Mind Mach*, 7(1), 1-37, F 97.

Herein we describe a network which displays strong semantic systematicity in response to Hebbian, connectionist training. During training, two-thirds of all nouns are presented only in a single syntactic position (either as grammatical subject or object). Yet, during testing, the network correctly interprets thousands of sentences containing those nouns in novel positions. In addition, the network generalizes to novel levels of embedding. Successful training requires a corpus of about 1000 sentences and network training is quite rapid. The architecture and learning algorithms are purely connectionist, but 'classical' insights are discernible in one respect, viz. that complex semantic representations spatially contain their semantic constituents. However, in other important respects, the architecture is distinctly nonclassical. (edited)

**Hayward, Tim**. Anthropocentrism: A Misunderstood Problem. *Environ Values*, 6(1), 49-63, F 97.

Anthropocentrism can intelligibly be criticized as an ontological error, be attempts to conceive of it as an ethical error are liable to conceptual and practical confusion. After noting the paradox that the clearest instances of overcoming anthropocentrism involve precisely the sort of objectivating knowledge which many ecological critics see as itself archetypically anthropocentric, the article presents the following arguments: there are some ways in which anthropocentrism is not objectionable; the defects associated with anthropocentrism in ethics are better understood as instances of speciesism and human chauvinism; it is unhelpful to call these defects anthropocentrism because there is an ineliminable element of anthropocentrism in any ethic at all; moreover, because the defects do not typically involve a concern with human interests as such, the rhetoric of antianthropocentrism is counterproductive in practice.

**Hazen, A P**. Actualism Again. *Phil Stud*, 84(2-3), 155-181, D 96.

Many people who call themselves actualists don't like Lewis's use of "counterparts" in intentional semantics, but actualism and anticounterpart theoreticism are logically independent positions. I give an actualistically acceptable semantics of modality that makes use of a generalization of the notion of a counterpart and ideas Lewis classifies as "linguistic ersatzism." The details are ugly, but I gain insight into the relation between semantic and metaphysical issues from the exercise.

**Headley, Clevis R**. Existential Phenomenology and the Problem of Race: A Critical Assessment of Lewis Gordon's *Bad Faith and Antiblack Racism*. *Phil Today*, 41(2), 334-345, Sum 97.

**Heal, Jane**. Simulation and Cognitive Penetrability. *Mind Lang*, 11(1), 44-67, Mr 96.

Stich, Nichols et al. assert that the process of deriving predictions by simulation must be cognitively impenetrable. Hence, they claim, the occurrence of certain errors in prediction provides empirical evidence against simulation theory. But it is false that simulation-derived prediction must be cognitively impenetrable. Moreover the errors they cite, which are instances of irrationality, are not evidence against the (very defensible) version of simulation theory that takes the central domain of simulation to be intelligible transitions between states with content.

**Healey, Richard**. Nonlocality and the Aharonov-Bohm Effect. *Phil Sci*, 64(1), 18-41, Mr 97.

At first sight the Aharonov-Bohm effect appears nonlocal, though not in the way EPR/Bell correlations are generally acknowledged to be nonlocal. This paper applies an analysis of nonlocality to the Aharonov-Bohm effect to show that its peculiarities may be blamed either on a failure of a principle of local action or on a failure of a principle of separability. Different interpretations of quantum mechanics disagree on how blame should be allocated. The parallel between the Aharonov-Bohm effect and violations of Bell inequalities turns out to be so close that a balanced assessment of the nature and significance of quantum nonlocality requires a detailed study of both effects.

**Heath, Joseph**. A Multi-Stage Game Model of Morals by Agreement. *Dialogue (Canada)*, 35(3), 529-552, Sum 96.

David Gauthier's claim that rational agents would choose to become "constrained maximizers" by adopting a special choice disposition suggests that they are concerned about the outcome of their actions for a series of future interactions. Unfortunately, he models this choice problem as a set of discrete one-shot games, when it should be represented as a decentralized multistage game. But in a multistage game, rational agents are able to secure cooperation without the need for any special choice disposition. This suggests that Gauthier's introduction of constrained maximization is merely an artifact of his failure to model the relevant decision problem correctly.

**Heath, Joseph**. Foundationalism and Practical Reason. *Mind*, 106(423), 451-473, Jl 97.

In this paper, I argue that Humean theories of moral motivation appear preferable to Kantian approaches only if one assumes a broadly foundationalist conception of rational justification. Like foundationalist approaches to justification generally, Humean psychology aims to counter the regress-of-justification argument by positing a set of ultimate regress-stoppers—in this case, unmotivated desires. If the need for regress-stoppers of this type in the realm of practical deliberation is accepted, desires do indeed appear to be the most likely candidate. But if this foundationalist strategy is rejected, there is no longer any reason to suppose that all motivation must be traceable to some extrarational incentive. This clears the way for a rehabilitation of the Kantian claim that reasons for action can take the form of categorical imperatives. (edited)

**Heath, Peter** (ed & trans) and Schneewind, J B (ed). *Lectures on Ethics*. New York, Cambridge Univ Pr, 1997.

The purpose of the Cambridge Edition is to offer translations of the best modern German edition of Kant's work in a uniform format suitable for Kant scholars. When complete (fourteen volumes are currently envisaged), the edition will include all of Kant's published writings and a generous selection of his unpublished writings such as the *Opus postumum, Handschriftliche Nachlass*, lectures, and correspondence. This volume contains four versions of the lecture notes taken by Kant's students in his university courses in ethics given regularly over a period of some thirty years. The notes are very comprehensive and expound not only Kant's views on ethics but many of his opinions on life and human nature as well. Much of this material has never before been translated into English. As in other volumes in the series, there are copious linguistic and explanatory notes and a glossary of key terms.

**Heavner, Eric K**. Malthus and the Secularization of Political Ideology. *Hist Polit Thought*, 17(3), 408-430, Autumn 96.

**Heberle, Renee**. Deconstructive Strategies and the Movement Against Sexual Violence. *Hypatia*, 11(4), 63-76, Fall 96.

This essay considers the social effects of the strategy of "speaking out" about sexual violence to transform rape culture. I articulate the paradox that women's identification as victims in the public sphere reinscribes the gendered norms that enable the victimization of women. I suggest we create a more diversified public narrative of sexual violence and sexuality within the context of the movement against sexual violence in order to deconstruct masculinist power in feminine victimization.

**Hébert, Michel**. Syntactic Characterizations of Closure under Pullbacks and of Locally Polypresentable Categories. *Annals Pure Applied Log*, 84(1), 73-95, Mr 97.

We give syntactic characterizations of 1) the (finitary) theories whose categories of models we closed under the formation of pullbacks, and of 2) (its categorical counterpart) the locally omega-polypresentable categories. A somewhat typical example is the category of algebraically closed fields. Case 1) is proved by classical model-theoretic methods; it solves a problem raised by H. Volger (with motivations from the theory of abstract data types). The solution of case 2) is in the spirit of the ones for the locally omega-presentable and omega-multipresentable cases found by M. Coste and P.T. Johnstone respectively. The problem 2) was raised in the context of *domain theory* by F. Lamarche.

**Heck Jr, Richard G**. "Definition by Induction in Frege's *Grundgesetze der Arithmetik*" in *Frege: Importance and Legacy*, Schirn, Matthias (ed), 200-233. Hawthorne, de Gruyter, 1996.

**Hedman, Carl**. Progressive and Regressive Uses of Reasonable Distrust. *J Soc Phil*, 28(1), 87-100, Spr 97.

After noting that those who are nonprivileged on racial, sexual or economic dimensions often have good reasons for distrusting white, economically-

privileged males, it is suggested that the various nonprivileged constituencies focus on different aspects of white, middle-class male privilege. It is concluded that while this specialization in distrust allows the super-privileged to preserve their position via divide and conquer maneuvers, it also has the potential to provide the basis for a coalition that attacks the super-privileged from all angels much as a gunnery crew triangulates its target by sighting it from various locations.

**Heesch, Matthias**. Religionsphilosophische Aspekte im Denken Husserls. *Theol Phil*, 72(1), 77-90, 1997.

E. Husserl intends a theory concerning the origins of phenomena. Therefore, he develops a theory of mind and its objects: Things come into existence when becoming phenomena. But if everything exists due to its appearance for mind, mind itself has to be described as a phenomenon. This means, that there must be a transcendental mind to which empirical mind appears. Every empirical mind depends on this relation towards the transcendental mind. Husserl calls this transcendental mind God, but he doesn't make clear, how anything about God as the transcendental subject could be known.

**Heesen, Berrie**. European Children Thinking Together in 100. *Thinking*, 13(2), 27-29, 1997.

**Heffernan, George**. An Essay in Epistemic Kuklophobia: Husserl's Critique of Descartes' Conception of Evidence. *Husserl Stud*, 13(2), 89-140, 1996-97.

**Hegel, G W F**. "Chi pensa astratto? traduzione e commento di Franca Mastromatteo e Leonardo Paganelli" in *Hegel e Aristotele,* Ferrarin, A, 403-416. Cagliari, Edizioni AV, 1997.

**Hegselmann, Rainer**. "Glaucons Herausforderung: Was ist Motiv und Lohn der Tugend?" in *Das weite Spektrum der analytischen Philosophie*, Lenzen, Wolfgang, 76-94. Hawthorne, de Gruyter, 1997.

The article analyses strategies to answer the question why to be moral. Contrary to some other reactions it is argued that this question should be taken as a non trivial and serious question. In a first step it is demonstrated by a functional analyses that all are better off if all have moral dispositions. Since there is a free riding problem that is no reason to become a moral agent. In a second step it is shown that agents with moral disposition are in a quite good position if they could confine their moral way of acting to those which act morally themselves.

**Heide, Gale Z**. The Nascent Noeticism of Narrative Theology: An Examination of the Relationship between Narrative and Metaphysics in Nicholas Lash. *Mod Theol*, 12(4), 459-481, O 96.

Taking into account Nicholas Lash's distrust of the foundations for most systematic theology and his affinity for a narrative epistemology, this article attempts to examine the plausibility of doing theology from a more strictly narrative framework. Lash's own method exemplifies a trend within many narrative theologians to use the retelling of the Christian story throughout history as a hermeneutical conscience for narrative construction. However, the narrative epistemology Lash develops appears to suffer from the same problems he attributes to systematic theology, prompting the question, "Is narrative theology still systematic?"

**Heidegger, Martin**. *Der Deutsche Idealismus (Fichte, Schelling, Hegel) und die philosophische Problemlage der Gegenwart*. Frankfurt/M, Klostermann, 1997.

Zur ersten Veröffentlichung gelangt Heideggers Vorlesungsausarbeitung für das Sommersemester 1929. Im Kern handelt es sich um eine Fichte-Vorlesung. Ausführlich interpretiert wird die Darstellung der drei Grundsätze der "Wissenschaftslehre" von 1794, sodann die Grundlagen des theoretischen Wissens und der Wissenschaft des Praktischen. Nach einer kurzen Zwischenbetrachtung über Schelling folgt als Einstieg in die Hegelsche Philosophie die Diskussion der "Differenzschrift". Abschliessend wird das Anfangsproblem in der Hegelschen Logik behandelt. (publisher,edited)

**Heidegger, Martin**. *Der Satz vom Grund*. Frankfurt/M, Klostermann, 1997.

Die Vorlesung *Der Satz vom Grund* wurde im Wintersemester 1955/56 von Martin Heidegger an der Freiburger Universität gehalten und 1957 im Verlag Günther Neske, Pfullingen, veröffentlicht. Dem unveränderten Vorlesungtext fügte Martin Heidegger damals für das Buch den am 25. Mai 1956 im Club zu Bremen gehaltenen und am 24. Oktober 1956 an der Universität Wien wiederholten Vortrag gleichen Titels bei. Der hier wiederabgedruckte, durchgesehene Text folgt der Heideggerschen Erstausgabe und ergänzt lediglich Randbemerkungen aus dem Handexemplar Heideggers. Heideggers Nachdenken über den *Satz vom Grund* weist diesen nicht nur als eine Aussage über das Seiende auf, sondern als ein Sagen vom Sein: Grund und Sein (*sind*) das Selbe. Der Anspruch dieses obersten Grundsatzes über das Seiende verdankt sich—seinsgeschichtlich gedacht—dem Entzug des Seins.

**Heidegger, Martin**. *Gesamtausgabe II. Abteilung: Vorlesungen (Band 27: Einleitung in die Philosophie)*. Frankfurt/M, Klostermann, 1996.

Die in diesem Band erstmals veröffentliche Vorlesung "Einleitung in die Philosophie: hielt Martin Heidegger im Wintersemester 1928/29 vierstündig an der Universität Freiburg. Der beabsichtige "Gang" der Einleitung umfasste drei Stadien bzw. Wege: "Philosophie und Wissenschaft", "Philosophie und Weltanschauung", "Philosophie und Geschichte". Der zweite Abschnitt gewann an Umfang durch eine eingehende Erörterung des Weltbegriffs von Kant, während der dritte Abschnitt "Philosophie und Geschichte" nicht zur Ausführung kam. (edited)

**Heidegger, Martin** and Borges-Duarte, Irene (trans). Carta al Padre William Richardson. *An Seminar Hist Filosof*, 13, 11-18, 1996.

**Heidegger, Martin** and Taft, Richard (trans). *Kant and the Problem of Metaphysics*. Bloomington, Indiana Univ Pr, 1997.

**Heidl, György**. Origen and Augustin on the *Hexaemeron* (in Czech). *Magyar Filozof Szemle*, 1-2, 115-152, 1997.

This paper is an attempt to prove that Augustine's interpretation of the six days of creation in his *De genesi contra manichaeos* directly depends on Origen's first homily on Genesis. Arguments for this thesis are based on a textual comparison of Augustine's commentary and Origen's homily. The literal and doctrinal parallels between the works in question indicate that Augustine had not simply heard about, as scholars generally think, the Origenian understanding of Genesis, but he had read the homily translated into Latin by Rufinus. (edited)

**Heidl, György**. Origen's First Homily on the Book of Genesis (in Hungarian). *Magyar Filozof Szemle*, 1-2, 337-354, 1997.

**Heidl, György**. Saint Augustin: Christian Struggle (in Hungarian). *Magyar Filozof Szemle*, 1-2, 356-382, 1997.

**Heil, John**. The Propositional Attitudes. *Protosoz*, 8/9, 53-67, 1996.

Traditionally conceived, rational action is action founded on reasons. Reasons involve the propositional attitudes—beliefs, desires, intentions, and the like. What are we to make of the propositional attitudes? One possibility, a possibility endorsed by Donald Davidson, is that an agent's possession of propositional attitudes is a matter of that agent's being interpretable in a particular way. Such a view accounts for the propositional content of the attitudes, but threatens to undercut their causal and explanatory roles. I examine Davidson's view and the suggestion that the explanatory value of appeals to propositional attitudes is best understood on analogy with measurement systems, and argue that, appearances to the contrary, this conception of the propositional attitudes can be reconciled with the idea that reasons are causes.

**Heilig, Steve**. Rebecca Reichmann on Womens' Health and Reproductive Rights in Brazil. *Cambridge Quart Healthcare Ethics*, 5(4), 579-581, Fall 96.

**Heilke, Thomas**. Nietzsche's Impatience: The Spiritual Necessities of Nietzsche's Politics. *Interpretation*, 24(2), 201-231, Wint 97.

**Heilke, Thomas**. On Being Ethical Without Moral Sadism: Two Readings of Augustine and the Beginnings of the Anabaptist Revolution. *Polit Theory*, 24(3), 493-517, Ag 96.

**Heilman, Madeline E**. Sex Discrimination and the Affirmative Action Remedy: The Role of Sex Stereotypes. *J Bus Ethics*, 16(9), 877-889, Je 97.

This paper explores the psychological phenomena of sex stereotypes and their consequences for the occurrence of sex discrimination in work settings. Differential conceptions of the attributes of women and men are shown to extend to women and men managers and the lack of fit model is used to explain how stereotypes about women can detrimentally affect their career progress. Commonly-occurring organizational conditions which facilitate the use of stereotypes in personnel decision making are identified and, lastly, data are provided demonstrating the way in which affirmative action programs and practices can act to promote the stereotyping of women. (edited)

**Heim, S Mark**. Orientational Pluralism in Religion. *Faith Phil*, 13(2), 201-215, AP 96.

Nicholas Rescher has advanced an account of philosophy which he calls orientational pluralism. It addresses the tension in philosophy between commitment to rational argument and the enduring lack of resolution of major issues. This article suggests that Rescher's view can be fruitfully transposed into a discussion of religious pluralism, illuminating the *status* of theories about religious diversity and providing grounds both for recognizing the legitimacy of diverse religious convictions and making a consistent argument in favor of one's own.

**Heinämaa, Sara**. What is a Woman? Butler and Beauvoir on the Foundations of the Sexual Difference. *Hypatia*, 12(1), 20-39, Wint 97.

The aim of this paper is to show that Simone de Beauvoir's *The Second Sex* has been mistakenly interpreted as a theory of gender, because interpreters have failed adequately to understand Beauvoir's aims. Beauvoir is not trying to explain facts, events, or states of affairs, but to reveal, unveil, or uncover (*découvrir*) meanings. She explicates the meanings of woman, female and feminine. Instead of a theory, Beauvoir's book presents a phenomenological description of the sexual difference.

**Heinz, Marion**. Die Fichte-Rezeption in der südwestdeutschen Schule des Neukantianismus. *Fichte-Studien*, 13, 109-129, 1997.

The purpose of this essay is to give an outline of the Fichte reception in southwest German neo-Kantianism. According to Rickert, Fichte's position marked a progression in relation to the philosophy of Kant in reference to the theory of the primacy of practical reason. Rickert maintains a close relationship to this Fichtean theory in his own philosophy of value. Even more important for the philosophy of the 20th century was Lask's interpretation of Fichte which included a critique of Rickert's philosophical programm. The center of Lask's Fichte reception lies in his concept of "Wertindividualität". According to Lask, Fichte succeeded in finding a method for analysing or conceptualising this topic.

**Hekman, Susan J** (ed). *Feminist Interpretations of Michel Foucault*. University Park, Pennsylvania Univ Pr, 1996.

Foucault's approach has raised serious questions about an equally crucial area of feminist thought—politics. Some feminist critics of Foucault have argued that his deconstruction of the concept "woman" also deconstructs the possibility of a feminist politics. Several essays explore the implications of this deconstruction for feminist politics and suggest that a Foucauldian feminist politics is not viable. Overall, this collection illustrates the range of interest Foucault's thought has generated among feminist thinkers and both the advantages and liabilities of his approach for the development of feminist theory and politics. (publisher, edited)

**Held, Klaus**. "Civic Prudence in Machiavelli: Toward the Paradigm Transformation in Philosophy in the Transition to Modernity" in *The Ancients and the Moderns*, Lilly, Reginald (ed), 115-129. Bloomington, Indiana Univ Pr, 1996.

**Held, Klaus**. Authentic Existence and the Political World. *Res Phenomenol*, 26, 38-53, 1996.

**Held, Klaus**. World, Emptiness, Nothingness: A Phenomenological Approach to the Religious Tradition of Japan. *Human Stud*, 20(2), 153-167, Ap 97.

**Held, Virginia**. Moral Prejudices: Essays on Ethics. *Phil Phenomenol Res*, 57(3), 703-707, S 97.

**Heldke, Lisa**. In Praise of Unreliability. *Hypatia*, 12(3), 174-182, Sum 97.

Bisexuality challenges familiar assumptions about love, family, and sexual desire that are shared by both heterosexual and homosexual communities. In particular, it challenges the assumption that a person's desire can and should run in only one direction. Furthermore, bisexuality questions the legitimacy, rigidity, and presumed ontological priority of the categories "heterosexual" and "homosexual." Bisexuals are often assumed to be dishonest and unreliable. I suggest that dishonesty and unreliability can be resources for undermining normative sexualities.

**Hella, Lauri**. Almost Everywhere Equivalence of Logics in Finite Model Theory. *Bull Sym Log*, 2(4), 422-443, D 96.

We introduce a new framework for classifying logics on finite structures and studying their expressive power. This framework is based on the concept of *almost everywhere equivalence of logics*, that is to say, two logics having the same expressive power on a class of asymptotic measure 1. Moreover, we explore connections with descriptive complexity theory and examine the status of certain classical results of model theory in the context of this new framework. (edited)

**Hella, Lauri** and Luosto, Kerkko and Väänänen, Jouko. The Hierarchy Theorem for Generalized Quantifiers. *J Sym Log*, 61(3), 802-817, S 96.

The concept of a generalized quantifier of a given similarity type was defined in [12]. Our main result says that on finite structures different similarity types give rise to different classes of generalized quantifiers. More exactly, for every similarity type $t$ there is a generalized quantifier of type $t$ which is not definable in the extension of first order logic by all generalized quantifiers of type smaller than $t$. This was proved for unary similarity types by Per Lindström [17] with a counting argument. We extend his method to arbitrary similarity types.

**Hella, Lauri** and Väänänen, Jouko and Westerståhl, Dag. Definability of Polyadic Lifts of Generalized Quantifiers. *J Log Lang Info*, 6(3), 305-335, Jl 97.

**Heller, Agnes**. Parmenides and the Battle of Stalingrad. *Grad Fac Phil J*, 19/20(2/1), 247-262, 1997.

**Heller, Agnes**. Tragedy as the Form of Existence (in Hungarian). *Magyar Filozof Szemle*, 4-5-6, 325-337, 1996.

In his essay on the metaphysics of tragedy Lukács experimented with a new antimetaphysical conception of the tragedy. The individual tragic hero is presented here as the only embodiment of the Platonic idea. This attempt is radical, in so far as it eliminates history and historicity on the one hand, psychology on the other, furthermore because it annuls time and the continuity between everyday life and the tragic "nunc stans." The paper argues that the philosophy presented in this essay is suicidal and occupies the existential borderline situation of total unrepeatability. This situation is, however, not an exception but will become paradigmatic for the representative radical philosophy of our century (Heidegger and Wittgenstein as examples.)

**Heller, Mark**. Ersatz Worlds and Ontological Disagreement. *Acta Analytica*, 35-44, 1996.

This paper is an attempt to tie together two different ontological questions. Concerning physical objects, I have declared myself a friend of four-dimensionalism. Concerning possible worlds, I advocate linguistic ersatzism; worlds are abstract representations. One difficulty for four-dimensionalism is that there seem to be many equally good competing ontologies of physical objects. One difficulty for linguistic ersatzism is that implicit representation seems to require primitive modality. I answer the latter problem by emphasizing the role of linguistic conventions in representation. That in turn provides a response to the former problem—the apparent competitors are just translations of one another.

**Hellman, Geoffrey**. Quantum Mechanical Unbounded Operators and Constructive Mathematics—A Rejoinder to Bridges. *J Phil Log*, 26(2), 121-127, Ap 97.

As argued in Hellman (1993), the theorem of Pour-El and Richards (1983) can be seen *by the classicist* as limiting constructivist efforts to recover the mathematics for quantum mechanics. Although Bridges (1995) may be right that the constructivist would work with a different definition of 'closed operator', this does not affect my point that neither the classical unbounded operators standardly recognized in quantum mechanics nor their restrictions to constructive arguments are recognizable as objects by the constructivist. Constructive substitutes that may still be possible necessarily involve additional 'incompleteness' in the mathematical representation of quantum phenomena. Concerning a second line of reasoning in Hellman (1993), its import is that constructivist practice is consistent with a 'liberal' stance but not with a 'radical', verificationist philosophical position. Whether such a position is actually espoused by certain leading constructivists, they are invited to clarify.

**Helm, Bennett**. Freedom of the Heart. *Pac Phil Quart*, 77(2), 71-87, Je 96.

Philosophical accounts of freedom typically fail to capture an important kind of freedom—freedom to change what one cares about—that is central to our understanding of what it is to be a person. This paper articulates this kind of freedom more clearly, distinguishing it from freedom of action and freedom of the will and gives an account of how it is possible. Central to this account is an understanding of the role of emotions in determining what we value, thus motivating a rethinking of the importance of emotions in the mental lives of persons.

**Helting, Holger**. Aristotelische Intellekttheorie und die "Sohnesgeburt" bei Meister Eckehart. *Theol Phil*, 71(3), 370-389, 1996.

over the past decades, the influence of the Aristotelian theory of intellect on Eckehart's thought has been frequently pointed out in scholarship. Even though there is an undeniable influence with regard to Eckehart's conception of how the intellect comes to understand the things within the world, this paper tries to emphasize that there is a radical difference between the two thinkers when Eckehart refers to the intellect as the "son being born in the soul". The relation between the intellect and its origin can no longer be understood within the Aristotelian theory.

**Hemaspaandra, Edith**. The Price of Universality. *Notre Dame J Form Log*, 37(2), 174-203, Spr 96.

We investigate the effect on the complexity of adding the universal modality and the reflexive transitive closure modality to modal logics. From the examples in the literature, one might conjecture that adding the reflexive transitive closure modality is at least as hard as adding the universal modality and that adding either of these modalities to a multimodal logic where the modalities do not interact can only increase the complexity to *Exptime*-complete. We show that the first conjecture holds under reasonable assumptions and that, except for a number of special cases which we fully characterize, the hardness part of the second conjecture is true. However, the upper bound part of the second conjecture fails miserably. (edited)

**Hemmenway, Scott R**. Pedagogy in the Myth of Plato's *Statesman*: Body and Soul in Relation to Philosophy and Politics. *Hist Phil Quart*, 11(3), 253-268, Jl 94.

Because the young Socrates has presuppositions typical of a mathematician about the independence of the mind from the body, he has to be led to a fuller appreciation of the human soul, i.e., embodied intelligence, in order to understand statesmanship. The Eleatic Stranger thus tells a myth about an age where men age backwards, are born out of the earth, and are cared for by shepherd/gods. This affords the opportunity to think quite radically about how the body shapes the soul and thus affects not only physical life, but also theoretical life and consequently both politics and philosophy.

**Hemmo, Meir**. Possible Worlds in the Modal Interpretation. *Proc Phil Sci Ass*, 3(Suppl), S330-S337, 1996.

**Hemmo, Meir** and Bacciagaluppi, Guido. Modal Interpretations, Decoherence and Measurements. *Stud Hist Phil Mod Physics*, 27B(3), 239-277, S 96.

We address Albert and Loewer's criticism of nonideal measurements in the modal interpretation, by examining the implications of the theory of decoherence for the modal interpretation. In the models originally considered by Albert and Loewer, the inclusion of decoherence provides an answer to their criticism. New problems seem to arise in different models and in situations more general than measurements.

**Henderson, David**. Epistemic Rationality, Epistemic Motivation, and Interpretive Charity. *Protosoz*, 8/9, 4-29, 1996.

On what has become the received view of the principle of charity, it is a fundamental methodological constraint on interpretation that we find peoples' intentional states patterned in ways that are characterized by norms of rationality. This recommended use of normative principles of rationality to inform intentional description is epistemically unmotivated. To say that the received view lacks epistemic motivation is to say that to interpret as it recommends would be epistemically irresponsible and, in important respects irrational. On the alternative that I recommend, descriptive psychological generalization are what properly inform interpretation. One can readily understand the epistemic motivations for so interpreting, for they are the familiar reasons for informing description with background descriptive information. No parallel motivations for the received view seems possible.

**Hendrickson, David C**. In Defense of Realism: A Commentary on *Just and Unjust Wars*. *Ethics Int Affairs*, 11, 19-53, 1997.

A significant portion of Walzer's *Just and Unjust Wars* is an argument "against realism." While Hendrickson applauds Walzer for his examination of the just war tradition, he nevertheless asserts that Walzer has characterized the tradition of political realism in a misleading way. Not simply the moral atheism it is portrayed to be, realism recognizes the moral reality of war while emphasizing state security and independence as the most important factors for the protection of citizens and the continuity of the political community. Indeed, Hendrickson identifies many realist aspects of Walzer's own moral arguments. However, he takes issue with Walzer's treatment of intervention, self-determination and the legitimate aims of war, stating that Walzer's framework is exceedingly permissive and ambiguous in these areas. Hendrickson concludes that the use of such a just war theory may lead to significant problems in the post-Cold War world.

**Hendrickson, John** and Kloppenburg, Jr, Jack and Stevenson, G W. Coming in to the Foodshed. *Agr Human Values*, 13(3), 33-42, Sum 96.

Bioregionalists have championed the utility of the concept of the watershed as an organizing framework for thought and action directed to understanding and implementing appropriate and respectful human interaction with particular pieces of land. In a creative analogue to the watershed, permaculturist Arthur Getz has recently introduced the term "foodshed" to facilitate critical thought about where our food is coming from and how it is getting to us. We find the "foodshed" to be a particularly rich and evocative metaphor; but it is much more than metaphor. Like its analogue the watershed, the foodshed can serve us as a conceptual and methodological unit of analysis that provides a frame for action as well as thought. (edited)

**Hendriks, Ruud**. Van woorden en wekkers: Temporele ordening op een leefgroep voor autistische jongeren. *Kennis Methode*, 20(4), 319-346, 1996.

In getting along with mentally handicapped autistic youths, it cannot be taken for granted that the progress and order of events and phenomena are understood in a common language. Besides or instead of words material objects are continuously put to the fore in the local establishment of temporal order. First, I will address these issues from a familiar, interpretative point of view. Next, I will suggest that this does not question familiar, nonautistic concepts radically enough and explore a more estranging vocabulary drawing on actor-network theory. Thus I intend to contribute to the repertoire of words and images which can be used to discuss a desirable future geography of this practice.

**Hengelbrock, Jürgen**. "The Relationship between African and European Philosophers" in *Philosophy and Democracy in Intercultural Perspective*, Kimmerle, Heinz (ed), 57-67. Amsterdam, Rodopi, 1997.

For understanding our own cultural horizon it is important to look at it from an exterior point of view, offered by intercultural communication. The knowledge of different cultural and social backgrounds will help us to see our own familiar ideas and habits in a new light. There is nothing more dangerous than fixed habits of thinking—African people have learned to organize themselves in a life of cultural contradictions and they know how to profit from these. This experience is useful for us Germans who should become more cosmopolitan in a period of new migrations of peoples.

**Henkel, Jacqueline M**. *The Language of Criticism: Linguistic Models and Literary Theory*. Ithaca, Cornell Univ Pr, 1996.

Henkel places problems of interdisciplinary borrowing in the foreground. Paying particular attention to the character of the original linguistic models, she outlines the process by which critics first import a language theory, complete with limitations and internal contradictions, and then repudiate it when it fails to solve a range of literary problems. Henkel argues that such unresolved conflicts within the borrowed models, between disciplines, and between the original and recreated theories, mean that critical discourse remains entangled in terms and issues based in linguistics. But she also calls tensions internal to models of language necessary and she points to the often productive results of the misreadings that inevitably attend their movement from one field to another. (publisher,edited)

**Hennigfeld, Jochem**. Schellings Identitätssystem von 1801 und Fichtes Wissenschaftslehre. *Fichte-Studien*, 12, 235-246, 1997.

The essay shows in which way Schelling's "Identitätssystem" from 1801 picks up and develops Fichte's "Wissenschaftslehre" (1794/95). Though Schelling's new attempt may be explained on the background of Fichte's analysis, it is obvious that Schelling's 'construction' (i.e., representation of things in the divine absolute) breaks with critical transcendental idealism. Nevertheless, Schelling is convinced that Fichte will go the same way (on account of his "Bestimmmung des Menschen"). Finally, the treatise resumes Fichte's critical commentary (in the posthumous works) of Schelling's system.

**Henrich, Dieter** and Förster, Eckart (ed). *The Course of Remembrance and Other Essays on Hölderlin*. Stanford, Stanford Univ Pr, 1997.

This volume includes six of Henrich's most important essays on Hölderlin's philosophical significance. Among the topics discussed are Hölderlin's motivation and methodological orientation in his work on German idealism, the intellectual atmosphere of Hölderlin's student years and the philosophical problems that occupied him, Hölderlin's attitude toward any first-principle philosophy and the complex personal and philosophical relationships between Hegel and Hölderlin. The last essay is a long, detailed interpretation of one of Hölderlin's greatest poems, "Remembrance."(publisher,edited)

**Henrich, Dieter** and Zöller, Günter (trans). "Self-Consciousness and Speculative Thinking" in *Figuring the Self: Subject, Absolute, and Others in Classical German Philosophy*, Zöller, Günter (ed), 99-133. Albany, SUNY Pr, 1997.

**Henriques, Fernanda**. É legítimo o Uso da Literatura no Processo de Transmissao da Filosofia?. *Philosophica (Portugal)*, 145-167, 1997.

Ce travail cherche, d'une part, à légitimer théoriquement l'articulation entre Philosophie et Littérature, moyennant la compréhension du sens du rapport philosophie-non philosophie chez Paul Ricoeur; d'autre part, il cherche à montrer la fécondité de ce rapport, dans un mode de transmission de la Philosophie qui ait en considération la nature épistémologique de cette discipline et qui, donc, configure cette transmission comme le développement d'un dialogue entre libertés. (edited)

**Henry, Barbara**. Aspetti del dibattito italiano sulla cittadinanza. *Iride*, 10(20), 145-154, Ap 97.

**Henry, Paget**. "African and Afro-Caribbean Existential Philosophies" in *Existence in Black: An Anthology of Black Existential Philosophy*, Gordon, Lewis R (ed), 13-36. New York, Routledge, 1997.

**Henry, Paget**. Rastafarianism and the Reality of Dread"" in *Existence in Black: An Anthology of Black Existential Philosophy*, Gordon, Lewis R (ed), 157-164. New York, Routledge, 1997.

**Hepburn, Elizabeth R**. The Situated but Directionless Self: The Postmetaphysical World of Benhabib's Discourse Ethics. *J Applied Phil*, 14(1), 59-68, 1997.

Drawing on the work of Furgen Habermas, Seyla Benhabib has developed a system of communicative or discourse ethics. Her approach is said to respect differences and to count context as important but she also claims that it is postmetaphysical. I dispute this claim on two grounds. First, I argue that any system of ethics must be grounded by metaphysical commitments. Second, I show that in using elements of both Kantian and Aristotelian theory, Benhabib has imported metaphysical underpinnings into her theory and that these implicit understandings of what the moral enterprise is about, ought to be made explicit. Finally, a brief exploration of some contemporary ethical reflection and problem solving suggests that a shared metaphysical foundation is essential to ethical discourse.

**Hepburn, Ronald W**. "Data and Theory in Aesthetics: Philosophical Understanding and Misunderstanding" in *Verstehen and Humane Understanding*, O'Hear, Anthony (ed), 235-252. New York, Cambridge Univ Pr, 1996.

The paper considers two contrasted understandings of the data of aesthetics and of how aesthetics should relate itself to its data. By 'data', should we mean not only works of art and critical interpretations, but also a philosophical vision of man and the world? Can an aesthetic theory legitimately appraise trends in the arts themselves? Or, should aesthetics play a much humbler, more circumscribed role, deferring to, and conceptually mapping the work of artists and critics, accepting their authority in the sphere of the arts? The second half of the paper turns to aesthetic appreciation of nature and asks questions about data and understanding in the different but important context.

**Hepburn, Ronald W**. Landscape and the Metaphysical Imagination. *Environ Values*, 5(3), 191-204, Ag 96.

Aesthetic appreciation of landscape is by no means limited to the sensuous enjoyment of sights and sounds. It very often has a reflective, cognitive element as well. This sometimes incorporates scientific knowledge, e.g., geological or ecological; but it can also manifest what this article will call 'metaphysical imagination', which sees or seems to see in a landscape some indication, some disclosure of how the world ultimately is. The article explores and critically appraises this concept of metaphysical imagination and some of the roles it can play in our aesthetic encounters.

**Herb, Karlfriedrich** and Ludwig, Bernd. Kants kritisches Staatsrecht. *Jahr Recht Ethik*, 2, 431-478, 1994.

Contrary to popular assumption, Kant's theory of state experienced a major transformation during the period between "On the Common Saying" of 1793 and the "Metaphysical First Principles of the Doctrine of Right" of 1797. This transformation is primarily expressed in the systematic new formulation of the relationship between "noumenal state" and "phenomenal state". Kant's new system permits him, on the one hand, to develop the idea of state a priori from his theory of private right and thus to systematically incorporate central elements of the modern tradition, including Rousseau's "Contrat social". On the other hand, it allows him to formulate the theory of state forms as a theory of the "phenomenal state", which in turn provides a tool for legal evaluation of the then current political events in revolutionary France. (edited)

**Herbert, Robert T**. One Short Sleep Past?. *Int J Phil Relig*, 40(2), 85-99, O 96.

**Herman, A L**. The Way of the Lotus: Critical Reflections on the Ethics of the *Saddharmapundarika* Sutra. *Asian Phil*, 7(1), 5-22, Mr 97.

Edward Conze once observed of the thirty-eight books constituting the Prajñāpāramitā Sūtras that their central message could be summed up in two sentences: 1) One should become a Bodhisattva (or Buddha-to-be), i.e., one who is content with nothing less than all-knowledge attained through the perfection of wisdom for the sake of all beings. 2) There is no such thing as a Bodhisattva or as all-knowledge or as a being or as the perfection of wisdom or as an attainment.

**Herman, Louis G**. Beyond Postmodernism: Restoring the Primal Quest for Meaning to Political Inquiry. *Human Stud*, 20(1), 75-94, Ja 97.

I use Eric Voegelin's notion of a multicivilizational "truth quest"—or search for meaning—to make a case for institutionalizing "extraordinary" or "revolutionary" political science. I attempt such a discipline by following Voegelin—reflecting on "the full amplitude of human experience." Such a meditation takes place within the "first reality of existence"—Plato's *metaxy* or the "in-between"—the experience of human existence between the sacred and the mundane. I bring to Voegelin's exploration of the *metaxy* the realm of experience which is most radically "other" for modernity—the primal political order of paleolithic and contemporary hunting-gathering societies. I argue that shamanic "*Urreligion*" and Socratic discussion share a boundary crossing logic which provides a basis for a discipline of "extraordinary political science." Finally I suggest that such a discipline is both the quest for, and, in a sense, a realization of, the '*good life*'—a source of order for the individual and society. (edited)

**Herman, Steward W**. Enlarging the Conversation. *Bus Ethics Quart*, 7(2), 5-20, Mr 97.

**Herman, Steward W** and Gross Schaefer, Arthur. Introduction. *Bus Ethics Quart*, 7(2), 1-3, Mr 97.

**Hermann, E**. Boolean Pairs Formed by the Delta$^0{}_n$-Sets. *Annals Pure Applied Log*, 87(2), 145-149, 15 S 97.

It will be shown that for all numbers *n* and *m* with *n is greater than* 1 the Boolean pairs have undecidable elementary theories. (edited)

**Hermans, Michel** and Klein, Michel. Ces *Exercices Spirituels* Que Descartes Aurait Pratiqués. *Arch Phil*, 59(3), 427-440, Jl-S 96.

This study concerns a single aspect of the education which Descartes received at the "College de La Flèche", i.e., his spiritual formation. Contemporary documents leave uncertain the exact form of the spiritual retreat proposed to Descartes, though they exclude any direct contact with the text of the Spiritual Exercises of St. Ignatius of Loyola. Rather, it is highly probable that Descartes experienced the Manuale Sodalitatis of Fr. François Véron, an example of the rationalizing tendency common to the entire Order.

**Herment, Michel** and Demri, Stéphane and Caferra, Ricardo. Framework for the Transfer of Proofs, Lemmas and Strategies from Classical to Non-Classical Logics. *Stud Log*, 52(2), 197-232, My 93.

There exist valuable methods for theorem proving in nonclassical logics based on translation from these logics into first-order classical logic (abbreviated henceforth FOL). The key notion in these approaches is *translation* from a *Source Logic* (henceforth abbreviated SL) to a *Target Logic* (henceforth abbreviated TL). These methods are concerned with the problem of *finding* a proof in TL by translating a formula in SL, but they do not address the very important problem of *presenting proofs* in SL via a backward translation. We propose a framework for presenting proofs in SL based on a partial backward translation of proofs obtained in a familiar TL: Order-Sorted Predicate Logic. (edited)

**Hermida, Pablo**. El mundo incuestionado (Ortega y Schütz). *Rev Filosof (Spain)*, 8(15), 67-95, 1996.

**Hernáez, Jesús**. Outline for a Theory of Action. *Rev Filosof (Venezuela)*, Supp(2-3), 115-120, 1996.

In this paper the author starts from Charles Thiebaut's approach to action in Aristotle to outline a theory on human action and its intrinsic relation to a theory of man.

**Hernández de Frutos, Teodoro**. La prospectiva de los grandes informes y la metodología Delphi. *Euridice*, 47-70, 1992.

Man has always been fascinated by the future, by his own future as a biopsychological necessity and by the shared future as a psychosocial interest. In his desire for accuracy, man has aimed to make the study of the weather as rigorous as possible and thus utopia, prophecy and futurology has given way to prevision, planning and finally to forecasting. In this context, in 1937 William Ogburn carried out a forecasting study and in 1960, Bertrand de Jouvenel, denominated as forecasting a study which he considered to be partly artistic. From then on, important institutes are created and macro studies on the future are carried out, among which "Limits of Growth" of the Club de Roma is worth mentioning due to its importance and influence. Later, this article will deal with the Delphi methodology used for the study of the future.

**Herráiz Martínez, Pedro José**. Tolerancia y escepticismo: el caso de J. Locke. *Dialogo Filosof*, 13(1), 55-62, Ja-Ap.

Se trata de exponer el modo en que se produce la articulación entre el escepticismo como actitud gnoseológica y la actitud de tolerancia, tal como esa articulación se presenta en el origen de la fundamentación teórica de esta última según la lleva a cabo Locke en el contexto político y social inglés del siglo XVII, marcado por el liberalismo; y cómo tal articulación desemboca en un concepto negativizado de la tolerancia, vacío de contenido por la relativización de su objeto—también de su sujeto—, y puramente formal, una tolerancia desde la indiferencia: el concepto moderno de tolerancia.

**Herrera, Christopher D**. A Historical Interpretation of Deceptive Experiments in American Psychology. *Hist Human Sci*, 10(1), 23-36, F 97.

In debate over the ethics of deceptive experiments in American psychology, commentators often provide an inaccurate history of these experiments. This happens especially where writers portray experimental deception as a necessary accompaniment to human experiments, rather than a conscious choice based on values attached to persons and scientific inquiry. Compounding the error, commentators typically give a misleading portrayal of psychologists' attitudes and procedures. Commentators frequently cite Stanley Milgram's work in the 1960s as a harbinger of changed attitudes towards deception and suggest that today's psychologists abide by more enlightened ethical practices. It is difficult to find evidence to support this portrayal.

**Herrera, Christopher D**. The Other Human-Subject Experiments. *J Med Phil*, 22(2), 161-171, Ap 97.

Although deceptive psychology experiments receive less attention than some forms of medical research, they pose similar moral challenges. These challenges mainly concern the use of human subjects and intentional deception. Psychologists provide an argument to justify this deception. But what is an essentially utilitarian argument too often includes faulty comparisons and dubious accounts of risks and benefits. Commentators in other areas of human-subject research might examine this argument and the assumptions behind it. Bioethics commentators seem especially well-positioned for this task.

**Herrera Ibáñez, Alejandro**. "Peirce and Scepticism" in *Scepticism in the History of Philosophy: A Pan-American Dialogue*, Popkin, Richard H (ed), 159-166. Dordrecht, Kluwer, 1996.

In this essay I show that Peirce's views of truth as an ideal limit and of inquiry as an endless approximation to truth are based on three of his doctrines: 1) the doctrine of the self-corrigibility of science, 2) the doctrine of fallibilism, and 3) the doctrine of synechism. Although Peirce's reflection on these topics seems mainly to be aimed at scientific truth and inquiry, some considerations show that what Peirce says in this regard, hold also for philosophical truth and inquiry. I examine some objections and finally, I see what sense Peirce can be called a sceptic.

**Herrera J, Rodolfo**. Algunas tesis sobre la tecnología. *Rev Filosof (Costa Rica)*, 34(83-84), 365-384, D 96.

In the following article some theses are developed that constitute a theoretical frame for the concept of technology. Based in a "criterio of practice" we make an analysis of the structure of the scientific and technological practices, showing the dialectic interrelation of the knowledge production process, and your objectification and materialization concrete in "artificial world", that allows us to make a critic to some idealist philosophical conceptions. (edited)

**Herrero, F Javier**. Sujeito e ética. *Kriterion*, 34(88), 87-97, Ag-D 93.

The author proposes to show how the current situation presents itself as a challenging ethical problem which requires a new articulation between intersubjectivity and ethics. The ethics of discourse which, beginning from language, articulates intersubjectivity with responsibility in a universal principle, is entitled to assume this challenge.

**Herrestad, Henning** and Krogh, Christen. "Getting Personal: Some Notes on the Relationship between Personal and Impersonal Obligation" in *Deontic Logic, Agency and Normative Systems,* Brown, Mark A (ed), 134-153. New York, Springer-Verlag, 1996.

The contribution of this paper lies in the analysis of the relationship between impersonal and personal deontic notions, keeping them as close to standard deontic logic as possible. In doing so, we offer arguments against reducing both personal notions to impersonal notions, and impersonal notions to personal notions. We discover that we need to introduce two new notions of impersonal obligation and permission. Finally we argue in favor of one particular representation of ought-to-do and permitted-to-do statements.

**Herrmann, Burghard**. Characterizing Equivalential and Algebraizable Logics by the Leibniz Operator. *Stud Log*, 58(2), 305-323, Mr 97.

In [14] we used the term "finitely algebraizable" for algebraizable logics in the sense of Blok and Pigozzi and we introduced "possibly infinitely algebraizable," for short, p.i.-algebraizable logics. In the present paper, we characterize the hierarchy of protoalgebraic, equivalential, finitely equivalential, p.i.-algebraizable, and finitely algebraizable logics by properties of the Leibniz operator. (edited)

**Herrmann, Burghard**. Equivalential and Algebraizable Logics. *Stud Log*, 57(2-3), 419-436, O 96.

The notion of an algebraizable logic in the sense of Blok and Pigozzi [3] is generalized to that of a *possibly infinitely algebraizable*, for short, p.i.-algebraizable logic by admitting infinite sets of equivalence formulas and defining equations. An example of the new class is given. Many ideas of this paper have been present in [3] and [4]. By a consequent matrix semantics approach the theory of algebraizable and p.i.-algebraizable logics is developed in a different way. It is related to the theory of equivalential logics in the sense of Prucnal and Wronski [18] and it is extended to nonfinitary logics. The main result states that a logic is algebraizable (p.i.-algebraizable) if it is finitely equivalential (equivalential) and the truth predicate in the reduced matrix models is equationally definable.

**Herron, Timothy**. C.S. Peirce's Theories of Infinitesimals. *Trans Peirce Soc*, 33(3), 590-645, Sum 97.

The paper explores Peirce's work on set-theoretic, numeric and algebraic systems of mathematical infinitesimals developed as an integral part of his ideas on synechism. Peirce held many ideas in common with contemporary proponents of infinitesimals: their use in simplifying mathematical reasoning and in expressing intuitions about continuity unexpressible in standard models of continuity. We also show that Peirce's desiderata for infinitesimals often differed from those current in Robinson's school of infinitesimal analysis: his insistence on tying together cardinality and possibility and on integrating fallibility and antifoundationalism into his theory. We also evaluate Peirce's theories for feasibility of their future development.

**Hersh, Reuben**. Prove-Once More and Again. *Phil Math*, 5, 153-165, Je 97.

There are two distinct meanings to 'mathematical proof'. The connection between them is an unsolved problem. The first step in attacking it is noticing that it is an unsolved problem.

**Hershfield, Jeffrey**. Searle's Regimen for Rediscovering the Mind. *Dialogue (Canada)*, 36(2), 361-374, Spr 97.

**Herzog, Katalin**. Een anatomie van de beeldende kunst. *Alg Ned Tijdschr Wijs*, 89(3), 234-239, Jl 97.

**Heschl, Adolf**. Who's Afraid of a Non-Metaphorical Evolutionary Epistemology?. *Phil Natur*, 34(1), 107-145, 1997.

The present contribution shows that epistemology can, in fact, be consistently integrated into modern evolutionary theory if one eliminates both the existing pure analogies and the more hidden Lamarckian elements. However, the final result of such a procedure—a scientific epistemology in the original sense of Darwin and Boltzmann—may force us to modify major parts of our self-understanding. (edited)

**Heslep, Robert D**. "The Moral Presuppositions of Multicultural Education" in *Philosophy of Education (1996),* Margonis, Frank (ed), 218-223. Urbana, Phil Education Soc, 1997.

The purpose of this paper is to look at a fundamental problem in multicultural education (ME): The failure to recognize the moral implications of tolerance and intolerance for ME in general. The argument of the paper proceeds with a consideration of ME's de-emphasis upon teaching tolerance and its emphasis upon teaching intolerance of so-called politically incorrect speech. The paper holds that ME's policy on teaching intolerance ultimately is indefensible. It then concludes by proposing that because ME conceptually implies a commitment to the norms of moral agency, it is committed to teaching cultural tolerance and intolerance according to those norms.

**Hetherington, Stephen Cade**. Scepticism on Scepticism. *Philosophia (Israel)*, 25(1-4), 323-330, Ap 97.

This paper argues for an internal refutation of external world scepticism. By his or her *own* evidential standard, the sceptic's argument fails. It therefore fails *simpliciter.*

**Hettema, Hinne**. Bohr's Theory of the Atom 1913-1923: A Case Study in the Progress of Scientific Research Programmes. *Stud Hist Phil Mod Physics*, 26B(3), 307-323, D 96.

This paper refines some aspect of Lakatos's rational reconstruction of atomic theory. It is argued that Bohr's initial problem was not the radiative instability of this atom. Also, the progress of Bohr's theory of the atom is described in terms of the 'thematically arranged theses' which have been proposed as testable hypotheses in a science of scientific change.

**Hettihewa, Samanthala** and Batten, Jonathan and Mellor, Robert. The Ethical Management Practices of Australian Firms. *J Bus Ethics*, 16(12-13), 1261-1271, S 97.

This paper addresses a number of important issues regarding the ethical practices and recent behaviour of large Australian firms in nine industries. These issues include whether firms have a written code of ethics, whether firms have a forum for the discussion of ethics, whether managers consider that their firm's activities have an environmental impact and whether there are any statistical relationships between the size, industry class, ownership, international involvement and location of the firm and its ethical management practices. These questions are examined by using data collected from a sample of 136 large firms operating in Australia.

**Hewitt, Peter**. Not-Knowing in the Work of Georges Bataille (in Serbo-Croatian). *Filozof Istraz*, 15(4), 845-873, 1995.

Dans le présent étude, l'auteur suit le développment de la pensée de Georges Bataille en l'examinant successivement à travers les concepts proposés par Bataille, à savoir: l'hétérogénéité, la souveraineté, le language de la souveraineté, le non-savoir, la conscience, la dépense, le monde de l'utilité, le sacrifice, l'érotisme, le sacré et le profane. Peter Hewitt y retrace la lutte que Bataille mène, d'un côté, contre son propre héritage philosophique—traditionnel et classique—s'appuyant sur le concept de l'unité du monde et du savoir, et, de l'autre côté, son engagement pour affirmer aussi bien le droit aux paradoxes insolubles de la philosophie que la légitimité de l'hétérogénéité qui en résulte. (edited)

**Heyd, David**. Experimenting with Embryos: Can Philosophy Help?. *Bioethics*, 10(4), 292-309, O 96.

This article discusses the limits of the force of the philosophical arguments in the formation of actual policies for regulating such practices as experimenting with embryos. The widely-shared fourteen-day limit is shown to be a sound practical compromise despite the difficulties in justifying it philosophically. (edited)

**Heyes, Cecilia**. A Tribute to Donald T. Campbell. *Biol Phil*, 12(3), 299-301, Jl 97.

**Heyes, Cressida**. Anti-Essentialism in Practice: Carol Gilligan and Feminist Philosophy. *Hypatia*, 12(3), 142-163, Sum 97.

Third wave antiessentialist critique has too often been used to dismiss second wave feminist projects. I examine claims that Carol Gilligan's work is "essentialist," and argue that her recent research requires this criticism be rethought. Antiessentialist feminist method should consist in attention to the relations of power that construct accounts of gendered identity in the course of different forms of empirical enquiry, not in rejecting any general claim about women or girls.

**Heymann, Ezra**. Filosofía Trascendental Mundaneizada. *Ideas Valores*, 37-47, Ap 96.

This paper offers support to Heidegger's first book on Kant insofar as the subject of knowledge is seen as an empirical being in the midst of beings and exposed to them. But in accordance with this view, it emphasizes experience as causal insertion in the world rather then (imaginative) intuition. Consequently, it emphasizes the realistic trend of the second edition of the CpR, a trend which is anticipated in the Analogies of Experience. In its last section, the paper supports Alberto Rosales's view that piecemeal synthesis is the existential basis of the transcendental unity of consciousness, whereas the later is the ideal basis of the former.

**Hichmann, Sandra K** (ed) and Hinchman, Lewis P (ed). *Memory, Identity, Community: The Idea of Narrative in the Human Sciences.* Albany, SUNY Pr, 1997.

This anthology documents the resurrection, in the last few decades, of the importance of narrative to the study of individuals and groups. The editors propose that the human sciences are undergoing a paradigm shift away from nomological models and toward a more humanistic language in which narrative plays a complex and controversial role. Narratives, they claim, help to make experience intelligible, to crystallize personal identity and to constitute and nurture community. The fifteen articles in this collection, organized into sections dealing with memory, identity and community, are by noted scholars representing a wide variety of disciplines, including philosophy, history, religion, communication, environmental studies, political science, sociology, anthropology, psychology and law. They advocate diverse political and ideological positions, supporting the editors' belief that because narrative has not been captured by any academic bloc, it has the potential to become a *lingua franca* of future debates in the human sciences. (publisher)

**Hick, John**. The Epistemological Challenge of Religious Pluralism. *Faith Phil*, 14(3), 277-286, Jl 97.

A critique of responses to the problem posed to Christian philosophy by the fact of religious plurality by Alvin Plantinga, Peter van Inwagen and George Mavrodes in the recent (Festschrift dedicated to William Alston and of Alston's own response to the challenge of religious diversity to his epistemology of religion. His argument that religious experience is a generally reliable basis for belief-formation is by implication transformed by his response to this problem into the principle that Christianity constitutes the sole exception to the general rule that religious experience is an *unreliable* basis for belief-formation, thus undermining his central thesis. Plantinga's and van Inwagen's defenses of the logical and moral permissability of Christian exclusivism fail to address the problem posed by the existence of other equally well-based religious belief-systems with equally valuable fruits in human life. Mavrodes's discussion of polytheism and his clarifying questions about religious pluralism, are also discussed.

**Hick, John**. The Possibility of Religious Pluralism: A Reply to Gavin D'Costa. *Relig Stud*, 33(2), 161-166, Je 97.

This paper is a reply to D'Costa's article (*Religious Studies*, 32, pp. 223-232) in which he argues that there is no such position as religious pluralism because in distinguishing between, e.g., Christianity or Buddhism and Nazism or the Jim Jones cult, a criterion is involved and to use a criterion is a form of exclusivism. In reply I point out that this sense of 'exclusivism', as consisting in the use of criteria, is self-destructive; that the pluralistic hypothesis, as a meta-theory about the religions, has a different logical status from the creeds of the historical religions; and I also show the origin of the ethnical criterion used by the religious pluralist who stands within one or other of the great world faiths.

**Hickman, Larry A**. "Nature as Culture: John Dewey's Pragmatic Naturalism" in *Environmental Pragmatism*, Light, Andrew (ed), 50-72. New York, Routledge, 1996.

This essay presents a comprehensive overview of John Dewey's naturalism and then compares the "guiding stars" of his environmental thought to the land ethic of Also Leopold. For Dewey, experiences of "nature-as-nature" are vague and immediate, but they are among the many materials from which "nature-as-culture" is constructed. It is "nature-as-culture," or nature as cultural artifact, that furnishes the basis for environmental decisions such as those involved in restoration ecology.

**Hierro, José S Pescador**. Problemas del empirismo en la filosofía de la mente. *Teorema*, 16(2), 35-49, 1997.

Experience of mental states becomes central as soon as we attempt to construe a science of the mind. Mental states appear irreducible to physical states in as far as they are neither public nor computable. From an epistemological point of view mental states are peculiar in that we have no knowledge proper to them, we simply have them. From the point of view of our experience, there are reasons to reject the physicalist explanation as well as the intentionalist account and also to reject the reducibility of mental states to brain states. Two different forms of experience are relevant: direct experience of one's own mental states and indirect experience of other people's through their behavior and speech.

**Higginbotham, James**. "Fodor's Concepts" in *Contents*, Villanueva, Enrique (ed), 25-37. Atascadero, Ridgeview, 1995.

**Higgins, Kathleen Marie**. "Musical Idiosyncrasy and Perspectival Listening" in *Music and Meaning*, Robinson, Jenefer (ed), 83-102. Ithaca, Cornell Univ Pr, 1997.

After indicating the ways in which the ideal of objectivity features in certain influential accounts within musical aesthetics, I will consider some characteristics of musical experience, both in non-Western cultures and in Western culture, which are not easily embraced by the Western "objective" paradigm. Idiosyncratic factors play a role in listeners' responses to music they value and those best educated to appreciate scores "objectively" often have the most idiosyncratic perspectives. "Idiosyncratic" experiences of music, I contend, are experiences of value that should be encouraged, not foreclosed, by philosophical analysis.

**Higgins, Kathleen Marie** and Solomon, Robert C. *A Passion for Wisdom: A Very Brief History of Philosophy*. New York, Oxford Univ Pr, 1997.

Without simplifying their subject, Solomon and Higgins tell the story of philosophy's development with great clarity and refreshing wit. They allow readers to see more clearly the connections and divergences between philosophers and their ideas as they change, reappear and evolve over time. They explore how, for example, the value of subjective experience is treated in Augustine, Luther, Descartes and Kierkegaard, how the idea of dynamic change appears in the work of Heraclitus, Darwin, Hegel and Nietzsche, and how the recurring dichotomies between faith and reason, belief and skepticism and mysticism and empiricism occupy philosophers from one generation to the next. (publisher, edited)

**Hill, Christopher S**. Imaginability, Conceivability, Possibility and the Mind-Body Problem. *Phil Stud*, 87(1), 61-85, Jl 97.

**Hill, Christopher S**. Lynne Rudder Baker, *Explaining Attitudes: A Practical Approach to the Mind*. Nous, 31(1), 132-142, Mr 97.

**Hill, Claire Ortiz**. *Rethinking Identity and Metaphysics: On the Foundations of Analytic Philosophy*. New Haven, Yale Univ Pr, 1997.

In this book, Claire Ortiz Hill offers a sophisticated rethinking of the foundations of twentieth-century analytic philosophy. She carefully uncovers the flaws of the central analytic tenet that philosophical discourse is reducible to identities. Closely examining the writings of the analytic philosophers Gottlob Frege, Bertrand Russell, and Willard Quine, she shows that the extensionalistic treatment of identity initiated by Frege and followed by the others has served as a hidden constraint on subsequent work in the mainstream of analytic philosophy. The result has been a flawed treatment of a range of philosophical problems, including necessity, objecthood, meaning, the ontology of mathematics, and Russell's paradox. Hill shows that heroic attempts by philosophers to free philosophical discourse from "intensions"—meanings, concepts, attributes—must fail. (publisher, edited)

**Hill, Greg**. Capitalism, Coordination, and Keynes: Rejoinder to Horwitz. *Crit Rev*, 10(3), 373-387, Sum 96.

In the ideal market of general equilibrium theory, choices are made in full knowledge of one another, and all expectations are fulfilled. This preharmonization of individual plans does not occur in real-world markets where decisions must be taken in ignorance of one another. The Austrian school grants this, but claims that real-world price systems are nonetheless effective in coordinating saving and investment decisions, which are motivated by disparate considerations. In contrast, Keynes held that without the

prereconciliation of individual plans, investment and employment would be less than optimal, and the resulting distribution of income arbitrary and inequitable.

**Hill, Greg**. The Moral Economy: Keynes's Critique of Capitalist Justice. *Crit Rev*, 10(1), 33-61, Wint 96.

Neoclassical and Austrian economic theory lend support to a conception of laissez-faire capitalism as an ideal scheme of cooperation in which individual decisions are harmonized and income is distributed according to one's productive contribution. Keynes's critique of this conception has an often-overlooked moral dimension, according to which the coordination problems that trouble real-world market economies produce an arbitrary and inequitable distribution of wealth and income.

**Hill, H Hamner**. John Dewey's Legal Pragmatism. *SW Phil Rev*, 13(1), 113-121, Ja 97.

Dewey's most direct treatment of law and legal theory, "Logical Method and Law," presents a sketch of a pragmatic theory of law. Dewey claims the law needs "a logic relevant to consequences, not antecedents." This paper unpacks Dewey's pragmatic theory of law and outlines some criticisms of Dewey's legal views set forth by the American Legal Realist Karl Llewellyn in an unpublished manuscript titled "John Dewey and Our Law." This paper aims to identify where Dewey and Llewellyn agree and where they, as representatives of major schools of thought, part company.

**Hill, Ronald Paul** and Keffer, Jane M. An Ethical Approach to Lobbying Activities of Businesses in the United States. *J Bus Ethics*, 16(12-13), 1371-1379, S 97.

This paper presents an ethical approach to the use of lobbying within the context of the relationships among U.S. organizations, their lobbyists and government officials. After providing a brief history of modern-day lobbying activities, lobbying is defined and described focusing on its role as a strategic marketing tool. Then ethical frameworks for understanding the impact of these practices on various *external* constituencies are delineated with an emphasis on the communitarian movement advanced by Etzioni. (edited)

**Hill, Susan**. Reason as the Foundation of *Eudaimonia* in the *Nicomachean Ethics*. *Phil Inq*, 18(1-2), 101-118, Wint-Spr 96.

The first stage of the article presents three arguments against Sarah Broadie's inclusivist interpretation of the *Nicomachean Ethics*. It is concluded that other inclusivist interpretations are likely to fall prey to some of the same arguments. The second stage of the article offers an alternative understanding of Aristotle's conception of happiness, one which is neither inclusivist nor intellectualist in character.

**Hill Jr, Thomas E**. "Respect for Humanity" in *The Tanner Lectures on Human Values, Volume 18, 1997*, Peterson, Grethe B (ed), 1-76. Salt Lake City, Univ of Utah Pr, 1997.

The first of two lectures, "Basic Respect and Cultural Diversity," reviews Kant's idea of respect for persons and its historical setting, proposes enriching it with contemporary ideas about how we develop values as individuals and as social beings, and then draws implications regarding cultural conflicts and "multiculturalism vs. canons" in universities. The second sketches Kantian grounds for respecting persons as human beings, independently of merit, then argues that respect cannot be entirely forfeited and that proper respect is compatible with self-protection, just punishment, and forceful moral censure. Animals, sociopaths and mental incompetents require special treatment.

**Hill Jr, Thomas E**. Kant on Responsibility for Consequences. *Jahr Recht Ethik*, 2, 159-176, 1994.

In der *Metaphysik der Sitten* nimmt Kant an, dass die schlechten Folgen einer pflichtwidrigen Handlung dem Handelnden stets zugerechnet werden können, im Gegensatz zu den schlechten Folgen pflichtgemässer Handlungen, die dem Handelnden niemals zugerechnet werden können. Obwohl es Kant im Kontext der *Metaphysik der Sitten* offensichtlich auf die juridische Zurechnung ankommt, geht es im vorstehenden Beitrag um die Frage, ob sich Kants Lehre auf die moralische Verantwortlichkeit für schlechte Folgen in denjenigen Fällen übertragen lässt, in denen eine juridische Normdurchsetzung unpassend ist. Und zwar geht es *erstens* um eine angemessene Interpretation der einschlägigen Textstellen selbst. (edited)

**Hill Jr, Thomas E**. Reasonable Self-Interest. *Soc Phil Pol*, 14(1), 52-85, Wint 97.

Common sense ideas of what is reasonable are compared and contrasted with philosophical ideas of rational choice: maximizing self-interest, efficiency and coherence in pursuit of one's ends, maximizing intrinsic value and efficient and coherent pursuits constrained by a Kantian ideal of colegislation. Contrary to usual assumptions, the last, it is argued, corresponds more closely to the common sense ideas than any of the other models. This is not proof of the Kantian ideal, or of common sense, but calls for rethinking assumptions. Morality and reasonable self-interest, it is suggested, are less sharply opposed than philosophers typically suppose.

**Hillman, Harold**. Honest Research. *Sci Eng Ethics*, 1(1), 49-58, J 95.

The origins of research projects, the duties of supervisors and research workers, the subjective elements in research and the difficulties of publication are reviewed, as a guide to the complexities of executing an honest research project. It is assumed that research carried out with maximal intellectual integrity will result in real advances.

**Hillman, Harold**. Parafraud in Biology. *Sci Eng Ethics*, 3(2), 121-136, Ap 97.

The concept of parafraud is described as "illogical or improper behaviour towards other peoples' views or publications," and 19 different kinds of common practices coming under this heading are listed. Ways of combating it are suggested.

**Hilton, Chadwick B** and Motes, William H and Dulek, Ronald E. Executive Perceptions of Superior and Subordinate Information Control: Practice Versus Ethics. *J Bus Ethics*, 16(11), 1175-1184, Ag 97.

This study examines executive perceptions of business information control. Specifically, the study explores a) whether executives perceive certain types of information control being practiced within their businesses; and, b) whether the executives regard such practices as ethical. In essence, the study suggests that both superiors and subordinates selectively practice information control. Even more importantly, however, executives see such practices as ethically acceptable on the part of superiors but as ethically questionable on the part of subordinates. A closer look at the responding executives' profile characteristics—age, gender, education and salary—reveals the complexity of these perceptions. Most importantly, gender and age emerge as two prime factors influencing executive perceptions regarding both the practice and the ethics of information control. Suggestions for future research are included at the end of the article.

**Himmer, Péter**. Contributions to the Reconstruction of the Later Lukacs's Philosophy (in Hungarian). *Magyar Filozof Szemle*, 4-5-6, 339-361, 1996.

Der Ausgangspunkt des Aufsatzes ist eine allbekannte Tatsache: die lukácssche philosophische Anschauung hat sich vom *Geschichte und Klassenbevusstsein*/1922/ bis *Zur Ontologie des gesellschftlichen Seins*/1971/ verändern. In der Reihe dieser Ursachen hat eine wichtige Rolle die Änderung des Verhältnis zu Hegel und Marx. Der Verfasser stellt diese Verhältnisse in den Mittelpunkt, und versucht die Änderungen als einen einheitlichen und zusammenhängenden Prozess darstellen, die kann man im Hauptlinien des philosophische Lebenswerk von Lukács sehen. (edited)

**Hinchman, Lewis P** (ed) and Hichmann, Sandra K (ed). *Memory, Identity, Community: The Idea of Narrative in the Human Sciences*. Albany, SUNY Pr, 1997.

This anthology documents the resurrection, in the last few decades, of the importance of narrative to the study of individuals and groups. The editors propose that the human sciences are undergoing a paradigm shift away from nomological models and toward a more humanistic language in which narrative plays a complex and controversial role. Narratives, they claim, help to make experience intelligible, to crystallize personal identity and to constitute and nurture community. The fifteen articles in this collection, organized into sections dealing with memory, identity and community, are by noted scholars representing a wide variety of disciplines, including philosophy, history, religion, communication, environmental studies, political science, sociology, anthropology, psychology and law. They advocate diverse political and ideological positions, supporting the editors' belief that because narrative has not been captured by any academic bloc, it has the potential to become a *lingua franca* of future debates in the human sciences. (publisher)

**Hinman, Lawrence M**. Are Appeals to the Emotions Necessarily Fallacious?. *Inquiry (USA)*, 15(1), 53-62, Fall 95.

**Hinman, Lawrence M**. The Virtual Seminar Room: Using a World Wide Web Site in Teaching Ethics. *Teach Phil*, 19(4), 319-329, D 96.

**Hinney, B** and Michelmann, H W. Ethical Reflections on the Status of the Preimplantation Embryo Leading to the German Embryo Protection Act. *Sci Eng Ethics*, 1(2), 145-150, A 95.

Ethical conflicts have always been connected with new techniques of reproductive medicine such as in vitro fertilization. The fundamental question is: When does human life begin and from which stage of development should the embryo be protected? This question cannot be solved by scientific findings only. In prenatal ontogenesis there is no moment during the development from the fertilized oocyte to a human being which could be recognized as an orientation point for all ethical problems connected with the question of the right to dispose of prenatal life (interruption of pregnancy, research on embryos). The protection of an individual human life must be valid for all in the same manner and from the very beginning on. It must not depend on value judgments or on stages of development, so-called grades of humanity, because these would then become selection criteria. Procreated life must have the right to be born. These were the essential ethical arguments which led to the German Embryo Protection Law.

**Hinshelwood, R D**. Primitive Mental Processes: Psychoanalysis and the Ethics of Integration. *Phil Psychiat Psych*, 4(2), 121-143, Je 97.

A person in two minds has to make choices. General ethics would accept that people can be influenced in their decisions both ethically and unethically. Divisions of the human mind occur in varying degrees: from ordinary conflict, to repression, to splitting. This paper describes these levels, as encountered in psychoanalytic observation. The primitive defense mechanisms of splitting, projection and introjection result in phenomena in which one person can perform the function of part of another person's mind. The interpersonal situation as found in the psychoanalytic setting can exemplify the diminishing of an individual's autonomy, not only in the practice of psychoanalysis but in the wider interpersonal social field. (edited)

**Hinshelwood, R D**. Response to the Commentaries. *Phil Psychiat Psych*, 4(2), 159-165, Je 97.

This response is a defense against several criticisms by Paul Sturdee, Chris Mace and Larry Thornton to my paper on ethical implications of psychoanalytic discoveries. I defend the validity of psychoanalysis itself and why Kleinian psychoanalysis is just the sort of theory for social issues such as ethics. Thornton questioned whether a technical process or measure (such as integration) can also be an ethical goal; to which I argue that in human 'science' every encounter has an ethical dimension simply because of the human nature of the subject. The Kleinian approach does not merely analyze a person's morality, but analyzes the person as a moral subject. And Sturdee's account of

the power-relations within a psychoanalysis is simplistic when the topic is in fact very intricate.

**Hinske, Norbert**. Fata ducunt. *Z Phil Praxis*, 4-6, 1996.

This contribution is the revised version of an address which was given by the author as a sign of gratitude for a most enchanting celebration of his 65th birthday. At the same time, it is a reflexion on a frequently quoted statement of Seneca's and on its influence in history. It seeks to clarify the internal connection that exists between the notions of fate and guidance. The assumption of such a connection has its origin in the paradoxical experience that frequently what is burdensome and causes suffering turns out to be a providential and fortunate juncture in one's life. Bad things, too, have their good sides.

**Hintikka, Jaakko**. "Jaako Hintikka Replies" in *Knowledge and Inquiry: Essays on Jaakko Hintikka's Epistemology and Philosophy of Science*, Sintonen, Matti (ed), 309-338. Amsterdam, Rodopi, 1997.

This is a series of answers to, and comments on, all the other contributions to the same volume. The topics touched on include Aristotle and plenitude; Aristotle's dialectic; theories of questions in German philosophy around 1900; relationship between Wittgenstein and Ramsey; inductive logic; the atomistic postulate; caution and nonmonotonic inference; identifiability; questions and natural kinds; structure of inquiry; semantics of questions; science and games; explanation; interrogative approach to inquiry; and the logical structure of learning models.

**Hintikka, Jaakko**. "The Place of C.S. Peirce in the History of Logical Theory" in *The Rule of Reason: The Philosophy of Charles Sanders Peirce*, Forster, Paul (ed), 13-33. Toronto, Univ of Toronto Pr, 1997.

In the grand contrast between language as the universal medium and the model-theoretical conception of language, Peirce belongs squarely to the latter camp. This is shown by his own testimony, his work in modal logic, his anticipation of game-theoretical semantics, his acceptance (and cultivation) of metalogic, his insistence on the iconicity of logic, and his theorematic vs. corollarial distinction. Peirce's model-theoretical approach is also a precondition of his idea that human action is constitutive of meaning and indeed a precondition of his entire pragmati(ci)sm. It distinguishes him sharply from such universalists as Frege, Wittgenstein and Quine.

**Hintikka, Jaakko**. A Revolution in the Foundations of Mathematics?. *Synthese*, 111(2), 155-170, My 97.

The received picture of the foundations of mathematics consists of (semantically complete) first-order logic supplemented by higher-order logic or, usually, set theory. But ordinary first-order logic involves needless restrictions on quantifier interplay whose removal results in a new *independence-friendly first-order logic*. It captures many mathematical notions (equicardinality, infinity, etc.) ordinary first-order logic does not capture. It is semantically incomplete, but it facilitates descriptively complete axiomatization of many mathematical theories. In a sense, any mathematical theorem is interpretable as a truth of this logic. In brief, it makes in principle set theory and higher-order logic largely dispensable.

**Hintikka, Jaakko**. Contemporary Philosophy and the Problem of Truth. *Filosof Cas*, 44(3), 369-387, 1996.

Twentieth-century philosophy has been dominated by a grand but largely tacit contrast. Universalists consider our actual language an unavoidable and irreplaceable medium of all thought. Hence semantics is ineffable, necessitating a special hermeneutical approach to our language and thought. The contrasting approach maintains the possibility of discursive thinking about our language and our thought. A veritable test case is the problem of the definability of truth. Tarski's indefinability result seemingly favors universalists. The author's recent results nevertheless vindicate the possibility of a truth-definition for a language in the language itself, thus overthrowing the universalist dogma.

**Hintikka, Jaakko**. Hilbert Vindicated?. *Synthese*, 110(1), 15-36, Ja 97.

The professed reasons for classifying Hilbert a formalist are largely mistaken. The only half-way valid reason is Hilbert's preference for concrete symbols as the objects dealt with in the foundations of mathematics. This preference was nevertheless only a small part of Hilbert's campaign against general concepts and for concrete individuals in logic and in the foundations. For Hilbert, mathematics is not a set-theoretical but a combinatorial enterprise. The same orientation is illustrated by Hilbert's use of the epsilon-symbol. Hilbert's ideas are partly vindicated by the author's independence-friendly first-order (and hence "nominalistic") logic to which all usual mathematical truths can in a sense be reduced.

**Hintikka, Jaakko**. *Lingua Universalis vs. Calculus Ratiocinator: An Ultimate Presupposition of Twentieth-Century Philosophy*. Dordrecht, Kluwer, 1997.

The essays collected here explore a fundamental contrast between two overall visions of language and its availability to self-examination. They can be characterized as "language as the universal medium" and "language as calculus" (or the model-theoretical view). The former normally includes the ineffability of semantics and a one-world ontology. This contrast has dominated twentieth-century philosophy but has scarcely been acknowledged before. Philosophers examined here from the vantage point of the contrast include Peirce, Frege, Wittgenstein, Carnap, Quine, Husserl and Heidegger. Tarski's famous result concerning the indefinability of truth seems to decide the issue in favor of the universalists. Hintikka nevertheless shows that Tarski's result is inconclusive and that truth can in fact be defined in languages which are in certain respects comparable to ordinary language. This unique volume is a must for every contemporary philosopher and for everyone interested in the semantics of our language. (publisher)

**Hintikka, Jaakko**. *Ludwig Wittgenstein: Half-Truths and One-and-a-Half-Truths*. Dordrecht, Kluwer, 1996.

Frequently, a genuine understanding of a thinker's ideas is possible only by following them further than he did himself. Wittgenstein's Viennese contemporary Karl Kraus spoke in a similar context of one-and-a-half truths in contradistinction to half-truths. In this volume of essays, Jaakko Hintikka examines in the spirit of Kraus's *bon not* the two grand visions concerning the interrelations of language, self and the world that guided Wittgenstein's thought at the different stages of his philosophical development. He shows how one of them, the so-called picture theory of language, was in reality a combination of several independent assumptions, while the other, the idea of language-games as the vehicles of meaning, was the end product of an intriguing development. Alas, the role of these two fundamental visions is in Wittgenstein's published books largely hidden by his legendary impatience as an expositor. To counter this impatience, Hintikka shows that many of Wittgenstein's best known ideas can, and must, be understood as defenses or rationalizations of his overall visions. In several essays, Wittgenstein's ideas are illuminated through comparisons with other philosophers, including Russell, Husserl and Carnap. (publisher)

**Hintikka, Jaakko**. *The Principles of Mathematics Revisited*. New York, Cambridge Univ Pr, 1996.

Jaako Hintikka proposes a new basic first-order logic and uses it to explore the foundations of mathematics. This new logic enables logicians to express on the first-order level such concepts as equicardinality, infinity and truth in the same language. The famous impossibility results by Gödel and Tarski that have dominated the field for the past sixty years turn out to be much less significant than has been thought. All of ordinary mathematics can in principle be done on this first-order level, thus dispensing with all problems concerning the existence of sets and other higher-order entities. (publisher,edited)

**Hinz, Evelyn J**. It's not the Principle, It's the Money!: An Economic Revisioning of Publishing Ethics. *J Infor Ethics*, 6(1), 22-33, Spr 97.

**Hiorth, Finngeir**. Criticism of Religion in Sweden. *Nature Soc Thought*, 9(2), 219-225, 1996.

The author reviews the work of leading Swedish freethinkers, especially highlighting the role of the philosopher Ingemar Hedenius and the principal critics of his views.

**Hirokawa, Sachio**. The Converse Principal Type-Scheme Theorem in Lambda Calculus. *Stud Log*, 51(1), 83-95, 1992.

This paper shows a simple proof for the theorem in *lambda*-calculus, by constructing an algorithm which transforms a type assignment to a *lambda*-term into a principal type assignment to another *lambda*-term that has the type as its principal type-scheme. The clearness of the algorithm is due to the characterization theorem of principal type-assignment figures. The algorithm is applicable to BCIW-*lambda*-terms as well. Thus a uniform proof is presented for the converse principal type-scheme theorem for general *lambda*-terms and BCIW-*lambda*-terms. (edited)

**Hirsch, Eli**. Complex Kinds. *Phil Papers*, 26(1), 47-70, Ap 97.

**Hirsch, Joachim**. Weltkapitalismus oder Nationalstaat—eine falsch gestellte Frage. *Das Argument*, 217(5-6), 725-728, 1996.

Jean Milios's article in this issue understands the relationship between global capitalism and the nation-state as a simple dichotomy when they are actually strictly contradictory. Analysis of their relationship requires theoretical tools unavailable in traditional Marxism.

**Hirsch, Robin** and Hodkinson, Ian. Step by Step—Building Representations in Algebraic Logic. *J Sym Log*, 62(1), 225-279, Mr 97.

We consider the problem of finding and classifying representations in algebraic logic. This is approached by letting two players build a representation using a game. Homogeneous and universal representations are characterized according to the outcome of certain games. The Lyndon conditions defining representable relation algebras (for the finite case) and a similar schema for cylindric algebras are derived. Finite relation algebras with homogeneous representations are characterized by first order formulas. Equivalence games are defined and are used to establish whether an algebra is *omega*-categorical. We have a simple proof that the perfect extension of a representable relation algebra is completely representable. (edited)

**Hirschbein, Ron**. Crisis and Narrativity. *Phil Cont World*, 2(1), 6-12, Spr 95.

Despite the dramatic changes in international politics it appears that crises—episodes in which decision-makers hazard urgent, perilous choices—will remain a prominent and dangerous feature of international relations. This realization prompts the question that informs this paper: why do American decision-makers define a situation as a crisis in the first place? I argue that prevailing theories do not adequately account for crises: the same situation (or perception of the situation) may be interpreted differently by various decision-makers. Specifically, it may be construed as an endurable problem to be resolved in due course, or an unendurable crisis demanding immediate resolution at considerable risk. I entertain the possibility that crises occur because crisis discourse has become the *lingua franca* in the halls of power. Taking a semiotic approach, I argue that crisis narratives are read into ambiguous situations to render them meaningful and dramatically self-valorizing.

**Hirschman, Albert O**. Melding the Public and Private Spheres: Taking Commensality Seriously. *Crit Rev*, 10(4), 533-550, Fall 96.

Tibor Scitovsky's *The Joyless Economy* distinguished the pleasure of moving from discomfort to comfort and the pleasure of replacing boredom with stimulation. I have argued that there are also pleasures distinctive to participating in public life. A third form of pleasure belongs to both the private and the public domain: the common meal leads to individual satiation and, as a result of *commensality*, has important social and public effects. A good example is the banquet in ancient Greece, closely connected to the lottery—the basic

mechanism of Athenian democracy. But the common meal can also lead to the degradation of human relations and political life.

**Hirst, Jeffry L** and Lempp, Steffen. Infinite Versions of Some Problems from Finite Complexity Theory. *Notre Dame J Form Log*, 37(4), 545-553, Fall 96.

Recently, several authors have explored the connections between NP-complete problems for finite objects and the complexity of their analogs for infinite objects. In this paper, we will categorize infinite versions of several problems arising from finite complexity theory in terms of their recursion theoretic complexity and proof theoretic strength. These infinite analogs can behave in a variety of unexpected ways.

**Hitchcock, Christopher Read**. The Mechanist and the Snail. *Phil Stud*, 84(1), 91-105, O 96.

**Hitchcock, David**. Did Jesus Commit a Fallacy?. *Inform Log*, 17(2), 297-302, Spr 95.

Jesus has been accused of committing a fallacy (of denying the antecedent) at John 8:47. Careful analysis of this text 1) reveals a hitherto unrecognized valid form of argument which can superficially look like the predicate-logic analogue of denying the antecedent; 2) shows that determining whether a published text can be fairly charged with committing a fallacy may require (but often does not get) extensive and detailed analysis; 3) acquits Jesus of the charge; and thereby 4) confirms a claim by Michael Burke that published arguments can seldom be fairly charged with denying the antecedent, or analogous fallacies.

**Hitoshi, Egawa**. Die Motive der Atmosphäre um 1820 von C.D. Friedrich: im Zusammenhang mit L. Howards Meteorologie. *Bigaku*, 48(1), 37-48, Sum 97.

Goethe wies im Jahre 1816 Caspar David Friedrich auf Howards Meteorologie hin und genau in dieser Zeit, bis 1824, entstanden viele Werke von Friedrich mit Atmosphären, wie Nebel oder Wolken, deren Gestalten typisch für die Klassifizierung nach Howards Meteorologie sind, wie z.B. Nebel odor Stratus in *Der Wanderer über dem Nebelmeer* (um 1818), Cumulus in *Neubrandenburg* (um 1816-17), Cirrus in *Abend* (1824), Nimbus in *Hünengrab im Herbst* (um 1820) usw. Howards Meteorologie verhalf Friedrichs Landschaftsmalerei zu einer bildnerischen Vielfalt der Atmosphärenmotive, die seine romantischen Forderungen erfüllten. (edited)

**Hiz, Henry**. "Peirce's Influence on Logic in Poland" in *Studies in the Logic of Charles Sanders Peirce*, Houser, Nathan (ed), 264-270. Bloomington, Indiana Univ Pr, 1997.

**Hjorth, Greg**. On Aleph₁ Many Minimal Models. *J Sym Log*, 61(3), 906-919, S 96.

The existence of a countable complete theory with exactly $Aleph_1$ many minimal models is independent of ZFC + not CH. (edited)

**Hjorth, Greg**. Some Applications of Coarse Inner Model Theory. *J Sym Log*, 62(2), 337-365, Je 97.

**Hjorth, Greg** and Hauser, Kai. Strong Cardinals in the Core Model. *Annals Pure Applied Log*, 83(2), 165-198, Ja 97.

We work with Steel's core model under the assumption that there is no inner class model for a Woodin cardinal. We also show in ZFC that set forcing cannot create class models with a given number of strongs. (edited)

**Hjorth, Greg** and Kechris, Alexander S. Borel Equivalence Relations and Classifications of Countable Models. *Annals Pure Applied Log*, 82(3), 221-272, D 96.

Using the theory of Borel equivalence relations we analyze the isomorphism relation on the countable models of a theory and develop a framework for measuring the complexity of possible complete invariants for isomorphism.

**Ho, Foo Nin** and Vitell, Scott J. Ethical Decision Making in Marketing: A Synthesis and Evaluation of Scales Measuring the Various Components of Decision Making in Ethical Situations. *J Bus Ethics*, 16(7), 699-717, My 97.

The authors present a comprehensive synthesis and evaluation of the published scales measuring the components of the decision making process in ethical situations using the Hunt-Vitell (1993) theory of ethics as a framework to guide the research. Suggestions for future scale development are also provided.

**Hoaglund, John**. Landmarks in Critical Thinking Series: Ennis on the Concept of Critical Thinking. *Inquiry (USA)*, 15(2), 1-19, Wint 95.

This excerpts and comments on Robert H. Ennis's 1962 *Harvard Educational Review* article, "A Concept of Critical Thinking." Ennis defines critical thinking as correctly assessing statements, and separates logical, criterial, and pragmatic dimensions. He then elaborates 12 aspects, e.g., grasping the meaning of a statement or judging whether an observation statement is reliable. His goal is to provide a basis for research into teaching and evaluating critical thinking. His current definition broadens in scope from assessing statements to reasonable reflective thinking about what to believe or do. In place of dimensions and aspects, the concept is now elaborated into dispositions and abilities.

**Hobart, Ann** and Jankélévitch, Vladimir. Do Not Listen to What They Say, Look at What They Do. *Crit Inquiry*, 22(3), 549-551, Spr 96.

**Hobart, Ann** and Jankélévitch, Vladimir. Should We Pardon Them?. *Crit Inquiry*, 22(3), 552-572, Spr 96.

**Hoch, David** and Hamilton III, J Brooke. Ethical Standards for Business Lobbying: Some Practical Suggestions. *Bus Ethics Quart*, 7(3), 117-129, Jl 97.

Rather than being inherently evil, business lobbying is a socially responsible activity which needs to be restrained by ethical standards. To be effective in a business environment, traditional ethical standards need to be translated into language which business persons can speak comfortably. Economical explanations must also be available to explain why ethical standards are appropriate in business. Eight such standards and their validating arguments are proposed with examples showing their use. (edited)

**Hochberg, Herbert**. Reference, Truth and Realism. *Acta Analytica*, 9-27, 1996.

John Searle sees previous philosophers as failing to distinguish between *intention-with-a-t* and *intension-with-an-s*. This, he believes, leads them to mistake properties of reports for properties of things reported, in their discussions of intentionality, since reports may be "intensional" while what is reported is "extensional". Thus, speaking about John's belief that King Arthur killed Sir Lancelot, he says: "It is completely extensional: it is true if there is a unique x such that x = King Arthur and there is a unique y such that y = Sir Lancelot and x killed y. That is as extensional as anything can get." But all Searle means by the claim that *the belief*, as opposed to *the report* of it, is completely extensional is that one gives the "truth condition" for *the belief*, by giving the truth condition for the sentence 'King Arthur killed Sir Lancelot'. Put simply, the sentence 'King Arthur killed Sir Lancelot' does not raise the familiar issues about substitution raised by 'John believes that King Arthur killed Sir Lancelot'. While this is true, the analysis of intentional contexts that lies behind it fails to adequately take up, let alone resolve, the familiar logical and ontological problems of intentionality that Searle purports to solve. (edited)

**Hoche, Hans-Ulrich**. Zur Komplementarität von Freiheit und Notwendigkeit des menschlichen Handelns. *Jahr Recht Ethik*, 2, 37-54, 1994.

Adopting an ontology of full concreteness, one has to distinguish between human action in the internal view of the actor himself and human action in the external view of a fellow human being, or spectator. As seen from the latter point of view, human action is nothing but observable behavior. As such, it belongs in the objective realm of natural necessity, as does any other macrophysical event. As seen from the former (internal) point of view, human action may be characterized as a system of nonindicative subjective traits of the actor's intentional objects, appealing to him, in the light of his motives, in a 'gerundive' way. (edited)

**Hocking, Richard**. "Emergence and Embodiment: A Dialectic within Process" in *The Recovery of Philosophy in America: Essays in Honor of John Edwin Smith,* Kasulis, Thomas P (ed), 155-165. Albany, SUNY Pr, 1997.

**Hocks, Elaine**. Dialectic and the "Two Forces of One Power": Reading Coleridge, Polanyi, and Bakhtin in a New Key. *Tradition Discovery*, 23(2), 4-16, 1996-97.

The focus of this essay is to read the nineteenth-century theories of poet and philosopher Samuel Taylor Coleridge against the twentieth century theories of chemist and philosopher of science Michael Polanyi and Russian philologist and critic Mikhail Bakhtin, showing their intellectual similarities and contrasts. My purpose in this essay is to redeem Coleridge's thought for rhetorical theory by linking him to modern thinkers who are respected within the field.

**Hodkinson, Ian** and Hirsch, Robin. Step by Step—Building Representations in Algebraic Logic. *J Sym Log*, 62(1), 225-279, Mr 97.

We consider the problem of finding and classifying representations in algebraic logic. This is approached by letting two players build a representation using a game. Homogeneous and universal representations are characterized according to the outcome of certain games. The Lyndon conditions defining representable relation algebras (for the finite case) and a similar schema for cylindric algebras are derived. Finite relation algebras with homogeneous representations are characterized by first order formulas. Equivalence games are defined and are used to establish whether an algebra is *omega*-categorical. We have a simple proof that the perfect extension of a representable relation algebra is completely representable. (edited)

**Hodkinson, Ian** and Simon, András. The *k*-Variable Property is Stronger than H-Dimension *k*. *J Phil Log*, 26(1), 81-101, F 97.

**Hoefer, Carl**. On Lewis's Objective Chance: "Humean Supervenience Debugged". *Mind*, 106(422), 321-334, Ap 97.

**Höffe, Otfried**. Der Kommunitarismus als Alternative? Nachbemerkungen zur Kritik am moralisch-politischen Liberalismus. *Z Phil Forsch*, 50(1/2), 92-112, Ja-Je 96.

The article takes stock of the Communitarian critique of Liberalism. First, it provides a conception of "moral-political Liberalism" by developing six "stages of justice" which represent general conditions regarding the constitution of a society. This conception could be supplemented by Communitarian theories in order to complete the conditions belonging to a good life. Communitarianism cannot present an alternative theory, because its objections to the status of justice in "moral-political Liberalism" are not convincing. The author considers justice as a common inheritance of mankind. He shows that Aristotle was not a Communitarian, that friendship is not an alternative to justice and that the myth of the "unencumbered self? originates from Sandels misunderstanding about Rawls's theory.

**Höffe, Otfried**. Una repubblica mondiale come ideale politico. *Iride*, 9(19), 623-649, S-D 96.

It is one of the surprising facts in the history of philosophy that a theory of international political justice is almost completely missing. Höffe's approach is to ask how much state is required and how much state can be permitted to realize international political justice. He distinguishes four types of state on an international level: 1) an ultra minimal state, 2) a minimal state, 3) a constitutional welfare state, and 4) an absolutistic state. Considering the problems such a state has to solve and the conditions which warrant its legitimacy, the world state can only be a world republic, having the competences of a minimal state.

**Hösle, Vittorio**. Hegel and Spinoza (in Dutch). *Tijdschr Filosof*, 59(1), 69-88, Mr 97.

The essay is not dedicated to Spinoza's factual influence on Hegel, but analyzes similitudes and differences between the philosophies of the two thinkers. Both philosophies are systematic-holistic and rationalistic, even if their concepts of rationality differ strongly. Further differences concern the lack of theory of forms and of a deduction of categories in Spinoza, the (probable) rejection of determinism in Hegel, his return to Aristotle with regard to the body-mind-problem, and finally, his theory of the social world. Nevertheless, a modified Spinozism can be recognized in the Hegelian rejection of the Kantian dualism of *is* and *ought* in the *Philosophy of Right*. Various allusions to the metaphysics of Leibniz and Kant enrich the comparison.

**Hösle, Vittorio**. Philosophy in an Age of Overinformation, or: What We Ought to Ignore in Order to Know What Really Matters. *Aquinas*, 39(2), 307-320, My-Ag 96.

**Hösle, Vittorio**. The Intellectual Background of Reiner Schürmann's Heidegger Interpretation. *Grad Fac Phil J*, 19/20(2/1), 263-285, 1997.

Purpose of the essay is an analysis and a critique of Schürmann's great book on Heidegger "From Principles to Anarchy." I accept the validity of Schürmann's attempt to give a systematic form to Heidegger's thought, but show that this system is inconsistent and incompatible with the most basic ethical insights. Heidegger is labeled "the greatest philosopher of national socialism" (in a double sense of the term); the psychological and social causes of Heidegger's attractiveness in postwar Germany are analyzed. Finally, Heidegger's lasting contribution to a diagnosis of modernity and to a philosophy of modernity is recognized.

**Hösle, Vittorio** and Hála, Vlastimil. Being and Subjectivity (and Commentary V. Hála) (in Czech). *Filosof Cas*, 45(3), 481-496, 1997.

**Hoff, Paul**. Fichte und die psychiatrische Forschung. *Fichte-Studien*, 13, 241-255, 1997.

**Hoffman, Joshua** and Rosenkrantz, Gary S. *Substance: Its Nature and Existence*. New York, Routledge, 1997.

Taking as their starting point the major philosophers in the historical debate—Aristotle, Descartes, Spinoza, Locke, and Hume—Joshua Hoffman and Gary S. Rosenkranz move on to a novel analysis of substance in terms of a kind of independence which insubstantial entities do not possess. The authors explore causal theories of the unity of the parts of inanimate objects and organisms; contemporary views about substance; the idea that the only existing physical substances are inanimate pieces of matter and living organisms, and that artifacts such as clocks, and natural formations like stars, do not really exist. (publisher,edited)

**Hoffman, Paul**. The Being of Leibnizian Phenomena. *Stud Leibniz*, 28(1), 108-118, 1996.

Robert M. Adams behauptet, dass Leibniz' zwei Konzeptionen der Körper als blosse Phänomene und als Aggregate von Substanzen konsistent und somit Bestandteile einer einzigen Theorie der Phänomene seien. Dagegen möchte ich hier zeigen, dass Adams' Strategie, Körper als intentionale Objekte der Perzeption zu verstehen—als objektive Realität von Ideen im kartesischen Sinn—nicht vereinbar damit ist, sie als Aggregate von Substanzen aufzufassen. Mit Adams stimme ich insofern überein, als Aggregate von Monaden sich nur im Geist als Einheit finden, ich bestreite jedoch, dass nur im Geist die Aggregate dann auch sind.

**Hoffmann, Michael** and Von Perger, Mischa. Ideen, Wissen und Wahrheit nach Platon: Neuere Monographien. *Phil Rundsch*, 44(2), 113-151, Je 97.

The review covers nine books on Plato that were published in the years 1987-1996: eight monographs (by Benitez, T. A. Blackson, L. Chen, Eming, Erler, v. Kutschera, Szaif) and one anthology (ed. by Kobusch & Mojsisch). Main issues are Plato's hypothesis that there exist "ideas", his supposed theory and teaching about them ("Ideenlehre") and the question what kind of knowledge could be elicited from them, especially knowledge concerning the ideas themselves. Statements about these matters turn out to be controversial even when restricted to single dialogues or to a group of works representing a certain state of Plato's thinking.

**Hoffmann, Thomas Sören**. Die *Grundlage der gesamten Wissenschaftslehre* und das Problem der Sprache bei Fichte. *Fichte-Studien*, 10, 17-33, 1997.

Die Abhandlung versucht nachzuzeichnen, inwiefern das Problem der Sprache bei Fichte als Problem der Individuation von Vernunft erscheint und dabei die Frage zu beantworten, welchen kategorialen Status im Rahmen der Prinzipienlehre von 1794/95 Sprache einzunehmen hätte. Die Ambivalenz der Sprache, zugleich transzendentaler wie empirischer Gegenstand zu sein, wird im Ausgang von der Sprachursprungsschrift über die Platner-Vorlesungen und die "Reden" bis in die Spätphilosophie hinein systematisch verfolgt. Das Problem, im Zeichen der Sprache eine antinomisch verfasste Identität von Ichheit und Individualität zu denken, wird im Rückgriff auf die GWL so gelöst, dass Sprache ihrer Idee nach die Form des "thetischen Urteils" erfüllt.

**Hofmann, Paul B**. Hospital Mergers and Acquisitions: A New Catalyst for Examining Organizational Ethics. *Bioethics Forum*, 12(2), 45-48, Sum 96.

Only recently has attention and emphasis been placed on organizational ethics in health care communities. The changing face of health care, including elements such as mergers and acquisitions, are forcing organizations to define clearly the ethical standards upon which the organization makes decisions and policies. The odds of successful integration in a health care merger situation are

AUTHOR INDEX 687 Holmes, Jeremy

enhanced when relationships are built on trust and when guidelines for ethical behavior are well-enunciated and adopted.

**Hogan, Pádraig**. Communicative Action, the Lifeworlds of Learning and the Dialogue that we Aren't. *Int J Phil Stud*, 4(2), 252-272, S 96.

The first section of the paper reviews the kind of action which unfolds in Plato's *Republic*, and argues that, from Book II onwards, its character shifts from a genuine dialogue (communicative action) to a more manipulative kind of intercourse (strategic action). While the former kind of action was characteristic of the educational activities of the historical Socrates, the case is made that this kind of action became largely eclipsed in Western education and superseded by the strategic concerns to which Platonist conceptions of learning gave prominence. An argument is presented in thirteen steps in the second section of the paper, to establish the case that the kind of action which properly describes the experience of teaching and learning is that of a cultural courtship. (edited)

**Hogan, Patrick Colm**. Reading for Ethos: Literary Study and Moral Thought. *J Aes Educ*, 27(3), 23-34, Fall 93.

The first section distinguishes between interpreting a literary work for its ethical themes and using a literary work to develop ethical reflection. The second section discusses how ethical reflection proceeds. Specifically, we have moral intuitions about specific cases and we articulate ethical generalizations. However, our particular intuitions and our generalizations are often mutually inconsistent. Ethical reflection is a process whereby we seek to uncover inconsistencies in order to clarify, reconcile, structure, and develop our own moral views. The final section discusses how one might use Shakespeare's *Measure for Measure* to develop ethical reflection in a class.

**Hogarth, Mark**. A Remark Concerning Prediction and Spacetime Singularities. *Stud Hist Phil Mod Physics*, 28B(1), 63-71, Mr 97.

Intuitively, singularities may be thought to oppose prediction, but in this paper it will be shown that in a sense the opposite is true: if the universe admits at least one 'predictable event' (as precisely defined by Geroch), then a singularity is expected to exist. The method of proof for this theorem is to show that every space-time that admits at least one predictable event must also admit a so-called 'trapped set'. A version of the Hawking-Penrose singularity theorem is then employed to show that this set signals geodesic incompleteness, i.e., a singularity. A further result shows that the singularity cannot reside within a well-defined region 'between' the event of prediction and the event predicted.

**Holbrook, Daniel**. The Consequentialistic Side of Environmental Ethics. *Environ Values*, 6(1), 87-96, F 97.

There are two principles often found in environmental ethics—self-realization and environmental preservation. I argue that these are two logically independent principles. An analysis of its essential features shows that the preservation principle should be based on actual consequentialism, for it is only the actual effects of our actions and policies that are important to the main issues of environmental preservation. Aldo Leopold's land ethic is found to be an example of a consequentialistic theory of environmental preservation.

**Holcomb III, Harmon R**. Just So Stories and Inference to the Best Explanation in Evolutionary Psychology. *Mind Mach*, 6(4), 525-540, N 96.

Evolutionary psychology is a science in the making, working toward the goal of showing how psychological adaptation underlies much human behavior. The knee-jerk reaction that sociobiology is unscientific because it tells "just-so stories" has become a common charge against evolutionary psychology as well. My main positive thesis is that inference to the best explanation is a proper method for evolutionary analyses, and it supplies a new perspective on the issues raised in Schlinger's (1996) just-so story critique. My main negative thesis is that, like many nonevolutionist critics, Schlinger's objections arise from misunderstandings of the evolutionary approach. (edited)

**Holder, John J**. The Early Buddhist Theory of Truth: A Contextualist Pragmatic Interpretation. *Int Phil Quart*, 36(4), 443-459, D 96.

In this essay, I argue that the early Buddhist theory of truth should be grounded on the doctrine of dependent arising. I carefully analyze the two most widely held interpretations of the early Buddhist theory of truth: the naive correspondence-theory and the simple utilitarian theory. The naive correspondence interpretation fails because it requires reference to a fixed reality that is ruled out by the doctrine of dependent arising. The simple utilitarian interpretation fails to preserve the objectivity of moral judgment. I show how a contextualist pragmatic interpretation preserves both correspondence and utility, and squares best with the doctrine of dependent arising.

**Holderegger, Adrian**. Zur Euthanasie-Diskussion in den USA: Eine kritische Einführung. *Frei Z Phil Theol*, 44(1-2), 137-151, 1997.

**Holemans, Dirk**. A Case Study of Conflicting Interests: Flemish Engineers Involved in Environmental Impact Assessment. *Sci Eng Ethics*, 2(1), 17-24, J 96.

This article reports of the activities of the working group, Ethics and Engineers, of the Royal Flemish Society of Engineers. More particularly, the ethical problems that engineers face in the preparation of an environmental report are illuminated. Irrespective to which party the engineer belongs, he or she is confronted with the difficult weighting of his or her personal interest, the interests of private companies and last but not least the common good. It is argued that the implementation of a code of ethics and the introduction of courses on engineering ethics into the education of engineers would strengthen the engineer in the fulfillment of his vocation.

**Holland, Kitty L**. Strongly Minimal Fusions of Vector Spaces. *Annals Pure Applied Log*, 83(1), 1-22, Ja 97.

We provide a simple and transparent construction of Hrushovski's strongly minimal fusions in the case where the fused strongly minimal sets are vector spaces. We strengthen Hrushovski's result by showing that the strongly minimal fusions are model complete.

**Holland, Nancy J** (ed). *Feminist Interpretations of Jacques Derrida*. University Park, Pennsylvania Univ Pr, 1997.

Much contemporary feminist theory continues to see itself as freeing women from patriarchal oppression so that they may realize their own inner truth. To be told by postmodern thinkers such as Jacques Derrida that the very possibility of such a truth must be submitted to the process of deconstruction thus seems to present a serious challenge to the feminist project. From a postmodern perspective, on the other hand, most feminist discourse remains deeply rooted, if not in essentialism, at least in the logocentrism of traditional philosophical and political thought. Stepping beyond the usual confines of this debate, the eleven thinkers whose ideas are represented in this volume take a deeper look at Derrida's work to consider its specific strengths and weaknesses as a model for feminist theory and practice. (publisher, edited)

**Holland, R F**. Fanciful Fates. *Phil Invest*, 20(3), 246-256, Jl 97.

**Hollander, Rachelle D** and Johnson, Deborah G and Beckwith, Jonathan R (& others). Why Teach Ethics in Science and Engineering?. *Sci Eng Ethics*, 1(1), 83-87, J 95.

**Hollenbach, S.J., David**. Social Ethics Under the Sign of the Cross. *Annu Soc Christ Ethics*, 3-18, 1996.

Social ethics faces a crisis in the postmodern period. Intellectually, this crisis rises from the loss of confidence in our ability to identify the human good and what a good society would be. Practically it is due to the bloody history of the twentieth century produced by the modern quest for control. The postmodern dilemma in ethics is ultimately religious: is the encompassing reality of human and cosmic existence hostile or friendly? An ethics under the sign of the cross risks interpreting the encompassing mystery—God—as a compassionate Friend who embraces human suffering. This interpretation leads to an ethic of active solidarity with those who suffer.

**Hollenberg, Marco**. An Equational Axiomatization of Dynamic Negation and Relational Composition. *J Log Lang Info*, 6(4), 381-401, O 97.

We consider algebras on binary relations with two main operators: relational composition and dynamic negation. Relational composition has its standard interpretation, while dynamic negation is an operator familiar to students of Dynamic Predicate Logic (DPL) (Groenendijk and Stokhof, 1991): given a relation *R* its dynamic negation ~ *R* is a *test* that contains precisely those pairs (*s*, *s*) for which *s* is not in the domain of *R*. These two operators comprise precisely the propositional part of DPL. This paper contains a finite equational axiomatization for these *dynamic relation algebras*. (edited)

**Holley, David M**. Breaking the Rules When Others Do. *J Applied Phil*, 14(2), 159-168, 1997.

People often speak as if the behaviour of others is relevant to the question of whether they are justified in violating a rule. This paper explores three lines of argument which might be used to justify rule violation on grounds appealing to what others do. The appeal to self-defence as a justification does not succeed, since it must expand the concept to involve a cumbersome weighing of harms. The argument that complying with a rule may involve two great a sacrifice in some cases needs to be developed by an account of when a sacrifice is morally significant. It is tempting, but problematic, to do this by weighing consequences of individual acts. An alternative approach is to argue that the behaviour of others is sometimes relevant to determining what rule is actually functioning in some context as a part of a particular moral system.

**Hollingdale, R J** (trans) and Nietzsche, Friedrich. *Human, All Too Human: A Book of Free Spirits*. New York, Cambridge Univ Pr, 1996.

**Hollinger, David A**. "James, Clifford, and the Scientific Conscience" in *The Cambridge Companion to William James*, Putnam, Ruth Anna (ed), 69-83. New York, Cambridge Univ Pr, 1997.

James in *The Will to Believe* misrepresented Clifford concerning the wrongness of believing on insufficient evidence. Clifford had endorsed the very trial-and-error method James defended. In 1896 James was still trying to protect religious belief from the critical scrutiny demanded by Clifford. James assigned religion a sphere of belief separate from science. In *Pragmatism* (1907) James abandoned this program and adopted a position similar to that of Clifford (and Peirce) to the effect that all belief was of a piece. Clifford understood the function of knowledge in a field of social power much more fully than James did.

**Hollinger, Dennis**. Theological Foundations for Death and Dying Issues. *Ethics Med*, 12(3), 60-65, 1996.

**Hollis, Martin**. "A Remarkable Change in Man" in *Jean-Jacques Rousseau and the Sources of the Self*, O'Hagan, Timothy (ed), 56-65. Brookfield, Avebury, 1997.

**Holly, Michael Ann**. Schapiro Style. *J Aes Art Crit*, 55(1), 6-10, Wint 97.

**Holmes, Arthur F**. *Fact, Value, and God*. Grand Rapids, Eerdmans, 1997.

Holmes surveys the historical ways of grounding moral values objectively in the nature of reality, pausing along the way to consider such major landmarks in Western thought as Plato, Aristotle, Augustine, Aquinas, Ockham, the Reformers, Kant, Hegel, and Nietzsche. Unconvinced that we live in a value-free universe, that face and value are ultimately unrelated, or that we have to create all our own values rather than discovering the good, Holmes here explores the fact-value connection in the larger context of metaphysical and theological views. What emerges is a pervasive—and convincing—link between religious and moral beliefs. (publisher, edited)

**Holmes, Jeremy**. Commentary on "Autobiography, Narrative, and the Freudian Concept of Life History". *Phil Psychiat Psych*, 4(3), 201-203, S 97.

**Holmes, Robert L**. Sexual Harassment and the University. *Monist*, 79(4), 499-518, O 96.

This article defines sexual harassment as repeated, unwanted sexual attention and argues that, so understood, sexual harassment is not, per se, sex discrimination; though in some contexts it may in fact constitute such discrimination (mainly by being a form of covert sexism). While recognizing that sexual harassment may be wrong for a variety of reasons, the article argues that it is always a violation of privacy and when practiced by faculty in a university is a betrayal of trust as well.

**Holmes, Susan** and Diaconis, Persi. Are There Still Things To Do in Bayesian Statistics?. *Erkenntnis*, 45(2 & 3), 145-158, Nov 96.

From the outside, Bayesian statistics may seem like a closed little corner of probability. Once a prior is specified you compute! From the inside the field is filled with problems, conceptual and otherwise. This paper surveys some of what remains to be done and gives examples of the work in progress via a Bayesian peek into Feller Volume I.

**Holowchak, Mark A**. Aristotle on Dreaming: What Goes On in Sleep When the 'Big Fire' Goes Out. *Ancient Phil*, 16(2), 405-423, Fall 96.

In three treatises on sleep and dreams in the *Parva Naturalia*, Aristotle gives an account of dreaming couched exclusively in terms of the material conditions of sleep. For Aristotle, dreams are not meaningful—in that all dreams are significant *in the same way* for each organism—and, therefore, serve no purpose for normal, healthy organisms. One should not, mistakenly conclude that he has no story to tell about dreams. For Aristotle, some dreams are morally or psychologically revelatory, some indicate bodily health, while others are predictive. In all, I argue, his account of dreams is one of the most fulfilling in antiquity.

**Holt, Jason**. A Comprehensivist Theory of Art. *Brit J Aes*, 36(4), 424-431, O 96.

Here I outline a theory of art based on separate accounts of artistic expression and aesthetic experience. Both the act of expression and the mental states that cause it are understood as "objectified" in artwork. Unlike experiences that typify mental life generally, aesthetic experience is understood as a "resolution" of, rather than as a conflict between, intellectual and emotional responses. The predicates 'objectified' and 'resolutive' are explicated, and art is understood as objectified expression elicitive of resolutive experience. Implications of this view are discussed and, I argue, largely intuitive.

**Holtman, Sarah Williams**. Toward Social Reform: Kant's Penal Theory Reinterpreted. *Utilitas*, 9(1), 3-21, Mr 97.

Here I set the stage for developing a Kantian account of punishment attuned to social and economic injustice and to the need for prison reform. I argue that we cannot appreciate Kant's own discussion of punishment unless we read it in light of the theory of justice of which it is a part and the fundamental commitments of that theory to freedom, autonomy and equality. As important, we cannot properly evaluate Kant's advocacy of the law of retribution unless we recognize his theory of justice as an ideal theory. Once we understand both Kant's larger account of justice and its relationship to his less basic commitments, we discover grounds to accept that larger theory, but reject components like the law of retribution with their basis in empirical conclusions we may not share with Kant. We also open the way to develop an account of punishment responsive to social circumstances.

**Holton, Richard**. Reason, Value and the Muggletonians. *Austl J Phil*, 74(3), 484-487, S 96.

Michael Smith has argued that to value an action is to believe that if one were fully rational one would desire that one perform it. I offer the Muggletonians as a counter-example. The Muggletonians, a 17th century English sect, believed that reason was the path of the Devil. They believed that their fully rational selves—rational in just Smith's sense—would have blasphemed against God; and that their rational selves would have wanted their actual selves to do likewise. But blaspheming against God was not what they valued.

**Holtug, Nils**. Altering Humans—The Case For and Against Human Gene Therapy. *Cambridge Quart Healthcare Ethics*, 6(2), 157-174, Spr 97.

It is argued that neither somatic nor germ-line gene therapy, nor even gene therapy for enhancement is inherently wrong, and that an adequate assessment should consist in weighing risks and benefits. Furthermore, it is argued that we have technologies that make germ-line therapy superfluous, unless we want to engage in enhancement engineering; and that although we should be extremely cautious if we were to engage in enhancement engineering, we cannot categorically rule out that there might be cases in which this kind of therapy should be applied.

**Holtug, Nils**. Who Benefits? Why Personal Identity Does Not Matter in a Moral Evaluation of Germ-Line Gene Therapy. *J Applied Phil*, 13(2), 157-166, 1996.

Recently it has been argued that some instances of germ-line gene therapy will change the identity of the person who receives the benefit of therapy, and that in these instances there is no good moral reason to conduct germ-line gene therapy. Against this we argue that even if gene therapy should have an effect on the identity of the resulting person, this would not diminish the urgency of the therapy. Not only would impersonal moral reasons speak in favour of such radical gene therapy, there would also be person-affecting reasons to perform it.

**Holtug, Nils** and Sandoe, Peter and Simonsen, H B. Ethical Limits to Domestication. *J Agr Environ Ethics*, 9(2), 114-122, 1996.

Through the process of domestication the genetic make-up of farm animals can be changed by means of either selective breeding or genetic engineering. This paper is about the ethical limits to such genetic changes. It is suggested that the ethical significance of domestication has become clear recently in the light of genetic engineering, but that the problem has been there all along. Two ethical approaches to domestication are presented, genetic integrity and animal welfare. It is argued that the welfare approach is superior. Finally, five ethical hypotheses based on the welfare approach are presented.

**Holtzapple, Mark** and Pritchard, Michael S. Responsible Engineering: *Gilbane Gold* Revisited. *Sci Eng Ethics*, 3(2), 217-230, Ap 97.

**Honderich, Ted**. Compatibilism, Incompatibilism, and the Smart Aleck. *Phil Phenomenol Res*, 56(4), 855-862, D 96.

**Honderich, Ted**. Consequentialism, Moralities of Concern, and Selfishness. *Philosophy*, 71(278), 499-520, O 96.

1) Consequentialism and nonconsequentialism are best identified ostensively, by giving groups of reasons for the rightness of actions. Concentration on utilitarianism distorts understanding of the first group. 2) Traditional causal conceptions of the two groups are inadequate and unenlightening. 3) So with newer conceptions. 4) Reasons of the first group are best understood in terms of satisfaction and frustration of desires and giving a priority to reducing frustration. They come from moralities of concern. 5) Reasons of the second group, including agent-relative reasons, cannot be defended by collapsing the question of right action into that of the goodness of an agent. 6) Reasons of the second group, if take as not involving satisfaction and frustration, are not reasons for action and hence not reasons for the rightness of action. 7) Reasons of this group, taken as involving satisfaction and frustration, face a judgement of selfishness.

**Hong, Tzung-Pei** and Chang, Kuo-Chin and Tseng, Shian-Shyong. Machine Learning by Imitating Human Learning. *Mind Mach*, 6(2), 203-228, My 96.

Learning general concepts in imperfect environments is difficult since training instances often include noisy data, inconclusive data, incomplete data, unknown attributes, unknown attribute values and other barriers to effective learning. It is well-known that people can learn effectively in imperfect environments and can manage to process very large amounts of data. Imitating human learning behavior, therefore, provides a useful model for machine learning in real-world applications. This paper proposes a new, more effective way to represent imperfect training instances and rules and based on the new representation, a Human-Like Learning (HULL) algorithm for incrementally learning concepts well in imperfect training environments. Several examples are given to make the algorithm clearer. Finally, experimental results are presented that show the proposed learning algorithm works well in imperfect learning environments

**Honig, Bonnie**. Ruth, The Model Emigrée: Mourning and the Symbolic Politics of Immigration. *Polit Theory*, 25(1), 112-136, F 97.

Are foreigners or strangers a threat to the social unity that democracy requires, as Jean-Jacques Rousseau thought? What are the implications of that belief, still popular today, for the contemporary politics of immigration? A reading of the contemporary symbolic politics of immigration in the U.S. and France, in combination with a reading of the Biblical *Book of Ruth*, and its interpreters (Ruth is an immigration story recently redeployed by Cynthia Ozick and Julia Kristeva), shows that foreigners play a complicated role in both hindering *and* fostering the development of shared identities, institutions and democratic commitments. Some psychoanalytic theories of mourning and loss may help us see the unattainability of the social unity upon which democracy supposedly depends. Rethinking democracy in relation to cosmopolitanism rather than the nation-state softens concerns about social unity while opening up new possibilities of alien political activity, from social movement politics to alien suffrage.

**Honneth, Axel**. Anerkennung und moralische Verpflichtung. *Z Phil Forsch*, 51(1), 25-41, Ja-Mr 97.

**Honneth, Axel**. Patologie del sociale: Tradizione e attualità della filosofia sociale. *Iride*, 9(18), 295-328, Ag 96.

L'articolo si propone di descrivere i compiti della "filosofia sociale", chiarendo il suo rapporto con campi di ricerca attigui come la filosofia politica o la filosofia morale, e di ricostruire la tradizione di pensiero che le ha assegnato la funzione di una diagnosi delle patologie sociali. Dal "fondatore" Jean-Jacques Rousseau, attraverso Hegel, Marx e Nietzsche (1) la filosofia sociale giunge al nostro secolo, quando acquisisce un significato particolare, dopo la nascita della sociologia, dall'esperienza storica del fascismo e dello stalinismo, nelle analisi che da Hannah Arendt conducono a Michel Foucault, Jürgen Habermas e Charles Taylor (2). In conclusione, viene messa a fuoco la domanda specifica della filosofia sociale, intorno alla possibilità etica di individuare in una società data i processi che vengono percepiti come pregiudizi alla possibilità di una vita buona, per individuarne i compiti futuri (3).

**Honneth, Axel** and Velek, Josef. Integrity and Disrespect (and J. Velek Commentary) (in Czech). *Filosof Cas*, 45(2), 297-309, 1997.

**Hoogland, Jan**. "The Vulnerability of Democracy" in *Philosophy and Democracy in Intercultural Perspective*, Kimmerle, Heinz (ed), 133-139. Amsterdam, Rodopi, 1997.

One can make a distinction between the democratic intention and the concrete rules and procedures in which democratic systems have got their shape. But it is impossible to find a unambiguous definition of the democratic intention to check the quality of real existing democracies. Must the democratic intention be interpreted as a regulative ideal in a Kantian sense? Or is it rather a law in the sense of Derrida? And what can be the contribution of African points of view (Wamba-dia-Wamba and others) to solve this problem concerning the relation between the democratic intention and real existing democracies?

**Hoogland, Jan**. On the Meaning of an Intercultural Philosophy (With Reply from H. Kimmerle). *Tijdschr Filosof*, 58(3), 519-546, S 96.

Often one experiences a tension between doing justice to the 'otherness' of (the philosophies of) other cultures on the one hand and claiming universal validity

AUTHOR INDEX 689 Horák, Petr

for one's own standards of rationality on the other. Therefore a plea for the acknowledgement of the intercultural dimension of philosophy and the necessity of intercultural dialogue seems to involve the rejection of universalistic claims. In my paper, I argue that this view is as indefensible as the universalistic one. Both views are characterized by a common, but often unnoticed presupposition, viz. that one is entitled to claims to truth and universal validity if one is able to justify one's claims rationally, and if not one's claims are no more than a personal, subjective and relative opinion. I argue that the claims of our basic beliefs which are regulative for our 'way of life' are scarcely justified rationally, although they are often of a rather universalistic character.

**Hook, Sidney**. *The Metaphysics of Pragmatism.* Amherst, Prometheus, 1996.

'Pragmatism' has become a debased word in the linguistic exchange of contemporary philosophy. Its one indisputable signification is that of a militant method of approaching and settling philosophic problems—some say by ignoring them, others say by calling familiar assumptions into question. But unless pragmatism is to experience the same fate which has befallen the positivism of Comte and the phenomenalism of March—philosophies proudly and avowedly antimetaphysical—it must analyze the implications of what it means to have a method and examine the generic traits of existence which make that method a fruitful one in revealing them. Identified as it commonly is with what is merely instrumental, it must start with a consideration of 'the instrument' and follow its lead into the subject matter which is, so to speak, instrumentalized. This emphasis on 'the instrument' is not an evasion of a metaphysics but a challenge to one."(publisher, edited)

**Hooker, Brad**. Ross-Style Pluralism versus Rule-Consequentialism. *Mind*, 105(420), 531-552, O 96.

This paper employs (and defends where needed) a familiar four-part methodology for assessing moral theories. This methodology makes the most popular kind of moral pluralism—here called Ross-style pluralism—look extremely attractive. The paper contends, however, that, if rule-consequentialism's implications match our considered moral convictions as well as Ross-style pluralism's implications do, the methodology makes rule-consequentialism look even more attractive than Ross-style pluralism. The paper then attacks two arguments recently put forward in defence of Ross-style pluralism. One of these arguments is that no moral theory containing some single normative principle to justify general pro tanto duties can do justice to the ineliminable role of judgment in moral thinking. The other argument is that no such theory is plausible in light of the fact that our moral ideas come from disparate historical sources.

**Hooker, Cliff A**. Dynamical Systems in Development: Review Essay of Linda V. Smith and Esther Thelen (Eds) *A Dynamics Systems Approach to Development: Applications. Phil Psych*, 10(1), 103-112, Mr 97.

This book focuses on showing how the ideas central to the new wave of dynamic systems studies may also form the basis for a new and distinctive theory of human development where both global order and local variability in behavior emerge together from the same organizing dynamical interactions. This also sharpens our understanding of the weaknesses of the traditional formal, structuralist theories. Conversely, dynamical models have their own matching set of problems, many of which are consciously explored here. Less readily acknowledged, the youthfulness of this field means that many of the studies presented here struggle to pass beyond speculative metaphor. Nonetheless, the field is shown to be one of vigor, intelligence and great promise.

**Hookway, Christopher**. "Logical Principles and Philosophical Attitudes: Peirce's Response to James's Pragmatism" in *The Cambridge Companion to William James,* Putnam, Ruth Anna (ed), 145-165. New York, Cambridge Univ Pr, 1997.

**Hookway, Christopher**. "Sentiment and Self-Control" in *The Rule of Reason: The Philosophy of Charles Sanders Peirce,* Forster, Paul (ed), 201-222. Toronto, Univ of Toronto Pr, 1997.

Peirce argues that logic and responsible reasoning are grounded in sentiment. He also says that scientific rationality depends upon altruistic sentiments. The essay explores these themes in Peirce's thought, showing how sentiments and emotions can contribute to the rationality of our deliberations by providing a vehicle for immediate evaluations which are not subject to self criticism. It also considers in detail Peirce's response to the problem of how a frequentist can account for the rationality of going by probabilities in particular cases.

**Hookway, Christopher**. Design and Chance: The Evolution of Peirce's Evolutionary Cosmology. *Trans Peirce Soc*, 33(1), 1-34, Wint 97.

After 1880, Peirce worked on a system of scientific metaphysics, an evolutionary cosmology which issued in six papers in The Monist after 1890. Examining several texts from the 1880s the paper asks why Peirce's thought took this new direction. After considering the suggestion that it is needed to explain why true laws and theories are 'salient' for us, it turns to his claim that fundamental logical and metaphysical axioms are only approximately true. The conclusion is that this development was required by Peirce's realism and by his claim that efficient inquiry is fated, eventually, to arrive at the truth.

**Hoover, Jeffrey L**. "Appropriating Selfhood: Schleiermacher and Hegel on Subjectivity as Mediated Activity" in *Figuring the Self: Subject, Absolute, and Others in Classical German Philosophy,* Zöller, Günter (ed), 206-226. Albany, SUNY Pr, 1997.

Schleiermacher and Hegel reject the conception of a pure, spontaneous ego that is immediately aware of itself and foundational for empirical consciousness. Instead, self-consciousness is viewed by these thinkers as the result of an empirical consciousness coming to distinguish itself from others within a community of language and action. Here I explore the essential role that both thinkers assign to property in the development of self-consciousness. Despite their general agreement on the necessity of the practical activity of appropriation for achieving an awareness of self, they provide opposing accounts of the nature and role of property in this process.

**Hoover, Randy L** and Kindsvatter, Richard. *Democratic Discipline: Foundation and Practice.* Englewood Cliffs, Prentice Hall, 1997.

We have conceived this book as a primary text for courses on classroom management and discipline as well as a supplemental text for either general methods classes and certain foundations classes related to examining democratic perspectives on schooling and teaching. We also believe that elements of this text can be used effectively in a variety of graduate-level professional development courses where the focus is school reform, critical reflectivity, curriculum development, or instructional development. (publisher, edited)

**Hopkins, Jasper**. *Glaube und Vernunft im Denken des Nikolaus von Kues: Prolegomena zu einem Umri_ seiner Auffassung.* Trier, Paulinus Verlag, 1996.

The author considers four interpretations which imply that Nicholas of Cusa's writings contain no consistently articulable conception of the relationship between faith and reason. After calling these interpretations into question, he goes on to sketch what he regards as the quintessence of Cusa's view.

**Hopkins, Patrick D**. Why Does Removing Machines Count as "Passive" Euthanasia?. *Hastings Center Rep*, 27(3), 29-37, My-Je 97.

The distinction between "passive" and "active" euthanasia, though problematic and highly criticized, retains a certain intuitive appeal. When a patient is allowed to die, nature appears simply to be taking its course. Yet when a patient is killed by, say, a lethal injection, humans appear to be causing his or her death. Guilt seems to follow naturally from the latter act while not from the former. Yet this view only holds up if age-old and vague ideas about "nature" and "artifice" go unscrutinized.

**Hopkins, Patrick D** (ed) and Strikwerda, Robert (ed) and May, Larry (ed). *Rethinking Masculinity: Philosophical Explorations in Light of Feminism.* Lanham, Rowman & Littlefield, 1996.

The new edition of this popular book is reorganized to present pairs of contrasting views on what it means to be a man in contemporary Western culture. Addressing such issues as sex differences, fatherhood, intimacy, homosexuality and oppression, the collection also includes new discussions of paternity, pornography, mixed race marriage, impotence and violence. Still the only philosophically-oriented collection on the subject, Rethinking Masculinity is an excellent text for gender studies, ethics and social philosophy courses. (publisher)

**Hopkins, Robert**. Pictures and Beauty. *Proc Aris Soc*, 97, 177-194, 1997.

Why do we care about pictures? Is there any reason for taking an aesthetic interest in pictorial art which does not apply to other art forms? I argue that pictures, but not literary works, allow the beauty of what they represent to engage our aesthetic sensibilities. To explain how they do this, we need to appeal not to what pictures represent, but to how they do so—to the form of representation involved. I reject some simple minded accounts of how pictorial representation has the capacity noted and conclude with some comments on the aesthetic significance of the phenomenon.

**Horák, Petr**. On the Main Articles in this Issue. *Filosof Cas*, 44(3), 359-361, 1996.

In the introduction to this year's third issue of *Filosoficky casopis*, the editors are drawing the readers' attention to the excellent articles included under the title *The Meeting of the International Institute of Philosophy*—Helsinki 1995. These articles were presented at the annual meeting of this institute, which is based in Paris but holds its annual meetings in different countries from which it has members. (edited)

**Horák, Petr**. Philosophy and Democracy in the World (in Czech). *Filosof Cas*, 45(2), 310-314, 1997.

*Philosophy and Democracy in the World* gives a short account of the book *Philosophie et Démocratie dans le monde* (Roger-Pol Droit ed.), which was published by UNESCO, Paris 1995 as a result of an exhaustive field research work sponsored and conducted by UNESCO in 184 countries with the aim to obtain a better view at the relationship between the philosophy status and teaching, and the democracy in the world. The author has enlarged his short report about the above mentioned book by a translation of the so-called *Declaration in favour of the philosophy* as it was adopted by UNESCO in Paris on February 15th and 11th, 1995 from the French into the Czech language.

**Horák, Petr** (trans) and Descartes, René. Letters to Elizabeth of Palatinate: (P. Horák: Commentary) (in Czech). *Filosof Cas*, 44(5), 717-730, 1996.

The A. has translated for the first time in to the Czech language four letters by René Descartes to Elisabeth of Palatinate dated by October 6th, 1645, November 3rd 1645, May 1646 and May 1648. The A. has chosen these four letters to illustrate the René Descartes's interest for the moral problems treated by him in his book *Les Passions de l'Ame* (1649).

**Horák, Petr** and Rivenc, François. The Heritage of Léon Brunschvicg (and Commentary by P. Horák) (in Czech). *Filosof Cas*, 45(2), 261-281, 1997.

G.-G. Granger's philosophical work is fully rooted in the tradition which the present paper proposes to identify as the *epistemology à la française*. This tradition goes back to the fundamental work by Léon Brunschvicg and as the author does suggest in his paper, its characteristic sings are some very topical philosophical categories like the object and the subject dialectics, the solidarity of the experiment and the theory, the discontinuity which does accompany the resolving of the problems by the means of the new conceptualizations. G.-G. Granger's work represents an attempt to give some substance to this dialectical categories with this result that the philosophy obtains a paradoxical status to be a knowledge without my object. The paper does suggest that this particular philosophical tradition represents a modern form of the idealism.

**Horder, Jeremy**. Reasons for Anger: A Response to Narayan and von Hirsch's Provocation Theory. *Crim Just Ethics*, 15(2), 63-75, Sum-Fall 96.

**Horgan, Terence**. Connectionism and the Philosophical Foundations of Cognitive Science. *Metaphilosophy*, 28(1-2), 1-30, Ja-Ap 97.

This is an overview of recent philosophical discussion about connectionism and the foundations of cognitive science. Connectionist modelling in cognitive science is described. Three broad conceptions of the mind are characterized and their comparative strengths and weaknesses are discussed: 1) the classical computational conception in cognitive science; 2) a popular foundational interpretation of connectionism that John Tienson and I call "nonsentential computationalism"; and 3) an alternative interpretation of connectionism attempts to enlist connectionism in defense of eliminativism about folk psychology.

**Horgan, Terence**. Kim on the Mind—Body Problem. *Brit J Phil Sci*, 47(4), 579-607, D 96.

For three decades the writings of Jaegwon Kim have had a major influence in philosophy of mind and in metaphysics. Sixteen of his philosophical papers, together with several new postscripts, are collected in Kim [1993]. The publication of this collection prompts the present essay. After some preliminary remarks in the opening section, in Section 2 I will briefly describe Kim's philosophical 'big picture' about the relation between the mental and the physical. In the remainder of the paper I will focus on two issues at the heart of his position, with particular attention to what he says about them in some of the more recent papers and the postscripts in Kim [1993]. First, how should a materialist understand the notion that the mental is 'determined' by the physical? Second, need a viable materialism assert that mentalistic psychology is reducible to neurobiology (and ultimately to physics)?(edited)

**Horgan, Terence**. The Perils of Epistemic Reductionism. *Phil Phenomenol Res*, 56(4), 891-897, D 96.

This is a contribution to a symposium on Crispin Wright's *Truth and Objectivity*. I distinguish between 1) Wright's generic approach to truth and to realism/antirealism debates about various kinds of discourse (e.g., humor discourse, moral discourse, mathematical discourse) and 2) an epistemically reductionist implementation of the generic view that he apparently favors. I sketch an alternative, nonepistemic, implementation and I argue against epistemically reductive versions. According to the view I sketch, truth is *correct assertibility*. Unlike Putnam's "ideal warranted assertibility" or Wright's "superassertibility," correct assertibility is not a concept constructible from the notion of epistemic warrant.

**Horgan, Terence** and Tienson, John. "Connectionism and the Commitments of Folk Psychology" in *AI, Connectionism and Philosophical Psychology, 1995*, Tomberlin, James E (ed), 127-152. Atascadero, Ridgeview, 1995.

William Ramsey, Stephen Stich, and Joseph Garon argue that folk psychology (FP) is committed to a feature of mental states they call "modularity," that this feature is incompatible with certain connectionist models, and hence that those models support eliminativism. We offer three replies. First, FP is clearly committed only to a weak form of modularity that connectionism accommodates easily. Second, even if FP were committed to other forms of modularity not manifested in human cognition, this would not mean that FP is so radically false that there are no beliefs and desires. Third, connectionism actually can accommodate various other forms of modularity anyway.

**Horgan, Terence** and Timmons, Mark. From Moral Realism to Moral Relativism in One Easy Step. *Critica*, 28(83), 3-39, Ag 96.

In recent years, defenses of moral realism have embraced what we call 'new wave moral semantics', which construes the semantic workings of moral terms like 'good' and 'right' as akin to the semantic workings of natural-kind terms in science and also takes inspiration from functionalist themes in the philosophy of mind. This sort of semantic view which we find in the metaethical views of David Brink, Richard Boyd, Peter Railton, is the crucial semantical underpinning of a naturalistic brand of moral realism that these philosophers favor—a view that promises to deliver a robust form of moral realism. We argue that new wave moral semantics leads, in one way or another, to moral relativism—a view that is incompatible with the kind of moral realism these philosophers aim to defend.

**Horgan, Terence** and Timmons, Mark. Troubles for Michael Smith's Metaethical Rationalism. *Phil Papers*, 25(3), 203-231, N 96.

In his recent book, *The Moral Problem*, Michael Smith defends as anti-Humean, rationalist account of normative reasons in terms of which he analyzes moral judgments of rightness. We argue that 1) if Smith's analysis of normative reasons is correct, then there is good reason to be skeptical about there being normative moral reasons, which would force one to accept an error theory of moral discourse; however we go on to argue that 2) there are serious problems with Smith's analysis of normative reasons and that 3) a kind of irrealist metaethical theory, not considered by Smith and not usually recognized as a metaethical option, has serious potential for solving what Smith call 'the moral problem'.

**Horn, Christoph**. Augustinus und die Entstehung des philosophischen Willensbegriffs. *Z Phil Forsch*, 50(1/2), 113-132, Ja-Je 96.

Is the philosophical concept of the will known in classical antiquity? Or has it been discovered by Judaeo-Christian authors, especially by Augustine? To find a solution for this question—still unresolved among classical scholars and philosophers—the article employs two criteria: an author disposes of the concept of the will if he accepts 1) a faculty of doing the wrong despite of

knowing the right, and 2) an ability of acting without being forced by any cause. While Plato and Aristotle do not fully possess such a concept, it is interesting to see that Augustine has exactly these conditions in mind which he speaks of *liberum arbitrium voluntatis*.

**Horn, Christoph**. Selbstbewusstsein in der Spätantike: Neuere Untersuchungen zu Plotins Schrift V 3 [49]. *Phil Rundsch*, 44(1), 33-43, Mr 97.

The discussion-note compares three recent commentaries on Plotinus on self-knowledge and self-consciousness (*Enneads*, V3 [49]). The main question is: In late antiquity, what is a theory of self-consciousness about? Apparently, there are great differences between the Plotinian conception and both that of Descartes and of Wittgenstein or Heidegger. Plotinus's theory is adequately to be compared to Fichte's notion of *Ich* or Hegel's notion of *Geist*.

**Horner, John M**. If the Eye Were an Animal...: The Problem of Representation in Understanding, Meaning and Intelligence. *J Consciousness Stud*, 3(2), 127-138, 1996.

Theories of epistemology have come a long way since Leucippus's account of objects emitting copies of themselves that are taken up by the senses and presented to the soul, but much of modern psychology and epistemology are still based upon a representational theory of knowledge—that there is something in our head which 'stands for' the things in our world. This view has been challenged since Aristotle by an alternative view that knowledge is simply a change in the organism such that the organism better fits within its world—in short, knowledge as an adaptation. Recent advances in philosophy, psychology and artificial intelligence reinforce this functional conception of knowledge and give us a valid and consistent way of understanding meaning and intelligence. In this paper, I articulate this alternative epistemology and lay out its implications for intelligences of the artificial kind.

**Horner, Richard**. A Pragmatist in Paris: Fréderic Rauh's "Task of Dissolution". *J Hist Ideas*, 58(2), 289-308, Ap 97.

**Hornsby, Jennifer**. Collectives and Intentionality. *Phil Phenomenol Res*, 57(2), 429-434, Je 97.

**Hornsby, Jennifer**. Simple Mindedness: In Defense of Naive Naturalism in the Philosophy of Mind. Cambridge, Harvard Univ Pr, 1997.

Jennifer Hornsby sets naive naturalism against dualism, but without advancing the claims of "materialism," "physicalism," or "naturalism" as these have come to be known. She shows how we can, and why we should, abandon the view that thoughts and actions, to be seen as real, must be subject to scientific explanation. (publisher, edited)

**Hornsby, Jennifer**. Truth: The Identity Theory. *Proc Aris Soc*, 97, 1-24, 1997.

The paper promotes "the identity theory of truth". It is argued that this theory: 1) treats truth as a *sui generis* norm; 2) lets us shun correspondence theories; 3) leaves us well placed to make out or title to commonsense realism. It is shown that those advocates of a minimal theory of truth who say distinctively and genuinely deflationary things about truth deny us our title to commonsense realism.

**Horowitz, Gregg M**. "Art History and Autonomy" in *The Semblance of Subjectivity*, Huhn, Tom (ed), 259-285. Cambridge, MIT Pr, 1997.

Paradoxes in Kant's theory of art are addressed with the aid of Adorno's account of art's relation to instrumental rationality. Kant argues that artistic work is a mode of labor which is resistant to necessity and so generates the appearance of autonomy, but also that such an appearance is incompatible with the attaining of genuine freedom from necessity. The history of autonomous art thus should be understood as a history of nonreconciliation to the failure to escape instrumental rationality. On this basis, an argument is mounted against historicist repudiations of the autonomy of art.

**Horowitz, Irving Louis**. Publishing Programs and Moral Dilemmas. *J Infor Ethics*, 6(1), 13-21, Spr 97.

The aim of this paper is to provide an empirical grounding to ethical concerns with respect to a variety of issues: multiple authorship; peer review process; editorial networks and quirks; misconduct on the part of authors; dishonesty on the part of publishers; and summary remarks on everyday considerations that enter into scholarly publishing. The overall findings, entirely informal, based on more than forty years experience in the publishing environment, and comparing them with the situation of others in the field, is that moral behavior is uncommonly high—insured by a series of academic checks and balances that do not obtain in purely commercial publishing.

**Horsten, Leon**. Reflecting in Epistemic Arithmetic. *J Sym Log*, 61(3), 788-801, S 96.

An epistemic formalization of arithmetic is constructed in which certain nontrivial metatheoretical inferences about the system itself can be made. These inferences involve the notion of *provability in principle* and cannot be made in any consistent extensions of Steward Shapiro's system of epistemic arithmetic. The system constructed in the paper can be given a modal-structural interpretation.

**Horsten, Leon** (& others) and Douven, Igor and Ladyman, James. A Defence of Van Fraassen's Critique of Abductive Inference: Reply to Psillos. *Phil Quart*, 47(188), 305-321, Jl 97.

**Horster, Detlef**. Die komplementäre disparater Ethikbegründungen in der Gegenwart: Über Martin Seels Buch *Versuch über die Form des Glücks*. *Z Phil Forsch*, 50(4), 611-617, O-D 96.

**Horth, David M** and Palus, Charles J. Leading Creatively: The Art of Making Sense. *J Aes Educ*, 30(4), 53-68, Wint 96.

**Horton, John**. The Good, the Bad, and the Impartial. *Utilitas*, 8(3), 307-328, N 96.

A critique of Brian Barry's *Justice as Impartiality*. The principal argument is that the theoretical structure of justice as impartiality is insufficient to generate substantive liberal egalitarian principles of justice. In so far as Barry does justify such principles, they illicitly depend upon controversial moral or empirical contentions smuggled into the idea of 'reasonable agreement'. Problems are identified and explored in relation to Barry's treatment of the agreement motive, moderate scepticism, conceptions of the good and the role of harm.

**Horty, John F**. "Combining Agency and Obligation (Preliminary Version)" in *Deontic Logic, Agency and Normative Systems,* Brown, Mark A (ed), 98-122. New York, Springer-Verlag, 1996.

The purpose of this paper is to explore a new deontic operator for representing what an agent ought to do; the operator is cast against the background of a modal treatment of action developed by Nuel Belnap and Michael Perloff, which itself relies on Arthur Prior's indeterministic tense logic. The analysis developed here of what an agent ought to do is based on a dominance ordering adapted from the decision theoretic study of choice under uncertainty to the present account of action. It is shown that this analysis gives rise to a normal deontic operator and that the result is superior to an analysis that identifies what an agent ought to do with what it ought to be that the agent does.

**Horty, John F**. "Combining Agency and Obligation (Preliminary Version)" in *Deontic Logic, Agency and Normative Systems,* Brown, Mark A (ed), 98-122. New York, Springer-Verlag, 1996.

The purpose of this paper is to explore a new deontic operator for representing what an agent ought to do; the operator is cast against the background of a modal treatment of action developed by Nuel Belnap and Michael Perloff, which itself relies on Arthur Prior's indeterministic tense logic. The analysis developed here of what an agent ought to do is based on a dominance ordering adapted from the decision theoretic study of choice under uncertainty to the present account of action. It is shown that this analysis gives rise to a normal deontic operator, and that the result is superior to an analysis that identifies what an agent ought to do with what it ought to be that the agent does.

**Horty, John F**. Agency and Obligation. *Synthese*, 108(2), 269-307, Ag 96.

The purpose of this paper is to explore a new deontic operator for representing what an agent ought to do; the operator is cast against the background of a modal treatment of action developed by Nuel Belnap and Michael Perloff, which itself relies on Arthur Prior's indeterministic tense logic. The analysis developed here of what an agent ought to do is based on a dominance ordering adapted from the decision theoretic study of choice under uncertainty to the present account of action. It is shown that this analysis gives rise to a normal deontic operator and that the result is superior to an analysis that identifies what an agent ought to do with what it ought to be that the agent does.

**Horvath, Christopher D**. Discussion: Phylogenetic Species Concept: Pluralism, Monism, and History. *Biol Phil*, 12(2), 225-232, Ap 97.

Species serve as both the basic units of macroevolutionary studies and as the basic units of taxonomic classification. In this paper I argue that the taxa identified as species by the *Phylogenetic Species Concept* (Mishler and Brandon 1987) are the units of biological organization most causally relevant to the evolutionary process, but that such "units" exist at multiple levels within the hierarchy of any phylogenetic lineage. The PSC gives us no way of identifying one of these levels as the privileged level on which taxonomic classifications can be based.

**Horvath, Tibor**. Theodore Karman, Paul Wigner, John Neumann, Leo Szilard, Edward Teller and Their Ideas of Ultimate Reality and Meaning. *Ultim Real Mean*, 20(2 & 3), 123-146, Je-S 97.

In the article, one of the great aeronautical scientists and the four Hungarian members of the "Manhattan projects" come alive and talk about: (a) their general idea as well as (b) their specific idea of ultimate reality and meaning in science. Theodore Kalman: (a) God will do right by us and we will survive the spirit of destruction, (b) equilibrium expressed by mathematical analysis as quantitative, experimentally testable result about vortex behavior which could be readily applied to many mechanical problems: Paul Wagner: be reasonable, kind, cooperative and helpful, everything will turn out all right, (b) symmetry and group theory; John Neumann: (a) new mathematics as ultimate in the light of which one understands whatever one can understand; Leo Szilard: God who exists, (b) belief in the perfection of creation; Edward Teller: (a) an everlasting God always has more secrets to be discovered through never ending surprises, (b) complementarity, the adjustment of two mutually exclusive approaches drawn from the pursuit of simplicity. (edited)

**Horwich, Paul**. "Comment on Dretske" in *Perception,* Villanueva, Enrique (ed), 167-170. Atascadero, Ridgeview, 1996.

This essay is a response to Fred Dretske's "Phenomenal Externalism" (published in the same volume). It criticizes his attempt to undermine the prevalent assumption that a person's sensations (unlike her beliefs) supervene on her internal state, arguing that Dretske's line of thought begs the question.

**Horwich, Paul**. "Disquotation and Cause in the Theory of Reference" in *Contents,* Villanueva, Enrique (ed), 73-78. Atascadero, Ridgeview, 1995.

This essay is a response to Brian Loar's defense of a causal theory of reference in his "Reference from the First Person Perspective" (published in the same volume). It is argued, contrary to Loar, that insofar as our concept of reference is captured by the disquotation schema (roughly: "N" refers to N), then the use and utility of that concept can be fully explained without invoking any causal analysis (however, liberal or disjunctive), and so there is no reason to anticipate such an account.

**Horwich, Paul**. Realism Minus Truth. *Phil Phenomenol Res*, 56(4), 877-881, D 96.

This essay is a critique of the account of truth given by Crispin Wright in his book, *Truth and Objectivity* (Harvard University Press, 1992). It combats Wright's

allegation that the deflationary view of truth (presented in Paul Horwich's *Truth* (Blackwell, 1990) is incoherent. And it takes issue with Wright's pluralistic thesis that we employ different conceptions of truth in different domains of discourse.

**Horwitz, Steven**. Keynes on Capitalism: Reply to Hill. *Crit Rev*, 10(3), 353-372, Sum 96.

Greg Hill's recent article voices the Keynesian complaint that capitalism produces unemployment because there is no mechanism that coordinates decisions to save with decisions to invest. But resources that are not spent on current consumption are either "invested" as bank deposits or "hoarded' as cash. Deposits are lent out by banks to investors, who are informed by interest rates as to the degree of saving for future consumption that is taking place. And wage/price flexibility, as well as increases in the supply of cash, can avoid declines in real income and employment caused by increased cash holdings.

**Hoshmand, Lisa Tsoi**. Cultural Psychology as Metatheory. *J Theor Phil Psych*, 16(1), 30-48, Spr 96.

The nature and uses of metatheory are examined. Current needs for metatheoretical understanding are discussed in the context of increased skepticism about grand narratives. A focus on the lived meanings of existing metatheory and metadiscourse points to the importance of cultural psychology in addressing some of the conceptual, methodological, and axiological problems we face. It is proposed that cultural psychology can illuminate the semantic sources and pragmatics of academic discourse in the social sciences and facilitate a reflexive understanding of our ways of being and knowing.

**Hosoi, Tsutomu** and Masuda, Isao. A Study of Intermediate Propositional Logics on the Third Slice. *Stud Log*, 52(1), 15-21, F 93.

The intermediate logics have been classified into slices (cf. Hosoi [1]), but the detailed structure of slices has been studied only for the first two slices (cf. Hosoi and Ono [2]). In order to study the structure of slices, we give a method of a finer classification of slice. Here we treat only the third slice as an example, but the method can be extended to other slices in an obvious way. It is proved that each subslice contains continuum of logics. A characterization of logics in each subslice is given in terms of the form of models. (edited)

**Hotel, Carla** and Brockman, Joan. Legal Ethics in the Practice of Family Law: Playing Chess While Mountain Climbing. *J Bus Ethics*, 16(8), 809-816, Je 97.

Current literature suggests that the adversarial legal system may undergo some changes or may even be transformed by a recent influx of women lawyers into the profession. Such research indicates that women may approach ethical problems differently than men. This paper examines the responses of family law lawyers in Vancouver, British Columbia and the surrounding lower mainland to a hypothetical case which requires an assessment of professional responsibilities in light of potential conflicts in personal moral values.

**Hough, Williston S** (ed & trans) and Erdmann, Johann Eduard. *A History of Philosophy: Volume I*. Bristol, Thoemmes, 1997.

The present translation of Erdmann's *Grundriss der Geschichte der Philosophie* has been made from the third and last edition (Berlin, 1878), and executed by different hands. (publisher, edited)

**Hough, Williston S** (ed & trans) and Erdmann, Johann Eduard. *A History of Philosophy: Volume II*. Bristol, Thoemmes, 1997.

**Hough, Williston S** (ed & trans) and Erdmann, Johann Eduard. *A History of Philosophy: Volume III*. Bristol, Thoemmes, 1997.

**Houghton, David**. Mental Content and External Representations. *Phil Quart*, 47(187), 159-177, Ap 97.

**Houlgate, Stephen**. Hegel's Critique of the Triumph of *Verstand* in Modernity. *Bull Hegel Soc Gt Brit*, 35, 54-70, Spr-Sum 97.

In this essay I examine Hegel's account of the monarchy and the legislature in his *Philosophy of Right*. I consider why he believes upholding monarchy and granting legislative rights to corporations and the landed nobility are essential to a rational, modern state, and why he thinks that *enlightenment* understanding or *Verstand* inevitably *mis*understands this fact. The essay concludes with an analysis of Marx's critique of Hegel's account of the political constitution, in which I argue that, from Hegel's perspective, Marx's wish to exclude determination by nature from the modern state represents the position of the understanding, rather than reason.

**Hountondji, Paulin J** and Evans, Henri (trans). *African Philosophy: Myth and Reality*. Bloomington, Indiana Univ Pr, 1996.

In this seminal exploration of the nature and future of African philosophy, Paulin J. Hountondji attacks a myth popularized by ethnophilosophers such as Placide Tempels and Alexis Kagamé that there is an indigenous, collective African philosophy separate and distinct from the Western philosophical tradition. Hountondji contends that ideological manifestations of this view that stress the uniqueness of the African experience are protonationalist reactions against colonialism conducted, paradoxically, in the terms of colonialist discourse. Hountondji argues that a genuine African philosophy must assimilate and transcend the theoretical heritage of Western philosophy and must reflect a rigorous process of independent scientific inquiry. This edition is updated with a new preface in which Hountondji responds to his critics and clarifies misunderstandings about the book's conceptual framework. (publisher, edited)

**Houser, Nathan**. "Introduction: Peirce as Logician" in *Studies in the Logic of Charles Sanders Peirce,* Houser, Nathan (ed), 1-22. Bloomington, Indiana Univ Pr, 1997.

Readers are introduced to Charles S. Peirce *as Logician* and to a collection of essays that grew out of the logic symposium of the Peirce Sesquicentennial International Congress held at Harvard in 1989. This paper and the book it introduces, records important contributions Peirce made to modern logic and discusses their relevance for research today. It is argued that Peirce was not a logicist—he did not think of logic as the foundation for mathematics—though he made significant contributions to foundations. Nevertheless, for Peirce logic is a normative science, much broader than mathematical logical today.

**Houser, Nathan** (ed) and Roberts, Don D (ed) and Van Evra, James (ed). *Studies in the Logic of Charles Sanders Peirce.* Bloomington, Indiana Univ Pr, 1997.

This volume provides a comprehensive exploration of Charles Sanders Peirce's work in mathematics and formal logic, highlighting linkages between Peirce's work and present developments in the science and history of logic. The essays are collected from an internationally distinguished group of scholars who gathered at Harvard University in 1989 to commemorate Peirce's birth in 1839. Not just of historical interest, *Studies in the Logic of Charles Sanders Peirce* shows the considerable relevance of Peirce's work for current research. The stimulating depth and originality of Peirce's thought and the continuing importance and usefulness of his ideas are brought out by this major volume. (publisher)

**Housman, David E** and Bird, Stephanie J. Conducting and Reporting Research. *Prof Ethics*, 4(3-4), 127-154, Spr-Sum 95.

**Housman, David E** and Bird, Stephanie J. Trust and the Collection, Selection, Analysis and Interpretation of Data: A Scientist's View. *Sci Eng Ethics*, 1(4), 371-382, O 95.

Trust is a critical component of research: trust in the work of coworkers and colleagues within the scientific community; trust in the work of research scientists by the nonresearch community. A wide range of factors, including internally and externally generated pressures and practical and personal limitations, affect the research process. The extent to which these factors are understood and appreciated influence the development of trust in scientific research findings.

**Houston, Barbara**. "Multiculturalism and a Politics of Persistence" in *Philosophy of Education (1996)*, Margonis, Frank (ed), 190-196. Urbana, Phil Education Soc, 1997.

**Houtman, Dick**. Science, Religion, and Modernity: Values and Lifestyles of University Professors. *Darshana Int*, 36(1/141), 63-84, Ja 96.

**Howard, Don**. "Relativity, *Eindeutigkeit*, and Monomorphism: Rudolph Carnap and the Development of the Categoricity Concept in Formal Semantics" in *Origins of Logical Empiricism*, Giere, Ronald N (ed), 115-164. Minneapolis, Univ of Minnesota Pr, 1996.

**Howard, V A**. The Aesthetic Face of Leadership. *J Aes Educ*, 30(4), 21-37, Wint 96.

The article examines some of unwarranted assumptions of social science approaches to leadership and of leadership training programmes based upon those approaches. For example, the tendencies 1) to reify leadership as a univocal concept; 2) to bury it under theoretical abstractions; 3) to confuse leadership and influence; and 4) to equate leading (having a directorial role) with achieving leadership in that role. The article stresses that leadership is less a process or thing-in-itself than a matter of performance success. Hence, however many "skills" of *leading* we may identify, however much we may learn *about* leading and leadership from the experiences of others, leadership as an achievement, like virtuosity in musical performance, cannot be taught.

**Howard, Vernon A**. Virtuosity as a Performance Concept: A Philosophical Analysis. *Phil Music Educ Rev*, 5(1), 42-54, Spr 97.

**Howard-Snyder, Daniel**. The Argument from Divine Hiddenness. *Can J Phil*, 26(3), 433-453, S 96.

If a perfectly loving God exists, then anyone capable of a personal relationship with Him will have reasonable grounds to believe that He exists, unless they culpably lack theistic belief or God has good enough reason to permit them to lack theistic belief inculpably. One might infer that there very likely is no God since some capable persons inculpably lack theistic belief and there is no good reason for God to permit it. I argue that there is a prima facie good reason for God to refrain from entering into a personal relationship with inculpable nonbelievers and hence that there is prima facie good reason for God to permit inculpable nonbelief.

**Howard-Snyder, Daniel** and Howard-Snyder, Frances. The *Real* Problem of No Best World. *Faith Phil*, 13(3), 422-425, Jl 96.

Jove, an essentially omnipotent, essentially omniscient and morally good being, faced with a choice of which world to create (where for any he might create there is a better) randomly selects no. 777. Is he, therefore, morally surpassable? William Rowe says "yes". For Thor, an essentially omnipotent and essentially omniscient being in Jove's predicament who does not randomly create but selects no. 888 because he is prepared to select no world less than no. 888, has a degree of moral goodness that exceeds Jove's. By exploring two options—either Thor has a reason for being so prepared or he doesn't—we question the coherency of Rowe's Thor.

**Howard-Snyder, Frances**. The Rejection of Objective Consequentialism. *Utilitas*, 9(2), 241-248, Jl 97.

Objective consequentialism is often criticized because it is impossible to know which of our actions will have the best consequences. Why exactly does this undermine objective consequentialism? I offer a new link between the claim that our knowledge of the future is limited and the rejection of objective consequentialism: that 'ought' implies 'can' and we cannot produce the best consequences available to us. I support this apparently paradoxical contention by way of an analogy. I cannot beat Karpov at chess in spite of the fact that I can make each of many series of moves, at least one of which would beat him. I then respond to a series of objections. In the process I develop an account of the 'can' of ability. I conclude with some remarks about the bearing this attack has on subjective consequentialism.

**Howard-Snyder, Frances** and Howard-Snyder, Daniel. The *Real* Problem of No Best World. *Faith Phil*, 13(3), 422-425, Jl 96.

Jove, an essentially omnipotent, essentially omniscient and morally good being, faced with a choice of which world to create (where for any he might create there is a better) randomly selects no. 777. Is he, therefore, morally surpassable? William Rowe says "yes". For Thor, an essentially omnipotent and essentially omniscient being in Jove's predicament who does not randomly create but selects no. 888 because he is prepared to select no world less than no. 888, has a degree of moral goodness that exceeds Jove's. By exploring two options—either Thor has a reason for being so prepared or he doesn't—we question the coherency of Rowe's Thor.

**Howe, Dianne S**. *Individuality and Expression: The Aesthetics of the New German Dance, 1908-1936.* New York, Lang, 1996.

While much has been written about the visual artists and playwrights of early 20th century Germany—Nolde, Kandinsky, Kikoschka and others—their equally innovative contemporaries in dance have not been studied so extensively. The development of the New Dance, also called *Ausdruckstanz*, paralleled that of expressionist art and drama. This study focuses on nine choreographers whose theories, work, aesthetic values and artistic intent convey the variations and commonalities of this dance form. They are Mary Wigman, Gret Palucca, Harald Kreutzberg, Ivonne Georgi, Vera Skoronel, Berthe Trümpy, Niddy Impekoven, Grete Wiesenthal and Valeska Gert. (publisher)

**Howe, Edmund G**. Everyday Heroes in Ethics: Part I. *J Clin Ethics*, 7(4), 291-296, Wint 96.

**Howe, Edmund G**. Everyday Heroes, Part 2: Should Careproviders Ever Be Quintilian?. *J Clin Ethics*, 8(2), 115-123, Sum 97.

**Howe, Edmund G**. The Three Deadly Sins of Ethics Consultation. *J Clin Ethics*, 7(2), 99-108, Sum 96.

**Howe, Edmund G**. When Some Careproviders Have More Power than Others. *J Clin Ethics*, 8(1), 3-5, Spr 97.

**Howe, Ken** and Miramontes, Ofelia B. *The Ethics of Special Education.* New York, Teachers College Pr, 1992.

The authors delineate the ethical issues most salient and pressing to special education and provide a philosophically grounded framework for their discussion. Using the case method, the book presents 35 real-life situations that raise personal, institutional and policy issues; 23 of the cases are accompanied by analyses and the remaining 12 are provided for further exploration. This approach allows students to reason and collaborate about ethical issues rather than simply to master a set of principles and precepts. (publisher, edited)

**Howe, Lawrence W**. Process: An Answer to Lacey on Bergson. *Mod Sch*, 74(1), 43-54, N 96.

This paper discusses A.R. Lacey's interpretation of Bergson's theory of change in his 1989 study of the French philosopher. I argue that Bergson developed an account of the morphology of change which overcomes problems associated with radical doctrines of flux.

**Howeidy, Yehia**. "Islam and Enlightenment" in *Averroës and the Enlightenment*, Wahba, Mourad (ed), 227-228. Amherst, Prometheus, 1996.

**Howell, Nancy R**. Ecofeminism: What One Needs to Know. *Zygon*, 32(2), 231-241, Je 97.

Ecofeminism refers to feminist theory and activism informed by ecology. Ecofeminism is concerned with connections between the domination of women and the domination of nature. Although ecofeminism is a diverse movement, ecofeminist theorists share the presuppositions that social transformation is necessary for ecological survival, that intellectual transformation of dominant modes of thought must accompany social transformation, that nature teaches nondualistic and nonhierarchial systems of relation that are models for social transformation of values and that human and cultural diversity are values in social transformation. (edited)

**Howell, Robert**. Essay: Kendall L. Walton, *Mimesis as Make-Believe*. *Synthese*, 109(3), 413-434, D 96.

I focus on Walton's accounts of pictorial representation and of fiction. For Walton, viewers penetratively imagine, *of* their perceptual acts directed at a pictorial representation, that those acts grasp, as their real object, the thing depicted. I argue that Walton's notion of penetration is circular or uninformative; depiction turns on shared perceptual cues. Again, for Walton, our reference, via the term "Hamlet," to a purely fictional object is simply a make-believe reference. But this idea fails to capture the fact that the selfsame character can appear in different works of fiction. Nevertheless, Walton's work represents a deep theoretical advance.

**Howie, John**. Human-Centered or Ecocentric Environmental Ethics?. *Phil Cont World*, 2(3), 1-7, Fall 95.

Are ethical principles that guide human behavior suitable for the array of complex new environmental problems? Justice, nonmaleficence, noninterference and fidelity seem by extension to apply. Conflicts between the principles of humanistic ethics and environmental ethics may perhaps be resolved, as Paul W. Taylor indicates, through the application of such "priority principles" as "self-defense," "proportionality," "minimum wrong," and "restitutive justice." Taylor suggests that these principles would forbid moral agents from perpetrating harm through direct killing, habitat destruction, environmental contamination and pollution.

**Howse, Robert** and Frost, Bryan-Paul. The Specificity and Autonomy of Right: Alexandre Kojève's Legal Philosophy. *Interpretation*, 24(1), 25-65, Fall 96.

The article is a translation of the third chapter of the first section of Alexandre Kojève's *Esquisse d'une phénoménologie du droit (Outline of a Phenomenology*

AUTHOR INDEX 693 Hubert, Bernard

of Right). We believe that this chapter raises and addresses fundamental questions in legal and political theory; and even though we do not always agree with Kojève's conclusions, we would argue that his bold and often provocative understanding of right and justice, law and politics and religion and morality merits sustained critical scrutiny today. In this brief introduction, we give a short synopsis of Kojève's career; situate the *Esquisse* in his work as a whole; and provide a short summary of the chapters preceding the translated passage. (edited)

**Howson, Colin**. Bayesian Rules of Updating. *Erkenntnis*, 45(2 & 3), 195-208, Nov 96.

This paper discusses the Bayesian updating rules of ordinary and Jeffrey conditionalisation. Their justification has been a topic of interest for the last quarter century, and several strategies proposed. None has been accepted as conclusive and it is argued here that this is for a good reason; for by extending the domain of the probability function to include propositions describing the agent's present and future degrees of belief one can systematically generate a class of counterexamples to the rules. Dynamic Dutch Book and other arguments for them are examined critically. A concluding discussion attempts to put these results in perspective within the Bayesian approach.

**Howson, Colin**. *Logic with Trees: An Introduction to Symbolic Logic*. New York, Routledge, 1997.

The book is an introduction to modern formal logic. Howson covers all the key methods in both truth-functional and full first order logic, using the truth-tree, or semantic tableau, approach throughout. In addition, he discusses alternative deductive systems, transfinite numbers and the famous theorems of Gödel and church. He concludes with an analysis of the liar paradox and of the weaknesses of the truth-functional account of conditionals. (publisher, edited)

**Howson, Colin**. On Chihara's 'The Howson-Urbach Proofs of Bayesian Principles'. *Brit J Phil Sci*, 48(1), 83-90, Mr 97.

This paper discusses and rejects some objections raised by Chihara to the book *Scientific Reasoning: the Bayesian Approach*, by Howson and Urbach. Some of Chihara's objections are of independent interest because they reflect widespread misconceptions. One in particular, that the Bayesian theory presupposes logical omniscience, is widely regarded as being fatal to the entire Bayesian enterprise. It is argued here that this is no more true than the parallel charge that the theory of deductive logic is fatally comprised because it presupposes logical omniscience. Neither theory presupposes logical omniscience.

**Hoy, David Couzens**. Debating Critical Theory. *Constellations*, 3(1), 105-114, Ap 96.

**Hoyningen-Huene, Paul**. Die neuzeitliche Naturerkenntnis zerstört die Natur: Zu Georg Pichts Theorie der modernen Naturwissenschaften. *Z Phil Forsch*, 51(1), 103-114, Ja-Mr 97.

The paper discusses critically Georg Picht's theory of the natural science contained in a series of lectures held by Picht in 1973-74 and published (in German) in 1989 as *the concept of nature and its history.* Picht contends that there is a conceptual link between the imminent destruction of our environment and the nature of modern science. The result of the analysis of Picht's argument is that his claim is inaccurate and that an alternative diagnosis of the roots of our environmental problems must be given.

**Hoyningen-Huene, Paul**. Niels Bohrs Argument für die Nicht-reduzierbarkeit der Biologie auf die Physik. *Phil Natur*, 29(2), 229-267, 1992.

Der Aufsatz analysiert das Argument für die Nichtreduzierbarkeit der Biologie auf die Physik, das Bohr in seinem Vortrag "Licht und Leben" entwickelt hat und das ein wesentlicher Ausgangspunkt für die Entwicklung der Molekularbiologie war. Zunächst wird die Bohrsche antireduktionistische Behauptung geklärt. Anschliessend werden die Prämissen und die Struktur des Arguments untersucht, das diese Behauptung begründen soll. Schliesslich wird das Argument kritisiert.

**Hoyos Vásquez, Guillermo**. "Liberalismo y Comunitarismo en diálogo sobre los Derechos Humanos" in *Liberalismo y Comunitarismo: Derechos Humanos y Democracia,* Monsalve Solórzano, Alfonso (ed), 147-169. 36-46003 València, Alfons el Magnànim, 1996.

In this essay, the fundamental relationship between liberalism and communitarianism is explored in terms of the phenomenology of morals (Husserl and Strawson). In examining this relationship, the theory of communicative action (Habermas) is adopted in order to refer to a dialogue through which the meaning of the ethics of discourse becomes more apparent. The possibilities for this dialogue are examined in terms of one aspect of the ethical-political problematic which seems to give this discussion its specific character in certain democracies: social-economic rights, whose absence implies greater inequity, higher levels of violence and, as a result, less humanity.

**Hoyos Vásquez, Guillermo**. Phenomenological Ethics and Moral Sentiments (Spanish). *Rev Filosof (Venezuela)*, Supp(2-3), 139-154, 1996.

This paper analyzes the recent discussion of moral sentiments, based on Strawsons's book *Freedom and Resentment.* The author presents on the one hand Habermas's and Tugendhat's, although with some differences, which assumes that the phenomenology of moral sentiments justifies ethical norms; and on the other hand, Husserl's approach, in which to avoid the danger of moral relativism and ethical scepticism, considers psychology as the basis of ethics understood as the individual's historical and cultural responsibility.

**Hríbek, Tomás**. Against Coady on Hume on Testimony. *Acta Analytica*, 189-200, 1996.

The paper critically examines C.A.J. Coady's analysis of testimony, concentrating on his interpretation of the views of David Hume. The author tries to show that not only is Coady's interpretation of Hume inadequate, but that Hume's conception of testimony is in fact superior to that of Coady. Coady sees Hume as the originator of the individualistic, first-person view of testimony, according to which the reports of other people must be confirmed on the basis of an individualistically interpreted perception. Coady argues against the first-person view that it undermines the very possibility of communication. Drawing on the ideas of Wittgenstein and Davidson, he argues that a good many beliefs must be true for the communication to be possible. The author provides evidence that Hume was a third-person theorist himself, even if he did not think that the truth of the majority of beliefs must be presupposed. Moreover, Wittgenstein and perhaps Davidson are also Humean in their belief that it suffices for beliefs to be generally correct rather than true.

**Hríbek, Tomás**. Descartes, Davidson and the Causal Impotence of Thought (in Czech). *Filosof Cas*, 44(5), 863-884, 1996.

The paper deals with the mind-body problem understood as the problem of mental causation. The paper has three parts. In the first part, the author discusses the origins of the problem in Descartes. Three alternative interpretations of his notion of causal efficiency are proposed: strong dualism, moderate dualism and eliminativism. It is argued that strong dualism makes causal efficiency of the mental mysterious; moderate dualism makes the mental epiphenomenal; and eliminativism wipes it out. The remaining two parts of the paper examine those current theories that want to avoid both dualism and eliminativist materialism. The most important among them is Davidson's anomalous monism which is examined in the second part. (edited)

**Hroch, Jaroslav**. Theories of Understanding and Hermeneutical Problematic in Contemporary Anglo-American Philosophy (Czech). *Filosof Cas*, 45(1), 3-23, 1997.

The article deals with the conceptions of understanding in the philosophy of P. Winch, Ch. Taylor, P. de Man, H. Bloom and R. Rorty. Special attention is paid to analysis of epistemological, methodological, socio-cultural and ethical dimension of understanding and its relation to cultural tradition. In this connection there is also reflected the influence of Wittgenstein's later philosophy, hermeneutics and postmodernism to contemporary Anglo-American postanalytic philosophy.

**Hruschka, Joachim**. Das Opferverhalten als Schlüssel zum System der Sachentziehungsdelikte. *Jahr Recht Ethik*, 2, 177-190, 1994.

The article first discusses the structures of imputation, which were primarily developed during the eighteenth century. It sketches the differences between two levels of imputation and between ordinary and extraordinary imputation, indicating the reasons for excluding ordinary imputation. The article then considers various types of property crimes, all involving the deprivation of possession of a movable object. The claim is made that these crimes can be distinguished on the basis of whether the victim's participation can be imputed to him on the first or second level of imputation. Contemporary German law differentiates between *Diebstahl, Erpressung* and *Betrug* (approximately, simple theft, extortion and fraud) thus covering most of the relevant cases in the three groups. (edited)

**Huang, Xiaodan**. "Counter the Dangers of Education" in *Philosophy of Education (1996),* Margonis, Frank (ed), 303-306. Urbana, Phil Education Soc, 1997.

**Huang, Yong**. God as Absolute Spirit: A Heideggerian Interpretation of Hegel's God-Talk. *Relig Stud*, 32(4), 489-505, D 96.

Though this is not a comparative study of Hegel and Heidegger, this article brings Heidegger's thinking of Being to shed light on some ambiguous parts of Hegel's God-talk, which is fundamentally postmodern. Its main arguments are 1) as real, Hegel's God is not a metaphysical Being but an absolute activity; 2) as transcendent, Hegel's God is not beyond this world but immanent in this world to bring it beyond itself; and 3) as revealing, God is not external but internal to human knowing. Largely a textual reinterpretation of Hegel in light of Heidegger, this article has in mind a theology that can take our postmodern condition into serious account.

**Huang, Yong**. The Father of Modern Hermeneutics in a Postmodern Age: A Reinterpretation of Schleiermacher's Hermeneutics. *Phil Today*, 40(2), 251-262, Sum 96.

It is widely believed that Schleiermacher's hermeneutics is a psychological one, doubly mistaken from a postmodern perspective: appealing to the myth of the given and being ahistorical. This essay aims to challenge this belief. Its central theme is that Schleiermacher's unique contribution is neither his grammatical nor psychological interpretation (which is neither prelinguistic nor ahistorical) but his idea of hermeneutics as an artful movement between the two. Its conclusion is that the predominating Gadamerian postmodern hermeneutics goes to the extreme in criticizing psychologism, the evil twin of Schleiermacher's hermeneutics, while Schleiermacher's hermeneutics itself, properly understood, can be a perfect antidote to both evils.

**Huang, Zhisheng** and Masuch, Michael. The Logic of Permission and Obligation in the Framework of ALX.3: How to avoid the Paradoxes of Deontic Logics. *Log Anal*, 38(149), 55-74, Mr 95.

Standard deontic logic features fairly serious so-called "paradoxes" (technically: counterintuitive validities). Much energy in deontic logic has been spent on avoiding these "paradoxes". We suggest a reformulation of deontic logic in terms of a multi-agent logic, ALX.3, where a "super-agent" (think of a legislature) lays down the law of the land and other agents have to follow its rules. In particular, obligations are reformulated in terms of "preferences" of the superagent. We can show that our approach avoids the classical "paradoxes" of deontic logic, thanks to the properties of the preference operator of ALX.3.

**Hubert, Bernard**. Le devenir, le moteur et l'argent dans la philosophie de la nature d'Aristote. *Rev Thomiste*, 96(4), 617-632, O-D 96.

**Hudelson, Richard**. Is Marxism Totalitarian?. *Phil Soc Sci*, 27(2), 206-208, Je 97.

This discussion note is a reply to Stephen Louw, "Unity and Development etc." published in the same number of *Philosophy of the Social Science*. Louw argues that totalitarian political consequences are inherent in Marx's metaphysics of history. I hold that Louw's argument turns on a misunderstanding of Hegel.

**Hudson, Deal**. Was the Peasant of the Garonne a Mistake?. *Maritain Stud*, 8, 70-84, 1992.

**Hudson, Hud**. Brute Facts. *Austl J Phil*, 75(1), 77-82, Mr 97.

Despite its historical popularity, the *principle of sufficient reason* has recently come under attack. The objection launched against PSR is that it leads to the unappealing consequence that every truth is a necessary truth. To escape this consequence it appears that we must tolerate brute facts, i.e., true propositions for which there is no sufficient reason. In this paper I formulate this objection and then I show how David Lewis's extreme modal realism together with its reductive analysis of modality provides the resources to respond to the objection. Accordingly, I conclude that one can accept both PSR and contingency, if one is willing to be an extreme modal realist.

**Hudson, Hud**. Feinberg on the Criterion of Moral Personhood. *J Applied Phil*, 13(3), 311-317, 1996.

In a very influential paper, *Abortion*, Joel Feinberg offers a series of arguments against four popular proposals for the criterion of moral personhood and defends a fifth proposal. In this paper, I demonstrate that two widely-accepted arguments employed by Feinberg against the modified species criterion and the strict potentiality criterion, respectively, are unsound. Moreover, I argue that there is a general feature of his inquiry into the criteria for moral personhood which undermines his efforts to argue convincingly either in favour of his own candidate or against other candidates.

**Hudson, Robert**. The Tapestry of Alternative Healing. *Bioethics Forum*, 12(4), 3-13, Wint 96.

Contrary to some thinking, traditional medicine did not become monolithic in theory and practice until the first half of the twentieth century. Before that its history was one of the alternative systems of causation and treatment following one after the other. In this paper, alternative medicine includes folk medicine, quackery, and "sectarians" such as osteopathy, chiropractic, and naturopathy. These categories of healers have not had discrete existences apart from each other and traditional medicine. Rather they all have edges where they have interacted with each other, at times competitively, at times cooperatively. The best tool society has to evaluate the validity of alternative medicines is science. Science, however, has not been very effective in this regard.

**Hudson, Robert G**. Classical Physics and Early Quantum Theory: A Legitimate Case of Theoretical Underdetermination. *Synthese*, 110(2), 217-256, F 97.

My goal is to dispute Norton's claim that there is no theoretical underdetermination problem arising between classical physics and early quantum theory. The strategy I use in defending my view is to adopt a suggestion made by Jarrett Leplin and Larry Laudan on how to assess the relative merits of competing theoretical alternatives, where each alternative has an equal capacity to 'save the phenomena'. In the course of the paper, I distinguish between two branches of classical physics: classical mechanics and classical electromagnetism. The former is claimed by Norton and Poincaré to be determinately ruled out by the black body evidence; and it is the former that I argue is compatible with this evidence. (edited)

**Hühn, Lore**. Das Schweben der Einbildungskraft: Eine frühromantische Metapher in Rücksicht auf Fichte. *Fichte-Studien*, 12, 127-151, 1997.

**Huemer, Michael**. Rawls's Problem of Stability. *Soc Theor Pract*, 22(3), 375-395, Fall 96.

I argue that Rawls's conception of justice cannot attain the kind of overlapping consensus that he describes in *Political Liberalism*. I show this by considering one example of a comprehensive moral and religious view, that a Christian fundamentalism, whose political implications are fundamentally in conflict with the requirements of justice as fairness. The adherents of this view could not be convinced to give up their comprehensive doctrine and no considerations outside their comprehensive doctrine could plausibly be claimed to override it. Furthermore, I argue, if one believes Christian fundamentalism, it would be irrational to set that belief aside in a political context. The broader argument is that it will always be irrational for a person to set aside his comprehensive religious, moral, or philosophical view in political theorizing, given that he takes it to be the truth.

**Huenemann, Charles**. Predicative Interpretations of Spinoza's Divine Extension. *Hist Phil Quart*, 14(1), 53-75, Ja 97.

The paper is a critical investigation of how bodies are modally related to extension in Spinoza's metaphysics. It includes an argument against Bennett's field-metaphysics interpretation.

**Hüntelmann, Rafael**. On the Ontological Determination of the States of Affairs (in German). *Prima Philosophia*, 10(3), 307-318, 1997.

By new ontological approaches rooted in analytical philosophy, the states of affairs became important for ontology. They are the ontological correlate to propositions. Different from entitative conceptions, H.-E. Hengstenberg propounded the states of affairs to be "transentitative." Hengstenberg's approach of interpretation is developed and discussed comparatively to more recent ontologies of the states of affairs. Finally, a principal problem of all ontologies of the states of affairs is pointed out. It consists in its formalism, excluding aspects of essence.

**Huerga Melcón, Pablo**. Newton, *El templo de Salomón* (Editorial Debate, Madrid 1996). *El Basilisco*, 22, 95-100, Jl-D 96.

**Hüttemann, Andreas**. *Idealisierungen und das Ziel der Physik: Eine Untersuchung zum Realismus, Empirismus und Konstruktivismus in der Wissenschaftstheorie*. Hawthorne, de Gruyter, 1996.

Die vorliegende Arbeit ist der Frage gewidmet, welches Ziel die Physik hat. Das wesentliche Ergebnis derselben ist die Ablehnung traditioneller Vorschläge für eine solches Ziel zugunsten eines neuen Vorschlages. Sowohl bei der Ablehnung der älteren als auch bei der Bestätigung des neuen Zielvorschlags stütze ich mich auf eine in der Physik weit verbreitete Praxis—die Praxis der Idealisierung. Traditionelle Zielvorschläge müssen deshalb aufgegeben werden, weil sie diese Praxis nicht zu erklären vermögen, mein eigener Vorschlag wird dadurch gestützt, dass nachgewiesen werden kann, dass er die Praxis der Idealisierung erklären kann. (edited)

**Hüttemann, Andreas**. Über das Verhältnis von Metaphysik und Physik bei Descartes. *Stud Leibniz*, 28(1), 93-107, 1996.

According to Descartes, physics rests on metaphysics. Various possible interpretations of this metaphor are considered. I will show that only a weak interpretation can be brought into accordance with other parts of Descartes' philosophy. According to the weak interpretation, physics has to presuppose metaphysics because the latter shows that contrary to widespread contemporary arguments the concepts of mathematical physics are adequate to describe nature. It is argued for this position by comparing the *Regulae*, where Descartes did not make use of metaphysical arguments, with the *Principia*, where he did.

**Huey-li, Li**. "On the Nature of Environmental Education: Anthropocentrism versus Non-Anthropocentrism: The Irrelevant Debate" in *Philosophy of Education (1996)*, Margonis, Frank (ed), 256-263. Urbana, Phil Education Soc, 1997.

This paper examines Aldo Leopold's land ethic and Arne Naess's deep ecology. I point out that the values of natural objects and processes cannot be independent from human moral reasoning and that a recognition of the integrated relationship between the values of nature and human values can be a double-edged sword for us in addressing today's ecological problems. In other words, understanding the cultural roots could lead us to assume our responsibilities and help us to articulate ecologically congenial cultural values.

**Huff, Chuck** and Anderson, Ronald E and Little, Joyce Currie (& others). Integrating the Ethical and Social Context of Computing into the Computer Science Curriculum. *Sci Eng Ethics*, 2(2), 211-224, A 96.

This paper describes the major components of ImpactCS, a program to develop strategies and curriculum materials for integrating social and ethical considerations into the computer science curriculum. It presents, in particular, the content recommendations of a subcommittee of ImpactCS; and it illustrates the interdisciplinary nature of the field, drawing upon concepts from computer science, sociology, philosophy, psychology, history and economics.

**Hufnagel, Erwin**. The Idea of the University and the Role of Philosophy. *Filozof Istraz*, 16(3), 727-740, 1996.

Ausgehend von der Rekonstruierung der Entstehungsgeschichte der Universität als eines komplexen kulturell-wissenschaftlichen Phänomens im europäischen geistig-wissenschaftlichen und sozio-politischen Kontext, untersucht der Verfasser wesentliche Aspekte von Struktur, Funktion und Zielen der Institution der Universität. Verfolgt wird ihre geschichtliche Dynamik, innerhalb derer als konstante Merkmale die Grundbestimmungen der Universität zu erkennen sind. (edited)

**Huggett, Nick**. Identity, Quantum Mechanics and Common Sense. *Monist*, 80(1), 118-130, Ja 97.

Commentators have argued that Quantum Mechanics (QM) challenges our classical 'common sense' intuitions about identity in a variety of ways. This paper is an introduction to the various ideas and arguments raised in the recent literature, at a level that does not presuppose much familiarity with QM. It focusses on the absence of definite trajectories, the indistinguishability of quanta, the consequences of 'Bose-Einstein' statistics and Bohm's interpretation. The paper also argues that the concepts of identity appropriate for QM may be much closer to those appropriate for classical physics than is usually appreciated.

**Huggett, Nick** and Weingard, Robert. Exposing the Machinery of Infinite Renormalization. *Proc Phil Sci Ass*, 3(Suppl), S159-S167, 1996.

This paper sets out the problem of renormalization in perturbative quantum field theory, and offers a transparent model as a clear counter example to the idea that the need for renormalization shows a theory to be inconsistent. The model is not of a quantum field but liquid diffusion through a porous medium: though the systems are physically dissimilar, their formal properties are identical, as we demonstrate. Since the model system is much easier to understand, we can see the meaning of renormalization much more clearly and, we claim, draw lessons about renormalization in field theory.

**Hughes, Charles T**. Belief, Foreknowledge, and Theological Fatalism. *Faith Phil*, 14(3), 378-387, Jl 97.

David Hunt has recently developed a new strategy called the "dispositional omniscience scenario," or (DOS), which is designed to defeat theological fatalism by showing the *compatibility* of divine foreknowledge and human (libertarian) free agency. But I argue that Hunt fails to establish his compatibility claim because (DOS) is based on a defective analysis of dispositional belief that is too weak to sustain *any* divine foreknowledge of future free actions.

**Hughes, Christopher**. Giving the Skeptic Her Due?. *Epistemologia*, 19(2), 309-326, Jl-D 96.

Robert Nozick propone una definizione di conoscenza secondo la quale qualcuno sa che *P* se e solo se la sua credenza che *P* covaria col fatto che *P*. Facendo uso di una tale definizione, egli offre una risposta nuova e ingegnosa allo scettico per cui quest'ultimo ha ragione nell'asserire che, per qualsiasi proposizione contingente *P* riguardante il mondo esterno, io non so di non sognare che *P*, ma è nel torto nell'inferire che, sempre per qualsiasi proposizione contingente *P* riguardante il mondo esterno, io non so che *P*. Nozick ritiene così di dare il dovuto allo scettico—accettando le sue premesse (plausibili), pur negando la sua (incredibile) conclusione. In questo articolo vengono presentate due argomentazioni al fine di mostrare che la definizione di conoscenza offerta da Nozick non è tale da consentirgli di dare il dovuto allo scettico. La prima di esse risulta plausibile ma inconcludente, mentre la seconda risulta concludente oltre che plausibile.

**Hughes, Christopher**. Same-Kind Coincidence and the Ship of Theseus. *Mind*, 106(421), 53-67, Ja 97.

Locke thought that it was impossible for there to be two things of the same kind in the same place at the same time. I offer (what looks to me like) a counterexample to that principle, involving two ships in the same place at the same time. I then consider two ways of explaining away, and one way of denying, the apparent counterexample of Locke's principle, and I argue that none is successful. I conclude that, although the case under discussion does not refute Locke's principle, it constitutes a serious challenge to it.

**Hughes, G E** and Cresswell, M J. *A New Introduction to Modal Logic*. New York, Routledge, 1996.

The book takes readers from the most basic systems of modal propositional logic right up to systems of modal predicate logic with identity. It covers both technical developments—such as completeness and incompleteness, and finite and infinite models—and their philosophical applications, especially in the area of modal predicate logic. (publisher,edited)

**Hughes, Paul**. Taking Ethics Seriously: Virtue, Validity, and the Art of Moral Reasoning. *Teach Phil*, 19(3), 219-232, S 96.

In this essay I show how Bishop Butler's moral theory may be used to teach students how to take morality seriously. Specifically, Butler's theory richly illustrates the importance of clarifying the meaning of key terms in a philosophical thesis, the connection between meaning and truth in philosophical theories and the role of formal arguments in moral theory. Stressing these methodological points while exploring paradoxical aspects of Butler's theory prepares students to confront the widespread but uncritical attitude of moral skepticism with which they often begin their study of philosophical ethics.

**Hughes, Paul M**. What is Involved in Forgiving?. *Philosophia (Israel)*, 25(1-4), 33-49, Ap 97.

In this article I argue that an important type of forgiving involves overcoming personal moral anger directed at another you regard as having wronged you. Since personal moral anger is anger partially constituted by the belief that you have been wrongfully harmed, and resentment is a paradigm case of such anger, forgiveness in the sense at issue typically involves overcoming resentment. Other forms of moral anger (e.g., indignation), insofar as they are not (necessarily) constituted by the belief that you have been wronged, are not usually involved in forgiveness. Moreover, nonangry emotions such as disappointment and sadness may be involved in forgiveness just in case they are partly constituted by the belief that you have been wrongfully harmed.

**Huhn, Tom**. "Kant, Adorno, and the Social Opacity of the Aesthetic" in *The Semblance of Subjectivity*, Huhn, Tom (ed), 237-257. Cambridge, MIT Pr, 1997.

Theodor Adorno's *Aesthetic Theory* is here presented as a transposition of themes from Kant's *Critique of Judgment*. The linkage between them occurs in the formulation of what is elaborated here as the opaque *yet* social character of the aesthetic. While Kant finds such opacity in aesthetic *judgments*, specifically those in regard to natural beauty, Adorno instead theorizes that social opacity has—as a result of the failed histories of subjectivity during the last 200 years—migrated into aesthetic *objects*, which is to say artworks. The essay shows that the key to understanding this migration lies in an interpretation of Kant's sublime.

**Huhn, Tom**. A Lack of Feeling in Kant: Response to Patricia M. Matthews. *J Aes Art Crit*, 55(1), 57-58, Wint 97.

Patricia Matthews's essay "Kant's Sublime: A Form of Pure Aesthetic Reflective Judgment," attempts to defend the purity of the sublime despite the claims by Schaper, Crawford, and Crowther of an affinity between judgments of the sublime and moral judgments. I question why Matthews argues for the purity of the sublime since in the end she asserts a deep, original, and shared intimacy between it and moral judgment. I contest her assimilation as well as her collapsing together of feeling and reflective judgment in Kant. I argue instead that Kantian taste is a problem of neither communication nor ethics.

**Huhn, Tom** (ed) and Zuidervaart, Lambert (ed). *The Semblance of Subjectivity*. Cambridge, MIT Pr, 1997.

The essays in the volume, by many of the major Adorno scholars in the United States and Germany, are organized around the twin themes of semblance and subjectivity. Whereas the concept of semblance, or illusion, points to Adorno's links with Marx, Nietzsche, and Freud, the concept of subjectivity recalls his lifelong struggle with a philosophy of consciousness stemming from Kant, Hegel, and Lukács. Adorno's elaboration of the two concepts takes many dialectical twists. Art, despite the taint of illusion that it has carried since Plato's *Republic*, turns out in Adorno's account of modernism to have a sophisticated capacity to critique illusion, including its own. Adorno's aesthetics emphasizes the connection between aesthetic theory and many other aspects of social theory. The paradoxical genius of *Aesthetic Theory* is that it turns traditional concepts into a theoretical cutting edge. (publisher, edited)

**Hulac, Peter** and Barbour, Elizabeth. Futile Care in Neonatology: An Interim Report from Colorado. *Bioethics Forum*, 11(1), 42-48, Spr 95.

A group of Colorado citizens, parents and health care professionals has begun work on the problem of aggressive medical treatment in cases when such care

appears futile or inappropriate. The group is part of a larger project called GUIDe (Guidelines for Intensive Care in Denver). The committee has studied lethal medical conditions, the role of a consultation structure, care of very premature infants and developed some guidelines about newborns with life-threatening conditions.

**Hull, Carrie L**. Materiality in Theodor W. Adorno and Judith Butler. *Rad Phil*, 84, 22-35, Jl-Ag 97.

This paper analyzes Judith Butler's *Bodies That Matter* from the perspective of Theodor Adorno's essay "Subject and Object," and book *Negative Dialectics*. The epistemological issues raised by Adorno and Butler are discussed, revealing that both thinkers are working within the Kant-Hegel horizon. Adorno's explicit recognition of this tradition, however, places him in a better position to evaluate its strengths and weaknesses. The political implications of Adorno and Butler's arguments are then scrutinized. It is concluded that Adorno's materialism permits a more explicit social commentary, while still leaving room for a potent feminism.

**Hull, Gordon**. The Jewish Question Revisited: Marx, Derrida and Ethnic Nationalism. *Phil Soc Crit*, 23(2), 47-77, Mr 97.

The question of nationalism as spoken about in contemporary circles is structurally the same as Marx's "Jewish Question". Through a reading of Marx's early writings, particularly the "Jewish Question" essay, guided by Derrida's *Specters of Marx* and Benedict Anderson's *Imagined Communities*, it is possible to begin to rethink the nationalist question. In this light, nationalism emerges as the by-product of the reduction of heterogeneous 'people' into a homogeneous 'state'; such 'excessive' voices occupy an ontological space outside of the categories within which the state operates, and thus return, in Derrida's terms, to 'haunt' it. When the nationalist question is viewed in this way, contemporary solutions that depend on reproducing this reduction are called into question.

**Hull, Richard T**. "The Just Claims of Dyslexic Children" in *Reproduction, Technology, and Rights: Biomedical Ethics Reviews*, Humber, James M (ed), 139-151. Clifton, Humana Pr, 1996.

**Hull, Richard T**. No Fear: How a Humanist Faces Science's New Creation. *Free Inq*, 17(3), 18-20, Sum 97.

**Hullot-Kentor, Robert**. "The Philosophy of Dissonance: Adorno and Schoenberg" in *The Semblance of Subjectivity*, Huhn, Tom (ed), 309-319. Cambridge, MIT Pr, 1997.

**Hullot-Kentor, Robert** (ed & trans) and Adorno, Gretel (ed) and Tiedemann, Rolf (ed). *Aesthetic Theory: Theodore W. Adorno*. Minneapolis, Univ of Minn Pr, 1997.

The culmination of a lifetime of aesthetic investigation, *Aesthetic Theory* is Adorno's major work, a defense of modernism that is paradoxical in its defense of illusion. In it, Adorno takes up the problem of art in a day when "it goes without saying that nothing concerning art goes without saying." In the course of Adorno's discussion, he revisits such concepts as the sublime, the ugly, and the beautiful, demonstrating that concepts such as these are reservoirs of human experience. These experiences ultimately underlie aesthetics, for in Adorno's formulation "art is the sedimented history of human misery."(publisher,edited)

**Hulswit, Menno**. Peirce's Teleological Approach to Natural Classes. *Trans Peirce Soc*, 33(3), 722-772, Sum 97.

**Humber, James M**. "Maternity, Paternity, and Equality" in *Reproduction, Technology, and Rights: Biomedical Ethics Reviews*, Humber, James M (ed), 27-41. Clifton, Humana Pr, 1996.

In "Abortion and Fathers' Rights" Steven Hales argues that because women have a right to abort, men should be seen as having a corresponding right to refuse child support. In this essay I attack Hales's argument and contend that it is not unjust to grant women a right to abort and at the same time insist that men have an absolute obligation to support their children once they are born.

**Humber, James M** (ed) and Almeder, Robert F (ed). *Reproduction, Technology, and Rights: Biomedical Ethics Reviews*. Clifton, Humana Pr, 1996.

In the book philosophers and ethicists debate the central moral issues and problems raised by the revolution in reproductive technology. Leading issues discussed include the ethics of paternal obligations to children, the place of in vitro fertilization in the allocation of health care resources, and the ethical implications of such new technologies as blastomere separation and cloning. Also considered are how parents and society should respond to knowledge gained from prenatal testing and whether or not the right to abort should relieve men of the duty to support unwanted children. (publisher, edited)

**Humberstone, I Lloyd**. A Basic System of Congruential-to-Monotone Bimodal Logic and Two of its Extensions. *Notre Dame J Form Log*, 37(4), 602-612, Fall 96.

If what is known need not be closed under logical consequence, then a distinction arises between something's being known to be the case (by a specific agent) and its following from something known (to that subject). When each of these notions is represented by a sentence operator, we get a bimodal logic in which to explore the relations between the two notions.

**Humberstone, I Lloyd**. Intrinsic/Extrinsic. *Synthese*, 108(2), 205-267, Ag 96.

Several intrinsic/extrinsic distinctions amongst properties, current in the literature, are discussed and contrasted. The proponents of such distinctions tend to present them as competing, but it is suggested here that at least three of the relevant distinctions (including here that between nonrelational and relational properties) arise out of separate perfectly legitimate intuitive considerations: though of course different proposed explications of the informal distinctions involved in any one case may well conflict. Special attention is paid to the question of whether a single notion of property is capable of supporting the various distinctions.

**Humberstone, I Lloyd**. Singular Extensional Connectives: A Closer Look. *J Phil Log*, 26(3), 341-356, Je 97.

The totality of extensional 1-ary connectives distinguishable in a logical framework allowing sequents with multiple or empty (alongside singleton) succedents form a lattice under a natural partial ordering relating one connective to another if all the inferential properties of the former are possessed by the latter. Here we give a complete description of that lattice. (edited)

**Humberstone, I Lloyd**. Two Types of Circularity. *Phil Phenomenol Res*, 57(2), 249-280, Je 97.

For the claim that the satisfaction of certain conditions is sufficient for the application of some concept to serve as part of the ('reductive') analysis of that concept, we require the conditions to be specified without employing that very concept. An account of the application conditions of a concept not meeting this requirement, we call *analytically* circular. For such a claim to be usable in determining the extension of the concept, however, such circularity may not matter, since if the concept figures in a certain kind of intensional context in the specification of the conditions, the satisfaction of those conditions may not itself depend on the extension of the concept. We put this by saying that although analytically circular, the account may yet not be *inferentially* circular.

**Humberstone, I Lloyd**. Valuational Semantics of Rule Derivability. *J Phil Log*, 25(5), 451-461, O 96.

If a certain semantic relation (which we call 'local consequence') is allowed to guide expectations about which rules are derivable from other rules, these expectations will not always be fulfilled, as we illustrate. An alternative semantic criterion (based on a relation we call 'global consequence'), suggested by work of J W Garson, turns out to provide a much better—indeed a perfectly accurate—guide to derivability.

**Humphrey, Robert L**. Human Nature's Natural Law. *Vera Lex*, 14(1-2), 8-16, 1994.

The author centers on two value assumptions of natural law, duty and equality. He correlates these values with what we would regard as an empirical fact: Species, and so also, our human species, tend to engage in self-preserving behaviors. If these values are naturally felt, as Humphrey believes, then their means are also natural: 1) we can really perceive all of humankind as of one species, and therefore equal; 2) we can enact when necessary our duties of self-discipline or self-giving toward others. These duties preserve our species. (publisher,edited)

**Humphreys, Paul**. How Properties Emerge. *Phil Sci*, 64(1), 1-17, Mr 97.

A framework for representing a specific kind of emergent property instance is given. A solution to a generalized version of the exclusion argument is then provided and it is shown that upwards and downwards causation is unproblematical for that kind of emergence. One real example of this kind of emergence is briefly described and the suggestion made that emergence may be more common than current opinions allow.

**Humphries, Christopher J** and Scotland, Robert W and Williams, David M. Confusion in Philosophy: A Comment on Williams (1992). *Synthese*, 108(1), 127-136, Jl 96.

Patricia Williams made a number of claims concerning the methods and practice of cladistic analysis and classification. Her argument rests upon the distinction of two kinds of hierarchy: a 'divisional hierarchy' depicting 'evolutionary' descent and the Linnean hierarchy describing taxonomic groups in a classification. Williams goes on to outline five problems with cladistics that lead her to the conclusion that systematists should "eliminate cladism as a school of biological taxonomy and to replace it either with something that is philosophically coherent or to replace it with 'pure' methodology, untainted by theory" (Williams 1992, 151). Williams makes a number of points which she feels collectively add up to insurmountable problems for cladistics. We examine Williams's views concerning the 'two hierarchies' and consider what cladists currently understand about the status of ancestors. We will demonstrate that Williams has seriously misunderstood many modern commentators on this subject and all of her "five persistent problems" are derivable from this misunderstanding.

**Hund, John**. H.L.A. Hart's Contribution to Legal Anthropology. *J Theor Soc Behav*, 26(3), 275-292, S 96.

This is the first part of a two-part paper. This part amplifies and applies Hart's theory of rules to problems of agency and behaviourism in legal anthropology. Hart's theory is also applied to the problem of rule scepticism in legal anthropology and view that "customary law is what the people say it is." Llewellyn and Hoebel's theory of investigation is discussed in connection with Hart's theory of rules and law.

**Hunt, David P**. Frankfurt Counterexamples: Some Comments on the Widerker-Fischer Debate. *Faith Phil*, 13(3), 395-401, Jl 96.

One strategy in recent discussions of theological fatalism is to draw on Harry Frankfurt's famous counterexamples to the principle of alternate possibilities (PAP) to defend human freedom from divine foreknowledge. For those who endorse this line, "Frankfurt counterexamples" are supposed to *show* that PAP is false and this conclusion is then extended to the foreknowledge case. This makes it critical to determine whether Frankfurt counterexamples perform as advertised, an issue recently debated in this journal *via* a pair of articles by David Widerker and John Martin Fischer. I suggest that this debate can be avoided: divine foreknowledge is itself a paradigmatic counterexample to PAP, requiring no support from suspect Frankfurt counterexamples.

**Hunt, David P**. How (Not) to Exempt Platonic Forms from *Parmenides'* Third Man. *Phronesis*, 42(1), 1-20, 1997.

One response to Plato's Third Man Argument is that *forms* are exempt from the principles driving the argument. Call this the "Exemption Defense." This paper focuses on the question whether the exemption defense is in fact available. In pursuing this question, the paper develops the most plausible version of the exemption defense and argues that it successfully repels an important attack on the theory of forms; but the paper also suggests that this is not the attack being made in the *Parmenides*. There is a brief concluding discussion of the actual attack and its legacy for the Platonic project.

**Hunt, David P**. Two Problems with Knowing the Future. *Amer Phil Quart*, 34(2), 273-285, Ap 97.

This paper explores connections between two famous foreknowledge problems—the "Problem of Agency" (antecedent belief stultifies intentional agency) and the "Problem of Freedom" (infallible foreknowledge precludes libertarian freedom)—which are usually looked at in isolation from each other. It argues, in particular, that 1) the Problem of Agency is parasitic on the Problem of Freedom, 2) the Problem of Agency does not impose a general structure on (rational) agency, 3) the Problem of Freedom threatens more than libertarianly free agency, and 4) the Problem of Agency is not necessarily more serious for the theistic God than it is for human beings.

**Hunt, Tammy G** and Jennings, Daniel F. Ethics and Performance: A Simulation Analysis of Team Decision Making. *J Bus Ethics*, 16(2), 195-203, F 97.

The interrelationships among a number of variables and their effect on ethical decision making was explored. Teams of students and managers participated in a competitive management simulation. Based on prior research, the effects of performance, environmental change, team age and type of team on the level of ethical behavior were hypothesized. The findings indicate that multiple variable may interact in such a fashion that significance is lost.

**Hunter, David A**. Definition in Frege's *Foundations of Arithmetic*. *Pac Phil Quart*, 77(2), 88-107, Je 96.

**Hunter, David A**. Understanding, Justification and the A Priori. *Phil Stud*, 87(2), 119-141, Ag 97.

**Hunter, Graeme**. What Leibniz Thought Perennial. *Maritain Stud*, 10, 44-56, 1994.

**Hunter, Kathryn**. "Don't Think Zebras": Uncertainty, Interpretation, and the Place of Paradox in Clinical Education. *Theor Med*, 17(3), 225-241, S 96.

Working retrospectively in an uncertain field of knowledge, physicians are engaged in an interpretive practice that is guided by counterweighted, competing, sometimes paradoxical maxims. "When you hear hoofbeats, don't think zebras," is the chief of these, the epitome of medicine's practical wisdom, its hermeneutic rule. The accumulated and contradictory wisdom distilled in clinical maxims arises necessarily from the case-based nature of medical practice and the narrative rationality that good practice requires. That these maxims all have their opposites enforces in students and physicians a practical skepticism that encourages them to question their expectations, interrupt patterns, and adjust to new developments as a case unfolds. Yet medicine resolutely ignores both the maxims and the tension between the practical reasoning they represent and the claim that medicine is a science. Indeed, resolute epistemological naiveté is part of medicine's accommodation to uncertainty; counterweighted, competing, apparently paradoxical (but always situational) rules enable physicians simultaneously to express and to ignore the practical reason that characterizes their practice.

**Hunter, Michael** (ed) and Davis, Edward B (ed) and Boyle, Robert. *A Free Enquiry into the Vulgarly Received Notion of Nature*. New York, Cambridge Univ Pr, 1996.

In this book, published in 1686, the scientist Robert Boyle (1627-91) attacked prevailing notions of the natural world which depicted 'Nature' as a wise, benevolent and purposeful being. Boyle, one of the leading mechanical philosophers of his day, believed that the world was best understood as a vast, impersonal machine, fashioned by an infinite, personal God. In this cogent treatise, he drew on his scientific findings, his knowledge of contemporary medicine and his deep reflection on theological and philosophical issues, arguing that it was inappropriate both theologically and scientifically to speak of Nature as if it had a mind of its own: instead, the only true efficient causes of things were the properties and powers given to matter by God. As such, *A Free Enquiry into the Vaguely Received Notion of Nature* represents one of the subtlest statements concerning the philosophical issues raised by the mechanical philosophy to emerge from the period of the scientific revolution. (publisher, edited)

**Huntington, Patricia J**. "Fragmentation, Race, and Gender: Building Solidarity in the Postmodern Era" in *Existence in Black: An Anthology of Black Existential Philosophy*, Gordon, Lewis R (ed), 185-202. New York, Routledge, 1997.

**Hurka, Thomas**. "The Justification of National Partiality" in *The Morality of Nationalism*, McKim, Robert (ed), 139-157. New York, Oxford Univ Pr, 1997.

Nationalism involves partiality, or caring more about one's own nation than about other nations. This paper examines the moral justification of such partiality. It first criticizes arguments of Sandel, McIntyre and others attempting to ground national partiality in theses about the social embeddedness of selves. It then argues that nationalism typically involves two quite different forms of partiality: to one's individual conationals as individuals and to one's nation's impersonal good, e.g., its survival as a nation. The paper concludes by offering a moral justification of partiality to one's conationals, one based on historical facts about the benefits one has produced with these individuals using the political and other institutions of the nation.

**Hurka, Thomas**. Self-Interest, Altruism, and Virtue. *Soc Phil Pol*, 14(1), 286-307, Wint 97.

This paper evaluates self-interest and altruism within a general theory of the intrinsic value of attitudes to goods and evils. It argues that each of self-interest and altruism is intrinsically good, because it involves concern for some person's good. But each can also be instrumentally evil and in either of two ways, if by being too intense it prevents a person from dividing his concerns proportionally between his own and others' good. (Excessive self-interest makes for a failing of selfishness, excessive altruism for one of self-abnegation.) The paper concludes by examining a subtle asymmetry in the common-sense view of these attitudes, one that makes some forms of self-abnegation not a failing.

**Hurst, Andrea**. Lyotard: Modern Postmodernist?. *S Afr J Phil*, 16(2), 51-54, My 97.

In this article the author examines the question of Lyotard's position *vis-à-vis* the paradigms of modernism and postmodernism respectively. Focusing mainly, but not exclusively on *The postmodern condition*, the argument uncovers and elaborates on an ambivalence in his thought which mirrors the tension between 'being' and 'becoming' characteristic of the relationship between modernity and postmodernity. Specifically, it is argued that to position Lyotard's work at either extreme of a crude polarization of the 'being/becoming' opposition is to distort or misrepresent his thinking, particularly in view of his own formulation of postmodernism as an oppositional movement within and integral to, modernism itself. An examination of Lyotard's views on questions concerning: the legitimation of diverse language-games or discourses; justice in the face of cultural fragmentation; increasingly unrepresentable social complexity; and the tension between determinacy and indeterminacy in human subjectivity, uncovers an unresolvable tension in his work between his acceptance of the universal as inevitable and necessary and his resistance to the homogenization it represents by activating the particular. Hence Lyotard's work seems, in the final analysis, to oscillate interminably between the universalist striving of modernism, and postmodernism's particularizing resistances. In light of this, he can neither properly be called a modernist, nor indeed a postmodernist. His ambivalence seems, therefore, to be aptly captured in the phrase modern postmodernist.

**Hurst, Andrea**. The Sublime and Human Existence. *S Afr J Phil*, 15(4), 144-148, N 96.

This article investigates the notion of the sublime in the context of human existence. This means that, rather than restricting it to a customary aesthetic perspective, what is termed sublime passion is examined as an experiential phenomenon. In the first instance, Heidegger's death analysis is shown to reveal surprising insights regarding sublime passion, while the practice of sado-masochism divulges insights into a similarly structured experience. An upshot of the investigation is the isomorphism, paradoxically, between an awareness of the radical finitude of the subject and its radical infinity, both of which may lead to sublime passion by provoking a confrontation with dread. (edited)

**Hurtado, Guillermo**. El (Supuesto) Trilema del Saber. *Critica*, 28(83), 131-136, Ag 96.

**Husak, Douglas**. The "But-Everyone-Does-That!" Defense. *Pub Affairs Quart*, 10(4), 307-334, O 96.

I describe a number of circumstances in which I argue that persons are exempted from blame—in both a moral and criminal context—because *other* persons would have done what they did.

**Husock, Howard**. Standards Versus Struggle: The Failure of Public Housing and the Welfare-State Impulse. *Soc Phil Pol*, 14(2), 69-94, Sum 97.

**Huspek, Michael** (ed) and Radford, Gary P (ed). *Transgressing Discourses: Communication and the Voice of Other*. Albany, SUNY Pr, 1997.

An essential theme running through this volume is the idea that our efforts to engage, as well as other's efforts to engage us, have been seriously impaired because of problems which are fundamentally communicative in nature. More specifically, there is general agreement among the contributors that the voice of others has not been sufficiently heard, and this on account of how discourses of the human sciences, as well as other dominant discourses (e.g., law) have structured our interaction with other. Each of the essays helps to clarify the nature of the communicative failing and to develop an appropriate corrective action. (publisher, edited)

**Husted, Jorgen**. "Autonomy and a Right not to Know" in *The Right to Know and the Right not to Know*, Chadwick, Ruth (ed), 55-68. Brookfield, Avebury, 1997.

**Hut, Piet** and Shepard, Roger N. Turning 'The Hard Problem' Upside Down & Sideways. *J Consciousness Stud*, 3(4), 313-329, 1996.

Instead of speaking of conscious experience as arising in a brain, we prefer to speak of a brain as arising in conscious experience. From an epistemological standpoint, starting from direct experiences strikes us as more justified. As a first option, we reconsider the 'hard problem' of the relation between conscious experience and the physical world by thus turning that problem upside down. We also consider a second option: turning the hard problem sideways. Rather than starting with the third-person approach used in physics, or the first-person approach of starting with individual conscious experience, we consider starting from an I-and-you basis, centered around the second-person. Finally, we present a candidate for what could be considered to underlie conscious experience: 'sense'. (edited)

**Hutchings, Kimberly**. *Kant, Critique and Politics*. New York, Routledge, 1996.

Kant's critical project continues to structure debates in contemporary philosophy, international relations and feminist theory. *Kant, Critique and Politics* examines this influence in the work of such diverse theorists as Habermas, Arendt, Foucault and Lyotard. Reading the Kantian critique as a *political* practice, Kimberly Hutchings demonstrates that a common Kantian heritage links modernist and postmodernist theorists. (publisher, edited)

**Hutchinson, D S** (ed) and Cooper, John M (ed). *Plato: Complete Works*. Indianapolis, Hackett, 1997.

Outstanding translations by leading contemporary scholars—many commissioned especially for this volume—are presented here in the first single edition to include the entire surviving corpus of works attributed to Plato in antiquity. In his introductory essay, John Cooper explains the presentation of these works, discusses questions concerning the chronology of their composition, comments on the dialogue form in which Plato wrote and offers guidance on approaching the reading and study of Plato's works. Also included are concise introductions by Cooper and Hutchinson to each translation, meticulous annotation designed to serve both scholar and general reader and a comprehensive index. This handsome volume offers fine paper and a high-quality Smyth-sewn cloth binding in a sturdy, elegant edition. (publisher)

**Hutchinson, Jaylynne N**. "A Revolution by Any Other Name" in *Philosophy of Education (1996)*, Margonis, Frank (ed), 421-424. Urbana, Phil Education Soc, 1997.

**Hutter, Axel**. Dem blinden Trieb ein Auge einsetzen?: Die Verkehrung von Fichtes ursprünglicher Intention in seiner Auseinandersetzung mit Kant. *Fichte-Studien*, 9, 163-180, 1997.

**Hutto, J D D**. "The Story of the Self: The Narrative Basis of Self-Development" in *Critical Studies: Ethics and the Subject*, Simms, Karl (ed), 61-75. Amsterdam, Rodopi, 1997.

This paper makes a provisional case for the post-Cartesian view that selves are formed by our linguistic practices—specifically our capacity to compose narratives. After considering various options in the debate between theory-theorists and simulation theorists, it is claimed that narrative plays is an essential ingredient in our capacity to interpret other minds and make intentional ascriptions. Given this, and assuming that first and third personal intentional ascription is symmetrical, it is argued that we have reason to prefer a post-Cartesian conception of self on grounds which are independent of arguments arising from the philosophy of language alone.

**Hutton, Sarah**. "Henry More and Anne Conway on Preexistence and Universal Salvation" in *Mind Senior to the World*, Baldi, Marialuisa, 113-125. Milano, FrancoAngeli, 1996.

**Hutton, Sarah**. La philosophie comme *ancilla theologiae* chez Stillingfleet. *Rev Phil Fr*, 1, 21-31, Ja-Mr 97.

**Hutton, Sarah** (ed) and Cudworth, Ralph. *A Treatise Concerning Eternal and Immutable Morality* with *A Treatise of Freewill*. New York, Cambridge Univ Pr, 1996.

Ralph Cudworth (1617-88) deserves recognition as one of the most important English seventeenth-century philosophers after Hobbes and Locke. In opposition to Hobbes, Cudworth proposes an innatist theory of knowledge which may be contrasted with the empirical position of his younger contemporary Locke, and in moral philosophy he anticipates the ethical rationalists of the eighteenth century. *A Treatise Concerning Eternal and Immutable Morality* is his most important discussion of epistemology and ethics and this volume makes it available, together with his shorter *Treatise of Freewill*, in its first modern edition, with a historical introduction, a chronology of his life, and a guide to further reading. (publisher, edited)

**Huxley, Andrew**. When Many Met Mahasammata. *J Indian Phil*, 24(6), 593-621, D 96.

**Huxley, Andrew** and Collins, Steven. The Post-Canonical Adventures of Mahasammata. *J Indian Phil*, 24(6), 623-648, D 96.

**Hyde, Charles E**. Bargaining and Delay: The Role of External Information. *Theor Decis*, 42(1), 81-104, Ja 97.

This paper examines the notion that delay in reaching agreement in bargaining may be caused by learning that is independent of the bargaining procedure. In particular, learning is not due to inference from the observed offers and responses of the opponent, but derives from observation of an exogenous, costly signal—we call this 'investigation'. First we observe that even if learning is costless and perfectly informative, investigation may not occur in equilibrium. Under more general conditions, however, uninformed agents typically have an incentive to try to manipulate their prior beliefs through investigation. The main result is that investigation by an uninformed agent may result in significant delay occurring before agreement is reached. (edited)

**Hylton, Peter**. "Functions, Operations, and Sense in Wittgenstein's Tractatus" in *Early Analytic Philosophy*, Tait, William W (ed), 91-105. Chicago, Open Court, 1997.

**Hymers, Michael**. Internal Relations and Analyticity: Wittgenstein and Quine. *Can J Phil*, 26(4), 591-612, D 96.

**Hymers, Michael**. Realism and Self-Knowledge: A Problem for Burge. *Phil Stud*, 86(3), 303-325, Je 97.

Tyler Burge says that first-person authority can be reconciled with anti-individualism about the intentional by denying part of the "Cartesian conception" of authority, which claims that I am *actually* authoritative about my intentional attitudes in *counterfactual* situations. This clause, he says, wrongly conflates the evaluation-conditions for sceptical doubts about the "external" world with the conditions for classifying intentional attitudes in counterfactual situations. This paper argues that the kind of possibility needed to understand external-world scepticism justifies the conflation and that Burge can reject the Cartesian conception only if he rejects either metaphysical realism or anti-individualism.

**Hymers, Michael**. Truth and Metaphor in Rorty's Liberalism. *Int Stud Phil*, 28(4), 1-21, 1996.

Richard Rorty has cited considerations about truth, justification and metaphor to argue that the social critic must focus on a) public proposals for the reform of liberal norms and institutions, or b) the private creation of metaphors that will slowly work their way into public practice, changing standards of justification. This paper clarifies Rorty's views on truth and metaphor in order to show how the radical critic can respond to Rorty. Rorty is neither a relativist nor an idealist, but his critique of the radical theorist attributes views about truth, ideology and critique to her that she need not hold.

**Hyppolite, Jean** and Sen, Amit (trans) and Lawlor, Leonard (trans). *Logic and Existence*. Albany, SUNY Pr, 1997.

*Logic and Existence*, which originally appeared in 1952, completes the project Hyppolite began with *Genesis and Structure of Hegel's "Phenomenology of Spirit."* Taking up successively the role of language, reflection, and categories in Hegel's *Science of Logic*, Hyppolite illuminates Hegelianism's most obscure dialectical synthesis: the relation between the phenomenology and the logic. (publisher, edited)

**Iachkina, Galina**. An Essay in the Applied Philosophy of Political Economy. *Int J Applied Phil*, 11(1), 63-69, Sum-Fall 96.

**Iagulli, Paolo**. Per una teoria del diritto ambientale: considerazioni a partire da un libro recente. *Riv Int Filosof Diritto*, 74(1), 129-135, Ja-Mr 97.

**Ianovskii, Rudol'f Grigor'evich** and Perminova, Alla Ivanovna and Mel'nikova, Tatiana A. Women and Society in Russia. *Russian Stud Phil*, 34(2), 66-72, Fall 95.

**Ibán, Iván C**. Religious Tolerance and Freedom in Continental Europe. *Ratio Juris*, 10(1), 90-107, Mr 97.

The author analyzes the problems faced by continental Europe's legal systems as a result of the appearance of the so-called new religious movements. He is of the opinion that the expected change towards the achievement of full legal neutrality regarding the religious phenomena cannot be based on the sole assumption that each and every religion deserves protection. In fact, he considers that any system of equality should be aimed at protecting the legitimate expression of the individual's free will; that is to say, neither a particular religion nor all of them, but the person considered as a citizen, regardless of whether he believes or not.

**Ibarra, Andoni** and Eizagirre, Xabier and Bengoetxea, Juan B. "Un escenario pragmático para la verdad en la ciencia" in *Verdad: lógica, representación y mundo*, Villegas Forero, L, 455-465. Santiago de Compostela, Univ Santiago Comp, 1996.

According to Cartwright fundamental laws do not tell the truth, do not describe objects in reality, but they have superior explanatory power. Others have argued that the notion of truth is unsubstantial for providing an adequate analysis of science, and instead of it they plea for the introduction of other epistemic values. We think that using an adequate notion of truth allows us to make sense of intuitions of scientists; truth is taken by them as something worth pursuing. Accordingly, we propose a pragmatic account of truth able to understand the specific aspect of scientific practice, i.e., the activity of idealizations and approximations. (edited)

**Iber, Christian**. Eros and Philosophy: The "Spherical-Man-Myth" of Aristophanes in Plato's Symposion (in German). *Prima Philosophia*, 10(3), 245-262, 1997.

In Plato's erotology Eros and philosophy mutually become evident. The myth of Aristophanes examines the dialectical structure of Eros and the status of sexuality. Diotima's doctrine of Eros demonstrates, that philosophy is itself determined by the dialectical structure of Eros. Philosophy is based on the irrationality of Eros, which results in the rational structure of reason. The erotical foundation of philosophy is accompanied by the sublimation of Eros. Eros is not only purified of its sexual but also of its intersubjective moments and transformed into a monistic, self-relating subjectivity of thinking, in which the dialectical restlessness of Eros dies away. This immanent self-contradiction in Plato's doctrine of Eros is illuminated in the light of a concept of dialogical Eros.

**Iber, Christian**. Frühromantische Subjektkritik. *Fichte-Studien*, 12, 111-126, 1997.

**Ichijo, Kazuhiko**. On the Limit of Iconology through the "Mental Habit"—Comparison between E. Panofsky's "Mental Habit" and P. Bourdieu's "Habitus" (in Japanese). *Bigaku*, 47(3), 1-11, Winter 96.

E. Panofsky's "Mental Habit," insisted in his book, *Gothic Architecture and Scholasticism* (1951), meant the tendency, peculiar to a certain era, formed habitually so as to regulate the conduct. He thought it to explain analogies among cultural phenomena at that era. My papers have pointed out that the "Mental Habit" was an arrival point in his art history study, located on the extending line of the iconology, through the clarification as to what Panofsky's iconology was. Further, my papers also have clarified how P. Bourdieu's "Habitus" was formed as compared with Panofsky's "Mental Habit."(edited)

**Ichimura, Shohei**. Contemporary Significance of Chinese Buddhist Philosophy. *J Chin Phil*, 24(1), 75-106, Mr 97.

**Idt, Geneviève**. L'engagement dans le *Journale de guerre I* de Jean-Paul Sartre. *Rev Phil Fr*, 3, 383-403, Jl-S 96.

**Idziak, Katarzyna**. Quasivarieties of Equivalential Algebras. *Rep Math Log*, 29, 81-85, 1995.

The expressive power of constants in the quasiequational logic is considered. We describe three 3 element algebras $A_1$, $A_2$, $A_3$ such that $A_{i+1}$ is obtained from $A_{iD}$ by adding one constant to the signature and such that the quasivariety generated by A2 has infinitely many subquasivarieties while both $A_1$ and $A_3$ generate quasivarieties with finitely many subquasivarieties. Moreover, each of the $A_i$'s generates a congruence permutable variety.

**Iglesias, Mercedes**. Otherness in J.P. Sartre's *Being and Nothingness* (Spanish). *Rev Filosof (Venezuela)*, 24(2), 29-46, Jl-D 96.

This paper examines the *other* in Sartre's *Being and Nothingness*. The author criticizes not only metaphysical positions (idealism and realism) but epistemological positions as well to take into account the existence and evidence of the *other*. He supports that the only way to having access to the *other* is via the ontological dimension and this is obtained through the perspective of the 'glance'. This paper briefly describes the concrete relationships with others as well as considering what kind of ethical position could be assumed taking into account the ontological considerations.

**Ignatow, Assen**. Die Marxismus—Debatte im "Silbernen Zeitalter". *Stud East Euro Thought*, 49(3), 187-225, S 97.

Im Anfang des 20.Jahrhunderts unterzog eine Reihe von jungen, später berühmt gewordenen Philosophen den Marxismus einer tiefen Kritik. Ihnen ist es gelungen, wichtige Defekte der revolutionären Doktrinen aufzudecken und ihre verhängnivsollen Konsequenzen vorwegzunehmen. Diese Kritik ist auch für die gegenwärtige geistig-politische Situation aktuell.

**Ihde, Don**. Whole Earth Measurements: How Many Phenomenologists Does It Take to Detect a "Greenhouse Effect"?. *Phil Today*, 41(1-4), 128-134, Spr 97.

This article argues that early phenomenology (Husserl), not unlike other early 20th century philosophies, misconstrued science in a theory-biased and disembodied mode. I argue that science praxis must be construed as a technologically embodied praxis, which particularly through imaging technologies can measure and perceive phenomena associated with events like a *greenhouse effect*. Similarly, although Heidegger did discern the role of instrumentation, his concept of world as Earth, misconstrues the perspectives from which measuring perceptions can show *greenhouse effects*. I reconstruct science praxis on a perceptual, technologically mediated basis to attain these results.

**Ihde, Don**. Why Not Science Critics?. *Int Stud Phil*, 29(1), 45-54, 1997.

Philosophers writing articles critical of science or technology are often tarred with "anti-science" or "anti-technology" responses. Contrarily, in arts and literary disciplines the art of literary critic is seldom, if ever, accused of being "anti-art" or "anti-Lit." This article argues that there should be the growth of something like the informed amateur, institutionalized approach of arts criticism with respect to science and technology. In addition, the essay argues that too often philosophers are expected to fill "ambulance corps" roles with respect to ethical applications after a technology is in place. Here the argument is that a better placing would be at the research and development stage, with prospective and proactive roles for philosophy of science and technology.

**Ihmig, Karl-Norbert**. Trägheit und Massebegriff bei Johannes Kepler. *Phil Natur*, 27(2), 156-205, 1990.

This article attempts to throw new light on the relationship between Kepler's and Newton's celestial mechanics. Following the traces of G. M. Bose (a widely unknown 18th century physicist and philosopher) the *dynamical* foundations of Newton's astronomy are compared with some fundamental conceptions used by Kepler in order to explain the planetary motions in causal terms. It turns out that there are interesting resemblances concerning the following points. Kepler *and* Newton maintained that "inertia" is an essential quality of matter and both treated "inertia" as a "vis insita". Furthermore they reveal similar definitions of "mass" and introduce a proportionality between the quantity of matter and the quantity of force.

**Ikuenobe, Polycarp**. The Parochial Universalist Conception of 'Philosophy' and 'African Philosophy'. *Phil East West*, 47(2), 189-210, Ap 97.

The universalists argue that there is currently no African philosophy. Compared to Western philosophy, African philosophy does not have the requisite features of a writing tradition and a rigorous and critical analytical approach to debates over universal conceptual issues, engaged in by individuals. This stance, it is argued here, involves a parochial conception of 'philosophy' that is applied to African philosophy and captures only the contemporary analytic tradition of Western philosophy—while the ancient and medieval periods indicate that other speculative, constructive, and normative approaches to philosophy exist that are not captured by this conception. Moreover, African philosophy that is equivalent to the ancient and medieval periods does exist, and this African equivalent is a precursor to the contemporary analytic philosophy that the universalists are looking for in Africa.

**Iliescu, Adrian-Paul**. Rational Reconstruction: Preconditions and Limits. *Theoria (Spain)*, 11(27), 33-47, S 96.

The aim of this paper is to investigate the preconditions and the limits of rational reconstruction in the philosophy of language, as these preconditions and limits can be deduced from Wittgenstein's arguments against philosophical constructivism. It will be shown that a main precondition of reconstructions in the field of language is the existence of nonarbitrary patterns of linguistic use, while the limits of this kind of theoretical enterprise derive precisely from the absence of such patterns.

**Iliff, Alan J**. "The Role of the Matrix Representation in Peirce's Development of the Quantifiers" in *Studies in the Logic of Charles Sanders Peirce*, Houser, Nathan (ed), 193-205. Bloomington, Indiana Univ Pr, 1997.

**Illich, Ivan**. Philosophy...Artifacts...Friendship—and the History of the Gaze. *Amer Cath Phil Quart*, 70(Supp), 59-77, 1996.

**Imamichi, Tomonobu**. "The Night as Category One Angle of Comparative Study in Aesthetics" in *East and West in Aesthetics*, Marchianò, Grazia (ed), 53-64. Pisa, Istituti Editoriali, 1997.

**Imbach, Ruedi**. L'antithomisme de Thierry de Freiberg. *Rev Thomiste*, 97(1), 245-258, Ja-Mr 97.

**Imbach, Ruedi**. Notule sur le commentaire du *Liber de causis* de Siger de Brabant et ses rapports avec Thomas d'Aquin. *Frei Z Phil Theol*, 43(3), 304-323, 1996.

**Imbert, Jean**. Toleration and Law: Historical Aspects. *Ratio Juris*, 10(1), 13-24, Mr 97.

Strictly speaking the law cannot admit toleration: It cannot tolerate ideas or behavior which are contrary to its requirements. This logic explains why for centuries civilizations found no place for toleration. Then in the seventeenth and eighteenth centuries, philosophers and thinkers such as Spinoza, Locke, Bayle and later Voltaire or Malesherbes advocated tolerance, certain aspects of which were to be introduced into the legislation of many countries: freedom of opinion, the free movement of persons, freedom of assembly and of religion.

**Imbo, Samuel Oluoch**. The Special Political Responsibilities of African Philosophers. *Int Stud Phil*, 29(1), 55-67, 1997.

In this paper I argue that the practice of philosophy in Third World countries differs significantly from that in the West. To develop this argument, I examine and use as an example the debate surrounding the existence, nature and definitions of African philosophy. Philosophers everywhere share the gadfly's role articulated by Socrates. I argue that African philosophers by virtue of special historical circumstances of colonialism have an added political dimension to their practice. In challenging the hegemonic constructions of the West and its canonical texts, African philosophy must recognize its allies in other deconstructive movements like feminism and Black studies.

**Imbruglia, Girolamo**. "L'ombra dei lumi: Il problema della storia universale in Francia tra Settecento e Ottocento" in *Lo Storicismo e la Sua Storia: Temi, Problemi, Prospettive,* Cacciatore, Giuseppe (ed), 128-138. Milano, Guerini, 1997.

**Imlay, Robert A**. Freedom, the Self and Epistemic Voluntarism in Descartes. *Stud Leibniz*, 28(2), 211-224, 1996.

J'essaie de montrer qu'il y a incompatibilité entre la liberté d'indifférence positive chez Descartes d'une part et la liberté de spontanéité chez ce même Descartes de l'autre part. Celui-ci à mon avis devrait, ne serait-ce que pour des raisons d'ordre systématique, trancher en faveur de la liberté de spontanéité. En même temps je plaide pour une interprétation pragmatique et non pas sémantique du pronom tel que le sous-entend *Cogito*. Finalement, j'essaie de défendre une forme limitée du volontarisme épistémologique que prône Descartes.

**Immerwahr, John**. Hume's Aesthetic Theism. *Hume Stud*, 22(2), 325-337, N 96.

This articles takes seriously Hume's claim that there is a "true religion" or "genuine theism" and tries to explain what, for Hume, is true about it. For Hume, true religion is epistemologically no sounder than any other form of religion such as superstition or enthusiasm. Because superstition and enthusiasm are invariably grounded in violent passions (especially hope and fear) they typically have a negative influence on morality. Genuine theism, by contrast, is based on an aesthetic appreciation of the workings of nature and is thus grounded in the calm passions. It alone, according to Hume, is able to perform the "proper office of religion" which is to have a positive moral impact on human life.

**Inácio Filho, Geraldo** and Gonçalves Neto, Wenceslau and Souza Araújo, José Carlos. Notícia sobre a Pesquisa de Fontes Histórico-educacionais no Triângualo Mineiro e Alto Paranaíba. *Educ Filosof*, 10(19), 115-127, Ja-Je 96.

A group of teachers at the Federal University of Uberlândia made, from 1994 to 1996, a survey and a catalogue of valuable primary and secondary sources for researchers dealing with the history of Brazilian education in the West region of the state of Minas Gerais, called Triâgulo Mineiro. The same research program is now being developed in eighteen other regions of Brazil. This activity, included in a group of studies and research entitled *History, Education and Society in Brazil,* aims to, among other goals, give support to the research activities of the postgraduation program in education of the university, that focuses on Brazilian education.

**Inada, Kenneth K**. "Buddhi-Taoist and Western Metaphysics of the Self" in *Culture and Self,* Allen, Douglas (ed), 83-93. Boulder, Westview Pr, 1997.

**Inada, Kenneth K**. A Theory of Oriental Aesthetics: A Prolegomenon. *Phil East West*, 47(2), 117-131, Ap 97.

Oriental thought requires the introduction of a novel metaphysical concept of nonbeing, along with being, so to exhibit the dynamics of becoming. The initial contact of being and nonbeing is the basis of aesthetic nature and the fountainhead of Oriental aesthetics.

**Inada, Kenneth K**. The Chinese Doctrinal Acceptance of Buddhism. *J Chin Phil*, 24(1), 5-17, Mr 97.

It is a historical fact that alien Buddhist thought permeated the Chinese mind despite the dominant presence of well-established Confucian and Taoist ways of life. The essay explores and exhibits certain fundamental ideas in Confucian/Taoist and Buddhist thought that do not oppose each other but instead run parallel and are conducive to the eventual acceptance of Buddhist essentials by the Chinese mind. The transformation of this mind may well be one of the creative cultural wonders of the world.

**Incardona, Nunzio**. Essere e tempo: Il primordio dell'anientamento. *G Metaf*, 18(1-2), 5-28, Ja-Ag 96.

**Incardona, Nunzio**. I sandali di Ermes e lo spazio di De Kooning: Appunti per una possibile negazione dell'epelysìa di metaphysikà. *G Metaf*, 19(1), 101-130, Ja-Ap 97.

**Inda, Caridad**. Between Apathy and Revolution: Nonviolent Action in Contemporary Mexico. *Acorn*, 5-2 &(6-1), 12-20, S 90 - Mr 91.

**Inés Mudrovcic, María**. "Racionalidad y *poiesis*: los límites de la praxis histórica" in *La racionalidad: su poder y sus límites,* Nudler, Oscar (ed), 495-504. Barcelona, Ed Paidos, 1996.

The first aim of this paper is to discuss the criteria on which the scientific-rational character of history lies. Secondly, I intend to point out the insufficiency of such criteria as G. Iggers and P. Zagorin characterize them. Lastly, I will try to show the fact that the literary dimension of the historical discourse is related to its pragmatic dimension. Hence the way in which history is cast is the borderline of any rational foundation and by it history can be said a poietic activity.

**Infinito-Allocco, Justen**. Philosophy and Shifting Morality. *Thinking*, 13(2), 48-49, 1997.

**Ingarden, Roman** and Jadczak, Ryszard. Some Tendencies in Modern Epistemology (in Polish). *Kwartalnik Filozof*, 24(3), 135-147, 1996.

**Ingham, Nicholas**. The Rectitude of Inclination. *Thomist*, 60(3), 417-437, Jl 96.

**Inglehart, Ronald**. The Diminishing Utility of Economic Growth: From Maximizing Security Toward Maximizing Subjective Well-Being. *Crit Rev*, 10(4), 509-531, Fall 96.

Twenty years ago, Tibor Scitovsky questioned the assumption embedded in neoclassical economics, that human happiness will be augmented if the level of consumption either rises or becomes more uniform over time. Evidence from the 1990-1993 World Values Survey suggests that his doubts were well-founded: although economic gains apparently make a major contribution to subjective well-being as one moves from societies at the subsistence level to those with moderate levels of economic development, further economic growth seems to have little or no impact on subjective well-being. This transition seems to reflect a basic cultural change that results in the diminishing marginal utility of economic growth.

**Inglis, John**. Philosophical Autonomy and the Historiography of Medieval Philosophy. *Brit J Hist Phil*, 5(1), 21-53, Mr 97.

This article uncovers the nineteenth-century philosophical and political origins of how we have come to interpret medieval philosophy according to the standard branches of philosophy, that is, according to such categories as logic, epistemology, metaphysics, natural philosophy, psychology, and morality. With a focus on the significant histories of medieval philosophy written up to the present, Inglis demonstrates how we continue to follow this interpretation today. By keeping such historiography in mind and paying attention to the context in which the medievals actually wrote, he raises serious questions concerning the accuracy of the dominant model and proposes an alternative.

**Inglis, Sam**. A Priori Knowledge. *Acta Analytica*, 213-222, 1996.

In this paper I consider some of the ways in which knowledge can be said to be independent of experience and argue that our intuitions about the epistemological significance of experience do not support a division of all knowledge into *a priori* and *a posteriori*. Following Philip Kitcher, I argue that the natural way to locate 'independence from experience' is in the cognitive processes through which knowledge is acquired. However, Kitcher's account seems to make the division between *a priori* and *a posteriori* ultimately an arbitrary one. I conclude that it would be better to abandon the attempt to classify all knowledge using these two categories; instead I think that the epistemological significance of experience is best seen in each individual case as context-dependent and interest-relative.

**Ingram, Attracta**. Constitutional Patriotism. *Phil Soc Crit*, 22(6), 1-18, N 96.

In this paper, I want to look at some questions that arise when we try to abandon the conceptual and political framework of the nation-state. Is it impossible to conceive the unity of the state apart from the unity of the nation? Are shared political values insufficient to account for the existence of bounded states and special duties to one's own country? In the first section I will discuss the view that the idea of the modern state is incoherent and that it tacitly relies on the social idea of membership provided by the nation. The following section will give an alternative to the nationalist account of the existence of bounded communities and suggest why Habermasians and Rawlsians are right in thinking that the shared value of justice can be sufficient for political unity. Finally, I give a brief indication of the relevance of this discussion to the idea of European Union.

**Ingram, Thomas N** and Schwepker, Jr, Charles H. Improving Sales Performance through Ethics: The Relationship Between Salesperson Moral Judgment and Job Performance. *J Bus Ethics*, 15(11), 1151-1160, N 96.

This study examines the relationship between salespeople's moral judgment and their job performance. Results indicate a positive relationship between moral judgment and job performance when certain characteristics are present. Implications for sales managers and sales researchers are provided. Additionally, directions for future research are given.

**Inman, Patricia**. Themes of Ivan Illich: An Intellectual Biography. *J Thought*, 32(3), 53-64, Fall 97.

Ivan Illich has written a number of essays and books providing an analysis of this societal institutions in crisis and has suggested a number of implications. Born in 1926, Illich is a historian, philosopher, educator and social critic. He has had a public career as a priest of an Irish-Puerto Rican parish in New York City, vice-rector of the Catholic University of Puerto Rico, founder of the Centre for Intercultural Documentation in Cuernavaca, Mexico and since 1986 a lecturer at Pennsylvania State University. This article analyzes his publications to discover emerging themes.

**Innala, Heikki-Pekka**. An Indefinability Argument for Conditional Obligation. *Log Anal*, 37(147-8), 295-302, S-D 94.

We present a relatively simple model-theoretic argument to the effect that the conditional obligation of deontic logic is indefinable in the sense that it cannot be expressed in terms of a nondeontic conditional and a deontic operator.

**Innerarity, Carmen**. "Aportación de la Ética a la Paz Perpetua" in *Kant: La paz perpetua, doscientos años después,* Martínez Guzmán, Vicent (ed), 101-117. Valencia, Nau Llibres, 1997.

**Innerarity, Daniel**. Pensar frente al exceso. *Dialogo Filosof*, 13(1), 63-72, Ja-Ap.

La queja contra el exceso es tan antigua como la misma cultura. Pero el saber no se rige únicamente por una ley de acumulación cuantitativa; saber significa también reducir. Una teoría hermenéutica del conocimiento escapa mejor a las aporías del exceso que una descripción positivista de la realidad. Desde esta economía de la significación cabe defender la interdisciplinariedad de los saberes como un ahorro y no como una suerte de complicación de las perspectivas sobre la realidad.

**Inoué, Takao**. On the Härtig-Style Axiomatization of Unprovable and Satisfiable Formulas of Bernays and Schönfinkel's Classes. *Log Anal*, 36(144), 261-309, S-D 93.

We give Härtig-style axiomatizations of unprovable and satisfiable formulas of Bernay's and Schönfinkel's classes. The characterization theorem, in other words, the completeness theorem for them is proved. We propose the notion of the absolute atomic formula property which is similar to that of the atomic formula property. The proposed systems have the absolute atomic formula property as well as the atomic formula property. We show the relation among the proposed property, the atomic formula property and the subformula property. We also consider the axiomatization of provable formulas and contradictions of the classes, for which the subformula property holds. In the last section, some open problem is given as well as our methodology for further studies of axiomatizing unprovable and satisfiable formulas. (edited)

**Insall, Matt**. Hyperalgebraic Primitive Elements for Relational Algebraic and Topological Algebraic Models. *Stud Log*, 57(2-3), 409-418, O 96.

Using nonstandard methods, we generalize the notion of an algebraic primitive element to that of an *hyperalgebraic primitive element* and show that under mild restrictions, such elements can be found *infinitesimally close to any given element of a topological field.*

**Introna, Lucas D**. Privacy and the Computer: Why we need Privacy in the Information Society. *Metaphilosophy*, 28(3), 259-275, Jl 97.

In this paper I want to argue that there is something fundamental in the notion of privacy and that due to the profoundness of the notion it merits extraordinary measures of protection and overt support. I will also argue that the notion of transparency (as advocated by Wasserstrom) is a useless concept without privacy and that accountability and transparency can only be meaningful if encapsulated in the concept of privacy. From philosophical and legal literature I will discuss and argue the value of privacy as the essential context and foundation of human autonomy in social relationships. In the conclusion of the paper I will discuss implications of this notion of privacy for the information society in general and for the discipline of information systems in particular. (edited)

**Iofrida, Manlio**. Derrida e la rivendicazione dello spirito del marxismo. *Iride*, 8(14), 197-211, Ap 95.

*Spectres de Marx* by Jacques Derrida (Paris, 1993) is analyzed, in order a) to state the problem of the relation between deconstruction and Marxism; b) to evaluate the meaning of Derrida's thought in relation to the present political and cultural situation. The key-concept of *ghost*, with its Husserlian and Heideggerian references, is analyzed. To confront oneself with Marx's ghost means to assume his *heritage*, i.e., to accept some aspects of his thought and to refuse other (totalitarian) aspects. The current interpretation of Derrida's thought as "postmodern" is showed to be untenable.

**Ioppolo, Anna Maria**. Fidelity to Zeno's Theory. *Diotima*, 25, 62-73, 1997.

**Iovino, José**. Definability in Functional Analysis. *J Sym Log*, 62(2), 493-505, Je 97.

The role played by real-valued functions in functional analysis is fundamental. One often considers metrics, or seminorms, or linear functionals, to mention some important examples. We introduce the notion of definable real-valued function in functional analysis: a real-valued function *f* defined on a structure of functional analysis is *definable* if it can be "approximated" by formulas which do not involve *f*. We characterize definability of real-valued functions in terms of a purely topological condition which does not involve logic.

**Iovino, José**. The Morley Rank of a Banach Space. *J Sym Log*, 61(3), 928-941, S 96.

We introduce the concepts of Morley rank and Morley degree for structures based on Banach spaces. We characterize *omega*-stability in terms of Morley rank and prove the existence of prime models for *omega*-stable theories.

**Iovino, Serenella**. L'ethos dell'intersoggettività nei romanzi di Friedrich Heinrich Jacobi. *Teoria*, 16(2), 65-106, 1996.

**Ipperciel, Donald**. Théorie des préjugés selon Descartes et Gadamer. *Horiz Phil*, 7(2), 43-57, Spr 97.

En plus de faire violence à la pensée de Descartes, l'aspect polémique et rhétorique de la réhabilitation des préjugés chez Gadamer occulte le sens

profond de sa théorie des préjugés. Afin d'accéder à une compréhension plus juste de cette dernière, il faudrait, selon l'auteur, dégager les éléments qui renvoient aux thèmes de la Kehre heideggérienne, de même qu'aux principes herméneutiques proprement gadamériens, tels la tradition et le langage.

**Iranzo, Valeriano**. "Inducción pesimista y verdad" in *Verdad: lógica, representación y mundo,* Villegas Forero, L, 481-487. Santiago de Compostela, Univ Santiago Comp, 1996.

The pessimistic induction (PI) is a well-known argument against the realist picture of scientific progress. I claim that PI is committed with an ultraholistic notion of evidence. I put forward an argument to show that it violates the conditions under which it is reasonable to take the falsity of TI in favor of the falsity of T2 (being T1 a discarded theory and T2 a current scientific theory). Even though this argument does not avoid working out a detailed account of "approximate truth"—if we are full-fledged realists—, it may be a more neutral policy against PI.

**Irfan, Ghazala**. "Enlightenment in the Islamic World: Muslims—Victims of Mneumonic Success" in *Averroës and the Enlightenment,* Wahba, Mourad (ed), 177-188. Amherst, Prometheus, 1996.

Mnemonic devices have a special place in Islamic theology for the preservation, perpetuation and propagation of Islam was dependent on one cognitive process-Memory. It becomes fundamental since imagery was taboo and icons a blasphemy. The paradox is that the acquisition of memory skills do not promote either the transfer or the application and use of knowledge in other areas. Mnemonic success in the Muslim world did not increase comprehension or problem solving strategies. It did not dwell in the higher order off cognition, i.e., intelligence, concept formation, thinking and logical activity. In analyzing and prescribing a perspective for enlightenment it is imperative that there be a paradigmatic shift from memory to creativity.

**Iribarne, Julia V**. Para una fenomenología de la muerte. *Cuad Etica*, 21-22, 45-59, 1996.

This paper deals with a phenomenological approach to death. It concerns a difficult task, i.e., the exposition of an experience of consciousness (dying) whose essence is supposed to be a total loss of consciousness. A meditation on Shakespeare's comparison of death and sleep leads the author to recall the same relationship thought of by E. Husserl and his assertion regards "the beginningless and endless nature of the transcendental I" as well. J. Hart's interpretation of Husserl's thought on this matter is recalled. The author points out to a second possible relationship between Aristotle and Husserl which should be taken into consideration in addition to the one highlighted by J. Hart. By means of a new reading of the Ms A V 21 a different stance towards death by Husserl is shown.

**Irrgang, Bernhard**. "Genethik" in *Angewandte Ethik: Die Bereichsethiken und ihre theoretische Fundierung,* Nida-Rümelin, Julian (ed), 510-551. Stuttgart, Alfred Kröner, 1996.

**Irvine, A D**. Bertrand Russell and Academic Freedom. *Russell*, 16(1), 5-36, Sum 96.

Bertrand Russell represents a unique focal point for the discussion of issues relating to academic freedom. Throughout most of his adult life he personified the type of outspoken public intellectual which principles of academic freedom have been designed to protect. Additionally, he was a forceful and articulate advocate of free speech and academic freedom in his own right. More than once throughout his long career on both sides of the Atlantic, he found himself forced to choose between his own freedom of expression and varying degrees of personal hardship. Russell's views concerning free speech and academic freedom turn out to be connected, not so much to political first principles, but to his views on the nature and utility of knowledge. After reviewing some of Russell's many personal battles relating to free speech and academic freedom, this article explores a tension that exists between Russell's defense of academic freedom and his views concerning the utility of scientific knowledge.

**Irwin, Ronald R**. Using Computer-Assisted Instruction and Developmental Theory to Improve Argumentative Writing. *Inform Log*, 17(2), 235-248, Spr 95.

A study is described in which the effectiveness of a computer program (Hermes) on improving argumentative writing is tested. It is concluded that argumentative writing operationalized here as dialectical writing, can be improved by computer-assisted instruction, but that attempts to teach such forms of thinking and writing need to take into account students' capacity to benefit from such instruction. Such capacity is defined here as intellectual development. (edited)

**Irwin, Terence H**. Art and Philosophy in Plato's Dialogues. *Phronesis*, 41(3), 335-350, 1996.

**Irwin, Terence H** (trans) and Fine, Gail (trans). *Aristotle: Introductory Readings.* Indianapolis, Hackett, 1996.

Adapted from Irwin and Fine's more comprehensive *Aristotle: Selections* (Hackett, 1995), *Introductory Readings* offers central works of Aristotle in a volume designed especially with the needs of beginning students in mind. The translation renders Aristotle's arguments clearly and accurately, with careful attention to technical terms. Brief clarifying and explanatory notes on selected passages are appended. An extensive Glossary explains some crucial terms and concepts, comments on questions of translation, and provides cross-references. (publisher, edited)

**Isaac, Jeffrey C**. Political Theory of and in America. *Polit Theory*, 25(3), 455-463, Je 97.

**Isaacs, Tracy**. Cultural Context and Moral Responsibility. *Ethics*, 107(4), 670-684, Jl 97.

**Isaacs, Tracy** (ed) and Brennan, Samantha (ed) and Milde, Michael (ed). *A Question of Values: New Canadian Perspectives in Ethics and Political Philosophy.* Amsterdam, Rodopi, 1994.

This book reflects a cross-section of the issues concerning values that are of contemporary philosophical interest in Canada and the United States. In the three parts of the book, ten philosophers bring fresh perspectives to bear upon questions of metaethics, freedom and autonomy and political philosophy. The studies concentrate upon acts, values and human lives; moral character, moral behavior and moral imagination; the limits of liberalism and communitarianism; social contract and institutions; and the morality of nationalism. (publisher)

**Isaacs, Tracy** and Milde, Michael (ed). "Acts and Value" in *A Question of Values: New Canadian Perspectives in Ethics and Political Philosophy*, Brennan, Samantha (ed), 17-27. Amsterdam, Rodopi, 1997.

Isn't it obvious that some acts are good or bad in themselves? Is this value intrinsic? If we follow Judith Thomson in understanding intrinsic value as value that a thing has independently of what it causes and what causes it, then acts do not have it. I argue that there is an account of conditional value, borrowed from Christine Korsgaard's work, in which acts can have value in themselves that nevertheless depends on the causal relations in which they stand. Though not intrinsic in Thomson's sense, this value is distinct from the value of the causes and effects and is objective.

**Isaacs, Tracy L** and Jeske, Diane. Moral Deliberations, Nonmoral Ends, and the Virtuous Agent. *Ethics*, 107(3), 486-500, Ap 97.

Some maintain that an agent with an agent with an overriding commitment to do as morality requires will be unable to pursue and develop nonmoral ends, such as friendships, that would give her life meaning and substance. We respond, arguing that placing overriding importance on moral ends is compatible with being noninstrumentally committed to nonmoral ends. Even in morally charged situations, agents may appeal to extramoral reasons to settle their deliberations. We argue that it is permissible and appropriate for the agent to appeal to such reasons in these situations, and that she will be better off if she makes such an appeal.

**Iseminger, Gary**. Actual Intentionalism vs. Hypothetical Intentionalism. *J Aes Art Crit*, 54(4), 319-326, Fall 96.

I defend the view that the actual intentions of the author are determinative of meaning, argued for in my "An Intentional Demonstration?" (*Intention and Interpretation*, ed. G. Iseminger, Temple U.D. 1992), against the alternative hypothetical intentionalism of Jerrold Levinson (also in *Intention and Interpretation*).

**Iserson, Kenneth V**. Staring at Our Future. *Cambridge Quart Healthcare Ethics*, 6(2), 243-244, Spr 97.

Western medicine arrogantly proceeds apace, cutting patient care services to save money, while some within this medical-industrial complex reap huge profits. The ideal expectation is that health care providers will remain above the fray, providing quality care without abusing their powers. The Sri Lanka medical system demonstrates what happens when self-enrichment, cost-cutting, and unhampered privatization predominate. Western medical systems, if they cannot mix economic necessities with moral controls, run the risk of developing the same type of decaying and corrupt medical environment he describes.

**Isham, George F**. Is God Exclusively a Father?. *Faith Phil*, 13(2), 266-271, AP 96.

William Harper presents five reasons for concluding that God should be referred to exclusively in male terms. To the contrary, I argue that: 1) by devaluating the feminine gender, Harper is guilty of the same reductionist and dichotomous thinking as his protagonists, 2) Harper's view of God is contrary to "the Biblical example," and 3) Harper's position rests on a number of logical confusions. I conclude that Harper's view should be rejected by both men and women of Christian convictions.

**Ishigami-Iagolnitzer, Mitchiko**. The Self and the Person as Treated in Some Buddhist Texts [1]. *Asian Phil*, 7(1), 37-45, Mr 97.

The theme of our conference is "The Concept of a Person." One of the most original attitudes of the Buddha towards this problem was to have dissuaded his followers from clinging to the concept of "person." The word "person" in Pāli is *puggala* (=individual), which represents in early middle Indian dialect *puthakala*, a derivation of Sanskrit: *prithak* (=prith or prath + añc = separately, one by one). *Puggala* means person or man, an individual as opposed to a group. Its equivalent in Sanskrit is *pudgala*, which means a personal entity or an individual. If there were any unique and permanent substance unifying this personal entity, it would be the self or the soul, *attan* in Pāli and *ātman* in Sanskrit. The self and the person are closely related to each other. I will trace the evolution of these two notions. (edited)

**Islam, Kazi Nurul**. Some Observations on the Revelation of the Qu'ran. *J Dharma*, 21(4), 395-406, O-D 96.

The purpose of the paper is to examine the charges against the authority of the Qur'an. From the discussion made in the paper it is evident that the Qur'an was not composed by any human being. It is neither the product of any creative imagination nor even an auditory visual hallucinatior or an Arabized version of Judaism and Christianity. Had the Qur'an been the product of any human being it would not be so immune from flaws. No man fourteen centuries ago could have been in such a position to have guessed, Conceived or known the scientific facts which are stated in the Qur'an.

**Isles, David**. A Finite Analog to the Löwenheim-Skolem Theorem. *Stud Log*, 53(4), 503-532, N 94.

The traditional model theory of first-order logic assumes that the interpretation of a formula can be given without reference to its deductive context. This paper investigates an interpretation which depends on a formula's location within a

derivation. The key step is to drop the assumption that all quantified variables must have the same range and to require only that the ranges of variables in a derivation must be related in such way as to preserve the soundness of the inference rules. (edited)

**Ismael, Jenann**. Curie's Principle. *Synthese*, 110(2), 167-190, F 97.

A reading is given of Curie's principle that the symmetry of a cause is always preserved in its effects. The truth of the principle is demonstrated and its importance under the proposed reading is defended.

**Isoda, Eiko**. Kripke Bundle Semantics and C-set Semantics. *Stud Log*, 58(3), 395-401, My 97.

Kripke bundle and C-set semantics are known as semantics which generalize standard Kripke semantics. In this paper, we show that Q-S4.1 is not Kripke bundle complete via C-set models. As a corollary we can give a simple proof showing that C-set semantics for modal logics are stronger than Kripke bundle semantics. (edited)

**Israel, M**. Polarity Sensitivity as Lexical Semantics. *Ling Phil*, 19(6), 619-666, D 96.

This paper offers a lexical semantic explanation for the distribution of negative and positive polarity items in English and other languages. Polarity items are analyzed as a special class of scalar operator conventionally specified for both quantitative and informative value. The simultaneous encoding of these two scalar properties makes these forms sensitive to pragmatic entailments within a scalar model and so creates the effect of polarity sensitivity. The proposed account offers empirical advantages over alternatives based on negative implicature or monotonicity and provides a natural pragmatic motivation for the existence of this widespread, but apparently useless feature of natural language.

**Itkonen, Matti**. Dialogic or Dialogistic? Dialogicity or Dialogism? A Word of Warning against Rigor Metodologiae. *Human Stud*, 20(1), 47-58, Ja 97.

Probing into the fundamentals of any phenomenon, we come upon a secret in the very moment of its inception—a bond with the multiplicity of the world. If anything in our world is detached from its foundations, this ontological lifeline is severed—being and Being are confounded. The ontic preexists language, it pre-empts all conceptualization. The world is in flux and lies always beyond the confines of any system; something of it always escapes. Only when this is conceded can beginning begin, only then can we set about the work of phenomenalizing our world; only then is it possible to seek answers to questions such as "Who am I?", "And you?", "What is the nature of responsibility, reflection, dialogicity and intersubjectivity?" Perhaps after all some notion can be netted in.

**Ito, Hisae**. Methode der Musikgeschichte von Guido Adler. *Bigaku*, 47(4), 46-57, Spr 97.

In der letzten Hälfte des 19. Jahrhunderts sind verschiedenartige Kunstwissenschaften wie die Wissenschaft für bildende Kunst erschienen. Man kann auch sagen, dass die empirischen, positiven Kunstwissenschaften der traditionellen Ästhetik überlegen geworden sind. Guido Adler (1855-1941) war einer der Musiwissenschaftler, die in dieser Zeit gelebt haben und versucht haben, Musikgeschichte als "Wissenschaft" zu systematisieren. (edited)

**Iuculano, John** and Burkum, Keith. The Humanism of Sartre: Toward a Psychology of Dignity. *J Theor Phil Psych*, 16(1), 19-29, Spr 96.

This paper is an attempt to make more explicit what we believe is the significance of the concept of dignity for psychology. The paper is grounded in the writings of Husserl and the humanism of Sartre and examines the humanistic position underlying psychology with that of positivism and determinism. Through an examination of Sartre's formulation of the cogito and intersubjectivity, we argue, that humanism more than any other orientation current in psychology is concerned with the human status of the individual and the recognition of dignity as central to that status. We argue that dignity is fundamental to the structure of human existence and is achieved only by holding the other as human in status rather than reduced to the status of an object.

**Iulina, Nina S**. Women, the Family, and Society: Discussions in the Feminist Thought of the United States. *Russian Stud Phil*, 34(2), 73-96, Fall 95.

**Ivaldo, Marco**. Transzendentale Lebenslehre: Zur Königsberger Wissenschaftslehre 1807. *Perspekt Phil*, 22, 167-188, 1996.

**Ivanov, A V**. The Philosophical-Theological Idea of Sophia: The Contemporary Context of Interpretation. *Russian Stud Phil*, 35(4), 6-23, Spr 97.

The main purpose of the work was to show the philosophical and cultural sources of the idea of Sophia in Russian philosophy, its metaphysical and methodological efficiency in the solution of such key-problems as mind-body problem, the genesis of the psychics, the relations between energetical and informative processes. From the modern point of view Sophia could be understood as a binary substance of Universe,—both spiritual and material, informative and energetical, which manifests itself on several ontological levels, correlative to different states of human consciousness. The idea of Sophia, in its rational interpretation, could explain some results in physics/the theory of torsion fields/and transpersonal psychology.

**Ivison, Duncan**. The Secret History of Public Reason: Hobbes to Rawls. *Hist Polit Thought*, 18(1), 125-147, Spr 97.

The problem of public reason became central to the political theory of the early modern period, and continues to be in ours. However, the solutions we have inherited and developed since then are increasingly under pressure. Modes of public justification can take alternative and conflicting forms. However, much justification is theoretically unlimited—however, much 'reasons for *us*' are always contestable and defeasible—it is always at the same time historically patterned and thus limited. I distinguish between three different modes of public justification, and suggest an alternative way of conceiving of the nature of political disagreement given deep social and political diversity.

**Ivry, Alfred**. "Ibn Rushd's Use of Allegory" in *Averroës and the Enlightenment*, Wahba, Mourad (ed), 113-125. Amherst, Prometheus, 1996.

**Iwand, Hans-Joachim**. Letter to Georg Lukács and Karl Barth (in Hungarian). *Magyar Filozof Szemle*, 4-5-6, 538-543, 1996.

**Izumi, Lance T**. Confounding the Paradigm: Asian Americans and Race Preferences. *Notre Dame J Law Ethics*, 11(1), 121-138, 1997.

**Jacinto Z, Agustin**. Conferencias de Einstein. *Mathesis*, 10(1), 115-125, F 94.

**Jackson, Arthur F**. Nature and Human Nature in an Existential Perspective. *Cont Phil*, 18(4 & 5), 3-6, Jl-Ag/S-O 96.

Reality exists as the total of its individual existents and these can be understood both as entities and as events. Considering them as events reinforces a dynamic view of reality and emphasizes the relatedness of all existents. This existential context is an ongoing, purposeful evolutionary process and humans, as that part of the process which is conscious of its evolving nature, have a moral obligation to contribute to the flourishing of this interconnected web of natural beings.

**Jackson, Frank** and Price, Huw. Naturalism and the Fate of the M-Worlds. *Aris Soc*, Supp(71), 247-282, 1997.

Concepts such as those of morality, modality, meaning and the mental are difficult to "place" in a naturalistic world view. This paper offers a novel placement strategy, based on a naturalistic pluralism about the functions of descriptive discourse. It is argued that this functional pluralism is more attractive than familiar alternatives, such as naturalistic reductionism, nonnaturalism, noncognitivism and eliminativism. The strategy exploits on Carnap's views about the nature of ontological issues.

**Jackson, Kevin T**. Globalizing Corporate Ethics Programs: Perils and Prospects. *J Bus Ethics*, 16(12-13), 1227-1235, S 97.

Establishing a cosmopolitan ethical culture for a multinational company requires special effort above and beyond that needed for standard domestic ethics initiatives. This articles discusses some of the perils and prospects involved in international corporate ethics programs and recommends some key guiding principles.

**Jackson, Michael**. Socrates' Soul and Our Own. *J Value Inq*, 31(2), 167-176, Je 97.

Socrates argued that the soul is immortal. After reviewing these arguments, I conclude they are not convincing, and yet Socrates' soul is immortal. Immortality is the legacy of Socrates in matters of judgment. At this point I use Hannah Arendt's distinction between thinking and judging. We cannot judge without thinking, but thinking is not judging. Judging descends to particulars that are often missed in our pursuit of universal criteria.

**Jackson, Peter** and Pais, John. Partial Monotonicity and a New Version of the Ramsey Test. *Stud Log*, 51(1), 21-47, 1992.

We introduce two new belief revision axioms: *partial monotonicity and consequence correctness*. We show that partial monotonicity is consistent with but independent of the full set of axioms for a *Gärdenfors belief revision system*. In contrast to the Gädenfors inconsistency results for certain monotonicity principles, we use partial monotonicity to inform a consistent formalization of the Ramsey test within a belief revision system extended by a conditional operator. We take this to be a technical dissolution of the well-known Gärdenfors dilemma. (edited)

**Jackson, Sally**. "Fallacies and Heuristics" in *Logic and Argumentation*, Van Eemeren, Frans H (ed), 101-114. Amsterdam, North-Holland, 1994.

In this paper, an explanation is proposed for the persuasiveness of fallacies. Most discourse is dependent on a broad presumption of acceptability that limits evaluation of claims to noticed trouble-spots: evaluation is triggered by identifiable symptoms of something wrong. Furthermore, the evaluation of claims occurs at varying levels of depth, depending on the level of suspicion aroused and the amount of effort the evaluator is willing to spend on the evaluation. The main implication of this is that fallacies are not incorrect argument schemes, or correct argument schemes applied incorrectly, but products of evaluation heuristics that can be given good defense as diagnostic tools.

**Jackson, Terence** and Calafell Artola, Marian. Ethical Beliefs and Management Behaviour: A Cross-Cultural Comparison. *J Bus Ethics*, 16(11), 1163-1173, Ag 97.

A cross-cultural empirical study is reported in this article which looks at ethical beliefs and behaviours among French and German managers and compares this with previous studies of U.S. and Israeli managers using a similar questionnaire. Significant differences are found by national ownership of the company rather than the country in which it is situated. Significant differences are found, for both individual managers by nationality and for companies by nationality of parents, in the area of 'organizational loyalty'. The attitude towards accepting gifts and favors in exchange for preferential treatment, as a measure of 'societal values', is also found to show significant differences between national groups. However, no significant differences are found for measures for 'group loyalty', 'conflict between organizational and group loyalty' and for 'conflicts between self and group/organization'. (edited)

**Jacob, Alexander**. The Metaphysical Systems of Henry More and Isaac Newton. *Phil Natur*, 29(1), 69-93, 1992.

**Jacob, Pierre**. "Can Semantic Properties Be Non-Causal?" in *Contents*, Villanueva, Enrique (ed), 44-51. Atascadero, Ridgeview, 1995.

**Jacob, Pierre**. State Consciousness Revisited. *Acta Analytica*, 29-54, 1996.

My goal in this paper is to defend the so-called "higher-order thought" theory of conscious mental states, which has been presented in various places by Rosenthal, from a pair of objections recently advanced by Dretske. According to the version of the "higher-order thought" (henceforth HOT) theory of conscious states which I have in mind, none of my mental states will be a conscious state unless I am conscious of it. The intuition behind this view—which I find appealing—is that a mental state of which a person is completely unaware counts as a nonconscious mental state. I think that some of the intuitions underlying Dretske's views can be reconciled with an amended version of the HOT theory. In particular, I will recommend the incorporation into the HOT theory of the concept of a state *of* consciousness intermediary between the concept of creature consciousness and the concept of state consciousness. (edited)

**Jacob, Pierre**. The Cognitive Turn in Philosophy (in Czech). *Filosof Cas*, 44(6), 895-902, 1996.

**Jacobelli, Angela Maria Isoldi**. Criticismo trascendentale, trascendenza, religione. *G Metaf*, 18(3), 321-338, S-D 96.

**Jacobi, Klaus** and King, Peter and Strub, Christian. From *intellectus verus/falsus* to the *dictum propositionis*: The Semantics of Peter Abelard and his Circle. *Vivarium*, 34(1), 15-40, My 96.

**Jacobs, Jonathan**. The Virtues of Externalism. *S J Phil*, 34(3), 285-299, Fall 96.

I explicate what I call Aristotle's *externalism* about both voluntariness and good. Externalism about good is the view that there are objective criteria for whether an individual is an excellent one of its kind and so there are grounds for being correct or mistaken (even in one's own case) about whether one is leading a good life. Externalism about voluntariness is the view that because one's character is shaped by activity that is self-moving (whether self-consciously deliberate or not), individuals are responsible for their characters, including their habits.

**Jacobs, Lesley A**. Can An Egalitarian Justify Universal Access to Health Care?. *Soc Theor Pract*, 22(3), 315-348, Fall 96.

The idea that in a just society all citizens should have secure access to some minimal standard of health care is a powerful one. This paper is concerned with identifying the normative foundations for providing this level of access to health care, which I call universal access to health care. Among political philosophers it is generally believed that some sort of general principle of distributional equality can provide solid moral foundations for universal access to health care. The purpose of this paper is to put pressure on this received view by showing how the egalitarian theories of justice in health care defended by Ronald Dworkin, Norman Daniels and Thomas Pogge each fail to ground a commitment to universal access.

**Jacobsen, Jans Jorgen**. On the Foundations of Nash Equilibrium. *Econ Phil*, 12(1), 67-88, Ap 96.

**Jacobsen, Rockney**. Self-Quotation and Self-Knowledge. *Synthese*, 110(3), 419-445, Mr 97.

I argue that indirect quotation in the first person simple present tense ("self-quotation") provides a class of infallible assertions. The defense of this conclusion examines the joint descriptive and constitutive functions of performance utterances and argues that a parallel treatment of belief ascription is in order. The parallel account yields a class of infallible belief ascriptions that makes no appeal to privileged modes of access. Confronting a dilemma formulated by Crispin Wright for theories of self-knowledge gives an epistemological setting for the account of infallible belief ascription.

**Jacobson, Daniel**. Sir Philip Sidney's Dilemma: On the Ethical Function of Narrative Art. *J Aes Art Crit*, 54(4), 327-336, Fall 96.

Sidney had both a positive and a negative task, in defending poetry. To satisfy his puritan opponents, he needed to find a nonhedonic value for poetry; and also to defend it against their charge that the poet is by nature a liar. Sidney's famous reply is that poets cannot lie, because they never assert. But he also held that the positive value of poetry lies in its ethical function of showing "what should be." I propose a model of the ethical function of art, in the spirit of Sidney's defense, which can resolve the tension between these two ideas.

**Jacobson, Stephen**. Externalism and Action-Guiding Epistemic Norms. *Synthese*, 110(3), 381-397, Mr 97.

In this book, *Contemporary Theories of Knowledge*, John Pollock argues that all externalist theories of justification should be rejected on the grounds that they do not do justice to the action-guiding character of epistemic norms. I reply that Pollock's argument is ineffective—because not all externalisms are intended to involve action-guiding norms, and because Pollock does not give a good reason for thinking that action-guiding norms must be internalist norms. Second, I consider rehabilitating Pollock's argument by restricting his conclusion to theories that do involve action-guiding norms and providing a better reason to think that action-guiding norms must be internalist norms. But I claim that if Pollock's argument is made strong enough to rule out all externalisms, it rules out too much, namely, any plausible conception of epistemic norms.

**Jaconelli, Joseph**. Rights Theories and Public Trial. *J Applied Phil*, 14(2), 169-175, 1997.

Most rights claims are capable of being analysed in terms of both the competing theories of rights, the will theory and the interest theory. Discussion hitherto has concentrated on particular instances of rights claims which are easily accommodated by the one theory but accommodated only with difficulty (if at all) by the other. Such problematic examples have served to illuminate what is at stake between the rival theories. However, in the case of the right to a public trial, I argue that neither theory is capable of accommodating that particular 'right'.

**Jacques, T Carlos**. From Savages and Barbarians to Primitives: Africa, Social Typologies, and History in Eighteenth-Century French Philosophy. *Hist Theor*, 36(2), 190-215, My 97.

This article describes the conceptual framework (what I call a "style of reasoning") within which knowledge about Africa was legitimized in eighteenth-century French philosophy. The article traces a shift or rupture in this conceptual framework which, at the end of the eighteenth century, led to the emergence of new conditions for knowledge legitimation that altered Europe's perception of Africa. The article examines these two conceptual frameworks within the context of a discussion of the social theory of the time, which categorized Africans first as savages, and then, with the advent of our modern "style of reasoning," as primitives. The argument used to demonstrate this change in categorizations is historical. (edited)

**Jacquette, Dale**. Is Nondefectively Justified True Belief Knowledge?. *Ratio*, 9(2), 115-127, S 96.

An alternative analysis of knowledge is proposed, according to which the potential loophole between the state of affairs that justifies belief in a proposition and the state of affairs that makes the proposition true, permitted by the traditional concept of knowledge and discovered by Gettier's counterexamples, is closed by redefining knowledge as semantically-epistemically evidentially relevant justified true belief. (edited)

**Jacquette, Dale**. *Meinongian Logic: The Semantics of Existence and Nonexistence*. Hawthorne, de Gruyter, 1996.

This book offers a systematic revisionary exposition of Meinongian logic and semantics. The logic developed provides the basis for a formal interpretation of intensional languages in which reference and true predication of properties to existent and nonexistent objects is possible, inspired by the *Gegenstandstheorie* or object theory logic and semantics of the Austrian philosopher, Alexius Meinong (1853-1920). The logic integrates a three-valued formalization of type-unordered predicate-quantificational object theory with abstract, modal and non-Russellian definite description subtheory. Applications of the logic include a refutation of Twardowski's exclusive distinction between the content and object of thought, a formal analysis of Wittgenstein's private language argument, critique of Anselm's ontological proof for the existence of God, Meinongian modelling of the logic of scientific law and of the logic of fiction and a formal resolution of the paradox of analysis.

**Jacquette, Dale**. Object Theory Foundations for Intensional Logic. *Acta Analytica*, 33-63, 1995.

The logic of existent and nonexistent objects provides a formal theory of reference and true predication for ordinary discourse, the semantics of ontological commitment, and logic of fiction. The intensional logic proposed in what follows offers a rigorous object theory semantics with nonstandard propositional and predicate inference machinery. The system is distinguished from previous formalizations of object theory by formal criteria for nuclear (constitutive) and extranuclear (nonconstitutive) properties, three-valued propositional semantics for predications of nuclear properties to incomplete nonexistent objects for which the objects ostensibly are undetermined, nonstandard set theory semantics with unrestricted comprehension for object theory predicate semantics (licensed by existence restrictions on abstraction equivalence), demonstrations of internal determinacy, consistency, and Henkin completeness, nonstandard deduction theorem, and consistency considerations in light of free assumption and unrestricted comprehension.

**Jacquette, Dale**. The Validity Paradox in Modal $S_5$. *Synthese*, 109(1), 47-62, O 96.

The standard definition of validity is challenged by the validity or Pseudo-Scotus paradox. To argue that this argument is valid, therefore, this argument is invalid, seems to constitute a counterexample to the definition that an argument is valid if and only if it is impossible for its assumptions to be true and its conclusions false (or such that if its assumptions are true then its conclusions must be true). The paradox is shown to rest on a modal fallacy in systems weaker than $S_5$, in the derivation of the second or invalidity horn of the paradox dilemma. But it is demonstrated that the paradox holds in modal system $S_5$ and its normal conservative extensions containing the characteristic axioms. The problematic choice presented by this result is either to modify the traditional definition of validity for modal $S_5$ and stronger logics, or to regard deductive inference in all such formal systems as logically suspect.

**Jadacki, Jacek Juliusz**. "Warsaw: The Rise and Decline of Modern Scientific Philosophy in the Capital City of Poland" in *In Itinere* European Cities and the Birth of Modern Scientific Philosophy, Poli, Roberto (ed), 145-160. Amsterdam, Rodopi, 1997.

**Jadczak, Ryszard**. Roman Ingarden's First Lecture at the University of Lvov (in Polish). *Kwartalnik Filozof*, 24(3), 133-134, 1996.

**Jadczak, Ryszard** and Ingarden, Roman. Some Tendencies in Modern Epistemology (in Polish). *Kwartalnik Filozof*, 24(3), 135-147, 1996.

**Jaeger, Suzanne M**. Beauty and the Breast: Dispelling Significations of Feminine Sensuality in the Aesthetics of Dance. *Phil Today*, 41(2), 270-276, Sum 97.

Using a phenomenological methodology, I examine alternative significations of feminine sensuality in artistic dance. Rather than the dancer's body being a product of values imminent to linguistic structure, I argue for an ethic of bodily integrity. My claim is that while there are reasons for rejecting feminine sensuality as it is constructed in classical ballet, the *presence* of bodily being is a constitutive aspect of even the ballet dancer's *becoming-feminine*. Thus, in comparison with strictly semiotic readings, the phenomenology of bodily

*presence* describes a deeper lying *pre-objective* and meaningful structuring of human existence as embodied.

**Jaeschke, Walter**. "Absolute Subject and Absolute Subjectivity in Hegel" in *Figuring the Self: Subject, Absolute, and Others in Classical German Philosophy*, Zöller, Günter (ed), 193-205. Albany, SUNY Pr, 1997.

**Jaffe, Arthur**. Proof and the Evolution of Mathematics. *Synthese*, 111(2), 133-146, My 97.

**Jaggar, Alison**. Gender, Race, and Difference: Individual Consideration versus Group-Based Affirmative Action in Admission to Higher Education. *S J Phil*, 34(Supp), 21-51, 1996.

**Jaggar, Alison**. Regendering the U.S. Abortion Debate. *J Soc Phil*, 28(1), 127-140, Spr 97.

**Jain, Renu** and Thomasma, David C. Discontinuing Life Support in an Infant of a Drug-Addicted Mother: Whose Decision Is It?. *Cambridge Quart Healthcare Ethics*, 6(1), 48-54, Winter 97.

**Jain, Sanjay** and Sharma, Arun. Characterizing Language Identification in Terms of Computable Numberings. *Annals Pure Applied Log*, 84(1), 51-72, Mr 97.

Identification of programs for computable functions from their graphs and identification of grammars (r.e., indices) for recursively enumerable languages from positive data are two extensively studied problems in the recursion theoretic framework of inductive inference. In the context of function identification, Freivalds et al. (1984) have shown that only those collections of functions, $L$, are identifiable in the limit for which there exists a 1-1 computable numbering Psi and a discrimination function $d$ such that a) for each $f$ "is an element of" $L$, the number of indices $i$ such that $\text{Psi}_i = f$ is exactly one and b) for each $f$ "is an element of" $L$, there are only finitely many indices $i$ such that $f$ and $\text{Psi}_i$ agree on the first $d(i)$ arguments. A similar characterization for language identification in the limit has turned out to be difficult. A partial answer is provided in this paper. Several new techniques are introduced which have found use in other investigations on language identification. (edited)

**Jaini, Padmanabh S**. Pandava-Purana of Vadicandra: Text and Translation. *J Indian Phil*, 25(1), 91-127, F 97.

**Jakob, Eric**. *Martin Heidegger und Hans Jonas: Die Metaphysik der Subjektivität und die Krise der technologischen Zivilisation*. Tubingen, Francke, 1996.

Themen der Untersuchung sind Martin Heideggers und Hans Jonas' Philosophie der Technik. Bei beiden Denkern erfolgt die Thematisierung der Technik auf dem Hintergrund der Abkehr von der neuzeitlichen Erkenntnistheorie, der "Metaphysik der Subjektivität". (publisher)

**Jakovleva, L E**. José L. Abellán y la *especificidad* de la filosofía española. *An Seminar Hist Filosof*, 13, 305-318, 1996.

**Jakovljevic, Dragan**. Bemerkungen zur Natur der Angewandten Ethik (in Serbo-Croatian). *Theoria (Yugoslavia)*, 38(4), 29-34, D 95.

Angewandte Ethik kann annäherungsweise als eine Abart der normativ-ethischen Betrachtung bestimmt werden, die sich der systematischen Untersuchung von unmittelbar an gewisse, zur moralischen Bewertung fähige Lebenslagentypen und ihre individuell geprägte Einzelfälle haftenden moralischen Fragen widmet, dabei Bewertungen formulierend und begründend, mit denen richtige Handlungsweisen ausgesondert werden. Allgemeine normative Ethik und Angewandte Ethik unterscheiden sich vornehmlich nach ihren Untersuchungsgegenständen, während in der Form der Betrachtung weitgehende Einheitlichkeit mit einigen graduellen Differenzen zu verzeichnen ist. Eine folgenschwere Öffnung des ethischen referenziellen Systems und begriffliche Erschliessung von neuartigen moralischen Aspekten des gegenwärtigen Lebens sind die Hauptbeiträge die Angewandte Ethik zur Moralphilosophie geleistet hat.

**Jakovljevic, Goran**. Zum wirkungsgeschichtlichen Bewusstsein (in Serbo-Croatian). *Theoria (Yugoslavia)*, 38(3), 47-61, S 95.

Ausgehend von einer verwickelten aber fruchtbaren gadamerschen "Definition" des Wirkungsgeschichtlichen Bewusstseins, unterscheidet der Verfasser zwei Aspekte dieses Begriffs: den der Substantialität und den Aspekt der Reflexivität. Sich an Heidegger anknüpfend, bestimmt Gadamer das Wirkungsgeschichtliche Bewusstsein als Bewusstsein der hermeneutischen Situation; im Anschluss an Hegel auch als Bewusstsein der Wirkungsgeschichte. Der in beiden Bestimmungen verwendete sujektiv-objektive Genitiv soll den Doppelaspekt des Begriffs andeuten: das Wirkungsgeschichtliche Bewusstsein ist einerseits das durch die hermeneutische Situation bzw. Wirkungsgeschichte *bewirkte* substantielle wirkungsgeschichtliche Bewusstsein und andrerseits das auf die hermeneutische Situation bzw. Wirkungsgeschichte *Wirkende* reflexive wirkungsgeschichtlichen Bewusstseins bekämpft Gadamer zuerst das historische Bewusstsein das den Moment der Wirkungsgeschichte vernachlässigt. Eine wichtige Rolle spielt dieser Begriff auch in Gadamers Auseinandersetzung mit Habermas und Apel.

**Jalbert, John E**. Habermas, Fichte and the Question of Technological Determinism. *Amer Cath Phil Quart*, 70(Supp), 209-218, 1996.

**Jalil, Abdul A K** and Pavri, Francis and Wimalasiri, Jayantha S. An Empirical Study of Moral Reasoning Among Managers in Singapore. *J Bus Ethics*, 15(12), 1331-1341, D 96.

The study reported here sought to examine the ethical orientations of business managers and business students in Singapore. Data were obtained using Defining Issue Test. Analysis of Variance revealed that age, education and religious affiliation had influenced cognitive moral development stages of the respondents. Vocation, gender and ethnicity did not seem to have affected moral judgment of the subjects. Contrary to the general view both business students and business managers demonstrated the same level of sensitivity to ethical dimensions of decision-making. Implications of the findings and limitations of the study are discussed.

**James, Joy Ann**. "Black Feminism: Liberation Limbos and Existence in Gray" in *Existence in Black: An Anthology of Black Existential Philosophy,* Gordon, Lewis R (ed), 215-224. New York, Routledge, 1997.

**James, William** and Levinson, Henry Samuel. *A Pluralistic Universe.* Lincoln, Univ of Nebraska Pr, 1996.

James argues for a metaphysical view he called 'pluralistic pantheism'. In *The Varieties of Religious Experience*, he argued that diverse religious experiences testified to a 'wider self through which saving experiences come'. But he thought he needed to transform that testimony into evidence by showing how this 'wider self' or selves entered into 'cosmic relations' which let people predict 'remote objective consequences' exceeding those reported in conversion narratives. *A Pluralistic Universe* suggests a mapping of relevant relations and consequences that James finds plausible. Levinson provides an introduction which shows how this work links up with James's most representative ideas.

**Jameson, Valerie** and Wall, Hershel P and Strong, Carson. A Model Policy Addressing Mistreatment of Medical Students. *J Clin Ethics*, 7(4), 341-346, Wint 96.

The University of Tennessee College of Medicine developed a policy on student mistreatment that has three main components. First, a statement of standards of behavior was set forth that affirms the importance of mutual respect among teachers and students and asserts that the College will not condone mistreatment. Second, methods were developed for ongoing education of the college community concerning the standards of behavior and the process by which they are upheld. This educational process is directed toward preclinical and clinical students and faculty, residents, fellows and nurses. It attempts to promote a positive environment for learning by increasing sensitivity concerning the issue of mistreatment. It also informs persons who believe they have been mistreated that avenues for seeking redress are available. Third, a process for responding to allegations of mistreatment was established. This process, designed to be fair and to respect the rights of accuser and accused, involves use of a "mediator" and a "conflict-resolution council" to deal with alleged and actual mistreatment and promote reconciliation between conflicting parties. This approach has been implemented and its effectiveness will be assessed.

**Jamieson, Dale**. Teaching Ethics in Science and Engineering: Animals in Research. *Sci Eng Ethics*, 1(2), 185-186, A 95.

**Jamieson, Dale**. What Society Will Expect from the Future Research Community. *Sci Eng Ethics*, 1(1), 73-80, J 95.

In the post-Cold War period of shrinking budgets, science will increasingly be subject to contradictory demands for Snappy, telegence big science but no pork barrell projects; better science education and lower taxes; wars in various diseases and disorders coupled with deficit reduction; more-mission-oriented research and less government interference. I offer same suggestions about how these troubled waters may be navigated.

**Jamme, Christoph**. Cross-cultural Understanding: Its Philosophical and Anthropological Problems. *Int J Phil Stud*, 4(2), 292-308, S 96.

In this paper I shall attempt to outline a double thesis: a) the philosophical theory of the experience of something other requires the challenge of ethnology as the science of the stranger; and b) conversely, however, ethnology itself requires a theory of cultural strangeness, which although always presupposed is never developed. (edited)

**Janaway, Christopher**. Two Kinds of Artistic Duplication. *Brit J Aes*, 37(1), 1-14, Ja 97.

The paper takes two much-discussed claims—Goodman's that one could not falsely pass off an indistinguishable copy of apiece of music or literary work as the work itself and Danto's that two verbally identical texts could be distinct works—and seeks to reconcile them. Any description of the relevant kind of forgery presupposes a scenario which contains an instruction to regard the fraudulent copy as work *W* by artist *S*. The paper argues that in such a context something notationally equivalent to *W* must fail to be a forgery, because it cannot be functionally distinct from *W*.

**Jané, Ignacio**. Theoremhood and Logical Consequence. *Theoria (Spain)*, 12(28), 139-160, Ja 97.

In this paper, Tarski's notion of logical consequence is viewed as a special case of the more general notion of being a theorem of an axiomatic theory. As was recognized by Tarski, the material adequacy of his definition depends on having the distinction between logical and non- logical constants right, but we find Tarski's analysis persuasive even if we don't agree on what constants are logical. This accords with the view put forward in this paper that Tarski indeed captures the more inclusive notion of theoremhood in an axiomatic theory. The approach to logical consequence via axiomatic theories leads us to grant centrality to inference schemas rather than to full-fledged arguments and to view the logically valid schemas as a subclass of generally valid schemas.

**Janeira, Ana Luisa**. A Ciência e a Virtude No Noviciado da Cotovia (1603-1759): Organizaçao do Espaço, Produçao do Discurso e Sistema Epistémico. *Rev Port Filosof*, 52(1-4), 441-447, Ja-D 96.

**Jang, In Ha**. The Problematic Character of Socrates' Defense of Justice in Plato's *Republic. Interpretation*, 24(1), 85-107, Fall 96.

**Janiaud, Joël**. Here I Am! Kierkegaard and Levinas: The Tensions of Responsibility (in French). *Arch Phil*, 60(1), 87-108, Ja-Mr 97.

In his reading of Kierkegaard, Levinas charges the former with irresponsibility, symbolized by the suspension of ethics by Abraham in *Crainte et tremblement*. This criticism places us squarely before the ambiguity of an election which

Kierkegaard based upon a secret and an interiority rather than on a meeting with others. This confrontation allows us to examine the larger question of Kierkegaardian responsibility and the subtle connections between the testimonial desires of these two philosophers.

**Janicaud, Dominique**. Back to a Monstrous Site: Reiner Schürmann's Reading of Heidegger's *Beiträge. Grad Fac Phil J*, 19/20(2/1), 287-297, 1997.

**Janke, Wolfgang**. "Das Wissen ist an sich die absolute Existenz": Der oberste Grundsatz in Fichtes 4: Vortrag der Wissenschaftslehre: Erlangen im Sommer 1805. *Perspekt Phil*, 22, 189-230, 1996.

**Janke, Wolfgang**. Fichte, Novalis, Hölderlin: die Nacht des gegenwärtigen Zeitalters. *Fichte-Studien*, 12, 1-24, 1997.

**Jankélévitch, Vladimir** and Hobart, Ann. Do Not Listen to What They Say, Look at What They Do. *Crit Inquiry*, 22(3), 549-551, Spr 96.

**Jankélévitch, Vladimir** and Hobart, Ann. Should We Pardon Them?. *Crit Inquiry*, 22(3), 552-572, Spr 96.

**Jankowski, Andrzej W**. An Algebraic Approach to Logics in Research Work of Helena Rasiowa and Cecylia Rauszer. *Bull Sec Log*, 25(3/4), 139-146, O-D 96.

**Jánossy, A** and Kurucz, A and Eiben, A. E. Combining Algebraizable Logics. *Notre Dame J Form Log*, 37(2), 366-380, Spr 96.

The general methodology of "algebraizing" logics is used here for combining different logics. The combination of logics is represented as taking the colimit of the constituent logics in the category of algebaizable logics. The cocompleteness of this category as well as its isomorphism to the corresponding category of certain first-order theories are proved.

**Jansana, Ramon** and Dellunde, Pilar. "Characterization Theorems for Infinitary Universal Horn Logic" in *Verdad: lógica, representación y mundo,* Villegas Forero, L, 193-199. Santiago de Compostela, Univ Santiago Comp, 1996.

The purpose of this paper is to characterize the classes of structures axiomatizable by a set of universal Horn sentences and the classes axiomatizable by a set of universal Horn sentences without equality of an arbitrary infinitary language. (edited)

**Jansana, Ramon** and Dellunde, Pilar. Some Characterization Theorems for Infinitary Universal Horn Logic without Equality. *J Sym Log*, 61(4), 1242-1260, D 96.

In the paper we mainly study preservation theorems for the universal strict Horn fragment of the infinitary languages without the equality symbol. We obtain definability, joint consistency and interpolation results for the mentioned fragments. We apply the results to obtain some generalizations of know theorems on the field of abstract algebraic logic.

**Jansana, Ramon** and Dellunde, Pilar and Casanovas, E. On Elementary Equivalence for Equality-free Logic. *Notre Dame J Form Log*, 37(3), 506-522, Sum 96.

This paper is a contribution to the study of equality-free logic, that is, first-order logic without equality. We mainly devote ourselves to the study of algebraic characterizations of its relation of elementary equivalence by providing some Keisler-Shelah type ultrapower theorems and an Ehrenfeucht-Fraïssé type theorem. We also give characterizations of elementary classes in equality-free logic. As a by-product we characterize the sentences that are logically equivalent to an equality-free one.

**Jantzen, Grace M**. Feminism and Pantheism. *Monist*, 80(2), 266-285, Ap 97.

Because of the historically oppressive consequences of Western religion, a disruption and rethinking of the religious symbolic is overdue. Pantheism offers an imaginative alternative symbolic. Although pantheism has been feared as the abyss in which all things would be a variant of the same, in fact pantheism can be shown to open the way to alterities of every sort. The contours of a pantheist imaginary offer creative potential for a sensible transcendental as discussed by Luce Irigaray and for an embodied freedom. The force of the symbolic in what is religiously thinkable is prior to the question of truth: although philosophers and religious thinkers are prone to insist on truth conditions, the truth question prematurely asked can foreclose the very possibilities of a creative symbolic.

**Jantzen, Grace M**. What's the Difference? Knowledge and Gender in (Post)Modern Philosophy of Religion. *Relig Stud*, 32(4), 431-448, D 96.

Although there is a deep channel dividing British philosophy of religion from French thought associated with poststructuralism, much is to be gained from communication between the two. In this paper I explore three central areas of difference: the understanding of the subject, of language and of God/religion. In each case I show that continental philosophy pursues these areas in ways which make issues of gender central to their understanding; and suggest that, while continental thought is neither monolithic nor beyond criticism, its understandings of difference are of great value to religious thought.

**Japaridze, Giorgi**. A Constructive Game Semantics for the Language of Linear Logic. *Annals Pure Applied Log*, 85(2), 87-156, My 97.

I present a semantics for the language of first-order additive-multiplicative linear logic, i.e., the language of classical first-order logic with two sorts of disjunction and conjunction. The semantics allows us to capture intuitions often associated with linear logic or constructivism such as *sentences=games, sentences=resources* or *sentences=problems*, where "truth" means existence of an effective winning (resource-using, problem-solving) strategy. The paper introduces a decidable first-order logic *ET* in the above language and gives a proof of its soundness and completeness (in the full language) with respect to this semantics. Allowing noneffective strategies in the latter is shown to lead to classical logic. (edited)

AUTHOR INDEX 705 Jemelka, Petr

**Jardine, Nick** and Frasca-Spada, Marina. Splendours and Miseries of the Science Wars. *Stud Hist Phil Sci*, 28(2), 219-235, Je 97.

Paul Gross and Norman Levitt's *Higher Superstition* (Baltimore, MD, 1994) and Alan Sokal's spoof 'Transgressing the Boundaries: Toward a Transformation Hermeneutics of Quantum Gravity' (*Social Text*, special 'Science Wars' double issue, 1996) have sparked off extensive and sharp exchanges concerning the credentials of history, philosophy, and social studies of science. Where others have bewailed these 'Science Wars', in this editorial article we celebrate, from a moderate sceptical and pragmatist standpoint, the dialogue with scientists that they have provoked and the publicity they have given to issues of outstanding concern for the future of our culture.

**Jarrett, Greg**. Analyzing Mental Demonstratives. *Phil Stud*, 84(1), 49-62, O 96.

**Jarvie, Ian** (ed) and Hall, John A (ed). *The Social Philosophy of Ernest Gellner*. Amsterdam, Rodopi, 1996.

A large collection of critical papers about the thought of the late Ernest Gellner, with a lengthy "Reply to Critics" and a definitive bibliography of his writings.

**Jasanoff, Sheila**. Is Science Socially Constructed—And Can It Still Inform Public Policy. *Sci Eng Ethics*, 2(3), 263-276, Jl 96.

This paper addresses, and seeks to correct, some frequent misunderstandings concerning the claim that science is socially constructed. It describes several features of scientific inquiry that have been usefully illuminated by constructivist studies of science, including the mundane or tacit skills involved in research, the social relationships in scientific laboratories, the causes of scientific controversy, and the interconnection of science and culture. Social construction, the paper argues, should be seen not as an alternative to but an enhancement of scientists' own professional understanding of how science is done. The richer, more finely textured accounts of scientific practice that the constructivist approach provides are potentially of great relevance to public policy.

**Jay, Martin**. "Mimesis and Mimetology: Adorno and Lacoue-Labarthe" in *The Semblance of Subjectivity*, Huhn, Tom (ed), 29-53. Cambridge, MIT Pr, 1997.

Against the poststructuralist critique of mimesis as the premise of a problematic aesthetic of imitative realism unable to register semiotic opacity, this paper explores a more nuanced and favorable notion of mimesis in the work of Adorno and Lacoue-Labarthe. Both defend mimesis as an alternative to the domination of conceptual subsumption, an alternative which preserves the claims of the body against the hegemony of abstract reason and the subject who claims to possess it. Both understand it as an obstacle to the desire of the speculative dialectics to sublate all otherness and nonidentity. Both see it as a means to avoid privileging an alleged origin over its mere copy, providing instead an endless oscillation between the two. However, unlike Lacoue-Labarthe, who criticized any attempt to coordinate reason and mimesis as a problematic "mimetology," Adorno sought a balance between the two.

**Jay, Martin**. The Limits of Limit Experience: Bataille and Foucault. *Constellations*, 2(2), 155-174, O 95.

Contrary to the conventional wisdom that assumes poststructuralist thought is hostile to the concept of experience, which it dissolves into discursive networks, this essay seeks to explore a more positive understanding of the term in the work of Georges Bataille and Michel Foucault. But examining their concepts of "inner experience" and "limit-experience," it probes a notion of experience that is liberated from a strong notion of a centered subject. It concludes by considering the implications for a theory of community of these notions of experience.

**Jayashanmukham, N**. The Atmahano Janāh of the Isāvāsya Upanisad. *J Indian Counc Phil Res*, 13(2), 151-162, Ja-Ap 96.

The article is concerned to determine the exact significance *of* ātmahano janāh in the Īsāvāsya Upanisad. Many scholars have tried to find out the right sense of the phrase. In my opinion the interpretation of the phrase by Sri Aurobindo is the best. According to him, the phrase refers to "*those who slay their souls*" either by keeping the souls in ignorance or by violently separating them from the bodies or by both. It seems to me that the phrase is introduced with a view to glorify those who arrive at fulfillment of their souls by liberated works, *ātmavanto narāH*.

**Jeavons, John S**. An Alternative Linear Semantics for Allowed Logic Programs. *Annals Pure Applied Log*, 84(1), 3-16, Mr 97.

We give a declarative semantics for allowed logic programs using pure linear logic. Previous proposals have used linear logic with weakening and interpret the comma in a logic program as conjunction. In our semantics the comma is interpreted as the multiplicative tensor product of linear logic.

**Jeavons, John S** and Crossley, John N. A Logic-Based Modelling of Prolog Resulation Sequences Including the Negation as Failure Rule. *Log Anal*, 37(147-8), 379-406, S-D 94.

In a previous paper, (Jeavons, J.S. and Crossley, J.N., "A Logic Based Modelling of Prolog Resolution Sequences," *Logique et Analyse*, 137-138: pp. 189-205, 1992) we gave a logic-based model for the procedural aspect of resolution-based logic programming. In this paper we extend the analysis to include the use of the negation as failure rule.

**Jech, Thomas** and Shelah, Saharon. On Countably Closed Complete Boolean Algebras. *J Sym Log*, 61(4), 1380-1386, D 96.

It is unprovable that every complete subalgebra of a countably closed complete Boolean algebra is countably closed.

**Jeck, Udo Reinhold**. Parmenides—Platon—Hermes Trismegistus: Bemerkungen zu einer *hermetischen* Reflexion in Heideggers Hegel-Traktat *Die Negativität*. *Bochumer Phil Jrbh*, 1, 153-178, 1996.

Heidegger's many observations about the philosophical thought of the Middle Ages, while often controversial, are deserving of attention. One of the lesser known of these observations reflects his interest in hermetic philosophy, as found in his posthumously published treatise *Die Negativität (1938/39), a critical engagement with Hegel with regard to the nature and ontological status of negation. Therein, Heidegger associates the "sphaira" of Parmenides with the sphaera intelligibilis* of Hermes Trismegistus and the *absolute Idee* of Hegel and therewith Plato's doctrine of the ideas in its absolute-idealist modification. Heidegger weaves these various strands of the tradition into a web of manifold significations representative of different yet related philosophical intentions.

**Jeck, Udo Reinhold**. Sieben Jenaer Reflexionen Hegels über Homer. *Jahr Hegelforschung*, 2, 55-97, 1996.

**Jecker, Nancy S**. Caring for "Socially Undesirable" Patients. *Cambridge Quart Healthcare Ethics*, 5(4), 500-510, Fall 96.

This paper reviews the history and ethics of using patients' social worth as a basis for rationing scarce health care resources. It also considers whether a patient's social worth should influence quality of life or medical futility judgments. Among its conclusions are 1) there is widespread agreement that the application of social worth fell prey to historical abuses; 2) if social worth is used as a rationing standard, it should be applied to a narrow range of cases, not used as a general rationing standard; and 3) social worth is irrelevant to medical futility judgments.

**Jeffrey, Andrew V**. Gale on Reference and Religious Experience. *Faith Phil*, 13(1), 91-112, Ja 96.

Richard Gale, in *On the Nature and Existence of God*, offers several reasons why a "historical-cum-indexical" theory of reference cannot be appropriate in explaining how people refer to God. The present paper identifies five distinct lines of argument in Gale, attempts to clarify several important desiderata for a successful theory of reference, and argues that Gale fails to discharge the burden of proof he has assumed, leaving the most important features of Alston's "direct reference" theory untouched. Nevertheless, it is conceded that some consequences of Alston's theory are quite counterintuitive. The paper, therefore, concludes with a consideration of two alternatives: either taking a hard, Alstonian line in conflict with people's linguistic intuitions, or striking a compromise with descriptivism along lines similar to those found in Gareth Evans's paper, "The Causal Theory of Names."

**Jeffrey, Richard**. Unknown Probabilities. *Erkenntnis*, 45(2 & 3), 327-335, Nov 96.

From a point of view like de Finetti's, what is the judgmental reality underlying the objectivistic claim that a physical magnitude *X* determines the objective probability that a hypothesis *H* is true? When you have definite conditional judgmental probabilities for *H* given the various unknown values of *X*, a plausible answer is sufficiency, i.e., invariance of those conditional probabilities as your probability distribution over the values of *X* varies. A different answer, in terms of conditional exchangeability, is offered for use when such definite conditional probabilities are absent.

**Jegstrup, Elsebet**. Kierkegaard on Tragedy: The Aporias of Interpretation. *Phil Today*, 40(2), 289-300, Sum 96.

Kierkegaard's *Either/Or* is examined for purposes of coming to understand how this complex two-volume work must be read, and the guide is the essay on tragedy. The teleological nature of tragedy is its ultimate purpose, meaning that tragedy makes more than aesthetic claims, it posits an ethic. Thus one must read Kierkegaard's use of tragedy as an indirect communication that discloses its thematic approach. Kierkegaard conceals himself forcing the reader to concentrate on the indirect communication, therefore the pseudonym. Its Latinized presentation unconceals the problem of the age revealed in the essay on tragedy, namely the isolation of the modern individual.

**Jemelka, Petr**. Environmental Ethics, Anthropocentrism and Rationality (in Czech). *Filosof Cas*, 45(3), 459-468, 1997.

The basic question here is the problem of anthropocentrism as an element in a criticized paradigm of modern civilization. The possibility of rejecting this does, however, call for consideration of other alternatives. The opposing biocentric pole clearly does not offer a problem-free solution for the emergence of new relations to the world of nature. The problem of the legitimacy and truth of a nonanthropocentrically formulated philosophy is fundamental. This leads to the critical point that the systematic implementation of this version is not merely a rejection of the human view of the problems of the modern world, but also the resignation to human responsibility. An even more fundamental question is the real acceptability of such concepts—their practical consequences (moral, political and technical). Biocentrism can be criticized primarily for its inability to offer concrete proposals in a form in which they can be put into practice. (edited)

**Jemelka, Petr**. Nature, Technology and Man in the Works of Dominik Pecka (in Czech). *Filosof Cas*, 44(6), 937-942, 1996.

This year was the 15th anniversary of the death of the theologian, philosopher and pedagogue, Dominik Pecka. The breadth of his work, and in particular his search for an answer to the question of man's place and role in the world give him a noteworthy place in Czech thought. Pecka's Christian humanism was critical of the modern era, noting the loss of man's natural link with the order of the world. This result of man's striving for individual emancipation is not, however, insuperable, although whether for good or evil depends on our free choice. The phenomenon of technology holds an important place in Pecka's thought, as something which (with the presupposition of experience and understanding of the transcendental meaning of human existence) can be of great help in rediscovering our roots in the world—primarily as a means for examining nature in detail. Pecka's formulation of the traditional version of humanism (primarily in terms of the so-called lordship of nature) can prove problematic in today's context. However, his call for a deeper understanding of the world and man in order to discover truly meaningful human activity was a valuable contribution for the debate on this question which was only beginning during his lifetime. For this too he holds an important position in Czech philosophy.

**Jenei, Ilona**. Prospective Payment System and the Traditional Medical Ethics in Hungary. *Ethics Med*, 13(1), 19-22, 1997.

This article aims at examining causes of the Hungarian health care reform, connected to the roots of the medical sense vocation and the moral premises of the reform. The DRGs - Based Payment system was introduced in Hungarian hospitals in 1993 which the majority of physicians received reservedly with referring to traditional medical ethics. The new financing system is closer to utilitarian thinking than to the traditional medical ethics of duty. It can be described as a conflict between the injunction to 'do no harm' and the injunction 'not to waste money'. Ethically it can be interpreted as a question of how much may be preserved from the values of traditional ethics during the costly development of modern medicine.

**Jenkins, Joyce L**. Desires and Human Nature in J.S. Mill. *Hist Phil Quart*, 14(2), 219-234, Ap 97.

It is argued that the best way to reconcile the tensions in Mill's theory of value is to construe him as a desire-satisfaction theorist. The largest difficulty for a desire-satisfaction reading is the implausibility of equating happiness and pleasure with desire-satisfaction. However, it is argued that Mill should be construed as speaking loosely when he says that the end of human conduct is pleasure. He thinks that feelings of pleasure play a role in forming desires, but he does not think that feelings of pleasure are the object of all desires.

**Jenkins, Joyce L**. Marx on Full and Free Development. *Soc Theor Pract*, 22(2), 181-192, Sum 96.

In "Marx on Full and Free Development," I argue that the commonly accepted interpretation of Marx's ideal of full and free human development is incorrect. I show, first, that Marx does not think that full development requires the development of every potential talent of the individual. Second, I argue that in spite of some misleading passages in the *Grundrisse*, and *Capital III* Marx does think that labor activity can be free activity. Thus, my view is that Marx's consistent position is that under communism labor would become "life's prime want."

**Jenni, Kathie**. The Ethics of Awareness: Inattention and Integrity. *Cont Phil*, 18(4 & 5), 30-36, Jl-Ag/S-O 96.

This essay examines errors of inattention that contribute to tolerance of evil. While I use tolerance of animal abuse as a focus, similar failures of attentiveness can be seen in our responses (or lack thereof) to child abuse, environmental degradation, world hunger—almost any social problem one can name. Section One catalogues ways in which we avoid undesired awareness and cultural factors that encourage this. Section Two offers a moral diagnosis of what is problematic about pervasive inattention: (a) it obscures responsibilities to prevent harm, (b) it subverts autonomy and responsible agency and c) it undermines integrity. Section Three makes suggestions concerning how to change a social climate that fosters inattention: a) that we revive thought about moral self-improvement and b) that we change our conception of awareness to encompass the notion (long embraced in Asian traditions) that consciousness.

**Jennings, Bruce** and Hanson, Mark J. Commodity or Public Work? Two Perspectives on Health Care. *Bioethics Forum*, 11(3), 3-11, Fall 95.

Much of today's debate over health care reform implicitly views health care services as commodities. This economic point of view obscures morally important features of health care and of the medical profession. By viewing health care service instead as a public work—a civic activity—we recapture its true purposes and are better prepared to debate health policy, health reform and ethical medical practice meaningfully.

**Jennings, Daniel F** and Hunt, Tammy G. Ethics and Performance: A Simulation Analysis of Team Decision Making. *J Bus Ethics*, 16(2), 195-203, F 97.

The interrelationships among a number of variables and their effect on ethical decision making was explored. Teams of students and managers participated in a competitive management simulation. Based on prior research, the effects of performance, environmental change, team age and type of team on the level of ethical behavior were hypothesized. The findings indicate that multiple variable may interact in such a fashion that significance is lost.

**Jennings, Ian**. Autonomy and Hierarchical Compatibilism. *S Afr J Phil*, 16(2), 44-50, My 97.

In this article I aim to show that theories of personal autonomy which identify the autonomous or free self as being one which meets certain conditions of self-appraisal—theories I have dubbed 'internalist theories of autonomy'—must necessarily fail, leaving open the possibility that the only coherent view of autonomy is one which stipulates certain objective features which must be present for the agent in question to be regarded as autonomous. The first reason I put forward for rejecting internalist theories of autonomy lies in the fact that such views must identify a particular mental item as the *self*, whose blessing confers autonomy on the desires and actions which flow from it in the specified way. In doing so, internalist theories of autonomy face the apparently insurmountable difficulty of identifying a mental item from which an agent *cannot* be alienated. The second reason I put forward is the fact that internalist theories of autonomy appear to be committed to regarding obviously pathological or heteronomous selves as the sources of autonomous desires and actions.

**Jennings, Jeremy**. The Return of the Political? New French Journals in the History of Political Thought. *Hist Polit Thought*, 18(1), 148-156, Spr 97.

**Jennings, Michael W** (ed) and Bullock, Marcus (ed). *Walter Benjamin: Selected Writings Volume 1 1913-1926*. Cambridge, Harvard Univ Pr, 1997.

Volume I of the *Selected Writings* brings together essays long and short, academic treatises, reviews, fragments, and privately circulated pronouncements. Fully five-sixths of this material has never before been translated into English. The contents begin in 1813, when Benjamin, as an undergraduate in imperial Germany, was president of a radical youth group, and take us through 1926, when he had already begun, with his explorations of the world of mass culture, to emerge as a critical voice in Weimar Germany's most influential journals. The volume includes a number of his most important works, including "Two Poems by Friedrich Hölderlin," "Goethe's Elective Affinities," "The Concept of Criticism in German Romanticism," "The Task of the Translator," and "One-Way Street." He is as compelling and insightful when musing on riddles or children's books as he is when dealing with weightier issues such as the philosophy of language, symbolic logic, or epistemology. We meet Benjamin the youthful idealist, the sober moralist, the political theorist, the experimentalist, the translator, and, above all, the virtual king of criticism, with his magisterial exposition of the basic problems of aesthetics. (publisher,edited)

**Jensen, Hans Siggaard**. Visual Metaphors. *Dan Yrbk Phil*, 31, 111-124, 1996.

**Jensen, Steven J**. A Defense of Physicalism. *Thomist*, 61(3), 377-404, Jl 97.

I argue that Thomas Aquinas upheld the view of physicalism against the claims of Abelardianism. Physicalism is the view that actions are good or evil in themselves, apart from the agent's will (intentions or motives); Abelardianism is the view that intentions and motives are good or evil first of all and that actions take their moral character from intentions. Aquinas holds that actions are good or evil first from their object. While intentions are essential for determining the character of any concrete action, they themselves receive their moral qualification from the action considered in itself.

**Jeong, Ho-Won**. Politics of Discourse on Liberal Economic Reform: The Case of Africa. *Quest*, 9(2), 172-195, D 96.

Analysant la politique du discours de la réforme économique libérale, cette étude premièrement traite la manière dont la communauté politique internationale discute le développement africain. Après une analyse de l'ajustement structurel elle cherche des politiques alternatives. Les stratégies économiques, néolibérales ainsi qu'orientées vers les besoins humains, sont discutées en relation avec leurs implications pour la bien-être des pauvres. La dernière partie de l'étude traite la discussion sur les réponses indigènes à la crise économique en Afrique et la nature du discours de l'ajustement économique. L'argumentation principale de l'étude est qu'un modèle économique néoclassique a été imposé à l'Afrique, ce qui est dû aux relations disproportionnées de pouvoir entre institutions financières internationaux et pays africains, plutôt qu'à une décision à la base d'une logique économique ou d'un intérêt au bien-être de l'humanité.

**Jergius, Holger**. Fichtes *geometrische* Semantik. *Fichte-Studien*, 10, 51-63, 1997.

**Jerphagnon, Lucien**. Le stoïcisme ou la conscience de Rome. *Diotima*, 25, 125-129, 1997.

**Jervolino, D**. Il *cogito* ferito e l'ontologia problematica dell'ultimo Ricoeur. *Aquinas*, 39(2), 369-380, My-Ag 96.

**Jerzak-Gierszewska, Teresa**. "Three Types of Theories of Religion and Magic" in *Epistemology and History*, Zeidler-Janiszewska, Anna (ed), 419-428. Amsterdam, Rodopi, 1996.

The paper's aim is to systematize the theories of religion and magic developed within anthropological evolutionism and the French sociological school with regard to their premises. According to the received view, these theories can be divided into psychological and sociological, the former being further divided into intellectualist and emotionalist. This view is analyzed and rejected as misconstruing the resemblances between them. The author argues that all traditionally distinguished forms of the theories involved can be more properly construed as a typology. Such a typology may include many types of theories of religion and/or magic, from purely intellectualist ones (Tylor, Frazer), through intermediate intellectualist-emotionalist theories (Lubbock) and emotionalist theories (Marett) to sociological theories (Hubert-Mauss-Durkheim).

**Jeske, Diane**. Associative Obligations, Voluntarism, and Equality. *Pac Phil Quart*, 77(4), 289-309, D 96.

Samuel Scheffler has identified two important objections to associative obligations, the voluntarist objection and the distributivist objection. The voluntarist is concerned about protecting the autonomy of the agent who is supposed to have associative obligations. However, the appropriate account of the source of associative obligations reveals that they pose no threat to autonomy, if we understand autonomy in a weak rather than a strong sense. The distributivist is worried about the claims of outsiders being ignored as the result of insiders having associative obligations to one another. This objection loses much of its force when we understand the genuine implications of associative obligations.

**Jeske, Diane**. Friedship, Virtue, and Impartiality. *Phil Phenomenol Res*, 57(1), 51-72, Mr 97.

The two dominant contemporary moral theories, Kantianism and utilitarianism, have difficulty accommodating our commonsense understanding of friendship as a relationship with significant moral implications. The difficulty seems to arise from their underlying commitment to impartiality, to the claim that all persons are equally worthy of concern. Aristotelian accounts of friendship are partialist in so far as they defend certain types of friendship by appeal to the claim that some persons, the virtuous, are in fact more worthy of concern than are other persons. This article argues that we can preserve the underlying impartiality of Kantianism and utilitarianism, while also preserving a certain partiality with respect to our friends: the partiality of commonsense only seems objectionable if we fail to understand the true grounds, nature and implications of such partiality. Neo-Aristotelian partiality should be rejected in favor of commonsense partiality.

**AUTHOR INDEX** 707 **Jin, Renling**

**Jeske, Diane**. Libertarianism, Self-Ownership, and Motherhood. *Soc Theor Pract*, 22(2), 137-160, Sum 96.

Susan Moller Okin has argued (in *Justice, Gender, and the Family*, 1989), that Robert Nozick's libertarianism leads to morally objectionable conclusions once we take account of the fact that human beings are produced by other human beings, namely, by women. She concludes that we must abandon Nozick's fundamental presupposition of self-ownership. I argue that an appropriately formulated and correctly understood conception of self-ownership does not lead to objectionable conclusions and that, in fact, such a notion can be used to support, for example, women's rights to have abortions and mothers' presumptive rights to care for their children.

**Jeske, Diane**. Perfection, Happiness, and Duties to Self. *Amer Phil Quart*, 33(3), 263-276, Jl 96.

Kant claimed that the content of our duties to ourselves differs from the content of our duties to others: whereas we have duties to promote others' happiness but no duties to promote their perfection, we have duties to promote our own perfection but not our own happiness. We should, however, reverse Kant's claim: we have duties to promote our own happiness but not the happiness of others and we have duties to promote others (and our own) perfection. In exploring why we should reject Kant's claims, we can see why the notion of a duty to self deserves an important place in moral theory.

**Jeske, Diane** and Fumerton, Richard. Relatives and Relativism. *Phil Stud*, 87(2), 143-157, Ag 97.

Many critics would claim that the most compelling objection to consequentialism is the "special obligations" objection, i.e., the claim that consequentialism is unable to accommodate the special obligations that we have to intimates, obligations that play a central role in commonsense morality. Despite the attention that it has received, we do not think that the implications of the objection regarding special obligations have been appreciated. We argue that one must either abandon consequentialism in favor of a deontological view, or, if one retains consequentialism, adopt a radical, relativistic conception of value.

**Jeske, Diane** and Isaacs, Tracy L. Moral Deliberations, Nonmoral Ends, and the Virtuous Agent. *Ethics*, 107(3), 486-500, Ap 97.

Some maintain that an agent with an agent with an overriding commitment to do as morality requires will be unable to pursue and develop nonmoral ends, such as friendships, that would give her life meaning and substance. We respond, arguing that placing overriding importance on moral ends is compatible with being noninstrumentally committed to nonmoral ends. Even in morally charged situations, agents may appeal to extramoral reasons to settle their deliberations. We argue that it is permissible and appropriate for the agent to appeal to such reasons in these situations, and that she will be better off if she makes such an appeal.

**Jespers, F P M**. Can Religion Survive the Rationalization? Questions at Habermas's Theory of Culture (in Dutch). *Bijdragen*, 57(3), 264-280, 1996.

In his early books and the *Theorie des kommunikativen Handelns* Habermas has criticized religion as a premodern form of life. But in later texts, especially *Nachmetaphysisches Denken*, he acknowledges religious intuitions as indispensable for the critical continuation of culture. On the base of an accurate analysis of his propositions on transcendence, metaphysics and metaphors we can conclude, that he thinks too quick to have a rational and objectivating grip on these matters. At the same time metaphors function in his theory and the life world gets a transcendent status. Further his very rational discourse ethics are a more abstract and less human way of life that religious morality. Habermas's conception of religion could be made consistent, if we situate religion immediately next to the life world, which is neither premodern nor modern. (edited)

**Jeurissen, Ronald**. De sociale functie van ethiek in de onderneming. *Alg Ned Tijdschr Wijs*, 89(2), 125-146, Ap 97.

The article presents a social philosophical perspective on business ethics. In a modern society, characterized by the differentiation of social subsystems, the task of business ethics is to reflect on processes of integration of the economic and the bureaucratic subsystems with the socio-cultural sphere of society. Contrary to widely held views, business organizations are not uniquely located in the economic and bureaucratic spheres of society. Social interaction in the context of business involves cultural and integrative elements as well. Drawing on Talcott Parson's systems theory, this configuration is explored, in order to develop a theoretical foundation of business ethics. The main conclusion is that ethics serves an indispensable function in business, on the borderlines between the cultural and integrative subsystems of the business organization.

**Jevremovic, Petar**. The Notion of Imagination in the Context of Aristotle's Practical Philosophy (in Serbo-Croatian). *Theoria (Yugoslavia)*, 38(1), 29-40, Mr 95.

The basic aim of this paper is in establishing an ontological perspective for an understanding of the concept of *phantasia* in Aristotle's practical philosophy. It is claimed that no desire should exist before the desirable has been imagined in the mind (De an. 433b 31-32), and also that no one really could reach full mastery over his own *phantasia* (EN 114a 32). Unpredictability of desire is deeply rooted in unpredictability of *phantasa*. *Phantasia* is by itself constitutive for every possible object of desire.

**Jhingran, Saral**. An Inquiry into Ethical Relativism in Hindu Thought. *Indian Phil Quart*, 23(3-4), 363-378, Jl-O 96.

The article argues that though Hindu ethics acknowledges and even emphasizes universal virtues and duties (sādhārana dharma) it is basically relativistic. Not only one's duty, but also one's entire way of life, is expected to be determined by one's caste (*varna*), stage of life (āsrama), and gender, as well as by one's place (*desa*) and time (*yuga*). Also, Aryans, eager to accommodate different ethnic groups into their society, advocated a policy of total tolerance for the socio-moral customs and ways (ācāra) of these groups, which may well mean a relativistic approach to ethics.

**Jiang, Yue J**. An Intensional Epistemic Logic. *Stud Log*, 52(2), 259-280, My 93.

One of the fundamental properties in *classical* equational reasoning is *Leibniz's principle of substitution*. Unfortunately, this property *does not* hold in *standard epistemic logic*. Furthermore, *Herbrand's lifting theorem* which is *essential* to the *completeness of resolution* and *paramodulation* in the *classical* first order logic (FOL), turns out to be invalid in standard epistemic logic. In particular, unlike classical logic, there is no Skolemization normal form for standard epistemic logic. To solve these problems, we introduce an *intensional epistemic logic*, based on a *variation of Kripke's possible-worlds semantics that need not have a constant domain*. We show how a weaker notion of substitution through indexed terms can retain the Herbrand theorem. We prove how the logic can yield a satisfiability preserving Skolemization form. In particular, we present an intensional principle form unifying indexed terms. Finally, we describe a *sound* and *complete* inference system for a Horn subset of the logic with *equality*, based on *epistemic SLD-resolution*.

**Jiménez, Jorge**. De Platón a Michael Jackson: Entresijos del imaginario andrógino. *Rev Filosof (Costa Rica)*, 34(83-84), 227-236, D 96.

I examine androgynism in its histrionic and hysterical double gesturing at the edge of ambiguity: between the psyche and its aesthetic magnification. The androgynous element is present in the mythical roots of Western culture and at present the manufactures of culture and the mass media profit from the androgynous semiotic as a variant of symbolic domination.

**Jiménez García, Antonio**. El krausopositivismo psicológico y sociológico en la obra de U. González Serrano. *An Seminar Hist Filosof*, 10, 73-92, 1993.

La evolución de la filosofía krausista, a partir de 1875, al entrar en contacto con las nuevas corrientes del pensamiento procedentes de Europa va a dar lugar a un movimiento denominado *krausopositivismo*, en el que se sintetizan armónicamente dos tendencias en principio opuestas: la idealista, defensora del método especulativo-abstracto, y la positivista, partidaria del método experimental. Iniciado dicho movimiento por Nicolás Salmerón, tiene en su discípulo Urbano González Serrano al representante más cualificado dentro de la psicología y la sociología, propiciando junto con Giner, Posada, Sales y Ferré, Azcárate y otros el desarrollo de las ciencias sociales en España.

**Jiménez Matarrita, Alexander**. El libro de filosofía en Costa Rica (1940-1995). *Rev Filosof (Costa Rica)*, 34(83-84), 465-467, D 96.

The article is the first step of a wider research project about the history and systematization of philosophical work in Costa Rica. As such, it describes the objectives and gives some provisional conclusions of this ongoing investigation. The period under study covers the production of philosophical texts in Costa Rica from 1940 to 1995. The final results will be published in an extraordinary issue of the magazine *Revista de Filosofia*, in 1998. This issue will include indexes of all the books published, ordered by author, year of publication and subject. There will also be a complimentary biographical index of authors. [The work will include a brief review of all the texts, which add to approximately 350, in such areas as Metaphysics, Ethics, History of Thought, Social and Political Philosophy, Epistemology, Philosophy of Science and Aesthetic Theory. This will be the basis for a future critical analysis of costarican philosophical production.]

**Jiménez Moreno, Luis**. Crisis de la modernidad en el pensamiento español: desde el Barroco y en la europeización del siglo XX. *An Seminar Hist Filosof*, 10, 93-118, 1993.

Against the epistemic pattern of modernity, "clear and distinct ideas", "ordine geometrico", in Spanish baroque prevails a symbolic expression with regard to values, nothing, life, temporality, dreams, intuitive and projective wisdom: Saint John of the Cross, Quevedo, Calderon.... Also in the XXth century, the way for understanding "European" and "modern" is different. Unamuno writes about the "passion-method" and "wisdom against science"; Ortega y Gasset of the "Spanish interpretation of the world" and of "reason in service to life"; the poet A. Machado invokes "cordial visions and sense-opinions instead of conceptual definitions". These are other ways to see modernity.

**Jimérez-Redondo, Manuel**. Der Begriff des Grundes in Fichtes Wissenschaftslehre. *Fichte-Studien*, 10, 299-316, 1997.

The development of the initial notion of *Ich* as *Grund* in the different versions of the *Wissenschaftslehre*, up to 1805, is analyzed. Fichte, searching for a rigorous articulation of the concepts of "subject," "ground," and "Absolute," submits Descartes's and Kant's *Ego cogito* to such a dissection that, through the themes of facticity, ontological difference, and the *als*-structure of appearances, he gets unwillingly entangled in problems that will only reappear in Heidegger's *Sein und Zeit*.

**Jimérez-Redondo, Manuel**. Fichte und die Metaphysik des deutschen Idealismus. *Perspekt Phil*, 22, 231-265, 1996.

Starting from Husserl's remarks on Fichte, the problems that lead from Husserl to Heidegger's *Sein und Zeit* are analysed in order to construct an interpretative framework for the versions of the *Wissenschaftslehre* written by Fichte between 1804 and 1807. The paper shows that Fichte analyses the "I think" so radically that he ends up hitting on those same problems. German idealism is a landmark of Western metaphysics: Husserl and Heidegger are its consequences in the twentieth century. Those consequences are already discerned and sometimes even expressly stated, in the very origin of that philosophical movement.

**Jin, Renling** and Shelah, Saharon. Can a Small Forcing Create Kurepa Trees. *Annals Pure Applied Log*, 85(1), 47-68, Ap 97.

In this paper we probe the possibilities of creating a Kurepa tree in a generic extension of a ground model of *CH* plus no Kurepa trees by an omega₁-preserving forcing notion of size at most omega₁. In Section I we show that in the Lévy model obtained by collapsing all cardinals between omega₁ and a strongly inaccessible cardinal by forcing with a countable support Lévy collapsing order, many omega₁-preserving forcing notions of size at most omega₁ including all omega-proper forcing notions and some proper but not omega-proper forcing notions of size at most omega₁ do not create Kurepa trees. In Section 2 we construct a model of *CH* plus no Kurepa trees, in which there is an omega-distributive Aronszajn tree such that forcing with that Aronszajn tree does create a Kurepa tree in the generic extension. At the end of the paper we ask three questions.

**Joao Correia, Carlos**. Thomas Mann e A Montanha Mágica. *Philosophica (Portugal)*, 123-131, 1997.

In this article, we analyse the symbolic meaning of Thomas Mann's novel, *The Magic Mountain*. We try to see the scope of the interpretations that consider the metaphors of death, time and culture as the main subject of the novel. Finally, we sustain the idea that Thomas Mann wants to tell us that beauty and perfection are the reverse of death and suffering.

**Joerden, Jan C**. Muss dieses Buch gelesen werden?—Zum Erscheinen der deutschen Ausgabe von Helga Kuhse/Peter Singer: *Should the Baby Live?. Jahr Recht Ethik*, 2, 529-537, 1994.

The article discusses the theories of H. Kuhse and Peter Singer detailed in their book "Should the Baby Live." The following criticisms are made: 1) the solutions offered to the problems concerning seriously disabled new born babies are not adequate; 2) the "slippery slope" argument is not properly utilized; 3) there is inappropriate use of the argument concerning speciesism; and 4) the terms of expression used are often unsuitable for such a sensitive area. In general the article welcomes the fact that the authors have raised such controversial issues.

**Joerden, Jan C**. Wesentliche und unwesentliche Abweichungen zurechnungsrelevanter Urteile des Täters von denen des Richters. *Jahr Recht Ethik*, 2, 307-325, 1994.

This article proceeds on the assumption that every criminal law judgment to impute is actually composed of four elements. Two of these are judgments reached by the judge and two are judgments reached by the defendant, namely the judge's and defendant's judgments as to the imputation of an occurrence as an act or omission and the judge's and defendant's judgments as to evaluation of the act or omission as wrongful. Each of these judgments presumes the existence of a rule as the standard of judgment. (edited)

**Joffe, Hélène**. The Shock of the New: A Psycho-Dynamic Extension of Social Representational Theory. *J Theor Soc Behav*, 26(2), 197-219, Je 96.

This paper draws on a) psycho-dynamic theory b) social identity theory and c) cultural theory in order to explain the pattern of people's social representations of crises ranging from AIDS to mental illness, from environmental and economic disaster to political turmoil. The focus is upon the processes whereby representations of large-scale crises link them to 'the other'. Making the link to 'the other' allays the sense of threat or 'shock' experienced by the individual. The paper shows that the way in which 'self' is protected against anxiety develops in infancy. Yet group identities, as well as historical anchors and contemporary cultural currents interact with early mental operations in the contents of the representations which calm the 'self' by indicating 'the other' when crises occur. The paper evaluates whether psycho-dynamic concepts, which have been derived clinically, can be transposed to the social scientific setting, as well as whether humans are able to represent large-scale crises without resorting to representations of a decorous 'us' versus an immoral 'them'. It resolves both issues in the affirmative.

**Johanson, Arnold A**. "The Logic of Normative Systems" in *Deontic Logic, Agency and Normative Systems*, Brown, Mark A (ed), 123-133. New York, Springer-Verlag, 1996.

This paper exploits the properties of "adjointness" to develop a theory of norms. The adjoints are a pair of mappings between two logics, one called *Imp*, a logic of imperatives and another called *Prop*, which is ordinary logic. In particular, L is a mapping from *Prop* to *Imp* and it has a *Right Adjoint R* from *Imp* to *Prop*. Norms are defined, formally, as statements that contain occurrences of RU where U is in *Imp*. A sample theorem (reminiscent of Kant's "ought implies can"): *Responsibility implies power and, moreover, incapacity implies immunity*)

**Johanson, Arnold A**. "The Logic of Normative Systems" in *Deontic Logic, Agency and Normative Systems*, Brown, Mark A (ed), 123-133. New York, Springer-Verlag, 1996.

This paper exploits the properties of adjointness to develop a theory of norms. The adjoints are a pair of mappings between two logics, one called IMP, a logic of imperatives, and another called PROP, which is ordinary logic. In particular, *L* is a mapping form PROP to IMP and it has a right adjoint *R* from IMP to PROP. Norms are defined, formally, as statements that contain occurrences of *RU* where *U* is in IMP. A sample theorem (reminiscent of Kant's "*ought* implies *can*"): Responsibility implies power and, moreover, incapacity implies immunity.

**Johnnie, Palmer B**. Formal Organizations: A Philosophical Review of Perspectives and Behaviour Dynamics. *J Indian Counc Phil Res*, 13(2), 45-67, Ja-Ap 96.

**Johns, Roger** and Pincus, Laura. Private Parts: A Global Analysis of Privacy Protection Schemes and a Proposed Innovation for their Comparative Evaluation. *J Bus Ethics*, 16(12-13), 1237-1260, S 97.

Pursuant to a Directive adopted by the European Union, privacy protections throughout the EU must become more stringent and consistent throughout EU member countries. One area of great concern to the United States is the Directive's requirement for certain minimum standards of privacy protection in countries receiving information from member countries. Given the limited

protections available in the United States, it does not appear that the United States meets these minimum standards. The purpose of this paper is to critically analyze the existing measurements of global privacy protections and to propose a new model which allows for their comparative evaluation. (edited)

**Johnsen, Bredo**. Dennett on Qualia and Consciousness: A Critique. *Can J Phil*, 27(1), 47-82, Mr 97.

I argue that none of Dennett's attacks on qualia—conceptually, experimentally or clinically based—succeeds in making any case at all against the view that there are qualia and subjective streams of consciousness, in part by distinguishing that view from numerous others with which he entangles it. I show that in defending his own "multiple drafts" theory he unwittingly and unnecessarily rejects the law of excluded middle, and propose a way out, which helps make clear that theory's compatibility with the existence of qualia. I urge that we abandon a priori arguments, pro and con, concerning the existence of qualia, and resolve the matter as we should any ontological question—by appeal to overall reflective equilibrium.

**Johnson, Christopher**. Anthropology and the *Sciences Humaines*: The Voice of Lévi-Strauss. *Hist Human Sci*, 10(3), 122-133, Ag 97.

The Neolithic metaphor not only allows Lévi-Strauss to explain the profound necessity of his vocation, it also forms part of a complex of concepts and values basic to his thought. To this extent the metaphor is an overdetermined one, objectively unacceptable but subjectively necessary for the construction of a coherent mythology of the ethnographic vocation. It is both a translation of the individual voice of Lévi-Strauss and part of a more general paradigm of the prehistoric utopia. (edited)

**Johnson, Clarence Sholé**. "Cornel West as Pragmatist and Existentialist" in *Existence in Black: An Anthology of Black Existential Philosophy*, Gordon, Lewis R (ed), 243-261. New York, Routledge, 1997.

This study delineates Cornel West's "prophetic pragmatism" as a contemporary variant of John Dewey's form of the pragmatic doctrine. It is demonstrated that West's engagement of what he considers some of the major social and political issues facing contemporary America is informed by his prophetic pragmatism. A discussion is then undertaken of what West describes as a specific crisis facing Black America, namely, the nihilistic threat to (the existence of) Black America. It is argued that prophetic pragmatism only partially provides a solution to the threat in question.

**Johnson, Clarence Sholé**. An Analysis of John Mbiti's Treatment of the Concept of Event in African Ontologies. *Quest*, 9(2), 138-157, D 96.

John Mbiti's supposed description of the nature of even and time in African ontologies as anaphoric is challenged on conceptual and axiological grounds. Conceptually, the account is shown to entail certain logical absurdities which demonstrate the impossibility of it being representative of the view of time and event of Africans. Axiologically, the account is shown to be at variance with the practices in both traditional and nontraditional (or contemporary) African societies. Thus, it is argued, Mbiti's account is to be rejected.

**Johnson, David E** and Lappin, Shalom. A Critique of the Minimalist Program. *Ling Phil*, 20(3), 273-333, Je 97.

The paper attempts to clarify the primary formal properties of Chomsky's (1995) minimalist program *MP* model of grammar and clarify some of its computational and empirical consequences. We argue that the global economy conditions of the MP raise serious complexity problems and lack either computational or linguistic motivation. They can either be replaced by local constraints on simply discarded without loss of coverage of the data. We compare the resulting "local" minimalist model with a local constraint-based typed feature structure grammar and provide empirical arguments for preferring the latter approach.

**Johnson, David E** and Moss, Lawrence S. Dynamic Interpretations of Constraint-Based Grammar Formalisms. *J Log Lang Info*, 4(1), 61-79, 1995.

We present a rendering of some common grammatical formalisms in terms of evolving algebras. Though our main concern in this paper is on constraint-based formalisms, we also discuss the more basic case of context-free grammars. Our aim throughout is to highlight the use of evolving algebras as a specification tool to obtain grammar formalisms.

**Johnson, David Kenneth**. Confessions of a Sentimental Philosopher: Science, Animal Rights, and the Demands of Rational Inquiry. *Inquiry (USA)*, 14(1), 76-83, Fall 94.

**Johnson, David Kenneth**. Hypothesis and Realism: A Comment on Sutton. *Inquiry (USA)*, 15(1), 80-85, Fall 95.

**Johnson, David Kenneth**. The Ought-Is Question: Discovering The Modern in Post-Modernism. *Inquiry (USA)*, 14(4), 74-79, Sum 95.

**Johnson, Deborah G** and Hollander, Rachelle D and Beckwith, Jonathan R (& others). Why Teach Ethics in Science and Engineering?. *Sci Eng Ethics*, 1(1), 83-87, J 95.

**Johnson, Fred**. Extended Gergonne Syllogisms. *J Phil Log*, 26(5), 553-567, O 97.

Syllogisms with or without negative terms are studied by using Gergonne's ideas. Soundness, completeness and decidability results are given.

**Johnson, J Prescott**. Spirituality and Community. *J Speculative Phil*, 11(1), 20-39, 1997.

This article is a consideration of the spiritual basis of society. First, attention is given to the question of the relation between *church* and *state* in our early American history. Jefferson's critical response to the claims of a biblical commonwealth and, further, his positive view of the spiritual foundations of society are considered in some detail. His individualistic and utilitarian presuppositions, shared to considerable extent by seventeenth-century and eighteenth-century European political thought, is appraised critically. Second, a concept of spirituality, which emphasizes self-awareness in the focus of social cohesion, is set forth. It is argued that such a concept of spirituality provides the conditions of community without the negative affects of imposed religious beliefs.

**Johnson, James**. Communication, Criticism, and the Postmodern Consensus: An Unfashionable Interpretation of Michel Foucault. *Polit Theory*, 25(4), 559-583, Ag 97.

**Johnson, Jeffery L**. Personal Survival and the Closest-Continuer Theory. *Int J Phil Relig*, 41(1), 13-23, F 97.

**Johnson, Kent**. Luck and Good Fortune in the *Eudemian Ethics*. *Ancient Phil*, 17(2), 85-102, Spr 97.

It is argued that Aristotle's discussion of luck (*tuche*) and good fortune (*eutuchia*) in the *Eudemian Ethics* should be understood as an application of the theory of luck found in the *Physics*. I also argue that Aristotle distinguishes between luck and good fortune. This distinction appears to be telling against Anthony Kenny's interpretation and it suggests a characteristically Aristotelian interpretation of the penultimate chapter of the *EE*.

**Johnson, Pauline**. Nietzsche Reception Today. *Rad Phil*, 80, 24-33, N-D 96.

**Johnson, Phil** and Cassell, Cathy and Smith, Ken. Opening the Black Box: Corporate Codes of Ethics in Their Organizational Context. *J Bus Ethics*, 16(10), 1077-1093, Jl 97.

A review of the literature on Corporate Codes of Ethics suggests that while there exists an informative body of literature concerning the prevalence of such codes, their design, implementation and promulgation, it is also evident that there is a relative lack of consideration of their impact upon members' everyday organizational behaviour. By drawing upon organizational sociology and psychology this paper constructs a contextualist and interpretive model which seeks to enable an analysis and evaluation of their effects upon individual, group and organizational behaviour.

**Johnson, Ralph H**. Critical Thinking and Command of Language. *Inquiry (USA)*, 16(2), 78-92, Wint 96.

The general thesis explored in this article is that critical thinking requires a command of language. First, I discuss the importance of clarity at the level of concepts and ideas: what that means and how it may be achieved, relying on reflections from philosophers who have thought about these matters: Peirce, James, and Wittgenstein. Next I turn to a discussion of the importance of clarity of expression. I identify and discuss six obstacles to achieving clarity that are found in this culture.

**Johnson, Ralph H**. The Principle of Vulnerability. *Inform Log*, 17(2), 259-269, Spr 95.

This paper seeks to articulate and defend the principle that every argument is susceptible to criticism and hence the arguer must not seek to immunize the argument from criticism. Considerations both in support of and opposed to, the principle are considered.

**Johnson, Robert Neal**. Kant's Conception of Merit. *Pac Phil Quart*, 77(4), 310-334, D 96.

It is standard to attribute to Kant the view that actions from motives other than duty deserve no positive moral evaluation. I argue that the standard view is mistaken. Kant's account of merit in the *Metaphysics of Morals* shows that he believes actions not performed from duty can be meritorious. Moreover, the grounds for attributing merit to an action are different from those for attributing moral worth to it. This is significant because it shows both that his views are reasonably consistent with our ordinary views and that he recognized a variety of purposes in evaluating actions, many of which are not furthered by determining whether they were motivated by duty.

**Johnson, Robert Neal**. Reasons and Advice for the Practically Rational. *Phil Phenomenol Res*, 57(3), 619-625, S 97.

This paper defends a model of the internalism requirement against Michael Smith's recent criticisms of it. On this "example model," what we have reason to do is what we would be motivated to do were we rational. After criticizing the example model, Smith argues that his "advice model," that what we have reason to do is what we would *advise* ourselves to do were we rational, is obviously preferable. The author argues that Smith's criticisms can quite easily be accommodated by the example model. Moreover, to the extent that his model connects reasons to advice, it is not a model of the internalism requirement at all. Yet, to the extent that it connects reasons to motivation, his model collapses into the example model. The author ends by arguing that Smith's view simply proposes an unambitious conception of practical rationality, not an alternative construal of the internalism requirement.

**Johnson, Ronald R**. The Logic of Leaping: Kierkegaard's Use of Hegelian Sublation. *Hist Phil Quart*, 14(1), 155-170, Ja 97.

M. Jamie Ferreira has argued that Kierkegaardian leaps are acts of imagination which do not significantly involve the will. This paper attempts to show that Kierkegaard's notion of the leap is both a reaction against and an appropriation of Hegelian sublation, and that, as such, it does depend heavily on the will. Ferreira is right, however, in combating the notion that the leap is irrational, for Kierkegaard maintains that any reasoning that is not tautological must include some kind of leap.

**Johnson, Steve** and Gardner, Peter. Thinking Critically About Critical Thinking: An Unskilled Inquiry into Quinn and McPeck. *J Phil Educ*, 30(3), 441-456, N 96.

Victor Quinn advocates teaching critical thinking as a curriculum subject. He has accused Professor John E. McPeck, a vehement critic of such proposals,

not only of being wrong but also of being in need of such a critical thinking course himself. In this paper we examine the five supposed critical thinking weaknesses of which McPeck is accused and consider what Quinn's arguments tell us about critical thinking, its skills, its priorities and its claims to subject status.

**Johnston, D Kay**. Cheating: Limits of Individual Integrity. *J Moral Educ*, 25(2), 159-171, Je 96.

Cheating is an issue with which most students deal in their school years. In this paper, college students who have taken a mid-term exam in which cheating occured are interviewed about their views of this incident. Their words reveal not only their individual responses and solutions to this dilemma, but also their views of what teachers can and could do. They also reveal the limitations of seeing the dilemma only in dichotomous terms, cheaters vs. noncheaters, teacher vs. students, or in terms of only individual responsibility.

**Johnston, David**. Hayek's Attack on Social Justice. *Crit Rev*, 11(1), 81-100, Wint 97.

Hayek assailed the idea of social justice by arguing that any effort to realize it would transform society into an oppressive organization, stifling liberty. Hayek's view is marred by two omissions. First, he fails to consider that the goal of social justice, like the goal of wealth generation, might be promoted by strategies of indirection that do not entail oppressive organization. Second, he underestimates the tendency of the market order itself to generate oppressive organization and consequently sees advantages in the market order that it may not possess.

**Johnston, David**. *The Idea of a Liberal Theory: A Critique and Reconstruction*. Princeton, Princeton Univ Pr, 1996.

Liberalism, the founding philosophy of many constitutional democracies, has been criticized in recent years from both the left and the right for placing too much faith in individual rights and distributive justice. David Johnston argues for a reinterpretation of liberal principles that he contends will restore liberalism to a position of intellectual leadership from which it can guide political and social reforms. He begins by surveying the three major contemporary schools of liberal political thought—rights-based, perfectionist and political liberalism—and then, by weeding out their weaknesses, sketches a new approach he calls humanist liberalism. (publisher)

**Johnston, Mark**. "A Mind-Body Problem at the Surface of Objects" in *Perception*, Villanueva, Enrique (ed), 219-229. Atascadero, Ridgeview, 1996.

**Johnston, Mark**. "Is the External World Invisible?" in *Perception*, Villanueva, Enrique (ed), 185-198. Atascadero, Ridgeview, 1996.

**Johnstone, Albert A**. Oneself as Oneself and Not as Another. *Husserl Stud*, 13(1), 1-17, 1996.

**Joisten, Karen**. Ressentiment (in Serbo-Croatian). *Filozof Istraz*, 15(4), 697-707, 1995.

Der vorliegende Beitrag arbeitet die Bedeutung des Ressentiments, das allgemein gesagt als das ohnmächtige Gefühl eines Unterlegenen verstanden werden kann, im Denken Nietzsches und Schelers heraus. Bei Nietzsche hat das Ressentiment eine zentrale Funktion, denn der Vorgang der Genealogie der Moral ist gleichbedeutend mit dem Vorgang der Genealogie des Ressentiments. Auf diese Weise kann im Aufweis der inhaltlichen Kennzeichnung des Ressentiments, genauer gesagt, in dem Aufweis der einzelnen Strukturelemente des Ressentiments der Übergang von der Phase der Vor-Moral in die der Moral erhellt werden. Bei Scheler liegt demgegenüber eine untrennbare Verbindung zwischen Ressentiment und Wertlehre vor.

**Jokic, Aleksandar**. Consequentialism, Deontological Ethics, and Terrorism (in Serbo-Croatian). *Theoria (Yugoslavia)*, 38(2), 135-146, Je 95.

On the fact of it, consequentialist ethics can be said to imply that terrorism might be morally justifiable whenever such acts would lead to the greatest good, while deontological ethics appears not to ever allow for terrorism. Yet philosophers of consequentialist bent have repeatedly tried to show that their theory cannot be used to justify terrorist acts. More surprisingly, recently some deontologists have tried to show how, in some extreme situations, even their theory might allow for terrorist actions. One such argument by Virginia Held is the topic of this article. It is claimed that her argument that rights oriented ethics might justify terrorism works only if rights oriented ethical theory is interpreted as a version of consequentialism. This argument is discussed in connection to the so-called Paradox of Deontology, and it is argued that it provides no hope for a solution to this paradox.

**Jonathan, Ruth**. Illusory Freedoms: Liberalism, Education and the Market. *J Phil Educ*, 31(1), 1-220, Mr 97.

**Jones, Coy A** and Wyld, David. The Importance of Context: The Ethical Work Climate Construct and Models of Ethical Decision Making—An Agenda for Research. *J Bus Ethics*, 16(4), 465-472, Mr 97.

This paper examines the role which organizational context factors play in individual ethical decision making. Two general propositions are set forth, examining the linkage between ethical work climate and decision making. An agenda for research and the potential implications of the study and practice of managerial ethics are then discussed.

**Jones, Dorothy V**. The League of Nations Experiment in International Protection. *Ethics Int Affairs*, 8, 77-95, 1994.

**Jones, John D**. St. Thomas Aquinas and the Defense of Mendicant Poverty. *Amer Cath Phil Quart*, 70(Supp), 179-191, 1996.

The paper examines Aquinas's analysis of whether religious orders can renounce common possession of all things including things consumed in use.

**Jones, Karen** 710 **AUTHOR INDEX**

The principal texts considered are the *Contra impugnantes dei religionem et cultum* and the *Contra pestiferam doctrinam retrahentium homines a religionis ingressu.* The first section considers texts in which Aquinas seems to accept such renunciation and, thus, the Franciscan position on the matter. The second section considers texts in which Aquinas appears to reject such renunciation. The third section offers further exploration of Aquinas's ambiguous treatment of this matter. Aquinas's discussions are also linked with some relevant texts of St. Bonaventure and Hervaeus Natalis, a 14th Dominican.

**Jones, Karen**. Trust as an Affective Attitude. *Ethics*, 107(1), 4-25, O 96.

In this article I defend an account of trust according to which trust is an attitude of optimism that the goodwill and competence of another will extend to cover the domain of our interaction with her, together with the expectation that the one trusted will be directly and favorably moved by the thought that we are counting on her. The attitude of optimism is to be cashed out not primarily in terms of beliefs about the other's trustworthiness, but rather—in accordance with certain contemporary accounts of the emotions—in terms of a distinctive, and affectively loaded, way of seeing the one trusted. This way of seeing the other, with its constitutive patterns of attention and tendencies of interpretation, explains the willingness of trusters to let those trusted get dangerously near the things they care about. (edited)

**Jones, Leslie E**. An Argument against Techno-Privacy. *SW Phil Rev*, 13(1), 155-162, Ja 97.

**Jones, Robert E**. Popular Biography, Plagiarism, and Persecution. *J Infor Ethics*, 3(1), 80-82, Spr 94.

**Jones, Todd**. Methodological Individualism in Proper Perspective. *Behavior Phil*, 24(2), 119-128, Fall 96.

"Methodological individualism" is the doctrine that all social phenomena should ultimately be understood in terms of the behavioral propensities of individuals. It has been steadfastly opposed by social scientists and philosophers who hold, like Emile Durkheim (1938), that social inquiry should focus on "social facts" that can't be reduced to individual behavioral propensities. I will argue that while one *can* explain any set of social events given sufficient information about individual behavior, nonindividualistic accounts of the social are, nevertheless, often preferable.

**Jones, III, Joe Frank**. Moral Growth in Children's Literature: A Primer with Examples. *Phil Cont World*, 1(4), 10-19, Wint 94.

This essay applies a plausible model for moral growth to examples of secular and religious children's literature. The point is that moral maturation, given this model, requires imaginary worlds on both secular and religious presuppositions. Trying to guide a child's reading toward either religious or secular books rather than toward good literature is shown, therefore, to miss the mark of good parenting.

**Jonkers, Peter**. Looking for a Truth that Obliges (in Dutch). *Bijdragen*, 58(2), 194-205, 1997.

In this paper I want to query L. Boeve's postmodern notion of truth as deficiency and radical plurality. In order to do so, I depart from a general analysis of truth and its ethical implications, especially with regard to the relation between universality and particularity. By stressing the practical dimension of truth, it becomes possible to overcome the dominant opposition between the universal truth of positive science and the particularity of opinions and beliefs with (religious) traditions. In this way, the question of the specific truth of traditions and its relation to other dimensions of truth can be approached from a new perspective. (edited)

**Jonsen, Albert R**. "Morally Appreciated Circumstances: A Theoretical Problem for Casuistry" in *Philosophical Perspectives on Bioethics*, Sumner, L W (ed), 37-49. Toronto, Univ of Toronto Pr, 1996.

**Jónsson, Bjarni**. On the Canonicity of Sahlqvist Identities. *Stud Log*, 53(4), 473-491, N 94.

We give a simple proof of the canonicity of Sahlqvist identities, using methods that were introduced in a paper by Jónsson and Tarski in 1951.

**Joos, Erich**. Die Begründung klassischer Eigenschaften aus der Quantentheorie. *Phil Natur*, 27(1), 31-42, 1990.

Die Quantentheorie wird heute als Grundlage aller physikalischen Theorien angesehen. Ursprünglich nur als Modell für die Atomhülle entworfen, hat sie sich als grundlegende Struktur mit praktisch uneingeschränktem Anwendungsbereich erwiesen. Trotz dieses in der Geschichte der Naturforschung einzigartigen Erfolges blieb die Interpretation der Quantenmechanik bis heute umstritten. Der Grund hierfür liegt in einer eigenartigen Schwäche der Theorie: Sie liefert Aussagen über Messergebnisse, kann aber nicht definieren, was eine Messung überhaupt ist. Übereinstimmung scheint zumindest darin zu bestehen, dass ein "Messgerät" ein "klassisches, makroskopisches" System sein soll. Doch was ist ein "makroskopisches System"? Erlaubt die Quantentheorie überhaupt solche Objekte? Diese Frage soll im folgenden diskutiert werden unter der Annahme einer uneingeschränkten Gültigkeit der Quantentheorie.

**Joós, Jean-Ernest**. Norm and End: A Kantian Theory of Action (in French). *Arch Phil*, 59(4), 555-575, O-D 96.

Once the rational norm is defined, Kant's theory of agency determines the subjective conditions which allow actions to occur. But, as those conditions happen to be necessary ones, Kant has to redefine the rationality of action, from a finite point of view, in order to "fit" it into finite subjectivity. Thus, the rational agency is decentered, and notions such as orientation and *Fürwahrhalten* become essential to understand how reason can effect a finite agent.

**Jopling, David A**. Philosophical Counselling, Truth and Self-Interpretation. *J Applied Phil*, 13(3), 297-310, 1996.

Philosophical counselling, Ran Lahav and others claim, helps clients deepen their philosophical self-understanding. The counsellor's role is the minimalist one of providing the client with the philosophical tools needed for reflective self-evaluation. I argue that this view, which is informed by an antirealist account of self and life-history, undermines the distinction between self-knowledge and self-deception. I defend the view that truth matters in philosophical counselling; more specifically, that there is a basic distinction between true and false forms of self-understanding. To do this, I offer a broadly realist account of self and reflective self-evaluation. (edited)

**Jopling, David A**. Sub-Phenomenology. *Human Stud*, 19(2), 153-173, Ap 96.

This paper outlines the historical roots of cognitive dualism, showing how it has come to recapitulate a number of puzzling conceptual dichotomies that have hindered scientific and philosophical psychology since Kantian constructivism. It then defends the view that cognitive psychology's commitment to the subpersonal explanatory level leads to exaggerated deflationary claims about the explanatory significance of phenomenology and the person-level framework. It is argued that phenomenological description must function as a constraint upon and guide for, theory formation in cognitive psychology (as illustrated in the work of the cognitive neuro-psychologist A.R. Luria). Phenomenology must be brought into a kind of reflective equilibrium with the cognitive and neuro-sciences. (edited)

**Jordan, Jeff**. "Concerning Moral Toleration" in *Philosophy, Religion, and the Question of Intolerance,* Ambuel, David (ed), 212-229. Albany, SUNY Pr, 1997.

**Jordan, Jeff**. Pragmatic Arguments and Belief. *Amer Phil Quart*, 33(4), 409-420, O 96.

A pragmatic argument is an argument which is intended to motivate the formation and maintenance of a certain belief, primarily because of the benefits of holding that belief. This essay consists of an argument that there are occasions in which it is permissible, morally and rationally, to form beliefs not on the basis of evidence, but on the basis of a pragmatic argument. Two permissibility-conditions are proposed and defended as regulators of pragmatic belief inducement.

**Jordan, Jeff**. Religious Reasons and Public Reasons. *Pub Affairs Quart*, 11(3), 245-254, Jl 97.

It is a common enough charge that liberalism, as a political philosophy, privileges some political discourse and silences others. Persons with strong religious convictions have recently joined in the making of that charge. That governmental institutions should be neutral with regard to the establishment of religion and the free exercise of religious belief is a commonplace in American political thought. The idea that persons have a similar duty when advocating or supporting a political view, while perhaps not as common an idea, has become a widely held belief. More precisely, the idea is that persons when advocating, or supporting a divisive political view have a duty to advocate, or support on the basis of a secular reason and not on the basis on only a religious one. The idea that citizens have a duty to refrain from using only religious reasons as the basis of their political advocacy is, I argue, pernicious. It is pernicious since it implies an epistemically disastrous consequence and because its practical demands are likely to drive some citizens out of the political arena.

**Jorgensen, Estelle R**. "Justifying Music in General Education: Belief in Search of Reason" in *Philosophy of Education (1996),* Margonis, Frank (ed), 228-236. Urbana, Phil Education Soc, 1997.

In this essay arguments traditionally advanced in support of music (and the arts) in general education are found to be problematical. Drawing on Israel Scheffler's tests for curricular justification and Peter Kivy's notion of music as "tribal ritual," two principles are proposed as a starting point for developing a more defensible philosophical basis for music in general education. Justifications on the basis of artistic value and role of the arts in social and cultural life that emphasize the commonality and divergence of the arts with other aspects of general education may be in dialectic and, therefore, also problematical.

**José Martínez, Francisco**. La filosofía materialista en la época de la Revolución Francesa. *Euridice*, 141-157, 1992.

Ce travail analyse a) les fondements philosophiques et politiques de la philosophie matérialiste dans les ans de la Révolution Française; b) l'importance de la littérature clandestine comme moyen essentiel de diffusion de cette philosophie matérialiste et athée et c) l'opposition dans cette même philosophie d'un pole technocratique (Idéologues) et un pole utopique-révolutionnaire (Sade, Roux, Marat) mis en scène d'une façon magistrale par l'oeuvre de P. Weiss, *Marat-Sade*. (edited)

**Josefson, Jim** and Bach, Jonathan. A Critique of Rawls's Hermeneutics as Translation. *Phil Soc Crit*, 23(1), 99-124, 1997.

This paper seeks to demonstrate that hermeneutics is a powerful conceptual tool for exploring the current trend towards theorizing justice as a conversation. Specifically we explore the work of John Rawls in order to describe the particular variety of hermeneutics at work in both 'political liberalism' and 'justice as fairness' and to critique this hermeneutics from the perspective of the ontological hermeneutics of Hans-Georg Gadamer. Using the critique of Quinean pragmatism found in Joseph Rouse's epistemology, we draw a parallel between the 'hermeneutics as translation' in Quine and Rawls's public reason. This parallel, we argue, helps us better understand the features and the limitations of political liberalism, especially when Rawls's hermeneutics is contrasted with the possibility of a theory of justice inspired by Gadamer.

**Joshi Jubert, Ujala**. Actio libera in causa: Ordentliche oder ausserordentliche Zurechnung?. *Jahr Recht Ethik*, 2, 327-338, 1994.

The article considers the justification for punishing an "actio libera in causa". It proceeds from a broad notion of "actio libera in causs", whereby the term relates to all offense elements whose existence or nonexistence can be brought about by the actor. The author is of the opinion that the problem presented here cannot be solved by assuming a purely dogmatic perspective or by relying merely on the concept of culpability. A multitude of difficulties confront even a normative theoretical approach. The author contends that punishing an "actio libera in causa" can only be justified if one can show that the actio libera in causa represents an attack on, and a danger for, a legally protected interest in the same sense as is represented by the "actio libera in se". (edited)

**Jospe, Raphael**. Philosophic Approaches to Sacred Scripture in Judaism. *J Dharma*, 21(4), 345-363, O-D 96.

Philosophic exegesis of the Bible is a way of understanding scripture philosophically and reconciling philosophic doctrines with the requirements of revealed religion. Bible exegesis as a philosophic literary genre follows from the very nature of Western religious philosophy, which, according to Harry Wolfson, is Philonic in its commitment to both scriptural faith and reason as sources of truth. Abraham ibn Ezra (Spain, twelfth century) and Moses Mendelssohn (Germany, eighteenth century) exemplify diverse Jewish philosophical approaches to scripture. Paradoxically, the medieval Ibn Ezra is often far more radical (e.g., his critical attitude towards the Mosaic authorship of the Torah) than is the modern Mendelssohn.

**Jovchelovitch, Sandra**. In Defence of Representations. *J Theor Soc Behav*, 26(2), 121-135, Je 96.

In this paper I reaffirm the notion of representation and its relevance for understanding the relationship between the individual and society. I do so by presenting some ideas related to the development of the theory of social representations, and by taking issue with postmodern positions that reject and/or misconceive representations. I argue that the trade-offs between societal forces and the agency of social subjects are central for understanding both the structure and social functioning of social representations, and the mediating nature of representations. I suggest that the failure of postmodern versions of social constructionism to conceptualize representations as constructions forged by the relationship between the subject and society reintroduces a new form of behaviourism, whilst legitimizing mainstream cognitive approaches to representation.

**Joven, Fernando**. The Infinitesimals as Useful Fictions for Leibniz: The Controversy in the Paris Academy of Sciences (Spanish). *Theoria (Spain)*, 12(29), 257-279, My 97.

In the beginning of the XVIII century arises a discussion in the Paris Academy of Sciences about the justification of infinitesimal calculus. In this line, Leibniz will present infinitesimals as useful fictions, a problematic notion that requires an accurate meaning. Leibniz does not accept the infinitesimal concept of his French followers. The result of the controversy was a triumph for calculus, but a pause in its justification.

**Jowett, Benjamin**. *The Dialogues of Plato: Volume I*. Bristol, Thoemmes, 1997.

This is a Classic late Victorian English translation of the dialogues of Plato (for all five volumes). (edited)

**Jowett, Benjamin**. *The Dialogues of Plato: Volume II*. Bristol, Thoemmes, 1997.

**Jowett, Benjamin**. *The Dialogues of Plato: Volume III*. Bristol, Thoemmes, 1997.

**Jowett, Benjamin**. *The Dialogues of Plato: Volume IV*. Bristol, Thoemmes, 1997.

**Jowett, Benjamin**. *The Dialogues of Plato: Volume V*. Bristol, Thoemmes, 1997.

**Jubien, Michael**. Actualism and Iterated Modalities. *Phil Stud*, 84(2-3), 109-125, D 96.

Accounts of modality that depend on "abstract" possible worlds, such as maximal consistent propositions, seem unable to deal appropriately with certain statements involving iterations of modalities. (For example, "The Clintons might have had a son who played saxophone, but who might not have played saxophone.") This paper shows that the problem of iterated modalities does not affect the property-theoretic account of modality that I offered in *Ontology, Modality, and the Fallacy of Reference*.

**Judkins, Jennifer**. The Aesthetics of Silence in Live Musical Performance. *J Aes Educ*, 31(3), 39-53, Fall 97.

The determination and characterization of musical silence is one of the most crucial 'live' decisions made by musicians on stage. For aestheticians, beyond exposing some of the process of live performance, silences are of particular interest as framing devices and as musical voids. When do musical works begin and end? How is on-goingness maintained through moments of 'empty' time? In this article, I venture that long unmeasured silences are given individual meaning and form by the tonal and rhythmic material surrounding them (their musical edges) and are characterized both by these edges and physical gesture in performance.

**Juengst, Eric T**. Can Enhancement Be Distinguished from Prevention in Genetic Medicine?. *J Med Phil*, 22(2), 125-142, Ap 97.

In this paper, I argue that a line *can* be drawn between prevention and enhancement for gene therapy (and thus between properly medical and nonmedical uses of gene therapy), but only if one is willing to accept two rather old-fashioned claims: 1) Some health problems are best understood as if they were entities in their own right, reifiable as processes or parts in a biological system, with at least as much ontological objectivity and theoretical significance as the functions that they inhibit. 2) Legitimate preventive genetic health care should be limited to efforts to defend people from attack by these more robust pathological entities, rather than changing their bodies to evade social injustices. (edited)

**Juengst, Eric T** and Whitehouse, Peter J and Mehlman, Maxwell (& others). Enhancing Cognition in the Intellectually Intact. *Hastings Center Rep*, 27(3), 14-22, My-Je 97.

As science learns more about how the brain works and fails to work, the possibility for developing "cognition enhancers" becomes more plausible. The success of drugs like Ritalin points to an eager demand for drugs that can help us think faster, remember more and focus more keenly. Whether such drugs are good for individuals, or for society, is an open question, one that demands far more public discussion.

**Jürgensen, Sven**. Hölderlins Trennung von Fichte. *Fichte-Studien*, 12, 71-90, 1997.

**Juhl, Cory F**. A Context-Sensitive Liar. *Analysis*, 57(3), 202-204, Jl 97.

Context-sensitive approaches to the liar paradox assign 'levels' to occurrences of 'is true' in sentence tokens. A clever attempt to handle strengthened liars that quantify over 'levels' proposes that domains of quantification are themselves context-sensitive. We show that the context-sensitive approach shares a common feature with others: either some things that can be said in a metalanguage cannot be said in the object language, or the theory is inconsistent. To show this, we assume that the full context-sensitive theory, including the way domains of quantification depend on context, is expressed in the language. Then we construct a strengthened liar for the full theory.

**Juhl, Cory F**. Objectively Reliable Subjective Probabilities. *Synthese*, 109(3), 293-309, D 96.

Subjective Bayesians typically find the following objection difficult to answer: some joint probability measures lead to intuitively irrational inductive behavior, even in the long run. Yet well-motivated ways to restrict the set of "reasonable" prior joint measures have not been forthcoming. In this paper I propose a way to restrict the set of prior joint probability measures in particular inductive settings. My proposal is the following: where there exists some successful inductive method for getting to the truth in some situation, we ought to employ a (joint) probability measure that is inductively successful in that situation, if such a measure exists. In order to do show that the restriction is possible to meet in a broad class of cases, I prove a "Bayesian Completeness Theorem", which says that for any solvable inductive problem of a certain broad type, there exist probability measures that a Bayesian could use to solve the problem. I then briefly compare the merits of my proposal with two other well-known proposals for constraining the class of "admissible" subjective probability measures, the "leave the door ajar" condition and the "maximize entropy" condition.

**Juncos-Rabadán, Onésimo**. "Processing of Negative Sentences by Adults with Unilateral Cerebral Lesions" in *Verdad: lógica, representación y mundo*, Villegas Forero, L, 311-322. Santiago de Compostela, Univ Santiago Comp, 1996.

We studied the processing of true and false negative sentences by 25 adults with left temporal brain lesions (fluent aphasics), 25 with right temporal lesions and 25 normal volunteers by recording their reaction times and error rates in sentence verification experiments. Left temporal lesions were associated with alteration of logico-semantic processing of negative sentences, especially false negative sentences. The performance of subjects with right temporal lesions did not differ significantly from that of the controls. These findings suggest 1) that the right hemisphere plays no important role in the logico-semantic processing of negative sentences; and 2) that Clark's (1977) comparative processing theory is not a fitting model of the comprehension of negative sentences in sentence verification tasks by individuals with brain lesions, especially in the case of those suffering from Wernicke's aphasia.

**Jung, Werner**. Everydayness, Aesthetics, Ontology: Notes on the Later Lukács (in Hungarian). *Magyar Filozof Szemle*, 4-5-6, 373-384, 1996.

Lukács selbst hat bekanntlich seine intellektuelle Entwicklung in der autobiographischen Skizze "Gelebtes Denken" und in sich darauf beziehenden Interviews dargetan. Es ist eine wechselvolle, spannungsreiche, zugleich jedoch eine deutliche Kontinuität im Wandel spiegelnde Entwicklung. Da gibt es einerseits das prämarxistische, weitgehend um Fragen und Probleme der Ästhetik kreisende Frühwerk, dann die frühen marxistischen Schriften, noch auf dem Weg zu Marx, da gibt es andererseits—nun an der Seite Marxens—das umfangreiche marxistische Oeuvre. (edited)

**Junqueira Smith, Plínio**. "Terapia y vida común" in *La racionalidad: su poder y sus límites*, Nudler, Oscar (ed), 153-177. Barcelona, Ed Paidos, 1996.

**Junqueira Smith, Plinio**. Sao os Problemas Filosóficos Tradicionais Confusoes Lingüísticas ou Investigaçoes Legítimas Sobre as Coisas?. *Cad Hist Filosof Cie*, 6(Spec), 201-263, Ja-D 96.

Analytical philosophy seems to have changed its view on the existence of philosophical problems since they are no longer considered as meaningless. Following the more recent tendency, I argue against the conception that philosophical problems are merely linguistic. Afterwards, I propose my own conception of what is a philosophical problem in which the ideas of conflict of opinions and arguments, as well as of a collective investigation, are central to it. Finally, I reject the ideas that philosophical problems are subjective, internal to a given philosophical system or always contextual in the sense that there are no permanent problems since the Greeks. (edited)

**Jutronic-Tihomirovic, Dunja**. Is Language an *A Priori* Accessible Platonic Object?. *Acta Analytica*, 131-143, 1995.

The author examines Katz's claim that linguistics is about Platonic objects like mathematics and logic presumably are. Why should we assume that mathematical objects and language are the same kind of entities? The author presents arguments to show that we should not view mathematics and language to be the same kind entities. Katz's comparison between language and mathematics is not valid and the author offers three sets of arguments for her claim: 1) general arguments; 2) arguments from learning; and 3) epistemological arguments. Furthermore, the author presents a number of arguments to show that language is not an *a priori* accessible and a solely intuition-based object, as Katz claims language to be.

**Kaboré, Boniface**. Paul Ricoeur et la question de la preuve en psychanalyse. *De Phil*, 11, 31-48, 1994-1995.

**Kacmar, K Michele** and Carlson, Dawn S. Perceptions of Ethics Across Situations: A View Through Three Different Lenses. *J Bus Ethics*, 16(2), 147-160, F 97.

This paper examined three approaches for understanding perceptions of ethics: moral philosophies, cognitive moral development and ethical value systems. First, the dimensionality of the moral philosophy approach was examined. Next, an attempt was made to integrate the models. Finally, each of the model's various components were used in a regression equation to isolate the best predictors of ethicality. Results indicated that the moral philosophies can be considered distinct entities, but the common underlying theme between the approaches was not as predicted. Also, individuals used a variety of approaches, not always the same ones, to determine the ethicalness of situations.

**Kaczor, Christopher**. Exceptionless Norms in Aristotle?: Thomas Aquinas and Twentieth-Century Interpreters of the *Nicomachean Ethics*. *Thomist*, 61(1), 33-62, Ja 97.

Within the context of larger debates in Thomistic ethics, the author presents the arguments of Martha Nussbaum, Nancy Sherman and W. F. R. Hardie that either explicitly or implicitly undermine the possibility of exceptionless norms in Aristotle's "Nicomachean Ethics". Next, Thomas Aquinas's reading of the "Nicomachean Ethics" in his "Sententia libri ethicorum" is contrasted with these modern interpreters of Aristotle. The very analogies used by Aristotle suggest a place for exceptionless norms as does the explicit teaching of "Nicomachean Ethics" II, 6. Some possible responses to Nussbaum, Sherman and Hardie are presented in the final section.

**Kadane, Joseph B** and Seidenfeld, Teddy and Schervish, Mark J. When Several Bayesians Agree That There Will Be No Reasoning to a Foregone Conclusion. *Proc Phil Sci Ass*, 3(Suppl), S281-S289, 1996.

When can a Bayesian investigator select an hypothesis H and design an experiment (or a sequence of experiments) to make certain that, given the experimental outcome(s), the posterior probability of H will be lower than its prior probability? We report an elementary result which establishes sufficient conditions under which this reasoning to a foregone conclusion cannot occur. Through an example, we discuss how this result extends to the perspective of an onlooker who agrees with the investigator about the statistical model for the data but who holds a different prior probability for the statistical parameters of that model. We consider, specifically, one-sided and two-sided statistical hypotheses involving i.i.d. normal data with conjugate priors. In a concluding section, using an "improper" prior, we illustrate how the preceding results depend upon the assumption that probability is countably additive.

**Kaeser, Eduard**. Gehirn und Ich: Zwei Hauptakteure des Geistes?. *Phil Natur*, 33(1), 83-117, 1996.

Proceeding from recent developments in Artificial Intelligence and neurobiology, I argue that any claim to understand human action in terms of neurophysiological and cognitive processes is intrinsically incomplete. Particularly, considering the fact that action is a performance by an embodied self, a person. Therefore, we need an additional stance to the objective point of view, taking into account these essentially subjective or personal features of human action. This stance is not reducible, but complementary to the scientific outlook. I plea for a complementaristic concept of the human body as a base for a nonreductive naturalism of the mental.

**Kagan, Shelly** and Vallentyne, Peter. Infinite Value and Finitely Additive Value Theory. *J Phil*, 94(1), 5-26, Ja 97.

Finitely additive value theories evaluate worlds containing a finite number of locations of value (people, times, etc.) by adding together the values at each location. A puzzle can arise when finitely additive value theories are applied to worlds involving an infinite number of locations. For such cases the totals will often be infinite. The article develops and defends some principles for finitely additive value theories that imply that some worlds with infinite totals are better than other worlds with infinite totals.

**Kahana, Eva** and Midlarsky, Elizabeth. *Altruism in Later Life*. Newbury Park, Sage, 1994.

Why are the elderly so often perceived as burdensome and unproductive members of our society? *Altruism in Later Life* explores and refutes this view with cogent, empirical data. Authors Elizabeth Midlarsky and Eva Kahana introduce the results of a series of investigations on assistance offered by—rather than to—the elderly, in the context of historical, philosophical, and theoretical trends in gerontology and altruism research. Following a brief but inclusive historical survey of aging treatments, they present their own theoretical model of successful aging: Based on a carefully applied methodological review of research focusing on altruism and the elderly, the results reveal the relative frequency, nature, correlates, and ramifications of the contributions they make. (publisher, edited)

**Kahnert, Klaus**. "Sprachursprung und Sprache bei J.G. Fichte" in *Sein—Reflexion—Freiheit: Aspekte der Philosophie Johann Gottlieb Fichtes*, Asmuth, Christoph (ed), 191-219. Amsterdam, Gruner, 1997.

**Kail, Michel**. La conscience n'est pas suject: pour un matérialisme authentique. *Rev Phil Fr*, 3, 339-354, Jl-S 96.

**Kainz, Howard**. *Democracy and the "Kingdom of God"*. Milwaukee, Marquette Univ Pr, 1995.

There is a consensus among Christian theologians that the symbol of the "kingdom of God," inherited from the Judaic tradition, is the key to understanding Christianity. But theologians have for millennia differed among themselves as to the interpretation of this symbol. Political ramifications of, or reactions to, this Judaeo-Christian idea have included the Holy Roman Empire, the Crusades, the "Third Rome," American Manifest Destiny, Zionism, the Third Reich and Liberation Theology. This book focuses on the question implementations and its possible implications for democracy and democratic theory. It examines the development of the symbol in the Old and New Testaments, the diversity of related theological interpretations and political concomitants and the significance of the "kingdom of God" in the development of present and future political formations and political theory. (publisher)

**Kakade, R M**. Confession of Sin: A Catharsis!. *Darshana Int*, 36(3/143), 43-48, Ap 96.

The purpose of the work is to highlight the significance of the concept of confession of sin as a spiritual exercise and a restorative and recuperative technique in Judaism, Christianity, psychotherapy and psychopathology. Confession is not only an empty exterior sign of repentance or consolation for forgiveness of sins but also a converting ordinance inspiring conversion of the sinner. Like catharsis it serves as an outlet for repressed guilts by orally revealing the malice. Humble, *sincere and voluntary* confession is a commendable and useful tonic for the soul and a remedy for troubled consciences. It is a treasure-trove bringing serenity and joy.

**Kakkuri-Knuuttila, Marja-Liisa**. "What Can the Sciences of Man Learn from Aristotle?" in *Knowledge and Inquiry: Essays on Jaakko Hintikka's Epistemology and Philosophy of Science*, Sintonen, Matti (ed), 19-39. Amsterdam, Rodopi, 1997.

This paper argues that both Aristotle's notion of rhetoric and dialectic, as well as his epistemological and methodological views have a greater contribution to offer to modern research in the sciences of man than recognized so far. Having presented some basic concepts of dialectic and rhetoric, the author shows with the help of a paradigmatic example the relevance of the Aristotelian model of rhetorical speech to traditional narrative historical research. She also elaborates in which ways Kuhn's conception of interparadigmatic choice corresponds to the Aristotelian view of decision making in rhetorical situations. In the last section, she claims that the Aristotelian concept of reputable opinions (*endoxa*) and the method of *saving the phenomena* provide fundamental epistemological solutions to problems raised by the recent criticism of positivistic philosophy of science.

**Kalderon, Mark Eli**. The Transparency of Truth. *Mind*, 106(423), 475-497, Jl 97.

Transparency is the following (alleged) property of truth; if one possesses the concept of truth, then to assert, believe, inquire whether it is true that S just is to assert, believe, inquire whether S (and conversely). It might appear (as it did to Frege in "Thoughts") that if truth ascriptions were transparent, then the truth predicate must be redundant; but the fact that some truth ascriptions are not transparent—for instance, those that quantify over, name, or describe the proposition(s) to which truth is ascribed—shows that the truth predicate could not be redundant. It is argued that the apparent paradox is resolved by treating content as more basic than truth. This strategy is illustrated by three candidate analyses, each of which treats the truth predicate as nonredundant but can, nevertheless, account for transparency. (edited)

**Kalligas, Paul**. Forms of Individuals in Plotinus: A Re-Examination. *Phronesis*, 42(2), 206-227, 1997.

**Kamareddine, Fairouz**. A Type Free Theory and Collective/Distributive Predication. *J Log Lang Info*, 4(2), 85-109, 1995.

The purpose of this paper is to provide a simple type-free set theory which can be used to give the various readings of collective/distributive sentences.

**Kambouchner, Denis**. Descartes and the Communication of Passions (in Czech). *Filosof Cas*, 44(5), 731-750, 1996.

This study is based around the fourth part of the work Descartes published in 1643 in reply to attacks and denunciations of G. Voetius, pastor of the reformed church and rector of the University of Utrecht. The text is newly translated into French and analyzed from the point of view of Descartes's conception of passions and the possibility of communicating them to individuals grouped in crowds, who are thus subject to the same effects. In this case, it is the effects of preaching which makes use of the pregiven disposition to certain passionate movements. Kambouchner's analysis shows that in Descartes's conception, only the inner stimulation to a certain passion can be communicated in a basically mechanical way, but that the soul must make a specific act of consent with this. (edited)

**Kamen, Henry**. Toleration and the Law in the West 1500-1700. *Ratio Juris*, 10(1), 36-44, Mr 97.

Before the emergence of the concept of individual rights, in the eighteenth century, toleration was conceded by states only to the corporations that constituted the state. Many states that, like France after the Edict of Nantes, conceded a form of toleration, did so without accepting the principle of toleration. The recognition or toleration of rights for individuals first became possible only in a wholly secularized society such as that of colonial North America.

**Kamenskii, Z A**. The *Philosophical Encyclopedia* Is Twenty-Five. *Russian Stud Phil*, 35(4), 60-91, Spr 97.

**Kaminski, Michael**. The Elimination of *De Re* Formulas. *J Phil Log*, 26(4), 411-422, Ag 97.

**Kamlah, Andreas**. "Die Logik der Überzeugungen und das Leib-Seele-Problem" in *Das weite Spektrum der analytischen Philosophie,* Lenzen, Wolfgang, 95-111. Hawthorne, de Gruyter, 1997.

**Kamp, Hans** and Beyle, Uwe. A Calculus for First Order Discourse Representation Structures. *J Log Lang Info*, 5(3-4), 297-348, O 96.

This paper presents a sound and complete proof systems for the first order fragment of Discourse Representation Theory. Since the inferences that human language users draw from the verbal input they receive for the most transcend the capacities of such a system, it can be no more than a basis on which more powerful systems, which are capable of producing those inferences, may then be built. Nevertheless, even within the general setting of first order logic the structure of the "formulas" of DRS-languages, i.e., of the Discourse Representation Structures suggest for the components of such a system inference rules that differ somewhat from those usually found in proof systems for the first order predicate calculus and which are, we believe, more in keeping with inference patterns that are actually employed in common sense reasoning. (edited)

**Kamuf, Peggy** (trans) and Derrida, Jacques. History of the Lie: Prolegomena. *Grad Fac Phil J*, 19/20(2/1), 129-161, 1997.

**Kanamori, Akihiro** and Dreben, Burton. Hilbert and Set Theory. *Synthese*, 110(1), 77-125, Ja 97.

**Kanazawa, Makoto**. Identification in the Limit of Categorial Grammars. *J Log Lang Info*, 5(2), 115-155, 1996.

It is proved that for any *k*, the class of classical categorial grammars that assign at most *k* types to each symbol in the alphabet is learnable, in the Gold (1967) sense of identification in the limit from positive data. The proof crucially relies on the fact that the concept known as finite elasticity in the inductive inference literature is preserved under the inverse image of a finite-valued relation. The learning algorithm presented here incorporates Buszkowski and Penn's (1990) algorithm for determining categorial grammars from input consisting of functor-argument structures.

**Kane, Gregory C**. Suicide and Advance Directives: One Doctor's Dilemma. *J Med Human*, 17(3), 191-193, Fall 96.

This paper describes a physician's reaction when treating a patient with advanced AIDS who had just attempted suicide and was brought to the hospital emergency room by his life partner. The dilemma for the treating physicians was how to react to the suicide attempt when the patient's living will clearly described the patient's wish not to receive heroic therapy including mechanical ventilation. This dilemma was finally resolved after investigation of the extent of the patient's underlying advanced illness (AIDS) through detailed discussion with the patient's life partner and durable power-of-attorney for health care.

**Kane, John**. Basal Inequalities: Reply to Sen. *Polit Theory*, 24(3), 401-406, Ag 96.

Amartya Sen claims he does not defend (as I implied in "Justice, Impartiality and Equality") a logical connection between the concept of justice and a principle of equality, merely an historically contingent one requiring some 'basal equality' of human beings as a foundation for theories of justice. But he also asserts that the view of justice as proportionality falls within the general category of such basal-egalitarian rules. He thus conflates equal treatment for equal cases with a general principle of human equality. The basal equality position *starts* from an assumption of the moral equality of human beings and tries to construct principles of justice that respect and safeguard it. But it is possible and historically common to begin with an assumption of some *basal inequality* of human beings and derive principles of justice which nevertheless treat equal cases equally. I reiterate that a principle of the moral equality of human beings must be logically separate from, and prior to, any conception of justice which incorporates it.

**Kane, John**. Justice, Impartiality, and Equality: Why the Concept of Justice Does Not Presume Equality. *Polit Theory*, 24(3), 375-393, Ag 96.

It is commonly believed that some notion of equality is logically implied in the concept of justice. The principle of equal treatment is taken as self-evidently just, so that only *departures* from a fundamental norm of equality appear to require moral justification. Defenders point to the alleged 'impartiality' of moral reason as translating, in matters of justice into a fundamental principle of 'presumptive equality' which Amartya Sen argues is implicit in many modern theories of justice. Acceptance of the principle has also led to the claim that there may in fact be *two* fundamental principles of justice in potential conflict with one another, one of comparative and one of noncomparative justice. However, the formal concept of justice is in fact unitary and implies no principle of equality, presumptive or otherwise. To presume the contrary is to smuggle an undefended substantive view into a theory of justice under the guise of definition, and to eschew many difficult positive arguments about the moral status of human beings relative to one another.

**Kane, Robert**. *The Significance of Free Will.* New York, Oxford Univ Pr, 1996.

In the past quarter-century, there has been a resurgence of interest in traditional philosophical questions about free will. The first of this book's aims is to explore the significance of this recent work, both for the advancement of understanding in one of philosophy's most perennially challenging areas, and for broad contemporary concerns in ethics, politics, science, religion, and humanistic studies. The book's second goal is to defend a classic "incompatibilist" or "libertarian" conception of free will in ways that are both new to philosophy and that respond to contemporary scientific learning. Incompatibilist or libertarian accounts of freedom are often criticized for being unintelligible or for having no place in the modern scientific picture of the world. Kane asserts to the contrary that a traditional view of free will can be supported without the usual appeals to obscure or mysterious forms of agency and can be reconciled with recent developments in the sciences—physical, biological, neurological, cognitive, and behavioral. (publisher, edited)

**Kaneko, Mamoru** and Nagashima, Takashi. Game Logic and its Applications I. *Stud Log*, 57(2-3), 325-354, O 96.

This paper provides a logic framework for investigations of game theoretical problems. We adopt an infinitary extension of classical predicate logic as the base logic of the framework. The reason for an infinitary extension is to express the common knowledge concept explicitly. Depending upon the choice of axioms on the knowledge operators, there is a hierarchy of logics. The limit case is an infinitary predicate extension of modal propositional logic $KD_4$ and is of special interest in applications. In Part I, we develop the basic framework and show some applications: an epistemic axiomatization of Nash equilibrium and formal undecidability on the playability of a game. To show the formal undecidability, we use a term existence theorem, which will be proved in Part II.

**Kaneko, Mamoru** and Nagashima, Takashi. Game Logic and Its Applications II. *Stud Log*, 58(2), 273-303, Mr 97.

This paper provides a Genzten-style formulation of the game logic framework $GL_m$ (0 "is less than or equal to" m "is less than or equal to" omega), and proves the cut-elimination theorem for $GL_{omega}$ used in Part I. (edited)

**Kant, Immanuel**. *Übergang Von Den Metaphysischen Anfangsgründen Der Naturwissenschaft Zur Physik.* Zürich, Georg Olms, 1996.

**Kant, Immanuel** and Ceñal Lorente, Ramón (trans) and Gómez Caffarena, José (ed). *Immanuel Kant: Principios Formales del Mundo Sensible y del Inteligible (Disertación de 1770).* Madrid, CSIC, 1996.

"Principios formales del mundo sensible" (que hacen *un todo* intuitivo de los múltiples datos de percepción sensorial) son el espacio y el tiempo. Para Kant desde 1770 son la estructura constitutiva (*a priori*) de la sensibilidad humana. "Principio formal del mundo inteligible" le parecía en 1770 ser Dios mismo, clave última de los múltiples procesos causales del cosmos. En los años sucesivos se le problematizó el alcance del conocer intelectual humano: las "formas *a priori*" del entendimiento—las categorías—sólo dan conocimiento "esquematizadas", o sea, adaptadas a la percepción sensorial: el "mundo inteligible" es, pues, en primera instancia función del "sensible". Ahora bien, el sujeto y su vivencia moral abren a una afirmación puramente intelectual (*noumenal*) de la libertad y Dios puede ser postulado en "fe racional" como clave última de unidad teleológica: retorna así un "principio formal del mundo inteligible", aunque en figura más modesta. (publisher)

**Kant, Immanuel** and Gregor, Mary (ed & trans). *The Metaphysics of Morals.* New York, Cambridge Univ Pr, 1996.

*The Metaphysics of Morals* is Kant's major work in applied moral philosophy in which he deals with the basic principles of rights and of virtues. It comprises two parts: 'The Doctrine of Right', which deals with the juridical rights which persons have or can acquire, and the 'Doctrine of Virtue', which deals with the virtues they ought to acquire. Mary Gregor's translation, revised publication in Cambridge *Texts in the History of Philosophy,* is the only complete translation of the whole text and includes extensive annotation on Kant's difficult and sometimes unfamiliar vocabulary. A new introduction by Roger Sullivan sets the work within the context of the rest of Kant's moral writings. (publisher, edited)

**Kant, Immanuel** and Hatfield, Gary (ed & trans). *Prolegomena to Any Future Metaphysics.* New York, Cambridge Univ Pr, 1997.

This new translation, the first in nearly fifty years, presents Kant's thought with special attention to the original sentence structure and vocabulary. The volume is intended for student use. It includes selections from the *Critique of Pure Reason*, which fill out some of Kant's arguments and in which Kant introduces some special terminology. Included also are a historical and philosophical introduction, explanatory notes, a chronology, a guide to further reading and a detailed index.

**Kant, Immanuel** and Naragon, Steve (ed & trans) and Ameriks, Karl (ed & trans). *The Cambridge Edition of the Works of Immanuel Kant: Lectures on Metaphysics.* New York, Cambridge Univ Pr, 1997.

This volume contains the first translation into English of notes from Kant's lectures on metaphysics. These lectures, dating from the 1760s to the 1790s, touch on all the major topics and phases of Kant's philosophy. Most of these notes appeared only recently in the German Academy's edition; this translation offers many corrections of that edition. (publisher, edited)

**Kant, Immanuel** and Pluhar, Werner S (trans). *Critique of Pure Reason: Unified Edition (With All Variants from the 1781 and 1787 Editions).* Indianapolis, Hackett, 1996.

Eminently suited for use by both scholars and students, this richly annotated volume offers translations of the complete texts of both the First (A) and Second (B) editions, as well as Kant's own notes. Extensive editorial notes by Werner Pluhar and James Ellington supply explanatory and terminological comments, translations of Latin and other foreign expressions, variant readings, cross-references to other passages in the text and in other writings of Kant, and references to secondary works. An extensive bibliography, glossary, and detailed index are included. (publisher,edited)

**Kanthamani, A**. Do Wittgenstein's Forms of Life Inaugurate a Kantian Project of Transcendental Idealism?. *J Indian Counc Phil Res*, 13(3), 137-139, My-Ag 96.

Seen in the context of Pradhan's transcendental interpretation of 'forms of life' as *a priori*, the critique exposes the *ignoratio elenchi* behind saying that since there is no metaphysical self in Wittgenstein, there must be a transcendental self. The vulnerability of the position is seen more due to the lack of any precise argumentation on the part of the author. Further, it shows that neither 'transcendental logic' nor 'transcendental ethics', in Wittgenstein's sense, embodies a Kantian idealism.

**Kanthamani, A**. Does the Grammar of Seeing Aspects Imply a Kantian Concept?. *J Indian Counc Phil Res*, 14(2), 133-138, Ja-Ap 97.

**Kanthamani, A**. Is Chomsky's Linguistics Non-Empirical?. *J Indian Counc Phil Res*, 13(2), 145-151, Ja-Ap 96.

The paper attempts to defend the empirical credentials of Chomsky's linguistics against an uncharitable reading. It reiterates Chomsky's own claims in an effort to show that the uncharitable reading deviates a great deal from Chomsky's claims. The criticism against Chomsky is totally misplaced.

**Kantor, Alon**. Time of Ethics: Levinas and the *éclectement* of time. *Phil Soc Crit*, 22(6), 19-53, N 96.

Our essay examines Levinas's ideas of time and their relation to his ethical discourse. We read 'his' texts deconstructively and show how the notions of time and of the ethical are closely interconnected. We argue that Levinas deconstructs the concept of time, as it is traditionally developed by Western philosophy and that this concept is part and parcel of and cannot be detached from his philosophical venture. By following two major shibboleths, jouissance and language, we trace the deconstructive effort of Levinas to dismantle Western philosophy's traditional conceptualization of time. Our discussion points not to the failure of Levinas's toil but rather to the aporetic structure of his itinerary and to the ethical significance of this aporia.

**Kapitan, Tomis**. "Peirce and the Structure of Abductive Inference" in *Studies in the Logic of Charles Sanders Peirce*, Houser, Nathan (ed), 477-496. Bloomington, Indiana Univ Pr, 1997.

Peirce argued that abductive inference differs from deduction and induction not only in its characteristic form and the purpose for which it is used, but also in terms of its distinct type of argument validity or correctness. Before Peirce's claim for the autonomy of abductive inference must be clarified. This paper, discusses various forms of abductive inference, with emphasis upon Peirce's post-1900 writings, published and unpublished. In explicating the autonomy thesis, it concludes that Peirce did not develop a convincing defense of the tripartite division of argument validity.

**Kaplan, Caren**. *Questions of Travel: Postmodern Discourses of Displacement*. Durham, Duke Univ Pr, 1996.

In this book the author explores the various metaphoric uses of travel and displacement of this "traveling theory," and shows how various discourses of displacement link, rather than separate, modernism and postmodernism. (edited)

**Kaplan, Charles** and Kaplan, Laura Duhan. Democracy, Meritocracy, and the Cognitive Elite: The Real Thesis of *The Bell Curve*. *Educ Theor*, 47(3), 425-431, Sum 97.

Drawing on Herrnstein and Murray's *The Bell Curve* and Christopher Lasch's *Revolt of the Elites and the Betrayal of Democracy*, the authors argue that contemporary social reality in the United States has moved away from democracy towards meritocracy, in which a small but elite minority dominates economic and social decision making. The new elite can be defined as the group of people who occupy the most cognitively demanding professions and who have been selected on the basis of IQ. To as great an extent as possible, the elites have created a life independent of the public square and abandoned the underclasses.

**Kaplan, Laura Duhan** and Kaplan, Charles. Democracy, Meritocracy, and the Cognitive Elite: The Real Thesis of *The Bell Curve*. *Educ Theor*, 47(3), 425-431, Sum 97.

Drawing on Herrnstein and Murray's *The Bell Curve* and Christopher Lasch's *Revolt of the Elites and the Betrayal of Democracy*, the authors argue that contemporary social reality in the United States has moved away from democracy towards meritocracy, in which a small but elite minority dominates economic and social decision-making. The new elite can be defined as the group of people who occupy the most cognitively demanding professions and who have been selected on the basis of IQ. To as great an extent as possible, the elites have created a life independent of the public square and abandoned the underclasses.

**Kaplan, Mark**. Skepticism and Pyrotechnics. *Acta Analytica*, 157-169, 1996.

Can one construct, from elements of Descartes's dream argument in the First Meditation, a genuinely disturbing skeptical argument? In "Scepticism and Dreaming: Imploding the Demon," Crispin Wright tries to show that one can. Crucial to his undertaking is the task of motivating of the premise that you have available no warrant to believe the proposition that you are not dreaming. It is, I maintain, a task he does not successfully complete. My nominal purpose is to explain why I think this is so. My more substantial aim is to draw attention to a fundamental difficulty inherent in the suspension of our ordinary methodological standards demanded by those who would have us take skeptical arguments seriously.

**Kaplan, Morris B**. Liberté! Egalité! Sexualité!: Theorizing Lesbian and Gay Politics. *Polit Theory*, 25(3), 401-433, Je 97.

**Kaplan, Robert M** and Schneiderman, Lawrence J and Rosenberg, Esther (& others). Do Physicians' Own Preferences for Life-Sustaining Treatment Influence Their Perceptions of Patients' Preferences? A Second Look. *Cambridge Quart Healthcare Ethics*, 6(2), 131-137, Spr 97.

Purpose: To follow up previous observations that physicians' predictions of their patients end-of-life treatment choices are closer to the choices they would make for themselves than to the choices expressed by their patients. Study: One hundred and eleven patients and 28 physicians completed two advance directive instruments—a procedure-oriented questionnaire and a quality of life questionnaire. The patients expressed their own preferences. Their physicians were asked to complete these instruments in terms of what they thought their patients would want and also what they would want for themselves, if they were in the same situation as their patient. Conclusion: The results show again that physicians perceptions of their patients wishes for treatment are influenced by what they would want for themselves.

**Kaposi, Márton**. Georg Lukács and Lajos Fülep Dante (in Hungarian). *Magyar Filozof Szemle*, 4-5-6, 303-323, 1996.

Lukács hielt Dante immer für einen ausgezeichneten und mit vielen theoretischen Lehren aufwartenden Autor, ausführlicher setzte er sich jedoch nur in zwei Perioden seiner Laufbahn—unter Anwendung der Erkenntnisse der deutschen Dantistik—mit Dantes Kunst auseinander: im zweiten Jahrzehnt dieses Jahrhunderts bei der Arbeit am geplanten Dostojewski-Band, bzw. während er an seinem Werk *Die Theorie des Romans* arbeitete sowie ab Mitte der 50er Jahre, als er seine ästhetische Synthese in *Die Eigenart des Aesthetischen* und *über die Besonderheitals Kategorie der Ästhetik* darlegte. (edited)

**Kappel, Klemens**. Equality, Priority, and Time. *Utilitas*, 9(2), 203-225, Jl 97.

The lifetime equality view (the view that it is good if people's lives on the whole are equally worth living) has recently been met with the objection that it does not rule out simultaneous inequality: two persons may lead equally good lives on the whole and yet there may at any time be great differences in their level of well-being. And simultaneous inequality, it is held, ought to be a concern of egalitarians. The paper discusses this and related objections to the lifetime equality view. It is argued that rather than leading to a revision of the lifetime equality view, these objections, if taken seriously, should make us account for our egalitarian concerns in terms of the priority view rather than the equality view. The priority view claims that there is a greater moral value to benefiting the worse off. Several versions of the priority view are also distinguished.

**Karakostas, Vassilios**. On the Brussels School's Arrow of Time in Quantum Theory. *Phil Sci*, 63(3), 374-400, S 96.

This paper examines the problem of founding irreversibility on reversible equations of motion from the point-of-view of the Brussels school's recent developments in the foundations of quantum statistical mechanics. A detailed critique of both their 'subdynamics' and 'transformation' theory is given. It is argued that the subdynamics approach involves a generalized form of 'coarse-graining' description, whereas, transformation theory cannot lead to truly irreversible processes pointing to a preferred direction of time. It is concluded that the Brussels school's conception of microscopic temporal irreversibility, as such, is tacitly assumed at the macroscopic level. Finally a logical argument is provided which shows, independently of the mathematical formalism of the theory concerned, that statistical reasoning alone is not sufficient to explain the arrow of time.

**Karambayya, Rekha**. In Shouts and Whispers: Paradoxes Facing Women of Colour in Organizations. *J Bus Ethics*, 16(9), 891-897, Je 97.

This paper draws attention to issues of race and gender and their intersections. The choices faced by women of colour are framed as a series of paradoxes that need to be acknowledged, if not resolved. The implications of a paradoxical perspective for research on race and gender are explored.

**Karasev, L V**. Down the Slope. *Russian Stud Phil*, 35(3), 65-95, Wint 96-97.

The work presents a special ontological aspect of the writings of the Russian writer Andrei Platonov. A new original method of reflection named "ontologica poetics" is used here. Ontological poetics makes it possible to reveal ontological structure of the Platonov's writings where the emptiness and the substance appear to be the main opposition. According to Platonov, emptiness corresponds to death while substance means life. An attempt to reconcile the antithesis brings Platonov to the idea of water which is related both to emptiness and substance. So the point of the work is that water is the main "hero" of Platonov. It is water that really "fills" his writings. The Platonov's heroes aspire to sink into lakes, sea, rivers, to be the part of water. The idea of water corresponds here to the idea of the prenatal condition they dream to get back. They move down the slope like water does attempting to find the way back to their prenatal condition and thus avoid death in accordance with the Russian idea of immortality.

**Karcher, Julia N**. Auditors' Ability to Discern the Presence of Ethical Problems. *J Bus Ethics*, 15(10), 1033-1050, O 96.

Recently, society and the accounting profession have become increasingly concerned with ethics. Accounting researchers have responded by attempting to investigate and analyze the ethical behavior of accountants. While the current state of ethical behavior among practitioners is important, the ability of accountants to detect ethical problems that may not be obvious should also be studied and understood. This study addresses three questions: 1) are auditors alert to ethical issues; 2) if so, how important do they perceive them to be; and 3) what factors affect their sensitivity threshold and their perceptions of the importance of the issues?(edited)

**Karger, Elizabeth**. Mental Sentences According to Burley and to the Early Ockham. *Vivarium*, 34(2), 192-230, N 96.

**Karger, Elizabeth**. Some 15th and Early 16th Century Logicians on the Quantification of Categorical Sentences. *Topoi*, 16(1), 65-76, Mr 97.

**Karlawish, Jason H T** and Lantos, John. Community Equipoise and the Architecture of Clinical Research. *Cambridge Quart Healthcare Ethics*, 6(4), 385-396, Fall 97.

**Karlsson, Gunnar**. The Experience of Spatiality for Congenitally Blind People: A Phenomenological-Psychological Study. *Human Stud*, 19(3), 303-330, Jl 96.

This phenomenological-psychological study aims at discovering the essential constituents involved in congenitally blind people's spatial experiences. Nine congenitally blind persons took part in this study. The data were made up of half structured (thorough) interviews. The analysis of the data yielded the following three comprehension forms of spatiality; I) Comprehension in terms of image-experience; II) Comprehension in terms of notions; III) Comprehension in terms of knowledge. (edited)

**Kasely, Terry S**. The Method of the Geometer: A New Angle on Husserl's Cartesianism. *Husserl Stud*, 13(2), 141-154, 1996-97.

Husserl's references to Descartes have motivated some scholars to dispute Husserl's methodic rigor and misunderstand the *Fifth Meditation*. I approach Husserl's Cartesian heritage by showing how each thinker models the method of the geometer to develop a universal method—the *eidetic* method. Husserl rigorously employs this method as delineated by Descartes in his *Rules*. This thesis supports the claim that Husserl's *Fifth Meditation* is his defense of both the eidetic method and positive science. Husserl encounters, and ultimately reveals, the limitations of the eidetic method and describes the ground of positive science as the essence of transcendental intersubjectivity.

**Kasher, Asa**. Life Sciences, Medicine and the Normative Communities: Early Cooperation. *Philosophia (Israel)*, 25(1-4), 69-70, Ap 97.

**Kashima, Ryo**. Contraction-Elimination for Implicational Logics. *Annals Pure Applied Log*, 84(1), 17-39, Mr 97.

We prove a "contraction-elimination theorem": If a sequent is provable in the implicational fragment of the Gentzen's sequent calculus LK (resp. LJ) and if it satisfies a certain condition on the number of the occurrences of propositional variables, then it is provable without the right (resp. left) contraction rule. This implies the following. If an implicational formula is a theorem of classical (resp. intuitionistic) logic and is not a theorem of intuitionistic (resp. BCK) logic, then there is a propositional variable which occurs at least once (resp. twice) positively and at least twice (resp. once) negatively in the formula.

**Kashima, Ryo**. Cut-Free Sequent Calculi for Some Tense Logics. *Stud Log*, 53(1), 119-135, F 94.

We introduce certain enhanced systems of sequent calculi for tense logics, and prove their completeness with respect to Kripke-type semantics.

**Kass, Nancy E** and Sugarman, Jeremy and Faden, Ruth. Trust: The Fragile Foundation of Contemporary Biomedical Research. *Hastings Center Rep*, 26(5), 25-29, S-O 96.

It is widely assumed that informing prospective subjects about the risks and possible benefits of research not only protects their rights, but empowers them to protect their interests. Yet interviews with patient-subjects suggest this is not always the case. Patient-subjects often trust their physician to guide them through decisions.

**Kassavine, Illia**. Berkeley Revised: On the New Metaphysics for Social Epistemology. 90 Years After "Materialism and Empiriocrticism". *Epistemologia*, 19(1), 157-174, Ja-Je 96.

Le idee di Berkeley concernenti la teoria della conoscenza—criticate da Lenin in *Materialismo ed empiriocriticismo* quale paradigma di soggettivismo e relativismo—vengono considerate come una possibile sorgente cui attingere in vista di una "umanizzazione" della filosofia russa contemporanea, dal momento che in quest'ultima vi è un'urgente necessità di una nuova teoria della conoscenza e di un nuovo individualismo. L'interpretazione moderna di queste idee nel senso di recenti sviluppi filosofici e scientifici conduce alla costruzione di una sorta di culturologia gnoseologica che unifica alcune idee strutturali e alcuni metodi della fenomenologia e dell'aritmetica. Questa culturologia viene considerata da un punto di vista che presenta nuove soluzioni ai problemi dell'accumulazione e del cambiamento della conoscenza, nonché ai problemi della creatività, a quelli emersi nella disputa sul rapporto fra società e persona, ecc.

**Kastely, James L**. *Rethinking the Rhetorical Tradition: From Plato to Postmodernism*. New Haven, Yale Univ Pr, 1997.

What is the role of rhetoric in a civil society? In this thought-provoking book, James L. Kastely examines works by writers from Plato to Jane Austin to Sartre and locates a line of thinking that values rhetoric but also raises questions about the viability of rhetorical practice. While dealing principally with literary theory, rhetoric, and philosophy, the author's arguments extend to practical concerns and open up the way to deeper thinking about individual responsibility for existing injustices, for inadvertently injuring others, and for silencing those without power. (publisher, edited)

**Kasulis, Thomas P**. "Intimations of Religious Experience and Interreligious Truth" in *The Recovery of Philosophy in America: Essays in Honor of John Edwin Smith*, Kasulis, Thomas P (ed), 39-57. Albany, SUNY Pr, 1997.

**Kasulis, Thomas P** (ed) and Neville, Robert Cummings (ed). *The Recovery of Philosophy in America: Essays in Honor of John Edwin Smith*. Albany, SUNY Pr, 1997.

John Edwin Smith, through a long publishing and teaching career at Yale, has championed the rich American conceptions of experience and speculative reason and it seems that at the end of this century they are returning in triumph. This book celebrates the recovery and new growth of American philosophy in a stunning variety of connected and vital intellectual projects represented by its contributors: George Allan, Douglas R. Anderson, Lewis S. Ford, Errol Harris, Richard Hocking, Thomas P. Kasulis, George R. Lucas, Jr., Robert Cummings Neville, Donald W. Sherburne, Merold Westphal, Kuang-ming Wu, and Carl G. Vaught. Displaying philosophy's recovery in America, this book also honors John Edwin Smith, who has kept the history and trajectory of philosophy in America in sight and who contributes a prophetic commentary on the other essays.

**Kather, Regine**. Selbsterschaffung und die Irreversibilität der Zeit bei A.N. Whitehead. *Phil Natur*, 29(1), 135-159, 1992.

**Kato, Tetsuhiro**. Toward Art beyond the Modern World: Aby Warburg and the Comparative Study of Art. *Bigaku*, 47(4), 36-45, Spr 97.

To the present day there remains a regrettable lack of insight in the comparative study of art. The objects examined are usually limited to works of art from the "highly civilized" zones of the old world. Even if eyes are raised to the art of other cultures, the standard of judgment is unchanged, i.e., the modern aesthetic principle of plasticity. What is needed for the comparative study of art today is a tolerant multiculturalism, which goes beyond the narrow framework of conventional aesthetics toward "art outside the modern world." I believe that Warburg's version of the "musée imaginaire" gives us many valuable suggestions for the solution of the problems with which we are now faced. (edited)

**Katz, Albert N**. Pragmatics and the Processing of Metaphors: Category Dissimilarity in Topic and Vehicle Asymmetry. *Prag Cognition*, 4(2), 265-304, 1996.

A model of metaphor processing is suggested based on the application of pragmatic principles to the type of semantic information easy to access. It is argued that, with metaphor, higher-order categorical knowledge is given processing preference over instance-specific knowledge in an attempt to recover likely intended meaning. Instance-specific information is used more often when the higher-order knowledge is taken to violate conversational postulates. One such violation occurs when the categories implicated by metaphor topic and vehicle are similar and thus unlikely to provide new or relevant information. It is argued further that these differences could, in part, explain at least one condition that produces the asymmetry observed in metaphor when topic and vehicle are reversed. Predictions supportive of the model were obtained in three studies, employing different methodologies: feature listing, recognition memory and a vehicle choice task.

**Katz, Bernard D** and Kremer, Elmar J. The Cosmological Argument Without the Principle of Sufficient Reason. *Faith Phil*, 14(1), 62-70, Ja 97.

We formulate a version of the *cosmological argument* that deploys an epistemic principle of explanation in place of the traditional *principle of sufficient reason*. The epistemic principle asserts that if there is a possible explanation of a fact, and some proposition is entailed by that explanation and by every other possible explanation of that fact, it is reasonable to accept that proposition. We try to show that there is a possible explanation of the fact that there are contingent beings and that any possible explanation of this fact presupposes that there is a necessary being. We conclude that it is reasonable to believe that there is a necessary being.

**Katz, Eric**. "Nature's Presence: Reflections on Healing and Domination" in *Philosophy and Geography I: Space, Place, and Environmental Ethics*, Light, Andrew (ed), 49-61. Lanham, Rowman & Littlefield, 1997.

In this essay, I reflect on the experience of places of human evil. Specifically, I consider the relationship between the contemporary environmental crisis and the Holocaust by analyzing the healing process of nature in several Eastern European landscapes. The concept of domination connects these two areas of inquiry, for in both genocide and the destruction of the environment we interfere with the autonomous self-development of our victims. I compare the healing process of nature with the human attempt to restore damaged ecosystems, and conclude that even healing, as an interference in self-development, can be considered another form of domination.

**Katz, Eric**. "Searching for Intrinsic Value: Pragmatism and Despair in Environmental Ethics" in *Environmental Pragmatism*, Light, Andrew (ed), 307-318. New York, Routledge, 1996.

Anthony Weston criticizes the place of "intrinsic value" in the development of an environmental ethic and recommends a "pragmatic shift" toward a plurality of values based on human experiences. I argue that Weston is mistaken for two reasons: 1) his view of the methodology of environmental ethics is distorted, for the intrinsic value of natural entities is not the ground of all moral obligations regarding the environment; and 2) his pragmatic theory of value is too anthropocentric and subjective for the development of a reliable and adequate environmental ethic.

**Katz, Eric**. *Nature as Subject: Human Obligation and Natural Community*. Lanham, Rowman & Littlefield, 1997.

Written by one of the instrumental figures in environmental ethics, *Nature as Subject* traces the development of an ethical policy that is not centered on human beings. Katz argues that Nature is worthy of direct moral consideration and examines the theoretical and philosophical problems with this idea. He applies this idea to contemporary environmental problems, introducing themes of justice, domination, imperialism and the Holocaust. *Nature as Subject* should serve as a foundational work for environmental philosophers, government and industry policy makers, activists and students in advanced philosophy and environmental studies courses. (publisher)

**Katz, Eric** (ed) and Light, Andrew (ed). *Environmental Pragmatism*. New York, Routledge, 1996.

Environmental pragmatism is a new strategy in environmental thought: it argues that theoretical debates are hindering the ability of the environmental movement to forge agreement on basic policy imperatives. This new direction in environmental philosophy moves beyond theory, advocating a serious inquiry into the practical merits of moral pluralism. Environmental pragmatism, as a coherent philosophical position, connects the methodology of classical American pragmatist thought to the explanation, solution and discussion of real issues. (edited)

**Katz, Eric** and Weston, Anthony. "Unfair to Swamps: A Reply to Katz Unfair to Foundations? A Reply to Weston" in *Environmental Pragmatism*, Light, Andrew (ed), 319-324. New York, Routledge, 1996.

**Katz, Jay** and Brody, Baruch A and Dula, Annette. In Case of Emergency: No Need for Consent. *Hastings Center Rep*, 27(1), 7-12, Ja-F 97.

This article offers a philosophical analysis of the FDA's recent regulations on emergency room research. It argues that these regulations are based upon an appropriate ethical balancing of competing legitimate values. It also argues that two important problems (use of placebo controls and definition of when informal convent is impractical) have not been adequately addressed in these regulations.

**Katz, Jerrold J**. Analyticity, Necessity, and the Epistemology of Semantics. *Phil Phenomenol Res*, 57(1), 1-28, Mr 97.

Contemporary philosophy standardly accepts Frege's conceptions of sense as the determiner of reference and of analyticity as (necessary) truth in virtue of meaning. This paper argues that those conceptions are mistaken. It develops referentially autonomous notions of sense and analyticity and applies them to the semantics of natural kind terms. The arguments of Donnellan, Putnam and Kripke concerning natural kind terms are widely taken to refute internalist and rationalist theories of meaning. This paper shows that the counter-intuitive consequences about the reference of natural kind terms depend as much on Frege's conceptions of sense and analyticity as on what such theories of meaning say about the senses of natural kind terms. Rather than refuting the internalist and rationalist theories of meaning, the arguments of Donnellan, Putnam and Kripke are best recast as refutations of their own Fregean assumptions. The paper also shows how autonomous notions of sense and analyticity enable us to reconstruct such theories, formulate an internalist/rationalist account of semantic knowledge and preserve Donnellan's, Putnam's and Kripke's insights about reference.

**Katz, Jerrold J**. The Unfinished Chomskyan Revolution. *Mind Lang*, 11(3), 270-294, S 96.

Chomsky's criticism of Bloomfieldian structuralism's conception of linguistic reality applies equally to his own conception of linguistic reality. There are too many sentences in a natural language for them to have either concrete acoustic reality or concrete psychological or neural reality. Sentences have to be types, which, by Peirce's generally accepted definition, means that they are abstract objects. Given that sentences are abstract objects, Chomsky's generativism as well as his psychologism have to be given up. Langendoen's and Postal's argument in *The Vastness of Natural Languages* to show that there are more than denumerably many sentences is flawed. But, with the view that sentences are abstract objects, the flaws can be corrected. Once psychologism and generativism are abandoned, the revolution against Bloomfieldian structuralism can be brought to completion and linguistics can be put on a sound philosophical basis.

**Katz, Leo**. Evading Responsibility: The Ethics of Ingenuity. *Jahr Recht Ethik*, 2, 191-223, 1994.

Der Aufsatz bietet eine Einblick in die Möglichkeiten, Normen zu umgehen—einer Praxis mit, wie gezeigt wird, langer Tradition. Die dargestellten Methoden reichen von einer Beeinflussung des Wissens des Täters, über das Heranziehen "anderer", seien es Menschen oder Maschinen, um die gewünschte aber verbotene Handlung vorzunehmen, bis hin zu Änderungen in den Kausalverläufen. Der Grund für diese Umgehungsmöglichkeiten liegt im Formalismus deontologischer Systeme, die im Gegensatz zu utilitaristischen Positionen gerade nicht auf die Folgen einer Handlung abstellen.

**Katz, Michael S**. "Moral Stories: How Much Can We Learn from Them and Is It Enough?" in *Philosophy of Education (1996)*, Margonis, Frank (ed), 12-17. Urbana, Phil Education Soc, 1997.

**Katzner, James** and Weiss, Andrea. Learning Philosophy Collaboratively with a Student. *Thinking*, 13(2), 23-26, 1997.

**Katzoff, Charlotte**. Epistemic Obligation and Rationality Constraints. *S J Phil*, 34(4), 455-470, Wint 96.

On one interpretation, the notion of epistemic obligation refers to the moment at which a subject is considering a particular proposition and requires him to try, at that time, to believe the proposition if and only if it is true. Attempts to discredit this notion based on our alleged inability to believe at will are inconclusive. In light of the strong rationality constraints which govern belief, however, the above notion proves impossible, not because one cannot believe at will, but because no case of trying to believe at will could count as a case of fulfilling that epistemic obligation.

**Katzoff, Charlotte**. When is Knowledge a Matter of Luck?. *Grazer Phil Stud*, 51, 105-120, 1996.

It is quite common that a claim to knowledge is dismissed as a matter of luck. It is demonstrated that when one cites as the reason for rejecting a true belief that it is merely lucky, this is typically because the belief has not satisfied the requirements of one's theory. So disputes on luck in fact turn out to be disputes on deep epistemological issues. Criteria for epistemological luck suggested by Thomas Nagel, Nicolas Rescher, Alvin Goldman, Mylan Engel and Richard Foley are analyzed and reconstructed and compared with accounts on luck in the moral sphere.

**Katzoff, Charlotte** and Widerker, David. Avoidability and Libertarianism: A Response to Fischer. *Faith Phil*, 13(3), 415-421, Jl 96.

Recently, Widerker has attacked Fischer's contention that one could use Frankfurt-type counterexamples to the principle of alternative possibilities to show that even from a libertarian viewpoint an agent might be morally responsible for a decision that he could not have avoided. Fischer has responded by: a) arguing that Widerker's criticism presupposes the falsity of Molinism and b) presenting a version of libertarianism which avoids Widerker's criticism. Here we argue that : I) Fischer's first response is unconvincing and undermines Molinism itself; II) the version of libertarianism he presents is fallacious, and III) even on the version of libertarianism he proposes, avoidability remains a necessary condition for moral responsibility.

**Kaufert, Joseph M** and Putsch, Robert W. Communication through Interpreters in Health Care: Ethical Dilemmas Arising from Differences in Class, Culture, Language, and Power. *J Clin Ethics*, 8(1), 71-87, Spr 97.

This article considers the problems faced by medical interpreters as they facilitate communication in informed consent and end-of-life decisions. It examines power relationships between participants who hold different interpretations of illness and treatment, disparate values in relation to death and dying and use language or decision-making frameworks differently. Cases drawn from our ethnographic research on the health interpreters in Winnipeg, Canada and Seattle are used to examine the ethical dimension of the work of interpreters. The article considers the evolution and regulation of the role of the healthcare interpreter and their relationships with other healthcare providers.

**Kaufman, Gordon D**. The Epic of Evolution as a Framework for Human Orientation in Life. *Zygon*, 32(2), 175-188, Je 97.

This article sketches what is required of a world picture (religious or nonreligious) that is intended to provide orientation in the world for ongoing human life today. How do we move from conceptions and theories prominent in the modern sciences—such as cosmic and biological evolution—to an overall picture or cosmology which can *orient* us for the effective address of today's deepest human problems? A *biohistorical* conception of the human is proposed in answer to this question.

**Kaufmann, Matthias**. Imputabilitas als Merkmal des Moralischen: Die Diskussion bei Duns Scotus und Wilhelm von Ockham. *Jahr Recht Ethik*, 2, 55-66, 1994.

John Duns Scotus deals with a question which is still of importance for modern ethical debate, namely what is the difference between a good deed which is intended but may be hindered by the circumstances and a good deed which is both intended and consummated? Scotus discusses this issue in connection with the question of whether moral goodness or badness can be assigned to the external act, which depends on physical capability. In his investigation, he determines that the imputability (imputabilitas) of acts, i.e., the fact that the actor had free power of disposition over them, is a criterion for being able to morally qualify them as good or bad. (edited)

**Kaufmann, Walter** and Baird, Forrest E (ed). *Ancient Philosophy, 2nd Edition*. Upper Saddle River, Prentice Hall, 1997.

An anthology of ancient philosophy including extensive selections from the pre-Socratics, the writings of the most important Greek philosophers (including almost 400 pages from Plato and Aristotle); along with shorter selections from the Hellenistic and Roman philosophers Epicurus, Zeno of Citium, Cleanthes, Epictetus, Lucretius, Marcus Aurelius, Pyrrho and Sextus Empiricus, and Plotinus. In choosing texts for this volume I have tried wherever possible to follow three principles: 1) to use complete works or, where more appropriate, complete sections of works 2) in clear translations 3) of texts central to the thinker's philosophy or widely accepted as part of the "canon."

**Kaufmann, Walter** and Baird, Forrest E (ed). *From Plato to Nietzsche, 2nd Edition*. Upper Saddle River, Prentice Hall, 1997.

An anthology of Western philosophy including extensive selections from ancient Greek philosophy (Plato, Aristotle), Hellenistic philosophy (Epicurus, Epictetus, Plotinus), medieval philosophy (Augustine, Thomas Aquinas, William of Ockham, and numerous others), modern philosophy (Bacon, Descartes, Hobbes, Spinoza, Locke, Leibniz, Berkeley, Hume, Kant), and nineteenth-century philosophy (Hegel, Mill, Kierkegaard, Marx, and Nietzsche). In choosing texts for this volume I have tried wherever possible to follow three principles: 1) to use complete works or, where more appropriate, complete sections of works, 2) in clear translations, 3) of texts central to the thinker's philosophy or widely accepted as part of the "canon."

**Kaufmann, Walter** and Baird, Forrest E (ed). *Medieval Philosophy, 2nd Edition*. Upper Saddle River, Prentice Hall, 1997.

An anthology of Medieval philosophy including extensive selections from Augustine, Thomas Aquinas, and William of Ockham, along with representative texts from Boethius, Eriugena, Anselm (and Guanilo), Abelard, Hildegard of Bingen, John of Salisbury, Avicenna, Averroes, Maimonides, Grosseteste, Roger Bacon, Bonaventure, Duns Scotus, Eckhart, Catherine of Siena, Nicholas Cusanas, and Pico and others. In choosing texts for this volume I have tried wherever possible to follow three principles: 1) to use complete works or, where more appropriate, complete sections of works 2) in clear translations 3) of texts central to the thinker's philosophy or widely accepted as part of the "canon."

**Kaufmann, Walter** and Baird, Forrest E (ed). *Modern Philosophy, 2nd Edition*. Upper Saddle River, Prentice Hall, 1997.

An anthology of modern philosophy including extensive selections from the "British Empiricists" (Francis Bacon, Thomas Hobbes, John Locke, George Berkeley, David Hume, Thomas Reid, and Mary Wollstonecraft) and the "Continental Rationalists" (Rene Descartes, Baruch Spinoza, and Gottfried Leibniz), together with almost 160 pages from the great synthesizer, Immanuel Kant. In choosing texts for this volume I have tried wherever possible to follow three principles: 1) to use complete works or, where more appropriate, complete sections of works, 2) in clear translations, 3) of texts central to the thinker's philosophy or widely accepted as part of the "canon."

**Kaufmann, Walter** and Baird, Forrest E (ed). *Nineteenth-Century Philosophy*. Upper Saddle River, Prentice Hall, 1997.

An anthology of both Continental and Anglo-American philosophy in the nineteenth century. Continental thinkers include Fichte, Hegel, Schopenhauer, Comte, Kierkegaard, Marx and Nietzsche. Anglo-American philosophers

AUTHOR INDEX 717 Keita Cha-Jua, Sundiata

include Bentham, Mill, Peirce, James, and Dewey. In choosing texts for this volume I have tried wherever possible to follow three principles: 1) to use complete works or, where more appropriate, complete sections of works, 2) in clear translations, and 3) of texts central to the thinker's philosophy or widely accepted as part of the "canon."

**Kaufmann, Walter** and Baird, Forrest E (ed). *Twentieth-Century Philosophy.* Upper Saddle River, Prentice Hall, 1997.

An anthology of both continental and Anglo-American philosophy in the twentieth century. Continental thinkers include Husserl, Heidegger, Gadamer, Sartre, de Beauvoir, Merleau-Ponty, Foucault, Derrida, Irigaray, and Habermas. Anglo-American philosophers include Dewey, Whitehead, DuBois, Russell, Moore, Wittgenstein, Carnap, Quine, Austin, Davidson, Rorty, Putnam, and Taylor. In choosing texts for this volume I have tried to follow three principles: 1) use complete works or, where more appropriate, complete sections of works, 2) in clear translations, 3) of texts central to the thinker's philosophy or widely accepted as part of the "canon" (though some recent philosophy criticizes the very notion of a canon).

**Kaul, R K**. Historiography of Civilizations: A Review. *J Indian Counc Phil Res*, 14(1), 174-179, S-D 96.

**Kaye, Sharon**. Against a Straussian Interpretation of Marsilius of Padua's Poverty Thesis. *Hist Phil Quart*, 11(3), 269-279, Jl 94.

Central to Marsilius of Padua's *Defensor Pacis* is the claim that priests should relinquish all property rights. This paper argues that Marsilius had both political and theological reasons for adopting this radical view. Aristotle demonstrates that priests have no political role and the life of Jesus confirms this; therefore, priests should give up the wealth which enables them to wield coercive authority. According to a recent Straussian interpretation, the *Defensor* is incoherent when read literally, but when read esoterically, constitutes a defense of aristocracy. This thesis not only distorts Marsilius's argument but also neglects the historical circumstances surrounding the work.

**Kazmi, Y**. Foucault's Genealogy and Teaching Multiculturalism as a Subversive Activity. *Stud Phil Educ*, 16(3), 331-345, Jl 97.

It is being argued, in this article, that multicultural education is subversive because it challenges the assumed inevitability and superiority of the dominant culture by presenting alternatives to it. For multicultural education to be subversive, however, culture has to be understood as an order of things mapped across truth and power axis à la Foucault. These order of things are suppressed by the dominant culture in order to maintain its hegemony. It is being further argued that with the help of Foucault's genealogy we can understand how multicultural education can liberate subjugated order of things.

**Kaznacheev, Vlail' Petrovich**. An Achievement of Humanity. *Russian Stud Phil*, 34(1), 7-13, Sum 95.

**Keaney, Michael**. The Poverty of Rhetoricism: Popper, Mises and the Riches of Historicism. *Hist Human Sci*, 10(1), 1-22, F 97.

The attacks on historicism by radical individualists such as Popper and Mises have had lasting repercussions in the social sciences. Specifically, the term is used to connote deterministic, teleological theories of history, associated with Hegelian notions of destiny and positivist ideas of historical laws. This article argues that historicism is very different in character, in that it essentially amounts to the belief that social science and history are one and the same, whilst emphasizing the separate epistemology of natural science. It rejects the fictitious historicism invented by Popper in his famous polemic and challenges the idea of a value-free social science posited by Mises, who saw history and human action as logically distinct entities. In conclusion, it is argued that the mechanistic rationalism that characterizes much of social science, particularly modern economics, should be supplementary, if anything, to the primacy of history. The notion of transcendent, value-free criteria upon which to construct social science is refuted.

**Kearney, Richard**. The Crisis of Narrative in Contemporary Culture. *Metaphilosophy*, 28(3), 183-195, Jl 97.

This article explores the crisis of narrative in contemporary culture. It begins by examining the challenge represented by the mass media for the continuing art of storytelling. Taking up Walter Benjamin's warning that we are moving from an age of narrative experience to an age of instant information, it analyses the implications of the postmodern 'cult of simulation' for education, historiography and ethics. The paper concludes by advocating a critical hermeneutic approach as the most apt response to this contemporary dilemma. Only by means of such hermeneutic retrieval, inspired by the work of Ricoeur and Gadamer, can we avoid the current reduction of temporal experience to a 'depthless present' without past or future, thereby reaffirming the crucial narrative dimensions of historical memory and hope.

**Kearns, John T**. "The Nonrepresentational Use of Language" in *Verdad: lógica, representación y mundo,* Villegas Forero, L, 323-332. Santiago de Compostela, Univ Santiago Comp, 1996.

This paper provides an analysis of representing which distinguishes the use of an image or expression to represent objects from its use to direct one's attention to (to *identify*) particular objects in the world. It is possible to use expressions to identify objects and to predicate concepts of objects without representing anything. It is also possible to use language to represent objects of a kind. The two uses of language are illustrated and explained and their differing truth conditions are characterized.

**Kearns, John T**. Thinking Machines: Some Fundamental Confusions. *Mind Mach*, 7(2), 269-287, My 97.

This paper explores Church's thesis and related claims made by Turing. Church's thesis concerns computable numerical functions, while Turing's claims concern both procedures for manipulating uninterpreted marks and machines that generate the results that these procedures would yield. It is argued that Turing's claims are true and that they support (the truth of) Church's thesis. It is further argued that the truth of Turing's and Church's theses have no interesting consequences for human cognition or cognitive abilities. The theses don't even mean that computers can do as much as people can when it comes to carrying out effective procedures. For carrying out a procedure is a purposive, intentional activity. No actual machines does, or can do, as much.

**Kechris, Alexander S** and Hjorth, Greg. Borel Equivalence Relations and Classifications of Countable Models. *Annals Pure Applied Log*, 82(3), 221-272, D 96.

Using the theory of Borel equivalence relations we analyze the isomorphism relation on the countable models of a theory and develop a framework for measuring the complexity of possible complete invariants for isomorphism.

**Keefer, Matthew Wilks**. The Inseparability of Morality and Well-Being: The Duty/Virtue Debate Revisited. *J Moral Educ*, 25(3), 277-290, S 96.

One characterisation of the duty/virtue debate contrasts an ethics of duty that provides us with the moral knowledge to know what is right because it is right, to an ethics of virtue that enables us to choose what is right only because we want to, and not because we know that we must (*Baron*, 1985). This paper provides an account of the practical reasoning that moral agents employ in the pursuit of valuable goals based on Raz (1986) that undermines the basis for this contrast. The account shows how acquiring practical knowledge of our own valuable pursuits instructs us in the duties that we owe to others, just as being able to identify the duties we owe to others requires knowing what is necessary for living a meaningful and fulfilling life. It is argued that the interdependence of these two important aspects of moral development puts into question attempts by moral educators to distinguish sharply between them.

**Keffer, Jane M** and Hill, Ronald Paul. An Ethical Approach to Lobbying Activities of Businesses in the United States. *J Bus Ethics*, 16(12-13), 1371-1379, S 97.

This paper presents an ethical approach to the use of lobbying within the context of the relationships among U.S. organizations, their lobbyists and government officials. After providing a brief history of modern-day lobbying activities, lobbying is defined and described focusing on its role as a strategic marketing tool. Then ethical frameworks for understanding the impact of these practices on various *external* constituencies are delineated with an emphasis on the communitarian movement advanced by Etzioni. (edited)

**Keijzer, Fred A** and Bem, Sacha. Behavioral Systems Interpreted as Autonomous Agents and as Coupled Dynamical Systems: A Criticism. *Phil Psych*, 9(3), 323-346, S 96.

We will discuss two contexts in which the behavioural systems idea is being developed. Autonomous Agents Research is the enterprise of building behaviour-based robots. Dynamical Systems Theory provides a mathematical framework well suited for describing the interactions between complex systems. We will conclude that both enterprises provide important contributions to the behavioural systems idea. But neither turns it into a full conceptual alternative which will initiate a major paradigm switch in cognitive science. The concept will need a lot of fleshing out before it can assume that role. (edited)

**Keil, Geert**. *Kritik des Naturalismus.* Hawthorne, de Gruyter, 1993.

The distinguishing feature of philosophical naturalism is its hostility to a realistic and literal understanding of the intentional notions of belief-desire psychology. In attacking the intentional idiom, the naturalist has got three options: outright elimination, instrumentalism, or providing sufficient conditions for intentional phenomena in nonmentalistic, nonsemantic and nonteleological vocabulary. It is argued in detail that none of these projects has been successful so far. Special attention is paid to the intentional *presuppositions* of putative naturalistic analyses. Typically, such presuppositions manifest themselves in the use of anthropomorphic metaphors, in the positing of homunculi and in category mistakes. The most part of the book is devoted to conceptual analyses, aiming at the detection of intentionalistic contaminations of prominent naturalistic theories.

**Keita, L D**. Neoclassical Economics and the Last Dogma of Positivism: Is the Normative-Positive Distinction Justified?. *Metaphilosophy*, 28(1-2), 81-101, Ja-Ap 97.

Neoclassical economic theory in its pretensions to scientific status is founded on one of the variants of a now discredited positivism. Neoclassical economic theory claims that there are two distinct areas of economic research: positive economics and normative economics. The former is assumed to deal with the cognitive as scientific content of economics while the later focuses on welfare or equity issues. I argue that the reliance of the whole theoretical structure of economics on the normative postulate of rationality renders neoclassical economics a normative discipline. I also argue that neoclassical economics should thus be viewed as an instance of applied ethics rather than as applied mathematics, say. Finally, it is suggested that neoclassical economics, if its scientific pretensions are to be taken seriously, should be absorbed theoretically into general anthropology.

**Keita, L D**. Winch and Instrumental Pluralism: A Reply to B. D. Lerner. *Phil Soc Sci*, 27(1), 80-82, Mr 97.

**Keita Cha-Jua, Sundiata**. Air Raid over Harlem: Langston Hughes's Left Nationalist Poetics, 1927-1936. *Nature Soc Thought*, 8(4), 433-455, 1995.

This paper explicates Hughes's understanding of race and class. Between 1927-1936 Hughes transcended the race/class dichotomy and examined the intertwining of race and class, or the *racialclass* problematic. Poems written in Hughes's *left nationalist* voice exposed capitalist exploitation, opposed white supremacy, challenged bourgeois Black leadership and advocated militant resistance. Responding to the 1935 Harlem Revolt Hughes wrote "Air Raid Over Harlem." Just as the insurrection heralded a new tactic in Black politics, "Air Raid" rearticulated orthodox Marxist understanding of the relationship between race and class; it reflected Hughes's new perception that African Americans could spark the socialist revolution.

**Keith, Heather** and DeTar, Richard. Interview with Martha Nussbaum. *Kinesis*, 23(2), 3-15, Fall 96.

This work is one in a series of interviews with philosophers published by *Kinesis*. It is an attempt to detail Martha Nussbaum's views concerning her own work, interpretations of her work, her continuing philosophical interests and goals, and her evaluation of various schools of social and political thought. It also includes autobiographical statements regarding Nussbaum's involvement in philosophy.

**Keizer, H M**. Hellenization and Keeping Body and Soul Together. *Phil Reform*, 62(1), 99-111, 1997.

The article evaluates *Hellenization Revisited: Shaping a Christian Response within the Greco-Roman World* (W.E. Helleman ed., University Press of American, 1994, 554 pp.—proceedings of a conference held in Toronto, 1991). First, the book's point of departure (Adolf von Harnack's thesis that Gnosticism represents the acute, Catholicism the gradual Hellenising of Christianity) and varied contents are described. Then, focusing on the book's revaluation and criticism of Harnack and on "Hellenization" as an influence on thought, the author suggests that "Hellenization" might be observed and studied best in attitudes towards the Old Testament and be characterized as abstracting spirit from body.

**Kekes, John**. A Question for Egalitarians. *Ethics*, 107(4), 658-669, Jl 97.

Statistical evidence indicates that the life expectancy of men is about one-tenth shorter than the life expectancy of women. This is clearly a case of unjustified inequality in the possession of the primary good of life. There are readily available policies for reducing this inequality. Yet these policies are absurd; no one could seriously advocate them. The question for egalitarians is why this absurdity does not carry over to policies that they do advocate. Several egalitarian answers are considered and rejected as indefensible.

**Kekes, John**. Academic Corruption. *Monist*, 79(4), 564-576, O 96.

Academics have the primary responsibility to uphold the truth through teaching and research and the secondary responsibility to participate in the administration of their institutions. American higher education is in a bad state partly because academic routinely discharge their secondary responsibility in a way that systematically undermines their primary responsibility. Current practices in publishing, evaluating research and teaching, hiring, tenuring and promoting academics are used as illustrations.

**Kekes, John**. *Against Liberalism*. Ithaca, Cornell Univ Pr, 1997.

Liberalism is doomed to failure, John Kekes argues in this criticism of its basic assumptions. Liberals favor individual autonomy, a wide plurality of choices and equal rights and resources, seeing them as essential for good lives. They oppose such evils as selfishness, intolerance, cruelty and greed. Yet the more autonomy, equality and pluralism there is, Kekes contends, the greater is the scope for evil. According to Kekes, liberalism is inconsistent because the conditions liberals regard as essential for good lives actually foster the very evils liberals want to avoid and avoiding those evils depends on conditions contrary to the ones liberals favor. (edited)

**Kekes, John**. What is Conservatism?. *Philosophy*, 72(281), 351-374, Jl 97.

Conservatism is a political morality. It is political because it is a view about the political arrangements that make a society good and it is moral because it takes it to be the justification of these arrangements that they make good lives possible. The argument identifies the constitutive features of conservatism as skepticism, pluralism, traditionalism, and pessimism. These features jointly define the strongest version of conservatism and distinguish it from other versions of conservatism, as well as from other political moralities.

**Kélessidou, Anna**. Autarcie et logos conciliateur chez Zénon de Cittium. *Diotima*, 25, 90-94, 1997.

L'independance de Zenon par rapport aux besoins et aux difficultés extérieures traduit son autarcie intérieure; cette indépendance n'est pas exempte de conflits avec la nécessité historique; la satisfaction des besoins auquels la société ne peut plus répondre impose l'impératif de se déterminer par sa raison et de suivre le cours bien réglé de la vie, impératif qui sauve l'individualité et garantit l'ordre de la vie en commun. L'expérience actuelle du renversement des principes de rationalité et d'objectivité par des volontés perverties remet en vigeur trois thèses zénoniennes qui se compénètrent: que la passion est un mouvement de l'âme déraisonnable, contraire à la nature; que le convenable est l'action, qui, une fois accomplie, peut se défendre raisonnablement; que toutes les vertus se ramènent à la "phronesis" (courage, tempérance ou justice).

**Kellenberger, J**. *Kierkegaard and Nietzsche: Faith and Eternal Acceptance*. New York, Macmillan, 1997.

For Kierkegaard, in *Fear and Trembling*, a joyful acceptance of life, as it is shown to us by Abraham and other "knights of faith', flows from the certitude of faith. For Nietzsche, in *Thus Spoke Zarathustra*, it is an acceptance of the eternal recurrence of life, and is ultimately a matter of will. J. Kellenberger examines the ways in which these contrasting visions connect to other parts of Kierkegaard's and Nietzsche's thinking, especially regarding the place of religious belief and the place of morality in a fully realized life. Furthermore, he examines the presuppositions of each vision for our modern and postmodern world. (publisher, edited)

**Keller, Evelyn Fox**. C'è un organismo in questo testo?. *Iride*, 9(19), 650-666, S-D 96.

**Kelley, Andrew**. Intuition and Immediacy in Kant's *Critique of Pure Reason*. *J Phil Res*, 22, 289-298, Ap 97.

In this paper, I provide an account of what Kant means by "intuition" (*Anschauung*) in the *Critique of Pure Reason*. The issue is whether "*intuition*" should be understood in terms of 1) singularity (e.g., singular concepts, singular representation, etc.), or 2) immediacy in knowledge. By considering issues internal to the *Critique*, such as the nature of transcendental logic, the type of intuition God exhibits, and Kant's use of the term "*Anschauung*," I argue that the most fundamental way to view intuition is in terms of immediacy. More specifically, "*immediacy*" means that intuition is that through which the existence of an object, or the matter that goes into making an object, is given to the mind.

**Kelley, Donald R**. The Old Cultural History. *Hist Human Sci*, 9(3), 101-126, Ag 96.

This essay traces the tradition of German cultural history (*Kulturgeschichte*) from its founding in the 1780s in the work of Adelung, Herder and others, through its nineteenth-century stages (Gustav Klemm, G. F. Kolb, Friedrich Hellwald, Otto Henne am Rhyn et al.), intersections with modern anthropology and Darwinism and emergence as a discipline, down to the controversial work of Karl Lamprecht in the early twentieth century and its aftermath, including the "new histories" in France and the United States.

**Kelly, David F**. Karl Rahner and Genetic Engineering: The Use of Theological Principles in Moral Analysis. *Phil Theol*, 9(1-2), 177-200, 1995.

Karl Rahner's analysis of genetic manipulation is found most explicitly in two articles written in 1966 and 1968: "The Experiment with Man," and "The Problem of Genetic Manipulation." The articles have received some attention in ethical literature. The present paper analyzes Rahner's use of theological and ethical principles, comparing and contrasting the two articles. In the first article, Rahner emphasizes humankind's essential openness to self-creativity. (edited)

**Kelly, Eugene**. *Structure and Diversity: Studies in the Phenomenological Philosophy of Max Scheler*. Dordrecht, Kluwer, 1997.

This book explores some foundational concepts of Scheler's phenomenological philosophy. Seldom or inadequately explored features of his thought, such as the concept of essence, the notion of fate and milieu as foundational of the human person, and the pedagogical and historical implications of his vision of a balancing-out of world cultures are each related to the phenomenological procedures that Scheler adapted from E. Husserl. This is the first contribution to the specifically phenomenological aspects of Scheler's philosophy since E. W. Ranly's *Scheler's Phenomenology of Community* published in 1966, and the only one to develop a global reading of Scheler's thought based upon the manuscripts by Scheler that have been published since 1972. (publisher, edited)

**Kelly, L G**. A Fragment of Michael de Marbasio, Summa de modis significandi. *Vivarium*, 34(2), 268-269, N 96.

**Kelly, P J**. Introduction. *Utilitas*, 8(3), 261, N 96.

**Kelly, P J**. Taking Utilitarianism Seriously. *Utilitas*, 8(3), 341-355, N 96.

**Kelly, Susan E** and Marshall, Patricia A and Sanders, Lee M (& others). Understanding the Practice of Ethics Consultation: Results of an Ethnographic Multi-Site Study. *J Clin Ethics*, 8(2), 136-149, Sum 97.

**Kelly, Thomas A F**. *Ex Possibili et Necessario*: A Re-Examination of Aquinas's Third Way. *Thomist*, 61(1), 63-84, Ja 97.

This article discusses Aquinas's version of that argument for God's existence which takes the contingency of the world as its starting point. Aquinas's argument is restructured in the light of an analysis of the three principles which are contained in it. The conclusion of the article is that a valid argument from contingency for God's existence can be constructed on the basis of these principles, an argument which, though no longer identical with Aquinas's formulation, is immune from the criticisms usually levelled at this type of argument.

**Kemal, Salim**. *Kant's Aesthetic Theory*. New York, St Martin's Pr, 1997.

This authoritative and accessible book explains the argument and strategy of Kant's analysis of beauty. Kant's theory of knowledge deprived previous aesthetic theories of their basis and led him to a distinctive understanding of aesthetic claims, in keeping with his critical philosophy. Salim Kemal clarifies the nature of aesthetic judgements and their epistemological status and examines the scope of Kant's justification of their validity. The latter, Kemal shows, led Kant to investigate the relationship between beautiful objects, subjects and morality. The author discusses a number of issues—among them the distinction and relation between natural beauty and fine art, pure and dependent beauty, disinterestedness and universality, form and expression, beauty and morality, transcendental and empirical necessity, individual and community—and links Kant's theory and contemporary commentaries, including those by Donald Crawford, Paul Crowther, Jacques Derrida, Paul Guyer, Rudolph Makkreel, Mary McCloskey, Kenneth Rogerson and John Zammito.

**Kemal, Salim**. The Need for Plans, Projects and Reasoning about Ends: Kant and Williams. *Int J Phil Stud*, 5(2), 187-215, Je 97.

Critics deny that Kant's moral theory has the resources it needs to guide our actual actions. They reject the power of reason to establish moral rules and they propose alternative notions of person and project. This paper first develops aspects of Kant's moral theory, setting out briefly his notions of personality and the primacy of moral reason. Second it considers an alternative account that has been influential in recent Anglo-American philosophy to show that its understanding of persons and projects fails to blunt the need for moral reasoning identified by Kant.

**Kemmerling, Andreas**. "Die (sei's auch metaphorische) These vom Geist als Computer" in *Das weite Spektrum der analytischen Philosophie*, Lenzen, Wolfgang, 112-134. Hawthorne, de Gruyter, 1997.

**Kemmerling, Andreas**. Frege über den Sinn des Wortes "Ich". *Grazer Phil Stud*, 51, 1-22, 1996.

Frege über den Sinn des Wortes "Ich" Frege hat an seiner metaphysischen und semantischen Lehre der frühen 90er Jahre Veränderungen vorgenommen, um Besonderheiten des Sinns von "ich" Rechnung zu tragen. Diese Veränderungen betreffen zum einen den Status von Gedanken als objektiven Entitäten, zum andern betreffen sie die sprachlogische Behandlung von Ausdrücken, deren Sinn erst im Zusammenspiel mit dem Verwendungskontext einen selbständigen Gedankenteil ergibt. (edited)

**Kemp, Kenneth**. Punishment As Just Cause for War. *Pub Affairs Quart*, 10(4), 335-353, O 96.

**Kemp, Martin**. "Temples of the Body and Temples of the Cosmos: Vision and Visualization in the Vesalian and Copernican Revolutions" in *Picturing Knowledge*, Baigrie, Brian S (ed), 40-85. Toronto, Univ of Toronto Pr, 1996.

The revolutions in the sciences of anatomy and astronomy both involve the fundamental revisions to visual models of the seen world. However, anatomy involves pictorial representation, whereas astronomy does not, except in the field of instrumentation. In spite of the differences, the visual models used by Andreas Versalius, Nicholas Copernicus and their successors shared crucial aspects of visual rhetoric and a series of common metaphors. Versalius used new Renaissance systems of depictions to stress the reality of his enterprise, while Tycho Brahe's illustrations of instruments and Johannes Kepler's image of the orbits of the planets in terms of geometrical solids bring "the real" into astronomical representation.

**Kemp, Peter**. Anthropo-centrifugal Ethics (in Czech). *Filosof Cas*, 45(3), 469-480, 1997.

In his present paper, the *Anthropo-centrifugal Ethics*, the author discusses first of all the concept of bioethics. This concept is relatively new and the author thinks that we must distinguish between a more comprehensive "bioethics" and a more specialized "medical ethics"; he thinks also that we must arrive to a more broad concept of bioethics as embracing the whole of the living nature. But he thinks at the same time that if it is true that the bioethics must be grounded on an idea of the inviolability and of the irreplaceability of the all kinds of life, this same idea cannot be derived from the impossible *experience* to encounter with the living nature as such. He does stress, therefore, that our consideration toward nature and for the nature's own life must be understood and asserted as an extension of the idea of the human person's inviolability and irreplaceability, so that it grows into the idea of the inviobility of the whole living world. In this way ethics does have to be *anthropocentrifugal* (moving outward from respect for man). (edited)

**Kempson, Ruth** and Gabbay, Dov. Language and Proof Theory. *J Log Lang Info*, 5(3-4), 247-251, O 96.

**Kennedy, David**. The Five Communities. *Inquiry (USA)*, 16(4), 66-86, Sum 97.

**Kennedy, Kevin E**. Paul Weiss's Methods(s) and System(s). *Rev Metaph*, 50(1), 5-33, S 96.

The purpose of this article is to identify the single method employed in the apparent plurality of metaphysical systems generated by Paul Weiss. After summarizing his latest effort (*Being and Other Realities*, Open Court, 1995), a number of Weiss's characteristic moves and methods are discussed. The method of indication, contemplation and adumbration, based on Weiss's early interpretation of the propositions of perceptual judgment (*Reality*, 1938), is then introduced. This method's successive focus on these three elements of experience is shown to have lead to the gradual unfolding of Weiss's unique philosophic vision.

**Kennett, Jeanette** and Smith, Michael. Synchronic Self-Control is Always Non-Actional. *Analysis*, 57(2), 123-131, Ap 97.

Self-control can be exercised at the very moment that agents are out of control (this is synchronic self-control), or it can be exercised prior to their losing control, so preventing the loss of control from ever arising (this is diachronic self-control). Though agents may exercise diachronic self-control by performing intentional actions, we argue that they never exercise synchronic self-control by performing intentional actions. Our paper is a reply to Alfred Mele's "Kennett and Smith on Frog and Toad" which appears in the same issue of *Analysis*.

**Kennett, Stephen** and Russell, Robert and Price, Thomas. Interview with A. J. Ayer. *Kinesis*, 23(1), 4-25, Sum 96.

**Kenny, Anthony**. History of Philosophy: Historical and Rational Reconstruction. *Filosof Cas*, 44(3), 395-412, 1996.

**Kent, Beverley**. "The Interconnectedness of Peirce's Diagrammatic Thought" in *Studies in the Logic of Charles Sanders Peirce*, Houser, Nathan (ed), 445-459. Bloomington, Indiana Univ Pr, 1997.

Peirce conceived pragmatism as a philosophy in which thinking involves manipulating diagrams to examine questions. He believed his *Existential Graphs* would allow logical relationships to be displayed in an iconic way yielding solutions to problems which had defied analysis by algebraic logics. Three dimensional imagery is also involved in his natural classification of the sciences. I suggest that diagrammatic thought in Peirce's pragmaticism, *Existential Graphs*, and classification of the sciences is interrelated in such a way that each sheds light on the other; and advances in one area further advances in another.

**Kente, Maria G**. "Ethical Elements in a Democratic State: Tanzania" in *Philosophy and Democracy in Intercultural Perspective*, Kimmerle, Heinz (ed), 221-223. Amsterdam, Rodopi, 1997.

**Keon, Thomas L** and Sims, Randi L. Ethical Work Climate as a Factor in the Development of Person-Organization Fit. *J Bus Ethics*, 16(11), 1095-1105, Ag 97.

The purpose of this study was to determine if there is a relationship between the ethical climate of the organization and the development of person-organization fit. The relationship between an individual's stage of moral development and his/her perceived ethical work environment was examined using a sample of 86 working students. Results indicate that a match between individual preferences and present position proved most satisfying. Subjects expressing a match between their preferences for an ethical work climate and their present ethical work climate indicated that they were less likely to leave their positions.

**Kerckhove, Lee**. Emancipatory Social Science: Habermas on Nietzsche. *Phil Cont World*, 2(1), 19-26, Spr 95.

I argue that Habermas's critique of Nietzsche overlooks the similarities between his conception of an emancipatory social science and Nietzsche's conception of genealogy. I conclude that it is necessary to disagree with Habermas's contention that with Nietzsche the critique of modernity abandons its emancipatory content.

**Kerin, Jacinta** (& others) and Stein, Edward and Schüklenk, Udo. The Ethics of Genetic Research on Sexual Orientation. *Hastings Center Rep*, 27(4), 6-13, Jl-Ag 97.

Research into the genetic component of some complex behaviors often causes controversy, depending on the social meaning and significance of the behavior. Research into sexual orientation—simplistically referred to as "gay gene" research—is an example of research that provokes intense controversy. This research is worrisome for many reasons, including a long history of abuse against homosexuals. But there are other reasons to worry. The very motivation for seeking an "origin" of homosexuality reveals homophobia. Moreover, such research may lead to prenatal tests that claim to predict for homosexuality.

**Kerkhoff, Manfred**. La pauta del muro: re-convocaciones del pensamiento de José Echeverría. *Dialogos*, 32(69), 63-96, Ja 97.

**Kerlin, Michael J**. From Kerlin's Pizzeria to MJK Reynolds: A Socratic and Cartesian Approach to Business Ethics. *J Bus Ethics*, 16(3), 275-278, F 97.

Like politics, all ethics is local. The key to understanding the most difficult ethical issues is in the relationships of neighbors. Consequently, in studying and teaching business ethics, we rightly begin with the microsetting of the neighborhood and work outward and upward in complexity and challenge. The author has found the operations of a small, imaginary pizzeria on his real street an ideal (in both senses) entry to all the issues of hiring, liability, environment and so on. The method of proceeding is Socratic inasmuch as it proceeds by conversation and takes for granted an elemental understanding on the part of all conversants. It is Cartesian inasmuch as it moves carefully from the simple situations to the most intricate organizational puzzles without ever forgetting the insights garnered at the outset.

**Kerlin, Michael J**. Peter French, Corporate Ethics and The Wizard of Oz. *J Bus Ethics*, 16(12-13), 1431-1438, S 97.

For more than two decades, Peter French has been arguing in books, articles and symposia that corporations are genuine actors in the moral universe. Like adult human beings, they can and should take moral responsibility for their actions and be held accountable by the other actors in this universe. I have always argued with my students that the position is both metaphysically incorrect and practically harmful. Now (1995) French has redeveloped his position through 380 pages in *Corporate Ethics*. In the essay, I explore *Corporate Ethics* both on the metaphysical and the practical level. (edited)

**Kernisky, Debra A**. Proactive Crisis Management and Ethical Discourse: Dow Chemical's Issues Management Bulletins 1979-1990. *J Bus Ethics*, 16(8), 843-853, Je 97.

This study employed a Discourse Ethicality Survey instrument to analyze the legitimacy and ethicality of one of Dow Chemical's externally focused, rhetorical, crisis management strategies. A stratified random sample of the issues management bulletin *The Point Is...*, published over a ten year period, was evaluated. The results showed that at the height of external criticism from the media and public interest groups in the early 80's, Dow's response was characterized as antagonistic and focused on technological arguments. By the late 1980's, the bulletins range of issues had broadened considerably, were perceived as less antagonistic in tone and focused more on issues and projects that may be described as socially conscious. (edited)

**Kerr, Andrew J**. Ethical Status of the Ecosystem in Whitehead's Philosophy. *Process Stud*, 24, 76-89, 1995.

The paper attempts to explain the intuition that conscious experience of the biotic community evokes good character. The paper seeks to describe a complementarity between the metaphysics of Alfred North Whitehead, especially his notion of living societies, and ecological science. This complementarity implies that ecological processes reveal moral norms, allowing for a normative redescription of these ecological processes. Thus, ecological 'law' is likewise moral 'law'.

**Kerr, Donna H** and Buchmann, Margret. On Avoiding Domination in Philosophical Counseling. *J Chin Phil*, 23(3), 341-351, S 96.

**Kerr-Lawson, Angus**. "Peirce's Pre-Logistic Account of Mathematics" in *Studies in the Logic of Charles Sanders Peirce*, Houser, Nathan (ed), 77-84. Bloomington, Indiana Univ Pr, 1997.

An analogy exists between Charles Peirce's philosophy of mathematics and the position held by many practicing mathematicians. This shared view finds few difficulties with the epistemology of mathematics. It differs also with the views of contemporary philosophers of mathematics, who insist that if mathematical entities are to be allowed, they must be given the fullest existential status. Peirce with his possibilities and mathematicians with their structures, admit a level of existence secondary to that of actual things. The paper tries to bring out the close bond between allowing a second level of existence and a relaxed attitude towards epistemological questions.

Kerr-Lawson, Angus 720 AUTHOR INDEX

**Kerr-Lawson, Angus**. Truth and Idiomatic Truth in Santayana. *Trans Peirce Soc*, 33(1), 91-111, Wint 97.

Sprigge notes (in *Santayana*, Routledge 1995) that when Santayana deals with truths which involve changing events, he alters his terminology somewhat. I argue that an appeal to *The Realm of Matter* clarifies what Santayana has in mind. Also, in Sprigge's eyes, the absence of the important notion of a proposition represents a deficiency in the system. I seek to clarify this question by turning to Santayana's notion of "idiomatic" truth; whereas truths describe the configuration of existing things, idiomatic truths (logical or mathematical) describe relations within the realm of essence.

**Kershnar, Stephen**. George Sher's Theory of Deserved Punishment, and the Victimized Wrongdoer. *Soc Theor Pract*, 23(1), 75-91, Spr 97.

George Sher's theory of deserved punishment is an attempt to link punishment to distributive justice. His theory builds on the notion that punishment is deserved insofar as it removes the unfair advantage that the wrongdoer gains through her act. I shall argue that Sher's theory fails because it does not account for ways besides state punishment in which the unfair advantage can be offset. When the theory is modified so as to account for these other ways, it fails to meet our intuitions.

**Kerstein, Samuel**. Justifying Kant's Principles of Justice. *Dialogue (Canada)*, 36(2), 401-407, Spr 97.

A critical discussion of Allen Rosen's *Kant's Theory of Justice*, this paper focuses on Rosen's claim that, with the help of the *Categorical Imperative*, Kant justifies the ideals of civil and political liberty. According to the former ideal, each individual has the right to pursue her own happiness, provided that she does not fraudulently or violently interfere with the freedom of others to pursue theirs; according to the latter, all legislative authority ought to lie in the united will of the people. The paper argues that, though Rosen's efforts are instructive, he fails to show that Kant vindicates these ideals.

**Kerszberg, Pierre**. *Critique and Totality.* Albany, SUNY Pr, 1997.

This book concerns the essential role that the issue of cosmology plays both in Kant's thought and those (especially in continental thought, Husserl and Heidegger) that Kant has affected. Both Husserl and Heidegger, still the most important thinkers in twentieth-century continental thought, briefly (but unsystematically) explored these topics for which now, thanks to the author, we have the details. The author's point is that Kant's project remains both more complicated and more fertile than either of these thinkers grasped, to the detriment of their own general philosophical positions. (publisher, edited)

**Kerszberg, Pierre**. Feeling and Coercion: Kant and the Deduction of Right. *Protosoz*, 8/9, 223-236, 1996.

Even though the concept of right is not empirical, Kant does not deduce right in a transcendental manner. If, in conformity with the rational principles of transcendental philosophy, we try to understand why this is so, the answer may be found in an analogy with aesthetic reflection. Indeed, aesthetic reflection might contain the transcendental ground of violence in civil society.

**Ketchum, Richard J**. On the Impossibility of Epistemology. *Phil Stud*, 88(1), 29-36, O 97.

Robert Almeder has attributed to me an argument which is reminiscent of the problem of the criterion but which is not mine. I first explain why I think the argument he attributes to me fails. I then clarify my argument for the conclusion that there is (can be) no correct analysis of justification. Any argument which uses a purported analysis of justification to support the conclusion that one is justified in believing it begs the question. I conclude that there is a relevant counter-factual conditional not supported by the analysis and thus, that the purported analysis is not an analysis.

**Kevorkian, Jack**. *Prescription: Medicine.* Amherst, Prometheus, 1995.

Kevorkian considers the loss of life a negative under all circumstances; he explains why the use of his suicide machine lightens the moral burden on doctors and emphasizes the freedom of the individual. He asserts that such procedures represent the first step toward a positive ethical stance by setting the stage for a new specialty, "obitiatry," which would offer concrete medical options under strictly controlled conditions, thereby allowing individuals to determine the real value of personal death. He concludes with reflections on how obitiatry can help medical science explore the mysteries of life and death.

**Keyes, C Don**. Crisis of Brain and Self. *Zygon*, 31(4), 583-595, D 96.

Neuroscientific evidence requires a monistic understanding of brain/mind. Truly appropriating what this means confronts us with the vulnerability of the human condition. Camus's absurd and Tillich's despair are extreme expressions of a similar confrontation. This crisis demands a type of courage that is consistent with scientific truth and does not undermine the spiritual dimension of life. That dimension is not a separate substance but the process by which brain/mind meaningfully wrestles with its crisis through aesthetic symbols, religious faith and ethical affirmation. The validity of these activities does not depend upon human autonomy but instead upon the fact that they exist. Furthermore, they constitute the self, which Dennett calls a "center of narrative gravity."

**Keyt, David**. Aristotle and the Ancient Roots of Anarchism. *Topoi*, 15(1), 129-142, Mr 96.

**Keyt, David**. Fred Miller on Aristotle's Political Naturalism. *Ancient Phil*, 16(2), 425-430, Fall 96.

**Keyton, Joann** and Rhodes, Steven C. Sexual Harassment: A Matter of Individual Ethics, Legal Definitions, or Organizational Policy?. *J Bus Ethics*, 16(2), 129-146, F 97.

Although interest in business ethics has rapidly increased, little attention has been drawn to the relationship between ethics and sexual harassment. While most companies have addressed the problem of sexual harassment at the organizational level with corporate codes of ethics or sexual harassment policies, no research has examined the ethical ideology of individual employees. This study investigates the relationship between the ethical ideology of individual employees and their ability to identify social-sexual behaviors in superior-subordinate interactions. The results indicate that ethical ideology does have an effect on employees' ability to identify verbal sexually harassing behaviors. This effect, however, is not demonstrated on nonverbal sexually harassing behaviors.

**Khalil, Elias L**. Economics, Biology, and Naturalism: Three Problems Concerning the Question of Individuality. *Biol Phil*, 12(2), 185-206, Ap 97.

The paper examines the ramifications of naturalism with regard to the question of individuality in economics and biology. Economic theory has to deal with whether households, firms, and states are individuals or are mere entities such as clubs, networks, and coalitions. Biological theory has to deal with the same question with regard to cells, organisms, family packs, and colonies. To wit, the question of individuality in both disciplines involves three separate problems: the metaphysical, phenomenist, and ontological. The metaphysical problem is concerned with purposeful action. The phenomenist problem is interested in the substantiality of essences. The ontological problem is related to the issue of reductionism. The paper finds that theoretical differences run along the naturalist/antinaturalist divide rather than along disciplinary specialization. Also, the paper finds that it is not inconsistent for the same theorist to be naturalist with regard to one problem and antinaturalist with respect to the other two problems. (edited)

**Khoruzhii, Sergei Sergeevich**. The Idea of Total-Unity from Heraclitus to Losev. *Russian Stud Phil*, 35(1), 32-69, Sum 96.

The first systematic reconstruction of the history of the concept "Total-Unity" is presented. Its genesis is characterized as the joining (visible already in Heraclitus) of two ideas of unity, the unity of all things (that of the Cosmos) and the inner structural unity (that of the Logos). Christianity states Mystical Church as a new, personalistic archetype for Total-Unity, instead of Platonic *cosmos noetos*. Conflict between the Platonic and Christian ideas of Total-Unity is traced through the medieval and Renaissance philosophy, the German idealism and the Russian metaphysics, for which the classification of all its Total-Unity systems by their historic roots is given.

**Khoruzhii, Sergei Sergeevich**. Transformations of the Slavophile Idea in the Twentieth Century. *Russian Stud Phil*, 34(2), 7-25, Fall 95.

Three influential currents in Russian thought of this century, having Slavophile roots, are analysed. The first is the idea advocated before the revolution by Vyacheslav Ivanov and Tadeusz Zielinski who stated that Russia should create the Slavonic Renaissance based, like the Italian one, on the Greek heritage. The second is the well-known Eurasian doctrine popular in Russian diaspora during the twenties. Finally, the third is the idea of Neopatristic Synthesis developed by Father George Florovsky and stressing the continuing formative and creative role of the Patristic Tradition for Russian culture. Prospects of these ideas and their mutual links are discussed.

**Khushf, George**. Why Bioethics Needs the Philosophy of Medicine: Some Implications of Reflection on Concepts of Health and Disease. *Theor Med*, 18(1-2), 145-163, Mr-Je 97.

Germund Hesslow has argued that concepts of health and disease serve no important scientific, clinical, or ethical function. However, this conclusion depends upon the particular concept of disease he espouses; namely, on Boorse's functional notion. The fact/value split embodied in the functional notion of disease leads to a sharp split between the "science" of medicine and bioethics, making the philosophy of medicine irrelevant for both. By placing this disease concept in the broader context of medical history, I shall show self-contradictory notion. By making explicit the value desiderate of medical nosologies, a reconfiguration of the relation between medicine, bioethics, and the philosophy of medicine is initiated. This, in turn, will involve a recovery of the caring dimensions of medicine, and thus a more humane practice.

**Kiang, Nelson Yuan-sheng**. How Are Scientific Corrections Made?. *Sci Eng Ethics*, 1(4), 347-356, O 95.

This paper provides examples drawn from the author's experience that support the conclusion that errors and deceptions in archival science are often not easily or quickly corrected. The difficulty in correcting errors and deceptions needs wider recognition if it is to be overcome. In addition, the paper discusses how subtle abuses introduce errors into the archival literature.

**Kiecker, P L** and Nelson, J E. Marketing Research Interviewers and Their Perceived Necessity of Moral Compromise. *J Bus Ethics*, 15(10), 1107-1117, O 96.

Marketing research interviewers often feel that they must compromise their own moral principles while executing work-related activities. This finding is based on analysis of data obtained from three focus group interviews and a mail survey of 173 telephone survey interviewers. Data from the mail survey were used to construct scales measuring interviewers' perceived necessity of moral compromise, moral character, and job satisfaction. The three scales then were used in a hierarchical regression analysis to predict incidences of interviewers' self-reported prescribed behaviors on the job, the latter being an index of behaviors known by interviewers to be "wrong." Results support all hypothesized relationships.

**Kiefer, Claus**. Der Zeitbegriff in der Quantengravitation. *Phil Natur*, 27(1), 43-65, 1990.

This article starts with a brief history of the physical concept of time from Newton to Einstein. The main part is devoted to a detailed conceptual discussion of canonical quantum gravity, one of the most promising attempts to reconcile quantum theory with the theory of general relativity. The fundamental equations in this approach are timeless—they don't contain any time parameter. It is then shown how the usual notion of time is recovered from these timeless equations as an approximate concept.

AUTHOR INDEX 721 Kim, Jaegwon

**Kiel, Albrecht**. Carl Schmitt und die Philosophie. *Prima Philosophia*, 10(2), 183-209, 1997.

Kant's critique of the Christian belief in divine revelation was nondenominational, as Hegel's was initially; only later on Hegel's sharp condemnation of Catholicism did contribute to the establishment of a Protestant political theology in the 19th century. This background needs to be borne in mind when one comes to evaluate the "katholische Verschärfung" (Catholic intensification) inherent in Carl Schmitt's political theology. At first it is dominated by a dualistic theory that has much in common with Nietzsche. The dualism is applied to anthropology, social doctrine, and the transcendental powers of good (Christ) and evil (Antichrist). This stems from a rationalistic approach which constitutes an inseparable mixture of the secular and the theological. (edited)

**Kielbasa, Jan**. Theory of Participation and Louis Lavelle's Philosophy (in Polish). *Kwartalnik Filozof*, 23(1), 97-127, 1995.

**Kielkopf, Charles F**. *A Kantian Condemnation of Atheistic Despair: A Declaration of Dependence*. New York, Lang, 1997.

William James's pattern of pragmatic argument is revised to defend contra-causal free will in the strong form of Kantian moral autonomy, which enables people to choose what they ought regardless of any contrary inclinations. With moral autonomy we have a moral theory under which we revised Kant's moral arguments into genuine moral arguments to give a moral condemnation of maxims to the effect: I will allow my reason to convince me that there can be no moral God who brings it about that it is as it ought to be with each human being. (publisher)

**Kielkopf, Charles F**. Masturbation: A Kantian Condemnation. *Philosophia (Israel)*, 25(1-4), 223-246, Ap 97.

It is argued that a typical male masturbator's maxim is inconsistent in a Kantian moral theory. The typical male masturbator's maxim is formulated as: With the aid of imagination and self-stimulation I may seek any sexual gratification to which I am inclined. An interpretation of Kant's moral theory is developed in which we have the obligatory end of being rule restricted satisfiers of sexual inclinations.

**Kienzler, Wolfgang** (ed) and Gabriel, Gottfried (ed) and Mendelsohn, Richard L (ed & trans). Diary: Written by Professor Dr. Gottlob *Frege in the Time from 10 March to 9. April 1924*. *Inquiry*, 39(3-4), 303-342, D 96.

**Kieran, Matthew**. A Divine Intimation: Appreciating Natural Beauty. *J Value Inq*, 31(1), 77-95, Mr 97.

Our appreciation of natural beauty is often thought to be subjective or dependent upon religious understanding. I critically examine recent arguments, in particular those offered by Terry Diffey and Allen Carlson, which defend a via media between these two extreme possibilities. Contrary to these positions I argue 1) that our aesthetic appreciation of nature is, necessarily, ineliminability subjective. 2) Appreciation of natural beauty is cognitively imbued. 3) Thus our appreciation of natural landscapes is typically relative. Nonetheless, a distinctive kind of aesthetic appreciation of nature is both objective and intimates a religious perspective upon the world.

**Kieran, Matthew**. Aesthetic Value: Beauty, Ugliness and Incoherence. *Philosophy*, 72. (281), 383-399, Jl 97.

Standardly, from Kant to Beardsley and Walton, an object is held to possess aesthetic value if it affords us a certain kind of pleasure. Yet, paradoxically, we apparently delight in unpleasant, ugly and incoherent artworks. Cognitivist retorts or emphasizing relational values won't do. Rather we should recognize that the brutal, ugly or incoherent can give rise to aesthetic pleasure. This saves the standard account but shows that aesthetic principles of evaluation derived from the paradigmatic case of beauty are flawed. The paper culminates with a discussion of the moral character of an aesthetic delight in the brutal, ugly and incoherent.

**Kieran, Matthew**. Art, Imagination, and the Cultivation of Morals. *J Aes Art Crit*, 54(4), 337-351, Fall 96.

Traditional aesthetics holds that artistic and moral value are unrelated. Why? We value artworks, like de Sade's *Juliette*, which are immoral and many morally sound works possess little artistic value. However, through an account of our imaginative engagement with artworks and the characters or scenes represented, I argue for a sophisticated form of ethicism which holds that artistic value and ethical value are intimately linked. Ethicism explains, as aestheticism cannot, why art is significant, in a way mere pleasures are not, why art should be 'true to life' and why our evaluation of works such as Pound's *Canto's* are problematic.

**Kieseppä, I A**. Akaike Information Criterion, Curve-Fitting, and the Philosophical Problem of Simplicity. *Brit J Phil Sci*, 48(1), 21-48, Mr 97.

The philosophical significance of the procedure of applying *Akaike information criterion* (AIC) to curve-fitting problems is evaluated. The theoretical justification for using AIC (the so-called Akaike's theorem) is presented in a rigorous way, and its range of validity is assessed by presenting both instances in which it is valid and counterexamples in which it is invalid. The philosophical relevance of the justification that this result gives for making one particular choice between simple and complicated hypothesis is emphasized. In addition, recent claims that the methods based on Akaike's theorem are relevant to other philosophical problems associated with the notion of simplicity are presented and evaluated.

**Kieve, Ronald A**. A Plaything in Their Hands: American Exceptionalism and the Failure of Socialism—A Reassessment. *Nature Soc Thought*, 9(1), 31-62, 1996.

**Kiikeri, Mika**. "On the Logical Structure of Learning Models" in *Knowledge and Inquiry: Essays on Jaakko Hintikka's Epistemology and Philosophy of Science*, Sintonen, Matti (ed), 287-307. Amsterdam, Rodopi, 1997.

This paper studies methodological issues in various learning models. The framework we adopt is the interrogative model of inquiry (I-model, for short), originally proposed and developed by Jaakko Hintikka. We shall first offer a survey of the structure of various contemporary learning models as well as discuss some methodological issues. Subsequently, the fundamentals of the I-model are presented and the interrogative notion of a learning process is introduced. Finally, we shall discuss some methodological problems which are prevalent in this context. For instance, it is interesting to study the problem of induction within this framework and some of the most usual methodological restrictions of learning models could be critically assessed.

**Kijima, Masaaki**. The Generalized Harmonic Mean and a Portfolio Problem with Dependent Assets. *Theor Decis*, 43(1), 71-87, Jl 97.

McEntire (1984) proved that, for a portfolio problem with independent assets, the generalized harmonic mean plays the role of a risk-free threshold. Based upon this property, he developed a criterion for including or excluding assets in an optimal portfolio and he proved an ordering theorem showing that an optimal portfolio always consists of positive amounts of the assets with the largest mean values. Also, some commonly used utility functions were shown to satisfy the property that the dominance of an asset over another is unaffected by the addition of other assets. In this paper we extend these results to the case where assets are dependent.

**Killoran, John B**. False and Genuine Knowledge: A Philosophical Look at the Peasant of the Garonne. *Maritain Stud*, 8, 85-100, 1992.

**Kilner, John F** (ed) and Miller, Arlene B (ed) and Pellegrino, Edmund D (ed). *Dignity and Dying: A Christian Appraisal*. Grand Rapids, Eerdmans, 1996.

The authors of the present volume engage matters of dignity and dying from a variety of perspectives. The three authors of the introduction root the book in the experience of dying itself. In Part I, the authors give careful attention to topics that provide guiding vision for approaches to dignity and dying: autonomy, death, suffering, and faithfulness. Four of the most pressing end-of-life challenges—forgoing treatment, medical futility, definition of death, and assisted-suicide/euthanasia—are then examined in some detail. Part III is devoted to investigations of key settings where people have wrestled with these challenges: i.e., Nazi Germany, Oregon (USA), North American legal systems, and The Netherlands. The book concludes, then, with discussions of five potentially constructive alternatives to the premature ending of life: hospice care, long-term care, wise advocacy, parish nursing and congregational ministry.(publisher, edited)

**Kilpi, Jukka**. Gearing Up, Crashing Loud: Should We Punish High-Flyers for Insolvency?. *J Bus Ethics*, 15(12), 1343-1354, D 96.

This paper argues that the hallmarks of high-flying provide neither retributive nor utilitarian grounds for punishing business bankrupts by limiting their access to discharge. Furthermore, it is argued that, from the point of view of distributive justice, wealth appropriated through leverage is ethically no worse than prosperity gained by hard work and parsimony—not even if the gearing eventually leads to insolvency.(edited)

**Kim, Hong-Gee**. A Psychologically Plausible Logical Model of Conceptualization. *Mind Mach*, 7(2), 249-267, My 97.

This paper discusses how we understand and use a concept or the meaning of a general term to identify objects falling under the term. There are two distinct approaches to research on the problems of concepts and meaning the psychological approach and the formal (or logical) approach. My major concern is to consider the possibility of reconciling these two different approaches, and for this I propose to build a psychologically plausible formal system of conceptualization. That is, I will develop a theory-based account of concepts and propose an explanation of how an agent activates a *perspective* (which consists of theories) in response to a situation in which reasoning using a concept is called for. Theories are represented as sets of facts and rules, both strict and defeasible. Each theory is organized in a coherent perspective which stands for an agent's mental state or an agent's model of another agent's perspective. Perspectives are organized into hierarchies and the theory for a concept in one perspective may defeat the theory for the same concept in another perspective. Which perspective is superior is context-dependent.

**Kim, Jaegwon**. "Dretske's Qualia Externalism" in *Perception*, Villanueva, Enrique (ed), 159-165. Atascadero, Ridgeview, 1996.

This paper discusses Fred Dretske's externalist account of sensory qualia in his "Phenomenal Externalism", *Philosophical Issues* 7 (1996).

**Kim, Jaegwon**. "Mental Causation: What? Me Worry?" in *Contents*, Villanueva, Enrique (ed), 123-151. Atascadero, Ridgeview, 1995.

The problem of mental causation has returned as a central issue in philosophy of mind. This paper discusses one popular deflationary reaction to this development: There is no need to worry about mental causation because the reasoning that leads to worries about mental causation can be generalized to show that there cannot be causation in chemistry, biology, geology, or any other science except basic microphysics. I show what's right and what's wrong about this "generalization argument" and along the way, discuss some issues concerning the "levels" or "orders" of properties and their relevance to the problem of macrocausation.

**Kim, Jaegwon**. Does the Problem of Mental Causation Generalize?. *Proc Aris Soc*, 97, 281-297, 1997.

One frequently heard response to the problem of mental causation is the observation that the problem generalized to all "higher-level" properties and that if mental causation is problematic, the same should hold for chemical, biological and geological and all other type of causation in the special sciences. Some take this to show the emptiness and triviality of the problem while others take this to show that we need an adequate account of causation at these higher levels in relation to causal processes at the basic physical level. The present paper discusses the extent to which the mental causation problem is generalizable.

**Kimbrough, Scott**. Belief Content and Compositionality. *SW Phil Rev*, 13(1), 175-185, Ja 97.

**Kimmerle, Heinz**. "The Philosophical Text in the African Oral Tradition" in *Philosophy and Democracy in Intercultural Perspective,* Kimmerle, Heinz (ed), 43-56. Amsterdam, Rodopi, 1997.

**Kimmerle, Heinz**. *Das Multiversum der Kulturen*. Amsterdam, Rodopi, 1996.

The editor of the volume shows in his 'Prolegomena' how in contemporary thought the intercultural dimension of philosophy is coming up. The coauthors examine how with certain authors of Western philosophy the openness for the philosophies of other cultures is prepared. In this respect D. Tiemersma is dealing with Merleau-Ponty, J. Hoogland with Habermas, A.W. Prins with Heidegger and H. Oosterling with Foucault, Barthes, Lyotard and Derrida. J. Van den Oord discusses the universality of human rights especially for women and F. Uyanne confronts Western and African models of democracy. C. Jacobs describes the intercultural dialogues in the field of visual art and finally E. de Schipper questions this whole approach to intercultural philosophy.

**Kimmerle, Heinz** (ed) and Wimmer, Franz M (ed). *Philosophy and Democracy in Intercultural Perspective*. Amsterdam, Rodopi, 1997.

**Kimsma, Gerrit K** and Quill, Timothy E. End-of-Life Care in the Netherlands and the United States: A Comparison of Values, Justifications, and Practices. *Cambridge Quart Healthcare Ethics*, 6(2), 189-204, Spr 97.

**Kimsma, Gerrit K** and Van Leeuwen, Evert. Philosophy of Medical Practice: A Discursive Approach. *Theor Med*, 18(1-2), 99-112, Mr-Je 97.

Medical practice is a discursive practice which is highly influenced by other discursive practices like science, law and economics. Philosophical analysis of those influences is needed to discern their effect on the goals of medicine and on the way in which the self-image of man may be changed. The nature of medical practice and discourse itself makes it necessary to include different philosophical disciplines, like philosophy of science, of law, ethics and epistemology. Possible scenario's of euthanasia and the human genome project in the USA and Europe are used to exemplify how philosophy of medicine can contribute to a realistic understanding of the problems which are related to the goals of medicine and health care.(edited)

**Kin'ya, Nishi**. "Form Should Not Be Tautological": Hegel and Adorno on Form (in Japanese). *Bigaku*, 47(1), 25-36, Sum 96.

This essay attempts to explore the structural role of "antitautology" in T.W. Adorno's form conception through examining his transformation of Hegelian form-content relation. First, I analyse how Hegel's logic bears on Adorno's self-reflective critique. Adorno assimilates Hegel's "movement against immediacy" as his critical method. This movement characterizes their logical structures and it enabled Hegel to elaborate the form-content relation. However, Hegel's formulation could never be sufficient for Adorno. I secondly thematize in which point the latter's formulation of form differs from that of the former. (edited)

**Kindhäuser, Urs**. Zur Rechtfertigung von Pflicht- und Obliegenheits-verletzungen im Strafrecht. *Jahr Recht Ethik*, 2, 339-352, 1994.

Criminal law behavioral norms provide the obligatory bases for actions. The addressee of a norm should avoid prohibited conduct to the extent of his ability. If at the time he is required to choose an alternative to violating the criminal law he is unable to do so, then his conduct generally may not be imputed to him as a violation of duty. The criminal law, however, does make an exception to this principle when the individual is responsible for being unable to act because he did not exercise the care expected of him regarding his ability to follow the norm (= negligence). This aspect of responsibility can be referred to as the failure to fulfill a condition precedent for obeying a norm as opposed to a violation of the norm itself. (edited)

**Kindsvatter, Richard** and Hoover, Randy L. *Democratic Discipline: Foundation and Practice*. Englewood Cliffs, Prentice Hall, 1997.

We have conceived this book as a primary text for courses on classroom management and discipline as well as a supplemental text for either general methods classes and certain foundations classes related to examining democratic perspectives on schooling and teaching. We also believe that elements of this text can be used effectively in a variety of graduate-level professional development courses where the focus is school reform, critical reflectivity, curriculum development, or instructional development. (publisher, edited)

**King, David**. Is the Human Mind a Turing Machine?. *Synthese*, 108(3), 379-389, S 96.

In this paper I discuss the topics of mechanism and algorithmicity. I emphasise that a characterisation of algorithmicity such as the Turing machine is iterative; and I argue that if the human mind can solve problems that no Turing machine can, the mind must depend on some noniterative principle—in fact, Cantor's second principle of generation, a principle of the actual infinite rather than the potential infinite of Turing machines. But as there has been theorisation that all physical systems can be represented by Turing machines, I investigate claims that seem to contradict this: specifically, claims that there are noncomputable phenomena. One conclusion I reach is that if it is believed that the human mind is more than a Turing machine, a belief in a kind of Cartesian dualist gulf between the mental and the physical is concomitant.

**King, G Heath** and Kircher, Timothy (ed). *Existence, Thought, Style: Perspectives of a Primary Relation: Portrayed through the Work of Soren Kierkegaard*. Milwaukee, Marquette Univ Pr, 1996.

The book brings forth and elaborates a new hermeneutic. King uncovers the first clues of this way of understanding and evaluating texts and their authors in Kierkegaard's writings, and he develops a new range of criteria for this

undertaking. The reader encounters a method of interpretation that brings the widest degree of authorial qualities into unified view: style, thought and the author's own relation to existence. (publisher, edited)

**King, James R**. *Remaking the World: Modeling in Human Experience*. Champaign, Univ of Illinois Pr, 1996.

In *Remaking the World*, James Roy King weaves together strands of thought creating a tapestry that mirrors John Dewey's pragmatism of sufficiencies. King uses the concept of activity sets—relatively stable combinations of activities that characterize every large-scale human enterprise—to explain how modelling can help people make sense of the world around them. The author also looks at working with small sizes and dealing with a variety of technical details, problems related to collecting and displaying models, and their commercial and aesthetic aspects. Appendixes give information about manufacturers of kits and modelling organizations. (publisher,edited)

**King, Jeffrey C**. Structured Propositions and Sentence Structure. *J Phil Log*, 25(5), 495-521, O 96.

It is argued that taken together, two widely held claims I) sentences express structured propositions whose structures are functions of the structures of sentences expressing them; and II) sentences have underlying structures that are the input to semantic interpretation) suggest a simple, plausible theory of propositional structure. According to this theory, the structures of propositions are the same as the structures of the syntactic inputs to semantics they are expressed by. The theory is defended against a variety of objections.

**King, Jonathan B**. An Exercise in Moral Philosophy: Seeking to Understand "Nobody". *Teach Bus Ethics*, 1(1), 63-91, 1997.

The late Hannah Arendt proposed that many, perhaps most monstrous deeds are not committed by moral monsters but by individuals who do not "think." However, understanding the significance of "activity of thinking as such" requires a moral philosophy that transcends rational actor assumptions and instrumental reason centering, instead, on the conditions of self-knowledge. The ubiquitous and often lethal phenomenon of information distortions provides a vehicle for expanding our understandings of individual moral response-abilities in our modern times.

**King, Peter** and Jacobi, Klaus and Strub, Christian. From *intellectus verus/falsus* to the *dictum propositionis*: The Semantics of Peter Abelard and his Circle. *Vivarium*, 34(1), 15-40, My 96.

**King, Roger**. "Critical Reflections on Biocentric Environmental Ethics: Is It an Alternative to Anthropocentrism?" in *Philosophy and Geography I: Space, Place, and Environmental Ethics*, Light, Andrew (ed), 209-230. Lanham, Rowman & Littlefield, 1997.

This article challenges the view that biocentrism is an adequate alternative to anthropocentric ethics. It also rejects the adequacy of anthropocentric views of nature. Anthropocentrism has supported cultural neglect of the environment. But biocentrism's efforts to redress this leave no defensible space for human aspirations and the domesticated landscape. Biocentrism becomes an untenable "view from nowhere." A third alternative is sketched which draw on ecofeminist discussions of narrative and relationship. The goal is to make intellectual space in environmental ethics for both the wild and the domesticated and to situate human reflections on nature's value.

**Kingwell, Mark**. "*Phronesis* and Political Dialogue" in *Political Dialogue: Theories and Practices,* Esquith, Stephen L (ed), 167-182. Amsterdam, Rodopi, 1996.

Objections to political dialogue, especially in forms influenced by Habermas's discourse ethics, often turn on a charge of practical emptiness: no meaningful results are generated by the transcendental regulations of the ideal speech situation. The solution to this difficulty is just as often thought to be some form of the Aristotelian virtue of *phronesis*, or practical wisdom. The hope is that *phronesis* will bridge the gap between formalistic justification and political application. In this paper I assess this charge against Habermas, his attempted refutation and the prospects that exist for recovering *phronesis* in political dialogue.

**Kinlaw, Kathleen** and Hanford, Russell and DeHaan, Robert. Promoting Ethical Reasoning, Affect and Behaviour Among High School Students: An Evaluation of Three Teaching Strategies. *J Moral Educ*, 26(1), 5-20, Mr 97.

Ethics education should aim to promote students' maturity across a broad spectrum of moral functioning, including moral reasoning, moral affect and moral behaviour. To identify the most effective strategy for promoting the comprehensive moral maturity of high school students, we enrolled students in one of four groups: an introductory ethics class, a blended economics-ethics class, a role-model ethics class taught by graduate students and a nonethics comparison class. Pretest and post-test instruments measured the ways students a) reason, b) feel and c) act with regard to ethical-normative issues. The results indicated that the approaches to teaching ethics varied considerably in terms of their ability to promote significant positive changes in students' moral reasoning, empathy and behaviour.

**Kipnis, Kenneth**. Confessions of an Expert Ethics Witness. *J Med Phil*, 22(4), 325-343, Ag 97.

The aim of this essay is to describe and reflect upon the concrete particulars of one academician's work as an expert ethics witness. The commentary on my practices and the narrative descriptions of three cases are offered as evidence for the thesis that it is possible to act honorably within a role that some have considered to be inherently illicit. Practical measures are described for avoiding some of the best known pitfalls. The discussion concludes with a listing of the distinctive competencies and understandings that are useful in serving as an expert ethics witness.

**Kirby, John T**. A Classicist's Approach to Rhetoric in Plato. *Phil Rhet*, 30(2), 190-202, 1997.

This article is written most especially for the student of rhetoric who has not studied Plato or ancient philosophy—who perhaps does not know Greek—but who wishes to investigate the Platonic corpus for material on ancient rhetorical theory or practice. In fact, however, the article could serve as a summary of basic topics in Plato studies. It consists of a ten-point checklist that includes such items as The Socratic Question, The Chronology of the Dialogues, Socratic (and Platonic) Irony, Specifics of Platonic Philosophy, The Development of Plato's Thought, Platonic vs. Socratic Doctrines, The Greek Language and Modern Scholarship.

**Kircher, Timothy** (ed) and King, G Heath. *Existence, Thought, Style: Perspectives of a Primary Relation: Portrayed through the Work of Soren Kierkegaard*. Milwaukee, Marquette Univ Pr, 1996.

The book brings forth and elaborates a new hermeneutic. King uncovers the first clues of this way of understanding and evaluating texts and their authors in Kierkegaard's writings, and he develops a new range of criteria for this undertaking. The reader encounters a method of interpretation that brings the widest degree of authorial qualities into unified view: style, thought and the author's own relation to existence. (publisher, edited)

**Kirchhoff, Evan** and Matheson, Carl. Chaos and Literature. *Phil Lit*, 21(1), 28-45, Ap 97.

Many literary theorists have made bold claims for the supposed "new paradigm" of chaos theory. Katherine Hayles and other theorists allege variously that: i) chaos mathematics and poststructuralist literary theory are significantly similar; ii) chaos theory and contemporary literary criticism are actually two formulations of the same concept; and iii) the science of chaos can be a useful tool for the study of literature. We argue that these claims are overblown, unwarranted, or empirically false.

**Kirk, Robert**. How Physicalists Can Avoid Reductionism. *Synthese*, 108(2), 157-170, Ag 96.

Kim maintains that "a physicalist has only two genuine options, eliminativism and reductionism". But physicalists can reject both by using the *Strict Implication* thesis (SI). Discussing his arguments will help to show what useful work SI can do. 1) His discussion of anomalous monism depends on an unexamined assumption to the effect that SI is false. 2) His conclusion on multiple realizability is much stronger than his reasoning warrants. 3) In discussing supervenience, he is wrong to assume that the only approach to explaining why "physical truths determine all the truths" must be via psychophysical laws. 4) His general argument rests on a mistaken assumption that the only alternative to psychophysical identity theses is to accept "supervenient causal relations".

**Kirkland, Anna** and Tong, Rosemarie. Working within Contradiction: The Possibility of Feminist Cosmetic Surgery. *J Clin Ethics*, 7(2), 151-159, Sum 96.

**Kirsch, Guy**. "Das Kalkül der Moral" in *Ökonomie und Moral: Beiträge zur Theorie ökonomischer Rationalität*, Lohmann, Karl Reinhard (ed), 49-64. München, Oldenbourg, 1997.

**Kirscher, Gilbert**. The Figures of Subjectivity in Éric Weil's *Logique de la philosophie* (in French). *Arch Phil*, 59(4), 607-628, O-D 96.

Contrary to any ontology of the subject or the self, Eric Weil's *Logique de la Philosophie* (Paris, 1950) conceives a plurality of possible discourses, a diversity of philosophical categories, in which subjectivity represents and stands for itself, such that none of the categories can be considered to be knowledge of the subject in any absolute sense.

**Kisiel, Theodore J**. The New Translation of *Sein und Zeit*: A Grammatological Lexicographer's Commentary. *Man World*, 30(2), 239-258, Ap 97.

The one merit of this "new" translation by Joan Stambaugh is the inclusion of Heidegger's later marginal notes from his "cabin copy" at the bottom of the pages. Not so meritorious are the numerous minor mistakes that still riddle the text and original notes. Some of the new translations of basic terms are questioned: the *Umgang* with things as "association," *Besorgen* as "taking care/heedfulness" rather than the familiar "concern," which now becomes the translation for *Fuersorge*, "solicitude," *Befindlichkeit* as "attunement" instead of "disposedness," *Bewandtnis* as "relevance" instead of "appliance," etc. The *Lexicon* by Theodore Kisiel expands upon Macquarrie & Robinson's fine *Index*, whose scholarly quality is now sorely missed. But the tendency toward simpler sentences in ordinary language, though not carried through completely is much appreciated.

**Kiss, Endre**. Zur Fichte-Darstellung in Hegels *Differenzschrift*. *Fichte-Studien*, 12, 247-256, 1997.

The main topic of this study is a reconstruction of Hegel's *Differenzschrift* with his central regard to the Fichte-interpretation. Hegel appears here as the organizer of the new post-Kantian paradigm of the philosophy. Hegel's strategy lies in a double decision. On the one hand he ascribes the begins of the new speculation not to Fichte but to Kant himself. On the other hand he attacks Fichte's conception of the *Verstand* and the new notion of identity. The study makes an interpretation of Hegel's decisions as a strategy of conscious founder of the new discourse of the post-Kantian philosophy.

**Kistler, Max**. On the Content of Natural Kind Concepts. *Acta Analytica*, 55-79, 1996.

The search for a nomological account of what determines the content of concepts as they are represented in cognitive systems, is an important part of the general project of explaining intentional phenomena in naturalistic terms. I examine Fodor's "Theory of Content" and criticize his strategy of combining constraints in nomological terms with constraints in terms of actual causal relations. The paper focuses on the problem of the indeterminacy of the content of natural kind concepts. (edited)

**Kitchen, Gary**. Alasdair MacIntyre: The Epitaph of Modernity. *Phil Soc Crit*, 23(1), 71-98, 1997.

At the heart of MacIntyre's critique of modernity is the problem of moral truth. He argues that the 'Enlightenment project' of justifying morality has failed due to the breakdown of a conceptual scheme inherited from Aristotle, in which the idea of an essential human nature or function played a crucial part. Where modernity trades on moral fictions such as 'utility' and 'natural rights', Aristotle's scheme allows moral judgements to be matters of fact. MacIntyre's denigration of modernity draws attention to his own positive account of moral justification, which I examine from a position of scepticism about moral knowledge. I argue that, while there is much of value in his work—his critique of modern moral philosophy is remarkably cogent and helps clarify what is at stake in discussion of modernity—his account of the good life seems to be circular and his notion of rational progress is unpersuasive.

**Kitchen, Gary**. Habermas's Moral Cognitivism. *Proc Aris Soc*, 97, 317-324, 1997.

This paper evaluates Habermas's moral cognitivism as expressed in the 'principle of universalization'. It suggests that there are at least four grounds on which this principle might fail to produce something analogous to 'moral knowledge': firstly, it might not lead to agreement on norms as a matter of fact; secondly, there is reason to think it might fail to lead to agreement in principle; thirdly, any convergence it brings about is likely to be unstable and ephemeral; and fourthly, it might not itself be justified.

**Kitcher, Philip**. An Argument About Free Inquiry. *Nous*, 31(3), 279-306, S 97.

**Kitcher, Philip**. Critical Notice of Philip Kitcher: *The Advancement of Science: Science without Legend, Objectivity without Illusions*. *Can J Phil*, 26(3), 463-489, S 96.

**Kittay, Eva Felder**. Ah! My Foolish Heart: A Reply to Alan Soble's "Antioch's 'Sexual Offense Policy': A Philosophical Exploration". *J Soc Phil*, 28(2), 153-159, Fall 97.

In this commentary I examine the three grounds, pleasure, body talk and consent, on which Alan soble bases his objection to the Antioch *Sexual Offense Policy*. I question his interpretation of the policy, suggesting that it less rigid than he supposes. I conclude that some his criticisms might be justified were the policy to apply to more generally than Antioch intended. The policy is one student body's pedagogic-minded self-governing choice. It takes effect in a small community that encourage discussion of sexual offense and constant reevaluation of the policy. Finally, I consider what consent means in the context of sexual relations and how Antioch's policy should be understood in light of this context of consent.

**Kivy, Peter**. *Philosophies of Arts: An Essay in Differences*. New York, Cambridge Univ Pr, 1997.

Since the beginning of the eighteenth century the philosophy of art has been engaged in the project of finding out what the fine arts might have in common, and thus how they might be defined. Peter Kivy's purpose in this very accessible and lucid book is to trace the history of that enterprise and then to argue that the definitional project has been unsuccessful, with absolute music as the continual stumbling block. He offers what he believes is a fruitful change of strategy: instead of undertaking an obsessive quest for sameness, let us explore the differences among the arts. He presents five case studies of such differences, three from literature, two from music. With its combination of historical and analytic approaches this book will appeal to a wide range of readers in philosophy, literary studies, and music, as well as to nonacademic readers with an interest in the arts. Its vivid style requires no technical knowledge of music on the part of the reader.

**Kiyokazu, Nishimura**. Photography as Narrative (in Japanese). *Bigaku*, 47(1), 1-12, Sum 96.

The invention of photography definitely changed our way of representing the world and the self. In this paper I try to show a portion of such transformation by way of regarding photography as a kind of narrative act. Painting is a 'depiction' by human eyes and hands and depends on the particular cultural code of representation. But photography is the direct 'trace' of nature. According to C.S. Peirce, we could call the semiotic status of photographic image 'icon=index'. (edited)

**Klappenbach, Augusto** and Vegas González, Serafín and Núñez Tomás, Paloma. *Razón, Naturaleza y Libertad: En Torno a La Crítica de la Razón Práctica* Kantiana. X, Unknown, 1996.

**Klausen, Jytte** and Wolfe, Alan. Identity Politics and the Welfare State. *Soc Phil Pol*, 14(2), 231-255, Sum 97.

**Klausen, Soren Harnow**. Die Ontologie des Intentionalen. *Dan Yrbk Phil*, 29, 114-128, 1994.

Basically a review of Dan Zahavi's book *Intentionalität und Konstitution* (Kopenhagen 1992), the article discusses the question whether Husserl in his early *Logical Investigations* defended a realist or an idealist ontology and concludes with Zahavi that he remained neutral on the question of realism, dismissing it as a kind pseudo-question. Against Zahavi it is argued that Husserl's criticism of psychologism is unconvincing and that Husserl himself later realized this and adopted a less Platonic view on abstract entities. Finally, questions are raised as to the ontological implications of Husserl's later concept of constitution.

**Kleefield, Sharon F** (& others) and Hauser, Joshua M and Fischbach, Ruth L. Minority Populations and Advance Directives: Insights from a Focus Group Methodology. *Cambridge Quart Healthcare Ethics*, 6(1), 58-71, Winter 97.

Motivated by the significantly lower prevalence of advance directives among African-American and Hispanic patients at one urban teaching hospital (18% for Caucasians, 4% for African-Americans, and 2% for Hispanics), we used a focus group methodology to examine ways in which diverse populations of patients view the medical, philosophical, and practical issues surrounding advance directives. Our premise was that African-American and Hispanic populations who have higher rates of morbidity and mortality across numerous disease categories, and historically have had limited access to care and opportunities to discuss health concerns, may be more suspicious about the right of autonomy that an advance directive is designed to ensure. Our premise was supported by our data.

**Klein, E R**. Philosophers as Experts: A Response to Pfeifer. *Inquiry (USA)*, 15(1), 86-91, Fall 95.

The great leap Pfeifer makes between the imperfect nature of the above three accounts of "philosophical counseling" and his pessimism about philosophical training in general is unwarranted. His narrow account of the philosophical enterprise and its experts caricatures a most noble profession. Pfeifer's biased attitude seems to have its origin in his limited philosophical education. Now I realize that it's an empirical point whether trained philosophers will make the best counselors, attorneys, physicians, or what have you. But until society as a whole ceases to view us, as it has for the last 2,500 years—as worthless rogues, we will never have the chance to do the test. It may be that philosophy has no place outside the academy. But it may also be, as Plato claimed, that the lack of respect for philosophy is indicated of a naive and/or corrupt state. After all, a contemplative existence is only meaningful when the examiner is philosophically estimable.

**Klein, Felix**. Consideraciones comparativas sobre nuevas investigaciones geométricas. *Mathesis*, 11(4), 331-370, N 95.

**Klein, John P** and Shapiro, Robyn S and Tym, Kristen A. Wisconsin Healthcare Ethics Committees. *Cambridge Quart Healthcare Ethics*, 6(3), 288-292, Sum 97.

**Klein, Michel** and Hermans, Michel. Ces *Exercices Spirituels* Que Descartes Aurait Pratiqués. *Arch Phil*, 59(3), 427-440, Jl-S 96.

This study concerns a single aspect of the education which Descartes received at the "Collège de La Flèche", i.e., his spiritual formation. Contemporary documents leave uncertain the exact form of the spiritual retreat proposed to Descartes, though they exclude any direct contact with the text of the Spiritual Exercises of St. Ignatius of Loyola. Rather, it is highly probable that Descartes experienced the Manuale Sodalitatis of Fr. François Véron, an example of the rationalizing tendency common to the entire Order.

**Klein, Ursula**. Experiment, Spiritus und okkulte Qualitäten in der Philosophie Francis Bacons. *Phil Natur*, 33(2), 289-315, 1996.

Bacons Beschäftigung mit Phänomenen, die die peripatetische Philosophie als "okkulte Qualitäten" aus den Wissenschaften ausschloss, hat das Ziel, eine neue Strategie zur empirischen Erforschung dieser Phänomene zu entwickeln. Als eine solche Strategie erweist sich das Experiment, worunter Bacon in erster Linie intervenierende Operationen versteht. Bacon sieht in Experimenten Vermittlungsinstanzen, denen die Aufgabe zukommt, das "Verborgene" der Natur und darunter auch die "okkulten Qualitäten" den Sinnen zugänglich zu machen. Die Funktionsweise solcher Vermittlungsinstanzen kann exemplarisch an Bacons experimenteller Untermauerung des Spiritusbegriffs nachvollzogen werden. (edited)

**Klein, Wayne**. *Nietzsche and the Promise of Philosophy*. Albany, SUNY Pr, 1997.

This book questions the consensus about the meaning and importance of Nietzsche's philosophy that has developed in the United States and Britain during the last thirty years and re-establishes close reading as the ground of interpretation. Arguing that there is greater continuity in Nietzsche's thought than is usually recognized, Klein focuses particularly on the genesis and nature of Nietzsche's theory of language and rhetoric, exploring the relationship between his early theory of language, expressed in *The Birth of Tragedy*, and the canonical writings of the late 1880s. Other topics considered include the relationship between style and subjectivity, the semiological underpinnings of Nietzsche's theory of tragedy and Nietzsche's naturalism. (publisher, edited)

**Kleiner, Deborah S** and Maury, Mary D. Thou Shalt and Shalt Not: An Alternative to the Ten Commandments Approach to Developing a Code of Ethics for Schools of Business. *J Bus Ethics*, 16(3), 331-336, F 97.

The authors' previous research indicates that there is a perceived need for a code of ethics for business schools. Currently, relatively few schools have in fact adopted codes of ethics applicable to all the constituents of the institution. Proposals made to businesses to help them determine which values should be included in a corporate code do not appear to adequately address the distinctive issues faced in an academic environment. (edited)

**Kleiner, Scott A**. "The Structure of Inquiry in Developmental Biology" in *Knowledge and Inquiry: Essays on Jaakko Hintikka's Epistemology and Philosophy of Science*, Sintonen, Matti (ed), 165-180. Amsterdam, Rodopi, 1997.

What are judged to be the most important questions from a survey of researchers in developmental biology are analyzed in the context of a cytological model of development and in the context of a molecular regulative model for gene expression. These models provide interpretations and a rational ordering of these questions that supersede the intuitively based opinions surveyed. The rational support behind molecular developmental genetics

comes from the epistemic import of explaining cell differentiation in embryology, discovering interfield and interlevel relations, and explaining variation, physiological stability and gene conservation in evolution.

**Kleinig, John**. Police Loyalties: A Refuge for Scoundrels?. *Prof Ethics*, 5(1-2), 29-42, Spr-Sum 96.

The Janus-like character of loyalty is approached via the specific phenomenon of police loyalty, which manifests itself, on the one hand, in heroic support, and on the other, in the code of silence. I argue that focusing on the latter, as loyalty's detractors do, overlooks the important communal value that loyalty has as a curb on the ravages of self-interest and self-assertion. Nevertheless, loyalty is not absolute and must be moderated by other values.

**Klemm, David E**. "Schleiermacher on the Self: Immediate Self-Consciousness as Feeling and as Thinking" in *Figuring the Self: Subject, Absolute, and Others in Classical German Philosophy*, Zöller, Günter (ed), 169-190. Albany, SUNY Pr, 1997.

**Klemm, David E** (ed) and Zöller, Günter (ed). *Figuring the Self: Subject, Absolute, and Others in Classical German Philosophy*. Albany, SUNY Pr, 1997.

The book consists of twelve essays which present, discuss and assess the principal accounts of the self in classical German philosophy, focusing on the period around 1800 and covering Kant, Fichte, Hölderlin, Novalis, Schelling, Schleiermacher and Hegel. (publisher)

**Klempay DiBlasio, Margaret**. Harvesting the Cognitive Revolution: Reflections on *The Arts, Education, and Aesthetic Knowing*. *J Aes Educ*, 31(1), 95-110, Spr 97.

**Klempe, Hroar**. Musicalisation of Metaphor and Metaphoricalness in Music. *Dan Yrbk Phil*, 31, 125-136, 1996.

The author discusses structural similarities and differences between music and language. From this perspective, metaphor is regarded as a borderline. On the one hand, it is a condensed expression and, therefore, represents a challenge to linguistic system. But on the other hand, condensation is a salient trait of musical polyphony. By referring to Freud's analysis of an enjoyable slip of the tongue, which is revealed as two utterances condensed into one, the author concludes that multidimensional simultaneity contradicts discursive rationality. In metaphor and music, therefore, meaning does not primarily lie in signification, but in structural and formal qualities.

**Klepper, Howard**. Intimacy and Parental Authority in the Philosophy of Ferdinand Schoeman. *Int J Applied Phil*, 11(1), 35-39, Sum-Fall 96.

**Klepper, Howard**. Mandatory Rights and Compulsory Education. *Law Phil*, 15(2), 149-158, 96.

**Klepper, Howard**. Treating the Patient to Benefit Others. *Cambridge Quart Healthcare Ethics*, 6(3), 306-313, Sum 97.

**Kleszcz, Ryszard**. Razón y Lógica: La Tradición Analítica en Polonia. *Agora (Spain)*, 14(2), 41-53, 1995.

This paper surveys the Polish tradition in analytical philosophy, the so-called Lvov-Varsovia School, that flourished in Poland from the end of XIX Century to the second World War. The aim of the paper is to show, beyond usual topics, that the common acceptance of a criterion for philosophical methodology by all members of the School was compatible with an internal radical liberalism at the time of selecting traditional philosophical problems and facing their solutions. Likewise, philosophical and metaphilosophical fundamental contributions of some of its most relevant members like Twardowski (the founder of the School), Ajdukiewicz or Lukasiewicz are presented and discussed.

**Klinger, Cornelia**. The Concepts of the Sublime and the Beautiful in Kant and Lyotard. *Constellations*, 2(2), 207-223, O 95.

**Klinger, Gerwin** and Ernst, Anna-Sabine. Socialist Socrates: Ernst Bloch in the GDR. *Rad Phil*, 84, 6-21, Jl-Ag 97.

**Klonoski, Richard J**. Homonoia in Aristotle's Ethics and Politics. *Hist Polit Thought*, 17(3), 313-325, Autumn 96.

The author argues that in the Nichomachean Ethics and in the Eudemian Ethics Aristotle views *homonoia* or concord as more than simply an expedient and/or pragmatic form of civic friendship. Rather concord is a primordial political gathering which unifies the wishes and purposes of the decent and the common people in Aristotle's most practicable political regime, the mixed polity. Moreover, concord functions in the city in much the same way love functions in the perfect friendship of individuals. Both *homonoia* and *philia* foster self-understanding, self-love, and self-sufficiency and thus both promote morally and politically responsible behavior.

**Kloppenburg, Jr, Jack** and Hendrickson, John and Stevenson, G W. Coming in to the Foodshed. *Agr Human Values*, 13(3), 33-42, Sum 96.

Bioregionalists have championed the utility of the concept of the watershed as an organizing framework for thought and action directed to understanding and implementing appropriate and respectful human interaction with particular pieces of land. In a creative analogue to the watershed, permaculturist Arthur Getz has recently introduced the term "foodshed" to facilitate critical thought about where our food is coming from and how it is getting to us. We find the "foodshed" to be a particularly rich and evocative metaphor; but it is much more than metaphor. Like its analogue the watershed, the foodshed can serve us as a conceptual and methodological unit of analysis that provides a frame for action as well as thought. (edited)

**Klosko, George**. Liberalism and Pluralism. *Soc Theor Pract*, 22(2), 251-269, Sum 96.

**Klosko, George**. Popper's Plato: An Assessment. *Phil Soc Sci*, 26(4), 509-527, D 96.

The author examines Karl Popper's contribution to the study of Plato in *The Open Society and Its Enemies*. Assessment of Popper's claims that Plato is a totalitarian, a historicist and a racist confirms what has become the general opinion of the work, that it played a major role in changing perceptions of Plato's political theory, in spite of significant problems with many of Popper's claims and the evidence he uses to support them.

**Klotz, Christian**. Der Ichbegriff in Fichtes Erörterung der Substantialität. *Fichte-Studien*, 10, 157-173, 1997.

**Klotzko, Arlene Judith**. What Kind of Life? What Kind of Death? An Interview with Dr. Henk Prins. *Bioethics*, 11(1), 24-42, Ja 97.

**Kluback, William**. *Léopold Sédar Senghor: From Politics to Poetry.* New York, Lang, 1997.

An exchange of letters, such as those between Leonard Woolf and his friends or between Harry Truman and his wife, however different the writers, offers a revealing view of relationships among people, of individual reflection and change over time, and thus an unequaled view of the human personality. Yet a third possibility for personal exchange is illustrated by this book. It presents us with the kind of conversation that can take place in the study when, at peace and at leisure, a curious and careful reader puts questions to the writers and philosophers of the past, searching their work for answers to problems that preoccupy him. Rarely are such conversations overheard, but Professor William Kluback, a philosopher who has written on connections between philosophy, religion, and poetry, has decided to put his conversations in print. (edited)

**Kluback, William** and Finkenthal, Michael. *The Temptations of Emile Cioran.* New York, Lang, 1997.

The Romanian-born Emile Cioran is one of the most important figures of modern French philosophy and literature. Even though most of his French works have been translated into English, this is the first attempt to produce a comprehensive presentation and appraisal of his work to an English-speaking public. Written in the form of a dialogue between two skeptical minds, this book discusses both the prewar Romanian and postwar French works of Cioran. (publisher)

**Kluyskens, Jups**. "Between Postcoloniality and Postcolonialism" in *Philosophy and Democracy in Intercultural Perspective,* Kimmerle, Heinz (ed), 69-84. Amsterdam, Rodopi, 1997.

**Kmiec, Douglas W**. The Abolition of Public Racial Preference—An Invitation to Private Racial Sensitivity. *Notre Dame J Law Ethics*, 11(1), 1-13, 1997.

**Kmita, Jerzy**. "Is a 'Creative Man of Knowledge' Needed in University Teaching" in *The Idea of University,* Brzezinski, Jerzy (ed), 179-190. Amsterdam, Rodopi, 1997.

The paper is an attempt to answer the title question. The answer argues F. Znaniecki's point. This point is that the university education requires exclusively "the erudite men of knowledge" who have mastered the whole of an accepted knowledge of respective subject, are able to argue for it and apply it to particular cases. On the other hand, "the creative men of knowledge" invent new ideas (like artists), but are not able to argue for them openly. They use "metaphors" (in Rorty's sense). Here is the answer: "the creative men of knowledge" use "metaphors", but can argue for them openly. This is why they are necessarily required as the university educators: they show how to maintain new scientific ideas intersubjectively.

**Kmita, Jerzy**. "Towards Cultural Relativism 'With a Small *R*'" in *Epistemology and History,* Zeidler-Janiszewska, Anna (ed), 541-614. Amsterdam, Rodopi, 1996.

The position that the author assumes and attempts to develop and that he terms cultural relativism "with a small 'r'" is located outside the dispute over cultural relativism "with a capital 'R'". That is the position according to which different reconstructions of particular cultures (as well as the conceptual systems connected with them) can be comparatively evaluated from the point of view of the scope of the interpretive and predictive possibilities of those reconstructions. What is at stake is the possibility of interpretation and prediction of intentional actions that are regulated by the culture being reconstructed. These reconstructions, obviously, are performed within particular cultures. Minimal or null interpretive and predictive possibilities of all reconstructions of the culture *A* that come into play within the culture *B* testify to untranslatability of (a conceptual system) of the culture *A* into the culture *B*. (edited)

**Knabenschuh de Porta, Sabine**. Maniobras doctrinales de un tomista colonial: tiempo y lugar según Suárez de Urbina. *Analogia*, 11(1), 127-149, Ja-Je 97.

**Knabenschuh de Porta, Sabine**. Notes on Suárez de Urbina's Cosmological Texts (Spanish). *Rev Filosof (Venezuela)*, 24(2), 93-108, Jl-D 96.

In order to contribute to the *Rediscovery Program of Colonial Thought* (Programa de Rescate del Pensamiento Colonial), some preliminary observations are presented concerning the cosmological texts that belong to the *Cursus Philosophicus* of the Venezuelan university professor Antonio José Suárez de Urbina (1730-1799). The research is centered on some "surface" features, such as the contextual configuration, the structure of the specific texts, and the manner of handling sources. It is shown that, notwithstanding the fact that this work belongs to the so-called colonial *Second Scholastics*, the author demonstrates as well certain inclinations which are compatible with the modern spirit of *new science*. In this regard, Suárez de Urbina seems to represent a generation that happens to be doubly decisive within the development of cosmological-philosophical tradition in Venezuela.

**Knabenschuh de Porta, Sabine**. Ontología del Movimiento en la Cosmología Venezolana del Siglo XVIII. *Ideas Valores*, 100-116, Ag 96.

The conceptualization of *motion* which is presented by the Venezuelan university professor Suárez de Urbina in his *Cursus Philosophicus* (1758) shows the following particularities: In principle the author follows the *Aristotelian-Thomistic* tradition of searching for an ontological explanation of motion and of constructing an *intensional* or essentialistic cosmology. However, his exposé reveals a certain doctrinal flexibility as it incorporates *post-Thomistic* ideas which already contain the germ of an *extensional* conception of motion. Such observations indicate that Venezuelan colonial cosmology presents, notwithstanding the fact that it belongs to the Spanish-American Second Scholastics, a certain receptivity towards quasi-modern view-points.

**Knebel, Sven K** (ed & trans). Agustin de Herrera, A Treatise on Aleatory Probability *De Necessitate Morali in Genere. Mod Sch*, 73(3), 199-264, Mr 96.

Ian Hacking's *Emergence of Probability* as well as its critics entirely ignored major trends in 17th-century scholasticism to deal with probability in terms of chances. In 1673, the Jesuit Herrera (1623-84) in defense of hypothetical optimism gave an account of probability which I suggest should be read as the most sophisticated attempt prior to Auguste Cournot in mid-19th century to establish objective vs. subjective probabilities. This reedition of an important piece of early modern philosophy also elucidates the broader context of the flourishing Molinist theology of the time and, incidentally, the scholastic background of Leibniz's notion 'moral necessity'.

**Knebel, Sven K**. Leibniz, Middle Knowledge, and the Intricacies of World Design. *Stud Leibniz*, 28(2), 199-210, 1996.

Im Zentrum des Streits zwischen Leibniz und Arnauld um die individuellen Begriffe steht die theologische Frage, ob sich dergleichen nur auf der Basis von Gottes Wirklichkeitswissen (scientia visionis) konzipieren lässt oder nicht. Arnauld behauptet das, Leibniz als Molinist bestreitet es. Nun war aber erstens die Reichweite der Scientia Media für die göttliche Weltplanung unter den Jesuiten des 17. Jahrhunderts selbst kontrovers. Zweitens hat Leibniz von den Gegnern der These, die göttliche Weltplanung komme mit der Scientia Media aus, bestimmte Ideen auch übernommen ('Adam vague'). Das führt schliesslich zu der Vermutung, dass das Lehrstück der Prästabilierten Harmonie eine Schwäche der Scientia-Media-Hypothese zu kompensieren bestimmt gewesen ist.

**Knebel, Sven K**. Scotists vs. Thomists: What Seventeenth-Century Scholastic Psychology was About. *Mod Sch*, 74(3), 219-226, Mr 97.

**Kneller, Jane E**. "Romantic Conceptions of the Self in Hölderlin and Novalis" in *Figuring the Self: Subject, Absolute, and Others in Classical German Philosophy,* Zöller, Günter (ed), 134-148. Albany, SUNY Pr, 1997.

**Knight, Christopher**. Psychology, Revelation and Interfaith Dialogue. *Int J Phil Relig*, 40(3), 147-157, D 96.

The status of the apparent referential content of revelatory religious experience is examined in the context of a nonreductionist psychological model of that experience. The cultural conditioning of such experience is found to have important implications for interfaith dialogue conceived in terms of convergent pluralism in relation to the sacramental penentheism of strands of the current dialogue of science and theology, this may be analyzed in terms of spontaneous development within psychocultural niches, analogous to the development of species within ecological niches.

**Knight, David**. "Illustrating Chemistry" in *Picturing Knowledge,* Baigrie, Brian S (ed), 135-163. Toronto, Univ of Toronto Pr, 1996.

**Knight, Deborah**. A Poetics of Psychological Explanation. *Metaphilosophy*, 28(1-2), 63-80, Ja-Ap 97.

I argue that psychological explanation is an agent-centered, narrative-based interpretive practice. To make my case, I present a *poetics* of psychological explanation: seven elements which collectively describe what makes psychological explanations work. After establishing the seven elements of the poetics, I address the objection that narrative-based accounts of intentional action are not properly explanatory. (edited)

**Knight, Deborah**. Back to Basics: Film/Theory/Aesthetics. *J Aes Educ*, 31(2), 37-44, Sum 97.

**Knight, Deborah** and McNight, George. The Case of the Disappearing Enigma. *Phil Lit*, 21(1), 123-138, Ap 97.

The argument is that the sort of comprehension required of detection narratives is pragmatical and hermeneutical. Understanding is directed by questioning and by the revision of hypothesis relative to what at each stage we believe has been going on. What allows the first-order mystery or enigma to disappear is a second-order, explanatory story that dispels the confusion or puzzle which the initial mystery represents. We discuss five films as our key examples.

**Knight, Gordon**. Universalism and the Greater Good: A Response to Talbott. *Faith Phil*, 14(1), 98-103, Ja 97.

Thomas Talbott has recently argued in this journal that the three propositions (1) God wills universal salvation, (2) God has the power to produce universal salvation, and (3) some persons are not saved, are inconsistent. I contend that this claim is only true if God has no overriding purposes that would place restrictions on the means God uses to achieve God's ends. One possible example of such an overriding purpose would be God's aim to produce the most good. I end by suggesting that while God's purpose of universal salvation does render the achievement of this end probable, it is by no means necessary.

**Knight, J F** and Ash, C J. Possible Degrees in Recursive Copies II. *Annals Pure Applied Log*, 87(2), 151-165, 15 S 97.

We extend results of Harizanov and Barker. For a relation *R* on a recursive structure *A*, we give conditions guaranteeing that the image of *R* in a recursive copy of *A* can be made to have arbitrary Sigma$^{o}_{x}$ degree over Delta $^{o}_{x}$. We give stronger conditions under which the image of *R* can be made Sigma$^{o}_{x}$ degree as well. The degrees over Delta$^{o}_{x}$ can be replaced by certain more general classes. We also generalize the Friedberg-Muchnik Theorem, giving conditions on a pair of relations *R* and *S* under which the images of *R* and *S* can be made Sigma$^{o}_{x}$ and independent over Delta$^{o}_{x}$ in a recursive copy of *A*.

**Knight, J F** and Cholak, P and Ash, C J. Permitting, Forcing, and Copying of a given Recursive Relation. *Annals Pure Applied Log*, 86(3), 219-236, Jl 97.

**Knight, J F** and Remmel, J B and Ash, C J. Quasi-Simple Relations in Copies of a given Recursive Structure. *Annals Pure Applied Log*, 86(3), 203-218, Jl 97.

**Knoepffler, Nikolaus**. Blondels *Action* von 1893 und Rahners transzendentaler Ansatz im *Grundkurs*—eine unterirdische Wirkungsgeschichte. *Theol Phil*, 72(1), 91-96, 1997.

Fassen wir zusammen: Die *Action* hat in mehrfacher Weise unterirdisch auf Rahners transzendentalen Ansatz im *Grundkurs* eingewirkt. Über Maréchal beeinflusst Blondel Rahners Ansetzen beim dynamischen Charakter menschlichen Erkennens und seine Auseinandersetzung mit Kant. Durch Arbeiten französischer Theologen vermittelt, wird sie gnadentheologisch wirksam. Rahners Bestimmungen der transzendentalen Erfahrung als übernatürlicher rührt von hier her. Auch sein Sprechen vom mensch-gewordenen Logos als Finalursache und absolutem Symbol Gottes ist durch den Panchristismus Blondels vorweggenommen. Dennoch hatten wir auch wesentliche Unterschiede festgestellt. Rahner argumentiert vom Erkennen her und gibt durch sein Theorem der transzendentalen Offenbarung Blondels philosophischen Ansatz auf. Dadurch bekommt auch die Deutung des Christusereignisses eine neue Ausformung. Letztlich versucht Rahner eine "Einführung in den Begriff des Christentums", während es Blondel um eine "Kritik des Lebens" und eine "Wissenschaft der Praxis" geht. Zuletzt wagten wir einen Ausblick auf eine relationale Ontologie des Faktums. Sie setzt mit Blondel philosophisch an und deutet zugleich mit Rahner den Menschen als Ereignis. Sie ruft zur Entscheidung im Angesicht des Faktums der Kreuzigung Jesu auf.

**Knoll, Victor**. On the Question of *Mimesis* (in Spanish). *Discurso*, 27, 61-81, 1996.

The issue of this article is to elucidate the Aristotelian notion of *mimesis*, referring it to the Hegel and Heidegger's point of view about the work of art. Our goal is to interpret the propositions of these authors according to the Aristotelian sense of *mimesis*.

**Knorpp Jr, William Max**. The Relevance of Logic to Reasoning and Belief Revision: Harman on 'Change in View'. *Pac Phil Quart*, 78(1), 78-92, Mr 97.

In *Change of View: Principles of Reasoning*, Gilbert Harman argues that i) all genuine reasoning is a matter of belief revision, and that, since ii) logic is not "specially relevant" to belief revision, iii) logic is not specially relevant to reasoning either. Thus, Harman suggests, what is needed is a "theory of reasoning"—which, incidentally, will be psychologistic, telling us both how we do and how we should reason. I argue that Harman fails to establish the need for such a theory, because a) reasoning is not always a matter of belief revision, and b) logic is, in fact, of the utmost relevance to both reasoning and belief revision.

**Knuuttila, Simo** and Hallamaa, Olli. Roger Roseth and Medieval Deontic Logic. *Log Anal*, 38(149), 75-87, Mr 95.

The elements of deontic logic were developed as part of philosophical modal logic in early fourteenth century. Roger Roseth wrote an extensive treatise on the rationality of norms c. 1335. The paper includes an analysis of Roseth's discussions of the types of deontic terms, deontic consequences and conditional norms with an English translation of the main tenets of Roseth's theory.

**Kober, Michael**. "Certainties of a World-Picture: The Epistemological Investigations on *On Certainty*" in *The Cambridge Companion to Wittgenstein*, Sluga, Hans (ed), 411-441. Needham Heights, Cambridge, 1996.

Wittgenstein's *On Certainty* provides a philosophically illuminating picture of the epistemic structure of language-games. In contrast to knowledge claims, certainties like "This is a hand" can be seen as constitutive rules of language games, such that they are unjustifiable, undeniable and serving as obliging standards of truth and rationality for members of a community engaging in the respective practices. Certainties are not fixed, but may change like any other component of a world-picture. Our certainties are drilled into us during our education. Cultural relativism cannot be justified. However, scepticism cannot be dissolved by means of that picture.

**Kobes, Bernard W**. "Telic Higher-Order Thoughts and Moore's Paradox" in *AI, Connectionism and Philosophical Psychology, 1995*, Tomberlin, James E (ed), 291-312. Atascadero, Ridgeview, 1995.

It is argued that a mental event's being conscious consists in its being the object of a higher-order thought (HOT) that contains the first-order mental event as a token constituent. HOTs may have telic (act-like) force; e.g., a HOT's representing a first-order thought as a *belief* can explain that thought's playing the role in virtue of which it *is* a belief. A certain kind of spontaneous, direct self-knowledge normally accompanies telic HOTs and helps constitute the unity of the self. Some imaginable sincere thoughts of Moore-Paradoxical form are described and understood as pathologies in which these normal processes fail.

**Kobes, Bernard W**. Metacognition and Consciousness: Review Essay of Janet Metcalfe and Arthur P. Shimamura (Eds) *Metacognition: Knowing about Knowing*. *Phil Psych*, 10(1), 93-102, Mr 97.

The field of metacognition, richly sampled in the book under review, is recognized as an important and growing branch of psychology. However, the field stands in need of a general theory that 1) provides a unified framework for understanding the variety of metacognitive processes, 2) articulates the relation between metacognition and consciousness, and 3) tells us something about the form of metalevel representations and their relations to object-level representations. It is argued that the higher-order thought theory of

consciousness supplies us with the rudiments of a theory that meets these desiderata and integrates the principal findings reported in this collection.

**Koch, Donald F**. "Dialogue: An Essay in the Instrumentalist Tradition" in *Political Dialogue: Theories and Practices*, Esquith, Stephen L (ed), 93-114. Amsterdam, Rodopi, 1996.

Dialogue is a major tool in the resolution of conflict situations. Its effectiveness is a function of our ability to utilize elements within the conflict situation that draws the participants into discussion. The goal is practical: to work towards the resolution of the problem. Effective dialogue uses the authority of the life process as a guide. It takes up any facts or aspects of the situation that are relevant to the solution of the conflict. Theoretical inquiry and face-to-face dialogue are not divorced from each other. They are factors in a continuum of inquiry that eventually leads us to focus upon the practical problem.

**Koch, Tom**. Principles and Purpose: The Patient Surrogate's Perspective and Role. *Cambridge Quart Healthcare Ethics*, 6(4), 461-469, Fall 97.

**Kocikowski, Andrzej**. Geography and Computer Ethics: An Eastern European Perspective. *Sci Eng Ethics*, 2(2), 201-210, A 96.

Several context-specific social and political factors in Eastern and Central Europe are described—factors that must be considered while developing strategies to introduce computer ethics. Poland is used as a primary example. GNP per capita, the cost of hardware and software, uneven and scan distribution of computing resources and attitudes toward work and authority are discussed. Such "geographical factors" must be taken into account as the new field of computer ethics develops.

**Koczwara, Bogda M** and Madigan, Timothy J. The Heterogeneity of Clinical Ethics: The State of the Field as Reflected in the *Encyclopedia of Bioethics*. *J Med Phil*, 22(1), 75-88, F 97.

The 1995 *Encyclopedia of Bioethics* is an almost complete reworking of the original 1978 edition, due to the expanding nature of the field. The following article focuses on how the second edition of the *Encyclopedia* deals with the topic of "clinical ethics" and three related topics: "nursing ethics," "trust," and "conflict of interest." We assess their relevance to the current developments in these fields and the *Encyclopedia*'s usefulness as a resource to ethics consultants, researchers and clinicians. We emphasize the heterogeneity of clinical ethics as a still new and evolving field.

**Köchy, Kristian**. Perspektiven der Welt: Vielfalt und Einheit im Weltbild der Deutschen Romantik. *Phil Natur*, 33(2), 317-342, 1996.

A characteristic trait of postmodern philosophy is the concept of perspectives: a pluralistic declaration of war on totalitarianism. From this point of view the philosophy of German Romanticism seems to be a dogmatic and unifying approach. A detailed study of romantic thinking shows, however, that such a simple reconstruction is wrong. The objective of Romanticism is not an egalitarian tyranny but a harmonic integration of different perspectives. We show that romantic philosophy propagates a specific "representation" model postulating an organic connexion on three different levels: 1) between the parts of nature, 2) between facts and thinking, 3) between the elements of theoretical systems.

**Köhler, Dietmar**. Die Einbildungskraft und das Schematismusproblem. *Fichte-Studien*, 13, 19-34, 1997.

The purpose of this paper is to trace the development of the concept of the faculty of the imagination from Kant to Fichte and finally in Heidegger's interpretation of Kant. The status of the faculty of the imagination remains ambiguous in Kant's *Critique of Pure Reason*. In Fichte's 1894 *Wissenschaftslehre*, however, the faculty of the imagination plays a central role: It is the basis for the unity of subjectivity as well as for cognition. In his interpretation of Kant, Heidegger identifies the power of the imagination with "original temporality"; in this, he may have had recourse to Fichte's reformulation of the imagination's role. Heidegger's reading of Kant's schematism leads him to the main systematic purpose of *Being and Time*: A structural analysis of the meaning of being through temporal schemata.

**Koehn, Daryl**. Business and Game-Playing: The False Analogy. *J Bus Ethics*, 16(12-13), 1447-1452, S 97.

A number of business writers have argued that business is a game and, like a game, possesses its own special rules for acting. While we do not normally tolerate deceit, bluffing is not merely acceptable but also expected within the game of poker. Similarly, lies of omission, overstatements, puffery and bluffs are morally acceptable within business because it, like a game, has a special ethic which permits these normally immoral practices. This paper argues that this analogy is quite weak and incapable of either providing much insight into business or of offering a reason to think that the ethics of business are, or even could be, like those of a game. (edited)

**Köker, Levent**. Political Toleration or Politics or Recognition: The Headscarves Affair Revisited. *Polit Theory*, 24(2), 315-320, My 96.

**Kölbel, Max**. Wright's Argument from Neutrality. *Ratio*, 10(1), 35-47, Ap 97.

In the first chapter of his book *Truth and Objectivity* (1992), Crispin Wright puts forward what he regards as 'a fundamental and decisive objection' to deflationism about truth (p. 21). His objection proceeds by an argument to the conclusion that truth and warranted assertibility coincide in normative force and potentially diverge in extension (I call this the 'argument from neutrality'). This argument has already received some attention. However, I do not believe that it has been fully understood yet. In this short paper, I shall assess the cogency of Wright's objection in some detail. My agenda is as follows. First, I give what I believe to be an adequate rendering of the objection. Secondly, I reveal the real force of the neutrality argument and say thirdly why it does not, as Wright thinks, refute deflationism. Finally, I argue that Wright's insistence that truth is a 'substantial property' is uncongenial to the overall project of his book.

**Koenig, Bernie**. Natural Law and the Scientific Revolution. *Vera Lex*, 14(1-2), 60-64, 1994.

This is the third article in the series, "Ethics and Science." The first article in the series was "Is Natural Law Ethics Obsolete?" (Vol.IX, No.1, 1989). The second was Wesley Paul Bois's "The Underpinnings of Natural Law" (Vol.XII, No.2, 1992) which parallels this science theme. When natural law as a moral theory was developed, Koenig believes that the medieval world view was dominant and influential. But now natural law proponents should acknowledge that certain discoveries made possible by contemporary science put the medieval world view into doubt. We have to "move into a new house," says Koenig. Nevertheless, natural law can meet the challenge of new discoveries without losing its moral force. Also in this issue, "Natural Law, Nature, and Biology: A Modern Synthesis," by the late Richard Shelly Hartigan, and Roger E. Bissell's review of the pathbreaking *Science and Moral Priority* by the neuropsychologist Roger Sperry, Nobel Laureate in Medicine, carry forward the theme of natural law and science.

**König, Esther** and Dörre, Jochen and Gabbay, Dov. Fibred Semantics for Feature-Based Grammar Logic. *J Log Lang Info*, 5(3-4), 387-422, O 96.

This paper gives a simple method for providing categorial brands of feature-based unification grammars with a model-theoretic semantics. The key idea is to apply the paradigm of fibred semantics (or layered logics, see Gabbay, 1990) in order to combine the two components of a feature-based grammar logic. We demonstrate the method for the augmentation of Lambek categorial grammar with Kasper/Rounds-style feature logic. These are combined by replacing (or annotating) atomic formulas of the first logic, i.e., the basic syntactic types, by formulas of the second. Modelling such a combined logic is less trivial than one might expect. The direct application of the fibred semantics method where a combined atomic formula like *np (num:sg & pers:3rd)* denotes those strings which have the indicated property and the categorial operators denote the usual left- and right-residuals of these string sets, does not match the intuitive, unification-based proof theory. Unification implements a global bookkeeping with respect to a proof whereas the direct fibring method restricts its view to the atoms of the grammar logic. The solution is to interpret the (embedded) feature terms as global feature constraints while maintaining the same kind of fibred structures. For this adjusted semantics, the anticipated proof system is sound and complete.

**Koenigsberg, Ernest** and Van Gigch, John P and Dean, Burton V. In Search of an Ethical Science: An Interview with C. West Churchman: An 80th Birthday Celebration. *J Bus Ethics*, 16(7), 731-744, My 97.

**Königshausen, Johann-Heinrich**. Paralelismos entre el "Sofista" de Platón y el libro *Gamma* de la "Metafísica" de Aristóteles?. *An Seminar Hist Filosof*, 10, 157-171, 1993.

Der Verfasser weist Parallelen auf zwischen Platons *Sophistes* und Aristoteles' *Metaphysik* IV, die sowohl inhaltliche philosophische Lehrstücke, methodische Argumentgänge sowie die Funktion bestimmter Argumente in der Kritik an vorsokratischen Lehren, sowie sprachliche Parallelen betreffen. Die systematische Bedeutung dieser antiken "Transzendentalien". Lehre zeigt sich daran, dass sie vor der Differenz der ontologische Konzepte beider (Platons Ideenlehre und Aristoteles' Substanzlehre) steht. Aristoteles greift in *Met.* IV die spätplatonische Lehre von den transgenerischen Begriffen zustimmend auf und diese Lehre ist gemeinsames Fundament der ontologisch differenten Theorien. Die alte Frage nach dem Verhältnis beider Grundfiguren der abendländischen Philosophie wird mit dieser bisher zu unberücksichtigten Thematik neu intensiviert.

**Koethe, John**. *The Continuity of Wittgenstein's Thought*. Ithaca, Cornell Univ Pr, 1996.

Ludwig Wittgenstein's philosophical work is informed throughout by a particular broad theme: that the semantic and mentalistic attributes of language and human life are shown by verbal and nonverbal conduct, but that they resist incorporation into the domain of the straightforwardly factual. So argues John Koethe, in contrast to the standard view that Wittgenstein's earlier and later philosophical positions are sharply opposed. (publisher,edited)

**Köveker, Dietmar**. The Constitution of the World of Experience and the Problem of the New (in German). *Prima Philosophia*, 10(3), 319-333, 1997.

The 'official' interpretation of Kant's *Critique of Pure Reason* parallels its division into a '*transcendental analytic*' and a '*transcendental dialectic*' with the elaboration of '*constitutive principles of the understanding*' on the one hand and '*regulative principles of reason*' on the other. Now it is no matter of question that even the '*transcendental analytic*' contains *regulative* principles. This fact requires further distinction between the 'regulative principle', solving the cosmological 'antimony' and 'regulative ideas', as well as several other observations concerning the general 'architectonic' structure of the '*Critique of Pure Reason*' are indicating its deeply-rooted 'regulative-constitutive double-structure'. In this article it is interpreted as the theoretical sublimation of cognition's characteristic *processuality*.

**Kohák, Erazim**. Phenomenology and Ecology—Support and Interdependence (in Czech). *Filosof Cas*, 45(3), 363-379, 1997.

The author claims that in their original intent as a call to life in responsibility, phenomenology (Husserl's *Wiener Vortrag*) and ecology (Hans Jonas in *Das Prinzip Verantwortung*) support each other. However, in their romantic form (Heidegger's *Die Frage nach der Technik*, John Seed et al., *Thinking like a Mountain*) they form a codependency. The author defines romanticism as a quest for a return to primordial innocence which fails in (romantic) ecology's attempt to return to nature but draws another lease on life from (romantic) phenomenology's quest for innocence in an inner nature. The author expresses the hope that the experience of human ability to destroy nature (nuclear explosion, population explosion, consumption explosion) might yet awaken humankind from dreams of innocence regained to responsibility accepted, vindicating phenomenology and ecology in their original intent.

**Kohák, Erazim**. Varieties of Ecological Experience. *Environ Ethics*, 19(2), 153-171, Sum 97.

I draw on the resources of Husserlian phenomenology to argue that the way humans constitute nature as a meaningful whole by their purposive presence as hunter/gatherers (nature as *mysterium tremendum*), as herdsmen/farmers (nature as partner) and as producer/consumers (nature as resource) affects the way they respond to its distress—as to a resource failure, as a to flawed relationship, or as to a fate from which "only a god could save us." I find all three responses wanting and look to a different experience, that of nature as an endangered species, as the ground for a more adequate response of accepting responsibility for our freedom, with the consequence of imposing ethical limits on the way that humans relate to all being, not to humans alone.

**Kohl, Marvin**. Gandhi on Love: A Reply to Ian M. Harris. *Acorn*, 8(1), 24-26, Spr-Sum 93.

Harris ["The Conditional Quality of Gandhi's Love," *The Acorn* Spring-Summer, 1992, 7-18] attempts to improve upon Gandhi's theory by combining four kinds of love. By way of reply it is suggested this effort is not and perhaps cannot be, successful. After distinguishing self-love from agape, love from loving the right things and caring love from nonviolence, two other conclusions are drawn: first, that fluent speakers would not be inclined to say that a person caringly loves another person if we thought he would never use force and deadly force, if necessary, to protect his beloved; second, there also remains the moral problem of how to successfully reconcile the obligation to protect a beloved with an unconditional love which, when it is a matter of habit, demands that we love those that hate or harm us.

**Kohlenbach, Michael** (ed) and Groddeck, Wolfram (ed). *Nietzsche Werke Kritische Gesamtausgabe: III 5/1*. Hawthorne, de Gruyter, 1996.

**Kohlenbach, Michael** (ed) and Groddeck, Wolfram (ed). *Nietzsche Werke Kritische Gesamtausgabe: III 5/2*. Hawthorne, de Gruyter, 1996.

**Kohli, Wendy**. "Teaching In/For the Enunciative Present" in *Philosophy of Education (1996)*, Margonis, Frank (ed), 252-255. Urbana, Phil Education Soc, 1997.

**Kohn Wacher, Carlos**. Los Substratos 'Metafísicos' de la Teoría Demo-Liberal: Prolegómenos. *Rev Filosof (Venezuela)*, 23(1), 93-113, 1996.

This work provides some preliminary results regarding the sorts of fundaments upon which lay most of the liberal theories that deal with the nature of democracy. My point of departure is that, under the façade that it depends the so-called "basic liberties" or "liberal principles" (*The Human Rights*), liberalism, both in its classical and contemporary versions, holds that it is indeed the only doctrine capable of preserving and developing a democratic regime of government. Furthermore, that it possesses the key for "an *impartial* or at least a *fair* distribution of justice" (RAWLS), while, in fact, what it pursues is the establishment of a "rightful" *suprasocial order*. In sum, I shall try to demonstrate that the *telos* of Fukuyama's famous thesis: "The 'end of history' is rooted on the globalization of the market system of society," is not the outset of "the realm of freedom", but of a "neutral" *Leviathan*.

**Kohut, Nitsa** and Singer, Peter A and Sam, Mehran (& others). Stability of Treatment Preferences: Although Most Preferences Do Not Change, Most People Change Some of Their Preferences. *J Clin Ethics*, 8(2), 124-135, Sum 97.

**Koj, Leon**. "Science, Teaching, and Values" in *The Idea of University*, Brzezinski, Jerzy (ed), 117-128. Amsterdam, Rodopi, 1997.

**Kolaitis, Phokion G** and Grädel, Erich and Vardi, Moshe Y. On the Decision Problem for Two-Variable First-Order Logic. *Bull Sym Log*, 3(1), 53-69, Mr 97.

We identify the computational complexity of the satisfiability problem for $FO^2$, the fragment of first-order logic consisting of all relational first-order sentences with at most two distinct variables. Although this fragment was shown to be decidable a long time ago, the computational complexity of its decision problem has not been pinpointed so far. In 1975 Mortimer proved that $FO^2$ has the *finite-model property*, which means that if an $FO^2$-sentence is satisfiable, then it has a finite model. Moreover, Mortimer showed that every satisfiable $FO^2$-sentence has a model whose size is at most doubly exponential in the size of the sentence. In this paper, we improve Mortimer's bound by one exponential and show that every satisfiable $FO^2$-sentence has a model whose size is at most exponential in the size of the sentence. As a consequence, we establish that the satisfiability problem for $FO^2$ is NEXPTIME-complete.

**Kolakowski, Leszek**. "What Are Universities For?" in *The Idea of University*, Brzezinski, Jerzy (ed), 27-33. Amsterdam, Rodopi, 1997.

**Kolany, Adam**. Consequence Operations Based on Hypergraph Satisfiability. *Stud Log*, 58(2), 261-272, Mr 97.

Four consequence operators based on hypergraph satisfiability are defined. Their properties are explored and interconnections are displayed. Finally their relation to the case of the *classical propositional calculus* is shown.

**Kolany, Adam**. Representation Theorems for Hypergraph Satisfiability. *Bull Sec Log*, 26(1), 12-19, Mr 97.

Given a set of propositions, one can consider its inconsistency hypergraph. Then the satisfiability of sets of clauses with respect to that hypergraph turns out to be the usual satisfiability. The problem is which hypergraphs can be obtained from sets of formulas as inconsistency hypergraphs. In the present paper it is shown that this can be done for all hypergraphs with countably many vertices and pairwise incomparable edges. Then, a general method of transforming the combinatorial problems into the satisfiability problem is shown.

**Kolársky, Rudolf**. Deep Ecology and its Significance for Philosophical Thought (in Czech). *Filosof Cas*, 45(3), 411-425, 1997.

The article concentrates on the question of what is the "deepness" of deep ecology. Its founder, A. Naess, sees the current ecological crisis as having deep-reaching effects on the life of people today, so that overcoming this crisis calls for deep-reaching changes. The depths of deep ecology can be understood in connection with the proposal for radical changes in the platform of the deep ecology movement, with Naess's thesis that the deep ecology movement is distinguished by a deeper questioning and with the concept of personal self-realization as identification with other people and with nature. The radical nature of the proposed changes and the depth of experience of identity with nature can be seen as a call to new "deeper" questions and so calls for radical questioning.

**Kolársky, Rudolf**. Environmental Ethics and the Critique of Anthropocentrism (Czech). *Filosof Cas*, 45(1), 73-88, 1997.

The paper is intended as a step towards clarifying the importance of the critique of anthropocentrism for environmental ethics. It concentrates on the question of the possibilities and means for bringing anthropocentrism and biocentrism closer together. It sees the relationship between these two as marked by moves towards each other, by complementing each other and by the lack of negotiation. The relation can be described as mutual amendment which prevents the extremes of either party increasing their influence.

**Kolas, Pawel**. The God and a Man-Philosopher: Vocation for Philosophy on the Basis of F.W.I. Schelling's Anthropotheology (in Polish). *Kwartalnik Filozof*, 23(1), 79-96, 1995.

**Komorowski, Jan** and Polkowski, Lech T and Skowron, Andrzej. Towards a Rough Mereology-Based Logic for Approximate Solution. *Stud Log*, 58(1), 143-184, 1997.

We are concerned with formal models of reasoning under uncertainty. Many approaches to this problem are known in the literature, e.g., Dempster-Shafer theory, Bayesian-based reasoning, belief networks, many-valued logics and fuzzy logics, nonmonotonic logics, neural network logics. We propose rough mereology developed by the last two authors as a foundation for approximate reasoning about complex objects. Our notion of a complex object includes, among others, proofs understood as schemes constructed in order to support within our knowledge assertions/hypotheses about reality described by our knowledge incompletely.

**Konaté, Yacouba**. "Parole et démocratie" in *Philosophy and Democracy in Intercultural Perspective*, Kimmerle, Heinz (ed), 141-158. Amsterdam, Rodopi, 1997.

**Kondratowicz, Diane M**. Approaches Responsive to Reproductive Technologies: A Need for Critical Assessment and Directions for Further Study. *Cambridge Quart Healthcare Ethics*, 6(2), 148-156, Spr 97.

Technological intervention in human reproduction has long been a subject of controversy. In addition to identifying two focal points of debate, this paper delineates a number of approaches that have been formulated by scholars in response to a host of problems reproductive technologies allegedly pose. Maintaining that critical assessment of these approaches is necessary, this paper identifies two areas of inquiry that deserve attention, notably, whether these approaches are warranted and, if so, which if any provide an appropriate and sufficient response to the problems scholars identify. Directions that might guide this inquiry are sketched.

**Konikowska, Beata**. A Logic for Reasoning about Relative Similarity. *Stud Log*, 58(1), 185-226, 1997.

A similarity relation is a reflexive and symmetric binary relation between objects. Similarity is relative: it depends on the set of properties of objects used in determining their similarity or dissimilarity. A multimodal logical language for reasoning about relative similarities is presented. The modalities correspond semantically to the upper and lower approximations of a set of objects by similarity relations corresponding to all subsets of a given set of properties of objects. A complete deduction system for the language is presented.

**Kontos, Pavlos**. L'éthique aristotélicienne et le chemin de Heidegger. *Rev Phil Louvain*, 95(1), 130-143, F 97.

The Heideggerian *Sophistes* offers an interpretation to Aristotelian ethics in the light of the existentials of *Being and Time*. Confronting two classical approaches of this topic (these of F. Volpi and J. Taminiaux), we pay attention to the triple structure: techne, phronesis, sophia and its possible projection on the terms: inauthenticity, care, authenticity. This strategy procures a deep explanation of techne in his neighbouring with the ready-on-hand (*Zuhandenheit*) and overall the chance to distinguish the care/phronesis from the supreme authenticity, economizing her ontologization.

**Kontostathis, Kyriakos**. The Combinatorics of the Splitting Theorem. *J Sym Log*, 62(1), 197-224, Mr 97.

**Koons, Robert C**. A New Look at the Cosmological Argument. *Amer Phil Quart*, 34(2), 193-211, Ap 97.

The article presents a new version of a classical argument: the cosmological argument from contingency. This version of the argument is unique in several respects: i) in its application of the theory of mereology to facts, ii) in its use of recent research on defeasible reasoning and causal inference, and iii) its use of a new concept, that of "wholly contingent" facts, in formulating a principle of universal causation. Standard objections to the cosmological argument (such as those of Ross and Rowe) fail against the new version. Finally, a successful cosmological argument provides strong support for the argument from design.

**Koontz, Theodore J**. Noncombatant Immunity in Michael Walzer's *Just and Unjust Wars*. *Ethics Int Affairs*, 11, 55-82, 1997.

Issues of immunity from attack and the assignment of responsibility for civilian deaths are central to the modern war convention. Koontz addresses several difficulties with Walzer's treatment of noncombatant immunity in *Just and Unjust Wars*. Walzer's theory of noncombatant immunity states that immunity from attack is a fundamental human right that can only be lost once a person becomes a direct threat or consents to give up his or her right to immunity. Using a deontological approach, Koontz cites inconsistencies in Walzer's method of determining the immunity of soldiers and civilians. Koontz argues that there can be no other form of consent to the loss of immunity besides the direct threat posed by a civilian, thereby eliminating inconsistencies and strengthening noncombatant protection.

**Kopelman, Loretta M**. Children and Bioethics: Uses and Abuses of The Best-Interest Standard: Introduction. *J Med Phil*, 22(3), 213-217, Je 97.

The best interest standard is used to guide moral, social, and legal decisions for children, as well as other incompetent persons. For example, it directs us how to select from among treatment options for a sick or dying child, settle custody disputes, allocate health care, and decide when children can participate in research. It is under attack, however, as self-defeating, individualistic, unknowable, vague, dangerous, and open to abuse. Contributors either question or defend its use as a guidance principle in certain contexts for clinicians, policy-makers, or surrogates making decisions for children individually or collectively. These authors examine whether this is one standard at all, and whether it permits clinicians to honor such choices as parental requests to screen children for late-onset genetic diseases.

**Kopelman, Loretta M**. The Best-Interests Standard as Threshold, Ideal, and Standard of Reasonableness. *J Med Phil*, 22(3), 271-289, Je 97.

The best-interest standards is a widely used ethical, legal, social basis for policy and decision-making involving children and other incompetent persons. It is under attack, however, as self-defeating, individualistic, unknowable, vague, dangerous, and open to abuse. The author defends this standard by identifying its employment, first, as a threshold for intervention and judgment (as in child abuse and neglect rulings), second, as an ideal to establish policies or *prima facie* duties, and, third, as a standard of reasonableness. Criticisms of the best-interests standard are reconsidered after clarifying these different meanings.

**Koppe, Simo** and Emmeche, Claus and Stjernfelt, Frederik. Explaining Emergence: Towards an Ontology of Levels. *J Gen Phil Sci*, 28(1), 83-119, 1997.

The vitalism/reductionism debate in the life sciences shows that the idea of emergence as something principally unexplainable will often be falsified by the development of science. Nevertheless, the concept of emergence keeps reappearing in various sciences and cannot easily be dispensed with in an evolutionary world-view. We argue that what is needed is an ontological nonreductionist theory of levels of reality which includes a concept of emergence and which can support an evolutionary account of the origin of levels. (edited)

**Koppelberg, Dirk**. Was macht eine Erkenntnistheorie naturalistisch?. *J Gen Phil Sci*, 27(1), 71-90, 1996.

"On What Makes an Epistemology Naturalistic." Since the publication of W. V. Quine's classic paper "Epistemology Naturalized" there have been many discussions on the virtues and vices of naturalistic epistemology. Within these discussions not much attention has been paid to a basic question: What makes an epistemology naturalistic? I give an answer by providing a logical geography of competing naturalistic positions. Then I defend naturalistic epistemology against the charge of the so-called causal fallacy. Finally I give a critical appraisal of different naturalistic theories of knowledge and introduce cooperative naturalism as the most promising research strategy.

**Korcz, Keith Allen**. Recent Work on the Basing Relation. *Amer Phil Quart*, 34(2), 171-191, Ap 97.

**Korey, William**. Minority Rights After Helsinki. *Ethics Int Affairs*, 8, 119-139, 1994.

**Korey, William**. The United States and the Genocide Convention: Leading Advocate and Leading Obstacle. *Ethics Int Affairs*, 11, 271-290, 1997.

While the United States is now an international leader in the fight against genocide and human rights abuses, it only recently ratified the Convention on the Prevention and Punishment of the Crime of Genocide—forty years after the convention's unanimous adoption by the United Nations General Assembly. Korey provides a description of the long struggle for ratification of the Genocide Convention, detailing decades of work by a committee of fifty-two nongovernmental organizations lobbying the Senate and the American Bar Association, the treaty's key opponent. Despite the public support for the United Nations and human rights by the United States, failure to ratify the Genocide Convention stemmed primarily from the fear that international covenants were threats to U.S. sovereignty. The United States finally overcame this fear with the final ratification of the Genocide Convention in 1988 which subsequently opened the doors to U.S. leadership against genocide and the advancement of the rule of law.

**Korn, James H** and Nicks, Sandra D and Mainieri, Tina. The Rise and Fall of Deception in Social Psychology and Personality Research, 1921 to 1994. *Ethics Behavior*, 7(1), 69-77, 1997.

The frequency of the use of deception in American psychological research was studied by reviewing articles from journals in personality and social psychology from 1921 to 1994. Deception was used rarely during the developmental years of social psychology into the 1930s, then grew gradually and irregularly until the 1950s. Between the 1950s and 1970s the use of deception increased significantly. This increase is attributed to changes in experimental methods, the popularity of realistic impact experiments, and the influence of cognitive dissonance theory. Since 1980 there appears to have been a decrease in the use of deception as compared to previous decades which is related to changes in theory, methods, ethical standards, and federal regulation of research.

**Kornblith, Hilary** and Christensen, David. Testimony, Memory and the Limits of the *A Priori*. *Phil Stud*, 86(1), 1-20, Ap 97.

Tyler Burge compares perception's role in testimony-based beliefs to its role in diagram-based mathematical proofs, arguing that testimonial beliefs can be *a priori* warranted. We argue that disanalogies undermine Burge's argument and that perception's role in testimonial beliefs is more closely analogous to its role in clearly *a posteriori* beliefs such as those based on reading clocks. Testimonial beliefs are not *a priori* in any interesting sense. Burge also emphasizes that memory, though only contingently reliable, plays a role in mathematical reasoning. We examine the extent to which human memory's heavy reliance on background beliefs renders memory-based beliefs *a posteriori*.

**Kornfeld, Donald S**. Commentary on "A Model Policy Addressing Mistreatment of Students". *J Clin Ethics*, 7(4), 347-348, Wint 96.

**Kosciuszko, Krzysztof**. Witkacy and Eddington—Two Conceptions of Metaphysics (in Polish). *Kwartalnik Filozof*, 24(4), 69-84, 1996.

**Koselleck, Reinhart**. "Remarks on the History of the Concept of Crisis" in *The Ancients and the Moderns*, Lilly, Reginald (ed), 148-158. Bloomington, Indiana Univ Pr, 1996.

**Koslicki, Kathrin**. Four-Eighths Hephaistos: Artifacts and Living Things in Aristotle. *Hist Phil Quart*, 14(1), 77-98, Ja 97.

The view that artifact-forms are related to their matter in a way crucially different from that of natural forms has a long tradition. This tradition has recently been called into question by the so-called functionalist interpretation of Aristotle's "philosophy of mind", initially proposed by Hilary Putnam and Martha Nussbaum. As against the functionalist interpretation, I argue that living things, according to Aristotle, must be made of the particular kind of matter of which they are actually made. Multiple realizability, hence, does not apply to living things.

**Kosman, Admiel**. Comments on the Paradox of Modesty (in Hebrew). *Iyyun*, 46, 209-220, Ap 97.

**Kossler, Matthias**. Empire, Transzendentalismus und Transzendenz: Neue Literatur zu Arthur Schopenhauer. *Phil Rundsch*, 43(4), 273-296, D 96.

**Kossovitch, Leon**. Permanence and Renovation in Arts (in Portuguese). *Discurso*, 26, 83-92, 1996.

The combination of rhetorical topics is to the constitution of the doctrines in arts. The nuclear *topoi* of Antiquity and Renaissance are presented as selected in the previous field of *inventio*; the 19th and 20th centuries art discourse is considered as euphoric and noncritical, for, as desire, it seeks future.

**Kostelanetz, Richard**. Some Notes about the Ethics of Editing Book Anthologies. *J Infor Ethics*, 6(1), 44-46, Spr 97.

Drawing upon my experience editing over three dozen anthologies of literature, criticism, and social thought, I have developed some general principles regarding purpose of such books, several strict rules for inclusion/exclusion, fair and generous methods for the crediting and payment of contributors, etc. that I hope might be generally applicable.

**Kostoff, Ronald N**. The Principles and Practices of Peer Review. *Sci Eng Ethics*, 3(1), 19-34, Ja 97.

The principles and practices of research peer review are described. While the principles are fundamentally generic and apply to peer review across the full spectrum of performing institutions as well as to manuscript/proposal/program peer review, the focus of this paper is peer review of proposed and ongoing programs in federal agencies. The paper describes desirable characteristics and important intangible factors in successful peer review. Also presented is a heuristic protocol for the conduct of successful peer review research evaluations and impact assessments. Problems with peer review are then outlined, followed by examples of peer review of proposed and existing programs in selected federal agencies. Some peer review variants, such as the *science court*, are described, and then research requirements to improve peer review are discussed.

**Kostoff, Ronald N**. Use and Misuse of Metrics in Research Evaluation. *Sci Eng Ethics*, 3(2), 109-120, Ap 97.

This paper addresses some critical issues in the applicability of quantitative performance measures (including bibliometric, economic and co-occurrence measures) to the assessment of basic research. The strengths and weaknesses of metrics applied as research performance measures are examined. It is concluded that metrics have a useful role to play in the evaluation of research. (edited)

**Kostyrko, Teresa**. "The 'Transhistoricity' of the Structure of a Work of Art and the Process of Value Transmission in Culture" in *Epistemology and History*, Zeidler-Janiszewska, Anna (ed), 509-516. Amsterdam, Rodopi, 1996.

In this paper I propose to conceive a work of art as a "transhistorical structure". This structure is a distinctive "humanistic structure" (in Kmita's sense of the term) corresponding to, what we call intuitively, the "proper work of art" and having a particular "constancy". A transhistorical structure is a set of successive historical-social alternative interpretative formulations of the same physical artistic product. The reality of the "transhistorical structure" is connected with the

intersubjective character of the rules of symbolic culture. A work of art in the sense presented here is also a result from our memory of interpretations previously made. Thus, it can be said that the "transhistoricity" of the structure of a work of art consists in the fact, that due to various interpretations, the process of transmitting values is maintained.

**Kotas, Jerzy** and Wojtylak, Piotr. Finite Distributive Lattices as Sums of Boolean Algebras. *Rep Math Log*, 29, 35-40, 1995.

**Kotin, Anthony M**. Do No Harm. *Bioethics Forum*, 12(2), 21-26, Sum 96.

Difficult ethical issues that require attention on the organizational level are emphasized here through the use of case scenarios. Only through adherence to a strong vision of the organization's role in the health care marketplace and a mission to do what is right for those for whom it cares can the organization consistently make appropriate ethical decisions in difficult situations such as these.

**Kotowa, Barbara**. "Humanistic Valuation and Some Social Functions of the Humanities" in *Epistemology and History*, Zeidler-Janiszewska, Anna (ed), 197-205. Amsterdam, Rodopi, 1996.

This article discusses the still ongoing controversy between scientists and antiscientists as to the cognitive status of value-judgments in the humanities. The cognitive standpoint adopted in this paper refers to certain ideas of Marxian historical materialism and employs the assumptions of the social-regulative conception of culture proposed by Jerzy Kmita. The object of this controversy is examined in terms of the (objective) social functions of particular disciplines performed within the humanities at various stages of their historical development.

**Kotva, Joseph J**. The Christian Case for Virtue Ethics. Washington, Georgetown Univ Pr, 1996.

This book is an entry into the current debate about the merits of virtue theory. I will argue for the Christian adoption of a neo-Aristotelian virtue framework by showing that it is compatible with, readily amended to, and useful in expressing Christian convictions and modes of moral reasoning. I will contend that, when evaluated in light of Christian theology and Scripture, virtue theory emerges as a particularly promising way of understanding the moral life. (publisher,edited)

**Kovach, Adam**. Deflationism and the Derivation Game. *Mind*, 106(423), 575-579, Jl 97.

The deflationary theory of truth for propositions aims to explain everything that needs to be explained about truth of propositions by reference to the propositional truth schema, *it is true that* p, *if and only if* p. Previous formulations of the theory, e.g., Horwich's *minimalism*, have failed to provide adequate explanatory derivations of general facts about truth. Matthew McGrath's *weak deflationism* attempts to correct this failure. It is shown that weak deflationism does not provide adequate derivations of general facts about truth.

**Kovach, Adam**. Why We should Lose Our Natural Ontological Attitudes. *S J Phil*, 35(1), 57-74, Spr 97.

Arthur Fine's influential "natural ontological attitude" (NOA) presents a challenge to scientific realists and antirealists alike. According to NOA, metaphysical and epistemological interpretations of science are pointless and we are practically better off without them. NOA especially opposes metaphysical theories of truth. This article clarifies this philosophical attitude. It assesses Fine's arguments against the possibility of a theory of truth. It exposes some difficulties facing NOA. This provides a practical incentive to lose the attitude.

**Kovacs, George**. The Meaning of History: A Further Contribution to URAM Buber Studies (URAM 17:33-49). *Ultim Real Mean*, 19(4), 285-291, D 96.

This essay argues that history has a meaning and that this meaning has contemporary relevance; it shows that history is not a random cycle of irrational forces, but a life of tension between the "forces of closure" and the "deeds of freedom." It develops these claims in light of Martin Buber's philosophy of history, together with the assessment of Buber's thesis on ultimate meaning in history.

**Kowalski, Ludwik**. An Exploration into Teaching with Computers. *Inquiry (USA)*, 14(3), 64-71, Spr 95.

**Kowalski, Tomasz**. A Syntactic Proof of a Conjecture of Andrzej Wronski. *Rep Math Log*, 28, 81-86, 1994.

A syntactic derivation of Cornish identity (J) from the axioms of HBCK is presented which amounts to a syntactic proof of Wronski's conjecture that naturally ordered BCK-algebras form a variety.

**Kowalski, Tomasz**. The Bottom of the Lattice of BCK-Varieties. *Rep Math Log*, 29, 87-93, 1995.

**Kozak, Ellen M**. Towards a Definition of Plagiarism: The Bray/Oates Controversy Revisited. *J Infor Ethics*, 3(1), 70-75, Spr 94.

**Kozel, Susan**. The Diabolical Strategy of Mimesis: Luce Irigaray's Reading of Maurice Merleau-Ponty. *Hypatia*, 11(3), 114-129, Sum 96.

In this essay I explore the dynamic between Luce Irigaray and Maurice Merleau-Ponty as it unfolds in *An Ethics of Sexual Difference* (1993). Irigaray's strategy of mimesis is a powerful feminist tool, both philosophically and politically. Regarding textual engagement as analogous for relations between self and other beyond the text, I deliver a cautionary message: mimetic strategy is powerful but runs the risk of silencing the voice of the other.

**Krabbe, Erik C W**. "Can we Ever Pin One Down to a Formal Fallacy?" in *Logic and Argumentation*, Van Eemeren, Frans H (ed), 129-141. Amsterdam, North-Holland, 1994.

In this paper, some circumstances are discussed in which it is possible to track down a formal fallacy. Charges of formal fallaciousness often seem impotent as instruments of argument evaluation and criticism. In a special dialogical setting, however, it does seem possible to pin down a formal fallacy. In order to show that, the Oliver-Massey asymmetry needs to be neutralized.

**Kracht, Marcus**. Syntactic Codes and Grammar Refinement. *J Log Lang Info*, 4(1), 41-60, 1995.

We call *syntactic coding* a technique which converts syntactic principles or constraints on representations into grammatical rules which can be implemented in any given rule grammar. In this paper we show that any principle or constraint on output trees formalizable in a certain fragment of dynamic logic over trees can be coded in this sense. This allows to reduce in a mechanical fashion most of the current theories of government and binding into GPSG-style grammars. This will be exemplified with Rizzi's *Relativized Minimality*.

**Krämer, Felix**. "Fichtes frühe Wissenschaftslehre als dialektische Erörterung" in *Sein—Reflexion—Freiheit: Aspekte der Philosophie Johann Gottlieb Fichtes,* Asmuth, Christoph (ed), 143-158. Amsterdam, Gruner, 1997.

**Krämer, Felix**. Parallelen zwischen Maimon und dem frühen Fichte. *Fichte-Studien*, 9, 275-290, 1997.

**Krämer, Hans**. Die Idee der Einheit in Platons Timaios. *Perspekt Phil*, 22, 287-304, 1996.

Six meanings of unity are to be found in Plato's *Timaeus* (singularity, uniqueness, totality/wholeness, simplicity/indivisibility, unity in plurality, identity). The metaphor of world-making hints at the world-order's teleological status, which is unity in plurality. Also the triangles of the world's substrate have a high degree of unity by virtue of symmetry and simplicity. There is an isomorphy between the levels of being. As Xenocrates' interpretation of Plato's physics shows, the regional ontology of the *Timaeus* was inserted in a system of derivation founded in the two principles and anticipating the modern program of a "deductive physics" (V. Weizsäcker).

**Krämer, Hans**. Überlegungen zur Anwendungsdimension der Philosophie. *Z Phil Praxis*, 10-12, 1995.

Application is essential for practical philosophy and reasoning, in contrast to a self-sufficient, autarchic philosophical theory as well as, on the other side, to an isolated sphere of "application", without an applied, in singular situations. Instead, practical reason applies general rules, modified and amplified by specific additions. Exercise of practical *judice* (competence of application) is possible by means of artificial scenarios and models. Application is different from improvisation, which goes far beyond and is not bound to an applicable, but can be improved in a similar way.

**Krämer, Hans Joachim**. The New View of Plato. *Grad Fac Phil J*, 19(1), 25-41, 1996.

**Krämer, Sybille**. Über das Verhältnis von Algebra und Geometrie in Descartes'"Geometrie". *Phil Natur*, 26(1), 19-40, 1989.

**Krämer, Sybille**. Zur Begründung des Infinitesimalkalküls durch Leibniz, *Phil Natur*, 28(2), 117-146, 1991.

**Krajicek, J**. Interpolation Theorems, Lower Bounds for Proof Systems, and Independence Results for Bounded Arithmetic. *J Sym Log*, 62(2), 457-486, Je 97.

A proof of the (propositional) Craig interpolation theorem for cut-free sequent calculus yields that a sequent with a cut-free proof (or with a proof with cut-formulas of restricted form; in particular, with only analytic cuts) with *k* inferences has an interpolant whose circuit-size is at most *k*. We give a new proof of the interpolation theorem based on a communication complexity approach which allows a similar estimate for a larger class of proofs. (edited)

**Kramer, Eric Mark**. *Modern/Postmodern: Off the Beaten Path of Antimodernism*. Westport, Praeger, 1997.

In this book Eric Kramer introduces his theory of dimensional accrual/dissociation to explain the difference between modernity and postmodernity. He also argues that social scientific operational definitions are useful but very often arbitrary. Thus, realities based on them are available for creative (alternative) validities. Kramer applies this position to the concepts of modernity and postmodernity, providing a painstaking review of the origins, key thinkers and current status of these ideas. By reviewing the development of these ideas and providing clear definitions of these concepts, Kramer helps scholars and researchers in the social sciences and humanities better understand applications and limitations of these key approaches in late twentieth-century scholarship. (publisher)

**Kramer, Lloyd**. Historical Narratives and the Meaning of Nationalism. *J Hist Ideas*, 58(3), 525-545, Jl 97.

**Kramer, Matthew H** and Simmonds, Nigel E. Reason Without Reasons: A Critique of Alan Gewirth's Moral Philosophy. *S J Phil*, 34(3), 301-315, Fall 96.

Alan Gewirth in numerous important writings has attempted to show that every purposive agent, simply by dint of being such an agent, is logically committed to a supreme moral principle—a principle which enjoins every agent to respect the fundamental well-being of every other agent. This essay refutes Gewirth's argument by exposing his repeated failure to attend to the distinction between not having a reason for action and not acknowledging a reason for action. When that distinction is properly heeded, Gewirth's derivation of a moral precept from the pre-moral posture of agency turns out to be untenable.

**Krámsky, David**. The Harmony of the World and its Greek Connection (in Czech). *Filosof Cas*, 45(2), 237-259, 1997.

In Greek mythology the origin of harmony appears in its link with music and light, through which it resolves antitheses. In harmony music and light are one and the same. Thus Orpheus's miraculous music brought peace between animals which are natural predators and prey, and Apollo's light joined Dionysus' *fysis* and the

Apollonian being or lack of control in a single rational whole. "Light" penetrates temporality and creates coherence/continuity. The existence of coherence/continuity makes situation and orientation possible, just as orientation lays the groundwork for communication and social relationships. Orientation also creates similarity itself; thus people are alike in their similar orientation to the world. (edited)

**Krasnoff, Larry**. The Fact of Politics: History and Teleology in Kant. *Euro J Phil*, 2(1), 22-40, Ap 94.

**Kratochvíl, Zdenek**. Religious Studies and Theology. Ethics and Philosophy (in Czech). *Filosof Cas*, 45(2), 321-324, 1997.

**Kraus, Jody S**. A Non-Solution to a Non-Problem: A Comment on Alan Strudler's "Mass Torts and Moral Principles". *Law Phil*, 16(1), 91-100, 97.

**Krause, Décio** and Da Costa, Newton C A. Schrödinger Logics. *Stud Log*, 53(4), 533-550, N 94.

Schrödinger logics are logical systems in which the principle of identity is not true in general. The intuitive motivation for these logics is both Erwin Schrödinger's thesis (which has been advanced by other authors) that identity lacks sense for elementary particles of modern physics, and the way which physicists deal with this concept; normally they understand *identity* as meaning *indistinguishabilty* (agreement with respect to attributes). Observing that these concepts are equivalent in classical logic and mathematics, which underly the usual physical theories, we present a higher-order logical system in which these concepts are systematically separated. A 'classical' semantics for the system is presented and some philosophical related questions are mentioned. (edited)

**Krause, Décio** and French, Steven. Quantum Objects are Vague Objects. *Sorites*, 21-33, Ag 96.

Is there vagueness in the world? This is the central question that we are concerned with. Focusing on identity statements around which much of the recent debate has centred, we argue that 'vague identity' arises in quantum mechanics in one of two ways. First, quantum particles may be described as individuals, with 'entangled' states understood in terms of nonsupervenient relations. In this case, the vagueness is ontic but exists at the level of these relations which act as a kind of 'veil'. Secondly, the particles can be regarded as nonindividuals, where this is understood as a lack of self-identity and given formal expression in terms of quasi-set theory. Here we have ontic vagueness at perhaps the most basic metaphysical level. Our conclusion is that there is genuine vagueness 'in the world' but how it is understood depends on the metaphysical package adopted.

**Krausz, Joshua** and Pava, Moses L. Criteria for Evaluating the Legitimacy of Corporate Social Responsibility. *J Bus Ethics*, 16(3), 337-347, F 97.

The goal of this paper is to provide a general discussion about the legitimacy of corporate social responsibility. Given that social responsibility projects entail costs, it is not always obvious under what precise conditions managers will have a responsibility to engage in activities primarily designed to promote societal goals. (edited)

**Krebs, Angelika**. "Ökologische Ethik I: Grundlagen und Grundbegriffe" in *Angewandte Ethik: Die Bereichsethiken und ihre theoretische Fundierung*, Nida-Rümelin, Julian (ed), 346-385. Stuttgart, Alfred Kröner, 1996.

This article presents a critical taxonomy of arguments for the conservation of nature. Six physiocentric and seven anthropocentric arguments are distinguished. The physiocentric arguments are: the pathocentric, teleological, reverence-for-life, naturam-sequi, theological and holistic argument. Of these arguments only the first one is found to be valid. The anthropocentric arguments are: the basic-needs, aisthesis, aesthetic-contemplation, natural-design, "Heimat", pedagogic argument and the argument from the meaning of life. All of the anthropocentric arguments are found to be valid. The position advocated is thus a rich version of anthropocentrism (according nature not only instrumental, but also intrinsic value (e.g., intrinsic aesthetic value) plus pathocentrism (according sentient nature intrinsic moral value).

**Krebs, Angelika**. Discourse Ethics and Nature. *Environ Values*, 6(3), 269-279, Ag 97.

The question this paper examines is whether or not discourse ethics is an environmentally attractive moral theory. The answer reached is: no. For firstly, nature has nothing to gain from the discourse ethical shift from monological moral reflection to discourse, as nature cannot partake in discourse. And secondly, nature (even sentient animal nature) has no sociopersonal integrity, which, according to discourse ethics, it is the function of morality to protect. Discourse ethics is a thoroughly anthropocentric moral theory.

**Krebs, Angelika**. Moral und Gemeinschaft: Eine Kritik an Tugendhat. *Z Phil Forsch*, 51(1), 93-102, Ja-Mr 97.

In seinen *Vorlesungen über Ethik* (1993) tritt Ernst Tugendhat u.a. dafür ein, dass sich das moralische "alle" auf alle kooperationsfähigen Wesen bezieht. Hätte Tugendhat recht, gehörten z.B. Tiere und Foeten nicht zum moralischen Universum. Wer ihnen Leid zufügte, täte ihnen kein Unrecht. Die These dieses Artikels ist, dass Tugendhat in dieser Sache fehlgeht. Das moralische "alle" bezieht sich auf alle leidensfähigen und nicht nur auf alle kooperationsfähigen Wesen. Der Artikel sucht den Fehler in Tugendhats Argumentation, findet ihn in einem doppeldeutigen Gebrauch des Begriffes "Kooperation" und ziegt auf hier ansonsten Tugendhatscher Basis, dass alle leidensfähigen Wesen zum moralischen Universum gehören. Das heisst dann aber auch, dass die alte Kantische und auch Tugendhatsche Dichotomie von "Pflichten in Ansehung" versus "Pflichten gegenüber" durch eine Trichotomie ersetzt werden muss.

**Krebs, Dennis L** and Denton, Kathy and Wark, Gillian. The Forms and Functions of Real-Life Moral Decision-Making. *J Moral Educ*, 26(2), 131-145, Je 97.

People rarely make the types of moral judgement evoked by Kohlberg's test when they make moral decisions in their everyday lives. The anticipated consequences of real-life moral decisions, to self and to others, may influence moral choices and the structure of moral reasoning. To understand real-life moral judgement we must attend to its functions, which, although they occasionally involve resolving hypothetical moral dilemmas like those on Kohlberg's test, more often involve promoting good social relations, upholding favourable self-concepts and justifying self-interested behaviour. We argue that a functional model of moral judgement and moral behaviour derived from evolutionary theory may supply a better account of real-life morality than the Kohlbergian model.

**Krebs, Víctor J**. El Naturalismo Trascendental del Ultimo Wittgenstein. *Ideas Valores*, 61-75, Ap 96.

The present article considers an internal tension in Wittgenstein's late philosophy. In what I call his 'naturalism', Wittgenstein circumscribes philosophical reflection to natural objects, to "making natural history". In his 'transcendentalism', he focuses on the "possibility of phenomena" and distinguishes philosophical method from the method of the natural sciences. I show that his 'transcendentalism' is present in his discussion of rules and private language, arguing for an interpretation in terms of a Kantian type of transcendental synthesis. But far from contradicting his 'naturalism', both tendencies are inseparable and essential to the main purpose of his *Philosophical Investigations*.

**Kreimendahl, Lothar**. Zur Geschichte des ontologischen Gottesbeweises. *Phil Rundsch*, 44(1), 44-51, Mr 97.

This is a critical review of Wolfgang Röd's *Der Gott der reinen Vernunft*, (München, 1992). Special attention is given to the proofs presented by Anselm, Descartes, Leibniz, Spinoza, Hume's criticisms as well as Kant's presentation and critique of it. It is shown that Röd's main thesis concerning the function of ontological proofs in all rationalistic systems has to be refused.

**Kremer, Elmar J** and Katz, Bernard D. The Cosmological Argument Without the Principle of Sufficient Reason. *Faith Phil*, 14(1), 62-70, Ja 97.

We formulate a version of the *cosmological argument* that deploys an epistemic principle of explanation in place of the traditional *principle of sufficient reason*. The epistemic principle asserts that if there is a possible explanation of a fact, and some proposition is entailed by that explanation and by every other possible explanation of that fact, it is reasonable to accept that proposition. We try to show that there is a possible explanation of the fact that there are contingent beings and that any possible explanation of this fact presupposes that there is a necessary being. We conclude that it is reasonable to believe that there is a necessary being.

**Kremer, Philip**. On the Complexity of Propositional Quantification in Intuitionistic Logic. *J Sym Log*, 62(2), 529-544, Je 97.

We define a propositionally quantified intuitionistic logic H*sub-pi+* by a natural extension of Kripke's semantics for propositional intuitionistic logic. We then show that H*sub-pi+* is recursively isomorphic to full second order classical logic. H*sub-pi+* is the intuitionistic analogue of the modal systems S5*sub-pi+*, S4*sub-pi+*, S4.2*sub-pi+*, K4*sub-pi+*, T*sub-pi+*, K*sub-pi+* and B*sub-pi+*, studied by Fine.

**Krentz, Arthur A**. Kierkegaard's Dialectical Image of Human Existence in *The Concluding Unscientific Postscript to the Philosophical Fragments*. *Phil Today*, 41(2), 277-287, Sum 97.

This paper explores the philosophical anthropology of Kierkegaard's *Postscript* which is shaped by Diotima/Socrates' account of the birth of Eros/existence in Plato's *Symposium*. The character of Eros is derived from the genetic legacy his divine and human parent—resource and need. Based on this narrative, Kierkegaard describes existence as a "dialectical" synthesis of the opposed characteristics of the infinite, the eternal and the temporal. The paper explores the adequacy of this account of the dialectic of human existence and how it is manifested in Kierkegaard's aesthetic, ethical and religious "stages of existence."

**Kresse, Kai**. Interview with Professor Henry Odera Oruka. *Quest*, 9(2), 22-31, D 96.

**Kresse, Kai** (ed) and Graness, Anke (ed). *Sagacious Reasoning: Henry Odera Oruka in Memoriam*. New York, Lang, 1997.

The tragic death of H. Odera Oruka on December 9th 1995 was a big loss for African philosophy and world philosophy on the whole. This book commemorates the important philosopher by presenting and discussing eminent contributions of his to the African and global philosophical debate, among others his projects of sage philosophy, a philosophy of foreign aid and parental earth ethics.

**Kretzmann, Norman**. *The Metaphysics of Theism: Aquinas's Natural Theology in Summa contra gentiles* I. New York, Clarendon/Oxford Pr, 1997.

Professor Kretzmann follows Aquinas in seeing natural theology as the means of integrating philosophy and theology. What makes this enterprise *natural* theology is its forgoing of appeals to revelation as evidence for the truth of propositions. What makes it natural *theology* is its agenda: to investigate, by means of analysis and argument, not only the existence and nature of God but also the relation of everything else—especially human nature and behavior—to God considered as reality's first principle. Professor Kretzmann argues that natural theology offers the most appropriate route by which philosophers can, as philosophers, approach theological propositions, and that the one presented in this book is the best available natural theology. (publisher, edited)

**Kretzmann, Norman** and Stump, Eleonore. An Objection to Swinburne's Argument for Dualism. *Faith Phil*, 13(3), 405-412, Jl 96.

In response to published objections, Swinburne has recently defended his 1984 argument for Cartesian dualism ("Dualism Intact," *Faith and Philosophy* 13

(1996)). We raise an objection that has not yet appeared in the literature and is fatal to the argument. We show that, viewed from more than one angle, the argument is either invalid, or unsound because the second of its three premises is false. We also emphasize that our criticisms don't constitute or even contribute to an argument against dualism generally.

**Kreysing, Helmuth**. Boris Uexkülls Aufzeichnungen Zum Subjektiven Geist—Eine Vorlesungsnachschrift?. *Jahr Hegelforschung*, 2, 5-25, 1996.

**Krifka, Manfred**. Parametrized Sum Individuals for Plural Anaphora. *Ling Phil*, 19(6), 555-598, D 96.

A theory of direct dynamic interpretation is proposed for anaphora with singular and plural pronouns under collective and distributive readings, as in "Three students (each) wrote an article. They (each) sent it/them to a journal," or in "Most of the students that wrote an article liked it." It makes use of the concept of a parameterized individual proposed by Barwise (1985), and of a sum individual proposed by Link (1983). The resulting framework is more restrictive than Discourse Representation Theory (Kamp & Reyle 1993), and allows for a compositional derivation of the meanings of sentences and texts.

**Krimsky, Sheldon**. Commentary: "On the Hazards of Whistleblowers and on Some Problems of Young Biomedical Scientists in our Time". *Sci Eng Ethics*, 1(4), 341-344, O 95.

Two case studies illustrate the complexities of whistleblowing protection. The first case portends a dangerous trend of companies that charge investigators with scientific misconduct when their results adversely affect company profits. A second case highlights the conflicts of interest of academic institutions in their investigations of misconduct allegations by whistleblowers within their institution. The essay concludes with an argument that it is a mistake to view the concept of "freedom of inquiry" in science ahistorically as new corporate values define the university. A recalibration of the social contract of scientific autonomy is in order.

**Krimsky, Sheldon** and Rothenberg, L S and Stott, P. Financial Interests of Authors in Scientific Journals: A Pilot Study of 14 Publications. *Sci Eng Ethics*, 2(4), 395-410, O 96.

This paper measures the frequency of selected financial interests held among authors of certain types of scientific publications and assesses disclosure practices of authors. We examined 1105 university authors (first and last cited) from Massachusetts institutions whose 789 articles, published in 1992, appeared in 14 scientific and medical journals. (edited)

**Krishna, Daya**. Can Navya Nyaya Analysis Make a Distinction between Sense and Reference. *J Indian Counc Phil Res*, 13(3), 151, My-Ag 96.

The issue relates to the Nyaya contention that if the *anuyogi* and the *pratiyogi* are different in a sentence then the 'state of affairs' mentioned by them is also different. But, if this is accepted, then there will remain no difference between the 'sense' of a sentence and the 'fact' it is supposed to refer to. This, however, will be a purely idealist position which normally the Nyayika is not supposed to hold.

**Krishna, Daya**. Indian Philosophy in the First Millennium AD: Fact and Fiction. *J Indian Counc Phil Res*, 13(3), 127-135, My-Ag 96.

The article argues that the currently accepted picture of Indian philosophy in the first millennium A.D. is unduly weighted in favor of the so-called 'orthodox' systems of Indian philosophy, ignoring the dominant presence of the Buddhist thinkers who far outnumber both in quantity and quality the combined strength of *all* the other schools of Indian philosophy including the Jains.

**Krishna, Daya**. Is Udayana a *pracchanna advaitin*?. *J Indian Counc Phil Res*, 13(3), 151, My-Ag 96.

The issue raised relates to Udayana's *Atmatattvaviveka* where he places the Advaitin's realization as second only to that of the Nayayika on the ground that, in the former, some difference still remains because of the fact of self-consciousness, while in the latter, even that too is transcended. Thus, his objection to the Advaitin's position is that it is not Advaitic enough, for if it were to be so, it will be just like the Nyāya position.

**Krishnamurti, J** and Martin, Raymond (ed). *Krishnamurti: Reflections on the Self*. Chicago, Open Court, 1997.

The book is a collection of Krishnamurti's writings and lectures about the individual in relation to society. In *Reflections*, he examines the importance of inquiry, the role of emotions, the relations between experience and the self, the observer/observed distinction, the nature of freedom, and other philosophical ideas. (publisher, edited)

**Krivine, Jean-Louis**. Une Preuve Formelle et Intuitionniste du Théorème de Complétude de la Logique Classique. *Bull Sym Log*, 2(4), 405-421, D 96.

The *Curry-Howard correspondence* associates a program with each formal proof, and, therefore, a specification of programs with each theorem. But the problem of finding this specification for a given theorem is, in general, absolutely not trivial. This problem is solved here for the Gödel completeness theorem of classical logic. As a by-product, it is shown that this theorem is intuitionistically provable. The specification associated with the completeness theorem is somewhat unexpected: it is a well-known utility for programmers, namely an *interactive disassembler*. Surprisingly enough, the system call protection device, usually implemented in this kind of program, is actually present. The epistemological meaning of these facts will be treated elsewhere.

**Krkac, Kristijan**. Heraclitus of Ephesus on Knowledge. *Filozof Istraz*, 16(3), 761-769, 1996.

In the article the author tries to give some crucial denotations on Heraclitus's concept of knowledge. He tries to justify the use of the concept of 'pre-Socratic epistemology' in the relevant extension of course. Finally, he tries to show the importance of Heraclitus's standpoint by analysing the relevant epistemological fragments of his philosophy.

**Krochmalnik, Daniel** and Stegmaier, Werner. *Jüdischer Nietzscheanismus*. Hawthorne, de Gruyter, 1997.

Der Nationalsozialismus hat in Vergessenheit geraten lassen, dass es zum grossen Teil jüdische Intellektuelle waren, die sich zuerst für Nietzsche begeisterten; mit ihnen begann die Nietzsche-Rezeption überhaupt. Nietzsche hatte, gegen den verbreiteten Antisemitismus seiner Zeit, das Judentum hoch geschätzt, und viele Juden schätzten ihn dafür hoch. Sie erwarteten von seinem Denken starke Anstösse für die Erneuerung des Judentums selbst. Unter dem Begriff "Jüdischer Nietzscheanismus" werden jüdische Intellektuelle zusammengefasst, die sich mit Nietzsche im Blick auf ihr Judentum auseinandersetzten, von 1888 an bis zur Gegenwart. Der Band legt dabei das Schwergewicht auf die philosophische Auseinandersetzung mit Nietzsche.

**Krogh, Christen**. "Getting Personal: Some Notes on the Relationship between Personal and Impersonal Obligation" in *Deontic Logic, Agency and Normative Systems,* Brown, Mark A (ed), 134-153. New York, Springer-Verlag, 1996.

The contribution of this paper lies in the analysis of the relationship between impersonal and personal deontic notions, keeping them as close to standard deontic logic as possible. In doing so, arguments are offered against reducing both personal notions to impersonal notions and impersonal notions to personal notions. It is observed that to two new notions of impersonal obligation and permission must be introduced. Finally, an argument is forwarded in favour of one particular representation of ought—to-do and permitted-to—do statements in terms of a personal deontic operator and an action operator.

**Krogh, Christen** and Herrestad, Henning. "Getting Personal: Some Notes on the Relationship between Personal and Impersonal Obligation" in *Deontic Logic, Agency and Normative Systems,* Brown, Mark A (ed), 134-153. New York, Springer-Verlag, 1996.

The contribution of this paper lies in the analysis of the relationship between impersonal and personal deontic notions, keeping them as close to standard deontic logic as possible. In doing so, we offer arguments against reducing both personal notions to impersonal notions, and impersonal notions to personal notions. We discover that we need to introduce two new notions of impersonal obligation and permission. Finally we argue in favor of one particular representation of ought-to-do and permitted-to-do statements.

**Kronen, John D**. Critical Notice of J. Gracia's *Individuation and Identity in Early Modern Philosophy. Sorites*, 34-60, Ag 96.

This review examines, in depth, a number of the articles contained in this collection on the theories of individuation and identity propounded by early modern philosophers. Since many of the articles give philosophical assessments of the theories discussed, the review critically examines, not only the scholarship of the contributors, but their philosophical conclusions as well. Included are lengthy discussions of the articles on the Cartesians, Locke, Leibniz, Hume, Wolf and Kant.

**Kronen, John D**. Substances are not Windowless: A Suarézian Critique of Monadism. *Amer Cath Phil Quart*, 71(1), 59-81, Wint 97.

Recently, Thomas Huffman has defended Leibniz's metaphysics of substance. In this paper I offer a critique of that metaphysics from the point of view of the metaphysics of Leibniz's near contemporary, Francis Suarez. In my critique I show that Suarez's Aristotelianism is better able to account for the existence of composite substances than is Leibniz's metaphysics and that Leibniz's implicit arguments against the Suarezian account of substance fail. I conclude, based upon this, that Suarez's metaphysics should be preferred to Leibniz's since it better accords with the common sense notion that things such as humans and cats are true substances and not mere aggregates.

**Kroon, Frederick W**. Characterizing Non-Existents. *Grazer Phil Stud*, 51, 163-193, 1996.

Consider predicates like 'is a fictional character' and 'is a mythical object'. Since their ascription entails a corresponding *negative existential* claim, call these 'NE-characterizing predicates'. Objectualists such as Parsons, Sylvan, van Inwagen and Zalta think that NE-characterizing properties are genuine properties of genuinely nonexistent objects. But how, then, to make room for statements like 'Vulcan is a failed posit' and 'that little green man is a trick of the light'? The present paper claims that while Walton's view thereby gains an important advantage over objectualism, the solution faces problems of its own. The rest of the paper describes another solution, one that assigns a large role to the idea of metaphor. (edited)

**Kroon, Frederick W**. God's Blindspot. *Dialogue (Canada)*, 35(4), 721-734, Fall 96.

Consider the puzzle of belief-instability: how can a rational agent choose between believing p and not believing p when he also accepts that p is true just when he doesn't believe it to be true? I argue that this puzzle resists satisfactory solution once we insist that the rational agent in question is not only supposed to be ideally rational but is supposed to have infallible knowledge of his ideal rationality. Since the usual conception of God requires God to have such knowledge, the argument suggests that there can't be a God meeting this traditional conception.

**Kruse, Felicia E**. "Peirce's Sign and the Process of Interpretation" in *Philosophy in Experience: American Philosophy in Transition,* Hart, Richard (ed), 128-152. New York, Fordham Univ Pr, 1997.

**Kruse, Michael**. Variation and the Accuracy of Predictions. *Brit J Phil Sci*, 48(2), 181-193, Je 97.

I present a justification for the intuition that more-varied data are more valuable than the same number of less-varied data by showing that the more-varied data help to improve the accuracy of our predictions.

**Kuçuradi, Ioanna**. "Secularization in Turkey" in *Averroës and the Enlightenment,* Wahba, Mourad (ed), 171-176. Amherst, Prometheus, 1996.

In this paper the author tries to show that Atatürk's revolution is a *cultural revolution,* aiming at *secularizing thinking* in Turkey, by introducing the ideas of enlightenment, through the secularization of law and education. She calls the readers' attention to recent attempts to desecularize thinking in Turkey and other regions of the world, made by religious fundamentalisms and promoted by postmodernism and the demand to respect equally all cultures. Thus, at the turn of the millennium we stand before a crucial choice: either to put enlightenment as one of the main objectives of education, or, to let the natural course of events lead where it runs: to a new Middle Ages.

**Kuczewski, Mark**. "Critical Thinking" as a Teaching Methodology: A Questionable Idea at the Wrong Time. *Inquiry (USA)*, 16(3), 42-44, Spr 97.

This essay questions whether certain kinds of philosophy courses designed to promote critical thinking are a good idea. The author argues that courses that purport to teach critical methods irrespective of content turn students into cynics rather than critical thinkers. These approaches are particularly ill-suited to the current crop of college students who are better served by historical and contextual studies.

**Kügler, Peter**. Pragmatische Bedingungen des wissenschaftlichen Realismus. *Phil Natur*, 33(2), 265-287, 1996.

Der wissenschaftliche Realismus wird in diesem Aufsatz als metaphysischer Realismus verstanden. Laut Hilary Putnam beinhaltet dieser die These, dass epistemisch ideale Theorien falsch sein können. Zunächst beschreibe ich das Scheitern von Putnams wichtigstem Argument gegen diese These. Danach entwickle ich eine externalistische Semantik wissenschaftlicher Ausdrücke, der durch pragmatische Überlegungen einiges von ihrer Unbekömmlichkeit genommen wird. Diese Überlegungen stützen sich auf die Begriffe des semantischen Paradigmas und der pragmatischen Angemessenheit von Kausalketten.

**Kuehn, Glenn** and Siliceo-Roman, Laura and Salyards, Jane. Interview with Richard Rorty. *Kinesis*, 23(1), 51-64, Sum 96.

**Kühn, Rolf**. Zur Phänomenologie der Technikentwicklung. *Phil Natur*, 28(2), 257-266, 1991.

**Kühnlein, Michael**. Aufhebung des Religiösen durch Versprachlichung? Eine religionsphilosophische Untersuchung des Rationalitätskonzeptes von Jürgen Habermas. *Theol Phil*, 71(3), 390-409, 1996.

**Küng, Hans**. A Global Ethic in an Age of Globalization. *Bus Ethics Quart*, 7(3), 17-32, Jl 97.

Starting from the four theses that globalization is unavoidable, ambivalent, incalculable, and can be controlled rationally, ethics has an indispensable and important role to play in the process of globalization. Indeed, a number of international documents published in the 1900s not only acknowledge human rights but also speak explicitly of human responsibilities. The author pleads for the primacy of ethics over politics and economics and, in reviewing both the Interfaith Declaration for Jews, Christians, and Muslims, and the Caux Roundtable Principles for Business Conduct, he raises the question about the foundation for the unconditional validity of particular basic ethical values and attitudes. (edited)

**Kuenning, Matthew**. Gadamer's Hermeneutic Externalism. *S J Phil*, 35(2), 179-201, Sum 97.

If the arguments of this paper are sound, Brink is at least tentatively sympathetic to two possible arguments for imposing the burden of argument on the moral antirealist, viz., the PC Argument, and the PC* Argument. Neither of these arguments justify Brink's dialectical stance. (edited)

**Kuhse, Helga** and McKie, John and Richardson, Jeff. Allocating Healthcare By QALYs: The Relevance of Age. *Cambridge Quart Healthcare Ethics*, 5(4), 534-545, Fall 96.

The QALY method ranks health care programs according to the Quality-Adjusted Life-Years they are expected to produce for each available health care dollar. According to some critics, this involves a comprehensive bias against the aged, since the aged have fewer remaining life years than the young. Some ways of defending the QALY approach against the criticism—e.g., by arguing that the aged have already had a "fair innings"—are incompatible with the QALY approach. In contrast, the authors defend the QALY approach by placing it within the context of utilitarian ethics. If discriminating against the aged in the distribution of health care threatens to decrease utility overall, the QALYs of the aged can be given a greater weight in comparison with other groups.

**Kuipers, Ronald A**. "Singular Interruptions: Rortian Liberalism and the Ethics of Deconstruction" in *Knowing Other-Wise: Philosophy at the Threshold of Spirituality,* Olthuis, James H (ed), 105-130. New York, Fordham Univ Pr, 1997.

One consequence of the private/public distinction in Rorty's thought is that his romantic emphasis on the private leads him to disregard the public, ethical impulse at work in deconstructionist philosophy. Yet Derrida, following Levinas, argues that in order to promote justice in a radically plural world we must remain open to the permanent possibility of interruption in our private lives by the singular call that issues from the face of the suffering stranger. To the extent that Rorty's texts show an unwillingness to submit to such an interpretation, his vision for a postphilosophical liberal utopia is found wanting.

**Kuipers, Theo A F**. "Explanation by Intentional, Functional, and Causal Specification" in *Epistemology and History,* Zeidler-Janiszewska, Anna (ed), 209-236. Amsterdam, Rodopi, 1996.

It is argued that intentional, functional and a special kind of causal explanation are of a different nature than explanations by subsumption under a law or theory and that they nevertheless have a sound logical structure and a substantive information content. In contrast to most defences of such claims, it is not argued that these explanations compete with eventual nomological explanation of the same facts. On the contrary, they are only, though highly informative, not so pretentious.

**Kuipers, Theo A F**. "The Carnap-Hintikka Programme in Inductive Logic" in *Knowledge and Inquiry: Essays on Jaakko Hintikka's Epistemology and Philosophy of Science,* Sintonen, Matti (ed), 87-99. Amsterdam, Rodopi, 1997.

Rudolf Carnap initiated a research program in quantitative confirmation theory, also called inductive probability theory, or inductive logic, by designing a continuum of systems for individual hypothesis. It has guided the search for optimum systems and for systems that take analogy into account. Carnapian systems, however, assign zero probability to universal hypotheses. Jaakko Hintikka was the first to reconsider their confirmation. His way of using Carnap's continuum for this purpose has set the stage for a whole spectrum of inductive systems of this type. The Carnap-Hintikka program clearly has many internal dynamics; as will be indicated, its results can also be applied in several directions.

**Kukla, André**. Antirealist Explanations of the Success of Science. *Proc Phil Sci Ass*, 3(Suppl), S298-S305, 1996.

Scientific realists have argued that the truth (likeness) of our theories provides the only explanation for the success of science. I consider alternative explanations proposed by antirealists. I endorse Leplin's contention that neither van Fraassen's Darwinist explanation nor Laudan's methodological explanation provides the sort of explanatory alternative which is called for in this debate. Fine's suggestion—that the empirical adequacy of our theories already explains their success—is more promising for antirealists. Leplin claims that this putative explanation collapses into realism on one reading and into vacuity on another reading. But his analysis conflates three doctrines into two and one of the three avoids both realism and vacuity.

**Kukla, André**. The Theory-Observation Distinction. *Phil Rev*, 105(2), 173-230, Ap 96.

Antirealists like van Fraassen must rely on a distinction between the observational and the nonobservational to formulate their thesis. Additionally, Fodor has argued that scientific realists also need an observational-nonobservational distinction to defend themselves against Kuhnian relativism. I argue that realists don't need the distinction after all and that neither van Fraassen's nor Fodor's manner of making the distinction will serve the purposes of the antirealists. However, there is a third way of making the distinction which may allow antirealists to formulate a coherent version of their thesis.

**Kukla, Rebecca**. "The Coupling of Human Souls: Rousseau and the Problem of Gender Relations" in *Political Dialogue: Theories and Practices,* Esquith, Stephen L (ed), 57-91. Amsterdam, Rodopi, 1996.

Rousseau can help us understand the different forms of private dialogue and interaction that take place between and within the genders. His analysis has implications for political dialogue on a more public scale. Although most critics read Rousseau as committed to a single account of gender relations, we can identify at least three possible forms of relationship that he explores: romantic love relationships dominated by feminine principles, relationships of mastery and slavery dominated by masculine principles and relationships of conjugal affection, which depend upon a fragile balance of power between the genders. This paper ends by problematizing Rousseau's assumption that the citizen of the public domain and the representative of the family unit is necessarily masculine. It suggests that Rousseau's ultimate dissatisfaction with his own attempts to theorize the possibility of social harmony may stem from his failure to question this assumption and explore its alternatives.

**Kulka, Tomas**. *Kitsch and Art.* University Park, Pennsylvania Univ Pr, 1996.

Tomas Kulka examines kitsch in the visual arts, literature, music and architecture. To distinguish kitsch from art, Kulka proposes that kitsch depicts instantly identifiable, emotionally charged objects or themes, but that it does not substantially enrich our associations relating to the depicted objects or themes. He then addresses the deceptive nature of kitsch by examining the make up of its artistic and aesthetic worthlessness. Ultimately Kulka argues that the mass appeal of kitsch cannot be regarded as aesthetic appeal, but that its analysis can illuminate the nature of art appreciation. (publisher)

**Kulstad, Mark A**. Spinoza's Demonstration of Monism: A New Line of Defense. *Hist Phil Quart*, 13(3), 299-316, Jl 96.

This article presents a new interpretation of Spinoza's demonstration of monism in IP14 of his *Ethics*, one that makes possible a defense of this demonstration against two serious challenges to initially plausible interpretations of that demonstration. The interpretation is based in part on ideas initially presented by Martial Guéroult and developed by Louis Loeb. The challenges involve the notion that initially plausible interpretations of the demonstration of monism would commit Spinoza to contradictory theses in Part One of the *Ethics*, that is, to inconsistency in the system of the *Ethics*. Discussion along the way may shed new light on IP5 and IP11, as well as on related discussions of Jonathan Bennett and Don Garrett.

**Kumabe, Masahiro**. Minimal Complementation Below Uniform Upper Bounds for the Arithmetical Degrees. *J Sym Log*, 61(4), 1158-1192, D 96.

It is known that uniform upper bounds for the arithmetical degrees are Turing jumps of upper bounds for the arithmetical degrees. Given a uniform upper bound for the arithmetical degrees, we prove minimal complementation theorem for the upper bounds for the arithmetical degrees below it. We prove this theorem by different methods depending on whether it has a function which is not dominated by any arithmetical function.

**Kumar Giri, Ananta**. The Condition of Postmodernity and the Discourse of the Body. *J Indian Counc Phil Res*, 13(3), 1-23, My-Ag 96.

**Kunin, Howard**. Ethical Issues in Pediatric Life-Threatening Illness: Dilemmas of Consent, Assent, and Communication. *Ethics Behavior*, 7(1), 43-57, 1997.

The treatment of life-threatening illnesses in childhood is replete with ethical issues and with clinical issues that have ethical implications. The central issues are those involved with a child's participation in the decision-making process and with communication of information about the illness and treatments to children. This article examines the questions of patient autonomy and of parental responsibility and prerogative in the context of pediatric oncology. Included in this examination of the ethical dimensions of pediatric life-threatening illness is a discussion of the many related aspects involved, including medical, cultural, psychosocial, legal, and developmental. A multidimensional approach that considers the ways in which these multiple aspects interact with one another, and which focuses on establishing a strong working alliance between the health care team and the pediatric patient's family, can help to avoid or resolve potential ethical and clinical conflicts.

**Kunszt, György**. The Word as Ultimate Reality: The Christian Dialogical Personalism of Ferdinand Ebner. *Ultim Real Mean*, 20(2 & 3), 93-98, Je-S 97.

Buber, Rosenzweig and Lévinas are celebrated representants of Jewish dialogical personalism, while the Catholic Ebner is almost unknown, although Buber proclaimed Ebner's outstanding achievement in dialogical personalism very strongly. Ebner's principal work "The Word and the Spiritual Realities" (1921) reveals the substantial role of the "Word" in creating the "I" and the "Thou" to doubtless realities. On this point Ebner alludes to the "Word" as revealed at the beginning of John's Gospel. This somewhat Gnostic approach may be a cause of the reserved Catholic attitude towards him, although his thinking may become a starting point in further Catholic revival.

**Kuper, Jan**. "Productive Abstraction for Sets" in *Verdad: lógica, representación y mundo,* Villegas Forero, L, 263-272. Santiago de Compostela, Univ Santiago Comp, 1996.

We analyse mathematical abstraction in the case of sets. Our analysis leads to the concept of representation, which means that in mathematical thinking sets exist in two different forms: as ordinary, informal sets (in this paper called *collections*), as formal, mathematical objects (in this paper called *sets*, where the latter "represent" the former. Since these formal objects are produced during the process of mathematical abstraction, we speak of "productive abstraction". We treat four aspects of the idea of representation, each leading to a conceptual understanding of usually highly technical problems and techniques, such as the notion of forcing and the possibility of non-well-founded sets.

**Kupfer, Joseph H**. Swift Things Are Beautiful: Contrast in the Natural Aesthetic. *J Aes Educ*, 31(3), 1-14, Fall 97.

Examining pairs of contrasting categories furthers our understanding of the natural aesthetic. Some categories emphasize the natural phenomena, others stress the appreciator's role in aesthetic experience. Among the first kind are profusion and simplicity. Contrasts stressing the appreciator's role include the noetic and perceptual, such as knowing the age or distance of a star vs. simply enjoying the patterns of veins in a leaf. The essay concludes by focusing on contrast in wintry precipitation. Where snow blatantly unites everything with a rounding, bleaching canopy, for example, fog is subtle and deceptive, shrinking and blurring our visual field.

**Kupfer, Joseph H**. The Sentimental Self. *Can J Phil*, 26(4), 543-560, D 96.

Because the self is the object as well as the subject of sentimentalizing activity, sentimentality is a more serious vice than usually thought. Sentimentalizing begins with simplification and embellishment, producing such uncomplicated emotions as compassion and admiration which support an ennobled view of ourselves. Sentimental idealizing reinforces an entrenched, unambiguous moral perspective on the world. Unsentimental idealizations include reality's ugliness and the difficulty of attaining the ideal. They prompt imaginative reconstructions of unfamiliar life histories, and inquiries into our values. Sentimentalizing the self inhibits self-examination and results from its inhibition. The self-absorption which feeds off the blatant emotional absorption makes sentimentality a deceptive, dangerous vice.

**Kupperman, Joel J**. Autonomy and the Very Limited Role of Advocacy in the Classroom. *Monist*, 79(4), 488-498, O 96.

The thesis of the paper is that advocacy in the college classroom is rarely appropriate in relation to contentious moral, political, or social issues. The main reason is that the aims of higher education include development and protection of students' autonomy. In the sense in which autonomy is a matter of control over one's own life and ability to think for oneself, it is a matter of degree. College education should promote skills of autonomy and advocacy in the classroom can undermine this process.

**Kupperman, Joel J**. Felt and Unfelt Emotions: A Rejoinder to Dalgleish. *Phil Psych*, 10(1), 91, Mr 97.

Dalgleish responds to my paper that appeared in *Philosophical Psychology*, December 1995. This had argued that, while paradigmatic emotions involve feelings, judgments or construals of objects and also motivational thrust, none of these is necessarily to be found in every case of emotion. Dalgleish objects that there can be both feelings and unintentional objects of which the person who has the emotion can be unaware. The rejoinder grants this, but denies that what is sometimes true is universally true: e.g., not all cases in which people experience ecstacy with no sense of what they are ecstatic about involve a hidden intentional object.

**Kurasha, Jameson**. "The African Concept of Personality as a Possible Contribution to Global Reconciliation" in *Kreativer Friede durch Begegnung der Weltkulturen,* Beck, Heinrich (ed), 215-225. New York, Lang, 1995.

**Kurtonina, Natasha** and De Rijke, Maarten. Bisimulations for Temporal Logic. *J Log Lang Info*, 6(4), 403-425, O 97.

We define bisimulations for temporal logic with *since* and *until*. This new notion is compared to existing notions of bisimulations and then used to develop the basic model theory of temporal logic with *since* and *until*. Our results concern both invariance and definability. We conclude with a brief discussion of the wider applicability of our ideas.

**Kurtz, Paul**. "Free Inquiry and Islamic Philosophy: The Significance of George Hourani" in *Averroës and the Enlightenment,* Wahba, Mourad (ed), 233-241. Amherst, Prometheus, 1996.

**Kurtz, Paul**. "Intellectual Freedom, Rationality, and Enlightenment: The Contributions of Averroës" in *Averroës and the Enlightenment,* Wahba, Mourad (ed), 29-40. Amherst, Prometheus, 1996.

**Kurtz, Paul**. The Infomedia Revolution: Opportunities for Global Humanism. *Free Inq*, 17(1), 34-37, Wint 96/97.

**Kurtz, Paul**. The Limits of Tolerance. *Free Inq*, 16(1), 16-19, Wint 95/96.

**Kurucz, A** and Jánossy, A and Eiben, A E. Combining Algebraizable Logics. *Notre Dame J Form Log*, 37(2), 366-380, Spr 96.

The general methodology of "algebraizing" logics is used here for combining different logics. The combination of logics is represented as taking the colimit of the constituent logics in the category of algebaizable logics. The cocompleteness of this category as well as its isomorphism to the corresponding category of certain first-order theories are proved.

**Kurucz, Agnes** and Németi, István and Sain, Ildikó (& others). Decidable and Undecidable Logics with a Binary Modality. *J Log Lang Info*, 4(3), 191-206, 1995.

We give an overview of decidability results for modal logics having a binary modality. We put an emphasis on the demonstration of proof-techniques and hope that this will also help in finding the borderlines between decidable and undecidable fragments of usual first-order logic.

**Kurzweil, Edith**. *The Age of Structuralism: From Lévi-Strauss to Foucault.* New Brunswick, Transaction Pub, 1996.

Structuralism began in Saussurean linguistics and was enlarged by Claude Lévi-Strauss into a new way of thinking that views our world as consisting of relationships between structures we create rather than of objective realities. *The Age of Structuralism* examines the work of seven writers who either expanded upon or reacted against Lévi-Strauss. (edited)

**Kusak, Leszek**. A Sketch of Nietzschean Theory of "Superman" (in Polish). *Kwartalnik Filozof*, 23(1), 63-77, 1995.

This article is an attempt to answer the question about the origin and form of the Nietzschean idea of "superman". The idea of "superman" already appeared with the sophists, Plato, early Christian anthropology and then with Machiavelli, Goethe and Stirner. In the modern culture it exists under the shape given to it by Nietzsche. The Nietzschean "superman" is a particularly successful kind of man/and not a new species/, which accidentally emerged already in the past. It constitutes the aim of our conscious actions/breading understood as sublimation of impulses and as biological selection of desired traits/, because only he is able to overcome the crisis of the culture.

**Kusch, Martin**. "Theories of Questions in German-Speaking Philosophy" in *Knowledge and Inquiry: Essays on Jaakko Hintikka's Epistemology and Philosophy of Science,* Sintonen, Matti (ed), 41-60. Amsterdam, Rodopi, 1997.

Around the turn of the century, German-speaking philosophers displayed a lively interest in the nature of questions. Theorizing concentrated on the relation between questions and judgments, the distinction between propositional and wh-questions, various further taxonomies, the problem of answerhood, and attempts to describe knowledge-acquisition as an interrogative process. Interest in question theory ran high because logical inquiry was nonformal and close to psychology, and because both applied and theoretical (experimental) psychology had independent reasons for focusing on the study of questions. Kant's use of question-theoretical terms was an important resource for neo-Kantian philosophers.

**Kusch, Martin**. The Sociophilosophy of Folk Psychology. *Stud Hist Phil Sci*, 28(1), 1-25, Mr 96.

**Kushmerick, Nicholas**. Software Agents and Their Bodies. *Mind Mach*, 7(2), 227-247, My 97.

Within artificial intelligence and the philosophy of mind, there is considerable disagreement over the relationship between an agent's body and its capacity for intelligent behavior. Some treat the body as peripheral and tangential to intelligence; others argue that embodiment and intelligence are inextricably linked. Software agents—computer programs that interact with software environments such as the Internet—provide an ideal context in which to study this tension. I develop a computational framework for analyzing embodiment. The framework generalizes the notion of a body beyond merely having a physical presence. My analysis sheds light on certain claims made about the relevance of the body to intelligence, as well as on embodiment in software worlds.

**Kuznetsov, V G**. Introduction to the Publication of G.G. Shpet's "A Work on Philosophy". *Russian Stud Phil*, 35(4), 39-42, Spr 97.

The publication of Shepet's archives (he was the student of E. Gusserl), is a substantial addition to his works already published, since it makes possible to

trace the origins and evolution of his phenomenological ideas. The main problem is the nature of philosophical concepts. Contemporary philosophy exists as a positive and as a negative one. The principles of positive philosophy were formulated by Plato and the principles of the negative—by Kant. Negative philosophy regards itself as being "scientific" one, borrowing the patterns of being "science" from scientific disciplines. Relativism and reductionism are it's inherent features. Positive philosophy is purely theoretical knowledge of the general foundations of being, which can be discovered by intuition of the mind.

**Kvanvig, Jonathan**. In Defense of Coherentism. *J Phil Res*, 22, 299-306, Ap 97.

Alvin Plantinga and John Pollock both think that coherentism is a mistaken theory of justification, and they do so for different reasons. In spite of these differences, there are remarkable connections between their criticisms. Part of my goal here is to show what these connections are. I will show that Plantinga's construal of coherentism presupposes Pollock's arguments against that view, and I will argue that coherentists need not breathe their last in response to the contentions of either. Coherentism may be a mistaken theory of justification, but if it is, it is not shown to be so by either Plantinga or Pollock.

**Kvasz, Ladislav**. An Outline of the Analytical Theory of the Subject. *Filosof Cas*, 44(4), 617-640, 1996.

Having taken the development of synthetic geometry as an example, we indicated the gradual changes leading from Euclidean geometry to Klein's Erlangen Programme. Should we provide a concise description of the essence of these changes, we could say that it consisted in the change of the epistemic subject which a corresponding language is built on. We can see that the ever richer structures of the subject are being gradually built into language. First of all, the subject has a form of a point of view founding the subjectivity of the gaze; then, the subject is an interpretation founding the subjectivity of signification; and, finally, the subject appears as potentionality of the possible points of view. We cannot deny that our subjectivity has all these qualities. We carry a unique point of view with us all the time, we possess a unique interpretation of reality; we incorporate a potentionality of possibilities. That is why the source, which geometry has drawn on during its development, is ourselves, our own subjectivity.

**Kwant, Remigius C**. Eindigen met een nieuw begin: Zien en denken in de laatste geschriften van M. Merleau-Ponty. *Tijdschr Filosof*, 58(4), 716-734, D 96.

In his self-critical book *The Visible and the Invisible* on p. 190—almost the end of the text—Merleau-Ponty ends an alinea with the words: "...the insertion of speaking and thinking into the field of silence." He adds a critical note in which he advances that seeing itself is already thinking, because it evidently is awareness of being. This implies an important renewal almost at the end of his life. So he ended with a new start: the soul, the mind, the spirit ("esprit") is "the other side of the body," i.e., corporeal. Merleau-Ponty did not have the time to work out the implications of his new philosophy. We find some of its implications in the latest parts of *The Visible and the Invisible* and in *The Eye and the Mind* (written in July-August 1960). The article describes some basic lines of Merleau-Ponty's latest philosophy.

**Kwiecinski, Zbigniew**. "The Decahedron of Education (Components and Aspects): The Need for a Comprehensive Approach" in *Epistemology and History,* Zeidler-Janiszewska, Anna (ed), 365-372. Amsterdam, Rodopi, 1996.

Education is seen as the totality of processes and actions which are conducive to individual development. Education in its broadest sense encompasses ten processes: 1) globalisation (introduction into global problems of humanity); 2) etatisation (instilling acceptance of the state): 3) nationalisation (in the ethnic sense, seen as the assimilation of national/ethnic traditions and national/ethnic distinctiveness); 4) collectivisation or secondary socialisation (growing into the traditions and interests of one's social class or social group); 5) professionalisation (introduction into organised social structures and vocational/professional roles); 6)primary socialisation and nurture (growing into norms and roles within primary groups); 7) enculturation and personalisation (growing into culture; reaching autonomy of moral choices which constitute personal identity); 8) education for citizenship and law (introduction into citizen roles, the shaping of legal awareness); 9) instruction and humanisation (transmission of knowledge, skills and communicative competence); 10) hominisation (instillation of habits pertaining to hygiene and health). A harmonious balance between the processes is decisive for an individual's successful development. Conversely, an imbalance between the constituent processes results in developmental pathologies falling into two basic categories: pathologies of excess and pathologies of deficit.

**Kyburg Jr, Henry E**. Thinking about Reasoning about Knowledge. *Mind Mach*, 7(1), 103-112, F 97.

This is an extended review of the book, *Reasoning about Knowledge* by Fagin and Halpern. The emphasis of the discussion is primarily philosophical. A number of issues of historical philosophical importance, are treated casually or not at all by the authors, and an effort is made to redress the balance, at the same time suggesting that the issues are of importance to AI as well as to philosophy.

**Kyburg, Jr, Henry E**. The Rule of Adjunction and Reasonable Inference. *J Phil*, 94(3), 109-125, Mr 97.

Although the rule of adjunction is one of the standard rules of first order logic, there are a number of reasons to be skeptical of its role in practical reason: for example, doxastic obligation does not seem to be closed under conjunction; the so-called lottery paradox cautions against conjunction. Even systems of logic that tolerate contradiction—paraconsistent logics—are found not to provide a satisfactory treatment of conjunction. The cost to logical practice of eschewing adjunction are explored and found to be relatively minor; and some unsuspected advantages in dealing with questionable arguments are revealed.

**Kymlicka, Will**. "Moral Philosophy and Public Policy: The Case of New Reproductive Technologies" in *Philosophical Perspectives on Bioethics*, Sumner, L W (ed), 244-270. Toronto, Univ of Toronto Pr, 1996.

This paper discusses two common views about the role that moral philosophers can play in public policy-making bodies, such as government commissions into reproductive technologies. The ambitious view says that philosophers should encourage commissioners to adopt the best comprehensive moral theory (e.g., utilitarianism or contractarianism), and then apply it to policy choices. The moderate view says that philosophers should identify inconsistencies within the commission's arguments, without influencing the underlying theory. I reject the first view as unrealistic and the second as inadequate to ensure morally responsible recommendations. I then discuss a third "guiding principles" approach that relies less on philosophical sophistication and more on sensitivity to the actual impact of policies on all relevant parties.

**Kymlicka, Will**. "The Sources of Nationalism: Commentary on Taylor" in *The Morality of Nationalism*, McKim, Robert (ed), 56-65. New York, Oxford Univ Pr, 1997.

My paper is a response to Charles Taylor's chapter in the same volume. Taylor's paper has two main sections: an account of the "context" of nationalism, emphasizing the centrality of nation-building to modern states; and an account of the "sources" of nationalism, which elaborates Taylor's earlier ideas about the importance of "recognition". I agree with Taylor's account of the context of nationalism, but I argue that his account of the "sources" of nationalism is less successful. In particular, Taylor's emphasis on "recognition" cannot explain the specificity of nationalist mobilization.

**Kymlicka, Will**. Do We Need a Liberal Theory of Minority Rights? Reply to Carens, Young, Parekh and Forst. *Constellations*, 4(1), 72-87, Ap 97.

In their critiques of my book on *Multicultural Citizenship*, Iris Young, Joseph Carens, Bhikhu Parekh and Rainer Forst raise several important issues. In this response, I focus on two of them. First, whereas I tried to draw a sharp distinction between immigrants and national minorities, my critics argue that we should think of ethnocultural groups on a more fluid continuum. Second, whereas I tried to ground a theory of minority rights on specifically *liberal* principles, my critics argue that such an approach is unduly intolerant of nonliberal groups. In response to these questions, I try to clarify and strengthen the positions taken in my book.

**Kyte, Richard**. Moral Reasoning as Perception: A Reading of Carol Gilligan. *Hypatia*, 11(3), 97-113, Sum 96.

Gilligan's understanding of moral reasoning as a kind of perception has its roots in the conception of moral experience espoused by Simone Weil and Iris Murdoch. A clear understanding of that conception, however, reveals grave difficulties with Gilligan's descriptions of the care perspective and justice perspective. In particular, we can see that the two perspectives are not mutually exclusive once we recognize that attention does not require attachment and that impartiality does not require detachment.

**La Forge, Paul G**. Teaching Business Ethics Through Meditation. *J Bus Ethics*, 16(12-13), 1283-1295, S 97.

The purpose of this article is to show how meditation can be used to help a student to become an ethical person. Discursive and nondiscursive meditation give the student an awareness of ethical issues and lead to the discovery and application of models of ethical conduct. In part one, the student is led through nondiscursive meditation to discover him/her self as an ethical person. Part two discusses a transition stage from nondiscursive to discursive meditation. Part three discusses four elements in the construction of an ethical vision with discursive meditation. (edited)

**La Puma, John**. Cultural Diversity in Medicine and Medical Ethics: What Are the Key Questions?. *Bioethics Forum*, 11(2), 3-8, Sum 95.

Culture, cultural diversity and value choices are 1990s buzz words that are likely to have lasting meaning for American medicine. To understand cultural diversity and to help patients and institutions into the twenty-first century, bioethics should not make the same mistake as it has in medicine as a whole. It should not leave discovering the facts of a case to others. Instead, it must go to the patient's side, where death and dying, managed care and family decision making will be key crossover areas of expertise for institutional ethics committees.

**La Rocca, Claudio**. Kant und die Methode der Philosophie Zur Kant-Interpretation Massimo Barales. *Kantstudien*, 87(4), 436-447, 1996.

**La Torre, Massimo**. Rules, Institutions, Transformations: Considerations on the "Evolution of Law" Paradigm. *Ratio Juris*, 10(3), 316-350, S 97.

The article's main objective is to test the merits of the evolutionary paradigm as it has been applied first to social phenomena and then more specifically to the legal domain. In a preliminary move, a set of the available concepts of law is worked out. A discussion of the idea of evolution and of its use in the social sciences follows. Functionalism and systems' theory are scrutinized, with a close eye to the new doctrine of "autopoiesis". Once an institutional and normative concept of law is agreed upon, attempts to introduce an "evolutionary" paradigm are deemed—the article contends—to be unfruitful. The article concludes that, if law needs a metaphysics, it should be one which allows for change, transformation and the emergence of the radically new. (edited)

**Laan, Twan** and Nederpelt, Rob. A Modern Elaboration of the Ramified Theory of Types. *Stud Log*, 57(2-3), 243-278, O 96.

The paper first formalizes the ramified type theory as (informally) described in the Principia Mathematica [32]. This formalization is close to the ideas of the Principia, but also meets contemporary requirements on formality and accuracy

and therefore is a new supply to the known literature on the Principia (like [25], [19], [6] and [7]). As an alternative, notions from the ramified type theory are expressed in a lambda calculus style. This situates the type system of Russell and Whitehead in a modern setting. Both formalizations are inspired by current developments in research on type theory and typed lambda calculus; see [3].

**Laberge, Jean**. La *méthode* de Lipman: un outil dangereux de propagande auprès des enfants? Une réplique à Pierre Desjardins. *Philosopher*, 19, 83-92, 1996.

**Laberge, Yves**. De la culture aux cultures: Délimitations d'un concept pluri-sémantique. *Laval Theol Phil*, 52(3), 805-825, O 96.

The term "culture" has so many definitions that its precise meaning must be determined before its different uses in a variety of disciplines can be studied. The following text is guided by the works of Fernand Dumont, Abram Kardiner and Edgar Morin; it considers such terms as popular and learned culture, primary and secondary culture, mass culture and counterculture and attempts to shed light on those different forms of culture in philosophy, anthropology, communication science and sociology.

**Labica, Georges**. Frederick Engels: Scholar and Revolutionary. *Nature Soc Thought*, 8(4), 457-462, 1995.

On the occasion of the centenary of the death of Friedrich Engels, this book, which is the result of an international symposium of the University of Paris-X Nanterre (France), aims to provide an introduction to the thought and political theory of F. Engels. It presents the principle themes of Engels's work in four sections: the formation of Marxism and the workers' movement; politics, democracy and revolution; between sciences and philosophy; Engels, heir and theoretician of Marxism. This book is supplemented by a biography and an ample bibliography.

**LaBossiere, Michael C**. Cracking The Division Bell: A Philosophic Attack On *The Bell Curve*. *Int J Applied Phil*, 10(2), 25-33, Wint-Spr 96.

**Lacey, Hugh**. Neutrality in the Social Sciences: On Bhaskar's Argument for an Essential Emancipatory Impulse in Social Science. *J Theor Soc Behav*, 27(2-3), 213-241, Je-S 97.

Suppose that one accepts a theory that proposes that a certain group's holding of a false belief is cocaused, for example, by a specified social structure. Then, Bhaskar has argued, one is rationally committed, *ceteris paribus*, to adopting a negative value judgment of that structure (the theory is not value neutral) and a positive value judgment of activity directed towards removing it (the theory is partial towards emancipation). Contrary to Bhaskar, I argue that any rational move from accepting a theory to value judgments is mediated either by further value judgments, or by the role played by value-impregnated theoretical terms. Furthermore, I argue (drawing upon a well-known argument of Rudner), Bhaskar's argument tends not to be applicable in the case of theories that assign certain kinds of causal roles to social structures. Reflection on Bhaskar's argument, however, leads to a deeper grasp of the relations between accepting theories in the social sciences and adopting value judgments. (edited)

**Lachterman, David**. The Ontology of Production in Marx: The Paradox of Labor and the Enigma of *Praxis*. *Grad Fac Phil J*, 19(1), 3-24, 1996.

**Lackey, Douglas**. Reply to Perkins on "Conditional Preventive War". *Russell*, 16(1), 85-88, Sum 96.

**Lackey, Douglas**. Self-Determination and Just War. *Phil Forum*, 28(1-2), 100-110, Fall-Wint 97.

**Laclau, Ernesto**. "Deconstruction, Pragmatism, Hegemony" in *Deconstruction and Pragmatism*, Mouffe, Chantal (ed), 47-67. New York, Routledge, 1996.

**Lacoste, Jean-Yves**. Du phénomène de la valeur au discours de la norme. *Frei Z Phil Theol*, 44(1-2), 87-103, 1997.

**Lacoue-Labarthe, Philippe**. "Phrase VII" in *On Jean-Luc Nancy: The Sense of Philosophy*, Sheppard, Darren (ed), 1-11. New York, Routledge, 1997.

**Lacy, William B**. Research, Extension, and User Partnerships: Models for Collaboration and Strategies for Change. *Agr Human Values*, 13(2), 33-41, Spr 96.

Increasing pragmatic and ethical concerns have been raised about the inadequacies of conventional approaches to agricultural research and extension worldwide and the lack of integrated efforts among researchers, extension educators, and users. This paper examines three models of these relationships: the diffusion or supply model; the induced innovation or demand model; and the synthesis triangular or supply/demand model. (edited)

**Ladenson, Robert F**. What is a Disability?. *Int J Applied Phil*, 11(1), 1-10, Sum-Fall 96.

This paper considers the question of what conditions count as disabilities under the Americans with Disabilities Act (ADA). The paper begins by posing issues of justice often implicit in requests for special modifications under the ADA. The paper then considers utilitarian and Kantian frameworks of analysis for resolving them, but concludes that neither approach provides the necessary guidance. The paper suggests an account according to which questions of justice, associated with the issue of what conditions count as disabilities under the ADA, require a critical focus of attention upon the appropriate procedures for society to use in resolving them.

**Ladeur, Karl-Heinz**. Superamento della complessità attraverso la capacità di apprendimento del diritto: L'adeguamento del diritto alle condizioni del Postmoderno. *Riv Int Filosof Diritto*, 73(3), 480-511, Jl-S 96.

**Ladyman, James** and Douven, Igor and Horsten, Leon (& others). A Defence of Van Fraassen's Critique of Abductive Inference: Reply to Psillos. *Phil Quart*, 47(188), 305-321, Jl 97.

**Laflamme, Claude**. A Few Special Ordinal Ultrafilters. *J Sym Log*, 61(3), 920-927, S 96.

We prove various results on the notion of ordinal ultrafilters introduced by J. Baumgartner. In particular, we show that this notion of ultrafilter complexity is independent of the more familiar Rudin-Keisler ordering.

**LaFollette, Hugh** and Shanks, Niall. *Brute Science: Dilemmas of Animal Experimentation*. New York, Routledge, 1996.

Are humans morally justified in conducting sometimes painful experiments on animals in their search for a cure for cancer, heart disease and AIDS? Apologists for animal experimentation claim for practice is morally justified, because humans are more valuable than animals and scientifically justified, because the data derived from these experiments profoundly benefits humans. *Brute Science* investigates this standard defense of animal experimentation. The authors show, on methodological and empirical grounds, that defenders of animal experimentation seriously exaggerate its benefits. Consequently, we need to reassess, scientifically and morally, our use of animals in biomedical experimentation. (edited)

**LaFortune, Louise** and Daniel, Marie-France and Pallascio, Richard (& others). Y a-t-il de la place pour philosopher sur les mathématiques au collégial?. *Philosopher*, 18, 107-126, 1995.

Dans cet article, nous explorons l'idée de transférer l'approche de *Philosophie pour enfants* adaptée aux mathématiques à l'enseignement post-secondaire. Dans une expérience où cette approche a été utilisée auprès de jeunes du primaire, les élèves approfondissent grâce aux communautés de recherche, certains concepts utilisés en mathématiques (infini, abstrait, zéro, géométrie, définition, preuve, existence, découverte...). Nous proposons des idées de plans de discussion et d'activités pouvant être transférées à l'enseignement post-secondaire et portant sur: abstrait-concret, figures géométriques, comprendre et connaître. De cette réflexion, nous concluons que différentes disciplines comme les mathématiques auraient avantage à intégrer des éléments d'une approche philosophique et à organiser des communautés de recherche dans leurs cours afin de susciter le processus de réflexion critique des élèves sur les notions enseignées, mais aussi sur leurs apprentissages.

**Laganà, Antonino**. Fondazione metafisica e fondazione teoretica. *G Metaf*, 18(1-2), 151-153, Ja-Ag 96.

**Laganà, Antonio**. Trascendentalità della metafisica. *G Metaf*, 18(1-2), 227-231, Ja-Ag 96.

**Lagrée, Jacqueline**. "Lumière naturelle et notions communes: Herbert de Cherbury and Culverwell" in *Mind Senior to the World*, Baldi, Marialuisa, 35-54. Milano, FrancoAngeli, 1996.

The purpose of this paper is to present and analyze the long commentary by Culverwell of the biblical statement: "the understanding of man is the candle of the Lord" and to determine the part of reason in faith. The work studies how Culverwell uses the Stoic concepts of common notions, law of nature and right reason in the understanding of faith. It compares Culverwell and Herbert of Cherbury on their conception and use of common notions (and which ones) and natural light in religion; and it examines the power and weakness of reason so as to determine the theological, philosophical and political issues of this kind of religious rationalism.

**Lagrée, Jacqueline**. Arianisme mitigé ou apologétique nouvelle?. *Rev Phil Fr*, 1, 5-8, Ja-Mr 97.

**Lahav, Ran**. Philosophical Counseling and Taoism: Wisdom and Lived Philosophical Understanding. *J Chin Phil*, 23(3), 259-276, S 96.

This paper argues that philosophical counseling manages to relate philosophy to the individual's everyday concerns because of its conception of the nature of philosophical understanding. Unlike mainstream Western thought, philosophical counseling regards philosophical understanding as embodied not only in our thoughts but in our entire way of being. A parallel connection between everyday life and philosophical understanding is found in traditional Oriental philosophy, specifically in Taoism. This suggests that it may be fruitful for the former to examine the foundations of the latter, older tradition.

**Lahav, Ran**. What is Philosophical in Philosophical Counselling?. *J Applied Phil*, 13(3), 259-278, 1996.

After a short description of the nature of philosophical counselling, this paper suggests that what makes philosophical counselling philosophical is that it helps the counsellee in philosophical self-investigations. These are critical nonempirical investigations of the fundamental principles underlying the counsellee's 'lived understanding' (i.e., conceptions which the counsellee lives by, though not necessarily articulates in words), aimed at the development of wisdom. In order to illustrate the nature of philosophical self-investigation, two case studies are presented. The nature and measurability of success in philosophical counselling is then discussed. A questionnaire filled out by a counsellee is quoted as an illustration of the possible effects and success of philosophical counselling.

**Lahey, Stephen E**. Wyclif on Rights. *J Hist Ideas*, 58(1), 1-20, J 97.

John Wyclif's political philosophy was reliant on the traditional, "objective" right, rather than on the then-developing "subjective" right, yet it can be argued to be as innovative as that of better known fourteenth-century advocates of the "subjective" right. Wyclif's conception of *ius*, or right, expressed in his *De Mandatis Divinis*, is rooted securely in his doctrine of Grace-founded *dominium* as it appears in *De Dominio Divino* and an understanding of these two works provides a basis for understanding the aspects of toleration and progressivity apparent in *De Civili Dominio* and *De Officio Regis*.

**Lahlou, Saadi**. The Propagation of Social Representations. *J Theor Soc Behav*, 26(2), 157-175, Je 96.

Based on a minimal formalism of social representations as a set of associated cognems, a simple model of propagation of representations is presented.

Assuming that subjects share the constitutive cognems, the model proposes that mere focused attention on the set of cognems in the field of common conscience may replicate the pattern of representation from context into subjects, or, from subject to subject, through actualization by language, where cognems are represented by verbal signs. Limits of the model are discussed, and evolutionist perspectives are presented with the support of field data.

**Lai, Whalen**. Kung-sun Lung on the Point of Pointing: The Moral Rhetoric of Names. *Asian Phil*, 7(1), 47-58, Mr 97.

Graham compares Kung-sun Lung's "White Horse not Horse" [Graham, A.C. (1990) *Studies in Chinese Philosophy and Philosophical Literature* (Albany, SUNY Press)] with the use of a synedoche in English, "Sword is not Blade." The blade as part stands in here for the whole which is the sword. But just as sword as 'hilt plus blade' is more than blade, then *via analogia*, *white horse* as 'white plus horse' is more than the part that is just 'horse'. Graham had taken over this part/whole argument from Chad Hansen who argues that since Chinese does not require the word *ma* for 'horse/horses' to be used with prefixed articles or numerals, *ma* is a 'mass-noun' similar to certain English mass-nouns like 'sand' which also has no plural form unlike the count-noun 'horse' [Hansen, Chad, (1983) *Language and Logic in Ancient China* (Ann Arbor, University of Michigan Press)].

**Laidlaw-Johnson, Elizabeth A**. *Plato's Epistemology: How Hard Is It to Know?*. New York, Lang, 1996.

Plato's thought evolves from the epistemology of the *Meno*, *Phaedo* and *Republic* to the combined doctrine of the *Theaetetus*. The combined doctrine maintains that both forms and certain objects rooted in perception are objects of knowledge. Dialectic results in apprehension of the good and consequently of being, which brings about a permanent change in a person's state of mind enabling one to know what one previously believed. The combined doctrine resolves the paradoxes of the refutations of the *Theaetetus*. It turns out that the difference between true belief and knowledge for Plato amounts to difference in states of mind. (publisher)

**Laidlaw-Johnson, Elizabeth A**. The Ethics of Information Transfer in the Electronic Age: Scholars Unite!. *J Infor Ethics*, 5(2), 29-38, Fall 96.

The essay considers whether the current set of copyright regulations, which favor the owners of intellectual property, treats the originators of that property in ways that allow the academic community to progress. I suggest improvements to the current systems of protecting intellectual property's markets, its producers and its users. These suggestions aim at treating each of the individual players in the intellectual property system more fairly.

**Laing, Jacqueline A**. "Innocence and Consequentialism: Inconsistency, Equivocation and Contradiction in the Philosophy of P. Singer" in *Human Lives: Critical Essays on Consequentialist Bioethics*, Oderberg, David S (ed), 196-224. New York, Macmillan, 1997.

On several occasions, the lectures and speeches of Peter Singer have been disrupted and subject to protest by the disabled as well as others who find his views morally repugnant. Singer claims he has been misunderstood. In this paper his writings are examined to see whether he has been misunderstood. In this paper his writings are examined to see whether he has indeed been misinterpreted. His technical concept of a 'person' is discussed; so is his rejection of potentiality, his rejection of the importance of commonness of kind and his apparent repudiation of restrictions on third party desire. It is shown that these ideas do indeed lead to the views seen as repugnant by his opponents. He is also shown inconsistently to rely on precisely the notions he seeks to eliminate from moral theory. Central to Singer's philosophy is an attack on the value of innocence, which no plausible moral theory can do without.

**Laing, Jacqueline A** (ed) and Oderberg, David S (ed). *Human Lives: Critical Essays on Consequentialist Bioethics*. New York, Macmillan, 1997.

*Critical Essays on Consequentialist Bioethics* is a collection of original papers by philosophers from Britain, the USA and Australia. The aim of the book is to redress the imbalance in moral philosophy created by the dominance of consequentialism, the view that the criterion of morality is the maximization of good effects over bad, without regard for basic right or wrong. This approach has become the orthodoxy over the last few decades, particularly in the field of bioethics, where moral theory is applied to matters of life and death. The essays in *Human Lives* critically examine the assumptions and arguments of consequentialism, in the process reviving important concepts such as rights, justice, innocence, natural integrity, flourishing, the virtues and the fundamental value of human life.

**Laitko, Hubert**. "Chemie und Philosophie: Anmerkungen zur Entwicklung des Gebietes in der Geschichte der DDR" in *Philosophie der Chemie: Bestandsaufnahme und Ausblick*, Schummer, Joachim (ed), 37-58. Wurzburg, Koenigshausen, 1996.

**Laks, André**. Between Religion and Philosophy: Allegorical Interpretation in Derveni Papyrus (in Czech). *Magyar Filozof Szemle*, 1-2, 1-23, 1997.

Describing the content of the Derveni allegory as "physical" may turn out to be inadequate. The Derveni author does not have much interest in the cosmological details. His physics is minimalist, because it is subordinated to a theological thesis that culminates in the affirmation of divine rationality. This, by itself, would be enough to explain why the Derveni author could be led to assume that the Orphic theogony and pre-Socratic philosophy were saying the same thing and to understand the use he makes of allegory. That he *had* to assume just this is quite another matter. Later developments in the story of allegory can help here. (edited)

**Laks, André**. Between Religion and Philosophy: The Function of Allegory in the Derveni Papyrus. *Phronesis*, 42(2), 121-142, 1997.

**Lalitha, Ch**. The Jain Conception of Liberation with Special Reference to the Sutrakrtanga. *Darshana Int*, 36(3/143), 57-63, Ap 96.

This paper aims to study the Jain conception of liberation as depicted in the Sutrakrtanga which is the second among the eleven extant Jain Angas and is also supposed to have been preached by Lord Mahavira. It is collated into three parts. The *first part* deals with the Jain object of liberation which is nothing but aiming to get complete deliverance of the soul from all evil and covering of Karma. The *second part* provides various means of liberation in general and the goal of moksa in particular. The *third part* deals with fruits of stages in spiritual realization which ultimately leads a spiritual aspirant to attain the ultimate of Kevalajnana.

**Lally, Laura**. Privacy Versus Accessibility: The Impact of Situationally Conditioned Belief. *J Bus Ethics*, 15(11), 1221-1226, N 96.

This paper proposes that the conflict is likely to be a function of the role the individual plays in the decision making situation—*situationally conditioned belief* (SCB)—rather than a function of the person's underlying ethical values. This paper presents an empirical study involving information privacy and accessibility in routine business and market decisions, designed to reveal the presence of SCBs. The results indicate that SCBs cause a gap in beliefs about information accessibility and privacy. Impacts of the SCB gap are discussed. A negotiation technique called information exchange is suggested as a means of closing the SCB gap in routine business and market transactions. (edited)

**Lalor, Brendan J**. It *is* What You Think: Intentional Potency and Anti-Individualism. *Phil Psych*, 10(2), 165-178, Je 97.

In this paper I argue against the worried view that intentional properties might be epiphenomenal. In naturalizing intentionality we ought to reject both the idea that causal powers of intentional states must supervene on local microstructures and the idea that local supervenience justifies worries about intentional epiphenomenality since our states could counterfactually lack their intentional properties and yet have the same effects. I contend that what's wrong with even the good guys (e.g., Dennett, Dretske, Allen) is that they implicitly grant that causal powers supervene locally. Finally, I argue that once we see the truth of an anti-individualism which sees cognition as a fundamentally embedded activity, it becomes clear both that granting local supervenience is granting too much and that intentional properties do work that mere neurological properties could never do. I also suggest how a transcendental argument for intentional potency might go.

**Lamau, M L** and Cadore, B and Boitte, P. From "The Ethical Treatment of Patients in a Persistent Vegetative State" To a Philosophical Reflection on Contemporary Medicine. *Theor Med*, 18(3), 237-262, S 97.

The reflections put forward in this text concern the clinical and practical difficulties posed by the existence of patients in PVS and the essential ethical issues raised, combining these ethical questions with practical and theoretical experience. Section 1 presents the methodology of the ethical reflection as we see it. Section 2 describes the clinical condition of patients in PVS. Section 3 develops the ethical difficulties relative to PVS from the French point of view. Section 4 illustrates the relevance of debating the ethical significance of such problematic situations, whilst defending a practical position based on a philosophical conviction. Section 5 points out the limits of ethical reflection in a biomedical context, and calls for reflection closer to the source of the problems described. (edited)

**Lamb, David**. *Death, Brain Death and Ethics*. Brookfield, Avebury, 1996.

This book examines the concept of death against the background of dramatic changes in medical technology. Developments in resuscitation techniques and the ability of machines to take over such vital functions as spontaneous breathing challenge traditional ways of diagnosing death. As a result physicians have employed brain-related criteria in certain cases where vital processes are being maintained by artificial means. While tests for the death of the brain are continually improving very little work has been done to explain why the death of the brain if a necessary and sufficient condition for the death of a human being. In fact, the very concept of 'brain death' has remained unclear in most of the medical literature related to this subject. Is brain death a new concept of death? Is it a new set of criteria for diagnosing death? Does it imply an alternative definition of death? It is clear that the term has arisen in the context of modern medical science but how does it stand in relation to older accounts of death? Can brain death be defined? Some philosophers have argued that it should not be defined, but left undetermined. (publisher, edited)

**Lamb, David**. *Organ Transplants and Ethics*. Brookfield, Avebury, 1996.

This book does not offer any solution to the problem of how to provide the maximum benefits of medicine, in particular organ transplantation. But it does express the view that, whatever benefits transplantation can provide, the procurement and allocation of organs should proceed according to principles of equity together with policies which maintain respect for the human body. To this end Chapter 4 examines ethical problems raised by proposals to procure fetal tissue for transplantation purposes. Chapter 5 examines the problems inherent in recent proposals to procure organs from dying neonates, whilst Chapter 6 examines the problems of cadaveric organ procurement as well as policies for obtaining replacement organs and tissues from living humans and various nonhuman sources. The final chapter assesses policy options for the procurement and allocation of organs, some of which are under consideration for adoption in the form of legal directives in several countries. (publisher, edited)

**Lamb, Roger E**. "Love and Rationality" in *Love Analyzed*, Lamb, Roger E, 23-47. Boulder, Westview Pr, 1997.

Our taking up of attitudes (e.g., pity, admiration, disdain) towards others is typically a function of various properties, features, or traits, which those others manifestly have or are believed to have. A consequence of this is that such attitudes are universalizable. Yet our loving another, in spite of often being, similarly, a function of properties of the beloved, is usually thought not to be universalizable. I consider the proposition that that thought might be mistaken, taking up discussions involving commitment, exclusivity, loyalty, replaceability and senses of 'universalizability'. I conclude that there is a robust sense of universalizability such that love is universalizable.

**Lamb, Roger E**. *Love Analyzed*. Boulder, Westview Pr, 1997.

Philosophers have turned their attention in recent years to many previously unmined topics, among them love and friendship. In this collection of new essays in philosophical and moral psychology, philosophers turn their analytic tools to a topic perhaps most resistant to reasoned analysis: erotic love. Also included is one previously published paper by Martha Nussbaum. Among the problems discussed are the role that qualities of the beloved play in love, the so-called union theory of love, intentionality and autonomy in love, and traditional issues surrounding jealously and morality. (publisher, edited)

**Lamb, Sharon**. Sex Education as Moral Education: Teaching for Pleasure, about Fantasy, and against Abuse. *J Moral Educ*, 26(3), 301-315, S 97.

This paper argues for an integration of moral education and sex education curricula. In such an integration, the primary values that would be taught would not be those relating to specific sexual behaviour but those relating to the general treatment of human beings, suggesting that sex that involves coercion or exploitation as well as sex that causes harm is wrong. Sex educators must take as their goal the prevention of abuse, not by placing responsibility on girls to avoid victimization but by teaching boys how to express themselves sexually in moral—that is, considerate and respectful—ways. The paper discusses differential gender role socialization and why integration of such material must be a part of every sex education curriculum. The paper also discusses how physical pleasure in not only a biological phenomenon but one that is culturally constructed, the discussion of which would be important to sex education. Finally, teaching about fantasy as well as sexual "deviance" (in terms of the moral behaviours discussed above) may be the most important aspect of sex education to prepare or retrain boys to be "good" sex partners rather than perpetrators of abuse.

**Lambek, J**. An Extension of the Formulas-as-Types Paradigm. *Dialogue (Canada)*, 36(1), 33-43, Wint 97.

Un paradigme en vogue en informatique théorique exploite l'analogie entre les formules et les types et traite une déduction $A_1 \ldots A_n$ infers B comme une opération plurisortale. On propose ici d'étendre cette analogie aux déductions de la forme $A_1 \ldots A_n$ infers, où la place à droite de la flèche est vide. D'un point de vue logique, une telle déduction constitue une réfutation de la conjonction des formules qui se trouvent à gauche de la flèche. On défend l'idée qu'il faut, selon ce paradigme étendu, interpréter la flèche comme assignant à n'importe quelle séquence $a_1 \ldots a_n$, où $a_i$ est de type $A_i$, le type des valeurs de vérité correspondantes. Pour que cela fonctionne, cependant, il faut abandonner la règle structurale de l'affaiblissement à droite de la flèche (cette règle est entièrement abandonnée en logique de la pertinence). La négation de *A* est alors interprétée comme l'ensemble puissance de *A* et la complétude fonctionnelle habituelle s'identifie au schème de compréhension avec extensionnalité.

**Lambert, Karel**. "Nonextensionality" in *Das weite Spektrum der analytischen Philosophie*, Lenzen, Wolfgang, 135-148. Hawthorne, de Gruyter, 1997.

**Lambert, Maria de Fátima**. Antero: As Imagens: Contexto Estético e Antropológico. *Rev Port Filosof*, 52(1-4), 449-474, Ja-D 96.

**Lamberth, David C**. "Interpreting the Universe after a Social Analogy: Intimacy, Panpsychism, and a Finite God in a Pluralistic Universe" in *The Cambridge Companion to William James*, Putnam, Ruth Anna (ed), 237-259. New York, Cambridge Univ Pr, 1997.

This article interprets William James's late philosophical world-view through his notion of "intimacy" found in *A Pluralistic Universe*. I note three distinct uses of intimacy: (a) a phenomenological use—intimacy as an affect; (b) a metaphysical use wherein intimacy is related to the constitutive factual relations of radical empiricism; (c) an ideal notion of intimacy-in-the-making construed after sociality or reciprocity. Next I explore three substantive commitments of James corresponding to these senses: (a) James's substitution of intimacy for rationality as a philosophical criterion; (b) James's metaphysical commitment to "pluralistic panpsychism"; (c) James's understanding of supernaturalism, religious experience and theism.

**Lamblin, Robert**. Le mal moral, pierre de touche de l'ontologie: Monisme idéal et dualisme réel du sens de l'être. *Rev Phil Fr*, 2, 209-222, Ap-Je 96.

I should want to prove, by admitting the reality of a voluntary and free evil, that there is a contradiction between the demand by the mind for a monist sense which would integrate and subordinate the natural sense to the spiritual sense and the obviousness that nature is in herself indifferent to this sense. Hence derives the possibility for freedom to doubt her own value and submit herself to a nature she erects as an absolute principle of her existence and her action by constituting through her union with her a right she opposes the illusory spiritual right. In the absence of any divine guarantee, liberty must assume this contradiction and maintain the value of her own demand by setting herself against evil, practically and theoretically.

**Lami, Gian Franco**. I rischi di una società dei "giusti". *Riv Int Filosof Diritto*, 73(3), 546-554, Jl-S 96.

**Lamm, Julia A**. *The Living God: Schleiermacher's Theological Appropriation of Spinoza*. University Park, Pennsylvania Univ Pr, 1996.

**Lammi, Walter**. "Hegel, Heidegger, and Hermeneutical Experience" in *Hegel, History, and Interpretation,* Gallagher, Shaun, 43-58. Albany, SUNY Pr, 1997.

Although Gadamer calls the concept of 'experience' "one of the most obscure we have," and it is famously so in Hegel and Heidegger, 'experience' is also a key—perhaps *the* key—to understanding the philosophical relationship among these thinkers. In what seems to be a mediation of Hegel and Heidegger, Gadamer has been criticized for having a tendency to "pick and choose" between them to suit his own purposes. This article answers this charge through a comparative study of philosophical 'experience' in Hegel, Heidegger, and Gadamer. I conclude that hermeneutical experience is a phenomenological rather than syncretist concept.

**Lamont, John**. Believing That God Exists Because the Bible Says So. *Faith Phil*, 13(1), 121-124, Ja 96.

The paper considers Reneé Descartes's assertion that believing that God exists because the Bible says so, and believing that what the Bible says is true because God says it, involves circular reasoning. It argues that there is no circularity involved in holding these beliefs, and maintains that the appearance of circularity results from an equivocation. It considers a line of argument that would defend the rationality of holding these beliefs, but does not try to prove its soundness.

**Lamont, John R T**. Newman on Faith and Rationality. *Int J Phil Relig*, 40(2), 63-84, O 96.

**Lampe, Marc**. Increasing Effectiveness in Teaching Ethics to Undergraduate Business Students. *Teach Bus Ethics*, 1(1), 3-19, 1997.

Undergraduate business students present special needs and challenges in respect to the teaching of ethics. Traditional methods of teaching this topic are the subject of criticism in the literature. This paper considers the nature of the target audience while advancing the complementary goals of convincing undergraduate business students that ethical behavior in business is important and increasing the likelihood that these students will make ethical choices in the future. Shortcomings of approaches commonly used to teach this topic are discussed. Specific instructional techniques to supplement or replace traditional pedagogy are suggested.

**Lampert, Jay**. Origen on Time. *Laval Theol Phil*, 52(3), 649-664, O 96.

Neo-Platonic concepts of emanation and return suggest a philosophy of history comparable to Hegel's, but in a purely formal way. Origen introduces some actual events into the form of history: the creation, the fall and the writing of scripture. His rewritings of the neo-Platonic hypostasis—the One, the Intellect and the Soul—as World, Will and Interpretation, show how historical events achieve transcendental significance.

**Lamping, John** and Dalrymple, Mary and Pereira, Fernando (& others). Quantifiers, Anaphora, and Intensionality. *J Log Lang Info*, 6(3), 219-273, Jl 97.

The relationship between Lexical-Functional Grammar (LFG) *functional structures* (f-structures) for sentences and their semantic interpretations can be formalized in *linear logic* in a way that correctly explains the observed interactions between quantifier scope ambiguity, bound anaphora and intensionality. While our approach resembles current categorial approaches in important ways (Moortgat, 1988, 1992a; Carpenter, 1993; Morrill, 1994) it differs from them in allowing the greater compositional flexibility of categorial semantics (van Benthem, 1991) while maintaining a precise connection to syntax. As a result, we are able to provide derivations for certain readings of sentences with intensional verbs and complex direct objects whose derivation in purely categorial accounts of the syntax-semantics interface appears to require otherwise unnecessary semantic decompositions of lexical entries. (publisher, edited)

**Lan, Conrado Eggers**. Etica y matemática en Platón. *Cuad Etica*, 19-20, 63-72, 1995.

In the allegory of the *Republic* of the *line*, Plato tells us that in the first part of the intelligible section the soul is compelled to investigate not by starting from assumptions up to a principle but down to a conclusion, while in the second part the mind advances from an assumption up towards a principle which is not hypothetical. This nonhypothetical principle is the Idea of the Good. The criticism by Richard Hare and others who say that the notion of goodness has nothing to do with mathematics overlooks the meaning of Greek notions such as *arete* and *aristos*.

**Lanceros, Patxi**. Dominio de sí, tecnologías del yo y hermenéutica del sujeto. *Dialogos*, 31(68), 29-56, Jl 96.

**Lanceros, Patxi**. La Modernidad cansada (o ¿para qué aún filosofía). *Euridice*, 71-88, 1992.

The author takes into account in this paper an interpretation in which, without forgetting the rational element and its importance, it pretends to underly the necessity of the passional factor in order to understand the beginning and the process of modernization and its crisis. The article starts with an analysis of the *enthusiasm* concept, focusing on the Kant and Hegel writings—assuming also the philosophies of Foucault and Benjamin. Finally, it shows the *critique* as the fundamental characteristic of modernity.

**Lanczkowski, Miroslaw** and Wittwer, Roland. Les *Evidentiae contra Durandum* de Durandellus. *Rev Thomiste*, 97(1), 143-156, Ja-Mr 97.

**Landau, Iddo**. Good Women and Bad Men: A Bias in Feminist Research. *J Soc Phil*, 28(1), 141-150, Spr 97.

The aim of this paper is to point out a prejudice which has not yet received sufficient attention, although it lies at the base of a fair amount of feminist research: the bias that whereas men are bad and aggressive, women are good and peaceful. Although as an explicit view this contention has been debated, its distortive influence on feminist research has so far remained undiscussed. In what follows I present examples of the effect of this bias on feminist research. Then I suggest why the bias has not yet been discussed. Finally, I argue that feminist research should be as critically received and treat as any other. (edited)

**Landau, Iddo**. Mendus on Philosophy and Pervasiveness. *Phil Quart*, 47(186), 89-93, Ja 97.

This is a rejoinder to Susan Mendus's "How Androcentric is Western Philosophy? a Reply", The Philosophical Quarterly, 46 1996), pp. 60-66, which addresses my "How Androcentric is Western Philosophy?", ib., pp. 48-59. The viability of the distinction between pervasive and nonpervasive androcentrism is defended, but I claim that most claims in the original paper do not presuppose it. Moreover, the original paper does not presuppose that there is a clear demarcation line between pervasive and nonpervasive androcentrism. I argue further that one can make use of some parts of philosophical systems while rejecting others, that Gilligan does see ethics as pervasively androcentric and that Rawls's theory is not a good example of pervasive androcentrism. (publisher)

**Landau, Iddo**. Why has the Question of the Meaning of Life Arisen in the Last Two and a Half Centuries?. *Phil Today*, 41(2), 263-269, Sum 97.

Questioning the meaning of life is a relatively recent phenomenon, by and large a matter of the last two hundred and fifty years. In this paper I try to explain why this is so. First, I investigate the nature of this questioning by identifying what is essential to it. Next, I link the analysis with cultural, social and economic features typical of the decades. Finally, I try to predict, on the basis of this analysis, whether the problem of the meaning of life will become even more prevailingly felt in the future or, alternately, will simply fade away.

**Landim Filho, Raul**. Pode o *Cogito* Ser Posto em Questao?. *Discurso*, 24, 9-30, 1994.

Este artigo pretende analisar o estatuto do *cogito* antes da prova da Veracidade Divina: é ele uma verdade ca ciência ("*scientia*"), "o primeiro princípio *verdadeiro* da filosofia", que escapa a qualquer dúvida, ou é apenas uma verdade momentânea e fugaz (uma "*persuasio*"), que nao resiste à dúvida metafísica, embora possa dela emergir? Para esclarecer esta questao, sao analisadas, no *Discurso do Método* e nas *Meditaçoes Metafísicas*, as noçoes cartesianas de ciência (que envolve as noçoes de verdade, certeza e Regra Geral de Verdade) e de Veracidade Divina. O artigo conclui que, antes da prova da Veracidade Divina, embora o *cogito* nao possa ser considerado como a primeira verdade da ciência, é, no entanto, o primeiro princípio da filosofia que permite a descoberta de outros conhecimentos verdadeiros.

**Landini, Gregory**. Logic in Russell's *Principles of Mathematics*. *Notre Dame J Form Log*, 37(4), 554-584, Fall 96.

Unaware of Frege's 1879 *Begriffsschrift*, Russell's 1903 *The Principles of Mathematics* set out a calculus for logic whose foundation was the doctrine that any such calculus must adopt only one style of variables—entity (individual) variables. The idea was that logic is a universal and all-encompassing science, applying alike to whatever there is—propositions, universals, classes, concrete particulars. Unfortunately, Russell's early calculus has appeared archaic if not completely obscure. This paper is an attempt to recover the formal system, showing its philosophical background and its semantic completeness with respect to the tautologies of a modern sentential calculus.

**Landini, Gregory**. The *Definability* of the Set of Natural Numbers in the 1925 *Principia Mathematica*. *J Phil Log*, 25(6), 597-615, D 96.

In his new introduction to the 1925 second edition of *Principia Mathematica*, Russell maintained that by adopting Wittgenstein's idea that a logically perfect language should be extensional mathematical induction could be rectified for finite cardinals without the axiom of reducibility. In an Appendix B, Russell set forth a proof. Gödel caught a defect in the proof at *89.16, so that the matter of rectification remained open. Myhill later arrived at a negative result: *Principia* with extensionality principles and without reducibility cannot recover mathematical induction. The finite cardinals are indefinable in it. This paper shows that while Gödel and Myhill are correct, Russell was not wrong. The 1925 system employs a different grammar than the original *Principia*. A new proof for *89.16 is given and induction is recovered.

**Landini, Paolo** and Figallo, Aldo V. On Generalizaed I-Algebras and 4-Valued Modal Algebras. *Rep Math Log*, 29, 3-18, 1995.

In this paper we establish a new characterization of 4-valued modal algebras considered by A. Monteiro. In order to obtain this characterization we introduce a new class of algebras named generalized *I*-algebras. This class contains strictly the class of C-algebras defined by Y. Komori as an algebraic counterpart of the infinite-valued implicative Lukasiewicz propositional calculus. On the other hand, the relationship between *I*-algebras and commutative BACK-algebras, defined by S. Tanaka in 1975, allows us to say that in a certain sense G-algebras are also a generalization of these latter algebras.

**Landsberg, Peter T**. Irreversibility and Time's Arrow. *Dialectica*, 50(4), 247-258, 1996.

This paper is based on a talk given at the meeting of the Portuguese Physical Society 19-23 September 1994 at Covilha, Portugal. In it we review the physicist's key problems regarding the arrow of time. For this purpose it is convenient to introduce six demons and a short way of characterising them, which will be clarified in the paper: D1 1812 Laplace: All-Knowing (Section11), D2 1867 Maxwell: Antiheat conduction (Section4), D3 1869 Loschmidt: Velocity reversal (Section 4), D4 1936 Eddington: particle count (Section 16), D5 1937 Dirac: Decrease of the gravitational "constant" (Section 17), D6 1970 Landsberg: Expansion or Contraction? (Section 14).

**Lane, Arline** and Dubler, Nancy Neveloff. The Health Care Agent: Selected but Neglected. *Bioethics Forum*, 13(2), 17-21, Sum 97.

The health care agent or "proxy" whose involvement in medical treatment decision making is triggered by the patient's incapacity, frequently faces a potentially awesome responsibility alone and unprepared. Often neglected or excluded from patient-care planning, the proxy has informational and emotional needs that must be met by the health care team in the very same manner as would those of the patient. By establishing a triad of provider, patient, and proxy early in the patient's care, much of the angst of proxy decision making could be eased.

**Lane, Harlan** and Grodin, Michael. Ethical Issues in Cochlear Implant Surgery: An Exploration into Disease, Disability, and the Best Interests of the Child. *Kennedy Inst Ethics J*, 7(3), 231-251, S 97.

This paper examines ethical issues related to medical practices with children and adults who are members of a linguistic and cultural minority known as the *Deaf-World*. Members of that culture characteristically have hearing parents and are treated by hearing professionals whose values, particularly concerning language, speech and hearing, are typically quite different from their own. That disparity has long fueled a debate on several ethical issues, most recently the merits of cochlear implant surgery for *Deaf* children. We explore whether that surgery would be ethical if implants could deliver close to normal hearing for most implanted children, thereby diminishing the ranks of the *Deaf-World*. The ethical implications of eugenic practices with the *Deaf* are explored, as are ethical quandaries in parental surrogacy for *Deaf* children and their parallels in transracial adoption.

**Lane, Neal**. "Prospect for Science and Technology" in *The American University: National Treasure or Endangered Species?*, Ehrenberg, Ronald G (ed), 128-140. Ithaca, Cornell Univ Pr, 1997.

**Lane, Robert**. Peirce's "Entanglement" with the Principles of Excluded Middle and Contradiction. *Trans Peirce Soc*, 33(3), 680-703, Sum 97.

Charles Peirce claimed that "anything is *general* in so far as the principle of excluded middle does not apply to it and is *vague* in so far as the principle of contradiction does not apply to it." This seems to imply that general propositions are neither true nor false and that vague propositions are both true and false. But this is not the case. I argue that Peirce's claim was intended to underscore relatively simple facts about quantification and negation, and that it implies neither that general propositions are neither true nor false nor that vague propositions are both true and false.

**Lang, André**. La place du politique dans le système stoïcien. *Diotima*, 25, 95-100, 1997.

**Lang, André**. Survol du Colloque. *Diotima*, 25, 130-132, 1997.

**Lang, Berel**. *Heidegger's Silence*. Ithaca, Cornell Univ Pr, 1996.

Heidegger was silent about Nazi crimes in general and the genocide against the Jews in particular not only when they were perpetrated but in the thirty productive years of his life after the end of World War II. The question is addressed here of what relation there is between this deliberate—and telling—silence and his philosophical thought. Disputing the view that his reaction was a matter only of personal biography or prejudice, the book attempts to show that the role Heidegger ascribes philosophically to the "Volk" in his concepts of history and the self accounted also for his sustained silence on the "Jewish Question."

**Lang, Berel**. The Ethics of Philosophical Discourse. *Iyyun*, 45, 85-101, Jl 96.

The claim is made here that philosophical writing—of course including writing on ethics—has itself ethical presuppositions or commitments. These emerge from the application of standard literary categories; e.g., the status of the 'implied reader' or the author's 'point of view' and then in the relation between them on the basis of which writing can be judged as an action. Thus the ethical relation between author and reader differs significantly in passages quoted from William James, on the one hand and A J Ayer on the other. A typology of discourse based on such ethical parameters is then proposed; the attempt is also made to correlate that typology with the ethical positions *asserted* by the authors.

**Lang, Helen S**. Thomas Aquinas and the Problem of Nature in Physics II, I. *Hist Phil Quart*, 13(4), 411-432, O 96.

This article considers the definition of nature as given by Aristotle in *Physics* II and the commentaries on it by Philoponus and Thomas Aquinas. Through Aristotle's definition and its treatment in two commentaries, we can see how each philosopher defines philosophy as an enterprise and the problems encompassed by it. I conclude that the conception of philosophy, and consequently its problems, is quite distinct in each case and should be considered as such; as a further consequence, the whole notion of "commentaries" should be rethought.

**Lang, Helen S**. Topics and Investigations: Aristotle's *Physics* and *Metaphysics*. *Phil Rhet*, 29(4), 416-435, 1996.

Although I recognize at the outset that there is no absolutely certain way to recover "Aristotle's meaning" (referring not to some historical person, but to the arguments generally referred to as "written by Aristotle"), my primary goal is to suggest a systematic approach to Aristotle's writings that will at least allow some clearness or exactness for the problem of establishing a position within the history of philosophy and by so doing to suggest a model for the broader problem of reading philosophy.

**Láng, Benedek**. Raimundus Lullus and His *Ars Magna,D (in Czech)*. *Magyar Filozof Szemle*, 1-2, 187-216, 1997.

The author's aim in this article is to give a description of the *Ars Magna* of Ramon Llull and to rethink some questions raised about it. These questions concern the intellectual milieu of the birth of this art, its possible relation to the Jewish Kabbala and the seldom raised issue of the real competence of this (as its inventor claims:) universal ontological logic that would be capable of solving any question. (edited)

**Lang'at, Wilson K A**. A Comparative Study between Comte's and Mill's View on Women. *Darshana Int*, 36(2/142), 40-45, Ap 96.

**Lang'at, Wilson K A**. A Critical Examination of Schleiermacher's Interpretation of Self-Consciousness. *Darshana Int*, 36(4/144), 4-17, O 96.

**Lange, Marc**. Inductive Confirmation, Counterfactual Conditionals, and Laws of Nature. *Phil Stud*, 85(1), 1-36, Ja 97.

Many philosophers (e.g., Goodman, Reichenbach, Mackie, Dretske) argue that there is a special way in which a hypothesis can be confirmed only if it is believed that this hypothesis may state a natural law—roughly, instances can confirm its predictive accuracy. Other philosophers (e.g., Carnap, Hempel, van Fraassen, Sober) have offered apparent counterexamples to such views. Here this dispute is settled: the relevant intuitions are cashed out, and the special sort of confirmation shown to be available only to hypotheses believed lawlike is revealed to account for the special relation between natural laws and counterfactual conditionals.

**Lange, Marc**. Laws of Nature, Cosmic Coincidences and Scientific Realism. *Austl J Phil*, 74(4), 614-637, D 96.

Realists argue that if an unobservable entity P posited by our best theories is unreal, then that phenomena can be saved by a P-theory must be a coincidence, which is very unlikely. Though this argument cannot persuade antirealists, it suggests that P is unreal if it is an accident, rather than a natural law, that those phenomena are as if there were P. This suggests an argument for realism appealing only to the antirealists' austere conception of science's goal, and a conception of what it is for a posited unobservable to be real rather than a useful fiction.

**Langerak, Edward**. "Disagreement: Appreciating the Dark Side of Tolerance" in *Philosophy, Religion, and the Question of Intolerance*, Ambuel, David (ed), 111-124. Albany, SUNY Pr, 1997.

I argue that tolerance, as well as toleration, involves enduring the disagreeable on matters that one cares about and, therefore, must be sharply distinguished from broad-minded celebration of diversity, which some writers are associating with true tolerance. Although tolerance should retain the connotation of "putting up with" rather than affirming, one should also recognize the appropriateness of respecting views that one regards as disagreeable but as reasonable. One can even be intolerant of actions that are motivated by views one respects as reasonable (though wrong).

**Langewand, Alfred**. Die Fichte-Lektüre des jungen Herbart (1796-1798). *Fichte-Studien*, 12, 273-284, 1997.

**Langford, Duncan**. Ethics and the Internet: Appropriate Behavior in Electronic Communication. *Ethics Behavior*, 6(2), 91-106, 1996.

The creation of global computer networks has given individuals the ability to communicate directly with each other, linking across national and international boundaries as easily as across the street. Global publication is surprisingly easy; this means, for example, that views that may be abhorrent to large numbers of individuals can be propagated an automatically distributed. Material such as pornography is, potentially, freely available everywhere. However, despite the wishes of politicians and others, it is technically and realistically impossible to censor or otherwise limit electronically published material. The fabric of global computer networks known generically as the Internet is, quite literally, out of political control. Drawing upon research carried out for a recent book on computer ethics, this article examines the current situation.

**Langiulli, Nino** (ed). *European Existentialism*. New Brunswick, Transaction Pub, 1997.

*European Existentialism* is a rich collection of major texts and is made all the more significant by the range and depth of its contributions. This book aims to give greater intelligibility to existentialism by providing samples from antecedents of and influences upon it. Although existentialism is regarded as an example of twentieth-century philosophizing, the book presents nineteenth-century thinkers such as Kierkegaard and Nietzsche as its forerunners. Thinkers, such as Dilthey, Husserl, and Scheler, frequently associated with other trends in philosophy, such as historicism and phenomenology, are included because of their influence upon existentialism. Informative biographies of each author represented are also included. (publisher, edited)

**Langsam, Harold**. How to Combat Nihilism: Reflections on Nietzsche's Critique of Morality. *Hist Phil Quart*, 14(2), 235-253, Ap 97.

Nietzsche's intended audience for his critique of morality are not the believers in morality, but those who have rejected morality in favor of nihilism. Nietzsche's point is that the rejection of morality need not result in nihilism, it can lead to an acceptance of the value of creating value. People embrace nihilism because they believe that only objective values can be legitimate values, and they have ceased to believe in objective values; Nietzsche, through his critique of morality, wants to show the nihilist that the claim that only objective values can be legitimate values is itself a lie of Christianity.

**Langsam, Harold**. The Theory of Appearing Defended. *Phil Stud*, 87(1), 33-59, Jl 97.

I defend the view that the phenomenal features of perceptual experience are relations between material objects and minds (the "theory of appearing"); this view is opposed to views that hold that phenomenal features are intrinsic properties, whether of mental objects, brain states, or material objects. I argue that the theory of appearing is part of our commonsense thinking about the world and that it can adequately respond to the standard philosophical arguments against it: the argument from hallucination, the causal argument and the time-gap argument.

**Langston, Douglas**. The Spark of Conscience: Bonaventure's View of Conscience and Synderesis. *Fran Stud*, 53, 79-95, 1993.

Unlike some of his predecessors and contemporaries, Bonaventure located the synderesis in the affective order. He understood conscience to be in the intellectual order, but, because he did not completely separate the two orders from one another, many of the activities of conscience were seen by him to be expressions of synderesis. In fact, he saw synderesis as the driving force (the spark) of conscience. Moreover, he presented a dynamic view of conscience by viewing it as capable of formulating general rules of behavior derived from experience.

**Langton, Rae**. "Love and Solipsism" in *Love Analyzed*, Lamb, Roger E, 123-152. Boulder, Westview Pr, 1997.

Suppose I lived in a solipsistic world but believed I did not; I would treat things as if they were people. Suppose I lived in a peopled world but believed I was alone; I would treat people as if they were things. These two solipsisms—and their epistemic, metaphysical, and moral aspects—are used (with the help of an example from Proust) to illumine Kant's suggestion in *Lectures on Ethics* that 'sexual love makes of the loved person an object of appetite', and that thereby a 'person becomes a thing and can be treated and used as such'.

**Langtry, Bruce**. Eyeballing Evil: Some Epistemic Principles. *Phil Papers*, 25(2), 127-137, Ag 96.

Objections from evil to the existence of God often centre on some such inference as this: 1) There are evils such that no good state of affairs we know of justifies God's permitting those evils. 2) Therefore, there are evils such that no good state of affairs justifies God's permitting those evils. But when should we infer 'There is no X' from 'There is no X we know of'? My paper is a contribution to the current debate on the issue in the philosophy of religion literature.

**Langtry, Bruce**. God and the Best. *Faith Phil*, 13(3), 311-328, Jl 96.

The paper reaches two main conclusions: Firstly, even if there are one or more possible worlds than which there are none better, God cannot actualise any of them. Secondly, if there are possible worlds which God can actualise and than which God can actualise none better, then God must actualise one of them. The paper is neutral between compatibilist and libertarian views of creaturely freedom.

**Lant, Christopher L** and Akama, John S and Burnett, G Wesley. A Political-Ecology Approach to Wildlife Conservation in Kenya. *Environ Values*, 5(4), 335-347, N 96.

This essay uses a political-ecological framework in the analysis of the social factors of wildlife conservation in Kenya. It postulates that the overriding socio-economic issue impacting wildlife conservation in Kenya is underdevelopment. The problem of underdevelopment is manifested in forms of increasing levels of poverty, famine and malnutrition. The long term survival of Kenya's wildlife depends on social and ecological solutions to the problems of underdevelopment. (edited)

**Lanteigne, Josette**. La question du suicide. *Horiz Phil*, 7(1), 17-24, Fall 96.

**Lantos, John** and Karlawish, Jason H T. Community Equipoise and the Architecture of Clinical Research. *Cambridge Quart Healthcare Ethics*, 6(4), 385-396, Fall 97.

**Lantos, John D**. Ethics Committees and Resource Allocation. *Bioethics Forum*, 10(4), 27-29, Fall 94.

Nobody, including most bioethicists, seeks or wants the job of allocating scarce resources. Instead, bioethicists have focused on the rights of patients to health care resources and the obligation of providers and of society to maintain an adequate supply of resources to meet patients' demands. The current health care system diffuses responsibility and hides accountability for resource allocation decisions. Ethical theory and moral deliberation could only guide allocation decisions in a health care system in which resource allocation decisions could be made in an open and explicit way.

**Lantos, John D**. Seeking Justice for Priscilla. *Cambridge Quart Healthcare Ethics*, 5(4), 485-492, Fall 96.

**Lanz, Peter**. *Das phänomenale Bewusstsein: Eine Verteidigung*. Frankfurt/M, Klostermann, 1996.

Thema dieser philosophischen Untersuchung ist das phänomenale oder sinnliche Bewusstsein. Darunter fallen die mit Hören, Sehen, Schmekken, Riechen, Tasten und Fühlen gegebenen Erfahrungen oder Erlebnisse. Die folgenden beiden Thesen werden verteidigt: 1) Konstitutiv für *sinnliches* Bewusstsein (im Unterschied zu dem mit Denken, Meinen oder blossem Vorstellen verbundenen Bewusstsein) ist die unmittelbare Präsenz sinnlicher Qualitäten: Töne beim Hören, Farben beim Sehen, Geschmack beim Schmecken, Geruch beim Riechen, Druck-, Temperaturund Schmerzempfindungen beim Tasten. 2) Diese für das sinnliche Bewusstsein konstitutiven Qualitäten treten nicht *vor* oder *jenseits* der Sinnesorgane auf, sondern sind bloss im Bewusstsein exemplifiziert. Letzteres wird so begründet: Die mit jeder einzelnen Sinnesmodalität gegebenen sinnlichen Qualitäten bilden jeweils spezifische Strukturen (Beziehungen der Ähnlichkeit, des Ausschlusses, der Anordnung/Abfolge), die wesentlich für die sinnlichen Qualitäten sind. (edited)

**Lanz, Peter**. *Das phänomenale Bewusstsein: Eine Verteidigung*. Frankfurt/M, Klostermann, 1996.

Auch die zur "Dekade des Gehirns" erhobenen letzten zehn Jahre des Jahrhunderts werden nur wenig Licht in das Dunkel bringen, in welches die Korrelationen zwischen neuralem "Gehirngeschehen" und "bewusstem mentalem Leben" gehüllt sind. *Dass* es da Verbindungen gebe, ist unbestritten; *wie* sie beschaffen seien, ist freilich eine Frage, auf die die naturwissenschaftliche Hirnforschung (bisher?) keine zureichende Antwort zu geben vermag. In den offerierten Antworten erkennen wir die uns vertrauten *Phänomene* wachen Bewusstseins—Gedanken, Empfindungen, Sinneseindrükke, Stimmungen, Emotionen—nicht wieder. Solange dies der Preis des wissenschaftlichen Fortschritts ist, ist er keiner. Dies jedenfalls legt die hier anzuzeigende Studie über das "phänomenale Bewusstsein" nahe. (edited)

**Lapierre, Serge**. Structured Meanings and Reflexive Domains. *Stud Log*, 51(2), 215-239, 1992.

This paper is about the most important technical problem faced by structured meanings semantics: the reiteration of hyperintensional functors (i.e., functors of *Theta*-categorial languages of the sort defined by Max Cresswell in [6]). A way to solve this problem in a general and natural way by using Scott's Domains is both suggested and carried through. The result is a semantics which unrestrictedly allows reiterations of hyperintensional functors. The semantics is also extended to accommodate *Theta*-categorial languages with variables.

**Laplanche, Jean**. La psychanalyse: mythe et théorie. *Rev Phil Fr*, 2, 205-224, Ap-Je 97.

**Laplanche, Jean** and Thurston, Luke (trans). Psychoanalysis as Anti-Hermeneutics. *Rad Phil*, 79, 7-12, S-O 96.

**LaPorte, Joseph**. Essential Membership. *Phil Sci*, 64(1), 96-112, Mr 97.

In this paper I take issue with the doctrine that organisms belong of their very essence to the natural kinds (or biological taxa, if these are not kinds) to which they belong. This view holds that any human essentially belongs to the species *Homo sapiens*, any feline essentially belongs to the cat family, and so on. I survey the various competing views in biological systematics. These offer different explanations for what it is that makes a member of one species, family, etc., a member of that taxon. Unfortunately, none of them offers an explanation that is compatible with the essentialism in question.

**Lappin, Shalom** and Johnson, David E. A Critique of the Minimalist Program. *Ling Phil*, 20(3), 273-333, Je 97.

The paper attempts to clarify the primary formal properties of Chomsky's (1995) minimalist program *MP* model of grammar and clarify some of its computational and empirical consequences. We argue that the global economy conditions of the MP raise serious complexity problems and lack either computational on linguistic motivation. They can either be replaced by local constraints on simply discarded without loss of coverage of the data. We compare the resulting "local" minimalist model with a local constraint-based typed feature structure grammar and provide empirical arguments for preferring the latter approach.

**Laraudogoitia, Jon Perez**. Classical Particle Dynamics, Indeterminism and a Supertask. *Brit J Phil Sci*, 48(1), 49-54, Mr 97.

In this paper a model in particle dynamics of a well-known supertask is constructed. As a consequence, a new and simple result about the failure of determinism of classical particle dynamics can be proved which is related to the nonexistence of boundary conditions at spatial infinity. This result is much more accessible to the nontechnical reader than similar ones in the scientific literature.

**Lardic, Jean-Marie**. Malebranche et l'argument ontologique. *Rev Phil Fr*, 4, 503-519, O-D 96.

**Largeault, Jean**. Can We Speak of Regional Logics? (in French). *Arch Phil*, 60(1), 129-134, Ja-Mr 97.

**Larmer, Robert**. The Ethics of Investing: A Reply to William Irvine. *J Bus Ethics*, 16(4), 397-400, Mr 97.

In a recent article in this journal entitled "The Ethics of Investing," William Irvine argues that what he calls the '*evil-company principle*' is an adequate guide to ethical investing. In its place, he proposes what he calls the '*enablement principle*'. In reply, I argue that his rejection of the evil-company principle is premature and that his enablement principle presupposes acceptance of the evil-company principle.

**Larochelle, Gilbert** and Mineau, André. Éthique et idéologie: frontière et médiation sémantique par la morale. *Laval Theol Phil*, 52(3), 827-836, O 96.

The article seeks to bring out how the notions of ethics and of ideology can be defined one with respect to the other. Its aim is to explore conceptually the influence of these categories, their corollary, the conditions under which they operate, the moral ground on which they meet.

**Larsen, Svend Erik**. Metaphor—A Semiotic Perspective. *Dan Yrbk Phil*, 31, 137-156, 1996.

The paper sets out to define and apply metaphor in a semiotic framework. With Charles S. Peirce and Karl Bühler as the main references metaphor is defined as an iconic function in an inferential sign process specifying a presupposed likeness between objects. In this context metaphor is not seen as predominantly verbal, but as involving both verbal and nonverbal sign systems. The opening scene of *Romeo and Juliet* serves as the basis for an application, showing how metaphors occur, change and function as a textual device that articulates the iconic dimension of the polysemiotic dramatic text.

**Larvor, Brendan P**. Lakatos as Historian of Mathematics. *Phil Math*, 5, 42-64, F 97.

This paper discusses the connection between the actual history of mathematics and Lakatos's philosophy of mathematics, in three parts. The first points to studies by Lakatos and others which support his conception of mathematics and its history. In the second I suggest that the apparent poverty of Lakatosian examples may be due to the way in which the history of mathematics is usually written. The third part argues that Lakatos is right to hold philosophy accountable to history, even if Lakatos's own view of mathematics fails that test.

**Lasaga Medina, José**. Cultura y reflexión en torno a Meditaciones del Quijote. *El Basilisco*, 22, 77-82, Jl-D 96.

**Laserna Pinzón, Mario**. "Analytic Geometry, Experimental Truth and Metaphysics in Descartes" in *Memorias Del Seminario En Conmemoración De Los 400 Años Del Nacimiento De René Descartes*, Albis, Víctor S (ed), 51-92. Sankt Augustin, Academia, 1997.

**Lasic, Hrvoje**. Maurice Blondel: A Philosopher of Tolerance and Human Dignity. *Filozof Istraz*, 16(3), 587-599, 1996.

Se basant sur l'étude des écrits philosophiques de Maurice Blondel et de sa riche correspondance avec les théologues et les philosophes à l'époque de la crise du modernisme, par une analyse critique, l'auteur tente de découvrir les fondements du concept que Blondel s'est formé de la tolérance et de la dignité humaine, ainsi que sa connaissance des sources théologiques qui contribuèrent à la formation d'un tel concept. Ces recherches ont porté l'auteur à conclure que le concept de Blondel concernant la tolérance et la dignité humaine découle de l'Idée qu'il se fait de l'homme-créature, être contingent par rapport à Dieu-créateur, seul "Etre nécessaire". (edited)

**Laskowski, Michael C** and Mayer, Laura L. Stable Structures with Few Substructures. *J Sym Log*, 61(3), 985-1005, S 96.

A countable, atomically stable structure U in a finite, relational language has fewer than $2^{\omega}$ nonisomorphic substructures if and only if U is cellular. An example shows that the finiteness of the language is necessary. (edited)

**Laskowski, Michael C** and Shelah, Saharon. Forcing Isomorphism II. *J Sym Log*, 61. (4), 1305-1320, D 96.

**Laso Prieto, José Maria**. Jack London y El Talón de Hierro. *El Basilisco*, 22, 83-94, Jl-D 96.

**Lata** and Bhandari, D R. Concept of Duty: A Study in Indian and Western Philosophy. *Darshana Int*, 36(1/141), 44-47, Ja 96.

The notion duty is essentially implied in every ethical theory. A duty means what we ought to perform as 'moral beings'. From Plato to Kant, Moore, Bradley etc. there have been very serious discussions regarding the concept of duty. It has individual as well as social aspect. In ancient Indian philosophical, social and ethical sphere it is said that whole universe is founded on moral law called Rita or Dharma or Duty. Human duties as laid down by the Bhagwad Gita are determined by a man's reaction to the outer World. A man is warned to persue his own Dharma or Duty. Here we find a striking similarity between these ideas of Gita and that of Plato's ideas regarding the concept of Duty.

**Lathrop, Anna** and Connolly, Maureen. Maurice Merleau-Ponty and Rudolf Laban—An Interactive Appropriation of Parallels and Resonances. *Human Stud*, 20(1), 27-45, Ja 97.

In this paper we propose an examination of the shared connections between the French philosopher Maurice Merleau-Ponty and the Austro-Hungarian movement theorist Rudolf Laban. In many ways Merleau-Ponty's philosophy demonstrates a synthesis of the best in existentialism and phenomenology. In like manner, Rudolf Laban was a synthesizer of experiences and theories of movement. We propose to examine the parallels and resonances of their theory with the forum of a hypothetical collegial conversation.(edited)

**Latzer, Michael**. The Proofs for the Existence of God: Henry of Ghent and Duns Scotus as Precursors of Leibniz. *Mod Sch*, 74(2), 143-160, Ja 97.

When Leibniz writes in section 45 of the *Monadology* that "God alone, or the Necessary Being, has this prerogative, that he must necessarily exist, if he is possible...", he is not presenting an original insight but is instead echoing a proof for the existence of God worked out in the monumental natural theologies of Henry of Ghent and Duns Scotus. In this paper I trace the striking parallels between Leibniz's proofs for the existence of God and of these two medieval doctors.(edited)

**Laudisa, Federico**. Non-Locality: A Defense of Widespread Beliefs. *Stud Hist Phil Mod Physics*, 27B(3), 297-313, S 96.

It has been argued, on the basis of an equivalence between the existence of a joint probability distribution for incompatible observables and the satisfaction of the Bell inequalities, that these inequalities are irrelevant to the issue of (non)locality; and that this issue arises only if we adhere to a notion of objectivity in the description of physical systems that is not justified in quantum mechanics. These arguments are discussed in the orthodox and in the unsharp approach to quantum mechanics and found defective: the Bell inequalities turn out to be relevant both in the orthodox and in the unsharp approach.

**Laudisa, Federico**. Still in Defence: A Short Reply on Non-Locality and Widespread Beliefs. *Stud Hist Phil Mod Physics*, 27B(3), 331-335, S 96.

In his (1996) Willem M. de Muynck takes issue with some arguments I have advanced in Laudisa (1996). He aims to show that my defence of the relevance of the Bell inequalities to the problem of nonlocality in quantum mechanics is not well-founded or—at least—is unduly restrictive. Several points in de Muynck's paper deserve discussion, but I would like just to comment on what seem to me the main ones. Accordingly I will focus on: 1) definitions of (non)locality; 2) nonobjectivism, contextualism and the Bell inequalities; 3) causal interpretation of quantum mechanics, explanation and metaphysics; and 4) joint measurements, locality and the Bell inequalities.

**Lauer, Henle**. Treating Race as a Social Construction. *J Value Inq*, 30(3), 445-451, S 96.

**Laufer, William S** and Robertson, Diana C. Corporate Ethics Initiatives as Social Control. *J Bus Ethics*, 16(10), 1029-1048, Jl 97.

Efforts to institutionalize ethics in corporations have been discussed without first addressing the desirability of norm conformity or the possibility that the means used to elicit conformity will be coercive. This article presents a theoretical context, grounded in models of social control, within which ethics initiatives may be evaluated. Ethics initiatives are discussed in relation to variables that already

exert control in the workplace, such as environmental controls, organizational controls and personal controls.

**Laura, Ronald S**. Reflections on Israel Scheffler's Philosophy of Religion. *Stud Phil Educ*, 16(1-2), 225-240, Ja-Ap 97.

The burden of this piece is to draw together into a coherent whole the somewhat diverse strands of Israel Scheffler's thought on the philosophy of religion. Extrapolating from personal discussions with Professor Scheffler, various of his books, articles, and other unpublished materials authored and kindly provided by him, I contend that he adumbrates a postempiricist rendering of religious belief which masterfully avoids some philosophical problems, while unwittingly giving rise to others. Committed to the view that the methodology of science—in one or other of its more acceptable guises—provides the most reliable measure of the content and structure of reality, Scheffler is bound conceptually to redefine Jewish belief in such a way that the traditional conflict between religion and science never emerges. Consistent with this end, he is concerned to divest traditional Judaism of its metaphysical garb, so that what remains are simply the matters of living to which religion ought properly on his view address itself.(edited)

**Laura, Ronald S** and Leahy, Michael. Religious 'Doctrines' and the Closure of Minds. *J Phil Educ*, 31(2), 329-343, Jl 97.

In a recent essay, Tasos Kazepides has used the later Wittgenstein's account of religious beliefs as either 'superstitions' or nonrational to condemn such beliefs as 'doctrines.' By this term he means teachings which close minds to alternative truth-claims. In this paper we criticize his interpretation and use of Wittgenstein and argue that, far from closing minds to possible realms of existence unconsidered in other subjects of the curriculum.

**Laurence, Stephen** and Margolis, Eric. Regress Arguments against the Language of Thought. *Analysis*, 57(1), 60-66, Ja 97.

The language of thought hypothesis is sometimes taken to be refuted by a familiar sort of argument: "The language of thought is appealed to in order to explain some feature of natural language (such as its learnability, or meaningfulness), but, in order to explain this feature, the language of thought must also have the feature. Thus a regress." We argue that such arguments rely on the assumption that the entire motivation for the language of thought is the explanandum that allegedly generates the regress. But this assumption is simply false.

**Laursen, John Christian** and Popkin, Richard H and Briscoe, Peter. Hume in the Prussian Academy: Jean Bernard Mérian's "On the Phenomenalism of David Hume". *Hume Stud*, 23(1), 153-191, Ap 97.

This article contains a transcription and translation of an important eighteenth-century interpretation of Hume's phenomenalism. A substantial introduction reviews interest in Hume at the Prussian Academy, Jean Bernard Mérian's engagement with skepticism and questions of the self and personal identity and analyzes Mérian's conclusions. Notes draw attention to Mérian's critique of Kant and to some of the later influence of Mérian on Victor Cousin and Maine de Biran.

**Lauth, Bernhard**. New Blades for Occam's Razor. *Erkenntnis*, 46(2), 241-267, Mr 97.

**Lauth, Reinhard**. "El progreso cognoscitivo en la primera Doctrina de la Ciencia de Fichte" in *El inicio del Idealismo alemán*, Market, Oswaldo, 35-49. Madrid, Ed Complutense, 1996.

La decisiva contribución de la primera Doctrina de la Ciencia no es la "decapitación" de la cosa en sí, ni tampoco la centralidad del Yo, sino la unificación de toda la razón (teórica y práctica) en la autoconstitución o autoposición de la libertad y el ascenso al Yo absoluto del primer principio, más allá de toda doctrina de la relación, en donde permanecieron sus contemporáneos. Por consiguiente, ese poner absoluto que se describe en la Doctrina de la Ciencia, y que funda todo poner relacional, es un principio sistemático peculiar de Fichte, dado que después no ha sido retomado ni comprendido, pues tanto Schelling como Hegel volvieron a objetivarlo.

**Lauth, Reinhard**. Leibniz im Verständnis Fichtes. *Kantstudien*, 87(4), 396-422, 1996.

**Lauwers, Luc**. Infinite Utility: Insisting on Strong Monotonicity. *Austl J Phil*, 75(2), 222-233, Je 97.

The note addresses the problem of how utilitarianism and other finitely additive theories of value should evaluate infinitely long utility streams. We use the axiomatic approach and show that finite anonymity does not apply in an infinite framework. A stronger anonymity demand (fixed step anonymity) is proposed and motivated. Finally, we construct an ordering criterion that combines fixed step anonymity and strong monotonicity.

**Lauzier Stone, Denise**. Preservice Art Education and Learning in Art Museums. *J Aes Educ*, 30(3), 83-96, Fall 96.

**Lauzon, Jean**. Sujet(s) à interprétation(s): sur la relative transparence d'une photographie positiviste. *Horiz Phil*, 7(2), 127-139, Spr 97.

Le XIXe siècle positiviste voit naître la photographie. L'auteur note que la faculté d'enregistrement objectif du réel attribuée à la photographie correspond à l'attitude positiviste voulant que de la stricte observation du monde, on puisse déduire ses lois générales de fonctionnement. Le statut indicaire du processus photographique semblait autoriser que l'on puisse oublier cet intermédiaire et ainsi croire en sa transparence absolue. Après avoir fait état d'une série de pratiques photographiques positivistes à prétention scientifique, l'auteur note l'existence de nombreux protocoles interprétatifs mis en oeuvre pour traduire leurs différents résultats. L'auteur conclut que la photographie ne saurait donc s'effacer devant ce qu'elle représente. On souligne ainsi que l'opacité du langage photographique doit faire l'objet d'une appréhension au moins aussi importante que sa présumée transparence.

**Lavaroni, Charles**. Self-Evaluation: A Learned Process. *Inquiry (USA)*, 14(2), 52-57, Wint 94.

**Lavers, Peter**. Generalising Tautological Entailment. *Log Anal*, 37(147-8), 367-377, S-D 94.

The first degree fragment of relevant logics, "Tautological Entailment," corresponds to variable sharing as described by Anderson and Belnap. I show how variable sharing can be generalized to entailments of arbitrary degree. Furthermore, in general the full degree "variable sharing" logics are strictly weaker than the "standard" relevant logics.

**Lawler, James**. Originalism, Moralism and the Public Opinion State of Mitchell Franklin. *Trans Peirce Soc*, 33(2), 446-487, Spr 97.

**Lawlor, Leonard** (trans) and Sen, Amit (trans) and Hyppolite, Jean. *Logic and Existence*. Albany, SUNY Pr, 1997.

*Logic and Existence*, which originally appeared in 1952, completes the project Hyppolite began with *Genesis and Structure of Hegel's "Phenomenology of Spirit."* Taking up successively the role of language, reflection, and categories in Hegel's *Science of Logic*, Hyppolite illuminates Hegelianism's most obscure dialectical synthesis: the relation between the phenomenology and the logic.(publisher, edited)

**Lawrence, Gavin**. Nonaggregatability, Inclusiveness, and the Theory of Focal Value: *Nichomachean Ethics* 1.7.1097b16-20. *Phronesis*, 42(1), 32-76, 1997.

**Lawrence, Matthew**. Pluralism, Liberalism, and the Role of Overriding Values. *Pac Phil Quart*, 77(4), 335-350, D 96.

While it is often thought that pluralism is best accommodated by a liberal state, John Kekes has recently argued that pluralism and liberalism involve inconsistent commitments. He maintains that liberalism is committed to the idea that one or more of the "liberal values" must override all other values, while pluralism is committed to the idea that there are no overriding values whatsoever. In this paper I challenge Kekes's position by arguing that ethical pluralism does not require an absence of overriding values and that liberalism does not require that one or more of the liberal values must override all others.

**Lawson, Bill E**. "On Disappointment in the Black Context" in *Existence in Black: An Anthology of Black Existential Philosophy,* Gordon, Lewis R (ed), 149-156. New York, Routledge, 1997.

We have many examples of disappointments in our personal lives. However, I want to consider the experience of disappointment in the more specific context of the lives of blacks in the U.S. I am concerned not with the day-to-day experiences of disappointments, but with the experience of disappointment that comes from the failure of the government to satisfy the expectations of the majority of blacks. I call this type of disappointment "social disappointment." It is my contention that given the social realities of the black experience, any definitive claims about the impact of the experience of social disappointment on the black collective view of self should be viewed as suspect.

**Laycock, Steven W**. The Dialectics of Nothingness: A Reexamination of Shen-hsiu and Hui-neng. *J Chin Phil*, 24(1), 19-41, Mr 97.

**Lazar, Philippe**. "The Idea of Progress in Human Health" in *The Idea of Progress,* McLaughlin, Peter (ed), 219-229. Hawthorne, de Gruyter, 1997.

**Lazere, Donald**. Critical Thinking in College English Studies. *Inquiry (USA)*, 14(1), 84-88, Fall 94.

**Lazich, Michael C**. Reason as Antithesis: Dialectical Theology and the Crisis of Modern Culture. *Int Stud Phil*, 28(4), 23-40, 1996.

**Lazzari, Alessandro**. Fichtes Entwicklung von der zweiten Auflage der Offenbarungskritik bis zur Rezeption von Schulzes *Aenesidemus*. *Fichte-Studien*, 9, 181-196, 1997.

**Le Poidevin, Robin**. *Arguing for Atheism: An Introduction to the Philosophy of Religion*. New York, Routledge, 1996.

The book addresses the question of whether theism—the view that there is a personal, transcendent creator of the universe—solves the deepest mysteries of existence. Theistic and atheistic approaches to the following questions are explored: why the universe exists, why the laws of nature are compatible with the emergence of life and how there can be objective moral values. Finally, a way of interpreting religious discourse is presented which allows us to make sense of the role of religion in our spiritual and moral lives but which treats talk apparently about God as non-fact-stating.

**Le Poidevin, Robin**. Time and the Static Image. *Philosophy*, 72(280), 175-188, Ap 97.

Can static images such as paintings and photographs represent the passage of time? Or are they confined, as the traditional view has it, to a single instantaneous moment? In *Moment and Movement in Art*, Ernst Gombrich attacks the traditional view and argues that the very notion of an instant is incoherent. The present paper looks critically at Gombrich's arguments, defending the notion of an instant and arguing that it does not commit us to dubious theses about how we perceive time and change. Finally, it concludes that static images are capable of nondepictively representing instants.

**Le Poidevin, Robin**. Time, Tense and Topology. *Phil Quart*, 46(185), 467-481, O 96.

A central contention of the tensed theory of time is that the 'B-series' relations of temporal precedence and simultaneity are reducible to the 'A-series' determinations of pastness, presentness and futurity. This paper examines the compatibility of this reductionist thesis with two topological structures for time, namely disunified time and branching time. It is argued that, despite initial appearances, disunified time need pose no problems for tensed theory. However, the tensed theorist has no nonquestion-begging argument against the coherence of branching time and no satisfactory reduction of the B-series to the A-series can be given which is compatible with branching time.

**Leader, Sheldon**. Toleration without Liberal Foundations. *Ratio Juris*, 10(2), 139-164, Je 97.

The author's aim to find principles grounding and limiting toleration that are sufficiently sensitive to the variety of distinct settings in which concrete problems arise, and to produce principles which can appeal both to liberals and to nonliberals. The range of settings is covered by fixing the nature of three distinct species of the genus right to toleration. Once these rights are analyzed, an attempt is made to see what agreement about them can be reached by liberals and nonliberals if they have a common commitment to democracy. A definition of democracy is produced that, it is argued, liberals and nonliberals would have difficulty rejecting. It is then explored as a definition that has definite consequences over the three rights to toleration, putting the opponents before a choice: either to accept their preferred content for the right to toleration, or to support a democratic policy.

**Leahy, Michael**. "Afterword" in *The Liberation Debate: Rights at Issue*, Leahy, Michael (ed), 246-260. New York, Routledge, 1996.

The book offers polemical essays by philosophers for and against the six most controversial areas typified by claims for 'liberation' and/or 'rights': women, blacks, gays, children, animals, and the third world. The *Afterword* reflects upon common themes (e.g., the preferential rhetoric of the two claims, the theories, justification, and terminology of discrimination—sexism, racism, homophobia, ageism, speciesism, etc.) which emphasize similarities between the six topics. Leahy also presents his views, which often hints at an adjudication between the warring parties. Flew is impatient of Hampton's feminism, Levin devastates Boxill (but in an unpopular cause), Scruton's subtlety fails to dislodge Nussbaum's statistics on gay goings-on, and Purdy's commonsense refutes the extravagances of allowing young teenagers to rule the roost. And speciesism does *not* rule the roost.

**Leahy, Michael**. "Brute Equivocation" in *The Liberation Debate: Rights at Issue,* Leahy, Michael (ed), 188-204. New York, Routledge, 1996.

Leahy argues that animals are primitive beings. They are conscious, sometimes trainable, and superior to plants. They are 'primitive' in that, lacking language, their over-praised rationality and emotional lives are mere shadows. Where they *appear* otherwise (e.g., guilty, frightened, hoping) we are observing prototypical instinctive behaviour. Human beings are able, by contrast, to rationalize these instincts; even chimps are not. Liberationists treat animals with ignorant sentimentality because, being often mammals like us, it is assumed that they suffer as humans can. This is nonsense. A chimp suffers *pain* but little more. It cannot worry about a diagnosis or prognosis as we do since we can understand such concepts as 'death'. There are no 'animal rights' as yet. But animals are protected from pain and exploitation by *legal* rights. Human babies and the mentally disabled are in much the same boat. But the planet would be a sad place without wild animals.

**Leahy, Michael** (ed) and Cohn-Sherbok, Dan (ed). *The Liberation Debate: Rights at Issue*. New York, Routledge, 1996.

Liberation movements of many kinds have exploded onto the contemporary scene, especially in the West. Convinced of their cause they often violently agitate for so-called rights and emancipation. Some regard these rights campaigners as noble; others view with horror their impact upon society. When groups are liberated their ammunition is the rhetoric of 'rights'. This polemical book leaves adversaries to fight it out. It will displease many; particularly on the issues of race and women. Four other topics are fought over, viz. the claims and counterclaims on behalf of gays, children, animals, and the poor. The format consists of original commissions from distinguished experts in the six areas. In each case there is a protagonist, an antagonist, a right to reply, and an element of adjudication in a final overview by the editors.

**Leahy, Michael** and Laura, Ronald S. Religious 'Doctrines' and the Closure of Minds. *J Phil Educ*, 31(2), 329-343, Jl 97.

In a recent essay, Tasos Kazepides has used the later Wittgenstein's account of religious beliefs as either 'superstitions' or nonrational to condemn such beliefs as 'doctrines'. By this term he means teachings which close minds to alternative truth-claims. In this paper we criticize his interpretation and use of Wittgenstein and argue that, far from closing minds to possible realms of existence unconsidered in other subjects of the curriculum.

**Leaman, Oliver**. "Averroës and the West" in *Averroës and the Enlightenment*, Wahba, Mourad (ed), 53-67. Amherst, Prometheus, 1996.

The Averroes of the West and the Islamic thinker are not as distinct as has often been argued. It is often claimed that the ways in which Christian and Jewish Europe interpreted Ibn Rushd is not an accurate guide to his thought and is more radical in its Aristotelianism than was actually present in the thought of Ibn Rushd himself. This position is challenged and evidence is produced to argue that the ways in which Ibn Rushd's philosophy was interpreted in its non-Islamic environment is faithful to his original thought.

**Leash, Evangeline** (& others) and Derish, Pamela and Eastwood, Susan. Ethical Issues in Biomedical Research: Perceptions and Practices of Postdoctoral Research Fellows Responding to a Survey. *Sci Eng Ethics*, 2(1), 89-114, J 96.

We surveyed 1005 postdoctoral fellows by questionnaire about ethical matters related to biomedical research and publishing; 33% responded. About 18% of respondents said they had taken a course in research ethics and about 31% said they had had a course that devoted some time to research ethics. A substantial majority stated willingness to grant other investigators, except competitors, access to their data before publication and to share research materials. Respondents' opinions about contributions justifying authorship of research papers were mainly consistent but at variance with those of many biomedical journal editors. (edited)

**Leavitt, Fred**. Resolving Hempel's Raven Paradox. *Phil Inq*, 18(3-4), 116, Sum-Fall 96.

**Leblanc, Hughes**. Commentary on W.V. Quine's "Free Logic, Description, and Virtual Classes". *Dialogue (Canada)*, 36(1), 109-112, Wint 97.

**Leblanc, Hughes** and Roeper, Peter. De *A* et *B*, de leur indépendance logique, et de ce qu'ils n'ont aucun contenu factuel commun. *Dialogue (Canada)*, 36(1), 137-155, Wint 97.

The logical independence of two statements is tantamount to their probabilistic independence, the latter understood in a sense that derives from stochastic independence. And analogous logical and probabilistic senses of having the same factual content similarly coincide. These results are extended to notions of nonsymmetrical independence and independence among more than two statements.

**LeBlanc, Albert**. Building Theory in Music Education: A Personal Account. *Phil Music Educ Rev*, 4(2), 107-116, Fall 96.

This article describes the development of the author's theories of the acquisition of individual music listening preferences and of music performance anxiety. The author's theory of music preference is discussed in detail.

**Lecaldano, Eugenio**. "L'influenza della logica sulla ricerca storiografica su Hume" in *Momenti di Storia della Logica e di Storia della Filosofia*, Guetti, Carla (ed), 95-111. Roma, Aracne Editrice, 1996.

**Lecaldano, Eugenio**. L'etica laica e l'enciclica "Evangelium vitae". *Iride*, 8(15), 274-282, Ag 95.

Il laico non può aspettarsi da chi si uniforma all'atteggiamento pontificio un rispetto per la propria etica analogo a quello che egli è pronto a dare alla morale cattolica. Non meno chiusa l'enciclica risulta nei confronti delle istituzioni politiche liberali e democratiche quando si sostiene che né il rispetto dell'altrui libertà, né l'esigenza della pace sociale possono giustificare la lealtà nei confronti di leggi che si allontanano dalla versione papale dell'etica della difesa della vita. Aperture si trovano solo in quei passi dell'enciclica in cui si ammette una graduazione della gravità morale dei diversi attentati al vangelo della vita.

**Lecaldano, Eugenio** and Schneewind, J B and Vacatello, Marzio. I metodi dell'etica di Henry Sidgwick. *Iride*, 9(18), 495-511, Ag 96.

Dopo 120 anni dalla pubblicazione dei *Metodi dell'etica* di H. Sidgwick, risaltano con maggiore evidenza i nuclei più originali e significativi delle analisi che vi sono sviluppate. In particolare la presentazione di una dimostrazione razionale dell'utilitarismo che, oltre ad essere del tutto nuova a suo tempo, risulta tuttora come riconoscibile e inconfondibile nella storia di questa concezione normativa. Inoltre la delineazione di un programma di ricerca per la teoria etica che era allora del tutto nuovo, ma che alla fine del XX secolo possiamo riconoscere come fertile e operante malgrado alcuni suoi limiti. (edited)

**Lecci, Bernardo** and Sparti, Davide. Scetticismo, riconoscimento, riscoperta dell'ordinario: La filosofia di Stanley Cavell. *Iride*, 10(20), 135-144, Ap 97.

**Lecourt, Dominique**. Crítica del llamado de Heidelberg. *Cuad Etica*, 21-22, 61-73, 1996.

This text is an analysis of the "Heidelberg Calling," which was sent to the participation governments in the UN's Conference about environment and development, in 1992. The Calling gave impulse to an interesting debate about the relationship between science and society. Lecourt sustains that the Calling repeats the mistakes of classical rationalism, because it assumes that ignorance and oppression are still the main problems of science. This position implies the belief that scientific progress will be able to resolve social and political conflicts. The author ends his paper criticizing the modern meaning of rationality.

**Lécrivain, André**. Phenomenology of Spirit and Logic (in French). *Arch Phil*, 60(2), 179-196, Ap-Je 97.

For a period of more than one decade, 1804/5 to 1816, Hegel's interest in logic never wained as is shown by *The Logic* at Jena, his correspondence, the courses in Nürnberg and lastly the publication of *The Science of Logic*. However, in this same period, 1807, came *The Phenomenology of Spirit*. What links does this work have with the logical texts which precede it and which follow it and what is the logic actually found at work, governing from the inside this monumental dialectical exposition of the cultural and spiritual development of consciousness? Finally, in what way did this book impel a shift in Hegel's logical reflection and enable the writing and publication of *The Science of Logic*?

**Leddy, Thomas**. Sparkle and Shine. *Brit J Aes*, 37(3), 259-273, Jl 97.

The qualities of sparkle and shine have not been much discussed in recent aesthetics and yet are central to aesthetics of the natural environment, everyday life and the arts. This neglect can be traced to matters of class, culture and age. Although inspired by Sircello's vivid examples, I reject his "fragmentarian" theory of beauty. I argue that sparkle and shine are at the core of the concept of beauty, which itself is paradigmatic for aesthetics. I distinguish "core" from necessary and sufficient conditions, and argue that although sparkle and shine are not literally necessary for beauty they are metaphorically so.

**Lee, Chung-Yeong** and Yoshihara, Hideki. Business Ethics of Korean and Japanese Managers. *J Bus Ethics*, 16(1), 7-21, Ja 97.

This is a study of 288 Korean and 323 Japanese business executives. The result indicates that 1) the business executives believe basically in higher level business ethics, but 2) they occasionally have to make unethical business decisions which conflict with their personal values because of prevailing business practices. 3) However, they think higher ethical standards are useful for long-term profit and for improving workers' attitudes and the standards can be improved, and 4) to improve ethical standards, model setting by superiors is the most important and clear-cut company policies and code of ethics are essential.

**Lee, Kam-lun Edwin**. The Correspondence between Human Intelligibility Physical Intelligibility: The View of Jean Ladrière. *Zygon*, 32(1), 65-81, Mr 97.

This article seeks to explain the correspondence between human intelligibility and that of the physical world by synthesizing the contributions of Jean Ladrière. Ladrière shows that the objectification function of formal symbolism in mathematics as an artificial language has operative power acquired through algorithm to represent physical reality. In physical theories, mathematics relates to observations through theoretic and empirical languages mutually interacting in a methodological circle and nonmathematical anticipatory intention guides mathematical algorithmic exploration. Ladrière reasons that mathematics can make the physical world comprehensible because of the presence of a rational principle in both kinds of intelligibility.

**Lee, Patrick**. Human Beings Are Animals. *Int Phil Quart*, 37(3), 291-303, S 97.

**Lee, Sandra S** and Schonberg, Sue E. Identifying the Real EAP Client: Ensuing Ethical Dilemmas. *Ethics Behavior*, 6(3), 203-212, 1996.

As employee assistance programs (EAPs) have evolved and expanded their scope in the past decade, many factors have contributed to meeting the demands of conflicting client constituencies in a multifaceted client environment. This article enumerates several of these factors, notes consequences of ensuing conflicts, and ultimately proposes some methods to counter some of these ethical dilemmas in the future. It is the hope that greater recognition and understanding of ethical conflicts in client loyalty within a host organization will foster increased sensitivity on the part of the EAP practitioner toward resolving these conflicts.

**Lee, Young Sook**. Spirit and Beauty. *J Aes Educ*, 31(3), 15-23, Fall 97.

Spirit plays a crucial role in explaining artistic beauty in general. Concerning natural beauty, however, the case is somewhat different: Hegel and Adorno have different opinions about it. For Adorno, spirit is very important in natural beauty as well. For Hegel, on the other hand, spirit is associated with the works of art only, not with nature. That is to say, spirit is a substance of art, not of nature. What makes this difference? Which view is correct? I tried to find an answer to this question in the first part of this paper, introducing some ideas of the Easterner's view of spirit. In the second part, I sought for an appropriate characterization of spirit which can give a plausible account on the beautiful in general: namely, 'the spirit of no-self.' Then, I showed that this characteristic of spirit, the spirit of no-self, was to be found not only in the beautiful but also in other phenomena such as the true or the good.

**Lee, Zosimo E**. Lui's Complaint. *Thinking*, 13(2), 45-47, 1997.

This is a philosophical short story depicting a discussion within a Filipino family about the distinctions and relationships among the concepts of 'chore', 'work' and 'labor'. The discussion also reaches the concept of 'exploitation' and later, the meaning of 'craft' and what a craftsman is. Full knowledge and recreation of self are important dimensions of what it means to be a craftsman. This story is meant to be read within a small group and is also intended to stimulate dialogue about the ideas articulated.

**Lee-Lampshire, Wendy**. "Women-Animals-Machines: A Grammar for a Wittgensteinian Ecofeminism" in *Ecofeminism: Women, Culture, Nature*, Warren, Karen J (ed), 412-424. Bloomington, Indiana Univ Pr, 1997.

Originally published in the *Journal of Value Inquiry* (29.1), this essay attempts to construct a viable naturalist ecofeminist standpoint which neither appeals (tacitly or otherwise) to Cartesian dualism nor concedes to the eliminativists who argue that the use of folk psychological terms (critical to the articulation of such a standpoint) has been antiquated by the advent of neurophysiology and its accompanying lexicon. Following the lead of later Wittgenstein, I argue that the use of terms like "belief" or "intention" can be utilized heuristically to describe subjects not traditionally so conceived, for example nonhuman animals, women, and computing machines.

**Leeds, Stephen**. Brains in Vats Revisited. *Pac Phil Quart*, 77(2), 108-131, Je 96.

**Leeds, Stephen**. Incommensurability and Vagueness. *Nous*, 31(3), 385-407, S 97.

**Leeman, Cavin P** and Fletcher, John C and Spencer, Edward M (& others). Quality Control for Hospitals' Clinical Ethics Services: Proposed Standards. *Cambridge Quart Healthcare Ethics*, 6(3), 257-268, Sum 97.

As hospital ethics committees have proliferated, problems in the way in which they operate have become increasingly apparent. In response, the authors propose two sets of standards. Standards for procedure and process are intended to help ensure that clinical ethics services are provided in ways which are fair, open, and procedurally consistent and predictable. Standards for education and training are designed to ensure that the people who provide clinical ethics services have the skills and expertise needed to do so competently, and to engender confidence in them. The standards are discussed, and examples of ways to meet them are offered.

**Leeser, Jaimie M**. Old Fashioned Normativity: Just What the Doctor Ordered. *Dialogue (PST)*, 38(2-3), 56-68, Ap 96.

**Leeser, Jamie**. Justified, True Belief: Is it Relevant to Knowledge?. *Auslegung*, 21(2), 107-124, Sum 96.

**Legemaate, Johan** and Gevers, J K M. Physician-Assisted Suicide in Psychiatry: Developments in the Netherlands. *Cambridge Quart Healthcare Ethics*, 6(2), 175-188, Spr 97.

**Legutko, Ryszard**. Was Hayek an Instrumentalist?. *Crit Rev*, 11(1), 145-164, Wint 97.

**Lehman, Paul R**. Who Benefits from the National Standards: A Response to Catherine M. Schmidt's "Who Benefits? Music Education and the National Standards.". *Phil Music Educ Rev*, 5(1), 55-57, Spr 97.

Schmidt contends that the Department of Education has used the standards movement to manipulate professional associations and others in order to impose a hidden agenda of top-down education reform reflecting a right-wing ideology. It's merely an illusion, she argues, to think that the standards-development process was open and broadly inclusive. As chair of the committee that developed the music standards, I can assure readers that this was no illusion. The music standards are based on a two-year effort to solicit advice and suggestions from every constituency in America with an interest in arts education. If there was ever a grassroots effort at bottom-up reform, this was it.

**Lehmann, Daniel** and Freund, Michael. Nonmonotonic Reasoning: From Finitary Relations to Infinitary Inference Operations. *Stud Log*, 53(2), 161-201, My 94.

A. Tarski [22] proposed the study of infinitary consequence operations as the central topic of mathematical logic. He considered monotonicity to be a property of all such operations. In this paper, we weaken the monotonicity requirement and consider more general operations, inference operations. These operations describe the nonmonotonic logics both humans and machines seem to be using when inferring defeasible information from incomplete knowledge. We single out a number of interesting families of inference operations. This study of infinitary inference operations is inspired by the results of [12] on nonmonotonic inference relations and relies on some of the definitions found there.

**Lehner, Christoph**. What It Feels Like To Be in a Superposition and Why. *Synthese*, 110(2), 191-216, F 97.

This paper attempts an interpretation of Everett's relative state formulation of quantum mechanics that avoids the commitment to new metaphysical entities like 'worlds' or 'minds'. Starting from Everett's quantum mechanical model of an observer, it is argued that an observer's belief to be in an *eigenstate* of the measurement (corresponding to the observation of a well-defined measurement outcome) is consistent with the fact that she objectively is in a superposition of such states. "Subjective states" corresponding to such beliefs are constructed. From an analysis of these subjective states and their dynamics it is argued that Everett's pure wave mechanics is subjectively consistent with von Neumann's classical formulation of quantum mechanics. It follows from the argument that the objective state of a system is in principle unobservable. Nevertheless, an adequate concept of empirical reality can be constructed.

**Lehrer, Keith**. "Love and Autonomy" in *Love Analyzed*, Lamb, Roger E, 107-121. Boulder, Westview Pr, 1997.

Extreme romantic love involves a desire for the satisfaction of the desires of the loved one, and when this is reciprocal, a kind of magic results in which each lover receives what they desire. However, this form of loved based on desire can lead to manipulation and disillusion when reciprocity fails and one is enslaved to the desires of the other. An alternative mode of love, autonomous love, based on autonomous preferences rather than desire is proposed. Autonomous preference is preference that a person has because he or she prefers to have it; and therefore, is not subject to manipulation.

**Lehrer, Keith**. Rationality and Trustworthiness. *Protosoz*, 8/9, 183-196, 1996.

Our rationality depends on the reasons we have for accepting and preferring what we do. But where do reasons come from? What makes what I accept a reason for a conclusion or what I prefer a reason for action? We can explain where reasons come from without postulation or regress. The explanation rests on our trustworthiness combined with our acceptance of it and our preference for it. The explanation reveals that theoretical and practical reason are intertwined in a loop of trustworthiness in what we accept, what we prefer and how we reason. The loop is the keystone of our rationality.

**Lehrer, Keith**. *Self-Trust: A Study of Reason, Knowledge and Autonomy*. New York, Clarendon/Oxford Pr, 1997.

Keith Lehrer offers an original philosophical view of principal aspects of the human condition, such as reason, knowledge, wisdom, autonomy, love, consensus, and consciousness. Three unifying ideas run through the book. The first is that what is uniquely human is the capacity for metamental ascent, the ability to consider and evaluate first-order mental states (such as beliefs and desires) that arise naturally within us. The second unifying idea is that we have a system for such reflective evaluation which yields acceptance (in relation to beliefs) or preference (in relation to the objects of desires). The third unifying idea is that there are 'keystones' of evaluation in this system: loops of trustworthiness that are themselves supported by the structure that they hold together. Self-trust is the basis of our trustworthiness, on which reason, knowledge, and wisdom are grounded. (publisher, edited)

**Leiber, Justin**. Nature's Experiments, Society's Closures. *J Theor Soc Behav*, 27(2-3), 325-343, Je-S 97.

The Wild Child, who lives through much of childhood without exposure to language or culture, is exceedingly rare. I examine three of the most famous and most well authenticated cases: Helen Keller, who was isolated from eighteen months until her seventh year; 'Victor', the wild boy of the forest near Aveyron, whom Itard studied; and 'Genie,' who was isolated from language from age two until the middle of her thirteenth year. Attention is paid both to the development of these individuals and to the conduct and misconceptions of those who examined and trained them. Various morals are drawn, which might also have application to research on nonhuman primates.

**Leiber, Justin**. On What Sort of Speech Act Wittgenstein's *Investigations* Is and Why It Matters. *Phil Forum*, 28(3), 232-267, Spr 97.

While philosophers concerned with speech acts fix on a few words, such as Wittgenstein's "five red apples," longer forms—meditations, confessions, dialogues—are speech acts as well. Descartes's first person *Meditations* adapts a churchly form to cognitive and philosophical uses. Wittgenstein's *Investigations* is an adaptation of the confessional mode, with the *tractatus* "I" and readerly "you" taking the confessant role, while the mature Wittgenstein "I" and "we" takes the confessor role, instructing, hearing, correcting. Such a reading makes best sense of the form and force of *Investigations*—it could no more be written without its panoply of personal voices than *Meditations* could be written in the third person. There are also textual indications that Wittgenstein understood his mode to be confessional. This will also help us to see that *Investigations* usefully dis-spells philosophical bewitchments *and* provides an unprejudiced survey of phenomena that call out for explanation in what Wittgenstein called "natural science" and we now call "cognitive science."

**Leiber, Theodor**. Chaos, Berechnungskomplexität und Physik: Neue Grenzen wissenschaftlicher Erkenntnis?. *Phil Natur*, 33(1), 23-54, 1996.

Problems of effective computability and logical undecidability in complex systems are discussed from mathematical, logical and physical points of view. While (some) postmodernists after the end of all metaphysics now also take an oath on the end of all natural science the scientists themselves estimate the corresponding problems more carefully. The result of their considerations is the scientifically well grounded, matter-of-fact oriented insight (possibly within the framework of the sciences of complexity of the 21st century) into the effective limitations of numerical computation procedures as well as into the overloaded interpretations of such limitations by uninformed and antiscientific tendencies.

**Leigh, David J**. Alexander Pope and Eighteenth Century Conflicts about Ultimacy. *Ultim Real Mean*, 20(1), 23-40, Mr 97.

Although influenced by the deistic and empiricist controversies of his age, and by the nonsacramental poetry of Vaughan, Milton, and Dryden, Alexander Pope throughout his works celebrated the importance of poetry and satire as necessary supports for the aesthetic, moral, cultural, and religious values of a humanistic civilization. The philosophical and religious imagery in *The Dunciad* reinforced the role of the "word" in preserving meaning in human life and society. In *An Essay of Man*, Pope's metaphors of the *chain of being*, of *organic growth*, and of *harmonious tension* are used to express the analogical order of the universe, the individual, society, and the pursuit of happiness. Finally, he undergirds this poem with allusions to Aristotle's four causes and to biblical patterns of creation, fall, and redemption.

**Leijenhorst, Cees**. Hobbes and Fracastoro. *Hobbes Stud*, 9, 98-128, 1996.

The article explores the relation between the natural philosophies of Thomas Hobbes and Girolamo Fracastoro (1475/6-1553), the inventor of the term *syphilis*, but also author of highly interesting works on natural philosophy and epistemology, which were cited by Descartes, Bacon and Mersenne. Leijenhorst argues that Hobbes's account of sensible species and his epistemology in the *Short Tract*, Hobbes's earliest philosophical manuscript, were very probably inspired by Fracastoro. Moreover, even in its ripe phase Hobbes's mechanistic natural philosophy and epistemology are far from incompatible with Fracastorian naturalism, a conclusion which urges us to reconsider the "modernity" of mechanistic philosophy.

**Leijenhorst, Cees**. Hobbes's Theory of Causality and Its Aristotelian Background. *Monist*, 79(3), 426-447, Jl 96.

The author argues that, although Thomas Hobbes tries to offer a mechanistic alternative to Aristotelian teleology, his own view incorporates important scholastic arguments, albeit suited to his own purposes. Hobbes's early definition of causality combines an anti-Aristotelian reduction of change to local motion with Aristotelian agent—patient and potency—act distinctions which his later account tries to discard. Moreover, Hobbes's radical determinism takes up the Aristotelian concept of absolute necessity, while omitting the Aristotelian finalist framework. Finally, the author suggests that Hobbes's notion of causality can help elucidate the problematic status of the so-called *accidentia communia* (magnitude/motion).

**Leinkauf, Thomas**. Diversitas identitate compensata: Ein Grundtheorem in Leibniz' Denken und seine Voraussetzungen in der frühen Neuzeit. *Stud Leibniz*, 28(1), 58-83, 1996.

Leibniz's basic concept of 'harmony' as a 'diversitas identitate compensata' is not only a type of hermeneutical key to nearly all of his philosophical writings and of his thinking in general that he gave us since, let's say, the early *Confessio philosophi* from about 1672. Rather it is, as I will try to make evident in the following paper, an expression of a thoroughgoing concept of thinking in early modern philosophy from the Renaissance onwards. I will try to outline here three main topics which independently from the fact that we will find all of these topics included in the 'quaestiones' and 'articuli' of an ordinary 'cursus philosophicus' in this period worked as a framework in particular in the philosophical discussion of nonscholastic thinkers, namely 1) the theory of mind, 2) cosmology, and 3) universal science or 'mathesis universalis'. In each of them I will analyse influences, at least possible influences, on the thinking of Leibniz. (edited)

**Leiser, Eckart**. Sobre algunos rasgos distintos del estructuralismo. *Mathesis*, 11(1), 23-35, F 95.

In this paper, I intend to outline, in an orientative manner, the fundamental properties of the structuralistic approach, by which it can be distinguished from the remaining scientific concepts of empiristic as well as holistic cut. On one hand, it examines the methodical arguments for taking an interest in structures; on the other hand, it enters into the question of the theoretical fruitfulness of introducing 'structures' as a key concept to comprehend the phenomena which constitute the matter of natural and human sciences. In the following, the paper restricts itself to structuralism in the framework of the human sciences, comprising a sufficiently large scope of its different manifestations to make appear a kind of common denominator. Starting with the linguistic structuralism of De Saussure, it passes on to the structural anthropology of Lévi-Strauss to conclude with Lacan and his structuralistic reinterpretation of psychoanalysis.

**Leisman, Gerald** and Nagatomo, Shigenori. An East Asian Perspective of Mind-Body. *J Med Phil*, 21(4), 439-466, Ag 96.

The paper examines states of conscious experience from an East Asian perspective allowing analysis on achieved supernormal consciousness rather than a focus on "normal" or "subnormal." The nature of the "transformation" of human consciousness will be studied both philosophically, as a transformation from "provisional" dualism to nondualism, and neurophysiologically. The theoretical structure of the transformation will, in part, be examined through the model provided by a Japanese medieval Zen master, Takuan Sôhô. (edited)

**Leist, Anton**. "Ökologische Ethik II: Gerechtigkeit, Ökonomie, Politik" in *Angewandte Ethik: Die Bereichsethiken und ihre theoretische Fundierung,* Nida-Rümelin, Julian (ed), 386-456. Stuttgart, Alfred Kröner, 1996.

This paper wants to give an overview on that part of ecological ethics not to be captured under the heading 'anthropocentricism vs. biocentrism'. How can ecological matters be taken up within a conception of social justice? How do ecological values link up with economic methodologies, especially cost-benefit-analysis? What could be the most important principles of an ecologically enlightened politics? A principle of sustainability is discussed and elaborated upon under this last heading. The paper closes with a sketch of several dilemmata inherent in present ecological politics.

**Leist, Anton**. Gibt es eine universelle Moral?. *Conceptus*, 29(74), 63-85, 1996.

According to the article's central thesis there are only three options how to give rational foundation to a universal morality that provides strong security to its subjects: reasoning according to contract theory, utilitarianism and Kantianism. Following a recent argument by E. Tugendhat, only the latter promises to be successful. To give Tugendhat's argument an additional twist, a value-theoretic reading of Kant is suggested, enlarged by a programmatic sketch of how human capabilities may provide the foundation for an attitude of universal moral respect.

**Leite, Lucimara** and Davi Maced, Dion. O Arco e a Lira—O inaudito na Erótica de Safo. *Educ Filosof*, 9(17), 91-111, Ja-Je 95.

**Leite, Sérgio Celani**. Política Educacional Rural. *Educ Filosof*, 10(19), 163-174, Ja-Je 96.

**Leiter, Brian**. Nietzsche and the Morality Critics. *Ethics*, 107(2), 250-285, Ja 97.

**LeJeune, Michel** (ed) and Rosemann, Philipp W (ed). *Business Ethics in the African Context Today*. Kampala, Uganda, 1996.

This book brings together contributions from ten outstanding experts in business and ethics, combining theoretical with eminently practical perspectives. In the first part, it examines the possibility of founding business ethics theologically, in the principles of Christianity. In the second part, it analyses concrete problems of business ethics in contemporary Africa and, especially, Uganda: corruption and bribery, the ethics of banking, and, international finance, the role of women in the African business world.

**Lekan, Todd**. The Normative Force of Genealogy in Ethics. *Int Phil Quart*, 37(1), 83-93, Mr 97.

**Lema-Hincapié, Andrés**. Le cosmopolitisme kantien. *De Phil*, 11, 65-86, 1994-1995.

**Lemert, Charles**. Social Ethics?. *J Theor Soc Behav*, 27(2-3), 277-287, Je-S 97.

Most of the sciences of social behavior arose initially out of social ethics. The question asked is whether social ethics can revive itself as a central occupation of social thought. Such a revival faces the challenge of rethinking the normative foundations of late modern, global conditions which themselves are seen as inhospitable to the classic terms of philosophical and social ethic reflection. Though the privileged doubt it, the world is in fact inclining towards stark conditions of economic and natural instability, to say nothing of social discord—towards ethics able to sustain itself, in the absence of global cultural accords, against a world in which social ideals of the good are uncertain, if not impossible.

**LeMoncheck, Linda**. Academic Feminism and Applied Ethics: Closing the Gap between Private Scholarship and Public Policy. *Int Stud Phil*, 29(1), 69-77, 1997.

The purpose of this paper is to explore how a feminist applied ethics can enhance philosophy's contribution to the formulation and execution of public policy. The feminist perspective put forth speaks to the lived experience of both women and men by appreciating the cultural, historical, and political context in which individual women and men conceptualize moral problems and resolve moral conflict. An outline of how to formulate guidelines and implement procedures for handling sexual harassment claims is offered to show how a feminist approach to applied ethics is effective in providing workable and sustainable public policy.

**LeMoncheck, Linda**. Philosophy, Gender Politics, and In Vitro Fertilization: A Feminist Ethics of Reproductive Healthcare. *J Clin Ethics*, 7(2), 160-176, Sum 96.

This paper outlines a feminist reproductive ethics that encourages health maintenance organizations and private clinicians to treat patients with an empathy and sensitivity to gender politics that can promote the reproductive interests of both their patients and women as a class. It is argued that neither a Kantian, utilitarian, nor virtue ethics can motivate in vitro fertilization practitioners

to particularize and politicize their treatment of women in ways that are essential to maximizing women's reproductive agency. It is contended that such agency can be encouraged by a feminist ethics that appreciates both the oppressive and liberating potential of new reproductive technologies in women's lives.

**LeMoncheck, Linda** and Hajdin, Mane. *Sexual Harassment: A Debate*. Lanham, Rowman & Littlefield, 1997.

In this uncompromising yet respectful debate, two philosophers of widely divergent views present clear arguments and then respond directly to each other's reasoning. LeMoncheck argues for a feminist perspective on sexual harassment that is sensitive to the politics of gender. Hajdin contends that this perspective is both morally confusing and legally problematic, and sexual harassment can be better addressed by traditional moral and legal categories. (publisher, edited)

**Lemos, John**. Moral Crutches and Nazi Theists: A Defense of and Reservations about Undertaking Theism. *SW Phil Rev*, 13(1), 147-154, Ja 97.

In this paper I defend the view that there are morally good reasons to undertake theism, but that we must be careful to undertake it in such a way that we are not made morally worse in so doing. In defending this view, I explain and critically address recent work by Douglas Drabkin, who has argued that there are morally good reasons to undertake theism.* There are various important objections to Drabkin's argument that need addressing before it can be made convincing to the skeptical reader. My paper takes up these objections and provides answers to them. *See Douglas Drabkin, "A Moral Argument for Undertaking Theism," *American Philosophical Quarterly*, 31 (1994), pp. 169-175.

**Lemos, John**. Virtue, Happiness, and Intelligibility. *J Phil Res*, 22, 307-320, Ap 97.

In such works as *A Short History of Ethics*, *Against the Self-Images of the Age*, and *After Virtue*, Alasdair MacIntyre has argued that the intelligibility of the moral life hinges upon viewing the moral life as essential to the happy life, or *eudaimonia*. In my article I examine the reasons he gives for saying this, arguing that this thesis is not sufficiently defended by MacIntyre. I also draw connections between this thesis about the intelligibility of the moral life and other aspects of MacIntyre's thought, such as his communitarianism. In concluding, I note that several of MacIntyre's more significant claims about morality might well be true even if his thesis about the intelligibility of the moral life is false.

**Lempp, Steffen** (& others) and Fejer, Peter A and Ambos-Spies, Klaus. Decidability of the Two-Quantifier Theory of the Recursive Enumerable Weak Truth-Table Degrees and Other Distributive Semi-Lattices. *J Sym Log*, 61(3), 880-905, S 96.

We formulate general criteria that allow one to conclude that a distributive upper semilattice has a decidable two-quantifier theory. These criteria are applied not only to the weak truth-table degrees of the recursively enumerable sets but also to various substructures of the polynomial many-one ($pm$) degrees of the recursive sets. These applications to the $pm$ degrees require no new complexity-theoretic results. The fact that the $pm$-degrees of the recursive sets have a decidable two-quantifier theory answers a question raised by Shore and Slaman. (edited)

**Lempp, Steffen** and Hirst, Jeffry L. Infinite Versions of Some Problems from Finite Complexity Theory. *Notre Dame J Form Log*, 37(4), 545-553, Fall 96.

Recently, several authors have explored the connections between NP-complete problems for finite objects and the complexity of their analogs for infinite objects. In this paper, we will categorize infinite versions of several problems arising from finite complexity theory in terms of their recursion theoretic complexity and proof theoretic strength. These infinite analogs can behave in a variety of unexpected ways.

**Lempp, Steffen** and Lerman, Manuel. A Finite Lattice without Critical Triple That Cannot Be Embedded into the Enumerable Turing Degrees. *Annals Pure Applied Log*, 87(2), 167-185, 15 S 97.

We exhibit a finite lattice without critical triple that cannot be embedded into the enumerable Turing degrees. Our method promises to lead to a full characterization of the finite lattices embeddable into the enumerable Turing degrees.

**Lenk, Hans**. "Realistischer Realismus als ein methodologischer und pragmatischer Interpretationismus" in *Das weite Spektrum der analytischen Philosophie,* Lenzen, Wolfgang, 149-159. Hawthorne, de Gruyter, 1997.

**Lenk, Hans**. Philosophie als kreatives Interpretieren. *Z Phil Forsch*, 50(4), 585-600, O-D 96.

**Lenk, Hans** and Maring, Matthias. Responsibility and Social Traps. *Int J Applied Phil*, 11(1), 51-61, Sum-Fall 96.

In highly developed societies individual actions are less important than collective and corporate actions. The individualistic concepts of ethics are generally not sufficient to tackle the problem of distributing responsibility for untoward (e.g., ecological) consequences of such actions, especially in social trap constellations. With respect to moral evaluation many participating and contributing individuals have to bear a certain correspondibility for emerging supraindividual effects. A moral reorientation of individuals to cope with the problems of this new situation is necessary, but not sufficient. We also need structural incentives, social mechanisms for sanctioning as well as the pertaining institutional measures, e.g., legal and political arrangements.

**Lenk, Hans** and Maring, Matthias. Technology in Opposition Power—Must (Czech). *Filosof Cas*, 45(1), 113-138, 1997.

The notion of individual is even in our current era of institutional and corporate decisions and enterprises of much import and of particular importance for technology. However, problems of collective and corporate responsibility are becoming and still will become more and more topical. Engineering ethics codes should be developed, improved and operationally implemented in the future. The rules sketched out here of priorities for handling responsibility conflicts have subsequently to be elaborated much further. All this, then, would be necessary to meet the ideal requirements of our joint and individual responsibility for technology in our society.

**Lenka, Laxminarayan**. A Dialogue between L1 and L2: Discussing on Seven Kinds of Privacy. *Darshana Int*, 36(1/141), 25-43, Ja 96.

This anti-Wittgensteinian paper attempts to establish the possibility of private language and explains the plausibility of seven kinds of privacy which are philosophically interesting.

**Lenka, Laxminarayan**. Linguistic Solipsism. *Indian Phil Quart*, 23(3-4), 474-475, Jl-O 96.

**Lenman, James**. Belief, Desire and Motivation: An Essay in Quasi-Hydraulics. *Amer Phil Quart*, 33(3), 291-301, Jl 96.

Following Nagel, a number of writers, while conceding that desires must always play a part in the rational motivation of action, insist that these in turn may be motivated simply by beliefs. However, the same teleological considerations that inform the concession are shown to tell equally against this sophisticated anti-Humean strategy. There might certainly be a *causal* process that take us from beliefs, and only beliefs, to desires but this could not be a *rational* process, a process of motivation by reasons. This defence of a Humean position is developed with reference to recent work by Darwall, Wallace and Smith.

**Lennon, Kathleen** and Longino, Helen E. Feminist Epistemology as a Local Epistemology. *Aris Soc*, Supp(71), 19-54, 1997.

A set of theoretical virtues drawn from feminist writings in and about the sciences contrasts interestingly with virtues described as scientific, cognitive, or epistemic in more conventional philosophy of science. The paper considers the sense in which they (or comparable candidates) could constitute elements of a feminist epistemology. It proposes that a feminist epistemology in this sense would be a local epistemology with normative force only for those who endorse its values. Local epistemology is contrasted with general epistemology.

**Lenoir, Noëlle**. UNESCO, Genetics, and Human Rights. *Kennedy Inst Ethics J*, 7(1), 31-42, Mr 97.

In response to a mandate conferred on the International Bioethics Committee (IBC) of UNESCO in November 1993, the IBC has drafted a "universal declaration on the human genome and human rights," which will be considered by the General Conference of UNESCO in November 1997. This article discusses the development of the document and provides the text of the "revised preliminary draft" of the declaration.

**Lentz, William**. The Problem of Motion in the *Sophist*. *Apeiron*, 30(2), 89-108, Je 97.

**Lenzen, Wolfgang**. "Die Newcomb-Paradoxie—und ihre Lösung" in *Das weite Spektrum der analytischen Philosophie*, Lenzen, Wolfgang, 160-177. Hawthorne, de Gruyter, 1997.

This paper takes a fresh view of "Newcomb's paradox", a well-known puzzle in the theory of decision. Two versions of the problem are distinguished depending on whether the Newcomb-predictor is assumed to be either absolutely infallible or only reliable to a high degree. It is argued that in the first case the premises of Newcomb's paradox presuppose a strict (nomic) entailment between 1) certain psychophysical states of the players prior to the prediction and 2) corresponding "decisions" afterwards. Such a strong deterministic behaviour, however, does not give rise to any problem of *decision* at all. If however, in the second case, the players' former states (or the predictions based upon these states) do not necessitate the subsequent decision, i.e., if a real decision is possible at all, then it is rational to choose both boxes even though the construction of the puzzle is intended to make one believe that the predictor awards just those players who take only one box.

**Lenzen, Wolfgang**. "Hommage und Einleitung" in *Das weite Spektrum der analytischen Philosophie*, Lenzen, Wolfgang, 1-7. Hawthorne, de Gruyter, 1997.

Franz von Kutschera's philosophical work is characterized by (and praised for) its extraordinary breadth and depth. During the past three decades he has published—besides numerous articles covering the entire field of analytic philosophy—no less than sixteen substantial books on authors such as Husserl, Frege and Plato and on topics such as logic, intensional semantics, philosophy of language, philosophy of science, epistemology, ethics, aesthetics and philosophy of religion.

**Lenzen, Wolfgang**. *Das weite Spektrum der analytischen Philosophie*. Hawthorne, de Gruyter, 1997.

This anthology is a "Festschrift" dedicated to Prof. Franz von Kutschera, Regensburg, on the occasion of his 65th anniversary. Besides a homage and a current bibliography of von Kutschera's philosophical work, the volume contains 27 contributions (in German and English) written by distinguished philosophers from Germany, Sweden, Italy, Austria, America, Venezuela, Poland and England. The articles reflect the broad range of von Kutschera's philosophical interests by dealing with diverse issues in deontic, intensional and temporal logic, history of logic, philosophy of mathematics, philosophy of science, philosophy of action, philosophy of language, philosophy of mind, epistemology, ethics, anthropology, ontology and the history of philosophy (Plato, Frege).

**Lenzi, Mary**. Platonic Polypsychic Pantheism. *Monist*, 80(2), 232-250, Ap 97.

This version of Platonic pantheism diverges not only from common interpretations of Plato, but also breaks away from a long Western tradition of seeing pantheism as a divine, monistic world-vision. The author speculates upon the Platonic pantheistic universe as a heterogeneously ensouled divine being, in which both *rational* and *irrational world-souls* are necessary to portray a pantheism better befitting our conflicting, pluralistic reality. Under this form of pantheism, Platonic polymorphism and polypsychism show that all (Platonic) Gods, by definition, are not morally good, albeit necessary to ensure the diversely ensouled divine nature of all things.

**Leocata, Francisco**. Malebranche y el *libertinage érudit*. *Sapientia*, 52(201), 41-74, 1997.

El pensamiento filosófico de Malebranche se caracteriza por un acentuado teocentrismo ontológico. Esto a su vez no puede explicarse tan sólo como una derivación de algunas tesis cartesianas llevadas a algunas de sus posibles consecuencias "racionalistas". Es preciso tener en cuenta además el contexto cultural europeo del siglo XVII, y en particular la difusión del llamado "libertinage érudit". Los textos malebranchianos abundan en referencias polémicas implícitas y explícitas contra este movimiento. Por lo cual su ontología aparece como una contrapartida a esas tendencias y una reelaboración del agustinismo en la época postcartesiana. Esta interpretación permite dilucidar mejor el alcance del clima cultural que precedió el iluminismo, y apreciar los motivos y la coherencia interna del ontologismo de Malebranche.

**León, Virgilio C**. El concepto de 'trabajo' en Hegel. *Dialogos*, 31(68), 63-82, Jl 96.

**Leonhardi, Steven D**. Generalized Nonsplitting in the Recursively Enumerable Degrees. *J Sym Log*, 62(2), 397-437, Je 97.

We investigate the algebraic structure of the upper semilattice formed by the recursively enumerable Turing degrees. A strong generalization of Lachlan's Nonsplitting Theorem is proved. This theorem is the dual of a theorem of Ambos-Spies and Soare and yields an alternative proof of their result that the theory of R has infinitely many one-types. (edited)

**Leopoldo e Silva, Franklin**. Transformaçao da Noçao de Beatitude em Descartes. *Discurso*, 24, 31-46, 1994.

Este texto pretende indicar alguns aspectos da trajetória da noçao de beatitude, de Agostinho a Descartes. Através da transformaçao semântico-conceitual da expressao *homo capax Dei*, podemos observar que, de Agostinho a Tomás de Aquino e deste a Suarez e a Descartes, a beatitude vai progressivamente deixando de ser entendida como capacidade de "conter" Deus e torna-se cada vez mais a capacidade racional-"natural"-de "pensar" Deus.

**Lepage, François**. Conditionals, Imaging, and Subjunctive Probability. *Dialogue (Canada)*, 36(1), 113-135, Wint 97.

On montre d'abord que la technique de révision des probabilités appelée *imagerie*, qui a été introduite par Lewis pour la logique des conditionnels de Stalnaker (la probabilité d'un conditionnel est la probabilité du conséquent après projection de la probabilité d'un monde donné sur le monde le plus rapproché dans lequel l'antécédent est vrai), peut être généralisée à la sémantique des systèmes de sphères de Lewis si l'on permet aux énoncés conditionnels d'avoir des valeurs de vérité fractionnaires. Un système est proposé.

**Leplin, Jarrett**. *A Novel Defense of Scientific Realism*. New York, Oxford Univ Pr, 1997.

Arguing that explanatory uniqueness warrants inference and exposing flaws in contending philosophical positions that sever explanatory power from epistemic justification, Leplin holds that abductive, or explanatory inference is a fundamental as enumerative or eliminative inference and contends that neither induction nor abduction can proceed without the other on pain of generating paradoxes.

**Lepore, Ernest**. Conditions on Understanding Language. *Proc Aris Soc*, 97, 41-60, 1997.

**Lepore, Ernest**. Donald Davidson: L'incontro con la filosofia e la definizione del progetto teorico. *Iride*, 8(15), 295-331, Ag 95.

Donald Davidson è un filosofo analitico nella tradizione di Wittgenstein e di Quine e le sue teorie sull'azione, la verità e l'interazione comunicativa hanno generato un dibattito considerevole nei circoli filosofici di tutto il mondo. Nell'intervista con E. Lepore (Università di Rutgers) traccia per la prima volta la sua autobiografia intellettuale, offrendoci uno spaccato della sua personalità umana e dell'ambiente universitario americano, ricordando gli anni della formazione e chiarendo alcuni concetti centrali del suo pensiero.

**Lepore, Ernest** and Cappelen, Herman. Varieties of Quotation. *Mind*, 106(423), 429-450, Jl 97.

**Lepore, Ernest** and Fodor, Jerry A. What Cannot Be Evaluated Cannot Be Evaluated, and it Cannot Be Supervalued Either. *J Phil*, 93(10), 516-535, O 96.

Van Fraassen and Fine, among many others, now argue that you can both deny the law of bivalence, thereby doing justice to the intuitions about the present king of France being bald, and hold onto excluded middle, thereby placating the classical logicians. Moreover, it's suggested that the mechanisms that allow you to do this make clear how sentences that lack truth-values can, as it were, be meaningful in virtue of their potential for having them, thereby solving the first problem as well as the second. All this relies essentially on the method of supervaluations. In this paper, we'll argue that there is something fundamentally wrong with using supervaluation techniques either for preserving classical logic or for providing a semantics for linguistic expressions ordinarily thought to produce truth-value gaps. (edited)

**Lerman, Manuel** and Lempp, Steffen. A Finite Lattice without Critical Triple That Cannot Be Embedded into the Enumerable Turing Degrees. *Annals Pure Applied Log*, 87(2), 167-185, 15 S 97.

We exhibit a finite lattice without critical triple that cannot be embedded into the enumerable Turing degrees. Our method promises to lead to a full characterization of the finite lattices embeddable into the enumerable Turing degrees.

**Leroux, François**. Entrevue avec Monique Séguin. *Horiz Phil*, 7(1), 65-76, Fall 96.

**Leroux, François**. Entrevue avec Richard Carpentier. *Horiz Phil*, 7(1), 51-64, Fall 96.

**Lértora Mendoza, Celina A**. Fuentes para la historia de la astronomia de los siglos XIV y XV. Eclipses y tablas. *Mathesis*, 10(3), 291-312, Ag 94.

Presento a continuación un proyecto de investigación sobre un período particularmente importante para la historia de la ciencia moderna: la crisis del paradigma ptolemaico que precedió a la teoría copernicana. Esta investigación aporta datos para la historia de las ciencias físicas, pero desde otro punto de vista es significativa para la historia de la matemática. En la primera parte del trabajo expondré la investigación sobre fuentes, y en la segunda discutiré sus implicancias matemáticas.

**Leschke, Martin**. "Das Problem der Steuerhinterziehung: Eine moral ökonomische Analyse" in *Ökonomie und Moral: Beiträge zur Theorie ökonomischer Rationalität*, Lohmann, Karl Reinhard (ed), 157-174. München, Oldenbourg, 1997.

The paper deals with the problem of tax evasion. It is argued that the neoclassical model of tax evasion has only little power of explanation. Additional aspects must be regarded to understand why people (do not) pay taxes. Empirical research shows that besides direct sanctions tax morale plays a very important role.

**Leshowitz, Barry** and Yoshikawa, Elaine. An Instructional Model for Critical Thinking. *Inquiry (USA)*, 15(3), 17-37, Spr 96.

This paper describes a college-level instructional program in critical thinking emphasizing the practical application of scientific (methodological) reasoning to controversial, often emotional, everyday-life situations. Also included in the intervention is instruction on the role of cost/benefit analysis, personal values, and ethical and moral beliefs in optimizing decisions and taking effective action. The program was evaluated in a pre-post experimental design: Methodological reasoning and metacognitive processing were measured at the beginning and the end of the semester for a control group of students and for a treatment group enrolled in the critical thinking course. A statistical mediational model showed that the observed changes in metacognitive processing of the group participating in the instructional intervention were causally related to improvements in their methodological reasoning. A three-stage instructional model is introduced to provide a descriptive account of the changes in "ways of knowing" and decision making evinced by most students over the course of the intervention.

**Leslie, John**. A Neoplatonist's Pantheism. *Monist*, 80(2), 218-231, Ap 97.

The ethical requirement that there exists a good universe is eternal, unconditional. It may be necessary—synthetically, not analytically and provably—that the requirement is creatively effective. The universe might consist of a divine mind, your thoughts being simply elements in its knowledge. Or, perhaps infinitely better, it might consist of infinitely many such minds. These ideas can explain the world's existence and its life-generating causal orderliness. Experience cannot refute them. Not only all the richness of a physicist's perceptions, but all the structure of the surrounding physical world (and of countless others) could be present in divine experiences.

**Lessa, Sergio**. Lukács: Ontology and Historicity (in Portuguese). *Trans/Form/Acao*, 19, 87-101, 1996.

The article argues that one of the main moments of Lukács's rupture with the preceding ontologies is his original distinction between essence and phenomenon from the peculiar relation of each one with the category of continuity. Doing so, Lukács could recover the radical historicity of the human realm.

**Létourneau, Alain**. Un aperçu de la "logique de la vie morale" chez Maurice Blondel. *Laval Theol Phil*, 52(3), 703-718, O 96.

In his thesis, *L'Action* (1893), Maurice Blondel offers some reflections on a "logic of action"; however, it is mostly in the article "Principe élémentaire d'une logique de la vie morale" (1903) that he develops his ideas on this topic. We review in detail this article, on one side showing how formal logic in its specific terms has its origin in action and how on the other side action always presupposes some principles, namely the principle of contradiction, to be able to exert itself.

**Letson, Ben H**. *Davidson's Theory of Truth and Its Implications for Rorty's Pragmatism*. New York, Lang, 1997.

One of the most exciting and controversial philosophers of our time, Richard Rorty has developed a radical pragmatism that criticizes the attempt to provide foundations for our standards of rationality. Rorty believes that the history of philosophy illustrates the futility of attempting to develop a theory of truth or justification that will enable us to be more rational in our activities and beliefs. This study focuses on the support that such a view might receive from Donald Davidson's work on truth and translation. Davidson's work is used to show that the apparent relativism in Rorty's account of truth can be avoided if we focus on the dynamics of translation. Davidson thus offers hope that we can defend objectivity without appealing to traditional views of truth and meaning. (publisher)

**Levey, Ann**. "Liberalism, Property, and Freedom" in *A Question of Values: New Canadian Perspectives in Ethics and Political Philosophy*, Brennan, Samantha (ed), 87-105. Amsterdam, Rodopi, 1997.

**Levey, Goeffrey Brahm**. Equality, Autonomy, and Cultural Rights. *Polit Theory*, 25(2), 215-248, Ap 97.

Will Kymlicka has advanced perhaps the most developed liberal theory of minority cultural rights. I argue that his appeal to "equally and cultural disadvantage" ill serves as a basis for discriminating among claims to cultural rights and that he scarcely honors the relations his own theory posits between individual autonomy, identity and cultural membership. I sketch an alternative route to relating cultural rights claims to the value of autonomy, one which sees them as flowing directly from the exercise of autonomy. This involves rescuing the distinction between cultural rights exercised by individuals and by collectives. I try to show why this distinction is important and how it orientates the discussion of the justification of particular cultural rights claims.

**Levey, Samuel**. Coincidence and Principles of Composition. *Analysis*, 57(1), 1-10, Ja 97.

**Levi, A H T**. The Heythrop Journal (1960-1996): From In-House Review to International Journal. *Heythrop J*, 37(3), 250-257, Jl 96.

**Levi, Don S**. The Unbearable Vagueness of Being. *S J Phil*, 34(4), 471-492, Wint 96.

**Levi, Isaac**. "Caution and Nonmonotonic Inference" in *Knowledge and Inquiry: Essays on Jaakko Hintikka's Epistemology and Philosophy of Science*, Sintonen, Matti (ed), 101-115. Amsterdam, Rodopi, 1997.

Default reasoning is that species of nonmonotonic reasoning that is *ampliative*. The other type of nonmonotonic reasoning is *belief contravening* as in reasoning from suppositions. It is commonly held that these two kinds of nonmonotonic reasoning share the same formal properties. According to the decision theoretic approach to ampliative reasoning shared by Hintikka, Hilpinen, Niiniluoto, Pietarinen and myself, formal similarity holds only when ampliative inferences are drawn with maximum boldness and when iterating the use of rules for inductive inference can yield no new information. Such "bookkeeping" with maximum boldness is hard to defend raising doubts about an important assumption made by the majority of students of nonmonotonic reasoning.

**Levi, Isaac**. "Inference and Logic According to Peirce" in *The Rule of Reason: The Philosophy of Charles Sanders Peirce*, Forster, Paul (ed), 34-56. Toronto, Univ of Toronto Pr, 1997.

Peirce's classification of logic underwent significant changes from the 1860s to the 1900s. This paper offers a conjecture as to why Peirce changed his views suggesting that the change may have been related to changes in his views about induction.

**Levi, Isaac** and Costa, Horacio A. Two Notions of Epistemic Validity: Epistemic Models for Ramsey's Conditionals. *Synthese*, 109(2), 217-262, N 96.

(RT) 'If A, then B' must be accepted with respect to the current epistemic state iff the minimal hypothetical change of it needed to accept A also requires accepting B. In this article we propose a formulation of (RT), which unlike some of its predecessors, is compatible with our best theory of belief revision, the so-called AGM theory (see Gärdenfors 1988), chapters 1-5 for a survey). The new test, which, we claim, encodes some of the crucial insights defended by F.P. Ramsey in (Ramsey 1990), is used to study the conditionals *epistemically validated* by the AGM postulates. Our notion of validity (PV) is compared with the notion of *negative validity* (NV) used by Gärdenfors in (Gärdenfors 1988). It is observed that the notions of PV and NV will in general differ and that when these differences arise it is the notion of PV that is preferable. Finally we compare our formulation of the Ramsey test with a previous formulation offered by Gärdenfors (GRT). We show that any attempt to interpret (GRT) as delivering acceptance conditions for Ramsey's conditionals is doomed to failure.

**Levin, David Michael**. "Keeping Foucault and Derrida in Sight: Panopticism and the Politics of Subversion" in *Sites of Vision*, Levin, David Michael (ed), 397-465. Cambridge, MIT Pr, 1997.

I argue that both Foucault and Derrida undertake a critique of panopticism and ocularcentrism, especially with regard to the history of philosophy and show how they deploy textual strategies that turn the gaze against itself, making the gaze inscribed in their writing deconstruct or subvert the gaze which, since Plato, has dominated philosophical thought and supported a metaphysics of presence. In their writings, the reader's gaze is turned away from conventional objects to see what the dominant gaze has overlooked and excluded. In Derrida's writings, the gaze also assumes an opticality that subverts the presence and dominance of the voice.

**Levin, David Michael**. Liberating Experience from the Vice of Structuralism: The Methods of Merleau-Ponty and Nagarjuna. *Phil Today*, 41(1-4), 96-111, Spr 97.

There is a convergence between the "deconstructive" logic of Nagarjuna, the greatest philosopher of Buddhism India produced, and the phenomenology of Merleau-Ponty: both attempted, through their respective methodologies, to liberate experience from conceptual reification, from enclosure and fixation within our concepts. Both return us to the aliveness of experiencing as lived. Both worked to compel critical reflection on the doctrines, conceptual structures and theoretical frameworks in terms of which we handle philosophical questions, opening philosophical thought to the radical logic of an experiencing that exceeds whatever conceptual structures we may have. Both, therefore, propose a "third way" between rationalism and empiricism.

**Levin, David Michael** (ed). *Sites of Vision*. Cambridge, MIT Pr, 1997.

The fourteen contributors to *Sites of Vision* explore the hypothesis that the nature of visual perception about which philosophers talk must be explicitly recognized as a discursive construction, indeed a historical construction, in philosophical discourse. The essays begin with the work of Aristotle and extend through Descartes, Malebranche, Leibniz, Berkeley, Vico, Hegel, Husserl, Wittgenstein, Dewey, Benjamin, and Arendt to Foucault, Derrida, and Deleuze, the recent French philosophers who have focused so intently on sight. Together they constitute a new way of looking at the history of philosophy. (publisher, edited)

**Levin, David Michael**. What-Is? On Mimesis and the Logic of Identity and Difference in Heidegger and the Frankfurt School. *Int Stud Phil*, 28(4), 41-60, 1996.

This study examines the intricacies and ambiguities surrounding the concept of mimesis in relation to the philosophical thought of what is. At the center of this problematic is the question of truth: What is truth? Is truth determinable in the way that the correspondence theory assumes? The study also touches on the implications for our ethical and moral life.

**Levin, Janet**. Consciousness Disputed. *Brit J Phil Sci*, 48(1), 91-107, Mr 97.

This article is a critical review of three recent books on consciousness: David Chalmers's *The Conscious Mind: In Search of a Fundamental Theory*, Fred Dretske's *Naturalizing the Mind* and Michael Tye's *Ten Problems of Consciousness: A Representational Theory of the Phenomenal Mind*.

**Levin, Janet**. Folk Psychology and the Simulationist Challenge. *Acta Analytica*, 77-100, 1995.

In this paper it is suggested that, though simulation theory seems plausible for certain sorts of cases, it cannot provide a general account of our predictions and explanations of others. It is also argued that folk psychology provides a more plausible account of our self-ascription of mental states. (edited)

**Levin, Michael**. "Blacks Don't Need Liberating" in *The Liberation Debate: Rights at Issue,* Leahy, Michael (ed), 65-81. New York, Routledge, 1996.

It is argued that the alleged oppression faced by blacks is at worst trivial, and that such widely advertised indignities as being passed up by taxicabs should properly be blamed on the high black crime rate. It is further argued that the actual underlying cause of the black attainment deficity is the lower average intelligence of blacks, which is most likely largely genetic in origin.

**Levin, Michael**. Natural Subordination, Aristotle On. *Philosophy*, 72(280), 241-257, Ap 97.

This paper defends Aristotle's famous claims that some individuals and groups are naturally subordinate to others. The main problem lies in Aristotle's teleological metaphysics, according to which what is natural is what always happens, yet putatively subordinate groups can live undomined. I construe natural dominance as dispositional and counterfactual, eventually explicated in terms of selection for traits that give rise to dominance patterns.

**Levin, Michael**. Plantinga on Functions and the Theory of Evolution. *Austl J Phil*, 75(1), 83-98, Mr 97.

Since being justified entails that our cognitive faculties are functioning properly, and "function" is not definable naturalistically, Plantinga argues, God exists if any beliefs are warranted. I show that Wright's definition of "function" suitably generalized survives the counterexamples of Plantinga and Boorse. Plantinga also argues that the theory of evolution implies that our faculties are unreliable, thus undercutting itself. It is shown that evolution implies no such thing. The case against evolutionary epistemology is much weaker than is usually thought.

**Levin, Michael**. Putnam on Reference and Constructible Sets. *Brit J Phil Sci*, 48(1), 55-67, Mr 97.

Putnam argues that, by 'reinterpretation', the *axiom of constructibility* can be saved from empirical refutation. This paper contends that this argument fails, a failure which leaves Putnam's sweeping appeal to the Lowenheim-Skolem Theorem inadequately motivated.

**Levin, Michael**. You Can Always Count on Reliabilism. *Phil Phenomenol Res*, 57(3), 607-617, S 97.

This article considers some recent objections to reliabilism, particularly those of Susan Haack in *Evidence and Inquiry.* Haack complains that reliabilism solves the "ratification" problem trivially, making it analytic that evidence relates to truth; this paper defends an analytic solution to this problem. It argues as well that reliabilism is not tacitly committed to "evidentialism." Familiar counterexamples to and repairs of reliabilism are reviewed, with an eye to finding their rationale. Finally, it suggests that the underlying dispute between reliabilism and its critics is the existence of a priori relations between evidence and hypotheses.

**Levin, Yakir**. Mind and World according to Kant (in Hebrew). *Iyyun*, 46, 139-154, Ap 97.

The paper consists of a new reconstruction of Kant's transcendental idealism and of his transcendental deduction. A main feature of the reconstruction is that it shows how both transcendental idealism and the transcendental deduction may be taken to stem from Kant's innovative distinction between the sensual and the conceptual.

**Levin-Waldman, Oren M**. Can Locke's Theory of Property Inform the Court on Fifth Amendment "Takings" Law?. *Pub Affairs Quart*, 10(4), 355-377, O 96.

Locke's theory of property has often been understood to be a defense of the minimalist state, in which property owners may pursue their interests unfettered by governmental control so long as no harm comes to others. And yet, a broader reading of Locke might suggest otherwise; that property serves a more utilitarian function in the protection of human agency. Given that the line between regulation aimed at furthering the public interest and regulation tantamount to a 'taking' hasn't always been clear, this paper seeks guidance by appealing to Locke. The Lockean framework is actually one designed to protect against arbitrary governmental action, and this framework would appear to be consistent with much of Fifth Amendment 'takings' law. And yet, the Supreme Court's ruling in *Lucas v. South Carolina Coastal Council* appears to be a departure.

**Levinas, Emmanuel** and Nicolás, Juan A (trans). Verdad del desvelamiento y verdad del testimonio. *Dialogo Filosof*, 13(2), 179-188, My-Ag 97.

Se distingue en primer lugar la verdad originaria del ser—fundamento de todo noción de verdad en la tradición griega—frente a la conciencia, la tematización

de la verdad frente a la manifestación en la inteligibilidad. Toda expresión de verdad—sentido—remite a un desvelamiento previo del ser. El testimonio, en cuanto confesión de un saber o experiencia por un sujeto, está referido al ser desvelado y gobernado por él. En cierto modo, el sujeto del saber queda anulado. Pero el testimonio, además de expresar el ser, apunta también más allá de él. La conciencia está estructuralmente abierta al ámbito de lo no-representable, de la responsabilidad para con el otro, previa a toda decisión subjetiva. La responsabilidad testimonia la relación con un infinito no tematizable, ambiguamente presente en el profeta.

**Levinas, Emmanuel** and Smith, Michael B (trans). *Proper Names*. Stanford, Stanford Univ Pr, 1996.

Combining elements from Heidegger's philosophy of "being-in-the-world" and the tradition of Jewish theology, Levinas evolved a new type of ethics based on a concept of "the Other" in two different but complementary aspects. He describes his encounters with those philosophers and literary authors (most of them his contemporaries) whose writings have most significantly contributed to the construction of his own philosophy of "Otherness": Agnon, Buber, Celan, Delhomme, Derrida, Jabès, Kierkegaard, Lacroix, Laporte, Picard, Proust, Van Breda, Wahl and most notably Blanchor. (publisher)

**Levine, James P**. Jury Wisdom: Norman J. Finkel, *Commonsense Justice: Juror's Notions of the Law*. *Crim Just Ethics*, 16(1), 49-58, Win-Spr 97.

This essay addresses the wisdom of jury reliance on popular conceptions of justice which according to social psychologist Norman Finkel is a standard part of the process of reaching verdicts. This approach is generally praised insofar as it brings broader contexts, practical experience and subtle strains of public opinion to bear in determining whether defendants should be exculpated. Pitfalls of this liberated role for the jury are discussed, including the potential for moral blunders, the intrusion of prejudice and the problem of reconciling juror subjectivity with a pluralist society encompassing a range of moral codes.

**Levine, Joe**. SwampJoe: Mind or Simulation?. *Mind Lang*, 11(1), 86-91, Mr 96.

**Levine, Joseph**. "On What It Is Like To Grasp a Concept" in *Contents*, Villanueva, Enrique (ed), 38-43. Atascadero, Ridgeview, 1995.

**Levine, Joseph**. Are Qualia Just Representations? A Critical Notice of Michael Tye's *Ten Problems of Consciousness*. *Mind Lang*, 12(1), 101-113, Mr 97.

Michael Tye defends a representational theory of qualia, according to which qualia are identified with internal representations of objective properties of external objects. I criticize his theory on two grounds. First, it doesn't solve the problems of subjectivity and the explanatory gap, as it is supposed to. Second, the externalist version of representation he endorses produces unacceptable consequences.

**Levine, Michael**. Must God Create the Best?. *Sophia (Australia)*, 35(1), 28-34, Mr-Ap 96.

R.M. Adams has based a kind of theodicy on contentious assumptions concerning what God can possibly do. His argument also rests on dubious criteria of personal identity. Adams argues that a "creator would [not] necessarily wrong someone (violate someone's rights), or be less kind to someone than a perfectly moral agent must be, if he knowingly created a less excellent world instead of the best that he could.") But the issue is not, as Adams would have it, whether a merely possible being can be wronged, but whether in not creating a better world (or the best), God is not wronging beings that do exist. To treat the issue otherwise is to obfuscate it.

**Levine, Peter**. *Nietzsche and the Modern Crisis of the Humanities*. Albany, SUNY Pr, 1995.

Levine argues that Strauss and Derrida have much in common, including an idealist, reified concept of culture that both inherited from Nietzsche. Levine interprets all of Nietzsche's basic doctrines in terms of this concept. Nietzsche's definition of culture produced epistemological and moral dilemmas for him and his followers and encouraged them to devise alternatives to mainstream humanities. Levine, however, offers an alternative paradigm of culture that better fits the data and allows us to understand and defend the humanities as a source of value. (publisher)

**Levine, Robert J**. Some Reflections on Postgraduate Medical Ethics Education. *Ethics Behavior*, 7(1), 15-26, 1997.

Three goals of teaching medical ethics to physicians are reviewed. Components of a basic course in medical ethics are described with special attention to the roles of case conferences, ethics rounds, and role modeling. Obstacles to teaching ethics are also addressed.

**Levinson, Henry Samuel** and James, William. *A Pluralistic Universe*. Lincoln, Univ of Nebraska Pr, 1996.

James argues for a metaphysical view he called 'pluralistic pantheism'. In *The Varieties of Religious Experience*, he argued that diverse religious experiences testified to a 'wider self through which saving experiences come'. But he thought he needed to transform that testimony into evidence by showing how this 'wider self' or selves entered into 'cosmic relations' which let people predict 'remote objective consequences' exceeding those reported in conversion narratives. *A Pluralistic Universe* suggests a mapping of relevant relations and consequences that James finds plausible. Levinson provides an introduction which shows how this work links up with James's most representative ideas.

**Levinson, Jerrold**. "Music and Negative Emotion" in *Music and Meaning,* Robinson, Jenefer (ed), 215-241. Ithaca, Cornell Univ Pr, 1997.

**Levinson, Jerrold**. Art, Value, and Philosophy. *Mind*, 105(420), 667-682, O 96.

The book consists of four chapters, the first devoted to the notion of artistic value in general and the remaining chapters devoted to the ways and means of artistic value in three particular artforms. Budd's treatment of these matters is eminently sane and judicious, even wise, and deserves the attention of all philosophers concerned with the question of what makes art valuable. (edited)

**Levinson, Jerrold**. Evaluating Music. *Rev Int Phil*, 50(198), 593-614, 1996.

This paper explores the issue of the value of individual pieces of music and suggests the form that the core principles of musical evaluation arguably must take. Though the core value of music is both experiential and intrinsic, there are dimensions of musical value that are not experiential at all, and ones that, while experiential, are instrumental in nature. The paper explores those issues as well.

**Levinson, Natasha**. "Beginning Again: Teaching, Natality and Social Transformation" in *Philosophy of Education (1996)*, Margonis, Frank (ed), 241-251. Urbana, Phil Education Soc, 1997.

**Levitt, Mairi**. "Sociological Perspectives on the Right to Know and the Right not to Know" in *The Right to Know and the Right not to Know*, Chadwick, Ruth (ed), 29-36. Brookfield, Avebury, 1997.

**Levitt, Mairi** and Chadwick, Ruth. "Mass Media and Public Discussion in Bioethics" in *The Right to Know and the Right not to Know*, Chadwick, Ruth (ed), 79-86. Brookfield, Avebury, 1997.

This paper is based on a manual search of coverage of genetic screening in the UK, mainly using the quality press, from 1982 to 1996. New techniques were found to be reported uncritically, not because of journalistic simplifications but because the scientific and medical professions are used as the source of information. Once specific programmes are underway there is a gradual shift to more critical coverage as patients' experiences are incorporated and 'simple tests' turn out to be more complicated in practice than was predicted. It is in the negative coverage that the ethical issues begin to be discussed.

**Levitt, Mairi** (ed) and Chadwick, Ruth (ed) and Shickle, Darren (ed). *The Right to Know and the Right not to Know*. Brookfield, Avebury, 1997.

Developments in genetics raise questions about the ability of traditional principles of biomedical ethics to deal with the complexity of the issues. Of central importance is the debate about the right to know versus the right not to know genetic information. Claims to a right *not* to know challenge the view that access to information is of value in facilitating choice and self-determination. This multidisciplinary collection of essays examines the issues from the perspectives of philosophy, sociology, history, law and public health. The volume goes beyond an examination of individual rights in considering the right of *society* not to know.

**Levy, Jacob T**. The Multiculturalism of Fear. *Crit Rev*, 10(2), 271-283, Spr 96.

The liberalism of fear urged by Judith Shklar emphasizes the dangers of political violence, cruelty and humiliation. Those dangers clearly mark ethnic and cultural conflicts, so the liberalism of fear is an especially appropriate political ethic for an age marked by such conflicts. A multiculturalism of fear keeps its attention on those central political dangers while also noting that some kinds of cruelty and humiliation might not be appreciated without reference to the larger ethnic and cultural context and that treating ethnicity and culture as completely outside of politics is not the best way to prevent cruelty.

**Levy, Jonathan**. Theatre and Moral Education. *J Aes Educ*, 31(3), 65-75, Fall 97.

**Levy, Sanford S**. Utilitarian Alternatives to Act Utilitarianism. *Pac Phil Quart*, 78(1), 93-112, Mr 97.

One problem for any utilitarian alternative to act utilitarianism, such as rule utilitarianism, is the feeling that act utilitarianism is the most natural form of utilitarianism. Other forms seem unmotivated, inconsistent, or irrational. This argument is found in Smart, Foot and Slote. It turns on the assumption that utilitarianism must be motivated by the "teleological motivation," the idea that one must derive one's entire moral theory from the notion of the good. I respond that act utilitarianism itself has a problem from the point of view of the teleological motivation, a problem solved, surprisingly, by several utilitarian alternatives including rule utilitarianism.

**Levy, Stephen H**. "Peirce's Theoremic/Corollarial Distinction and the Interconnections between Mathematics and Logic" in *Studies in the Logic of Charles Sanders Peirce*, Houser, Nathan (ed), 85-110. Bloomington, Indiana Univ Pr, 1997.

**Lewin, Renato A** and Mikenberg, Irene F and Schwarze, Maria G. P1 Algebras. *Stud Log*, 53(1), 21-28, F 94.

In [3] the authors proved that the deductive system P1 introduced by Sette in [6] is algebraizable. In this paper we study the main features of the class of algebras thus obtained. The main results are a complete description of the free algebras in *n* generators and that this is not a congruence modular quasi-variety.

**Lewis, Brian L**. Self-Deception: A Postmodern Reflection. *J Theor Phil Psych*, 16(1), 49-66, Spr 96.

The traditional perspective on self-deception, which assumes that the mind can be simultaneously involved in contradictory stories, and that there is an integrated understanding of the "truth" somewhere inside, is apparent in most contemporary theories of psychology. A critique of the phenomenon from a postmodern perspective raises questions regarding these assumptions. Ideas from evolutionary biology and research concerning hypnotically induced amnesia are used to support the thesis that self-deception is more a cultural phenomenon maintained by the observer, than a natural phenomenon situated in the individual mind.

**Lewis, David**. Elusive Knowledge. *Austl J Phil*, 74(4), 549-567, D 96.

The analysis of knowledge is simple: S knows that P if S's evidence eliminates every possibility in which not-P—except for those possibilities that we are

properly ignoring. What is complicated, however, is the set of pragmatic rules governing proper ignoring. For one thing, you may not properly ignore a possibility which your conversational partner is right now calling to your attention. So when the sceptic draws your attention to some far-fetched possibility of error, he thereby destroys your knowledge—but only temporarily.

**Lewis, David**. Finkish Dispositions. *Phil Quart*, 47(187), 143-158, Ap 97.

C. B. Martin has refuted the simple conditional analysis of dispositions: maybe a certain fragile thing would not break if struck, because maybe it would lose its fragility if struck. Yet there is a reformed conditional analysis; because even such a thing has some intrinsic property such that if it were struck and it nevertheless retained that property, it would thereby be caused to break.

**Lewis, David**. Maudlin and Modal Mystery. *Austl J Phil*, 74(4), 683-684, D 96.

An alleged refutation of modal realism by Tim Maudlin relies upon an 'Aristotelian' principle: whatever cannot be refuted is possibly true. If that principle is disambiguated in the way that meets the needs of Maudlin's argument, it will engender contradiction in all manner of theories of modality, realist or not; wherefore it should be rejected.

**Lewis, Eric** (trans). *Alexander of Aphrodisias: On Aristotle's Meteorology 4*. Ithaca, Cornell Univ Pr, 1996.

Aristotle's *Meteorology* Book 4 provides an account of the formation of minerals, metals, and other homogeneous stuffs. Eric Lewis argues that, in doing so, it offers fresh insight into Aristotle's conception of matter. The four elements (earth, air, fire, and water) do have matter, and their matter is the contraries—hot and cold, moist and dry. Lewis further argues that in the text translated here, the only extant ancient commentary on the *Meteorology*, Alexander of Aphrodisias supports this interpretation of Aristotle. (publisher,edited)

**Lewis, Frank A**. Self-Knowledge in Aristotle. *Topoi*, 15(1), 39-58, Mr 96.

**Lewis, Paul**. Polanyian Reflections on Embodiment, the Human Genome Initiative and Theological Anthropology. *Tradition Discovery*, 23(2), 5-14, 1996-97.

The *Human Genome Initiative* represents an ambitious attempt to map the genetic structure of the human species (an estimated 100,000 genes). The project has generated a vast amount of theological and ethical literature, none of which discusses the impact of the project on understandings of embodiment. This gap is surprising since Michael Polanyi and, more recently, feminist thinkers have argued that embodiment is central to human existence. I argue that theologians and scientists can teach one another some important lessons about embodiment by exploring some of the literature produced by the project and the anthropologies of Karl Rahner, Wolfhart Pannenberg, Stanley Hauerwas and James McClendon.

**Lewis, Phillip V** and Butz, Clarence E. Correlation of Gender-Related Values of Independence and Relationship and Leadership Orientation. *J Bus Ethics*, 15(11), 1141-1149, N 96.

This study compares the relationship between the moral reasoning modes and leadership orientation of males versus females, and managers versus engineers/scientists. A questionnaire developed by Worthley (1987) was used to measure the degree of each participants' respective independence and justice, and relationships and caring moral reasoning modes. Leadership orientation values and attitudes were measured using the Fiedler and Chemers (1984) Least Preferred Coworker Scale. The results suggest that, although males differ from female in their dominant moral reasoning modes, managers are not distinguishable from the engineers/scientists they manage in terms of their moral reasoning mode or Least Preferred Coworker score.

**Lewis, Wendy** (trans) and Barney, Stephen (trans) and Normore, Calvin G (& other trans). On the Properties of Discourse: A Translation of *Tractatus de Proprietatibus Sermonum* (Author Anonymous). *Topoi*, 16(1), 77-93, Mr 97.

This is a translation of part of an anonymous early thirteenth tract on medieval semantics. The author discusses signification, supposition and appellation, including the division of supposition into determinate, distributive and merely confused. Causes of confusion are covered; sophisms are solved by applying the theory. Also covered: ampliation of terms by tenses and modalities.

**Lewis, William F** and DeConinck, James B. The Influence of Deontological and Teleological Considerations and Ethical Climate on Sales Managers' Intentions to Reward or Punish Sales Force Behavior. *J Bus Ethics*, 16(5), 497-506, Ap 97.

This study examined how sales managers react to ethical and unethical acts by their salespeople. Deontological considerations and, to a much lesser extent, teleological considerations predicted sales managers' ethical judgments. Sales managers' intentions to reward or discipline ethical or unethical sales force behavior were primarily determined by their ethical judgments. An organization's perceived ethical work climate was not a significant predictor of sales managers' intentions to intervene when ethical and unethical sales force behavior was encountered.

**Leydesdorff, Loet**. The Possibility of a Mathematical Sociology of Scientific Communication. *J Gen Phil Sci*, 27(2), 243-265, 1996.

The focus on discourse and communication in the recent sociology of scientific knowledge offers new perspectives for an integration of qualitative and quantitative approaches in science studies. The common point of interest is the question of how reflexive communication systems communicate. The elaboration of the mathematical theory of communication into a theory of potentially self-organizing entropical systems enables us to distinguish the various layers of communication and to specify the dynamic changes in these configurations over time. For example, a paradigmatic discourse can be considered as a virtual communication system at the supraindividual level.

Communication systems, however, cannot be directly observed. One observes only their instantaneous operations. The reflexive analyst is able to attribute the observed uncertainty to hypothesized systems that interact in the events. The implications of this perspective for various programmes in the sociology of scientific knowledge are discussed.

**Leydet, Dominique**. Thinking Critical History: Young Hegel and the German Constitution (in French). *Arch Phil*, 60(2), 197-215, Ap-Je 97.

Hegel's series of pamphlets called *The German Constitution* contains a critical conception of history. The object of this article is to illuminate its development by relating Hegel's unfinished work on the German constitution to the other philosophical fragments from the end of the Frankfurt period to the beginning of his stay in Jena. My analysis shows that it is Hegel's coming to question the main categories of his ontology that made it possible for him to think of history in this way.

**Lhoták, Kamil** and Vlasáková, Marta. The Reflecting Symmetry of Subjective and Extra-Subjective Processes (and To Theme... M. Vlasáková) (in Czech). *Filosof Cas*, 45(2), 315-320, 1997.

**Li, Chenyang**. Confucian Value and Democratic Value. *J Value Inq*, 31(2), 183-193, Je 97.

Today Confucianism and democracy can only possibly conflict as two systems of value. Against contemporary new-Confucians' attempt to democratize Confucianism, I argue that the two cannot be integrated into a single coherent value system without severely undermining Confucianism. I also disagree with Samuel Hungtinton, who advocates democratic values superseding undemocratic Confucian values. Borrowing from the model of Confucianism, Buddhism, and Taoism coexistence, I argue for the desirability and possibility for the two to coexist as two independent value systems in China.

**Li, Chenyang**. Shifting Perspectives: Filial Morality Revisited. *Phil East West*, 47(2), 211-232, Ap 97.

Does morality require the filial obligation of grown children toward their aged parents? First, problems with some accounts of filial morality that have been put forth in recent years in the West are examined (Jane English, Jeffrey Blustein, and others), and then it is shown how Confucianism provides a sensible alternative perspective.

**Li, Hon-Lam**. Abortion and Degrees of Personhood: Understanding Why the Abortion Problem (and the Animal Rights Problem) are Irresolvable. *Pub Affairs Quart*, 11(1), 1-19, Ja 97.

The aim of this article is to understand the apparent impasse in the problem of abortion. Its conclusion is that the problem of abortion—and that of animal rights—are irresolvable. In arriving at such a conclusion, the author argues that both a) the mother's and the fetus's intrinsic values, and b) their competing types of claims (i.e., life versus freedom), are relevant and important considerations to the abortion problem. Yet we do not know how to weigh and compare a mother's claim to freedom and a fetus's claim to life. Similarly, we do not know how to compare a nonvegetarian's claim to tasting a steak and a cow's claim to its life. This is because we do not have any ethical calculus or conceptual apparatus for comparing the lesser claim of a greater being (e.g., a mother's freedom, a nonvegetarian's taste) and the greater claim of a lesser being (e.g., a fetus's life, a cow's life). Because these competing claims seem incommensurable, the problems of abortion and animal rights are irresolvable. At least, the difficulties of these problems have a deeper source than we have so far acknowledged.

**Libardi, Massimo**. "*In Itinere*: Vienna 1870-1918" in *In Itinere* European Cities and the Birth of Modern Scientific Philosophy, Poli, Roberto (ed), 53-78. Amsterdam, Rodopi, 1997.

**Liberman, Gauthier**. La Dialectique Ascendante du *Banquet* de Platon. *Arch Phil*, 59(3), 455-462, Jl-S 96.

This essay treats an extract from Plato's *Symposium* wherein is considered the movement from the love of a beautiful object to an intuition of the beautiful. The author highlights the structure and the functioning of this ascent and examines the various states of this movement as well as this movement itself.

**Liberman, Kenneth**. "Universal Reason" as a Local Organizational Method: Announcement of a Study. *Human Stud*, 19(3), 289-301, Jl 96.

This article announces an ethnomethodological study of the formal analytic practices of Tibetan philosophers engaged in the collaborative work of producing correct philosophical debates. Tibetan scholar-monks address themselves to the work of sustaining an argument, providing formal warrants for authorizing truth and correctness, objectivating their accounts and disengaging those accounts from their local organizational practices. At the same time, it is the concern of the Tibetans' dialectics to avoid naive acceptance of reified accounts. The announced study proposes to describe their philosophical activities and to locate what originality may affect resolving the tension between formal analytic work and philosophical insight into truth.

**Librett, Jeffrey S**. "Interruptions of Necessity: Being Between Meaning and Power in Jean-Luc Nancy" in *On Jean-Luc Nancy: The Sense of Philosophy*, Sheppard, Darren (ed), 103-139. New York, Routledge, 1997.

**Lichtenberg, Judith**. "Nationalism, For and (Mainly) Against" in *The Morality of Nationalism*, McKim, Robert (ed), 158-175. New York, Oxford Univ Pr, 1997.

**Lichtenberg, Judith**. Consuming Because Others Consume. *Soc Theor Pract*, 22(3), 273-297, Fall 96.

I argue that, to a large extent, people consume because others around them do. The thesis has implications of two kinds, which I explore. One is practical: to the extent that one consumes because others do, one could consume less if others did, without diminishing one's well-being. The other is moral: despite the bad connotations of "consuming because others do," an appreciation of the

complexities of consumption shows why such behavior is often reasonable and even respectable. (edited)

**Lichtenberg, Judith**. How Liberal Can Nationalism Be?. *Phil Forum*, 28(1-2), 53-72, Fall-Wint 97.

**Liddy, Richard M**. Susanne K. Langer's Philosophy of Mind. *Trans Peirce Soc*, 33(1), 149-160, Wint 97.

This article analyzes the significant shift in Susanne K. Langer's philosophy of mind from her earlier *Philosophy in a New Key* and *Feeling and Form* to her later *Mind: An Essay on Human Understanding*. In her early work she emphasized the activity of understanding the "forms" of things, particularly symbols and works of art. Later she neglected the activity of understanding in favor of biological analyses of mind. The result is an unfortunate tendency to reduce mind to biological process. Langer's work is analyzed from the viewpoint of Bernard Lonergan's *Insight: An Essay on Human Understanding*.

**Lieberman, Marcel**. The Limits of Comparison: Kant and Sartre on the Fundamental Project. *Hist Phil Quart*, 14(2), 207-217, Ap 97.

**Lifsches, Shmuel** and Shelah, Saharon. Uniformization, Choice Functions and Well Orders in the Class of Trees. *J Sym Log*, 61(4), 1206-1227, D 96.

The monadic second-order theory of trees allows quantification over elements and over arbitrary subsets. We classify the class of trees with respect to the question: does a tree $T$ have a definable choice function (by a monadic formula with parameters)? A natural dichotomy arises where the trees that fall in the first class don't have a definable choice function and the trees in the second class have even a definable well ordering of their elements. This has a close connection to the uniformization problem.

**Light, Andrew**. "Compatibilism in Political Ecology" in *Environmental Pragmatism*, Light, Andrew (ed), 161-184. New York, Routledge, 1996.

Expanded version of "Materialists, Ontologists, and Environmental Pragmatists," *Social Theory and Practice* 21:2, 1995. Develops a strategy for resolving competing claims within environmental political theory, focusing on the debates between two different kinds of theorists: ontologists—such as deep ecologists—and materialist—such as Murray Bookchin's social ecologists. The urgency of the ecological crisis requires a form of metatheoretical compatibilism between these two types of theories. The argument is derived from a selective and critical reading of Rorty's neopragmatism concerning the distinction between public and private philosophical practice.

**Light, Andrew**. "Environmental Pragmatism as Philosophy or Metaphilosophy? On Weston-Katz Debate" in *Environmental Pragmatism*, Light, Andrew (ed), 325-338. New York, Routledge, 1996.

Examines the debate in *Environmental Ethics* between Anthony Weston and Eric Katz (vols 7:4, 9:3 and 10:3) on the issue of the relationship between pragmatism and environmental ethics. Argues that given a distinction between two different approaches to pragmatism in environmental ethics (philosophical and metaphilosophical), both Katz and Weston (contra Katz's assessment) are environmental pragmatists. A comparison is made between Katz and Weston on the one hand and J Baird Callicott on the other. It is argued that Callicott is not an environmental pragmatist in either sense. The paper includes a discussion of cultural pluralism and environmental ethics.

**Light, Andrew**. Wim Wenders and the Everyday Aesthetics of Technology and Space. *J Aes Art Crit*, 55(2), 215-229, Spring 97.

This paper argues that at least one of Wim Wenders's films provides a claim for the rethinking of the aesthetics of built space. This argument depends on two assumptions: 1) that the characteristics of built spaces are in part the result of the characteristics of their component material parts, and 2) that an engagement in the technological world with "focal things" provides a capacity to create a renewed sense of place. Finally, the paper examines how Wenders's work provides an occasion to consider the relationship between film as an art form and its technological form of reproduction.

**Light, Andrew** (ed) and Katz, Eric (ed). *Environmental Pragmatism*. New York, Routledge, 1996.

Environmental pragmatism is a new strategy in environmental thought: it argues that theoretical debates are hindering the ability of the environmental movement to forge agreement on basic policy imperatives. This new direction in environmental philosophy moves beyond theory, advocating a serious inquiry into the practical merits of moral pluralism. Environmental pragmatism, as a coherent philosophical position, connects the methodology of classical American pragmatist thought to the explanation, solution and discussion of real issues. (edited)

**Light, Andrew** (ed) and Smith, Jonathan M (ed). *Philosophy and Geography I: Space, Place, and Environmental Ethics*. Lanham, Rowman & Littlefield, 1997.

The inaugural collection in an exciting new exchange between philosophers and geographers, this volume provides interdisciplinary approaches to the environment as space, place and idea. Never before have philosophers and geographers approached each other's subjects in such a strong spirit of mutual understanding. The result is one of the most concrete explorations of the human-nature relationship, eschewing esoterica, while embracing strong normative approaches to environmental problems. While grounded in philosophy and geography, the essays also will interest readers in political theory, environmental studies, public policy and other disciplines. (publisher)

**Lightner, D Tycerium**. Hume on Conceivability and Inconceivability. *Hume Stud*, 23(1), 113-132, Ap 97.

**Lillehammer, Hallvard**. Smith on Moral Fetishism. *Analysis*, 57(3), 187-195, Jl 97.

The paper examines Smith's claim that externalism accounts for the reliable connection between moral judgement and motivation in good and strong-willed persons by attributing to them a fetishistic desire to do what is right, where this is read *de dicto*, not *de re*. It is argued that *de dicto* desires to do what is right do not amount to fetishism, that externalism can attribute *de re* desires to do what is right to good and strong-willed persons and that there are agents for whom it is not irrational not to be motivated in accordance with their moral judgement.

**Lilly, Reginald** (ed). *The Ancients and the Moderns*. Bloomington, Indiana Univ Pr, 1996.

Part One emphasizes the politics and experience of crisis. Manfred Riedel, Cornelius Castoriadis, John Sallis and Christian Meier examine the structures and issues that defined the Greek *polis*. Rüdiger Bubner, Reidel, Klaus Held, Paul Ricoeur, Reinhart Koselleck, Castoriadis, and Wolfgang Hardtwig focus on the historical crisis out of which modernity emerged. Part Two develops a critique of modernity, especially in light of Martin Heidegger's thought. Jean-Luc Marion, Jacques Taminiaux, Giorgio Agamben, and Rémi Brague find that Heidegger's thinking about the legacy of Greek and modern philosophy is compelling but that his understanding of philosophy and its history must be questioned. Victor Bourevitch, Frank Ankersmit, Heinrich Mohr and James Mensch explore the schism between philosophy and literature from Renaissance and contemporary perspectives. At issue here is the very emergence of the modern intellectual world with its distinctive concepts of subjectivity, history and knowledge. (publisher)

**Lim, Tock Keng**. Daughters of a Better Age. *Thinking*, 13(1), 23-25, 1997.

**Lincoln, Patrick D** and Mitchell, John C and Scedrov, Andre. Linear Logic Proof Games and Optimization. *Bull Sym Log*, 2(3), 322-338, S 96.

**Lincoln, Yvonna S** (ed) and Tierney, William G (ed). *Representation and the Text: Re-Framing the Narrative Voice*. Albany, SUNY Pr, 1997.

This book focuses on representations of contested realities in qualitative research. The authors examine two separate, but interrelated, issues: criticisms of how researchers use "voice," and suggestions about how to develop experimental voices that expand the range of narrative strategies. (publisher, edited)

**Lind, Richard**. A Micro-Phenomenology of Consonance and Dissonance. *J Phil Res*, 22, 321-355, Ap 97.

Using microphenomenology, I hypothesize that a consonant tonal interval is simply one that can be subliminally discriminated with relative ease and a dissonant interval is one that is relatively indiscriminable. Predictions implied by the hypothesis can be shown consistent with musical experience. If the theory is true, the affective character of harmonic progression is more the result of the need to discriminate tonal proportionality than the effect of expectation. (edited)

**Lind, Richard**. Art as Aesthetic Statement. *J Aes Educ*, 27(3), 1-21, Fall 93.

Art *can* be defined. First, all art is "aesthetic," i.e., capable of arousing and satisfying our interest in making the object perceptually intelligible. This condition applies not only to traditional art forms but to all the problematic works of recent history. Secondly, all art makes some sort of "statement," as Danto argued. Authorial meaning distinguishes art from the aesthetic in nature. Finally, in all art the authorial statement *subserves* the aesthetic effect. That is what distinguishes art from such other aesthetic statements as propaganda and rhetoric.

**Lind, Richard**. Micro-Phenomenology: Toward a Hypothetico-Inductive Science of Experience. *Int Phil Quart*, 36(4), 429-442, D 96.

Husserlian phenomenology, which has failed in its promise of apodictic knowledge, can be revitalized by a new methodology. The most crucial phenomena have proven inaccessible to reflective consciousness. Microphenomenology, which parallels the hypothetico-deductive method of the natural sciences, would enable us to propose testable hypotheses about elusive straight-forward conscious events. By predicting what should be explicit if our hypotheses were true, we can support them inductively by partial observations of what is postulated. Though we shall never know absolutely whether our theories are true, microphenomenology at least enables us to make progress towards an understanding of vital phenomena.

**Lindahl, Hans**. La Política de la Razón (In)suficiente. *Ideas Valores*, 24-41, Ag 96.

This paper argues that the normative concepts of legitimacy, political practice and democracy enjoined by Habermas's theory of communicative action are a political concretization of the principle of sufficient reason. Yet that a practically sufficient reason must be given of society presupposes that such a reason can be rendered. But can it? This question is *de iure*, not *de facto*; it concerns the regulative claim raised by the principle of reason, not the vicissitudes of empirical politics. Closer consideration suggests that a principle of *in*sufficient reason is the orienting principle of modern politics.

**Lindblom, Cristi K** and Ruland, Robert G. Functionalist and Conflict Views of AICPA Code of Conduct: Public Interest vs. Self Interest. *J Bus Ethics*, 16(5), 573-582, Ap 97.

The sociological model of functionalism and conflict are introduced and utilized to analyze professionalism in the accounting profession as it is manifest in the American Institute of Certified Public Accountant's Code of Conduct. Rule 203 of the code and provisions of the code related to the public interest are examined using semiotic analysis to determine if they are most consistent with the functionalist or conflict models. While the analysis does not address intent of the code, it is determined that the code contains semantic defects which result in different interpretations of the code to different readers. The defects found are most consistent with the conflict model of professionalism. This has implications for the public and for individuals within the profession, making the code less useful to both groups. The defects are seen as a potential battleground for the self-interest vs. the public interest orientation of the accounting profession.

**Lindén, Johan** and Dufwenberg, Martin. Inconsistencies in Extensive Games. *Erkenntnis*, 45(1), 103-114, Jl 96.

In certain finite extensive games with perfect information, Cristina Bicchieri (1989) derives a logical contradiction from the assumptions that players are rational and that they have common knowledge of the theory of the game. She argues that this may account for play outside the Nash equilibrium. She also claims that no inconsistency arises if the players have the minimal beliefs necessary to perform backward induction. We here show that another contradiction can be derived even with minimal beliefs, so there is no paradox of common knowledge specifically. These inconsistencies do not make play outside Nash equilibrium plausible, but rather indicate that the epistemic specification must incorporate a system for belief revision. Whether rationality is common knowledge is not the issue.

**Lindner, Konrad**. Vom Begriff der Freiheit: Fichtes Leipziger Kant-Studien (1790). *Fichte-Studien*, 9, 19-26, 1997.

**Lindop, Clive**. Wisdom and Intelligence in Philosophy for Children. *Thinking*, 13(2), 8-10, 1997.

Philosophy for children aims to encourage children to think about the quality of their thinking. By modelling and exercising children in formal and informal reasoning, it aims to develop excellence in judgment. This being so, philosophy for children can be expected to contribute to more intelligent behavior. In this paper, Sternberg's concept of the triarchic mind is used to scrutinize the philosophy for children program for the extent to which it exercises children in the three kinds of mental processes he considers essential for intelligent functioning. (edited)

**Lindquist, Stanton C** and McKendall, Marie A. True Colors: The Response of Business Schools to Declining Enrollment. *J Bus Ethics*, 16(8), 867-872, Je 97.

During the last several decades, business schools have increasingly portrayed themselves as the advocates and teachers of business ethics. In this context, educators have examined, criticized and written about the questionable actions of many organizations. Business schools are, however, currently facing their own unprecedented crisis in the form of dramatically declining enrollments. This paper examines the morality of the various possible response strategies and argue that how business schools respond to this crisis will serve as a clear indication of their own organizational ethics and values.

**Lindsay, Ronald A**. Assisted Suicide: Will the Supreme Court Respect the Autonomy Rights of Dying Patients?. *Free Inq*, 17(1), 4-5, Wint 96/97.

This article argues that assisted suicide is not only morally permissible, but that there is a fundamental liberty interest in being able to end one's own life. Because some, including, but not limited to, the terminally ill, are incapable of bringing about their own deaths effectively, an absolute ban on assisted suicide violates this fundamental liberty interest. When the State compels someone to live, it has appropriated that person's life and eliminated her autonomy. Legitimate concerns about assisted suicide's attendant abuses justify regulation, not an absolute ban.

**Lindsay, Ronald A**. Taboos Without a Clue: Sizing up Religious Objections to Cloning. *Free Inq*, 17(3), 15-17, Sum 97.

This article discusses religious objections to human cloning, especially as they were presented to the National Bioethics Advisory Commission by various theologians. Two arguments are made against these religious objections. The first argument, familiar to many philosophers, contends that divine commands cannot provide us with moral guidance and theologians *qua* theologians have nothing to contribute to the ethical debate on human cloning. The second argument then addresses specific religious objections and finds them to be question-begging and uninformative even within the context of the religious traditions in which these objections are formulated.

**Lindstedt, David**. The Progression and Regression of Slave Morality in Nietzsche's *Genealogy*: The Moralization of Bad Conscience and Indebtedness. *Man World*, 30(1), 83-105, Ja 97.

With the advent of slave morality and the belief system it entails, human beings alone begin to advance to a level beyond that of simple, brute, animal nature. While Christianity and its belief system generate a progression, however, allowing human beings to become interesting for the first time, Nietzsche also maintains in the *Genealogy* that slave morality is a regression, somehow lowering or bringing them down from a possible higher level. In this paper I will argue that this is not a mere inconsistency in Nietzsche's writing, but is instead an important clue to a correct interpretation of the *Genealogy*.

**Linell, Per** and Marková, Ivana. Coding Elementary Contributions to Dialogue: Individual Acts versus Dialogical Interaction. *J Theor Soc Behav*, 26(4), 353-373, D 96.

Coding as a method of dialogue analysis has often failed to distinguish between individual acts and dialogical interactions. The purpose of this paper was to draw attention to conceptual problems involved in providing coding systems for interactions that could preserve dialogicality, i.e., the joint construction of meaning, sequentiality and act-activity interdependence and the reflexive nature of interactions. We show that some aspects of dialogicality are already built into a few existing systems. We argue that building on these dialogical characteristics, more suitable dialogically orientated coding systems can be developed and that such systems have their important role in diagnostic practices.

**Lingis, Alphonso**. "Anger" in *On Jean-Luc Nancy: The Sense of Philosophy*, Sheppard, Darren (ed), 197-215. New York, Routledge, 1997.

Anger, Jean-Luc Nancy wrote, is the political emotion par excellence. In our world, where national markets and nation-states are giving place to a transnational technocratic-commercial archipelago, more and more divided from the outer zone of underdevelopment, what political agenda has to be formulated, what political forces assembled? How is such a new politics to be driven by anger?

**Lingis, Alphonso F**. Joy in Dying. *Grad Fac Phil J*, 19(1), 99-112, 1996.

**Linhe, Han**. Philosophy as Experience, as Elucidation and as Profession: An Attempt to Reconstruct Early Wittgenstein's Philosophy. *Grazer Phil Stud*, 51, 23-46, 1996.

Wittgenstein uses the word "philosophy" in the *Tractatus* in three different senses: philosophy as experience (Erlebnis) aiming at solving the problem of the meaning of life and world, philosophy as elucidation (Erläuterung) aiming at determining the nature of philosophy, clearly demarcating what can be said from what cannot and philosophy as profession. The latter only consists in the work of analyzing the propositions brought about by philosophy as experience—which cannot be pursued professionally as well as philosophy as elucidation—and in pointing out the nonsensicalness of these propositions.

**Linsky, Bernard**. The Vienna Circle and German Speaking Culture Before and After World War II. *Acta Analytica*, 189-194, 1995.

**Linsky, Bernard** and Zalta, Edward. In Defense of the Contingently Nonconcrete. *Phil Stud*, 84(2-3), 283-294, D 96.

In our "In Defense of the Simplest Quantified Modal Logic" (*Philosophical Perspectives 8: Philosophy of Logic and Language*, Atascadero, CA: Ridgeview, pp. 431-458), we introduced the notion of contingently nonconcrete objects to provide an actualist interpretation of modal logic with the Barcan formulas. In "Actualism or Possibilism?" (this volume), James Tomberlin accepts that this work accounts for the truth of certain puzzling sentences, but objects to our understanding of essential properties and contingent existence. In this paper we respond to Tomberlin's objections. We first correct his account of our position by sharply distinguishing between possibilities and objects of intentional attitudes and then argue that our understanding of essential properties and contingent existence preserves ordinary intuitions about modal reality.

**Linzey, Andrew**. "For Animal Rights" in *The Liberation Debate: Rights at Issue*, Leahy, Michael (ed), 171-187. New York, Routledge, 1996.

**Linzey, Andrew**. "Linzey's Reply" in *The Liberation Debate: Rights at Issue*, Leahy, Michael (ed), 205-207. New York, Routledge, 1996.

**Lipari, Maria Chiara**. I confini del fondamento. *Riv Int Filosof Diritto*, 74(4), 319-337, Ap-Je 97.

**Lipman, Matthew**. Caring as Thinking. *Inquiry (USA)*, 15(1), 1-13, Fall 95.

In recent years, a number of authors have proposed sets of criteria with which to identify critical thinking. At the same time, there has been a concerted push to get educators to recognize the desirability of teaching for thinking and not just for knowledge. Since thinking is presumably something students do already, it has become desirable to insist that education be aimed at the production of "higher-order thinking." What, then, is the connection between critical thinking and higher-order thinking? Many writers have advocated that higher-order thinking be understood as a combination of critical and creative thinking. This is unobjectionable, but I would like to show here that there is such a thing as *caring thinking* and that it is the third prerequisite to higher-order thinking.

**Lipman, Matthew**. Good Thinking. *Inquiry (USA)*, 15(2), 37-41, Wint 95.

The paper begins with an explanation of complex thinking as concerned with both subject-matter and method simultaneously (as in the *Euthyphro*. It proceeds to discuss higher-order thinking as critical, creative, responsible, etc. Finally, definitions are proposed for critical and creative thinking.

**Lipman, Matthew**. Thinking in Community. *Inquiry (USA)*, 16(4), 6-21, Sum 97.

A consideration of the process by which a classroom of students becomes converted to a *community of inquiry*. Among the aspects of this conversion to be discussed are: the logic of conversational discourse, the structure of dialogue, thinking moves and mental acts will learn from the experience of others.

**Lippert-Rasmussen, Kasper**. Moral Status and the Impermissibility of Minimizing Violations. *Phil Pub Affairs*, 25(4), 333-350, Fall 96.

Agent-relative restrictions on behaviour seem puzzling to many, since they forbid us to violate them even when doing so will minimize the overall number of violations, i.e., they forbid us to perform minimizing violations. The article discusses and criticizes various attempts, notably Frances Kamm's, to account for the impermissibility of minimizing violations in terms of considerations about moral status. Specifically, the article argues that it is hard to combine Kamm's account with the view that it is impermissible to perform minimizing violations of the doctrine of doing and allowing and the doctrine of the double effect.

**Lippitt, John**. A Funny Thing Happened to Me on the Way to Salvation: Climacus as Humorist in Kierkegaard's *Concluding Unscientific Postscript*. *Relig Stud*, 33(2), 181-202, Je 97.

According to James Conant, the 'revocations' made of the *Concluding Unscientific Postscript* and the *Tractatus* by their authors mean that we should view these texts as containing 'simple nonsense'. I firstly criticize the reading of the *Postscript*'s 'revocation' which leads Conant to this conclusion. Next, I aim to show why we shall better understand the revocation's significance if we pay close attention to two factors: the pseudonymous author Johannes Climacus's description of himself as a 'humorist'; and, more importantly, what the text tells us about 'humour' as an entire existential life-view; one given much less attention in Kierkegaard scholarship than the much better-known 'aesthetic', 'ethical' and 'religious' views of life.

**Lippke, Richard L**. Should States Be in the Gambling Business?. *Pub Affairs Quart*, 11(1), 57-73, Ja 97.

Five arguments against state sponsorship of gambling are analyzed critically and linked to deeper issues in political theory. The arguments are that state-sponsored gambling 1) encourages undesirable attitudes and character-traits in citizens; 2) produces more social costs than benefits; 3) is an especially regressive form of taxation; 4) is an illicit form of state activity; and 5) contributes to the increasing commercialization of play. I suggest that, taken together, these arguments make a strong case against state sponsorship of gambling.

**Lippke, Richard L**. Thinking about Private Prisons. *Crim Just Ethics*, 16(1), 26-38, Win-Spr 97.

States with burgeoning prison populations are increasingly contracting with private companies to house convicted offenders. I first consider the extent to which the administration of legal punishment by private institutions coheres with traditional theories of punishment. I then provide a brief overview of the contemporary reality of crime and punishment in the United States. I suggest that how we should think about private prisons is a complicated function of a theory of punishment, an understanding of the contemporary reality of crime and punishment and an analysis of how far any theory of punishment can take us in justifying current penal practices, including private prisons.

**Liquin, Deng**. On Freedom. *Chin Stud Phil*, 28(1), 78-88, Fall 96.

**Liquori, Luigi** and Van Bakel, Steffen and Ronchi della Rocca, Simona (& others). Comparing Cubes of Typed and Type Assignment Systems. *Annals Pure Applied Log*, 86(3), 267-303, Jl 97.

We study the *cube of type assignment systems*, as introduced in Giannini et al. (Fund. Inform. 19 (1993) 87-126) and confront it with Barendregt's typed *Lambda*-cube (Barendregt, in: *Handbook of Logic in Computer Science*, Vol. 2, Clarenden Press, Oxford, 1992). The first is obtained from the latter through applying a natural type erasing function *E* to derivation rules, that erases type information from terms. In particular, we address the question whether a judgement, derivable in a type assignment system, is always an erasure of a derivable judgement in a corresponding typed system; we show that this property holds only for systems without polymorphism. The type assignment systems we consider satisfy the properties 'subject reduction' and 'strong normalization'. Moreover, we define a new type assignment cube that is isomorphic to the typed one.

**Lisi, Francisco L**. El debate sobre la filosofía de la naturaleza y de la historia de Platón: el IV Symposium Platonicum. *An Seminar Hist Filosof*, 13, 293-303, 1996.

**Liske, Michael-Thomas**. Für und Wider den Essentialismus: Zu Rudolf-Peter Häglers *Kritik des neuen Essentialismus*. *Z Phil Forsch*, 50(4), 618-623, O-D 96.

A serious criticism of essentialism should refute the proposition that there are absolutely fundamental descriptions. One can take an intermediary position between the theory that there are sufficient qualitative or descriptive conditions of reference and Kripke's claim that descriptions are not even necessary conditions: in the Aristotelian view, sortals are only necessary conditions of reference. Distinctions like the distinction of 'analytic' and 'synthetic' do not define mutually exclusive classes, but only different aspects. This is not what an abstract scientific approach aims at, but it is adequate for a nonreductive ordinary-language approach to our complex reality.

**Lissa, Giuseppe**. "Piovani e lo storicismo" in *Lo Storicismo e la Sua Storia: Temi, Problemi, Prospettive*, Cacciatore, Giuseppe (ed), 557-581. Milano, Guerini, 1997.

This work aims to verify the contribution of Pietro Piovani to the developments of historicism. Piovani means to distinguish precisely two forms of historicism: a historicism "absolute" that brings the individuality of human representations back to philosophy of history; and a historicism "critical and problematical" that, sensible to the developments of modernity, is instead inclined to favour the plurality. That has, then, a deep ethical valence since it searches to reform the values and, respecting human individualities, to connect the link *rule-universality*. In that sense, Piovani feels himself obliged to react to Heidegger's challenge. The historicism "critical and problematical" aims, in fact, to the equation of *being* and *time*, but, unlike Heidegger who solves it in the *oneness* and in a *history of being*, Piovani seeks the recognition of the *otherness* and *plurality*.

**Lissa, Giuseppe** (ed) and Cantillo, Giuseppe (ed) and Cacciatore, Giuseppe (ed). *Lo Storicismo e la Sua Storia: Temi, Problemi, Prospettive*. Milano, Guerini, 1997.

Testimonianza dell'affetto dei suoi allievi, questo libro riflette, nell'impostazione e negli esiti, i motivi ispiratori dell'insegnamento e dell'attività scientifica e culturale di Fulvio Tessitore. Gli autori, uniti da una comunanza di ricerca e di studio, si muovono lungo una pluralità di percorsi tematici che mettono a fuoco le diverse dimensioni teoriche e storiche dello storicismo. Ne emerge una ben determinata visione teoretico-filosofica dello storicismo (lo *storicismo criticoproblematico*, il *nuovo* storicismo) e, insieme, una ricostruzione storiografica della sua genesi e delle connessioni che lo legano ai principali orientamenti filosofici contemporanei. (publisher, edited)

**List, Peter** and Gruen, Lori and Chorover, Stephan L. Commentary On: "There is no Such Thing as Environmental Ethics". *Sci Eng Ethics*, 2(3), 319-334, Jl 96.

**Little, Daniel**. Introduction: Recent Currents in Marxist Philosophy. *Topoi*, 15(2), 143-148, S 96.

**Little, Joyce Currie** (& others) and Anderson, Ronald E and Huff, Chuck. Integrating the Ethical and Social Context of Computing into the Computer Science Curriculum. *Sci Eng Ethics*, 2(2), 211-224, A 96.

This paper describes the major components of ImpactCS, a program to develop strategies and curriculum materials for integrating social and ethical considerations into the computer science curriculum. It presents, in particular, the content recommendations of a subcommittee of ImpactCS; and it illustrates the interdisciplinary nature of the field, drawing upon concepts from computer science, sociology, philosophy, psychology, history and economics.

**Little, Margaret Olivia**. Virtue as Knowledge: Objections from the Philosophy of Mind. *Nous*, 31(1), 59-79, Mr 97.

There has lately been a tendency to regard the idea of equating virtue and moral knowledge as one that can be cleanly and quickly dismissed on the grounds that it contravenes certain basic tenets of our philosophy of mind and moral psychology. I argue that this view, advanced most notably by Michael Smith, is simply barking up the wrong tree. There is nothing in the mere idea of belief and desire, or in our lived moral experience, to argue against equating virtue and knowledge; arguments that seem to indicate they do rely, it turns out, on further, smuggled, substantive assumptions about issues that lie well outside the philosophy of mind and psychology.

**Littlejohn, Murray**. Augustinian Wisdom and the Law of the Heart. *Maritain Stud*, 12, 77-97, 1996.

**Litz, Reginald A**. A Resource-Based-View of the Socially Responsible Firm: Stakeholder Interdependence, Ethical Awareness, and Issue Responsiveness as Strategic Assets. *J Bus Ethics*, 15(12), 1355-1363, D 96.

In recent years the resource-based view of the firm has made significant headway in explaining differences in interfirm performance. However, this perspective has not considered the social and ethical dimensions of organizational resources. This paper seeks to provide such an integration. Using Kuhn's three stage model of adaptive behaviour, the resource worthiness of stakeholder management, business ethics, and issues management are explored. The paper concludes by drawing on prospect theory to understand the reasons for this conceptual lacuna.

**Liu, Chuang**. Gauge Invariance, Cauchy Problem, Indeterminism, and Symmetry Breaking. *Proc Phil Sci Ass*, 3(Suppl), S71-S79, 1996.

The concepts in the title refer to properties of physical theories (which are given, in this paper, a model-theoretic formulation and appropriate idealizations) and this paper investigates their nature and relations. The first three concepts, especially gauge invariance and indeterminism, have been widely discussed in connection to space-time theories and the hole argument. Since the gauge invariance principle is at the crux of the issue, this paper aims at clarifying the nature of gauge invariance (either in general or as general covariance). I first explore the following chain of relations: gauge invariance implies the conservation laws implies the Cauchy problem implies indeterminism. Then I discuss gauge invariance in light of our understanding of the above relations and the possibility of spontaneous symmetry breaking. (edited)

**Liu, Chuang**. Holism vs. Particularism: A Lesson from Classical and Quantum Physics. *J Gen Phil Sci*, 27(2), 267-279, 1996.

The present essay aims at broadening the recent discussion on the issue of holism vs. particularism in quantum physics. I begin with a clarification of the relation between the holism/particularism debate and the discussion of supervenience relation. I then defend particularism in physics (including quantum physics) by considering a new classification of properties of physical systems. With such a classification, the results in the Bell theorem are shown to violate spatial separability but not physical particularism.

**Liu, Chuang**. Potential, Propensity, and Categorical Realism. *Erkenntnis*, 45(1), 45-68, Jl 96.

I argue that categorical realism, contrary to what most believe today, holds for quantum (and indeed for all) objects and substances. The main argument consists of two steps: I) the recent experimental verification of the AB affect gives strong empirical evidence for taking quantum potentials as physically real (or substantival), which suggests a change of the data upon which any viable interpretation of quantum theory must rely and II) quantum potentials may be consistently taken as the categorical properties of quantum objects so that categorical realism can be restored.

**Liu, Chuang**. Realism and Spacetime: Of Arguments Against Metaphysical Realism and Manifold Realism. *Phil Natur*, 33(2), 243-263, 1996.

In this essay I explore the relation between Putnam's model-theoretic argument against metaphysical realism and the hole argument against space time manifold realism. It is shown that the hole argument is really Putnam's argument restricted to space time predicates. This is because the gauge theorem is about inscrutability of reference, not about the indeterminacy of possible worlds. Thus, the gauge freedom in space time theories expresses a semantic fact rather than one about ontology; and the hole argument is really against the metaphysical determinacy of reference. Thus, the indeterminism crisis does not even arise. I then defend my construal of the hole argument by refuting a dualist view of the physical world and an incorrect version of the relationism-substantivalism debate.

**Liu, Nianzheng**. Analytic Cell Decomposition and the Closure of *p*-ADIC Semianalytic Sets. *J Sym Log*, 62(1), 285-303, Mr 97.

The main result of this article is that the closure of a p-adic semianalytic set is also semianalytic. The proof is based on an analytic cell decomposition theorem, proved in the article, which allows one to partition p-adic semianalytic sets into cells defined in a simple way. Cell decompositions play a central role in the theory of semi-algebraic and semi-analytic sets.

**Livesley, W John**. Commentary on "Epistemic Value Commitments". *Phil Psychiat Psych*, 3(3), 223-226, S 96.

**Livingston, Paisley**. Arguing over Intentions. *Rev Int Phil*, 50(198), 615-633, 1996.

**Livingston, Paisley**. From Work to Work. *Phil Lit*, 20(2), 436-454, O 96.

I argue, contra various post-structuralist, that much can be learned by interpreting a work of art in terms of its place within the actual author's life-work. Beginning with Jerrold Levinson's discussion of intended work/life-work relations, I defend the critical relevance of retrospective and retroactive relations—including some unintended relations—between works in a writer's corpus. Various examples are used to show that a genetic, actual intentionalist perspective on an artist's dynamic activity can reveal important dimensions of the movement from work to work, including the artist's response to the "Bratmanian" dilemma of planning.

**Liz, Manuel**. "Las variedades del escepticismo" in *La racionalidad: su poder y sus límites,* Nudler, Oscar (ed), 179-210. Barcelona, Ed Paidos, 1996.

Four general varieties of sceptical arguments are distinguished according to their different scope and modal force. Radical varieties of scepticism would have the greatest scope, modal force, or both. We argue that they can be answered from a fallibilist perspective and that some relevant epistemic features need to be admitted. Namely, that our justification does not require any previous knowledge and that the possibilities displayed in radical sceptical scenarios must be considered only mere possibilities. Questions opened by Barry Stroud's recent book *The Significance of Philosophical Scepticism* are also discussed in relation with the fallibilist perspective adopted.

**Liz, Manuel**. La estructura de las representaciones mentales: una perspectiva integradora. *Analisis Filosof*, 15(1-2), 135-166, My-N 95.

Some of the more representative recent issues in cognitive sciences share the thesis that all mental representations must have in an essential way some determinate and specific structure. For classical computationalism that structure must be symbolic and it is based on relations of constituency obtained through a syntax. Noneliminativist connectionism rejects the appeal of a syntax. It postulates only causal relations of connectedness and, perhaps, some sort of semantical relationships other than the ones posited by classical computationalism. In this paper, I examine both positions defending that it is not necessary for mental representations, in general, to have any determinate and specific structure. Moreover, I argue that the symbolic structure that some mental representations seem to have only emerged under a set of very special conditions among which it must be included the fact that these mental representations have other nonsymbolic structures. (edited)

**Llano, Carlos** and Aspe A, Virginia and Mier y Terán, Rocío. *Ensayos Aristotélicos*. Mexico, Univ Panamericana, 1996.

**Llano Alonso, Fernando H**. Guida Fassò: Estudios en torno a Giambattista Vico. *Cuad Vico*, 5/6, 67-82, 1995/96.

In this paper we expose the studies that Professor Guido Fassò carried out concerning Vico's thinking, in particular the interpretation of his works made by his first translator, Jule Michelet. We present as well an approach to the historical and logical genesis of the *Scienza Nuova*, which have been eulogized by Benedetto Croce, Giovanni Gentile and Felice Battaglia.

**Llano Alonso, Fernando H**. La influencia del jusnaturalismo racionalista en la génesis de la moral cristiana pre-evangélica. *Rev Espan Filosof Med*, 4, 123-129, 1997.

This essay tries to present an analysis in prospective terms of the main keys and questions risen from one of the most enigmatic stages in the history of classical philosophy: the genesis of postevangelical Christian morality in which it is possible to find indissoluble bonds with the iusnatualist Greco-Latin tradition.

**Llano Cifuentes, Carlos**. "La reflexión de la *proairesis* aristotélica" in *Ensayos Aristotélicos,* Rivera, José Luis (ed), 29-47. Mexico, Univ Panamericana, 1996.

This paper concerns to the problem of attributing choice to a "desiring intelligence" or to an "intelligent will", according to *Nichomachean Ethics* VI 2, 1139b 5, as well as to the role of intelligence and will in free choice. Llano emphasizes the importance of the integral (human) agent, stating the principle that neither intelligence nor will are who properly choose, but the whole individual through these powers.

**Llano Cifuentes, Carlos**. Función, plan y proyecto. *Topicos*, 25-59, 1996.

After a brief criticism of some aspects of Luhmann's social theory (based on the concept of *function*), the author proposes a description of social development emphasizing the relevance of personal participation, using Ackoff's idea of "planning" and Donati's theory of "project".

**Lloyd, Dan**. Commentary on "Searle and the 'Deep Unconscious'". *Phil Psychiat Psych*, 3(3), 201-202, S 96.

**Lloyd, Genevieve**. *Spinoza and the Ethics*. New York, Routledge, 1996.

Written for students coming to Spinoza for the first time, *Spinoza and the Ethics* is the ideal guide to this rich and illuminating work. This book provides an overview of the critical interpretations, relating the *Ethics* to its intellectual context; considers its historical reception; and highlights why the work continues to be relevant today. In addition, the most intriguing final sections of the *Ethics*, usually ignored in introductory commentaries, are given special attention and illuminated as the climax of the work. (edited)

**Lo Bue, Elisabetta**. Enigma e relazione: Da Apollo a Edipo. *G Metaf*, 19(1), 57-73, Ja-Ap 97.

**Lo Monaco, Vicenzo P**. Sobre referencia y causalidad. *Rev Filosof (Venezuela)*, 23(1), 49-65, 1996.

This article challenges Kripke's claim that the causal theory of manes may give a semantic account of reference in terms of causal channels. A distinction is made between referential and causal perspectives and it is argued that genetic character of proper names does not necessarily support its referential adequation. It is maintained that referential use of any name depends on the semantic structures which underlie many linguistic elements of referential individuation—than on causal processes of its acquisition. The philosophical correlate of this argument is that there is no referential link as a causal channel: Types of causal relationships that share a common semantic link between names and objects provide referential contents of names. The character of causal theory is also considered from a Kripkean structure-models perspective. (edited)

**Loader, Ralph**. Equational Theories for Inductive Types. *Annals Pure Applied Log*, 84(2), 175-217, Mr 97.

This paper provides characterizations of the equational theory of the PER model of a typed lambda calculus with inductive types. The characterization may be cast as a *full abstraction* result, in other words, we show that the equations between terms valid in this model coincides with a certain syntactically defined equivalence relation. Along the way we give other characterizations of this equivalence; from below, from above, and from a domain model, a version of Kreisel-Lacombe-Schoenfield theorem allows us to transfer the result from the domain model to the PER model.

**Loar, Brian**. "Comments on John Campbell, 'Molineux's Question'" in *Perception,* Villanueva, Enrique (ed), 319-324. Atascadero, Ridgeview, 1996.

**Loar, Brian**. "Reference from the First Person Perspective" in *Contents,* Villanueva, Enrique (ed), 53-72. Atascadero, Ridgeview, 1995.

**Lobato, Abelardo**. La dignidad humana desde una perspectiva metafísica. *Sapientia,* 51(200), 309-326, 1996.

**Locke, John** and Winkler, Kenneth P (ed). *John Locke: An Essay Concerning Human Understanding.* Indianapolis, Hackett, 1996.

Kenneth Winkler's abridgment of Locke's *Essay Concerning Human Understanding* includes generous selections from the *Essay,* topically arranged passages from the replies to Stillingfleet, a chronology, a bibliography, a glossary, and an index based on the entries that Locke himself devised. His introduction provides the reader with both a historical and a philosophical context in which to assess Locke's masterwork. (publisher, edited)

**Lockwood, Michael**. "The Grain Problem" in *Objections to Physicalism,* Robinson, Howard (ed), 271-291. New York, Clarendon/Oxford Pr, 1996.

Russell advocated a form of the identity theory, according to which qualia are a manifestation of the intrinsic nature of our own brain states. An obvious obstacle to this view is the ostensible *structural* mismatch between brain states, as revealed by neuroscience and conscious states, as revealed by introspection. This is the *grain problem.* Here, it is suggested that the grain problem is rooted in a *classical* way of thinking and that the problem might be resolved if we instead conceptualize the brain in the way quantum mechanics conceptualizes physical systems in general.

**Lockwood, Michael**. 'Many Minds' Interpretations of Quantum Mechanics: Replies to Replies. *Brit J Phil Sci,* 47(3), 445-461, S 96.

**Loeb, Stephen E** and Ostas, Daniel T. A Business Ethics Experiential Learning Module: The Maryland Business School Experience. *Teach Bus Ethics,* 1(1), 21-32, 1997.

In this paper we describe the principal activities of the initial implementation in May of 1996 of one of the "Experiential Learning Modules (ELMs)' entitled "Business Ethics" (UMCP 1995, p. 7) that is part of the full-time MBA program at the College of Business and Management (Maryland Business School) of the University of Maryland at College Park (UMCP). Additionally, we briefly consider the location of this Business Ethics ELM in the curriculum of the Maryland Business School's full-time MBA program. We also outline how the Business Ethics ELM was developed. Further, we provide a discussion and a short conclusion.

**Loeck, Gisela**. Epistemische Leistungen technischer Simulationen. *Phil Natur,* 26(2), 202-245, 1989.

This paper investigates the epistemic achievements of technical simulation providing explanations for nontechnical systems. It aims to show that there exist simulations whose simulators and explananda are identical that provide nevertheless different explanations, presenting as an example the simulation of living systems by gear wheel mechanisms in the biology of Aristotle and Descartes. It presents a conceptual frame employing 'explanatory system', 'explanatory pattern', 'reference entity' and 'C-C-relation'. (edited)

**Loetscher, Catherine**. Une guerre juste est-elle possible?. *Rev Theol Phil,* 128(4), 339-356, 1996.

Just war theory appears to be a reasonable middle way between the amorality of the warmongers and naïve pacifism. It is based on the analogy that the right of individuals to the use of violence, under particular circumstances, applies equally to states. However, not only is this analogy questionable in itself, accepting the doctrine of a just war leads to a series of problematic consequences. (edited)

**Loevinger, Lee**. Enforcing Ethical Standards of Professional Associations. *Prof Ethics,* 5(1-2), 157-166, Spr-Sum 96.

**Loewenstein, Bedrich**. Animal symbolicum?. *Filosof Cas,* 44(4), 535-564, 1996.

This article considers the ever-present nature of symbols in the human world and their specific nature in comparison with discursive signs, considering the "use and harm (good and bad) of symbolic orientations" in secular society. Symbols are dramatized images which contain deeply rooted inherited experience and recall forgotten practices for certain situations, reinforce the system of faith and other forms of collective identity. The article also looks at the symbolic quality of the subjects and activities of everyday life—from home and car to football. Those recreational activities, which fall within the symbolic rule of a limited field, seem to have an eminent civilizing function. Symbols do,

however, create an imaginary field of power, coherence, legitimacy, a certain order, a barrier against chaos, "a sign of quality."(edited)

**Löwith, Karl** and Lomax, J Harvey (trans). *Nietzsche's Philosophy of the Eternal Recurrence of the Same.* Berkeley, Univ of Calif Pr, 1997.

Criticizing the tendency to treat Nietzsche as a literary figure or as a vitalist in the tradition of Bergson, Simmel, and Klages, Löwith situates Nietzsche squarely within the history of Western philosophy. He takes issue with the position of Jaspers that Nietzsche is best read as a rejection of all philosophical certainties and challenges Heidegger's view that Nietzsche was the last metaphysician of the West. For Löwith, the centerpiece of Nietzsche's thought is the doctrine of eternal recurrence, a notion which Löwith, unlike Heidegger, deems incompatible with the will to power. (publisher, edited)

**Loewy, Erich H**. Developing Habits and Knowing What Habits to Develop: A Look at the Role of Virtue in Ethics. *Cambridge Quart Healthcare Ethics,* 6(3), 347-355, Sum 97.

**Loewy, Erich H**. Finding an Appropriate Ethic in a World of Moral Acquaintances. *Theor Med,* 18(1-2), 79-97, Mr-Je 97.

This paper discusses the possibility of finding an ethic of at least partial and perhaps ever-growing content in a world not that of moral strangers (where we have nothing except our desire to live freely to unite us) and one of moral friends (in which values, goals and ways of doing things are held in common). I argue that both the world of moral strangers which Engelhardt's world view would support, as the world of moral friends which is the one Pellegrino seeks both are untenable and that furthermore both can lead to a similar state of affairs. I suggest a dynamic world of moral acquaintances in which different belief systems and ways of doing things can come to some broad agreements about some essential thing. This is made possible because although we do not share the intimate framework Pellegrino might suggest, yet we are united by a much broader framework than the one moral strangers share.

**Loewy, Erich H**. Justice, Society, Physicians and Ethics Committees: Incorporating Ideas of Justice into Patient Care Decisions. *Cambridge Quart Healthcare Ethics,* 5(4), 559-569, Fall 96.

This paper seeks to make a distinction between two contingent but nevertheless quite distinguishable senses of the concept "justice:" the formal and what is here called the operative concept. The reason why physicians, for example, have felt that justice is "misplaced at the bed-side" is that justice has been viewed in an entirely too formalistic way. I argue that it is possible to allow considerations of relationships, compassion and interests to flesh out the formal concept and in this manner provide a far more flexible and realistic view of the concept then can be expected by using the formal approach alone.

**Loewy, Erich H** and Thomasma, David C. A Dialogue on Species-Specific Rights: Humans and Animals in Bioethics. *Cambridge Quart Healthcare Ethics,* 6(4), 435-444, Fall 97.

**Löwy, Ilana**. The Legislation of Things. *Stud Hist Phil Sci,* 28(3), 533-543, S 97.

Until recently technology, unlike science, was not viewed as an important topic for a philosophical inquiry. Recent changes in the status of the philosophy of technology are documented in two books, *Alternative Modernity* by Andrew Feenberg (Berkeley, 1995), and *Living in Technological Culture,* by Mary Tiles and Hans Oberdiek (London, 1995). These books study the ways technology makes values and interests invisible through their incorporation into things and accomplishes political tasks through the attribution of symbolic and ideological meaning to technical devices and the construction of interconnected technological networks.

**Löwy, Michael**. Utopia or Reconciliation with Reality—Lukács's 1922-23 Literary Essays (in Hungarian). *Magyar Filozof Szemle,* 4-5-6, 583-589, 1996.

During the years 1922-23 Georg Lukacs published several literary essays in the *Rote Fahne,* the periodical of the German communists. The main topic of the articles is, as in his earlier book *Theory of the Novel* (1916), the opposition between utopia and reconciliation with reality. The utopia of a human kingdom is represented by Lessing's piece "Nathan the Wise" as well as by Dostoievsky's novels, while Goethe's "Torquato Tasso"—in spite of its literary superiority—is a sort of "regression to philistinism" and a conformist acceptance of German reality. Instead of emphasizing—as in his later works, from the 30's on—"realism", the young Lukacs celebrates the utopian dimension in literature, its capacity to anticipate a new, emancipated world, beyond the inhuman and reified reality of capitalism.

**Löwy, Michael** and Macey, David (trans). Walter Benjamin and Surrealism: The Story of a Revolutionary Spell. *Rad Phil,* 80, 17-23, N-D 96.

Walter Benjamin shared with the surrealists a sort of "Gothic Marxism", i.e., a historical materialism sensitive to the *magical* dimension of past cultures, to the "black" moment of revolt and to the illumination that rends the sky of revolutionary action like a bolt of lightning. "Gothic" should also be understood literally as a positive reference to certain key moments in profane medieval culture: both Benjamin and André Breton admired the courtly love of medieval Provence. Benjamin understood perfectly that surrealism is not just an "artistic movement" but a set of magical experiments with revolutionary implications, both profoundly libertarian and in search of convergence with communism.

**Logan, Beryl**. *Immanuel Kant's Prolegomena to Any Future Metaphysics.* New York, Routledge, 1996.

This book provides the student of philosophy with an invaluable overview of some issues and problems raised by Kant. In addition to the Carus translation of Kant's work, it offers a substantive new introduction, six seminal essays on the *Prolegomena* never before published together and an extensive bibliography.

Special attention is paid to the relationship between Kant and David Hume, whose treatment of causality, according to Kant's famous quote, first interrupted Kant's "dogmatic slumber". (publisher)

**Logan, John E** (& others) and Bumpus, Minnette A and Glover, Saundra H. Re-Examining the Influence of Individual Values on Ethical Decision Making. *J Bus Ethics*, 16(12-13), 1319-1329, S 97.

This paper presents the results of five years of research involving three studies. The first two studies investigated the impact of the value honesty/integrity on the ethical decision choice an individual makes, as moderated by the individual personality traits of self-monitoring and private self-consciousness. The third study, which is the focus of this paper, expanded the two earlier studies by varying the level of moral intensity and including the influence of demographical factors and other workplace values; achievement, fairness and concern for others on the ethical decision process. (edited)

**Logsdon, Jeanne M** and Yuthas, Kristi. Corporate Social Performance, Stakeholder Orientation, and Organizational Moral Development. *J Bus Ethics*, 16(12-13), 1213-1226, S 97.

This article begins with an explanation of how moral development for organizations has parallels to Kohlberg's categorization of the levels of individual moral development. Then the levels of organizational moral development are integrated into the literature on corporate social performance by relating them to different stakeholder orientations. Finally, the authors propose a model of organizational moral development that emphasizes the role of top management in creating organizational processes that shape the organizational and institutional components of corporate social performance. This article represents one approach to linking the distinct streams of business ethics and business-and-society research into a more complete understanding of how managers and firms address complex ethical and social issues.

**Lohmann, Karl R**. "Vom Versuch angewandter Philosophie: Warum sich Philosophen mit Managern unterhalten" in *Werte und Entscheidungen im Management,* Schmidt, Thomas, 19-27. Marburg, Metropolis, 1996.

**Lohmann, Karl R**. "Zur Integration von Werten in Entscheidungen: Entscheidungsorientierung und eine liberale Theorie der Werte" in *Werte und Entscheidungen im Management,* Schmidt, Thomas, 137-194. Marburg, Metropolis, 1996.

**Lohmann, Karl R**. *Darf Pedro sein Land verkaufen? Versuch einer sozialwissenschaftlichen Perspektive in der Ökonomik.* Marburg, Metropolis, 1995.

Der Autor macht den Versuch einer Antwort, die über das konkrete Fallbeispiel des honduranischen Bodenmarktes hinaus für die ökonomische Theoriebildung relevant ist. In einem erweiterten entscheidungstheoretischen Ansatz wird die betriebswirtschaftliche Perspektive mit der Perspektive der Wohlfahrtsökonomik verbunden. Dieser Ansatz erlaubt es, verschiedene Informationen differenziert zuzuordnen, Kooperation methodisch zu berücksichtigen und schliesslich einen differenzierten ökonomischen Begriff der Person zu setzen. Abschliessend wird gezeigt, in welcher Weise eine solche sozialwissenschaftliche Perspektive der Ökonomik in besonderer Weise Vorhersagen und politische Empfehlungen erlaubt.

**Lohmann, Karl R** and Schmidt, Thomas. *Werte und Entscheidungen im Management.* Marburg, Metropolis, 1996.

In der zeitgenössischen unternehmensethischen Debatte wird in erster Linie die Möglichkeit und der Sinn von Ethik-Programmen diskutiert. In der Untersuchung *Werte und Entscheidungen im Management* wurde ein anderer Ansatz gewählt. Die Autoren analysieren, wie Werte und moralische Überzeugungen von Personen in die Struktur individueller Entscheidungen integrierbar sind. In dem Buch werden der Verlauf der empirisch gestützten Studie, die verwendeten Instrumente und ihre Ergebnisse dargestellt. Die Ergebnisse sind für Theoretiker und Praktiker gleichermassen interessant. Zum einen muss in Theorie und Praxis der Organisationsentwicklung die Struktur individueller Entscheidungen berücksichtigt werden. Zum anderen bildet eben diese Struktur die Grundlage jeder Personalpolitik und jedes erfolgreichen Personaltrainings. (publisher, edited)

**Lohmann, Karl Reinhard**. "Moralische Überzeugung und wirt-schaftliche Wahl" in *Ökonomie und Moral: Beiträge zur Theorie ökonomischer Rationalität,* Lohmann, Karl Reinhard (ed), 113-133. München, Oldenbourg, 1997.

**Lohmann, Karl Reinhard** (ed) and Priddat, Birger P (ed). *Ökonomie und Moral: Beiträge zur Theorie ökonomischer Rationalität.* München, Oldenbourg, 1997.

This edition on economics and morals contains 10 papers by philosophers as well as economists. In Germany the discussion in the philosophy of economics is very much limited to questions concerning the institutional constraints of economic development. The focus of this edition on the contrary is on the economic theory of rationality. The contributors discuss both minor modifications of standard consequentialism as well as alternative approaches that allow morals to be integrated in economic analysis. All contributions stress the importance of broadening the economic calculus towards other person's interests.

**Lohmar, Dieter**. Zu der Enstehung und den Ausgangsmaterialien von Edmund Husserls Werk *Erfahrung und Urteil. Husserl Stud*, 13(1), 31-71, 1996.

**Lojacono, Ettore**. L'arrivo del *Discours* e dei *Principia,D* in Italia: prime letture dei testi cartesiani a Napoli. *G Crit Filosof Ital*, 16(3), 395-454, S-D 96.

**Lokhorst, Gert-Jan C**. Aristotle on Reflective Awareness. *Log Anal*, 37(146), 129-143, Je 94.

We present a logical reconstruction of Aristotle's views on reflective awareness (*De Anima* III.2, 425b12-25, and *De Somno* 2, 455a12-22).

**Lokhorst, Gert-Jan C**. Maarten Doormans kwantitatieve argumenten voor vooruitgang in de kunst. *Alg Ned Tijdschr Wijs*, 89(3), 230-231, Jl 97.

In his book *Steeds mooier* (Amsterdam 1994), Maarten Doorman put forward three so-called quantitative arguments for the thesis that there is progress in art. We present a formal analysis of these arguments according to which they are valid, but utterly trivial.

**Lolas, Fernando**. Theoretical Medicine: A Proposal for Reconceptualizing Medicine as a Science of Actions. *J Med Phil*, 21(6), 659-670, D 96.

The main task of a critical theory of medicine should be to develop a perspectival, context-fair and multidimensional science of actions which integrates both diversity and heterogeneity within medicine without eliminating either one. Such a theory should employ diversity in the following areas: 1) in systems, subsystems and professions, because different medical professions embody different health-care subsystems, thereby influencing the way manpower is utilized, 2) in actors, (e.g., patients, health-care experts and society), processes and situations, because each actor potentially conceptualizes health, illness and desired outcomes differently; and 3) in models of medicine (i.e., as an object science versus an action science). Situational influences modify concepts and explanatory models; even the particular terms, such as illness, disease, and sickness, are not necessarily concordant with each other.

**Lolli, Gabriele**. "Storia del teorema di completezza" in *Momenti di Storia della Logica e di Storia della Filosofia,* Guetti, Carla (ed), 187-235. Roma, Aracne Editrice, 1996.

**Lomax, J Harvey** (trans) and Löwith, Karl. *Nietzsche's Philosophy of the Eternal Recurrence of the Same.* Berkeley, Univ of Calif Pr, 1997.

Criticizing the tendency to treat Nietzsche as a literary figure or as a vitalist in the tradition of Bergson, Simmel, and Klages, Löwith situates Nietzsche squarely within the history of Western philosophy. He takes issue with the position of Jaspers that Nietzsche is best read as a rejection of all philosophical certainties and challenges Heidegger's view that Nietzsche was the last metaphysician of the West. For Löwith, the centerpiece of Nietzsche's thought is the doctrine of eternal recurrence, a notion which Löwith, unlike Heidegger, deems incompatible with the will to power. (publisher, edited)

**Lomba, Joaquín**. *La raíz semítica de lo europeo: Islam y judaísmo medievales.* Madrid, Ed Akal, 1997.

Si se quiere entender en profundidad el ser de Europa, no basta con volver la mirada a Grecia y Roma para encontrar en ellas sus raíces. El mundo semita, en su vertiente musulmana y judía, constituye una de las bases fundamentales de nuestra historia y cultura. No en vano "Europa", en la mitología griega, era de ascendencia fenicia. (edited)

**Lombardi, Joseph L**. James Rachels on Kant's Basic Idea. *Amer Cath Phil Quart*, 71(1), 53-58, Wint 97.

In *The Elements of Moral Philosophy* (McGraw-Hill, 1986/1993), James Rachels claims to have isolated the "basic idea" undergirding Kantian morality. Thus, someone who accepts that certain considerations constitute good reasons for her acting in a particular way must agree that anyone similarly situated has good reasons to act likewise. The article supplies an argument articulating Rachels's presumed insight. It incorporates the "basic idea" and concludes that reason demands conformity to the categorical imperative. Unfortunately, the argument commits the "quantifier shift" fallacy. Implicit is a challenge to any attempt at deriving the universalizability requirement from the "basic idea."

**Lombo, José Angel**. La Persona y su naturaleza: Tomás de Aquino y Leonardo Polo. *Anu Filosof*, 29(2), 721-739, 1996.

Polo's philosophy is deeply rooted in Aquinas's distinction between being and essence. The author applies a circular hermeneutic. Aquinas philosophy of the person is read from the perspective of Polo's account in order to elucidate Polo's own transcendental anthropology. The exposition is structured in two parts, each one describing a fundamental thesis. The first concerns the notion of person in Thomas, which appears in his discussion of Boethius's definition. The second one deals with the problem of conciliating mind as form of the body and as a spiritual substance.

**Lomonaco, Fabrizio**. "Herder, Kant e la storia" in *Lo Storicismo e la Sua Storia: Temi, Problemi, Prospettive,* Cacciatore, Giuseppe (ed), 98-111. Milano, Guerini, 1997.

In this essay, the author compares several J.G. Herder's ideas on poetry, language and history to Kantian analysis of history. The main direction is Herder's "genetic" method which elaborates a conception of "organic force" and explains the dynamic connection between nature, religion, language and history (*Älteste Urkunde des Menschengeschlechts* 1774-1776 and *Ideen zur Philosophie der Geschichte der Menschheit*, 1784-1791). Kant views history as a necessary development toward rationality and freedom (*Idee zu einer allgemeine Geshichte in weltbürgerlicher Absicht*, 1784 and *Muthmasslicher Anfang der Menschengeschichte*, 1786, *Recensionen von J.G. Herders Ideen...*, 1785). His view of history does not seem incompatible with the substance of his philosophy (*Kritik der praktischen Vernunft*, 1788 and *Kritik der Urteilskraft*, 1790).

**Lomonaco, Fabrizio**. A propósito de *Giusnaturalismo ed etica moderna*: Notas sobre Grocio y Vico en la Vª Orazione Inaugurale V (1705). *Cuad Vico*, 5/6, 253-260, 1995/96.

From the study of Piovani's *Giusnaturalismo ed etica moderna* (Bari, Laterza, 1961)—although the core of the analysis is based on Grotius's *De iure belli ac pacis*, an author whom Vico explicitly acknowledges as one of his sources—the interconnections between philosophical reflection and legal practice are emphasized. The aim is to outline some ideas about the problems involved with the wide relationship between law-nature-history, which from a Grocian-Vichian point of view leads to a deep transformation of anthropological patterns along the lines of the universalist humanism's principles.

**Lomonaco, Fabrizio**. *Le Orationes* Di G. Gravina: Scienza, Sapienza e Diritto. Naples, La Città del Sole, 1997.

Delle *Orationes* di Gianvincenzo Gravina questo studio intende sottolineare—dal punto di vista filosofico e giuridico—i principali nuclei problematici e, in particolare, il significato del loro cartesianesimo contrassegnato da interessi pedagogico-civili. Un tema, quest'ultimo, poco frequentato dalla letteratura critica che, com'è noto, ha spesso limitato il giudizio sul Cartesio del pensatore calabrese ai soli *Originum iuris civilis libri tres*. (edited)

**Lomonaco, Fabrizio**. *Lex Regia*. Napoli, Guida, 1990.

The book consists of an introduction, three chapters, respectively dedicated to Johannes Fredericus Gronovius, Ulricus Huber and Jacobus Perizonius, an appendix that contains the first modern edition of Martin Schoock's *De figmento Legis Regiae* and an index of names. The author concentrates his inquiry on the "royal law concerning Vespasian's empire," an inscription containing the final part of an act which sanctioned the imperial power bestowed by "Senate and the People of Rome" upon Vespasian. This text dealt with crucial problems such as the origins of absolutism and the conflict between liberty and authority. In this polemic, Grotius's *De iure belli ac pacis* played an important role. The validity of Grotius's thought was questioned on the basis of the ideas of other thinkers such as Bodin, Althusius, Hobbes and Spinoza. Dutch Cartesians contributed more than other philosophers to sharpen the intellectual arguments of Dutch erudites.

**Lonergan, Bernard J F** and Sierra-Gutiérrez, Francisco (trans). La filosofía y el fenómeno religioso. *Univ Phil*, 14(27), 131-158, D 96.

Shifting from a "metaphysics of objects" to a "theory of our conscious and intentional operations," Lonergan conceives a philosophy of religion as the foundational methodology of religious studies. Momentous to this heuristic structure is Lonergan's distinction between authenticity and inauthenticity, the level of symbolic operations, interpersonal relations and religious conversion. Also, his account and ordering of the various contexts in which religious living occurs and investigations of religious living are undertaken. This is a genuine approach to the academic integrity of religious studies; a very illumination of the function religions play out in various social and cultural contexts.

**Long, A A** (ed) and Dillon, John M (ed). *The Question of "Eclecticism": Studies in Later Greek Philosophy*. Berkeley, Univ of Calif Pr, 1996.

This collection of essays is addressed to the growing number of philosophers, classicists, and intellectual historians interested in the development of Greek thought after Aristotle. In nine original studies, the authors explore the meaning and history of "eclecticism" in the context of ancient philosophy. This book casts fresh light on the methodology of such central figures as Cicero, Philo, Plutarch, Sextus, Empiricus, and Ptolemy, and also illuminates many of the conceptual issues discussed most creatively in this period. (publisher, edited)

**Long, Steven A**. Obediential Potency, Human Knowledge, and the Natural Desire for God. *Int Phil Quart*, 37(1), 45-63,, Mr 97.

**Long, Steven A**. Personal Receptivity and Act: A Thomistic Critique. *Thomist*, 61(1), 1-31, Ja 97.

**Long, Steven A**. Reply. *Thomist*, 61(3), 373-376, Jl 97.

**Longacre, Jay**. Secular Perspective of Salvation. *J Dharma*, 22(2), 111-127, Ap-Je 97.

This is a brief study of the positive value of secularization and secularity in trying to find answers to human problems away from ecclesiastical tradition and ecclesiastical control. Truth can be found in the everyday, understandable language and human areas of thought—politics, sociology, psychology, philosophy, to name just a few. Theological implications underlie every area of human discourse.

**Longega, Andrea**. Sul contrattualismo di Hobbes: una recente interpretazione. *G Crit Filosof Ital*, 17(1), 112-116, Ja-Ap 97.

**Longhini, Carlos Guillermo**. Una perspectiva sobre la relación entre historia y violencia. *Cuad Etica*, 17-18, 131-138, 1994.

This paper deals with the problematic relationship between history and violence. In doing so, it makes use of *certain* analytical categories established by M. Foucault in *some of* his works, in order to think history and power from the war-model point of view. This approach leads to reexamine the different notions of "power" which have played a decisive and influential role in accounting for historical phenomena. The consideration of the model of "politics as war continued by other means" opens a new theoretic space to disclose what is the role concerning the main notions that practical philosophy has been developed since *ancient* Greek *philosophers* to date.

**Longino, Helen E** and Lennon, Kathleen. Feminist Epistemology as a Local Epistemology. *Aris Soc*, Supp(71), 19-54, 1997.

A set of theoretical virtues drawn from feminist writings in and about the sciences contrasts interestingly with virtues described as scientific, cognitive, or epistemic in more conventional philosophy of science. The paper considers the sense in which they (or comparable candidates) could constitute elements of a feminist epistemology. It proposes that a feminist epistemology in this sense would be a local epistemology with normative force only for those who endorse its values. Local epistemology is contrasted with general epistemology.

**Longo, Rosaria**. "Il tempo nell'eternità" in *Il Concetto di Tempo: Atti del XXXII Congresso Nazionale della Società Filosofica Italiana*, Casertano, Giovanni (ed), 285-292. Napoli, Loffredo, 1997.

**Loock, Reinhard**. Gefühl und Realität: Fichtes Auseinandersetzung mit Jacobi in der *Grundlage der Wissenschaft des Praktischen*. *Fichte-Studien*, 10, 219-237, 1997.

In this essay the critical transfiguration from Jacobi's philosophy to Fichte's *Grundlage* is analyzed. In Fichte's transcendental deduction it is pointed out that the system of sentiments can only be produced by the necessary reflection of reason onto its preconscious striving. Because of this specific identity of reflection and sentiment he is able to comprehend the immediacy within the speculative system, just that immediacy that constitutes according to Jacobi the essence of reason in whole. This presented solution of the post-Kantian problem of (reflected) immediacy is in itself a fundamental contribution to the genesis of absolute idealism.

**Loparic, Zeljko**. Descartes Desconstruído. *Cad Hist Filosof Cie*, 5(1-2), 183-203, Ja-D 95.

The present article offers a schematic study of the way Heidegger reads Descartes. It begins by showing the differences between traditional methods of text interpretation and the "desconstruction" of metaphysics as practiced by Heidegger. Next, it examines the opposition between the Cartesian concept of *res extensa* and the concept of the world as an element of the structure of Being-there, in the sense of Heidegger I. Finally, it explains the main moments of the history of metaphysics in the sense of Heidegger II, namely, as a history of oblivion of the question about the sense of Being, with special attention to the position and role of Cartesian metaphysics in this happening.

**López, Bernardo Correa**. Between Ethics and Epistemology: Sartre and Bachelard, Readers of Descartes (Spanish). *Rev Filosof (Venezuela)*, Supp(2-3), 173-189, 1996.

The problem of the possibility of evaluating two types of philosophy or perhaps two types of commitment—the existentialist commitment and the rationalist commitment (Sartre-Bachelard)—serves as crux for the author's analysis of the way in which the Cartesian *cogito* is assumed. To answer the question as to which type of rationality should be used to confront the problem of ethics, scientific reason is analyzed as a model of liberty and responsibility (Bachelard) and the revindication of the common man (Sartre) in that his life is an affirmation of liberty which is at the same time both absolute and contingent.

**López Castellón, Enrique**. Autonomía y Comunidad: Sobre el debate entre comunitaristas y liberales. *Rev Filosof (Spain)*, 8(15), 183-207, 1996.

**López de Dicastillo, Luis**. La Paideia Durkheimiana: una teoría general de la educación. *Euridice*, 35-64, 1995.

The article defends that Durkheim's sociology of education has theoretical elements and practical proposals apt to interpret and participate in the generalized crises of the present cultural moment. The study, immerse in a strongly organicist general theory, is centred in education because the educative function send us to the structure and this to the mediators elements between individuals and it: the values. The work finishes with some notes that appreciate more the modernity sense and the possibilities of Durkheim's sociology to found a general updated theory of education.

**López de Dicastillo, Luis**. Marcuse: La última utopía. *Euridice*, 89-117, 1992.

Pendant la jeunesse de Marcuse les procès révolutionnaires étaient en train d'échouer. Marcuse ne cherche pas la cause de ces échecs dans l'absence de contrôle des forces objectives qui y intervenaient, mais dans les conditions psychologiques des sujets de la Révolution. L'anthropologie de Freud et la dialectique de ses topiques semble pouvoir expliquer ce qui s'ést passé et donner des orientations pour éviter des échecs à venir. La clé de l'interpretation que Marcuse fait de Freud se trouve dans la torsion, selon laquelle le principe de réalité de celui-ci devient le principe d'action de celui-là. Évidemment avec l'aide de Marx. Une fois réalisé le changement, il ne reste qu'à savoir si la même activité de l'homme est capable d'éliminer les éléments répréssifs que la principe d'action a impliqué historiquement. Marcuse considère que les sociéte industrielles avancées peuvent y réussir. Thanatos (guerre, destruction, suicide...) s'en va et Eros arrive. A quoi attendre pour accélérer sa venue? Il faut se mettre à l'oeuvre pour obtenir des sujets prêts à faire la Révolution.

**Lopez de la Vieja, Maria Teresa** (ed). *Política y Sociedad en José Ortega y Gasset: En Torno a "Vieja y Nueva Política"*. Barcelona, Anthropos, 1997.

Los artículos del texto inciden de forma especial en la vigencia de la Filosofía política de Ortega, en lo que respecta a la Teoría de la democracia, la actividad política como actividad formativa, la modernización de la sociedad, cuestiones que hoy, en efecto, interesan al lector como *ciudadano*. (publisher, edited)

**López de la Vieja, Maria Teresa**. "Élites Sin Privilegio" in *Política y Sociedad en José Ortega y Gasset: En Torno a "Vieja y Nueva Política"*, Lopez de la Vieja, Maria Teresa (ed), 141-165. Barcelona, Anthropos, 1997.

The purpose of this paper is to analyze the most relevant ideas about *Society and Politics* in the early writing of the philosopher J. Ortega y Gasset, especially concerning his theory of the elites. "Vieja y Nueva Política" focused on the role and responsibilities of the minority, who received and increased cultural goods. For this reason his theory was advocating the role of elites in the field of culture and in the public sphere. Meanwhile the political role of the elites had to be limited in democratic systems. The conclusion of the article is that, at the present time, the field of cultural activities would be implemented by minorities, but the political role had to be restricted within the rules of liberal democracy.

**López de la Vieja, Maria Teresa**. *Ética: Procedimientos Razonables*. Padrón, Novo Século, 1996.

En la Etica contemporánea los procedimientos tienden a ocupar un lugar destacado, a causa de la expansión de los elementos reflexivos que cobraron importancia desde la Filosofía moderna. La racionalidad práctica resulta a veces poco explícita sobre cuestiones más sustantivas, al ocuparse ante todo de la justificación de los principios. El presente trabajo llama la atención sobre principios y procedimientos complementarios en la la Filosofía moral. Los *procedimientos razonables* configuran un espacio en el cual la crítica de los sistemas de dominio, las voces de la diferencia, la comprensión de otras pautas de cultura, la relevancia de los contextos, la moral de las profesiones, la construcción de una cultura europea, la recepción de teorías, el cuestionamiento del pasado o bien la complejidad del presente, responden aún al despliegue de la razón en la Etica. (publisher)

**López de la Vieja, Maria Teresa** (ed). *Figuras del Logos: Entre la Filosofía y la Literatura*. Madrid, Fondo de Cultura, 1994.

¿Qué es o qué debe ser la Filosofía? ¿Cuáles han sido y cuáles pueden ser sus relaciones con otras disciplinas? La perspectiva simultánea de Filosofía y Literatura permite valorar qué grado de conocimiento hay en la ficción, cómo se construyen subjetividad y texto, mundo y lenguaje. *Figuras del logos: Ensayos entre la Filosofía y la Literatura* muestra las posibilidades, teóricas y prácticas, de la relación interna entre diferentes espacios argumentativos. Entre actividades que poseen una vertiente creativa y, a la vez, una importante faceta reflexiva. Han colaborado en el texto especialistas de distinta formación y procedencia: la Universidad Autónoma de México, Universidad de Konstanz, de Bochum, State University de Nueva York, la Universidad Complutense de Madrid, Autónoma de Barcelona, C.S.I.C. de Madrid, Universidad de Salamanca. (publisher)

**López Fernández, Alvaro**. Constativas kantianas y realizativas cartesianas: el yo pienso como emisión realizativa. *Dialogos*, 32(69), 175-201, Ja 97.

The central theme of the investigation is the Kantian concept of the *I think (Ich denke)*. Some differences between the Cartesian *ego cogito* and the Kantian *Ich denke* are considered. The Kantian *Ich denke* can be partially understood with the help of a concept which I call *epistemic I think*. The Kantian *I think* is analyzed in the light of Austin's division of emissions in *constative* and *performative*, and of the Kantian classification of analytic and synthetic judgments. This allows one to introduce the concept of *Kantian constatives* and *Cartesian performatives*. These last constitute an essential feature of the Kantian *Ich denke*.

**López Fernández, Alvaro**. La paradoja de la unidad originaria de la conciencia en la intuición pura y de la multiplicidad a priori de la sensibilidad. *Dialogos*, 31(68), 83-117, Jl 96.

**López Frías, Francisco**. La recepción del Utilitarismo en el mundo hispánico: El caso de Ortega y Gasset. *Telos (Spain)*, 1(3), 111-144, O 92.

**López Gil, Marta**. La noción de inconmensurabilidad y la realidad de los otros o el derecho a la diferencia. *Cuad Etica*, 21-22, 75-82, 1996.

Recurrir a la noción de *diferencia* no es ni sencillo ni convincente cuando se trata de defender una ética distinta a la absolutista y/o universalista propia de la modernidad (no de toda: siempre hubo un contradiscurso imposible de ignorar). Adoptar la *inconmensurabilidad* como un concepto más agregado al anterio complica también las cosas. Sin embargo, trabajo con esos conceptos a los cuales sumo el de *conflicto* en un intento teórico de pensar la ética desde una óptica que satisfaga más mi perplejidad actual en este mundo complejo, multicultural, inabarcable para un individuo angustiado y tentado de "encerrarse en su corazón" y abandonar el ruedo público.

**López Lloret, Jorge**. Más allá del bosque (Reflexiones agoralógicas en torno a Vico). *Cuad Vico*, 7/8, 377-389, 1997.

At present it is research into the complex relation between country and city. However, country and city are in fact urban ways of life. This can be inferred from Vico's words. Actually the opposition is between the woodland life and the urban life. The man as urban being is the being that has got word and the being that have got history. From this Vichian point of view, we will understand that the barbarity of reason is waiting for us.

**López Sáenz, Maria Carmen**. El paradigma del texto en la filosofía hermenéutica. *Pensamiento*, 53(206), 215-242, My-Ag 97.

La hermenéutica ontológica contemporánea considera que el ser es comprensión y que la interpretación forma parte integrante de éste. Hoy en día la interpretación se entiende como un componente de todo tipo de saber; de ahí el auge de la hermenéutica. En este artículo damos cuenta de este hecho al analizar la aproximación de H. G. Gadamer al problema del texto y de su interpretación y confrontaria con la de P. Ricoeur. El texto ocupa un puesto central en la estructura universal de la lingüisticidad y sirve, además, como paradigma de las ciencias humanas y sociales. Gadamer define el texto eminente como aquél que precisa interpretación; ésta es inseparable de la comprensión y de la aplicación a nuestra situación. Interpretar un texto es comprender su verdad abriéndose al mundo que ofrece. (edited)

**López-Domínguez, Virginia**. "Del Yo a la naturaleza por el camino del arte" in *El inicio del Idealismo alemán,* Market, Oswaldo, 281-289. Madrid, Ed Complutense, 1996.

Schelling's conception of nature rises not only in opposition to Fichte's ethical idealism but also as a result of a radical appropriation of his thought, in particular, of the idea of freedom. Schelling assumes the idealism from a mystical intuition of freedom that requires, from the beginning, an overcoming of the moral sphere that conducts him to an aesthetical view of world, explicitly affirmed since 1800. This view, latent in his first writings, obliges him to reformulate the function of nature and is present in the configuration of his conception of intellectual intuition.

**López-Domínguez, Virginia**. Die Deduktion des Gefühls in der *Grundlage der gesamten Wissenschaftslehre*. *Fichte-Studien*, 10, 209-218, 1997.

The study on feeling made in the *Grundlage* is presented as union nexus for Fichte's philosophy on three different levels: There is a parallelism between it

and the deduction of representation. Both concern to the I series, in which the I becomes conscious of both his practical and theoretical products respectively. Feeling constitutes the intimate aspect of action, while it apports contents to knowledge and formal ethics. As a result, it is neither purely accidental nor irrational and can grant unity to the entire human being. Finally, feeling (love) serves as a bridge to the mature theory of religion.

**Loptson, Peter J**. Critical Notice of J.J. MacIntosh and H.A. Meynell, eds. *Faith, Scepticism and Personal Identity: A Festschrift for Terence Penelhum. Can J Phil*, 27(1), 111-132, Mr 97.

**Lorca, Andrés Martínez**. El concepto de *civitas* en la teoría política de Tomás de Aquino. *Analogia*, 10(2), 139-150, 1996.

**Lorca, Daniel**. Kant Was Not Able to Distinguish True from False Experiences. *Dialogue (PST)*, 38(2-3), 33-42, Ap 96.

**Lorente Tallada, Juan Manuel** and Ubeda Rives, José Pedro. "Representación de la relación de afianzamiento epistémico en *Prolog*" in *Verdad: lógica, representación y mundo*, Villegas Forero, L, 355-367. Santiago de Compostela, Univ Santiago Comp, 1996.

Within the framework of the model of belief change of Alchourrón, Gärdenfors, Makinson [1985], Gärdenfors [1988] proposes the relation of epistemic entrenchment between sentences as a procedure to uniquely determine the contraction and revision function for an arbitrary theory. In this paper this relation is analyzed when the language of sentences is PROLOG and a procedure is presented to represent this relation in PROLOG.

**Lorentzen, Lois Ann** (& others) and Mendieta, Eduardo and Batstone, David. *Liberation Theologies, Postmodernity, and the Americas*. New York, Routledge, 1997.

Over the last thirty years, liberation theology has irrevocably altered religious thinking and practice throughout the Americas. Liberation theology rises up at the margins of social power. Drawing its energies from the black community in the United States, grassroots religious communities in Latin America and feminist circles in North Atlantic countries, theologies of liberation have emerged as a resource and inspiration for people seeking social and political freedom. (publisher, edited)

**Lorenzi-Cioldi, Fabio**. Psychological Androgyny: A Concept in Seach of Lesser Substance. Towards the Understanding of the Transformation of a Social Representation. *J Theor Soc Behav*, 26(2), 137-155, Je 96.

The term 'androgyny' has been given a variety of meanings, in psychology as well as in popular thinking. This paper aims at distinguishing the most important meanings of this term, and at showing that scientific and lay conceptions of what is or should be an androgynous person share many features, but less and less so. It then elaborates on this striking similarity between scientific and lay psychology by demonstrating that: a) Three conceptions of androgyny have prevailed over the time; b) This evolution has been prompted by a need to counteract the objectification of the androgynous individual into the sexually ambiguous individual; c) The inaugural conception of psychological androgyny was concerned with the content of the androgynous personality, whereas a marked cognitive orientation characterized later conceptions; d) As a consequence, the concept of psychological androgyny has evolved towards lesser substance. Presently, this concept has succeeded in departing from lay representations of the sexually ambiguous individual, but it has lost its anchoring in the social group. This evolution of the concept of psychological androgyny is discussed in light of the process of objectification propounded by the theory of social representations.

**Loretoni, Anna**. Un discorso morale sulla guerra. *Iride*, 8(15), 422-430, Ag 95.

La teoria di Walzer dei diritti degli stati (integrità territoriale e sovranità giuridica) offre una sorta di "paradigma giuridico" per regolamentare la società internazionale secondo il principio della *domestic analogy.* Secondo l'Autrice però il discorso morale di Walzer mostra la sua inefficacia politica qualora venga inteso come svincolato dagli assetti istituzionali e dalla revisione critica della sovranità istituzionale.

**Lories, Danielle**. Du bon sens le mieux partagé.... *Rev Phil Louvain*, 94(2), 243-270, My 96.

This article sets out to contrast Cartesian generosity with the *phronesis* of the *Nicomachean Ethics* under four headings. 1) The two virtues confront the contingency of a situation and seek to bring together its particularity with a universal; hence the certainty of the judgment in question is of a different order to that in science. 2) These virtues have a normative relationship to the ethical virtues and determine for them a measure which is the right middlepoint. 3) They have a twofold aspect, intellectual and more truly moral, the components of which are circular. 4) They portray a respectful, favourable and friendly relationship with other people. What generosity reveals in this way is that it is Cartesian to recognize the impossibility of laying down general laws of human action as one lays down laws of nature, to admit that the wisest thing to do is to rely in the order of action on the good will that is at least possible in each individual and on its judgment, thus to attain the greatest importance to individual *freedom* and its absoluteness in each of us.

**Lorini, Giuseppe**. Deontica in Rose Rand. *Riv Int Filosof Diritto*, 74(4), 197-251, Ap-Je 97.

**Lorite Mena, José**. Antropología y alteridad: De la naturaleza humana a la normalidad social. *Daimon Rev Filosof*, 12, 79-91, Ja-Je 96.

L'Anthropologie, en tant que "science de la culture", naît comme un regard vers l'*autre*. La composition de ce regard est soutenue par la nouvelle distribution que la pensée européenne fait du normal et du pathologique dans son propre espace. Dans cette visibilité de l'altérité jouent un rôle décisif et symétrique la Médecine et la Mythologie.

**Lorite Mena, José**. *Sociedades sin Estado: El Pensamiento de los Otros*. Madrid, Ed Akal, 1995.

Parece adecuado que una Historia de la Cultura comience por un deslindamiento que impida la confusión (es decir, tanto la invasión como la transgresión). Y ese deslindamiento comporta necesariamente el trazado de *señas de identidad*. La propia definición de lo Otro como *sociedades sin estado* muestra que sólo negativamente, en un doble movimiento de rechazo y reconversión violenta (entre la nostalgia de lo que *podríamos haber sido* y el terror ante lo que *nunca deberíamos ser*: salvajes, primitivos), hemos dado cuenta del Otro—hemos suprimido su radical alteridad. (edited)

**Lorite-Mena, José**. *La metáfora moderna del pensamiento*. Murcia, Murcia, 1996.

The text stems from an assertion and develops with a proposal. The assertion is the rupture that has occurred since Kant and Nietzsche in the ways that the foundation of reality in philosophy and science are seen (First part). The proposal is the need to change realism (i.e., common sense) in our various cultural forms (Second part). Evolution, relativity, thermodynamics..., are not only scientific theories but, in fact, they also require the inclusion of man in the world in a different way (*a new alliance*: Prigogine).

**Losonsky, Michael**. John Locke on Passion, Will and Belief. *Brit J Hist Phil*, 4(2), 267-283, S 96.

**Losurdo, Domenico**. Marx, Columbus, and the October Revolution: Historical Materialism and the Analysis of Revolutions. *Nature Soc Thought*, 9(1), 65-86, 1996.

The October Revolution did not achieve its declared objectives, (Abolition of social classes, of states, of nations, of the market, of religion). Was it a failure? The Jacobites didn't restore the ancient polis; the American revolutions did not create the society of small farmers and producers. The case of Columbus who set off in search of the Indies but discovered America will serve as a metaphor to understand the dialectic of revolution. This was emphasized by Marx and Engels. The methodology they devised also has to be applied to a revolution which they inspired. What is the new continent discovered by the October Revolution?

**Lotringer, Sylvère**. A Conversation with Sylvère Lotringer. *Conference*, 6(1), 3-14, Sum 95.

**Lottenbach, Hans**. Monkish Virtues, Artificial Lives: On Hume's Genealogy of Morals. *Can J Phil*, 26(3), 367-388, S 96.

Hume's moral philosophy is often interpreted as an example of a naturalistic approach to ethics (in terms of general psychological or sociological laws). But if Hume is developing a general explanatory theory of moral sentiments, he must give an account of the apparent counterexamples to this theory: the approbation of 'useless' or 'monkish' virtues. An examination of how Hume (in the *Treatise*, the second *Enquiry*, and the *Essays*) deals with these counterexamples leads us to a reinterpretation of his 'experimental method' and to a new understanding of his ethics (as a position and self-enforcing genealogy of morals).

**Lottenbach, Hans**. Subjectivism, Utility, and Autonomy. *Pac Phil Quart*, 77(1), 19-35, Mr 96.

Taking as a starting point a thesis of David Gauthier's about the status of Rational Choice Theory, I discuss the relation between a subjectivist theory of value and an account of rational agency that leaves room for autonomy. I argue that if autonomy presupposes an activity of practical reason, the maximization of subjective expected utility (as prescribed by Rational Choice Theory) cannot serve as the principle of practical reason.

**Louch, Alfred**. Sick with Passion. *Phil Lit*, 21(1), 155-166, Ap 97.

Death, particularly of divas, has always been standard operatic fare. That they sometimes succumb to disease is also not surprising, since that process affords composer and librettist maximum opportunities for the display of melancholy emotions. The Hucheons, in *Opera: Desire, Disease, Death*, think to add a dimension to our understanding or appreciation of select operas by adding clinical diagnoses and medical sociology. Alas, in some cases opera buffs are in the know already and in the rest the diagnoses seem unwarranted.

**Louden, Robert B**. What is Moral Authority?. *Ancient Phil*, 17(2), 103-118, Spr 97.

In this essay I explore three underappreciated intellectual virtues concerned with conduct which are discussed briefly by Aristotle in *Nicomachean Ethics* VI.9-11: *euboulia* (good deliberation), *sunesis* (comprehension) and *gnomē* (judgment). By comparing and contrasting them to one another as well as to the most significant and comprehensive intellectual virtue concerned with conduct (*phronēsis*, practical wisdom), I show that significant remainders exist in the latter once these three subordinate virtues are peeled away from it. A fuller picture of *phronēsis* is thereby arrived at.

**Loui, Michael**. Commentary on "Better Communication between Engineers and Managers. *Sci Eng Ethics*, 3(2), 215-216, Ap 97.

**Loui, Michael** and Bakker II, Willem. Can Designing and Selling Low-Quality Products Be Ethical?. *Sci Eng Ethics*, 3(2), 153-170, Ap 97.

Whereas previous studies have criticized low-quality products for inadequate safety, this paper considers only safe products and it examines the ethics of designing and selling low-quality products. Product quality is defined as suitability to a general purpose. The duty that companies owe to consumers is summarized in the Consumer-Oriented Process principle: "to place an increase in the consumer's quality of life as the primary goal for producing products." This principle is applied in analyzing the primary ethical justifications for low-quality products: availability and applicability. Finally, a low-quality product should be designed afresh, not by altering an existing high-quality product.

**Louis, Desmeules** and Desjardins, Richard. A propos de l'Éducation et de l'Institution scolaire au Québec. *Philosopher*, 18, 25-36, 1995.

Cet article vise à établir des distinction, à poser des questions et, ultimement à énoncer des thèses sur l'éducation et l'institution scolaire au Québec. Il s'agit de cerner l'importance des forces économiques qui travaillent le pouvoir de l'État, nous devons aussi reconnaître que l'exercice du pouvoir de l'État s'articule sur d'autres rapports de forces de grande importance, principalement de nature idéologique. Nous croyons que l'institution scolaire, tout comme l'institution des services de santé, subit actuellement les contrecoups d'une réorganisation des économies occidentales capitalistes que les réformes actuelles servent tout à la fois à occulter et à justifier.

**Louw, Stephen**. Response to Richard Hudelson. *Phil Soc Sci*, 27(2), 209-211, Je 97.

**Louw, Stephen**. Unity and Development: Social Homogeneity, the Totalitarian Imaginary, and the Classical Marxist Tradition. *Phil Soc Sci*, 27(2), 180-205, Je 97.

This article examines the relationship between the classical Marxist tradition and the conceptual roots of totalitarianism. Here totalitarianism is understood to entail the attempt to frame the developmental impulses of modernity within the logic of a premodern political imaginary—defined as internally homogeneous and transparent to itself. In the first part, we take issue with those who try to distinguish between the thought of Marx and Engels, and who insist that it is only in Engels's thought that the traces of a totalitarian politics might be found. In the second section, we outline briefly the context within which Marx's thought was developed, after which we argue that Marx's vision of communism is dependent on the three-phase vision of historical process which he inherited from Hegel. Without denying the historical peculiarities of the imposition of communism in Russia, we conclude that it is out of this latter vision of history that the conceptual roots of totalitarianism must be located.

**Louw, Tobias J G**. "Democracy in an Ethical Community" in *Philosophy and Democracy in Intercultural Perspective*, Kimmerle, Heinz (ed), 203-219. Amsterdam, Rodopi, 1997.

**Loux, Michael J**. Kinds and Categories: Proceedings of the Twentieth Annual Greensboro Symposium in Philosophy. *Phil Papers*, 26(1), 3-28, Ap 97.

**Love, Jim L** and Plumly, L Wayne and Ostapski, S Andrew. The Ethical and Economic Implications of Smoking in Enclosed Public Facilities: A Resolution of Conflicting Rights. *J Bus Ethics*, 16(4), 377-384, Mr 97.

Smokers and nonsmokers possess equal rights but those rights conflict with each other in the use of shared facilities. Medical research has established that smoking harms not only those who use the product but also those who are passively exposed to it. Laws and private regulation of smoking in shared facilities have resulted in the segregation of smokers from nonsmokers to an outright ban of tobacco use. Such controls have provided unsatisfactory results to both groups. An acceptable ethical solution, based on reduction of harm and compensation, can be derived by applying *moral audit* principles, supported by economic analysis, which does not unduly curtail the rights of both parties as to the use of tobacco products.

**Loveys, James** and Chowdhury, Ambar and Tanovic, Predrag. A Definable Continuous Rank for Nonmultidimensional Superstable Theories. *J Sym Log*, 61(3), 967-984, S 96.

**Loveys, James** and Tanovic, Predrag. Countable Model of Trivial Theories Which Admit Finite Coding. *J Sym Log*, 61(4), 1279-1286, D 96.

We prove: *Theorem*. A complete first order theory in a countable language which is strictly stable, trivial and which admits finite coding has $2^{\aleph_0}$ nonisomorphic countable models. Combined with the corresponding result or superstable theories from our result confirms the Vaught conjecture for trivial theories which admit finite coding.

**Lovibond, Sabina**. The 'Late Seriousness' of Cora Diamond. *J Phil Res*, 22, 43-55, Ap 97.

**Low, Douglas**. Merleau-Ponty and the Liberal/Communitarian Debate. *J Phil Res*, 22, 357-386, Ap 97.

The main goal of this essay is to bring the works of Merleau-Ponty to bear on the liberal/communitarian debate. His works antedate and in many ways anticipate the themes currently being raised by this debate. I hope to show that Merleau-Ponty comes between liberalism and communitarianism. On the one hand, he supports liberalism's claim about the importance of individual rights, yet on the other hand, he supports communitarianism by claiming that without certain social and political communities, to which we owe allegiance, these rights would be nonexistent.

**Lowe, E J**. Conditional Probability and Conditional Beliefs. *Mind*, 105(420), 603-615, O 96.

Much philosophical ink has been spilt on the relationship between conditional statements and conditional probability, including a proof by David Lewis that the probability of a conditional's being true cannot on pain of triviality be identified with a conditional probability, and a defence by Dorothy Edgington of the thesis that, for this very reason, conditional statements do not express propositions and do not have truth-conditions. It is Edgington's position that I particularly wish to examine in this paper, though I also have more general points to make both about conditionals and about the notion of conditional probability. (edited)

**Lowe, E J**. Ontological Categories and Natural Kinds. *Phil Papers*, 26(1), 29-46, Ap 97.

The aim of this paper is to examine the ways in which the a priori categorial distinctions of ontology combine with the a posteriori deliverances of observation and scientific theory to yield and justify our conception of the world as constituted by individual substances belonging to discrete natural kinds. The issue is approached through a consideration of the problem of substantial change, since a principled differentiation of kinds presupposes a solution to this problem.

**Lowe, E J**. Reply to Noonan on Vague Identity. *Analysis*, 57(1), 88-91, Ja 97.

Harold Noonan concedes the force of an objection I raise against Gareth Evans's argument that there cannot be ontically indeterminate identity statements, but tries to establish the same conclusion by another line of reasoning which does not appeal to identity-involving properties. However, it can be seen that Noonan's new argument is no more satisfactory than Evans's, once due account is taken of the tensed character of properties of the kind to which Noonan appeals.

**Lowenthal, David**. Forgiare e dimenticare: i doveri dell'oblio. *Iride*, 8(14), 95-109, Ap 95.

**Lucas, John R**. The Unity of Science without Reductionism. *Acta Analytica*, 89-95, 1996.

The unity of science is often thought to be reductionist, but this is because we fail to distinguish questions from answers. The questions asked by different sciences are different—the biologist is interested in different topics from the physicist and seeks different explanations—but the answers are not peculiar to each particular science and can range over the whole of scientific knowledge. The biologist is interested in organisms—concept unknown to physics—but explains physiological processes in terms of chemistry, not a mysterious vital force. The replacement of Laplacian determinism by quantum mechanics further erodes the tendency towards reductionism. The answers given in different explanations are not subsumed under one complete theory; and quantum mechanics does not have a concept of haecceitas, "this-i-ness" which would make its entities the fundamental constituents of everything.

**Lucas Jr, George R**. "Philosophy's Recovery of Its History: A Tribute to John E. Smith" in *The Recovery of Philosophy in America: Essays in Honor of John Edwin Smith*, Kasulis, Thomas P (ed), 11-37. Albany, SUNY Pr, 1997.

**Lucas Jr, George R**. "Recollection, Forgetting, and the Hermeneutics of History: Meditations on a Theme from Hegel" in *Hegel, History, and Interpretation*, Gallagher, Shaun, 97-115. Albany, SUNY Pr, 1997.

**Lucas Jr, George R**. The Seventh Seal: On the Fate of Whitehead's Proposed Rehabilitation. *Process Stud*, 25, 104-116, 1996.

Using the imagery of Ingmar Bergman's apocalyptic film of this title, the author argues that scholars of Whitehead's work and followers of process philosophy generally have, like Bergman's medieval knight, a "god obsession" that blinds them to the threat of the pending historical oblivion of their other philosophical interests. Comparing Whitehead to Aristotle, the author argues that theology played a relatively minor role in his cosmology; comparing contemporary Whiteheadians to Thomists, the author argues that these subsequent followers have distorted or lost the broad cosmological perspective that originally made Whitehead's work interesting. In particular, discussing critical reception of his 1989 book, *The Rehabilitation of Whitehead*, the author calls attention to numerous contemporary themes in analytic and continental philosophy to which Whitehead's own thought makes substantial, original, plausible and construction contributions.

**Lucey, Kenneth G** (ed). *On Knowing and the Known: Introductory Readings in Epistemology*. Amherst, Prometheus, 1996.

What do we mean when we say we "know" something? What is knowledge and how do we come by it? What counts as an object of knowledge and how can we tell when someone's knowledge claim lacks foundation? How can we distinguish "knowing" from "believing," "understanding," "feeling sure," "being certain," "having adequate evidence for," "being justified in believing," and the like? On what basis do we defend our claims to know this or that against skeptics who deny that knowledge is possible or who contend that the criteria for knowing can never be satisfied? These questions and many others are addressed in this fascinating collection of essays featuring leading philosophers who discuss the nature, meaning, and extent of human knowledge. (publisher,edited)

**Luckner, Kleia R** and Weinfeld, Irwin J. Informed Consent as a Parent Involvement Model in the NICU. *Bioethics Forum*, 11(1), 35-41, Spr 95.

The informed consent doctrine can be a viable model that ensures and enhances parental input in the decision-making process in the neonatal intensive care unit (NICU). Throughout medical history the purpose and practice of informed consent and patient disclosure has often been to encourage the patient to agree to what the physician wanted to do. A new understanding of this doctrine is necessary for both health care givers and patients, one that views informed consent as a process of mutual discovery, shared options and dialogue.

**Ludlow, Peter** (ed). *Readings in the Philosophy of Language*. Cambridge, MIT Pr, 1997.

A central theme of this collection is that the philosophy of language, or at least a core portion of it, has matured to the point where it is now being spun off into linguistic theory. Each section of the book contains historical (twentieth-century) readings and, where available, recent attempts to apply the resources of contemporary linguistic theory to the problems under discussion. This approach helps to root the naturalization project in the leading questions of analytic philosophy. Although the older readings predate the current naturalization project, they help to lay its conceptual foundations. The main sections of the book, each of which is preceded by an introduction, are "Language and Meaning," "Logical Form and Grammatical Form," "Definite and Indefinite Descriptions," "Names," "Demonstratives," and "Attitude Reports."(publisher, edited)

**Ludlow, Peter**. Social Externalism and Memory: A Problem?. *Acta Analytica*, 69-76, 1995.

In this note some of the consequences of externalism (setting aside the question of its truth or falsity) are pursued. One of the most interesting threads in this pursuit has been the question of what consequences externalism may have (if any) for the doctrine that we have a priori knowledge of our mental states. In a recent paper, I argued that certain problems about social externalism and self-knowledge might be avoided if one adopted an externalist view about the nature of memory. Since then, Frank Hofmann has observed that the view of memory I suggested itself gives rise to a number of unwelcome consequences. In this note, I comment on these alleged consequences and to offer one possible solution. (edited)

**Ludwig, Bernd**. Will die Natur unwiderstehlich die Republik? Einige Reflexionen anlässlich einer rätselhaften Textpassage in Kants Friedensschrift. *Kantstudien*, 88(2), 218-228, 1997.

The famous proverb 'If the reed is bent too far, it breaks; and he who wants too much gets nothing' does not make sense at its original place in Kant's 'Perpetual Peace'. The correct place of the proverb is indicated and thus the way is prepared for an adequate interpretation of 'nature's guarantee of perpetual peace'.

**Ludwig, Bernd** and Herb, Karlfriedrich. Kants kritisches Staatsrecht. *Jahr Recht Ethik*, 2, 431-478, 1994.

Contrary to popular assumption, Kant's theory of state experienced a major transformation during the period between "On the Common Saying" of 1793 and the "Metaphysical First Principles of the Doctrine of Right" of 1797. This transformation is primarily expressed in the systematic new formulation of the relationship between "noumenal state" and "phenomenal state". Kant's new system permits him, on the one hand, to develop the idea of state a priori from his theory of private right and thus to systematically incorporate central elements of the modern tradition, including Rousseau's "Contrat social". On the other hand, it allows him to formulate the theory of state forms as a theory of the "phenomenal state", which in turn provides a tool for legal evaluation of the then current political events in revolutionary France. (edited)

**Ludwig, Kirk A**. "Shape Properties and Perception" in *Perception*, Villanueva, Enrique (ed), 325-350. Atascadero, Ridgeview, 1996.

This paper responds to John Campbell's "Molyneux's Problem." Campbell argues for three claims: if shape properties are categorical, then perception of shape is externalist; if perception of shape properties is externalist, then there is no difference in the phenomenal character of shape experience in sight and touch; if externalism about shape perception is correct, then cross modal transfer of information is rational. I argue that shape properties are categorical, that the cross modal transfer of information is rational, and that none of these conditionals, contrary to Campbell's claims, can be shown to be true on nontruth functional grounds.

**Ludwig, Kirk A**. Duplicating Thoughts. *Mind Lang*, 11(1), 92-102, Mr 96.

i) Would a duplicate of me have the same thoughts I do? ii) Would it speak my language? iii) Would it have any thoughts, or iv) speak any language at all? I give a taxonomy of views on content determination, classify arguments for externalism, and argue for the following theses. Standard semantical arguments unwarrantedly assume that if attitudes attributed using sentences for natural languages are relationally individuated, then all thoughts are individuated relationally. The answers to i) and ii) are 'no', but questions iii) and iv) are empirical questions.

**Lübbe, Hermann**. Netzverdichtung: Zur Philosophie industrie-gesellschaftlicher Entwicklungen. *Z Phil Forsch*, 50(1/2), 133-150, Ja-Je 96.

**Lueken, Geert-Lueke**. On Showing in Argumentation. *Phil Invest*, 20(3), 205-223, Jl 97.

There is a relation between the way we analyse argument and how we view the role of showing in argumentation. The concept of showing covers different ideas. Different kinds of showing are present in argumentative practice. This can be exemplified by reference to sensory evidence, logical inference and analogical arguments. If showing plays an essential role in the argumentative use of language, an analysis trying to completely replace what is shown by something explicitly said distorts what it is trying to grasp. Analysing an argument is interpreting and continuing argumentative practice; it does not operate on a separate level.

**Lüthe, Rudolf**. "Die Unterstellung von Vernunft in der Geschichte: Vorläufiger kritischer Versuch über einen Aspekt von Kants Geschichtsphilosophie" in *Grenzen der kritischen Vernunft*, Schmid, Peter A, 243-256. Basel, Schwabe Verlag, 1997.

**Lütterfelds, Wilhelm**. Das *objektive Selbst* (Nagel)—Eine Destruktion oder Rekonstruktion transzendentaler Subjektivität?. *Fichte-Studien*, 13, 161-171, 1997.

In seinem Buch "Der Blick von nirgendwo" (Frankfurt a. M. 1992) hat Thomas Nagel eine Konzeption des Subjekts vorgelegt, die unter dem Titel des "objektiven Selbst" nicht nur verblüffende und detaillierte Ähnlichkeiten mit der idealistischen Theorie des transzendenten Subjekts aufweist. Vielmehr scheint auch der Idealismus-externe Ausgangspunkt der Nagelschen Analysen eine phänomenale Basis dafür zu bieten, dass sich der Begriff des transzendentalen Subjekts auch im normalen Selbstverständnis des Alltags verankern lässt und somit im Rückgriff auf nicht-idealistische Theoriezusammenhänge gerechtfertigt werden kann.

**Lütterfelds, Wilhelm**. Kant oder Berkeley? Zum aktuellen Streit um den korrekten Realismus. *Perspekt Phil*, 22, 305-340, 1996.

Für die aktuelle Diskussion um ein korrektes Konzept des Aussenwelt-Realismus ist die Gegenüberstellung der Theorien von Kant und Berkeley hilfreich. Während Kant einen empirischen Aussenwelt-Realismus mit dessen idealistischer Begründung verbindet, reduziert Berkeley die erfahrbare Welt in

Raum, und Zeit auf den psychischen Vorstellungsinhalt eines weltimmanenten Subjekts und seiner Ideen. Dieser empirische Idealismus Berkeleys ist jedoch selbstwidersprüchlich und mündet in einer absurden Interpretation der perspektivischen Wahrnehmung realer Dinge ausser uns.

**Luft, Sandra Rudnick**. "Embodying the Eye of Humanism: Giambattista Vico and the Eye of *Ingenium*" in *Sites of Vision,* Levin, David Michael (ed), 167-197. Cambridge, MIT Pr, 1997.

If, as Heidegger asserts, the Greek ennobling of intellectual vision culminated in Descartes's epistemological subject, Vico's *New Science* presented an alternative—a poetic science of a human world made by the "seeing" of the eye of *ingenium*, the imaginative capacity of corporeal beings. "Seeing" was, metaphorically, the activity of an originary, ontologically constructive metaphoric language which made the true—the social world—by "seeing" what did not exist. This paper argues *verum-factum* is not an epistemological but ontological principle asserting the true is artefactual, "knowing" a hermeneutic of making: and discusses affinities between Heidegger's hermeneutic ontology and Vico's ontology of poetic making.

**Lukac de Stier, María L**. El aristotelismo y el tomismo frente al egoísmo psicológico. *Sapientia*, 52(201), 3-13, 1997.

**Lukács, Georg**. Chvostism and Dialectics (Introduced and Commentaries by László Illés) (in Hungarian). *Magyar Filozof Szemle*, 4-5-6, 459-537, 1996.

**Lukasiewicz, Dariusz**. The Category of the State of Things in Husserl's *Logical Investigations* (in Polish). *Kwartalnik Filozof*, 24(3), 63-87, 1996.

**Luke, Andrew**. Tackling Crime by Other Means. *J Applied Phil*, 13(2), 179-188, 1996.

If crime is a social problem, then ways of preventing it must be sought. Punishment has been the traditional approach to preventing crime, either as a deterrent, or a means of reforming the offender. Neither of these approaches is wholly acceptable. Even if deterrence punishment, as grounded in utilitarianism, effectively prevents crime, there may be other methods which produce better results. Reform fails to justify any form of punishment since not only does punishment not reform, but it interferes with the reformative process. Reform is limited in scope to those people who commit crimes and are caught. If crime is to be prevented, then it is necessary to go beyond the crime and the criminal and consider the social contexts in which people act, and the ways in which they learn to react to them. By shaping both the environment and people's responses to it, society can solve the problem of preventing crime, without the need for punishment.

**Luke, Brian**. A Critical Analysis of Hunters' Ethics. *Environ Ethics*, 19(1), 25-44, Spr 97.

I analyze the "Sportsman's Code," arguing that several of its rules presuppose a respect for animals that renders hunting a *prima facie* wrong. I summarize the main arguments used to justify hunting and consider them in relation to the *prima facie* case against hunting entailed by the sportsman's code. Sport hunters, I argue are in a paradoxical position—the more conscientiously they follow the code, the more strongly their behavior exemplifies a respect for animals that undermines the possibilities of justifying hunting altogether. I consider several responses, including embracing the paradox, renouncing the code, and renouncing hunting.

**Luke, Carmen**. Feminist Pedagogy Theory: Reflections on Power and Authority. *Educ Theor*, 46(3), 283-302, Sum 96.

**Lukes, Steven**. Social Justice: The Hayekian Challenge. *Crit Rev*, 11(1), 65-80, Wint 97.

Hayek's argument that social justice is a mirage consists of six claims: that the very idea of social justice is meaningless, religious, self-contradictory and ideological; that realizing any degree of social justice is unfeasible; and that aiming to do so must destroy all liberty. These claims are examined in the light of contemporary theories and debates concerning social justice in order to assess whether the argument's persuasive power is due to sound reasoning and to what extent contemporary theories of justice meet or escape the Hayekian challenge.

**Lukes, Steven**. Toleration and Recognition. *Ratio Juris*, 10(2), 213-222, Je 97.

The author asks: Is there a case for redefining toleration as the recognition of excluded identities? He is inclined to answer no. Liberal democratic states should of course recognize disfavored groups by registering the normality of their members and the justice of their claims but must resist recognition in any stronger sense. Appropriate recognition consists in confronting the live contemporary issues of exclusion and of ethnic and national injustice by compensatory policies and constitutional innovations.

**Luksic, Branimir**. Difference and Consensus. *Filozof Istraz*, 16(3), 641-651, 1996.

The author contends that in a world of radical ontological and epistemic difference tolerance means indifference to such difference owing to the alleged total incommensurability of differing values and opinions. He then analyses some makeshifts intended to redress this radical difference of truth and value, like the so-called consensual theory of truth and Habermas's ethics of discourse and universal pragmatics and he finds them insufficient as a basis for an ethical consensus which is today urgently needed for the survival of mankind. The author suggests that such a pragmatic consensus could perhaps be established recognizing the common nature of human beings, their biological, mental and spiritual values. (edited)

**Lumer, Christoph**. Habermas' Diskursethik. *Z Phil Forsch*, 51(1), 42-64, Ja-Mr 97.

First, the main theses of Habermas's discourse ethics are presented, especially the principle of universalization U, and the principle of discourse ethics D. 2)

Then a detailed analysis shows that Habermas's arguments for these principles are fallacious in various respects. The consideration of earlier versions of these arguments and later comments by Habermas reveals in Habermas some turning away from transcendental pragmatics towards intuitionism and that he weakens to zero his claim to have founded those principles. 3) A criticism of four interpretations of U and 4) of the two main interpretations of D shows that these criteria of morality are unsuitable in many respects and that they are only verbal combinations of ideals difficult to combine.

**Lumpkin, James R** and Hamilton III, J Brooke and Strutton, David. An Essay on When to Fully Disclose in Sales Relationships: Applying Two Practical Guidelines for Addressing Truth-Telling Problems. *J Bus Ethics*, 16(5), 545-560, Ap 97.

Salespeople have a moral obligation to prospect/customer, company and self. As such, they continually encounter truth-telling dilemmas. "Ignorance" and "conflict" often block the path to morally correct sales behaviors. Academics and practitioners agree that adoption of ethical codes is the most effective measure for encouraging ethical sales behaviors. Yet no ethical code has been offered which can be conveniently used to overcome the unique circumstances that contribute to the moral dilemmas often encountered in personal selling. An ethical code is developed that charts ethical paths across a variety of sales settings (addressing "ignorance") while illustrating why the cost associated with acting morally is generally reasonable (addressing "conflict"). (edited)

**Lumsden, David**. How Well does Direct Reference Semantics Fit with Pragmatics?. *Phil Papers*, 25(2), 139-147, Ag 96.

**Luna, Florencia**. Vulnerable Populations and Morally Tainted Experiments. *Bioethics*, 11(3-4), 256-264, Jl 97.

This article addresses the dilemma facing an editor when he or she has to decide whether or not to publish a manuscript that describes unethical research. I will explore three options the editor may follow: a) publish the unethical research; b) publish it with an explicit condemnation of the methods used; c) reject the article on moral grounds. I will consider the importance of deterring unethical research, why the deterrence argument has been overlooked and the relevance it has in developing countries which seem to be more exposed to morally tainted experiments. (edited)

**Luna Alcoba, Manuel**. El problema del continuo en la escolástica española: Francisco de Oviedo (1602-1651). *Daimon Rev Filosof*, 12, 37-47, Ja-Je 96.

Puede decirse, con escaso margen para la discusión, que las propuestas modernas sobre el continuo tienen su comienzo en la figura de G. W. Leibniz, inventor del cálculo infinitesimal y primero en enunciar la ley de continuidad. Este artículo trata de mostar cómo en los textos de Oviedo existe una serie de análisis que, si bien restringidos por la imposibilidad de introducir la matemática en el aristotelismo, sientan bases metafísicas para las teorías modernas del continuo.

**Luna Alcoba, Manuel**. G.W. Leibniz: *Geschichte des Kontinuumproblems*. *Stud Leibniz*, 28(2), 183-198, 1996.

L'inédite que nous offrons ici, c'est un écrit de Leibniz où il fait mention des affirmations et problèmes qu'il a eu présent dans sa théorie de la continuité. Il est donc un inventaire détaillé des fonts leibniziennes avec rapport au continu. Nonobstant, plus que fermer les discussions autour de ce qu'on a coutume d'appeler les *influences* que Leibniz a reçu, cette édition peut ouvrir nouvelles lignes de recherche, à cause de la nature, quelque fois surprenant, des fonts cités.

**Luna Alcoba, Manuel**. G.W. Leibniz: Consequence de l'Hypothese generalle publiée il y a quelque temps, pour expliquer le Phenomene de l'attachement dans le vuide, ou dans une place dont l'air a esté tiré. *Stud Leibniz*, 28(1), 1-16, 1996.

La *Consequence de l'Hypothese generalle* écrit à l'entoure de 1673-1675 c'est un texte sur problèmes de pneumatique où Leibniz énonce par première fois sa "loix de la continuation des corps sensibles". Malgré qu'on peut discuter si nous sommes, en parlant strictement, face à un cas de la loi de continuité, cette loi, oubliée par les spécialistes et, il semble, par Leibniz lui même, doi nous obliger à nous retracer en grand part l'interprétation traditionnelle sur le continu chez Leibniz.

**Lund, William**. Egalitarian Liberalism and the Fact of Pluralism. *J Soc Phil*, 27(3), 61-80, Wint 96.

Against recent critics, this article argues that the egalitarian liberalism of Rawls and Dworkin is compatible with ethical pluralism. They reject monism and assume ineliminable intra- and interpersonal conflicts of incommensurable values, but go on to impose a commitment to equality as a constraint on the process by which we create public answers to such conflicts. While that commitment is overriding, it both reflects our equal liability to ethical dilemmas and leaves space for their private and varying resolution. Thus, their view is both consistent with ethical pluralism and more hospitable to it than intuitionistic or conservative alternatives.

**Luntley, Michael**. "The Disciplinary Conception of Truth" in *Verdad: lógica, representación y mundo*, Villegas Forero, L, 65-81. Santiago de Compostela, Univ Santiago Comp, 1996.

This paper starts with the assumption that whatever else we say about content, content is that which is to be assessed as correct/incorrect. The paper then explores how much has to go into our notion of correctness/incorrectness (truth and falsity) in order to capture the idea of content. I argue for the following claims: First, a minimal requirement on our concept of truth is that truth is that which *disciplines* content. Second, a concept of truth adequate to capture this normativity of content is a realist concept in one of the many senses of that overused classification. The conclusion of this argument can be summed up in the slogan 'Ontology disciplines semantics'. (edited)

**Luntley, Michael**. An Engaging Practice?. *Inquiry*, 40(3), 357-374, S 97.

**Luntley, Michael**. Commentary on "Epistemic Value Commitments". *Phil Psychiat Psych*, 3(3), 227-229, S 96.

**Luosto, Kerkko** and Hella, Lauri and Väänänen, Jouko. The Hierarchy Theorem for Generalized Quantifiers. *J Sym Log*, 61(3), 802-817, S 96.

The concept of a generalized quantifier of a given similarity type was defined in [12]. Our main result says that on finite structures different similarity types give rise to different classes of generalized quantifiers. More exactly, for every similarity type *t* there is a generalized quantifier of type *t* which is not definable in the extension of first order logic by all generalized quantifiers of type smaller than *t*. This was proved for unary similarity types by Per Lindström [17] with a counting argument. We extend his method to arbitrary similarity types.

**Lupoli, Agostino**. "L'*Account of the Nature and the Extent of the Divine Dominion and Goodnesses* di Samuel Parker: dalla teologia alla filosofia politica" in *Mind Senior to the World*, Baldi, Marialuisa, 205-254. Milano, FrancoAngeli, 1996.

**Luscombe, David**. *Medieval Thought*. New York, Oxford Univ Pr, 1997.

The book steers a clear path through this long period, beginning with three great influences on medieval philosophy: Augustine, Boethius, and Pseudo-Denis, and focusing on Alcuin, then Anselm, Abelard, Aquinas, Ockham, Duns Scotus, and Eckhart amongst others from the twelfth to the fifteenth century. Medieval philosophy is widely regarded as having a theological and religious orientation, but more recently attention has been given to the early study of logic, language, and the philosophy of science. This history, therefore, gives a fascinating insight into medieval views on aspects such as astronomy, materialism, perception, and the nature of the soul, as well as of God. (publisher, edited)

**Luthar, Harsh K** and DiBattista, Ron A and Gautschi, Theodore. Perception of What the Ethical Climate Is and What It Should Be: The Role of Gender, Academic Status, and Ethical Education. *J Bus Ethics*, 16(2), 205-217, F 97.

This study examined ethical attitudes and perceptions of 691 undergraduate seniors and freshmen in a college of business. Gender was found to be correlated to perceptions of "what the ethical climate should be" with female subjects showing significantly more favorable attitude towards ethical behaviors than males. Further, seniors had a more cynical view of the current ethical climate than freshmen. Freshmen were significantly more likely than seniors to believe that good business ethics is positively related to successful business outcomes. Ethical education was significantly correlated to both perceptions of "current ethical climate" as well as "what the ethical climate should be". Students who had been exposed to ethical issues in a course were more likely to believe both, that ethical behavior is, and should be, positively associated with successful business outcomes.

**Lutz Müller, Marcos**. The Negative Dialectic of Modernity and the Speculative Resolution of the Contradiction of Modern Moral Consciousness (in Spanish). *Discurso*, 27, 83-116, 1996.

In this essay we show that the presentation of the constitution of modern moral consciousness, in Hegel, that results from the dialectic-speculative reformulation of Kantian moral autonomy, is essentially critical and condenses to a "negative dialectic".

**Lúzon, Diego-Manuel**. Actio illicita in causa und Zurechnung zum Vorverhalten bei Provokation von Rechtfertigungsgründen. *Jahr Recht Ethik*, 2, 353-374, 1994.

After discussing the divergent scholarly opinions on the general validity or invalidity of the *actio illicita in causa* construction, the author makes the following two claims: 1) From a substantive point of view, namely one that considers the actual wrong inherent to the conduct as well as the criminal policy issues involved, the concept of the *actio illicita in causa* cannot be employed with respect to the provocation of justifying circumstances when the justification excludes the wrong otherwise inherent to the consequences of the act. 2) From a formal point of view with respect to the act as satisfying the elements of the offense definition, one has to distinguish two separate subclasses within this latter class. (edited)

**Lycan, William G**. "Consciousness as Internal Monitoring, I" in *AI, Connectionism and Philosophical Psychology, 1995,* Tomberlin, James E (ed), 1-14. Atascadero, Ridgeview, 1995.

This paper defends the view, due in this century to Armstrong, that what it is for a mental state to be a conscious state (in the sense of: a state one is aware of being in) is for the subject to be monitoring or scanning the state by means of an internal attention mechanism. Several common objections are rebutted, as is a particularly ingenious criticism of Georges Rey's.

**Lycan, William G**. "Layered Perceptual Representation" in *Perception,* Villanueva, Enrique (ed), 81-100. Atascadero, Ridgeview, 1996.

This paper defends the *representational theory* of qualia against objections by Ned Block and Christopher Peacocke. It also argues that a given perceptual state has multiple intentional objects, representing some of those objects by representing others.

**Lycan, William G**. "On Sosa's 'Fregean Reference Defended'" in *Contents,* Villanueva, Enrique (ed), 100-103. Atascadero, Ridgeview, 1995.

This paper is a discussion note on Sosa's article and argues that Sosa's theory of mental reference succumbs to a particular sort of counterexample.

**Lycan, William G**. "Replies to Tomberlin, Tye, Stalnaker and Block" in *Perception,* Villanueva, Enrique (ed), 127-142. Atascadero, Ridgeview, 1996.

This paper replies to critical commentary on the author's "Layered Perceptual Representation."

**Lycos, Kimon**. Making Things with Words: Plato on Mimesis in *Republic*. *Phil Inq*, 18(3-4), 1-19, Sum-Fall 96.

**Lynch, Cecelia**. Kant, the Republican Peace, and Moral Guidance in International Law. *Ethics Int Affairs*, 8, 39-58, 1994.

**Lynch, James F**. Infinitary Logics and Very Sparse Random Graphs. *J Sym Log*, 62(2), 609-623, Je 97.

Let *L* be the infinitary language obtained from the first-order language of graphs by closure under conjunctions and disjunctions of arbitrary sets of formulas, provided only finitely many distinct variables occur among the formulas. Let a random graph on *n* vertices be constructed by choosing independently, for each pair of vertices, that there is an edge between them with probability *p(n)*. It is shown that if *p(n)* satisfies certain simple conditions on its growth rate, then for every sentence in *L*, the probability that the sentence holds for the random graph on *n* vertices converges as *n* grows. Results on the difficulty of computing this asymptotic probability are given.

**Lynch, Joseph J**. Wittgenstein and Animal Minds. *Between Species*, 12(1-2), 47-52, Wint-Spr 96.

Wittgenstein has often been associated with the view that there is a radical discontinuity between human and animal mental lives. Naturally, this view has serious moral implications. I argue that efforts to draw a clear line between animal and human mentality are misguided and that emphasis on psychological continuity between the species is evidenced in Wittgenstein's own work. I then make some suggestions, in a Wittgensteinian spirit, concerning animal minds and human obligations.

**Lynch, Michael**. A So-Called 'Fraud': Moral Modulations in a Literary Scandal. *Hist Human Sci*, 10(3), 9-21, Ag 97.

Physicist Alan Sokal achieved a moment of fame by announcing that he had succeeded in publishing an article in the cultural studies journal *Social Text*, which was 'sprinkled with nonsense' about developments in quantum gravity physics that supposedly converge with postmodernist themes. Sokal announced his hoax in an article in the literary magazine *Lingua Franca*. In this paper, I suggest that the *Lingua Franca* article also achieved a parody and that those who took Sokal seriously were once again taken in by the voice of scientific authority. (edited)

**Lynch, Michael P**. Relativism and Truth: A Reply to Steven Rappaport. *Philosophia (Israel)*, 25(1-4), 417-421, Ap 97.

While I agree with Rappaport that metaphysical relativism—relativism with regard to the nature of reality—is consistent with a nonrelativistic view of truth, I argue that Rappaport has not shown this to be the case. The deflationary conception of truth advocated in Rappaport's original paper ends up implying a type of relativism about truth.

**Lynch, Michael W**. Affirmative Action at the University of California. *Notre Dame J Law Ethics*, 11(1), 139-158, 1997.

**Lynn, Joanne** and Harrold, Joan and Ayers, Elise. A Good Death: Improving Care Inch-by-Inch. *Bioethics Forum*, 13(1), 38-40, Spr 97.

As people live longer with chronic diseases before dying, it is increasingly important to define a "good death." This may include freedom from pain, preservation of dignity and family and spiritual reconciliation—goals our health care system rarely recognizes. To ensure a good death, we must measure and improve the quality of end of life care. Ten domains for measurement have been identified: symptom relief; support of function and autonomy; advance care planning; use of aggressive care and appropriate site of death; patient and family satisfaction; global quality of life; family burden; survival time; provider continuity and skill; and bereavement.

**Lyons, Jack**. Testimony, Induction and Folk Psychology. *Austl J Phil*, 75(2), 163-178, Je 97.

Several recent authors have argued that beliefs held on the basis of testimony could not possibly be justified via simple induction. This paper argues against this view. I try to show that C.A.J. Coady's recent arguments for this position rest on a flawed general conception of induction. Other authors hold that we simply haven't had enough experience checking reports against facts to have any adequate inductive evidence for the accuracy of testimony. Against this claim, I argue that the mechanisms operative in the production of our folk psychological beliefs could serve to provide a sort of indirect inductive evidence for the reliability of testimony.

**Lysaught, M Therese**. Suffering, Ethics, and the Body of Christ: Anointing as a Strategic Alternative Practice. *Christian Bioethics*, 2(2), 172-201, Ag 96.

Within the moral/social order maintained and reproduced by biomedical ethics (i.e., the "peaceable community"), suffering is a senseless accident with no value. Insofar as suffering compromises the fundamental pillar of this order, namely, autonomy, it threatens the existence of the "peaceable community." Consequently, biomedical ethics is only able to offer those who suffer one moral or practical response: that of elimination, embodied most vividly in the increasingly approved practice of assisted-suicide. Another moral/social order, however, the "peaceable Kingdom" or the "Body of Christ," provides an alternative understanding of the meaning purpose and significance of suffering through the Roman Catholic sacrament of anointing of the sick. Recognizing the power of sickness and suffering to dis-inscribe" bodies of their normative self-understandings, the Church responds with a set of liturgical practices which intend to respond to the dynamics of suffering, reinscribe these bodies, and assist persons in fulfilling the vocation of "participating in Christ's suffering for the salvation of the world."

**Mac Lane, Saunders**. Despite Physicists, Proof is Essential in Mathematics. *Synthese*, 111(2), 147-154, My 97.

**Macbeth, Douglas**. The Discovery of Situated Worlds: Analytic Commitments, or Moral Orders?. *Human Stud*, 19(3), 267-287, Jl 96.

The discovery of social phenomena by a discipline whose roots are abidingly psychological has been a singular development in American educational research. Formulations of "situatedness" are emblematic of this rethinking and depending on our understanding of it, we have in situatedness the possibility of a distinctive set of analytic commitments. This paper discusses these possibilities and their development in the educational research literature, in the particulars of the Brown, Collins and Duguid (1989) publication "Situated Cognition." In the end, situatedness is understood as a unifying formulation. And while it opens a huge domain of topics for inquiry, it also proves, *as* its inclusiveness, of no use whatsoever as a parsing device. Situated cognition, for example, could not be, nor has ever been, otherwise.

**MacCormick, Neil**. Democracy, Subsidiarity, and Citizenship in the 'European Commonwealth'. *Law Phil*, 16(4), 331-356, Jl 97.

The suggestion offered is that there is a legally constituted order and that a suitable term to apply to it is a 'commonwealth', comprising a commonwealth of 'postsovereign' states. Is it a democratic commonwealth and can it be? Is there sufficiently a *demos* or 'people' for democracy to be possible? If not democratic, what is it? Monarchy, oligarchy, or democracy, or a 'mixed constitution'? Argued: there is a mixed constitution containing a reasonable element of democratic rule. The value of democracy is then explored in terms of individualistic versus holistic evaluation and instrumental versus intrinsic value. Subsidiarity can be considered in a similar light, suggestively in terms of forms of democracy appropriate to different levels of self-government. The conclusion is that there is no absolute democratic deficit in the European commonwealth. (edited)

**Macdonald, Amie A**. A Critique of Academic Nationalism. *Int Stud Phil*, 29(1), 79-90, 1997.

It is my position that what is fundamentally at issue in the controversy over curricular reform is the struggle over national identity. Thus I consider the relationship between identity and ideology, between formal intellectual activity in the academy and nationalism. I argue that the curriculum envisioned by the traditionalists preserves an identifiably homogeneous version of national culture. By regulating national culture in this way, the traditionalists are actually fortifying their notion of national identity. And mediating between this ideal of national identity and this manipulation of national culture is nationalism, a sentiment completely antithetical to the mission of the university.

**Macdonald, Cynthia**. *Connectionism and Eliminativism: Reply to Stephen Mills in Vol. 5, No. 1*. *Int J Phil Stud*, 5(2), 316-322, Je 97.

**MacDonald, Chris J** and Danielson, Peter A. Hard Cases in Hard Places: Singer's Agenda for Applied Ethics. *Dialogue (Canada)*, 35(3), 599-610, Sum 96.

This is a critical notice of the second edition of Singer's deservedly influential book, *Practical Ethics*. First we consider Singer's appeal to a principle of equality as definitive of ethics and subject it to a contractarian criticism. Second, we argue that Singer's discussion of environmental ethics makes clear that he lacks an adequate theory of value. Next, we discuss Singer's involvement in the controversy over euthanasian in the German-speaking countries, and suggest that his analysis is at odds with his earlier discussion of civil disobedience. Finally, we consider Singer's ill-fated attempt to justify the moral life in self-interested terms.

**Mace, Chris**. Commentary on "Primitive Mental Processes". *Phil Psychiat Psych*, 4(2), 145-149, Je 97.

Hinshelwood's proposal that a "principle of integration" would resolve ethical dilemmas raised by the existence of primitive mental processes is critically examined. Evidence is presented that, as formulated, this principle is susceptible to misuse, confuses stated intentions with their consequences and is inconsistent with premises concerning the fluidity of personal identity that Hinshelwood's account of primitive processes assumes.

**Macedo, Stephen**. "Sexuality and Liberty: Making Room for Nature and Tradition?" in *Sex, Preference, and Family: Essays on Law and Nature*, Nussbaum, Martha C (ed), 86-101. New York, Oxford Univ Pr, 1997.

**Macedo Lourenço, Joao**. A intencionalidade na filosofia de Levinas. *Rev Port Filosof*, 53(1), 71-84, Ja-Mr 97.

Intentionality is a fundamental concept in Emmanuel Levinas's philosophy. Based on Husserl, the Lithuanian philosopher understands this concept not only as objectifying and as such, as identification and representation, but also as sense: the relation subject-object appears, therefore, as transitivity. In proclaiming this new sense of intentionality, Levinas departs from the traditional philosophy of being, of same and in affirming the discontinuity of subjective time he assumes the relation I-Other as fruition, on the one hand and as responsibility, on the other hand. At the same time, alterity affirms itself and becomes more radical. The sense of intentionality is then reversed and acquires a new dimension, since it now becomes responsibility, heteronomy, the Other's call. The Other appears in its concrete aspects as face and as Enigma, Infinite. Ethics becomes acquired primacy.

**Macey, David** (trans) and Löwy, Michael. Walter Benjamin and Surrealism: The Story of a Revolutionary Spell. *Rad Phil*, 80, 17-23, N-D 96.

Walter Benjamin shared with the surrealists a sort of "Gothic Marxism", i.e., a historical materialism sensitive to the *magical* dimension of past cultures, to the "black" moment of revolt and to the illumination that rends the sky of revolutionary action like a bolt of lightning. "Gothic" should also be understood literally as a positive reference to certain key moments in profane medieval culture: both Benjamin and André Breton admired the courtly love of medieval Provence. Benjamin understood perfectly that surrealism is not just an "artistic movement" but a set of magical experiments with revolutionary implications, both profoundly libertarian and in search of convergence with communism.

**MacGregor, David**. *Hegel, Marx, and the English State*. Toronto, Univ of Toronto Pr, 1996.

This work, now brought back into print, is an insightful intellectual portrait of Hegel and Marx that challenges standard interpretations of their political theory and places their political thought directly into social and historical context. David MacGregor reveals the revolutionary content of Hegel's social theory and the Hegelian themes that underlie Marx's analysis of the English state in *Capital*, shows how the transformation of the Victorian state in the nineteenth century influenced the mature Marx to reclaim Hegelian arguments he had earlier abandoned. These ideas included a theory of politics and social class that coloured Marx's view of capitalist and working-class opposition to government reform initiatives. (edited)

**MacGuigan, Mark R**. World Order: Maritain and Now. *Maritain Stud*, 8, 104-111, 1992.

**Machalová, Tatiana**. Two Concepts of the Ethics of Responsibility: H. Jonas and K.-O. Apel (in Czech). *Filosof Cas*, 45(3), 443-458, 1997.

The article considers two contemporary concepts of the ethics of responsibility: the ethics of the future put forward by H. Jonas's and K.-O. Apel's discursive-ethical model of responsibility. The author seeks to highlight the points at which both concepts introduce marked dissonances with the traditional concept of responsibility. Neither Jonas nor Apel sees responsibility as simply a quality which directs our behaviour, but rather as a capacity of the real human substance. Both philosophers, however, reach this point at the price of a reduction of morality and the moral point of view. The author suggests that a starting point for the discussion of morals could be the possibility of further reconstruction of the necessary conditions of human existence and the discussion of needs.

**Machan, Tibor R**. "Individualism and Political Dialogue" in *Political Dialogue: Theories and Practices*, Esquith, Stephen L (ed), 45-55. Amsterdam, Rodopi, 1996.

Lockean individualism is a crucial value for developing a theory of dialogical practical reason. Any discourse ethic, including a Habermasian one, must avoid collectivism and ground its principles on an individualist conception of human action.

**Machan, Tibor R**. Communication From One Feminist. *J Soc Phil*, 28(1), 54-61, Spr 97.

This paper responds to some of Alison Jaggar's views on how men and women tend to communicate. It attempts to be more expressive than argumentative, mainly because it seems to be a thesis of Jaggar that men do not communicate expressively whereas women do. By "expressive" is meant "giving one's emotions verbal representation." I found Jaggar's claims about men to be insensitive, prejudiced, insulting, biased and certainly irritating to anyone with a sense of justice. I wanted her and others to realize that a man can feel every bit as hurt and upset as any woman can and that her caricaturing of how men communicate easily results in simply upsetting people, not in shedding much light on anything.

**MacIntosh, David**. The Moral Art of Being a Good Doctor. *Bioethics*, 10(4), 331-333, O 96.

**MacIntosh, J J**. Animals, Morality and Robert Boyle. *Dialogue (Canada)*, 35(3), 435-472, Sum 96.

In early life, the philosopher, theologian, and natural philosopher Robert Boyle (1627-1691) wrote extensively on moral matters. In an early manuscript (probably written about 1647) Boyle offered a number of arguments for extending moral concern to nonhuman animals. Since the later Boyle routinely vivisected or otherwise killed animals in his scientific experiments we are left with the biographical questions, did his views change, and if so, why, as well as with the philosophical questions, what were his arguments and how good are they? In this paper I try to answer those questions.

**MacIntyre, Alasdair** and Will, Frederick L and Westphal, Kenneth R (ed). *Pragmatism and Realism*. Lanham, Rowman & Littlefield, 1997.

Will demonstrates that a social account of human knowledge is consistent with, and ultimately requires, realism. The book culminates in a naturalistic account of the generation, assessment and revision of cognitive, moral and social norms. It is written clearly enough for undergraduates and makes a timely contribution to current debates. A critical introduction by the editor discusses the bearing of Will's views on current issues in analytic epistemology, philosophy of science, and moral theory. Will's work "is one of the more remarkable achievements of 20th-century North American philosophy."—Alasdair MacIntyre. (publisher)

**Mackay, Robin**. "Capitalism and Schizophrenia: Wildstyle in Full Effect" in *Deleuze and Philosophy: The Difference Engineer*, Ansell Pearson, Keith (ed), 247-269. New York, Routledge, 1997.

**MacKellar, Calum**. The Biological Child. *Ethics Med*, 12(3), 65-69, 1996.

During the last decades the issues concerning techniques of assisted conception have grown both in number and complexity. New possibilities provided by scientific research have raised the hope of many infertile couples and individuals to fulfill their deepest aspirations of giving birth to a child. Although the possible pain, psychological pressure, deception and, in some countries, financial burden, accepted by the hopeful parents are generally of extreme severity, the hope of obtaining a child containing as much of their own biological material as possible is the reason for the popularity of these new developments in procreation. Biological children have indeed generally been preferred to nonbiological adopted children for reasons the present paper seeks to explore.

**Mackie, David**. The Individuation of Actions. *Phil Quart*, 47(186), 38-54, Ja 97.

I argue against a view of the individuation of actions endorsed most notably by Hornsby and Davidson. This is the view that in, for example, Anscombe's case of the pumping man, we have a single action which can be described, variously, as a pumping, a poisoning and so on. I argue that, even in the area of the standard arguments against this view, such as that based on the logic of 'by' and the argument from temporal dimensions, the case against the Davidson-Hornsby view has not been made as strong as it ought to have been. I show how those standard arguments can be strengthened; and I argue that the principal considerations adduced in support of the view do not in fact lend it the support that they have been widely thought to lend it. I conclude that the view should be rejected.

**MacKinnon, Catherine A**. "Pornography Left and Right" in *Sex, Preference, and Family: Essays on Law and Nature,* Nussbaum, Martha C (ed), 102-125. New York, Oxford Univ Pr, 1997.

Two books are critically discussed that defend pornography on essentially the same grounds, one form the left (Edward DeGrazin, *Girls Lean Back Everywhere* and one from the right (Richard Posner, *Sex and Reason.*

**MacKinnon, John E**. Advocacy, Therapy, and Pedagogy. *Phil Lit*, 20(2), 492-500, O 96.

In this critical discussion, I review *Beyond Political Correctness: Toward the Inclusive University* (University of Toronto Press: 1995), a collection of essays concerned with the current state and future prospects of Canadian universities. The title is somewhat misleading. It is not that the contributors believe that Canadian universities ought to get beyond the implementation of policies that have come to be identified as politically correct (e.g., preferential hiring policies, campus speech codes and so on), but rather that all of us ought to get beyond the use of the term "politically correct" as an epithet to deride such policies. The status quo is oppressive, they contend, the policies themselves enlightened. I quote many of the contributors at length, the best way to expose the failings of a truly shoddy book.

**Macklin, Ruth** and Beer, Douglas A and Robinson, Walter (& others). Bad Night in the ER—Patients' Preferences and Reasonable Accommodation: Discussed by Douglas A. Beer, Ruth Macklin, Walter Robinson, and Philip Wang. *Ethics Behavior*, 6(4), 371-383, 1996.

**Mackor, Anne Ruth** and Peijnenburg, Jeanne. Chief Bumbu en de Verklaring van Menselijk Gedrag. *Alg Ned Tijdschr Wijs*, 88(3), 208-215, Jl 96.

The paper is a review of the conference 'Human action and causality', held April 1996 at the University of Utrecht in The Netherlands. Contributions of speakers (J. Kim, P. Pettit, F. Dretske, among others) are summarized and critically discussed. (The papers will be published in Proceedings.)

**Maclachlan, Lorne**. "F.H. Bradley and C.A. Campbell" in *Philosophy after F.H. Bradley,* Bradley, James (ed), 73-90. Bristol, Thoemmes, 1996.

Although C.A. Campbell is most widely known as a champion of freewill, he conceived his main contribution to philosophy to be the discussion and development of the Suprarationalism of F.H. Bradley. Campbell follows Bradley in rejecting all products of thought as intellectually unsatisfactory. The *real* is not the *rational* but the *suprarational*. But Campbell's austere conception of reality disallows Bradley's idea that the Absolute is a harmonious whole of experience. Campbell also attacks Bradley's doctrine of degrees of truth and introduces a category of final phenomenal truths which although not intellectually satisfactory are intellectually incorrigible. The belief in freewill belongs to this group.

**MacLellan, Cheryl** and Dobson, John. Women, Ethics, and MBAs. *J Bus Ethics*, 16(11), 1201-1209, Ag 97.

We argue that the declining female enrollment in graduate business schools is a manifestation of gender bias in business education. The extant conceptual foundation of business education is one which views business activity in terms of a game with fixed and wholly material objectives. This concept betrays an underlying value system that reflects a male orientation. Business education is not merely amoral, therefore, but is gender biased. We suggest that business educators adopt a broadened behavioral rubric. Virtue-ethics theory provides such a rubric.

**MacLennan, Bruce**. The Elements of Consciousness and their Neurodynamical Correlates. *J Consciousness Stud*, 3(5-6), 409-424, 1996.

The 'hard problem' is hard because of the special epistemological status of consciousness, which does not, however, preclude its scientific investigation. Data from phenomenologically trained observers can be combined with neurological investigations to establish the relation between experience and neurodynamics. Although experience cannot be reduced to physical phenomena, parallel phenomenological and neurological analyses allow the structure of experience to be related to the structure of the brain. Such an analysis suggests a theoretical entity, an elementary unit of experience, the protophenomenon, which corresponds to an activity site (such as a synapse) in the brain. The structure of experience is determined by connections (e.g., dendrites) between these activity sites; the connections correspond to temporal patterns among the elementary units of experience, which can be expressed mathematically. This theoretical framework illuminates several issues, including degrees of consciousness, nonbiological consciousness, sensory inversions, unity of consciousness and the unconscious mind.

**Macmillan, C J B**. "The Freedom of the Playpen" in *Philosophy of Education (1996),* Margonis, Frank (ed), 43-47. Urbana, Phil Education Soc, 1997.

**MacNiven, Don**. "Bradley and MacIntyre: A Comparison" in *Philosophy after F.H. Bradley,* Bradley, James (ed), 349-365. Bristol, Thoemmes, 1996.

The article develops a philosophical comparison between the idealistic ethics of F.H. Bradley (*Ethical Studies*, 1876/1727), and Alasdair MacIntyre (*After Virtue*, 1984). The article argues that MacIntyre shares with idealists like Bradley, the

views that the philosophy of the enlightenment was bankrupt and that its philosophy was marked by several characteristic viewpoints; foundationalism, radical individualism, individual liberty and equality, natural rights, liberal democracy and the fact/value dichotomy. However they differ as to how these viewpoints are related to each other. MacIntyre appears to hold that they logically entail one another, hence if one aspect of the Enlightenment is rejected the whole package must go. Bradley, on the other hand, holds that these viewpoints are historically, rather than logically related, hence a commitment to idealism does not imply a wholesale rejection of the Enlightenment.

**Macpherson, Jay** and Anderson Silber, C. Francis Sparshott, Poet. *J Aes Educ*, 31(2), 31-36, Sum 97.

Sparshott is rare in being an aesthetician who seriously practices an art. A two-page introduction to three of his poems (previously unpublished) characterizes his poetry and invites its reading.

**Maczynski, M J**. Non-Classical Logics in Quantum Mechanics and Physics. *Bull Sec Log*, 25(3/4), 161-165, O-D 96.

The aim of this presentation is to discuss the role played by the works of Helena Rasiowa in the theory of logics suitable for quantum mechanics and physics. It is shown that the method used by H. Rasiowa to prove algebraically the completeness theorem in classical logic by constructing the Lindenbaum-Tarski algebra of a formalized theory can be also used to define quantum logic from a formalized system of experimental propositions. It is shown that the quantum nonclassical logic can be viewed as built from a system of Boolean (classical) logics. In conclusion, the importance of the monograph of H. Rasiowa's *Algebraic Methods in Non-Classical Logics* for the theory of quantum logic indicated and stressed.

**Madanes, Leiser**. "*Recta ratio* y arbitrariedad en la filosofía política de Hobbes" in *La racionalidad: su poder y sus límites,* Nudler, Oscar (ed), 383-396. Barcelona, Ed Paidos, 1996.

**Madanes, Leiser**. "Hobbes on Peace and Truth" in *Scepticism in the History of Philosophy: A Pan-American Dialogue,* Popkin, Richard H (ed), 45-52. Dordrecht, Kluwer, 1996.

**Madanes, Leiser**. Descartes: La Libertad de Pensamiento, Fundamento de La Moral Provisional. *Cad Hist Filosof Cie*, 5(1-2), 125-162, Ja-D 95.

Descartes wrote three or four provisional moral rules to be observed while a definitive morality could be well-founded on certainty. It is often discussed if he ever achieved this task and, if so, which are those final moral rules. This paper purports to show that Descartes found a new object of moral inquiry, i.e., freedom of thought. This freedom of thought is also the ground of his epistemological project. Paulo Faria's interpretation of Descartes provisional morality is discussed in the second part of this paper.

**Madden, Edward H**. William Ellery Channing: Philosopher, Critic of Orthodoxy, and Cautious Reformer. *Trans Peirce Soc*, 33(3), 558-588, Sum 97.

In spite of previous conflicting estimates of the philosophy and theology of William Ellery Channing I try to show that he was, in fact, a consistent philosopher and theologian: I characterize him as more Reidian and less transcendental, a liberal Unitarian who, nevertheless, accepted those parts of Christianity not connected with the incarnation, a significant reformer in penological and other social matters and a psychologically complex man who could express his care and love in letters to friends but seemed remote when he was with them.

**Madell, Geoffrey** and Ridley, Aaron. Emotion and Feeling. *Aris Soc*, Supp(71), 147-176, 1997.

**Màdera, Romano**. "La Libertà Della Contraddizione" in *Soggetto E Verità: La questione dell'uomo nella filosofia contemporanea,* Fagiuoli, Ettore, 103-110. 20136 Milano, Mimesis, 1996.

Contradiction does not sign the last limit of the human capacity of meaningful language. On the contrary, the possibility to contradict oneself arouses from the wickness of instinctual endowment of our species. Culture transforms and substitutes instincts, providing customs and institutions to manage human drives and behaviors. This is the base of the historical and ecological alternatives. The possibility to contradict oneself is the symptom of the possibility to choice among different but comparable alternatives, a fact that is constitutive of the freedom of human culture.

**Madigan, Timothy J**. "Averroës and Inquiry: The Need for an Enlightened Community" in *Averroës and the Enlightenment,* Wahba, Mourad (ed), 69-77. Amherst, Prometheus, 1996.

This is a comparison between Averroes's defense of a scholarly community and Charles Peirce's notion of a community of inquiries.

**Madigan, Timothy J** and Koczwara, Bogda M. The Heterogeneity of Clinical Ethics: The State of the Field as Reflected in the *Encyclopedia of Bioethics*. *J Med Phil*, 22(1), 75-88, F 97.

The 1995 *Encyclopedia of Bioethics* is an almost complete reworking of the original 1978 edition, due to the expanding nature of the field. The following article focuses on how the second edition of the *Encyclopedia* deals with the topic of "clinical ethics" and three related topics: "nursing ethics," "trust," and "conflict of interest." We assess their relevance to the current developments in these fields and the *Encyclopedia*'s usefulness as a resource to ethics consultants, researchers and clinicians. We emphasize the heterogeneity of clinical ethics as a still new and evolving field.

**Mäki, Uskali**. Universals and the *Methodenstreit*: a Re-examination of Carl Menger's Conception of Economics as an Exact Science. *Stud Hist Phil Sci*, 28(3), 475-495, S 97.

The precise positions of the antagonists in the legendary *Methodenstreit* between Menger and Schomoller and their allies are not well understood. A novel interpretation of Menger's (1883) view of exact types and exact laws is formulated in terms of an immanent realist theory of universals drawn from Armstrong and others. Menger's exact types (money, economic man, economic price) can be interpreted as economic universals; i.e., universals involving economizing action by individuals. Exact laws (law of demand, etc.) can in turn be understood as relationships between such first-order universals. This reveals problems involved in Menger's statements (such as that exact laws hold without exception).

**Maesschalck, Marc**. Fichte et la question nationale. *Arch Phil*, 59(3), 355-380, Jl-S 96.

The originality of Fichte's reflections concerning the nation have been obscured by the passage of time. The return of nationalism in contemporary politics is perhaps the occasion for a retrieval of this political philosophy which transcends angelic cosmopolitanism and the messianic fervor of cultural regeneration. Fichte envisions a "deterritorialized" patriotism based upon the multicultural construction of a common political identity.

**Maffettone, Sebastiano**. Bioetica Laica. *Iride*, 9(19), 554-562, S-D 96.

**Maffie, James**. Just-So Stories about "Inner Cognitive Africa": Some Doubts about Sorensen's Evolutionary Epistemology of Thought Experiments. *Biol Phil*, 12(2), 207-224, Ap 97.

Roy Sorensen advances an evolutionary explanation of our capacity for thought experiments which doubles as a naturalized epistemological justification. I argue Sorensen's explanation fails to satisfy key elements of environmental-selectionist explanations and so fails to carry epistemic force. I then argue that even if Sorensen succeeds in showing the adaptive utility of our capacity, he still fails to establish its reliability and hence epistemic utility. I conclude Sorensen's account comes to little more than a "just-so story."

**Magee, Joseph M**. Eternal Truths in Aristotle's Posterior Analytics, 1, 8. *Dialogue (PST)*, 39(1), 30-35, O 96.

Consulting the commentaries of Aquinas, Barnes and McKirahan, this paper investigates Aristotle's claim at 75b22 that scientific knowledge of perishable things is eternal. Since *APo* I, 8 is part of his argument against Platonic dialectic, what Aristotle means by eternal conclusions is not that their subjects always exist, but that the connection between subject and predicate was proved to be a *per se* connection, i.e., drawn from the commensurately universal and not merely what is *dici de omni*.

**Magendzo, Abraham** and Misgeld, Dieter. Human Rights Education, Moral Education and Modernisation: The General Relevance of Some Latin American Experiences: A Conversation. *J Moral Educ*, 26(2), 151-168, Je 97.

**Magidor, Menachem** and Foreman, Matthew. A Very Weak Square Principle. *J Sym Log*, 62(1), 175-196, Mr 97.

**Magill, Kevin**. *Freedom and Experience: Self-Determination without Illusions*. New York, Macmillan, 1997.

Several contemporary philosophers have argued that the intractability of the old argument about whether causal determinism is compatible with free will is caused by deep rooted illusions and inconsistencies in our unreflective attitudes about moral responsibility and freedom to act. Kevin Magill challenges this view and argues that the philosophical stalemate about free will has arisen through lack of attention to the content of the experiences that shape our understanding of free will and agency, and through a mistaken belief that the concept of moral responsibility calls for a moral and metaphysical justification. The book sets out an original account of the various ways we experience choosing, deciding and acting, which reconciles the apparently opposing intuitions that have fueled the traditional dispute.

**Magnani, Lorenzo**. "Filosofi Artificiali" in *Soggetto E Verità: La questione dell'uomo nella filosofia contemporanea*, Fagiuoli, Ettore, 111-118. 20136 Milano, Mimesis, 1996.

The purpose of this paper is to consider the impact of some computational systems (the "artificial philosophers") on the epistemological problems of *scientific discovery* and *explanatory reasoning*. After illustrating some epistemological aspects that concern the fundamental relationship between these systems and the problem of discovering and explaining, I will explore the creative role of *abduction* in reasoning and the role of the so-called *explanatory coherence*, that applies to the acceptance and rejection of hypotheses in both scientific theories and reasoning in everyday life, and involves a dynamic set of criteria having a multidimensional character.

**Magnani, Lorenzo**. *Ingegnerie della Conoscenza: Introduzione alla Filosofia Computazionale*. Milano, Marcos y Marcos, 1997.

The purpose of this book is to consider the impact of some computational systems on the epistemological problems of scientific discovery and explanatory, temporal, analogical and visual reasoning: the aim is to design the whole area of the so-called computational philosophy. The author systematically describes some philosophical aspects that concern the relationship between these systems and the problem of discovering and explaining, including the creative role of abduction and the role of the so-called explanatory coherence, that applies to the acceptance and rejection of hypothesis in both scientific theories and reasoning in everyday life.

**Magnus, David**. Heuristics and Biases in Evolutionary Biology. *Biol Phil*, 12(1), 21-38, Ja 97.

Approaching science by considering the epistemological virtues which scientists see as constitutive of good science and the way these virtues trade-off against one another, makes it possible to capture action that may be lost by approaches which focus on either the theoretical or institutional level. Following Wimsatt (1984) I use the notion of heuristics and biases to help explore a case

study from the history of biology. Early in the 20th century, mutation theorists and natural historians fought over the role that isolation plays in evolution. This debate was principally about whether replication was the central scientific virtue (and hence the ultimate goal of science to replace nonexperimental evidence with experimental evidence) or whether consilience of inductions was the central virtue (and hence, as many kinds of evidence as possible should be pursued).

**Magnus, David**. Theory, Practice, and Epistemology in the Development of Species Concepts. *Stud Hist Phil Sci*, 27(4), 521-545, D 96.

Species concepts are obviously influenced by the types of organisms that biologists work on, the kinds of research they engage in, as well as the theoretical views they hold about how they are produced. In addition, epistemological differences over which virtues are central to good science will influence species concepts. At the same time, species concepts can be wielded as rhetorical devices in debates about each of these issues. The complex interplay between these forces can be seen at work in early twentieth century biology and in the development of the (surprisingly divergent) species concepts of Ernst Mayr and Theodosius Dobzhansky during the evolutionary synthesis.

**Magri, Tito**. Natural Obligation and Normative Motivation in Hume's *Treatise*. *Hume Stud*, 22(2), 231-253, N 96.

A systematic reconstruction of Hume's views of rational motivation is offered, by pointing a different occurrences of the concept of "natural obligation" in the *Treatise of Human Nature*. Particular emphasis is put on the naturalized concept of reason underlying Hume's theory and on its consequences for the sequential evaluation and choice of goods.

**Maguire, Stephen**. Business Ethics: A Compromise Between Politics and Virtue. *J Bus Ethics*, 16(12-13), 1411-1418, S 97.

This article examines and synthesizes two different approaches to determining the content of business ethics courses and the manner in which they ought to be taught. The first approach, from a political perspective, argues that the institutional framework within which business operates ought to be tested by theories of distributive justice. The second approach, from the perspective of virtue theory, argues that we ought to examine the character of individual employees and the responsibilities associated with the roles which these individuals play within organizations. I argue that Gadamer's interpretation of Aristotle's notion of *phronesis* showns an inseparable, bidirectional, conceptual link between the approaches of politics and virtue as well as providing insight into how business ethics might best be taught.

**Maher, Patrick**. The Hole in the Ground of Induction. *Austl J Phil*, 74(3), 423-432, S 96.

In *The Ground of Induction*, Donald Williams claimed to have justified induction by proving the following: If in a large sample the proportion of $Fs$ that are $G$ is $r$, then given no other relevant information it is probable that the proportion of all $Fs$ that are $G$ is near $r$. Williams's argument has been endorsed—with relatively minor qualification—by David Stove and Keith Campbell. Others have been sceptical but have not correctly identified a flaw in the justification. In this paper I show what is wrong with this putative justification of induction.

**Mahoney, Timothy A**. Aspiring to the Divine: Love and Grace. *Apeiron*, 30(1), 63-71, Mr 97.

This is a critical notice of Catherine Osborne's *Eros Unveiled: Plato and the God of Love* (Oxford, 1994). In a wide-ranging survey of ancient works, Osborne argues that the "ancient tradition" conceives of love as something inexplicable in itself but which explains desire and admiration. She has convincing arguments in the case of Christian love, but not in the more controversial case of Platonic love. But Osborne is right in claiming Christian and Platonic loves are importantly alike. I suggest that the proper parallel is between Platonic eros and Christian grace, rather than between Platonic eros and Christian agape.

**Mahoney, Timothy A**. Plato's Practical Political-Rhetorical Project: The Example of the *Republic*. *Polis*, 14(1-2), 30-52, 1995.

I examine Plato's conception of politics as it is found in early dialogues, and argue that in light of this conception we can attribute to Plato a well-conceived practical political project which he actually carried out. I argue that we can understand Plato's peculiar conception of politics from the evidence of the early dialogues, and that Plato formulated a project to fill the political void he saw in Greek society. I demonstrate how the drama and dialectic of the *Republic* are, in part, designed to overcome important obstacles that this project faces.

**Mahowald, Mary B**. A Feminist Standpoint for Genetics. *J Clin Ethics*, 7(4), 333-340, Wint 96.

A feminist standpoint provides a means of reducing gender inequities in genetics by imputing privileged status to input from women in clinical and policy decisions. An egalitarian version of feminism applies this strategy not only to women but to others besides women and others besides feminists. After delineating meanings of standpoint, standpoint theory, and feminist standpoint theory, this paper illustrates an egalitarian application of feminist standpoint theory through consideration of a case involving maternal phenykletonuria (PKU), a genetic disease associated with diet during pregnancy.

**Mahowald, Mary B**. The Brain and the I: Neurodevelopment and Personal Identity. *J Soc Phil*, 27(3), 49-60, Wint 96.

**Mahowald, Mary B**. What Classical American Philosophers Missed: Jane Addams, Critical Pragmatism, and Cultural Feminism. *J Value Inq*, 31(1), 39-54, Mr 97.

In this essay, my overall goal is to provide an account of two topics that classical American philosophers have virtually ignored: gender relations and the experience of women. I begin by examining feminism, pragmatism and

American philosophy and discuss possible reasons for the neglect of women in classical American philosophy. I then consider two themes attributed to the work of Jane Addams, who was closely associated with leading American pragmatists. The first theme, critical pragmatism, involves a critique of gender injustice. The second, cultural feminism, focuses on women's experience as a source of knowledge about ourselves and the world. Finally, I consider "standpoint theory" as suggestive of a strategy for overcoming the neglect of nondominant views in classical American philosophy.

**Mahowald, Mary B** and Nora, Lois Margaret. Neural Fetal Tissue Transplants: Old and New Issues. *Zygon*, 31(4), 615-633, D 96.

Neural fetal tissue transplantation offers promise as a treatment for devasting neurologic conditions such as Parkinson's disease. Two types of issues arise from this procedure: those associated with the use of fetuses and those associated with the use of neural tissue. The former issues have been examined in many forums; the latter have not. This paper reviews issues and arguments raised by the use of fetal tissue in general, but focuses on the implications of the use of neural tissue for basic concepts of personhood and personal identity.

**Maia Neto, José R**. "Kierkegaard's Distinction between Modern and Ancient Scepticism" in *Scepticism in the History of Philosophy: A Pan-American Dialogue*, Popkin, Richard H (ed), 135-158. Dordrecht, Kluwer, 1996.

**Maia Neto, José R**. Academic Skepticism in Early Modern Philosophy. *J Hist Ideas*, 58(2), 199-220, Ap 97.

Although the skeptical crisis at the dawn of modern philosophy can be properly labelled Pyrrhonian specific features of the academic school of skepticism played an important role in this crisis. Academic skepticism becomes even more influential in post-Cartesian skepticism from Foucher to Hume.

**Maia Neto, José R**. Pascal e as Grandes Questoes do seu Tempo. *Cad Hist Filosof Cie*, 5(1-2), 205-220, Ja-D 95.

In the article, I show Pascal's engagement and position in three major debates that occurred in the 17th century: the battle between the new and the "old" peripatetic science, the struggle between Jesuits and Jansenists in the theological field and the reaction by apologists of the Christian religion to deistic and atheistic movements. The most remarkable feature of Pascal's engagement in these debates is his use of humanist and secularizing intellectual movements to ground a Christian anthropology that emphasizes the corruption of nature.

**Maier, Mark**. Gender Equity, Organizational Transformation and Challenger. *J Bus Ethics*, 16(9), 943-962, Je 97.

The concept of the "unlevel playing field" is critiqued for its tendency to take the prevailing masculinist managerial paradigm for granted. Rather than assume that both men and women should assimilate to corporate masculinity, feminist alternatives are suggested. The pervasiveness of the masculine ethic and the "myth of meritocracy" in organizations are reviewed, with the space shuttle Challenger disaster serving as a focal point to demonstrate the dysfunctionality of masculine management and the rationale for feminist-based organizational transformation to promote not only gender equity, but more effective and ethical organizational behavior.

**Maierù, Alfonso**. "Il linguaggio mentale tra logica e grammatica nel medioevo: il contesto di Ockam" in *Momenti di Storia della Logica e di Storia della Filosofia*, Guetti, Carla (ed), 69-94. Roma, Aracne Editrice, 1996.

**Maimoni, Eulália Henrique**. Relato Verbal e Julgamento da Professora sobre o Rendimento do aluno: Relaçao com os Comportamentos Observados em Sala de Aula. *Educ Filosof*, 9(17), 53-77, Ja-Je 95.

The objective of this study was verified, partly by structured interviews as well as the teacher's perception about her students and the relationship between the teacher's judgments and the behavior of the student in the classroom. Four classrooms of two public schools were observed (two special education and two regular education) composed of delayed-reading students in the first grade. The teachers were asked to classify their students and the subjects of this study were selected from the extremes: half of the subjects presenting low academic achievement and half with good academic achievement according to the teacher's perception. (edited)

**Main, Thomas J**. Does Political Theory Matter for Policy Outcomes? The Case of Homeless Policy in the 1980s. *Pub Affairs Quart*, 11(2), 183-201, Ap 97.

**Mainberger, Gonsalv K**. "*Ewiger Friede*: Warum ein Beweismittel in Kants philosophischem Entwurf?" in *Grenzen der kritischen Vernunft*, Schmid, Peter A, 257-272. Basel, Schwabe Verlag, 1997.

**Mainetti, Joé Alberto**. In Search of Bioethics: A Personal Postscript. *J Med Phil*, 21(6), 671-679, D 96.

*De nobis ipsis silemus*: About ourselves—we keep silent. If we violate this prudent rule by the least modest of literary exercises—the autobiography—we must be able to say that we do so to bear witness. From my intellectual vocation of physician and philosopher, I have receive the Chinese blessing of "living in interesting times." I received two degrees in 1962 and spent thirty years developing a previously unimaginable encounter between medicine and humanism. That which follows tells the story of the development of bioethics in Ibero-America from the perspective of a testifying witness.

**Mainieri, Tina** and Nicks, Sandra D and Korn, James H. The Rise and Fall of Deception in Social Psychology and Personality Research, 1921 to 1994. *Ethics Behavior*, 7(1), 69-77, 1997.

The frequency of the use of deception in American psychological research was studied by reviewing articles from journals in personality and social psychology

from 1921 to 1994. Deception was used rarely during the developmental years of social psychology into the 1930s, then grew gradually and irregularly until the 1950s. Between the 1950s and 1970s the use of deception increased significantly. This increase is attributed to changes in experimental methods, the popularity of realistic impact experiments, and the influence of cognitive dissonance theory. Since 1980 there appears to have been a decrease in the use of deception as compared to previous decades which is related to changes in theory, methods, ethical standards, and federal regulation of research.

**Maitland, Ian**. Virtuous Markets: The Market as School of the Virtues. *Bus Ethics Quart*, 7(1), 17-31, Ja 97.

This paper addresses the character forming effects of the market—and, specifically its impact on the "virtues." There is a long tradition of viewing commerce as subversive of the virtues. In this view, the market is held to have legitimated the pursuit of narrow self-interest at the expense of social and civic obligations and moral restraints. But, as Albert Hirschman has shown, many enlightenment moralists saw commercial society as a moralizing force. Which view is right? This paper examines how many of the character traits that we commonly call virtues are rewarded—and so presumably reinforced and diffused—by the market. (edited)

**Maitzen, Stephen**. Diversity in the Classroom. *Stud Phil Educ*, 16(3), 293-302, Jl 97.

It is important to appreciate how the battle between multiculturalist and individualist theories of education has shaped the pedagogical advice that some institutions of higher learning now give their instructors. In an important sense, that advice invites college and university teachers to pursue conflicting, irreconcilable goals in their teaching. By examining a particular North American example of such advice, I try to explain why the understandable attempt to accommodate both multiculturalism and individualism in the classroom inevitably makes for incoherent pedagogy.

**Maiza Ozcoidi, Idoia**. Averroes, filósofo y teólogo. *Euridice*, 119-139, 1992.

Cet article prétend montrer qu'Averroes n'a pas été seulement le meilleur interprète du *Corpus aristotelicum* et le plus influent aristotélicien au Moyen Age et au Renaissance. Il a été aussi un penseur originel qui a recrée le légat grec classique en l'enrichissant avec les apports de la culture islamique. L'originalité d'Averroes est de mettre aussi l'accent sur l'adhesion à la verité en suivant une méthodologie fort rigoureuse, et de s'élever comme un genial innovateur, pour établir la posibilité d'être scientifique et philosophe, et en plus, croyant. (edited)

**Majer, Ulrich**. Husserl and Hilbert on Completeness: A Neglected Chapter in Early Twentieth Century Foundations of Mathematics. *Synthese*, 110(1), 37-56, Ja 97.

**Major, Ladislav**. Descartes in the Context of Husserl's and Patocka's Phenomenology (in Czech). *Filosof Cas*, 44(5), 841-861, 1996.

Descartes is according to Husserl an author of two significant steps. Firstly, he renewed the demand that philosophy must be a universal science from the absolute evidence. Secondly, he discovered this absolute evidence in the turn to subject and that's why he initiated the passage from the naive objectivism to the transcendental subjectivism. But simultaneously Descartes committed two basic errors, depreciating his important contribution. Instead of the transcendental subjectivism he created a nonsense transcendental realism. (edited)

**Major, Ladislav**. Patocka's Phenomenology of Meaning and Heidegger. *Filosof Cas*, 44(4), 605-616, 1996.

Patocka's late nonsubjective phenomenology is well-known. One of its important aspects is not properly analysed up to this time—i.e., the outline of phenomenology of meaning. It can be explained by the fact that the demand to elaborate the real philosophy of meaning was pronounced in his late essay *About Masaryk's Philosophy of Religion* (1976). But some basic ideas of his own theory was mentioned sooner. Patocka deals very thoroughly with Kant's conception of meaning of human life. Kant's solution is according to him wrong, because it puts together meaning with purpose, i.e., with causality. The notion of causality is however only ontic, while the notion of meaning must be understood as ontological. (edited)

**Makkreel, Rudolph A**. Philosophical Hermeneutics and Hermeneutical Philosophy (in Dutch). *Tijdschr Filosof*, 59(1), 3-27, Mr 97.

Gadamer's distinction between traditional and philosophical hermeneutics is challenged in order to consider a variety of ways in which philosophy and hermeneutics have intersected since the eighteenth century. Not only has philosophy influenced hermeneutics (as in Dilthey's inquiry into the conditions of understanding), but hermeneutical considerations have also influenced philosophy (as in Nietzsche's perspectivism). Practical and moral concerns are shown to provide an important background for the philosophical reflections on interpretation found in Kant, Schleiermacher, Droysen, and Dilthey. Although the hermeneutical views of Dilthey and Heidegger display certain affinities with Aristotle, they part ways on the role of judgment in interpretation. By relating Dilthey, Heidegger and Gadamer back to Kant, it becomes possible to distinguish two complementary philosophical approaches to hermeneutics, one that roots interpretation in prejudgment and seeks authentic disclosure, and one that aligns interpretation with reflective judgment and aims at authentic critique.

**Makkuni, Santosh**. Moral Luck and Practical Judgment. *J Speculative Phil*, 10(3), 199-209, 1996.

**Makowski, François**. "Il provincialismo filosofico" in *Geofilosofia*, Bonesio, Luisa (ed), 39-55. Sondrio, Lyasis, 1996.

"Socrate, d'où viens tu et où vas-tu?" (*Lysis*, 203a)? Nous posons ces questions à Socrate, Kant et Heidegger. "Dans quel lieu s'enracine leur réflexion?", "en quel lieu sont-ils arrivés?", "comment, entre ces deux lieux, cheminent-ils?". Nos

Makus, Robert 766 AUTHOR INDEX

philosophes présentent indentiquement la pensée comme activité, chemin à tracer et habitation à construire. Ontiquement: ils sont des modèles de sédentarité. Ontologiquement, la problématique développe les rapports de la pensée et du spatial de façon non *métaphorique*. Exercer la philosophie, c'est cheminer et bâtir une province, atopique lieu du repos. Philosopher, bâtir, habiter, c'est s'approprier l'inappropriable, car nous ne sommes finalement nulle part, atopiques.

**Makus, Robert**. Response to Gregory Pence's Case Study in the Teaching of Ethics. *Teach Phil*, 19(3), 280-282, S 96.

**Malard, Letícia**. Ficçao e História na Narrativa Contemporânea. *Educ Filosof*, 10(19), 105-113, Ja-Je 96.

The purpose of this work is analyzing the relationship between history and fiction, building upon the thought of some novelists and historians about this subject. On a second level, the work intends to demonstrate how one can study that relationship in novels, not necessarily checking the presence or absence of historical facts in them. The fundamental is to understand how writers fictionalize the history of literary procedures. It is also to verify which borderlines are imposed by the real events and how the veto at the pure historic discourse is configured. (edited)

**Malatesta, Michele**. *The Primary Logic: Instruments for a Dialogue between the Two Cultures*. Roma, Millennium Romae, 1997.

The present work on symbolic logic differs from more widely diffused and better-known ones because of the generous space devoted to the philosophical problems of language. Without an adequate understanding of these problems, there is a risk of losing sight of the value—and at the same time of the utility—of a technique which, far from being an end in itself, has proved to be an irreplaceable instrument for approaching the most difficult philosophical questions. A second point in which the present work differs from others is that it introduces the reader not only to standard symbology and those of the *Principia Mathematica* and of Hilbert, but also to the symbology of Jan Lukasiewicz. (publisher, edited)

**Malcolm, Norman** and Von Wright, Georg Henrik (ed). *Wittgensteinian Themes: Essays 1978-1989*. Ithaca, Cornell Univ Pr, 1995.

The book demonstrates the clarity and accessibility for which Malcolm's writing is renowned. Like most of his work, the essays examine basic issues in philosophy of language and philosophy of mind. Himself a noted philosopher, Georg Henrik von Wright has chosen the papers included here and appended to the volume his eloquent Memorial Address for Norman Malcolm, delivered at King's College, London, in November 1990. Professor von Wright has also supplied a brief preface. (publisher, edited)

**Maldamé, Jean-Michel**. Évolution et Création: La Théorie de L'évolution: Ses Rapports avec la Philosophie de la Nature et la Théologie de la Création. *Rev Thomiste*, 96(4), 575-616, O-D 96.

The purpose of the present study is to give a proof that it is not any conflict between science and theology about evolution and creation. In the first part, the study indicates the meaning of fact, theory, paradigm and principle. After those epistemological accuracies, the second part shows the philosophical implications and ground of evolutionism. Then the theological part studies and examines how the action from God and natural laws work in harmony.

**Malet, Antoni**. Isaac Barrow on the Mathematization of Nature: Theological Voluntarism and the Rise of Geometrical Optics. *J Hist Ideas*, 58(2), 265-287, Ap 97.

This paper suggests that Barrow introduced a novel philosophy of the mathematical sciences—one in which theological voluntarism played a key grounding role. Barrow argued that the principles of mathematical sciences need not be self-evidently true, nor need they be true when applied to "this world," for they only must be free from contradiction. He also introduced an explicit distinction between mathematical and physical truths, characterizing the former as truths that apply to imaginary worlds, perhaps nonexistent now, that God might have created nonetheless. Barrow's geometrical optics was an attempt to provide a mathematization of nature inspired by his new philosophy of the mathematical sciences.

**Malherbe, Michel**. Hobbes et la mort du Léviathan: opinion, sédition et dissolution. *Hobbes Stud*, 9, 11-20, 1996.

**Malhotra, Ashok K**. "Sartre and Samkhya-Yoga on Self" in *Culture and Self*, Allen, Douglas (ed), 111-128. Boulder, Westview Pr, 1997.

In Chapter 7, "Sartre and Samkhya-Yoga on Self," Ashok Malhotra delineates six perspectives on the self as presented by Jean-Paul Sartre in his work *Being and Nothingness*. Sartre views the self as a consciousness, an ego, a body, a social entity, a value, and an *ego-less* being. Professor Malhotra compares and contrasts Sartre's position with that of the Samkhya-Yoga view which understands self as consciousness, *buddhi*, *ahamkara*, *manas*, sense-motor organ complex, and an *ego-less* reality. Though there are major ontological differences between the two positions, Malhotra submits that they are similar in spirit. This chapter is divided into three parts: a presentation of Sartre's six perspectives on the shelf; an explication of the Samkhya-Yoga view in terms of the transcendental and empirical selves; and a comparative analysis of the two positions.

**Malhotra, Ashok K** and Allen, Douglas (ed). *Culture and Self*. Boulder, Westview Pr, 1997.

Traditional scholars of philosophy and religion, both East and West, often place a major emphasis on analyzing the nature of "the self." In recent decades, there has been a renewed interest in analyzing self, but most scholars have not claimed knowledge of an ahistorical, objective, essential self free from all cultural determinants. The contributors of this volume recognize the need to contextualize specific views of self and to analyze such views in terms of the dynamic, dialectical relations between self and culture. An unusual feature of this book is that all of the chapters not only focus on traditions and individuals, East and West, but include as primary emphases comparative philosophy, religion and culture, reinforcing individual and cultural creativity. Each chapter brings specific Eastern and Western perspectives into a dynamic, comparative relation. This comparative orientation emphasizes our growing sense of interrelatedness and interdependency. (publisher)

**Maliandi, Ricardo**. "Cinco tesis sobre la racionalidad de la acción" in *La racionalidad: su poder y sus límites*, Nudler, Oscar (ed), 353-360. Barcelona, Ed Paidos, 1996.

**Malinowski, Jacek**. Strong Versus Weak Quantum Consequence Operations. *Stud Log*, 51(1), 113-123, 1992.

This paper is a study of similarities and differences between strong and weak quantum consequence operations determined by a given class of ortholattices. We prove that the only strong orthologics which admits the deduction theorem (the only strong orthologics with algebraic semantics, the only equivalential strong orthologics, respectively) is the classical logic.

**Mall, Ram Adhar**. "Spezifisch indischer Beitrag zur Interkulturalität und Interreligiosität als ein möglicher Weg zum Weltfrieden" in *Kreativer Friede durch Begegnung der Weltkulturen*, Beck, Heinrich (ed), 261-275. New York, Lang, 1995.

The paper proposes to delineate the two concepts of interculturally and interreligiosity from an Asian perspective. In doing so the author works out an 'analogous concept of hermeneutics' and critically discusses the different intercultural encounters and clashes of civilizations in history of humanity and asks for their reasons of their more or less destructive outcome. The conclusion reached is: Neither the one *philosophia perennis* nor the one *religio perennis* is an exclusive possession of any one philosophical or religious tradition. Such an insight helps us to give up our absolutistic truth claims which are productive of conflicts and which jeopardize mutual understanding.

**Malo, Antonio**. Il desiderio: precedenti storici e concettualizzazione platonica. *Acta Phil*, 5(2), 317-337, 1996.

The main point of this study is to show the relation between different pre-Socratic views on the desire and the Platonic notion of *thymos*, that is a synthesis of preceding intuitions. The *thymos* is the essence of the human desire, because it is the place in which there are always present two opposite desires: the desire of life (*epithymia*) and the desire of beauty and immortality (*eros*). For that the *thymos* reveals the impossibility to unify human desires and at the same time appears as the field of ethics. In fact the *eros* can indirectly manage the *epithymia* through the *thymos*, promoting in that way the birth of virtues.

**Malone, Michael J**. Donagan on Cases of Necessity. *Amer Cath Phil Quart*, 70(Supp), 229-236, 1996.

Alan Donagan in *The Theory of Morality* permits the intentional killing of innocent persons in a certain kind of situation. I argue that Donagan erred when he granted this permission. There is no morally relevant difference between this kind of case and others he considers impermissible. Killing the innocent in this kind of case contraverts his fundamental principle and its moral foundation.

**Malone, Patricia**. Expanding Diversity Education for Preservice Teachers: Teaching about Racial Isolation in Urban Schools. *J Thought*, 32(3), 97-111, Fall 97.

**Maloney, Philip J**. Infinity and the Relation: The Emergence of a Notion of Infinity in Derrida's Reading of Husserl. *Phil Today*, 40(3), 418-429, Fall 96.

This essay elaborates the Husserlian contexts of Derrida's understanding of infinity. Despite the Hegelian tone of Derrida's discussions of infinity, most notably in "The Double Session," many of the structural elements of the incessant supplementarity articulated by Derrida in this essay are first noted in his early work on Husserl. Turning first to Derrida's problematization of Husserl's evocation of the Idea in the Kantian sense in his introduction to Husserl's *The Origin of Geometry*, the author focuses in the last two sections on the quasi-transcendental supplementarity articulated by Derrida in *Speech and Phenomena*. Taken together, these two discussions point toward an incessant supplementation that is not transcended by an absolute infinity but is rather constituted by an essential finitude. It is thus a notion of infinity proper to *Différance*.

**Maloney, Philip J**. Levinas, Substitution, and Transcendental Subjectivity. *Man World*, 30(1), 49-64, Ja 97.

The task of this paper is to clarify the status and implications of Levinas's insistence on the necessity of subjectivity to the ethical relation. Focusing in particular on the discussion of substitution in *Otherwise than Being*, it is argued that the description of subjectivity as substitution enables Levinas to articulate the necessity of the subject to the approach of the other in a manner which avoids the transcendental character which such claims to necessity usually embody. This argument proceeds from an initial characterization of substitution within the constellation of themes pursued by Levinas in *Otherwise than Being* to a detailed examination of the first four sections of the "Substitution" chapter. The essay concludes by noting the unity of the ethical exceeding of the transcendental character of subjectivity with the project which animates Levinas's work from its beginnings: the exceeding of the ontological by the ethical.

**Malpas, Jeff**. Space and Sociality. *Int J Phil Stud*, 5(1), 53-79, Mr 97.

To what extent is our being as social creatures dependent on our having a grasp of sociality? Is a purely solipsistic space, a space that can be grasped without any grasp of the existence of others, possible? These questions are examined and the possible connection between space and sociality explored. The central claim is that there is indeed an intimate relation between the concept of space

AUTHOR INDEX 767 Manning, Richard N

and the idea of the social: that any creature that has a grasp of the concept of space must also be a creature that has a grasp of sociality in the sense of having a grasp of itself as one creature existing alongside a multiplicity of other creatures.

**Malpas, Jeff**. The Transcendental Circle. *Austl J Phil*, 75(1), 1-20, Mr 97.

Circularity has often been cited as a basic flaw in 'transcendental' arguments. Drawing on the work of Kant and Heidegger, this paper argues that the circularity that is evident in transcendental arguments is an essential feature of the transcendental as such (and indicative of an important connection between the transcendental and the hermeneutical) and that transcendental circularity need not be viewed as undermining the viability of transcendental forms of reasoning.

**Maltese, Giulio** and Orlando, Lucia. The Definition of Rigidity in the Special Theory of Relativity and the Genesis of the General Theory of Relativity. *Stud Hist Phil Mod Physics*, 26B(3), 263-306, D 96.

**Man Ling Lee, Theresa**. *Politics and Truth: Political Theory and the Postmodernist Challenge*. Albany, SUNY Pr, 1997.

Postmodernism maintains that the philosophical validation of ideas by way of truth is intrinsically linked to the legitimation of power. In this political context Lee considers a series of related questions. Why does it matter politically how truth is validated? Does the claim to having truth necessarily imply a certain claim to authority by those who possess truth? Is truth therefore power? Is a foundationalist notion of truth antidemocratic by implication? Is a contextualist notion necessarily democratic, as the postmodernists suggest? *Politics and Truth* examines the treatment of these problems in the work of thinkers ranging from Plato and Hobbes to Weber, Foucault, and Arendt. The book concludes with a consideration of ideology in post-Mao China that shows the elusive if not illusory openness of contextualism. (published, edited)

**Mancini, Sandro**. Merleau-Ponty's Phenomenology as a Dialectical Philosophy of Expression. *Int Phil Quart*, 36(4), 389-398, D 96.

The article show that the purpose of the final elaboration of Merleau-Ponty is thus to find a new idea of philosophy in which both Hegelian and Husserlian phenomenology can converge. But this tension in no way constitutes an element of rupture in the theoretical continuity of the Merleau-Pontian philosophy.

**Mandelbrote, Scott**. History, Narrative, and Time. *Hist Euro Ideas*, 22(5-6), 337-350, S-N 96.

During the summer of 1992, Robert Smith and I organised a series of lectures in Oxford on the theme 'History and Narrative'. This essay was originally prepared to accompany those lectures in print, but, sadly, their publication has been prevented by differences of opinion among the contributors. I am, however, extremely grateful to Lisa Jardine, Robert Young, Marina Warner, Terence Ranger, Marilyn Butler, Michael Gilsenan, Antonia Byatt, Frank Romany and the late Louis Marin for the inspiration with which they have provided me. Brian Young gave me the opportunity to deliver an earlier version of this essay as a paper at the University of Sussex; a number of those who raised points at that seminar, or who have read drafts for me, also deserve thanks: Mishtooni Bose, Robin Briggs, John Burrow, Mark Collier, Saul Dubow, Clare Griffiths, Giles Mandelbrote, James McConica, Joad Raymond, Peter Sarris and Martin van Gelderen.

**Mander, W J**. McTaggart's Argument for Idealism. *J Speculative Phil*, 11(1), 53-72, 1997.

McTaggart deserves to be remembered as more than just the originator of an unsettling paradox about the nature of time, for he was also the creator of an original and perplexing argument, now largely forgotten, in support of philosophical idealism. The reasons why it has been ignored, though understandable, are unjust, and my aim in this paper is to show that, despite initial appearances, McTaggart's argument for idealism has a serious and troubling core that, like his more famous argument about time, cannot be simply ignored by anyone who wishes to arrive at a coherent overall theory of reality.

**Mandt, A J**. Fichte, Kant's Legacy, and the Meaning of Modern Philosophy. *Rev Metaph*, 50(3), 591-633, Mr 97.

**Maner, Walter**. Unique Ethical Problems in Information Technology. *Sci Eng Ethics*, 2(2), 137-154, A 96.

A distinction is made between moral indoctrination and instruction in ethics. It is argued that the legitimate and important field of computer ethics should not be permitted to become mere moral indoctrination. Computer ethics is an academic field in its own right with unique ethical issues that would not have existed if computer technology had not been invented. Several example issues are presented to illustrate this point. The failure to find satisfactory noncomputer analogies testifies to the uniqueness of computer ethics. Lack of an effective analogy forces us to discover new moral values, formulate new moral principles, develop new policies and find new ways to think about the issues presented to us. For all of these reasons, the kind of issues presented deserve to be addressed separately from others that might at first appear similar. At the very least, they have been so transformed by computing technology that their altered form demands special attention.

**Mangiafico, James**. Nietzsche and the Value of Truth. *Phil Today*, 41(1-4), 174-180, Spr 97.

Challenging the view that Nietzsche's work ultimately reinforces what he calls the "will to truth" (the conviction that nothing is needed more than truth and that everything else has only second-rate value), I argue that Nietzsche shows such faith in truth to be self-defeating. The result of a moral imperative to avoid deceiving, the unconditional value of truth culminates in modern science and the rejection of the metaphysics underlying its founding morality. Having led truthfulness to infer its own demise, Nietzsche attempts to foster a love of surfaces in the spirit of the Greeks, who were "superficial out of profundity."

**Manicas, Peter T**. Explanation, Understanding and Typical Action. *J Theor Soc Behav*, 27(2-3), 193-212, Je-S 97.

There are immense differences in the social sciences both as regards what is to be explained and how it is to be explained. I make an initial distinction between the understanding, construed roughly as acquiring a grasp of the generative mechanisms and structures at work in the world, natural and social and explanation, which I construe as causal. I clarify several candidates for the objects of explanation and reject the idea that the "explanation of behavior"—if that means the acts of concrete situated persons—is ever the proper object of explanation. Critical to my account is the idea of a typical actor, created for purposes of explanation. I conclude by applying this analysis to the explanation of crime.

**Manimala, Varghes**. The Revolutionary Humanism of Jayaprakash Narayan. *J Dharma*, 22(1), 18-34, Ja-Mr 97.

The purpose of this article was to highlight the philosophical basis of the revolutionary thought of Jayaprakash. It tries to spell out the character of Jayaprakash and the struggles he faced to achieve the idealistic goals he placed before himself and the society. Jayaprakash, a revolutionary by nature, was not satisfied with the ordinary. He sought a transformation of society by trying to infuse an ethical quideline in the political life of the day. Remaining a nonseeker of power he questioned the structures that contribute towards the dehumanisation of humankind. In order to restore human beings their dignity what is needed is not a piece-meal approach, but a *sanatio in radice*, a *total revolution*. It is a process and continuous struggle, based primarily on moral principles, while it stresses the internal as well as the external transformation, through people's participation. Total revolution is a nonviolent struggle aimed at genuine democracy with a decentralised power structure. Jayaprakash also suggested the agents and methods of total revolution.

**Mann, David W**. The Virtues in Psychiatric Practice. *Theor Med*, 18(1-2), 21-30, Mr-Je 97.

Using as a guide Pellegrino and Thomasma's "end-oriented beneficence model" of the virtues in medical practice, the author derives from the cardinal forms of psychiatric treatment a set of virtues particular to this field. Prior work from Jung, Havens and Menzer-Benaron helps to clarify the analysis.

**Mann, Doug**. Porn Revisited. *J Soc Phil*, 28(1), 77-86, Spr 97.

In this paper I will revisit the debate over pornography by doing three things: a) I will suggest a more sophisticated, two-dimensional set of distinctions between positions in the debate; b) I will then go on to attack both libertarians and the group I call "repressive feminists"; and c) I will conclude by suggesting that by means of Hume's theory of sympathy we could support a limited form of censorship to bring women more fully into our moral and political community. I turn first to the labors of definition.

**Mann, Doug**. The Body as an "Object" of Historical Knowledge. *Dialogue (Canada)*, 35(4), 753-776, Fall 96.

In this paper I try to unearth the sociological roots of "body theory" in history, sociology and philosophy in terms of postmodernist and feminist reactions to consumer culture. I argue that the notion of a constructed body (and, in a similar sense, of gender as pure construction) comes out of a *culture of narcissism* and not out of a quest for an objective understanding of the human condition. I conclude by arguing *against* Foucault's power/knowledge equation and *for* the continued relevance of an idealist hermeneutic (along Collingwoodian or Winchian lines) for understanding the human body as a social or historical thing.

**Mann, Golo**. Bertrand Russell (in Polish). *Kwartalnik Filozof*, 24(4), 175-206, 1996.

**Mann, Jonathan M**. Medicine and Public Health, Ethics and Human Rights. *Hastings Center Rep*, 27(3), 6-13, My-Je 97.

There is more to modern health than new scientific discoveries, the development of new technologies, or emerging or re-emerging diseases. World events and experiences, such as the AIDS epidemic and the humanitarian emergencies in Bosnia and Rwanda, have made this evident by creating new relationships among medicine, public health, ethics and human rights. Each domain has seeped into the other, making allies of public health and human rights, pressing the need for an ethics of public health and revealing the rights-related responsibilities of physicians and other health care workers.

**Mannath, Joe**. The Political Philosophy of Martin Luther King Jr.. *J Dharma*, 22(1), 49-73, Ja-Mr 97.

This article presents King's work and political philosophy. Part one introduces King's person and work. Part two explains the steps by which he was thrust more and more deeply into the Civil Rights Movement, became its most influential leader and went on to attack America's war in Vietnam and criticize U.S. culture radically. The third part examines King's political philosophy, particularly the meaning and elements of the militant nonviolence which he advocated. King's achievement lies in finding a path between apathy and violence. How deep and lasting his contribution is, remains a moot point, since the racial divide is still strong.

**Manning, Richard N**. Biological Function, Selection, and Reduction. *Brit J Phil Sci*, 48(1), 69-82, Mr 97.

It is widely assumed that selection history accounts of function can support a fully reductive naturalization of functional properties. I argue that this assumption is false. A problem with the alternative causal role account of function in this context is that it invokes the teleological notion of a goal in analyzing real function. The selection history account, if it is to have reductive status, must not do the same. But attention to certain cases of selection history in biology, specifically those involving meiotic drive, shows that selection historical explanations are available in the case of items without any plausible function. Making contributions to goals, here fitness, must be introduced as an additional constraint in the analysis, either explicitly, or implicitly by appeal to individual functions or the selection-of/selection-for distinction.

**Manning, Rita C**. Liberal and Communitarian Defenses of Workplace Privacy. *J Bus Ethics*, 16(8), 817-823, Je 97.

In this paper, I survey liberal and communitarian defenses of privacy, paying particular attention to defenses of privacy in the workplace. I argue that liberalism cannot explain all of our intuitions about the wrongness of workplace invasions of privacy. Communitarianism, on the other hand, is able to account for these intuitions.

**Manning, Robert J S**. Openings: Derrida, *Différance*, and the Production of Justice. *Phil Today*, 40(3), 405-417, Fall 96.

**Manning, Sharyn** and Schneiderman, Lawrence J. The Baby K Case: A Search for the Elusive Standard of Medical Care. *Cambridge Quart Healthcare Ethics*, 6(1), 9-18, Winter 97.

A hospital resisted providing life-sustaining treatments for an anencephalic infant on the grounds that such treatment did not fall within the "prevailing standard of medical care." We conducted a phone survey of children's hospitals' physicians and reviewed guidelines and consensus statements by authoritative medical societies. Although there was universal condemnation of prolonged life support of an anencephalic baby, there was little evidence that the hospitals would resist such treatment if parents demanded it. Furthermore, guidelines by professional societies provide no grounds for refusing to treat an anencephalic infant on parental demand. There appears to be little to support the hospital's claim that in the face of parental demand for prolonged life support of an anencephalic infant a "prevailing standard of medical care" exists that rejects such treatment. Instead there appears to be a serious gap between the attitudes of the physicians interviewed as to what constitutes acceptable practice and the declarations of the professional leadership.

**Manno, Ambrogio Giacomo**. La Volontà di Potenza in Nietzsche e la Storia dell'Europa negli Ultimi Tempi. L'Aquila, Japadre, 1996.

**Manno, Ambrogio Giacomo**. Nuove frontiere della scienza. *Sapienza*, 49(3), 351-366, 1996.

**Mansbach, Abraham**. Overcoming Anthropocentrism: Heidegger on the Heroic Role of the Works of Art. *Ratio*, 10(2), 157-168, S 97.

In this paper I argue that although Heidegger's *Being and Time* and 'The Origin of the Work of Art,' seem to deal with different topics, there is continuity between these two texts. In the latter Heidegger was trying to solve a central problem that arose in the former: how to account for authentic existence and at the same time overcome the anthropocentrism of traditional philosophy. (edited)

**Mansbach, Abraham**. Strange Epoch! From Modernism to Postmodernism (in Hebrew). *Iyyun*, 46, 193-208, Ap 97.

There is general agreement in Western intellectual circles that our familiar ways of knowing, representing and reading have changed unrecognizably in recent years. But there is confusion regarding the meaning and implications of this changes for major issues in our culture: art, ethics and philosophy. In this paper I delineate the source of the confusion by analyzing some of Heidegger's contributions to the destruction of modern thinking and by arguing that there are three main factors to this confusion. One is the breakdown of the hierarchy of the dualist structures. The second factor is the misconception of this breakdown by postmodern thinkers. Lastly, that part of Heidegger's own critique of the philosophical tradition is open to the same criticisms that it levels.

**Mansbridge, Jane**. Taking Coercion Seriously. *Constellations*, 3(3), 407-416, Ja 97.

Democracies need coercion to avoid illegitimately privileging the status quo. Incorporating "partially legitimate coercion" (not Haugaard's "noncoercively based power conflict") into ideal democratic theory recognizes the always unsettled nature of interactions in which some parties succeed in imposing their will upon others. No single set of procedural principles to govern coercion—not even a single set of interpretations of the principle of equal power—can even hypothetically command agreement (or meet the criteria of Benhabib and Habermas for "general rules of action and institutional arrangements"). Other equally valid sets of procedural principles will produce other results.

**Mansilla, H C Felipe**. El disciplinamiento social como factor del desarrollo histórico: Una visión heterodoxa desde el tercer mundo (Primera parte). *Rev Filosof (Costa Rica)*, 34(83-84), 213-225, D 96.

Departing from diverging perspectives, Sigmund Freud, Norbert Elias and even the Frankfurt School have perceived the disciplization of instincts and passion as a fundamental civilizatory element. Taking into account the not very positive results of this process in the Third World (universal standardization, decline of spontaneity and the individual), the author advances a critical revision of those approaches.

**Mantovani, Paolo** (& others) and Fiorentini, Camillo and Avelone, Alessandro. On Maximal Intermediate Predicate Constructive Logics. *Stud Log*, 57(2-3), 373-408, O 96.

We extend to the predicate frame a previous characterization of the maximal intermediate propositional constructive logics. This provides a technique to get maximal intermediate predicate constructive logics starting from suitable sets of classically valid predicate formulae we call maximal nonstandard predicate constructive logics. As an example of this technique, we exhibit two maximal intermediate predicate constructive logics, yet leaving open the problem of stating whether the two logics are distinct. Further properties of these logics will be also investigated.

**Manyà Serres, Felip** and Escalda-Imaz, Gonzalo and Sobrino, Alejandro. Principles of Logic Programming with Uncertain Information: Description of Some of the Most Relevant Systems (in Spanish). *Theoria (Spain)*, 11(27), 123-148, S 96.

The purpose of this paper is to present the principles of the fuzzy logic programming, exemplifying them by a couple of proposals that we think are representatives of the advances in this field. We include also the description of another systems' programming with uncertain information that are based on other logics of uncertainty which are different from fuzzy logic. This article only presupposes an elementary knowledge of the classical first-order logic.

**Manzer, Robert A**. The Promise of Peace? Hume and Smith on the Effects of Commerce on War and Peace. *Hume Stud*, 22(2), 369-382, N 96.

With the demise of Marxist communism, the prospects for international peace seem greater than ever;; this essay explores the role commerce and the commercial spirit might play in promoting this end. A deeper perspective on this problem is sought by examining the thought of two highly insightful early advocates of the commercial way of life, David Hume and Adam Smith. Their thoughts on commerce and war qualify in important ways the prevailing scholarly view that commerce is a force for peace—via international cooperation or the pacific passion of interest—while showing us why peace is more likely in a commercial world. Drawing attention to the psychological underpinnings of commerce and war and to changes in the way nations make war brought on by commerce, they help deepen our understanding of the complex relation between commerce and international behavior while determining more precisely the significance of the commercial ethos for human behavior in general.

**Manzi, Attilio**. Las parábolas ficinianas del bosque y el jardín en las Stanze per la Giostra de Angelo Poliziano. *Cuad Vico*, 7/8, 323-331, 1997.

With the work of Poliziano the idea of a *topos* adopted by several artists who so adhere the Platonical conception of nature as a metaphysical place, ideal and abstract, becomes stronger. The "garden", instrumental and rationalized model, shows the taste of the late 15th century. This taste impregnates every ambit of creativity in such a way that nature amounts to a creation of the human mind. The author emphasizes how the aesthetical and philosophical horizon of Poliziano in his *Stanze*—the values and the taste of which are recreated—can be considered as a key for opening the extreme complexity of the 15th century.

**Mar, Gary**. The Modal Unity of Anselm's *Proslogion*. *Faith Phil*, 13(1), 50-67, Ja 96.

Anselm claimed that his *Proslogion* was a "single argument" sufficient to prove "that God truly exists," that God is "the supreme good requiring nothing else," as well as prove "whatever we believe regarding the divine Being." In this paper we show how Anselm's argument in the *Proslogion* and in his *Reply to Gaunillo* can be reconstructed as a single argument. A logically elegant result is that the various stages of Anselm's argument are validated by standard axioms from contemporary modal logic.

**Mara, Gerald M**. *Socrates's Discursive Democracy: Logos* and *Ergon* in Platonic Political Philosophy. Albany, SUNY Pr, 1997.

This book is intended to contribute to what I believe is an important conversation about the importance of Platonic political philosophy for contemporary political theory, especially democratic theory. My goal is not to try to say the last word on Plato's contributions, but to try to encourage others to engage the Platonic dialogues in a way that is open to the possibility of discovering a variety, indeed a wealth, of contributions. It would be, in fact, surprising if such engagements did not generate substantive interpretations of particular dialogues that were often very different from the ones presented here. My own debt to interpreters who have said other, different things about Plato should be apparent throughout. I hope that it is also clear that I owe at least as much to those with whom I disagree as I do to those whose views I share. (publisher)

**Marbach, Eduard**. Understanding the Representational Mind: A Phenomenological Perspective. *Human Stud*, 19(2), 137-152, Ap 96.

This paper reflects on the relationship between Husserlian phenomenology and scientific psychology. It tries to show how phenomenological results have relevance and validity for present-day cognitive developmental psychology by arguing that consciousness matters in the study of the representational mind. The paper presents some methodological remarks concerning empirical or applied phenomenology; it describes the conception of an exploratory developmental study with 3 to 9-year-old children viewing a complex pictorial display; it then illustrates how a phenomenological interpretation of the data works; in conclusion, it sketches a view of realism about conscious experiences which is taken to be inherent in the phenomenological perspective of understanding the representational mind.

**Marcenaro, Alessandro**. "Geometrie dell'Aperto" in *Geofilosofia*, Bonesio, Luisa (ed), 57-76. Sondrio, Lyasis, 1996.

**Marchianò, Grazia**. "The Flowers of the *Noh* and the Aesthetics of *Iki*" in *East and West in Aesthetics*, Marchianò, Grazia (ed), 99-106. Pisa, Istituti Editoriali, 1997.

**Marchianò, Grazia** (ed). *East and West in Aesthetics*. Pisa, Istituti Editoriali, 1997.

Aesthetic theory in Asia, viewed as a coessential part of aesthetic theory in general, is the issue proposed by the editor in her introduction, where the enlarging of the aesthetic ecumenism in the last fifty years (1947-1997) is critically examined. The book consists of nine original essays by five specialists—three of whom Asiatic—in oriental aesthetics and by four Western scholars dealing with interdisciplinary approaches to aesthetic problems. The 200 page text brings to a sharp focus issues of mutual concern to aestheticians throughout the world. (edited)

**Marchini, Pier Paolo**. Recenti interpretazioni di J.S. Mill. *G Crit Filosof Ital*, 16(2), 185-222, My-Ag 96.

**Marchis, Vittorio**. Protesi, ovvero la metamorfosi. *Iride*, 9(19), 703-715, S-D 96.

**Marcialis, Maria Teresa**. Genovesi e Cartesio. *G Crit Filosof Ital*, 16(3), 455-475, S-D 96.

**Marciniec, Jacek**. Infinite Set Unification with Application to Categorical Grammar. *Stud Log*, 58(3), 339-355, My 97.

In this paper the notion of unifier is extended to the infinite set case. The proof of existence of the most general unifier of any infinite, unifiable set of types (terms) is presented. Learning procedure, based on infinite set unification, is described.

**Marcos, Alfredo**. The Tension between Aristotle's Theories and Uses of Metaphor. *Stud Hist Phil Sci*, 28(1), 123-139, Mr 97.

There is a debate concerning the cognitive role of metaphor. Aristotle's work is one of the most interesting case studies in history. The purpose here is an interpretation of Aristotelian passages and an explanation of their relevance to some contemporary philosophical problems. A reading of Aristotelian texts with an *interpretative view of metaphor* is suggested. Every good metaphor has its own *heuristic inertia*. We need to create conjectures and challenge their functionality: no automatic rules, no special faculties. A good metaphor uncovers *objective potential similarities* existing between entities in the world, a *discovery* which is, however, a *creative* one.

**Marcus, Jacqueline**. Brief Takes From the Horizon. *Teach Phil*, 19(3), 259-261, S 96.

Six skits/satires in the vein of Monty Python humor on Socrates, Nietzsche, Heidegger, Kant, Descartes and Hegel.

**Marcus, Ruth Barcan**. Are Possible, Non Actual Objects Real?. *Rev Int Phil*, 51(200), 251-257, Je 97.

A critique of versions of modal realism which countenance possible but nonactual individuals. It is claimed that a sentence which purports to be about a properly named nonactual individual is best understood as nonfully interpreted and without a truth value, since such syntactic names are not descriptive and are nonreferring. Possible or alternative worlds which are nonactual are taken as those whose domains include actual objects but which vary from the actual with respect to their histories. Some particular attention is given to an analysis of belief contexts where the sentence following the propositional attitude verb contains nonreferring syntactic names.

**Mares, Edwin D**. Mostly Meyer Modal Models. *Log Anal*, 37(146), 119-128, Je 94.

In this paper, it is shown that several modal relevant logics are complete over a semantics in which the truth conditions for the modal operators are the standard Kripkean truth conditions.... This proof confirms *most* of a conjecture made by Meyer in Routley and his "Semantics of Entailment II" (*Journal of Philosophical Logic* 1, 1973). (edited)

**Mares, Edwin D**. Relevant Logic and the Theory of Information. *Synthese*, 109(3), 345-360, D 96.

This paper provides an interpretation of the Routley-Meyer semantics for a weak negation-free relevant logic using Israel and Perry's theory of information. In particular, Routley and Meyer's ternary accessibility relation is given an interpretation in information-theoretic terms.

**Mares, Edwin D**. Semantics for Relevance Logic with Identity. *Stud Log*, 51(1), 1-20, 1992.

Models are constructed for a variety of systems of quantified relevance logic with identity. Models are given for systems with different principles governing the transitivity of identity and substitution and the relative merits of these principles are discussed. The models in this paper are all extensions of the semantics of Fine's "Semantics for Quantified Relevance Logic".

**Mares, Edwin D** and Fuhrmann, André. On S. *Stud Log*, 53(1), 75-91, F 94.

The sentential logic S extends classical logic by an implication-like connective. The logic was first presented by Chellas as the smallest system modelled by constraining the Stalnaker-Lewis semantics for counterfactual conditionals such that the conditional is effectively evaluated as in the ternary relations semantics for relevant logics. The resulting logic occupies a key position among modal and substructural logics. We prove completeness results and study conditions for proceeding from one family of logics to another.

**Margalit, Avishai**. "The Moral Psychology of Nationalism" in *The Morality of Nationalism*, McKim, Robert (ed), 74-87. New York, Oxford Univ Pr, 1997.

**Margolis, Eric** and Laurence, Stephen. Regress Arguments against the Language of Thought. *Analysis*, 57(1), 60-66, Ja 97.

The language of thought hypothesis is sometimes taken to be refuted by a familiar sort of argument: "The language of thought is appealed to in order to explain some feature of natural language (such as its learnability, or meaningfulness), but, in order to explain this feature, the language of thought must also have the feature. Thus a regress." We argue that such arguments rely on the assumption that the entire motivation for the language of thought is the explanandum that allegedly generates the regress. But this assumption is simply false.

**Margolis, Joseph**. "The Declension of Progressivism" in *Epistemology and History*, Zeidler-Janiszewska, Anna (ed), 383-404. Amsterdam, Rodopi, 1996.

Several versions of progressivism are presented and discussed (C S Peirce, K R Popper, Th Kuhn, I Lakatos, L Laudan). Peirce's doctrine (fallibilism) is subjected to analysis and critique (Quine) as well as Hegel's philosophy in this matter. Hempel and Putnam are referred to as representatives of progressivism in science. A discussion on Popper's views as confronted with Kuhn's theory closes the article.

**Margolis, Joseph**. Remarks on History and Interpretation: Replies to Casey, Carr, and Rockmore. *Man World*, 30(2), 151-157, Ap 97.

**Margolis, Joseph**. Some Remarks on Sparshott on the Dance. *J Aes Educ*, 31(2), 45-50, Sum 97.

**Margolis, Joseph**. Two Paradoxes in Heidegger. *Phil Today*, 41(1-4), 189-198, Spr 97.

**Margonis, Frank** (ed) and Boler, Megan (ed) and Callan, Eamonn (ed). *Philosophy of Education (1996)*. Urbana, Phil Education Soc, 1997.

**Margot, Jean-Paul**. "La creación de las verdades eternas y la fábula del mundo" in *Memorias Del Seminario En Conmemoración De Los 400 Anos Del Nacimiento De René Descartes*, Albis, Víctor S (ed), 93-109. Sankt Augustin, Academia, 1997.

La carta a Mersenne del 15 de abril de 1630 que afirma el encadenamiento de "todas las dificultades de fisica" respecto a las cuales Descartes "tomó partido", de tal manera que (le) resultaría imposible "demostrar una sin demostrarlas todas juntas", muestra que, sin las reflexiones que pertenecen al *Tratado de Metafisica de 1629*, Descartes "no hubiese podido encontrar los fundamentos de la Física". Introduce "cuestiones metafísicas relacionadas con la física", particularmente "la creación de las verdades eternas". Cabe entonces preguntarse en qué medida *El Mundo o el Tratado de la Luz*, es decir, el discurso cartesiano sobre la naturaleza, está en deuda con la doctrina de la creación de las verdades eternas. Creemos que lejos de ser circunstancial, la doctrina de las verdades eternas creadas está en el corazón mismo de la articulación de la física y la metafísica.

**Margreiter, Reinhard**. The Internal Connectedness of Philosophy of History and Philosophy of Language in Nietzsche's Early Writings (in Serbo-Croatian). *Filozof Istraz*, 15(4), 643-654, 1995.

Gezeigt werden soll der systematische Zusammenhang von Geschichtsund Sprachphilosophie beim frühen Nietzsche. Referenztexte sind die "Zweite Unzeitgemässe Betrachtung" (*Vom Nutzen und Nachteil der Historie für das Leben*) und das Fragment "Über Wahrheit und Lüge im aussenmoralischen Sinne". Ein Brennpunkt der zentralen Themen, die sowohl in diesen beiden Schriften wie auch in der *Geburt der Tragödie* verfolgt werden, ist die Frage nach dem Verhältnis von Wissenschaft und Leben. Dabei werden sowohl der Wissenschafts-wie der Lebensbegriff problematisiert. Zuerst wird Nietzsches Konzeption der Geschichte im Kontext seiner Konzeption von Wissenschaft dargelegt, darauffolgend seine erkenntnis-und sprachphilosophische Position (auf der seine Wissenschaftskonzeption aufbaut) und abschliessend der innere Zusammenhang von Geschichte und Sprache. (edited)

**Margutti Pinto, Paolo Roberto**. Há Problemas Filosóficos? Uma Avaliaçao da Resposta do Pirronismo. *Cad Hist Filosof Cie*, 6(Spec), 159-178, Ja-D 96.

The purpose of this work is to clarify some mistakes in the current controversy about Pyrrhonism. An interpretation and an assessment of the Pyrrhonean response to the question concerning the existence of philosophical problems is presented. It is suggested that the Pyrrhonean response is ambiguous and outdated, requiring important adaptations in order to fit the current philosophical needs.

**Mari, Enrique E**. Las teoría y su influencia política y socio-jurídica en los problemas de la democracia. *Cuad Etica*, 19-20, 87-104, 1995.

In the ancient ages the "theorei" had to communicate to the Polis the results of their visits to other countries and the counsel they gave to the authorities concerning rules in the fields of education, law, etc., represented a great political influence for them. This paper examines the influence enjoyed in the present time by hegemonic economical and social theories, which guide the policies of the globalized market economy in a sense which is neither democratic nor participative. The ideas of Robert Musil are thought to be especially suitable for the present situation.

**Marín, R** and Taboada, M. What's the Fuzzy Temporary Reasoning? (in Spanish). *Agora (Spain)*, 15(2), 83-96, 1996.

In this work we analyze the role of fuzzy logic in the field of temporal reasoning. The basic problems associated with the representation and management of time dependent information in expert systems are addressed and the basic strategies used to formally model temporal imprecision present in multiple domains are introduced. The foundations of time modelling through fuzzy temporal constraint networks are introduced and some examples are presented.

**Marín-Casanova, José Antonio**. Nada existe donde faltan las palabras: La *quidditas* retórica de Vico y la metafísica de la evidencia. *Cuad Vico*, 7/8, 75-99, 1997.

(I) Metaphysics of evidence, which most conspicuous expression is the Cartesian *mathesis universalis*, looks for the urgent and necessary, the fundament or foundation of things, which is regarded as independent of the form and accessible without assumptions to knowledge: rhetoric is the dispensable *qualitas* of philosophy. (II) Vico's way of thinking, in opposition to that view, could be considered as its retorsion: by reveling its hidden presuppositions, refuses them. (III) Vico's tropology, by proposing the tropical univocity, makes a rhetoric philosophy and a philosophical rhetoric: rhetoric is the indispensable *quidditas* of philosophy.

**Marín-Casanova, José Antonio**. Nihilismo y metáfora: La fábula imaginera en Vico y Nietzsche. *Cuad Vico*, 5/6, 83-104, 1995/96.

*Nihilism and Metaphor: The Imaginative Fable of Vico and Nietzsche* fancies a reading of the "new" science as "gay" science imagining that the rather common metaphor of Vico's *Scienza Nuova* and of Nietzsche's *Über Wahrheit und Lüge im aussermoralischen Sinn* answers to the problem of nihilism: to introduce meaning into a world characterized by God's absence. Vico and Nietzsche show that the meaning of existence cannot be described but only fabled: every authenticity is always a trophic one. With this paradoxical result the article aims to provide a reflection of the significance of rhetoric for contemporary philosophical debate. (edited)

**Marín-Casanova, José Antonio**. Vico y la retórica que no cesa. *Cuad Vico*, 7/8, 413-422, 1997.

Our time is not an exception to the rule that identifies rhetoric and crisis, especially the crisis of the monological accounts. [Today, the very Western canon becomes suspicious and thought, pluralist, philosophical rhetoric appears as *locus* for a reason which does not desire to manage the world, but to inhabit it "poetically"]. (Hence, the present acme of Vico's rhetoric philosophy, which was a reaction—by no means resentful—against Cartesianism, is at the *impasse* of that rationality symbolized by Descartes). Battistini's reflections in *New Vico Studies* (1994) and the publication of Vico's *The Art of Rhetoric* give a convincing proof of it.

**Marinabarreto, Luz**. Es Posible una Ética de las Emociones?. *Ideas Valores*, 3-20, Ap 97.

I analyze two different ways to conceive the relationship between emotions and morality. The first one consists in understanding moral sense as an expression of moral feelings. The second one emphasizes that moral convictions may control our emotions and that rational justification of emotional states is possible. Although moral motivation is not necessarily a rational one, I stress that moral choice is possible, based on the internal coherence of our convictions about the kind of person we want to be and what motivations we think are worth having. I suggest that this reflective attitude concerning moral choice applies also to emotions, including those (irrational ones) such as love, hate, etc.

**Marincevic, Juan** and Becerra Batán, Marcela. Elecciones epistemológicas y práctica docente. *Rev Latin de Filosof*, 22(2), 367-374, 1996.

This work purports to give an account of a teaching experience regarding problems of scientific knowledge, which has taken place at the School of Humanistic Sciences of the State University in San Luis. The starting point of this experience was determined by certain positions suggested hypothetically. To begin with, we believe that the "transmission" of knowledge is determined by the epistemological elections. We regard knowledge as a construction and we conceive scientific knowledge as processes historically and culturally situated. The teaching practice consistent with this choice, will permit the reconstruction of relations with the knowledge and with the pupils, active subjects in the process of appropriation and recreation of knowledge.

**Maríñez Navarro, Freddy**. Postmodernity: the End of Modernism or the End of Diversity? (Spanish). *Rev Filosof (Venezuela)*, 24(2), 81-92, Jl-D 96.

This work specifies the elements of the present sociohistoric process characterized by economic as well as social globalization. In this sense, it analyzes two opposite viewpoints on social change: as postmodern homogeneity and as utopia of diversity.

**Maring, Matthias** and Lenk, Hans. Responsibility and Social Traps. *Int J Applied Phil*, 11(1), 51-61, Sum-Fall 96.

In highly developed societies individual actions are less important than collective and corporate actions. The individualistic concepts of ethics are generally not sufficient to tackle the problem of distributing responsibility for untoward (e.g., ecological) consequences of such actions, especially in social trap constellations. With respect to moral evaluation many participating and contributing individuals have to bear a certain corresponsibility for emerging supraindividual effects. A moral reorientation of individuals to cope with the problems of this new situation is necessary, but not sufficient. We also need structural incentives, social mechanisms for sanctioning as well as the pertaining institutional measures, e.g., legal and political arrangements.

**Maring, Matthias** and Lenk, Hans. Technology in Opposition Power—Must (Czech). *Filosof Cas*, 45(1), 113-138, 1997.

The notion of individual is even in our current era of institutional and corporate decisions and enterprises of much import and of particular importance for technology. However, problems of collective and corporate responsibility are becoming and still will become more and more topical. Engineering ethics codes should be developed, improved and operationally implemented in the future. The rules sketched out here of priorities for handling responsibility conflicts have subsequently to be elaborated much further. All this, then, would be necessary to meet the ideal requirements of our joint and individual responsibility for technology in our society.

**Marinho Sampaio, Tânia Maria**. A Práxis Freireana na Educaçao. *Educ Filosof*, 10(19), 7-16, Ja-Je 96.

**Marinho Sampaio, Tânia Maria**. A Questao Freireana da Educaçao como Práxis Político-Filosófica. *Educ Filosof*, 9(17), 79-89, Ja-Je 95.

**Marion, Jean-Luc**. "Nothing and Nothing Else" in *The Ancients and the Moderns*, Lilly, Reginald (ed), 183-195. Bloomington, Indiana Univ Pr, 1996.

**Marion, Mathieu**. Wittgenstein et son oeuvre posthume. *Dialogue (Canada)*, 35(4), 777-789, Fall 96.

Critical study of Wittgenstein's *Wiener Ausgabe*, volumes 1 and 2. After recalling the story of this edition of Wittgenstein's posthumous writings, the authors discuss issues in philosophy of mathematics raised in these volumes and Wittgenstein's rejection of his own 'phenomenology'.

**Markell, Patchen**. Contesting Consensus: Rereading Habermas on the Public Sphere. *Constellations*, 3(3), 377-400, Ja 97.

Comparisons of Arendt's and Habermas's accounts of the "public sphere" suggest that Arendtian politics preserves contestation while resisting consensus, and that the Habermasian public sphere represses contestation in its pursuit of consensus. These claims are mistaken. Arendt's and Habermas's critiques of Rousseau demonstrate their shared concern with preserving spaces of contestation against the aspiration to universal agreement. Attention to Habermas's use of the concepts of understanding, agreement, and consensus reveals that his description of the communicative action as "action oriented toward agreement" does not demand the suppression of contestatory action. Finally, Habermas's own account suggests (in ways he does not clearly acknowledge) that a vigorously contestatory public sphere is a necessary condition of democratic legitimacy.

**Market, Oswaldo**. "Fichte y el modelo del Ser" in *El inicio del Idealismo alemán*, Market, Oswaldo, 13-34. Madrid, Ed Complutense, 1996.

El inicio de la nueva y radical andadura del filosofar, la del Idealismo alemán, arranca de la defensa fichteana del *Ich bin*, como principio supremo. Éste implica, según piensa el autor, la vivencia del estar siendo, por lo tanto la de *ser en cuanto actividad del sujeto*, al margen de todo uso copulativo y meramente intelectual del "es" o del "soy". Comprender al ser como sujeto, se defiende igualmente, fue el hallazgo de Aristóteles en su concepción de la *ousía*. La conferencia propone la contraposición pensar y entender y concluye que el único camino abierto a la meditación del ser es la de comprenderlo en el convivir de la intersubjetividad.

**Market, Oswaldo**. Vida y concepción del Mundo: Un texto olvidado de Karl Ernst von Baer (1860). *An Seminar Hist Filosof*, 13, 209-234, 1996.

Zentrale Texte des Vortrages von 1860, den K.E. v. Baer in Petesbrug hielt, nach der seltenen Ausgabe von 1862, sowie ihre spanische Übersetzung sind hier herausgegeben. Seine imaginative Darstellung der ganz verschiedenen Auffasung der Natur nach der Veränderung des Raum-Zeit-Massstabes gelten immer noch als Anregung einer fruchtbaren Reflexion, überhaupt in Zeiten des sogenannten Konstruktivismus.

**Market, Oswaldo** and Rivera de Rosales, Jacinto. *El inicio del Idealismo alemán*. Madrid, Ed Complutense, 1996.

**Markham, Steven E** and Shepard, Jon M and Wimbush, James C. An Empirical Examination of the Multi-Dimensionality of Ethical Climate in Organizations. *J Bus Ethics*, 16(1), 67-77, Ja 97.

The purpose of this study was to determine whether the ethical climate dimensions identified by Victor and Cullen (1987, 1988) could be replicated in the subunits of a multiunit organization and if so, were the dimensions associated with particular types of operating units. We identified three of the dimensions of ethical climate found by Victor and Cullen and also found a new dimension of ethical climate related to service. Partial support was found for Victor and Cullen's hypothesis that certain ethical climate dimensions are associated with particular forms of organizational governance and control.

**Markic, Olga**. Finding the Right Level for Connectionist Representations (A Critical Note on Ramsey's Paper). *Acta Analytica*, 27-35, 1995.

The paper discusses Ramsey's suggestion that the fully distributed character of representations in connectionist models supports the antirepresentationalist position. It is argued that if we take into account learning, the higher-level descriptions of the connectionist networks and the possibility of holistic inference, then the fully distributed character of connectionist representations does not give a cogent reason to deny them the status of representation.

**Markie, Peter J**. Goldman's New Reliabilism. *Phil Phenomenol Res*, 56(4), 799-817, D 96.

**Markie, Peter J**. In Defense of One Form of Traditional Epistemology. *Phil Stud*, 85(1), 37-55, Ja 97.

**Markosian, Ned**. The Paradox of the Question. *Analysis*, 57(2), 95-97, Ap 97.

**Marková, Ivana**. Language and Authenticity. *J Theor Soc Behav*, 27(2-3), 265-275, Je-S 97.

It is argued that the analysis of language should play a central role in the study of social psychological phenomenon. For example, there is evidence that habitual inauthenticity in the use of language which was practiced in the Eastern and Central European totalitarian systems was partly related to the breakdown of moral principles and to the loss of identity. Using two sentences, 'Proletarians of the whole world—unite' and 'The Bororo are arara', it is shown that they can carry content which goes beyond their semantic meanings. In the given examples, the former sentence is analysed in terms of an ideology and the latter in terms of a social representation. It is pointed out that subjectivation, which is a pervasive feature of modern individualism, just as totalitarianism, represents a threat to authenticity in language.

**Marková, Ivana**. Towards an Epistemology of Social Representations. *J Theor Soc Behav*, 26(2), 177-196, Je 96.

The theory of social representations is primarily a theory of lay knowledge. It is argued that it employs polar concepts of the post-Hegelian social science in which the opposite components of such concepts are mutually interdependent. The focus of this paper is on polarities such as individual/social, implicit/explicit and unconscious/conscious. The theory of social representations is conceptually compatible with the sociocultural theories of knowledge imply that in order to become an independent thinker, the child or the scientist must conceptually free themselves, at least partly, from the constraints of their symbolic social environment. The theory of social representations, in contrast, studies how the social symbolic social environment arrests the individual in the existing forms of thinking, prohibits him or her from independent thought and enforces a particular manner of conceiving the world, events and objects. Finally, attention is drawn to the multilayered nature of thought and to its methodological implications.

**Marková, Ivana** and Linell, Per. Coding Elementary Contributions to Dialogue: Individual Acts versus Dialogical Interaction. *J Theor Soc Behav*, 26(4), 353-373, D 96.

Coding as a method of dialogue analysis has often failed to distinguish between individual acts and dialogical interactions. The purpose of this paper was to draw attention to conceptual problems involved in providing coding systems for interactions that could preserve dialogicality, i.e., the joint construction of meaning, sequentiality and act-activity interdependence and the reflexive nature of interactions. We show that some aspects of dialogicality are already built into a few existing systems. We argue that building on these dialogical characteristics, more suitable dialogically orientated coding systems can be developed and that such systems have their important role in diagnostic practices.

**Marks, Amy S** and Morris, Michael H and Allen, Jeffrey A. Modeling Ethical Attitudes and Behaviors under Conditions of Environmental Turbulence: The Case of South Africa. *J Bus Ethics*, 15(10), 1119-1130, O 96.

This study explores the impact of environmental turbulence on relationships between personal and organizational characteristics, personal values, ethical perceptions, and behavioral intentions. A causal model is tested using data obtained from a national sample of marketing research professionals in South Africa. The findings suggest turbulent conditions lead professionals to report stronger values and ethical norms, but less ethical behavioral intentions. Implications are drawn for organizations confronting growing turbulence in their external environments. A number of suggestions are made for ongoing research.

**Marks, Joel**. The Trivialization of Ethics or Ethics Programs in the Workplace: A Cautionary Tale. *Acorn*, 6(2), 29-31, Fall 91.

Is an ethics program in a workplace setting really an *ethics* program if it does not consider, among other issues, the ethics of the business or industry itself (for example, manufacturing weapons)? In order to apply the category of ethics properly to their own workplace, directors of nonacademic ethics programs would do well to have an academic background in ethics, i.e., the study of the nature of ethics.

**Markus, György**. Hegel and the End of Art. *Lit Aes*, 6, 7-26, O 96.

The paper situates the Hegelian conception of the "end of art" in the context of his philosophy of history. It distinguishes the philosophical and empirical notions of art in Hegel. In the first sense art ends in modernity, since by becoming autonomous, i.e., solely and truly art, it looses its function to make sensuously manifest the highest values, the Absolute for a historical community. In its empirical sense, however, art will continue to exist and even reach new perfections, but now each work of art has to win for itself some sort of (limited) social significance and whether it succeeds in this endeavour, this depends partly on accidental circumstances.

**Marlangeon, Mauricio Pablo**. Capitalizer of Binary Relations and the Fork Operator as Image of a General Disjoint Union-Function of Cartesian Product Functions. *Bull Sec Log*, 26(1), 31-38, Mr 97.

The fork operator is conceived here as a slight generalization of that defined in [1]. In the present paper the composition $f \circ g$ of two binary relations $f$ and $g$ is taken as of they were functions. In general $f$ and $g$ are incoherent and heterogeneous, in a sense specified below. The concept of catalyzer of that composition is introduced and the compatibility relation of catalyzing the same ordered pair of $f \circ g$ is indicated. Next a bijection between that covering and $f \circ g$ itself is established. (edited)

**Marletti, Carlo**. Note su conoscenza e grammatica. *Teoria*, 16(1), 93-99, 1996.

**Marmor, Andrei**. On the Limits of Rights. *Law Phil*, 16(1), 1-18, 97.

**Marmura, M E**. "Some Remarks on Averroës's Statements on the Soul" in *Averroës and the Enlightenment,* Wahba, Mourad (ed), 279-291. Amherst, Prometheus, 1996.

**Maróstica, Ana H**. "A Nonmonotonic Approach to Tychist Logic" in *Studies in the Logic of Charles Sanders Peirce,* Houser, Nathan (ed), 535-559. Bloomington, Indiana Univ Pr, 1997.

**Marqués, Gustavo L**. A propósito de la crítica de Feyerabend al racionalismo crítico. *Analisis Filosof*, 16(1), 17-26, My 96.

In this work I wish to defend the following thesis: 1) The criticism that Feyerabend makes against the critical rationalism is based on certain aspects of the evidence which affects not only to its prescriptive aim, but also to the evaluative task of methodology. 2) It is possible to find an argument against prescriptivism that is independent of any consideration about evidence, avoiding in this way the undesirable consequences about evaluation. 3) The notions of certainty and elimination are connected in a way that poses serious problems for the critical rationalism. (edited)

**Marques Veríssimo, Mara Rúba Alves**. A Articulaçao entre Infância, Cidadania e História: Uma Questao para a Pedagogia. *Educ Filosof*, 9(17), 191-207, Ja-Je 95.

This work presupposes that the current challenging to the pedagogy should be the consideration about what kind of man it intends to form. The work also criticises traditional basis of classical modern pedagogy, which led to an increasing dissociation between school cultural context and concrete social world, as a way of protecting the child. From the reviewing of modern basis of childhood construction, and from the analysis of other citizenship and history conceptions, it proposes teaching theoretical-methodological alternatives to articulate the child to adult-social world.

**Marques Veríssimo, Mara Rúba Alves**. O Materialismo Histórico e Dialético nas Abordagens de Vigotsky e Wallon acerca do Pensamento e da Linguagem. *Educ Filosof*, 10(19), 129-143, Ja-Je 96.

This work discusses about the contribution of the theory of history for the social psychology field, helping on the yielding of a new theory of knowledgement. After approaching the basic aspects of historical and dialectical materialism, we identified the influence of Marxist's theoretical assumptions about man and history in Vigotsky and Wallon works, which deals with psychogenesis. To emphasize methodological aspects, to the detriment of conceptual analysis, we delineated some of the consequences of the referred approaches in the pedagogical field.

**Márquez, Alvaro**. The Modernity Crisis and the Pedagogical Reason (Spanish). *Fronesis*, 2(2), 1-21, D 95.

The pedagogical reason is an "order" of the knowledge-power (Foucault) which systematizes, regulates and performs the discourse of rationality underlying the historic knowledges; then, it could be part of the critique that: 1) finds out which philosophy of the technique these knowledges are rationalized with, and 2) it tries to create the public nonvirtual-space where the crisis of the modern human being's reason is faced and suppressed. (edited)

**Marquis, Don**. Fred Feldman's *Confrontations with the Reaper: A Philosophical Study of the Nature and Value of Death. Nous*, 30(3), 401-410, S 96.

Fred Feldman's book contains careful, interesting and provocative analyses of the concepts of life, death, and dying. His account of the nature of the misfortune of death is sound. His account of the wrongness of killing is an attempt at an account of the wrongness of all killings that are wrong. Such an overly ambitious analysis is both vague and circular. He attempts to provide a gradualist account of the wrongness of abortion such that early abortions are "not very bad" and late abortions are morally "horrendous." This fails too.

**Marquit, Erwin**. Some Comments on Dialectical and Logical Contradictions. *Nature Soc Thought*, 8(2), 155-159, 1995.

The commentary relates to an attempt to obscure the fact that an element of Hegelian idealism was uncritically brought into the classics of Marxism, which, in turn, gave rise to the illusion that dialectical materialists accept the possibility of objectively existing logical contradictions. Hegel extended the concept of identity of opposites from a dialectical identity in difference, which is a necessary characteristic of a dialectical contradiction, to the absolutized identity of opposites as a logical contradiction. Materialist dialectics does not need, nor can it accept, this absolutizing of the identity of opposites.

**Marra, Bruno**. Consapevolezza etica ed esperienza della virtù. *Sapienza*, 49(4), 455-461, 1996.

L'etica deve elaborare una tipologia salvifica adeguata per la società composta più da agglomerati socioistituzionali che da soggetti. F. Ferrarotti afferma che esiste una storicizzazione dei valori in rapporto alla consapevolezza soggettiva. Per A. Da Re la fenomenologia del comportamento umano e la descrizione dei contenuti materiali delle virtù costituiscono la base dell'esigenza etica. Per G. Piana il ricupero della virtù è essenziale per dare pieno sviluppo ad un'etica della responsabilità. In conclusione il vissuto è un accadimento che dà al soggetto la certezza di un ethos prive di sentenze. Il percorse virtuoso deve essere compenetrato dallo svuotamento per essere al riparo da contraffazioni. Nulla verrà concesso al soggetto che non sia giustiziato dallo stesso esistere.

**Marras, Ausonio**. The Causal Relevance of Mental Properties. *Philosophia (Israel)*, 25(1-4), 389-400, Ap 97.

I argue that (strong) psychophysical supervenience, properly understood as a metaphysical dependence or determination relation, helps to account for the causal/explanatory relevance of mental properties because (1) it blocks a standard epiphenomenalist objection to the effect that an event's mental properties are 'screened off' by their physical properties: (2) it accounts for the *causal* (and not merely *normative* or merely *nomological)* status of commonsense psychological generalizations; (3) it accounts for the *nonredundancy* and *irreducibility* of psychological explanations.

**Marsden, Jill**. Virtual Sexes and Feminist Futures: The Philosophy of 'Cyberfeminism'. *Rad Phil*, 78, 6-16, Jl-Ag 96.

**Marsden, John**. Liberation Theology and the Search for Peace in Ireland. *Heythrop J*, 37(4), 399-420, O 96.

The article examines the conflict over competing conceptions of political identity and identifies the various strands in the nationalist and unionist traditions. A political analysis using a noneconomistic historical materialism and theoretical reflections on nationalism is offered. Modern nationalism is traced to two sources: the democractic nationalism associated with the notion of popular sovereignty and nineteenth-century romantic nationalism. More culturally inclusive conceptions of political identity are needed in Irish society. The churches have reinforced cultural divisions and helped foster sectarianism. The Protestant churches must break with the *Orange Order*, and on the Roman Catholic side a plea is made for eucharistic sharing.

**Marshall, Bev** and Dewe, Philip. An Investigation of the Components of Moral Intensity. *J Bus Ethics*, 16(5), 521-530, Ap 97.

While there is a considerable interest in the topic of business ethics, much of the research moves towards measuring components with a view to predicting ethical behavior. To date there has not been a satisfactory definition of business ethics, nor has there been any real attempt to understand the components of a situation that may influence an individual's assessment of that situation as ethical or otherwise. Using Jones's (1991) construct of moral intensity as a basis for investigation, this paper presents some exploratory analysis on the context within which ethical decisions are assessed. The findings reveal that individuals differ in their assessments of the same situation and often use a number of complex reasons to explain whether a situation poses an ethical problem for them. These findings are discussed within a framework of measurement issues and future directions for research.

**Marshall, Graeme**. "Love's Truths" in *Love Analyzed,* Lamb, Roger E, 243-256. Boulder, Westview Pr, 1997.

Cleopatra dreamed there was an Emperor Antony. Her hyperboles are one of love's glories. There is a truthfulness in her seeing which a theory of interpretation for lovers enables us to uncover. Such a theory begins with beauty. Part II applies to aesthetic perception Wittgenstein's remarks about aspects in order to account for the perceptions of lovers. Part III is concerned with what is desired in love and the effects of it on the perception of the beloved. Part IV addresses the truths love reveals and how they might be known.

**Marshall, James D**. "Education in the Mode of Information: Some Philosophical Considerations" in *Philosophy of Education (1996)*, Margonis, Frank (ed), 268-276. Urbana, Phil Education Soc, 1997.

**Marshall, Patricia A** and Kelly, Susan E and Sanders, Lee M (& others). Understanding the Practice of Ethics Consultation: Results of an Ethnographic Multi-Site Study. *J Clin Ethics*, 8(2), 136-149, Sum 97.

**Marsonet, Michele**. I rapporti tra scienza e metafisica. *Acta Phil*, 5(2), 251-268, 1996.

Despite the neopositivistic efforts to eliminate metaphysics, the relation between science and metaphysics remains one of the great themes of philosophical discussion. Still, logical neopositivism, even in its decline, continues to have influence. The recent publication of E. Agazzi's *Filosofia della natura* offers an opportunity to reflect on this topic. The aim of the present article is to show, first of all, that science itself has its own metaphysics: the image of the scientist who investigates without having metaphysical hypotheses in mind is a myth. Moreover, if we understand metaphysics as the explication of the general conditions of the intelligibility of the real, it is easy to perceive that science is based upon certain presuppositions that have a transcendental character. From this it follows that there is a minimal sense of the term "metaphysics" which proves impossible to renounce. Since no one can exempt himself from having certain fundamental ideas about the real, neither are scientists exempt from this rule; at most, one may acknowledge that the metaphysical framework which some of them adopt is merely implicit.

**Marsoobian, Armen T**. "Aesthetic Form Revisited: John Dewey's Metaphysics of Art" in *Philosophy in Experience: American Philosophy in Transition,* Hart, Richard (ed), 195-221. New York, Fordham Univ Pr, 1997.

**Martens, Ekkehard**. La Filosofía como cuarta destreza cultural para la realización humana de la vida. *Dialogo Filosof*, 13(2), 233-238, My-Ag 97.

**Martí, Genoveva**. "Rigidity and Genuine Reference" in *Verdad: lógica, representación y mundo,* Villegas Forero, L, 401-411. Santiago de Compostela, Univ Santiago Comp, 1996.

I have argued elsewhere that these two days of identifying genuine reference are not just two different depictions of the same underlying idea; they respond to separate intuitions, they rely on different tools and they end up generating conflicting classifications of terms as genuinely referential. My purpose now is to continue exploring the chasm between these two conceptions of genuine reference. Here I will focus on the answer that each approach gives to the old question of the relation between genuine reference and rigidity. (edited)

**Martin, Brian**. Critics of Pesticides: Whistleblowing or Suppression of Dissent?. *Phil Soc Act*, 22(3), 33-55, Jl-S 96.

Many dissident experts are subject to dismissal, transfer and blocking of appointments, research grants and publications. Cases of attack on critics of pesticides illustrate the advantages of analysing this phenomenon using the concept of "suppression of dissent" rather than the concept of "whistleblowing."

**Martin, C B**. "Final Replies to Place and Armstrong" in *Dispositions: A Debate,* Armstrong, D M, 163-192. New York, Routledge, 1996.

**Martin, C B**. "Properties and Dispositions" in *Dispositions: A Debate,* Armstrong, D M, 71-87. New York, Routledge, 1996.

**Martin, C B**. "Replies to Armstrong and Place" in *Dispositions: A Debate,* Armstrong, D M, 126-146. New York, Routledge, 1996.

**Martin, C B** and Armstrong, D M and Place, Ullin T. *Dispositions: A Debate*. New York, Routledge, 1996.

In this book, first Place and Armstrong debate the ontological nature of dispositions, each setting out their view, and each in a second contribution criticizing the other and expanding their own view. In the second part of the book the debate becomes three-cornered, with three contributions from Martin, and two each from Armstrong and Place. An introduction by Tim Crane summarizes and surveys the debate.

**Martin, Christopher F J**. *An Introduction to Medieval Philosophy*. Edinburgh, Edinburgh Univ Pr, 1996.

Emphasizing the relationship between reason and faith, the author describes how and why Medieval philosophers saw their task as the development of a tradition handed down authoritatively. The first general introduction of its kind, this book will give students from a wide range of disciplines an essential philosophical understanding of the Medieval period. (publisher, edited)

**Martin, Dan**. Beyond Acceptance and Rejection?. *J Indian Phil*, 25(3), 263-305, Je 97.

**Martin, David S**. Critical Comparisons of Thinking Skills Programs: Making Curriculum Decisions. *Inquiry (USA)*, 14(2), 11-16, Wint 94.

The multiplicity of published programs in the field of education today that purport to enable teachers to teach for higher-order thinking strategies, demands a set of objective criteria for intelligent adoption decisions by schools and educators. A set of criteria by which decision-makers and teachers may make a judgment on adoption are presented, together with a rationale and procedure. Absolute indicators of quality and relative indicators for individual school settings are included.

**Martin, Dean M**. God and Objects: Beginning with Existence. *Int J Phil Relig*, 41(1), 1-11, F 97.

In *On Certainty*, Ludwig Wittgenstein shows that the certainty with which people think and act toward ordinary objects is neither grounded nor does it need

grounds. This paper proposes that the certainty exhibited by religious believers as they worship, pray, etc. with reference to God is logically similar and primitive in this respect. Nonetheless, there are important differences between the way certainty about God accrues for believers as compared to sureness about physical objects. Ultimately, the differences are traceable to the distinctive practices and passions that are intrinsic to the religious life itself.

**Martin, Jack**. Psychological Research as the Formulation, Demonstration, and Critique of Psychological Theories. *J Theor Phil Psych*, 16(1), 1-18, Spr 96.

The subject matter of psychology is humans and their experiences and actions. This subject matter differs from the subject matter of physical science by being more highly contextualized, uncertain, and morally saturated. As a consequence, psychological theory must concern itself with context and moral significance, and with the formulation of principles rather than causal laws. The development of psychological theory can be assisted by programs of inquiry that emphasize conceptual clarification and moral consideration, in addition to empirical demonstration. Programs of inquiry in psychology also should place a high value on reasoned criticism derivative from a wider array of scholarly methods and traditions. In all of this, psychology should be guided first and foremost by the nature of its subject matter. A desired implication of these proposals is a vision of psychology as a more broadly based scholarly discipline in which psychologists would identify themselves, and act as scholars and scholar-practitioners.

**Martin, Jack** and Sugarman, Jeff. Bridging Social Constructionism and Cognitive Constructivism: A Psychology of Human Possibility and Constraint. *J Mind Behav*, 17(4), 291-320, Autumn 96.

A theory intended to bridge social constructionist and cognitive constructivist thought is presented and some of its implications for psychotherapy and education are considered. The theory is mostly concerned with understanding the emergence and development of the psychological (mind, selfhood, intentionality, agency) from its biological and sociocultural origins. It is argued that the psychological is underdetermined by the biological and sociocultural, and possesses a shifting, dynamic ontology that emerges within a developmental context. Increasingly sophisticated capabilities of memory and imagination mediate and support the emergence of genuinely agentic psychological phenomena from appropriated sociocultural forms and practices.

**Martin, James**. Hegemony and the Crisis of Legitimacy in Gramsci. *Hist Human Sci*, 10(1), 37-56, F 97.

Gramsci's concept of hegemony is often believed to be a political account of legitimation. His Marxist critics go on to accuse him of failing to offer a properly structural account of bourgeois legitimation. I argue that Gramsci's theory attempted to straddle both economic and political accounts. In so doing, he presupposed the absence of effective authority in the Italian state. In such conditions, his project was to theorize the way in which economic classes became agents that would institute political order. The difficulties in applying Gramsci's formulation today lie in this combined economic and political account and the assumption of 'organic crisis' that supported it.

**Martin, John N**. Whether Logic Should Satisfy the Humanities Requirement. *Teach Phil*, 19(4), 385-396, D 96.

The arguments for logic as satisfying college humanities requirements, presenting both sides of the question. Originally written to be engaging for faculty outside philosophy, it employs the style of a mediaeval disposition. The humanities, liberal arts and fine arts are defined. The liberal arts are defined as usual in terms of theory; logic's role as the "art of arts" follows. The humanities are defined as in the Renaissance in terms of moral issues, as stressed by modern scholars like Garin. Logic's value then consists of its contribution to moral reasoning, the first serious developments in "informal" logic taking place during that period. It is explained how the two contribute to Cardinal Newman's ideal of the university education as knowledge-for-itself.

**Martin, Kathleen** and Reynolds, Sherrie. Educational Reform: A Complex Matter. *J Thought*, 32(1), 77-86, Spr 97.

This research suggests an approach to educational reform which honors the complexity of classrooms and schools. The authors call for ways of thinking about change which are consonant with what is known about the behavior of complex systems. They discuss the initial conditions which facilitate the emergence of spontaneously self-organizing systems appropriate for learning and the conditions which permit the continued functioning of such systems in adaptive, dynamic ways.

**Martin, M G F**. Self-Observation. *Euro J Phil*, 5(2), 119-140, Ag 97.

**Martin, M G F** and Campbell, John. Sense, Reference and Selective Attention. *Aris Soc*, Supp(71), 55-98, 1997.

**Martin, Michael**. *Legal Realism: American and Scandinavian*. New York, Lang, 1997.

As one of the most important movements in twentieth century legal thought, legal realism continues to be a source of controversy and inspiration. This study provides the first critical comparison and evaluation of American and Scandinavian legal realism. Presenting, evaluating and reformulating the basic ideas of American legal realists such as Karl Llewllyn, Walter Wheeler Cook, Herman Oliphant, Jerome Frank and Underhill Moore in the first part of the book, the author devotes the second part to a critical appraisal and reformulation of the major doctrines of Scandinavian legal realists such as Axel Hägerström, A. V. Lundstedt, Karl Olivecrona and Alf Ross. The book also reveals the misunderstanding of legal realism by legal philosophers such as H. L. A. Hart and Ronald Dworkin and the connections of legal realism to the critical legal studies movement. (publisher)

**Martin, Mike W**. Advocating Values: Professionalism in Teaching Ethics. *Teach Phil*, 20(1), 19-34, Mr 97.

I argue that professional responsibilities justify professors in advocating their personal ideals and value commitments pertinent to their disciplines. It follows that much advocacy is inevitable and desirable. The challenge is to distinguish acceptable from unacceptable forms, especially in the gray areas of undue influence where inappropriate pressures distort the learning process without amounting to overt coercion, indoctrination, or proselytizing. (edited)

**Martin, Mike W**. Personal Ideals in Professional Ethics. *Prof Ethics*, 5(1-2), 3-27, Spr-Sum 96.

According to the consensus paradigm, professional ethics consists in the set of responsibilities developed as a consensus within a profession and incumbent on all its members. After acknowledging the large element of truth in the paradigm, I argue that the paradigm is constricting and misleading. In doing so, I affirm the importance of personal commitments to ideals that are morally valuable but transcend minimum requirements. Personal ideals guide and motivate individuals in the professions, not only in career choices and matters of supererogation, but also in interpreting shared responsibilities such as confidentiality, loyality, and respect for clients.

**Martin, Raymond**. The Essential Difference between History and Science. *Hist Theor*, 36(1), 1-14, 1997.

My thesis is that there is a deep, intractable difference, not between history and science *per se*, but between paradigmatically central kinds of historical interpretations—call them *humanistic historical interpretations*—and theories of any sort that are characteristic of the physical sciences. The difference is that unlike theories in the physical sciences good humanistic historical interpretations (purport to) reveal subjectivity, agency and meaning. I use the controversy provoked by Gordon Wood's recent reinterpretation of the American Revolution to illustrate and substantiate this thesis. I also use it to support the claim that unless one attends to the ways in which humanistic historical interpretations reveal subjectivity, agency and meaning one has no hope whatsoever of getting the epistemology of historical studies right.

**Martin, Raymond** (ed) and Krishnamurti, J. *Krishnamurti: Reflections on the Self*. Chicago, Open Court, 1997.

The book is a collection of Krishnamurti's writings and lectures about the individual in relation to society. In *Reflections*, he examines the importance of inquiry, the role of emotions, the relations between experience and the self, the observer/observed distinction, the nature of freedom, and other philosophical ideas. (publisher, edited)

**Martin, Ursula** and Scott, Elizabeth. The Order Types of Termination Orderings on Monadic Terms, Strings and Multisets. *J Sym Log*, 62(2), 624-635, Je 97.

We consider total well-founded orderings on monadic terms satisfying the replacement and full invariance properties. We show that any such ordering on monadic terms in one variable and two unary function symbols must have order type *omega*, $omega^2$ or $omega^{omega}$. We show that a familiar construction gives rise to continuum many such orderings of order type *omega*. We construct a new family of such orderings of order type $omega^2$ and show that there are continuum many of these. We show that there are only four such orderings of order type $omega^{omega}$, the two familiar recursive path orderings and two closely related orderings. We consider also total well-founded orderings on $N^n$ which are preserved under vector addition. We show that any such ordering must have order type $omega^k$ for some 1 equal to or less then *k* equal to or less then *n*. We show that if *k* equal to *n* there are continuum many such orderings, and if *k* = *n* there are only *n!*, the *n!* lexicographic orderings.

**Martindale, Colin**. Empirical Questions Deserve Empirical Answers. *Phil Lit*, 20(2), 347-361, O 96.

**Martines, Paulo Ricardo**. Karl Barth's Interpretation of the *Proslogion* (in Portuguese). *Trans/Form/Acao*, 19, 231-239, 1996.

The chief aim of this paper is to present some essential elements of the interpretation to the *Proslogion* carried out by Karl Barth in his book, *S. Anselme, Fides Quaerens Intellectum, La preuve de l'existence de Dieu* (French translation). Taking Anselm's "theological programme" as a point of departure, Barth identifies the central lines for the reading of chapters 2-4 of the *Proslogion*. We shall attempt to point out both the significance and the achievement of that interpretation as a contribution to the historiography of the Anselmian thought.

**Martinez, Roy**. Speech-Acts, Kierkegaard, and Postmodern Thought. *Int Phil Quart*, 37(2), 149-159, Je 97.

According to Ronald L. Hall, there is a point of intersection between Austin and Kierkegaard; namely, the role played by language in interpersonal exchanges. For, whereas Austin's *How To Do Things with Words* analyzes certain classes of statements in ordinary language, Kierkegaard's *Either/Or* treats, however indirectly, the moral requirements imposed on us by the language we use. In this study I analyze the arguments Hall conducts in his book, *Word and Spirit*. I attempt to show that while Hall's reading of *Either/Or* from a linguistic point of view is tenable, neither his attempt to inscribe deontological characteristics within the pseudonymous strategy nor his ascription of a monistic ontology to Kierkegaard finds support in the corpus. For the linguistic practices of the works, instead of claiming to report or reflect facts, states of affairs in the world, or represent reality itself, derive their meaning of justification from the consistency of their own internal logic and the force of their rhetoric.

**Martínez Barrera, Jorge**. Los fundamentos de la bioética de H. Tristram Engelhardt. *Sapientia*, 52(201), 99-115, 1997.

**Martínez Barrera, Jorge**. Psicología de la libertad política en Aristóteles (comentario de *Política*, I, 4-7 y I, 13). *Analogia*, 11(1), 167-185, Ja-Je 97.

**Martínez Barrera, Jorge**. Significación contemporánea de las nociones de experiencia y derecho natural según Santo Tomás de Aquino. *Sapientia*, 51(200), 475-484, 1996.

**Martínez Guzmán, Vicent**. "Reconstruir la paz doscientos años después: Una Filosofía Transkantiana para la Paz" in *Kant: La paz perpetua, doscientos años después*, Martínez Guzmán, Vicent (ed), 119-144. Valencia, Nau Llibres, 1997.

The purpose of the work is to update the Kantian reflection about *peace*. First of all, it reconstructs the scholastic and cosmical concepts of philosophy focusing on the commitment to the regulative idea of peace. Secondly, from a realist point of view, it takes into account the role of the hard experience according to which human relationships are featured by an unsocial sociability. Thirdly, despite this hard experience, human beings are capable of reconstructing transcendentally the ideal of peace, that should be communicable and valid for all human reason and submitted to the publicity of the critique of this reason itself. Finally, from the perspective of pragmatic anthropology it reviews human capacities in the framework of which appears the moral predisposition as a guide to develop a cosmopolitan democracy and a universal civil society.

**Martínez Guzmán, Vicent** (ed). *Kant: La paz perpetua, doscientos años después*. Valencia, Nau Llibres, 1997.

**Martínez Marzoa, Felipe**. "Seyn" y "Ur-teilung" in *El inicio del Idealismo alemán*, Market, Oswaldo, 335-342. Madrid, Ed Complutense, 1996.

Con base en ciertos rasgos del uso kantiano del lenguaje se maneja aquí el término *reflexión* en un sentido que señala hacia la totalidad de la obra crítica de Kant, a la vez que sirve de punto de partida para interpretar las expresiones "Ur-theilung" y "Seyn", usadas por el joven Hölderlin. Algunos aspectos de la Lógica hegeliana son igualmente abordados por esta vía.

**Martínez Velasco, Jesús**. Monismo metodológico y metafísico en Spinoza: la mente como idea del cuerpo. *Pensamiento*, 53(206), 263-269, My-Ag 97.

The purpose of this work is to justify Spinoza's conception of the mind within a scientific framework that surpasses Descartes's unacceptable dualism. Spinoza outlined a less capricious philosophical model than the one devised by Descartes by means of his thesis of a unique substance, but with different attributes. He proposed an ontological and methodological monism, in which body and soul expressed the same event *simul*: the nature or the substance. Between mind and body there is an epistemic relationship; and, consequently, to know the mind implies to know more and better the body, the idea of which is the mind. The relationship is, then, an organic one. Spinoza refuses to regard the mind as an spiritual principle autonomous from the body and conscribes it as the idea of the body.

**Martínez Vidal, C** and Villegas Forero, L and Rivas Monroy, Uxía. *Verdad: lógica, representación y mundo*. Santiago de Compostela, Univ Santiago Comp, 1996.

This book corresponds to the Proceedings of the Symposium "Truth: Logic, Representation and World" (Santiago de Compostela, Spain, January 1996, from 17th to 20th). The volume is divided into the following sections: Truth Theories, Philosophy of Mathematics, Philosophy of Science, Philosophy of Language, Cognitive Sciences and Philosophy of Mind and Logic. The papers included in the different sections reflect the general and omnipresent character of the problem of truth in relation to research studies in semantics, representation and ontology.

**Martínez-Solano, José Francisco**. "Variations in the Notion of "Truth" in *K. R. Popper's Philosophy" in Verdad: lógica, representación y mundo*, Villegas Forero, L, 83-94. Santiago de Compostela, Univ Santiago Comp, 1996.

The notions of 'truth' and 'truthlikeness' in Karl Popper has been analyzed by I. Grattan-Guinness, S. Haack, D. Miller, G. Anderson or H. Albert. However, they interpret them in different ways: some of them hold that Popper does not make good use of the theory of truth as 'correspondence'; others, having based on how Tarski influences Popper's work, maintain that Tarski did not defend about truth what Sir Karl ascribes to him; finally, the rest of them do not only agree with Popper, but also add important arguments in his favor. Nevertheless, the question of whether Popper modified or developed his conception about the 'truth' has been dealt with only a few times. This paper tries to shed light on this issue. (edited)

**Martinich, A P**. *Thomas Hobbes*. New York, St Martin's Pr, 1997.

Thomas Hobbes is one of the greatest philosophers and political theorists of the last three hundred years. His life and thought are an intriguing blend of conservatism and radicalism and possibly subterfuge. He was both a conservative supporter of the Stuart monarchy and absolute sovereignty and also a radical democratic theorist. In religion, he was an astute biblical critic, being the first person to argue that Moses could have written only a small part of the Pentateuch. (publisher,edited)

**Martins, António Manuel**. O Conimbricense Manuel Góis e a Eternidade do Mundo. *Rev Port Filosof*, 52(1-4), 487-499, Ja-D 96.

**Martins, J. Cândido**. Filosofia do *Carnival* Surrealista. *Rev Port Filosof*, 52(1-4), 501-522, Ja-D 96.

Employing as theoretical matrix Bakhtine's thought on "carnivalesque" parody, the author analyses the parodistic aspect of Portuguese surrealist poetry in the 50's and 60's. Surrealism is presented as shock-aesthetics. The article shows black humor as a form of liberating laughter, while illustrating the "carnivalesque" worldview with parodistic rhetoric and inferring the interrelationship between surrealist aesthetics and vital praxis. Finally, there is a reflection on the paradoxical officialization of this avant-garde movement.

**Martirano, Maurizio**. "Ernst Cassirer e il problema dell'oggettività nelle scienze della cultura" in *Lo Storicismo e la Sua Storia: Temi, Problemi, Prospettive,* Cacciatore, Giuseppe (ed), 396-408. Milano, Guerini, 1997.

**Marton, Scarlett**. Pascal: A Busca do Ponto Fixo e a Prática da Anatomia Moral. *Discurso,* 24, 159-172, 1994.

O objetivo deste artigo é discutir dois aspectos centrais da filosofia de Pascal. Explorando o paradoxo da condiçao humana, mostra-se a necessidade da busca do ponto fixo. Aplicando o *renversement du pour au contre* ao conceito de eu, revela-se a importância da prática da anatomia moral.

**Martone, Arturo**. L'Istoria dell'Uomo dipinta ne' linguaggi: Il Vico di Diego Colao Agata. *Stud Filosofici,* 301-330, 1995.

This work provides some essential features of the text Diego Colao Agata's, *Piano ovvero Ricerche filosofiche sulle lingue* (Napoli, 1774), that will be published at the end of 1997 and that shows the influence of G.B. Vico and A. Genovesi.

**Marturano, Antonio**. Filosofia e realtà virtuale. *Iride,* 9(19), 769-772, S-D 96.

**Marty, Gisèle** and Cela-Conde, Camilo J. Mind Architecture and Brain Architecture. *Biol Phil,* 12(3), 327-340, Jl 97.

The use of the computer metaphor has led to the proposal of "mind architecture" (Pylyshyn 1984; Newell 1990) as a model of the organization of the mind. The dualist computational model, however, has, since the earliest days of psychological functionalism, required that the concepts "mind architecture" and "brain architecture" be remote from each other. The development of both connectionism and neurocomputational science, has sought to dispense with this dualism and provide general models of consciousness—a "uniform cognitive architecture"—, which is in general reductionist, but which retains the computer metaphor. This paper examines, in the first place, the concepts of mind architecture and brain architecture, in order to evaluate the syntheses which have recently been offered. (edited)

**Marx, Maarten** and Mikulás, Szabolcs and Németi, István. Taming Logic. *J Log Lang Info,* 4(3), 207-226, 1995.

In this paper, we introduce a general technology, called *taming,* for finding well-behaved versions of well-investigated logics. Further, we state completeness, decidability, definability and interpolation results for a multimodal logic, called *arrow logic,* with additional operators such as the *difference operator* and *graded modalities.* Finally, we give a completeness proof for a strong version of arrow logic.

**Marzocchi, Virginio**. E possibile decidere argomentativamente il linguaggio in cui argomentiamo? La svolta linguistica di K.-O. Apel. *Iride,* 8(14), 28-45, Ap 95.

**Mas Torres, Salvador**. El tema de la virtud: A. Macintyre, lector de Aristóteles. *Rev Filosof (Spain),* 8(15), 159-181, 1996.

This essay analyzes AM's arguments in the light of two main subjects. First, his roots in the cultural tradition of which he considers himself an heir; in this sense, my contention is that AM's Aristotle is extremely personal, since besides being an Aristotle who is already acquainted with the Hellenistic, AM approaches him from an Augustinian standpoint. Briefly stated, it is an ad hoc Aristotle, read in the light of an ethics of virtue. Second, I compare AM's points of view with others which also claim to be Aristotelian, specially within the German context, and which I consider more coherent since they do without AM's "liberal" biases, hardly compatible with his own reading of Aristotle. In short, I reach the following conclusions: a) AM only manages to show the possibility of an Aristotelian-Tomist narrative, b) to demonstrate this possibility does not mean to show that this narrative is true and correct and its alternatives are false and incorrect, c) AM has taken this step at the cost of reinterpreting the tradition which permits his narrative.

**Masi, Giuiseppe**. Antonio Rosmini: Aristotele Esposto ed Esaminato. *Aquinas,* 39(3), 551-555, S-D 96.

**Masi, Giuseppe**. Trascendenza e trascendentalità in Kant. *G Metaf,* 18(1-2), 233-242, Ja-Ag 96.

**Masi, Giuseppe**. Ulteriorità del pensare. *G Metaf,* 18(1-2), 87-94, Ja-Ag 96.

**Mason, Andrew**. Justice, Contestability, and Conceptions of the Good. *Utilitas,* 8(3), 295-305, N 96.

**Mason, Andrew**. Special Obligations to Compatriots. *Ethics,* 107(3), 427-447, Ap 97.

Many political philosophers believe that we have a range of special obligations to our compatriots. There is considerable disagreement about the best way to justify these obligations, however. Some argue that they derive from general moral principles, while others maintain that they have a more immediate basis in the relationships themselves. I shall question the ideal that all these special obligations can be grounded in general moral principles, but I shall also argue that the most popular alternative, which seeks to generate them from constitutive attachments alone, suffers from grave problems. (edited)

**Mason, E Sharon** and Mudrack, Peter E. Do Complex Moral Reasoners Experience Greater Ethical Work Conflict?. *J Bus Ethics,* 16(12-13), 1311-1318, S 97.

Individuals who disagree that organizational interests legitimately supersede those of the wider society may experience conflict between their personal standards of ethics and those demanded by an employing organization, a conflict that is well documented. An additional question is whether or not individuals capable of complex moral reasoning experience greater conflict than those reasoning at a less developed level. This question was first positioned in a theoretical framework and then investigated using 115 survey responses from a student sample. Correlational analysis and hierarchical regression indicated that individuals scoring high on the Defining Issues Test measure of Kohlberg's stages of moral development experienced significantly greater workplace ethical conflict then low scorers. (edited)

**Mason, Franklin C**. The Presence of Experience and Two Theses About Time. *S J Phil,* 35(1), 75-89, Spr 97.

**Mason, John Hope**. "Originality: Moral Good, Private Vice, or Self-Enchantment" in *Jean-Jacques Rousseau and the Sources of the Self,* O'Hagan, Timothy (ed), 37-55. Brookfield, Avebury, 1997.

Three different ways in which "originality" became significant in mid-18th c. Britain and France. First, derived from stoic thought, was a moral demand, to be true to your own (original) self. Second, a literary/economic need, as a result of the development of copyright: to claim title in a literary work a writer had to demonstrate individual novelty. Third, evident in Rousseau's *Reveries,* was a claim to individual valve, self-sufficient *because* unique.

**Mason, Jonathan**. Jesus is Offensive: Contemporaneity, Freedom, and Joy in Kierkegaard. *Dialogue (PST),* 39(1), 21-29, O 96.

Kierkegaard has often been accused of allowing his melancholy to dominate his philosophy. His harsh critique of Christendom and his insightful investigation of the paradox of Jesus Christ point to a life of suffering. Is there a release for Kierkegaard? In this essay it will be argued that genuine Christianity is made joyful by the fact that it is the individual's choice. Being in truth, regardless of the consequences, is always joyful.

**Mason, Michael**. Democratising Nature? The Political Morality of Wilderness Preservationists. *Environ Values,* 6(3), 281-306, Ag 97.

Deep ecological appeals for wilderness preservation commonly conjoin arguments for participatory land use decision-making with their central championing of natural areas protection. As an articulation of the normative meaning of participatory democracy, the discourse ethics advanced by Jürgen Habermas is employed to highlight the consistency and justifiability of this dual claim. I argue that Habermasian moral theory reveals a key tension between, on the one hand, an ethical commitment to wilderness preservation informed by deep ecological and bioregional principles that is oriented to a naturalistic value order and, on the other, the procedural norms of democratic participation. (edited)

**Mason, Richard**. Getting Around Language. *Philosophy,* 72(280), 259-268, Ap 97.

Opposing views that language either does or does not get between us and reality are both ancient and persistent. They are also equally misguided. We can ask how language—what we say—relates to the rest of reality—what is so—and we can get different answers from opposite starting-points. Starting from what we say, we get problems about meaning and truth: Dummett provides an example. Starting from what is known to be so, we may not. (Aquinas was illuminating on this, without getting enmeshed in *de re*—*de dicto* complications.) The suggestion is that some problems about meaning and truth may be created by the direction from which they are addressed. They may matter less from a different approach.

**Mason, Richard**. How Things Happen: Divine-Natural Law in Spinoza. *Stud Leibniz,* 28(1), 17-36, 1996.

Niemand bezweifelt, dass nach Spinoza der Lauf der Dinge nicht auf übernatürliche Weise, d. h. durch irgend etwas ausserhalb der Natur erklärt werden kann. Aber weniger klar ist, wie radikal seine Sicht der Naturgesetze zu verstehen ist und wie sein Erklärungsapparat arbeiten soll. Können wir zum Beispiel von einem göttlichen Gesetzgeber absehen und doch die Naturgesetze als herrschende Regeln akzeptieren—vielleicht in Verbindung mit den unendlichen Modi? Dieser Aufsatz legt eine andere Sicht dar. Spinoza schrieb von, Gesetzen oder der Natur'. Nicht Gesetze sind es für ihn, die die Dinge geschehen lassen, sondern Ursachen; sie sollten somit bei der Erklärung, warum etwas geschieht, Berücksichtigung finden. Von Naturgesetzen können wir sprechen, sofern wir nicht der Vorstellung erliegen, sie seien getrennt vom Lauf der Dinge. Spinozas Position legt nahe, dass es auf das ankommt, was in der Natur geschieht: Fragen zum Status der Gesetze und ihrer Beziehung zu Dingen und Ereignissen sollten sich folglich nicht mehr stellen.

**Mason, Richard**. *The God of Spinoza.* New York, Cambridge Univ Pr, 1997.

This study brings together his fundamental philosophical thinking with his conclusions about God and religion. Spinoza was born a Jew but chose to live outside any religious community. He was deeply engaged both in traditional Hebrew learning and in contemporary physical science. He identified God with nature or substance: a theme which runs through his work, enabling him to naturalize religion but—equally important—to divinize nature. He emerges not as a rationalist precursor of the Enlightenment but as a thinker of the highest importance in his own right, both in philosophy and in religion. (publisher, edited)

**Massey, Joe B** and Ganss Gibson, Kathleen. "Ethical Considerations in the Multiplication of Human Embryos" in *Reproduction, Technology, and Rights: Biomedical Ethics Reviews,* Humber, James M (ed), 55-71. Clifton, Humana Pr, 1996.

**Massimilla, Edoardo**. "Vita e storia nella 'nuova scienza' del George-Kreis" in *Lo Storicismo e la Sua Storia: Temi, Problemi, Prospetive,* Cacciatore, Giuseppe (ed), 435-442. Milano, Guerini, 1997.

**Massini Correas, Carlos Ignacio**. El pensamiento práctico: Consideraciones metodológicas a partir de Tomás de Aquino. *Analogia,* 10(2), 31-54, 1996.

**Massini Correas, Carlos Ignacio**. Ensayo de síntesis acerca de la distinción especulativo-práctico y su estructuración metodolón metodológica. *Sapientia*, 51(200), 429-451, 1996.

**Masters, Roger D**. *Machiavelli, Leonardo, and the Science of Power*. Notre Dame, Univ Notre Dame Pr, 1996.

After introducing historical evidence of the circumstances in which da Vinci and Machiavelli probably met, Masters reinterprets *The Prince* in the light of Machiavelli's political experiences and da Vinci's invention of what came to be modern science. Masters presents a comprehensive account of Machiavelli's teaching as a scientific approach to human nature and politics. In this reading, the "lion, fox, and wolves" symbolize principles studied in contemporary biology, whereas the "dikes and dams" controlling the river of "fortune" describe Machiavelli's experience of diverting the Arno River, apparently aided by Leonardo's expertise, in hopes of winning a war with Pisa. Masters relates Machiavelli's views to the history of centralized governments, to models in rational choice or game theory, and to neo-Darwinian evolutionary theory. This approach shows how Machiavelli's view of leadership clarifies the role of television in industrialized societies and the profound transformations in contemporary politics. (publisher,edited)

**Masterson, David L**. The Educational Contributions of Sir Thomas More. *J Thought*, 32(2), 25-36, Sum 97.

**Masuch, Michael** and Huang, Zhisheng. The Logic of Permission and Obligation in the Framework of ALX.3: How to avoid the Paradoxes of Deontic Logics. *Log Anal*, 38(149), 55-74, Mr 95.

Standard deontic logic features fairly serious so-called "paradoxes" (technically: counterintuitive validities). Much energy in deontic logic has been spent on avoiding these "paradoxes". We suggest a reformulation of deontic logic in terms of a multi-agent logic, ALX.3, where a "super-agent" (think of a legislature) lays down the law of the land and other agents have to follow its rules. In particular, obligations are reformulated in terms of "preferences" of the superagent. We can show that our approach avoids the classical "paradoxes" of deontic logic, thanks to the properties of the preference operator of ALX.3.

**Masuda, Isao** and Hosoi, Tsutomu. A Study of Intermediate Propositional Logics on the Third Slice. *Stud Log*, 52(1), 15-21, F 93.

The intermediate logics have been classified into slices (cf. Hosoi [1]), but the detailed structure of slices has been studied only for the first two slices (cf. Hosoi and Ono [2]). In order to study the structure of slices, we give a method of a finer classification of slice. Here we treat only the third slice as an example, but the method can be extended to other slices in an obvious way. It is proved that each subslice contains continuum of logics. A characterization of logics in each subslice is given in terms of the form of models. (edited)

**Masugi, Ken**. Race, the Rule of Law, and *The Merchant of Venice*: From Slavery to Citizenship. *Notre Dame J Law Ethics*, 11(1), 197-223, 1997.

**Masullo, Aldo**. "Il tempo e l'etica" in *Il Concetto di Tempo: Atti del XXXII Congresso Nazionale della Società Filosofica Italiana*, Casertano, Giovanni (ed), 105-128. Napoli, Loffredo, 1997.

**Mate, Reyes**. Sendas Perdidas de la Razon (Cuando "el sueño de la razón produce monstruos"). *Ideas Valores*, 76-92, Ap 96.

The author resorts to the Weber-Scheme, which explains rationality on the basis of an underlying *religiöses Weltbild* (ascetic Protestantism in the case of Western rationality). In view of the crisis of Western rationality, the author asks himself what would happen if one would resort to some other *religiöses Weltbild*, as for example Judaism, to face the great challenges of the *Aufklärung*. He then pleads for an *anamnetische Vernunft*, upheld by Spinoza (the "*Marrano* of reason") and the Jewish-German philosophers H. Cohen, F. Rosenszweig and W. Benjamin.

**Mateo Gambarte, Eduardo**. La Ideología del primer franquismo y los intelectuales. *Euridice*, 81-111, 1995.

During the 30's and 40's, the intellectual is an enemy of the *Falange*, even to the traditionalist and the Catholic Church. For all of them, the intellectual is synonymous with pro-European, liberal, republican, intriguing, democrat, free-thinker..., The anti-intellectual disdain may be captured in the apodictic judgement made by the *Caudillo* at the end of his monologues: *With the characteristics arrogant pride of the intellectuals....*

**Matet, Pierre**. Combinatorics and Forcing with Distributive Ideals. *Annals Pure Applied Log*, 86(2), 137-201, 16 Je 97.

We present a version of Kappa-distributive ideals over a regular infinite cardinal Kappa of some of the combinatorial results of Mathias on happy families. We also study an associated notion of forcing which is a generalization of Mathias forcing and of Prikry forcing.

**Matheson, Carl** and Kirchhoff, Evan. Chaos and Literature. *Phil Lit*, 21(1), 28-45, Ap 97.

Many literary theorists have made bold claims for the supposed "new paradigm" of chaos theory. Katherine Hayles and other theorists allege variously that: i) chaos mathematics and poststructuralist literary theory are significantly similar; ii) chaos theory and contemporary literary criticism are actually two formulations of the same concept; and iii) the science of chaos can be a useful tool for the study of literature. We argue that these claims are overblown, unwarranted, or empirically false.

**Matos de Noronha, Nelson**. Arqueologia da Gramática Geral: O Estatuto da Linguagem no Saber da idade Clássica. *Cad Hist Filosof Cie*, 5(1-2), 261-280, Ja-D 95.

We present a reconstruction of Michel Foucault's analysis of the existence and function of language in the 17th and 18th centuries, when general grammar became at the same time a science of language and a theory of knowledge.

Through an analysis of the conception of knowledge we raise the question of the role of language in the organization of thought and the formation of the empirical sciences in this period. Some comparisons are also made between knowledge in the Renaissance and in the modern age.

**Matravers, Matt**. What's 'Wrong' in Contractualism?. *Utilitas*, 8(3), 329-340, N 96.

This paper is a critical commentary on Brian Barry's *Justice as Impartiality* and examines the relationship between contractual theories of justice and moral theory. The paper alleges that Barry cannot maintain his central thesis that public rules must be justified without appeal to any particular conception of the good. First, Barry only avoids justice as mutual advantage by committing himself to the equal worth of human beings independent of the features they possess. Second, Barry has a conception of wrong (specifically, the wrongness of harm) that is independent of his contractualism and from which nonimpartial rules of justice can be derived directly.

**Matsubara, Yo** and Burke, Douglas. Ideals and Combinatorial Principles. *J Sym Log*, 62(1), 117-122, Mr 97.

**Mattéi, Jean-François**. Le système stoïcien: monde et langage. *Diotima*, 25, 74-85, 1997.

**Matthen, Mohan**. Teleology and the Product Analogy. *Austl J Phil*, 75(1), 21-37, Mr 97.

Philosophers account for the currency of teleology in contemporary science by reducing it to some acceptable explanatory schema, usually Darwinian. Such reductions do not work, it is argued, a) because, as a number of examples show, there is a multiplicity of explanatory schema that could underwrite teleology and b) because teleology appeals to an analogy with human products. It is proposed that the product analogy has an objective basis that sufficiently accounts for its contemporary uses. However, because of a) above, it would be wrong to think that teleology serves an explanatory purpose. Teleology is analogical and descriptive, not explanatory.

**Matthews, Gareth B**. Perplexity in Plato, Aristotle, and Tarski. *Phil Stud*, 85(2-3), 213-228, Mr 97.

The role Plato assigns to perplexity (*aporía*) shifts from the early dialogues, such as the *Euthyphro* and the *Meno*, to such middle dialogues as the *Phaedo* and the *Republic*. There is a further shift in the *Parmenides* and the *Theaetetus*. With these shifts seem to go changes in philosophical methodology and even perhaps a change in the conception of philosophy Plato presents. The methodological role of perplexity in Aristotle is a natural development from Plato. Perplexity in Aristotle can be usefully compared with the role the antinomy of the liar plays in Tarski's treatment of truth.

**Matthews, Gareth B**. Two Theories of Supposition?. *Topoi*, 16(1), 35-40, Mr 97.

In a recent paper Paul Vincent Spade suggests that, although the medieval doctrine of the modes of personal supposition originally had something to do with the rest of the theory of supposition, it became, by the 14th century, an unrelated theory with no question to answer. By contrast, I argue that the theory of the modes of personal supposition was meant to provide a way of making understandable the idea that a general term in a categorical proposition can be used to refer to the individual things that fall under it. Once that idea had been made acceptable, truth conditions for the various forms of categorical proposition could be given without any specific appeal to the ideas of descent and ascent in terms of which the modes had been defined.

**Matthews, Michael R**. Scheffler Revisited on the Role of History and Philosophy of Science in Science Teacher Education. *Stud Phil Educ*, 16(1-2), 159-173, Ja-Ap 97.

Twenty-five years ago Israel Scheffler argued for the inclusion of philosophy of science in the preparation of science teachers. It was part of his wider argument for the inclusion of courses in the philosophy of the discipline in programmes that are preparing people to teach that discipline. For the most part Scheffler's suggestion, at least as far as science education is concerned, went unheeded. Pleasingly, in recent times there has been some rapprochement between these fields. This paper will restate parts of Scheffler's argument, it will develop some additional considerations pertaining to it, and it will set the discussion in the context of contemporary debate about science, science education and teacher training. With changed time and circumstances, Scheffler's arguments might find more adherents than when they were initially proposed. My revision of Scheffler's argument has two planks: first pedagogical, second professional.

**Matthews, Patricia M**. Feeling and Aesthetic Judgment: A Rejoinder to Tom Huhn. *J Aes Art Crit*, 55(1), 58-60, Wint 97.

I defend my paper, "Kant's Sublime," against the charges that it reduces judgments of the sublime to moral judgments and collapses feeling and reflective judgment. Against the first charge I argue that just as judgments of taste are not cognitive judgments just because they are based on a condition of cognition, judgments of the sublime are not moral judgments just because they are based on a condition of moral judgment. Against the latter charge I argue that I do not collapse feeling and reflective judgment, but my account does rightly focus on feeling as the basis of reflective judgment.

**Mattick, Paul**. Form and Theory: Meyer Schapiro's *Theory and Philosophy of Art*. *J Aes Art Crit*, 55(1), 16-18, Wint 97.

**Maudlin, Tim**. Descrying the World in the Wave Function. *Monist*, 80(1), 3-23, Ja 97.

This essay examines the relationship between the theoretical description of the world given in physics and the evidence one has for the theory. Drawing on work of Wilfrid Sellars, I argue that Bohm's theory provides a clear example of how to solve the "reality problem" in quantum physics by linking the scientific and manifest images of the world. I also show that the connection between these two images can be made in many ways, with different possibilities illustrated by collapse theories and the many-minds theory.

**Maudlin, Tim**. On the Impossibility of David Lewis' Modal Realism. *Austl J Phil*, 74(4), 669-682, D 96.

In this paper, it is shown that David Lewis's conception of possible worlds as concrete particulars isolated by lack of spatio-temporal connectedness cannot be maintained. Such worlds could possibly differ *solo numero* and hence do differ *solo numero* (on Lewis's view). But no matter how many copies of such indiscernible worlds there are, there could have been more, a possibility which Lewis's theory cannot represent.

**Maurin, Françoise**. The Theory of Integer Multiplication with Order Restricted to Primes is Decidable. *J Sym Log*, 62(1), 123-130, Mr 97.

We show here that the first order theory of the positive integers equipped with multiplication remains decidable when one adds to the language the usual order restricted to the prime numbers. We see, moreover, that the complexity of the latter theory is a tower of exponentials, of height *O(n)*.

**Maury, Mary D** and Kleiner, Deborah S. Thou Shalt and Shalt Not: An Alternative to the Ten Commandments Approach to Developing a Code of Ethics for Schools of Business. *J Bus Ethics*, 16(3), 331-336, F 97.

The authors' previous research indicates that there is a perceived need for a code of ethics for business schools. Currently, relatively few schools have in fact adopted codes of ethics applicable to all the constituents of the institution. Proposals made to businesses to help them determine which values should be included in a corporate code do not appear to adequately address the distinctive issues faced in an academic environment. (edited)

**Maus, Fred Everett**. Narrative, Drama, and Emotion in Instrumental Music. *J Aes Art Crit*, 55(3), 293-303, Sum 97.

**Mavrodes, George I**. A Response to John Hick. *Faith Phil*, 14(3), 289-294, Jl 97.

Hick professes now to be a "poly-something" and a "mono-something." Most of my response is directed to these claims. I suggest that (contrary to my earlier assumption) Hick does not take any of the gods of the actual religions to be real. They are much more like fictional characters than like Kantian phenomena. He is "poly" about these *insubstantia*. I argue that Hick is not "mono" about anything at all of religious significance. In particular, he is not a mono-realist. I conclude by arguing that Hick has no satisfactory support for the sort of ineffability which he attributes to the real.

**Mavrodes, George I**. Are PSI Effects Natural? A Preliminary Investigation. *Darshana Int*, 35(3/139), 48-57, Jl 95.

I argue against an "invariant regularity" account of natural law, and in favor of some necessitarian view. I explore some consequences—e.g., an event might exemplify a law relative to some property and violate a law relative to another property (and so might be both natural and nonnatural) and an event might exemplify a law relative to some property and violate a (different) law relative to the same property (i.e., the operative laws of nature are nomologically inconsistent). I argue that these are genuine possibilities and that we have no strong empirical data against them.

**Mawby, Ronald**. The Dying Vine. *J Thought*, 32(1), 49-68, Spr 97.

Liberal education is difficult for three reasons. Students naturally lack skills, habits and attitudes that would make liberal education easier, since liberal education succeeds when students acquire just those skills, habits and attitudes. Students often misconceive what education requires, as prior schooling, plus sloth, predispose them to passivity. Students have a vague but correct sense that education is dangerous to the established order of their lives. Ignorance may not be bliss, but it does seem to be a disease largely free of painful symptoms and so few are willing to undergo the radical and frightening transformation that is the cure.

**Maxwell, Vance**. Making God Go Away and Leave Us Alone. *Dialogue (Canada)*, 35(4), 805-819, Fall 96.

**May, Larry** and Bohman, James. Sexuality, Masculinity, and Confession. *Hypatia*, 12(1), 138-154, Wint 97.

The practice of confessing one's sexual sins has historically provided boys and men with mixed messages. Engaging in coercive sex is publicly condemned; yet it is treated as not significantly different from other transgressions that can be easily forgiven. We compare Catholic confessional practices to these of psychoanalytically oriented male writers on masculinity. We argue that the latter is no more justifiable than the former and propose a progressive confessional mode for discussing male sexuality.

**May, Larry** (ed) and Strikwerda, Robert (ed) and Hopkins, Patrick D (ed). *Rethinking Masculinity: Philosophical Explorations in Light of Feminism*. Lanham, Rowman & Littlefield, 1996.

The new edition of this popular book is reorganized to present pairs of contrasting views on what it means to be a man in contemporary Western culture. Addressing such issues as sex differences, fatherhood, intimacy, homosexuality and oppression, the collection also includes new discussions of paternity, pornography, mixed race marriage, impotence and violence. Still the only philosophically-oriented collection on the subject, Rethinking Masculinity is an excellent text for gender studies, ethics and social philosophy courses. (publisher)

**May, Reinhard** and Parkes, Graham (trans). *Heidegger's Hidden Sources: East Asian Influences on His Work*. New York, Routledge, 1996.

The book documents for the first time Heidegger's remarkable debt to East Asian philosophy. In this groundbreaking study, Reinhard May shows conclusively that Martin Heidegger borrowed some of the major ideas of his philosophy—on occasion almost word for word—from German translations of

Chinese Daoist and Zen Buddist classics. The discovery of this astonishing appropriation of non-Western sources will have important consequences for future interpretations of Heidegger's work. Moreover, it shows Heidegger as a pioneer of comparative philosophy and transcultural thinking. (publisher)

**May, Thomas**. On Raz and the Obligation to Obey the Law. *Law Phil*, 16(1), 19-36, 97.

**May, Thomas**. Reassessing the Reliability of Advance Directives. *Cambridge Quart Healthcare Ethics*, 6(3), 325-338, Sum 97.

**May, Todd**. Gilles Deleuze and the Politics of Time. *Man World*, 29(3), 293-304, Jl 96.

**May, Todd**. *Reconsidering Difference*. University Park, Pennsylvania Univ Pr, 1997.

*Reconsidering Difference* has a twofold task, the primary one critical and the secondary one reconstructive. The critical task is to show that these various privilegings are philosophical failures. They wind up, for reasons unique to each position, endorsing positions that are either incoherent or implausible. Todd May considers the incoherencies of each position and offers an alternative approach. His reconstructive task, which he calls "contingent holism," takes the phenomena under investigation—community, language, ethics, and ontology—and sketches a way of reconceiving them that preserves the motivations of the rejected positions without falling into the problems that beset them. (publisher, edited)

**May, William F**. Money and the Medical Profession. *Kennedy Inst Ethics J*, 7(1), 1-13, Mr 97.

Money motivates people, lubricates the movement of resources, mobilizes talent and breaks down some barriers. But money also has a darker side; it can distract, corrupt, distort and cruelly exclude. Money is a useful but unruly servant; sometimes, a hard master. The professional, at least in part, belongs to the world of money. We sometimes distinguish the amateur from the professional in that the amateur does it for love; the professional, for money. The professional has one foot in the marketplace, but also, purportedly, professes something else—beyond the bottom line. The following discussion explores the morally complex ties and tensions between money and the medical professions.

**May, William F**. *Testing the Medical Covenant: Active Euthanasia and Health Care Reform*. Grand Rapids, Eerdmans, 1996.

May begins with an incisive introduction that delineates the *covenantal*, or relational, nature of the practice of medicine over against the merely *contractual* view—the quid pro quos of the commercial buying and selling of professional services. In the subsequent chapters, May follows the implications of the medical covenant with respect to the related issues of euthanasia and health care reform. He also provides a covenantal view of professional character and virtue—what virtues we should look for in covenanted physicians and nurses—discusses the limits of the medical covenant in the face of "medical futility," and examines the implications of covenant keeping for the shape of future health care reform. (publisher, edited)

**May, Jr, Roy H**. Reconciliation: A Political Requirement for Latin America. *Annu Soc Christ Ethics*, 41-58, 1996.

Latin American countries are democratizing after years of military dictatorship and state terrorism. Wounds left by human rights abuses are not healed, endangering democracy. The historical subject of reconciliation are those who suffered human rights violations. As a process on their behalf, reconciliation requires truth and justice, apology and redress and repentance and forgiveness. Questions relating to amnesty and pardon are integral to this discussion. At the same time, the United States government must recognize its role in fomenting human rights abuses and join in the reconciliation process. Finally, although difficult, grass roots organizations are working to heal broken societies and bring about reconciliation.

**Maybee, Julie E**. Kierkegaard on the Madness of Reason. *Man World*, 29(4), 387-406, O 96.

**Maybon, Marie-Pierre**. Les Technologies de L'images: Nouveaux Instruments du Bio-Pouvoir. *Horiz Phil*, 7(1), 97-111, Fall 96.

The purpose of this paper is to explore the impact of technoculture upon the modern individual's subjectivity process from the perspective of the literary field. Our hypothesis is that political and ethical issues of a deconstruction of the subject through the use of particular technologies are at stake in contemporary occidental literature which may be considered as a "discourse of knowledge." First, image technologies reshape the relationships between the public and the private sphere, thus revealing new power stakes linked to the morcelling of the feminine subject. A second perspective investigates how, in the literary field, these problems of identity and difference are dealt with.

**Mayer, Laura L** and Laskowski, Michael C. Stable Structures with Few Substructures. *J Sym Log*, 61(3), 985-1005, S 96.

A countable, atomically stable structure U in a finite, relational language has fewer than $2^{omega}$ nonisomorphic substructures if and only if U is cellular. An example shows that the finiteness of the language is necessary. (edited)

**Mayer, Michael**. Das Subjekt jenseits seines Grundes—Emmanuel Lévinas' Deduktion des Selbstbewusstseins. *Prima Philosophia*, 10(2), 131-148, 1997.

One of the big, yet unresolved problems in the tradition of both German idealism and romanticism is the issue of identity, specifically identity of "Selbstbewusstsein" (selfconsciousness). The origin itself of identity of "Selbstbewusstsein," being the paradigm of all the different possibilities of identity, however, has remained to be enigmatic. One of the endeavors to resolve this problem is connected to the names of Dieter Henrich and, recently, Manfred Frank. Their efforts, however, to attribute identity of "Selbstbewusstsein" to basic, prereflexive and irrelational self-confidence,

AUTHOR INDEX 777 McBride, William L

ultimately only created new aporias. In dialogue with the late thinking of Emmanuel Lévinas the following essay constructs and reconstructs a surprising response to the question of identity of "Selbstbewusstsein." The central idea is, that within kind of "passive identity," which is an effect of the ethical situation: the confrontation of a "myself" with the absolute and irreducible otherness of the other.

**Mayer, Robert**. Plekhanov, Lenin and Working-Class Consciousness. *Stud East Euro Thought*, 49(3), 159-185, S 97.

According to the prevailing scholarly view, made popular by Neil Harding, Lenin is said to have derived his well-known theory of working-class consciousness in *What Is To Be Done?* from G. V. Plekhanov, the father of Russian Marxism. In this article I demonstrate, however, that Plekhanov and Lenin disagreed quite sharply on this question. Plekhanov did not believe that workers would fail to develop a socialist consciousness in the absence of external intervention. Indeed, Plekhanov was a thorough-going optimist about proletarian capacities and while he did assign an important role to the intelligentsia in the process of consciousness-raising, that role was carefully circumscribed. An exhaustive review of Plekhanov's writings before November 1903, when he broke with Lenin, reveals just how unorthodox Lenin's most famous argument was in the context of Russian social-democratic theory.

**Mayer, Robert**. The Status of a Classic Text: Lenin's *What Is To Be Done?* After 1902. *Hist Euro Ideas*, 22(4), 307-320, Jl 96.

It is often assumed that Lenin remained committed in subsequent years to the pessimistic argument about working-class abilities set forth in *What Is To Be Done?* and that this pessimism served as the justification for party dictatorship over the proletariat after 1917. In this paper, however, I show that Lenin's pessimistic argument was an aberration and did not reflect his mature conviction. Drawing on neglected sources, I reconstruct how Lenin arrived at his pessimistic view and then document his retreat from it in the face of intense criticism. The last section of the paper describes the very different legitimation strategy Lenin employed after 1917 in order to justify party dictatorship.

**Mayer-Sommer, Alan P** and Roshwalb, Alan. An Examination of the Relationship Between Ethical Behavior, Espoused Ethical Values and Financial Performance in the U S Defense Industry: 1988-1992. *J Bus Ethics*, 15(12), 1249-1274, D 96.

This paper tests the ethics-is-good-for-profits as well as the ethics-and-profits-are-joint-outcomes-of-good-management hypotheses in the context of the U.S. defense industry in the 1988-1992 period. Both ethical behaviors are compared with measures of profitability for the defense-oriented business segments of sixty-two major U.S. defense contractors. We found statistically significant, positive correlations between 1) our two measures of espoused ethical values and 2) both measures of espoused ethical values and violative ethical acts. (edited)

**Mayerfeld, Jamie**. The Incrementalist Argument for a Strong Duty To Prevent Suffering. *J Soc Phil*, 28(1), 5-21, Spr 97.

Several philosophers use an "incrementalist argument" to claim that affluent individuals should devote far more of their resources to the alleviation of suffering. This argument maintains that affluent individuals have repeated opportunities to prevent extreme suffering at slight cost to themselves. Since it seems wrong to neglect such an opportunity on any given occasion, affluent individuals should keep on preventing extreme suffering until they have incurred a large cumulative sacrifice. I argue that it is misleading to claim that affluent individuals can prevent extreme suffering at slight cost to themselves. However, we can repair the incrementalist argument if we appeal to the collective impact of many people's modest beneficent sacrifices and the small possibility that any one such sacrifice will succeed in preventing extreme suffering.

**Mayerfeld, Jamie**. The Moral Asymmetry of Happiness and Suffering. *S J Phil*, 34(3), 317-338, Fall 96.

**Mayhew, Robert**. Aristotle's Criticism of Plato's Communism of Women and Children. *Apeiron*, 29(3), 231-248, S 96.

Aristotle's criticism of Plato's communism of women and children were for many years neglected and the little that was written on them tended to be negative. Aristotle's opponents argue that whatever the merits of his criticisms, he is unfair to Plato and misses the point. Recently these criticisms have received a bit more attention, much of it sympathetic. I argue that Aristotle's criticisms *do* succeed, but that those who have defended them in the past have not sufficiently answered an important objection posed by his critics. Answering this objection requires going outside the *Politics* to Aristotle's ethical writings.

**Maynard, Patrick**. Introduction. *J Aes Art Crit*, 55(2), 95-106, Spring 97.

**Mayo, Cris**. "Performance Anxiety: Sexuality and School Controversy" in *Philosophy of Education (1996)*, Margonis, Frank (ed), 281-289. Urbana, Phil Education Soc, 1997.

**Mayo, Deborah G**. Severe Tests, Arguing from Error, and Methodological Underdetermination. *Phil Stud*, 86(3), 243-266, Je 97.

My task is to sketch an account of *severe tests* and show how it answers the "alternative hypothesis objection": that whatever rule is specified for positively appraising hypothesis *H*, there will always be rival hypotheses that satisfy the rule equally well. I argue that: 1) The existence of hypotheses alternative to *H* that accord with evidence *e* as well as *H* does, does not prevent *H* from passing a severe test with *e*; and 2) Even if there are alternative hypotheses that entail or fit evidence *e* as well as *H* does, there are not always alternatives equally severely tested by *e*.

**Mayos, Gonçal**. Fundamentación de la metafísica y gnoseología del sujeto en Descartes. *Pensamiento*, 205(53), 3-31, Ja-Ap 97.

Se parte de la ambivalente relación en el pensamiento cartesiano entre el yo y Dios para analizar su supremacía metafísica y/o gnoseológica, encarando las cuestiones del verdadero orden del discurso cartesiano, de la naturaleza humana, del papel calificable de finito o infinito del sujeto pensante, del papel jugado por la voluntad en la ruptura y fundamentación cartesiana. Todo ello conduce a la constitución de una compleja filosofía del sujeto que determina la especificidad de la fundamentación cartesiana de filosofía y ciencia e inaugura la idea moderna del sujeto a través de la astuta contraposición entre Dios y el yo.

**Mazhary, Djahanguir R**. "Contraintes socio-culturelles et conversions philosphiques chez Descartes..." in *Memorias Del Seminario En Conmemoración De Los 400 Anos Del Nacimiento De René Descartes*, Albis, Víctor S (ed), 111-133. Sankt Augustin, Academia, 1997.

**Mazumdar, Rinita**. Inference: Heuristic vs. Naturalistic Model. *Indian Phil Quart*, 23(3-4), 395-410, Jl-O 96.

**Mazur, B**. Conjecture. *Synthese*, 111(2), 197-210, My 97.

Much has been written about the formal logical structure of mathematics and the formulation of axioms, definitions, theorems, and proofs, in mathematical literature. But aside from foundational and logical issues there are elements of style and mode of presentation that have seldom been specifically commented upon. This article discusses one such element: the appearance of what could be called "architectural conjectures" in mathematical writing. Architectural conjectures are formally articulated constellations of conjectures which constitute theories in their own right and which can be thought of as detailed research projects.

**Mazza Farias, Itamar**. O Sentido do Trabalho como Principio Educativo na Concepçao Gramsciana. *Educ Filosof*, 9(17), 139-155, Ja-Je 95.

The present study takes the presupposition that school is a place of contradiction and myth creation about human work. Gramsci resumes the discipline as a tool in citizen formation, synthesizes the historical moment and the specific child's psychological dynamics, and establishes the modern industrial work as a general educational principle at school or in a family context. (edited)

**Mazzarella, Eugenio**. "De servo arbitrio: La fine della libertà in Martin Heidegger" in *Lo Storicismo e la Sua Storia: Temi, Problemi, Prospettive*, Cacciatore, Giuseppe (ed), 516-523. Milano, Guerini, 1997.

**Mazziotti, Stelio**. "Brevi note su liberalismo e storia in Constant e Tocqueville" in *Lo Storicismo e la Sua Storia: Temi, Problemi, Prospettive*, Cacciatore, Giuseppe (ed), 213-217. Milano, Guerini, 1997.

**McAdoo, Nick**. Hearing Musical Works in their Entirety. *Brit J Aes*, 37(1), 66-74, Ja 97.

This paper examines the paradox that while musical discourse presupposes our ability to hear temporally extended sound relationships, all that we actually seem to hear is one brief snatch of sound at a time. I contrast the views of 1) Edmund Gurney and Jerrold Levinson, who accept that large-scale aural *Gestalten* are impossible—which entails that musical analysis should concentrate on the fleeting moments of musical transition rather than on larger architectonic structures—with 2) Husserl and Merleau-Ponty, who take the opposite view that the "now moment" contains within itself the whole "presence" of the piece from start to finish.

**McAleer, Graham**. Matter and the Unity of Being in the Philosophical Theology of Saint Thomas Aquinas. *Thomist*, 61(2), 257-277, Ap 97.

The essay has a historical and philosophical argument. Historically, the essay contests the twentieth century interpretation that Averroes and Thomas share the same concept of matter. Philosophically, the argument is made that medieval theories of matter were theories of desire. Thomas's theory of desire was developed to both defend his belief in the bodily resurrection and to develop a metaphysics of hope for this belief. Averroes's theory of desire does not have such aims. The essay includes an additional argument that Paul Ricoeur's theory of desire is close to Averroes's and therefore, it cannot sustain hope in the bodily resurrection.

**McAleer, Graham**. Saint Anselm: An Ethics of *Caritas* for a Relativist Age. *Amer Cath Phil Quart*, 70(Supp), 163-178, 1996.

The argument is made that Anselm's treatment of charity can match the strictures for an ethics demanded by relativism and can also address some of the problems inherent to relativism. The ontologies of difference articulated by Foucault and Heidegger provide the framework for the discussion of relativism in Part I. Part II is a philosophical treatment of Anselm's position on why the devil fell and understands Anselm to be addressing an ontology of difference.

**McAvoy, Martin**. "Carnal Knowledge in the *Charmides*" in *Dialogues with Plato*, Benitez, Eugenio (ed), 63-103. Edmonton, Academic, 1996.

**McAvoy, Martin**. Carnal Knowledge in the *Charmides*. *Apeiron*, 29(4), 63-103, D 96.

The *Charmides'* Socrates is professor of ignorance par excellence and he encourages his interlocutors to profess theirs. This they fail to do with any conviction or depth of understanding. They lack *sôphrosúnê* while attempting to claim it or some knowledge of it, whereas Socrates embodies it while attempting to disclaim it or knowledge of it. The prologue enacts this paradox in encapsulated, carnal form—the body of Charmides, like the *Charmides* itself, is partially uncovered before the soul, though both lie under the questionable guardianship of Critias. The revelation of both reveals the ignorance of all, but Socrates' is special.

**McBride, William L**. Ontological "Proofs" in Descartes and Sartre: God, the "I," and the Group. *Amer Cath Phil Quart*, 70(4), 551-567, Autumn 96.

First, Sartre's "reversal" of Descartes's ontological proof is examined through some textual analysis of *Being and Nothingness*. Part 2 examines certain French scholars' explanations of Descartes's failure to deal with sociopolitical and historical matters and shows that Sartre remained crucially indebted to the Cartesian *cogito* even in his later, sociopolitically-oriented philosophy. Part 3 argues, against Descartes via Sartre's concept of "the group," that no clear dividing line can legitimately be drawn between philosophical treatments of the sociopolitical/historical domain and ontology, although the key entities of one's ontology may well be much more contingent, changeable and "detotalized" than were Descartes's.

**McCabe, Adam** and Friedman, Jeffrey. Preferences or Happiness? Tibor Scitovsky's Psychology of Human Needs. *Crit Rev*, 10(4), 471-480, Fall 96.

Tibor Scitovsky's psychological theory holds that human beings have a natural propensity to pursue comfort—the cessation of need and effort—which, he contends, is in its own way as conducive to unhappiness as pain is. This view, supported by a wealth of empirical data, raises troublesome questions for economics as well as for democratic and liberal theory, since it suggests a dichotomy between people's preferences—as expressed in their purchases, their votes and their exercise of autonomy—and their happiness.

**McCabe, David**. Patriotic Gore, Again. *S J Phil*, 35(2), 203-223, Sum 97.

**McCabe, Mary Margaret**. Chaos and Control: Reading Plato's *Politicus*. *Phronesis*, 42(1), 94-117, 1997.

**McCampbell, Atefeh Sadri** and Rood, Tina L. Ethics in Government: A Survey of Misuse of Position for Personal Gain and Its Implications for Developing Acquisition Strategy. *J Bus Ethics*, 16(11), 1107-1116, Ag 97.

This study surveys one element of the government standards of conduct, named "Misuse of Position for Personal Gain", assesses the results and compares various acquisition strategies to identify high risk procurement where individual misuse of position for personal gain may be more pervasive. It also provides a valuable historical summary of government standards of conduct. The study concludes with an assessment of enforcement mechanisms, or lack thereof, to ensure that government procurement is conducted in a manner which gains public trust and confidence.

**McCann, Dennis P**. Catholic Social Teaching in an Ara of Economic Globalization: A Resource for Business Ethics. *Bus Ethics Quart*, 7(2), 57-70, Mr 97.

The paper attempts to provide a basis for exploring the continued relevance of Catholic social teaching to business ethics, by interpreting the historic development of a Catholic work ethic and the traditions of Catholic social teaching in light of contemporary discussions of economic globalization, notably those of Robert Reich and Peter Drucker. The paper argues that the Catholic work ethic and the Church's tradition of social teaching has evolved dynamically in response to the structural changes involved in the history of modern economic development and thus is well poised to speak to the ethical challenges implicit in the advent of a knowledge-based society. (edited)

**McCann, Greg K** and DeMoss, Michelle A. Without a Care in the World: The Business Ethics Course and Its Exclusion of a Care Perspective. *J Bus Ethics*, 16(4), 435-443, Mr 97.

This article analyzes the impact of the rights-oriented business ethics course on student's ethical orientation. This approach, which is predominant in business schools, excludes the care-oriented approach used by a majority of women as well as some men and minorities. The results of this study showed that although students did not shift significantly in their ethical orientation, a majority of the men and an even greater majority of the women were care-oriented before and after a course in business ethics. If business schools are to address society's increasing diversity then the perspective of women and others who are care-oriented must be assimilated into the curriculum. This can only be done by rethinking how the business ethics course (and the entire business curriculum) are taught to include a care-oriented approach.

**McCanna, Tony**. A Practical Advance Directive Survey. *Bioethics Forum*, 13(2), 44-46, Sum 97.

A one-day survey done in eleven Kansas City hospitals—including both acute and skilled nursing units—revealed higher than average completion of advance directives. Furthermore, completion of treatment directives was higher in hospitals in which social workers distributed and explained the documents.

**McCarrick, Pat Milmoe** and Darragh, Martina. A Just Share: Justice and Fairness in Resource Allocation. *Kennedy Inst Ethics J*, 7(1), 81-102, Mr 97.

Scope Notes provide a current overview to a specific topic in biomedical ethics. This one, number 32 in the series, has a brief two page discussion of the concept of what "fair" or "just", or "fairness" or "justice" could mean in the provision of health care to all who need it. Its' bibliography is divided into seven categories: general works on justice and resource allocation, groups affected by rationing, applied justice, international perspectives, physicians as gatekeepers, organizational statements and references to early works.

**McCarthy, Christine**. "When You Know It, and I Know It, What is It We Know? Pragmatic Realism and the Epistemologically Absolute" in *Philosophy of Education (1996)*, Margonis, Frank (ed), 21-29. Urbana, Phil Education Soc, 1997.

**McCarthy, David**. Rights, Explanation, and Risks. *Ethics*, 107(2), 205-225, Ja 97.

Theories of rights seem well equipped to explain facts about the morality of causing harm. But can they explain moral facts about imposing risks of harm? Many think not. But a plausible theory of rights can if it says we have the right that others not impose risks of harm upon us. That is a good reason to believe we have that right and none of the many objections are sound. Among the topics covered are: the permissibility of rights infringements, trivial rights

infringements, the permissibility of risk impositions, the aggregation of rights, consent, self-defense, punishment and compensation.

**McCarthy, David** and Arntzenius, Frank. The Two Envelope Paradox and Infinite Expectations. *Analysis*, 57(1), 42-50, Ja 97.

We argue that the two envelope paradox can be dissolved by looking closely at the connection between conditional and unconditional expectation and by being careful when summing an infinite series of positive and negative terms. We argue that it is not another St. Petersburg paradox and that one does not need to ban talk of infinite expectation values in order to dissolve it. We end by posing a new puzzle.

**McCarthy, Erin**. Ningen: Intersubjectivity in the Ethics of Watsuji Tetsuro. *De Phil*, 11, 19-30, 1994-1995.

**McCarthy, Irene N**. Professional Ethics Code Conflict Situations: Ethical and Value Orientation of Collegiate Accounting Students. *J Bus Ethics*, 16(12-13), 1467-1473, S 97.

Public accounting in the United States is generally guided by the Code of Professional Conduct of the American Institute of Certified Public Accountants (AICPA). It has been suggested that education in understanding and accepting their ethical code would increase accountants' adherence and ethicality. This study was designed to examine the level of consensus to AICPA ethical standards by accounting students (ethical orientation). Situation ethics provided the theoretical rationale for this study. The results indicate that ethical orientation is not significantly improved through exposure to the AICPA Code of Conduct in collegiate courses in accounting. (edited)

**McCarthy, Thomas A**. Philosophy and Critical Theory: A Reply to Richard Rorty and Seyla Benhabib. *Constellations*, 3(1), 95-103, Ap 96.

**McCarthy, Thomas A**. The Philosophy of the Limit and its Other. *Constellations*, 2(2), 175-188, O 95.

**McCarthy Matzko, David**. Homosexuality and the Practices of Marriage. *Mod Theol*, 13(3), 371-397, Jl 97.

**McCarty, D C**. Undecidability and Intuitionistic Incompleteness. *J Phil Log*, 25(5), 559-565, O 96.

An immediate corollary is that the Tarski, Beth and Kripke weak completeness theorems for the negative fragment of intuitionistic predicate logic are unobtainable in second-order Heyting arithmetic. Second, each of these: weak completeness for classical predicate logic, weak completeness for the negative fragment of intuitionistic predicate logic and strong completeness for sentential logic implies Markov's Principle. Beth and Kripke completeness for intuitionistic predicate or sentential logic also entail Markov's Principle. These results give extensions of the theorem of Gödel and Kreisel that completeness for pure intuitionistic predicate logic requires Markov's Principle. The assumptions of Gödel and Kreisel's original proof included the Axiom of Dependent Choice and Herbrand's Theorem, no use of which is explicit in the present article. (edited)

**McCarty, Luise Prior**. Experience and the Postmodern Spirit. *Educ Theor*, 47(3), 377-394, Sum 97.

Attention to three postmodernist books in education reveals that contemporary postmodernism suffers a major defect of 19th Century romanticism. The books in question are Patrick Slattery's "Curriculum Development in the Postmodern Era," Robin Usher and Richard Edwards's "Postmodernism and Education" and the anthology "Education and the Postmodern Condition," edited by Michael Peters. The main argument that postmodern educational theory is pedagogically flawed derives from Hegel and Kierkegaard. It shows that postmodern education, like romanticism, ends because it cannot begin, because teaching and learning must begin with formative experience, which the postmoderns attempt to banish.

**McClellan, Jr, James E**. "Theoretical and Practical Reasoning: An Intractable Dualism?" in *Philosophy of Education (1996)*, Margonis, Frank (ed), 34-42. Urbana, Phil Education Soc, 1997.

**McComiskey, Bruce**. Gorgias, *On Non-Existence*: Sextus Empiricus, *Against the Logicians* 1.65-87, Translated from the Greek Text in Hermann Diels's *Die Fragmente der Vorsokratiker*. *Phil Rhet*, 30(1), 45-49, 1997.

McComiskey translates the Sextus Empiricus text of Gorgias's *On Non-Existence*, in which the sophist argues his famous trilemma: "first and foremost, that nothing exists; second, that even if existence exists, it is inapprehensible to humans; and, third, that even if existence is apprehensible, nevertheless, it is certainly not able to be communicated or interpreted for one's neighbors.

**McConnell, Terrance C**. *Moral Issues in Health Care: An Introduction to Medical Ethics*. Belmont, Wadsworth, 1997.

Here in seven succinct chapters, Terrance McConnell introduces readers to the oftentimes contentious debate surrounding bioethics. The book opens with a discussion of ethical theory, providing students and professionals with the moral reasoning skills needed to think about bioethics meaningfully. The book then presents case studies, background and analysis on several complex ethical issues—including confidentiality, organ procurement and abortion—that encourage readers to think about bioethics from an informed standpoint. The book also demonstrates the diversity of opinion that exists in medicine today. Through this balanced approach, readers can expect to understand morally complex situations better and to learn to think critically and compassionately about important medical issues. (publisher, edited)

**McConnell, Terrance C**. The Inalienable Right of Conscience: A Madisonian Argument. *Soc Theor Pract*, 22(3), 397-416, Fall 96.

Inalienable rights may not be transferred to others. So, if the right of conscience is inalienable, one may not bind oneself irrevocably to follow the commands of another. Madison argues for the inalienability of the right of conscience on grounds that agents cannot otherwise discharge their duties to render to the Creator such homage and only such as they believe to be acceptable to him. An extension of the Madisonian argument holds that agents may not commit themselves always to obey another because the content of the other's commands might be anything whatsoever. This implies that though consent may be necessary for political obligations, it is not alone sufficient. But this need not preclude some other basis for such obligations.

**McCormack, Robert**. Provider Disclosure of Financial Incentives in Managed Care: Pros and Cons. *Bioethics Forum*, 12(1), 21-24, Spr 96.

Financial incentives in managed care organizations are under scrutiny. The organization, rather than the physician, has the responsibility to explain these incentives to plan holders in a clear and understandable manner.

**McCormick, Richard A**. A Good Death—Oxymoron?. *Bioethics Forum*, 13(1), 5-10, Spr 97.

**McCree, Herbert L** and Bowyer, Carlton H. National Goals for Education and *The Language of Education*. *Stud Phil Educ*, 16(1-2), 139-148, Ja-Ap 97.

Schools have always been under pressure to change or reform. Recent public criticism of schools provoked an attempt to address weaknesses in American education. Goals 2000 is a legislative effort that would reform schools using national goals for education. Selected goals are highlighted and *The Language of Education* provides a structure to develop understanding of the goals. We contend that Scheffler's method for examining the discussion on education and policies developed from it is valid in the contemporary context. The analysis possible using *The Language of Education* would bring a missing sense of order to educational policy development and possibly give voice to those often disenfranchised by the process.

**McCulloch, Gregory**. Dismounting from the Seesaw: John McDowell *Mind and World*. *Int J Phil Stud*, 4(2), 309-320, S 96.

**McCullough, Laurence B**. John Gregory (1724-1773) and the Invention of Professional Relationships in Medicine. *J Clin Ethics*, 8(1), 11-21, Spr 97.

We take for granted the existence and ethical character of professional-patient relationships in health care, as if these relationships have been of long standing, back to Hippocrates. The purpose of this article is to show that this assumption is not well supported historically. Instead, the professional-patient relationship had to be invented and John Gregory (1724-1773) did so for medicine and medical ethics in the 18th century. By the 18th century in Britain medicine had become a largely entrepreneurial affair, with physicians busily pursuing self-interest in income, market share, prestige and power—often at the expense of patients' health and lives. Drawing on Hume's concept of sympathy and his own commitments to feminism—women of learning and virtue were the moral exemplars for physicians to follow, Gregory develops the concept of the physician as someone who commits himself to the life of service to patients—the physician as moral fiduciary of the patient.

**McCullough, Laurence B**. The Management of Instability and Incompleteness: Clinical Ethics and Abstract Expressionism. *J Med Phil*, 22(1), 1-10, F 97.

Central concepts and consensus views in clinical ethics are marked by instability. The papers in this number of the *Journal* take up two such central concepts, quality of life and moral status, and two such consensus views, that germ-line gene transfer should not be undertaken for the purposes of enhancement of human traits and that the ethical obligation of physicians to treat HIV-infected patients rests on consent of the physician. One outcome of these philosophical investigations is that these two concepts and consensus views are less stable than one might have thought. I explore the possibility of generalizing this outcome in a reflection on clinical ethics as the management of instability and incompleteness, including the instability and incompleteness of clinical ethics itself. (edited)

**McCumber, John**. "Aristotle and the Metaphysics of Intolerance" in *Philosophy, Religion, and the Question of Intolerance*, Ambuel, David (ed), 16-27. Albany, SUNY Pr, 1997.

**McCurdy, Christopher S I**. Humphreys's Paradox and the Interpretation of Inverse Conditional Propensities. *Synthese*, 108(1), 105-125, Jl 96.

The aim of this paper is to distinguish between and examine three issues surrounding "Humphreys's paradox" and interpretation of conditional propensities. The first issue involves the controversy over the interpretation of inverse conditional propensities—conditional propensities in which the conditioned event occurs before the conditioning event. The second issue is the consistency of the dispositional nature of the propensity interpretation and the inversion theorems of the probability calculus, where an inversion theorem is any theorem of probability that makes explicit (or implicit) appeal to a conditional probability and its corresponding inverse conditional probability. The third issue concerns the relationship between the notion of stochastic independence which is supported by the propensity interpretation and various notions of causal independence. In examining each of these issues, it is argued that the dispositional character of the propensity interpretation provides a consistent and useful interpretation of the probability calculus.

**McDermott, John J**. Symposium on Susanne K. Langer: A Foreward. *Trans Peirce Soc*, 33(1), 131-132, Wint 97.

**McDermott, John M**. Jesus: Parable or Sacrament of God?. *Gregorianum*, 78(3), 477-499, 1997.

Le livre excellent de E. Schweizer, intitulé *Jesus: The Parable of God*, offre une belle occasion pour un dialogue oecuménique. A la base de son exégèse profonde se trouve l'a priori théologique que Schweizer partage avec Karl Barth et Bultmann, ses maîtres. Il interprète Jésus comme *la* parabole de Dieu, le voyant comme la révélation définitive de Dieu et *plus qu'un homme*. Son hésitation à identifier Jésus comme Dieu a sa source dans son refus d'employer le langage objectivant de *substance*. Mais l'affirmation patristique de la nature divine de Jésus est basée sur sa relation filiale unique par rapport au Père telle qu'elle est révélée dans l'Ecriture. Le terme *sacrement de Dieu* n'exprimerait-il pas ce qui est dit par *parabole de Dieu*, en synthétisant mieux les thèmes néo-testamentaires? Cette suggestion introduit les questions théologiques sous-jacentes de l'analogie et de la liberté qui seront traitées dans la seconde partie de l'article.

**McDermott, John M** and Comandini, Glenn J. The Problem of Person and Jean Mouroux. *Sapientia*, 52(201), 75-97, 1997.

In Thomism person denotes "subsistent relation" (Trinity) and "individual subsistence" (Christology), perichoresis and incommunicability, a part and a whole. As freely dominating actions person contracts with nature, intrinsic principle of motion and free will. Building ascending series of integrating paradoxes upon the form-matter composition, Mouroux identified person with the soul's apex where meet existence-essence, spirit-matter, intellect-will, individual-species, activity-passivity, eternity-time and grace-nature. In love the person is most himself when joined to God and others, called in freedom to become who he is. Unclear are the soul's possession of existence and how Christ's infinite existence actuates a finite nature.

**McDonald, Michael**. Business Ethics in Canada: Integration and Interdisciplinarity. *J Bus Ethics*, 16(6), 635-643, Ap 97.

In 1989, the Social Sciences and Humanities Research Council of Canada established a strategic research theme on applied ethics—a theme which has been characterized by its welcome emphasis on the integration of theory and practice and interdisciplinarity. In the six competitions in that theme for research funding, bioethics has received more support than other areas of applied ethics including business ethics. Nonetheless, I argue that Canadian research in business and professional ethics has made significant strides over the past six years.

**McDonough, Kevin**. "The Complex Ethics of Separate Schools" in *Philosophy of Education (1996)*, Margonis, Frank (ed), 58-61. Urbana, Phil Education Soc, 1997.

**McDonough, Richard**. Hegel's Organic Account of Mind and Critique of Cognitive Science. *Grad Fac Phil J*, 19(1), 67-97, 1996.

**McDowell, Jean**. The Ethical Neutrality of Prospective Payments: Justice Issues. *Cambridge Quart Healthcare Ethics*, 5(4), 570-578, Fall 96.

**McDowell, John**. "Précis of *Mind and World*" in *Perception*, Villanueva, Enrique (ed), 231-239. Atascadero, Ridgeview, 1996.

**McDowell, John**. "Reply to Gibson, Byrne, and Brandom" in *Perception*, Villanueva, Enrique (ed), 283-300. Atascadero, Ridgeview, 1996.

**McDowell, John**. Brandom on Representation and Inference. *Phil Phenomenol Res*, 57(1), 157-162, Mr 97.

**McDowell, John**. Mind and World. *Phil Books*, 38(3), 169-181, Jl 97.

**McEvoy, James**. Zur Rezeption des Aristotelischen Freundschaftsbegriffs in der Scholastik. *Frei Z Phil Theol*, 43(3), 287-303, 1996.

The recovery of Aristotelian texts through Latin translation was extended to the *Nicomachean Ethics* by Robert Grosseteste, ca. 1245 whose translation, glosses and fragmentary commentary are described here. The reception of Books 8 and 9 of the *Nicomachean Ethics*, dedicated to philia in its various forms, is discussed. The character of the earliest commentaries, by Robert Grosseteste, Albert the Great and Thomas Aquinas, is brought out and the focus of each of them is indicated. The disputed question by Henry of Ghent, as to whether friendship is a virtue, is summarized. The political emphasis of the French glosses on N.E. 8 and 9 by Nicolas Oresme is noted. General conclusions concerning the reception of the work are formulated.

**McFarlane, Adrian Anthony**. A Grammar of Fear and Evil: A Husserlian-Wittgensteinian Hermeneutic. New York, Lang, 1996.

*A Grammar of Fear and Evil* examines the phenomenon of fear as a primary context for the problem of evil. It claims that whereas the locution "evil" is primarily a religious interpretation of life's troubling experiences, fear is the primary experience on which this interpretation builds. Thus, the problem of evil has to be seen in the light of the fears that inform our interpretations. A grammar of fear makes possible both the description and the modalization of fear. The one deals with the ongoing relations between self and world, while the other deals with the ways in which the relationships are approached. One of the ways of dealing with these relationships is to attribute ultimate significance—evil and good—to the threats and securities we experience. (publisher)

**McFee, Graham**. Meaning and the Art-Status of 'Music Alone'. *Brit J Aes*, 37(1), 31-46, Ja 97.

**McGary, Howard**. "On Violence in the Struggle for Liberation" in *Existence in Black: An Anthology of Black Existential Philosophy*, Gordon, Lewis R (ed), 263-272. New York, Routledge, 1997.

I contend that physical violence by members of an oppressed group, under certain conditions, can be used to combat prolonged and systematic psychological violence. I argue that the moral justification for such violence is the right to self-defense.

**McGee, Glenn**. Parenting in an Era of Genetics. *Hastings Center Rep*, 27(2), 16-22, Mr-Ap 97.

Most parents want to improve the lot of their children. And increasingly, parents or would-be parents are being offered genetic means for doing so. To whichever means parents turn, the road to enhancement is paved with some deadly and not-so-deadly sins that all parents and social stewards ought to learn to avoid.

**McGee, Glenn**. Phronesis in Clinical Ethics. *Theor Med*, 17(4), 317-328, D 96.

This essay argues that while we have examined clinical ethics quite extensively in the literature, too little attention has been paid to the complex question of how clinical ethics is learned. Competing approaches to ethics pedagogy have relied on outmoded understandings of the way moral learning takes place in ethics. It is argued that the better approach, framed in the work of Aristotle, is the idea of *phronesis*, which depends on a long-term mentorship in clinical medicine for either medical students or clinical ethics students. Such an approach is articulated and defended.

**McGee, Glenn**. *The Perfect Baby: A Pragmatic Approach to Genetics*. Lanham, Rowman & Littlefield, 1997.

*The Perfect Baby* is a clarion call for a more realistic discussion of biotechnology. McGee challenges the common assumption that we are essentially determined by a genetic blueprint. He denies the necessity of a new "Genethics," arguing that the wisdom we need can be found in the everyday experience of parents. The book dramatically alters the terms of the moral debate for parents, policymakers, scientists, philosophers, theologians and physicians. (publisher, edited)

**McGee, Vann**. Logical Operations. *J Phil Log*, 25(6), 567-580, D 96.

Tarski and Mautner proposed to characterize the "logical" operations on a given domain as those invariant under arbitrary permutations. These operations are the ones that can be obtained as combinations of the operations on the following list: identity; substitution of variable; negation; finite or infinite disjunction; and existential quantification with respect to a finite or infinite block of variables. Inasmuch as every operation on this list is intuitively "logical", this lends support to the Tarski-Mautner proposal.

**McGeer, Victoria**. Is "Self-Knowledge" an Empirical Problem? Renogotiating the Space of Philosophical Explanation. *J Phil*, 93(10), 483-515, O 96.

Our first-person authority with respect to intentional states has recently been challenged by both philosophers and psychologists. In philosophy, the challenge has centred on externalist accounts of content. Externalists, like Wright and Bilgrami, defend 1st-person authority by arguing for a nonepistemic account of self-knowledge. Their views are suggestive but not sufficiently developed to meet a deeper challenge increasingly presented by empirical findings in cognitive psychology. After describing these findings, I defend first-person authority by suggesting an account of intentional states that itself challenges the widely-held view of folk psychology as (just) a causal-explanatory protoscientific theory of mind.

**McGilvray, James**. Indexing Truths: A Critical Notice of John Campbell's *Past, Space, and Self*. *Mind Lang*, 11(4), 433-446, D 96.

Against Campbell's effort to defend a global realism that is committed to a uniform application of 'true' to claims made within different epistemic contexts, I defend the view that 'true' can be epistemically indexed.

**McGinn, Colin**. "Consciousness Evaded: Comments on Dennett" in *AI, Connectionism and Philosophical Psychology, 1995*, Tomberlin, James E (ed), 241-249. Atascadero, Ridgeview, 1995.

**McGinn, Colin**. Another Look at Color. *J Phil*, 93(11), 537-553, N 96.

**McGinn, Colin**. *The Character of Mind: An Introduction to the Philosophy of Mind*. New York, Oxford Univ Pr, 1996.

**McGinn, Marie**. The Writer and Society: An Interpretation of *Nausea*. *Brit J Aes*, 37(2), 118-128, Ap 97.

Interpretations of *Nausea* have focused on its metaphysical themes. While these themes are present, they do not provide a satisfying reading of the work as a whole. I offer an interpretation that connects *Nausea* with Sartre's psychological interest in the question of how someone becomes a writer and with his unresolved anxieties concerning the problem of the relation between the alienated bourgeois writer and the bourgeois society that produced him. Sartre uses Roquentin's extended crisis to explore themes that are central to his study of Flaubert. This reading brings out the negative elements in Sartre's portrait of Roquentin and draws together many of the apparently incidental aspects of the book into a coherent whole.

**McGinn, Marie**. *Wittgenstein and the Philosophical Investigations*. New York, Routledge, 1997.

Wittgenstein is the most important twentieth-century philosopher in the English-speaking world. In the *Philosophical Investigations* he undertakes a radical critique of the presuppositions that form the framework to analytical philosophy's approach to both the philosophy of language and the philosophy of mind. The book introduces and assesses: Wittgenstein's life and its connections with his thought, the principal ideas of the *Philosophical Investigations*, and Wittgenstein's philosophical method. (publisher, edited)

**McGinn, Robert E**. The Engineer's Moral Right to Reputational Fairness. *Sci Eng Ethics*, 1(3), 217-230, Jl 95.

This essay explores the issue of the moral rights of engineers. An historical case study is presented in which an accomplished, loyal, senior engineer was apparently wronged as a result of actions taken by his employer in pursuit of legitimate business interests. Belief that the engineer was wronged is justified by showing that what happened to him violated what can validly be termed one of his moral rights as an engineer: the right to reputational fairness. It is then argued that, this right notwithstanding, under certain circumstances it is morally permissible for employers to override it. The paper concludes by identifying two complementary facets of this right, discussing its scope, and indicating what is required of employers obliged to respect it in two types of action contexts.

**McGleenan, Tony**. "Rights to Know and not to Know: Is there a Need for a Genetic Privacy Law?" in *The Right to Know and the Right not to Know*, Chadwick, Ruth (ed), 43-54. Brookfield, Avebury, 1997.

**McGowan, Matthew K** and McGowan, Richard J. Ethics and MIS Education. *Phil Cont World*, 3(3), 12-17, Fall 96.

In this paper, we document the need for an education in ethics in management information systems (MIS) curricula, identify the gap in current curricula materials for MIS and propose material and an organization of material to include in MIS curricula. The paper contributes to the development of material on ethics for MIS curricula and also advances the discussion between people educated in MIS and people educated in ethics.

**McGowan, Richard J** and McGowan, Matthew K. Ethics and MIS Education. *Phil Cont World*, 3(3), 12-17, Fall 96.

In this paper, we document the need for an education in ethics in management information systems (MIS) curricula, identify the gap in current curricula materials for MIS and propose material and an organization of material to include in MIS curricula. The paper contributes to the development of material on ethics for MIS curricula and also advances the discussion between people educated in MIS and people educated in ethics.

**McGowan Tress, Daryl**. Aristotle's *Child*: Development Through *Genesis, Oikos*, and *Polis*. *Ancient Phil*, 17(2), 63-84, Spr 97.

The paper examines the concept of the *child* in Aristotle's biological, ethical and political treatises. In attempting to reconstruct a comprehensive notion of children's development from these works of the theoretical and practical sciences, Aristotle's principle of the division of the sciences must be heeded. It is argued that Aristotle conceives of children as unfinished and as having their source in a prior actuality and that these notions unify the biological, ethical and political treatments. At the same time, however, each science retains its separate integrity by means of its own *telos*, representing different—yet linked—stages of the child's development.

**McGrath, Matthew**. Reply to Kovach. *Mind*, 106(423), 581-586, Jl 97.

I defend deflationism about propositional truth against Adam Kovach's criticisms. I argue, first, that the logical principles I employ in my attempted explanations of general facts about truth are both fully general and do not stand in need of elucidation in terms of truth. Second, I show that even if material implication is analyzable in terms of truth, entailment is not, and that the deflationist, without loss, may forgo appeal to material implication in formulating deflationism and deriving explanatory consequences from it. Third, I formulate and explain the purported fact that true beliefs leads to successful behavior.

**McGrath, Matthew**. Weak Deflationism. *Mind*, 106(421), 69-98, Ja 97.

Is truth a substantial feature of truth-bearers? Correspondence theorists answer in the affirmative, deflationists in the negative. Correspondence theorists cite in their defense the dependence of truth on meaning or representational content. Deflationists in turn cite the conceptual centrality of simple equivalences such as "'Snow is white' is true iff snow is white" and "It is true that snow is white iff snow is white." The apparent facts to which these theorists appeal correspond to some of our firmest and most basic convictions about truth. An account of truth that fails to accommodate either sort of apparent fact is inadequacy by "deflating" truth for propositions but "inflating" truth for entities that express propositions, thus drawing from the insights of both deflationists and correspondence theorists.

**McGregor Wright, R K**. *No Place for Sovereignty: What's Wrong with Freewill Theism*. Downers Grove, InterVarsity Pr, 1996.

**McGrew, Lydia M**. Reason, Rhetoric and the Price of Linguistic Revision. *Pub Affairs Quart*, 11(3), 255-279, Jl 97.

**McGrew, Lydia M** and McGrew, Timothy J. Level Connections in Epistemology. *Amer Phil Quart*, 34(1), 85-94, Ja 97.

This paper argues that a posteriori epistemology cannot yield true epistemic principles and hence leads to skepticism. William Alston insists that a priori principles are unnecessary because the KK thesis is false; he concludes that an infinite metaregress of externalist principles is not vicious. But a more modest modal principle still rules out externalist principles. Even if a subject cannot argue for the principles underwriting his justification, it must be in principle possible to defend them decisively and stop the metaregress, or the subject is not justified. And only a priori epistemic principles can be thus defended.

**McGrew, Timothy J** and McGrew, Lydia M. Level Connections in Epistemology. *Amer Phil Quart*, 34(1), 85-94, Ja 97.

This paper argues that a posteriori epistemology cannot yield true epistemic principles and hence leads to skepticism. William Alston insists that a priori principles are unnecessary because the KK thesis is false; he concludes that an infinite metaregress of externalist principles is not vicious. But a more modest modal principle still rules out externalist principles. Even if a subject cannot argue for the principles underwriting his justification, it must be in principle possible to defend them decisively and stop the metaregress, or the subject is not justified. And only a priori epistemic principles can be thus defended.

**McGrew, Timothy J** and Shier, David and Silverstein, Harry S. The Two-Envelope Paradox Resolved. *Analysis*, 57(1), 28-33, Ja 97.

The two envelope paradox, this paper contends, arises from an ambiguity as to whether the amount of money in the first envelope or the amount in the entire game is taken to be a fixed sum. In the former case, the conclusion that one should swap envelopes is correct and unparadoxical; in the latter, it is mathematically demonstrable that there is no advantage to swapping. This paper lays out the proof and then addresses three possible objections to this solution.

**McHenry, Leemon B**. Descriptive and Revisionary Theories of Events. *Process Stud*, 25, 90-103, 1996.

Much of the current debate on the ontological status of events is conducted within the framework of what Strawson called "descriptive metaphysics."

Whether or not events gain the privileged status of 'particulars' along with primary substances depends essentially on an analysis of the logic of their grammar. Following the lead of Russell, Whitehead and Quine, this paper challenges the Aristotelian bias of the descriptive approach and argues for a revisionary event ontology. The conceptual scheme of ordinary language is thereby replaced with one that is more compatible with modern physics. Events, in this theory, replace Aristotelian substances as the primary constituents of the universe—they are conceived as units of space-time spreading throughout and overlapping within the electromagnetic field.

**McHenry, Leemon B**. Whitehead's Panpsychism as the Subjectivity of Prehension. *Process Stud*, 24, 1-14, 1995.

This essay draws a distinction between 'pure' and 'naturalized' metaphysics in order to evaluate critically Bradley's conception of metaphysics as a pure endeavor uncontaminated by the results of empirical science. Bradley's attempt to separate science and metaphysics leaves both in an impoverished state and especially the latter since it deprives itself of the most accurate knowledge we have at present.

**McHenry Jr, Henry D**. Education as Encounter: Buber's Pragmatic Ontology. *Educ Theor*, 47(3), 341-357, Sum 97.

**McInerny, Daniel**. Divinity Must Live Within Herself: Nussbaum and Aquinas on Transcending the Human. *Int Phil Quart*, 37(1), 65-82, Mr 97.

**McInerny, Daniel**. Electric Technology and Poetic Mimesis. *Amer Cath Phil Quart*, 70(Supp), 95-104, 1996.

**McInerny, Ralph**. History and Ethics. *Maritain Stud*, 11, 146-156, 1995.

**McIntosh, Donald**. Husserl, Weber, Freud, and the Method of the Human Sciences. *Phil Soc Sci*, 27(3), 328-353, S 97.

In the debate between the natural science and the phenomenological or hermeneutical approaches in the human sciences, a third alternative described by Husserl has been widely ignored. Contrary to frequent assumptions, Husserl believed that a purely phenomenological method is not generally the appropriate approach for the empirical human sciences. Rather, he held that although they can and should make important use of phenomenological analysis, such sciences should take their basic stance in the "natural attitude," the ordinary commonsense lifeworld mode of understanding which cuts across the divergent abstractive specializations of natural science and phenomenology. (edited)

**McIntyre, Lee**. Gould on Laws in Biological Science. *Biol Phil*, 12(3), 357-367, Jl 97.

Are there laws in evolutionary biology? Stephen J. Gould has argued that there are factors unique to biological theorizing which prevent the formulation of laws in biology, in contradistinction to the case in physics and chemistry. Gould offers the problem of "complexiti" as just such a fundamental barrier to biological laws in general and to Dollo's Law in particular. But I argue that Gould fails to demonstrate: 1) that Dollo's Law is not law-like, 2) that the alleged failure of Dollo's Law demonstrates why there cannot be laws in biological science, and 3) that "complexity" is a fundamental barrier to nomologicality.

**McIntyre, Lee** and Scerri, Eric R. The Case for the Philosophy of Chemistry. *Synthese*, 111(3), 213-232, Je 97.

The philosophy of chemistry has been sadly neglected by most contemporary literature in the philosophy of science. This paper argues that this neglect has been unfortunate and that there is much to be learned from paying greater philosophical attention to the set of issues defined by the philosophy of chemistry. The potential contribution of this field to such current topics as reduction, laws, explanation and supervenience is explored, as are possible applications of insights gained by such study to the philosophy of mind and the philosophy of social science.

**McKay, Alexander**. Accommodating Ideological Pluralism in Sexuality Education. *J Moral Educ*, 26(3), 285-300, S 97.

Because norms related to sexuality are an important determinant of the nature of society, sexuality education in schools is the subject of passionate debate. This discourse reflects a struggle between *restrictive* and *permissive* sexual ideologies. These ideologies compete for influence in shaping sexuality education. As a result, some sexuality education programs constitute ideological indoctrination. Many other programs, because of the ideological conflict surrounding sexuality, omit health information. The objective of this paper is to articulate the basic parameters of a democratic philosophy of sexuality education. The aim of this philosophy is to accommodate ideological pluralism related to sexuality while simultaneously ensuring that educational programs provide the necessary information and skills to facilitate the human right to sexual health. Based on Rawls's (1993) theory of political liberalism, this philosophy proposes that sexuality education ought to be centered upon the overlapping consensus within a democracy on the right to freedom of belief. (edited)

**McKay, Alexander** and Boyd, Dwight. "The Politics of the "Good" in *Good Sexuality Education" in Philosophy of Education (1996)*, Margonis, Frank (ed), 408-411. Urbana, Phil Education Soc, 1997.

**McKay, Brian W** and Souryal, Sam S. Personal Loyalty to Superiors in Public Service. *Crim Just Ethics*, 15(2), 44-62, Sum-Fall 96.

The purpose of this article is to expose the dangers of loyalty to the *person* of the superior. While one can and should be loyal to the organization, to the group, to authority, or to the profession, loyalty to the *person* of the superior in neither required nor is necessary. Two long arguments and six short ones are offered in support of this view. The arguments are philosophical in nature and attack the common, yet unsubstantiated, *belief* that loyalty to superiors is conducive to any good in public service. Indeed, it may lead to undesirable consequences.

**McKay, Thomas J**. Analogy and Argument. *Teach Phil*, 20(1), 49-60, Mr 97.

**McKendall, Marie A** and Lindquist, Stanton C. True Colors: The Response of Business Schools to Declining Enrollment. *J Bus Ethics*, 16(8), 867-872, Je 97.

During the last several decades, business schools have increasingly portrayed themselves as the advocates and teachers of business ethics. In this context, educators have examined, criticized and written about the questionable actions of many organizations. Business schools are, however, currently facing their own unprecedented crisis in the form of dramatically declining enrollments. This paper examines the morality of the various possible response strategies and argue that how business schools respond to this crisis will serve as a clear indication of their own organizational ethics and values.

**McKenna, Erin** and Hanks, J Craig. Fragmented Selves and Loss of Community. *Phil Cont World*, 3(3), 18-23, Fall 96.

In this paper we try to provide the beginning of an analysis of some of the crises of our time. We do so by arguing that a certain account of the individual blocks our ability to think about solutions at the individual and the social levels. As an example we take the industrialization of housework in the United States and its effects on women's identity and on notions of "home." We suggest that the rise of liberal individualism, the industrialization of public and private life and the predomination of capitalism are central to the disintegration of the individual/self and that they limit the possibilities of some to determine the content and direction of self change. We argue that a notion of self as integrated and in process is needed in order to address our rapidly changing world.

**McKenna, Michael S**. A Reply to McDonald: A Defense in Favor of Requirement Conflicts. *J Soc Phil*, 28(1), 151-157, Spr 97.

In "The Presumption in Favor of Requirement Conflicts", Julie McDonald argues that participants to the moral dilemmas debate wrongly elevate the status of requirement conflicts over conflicts involving ideals or partialities. She maintains that this is explained by two background assumptions: 1) Ideals and partialities can never trump requirements; 2) Judgments of moral fault and sentiments of guilt are only appropriate in connection with the failure to satisfy a moral requirement. By examining the nature of a moral requirement and the conditions which give rise to a moral dilemma, I argue that 1) and 2) do not explain the prominence accorded to requirement conflicts.

**McKeon, Matthew**. Logical Truth in Modal Logic. *Pac Phil Quart*, 77(4), 351-361, D 96.

In this paper, I consider the criticism due to Hartry Field, John Pollack, William Hanson and James Hawthorne that the Kripkean requirement that a logical truth in modal logic be true at all possible worlds in *all* quantified model structures is unmotivated and misses some logical truths. These authors do not see the basis for making the logical truth of a modal sentence turn on more than the model structure given by one reading of the modal operator(s) which occur in the sentence. The primary goal here is to motivate the Kripkean requirement.

**McKie, John** and Kuhse, Helga and Richardson, Jeff. Allocating Healthcare By QALYs: The Relevance of Age. *Cambridge Quart Healthcare Ethics*, 5(4), 534-545, Fall 96.

The QALY method ranks health care programs according to the Quality-Adjusted Life-Years they are expected to produce for each available health care dollar. According to some critics, this involves a comprehensive bias against the aged, since the aged have fewer remaining life years than the young. Some ways of defending the QALY approach against the criticism—e.g., by arguing that the aged have already had a "fair innings"—are incompatible with the QALY approach. In contrast, the authors defend the QALY approach by placing it within the context of utilitarian ethics. If discriminating against the aged in the distribution of health care threatens to decrease utility overall, the QALYs of the aged can be given a greater weight in comparison with other groups.

**McKim, Robert**. "National Identity and Respect among Nations" in *The Morality of Nationalism*, McKim, Robert (ed), 258-273. New York, Oxford Univ Pr, 1997.

**McKim, Robert** (ed) and McMahan, Jeff (ed). *The Morality of Nationalism*. New York, Oxford Univ Pr, 1997.

**McKinney, William J**. Prediction and Rolston's Environmental Ethics: Lessons from the Philosophy of Science. *Sci Eng Ethics*, 2(4), 429-440, O 96.

Rolston (1988) argues that in order to act ethically in the environment, moral agents must assume that their actions are potentially harmful, and then strive to prove otherwise before implementing that action. In order to determine whether or not an action in the environment is harmful requires the tools of applied epistemology in order to act in accord with Rolston's ethical prescription. This link between ethics and epistemology demands a closer look at the relationship between confirmation theory, particularly notions of plausibility, in the philosophy of science and environmental ethics. Upon taking this look, I conclude that, at least logically, we are not better off assuming that actions are maximally risky (Rolston) than when we assume minimal risk.

**McKinnon, Catriona**. Self-Respect and the Stefford Wives. *Proc Aris Soc*, 97, 325-330, 1997.

**McLanahan, Sara**. "The Consequences of Single Motherhood" in *Sex, Preference, and Family: Essays on Law and Nature*, Nussbaum, Martha C (ed), 306-318. New York, Oxford Univ Pr, 1997.

**McLane, Janice**. The Voice on the Skin: Self-Mutilation and Merleau-Ponty's Theory of Language. *Hypatia*, 11(4), 107-118, Fall 96.

Self-mutilation is generally seen only as a negative response to trauma. But when trauma cannot be expressed, other forms of communication become necessary. As gestural communication, self-mutilation can reorganize and stabilize the trauma victim's world, providing a "voice on the skin" when the actual voice is forbidden. This is a plausible extension of Merleau-Ponty's gestural theory of language and an interesting comment on his notion of "reversibility" as essential to linguistic communication.

**McLaren, Margaret A**. Foucault and the Subject of Feminism. *Soc Theor Pract*, 23(1), 109-128, Spr 97.

Many feminists argue that Foucault's refusal of the subject seriously compromises the usefulness of his work, while other feminists argue that his work on the subjected and disciplined body provides a way of understanding the incorporation of social norms. This paper argues that feminists can engage productively with Foucault. Feminists have paid little attention to his later works where he suggests a subjectivity that is constituted through social practices, but capable of resistance. I argue that this social self bears a resemblance to a notion of self in care ethics. However, I conclude that feminists should remain wary when engaging with Foucault.

**McLarty, Colin**. Poincaré: Mathematics & Logic & Intuition. *Phil Math*, 5, 97-115, Je 97.

Poincaré often insisted existence in mathematics means logical consistency and formal logic is the sole guarantor of rigor. The paper joins this to his view of intuition and his own mathematics. It looks at predicativity and the infinite, Poincaré's early endorsement of the axiom of choice and Cantor's set theory *versus* Zermelo's axioms. Poincaré discussed constructivism sympathetically only once a few months before his death and conspicuously avoided committing himself. We end with Poincaré on Couturat, Russell, and Hilbert.

**McLaughlin, Peter** (ed) and Burgen, Arnold (ed) and Mittelstrass, Jürgen (ed). *The Idea of Progress*. Hawthorne, de Gruyter, 1997.

This volume represents an interdisciplinary attempt to deal with the concept of progress as used in and as viewed by various disciplines, from musicology to physics. Many of the contributions are philosophical or historical analyses of the concept of progress itself. The philosophical essays discuss empirical and valuational aspects as well as the question of whether and how philosophy itself makes progress. Other areas dealt with are progress in time, evolution, politics, health and music.

**McLaughlin, Terence H**. Israel Scheffler on Religion, Reason and Education. *Stud Phil Educ*, 16(1-2), 201-223, Ja-Ap 97.

Israel Scheffler has only recently written directly about religion and education in religion, although these are matters in which he has a strong personal interest. Scheffler's views on these issues are outlined and critically appraised, with some reference to the views of R.S. Peters on similar questions. It is suggested that one of the major difficulties which arise in relation to Scheffler's position concern its account of the balance between 'acceptance' and 'critical search for clarity' needed on the part of students in their engagement with Jewish ritual. This difficulty brings into focus a number of central questions which arise concerning the reinterpretive account of Jewish tradition which Scheffler offers.

**McMahan, Jeff**. "The Limits of National Partiality" in *The Morality of Nationalism,* McKim, Robert (ed), 107-138. New York, Oxford Univ Pr, 1997.

**McMahan, Jeff** (ed) and McKim, Robert (ed). *The Morality of Nationalism*. New York, Oxford Univ Pr, 1997.

**McManus, Denis**. Error, Hallucination and the Concept of 'Ontology' in the Early Work of Heidegger. *Philosophy*, 71(278), 553-575, O 96.

**McMillan, John** and Anderson, Lynley. Knowledge and Power in the Clinical Setting. *Bioethics*, 11(3-4), 265-270, Jl 97.

In this paper we consider the three categories offered by Howard Brody for understanding power in medicine. In his book, *The Healer's Power* Brody separates out power in medicine into the categories of Aesculapian, social, and charismatic power. We examine these three categories and then apply them to a case. In this case set in an obstetric ward, a junior member of the medical staff makes a clinical decision about a patient. This clinical decision is overruled by a senior medical staff member who then carries out his plan with disastrous consequences for the woman and her baby. This case challenges the three categories of power offered by Brody and highlights the need for a further category of hierarchical power to be added to Brody's framework. We conclude by suggesting that there is a need to recognize the discrepancy in power not only between physician and patient but also between senior and junior staff in a clinical setting.

**McMurtry, John**. The Contradictions of Free Market Doctrine: Is There a Solution?. *J Bus Ethics*, 16(7), 645-662, My 97.

The article considers six standard arguments in favor of an unfettered free market: 1) the freedom to consume; 2) the freedom of the seller; 3) the freedom of the producer; 4) the freedom from government interference; 5) lower costs; 6) promotion of democracy. It demonstrates that each of these arguments turns out to be incoherent on closer examination. The ground of this incoherence it is shown, is the market doctrine's systematic omission of nonbusiness costs and benefits from its analysis, a methodological blindness which can only be overcome by a wider-lensed comprehension of economic value.

**McNair, Douglas**. In a Different Voice: Technology, Culture, and Post-Modern Bioethics. *Bioethics Forum*, 11(2), 35-44, Sum 95.

Technology inevitably challenges culture-bound values. When this happens in health care, values of individuals and organizations who speak for the dominant technological Western culture impinge upon the most personal aspects of life of people of different cultures. Those affected have difficulty resisting the infringements and, in some cases, even have difficulty recognizing them as infringements. This essay suggests how bioethics may evolve in years to come, in response to medicalized, bureaucratized and technology-mediated care, multiculturalism and postmodern trends in philosophy.

**McNair, Douglas**. My Quality is not Low!. *Bioethics Forum*, 12(3), 11-16, Fall 96.

Proponents of *quality of life* assessment often link QOL with contentment, a fact that may result in interference of the rights of people with disabilities. Instead, the voice of the client, his or her caregivers, and of society-at-large need to be listened to and respected.

**McNamara, Paul**. "Must I Do What I Ought? (Or Will the Least I Can Do Do?)" in *Deontic Logic, Agency and Normative Systems,* Brown, Mark A (ed), 154-173. New York, Springer-Verlag, 1996.

Some key pretheoretic semantic and pragmatic phenomena that support a negative answer to the main title question are identified and a conclusion of some significance is drawn: a pervasive bipartisan presupposition of twentieth century ethical theory and deontic logic is false. Next, an intuitive model-theoretic framework for "must" and "ought" is hypothesized. It is then shown how this hypothesis helps to explain and predict all the pretheoretic phenomena previously observed. Next, I show that the framework hypothesized possesses additional expressive and explanatory power, thus adding further confirmation that it is on the right track.

**McNaughton, David**. An Unconnected Heap of Duties?. *Phil Quart*, 46(185), 433-447, O 96.

Critics often accuse ethical intuitionism of being unsystematic: first, because it offers a heap of unconnected duties with no unifying rationale; second, because it provides no general guidance in cases of conflicts of duty. To the first charge, Ross has a complete answer: he offers a distinction between basic and derivative duties and a methodology for determining which is which Ross appears to offer an answer to the second charge by claiming that some duties are intrinsically more stringent than others. In fact, this part of his theory fails, but this is just as well, because Ross's account entails that moral theory cannot perform this task.

**McNight, George** and Knight, Deborah. The Case of the Disappearing Enigma. *Phil Lit*, 21(1), 123-138, Ap 97.

The argument is that the sort of comprehension required of detection narratives is pragmatical and hermeneutical. Understanding is directed by questioning and by the revision of hypothesis relative to what at each stage we believe has been going on. What allows the first-order mystery or enigma to disappear is a second-order, explanatory story that dispels the confusion or puzzle which the initial mystery represents. We discuss five films as our key examples.

**McOuat, Gordon R**. Species, Rules and Meaning: The Politics of Language and the Ends of Definitions in 19th Century Natural History. *Stud Hist Phil Sci*, 27(4), 473-519, D 96.

The standard claim that species definitions, which included fixed "essences," mattered in the pre-Darwinian period may be wholly wrong. This has strong implications to our understanding of the Darwinian revolution and to our theories of meaning in scientific change. This paper examines the debates over language and species terms in the immediate pre-Darwinian period, and finds that by the 1840s, naturalists had come to an agreement that species were defined by conventional rules of gentlemanly conduct. Debates over the philosophy of language in the early 19th century and radical challenges to accepted language rules are also addressed. Finally, a new interpretation of the place of species in biological discourse is offered. (edited)

**McPherran, Mark L**. *The Religion of Socrates*. University Park, Pennsylvania Univ Pr, 1996.

This study argues that to understand Socrates we must uncover and analyze his religious views, since his philosophical and religious views are part of one seamless whole. Mark McPherran provides a close analysis of the relevant Socratic texts, an analysis that yields a comprehensive and original account of Socrates' commitments to religion (e.g., the nature of the gods, the immortality of the soul). (publisher)

**McWhorter, Ladelle**. Foucault's Attack on Sex-Desire. *Phil Today*, 41(1-4), 160-165, Spr 97.

There are significant genealogical and, therefore, political or strategic differences between desire on the one hand and bodies and pleasures on the other. This article explicates those differences and argues that Foucault is right to assert the strategic superiority of bodies and pleasures above desire—not because bodies and pleasures are unproblematic but because desire is so very problematic and dangerous, given its place in structures of normalization and biopower.

**Mead, Lawrence M**. Citizenship and Social Policy: T.H. Marshall and Poverty. *Soc Phil Pol*, 14(2), 197-230, Sum 97.

This paper discusses the dilemma posed for the welfare state by nonworking poverty. T.H. Marshall said that the welfare state embodied a kind of social citizenship. But he tacitly assumed that those claiming benefits also observed social obligations such as work. Today's poor don't work enough to do that. The paper considers several ways that work levels among the poor might be raised. It argues that the most effective, and the most consistent with Marshall, is to enforce work within the welfare system.

**Meaney, Mark E**. Freedom and Democracy in Health Care Ethics: Is the Cart Before the Horse?. *Theor Med*, 17(4), 399-414, D 96.

**Meazza, Carmelino**. "Aristotele tra Hegel e Heidegger: tracce per una ricostruzione" in *Hegel e Aristotele,* Ferrarin, A, 295-334. Cagliari, Edizioni AV, 1997.

**Meckenstock, Günter**. Beobachtungen zur Methodik in Fichtes *Grundlage der gesamten Wissenschaftslehre. Fichte-Studien*, 10, 67-80, 1997.

**Medina Medina, Francisco**. "El idealismo transcendental como vía de superación del realismo e idealismo dogmáticos" in *El inicio del Idealismo alemán,* Market, Oswaldo, 127-135. Madrid, Ed Complutense, 1996.

Nous avons pour but de refléchir sur le projet trascendental fichtéen en tant que rectification, élargissement et parachément du projet kantien, et d'atteindre et résoudre le problème de la connaissance en evitant certains dogmatismes et en proposant au même temps un idéalisme réel ou un réalisme idéal, ce qui entraîne un déplacement du théorique vers la praxis, et le réaffermissement de la liberté, en outre.

**Medler, David A** and Dawson, Michael R W and Berkeley, Istvan S N. PDP Networks can Provide Models that are not Mere Implementations of Classical Theories. *Phil Psych*, 10(1), 25-40, Mr 97.

There is a widespread belief that connectionist networks are dramatically different from classical or symbolic models. However, connectionists rarely test this belief by interpreting the internal structure of their nets. A new approach to interpreting networks was recently introduced by Berkeley et al. (1995). The current paper examines two implications of applying this method: 1) that the internal structure of a connectionist network can have a very classical appearance, and 2) that this interpretation can provide a cognitive theory that cannot be dismissed as a mere implementation.

**Meeker, Kevin**. Should We Abandon Epistemic Justification?. *SW Phil Rev*, 13(1), 129-136, Ja 97.

William Alston has recently argued that there is not unique item called 'epistemic justification'. So he suggests that epistemologists should abandon discussions about the justification of belief. In this paper, I examine Alston's argument and offer two objections to his reasoning. First, I contend that from Alston's perspective it is difficult to explain how epistemologists' views about justification can change under the pressure of argument. Second, I show how Alston's reasoning likewise shows that there is no unique property of propositional knowledge—a conclusion that Alston explicitly admits is unacceptable.

**Meggle, Georg**. "Das Leben eine Reise" in *Das weite Spektrum der analytischen Philosophie*, Lenzen, Wolfgang, 178-192. Hawthorne, de Gruyter, 1997.

**Meheus, Joke**. Adaptive Logic in Scientific Discovery: The Case of Clausius. *Log Anal*, 36(144), 359-391, S-D 93.

It is the aim of this paper to review some logical systems with respect to their adequacy in a particular type of creative processes, namely those that involve inconsistent constraints. I shall show that these creative processes have some very interesting properties: they require *reasoning* (from inconsistent premises) in order to detect *specific* contradictions and to resolve them. I shall argue in detail that neither classical logic nor *mixed* nonmonotonic logics, nor Rescher-like mechanisms, nor monotonic paraconsistent logics are suitable to understand this kind of precesses. We need a logic that enables us to reason sensibly in the presence of (explicit and implicit) inconsistencies and that nevertheless is almost as powerful as classical logic, in other words an inconsistency-adaptive logic. (edited)

**Mehl, Peter J**. The Self Well Lost: Psychotherapeutic Interpretation and Nelson Goodman's Irrealism. *Phil Cont World*, 2(4), 16-21, Wint 95.

In this paper, I consider Goodman's philosophy in relation to psychotherapeutic interpretation. Goodman argues that we should understand our knowledge as a creative symbolic construction and not as a set of ideas that match reality. The notion of "the world" does no epistemological work. Using an example of psychotherapeutic interpretation found in Erik Erikson's writings, I argue that while Erikson suggests that he discovers in the patient's showings and telling the patient's message and its meaning, I argue (with Goodman) that Erikson creates a narrative identity for his patient. The self is not found but fashioned and it is deemed the true self because it coheres with Erikson's general theoretic standpoint and is found to be cognitively and practically helpful for the patient. The conclusion is that selves, like worlds, are largely creative constructs.

**Mehl, Peter J**. William James's Ethics and the New Casuistry. *Int J Applied Phil*, 11(1), 41-50, Sum-Fall 96.

In their recent work, *The Abuse of Casuistry*, Albert Jonsen and Stephen Toulmin note that the moral methodology of the pragmatists is an exception to the anticasuistic aspirations of much modern moral philosophy. In this essay I consider their suggestion by examining William James's moral thought. After I explicate the current casuistic approach to morality, I consider James's ethics through a close reading of his essay "The Moral Philosopher and the Moral Life." I argue that James's moral thought does have a deep affinity to the approach of the "new casuistry," and I develop a number of connections here.

**Mehlman, Maxwell** (& others) and Whitehouse, Peter J and Juengst, Eric T. Enhancing Cognition in the Intellectually Intact. *Hastings Center Rep*, 27(3), 14-22, My-Je 97.

As science learns more about how the brain works and fails to work, the possibility for developing "cognition enhancers" becomes more plausible. The success of drugs like Ritalin points to an eager demand for drugs that can help us think faster, remember more and focus more keenly. Whether such drugs are good for individuals, or for society, is an open question, one that demands far more public discussion.

**Mehtonen, Päivi**. Obscurity as a Linguistic Device: Introductory and Historical Notes. *Dan Yrbk Phil*, 31, 157-168, 1996.

**Meier, Christian**. "Freedom of Choice and the Choice of Freedom on the Path to Democracy" in *The Ancients and the Moderns*, Lilly, Reginald (ed), 72-89. Bloomington, Indiana Univ Pr, 1996.

**Meijers, Anthonie**. De structuur van Searles filosofische project. *Alg Ned Tijdschr Wijs*, 89(2), 106-124, Ap 97.

The article aims at a rational reconstruction of Searle's philosophical project. It is conceived as a project driven by a central ontological question with two types of answers. The question is: "How does our language, mind and social institutions relate to the world of physics and biology?" The answers are given in terms of

the principle of emergence 'X constitutes Y in context C' and the principle of the transfer of intentionality 'X counts as Y in context C'. It is concluded that Searle's project is highly consistent, but raises serious questions with regard to the formal nature of the answers given.

**Meijsing, Monica**. Cuypers' Persoonlijke aangelegenheden. *Tijdschr Filosof*, 59(2), 329-343, Je 97.

Cuypers's book *Persoonlijke aangelegenheden* is critically reviewed. The criticism focuses on two points. The first point is the question how the double structure of bodily identity and actor or narrative identity can handle cases of Multiple Personality Disorder and especially of split brain, where both kinds of identity diverge. The second point is a on a meta-level. It concerns the much too apologetic description of analytical philosophy—and Cuypers's own analytical anthropology—as "superficial" and "impoverished".

**Meilaender, Gilbert**. Products of the Will: Robertson's *Children of Choice*. *Ethics Med*, 13(1), 11-19, 1997.

**Meir, Ephraim**. War and Peace in Levinas (in Hebrew). *Iyyun*, 45, 471-479, O 96.

The article discusses the themes of peace and war in the philosophy of Levinas. In his ethical metaphysics, peace as nonindifference and responsibility is conceived of as the root of truth. This concept of peace implies a series of phenomenological reflections on the precise relation between Jerusalem and Athens or between ethics and politics. The said concept of peace and its implications are carefully analysed and finally applied to the concrete situation in Israel.

**Meister, Robert**. Beyond Satisfaction: Desire, Consumption, and the Future of Socialism. *Topoi*, 15(2), 189-210, S 96.

**Meixner, Uwe**. "It is NOW" in *Das weite Spektrum der analytischen Philosophie*, Lenzen, Wolfgang, 193-202. Hawthorne, de Gruyter, 1997.

The article introduces a new tense-logical operator, N*A ("It is NOW that A"), which in combination with P (Past) and F (Future) enables one to provide formulas that express the irreflexivity and linearity of time—something that cannot be done with P and F alone. Various ways of stating the semantics of N* are presented and compared, the mentioned expressibility results are proven, a calculus for N* is stated, and N* is compared with Kamp's *now*.

**Meixner, Uwe**. Eine Explikation des Begriffes der Zurechnung. *Jahr Recht Ethik*, 2, 479-503, 1994.

This article provides an explication of the concept "imputation". On the one hand, this explication takes account of the common meaning of the concept and its generally intended range of application. On the other hand, it also provides a definition of the meaning of "y is to be imputed to x", which is precise (excluding ambiguity and incoherence and minimizing vagueness) and fruitful ("comprising that which is essential"). The adequacy of this definition of "imputation" is justified in detail, in the light of the standards for explications. (edited)

**Mejbaum, Waclaw**. "Explaining Social Phenomena" in *Epistemology and History*, Zeidler-Janiszewska, Anna (ed), 313-324. Amsterdam, Rodopi, 1996.

I deal with the concept of "functional determination" in Kmita's works. Some of the weak points of the conception are discussed. The problem of methodological individualism and some questions concerning Marxist tradition in Kmita's philosophy are also examined.

**Mejía Quintana, Oscar**. La Teoría del Derecho y la Democracia en Jürgen Habermas: En torno a *Faktizität und Geltung*. *Ideas Valores*, 32-52, Ap 97.

This essay presents an interpretation of the theories of law and democracy developed in J. Habermas's *Faktizität und Geltung* (1992) as a product of four complementary theoretical strategies. Habermas conceives the law as the only postconventional medium through which the disintegrated social bond can be remade. The discursive reconstruction of the law and of constitutional democracy—based upon a new procedural paradigm that reflects the communicative power of public opinion in both cases—, constitutes the most appropriate option for resolving the dichotomies between system and lifeworld, facts and norms and the problems of legitimization characteristic of contemporary societies, both postliberal and traditional.

**Mel'nikova, Tatiana A** and Perminova, Alla Ivanovna and Ianovskii, Rudol'f Grigor'evich. Women and Society in Russia. *Russian Stud Phil*, 34(2), 66-72, Fall 95.

**Melander, Peter**. *Analyzing Functions: An Essay on a Fundamental Notion in Biology*. Stockholm, Almqvist och Wiksell, 1997.

This study is about the notion of function in modern biology. Various recent analyses of function ascriptions and functional explanation are presented and criticized (the deductive-nomological analysis of Ernest Nagel and Carl Hempel, the etiological analyses of Larry Wright and his followers, the intrasystemic role analyses of Robert Cummins and his followers, and Mark Bedau's value-centered analysis). It is argued that a fundamental reason for the failure of these analyses is that they do not recognize that modern biology employs two different notions of function. In the final chapter these two notions are spelled out, and it is shown that on this analysis all the philosophical problems concerning the notion of function in biology are solved.

**Melaney, William D**. Art as a Form of Negative Dialectics: 'Theory' in Adorno's *Aesthetic Theory*. *J Speculative Phil*, 11(1), 40-52, 1997.

The paper demonstrates that Theodor Adorno's *Aesthetic Theory* combines Kant's belief in autonomy with Hegel's emphasis on historicity in order to develop a dialectical approach to art. A new conception of artistic truth underlies a concern for content that goes beyond formalism and respects art's utopian promise. Hence, "negative dialectics" has sociological implications and can be used to reappraise twentieth-century modernism. Finally, Adorno's philosophical aesthetics provides a basis for surpassing enlightenment rationality, and, in this way, supports the goal of political change.

**Melby, Alan K** and Warner, C Terry. *The Possibility of Language: A Discussion of the Nature of Language, with Implications for Human and Machine Translation*. Amsterdam, J Benjamins, 1995.

We attempt to address several open issues by examining the intellectual tradition of mainstream linguistics and philosophy and to identify why this tradition has failed to provide an adequate theoretical framework for some of the goals of machine translation. In the course of this investigation, we present an alternative view of how human language is possible. We then trace some of the implications of this view for the shape of translation theories, the practice of human translation and the future of translation technology, including both machine translation and computer-based tools for human translators. (publisher, edited)

**Melchior, Timothy**. Counterpoint Thinking: Connecting Learning and Thinking in Schools. *Inquiry (USA)*, 14(3), 82-90, Spr 95.

**Mele, Alfred R**. Addiction and Self-Control. *Behavior Phil*, 24(2), 99-117, Fall 96.

Addicts often are portrayed as agents driven by irresistible desires in the philosophical literature on free will. Although this portrayal is faithful to a popular conception of addiction, that conception has encountered opposition from a variety of quarters (e.g., Bakalar & Grinspoon, 1984; Becker & Murphy, 1988; Peele, 1985 and 1989; Szasz, 1974). My concern here is some theoretical issues surrounding a strategy for self-control of potential use to addicts on the assumption that their pertinent desires *fall short* of irresistibility. I offer no defense of this assumption; rather, I treat it as a point of departure for one approach to understanding addiction in action. (edited)

**Mele, Alfred R**. Rational Intentions and the Toxin Puzzle. *Protosoz*, 8/9, 39-52, 1996.

Gregory Kavka's toxin puzzle has spawned a lively literature about the nature of intention and of rational intention in particular. This paper is largely a critique of a pair of recent responses to the puzzle that focus on the connection between rationally forming an intention to A and rationally A-ing, one by David Gauthier and the other by Edward McClennen. It also critically assesses the two main morals Kavka takes reflection on the puzzle to support, morals about the nature of intention and the consequences of a divergence between "reasons for intending and reasons for acting."

**Mele, Alfred R**. Socratic Akratic Action. *Phil Papers*, 25(3), 149-159, N 96.

In this attempt at a diagnosis of what really happens in scenarios commonly regarded as involving paradigmatic *akrasia* or "weakness of will" (*Protagoras* 352b-358d), Socrates identifies a phenomenon that arguably exhibits nonparadigmatic *akrasia*. In some cases of backsliding, we act as we judge best, but the judgment itself is akratically formed. Attention to recent work in social psychology and psychiatry provides support for this thesis.

**Mele, Alfred R**. Strength of Motivation and Being in Control. *Amer Phil Quart*, 34(3), 319-332, Jl 97.

Some theorists claim that if (1) whenever we act intentionally, we do, or try to do, what we are most strongly motivated to do at the time, then (2) we are at the mercy of whatever desire happens to be strongest then. This paper exploits the results of some well-known experiments by physiologist Benjamin Libet in arguing that (1) does not imply (2). The paper develops an interpretation of Libet's results that is sensitive to important conceptual distinctions that he ignores and it moves beyond Libet's laboratory setting to some garden-variety cases of self-control.

**Mele, Alfred R**. Underestimating Self-Control: Kennett and Smith on Frog and Toad. *Analysis*, 57(2), 119-123, Ap 97.

In "Frog and Toad Lose Control" (*Analysis*, 1996), Jeannette Kennett and Michael Smith propose a resolution to a puzzle about exercising self-control in support of one's doing A at a time at which one wants most to do something other than A. Their resolution features alleges exercises of self-control that are not actions. This paper defends a resolution according to which a more robust, *actional* exercise of self-control is open to agents in scenarios of this kind.

**Meléndez, Germán**. Acerca del Pensador Profesional de Schumacher. *Ideas Valores*, 53-66, Ag 97.

**Meléndez, Germán**. El *Nacimiento de la Tragedia* como Introducción a la Filosofía Posterior de Nietzsche. *Ideas Valores*, 54-73, D 96.

The purpose of this paper is to introduce the main ideas and theses of Nietzsche's *The Birth of Tragedy* in a way that allows to perceive a continuity between them and the central doctrines of his later thought. Following some indications given by Nietzsche in his *Posthumous Fragments*, I attempt to show that the idea of eternal recurrence (as perfection of nihilism) plays an analogous role to that previously attributed to pessimism, namely that of affording a most indispensable condition (the inclusion of the negative) for the superlative affirmation of existence.

**Melina, Livio**. Desire for Happiness and the Commandments in the First Chapter of *Veritatis Splendor*. *Thomist*, 60(3), 341-359, Jl 96.

Starting from the indications of the Encyclical *Veritatis splendor*, the article focuses the relationship that moral theology must establish between desire for happiness and commandments. In the perspective of an "ethics of the first person", the desire for happiness is freed from his constitutive ambiguity through the moment of truth about the good. The commandments educate the desire, favouring his integration in the moral virtues. At the theological level, the desire for happiness finds his interpretation and superabundant fulfillment in the

encounter with Jesus, whereas the commandments in their christological dimension, become paths towards the perfection of one's personal vocation.

**Melissidis, N S**. Poiesis and Praxis in Aristotle's *Poetics*. *Phil Inq*, 18(1-2), 143-150, Wint-Spr 96.

Plato's view on poetry follows from his anthropological doctrine; namely that ethical-political correctness precedes any aesthetic judgment and determines the artistic correctness, and consequently the position of poetry in his ideal city. That means that a political-intellectual élite should protect youth and preserve citizens' good life from harmful influence of poetry by fixing the specifications of "correct" poetic works. Unlike Plato, Aristotle inquires the literary correctness itself, according to its own intrinsic rules, and then he looks into its artistic value through the organic structures that make up the ideal poetic work in general, without any ethical-political influence on the audience being involved. (edited)

**Mellor, D H**. The Facts of Causation. *Phil Books*, 38(1), 1-11, Ja 97.

This book develops a new metaphysical theory of causation, including indeterministic causation. It is based on a concept of objective chance, and shows why causes are evidence for, explains, are means to, and must precede their effects. It covers causation between facts and particulars, the difference between facts and particulars, the difference between causing something and affecting it, and shows how causation can be either opaque or transparent. It includes a new theory of laws and properties and shows how time, defined as the causal dimension of space-time, can also be Kant's 'form of inner sense.'

**Mellor, D H** (ed) and Oliver, Alex (ed). *Properties*. New York, Oxford Univ Pr, 1997.

This volume offers a selection of the most interesting and important readings on properties beginning with the work of Frege, Russell and Ramsey. In particular, it makes accessible for the first time contributions to the contemporary controversy about the nature and roles of properties: Do they differ from particulars? Are they universals, sets or tropes? How are properties involved with causation, laws and semantics? The editors' introduction guides the novice through these issues and critically discusses the readings.

**Mellor, Robert** and Hettihewa, Samanthala and Batten, Jonathan. The Ethical Management Practices of Australian Firms. *J Bus Ethics*, 16(12-13), 1261-1271, S 97.

This paper addresses a number of important issues regarding the ethical practices and recent behaviour of large Australian firms in nine industries. These issues include whether firms have a written code of ethics, whether firms have a forum for the discussion of ethics, whether managers consider that their firm's activities have an environmental impact and whether there are any statistical relationships between the size, industry class, ownership, international involvement and location of the firm and its ethical management practices. These questions are examined by using data collected from a sample of 136 large firms operating in Australia.

**Melnick, Arthur**. *Representation of the World: A Naturalized Semantics*. New York, Lang, 1997.

We have thoughts of the world by having thoughts of spatio-temporal positioning which, as naturalized, are mechanisms for spatio-temporal constructive output. Even thoughts of past time are such thoughts of positioning by being mechanisms for being beyond stages of temporal constructions. This allows a naturalized realist semantics in which the content of thoughts that are in the head is purported existence anywhere in space and time. A correspondence theory of truth and a truth-conditional theory of meaning derive naturalistically from this basis. (publisher, edited)

**Melnyk, Andrew**. On the Metaphysical Utility of Claims of Global Supervenience. *Phil Stud*, 87(3), 277-308, S 97.

I argue that there is a kind of metaphysical utility that claims of global supervenience lack; they cannot play a truly explanatory role in a metaphysically illuminating account of interlevel property relations. Claims of supervenience can assume different metaphysical pictures of what it is in the world that makes the claims true, and my arguments for thinking that claims of global supervenience cannot play this role depend upon which picture is assumed. The four pictures I distinguish are Lewisian modal realism, ersatzism, the Truthmaker Picture, and the Superglue Picture.

**Melnyk, Andrew**. Searle's Abstract Argument Against Strong AI. *Synthese*, 108(3), 391-419, S 96.

Discussion of Searle's case against strong AI has usually focused upon his Chinese Room thought-experiment. In this paper, however, I expound and then try to refute what I call his abstract argument against strong AI, an argument which turns upon quite general considerations concerning programs, syntax and semantics and which seems not to depend on intuitions about the Chinese Room. I claim that this argument fails, since it assumes one particular account of what a program is. I suggest an alternative account which, however, cannot play a role in a Searle-type argument and argue that Searle gives no good reason for favoring his account, which allows the abstract argument to work, over the alternative, which doesn't. This response to Searle's abstract argument also, incidentally, enables the Robot Reply to the Chinese Room to defend itself against objections Searle makes to it.

**Melnyk, Andrew**. Testament of a Recovering Eliminativist. *Proc Phil Sci Ass*, 3(Suppl), S185-S193, 1996.

If physicalism is true (e.g., if every event is a fundamental-physical event), then it looks as if there is a fundamental-physical explanation of everything. If so, then what is to become of special scientific explanations? They seem to be excluded by the fundamental-physical ones, and indeed to be excellent candidates for elimination. I argue that, if physicalism is true, there probably is a fundamental-physical explanation of everything, but that nevertheless there can perfectly well be special scientific explanations as well, notwithstanding eliminativist scruples concerning overdetermination and Ockham's Razor.

**Melnyk, Andrew**. The Prospects for Dretske's Account of the Explanatory Role of Belief. *Mind Lang*, 11(2), 203-215, Je 96.

When a belief is cited as part of the explanation of an agent's behaviour, it seems that the belief is explanatorily relevant in virtue of its content. In his *Explaining Behavior*, Dretske presents an account of belief, content and explanation according to which this can be so. I supply some examples of beliefs whose explanatory relevance in virtue of content apparently cannot be accounted for in the Dretskean way. After considering some possible responses to this challenge, I end by discussing how serious these counterexamples are for Dretske's account.

**Melo, António**. A *Areté* Helénica nos Jogos Olímpicos. *Rev Port Filosof*, 52(1-4), 523-537, Ja-D 96.

**Meloni, Giancarlo** and Ghilardi, Silvio. Constructive Canonicity in Non-Classical Logics. *Annals Pure Applied Log*, 86(1), 1-32, Je 97.

Sufficient syntactic conditions for canonicity in intermediate and intuitionistic modal logics are given. We present a new technique which does not require semantic first-order reduction and which is constructive in the sense that it works in an intuitionistic metatheory through a model without points which is classically isomorphic to the usual canonical model.

**Meloni, Giancarlo** and Ghilardi, Silvio. Relational and Partial Variable Sets and Basic Predicate Logic. *J Sym Log*, 61(3), 843-872, S 96.

In this paper we study the logic of relational and partial variable sets, seen as a generalization of set-valued presheaves, allowing transition functions to be arbitrary relations or arbitrary partial functions. We find that such a logic is the usual intuitionistic and cointuitionistic first order logic without Beck and Frobenius conditions relative to quantifiers along arbitrary terms. The important case of partial variable sets is axiomatizable by means of the substitutivity schema for equality. Furthermore, completeness, incompleteness and independence results are obtained for different kinds of Beck and Frobenius conditions.

**Mendelsohn, Richard L**. "Frege's Treatment of Indirect Reference" in *Frege: Importance and Legacy*, Schirn, Matthias (ed), 410-437. Hawthorne, de Gruyter, 1996.

**Mendelsohn, Richard L** (ed & trans) and Gabriel, Gottfried (ed) and Kienzler, Wolfgang (ed). Diary: Written by Professor Dr. Gottlob *Frege in the Time from 10 March to 9. April 1924*. Inquiry, 39(3-4), 303-342, D 96.

**Mendenhall, Vance**. On Grading Apples and Arguments. *Inquiry (USA)*, 16(3), 45-63, Spr 97.

**Mendenhall, Vance**. When Is An Excuse A Reason?. *Inquiry (USA)*, 15(2), 72-82, Wint 95.

**Méndez Lloret, Isabel**. La teología epicúrea: la concepción de la divinidad y su incidencia en la vida humana. *Pensamiento*, 205(53), 33-52, Ja-Ap 97.

La *teología* epicúrea es, además de coherente, consecuente con su *física* y su *canónica*. La originalidad con la que Epicuro trata a los dioses se sigue de su intento de liberar al hombre de sus miedos y conseguir la *autarquía*. Los dioses son compuestos atómicos; no son ingénitos, aunque sí inmortales. Su inmortalidad es fruto de una conquista consistente en seguir un régimen alimenticio sano, despreciando lo ajeno y acogiendo lo propio. Los dioses son el paradigma para el hombre quien, para asimilarse a lo divino, debe imitar la vida divina, acogiendo la correcta *prólepsis* y rechazando las falsas nociones acerca de los dioses.

**Mendieta, Eduardo** (ed). *Karl-Otto Apel: Selected Essays*. Atlantic Highlands, Humanities Pr, 1996.

This second volume of Karl-Otto Apel's selected essays gathers his most important work on discourse ethics and the communicative theory of rationality, both of which he has been elaborating since the late 1960s with Jürgen Habermas. The book contributes greatly to the understanding of the difference between Apel's and Habermas's versions of discourse ethics. Most important, the book clearly illustrates how a theory of rationality presupposes a theory of ethics and vice versa. This collection will be indispensable for all scholars concerned with contemporary moral and ethical problems, contemporary history of philosophy, and the convergence of analytical philosophy, pragmatism, and Continental philosophy. (publisher,edited)

**Mendieta, Eduardo**. Modernity, Postmodernity and Transmodernity: Hope in Search of Time (in Spanish). *Univ Phil*, 14(27), 63-86, D 96.

This essay offers a critical appraisal of the relationship between modernity, postmodernity and transmodernity (and the postcolonial). It begins with a genealogy of the fundamental notions underpinning the temporal regimes of modernity. Foucault's notion of the panopticon is reformulated not in terms of optics or oculocentrism, but in terms of temporal and spatial mappings. Underlying Christendom, modernity, postmodernity, the author argues, is a particular chronotopology that regiments transcendence and social life in terms of a calculus of the teleological. This chronotope has assumed different chronograms, i.e., the modern, postmodern and postcolonial. The essay concludes offering a practical example of how the chronotopology of modernity works itself out in the case of biotechnology and genetic colonization.

**Mendieta, Eduardo** and Batstone, David and Lorentzen, Lois Ann (& others). *Liberation Theologies, Postmodernity, and the Americas*. New York, Routledge, 1997.

Over the last thirty years, liberation theology has irrevocably altered religious thinking and practice throughout the Americas. Liberation theology rises up at the margins of social power. Drawing its energies from the black community in the United States, grassroots religious communities in Latin America and feminist circles in North Atlantic countries, theologies of liberation have emerged as a resource and inspiration for people seeking social and political freedom. (publisher, edited)

**Mendik, Xavier**. "Transgressive Bodies: Destruction and Excessive Display of the Human Form in the Horror Film" in *Critical Studies: Ethics and the Subject*, Simms, Karl (ed), 189-202. Amsterdam, Rodopi, 1997.

**Menéndez Alzamora, Manuel**. "Vieja y Nueva Política y el Semanario *España* en el Nacimiento" in *Política y Sociedad en José Ortega y Gasset: En Torno a "Vieja y Nueva Política"*, Lopez de la Vieja, Maria Teresa (ed), 185-193. Barcelona, Anthropos, 1997.

**Menezes, Flavio M** and Monteiro, Paulo K. Sequential Asymmetric Auctions with Endogenous Participation. *Theor Decis*, 43(2), 187-202, S 97.

In this paper we suggest a model of sequential auctions with endogenous participation where each bidder conjectures about the number of participants at each round. Then, after learning his value, each bidder decides whether or not to participate in the auction. In the calculation of his expected value, each bidder uses his conjectures about the number of participants for each possible subgroup. In equilibrium, the conjectured probability is compatible with the probability of staying in the auction. (edited)

**Mensch, James Richard**. "Postnormative Subjectivity" in *The Ancients and the Moderns*, Lilly, Reginald (ed), 311-321. Bloomington, Indiana Univ Pr, 1996.

Modern philosophy does not just attempt to say in advance how things must be, it bases its normative assertions on its analyses of the subject. Historically, the result has been a plurality of absolute, yet contradictory claims. The reason for this is that the subject itself has no definite content. Its "openness" is such that it draws its content from the situations it finds itself in. As a result, the subject appears, in its content, to support every possible analysis, every possible normative structure, from the Kantian to the Freudian. Given that the "openness" of the subject is ultimately that of time, the conception of a genuine postnormative subjectivity requires our rethinking and renewing the pre-Cartesian claim that subjective time is dependent on being.

**Mensch, James Richard**. Presence and Post-Modernism. *Amer Cath Phil Quart*, 71(2), 145-156, Spr 97.

The postmodern, postenlightenment debate on the nature of being begins with Heidegger's assertion that the "ancient interpretation of the being of beings" is informed by "the determination of the sense of being as ... 'presence.'" At its origin is supposedly "Aristotle's treatment of time," which has "determined every subsequent account of time," Kant's included. I argue that this is not the case. The enlightenment project, as exemplified by both Kant and Heidegger, actually reverses Aristotle's position. Given this, the failure of the enlightenment project cannot be traced to a failure of the metaphysics of presence as such, but only to the modern version of it. My claim, then, is that the postmodern critique of philosophy is undermined by a faulty historical analysis.

**Menssen, Sandra**. Grading Worlds. *Amer Cath Phil Quart*, 70(Supp), 149-161, 1996.

**Menta, Timothy**. Response: What Does Evolutionary Theory Tell Us about the Moral Status of Animals?. *Between Species*, 12(1-2), 64-66, Wint-Spr 96.

**Mercier, Jean L**. For a Minimal Theory of Truth. *Indian Phil Quart*, 23(3-4), 429-437, Jl-O 96.

**Mercier, Sean L**. The Three Meanings of Truth in Religion. *J Dharma*, 21(2), 141-162, Ap-Je 96.

**Merino, Magdalena**. Cogito ergo sum como conculcación al axioma A. *Anu Filosof*, 29(2), 741-750, 1996.

The purpose of this work is to explain how, with the proposition "cogito ergo sum", Descartes contradicts the A axiom from the theory of knowledge of Leonardo Polo, by accepting the passiveness of the knowledge and denying it as an operation of knowing an object, in which the cognizant and the cognizance are one in act.

**Merks, Karl-Wilhelm**. The Sirens' Song of the Traditions: A plea for a Universal Ethics (in Dutch). *Bijdragen*, 58(2), 122-143, 1997.

To what extent can tradition legitimize morality? With the help of three questions, the author elaborates his answer: 1) Why is tradition unable to provide a basis for morality? The answer is: because of the moral ambiguity of tradition. Tradition can offer a wealth of moral experience, but can equally turn out to be a conglomerate of moral petrifaction. Therefore, tradition as such is absolutely no legitimizing agency of moral truth. 2) Where can a measuring rod for the morality of tradition be found? The answer is: properly speaking the human person himself is the measure of morality. 3) What moral significance of tradition remains in a universal ethics "which has the human person as its measure"? The answer is: the moral significance of tradition cannot be seen in a function of legitimizing morality. Tradition is measured by ethics, but ethics is not measured by tradition. (edited)

**Merlini, Fabio**. "Per Una Genealogia Della Coscienza Storica" in *Soggetto E Verità: La questione dell'uomo nella filosofia contemporanea*, Fagiuoli, Ettore, 267-276. 20136 Milano, Mimesis, 1996.

The essay examines the "theorem" of "the end of history" in its outcomes regarding the reformulation of the concept of subjectivity. By examining the hermeneutical ontology by Hans-Georg Gadamer, the author points out the crisis of the idea of the superimposition of "world" and "history." Beyond Gadamer's thesis (in which Merlini sees the same notion of history typical of the historicism) the essay proposes to replace the problem of the essence of history with the one of the genealogy of historical conscience, that is with the problem of the subject experiencing history.

**Merrell, Floyd**. *Peirce, Signs, and Meaning*. Toronto, Univ of Toronto Pr, 1997.

Merrell discusses Peirce's thought in relation to that of early twentieth-century philosophers such as Frege, Russell, and Quine, and contemporaries, such as Goodman, Putnam, Davidson, and Rorty. In doing so, Merrell demonstrates how quests for meaning inevitably fall victim to vagueness in pursuit of generality, and how vagueness manifests an inevitable tinge of inconsistency, just as generalities always remain incomplete. He suggests that vagueness and incompleteness/generality, overdetermination and underdetermination, and Peirce's phenomenological categories of *firstness*, *secondness*, and *thirdness* must be incorporated into notions of sign structure for proper treatment of meaning. He also argues that the twentieth-century search for meaning has placed overbearing stress on language while ignoring nonlinguistic sign modes and means. (edited)

**Merricks, Trenton**. More On Warrant's Entailing Truth. *Phil Phenomenol Res*, 57(3), 627-631, S 97.

Warrant is that, whatever it is, which makes the difference between knowledge and mere truth belief. In "Warrant Entails Truth" (*PPR*, December 1995), I argued that it is impossible that a false belief is warranted. Sharon Ryan attacked the argument of that paper in her "Does Warrant Entail Truth?" (*PPR*, March 1996). In "More on Warrant's Entailing Truth" I present arguments for the claim that warrant entails truth that are, I think, significantly more compelling than the arguments of my original "Warrant Entails Truth." This paper responds to Ryan's objections, but it is not merely a reply to Ryan's article. It is, rather, a free-standing defense of warrant's entailing truth that is the product of discussion and argument for over two years with many philosophers including Ryan, over the arguments contained in my original paper.

**Merridale, Catherine**. English-Language History and the Creation of Historical Paradigm. *Hist Human Sci*, 9(4), 81-98, N 96.

**Merrill, Daniel D**. "Relations and Quantification in Peirce's Logic, 1870-1885" in *Studies in the Logic of Charles Sanders Peirce*, Houser, Nathan (ed), 158-172. Bloomington, Indiana Univ Pr, 1997.

**Merritt, Suzanne** and DeGraff, Jeff. The Revisionary Visionary: Leadership and the Aesthetics of Adaptability. *J Aes Educ*, 30(4), 69-85, Wint 96.

**Mertens, Thomas**. "Las tesis de Hegel sobre la guerra y el derecho internacional" in *Kant: La paz perpetua, doscientos años después*, Martínez Guzmán, Vicent (ed), 145-160. Valencia, Nau Llibres, 1997.

In this essay Hegel's account of war and international law is interpreted as mainly a direct reply to Kant's views on international law, which consists of both criticism and approval. The first part of this essay discusses Hegel's criticism. According to Hegel complete absence of war is undesirable and impossible to achieve. The second part discusses to what extent Hegel agrees with Kant. Hegel thought that war should be limited and temporary affair. Yet, instead of arguing in favor of the establishment of international humanitarian law like Kant, Hegel argues that the establishment of a well-trained army can guarantee that war should not exceed its limits. Finally, the consistency of Hegel's solution is tested.

**Mertens, Thomas**. Cosmopolitanism and Citizenship: Kant Against Habermas. *Euro J Phil*, 4(3), 328-347, D 96.

This article discusses the ways in which cosmopolitanism and citizenship are conceived in the writings of Kant and Habermas. With regard to Kant it focusses on an interpretation of the third definitive article in his "Toward Perpetual Peace": the cosmopolitan right. With regard to Habermas it analyzes his "Citizenship and National Identity." The article provides a detailed account of the contrasts between Kant's state-based conception of cosmopolitanism and Habermas's account of constitutional patriotism and his requirement of the dissolution of the nation-state. The positions taken by Kant and Habermas are compared with both communitarian and liberal authors on the subject. Finally, the article summarizes the arguments Kant uses in favor of a lasting separation of nations.

**Merz-Benz, Peter-Ulrich**. "Die Stufen zum Vernunftvermögen: Richard Hönigswalds Begriff der monas als Gegenstand erkenntniskritischer Reflexion" in *Grenzen der kritischen Vernunft*, Schmid, Peter A, 133-157. Basel, Schwabe Verlag, 1997.

**Meslin, Eric M** and Thomson, Elizabeth J and Boyer, Joy T. The Ethical, Legal, and Social Implications Research Program at the National Human Genome Research Institute. *Kennedy Inst Ethics J*, 7(3), 291-298, S 97.

**Mesman, Jessica**. Dwingende feiten en hun verborgen moraal: Over doen en laten in de neonatologiepraktijk. *Kennis Methode*, 20(4), 377-397, 1996.

The focus of this article is on nontreatment decisions in a Neonatal Intensive Care Unit (NICU). A detailed ethnographic analysis of this moral decision shows that facts instead of morality is the matter of dispute. When hard facts are available the problem is solved for hard facts embody an imperative of act. Facts are decisive, not because they overrule morality, but because they embody morality. "What to do?" and "what is the matter?" are not two separate questions, but are answered in the same process. Factuality-in-the-making is tight up with morality-in-the-making.

**Mesquita, António Pedro**. Da Filosofia como Universalizaçao: Universalidade e Situaçao da Filosofia num Passo Nuclear de *A Razao Experimental* de Leonardo Coimbra. *Rev Port Filosof*, 52(1-4), 539-553, Ja-D 96.

Leonardo Coimbra=92s philosophy (the "criacionismo") is based on three main principles: the recognition of the dynamic structure of reality; the importance given to science as an essential starting point of the conceptual dialectic which includes philosophy as its concluding goal; and the centrality of man both as a factor of this dialectic and the ultimate subject of philosophic reflection. In this article we investigate the notion of philosophy he exposes in one of his chief

works, "A Raz=E3o Experimental", showing, through the analysis of the concepts "freedom", "love" and "history", that, beyond its interpretation under the duality universality/concretion, philosophy should be conceived as the process by which universality itself becomes continuously concrete.

**Mesquita, António Pedro**. O argumento ontológico em Platao: (I) O problema da imortalidade. *Philosophica (Portugal)*, 31-42, 1993.

This article, *The ontological argument in Plato: 1) the problem of immortality*, discusses the interpretation of Socrates' last demonstration of the immortality of the soul in the *Phaedo* as an "ontological argument" and tries to refute this interpretation through an examination of the concept of immortality in Plato and its implications on the central relation soul/life. At the same time, it argues that the ontological argument should be seen as the very back-bone of Plato's ontology, a point of view which will be developed in a forthcoming paper.

**Mesquita, António Pedro**. O argumento ontológico em Platao: (II) A imortalidade do problema. *Philosophica (Portugal)*, 85-109, 1994.

The first part of this article attempted to refute the interpretation of *Phd*. 102a-107a as being the canonic place of the ontological argument in Platonic thought. The second part of this article will attempt to outline three objectives: 1) to show that the ontological argument intervenes in Plato's thought not as a strict demonstration but as a central and permanent structure whereby the idea is necessarily deduced from the sensible; 2) to show that this structure is also present in Saint Anselm's ontological argument as its philosophical meaning; 3) to elucidate how Parmenides' ontology is the paradigm which inspired both Plato and Saint Anselm.

**Mesquita, António Pedro**. O que é a Filosofia? Sentido filosófico e virtualidades pedagógicas de uma definiçao de filosofia. *Philosophica (Portugal)*, 111-141, 1996.

Dans un article précédent, nous avons essayé de réfuter la thèse selon laquelle la philosophie possède une nature essentiellement indéfinissable. En utilisant cette fois une voie positive, nous cherchons d'établir les conditions d'une définition de la philosophie qui contienne organiquement les éléments suivants: d'abord, la philosophie en tant qu'activité et en tant qu'ensemble de problèmes; deuxièmement, la philosophie et sa nature radicalement créatrice; en dernier lieu, l'identification de la philosophie avec un intérêt irréductiblement philosophique de la raison elle-même. Après la présentation philosophique de la définition proposée, il y a lieu a une discussion de ses virtualités pédagogiques.

**Messeri, Marco**. Ancora su nuvole ed orologi. *Epistemologia*, 19(1), 3-32, Ja-Je 96.

This paper undertakes a critical evaluation of the problem of freedom and determinism, aiming to show that determinism is vitiated by conceptual inconsistency, stemming from the gratuitous application of a space and time structure appropriate for idealized physical systems to all entities. This paper aims to show particularly that the time structure of actions and mental states is essentially unsaturable, and thus that the whole alternative of determinism and indeterminism makes no sense if referred to our mental and practical life. First of all, the theoretical content of philosophical determinism is taken into consideration, and it is argued that only a physical determinism (the claim that the state of the world at every time is determined by the former ones) is relevant to the issue of freedom, while a metaphysical determinism (the claim that the state of the world at every time is determined by some nontime entity, like God's will or Leibnitian "complete notion") is not. Next, the variety of time structures acknowledge in our conceptual framework is emphasized. (edited)

**Messerly, John G**. Psychogenesis and the History of Science: Piaget and the Problem of Scientific Change. *Mod Sch*, 73(4), 295-307, M 96.

**Messina, Gaetano**. La critica rosminiana alla cosmologia di Aristotele. *G Metaf*, 19(1), 3-47, Ja-Ap 97.

**Messuti, Ana**. Obligaciones humanas Apuntes para la formulación de una idea. *Riv Int Filosof Diritto*, 74(4), 345-359, Ap-Je 97.

**Mészáros, István**. The Tragedy of Lukács and the Problem of Alternatives (in Hungarian). *Magyar Filozof Szemle*, 4-5-6, 610-640, 1996.

**Meyer, John-Jules Ch** and Dignum, Frank and Wieringa, Roel J (& others). "A Modal Approach to Intentions, Commitments and Obligations: Intention Plus Commitment Yields Obligation" in *Deontic Logic, Agency and Normative Systems*, Brown, Mark A (ed), 80-97. New York, Springer-Verlag, 1996.

In this paper we introduce some new operators into our framework that make it possible to reason about decisions and commitments to do actions. In our framework, a decision leads to an intention to do an action. The decision in itself does not change the state of the world, but only the relation to possible future worlds. A commitment to actually perform the intended action changes the deontic state of the world such that the intended action becomes obligated. Of course, the obligated action may never actually occur. In our semantic structure, we use static (ought-to-be) and dynamic (ought-to-do) obligation operators. The static operator resembles the classical conception of obligation as truth in ideal worlds, except that it takes the current state as well as the past history of the world into account. This is necessary because it allows us to compare the way a state is actually reached with the way we committed ourselves to reach it. We show that some situations that could formerly not be expressed easily in deontic logic can be described in a natural way using the extended logic described in this paper.

**Meyer, Robert K** and Ono, Hiroakira. The Finite Model Property for BCK and BCIW. *Stud Log*, 53(1), 107-118, F 94.

Ono raised in conversation the question whether the Finite Model Property (henceforth FMP) could be established for the pure implicational logic BCK. Meyer responded that, adapting an argument of Kripke, the FMP could certainly

AUTHOR INDEX 787 Michelini, Dorando J

be shown for Church's weak theory BCIW of implication. Dualizing, it turned out that what is almost the same argument works also for BCK. Left open was the question of the FMP for pure implicational BCI. (This BCI problem has since been solved affirmatively and independently by Buszkowski and by Lafont. With Massey, we have subsequently generalized Lafont's argument to show the FMP for a host of systems.)

**Meyer, William J**. Ethics, Theism and Metaphysics: An Analysis of the Theocentric Ethics of James Gustafson. *Int J Phil Relig*, 41(3), 149-178, Je 97.

Modern ethics has been shaped by two dominant philosophical assumptions: 1) that there can be no theoretical knowledge of God, i.e., denial of metaphysics, and 2) that moral claims can be redeemed independently of theistic affirmations, i.e., morality does not require theism. These assumptions have influenced much of modern theological ethics. Yet, insofar as theological ethics accepts that morality does not require any explicit or implicit religious beliefs, it affirms that a secularistic morality is possible. But this affirmation is directly at odds with the essence of theism, namely that God is the source and end of all things, including the moral life. By accepting the dominant consensus, therefore, theological ethics undermines its fundamental theistic claim. Focusing on James Gustafson's theocentric ethics, I seek to show the price that theological ethics pays for subscribing to the dominant consensus. I argue that: 1) Gustafson embraces an inconsistent self-understanding, which undermines his theocentric claim, 2) this is due to his dismissal of metaphysics, and 3) his theocentric ethic would be more compelling if formulated in terms of Whitehead's process metaphysics.

**Meyering, Theo C**. Fodor's Information Semantics between Naturalism and Mentalism. *Inquiry*, 40(2), 187-207, Je 97.

**Meyering, Theo C**. Philosophical Psychology in Historical Perspective: Review Essay of J.-C. Smith (Ed.), *Historical Foundations of Cognitive Science*. *Phil Psych*, 9(3), 381-390, S 96.

Historiography of science faces a preliminary question of strategy. A *continuist* conception of the history of science poses research problems different from those of a *dynamic* conception, which acknowledges that not only our theoretical knowledge but also the *explananda* themselves may change under the influence of new scientific insights. Whereas continuist historiography may advance our understanding of (the historical background of) current theoretical problems, dynamic historiography may also make a creative contribution to the *progress* of present-day research. This fact is illustrated in a discussion of the various treatments of paradigmatic episodes in the history of philosophical psychology collected in the book under review, ranging from Socratic and Platonic sources of cognitivism, through medieval and modern views on mental language, representation and consciousness, to such 20th-century contributions as those of Husserl, Titchener and analytic philosophy.

**Meyering, Theo C**. Representation and Resemblance: A Review Essay of Richard A. Watson's *Representational Ideas: From Plato to Patricia Churchland*. *Phil Psych*, 10(2), 221-230, Je 97.

Are experience and stimulus necessarily alike? Wertheimer spoke of this as an "insidious and insistent belief". By contrast, Watson devotes an entire book to the defense of the thesis that representation necessarily requires resemblance. I argue that this bold and important thesis is ambiguous between a historical and a systematic reading and that in either one of these readings the thesis, for different reasons, will be found wanting. Second, a proper evaluation of it in either one of its possible interpretations requires a careful analysis of the notion of resemblance. I proceed to supply some necessary distinctions and argue that, given such an analysis, Watson's thesis may be historically applicable only to ancient and medieval philosophy, while its systematic import is untenable.

**Meynell, Hugo**. Justifying the Perennial Philosophy. *Maritain Stud*, 10, 34-43, 1994.

**Meynell, Hugo**. Scientism, Deconstruction, Atheism. *Heythrop J*, 37(3), 336-347, Jl 96.

Scientism and deconstruction are totally opposed; but both culminate in atheism, and are as self-destructive as fashionable. Scientism is incompatible with science, which depends on scientists making judgments on the basis of evidence. This is impossible if the movements of their brains are totally determined by physical laws. Deconstruction subverts all grounds of reasonable judgment—even to the effect that the judgments presupposed by deconstruction are well-founded. The combined best insights of both movements lead to belief in a 'mind-shaped' world—knowable through the free play of intelligence (deconstruction) together with strict corroboration in experience (science)—and so to theism.

**Meynell, Hugo** (ed) and Stoeber, Michael (ed). *Critical Reflections on the Paranormal*. Albany, SUNY Pr, 1996.

The book discusses various aspects of paranormal phenomena such as telepathy, psychokinesis, transmediumship, near death experiences, and past-life memories. It reflects on what is reasonable to believe about them and why; and it suggests what changes they might demand in our worldview if these phenomena are accepted as genuine. The collection includes essays, written by Susan Armstrong, Heather Botting, Stephen Braude, Don Evans, David Ray Griffin, James Horne, Terence Penelhum, and the editors. (publisher,edited)

**Mi, Michael C**. The Spread of Aristotle's Political Theory in China. *Polit Theory*, 25(2), 249-257, Ap 97.

It was together with Christianity that Aristotle's political theory spread into China. Jesuits set off an upsurge of introducing Western culture into China through translating or adapting original Western books during 1583-1720. Since the persecution of Christianity, the government gathered and prohibited many so-called heretical books under the guise of collecting books in order to compile the *Complete Collection of Four Categories of Books* and some Western books have been even more distorted and inveighed against by the *Overall Bibliography* and its *Comments of the CCFCB*. From the end of the Qing dynasty, and especially in the 1930s, a new tide of introducing Aristotle flowed into China. The complete translated Chinese edition of *Aristotle's Political Theory* by Wu Shoupeng which was published in the 1960s marked the beginning of a ripe period in that subject's development. In fact all human knowledge is an organic body, we could not cut off any links or the trunk from it. The cultural interchange between nations should be in whole disciplines and subjects. The result of anyone or any authority in any time who wants to act willfully or cling obstinately to his course, must be the failure to achieve his aim. (edited)

**Miano, Francesco**. "Esistenza, storia e storia della filosofia nel pensiero di Karl Jaspers" in *Lo Storicismo e la Sua Storia: Temi, Problemi, Prospettive*, Cacciatore, Giuseppe (ed), 496-505. Milano, Guerini, 1997.

**Michael, Mark A**. Environmental Egalitarianism and 'Who do you Save?' Dilemmas. *Environ Values*, 6(3), 307-325, Ag 97.

I argue that one can distinguish two distinct versions of equality, one based on the idea of equal treatment, the other on the idea of equally valuable lives. I look at a lifeboat case where one must choose between saving a human and saving a dog and using the work of Peter Singer and Tom Regan, I show why equality understood as equal treatment does not entail that lifeboat cases are moral toss-ups. But the view that all lives are equally valuable does entail this and so egalitarians should reject this alternative account of equality. The upshot is that egalitarians need to be more careful about distinguishing between these two versions of equality. The failure to insist on this distinction has led many to believe that egalitarianism generally has counter-intuitive implications when in fact only one version of egalitarianism has this problem. (edited)

**Michael, Mark A**. Redistributive Taxation, Self-Ownership and the Fruit of Labour. *J Applied Phil*, 14(2), 137-146, 1997.

Libertarians such as Nozick have argued that any redistributive tax scheme intended to achieve and maintain an egalitarian distributive pattern will violate self-ownership. Furthermore, since self-ownership is a central component of the idea of freedom, instituting an egalitarian distribution makes a society less rather than more free. All this turns on the claim, accepted by both libertarians and their critics, that a redistributive tax will violate self-ownership because it must expropriate the fruit of a person's labour. I show here that there is no reason to accept this claim. The libertarian argument works only if the fruit of one's labour must be understood to include everything that a person produces through his labour. But there is an alternative reading of the fruit of labour which identifies it with that subset of the total product of one's labour which is due to his choices rather than luck. (edited)

**Michael, S M**. Theoretical Issues in Social Movements. *J Dharma*, 22(1), 5-17, Ja-Mr 97.

**Michalos, Alex C**. Issues for Business Ethics in the Nineties and Beyond. *J Bus Ethics*, 16(3), 219-230, F 97.

Nine issues of fundamental importance for business ethics are examined with a view to encouraging researchers in the field to direct their attention to them in the 1990s and beyond. The issues are related to organized labor, social dumping, international finance and third world debt, tobacco promotion, arms trade, wealth concentration and taxation, pollution and resource depletion, international trading blocks, and the Canadian Business Council on National Issues and other business organizations.

**Michalos, Alex C**. Non-Academic Critics of Business Ethics in Canada. *J Bus Ethics*, 16(6), 611-619, Ap 97.

This paper shows that there are contemporary moral appraisals of business ethics in Canada published in periodicals that would not ordinarily be regarded as scholarly in substance or format. Because there is so much important material in these nonacademic periodicals, scholars interested in business ethics in Canada ought to give them serious consideration in any overall review of the field here.

**Michalos, Alex C**. The Best Teacher I Ever Had Was... J. Coert Rylaarsdam. *Teach Bus Ethics*, 1(1), 93-95, 1997.

This is a brief sketch of an extraordinary teacher.

**Michalski, Krzysztof**. On Historicity of History and Stupidity of Concepts: Nietzsche's Nihilism (in Polish). *Kwartalnik Filozof*, 23(1), 45-61, 1995.

**Michalson, Gordon E**. The Problem of Salvation in Kant's *Religion within the Limits of Reason Alone*. *Int Phil Quart*, 37(3), 319-328, S 97.

**Michel, Vicki**. Reflections on Cultural Difference and Advance Directives. *Bioethics Forum*, 13(2), 22-26, Sum 97.

Advance care planning cannot assume a single meaning of autonomy. Even when autonomy is apparently employed in the traditional white, middle class, American sense, personal interviews uncover nuances that are based on cultural differences.

**Micheletti, Mario**. "Giustizia divina e apocatastasi in John Smith, platonico di Cambridge" in *Mind Senior to the World*, Baldi, Marialuisa, 89-111. Milano, FrancoAngeli, 1996.

**Michelini, Dorando J**. Conciencia subjetiva y conciencia comunicativa en el discurso ético. *Cuad Etica*, 19-20, 105-116, 1995.

The concept of "moral conscience" is a clue for ethical-philosophical thought. Traditionally, the concept of "moral conscience" has been interpreted in a monological way, as an ultimate and "unsurpassable" instance for the ethical reflection. This paper shows the extent and limits of a monological conception of moral conscience and tries to find some kind of intersubjective-communicative conscience, which should be able to detect moral problems and conflicts and to examine both the validity of individual convictions and maxims of agency and the direct and indirect consequences of human actions.

**Michelis, Angela**. *Carlo Michelstaedter: il coraggio dell'impossibile*. Rome, Citta Nuova Ed, 1997.

Il pensiero di Michelstaedter (1887-1910) esaminato nelle sue varie componenti con grande aderenza ai testi e precisa attenzione ai rapporti con il contesto esistenziale e culturale: il mondo mitteleuropeo nel difficile passaggio di secolo e quello ebraico sospeso fra emancipazione e assimilazione. (publisher, editor)

**Michell, Joel**. Bertrand Russell's 1897 Critique of the Traditional Theory of Measurement. *Synthese*, 110(2), 257-276, F 97.

The transition from the traditional to the representational theory of measurement around the turn of the century was accompanied by little sustained criticism of the former. The most forceful critique was Bertrand Russell's 1897 *Mind* paper, "On the Relations of Number and Quantity." The traditional theory has it that real numbers unfold from the concept of continuous quantity. Russell's critique identified two serious problems for this theory: 1) can magnitudes of a continuous quantity be defined without infinite regress; and 2) can additive relations between such magnitudes exist if magnitudes are not divisible? The present paper shows how the traditional theory answers these questions and compares the traditional and representational theories as contributions to our understanding of the logic of application.

**Michelman, Frank I**. Must Constitutional Democracy Be "Responsive"?. *Ethics*, 107(4), 706-723, Jl 97.

Constitutional government requires acceptance of nonconsensual resolutions of important practical questions. "Responsive," "identificational," and "epistemic" conceptions of democracy are brought forth as answers to the problem of harmonizing this fact with individual self-government. A comparative study of these conceptions, with special attention to the use by Robert Post, in *Constitutional Domains*, of the "responsive" and "identificational" conceptions, issues in a conclusion that commitment to democracy fails to provide a convincing explanation for certain aspects of the prevailing American legal doctrine of freedom of speech.

**Michelman, Frank I**. Parsing "A Right to Have Rights". *Constellations*, 3(2), 200-208, O 96.

**Michelmann, H W** and Hinney, B. Ethical Reflections on the Status of the Preimplantation Embryo Leading to the German Embryo Protection Act. *Sci Eng Ethics*, 1(2), 145-150, A 95.

Ethical conflicts have always been connected with new techniques of reproductive medicine such as in vitro fertilization. The fundamental question is: When does human life begin and from which stage of development should the embryo be protected? This question cannot be solved by scientific findings only. In prenatal ontogenesis there is no moment during the development from the fertilized oocyte to a human being which could be recognized as an orientation point for all ethical problems connected with the question of the right to dispose of prenatal life (interruption of pregnancy, research on embryos). The protection of an individual human life must be valid for all in the same manner and from the very beginning on. It must not depend on value judgments or on stages of development, so-called grades of humanity, because these would then become selection criteria. Procreated life must have the right to be born. These were the essential ethical arguments which led to the German Embryo Protection Law.

**Midgley, Mary**. One World, But a Big One. *J Consciousness Stud*, 3(5-6), 500-514, 1996.

But an item which plays as central a role in our life and thought as consciousness does is too large to be 'explained' by being annexed to a particular physical science in this way. Nor does it need to be. The difficulty that we feel about consciousness is not a local one that can be resolved by relating it directly to physics. It is one of relating our whole inner and outer viewpoint—of finding a context in which the subjective and objective aspects of life can be intelligibly connected. To some extent this is a real, unavoidable, general difficulty which can only be handled by constant adjustment in our lives. This adjustment is attempted by all cultures and is a topic which, so far, is usually viewed as the business of serious literature, of history and of philosophy rather than of the physical sciences. (edited)

**Midlarsky, Elizabeth** and Kahana, Eva. *Altruism in Later Life*. Newbury Park, Sage, 1994.

Why are the elderly so often perceived as burdensome and unproductive members of our society? *Altruism in Later Life* explores and refutes this view with cogent, empirical data. Authors Elizabeth Midlarsky and Eva Kahana introduce the results of a series of investigations on assistance offered by—rather than to—the elderly, in the context of historical, philosophical, and theoretical trends in gerontology and altruism research. Following a brief but inclusive historical survey of aging treatments, they present their own theoretical model of successful aging: Based on a carefully applied methodological review of research focusing on altruism and the elderly, the results reveal the relative frequency, nature, correlates, and ramifications of the contributions they make. (publisher, edited)

**Mielke, Eckehard W**. Bemerkung zu: "Epistemologische Aspekte der neuen Entwicklungen in der Physik" von G. Münster. *Phil Natur*, 28(2), 267-268, 1991.

As a comment on a paper of G. Munster (ibid {bf 27}) (1990) 83), it is pointed out that the German poet and cartonist Wilhelm Busch has already 1883 a vision of the 4-dimensional spacetime of Einstein, the 5-dimensional generalizations of Kaluza and Klein, as well as of the "ghost" states of modern quantum field theory. This ironic critic has itself the form of a poem.

**Mier y Terán, Rocío**. "Prioridad del acto en la génesis de los hábitos operativos" in *Ensayos Aristotélicos*, Aspe, Virginia, 49-59. Mexico, Univ Panamericana, 1996.

Aristotle claims that the operations are the cause of operative habits; but though this opinion can be correct, it cannot explain completely their origin. There

seems to be, instead, a previous "working" principle in activity, which along with operations makes the achievement of habits possible. (publisher)

**Mier y Terán, Rocío**. "Prioridad del acto en la génesis de los hábitos operativos" in *Ensayos Aristotélicos*, Rivera, José Luis (ed), 49-59. Mexico, Univ Panamericana, 1996. ¿

Aristotle claims that the operations are the cause of operative habits; but though this opinion can be correct, it cannot explain completely their origin. There seems to be, instead, a previous "working" principle in activity, which along with operations makes possible the achievement of habits.

**Mier y Terán, Rocío** and Llano, Carlos and Aspe A, Virginia. *Ensayos Aristotélicos*. Mexico, Univ Panamericana, 1996.

**Mignucci, Mario**. "Che cos'è un sillogismo aristotelico?" in *Momenti di Storia della Logica e di Storia della Filosofia*, Guetti, Carla (ed), 39-58. Roma, Aracne Editrice, 1996.

**Mignucci, Mario**. "L'interpretazione hegeliana della logica di Aristotele" in *Hegel e Aristotele*, Ferrarin, A, 29-49. Cagliari, Edizioni AV, 1997.

**Miguel-Alfonso, Ricardo** (ed). *Powerless Fictions? Ethics, Cultural Critique, and American Fiction in the Age of Postmodernism*. Amsterdam, Rodopi, 1996.

**Migura, Fernando**. Información y Bases de Datos Situadas. *Manuscrito*, 19(2), 45-91, O 96.

The aim of this paper is to show some of the features of a "situated approach" (understood in terms of situation theory) to inference, information and knowledge representation. As we know the logical view gives an account of them by means of concepts like "logical form" or "model" and their mutual relations. However, situation theory, taken as a general and qualitative theory of information gives us a framework in which we can analyze the relationship between representation schemes and their informational contents, taking as starting point the study of the structure of the informational relations postulated for the explanation of the flow of information. Having introduced the basic concepts of the theory, we seek an application in the field of representation in data bases, in order to eventually improve the limits of the very idea of representation.

**Mikenberg, Irene F** and Lewin, Renato A and Schwarze, Maria G. P1 Algebras. *Stud Log*, 53(1), 21-28, F 94.

In [3] the authors proved that the deductive system P1 introduced by Sette in [6] is algebraizable. In this paper we study the main features of the class of algebras thus obtained. The main results are a complete description of the free algebras in $n$ generators and that this is not a congruence modular quasi-variety.

**Mikkelson, Douglas K**. Who is arguing about the Cat? Moral Action and Enlightenment according to Dōgen. *Phil East West*, 47(3), 383-397, Jl 97.

This essay is an analysis of Dōgen's commentary on "Nan-ch'üan's Cutting of the Cat" as found in section I.6 of the *Shōbōgenzō* Zuimonki. It argues that Dōgen's conception of *hishiryō* ("without-thinking") is the starting point for understanding Dōgen's moral vision and employs this idea in the interpretation of the passage.

**Mikkelson, Gregory M**. Stretched Lines, Averted Leaps, and Excluded Competition: A Theory of Scientific Counterfactuals. *Proc Phil Sci Ass*, 3(Suppl), S194-S201, 1996.

Lewis's argument against the Limit Assumption and Pollock's Generalized Consequence Principle together suggest that "minimal-change" theories of counterfactuals are wrong. The "small-change" theories presented by Nute do not say enough. While these theories rely on closeness between possible worlds, I base an alternative on the ceteris paribus concept. My theory solves a problem that the above cannot and is more relevant to the philosophy of science. Ceteris paribus conditions should normally include the causes, but exclude the effects, of the negated antecedent. An example from community ecology, the debate over null models in island-biogeographical studies of competition, supports these arguments.

**Mikulás, Szabolcs** and Marx, Maarten and Németi, István. Taming Logic. *J Log Lang Info*, 4(3), 207-226, 1995.

In this paper, we introduce a general technology, called *taming*, for finding well-behaved versions of well-investigated logics. Further, we state completeness, decidability, definability and interpolation results for a multimodal logic, called *arrow logic*, with additional operators such as the *difference operator* and *graded modalities*. Finally, we give a completeness proof for a strong version of arrow logic.

**Mil'don, Valerii Il'ich**. The Russian Idea at the End of the Twentieth Century. *Russian Stud Phil*, 35(4), 24-38, Spr 97.

The Russian idea is a conception of the Russian exceptionalism. It contains the preference of common interests (of state, people) to personal, the predomination of intuitive methods of cognition over logical analysis, the conviction that the Catholic West is in the crisis and the Orthodox Russia mission is to save it and all the world. The Russian idea was formed by the end of the 15th century. At the end of the 19th century the philosophers V.S. Solov'ev, V.I. Nesmelov recognized the falsity of the conception. N.A. Berd'aev, G.P. Phedotov proved that the Russia would be able to maintain its role in the world only if it overcomed this intellectual heritage of five hundred years. The modern meaning of the Russian idea should include the concept of individual freedom which is not characteristic for the Russian historical experience.

**Milavec, Aaron**. Religious Pedagogy from Tender to Twilight Years: Parenting, Mentoring, and Pioneering Discoveries by Religious Masters as Viewed from within Polanyi's Sociology and Epistemology of Science. *Tradition Discovery*, 23(2), 15-36, 1996-97.

AUTHOR INDEX 789 Miller, Franklin G

My study puts forward seven theses designed to demonstrate that everything which Polanyi put forward regarding the transmission of a scientific heritage through a successive series of apprenticeships can be seen as functioning within the religious enterprise as well. Then, when it comes to the role of masters in pursuing lines of inquiry which sometimes lead to self-transforming acts of discovery, such feats can be understood as defining the function of creative theologians and pastors who both exhibit and transform the tradition in which they dwell. In conclusion, my inquiry will attempt to show that, when Polanyi's own inadequate assessment of religion is set aside, one comes to a proper understanding as to how religious pedagogy actually functions within the Christian enterprise. (edited)

**Milbank, John**. The Sublime in Kierkegaard. *Heythrop J*, 37(3), 298-321, Jl 96.

**Milde, Michael**. "Justice, Gender, The Family, and The Practice of Political Philosophy" in *A Question of Values: New Canadian Perspectives in Ethics and Political Philosophy*, Brennan, Samantha (ed), 175-187. Amsterdam, Rodopi, 1997.

**Milde, Michael** (ed) and Isaacs, Tracy. "Acts and Value" in *A Question of Values: New Canadian Perspectives in Ethics and Political Philosophy*, Brennan, Samantha (ed), 17-27. Amsterdam, Rodopi, 1997.

Isn't it obvious that some acts are good or bad in themselves? Is this value intrinsic? If we follow Judith Thomson in understanding intrinsic value as value that a thing has independently of what it causes and what causes it, then acts do not have it. I argue that there is an account of conditional value, borrowed from Christine Korsgaard's work, in which acts can have value in themselves that nevertheless depends on the causal relations in which they stand. Though not intrinsic in Thomson's sense, this value is distinct from the value of the causes and effects and is objective.

**Milde, Michael** (ed) and Isaacs, Tracy (ed) and Brennan, Samantha (ed). *A Question of Values: New Canadian Perspectives in Ethics and Political Philosophy*. Amsterdam, Rodopi, 1994.

This book reflects a cross-section of the issues concerning values that are of contemporary philosophical interest in Canada and the United States. In the three parts of the book, ten philosophers bring fresh perspectives to bear upon questions of metaethics, freedom and autonomy and political philosophy. The studies concentrate upon acts, values and human lives; moral character, moral behavior and moral imagination; the limits of liberalism and communitarianism; social contract and institutions; and the morality of nationalism. (publisher)

**Milet, Jean-Philippe**. Horizon and Region in Heidegger (in French). *Arch Phil*, 59(4), 577-606, O-D 96.

In the relationship between the themes of "horizon" and "region" in the thought of Heidegger, we find a radicalized consideration of the finitude of being. *Horizon*, for example that of time, constitutes the ontological possibility for the appearance of all being as world. *Region* designates the temporal and spatial dimension of nearness, i.e., the "letting be" which commences the world-game. Horizon's structure is subject to the metaphysical primacy of representation and will; region is an openness to that which cannot be anticipated. Hence the sense involved in overcoming (*Ueberwindung*) the question of horizon toward that of motive, more original than that of region, needs reconsideration.

**Milikan, Ruth Garrett**. "Pushmi-Pullyu Representations" in *AI, Connectionism and Philosophical Psychology, 1995*, Tomberlin, James E (ed), 185-200. Atascadero, Ridgeview, 1995.

Many representations are both descriptive and directive: "pushmi-pullyu representations" or PPRs. Most obvious are simple signals to conspecifics employed by various animals. PPRs appear in human language: "No Johnny, we don't eat peas with our fingers," "The meeting is (hereby) adjourned." Human intentions are PPRs in thought, as are perceptual representations representing affordances. Inner representations of the social roles that we play as we play them are PPRs, as we fall into doing "what one does." These primitive ways of thinking are an essential glue holding human societies together. PPRs are viewed from within a general theory of representations developed elsewhere but reviewed here.

**Milios, Jean**. Internationalisierung des Kapitals, Gesamtkapital und nationalstaat. *Das Argument*, 217(5-6), 713-724, 1996.

For many Marxists, "world capitalism" entails worldwide capitalist and laboring classes. This both underestimates the role of political class power and the capitalist state and misunderstands the "national segmentation" of the world economy. This segmentation arises not only from limited international labor mobility and state protectionist policies in favor of national markets, but also from the absence of a unique international currency. In the world market, fluctuating currency rates resulting from each country's unequally changing economic position modify the functioning of the law of value. These unequally developed (capitalist) formations behave like what Lenin called an "imperialist chain".

**Millar, Alan**. Sensibility and Understanding. *Inquiry*, 39(3-4), 459-478, D 96.

The article is a critical study of John McDowell's *Mind and World*. McDowell links problems about the relation between sensibility and understanding to a wider theme concerning how reason relates to nature. The primary focus of the article is on his treatment of how thought can be rationally constrained by experience if experience is conceived as lying outside the sphere of concepts. It is argued, against McDowell, that there is a way of understanding how experience constrains thought which avoids the Myth of the Given and yet sharply distinguishes between sensibility and understanding, taking sensibility to be nonconceptual and thought to be conceptual.

**Miller, Alexander**. An Objection to Smith's Argument for Internalism. *Analysis*, 56(3), 169-174, Jl 96.

In Chapter 3 of *The Moral Problem*, Michael Smith develops a novel and interesting argument in favour of internalism about moral motivation. In this paper I argue that Smith's argument is unsuccessful.

**Miller, Alexander**. Boghossian on Reductive Dispositionalism about Content: The Case Strengthened. *Mind Lang*, 12(1), 1-10, Mr 97.

Paul Boghossian has recently argued against reductive dispositionalism concerning mental content. However, there is a powerful version of reductive dispositionalism—based on work by Ramsey and Lewis—that Boghossian does not consider. In this paper I argue that Boghossian's arguments can be adapted to apply even to this stronger version of reductionism.

**Miller, Alexander**. More Responses to the Missing-Explanation Argument. *Philosophia (Israel)*, 25(1-4), 331-349, Ap 97.

In this paper, I broaden and develop further the attack on Mark Johnston's "Missing-Explanation Argument", which I started in my "Objectivity Disfigured" (*Philosophy and Phenomenological Research* (1993)). In particular, I argue that Johnston's argument would undermine the account of natural kind terms promulgated by Kripke and Putnam, and defend some of Crispin Wright's objections to Johnston.

**Miller, Arlene B** (ed) and Kilner, John F (ed) and Pellegrino, Edmund D (ed). *Dignity and Dying: A Christian Appraisal*. Grand Rapids, Eerdmans, 1996.

The authors of the present volume engage matters of dignity and dying from a variety of perspectives. The three authors of the introduction root the book in the experience of dying itself. In Part I, the authors give careful attention to topics that provide guiding vision for approaches to dignity and dying: autonomy, death, suffering, and faithfulness. Four of the most pressing end-of-life challenges—forgoing treatment, medical futility, definition of death, and assisted-suicide/euthanasia—are then examined in some detail. Part III is devoted to investigations of key settings where people have wrestled with these challenges: i.e., Nazi Germany, Oregon (USA), North American legal systems, and The Netherlands. The book concludes, then, with discussions of five potentially constructive alternatives to the premature ending of life: hospice care, long-term care, wise advocacy, parish nursing and congregational ministry. (publisher, edited)

**Miller, Chris**. A Comment on 'Radiation Protection and Moral Theory'. *Environ Values*, 6(1), 97-103, F 97.

A paper in an earlier volume [4 (3) pp. 241-256] of *Environmental Values* was concerned with certain moral consequences of the absence of a threshold in the dose-response relationship for ionizing radiation. These could be reduced to two propositions: 1) licensing procedures which, by permitting nonzero radiation in nuclear installations, implicitly accept radiation-induced cancers are morally wrong; 2) radiation-induced cancers constitute a moral 'special-case'. Proposition 2 is refuted by empirical evidence on the existence of other environmental pollutants with similar properties. Proposition 1, especially the impossibility of distinguishing radiation-induced cancers from those attributable to other causes, is critically examined.

**Miller, Chris**. Attributing 'Priority' to Habitats. *Environ Values*, 6(3), 341-353, Ag 97.

A close scrutiny of a European community directive on habitats and of the statutory instrument by which it is implemented in Britain reveals small but nevertheless significant concessions towards an eccentric approach. Planning law now allows interference in the habitats of protected species only when human interests are demonstrably overriding. Recent decisions of the European Court of Justice have given a very restrictive interpretation of the circumstances in which such interference may be permitted. The implications for further eccentric influence in environmental law are discussed.

**Miller, David**. Nationality: Some Replies. *J Applied Phil*, 14(1), 69-82, 1997.

This paper [1] defends the principle of nationality against a number of critical objections made in recent issues of the journal. It starts from the claim that national solidarity has served and continues to serve as an essential support to liberal democratic institutions and practices of social justice. Such national allegiances are not easy to defend if one begins from a cosmopolitan standpoint. But defending them does not mean embracing everything that people ordinarily believe—a political philosophy that begins from existing national sentiments can be sharply critical of the practices that are said to embody those sentiments. In particular justice, although its principles are context-dependent, is more than merely subjective. (edited)

**Miller, David**. What Use Is Empirical Confirmation?. *Econ Phil*, 12(1), 197-206, Ap 96.

Although he repudiates it, Daniel Hausman (in *The Inexact & Separate Science of Economics*, Cambridge 1992) recognizes the magnitude of the problem shift in epistemology proposed by Popper's falsificationist challenge to traditional inductivism. This review article of Hausman's book sets out again the main lines of the falsificationist position, concentrating especially on the doctrine that empirical confirmation, or inductive support, even if it could be obtained, would be intellectually valueless. As Popper stressed, only critical arguments count.

**Miller, Eric**. Is Literature Self-Referential?. *Phil Lit*, 20(2), 475-486, O 96.

Most contemporary theorists of literature believe that literary language is necessarily self-referential and thus paradoxical. This belief is false. Their desire to believe is rooted in a distorted sense of competition with the rational-empirical method of the natural sciences. Their actual arguments for it depend on a series of ambiguities and misunderstandings in their uses of the concept of reference.

**Miller, Franklin G**. A Communitarian Approach to Physician-Assisted Death. *Cambridge Quart Healthcare Ethics*, 6(1), 78-87, Winter 97.

The standard ethical argument for physician-assisted suicide and voluntary active euthanasia, which appeals to the individualistic grounds of personal self-determination and well-being, is vulnerable to the challenge that it fails to address the relevant values of community. To meet this challenge, a communitarian approach to physician-assisted death is developed. The article defends voluntary physician-assisted death as a compassionate measure of last resort in terms of reciprocal responsibilities between dying patients and their caregivers and the responsibility of society not to abandon dying patients. Three objections to this position are critically examined.

**Miller, Franklin G** and Bacchetta, Matthew D and Fins, Joseph J. Clinical Pragmatism: A Method of Moral Problem Solving. *Kennedy Inst Ethics J*, 7(2), 129-145, Je 97.

This paper presents a method of moral problem solving in clinical practice that is inspired by the philosophy of John Dewey. This method, called "clinical pragmatism," integrates clinical and ethical decision making. Clinical pragmatism focuses on the interpersonal processes of assessment and consensus formation as well as the ethical analysis of relevant moral considerations. The steps in this method are delineated and then illustrated through a detailed case study. The implications of clinical pragmatism for the use of principles in moral problem solving are discussed.

**Miller, Fred D** (ed) and Paul, Ellen Frankel (ed) and Paul, Jeffrey (ed). *The Welfare State*. New York, Cambridge Univ Pr, 1997.

These twelve essays—written from a range of viewpoints by philosophers, historians, economists, and political and legal theorists—offer valuable insights into the history of the welfare state, the proper role of government in ameliorating distress, and the nature of individual and collective responsibility. (publisher, edited)

**Miller, Hugh**. Phenomenology, Dialectic, and Time in Levinas's *Time and the Other*. *Phil Today*, 40(2), 219-234, Sum 96.

**Miller, Jerome A**. Intelligibility and the Ethical. *Amer Cath Phil Quart*, 71(1), 101-112, Wint 97.

In arguing that knowledge works a kind of violence on the *other*, Levinas contests the traditional analogy between intelligibility and the good. However, incorporating the *other* into an already existing cognitive framework contrasts with the kind of understanding that can emerge by allowing the *otherness* of the *other* to shatter one's framework. This shattering can give rise to an insight that does not violate the *other* but participates in the intelligibility immanent within the *other*—though we can "know" in this way only by relinquishing all that we know in the ordinary sense, as we are commanded to do by the ethical.

**Miller, Leigh** and Myers, Michael D. Ethical Dilemmas in the Use of Information Technology: An Aristotelian Perspective. *Ethics Behavior*, 6(2), 153-160, 1996.

In this article the authors suggest that a fruitful and interesting way to conceptualize some of these moral and ethical issues associated with the use of information technology is to apply the principles of Aristotle's ethics to this topic. They argue that framing the moral and ethical choices associated with information technology in Aristotelian terms draws attention to the fact that there are fundamental *dilemmas* to be addressed. These dilemmas are discussed in relation to the four areas suggested by Dejoie, Fowler, and Paradice (1991): a) privacy, b) information accuracy, c) access to information, and d) intellectual property rights. The dilemmas associated with all four areas are illustrated with references to recent legal developments in Australia and New Zealand. (edited)

**Miller, Linda B**. Millennium Approaches: Previewing the Twenty-first Century. *Ethics Int Affairs*, 8, 203-214, 1994.

**Miller, Mara**. "Views of Japanese Selfhood: Japanese and Western Perspectives" in *Culture and Self*, Allen, Douglas (ed), 145-162. Boulder, Westview Pr, 1997.

This paper examines the arguments that a) Japanese and Western selfhood differ fundamentally and b) Japanese identification with the group entails that individuality, originality, independence and moral autonomy are nonexistent or devalued. While agreeing with the first, it refutes the second argument, through evidence establishing the existence and valuing of these qualities in three traditional Japanese contexts: Buddhism (internally—versus externally based salvation (*jirikiltariki*), emphasis on the *individual's* enlightenment and karma and Zen's emphasis on individuality among artists and portrait subjects); Confucianism (relational selves, conflicting duties, self-cultivation and the arts of the brush); and natural language (where the systems of honorifics and politeness demand autonomous speaking).

**Miller, Patrick**. Struggle. *Bioethics Forum*, 13(1), 41-45, Spr 97.

**Miller, Peter N**. Citizenship and Culture in Early Modern Europe. *J Hist Ideas*, 57(4), 725-742, O 96.

**Miller, Richard B**. Love and Death in a Pediatric Intensive Care Unit. *Annu Soc Christ Ethics*, 21-39, 1996.

This essay attempts to discern aspects of the moral world of pediatric medicine. The author pays attention to health care workers' efforts to be neither judgmental nor nondirective in their relations with patients, and discusses this fact in light of recent attempts to view professional responsibility in "transformational" terms. The essay also calls attention to social etiologies of disease, and how health care providers seek on a regular basis to cope with the suffering of the innocent and their families. The author uses a method that joins ethnography with social and cultural criticism.

**Miller, Richard B**. One Bad and One Not Very Good Argument Against Holism. *Austl J Phil*, 75(2), 234-240, Je 97.

**Miller, Richard W**. Externalist Self-Knowledge and the Scope of the A Priori. *Analysis*, 57(1), 67-75, Ja 97.

**Miller, Seumas** and Alexandra, Andrew. Needs, Moral Self-Consciousness, and Professional Roles. *Prof Ethics*, 5(1-2), 43-61, Spr-Sum 96.

We aim to give a unified account of the concept of a professional role, claiming that the *telos* definitive of this role is the satisfaction of certain kinds of fundamental needs. Having explicated the concept of a fundamental need, we explore the implications of this claim, including the obligation of professionals to develop a high degree of moral self-consciousness, and to organize in distinctive occupational groupings in ways that facilitate the achievement of their *telos*.

**Miller, Seumas** and Collingridge, Michael. Filial Responsibility and the Care of the Aged. *J Applied Phil*, 14(2), 119-128, 1997.

What obligations and responsibilities, if any, do adult children have with respect to their aged parents? This paper briefly considers the sociohistorical and legal bases for filial obligations and suggests there is a mismatch between perceptions in the community over what they see as their obligations, what policy makers would like to impose and how philosophers identify and ground these obligations. Examining four philosophical models of filial obligation, we conclude that no one account provides an adequate justification for the types of responsibility that might be assumed in a family relationship.

**Miller, Ted** and Strong, Tracy B. Meanings and Contexts: Mr. Skinner's Hobbes and the English Mode of Political Theory. *Inquiry*, 40(3), 323-356, S 97.

Skinner's approach to political theory, while important and interesting, rests on a particular thin version of his reading of Austin and Collingwood. In turn this affects both his analysis of rhetoric in the XVIIth century and his understanding of Hobbes's intentions for his various texts. Therewith, we argue against Skinner that Hobbes did not reverse himself on rhetoric. Instead, the differences between Hobbes's three iterations of his doctrine reflect efforts to prove its worth before distinct audiences: political opponents, potential students and the sovereign that might have made his doctrine the state's official teaching. Finally, Skinner's deficiencies on Hobbes show some of the problems of the "English Mode of Political Theory."

**Miller, Tyrus**. From City-Dreams to the Dreaming Collective. *Phil Soc Crit*, 22(6), 87-111, N 96.

This essay discusses Walter Benjamin's development of 'dream' as a model for understanding 19th- and 20th-century urban culture. Benjamin's interpretative use of the dream cuts across Ricoeur's distinction between the hermeneutics of 'recollection' and the hermeneutics of 'suspicion'. The political dream analyst seeks to discharge the 'fatal powers' of the ideological dream, while at the same time fostering the experience of waking in which dream elements may recollectively be grasped. Benjamin extends this dialectic of dreaming, interpreting and waking to the relation between historical epochs and the tasks of the materialist historian. (edited)

**Miller Jr, Fred D**. A Reply to David Keyt and David Gill. *Ancient Phil*, 16(2), 443-454, Fall 96.

This essay responds to two critics of my book, *Nature, Justice, and Rights in Aristotle's Politics* (Oxford, 1995). Against David Keyt, who held that Aristotle's use of 'nature' (*phusis*) in the *Politics* is fallacious, I argued that Aristotle uses 'nature' in an extended sense in the *Politics* so that his arguments are valid although ultimately dependent on his teleological metaphysics. Here I demonstrate that this does not have the implication that Keyt alleges, namely a collapse of the natural/artificial distinction. Against David Gill I show that Aristotle's linkage of political justice with the common advantage supports claims of political rights and not merely duties.

**Millett, Nick**. The Trick of Singularity. *Theor Cult Soc*, 14(2), 51-66, My 97.

**Millett, Nick** and Deleuze, Gilles. Immanence: A Life.... *Theor Cult Soc*, 14(2), 3-7, My 97.

**Millgram, Elijah**. *Practical Induction*. Cambridge, Harvard Univ Pr, 1997.

In *Practical Induction* Elijah Millgram argues that experience plays a central role in this process of deciding what is or is not important or worth pursuing. He takes aim at instrumentalism, a view predominant among philosophers today, which holds that the goals of practical reasoning are basic in the sense that they are given by desires that are not themselves the product of practical reasoning. The view Millgram defends is "practical induction," a method of reasoning from experience similar to theoretical induction. (publisher,edited)

**Millgram, Elijah** and Thagard, Paul. Deliberative Coherence. *Synthese*, 108(1), 63-88, Jl 96.

Choosing the right plan is often choosing the more coherent plan: but what is coherence? We argue that coherence-directed practical inference ought to be represented computationally. To that end, we advance a theory of deliberative coherence and describe its implementation in a program modelled on Thagard's ECHO. We explain how the theory can be tested and extended and consider its bearing on instrumentalist accounts of practical rationality.

**Millikan, Ruth Garrett**. Images of Identity: In Search of Modes of Presentation. *Mind*, 106(423), 499-519, Jl 97.

There are many alternative ways that a mind or brain might represent that two of its representations were of the same object or property, the "Strawson" model, the "duplicates" model, the "synchrony" model, the "Christmas lights" model, the "anaphor" model, and so forth. I first discuss what would *constitute* that a mind or brain was using one of these systems of identity marking rather than another. I then discuss devastating effects that adopting the Strawson model has on the notion that there are such things as modes of presentation in thought. Next I argue that Evans's idea that there are "dynamic Fregean thoughts" has exactly the same implications. I argue further that all of the other models of thought discussed earlier are in fact isomorphic to the Strawson model. (edited)

**Millikan, Ruth Garrett**. On Swampkinds. *Mind Lang*, 11(1), 103-117, Mr 96.

Does the science of psychology range over Swampman, Davidson's imagined, accidentally created, molecule-for-molecule-identical, double? It does not. The principle by which the members of the human race fall under the same natural or 'real' kind is importantly different from that by which Davidson and Swampman do. You, I, and Swampman cannot all fall under the same natural science. (Besides, there is reason to suppose that Swampman is not just rediculously improbable but actually is physically impossible.)

**Millikan, Ruth Garrett**. Troubles with Wagner's Reading of Millikan. *Phil Stud*, 86(1), 93-96, Ap 97.

A dozen serious errors in Wagner's interpretation of Millikan's position in his "Teleosemantics and the Troubles with Naturalism" (*Philosophical Studies* April 1996) are corrected and relevant references to the Millikan Corpus supplied.

**Mills, Charles W**. "Carnal Knowledges: Beyond Rawls and Sandel" in *A Question of Values: New Canadian Perspectives in Ethics and Political Philosophy,* Brennan, Samantha (ed), 155-174. Amsterdam, Rodopi, 1997.

Radical democratic theory has traditionally found it necessary to critique not merely the political sociology of orthodox theory, but also its social ontology and epistemology. In this paper I argue that those seeking theoretical models to conceptualize social subordination need to distance themselves from both John Rawls's contractarianism and the communitarianism of Michael Sandel. "Carnal Knowledges" is meant to register this double opposition, (objective) knowledge as against the relativism of communitarians, but a knowledge that is plurally located, situated, embodied, as against the ethereally undifferentiated residents of the epistemic ghost towns of traditional contractarian theory.

**Mills, Claudia**. Should We Boycott Boycotts?. *J Soc Phil*, 27(3), 136-148, Wint 96.

I first distinguish political, commercial, and mixed boycotts. I then examine two different justifications for boycotts: 1) strategic justifications, which appeal to the efficacy of boycotts as an instrumental tool of change; and 2) shunning justifications, which defend boycotts on grounds of moral integrity. I argue that, however appealing each justification may be separately, they are only uneasily combined. It is unwise to bolster one by appeal to the other, for rather than complementing each other, they are in some fundamental sense contradictory. Moreover, on both justifications, boycotts may inherently fail to achieve—indeed, may work against achieving—their own deepest objectives.

**Mills, Eugene**. Interactionism and Physicality. *Ratio*, 10(2), 169-183, S 97.

Substance-dualist interactionism faces two sorts of challenge. One is empirical, involving the alleged incompatibility between interactionism and the supposed closure of the physical world. Although widely considered successful, this challenge gives no reason for preferring materialism to dualism. The other sort of challenge holds that interactionism is *conceptually* impossible. The historically influential version of the conceptual challenge is now discredited, but recent discussions by Chomsky and by Crane and Mellor suggest a new version. In brief, the argument is that anything that interacts causally with physical things would have to be sanctioned by physics and anything sanctioned by physics is ipso facto (as a matter of conceptual necessity) physical. I focus on the second premise. I show that plausible arguments for it are in fact fallacious and that counterexamples undermine it. Thus the argument fails: substance-dualist interactionism cannot be ruled out on conceptual grounds alone.

**Mills, Jon**. Hegel on the Unconscious Abyss: Implications for Psychoanalysis. *Owl Minerva*, 28(1), 59-75, Fall 96.

**Mills, Stephen**. Cynthia Macdonald and Graham Macdonald (eds), *Connectionism: Debates on Psychological Explanation, Volume Two. Int J Phil Stud*, 5(1), 95-105, Mr 97.

Papers in *Connectionism* address either Fodor and Pylyshyn's argument that connectionism can do no better than implement classical cognitive models or Ramsey, Stich and Garon's argument that the success of connectionist models would reasonably imply eliminativism about folk psychological propositional attitudes. The notice concentrates upon Stich and Warfield's argument that while connectionist success would imply serious folk psychological error it would not justify the eliminativist conclusion. It is argued that Stich and Warfield's argument against the eliminativist conclusion should be rejected as such too strong and an alternative account of the justification of eliminativist conclusions is sketched.

**Millstein, Roberta L**. Random Drift and the Omniscient Viewpoint. *Proc Phil Sci Ass*, 3(Suppl), S10-S18, 1996.

Alexander Rosenberg (1994) claims that the omniscient viewpoint of the evolutionary process would have no need for the concept of random drift. However, his argument fails to take into account all of the processes which are considered to be instances of random drift. A consideration of these processes shows that random drift is not eliminable even given a position of omniscience. Furthermore, Rosenberg must take these processes into account in order to support his claims that evolution is deterministic and that evolutionary biology is an instrumental science.

**Millucci, Marco**. La "Freiheitsschrift" del 1809 come momento decisivo tra la filosofia dell'identità e il rilievo dell'esistenza nel pensiero di Schelling. *Riv Filosof Neo-Scolas*, 88(2), 205-222, Ap-Je 96.

**Milne, Peter**. Bruno de Finetti and the Logic of Conditional Events. *Brit J Phil Sci*, 48(2), 195-232, Je 97.

This article begins by outlining some of the history—beginning with brief remarks of Quine's—of work on conditional assertions and conditional events. The upshot of the historical narrative is that diverse works from various starting points have circled around a nexus of ideas without convincingly tying them together. Section 3 shows how ideas contained in a neglected article of de Finetti's lead to a unified treatment of the topics based on the identification of conditional events as the objects of conditional bets. The penultimate section explores some of the consequences of the resulting logic of conditional events while the last defends it.

**Milne, Peter**. Quick Triviality Proofs for Probabilities of Conditionals. *Analysis*, 57(1), 75-80, Ja 97.

**Milner, Benjamin**. Francis Bacon: The Theological Foundations of *Valerius Terminus. J Hist Ideas*, 58(2), 245-264, Ap 97.

**Milosavljevic, Boris**. An Objectivistic Critic of Phenomenological Hermeneutics (in Serbo-Croatian). *Theoria (Yugoslavia)*, 38(3), 63-76, S 95.

Traditional hermeneutics presupposes a complete objective interpretation. In its detailed study of hermeneutic methods and rules of interpretation, traditional hermeneutics has ignored the role of interpreter and his hermeneutic situation. Phenomenological approach to hermeneutics satisfies the objectivity requirement, because it throws a light on the interpreter's viewpoint and hermeneutic situation. By recognizing and removing his own prejudices and by pursuing careful and objective investigation, the interpreter gets closer to the correct understanding of a historical horizon.

**Milov, Yury P** and Girnyk, Andryi and Salamatov, Vladimir. The Chaos-Cosmos Transformation Cycle with Special Reference to the Chernobyl Disaster: Toward the Ultimate Reality and Meaning of the Ukraine. *Ultim Real Mean*, 20(2 & 3), 196-204, Je-S 97.

**Milovic, Miroslav**. Ideología y comunicación (Yugoslavia como problema). *Daimon Rev Filosof*, 12, 93-102, Ja-Je 96.

In Yugoslavia, the new transcendental, constitutive subject in the Kantian sense became a national state. This particularity of establishing social sense resulted with catastrophe.

**Milovic, Miroslav** (trans) and Saez Rueda, Luis. For Non-Relative Difference and Non-Coercive Dialogue (in Serbo-Croatian). *Theoria (Yugoslavia)*, 38(4), 7-21, D 95.

The aim of this article is to show that there are reasons for affirming the difference against the identity in a critical and nonrelative way. First, the author explains how the modern thinking of difference led to pluralism and relativism. Then he exposes Habermas's and Apel's thesis that "spiritual unity" cannot stem either from metaphysics nor from religion. He criticizes their "dialogical" solution and examines postmodern alternative. Finally, he defends his own, nonrelativistic view which relies on the so-called "tragic" conception of rationality.

**Milton, J R**. Lockean Political Apocrypha. *Brit J Hist Phil*, 4(2), 247-266, S 96.

**Minazzi, Fabio**. "The Presence of Phenomenology in Milan Between the Two World Wars" in *In Itinere* European Cities and the Birth of Modern Scientific Philosophy, Poli, Roberto (ed), 213-232. Amsterdam, Rodopi, 1997.

**Minazzoli, Agnès**. *L'Homme sans image: Une anthropologie négative.* Paris, Pr Univ France, 1996.

Une définition de l'humain est-elle possible? Chaque homme est singulier. Multiple. Pour saisir tous ses visages, l'image ne suffit pas. Autrefois, la Théologie négative prêtait au divin toutes les formes et ne lui en reconnaissait aucune. Ainsi traduisait-elle la disproportion de l'homme à Dieu, le rapport du fini à l'infini. De l'homme à l'homme, la relation diffère: de l'un au multiple, une anthropologie, elle aussi négative, permettrait de concevoir l'humain sous toutes ses formes, quitte à n'en retenir aucune. A quoi tient la forme humaine? La question est ouverte. (publisher, edited)

**Mineau, André** and Giroux, Guy and Boisvert, Yves. De l'usage social de l'éthique. *Philosopher*, 19, 9-22, 1996.

Lorsqu'un tel phénomène se produit, il est la résultante de l'usage social que l'on fait de l'éthique à l'intérieur de ces appareils. Il repose sur l'introduction de *codes de conduite* dont l'ultime finalité en est ce contrôle social. Il s'ensuit que la demande d'éthique que nous connaissons aujourd'hui est susceptible de provoquer un effet pervers important. "Ce serait le cas dès lors qu'elle serait interprétée comme un appel en faveur d'un contrôle à exercer sur la société et sur les individus qui la composent, plutôt que de représenter un contrôle de la société par elle-même, d'abord au niveau des individus, puis au niveau de leurs unités d'appartenance, communautaires ou organisationnelles". (edited)

**Mineau, André** and Larochelle, Gilbert. Éthique et idéologie: frontière et médiation sémantique par la morale. *Laval Theol Phil*, 52(3), 827-836, O 96.

The article seeks to bring out how the notions of ethics and of ideology can be defined one with respect to the other. Its aim is to explore conceptually the influence of these categories, their corollary, the conditions under which they operate, the moral ground on which they meet.

**Miniotaite, Grazina**. Civil Disobedience: Justice against Legality. *Acorn*, 5-2 &(6-1), 21-23, S 90 - Mr 91.

The paper deals with the problem of the moral justification of civil disobedience. It is claimed that civil disobedience is premised on the distinction between justice and legality. The premise is also at the basis of the Kantian philosophy of law that laid the moral foundations for the law. It is concluded that Kantian practical philosophy contains all the elements for the contemporary notion of civil disobedience. Next, an attempt is made to show that the Lithuanian independence movement "Sajudis" was conceived and shaped in 1988-89 as a moral opposition to the authorities and that its universalist character was essential in uniting Lithuania's people for mass actions of civil disobedience.

**Minogue, Kenneth**. The Christian Roots of a Free Society. *Riv Int Filosof Diritto*, 73(4), 639-650, O-D 96.

Christianity is often taken as hostile to freedom, especially freedom of thought, as in the famous Galileo case. At a deeper level of thought, however, both civil and intellectual freedom have arisen from the Christian doctrine of individuality. It is the root of both the market and constitutional liberal democracy. A false justification of these institutions points to their consequence (if such it is) of prosperity, but this aim more precisely corresponds to the socialist doctrine that the point of human life is the satisfaction of needs. Christianity takes life's point to be moral challenge, which has generated Western adversariality.

**Minow, Martha**. "All in the Family and In All Families: Membership, Loving, and Owing" in *Sex, Preference, and Family: Essays on Law and Nature*, Nussbaum, Martha C (ed), 249-276. New York, Oxford Univ Pr, 1997.

Growing diversity in groups across this nation who claim to be families, including single parent households, blended families, gay and lesbian families and extended families, as well as growing diversity within families, such as religious and racial diversity, have consequences for the basic issues of family law: Who is in "the family"? What benefits accompany family membership? What obligations accompany family roles? Part One of this article addresses what considerations should guide legal definitions of families and distributions of benefits based on family status. In Part Two, I reconsider this discussion while examining legal obligations based on family status.

**Mintoff, Joe**. Rational Cooperation, Intention, and Reconsideration. *Ethics*, 107(4), 612-643, Jl 97.

This paper examines the rationality of forming and acting on, intentions. I introduce Gauthier's discussion in his "Assure and Threaten" and propose an alternative account. Unlike the standard maximizing theory, this account respects the intuition that it is rational to act on a rationally formed and rationally not-reconsidered intention; unlike Gauthier's it departs from this theory only by the minimal amount required to respect this intuition. As a result, it also respects intuitions about various cases: it can explain why straightforward cooperation and modest forms of deterrence are rational, and why more extreme types of constraint are not.

**Mintoff, Joe**. Slote on Rational Dilemmas and Rational Supererogation. *Erkenntnis*, 46(1), 111-126, Ja 97.

The so-called optimizing conception of rationality includes (amongst other things) the following two claims: I) that it is irrational to choose an option if you know there is a better one, and II) there are no situations in which an agent, through no practical fault of her own, cannot avoid acting irrationally. As part of his ongoing attempt to explain why we need to go beyond the optimizing conception, Michael Slote discusses a number of examples in which it seems that I) and II) are inconsistent. According to Slote, these situations seem to involve the existence of rational supererogation (a denial of I), or rational dilemmas (a denial of II). The purpose of this paper is to examine Slote's arguments for these claims and to propose an alternative solution to the problem he presents.

**Mints, Grigori**. Strong Termination for the Epsilon Substitution Method. *J Sym Log*, 61(4), 1193-1205, D 96.

Ackermann proved termination for a special order of reductions in Hilbert's epsilon substitution method for the first order arithmetic. We establish termination for arbitrary order of reductions.

**Mir Puig, Santiago**. Die Zurechnung im Strafrecht eines entwickelten sozialen und demokratischen Rechtsstaates. *Jahr Recht Ethik*, 2, 225-237, 1994.

This article considers the prerequisites for criminal law imputation of action undertaken within complex organizational structures. The assumption is that rules of imputation, like rules of conduct, are determined by historical and cultural factors. Accordingly, they are not objectively given but rather are relative, depending to a considerable extent on changes in values. The content of rules of imputation cannot be established until one specifies the cultural background and functions of the criminal law. In Europe, this cultural background is defined by principles intrinsic to a democratic, social welfare state governed by the rule of law and by the technical needs of a developed society. (edited)

**Miraglia, Pierluigi**. A Note on Truth, Deflationism and Irrealism. *Sorites*, 48-63, N 95.

The paper deals with a problem about irrealist doctrines of content, according to which there are no real properties answering to content-attributing expressions. The central claim of the paper is that the distinction between factual and nonfactual discourse (key to irrealism) is independent from particular conceptions of truth and is thus compatible with a deflationary conception. This claim is sustained by an examination of what I take to be significant aspects of the deflationary conception. I argue, therefore, directly against Paul Boghossian's paper "The Status of Content", which attempted to show that irrealism about content is inconsistent.

**Miralbell, Ignacio**. La gnoseología escotista como transformación de la aristotélica: Un análisis desde la axiomática de Polo. *Anu Filosof*, 29(2), 751-771, 1996.

In this paper I am trying to show the differential points of view between the escotistic theory of knowledge—which is a peculiar derivation of Augustinianism—and the axiomatic gnosiology of L. Polo, which has his inspiration in Aristotle. The univocist conceptualism together with the intuitionism of Duns Scotus leads to a primacy of the mental presency, which is just what Polo tries to overcome.

**Miramontes, Ofelia B** and Howe, Ken. *The Ethics of Special Education*. New York, Teachers College Pr, 1992.

The authors delineate the ethical issues most salient and pressing to special education and provide a philosophically grounded framework for their discussion. Using the case method, the book presents 35 real-life situations that raise personal, institutional and policy issues; 23 of the cases are accompanied by analyses and the remaining 12 are provided for further exploration. This approach allows students to reason and collaborate about ethical issues rather than simply to master a set of principles and precepts. (publisher, edited)

**Miranda Carrao, Eduardo Vitor**. Informática na Educaçao: Perspectivas. *Educ Filosof*, 10(19), 145-151, Ja-Je 96.

**Mirek, Ryszard**. The Problem of Justification of Abduction in C.S. Peirce in the Light of Tadeusz Czezowski's Views (in Polish). *Kwartalnik Filozof*, 24(4), 85-95, 1996.

**Mirkes, Renée**. Aquinas's Doctrine of Moral Virtue and Its Significance for Theories of Facility. *Thomist*, 61(2), 189-218, Ap 97.

**Miroiu, Adrian**. Global Warming and Moral Theorizing. *Theoria (Spain)*, 11(27), 61-81, S 96.

The aim of my paper is to explore in some detail some epistemological issues concerning moral theorizing on global warming. First, I consider the issue of the structure of the theoretical approach in a field of inquiry requiring normative assessments. How do theoretical principles work here? What is to be regarded as a normative evidence for such a theory? Second, the criteria to determine which part, if any, of the theory gets normatively constrained, and which does not, are discussed. Third, I focus on the procedures to reach an equilibrium between such a theory and its evidence and to reach it, changes might be required on the normative side of the theory, rather than on its nonnormative one.

**Miscevic, Nenad**. The Skeptic and the Hoverfly (A Teleo-Computational View of Rule-Following). *Acta Analytica*, 171-187, 1996.

The paper proposes a solution to the quus-plus puzzle raised in Kripke's reading of Wittgenstein. The solution builds upon two lines of thought to be found in the literature: upon a dispositionalist proposal for ascertaining the actual propensities of the would-be added and a teleological proposal for explaining the normativity of meaning. The dispositionalist line of thought is briefly developed in a computational direction. The center-state, however, is occupied by the teleological line. The original teleological strategy, invented by R.G. Millikan is discussed; her main idea is endorsed, but tentatively modified and supplemented with computational considerations. The main criticisms of Millikan presented here are geared to showing that such supplementation is needed. It is argued that the integrated, teleo-computationalist proposal successfully handles the puzzle.

**Misgeld, Dieter** and Magendzo, Abraham. Human Rights Education, Moral Education and Modernisation: The General Relevance of Some Latin American Experiences: A Conversation. *J Moral Educ*, 26(2), 151-168, Je 97.

**Mishara, Aaron L**. Commentary on "Wilhelm Griesinger". *Phil Psychiat Psych*, 3(3), 165-167, S 96.

**Mishra, Amarendra**. Why God. *Darshana Int*, 36(2/142), 53-56, Ap 96.

The concept of "God" is not inherent from birth. Babies and children depend upon parents for their basic needs. Adults substitute concept of God for parental figures to seek moral and spiritual support from. Ancient Indian philosophy including Sankhya, Buddhism and Vedanta propound that one's station in life depends on his deeds (Karma) and God does not interfere in mundane affairs. This concept is not readily grasped by the common man who prefers to see God as a tangible supreme power, to be depended upon in adversity. This psychological assurance is an important concept for peace within the individual and harmony in society.

**Missac, Pierre** and Nicholsen, Shierry Weber (trans). *Walter Benjamin's Passages*. Cambridge, MIT Pr, 1995.

Taking a cue from his subject, Missac adopts a form of indirect critique in which independent details examined seemingly in passing emerge over the course of the book as parts of larger patterns of understanding. The interlocked essays move among such topics as reading and writing, collecting, the dialectic and time and history. Many of the subjects are standard in Benjamin studies, but the freshness and directness of Missac's response to them makes this book compelling. It is a work of sophisticated and imaginative criticism that shows how Benjamin's work anticipated the future and how it can be fruitfully extended. (publisher, edited)

**Missimer, Connie**. Darwin's Origin and Mill's Subjection. *Inquiry (USA)*, 16(3), 10-24, Spr 97.

**Missimer, Connie**. The Case that Alternative Argumentation Drives the Growth of Knowledge—Some Preliminary Evidence. *Inform Log*, 17(2), 201-211, Spr 95.

Argumentation theorists can make a much larger case for the significance of their discipline than they appear to do. This larger case entails asking the overarching question, "How is knowledge driven?" and seeking the answer in arguments for which there is near universal agreement that they drove the growth of knowledge. Three such benchmark arguments are Newton's on motion, Darwin's on evolution and Mill's on women's intellectual equality to men. These and other seminal historical arguments suggest that alternative argumentation in light of evidence is the mechanism that drives the growth of knowledge. There are also a number of surprising results, among them that even the most epistemically salient arguments contain significant errors and that what is "reasonable" is a constantly changing intuition which is biased against superior but novel ideas. This approach suggests a new fallacy as well, the intuitive fallacy of believing that plausibility is evidence for likelihood.

**Missimer, Connie**. Where's the Evidence?. *Inquiry (USA)*, 14(4), 1-18, Sum 95.

Many claims about critical thinking are intuitively appealing yet lack evidentiary support. For example, Harvey Siegel has claimed that a person must display six traits. Using two uncontroversial examples of great critical thought, Darwin's *Origins of Species* and Newton's *Principia*, this paper demonstrates that Siegel's view contains serious anomalies: He must either revise his claims or declare these seminal works excluded from the corpus of critical thought. The paper also offers examples showing how an argument can be constructed to make any view seem trivial or false, including Newton's on motion, as well as Siegel's or Missimer's on critical thinking.

**Mitcham, Carl**. Computers, Information and Ethics: A Review of Issues and Literature. *Sci Eng Ethics*, 1(2), 113-132, A 95.

The following bibliographic survey of computer ethics is intended as a general introduction useful to guide both preliminary research and course development. It is the first of a series that Carl Mitcham will be doing on a number of specific discussions of ethics in science and technology. Future installments are projected on nuclear ethics, engineering ethics, ethics in scientific research, and biomedical ethics.

**Mitcham, Carl**. Ethics, Standards, Diversity: Dimensions of the Social Construction of Responsibility. *Prof Ethics*, 5(1-2), 167-177, Spr-Sum 96.

The move from the development of ethics "guidelines" to ethics "standards" builds a bridge between the social control of technoscience by means of technical standards and legal regulation to professional ethics. Related connections can be found in professional ethics development outside the US, e.g., Chile, Costa Rica, Germany, Japan and Hong Kong.

**Mitcham, Carl**. The Philosophical Challenge of Technology. *Amer Cath Phil Quart*, 70(Supp), 45-58, 1996.

To think technology is a struggle between two different ways of thinking the presence of the making and using of artifacts. One is the effort of engineering philosophy to think the world and experience in technological terms. The other is the effort of humanities philosophy to think technology as limited to some aspect of the world or human experience. In the first instance, then, the challenge of technology to philosophy is the confrontation of these two efforts: How is technology to be thought? In a second instance, however, the challenge is to recognize the extent to which this confrontation has been surpassed by what can be termed the meta-technological world in which we now reside.

**Mitchell, Jeff**. Reason's Different Tastes. *S J Phil*, 34(4), 493-505, Wint 96.

In this article I am interested in taste as a deliberative and critical capacity. Building on John Dewey's social psychology and theory of valuation, I argue that taste is a personal constellation of habits which, when combined with intelligence, constitutes deliberation. Taste signifies the individual's acquired mental dispositions and predispositions or cast of mind that regularly enter into decision making. In the last part of the essay, I consider the role taste plays in different areas of inquiry.

**Mitchell, John C** and Lincoln, Patrick D and Scedrov, Andre. Linear Logic Proof Games and Optimization. *Bull Sym Log*, 2(3), 322-338, S 96.

**Mitchell, Robert W**. Kinesthetic-Visual Matching and the Self-Concept as Explanations of Mirror-Self-Recognition. *J Theor Soc Behav*, 27(1), 17-39, Mr 97.

Since its inception as a topic of inquiry, mirror-self-recognition has usually been explained by two models: one, initiated by Guillaume, proposes that mirror-self-recognition depends upon kinesthetic-visual matching, and the other, initiated by Gallup, that self-recognition depends upon a self-concept. These two models are examined historically and conceptually. This examination suggests that the kinesthetic-visual matching model is conceptually coherent and makes reasonable and accurate predictions; and that the self-concept model is conceptually incoherent and makes inaccurate predictions from premises which are themselves inaccurate. From a theoretical (and empirical) standpoint, the kinesthetic-visual matching model is the better explanation of self-recognition.

**Mitchell, William J** and Gitik, Moti. Indiscernible Sequences for Extenders, and the Singular Cardinal Hypothesis. *Annals Pure Applied Log*, 82(3), 273-316, D 96.

We prove several results giving lower bounds for the large cardinal strength of a failure of the singular cardinal hypothesis. The main result is the following theorem: ...In order to prove these theorems we give a detailed analysis of the sequences of indiscernibles which come from applying the covering lemma to nonoverlapping sequences of extenders. (edited)

**Mitchell, William J** and Schimmerling, E and Steel, J R. The Covering Lemma Up to a Woodin Cardinal. *Annals Pure Applied Log*, 84(2), 219-255, Mr 97.

It is proven that if there is no model with a Woodin cardinal and the Steel core model K exists, then the weak covering lemma holds at strong limit cardinals, that is, if lambda is a singular cardinal such that no smaller cardinal has lambda many countable subsets, then the successor of lambda is K is the same as the true successor of lambda.

**Mitias, Michael H**. "How Does a Building Mean?" in *East and West in Aesthetics*, Marchianò, Grazia (ed), 131-154. Pisa, Istituti Editoriali, 1997.

Contrary to Nelson Goodman's claim, a building does not mean by exemplifying the qualities it possesses but by expressing these qualities. The essay presents (1) a critical analysis of exemplification as a principle of aesthetic explanation in architecture and (2) a defense of the view that the relation which holds between a building as a physical object and the aesthetic qualities it has is one of expression.

**Mitra, Kumar**. Euthanasia. *J Indian Counc Phil Res*, 14(1), 157-163, S-D 96.

**Mitsis, Phillip T** (ed) and Devereux, Daniel T (ed). *Encyclopedia of Classical Philosophy*. Westport, Greenwood Pr, 1997.

*The Encyclopedia of Classical Philosophy* is a reference work in the philosophy of Greek and Roman antiquity. As such, its subject matter comprises subjects and figures from the dawn of philosophy in Ionia (on the west coast of modern Turkey) in the sixth century B.C.E. to the decline of the Academy of Athens in the sixth century C.E. (publisher, edited)

**Mittelstrass, Jürgen** (ed) and Burgen, Arnold (ed) and McLaughlin, Peter (ed). *The Idea of Progress*. Hawthorne, de Gruyter, 1997.

This volume represents an interdisciplinary attempt to deal with the concept of progress as used in and as viewed by various disciplines, from musicology to physics. Many of the contributions are philosophical or historical analyses of the concept of progress itself. The philosophical essays discuss empirical and valuational aspects as well as the question of whether and how philosophy itself makes progress. Other areas dealt with are progress in time, evolution, politics, health and music.

**Mittmann, Jörg-Peter**. "Über die präreflexive Existenz meiner selbst" in *Sein—Reflexion—Freiheit: Aspekte der Philosophie Johann Gottlieb Fichtes*, Asmuth, Christoph (ed), 159-171. Amsterdam, Gruner, 1997.

**Mittmann, Jörg-Peter**. Vom sprachlichen Zugang zum Absoluten. *Phil Rundsch*, 44(1), 64-73, Mr 97.

**Mitzman, Arthur**. Michelet and Social Romanticism: Religion, Revolution, Nature. *J Hist Ideas*, 57(4), 659-682, O 96.

**Mixie, Joseph**. The Causal Closure Principle of the Physical Domain and Quantum Mechanics. *Dialogos*, 31(68), 119-125, Jl 96.

**Mizrahi, Esteban**. Persona, propiedad y reconocimiento intersubjetivo: Una interpretación de los fundamentos normativos del estado de derecho hegeliano. *Cuad Etica*, 21-22, 83-115, 1996.

In this paper I analyze the ethical and juridical sense of the concepts of person and property in Hegel's *Philosophy of Right*. The development is centred in the source of legitimacy of those concepts and in the normative consequences they imply. It's not possible to develop this task, I argue, without approaching the Hegelian concept of the intersubjective recognition to which both concepts are narrowly linked from a systematical and phenomenological point of view. The central thesis is that the person as an ethical and juridical category is founded in a double legitimacy structure, on one hand, in the self-reflexive structure of the self, and on the other, in the intersubjective recognition. (edited)

**Moberg, Dennis**. Virtuous Peers in Work Organizations. *Bus Ethics Quart*, 7(1), 67-85, Ja 97.

It is argued that virtuous peers in work organizations have two elements of character no matter what the nature of the goods the organization produces: loyalty to common projects for their own sake and trustworthiness. Each of these is shown to be a uniquely human attribute, an element of character that contributes to a life well lived, and a trait that leads to the flourishing of an entire work community.

**Mock, Verena**. Common Sense und Logik in Jan Smedslunds 'Psychologik'. *J Gen Phil Sci*, 27(2), 281-306, 1996.

This paper is about the efforts the Norwegian psychologist Jan Smedslund made in analyzing and checking philosophically his theory called 'Psycho-logic'. I am going to reconstruct and discuss the debates between Smedslund and several critics, which have been going on since about 1978, mainly in the "Scandinavian Journal of Psychology". A result will be that the kind of modal logics Smedslund uses—a type with realistic semantics and epistemology—is not the proper one for the analysis of 'Psycho-logic'.

**Moellendorf, Darrel**. Constructing the Law of Peoples. *Pac Phil Quart*, 77(2), 132-154, Je 96.

In this paper I shall argue that due to the constructivist procedure which John Rawls employs in "The Law of Peoples," he is unable to justify his claim that there is a relationship between limiting the internal and external sovereignty of states. An alternative constructivist procedure is viable, but it extends the ideal theory of international justice to include liberal democratic and egalitarian principles. The procedure and principles have significant implications for nonideal theory as well, insofar as they justify a principle of international resource redistribution and weaken general prohibitions against intervention.

**Moellendorf, Darrel**. Liberalism, Nationalism, and the Right to Secede. *Phil Forum*, 28(1-2), 87-99, Fall-Wint 97.

This paper argues that a right of nations to secede is defensible even on the liberal assumption of state neutrality. The right is a group right, but its value derives from its service to important individual interests, in particular to be governed by a state to which one consents and to utilize one's cultural context in rationally revising one's life plans. The right is nonremedial, but constrained by other considerations of justice.

**Möller, Hans Georg**. The Chinese Theory of Forms and Names (*xingming zhi xue*) and Its Relation to "Philosophy of Signs". *J Chin Phil*, 24(2), 179-190, Je 97.

**Moffat, Robert C L** (ed) and Griffin, Stephen M (ed). *Radical Critiques of the Law*. Lawrence, Univ Pr Kansas, 1997.

The authors consider whether the critiques advanced in recent legal theory can truly be called radical and what form a radical critique of American law should take. Writing at the cutting edge of the critique of critical legal theory, they offer insights first on critical legal scholarship, then on feminist political and legal theory. A third group of contributions questions the radicalness of these approaches in light of their failure to challenge fundamental aspects of liberalism, while a final section focuses on current issues of legal reform through critical views on criminal punishment, including observations on rape and hate speech. (publisher, edited)

**Mogyoródi, Emese**. Mythical Perspective and Philosophical Speculation in Late Greek Philosophy (in Czech). *Magyar Filozof Szemle*, 1-2, 383-412, 1997.

**Mohanta, Dilip Kumar**. A Note on the Concept of Alienation. *Darshana Int*, 36(3/143), 69-74, Ap 96.

**Mohanty, J N**. Kant and Husserl. *Husserl Stud*, 13(1), 19-30, 1996.

**Mohr, Heinrich**. "Death and Nothingness in Literature" in *The Ancients and the Moderns,* Lilly, Reginald (ed), 295-310. Bloomington, Indiana Univ Pr, 1996.

**Mohr-Lane, Jana**. Voices in the Classroom: Girls and Philosophy for Children. *Thinking*, 13(1), 9-12, 1997.

Philosophical inquiry can help to create a classroom environment that addresses the disadvantages girls face in school, where there are often expectations (mirroring the conditions of girls' lives in the larger community) that girls should be pleasant and conciliatory, while boys should be assertive and confident. A rich philosophical dialogue must involve an openness to the diversity of the participants' voices: the point is not who has the right answer, but whether there is a thoughtful, deep discussion that engages the group. This requires the participation of the whole class, each student claiming his or her individual, unique voice.

**Mojsisch, Burkhard**. "Dieses Ich: Meister Eckharts Ich-Konzeption: Ein Beitrag zur 'Aufklärung' im Mittelalter" in *Sein—Reflexion—Freiheit: Aspekte der Philosophie Johann Gottlieb Fichtes,* Asmuth, Christoph (ed), 239-252. Amsterdam, Gruner, 1997.

In conceiving the I as such in place of the Godhead, Meister Eckhart employs motifs of the Aristotelian possible intellect in order to define the I as the uncreated and uncreatable ground of the soul—an otherwise unheard—of thought in the Middle Ages. Exemplary of Eckhart's interpretation of self-reflexive consciousness as univocal correlationality is his German Sermon 52, which through its reflection on willing, knowing and being nothing advances the absolute reality of the I before the secondarily relational concept of God. Unthought by Eckhart, however, is the infinite regress of possibility as the condition of all positing, including self-positing.

**Mojsisch, Burkhard**. Marsilius Ficinus: In *Theaetetum* Platonis vel *De scientia* ad Petrum Medicem, patriae patrem: Epitome. *Bochumer Phil Jrbh*, 1, 179-194, 1996.

This is the corrected Latin text of Marsilio Ficino's *Epitome* of the Platonic dialogue *Theaetetus*; it is followed by a separate German translation. With reference to Plato and Neoplatonic thought as well as Hermes Trismegistos and Thomas Aquinas, Ficino develops here his own syncretic epistemology. Beyond the aporia of the dialogue, Ficino connects some of Plato's suggestions about the essence of knowledge, especially the sixth book of the *Politeia*, with theories from Aristotle and the Peripatetics on one hand and Plotinus and Proclus on the other, eliminating nonbeing from the canon of universal contents and rendering knowledge certain, yet graced, comprehension of the divine.

**Mojsisch, Burkhard**. The Epistemology of Humanism. *Bochumer Phil Jrbh*, 1, 127-152, 1996.

This essay explores the interconnections among the humanistic epistemological theories of Ficino, Pomponazzi and Cusanus apparent in the context of their reception of ancient Greek and medieval philosophy, especially Plato's *Theaetetus* and Aristotle's *De anima*. It shows that preceding the opposition between the neo-Platonic scheme of knowledge favored by Ficino and the Aristotelian account of the intellect championed by Pomponazzi, Cusanus attempted to articulate the nature of the mind (*mens*) as such which all modes of knowledge presuppose. Central to this project is his work *De coniecturis* with its theory of the unity of the divine, reason, the understanding and the body, by means of which Cusanus undertook to show how all modes of knowledge are immanent in the mind even as knowledge itself is a process. Concluding critical remarks expound upon the principal significance for knowledge of the thought of nothing, which fundamentally defines the relation to self and other and therewith the horizon of the possible truth of knowledge.

**Mojsisch, Burkhard**. Zu Platons *Theaetet* oder *Über das Wissen*: An Petrus Medices, den Retter des Vaterlandes: Epitome. *Bochumer Phil Jrbh*, 1, 195-215, 1996.

This is a German translation of the corrected Latin text—preceding separately—of Marsilio Ficino's *Epitome* of the Platonic dialogue *Theaetetus*. With reference to Plato and Neoplatonic thought as well as Hermes Trismegistos and Thomas Aquinas, Ficino develops here his own syncretic epistemology. Beyond the aporia of the dialogue, Ficino connects some of Plato's suggestions about the essence of knowledge, especially the sixth book of the *Politeia*, with theories from Aristotle and the Peripatetics on one hand and Plotinus and Proclus on the other, eliminating nonbeing from the canon of universal contents and rendering knowledge certain, yet graced, comprehension of the divine.

**Mokdad, Arfa Mensia**. "Ibn Rushd in the Islamic Context" in *Averroës and the Enlightenment,* Wahba, Mourad (ed), 91-92. Amherst, Prometheus, 1996.

**Mokhov, V V**. Aleksei Fedorovich Losev and Orthodoxy. *Russian Stud Phil*, 35(1), 86-91, Sum 96.

**Mol, Annemarie** and Pols, Jeannette. Ziekte leven: Bouwstenen voor een medische sociologie zonder *disease/illness*-onderscheid. *Kennis Methode*, 20(4), 347-361, 1996.

**Molina, Katiuska**. El Concepto de "Hombre Natural" en Rousseau (Consideraciones Etico-Educativas). *Rev Filosof (Venezuela)*, 23(1), 31-48, 1996.

In this paper we pursue only one objective: to examine the concept of "natural man" in three of his most fundamental works: *The Emile*, *The New Eloise* and the *Discourse on Inequality*. This concept is analyzed exegetically with the purpose of understanding the meaning of the three individual correlative concepts of individual, society and education. In order to proceed with this analysis, the principles of hermeneutic interpretation are accepted and explained in the introduction of this paper. (edited)

**Molina Delgada, Mauricio**. Discusiones filosóficas en torno a la creatividad. *Rev Filosof (Costa Rica)*, 34(83-84), 401-414, D 96.

This paper deals with different psychological approaches to creativity and their philosophical background. It strongly supports that it is necessary to integrate those approaches in spite of their apparent contradictions.

**Molina Pérez, Francisco**. Sindéresis y conciencia moral. *Anu Filosof*, 29(2), 773-785, 1996.

Man's cognoscitive acts study can improve a better understanding of intellectual habits. The sinderesis and conscience notions are, in this way, notoriously lightened.

**Molino, Jean**. Après l'herméneutique: Analyse et interprétation des traces et des oeuvres. *Horiz Phil*, 7(2), 1-32, Spr 97.

**Molinuevo, José Luis**. "La Crisis del Socialism Ético en Ortega" in *Política y Sociedad en José Ortega y Gasset: En Torno a "Vieja y Nueva Política",* Lopez de la Vieja, Maria Teresa (ed), 23-50. Barcelona, Anthropos, 1997.

The aim of this article is to examine the meaning of "Ethical Socialism" and its many faces in the work of Ortega y Gasset. The article concludes that, in spite of the current trends in the interpretation, a wide crisis had modified the concept of "ethical" socialism, originating in neo-Kantism. During a long period of his political and intellectual life, that is to say beyond the period between 1914 and 1919, Ortega y Gasset was trying to define his own Socialism. "Vieja y Nueva Politica" and other writings demonstrated how his main ideas about culture and moral aristocracy had taken place in modified socialism.

**Molinuevo, José Luis** (ed). *Deshumanización del Arte?: (Arte y Escritura II)*. Salamanca, Ed Univ de Salamanca, 1996.

Este libro forma parte del proyecto *Arte y Escritura*, que opera en los territorios intermedios de la cultura tendiendo un puente entre la reflexión y la creación artística y literaria. Trata de la pintura, escultura y arquitectura que, desde las vanguardias hasta ahora, están ocupados en diseñar aquello que preocupó a este siglo y a un reto para el venidero: el espacio habitable de lo humano. Colaboran en él: José Luis Pardo, Félix Duque, Fernando Castro, Javier Maderuelo, Kosme de Barañano, José Luis Molinuevo.

**Molinuevo, José Luis**. *Die Zweideutigkeit des Ursprünglichen bei Martin Heidegger*. New York, Lang, 1996.

Das Buch behandelt ein sehr aktuelles Thema des 20.Jahrhunderts: die Rückkehr des Ursprünglichen nach den Krisen der Vernunft, im Sinne der Moderne. Ansatt das Bild eines postmodernen Heideggers zu zeichnen, zeigt das Buch auf, dass er schon früh das "Programm des wesentlichen Menschen" entwarf, das existentiale Veränderung verlangt. Die Zweideutigkeit der Erfahrung des Seins erfüllt jegliches Unternehmen mit einem tragischen Ethos und verhindert ein Zurückgreifen auf eine Ethik der Verantwortung. (publisher)

**Molinuevo, José Luis**. *La Ambigüedad de lo Originario en Martin Heidegger*. Padrón, Novo Século, 1994.

En *Ser y Tiempo* nos presenta Heidegger el ideal del hombre esencial, esto es, decidido, que asume su destino histórico individual en el destino colectivo, y en la *Carta sobre el humanismo* insiste frente a Sartre que es preciso decidirse o por el hombre o por el Ser. La descalificación global del presente juzgado como inauténtico, la culpabilidad del espíritu ilustrado y moderno en ello, junto con el apremio a que se tome la decisión por una vida auténtica dirigida por instancias salvadoras superiores al hombre, ese es el núcleo del mensaje de Heidegger. Pero al mismo tiempo advierte que sólo se puede ser auténtico en la inautenticidad, es decir, dentro y contra ella, en la ambigüedad de una existencia que incorpora la inautenticidad como componente ontológico suyo. El libro es el eco de esa paradoja: de la exigencia irresponsable de una responsabilidad. (publisher)

**Molinuevo, José Luis**. *La Estética de lo Originario en Jünger*. Madrid, Tecnos, 1994.

La dilatada obra de Jünger (Heidelberg, 1895) es un testimonio caleidoscópico del siglo XX. Arte, Literatura y Filosofía se enhebran en su discurso estético de la historia, a través del cual se da cuenta de nuestro tiempo presente en una narración del tiempo originario. Las imágenes de nuestra época adquieren así una textura arcaica, como sueños de lo Elemental en la materia, que se expresa sensiblemente en figuras, tipos, formas...De ellas se destacan cuatro en el libro: el Soldado Desconocido, el Trabajador, el Emboscado y el Anarca. Su recorrido coincide con lo que Jünger define como el "núcleo de la autoría": una particular forma de resistencia hoy en el retorno a las imágenes, a la palabra. (publisher)

**Molivas, Gregory I**. Richard Price, the Debate on Free Will, and Natural Rights. *J Hist Ideas*, 58(1), 105-123, J 97.

**Molivas, Gregory I**. The Influence of Utilitarianism on Natural Rights Doctrines. *Utilitas*, 9(2), 183-202, Jl 97.

This paper shows that the perceived difference between utilitarianism and natural rights theories in the eighteenth century was much less sharp than that in the twentieth century. This is demonstrated by exploring Josiah Tucker's critique of Locke and his disciples and the way in which the latter responded to it. Tucker's critique of Locke was based on a sharp distinction between a conception of natural rights as individual entitlements and the conception of the public good. The disciples of Locke did not share Tucker's views and his interpretation of Locke. In defending natural rights they appealed less to the notion of moral agency and more to utilitarian ideas. The extent to which the advocates of the rights of man employed utilitarian ideas is obscured by the fact that they never divested themselves of the political advantage of using the words 'natural rights' even when their arguments were closer to the principle of utility.

**Molnár, Péter**. Amicitia Politica: Thomas Aquinas on Political Cohesion in Society (in Czech). *Magyar Filozof Szemle*, 1-2, 173-186, 1997.

A la différence du discours moderne, dans lequel l'amitié n'est qu'un sentiment privé, la philosophie médiévale connut la notion d'*amicitia* en tant qu'une des caractéristiques unissant les membres de la communauté politique. Chez saint Thomas d'Aquin on peut révéler le développement détaillé de cette conception, celui qui s'inscrit, en même temps, dans le processus de l'harmonisation des idées chrétiennes et aristotéliciennes concernant la question de l'amitié. Nonobstant que dans l'oeuvre du *Doctor Angelicus* l'amitié spirituelle occupe un rôle supérieur par rapport à l'amitié politique, cette dernière ne cesse pas de s'affirmer comme l'une des conceptions-clés dans la pensée politique de l'auteur. (edited)

**Moltchanov, Viktor I**. Bewusstsein, Erfahrung und Unterschneidensleistung. *Prima Philosophia*, 10(1), 3-22, 1997.

**Mondal, Parthasarathi**. Body-Subjectivity in Psychiatry: The Initial Argument. *J Indian Counc Phil Res*, 13(3), 53-71, My-Ag 96.

**Mondin, Battista**. La teologia esistenziale di S. Kierkegaard. *Sapienza*, 49(4), 397-416, 1996.

Theology by its very nature is not just a speculative but also an existential discipline. The existential approach, already familiar to Augustine, Bonaventure and Luther, becomes prominent in S. Kierkegaard. For him faith is mainly an existential event, that takes place when man gives up to all certainties of his reason, becomes aware of his sinful condition and gladly accepts the paradox of Christ—the Man-God, "the absolute paradox". In the existential theology of S. Kierkegaard there is a twofold radicalism: a "theological" radicalism, which concerns his total, unlimited, all-embracing faith in God and a "Christian" radicalism which regards his passionate and devoted love for Christ the Crucified. In this twofold radicalism consists the originality of Kierkegaard's theology. Like Nietzsche, Kierkegaard is *anti-modern*. But whereas Nietzsche fights against modernity in the name of the Anti-Christ; Kierkegaard fights against it in the name of Christ.

**Moneti, Maria** and Boella, Laura and Schmidt, Burghart. Discutono *Il principio speranza*, di Ernst Bloch. *Iride*, 8(15), 466-482, Ag 95.

Il ritardo della traduzione italiana del capolavoro di E. Bloch, pubblicato in Germania alla fine degli anni cinquanta, probabilmente "offre oggi i vantaggi della maturazione tardiva o persino dell'inattualità permanente che tutti i grandi testi filosofici posseggono" (R. Bodei, *Introduzione*). I tre interventi che seguono rilevano e discutono aspetti essenziali del libro. L. Boella instaura un parallelo tra i "fantasmi" di Derrida e l'utopia di Bloch al fine di rilevare la stringente attualità della questione del presente in entrambi i pensatori; M. Moneti si sofferma su alcune nozioni centrali del *Principio speranza* sottolineandone una "certa debolezza teorica"; B. Schmidt, Presidente della *Ernst Bloch-Gesellschaft* a Ludwigshafen, approfondisce il nesso rintracciabile in Bloch tra ontologia e teoria critica della società.

**Monk, Nicholas A M**. Conceptions of Space—Time: Problems and Possible Solutions. *Stud Hist Phil Mod Physics*, 28B(1), 1-34, Mr 97.

In this paper, the implications of quantum mechanics and general relativity for the understanding of space-time are discussed. There are strong indications that classical notions of space-time are inadequate as a basis for these theories. A number of proposals for nonclassical space-time structures are reviewed. Bohm's framework for the description of natural phenomena based on the notion of process is described. Here, space-time is no longer taken as basic; rather it is a derived feature of the underlying process. This approach opens up the possibility of investigating space-time problems from a new angle, where the nature of space-time is determined by the system under study.

**Monk, Ray**. Was Russell an Analytical Philosopher?. *Ratio*, 9(3), 227-242, D 96.

**Monsalve, Alfonso**. Argumentation, Values, and Ethics. *Sorites*, 24-32, Je 97.

Moral concepts are argumentative values with claims to universal acceptance, they express beliefs that are formed in dialogical exchange. The paper defines conditions of acceptability of this kind of beliefs and its limitations.

**Monsalve, Luisa**. La noción de acto ilocucionario en Austin y Searle. *Franciscanum*, 37(111), 451-464, S-D 95.

**Monsalve Solórzano, Alfonso**. "La idea del Consenso en Rawls: Una exposición crítica" in *Liberalismo y Comunitarismo: Derechos Humanos y Democracia*, Monsalve Solórzano, Alfonso (ed), 211-229. 36-46003 València, Alfons el Magnànim, 1996.

**Monsalve Solórzano, Alfonso** (ed) and Cortés Rodas, Francisco (ed). *Liberalismo y Comunitarismo: Derechos Humanos y Democracia*. 36-46003 València, Alfons el Magnànim, 1996.

**Monshipouri, Mahmood**. State Prerogatives, Civil Society, and Liberalization: The Paradoxes of the Late Twentieth Century in the Third World. *Ethics Int Affairs*, 11, 233-251, 1997.

The end of the Cold War has left the international system in a state of paradox, most prominently in the growing conflict between the legal-political global order and the growth of civil society. Monshipouri identifies and discusses three paradoxes that exemplify this central conflict: state-building versus democratization; economic liberalization versus political liberalization; and human rights versus state sovereignty. In discussing each of these paradoxes, the author describes the difficulties and ethical questions involved in making economic and political reforms without the necessary means and institutional resources. Monshipouri concludes that in order to manage such dilemmas, Third World states must find a delicate balance between global economic reforms and an ethically sensitive international political and legal order.

**Montague, Phillip**. Government, the Press, and the People's Right to Know. *J Soc Phil*, 28(2), 68-78, Fall 97.

This paper addresses the question of whether establishing a legal right to freedom of the press—regardless of how it might be limited—is justifiable on moral grounds. In pursuing this investigation, special attention is devoted to familiar claims about the relation between press rights on the one hand and "the people's right to know" on the other.

**Montague, Phillip**. *Punishment as Societal-Defense*. Lanham, Rowman & Littlefield, 1995.

The book develops and defends a justification of legal punishment based on a principle of distributive justice that also justifies individual self-defense. Individuals who will be harmed by culpable aggressors if they do not harm the aggressors must choose how to distribute harm and the aggressors are to blame for their having to do so. The targets of aggression are therefore justified in harming the aggressors. Similarly, a society is justified in establishing a system of punishment as the only means of justly distributing harm to those whose fault it is that that harm must be distributed. (publisher)

**Montague, Phillip**. The "Negative" and "Positive" Arguments of Moral Moderates. *Pac Phil Quart*, 77(1), 37-44, Mr 96.

According to Shelly Kagan, "ordinary" or "moderate" moralists must establish the existence of "options." Kagan considers a "negative" and a "positive" argument, which he regards as the most promising means by which moral moderates might establish their position. He offers objections to both, and he concludes that the moderate position is indefensible. I argue that Kagan fails in his attempt to discredit the negative argument. I also argue that the positive argument is so implausible that Kagan's elaborate criticism of it is unnecessary. The positive argument is interesting nevertheless, because of why it cannot serve the moderate's purposes.

**Montanari, Angelo** and Policriti, Alberto. Decidability Results for Metric and Layered Temporal Logics. *Notre Dame J Form Log*, 37(2), 260-282, Spr 96.

We study the decidability problem for metric and layered temporal logics. The logics we consider are suitable to model time granularity in various contexts and they allow one to build granular temporal models by referring to the "natural scale" in any component of the model and by properly constraining the interactions between differently-grained components. A monadic second-order language combining operators such as temporal contextualization and projection, together with the usual displacement operator of metric temporal logics, is considered and the theory of finitely-layered metric temporal structures, is shown to be decidable.

**Monteiro, Joao Paulo**. Perspectivismo Mitigado. *Philosophica (Portugal)*, 11-20, 1993.

A coherent perspectivism should be moderate—or mitigated. It only becomes meaningful against a transperspective background, which is part of both Hume's and Nietzsche's legacies, a "minimalist" conception of causation. Metaphysical necessity must be excluded, but not a naturalistic, Humean harmony between causal thinking and the real world. One without which even Nietzsche's "mistakes with survival value" would hardly make any sense. It is thus that a plausible perspectivism may distinguish itself from mere rhetoric, scepticism, or relativism.

**Monteiro, Paulo K** and Menezes, Flavio M. Sequential Asymmetric Auctions with Endogenous Participation. *Theor Decis*, 43(2), 187-202, S 97.

In this paper we suggest a model of sequential auctions with endogenous participation where each bidder conjectures about the number of participants at each round. Then, after learning his value, each bidder decides whether or not to participate in the auction. In the calculation of his expected value, each bidder uses his conjectures about the number of participants for each possible subgroup. In equilibrium, the conjectured probability is compatible with the probability of staying in the auction. (edited)

**Montepaone, Claudia**. "Storia e filologia in Niebuhr" in *Lo Storicismo e la Sua Storia: Temi, Problemi, Prospettive*, Cacciatore, Giuseppe (ed), 150-158. Milano, Guerini, 1997.

**Montero Anzola, Jaime**. Reflexiones en torno a ser y tiempo de Martín Heidegger. *Franciscanum*, 37(112), 19-45, Ja-Ap 96.

**Montero Moliner, Fernando**. Kant y Husserl: El Problema de la Subjetividad. *Agora (Spain)*, 14(2), 5-22, 1995.

In this paper an account of the Kantian and Husserlian subjectivity theories is carried out involving its twofold empirical and transcendental facet. This account allows to show the deep affinities between the Kantian and the Husserlian systems and how this twofold dimension of subjectivity opens phenomenological perspectives in Kant's philosophy that will reach their plenitude in Husserl's work.

**Montesinos, José**. El seminario 'Orotava' de historia de la ciencia. *Mathesis*, 10(4), 375-380, N 94.

**Montiel, Luis**. "Más allá de "El nacimiento de la clínica": La comprensión de la "Anatomía General" de Bichat desde la *Naturphilosophie* de Schelling" in *El inicio del Idealismo alemán*, Market, Oswaldo, 315-324. Madrid, Ed Complutense, 1996.

La publicación de *Naissance de la clinique*, de Michel Foucault, representó una sacudida en el ámbito del pensamiento y, en particular, en la historiografía médica. Su tema, el análisis de la revolución epistemológica suscitada en la medicina europea por la obra de Bichat, es abordado en el presente trabajo con el fin de mostrar la perfecta comprensión del significado de la misma por parte de un médico alemán, Philipp Franz von Walther, gracias a su formación en la *Naturphilosophie* de Schelling.

**Montini, Pierino**. La metafisica dell'ermetismo. *Sapienza*, 50(1), 103-108, 1997.

**Montminy, Jacques**. Les limites de la rationalité humaine: une introduction. *Philosopher*, 18, 37-42, 1995.

Being rational is not easy nor common. The following article shows this by using a very simple definition and a minimum of abstract ideas. It also makes a basic distinction between rationality and truth, stressing the fact that rationality has more to do with the structure of thought rather than its content.

**Montminy, Martin**. Les conditions de l'interprétation. *Dialogue (Canada)*, 35(3), 505-527, Sum 96.

I defend Davidson's principle of charity against criticisms that were voiced by proponents of the principle of humanity. Then I raise my own objections. First, I point out that it cannot be conceived as *necessary* to interpretation and cannot be used to launch a transcendental argument against skepticism. Second, I argue that agreement between the agent and the interpreter is not sought on *all* sentences, but on a particular class of them, namely, the ones whose truth would be accepted by all competent speakers of the relevant communities.

**Montoya, José**. Bentham y los derechos humanos. *Telos (Spain)*, 5(1), 9-24, Je 96.

Bentham's critical statements on the *Declaration of Human Rights* of the French revolutionaries are supposed to be merely of historical value, as directed against a dated formulation. Against this, it is argued that the essential point of Bentham's argument is valid against any intuitivist interpretation of human rights (that is, against interpretations that take Human Rights as ultimate, absolute data) but are agreeable with an interpretation that takes Human Rights to be preferred lines of action that are normally conducive to the greatest general happiness.

**Montoya Saenz, José**. La filosofía política en el final de siglo. *Agora (Spain)*, 15(1), 7-29, 1996.

This article intends to present the main currents in political philosophy that remain alive after the decline and fall of the authoritarian regimes in Europe. After some brief considerations about the nature of political philosophy in the modern age, three theories (traditionalism, socialism and liberalism) are studied in their newest avatars. The author, while intending to be just to what is important in every theory, prones towards a soft version of classical liberalism.

**Moody, Todd C**. *Does God Exist?: A Dialogue*. Indianapolis, Hackett, 1996.

In this provocative new introductory dialogue among three fictional college companions, Moody maps the spectrum of philosophical arguments and counterarguments for the existence of God. Structuring their colloquial conversations along classical lines, he presents an accessible and concrete display of the concerns central to theist and atheist thinking, including consecutive discussions on the burden of proof, the first cause, a necessary being, the natural order, suffering, miracles, experience as knowledge, and rationality without proof. A short preface explains the purpose of the dialogue form, and an afterword suggests further readings of contemporary and classical sources. (publisher, edited)

**Moody-Adams, Michele M**. "The Social Construction and Reconstruction of Care" in *Sex, Preference, and Family: Essays on Law and Nature*, Nussbaum, Martha C (ed), 3-16. New York, Oxford Univ Pr, 1997.

**Moore, A W**. Solipsism and Subjectivity. *Euro J Phil*, 4(2), 220-234, Ag 96.

A formulation of solipsism is proposed, inspired by a Quinean combination of naturalism and empiricism. An objection to this position, based on Putnam's argument that we are not brains in a vat, is first outlined and then pitted against a series of counterobjections. This objection is eventually endorsed, but only at the price of showing that the proposed formulation of solipsism is not, after all, a satisfactory formulation. This leads to further speculation about the status of solipsism itself. Two of the possibilities considered are, firstly, that it is incoherent and, secondly, that it is inexpressible.

**Moore, A W**. The Underdetermination/Indeterminacy Distinction and the Analytic/Synthetic Distinction. *Erkenntnis*, 46(1), 5-32, Ja 97.

Two of W. V. Quine's most familiar doctrines are his endorsement of the distinction between underdetermination and indeterminacy and his rejection of the distinction between analytic and synthetic truths. The author argues that these two doctrines are incompatible. In terms wholly acceptable to Quine and based on the underdetermination/indeterminacy distinction, the author draws an exhaustive and exclusive distinction between two kinds of true sentences and then argues that this corresponds to the traditional analytic/synthetic distinction. In an appendix the author expands on one aspect of the underdetermination/indeterminacy distinction, as construed here, and discusses, in passing, some of Quine's more general views on truth.

**Moore, Andrew**. Commentary on "Psychological Courage". *Phil Psychiat Psych*, 4(1), 13-14, Mr 97.

**Moore, Andrew** and Crisp, Roger. Welfarism in Moral Theory. *Austl J Phil*, 74(4), 598-613, D 96.

We take welfarism in moral theory to be the claim that the well-being of individuals matters and is the only consideration that fundamentally matters, from a moral point of view. We argue that criticisms of welfarism due to G.E.

Moore, Donald Regan, Charles Taylor and Amartya Sen all fail. The final section of our paper is a critical survey of the problems which remain for welfarists in moral theory.

**Moore, Gregory H**. Hilbert and the Emergence of Modern Mathematical Logic. *Theoria (Spain)*, 12(28), 65-90, Ja 97.

Hilbert's unpublished 1917 lectures on logic, analyzed here, are the beginning of modern metalogic. In them he proved the consistency and postcompleteness (maximal consistency) of propositional logic—results traditionally credited to Bernays (1918) and Post (1921). These lectures contain the first formal treatment of first-order logic and form the core of Hilbert's famous 1928 book with Ackermann. What Berneys, influenced by those lectures, did in 1918 was to change the emphasis from the consistency and postcompleteness of a logic to its soundness and completeness: a sentence is provable if and only if valid. By 1917, strongly influenced by *PM*, Hilbert accepted the theory of types and logicism—a surprising shift. But by 1922 he abandoned the axiom of reducibility and then drew back from logicism, returning to his 1905 approach of trying to prove the consistency of number theory syntactically.

**Moore, Jay**. On the Relation between Behaviorism and Cognitive Psychology. *J Mind Behav*, 17(4), 345-368, Autumn 96.

Cognitive psychology and behaviorism are often held to be competing, mutually exclusive paradigms in contemporary psychology. The present paper argues that cognitive psychology is actually quite compatible with the most widely recognized version of behaviorism, here designated as mediational S-O-R neobehaviorism. The paper argues this case by suggesting that neobehaviorist theoretical terms have tended to be interpreted as "hypothetical constructs." Such an interpretation permits neobehaviorist theoretical terms to refer to a wide variety of nonbehavioral acts, states, mechanisms, and processes, with extensive "surplus meaning." Consequently, an interpretation of neobehaviorist theoretical terms as hypothetical constructs can readily accommodate the kind of mental entities postulated by cognitive psychology.

**Moore, Margaret**. On Reasonableness. *J Applied Phil*, 13(2), 167-178, 1996.

This essay argues that the concept of 'reasonableness' plays an important role in Scanlon's, Rawls's, and Barry's theories of justice (or morality). The relationship between moral motivation and reasonableness is critically analysed. Specifically, the paper questions whether it is plausible to impute to the agents of construction the desire 'to justify our actions to others on impartial terms'. It also argues that most of the work is done by the assumption that people are reasonable rather than by the contractarian formulation. Indeed, the paper argues, the argument could proceed entirely by making explicit and arguing for the moral assumptions embedded in the concept of reasonableness.

**Moore, Mick** and Robinson, Mark. Can Foreign Aid Be Used to Promote Good Government in Developing Countries?. *Ethics Int Affairs*, 8, 142-158, 1994.

**Moore, Ronald**. Aesthetic Case Studies and Discipline-Based Art Education. *J Aes Educ*, 27(3), 51-62, Fall 93.

**Moore, Ronald**. The Nightmare Science and Its Daytime Uses. *J Aes Educ*, 30(4), 5-20, Wint 96.

**Moortgat, Michael**. Multimodal Linguistic Inference. *J Log Lang Info*, 5(3-4), 349-385, O 96.

In this paper we compare grammatical inference in the context of *simple* and of *mixed* Lambek systems. Simple Lambek systems are obtained by taking the logic of residuation for a family of multiplicative connectives /, "dot", \, together with a package of structural postulates characterizing the resource management properties of the "dot" connective. Different choices for Associativity and Commutativity yield the familiar logics *NL, L, NLP, LP*. Semantically, a simple Lambek system is a unimodal logic: the connectives get a Kripke style interpretation in terms of a single ternary accessibility relation modelling the notion of linguistic composition for each individual system. The simple systems each have their virtues in linguistic analysis. But none of them in isolation provides a basis for a full theory of grammar. In the second part of the paper, we consider two types of *mixed* Lambek systems. (edited)

**Mora, José Luis**. Filosofía española en el bachillerato?. *Dialogo Filosof*, 13(1), 73-80, Ja-Ap.

¿Qué significa hoy plantearnos la presencia de la filosofía española en el bachillerato? ¿Qué sentido tiene hacerse esta pregunta? ¿Por qué es necesario hacérsela? La respuesta a estas cuestiones es muy importante a la hora de buscar el sentido de la presencia o ausencia de la filosofía en nuestro bachillerato.

**Morais, Carlos Bizarro**. A Institucionalizaçao da Arte e o Esvaziamento da *Aisthesis*: Interpretaçao do Ponto de Vista de Mikel Dufrenne. *Rev Port Filosof*, 52(1-4), 555-577, Ja-D 96.

Taking M. Dufrenne's texts as a starting point, this paper tries to identify the procedures by which art has achieved its status as a top institution within culture, raising questions concerning its consequences within the sphere of a theory of aesthetic experience. Presupposing the aesthetic experience as an original and integrative experience of the human subject in the world, the author shows how the dominant culture has a tendency to attenuate and to neutralise the power resulting from art and the aesthetic experience; the more art gains in institutional perceptibility, the more the dominant culture succeeds in its aim. (edited)

**Morales, Maria H**. *Perfect Equality: John Stuart Mill on Well-Constituted Communities*. Lanham, Rowman & Littlefield, 1996.

Maria Morales demonstrates that Mill was fundamentally concerned with how the exercise of unjust or arbitrary power by some individuals over others sabotages the possibility of human well-being and social improvement. Mill therefore believed that "perfect equality"—more than liberty—was the foundation of democracy and that democracy was a moral ideal for the organization of human life in all of its dimensions. By reinterpreting Mill, Morales also challenges twentieth-century views of liberalism, and addresses contemporary communitarian and feminist criticisms of liberalism. She argues that, because the progressiveness of Mill's moral and political ideals has been obscured, so has an important strand of the liberal tradition. Liberalism need not be based on an abstract, atomistic, individualistic model of social life. *Perfect Equality* is clearly and elegantly written, making it an excellent text for students as well as scholars of Mill, women's studies, political theory, the history of feminism, and social and political philosophy. (publisher,edited)

**Morales Manzur, Juan Carlos**. The Centrifugal Forces of Latin American Integration. *Fronesis*, 3(1), 97-111, Ap 96.

This study analyzes and constrasts associating and disassociating factors of the Latin American integration process under a historical-political and economic perspective, where the tendencies to the regionalization that have prevailed until the present economical dynamization and the advances of the integrationist process can be identified. By virtue of this, the colonial past, the political, ideological and economical structural disarticulation during the XIXth century, the intention to consolidate integrationist groups during this century and the present and future perspectives that orient the Latin American integrationism were taken as a reference point. (edited)

**Morales Moya, Antonio**. "Vieja y Nueva Política: La Circunstancia Histórica" in *Política y Sociedad en José Ortega y Gasset: En Torno a "Vieja y Nueva Política"*, Lopez de la Vieja, Maria Teresa (ed), 69-100. Barcelona, Anthropos, 1997.

**Moran, Dermot** (trans) and Taminiaux, Jacques. *Bios politikos* and *bios theoretikos* in the Phenomenology of Hannah Arendt. *Int J Phil Stud*, 4(2), 215-232, S 96.

Hannah Arendt frequently referred to herself as a phenomenologist in that she wished to reveal how *action*, in the Greek sense of *praxis*, engenders a public space of appearances or of phenomenality. The life of the Greek city-state, of the *polis*, was made possible through this activity, this *bios politikos*. However, beginning with Plato and continuing right down to Hegel and Heidegger, there has been a sustained attempt to cover up and conceal the specific phenomenality of the *bios politikos* in favour of the *bio theoretikos*, involving the substitution of *poiesis* and *theoria* for the life of *praxis*. At the roots of this concealment of the active life is a misunderstanding of the true nature of the theoretical and its highest form, namely, thinking.

**Moran, Richard**. Self-Knowledge: Discovery, Resolution, and Undoing. *Euro J Phil*, 5(2), 141-161, Ag 97.

**Morán y Castellanos, Jorge**. "Los momentos metodológicos en Aristóteles" in *Ensayos Aristotélicos*, Rivera, José Luis (ed), 61-95. Mexico, Univ Panamericana, 1996.

After an overview of some methodological reflections excerpted from different works, it cannot be said that the "Aristotelian method" is either unique or unidimensional. Instead, it is constituted by many different interlinked attitudes which, as a whole, could be called "pathways to reality".

**Morán y Castellanos, Jorge**. Los primeros principios; interpretación de Polo de Aristóteles. *Anu Filosof*, 29(2), 787-803, 1996.

The author studies the theory of "first principles" in Leonardo Polo's philosophy (in the book *El conocimiento habitual de los primeros principios*) and Aristotle's thought. He criticizes Polo's theory of first principles in using Aristotelian concepts from *Metafísica*, III, IV and IX. (edited)

**Moravcsik, Julius M**. The Nature of Ethical Theorizing in the *Eudemian Ethics*. *Topoi*, 15(1), 81-88, Mr 96.

**Morawski, Stefan**. "Theses on the 20th Century Crisis of Art and Culture" in *Epistemology and History*, Zeidler-Janiszewska, Anna (ed), 451-467. Amsterdam, Rodopi, 1996.

This essay written in 1988 takes the problem of the modern artist in his (her) relation to the social world which underwent criticisms from many sides at least from Spengler on. The author explains what is to be understood by culture versus civilisation, and by the concept of crisis. Four main attitudes of the artist are distinguished, namely: bearing witness to the crisis, contesting the *status quo*, safeguarding art's sovereignty and dignity by the continuation of its heritage, or resisting the ways of things around by bidding farewell to artistic practice in the shape established for centuries. These attitudes are confronted with the philosophic conceptions of the interwar period and the sociological ideas after World War II from the 50s to the 70s. (edited)

**More, Ellen S**. Empathy as a Hermeneutic Practice. *Theor Med*, 17(3), 243-254, S 96.

This essay will argue for the centrality of empathy in the doctor-patient relationship—as a core of ethically sound, responsible therapeutics. By "empathy," I intend an explicitly hermeneutic practice, informed by a reflexive understanding of patient and self. After providing an overview of the history of the concept of empathy in clinical medicine, I discuss current definitions and the use of Balint groups in residency training as a way to develop empathic competence in novice physicians.

**Morehead Dworkin, Terry** and Near, Janet P. A Better Statutory Approach to Whistle-Blowing. *Bus Ethics Quart*, 7(1), 1-16, Ja 97.

Statutory approaches toward whistle-blowing currently appear to be based on the assumption that most observers of wrongdoing will report it unless deterred from doing so by fear of retaliation. Yet our review of research from studies of whistle-blowing behavior suggests that this assumption is unwarranted. We propose that an alternative legislative approach would prove more successful in encouraging valid whistle-blowing and describe a model for such legislation that would increase self-monitoring of ethical behavior by organizations, with obvious benefits to society at large. (edited)

**Moreira, Isabel**. Augustine's Three Visions and Three Heavens in Some Early Medieval Florilegia. *Vivarium*, 34(1), 1-14, My 96.

In examining the contribution of florilegial literature to our understanding of the early medieval approach to patristic texts, this article emphasizes the need to move beyond a focus on the "vertical" relationship between pseudonymous text and original source text and towards a "horizontal" investigation of themes across a wide spectrum of medieval *florilegia*. Focusing on the transmission of Augustine's three visions theme, the paper examines how Augustine's famous epistemological formulation was used, transformed and given new meanings and contexts in early medieval Insular and Continental *florilegia*. The date and authorship of the important pseudo-Augustinian "*Dialogus quaestionum LXV*" is also discussed.

**Moreland, J P**. A Critique of Campbell's Refurbished Nominalism. *S J Phil*, 35(2), 225-246, Sum 97.

Keith Campbell is the leading exponent of nominalism, the view that properties exist and are abstract particulars called tropes. Campbell's nominalism has evolved from an earlier view to his most recent position. I sketch out his earlier view, show what criticisms cause him to abandon it in favor of his refurbished nominalism, and go on to argue that his current position is less acceptable than the view he has abandoned. Among other things, I argue that the central problematic feature of trope nominalism is the simplicity of a basic trope and not the role of space-time in a trope's analysis.

**Morelli, Elizabeth A** (ed) and Morelli, Mark (ed). *The Lonergan Reader*. Toronto, Univ of Toronto Pr, 1997.

*The Lonergan Reader* includes an abridgment of Lonergan's massive foundational work, *Insight*, and extensive selections from his last major work, *Method in Theology*. In addition, the collection contains the complete texts of several articles that expanded and transformed his original positions, as well as a broad range of shorter selections. The volume not only highlights Lonergan's essential philosophical writings, but also reveals the larger cultural and theological dimensions of his work. (edited)

**Morelli, Mark** (ed) and Morelli, Elizabeth A (ed). *The Lonergan Reader*. Toronto, Univ of Toronto Pr, 1997.

*The Lonergan Reader* includes an abridgment of Lonergan's massive foundational work, *Insight*, and extensive selections from his last major work, *Method in Theology*. In addition, the collection contains the complete texts of several articles that expanded and transformed his original positions, as well as a broad range of shorter selections. The volume not only highlights Lonergan's essential philosophical writings, but also reveals the larger cultural and theological dimensions of his work. (edited)

**Moreno, Jonathan D**. Recapturing Justice in the Managed Care Era. *Cambridge Quart Healthcare Ethics*, 5(4), 493-499, Fall 96.

**Moreno, Jonathan D**. The Only Feasible Means: The Pentagon's Ambivalent Relationship with the Nuremberg Code. *Hastings Center Rep*, 26(5), 11-19, S-O 96.

In the early 1950s the U.S. Department of Defense promulgated a policy governing human experimentation based on the Nuremberg Code. Yet the policymaking process focused on the abstract issue of whether human experiments should go forward at all, ignoring the reality of human subjects research already under way and leaving unanswered many ethical questions. newly released documents tell the story of the Pentagon policy.

**Moreno, Luis Fernández**. Truth in Pure Semantics: A Reply to Putnam. *Sorites*, 15-23, Je 97.

In his book *Representation and Reality* Hilary Putnam raises a number of objections against the semantical conception of truth. According to Putnam two particularly undesirable consequences of the semantical conception of truth are that the equivalences of the form (T) are logically necessary and that the truth of a sentence does not depend on its meaning. In this paper I examine these two objections of Putnam with respect to Carnap's formulation of the semantical conception of truth.

**Moreno Chumillas, Evelio**. Las Utopías de la Mediocridad. *Agora (Spain)*, 14(2), 99-111, 1995.

**Morenz, Barry** and Sales, Bruce. Complexity of Ethical Decision Making in Psychiatry. *Ethics Behavior*, 7(1), 1-14, 1997.

Psychiatric residents and psychiatrists have little difficulty in making judgments about a clinical course of action to take with patients. However, making ethical clinical decisions is more challenging, because psychiatric residents are usually provided little formal training in ethics. Further, many ethical dilemmas are complex, requiring knowledge of the psychiatric profession's ethics code, moral principles, law and practice standards and of how they should be weighed in the decision-making process. The purpose of this article is to demonstrate this complexity in regard to the identification of potential ethical dilemmas, understanding the issues that these dilemmas raise and formulating potential solutions to them. Two common but important areas of treatment in which ethical dilemmas arise (informed consent and competence of care) are used as examples for our presentation. The article demonstrates that to successfully engage in ethical analysis in psychiatry is impossible without substantial formal training in the process.

**Moreso, José Juan** and Navarro, Pablo E. Applicability and Effectiveness of Legal Norms. *Law Phil*, 16(2), 201-219, 97.

We analyse the relationship between applicability and effectiveness of legal norms from a philosophical perspective. In particular, we distinguish between two concepts of applicability. The external applicability of norms refers to

Moreso, José Juan 798 AUTHOR INDEX

institutional duties; a norm N is externally applicable if and only if a judge is legally obliged to apply N to some case c. Internal applicability refers instead to the sphere of validity of legal norms. A norm N is internally applicable to actions regulated by its sphere of validity. We also explore the consequences of a thesis which maintain that applicability restricts the concept of effectiveness, so that only applicable norms can be considered effective. Our analysis illustrates that a proper reconstruction of the concept of applicability is of great importance not only for understanding the concept of effectiveness but also for providing insight into the nature of law.

**Moreso, José Juan** and Navarro, Pablo E. The Dynamics of Legal Positivism: Some Remarks on Shiner's *Norm and Nature*. *Ratio Juris*, 10(3), 288-299, S 97.

In a recently published book, Roger Shiner shows that understanding the fundamental discrepancies between different legal theories is important for a better understanding of law itself. He argues that one of the most important tasks of legal philosophers is to take into account the dynamics or conceptual movements generated by positivism and antipositivism. Our paper intends to show that Shiner's analysis can be developed and modified when other relevant elements are introduced into the universe of discourse. We emphasize the importance of a positivistic conception of legal science. (edited)

**Moretti, Anna M**. Advocating for the Dying: The View of Family and Friends. *Bioethics Forum*, 13(2), 27-31, Sum 97.

**Moretto, Antonio**. "Sul problema della considerazione matematica dell'infinito e del continuo in Aristotele e Hegel" in *Hegel e Aristotele*, Ferrarin, A, 51-101. Cagliari, Edizioni AV, 1997.

Antonio Moretto's essay goes through the mathematical content of Aristotles thought in the *Physics* on the concept of infinite and continuous. In the same way it deals with the mathematical importance of same subject in Hegel's *Science of logic* and *Encyclopaedia*. The essay points out the importance of the Aristotelian thought for the philosophy of mathematics, where the themes of convergence and divergence of series are dealt with and the concept of continuous is linked to that of infinitesimal functions. It also emphasizes the importance of Hegel's thought, which revalues the concept of actual infinite taking into account some new points of view of modern mathematics.

**Moretto, Giovanni**. "Etica e storia in Schleiermacher" in *Lo Storicismo e la Sua Storia: Temi, Problemi, Prospettive*, Cacciatore, Giuseppe (ed), 172-181. Milano, Guerini, 1997.

**Moretto, Giovanni**. Schleiermacher: edizione critica e bibliografia. *G Metaf*, 19(1), 167-181, Ja-Ap 97.

**Morgan, Kathryn Pauly**. "Gender Rites and Rights: The Biopolitics of Beauty and Fertility" in *Philosophical Perspectives on Bioethics*, Sumner, L W (ed), 210-243. Toronto, Univ of Toronto Pr, 1996.

Having set out moral questions to guide the search for a framework to assess elective cosmetic surgery decisions, the author first examines a *rights framework*. Having examined five central rights-maxims the author concludes that this framework provides little illumination and serves to camouflage systematically oppressive practices and political contexts within which individual decisions are made. She argues that a critical paradigm shift is needed in the direction of a more Foucauldian framework of bioethical politics involving a critical examination of the role of technology, body-artifacts, epistemic experts, and the phenomenological experience of coerced voluntarism. She concludes by drawing analogies between the technologies of cosmetic surgery, genetic engineering, and reproduction, highlighting three paradoxes of choice which arise.

**Morgan, Kathryn Pauly**. "Humpty Dumpty An Ovular Model of Resistance to Modernist Recidivism" in *Philosophy of Education (1996)*, Margonis, Frank (ed), 124-129. Urbana, Phil Education Soc, 1997.

This is a critical engagement with Nick Burbules's views regarding the methodological, pedagogical, and political value of *difference theory*. The author agrees that *difference theory* reveals the pseudonaturalness of categories, renders privilege and oppression visible in the construction of 'the same' and 'the different', and demonstrates that differences need to be critically re-examined not merely tolerated or simplistically celebrated. The author disagrees with Burbules in three areas: 1) whether *difference theory* entails a commitment to social change, 2) whether emphasizing difference carries the same dangerous political consequences as emphasizing sameness, and 3) Burbules's model of multiculturalism. The author maintains that by privileging sameness, Burbules is really a 'modernist recidivist'. The article concludes with a conceptual/metaphorical exploration of Humpty Dumpty symbolizing, by nature, the coalescences, resemblances, positionings, blendings, and emergences of a multipositional subject.

**Morgan, Lynn M**. Fetal Relationality in Feminist Philosophy: An Anthropological Critique. *Hypatia*, 11(3), 47-70, Sum 96.

This essay critiques feminist treatments of maternal-fetal "relationality" that unwittingly replicate features of Western individualism (for example, the Cartesian division between the asocial body and the social-cognitive person, or the conflation of social and biological birth). I argue for a more reflexive perspective on relationality that would acknowledge how we produce persons through our actions and rhetoric. Personhood and relationality can be better analyzed as dynamic, negotiated qualities realized through social practice.

**Morgan, Michael L** (ed) and Fackenheim, Emil L. *Jewish Philosophers and Jewish Philosophy*. Bloomington, Indiana Univ Pr, 1996.

If, in content and in method, philosophy and religion conflict, can there be a Jewish philosophy? What makes a Jewish thinker a philosopher? Emil L. Fackenheim confronts these questions in a series of essays on the great Jewish thinkers from Maimonides through Hermann Cohen, Martin Buber, Franz Rosenzweig, and Leo Strauss. Fackenheim also contemplates the task of Jewish philosophy after the Holocaust. While providing access to key Jewish thinkers of the past, this volume highlights the exciting achievements of one of today's most creative and most important Jewish philosophers. (publisher, edited)

**Morgan, Paul**. "Reconceiving the Foundations of Education: An Ecological Model" in *Philosophy of Education (1996)*, Margonis, Frank (ed), 294-302. Urbana, Phil Education Soc, 1997.

**Morgan, Vance G**. An Aspect of Love: Descartes on Friendship. *Amer Cath Phil Quart*, 71(1), 83-100, Wint 97.

This essay focuses on Descartes's analysis of friendship, an aspect of the passion of love that he describes as "a sacred thing" and "the chief good of life". Descartes's treatment of friendship provides a clear example of his methodical attempts to understand and utilize the passions, always recognizing their inherent power and capacity to frustrate, deceive and override reason. Properly identified and understood, the passion underlying friendship, the passion of love, is the most beneficial passion in social and practical contexts; improperly identified and understood, it is a source of confusion, irrationality and ultimate frustration. Understanding friendship and love is not only fundamentally important to understanding human relationships on the individual level, but, Descartes will argue, is crucial to understanding the proper foundations of human communities and societies at large.

**Morgenstern, Mira**. *Rousseau and the Politics of Ambiguity: Self, Culture, and Society*. University Park, Pennsylvania Univ Pr, 1996.

Ultimately, what makes Rousseau worth reading today, argues Morgenstern, is his ability to illuminate critical weaknesses in the dualisms of liberal political theory and his pointing out, if only by implication, alternative ways of reaching the full measure of our individual and communal humanity. In honoring the traditional liberal emphasis on individual liberty and self-development, Rousseau's meditations on the proper aim of political life are especially helpful to those today who seek ways to expand liberalism's promise of freedom and authenticity, while not losing sight of the common threads of meaning and community that continue to bind us together. (publisher, edited)

**Mori, Gianluca**. Pierre Bayle, the Rights of the Conscience, the "Remedy" of Toleration. *Ratio Juris*, 10(1), 45-60, Mr 97.

Pierre Bayle (1647-1706) is often considered one of the staunchest defenders of toleration, especially in the domain of religion. His *Commentaire philosophique* published in 1686, one year after the revocation of the Edict of Nantes, argued for a broad idea of toleration, to be extended with no exceptions to all sects and religions. However, his thought can hardly be reduced to an exaltation of the "rights of the conscience," for he realized very soon that such an exaltation risks bringing forth religious fanaticism, which in turn is the cause of religious wars and acts of violence. Toleration, in these conditions, is only a political remedy for the sickness of the human mind.

**Mori, Maurizio**. Che cosa ha veramente detto il Comitato Nazionale per la Bioetica sull'individualità dell'embrione?. *Iride*, 9(19), 563-570, S-D 96.

**Morissette, Yves**. De la volonté générale et des lois. *Philosopher*, 18, 97-104, 1995.

**Morito, Bruce**. Aboriginal Right: A Conciliatory Concept. *J Applied Phil*, 13(2), 123-139, 1996.

The confusion that persists over Aboriginal claim in North America calls for close examination. The paper begins by sorting out various versions of 'Aboriginal right' and some of the main factors that govern its use. Confusion is analysed as the result of conflating different frames of reference which determine different sets of expectations by Aboriginal and government representatives. To appreciate the significance of this conflation, it is helpful if not necessary to view the move to use the concept 'Aboriginal right' as a strategic rather than a legally substantive one. Understanding the move in this way helps to explain why it is that definitions remain elusive. The effect of using the concept has indeed been to enable Aboriginals finally and effectively to table their claim. However, the strategy has its cost. Using the language of the courts places Aboriginal negotiators at a disadvantage, since that language is ineluctably tied to European social and legal sensibilities that militate against understanding Aboriginal claim. If in the end, we understand that the move to use the language of the courts has been conciliatory, we can better recognise the nature of Aboriginal claim. We can begin to understand that it involves a complex web of responsibilities and commitments, most of which have either been forgotten or perverted to suit government agendas. We can begin to see that it has to do with restoring a relationship of mutual respect and protection.

**Moros Claramunt, Enrique R**. La demostración de la existencia de Dios a partir de la libertad. *Anu Filosof*, 29(2), 805-814, 1996.

In this paper I analyse an argument for God's existence from the liberty proposed by Prof. Polo. I think that an examination of his transcendental anthropology will yield some important insights concerning person and liberty. I argue this argument is sound and illuminating our concept of God.

**Morreau, Michael**. Fainthearted Conditionals. *J Phil*, 94(4), 187-211, Ap 97.

Heat a dry piece of wood thoroughly and you can expect it to burn. What sets this expectation apart from other, unreasonable ones? That the wood is combustible guarantees the truth of: If it is heated thoroughly, then provided conditions are suitable the wood will burn. But this sentence does not entail that the wood will burn, given only that it is thoroughly heated, so it appears that *entailment* does not set this reasonable expectation apart. This article is about conditional sentences with modifiers including 'normally', 'other things being equal' and 'provided conditions are suitable'. To characterize reasonable expectations it introduces *allowed arguments*, which lead beyond the logical consequences of premises.

AUTHOR INDEX 799 Mortensen, Preben

**Morreim, E Haavi**. Bioethics, Expertise, and the Courts: An Overview and an Argument for Inevitability. *J Med Phil*, 22(4), 291-295, Ag 97.

**Morris, Katherine J**. Ambiguity and Bad Faith. *Amer Cath Phil Quart*, 70(4), 467-484, Autumn 96.

Against McCulloch, who claims that the ambiguity central to Sartrean bad faith is a verbal ambiguity between two senses of the verb 'to be', I argue that the central ambiguity is 'existential'. This 'existential ambiguity', expressed by Sartre as the claim that human reality "is what it is not and is not what it is", is exhibited as the condition for the possibility of self-deception. An analogy between existential ambiguity and the ambiguity of certain pictures elucidates Sartre's claim that evidence in the realm of human reality is 'nonpersuasive' and clarifies the role which this plays in Sartre's positive account of bad faith.

**Morris, Katherine J** and Baker, Gordon. *Descartes' Dualism*. New York, Routledge, 1996.

The position of Cartesian dualism has come to be accepted as a view of the mind as an inner world of private 'objects' and of the body as an insentient machine; according to the authors, Descartes did not subscribe to this doctrine. Indeed, he could not have done since, Baker and Morris argue, such a view is inconsistent with the logical, scientific, theological and metaphysical frameworks of his thinking. The book has two central aims: the first is to argue for a radically different interpretation of Descartes's doctrine. The second aim is to clarify the philosophical interest of looking at Descartes's actual concept of a person. This is meant to shake complacency about the presuppositions underlying current investigations in areas as diverse as logic, cognitive science and animal rights. (publisher, edited)

**Morris, Katherine J** and Baker, Gordon. Descartes's Dualism?. *Phil Books*, 38(3), 157-169, Jl 97.

Nadler gives an informative, lucid and balanced account of our book, and raises some challenging objections. However, he focuses exclusively on our 'first-order' aim of presenting an alternative to the standard Anglo-American interpretation of Descartes's dualism, at the expense of our 'second-order' aim of showing the *philosophical* interest of such historical explorations. His principal criticisms centre on our account of mind-body interaction; these rest, we argue, on the challengeable axiom that for Descartes, 'the mind alone is active'; on misunderstandings of Descartes's notions of intelligibility and resemblance; and on misrepresentations of the background of scholastic doctrines of causation.

**Morris, Michael H** and Marks, Amy S and Allen, Jeffrey A. Modeling Ethical Attitudes and Behaviors under Conditions of Environmental Turbulence: The Case of South Africa. *J Bus Ethics*, 15(10), 1119-1130, O 96.

This study explores the impact of environmental turbulence on relationships between personal and organizational characteristics, personal values, ethical perceptions, and behavioral intentions. A causal model is tested using data obtained from a national sample of marketing research professionals in South Africa. The findings suggest turbulent conditions lead professionals to report stronger values and ethical norms, but less ethical behavioral intentions. Implications are drawn for organizations confronting growing turbulence in their external environments. A number of suggestions are made for ongoing research.

**Morris, Nancy A**. The Status of the *Dimensiones Interminatae* in the Thomasian Principle of Individuation. *Aquinas*, 39(2), 321-338, My-Ag 96.

**Morris, Phyllis Sutton**. Self-Creating Selves: Sartre and Foucault. *Amer Cath Phil Quart*, 70(4), 537-549, Autumn 96.

Sartre's claim that individuals create themselves is philosophically puzzling, for it would seem that the self must preexist itself in order to form the self. Several different senses of "self" within Sartre's early writings are distinguished to resolve the ensuing puzzles. Foucault's late work takes self-creation of the subject as a theme, building on techniques he had identified in earlier works as socially imposed to produce "docile bodies." These two approaches are seen as working at different levels of self-creativity.

**Morris, R C**. Intentions, Self-Monitoring and Abnormal Experiences. *Phil Psych*, 10(1), 77-83, Mr 97.

Conscious awareness of intentionality is considered to be a product of specialized monitoring processes which distinguish intentional, goal-directed actions from unintentional, passive/reactive actions. When goals are not met or unfavorable conditions arise, this ability to distinguish intentional and unintentional enables us to direct adaptive efforts towards either changing plans and goals or towards altering the environment. The formulation is discussed in relation to monitoring theories of consciousness and the concept of 'locus of control', and is developed to explain several common psychological disorders in terms of dysfunctional monitoring of intentions. It is suggested that it could provide a theoretical basis for psychological treatment methods.

**Morris, Robert**. Professional Rules. *Crit Inquiry*, 23(2), 298-322, Wint 97.

**Morris, Ronald**. Myths of Sexuality Education. *J Moral Educ*, 26(3), 353-361, S 97.

This paper suggests that sexuality education needs to take into account the myths by which teachers educate and students learn. Here myth is understood as a narrative, paradigm or vision. The paper does not argue against myth. Rather, it argues that myth or narrative provides a much needed depth dimension to sexuality education. It does argue, however, that the existing myths serve sexuality education poorly. The final section of the paper proposes three narratives which provide rich alternatives to the dominant myth.

**Morris, Stephen**. Risk, Uncertainty and Hidden Information. *Theor Decis*, 42(3), 235-269, My 97.

People are less willing to accept bets about an event when they do not know the true probability of that event. Such "uncertainty aversion" has been used to explain certain economic phenomena. This paper considers how far standard private information explanations (with strategic decisions to accept bets) can go in explaining phenomena attributed to uncertainty aversion. This paper shows that if two individuals have different prior beliefs about some event, and two-sided private information, then each individual's willingness to bet will exhibit a bid-ask-spread property. Each individual is prepared to bet for the event, at sufficiently favorable odds, and against, at sufficiently favorable odds, but there is an intermediate range of odds where each individual is not prepared to bet either way. This is only true if signals are distributed continuously and sufficiently smoothly. It is *not* true, for example, in a finite signal model.

**Morris, Stephen** and Shin, Hyun Song. Approximate Common Knowledge and Co-Ordination: Recent Lessons from Game Theory. *J Log Lang Info*, 6(2), 171-190, Ap 97.

The importance of the notion of common knowledge in sustaining cooperative outcomes in strategic situations is well appreciated. However, the systematic analysis of the extent to which small departures from common knowledge affect equilibrium in games has only recently been attempted. We review the main themes in this literature, in particular, the notion of common *p*-belief. We outline both the analytical issues raised and the potential applicability of such ideas to game theory, computer science and the philosophy of language.

**Morris, William E**. The Hume Literature, 1995. *Hume Stud*, 22(2), 387-400, N 96.

A comprehensive bibliography of the Hume literature from 1995, with additions and corrections to my previous bibliographies (1986-1993, *Hume Studies*, November 1994, and 1994, *Hume Studies*, November 1995). This bibliography also includes a listing of relevant doctoral dissertations, 1986-1995. It does *not* include articles and reviews published in *Hume Studies*, which are now indexed in the November issue of each volume beginning with November 1993. Additions and corrections to this bibliography are encouraged.

**Morrison, Margaret**. Whewell on the Ultimate Problem of Philosophy. *Stud Hist Phil Sci*, 28(3), 417-437, S 97.

**Morrison II, Roy D**. "Self-Transformation in American Blacks: The Harlem Renaissance and Black Theology" in *Existence in Black: An Anthology of Black Existential Philosophy*, Gordon, Lewis R (ed), 37-47. New York, Routledge, 1997.

**Morriss, Peter**. Blurred Boundaries. *Inquiry*, 40(3), 259-290, S 97.

Since 1990 it has been illegal in Britain to create human/animal hybrids. But what is the objection to hybrids? A proposal based on a fear of blurring conceptual boundaries is offered; this fear also seems to underlie several other of our deep-seated taboos, such as incest and bestiality, which are often explained in other, quite inappropriate, ways. The new law shows that the boundary between the human and the animal is still thought of as crucial and untransgressible in modern Britain, yet it is not clear why; the world-views that in the past justified protecting this particular boundary are usually thought of as having been abandoned centuries ago. Thus it would seem that within our culture there are firmly entrenched taboos that are not readily justifiable from within that culture; the taboo against blurring the human/animal boundary is one such. This raises the question whether this human/animal boundary is one we should still want to protect in this way.

**Morrissey, John M** and Stadler, Holly A and Tucker, Joycelyn E. Nurses' Perspectives of Hospital Ethics Committees. *Bioethics Forum*, 10(4), 61-65, Fall 94.

The Midwest Bioethics Center (MBC) commissioned a survey of nurses' attitudes and needs regarding Hospital Ethics Committees (HECs) to guide its Ethics Committee Consortium. The survey examined three areas related to nurse utilization of and participation on HECs: 1) perception of HEC role and function; 2) perception of HEC case consultation function; 3) nurses' ethics training and continuing education. Important findings include nurses' reported lack of knowledge regarding HEC policies; a perception that their training in clinical ethics was inadequate; and a strong indication that HECs should be accessible to a wide range of health care professionals.

**Morselli, Graziella**. "Dobbiamo ancora pensare il tempo come finito?" in *Il Concetto di Tempo: Atti del XXXII Congresso Nazionale della Società Filosofica Italiana,* Casertano, Giovanni (ed), 339-344. Napoli, Loffredo, 1997.

**Mortensen, Chris**. The Leibniz Continuity Condition, Inconsistency and Quantum Dynamics. *J Phil Log*, 26(4), 377-389, Ag 97.

A principle of continuity due to Leibniz has recently been revived by Graham Priest in arguing for an inconsistent account of motion. This paper argues that the *Leibniz continuity condition* has a reasonable interpretation in a different, though still inconsistent, class of dynamical systems. The account is then applied to the quantum mechanical description of the hydrogen atom.

**Mortensen, Preben**. *Art in the Social Order: The Making of the Modern Conception of Art*. Albany, SUNY Pr, 1997.

For the first time, a historical examination of the origin of our ideas of art are related to questions in contemporary art theory. Mortensen shows that our conception of art emerged in the eighteenth century as part of new ideas of edification and of the presentation of the self. He examines the complex social and cultural context in which our ideas of art emerge in the eighteenth century. In a context of social, political, and cultural changes, knowledge about art and the display of taste come to indicate social distinctions and replace older notions of birth and rank. Mortensen connects these historical developments to contemporary discussions about the relationship between high art and popular art. (publisher,edited)

**Morton, Adam**. Can Edgington Gibbard Counterfactuals?. *Mind*, 106(421), 101-105, Ja 97.

I state objections to Edgington's claim ("On Conditionals' Mind," 1995) that counterfactual conditionals often lack truth values. I argue that her application of Giffard's examples of indicative conditionals without truth values ignores the fact that conditional excluded middle fails for counterfactuals.

**Morton, Adam**. Hypercomparatives. *Synthese*, 111(1), 97-114, Ap 97.

In natural language we rarely use relation-words with more than three argument places. This paper studies one systematic device, rooted in natural language, by which relations of greater adicity can be expressed. It is based on a higher-order relation between 1-place, 2-place, and 4-place relations (and so on) of which the relation between the positive and comparative degrees of predicate is a special case. Two formal languages are presented in this connection, one of which represents the language of communication and the other the contextual information against which the first language is interpreted. A semantical theory is described, which treats the two languages in an interdependent way. Logical consequence is noncompact. Connections with issues about vagueness are made.

**Morujao, Alexandre Fradique**. A Dialéctica da Acçao em L'Action (1893) de Maurice Blondel. *Rev Port Filosof*, 52(1-4), 579-588, Ja-D 96.

**Moscato, Alberto**. Metafisica e "transcendentali". *G Metaf*, 18(1-2), 157-193, Ja-Ag 96.

**Moscovici, Claudia**. *From Sex Objects to Sexual Subjects*. New York, Routledge, 1996.

Investigates various historical formulations of subjects and subjectivity as expressed in the works of Rousseau, Diderot and Kant in order to discuss several contemporary feminist and philosophical critiques of these theories. By tracing the continuities and ruptures between these eighteenth-century philosophical doctrines and the modern writings of Michel Foucault, Judith Butler, Luce Irigaray and others, Moscovici is able to trace the development of certain central debates that organize both current scholarly work and contemporary social life. (publisher)

**Moseley, Kathryn L** and Truesdell, Sandra. A Noncompliant Patient?. *J Clin Ethics*, 8(2), 176-177, Sum 97.

**Moser, Anton**. *Principia Ecologica* Eco-Principles as a Conceptual Framework for a New Ethics in Science and Technology. *Sci Eng Ethics*, 1(3), 241-260, Jl 95.

As a result of contemporary environmental problems, scientists are focusing their interests on developing a greater understanding of nature. Described in this paper is a view of life and the environment as a case of complex systems analysis; this analysis results in a series of general principles which are manifested in life and bioprocesses. These 'eco-principles' will be very useful as guidelines for the eco-restructuring of technology as well as the reorientation of human activities towards a sustainable lifestyle which includes the economy, society, management of industry, the university and even the church. The goal is a society which will be in harmony with the laws of nature ('*Principia Ecologica*').

**Moser, Edward**. Nihilism and the Continuing Crisis of Reason. *Int Stud Phil*, 29(1), 91-97, 1997.

One can read the *Crisis of European Sciences and Transcendental Phenomenology* as Husserl's attempt to confront the nihilism of the age. In contrast to Nietzsche's nihilistic account of nihilism, Husserl accepts the responsibility of seeking a rational account of nihilism. Reflecting on the pretheoretical world of everyday life can provide adequate reasons for rejecting nihilism.

**Moser, Paul K**. New Books on Philosophy of Religion. *Int J Phil Stud*, 5(1), 106-110, Mr 97.

This is a review of three books: J.L. Schellenberg, *Divine Hiddenness and Human Reason* (Cornell University Press, 1993); W.J. Wainwright, *Reason and the Heart* (Cornell University Press, 1995); T.D. Senor, ed., *The Rationality of Belief and the Plurality of Faith* (Cornell University Press, 1995). Schellenberg's argument for atheism receives most of the attention; his argument stems from the question of why a benevolent God would allow some rational people not to believe that he exists. I contend that Schellenberg's argument fails to give due attention to a distinctly Hebraic conception of knowing God.

**Moser, Paul K**. Physicalism and Mental Causes: Contra Papineau. *Analysis*, 56(4), 263-267, O 96.

This article raises a dilemma for versions of nonreductive physicalism that endorse the completeness of physics. The dilemma is: either affirm the causal impotence of the mental or reject the literal completeness of physics. This dilemma bears on various species of nonreductive physicalism now in circulation.

**Moser, Paul K**. The Relativity of Skepticism. *Phil Phenomenol Res*, 57(2), 401-406, Je 97.

This paper is part of a symposium on Robert Fogelin's book, *Pyrrhonian Reflections on Knowledge and Justification*. The paper argues that Pyrrhonian skeptics typically rely on epistemic standards that lack cogent, nonquestion begging epistemic support. This conclusion raises a serious challenge to Pyrrhonian skepticism, including that of Fogelin's book.

**Moser, Paul K** (ed) and Carson, Thomas L (ed). *Morality and the Good Life*. New York, Oxford Univ Pr, 1997.

The book is a comprehensive survey of contemporary ethical theory that collects thirty-four selections on morality and the theory of value. Emphasizing value theory, metaethics and normative ethics, it is nontechnical and accessible to a wide range of readers. Selections are organized under six main topics: 1) Concepts of Goodness, 2) What Things are Good? 3) Virtues and Ethics, 4)

Realism vs. Anti-Realism, 5) Value and Obligation, and 6) The Value and Meaning of Life. The text includes both a substantial general introduction featuring explanatory summaries of all the selections and an extensive topical bibliography, which enhance the volume's pedagogical and research utility. (publisher, edited)

**Moser, Paul K** and Yandell, David. Against Naturalizing Rationality. *Protosoz*, 8/9, 81-96, 1996.

Recent obituaries for traditional nonnaturalistic approaches to rationality are not just premature but demonstrably self-defeating. One such prominent obituary appears in the writings of W. V. Quine, whose pessimism about traditional epistemology stems from his scientism, the view that the natural sciences have a monopoly on legitimate theoretical explanation. Quine also offers an obituary for the a priori constraints on rationality found in "first philosophy", resting on his rejection of the "pernicious mentalism" of semantic theories of meaning. Quine's pronouncements of the death of traditional conceptions of rationality in epistemology and in the theory of meaning are, we contend, but misguided wishes for their death, wishes that face severe problems of self-defeat. In addition, Quine's naturalistic epistemology is subject to damaging skeptical worries, the force of which one cannot escape by ignoring them. (edited)

**Moser, Stephanie**. "Visual Representation in Archaeology: Depicting the Missing-Link in Human Origins" in *Picturing Knowledge*, Baigrie, Brian S (ed), 184-214. Toronto, Univ of Toronto Pr, 1996.

The topic of visual representation in the sciences has raised a number of significant problems in the discipline of prehistoric archaeology. This paper addresses how images of our earliest ancestors—the australopithecines—represent the attempt to distinguish between human and ape like traits. The reconstructions of these ancestors shows how palaeoanthropologists and archaeologists have come to understand human origins via visual modes of reasoning.

**Moses, Yoram** (& others) and Halpern, Joseph Y and Fagin, Ronald. Reasoning about Knowledge: A Response by the Authors. *Mind Mach*, 7(1), 113, F 97.

**Moshier, M Andrew**. A Rational Reconstruction of the Domain of Feature Structures. *J Log Lang Info*, 4(2), 111-143, 1995.

Feature structures are employed in various forms in many areas of linguistics. Informally, one can picture a feature structure as a sort of tree decorated with information about constraints requiring that specific subtrees be identical (isomorphic). Here I show that this informal picture of feature structures can be used to characterize exactly the class of feature structures under their usual subsumption ordering. Furthermore, once a precise definition of tree is fixed, this characterization makes use only of standard domain-theoretic notions regarding the information borne by elements in a domain, thus removing (or better, explaining) all apparently ad hoc choices in the original definition of feature structures. In addition, I show how this characterization can be parameterized in order to yield similar characterizations of various different notions of feature structure. (edited)

**Mosler, Karl**. De Minimis and Equity in Risk. *Theor Decis*, 42(3), 215-233, My 97.

Indices and orderings are developed for evaluating alternative strategies in the management of risk. They reflect the goals of reducing individual and collective risks, of increasing equity, and of assigning priority to the reduction and to the equity of high risks. Individual risk is defined as the (random or nonrandom) level of exposure to a danger. In particular the role of a lower negligibility level is investigated. A class of indices is proposed which involves two parameters, a negligibility level and a parameter of inequality aversion, and several interpretations of the indices are discussed. We provide a set of eight axioms which are necessary and sufficient for this class of indices, and we present an approach to deal with partial information on the parameters.

**Mosley, Albert G** and Capaldi, Nicholas. *Affirmative Action: Social Justice or Unfair Preference?*. Lanham, Rowman & Littlefield, 1996.

In this book, two distinguished philosophers debate one of the most controversial public policy issues of the late twentieth century. Each begins by making a case for or against affirmative action, laying out the major arguments on both sides. Each author then responds to the other's essay. Written in an engaging, accessible style, *Affirmative Action* is an excellent text for junior level philosophy, political theory, public policy and African-American studies courses as well as a guide for professionals navigating this important debate. (publisher, edited)

**Moss, Jean Dietz**. Reclaiming Aristotle's *Rhetoric*. *Rev Metaph*, 50(3), 635-646, Mr 97.

The author critiques four recent studies devoted to Aristotle's *Rhetoric*: Eugene Garver's *Aristotle's Rhetoric: A Rhetoric of Character*; *Aristotle's Rhetoric: Philosophical Essays*, edited by David J. Furley and Alexander Nehamas, *Essays on Aristotle's Rhetoric*, edited by Amelie Rorty; *Peripatetic Rhetoric after Aristotle*, edited by William W. Fortenbaugh and David C. Mirhady. The first three of these claim to redress the lack of attention paid to Aristotle's text by philosophers, while the fourth contains essays on the later fate of Aristotelian rhetoric. All four of these books are of considerable worth in assaying the unique contribution of the focal text.

**Moss, Lawrence S** and Johnson, David E. Dynamic Interpretations of Constraint-Based Grammar Formalisms. *J Log Lang Info*, 4(1), 61-79, 1995.

We present a rendering of some common grammatical formalisms in terms of evolving algebras. Though our main concern in this paper is on constraint-based formalisms, we also discuss the more basic case of context-free grammars. Our aim throughout is to highlight the use of evolving algebras as a specification tool to obtain grammar formalisms.

**Most, Glenn W**. Reading Raphael: *The School of Athens* and Its Pre-Text. *Crit Inquiry*, 23(1), 145-182, Fall 96.

Raphael's decision to represent philosophy by depicting the intellectual activities performed by philosophers was unprecedented: traditionally artists had depicted philosophy allegorically. Raphael seems to have been inspired not by a pictorial source, but by a written one: the scene in Plato's *Protagoras* (314E-316A) in which Socrates and Hippocrates come upon three sophists and their entourage in Callias's palace. Presumably the connection between Raphael and Plato was Giles of Viterbo. The building in which Raphael's philosophers are shown recalls the so-called Temple of Janus in Rome: for Giles Janus was both the initiator of philosophy and a fore-runner of Christianity.

**Motes, William H** and Dulek, Ronald E and Hilton, Chadwick B. Executive Perceptions of Superior and Subordinate Information Control: Practice Versus Ethics. *J Bus Ethics*, 16(11), 1175-1184, Ag 97.

This study examines executive perceptions of business information control. Specifically, the study explores a) whether executives perceive certain types of information control being practiced within their businesses; and, b) whether the executives regard such practices as ethical. In essence, the study suggests that both superiors and subordinates selectively practice information control. Even more importantly, however, executives see such practices as ethically acceptable on the part of superiors but as ethically questionable on the part of subordinates. A closer look at the responding executives' profile characteristics—age, gender, education and salary—reveals the complexity of these perceptions. Most importantly, gender and age emerge as two prime factors influencing executive perceptions regarding both the practice and the ethics of information control. Suggestions for future research are included at the end of the article.

**Mothersill, Mary**. In Defense of Hume and the Causal Theory of Taste. *J Aes Art Crit*, 55(3), 312-317, Sum 97.

**Motilal, Shashi**. The Intentionality of Mental Reference. *J Indian Counc Phil Res*, 13(3), 73-86, My-Ag 96.

**Motzkin, Gabriel**. The Invention of History and the Reinvention of Memory. *Iyyun*, 45, 15-39, Jl 96.

**Mouffe, Chantal**. "Deconstruction, Pragmatism and the Politics of Democracy" in *Deconstruction and Pragmatism*, Mouffe, Chantal (ed), 1-12. New York, Routledge, 1996.

Through a discussion of the work of Richard Rorty and Jacques Derrida, the article scrutinizes the relevance of pragmatism and deconstruction for politics. Rortyian pragmatism with the importance it gives to shared vocabularies is able to grasp better than universalist and rationalist theories the way in which democratic values can be fostered. However, his view of politics puts too much emphasis on consensus and he is unable to grasp the dimension of antagonism. This is where lies the importance of Derrida's work which brings to the fore the impossibility of establishing a consensus without exclusion. Thanks to such an insight we can acknowledge the need to always keep the democratic contestation alive.

**Mouffe, Chantal**. Decision, Deliberation, and Democratic Ethos. *Phil Today*, 41(1-4), 24-30, Spr 97.

By comparing the approaches of Richard Rorty and Jacques Derrida, the author aims at bringing to the fore how pragmatism and deconstruction can help grasping the nature of democracy. She argues that both approaches converge in undermining the rationalist attempt to provide philosophical foundations for democracy. Concurring with Rorty's move to separate the democratic political aspect of the Enlightenment from its epistemological framework, she nevertheless deplores the limited understanding of politics proposed by pragmatism. Deconstruction, on the contrary, thanks to the Derridean notions of undecidability and decision is seen as providing crucial insights for a pluralist democratic politics.

**Mouffe, Chantal** (ed). *Deconstruction and Pragmatism*. New York, Routledge, 1996.

Jacques Derrida and Richard Rorty are two of the most famous living philosophers. The current influence of deconstruction and pragmatism, two major intellectual traditions, would be unthinkable without their work. This ground-breaking book brings these two thinkers together in a critical confrontation between these two traditions. Derridean deconstruction and Rortian pragmatism are both accused by their enemies of undermining our ideas of truth and reason, but do their ideas lead to intellectual and political chaos? Both are committed to the democratic project but they reject the necessary link between universalism, rationalism and modern democracy and seek to clarify what is at stake intellectually and politically. Two other distinguished theorists, Simon Critchley and Ernesto Laclau, provide a critical context for their debate and bring out the importance of the convergences and differences between the two. (publisher)

**Moulin, Bernard** and Boury-Brisset, Anne-Claire. An Agent Model Integrating Multiple Reasoning Mechanisms. *Commun Cog—AI*, 13(1), 57-91, 1996.

In this paper we study various reasoning mechanisms that affect the way that a software agent makes decisions in a multiagent environment: hypothetical reasoning, generation of hypothesis and deduction of knowledge in hypothetical worlds: evolution of the content of hypothetical worlds in order to choose among them a solution that conforms to the agent's preferences; management of deontic modalities in relation to hypothetical reasoning; reasoning on other agents and belief revision.

**Moulines, C Ulises**. "Der epistemologische Kulturrelativismus: Eine dialogische Paralyse?" in *Das weite Spektrum der analytischen Philosophie*, Lenzen, Wolfgang, 203-215. Hawthorne, de Gruyter, 1997.

This is a critique of sociocultural relativism with respect to entral epistemic and semantic notions (knowledge and truth and its derivatives), as represented mainly by the Edinburgh School. It is shown that, assuming the principles of "reflexivity" and "symmetry" which are specific of this form of relativism, it is certainly not a self-refuting position (as some authors have claimed) but it leads to a sort of dialogical paralysis, where any argument becomes meaningless by principle.

**Moulines, C Ulises**. Gibt es etwas ausser mir selbst? Überlegungen zur semantischen Begründun des Realismus. *Z Phil Forsch*, 50(1/2), 151-166, Ja-Je 96.

To the question, 'Is there anything besides myself?', four answers are possible: 'Yes' (Realism), 'No' (Solipsism), 'I'll never know' (Skepticism) and 'Nonsense!' (Positivism). The cogency of each answer is examined from a semantical point of view and by using a hypothetical model situation based on Calderón's "Life is a Dream". It is shown that the positivistic answer lacks any semantical justification while the best semantical arguments in favor of realism produced so far have some prime facie plausibility but eventually fall short of attaining their goal.

**Moulines, C Ulises**. Structural Approach in Physics (in Spanish). *Agora (Spain)*, 15(2), 97-102, 1996.

According to the structural view of science (abbreviated as *structuralism*), the approximate nature of empirical theories in general and of physical theories in particular, is one of their essential components, which should not be neglected in any systematic metascientific analysis. Contrary to other metascientific approaches that have dealt with this problem area, structuralism sets forth to explicate the concept of 20 approximation not as a relation between statements but rather as a relation between models (i.e., structures). In this paper, the basic intuition behind this idea, the short history of its development until present times and some open questions are laid out.

**Moulines, Carlos Ulises**. Las ideas básicas del estructuralismo metacientífico. *Rev Filosof (Spain)*, 9(16), 93-104, 1996.

**Mounce, H O**. Philosophy, Solipsism and Thought. *Phil Quart*, 47(186), 1-18, Ja 97.

Wittgenstein's view of philosophy in the *Tractatus* presupposes that thought may be revealed without remainder in the use of signs. It is commonly held, however, that in the *Tractatus* he treated thought as logically prior to language. If this view, expressed most lucidly by Norman Malcolm, were correct, Wittgenstein would be inconsistent in holding that thought can be revealed without remainder in the use of signs. I argue that this is not correct. Thought may be prior to language in time but not in logic, for nonverbal symbols must have a logical structure in common with verbal ones. A view comparable with Malcolm's holds that Wittgenstein, under the influence of Schopenhauer, is committed to some form of solipsism. I argue that neither Schopenhauer nor Wittgenstein held any version of solipsism. For both philosophers, subject and object are correlative, so that it is incoherent to affirm the existence of the one without presupposing the existence of the other.

**Mounce, H O**. *The Two Pragmatisms: From Peirce to Rorty*. New York, Routledge, 1997.

*The Two Pragmatisms: From Peirce to Rorty* maps the main movements within the pragmatist tradition. Two distinct forms of pragmatism are identified: that of Peirce and that of the 'second' pragmatism stemming from James's interpretation of Peirce and seen in the work of Dewey and, above all, Rorty. Both the influential work of Rorty and the way in which he has transformed contemporary philosophy's understanding of pragmatism are clearly explained. (publisher, edited)

**Mount, Jr, Eric**. The Currency of Covenant. *Annu Soc Christ Ethics*, 295-310, 1996.

**Mourao, Luís**. Panlogismo, Pantagrismo, e o *Saber Mais* do Romance —Uma Leitura de *Mudança* de Vergílio Ferreira. *Rev Port Filosof*, 52(1-4), 589-601, Ja-D 96.

*Mudança* (1949) pretendia ser um romance exemplarmente neo-realista. O seu herói positivo saberia ler, no emaranhado dos acontecimentos negativos, a linha lógica do progresso inelutável da história. Mas ao longo da escrita do romance, as dúvidas da personagem pessimista impoem-se ao autor: a confiança na lógica da história cede lugar à visao do sofrimento implicado no processo histórico. Esta mudança deve-se à sabedoria da incerteza que o processo de escrita romanesca arrasta consigo, ainda que, nos termos da época, tenha sido lido como uma passagem do campo marxista para o campo existencialista.

**Moutsopoulos, Evanghélos**. Brahms-Bruckner: deux univers en dissonance. *Diotima*, 25, 163-164, 1997.

Tout chez Brahms est emporté par le courant puissant d'une inspiration calme plutôt qu'impétueuse, mais parfaitement maîtrisée: fluidité assurée par le recours à des artifices savants. Contre l'écoulement de la musique de Brahms, Bruckner dresse un constructivisme. Ses formes surgissent d'un emboîtement constant d'éléments, de phrases ou de parties entières, en réalité interchangeables. En raison de ce constructivisme, la musique de Bruckner, au demeurant savante au possible, fut jadis qualifiée de naïve. Le trait commun de ces deux musiques se situe cependant dans le fait que leurs deux créateurs sont hantés, chacun a sa manière, par le souci d'économie (à l'envers) dans l'utilisation de leurs ressources thématiques; a l'envers, car tout deux entendent entendent en tirer le *maximum* avant de procéder à l'exploitation d'une nouvelle filière, et ainsi de suite.

**Moutsopoulos, Evanghélos**. Kairos: Balance ou rasoir? La statue de Lysippe et l'épigramme de Poseidippos. *Diotima*, 25, 134-135, 1997.

There is an inadequacy between the sculptural representation of Kairos by Lysippus, holding a *balance* and the description of this status by the poet

Poseidippos who supposes that Kairos is holding a *razor*. A long argumentation leads to the conclusion that the poet had never seen Lysuppus's masterwork, but only read a literary description thereof, or rather *misread* it, understanding *xyros* (razor) instead of *zygos* (balance), a misreading paleographically easy to explain, but also due to the literary tradition (see E. Moutsopoulos, *Kairos.Lamise l'enjeu*, Paris, Vrin, 1991).

**Moutsopoulos, Evanghélos**. Modèles historique et modèles culturels. *Diotima*, 25, 143-147, 1997.

Once the existence of a historical process has been accepted as an undeniable reality, its nature, its structure and its significance for man may become an object of research. It is admitted that such a process is conceived of and interpreted in different ways according human societies. History has two faces: one of them results from its erection through human activity; the other results from its reconstitution through the labor of the historians. There are four categories of historical models, each one of them presenting particular structural aspects: a) *Political models* (mythical, ideological, Hesiodian); b) *Religious models*: Prophetic, Christian etc.; c) *Scientific models* (Condorcet, Comte); d) *Synthetical models* which are multidimensional and polyphonic structural conceptions which, after the example of Claude Lévi-Strauss, may refer to musical structures: *Serial* conception of history (R. Aron); *Fugical* conception of history (E. Moutsopoulos). These conceptions may also be applied to the history of ideas (see E. Moutsopoulos, *Possibilités et limites d'une histoire "sérielle"*, Diotima,7,1979, pp. 204-205).

**Movia, Giancarlo**. "L'Uno e i molti: Sulla logica hegeliana dell'Essere per sé" in *Hegel e Aristotele*, Ferrarin, A, 335-401. Cagliari, Edizioni AV, 1997.

This essay is the report presented during the convention on "Hegel interpreter of Aristotle," held at the University of Cagliari (Italy) in April 1994. The essay shows that Aristotle affirms the primary and immediate multiplicity of the *being* and of the *one*, a multiplicity that, nevertheless, requires unity, that is a relation to a single term, the *substance*. Hegel as well, in the chapter of the *Science of Logic* on the *being-for-self*, affirms the immediate, intrinsic, primary multiplicity of the *one*, that however, does not give rise to a plurality of meanings. In fact, the terms which the *one* refers to in its self-fragmentation, are themselves *ones*, so that the *one*, so that the *one* refers in them to itself.

**Movia, Giancarlo** (ed). *Hegel e Aristotele*. Cagliari, Edizioni AV, 1997.

**Moxley, Roy A**. The Import of Skinner's Three-Term Contingency. *Behavior Phil*, 24(2), 145-167, Fall 96.

The view presented here argues that Skinner's operant is integrated as a three-term unit within a selectionist tradition that has explanatory origins in probabilistic relations and random variation. This tradition is fundamentally opposed to a mechanistic tradition that has explanatory origins in determinism and its manifestations in paired connections of if-then necessity. (edited)

**Moya, Carlos J**. The Regress-Problem: A Reply to Vermazen. *Pac Phil Quart*, 77(2), 155-161, Je 96.

This paper is intended to meet some objections that Vermazen has raised about the treatment of the regress-problem in the author's book on the philosophy of action. This problem is shown to involve a skeptical claim about the very existence of actions as distinct from happenings. It is argued, against Vermazen's contention, that only one version of the problem is at work in that book and that, while Danto's basic actions, McCann's volitions and O'Shaughnessy's and Hornsby's tryings do not solve, after analysis, that version of the problem, the author's proposal does in fact provide a solution to it.

**Moya, Carlos J**. Was Descartes an Individualist? A Critical Discussion of W. Ferraiolo's "Individualism and Descartes". *Teorema*, 16(2), 77-85, 1997.

In his paper "Individualism and Descartes," William Ferraiolo puts into question the widely accepted interpretation of Descartes as an individualist about mental content. In this paper, I intend to defend this interpretation of Descartes's thinking against Ferraiolo's objections. I shall hold, firstly, that attributing to Descartes an individualist doctrine is not historically misguided. Secondly, I will try to show that Descartes's endorsement of anti-individualism would lead either to depriving sceptical hypotheses of their force or to rejecting the epistemological privilege of the first person. And, thirdly, I shall try to show that Ferraiolo's objections to the individualistic interpretation rest on two important errors: a misapprehension of the argumentative order of the *Mediations* and a confusion between the notions of causal and constitutive dependence of content on the external environment.

**Moya Bedoya, Juan Diego**. La ontología spinociana de las modalidades entitativas. *Rev Filosof (Costa Rica)*, 34(83-84), 445-453, D 96.

This paper deals with the Spinozistic ontology of real modalities: necessity and possibility. The author attempts to elucidate the domain where the concept of necessity works and to restore to Spinozistic ontology the idea of possibility.

**Moyes, Glen D** and Park, Kyungjoo. Chief Financial Officers' Perceptions Concerning the IMA's Standards of Ethical Conduct. *J Bus Ethics*, 16(2), 189-194, F 97.

Do chief financial officers (CFOs) of publicly held corporations agree with the Institute of Management Accountants' (IMA) Standards of Ethical Conduct and are they willing to adopt them? To address these issues, a survey was conducted concerning the standards. The IMA issued the Pronouncement of Standards in June, 1982. The surveyed CFOs agreed with the majority of the standards. However, many CFOs commented that some of the standards of Ethical Conduct were difficult to implement in the real world. The CFOs critically commented that all the Standards were too general, too vague, or did not cover the grey areas that occur in real world situations. (edited)

**Mudrack, Peter E** and Mason, E Sharon. Do Complex Moral Reasoners Experience Greater Ethical Work Conflict?. *J Bus Ethics*, 16(12-13), 1311-1318, S 97.

Individuals who disagree that organizational interests legitimately supersede those of the wider society may experience conflict between their personal standards of ethics and those demanded by an employing organization, a conflict that is well documented. An additional question is whether or not individuals capable of complex moral reasoning experience greater conflict than those reasoning at a less developed level. This question was first positioned in a theoretical framework and then investigated using 115 survey responses from a student sample. Correlational analysis and hierarchical regression indicated that individuals scoring high on the Defining Issues Test measure of Kohlberg's stages of moral development experienced significantly greater workplace ethical conflict than low scorers. (edited)

**Mudragei, Nellia Stepanovna**. The Rational and the Irrational: A Philosophical Problem (Reading Arthur Schopenhauer). *Russian Stud Phil*, 34(2), 46-65, Fall 95.

**Mudroch, Vilem**. "Vernunft und Empirie in Kants Natur-wissenschaftstheorie: Überlegungen zur Möglichkeit von Paradigmenwechseln bei Kant" in *Grenzen der kritischen Vernunft*, Schmid, Peter A, 290-304. Basel, Schwabe Verlag, 1997.

In his preface to the first critique Kant maintains that an examination of nature can be successful only when guided by concepts, without, however, specifying their exact status. A number of recent interpretations have claimed more or less explicitly that these concepts readily admit of paradigm changes in a Kuhnian sense. This paper argues that Kant's philosophy of science is instead best characterized by the conception of mature science as gradually approaching truth. It is suggested that in view of the many justified criticisms of Kuhn an understanding of Kant distancing itself from the idea of paradigm changes is preferable.

**Müller, Benito**. Introduction. *Dialectica*, 51(1), 5-15, 1997.

This introductory note to a collection of papers by Rom Harré, Jerrold Aronson, Nancy Cartwright and Richard Swinburne on the topic of 'Dispositions in Science' provides a short survey of treatment of dispositions and dispositional terms by Carnap, Ryle, Armstrong and Mellor and a summary of the views put forward by the four contributors.

**Müller, Benito** (ed & trans) and Brentano, Franz. *Descriptive Psychology*. New York, Routledge, 1995.

The book contains a first English translation of a lecture series given by Brentano at the University of Vienna between 1887 and 1891. In these lectures, Brentano presents the mature culmination of the ideas he initially published in his psychology from an Empirical Standpoint (1874). The topics dealt with are: Psychognosy and Genetic Psychology; Elements of Consciousness; The Correct Method of the Psychognost; The Components of Human Consciousness; The Components of Human Consciousness; Psychical Acts; The General Character of Sensations; Inner Perception; Descriptive Psychology or Descriptive Phenomenology; On the Content of Experiences; Psychognostic Sketch; Perceiving, Apperceiving, Clearly Apperceiving, Compounded Apperceiving, Transcendentally Apperceiving.

**Müller, Jan**. Carl Schmitt: An Occasional Nationalist?. *Hist Euro Ideas*, 23(1), 19-34, Ja 97.

**Müller, Vincent C** and Stein, Christian. "Epistemic Theories of Truth: The Justifiability Paradox Investigated" in *Verdad: lógica, representación y mundo*, Villegas Forero, L, 95-104. Santiago de Compostela, Univ Santiago Comp, 1996.

Epistemic theories of truth, such as those presumed to be typical for antirealism, can be characterized as saying that what is true can be known in principle. Analysis of the nature of the paradox shows that such statements refute epistemic theories of truth only if the antirealist motivation for epistemic theories of truth is not taken into account. The motivation in a link of understandability and meaningfulness suggests to change the above principle and to restrict the theory to logically simple sentences, in which case the paradox does not arise. This suggestion also allows to see the deep philosophical problems for antirealism those counterexamples are pointing at. (edited)

**Müller, Volkhard F**. Lokale Quantenfeldtheorie und Kontinuumslimes. *Phil Natur*, 27(1), 66-82, 1990.

A survey is given of a recent development in theoretical physics aiming at a nonperturbative construction of relativistic quantum field theories. This approach—initiated by K. Wilson in the early seventies—connects the Euclidean formulation of a quantum field theory with classical statistical mechanics. Its central idea is to construct the correlation functions of a quantum field theory via those of a mathematically well-defined lattice system which shows a phase transition of second order.

**Müller-Lauter, Wolfgang**. Heidegger e Nietzsche. *Teoria*, 16(1), 5-29, 1996.

**Müller-Lauter, Wolfgang**. Heidegger's Lecture on Nietzsche: On the Problem of Nihilism (in Serbo-Croatian). *Filozof Istraz*, 15(4), 749-755, 1995.

Heidegger deutet Nietzsches Philosophie als Metyphysik des Willens zur Macht und stellt sie in die Geschichte der abendländischen Metaphysik im Ganzen. Auf diese Weise kann er Nietzsches Philosophie als Vollendung des Nihilismus auslegen, insofern sie nicht zu der Frage nach dem Sein als Sein gelangt, vielmehr in der Unterscheidung zwischen Seiendheit und Seienden steckenbleibt. Die mehrschichtige Aus-einander-setzung Heideggers führt auch zu der Herausarbeitung verschiedener "Stufen und Gestalten" des Nihilismus, der bei Nietzsche oft nur knapp und keineswegs einheitlich gefasst wird. In den "Beiträgen zur Philosophie. Vom Ereignis" wird von Heidegger der Nihilismus Nietzsches darüberhinaus hinsichtlich der beiden Aspekte der Machenschaft und des Erlebnisses untersucht.

**Münnich, Susana**. En torno a la frase de Nietzsche *La verdad es mujer*. *Convivium*, 9, 77-91, 1996.

The aforementioned phrase gives rise for revising Nietzsche's criticisms of traditional philosophy and his sarcastic jeers at the most currently admitted conception of truth. His own ideas on the matter are also examined, especially with regard to such topics as feminity, feminism and its relations to democracy and socialism.

**Münnix, Gabriele**. Liberty—Equality—Fraternity—Justice (in Czech). *Filosof Cas*, 44(6), 1003-1020, 1996.

**Münster, Gernot**. Epistemologische Aspekte der neuen Entwicklungen in der Physik. *Phil Natur*, 27(1), 83-98, 1990.

**Múgica, Fernando**. El habitar y la técnica: Polo en diálogo con Marx. *Anu Filosof*, 29(2), 815-849, 1996.

Professor Leonardo Polo's theory about man as a dweller constitutes the framework for a dialogue with Marx. According to the latter, man realizes himself as species through work, creating his own conditions for survival by dwelling in the world. Furthermore this process presupposes that technical progress will have a historical culmination. According to Polo, neither can we view man as a finished product now nor in the future, nor can modern technology warrant such a culmination.

**Mukherji, Arundhati**. Habermas' Pragmatic Universals. *J Indian Counc Phil Res*, 14(2), 31-36, Ja-Ap 97.

The paper examines two alternative explanations of our linguistic behaviour. Chomsky's theory of *linguistic universals* which holds that the child is born with a knowledge of *universal grammar* that he uses in acquiring language, gives emphasis only on the syntactic aspect of language and not on performance factors or on communicative aspects of language. Habermas's theory of *pragmatic universals*, on the contrary, is better than that of Chomsky's, for it lays emphasis on the *communicative function of language*. The paper argues that everyday social interaction which is overtly strategic and covertly manipulative, does not fit Habermas's *ideal* communicative model.

**Muldoon, Mark S**. Ricoeur and Merleau-Ponty on Narrative Identity. *Amer Cath Phil Quart*, 71(1), 35-52, Wint 97.

One topic not covered sufficiently in the renewed interest in Merleau-Ponty's contributions to postmodern thought is the close approximation in his works to a current postmodern theme, namely, the notion of narrative identity proposed by Ricoeur. Although this topic is not thematized by Merleau-Ponty, many of the key elements that Ricoeur weaves into his hermeneutical discussion on narrative identity—such as lived body, the tension of linguistic sedimentation and innovation, and the act of reading—are of central concern to the earlier phenomenologist. The paper discusses some of these elements between the two French authors, concluding that Merleau-Ponty's recognition of 'the ambiguous self' is dramatically close to what Ricoeur has in mind when he employs the term 'narrative identity'.

**Muldoon, Mark S**. Silence Revisited: Taking the Sight Out of Auditory Qualities. *Rev Metaph*, 50(2), 275-298, D 96.

The purpose of the article is to point out certain shortcomings of previous studies on silence and to advance a more precise terminology with which to discuss silence philosophically. Silence, as a level of audition, is not taken seriously when it is forced to be studied under the traditional epistemological metaphors of vision that violate its very nature. It is therefore suggested that all transient auditory qualities that erupt in the totality of the life-world be called akoumena. An akoumenon typically means 'that which is to be listened to.' Given this new term, we can understand better how, as human beings, we organize akoumena and summon silence into perceptible existence.

**Mulgan, Tim**. One False Virtue of Rule Consequentialism, and One New Vice. *Pac Phil Quart*, 77(4), 362-373, D 96.

A common objection to *act consequentialism* (AC) is that it makes unreasonable demands on moral agents. *Rule consequentialism* (RC) is often presented as a less demanding alternative. It is argued that this alleged virtue of RC is false, as RC will not be any less demanding in practice than AC. It is then demonstrated that RC has an additional (hitherto unnoticed) vice, as it relies upon the undefended simplifying assumption that the best possible consequences would arise in a society in which everyone followed the same rules. Once this "homogeneity assumption" is rejected, RC is unable to provide a workable alternative to AC.

**Mulgan, Tim**. Two Conceptions of Benevolence. *Phil Pub Affairs*, 26(1), 62-79, Wint 97.

**Mulhall, Stephen**. "Can There be an Epistemology of Moods?" in *Verstehen and Humane Understanding*, O'Hear, Anthony (ed), 191-210. New York, Cambridge Univ Pr, 1996.

This article introduces and defends a Heideggerian account of moods as genuinely cognitive modes of human experience, in a manner directly influenced by Stanley Cavell's work on Wittgenstein, Heidegger and Emerson. It specifies a variety of connections between this Heideggerian account and those of influential contemporary analytical philosophers (Nussbaum, Taylor, McDowell), develops a Heideggerian critique of Kant's attempted definition of the subjectivity/objectivity distinction, and suggests a number of significant parallels between the Heideggerian position and views attributable to Wittgenstein with respect to the connections between moods, passivity, language and philosophical method.

**Mulhall, Stephen**. Constructing a Hall of Reflection. *Philosophy*, 72 (280), 219-239, Ap 97.

This article develops an interpretation of *Metaphysics as a Guide to Morals* as a perfectionist text in which Murdoch's moral vision multiply determines the form in which she presents it. For her, the moral duty of attention to reality entails the endless discarding of false unities of thought in favor of better ones, the ineliminability of metaphysical speculation in moral reflection and the subjection of the former to the latter—particularly with reference to its treatment of limited wholes such as (concepts of) world, self and language. Murdoch's book itself aims to attend properly to the complex structure of words and images through which those metaphysical treatments are handed down to us, and to constitute itself as a further element (or limited whole) in that inheritance.

**Mulhall, Stephen**. *Heidegger and Being and Time*. New York, Routledge, 1996.

This book guides the reader through the complexities of Heidegger's first major publication, *Being and Time*. One of the most important works of philosophy published this century, *Being and Time* has influenced numerous thinkers and philosophical movements over the last seventy years. Existentialism, hermeneutics and deconstruction are inconceivable without Heidegger's groundbreaking phenomenological work. (publisher, edited)

**Mulhall, Stephen**. Promising, Consent, and Citizenship. *Polit Theory*, 25(2), 171-192, Ap 97.

This article examines the dispute between Cavell and Rawls over the role of perfectionism in moral and political thought, in three phases. The first investigates Cavell's early argument that Rawls errs in thinking of promising as a practice; the second defends Cavell's claim that Rawls's theory of justice as fairness is based upon an unduly contractual notion of the social contract; and the third speculates as to how this claim might be made good against Rawlsian political liberalism—specifically its conception of the limits of the reasonable as settleable in advance of political debate.

**Mulhauser, Gregory R** and Dennett, Daniel C. In the Beginning, There Was Darwin: *Darwin's Dangerous Idea: Evolution and the Meanings of Life. Phil Books*, 38(2), 81-92, Ap 97.

**Mullarkey, John C**. Bergson and the Language of Process. *Process Stud*, 24, 44-58, 1995.

Contrary to the myth that Bergson has nothing positive to say about language, this essay demonstrates the centrality of language and symbolism both to the expression and the content of Bergson's process metaphysics. Another focus is the paradox of how to state any process philosophy when our language is seemingly formed through a substantialist conceptuality. In opposition to this view, Bergson shows us numerous strategies by which language can be subverted and turned against its natural course in order to instantiate the very processual reality its supposedly singular and rigid conceptual basis is meant to thwart.

**Mullarkey, John C**. Bergson: The Philosophy of *Durée-Différence. Phil Today*, 40(3), 367-380, Fall 96.

Through close examinations of the Bergsonian critique of negativity, his concept of 'dissociation', and his devastating analyses of perception and presence, a divergent and challenging understanding of Bergson is presented in the hope of placing in full view those radical aspects of his thinking which fly in the face of its current domesticated image. With his notions of the irreducibility and ontological priority of difference, the impossibility of subtracting representation from presence, and the denial of a temporal present, some inkling may be gained of the revolutionary character of Bergsonian thought, and with that, of the qualities which gained it such notoriety in the first decades of this century.

**Muller, F A**. The Equivalence Myth of Quantum Mechanics—Part I. *Stud Hist Phil Mod Physics*, 28B(1), 35-61, Mr 97.

The author endeavours to show two things: first, that Schrödinger's (and Eckart's) demonstration in March (September) 1926 of the equivalence of *matrix mechanics*, as created by Heisenberg, Born, Jordan and Dirac in 1925 and *wave mechanics*, as created by Schrödinger in 1926, is not foolproof; and second, that it could not have been foolproof, because at the time matrix mechanics and wave mechanics were neither mathematically nor empirically equivalent. That they were is the Equivalence Myth. (edited)

**Muller, Jerry Z** (ed). *Conservatism*. Princeton, Princeton Univ Pr, 1997.

This collection is a richly diverse, intelligently designed and helpfully annotated introduction to the world of conservative theory. No comparable collection that I know of is as broad and unparochial as this one. The introduction is in itself a substantial contribution to the history of political thought and the 'Afterword' is a brilliant and concise formulation of the fundamental dilemmas of conservative thought. (publisher)

**Mulligan, Kevin**. Percepción, particulares y predicados. *Rev Filosof (Spain)*, 9(16), 105-120, 1996.

A view of perception is outlined according to which seeing, as opposed to seeing-that, is not to believe, involves nonconceptual content and is of things, states and processes (monadic and relational tropes). It is then argued that this analysis is compatible with an analysis of reports of visual perception the complements of which are nonpropositional. It is suggested that to see is always to see in a nonconceptual way.

**Mulsow, Martin**. Eclecticism or Skepticism? A Problem of the Early Enlightenment. *J Hist Ideas*, 58(3), 465-477, Jl 97.

Fideistic Skepticism in the Early German Enlightenment could serve as a way of avoiding the constraints of dogmatic philosophy. For thinkers like Jakob Friedrich Reimmann (1668-1743), this strategy could better fulfil the purpose than the more common 'eclectic' philosophy. Eclecticism, he said, had already begun to emerge 'sectarian' features. On the other hand (especially in the work of Johann Franz Buddeus, 1667-1729) eclecticism was consolidated by its holistic emphasis on the history of philosophy—the importance of viewing the whole of history before selecting from it.

Mulvaney, Robert J 804 AUTHOR INDEX

**Mulvaney, Robert J**. Frederic Henry Hedge, H.A.P. Torrey, and the Early Reception of Leibniz in America. *Stud Leibniz*, 28(2), 163-182, 1996.

Leibniz' Bedeutung für die Entwicklung der amerikanischen Philosophie ist bisher wenig erforscht worden. In diesem Aufsatz untersuche ich den Beitrag zweier amerikanischer Idealisten der Mitte des 19. Jahrhunderts zur Leibniz-Forschung. Der erstere, Frederic Henry Hedge, ein enger Mitarbeiter Emersons und eine zentrale Figur der transcendentalist movement, legte die erste Übersetzung der *Monadologie* ins Englische vor und schrieb die erste wichtige wissenschaftliche Abhandlung über Leibniz in einer amerikanischen Zeitschrift. Der zweite, H.A.P. Torrey, von prägendem Einfluss auf die Gedanken John Deweys, schrieb eine Reihe kritischer Essays zur *Théodicée*, die Auswirkungen auf Deweys Buch über Leibniz hatten. In diesem Aufsatz gebe ich eine Überblick der Arbeiten von Hedge und Torrey, bewerte ihre Arbeiten zu Leibniz und untersuche einige Aspekte ihres Einflusses auf das amerikanische Denken. Ich folgere, dass Leibniz' Einfluss auf die amerikanische Philosophie grösser ist als allgemein angenommen und schlage weitere Forschungsmöglichkeiten vor.

**Munda, Giuseppe**. Environmental Economics, Ecological Economics, and the Concept of Sustainable Development. *Environ Values*, 6(2), 213-233, My 97.

This paper presents a systematic discussion, mainly for noneconomists, on economic approaches to the concept of sustainable development. As a first step, the concept of sustainability is extensively discussed. As a second step, the argument that it is not possible to consider sustainability only from an economic or ecological point of view is defended; issues such as economic-ecological integration, inter-generational and intra-generational equity are considered of fundamental importance. Two different economic approaches to environmental issues, i.e., neoclassical environmental economics and ecological economics, are compared. Some key differences such as weak versus strong sustainability, commensurability versus incommensurability and ethical neutrality versus different values acceptance are pointed out.

**Mundale, Jennifer** and Bechtel, William. Integrating Neuroscience, Psychology, and Evolutionary Biology through a Teleological Conception of Function. *Mind Mach*, 6(4), 481-505, N 96.

The idea of integrating evolutionary biology and psychology has great promise, but one that will be compromised if psychological functions are conceived too abstractly and neuroscience is not allowed to play a constructive role. We argue that the proper integration of neuroscience, psychology, and evolutionary biology requires a teleological as opposed to merely componential analysis of function. A teleological analysis is required in neuroscience itself; we point to traditional and current research methods in neuroscience, which make critical use of distinctly teleological functional considerations in brain cartography. Only by invoking teleological criteria can researchers distinguish the fruitful ways of identifying brain components from the myriad of possible ways. (edited)

**Mundici, Daniele** and Cignoli, Roberto. An Elementary Proof of Chang's Completeness Theorem for the Infinite-Valued Calculus of Lukasiewicz. *Stud Log*, 58(1), 79-97, 1997.

The interpretation of propositions in Lukasiewicz's infinite-valued calculus as answers in Ulam's game with lies—the Boolean case corresponding to the traditional *Twenty Questions* game—gives added interest to the completeness theorem. The literature contains several different proofs, but they invariably require technical prerequisites from such areas as model-theory, algebraic geometry, or the theory of ordered groups. The aim of this paper is to provide a self-contained proof, only requiring the rudiments of algebra and convexity in finite-dimensional vector spaces.

**Mundici, Daniele** and Sette, A M and Cifuentes, J C. Cauchy Completeness in Elementary Logic. *J Sym Log*, 61(4), 1153-1157, D 96.

**Munk, Axel** and Schmidt, Thomas and Nida-Rümelin, Julian. Interpersonal Dependency of Preferences. *Theor Decis*, 41(3), 257-280, N 96.

Standard decision theoretic models disregard the phenomenon of interpersonal dependency of preferences. In this paper it is argued that interpersonal dependency of preferences is a serious challenge for standard utility theory. First we sketch the more philosophical aspects of the problem and then, using a simple, formal model for the two-person case, we show that interpersonal dependency of preferences generally results in indeterminacy of preferences (resp. of subjective utility).

**Muñoz García, Angel**. La Meteorología de Suárez de Urbina: Filosofía, Filokalia, Cosmología o sólo "Folklórica"?. *Rev Filosof (Venezuela)*, 23(1), 5-20, 1996.

A fragment of the Second Part of the Philosophical Course of Suarez de Urbina (soon to be published) concerning his meteorology is analyzed. Due to the historical context of the author (1958), his faithfulness to Aristotle versus his acceptance of scientific experience is studied. Suárez de Urbina considers philosophy to be the study of beauty and the product of admiration.

**Munthe, Christian** and Welin, Stellan. The Morality of Scientific Openness. *Sci Eng Ethics*, 2(4), 411-428, O 96.

The ideal of scientific openness, i.e., the idea that scientific information should be freely accessible to interested parties, is strongly supported throughout the scientific community. At the same time, however, this ideal does not appear to be absolute in the everyday practice of science. In order to get the credit for new scientific advances, scientists often keep information to themselves. Also, it is common practice to withhold information obtained in commissioned research when the scientist has agreed with his or her employer to do so. The secrecy may be intended forever, as in the military area, but also temporarily until a patent application has been made. The paper explores to what extent such secrecy is undesirable, as seems to be suggested by the ideal of scientific openness. Should this ideal be interpreted as having certain exceptions which make the above-mentioned practices acceptable? Are there, on closer inspection, good arguments for the ideal of scientific openness, and for officially upholding it? Possible versions of the ideal of scientific openness are explored and the issue is found to be rather complex, allowing for wide variations depending on the acting parties, beneficiaries, types of information and moral requirements involved. We conclude that the arguments usually given in favor of this ideal are weaker than what seems to be generally believed, and that, on closer inspection, they have plenty of room for exceptions to it. These exceptions only partly cover the actual practice of withholding scientific information, and there may still be good reason to advocate, teach and enforce the ideal of scientific openness within the scientific community.

**Munz, Peter**. The Quixotic Element in *The Open Society*. *Phil Soc Sci*, 27(1), 39-55, Mr 97.

While the ethics and the sociology of *The open Society* can stand up to criticism after 50 years, it is argued that Popper's thesis that closed societies are prompted and promoted by "historicism" cannot. Moreover, Popper's conceptions of "historicism" and of "developmental law" are based on a misunderstanding of our knowledge of history, the practice of historical writing and the discipline of sociology. In conclusion there is an attempt to explain why, of all people Popper ever criticized for their historicism, Darwin alone was singled out by him for exoneration.

**Munzel, G Felicitas**. Reason's Practical Idea of Perpetual Peace, Human Character, and the Pedagogical Function of the Republican Constitution. *Ideal Stud*, 26(2), 101-134, Wint 96.

Interpreting the idea of perpetual peace as fundamentally a practical idea of reason, the essay 1) identifies the problematical nature of the concept in Kant's writings, 2) argues that as a moral task its essential reference is to human character; and 3) that its attainment consists in overcoming an internal source of conflict within human nature, one for which external war between peoples is but its worst manifestation. Thus the pedagogical function Kant claims for the republican constitution proves to be a negative and facilitating one in relation to what remains the individual's responsibility, the "virtue that cannot be taught."

**Muram, David** and Aiken, Margaret M and Strong, Carson. Children's Refusal of Gynecologic Examinations for Suspected Sexual Abuse. *J Clin Ethics*, 8(2), 158-164, Sum 97.

Cases are presented in which children refuse gynecologic examinations following suspected sexual abuse. Topics discussed include background concerning child sexual abuse, the purpose of the medical examination, and psychosocial aspects of such examinations. A framework for dealing with such refusals is presented that identifies relevant ethical values, distinguishes categories of decision-making capacity in children, and provides an interpretation of the principle of patient advocacy. Using this framework, the authors argue for proposed resolutions of the cases presented.

**Muray, Leslie A**. Ultimate Reality and Meaning as Portrayed in the Religious Symbolism of Aron Tamási. *Ultim Real Mean*, 20(2 & 3), 165-178, Je-S 97.

This article first presents a biographical sketch of Aron Tamasi, an ethnic Hungarian writer from Transylvania (1897-1966). Few writers have expressed as poignantly yet realistically the ethos of a people as has Tamasi the ethos of his own Szekely people, the ethnic Hungarians of Transylvania. Following the biographical sketch, I examine the indissolubility of religious and cultural symbols in his classic Abel trilogy. Themes explored include Abel as a primordial, mythical character who symbolizes innocence and the loss of innocence, who also represents the Szekely people and whose powerful sense of rootedness in the land is inseparably linked to the sense of a transcendent mystery immanent in the ambiguities of nature and history.

**Muresan, Valentin**. Transcendentalism, Nomicity and Modal Thought. *Theoria (Spain)*, 11(27), 49-59, S 96.

The main purpose of this paper is to show that Kant's transcendental philosophy is tacitly laden with the structures of modern modal thought. More exactly, the surprising parallelism which seems to exist between Kant's manner of defining *necessity* (and, on this basis, *nomicity*) and the modern approaches of the same concepts in the frame of "possible worlds philosophy" is stressed. A new interpretation of the Categorical Imperative is also offered on this basis.

**Murillo, José Ignacio**. La teoría de la cultura de Leonardo Polo. *Anu Filosof*, 29(2), 851-867, 1996.

Culture is a social and historical *continuatio ficta naturae* which represents the solution to the problem of a plurality of persons who share the same nature and dispose of the universe according to the limitation of their knowledge.

**Murmann, Sven** and Schefczyk, Michael. Bewusstes Leben und Metaphysik: Gespräch mit Dieter Henrich. *Z Phil Praxis*, 4-9, 1995.

In the interview mentioned above D. Henrich outlines ideas which are essential for his philosophical thinking. It becomes transparent that for Henrich genuine human self-understanding is based on nonmaterialist metaphysics. Towards the end of the interview he comes to a conclusion concerning *sense* and *non-sense* of philosophical counselling.

**Murphy, Arthur E** and Singer, Marcus G (ed). *Reason, Reality, and Speculative Philosophy*. Madison, Univ of Wisconsin Pr, 1996.

This book brings to publication the bulk of a previously unpublished manuscript which the author, who died in 1962, finished writing in 1940. In the course of his discussion of speculative philosophy and the main philosophical tendencies in the period 1890 to 1940, the author provides his own account of what a

AUTHOR INDEX 805 Myro, George

reasonable and sensible philosophy should be and do and what a reasonable philosophical method consists in. Among the topics discussed are Philosophy in the Contemporary World, The Rational Use of Ideas, The Standpoint of Philosophy, The Way Philosophies Work and The Life of Reason. The philosophies considered include idealism, Realism and the enterprise called Speculative Philosophy—its nature and character and major types and representatives. The author discusses, among other philosophers, Bradley, Bosanquet, Peirce, Russell, Whitehead, Alexander, R. W. Sellars, McTaggart, Gilson and Santayana, in the light of the ideas presented on what philosophy is and reasonably can accomplish. The book also presents an account of the nature of reason and reality and of critical philosophy as opposed to speculative philosophy and an argument for the method of operational or contextual analysis. The editor has provided a Preface, a Memoir of the author, an Introduction, Bibliographical Notes and explanatory comments where needed.

**Murphy, George L**. Fertility Technologies and Trans-Kin Altruism. *J Med Human*, 17(3), 195-202, Fall 96.

We consider the ethics of fertility technologies such as harvesting ova from aborted fetuses. Is provision of biological descendants for a couple so important that all technological measures are permissible in pursuit of that goal? "Genetic self-interest" is important in evolution, but the development of humanity is also marked by "trans-kin altruism", concern for individuals beyond bounds of close genetic relationship. If this is an aspect of genuine humanity, then in some cases we may encourage childless couples to adopt rather than conceive by ethically problematic technologies. Some practical suggestions in this direction are given.

**Murphy, Jeffrie G**. Cognitive and Moral Obstacles to Imputation. *Jahr Recht Ethik*, 2, 67-79, 1994.

Oftmals rechnen wir anderen Verantwortlichkeit zu, um durch Strafe Vergeltung zu üben—und dies manchmal in der Hoffnung, dass ihnen gerade der Grad an Leid zugefügt wird, der im rechten Verhältnis zu dem steht, was Kant "innere Bösartigkeit" nennt. Aber wissen wir eigentlich genug, um dies ohne grobe Fahrlässigkeit, und sind wir moralisch rein genug, um dies ohne Heuchelei tun zu können? Der vorliegende Beitrag befasst sich mit diesen beiden Fragen.

**Murphy, Liam B**. A Relatively Plausible Principle of Beneficence: Reply to Mulgan. *Phil Pub Affairs*, 26(1), 80-86, Wint 97.

**Murphy, Mark C**. Deviant Uses of "Obligation" in Hobbes' *Leviathan*. *Hist Phil Quart*, 11(3), 281-294, Jl 94.

In this paper I provide both a catalog of the uses of 'obligation' in *Leviathan* that do not accord with Hobbes's official definition and an explanation for those deviant uses of 'obligation'. I argue that Hobbes's deviant uses of 'obligation' correspond to two understandings of obligation prevalent in the scholastic natural law tradition. This correspondence suggests that Hobbes's deviant uses of 'obligation' are not mere accidents to be explained away; rather, they bring into focus tensions within Hobbes's moral theory that mark it both as continuous with and as moving beyond the scholastic natural law tradition.

**Murphy, Mark C**. Surrender of Judgment and the Consent Theory of Political Authority. *Law Phil*, 16(2), 115-143, 97.

The aim of this paper is to take the first steps toward providing a refurbished consent theory of political authority, one that rests in part on a reconception of the relationship between the surrender of judgment and the authoritativeness of political institutions. On the standard view, whatever grounds political authority implies that one ought to surrender one's judgment to that of one's political institutions. On the refurbished view, it is the surrender of one's judgment—which can plausibly be considered a form of consent—that makes political institutions practically authoritative.

**Murphy, Mark C**. The Conscience Principle. *J Phil Res*, 22, 387-407, Ap 97.

In the first part of this paper, I explain what I mean by "conscience" and "dictate of conscience," and I show that the notion that the conscience principle is inherently anti-authoritarian or inherently fanatical is mistaken. In the second part, I argue that the existence of mistaken conscience does not reduce the conscience principle to absurdity. In the third part, I present two arguments for the plausibility of that principle.

**Murphy, Michael R** and Veit, E Theodore. Ethics Violations: A Survey of Investment Analysts. *J Bus Ethics*, 15(12), 1287-1297, D 96.

The authors analyze the responses to a mail survey of securities analysts who were asked about their ethical behavior and the ethical behavior of people with whom they work. The findings show the types of ethical violations that occur and the frequency with which they occur. The findings also show how respondents deal with observed violations of ethical behavior. All responses are analyzed to determine if differences exist between the responses of analysts having different characteristics (gender, age, years of employment, and education) and differences in employment circumstances (firm size, firm type, buy side/sell side, U.S./Canada)

**Murray, Michael**. Intellect, Will, and Freedom: Leibniz and His Precursors. *Leibniz Soc Rev*, 6, 25-59, D 96.

Like his predecessors and contemporaries, Leibniz's account of the "mechanics" of free choosing was cast in terms of faculty psychology. From medieval to early modern times, explanations of free choice were cast in terms of the operations of intellect and will severally and upon one another. In this essay I survey certain psychological accounts of freedom offered by some important scholastic precursors of Leibniz's view. I argue that examination of these figures, especially seventeenth century Spanish figures, allows us to see exactly what Leibniz is after with his use of cryptic phrases such as "moral necessity" and "inclination without necessitation."

**Murray, Patrick** (ed). *Reflections on Commercial Life: An Anthology of Classic Texts from Plato to the Present*. New York, Routledge, 1997.

Is commercialization the mainspring of modernity? Do modern commercial forms represent an end state of social development—the "end of history"? *Reflections on Commercial Life*, an anthology of writings from the ancient Greeks to contemporary thinkers, poses these and related questions. It provides students, scholars and general readers an opportunity to develop a more self-conscious and critical relationship to commercial life, as it challenges the inattention of mainstream economics to the social forms that make up commercial life, such as money, the commodity, wage-labor and capital. Selections are drawn from seminal works of high intellectual and literary quality. *Reflections on Commercial Life* is an important anthology that offers the opportunity to explore, as never before, the history, nature, outcomes and alternatives to modern commercial life. (publisher)

**Murty, K Satchidananda**. Comment on "Vedānta in the First Millennium AD: Illusion or Reality?". *J Indian Counc Phil Res*, 13(3), 150, My-Ag 96.

**Muskin, Philip R**. Care, Support, and Concern for Noncompliant Patients. *J Clin Ethics*, 8(2), 178-180, Sum 97.

**Musschenga, Albert W**. The Relation between Concepts of Quality-of-Life, Health and Happiness. *J Med Phil*, 22(1), 11-28, F 97.

In this article I will, first, summarize the results of my explorations of the use and the meaning of the term "quality-of-life." The use and the meaning of the term turn out to depend on the contexts of medical decision making in which it is used. I will show that there are at least three different concepts of quality-of-life. Second, I will argue that the different concepts of quality-of-life are not unrelated. They point to different components of and/or conditions for happiness. Third, I will analyze the relation between the three concepts of quality-of-life, health and happiness. (edited)

**Mutanen, Arto**. "Theory of Identifiability" in *Knowledge and Inquiry: Essays on Jaakko Hintikka's Epistemology and Philosophy of Science*, Sintonen, Matti (ed), 133-146. Amsterdam, Rodopi, 1997.

In this paper I will introduce the notion of identifiability. The most basic properties of the notion will be stated. In my presentation I will follow, very carefully, Hintikka's ideas. The theory of identifiability is introduced in the framework of interrogative model of inquiry. We 'stabilize' interrogative process by using Abraham Robinson's diagram method. This helps us in presenting properties of the notion, and in seeing the interconnection between the notions of identifiability and definability.

**Myers, Gerald E**. "Pragmatism and Introspective Psychology" in *The Cambridge Companion to William James*, Putnam, Ruth Anna (ed), 11-24. New York, Cambridge Univ Pr, 1997.

**Myers, Michael D** and Miller, Leigh. Ethical Dilemmas in the Use of Information Technology: An Aristotelian Perspective. *Ethics Behavior*, 6(2), 153-160, 1996.

In this article the authors suggest that a fruitful and interesting way to conceptualize some of these moral and ethical issues associated with the use of information technology is to apply the principles of Aristotle's ethics to this topic. They argue that framing the moral and ethical choices associated with information technology in Aristotelian terms draws attention to the fact that there are fundamental *dilemmas* to be addressed. These dilemmas are discussed in relation to the four areas suggested by Dejoie, Fowler, and Paradice (1991): a) privacy, b) information accuracy, c) access to information, and d) intellectual property rights. The dilemmas associated with all four areas are illustrated with references to recent legal developments in Australia and New Zealand. (edited)

**Myers, Robert J**. Hans Morgenthau's Realism and American Foreign Policy. *Ethics Int Affairs*, 11, 253-270, 1997.

As the father of the realist theory of international relations, Hans Morgenthau consistently argued that international politics is governed by the competitive and conflictual nature of humankind. Myers discusses the history of American foreign policy and the ongoing debate over the continued relevance of realist thought in the post-Cold War era. He argues that despite vast changes in the international system, realism remains relevant as an accurate description of human nature and hence the interactions between nations. Analyzing Morgenthau's *Politics Among Nations*, Myers provides a point-by-point discussion of his theory. The end of the Cold War and collapse of the Soviet Union have renewed the idealist-realist debate. Myers concludes by stating that the relevance of realism will be seen particularly in the search for a new balance of power in the post-Cold War world.

**Myerson, George**. They Speak for Themselves, or else...: Human Voices and the Dreams of Knowledge. *Hist Human Sci*, 10(3), 134-150, Ag 97.

This article is about knowledge and argument. The purpose is to dramatize certain questions of knowledge: how and why does the better knowledge not become the better argument; what are the voices accessible to the claiming of new knowledge; what are the limits and destinies of contemporary expertise? The article is also an experiment in academic and intellectual forms, an experiment which corresponds to the central inquiry: how should knowledge speak now? There are three parts. The first part tells a story about enlightenment and persuasion. The second part is a dialogue between two voices which speak for the argumentative ethos of knowledge—Newtonian is a voice of the centre, and Paracelsan speaks from and for the margins. The third part is a dialogue between critic and speculator, a dialogue about the fate of knowledge in postmodernity. (edited)

**Myro, George**. "Thinking" in *Objections to Physicalism*, Robinson, Howard (ed), 27-38. New York, Clarendon/Oxford Pr, 1996.

**Myrvold, Wayne C**. Bayesianism and Diverse Evidence: A Reply to Andrew Wayne. *Phil Sci*, 63(4), 661-665, D 96.

Andrew Wayne (1995) discusses some recent attempts to account, within a Bayesian framework, for the "common methodological adage" that "diverse evidence better confirms a hypothesis than does the same amount of similar evidence" (112). One of the approaches considered by Wayne is that suggested by Howson and Urbach (1989/1993) and dubbed the "correlation approach" by Wayne. This approach is, indeed, incomplete, in that it neglects the role of the hypothesis under consideration in determining what diversity in a body of evidence is *relevant* diversity. In this paper, it is shown how this gap can be filled, resulting in a more satisfactory account of the evidential role of diversity of evidence. In addition, it is argued that Wayne's criticism of the correlation approach does not indicate a serious flaw in the approach.

**Naas, Michael B**. "Rashomon and the Sharing of Voices Between East and West" in *On Jean-Luc Nancy: The Sense of Philosophy,* Sheppard, Darren (ed), 63-90. New York, Routledge, 1997.

This essay takes as its inspiration and point of departure Jean-Luc Nancy's "Sharing Voices." It is conceived as a parallel reading of Heidegger's "A Dialogue on Language" in *On the Way to Language*. While Nancy's essay brilliantly demonstrates the role Plato's *Ion* plays in Heidegger's dialogue and the way a certain conception of interpretation on the margins of Plato's text accords with Heidegger's own conception, this work attempts to illuminate the very same issues of interpretation, communication, and the originary sharing out of voices by focusing on a reference on the margins of Heidegger's text—Akira Kurosawa's film *Rashomon.*

**Naas, Michael B**. Derrida's Watch/Foucault's Pendulum. *Phil Today*, 41(1-4), 141-152, Spr 97.

This paper re-examines the Foucault-Derrida debate that begins in 1963 with Derrida's essay "Cogito and the History of Madness" and ends, or would seem to end, with Derrida's 1992 essay "'To do Justice to Freud': The history of Madness in the Age of Psychoanalysis." After providing a brief summary of the history of the debate between Foucault and Derrida, the paper looks at how the terms at issue in the debate concerning the nature of madness (terms such as inclusion and exclusion, dialogue and silence, and, especially, mastery and discipleship) come to characterize the nature and history of the debate itself.

**Nacci, Michela**. Il gioco degli specchi. *Iride*, 9(18), 366-373, Ag 96.

In questo articolo si discutono i rapporti fra destra e sinistra: oggi è difficile distinguere i rispettivi temi e preferenze. Di questa realtà si ripercorrono la fenomenologia recente e alcune interpretazioni. La tesi che viene sostenuta è che destra e sinistra si sono modificate entrambe: sempre, ognuna di esse definisce se stessa in rapporto all'altra. Ma forse sono proprio i criteri con i quali destra e sinistra vengono distinte che vanno ridiscussi.

**Nacci, Michela**. Tecnopolitica: Le idee del cyberpunk. *Iride*, 9(19), 716-729, S-D 96.

**Nadler, Steven**. "No Necessary Connection": The Medieval Roots of the Occasionalist Roots of Hume. *Monist*, 79(3), 448-466, Jl 96.

This is an analysis of the "no necessary connection" argument in Hume and its antecedents in Malebranche, Al-Ghazali, and Nicholas of Autrecourt. (edited)

**Nadler, Steven**. Descartes's Demon and the Madness of Don Quixote. *J Hist Ideas*, 58(1), 41-55, J 97.

A comparison of the epistemological issues raised by Descartes in the *First Meditation* and by the predicament of Don Quixote—in the light of his belief in an evil enchanter—in Arvantes's novel. An analysis of the skeptical crisis faced in each work.

**Nagasawa, Kunihiko**. Eine neue Möglichkeit der Philosophie nach der *Grundlage der gesamten Wissenschaftslehre*. *Fichte-Studien*, 10, 115-123, 1997.

This paper tries to explore a new possibility of philosophy based on Fichte's *Grundlage der gesamten Wissenschaftslehre*. Part 1 analyzes the relation of philosopher and philosophy. Using the symbol of "Zirkel," Fichte describes how the thinking of the philosopher and the thinking of the self attempt to become one, and thus, in the process of philosophy, approach the infinite in the finite self. Part 2, starting from this double character of thinking, derives the uniqueness of Fichte's transcendental philosophy. Part 3 shows that Fichte's science of knowledge as metascience opens a new horizon for a new encounter between Eastern and Western thinking. (edited)

**Nagashima, Takashi** and Kaneko, Mamoru. Game Logic and its Applications I. *Stud Log*, 57(2-3), 325-354, O 96.

This paper provides a logic framework for investigations of game theoretical problems. We adopt an infinitary extension of classical predicate logic as the base logic of the framework. The reason for an infinitary extension is to express the common knowledge concept explicitly. Depending upon the choice of axioms on the knowledge operators, there is a hierarchy of logics. The limit case is an infinitary predicate extension of modal propositional logic $KD_4$ and is of special interest in applications. In Part I, we develop the basic framework and show some applications: an epistemic axiomatization of Nash equilibrium and formal undecidability on the playability of a game. To show the formal undecidability, we use a term existence theorem, which will be proved in Part II.

**Nagashima, Takashi** and Kaneko, Mamoru. Game Logic and Its Applications II. *Stud Log*, 58(2), 273-303, Mr 97.

This paper provides a Genzten-style formulation of the game logic framework $GL_m$ (0 "is less than or equal to" m "is less than or equal to" omega), and proves the cut-elimination theorem for $GL_{omega}$ used in Part I. (edited)

**Nagatomo, Shigenori** and Leisman, Gerald. An East Asian Perspective of Mind-Body. *J Med Phil*, 21(4), 439-466, Ag 96.

The paper examines states of conscious experience from an East Asian perspective allowing analysis on achieved supernormal consciousness rather than a focus on "normal" or "subnormal." The nature of the "transformation" of human consciousness will be studied both philosophically, as a transformation from "provisional" dualism to nondualism, and neurophysiologically. The theoretical structure of the transformation will, in part, be examined through the model provided by a Japanese medieval Zen master, Takuan Sôhô. (edited)

**Nagayama, Misao**. On a Property of BCK-Identities. *Stud Log*, 53(2), 227-234, My 94.

A BCK-algebra is an algebra in which the terms are generated by a set of variables, 1, and an arrow. We mean by a *BCK-identity* an equation valid in all BCK-algebras. In this paper using a syntactic method we show that for two terms *s* and *t*, if neither *s*=1 nor *t*=1 is a BCK-identity, and *s*=*t* is a BCK-identity, then the rightmost variables of the two terms are identical. The prove the main theorem, we use a Gentzen-type logical system for the BCK-algebras, introduced by Komori, which consists of the identity axiom, the right and the left introduction rules of the implication, the exchange rule, the weakening rule and the cut. As noted in [2], the cut-elimination theorem holds for this system. (edited)

**Nagel, Alexandra H M**. Are Plants Conscious?. *J Consciousness Stud*, 4(3), 215-230, 1997.

Views of 'plant consciousness' in the literature are classified on a scale ranging from descriptions of plant phenomena using consciousness as a metaphor, to explicit statements that plants are conscious beings. The idea of plant consciousness is far from new, but it has received a new impetus from recent claims by psychics to communicate with plants. The literature surveyed is widely scattered and very diverse, but it can teach us much about the views that various segments of society hold on plant consciousness.

**Nagel, Christopher P**. Hegelianism in Merleau-Ponty's Philosophy of History. *Phil Today*, 41(2), 288-298, Sum 97.

Despite his critical comments about Hegel, Merleau-Ponty's view of history derives from Hegel's. For both, the task of understanding history requires an account of action in the context of the developing, worldly reason underlying events. The chief difference between their views is Merleau-Ponty's emphasis on the contingency of these events and of reason itself, yet for Merleau-Ponty as well as for Hegel, reason can only appear contingent. Thus their views are far more similar than Merleau-Ponty admits.

**Nagel, Thomas**. *The Last Word*. New York, Oxford Univ Pr, 1997.

In *The Last Word*, Thomas Nagel, one of the most influential philosophers writing in English, presents a sustained defense of reason against the attacks of subjectivism, delivering systematic rebuttals of relativistic claims with respect to language, logic, science and ethics. He shows that the last word in disputes about the objective validity of any form of thought must lie in some unqualified thoughts about how things are—thoughts that we cannot regard from outside as mere psychological dispositions. His work sets a new standard in the debate on this crucially important question and should generate intense interest both within and outside the philosophical community. (publisher)

**Nagl-Docekal, Herta**. Seyla Benhabib and the Radical Future of the Enlightenment. *Phil Soc Crit*, 23(5), 63-78, S 97.

**Naik, A D**. A Proof of One Substance Monism. *Darshana Int*, 36(3/143), 75-80, Ap 96.

I argue that there cannot be more than one self-determining substance. The argument is that if there were more than one such substances then the relation of difference between them would not be determined by any substance. Since the relation of difference determines one's identity no substance would then be self-determined.

**Naik, A D**. Belief and Knowledge. *Darshana Int*, 36(1/141), 6-10, Ja 96.

First I distinguish belief from knowledge and argue that knowledge cannot be defined in terms of justified true belief. I then distinguish seventy three complex epistemic states which combine states of belief and knowledge.

**Naik, A D**. Belief and Knowledge. *Indian Phil Quart*, 23(3-4), 411-416, Jl-O 96.

**Naik, A D**. The Ontological Argument Revisited. *Darshana Int*, 35(3/139), 45-47, Jl 95.

**Naishtat, Francisco**. "El lugar de la decisión en la acción racional: de la decisión como deseo, cálculo y acto" in *La racionalidad: su poder y sus límites*, Nudler, Oscar (ed); 329-351. Barcelona, Ed Paidos, 1996.

**Naishtat, Francisco**. Entrevistas: René Descartes, Cuatrocientos años de actualidad. *Rev Latin de Filosof*, 22(2), 375-384, 1996.

**Naishtat, Francisco Samuel**. Los Filósofos y la Pregunta por la Existencia de los Problemas filosóficos. *Cad Hist Filosof Cie*, 6(Spec), 73-84, Ja-D 96.

This article argues for the existence of genuine philosophical problems. The neopositivists of the Vienna Circle sustained that philosophical problems were meaningless, but their opinion was based on an unacceptable verificationist theory of meaning. If we, instead, accepted a pragmatic theory of meaning as use, then philosophy would be meaningful. Its meaning, according to this perspective, would be to draw the limits of a given conceptual scheme or to help the transition to another conceptual scheme.

**Nakajima, Keita**. Dogen on *seppo* and *jodo*. *Bigaku*, 47(4), 25-35, Spr 97.

If the true experience of beauty in art appreciation is, as Kakuzo Okakura argues, presumed to derive from harmony with the whole universe, then works of art are considered to function as *seppo* (preaching of the Dharma, or the truth of the world) in the context of 'One is all, all one.' The purpose of this essay is to analyze Dogen's concept of *seppo* and *jodo* (achievement of the Way, or enlightenment) in order to explore the significance of the realization and enjoyment of works of art in the cosmological framework. Dogen is regarded as one of the major thinkers upon the one-is-all relationship among human beings and things. (edited)

**Nakamura, Yutaka**. Lexicographic Additivity for Multi-Attribute Preferences on Finite Sets. *Theor Decis*, 42(1), 1-19, Ja 97.

This paper explores lexicographically additive representations of multi-attributive preferences on finite sets. Lexicographic additivity combines a lexicographic feature with local value tradeoffs. Tradeoff structures are governed by either transitive or nontransitive additive conjoint measurement. Alternatives are locally traded off when they are close enough within threshold associated with a dominant subset of attributes.

**Nakayama, Shigeru**. "The Chinese "Cyclic" View of History vs. Japanese "Progress" in *The Idea of Progress,* McLaughlin, Peter (ed), 65-75. Hawthorne, de Gruyter, 1997.

**Nakhov, Isai**. Losev and Marxism: Lessons of a Life: 1893-1988. *Russian Stud Phil*, 35(1), 70-85, Sum 96.

**Nancarrow, Paul S**. Realism and Anti-Realism: A Whiteheadian Response to Richard Rorty Concerning Truth, Propositions, and Practice. *Process Stud*, 24, 59-75, 1995.

Alfred North Whitehead's theory of propositions offers a new approach to the postmodern debate over realism and antirealism. Because it combines elements of both a "coherence" and a "correspondence" theory of truth, the Whiteheadian approach can allow for genuine relationship between mind and extramental process, while at the same time affirming the importance of intersubjectivity and shared practice as contributing factors in what counts as truth. Philosophical ideas can be recognized, not only as "optional glosses" or "rhetorical flourishes" for social practices, but as "critics of abstraction" that play a constitutive role in social practices.

**Nancarrow, Paul S**. Wisdom's Information: Rereading a Biblical Image in the Light of Some Contemporary Science and Speculation. *Zygon*, 32(1), 51-64, Mr 97.

The biblical image of *wisdom* as the power who "orders all things well" in nature and in human life can be read in the light of contemporary information theory. Some current scientific speculation offers an interpretation of reality as a vast information-processing system, in which informational situations are continuously transformed through algorithmic operations. This interpretation finds a metaphysical counterpart in the distinction between "nature natured" and "nature naturing" in the philosophical theology of Samuel Taylor Coleridge. This confluence of religious, metaphysical and scientific imagery suggests a picture of the world in which the processes of "nature naturing," "human humaning," and "God Godding" inform and recur in each other.

**Nancy, Jean-Luc**. "Alla frontiera, figure e colori" in *Geofilosofia,* Bonesio, Luisa (ed), 177-188. Sondrio, Lyasis, 1996.

**Naragon, Steve** (ed & trans) and Ameriks, Karl (ed & trans) and Kant, Immanuel. *The Cambridge Edition of the Works of Immanuel Kant: Lectures on Metaphysics*. New York, Cambridge Univ Pr, 1997.

This volume contains the first translation into English of notes from Kant's lectures on metaphysics. These lectures, dating from the 1760s to the 1790s, touch on all the major topics and phases of Kant's philosophy. Most of these notes appeared only recently in the German Academy's edition; this translation offers many corrections of that edition. (publisher, edited)

**Narayan, Uma** (ed) and Shanley, Mary Lyndon (ed). *Reconstructing Political Theory: Feminist Perspectives*. University Park, Pennsylvania Univ Pr, 1997.

While some of the chapters discuss traditional concepts such as rights, power, freedom, and citizenship, others argue that less frequently discussed topics in political theory—such as the family, childhood, dependency, compassion, and suffering—are just as significant for an understanding of political life. The opening chapter by Narayan and Shanley shows how this diverse set of topics can be linked together and how feminist political theory can be elaborated systematically if it takes notions of independence and dependancy, public and private, and power and empowerment as central to its agenda. (publisher, edited)

**Narayanadas, V C** and Devi, S Sreekala. Dostoyevsky and the Problem of God. *Darshana Int*, 36(2/142), 57-63, Ap 96.

**Narbonne, Jean-Marc**. Aristotle and the Question of Being as Being: Reflections on S. Rosen's *The Question of Being* (in French). *Arch Phil*, 60(1), 5-24, Ja-Mr 97.

This article aims at showing the underlying proximity existing between Aristotelian ontology and Platonic henology and at the same time it attempts to bring out the inherent difficulties in the *metaphysical* orientation proposed by Heidegger.

**Narbonne, Jean-Marc**. Le réceptacle platonicien: nature, fonction, contenu. *Dialogue (Canada)*, 36(2), 253-279, Spr 97.

This paper will attempt to show that the interlude on necessity in the Timaeus narrative introduces a dualism into the Platonic cosmology, and that it is the material principle which is the positive cause of the disorder in the world. Furthermore, one can notice that in this work Plato is heading toward a concept of sensible substance that is close to the one which Aristotle will be defending.

**Nardone, Marco**. Il problema del 'Desiderium naturale videndi Deum' nell'ottica tomista della partecipazione secondo la prospettiva di Cornelio Fabro. *Sapienza*, 50(2), 173-240, 1997.

**Nardozza, Massimo**. Tradizione romanistica e dommatica moderna. *Riv Int Filosof Diritto*, 73(4), 651-703, O-D 96.

**Narendran, Paliath** and Pfenning, Frank and Statman, Richard. On the Unification Problem for Cartesian Closed Categories. *J Sym Log*, 62(2), 636-647, Je 97.

Cartesian closed categories (CCCs) have played and continue to play an important role in the study of the semantics of programming languages. An axiomatization of the isomorphisms which hold in all Cartesian closed categories discovered independently by Soloviev and Bruce, Di Cosmo and Longo leads to seven equalities. We show that the unification problem for this theory is undecidable, thus settling an open question. We also show that an important subcase, namely unification modulo the *linear isomorphisms*, is NP-complete. Furthermore, the problem of matching in CCCs is NP-complete when the subject term is irreducible. (edited)

**Nascimento, Maria das Graças S**. O Modelo Psicofisiológico Cartesiano e o Materialismo das Luzes. *Cad Hist Filosof Cie*, 5(1-2), 105-123, Ja-D 95.

Criticizing Descartes's dualism, French materialistic doctrines of the 18th century have curiously looked for inspiration in the psychophysiological model of explanation of the bodily machine and its relationships to the soul, as it is presented in *Passions of the Soul*. Such a procedure seeks to point out that it was unnecessary for Descartes to consider the soul as a substance.

**Nash, Andrew**. Wine-Farming, Heresy Trials and the 'Whole Personality': The Emergence of the Stellenbosch Philosophical Tradition, 1916-40. *S Afr J Phil*, 16(2), 55-65, My 97.

This is the first of a series of three articles on the development of a Socratic moment in the Stellenbosch philosophical tradition. This article seeks to describe and explain the emergence of a distinctive local philosophical tradition in the Stellenbosch context. To this end, it analyses the historical peculiarities of Afrikaner political and intellectual life in the Western Cape, showing how these prevented Stellenbosch philosophers both from identifying with capitalist modernity and from rejecting it in favour of premodern ideals. A distinctive response to this dilemma, seeking a philosophical reconciliation of modernity and tradition, was first articulated by Tobie Muller. But his arguments led away from the study of philosophy itself and towards the tasks of social and spiritual upliftment. Philosophy as a discipline only expended after the removal of Professor du Plessis from the theological seminary after repeated charges of heresy. The philosophical optimism propounded by du Plessis and *Het Zoeklicht* had suffered a decisive defeat and the next generation of philosophers turned toward more individualist and voluntarist themes.

**Nash, Robert J**. *"Real World" Ethics: Frameworks for Educators and Human Service Professionals*. New York, Teachers College Pr, 1996.

**Nasr, Seyyed Hossein**. "Metaphysical Roots of Tolerance and Intolerance: An Islamic Interpretation" in *Philosophy, Religion, and the Question of Intolerance*, Ambuel, David (ed), 43-56. Albany, SUNY Pr, 1997.

Only the Divine Principle can be said to be beyond all opposition for even in the Divine Order at the level of the Divine Names and Qualities there is an opposition which is the principle of all the opposition one meets in the world of manifestation. Tolerance and intolerance are in fact not only moral but also cosmic terms. Certain dualities whose principle is to be sought in the realm of the Divine Names and Qualities can be harmonized such as the male and female while others such as good and evil cannot be harmonized but only transcended as far as particular good and evil are concerned. Religion is fully aware of this reality and is always intolerant of the false and of evil. It is in the light of this metaphysical opposition that tolerance and intolerance must be reappraised and the current understanding on the basis of secular humanism criticized. Islam is often accused today of intolerance because of its uncompromising stance concerning the truth. But on the practical level Islam has shown a great deal of tolerance and especially Sufism has emphasized tolerance on the basis of universal truth which then transcends even the category of tolerance as usually understood. While the Age of Enlightenment absolutized reason and understood tolerance accordingly, Islam bases itself on the primacy of the Divine over the "merely" human. A living organism is always intolerant of that which threatens its life and much of the reaction of contemporary Islam must be seen in this light. The future depends on being "tolerant" towards the truth and not only towards error which is the case for the most part in the modern world.

**Nathan, N M L**. "Weak Materialism" in *Objections to Physicalism,* Robinson, Howard (ed), 207-224. New York, Clarendon/Oxford Pr, 1996.

**Nathan, N M L**. Admiration: A New Obstacle. *Philosophy*, 72(281), 453-459, Jl 97.

**Nathan, N M L**. Naturalism and Self-Defeat: Plantinga's Version. *Relig Stud*, 33(2), 135-142, Je 97.

In *Warrant and Proper Function* Plantinga argues that atheistic naturalism is self-defeating. What is the probability that our cognitive faculties are reliable, given this naturalism and an evolutionary explanation of their origins? Plantinga argues that if the naturalist is modest enough to believe that it is irrational to have any belief as to the value of this probability, then he is irrational even to believe his own naturalism. I suggest that Plantinga's argument has a false premise, and that even if his argument were sound, there would be reasons for doubting whether the naturalist should respond to it by abandoning his naturalism.

**Nathan, N M L**. Self and Will. *Int J Phil Stud*, 5(1), 81-94, Mr 97.

When do two mental items belong to the same life? We could be content with the answer—just when they have certain volitional qualities in common. An affinity is noted between that theory and Berkeley's early doctrine of the self. Some rivals of the volitional theory invoke a spiritual or physical owner of mental items. They run a risk either of empty formality or of causal superstition. Other rivals postulate a nontransitive and symmetrical relation in the set of mental items.

Nathan, Nicholas 808 AUTHOR INDEX

They must allow in consequence either for joint ownership of one and the same mental item, or for incompatible simultaneous decisions by one and the same person, or for new forms of death. This makes them disquieting. Another rival invokes a transitive and symmetrical relation defined in terms of coconsciousness. Even that allows for incongruous simultaneities. The volitional theory is free from such disadvantages.

**Nathan, Nicholas**. True and Ultimate Responsibility. *Philosophy*, 72(280), 297-302, Ap 97.

**Nathaniel, Alvita K** and Burkhardt, Margaret A. Patient Self-Determination and Complementary Therapies. *Bioethics Forum*, 12(4), 24-29, Wint 96.

Many people who seek health care from conventional biomedical health care providers utilize other healing modalities as well, which are often referred to as alternative or complementary therapies. When considering ethical issues regarding complementary therapies, attentiveness to patient self-determination is imperative. Although it is the patient's responsibility to seek information about complementary modalities and to make health choices in this regard, it is prudent for conventional providers to become knowledgeable about other modalities and to provide a nonjudgmental atmosphere in which patients can discuss and explore approaches to addressing their health care needs.

**Nathanson, Stephen**. "Nationalism and the Limits of Global Humanism" in *The Morality of Nationalism*, McKim, Robert (ed), 176-187. New York, Oxford Univ Pr, 1997.

**Natsoulas, Thomas**. Consciousness and Self-Awareness—Part I: $\text{Consciousness}_1$, $\text{Consciousness}_2$, and $\text{Consciousness}_3$. *J Mind Behav*, 18(1), 53-74, Wint 97.

Published in two parts, the present article addresses whether self-awareness is necessarily involved in each of the six kinds of consciousness that *The Oxford English Dictionary* identifies under the word *consciousness*. Part I inquires into how, if at all, self-awareness enters consciousness: a cognitive relation between people in which they have joint and mutual cognizance; consciousness: a psychological process of conceiving of oneself in certain sorts of respects on a firsthand evidentiary basis; and consciousness: being occurrently aware of anything at all, including nonexistent particulars. (edited)

**Natsoulas, Thomas**. Consciousness and Self-Awareness—Part II: $\text{Consciousness}_4$, $\text{Consciousness}_5$, and $\text{Consciousness}_6$. *J Mind Behav*, 18(1), 75-94, Wint 97.

Published in two parts, the present article addresses whether and how self-awareness is necessarily involved in each of the six kinds of consciousness that *The Oxford English Dictionary* identifies in its entry for the word *consciousness*. In this second part, I inquire into how self-awareness enters a) consciousness, or the immediate ("inner") awareness that we have of our mental-occurrence instances, b) consciousness, or the constitution of the totality of mental-occurrence instances which is the person's conscious being and c) consciousness, or the highly adaptive general mode of the mind's functioning that we instantiate for most of the time that we are aware. (edited)

**Natsoulas, Thomas**. The Case for Intrinsic Theory: I. An Introduction. *J Mind Behav*, 17(3), 267-286, Sum 96.

This is the introductory installment in a projected series of articles in which I shall be advancing the positive case for the "instrinsic" kind of explanatory account of "$\text{consciousness}_4$." "$\text{Consciousness}_4$" has reference to a property of individual mental-occurrence instances (the "$\text{conscious}_4$" ones) wherein there takes place an immediate awareness of them either upon their occurrence or as part of their very occurrence. In this article, I set the stage by a) rendering some of the relevant meanings explicit, b) spelling out my purpose and approach to making the case for intrinsic theory, c) providing some context for the discussions to follow, and d) mentioning important objections to intrinsic theory that have been voiced in the literature. (edited)

**Natsoulas, Thomas**. The Case for Intrinsic Theory: II. An Examination of a Conception of $\text{Consciousness}_4$ as Intrinsic, Necessary, and Concomitant. *J Mind Behav*, 17(4), 369-390, Autumn 96.

The present article is the second one in a series and begins to spell out the case for the intrinsic kind of theory of consciousness. According to such theory, a mental-occurrence instance is conscious (i.e., an immediate object of occurent awareness) on its own, that is, as part of its own internal structure. Considered here are a prominent phenomenologist's argument in favor of an intrinsic theory of consciousness, and his conception of how such inner awareness occurs in the case of objectivating mental acts, which are all conscious in his view. This article emphasizes the question of what property of outer awareness it is that necessarily, as has been claimed, brings along with it inner awareness of the respective objectivating act. Also, this article begins to argue that, in the very occurrence of any conscious objectivating act, inner awareness is "interwoven" with outer awareness. (edited)

**Natsoulas, Thomas**. The Presence of Environmental Objects to Perceptual Consciousness: Consideration of the Problem with Special Reference to Husserl's Phenomenological Account. *J Mind Behav*, 17(2), 161-184, Spr 96.

In the succession of states of consciousness that constitute James's stream of consciousness, there occur, among others, states of consciousness that are themselves, or that include, perceptual mental acts. It is assumed some of the latter states of consciousness are purely perceptual, lacking both imaginal and signitive contents. According to Husserl, purely perceptual acts present to consciousness, uniquely, their environmental objects in themselves, in person. They do not present, as imaginal mental acts do, an image or other representation of their object. Husserl's theory resembles Gibson's with respect to perception's being direct. Both theorists hold perceptual awareness of the environment is not a "founded" act; its proximate causation does not involve any other mental act. Both theorists contend that perceptual acts keep the perceiver directly in touch with the surrounding environment. The present article considers Husserl's account of this directness. (edited)

**Natsoulas, Thomas**. The Sciousness Hypothesis: Part I. *J Mind Behav*, 17(1), 45-66, Wint 96.

James seems to have been tempted by the Sciousness Hypothesis. And he adopted an account of inner awareness that is popular among present-day psychologists of consciousness, to the effect that awareness of a mental-occurrence instance never takes place from within its phenomenological structure, always from a certain distance, by means of a distinct mental-occurrence instance. This means that the immediacy of inner awareness can only be a temporal and causal immediacy, not the kind we seem to have, whereby we consciously participate in the occurrence of a mental state. The present article, which is published in two separate though continuous parts, clarifies and elaborates the Sciousness Hypothesis, and critically discusses it and the kind of account of inner awareness that seems closest to it. (edited)

**Natsoulas, Thomas**. The Sciousness Hypothesis: Part II. *J Mind Behav*, 17(2), 185-206, Spr 96.

James was tempted by the Sciousness Hypothesis; and he adopted the kind of account of inner awareness favored among present-day psychologists of consciousness: to the effect that awareness of a mental-occurrence instance does not take place from within its phenomenological structure, always from a certain distance, by means of a distinct mental-occurrence instance. This means that the immediacy of inner awareness can only be a temporal and causal immediacy, not the kind we seem actually to have, whereby we consciously participate in the occurrence of a mental state. The present article, which is published in two separate though continuous parts, clarifies and elaborates the Sciousness Hypothesis and critically discusses it and the kind of account of inner awareness that seems to be closest to it. (edited)

**Nattiez, Jean-Jacques**. Faits et interprétations en musicologie. *Horiz Phil*, 7(2), 33-42, Spr 97.

**Naudin, Jean** and Azorin, Jean-Michel. Commentary on "Edmund Husserl's Influence on Karl Jaspers's Phenomenology". *Phil Psychiat Psych*, 4(1), 37-39, Mr 97.

**Naumann, Ralf**. Internal Realism, Rationality and Dynamic Semantics. *Protosoz*, 8/9, 111-148, 1996.

Putnam's internal realism implies a form of conceptual relativity with respect to ontology. There can be different descriptions of the world which are based on distinct ontologies. It has been argued that this relativity forecloses any possibility of unifying our knowledge and can even lead to inconsistency. If this is true, internal realism should be abandoned because it is compatible with nonrational positions. We will argue that these objections can be dismissed if truth as idealized warranted assertibility is understood as stability of a belief state under new evidence. This view of truth is still compatible with the existence of distinct belief states expressing different views on the world. (edited)

**Naval, Concepción**. En torno a la sociabilidad humana en el pensamiento de Leonardo Polo. *Anu Filosof*, 29(2), 869-883, 1996.

Education is better thought of as an activity or social practice, from the individual praxis, whose main purpose is to help others become persons. The purpose of this paper is to offer a solid foundation for the natural human sociability, the social virtues and the ideal of cooperation, three areas currently invoked by thinkers of greatly divergent points of view. This paper is written along the lines of the classics and follows the thought of Prof. Polo.

**Navarro, Bernabé**. Los aspectos de ciencia moderna en la filosofía de Clavigero. *Dialogo Filosof*, 12(3), 385-398, S-D 96.

El jesuita mexicano del siglo XVIII Clavigero fue considerado como el pensador mas distinguido de su tiempo. Aquí se investiga su contribución a la introducción en México de la *fisica moderna*, considerada en su época como filosofía moderna.

**Navarro, Pablo E** and Moreso, José Juan. Applicability and Effectiveness of Legal Norms. *Law Phil*, 16(2), 201-219, 97.

We analyse the relationship between applicability and effectiveness of legal norms from a philosophical perspective. In particular, we distinguish between two concepts of applicability. The external applicability of norms refers to institutional duties; a norm N is externally applicable if and only if a judge is legally obliged to apply N to some case c. Internal applicability refers instead to the sphere of validity of legal norms. A norm N is internally applicable to actions regulated by its sphere of validity. We also explore the consequences of a thesis which maintain that applicability restricts the concept of effectiveness, so that only applicable norms can be considered effective. Our analysis illustrates that a proper reconstruction of the concept of applicability is of great importance not only for understanding the concept of effectiveness but also for providing insight into the nature of law.

**Navarro, Pablo E** and Moreso, José Juan. The Dynamics of Legal Positivism: Some Remarks on Shiner's *Norm and Nature*. *Ratio Juris*, 10(3), 288-299, S 97.

In a recently published book, Roger Shiner shows that understanding the fundamental discrepancies between different legal theories is important for a better understanding of law itself. He argues that one of the most important tasks of legal philosophers is to take into account the dynamics or conceptual movements generated by positivism and antipositivism. Our paper intends to show that Shiner's analysis can be developed and modified when other relevant elements are introduced into the universe of discourse. We emphasize the importance of a positivistic conception of legal science. (edited)

**Navarro, Rolando**. Remissions on Jacques Derrida's Work (Spanish). *Fronesis*, 2(2), 189-196, D 95.

This article deals with the main thoughts expressed by the French philosopher Jacques Derrida in his book *La Desconstrucción en las Fronteras de la Filosofía* (1989), which is divided into two sections: the first one deals with the distinction between the *proper sense* and the *metaphorical sense*. Derrida takes us through the evolution of metaphor since the Stoics, from Aristotle to Martin Heidegger and Paul Ricoeur. In the second section entitled *Envío*, Derrida analyzes the problem of representation as a translatability problem and distinguishes between the *praesentation* (act of presenting) and the *repraesentation* (act of becoming present).

**Navarro Pérez, Jorge**. El retorno de la referencia. *Daimon Rev Filosof*, 10, 117-126, Ja-Je 95.

This paper criticizes the interpretation of the history of German philosophy of language (J.G. Hamann, W. von Humboldt, M. Heidegger, H.G. Gadamer, and J. Habermas) that the Spanish scholar Cristina Lafont has propounded in a book from 1993. Against her ideas about "direct reference," the paper states that the extralinguistic concept of reference is a mere illusion.

**Nave, Alberto**. "Logica e filosofia nel pensiero contemporaneo" in *Momenti di Storia della Logica e di Storia della Filosofia,* Guetti, Carla (ed), 239-245. Roma, Aracne Editrice, 1996.

**Navia, Luis E**. *Classical Cynicism: A Critical Study.* Westport, Greenwood Pr, 1996.

The aim of this book is to present a historical review of the Cynic movement in all its aspects, with critical documentation related to ancient sources and modern scholarship. Emphasis is placed, of course, on the three major Cynic philosophers, namely Antisthenes, Diogenes of Sinope, and Crates of Thebes, for it is in them that we find the basis of everything that can be viewed as valuable in classical Cynicism. The many Cynics who emerged after these three philosophers merely carried on certain traditions, exemplified certain modes of living, and upheld certain convictions, all of which can be traced back in one way or another to the early stages of the Cynic movement; these stages are well represented in Antisthenes, Diogenes, and Crates. (edited)

**Nayak, Abhaya C** and Nelson, Paul and Polansky, Hanan. Belief Change as Change in Epistemic Entrenchment. *Synthese*, 109(2), 143-174, N 96.

In this paper, it is argued that both the belief state and its input should be represented as epistemic entrenchment (EE) relations. A belief revision operation is constructed that updates a given EE relation to a new one in light of an evidential EE relation, and an axiomatic characterization of this operation is given. Unlike most belief revision operations, the one developed here can handle both "multiple belief revision" and "iterated belief revision."

**Nayak, G C**. Approach of Hinduism to Its Scriptures. *J Dharma*, 21(4), 307-319, O-D 96.

**Nayak, G C**. Ethical Considerations in Vedanta—A Scientific Approach. *J Dharma*, 21(2), 204-209, Ap-Je 96.

**Neale, Stephen** and Dever, Josh. Slingshots and Boomerangs. *Mind*, 106(421), 144-168, Ja 97.

**Nealon, Jeffrey T**. Between Emergence and Possibility: Foucault, Derrida, and Judith Butler on Performative Identity. *Phil Today*, 40(3), 430-439, Fall 96.

**Neander, Karen**. Swampman Meets Swampcow. *Mind Lang*, 11(1), 118-129, Mr 96.

**Near, Janet P** and Morehead Dworkin, Terry. A Better Statutory Approach to Whistle-Blowing. *Bus Ethics Quart*, 7(1), 1-16, Ja 97.

Statutory approaches toward whistle-blowing currently appear to be based on the assumption that most observers of wrongdoing will report it unless deterred from doing so by fear of retaliation. Yet our review of research from studies of whistle-blowing behavior suggests that this assumption is unwarranted. We propose that an alternative legislative approach would prove more successful in encouraging valid whistle-blowing and describe a model for such legislation that would increase self-monitoring of ethical behavior by organizations, with obvious benefits to society at large. (edited)

**Nederman, Cary J**. Constitutionalism—Medieval and Modern: Against Neo-Figgisite Orthodoxy (Again). *Hist Polit Thought*, 17(2), 179-194, Sum 96.

Francis Oakley has argued (following the earlier work of John Neville Figgis) that medieval conciliar ecclesiology was a central source of later Western ideas about the "constitutional" limitation of the power of rulers. Several years ago, I challenged this neo-Figgisite approach in an article on the political thought of Jean Gerson, to which Oakley responded in an essay published in *History of Political Thought*, 16 (2). In reply to Oakley, I identify methodological problems with the neo-Figgisite stance. I also demonstrate that Oakley lacks appreciation for the points of intellectual congruence between conciliar theory and broader trends within medieval political thought.

**Nederman, Cary J**. The Meaning of "Aristotelianism" in Medieval Moral and Political Thought. *J Hist Ideas*, 57(4), 563-586, O 96.

"Aristotelian" and "Aristotelianism" are terms that scholars apply to medieval moral and political thought constantly and almost inescapably. Yet given the dominance of Christianity, medieval Aristotelianism could never be complete. "Aristotelianism" in the Middle Ages is thus ambiguous. A coherent definition of Aristotelianism in the political and moral writings of the Middle Ages is only possible by reference to a particular organization and orientation towards the kind of knowledge necessary for achieving human good. Aristotelianism posits the practical quality of the study of ethics and politics and hence the value of such knowledge insofar as it guides action.

**Nederpelt, Rob** and Laan, Twan. A Modern Elaboration of the Ramified Theory of Types. *Stud Log*, 57(2-3), 243-278, O 96.

The paper first formalizes the ramified type theory as (informally) described in the Principia Mathematica [32]. This formalization is close to the ideas of the Principia, but also meets contemporary requirements on formality and accuracy and therefore is a new supply to the known literature on the Principia (like [25], [19], [6] and [7]). As an alternative, notions from the ramified type theory are expressed in a lambda calculus style. This situates the type system of Russell and Whitehead in a modern setting. Both formalizations are inspired by current developments in research on type theory and typed lambda calculus; see [3].

**Need, Stephen W**. *Human Language and Knowledge in the Light of Chalcedon.* New York, Lang, 1996.

There have been many responses to the problem of how human language and knowledge function in relation to God. *Human Language and Knowledge in the Light of Chalcedon* breaks new ground by suggesting that the relation between humanity and divinity found in the *Chalcedonian Definition of the Faith* (A.D. 451) can make one of Christian theology's basic tasks look rather different. In the light of a dynamic reading of Chalcedonian christology, the author discusses analogy, metaphor, and symbol, as well as fundamental questions about human knowledge. Some old pitfalls are avoided and an essential link between Christology, language, and knowledge is exposed. (publisher, edited)

**Neeley, G Steven**. Nietzsche "On Apostates" and Divine Laughter. *Cont Phil*, 18(2-3), 28-33, Mr-Ap/My-Je 96.

Nietzsche triumphantly heralds the death of God. Yet the reports on the exact cause of death are inconsistent. In certain passages, Nietzsche suggests that God was murdered in the spirit of revenge. Elsewhere, we are told that God died out of pity. There is also a very curious passage in *Zarathustra* in which Nietzsche suggests that the "old gods" laughed themselves to death. While there is ample literature on Nietzsche's overall "Death-of-God" theme, the statement that the "old gods" laughed themselves to death has not been taken seriously. This paper will contend that the death of the "old gods" through laughter is a theme that should be taken seriously, as Nietzsche employs the motif to suggest that a "god-like" spirit of laughter is necessary to *overcome* indecisiveness regarding the ultimate fate of the Christian God as well as the otherwise debilitating limits of human knowledge.

**Nef, Frédéric**. La métaphysique du réalisme modal: régression ou enjeu véritable?. *Rev Int Phil*, 51(200), 231-250, Je 97.

J'ai défendu une solution actualiste avec des conditions strictes sur les domaines d'individus. Cette solution permet de distinguer parmi les *possibilia* des entités acceptables et des entités douteuses. La sémantique modale aurait le moyen interne d'éliminer les *possibilia* au sens fort qui échappent à l'exigence sémantique de désignation. Si c'est le cas, si le réalisme modal peut faire lui-même sa police métaphysique, on peut le laisser s'administrer lui-même. (edited)

**Negro, Paola**. Un *topos* in Hugo Grotius: *Etiamsi daremus non esse deum*. *Stud Filosofici*, 57-80, 1995.

The article examines possible precedents in mediaeval theology and Spanish scholastics for Grotius's celebrated hypothesis in the *Deiure belli ac pacis*: "All that we have said [the nature, based on self-evident principles] would have weight even if we were to admit—and this may only be admitted with maximum wickedness—that God does not exist or does not attend to the thing of men". It also examines the reasons his hypothesis was used with equanimity by the scholastics but caused scandal in the seventeenth and eighteenth centuries.

**Nehamas, Alexander**. Nietzsche as Self-Made Man. *Phil Lit*, 20(2), 487-491, O 96.

A short essay on Graham Parkes's *Composing the Soul: Reaches of Nietzsche's Psychology*. I praise the book for the thoroughness of its theoretical aspects, its treatment of Nietzsche's various metaphors for the complex structure he put in place of the traditional unitary soul. I take exception to Parkes's impersonal style which leaves the question what to do with Nietzsche's dissolution of the soul unanswered.

**Neill, Elizabeth**. Hume's Moral Sublime. *Brit J Aes*, 37(3), 246-258, Jl 97.

Through examining the respective roles of "pride" and "sympathy" in Hume's natural sublime experience and through comparing that analysis with the roles played by those concepts in his discussion of "heroic virtue," I demonstrate both that there is an element of the moral in natural sublimity and that Hume evokes a conception of sublimity as sometimes *distinctly* moral. Moral sublime experience entails the *un*-comfortably *un*-Humean possibility of sublimity inhering in the uniquely human object which makes that experience "moral." I detail how this radical claim is so and demonstrate how Hume's moral sublime deepens the pre-Kantian strain in his aesthetics.

**Neiman, Alven**. "No More Method! A (Polemical) Response to Audrey Thompson" in *Philosophy of Education (1996)*, Margonis, Frank (ed), 435-440. Urbana, Phil Education Soc, 1997.

In this article I defend Dewey and classical pragmatism in general, against those who would claim that it fails to take adequate account of the economic/political dimension. Such critics include authors ranging from C. Wright Mills to Cornel West, as well as Audrey Thompson. Against writers such as Mills, West and Thompson I argue that no science or "method" is necessary to allow writers such as James and Dewey to engage in the sort of "social critiques" needful of the times.

**Neiman, Alven**. Pragmatism, Thomism, and the Metaphysics of Desire: Two Rival Versions of Liberal Education. *Educ Theor*, 47(1), 91-117, Wint 97.

In this paper I attempt to suggest the plausibility of the philosophy of higher education implicit in Alasdair MacIntyre's *Three Rival Versions of Moral Inquiry*

(University of Notre Dame Press) against other recent contenders. Much space and time is spent elucidating that philosophy through 1) a comparison with pragmatist philosophy as exhibited in Benjamin Barber's *An Aristocracy of Everyone* and Rene Arcilla's *For the Love of Perfection—Richard Rorty and Liberal Education*; 2) a suggestion that perhaps only MacIntyre's grander Augustinian views, grounded as they are in a contemplative tradition allow us to make good sense of that yearning that ultimately maturates all education.

**Neimanis, George J**. Business Ethics in the Former Soviet Union: A Report. *J Bus Ethics*, 16(3), 357-362, F 97.

Transition from a planned command economy to a market economy means tearing down a socio-economic setting where everybody follows orders and nobody bears individual responsibility for anything. The absence of personal responsibility does not promote ethical behavior in any walk of life. Today, the malnourished business ethics in the former Soviet Union creates a critical obstacle to economic development. The first part of this paper surveys the most visible unethical business practices. The second part of the paper looks at ethical problems that have been under-reported.

**Nelson, Alan**. Descartes's Ontology of Thought. *Topoi*, 16(2), 163-178, S 97.

**Nelson, Craig E**. Skewered on the Unicorn's Horn. *Inquiry (USA)*, 15(3), 49-64, Spr 96.

**Nelson, David E**. Confirmation, Explanation, and Logical Strength. *Brit J Phil Sci*, 47(3), 399-413, S 96.

Van Fraassen argues that explanatory power cannot be a *conformational virtue*. In this paper I will show that informational features of scientific theories can be positively relevant to their levels of conformation. Thus, in the cases where the explanatory power of a theory is tied to an informational feature of the theory, it can still be the case that the explanatory power of the theory is positively relevant to its level of confirmation.

**Nelson, J E** and Kiecker, P L. Marketing Research Interviewers and Their Perceived Necessity of Moral Compromise. *J Bus Ethics*, 15(10), 1107-1117, O 96.

Marketing research interviewers often feel that they must compromise their own moral principles while executing work-related activities. This finding is based on analysis of data obtained from three focus group interviews and a mail survey of 173 telephone survey interviewers. Data from the mail survey were used to construct scales measuring interviewers' perceived necessity of moral compromise, moral character, and job satisfaction. The three scales then were used in a hierarchical regression analysis to predict incidences of interviewers' self-reported prescribed behaviors on the job, the latter being an index of behaviors known by interviewers to be "wrong." Results support all hypothesized relationships.

**Nelson, John O**. In Defence of a Radical Millianism. *Philosophy*, 71(278), 521-530, O 96.

**Nelson, John O**. The Myriad Faces of Personal Survival. *Darshana Int*, 35(4/140), 1-5, O 95.

The purpose of "The Myriad Faces of Personal Survival" is to provide a conception of *person* that allows possible veracity to those common views of personal survival, e.g., reincarnation, which resist assimilation to the stock philosophical models of personal survival, e.g., the theory of identity through time, the theory of psychological continuity and connectedness. It will finally be argued that the conception in question can also resolve the much bruited problems associated with hypothetical brain-fission.

**Nelson, Michael P**. Rethinking Wilderness: The Need for a New Idea of Wilderness. *Phil Cont World*, 3(2), 6-9, Sum 96.

The "received" concept of wilderness as a place apart from and untouched by humans is five-times flawed: it is not universalizable, it is ethnocentric, it is ecologically naive, it separates humans from nature and its referent is nonexistent. The received view of wilderness leads to dilemmas and unpalatable consequences, including the loss of designated wilderness areas by political and legislative authorities. What is needed is a more flexible notion of wilderness. Suggestions are made for a revised concept of wilderness.

**Nelson, Paul** and Nayak, Abhaya C and Polansky, Hanan. Belief Change as Change in Epistemic Entrenchment. *Synthese*, 109(2), 143-174, N 96.

In this paper, it is argued that both the belief state and its input should be represented as epistemic entrenchment (EE) relations. A belief revision operation is constructed that updates a given EE relation to a new one in light of an evidential EE relation, and an axiomatic characterization of this operation is given. Unlike most belief revision operations, the one developed here can handle both "multiple belief revision" and "iterated belief revision."

**Nelson, R J**. Proxy Functions, Truth and Reference. *Synthese*, 111(1), 73-95, Ap 97.

Quine's ontological relativity is related to Tarski's theory of truth in two ways: Quine "repudiates term-by-term-correspondence," as does Tarski's rule of truth; and Quine's proxy argument in support of relativity finds exact formulation in Tarski's truth definition. Unfortunately, relativity is threatened by the fact that the proxy argument doesn't comply with the rule of truth (Tarski's celebrated condition (T)). Despite Quine's express allegiance to (T), use of proxy schemes does not generate all of the true sentences condition (T) requires. A saving alternative is a theory of term-reference that appears in *Roots of Reference* and affords a return to behaviorism, and reinstatement of the proxy argument and relativity in a way compatible with Tarski's (T). (edited)

**Nelson, Ralph C**. Between Inconsistent Nominalists and Egalitarian Idealists. *Maritain Stud*, 12, 113-132, 1996.

What does being a nominalist, an idealist, or a realist entail in moral and political affairs? Three sets of philosophers, each corresponding to the three options, are

examined: Popper and Nozick, Rawls and Dworkin, Gewirth and Veatch. The issues are individualism, equality and rights. While Popper's position is ambivalent, Nozick, like Locke, is an inconsistent nominalist. It is argued that there are serious shortcomings in the idealist conception of justice. Reasons are then provided to support the realist option, for though the arguments for the derivation of human rights are flawed, they do seem to be on the right track.

**Nelson, Ralph C**. Beyond the Sovereignty of Good. *Maritain Stud*, 10, 124-141, 1994.

**Nelson, Ralph C**. History and the Advent of the Self. *Maritain Stud*, 8, 112-142, 1992.

**Németi, István** and Kurucz, Agnes and Sain, Ildikó (& others). Decidable and Undecidable Logics with a Binary Modality. *J Log Lang Info*, 4(3), 191-206, 1995.

We give an overview of decidability results for modal logics having a binary modality. We put an emphasis on the demonstration of proof-techniques and hope that this will also help in finding the borderlines between decidable and undecidable fragments of usual first-order logic.

**Németi, István** and Mikulás, Szabolcs and Marx, Maarten. Taming Logic. *J Log Lang Info*, 4(3), 207-226, 1995.

In this paper, we introduce a general technology, called *taming*, for finding well-behaved versions of well-investigated logics. Further, we state completeness, decidability, definability and interpolation results for a multimodal logic, called *arrow logic*, with additional operators such as the *difference operator* and *graded modalities*. Finally, we give a completeness proof for a strong version of arrow logic.

**Neocleous, Mark**. Friend or Enemy?: Reading Schmitt Politically. *Rad Phil*, 79, 13-23, S-O 96.

The article challenges some of the recent attempts to rehabilitate Carl Schmitt for a rethinking of socialist political thought. It explores the central aspects of Schmitt's thought and identifies the essentially fascist nature of his work. His account of democracy, concept of the political, and understanding of war all contain a fascist moment, and it is this fascist moment, rather than personal misjudgment, which explains his joining the Nazi Party. This makes the attempt to rehabilitate him not only intellectually naive but also politically dangerous.

**Nepomuceno Fernández, Angel**. "Modelos fregeanos intensionales" in *Verdad: lógica, representación y mundo*, Villegas Forero, L, 201-209. Santiago de Compostela, Univ Santiago Comp, 1996.

Extensional Fregean models are very interesting to study some linguistical structures. In this paper an intensional version of that is given. So, first of all, we define a second-order language with Lambda-abstraction. Secondly, we define an intensional frame by means of a family of domains (a nonempty domain and predicates and relations defined over it), a base for a postalgebra, a set of indices (context of uses), a set of functions (from the set of indices to the family of domains). Then an intensional Fregean model is viewed as an intensional frame and an interpretation of parameters and relaters of that language. Finally, some propositions are intended.

**Nepomuceno Fernández, Angel**. Lógica y práctica matemática. *Mathesis*, 11(3), 201-216, Ag 95.

Several logics are presupposed in mathematical practice, namely what has been called its underlying logics, that can be modelled by means of formal systems of logic. An important feature of mathematical practice is the method for introducing (mathematical) objects, starting from some propositions (postulates or axioms) to which deduction rules are applied. In this paper we shall refer to those parts of mathematics whose underlying logic is classical logic. Some extensions of first order logic may be appropriated (*omega*-logic, Q-logic, infinitary logic). If we focus on some postulates (usual in some practices), as completeness, replacement and induction, then we can choose first order logic as underlying logic or on the contrary second order logic. So option of second order logic represents one of the philosophical attitudes from which some mathematical practices may be studies.

**Nepomuceno Fernández, Angel**. Un Estudio Formal de Aspectos Relevantes de Estructuras Informativas. *Agora (Spain)*, 14(2), 23-30, 1995.

Informative content is obtained by means of joining logical content and lexical. Some inferential process may be represented in classical terms but "*m* is grandfather, therefore *m* is father" is a deduction that have to take into account the meaning of terms; that is to say, "*m* is grandfather" does not entail "*m* is father" in classical sense. In order to study informative content, we shall describe a formal language, its semantics, then informative systems will be defined. Those systems may have relevant characteristics, so we shall explore as B+—a basic relevant system—gives account of some consequences from premises whose informative content is well-known.

**Nerbonne, John**. Nominal Comparatives and Generalized Quantifiers. *J Log Lang Info*, 4(4), 273-300, 1995.

This work adopts the perspective of plural logic and measurement theory in order first to focus on the microstructure of comparative determiners; and second, to derive the properties of comparative determiners as these are studied in Generalized Quantifier Theory, locus of the most sophisticated semantic analysis of natural language determiners. The work here appears to be the first to examine comparatives within plural logic, a step which appears necessary, but which also harbors specific analytical problems examined here. (edited)

**Neri, Demetrio**. Privacy, autonomia e regole. *Iride*, 9(18), 458-465, Ag 96.

Questo intervento trae lo spunto dal libro di Stefano Rodotà *Tecnologie e diritti* (Bologna, Il Mulino, 1995) circa la radicalità della sfida posta dall'innovazione tecnologica in settori "sensibili" quali l'informazione o la medicina per sviluppare alcune riflessioni sul tema del rapporto tra *privacy* e autonomia e su alcune questioni di bioetica. Sullo sfondo c'è il tema, centrale nel discorso di Rodotà, di come costruire punti di riferimento normativi intorno a questioni sulle quali esistono profondi disaccordi morali.

**Nerlich, Brigitte** and Clarke, David D. *Language, Action, and Context: The Early History of Pragmatics in Europe and America, 1780-1930.* Amsterdam, J Benjamins, 1996.

This book explores the often neglected philosophical, psychological and linguistic foundations of modern linguistic pragmatics, which has its deepest roots in ancient rhetoric. The first part of the book describes the emergence of pragmatics in Britain, Germany and France in post-Lockian and post-Kantian philosophies of language. The second part explores pragmatic insights made between 1830 and 1880, when they were relegated to the philosophical and linguistic underground. In a last part the period between 1880 and 1930 is studied, when pragmatic ideas flourished.

**Nersessian, Nancy J**. Child's Play. *Phil Sci*, 63(4), 542-546, D 96.

**Nesher, Dan**. Peircean Realism: Truth as the Meaning of Cognitive Signs Representing External Reality. *Trans Peirce Soc*, 33(1), 201-257, Wint 97.

My purpose in this work is to show that within the Peircean philosophy the problem of our knowledge of external reality can be solved without getting outside our cognitive skins. I criticize the Humean and Kantian tradition that only what is given to us immediately can be known and show that we can know external reality only indirectly through our cognitions. By analyzing Peirce's description of our perceptual experience, I show that in error we detect the clash between our subjective expectations and objective reality, and that when the process of perception is harmonious our materialized expectations are true. Thus, in disharmonious and harmonious experience our cognitions are disproved and proved and thus "hook on" to external reality.

**Nessa, John**. About Signs and Symptoms: Can Semiotics Expand the View of Clinical Medicine?. *Theor Med*, 17(4), 363-377, D 96.

Semiotics, the theory of sign and meaning, may help physicians complement the project of interpreting signs and symptoms into diagnoses. A sign stands for something. We communicate indirectly through signs and make sense of our world by interpreting signs into meaning. Thus, through association and inference, we transform flowers into love, Othello into jealousy and chest pain into heart attack. Medical semiotics is part of general semiotics, which means the study of life of signs within society. With special reference to a case story, elements from general semiotics, together with two theoreticians of equal importance, the Swiss linguist Ferdinand de Saussure and the American logician Charles Sanders Peirce, are presented. Two different modes of understanding clinical medicine are contrasted to illustrate the external link between what we believe or suggest, on the one hand and the external reality on the other hand.

**Neta, Ram**. Stroud and Moore on Skepticism. *SW Phil Rev*, 13(1), 83-89, Ja 97.

**Neu, Carlos** and Sabin, James E. Real World Resource Allocation: The Concept of "Good-Enough" Psychotherapy. *Bioethics Forum*, 12(1), 3-9, Spr 96.

Principles can be established within a managed care plan to assist clinicians in managing resources. The concept of "good enough psychotherapy" is illustrated as a principle by which resources in a managed mental health program can be allocated in an ethically justifiable manner.

**Neubauer, Patrick**. Zur Rehabilitation des Unbewussten. *Z Phil Praxis*, 7-8, 1996.

In my essay, I give a critical discussion of two crucial notions within orthodox Freudian psychoanalytic methodology: "transference" and "resistance". I argue that psychoanalysis not only embeds the *specific* self-interpretation of the client into a *general* theory of etiology, but that it even interprets perspectives differing from psychoanalytic models *as* part of the problem to be cured by calling them "intellectualizing resistances". I conclude that psychoanalysis is a rationalistic enterprise which has unjustifiedly pathologized the unconscious.

**Neugebauer, Christian**. "Against Culture and the Aliens of Moderni- zation" in *Philosophy and Democracy in Intercultural Perspective*, Kimmerle, Heinz (ed), 95-113. Amsterdam, Rodopi, 1997.

**Neumann, Holger**. How Can Reality Be Proved?. *Phil Natur*, 28(1), 70-75, 1991.

**Neumann, Holger**. Objektive Beschreibung und Messprozess in der Quantenmechanik. *Phil Natur*, 27(1), 8-13, 1990.

Wir wollen weniger auf den Vergleich solcher verschiedenartiger Versuche eingehen, als vielmehr einen Versuch schildern, wie man ohne diese radikalen Umbrüche eine konsistente Quantentheorie formulieren kann und mit welchen "Verlusten" man diesen "Gewinn" bezahlen muss. (edited)

**Neumann, Ulfrid**. Die Moral des Rechts: Deontologische und konsequentialistische Argumentationen in Recht und Moral. *Jahr Recht Ethik*, 2, 81-94, 1994.

The distinction developed in moral philosophy between deontic and consequentialistic systems can be fruitfully employed in the analysis of value structures inherent to legal rules and institutions. Criminal law norms of conduct basically correspond to a deontic system of rules. Yet necessity as a justification (lesser evils, paragraph 34 German Criminal Code) represents a breakthrough, which permits consideration of the consequences of actions. Still German criminal law confronts the resulting danger of restructuring its norm-oriented system of conduct rules into a consequence-oriented system by including a double deontic corrective.

**Nevers, Patricia** and Gebhard, Ulrich and Billmann-Mahecha, Elfriede. Patterns of Reasoning Exhibited by Children and Adolescents in Response to Moral Dilemmas Involving Plants, Animals and Ecosystems. *J Moral Educ*, 26(2), 169-186, Je 97.

Traditional moral philosophy, developmental psychology and moral education have generally been concerned with relationships between human beings. However, moral philosophy has gradually expanded to include plants, animals and ecosystems as legitimate moral objects and aesthetics has rediscovered nature as an object of consideration. Thus it seems appropriate to begin to include this sphere in moral education and corresponding research as well. In this paper we wish to report on an investigation we have begun using children's philosophy as a hermeneutic tool to assess the morally relevant values and attitudes that children and adolescents hold with respect to nature and the patterns of reasoning with which they are expressed. In the first part of our presentation we will outline current positions in environmental ethics and aesthetics which provide a theoretical framework for such an investigation and the problems they present. Subsequently, the difficulties involved with applying contemporary theories of moral development to the problem at hand will be discussed. Finally, we will describe the project we have begun and summarize preliminary results derived from different age groups.

**Neves, Maria do Céu Patrao**. A Pessoa e o Seu Universo. *Rev Port Filosof*, 52(1-4), 603-615, Ja-D 96.

Man is the reality that is nearest to himself, most intimate and familiar yet, simultaneously, the most distant, foreign and unknown. For that reason the quest about himself goes on today with unprecedented demand and reach. "The Person and its Universe" traces the pathway of the query of man about himself and sketches the various images about himself he has successively construed. Three main axes have marked the history of understanding of himself that man has acquired: nature, God and man. Today, a new axis—that of community—appears to be arising; having been active several times in the past, it takes on now unprecedented preponderance.

**Neville, Robert Cummings**. "American Philosophy's Way around Modernism (and Postmodernism)" in *The Recovery of Philosophy in America: Essays in Honor of John Edwin Smith,* Kasulis, Thomas P (ed), 251-268. Albany, SUNY Pr, 1997.

The essay argues that the American conception of experience, in contrast to that of British empiricism, provides resources for avoiding the pitfalls of modernist philosophy. The work of John E. Smith is used to make this point.

**Neville, Robert Cummings**. "John E. Smith and Metaphysics" in *Reason, Experience, and God: John E. Smith in Dialogue,* Colapietro, Vincent M, 71-81. New York, Fordham Univ Pr, 1997.

A study of the philosophy of John E. Smith, arguing that his elaborate theory of experience is in fact a metaphysical position in a sense justified by his American empiricism.

**Neville, Robert Cummings**. "Political Tolerance in an Age of Renewed Religious Warfare" in *Philosophy, Religion, and the Question of Intolerance,* Ambuel, David (ed), 28-40. Albany, SUNY Pr, 1997.

A defense of four theses. (1) That religious wars show that religion has not been privatized. (2) That religion's civil function is to teach and justify a sense of obligation. (3) That religion's main role is to provide orientation to God or some ultimate principle, the infinite passion for which is often displaced onto civil matters. (4) A principle of tolerance needs to respect Thesis 3. (5) Public theology needs to adjudicate religious conflicts with regard to Theses 1-4.

**Neville, Robert Cummings**. "Reflections on Philosophic Recovery" in *The Recovery of Philosophy in America: Essays in Honor of John Edwin Smith,* Kasulis, Thomas P (ed), 1-10. Albany, SUNY Pr, 1997.

This essay traces the revival and considerable extension of the classic American philosophers among recent thinkers, most of whom have been colleagues or students of John E. Smith who has sparked the revival.

**Neville, Robert Cummings**. Commentary on the AAS Panel: Shun, Bloom, Cheng, and Birdwhistell. *Phil East West*, 47(1), 67-74, Ja 97.

**Neville, Robert Cummings** (ed) and Kasulis, Thomas P (ed). *The Recovery of Philosophy in America: Essays in Honor of John Edwin Smith.* Albany, SUNY Pr, 1997.

John Edwin Smith, through a long publishing and teaching career at Yale, has championed the rich American conceptions of experience and speculative reason and it seems that at the end of this century they are returning in triumph. This book celebrates the recovery and new growth of American philosophy in a stunning variety of connected and vital intellectual projects represented by its contributors: George Allan, Douglas R. Anderson, Lewis S. Ford, Errol Harris, Richard Hocking, Thomas P. Kasulis, George R. Lucas, Jr., Robert Cummings Neville, Donald W. Sherburne, Merold Westphal, Kuang-ming Wu, and Carl G. Vaught. Displaying philosophy's recovery in America, this book also honors John Edwin Smith, who has kept the history and trajectory of philosophy in America in sight and who contributes a prophetic commentary on the other essays.

**Nevo, Isaac**. The Practice of Philosophy. *Euro J Phil*, 5(1), 74-82, Ap 97.

**New, Kostja**. The Correspondence Theory of Truth. *Acta Analytica*, 57-67, 1995.

What gives the correspondence theory of truth its pretheoretic attraction is the thought that the value of a truthful statement or belief lies in its telling us how things are in a world conceived to be *not* of our own making and in that sense independent of us. It is argued that, contrary to expectations, the correspondence theory fails to capture this very idea. This means that whatever one's thoughts are about the value of truth, the correspondence theory can satisfy none. There are connections between language and independent objects in the world, but these connections do not amount to correspondence between representations and whatever representations are supposed to represent.

**Newberg, Andrew B**. Methods and Systematic Reflections: Unitary States, Free Will and Ultimate Reality. *Ultim Real Mean*, 19(4), 298-311, D 96.

**Newby, Mike**. Literary Development as Spiritual Development in the Common School. *J Phil Educ*, 31(2), 283-294, Jl 97.

The central task of this paper is to bring into focus a conception of spiritual development which is not, in essence, religious, and which, therefore, can express the meaning of personal and communal identity within the established climate of the age. Such a conception must accept cultural diversity, reflect democratic humanism and seek to promote life-chances for children and adults in a world of high stress and rapid change.

**Newey, Glen**. Against Thin-Property Reductivism: Toleration as Supererogatory. *J Value Inq*, 31(2), 231-249, Je 97.

**Newey, Glen**. Political Lying: A Defense. *Pub Affairs Quart*, 11(2), 93-116, Ap 97.

**Newey, Katherine**. The Aesthetics of the Marketplace: Women Playwrights, 1770-1850. *Lit Aes*, 6, 43-53, O 96.

**Newman, James**. Putting the Puzzle Together: Part I: Towards a General Theory of the Neural Correlates of Consciousness. *J Consciousness Stud*, 4(1), 47-66, 1997.

Despite the whirl of controversy surrounding consciousness studies, there is real progress being made in cognitive science towards establishing an empirically rigorous theory of mind, in both its conscious and nonconscious manifestations. In this two-part article, beginning with a broad overview of clinical and experimental findings bearing on the neural correlates of conscious processes, the author traces the development of several related models that appear to converge upon a central 'conscious system'. It is argued that the increasing convergence of models from clinical and experimental neuroscience is leading towards a general theory of consciousness which is both nondualist and nonreductionist. (edited)

**Newmyer, Stephen T**. Plutarch on the Treatment of Animals: The Argument from Marginal Cases. *Between Species*, 12(1-2), 40-46, Wint-Spr 96.

This article argues that the Greek essayist Plutarch anticipates, in his treatise *De sollertia animalium* (*On the Cleverness of Animals*), the argument from marginal cases employed in defense of animal rights. Maintaining that all creatures possess some degree of reason, Plutarch argues that one cannot deny rights to slaves on the grounds that they are not so virtuous as a Socrates or a Plato since they are not by nature capable of attaining pure reason, nor likewise can one deny rights to animals whose intellectual capacities may be as developed as those of some classes of humans, namely of such marginal cases as slaves. Thus animals must be accorded any rights that are given to such classes of humans.

**Neymeyr, Barbara**. *Ästhetische Autonomie als Abnormalität: Kritische Analysen zu Schopenhauers Ästhetik im Horizont seiner Willensmetaphysik*. Hawthorne, de Gruyter, 1996.

A systematic-critical analysis of the German philosopher Schopenhauer's (1788-1860) aesthetics within his metaphysics of will, examining his notion of aesthetic autonomy (i.e., the freedom of the will intellect from the will in his conception of aesthetic attitude) as abnormality. (publisher)

**Nichol, Lee** (ed) and Bohm, David. *On Dialogue*. New York, Routledge, 1996.

The question of how we communicate is at the heart of *On Dialogue*. This revised and expanded edition is the most comprehensive documentation to date of best-selling author David Bohm's dialogical world view. While the exercise of dialogue is as old as civilization itself, in recent times a profusion of practices, techniques and definitions has arisen around the term 'dialogue'. None of these approaches can claim to be the correct view, but it is possible to distinguish between them and to clarify the intention of each. To this end, the current edition of *On Dialogue* illuminates the underlying meaning, purpose and uniqueness of David Bohm's work in this field. (publisher)

**Nichols, Ray**. Maxims, "Practical Wisdom," and the Language of Action: Beyond Grand Theory. *Polit Theory*, 24(4), 687-705, N 96.

This article examines the elusive subject "practical wisdom" by exploring the neglected nature of "maxims"—short pretheoretical counsels of action. It outlines the commonplace maxim family (proverbs, aphorisms, apothegms, precepts, epigrams); profiles maxims against commands, rules, laws, and truisms; and compares commonplace maxims with those of François de la Rochfoucauld, Sir Henry Taylor, and Francesco Guicciardini. Since maxims are counsels of action, considering them involves considering action; and since the analysis focuses on the language of action, it involves both the philosophy and the rhetoric of action—especially the importance of irony. It suggests how bringing these matters together illuminates "practical" wisdom.

**Nicholsen, Shierry Weber**. "*Aesthetic Theory*'s Mimesis of Walter Benjamin" in *The Semblance of Subjectivity*, Huhn, Tom (ed), 55-91. Cambridge, MIT Pr, 1997.

**Nicholsen, Shierry Weber** (trans) and Missac, Pierre. *Walter Benjamin's Passages*. Cambridge, MIT Pr, 1995.

Taking a cue from his subject, Missac adopts a form of indirect critique in which independent details examined seemingly in passing emerge over the course of the book as parts of larger patterns of understanding. The interlocked essays move among such topics as reading and writing, collecting, the dialectic and

time and history. Many of the subjects are standard in Benjamin studies, but the freshness and directness of Missac's response to them makes this book compelling. It is a work of sophisticated and imaginative criticism that shows how Benjamin's work anticipated the future and how it can be fruitfully extended. (publisher, edited)

**Nicholson, Graeme**. The Ontological Difference. *Amer Phil Quart*, 33(4), 357-374, O 96.

Heidegger's discrimination of beings, entities, from the very being of those beings or entities. Anyone who is a doctor is aware of being a doctor, which incorporates not only the awareness of a social role but the awareness of being. This is one of several forms of the human "preontological awareness of being." The article seeks to demonstrate that every human consciousness includes such an awareness and therefore an awareness of the difference between being and beings. It defends this claim by a number of disputations, versus empiricism, dialectics and Aristotelianism.

**Nicholson, Linda** (ed). *The Second Wave: A Reader in Feminist Theory*. New York, Routledge, 1997.

This volume collects many of the major works of feminist theorists from diverse ethnic, disciplinary and theoretical backgrounds, demonstrating the wide range of ideas reflected by second wave feminist thought. The essays included here are those which have made key contributions to feminist theory over the past forty years and which have generated extensive and often heated discussion. (publisher, edited)

**Nicholson, Linda**. To Be or Not to Be: Charles Taylor and the Politics of Recognition. *Constellations*, 3(1), 1-16, Ap 96.

This article comments upon Charles Taylor's essay "The Politics of Recognition" in two stages. Firstly, it critiques the strain in Taylor's argument which describes identity and the need for its recognition as issues of "modernity," whose ethical and political implications are generalizable across a wide set of social struggles. I argue that even within the context of the very recent past, the meaning of identity and of recognition has varied widely. Secondly, it argues that certain understandings of identity and of recognition have emerged in the post 1960s feminist and African-American movements which highlight shortcomings in Taylor's analysis of multiculturalism. In contrast to Taylor's understanding of multiculturalism as a process where those with authority give preliminary credence to the claims of some of those whose previous claims for recognition have been denied, this essay argues for an understanding of multiculturalism which calls into question the very processes by which judgments of worth have often previously been made.

**Nicholson, Nigel** and Robertson, Diana C. Expressions of Corporate Social Responsibility in U.K. Firms. *J Bus Ethics*, 15(10), 1095-1106, O 96.

This study examines corporate publications of U.K. firms to investigate the nature of corporate social responsibility disclosure. Using a stakeholder approach to corporate social responsibility, our results suggest a hierarchical model of disclosure: from general rhetoric to specific endeavors to implementation and monitoring. Industry differences in attention to specific stakeholder groups are noted. These differences suggest the need to understand the effects on social responsibility disclosure of factors in a firm's immediate operating environment, such as the extent of government regulation and level of competitiveness in the industry.

**Nickel, James**. The Liberty Dimension of Historic and Contemporary Segregation. *Law Phil*, 16(3), 259-277, My 97.

Both historic and contemporary segregation involve significant infringements of equal basic liberties. The ideal of equal basic liberties supports a powerful indictment of both historic and contemporary segregation. The first section offers a description and analysis of racial segregation as it existed around the turn of the century in the United States. The second section develops in some detail the diagnosis of segregation as a violation of basic liberties, attending to both its legally and socially enforced components. The final section considers the extent to which the same diagnosis applies to contemporary racial segregation.

**Nicks, Sandra D** and Korn, James H and Mainieri, Tina. The Rise and Fall of Deception in Social Psychology and Personality Research, 1921 to 1994. *Ethics Behavior*, 7(1), 69-77, 1997.

The frequency of the use of deception in American psychological research was studied by reviewing articles from journals in personality and social psychology from 1921 to 1994. Deception was used rarely during the developmental years of social psychology into the 1930s, then grew gradually and irregularly until the 1950s. Between the 1950s and 1970s the use of deception increased significantly. This increase is attributed to changes in experimental methods, the popularity of realistic impact experiments, and the influence of cognitive dissonance theory. Since 1980 there appears to have been a decrease in the use of deception as compared to previous decades which is related to changes in theory, methods, ethical standards, and federal regulation of research.

**Nicolás, Juan A** and Frápolli, María José. Teorías actuales de la verdad. *Dialogo Filosof*, 13(2), 148-178, My-Ag 97.

Se aborda la delimitación de lo que una teoría de la verdad y la clasificación de las principales teorías elaboradas durante el siglo XX. Una teoría de la verdad ha de incluir al menos cuatro apartados: definición del concepto de verdad determinación del criterio de verdad, distinción de los tipos de verdad y fijación del lugar sistemático de la verdad y de la teoría de la verdad en el marco del saber y de la acción. En segundo lugar, se han clasificado las teorías de la verdad en siete grupos: teoría de la correspondencia (semánticas y no semánticas), teorías prooracionales, teorías fenomenológicas, teorías hermenéuticas, teorías coherenciales, teorías pragmáticas y teorías intersubjetivistas de la verdad.

**Nicolás, Juan A** (trans) and Levinas, Emmanuel. Verdad del desvelamiento y verdad del testimonio. *Dialogo Filosof*, 13(2), 179-188, My-Ag 97.

Se distingue en primer lugar la verdad originaria del ser—fundamento de toda noción de verdad en la tradición griega—frente a la conciencia, la tematización de la verdad frente a la manifestación en la inteligibilidad. Toda expresión de verdad—sentido—remite a un desvelamiento previo del ser. El testimonio, en cuanto confesión de un saber o experiencia por un sujeto, está referido al ser desvelado y gobernado por él. En cierto modo, el sujeto del saber queda anulado. Pero el testimonio, además de expresar el ser, apunta también más allá de él. La conciencia está estructuralmente abierta al ámbito de lo no-representable, de la responsabilidad para con el otro, previa a toda decisión subjetiva. La responsabilidad testimonia la relación con un infinito no tematizable, ambiguamente presente en el profeta.

**Nida-Rümelin, Julian**. "Ethik des Risikos" in *Angewandte Ethik: Die Bereichsethiken und ihre theoretische Fundierung,* Nida-Rümelin, Julian (ed), 806-830. Stuttgart, Alfred Kröner, 1996.

The article criticizes the mainstream consequentialist account of public policy facing technological risks and develops the core elements of a nonconsequentialist ethics of risk which requires constraints on optimizing behaviour in risky situations. These constraints are mainly constituted by individual rights which on their part can be waived by a consensus on collective decision procedures.

**Nida-Rümelin, Julian**. "Objektivität und Moral" in *Das weite Spektrum der analytischen Philosophie,* Lenzen, Wolfgang, 216-230. Hawthorne, de Gruyter, 1997.

The paper is antiseptic and argues in favor of an intentionalist version of moral objectivism.

**Nida-Rümelin, Julian**. "Ökonomische Optimierung in den Grenzen struktureller Rationalität" in *Ökonomie und Moral: Beiträge zur Theorie ökonomischer Rationalität,* Lohmann, Karl Reinhard (ed), 101-111. München, Oldenbourg, 1997.

It is argued that an adequate theory of practical rationality can neither do without optimization nor without rules. Optimization is rational within constraints which themselves can be justified as optimizing. This account of "structural rationality" allows for adequately integrating practical reasons.

**Nida-Rümelin, Julian**. "Politische Ethik I: Ethik der politischen Institutionen und der Bürgerschaft" in *Angewandte Ethik: Die Bereichsethiken und ihre theoretische Fundierung,* Nida-Rümelin, Julian (ed), 138-153. Stuttgart, Alfred Kröner, 1996.

This article gives an overview on political ethics in two parts: the ethics of political institutions and the ethics of citizenship.

**Nida-Rümelin, Julian**. "Theoretische und angewandte Ethik: Paradigmen, Begründungen, Bereiche" in *Angewandte Ethik: Die Bereichsethiken und ihre theoretische Fundierung,* Nida-Rümelin, Julian (ed), 2-85. Stuttgart, Alfred Kröner, 1996.

This first and introductory article of the *Handbook for Applied Ethics* presents the main paradigms of present-day normative ethics. It is argued that ethical justification requires no specific types of justification and faces no additional problems compared with other kinds of justification in every-day discourse in the humanities and in the sciences.

**Nida-Rümelin, Julian**. "Tierethik I: Zu den philosophischen und ethischen Grundlagen des Tierschutzes" in *Angewandte Ethik: Die Bereichsethiken und ihre theoretische Fundierung,* Nida-Rümelin, Julian (ed), 458-483. Stuttgart, Alfred Kröner, 1996.

The article develops the main philosophical and ethical foundations for the protection of animals. Different levels of mental capacities, the role of language and self-consciousness are discussed. It is argued in favour of an "extensionist" method for ethical judgement concerning animals. Since only parts of human morality are based on optimizing individual well-being, whereas other parts are depending on higher mental capacities like being responsible for one's actions, leading an autonomous life etc., which most animal species don't share, equal treatment of humans and nonhuman animals is limited.

**Nida-Rümelin, Julian**. "Wert des Lebens" in *Angewandte Ethik: Die Bereichsethiken und ihre theoretische Fundierung,* Nida-Rümelin, Julian (ed), 832-861. Stuttgart, Alfred Kröner, 1996.

In this last article of the *Handbook on Applied Ethics*, it is argued that only a deontological perspective is adequate in valuing human life.

**Nida-Rümelin, Julian**. "Wissenschaftsethik" in *Angewandte Ethik: Die Bereichsethiken und ihre theoretische Fundierung,* Nida-Rümelin, Julian (ed), 778-805. Stuttgart, Alfred Kröner, 1996.

In the first part, the ethos of epistemic rationality is developed historically and systematically as the core of research ethics. The second part argues for an extension of this core including an ethos of scientific responsibility. The last part argues for an integrated account of research ethics which focuses on duties of cooperation within the scientific community and in relation to the society in general. A broad institutionalization of ethical advice is argued for.

**Nida-Rümelin, Julian** (ed). *Angewandte Ethik: Die Bereichsethiken und ihre theoretische Fundierung.* Stuttgart, Alfred Kröner, 1996.

Das Handbuch stellt die einzelnen Bereichsethiken fundiert und informativ vor. Das ausführliche Einleitungskapitel führt in die Ethik und ihre zentralen Ansätze ein, die beiden Schlusskapitel *Ethik des Risikos* und *Ethik des Lebens* erörtern übergreifende Fragen, die in mehreren Bereichsethiken eine wesentliche Rolle spielen. Ein detailliertes Inhaltsverzeichnis, ein Personenregister sowie zahlreiche Literaturhinweise erhöhen den Informationswert des Handbuchs.

Der Band zieht erstmals eine differenzierte und allgemeinverständliche Bilanz über eines der derzeit lebendigsten und politisch aktuellsten Forschungsfelder der Philosophie. Namhafte Autorinnen und Autoren in der gegenwärtigen Forschungsdiskussion trugen dazu bei. (publisher)

**Nida-Rümelin, Julian**. Praktische Kohärenz. *Z Phil Forsch*, 51(2), 175-192, Ap-Je 97.

Practical coherence has two aspects: coherence of conative attitudes and coherence of action-guiding normative beliefs. The conception of practical coherence developed in this article is gradualistic and holistic. Practical reason is constituted by the coherence of the whole web constituted by the interdependencies of conative attitudes and normative beliefs. It is the task of ethics to reconstruct practical reasons. "Application" is, therefore, a genuine part of ethical "theory".

**Nida-Rümelin, Julian** and Schmidt, Thomas and Munk, Axel. Interpersonal Dependency of Preferences. *Theor Decis*, 41(3), 257-280, N 96.

Standard decision theoretic models disregard the phenomenon of interpersonal dependency of preferences. In this paper it is argued that interpersonal dependency of preferences is a serious challenge for standard utility theory. First we sketch the more philosophical aspects of the problem and then, using a simple, formal model for the two-person case, we show that interpersonal dependency of preferences generally results in indeterminacy of preferences (resp. of subjective utility).

**Nida-Rümelin, Julian** and Von der Pfordten, Dietmar. "Tierethik II: Zu den ethischen Grundlagen des Deutschen Tierschutzgesetzes" in *Angewandte Ethik: Die Bereichsethiken und ihre theoretische Fundierung,* Nida-Rümelin, Julian (ed), 484-509. Stuttgart, Alfred Kröner, 1996.

The article develops and criticizes the ethical foundations and implications of the German law regarding the treatment of animals. The original paper was presented at a hearing of the German National Parliament in October 1993.

**Niebuhr, Richard R**. "William James on Religious Experience" in *The Cambridge Companion to William James,* Putnam, Ruth Anna (ed), 214-236. New York, Cambridge Univ Pr, 1997.

**Nielsen, Kai**. Cultural Nationalism, Neither Ethnic Nor Civic. *Phil Forum*, 28(1-2), 42-52, Fall-Wint 97.

**Nielsen, Kai**. Habermas and Foucault: How to Carry Out the Enlightenment Project. *J Value Inq*, 31(1), 5-21, Mr 97.

**Niemann, Hans-Joachim**. Populismus in der Philosophie: Nicholas Reschers wissenschaftlicher Relativismus. *Conceptus*, 28(73), 271-300, 1995.

The influence of philosophical papers can be increased by matching the interests of two different groups of readers: the wide section of those generally interested in philosophical issues and, on the other hand, the professional philosophers. Often a kind of *ambiguous writing* is successfully used for this purpose, but not always sustained consistently. In such cases the message to their fellow philosophers is trivial, though it cannot be denied, whereas the other message to their fellow philosophers is trivial, though it cannot be denied, whereas the other message is exciting, but suffers a serious lack of justification. In addition, the arguments are put forward in a misleading way so as to let you think they would support the more interesting thesis. As a recent example of this artful and widespread philosophical populism a paper of Nicholas Rescher is discussed. His "scientific relativism" is scientifically defensible only in a very trivial interpretation. On the other hand, the second version occurring no less than 55 times would mean a revolution in philosophy of science and a really bad surprise to all scientists—if Rescher could give detailed reasons for it. But just that he fails to do. (publisher,edited)

**Nies, André** and Shore, Richard A and Slaman, Theodore A. Definability in the Recursively Enumerable Degrees. *Bull Sym Log*, 2(4), 392-404, D 96.

**Nieto Blanco, Carlos**. *La conciencia lingüística de la filosofía: Ensayo de una crítica de la razón lingüística.* Madrid, Trotta, 1997.

This work is split into three parts. In the first are presented the relationships among language and philosophy from Plato until Nietzsche. In the second is studied this topic in the principal philosophical traditions of our century, with special consideration to authors such as Wittgenstein, Heidegger, Gadamer and Habermas, among others. In the third are extracted the conclusions through a critique, proposing a new rational figure, agreed with the new philosophical situation, designated the *linguistics reason.* (edited)

**Nieto Blanco, Carlos**. *La filosofía en la encrucijada: Perfiles del pensamiento de José Ferrater Mora.* Barcelona, Serv de Pub U Autóno, 1985.

The book is the first study on the Spanish philosopher José Ferrater Mora (1912-1991), exile after the Civil War and resident in USA from 1947, known in the world for be the author of the better *Dictionary of Philosophy* written by an alone person. Though he has cultivated most of the philosophical genders, in addition to the narrative, his more relevant contributions belong to the field of the ontology. His conception of the world defends an emergent naturalism to which is arrived from logical-linguistics positions, within the supposed general of the analytical tradition. Proposes an ethics not anthropocentric, based on the freedom and in the solidarity.

**Nieto Blanco, Carlos** (ed). *Lecturas de Historia de la Filosofía.* Santander, Serv de Pub U Cantab, 1996.

This work was born in 1981 as of a series of meetings of philosophy teachers in the secondary level under the coordination of the University of Cantabria. The fundamental objective consists in presenting the history of philosophy through the reading of a series of classic texts of mean extension. The work includes a methodological chapter on the philosophical texts commentary, incorporating 14 texts of all the historical eras, from Plato until Foucault. The introductions that precede the texts are written by 14 different teachers and have a character eminently didactic thinking in the educational activity.

**Nieto Blanco, Carlos** (ed). *Saber, Sentir, Pensar: La cultura en la frontera de dos siglos*. Madrid, Debate, 1997.

My contribution in this book is double. As publisher, I accomplish a presentation of the work (pp. 9-15), in the one which collaborate relevant scientific and Spanish thinkers, on three large topics: the science, the feelings and the humanities, three large fields of the current culture, as well as three challenges for the education of the future. As author (pp. 251-274) I propose a reflection on the paper that it must play the philosophy from his critical conscience paper of the humanities.

**Nietzsche, Friedrich** and Handwerk, Gary (trans). *Human, All Too Human, I*. Stanford, Stanford Univ Pr, 1995.

This volume of *Human, All Too Human*, the first of two parts, is the earliest of Nietzsche's works in which his philosophical concerns and methodologies can be glimpsed. In this work Nietzsche began to establish the intellectual difference from his own cultural milieu and time that makes him our contemporary. Published in 1878, it marks both a stylistic and an intellectual shift away from Nietzsche's own youthful affiliation with Romantic excesses of German thought and culture typified by Wagnerian opera. (publisher, edited)

**Nietzsche, Friedrich** and Hollingdale, R J (trans). *Human, All Too Human: A Book of Free Spirits*. New York, Cambridge Univ Pr, 1996.

**Nietzsche, Friedrich** and Polt, Richard (trans). *Twilight of the Idols Or, How to Philosophize with the Hammer*. Indianapolis, Hackett, 1997.

*Twilight of the Idols*, which deals with what we worship and why, presents a vivid overview of many of Nietzsche's mature ideas—including his attack on Plato's Socrates and on the Platonic legacy in Western philosophy and culture—and anticipates his projected revaluation of all values. Accompanied by a fascinating Introduction by Tracy Strong, Richard Polt's new translation faithfully and beautifully renders this highly formal, even musical, late work of Nietzsche, which Nietzsche characterized as "a very sharp, precise and quick digest of my essential philosophical heterodoxies," and which offers such an excellent introduction to his thought. Includes select bibliography, notes, and index. (publisher)

**Nietzsche, Friedrich** and Smith, Douglas (trans). *On the Genealogy of Morals*. New York, Oxford Univ Pr, 1996.

**Niiniluoto, Ilkka**. "Inductive Logic, Atomism, and Observational Error" in *Knowledge and Inquiry: Essays on Jaakko Hintikka's Epistemology and Philosophy of Science*, Sintonen, Matti (ed), 117-131. Amsterdam, Rodopi, 1997.

Jaakko Hintikka has recently claimed that the traditional problem of inductive generalization occupies only a modest place in the interrogative logic of scientific inquiry. It is argued in this paper that the *atomistic postulate*, i.e., the restriction of nature's answers to atomic propositions and their negations, can be avoided only under very strong regularity conditions. In typical curve-fitting problems the desired function is not given by nature but discovered and supplied by the inquirer. On the other hand, Hintikka's own system of inductive logic is not tied to the *atomistic postulate*, since it can be (and has been) applied to situations where the evidence contains a universal theory. The second part of the paper outlines a system of inductive logic which allows for observational error. In analogy to Bayesian treatments of parameter estimation, the system is based upon a probabilistic error distribution for observations.

**Niiniluoto, Ilkka**. From Logic to Love: The Finnish Tradition in Philosophy. *Filosof Cas*, 44(3), 430-444, 1996.

**Niiniluoto, Ilkka**. Opening Words. *Filosof Cas*, 44(3), 362-368, 1996.

**Nikitovic, Aleksandar**. Hegels Differenzierung zwischen die "innere" und "aüssere" Philosophiegeschichte (in Serbo-Croatian). *Theoria (Yugoslavia)*, 38(3), 23-29, S 95.

Die Frage der Beziehung zwischen Wahrheit und Geschichte hat Hegel als Thema im Kontext der Widersprüche der Geschichte, die das Vergangene darstellt, was es nicht mehr gibt, und des wahrhaftigen Gedankens, der ewig ist. Der angegebene Widerspruch wird durch den lösenden Moment—durch die Geschichte der Selbsterfindung der Gedanken—aufgehoben. Der neue Begriff der Philosophiegeschichte stellt am wenigsten des dar "was es nicht mehr gibt", und er stellt die "innere" Geschichte als System der Begriffe und das Selbstbewusstsein des Weltgeistes dar. Der "inneren" Geschichte gegenüber steht die Vorstellung der Geschichte des gegebenen Widerspruches, wo die Geschichte eine vergängliche Gedankenform darstellt, die Hegel die "äussere" Philosophiegeschichte nennt.

**Niles, Ian**. Rescuing the Counterfactual Solution to Chisholm's Paradox. *Philosophia (Israel)*, 25(1-4), 351-371, Ap 97.

In his paper "On Chisholm's Paradox," Mott proposes an intuitively appealing solution to this paradox. However, Decew raises several potent objections to this proposal in her paper "Conditional Obligations and Counterfactuals." In this essay, I show that all but one of Decew's objections can be defeated without modifying Mott's counterfactual approach. I then argue that this approach is burdened with an extremely serious problem unrelated to Decew's objections. I then show that this problem can be met by augmenting Mott's system with Donald Davidson's theory of act-individuals. Finally, I argue that this modification resolves Decew's remaining objection.

**Nissenbaum, Helen**. Accountability in a Computerized Society. *Sci Eng Ethics*, 2(1), 25-42, J 96.

This essay warns of eroding accountability in computerized societies. It argues that assumptions about computing and features of situations in which computers are produced create barriers to accountability. Drawing on philosophical analyses of moral blame and responsibility, four barriers are identified: 1) the problem of many hands, 2) the problem of bugs, 3) blaming the computer, and 4) software ownership without liability. The paper concludes with ideas on how to reverse this trend.

**Nisters, Thomas**. Aquinas on Passions and Diminished Responsibility. *Jahr Recht Ethik*, 2, 239-257, 1994.

Gefühle können die Schwere der Schuld der Schuld beeinflussen. Bisweilen mindern sie die Schuldgrösse, manchmal vergrössern sie die Schuld und in einigen Fällen entschuldigen sie völlig. Ob ein Gefühl in die eine oder andere Richtung Einfluss nimmt, hängt nicht vom Gefühl selbst ab. Den Ausschlag gibt, wie sich das Gefühl zum Verstand und zum Willen verhält. Wenn das Gefühl dem Verstand und dem Willen folgt, dann erschwert es. Wenn das Gefühl jedoch vorhergeht, dann vermag es die freie Tatherrschaft einzuschränken und subjektive Schuld zu verringern, im Extremfall gar zu beseitigen.

**Niwinski, Damian** and Stolboushkin, Alexei. $y = 2x$ VS. $y = 3x$. *J Sym Log*, 62(2), 661-672, Je 97.

We show that no formula of first order logic using linear ordering and the logical relation $y = 2x$ can define the property that the size of a finite model is divisible by 3. This answers a long-standing question which may be of relevance to certain open problems in circuit complexity.

**Niznik, Jozef** (ed) and Sanders, John T (ed). *Debating the State of Philosophy: Habermas, Rorty, and Kolakowski*. Westport, Praeger, 1996.

Habermas begins with a comprehensive account of contextualism. According to him, contextualism is a new form of historicism. What are the merits of an approach that takes into account both a historical and a cultural context? Is the pragmatism promoted by Richard Rorty an acceptable criticism of our Platonic heritage? If so, does this mean the end of rationality as a regulative ideal of the human universe? Rorty's answer is "Yes." This world-renowned American thinker recommends putting a full stop at the end of a narrative which was useful in pursuit of our ancestors' purposes but is no longer useful for ours. Leszek Kolakowski attempts to undermine the alleged pragmatic merits of pragmatism from the position of an analytic philosopher who continues to value classical elements of philosophical tradition. Ernest Gellner also turns against Rorty's pragmatism, which he denounces as a product of the Enlightenment roots of American culture and its centuries of political and economic stability. The future of Western culture may depend on the answers to the questions asked by these authors. (publisher, edited)

**Nnoruka, Sylvanos I**. Alfred Schutz on the Social Distribution of Knowledge. *Darshana Int*, 36(1/141), 54-62, Ja 96.

**Nobre, Sergio**. La contribución de Christian Wolff (1679-1754) a la popularización de las matemáticas en la primera mitad del siglo XVIII. *Mathesis*, 10(2), 153-169, My 94.

This essay demonstrates the importance of the philosopher and mathematician Christian Wolff in the diffusion of the mathematics of his time in Germany. With the purpose that his books could be read for those who had not mastered the scientific language of the time, Wolff wrote his main mathematical books in German and many mathematical concepts which were usually presented in Latin or French were translated and are still in use. His scholar book—the most important mathematical book in the Germany of the first half of the 18th century—and his mathematical encyclopaedia—the first work of its kind to be published in German—are introduced in this text.

**Noddings, Nel**. On Community. *Educ Theor*, 46(3), 245-267, Sum 96.

This article responds to the call for community heard everywhere today. First, it provides background for understanding the tensions between views that emphasize the individual and those that focus on community. Then, noting that community is not an alloyed good (it has a dark side), it explores some of the problems and potential solutions in the quest for communities free of the dark side. Finally, some recommendations are made for educators interested in community.

**Noel, Jana**. "Physical and Cultural Dimensions of Horizon" in *Philosophy of Education (1996)*, Margonis, Frank (ed), 307-314. Urbana, Phil Education Soc, 1997.

This paper describes the physical and cultural dimensions of Gadamer's sense of horizon. It is proposed that physical dimensions such as geographic barriers are tied to cultural dimensions such as the active or lack of active examination of one's horizon. The city as a concentration of difference is proposed as a space within which horizon can be examined. A flaneur within the city, who does not seek the singular perspective that arises in a closed horizon but rather is open to the "beyond," demonstrates the movement in relation to one's cultural horizon that is encouraged in this paper.

**Noggle, Robert**. The Nature of Motivation (and Why it Matters Less to Ethics than One Might Think). *Phil Stud*, 87(1), 87-111, Jl 97.

Anti-Humeans claim that beliefs alone can produce motivation. Humeans deny this and claim that desires are necessary for motivation. Any plausible theory of motivation must account for the means-end structure of motives and the fact that sometimes motivation is subjectively irrational. I argue that given these plausibility constraints, plausible versions of Humeanism and anti-Humeanism are merely notational variants of each other. This thesis has implications for the moral realism debate, for it means that arguments against internalist moral realism cannot rest on the claim that moral judgements cannot be both beliefs and motivators as the same time.

**Noggle, Robert** and Brennan, Samantha. The Moral Status of Children: Children's Rights, Parents' Rights, and Family Justice. *Soc Theor Pract*, 23(1), 1-26, Spr 97.

This paper aims to provide a philosophical foundation for thinking about the moral status of children. Three plausible constraints on moral theorizing about children are put forward: The Equal Consideration Thesis, the Unequal Treatment Thesis and the Limited Parental Rights Thesis. While these claims underlie much common sense thinking about the moral status and treatment of children, the claims also appear to be inconsistent. A right-based theory of the moral status of children is proposed which both meets the three constraints and resolves their internal conflicts. A final section examines the policy implications of the proposed account.

**Nola, Robert** and Braddon-Mitchell, David. Ramsification and Glymour's Counterexample. *Analysis*, 57(3), 167-169, Jl 97.

**Nolan, Daniel**. Recombination Unbound. *Phil Stud*, 84(2-3), 239-262, D 96.

A basic formulation of the Principle of Recombination in the theory of possible worlds is that for any possible objects in any possible worlds, there is some particular world which contains any number of duplicates of each of those objects. David Lewis wants to add a qualification: "size and shape permitting". He appears to be driven to this by a cardinality objection raised by Peter Forrest and D.M. Armstrong. This paper argues that the Forrest/Armstrong argument fails and goes on to argue that Lewis's restriction of the principle of recombination should be dropped.

**Nolan, Daniel**. Three Problems for "Strong" Modal Fictionalism. *Phil Stud*, 87(3), 259-275, S 97.

Modal fictionalism, the theory that possible worlds do not literally exist but that our talk about them should be understood in the same way that we understand talk about fictional entities, is an increasingly popular approach to possible worlds. This paper will distinguish three versions of modal fictionalism and will show that the third, a version endorsed by some of the most prominent modal fictionalists, faces at least three serious objections: that it makes modality too artificial, the modal fiction does not have the representative resources it needs and the approach has trouble accounting for propositions.

**Nolan, Lawrence**. Reductionism and Nominalism in Descartes's Theory of Attributes. *Topoi*, 16(2), 129-140, S 97.

**Nolan, Lawrence**. The Ontological Status of Cartesian Natures. *Pac Phil Quart*, 78(2), 169-194, Je 97.

In the Fifth Meditation, Descartes makes a remarkable claim about the ontological status of geometrical figures. He asserts that an object such as a triangle has a 'true and immutable nature' that does not depend on the mind, yet has being even if there are no triangles existing in the world. This statement has led many commentators to assume that Descartes is a Platonist regarding essences and in the philosophy of mathematics. One problem with this seemingly natural reading is that it contradicts the conceptualist account of universals that one finds in the *Principles of Philosophy* and elsewhere. In this paper, I offer a novel interpretation of the notion of a true and immutable nature which reconciles the Fifth Meditation with the conceptualism of Descartes's other work. Specifically, I argue that Descartes takes natures to be innate ideas considered in terms of their so-called 'objective being'.

**Nolte, Ernst**. Ricordo e oblio: La Germania dopo le sconfitte nelle due guerre mondiali. *Iride*, 8(14), 110-122, Ap 95.

**Noonan, Jeff**. Philosophy in a Fragmented World. *Int Stud Phil*, 29(1), 99-109, 1997.

**Noone, Timothy B**. Alnwick on the Origin, Nature, and Function of the Formal Distinction. *Fran Stud*, 53, 231-245, 1993.

**Noordhof, Paul**. Accidental Associations, Local Potency, and a Dilemma for Dretske. *Mind Lang*, 11(2), 216-222, Je 96.

I argue that Fred Dretske's account of the causal relevance of content only works if another account works better, that put forward by Gabriel Segal and Elliot Sober. Dretske needs to appeal to it to deal with two problems he faces: one arising because he accepts that the mere association between indicators and indicated is causally relevant to the recruitment of indicators in causing behaviour, the other from the need to explain how a present token of a certain type of content is causally relevant. For this and other reasons their approach has clear advantages over Dretske's.

**Noordhof, Paul**. Making the Change: the Functionalist's Way. *Brit J Phil Sci*, 48(2), 233-250, Je 97.

The paper defends functionalism against the charge that it would make mental properties inefficacious. It outlines two ways of formulating the doctrine that mental properties are functional properties and shows that both allow mental properties to be efficacious. The first (Lewis) approach takes functional properties to be the *occupants* of causal roles. I show why this is not a problem. The second way of formulating the doctrine takes functional properties to be causal role properties. I claim that mental properties so understood would only be inefficacious if a *law-centred* rather than a *property-centred* approach is adopted to the introduction of efficacy into the world. I develop a property-centred account that explains how mental properties can be efficacious without introducing systematic overdetermination. (edited)

**Noordhof, Paul**. The Mysterious Grand Properties of Forrest. *Austl J Phil*, 75(1), 99-101, Mr 97.

Forrest argues that supervening properties are properties of properties (Forrest (1988)). He claims that this is a way of getting out of what he calls the *mystery or reduction* dilemma. Those supervenient properties that do not reduce to their supervenience-base stand in a mysterious relation to it. I argue that if one is worried about the mystery in this case, there is an analogous mystery that his own proposal introduces. Why is it that some properties essentially possess certain other properties?

**Noordhoof, Paul** and Ganeri, Jonardon and Ramachandran, Murali. Counterfactuals and Preemptive Causation. *Analysis*, 56(4), 219-225, O 96.

**Nootens, Geneviève**. Ontologie, philosophie et politique: la critique de la tradition épistémologique chez Charles Taylor. *Dialogue (Canada)*, 35(3), 553-569, Sum 96.

**Nora, Lois Margaret** and Mahowald, Mary B. Neural Fetal Tissue Transplants: Old and New Issues. *Zygon*, 31(4), 615-633, D 96.

Neural fetal tissue transplantation offers promise as a treatment for devasting neurologic conditions such as Parkinson's disease. Two types of issues arise from this procedure: those associated with the use of fetuses and those associated with the use of neural tissue. The former issues have been examined in many forums; the latter have not. This paper reviews issues and arguments raised by the use of fetal tissue in general, but focuses on the implications of the use of neural tissue for basic concepts of personhood and personal identity.

**Norcross, Alastair**. Comparing Harms: Headaches and Human Lives. *Phil Pub Affairs*, 26. (2), 135-167, Spr 97.

How might a consequentialist avoid the conclusion that there is some finite number of headaches, such that it is permissible to kill an innocent person to avoid them? I consider two possibilities: I) headaches and human lives are incomparable; II) the loss of an innocent life is worse than *any* number of headaches. The first possibility doesn't seem to capture our intuitions about the comparison and might even justify killing the innocent, depending on which formulation of the consequentialist criterion of permissibility we employ. The second possibility, when combined with some plausible assumptions, requires us to deny the transitivity of 'better than'. Such a denial of transitivity could accommodate moral dilemmas within a consequentialist framework, but is, in itself, so counterintuitive that it requires independent arguments. I consider an reject two such arguments, offered by Warren Quinn and Larry Temkin. Finally, I argue that most people accept at least some claims that are morally equivalent to the claim that it is permissible to kill an innocent person to avoid some finite number of headaches. (edited)

**Norcross, Alastair**. Trading Lives for Convenience: It's Not Just for Consequentialists. *SW Phil Rev*, 13(1), 29-37, Ja 97.

Consider the following case: a vast number of people are experiencing fairly minor headaches, which will continue unabated for another hour, unless an innocent person is killed, in which case they will cease immediately. Common-sense morality seems to tell us that we can't sacrifice the innocent person to save *any* number of headaches. But consequentialism tells us that, if even a minor headache has *some* disvalue, a large enough number of such headaches must equal the disvalue of a death. So consequentialism is sometimes accused of being committed to: *The unpleasant conclusion*: there is some finite number of headaches, such that it is permissible to kill an innocent person to avoid them. I argue that the *unpleasant conclusion* is not, after all, particularly unpleasant. In fact, I claim, most of us, consequentialists and nonconsequentialists alike, accept at least some other claims that do not differ significantly from the *unpleasant conclusion*.

**Nordenbo, Sven Erik**. Against Education. *J Phil Educ*, 30(3), 401-413, N 96.

The article analyses some of the central ideas of the Movement Against Education (die anti-Pädagogik). First the inspiration supplied by 'anti-psychiatry' is noted. Secondly, an example of everyday 'educational interference' is discussed from the perspective of the Movement's ideas. Thirdly, the elements of education the Movement considers outrageous, and so demands the abolition of all educational activity, are discussed. It is concluded that the Movement still raises questions about the general understanding of educational theory and practice today, in particular about the justification of educational intervention and compulsion in a context of scepticism about natural development, absolute values or the predictability of the future.

**Nordquist, Joan** (ed). *Emmanuel Levinas: A Bibliography.* Santa Cruz, Reference & Research, 1997.

The bibliography lists the essays and books of Emmanuel Levinas that have been reprinted in English with the original French sources noted. Critical literature about these books and essays is also included. The critical literature is arranged by author and dates from 1980 to 1997. Books, dissertations and theses, journal articles and articles within books are included.

**Nordquist, Joan** (ed). *French Feminist Theory (III): Luce Irigaray and Helene Cixous: A Bibliography.* Santa Cruz, Reference & Research, 1996.

The bibliography lists the essays and books of Luce Irigaray and Helene Cixous that have been reprinted in English with the original French sources noted. Critical literature about these books and essays is provided. The critical literature about the work of Irigaray and Cixous in general is arranged by author and dates from 1990 to 1996. Keyword-in-title indexes are provided. Books, theses and dissertations, journal articles and articles within books are included. (publisher)

**Nordquist, Joan** (ed). *Rosa Luxemburg and Emma Goldman: A Bibliography.* Santa Cruz, Reference & Research, 1996.

The bibliography lists the essays and books of Rosa Luxemburg that have been reprinted in English with the original German sources noted. The books and essays by Emma Goldman in English are also listed. Critical literature about these books and essays is provided. The critical literature about the work of Luxemburg and Goldman in general is arranged by author and dates from 1900 to 1996. Keyword-in-title indexes are provided. Books, dissertations and theses, journal articles and articles within books are included. (publisher)

**Nordquist, Joan**. *Social Theory: A Bibliographic Series, No. 42-Martin Heidegger (II): A Bibliography.* Santa Cruz, Reference & Research, 1996.

The bibliography lists the essays and books of Martin Heidegger that have been reprinted in English with the original German sources noted. Critical literature about these books and essays is also included. The critical literature about the work of Heidegger in general is arranged by author and dates from 1989 to 1996. Keyword-in-title indexes are provided. Books, dissertations and theses, journal articles and articles within books are included. This bibliography supplements an early bibliography (*Martin Heidegger: A Bibliography.* Social Theory: A Bibliographic Series, No. 17, 1990).

**Norman, Richard**. Cooperation and Equality: A Reply to Pojman. *Philosophy*, 72(279), 137-142, Ja 97.

**Norman, Richard**. Making Sense of Moral Realism. *Phil Invest*, 20(2), 117-135, Ap 97.

The article reviews the range of positions which have gone under the title of 'moral realism' in recent years. It examines the metaphor of 'vision' as one way of characterizing the nature of moral understanding and explores the merits of the alternative model of moral understanding as a matter of 'making sense of' or 'finding a meaning in' our experience. It considers the merits and shortcomings of the analogy with perception of secondary qualities and ends by suggesting that the important issues in this area are epistemological rather than ontological, but that the term 'moral realism' may nevertheless be a suitable label for a defensible position.

**Norman, Wayne**. "Prelude to a Liberal Morality of Nationalism" in *A Question of Values: New Canadian Perspectives in Ethics and Political Philosophy,* Brennan, Samantha (ed), 189-208. Amsterdam, Rodopi, 1997.

**Normore, Calvin G**. "David Savan: In Memoriam" in *The Rule of Reason: The Philosophy of Charles Sanders Peirce,* Forster, Paul (ed), 309-311. Toronto, Univ of Toronto Pr, 1997.

**Normore, Calvin G**. Material Supposition and the Mental Language of Ockham's *Summa Logicae. Topoi*, 16(1), 27-33, Mr 97.

**Normore, Calvin G** (& other trans) and Lewis, Wendy (trans) and Barney, Stephen (trans). On the Properties of Discourse: A Translation of *Tractatus de Proprietatibus Sermonum* (Author Anonymous). *Topoi*, 16(1), 77-93, Mr 97.

This is a translation of part of an anonymous early thirteenth tract on medieval semantics. The author discusses signification, supposition and appellation, including the division of supposition into determinate, distributive and merely confused. Causes of confusion are covered; sophisms are solved by applying the theory. Also covered: ampliation of terms by tenses and modalities.

**Norrie, Alan**. Commentary on "Pathological Autobiographies". *Phil Psychiat Psych*, 4(2), 115-118, Je 97.

**Norris, Christopher**. Doubting Castel or the Slough of Despond: Davidson and Schiffer on the Limits of Analysis. *Rev Metaph*, 50(2), 351-382, D 96.

This paper argues for a truth-based, propositional, and realist theory of meaning and belief. It also examines the retreat from that position manifest in the work of recent (arguably 'postanalytic') philosophers, among them Stephen Schiffer and Donald Davidson. With Schiffer it issues in an outlook of extreme pessimism with regard to his own earlier project, namely the attempt to specify meanings, attitudes, and belief-contents through a form of compositional semantics. With Davidson—in his essay "A Nice Derangement of Epitaphs"—it involves the idea that ad hoc 'passing theories' (rather than 'prior theories') are all we have to go on in most cases, since no generalized account of speaker—or listener-competence is adequate to cover the possible range of nuances, deviant meanings, or localized contextual clues and cues. Thus communicative uptake can only be a matter of intuitive 'wit, luck, and wisdom', eked out by more-or-less inspired or charitable guesswork. However, such notions cannot start to explain our most basic and everyday, let alone our more resourceful and inventive performances with language. I therefore bring together a range of alternative perspectives—from philosophical semantics and (unusually) William Empson's neglected book *The Structure of Complex Words*—which point a way beyond this false dilemma.

**Norris, Christopher**. Ontological Relativity and Meaning-Variance: A Critical-Constructive Review. *Inquiry*, 40(2), 139-173, Je 97.

This article offers a critical review of various ontological-relativist arguments, mostly deriving from the work of W.V. Quine and Thomas Kuhn. I maintain that these arguments are 1) internally contradictory, 2) incapable of accounting for our knowledge of the growth of scientific knowledge, and 3) shown up as fallacious from the standpoint of a causal-realist approach to issues of truth, meaning, and interpretation. Moreover, they have often been viewed as lending support to such programs as the 'strong' sociology of knowledge and the turn towards wholesale cultural-relativist doctrines, whether of the Wittgensteinian ('language-games') or Heideggerian (depth-hermeneutic) varieties. However, both thinkers have left themselves open to misconstrual by adopting a sceptical-relativist fallback position in response to the well-known problems with logical empiricism. This essay, therefore, reviews those problems with reference to alternative, more adequate accounts of what is involved in the process of scientific discovery and theory-change. (edited)

**Norris, Christopher**. Ontology according to Van Fraassen: Some Problems with Constructive Empiricism. *Metaphilosophy*, 28(3), 196-218, Jl 97.

This paper argues the case for ontological realism. In particular it takes issue with Richard Rorty's writings on philosophy of science and with Bas van Fraassen's more moderate 'constructive empiricist' approach. This latter entails ontological commitment to whatever shows up through trained observation or empirical research. However, it refuses to countenance realist claims concerning the existence of (as yet) unobserved entities and their role in explanatory theories premised on putative laws of nature. I maintain that van Fraassen's position is: (1) inadequate to account for our knowledge of the growth of scientific knowledge; (2) self-refuting since often undermined by examples which he himself supplies; and (3) incapable of mounting resistance

to other, more wholesale (e.g., Rortian) varieties of antirealist argument. Only by combining causal realism with a principle of inference to the best explanation can philosophy of science avoid these kinds of hyperinduced sceptical doubt. (edited)

**Norris, Christopher**. *Reclaiming Truth: Contribution to a Critique of Cultural Relativism.* Durham, Duke Univ Pr, 1996.

Norris presents his case in a series of closely argued chapters that take issue with the relativist position. He attempts to rehabilitate the value of truth in philosophy of science by restoring a lost distinction between concept and metaphor and argues that theoretical discourse, far from being an inconsequential activity, has very real consequences, particularly in ethics and politics. This debate has become skewed, he suggests, through the widespread and typically postmodern idea that truth-claims must always go along with a presumptive or authoritarian bid to silence opposing views. (publisher,edited)

**Norris, Christopher**. Why Strong Sociologists Abhor a Vacuum: Shapin and Schaffer on the Boyle/Hobbes Controversy. *Phil Soc Crit*, 23(4), 9-40, Jl 97.

This essay takes issue with the 'strong' programme in sociology of knowledge as applied to the history and philosophy of science. It focuses chiefly on a classic text of that movement, Shapin and Schaffer's *Leviathan and the Air-Pump.* I maintain that this approach is mistaken in principle and cannot be carried through without producing some contorted arguments and justifications. Moreover, their proclaimed even-handedness as between Boyle and Hobbes in fact ends up by espousing the Hobbesian (also Foucauldian) belief that knowledge is *always and everywhere* a product of power-interests concealed by a rhetoric of 'disinterested' truth-seeking inquiry. (edited)

**Nortmann, Ulrich**. Über einen vermuteten Zusammenhang von Müssen und Wollen—Diskussion der Monographie von Hans-Ulrich Hoche: *Elemente einer Anatomie der Verpflichtung. Jahr Recht Ethik*, 2, 539-551, 1994.

**Norton, Bryan G**. "Integration or Reduction: Two Approaches to Environmental Values" in *Environmental Pragmatism,* Light, Andrew (ed), 105-138. New York, Routledge, 1996.

Standard approaches to environmental values, whether anthropocentric or nonanthropocentric, are equally reductionist in the sense that they reduce all types of environmental values to a common currency. These approaches are contrasted with a pluralistic approach that recognizes human values that unfold on multiple scales of time and seeks time-sensitive integration of human valuations of the environment. The first half of the paper criticizes the nonanthropocentric, reductionist position of J B Callicott; the second half shows how a multiscalar approach to environmental values can be built upon the ideas of C S Peirce.

**Norton, Bryan G**. "The Constancy of Leopold's Land Ethic" in *Environmental Pragmatism,* Light, Andrew (ed), 84-102. New York, Routledge, 1996.

Aldo Leopold, in 1923, considered a range of theories of environmental value and concluded that, while nonanthropocentrism was attractive to him personally, a "sustainability" ethic, emphasizing obligations to posterity, provides the best basis for analyzing and advocating environmental policies. Influenced by A.T. Hadley (President of Yale University and a minor American pragmatist), Leopold applied a "pragmatic theory of truth" to societies: a society has the "truth" if it survives without destroying its resources. This approach allowed Leopold to criticize the Gifford Pinchot's production-orientation forestry while leaving open the intriguing question of nonanthropocentric values. Conclusion: adopting the land ethic does not require a conversion to nonanthropocentrism.

**Norton, Bryan G**. Convergence and Contextualism: Some Clarifications and a Reply to Steverson. *Environ Ethics*, 19(1), 87-100, Spr 97.

The convergence hypothesis asserts that, if one takes the full range of human values—present and future—into account, one will choose a set of policies that can also be accepted by an advocate of a consistent and reasonable nonanthropocentrism. Brian Steverson has attacked this hypothesis from a surprising direction. He attributes to deep ecologists the position that nonhuman nature has intrinsic value, interprets this position to mean that no species could ever be allowed to go extinct, and proceeds to show that my commitment to contextualism prohibits me from advocating the protection of species universally. In response, I show, by reference to recent scientific findings, how difficult it is to defend species preservation in all situations. (edited)

**Norton, Bryan G** and Hannon, Bruce. Environmental Values: A Place-Based Theory. *Environ Ethics*, 19(3), 227-245, Fall 97.

Several recent authors have recommended that "sense of place" should become an important concept in our evaluation of environmental policies. In this paper, we explore aspects of this concept, arguing that it may provide the basis for a new, "place-based" approach to environmental values. This approach is based on an empirical hypothesis that place orientation is a feature of all people's experience of their environment. We argue that place orientation requires, in addition to a home perspective, a sense of the space around the home place and that this dual aspect can be modeled using a "hierarchical" methodology. We propose a "triscalar," place-oriented system for the analysis of environmental values, explore the characteristics of place-orientation through several examples and employ these characteristics to distinguish acceptable and unacceptable aspects of the NIMBY (not-in-my-backyard) idea.

**Norton, John D**. Are Thought Experiments Just What You Thought?. *Can J Phil*, 26(3), 333-366, S 96.

I defend the view that thought experiments in science are merely picturesque arguments and criticize an alternative view of James Brown that thought experiments can provide access to a Platonic world of laws.

**Nussbaum, Martha C**. "Love and the Individual: Romantic Rightness and Platonic Aspiration" in *Love Analyzed,* Lamb, Roger E, 1-22. Boulder, Westview Pr, 1997.

**Nussbaum, Martha C**. "Nussbaum's Reply" in *The Liberation Debate: Rights at Issue,* Leahy, Michael (ed), 125-129. New York, Routledge, 1996.

**Nussbaum, Martha C**. *Wuthering Heights*: The Romantic Ascent. *Phil Lit*, 20(2), 362-382, O 96.

**Nussbaum, Martha C**. Gregory Vlastos: *Socratic Studies*. *J Phil*, 94(1), 27-45, Ja 97.

**Nussbaum, Martha C**. Is Nietzsche a Political Thinker?. *Int J Phil Stud*, 5(1), 1-13, Mr 97.

Nietzsche claimed to be a political thinker in *Ecce Homo* and elsewhere. He constantly compared his thought with other political theorists, chiefly Rousseau, Kant and Mill and he claimed to offer an alternative to the bankruptcy of Enlightenment liberalism. It is worthwhile re-examining Nietzsche's claim to offer serious criticisms of liberal political philosophy. I shall proceed by setting out seven criteria for serious political thought: understanding of material need; procedural justification; liberty and its worth; racial, ethnic and religious difference; gender and family; justice between nations; and moral psychology. I shall argue polemically that on the first six issues Nietzsche has nothing to offer, but that on the seventh, moral psychology, he makes a profound contribution. Serious political theory, however, needs to forget about Nietzsche and turn to those thinkers he found so boring—the liberal Enlightenment thinkers.

**Nussbaum, Martha C** (ed) and Estlund, David M (ed). *Sex, Preference, and Family: Essays on Law and Nature.* New York, Oxford Univ Pr, 1997.

From Dan Quayle's attack on TV's Murphy Brown for giving birth out of wedlock, to the referendum recently passed in Colorado that forbids local communities from enacting nondiscrimination laws for sexual orientation, the public furor over issues of same-sex marriages, gay rights, pornography and single-parent families has erupted with a passion not seen since the 1960s. It is a battle being fought, in large part, over where to draw the line between law and nature, between the political and the personal, the social and the biological. And it is an important struggle to resolve, for as we move into the next century our culture is redefining itself in fundamental ways. How we decide these questions will determine much about the kind of society we and our children will live in. (publisher)

**Nuyen, A T**. Education for Imaginative Knowledge. *J Thought*, 32(1), 37-47, Spr 97.

The paper argues for the addition of a category of knowledge, or knowing, namely knowing how to imagine. With reference to the works of Lyotard, it is argued that knowing how to imagine has an important role to play in avoiding, or minimizing, the wrongs of what Lyotard calls the differends. Education for imagination is then of crucial importance for the postmodern condition.

**Nuyen, A T**. Just Desert. *J Value Inq*, 31(2), 221-230, Je 97.

According to Feinberg, desert and justice belong to different parts of our ethical vocabularies. Against Feinberg, I argue that by separating the two we fail properly to understand the nature of desert. Taking justice in the sense of *dike* understood by the ancient Greeks, we can give an account of desert in terms of justice.

**Nuyen, A T**. The Nature of Temptation. *S J Phil*, 35(1), 91-103, Spr 97.

This paper makes a distinction between "the tempter," "the temptee," and "the tempted." It then stipulates and defends the necessary and sufficient conditions for someone to be a tempter, or a temptee, or a tempted. Finally, the paper argues that it is not always morally wrong to be either a tempter, or a temptee, or a tempted, by showing why it is wrong if it is wrong.

**Nuyen, A T**. The Sublimity of Evil. *Int J Phil Relig*, 41(3), 135-147, Je 97.

Borrowing from Kant, the paper argues that evil is sublime. This is not to say that there is something good about evil. It is to say that we are as a matter of fact confronted with evil as much as with raging torrents, stormy seas, huge mountains and so on, all of which evoke in us a Kantian sense of the sublime, allowing us to see our own form, namely freedom, particularly the freedom to resist the temptation to do evil or to succumb to its influence in other ways.

**Nuyen, A T**. The Trouble with Tolerance. *Amer Cath Phil Quart*, 71(1), 1-12, Wint 97.

The paper argues against the idea that tolerance requires that we see those we need to tolerate as "the same as us." This is to reduce difference to sameness and is to do violence to difference. The paper then argues for a postmodern ethics of difference in which tolerance requires that we respect difference as difference. The paper shows that the works of Levinas and Lyotard are illuminating in this respect.

**Nuzzo, Enrico**. "Vico e Bayle: Ancora una messa a punto" in *Pierre Bayle e l'Italia*, Bianchi, Lorenzo, 123-202. Napoli, Liguori Ed, 1996.

**Nuzzo, Enrico**. "Vico, la storia, lo storicismo" in *Lo Storicismo e la Sua Storia: Temi, Problemi, Prospettive*, Cacciatore, Giuseppe (ed), 50-68. Milano, Guerini, 1997.

**Nwachukwu, Saviour L S** and Vitell, Scott J. The Influence of Corporate Culture on Managerial Ethical Judgments. *J Bus Ethics*, 16(8), 757-776, Je 97.

The contention that organizational culture influences ethical decision making is not disputable. However, the extent to which it influences ethical decision making in the workplace is a topic for scholarly debate and investigation. There are scholars who argue that, though corporate values are a powerful force within organizations, these values are unperceived, unspoken, and taken for granted.

However, there are others who argue that the formalization of corporate values facilitates job and role clarity and is the key to influencing employee behavior. The purpose of this study is to examine the extent of the influence of organizational codes of ethics. The findings suggest that, depending upon the particular situation, corporate culture and ethics may mitigate individual personal moral convictions about right and wrong.

**Nye, Andrea**. Friendship Across Generations. *Hypatia*, 11(3), 154-160, Sum 96.

*Feminist Interpretations* of Hannah Arendt, edited by Bonnie Honig, a collection of critical feminist essays on Hannah Arendt, illustrates both the disorientation and the insights that can result when feminist philosophers come to terms with a canonical figure who is a woman.

**Nylan, Michael**. Han Classicists Writing in Dialogue about their Own Tradition. *Phil East West*, 47(2), 133-188, Ap 97.

Despite the scathing criticisms leveled at Han philosophy by orthodox neo-Confucians and their latter-day scholastic followers, the most accurate characterization of many extant pieces of Han philosophical writing would be "critical" (rather than "superstitious") and "probing" (rather than "derivative"). In defense of this statement, three major Han philosophical works are examined, with particular emphasis on the treatment in these works of classical tradition and classical learning. The three works are the *Fa yen* (ca. A.D. 9) by Yang Hsiung, the *Lun heng* (ca. A.D. 80) by Wang Ch'ung and the *Feng su t'ung yi* (ca. A.D. 200) by Ying Shao. (edited)

**O'Brien, Lucy F**. Solipsism and Self-Reference. *Euro J Phil*, 4(2), 175-194, Ag 96.

**O'Brien, Wendell**. Butler, Hobbes, and Human Nature. *Vera Lex*, 14(1-2), 89-95, 1994.

**O'Brien, Wendell**. Meaning and Mattering. *S J Phil*, 34(3), 339-360, Fall 96.

The notion of meaningfulness in "a meaningful life" cannot be defined in terms of the notion of importance or mattering. This is shown by (among other things) the fact that, in many traditions, a life of detachment is regarded as one of the most meaningful sorts of lives.

**O'Callaghan, John P**. The Problem of Language and Mental Representation in Aristotle and St. Thomas. *Rev Metaph*, 50(3), 499-545, Mr 97.

**O'Connell, Lenahan** and Betz, Michael and Shepard, Jon M. The Proactive Corporation: Its Nature and Causes. *J Bus Ethics*, 16(10), 1001-1010, Jl 97.

We argue that the stakeholder perspective on corporate social responsibility is in the process of being enlarged. Due to the process of institutional isomorphism, corporations are increasingly adopting organizational features designed to promote proactivity over mere reactivity in their stakeholder relationships. We identify two sources of pressure promoting the emergence of the proactive corporation—stakeholder activism and the recognition of the social embeddedness of the economy. The final section describes four organizational design dimensions being installed by the more proactive corporations today—cooperation, participation, negotiation, and direct anticipation.

**O'Connell, Robert J**. *Plato on the Human Paradox*. New York, Fordham Univ Pr, 1997.

Through Plato, Father O'Connell provides us here with an introduction to all philosophy. Designed for beginning students in philosophy, *Plato on the Human Paradox* examines and confronts human nature and the eternal questions concerning human nature through the dialogues of Plato, focusing on the *Apology*, *Phaedo*, Books *III-VI* of the *Republic*, *Meno*, *Symposium*, and O'Connell presents us here with an introduction to Plato through the philosopher's quest to define "human excellence" or *aretê* in terms of defining what "human being" is body and soul, focusing on Plato's preoccupations with the questions of how and what it means to have a "good life" in relation to or as opposed to a "moral life."(publisher, edited)

**O'Connell, Robert J**. *William James on The Courage to Believe*. New York, Fordham Univ Pr, 1997.

O'Connell contributes a fresh interpretation of James's argument. *William James on the Courage to Believe* contends that "The Will to Believe" should be viewed against James indebtedness to Pascal and Renouvier; that it works primarily to validate our "over-beliefs"; and most surprising perhaps, that James envisages our "passional nature" as intervening, not after, but before and throughout, our intellectual weighing of the evidence for belief. This eloquently written study provides a view of James's philosophy as not being limited to epistemological categories, but rather one that is in line with a Western philosophical tradition which wishes to transcend them. For this second edition, Father O'Connell has added extensively to sharpen his arguments: that James's "deontological streak" saves him from "wishful thinking" and weaves together the attitudes of right, readiness, willingness, and will to believe, and that "willing faith" lends "the facts" their aura of believability. (publisher, edited)

**O'Connell, Rory**. Natural Law: Alive and Kicking? A Look at the Constitutional Morality of Sexual Privacy in Ireland. *Ratio Juris*, 9(3), 258-282, S 96.

This article discusses the role of moral argument in the Constitutional case law of the Irish courts. It looks at the debate on the constitutional morality of sexuality in four major cases: a 1973 case protecting the right to use contraceptives; a 1984 case which upholds discrimination against gay men; a 1987 case limiting access to abortion information; and a 1992 case which finds a limited right to abortion in the Constitution. These cases show the role of the courts in contributing to a debate on political morality, both proposing new visions of political morality, and elaborating on the requirements of the current one.

**O'Connor, Peg**. Warning! Contents Under Heterosexual Pressure. *Hypatia*, 12(3), 183-188, Sum 97.

This essay examines some stereotypes of bisexuals held by some lesbians. I argue that the decision that a lesbian makes not to become involved with a bisexual woman because she is bisexual can recenter men in lesbian desire, a consequence many lesbians would find deeply problematic. The acceptance of these stereotypes also results in sex becoming the defining characteristic of one's sexual orientation, thus privileging sex over any emotional, affectional, and political commitments to women.

**O'Dea, Jane**. Integrity and the Feminist Teacher. *J Phil Educ*, 31(2), 267-282, Jl 97.

Our popular conception of integrity brings to mind uncompromising figures like Socrates or Sir Thomas Moore whose steadfast stands on matters of principle we accept and admire. The paper considers the implications of this for two committed feminists, both of whom are teachers. Their pedagogical philosophies are sufficiently different to lead one to charge the other with selling out her feminist principles. But is this a fair assessment? Is there room for compromise within the complex notion of integrity? How might feminist teachers rework the concept to do justice to the complexities involved?

**O'Grady, Paul**. Aquinas on Modal Propositions: Introduction, Text, and Translation. *Int Phil Quart*, 37(1), 13-27, Mr 97.

This paper presents a translation and study of a little known work by Aquinas. Situating the treatise "On Modal Propositions" in the context of the development of medieval logic and accounts of modality, the paper discusses its authenticity and analyzes its contents.

**O'Grady, Terence J**. Critical Perspectives on Early Twentieth-Century American Avant-Garde Composers. *J Aes Educ*, 27(2), 15-28, Sum 93.

**O'Hagan, Timothy**. "Amour-propre" in *Jean-Jacques Rousseau and the Sources of the Self,* O'Hagan, Timothy (ed), 66-84. Brookfield, Avebury, 1997.

In the *Emile*, Rousseau argues that amour-propre is the key to the formation of the adult personality endowed with morality and socially engaged. Yet amour propre is "a useful but dangerous tool" and Rousseau devotes much of his writing to analyzing its dangers, as it develops into a manipulative, exploitative passion. O'Hagan describes both the positive and negative forms of amour-propre and the mechanism of degeneration of the former into the latter. Unresolved tension remains at the heart of Rousseau's thinking. He is drawn both by a desire to construct a theory of social integration, in which amour-propre, suitably purified, would play a key role and also by a yearning for retreat and solitude in a world where the strenuous demands of moral engagements, mediated by amour-propre, would disappear.

**O'Hagan, Timothy** (ed). *Jean-Jacques Rousseau and the Sources of the Self*. Brookfield, Avebury, 1997.

"We see neither the soul of others, because it hides itself, nor our own, because we have no mirror in the mind", wrote Rousseau in 1757. In this collection of previously unpublished papers, David Gauthier, Martin Hollis, Robert Wokler, Nicholas Dent, John Hope Mason, Howard Caygill, Zev Trachtenberg and Timothy O'Hagan address the multi-faceted conceptions of the self elaborated by Rousseau, psychologist, pedagogue, literary theorist and political philosopher. Jean-Jacques emerges as a writer of extraordinary subtlety and sophistication, one of the first and most powerful critics of the myth of "man's glassy essence", of the idea that the self is a transparent, self-evident given.

**O'Hara, Kieron** and Scutt, Tom. There Is No Hard Problem of Consciousness. *J Consciousness Stud*, 3(4), 290-302, 1996.

The paper attempts to establish the importance of addressing what Chalmers (1995) calls the 'easy problems' of consciousness, at the expense of the 'hard problem'. One pragmatic argument and two philosophical arguments are presented to defend this approach to consciousness and three major theories of consciousness are criticized in this light. Finally, it is shown that concentration on the easy problems does not lead to eliminativism with respect to consciousness.

**O'Hara, Robert J**. "Representations of the Natural System in the Nineteenth Century" in *Picturing Knowledge,* Baigrie, Brian S (ed), 164-183. Toronto, Univ of Toronto Pr, 1996.

*The natural system* is the abstract notion of the order in living diversity. Representations of *the natural system* in the Nineteenth Century varied in overall form from stars, to circles, to maps, to trees and cross sections through trees. They differed in their depiction of affinity, analogy, continuity, directionality, symmetry, reticulation, branching, evolution and morphological convergence and divergence. Some representations were two-dimensional and some were three-dimensional; n-dimensional representations were discussed but never illustrated. The systematics controversies of the last thirty years have their roots in the conceptual problems that surrounded *the natural system* in the late 1800s.

**O'Hear, Anthony**. "Two Cultures' Revisited" in *Verstehen and Humane Understanding,* O'Hear, Anthony (ed), 1-16. New York, Cambridge Univ Pr, 1996.

An attempt is made to uncover the philosophical issues underlying the *Two Cultures* debate between C.P. Snow and F.R. Lewis. Science is by its nature unsuited to examining the human world, which is the province of nonscientific rationality. The question is then raised as to the specificity of cultural backgrounds and the extent to which a universal human nature underlies different cultures. (edited)

**O'Hear, Anthony** (ed). *Verstehen and Humane Understanding*. New York, Cambridge Univ Pr, 1996.

In the Royal Institute of Philosophy Lecture Series for 1995-96, the topic is whether there is a mode of discourse which is not scientific, but in its own way,

rational. The lectures are part historical, part thematic. Historical figures covered include Vico, Herder, Schleiermacher, Dilthey, Collingwood, and Weber; there are essays on aesthetics, religion, psychology and culture generally. (edited)

**O'Keefe, Daniel J**. "Argumentation Studies and Dual-Process Models of Persuasion" in *Logic and Argumentation,* Van Eemeren, Frans H (ed), 61-76. Amsterdam, North-Holland, 1994.

This essay discusses some interconnections between argumentation studies and persuasion effects research. Persuasion effects research is social-scientific work concerned with how and why persuasive messages have the effects they do; expressed broadly, such studies are concerned with identifying the factors influencing the effectiveness of persuasive messages and with constructing explanations of such effects. The focus of this essay is an attractive general picture of how persuasive messages work that has emerged from research on persuasion effect: "dual-process" models. I first describe this emerging general picture, and then display some interconnections between it and argumentation studies, discussing both what it has to offer to argumentation and what argumentation has to offer to it.

**O'Keefe, Timothy**. Does Epicurus Need the Swerve as an *Archê* of Collisions?. *Phronesis*, 41(3), 305-317, 1996.

**O'Keefe, Timothy**. The Ontological Status of Sensible Qualities for Democritus and Epicurus. *Ancient Phil*, 17(2), 119-134, Spr 97.

**O'Leary, Timothy**. Fat, Felt and Fascism: The Case of Joseph Beuys. *Lit Aes*, 6, 91-105, O 96.

This article considers the work of Joseph Beuys in the light of critiques claiming that any attempt to expand the concept of art into the political realm leads to some form of fascism. Through a reading of Walter Benjamin's "The Work of Art in the Age of Mechanical Reproduction" I show that if Beuys's thought is indeed in some sense fascist, this is not so much a result of the *fact* that he expands the concept of art, as a result of the *concept* of art which he expands. What I propose is a way of distinguishing between potentially fascist and nonfascist forms of the 'aestheticisation of politics'.

**O'Leary, Timothy**. Foucault, Politics and the Autonomy of the Aesthetic. *Int J Phil Stud*, 4(2), 273-291, S 96.

In this paper, I examine key accounts of the fascist 'aestheticization of politics'—from Walter Benjamin's classic essay, "The Work of Art in the Age of Mechanical Reproduction" (1936), to Philippe Lacoue-Labarthe's work on the relation between Heidegger's philosophy and the fascist theme of politics as the plastic art of the state. Through a discussion of Foucault's late work, the paper demonstrates the connection between Foucault's turn to ancient Greek ethical practices and his call for a contemporary renewal of the idea of ethics as an art of living. The aim of the paper is to show in what ways the ethico-political position which is presented in Foucault's late work, far from contributing to a fascist politics, in fact provides ways of thinking about the relationship between the aesthetic and the political which avoid both mindless radicalism and totalitarian narcissism. (edited)

**O'Leary-Hawthorne, Diane**. "Not-Being and Linguistic Deception" in *Dialogues with Plato,* Benitez, Eugenio (ed), 165-198. Edmonton, Academic, 1996.

**O'Leary-Hawthorne, Diane**. Not-Being and Linguistic Deception. *Apeiron*, 29(4), 165-198, D 96.

**O'Leary-Hawthorne, John**. The Epistemology of Possible Worlds: A Guided Tour. *Phil Stud*, 84(2-3), 183-202, D 96.

**O'Leary-Hawthorne, John** and Cover, J A. Framing the Thisness Issue. *Austl J Phil*, 75(1), 102-108, Mr 97.

**O'Leary-Hawthorne, John** and Oppy, Graham. Minimalism and Truth. *Nous*, 31(2), 170-196, Je 97.

Minimalism about truth has received considerable attention of late. We think that much of the discussion suffers from a pair of deficiencies. *First*, there has been a failure to discriminate different varieties and dimensions of minimalism about truth. *Second*, some serious and fundamental problems for the most popular varieties of minimalism about truth have not yet received sufficient attention. This paper aims to remedy those deficiencies. The paper is divided into three sections. In the first section, we distinguish six main varieties of minimalism about truth. In the second section, we identify four dimensions along which views about truth can be more or less minimal, thus clarifying the range of relevant notions of "minimality". In the third section, we critically discuss four minimalist theses.

**O'Leary-Hawthorne, John** and Petit, Philip. Strategies for Free Will Compatibilists. *Analysis*, 56(4), 191-201, O 96.

This essay is an attempt to redress the balance of attention and to offer an overview of the different broad strategies that compatibilists may pursue. We start from a formulaic account of what it is for an agent to do something freely which all or nearly all compatibilists can be expected to endorse. We go on to look, then, at the different ways in which this account may be interpreted by different compatibilists. And we offer a concluding remark on the nature of the contest between the different strategies.

**O'Loughlin, Marjorie**. Listening, Heeding, and Respecting the Ground at One's Feet: Knowledge and the Arts Across Cultures. *Phil Music Educ Rev*, 5(1), 14-24, Spr 97.

**O'Mathúna, Dónal P**. Did Paul Condone Suicide? Implications for Assisted Suicide and Active Euthanasia?. *Ethics Med*, 12(3), 55-60, 1996.

**O'Meara, William**. "Beyond Toleration" in *Philosophy, Religion, and the Question of Intolerance,* Ambuel, David (ed), 94-108. Albany, SUNY Pr, 1997.

**O'Neil, Rick**. Intrinsic Value, Moral Standing, and Species. *Environ Ethics*, 19(1), 45-52, Spr 97.

Environmental philosophers often conflate the concepts of intrinsic value and moral standing. As a result, individualists needlessly deny intrinsic value to species, while holists falsely attribute moral standing to species. Conceived either as classes or as historical individuals, at least some species possess intrinsic value. Nevertheless, even if a species has interests or a good of its own, it cannot have moral standing because species lack sentience. Although there is a basis for duties toward some species (in terms of their intrinsic value), it is not the one that the holists claim.

**O'Neill, John**. Cantona and Aquinas on Good and Evil. *J Applied Phil*, 14(2), 97-105, 1997.

An important but neglected difference between modern utilitarian and Kantian ethics on one side and virtues ethics on the other concerns the relation of good and evil. By taking virtues to be ethical primitives, standard versions of virtues ethics entail that some goods are logically evil-dependent. That is, at least some central virtues cannot be characterized without reference to the possible existence of an evil and cannot be exercised without the actual existence of that evil. Given this account on the logical relation of good and evil, can a virtues ethic be defended? In particular, does a virtues ethic sanction an inference from a virtue to the evil that is the occasion for its exercise? The paper examines some prima facie examples of such inferences and considers how they might be blocked from within a virtues ethics.

**O'Neill, John** (ed). *Freud and the Passions*. University Park, Pennsylvania Univ Pr, 1996.

Love, hate, anger, jealousy, envy, knowledge, and ignorance: the passions dominate infancy, adolescence, and adulthood, marking them with narcissism, murder, seduction, and self-destruction. They are both the soul's theater and the soul of theater, art, literature, and music. If fear, hate, envy, and jealousy rival love, beauty, and knowledge, or turn into one another, they just as surely expand the human heart. The original essays in this volume analyze the human passions in Freud's metapsychology, from the case histories of Dora, Rat Man, and Schreber to his studies of Leonardo da Vinci, *Gradiva* and the "Case of Homosexuality in a Woman."(publisher,edited)

**O'Neill, John**. Thinking Naturally. *Rad Phil*, 83, 36-39, My-Je 97.

The richness of the debates about the environment has its source in the fact that the environment lies at a point of convergence between a number of distinct lines of debate: between realism and constructivism; between the enlightenment and its critics; between humanism and antihumanism; on the relation of economy, culture and nature; on the future directions of radical politics; on the future direction of feminist thought and action. This paper explores the relations between these different arguments. It considers in particular the prospects for those positions that lie between 'nature-endorsing' and 'nature-sceptical' perspectives in social theory.

**O'Neill, John**. Who Won the Socialist Calculation Debate?. *Hist Polit Thought*, 17(3), 431-442, Autumn 96.

**O'Neill, Onora**. "Kant on Reason and Religion" in *The Tanner Lectures on Human Values, Volume 18, 1997*, Peterson, Grethe B (ed), 267-308. Salt Lake City, Univ of Utah Pr, 1997.

Lecture I, *Reasoned Hope*, explicates Kant's meagre conception of reason's authority and shows how it can be used to make sense of the accounts of otherworldly and of this-worldly hope that are fundamental in his writing on religion and on politics. Lecture II, *Reason and Interpretation*, discusses Kant's use of this conception of reason to distinguish between 'doctrinal' and 'authentic' interpretation of religious texts and seeks to show that the exuberant text of *Religion within the Limits of Reason Alone* deserves its austere title.

**O'Neill, Onora**. Environmental Values, Anthropocentrism and Speciesism. *Environ Values*, 6(2), 127-142, My 97.

Ethical reasoning of all types is anthropocentric, in that it is addressed to agents, but anthropocentric starting points vary in the preference they accord the human species. Realist claims about environmental values, utilitarian reasoning and rights-based reasoning all have difficulties in according ethical concern to certain all aspects of natural world. Obligation-based reasoning can provide quite strong if incomplete reasons to protect the natural world, including individual nonhuman animals. Although it cannot establish all the conclusions to which antispeciesists aspire, it may establish many of them with some clarity.

**O'Neill, Shane**. *Impartiality in Context: Grounding Justice in a Pluralist World*. Albany, SUNY Pr, 1997.

In this book, Shane O'Neill argues that the theory of justice must take seriously two dimensions of pluralism in the modern world. While it must acknowledge the plurality of individual conceptions of the good that is characteristic of every modern society, it must also reckon with the plurality of historically unique, culturally specific, political societies. (publisher, edited)

**O'Reilly-Meacock, Heather**. Kantian Ethics and a Theory of Justice; Reiman, Kaufman and MacIntyre. *Relig Stud*, 33(1), 93-103, Mr 97.

This paper examines recent contributions to moral philosophy by Jeffrey Reiman and Gordon Kaufman, which, while differing in that they derive from 'secular' and 'religious' world views, share certain common concerns and a common conviction of the universality of the moral principle of justice, rooted in a Kantian philosophical framework. I argue that these theories of justice provide ground for useful interfaith and secular/religious dialogue, against the view of MacIntyre, that morality itself is 'tradition specific'.

**O'Riordan, Tim**. Valuation as Revelation and Reconciliation. *Environ Values*, 6(2), 169-183, My 97.

Valuation is portrayed here as a dynamic and interactive process, not a static notion linked to willingness to pay. Valuation through economic measures can

be built upon by creating trusting and legitimizing procedures of stakeholder negotiation and mediation. This is a familiar practice in the US, but it is only beginning to be recognized as an environmental management tool in the UK. The introduction of strategic environmental and landuse appraisal plans for shorelines, estuaries, river catchments and rural landscapes, combined with the mobilization of protest around landuse proposals that are not seemingly justified on the basis of 'need' (incinerators, landfills, quarries, reservoirs, roads) suggest that a more legitimate participatory form of democracy is required to reveal valuation through consensual negotiation.

**O'Shea, James R**. Hume's Reflective Return to the Vulgar. *Brit J Hist Phil*, 4(2), 285-315, S 96.

Was Hume *primarily* a phenomenalist, a direct realist, an indirect realist, or a sceptic concerning the objects of perception? I argue (against current views) that Hume was neither 1) a phenomenalist, 2) an 'intentional realist', 3) a 'sceptical realist', nor 4) simply a 'sceptic in the study, realist in the street'. In the end Hume uses a deep and irresolvable theoretical scepticism to defend a pragmatic 'return to vulgar realism'. This is based not merely on the irresistibility of common sense beliefs, but rather on philosophical reflections concerning the possibility of a pragmatically coherent and reflectivity satisfying *system* of belief.

**O'Shea, James R**. Kantian Matters: The Structure of Permanence. *Acta Analytica*, 67-88, 1996.

In the *Critique of Pure Reason* Kant argues for a 'Principle of the Permanence of Substance' (A182, the 'First Analogy of Experience'). Put in the most general terms, Kant offers a transcendental argument for the conclusion that all the changing appearances we encounter in experience must be conceived as the alterations of absolutely permanent, forever abiding substance. I will be less concerned with the structure and validity of Kant's argument than with the correct interpretation of his unique conception of substance and material reality in general. I will then argue that correcting certain basic misconceptions concerning the *nature* of Kantian material substance serves to put his *argument* for absolute permanence in proper perspective. (edited)

**O'Shea, James R**. The Needs of Understanding: Kant on Empirical Laws and Regulative Ideals. *Int J Phil Stud*, 5(2), 216-254, Je 97.

This article examines the relationship in Kant between transcendental laws and empirical laws (focusing on causal laws) and then brings a particular interpretation of that issue to bear on familiar puzzles concerning the status of the regulative maxims of reason and reflective judgment. It is argued that the 'indeterminate objective validity' possessed by the regulative maxims derives ultimately from strictly constitutive demands of understanding.

**O'Toole, Robert**. "Contagium Vivum Philosophia: Schizophrenic Philosophy, Viral Empiricism and Deleuze" in *Deleuze and Philosophy: The Difference Engineer,* Ansell Pearson, Keith (ed), 163-179. New York, Routledge, 1997.

**Oakes, Robert**. God and Cosmos: Can the "Mystery of Mysteries" be Solved?. *Amer Phil Quart*, 33(3), 315-323, Jl 96.

**Oakes, Robert**. The Divine Infinity: Can Traditional Theists *Justifiably* Reject Pantheism?. *Monist*, 80(2), 251-265, Ap 97.

**Oaklander, L Nathan**. McTaggart's Paradox and Smith's Tensed Theory of Time. *Synthese*, 107(2), 205-221, My 96.

Since McTaggart first proposed his paradox asserting the unreality of time, numerous philosophers have attempted to defend the tensed theory of time against it. Certainly, one of the most highly developed and original is that put forth by Quentin Smith. Through discussing McTaggart's positive conception of time as well as his negative attack on its reality, I hope to clarify the dispute between those who believe in the existence of the transitory temporal properties of *pastness, presentness* and *futurity* and those who deny their existence. We shall see that the debate centers around the ontological status of *succession* and the B-relations of *earlier* and *later*. I shall argue that Smith's tensed theory fails because he cannot account for the sense in which events have their tensed properties successively and he cannot account for the direction of time.

**Oakley, Justin**. Varieties of Virtue Ethics. *Ratio*, 9(2), 128-152, S 96.

The revival of virtue ethics over the last thirty-five years has produced a bewildering diversity of theories, which on the face of it seem united only by their opposition to various features of more familiar Kantian and Utilitarian ethical theories. In this paper I present a systematic account of the main *positive* features of virtue ethics, by articulating the common ground shared by its different varieties. I do so not to offer a fresh defence of virtue ethics, but rather to provide a conceptual map that locates its main claims and arguments in relation to those of rival theories, and identifies its distinctive contribution to contemporary ethics. I set out *six* specific claims which are made by all forms of virtue ethics and I explain how these claims distinguish the theory from recent character-based forms of Kantian ethics and Utilitarianism. I then use this framework to briefly survey two main strands of virtue ethics which have been developed in the literature.

**Oakley III, Elwood F** and Smith, Patricia L. Gender-Related Differences in Ethical and Social Values of Business Students: Implications for Management. *J Bus Ethics*, 16(1), 37-45, Ja 97.

This study investigated gender-related differences in ethical attitudes of 318 graduate and undergraduate business students. Significant differences were observed in male and female responses to questions concerning ethics in social and personal relationships. No differences were noted for survey items concerning rules-based obligations. Implications for future management are discussed.

**Oaksford, Mike** and Chater, Nick. Deontic Reasoning, Modules and Innateness: A Second Look. *Mind Lang*, 11(2), 191-202, Je 96.

Cummins (this issue) puts the case for an innate module for deontic reasoning. We argue that this case is not persuasive. First, we claim that Cummins's evolutionary arguments are neutral regarding whether deontic reasoning is learned or innate. Second, we argue that task differences between deontic and indicative reasoning explain many of the phenomena that Cummins takes as evidence for a deontic module. Third, we argue against the suggestion that deontic reasoning is superior to indicative reasoning, either in adults or children. Finally, we reevaluate Cummins's interpretation of differences in children's performance on deontic and indicative versions of Wason's selection task.

**Oates, Stephen B**. "A Horse Chestnut Is Not a Chestnut Horse": A Refutation of Bray, Davis, MacGregor, and Wollan. *J Infor Ethics*, 3(1), 25-41, Spr 94.

**Obenauer, Klaus**. Zur subsistentia absoluta in der Trinitätstheologie. *Theol Phil*, 72(2), 188-215, 1997.

The subsistence of the unique essence as such by itself in the triune God and not only because of its identity with the three hypostases (so-called "subsistentia absoluta"), denied from near all of the modern theologians, is the subject of this short study. After investigating, which St. Bonaventure and St. Thomas Aquinas have to say to that theme, there is here attempted to trace out a speculative view, in which the subsistence of the essence as such by itself and that of the three persons in the triune God do not exclude, but incluse each other.

**Oberdan, Thomas**. "Postscript to Protocols: Reflections on Empiricism" in *Origins of Logical Empiricism*, Giere, Ronald N (ed), 269-291. Minneapolis, Univ of Minnesota Pr, 1996.

**Oberdiek, Hans** and Tiles, Mary. *Living in a Technological Culture: Human Tools and Human Values*. New York, Routledge, 1995.

This book is an introduction to the philosophy of technology, but assumes no background in philosophy. It explores the relations between science, technology and culture, and is designed to make us more mindful users of technology. It asks why it is that we are alternately dazzled by the prospect of apparently unlimited power that technological devices seems to offer, and threatened by the power that they have over our lives. In answering this question the book shows how our attitudes toward technology are intimately entangled with our aspirations as human beings and thus opens up a wider debate on whether or how we can shape the future.

**Oberhausen, Michael**. *Das neue Apriori: Kants Lehre von einer 'ursprünglichen Erwerbung' apriorischer Vorstellungen*. Stuttgart, Frommann-Holzboog, 1997.

According to Kant's theory of acquisition the a priori concepts arise from the logical rules of thought, from which they develop when these rules are applied to objects of the senses. This he said as early as 1770. As the logical rules are all well-known, they provide Kant with the 'Leitfaden', the clue, that enables him to define the a priori concepts completely. Kant derives the categories from the forms of judgments and the ideas from the forms of syllogism in the *Critique of Pure Reason*, on the basis of his theory of acquisition. He derives the transcendental faculty of pure concepts from the logical faculty of judgment and inferring, respectively, because the logical faculty is the origin of the transcendental one. In a systematic respect Kant's acquisition theory of knowledge is thus a key to the central question for the relationship of formal and transcendental logic and the reason of the basic logical structure of the *Critique of Pure Reason*. (edited)

**Oberman, Michelle**. Response to "Discounting Life Support in an Infant of a Drug Addicted Mother: Whose Decision Is It?" by Renu Jain and David C. Thomasma (CQ Vol 6, No 1). *Cambridge Quart Healthcare Ethics*, 6(2), 235-239, Spr 97.

**Oberschelp, Arnold**. "Intensionale Semantik und physikalische Grössen" in *Das weite Spektrum der analytischen Philosophie*, Lenzen, Wolfgang, 231-249. Hawthorne, de Gruyter, 1997.

**Ocaña García, Marcelino**. El contraluz de Vitoria en el Siglo de las Luces. *An Seminar Hist Filosof*, 13, 247-261, 1996.

The fact that the name of Francisco de Vitoria does not appear in the treatises and among the authors of the 18th century does not mean that his doctrine was unknown. On the contrary, his thesis although credited to Grotius was known and accepted by many important authors such as Locke or Kant.

**Ochieng'-Odhiambo, F**. An African Savant: Henry Odera Oruka. *Quest*, 9(2), 12-21, D 96.

The article is in honor of the late professor of philosophy, Henry Odera Oruka. It gives a brief biographical note of Odera Oruka from his childhood through to his academic and intellectual achievements prior to his death. The paper particularly highlights philosophical sagacity, a trend within African philosophy which was initiated by Odera Oruka in 1974. It also relates Odera Oruka's intellectual and academic disposition to the five mirrors explicated in his article "Cultural Fundamentals in Philosophy."

**Ochoa Henríquez, Haydée**. Crises and Way Outs of the Public Administration Theory. *Fronesis*, 2(2), 97-131, D 95.

The article explores the crisis and ways out of the public administration theory from its beginning up to our days. It is observed that the changes in the state have contributed to the crises in the mentioned theories, in which answers from different disciplines have favored the theoretic advance, but have not crystallized until now in a paradigm which explains the phenomenon in depth. The changes produced since the eighties bring new theoretic requirements and the ways out make evident a new crisis of the public administration theory. (edited)

**Oddo, Alfonso R**. A Framework for Teaching Business Ethics. *J Bus Ethics*, 16(3), 293-297, F 97.

What ethical framework should be used as a basis for teaching business ethics? Should business ethics be taught by ethicists in a separate course, by business

faculty in business courses, or perhaps by both? These are some of the issues this paper will address. The paper begins with a review of the literature concerning approaches to teaching business ethics. Next, some ethical frameworks for teaching business ethics are considered. Finally, the paper proposes that students should apply their own personal values to business ethical issues in the classroom, thus providing future business leaders with a process for resolving ethical dilemmas.

**Odegard, Douglas**. Locke as a Fallibilist. *Dialogue (Canada)*, 35(3), 473-484, Sum 96.

Locke's considered view is that knowledge excludes the possibility of error. But he offers no resources for claiming infallible knowledge and he needs fallibilism to preserve his program of intellectual toleration. Fortunately some of his remarks can be made to yield a distinction that, if added to his position, can allow him to claim certainty while denying infallibility. The distinction can also be used to make sense of his notion of degrees of certainty.

**Odegard, Douglas**. Neorationalist Epistemology. *Phil Phenomenol Res*, 57(3), 567-584, S 97.

Whether any beliefs are justified nonempirically is important in a debate with sceptics who deny empirical justification, if the parties involved in the debate claim that their position is justified. Sceptics must assume that their premises are justified nonempirically, to avoid begging the question. The main problem with advocating nonempirical justification is that accounts tend to be either too niggardly or too generous, implying either that nonempirical justification is impossible or that peer adversaries must be equally justified. The way to solve this problem is to recognize that justification involves satisfying two conditions: having reason to hold a belief and having a ground for being confident about one's reason. The reason can be nonempirical even though the ground is almost always empirical. This distinction can be used to resolve a number of familiar concerns.

**Oderberg, David S**. "Voluntary Euthanasia and Justice" in *Human Lives: Critical Essays on Consequentialist Bioethics*, Oderberg, David S (ed), 225-240. New York, Macmillan, 1997.

This paper sets out to answer the question: Does a person who kills another at the latter's request commit an injustice against that person? Defining justice in terms of rights, it is argued that the right to life is inalienable; hence, that voluntary euthanasia is always an injustice by the killer against the killed. Inalienability is justified in three ways. First, it is shown that there is nothing peculiar in the concept of an inalienable right and that even consequentialism must recognize at least one such right. Secondly, some plausible examples of inalienable rights are considered and a purported refutation of inalienability based on the analogy with property rights is dismissed. Thirdly, a positive account is outlined, according to which the right to life is seen as fundamental to a theory of human good.

**Oderberg, David S**. Coincidence under a Sortal. *Phil Rev*, 105(2), 145-171, Ap 96.

This paper defends the thesis (called the Substance Thesis) that no two substances belonging to the same substantial kind can be in the same place at the same time. First, weaker theses allowing certain types of coincidence are distinguished and demonstrated. Secondly, the Substance Thesis is elaborated and a failed attempt to refute it is discussed. Thirdly, the thesis is shown not to be refuted by cases (called Leibnizian) of coinciding, ontologically dependent objects. Fourthly, it is shown in terms of discussion of key examples why coincidence is impossible for substances. Finally, the Substance Thesis is applied to personal identity, to show why persons cannot coincide and to refute a recent attempt to prove that they can.

**Oderberg, David S** (ed) and Laing, Jacqueline A (ed). *Human Lives: Critical Essays on Consequentialist Bioethics*. New York, Macmillan, 1997.

*Critical Essays on Consequentialist Bioethics* is a collection of original papers by philosophers from Britain, the USA and Australia. The aim of the book is to redress the imbalance in moral philosophy created by the dominance of consequentialism, the view that the criterion of morality is the maximization of good effects over bad, without regard for basic right or wrong. This approach has become the orthodoxy over the last few decades, particularly in the field of bioethics, where moral theory is applied to matters of life and death. The essays in *Human Lives* critically examine the assumptions and arguments of consequentialism, in the process reviving important concepts such as rights, justice, innocence, natural integrity, flourishing, the virtues and the fundamental value of human life.

**Odero, José Miguel**. *Teología de la fe: Una aproximación al misterio de la fe cristiana*. Pamplona, Univ de Navarra, 1997.

Many books whose title designates the "Christian Faith" are only explanations of what Christians believe, and only some few words are said in them about what is *believing*. The object of this study is, on the contrary, to focus faith in its active meaning: as believing. To believe the *Christian revelation* (God's self-revelation) is a real foundation of Christian life. The faith of a Christian works as an acting element that becomes present at every moment of our life. Its influence converges to one sole goal: the divination of the believer, to endeavor his glory. Substantial faith stays, however, discreetly concealed. Its acting presence remains often hidden to the man's conscious life, and only gets revealed by some inner impulses to act as God's son. (edited)

**Öffenberger, Niels** and Bertók, Rozsa. Observations on the So-Called Practical Syllogism (Spanish). *Rev Filosof (Venezuela)*, 24(2), 47-52, Jl-D 96.

On analysis of the idea of practical syllogism as it is suggested by the Aristotelian texts on ethics, a comparison is made between this kind of syllogism and strictly formulated theoretical syllogisms. The research is mainly centered

**Öffenberger, Niels** 822 **AUTHOR INDEX**

on the background of imprudent action. It is stated that a practical syllogism presents the peculiarity of permitting contradictory conclusions, but that the derivability of false conclusions from true premises is only an apparent one.

**Öffenberger, Niels** and Bustos López, Javier. La negación de los juicios estrictamente particulares en la tetravalencia. *Rev Filosof (Venezuela)*, 23(1), 67-77, 1996.

In bivalent truth tables we find possible cases, but not conclusive ones; the only possible and conclusive case is the contradiction. In tetravalence, on the other hand, we find three conclusive cases for each relation. This truth table offers certain exceptions when resolving the negation of strictly particular judgements: (a) the negation of the judgement is possible in the qualitative statement itself; (b) the negation of a judgement is also possible in the quantitative statement itself; (c) the negation of a judgement with a truth value Fp is possible in a universal; quantitative judgement; (d) the negation of strictly particular judgements does not admit the possibility of contradictory statements as such; and (e) the tetravalent truth table does not possess universal validity.

**Öktem, Niyazi**. Tolerance and Law. *Ratio Juris*, 10(1), 114-123, Mr 97.

The aim of this study is to make a universal analysis of the concept of tolerance. To this end, the relations of state and religion in different systems will be briefly discussed. The main focus will be on tolerance in Islam. In this context, the Alaouite sect, which deserves special attention, will be presented from historical ideological and sociopolitical points of views.

**Oelkers, Jürgen**. Is There *a* "Language of Education?". *Stud Phil Educ*, 16(1-2), 125-138, Ja-Ap 97.

What Israel Scheffler analyzed in his *The Language of Education* was a corpus of slogans and metaphors which obviously influence public communication. But are these a language of "education"? The article argues that "language of education" is a historical enterprise that constitutes a special public discourse on and about *education*. The writings of the eminent educators developed and reflected this discourse, the language of education is composed out of typical arguments and suggestions not just of slogans and metaphors. And this corpus is historically very stable: The basic arguments are similar and there is little change in the basic creeds of what one can call the *public* language of education (to be opposed to philosophy of education).

**Oesch, Erna**. The Limits of Literal Meaning: New Models for Understanding Metaphor. *Dan Yrbk Phil*, 31, 169-180, 1996.

Drawing on the Augustinian notion of *verbum cordis* and Wilhelm von Humboldt's idea of language as *energeia* my article emphasizes the importance of metaphor for understanding the creative process of transforming thought into language. Inspired by the hermeneutic tradition I suggest a new definition of metaphor which stresses the ultimate openness of metaphorical meaning and gives an opportunity to investigate metaphor at both a functional and an interpretive level. I argue that a new understanding of metaphor is needed to be able to handle such contemporary metaphors as, for instance, *virtual reality* which seems to question both our classifications concerning reality and some of our basic concepts of understanding, like the concept of space.

**Österberg, Jan** and Rabinowicz, Wlodzimierz. Value Based On Preferences: On Two Interpretations of Preference Utilitarianism. *Econ Phil*, 12(1), 1-27, Ap 96.

Does intrinsic value, as understood by preference utilitarians, reside in i) it being the case *that* our (intrinsic) desires and preferences are satisfied (the *satisfaction* interpretation), or rather in ii) those states that are the *objects* of our (intrinsic) preferences and desires (the *object* interpretation)? The paper is a dialogue between Österberg who pleads for the former view, and Rabinowicz who finds the latter interpretation more plausible, even though it leads to a very nonstandard (nonindividualistic and nonmonistic) form of preference utilitarianism. To these two interpretations correspond, respectively, two different ways of viewing utilitarianism: the *spectator* and the *participant* models. According to the former, the utilitarian attitude is embodied in a detached and impartial benevolent spectator, while the latter puts forward as a utilitarian ideal an attitude of sympathetic identification with other people and their desires: What it recommends is not a detachment from subjectivity but instead its universalization.

**Oesterreich, Peter L**. Die Bedeutung von Fichtes Angewandter Philosophie für die Praktische Philosophie der Gegenwart. *Fichte-Studien*, 13, 223-239, 1997.

The article focuses on the applied philosophy of J. G. Fichte and its relevance for the present time. Fichte's applied philosophy tries to fulfill Kant's vision of a 'culture of reason'. She is opposed to the aesthetic nihilism of pure theoretical philosophy and invents a new philosophical rhetoric in order to provide a general change in history and the life of mankind. There are three arguments which stress the relevance of Fichte's conception of applied philosophy for the contemporary practical philosophy.

**Ogbogbo, C B N**. Some Problems in the Writing of the History of African Philosophy. *Quest*, 9(2), 159-171, D 96.

**Ohlsson, Ragnar**. *Morals Based on Needs*. Lanham, Univ Pr of America, 1995.

"Basic need" is defined in terms of "necessary and in the situation sufficient condition for an acceptable life", which as far as human beings are concerned means a conscious life without serious, uncompensated suffering, affording a certain amount of liberty and education. At least every human being has both a negative and a positive right to satisfaction of basic needs and a negative right to strive for satisfaction of her or his desires. Such a moral system seems to be in accordance with well entrenched moral intuitions, which can be both explained and justified in a naturalistic way.

**Oizerman, Teodor I**. Fundamental Principles of Marxism's Self-Criticism. *Russian Stud Phil*, 34(2), 26-45, Fall 95.

**Okada, Katsuaki**. Der erste Grundsatz und die Bildlehre. *Fichte-Studien*, 10, 127-141, 1997.

**Okafor, Fidelis U**. African Philosophy in Comparison with Western Philosophy. *J Value Inq*, 31(2), 251-267, Je 97.

**Okafor, Fidelis U**. In Defense of Afro-Japanese Ethnophilosophy. *Phil East West*, 47(3), 363-381, Jl 97.

Ethnophilosophy is so-called because its focus is on the thought that underlies the life patterns and belief system of a people. It is folk philosophy insofar as it is an exposition of the philosophical thought undergirding the way of life of a people as a collectivity. African and Japanese philosophy belong to this tradition. Western philosophy, however, is based on reason and logic; in contrast with ethnophilosophy, it developed ab initio as a critique of folk thought and worldviews. Both traditions are not contradictory but complementary. Each bears the marks of its peculiar culture and history.

**Okasha, Samir**. Laudan and Leplin on Empirical Equivalence. *Brit J Phil Sci*, 48(2), 251-256, Je 97.

In this paper, I explore Larry Laudan's and Jarrett Leplin's recent claim that empirically equivalent theories may be differentially confirmed. I show that their attempt to prise apart empirical equivalence and epistemic parity commits them to two principles of confirmation that Hempel demonstrated to be incompatible.

**Okin, Susan Moller**. "Sexual Orientation and Gender: Dichotomizing Differences" in *Sex, Preference, and Family: Essays on Law and Nature*, Nussbaum, Martha C (ed), 44-59. New York, Oxford Univ Pr, 1997.

**Okolova, Marina Dimitrieva** and Rendón Rojas, Miguel Angel. La re-presentación extrema del estetismo, del intelectualismo y del moralismo en política. *Analogia*, 10(2), 151-174, 1996.

The aestheticism with its cult for beauty, the intellectualism for truth, the moralism for goodness, can lead to political totalitarianism. This happens when one of these values (beauty, truth, goodness) becomes unlimited, without any kind of relation with the others, and on the other hand, when an excessive subjectivism takes a place and the leader's finite ego change to a transcendental ego representative or substitute of God. This political power legislates totally convinced that its special mission is to actualize the central value.

**Olafson, Frederick A**. Heidegger on Presence: A Reply. *Inquiry*, 39 (3-4), 421-426, D 96.

Taylor Carman has argued that the passages I submitted to him as proof that Heidegger identifies being with presence are really just his characterizations of a metaphysical conception of being that he repudiates. I show that he has misread these passages and has misunderstood the nature of the continuity that Heidegger himself recognizes between the views of Kant which are under discussion in the texts from which these passages are drawn and his own (Heidegger's) position which finds expression in them. I then cite other passages from anothers work by Heidegger that make the same point about being and presence just as emphatically and quite independently of any account of any other philosopher's views. Finally, I explain the difference between the ways Heidegger uses the word *Anwesenheit*—his word for presence. One of these is as a translation of the Greek *ousia* which he interprets as a concept of being as presence *sans* temporality; the other is the radicalized concept of being as presence toward which Heidegger was working in *Being and Time*.

**Olaso, Ezequiel de**. "Racionalidad y escepticismo" in *La racionalidad: su poder y sus límites,* Nudler, Oscar (ed), 143-152. Barcelona, Ed Paidos, 1996.

**Olberding, Amy**. Mourning, Memory, and Identity: A Comparative Study of the Constitution of the Self in Grief. *Int Phil Quart*, 37(1), 29-44, Mr 97.

**Olcina, Gonzalo**. Forward Induction in Games with an Outside Option. *Theor Decis*, 42(2), 177-192, Ja 97.

We provide eductive foundations for the concept of forward induction in the class of games with an outside option. The formulation presented tries to capture in a static notion the rest point of an introspective process, achievable from some restricted preliminary beliefs. The former requisite is met by requiring the rest point to be a Nash equilibrium that yields a higher payoff than the outside option. With respect to the beliefs, we propose the *incentive dominance criterion*. Players should consider one action more likely than another whenever the former is better than getting the outside option for more conjectures over his rival's actions. (edited)

**Olesen, Soren Gosvig**. L'Heritage Husserlien chez Koyré et Bachelard. *Dan Yrbk Phil*, 29, 7-43, 1994.

A partir du projet d'une "élucidation ontologique des sciences", tel qu'il se manifeste avec la phénoménologie husserlienne, il est ici traité de l'épistémologie française de façon à y faire apercevoir un renouveau de ce projet. Dans cette perspective, le rapprochement opéré par Koyré et Bachelard, de la théorie des sciences avec l'histoire des sciences, est considéré comme une historisation nécessaire de la question ontologique.

**Olivé, León**. Pluralismo epistemológico: Más sobre racionalidad, verdad y consenso. *Rev Latin de Filosof*, 22(2), 251-263, 1996.

**Oliveira Barra, Eduardo Salles De**. Em que Sentido Newton pode Dizer *Hypotheses Non Fingo*?. *Cad Hist Filosof Cie*, 5(1-2), 221-245, Ja-D 95.

Analysis of the Newton's famous statement 'hypotheses non fingo' in context of his divergences with those who advocated the method of hypotheses from the Cartesian physics. It is shown that such divergences had origins in the different scientific beliefs adopted by both sides in dispute. The meaning intended to Newton's statement is attached to the author's own methodological procedures concerning universal gravitation.

**Olivelle, Patrick**. Orgasmic Rapture and Divine Ecstasy: The Semantic History of Ānanda. *J Indian Phil*, 25(2), 153-180, Ap 97.

**Oliver, Alex** (ed) and Mellor, D H (ed). *Properties*. New York, Oxford Univ Pr, 1997.

This volume offers a selection of the most interesting and important readings on properties beginning with the work of Frege, Russell and Ramsey. In particular, it makes accessible for the first time contributions to the contemporary controversy about the nature and roles of properties: Do they differ from particulars? Are they universals, sets or tropes? How are properties involved with causation, laws and semantics? The editors' introduction guides the novice through these issues and critically discusses the readings.

**Oliver, Kelly**. *Family Values: Subjects Between Nature and Culture*. New York, Routledge, 1997.

*Family Values* offers groundbreaking analyses of age-old conceptions of maternity and paternity, woman and man, nature and culture, and subjectivity and ethics. The author shows how the contradictions within Western conceptions of maternity and paternity problematize our conceptions of ourselves and our relationships with others. *Family Values* overturns our traditional association of maternity with nature and paternity with culture. In reconceiving maternity and paternity, Oliver undercuts the recent return of the rhetoric of a "battle between the sexes" and offers hope for a truce. (publisher, edited)

**Oliver, Kelly**. The Gestation of the Other in Phenomenology. *Epoche*, 3(1 & 2), 79-116, 1995.

This essay traces phenomenology of intersubjectivity from Husserl, through Heidegger, Merleau-Ponty, Sartre and Levinas, to Kristena. I argue that alterity is at the heart of the phenomenological notion of the self from its inception. In addition, I point to the recurring use of metaphors of maternity to figure intersubjective relations throughout the history of phenomenology.

**Olivetti, Marco M**. Commentary to J. Hintikka's Lecture. *Filosof Cas*, 44(3), 388-394, 1996.

**Olivier, Bert**. The Sublime, Unpresentability and Postmodern Cultural Complexity. *S Afr J Phil*, 16(1), 7-13, F 97.

The present article examines the pertinence of the sublime for the understanding of postmodern culture, particularly with regard to its complexity. It begins by looking at Kant's notion of the 'mathematical *sublime*', with its structure of initial displeasure in the face of the unpresentable, followed by a feeling of pleasure on discovering a 'supersensible' faculty of cognition that surpasses the limitations of the sensible and the imaginative. It is then shown that Kant's insight may be applied, not only to vast, overwhelming natural phenomena, but to complex mathematical and cultural phenomena as well, in a manner that emphasizes the inconclusiveness of their apprehension as instances of the sublime, but also their intersubjectively shared intelligibility at the level of rational comprehension. (edited)

**Olkowski, Dorothea**. "Difference and the Ruin of Representation in Gilles Deleuze" in *Sites of Vision*, Levin, David Michael (ed), 467-491. Cambridge, MIT Pr, 1997.

**Olkowski, Dorothea**. Beside us, in Memory. *Man World*, 29(3), 283-292, Jl 96.

**Olkowski, Dorothea**. Materiality and Language: Butler's Interrogation of the History of Philosophy. *Phil Soc Crit*, 23(3), 37-53, My 97.

In *Bodies That Matter* Judith Butler reflects upon the relationship between women and materiality in the context of the history of philosophy. She points to the presumption of the material irreducibility of sex as the ground of feminist epistemology and ethics and analyses of gender. She also finds a similarity between Aristotle's principles of formativity and intelligibility and Foucault's discussion of how discourse materializes bodies. While Butler's analysis reveals much about the history of philosophy with regard to the discourse on matter and women, nonetheless, she appears to begin with the notion of bodies as largely passive, even negative entities. Additionally, her analysis also implies that principles of formativity and intelligibility are historically contingent. This essay seeks to undermine those two positions in preparation for inaugurating a positive theory of fluid structures.

**Ollig, Hans-Ludwig**. "Die Aktualität des Neukantianismus: Bemerkungen zu einem unumgänglichen Thema der Neukantianismusforschung" in *Grenzen der kritischen Vernunft*, Schmid, Peter A, 61-76. Basel, Schwabe Verlag, 1997.

**Olshewsky, Thomas M**. Reconstructing Deconstruction for a Prospectival Realism. *Hist Phil Quart*, 13(3), 375-388, Jl 96.

**Olson, Carl**. *The Indian Renouncer and Postmodern Poison: A Cross-Cultural Encounter*. New York, Lang, 1997.

In his essay on the pharmacy of Plato, Jacques Derrida discusses the ambivalence associated with the notion of *pharmakon* (drug, medicine, or poison) and its ability to either cure or destroy. By allowing the Indian renouncer and selected postmodern thinkers to share the medicine of each party in a cross-cultural exchange of ideas, this work will attempt to cure one's understanding about the several roles played by the renouncer as a stranger, hero figure androgynous being, and victim of self-sacrificial violence. (publisher, edited)

**Olson, Eric T**. Composition and Coincidence. *Pac Phil Quart*, 77(4), 374-403, D 96.

Many philosophers say that the same atoms may compose at once a statue and a lump of matter that could outlive the status. I reject this because no difference between the statue and the lump could explain why they have different persistence conditions. But if we say that the lump *is* the statue, it is difficult to

see how there could be any human beings. I argue that this and analogous problems about material objects admit only of solutions that at least appear to be radically at odds with our ordinary thinking.

**Olson, Eric T**. Dion's Foot. *J Phil*, 94(5), 260-265, My 97.

Michael Burke argues that your "foot-complement" ceases to exist when you lose your foot, for otherwise it would change, impossibly, from a nonperson to a person. I argue that Burke cannot consistently deny that a foot-complement is a person. Moreover, if he were right, there could be physically indistinguishable objects, only one of which was a person—in which case Burke's case for rejecting the "standard" solution to the "foot" puzzle collapses.

**Olson, Eric T**. *The Human Animal: Personal Identity without Psychology*. New York, Oxford Univ Pr, 1997.

Most philosophers writing about personal identity in recent years claim that what it takes for us to persist through time is a matter of psychology. Where some take the view that we persist by continuity of our mental *contents*, others tie our identity to the preservation of our mental *capacities*. Olson argues that both approaches face daunting ontological difficulties, and defends in their place a radically nonpsychological account of personal identity. You and I are biological organisms, he claims; and no psychological relation is either necessary or sufficient for an organism to persist through time. (publisher,edited)

**Olson, Eric T**. Was I Ever A Fetus?. *Phil Phenomenol Res*, 57(1), 95-110, Mr 97.

The standard view of personal identity says that someone who exists now can exist at another time only if there is continuity of her mental contents or capacities. But no person is psychologically continuous with a fetus, for a fetus, at least early in its career, has no mental features at all. So the standard view entails that no person was ever a fetus—contrary to the popular assumption that an unthinking fetus is a potential person. It is also mysterious what *does* ordinarily happen to a human fetus, if it does not come to be a person. Although an extremely complex variant of the standard view may allow one to persist without psychological continuity before one becomes a person but not afterwards, a far simpler solution is to accept a radically nonpsychological account of our identity.

**Olson, Ivan**. The Arts and Educational Reform: More Critical Thinking in the Classrooms of the Future?. *J Aes Educ*, 31(3), 107-117, Fall 97.

This article summarizes a survey of six major educational reform networks in order to establish an overview of their capacities to accommodate arts education in terms of quality, rigor, priorities and general educational objectives. Insights from the survey are used to consider such issues as the national educational agenda, quality research and increased rigor in programs, all of these coming together with two themes: cultural literacy and defining critical thinking. Conclusions, in general, point toward school reform groups for greater opportunity in maintaining a "language of aesthetics" which works toward increased understanding and "engagement" through a platform of experience modes: cognitive, instrumental, moral and aesthetic.

**Olthuis, James H**. "Crossing the Threshold: Sojourning Together in the Wild Spaces of Love" in *Knowing Other-Wise: Philosophy at the Threshold of Spirituality*, Olthuis, James H (ed), 235-257. New York, Fordham Univ Pr, 1997.

Confirming the postmodern critique of ontotheology (Heidegger, Levinas, Derrida), Olthuis, however, does not conclude (á là Mark Taylor) that we are left with the death of God and self. Rather, he suggests that when a vision of love—with its basic question, "to love or not to love"—replaces an ontology of being-as-power—with its question, "to be or not to be"—God and self return. In the priority of love, the human self is an intersubjectivity, an agency-with and a space opens up for sojourning with others in a mutuality ethics founded upon connection rather than control.

**Olthuis, James H**. "Face-to-Face: Ethical Asymmetry or the Symmetry of Mutuality?" in *Knowing Other-Wise: Philosophy at the Threshold of Spirituality*, Olthuis, James H (ed), 131-158. New York, Fordham Univ Pr, 1997.

Emmanuel Levinas's insistence on the ethical priority of the other is vulnerable to being misread as a plea for selflessness and self-sacrifice. The author suggests an alternative ethics of nonhierarchical mutuality in which "substitution" and self-sacrifice are seen not as the heart of ethics, but as an emergency compromise ethic because of the breakdown of mutuality.

**Olthuis, James H** (ed). *Knowing Other-Wise: Philosophy at the Threshold of Spirituality*. New York, Fordham Univ Pr, 1997.

The book calls into question the Western philosophical tradition of giving pride of place to reason in the acquisition of knowledge. Reasoning, the author offers, is only one of the many ways in which we engage, i.e., know, the world. We know more than we think. We know by touch, feel, taste, sight, sound, symbol, sex, trust—by means of every modality of human experience. Philosophy becomes, in the fashion of Levinas, "the wisdom of love at the service of love. Tracing connections between epistemology, ethics and spirituality—between "knowing" and the "other," between an other and the Other—all the essays serve as points of convergence between postmodern discussions and the Calvinian spirituality which is the home for writers in this collection. In particular, this collection explores the contributions of feminist thought and thinkers such as Emmanuel Levinas, Richard Rorty, Jacques Derrida, and John D. Caputo to a spiritually and ethically sensitive knowing. (publisher, edited)

**Olubi Sodipo, J** and Hallen, Barry. *Knowledge, Belief, and Witchcraft: Analytic Experiments in African Philosophy*. Stanford, Stanford Univ Pr, 1997.

First published in 1986, *Knowledge Belief, and Witchcraft* remains the only analysis of indigenous discourse about an African belief system undertaken from within the framework of Anglo-American analytical philosophy. Taking as its point of departure W.V.O. Quine's thesis about the indeterminacy of translation, the book investigates questions of Yoruba epistemology and of how knowledge is conceived in an oral culture. (publisher, edited)

**Oluwole, Sophie B.** "Culture, Nationalism and Philosophy" in *Philosophy and Democracy in Intercultural Perspective,* Kimmerle, Heinz (ed), 23-42. Amsterdam, Rodopi, 1997.

**Omine, Akira.** Das Verhältnis des Selbst zu Gott in Fichtes Wissenschaftslehre. *Fichte-Studien,* 12, 322-334, 1997.

**Ommerborn, Wolfgang.** *Mein Geist ist das Universum*: Ontologische und erkenntnistheoretische Aspekte in der Lehre des Lu Jiuyuan (1139-1193). *Bochumer Phil Jrbh,* 1, 57-80, 1996.

Lu Jiuyuan (1139-1193) is one of the most prominent philosophers of the Song dynasty. He belonged to the School of Mind (*Xin-Xue*), one of the two main schools of neo-Confucianism—the other being the School of Principle (*Li Xue*), of which Zhu Xi (1130-1200) is the outstanding figure. This essay investigates the ontological and epistemological teachings of Lu Jiuyuan and compares them with the thought of other neo-Confucian thinkers such as Zhu Xi. The most important term in Zhu Xi's philosophy is *li* (universal principle). Lu Jiuyuan equated *li* with the mind of man. He developed his philosophy on the basis of *li*—present in and apprehended by the mind—as the moral criterion of human conduct. For him, the purpose of study is to recognize *li* and return to the originally pure condition of the mind. Every man, he said, is responsible for the condition of his mind and must strive to attain knowledge of the truth. Lu refused to consider as important the acquisition of factual knowledge by external investigation, emphasizing instead that *li* is to be known intuitively. The realization of *li* is the result of inner, subjective self-examination.

**Oncina Coves, Faustino.** "Representación de la alteridad y Derecho desde la *aetas kantiana* a Fichte" in *El inicio del Idealismo alemán,* Market, Oswaldo, 167-178. Madrid, Ed Complutense, 1996.

Esta contribución aborda dos cuestiones: en primer lugar, la posición sistemática del Derecho en el seno de la *Doctrina de la Ciencia*; en segundo lugar, el papel del Derecho en la fundamentación de la intersubjetividad. Ambas cuestiones están vinculadas con el problema del fundamento de la representación, que ocupó a kantianos y antikantianos. Dos escépticos en particular, Schulze-Enesidemo y Maimon-Pirrón, destacaron la importancia de este problema para la filosofía en su conjunto. La exigencia de un tránsito de la teoría a la práctica, de la naturaleza a la libertad, en suma, que la razón teórica y la práctica sean causa eficiente en el mundo sensible, se torna un desafío para Fichte. Sin una fenomenología de la razón, de la libertad, resulta problemática la aplicabilidad del concepto de derecho.

**Oniang'o, Clement M P.** "The Relation to Nature, Time and Individuality as the Foundation of the African Concept of Harmony and Peace" in *Kreativer Friede durch Begegnung der Weltkulturen,* Beck, Heinrich (ed), 191-213. New York, Lang, 1995.

**Onigbinde, Akinyemi.** Of Existence and Serenity: An Essay in Nonconceptual Awareness. *Darshana Int,* 36(3/143), 25-35, Ap 96.

**Ono, Hiroakira** and Meyer, Robert K. The Finite Model Property for BCK and BCIW. *Stud Log,* 53(1), 107-118, F 94.

Ono raised in conversation the question whether the Finite Model Property (henceforth FMP) could be established for the pure implicational logic BCK. Meyer responded that, adapting an argument of Kripke, the FMP could certainly be shown for Church's weak theory BCIW of implication. Dualizing, it turned out that what is almost the same argument works also for BCK. Left open was the question of the FMP for pure implicational BCI. (This BCI problem has since been solved affirmatively and independently by Buszkowski and by Lafont. With Massey, we have subsequently generalized Lafont's argument to show the FMP for a host of systems.)

**Ono, Kent A** and Sloop, John M. Out-Law Discourse: The Critical Politics of Material Judgment. *Phil Rhet,* 30(1), 50-69, 1997.

Drawing upon recent poststructural investigations of judgment and justice, we argue that judgment is most profitably investigated from a rhetorical perspective, investigating not what judgment "should be," but instead investigating judgments as practiced by people in the context of their own experiences and using these judgments to disrupt and alter existing dominant logics. Ultimately, we argue that the role of theorists and critics is to develop strategies to disrupt the logics of judgment of the center and to highlight, enhance and create new judgments; critical practice should produce what we call "materialist conceptions of judgment," taking judgments made by (out)law communities in vernacular discourses and utilizing self-selected (out)law discourses as disruptive possibilities.

**Oosterling, Henk A F.** "Fascism as the Looming Shadow of Democracy" in *Philosophy and Democracy in Intercultural Perspective,* Kimmerle, Heinz (ed), 235-251. Amsterdam, Rodopi, 1997.

**Opalic, Petar.** Antinomies of Practice and Research of Group Psychotherapy (in Serbo-Croatian). *Theoria (Yugoslavia),* 38(4), 35-46, D 95.

This article exposes moral, ontological and practical antinomies of small group psychotherapy. Epistemological, methodological and cognitive antinomies of research in group-therapy are analyzed in more details. In the concluding section, the author outlines the theoretical framework of group therapy leading and investigating, within which the antinomnies could be more easily resolved.

**Oppy, Graham.** Gödelian Ontological Arguments. *Analysis,* 56(4), 226-230, O 96.

The main thesis of this paper is that Godel's ontological argument is subject to a kind of objection which has hitherto been overlooked, but which has often been

levelled at other ontological arguments, viz. that it can be paralleled by apparently equally persuasive proofs of the existence of beings in which no one should wish to believe. (Compare Gaunilo's objection to St. Anselm: No one should wish to believe in the existence of an island than which no greater island can be conceived.)

**Oppy, Graham.** Pantheism, Quantification and Mereology. *Monist,* 80(2), 320-336, Ap 97.

Pantheism divides into two doctrines, one ontological and one ideological. The ontological doctrine holds that there is a mereological sum of all beings—a being of which all beings are parts. I argue that, while controversial, this thesis admits of a reasonable defense. The ideological doctrine holds that the being of which all beings are parts is divine. I claim that it is hard to find good things to say on behalf of this doctrine.

**Oppy, Graham.** Pascal's Wager Is a Possible Bet (But Not a Very Good One): Reply to Harmon Holcomb III. *Int J Phil Relig,* 40(2), 101-116, O 96.

This paper is a reply to Harmon Holcomb III (1995) "To Bet The Impossible Bet", International Journal of Philosophy of Religion 35, pp. 65-79. Holcomb there argues that Pascal's Wager is "an inconceivable bet" and claims that my 1990 critique of Pascal's Wager—in "On Resche on Pascal's Wager" International Journal for Philosophy of Religion 30, pp. 159-168—is this mistaken. My paper substantiates and realism, my earlier critique.

**Oppy, Graham.** The Philosophical Insignificance of Gödel's Slingshot. *Mind,* 106(421), 121-141, Ja 97.

In "The Philosophical Significance of Godel's Slingshot" (*Mind* 104, 1995, 761-825) Stephen Neale claims that Godel's slingshot has important and unpleasant consequences for *all* theories of facts which endorse referential treatments of definite descriptions. I object: i) that it seems possible to construct theories of facts which endorse referential treatments of definite descriptions and yet which escape Godel's slingshot by escaping the substitution principle upon which the slingshot argument relies; and ii) that, in any case, it is clear that no Russellian ('logical atomist') theory of facts falls foul of Godel's slingshot, no matter what it says about definite descriptions.

**Oppy, Graham** and O'Leary-Hawthorne, John. Minimalism and Truth. *Nous,* 31(2), 170-196, Je 97.

Minimalism about truth has received considerable attention of late. We think that much of the discussion suffers from a pair of deficiencies. *First,* there has been a failure to discriminate different varieties and dimensions of minimalism about truth. *Second,* some serious and fundamental problems for the most popular varieties of minimalism about truth have not yet received sufficient attention. This paper aims to remedy those deficiencies. The paper is divided into three sections. In the first section, we distinguish six main varieties of minimalism about truth. In the second section, we identify four dimensions along which views about truth can be more or less minimal, thus clarifying the range of relevant notions of "minimality". In the third section, we critically discuss four minimalist theses.

**Orden Jiménez, Rafael.** "El problema de la introducción a la filosofía en el pensamiento de K. Chr. Krause en Jena (1797-1804)" in *El inicio del Idealismo alemán,* Market, Oswaldo, 397-414. Madrid, Ed Complutense, 1996.

Krause, estudiante de filosofía en la Universidad de Jena (1797-1801), asumió el proyecto fichteano de sistematizar toda la ciencia a partir de un único principio. Pero hubo de enfrentarse también con la cuestión de cómo sería posible una introducción a la filosofía y cómo justificar dicho principio. La urgencia de encontrar una solución se acrecentó cuando en su período de docente privado (1802-1804) optó por el mundo total como principio. Puesto que no pudo resolver el problema, inició su sistema con un principio dogmático. La solución la encontró en 1814 con una crítica que denominó "analítica".

**Orellana Benado, Miguel E.** "Scepticism Humor and the Archipelago of Knowledge" in *Scepticism in the History of Philosophy: A Pan-American Dialogue,* Popkin, Richard H (ed), 235-252. Dordrecht, Kluwer, 1996.

**Oretskin, Nancy A** and Sautter, Elise Truly. Tobacco Targeting: The Ethical Complexity of Marketing to Minorities. *J Bus Ethics,* 16(10), 1011-1017, Jl 97.

In recent years, there has been heightened concern regarding the marketing of potentially harmful products (PHPs) to disadvantaged markets. Three issues which commonly dominate discussions in this controversy are: 1) the potential for exploitation of vulnerable markets, 2) the tradeoff between protection of disadvantaged consumers and their rights to make informed choices, and 3) the appropriateness of using the commercial speech doctrine to settle the issue of targeting minority markets with PHPs. This paper examines the arguments raised in this debate so that interested parties will better appreciate the ethical complexity of marketing PHPs to minority segments.

**Orlando, Eleonora.** Sobre la interpretación deflacionaria de la teoría de Tarski. *Analisis Filosof,* 17(1), 49-73, My 97.

This paper is centered on the semantic theory of truth, formulated by Alfred Tarski. According to some authors, this theory is to be construed as a contemporary version of the traditional correspondence theory, namely, the one that defines truth as the correspondence between language and the world. In contrast, there are others who think that Tarski's theory reveals a deflationary conception of truth, according to which truth can be reduced to a linguistic resource for semantic ascent. Since I agree with the last group, I set out to support a special version—the so-called "semanticalist version"—of the deflationary interpretation of the semantic theory. In the first section, I characterize the two alternative conceptions of truth above mentioned, that is, correspondence and deflationism. The second section contains an exposition of the modal argument, which takes the Tarskian theory to inspire a syntacticalist version of the deflationary conception. In the third section, I criticize the argument in question and attempt to ground the above mentioned wide, semanticalist interpretation of deflationism.

**Orlando, Lucia** and Maltese, Giulio. The Definition of Rigidity in the Special Theory of Relativity and the Genesis of the General Theory of Relativity. *Stud Hist Phil Mod Physics*, 26B(3), 263-306, D 96.

**Orlans, F Barbara**. Ethical Decision Making About Animal Experiments. *Ethics Behavior*, 7(2), 163-171, 1997.

Laboratory animals, being vulnerable subjects, need the protection provided by adequate ethical review. This review falls primarily to Institutional Animal Care and Use Committees. A review committee's first duty is to identify which procedures ethically are unacceptable irrespective of any knowledge that might be derived. Examples are provided. These projects should be disapproved. Then, "on balance" judgments are assessed that weigh the animal harms against the potential benefits to humans. Several countries (but not the United States) use a classification system for ranking the degree of animal pain and distress. This type of assessment is essential for careful ethical analysis. Another way to enhance ethical discussion is to strive for a more balanced perspective of different viewpoints among member of decision making committees. Inclusion of representatives of animal welfare organizations and a greater proportion on nonanimal researchers would likely achieve this objective.

**Orlowska, Ewa**. "Semantic Considerations on Relevance" in *Das weite Spektrum der analytischen Philosophie*, Lenzen, Wolfgang, 250-261. Hawthorne, de Gruyter, 1997.

**Orlowska, Ewa**. Proof-Theoretical Investigations of Helena Rasiowa. *Bull Sec Log*, 25(3/4), 147-151, O-D 96.

**Orlowska, Ewa** and Demri, Stéphane. A Class of Modal Logics with a Finite Model Property with Respect to the Set of Possible-Formulae. *Bull Sec Log*, 26(1), 39-49, Mr 97.

We propose a formalism for presentation and classification of modal logics that admit a possible world semantics. We introduce a broad family of operators acting on binary relations and we show how various classes of accessibility relations from modal frames can be uniformly represented using these operators. Within this framework we define a class of modal logics that possess the finite model property with respect to the set of possible-formulae. (edited)

**Orlowska, Ewa** and Frias, Marcelo F. Equational Reasoning in Non-Classical Logics. *Bull Sec Log*, 26(1), 2-11, Mr 97.

In this paper it is shown that a broad class of propositional logics can be interpreted in an equational logic based on fork algebras. This interpretability enables us to develop a fork-algebraic formalization of these logics and, as a consequence, to simulate nonclassical means of reasoning with equational theories of fork algebras. As examples we showed how to reason equationally in modal, relevant, and dynamic logics.

**Orlowski, Hubert**. "Generationszugehörigkeit und Selbsterfahrung von (deutschen) Schriftstellern" in *Epistemology and History*, Zeidler-Janiszewska, Anna (ed), 497-508. Amsterdam, Rodopi, 1996.

The article aims at reconstruction of the auto-diagnosis of two literary generations: 1) authors whose first publications appeared in the late 20's, and 2) authors who had their debut in the years 1960-1980. The notion of generation status is defined in reference to Jerzy Kmita's conception. The author approaches the category of "generation" in accordance with Pinder's and Mannheim's conception of "simultaneous nonsimultaneousness". According to it a "generation" is a community whose discriminante feature is not the objective historic time but the subjective experience of the community. Two aspects of generation status—common experience of history and common estimation of values and objectives—correspond with two different models of interpretation.

**Orlowski, James P** and Vinicky, Janicemarie K and Shevlin Edwards, Sue. Conflicts of Interest, Conflicting Interests, and Interesting Conflicts, Part 3. *J Clin Ethics*, 7(2), 184-186, Sum 96.

**Orozco, Teresa**. Die Kunst der Anspielung: Hans-Georg Gadamers philosophische Interventionen im NS. *Das Argument*, 209(2-3), 311-324, Mr-Je 95.

Hans Georg Gadamer's writings on Plato during the Nazi period are interpreted against the background of manifold fascistic interpretations of Plato. In their indirectness, Gadamer's interpretations show how he supports the national conservative fraction without explicitly disarticulating himself from the "Volk"-type currents.

**Orozco, Teresa**. The Art of Allusion: Hans-Georg Gadamer's Philosophical Interventions under National Socialism. *Rad Phil*, 78, 17-26, Jl-Ag 96.

**Orozco Cantillo, Alvaro J**. *Valores Latinoamericanos y del Caribe: ¿Obstaculos o Ayudas para el Desarrollo?*. Barranquilla, Donado, 1996.

El trabajo, valores latinoamericanos y del caribe: obstáculos o ayudas para el desarrollo?, ampliado ahora e incorporado al corpus de este libro, fue leído en una de las sesiones del II Congreso Mundial sobre Etica del desarrollo, realizado en México y convocado por la Asociación Internacional de Etica del Desarrollo, cuyo director es el filósofo norteamericano David Crocker, profesor de Colorado State University. El citado congreso, al que asistió como invitado el autor de la presente obro, contó con la presencia activa de notables investigadores de la cultura, la ciencia y la filosofía, procedentes de diversas áreas del planeta. Parte del trabajo, arriba mencionado, fue publicado por la revista dominical del prestigioso diario El Heraldo, de Barranquilla, Columbia, Sur América, en agosto 6 de 1989. (publisher)

**Orr, Catherine M**. Charting the Currents of the Third Wave. *Hypatia*, 12(3), 29-45, Sum 97.

The term "third wave" within contemporary feminism presents some initial difficulties in scholarly investigation. Located in popular-press anthologies, zines, punk music, and cyberspace, many third wave discourses constitute themselves as a break with both second wave and academic feminisms; a break problematic for both generations of feminists. The emergence of third wave feminism offers academic feminists an opportunity to rethink the context of knowledge production and the mediums through which we disseminate our work.

**Orsucci, Andrea**. Gustav Teichmüller filologo e metafisico tra Italia e Germania: I) Teichmüller, Nietzsche e la critica delle 'mitologie scientifiche'. *G Crit Filosof Ital*, 17(1), 47-63, Ja-Ap 97.

**Orth, Ernst Wolfgang**. "Psyche und Psychologie bei Rudolph Hermann Lotze" in *Grenzen der kritischen Vernunft*, Schmid, Peter A, 117-132. Basel, Schwabe Verlag, 1997.

**Orth, Ernst Wolfgang**. Orientierung über Orientierung: Zur Medialität der Kultur als Welt des Menschen. *Z Phil Forsch*, 50(1/2), 167-182, Ja-Je 96.

**Ortiz-Osés, Andrés**. La redención oscura. *Dialogo Filosof*, 13(2), 215-232, My-Ag 97.

El autor ofrece un ramillete de aforismos de tono oscuro, pero no oscurantista. En ellos trata de apalabrar lo sombrío de la existencia humana.

**Ortiz-Osés, Andrés**. Religión entre Ilustración y Romanticismo. *Pensamiento*, 205(53), 127-134, Ja-Ap 97.

**Ortiz-Osés, Andrés**. Visiones del mundo: Lógica simbólica. *Rev Filosof (Spain)*, 8(15), 63-66, 1996.

**Orton, Robert E**. "Teacher Beliefs and Student Learning" in *Philosophy of Education (1996)*, Margonis, Frank (ed), 318-325. Urbana, Phil Education Soc, 1997.

**Orudzhev, Z M**. A Philosophical Analysis of the Regional Policy of Russia. *Russian Stud Phil*, 35(2), 76-92, Fall 96.

**Oruka, Odera**. "Reason and Action in Africa" in *Averroës and the Enlightenment*, Wahba, Mourad (ed), 127-132. Amherst, Prometheus, 1996.

**Osamu, Maekawa**. On Walter Benjamin and Modern Optical Phenomena. *Bigaku*, 48(1), 1-12, Sum 97.

The concept "taktil", which originally stemmed from physiological psychology, is closely related to the formation of new social mechanism. This mechanism abandons the distinction between the referent and the perception and divides and regulates the subject in a newly-formed unified plane. "Taktil" not only constitutes such certain reality, but also signifies the unrest caused by this new perceptual organization. Such unrest is evident, for example, in two optical devices widely permeated in the second half of 19th century: panorama and stereoscope. From this standpoint taken by Benjamin, we could relocate the actuality of "taktil" in a wider context, sociocultural discourses/praxis. (edited)

**Osborne, Catherine**. Love's Bitter Fruits: Martha C Nussbaum *The Therapy of Desire: Theory and Practice in Hellenistic Ethics*. *Phil Invest*, 19(4), 318-328, O 96.

A pugnacious attack on M.C. Nussbaum's assessment of Hellenistic views of the emotions. Osborne argues that Nussbaum is confused about the connections between love, anger, attachment to externals, risk and wrongdoing. By treating love as a self-centred attachment to possessions she takes love's vulnerability as a risk of loss and the consequent anger as bitterness and resentment, thereby concluding that love inevitably leads to vice. Osborne shows that love, by contrast, cares for the other, risks grief and anger at wrongs done to another, and that this is not vicious but central to any morally worthy response.

**Osborne, Thomas** and Rose, Nikolas. In the Name of Society, or Three Theses on the History of Social Thought. *Hist Human Sci*, 10(3), 87-104, Ag 97.

This paper is something of a preview of a projected attempt on the part of the authors to capture the voice of social thought in rather different terms. Our three theses are: 1) that those who speak 'in the name of society' have just as frequently been doctors and bureaucrats as opposed to 'social philosophers' or professional sociologists; correlatively, 2) that the creative voice of social thought has more often been technical, problem-centred and tied up with particular rationalities of government as opposed to being either exclusively theoretical or merely responsive to 'objective problems' in society; and, 3) that if sociology today struggles for a voice in which to speak this may be in some part due to the ways in which the past history of social thought has typically been conceived. (edited)

**Oser, Fritz K**. Kohlberg's Dormant Ghosts: The Case of Education. *J Moral Educ*, 25(3), 253-275, S 96.

**Osés Gorráiz, Jesús María**. El vivir y la fatiga: La fatiga de vivir. *Euridice*, 183-196, 1992.

Les formes de vie actuelles semblent ne rien avoir en commun avec la devise de l'Illustration *sapere aude!* (Kant), expliqué dans la trilogie autoconsciénce, autodétermination et autoréalisation (Habermas). C'est la hâte, la vitesse des changements, la mode de ce qui est éphémère: en somme l'hétéronomie, l'avoir et le parraître, qui s'imposent aujourd'hui. Ceci est à l'origine d'une fatigue vitale, sans précédents, dont la seule issue semble être l'établissement de projets rationnels et communautaires dans lesquels les hommes livres soient capables de mener à bien—ou au moins, d'en approcher—l'idéal illustré.

**Osés Gorráiz, Jesús María**. La influencia de la Revolución Francesa en el pensamiento de Bonald. *Euridice*, 127-152, 1995.

The French Revolution had a direct repercussion in the Louis de Bonald's life. The article analyzes not only the ideological and religious strongpoints that the French author suffered because of the revolution, but also the effect that it had in Bonald's personal and family aspects when he was forced to go into exile. Finally, it studies the scarce credibility that he places in the "Restoration" period. (edited)

**Oshana, Marina A L**. Ascriptions of Responsibility. *Amer Phil Quart*, 34(1), 71-83, Ja 97.

**Osler, Margaret J**. "Triangulating Divine Will: Henry More, Robert Boyle, and René Descartes on God's Relationship to the Creation" in *Mind Senior to the World*, Baldi, Marialuisa, 75-87. Milano, FrancoAngeli, 1996.

Descartes, Boyle, and More were each determined to preserve an important role for God in their philosophies of nature. Unlike Boyle and More, Descartes was not obsessed with proving God's ongoing providential relationship to the world. His understanding of God's relationship to the creation—his mitigated intellectualism—was, nevertheless, central to his philosophical project. Boyle's empiricist experimentalism was rooted in his voluntarism. In a similar way, More's Platonic intellectualism provided the foundation for his modifications of the mechanical philosophy, particularly the spirit of nature, which he thought would ensure God's providential role in the created world.

**Osler, Margaret J**. From Immanent Natures to Nature as Artifice: The Reinterpretation of Final Causes in Seventeenth-Century Natural Philosophy. *Monist*, 79(3), 388-407, Jl 96.

Examination of the writings of several key seventeenth-century natural philosophers—including Gassendi, Boyle, and Newton—demonstrates that final causes did not disappear at this time as the traditional historiography of the Scientific Revolution would have us believe. Rather they came to be reinterpreted in a way compatible with the underlying metaphysics of the mechanical philosophy, which reduced causality to the impact of material particles. Final causes were reinterpreted in terms of God's purposes which were thought to be reflected in the design of the creation.

**Osman, Mahmoud**. "The Third World and Enlightenment" in *Averroës and the Enlightenment*, Wahba, Mourad (ed), 221-226. Amherst, Prometheus, 1996.

**Ossorio, Peter G**. What There Is, How Things Are. *J Theor Soc Behav*, 27(2-3), 149-172, Je-S 97.

Ontology is critically assessed as being too narrowly based to contribute substantially to our understanding of the real world. Ontology reflects only what amounts to an extended notion of an object, whereas understanding the real world requires, in addition, the concepts of process, event and state of affairs. Formal relationships among the four reality concepts are presented and the privileging of any one of them is rejected, the use of the State of Affairs System (the conceptual system encompassing objects, processes, events and states of affairs) leads to a parsimonious formulation of the nature of persons as states of affairs rather than objects. In passing, the notion that states of affairs cannot be located is rejected and the significance of the State of Affairs System for scientific and metaphysical theorizing is noted.

**Ostanello, A**. Understanding and Structuring Complex Problems Within Organisational Contexts. *Commun Cog—AI*, 13(1), 31-56, 1996.

Several studies on Decision Aid in organizational contexts have pointed out that the client's demand refers, generally, to a complex situation in which various kinds of uncertainties make any clear 'action' conception very problematical, and the structuring of such a representation ('action'), that is acceptable in a pluralistic context, very difficult. This paper aims to give a contribution to such a line of research. A context/process framework is proposed and a *bipolar* model is defined for framing a structuring/validation process. This permits one to conceive a more general '*Action Space*' than the 'solution space' defined by mathematical works from *OR/DA* literature.

**Ostapski, S Andrew** and Plumly, L Wayne and Love, Jim L. The Ethical and Economic Implications of Smoking in Enclosed Public Facilities: A Resolution of Conflicting Rights. *J Bus Ethics*, 16(4), 377-384, Mr 97.

Smokers and nonsmokers possess equal rights but those rights conflict with each other in the use of shared facilities. Medical research has established that smoking harms not only those who use the product but also those who are passively exposed to it. Laws and private regulation of smoking in shared facilities have resulted in the segregation of smokers from nonsmokers to an outright ban of tobacco use. Such controls have provided unsatisfactory results to both groups. An acceptable ethical solution, based on reduction of harm and compensation, can be derived by applying *moral audit* principles, supported by economic analysis, which does not unduly curtail the rights of both parties as to the use of tobacco products.

**Ostas, Daniel T** and Loeb, Stephen E. A Business Ethics Experiential Learning Module: The Maryland Business School Experience. *Teach Bus Ethics*, 1(1), 21-32, 1997.

In this paper we describe the principal activities of the initial implementation in May of 1996 of one of the "Experiential Learning Modules (ELMs)' entitled "Business Ethics" (UMCP 1995, p. 7) that is part of the full-time MBA program at the College of Business and Management (Maryland Business School) of the University of Maryland at College Park (UMCP). Additionally, we briefly consider the location of this Business Ethics ELM in the curriculum of the Maryland Business School's full-time MBA program. We also outline how the Business Ethics ELM was developed. Further, we provide a discussion and a short conclusion.

**Ostovich, Steven T**. Messianic History in Benjamin and Metz. *Phil Theol*, 8(4), 271-289, Sum 94.

History is not the record of humanity's progress through otherwise empty time. It is rather to be conceived Messianically, i.e., in terms of God's eschatological promises and the interruptive capacity of dangerous memories of human suffering. This insight is contained in both the historical philosophy of Walter Benjamin and the political theology of Johann Baptist Metz. Metz's theological categories also contribute an understanding of messianic history that avoids the dualism of Benjamin's description of history in both messianic and materialist terms.

**Ostrowiecki, Hélène**. Le jeu de l'athéisme dans le *Theophrastus redivivus*. *Rev Phil Fr*, 2, 264-277, Ap-Je 96.

**Otabe, Tanehisa**. Originality and Its Origin in Modern Aesthetics (in Japanese). *Bigaku*, 47(4), 1-12, Spr 97.

The idea of 'originality' is one of the most important concepts in modern aesthetics. Few attempts, however, have been made so far at clarifying how and why this idea was established in the middle of the eighteenth-century. Our concern in this paper is to examine what motivated the idea of originality. (edited)

**Otero, Margarita** and Berarducci, Alessandro. A Recursive Nonstandard Model of Normal Open Induction. *J Sym Log*, 61(4), 1228-1241, D 96.

Models of normal open induction are those normal discretely ordered rings whose nonnegative part satisfy Peano's axioms for open formulas in the language of ordered semirings. (Where normal means integrally closed in its fraction field.) In 1964 Shepherdson gave a recursive nonstandard model of open induction. His model is not normal and does not have any infinite prime elements. In this paper we present a recursive nonstandard model of normal open induction with an unbounded set of infinite prime elements.

**Otsuka, Michael**. Quinn on Punishment and Using Persons as Means. *Law Phil*, 15(2), 201-208, 96.

In "The Right to Threaten and the Right to Punish," Warren Quinn justifies punishment on the ground that it can be derived from the rights of persons to protect themselves against crime. Quinn, however, denies that a right of self-protection justifies the punishment of an aggressor solely on the ground that such punishment deters others from harming the victim of that aggression or others. He believes that punishment so justified would constitute a morally objectionable instance of using the punished individual as a means. Contrary to Quinn, I argue that 1) an individual can, on the very ground of a right to self-protection that Quinn ultimately relies upon to justify punishment, justify the punishment of an individual as a means of deterring others from committing crimes; and that 2) an individual or individuals (including state officials) can, on the ground of vindicating the right of protection that others possess, justify the punishment of an individual as a means of deterring others from committing crimes.

**Ott, Konrad**. "Technik und Ethik" in *Angewandte Ethik: Die Bereichsethiken und ihre theoretische Fundierung*, Nida-Rümelin, Julian (ed), 650-717. Stuttgart, Alfred Kröner, 1996.

The article consists of five sections. First, notions are introduced and some explanations are given why technology has become a major topic of ethical reflection. A diagram is to be offered which allows for combinations of technological and moral premises in order to infer different kinds of value-judgements on technology. Second section surveys the history of an ethics of technology. Third section analyses contemporary German approaches to an ethics of technology. In the fourth section there is a distinction to be made between 1) an ethics of engineering and 2) the ethical idea of technology assessment. In the last section, the diagram is to be supplemented. Last, the idea of the "promise of technology" is to be renewed under the horizon of an ethics of technology.

**Ott, Konrad**. *Vom Begründen zum Handeln: Aufsätze zur angewandten Ethik*. Tübingen, Attempto Verlag, 1996.

Konrad Otts neues Buch enthält bislang unveröffentlichte Aufsätze zu Begründungs- und Anwendungsfragen der Ethik. Im Mittelpunkt der Abhandlungen steht die Frage nach konkreten Durchsetzungsmöglichkeiten einer anwendungsbezogenen Philosophie vor allem auf den Gebieten der Umweltethik und der Wissenschaftsethik. (publisher, edited)

**Otte, Michael**. Gegenstand und Methode in der Geschichte der Mathematik. *Phil Natur*, 29(1), 31-68, 1992.

**Otto, Martin**. Canonization for Two Variables and Puzzles on the Square. *Annals Pure Applied Log*, 85(3), 243-282, My 97.

We consider infinitary logic with only two variable symbols, both with and without counting quantifiers. The main result is that finite relational structures admit *PTIME* canonization with respect to $L^2$ and $C^2$: there are polynomial time computable functors mapping finite relational structures to unique representatives of their equivalence class with respect to indistinguishability in either of these logics. (edited)

**Ottonello, Pier Paolo**. Rosmini y Vico: la "filosofía italiana". *Cuad Vico*, 5/6, 105-113, 1995/96.

The author describes the Italian philosophy's renewing line, which begins with both Vico and Rosmini, "two well-established thinkers," though Vico might not be one of Rosmini's most mentioned authors. Such a renovated current gives rise to an anthropological all-out metaphysics, which nourishes the so-called "big-deep thinking" and is expected to cross the Italian borders and make a significant contribution to the renewal of civilization.

**Ottonello, Pier Paolo**. Vico en Sciacca. *Cuad Vico*, 5/6, 115-121, 1995/96.

Sciacca takes Vico as a representative of modernity in the Western culture. He

AUTHOR INDEX 827 Paden, Roger

aims to spell out his philosophical doctrine on the integrity through a continuous dialogue on the dynamics and the importance of the Italian thought with its more outstanding participants: Gentile and Spaventa. Vico's greatness—still brighter among the surrounding shadows-related to Rosmini's, should be used, according to the author, to avoid being caught by the so-called "darkening of the mind" into which both rationalism and nihilism makes us so easily prone to fall.

**Otxoterena, Juan M**. Dialéctica moderna y límite mental: el realismo como hallazgo en Leonardo Polo. *Anu Filosof*, 29(2), 885-900, 1996.

Against contemporary philosophy, Leonardo Polo's thought is a defense of *realism*. This realism is neither the forgetfulness of modern philosophy (mere approbation of classic philosophy) nor a critic-realism. The author calls "methodic realism". Between Modern Philosophy and traditional metaphysic, L. Polo's philosophy can be called metaphysics.

**Ouattara, Ibrahim S**. L'interprétation de la position originelle et la question de la fondation. *De Phil*, 10, 43-58, 1993.

What is the theoretical function of Rawls's original position? Through an analysis of the reception of Rawls's theory, the author argues that 1) despite the antifoundationalist tendencies noted by the "*methodological Rawlsians*," there is a residual foundationalism to Rawls's original position, 2) what divides the commentators on Rawls is precisely the question of philosophical justification, 3) on this last question, a foundationalist point of view is to be preferred to that of the antifoundationalists.

**Ouwerkerk, Cok** and Verbeke, Willem and Peelen, Ed. Exploring the Contextual and Individual Factors on Ethical Decision Making of Salespeople. *J Bus Ethics*, 15(11), 1175-1187, N 96.

This paper studies how salespeople make ethical decisions. For this purpose a structural model has been developed which configures how the organization's environment, the organization's climate, and personality traits affect ethical decision making. Internal communication and the choice of a control system especially affect ethical decision making. Internal communication also affects the attraction of salespeople with unethical personality traits (Machiavellism), while the control system affects the ethical climate. Ethical climate and salespeople's personality traits also affect the ethical decision making. In fact the study shows that ethical decision making can be influenced by management.

**Overall, Christine**. "Reflections of a Sceptical Bioethicist" in *Philosophical Perspectives on Bioethics,* Sumner, L W (ed), 163-186. Toronto, Univ of Toronto Pr, 1996.

In this paper I argue that there is a need for scepticism about 1) the existence of bioethics as a distinct field; 2) the success and acceptance of bioethics within medicine, academia, and the culture generally; and 3) the moral and political conservatism of bioethical theory. All of these characteristics are at least in part a function of contemporary bioethics' parasitism on health care as it is currently practiced; bioethics tends to reiterate the hierarchism, individualism, professionalism,, adultism, and separatism of medicine, and to co-opt the radical potential of progressive analyses of health care and the medical profession.

**Overall, Christine**. Feeling Fraudulent: Some Moral Quandaries of a Feminist Instructor. *Educ Theor*, 47(1), 1-13, Wint 97.

I explore, from a feminist perspective, some ethical dimensions of university teaching. I begin by examining the feeling of fraudulence. Tracing the origins of this feeling reveals moral quandaries in the situation of university instructors, especially feminist instructors. In particular, the academic system demands my complicity in enforcing in my students behaviors that conflict both with feminist ideals and with what I perceive to be my students' intellectual, social and personal growth. I conclude by sketching some ways of revisioning, if not resolving, the moral quandaries that the feeling of fraudulence reveals.

**Overdiek, Anja**. Ein Mann sieht vor lauter Welle das Wasser nicht. *Z Phil Praxis*, 24-25, 1996.

This text is a reply to the article of Phil Whyte on "Second Wave Feminism" in the same issue. It argues with central features of feminism concerning questions of epistemology and methodology. It shows why contemporary feminist theory as a whole can neither be called essentialist nor verificationist or perspectivist and explores further feminisms' relationship to humanism.

**Overenget, Einar**. The Presence of Husserl's Theory of Wholes and Parts in Heidegger's Phenomenology. *Res Phenomenol*, 26, 171-197, 1996.

In this paper I argue that Husserl's theory of wholes and parts plays an essential role in the phenomenological project Heidegger carries out in *Being and Time* (BT). I submit three theses. First, Heidegger uses the theory of wholes in accordance with the conventions Husserl establishes in the third of his *Logical Investigations*. Second, Heidegger uses this theory when he discusses the structural make-up of *Dasein*. Third, the importance of this theory for the *Daseinsanalytik* can be attributed to the fact that it plays a decisive role in Heidegger's approach to the *Seinsfrage* in BT. Acknowledging the presence of this theory will help us to more accurately appreciate the nature of Heidegger's fundamental ontology.

**Owen, B William**. On the Alleged Uniqueness and Incomprehensibility of the Holocaust. *Phil Cont World*, 2(3), 8-16, Fall 95.

A number of philosophers have argued that the Holocaust is incapable of philosophical analysis and explanation. There are two arguments for this view: 1) that it is unique and thus resists such analysis; and 2) that it is incomprehensible and thus incapable of being understood. In this article, several versions of both of these arguments are considered and shown not to support a conclusion that the Holocaust resists philosophical explanation. An alternative route to philosophical explanation is then suggested.

**Owen, David**. Philosophy and the Good Life: Hume's Defence of Probable Reasoning. *Dialogue (Canada)*, 35(3), 485-503, Sum 96.

Hume thinks that the wise person adjusts her beliefs according to the evidence. To not do so would be to go against the rules of just reasoning. But if beliefs are formed in the way Hume says they are, how can we adjust them? And if probable reasoning is not based on reason, how can there be rules of just reasoning? What grounds Hume's preference for reason over bigotry and superstition? In this paper I argue that Hume suggests that only an appeal to the good life, or what is better for a person and society, can ground this preference.

**Owolabi, Kolawole Aderemi**. African Philosophy and the African Crisis. *Quest*, 9(2), 32-43, D 96.

Cette étude traite le(s) rôle(s) que la philosophie pourrait jouer dans la résolution de la crise africaine. Premièrement l'état des affaires actuel de la philosophie en Afrique est présenté, disant que la philosophie africaine n'a pas contribué de manière pertinente au développement de la société africaine. Pour cette raison, l'essai suggère que la philosophie africaine puisse être plus valable pour la situation africaine en insistant sur l'essentiel traditionel de la discipline étant la critique de la culture, basé spécifiquement sur la théorie de ce journal que la crise africaine est essentiellement une crise culturelle. (edited)

**Ozdowski, Pawel**. "The Broken Bonds with the World" in *Epistemology and History,* Zeidler-Janiszewska, Anna (ed), 133-155. Amsterdam, Rodopi, 1996.

Kmita's views are placed in the context of the ongoing dialogue between Quine, Putnam and Davidson. The argument shows that an attempt to relativize truth or to relinquish the concept of truth cannot be consistent. The Weberian interpetive neutrality, this remnant of scientism that still afflicts Kmita's program, is not available to us if we realize that interpretation *inevitably* presupposes a normative appraisal of beliefs and actions against a *shared* background of truths. Bringing this to our attention may help us improve our understanding of others no matter how remote they seem. Let us, students of culture, take off the masks of social engineers and disclose the faces of *philosophers*.

**Pac, Andrea**. Gender and Social Awareness: A Story from Buenos Aires. *Thinking*, 13(1), 5-8, 1997.

**Pacheco, Décio**. Um Problema no Ensino de Ciências: organizaçao conceitual do conteúdo ou estudo dos fenômenos. *Educ Filosof*, 10(19), 63-81, Ja-Je 96.

This article is based on an educational experience that illustrates one of the main problems concerning the teaching of sciences. From this experience we can assume one of two different methodological orientations: the conceptual content organization, that is strongly connected to traditional teaching, or the study of phenomena, that leads to an innovative posture.

**Packer, Arnold H**. Arts and Earning a Living. *J Aes Educ*, 30(4), 99-114, Wint 96.

**Paden, Roger**. "Wilderness Management" in *Philosophy and Geography I: Space, Place, and Environmental Ethics,* Light, Andrew (ed), 175-187. Lanham, Rowman & Littlefield, 1997.

After discussing the history of wilderness management in the United States, this essay evaluates four types of wilderness management policies. These policies differ practically in terms of their normative details concerning what is to be protected, how extensive that protection is to be, and how conflicts are to be resolved. Moreover, the policies also differ theoretically in terms of their philosophical foundations. The essay demonstrates the relationship between the normative elements and the philosophical foundations, while critically evaluating those foundations.

**Paden, Roger**. Hare's Reductive Justification of Preference Utilitarianism. *S J Phil*, 34(3), 361-378, Fall 96.

This essay argues against "reductive" arguments for utilitarianism, according to which, the justification for utilitarianism depends essentially on "the reduction of interpersonal comparisons to intrapersonal ones by appeal to the judge's own preferences as to possible states of himself." This justification is based on an analogy between persons attempting to make public choices morally and persons attempting to make private choices rationally. According to this argument, in each case, people should choose that option which promises to maximize the satisfaction of interests, when those interests are judged, "strength for strength." Although some opponents of utilitarianism have objected to this analogy, I accept it, arguing that it cannot be used to support utilitarianism.

**Paden, Roger**. Liberalism and Consumerism. *Phil Cont World*, 3(4), 14-19, Wint 96.

Communitarians have argued that liberalism somehow causes or leads to a consumer society. Moreover, they have argued that consumer society is somehow morally suspect. Given the connection between liberalism and consumerism, they have argued that the moral problems they have found in consumer society give reason to oppose liberalism. In this paper, after defining "consumerism" and "liberalism," I examine the various communitarian arguments against consumerism and the various arguments that seek to connect liberalism to consumerism. I argue that only one of these arguments has any hope of establishing this connection.

**Paden, Roger**. Rawl's Just Savings Principle and the Sense of Justice. *Soc Theor Pract*, 23(1), 27-51, Spr 97.

In this essay, I defend Rawls's theory of intergenerational justice. I begin with a careful reconstruction of this theory which both clarifies its central principle, "the just savings principle," and places it within the overall structure of his theory. I then argue that none of the arguments that Rawls offers explicitly in support of it succeed. However, I argue that there is some evidence supporting the claim that there is another, implicit, argument for the just savings principle which grounds that principle on the concept of the "sense of justice." After developing and defending this argument, I critically assess it, arguing that careful attention to this theory of intergenerational justice casts new light on the foundations of Rawls's overall theory of justice.

**Paden, Roger**. Reconstructing Rawls's Law of Peoples. *Ethics Int Affairs*, 11, 215-232, 1997.

In his recent article "The Law of Peoples", John Rawls attempts to develop a theory of *international* justice. Paden contrasts "The Law of Peoples" with Rawls's earlier work, "A Theory of Justice." Paden reconstructs Rawls's new theory, in a way which he claims is more consistent with "A Theory of Justice." Paden finds Rawls's new theory lacking in the degree to which it attempts to respond to communitarian criticisms, those that advocate a different theory of good than that of liberal societies. Paden examines the various flaws in "The Law of Peoples" and goes back to "A Theory of Justice" to state that all societies seek one good, that is, the protection of their just institutions. In so doing, Paden provides a more expansive view of the interests of societies, which, he argues, ultimately is more consistent with "A Theory of Justice," conceptually simpler and avoids the flaws identified in the original argument.

**Paden, Roger**. Signaling Cooperation: Prisoner's Dilemmas and Psychological Dispositions in Hobbes's State of Nature. *Dialogos*, 32(70), 27-51, Jl 97.

Hobbes argued that, although life in the state of nature is both unacceptably dangerous and known to be so by its inhabitants, they can only escape from it by appointing an absolute sovereign. This appears to be paradoxical, as it would seem that rational people should be able to escape from a self-imposed danger without resorting to a dangerous form of indirect coercion. Because the Prisoner's Dilemma can make sense of this paradox, it has been used to explain the choices made by the people in the state of nature, but it is not clear that the two situations are analogous. Some have argued that there exist significant objective dissimilarities between the two situations that defeat the analogy. In this paper, after criticizing those arguments, I argue that there are several subjective factors that differentiate the two situations. This point suggests an interesting new interpretation of Hobbes's argument.

**Padial Benticuaga, Juan José**. Aspectos gnoseológicos de la noción de mundo. *Anu Filosof*, 29(2), 901-910, 1996.

Contemporary philosophy from Husserl focuses in the notion of world. Polo in his theory of knowledge explain a notion of world that solves some latent difficulties in the speeches of Husserl and Heidegger.

**Padilla-Gálvez, Jesús**. Die Rolle der vollständigen Induktion in der Theorie des Wahrheitsbegriffes. *Phil Natur*, 33(1), 1-21, 1996.

**Padilla-Gálvez, Jesús**. La metalógica en la propuesta de R. Carnap. *Mathesis*, 11(2), 113-136, My 95.

In this study we tackle the beginnings of metalogical research which was carried out around the Circle of Vienna during the thirties. More specifically, we propose a thorough analysis in a definite direction, that which was elaborated by Carnap in a series of conferences on metalogics which were put forward in the *Mathematischen Institut* on the 11th, 18th and 25th of June 1931 and which are translated below. Metalogics will clarify some key concepts of the work performed in this field. (edited)

**Paetzold, Heinz**. "Adorno's Notion of Natural Beauty: A Reconsideration" in *The Semblance of Subjectivity*, Huhn, Tom (ed), 213-235. Cambridge, MIT Pr, 1997.

The article proposes a new approach to Adorno's notion of natural beauty. On the one hand Adorno is confronted with Derrida's 'method' of deconstruction. On the other hand recently developed environmental aesthetics is outlined. Explicit references are made to the German environmental aesthetics by G. Böhme and M. Seel. But the article argues that we have to go back again to Adorno in order to avoid shortcomings of deconstruction as well as environmental aesthetics. There are still convincing arguments to be found in Adorno's materialism and in his conviction that we can't play off art against nature even if nature is understood as environment.

**Paetzold, Heinz**. "Mythos und Moderne in der *Philosophie der symbolischen Formen* Ernst Cassirers" in *Epistemology and History*, Zeidler-Janiszewska, Anna (ed), 429-439. Amsterdam, Rodopi, 1996.

The objective of the text is to relate Cassirer's philosophy of culture expounded in his *Philosophy of Culture* to the problems of community and modernity. The author approaches Cassirer's philosophy of culture as a theory of modernity, where differentiation of symbolic forms acts as a motor of modernization. In the ideal case, symbolic forms complete each other creating a merge of various perspectives allowing us to understand the world. The history of modernity, however, makes us aware of the continuous danger of social crises in which there appears a temptation to return to the mystical community spirit. This danger can be averted only through transformations of the mythical energies underlying each experience.

**Pagallo, Ugo**. Bacon, Hobbes and the Aphorisms at Chatsworth House. *Hobbes Stud*, 9, 21-31, 1996.

The extraordinary fortune that marks Hobbes's legal and political science throughout this century, largely coincides with the Inaktualitä5 that has contradistincted vice versa Bacon's civil philosophy. The dominant idea of the Lord Chancellor's negligible contribution to both the birth and development of modern legal and political thought has prevailed to such an extent that maybe a work published in 1936 by Leo Strauss appears as the last book dedicated in our century to Hobbes's philosophy, which confirming the full theoretical autonomy of its author, closely examines nevertheless the doctrine of the 'old Master'. That is one of the main reasons why the aphorisms of Chatsworth House are so important. For that manuscript offers a new opportunity in order to analyze with its twenty aphorisms some crucial principles of Bacon's civil

philosophy that would probably remain otherwise overshadowed by the contemporary image of a Veruram "Hobbesian without qualities".

**Page, Benjamin**. *Four Summers: A Czech Kaleidoscope*. Washington, IREX, 1994.

A gradually unfolding "slice" of atmosphere and opinion in the Czech Republic's first four post-Communist summers. Discussion partners—many present each year—include philosophers Milan Machovec and Zbynek Fiser (Egon Bondy); the granddaughters of philosopher and founding President T.G. Masaryk, rural and city folk, youth and professional social scientists, retirees, former dissidents, a still faithful party member and a Catholic leader. Topics range widely as discussants seek to understand the causes, nature and implications of the transition, for their own lives and their society, in contexts that move from the personal to the global, the practical to the ontological.

**Page, Carl**. Thumos and Thermopylae: Herodotus vii 238. *Ancient Phil*, 16(2), 301-331, Fall 96.

In the aftermath of Thermopylae, Xerxes desecrates the corpse of the Spartan general Leonidas. His anger belongs to a larger pattern of meaning concerning spiritedness (thumos), that touches on his kingly sense of glory, the struggle for hegemony between Persians and Greeks and the political place accorded spiritedness by the two ways of life. Having a care for the civilized whole, Xerxes emerges as a self-conscious and intelligently ambitious, though still seriously flawed monarch. The nomoi of the Persians fail in not giving spiritedness its proper, communal due and recognition.

**Page, James**. Unconfigured Tractarian Objects. *Phil Invest*, 20(1), 39-50, Ja 97.

According to Wittgenstein's *Tractatus*, the world consists of atomic objects arranged in various configurations and the ways the world might be are determined by the ways these objects can be configured. I question whether these very objects can be unconfigured as well. Black and Fogelin are nearly alone in their attention to this issue but reach opposite conclusions. Black asserts, essentially without argument, that atomic objects can be unconfigured, while Fogelin is committed to the view that they cannot. I think Black is right and my aim is to show why.

**Pages, Joan**. Armstrong on the Role of Laws in Counterfactual Supporting. *Theoria (Spain)*, 12(29), 337-342, My 97.

Armstrong (1983) poses two requirements that law-statements must satisfy in order to support the corresponding counterfactuals. He also argues that law-statements cannot satisfy one of these requirements if they merely express regularities, although both requirements are satisfied if law-statements are interpreted as expressing relations between universals. I try to show that Armstrong's argument can be raised against Armstrong's own solution by adding three premisses to it: the inference thesis, the contingency thesis and a principle whose rationality I also argue for. Finally, I offer a more reasonable alternative condition for nomic counterfactual supporting which is satisfied by law-statements if they are interpreted as expressing relations between universals, but not so if we interpret them as mere regularities.

**Pagin, Peter**. Is Compositionality Compatible with Holism?. *Mind Lang*, 12(1), 11-33, Mr 97.

This paper deals with three prima facie problems for the compatibility of the principle of semantic compositionality with semantic holism. The first problem concerns the order and mode of determination of the meaning of complex expressions. The second concerns the individuation of meanings and as a consequence, the possibility of communication. The third problem concerns the role of compositionality in explaining the understanding of new sentences and in conjunction with that, the possibility of language learning. It is argued that each has an acceptable solution.

**Painter, Mark**. The Loss of Practical Reason and Some Consequences for the Idea of Postmodernism. *SW Phil Rev*, 13(1), 39-46, Ja 97.

**Pais, John**. Revision Algebra Semantics for Conditional Logic. *Stud Log*, 51(2), 279-316, 1992.

The properties of belief revision operators are known to have an informal semantics which relates them to the axioms of conditional logic. The purpose of this paper is to make this connection precise via the model theory of conditional logic. A semantics for conditional logic is presented, which is expressed in terms of algebraic models constructed ultimately out of revision operators. In addition, it is shown that each algebraic model determines both a revision operator and a logic, that are related by virtue of the stable Ramsey test.

**Pais, John** and Jackson, Peter. Partial Monotonicity and a New Version of the Ramsey Test. *Stud Log*, 51(1), 21-47, 1992.

We introduce two new belief revision axioms: *partial monotonicity and consequence correctness*. We show that partial monotonicity is consistent with but independent of the full set of axioms for a *Gärdenfors belief revision system*. In contrast to the Gädenfors inconsistency results for certain monotonicity principles, we use partial monotonicity to inform a consistent formalization of the Ramsey test within a belief revision system extended by a conditional operator. We take this to be a technical dissolution of the well-known Gärdenfors dilemma. (edited)

**Paisana, Joao**. Discurso Científico e Poético na Filosofia de Aristóteles. *Philosophica (Portugal)*, 77-93, 1997.

Dans le présent travail on défend que le discours prédicatif (*Logos apophantikos*) est subordonné au discours non-prédicatif, qu'il présuppose. C'est l'étude de la structure "en tant que" (structure de l'expérience—*Als Struktur*) qui la montre. La structure "en tant que" apophantique s'enracine dans l'expérience de la substance. La structure "en tant que" herméneutique renvoye à une dimension communicative (tradition et pré-compréhension du monde). (edited)

AUTHOR INDEX 829 Palubicka, Anna

**Paisana, Joao**. Sartre e o pensamento de Marx. *Philosophica (Portugal)*, 83-97, 1993.

Après un rapide exposé du trajet politique de J.P. Sartre et de la revue *Temps Modernes* on se questionne sur les rapports tardifs entre la philosophie et la pensée politique chez le philosophe. Il faut donc revenir à *L'être et le néant* et essayer de comprendre pourquoi cet ouvrage s'est terminé avec une promesse qui n'a pas été soutenue par l'auteur: la formulation d'une *morale*. Selon *L'être et le néant* seulement une *morale de situation* est soutenable. D'une autre côté, *l'universalité* est l'exigence première pour la formulation de la morale. Ainsi, pour qu'une morale devienne possible il faut d'abord *universaliser la situation* de l'homme. Mais si on accepte, avec Marx, que dans une société divisée en classes c'est exactement cette division qui ne permet pas l'universalité de la situation, il devient clair que l'abolition des classes est la condition exigée par l'universalisation de la situation et, donc, par la morale. *L'engagement politique*, visant l'abolition des classes sociales, devient alors la condition préalable à la formulation de la morale. Pour Sartre le socialisme et la morale sont possibles, ils ne sont pas nécessaires; l'alternative est donc: socialisme ou barbarie.

**Palacios, Juan Miguel** and Rovira, Rogelio. Noticia sobre la edición de las *Obras Completas* de Manuel García Morente. *An Seminar Hist Filosof*, 13, 285-290, 1996.

**Palavecino, Sergio R**. Nota sobre la certeza: Una discusión con Samuel Cabanchik. *Rev Latin de Filosof*, 22(2), 281-286, 1996.

**Palazón M, María Rosa**. La literatura como juego. *Analogia*, 11(1), 109-125, Ja-Je 97.

Like the game, the literature provides joy when it is written, read or listened. The literature is a game, understood as a creative activity submitted to rules. Literature and game cover various theoretical-practical functions and also cover the esthetic function which considers as primordial the creative and recreative activity and its product as ends and not only as means. As the religious ceremonial games, the literature mixes fantasies and direct references to reality. The oral literature sometimes is competitive; the written one, never. I study this topic on the basis of Kant, Schiller, Eugen Fink and H. G. Gadamer.

**Palca, Joseph**. Scientific Misconduct: Ill-Defined, Redefined. *Hastings Center Rep*, 26(5), 4, S-O 96.

**Palcsó, Mária**. Georg Lukács's Plans for an Ethics (in Hungarian). *Magyar Filozof Szemle*, 4-5-6, 395-405, 1996.

Die Ethik, die Interesse für die ethische Probleme hat das ganze Werk von Lukács György begleitet, aber erst am Abend seines Lebens hat er sich zu Arbeit gemacht, eine systematische "wissenschaftliche" Ethik zu schreiben. Warum will der alte Lukács Ethik schreiben? Die Forschung hat zur Beantwortung dieser Frage verschiedene Typen an Hypothesen aufgestellt, aber meiner Meinung nach kann keine von diesen eine vollkommen zufriedenstellende Antwort präsentieren. Ich glaube, die wirklichen Gründe sind im Verhältnis von Lukács zum Marxismus, in der damaligen Situation des Marxismus sowie in der "Onthologisierung" seiner eigenen Denkweise zu suchen. (edited)

**Pallascio, Richard** (& others) and LaFortune, Louise and Daniel, Marie-France. Y a-t-il de la place pour philosopher sur les mathématiques au collégial?. *Philosopher*, 18, 107-126, 1995.

Dans cet article, nous explorons l'idée de transférer l'approche de *Philosophie pour enfants* adaptée aux mathématiques à l'enseignement post-secondaire. Dans une expérience où cette approche a été utilisée auprès de jeunes du primaire, les élèves approfondissent grâce aux communautés de recherche, certains concepts utilisés en mathématiques (infini, abstrait, zéro, géométrie, définition, preuve, existence, découverte...). Nous proposons des idées de plans de discussion et d'activités pouvant être transférées à l'enseignement post-secondaire et portant sur: abstrait-concret, figures géométriques, comprendre et connaître. De cette réflexion, nous concluons que différentes disciplines comme les mathématiques auraient avantage à intégrer des éléments d'une approche philosophique et à organiser des communautés de recherche dans leurs cours afin de susciter le processus de réflexion critique des élèves sur les notions enseignées, mais aussi sur leurs apprentissages.

**Palmer, Craig T** and Steadman, Lyle B. Myths as Instructions from Ancestors: The Example of Oedipus. *Zygon*, 32(3), 341-350, S 97.

This essay proposes that traditional stories, or myths, can be seen as a way in which ancestors influence their descendant-leaving success by influencing the behavior of many generations of their descendants. The myth of Oedipus is used as an example of a traditional story aimed at promoting proper behavior and cooperation among kin. This interpretation of the Oedipus myth is contrasted with Freudian and structuralist interpretations. (edited)

**Palmer, Daniel E**. Kant's Refutation of Idealism. *Dialogue (PST)*, 39(2-3), 49-55, Ap 97.

Commentators have often regarded Kant's two separate refutations of idealism in the *Critique of Pure Reason* as fundamentally different or even contradictory in nature. Thus, for instance, one interpreter has stated that "Kant proves the exact opposite of what is asserted in the first edition" in the second. However, in this paper I argue that a careful reading of the refutations, bearing in mind what Kant has already established earlier in the *Critique*, shows that the two versions both provide viable arguments against the type of idealism with which Kant is concerned, and, as such, are also in no way incompatible with each other. Indeed, I show that the two versions of the refutation merely approach the same problem from two different perspectives that can be taken within the critical philosophy. (edited)

**Palmer, Richard E**. Husserl's Debate with Heidegger in the Margins of *Kant and the Problem of Metaphysics*. *Man World*, 30(1), 5-33, Ja 97.

Husserl received from Martin Heidegger a copy of his *Kant and the Problem of Metaphysics* in the summer of 1929 not long before Husserl had determined to reread Heidegger's writings in order to arrive at a definitive position on Heidegger's philosophy. With this in view, Husserl reread and made extensive marginal comments in *Being and Time* and *Kant and the Problem of Metaphysics*. This essay by the translator of the remarks in *KPM* offers some historical background and comment on the importance of the remarks in *KPM* and attempts to describe Husserl's counterposition to Heidegger on six issues that divided the two major twentieth century philosophers.

**Palmer-Fernandez, Gabriel**. *Deterrence and the Crisis in Moral Theory: An Analysis of the Moral Literature on the Nuclear Arms Debate*. New York, Lang, 1996.

The primary aim of this study is to examine the dominant views on the subject of deterrence and the use of nuclear weapons, compare them with each other, and consider objections that have or might be made against them. A second, more substantive aim is to show that nuclear weapons and war-fighting plans engender some disturbing moral dilemmas that call into question fundamental ways of thinking about morality and some of our common intuitions on the relation of intentions and actions. *Deterrence and the Crisis in Moral Theory* points to a profound conflict in moral theory between the ideals of character and the moral claims of politics. (publisher)

**Palmgren, Erik**. A Sheaf-Theoretic Foundation for Nonstandard Analysis. *Annals Pure Applied Log*, 85(1), 69-86, Ap 97.

A new foundation for constructive nonstandard analysis is presented. It is based on an extension of a sheaf-theoretic model of nonstandard arithmetic due to I. Moerdijk. The model consists of representable sheaves over a site of filter bases. Nonstandard characterizations of various notions from analysis are obtained: modes of convergence, uniform continuity and differentiability, and some topological notions. We also obtain some additional results about the model. As in the classical case, the order type of the nonstandard natural numbers is a dense set of copies of the integers. Every standard set has a hyperfinite enumeration of its standard elements in the model. All arguments are carried out within a constructive and predicative metatheory: Martin-Löf's type theory.

**Palonen, Kari**. Quentin Skinner's *Rhetoric of Conceptual Change*. *Hist Human Sci*, 10(2), 61-80, My 97.

Although Quentin Skinner has only recently written explicitly on rhetoric, a sort of 'rhetorical turn' is present already in his early work. The Austinian speech act theory serves him both as a linguistic version of the Weberian nominalism and as an action-theory of language similar to rhetoric. Skinner's disinterest in 'truth' in historical inquiries signifies a further link to the rhetorical tradition. So does also his analysis of ideological changes from the perspective of legitimacy. Finally, the specificity of Skinner's perspective to conceptual change, especially when compared with that of Reinhart Koselleck, can be characterized as rhetorical.

**Pálsson, Gísli** (ed) and Descola, Philippe (ed). *Nature and Society: Anthropological Perspectives*. New York, Routledge, 1996.

*Nature and Society* looks critically at the nature/society dichotomy and its place in human ecology and social theory. Rethinking the dualism means rethinking ecological anthropology and its notion of the relation between person and environment. *Nature and Society* focuses on the issue of the environment and its relations to humans. By inviting concern for sustainability, ethics, indigenous knowledge, animal rights and social context of science, this book will appeal to students of anthropology, human ecology and sociology. (publisher,edited)

**Palti, Elías José**. Frederic Jameson: ¿El marxismo el el Mäelstrom textualista?. *Agora (Spain)*, 15(1), 69-87, 1996.

Frederic Jameson is, no doubt, the author of one of the most audacious and provocative intellectual projects of our times. Departing from a Marxist basis, he attempts to incorporate the major contributions of the latest textualist theories and, at the same time, to reveal and overcome their inherent limitations. Few authors discuss his penetration, as well as few of them (Marxists or not) are convinced about the success, and indeed the legitimacy, of his attempt at revealing Marxism as the "untranscendable horizon," infinitely expandable and (potentially) able to subsume all the rest. As this article shows, there are good reasons for both recognition and criticism. However, as it is also exposed in it, even those tensions and inconsistencies internal to Jameson's own work are significative for his contenders, since they make manifest broader problems, not exclusive to his concept, but intrinsic to the so-called "linguistic turn" today under way in the American academic milieu.

**Palti, Elías José**. Hans Blumenberg: sobre la modernidad, la historia y los límites de la razón. *Rev Latin de Filosof*, 22(2), 291-330, 1996.

**Palti, Elías José**. Time, Modernity and Time Irreversibility. *Phil Soc Crit*, 23(5), 27-62, S 97.

As soon as 'modernity' was defined as a particular way of conceiving of time (the so-called 'time of modernity'), the questions of temporality came to be situated at the heart of the ongoing debate regarding the legitimacy or illegitimacy of the 'modern age'. This has, in turn, readily led to a no less passionate search for the assessment of modernity's foundations which are thought to rest in its typical sense of experiencing temporality. This polemic instance, however, involves polarized perspectives (from both sides) and the consequent risk, always present in dichotomous approaches, of oversimplifying the concepts at stake and smoothing over the intricacies of their history and meaning. Does there really exist something like a 'time of modernity'? This is the central question that the present article examines.

**Palubicka, Anna**. "Pragmatist Holism as an Expression of Another 'Disenchantment of the World'" in *Epistemology and History*, Zeidler-Janiszewska, Anna (ed), 99-112. Amsterdam, Rodopi, 1996.

Rorty's holism has two aspects: "extrinsic," physical, and "intrinsic," semantic or intentional. I am interested in the latter aspect only. It is supposed to be

Palus, Charles J 830 AUTHOR INDEX

"irreducible" to an "extrinsic" aspect. The entirety of "beliefs and desires" expressed by a relevant text (texts) is gradually formed within a framework of interpretive procedures that assume the "disquotatively" seen "truth" of the majority of sentences being interpreted, their coherence and accordance with the rules of a given "linguistic game." Particular "true beliefs" assemble around objects that are "postulated" by them: "true" sentences supposed to express those "beliefs" cluster around "centers of gravity" constituted by proper terms. The notion of reference of these terms is unnecessary and misleading: it is not the world that provides references, nor does it make sentences "true." I basically agree with that idea and consider it to be another step in the "disenchantment of the world" (Weber). But I see the necessity of taking into account the fact that "intrinsic" entirety of "beliefs" is grounded by "intrinsic" causality that works in practice and that this fact is distinguished in culture precisely by the term "reference."

**Palus, Charles J** and Horth, David M. Leading Creatively: The Art of Making Sense. *J Aes Educ*, 30(4), 53-68, Wint 96.

**Paluzzi, Antonio**. "Temporalità e filosofia umana-soggettiva-esistenziale" in *Il Concetto di Tempo: Atti del XXXII Congresso Nazionale della Società Filosofica Italiana,* Casertano, Giovanni (ed), 345-350. Napoli, Loffredo, 1997.

**Panichas, George E** (ed) and Gruen, Lori (ed). *Sex, Morality, and the Law.* New York, Routledge, 1997.

The book combines legal opinions and philosophical analysis to explore the controversial issues surrounding state control of sexual and reproductive behavior. This unique anthology focuses on six topics of enduring moral, social and legal concern: lesbian and gay sex, prostitution, pornography, abortion, sexual harassment and rape. Each section includes introductions by the editors and substantial excerpts from influential court decisions, such as *Bowers v. Hardwock, Roe v. Wade,* and *American Booksellers v. Hudnut,* as well as recent court decisions *Romer v. Evans* and *Casey v. Planned Parenthood.* (publisher)

**Pannenberg, Wolfhart**. Geist als Feld—nur eine Metapher?. *Theol Phil*, 71(2), 257-260, 1996.

Against a merely metaphorical value of such language, however, it is argued that the fundamental requirement of a rigorously conceptual use of field concepts is only their relatedness to the concepts of space and time. If space and time have a theological dimension or even a theological basis, as it was affirmed since Plotinus for eternity as presupposed in any concept of time and for the divine immensity with relation to space, then it seems meaningful to speak of the divine "spirit" in terms of a comprehensive field, within which all finite events and entities occur. Such a use of the field concept does not confound theological and scientific conceptualities or realities, but rather points to the transcendental presupposition of physical fields as well as of geometrical and physical time and space. (edited)

**Pantaleo, Pasquale**. "Logica ed ermeneutica: Una precisazione necessaria nell'interpretazione dei contenuti della conoscenza" in *Momenti di Storia della Logica e di Storia della Filosofia,* Guetti, Carla (ed), 247-254. Roma, Aracne Editrice, 1996.

**Papa-Grimaldi, Alba**. Why Mathematical Solutions of Zeno's Paradoxes Miss the Point: Zeno's One and Many Relation and Parmenides' Prohibition. *Rev Metaph*, 50(2), 299-314, D 96.

Mathematical solutions to Zeno's paradoxes of motion have been proposed with regularity since their first formulation. This paper argues that such solutions miss, and always will miss, the point of Zeno's arguments—they ignore Zeno's concern for the one-many relation, or rather the lack of it and Parmenides' prohibition. To illustrate the argument two proposed mathematical solutions, involving infinitesimals and indeterminate forms are analysed. The main conclusion is that, concrete plurality remains unconceptualized and the mathematical plurality is just a repetition of the unit—despite the correctness of the mathematics, no metaphysical sense can be made out of mathematical sense and any claim to the contrary is unjustified.

**Papacchini, Angelo**. "Comunitarismo, Liberalismo y Derechos Humanos" in *Liberalismo y Comunitarismo: Derechos Humanos y Democracia,* Monsalve Solórzano, Alfonso (ed), 231-261. 36-46003 València, Alfons el Magnànim, 1996.

**Papacchini, Angelo**. The Right to Life and the Death Penalty (Spanish). *Rev Filosof (Venezuela)*, Supp(2-3), 49-77, 1996.

This paper covers a very controversial topic in Latin America where as quoted from the author, "violence often transforms life into a precarious commodity." Based on various writings it tries to establish the right to live as opposed to the establishment of capital punishment, recognizing life as a precious and privileged commodity which permits the exercise of other rights. The proposal considered here is the dialectic of recognition on which "the reasonable explanation of the obligation to respect the life of others" is based. This recognition underlies the nonviolent imperative and respect for life and liberty.

**Papastathis, Charalambos**. Tolerance and Law in Countries with an Established Church. *Ratio Juris*, 10(1), 108-113, Mr 97.

The author argues that the cohabitation of an established church and nonestablished ones is bound to generate unfair discrimination and abridges religious tolerance which is a European achievement and an indispensable part of Western political and constitutional culture. In defiance of the strong traditions that survive in certain European countries, the institution of the established church should wither away.

**Papastephanou, Marianna**. Communicative Action and Philosophical Foundations: Comments on the Apel-Habermas Debate. *Phil Soc Crit*, 23(4), 41-69, Jl 97.

Whereas Apel's controversial conclusions concerning foundationalism are widely debated in Germany, in the English-speaking world the few references to his work content themselves with merely presenting him as one of Habermas's associates. My exposition of the distinction between Apel's and Habermas's theories will be focused on their justification of the priority of communicative over strategic action, their divergent accounts of pragmatics and their different underlying anthropological assumptions. Finally, both theories are regarded as promising *alternatives* within the same paradigm of thought, as both critically engage with a number of pressing sociopolitical and philosophical issues. (edited)

**Pape, Helmut**. "The Logical Structure of Idealism: C.S. Peirce's Search for a Logic of Mental Processes" in *The Rule of Reason: The Philosophy of Charles Sanders Peirce,* Forster, Paul (ed), 153-184. Toronto, Univ of Toronto Pr, 1997.

The thesis of this paper is that one of Peirce's most important contribution to philosophy is a variety of idealistic metaphysics, which I call "logical idealism" (LI). LI claims that mental and physical processes have the same logical structure: there is a triadic structure exemplified both in experience and in matter. I argue that the requirements for structural unity of processes (e.g., sequential ordering in time, continuity) connect the logics and semantics Peirce's metaphysical and logical conception of mind. Using of logical, phenomenological and metaphysical arguments LI provides a logical basis for idealistic conception of reality understood as an evolving process.

**Pape, Helmut**. Love's Power and the Causality of Mind: C.S. Peirce on the Place of Mind and Culture in Evolution. *Trans Peirce Soc*, 33(1), 59-90, Wint 97.

Peirce's account of love as *agape* is interpreted as a theory of cultural evolution that extends his semiotics into a metaphysical account of the force and function of culture: Love is a sympathetic attraction exerted on people by other people, things or ideas that creates the social and cognitive habits of the heart that connects people and projects. Human culture develops only because of such a growth of sympathetic forces. Such a process of social communication and individual participation makes culture into an evolutionary force in the universe. Agapism is also explained in its relevance or contemporary problems in ethics, social and political philosophy.

**Pape, Helmut**. Perspectivity: G. W. Leibniz on the Representation of Ontological Structure. *J Speculative Phil*, 11(1), 1-19, 1997.

Leibniz uses in his ontological and epistemological writings the language of perspectivity: he speaks about point of view, and perspectival representations, reflections and projective transformations of pictures. This paper argues that this is not just a happy metaphor for the distribution and differentiation of knowledge. I try to show that Leibniz knew about the systematic unity of Desargues's projective geometry and that his concept of perspectivity is an interpretation of Desarguean geometry as a functional semantical model for his epistemic ontology. I claim that perspectivity gives us the *only* systematic and consistent explanation for the relation between monads and the infinity of knowledge they contain.

**Papi, Fulvio**. Per una ontologia del ricordare. *Iride*, 8(14), 123-130, Ap 95.

**Papineau, David**. Doubtful Intuitions. *Mind Lang*, 11(1), 130-132, Mr 96.

This note argues that intuitions about Swampman do not discredit teleological theories of representation. These intuitions are manifestations of hidden philosophical assumptions which teleo-semanticists can reject. (Aren't all philosophical assumptions ultimately backed by their conformity to intuitions? No. As central planks in overall scientific theory, they rest ultimately on empirical support.) Everyday intuition matters only when we ask whether teleosemantics eliminates or reduces our antecedent notion of representation. If the teleological theory disagreed with most everyday intuitions, it would eliminate the antecedent notion. Still, it could overturn a few intuitions, like those about Swampman, and still qualify as a reduction.

**Papineau, David**. Uncertain Decisions and the Many-Minds Interpretation of Quantum Mechanics. *Monist*, 80(1), 97-117, Ja 97.

Why act on probabilities? It seems obvious that we want a) desired results, not b) that desired results be maximally probable. But what then is the rationale for choosing actions that ensure (b), but not (a)? Notoriously, there is not good answer within conventional thought. However, this conundrum is dissolved within the many-minds interpretation of quantum mechanics. On the many-minds interpretation, all results with nonzero probability occur, and there is no further issue of which actually occurs. So (b) becomes the only criterion for successful action, and the tension with (a) falls away.

**Papineau, David** and Beebee, Helen. Probability as a Guide to Life. *J Phil*, 94(5), 217-243, My 97.

The article is concerned with the objective constraints on rational agents' degrees of belief. Views which regard single-case chances as the primary providers of objective constraints cannot accommodate agents whose information does not determine single-case chances. The authors argue that the degree of belief in an outcome should correspond instead to its objective probability relative to those relevant features of the world which the agent knows about. This avoids the central problem facing the single-case view, but nonetheless preserves the intuition that agents should set their degrees of belief equal to single-case chances when they are in a position to do so.

**Pappas, Gregory Fernando**. Dewey's Moral Theory: Experience as Method. *Trans Peirce Soc*, 33(3), 520-556, Sum 97.

I argue that without the background understanding of Dewey's philosophic method, one cannot understand how novel and distinct is Dewey's ethics from any other ethical theory in this century that might claim to be empirical. There is much to learn from Dewey about how to proceed in an empirical philosophical inquiry about morality.

**Pappin III, Joseph**. Freedom and Solidarity in Sartre and Simon. *Amer Cath Phil Quart*, 70(4), 569-584, Autumn 96.

**Papterra Limongi, Maria Isabel**. A Relaçao entre a Razao e as Paixoes na Antropologia Hobbesiana. *Discurso*, 24, 147-158, 1994.

Este texto pretende indicar que a teoria da soberania hobbesiana nao tem por funçao resolver, a favor da razao, um conflito entre ela e as paixoes anti-sociais, mas um desnível entre o cálculo prudencial e racional, entre os planos dos fatos e de sua expressao verbal, ou entre dois modos de o pensamento se colocar a serviço das paixoes.

**Papy, Jan**. Locke's Criticism on Robert Filmer about the Origin of Private Property. *Tijdschr Filosof*, 59(2), 253-275, Je 97.

Locke's philosophical statement concerning the status of private property and its consequences can be understood in a more proper way by replacing his views in their historical and philosophical context. In this way, Locke's "discourse on government" seems to be an ingenious adaptation of the discourse of 17th Century political philosophy. By indicating Locke's use of the natural right tradition and by contrasting Locke's views with Robert Filmer's *Patriarcha* (1680), one is able to see where his philosophical and political views are conventional or progressive. The question why Locke used and assimilated arguments from Grotius, Suarez and Pufendorf to reject Filmer's Adamite theory and to legitimate private property in a nonabsolutist way is, therefore, of central interest. So, Locke's natural right to *preservation* as fundamental for his right to revolution against absolutism, seems to be an appeal to a commonly accepted notion from natural law, turned upside down to an exclusive right in the framework of common property. (edited)

**Paquette, Éric**. Husserl et le *Ichprinzip*: Le tournant en question. *Horiz Phil*, 7(2), 91-105, Spr 97.

**Paracchini, Franco**. Sorpresa e giustificazione: Una discussione dell'esempio weberiano della madre intemperante. *Itinerari Filosof*, 3(5), 15-32, Ja-Ap 93.

**Parascandola, Mark**. Chances, Individuals and Toxic Torts. *J Applied Phil*, 14(2), 147-157, 1997.

In this paper I argue that the law has taken an ill-founded, skeptical stance towards statistical evidence for causation in toxic tort cases, making the task of plaintiffs unjustly difficult. I address two frequently cited skeptical claims about statistical evidence and argue that they are unfounded as applied in tort law. I conclude that the skeptical stance results from a failure to distinguish physical chances from epistemic probabilities and that such a distinction is necessary if plaintiffs are to have a chance of prevailing. (edited)

**Parascandola, Mark**. Evidence and Association: Epistemic Confusion in Toxic Tort Law. *Proc Phil Sci Ass*, 3(Suppl), S168-S176, 1996.

**Pardo Bazán, Emilia**. Stuart Mill. *Telos (Spain)*, 1(3), 145-158, O 92.

**Paredes Martín, M.ª del Carmen**. "El concepto de vida en el joven Hegel" in *El inicio del Idealismo alemán,* Market, Oswaldo, 415-425. Madrid, Ed Complutense, 1996.

This paper provides an analysis of Hegel's writings "Die Liebe" and "Der Geist des Christentums" (1798/99), from the Frankfurt period, on the concept of life. In the revised version of these texts there is the first occurrence of the Hegelian motion of life as a triadic circle which will be interesting for his later concept of dialectics. The comparison between the first and the revised versions of these texts as are known for the time being helps to understand Hegel's development in the metaphysical comprehension of life, under the influence of Hölderlin and Schelling.

**Pareira Martins, Lilian Al-Chueyr** and De Andrade Martins, Roberto. Lamarck's Method (in Portuguese). *Trans/Form/Acao*, 19, 115-140, 1996.

This paper studies Lamarck's scientific method both from the point of view of his methodological discourse and according to his scientific *praxis*. Lamarck's methodology is compared to Condillac's as well as to that of the idéologues—a group in which Lamarck is usually included. The analysis of this paper shows that Lamarck's methodological discourse is very similar to Condillac's, but his scientific *praxis* does not follow this view. Instead of following an empiricist approach, Lamarck's work is grounded upon general metaphysical principles concerning nature. Thus, from the idéologues' point of view, Lamarck's work should have been rejected—and that is what really happened—as being a mere metaphysical system (système)—in the pejorative sense employed by Condillac's followers. However, the present work argues that thus is in fact an important and innovative aspect of Lamarck's work and that it leads to the emergence of modern evolutionism.

**Parekh, Bhikhu**. Dilemmas of a Multicultural Theory of Citizenship. *Constellations*, 4(1), 54-62, Ap 97.

This article is a critical discussion of Will Kymlicka's new book, *Multicultural Citizenship*. The author argues that the book suffers from several limitations, arising mainly out of the fact that it is an attempt to articulate a liberal theory of multiculturalism. Since it is a liberal theory, it carries no conviction with nonliberals. Also, for that very reason it analyzes other cultures in liberal terms and distorts them. Kymlicka is able to defend other cultures in terms that they neither recognize nor respect. The author concludes by arguing that Will Kymlicka's discussion of the rights of national minorities, immigrants and so on suffers from a lack of coherent theory.

**Parent, David J** (trans) and Waldenfels, Bernhard. *Order in the Twilight*. Athens, Ohio Univ Pr, 1996.

Order in the twilight means that the idea of an all-encompassing or fundamental order comes to an end. Instead every order shows certain limits, selecting certain possibilities while excluding others. Closed orders are replaced by open-ended orders where interlocations and interactions take place, linking up and responding to the other's appeal or challenge in terms of responsive rationality. These events are no longer centered on a subject. New orders are inaugurated by deviation from existing orders, starting from certain key events. Finally, the ordinary continues to be perturbed by the extraordinary and the impossible. Possibility does not have the last word.

**Parent, William A** and Prior, William J. Thomson on the Moral Specification of Rights. *Phil Phenomenol Res*, 56(4), 837-845, D 96.

In this paper we offer a limited defense of the "moral specification" view of rights in response to criticisms of Judith Jarvis Thomson. The moral specification view states that moral rights embody principles of justice, so their meaning is specifiable by those principles. Our defense is limited in that we do not attempt to demonstrate the overall superiority of this view to others, including the view currently advocated by Thomson. We only attempt to show that the advocate of moral specifications (MS) has a plausible response to two objections she raises.

**Parentelli, Gladys**. Women of the Popular Sectors and Ecofeminist Ethics in Latin America (Spanish). *Fronesis*, 2(2), 171-188, D 95.

It has been tried to analyze the social condition of women of the popular sectors in Latin America and of the ethics of those women at fulfilling a role in preserving the environment. The author frames her analysis in elements which fall on the Latin American social condition, such as the consequences of the Spanish colonization and the political and economical powers ruling the area.

**Parfit, Derek**. Acts and Outcomes: A Reply to Boonin-Vail. *Phil Pub Affairs*, 25(4), 308-317, Fall 96.

**Parfit, Derek** and Broome, John. Reasons and Motivation. *Aris Soc*, Supp(71), 98-146, 1997.

**Pargetter, Robert** and Bigelow, John. The Validation of Induction. *Austl J Phil*, 75(1), 62-76, Mr 97.

**Parikh, Rohit**. Vague Predicates and Language Games. *Theoria (Spain)*, 11(27), 97-107, S 96.

Attempts to give a logic or semantics for vague predicates and to defuse the Sorites paradoxes have been largely a failure. We point out yet *another* problem with these predicates which has not been remarked on before, namely that different people do and must use these predicates in individuality different ways. Thus even if there *were* a semantics for vague predicates, people would not be able to *share* it. To explain the occurrence nonetheless of these troublesome predicates in language, we propose a different approach based on asking the question, "How do these vague predicates help people to communicate with each other?" We show that in general, even though different people assign different extensions to vague predicates, they usually benefit from receiving information framed in terms of them.

**Parini, Jay**. The Lessons of Theory. *Phil Lit*, 21(1), 91-101, Ap 97.

**Park, Kyungjoo** and Moyes, Glen D. Chief Financial Officers' Perceptions Concerning the IMA's Standards of Ethical Conduct. *J Bus Ethics*, 16(2), 189-194, F 97.

Do chief financial officers (CFOs) of publicly held corporations agree with the Institute of Management Accountants' (IMA) Standards of Ethical Conduct and are they willing to adopt them? To address these issues, a survey was conducted concerning the standards. The IMA issued the Pronouncement of Standards in June, 1982. The surveyed CFOs agreed with the majority of the standards. However, many CFOs commented that some of the standards of Ethical Conduct were difficult to implement in the real world. The CFOs critically commented that all the Standards were too general, too vague, or did not cover the grey areas that occur in real world situations. (edited)

**Park, Ynhui**. *Rationality* and *Human Dignity*—Confucius, Kant and Scheffler on the Ultimate Aim of Education. *Stud Phil Educ*, 16(1-2), 7-18, Ja-Ap 97.

This paper argues that certain influential views to the contrary, without an overall aim of education no philosophy of education is neither complete nor intelligible. On this assumption, it intends to show I) that in spite of the absence of the explicit statement, a certain view on the ultimate aim of education implicitly underlies all specific educational views of Professor Scheffler, which should be defined in terms of rationality constituting human dignity and which the author of the paper is convinced to be the most adequate among other competing views and II) that in this respect Professor Scheffler stands on the same line at least with two great philosophers of education: Confucius and Dewey.

**Parke, Dennis V**. Ethical Aspects of the Safety of Medicines and Other Social Chemicals. *Sci Eng Ethics*, 1(3), 283-298, Jl 95.

The historical background of the discovery of adverse health effects of medicines, food additives, pesticides, and other chemicals is reviewed, and the development of national and international regulations and testing procedures to protect the public against the toxic effects of these drugs and chemicals is outlined. Ethical considerations of the safety evaluation of drugs and chemicals by human experimentation and animal toxicity studies, ethical problems associated with clinical trials, with the falsification of clinical and toxicological data, and with inadequate experimental methodology, are reviewed, and the ethics of the marketing of drugs and their postmarketing surveillance, are similarly considered. These ethical problems are illustrated with many specific examples, including the drugs neoarsphenamine, chloramphenicol, thalidomide, diethyl stilboestrol and benoxaprofen.

**Parker, Kelly A**. "Pragmatism and Environmental Thought" in *Environmental Pragmatism,* Light, Andrew (ed), 21-37. New York, Routledge, 1996.

This essay introduces the key insight of "environmental pragmatism": classical American pragmatism is a philosophy of environments and, as such, is a fruitful framework for addressing issues in ecophilosophy. Part I of the essay outlines the main features of pragmatism. These features are presented as critical responses to familiar positions in epistemology, metaphysics and value theory. Part II offers critical consideration of the major issues in current ecophilosophy, from within the pragmatic framework. The question of a metaphysical grounding for environmental ethics is noted, in particular, as an area of environmental philosophy where pragmatism may have the most to offer.

**Parkes, Graham**. "Nietzsche and Nishitani on Nihilism and Tradition" in *Culture and Self,* Allen, Douglas (ed), 131-144. Boulder, Westview Pr, 1997.

Superficial accounts of Nietzsche's nihilism present him as a mere iconoclast who rejects and negates all cultural traditions. A reading of relevant sections of *The Self-Overcoming of Nihilism* (1949) by the Japanese philosopher Nishitani Keiji gives a different and more interesting picture. By focusing on the idea of *amor fati*, Nishitani shows how the break with the past that is necessary for the true self to emerge is followed in Nietzsche by a moment of creative appropriation of elements from the tradition. By considering Nishitani's application of Nietzsche's ideas about nihilism to the case of contemporary Japan, we can see how such creative appropriation might work between as well as within cultural traditions.

**Parkes, Graham**. The Putative Fascism of the Kyoto School and the Political Correctness of the Modern Academy. *Phil East West*, 47(3), 305-336, Jl 97.

There is a current fashion among some prominent Japanologists to brand Kyoto School philosophers as mere fascist or imperialist ideologues. This essay examines these charges and criticizes the critics, endeavoring thereby to encourage a more responsible evaluation of the relationship between philosophical and political discourse.

**Parkes, Graham** (trans) and May, Reinhard. *Heidegger's Hidden Sources: East Asian Influences on His Work*. New York, Routledge, 1996.

The book documents for the first time Heidegger's remarkable debt to East Asian philosophy. In this groundbreaking study, Reinhard May shows conclusively that Martin Heidegger borrowed some of the major ideas of his philosophy—on occasion almost word for word—from German translations of Chinese Daoist and Zen Buddist classics. The discovery of this astonishing appropriation of non-Western sources will have important consequences for future interpretations of Heidegger's work. Moreover, it shows Heidegger as a pioneer of comparative philosophy and transcultural thinking. (publisher)

**Parkin, Andrew C**. On the Practical Relevance of Habermas's Theory of Communicative Action. *Soc Theor Pract*, 22(3), 417-441, Fall 96.

**Parkinson, G H R**. Rethinking Leibniz. *Brit J Hist Phil*, 4(2), 399-407, S 96.

**Parra, Lisímaco**. Poder Pensar y "Poder Querer": Acerca de Moral y Prudencia en Kant. *Ideas Valores*, 112-119, D 96.

**Parra, Lisímaco**. Trabajo Filosófico y Comunidad Filosófica. *Ideas Valores*, 67-78, Ag 97.

**Parret, Herman**. Kant sur la musique. *Rev Phil Louvain*, 95(1), 24-43, F 97.

Music according to Kant in the *Critique of Judgment* has an ambiguous status in the hierarchy of the fine arts: it is valued highly as a language of the affects, but finds itself at the bottom of the classification due to its lack of durability and of "urbanity." The certainly intuitive musicology of Kant is based on fundamental options: music is above all a matter of sonority, and it is the tonality of sounds that accounts for their quality; pure sound is natural sound, that of the voice. Kant does not discuss the temporality essential to music nor the components of harmony, rhythm or tempo. The musicologist Christian Friedrich Michaelis made us of Kant's conception of music as early as 1795: he showed himself to be more Kantian than Kant himself. (edited)

**Parsons, Howard L**. The Philosophy of Barrows Dunham: The Progress of an American Radical. *Trans Peirce Soc*, 33(2), 410-444, Spr 97.

The thought of Dunham (1905-1995) was an independent, creative response to: his father, liberal minister and philosopher; Warner Fite at Princeton, the idealists, James, Whitehead, and the positivists; the 1929 stock market crash and the Great Depression; and Marx and Engels. *Man against Myth* (1949) analyzed social illustrations; *Giant in Chains* (1953) showed the bearing of philosophical thought on concrete problems of everyday life. Dismissed in 1953 by Temple University for refusing to testify before the House Unamerican Activities Committee but vindicated in the courts, Dunham was never rehired. His most comprehensive work was *Heroes and Heretics* (1964).

**Parsons, Terence**. "Fregean Theories of Truth and Meaning" in *Frege: Importance and Legacy,* Schirn, Matthias (ed), 371-409. Hawthorne, de Gruyter, 1996.

A semantic theory of natural language with indirect contexts is given that satisfies Tarski's material adequacy condition for truth and also yields a theory of meaning that satisfies the adequacy condition for meaning, entailing for every sentence S a statement of the form: 'S' means that S. The theory is independent of the doctrine that sense determines reference. (Frege's presentation relation is the reference of a term representing propositional truth.) Frege held that in a doubly embedded context there is a double shift in expressing and referring; a simpler view is that re-embedding a term causes no further semantic shifts and that a term has at most one (or two) distinct senses. Under certain conditions these theories satisfy a natural requirement of learnability and they are "outwardly equivalent" to one another.

**Parsons, Terence**. Supposition as Quantification *versus* Supposition as Global Quantificational Effect. *Topoi*, 16(1), 41-63, Mr 97.

This paper follows up a suggestion by Paul Vincent Spade that there were two medieval theories of the modes of personal supposition. I suggest that early

work by Sherwood and others was a study of quantifiers: their semantics and the effects of context on inferences that can be made from quantified terms. Later, in the hands of Burley and others, it changed into a study of something else, a study of what I call *global quantificational effect*. (edited)

**Parvu, Ilie**. The Unity of Scientific Knowledge in the Framework of a Typological Approach of Theories. *Theoria (Spain)*, 11(27), 7-17, S 96.

The paper proposes a typology of the scientific theories based on the modality of mathematizing (relying on the kind of mathematics which participates to the theory edification and the level of mathematical organizing of the theoretical frame). This gives us, like the classification of the geometries from the famous "Erlagen Program" initiated by Felix Klein, an internal principle for the connection of the different forms or levels of the theorizing, a constructive basis for the understanding of the complex structural nets of the mature scientific disciplines.

**Pasanen, Outi** and Sallis, John. Double Truths: An Interview with John Sallis. *Man World*, 30(1), 107-114, Ja 97.

This interview is devoted to such topics as the end of metaphysics, the role of imagination in addressing the limits of metaphysics and the implications for the concept of mimesis and for the understanding of art as mimesis. There are also discussions of John Sallis's current work on painting and on the *chora* in Plato's *Timaeus*.

**Pascalev, Assya**. Images of Death and Dying in the Intensive Care Unit. *J Med Human*, 17(4), 219-236, Wint 96.

The paper explores the two metaphors of death and dying that dominate the professional imagination of medical workers in the Intensive Care Unit—the war metaphor (representing death as the chief enemy of medicine), and the "Cheechee" metaphor (representing dying as torture). The cultural values and professional dispositions underlying the metaphors are identified, the correlation between the medical perceptions of death and medical practice is examined, and the effects of these perceptions on patients are evaluated. I argue that the metaphors display an inner tension and fail to serve the dying patients. The metaphors signal the need for reconsidering the priorities of medicine to meet the needs of the dying individuals.

**Pascual, José A**. "Ortega entre Literatos y Lingüistas" in *Política y Sociedad en José Ortega y Gasset: En Torno a "Vieja y Nueva Política",* Lopez de la Vieja, Maria Teresa (ed), 51-68. Barcelona, Anthropos, 1997.

**Pascucci, Enrico**. La providencia y la ubicación de Vico en la historia del pensamiento. *Cuad Vico*, 5/6, 313-321, 1995/96.

This paper attempts to provide a rough analysis of the manyfold ways according to which the Vichian notion of providence has been clarified. It endeavors to emphasize both the recurrent and still lasting antagonism between the immanent and the transcendent interpretation of Vico's thought. Also it is about the different approaches in which scholars have tried to assess his philosophical contribution. The purpose of this work was to summarize the main ideas of my doctoral thesis. (G.B. Vico: the establishment of the natural order through the notion of providence).

**Pasek, Joanna** and Beckerman, Wilfred. Plural Values and Environmental Valuation. *Environ Values*, 6(1), 65-86, F 97.

The paper discusses some of the criticisms of contingent valuation (CV) and allied techniques for estimating the intensity of peoples' preferences for the environment. The weakness of orthodox utilitarian assumptions in economics concerning the commensurability of all items entering into peoples' choices is discussed. The concept of commensurability is explored as is the problem of rational choice between incommensurate alternatives. While the frequent claim that the environment has some unique moral intrinsic value is unsustainable, its preservation often raises ethical and other motivations that are not commensurate with the values that people place on ordinary marketable goods. Nevertheless, CV is also claimed to have some advantages and it is concluded that little progress will be made in this area until both sides in the debate recognize what is valid in their opponents' arguments.

**Paske, Gerald H**. The Emancipation of Reason. *J Value Inq*, 30(3), 399-414, S 96.

**Pasnau, Robert**. Petri Iohannis Olivi Tractatus de Verbo (Peter John Olivi's Tractatus de Verbo). *Fran Stud*, 53, 121-153, 1993.

An edition of the beginning of Olivi's commentary on the Gospel of John, where he discusses at length his theory of the mental word (*verbum*). In an extended introduction to the text, I analyze the philosophical significance of Olivi's account for philosophy of mind.

**Pasnau, Robert**. *Theories of Cognition in the Later Middle Ages*. New York, Cambridge Univ Pr, 1997.

This book is a major contribution to the history of philosophy in the later medieval period (1250-1350). It focuses on cognitive theory, a subject of intense investigation during these years. In fact, many of the issues that dominate philosophy of mind and epistemology today—intentionality, mental representation, skepticism, realism—were hotly debated in the later medieval period. The book offers a careful analysis of these debates, primarily through the work of Thomas Aquinas, Peter John Olivi, and William Ockham. Both Olivi and Ockham attempt to reconceptualize cognition along direct realist lines, criticizing in the process standard Aristotelian accounts of the sort proposed by Aquinas. (publisher, edited)

**Pasnau, Robert**. Who Needs an Answer to Skepticism?. *Amer Phil Quart*, 33(4), 421-432, O 96.

**Pasniczek, Jacek**. "The Relational vs. Directional Conception of Intentionality" in *Epistemology and History,* Zeidler-Janiszewska, Anna (ed), 373-380. Amsterdam, Rodopi, 1996.

The paper presents two main theories of intentionality that can be an extension of Brentano's famous thesis. In particular, these theories correspond to two possible ways of comprehending Husserl's conception of intentionality (the Gurwitschian and Follesdalian one). The author argues that the two theories and thus the two interpretations of Husserl's views, are basically consistent with each other.

**Pasniczek, Jacek**. The Simplest Meinongian Logic. *Log Anal*, 36(144), 329-342, S-D 93.

The Meinongian logic is a logic which accommodates main principles of Meinong's theory of objects. This principles give rise to a very extensive ontology which contains various kind of nonexistent entities (e.g., incomplete and impossible ones). In the paper quite a simple Meinongian logic is developed. This logic has the following features: 1) it is extensional, 2) it differs slightly from the classical first-order logic, 3) it is a first-order system, 4) it is closer to the natural language than classical logic, 5) it is much more simple than Meinongian systems created by T. Parsons and E. Zalta.

**Pasquero, Jean**. Business Ethics and National Identity in Quebec: Distinctiveness and Directions. *J Bus Ethics*, 16(6), 621-633, Ap 97.

This essay will not present a survey of business ethics literature in Quebec; it will rather try to analyze the nature and meaning of this distinctiveness for both practice and theory. The critical difference is that, unlike the U.S. where it is defined largely in individual terms, in Quebec business ethics is tightly linked to one central issue, the preservation of a "national identity." Therefore, understanding the obligations of business people and firms requires to put them within a societal context. (edited)

**Passell, Dan**. Hume's Arguments for His Sceptical Doubts. *J Phil Res*, 22, 409-422, Ap 97.

In his *Enquiry Concerning Human Understanding*, Section 4, "Sceptical Doubts Concerning the Operations of the Understanding," Hume offers three conceptual arguments against causes necessitating their effects. These are a difference argument, a logical or relations of ideas argument, and a factual argument. I contend that the logical argument rests on the difference argument and that the factual argument, when seen for what it is, is simply the difference argument. In effect the three arguments reduce to one.

**Passell, Dan**. What Makes Something Practically Worth Thinking About. *Inquiry (USA)*, 15(3), 65-73, Spr 96.

In decision theory in order to decide on a rational strategy for action, one has to assign utilities to possible outcomes and to assign probabilities relating evidence to states of nature. Often one is not able to do either. Yet one may still wish to decide whether a given matter is worth thinking about. The standpoint of this paper is prior to that of decision theory. Its thesis is that there are four features to consider in making the whether-to-think decision: importance, uncertainty, amenability to reason and amenability to action.

**Passerin d'Entrèves, Maurizio**. Democracy: A Convergent Value? Comments on Sheldon Leader and Ernesto Garzón Valdés. *Ratio Juris*, 10(2), 193-198, Je 97.

In this paper, the author contends that Leader's attempt to ground the value of toleration on a common understanding of democracy faces a number of fundamental obstacles. Such obstacles could only be overcome if both liberals and their opponents were to reach an agreement on the value of democracy and thereby converge in their support of toleration. The author shows that far from providing a common ground that liberals and their opponents can share, the so-called "shareable understanding" of democracy appeals primarily to liberals. The author also argues that Garzón Valdés's thesis that democracy is the system best suited to the flourishing of toleration faces the same kind of difficulty, namely, that not every group in a liberal constitutional regime can be convinced of the priority of democratic principles over their other fundamental value-commitments.

**Passerin d'Entrèves, Maurizio** (ed) and Benhabib, Seyla (ed). *Habermas and the Unfinished Project of Modernity*. Cambridge, MIT Pr, 1997.

This collection of ten essays offers the first systematic assessment of *The Philosophical Discourse of Modernity*, Jürgen Habermas's masterful defense of the rational potential of the modern age. An opening essay by Maurizio Passerin d'Entrèves orients the debate between Habermas and the postmodernists by identifying two different senses of responsibility. Habermas's own essay discusses the themes of his book in the context of a critical engagement with neoconservative cultural and political trends. The main body of essays is divided into two sections—*Critical Rejoinders* and *Thematic Reformulations*. These essays offer an important set of perspectives on Habermas's position by philosophers, social scientists, intellectual historians, and literary critics. (publisher, edited)

**Pastor, Félix-Alejandro**. La cuestión de lo Incondicionado: Dialéctica y revelación de lo sagrado en Paul Tillich. *Gregorianum*, 78(2), 267-308, 1997.

La *question de l'Inconditionné* est développée par Paul Tillich dans une *Religionsphilosophie* pensée comme Logique de la raison religieuse et comme Théorie du sens, dans une perspective théonome. La présente étude analyse le projet du premier Tillich, après l'avoir situé en relation au paradigme de la Modernité. Tillich mène un double combat, face à l'*hybris religieuse* de l'hétéronomie et à l'*hybris culturelle* de la pure autonomie. Partant de la tension fondamentale entre identité mystique et différence éthique, le projet de Tillich souligne l'aspect paradoxal et dialectique de la religion, son vouloir d'atteindre le contenu inconditionné à travers des formes conditionnées, sa résistance à être pur objet et concept d'une science. Dépassant le paradigme de la Modernité, Tillich construit une Philosophie de la Religion située dans le système des sciences, mais non fondée sur le conditionné, mais au contraire sur l'Inconditionné. (edited)

**Pastor Pérez, Miguel Antonio**. Grocio, por derecho. *Cuad Vico*, 5/6, 351-355, 1995/96.

This is a critical study of Francesco M. De Sanctis's *Grozio: Diritto naturale e diritto civile*, published by Istituto Suor Orsola Benincasa, Naples, 1994, 56 pp. (edited)

**Pastor Pérez, Miguel Antonio**. Igualidad no es fraternidad. *Cuad Vico*, 5/6, 367-373, 1995/96.

This is a bibliographical study of Francesco de Sanctis's *Stato e Diritti* and introductory elements for the course of philosophy of law, Bulzioni Editore, Roma, 1994, 135 pp. (edited)

**Pastor Pérez, Miguel Antonio**. La insoportable liviandad del ser (político). *Cuad Vico*, 5/6, 325-337, 1995/96.

This is a critical bibliographical study of J.M. Bermudo's *Maquiavelo, consejero de prícipes*, prologue by J. Solé Tura, P.U.B. Barcelona, 1994. (edited)

**Pataki, Tamas**. Self-Deception and Wish-Fulfilment. *Philosophia (Israel)*, 25(1-4), 297-322, Ap 97.

Philosophers have had little to say about the psychoanalytic concept of wish-fulfillment, though this is not true of related concepts like self-deception and wishful thinking. I expound what I take to be central to the psychoanalytic conception and illustrate it. I argue that the most significant forms of wish-fulfillment—there is a variety of forms—are intentional and strategic and that these forms are themselves a subclass of self-caring or self-solicitous actions whose operation presupposes complex diremptions of the self. The central cases of self-deception, those which retain the essential characteristics of deception, are shown to be compartments of self-solicitude, close kin to wish-fulfillment, self-gratification, some forms of self-abasement and other intentional strategies in which the self takes itself as an object to be cared for.

**Patella, Giuseppe**. Giambattista Vico, la Universidad y el saber: el modelo retórico. *Cuad Vico*, 7/8, 101-113, 1997.

Vico's conception of University is studied regarding the function it performs in the construction of knowledge. In this frame the author places the claim for the rhetorical paradigm against the dissociative model of modernity. Vico is for an ideal paideia which rejects every specialism in order to achieve a methodological integration of all human faculties. That implies a marriage between imagination and understanding, between rhetorical reason and critical reason. As a result of it we obtain a dialectic of joint presence, integrity and reciprocal cooperation.

**Pateman, Trevor**. Space for the Imagination. *J Aes Educ*, 31(1), 1-8, Spr 97.

**Pathil, Kuncheria**. Scientific Study of Religions: Some Methodological Reflections. *J Dharma*, 21(2), 163-169, Ap-Je 96.

The purpose of the article is to provide some methodological guidelines for the scientific comparative study of religions and to warn against all superficial comparisons among the different religions of the world. The main objective of the study of religions has to be real understanding of the uniqueness of each religion. The uniqueness of a religion shows itself in all its parts or elements. Resemblances among religions need not necessarily mean dependence or borrowing, but rather their common source of one human nature. In explaining the religious phenomenon all reductionism must be avoided. At the heart of every religion there remains the core of a unique religious experience which is expressed in its creed, code and cult.

**Patiño A, Alejandro**. Malinowksi: La Importancia de la Pragmática y del Bla-bla-bla en la Comunicación. *Ideas Valores*, 55-63, Ag 96.

This paper intends to show the way in which Malinowski, in spite of not being known as a pragmatist of language, foresees some essential elements in this conception, later developed by thinkers such as Austin, Searle, Grice, Strawson and others. Malinowski explicitly acknowledges the relevance of speech acts for communication and introduces concepts as intentionality, convention, agreement, linguistic context and situation context. Moreover, he discovers the importance of phatic language in the performance of communication.

**Paton, David**. The Use of Backstreet Abortion Arguments in Favour of Legalized Abortion. *Ethics Med*, 13(1), 5-10, 1997.

Many people are in favor of legalized abortion because of the concerns about back-street abortion. This paper argues that the fetus's legal right to protection should not depend on such arguments. Further, reported estimates of illegal abortions and subsequent maternal deaths both in the West and in developing countries are shown often to be unfounded and sometimes simply made up, seemingly with the intention of shifting the tide of opinion in favor of legalized abortion. It is estimated that no more than about 25,000 illegal abortions per year took place in England and Wales in the early sixties. Legalizing abortion seems to have had little impact on the numbers of women dying from abortion in the U.K. Lastly, simple calculations are undertaken to show that the commonly quoted statistic that 200,000 women die every year from illegal abortion in developing countries is without foundation.

**Pator Pérez, Miguel A**. Post-reflexiones arteaguianas: análisis de *La Belleza Ideal*. *Cuad Vico*, 7/8, 333-353, 1997.

An analysis of *La belleza ideal* shows Arteaga being the link inside the Spanish thought between the 18th century aesthetics and the 19th one. Emerging from a rationalist tradition as regards the taste, he embraced a subjective point of view relaying on sentiment. The book appears as a compendium of every question debated in the 18th century, attempting to resolve them in an interesting and amusing way, but also anticipates questions and a sensibility which corresponded to a later time.

**Patrício, Manuel Ferreira**. Pela Construçao de uma Filosofia da Educaçao no Horizonte do Universal Concreto. *Rev Port Filosof*, 52(1-4), 633-666, Ja-D 96.

**Patt, Walter**. *Formen des Anti-Platonismus bei Kant, Nietzsche und Heidegger*. Frankfurt/M, Klostermann, 1997.

**Patterson, Wayne A**. The Logical Structure of Russell's Negative Facts. *Russell*, 16(1), 45-66, Sum 96.

This article uncovers the logical structure of Russell's negative facts, which he postulated in his 1919 lectures on logical atomism as a way of accounting for the truth of negative propositions. It is argued that he subsequently abandoned his belief in the existence of negative facts because the latter could not be reconciled with his Principle of Acquaintance, a fundamental corner stone of his logical atomism. A proposed fine tuning of this Principle shows that the postulation of negative facts represents the best solution to the problem of negation which his logical atomism must face.

**Patthey-Chavez, G Genevieve** and Gallimore, Ronald and Clare, Lindsay. Using Moral Dilemmas in Children's Literature as a Vehicle for Moral Education and Teaching Reading Comprehension. *J Moral Educ*, 25(3), 325-341, S 96.

Moral development research has previously demonstrated that more extended discourse is a vital element in effective moral education, although the difficulty of implementing this type of discourse into classroom practice has seldom been discussed. In this study, transcripts of lessons were examined of a teacher systematically assisted to develop a more conversational style. These lessons were taped over the course of the school year at different times, beginning in the fall of the year. In addition, writing samples from children who participated in the lessons were subject to content analysis for themes relating to moral questions. Analysis of the lesson transcripts suggests that young students initiate discussion of values-implications of the texts they read if opportunities for connected discourse are increased. Evidence of the impact of more "conversational" discussions was found in the essays written by students in the class of a teacher using a more conversational style but not in the essays of students who were taught using a conventional format.

**Patton, Paul**. Concept and Event. *Man World*, 29(3), 315-326, Jl 96.

This paper examines the definition of philosophy propounded by Deleuze and Guattari in *What is Philosophy?*, with particular attention to their claim that philosophy is the invention of concepts. After setting out their account of concepts and what is involved in the creation of concepts, it argues that philosophical concepts on this account are sui generis. For Deleuze and Guattari, concepts express events and thereby provide a peculiar kind of nonempirical 'knowledge'. Their position is defended against critical claims that it is incoherent of self-contradictory and some suggestions advanced with regard to the value of philosophy thus understood.

**Patton, Thomas E**. Explaining Referential/Attributive. *Mind*, 106(422), 245-261, Ap 97.

The theory recognizes both *singular* and *general* propositions, in Kaplan's senses. But reflecting one sense of such a doubly ambiguous sentence, two-stage theory would seem to need a proposition both singular and general with respect to a definite description attributively used. Since modal operators will come into rendering the problem sentences, an obvious idea is to let *scope* distinctions rescue two-stage theory from the apparent paradox. But while a rescue based on multiple renderings is proposed, it is not strictly a *scope* rescue, though different scopes are involved. Readers are asked to trust the author on missing formalities of an intuitively transparent two-sorted modal language that is employed. Two-stage theorists explicitly oppose scope treatments of modal ambiguities seeing them as rivals. Stalnaker, in particular, argues against them. But his arguments are shown not to count against the proposed rescue, on which the anticipated rivalry proves to be minimal. (edited)

**Paty, Michel**. "Mathesis universalis e inteligibilidad en Descartes" in *Memorias Del Seminario En Conmemoración De Los 400 Anos Del Nacimiento De René Descartes*, Albis, Víctor S (ed), 135-170. Sankt Augustin, Academia, 1997.

El problema de la inteligibilidad, corazón de la filosofía de Descartes, surge por primera vez en las *Reglas para la dirección del espíritu*, escritas nueve años antes que el *Discurso del Método*. Las *Reglas* se presentan como el primer movimiento de su pensamiento profundo sobre las matemáticas y sobre la cuestión de la certeza del conocimiento con relación a la subjetividad. La *mathesis universalis* resume, por así decirlo, su filosofía del conocimiento en lo que elle tiene de esencial.

**Pauen, Michael**. Wahrnehmung und Mentale Repräsentation. *Phil Rundsch*, 43(3), 243-264, S 96.

The paper gives a survey of recent discussions on mental representation and perception in the philosophy of mind. It is argued that, contrary to Fodor, Dretske and others, there is no necessity to 'naturalize content.' Since physical and semantic properties belong to two different and independent, levels of scientific explanation there is no reason to require that the properties of one level be reduced to the properties of another—presumably 'more basic'—level. This is confirmed by recent insights from the theory of perception which seem to indicate that even basic properties of perception (e.g., colors) can't be explained only in physical terms.

**Pauer-Studer, Herlinde**. "Ethik und Geschlechterdifferenz" in *Angewandte Ethik: Die Bereichsethiken und ihre theoretische Fundierung*, Nida-Rümelin, Julian (ed), 86-136. Stuttgart, Alfred Kröner, 1996.

The article gives an overview of feminist contributions to issues of applied ethics. After a general discussion of the feminist ethics debate, feminist perspectives on problems like abortion, in vitro fertilization, justice in the family and affirmative action are discussed.

**Paul, Ellen Frankel** (ed) and Miller, Fred D (ed) and Paul, Jeffrey (ed). *The Welfare State*. New York, Cambridge Univ Pr, 1997.

These twelve essays—written from a range of viewpoints by philosophers, historians, economists, and political and legal theorists—offer valuable insights into the history of the welfare state, the proper role of government in ameliorating distress, and the nature of individual and collective responsibility. (publisher, edited)

**Paul, Jeffrey** (ed) and Miller, Fred D (ed) and Paul, Ellen Frankel (ed). *The Welfare State*. New York, Cambridge Univ Pr, 1997.

These twelve essays—written from a range of viewpoints by philosophers, historians, economists, and political and legal theorists—offer valuable insights into the history of the welfare state, the proper role of government in ameliorating distress, and the nature of individual and collective responsibility. (publisher, edited)

**Paul, L A**. Truth Conditions of Tensed Sentence Types. *Synthese*, 111(1), 53-71, Ap 97.

Quentin Smith has argued that the new tenseless theory of time is faced with insurmountable problems and should be abandoned in favor of the tensed theory of time. Smith's main argument attacks the fundamental premise of the tenseless theory: that tenseless truth conditions for tokens of tensed sentences adequately capture the meaning of tensed sentences. His position is that tenseless truth conditions cannot explain the logical relations between tensed sentences, thus the tensed theory must be accepted. Against Smith, this paper adopts an alternative approach to the explanation of the entailment relations between sentences which contain indexicals. The approach drops the reliance upon tokens and instead relies on the evaluation of sentence types with respect to a context rather than upon actual or possible utterances of tokens of the types. This (new) version of the tenseless theory of time can adequately explain the relevant entailment relations between tensed sentences.

**Paul, Richard**. A "Third Wave" Manifesto: Keynotes of the Sonoma Conference. *Inquiry (USA)*, 16(2), 1-11, Wint 96.

**Paul, Richard**. Critical Thinking and the State of Education Today. *Inquiry (USA)*, 16(2), 12-34, Wint 96.

**Pautz, Adam**. An Argument against Armstrong's Analysis of the Resemblance of Universals. *Austl J Phil*, 75(1), 109-111, Mr 97.

**Pava, Moses L** and Krausz, Joshua. Criteria for Evaluating the Legitimacy of Corporate Social Responsibility. *J Bus Ethics*, 16(3), 337-347, F 97.

The goal of this paper is to provide a general discussion about the legitimacy of corporate social responsibility. Given that social responsibility projects entail costs, it is not always obvious under what precise conditions managers will have a responsibility to engage in activities primarily designed to promote societal goals. (edited)

**Pavan Baptista, Ligia**. O Estatuto da Paz na Teoria Política Hobbesiana. *Cad Hist Filosof Cie*, 5(1-2), 87-103, Ja-D 95.

As a mortal God, or Leviathan the state in Hobbes's political theory is, in the same sense as a human being, affected by several diseases; namely, conflicts. A civil war, that means, the state's death, should be avoided by accurate analysis of its causes. Based upon both empirical analysis on human nature and methodological concepts as the state of nature, Hobbes stresses the practical function of civil service, which is the search for peace. Peace, which should also be seen as the state's major aim, should be sought through proper education on political matters. The knowledge about the duties and the rights of both citizens and sovereigns should be precisely defined. To settle the preconditions for peace primarily within the state but also among the state is, therefore, the main goal of Hobbes's treatises on politics.

**Pavri, Francis** and Wimalasiri, Jayantha S and Jalil, Abdul A K. An Empirical Study of Moral Reasoning Among Managers in Singapore. *J Bus Ethics*, 15(12), 1331-1341, D 96.

The study reported here sought to examine the ethical orientations of business managers and business students in Singapore. Data were obtained using Defining Issue Test. Analysis of Variance revealed that age, education and religious affiliation had influenced cognitive moral development stages of the respondents. Vocation, gender and ethnicity did not seem to have affected moral judgment of the subjects. Contrary to the general view both business students and business managers demonstrated the same level of sensitivity to ethical dimensions of decision-making. Implications of the findings and limitations of the study are discussed.

**Pawelzig, Gerd** and Griese, Anneliese. Why Did Marx and Engels Concern Themselves with Natural Science?. *Nature Soc Thought*, 8(2), 125-137, 1995.

As work proceeds on the complete original writings of Marx and Engels for the *Marx-Engels Gesamtausgabe (MEGA)*, the extent to which they dealt with the natural sciences is quite striking. Since their interest in the natural sciences was not connected with professional ambitions in these areas, this interest must have been motivated by the connections they saw between developments in the natural sciences and their general sociotheoretical work connected with the working-class movement. Among the principal factors that contributed to their interest in the natural sciences was the need to draw upon the methodology of the natural sciences for the application of dialectical and historical materialism to the social sphere. The often made allegation that Engels's understanding of dialectics, especially in regard to the natural sciences, was incompatible with Marx's is sharply disputed.

**Pawlak, Zdzislaw** and Skowron, Andrzej. Helena Rasiowa and Cecylia Rauszer Research on Logical Foundations of Computer Science. *Bull Sec Log*, 25(3/4), 174-184, O-D 96.

It is an abstract of the talk presented on the session dedicated to the memory of

Professor Helena Rasiowa and Professor Cecylia Rauszer on June 10, 1995 in the Faculty of Mathematics, Computer Science and Mechanics at Warsaw University, Poland. It presents the results received by Professor Rasiowa and Professor Rauszer on logical and algebraic foundations of computer science and the influence of Professor Rasiowa on the development of research on mathematical foundations of computer science in Poland and other countries.

**Pazanin, Ante**. Practical Philosophy and the Human Sciences Today (in Serbo-Croatian). *Filozof Istraz*, 15(4), 887-900, 1995.

Der durch die phänomenologische und hermeneutische Philosophie in die Wege geleitete Rehabilitierungsprozess der praktischen Philosophie hat in den sechziger Jahren unseres Jahrhunderts zunächst mit der Rehabilitierung der klassischen Politikphilosophie begonnen. In den letzten fünfzehn Jahren ist die ethische Problematik Mittelpunkt diese Prozesses sowie des Interesses der zeitgenössischen Philosophie, sei es, dass ethische Untersuchungen in erster Linie prinzipiellen Fragen von Begründung und Kritik ethischer Normen und Prinzipien oder der systematischen Entwicklung der einzelnen Ethikrichtungen von der ökologischen und biomedizinischen über die Diskursethik bis zur hermeneutischen Philosophieethik und der Ethik des "Verantwortungsprinzips" gewidmet sind, sei es, dass man durch die Erforschung der Geschichte der antiken und neuzeitlichen praktischen Philosophie die praktische Philosophie auf den Spuren der Kantischen Trennung der Moral von Recht und Politik oder auf den Spuren der Aristotelischen Einheit von Ethik und Politik sowie der Hegelschen Philosophie des objektiven Geistes erneuert und weiterentwickelt. (edited)

**Peacocke, Christopher**. "Content, Computation and Externalism" in *Contents,* Villanueva, Enrique (ed), 227-264. Atascadero, Ridgeview, 1995.

**Peacocke, Christopher**. Metaphysical Necessity: Understanding, Truth and Epistemology. *Mind*, 106(423), 521-574, Jl 97.

This paper presents an account of the understanding of statements involving metaphysical modality, together with dovetailing theories of their truth conditions and epistemology. The account makes modal truth an objective matter, whilst avoiding both Lewisian modal realism and mind-dependent or expressivist treatments of the truth conditions of modal sentences. The theory proceeds by formulating constraints a world-description must meet if it is to represent a genuine possibility. Modal truth is fixed by the totality of the constraints. To understand modal discourse is to have tacit knowledge of the body of information stated in these constraints. Modal knowledge is attained by evaluating modal statements in accordance with the constraints. The question of the general relations between modal truth and knowability is also addressed. The paper includes a discussion of which modal logic is supported by the presented theory of truth conditions for modal statements.

**Pearce, Colin D**. Prescott's Conquests: Anthropophagy, Auto-da-Fe and Eternal Return. *Interpretation*, 24(3), 339-361, Spr 97.

**Pearlman, Robert A** and Back, Anthony L and Burack, Jeffrey H. Provoking Nonepileptic Seizures: The Ethics of Deceptive Diagnostic Testing. *Hastings Center Rep*, 27(4), 24-33, Jl-Ag 97.

The use of deception in medical care is highly suspect in this country. Yet there is one condition in which deception is often used as a diagnostic tool. Nonepileptic seizures, a psychiatric condition in which emotional or psychological conflicts manifest themselves unconsciously through bodily symptoms, are currently diagnosed by a procedure called "provocative saline infusion." The test is fundamentally deceptive, but without such deception the test might be useless.

**Pearn, John**. The Quiddity of Mercy—A Response. *Philosophy*, 71(278), 603-604, O 96.

**Pears, David**. The Originality of Wittgenstein's Investigation of Solipsism. *Euro J Phil*, 4(2), 124-136, Ag 96.

**Pearson, Allen T**. Teaching, Reason and Risk. *Stud Phil Educ*, 16(1-2), 103-111, Ja-Ap 97.

In his writings on teaching, Israel Scheffler has argued for the close connection between teaching and reason, an argument which can be summarized by, "Teaching is...an initiation into open rational discussion." This essay examines Scheffler's thesis in the light of criticisms drawn from feminist writings on teaching. It is argued that Scheffler's thesis is consistent with a view of teaching in which it can be achieved through "kindness, good example and the efficacy of unconscious imitation," characteristics of the private, reproductive processes typical of women. It is then argued that Scheffler's concept of teaching is compatible with views of education that try to do justice to both reason and emotion, mind and feeling.

**Pearson, Thomas D**. Interview with Alasdair MacIntyre. *Kinesis*, 23(1), 40-50, Sum 96.

**Pécharman, Martine**. La puissance propre de la volonté selon Pascal. *Rev Int Phil*, 51(199), 59-76, 1997.

**Peckhaus, Volker**. The Way of Logic into Mathematics. *Theoria (Spain)*, 12(28), 39-64, Ja 97.

Using a contextual method the specific development of logic between c. 1830 and 1930 is explained. A characteristic mark of this period is the decomposition of the complex traditional philosophical omnibus discipline logic into new philosophical subdisciplines and separate disciplines such as psychology, epistemology, philosophy of science and formal (symbolic, mathematical) logic. In the 19th century a growing foundational need in mathematics provoked the emergence of a structural view on mathematics and the reformulation of logic for mathematical means. As a result formal logic was taken over by mathematics in the beginning of the 20th century as is shown by sketching the German example.

**Pecnjak, Davor**. Remarks on Disembodied Existence. *Acta Analytica*, 209-213, 1995.

The author examines some claims about the possible existence of disembodied persons. Contrary to G.R. Gillett, it is shown that disembodied persons could be disembodied ab initio and that they could have disembodied "modules" for learning in addition to those for perceptual, tactile and telekinetic abilities.

**Peelen, Ed** and Ouwerkerk, Cok and Verbeke, Willem. Exploring the Contextual and Individual Factors on Ethical Decision Making of Salespeople. *J Bus Ethics*, 15(11), 1175-1187, N 96.

This paper studies how salespeople make ethical decisions. For this purpose a structural model has been developed which configures how the organization's environment, the organization's climate, and personality traits affect ethical decision making. Internal communication and the choice of a control system especially affect ethical decision making. Internal communication also affects the attraction of salespeople with unethical personality traits (Machiavellism), while the control system affects the ethical climate. Ethical climate and salespeople's personality traits also affect the ethical decision making. In fact the study shows that ethical decision making can be influenced by management.

**Peijnenburg, Jeanne** and Mackor, Anne Ruth. Chief Bumbu en de Verklaring van Menselijk Gedrag. *Alg Ned Tijdschr Wijs*, 88(3), 208-215, Jl 96.

The paper is a review of the conference 'Human action and causality', held April 1996 at the University of Utrecht in The Netherlands. Contributions of speakers (J. Kim, P. Pettit, F. Dretske, among others) are summarized and critically discussed. (The papers will be published in Proceedings.)

**Pejovic, Danilo**. Heidegger at the Turn of the Century (in Serbo-Croatian). *Filozof Istraz*, 15(4), 793-812, 1995.

Eine denkende Auseinandersetzung mit Martin Heidegger und seinem Werk gilt noch immer als eine Herausforderung und philosophische Aufgabe ersten Ranges, auch jetzt an der Jahrhundertwende, nach vielen Jahren grosser Wirkung und einer neigenden Abkehr. Er war doch ein philosophischer Denker von Weltruf und einer der führenden Geister im Gespräch der Zeit, ist noch immer Gegenstand philosophischer Diskussion und zugleich heftig umstritten. Deshalb schien uns ratsam, in diesem Aufsatz auf einige Marksteine in dieser Entwicklung hinzuweisen und diesen Versuch als einen Beitrag zur Heidegger-Bilanz zu betrachten. (edited)

**Pelayo, Francisco**. Creacionismo y evolucionismo en el siglo XIX: las repercusiones del Darwinismo en la comunidad científica española. *An Seminar Hist Filosof*, 13, 263-284, 1996.

Darwin's *Theory of Evolution* was received by the Spanish naturalist's community within a harmonic spirit between the natural sciences and the *Bible*. The weakest part of Darwin's theory, the fossil record, was interpreted from different creationist positions and became the main argument wielded by the anti-Darwinist.

**Pellegrino, Edmund D**. Ethical Issues in Managed Care: A Catholic Christian Perspective. *Christian Bioethics*, 3(1), 55-73, Mr 97.

A Christian analysis of the moral conflicts that exist among physicians and health care institutions requires a detailed treatment of the ethical issues in managed care. To be viable, managed care, as with any system of health care, must be economically sound and morally defensible. While managed care is *per se* a morally neutral concept, as it is currently practiced in the United States, it is morally dubious at best and in many instances is antithetical to a Catholic Christian ethics of health care. The moral status of any system of managed care ought to be judged with respect to its congruence with Gospel teachings about the care of the sick, Papal Encyclicals and the documents of the Second Vatican Council. In this essay, I look at the important conceptual or definitional issues of managed care, assess these concerns over against the source and content of a Catholic ethic of health care and outline the necessary moral requirements of any licit system of health care.

**Pellegrino, Edmund D** (ed) and Kilner, John F (ed) and Miller, Arlene B (ed). *Dignity and Dying: A Christian Appraisal*. Grand Rapids, Eerdmans, 1996.

The authors of the present volume engage matters of dignity and dying from a variety of perspectives. The three authors of the introduction root the book in the experience of dying itself. In Part I, the authors give careful attention to topics that provide guiding vision for approaches to dignity and dying: autonomy, death, suffering, and faithfulness. Four of the most pressing end-of-life challenges—forgoing treatment, medical futility, definition of death, and assisted-suicide/euthanasia—are then examined in some detail. Part III is devoted to investigations of key settings where people have wrestled with these challenges: i.e., Nazi Germany, Oregon (USA), North American legal systems, and The Netherlands. The book concludes, then, with discussions of five potentially constructive alternatives to the premature ending of life: hospice care, long-term care, wise advocacy, parish nursing and congregational ministry. (publisher, edited)

**Pellegrino, Edmund D** and Sharpe, Virginia A. Medical Ethics in the Courtroom: A Reappraisal. *J Med Phil*, 22(4), 373-379, Ag 97.

Following up on a 1989 paper on the subject, this essay revisits the question of ethical expertise in the court room. Informed by recent developments in the use of ethics experts, the authors argue (1) that the adversarial nature of court proceedings challenges the integrity of the ethicist's pedagogical role; (2) that the use of ethics experts as normative authorities remains dubious; (3) that clarification of the State's interest in "protecting the ethical integrity of the medical profession" is urgently required; and (4) that the expertise of the ethicist may be more appropriately used in advising the legislature than in influencing the court.

**Pelletier, Francis J**. Identity in Modal Logic Theorem Proving. *Stud Log*, 52(2), 291-308, My 93.

"Thinker" is an automated natural deduction first-order theorem proving program. This paper reports on how it was adapted so as to prove theorems in modal logic. The method employed is an "indirect semantic method", obtained by considering the semantic conditions involved in being a valid argument in these modal logics. The method is extended from propositional modal logic to predicate modal logic and issues concerning the domain of quantification and "existence in a world's domain" are discussed. Finally, we look at the very interesting issues involved with adding identity to the theorem proven in the realm of modal predicate logic. Various alternatives are discussed.

**Pelosse, Valentin**. Modes de proximités avec l'animal chez Montaigne. *Philosopher*, 18, 43-54, 1995.

**Pelton, Lou E** and Strutton, David and Ferrell, O C. Ethical Behavior in Retail Settings: Is There a Generation Gap?. *J Bus Ethics*, 16(1), 87-105, Ja 97.

A new generation, earmarked the Thirteeners, is an emerging force in the marketplace. The Thirteener cohort group, so designated since they are the thirteenth generation to know the American flag and constitution, encompass over 62 million adult consumers. All the former "Mall Rats" have grown up. The normative structures that these Thirteeners employ in both acquisition and disposition retail settings is empirically assessed in this study through the use of a national sample. The findings suggest that Thirteeners are more likely to attempt to rationalize away unethical retailing consumption behaviors than their parent's generation. The managerial and theoretical implications for the practice of retailing in the 1990s associated with these observations are discussed.

**Peña, Lorenzo**. Grados, franjas y líneas de demarcación. *Rev Filosof (Spain)*, 9(16), 121-149, 1996.

A property is fuzzy if, and only if, some entities both, to some extent, have the property and also, to some extent, lack the property. Fuzzy properties are qualities which come in degrees. Some of them give rise to sorites or slippery slope arguments. The sorites is solved by admitting that the property in question has a fringe, not a unique demarcation line. Out of any two entities lying in the fringe one has the property and the other does not. If two such entities are close, one of them has the property more than the other does. In fact, each entity in the fringe both has and does not have the property. While in sorites-related cases the principle of Chrisippus applies (either both entities have the property or else neither has it), the conditional formulation 'If either has the property so does the other' fails, since classical definition of 'if' is not correct for natural negation, the mere 'not'. On the other hand, disjunctive syllogism is in general not valid, so the sorites is stopped at the last stage: the last link in the chain is a couple of entities one of which has the property to some ever so small degree, whereas the other completely lacks the property.

**Peña, Lorenzo**. Graham Priest's "Dialectheism"—Is It Altogether True?. *Sorites*, 28-56, N 96.

Graham Priest's book *In Contradiction* is a bold defense of the existence of true contradictions. Although Priest's case is impressive and many of his arguments are correct, his approach is not the only one allowing for true contradictions. As against Priest's, there is at least one contradictorialist approach which establishes a link between true contradictions and degrees of truth. All in all, such an alternative is more conservative, closer to mainstream analytical philosophy. The two approaches differ as regards the floodgate problem. Priest espouses a confinement policy banning contradictions except in a few special domains, particularly those of pure semantics and set-theory (and perhaps arithmetics), whereas the alternative approach admits two negations—natural or weak negation and strong negation, the latter being classical; accordingly, the alternative approach prohibits any contradiction involving strong negation, thus providing a syntactic test of what contradictions have to be rejected.

**Peña, Lorenzo**. Raúl Orayen's Views on Philosophy of Logic. *Sorites*, 76-94, Jl 95.

Orayen proposes some kind of intensional approach in philosophy of logic, with meanings playing a central role in implementing the notion of logical truth. Orayen regards Quine as his main interlocutor. The major topic gone into through the book is logical form, validity and logical truth. As an outgrowth, Quine's operationalist view of language receives an extensive coverage and discussion. The investigation into the notion of logical truth and validity leads to a critical assessment of the relevantist challenge to the classical conception. This critical notice casts doubt on Orayen's defence of analyticity as a requirement for logical truth.

**Peña, Lorenzo** and Vásconez, Marcelo. What's a Gradual Ontology? (in Spanish). *Agora (Spain)*, 15(2), 29-48, 1996.

What makes fuzzy properties fuzzy is not vagueness but graduality. We argue that such graduality is objective, that there are degrees of truth which are as many degrees of existence of facts. We go on to uphold degrees of existence of other sorts of entities, such as artifacts and species. There is a thick fringe between what is and what is not at all, wherein entities both are and are not. Two different negations, *not* and *not... at all*, are distinguished. Disjunctive syllogism holds for the latter only. Thus, a gradualistic ontology successfully stops the disastrous final step of a sorites argument.

**Peña Vial, Jorge**. Narración y libertad. *Anu Filosof*, 29(2), 911-920, 1996.

What is called by Polo as "the native freedom" derives from the acceptance of the being offered and that is precisely known as such in the act of accepting it as a gift. This native freedom requires a destination to be unfolded. Freedom requires radicality as well as horizon. The radical freedom only exists where its horizon is open to big question putting the entire life at stake. The structure of the heroic myth illustrates the difficulties of the freedom. In the true free act we

choose at the same time that we consent. The dialectic of this time free act is illuminated by the basic confidence of the native freedom and the taking into account of the beneficiary (destination).

**Penati, Giancarlo**. Come pensare diversamente l'identico: incontrovertibilità dell'essere e irreversibilità del tempo. *G Metaf*, 18(1-2), 131-140, Ja-Ag 96.

The main purpose of this essay is to think a form of necessity which cannot be denied or excluded from the existential dimension of reality. As temporality, she is obliged to arise, pass and die, without return: this is the absolute necessity of *time* ("*fluit irremeabile tempus*"), the condition of his being and realisation. So *time* is not pure contingence and cannot be assumed as figure of "*nothing,*" but, in spite of all form of reduction, is itself an image of incontrovertibility of *being*, a shadow of its absolute principle, whose necessity (and analogical "*time*"), is *eternity.*

**Penati, Giancarlo**. Trascendentalità, inferenza e trascendenza: Dopo Kant e Heidegger. *G Metaf*, 18(1-2), 259-269, Ja-Ag 96.

**Penczek, Alan**. Counterfactuals with True Components. *Erkenntnis*, 46(1), 79-85, Ja 97.

One criticism of David Lewis's account of counterfactuals is that it sometimes assigns the wrong truth-value to a counterfactual when both antecedent and consequent happen to be true. Lewis has suggested a possible remedy to this situation, but commentators have found this to be unsatisfactory. I suggest an alternative solution which involves a modification of Lewis's truth conditions, but which confines itself to the resources already present in his account. This modification involves the device of embedding one counterfactual within another. On the revised set of truth conditions, counterfactuals with true components are sometimes true and sometimes false, in a way that is more in keeping with our intuitive judgments about such statements.

**Penczek, Alan**. Disjunctive Properties and Causal Efficacy. *Phil Stud*, 86(2), 203-219, My 97.

A pigeon has been conditioned to peck at red objects and has also been conditioned to peck at triangular objects. The pigeon is now presented with a red triangle and pecks. In virtue of which of the object's properties did the pigeon peck? I argue that the disjunctive property "red or triangular" best answers this question and that this in turn gives us reason to admit such disjunctive properties to our ontology. I also show how the criterion for causal efficacy that I employ, expressed in terms of counterfactual conditionals, works to preclude spurious disjunctive properties from counting as efficacious.

**Pendlebury, Michael**. The Role of Imagination in Perception. *S Afr J Phil*, 15(4), 133-138, N 96.

This article is an explication and defence of Kant's view that 'imagination is a necessary ingredient of perception itself' (*Critique of Pure Reason* A120, fn.). Imagination comes into perception at a far more basic level than Strawson allows, and is required for the constitution of intuitions (=sense experiences) out of sense impressions. It also plays an important part in explaining how it is possible for intuitions to have intentional contents. These functions do not involve the application of concepts, and I offer a schematic account of how they are carried out by preconceptual syntheses.

**Pendlebury, Shirley**. "Utopia Flawed? A Response to Reich on Rorty" in *Philosophy of Education (1996)*, Margonis, Frank (ed), 352-355. Urbana, Phil Education Soc, 1997.

**Penelhum, Terence**. Response to Chappell. *Relig Stud*, 33(1), 115-119, Mr 97.

I respond to two criticisms in Chappell's kind of review of my *Reason and Religious Faith*. 1) I defend the claim that the world is religiously ambiguous by emphasizing that such ambiguity consists in the existence of a number of worldviews that are capable of rational support, even though at most one can be true; and the fact that it is rational to assent to each of our great religious figures is constitutive of this ambiguity. 2) I defend the distinction between belief and belief-forming processes, and the view that belief is not voluntary although belief-forming processes may be.

**Penner, J E**. The Analysis of Rights. *Ratio Juris*, 10(3), 300-315, S 97.

The author argues that the interest theory of rights is clearly preferable to the choice theory of rights and that this is due in large part to the work of Raz and MacCormick. Critical scrutiny of their views, however, reveals a flawed conception of the way that rights reflect interests. The author contends that a superior relation between rights and interests can be formulated, in which rights are identified with a constellation of norms within a normative system which reflect the interests which justify them, but wherein rights are not coextensive with interests conceived as reasons for the imposition of duties.

**Penner, Terry**. Knowledge vs True Belief in the Socratic Psychology of Action. *Apeiron*, 29(3), 199-230, S 96.

It may be objected to my view of *Protagoras* 352b-357e (knowledge strong against pleasure, because stable; even *true* belief correspondingly weak: *AGP* 1996) that "True belief can be just as stubborn (involve as much will power) as knowledge." (Compare Aristotle) Reply: Desire in Socrates being always rational, the practical deliberative structures of contemplated alternatives involve virtually all one's ethical beliefs. With some true beliefs, some false, one may get different answers depending upon the route followed through the belief-structure. (Compare Socratic conversations on *theoretical* ethical beliefs.) Belief-akrasia, like elenchus, is the finding of weak spots in total ethical belief-structures.

**Pennock, Robert T**. Inappropriate Authorship in Collaborative Science Research. *Pub Affairs Quart*, 10(4), 379-393, O 96.

National scientific societies cite "inappropriate authorship" of scientific papers as one sort of ethical misconduct that concerns them, but there has been little

AUTHOR INDEX 837 Pereira Borges, J F

discussion of what it involves or what to do about it. I analyze varieties of improper authorship, showing that they involve failure to respect principles of truthfulness, responsibility and justice. I argue that many of the ethical problems arise not because of willful misconduct of scientists, but because of the vague and conflicting authorship conventions currently available for differentiating researcher contributions. I propose and defend a new credit attribution convention that could mitigate this sort of problem.

**Pensky, Max** (ed). *The Actuality of Adorno: Critical Essays on Adorno and the Postmodern.* Albany, SUNY Pr, 1997.

Always resistant to classification, the work of Theodor Adorno ranged from biting criticism of the emergent popular culture in the United States and Europe, through theories of contemporary music and literature and sociological analyses of the rise of fascism and anti-Semitism in Germany and elsewhere, to careful readings of modern Continental philosophers. As a leading member of the famous Frankfurt School of critical social theory, Adorno influenced current discussions in cultural studies and Continental philosophy. However, the various dimensions of Adorno's significance for the range of contemporary postmodern theory remained unclear. This book demonstrates the relevance and power of Adorno's work for the state of critical social theory today. (publisher)

**Penta, Leo J**. Hannah Arendt: On Power. *J Speculative Phil*, 10(3), 211-229, 1996.

**Pentus, Mati**. Product-Free Lambek Calculus and Context-Free Grammars. *J Sym Log*, 62(2), 648-660, Je 97.

In this paper we prove the Chomsky conjecture (all languages recognized by the Lambek calculus are context-free) for both the full Lambek calculus and its product-free fragment. For the latter case we present a construction of context-free grammars involving only product-free types.

**Pentzopoulou-Valadas, Thérèse**. Fichte et Husserl: Une lecture parallèle. *Fichte-Studien*, 13, 65-76, 1997.

**Peperzak, Adriaan Theodoor**. Judaism and Philosophy in Levinas. *Int J Phil Relig*, 40(3), 125-145, D 96.

To what extent is Levinas's philosophy Jewish? In order to ask this question, *first*, his conception of Judaism is presented; *second*, the question is answered to what extent his philosophy coincides with Judaism thus understood and whether it is still "pure" philosophy.

**Peperzak, Adriaan Theodoor**. Philosophia. *Faith Phil*, 14(3), 321-333, Jl 97.

This article defends the thesis that philosophy in the modern sense of the word never has been and cannot be autarkic because it cannot demonstrate the truth of the faith from which it draws its basic stance and orientation. If this faith is the faith of a Christian, it is impossible to draw a sharp distinction between the philosophical and the theological activities of such a philosopher. The stubborn attempt to restrict one's thought to autonomous philosophy wounds and paralyzes the thinking of Christians and destroys most of its relevance. The old synthetic conception of *philosophia*, upheld by Plato and the Stoics no less than by the fathers of the church, deserves a re-evaluation. Despite the profound differences between unscientific premodernity and modern scientificity, that old conception is a more adequate description of the philosophical practice performed in real human lives. (edited)

**Peperzak, Adriaan Theodoor** (ed) and Critchley, Simon (ed) and Bernasconi, Robert (ed). *Emmanuel Levinas: Basic Philosophical Writings*. Bloomington, Indiana Univ Pr, 1996.

This anthology of Levinas's key philosophical texts over a period of more than forty years provides an ideal introduction to his thought and offers insights into his most innovative ideas. Five of the ten essays included here appear in English for the first time. An introduction by Adriaan Peperzak outlines Levinas's philosophical development and the basic themes of his writings. Each essay is accompanied by a brief introduction and notes. (publisher,edited)

**Peppin, John F**. The Christian Physician in the Non-Christian Institution: Objections of Conscience and Physician Value Neutrality. *Christian Bioethics*, 3(1), 39-54, Mr 97.

Christian physicians are in danger of losing the right of conscientious objection in situations they deem immoral. The erosion of this right is bolstered by the doctrine of "physician value neutrality" (PVN) which may be an impetus for the push to require physicians to refer for procedures they find immoral. It is only a small step from referral to compelling performance of these same procedures. If no one particular value is more morally correct than any other (a foundational PVN premise) and a physician ought to be value neutral, than conscientious objection to morally objectionable actions becomes a thing of the past. However, the argument for PVN fails. Therefore, Christian physicians should state their values openly, which would allow patients the ability to choose like-minded physicians. (edited)

**Pequeno, Tarcisio** and Buchsbaum, Arthur. A Reasoning Method for a Paraconsistent Logic. *Stud Log*, 52(2), 281-289, My 93.

A proof method for automation of reasoning in a paraconsistent logic, the calculus C1 of da Costa, is presented. The method is analytical, using a specially designed tableau system. Actually two tableau systems were created. A first one, with a small number of rules in order to be mathematically convenient, is used to prove the soundness and the completeness of the method. The other one, which is equivalent to the former, is a system of derived rules designed to enhance computational efficiency. A prototype based on this second system was effectively implemented.

**Pequeno, Tarcisio** and Castro Martins, Ana Teresa. Proof-Theoretical Considerations about the Logic of Epistemic Inconsistency. *Log Anal*, 36(144), 245-260, S-D 93.

The *Logic of Epistemic Inconsistency* (LEI) provides an interesting example of a paraconsistent formal system from the proof theoretical point of view. Although *cut elimination* theorem for its sequent calculus can only be proved with a restriction, this does not damage its main desirable outcomes. Consistency and subformula property, for instance, are preserved. The motivation for LEI designing, its sequent calculus and most remarkable theorems are presented. The sole unremovable cut-proof pattern is analysed.

**Perczel, István**. Pseudo-Dionysius Areopagiticus and Saint Simon The New Theologian (in Czech). *Magyar Filozof Szemle*, 1-2, 153-172, 1997.

Dans le présent article l'Auteur se propose, d'une part, de démontrer qu'au cas de Syméon le Nouveau Théologien il faut compter avec une influence considérable de Denys l'Aréopagite, et cela en présentant quelques parallèles entre les textes des deux auteurs, concernant surtout l'illumination divine et l'union à Dieu. D'autre part—tâche bien plus difficile—il essaie d'apprécier la nature et l'ampleur de cette influence. (edited)

**Pereboom, Derk**. "Conceptual Structure and the Individuation of Content" in *AI, Connectionism and Philosophical Psychology, 1995*, Tomberlin, James E (ed), 401-428. Atascadero, Ridgeview, 1995.

Here I attempt to develop a strategy for individuating psychological content that is immune to deficiencies in fineness or coarseness of grain. My approach takes its cue from individuation of kinds in the natural sciences, where structural features of entities play a prominent role in characterizations of kinds. Recent studies in cognitive psychology suggest that psychological content also has structural features. I argue that individuation of content based on such features has a reasonable prospect of capturing our intuitions about psychological explanation and of providing principled criteria for identity of content and concept.

**Pereboom, Derk**. Kant on God, Evil, and Teleology. *Faith Phil*, 13(4), 508-533, O 96.

In his mature period Kant maintained that human beings have never devised a theory that shows how the existence of God is compatible with the evil that actually exists. But he also held that an argument could be developed that we human beings might well not have the cognitive capacity to understand the relation between God and the world and that, therefore, the existence of God might nevertheless be compatible with the evil that exists. At the core of Kant's position lies the claim that God's relation to the world might well not be purposive in the way we humans can genuinely understand such a relation. His strategy involves demonstrating that the teleological argument is unsound—for this argument would establish that the relation between God and the world is purposive in a way we can grasp—and showing that by way of a Spinozan conception we can catch an intellectual glimpse of an alternative picture of the relation between God and the world.

**Peregrin, Jaroslav** and Wheeler III, Samuel C. The Extension of Deconstruction and Commentary (in Czech). *Filosof Cas*, 44(6), 943-967, 1996.

**Pereira, Fernando** (& others) and Lamping, John and Dalrymple, Mary. Quantifiers, Anaphora, and Intensionality. *J Log Lang Info*, 6(3), 219-273, Jl 97.

The relationship between Lexical-Functional Grammar (LFG) *functional structures* (f-structures) for sentences and their semantic interpretations can be formalized in *linear logic* in a way that correctly explains the observed interactions between quantifier scope ambiguity, bound anaphora and intensionality. While our approach resembles current categorial approaches in important ways (Moortgat, 1988, 1992a; Carpenter, 1993; Morrill, 1994) it differs from them in allowing the greater compositional flexibility of categorial semantics (van Benthem, 1991) while maintaining a precise connection to syntax. As a result, we are able to provide derivations for certain readings of sentences with intensional verbs and complex direct objects whose derivation in purely categorial accounts of the syntax-semantics interface appears to require otherwise unnecessary semantic decompositions of lexical entries. (publisher, edited)

**Pereira, Luiz Carlos P D** and Poubel, Hardée Werneck. A Categorical Approach to Higher-Level Introduction and Elimination Rules. *Rep Math Log*, 28, 3-19, 1994.

The aim of the present work is to extend the well-known connections between proof theory and category theory to higher-level natural deduction. To be precise, we will show how an adjointness between Cartesian closed categories with finite coproducts can be associated, in a systematic way, with any operator Phi defined by the higher-level schemes. The objects in the categories will be rules instead of formulas. (edited)

**Pereira Arêdes, José de Almeida**. Foucault: *Da Morte do* Sujeito *Ao Sujeito da* Morte. *Philosophica (Portugal)*, 37-49, 1996.

In the context of the convention on *Descartes, Leibniz, and Modernity*, our aim is to show how Foucault followed a course which, although devoid of teleological intention, led him from *the criticism of the subject* to *the subject of criticism*. Starting from the criticism of Descartes and of *the thinking subject* as the basis of knowledge, we aim to show how Foucault first explores the death of the subject as the death of the substantial subject and how he is then urged to move from *subjection* (ontological hetero-constitution) to *subjectivation* (ontological self-constitution), thus showing the danger of the separation proposed by Descartes between *the subject of knowledge* and *the ethical subject*. This means the constitution of a subject that is *ethical* instead of moral, the exploration by Foucault of a subject that constructs itself through the practice of liberty, which is made possible through the technologies of *self-care*. *Melete thanatou*, or meditation on death, stands out among these technologies, as an exercise of detachment and practice of the self and the liberty.

**Pereira Borges, J F**. Poder político e liberdade. *Rev Port Filosof*, 53(1), 63-70, Ja-Mr 97.

Two among the main authors deserve a special attention in the context of political thought over the last centuries: John Locke and J. J. Rousseau. The

Pereira da Silva, Marcelo Soares 838 AUTHOR INDEX

former proposed a theory of powers separation and founded political society on the majority consensus. The majority commands and is free; the minority obeys and is enslaved. Obedience without justified assent is a certain form of slavery. J. J. Rousseau organized and founded political society on general will. Citizen's freedom is guaranteed by obedience and spontaneous agreement as to that will; in this way, individual freedom disappears. Such doctrines did not reconcile power and freedom. It is, therefore, urgent a more penetrating study of the relations between power and freedom, by clarifying the origin, nature and organization of political power. (edited)

**Pereira da Silva, Marcelo Soares**. Elementos para a Construçao Teórica da Historicidade das Práticas Educativas Escolares. *Educ Filosof*, 9(17), 173-183, Ja-Je 95.

**Pereira da Silva, Sérgio**. O "Romantismo", o "Enciclopedismo" e o "Criticismo" Manifestos no Magistério da Filosofia no Ensino Médio em Uberlândia. *Educ Filosof*, 10(19), 181-188, Ja-Je 96.

This article is a product of research about the teaching of philosophy, at high school, in Uberlândia. It tries to show some methodologies associated with conceptions called "romantic", "encyclopaedic" and "critic".

**Pereppaden, Jose**. Habermas' Philosophy of Liberation. *J Dharma*, 22(1), 74-85, Ja-Mr 97.

**Perez, Diana I**. Cualidades secundarias y autoconocimiento. *Analisis Filosof*, 17(1), 27-33, My 97.

After pointing particular difficulties about Vergara's argument against self-knowledge, I sketch an alternative to Vergara's way of posing the problem about self-knowledge. Firstly, I argue that it makes sense to affirm that we know our own states of mind. Secondly, I argue for the thesis of privileged access to our own states of mind—the thesis that our knowledge about our own states of mind is superior than our knowledge of other people—but deny that there exists a qualitative difference between first person and third person knowledge of the mental.

**Perez, Diana I** and Sabatés, Marcelo H. La noción de superveniencia en la visión estratificada del mundo. *Analisis Filosof*, 15(1-2), 181-199, My-N 95.

Arguably, the orthodox ontological doctrine of contemporary physicalism is the so-called "layered view of reality". According to this widespread but generally implicit or understated view, reality is hierarchically structured in a series of levels such that objects and properties characterizing higher layers depend on those that characterize lower layers. While the part-whole relation cements objects of different levels, supervenience is thought to be what ties properties of different strata. However, even though many alternative notions of supervenience have been proposed recently for diverse purposes, it is in no way clear whether any of these notions is apt to relate the properties of different layers. In this paper we: I) offer a brief but explicit statement of the layered view of reality, II) discuss the requirements a notion of supervenience has to meet in order to play a substantive role in such a view, and III) argue that a notion of supervenience that takes a particular side on issues such as strength, modal force, ontological import and composition of the supervenience base is a good starting point as the cementing relation between the properties of the different layers of reality.

**Perez, Diana Inés**. Variedades de Superveniencia. *Manuscrito*, 19(2), 165-199, O 96.

The notion of supervenience has been much discussed recently and employed in many different areas of philosophy. Supervenience is a relation between sets of properties and its major attraction is that it seems to provide the only way of formulating a stable form of nonreductive materialism. In this paper the various different versions of supervenience that have been proposed are distinguished (weak versus strong, local versus global, and ontological versus adscriptive). We conclude by examining the arguments for taking the notion of supervenience seriously and trying to make it precise.

**Pérez de Laborda, Alfonso**. Teoría de la verdad: sobre ciencia y verdad. *Dialogo Filosof*, 13(2), 203-214, My-Ag 97.

La verdad en cuanto ligada al lenguaje ha de ser concebida simultáneamente como coherencia y como correspondencia. Pero la palabra es siempre, a la vez, impotencia y fuerza creadora. Ahí es donde se sitúa realmente el tema de la verdad. La razón nos sitúa ante la responsabilidad de un proyecto y unos fines. La ciencia nos acerca a la verdad de lo que es la realidad en cuanto "acción racional de la razón práctica". Se trata de un proceso de "empastamiento" o progresiva coherencia, que no llega nunca a "tocar" la realidad. Hay una relación dialéctica entre nuestro juicio y la realidad. Nuestra imputación de realidad se nos convierte en un "juicio de verdad" hermenéuticamente desvelada.

**Pérez de Laborda, Miguel**. Sujeto, propio y esencia: el fundamento de la distinción aristotélica de modos de predicar. *Acta Phil*, 5(2), 269-292, 1996.

Sono vari i modi di attribuire qualcosa a un soggetto che appaiono nell'opera di Aristotele. In questo studio oltre a mostrare quali sono i principali modi di predicare, si tenta di cogliere il fondamento di queste divisioni. Si chiarisce in primo luogo la distinzione fra il predicare in senso proprio e altri modi non chiari o impropri, in particolare il predicare *per accidens*. Si spiegano anche i criteri secondo i quali Aristotele distingue la predicazione essenziale e la predicazione accidentale. E infine si presenta la nozione aristotelica di proprio, in rapporto al darsi "per lo più" o "per natura".

**Pérez de Tudela, Jorge**. "Los términos disposicionales: Una propuesta (abierta) de interpretación" in *Verdad: lógica, representación y mundo,* Villegas Forero, L, 489-502. Santiago de Compostela, Univ Santiago Comp, 1996.

The aim of this paper is to suggest that the discussion about the nature of the (so-called) "dispositional properties" may be attacked drawing a parallel between the "ontological" and the "juridical" sides of the problem of the "dispositions." This leads to the suggestion that the "dispositional properties" of the objective realities are as reducible to the laws of science as the "legal capacities" or "rights" of the human beings are reducible, according to certain interpretations, to the rules of law. That opens the field of an enlarged investigation about the next question: what is exactly the nature of a "rule"?

**Pérez Guerrero, Fco Javier**. La criatura es hecha como comienzo o principio. *Anu Filosof*, 29(2), 921-928, 1996.

Creation mustn't be considerated as a production whose term is creature. Creature as such isn't a term but a beginning. Abandonment of mental limit is a necessary method to reach such a knowledge of creature.

**Pérez Herranz, Fernando-M**. Para una ontología del continuo. *El Basilisco*, 22, 43-70, Jl-D 96.

**Pérez Luño, Antonio-Enrique**. Giambattista Vico y el actual debate sobre la argumentación jurídica. *Cuad Vico*, 5/6, 123-137, 1995/96.

Contrarily to the images purporting Vico as a thinker who paid little attention to methodological rigor, this paper aims to show: a) that there is a through concern along the Vichian thought with problems related with methodology; b) that Vico's philosophical contributions should be acknowledged particularly relevant in those subjects connected both with practical rationality and recent theories about legal reasonings; c) that Vico's methodological and legal approach can, nonetheless, hardly be labeled merely as "rhetoric," rather it entails a serious attempt to cast rational justifying principles onto the topic related with legal reasonings. In order to accomplish the above claims, three related questions should be addressed: i) the basic elements underlying the recent discussion on legal rationality and theories about patterns of reasonings in law; ii) the claim that Vico is to be regarded as a starting point in the new assessment of legal topic; iii) the meaning of the arguments inside the limits of the Vichian methodological reflections and the external connections they still keep with contemporary discussions.

**Perez Ruiz, Francisco**. Tres tratados "Sobre el maestro": Agustín, Buenaventura, Tomás de Aquino. *Pensamiento*, 53(206), 191-214, My-Ag 97.

La posibilidad de ensenar y aprender es un problema doctrinal e históricamente importante en la antropología filosófica y teológica. San Agustín le ha dedicado el último de sus diálogos filosóficos. Fuertemente influidos por él, también Buenaventura y Tomás de Aquino han tratado de este problema, cada cual a su modo. El examen del contenido de cada una de esas tres obras nos puede ayudar a profundizar diversos aspectos de este problema en sí mismo y en su desarrollo histórico.

**Pérez-Estévez, Antonio**. "The Other Through Dialogue: Latin-american Contribution to Intercultural Peace" in *Kreativer Friede durch Begegnung der Weltkulturen,* Beck, Heinrich (ed), 335-345. New York, Lang, 1995.

The author takes into account that dialogue in Western Platonic tradition is a discursive logical process towards intelligible ideas or truths. This Socratic-Platonic tradition does not point out the importance of the multiplicity of dialoguing persons and, therefore, the Other cannot enter into dialogue. This paper tries to develop a notion of 'existential dialogue' in which a few requisites are essential: 1) multiplicity of dialoguing persons, at least two. 2) Symmetry in the two moments of dialogue: talking and listening, with a stressing accent on the listening moment, so difficult to attain in our culture of vision. The listening moment is the moment of the Other by which his cultural world, folded by his words, invades mine. 3) The end or objective of dialogue is not any transcendental idea or truth but the dialoguing persons themselves and their performance as human beings. Dialoguing persons are not for ideas or truths, but ideas or truths are for dialoguing persons.

**Péréz-Estévez, Antonio**. Ciencia y docencia en Agustín y Tomás de Aquino: (Del maesto agustiniano al maestro tomista). *Rev Espan Filosof Med*, 4, 103-114, 1997.

Augustinian science of intelligible and eternal truths is acquired by a mental view of intellect and reason; it supposes the good will of knowing subject. Thomist science consists of a number of intelligible forms acquired from a deductive logic-necessary process that begins with the first obvious principles and axioms. For Augustin, there is only one teacher of intelligible truths that hides himself in the deepest of every rational soul and shows the Truth only to the interior man, that is, the one dominated by the good will. For Thomas Aquinas, there exist two different teachers: the main and interior one that is God and another external and human, with perfect and actual knowledge, who helps the disciple to get the ability and the habit of deducing notions and truths from the first obvious principles and axioms. For Augustin, we all are disciples of the unique teacher of Truth, Christ and we will be good or bad disciples according to our good or evil will. For Thomas Aquinas, every disciple has from the very beginning all the notions and truths that he is going to learn, but in potency or in their seminal reasons—the first obvious principles and axioms—; but he will try, with the important help of the teacher, to get the ability and the habit of deducing and developing all notions and truths enclosed within the first evident principles and axioms. (edited)

**Pérez-Wicht, Pablo Quintanilla**. Teoría de la acción y racionalidad en Donald Davidson. *Rev Latin de Filosof*, 23(1), 5-21, O 97.

This paper departs from an interpretation of Davidson's project of integrating the theory of action and the theory of communication. This shall allow me to consider, in the second part, to what extent this project culminates in a conception of the nature of rationality. Finally, in the third part, I will discuss to what extent this conception of rationality discards the possibility of accepting incommensurable rationalities.

AUTHOR INDEX 839 Perring, Christian

**Perine, Marcelo**. "Phronesis": Um Conceito Inoportuno?. *Kriterion*, 34(87), 31-55, Ja-Jl 93.

**Perine, Marcelo**. Ato e potência: implicaçoes éticas de uma doutrina metafísica. *Kriterion*, 37(94), 7-23, Jl-D 96.

Aristotle's book IX of *Metaphysics* comprises detailed study concerning concepts of potential and actuality. In IX 5, 1047b31 - 1048a24 Aristotle distinguishes between *acquired* and *congenital* potential and further develops the themes of determination of the potential and the diversity of rational potential relative to irrational, as regarding their actualization. The principle which decides the actualization of one of the opposites in the rational potential is *desire* and *rational choice*, although the law of determination of the all potential imposes to it a certain necessity. The present study intends to make explicit the importance of the metaphysical doctrine of actuality and potential for the comprehension of Aristotle's anthropology. (edited)

**Perini Santos, Ernesto**. 'Pseudo-Dionísio Areapagita' ou 'Dionísio Pseudo-Aeropagita'? Uma confusao a respeito de nomes e descriçoes definidas. *Kriterion*, 37(94), 91-96, Jl-D 96.

The paper analyzes '*pseudo-Denis the Areopagite*' as an abbreviated definite description and shows that one should use the above mentioned form, instead of '*Denis the pseudo-Areopagite*', also found in the literature.

**Perini Santos, Ernesto**. Suppositio and Significatio in Ockham's *Summa Logicae* (in Portuguese). *Trans/Form/Acao*, 19, 195-203, 1996.

*Significatio* and *suppositio* are central notions in Ockham's semantics; the former is propriety of isolated terms, the later, of terms in propositional contexts. Understanding the relation between both notions is important to determine the atomistic or propositional character of Ockham's semantics. The definition of each term refers to the other, not allowing any priority of one of them. Both terms exceed one another, covering cases which are outside the scope of the other. We identify, through the analysis of this excess the dominant term for the explanation of different kinds of linguistic phenomena. These different kinds of phenomena are identified with two different conceptual fields, each term (*suppositio* and *significatio*) being dominant in one field.

**Peris-Viñé, Luis M**. "The Grammar of Chomsky is not Mentalist" in *Verdad: lógica, representación y mundo,* Villegas Forero, L, 413-420. Santiago de Compostela, Univ Santiago Comp, 1996.

What is lingüistics all about? The conception of language of the *Chomskyan Trend,* CHT, is in general, *mentalist*, that is, it asserts that lingüistic theories are about mental entities. The first stage of CHT corresponds to Chomsky (1955) and (1957), and it is called *Grammar of Chomsky*, gch. To know this stage is fundamental for knowing CHT. Is gch mentalist? To answer this question we draw up the mentalist conception of CHT as it is presented in Chomsky (1986) and the conception of language of gch; we compare them and advance a answer. Finally we place the conception of gch in a no mentalist perspective by arguments coming from the logical reconstruction of gch.

**Peris-Viñé, Luis M**. Characterization of the Basic Notions of Chomsky's Grammar (in Spanish). *Agora (Spain)*, 15(2), 105-124, 1996.

We deal with relational basic notions of *Chomsky's grammar* (the linguistic theory exposed by Noam Chomsky in *The Logical Structure of Linguistic Theory*). First, we identify such notions (*phrase structure, transformed structure, phonemic representation* and *phonetic representation*) and we defend that all can be conceived as assigning representations to sentences. Second, we analyze their conceptual structure, defending that *phrase structure* is a ternary function with sentences and natural numbers as arguments, that *transformed structure* is a ternary function with sentences and phrase structures as arguments and that *phonemic representation* and *phonetic representation* are binary functions with sentences as arguments.

**Perkins, Mary Anne**. The Future and the History of Ideas. *Heythrop J*, 37(3), 322-335, Jl 96.

Written as a contribution to a *festschrift* edition of the *Heythrop Journal*, this is an apologetic for the history of ideas and attempts to communicate what Isaiah Berlin has called its 'surprises and rewards'. The author discusses differing definitions of the subject, and its potential contribution to other fields of study and discourse: for example, education, linguistics and law. The double-edged methodology (a polarity of history and philosophy) is presented as a valuable tool of criticism. The work of S.T. Coleridge is explored as having both anticipated the dangers and demonstrated the benefits of intellectual history.

**Perkins Jr, Ray**. Response to Lackey on "Conditional Preventive War". *Russell*, 16(2), 169-170, Wint 96-97.

Perkins responds to Douglas Lackey's claims that 1)there is no tenable distinction between conditional and unconditional war and 2) Russell's belief about the likelihood of war is not morally relevant to the question of his culpability for his advocacy of conditional preventive war against the Soviet Union in the 1945-1947 period.

**Perler, Dominik**. Abkehr vom Mythos: Descartes in der gegenwärtigen Diskussion. *Z Phil Forsch*, 51(2), 285-308, Ap-Je 97.

**Perler, Dominik**. *Repräsentation bei Descartes*. Frankfurt/M, Klostermann, 1996.

Descartes' Ideentheorie ist in der neueren Forschung immer wieder als Ausgangspunkt des neuzeitlichen *way of ideas* dargestellt worden, der in einen verhängnisvollen Repräsentationalismus mündet. Denn Cartesische Ideen scheinen so etwas wie mentale Objekte in einer "inneren Arena" zu sein. Da wir nur zu diesen mentalen Objekten einen unmittelbaren Zugang haben, können wir höchstens auf die Existenz äusserer Objekte schliessen, wir können sie aber nie unmittelbar erkennen. Stets sind wir in unserer inneren Arena gefangen. (publisher, edited)

**Perler, Dominik**. Things in the Mind: Fourteenth-Century Controversies over "Intelligible Species". *Vivarium*, 34(2), 231-253, N 96.

**Perler, Dominik**. War Aristoteles ein Funktionalist? Überlegungen zum Leib-Seele-Problem. *Z Phil Forsch*, 50(3), 341-363, Jl-S 96.

**Perloff, Michael** and Belnap, Nuel. The Way of the Agent. *Stud Log*, 51(3-4), 463-484, 1992.

The conditional, *if an agent did something, then the agent could have done otherwise*, is analyzed using *stit* theory, which is a logic of "seeing to it that" based on agents making choices in the context of branching time. The truth of the conditional is found to be a subtle matter that depends on how it is interpreted (e.g., on what "otherwise" refers to and on the difference between "could" and "might") and also on whether or not there are "busy choosers" that can make infinitely many choices in a finite span of time.

**Perminov, V Ya**. The Philosophical and Methodological Thought of N. I. Lobachevsky. *Phil Math*, 5, 3-20, F 97.

The article deals with the philosophical and methodological ideas of N.I. Lobachevsky—one of the creators of non-Euclidean geometries in the first half of the nineteenth century. The author shows that Lobachevsky elaborated a specific system of views on the nature of mathematical concepts and that these views were deeply involved in his mathematical investigation, especially in the creation and justification of the new geometry.

**Perminova, Alla Ivanovna** and Ianovskii, Rudol'f Grigor'evich and Mel'nikova, Tatiana A. Women and Society in Russia. *Russian Stud Phil*, 34(2), 66-72, Fall 95.

**Perna Marano, Enrica**. "Marcel Proust e i 'miracoli' della memoria involontaria" in *Il Concetto di Tempo: Atti del XXXII Congresso Nazionale della Società Filosofica Italiana,* Casertano, Giovanni (ed), 243-247. Napoli, Loffredo, 1997.

**Perreijn, Willem**. Kant, Smith and Locke: The Locksmith's Mending of Tradition: A Reaction to Mr. Fleischacker's Thesis. *Kantstudien*, 88(1), 105-118, 1997.

We reject Mr. Fleischacker's thesis according to which Smith did substantially influence Kant's ethics. A consideration of the main concepts involved in any comparison between them, shows these to be present in Kant's early writings even before anyone ever reported on Smith in German philosophy. Alternatives for key-notions like the spectator, impartiality, substitution and conscience are found in e.g., Locke, Burke, the Epistle of Paul, Leibniz, Wolff, Rousseau and Baumgarten.

**Perrett, Roy W**. Religion and Politics in India: Some Philosophical Perspectives. *Relig Stud*, 33(1), 1-14, Mr 97.

What is the traditional relation of religion to politics in India? Recent scholarly debate has generated at least two divergent answers. According to one view there is a long standing traditional opposition between religion and politics in India. According to another view a separation of religion from politics is contrary to Indian ways of thinking. I argue that from the perspective of classical Indian philosophy there is no *single* tradition on the issue of religion and politics. To be able to do so, however, I utilize too some work in Western philosophy.

**Perrett, Roy W**. Symbols, Icons and Stupas. *Brit J Aes*, 36(4), 432-438, O 96.

Jane Duran claims that the usual Western historian's description of the Buddhist reliquary stupa as a psycho-cosmic symbol is problematic (*BJA* January 1996), for our notion of a symbol suggests that symbols are heavily conventional and such a description is implausible in the Indian cultural context. Nor is the stupa symbolic in an iconic sense. I argue that the customary description of the Buddhist stupa as a symbol is not so very problematic. However, perhaps the most accurate description is that the stupa is a Peircean "hypoicon", i.e., a (semiotically) impure icon that is also a symbol.

**Perrett, Roy W**. The Analogical Argument for Animal Pain. *J Applied Phil*, 14(1), 49-58, 1997.

Philosophical defenders of animal liberation believe that we have direct duties to animals. Typically a presumption of that belief is that animals have the capacity to experience pain and suffering. Notoriously, however, a strand of Western scientific and philosophical thought has held animals to be incapable of experiencing pain and even today one frequently encounters in discussions of animal liberation expressions of scepticism about whether animals really experience pain. This article responds to this scepticism by claiming that it is just as reasonable for me to believe that animals feel pain, given my only evidence for this is shared behaviour and physiology, as it is for me to believe that other humans feel pain on the basis of similar evidence. In this paper I expound and defend this argument. (edited)

**Perrick, M** and Swart, H C M. Quantified Modal Logic, Reference and Essentialism. *Log Anal*, 36(144), 219-231, S-D 93.

After explaining in section 1 why modal contexts should be referentially transparent and extensionally opaque, we point out in section 2 that modal (necessity) contexts can only be referentially transparent if we take necessity as necessity de re, not de dicto. In section 3 we argue that quantified modal logic (as it appears in the literature) implies essentialism de dicto, in the sense that it limits the referring expressions to rigid designators. The arguments in the literature that "the Evening Star is the Morning Star" is a contingent truth are based on de dicto considerations and are not detrimental to the metaphysical (or de re) status of this sentence as a necessary truth. By making a distinction "de re—de dicto" we make it clear that essentialism (de re) and quantified modal logic (as conceived by Quine, Follesdal, Kripke and others) cannot be identified. Finally, we present two objections against the view that quantified modal logic presupposes that the referring terms are rigid designators.

**Perring, Christian**. Degrees of Personhood. *J Med Phil*, 22(2), 173-197, Ap 97.

In this paper I argue that a naturalist conception of personhood, such as the one defended by Derek Parfit, implies that there are degrees of personhood, i.e., that it makes sense to say one individual has a greater degree of personhood than another. I describe both criteria of general personhood, which distinguish between persons and nonpersons and criteria of particular personhood, which distinguish between one person and another. I examine some of the consequences for ethics, including the rights to life, self-determination and treatment. There may be circumstances in medicine where we have to judge the value of a patient's life in order to decide what medical treatment, if any, to provide, and although it may be emotionally difficult and politically dangerous, one relevant factor is what degree of personhood that individual has.

**Perring, Christian**. Medicating Children: The Case of Ritalin. *Bio- ethics*, 11(3-4), 228-240, Jl 97.

In response to recent concerns about the overmedication of children, this paper considers ethical and conceptual issues that arise in the issue of when children who are diagnosed with attention deficit hyperactivity disorder (ADHD) should be given stimulants such as the psychotropic drug Ritalin as part of their treatment. There is considerable resistance and worry about the possibility of overmedication. This is linked to the worry that the diagnosis of ADHD is overused, and the paper considers some reasons to worry about the overuse of the diagnosis itself. The paper then focuses on the resistance to the use of drugs, which is particularly strong for children in the gray area of diagnosis, where it is dubious whether the children really meet the strict diagnostic criteria. (edited)

**Perron, Louis**. L'idée de loi naturelle dans le contexte actuel de la raison pratique. *Maritain Stud*, 12, 98-112, 1996.

Largely inspired by the work of the Belgian philosopher Jean Ladrière, this article tries to reinterpret the idea of natural law from the perspective of the practical reason taken in its present historical context it examines successively three types of relations: first, the relation between practical reason and ethical normativity, second the relation between ethics and law and finally the relation between existence and nature. In conclusion, the article suggests that Ladrière's notion of an eschatological reason could provide the leading idea in reinterpretating the notion of natural law in a meaningful way from today's standpoint.

**Perron, Louis**. La paix perpétuelle chez Kant: du devoir à l'espérance. *De Phil*, 12, 179-194, 1995-1996.

This article focuses on the link between duty, hope and peace in Kant's essay on *Perpetual Peace*. It tries to answer two specific questions: 1) Why is perpetual peace a duty? 2) In which sense does this duty provide a ground for hope? Perpetual peace is a duty because it is rooted in the categorical imperative and because it is needed in order to achieve right and justice. This duty in its turn grounds the hope of peace because it is linked to the hope of reason itself.

**Perry, Clifton B**. Is Being a Carrier of a Disability, a Disability?. *Int J Applied Phil*, 11(1), 11-13, Sum-Fall 96.

It has been argued that the carrier of a recessive trait suffers from an impairment recognizable as a disability by the Americans with Disabilities Act. To demonstrate that such an argument is both deductively invalid an inductively weak shall be the purpose of this note.

**Perry, John**. Frege über indexikalische Ausdrücke. *Conceptus*, 28(73), 147-183, 1995.

The main thrust of this essay is to show that there is a fundamental and irreparable inconsistency in Frege's concept of *Sense*, although it is a flaw which is barely visible until one considers certain examples involving indexical expressions. The significance of this will be obvious to anyone interested in Frege or the Fregean tradition. The essay also provides an accessible introduction to the contemporary study of indexical reference, especially as it relates to direct, causal and informational theories of linguistic meaning. It may also provide a point of entry into the author's work in general (especially in light of a Postscript, which discusses the motivation behind this essay and it's relation to more recent work by the author). Much of this work may be unfamiliar to readers who have only encountered "situation semantics."(publisher,edited)

**Persson, Ingmar**. Genetic Therapy, Person-Regarding Reasons and the Determination of Identity: A Reply to Robert Elliot. *Bioethics*, 11(2), 161-169, Ap 97.

I have outlined two ways of defending the claim that there are so-called person-regarding reasons for practicing gene therapy on human conceptuses. One is metaphysical and concerns our nature and identity. The upshot of it is that, in cases of most interest, this therapy does not affect our identity, by bringing into existence anyone of our kind who would not otherwise have existed. The other defense is value theoretical and claims that even if genetic therapy were to affect the identity of beings our kind, there could still be person-regarding reasons for performing it, since we can be benefited and harmed by being caused to exist or not to exist. Robert Elliot has attacked both of these lines, and my present objective is to show how his criticisms can be deflected.

**Persson, Ingmar**. Hume—Not a "Humean" about Motivation. *Hist Phil Quart*, 14(2), 189-206, Ap 97.

A standard interpretation of Hume is that he regards beliefs alone as insufficient to produce an action: some "passion" or noncognitive state is also necessary. It is here argued that this interpretation clashes with central doctrines of his. Instead of taking Hume's claim to be about *manifestations* of reason, i.e., ideas or beliefs, not causing passion and action, this paper construes him as making a claim about the *faculty* of reason, to the effect that passions and actions cannot be manifestations of it because they are "original existences" lacking any "representative quality."

**Peruzzi, Alberto**. Debiti dello strutturalismo. *Teoria*, 16(2), 21-63, 1996.

Focus is on the definition of meaning as role-in-a-structure. The purpose is to show that European structuralism anticipated basic semantic problems and the

holistic solution to them proposed by many analytic philosophers. The structuralist version is even more clear. Thus, it's easier to see that the solution proposed is inadequate. The main steps in the history of structuralism are discussed, emphasizing that the symbiosis of structuralism and semiotics was a blind-alley. Linguistic relativism is a consequence of such symbiosis. A few data from psychology of perception and anthropology are mentioned, which contrasts with semantic structuralism.

**Peruzzi, Nico** and Canapary, Andrew and Bongar, Bruce. Physician-Assisted Suicide: The Role of Mental Health Professionals. *Ethics Behavior*, 6(4), 353-366, 1996.

A review of the literature was conducted to better understand the (potential) role of mental health professionals in physician-assisted suicide. Numerous studies indicate that depression is one of the most commonly encountered psychiatric illnesses in primary care settings. Yet, depression consistently goes undetected and undiagnosed by nonpsychiatrically trained primary care physicians. Noting the well-studied link between depression and suicide, it is necessary to question giving sole responsibility of assisting patients in making end-of-life treatment decisions to these physicians. Unfortunately, the use of mental health consultation by these physicians is not a common occurrence. Greater involvement of mental health professionals in this emerging and debated area is advocated. (edited)

**Pestana, Mark Stephen**. The Three Species of Freedom and the Six Species of Will Acts. *Mod Sch*, 74(1), 19-29, N 96.

The author contrasts the analyses of willing a complete human action provided by Aquinas's and Scotus's conceptions of freedom of will. Both conceptions of freedom are developed and their difference explicated. The constituent acts of will and intellect that make up a complete human action in Thomas's theory are explicated. The author demonstrates the difference that Thomas's and Scotus's conceptions of freedom make to the completion of the series of constituent acts. The paper concludes by showing how Scotus's account of the failure to finish the series of constituent acts better allows than does Thomas's account for a type of irrational inaction.

**Peters, Gary**. The Rhythm of Alterity: Levinas and Aesthetics. *Rad Phil*, 82, 9-16, Mr-Ap 97.

**Peters, John Durham**. "The Root of Humanity: Hegel on Communication and Language" in *Figuring the Self: Subject, Absolute, and Others in Classical German Philosophy*, Zöller, Günter (ed), 227-244. Albany, SUNY Pr, 1997.

Hegel's understanding of self and others offers rich ways to refigure the concept of communication from its current antinomies. Hegel's account of communication neither erases the curious fact of otherness at language's core nor the possibility of doing things with words. I focus especially on the treatment of recognition and language in the *Phenomenology of Spirit*. Here communication is not a psychological problem of private minds touching but a political-historical problem of creating conditions that make the mutual recognition of self-conscious individuals possible. This resonance of these ideas in the philosophies of Peirce and Royce is suggested in conclusion.

**Petersen, Karl**. Ergodic Theorems and the Basis of Science. *Synthese*, 108(2), 171-183, Ag 96.

New results in ergodic theory show that averages of repeated measurements will typically diverge with probability one if there are random errors in the measurement of time. Since mean-square convergence of the averages is not so susceptible to these anomalies, we are led again to compare the mean and pointwise ergodic theorems and to reconsider efforts to determine properties of a stochastic process from the study of a generic sample path. There are also implications for models of time and the interaction between observer and observable.

**Peterson, Douglas**. Cardinal Functions on Ultraproducts of Boolean Algebras. *J Sym Log*, 62(1), 43-59, Mr 97.

**Peterson, Gregory R**. Minds and Bodies: Human and Divine. *Zygon*, 32(2), 189-206, Je 97.

Does God have a mind? Western theism has traditionally construed God as an intentional agent who acts on creation and in relation to humankind. God loves, punishes and redeems. God's intentionality has traditionally been construed in analogy to human intentionality, which in turn has often presumed a supernatural dualism. Developments in cognitive science, however, render supernatural dualism suspect for explaining the human mind. How, then, can we speak of the mind of God? Borrowing from Daniel Dennett's intentional stance, I suggest that analogical reasoning regarding the mind of God be abandoned in favor of an ontologically agnostic approach that treats God as an intentional system. In this approach, God's purposive action is an explanatory feature of the believer's universe, a real pattern that informs our values and beliefs about the world and our place in it.

**Peterson, Grethe B** (ed). *The Tanner Lectures on Human Values, Volume 18, 1997*. Salt Lake City, Univ of Utah Pr, 1997.

*The Tanner Lectures on Human Values* were founded to advance and reflect upon the scholarly and scientific learning relating to human values. The purpose embraces the entire range of physical, moral, artistic, intellectual, and religious values pertinent to the human condition, interest, behavior, and aspiration. Appointment as a Tanner Lecturer is a recognition of uncommon capabilities and outstanding scholarly or leadership achievement in the field of human values. This year's volume includes Tanner Lectures given at Stanford University, Princeton University, the University of Utah, Cambridge University, the University of California at Riverside, and Harvard University.

**Peterson, John**. The Interdependence of Intellectual and Moral Virtue in Aquinas. *Thomist*, 61(3), 449-454, Jl 97.

Aquinas distinguishes the natural and the supernatural ends of persons. In both moral and intellectual virtue are interdependent. In the natural end, intellectual virtue (prudence) is the causal condition of moral virtue and moral virtue is logical condition of intellectual virtue (prudence). But in the supernatural end, it is just the converse of this. Intellectual virtue (the Beatific Vision) is the logical condition of moral virtue and moral virtue is the causal condition of intellectual virtue (the Beatific Vision).

**Peterson, John**. The Real and the Rational: Aquinas's Synthesis. *Int Phil Quart*, 37(2), 189-202, Je 97.

Aquinas avoids either reducing the real to the rational (extreme realism) or the rational to the real (nominalism). The first mistake identifies how something is with how it is known. The second identifies how something is known with how it is. But Aquinas keeps the distinction without so radically separating the two (Kantian conceptualism) that a transcendental turn is necessary to save the conformity of real and rational in which knowledge consists. That is how he escapes the Kantian error of splitting the tie that binds knowledge and truth on the one hand and reality on the other.

**Peterson, Philip L**. Singular (Non-)existence Propositions. *Acta Analytica*, 45-65, 1996.

Any *singular* existence proposition appears to be provable and, thereby, "necessary if true at all" (deemed "noncontingent", which contradicts a "nonnecessity" of the form "p & not-Nec-p"). *True* singular existence propositions are noncontingent and *false* ones are contingent! Singular existence propositions about fictional entities can't be about objects in merely possible worlds, since there are *impossible* fictional objects. The explanation of our only apparent success in expressing such propositions (e.g., that Cleo, the barber of Alcala who shaves all and only those who do not shave themselves, does not exist) is that we *pretend* that such propositions exist just as we *pretend* that fictional objects exist in playing the "make-believe games" (K. Walton) we routinely participate in when appreciating representational art.

**Peterson, Richard T**. "Democracy and Intellectual Mediation: After Liberalism and Socialism" in *Political Dialogue: Theories and Practices*, Esquith, Stephen L (ed), 183-213. Amsterdam, Rodopi, 1996.

The problem of democratically generated power is here addressed in terms of a communication conception that responds to issues posed by the contemporary division of labor. In the wake of Communism, the power of bureaucrats and experts has not been adequately addressed by triumphant liberalism, since liberalism promotes its own version of knowledge politics. Moreover, contemporary liberalism has not adequately responded to the productivist assumptions it shares with traditional socialism or to the limitations inherent in a nation-centered politics in the age of multinational capital and global mass culture. (edited)

**Peterson, Tarla Rai** and Gilbertz, Susan J and Varner, Gary E. "Teaching Environmental Ethics as a Method of Conflict Management" in *Environmental Pragmatism,* Light, Andrew (ed), 266-282. New York, Routledge, 1996.

Representatives of diverse interests in regional environmental disputes were brought together for two day workshops on environmental ethics. The workshops introduced participants to concepts and theories commonly discussed in college philosophy courses on the subject and presented them with opportunities to describe themselves and their perceived opponents in those terms. Content analysis of lengthy, unstructured interviews conducted months before and after suggest that such workshops affect participants' ways of framing environmental controversies and encourage related philosophical reflection.

**Petit, Philip** and O'Leary-Hawthorne, John. Strategies for Free Will Compatibilists. *Analysis*, 56(4), 191-201, O 96.

This essay is an attempt to redress the balance of attention and to offer an overview of the different broad strategies that compatibilists may pursue. We start from a formulaic account of what it is for an agent to do something freely which all or nearly all compatibilists can be expected to endorse. We go on to look, then, at the different ways in which this account may be interpreted by different compatibilists. And we offer a concluding remark on the nature of the contest between the different strategies.

**Petrícek Jr, Miroslav** and Waldenfels, Bernhard. The Mine and That of Others (and M. Petrícek Commentary). (in Czech). *Filosof Cas*, 45(2), 283-295, 1997.

**Petrone, Giuseppe Landolfi**. Vittorio Imbriani e il *Kant poeta*. *Stud Filosofici*, 127-155, 1995.

The article contains the reprint of a small paper which Vittorio Imbriani published in 1884 with the title *Epicedii del Kant* Imbriani's pap, which is introduced by a historical note by myself, gave the Italian translation of Kant's verses, composed on the occasion of the death of some of Kant's Koenisberg leagues. My historical note investigates Imbriani's paper in the context of the crisis of Neapolitan Hegelianism. My note sheds some light on Imbriani's controversial interest in German literature.

**Petru, Eduard**. The Harmonizing Influence of God in the Understanding of J.A. Comenius. *Ultim Real Mean*, 20(2 & 3), 99-106, Je-S 97.

J.A. Comenius's thinking is usually interpreted as an expression of the baroque conflict of irreconcilable contradictions. Although it is possible to find many examples of this understanding. *The Labyrinth of the World and the Paradise of the Heart* proves that it is necessary to see Comenius as a baroque humanist. According to him, the world is contradictory if it is interpreted with the help of insufficient reason, however, if it is judged from the viewpoint of God's order it gains the form of harmonic unity. The connection of humanistic and baroque ideas thus made it possible for Comenius not only to discover the harmony of the world but also to solve the contradiction in his thinking.

**Petrus, Klaus**. Analyse und Kontext des Wachsbeispiels bei Descartes. *Frei Z Phil Theol*, 43(3), 324-334, 1996.

**Petrus, Klaus**. *Genese und Analyse*. Hawthorne, de Gruyter, 1997.

**Petrus, Klaus**. Naturgemässe Klassifikation und Kontinuität, Wissenschaft und Geschichte: Überlegungen zu Pierre Duhem. *J Gen Phil Sci*, 27(2), 307-323, 1996.

Duhem is commonly held to have founded his view of history of science as continuous on the 'metaphysical assertion' of natural classification. With the help of a strict distinction between formal and material characterization of natural classification I try to show that this imputation is problematic, if not simply incorrect. My analysis opens alternative perspectives on Duhem's talk of continuity, the ideal form of theories and the rôle of 'bon sens'; moreover it emphasizes some aspects of Duhem's realism that play an important part in his philosophy of science.

**Pettit, Philip**. "Love and Its Place in Moral Discourse" in *Love Analyzed*, Lamb, Roger E, 153-163. Boulder, Westview Pr, 1997.

Love is not a virtue on a par with fairness and kindness: It does not connect in the manner of a virtue with motivation. But neither is love just a schema, like prudence, for explaining to others why we are moved by certain attachments. Love is represented in our discourse as itself a value that we expect to make a universal claim.

**Pettit, Philip**. Realism and Truth: A Comment on Crispin Wright's *Truth and Objectivity*. *Phil Phenomenol Res*, 56(4), 883-890, D 96.

Realism in any area of talk or thought requires a view of the discourse both as truth-seeking and in some of its positive claims, truth-attaining. But what else does it need? Crispin Wright suggests: a commitment to a heavyweight conception of what is involved in sentences of the discourse being true. I disagree. If anything else is needed, it is only that the true sentences of the discourse are made true—true, under a common conception of truth—by how things are in the world-at-large, not just by how things are with us or by how things relate to us.

**Pettit, Philip**. Republican Theory and Criminal Punishment. *Utilitas*, 9(1), 59-79, Mr 97.

Suppose we embrace the republican ideal of freedom as nondomination: freedom as immunity to arbitrary interference. In that case those acts that call uncontroversially for criminalization will usually be objectionable on three grounds: the offender assumes a dominating position in relation to the victim, the offender reduces the range or ease of undominated choice on the part of the victim and the offender raises a spectre of domination for others like the victim. And in that case, so it appears, the obvious role for punishment will be, so far as possible, to undo such evils: to rectify the effects of the crime that make it a repugnant republican act. This paper explores this theory of punishment as rectification, contrasting it with better established utilitarian and retributivist approaches.

**Pettit, Philip**. Three Aspects of Rational Explanation. *Protosoz*, 8/9, 170-182, 1996.

In this paper I want to draw attention to three distinct and progressively more specific, aspects of such rational explanation. I do so, because I believe that they are not always prised apart sufficiently. The first aspect of rational explanation is that it is a programming variety of explanation, in a phrase that Frank Jackson and I introduced some years ago (Jackson and Pettit 1988). The second is, in another neologism (Pettit 1986), that it is a normalising kind of explanation. And the third is that it is a variety of interpretation: if you like, it is a hermeneutic form of explanation. (edited)

**Pfeifer, Karl**. Laughter, Freshness, and Titillation. *Inquiry*, 40(3), 307-322, S 97.

Robert C. Roberts's suggestion that the conditions for laughter at humor (e.g., jokes) can best be captured with a notion of freshness, as opposed to surprise, is pursued. The relationship freshness has to setup and surprise is clarified and the place of freshness within a larger system of structuring metaphors is alluded to. The question of whether freshness can also cover laughter at the nonhumorous (e.g., tickling) is then taken up, it being determined that such coverage is possible but uneven. However, once the phenomenon of laughter in the absence of feelings of amusement or similarly pleasant psychological states is considered, it is seen that freshness cannot underpin a comprehensive account of laughter. The notion of titillation is then proposed for this role.

**Pfeifer, Karl**. Philosophy Outside the Academy: The Role of Philosophy in People-Oriented Professions and the Prospects for Philosophical Counseling. *Inquiry (USA)*, 14(2), 58-69, Wint 94.

I suggest that the current interest in philosophical counseling is comparable to the situation in the Sixties when many philosophy graduates entertained false hopes of nonacademic philosophical employment. I describe my own experience as a welfare worker, in the course of which my philosophical training proved useful in various ways; I maintain, though, that there was nothing especially philosophical in this. I then consider some ways in which philosophical counseling might be distinctively philosophical. I conclude that philosophical training, as we know it, is in any case inadequate for philosophical counseling and would need to be supplemented by psychological and other training.

**Pfeiffer, María Luisa**. La muerte, ese escándalo. *Cuad Etica*, 21-22, 117-134, 1996.

Death is a jump into emptiness, a mystery and this is why it is a cause of preoccupation for us human beings. In these times death appears mostly as failure and, therefore, as the greatest of scandals. To make death retreat has been the fantasy of all ages, and is the origin of medicine. Death and medicine are old enemies. This paper shows some medical and psychological points of view about death in the present time: conceptualization, medication, experience. Further philosophical approaches should continue this line of inquiry.

**Pfenning, Frank** and Narendran, Paliath and Statman, Richard. On the Unification Problem for Cartesian Closed Categories. *J Sym Log*, 62(2), 636-647, Je 97.

Cartesian closed categories (CCCs) have played and continue to play an important role in the study of the semantics of programming languages. An axiomatization of the isomorphisms which hold in all Cartesian closed categories discovered independently by Soloviev and Bruce, Di Cosmo and Longo leads to seven equalities. We show that the unification problem for this theory is undecidable, thus settling an open question. We also show that an important subcase, namely unification modulo the *linear isomorphisms*, is NP-complete. Furthermore, the problem of matching in CCCs is NP-complete when the subject term is irreducible. (edited)

**Pfitzner, Elvira**. Korrespondenten von G.W. Leibniz: Georg Samuel Dörffel, geb. 11 Oktober 1643 in Plauen/Vogtland—gest. 6. August 1688 in Weida. *Stud Leibniz*, 28(1), 119-122, 1996.

This letter investigates the question, whether Leibniz and Dörffel did really have that profound contacts as it was presumed for over 100 years. The pastor and dean Dörffel, contemporary of Leibniz, did intensive work in mathematics and astronomy. Apart from others, in 1680/81 he discovered the parabolic orbit of comets around the sun. The investigation shows that Leibniz and Dörffel were friends in their college time. Later on they lost their contacts. In the years 1679/80 a scientific correspondence between both did start. But this was interrupted by the restrictive quarantine measures against extension of the plague.

**Phelan, Shane**. Coyote Politics: Trickster Tales and Feminist Futures. *Hypatia*, 11(3), 130-149, Sum 96.

This essay is a first attempt at thinking through the ways in which Native American Coyote stories can illustrate options for lesbian and feminist politics. I follow the metaphors of trickery and shape-shifting common to the stories and recommend the laughter they evoke as we engage in feminist politics and philosophy.

**Philipose, Liz**. The Laws of War and Women's Human Rights. *Hypatia*, 11(4), 46-62, Fall 96.

This is a review of historical developments in international criminal law leading up to the inclusion of rape as a "crime against humanity" in the current war crimes tribunal for the ex-Yugoslavia. In addition to the need to understand the specificity of events and their impact on women, the laws of war must also be understood in their specificity and the ways in which even the humanitarian provisions of those laws privilege military needs.

**Philippe, Marie-Dominique**. Saint Thomas et le mystère de la création: une réponse aux interrogations de l'homme d'aujourd'hui. *Sapientia*, 52(201), 145-158, 1997.

Today, man seems to have lost the sense of his finality as a human person. If we look back in history, it seems that since the 14th century, final casuality has been considered as metaphorical. It is necessary to rediscover being-in-act and, thus, creation as one of the most important and urgent philosophical and theological problems of today. In *Aquinas's Commentary on the Sentences*, we can see the major points of St. Thomas conception of creation, although not in a fully developed way. It is in the *Summa* that we can see the full depth of Aquinas's view of creation.

**Philipse, Herman**. The End of Plasticity. *Inquiry*, 40(3), 291-306, S 97.

Paul Churchland has become famous for holding three controversial and interrelated doctrines which he put forward in early papers and in his first book, *Scientific Realism and the Plasticity of Mind* (1979): eliminative materialism, the doctrine of the plasticity of perception and a general network theory of language. In his latest book, *The Engine of Reason, the Seat of the Soul* (1995), Churchland aims to make some results of connectionist neuroscience available to the general public and explores the philosophical and social consequences that neuroscience is likely to have. I argue that these results of neuroscience refute the three doctrines that Churchland advocated in his earlier works. Yet youthful dreams do not die easily and Churchland is reluctant to relinquish his early views.

**Phillips, Barbara J**. In Defense of Advertising: A Social Perspective. *J Bus Ethics*, 16(2), 109-118, F 97.

Many critics have questioned the ethics of advertising as an institution in current American society. The purpose of this paper is to critically examine three negative social trends that have been attributed to advertising: a) the elevation of consumption over other social values, b) the increasing use of goods to satisfy social needs, and c) the increasing dissatisfaction of individual consumers. This explanation yields a defense of advertising which argues that the underlying cause of these negative trends is not advertising, but a larger social factor—capitalism. Solutions that address the capitalistic roots of these negative social trends are suggested.

**Phillips, Benjamin** and Wear, Stephen. Clinical Ethics and the Suffering Christian. *Christian Bioethics*, 2(2), 239-252, Ag 96.

Contrary to the ecumenical spirit of our time, the differences among the Christian religions bring into question what one can say or do in common with fellow Christians. This issue, echoing the program of this journal, accentuates those differences, specifically when we focus on the Christian who is ill and suffering. At the bedside, it is the specifics of a religion, including not only its doctrines, but its informing and sustaining narratives, that must particularly be brought into play for the sake of the patient. Given this, our focus in this article regards what such a view implies for the clinician who is caring for a Christian patient whose religion he may or may not share, in general or in its specifics. Our basic conclusion is that the tendency for the clinician to act as both the patient's spiritual counselor, as well as his clinician, is generally neither prudent nor appropriate. Both hats should be worn concurrently. This view is advanced not only because of concerns regarding patient vulnerability and the possible abuse of power, but also because the two roles may collide with or undermine each other.

**Phillips, D C**. (Re)Inventing Scheffler, or, Defending Objective Educational Research. *Stud Phil Educ*, 16(1-2), 149-158, Ja-Ap 97.

Israel Scheffler's book *Science and Subjectivity* (1967) was prescient: His criticisms of attacks on the traditional notions of objectivity and truth that underlie modern science are still relevant nearly thirty years later, when postmodernism and some varieties of feminist epistemology are winning many adherents. Two aspects of Scheffler's book are singled out for discussion—his philosophical style, which is marked by careful, well-developed and detailed argument (in contrast to many contemporary writers in education who have postmodernist leanings, who merely make assertions about objectivity and so forth); and the actual content of the positions for which he argues.

**Phillips, D E** (ed) and Rhees, Rush. Language as Emerging from Instinctive Behaviour. *Phil Invest*, 20(1), 1-14, Ja 97.

**Phillips, J W P**. "The Subject of the Other: Ordinary Language and Its Enigmatic Ground" in *Critical Studies: Ethics and the Subject*, Simms, Karl (ed), 29-42. Amsterdam, Rodopi, 1997.

**Phillips, James**. Commentary on "Non-Cartesian Frameworks". *Phil Psychiat Psych*, 3(3), 187-189, S 96.

**Phillips, Lisa**. "Wholeness in Manifoldness: Genealogical Methods and Conditions of Agency in Nietzsche and Foucault" in *Critical Studies: Ethics and the Subject*, Simms, Karl (ed), 127-137. Amsterdam, Rodopi, 1997.

**Phillips, Patrick J J**. Winch's Pluralist Tree and the Roots of Relativism. *Phil Soc Sci*, 27(1), 83-95, Mr 97.

In this paper I critically engage with Berel Dov Lerner's version of "Instrumental Pluralism" (Phil. Soc. Sci. Vol. 25, 1995). "Instrumental Pluralism" is the thesis that there are many different standards of rationality. Through the employment of Ludwig Wittgenstein's "Remarks On Frazer's *The Golden Bough*" I point out the methodological shortcomings of Lerner's thesis. I also argue that Lerner and Peter Winch both equate possessing rationality with possessing a language. I indicate that as a result of such a move, both Lerner and Winch generate a form of relativism that is destructive to their respective aims.

**Phillips, Robert A**. Stakeholder Theory and A Principle of Fairness. *Bus Ethics Quart*, 7(1), 51-66, Ja 97.

Stakeholder theory has become a central issue in the literature on business ethics/business and society. There are, however, a number of problems with stakeholder theory as currently understood. Among these are: 1) the lack of a coherent justificatory framework, 2) the problem of adjudicating between stakeholders, and 3) the problem of stakeholder identification. In this essay, I propose that a possible source of obligations to stakeholders is the principle of fairness (or fair play) as discussed in the political philosophic literature of Rawls, Simmons and Cullity among others. (edited)

**Piá Tarazona, Salvador**. De la criatura a Dios: La demostración de la existencia de Dios en la primera dimensión del abandono del límite mental. *Anu Filosof*, 29(2), 929-948, 1996.

Leonardo Polo proposes a new interpretation of the demonstration of God's existence. This demonstration is based on the awareness of the creature's being and it is reached in the first dimension of the abandon of the mental limit, the method proposed by L. Polo.

**Pía Tarazona, Salvador** and García-Valdecasas, Miguel. Relación de obras publicadas e inéditos de Leonardo Polo. *Anu Filosof*, 29(2), 323-331, 1996.

**Piar, Carlos R**. César Chávez and La Causa: Toward a Hispanic Christian Social Ethic. *Annu Soc Christ Ethics*, 103-120, 1996.

Using the narrative theology of James McClendon as a paradigm, especially his notion of "biography as theology," this paper analyzes the life of César Chavez to discover what "God was doing" amidst the Hispanic community during the years of *La Causa*, "The Cause." It examines Chavez's values, principles, and methods as union organizer in order to forge a Hispanic Christian social ethic suitable for present-day issues and concerns.

**Piazza, Mario**. "Propositional Constants in Classical and Linear Logic" in *Verdad: lógica, representación y mundo*, Villegas Forero, L, 211-217. Santiago de Compostela, Univ Santiago Comp, 1996.

The purpose of this paper is to show briefly the different role of propositional constants in linear logic and in classical logic. This difference is stressed by means of a model-theoretical approach.

**Pica Ciamarra, Leonardo**. "L'immagine di Goethe e il pensiero storico (per una discussione dell'interpretazione di Meinecke)" in *Lo Storicismo e la Sua Storia: Temi, Problemi, Prospettive*, Cacciatore, Giuseppe (ed), 139-149. Milano, Guerini, 1997.

**Picardi, Eva**. "Frege's Anti-Psychologism" in *Frege: Importance and Legacy*, Schirn, Matthias (ed), 307-328. Hawthorne, de Gruyter, 1996.

The paper argues that Frege took the chief defect of psychologism to reside in a mistaken picture of meaning, which turns the objectivity of sense and the communication of thoughts into a mystery. The link between Frege's criticism of psychologistic conceptions of logic and psychologistic accounts of meaning is to be found in his (realist) conception of truth. Contrary to what Sluga and Kitcher have suggested, Frege's concern with the issue of psychologism is essentially semantic in nature. Kantian epistemology offers no answer to Frege's questions.

**Picardi, Eva**. Sigwart, Husserl and Frege on Truth and Logic, or Is Psychologism Still a Threat?. *Euro J Phil*, 5(2), 162-182, Ag 97.

The paper argues that Husserl's criticism of Sigwart's normative conception of logical laws rests on an absolutist conception of truth and content which is itself

AUTHOR INDEX 843 Pigden, Charles R

in need of justification. Also the contrast between psychological laws of holding true and logical laws of being true used by Frege in his criticism of psychologism fails to explain the epistemological status of logical laws. A better understanding of the latter is to be found in Frege's conception of truth and justification. Sigwart's psychologism comes to the fore in the privileged role he assigned in his logic to judgments of recognition and naming. While the attention paid to the indexical component of certain utterances enables Sigwart to give an original account of the import of impersonal judgments, his concentration on a first-person account of sentence meaning prevents him from appreciating the public dimension of meaning, which alone renders communication possible.

**Picart, Caroline Joan S**. Metaphysics in Gaston Bachelard's "Reverie". *Human Stud*, 20(1), 59-73, Ja 97.

This paper aims to trace the evolution of Bachelard's thought as he gropes toward a concrete formulation of a philosophy of the imagination. Reverie, the creative daydream, occupies the central position in Bachelard's emerging metaphysic, which becomes increasingly "phenomenological" in a manner reminiscent of Husserl. This means that although Bachelard does not use Husserlian terms, he appropriates the following features of (Husserlian) phenomenology: 1) a desire to "embracket" the initial (rationalistic) impulse; and 2) an aspiration to apprehend in its entirety, the creative epiphany of an image. Ultimately, this paper aims to show that there is a sense in which Bachelard's metaphysical concerns in his poetics are an outgrowth of (rather than radical break from) his earlier scientific and epistemological concerns. (edited)

**Picart, Caroline Joan S**. Nietzsche as Mashed Romantic. *J Aes Art Crit*, 55(3), 273-291, Sum 97.

**Piccari, Paolo**. La prima scuola tomistica: Erveo di Nedellec e l'epistemologia teologica. *Sapienza*, 50(2), 147-162, 1997.

**Picchioni, Anthony**. The Kevorkian Challenge. *Phil Cont World*, 2(3), 17-22, Fall 95.

The problem of self-determination in the dying process confronts a dilemma regarding clients' desire to know and not to know. Ambivalence and guilt make "free choice" problematic in choosing the way to die. Telling dying clients the "whole truth" about their condition is an art or skill. The question of a meaningful death raises questions that philosophical analysis can help clarify.

**Piché, Claude**. Fichte und die Urteilstheorie Heinrich Rickerts. *Fichte-Studien*, 13, 143-160, 1997.

In this article, I explain that the occurrence of the expression "primacy of practical reason" in the second edition of *Der Gegenstand der Erkenntnis* (1904) has to be related to Fichte rather than to Kant. In fact Rickert, encouraged by his student Emil Lask, came into closer contact with Fichte's thought in second half of the 1890, so that the "aesthetic" paradigms at work in the theory of judgment of the first edition of his book (1892) was to be replaced in 1904 by Fichte's model of "practical" philosophy: the truth of a judgement is based on something like moral consciousness.

**Pichler, Hanns**. "Sozio-ökonomische Entwicklung unter humanitären Kriterien als Friedenspostulat" in *Kreativer Friede durch Begegnung der Weltkulturen,* Beck, Heinrich (ed), 103-117. New York, Lang, 1995.

Immer schon, so dünkt es, war man wohl sich der Problematik von "Arm" und "Reich" gewahr; schon von ihren frühen, insbesondere klassischen Ansätzen an befasste sich denn auch die Wirtschaftstheorie mit dem Phänomen der Entwicklung, mit Wachstum und Wohlstandsmehrung, wofür Adam Smith sein Basismodell lieferte. An darin liegendem Anspruch hat im Grundsätzlichen sich wenig geändert; geändert sehr wohl aber hat sich dessen Perspektive im Sinne von "Globalisierung", mit daraus sich ergebenden Folgerungen weltweit. (edited)

**Pickens, Donald K**. From Atlas to Adolph: Body Building, Physical Culture, and National Socialism. *Cont Phil*, 18(4 & 5), 42-45, Jl-Ag/S-O 96.

Using the scholarship of George Mosse and other leading historians of fascism, this essay explains that Nazism and the ideal of body building were linked via the modern concept of masculinity. This linkage indicated that the Nazis were reactionary modernists, a concept closely defined within the essay. The thesis is based on two major factors. First, nineteenth-century popular culture influenced a social fad in physical training and secondly, the ideological and economic disasters of the twentieth century—The Great War, the Great Depression, the rise of National Socialism—fixed the ideas of reactionary modernism in the Third Reich. These two developments are analyzed in the essay and lead to the conclusion that the Nazis did, indeed, embrace the body building fad, exemplified by Charles Atlas.

**Picotti, Dina**. Sobre "Filosofía intercultural": Comentario a una obra de R. Fornet Betancourt. *Stromata*, 52(3-4), 289-298, Ja-Je 96.

**Pieper, Annemarie**. Europa—ein utopisches Konstrukt. *Z Phil Forsch*, 50(1/2), 183-196, Ja-Je 96.

**Piercey, Robert**. The Spinoza-Intoxicated Man: Deleuze on Expression. *Man World*, 29(3), 269-281, Jl 96.

Deleuze calls himself a Spinozist, but it is difficult to see how Spinoza could have influenced this apparently very different thinker. I argue that Deleuze is a Spinozist in ontology: that Deleuze, like Spinoza, develops an ontology in which the concepts of expression and immanence are central. Deleuze's main ontological categories—being, the virtual and the actual—are exactly parallel to Spinoza's substance, attribute and mode. And Deleuze's differentiation and differenciation mirror exactly the two levels of expression found in Spinoza's metaphysics. I also argue that in some respects, Deleuze is a more Spinozistic philosopher than Spinoza himself.

**Pieretti, Antonio**. La filosofia tra presenza e ulteriorità. *G Metaf*, 18(1-2), 31-45, Ja-Ag 96.

The paper, starting from the analysis of the "ontological difference", in its Heideggerian meaning as well as in its Wittgensteinian terms, i.e., as difference between the ontological consistency of the world and its untranslatability in language, aims to analyse the status of philosophy between presence and ulteriority. Since there is an ulteriority which is ontologically different from the presence and does not allow to be expressed in the specific ways of scientific language, philosophy, as vocation to pure theoresis, must assume the task of nourishing and preserving such a difference, without claiming or aiming to totalize the whole of the experience.

**Pierris, A L**. The Origin of Stoic Fatalism. *Diotima*, 25, 21-30, 1997.

**Pierson, Robert**. Anything Goes: Goodman on Relevant Kinds. *Int Stud Phil*, 29(2), 47-56, 1997.

**Pieters, Toine**. Shaping a New Biological Factor, 'The Interferon', in Room 215 of the National Institute for Medical Research, 1956/57. *Stud Hist Phil Sci*, 28(1), 27-73, Mr 96.

The main purpose of the paper is to identify the material, social and literary practices whereby the cytokine 'interferon' as a current matter-of-fact was shaped in the late 1950's. The emphasis is on studying and analyzing how explanatory ideas and the objects with which they are concerned as well as those objects used to elaborate them, are coproduced as constitutive elements of an evolving experimental system. This clearly showed that the range and priority of hypotheses and research with which the experiments were associated was subsidiary to and dependent on the events at the laboratory bench.

**Pietroski, Paul M**. "Moral Causation" in *A Question of Values: New Canadian Perspectives in Ethics and Political Philosophy,* Brennan, Samantha (ed), 39-61. Amsterdam, Rodopi, 1997.

**Pietroski, Paul M**. Critical Notice of John McDowell *Mind and World*. *Can J Phil*, 26(4), 613-636, D 96.

**Pietroski, Paul M**. Fregean Innocence. *Mind Lang*, 11(4), 338-370, D 96.

Frege's account of opacity is based on two attractive ideas: every meaningful expression has a sense (*Sinn*) that determines the expression's semantic value (*Bedeutung*); and the semantic value of a 'that'-clause is the thought expressed by its embedded sentence. Considerations of compositionality led Frege to a more problematic view: inside 'that'-clauses, an expression does not have its customary *Bedeutung*. But contrary to initial appearances, compositionality does not entail a familiar substitutivity principle. And Fregeans can exploit this point in a way that lets them reject *Bedeutung*-shifting.

**Pietroski, Paul M** and Dwyer, Susan. Believing in Language. *Phil Sci*, 63(3), 338-373, S 96.

We propose that the generalizations of linguistic theory serve to ascribe beliefs to humans. Ordinary speakers would explicitly (and sincerely) deny having these rather esoteric beliefs about language—e.g., the belief that an anaphor must be bound in its governing category. Such ascriptions can also seem problematic in light of certain theoretical considerations having to do with concept possession, revisability, and so on. Nonetheless, we argue that ordinary speakers believe the propositions expressed by certain sentences of linguistic theory, and that linguistics can therefore teach us something about belief as well as language. Rather than insisting that ordinary speakers lack the linguistic beliefs in question, philosophers should try to show how these empirically motivated belief ascriptions can be correct. We argue that Stalnaker's (1984) "pragmatic" account—according to which beliefs are dispositions, and propositions are sets of possible worlds—does just this. Moreover, our construal of explanation in linguistics motivates (and helps provide) responses to two difficulties for the pragmatic account of belief: the phenomenon of opacity, and the so-called problem of deduction.

**Pietruszczak, Andrzej**. Cardinalities of Models for Pure Calculi of Names. *Rep Math Log*, 28, 87-102, 1994.

**Pievatolo, Maria Chiara**. Piccolo mondo antico: appunti sul problema dell'identificazione del soggetto morale. *Iride*, 9(18), 417-430, Ag 96.

L'articolo tenta di tracciare le coordinate del problema dell'identificazione del soggetto morale, interpretato come una questione di filosofia pratica e non di filosofia teoretica. L'interrogativo sul soggetto è una chiave analitica efficace perfino in un mondo etico particolaristico e non universalistico, come era quello greco classico—che qui presentiamo attraverso i testi di riferimento della *Lisistrata* di Aristofane e dell'*Eutifrone* di Platone. Da questa lettura critica si può ricavare un criterio tassonomico che permette di classificare le filosofie pratiche in due gruppi fondamentali, a seconda che scelgano di determinare il soggetto lasciando indeterminato il bene, o viceversa, di determinare il bene lasciando indeterminato il soggetto cui si rivolge.

**Pigden, Charles R** and Cheyne, Colin. Pythagorean Powers or A Challenge to Platonism. *Austl J Phil*, 74(4), 639-645, D 96.

Platonism contends that there are mathematical objects—sets and numbers—which lack locations and causal powers. The chief argument for such objects is that they are indispensable to science. Field replies by trying to construct a 'science without numbers', but so far he has not managed to exercise numbers from relativistic physics. But whether Field's project succeeds or fails, Platonism is in trouble. If Field succeeds, numbers can be dispensed with. If he fails, this shows that numbers play some part in the causal process and hence that they are possessed of causal powers. Platonism loses either way.

**Pigden, Charles R** and Gillet, Grant R. Milgram, Method and Morality. *J Applied Phil*, 13(3), 233-250, 1996.

In Milgram's experiments, subjects were induced to inflict what they believed to be electric shocks in obedience to a man in a white coat. This suggests that many can be persuaded to torture and perhaps kill, another person simply on the say-so of an authority figure. But the experiments have been attacked on methodological, moral and methodologico-moral grounds. Patten argues that the subjects probably were not taken in by the charade; Bok argues that lies should not be used in research; and Patten insists that any excuse for Milgram's conduct can be adapted on behalf of his subjects. (Either he was wrong to conduct the experiments or they do not establish the phenomenon of immoral obedience). We argue that the subjects were indeed taken in, that lies (though usually wrong) were in this case legitimate and that there were excuses available to Milgram which were not available to his subjects. So far from 'disrespecting' his subjects, Milgram enhanced their autonomy as rational agents. We concede, however, that it might be right to prohibit what it was right to do.

**Pignatelli, Frank**. "Narrowing the Gap Between Difference and Identity" in *Philosophy of Education (1996),* Margonis, Frank (ed), 99-101. Urbana, Phil Education Soc, 1997.

**Pihlström, Sami**. A Solipsist in a Real World. *Dialectica*, 50(4), 275-290, 1996.

It is trivially true that solipsism, the view that "the world is my world" and that whatever there is is ontologically dependent on my thought or language, cannot be conclusively refuted. The issue of solipsism is, however, an important one. The paper considers this issue mainly from the point of view of Wittgenstein's remarks on solipsism in the *Tractatus* and in his early Notebooks. It is argued that we should not accept the Wittgensteinian idea that solipsism eventually coincides with "pure realism". A position labeled "pragmatic realism" is briefly sketched in order to avoid both solipsism and what I call "credo realism". Thus, I try to show that the issue of solipsism vs. realism should not simply be dismissed and that it should be approached from a pragmatist perspective.

**Pillay, Anand**. Remarks on Galois Cohomology and Definability. *J Sym Log*, 62(2), 487-492, Je 97.

**Pimentel, David** and Shanks, Roland E and Rylander, Jason C. Bioethics of Fish Production: Energy and the Environment. *J Agr Environ Ethics*, 9(2), 144-164, 1996.

Aquatic ecosystems are vital to the structure and function of all environments on earth. Worldwide, approximately 95 million metric tons of fishery products are harvested from marine and freshwater habitats. A major problem in fisheries around the world is the bioethics of overfishing. A wide range of management techniques exists for fishery, managers and policy-makers to improve fishery production in the future. The best approach to limit overfishing is to have an effective, federally regulated fishery, based on environmental standards and fishery carrying capacity. Soon, overfishing is more likely to cause fish scarcity than fossil fuel shortages and high energy prices for fish harvesting. However, oil and other fuel are projected to influence future fishery policies and the productive capacity of the fishery industry. Overall, small-scale fishing systems are more energy efficient than large-scale systems. Aquaculture is not the solution to wild fishery production. The energy input/output ratio of aquacultural fish is much higher than that of the harvest of wild populations. In addition, the energy ratios for aquaculture systems are higher than those for most livestock systems.

**Pimentel, Manuel Cândido**. Elementos para uma Fenomenologia Literária do Texto Filosófico. *Philosophica (Portugal)*, 7-31, 1997.

La pluralité des théories sur le texte qui sortent de l'herméneutique philosophique et de la théorie littéraire contemporaines ressemblent à l'extrême complexité du labyrinthe, une image qui rappelle Thésée, l'interprète du sens qui questionne le sens, mais sans y trouver le fil d'Ariane. L'auteur, partant de ce mythe, s'adresse à l'étude du conflit des interprétations sous le nom de *complexe de Thésée*. La recherche suit la route critique des diverses théories du texte (de Dilthey a Gadamer, Ricoeur et Greimas) et parvient à détacher le sens heuristique du modèle rhétorique argumentatif de la philosophie qui jette sa lumière sur l'intentionalité spécifique du texte et du monde philosophique, en y voyant la clef de la distinction entre la philosophie et la littérature. (edited)

**Pimentel, Manuel Cândido**. Frei Manuel de S. Luís Escritor e Orador Açoriano dos Séculos XVII-XVIII (1660-1736). *Rev Port Filosof*, 52(1-4), 667-690, Ja-D 96.

The author studies the theological thinking of the Franciscan orator Friar Manuel de S. Luís—born in 1660. In his doctrine of enlightenment of the human conscience, he adopted a commitment between the intuitive access to the contemplation and his rationalist reasoning. The synthesis of will and understanding, and of love and intelligence, the ways through which the soul might reach a union with God, have contributed to the definition of his thought as an *intellectual voluntarism: knowledge* is regarded as a collaboration between love and reason. His reflections on mysticism, gnoseology, metaphysics and ethics resemble St. António de Lisboa, St. Bonaventura and Duns Scotus. (edited)

**Pinches, Charles** and Hauerwas, Stanley. Practicing Patience: How Christians Should Be Sick. *Christian Bioethics*, 2(2), 202-221, Ag 96.

In contemporary society nothing upsets us more than having to wait for our bodies. Our bodies serve us as we direct and when they break down we become angry that they have failed us. Christians, however, are called to be patient people even in illness. Indeed, impatience is a sin. Learning to be patient when sick requires practicing patience while healthy. First, we must learn that our bodies are finite—they will die. Second, we must learn to live with one another in patience as Christians with the love that the presence of others can and does create in us. Third, in life there is time for the acquisition of habits that come from worthy activities that require time and force us to take first one step and then another. In patience one can live with God.

**Pinckaers, Servais**. Rediscovering Virtue. *Thomist*, 60(3), 361-378, Jl 96.

A virtue centered morality, thanks to the intervention in prudential judgment of acquired experience and knowledge had by way of connaturality which that morality procures, leads to an enrichment and deepening of moral judgment in dealing with cases of conscience and in the conception and application of justice.

**Pincus, David**. The Dense Linear Ordering Principle. *J Sym Log*, 62(2), 438-456, Je 97.

Let DO denote the principle: Every infinite set has a dense linear ordering. DO is compared to other ordering principles such as O, the Linear Ordering principle, KW, the Kinna-Wagner Principle, and PI, the Prime Ideal Theorem, in ZF, Zermelo-Fraenkel set theory without AC, the Axiom of Choice. The main result is: Theorem. AC implies KW implies DO implies O, *and none of the implications is reversible in* ZF + PI. The first and third implications and their irreversibilities were known. The middle one is new. Along the way other results of interest are established. O, while not quite implying DO, does imply that every set differs finitely from a densely ordered set. The independence result for ZF is reduced to one for Fraenkel-Mostowski models by showing that DO falls into two of the known classes of statements automatically transferable from Fraenkel-Mostowski to ZF models. Finally, the proof of PI in the Fraenkel-Mostowski model leads naturally to versions of the Ramsey and Ehrenfeucht-Mostowski theorems involving sets that are both ordered and colored.

**Pincus, Laura**. Friedman with a Conscience?. *Bus Ethics Quart*, 7(1), 101-107, Ja 97.

**Pincus, Laura** and Johns, Roger. Private Parts: A Global Analysis of Privacy Protection Schemes and a Proposed Innovation for their Comparative Evaluation. *J Bus Ethics*, 16(12-13), 1237-1260, S 97.

Pursuant to a Directive adopted by the European Union, privacy protections throughout the EU must become more stringent and consistent throughout EU member countries. One area of great concern to the United States is the Directive's requirement for certain minimum standards of privacy protection in countries receiving information from member countries. Given the limited protections available in the United States, it does not appear that the United States meets these minimum standards. The purpose of this paper is to critically analyze the existing measurements of global privacy protections and to propose a new model which allows for their comparative evaluation. (edited)

**Pinilla Burgos, Ricardo**. "August Wilhelm Schlegel y sus lecciones de Jena sobre teoría del arte (1798)" in *El inicio del Idealismo alemán*, Market, Oswaldo, 381-395. Madrid, Ed Complutense, 1996.

Las lecciones jenenses de A. W. Schlegel sobre teoría del arte (1798), que nos llegan a través de una única edición con anotaciones de K.C.F. Krause, constituyen una fuente interesante y casi desconocida del romanticismo alemán. Partiendo de una radicalización del principio trascendental aplicado al campo estético, muestran estas lecciones a un A. W. Schlegel previo al impacto de la filosofía de Schelling en su formulación de 1800. Por ello contrastan con las lecciones posteriores de Berlín (1801-3). De otro lado, el estudio de las numerosas anotaciones de Krause demuestra la relevancia que éstas tuvieron en la gestación definitiva de la estética krausiana.

**Pink, Thomas**. Reason and Agency. *Proc Aris Soc*, 97, 263-280, 1997.

A *motivation-based* conception of human action, found in Hobbes or Davidson, characterizes action as something motivated by psychological attitudes that make it purposive or goal-directed. A *practical reason-based* conception, found in Aquinas or Kant, characterizes human action as the exercise of a capacity to apply (or misapply) a distinctively practical reason. Only the practical reason-based conception is consistent with the extension accorded 'is an intentional action' by common sense psychology. Despite this, the motivation-based conception gained ground from the early modern period onwards, supported by new developments in the theory of human rationality.

**Pinkard, Terry**. Romanticized Enlightenment? Enlightened Romanticism? Universalism and Particularism in Hegel's *Understanding of the Enlightenment*. *Bull Hegel Soc Gt Brit*, 35, 18-38, Spr-Sum 97.

**Pinkard, Terry**. What is the Non-Metaphysical Reading of Hegel? A Reply to Frederick Beiser. *Bull Hegel Soc Gt Brit*, 34, 13-20, Autumn-Wint 96.

**Pinkard, Terry** and Hardimon, Michael O and Dallmayr, Fred R. The New Hegel. *Polit Theory*, 25(4), 584-597, Ag 97.

**Pinker, Steven** and Prince, Alan. The Nature of Human Concepts/ Evidence from an Unusual Source. *Commun Cog*, 29(3/4), 307-362, 1996.

What kind of categories do human concepts represent? *Classical* categories are defined by necessary and sufficient criteria that determine whether an object is in a category or not in it. A popular contemporary view is that concepts correspond instead to *prototype* categories. *Prototype* categories lack necessary and sufficient conditions; their members need not be absolutely "in" or "out of" the category but can be members to greater or lesser degrees; their members display family resemblances in a number of characteristic properties rather than uniformly sharing a few defining properties; and they are organized around "prototypical" exemplars. This distinction raises several questions. Is one type of category psychologically real, the other an artifact? If both are psychologically real, do they serve different functions in cognition? Are they processed by the same kind of computational architecture? And do they correspond to fundamentally different kinds of things in the world? We suggest that some answers to these questions can be found in an unusual place: the English past tense system. (edited)

**Pinnick, Cassandra L**. Epistemology of Technology Assessment: Collingridge, Forecasting Methodologies, and Technological Control. *Phil Cont World*, 3(1), 14-18, Spr 96.

This paper criticizes Collingridge's arguments against an epistemology of technological control. Collingridge claims that because prediction mechanisms are inadequate, his "dilemma of control" demonstrates that the sociopolitical impact of new technologies cannot be forecasted and that, consequently, policy makers must concentrate their control measures on minimizing the costs required to alter entrenched technologies. I argue that Collingridge does not show on either horn that forecasting is impossible and that his criticisms of forecasting methods are self-defeating for they undercut his positive case for the control of entrenched technologies. Finally, I indicate an empirical base for forecasting risk that may define epistemic principles of technology assessment.

**Piñon G, Francisco**. Sociología y tipología del fenómeno religioso. *Analogia*, 11(1), 209-218, Ja-Je 97.

**Pintado, Patricia**. Sobre los sentidos objetivo y sujetivo del trabajo según Polo. *Anu Filosof*, 29(2), 949-959, 1996.

The present paper wants to show the "sense of work" (subjective and objective). It studies L. Polo's work in relation with some Encyclicals and documents about Social Doctrine of Catholic Church.

**Pinto, José Rui da Costa**. Amor e Morte: Meditaçao Antropológica. *Rev Port Filosof*, 52(1-4), 691-694, Ja-D 96.

**Pinto, Robert C**. "The Relation of Argument to Inference" in *Logic and Argumentation*, Van Eemeren, Frans H (ed), 163-178. Amsterdam, North-Holland, 1994.

This paper attempts to clarify the relationships that hold between 1) arguments and inferences, 2) the normative study of arguments and the normative study of inference, 3) logic as the normative study of inference and the study of argumentation. It aims to provide an alternative to a) standard formal logic textbook accounts of reasoning or inference, b) the pragma-dialectical theories of van Eemeren and Grootendorst and c) the views presented by Doug Walton in his paper "What is logic? What is reasoning?". More particularly, it argues that there is a normative study of inference that does not coincide either with formal logic or with the study of argumentation, but which must be presupposed by the study of argumentation.

**Pinto, Robert C**. Inconsistency, Rationality and Relativism. *Inform Log*, 17(2), 279-288, Spr 95.

In section 1, I argue that the principal reason why inconsistency is a fault is that it involves having at least one false belief. In section 2, I argue that inconsistency need not be a serious epistemic fault. The argument in section 2 is based on the notion that what matters epistemically is always in the final analysis an item's effect on attaining the goal of truth. In section 3 I describe two cases in which it is best from an epistemic point of view to knowingly retain inconsistent beliefs. In section 4 my goal is to put into perspective the charge that relativism ought to be rejected because it involves one in inconsistency.

**Pinto, Valeria**. "Autocoscienza e rivelazione: Solger e Schleiermacher di fronte alla storia" in *Lo Storicismo e la Sua Storia: Temi, Problemi, Prospettive*, Cacciatore, Giuseppe (ed), 182-196. Milano, Guerini, 1997.

**Pinto Furtado, Joao**. Educaçao e Movimento Social: a Questao da Qualidade do Ensino na Perspectiva de um Sindicato de Educadores. *Educ Filosof*, 9(17), 17-38, Ja-Je 95.

Este artigo discute o problema da qualidade do ensino no interior do sistema de ensino público de Minas Gerais a partir do tratamento dado à questao pela Uniao dos Trabalhadores do Ensino de Minas Gerais. Procuramos estabelecer uma relaçao entre as concepçoes pedagógicas propriamente ditas e as práticas políticas e sindicais mais amplas. Nesse sentido o artigo aborda ainda do ponto de vista sociológico, o problema da reorganizaçao do sistema produtivo e das condiçoes de trabalho em suas relaçoes com o movimento enfocado.

**Pinton, Giorgio A**. La Nápoles de Vico. *Cuad Vico*, 7/8, 115-139, 1997.

This paper proposes not only a topographic map of Vico's Naples but also the human map of interrelationships which Vico had with so many and different individuals. These two factors together, the topographic (city) and human (civility) maps, give us the civilizing city, our idea of the *great human race*. Visiting Vico's Naples will give us the enjoyment and thrill of knowing truly Vico as the Neapolitan he was and thus value his writings more intimately. This paper is a "guide" by means of which the reader will figure out, through his imagination, Vico's world-life; but it is as well a proposal to visit the Parthenopean city following this travelogue.

**Pintor-Ramos, Antonio**. Para qué la historia de la filosofía?. *Dialogo Filosof*, 13(1), 33-40, Ja-Ap.

Ante la variedad, inabarcable y algo caótica, de contenidos que hoy suelen cobijarse bajo la rúbrica de "historia de la filosofía", se presenta una somera reflexión sobre las exigencias que debería colmar cualquier historia de la filosofía que, siendo historia, pueda mantener el esencial interés filosófico.

**Pinzani, Alessandro**. Solidarietà e democrazia: Osservazioni su antropologia, diritto e legittimità nella teoria giuridica di Habermas. *Iride*, 9(18), 473-482, Ag 96.

L'autore delinea le premesse antropologiche della ricerca habermasiana e passa quindi ad un'analisi di *Faktizität und Geltung* soffermandosi sulle tre risorse di integrazione sociale che secondo Habermas operano nella società contemporanea: la solidarietà, il denaro e il potere amministrativo. In questo quadro l'assenza di valori condivisi fa assumere al diritto una funzione di cerniera tra sistema e mondo della vita grazie alla sua legittimazione attraverso la democrazia.

**Piozzi, Patrizia**. Between Libertarian Utopia and Political Realism: Godwin and Shelley on Revolution (in Portuguese). *Trans/Form/Acao*, 19, 35-46, 1996.

This article investigates Godwin's and Shelley's political ideas within the broad backdrop established by the emergence and crisis of the English "Jacobin"

radicalism. The following analysis explores the development of and problems faced by the libertarian ideals of those thinkers and their reactions to the dramatic social and political changes which took place between the end of the XVIIIth and beginnings of the XIXth centuries.

**Pipes, Randolph B**. Nonsexual Relationships between Psychotherapists and Their Former Clients: Obligations of Psychologists. *Ethics Behavior*, 7(1), 27-41, 1997.

This article examines the issue of nonsexual relationships between psychologists and their former therapy clients. What little research is available concerning nonsexual relationships with former clients suggests that psychologists have clear reservations about some of these relationships, especially personal ones and intentional social interactions. Relationships immediately following termination are seen as particularly suspect. Drawing on the literature dealing with multiple relationships in general, and sexual relationships with former clients in particular, a number of arguments are made outlining why psychologists should avoid significant nonsexual relationships with former clients for at least some period of time following termination.

**Pippin, Robert B**. Hegel on Historical Meaning: For Example, The Enlightenment. *Bull Hegel Soc Gt Brit*, 35, 1-17, Spr-Sum 97.

**Pippin, Robert B**. Horstmann, Siep, and German Idealism. *Euro J Phil*, 2(1), 85-96, Ap 94.

**Pippin, Robert B**. *Idealism as Modernism: Hegelian Variations*. New York, Cambridge Univ Pr, 1997.

"Modernity" has come to refer both to a contested historical category and to an even more contested philosophical and civilizational ideal. In this important collection of essays Robert Pippin takes issue with some prominent assessments of what is or is not philosophically at stake in the idea of a modern revolution in Western civilization, and presents an alternative view. Pippin disputes many traditional characterizations of the distinctiveness of modern philosophy. In their place he defends claims about agency, freedom, ethical life, and modernity itself that were central to the German idealist philosophical tradition and, in particular, to the writings of Hegel. Having considered the Hegelian version of these issues, the author explores other accounts as found in Habermas, Strauss, Blumenberg, Nietzsche, and Heidegger. Any serious student concerned with the question of modernism and postmodernism will want this major collection of essays. Dealing with a wide range of modern theorists, the volume will interest philosophers, literary theorists, and social and political theorists.

**Pippin, Robert B**. Medical Practice and Social Authority. *J Med Phil*, 21(4), 417-437, Ag 96.

Questions of medical ethics are often treated as especially difficult casuistical problems or as difficult cases illustrative of paradoxes or advantages in global moral theories. I argue here, in opposition to such approaches, for the inseparability of questions of social history and social theory from any normative assessment of medical practices. The focus of the discussion is the question of the legitimacy of the social authority exercised by physicians and the insufficiency of traditional defences of such authority in liberal societies (voluntarist, informed consent approaches), as well as traditional attacks on such strategies (ideology critique). Seeing such authority as institution bound and role based, it is argued, can help reframe, more broadly and more adequately, what is an "ethical problem" in medical practice and why.

**Pires, Francisco Videira**. Marx, Ideólogo dos Ideólogos. *Rev Port Filosof*, 52(1-4), 695-712, Ja-D 96.

**Pires Da Silva, Joao Carlos Salles**. Dialectics and Rhetoric in Peter Abelard (in Portuguese). *Trans/Form/Acao*, 19, 221-230, 1996.

Abelard is acknowledged as a dreaded arguer. In this paper we try to demonstrate how the refinement of his argumentative technique associates intimately and finds a theoretical justification in his work. (Thus, the resources (like the reduction to the absurd) that seem just to guarantee the success and survival of the itinerant master point to the philosophical defense of the independence of language;) therefore, those resources not only denounce the philosopher's extreme insertion in his historical context and his concern about his specific public, but they also condense elements of his intellectual autonomy and pioneering spirit.

**Pirri, Fiora** and Amati, Giambattista. A Uniform Tableau Method for Intuitionistic Modal Logics I. *Stud Log*, 53(1), 29-60, F 94.

We present tableau systems and sequent calculi for the intuitionistic analogues IK, ID, IT, IKB, IKDB, IB, IK4, IKD4, IS4, IKB4, IK5, IKD5, IK45, IKD45 and IS5 of the normal classical modal logics. We provide soundness and completeness theorems with respect to the models of intuitionistic logic enriched by a modal accessibility relation, as proposed by G. Fischer Servi. We then show the disjunction property for IK, ID, IT, IKB, IKDB, IB, IK4, IKD4, IS4, IKB4, IK5, IK45 and IS5. We also investigate the relationship of these logics with some other intuitionistic modal logics proposed in the literature.

**Pirrucello, Ann**. "Gravity" in the Thought of Simone Weil. *Phil Phenomenol Res*, 57(1), 73-93, Mr 97.

Simone Weil's concept of gravity (*la pésanteur*) has received attention from philosophers and interested readers at least since the 1947 publication of *La Pésanteur et la grâce*. "Gravity" is a key concept in Weil's moral and spiritual psychology, and despite the attention Weil's writings have received, there is ample need for a study that draws together Weil's scattered references to gravity and demonstrates their cohesion. This article develops a treatment of gravity that seeks to clarify one of the major scientific analogies Weil uses to develop her notion of moral gravity. It is hoped that this approach will furnish a point of departure for interpreting Weil's obscure and often fragmentary remarks on gravity. In addition, something important can be said about both the difficulties and the promise of Weil's analogy, and this article offers a few critical comments towards that end.

**Pitowsky, Itamar**. Laplace's Demon Consults an Oracle: The Computational Complexity of Prediction. *Stud Hist Phil Mod Physics*, 27B(2), 161-180, Je 96.

How much computation power is required in order to predict the future of a classical mechanical system? In the first part of the paper I describe in detail a recent result of Christopher Moore. He designed an idealized universal Turing machine (including its infinite tape) which is made of a single particle moving among a few mirrors. Simple questions about this system are computationally undecidable (for example, is the particle motion periodic?) The second part of the paper deals with the implications of Moore's construction to two (unrelated) philosophical issues: Laplacian determinism and the computational theories of cognition.

**Pitson, Tony**. Sympathy and Other Selves. *Hume Stud*, 22(2), 255-271, N 96.

This paper is concerned with Hume's theory of sympathy in relation to belief in the existence of others as the subjects of mental states. I argue that sympathy, as Hume introduces this notion, should not be viewed as a cognitive process; rather, it reflects the part played by propensities of the imagination in our attribution of mental states to others. It then provides the foundation for the more extended forms of sympathy which underlie our moral and aesthetic responses. As for belief in the existence of other minds or selves, this may be seen to belong to the category of 'natural' belief.

**Pitson, Tony**. The Dispositional Account of Colour. *Philosophia (Israel)*, 25(1-4), 247-266, Ap 97.

This paper defends a dispositional account of colour according to which the redness of an object consists in a disposition of the object to look red to normal perceivers under normal conditions. This account is contrasted with others which for various reasons appear unacceptable and it is defended against a number of objections: e.g., that it is circular, that it misdescribes the nature of colour experience and that the notion of normal conditions of perception may have no application. In so far as it survives these objections, the dispositional account appears to remain the most promising available.

**Pittman, John P** (ed). *African-American Perspectives and Philosophical Traditions*. New York, Routledge, 1997.

This book brings together twelve outstanding essays by distinguished scholars in the field of African-American philosophy. First published as a special issue of *The Philosophical Forum*, one of the most prestigious philosophical journals, this work is now available to a wider readership through its publication in book form. The volume includes twelve essays in three sections—Philosophical Traditions; the African-American Tradition; and Racism, Identity and Social Life and it includes an introduction by John P. Pittman. (publisher)

**Pittman, John P**. Punishment and Race. *Utilitas*, 9(1), 115-130, Mr 97.

This article criticizes the standard way philosophers pose issues about the core practices of criminal justice institutions. Attempting to get at some of the presuppositions of posing these issues in terms of punishment, I construct a revised version of Rawls's 'telishment' case, a revision based on actual features of contemporary criminal justice practices in the USA. In addressing the implications of 'racialment', as I call it, some connections are made to current philosophical discussions about race. I conclude with brief remarks about the importance of race to philosophical discussion as such.

**Piulats Riu, Octavi**. Las ideas de 'ciudadanía universal' y 'paz perpetua' en la *Metafísica de la costumbres* de Kant. *Convivium*, 10, 61-87, 1997.

The article concerns the ideas of 'perpetual peace' and 'universal community' by Kant, who defines their complex as the 'supreme political good' and the summit of the whole Doctrine of Right. The main purpose of this investigation is to reconstruct the whole complex of 'ewige Friede' and 'Weltbürgertum' through the texts of the *Metaphysik der Sitten*. The second goal of this construction tries to resolve the cognitive ambivalences of these ideas in connection with their practical development and also to explain the doubts and hesitations of Kant when in the Doctrine of Right he has to define this complex in his last issue. In order to achieve a true and immanent reconstruction of the philosophy of Kant, we use a genetical methodology of research and exposition.

**Pivcevic, Edo**. *What is Truth?*. Brookfield, Ashgate, 1997.

Contrary to the prevailing view, the book argues that truth is a complex notion and demands an approach on a broad front. What emerges is that truth has to do with the manner in which facts constitute themselves as facts within the horizon of knowledge, and strictly it does not exist until it occurs, and survives only as long as the requisite conditions are in place. The word 'truth' is comparable to a verbal noun, and designates a complex event, like *reading*. For a reading to take place certain conditions must be fulfilled which make such an event possible, but the event itself is not to be confused with any one of those conditions, and the same applies to truth.

**Pizzi, Claudio** and Williamson, Timothy. Strong Boethius' Thesis and Consequential Implication. *J Phil Log*, 26(5), 569-588, O 97.

The paper studies the relation between systems of modal logic and systems of consequential implication, a nonmaterial form of implication satisfying "Aristotle's Thesis" (*p* does not imply not *p*) and "Weak Boethius' Thesis" (if *p* implies *q*, then *p* does not imply not *q*). Definitions are given of consequential implication in terms of modal operators and of modal operators in terms of consequential implication. The modal equivalent of "Strong Boethius' Thesis" (that *p* implies *q* implies that *p* does not imply not *q*) is identified.

**Pizzi, Laura Cristina V**. A Organizaçao do Trabalho Escolar e os Especialistas da Educaçao. *Educ Filosof*, 10(19), 17-44, Ja-Je 96.

**Pizzorni, Reginaldo M**. Dio fondamento ultimo della morale e del diritto. *Sapienza*, 49(4), 435-448, 1996.

**Place, U T**. "A Conceptualist Ontology" in *Dispositions: A Debate*, Armstrong, D M, 49-67. New York, Routledge, 1996.

Nominalised predicates, opaque contexts and monadic relational predicates are cases where surface structure conceals an underlying complexity. A conceptualist picture theory of meaning allows different ways of carving up reality into atomic situations. To say that a universal exists means *either* that it has at least one instance *or* that some creature has that concept. Structural factors combine to cause dispositions. Dispositions combine with the relevant conditions to cause their manifestations. Type-identities begin as contingent hypotheses and become necessary when used in classification. The existence of individual dispositional properties, not Laws of Nature, are the truthmakers for causal counterfactuals.

**Place, U T**. "Conceptualism and the Ontological Independence of Cause and Effect" in *Dispositions: A Debate*, Armstrong, D M, 153-162. New York, Routledge, 1996.

If causal relations hold only between "distinct existences" (Hume), since the relation between structure and disposition is causal, they cannot be (aspects of) the same thing. Though causal relations are contingent, cause and effect are connected necessarily in that the causal counterfactual is true (Hume). Since causal counterfactuals can be deduced from statements ascribing dispositional properties to individuals (Goodman), the existence of a disposition is the only truthmaker they need. We must distinguish cases where both the universal *and* its instances are "mind-made" from cases where, on the conceptualist view, it is only the universals that are "mind-made."

**Place, U T**. "Dispositions as Intentional States" in *Dispositions: A Debate*, Armstrong, D M, 19-32. New York, Routledge, 1996.

All three authors agree that 'This glass is brittle' entails 'If it were suitably struck, it would break'. They also agree that such a statement, if true, requires a state of affairs whose existence makes it true (its truthmaker). They disagree as to its nature. For Place, it is an intentional state which "points towards" a possibly-never-to-exist future and a counterfactual past. In accordance with the *conceptualist theory of universals* and the *picture theory of meaning* which he outlines, such states are construed as properties of particulars. They provide Hume's "invisible glue" which sticks cause to effect.

**Place, U T**. "Structural Properties: Categorical, Dispositional or Both?" in *Dispositions: A Debate*, Armstrong, D M, 105-125. New York, Routledge, 1996.

Martin's "linguisticism" which converts existence into the truth of an existential statement is found in such doctrines as "To exist is to be the value of a variable," "Wanting is a propositional attitude," and "Causal conditionals are of the form 'If *p*, then *q*'." The (dispositional) properties of the whole are caused by, are often predictable from, but are not reducible to, the (categorical) arrangement of its parts and *their* dispositional properties. An unmanifested dispositional property is a law of the nature of the property-bearer which governs how it *would* behave, if its manifestation conditions *were to be* fulfilled.

**Place, U T**. Intentionality as the Mark of the Dispositional. *Dialectica*, 50(2), 91-120, 1996.

Martin and Pfeifer (1986) have claimed "that the most typical characterizations of intentionality...all fail to distinguish...mental states from...dispositional physical states." The evidence they present in support of this thesis is examined in the light of the possibility that what it shows is that intentionality is the mark, not of the mental, but of the dispositional. Of the five marks of intentionality they discuss a critical examination shows that three of them, Brentano's (1874) *inexistence* of the intentional object, Searle's (1983) *directedness* and Anscombe's (1965) *indeterminacy*, are features which distinguish T-intenTional/dispositional states, both mental and nonmental (physical), from nondispositional "categorical" states. The other two are either, as in the case of Chisholm's (1957) *permissible falsity* of a propositional attitude ascription, a feature of linguistic utterances too restricted in its scope to be of interest, or, as in the case of Frege's (1892) *indirect reference*/Quine's (1953) *referential opacity*, evidence that the S-intenSional locution is a quotation either of what someone *has said* in the past or *might be expected to say*, if the question were to arise at some time in the future.

**Place, Ullin T**. Metaphysics as the Empirical Study of the Interface between Language and Reality. *Acta Analytica*, 97-118, 1996.

The rules of syntax and semantics on conformity to which linguistic communication depends are construed as social conventions instilled and maintained by the error-correcting practices of a linguistic community. That conception argues for the revival of conceptual analysis construed as the empirical investigation of such conventions using the *ethnomethodological thought experiment* as its primary research tool and for a view of metaphysics as the empirical study of the interface between utterances and the reality they depict.

**Place, Ullin T** and Martin, C B and Armstrong, D M. *Dispositions: A Debate*. New York, Routledge, 1996.

In this book, first Place and Armstrong debate the ontological nature of dispositions, each setting out their view, and each in a second contribution criticizing the other and expanding their own view. In the second part of the book the debate becomes three-cornered, with three contributions from Martin, and two each from Armstrong and Place. An introduction by Tim Crane summarizes and surveys the debate.

**Placella, Vincenzo**. Vico e la Poesia. *Stud Filosofici*, 331-350, 1995.

**Plangesis, Yannis**. Deconstruction and Marxism: Jacques Derrida's Specters of Marx. *Phil Inq*, 18(3-4), 91-115, Sum-Fall 96.

The purpose of this paper is to discuss certain aspects of Jacques Derrida's book on Marx: in the first place, his critique of capitalism; secondly, his reception of the critical spirit of Marxism; thirdly, his alternative vision of the so-called "New International"; and lastly his use of Messianism and religion. The conclusion reached is that Derrida's analysis, though positive in certain respects, suffers from a fundamental misunderstanding of the Marxian thought. Thus, the utilization of its positive aspects cannot be conducted but through an *"Aufhebung of Deconstruction"* towards a renewed critical reception of the Marxist theory.

**Plantinga, Alvin**. Ad Hick. *Faith Phil*, 14(3), 295-298, Jl 97.

**Plantinga, Alvin**. Science: Augustinian or Duhemian?. *Faith Phil*, 13(3), 368-394, Jl 96.

This paper is a continuation of a discussion with Ernan McMullin; its topic is the question how theists (in particular, Christian theists) should think about modern science—the whole range of modern science, including economics, psychology, sociobiology and so on. Should they follow Augustine in thinking that many large scale scientific projects as well as intellectual projects generally are in the service of one or the other of the *civitates* Or should they follow Duhem, who (at least in the case of physics) held that proper science is independent of metaphysical, theological or (broadly) religious concerns? The focus of the discussion is biology; I support the Augustinian line of thought, while McMullin is more inclined to the Duhemian. I conclude by defending the idea that the epistemic probability of the Grand Evolutionary Scenario on Christian theism together with the empirical evidence is somewhat less than l/2.

**Plantinga, Alvin**. Warrant and Accidentally True Belief. *Analysis*, 57(2), 140-145, Ap 97.

**Platt, Anthony M**. The Rise and Fall of Affirmative Action. *Notre Dame J Law Ethics*, 11(1), 67-78, 1997.

**Platts, Mark**. *Ways of Meaning: An Introduction to a Philosophy of Language*. Cambridge, MIT Pr, 1997.

The philosophy of language is not an isolated philosophical discipline of merely technical interest to other philosophers. Rather, as Mark Platts shows, it can help to solve traditional problems in other areas of philosophy, such as metaphysics, epistemology and ethics. *Ways of Meaning* provides a clear, comprehensive introduction to such issues at the forefront of philosophy. Assuming only minimum knowledge of elementary formal logic, the book shows how taking truth as the central notion in the theory of meaning can clarify the relations between language, reality and knowledge and thus illuminate the nature of each. (publisher, edited)

**Platzer, Katrin** and Sinemus, Kristina and Bender, Wolfgang. On the Assessment of Genetic Technology: Reaching Ethical Judgments in the Light of Modern Technology. *Sci Eng Ethics*, 1(1), 21-32, J 95.

The "Model for Reaching Ethical Judgments in the Context of Modern Technologies—the Case of Genetic Technology," which is presented here, has arisen from the project "Ethical Criteria Bearing Upon Decisions Taken in the Field of Biotechnology." This project has been pursued since 1991 in the Zentrum für interdisziplinäre Technikforschung (ZIT) of the Technical University of Darmstadt, with the purpose of examining decision-making in selected activities involving the production of transgenic plants that have a useful application. The model is the basis of an outline for interviews to investigate how far decisions concerning the development of such plants with genetic techniques take ethical criteria into account. It was necessary to design this new model because other models for reaching judgments of this kind were not conceptually suited for concrete application. This model represents a problem related approach and combines methodological with substantive typology. In this it differs from comparable models for reaching ethical judgments.

**Pleasants, Nigel**. Nothing is Concealed: De-centring Tacit Knowledge and Rules from Social Theory. *J Theor Soc Behav*, 26(3), 233-255, S 96.

The concept of "tacit knowledge' as the means by which individuals interpret the "rules" of social interaction occupies a central role in contemporary theories of action and social structure. The major reference point for social theorists is Wittgenstein's discussion of rule-following in the *Philosophical Investigations*. Focusing on Giddens's incorporation of tacit knowledge and rules into his "theory of structuration", I argue that Wittgenstein's later work is steadfastly set against the latent cognitivism inherent in theories of tacit knowledge and tacit rules. I conclude that the idea of tacit knowledge and tacit rules is either incoherent or explanatorily vacuous.

**Pleasants, Nigel**. The Epistemological Argument Against Socialism: A Wittgensteinian Critique of Hayek and Giddens. *Inquiry*, 40(1), 23-45, Mr 97.

Hayek's and Mises's argument for the impossibility of socialist planning is once again popular. Their case against socialism is predicated on an account of the nature of knowledge and social interaction. Hayek refined Mises's original argument by developing a philosophical anthropology which depicts individuals as tacitly knowledgeable rule-followers embedded in a 'spontaneous order' of systems of rules. Giddens, whose social theory is informed by his reading of Wittgenstein, has recently added his sociological support to Hayek's 'epistemological argument' against socialism. With the aid of an interpretation of Wittgenstein which emphasizes his *philosophy of praxis*, I attempt to 'deconstruct' Giddens's and Hayek's 'picture' of tacit knowledge and rule-following on which their argument against socialism is predicated.

**Pleune, Ruud**. Strategies of Environmental Organisations in the Netherlands regarding the Ozone Depletion Problem. *Environ Values*, 5(3), 235-255, Ag 96.

Strategies of environmental organisations in the Netherlands regarding the ozone depletion problem have been analysed both at the cognitive level and at the operational level. The first objective of this analysis was to describe their strategies over a period of time. Secondly, it aimed to increase understanding of the linkage between cognitive and operational aspects of the strategies. The third objective was to find out to what extent strategies are constant features of an organisation and how far they are defined by particular problems. The results indicate that each of the organisations concerned with the ozone depletion problem adopted several different strategies, that the strategies of the organisations did not change much over time and that there was no one-to-one linking of different aspects of the strategy of the organisations. Strategies seem largely to be defined by the problem encountered.

**Plotke, David**. Representation is Democracy. *Constellations*, 4(1), 19-34, Ap 97.

During the Cold War, arguments about representation were a significant part of international debates about democracy. Proponents of minimal democracy dominated these arguments and their thin notions of representation became political common sense. I propose a view of representation that differs from the main views advocated during the Cold War. Representation has a central positive role in democratic politics: I gain political representation when my authorized representative tries to achieve my political aims, subject to dialogue about those aims and to the use of mutually acceptable procedures for gaining them. Thus the opposite of representation is not participation. The opposite of representation is exclusion—and the opposite of participation is abstention. Rather than opposing participation to representation, we should try to improve representative practices and forms to make them more open, effective, and fair.

**Pluhacek, Stephen** and Bostic, Heidi. Thinking Life as Relation: An Interview with Luce Irigaray. *Man World*, 29(4), 343-360, O 96.

This interview, conducted in Paris during the Spring of 1996, draws upon Luce Irigaray's recent work, including *I love to you, Je, tu, nous* and *Thinking the Difference*, as well as her 1995-96 seminar on "The question of the other" at the Ecole des Hautes Etudes en Sciences Sociales in Paris. The interview treats questions of nature vs. culture, sexual difference and relational identity.

**Pluhar, Werner S** (trans) and Kant, Immanuel. *Critique of Pure Reason: Unified Edition (With All Variants from the 1781 and 1787 Editions)*. Indianapolis, Hackett, 1996.

Eminently suited for use by both scholars and students, this richly annotated volume offers translations of the complete texts of both the First (A) and Second (B) editions, as well as Kant's own notes. Extensive editorial notes by Werner Pluhar and James Ellington supply explanatory and terminological comments, translations of Latin and other foreign expressions, variant readings, cross-references to other passages in the text and in other writings of Kant, and references to secondary works. An extensive bibliography, glossary, and detailed index are included. (publisher,edited)

**Plumly, L Wayne** and Ostapski, S Andrew and Love, Jim L. The Ethical and Economic Implications of Smoking in Enclosed Public Facilities: A Resolution of Conflicting Rights. *J Bus Ethics*, 16(4), 377-384, Mr 97.

Smokers and nonsmokers possess equal rights but those rights conflict with each other in the use of shared facilities. Medical research has established that smoking harms not only those who use the product but also those who are passively exposed to it. Laws and private regulation of smoking in shared facilities have resulted in the segregation of smokers from nonsmokers to an outright ban of tobacco use. Such controls have provided unsatisfactory results to both groups. An acceptable ethical solution, based on reduction of harm and compensation, can be derived by applying *moral audit* principles, supported by economic analysis, which does not unduly curtail the rights of both parties as to the use of tobacco products.

**Plumwood, Val**. "Androcentrism and Anthropocentrism: Parallels and Politics" in *Ecofeminism: Women, Culture, Nature,* Warren, Karen J (ed), 327-355. Bloomington, Indiana Univ Pr, 1997.

The critique of anthrocentrism has been one of the major tasks of ecophilosophy, whose characteristic general thesis has been that our frameworks of morality and rationality must be challenged to include consideration of nonhumans. But the core of anthrocentrism is embattled and its relationship to practical environmental activism is problematic. I shall argue here that although the criticisms that have been made of the core concept have some justice, the primary problem is not the framework challenge or the core concept itself, but rather certain problematic understandings of it which have develop in environmental philosophy. (edited)

**Pluta, Olaf**. Der Alexandrismus an den Universitäten im späten Mittelalter. *Bochumer Phil Jrbh*, 1, 81-109, 1996.

This essay outlines the history of Alexandrism in the Middle Ages, focusing on the reception of Alexander of Aphrodisias in the late-medieval universities. Alexander of Aphrodisias met with severe criticism in the 13th century from William of Auvergne, Albert the Great and Thomas of Aquinas among others, but in the 14th century this attitude changed completely with John Buridan, giving way to a positive and productive adoption of his theories. The centerpiece of the controversy was Alexander's doctrine that the human soul is similar to the animal soul and hence mortal "like the soul of a dog or a donkey."(edited)

**Poblette, Juan**. Rethinking Latinoamericanism: On the (Re)Articulations of the Global and the Local. *Int Stud Phil*, 29(1), 111-120, 1997.

**Pochelú, Alicia G**. El origen de la experiencia humana. *Pensamiento*, 205(53), 113-125, Ja-Ap 97.

Maurice Merleau-Ponty concede a la teoría de la percepción una importancia capital porque ella intenta una explicación que permite conocer un género de ser, en relación al cual el sujeto permanece inserto. La conciencia perceptiva se convierte en la noción clave de su investigación dado que ella es vivida en la experiencia del cuerpo propio y descrita en el mundo de la vida. La íntima afinidad de la existencia corporal con el mundo que ella asume, se comprende de una manera más adecuada desde lo visible y lo móvil, porque son los aspectos desde donde el cuerpo se despliega. En consecuencia, la existencia corporal por su visión y movimiento extiende las cosas a su alrededor, las constituye en su prolongación y, de esta forma, se atestigua la indivisión entre lo sentiente y lo sentido.

**Pöggler, Otto**. "L'europeizzazione come probleme europeo" in *Geofilosofia,* Bonesio, Luisa (ed), 189-203. Sondrio, Lyasis, 1996.

**Pörn, Ingmar**. "The Meaning of 'Rights' in the Right to Know Debate" in *The Right to Know and the Right not to Know,* Chadwick, Ruth (ed), 37-42. Brookfield, Avebury, 1997.

**Poesche, Jürgen S**. Punishment in Environmental Protection. *J Bus Ethics,* 15(10), 1071-1081, O 96.

The fundamental character of a punishment is the subject of this paper. Based on the assumed function of a punishment (deterrent), a punishment has to be perceived and experienced to be an adverse result by the punished and the public. The first factor in particular means that the courts have to have flexibility to sentence a person to such a punishment that is experienced as such. The legal question becomes how this customization of a punishment is acceptable from an equality standpoint. In the field of environmental protection, the administrative process poses serious problems. There may be administrative proceedings that result in substantial economic losses for individuals and groups alike.

**Pogge, Thomas W**. "Europa y una federación global: La visión de Kant" in *Kant: La paz perpetua, doscientos años después,* Martínez Guzmán, Vicent (ed), 161-177. Valencia, Nau Llibres, 1997.

In "Perpetual Peace," Kant officially endorses the ideal of a pacific federation of sovereign states, but then also states that such a federation is only a "negative surrogate" for a world republic and cannot make peace truly secure. The reason for his ambivalence is that both models are flawed: A federation fails to achieve a thoroughgoing juridical condition, while a world government is unrealistic and dangerous. Had Kant been able to shed his unsound belief in the indivisibility of sovereignty, he might have endorsed a superior intermediate ideal of a vertical (and horizontal) dispersal of sovereign powers. The emerging European Union exemplifies this intermediate model—though, from a Kantian point of view, it still needs to be perfected in four important respects before it can serve as an ideal for the world at large.

**Pogge, Thomas W**. Lebensstandards im Kontext der Gerechtig-keitslehre. *Z Phil Forsch,* 51(1), 1-24, Ja-Mr 97.

Defining the justice of social institutions in terms of how they treat the persons affected by them and noting the fact that the lives of individuals are increasingly affected by foreign and by supranational institutions, we need a globally sharable and hence, relatively modest and abstract criterion of justice through which different societies can assess one anothers as well as common social institutions. Such a criterion should be sensitive to whether persons, who may specify the subjective and the ethical value of human lives in a wide variety of ways, have reasonably secure access to minimally adequate shares of the goods that are essential to leading worthwhile lives. Contrary to received consequentialist and contractarian theories, such a criterion must also differentiate among the various ways in which social institutions may affect the lives of individuals (e.g., by mandating, authorizing, or insufficiently deterring certain harms). A somewhat unconventional understanding of human rights furnishes a promising candidate for such a criterion.

**Pohlenz, Gerd**. Teleologie und Teleonomie aus Sicht der philosophischen Qualia-Thematik. *Z Phil Forsch,* 51(2), 232-250, Ap-Je 97.

Die eigentümliche Natur der Qualia (z.B. Farben) wird expliziert. Konsequenzen dieser Explikation sind die *ontologische Festschreibung* der phänomenalen Objektwelt und die *absolute kognitive Unmittelbarkeit* im Wahrnehmen. Vereinbar mit den Naturwissenschaften sind derartige Konzepte durch a) den *grenztheoretischen* Charakter ihrer Interpretation, b) die *Zwischenstellung* der Qualia zwischen dem Organismus und seiner Umwelt, c) die *Inhärenz* der phänomenalen Leib-Umwelt-Struktur in den Qualia. Demnach müssen auch jene Qualia, die biologisch als 'subjektive' Zutaten des verhaltens*motivierenden* Apparates rekonstruiert werden (wie Schmerz, Duft), als *irreduzibel objektzugehörig* und *als solche* unmittelbar motivierend gelten. Die Welt steht so unter dem Titel absoluter Werthaftigkeit und des Sinnes(-in-sich). Unlösbar hiervon ist das Verständnis des Menschen als Selbstzweck. Die evolutionsbiologische *Teleonomie* gewinnt so den Aspekt hinzu, jener *modifiziert-teleologischen* grenztheoretischen Sicht *gemäss* zu sein.

**Poivet, Roger**. Compétence, survenance et émotion esthétique. *Rev Int Phil,* 50(198), 635-649, 1996.

**Pojman, Louis** (ed) and Westmoreland, Robert (ed). *Equality: Selected Readings.* New York, Oxford Univ Pr, 1997.

The book collects the most representative material on the subject of equality, providing critical analyses of the egalitarian principles which underlie contemporary debate on issues such as welfare, civil and human rights, affirmative action, and immigration. This volume includes a broad range of readings, from the classical works of Aristotle, Hobbes, and Rousseau to contemporary selections by John Rawls, Thomas Nagel, R.M. Hare, Harry Frankfurt, Wallace Matson, Robert Nozick, Michael Walzer, and others. Several important topics are covered in depth, including the concept of equality; equal opportunity; welfare egalitarianism; resource egalitarianism; complex equality; and equal human worth and human rights. A comprehensive introduction and bibliography are also included. (publisher, edited)

**Pokker, P K**. The Role of Marxism and Deconstruction in Demystifying Aesthetics. *Darshana Int,* 36(2/142), 1-5, Ap 96.

**Pokorny, Petr**. Oh Our Children! (in Czech). *Filosof Cas,* 44(6), 1021-1025, 1996.

The counter-arguments are: a) All Christians, Muslims etc. and also all convinced atheists are preoccupied. A totally indifferent view is impossible; b) The only way to prevent one sidedness is to be aware of each person's commitment and reflect it critically; and c) The anti-ideological bias of postmodern thought does not mean giving up personal convictions, but rather tolerance towards other attitudes and views.

**Polacik, Tomasz**. Second Order Propositional Operators Over Cantor Space. *Stud Log,* 53(1), 93-105, F 94.

We consider propositional operators defined by propositional quantification in intuitionistic logic. We relate topological interpretations of second order intuitionistic propositional logic over Cantor space with the interpretation of propositional quantifiers (as the strongest and weakest interpolant in Heyting calculus) suggested by A. Pitts. One of the merits of Pitts's interpretation is shown to be valid for the interpretation over Cantor space. (edited)

**Polansky, Hanan** and Nelson, Paul and Nayak, Abhaya C. Belief Change as Change in Epistemic Entrenchment. *Synthese,* 109(2), 143-174, N 96.

In this paper, it is argued that both the belief state and its input should be represented as epistemic entrenchment (EE) relations. A belief revision operation is constructed that updates a given EE relation to a new one in light of an evidential EE relation, and an axiomatic characterization of this operation is given. Unlike most belief revision operations, the one developed here can handle both "multiple belief revision" and "iterated belief revision."

**Polanyi, Michael** and Allen, R T (ed). *Society, Economics & Philosophy: Selected Papers.* New Brunswick, Transaction Pub, 1997.

*Society, Economics, and Philosophy* represents the full range of Polanyi's interests outside of his scientific work: economics, politics, society, philosophy of science, religion and positivist obstacles to it, and art. Polanyi's principal ideas are contained in three essays: on the scientific revolution, the creative imagination and the mind-body relation. Precisely because of Polanyi's work in the physical sciences, his writings have a unique dimension not found in the writings of other advocates of the market and too infrequently found even in the work of philosophers of science. (publisher, edited)

**Poli, Roberto**. "*In Itinere* Pictures from Central-European Philosophy" in *In Itinere* European Cities and the Birth of Modern Scientific Philosophy, Poli, Roberto (ed), 11-31. Amsterdam, Rodopi, 1997.

Two of the distinctive features of Central European culture were (1) the insistence on decomposition and on everything that highlights differences and multiplicities and (2) a concern to reconcile science and literature, analytical rigour and intensity of feeling. In this situation, philosophers active prior to the 1st World War developed their analyses within the context of a close connection between metaphysics and psychology, whereas scholars in the subsequent period concentrated instead on the relationship between ontology and logic. One of the principal effects of the shift from metaphysics to ontology has been the 'incommunicability' that has arisen between logic and psychology.

**Poli, Roberto** (ed). *In Itinere* European Cities and the Birth of Modern Scientific Philosophy. Amsterdam, Rodopi, 1997.

The papers collected in this volume are an improved version of the talks given at the conference "*In itinere.* European cities and the birth of modern scientific philosophy," which was organized by the *Istituto Mitteleuropeo di Cultura/Mitteleuropäisches Kulturinstitut* in Bolzano/Bozen on the 8th and 9th of September 1994. The conference was a fantastic virtual tour of the cities in which the Brentanians worked and lived, with a reconstruction of the intellectual climate of their time. A draft version of some of the contributions to the conference has been published in *Axiomathes* 1994, 2/3.

**Poli, Roberto**. The Activator. *Dialogos,* 31(68), 7-21, Jl 96.

**Poliakov, L V**. The Conservatism of Konstantin Leont'ev in Present-Day Russia. *Russian Stud Phil,* 35(2), 51-60, Fall 96.

**Policriti, Alberto** and Montanari, Angelo. Decidability Results for Metric and Layered Temporal Logics. *Notre Dame J Form Log,* 37(2), 260-282, Spr 96.

We study the decidability problem for metric and layered temporal logics. The logics we consider are suitable to model time granularity in various contexts and they allow one to build granular temporal models by referring to the "natural scale" in any component of the model and by properly constraining the interactions between differently-grained components. A monadic second-order language combining operators such as temporal contextualization and projection, together with the usual displacement operator of metric temporal logics, is considered and the theory of finitely-layered metric temporal structures is shown to be decidable.

**Polikarov, Asaria**. Über den Charakter von Einsteins philosophischem Realismus. *Phil Natur,* 26(1), 135-158, 1989.

Man sollte annehmen, dass die Frage nach den philosophischen Auschauungen des berühmten Physikers schon geklärt sei und dass es in dieser Hinsicht keine ernsthaften Meinungsverschiedenheiten gebe. Dem ist aber nicht so. Die jüngsten Publikationen zeigen das anhaltende Interesse an dieser Frage, und in einigen von ihnen tauchen u.E. überwundene Ansichten auf oder bestehende Auffassungen werden bestritten. Deswegen scheint es uns angebracht, Stellung zu derartigen Versuchen zu nehmen, indem wir die Frage umfassend behandeln.

**Politis, Vasilis**. The Apriority of the Starting-Point of Kant's Transcendental Epistemology. *Int J Phil Stud,* 5(2), 255-284, Je 97.

The paper raises two questions, which seem central to understanding Kant's transcendental epistemology in the first *Critique.* First, Kant claims that the conditions for the possibility of experience are also conditions for the possibility of the objects of experience (A158/B197). Second, in what sense is Kant's transcendental epistemology a priori? I argue that Kant's notion of an object of experience is the notion of an object of any possible experience, not the notion of an object of one specific kind of experience, human experience. It follows, I argue, that Kant's transcendental epistemology is a priori in the strong sense that its starting-point is a priori. If we deny strong a priority, we fail to account for Kant's move from the nature of experience to the nature of empirical reality: empirical reality as such, not empirical reality as experienced by a particular variety of creatures capable of experience. (edited)

**Polizzi, Gaspare**. Tempo e pensiero topologico tra scienza e filosofia. *Iride*, 8(15), 409-421, Ag 95.

Dopo aver individuato un passaggio dai tempi fisici a quelli biologici e a quelli storici, G. Polizzi, in discussione con M. Serres e G. Marramao, considera la contingenza e le circostanze nel quadro di una "filosofia topologica" nella quale si delinea una temporalità complessa in cui vige l'inclusione e la coesistenza del "locale" e del "globale".

**Polizzotti, Mark** (trans) and Breton, André. *The Lost Steps*. Lincoln, Univ of Nebraska Pr, 1996.

*The Lost Steps* (*Les Pas perdus*) is André Breton's first collection of critical and polemical essays. Composed between 1917 and 1923, these pieces trace his evolution during the years when he was emerging as a central figure in French (and European) intellectual life. They chronicle his tumultuous passage through the Dada movement, proclaim his explosive views on Modernism and its heroes, and herald the emergence of Surrealism itself. Along the way, we are given Breton's serious commentaries on his Modernist predecessors, Guillaume Apollinaire and Alfred Jarry, followed by his not-so-serious Dada manifestoes. (publisher,edited)

**Polkowski, Lech T** and Komorowski, Jan and Skowron, Andrzej. Towards a Rough Mereology-Based Logic for Approximate Solution. *Stud Log*, 58(1), 143-184, 1997.

We are concerned with formal models of reasoning under uncertainty. Many approaches to this problem are known in the literature, e.g., Dempster-Shafer theory, Bayesian-based reasoning, belief networks, many-valued logics and fuzzy logics, nonmonotonic logics, neural network logics. We propose rough mereology developed by the last two authors as a foundation for approximate reasoning about complex objects. Our notion of a complex object includes, among others, proofs understood as schemes constructed in order to support within our knowledge assertions/hypotheses about reality described by our knowledge incompletely.

**Pollard, Stephen**. Who Needs Mereology?. *Phil Math*, 5, 65-70, F 97.

This note examines the mereological component of Geoffrey Hellman's most recent version of modal structuralism. There are plausible forms of agnosticism that benefit only a little from Hellman's mereological turn.

**Pollock, John L**. "Practical Reasoning in Oscar" in *AI, Connectionism and Philosophical Psychology, 1995*, Tomberlin, James E (ed), 15-48. Atascadero, Ridgeview, 1995.

This describes the theory of practical cognition embodied in the OSCAR architecture for rationality agency. Practical cognition consists of the selection of goals and the adoption of plans for achieving those goals. It is argued that practical decisions cannot choose acts one at a time. They must be chosen as parts of plans. Rules are proposed for reasoning about the adaptability of plans.

**Pollock, John L**. Reasoning about Change and Persistence: A Solution to the Frame Problem. *Nous*, 31(2), 143-169, Je 97.

"The Frame Problem" concerns how to reason about change and persistence in a complex environment. This has traditionally been regarded as a problem for artificial intelligence, but it can equally be regarded as a problem for human epistemology. This paper proposes a solution to the *frame problem*, in the form of a set of reason schemas for reasoning defeasibly about change and persistence. These schemas have been tested by implementing them in the author's AI system OSCAR.

**Pols, Jeannette** and Mol, Annemarie. Ziekte leven: Bouwstenen voor een medische sociologie zonder *disease/illness*-onderscheid. *Kennis Methode*, 20(4), 347-361, 1996.

**Polt, Richard** (trans) and Nietzsche, Friedrich. *Twilight of the Idols Or, How to Philosophize with the Hammer*. Indianapolis, Hackett, 1997.

*Twilight of the Idols*, which deals with what we worship and why, presents a vivid overview of many of Nietzsche's mature ideas—including his attack on Plato's Socrates and on the Platonic legacy in Western philosophy and culture—and anticipates his projected revaluation of all values. Accompanied by a fascinating Introduction by Tracy Strong, Richard Polt's new translation faithfully and beautifully renders this highly formal, even musical, late work of Nietzsche, which Nietzsche characterized as "a very sharp, precise and quick digest of my essential philosophical heterodoxies," and which offers such an excellent introduction to his thought. Includes select bibliography, notes, and index. (publisher)

**Póltawski, Andrzej**. Phenomenological Personalism: Edith Stein and Karol Wojtyla (in Polish). *Kwartalnik Filozof*, 23(1), 33-44, 1995.

**Póltawski, Andrzej**. Phenomenology as Fundamental Moral Philosophy by Stephen Strasser (in Polish). *Kwartalnik Filozof*, 25(1), 175-194, 1997.

**Póltawski, Andrzej**. The Problems of "External" Experience in Roman Ingarden's Philosophy: Part I (in Polish). *Kwartalnik Filozof*, 24(3), 7-31, 1996.

**Póltawski, Andrzej**. The Problems of "External" Experience in Roman Ingarden's Philosophy: Part II (in Polish). *Kwartalnik Filozof*, 24(4), 97-123, 1996.

**Poltier, Hugues**. La justice peut-elle naître du contrat social?. *Rev Theol Phil*, 129(2), 141-160, 1997.

Après avoir établi qu'en toute rigueur, seules les théories d'inspiration hobbesienne peuvent être qualifiées de contractualistes, l'A., examinant deux de ses versions les plus récentes (Höffe et Gauthier), montre que le développement conséquent des prémisses du contractualisme débouche nécessairement sur des conclusions qui heurtent profondément notre sens de la justice. Il en conclut à la nécessité de renoncer à la tentation de fonder la justice sur un supposé contrat social.

**Poma, Andrea**. "Die kritische Vernunft in der Theodizee von Leibniz" in *Grenzen der kritischen Vernunft*, Schmid, Peter A, 305-314. Basel, Schwabe Verlag, 1997.

**Pompa, Leon**. "Vico and Metaphysical Hermeneutics" in *Verstehen and Humane Understanding*, O'Hear, Anthony (ed), 29-46. New York, Cambridge Univ Pr, 1996.

The aim is to establish the relationship between metaphysics and historical interpretation in Vico's later philosophy. It is concluded that in the *Scienza Nuova* of 1725, he tried to underpin interpretation by recourse to a metaphysical pattern of historical development, but that in the *Scienza Nuova* of 1744, he tried to establish it empirically by comparative historical research based upon an acceptable canon of rules of interpretation and substantial hypotheses about the possible course of historical development. The latter view is argued to be more fruitful than the former.

**Pompa, Leon**. Hermenéutica metafísica y metafísica hermenéutica. *Cuad Vico*, 7/8, 141-166, 1997.

Some of the difficulty in establishing how philosophy and philology are related in Vico's theory of hermeneutics arises from the fact that he vacillated between two different views about their relationship, resulting in two different conceptions of the relationship between metaphysics and hermeneutics: between *metaphysical hermeneutics* (more pronounced in *SNP*) and *hermeneutical metaphysics* (more pronounced in *SNS*). The former, according to Vico's wish to produce an "art of diagnosis", makes interpretation dependent upon metaphysics, which is unacceptable nowadays. The latter involves a much more complex relationship between interpretation and metaphysics and offers us a viable method of hermeneutical enquiry with philosophical significance at the present time.

**Pompa, Leon**. La función del legislador en Giambattista Vico. *Cuad Vico*, 5/6, 139-153, 1995/96.

The article makes explicit a theory of the function of the legislator which is largely implicit in Vico's work. The conclusion is that Vico's theory depends upon a historically developing dialectical relationship between positive and ideal law. Positive law provides the basis of actual judicial practice but deficiencies in this law, revealed in such practice, give rise to an awareness of higher ideals of justice. The function of the legislator is to embody these ideals in new versions of positive law from which new ideals again arise. Vico applies this conception only to private law but his conception of public law can easily be amended to incorporate it.

**Ponferrada, Gustavo Eloy**. Del acto de ser a la acción moral. *Sapientia*, 51(200), 287-308, 1996.

**Poniatowski, Larry** and Worth-Staten, Patricia A. Advance Directives and Patient Rights: A Joint Commission Perspective. *Bioethics Forum*, 13(2), 47-50, Sum 97.

Advance directives for health care are an inherent right from the perspective of the Joint Commission for the Accreditation of Healthcare's standards. Highlighting standards from the *Comprehensive Accreditation Manual of Hospitals: The Official Handbook*, the authors outline this right. They contrast barriers patients encounter to having their preferences respected.

**Ponton, Lionel**. La définition du droit naturel d'Ulpien: sa reprise par Thomas d'Aquin et son actualisation comme critique des droits de l'homme. *Laval Theol Phil*, 52(3), 845-861, O 96.

**Ponton, Lionel**. Le statut de l'éthique aristotélicienne dans la morale 'adéquatement prise' de Jacques Maritain. *Maritain Stud*, 12, 50-66, 1996.

In order better to establish the validity of what he called "adequately taken" ethics, or "ethics subordinated to theology", Jacques Maritain was gradually led to distance himself from Aristotle's practical philosophy. The more radically so as he would come to realize clearly through the years that the critiques levelled against his interpretation of the Thomist notion of the political common good were grounded in it.

**Ponzio, Augusto**. "Essere, Materia, Soggetto, Alterità: Per una critica filosofica della comunicazione mondializzata" in *Soggetto E Verità: La questione dell'uomo nella filosofia contemporanea*, Fagiuoli, Ettore, 53-70. 20136 Milano, Mimesis, 1996.

**Ponzio, Augusto**. *Augusto Ponzio: Bibliografia e Letture Critiche*. Modugno (Bari), Edizioni dal Sud, 1995.

**Poole, Ross**. Freedom, Citizenship, and National Identity. *Phil Forum*, 28(1-2), 125-148, Fall-Wint 97.

**Pope, Stephen J**. Neither Enemy nor Friend: Nature as Creation in the Theology of Saint Thomas Aquinas. *Zygon*, 32(2), 219-230, Je 97.

This paper traces three paradigmatic responses to the presence of evil in nature. Thomas Henry Huxley depicts nature as the enemy of humanity that morality combats "at every step." Henry Drummond views nature as benevolent, a friend of humanity and the ultimate basis for morality. The paper argues that a third view, that of Thomas Aquinas, regards nature as creation, capable of being neither enemy for friend of humanity but rather the context within which relations of enmity or friendship develop between human beings and God.

**Popkewitz, Thomas S** and Brennan, Marie. Restructuring of Social and Political Theory in Education: Foucault and a Social Epistemology of School Practices. *Educ Theor*, 47(3), 287-313, Sum 97.

**Popkin, Richard H**. Scepticism at the Time of Descartes. *Dialogos*, 32(69), 243-253, Ja 97.

**Popkin, Richard H** (ed). *Scepticism in the History of Philosophy: A Pan-American Dialogue*. Dordrecht, Kluwer, 1996.

*Scepticism in the History of Philosophy* is a dialogue between Latin American and North American scholars concerned with the history of scepticism from ancient times to present-day philosophy. The volume contains interesting discussions by a wide range of philosophers and historians of philosophy. It is unique in presenting in English the work of philosophers from Mexico, Brazil, Argentina and Chile who are not well-known to the English-speaking world. (publisher, edited)

**Popkin, Richard H** and Laursen, John Christian and Briscoe, Peter. Hume in the Prussian Academy: Jean Bernard Mérian's "On the Phenomenalism of David Hume". *Hume Stud*, 23(1), 153-191, Ap 97.

This article contains a transcription and translation of an important eighteenth-century interpretation of Hume's phenomenalism. A substantial introduction reviews interest in Hume at the Prussian Academy, Jean Bernard Mérian's engagement with scepticism and questions of the self and personal identity and analyzes Mérian's conclusions. Notes draw attention to Mérian's critique of Kant and to some of the later influence of Mérian on Victor Cousin and Maine de Biran.

**Popper, Karl** and Bennet, Laura J (trans). *In Search of a Better World: Lectures and Essays from Thirty Years*. New York, Routledge, 1996.

'I wish to begin by saying that I regard scientific knowledge as the most important kind of knowledge we have, though I am far from regarding it as the only one', writes Sir Karl Popper in the opening essay of this book. His subjects range from the beginnings of scientific speculation in classical Greece to the destructive effects of twentieth-century totalitarianism, from major figures of the Enlightenment such as Voltaire and Kant to the role of science and self-criticism in the arts. The essays offer striking new insights; including insights into the mind of their author, a fighter for freedom and one of the most forthright critics of Marxism and all totalitarian ideologies. (publisher,edited)

**Porchat Pereira, Oswaldo**. "Verdad, realismo y racionalidad escéptica" in *La racionalidad: su poder y sus límites,* Nudler, Oscar (ed), 99-141. Barcelona, Ed Paidos, 1996.

This paper tries to elaborate and develop a *sceptical conception of truth* and a notion of *sceptical realism* which, notwithstanding Sextus Empiricus's silence on those points, are claimed to be plainly compatible with the basic standpoints of the Pyrrhonian scepticism and at the same time to preserve the fundamental intuitions of our common sense.

**Porchat Pereira, Oswaldo**. O Ceticismo Pirrônico e os Problemas Filosóficos. *Cad Hist Filosof Cie*, 6(Spec), 97-157, Ja-D 96.

This paper develops two main themes: in the first place, one tries to make clear how, from the point of view of our contemporary philosophical ideas, a retrospective interpretation of Greek sceptic Pyrrhonism allows us to read it, not only as a questioning of the theses and arguments of dogmatic philosophy, but as a questioning, too, of the very legitimity of the traditional philosophical problems and philosophical language. But the second part of the text is a "positive" one, which proceeds to an analysis of the relation between a phenomenic and a dogmatic level of language and, then, explains how the idea of a philosophical investigation of problems formulated in the phenomenic level is plainly compatible with (neo)Pyrrhonic philosophy. And a discussion is undertaken of the relation between problems formulated in one and another levels.

**Porcheddu, Raimondo**. "L'idea aristotelica di natura nell'interpretazione di Hegel" in *Hegel e Aristotele*, Ferrarin, A, 111-133. Cagliari, Edizioni AV, 1997.

**Poreba, Marcin**. Das Problem der transzendentalen Freiheit in semantischer Formulierung (Dargestellt an Fichtes Jenaer Wissenschaftslehren). *Fichte-Studien*, 10, 273-283, 1997.

**Porée, Jérôme**. Normativité et vérification immanentes des valeurs chez Max Scheler. *Frei Z Phil Theol*, 44(1-2), 104-116, 1997.

Although Max Scheler bases norms on values considered as essences directly presented through a specific intuition, he remains fully aware of the requirement to communicate them and to validate them intersubjectively. However, besides the fact that this requirement itself presupposes such an intuition, the intuition provides the answer to the requirement. As personal values eminently prove, having a value means having duties and having duties implies sympathy.

**Porée, Jérôme**. Souffrance et temps: Esquisse phénoménologique. *Rev Phil Louvain*, 95(1), 103-129, F 97.

Suffering does not merely determine the content, but also affects the form of our experience. This is witnessed to by the upsets it brings about in temporality. The description of such upsets is the task of a phenomenology concerned as much to clarify from within the singular destiny of suffering consciousness as to find within it the key to an understanding profound itself of our temporal condition. It is true, thus, that what time teaches us about suffering cannot be separated from what suffering teaches us about time.

**Porpora, Douglas V**. The Caterpillar's Question: Contesting Anti-Humanism's Contestations. *J Theor Soc Behav*, 27(2-3), 243-263, Je-S 97.

The caterpillar's question is the question Wonderland's caterpillar posed to Alice: Who are you? This is a question Alice finds she cannot answer. According to postmodernist antihumanism, Alice cannot answer the question because

there is no coherent Alice there to answer it, no unitary subject of consciousness. This paper contests the anti-humanist denial of a coherent subject of experience. While it is conceded that phenomenologically, we may have difficulty today identifying who we are essentially, it is argued that, conceptually, we cannot do without the ontological category of the person as a unified center of consciousness.

**Portelli, John**. Democracy in Education: Beyond the Conservative or Progressivist Stances. *Inquiry (USA)*, 16(1), 9-21, Fall 96.

The general aim of this paper is to explore the relationship between democracy and education. There are several views that philosophers of education and educationists have put forth with regard to the relationship of these two contested concepts. In this paper I will focus on two major views: a) the conservative or traditional stance and b) the progressivist or student-centred stance. After offering a brief description of these positions and their corresponding assumptions, I will identify problems with both positions. My brief account and criticisms of these views will attempt to show that the difference in the stances taken about the role of democracy in education varies according to the different beliefs held about the nature of the child or the learner—beliefs which are really embedded in a certain ideological or political framework. (edited)

**Porter, Andrew P**. Science, Religious Language, and Analogy. *Faith Phil*, 13(1), 113-120, Ja 96.

Ian Barbour sees four ways to relate science and religion: 1) conflict, 2) disjunction or independence, 3) dialogue, and 4) synthesis or integration. David Burrell posits three ways to construe religious language, as a) univocal, b) equivocal, or c) analogous. The paper contends that Barbour's (1) and (4) presuppose Burrell's (a) Barbour's (2) presupposes Burrell's (b), and Barbour's (3) presupposes Burrell's (c), and it explores some of the implications for each alternative.

**Porter, James I**. "Aristotle and Specular Regimes: The Theater of Philosophical Discourse" in *Sites of Vision,* Levin, David Michael (ed), 93-115. Cambridge, MIT Pr, 1997.

A general discussion of visual language in Aristotle's *Metaphysics* and *Politics* leads to an insight into the discursive logic of Aristotle's philosophical regimes. Philosophy is best viewed as a discipline and method for organizing the perceptual field; the *Politics* emerges as the theory of this subordination and supervision of knowledges, techniques and discourses. Developing from Foucault, two forms of power can be detected in their mutual dependency in Aristotle (and in power relations in general), the one "classical" (frontal, spectacular, real) the other "postmodern" (oblique, panoptic, imaginary). *Politics* 5 is paradigmatic in both respects and Aristotle's "recommendations" to prospective tyrants have troubling implications for his ethical theory.

**Posada, Jorge Mario**. Sobre el sentido común y la percepción: Algunas sugerencias acerca de la facultad sensitiva central. *Anu Filosof*, 29(2), 961-984, 1996.

Standing upon Leonardo Polo's interpretation about Aristotle's doctrine on sensitive cognition, some aspects of the sensorial organical immutation required in it are examined and a thesis concerning the common sense as center and root of sensibility—not only exterior, but also interior—is suggested. According to this thesis, even the sensorial and organical immutations belonging to the other internal senses can return to the organ of the common sense, which becomes the central and radical organ. Therefore, all sensible objectivation should take place in the common sense. This conclusion does not agree with Polo's position.

**Posavac, Zlatko**. Arnold's Aesthetics and 19th Century Croatian Philosophy of History (in Serbo-Croatian). *Filozof Istraz*, 15(4), 901-917, 1995.

In der umfangreichen monographischen Darstellung der Ästhetik Gjuro Arnolds (1854-1941), erschienen in der Zeitschrift *Prilozi za istrazivanje hrvatske filozofske bastine*, Zagreb 1990-1994, Nr. 31-40, wurde dem Umstand Rechnung getragen, dass die ästhetischen Ansichten Arnolds (ausgehend!) in der "praktischen Philosophie" (Herbartismus), aus der Arnold seine Anschauung über die Geschichtsphilosophie herleitet, begründet sind. (edited)

**Poser, Hans**. Ontologie der Mathematik im Anschluss an Oskar Becker. *Acta Analytica*, 125-146, 1996.

Richtig ist, dass weder die Mathematik phänomenologische noch die Phänomenologie mathematische Erkenntnisse geben kann. Aufgabe der phänomenologischen Philosophie ist es, den *Sinn* der mathematischen Erkenntnisse zu erklären, nicht solche Erkenntnisse zu finden.

**Posner, Richard A**. "The Economic Approach to Homosexuality" in *Sex, Preference, and Family: Essays on Law and Nature,* Nussbaum, Martha C (ed), 173-191. New York, Oxford Univ Pr, 1997.

The purpose of this essay is to offer a rational-choice approach to homosexual orientation and activity. Sexual orientation is assumed given by the genes or early development, but the choice of sexual behaviors is determined by private costs and benefits, just as in the case of market behavior. This approach explains salient features of homosexual behavior and a framework for normative analysis of such behavior and of public policy toward it.

**Posner, Richard A**. Against Ethical Criticism. *Phil Lit*, 21(1), 1-27, Ap 97.

This article criticizes ethical or edifying criticism, as exemplified in recent work by Wayne Booth and Martha Nussbaum. The article argues the claims of the aesthetic tradition: that the moral content of a work of literature and the moral qualities of its author, are irrelevant to the literary significance of the work.

**Posnock, Ross**. "The Influence of William James on American Culture" in *The Cambridge Companion to William James,* Putnam, Ruth Anna (ed), 322-342. New York, Cambridge Univ Pr, 1997.

AUTHOR INDEX 851 Potter, Robert Lyman

**Posnock, Ross**. How It Feels to Be a Problem: Du Bois, Fanon, and the "Impossible Life" of the Black Intellectual. *Crit Inquiry*, 23(2), 323-349, Wint 97.

**Pospesel, Howard** and Rodes, Robert E. *Premises and Conclusions: Symbolic Logic for Legal Analysis*. Englewood Cliffs, Prentice Hall, 1997.

This volume presents the elements of contemporary symbolic logic and applies that powerful instrument to reasoning in the law. Deductive logic is employed to illuminate the structure of legal reasoning and clarify various legal problems. Attention has been given to the clear and orderly presentation of concepts and techniques, and to their illustration with practical examples including many legal cases and problems. Numerous exercises are provided so that readers can check their mastery of the material. (publisher, edited)

**Possenti, Vittorio**. Conoscenza metafisica dell'esistenza. *Riv Filosof Neo-Scolas*, 88(3), 483-509, Jl-S 96.

**Possenti, Vittorio**. *Dio e il male*. Torino, SEI, 1995.

Che cosa è il *male* e donde viene all'uomo? Dopo l'abisso di dolore della seconda guerra mondiale e dell'Olocausto, questi interrogativi sono riesplosi, sebbene non poca filosofia sia andata volgendosi verso teorie sofisticate e astratte, forse nell'infecondo tentativo di mettere fra parentesi la questione. Ma se anche l'uomo volesse abbandonare il male, questo non abbandonerà l'uomo. Un filone di pensatori (fra cui L. Pareyson e H. Jonas) si è posto dinanci all'enigma del male, chi vedendone un'antica traccia in Dio, chi considerando questi impotente nei suoi confronti. Tentativi generosi, ma forse impari al tema. Sembra piuttosto necessario, unendo la riflessione ontoteologica e la meditazione credente, porre l'interrogativo *dinanzi a Dio*, ed elevare la lotta contro il male a scelta umana centrale, L'uomo ha sempre e nuovamente bisogno di nutrirsi di liberazione dal male. (publisher)

**Postema, Gerald J**. Introduction: The Sins of Segregation. *Law Phil*, 16(3), 221-244, My 97.

**Poster, Mark**. *Cultural History and Postmodernity: Disciplinary Readings and Challenges*. New York, Columbia Univ Pr, 1997.

As Poster provides close reading of leading historians and theorists such as Lawrence Stone, François Furet, Michel de Certeau, and Michel Foucault, key themes animate his work: the often irreducible difference between past and present; the relationship of writing and representation to power and domination; the dissolving distinctions between high and low culture, production and consumption, and reality and fiction; and, most important, a new perspective on human agency and the construction of political subjects. (publisher, edited)

**Postgate, John**. Science, Morality and Religion: An Essay. *Sci Eng Ethics*, 2(1), 9-16, J 96.

The nonprescriptive, morally neutral, nature of science, in contrast to the prescriptive and dogmatic nature of religion, imposes open mindedness and probity among scientists, which spill over into their everyday moral and ethical outlooks. Scientists become significantly less susceptible to the religious imperatives which underlie the majority of today's wars, acts of terrorism, genocide and hatred, as well as to the growing fad for cults and mysticism. The antiscience posture now widespread among nonscientist intellectuals throughout the world may stem in part from an unacknowledged awareness of this moral superiority.

**Postow, B C**. Agent-Neutral Reasons: Are They for Everyone?. *Utilitas*, 9(2), 249-257, Jl 97.

According to both deontologists and consequentialists, if there is a reason to promote the general happiness—or to promote any other state of affairs unrelated to one's own projects or self-interest—then the reason must apply to everyone. This view seems almost self-evident; to challenge it is to challenge the way we think of moral reasons. I contend, however, that the view depends on the unwarranted assumption that the only way to restrict the application scope of a reason for action is by restricting it to those agents whose interests or projects are involved in the reason. In fact normative theories may coherently restrict application scopes in other ways. Thus we must take seriously the possibility that the reasons to promote the general happiness, although genuine, does not apply to everyone.

**Potepa, Maciej**. Die Wissenschaftslehre: Die Auseinandersetzung Schleiermachers mit Fichte. *Fichte-Studien*, 12, 285-294, 1997.

**Potrc, Matjaz**. Consciousness and Connectionism—The Problem of Compatability of Type Identity Theory and of Connectionism. *Acta Analytica*, 175-190, 1995.

U.T. Place repeatedly affirms that his approach is superior to others, particularly to token identity theorists, in that it fits recent developments of connectionism. It is therefore appropriate to find out what the claim of compatibility amounts to. U.T. Place's version of type identity thesis is compared with his assertions about compatibility with connectionism. The result is that arguing to this effect may still leave us wanting. Type identity thesis conceives consciousness to be a process in the brain, and this does not give any support for the straight semantic elasticity.

**Pott, Heleen**. Op zoek naar Mr. Spock: Kort commentaar op Apostel en Walry, 'Minimale rationaliteit van emoties en van overtuigingen'. *Alg Ned Tijdschr Wijs*, 89(2), 147-151, Ap 97.

**Potter, Jason** and Fisher, John Andrew. Technology, Appreciation, and the Historical View of Art. *J Aes Art Crit*, 55(2), 169-185, Spring 97.

Appreciative practices pose a difficult problem for historical-contextualist (HC) theorists of art (Danto, Levinson, Davies, etc.). Their theories suggest that historical artworks cannot be appropriately appreciated in contexts divorced from information about the artwork's context of creation, yet modern, technological appreciative practices presuppose the opposite. Either HC theories are wrong, or they must reject the idea that artworks are socially constructed in part by how we appreciate them. We rebut both disjuncts of this dilemma. We defend the role of appreciative practices in determining our common conception of the artwork. We defend HC theories by showing that this common conception contains the historical art object as a regulative idea, even in highly abstracted contexts of appreciation.

**Potter, Michael** and Sullivan, Peter. Hale on Caesar. *Phil Math*, 5, 135-152, Je 97.

Crispin Wright and Bob Hale have defended the strategy of defining the natural numbers contextually against the objection which led Frege himself to reject it, namely the so-called 'Julius Caesar problem'. To do this they have formulated principles (called sortal inclusion principles) designed to ensure that numbers are distinct from any objects, such as persons, a proper grasp of which could not be afforded by the contextual definition. We discuss whether either Hale or Wright has provided independent motivation for a defensible version of the sortal inclusion principle and whether they have succeeded in showing that numbers are *just* what the contextual definition says they are.

**Potter, Michael D**. Taming the Infinite. *Brit J Phil Sci*, 47(4), 609-619, D 96.

Shaughan Lavine's book *Understanding the Infinite* uses recent work of Jan Mycielski to interpret mathematics within theories of what he calls 'finite mathematics'. I describe the resulting trade-off between concepts and objects and argue that it does not solve the epistemological problem occasioned by our apparent grasp of the infinite in mathematics. In particular, Lavine pays insufficient attention to the difficulties involved in supposing that we can treat proofs which use instances of an axiom scheme as valid without being committed already to each instance of the scheme.

**Potter, Nancy**. Discretionary Power, Lies, and Broken Trust: Justification and Discomfort. *Theor Med*, 17(4), 329-352, D 96.

This paper explores the relationship between the bonds of practitioner/patient trust and the notion of a justified lie. The intersection of moral theories on lying which prioritize right action with institutional discretionary power allows practitioners to dismiss, or at least not take seriously enough, the harm done when a patient's trust is betrayed. Even when a lie can be shown to be justified, the trustworthiness of the practitioner may be called into question in ways that neither theories of right action nor contemporary discourse in health care attends to adequately. I set out features of full trustworthiness along Aristotelian lines.

**Potter, Nancy**. Loopholes, Gaps, and What is Held Fast: Democratic Epistemology and Claims to Recovered Memories. *Phil Psychiat Psych*, 3(4), 238-254, D 96.

This paper raises questions about who counts as a knower with regard to his or her own memories, what gets counted as a genuine memory, and who will affirm those memories within an epistemic community. I argue for a democratic epistemology informed by an understanding of relations of power. I investigate implications of the claim that knowledge is both social and political and suggest ways it is related to trust. Given the tendency of epistemology to draw lines that discriminate unfairly against some, it is vital that effects to create democratic epistemologies be sensitive to the potential for exploitation. Standards of credibility often favor members of dominant groups, and our ontological commitments may intersect with patterns of domination. While acknowledging difficulties in evaluating what counts as credible claims to memories, I argue that one's engagement with clients must be mapped onto the larger moral and political domain.

**Potter, Nelson**. Kant on Obligation and Motivation in Law and Ethics. *Jahr Recht Ethik*, 2, 95-111, 1994.

Der erste Teil in Kants Werk *Die Metaphysik der Sitten*, die *Rechtslehre*, wird üblicherweise als eine politische Abhandlung diskutiert. Aber es gibt Parallelen zwischen Recht (der äusseren Freiheit) und Ethik (der inneren Freiheit) bei Kant. Gesetzgebung ist in beiden Bereichen eine Kombination von Gesetz und Triebfeder. In den Arbeiten, die das eigentliche Herzstück von Kants Tugendlehre behandeln, ist die Freiheit eine innere ethische Freiheit, die auf einer rein moralischen Triebfeder basiert, deren Angemessenheit und Zulänglichkeit eine transzendentale Annahme dieses Teils von Kants Moralphilosophie ist. (edited)

**Potter, Robert Lyman**. From Clinical Ethics to Organizational Ethics: The Second Stage of the Evolution of Bioethics. *Bioethics Forum*, 12(2), 3-12, Sum 96.

Bioethics has succeeded to an important extent in clinical ethics. In order to meet the challenges of clinical ethics in a highly systematized health care industry, it will be necessary to move to a full engagement in organizational ethics. Re-engineering the institutional ethics committee as an integrated ethics program is one strategy for creating an ethical corporate culture where clinical ethics can flourish. This expansion from clinical to corporate ethics is a return to a broader vision of the goals of bioethics.

**Potter, Robert Lyman**. Learning to "Real/Hear": Narrative Ethics and Ethics Committee Education. *Bioethics Forum*, 10(4), 36-40, Fall 94.

Narrative ethics, a method of ethical analysis that focuses on an individual's character and virtues, is an alternative and supplemental approach to doing ethics in a clinical setting. A narrative ethics perspective provides ethics committees with an understanding of the complexity of agents and their actions. Members of ethics committees trained in narrative ethics learn to "read/hear" the patient in the context of his or her life and history, and are able, consequently, to anticipate probable futures and design interventions which can change the course of an illness in a positive way.

**Potter, Robert Lyman** and Schneider, Jennifer. Bioethical Analysis of an Integrated Medicine Clinic. *Bioethics Forum*, 12(4), 30-38, Wint 96.

This paper considers the bioethical analysis of an alternative medicine project: first, it proposes a "bioethics analysis grid" constructed from the principles, virtues, and goals established by the discipline of bioethics; second, it describes the development of a public clinic that integrates conventional and natural medicine, and third, it supports the conclusion that this unique project has a core set of values that generally comply with the standards of bioethics.

**Potter, Van Rensselaer**. Individuals Bear Responsibility. *Bioethics Forum*, 12(2), 27-28, Sum 96.

Organizational ethics ultimately can be reduced to the ethical norms of individuals within the organization itself. By their actions, the organization is formed and sustained; likewise, they bear the responsibility to improve the ability of the system to do good.

**Potter, Vincent G**. "John E. Smith and the Recovery of Religious Experience" in *Reason, Experience, and God: John E. Smith in Dialogue*, Colapietro, Vincent M, 7-18. New York, Fordham Univ Pr, 1997.

**Poubel, Hardée Werneck** and Pereira, Luiz Carlos P D. A Categorical Approach to Higher-Level Introduction and Elimination Rules. *Rep Math Log*, 28, 3-19, 1994.

The aim of the present work is to extend the well-known connections between proof theory and category theory to higher-level natural deduction. To be precise, we will show how an adjointness between Cartesian closed categories with finite coproducts can be associated, in a systematic way, with any operator Phi defined by the higher-level schemes. The objects in the categories will be rules instead of formulas. (edited)

**Poulakos, John**. The Letter and the Spirit of the Text: Two Translations of Gorgias's *On Non-Being or On Nature* (MXG). *Phil Rhet*, 30(1), 41-44, 1997.

**Pound, Roscoe** and Treviño, A Javier (ed). *Social Control Through Law*. New Brunswick, Transaction Pub, 1997.

In *Social Control Through Law* Roscoe Pound formulates a list of social-ethical principles with a three-fold purpose. First, they are meant to identify and explain human claims, demands, or interests of a given social order. Second, they express what the majority of individuals in a given society want the law to do. Third, they are meant to guide the courts in applying the law. Pound distinguishes between individual interests, public interests, and social interests. He warns that these three types of interests are overlapping and interdependent and that most claims, demands, and desires can be placed in all three categories. Pound's theory of social interests is crucial to his thinking about law and lies at the conceptual core of sociological jurisprudence. In the new introduction, A. Javier Treviño outlines the principle aspects of Roscoe Pound's legal philosophy. (publisher, edited)

**Poupard, Cardinal P**. Science et foi: pour un nouveau dialogue. *Laval Theol Phil*, 52(3), 761-776, O 96.

Since Galileo, the situation has changed in the relationship between science and faith. The time of scienticism has passed: scientists acknowledge the complementarity of different ways to the truth. As for the church, Vatican II holds to the autonomy of culture, especially of sciences. However, now discoveries in sciences raise up new challenges which should be addressed in a new dialogue, where science and faith acknowledge the difference and the complementarity of their own standpoint.

**Povar, Gail J**. The Quality of Primary Care/Consultant Relationships in Managed Care: Have We Gone Forward or Backward?. *J Clin Ethics*, 8(1), 66-70, Spr 97.

**Powell, Andrew**. Philosophy and Mathematics. *Teorema*, 16(2), 97-108, 1997.

This article is an English-language review of Christian Thiel's book *Philosophie und Mathematik*, itself a work which surveys many topics in the philosophy of mathematics. It examines some of the philosophical standpoints discussed (conventionalism and formalism), and furnishes an introduction to some of the book's more unusual topics by giving an overview of the "constructive philosophy" of Thiel's mentor, Paul Lorenzen. Sketches are provided of Lorenzen's foundational approaches to analysis, Euclidean geometry, and logic. The article ends by comparing Lorenzen's foundationalism with Thiel's more methodological approach to the philosophy of mathematics.

**Powers, Lawrence H**. The One Fallacy Theory. *Inform Log*, 17(2), 303-314, Spr 95.

My One Fallacy theory says there is only one fallacy: equivocation, or playing on an ambiguity. In this paper I explain how this theory arose from metaphilosophical concerns. And I contrast this theory with purely logical, dialectical and psychological notions of fallacy.

**Prabhakara Rao, M**. A Critique on Brahman-Realization. *J Indian Counc Phil Res*, 14(2), 71-82, Ja-Ap 97.

**Prade, Henri** and Dubois, Didier. New Trends and Open Problems in Fuzzy Logic and Approximate Reasoning. *Theoria (Spain)*, 11(27), 109-121, S 96.

This short paper about fuzzy set-based approximate reasoning first emphasizes the three main semantics for fuzzy sets: similarity, preference and uncertainty. The difference between truth-functional many-valued logics of vague or gradual propositions and nonfully compositional calculi such as possibilistic logic (which handles uncertainty) or similarity logics is stressed. Then, potentials of fuzzy set-based reasoning methods are briefly outlined for various kinds of approximate reasoning: deductive reasoning about flexible constraints, reasoning under uncertainty and inconsistency, hypothetical reasoning, exception-tolerant plausible reasoning using generic knowledge, interpolative reasoning, and abductive reasoning (under uncertainty). Open problems are listed in the conclusion.

**Prade, Henri** and Dubois, Didier and Benferhat, Salem. Some Syntactic Approaches to the Handling of Inconsistent Knowledge Bases: A Comparative Study. *Stud Log*, 58(1), 17-45, 1997.

This paper presents and discusses several methods for reasoning from inconsistent knowledge bases. A so-called argued consequence relation, taking into account the existence of consistent arguments in favor of a conclusion and the absence of consistent arguments in favor of its contrary, is particularly investigated. Flat knowledge bases, i.e., without any priority between their elements, are studied under different inconsistency-tolerant consequence relations, namely the so-called argumentative, free, universal, existential, cardinality-based, and paraconsistent consequence relations. The syntax-sensitivity of these consequence relations is studied. A companion paper is devoted to the case where priorities exist between the pieces of information in the knowledge base.

**Pradhan, R C**. Life, Culture and Value: Reflections on Wittgenstein's *Culture and Value*. *J Indian Counc Phil Res*, 13(2), 19-30, Ja-Ap 96.

Culture signifies the inward development of man whereas civilization pertains to the outward development of the material life. According to Wittgenstein, culture embodies the timeless values of life that to not follow from the so-called scientific attitude towards life. Science and values belong to two distinct realms; values belong to the transcendental realm. Wittgenstein's antiscientific argument reveals the fact that the value of life is beyond the measure of time and so has to be looked at *sub specie aeternitatis*. This paper thus makes an attempt to bring out the transcendental nature of values and their implications for culture.

**Pradhan, R C**. Response to Kanthamani's Comment. *J Indian Counc Phil Res*, 13(3), 139-143, My-Ag 96.

My response to Kanthamani's comments on my transcendental interpretation of Wittgenstein's philosophy is that notwithstanding Wittgenstein's emphasis on the naturalistic origin of language and forms of life, there is scope for a logical and transcendental perspective on them. The transcendental—not transcendent—perspective consists in presenting a grammatical overview of language, life and the world. This makes room for a "perspicious representation" of the essence of language and the world. Thus there is no denying the fact that Wittgenstein recommends a metaphysics of possibilities as the ultimate result of the grammatical way of understanding language and forms of life.

**Prado, José Hernández**. Sentido común "común" y sentido común "sensato". Una reivindicación de Thomas Reid. *Topicos*, 35-50, 1996.

This article attempts to show that Thomas Reid (1710-1796) especially argued not a "common" common sense, but a "sensible" one. In addition, it proposes that Reid's philosophy of common sense is quite important amongst those of its kind.

**Prado Júnior, Bento**. Gilda de Mello e Souza (in Portuguese). *Discurso*, 26, 15-17, 1996.

**Prandini, Riccardo**. La fiducia come forma di fede: Alcune riflessioni introduttive ad un problema sociologico. *Iride*, 10(20), 105-125, Ap 97.

**Prasad, Rajendra**. Applying Ethics: Modes, Motives, and Levels of Commitment. *J Indian Counc Phil Res*, 14(2), 1-30, Ja-Ap 97.

**Prawitz, Dag**. "Progress in Philosophy" in *The Idea of Progress*, McLaughlin, Peter (ed), 139-153. Hawthorne, de Gruyter, 1997.

**Predelli, Stefano**. Talk About Fiction. *Erkenntnis*, 46(1), 69-77, Ja 97.

I present a novel explanation of the apparent truth of certain remarks about fiction, such as an utterance of 'Salieri commissioned the *Requiem*' during a discussion of the movie *Amadeus*. I criticize the traditional view, which alleges that the uttered sentence abbreviates the longer sentence 'it is true in the movie *Amadeus* that Salieri commissioned the *Requiem*'. I propose a solution which appeals to some independently motivated results concerning the contexts relevant for the semantic evaluation of indexical expressions.

**Prendinger, Helmut** and Schurz, Gerhard. Reasoning about Action and Change. *J Log Lang Info*, 5(2), 209-245, 1996.

Reasoning about change is a central issue in research on human and robot planning. We study an approach to reasoning about action and change in a dynamic logic setting and provide a solution to problems which are related to the *frame problem*. Unlike most work on the frame problem the logic described in this paper is *monotonic*. It (implicitly) allows for the occurrence of actions of multiple agents by introducing nonstationary notions of waiting and test. The need to state a large number of "frame axioms" is alleviated by introducing a concept of *chronological preservation* to dynamic logic. As a side effect, this concept permits the encoding of *temporal* properties in a natural way. We compare the relative merits of our approach and nonmonotonic approaches as regards different aspects of the frame problem. Technically, we show that the resulting extended systems of propositional dynamic logic preserve (weak) completeness, finite model property and decidability.

**Presbey, Gail**. Hannah Arendt on Power, Consent, and Coercion: Some Parallels with Gandhi. *Acorn*, 7(2), 24-32, Fall-Wint 92-93.

**Press, Gerald A**. Continuities and Discontinuities in the History of *Republic* Interpretation. *Int Stud Phil*, 28(4), 61-78, 1996.

**Press, Gerald A**. The State of the Question in the Study of Plato. *S J Phil*, 34(4), 507-532, Wint 96.

Extensive review of the literature shows that the old consensus about a dogmatic, developmental, nonliterary interpretation of Plato no longer exists. Abandoning the assumption that Plato has doctrines, many now believe that Plato's 'philosophy' consists of something other than doctrines; the question is, *what*? The question is not *whether* to take literary and dramatic aspects into consideration, but *how*. Developmentalism is now a hypothesis needing defense as is the older belief that the dialogues' function simply to communicate Plato's doctrines. The question about the arguments is no longer simply whether they are valid, but what purposes Plato means than to serve.

AUTHOR INDEX 853 Primeaux, Patrick

**Preston, William A**. "Nietzsche on Blacks" in *Existence in Black: An Anthology of Black Existential Philosophy,* Gordon, Lewis R (ed), 167-172. New York, Routledge, 1997.

**Price, Daniel**. *Without a Woman to Read: Toward the Daughter in Postmodernism.* Albany, SUNY Pr, 1997.

*Without a Woman to Read* enacts a new metaphorical thinking of political and social space around the questions of silence and voice, reading and writing, maternity and paternity, faithless daughters and transcendent sons. Price's interrogations of the tradition find a new space between primary and secondary sources, orchestrating the conjunction and disjunction of political, social, and aesthetic themes within postmodernism. In that sense, the book belongs to several discourses—postmodern philosophy, political theory, feminism, psychoanalysis, and literary theory—at the same time that it transcends any particular discourse. (publisher, edited)

**Price, Huw** and Jackson, Frank. Naturalism and the Fate of the M-Worlds. *Aris Soc*, Supp(71), 247-282, 1997.

Concepts such as those of morality, modality, meaning and the mental are difficult to "place" in a naturalistic world view. This paper offers a novel placement strategy, based on a naturalistic pluralism about the functions of descriptive discourse. It is argued that this functional pluralism is more attractive than familiar alternatives, such as naturalistic reductionism, nonnaturalism, noncognitivism and eliminativism. The strategy exploits on Carnap's views about the nature of ontological issues.

**Price, Mark C**. Should We Expect To Feel As If We Understand Consciousness?. *J Consciousness Stud*, 3(4), 303-312, 1996.

We tend to assume that progress in answering the 'hard question' of consciousness will be accompanied by a subjective *feeling* of greater understanding. However, in order to feel we understand how one state of affairs arises from another, we have to deceive ourselves into thinking we have found a type of causal link which in reality may not exist (Rosch, 1994). I draw from and expand upon Rosch's model, which specifies the conditions under which this self-deceptive kind of causal attribution arises. I argue that the mind-body relationship may not meet these conditions, especially because of its potential novelty and uniqueness. We should *not*, therefore, expect to subjectively *feel* we understand consciousness.

**Price, Thomas** and Russell, Robert and Kennett, Stephen. Interview with A. J. Ayer. *Kinesis*, 23(1), 4-25, Sum 96.

**Priddat, Birger P**. "Moralischer Konsum: Über das Verhältnis von Rationalität, Präferenzen und Personen" in *Ökonomie und Moral: Beiträge zur Theorie ökonomischer Rationalität,* Lohmann, Karl Reinhard (ed), 175-193. München, Oldenbourg, 1997.

**Priddat, Birger P** (ed) and Lohmann, Karl Reinhard (ed). *Ökonomie und Moral: Beiträge zur Theorie ökonomischer Rationalität.* München, Oldenbourg, 1997.

This edition on economics and morals contains 10 papers by philosophers as well as economists. In Germany the discussion in the philosophy of economics is very much limited to questions concerning the institutional constraints of economic development. The focus of this edition on the contrary is on the economic theory of rationality. The contributors discuss both minor modifications of standard consequentialism as well as alternative approaches that allow morals to be integrated in economic analysis. All contributions stress the importance of broadening the economic calculus towards other person's interests.

**Priest, Graham**. Everett's Trilogy. *Mind*, 105(420), 631-647, O 96.

In three recent papers, Anthony Everett (1993, 1994 and 1996) has produced a number of interesting and interrelated arguments against a dialetheic solution to the semantic paradoxes. The purpose of this paper is to assess the effectiveness of these arguments. The relationship between the papers is roughly this: Everett (1994) argues that a dialetheic solution to the paradoxes falls foul of certain kinds of Curry paradox (left pincer); Everett (1993) argues that it falls foul of extended paradoxes (right pincer); Everett (1996) argues that any way of avoiding one pincer drives one firmly into the other (the fork). In the next section I will set up the background for the discussion. I will then take the papers in turn. I will argue that Everett's strategic onslaught fails, on all fronts. There are, however, interesting lessons to be learned from his campaign. (edited)

**Priest, Graham**. Inconsistent Models of Arithmetic Part I: Finite Models. *J Phil Log*, 26(2), 223-235, Ap 97.

The paper concerns interpretations of the paraconsistent logic *LP* which model theories properly containing all the sentences of first order arithmetic. The paper demonstrates the existence of such models and provides a complete taxonomy of the finite ones.

**Priest, Graham**. On a Paradox of Hilbert and Bernays. *J Phil Log*, 26(1), 45-56, F 97.

The paper is a discussion of a result of Hilbert and Bernays in their *Grundlagen der Mathematik.* Their interpretation of the result is similar to the standard interpretation of Tarski's theorem. This and other interpretations are discussed and shown to be inadequate. Instead, it is argued, the result refutes certain versions of Meinongianism. In addition, it poses new problems for classical logic that are solved by dialetheism.

**Priest, Graham**. On Inconsistent Arithmetics: A Reply to Denyer. *Mind*, 105(420), 649-659, O 96.

In "Is Arithmetic Consistent?" (1994a—hereafter, IAC) I drew attention to the fact that there are inconsistent but nontrivial theories that contain all the sentences true in the standard model of arithmetic, *N*. The theories are not, of course, classical theories, but paraconsistent ones. I also argued that it is not as obvious that *N* is the correct arithmetic as one might suppose and that there are reasons for taking one of the inconsistent arithmetics, *M*, with least inconsistent number, *m*, to be the correct one. Two reasons were given. The first was a direct one; the second an indirect one, to the effect that *M* avoids most of the limitative theorems of classical metatheory. In "Priest's Paraconsistent Arithmetic" (1995—hereafter PPA), Nicholas Denyer gives a critique of the paper. The first four sections attack the indirect argument, the fifth the direct argument, and the sixth and final, section is an *ad hominem* attack. The paper is a mixture of insightful criticism, over-swift argument and misreading. The purpose of this note is to point out which parts are which.

**Prigogine, Ilya** and Cornelis, Gustaaf C. Unity of Science and Culture. *Commun Cog*, 29(2), 239-248, 1996.

**Prijatelj, Andreja**. Bounded Contraction and Gentzen-style Formulation of Lukasiewicz Logics. *Stud Log*, 57(2-3), 437-456, O 96.

In this paper, we consider multiplicative-additive fragments of affine propositional classical linear logic extended with *n*-contraction. To be specific, *n*-contraction (n is greater than or equal to 2) is a version of the contraction rule where (n + 1) occurrences of a formula may be contracted to *n* occurrences. We show that expansions of the linear models for (n + 1)-valued Lukasiewicz logic are models for the multiplicative-additive classical linear logic, its affine version and their extensions with *n*-contraction. We prove the finite axiomatizability for the classes of finite models, as well as for the class of infinite linear models based on the set of rational numbers in the interval [0,1]. The axiomatizations obtained in a Gentzen-style formulation are equivalent to finite and infinite-valued Lukasiewicz logics. (edited)

**Prijateljz, Andreja**. Lambek Calculus with Restricted Contraction and Expansion. *Stud Log*, 51(1), 125-143, 1992.

This paper deals with some strengthenings of the nondirectional product-free Lambek calculus by means of additional structural rules. In fact, the rules contraction and expansion are restricted to basic types. For each of the presented systems the usual proof-theoretic notions are discussed, some new concepts especially designed for these calculi are introduced reflecting their intermediate position between the weaker and the stronger sequent-systems.

**Prijic-Samarzija, Snjezana**. Testimony and Perception. *Acta Analytica*, 201-212, 1996.

C.A.J. Coady ascribes the equally primitive epistemic status to testimony and perception. His thesis grounded on allegedly direct and noninferential nature of both perception and testimony. Precisely, Coady builds his antireductionism on the comparison between perception and testimony geared to establishing their equality with regard to (primitive) epistemic status: the testimony is as direct and noninferential as perception. Unfortunately, he does not precisely determine the meaning of these crucial concepts. We offer several ways of making it precise. Our purpose is to show that vagueness, at first glance nonessential, hides serious inconsistencies in his own epistemology of testimony.

**Prilleltensky, Isaac** and Rossiter, Amy and Walsh-Bowers, Richard. Preventing Harm and Promoting Ethical Discourse in the Helping Professions: Conceptual, Research, Analytical, and Action Frameworks. *Ethics Behavior*, 6(4), 287-306, 1996.

The first in a series of four articles, this article provides an overview of the concepts and methods developed by a team of researchers concerned with preventing harm and promoting ethical discourse in the helping professions. In this article we introduce conceptual, research, analytical and action frameworks employed to promote the centrality of ethical discourse in mental health practice. We employ recursive processes whereby knowledge gained from case studies refines our emerging conceptual model of applied ethics. Our *participatory* conceptual framework differs markedly from the *restrictive* model typically used in applied ethics. (edited)

**Prilleltensky, Isaac** and Rossiter, Amy and Walsh-Bowers, Richard. The Personal Is the Organizational in the Ethics of Hospital Social Workers. *Ethics Behavior*, 6(4), 321-335, 1996.

Understanding the social context of clinical ethics is vital for making ethical discourse central in professional practice and for preventing harm. In this paper we present findings about clinical ethics from in-depth interviews and consultation with seven members of a hospital social work department. Workers gave different accounts of ethical dilemmas and resources for ethical decision making than did their managers, whereas workers and managers agreed on core-guiding ethical principles and on ideal situations for ethical discourse. We discuss the research team's initial interpretations, the relevance of the extant ethics literature to organizational structures and dynamics, and alternative perspectives on clinical ethics.

**Prilleltensky, Isaac** and Walsh-Bowers, Richard and Rossiter, Amy. Learning from Broken Rules: Individualism, Bureaucracy, and Ethics. *Ethics Behavior*, 6(4), 307-320, 1996.

The authors discuss findings from a qualitative research project concerning applied ethics that was undertaken at a general family counseling agency in southern Ontario. Interview data suggested that workers need to dialogue about ethical dilemmas, but that such dialogue demands a high level of risk taking that feels unsafe in the organization. This finding led the researchers to examine their own sense of "breaking rules" by suggesting an intersubjective view of ethics that requires a "safe space" for ethical dialogue. The authors critique the individualistic tendency of professional ethics as an effect of power that is tied to the history of professionalism and discuss the role of bureaucracies in diminishing a central role for ethics in helping services. (edited)

**Primeaux, Patrick**. Business Ethics in Theory and Practice: Diagnostic Notes B: A Prescription for Profit Maximization. *J Bus Ethics*, 16(3), 315-322, F 97.

**Primeaux, Patrick** and Stieber, John. Managing Business Ethics and Opportunity Costs. *J Bus Ethics*, 16(8), 835-842, Je 97.

Economic profits differ from accounting profits. Accounting profits are usually defined as revenues minus costs and those costs as fixed and variable. Economic profits enlist a third cost, opportunity costs. While these costs are difficult to determine with mathematical precision, they are nonetheless significant, especially for decision making in business. They reflect social costs and benefits, tensions between individual and corporate interests, and all internal and external considerations which enter into decision making in business. It is precisely within opportunity cost decision making that Primeaux and Stieber situate business ethics.

**Primorac, Igor**. On Tolerance. *Filozof Istraz*, 16(3), 571-577, 1996.

The paper offers a brief review of the main arguments for tolerance in general, i.e., arguments that are meant to support tolerance in every area of personal and social life where the issue of tolerance vs. intolerance and persecution comes up, rather than merely in some particular field such as religion or politics. The author looks into seven such arguments: 1) from liberty, 2) from diversity, 3) from human fallibility, 4) from social progress, 5) from the ineffectiveness of intolerance and persecution, 6) from the Golden Rule, and 7) from nonviolent and rational, rather than violent and irrational, ways of coping with social problems.

**Primorac, Zoran**. Contributions of V. Varicak to the Interpretation of the Theory of Relativity in Lobachevski-Bolyái Geometry. *Filozof Istraz*, 16(3), 713-726, 1996.

At the time Varicak interpreted Einstein's formulae in a non-Euclidean way, but only a year later, 1911, he perceived the relation between the geometry of Lobachevski and the theory of relativity and as he himself puts it, he derived Einstein's formulae the other way round. He assumes that all phenomena occur in the space of Lobachevski and on the basis of this assumption and meditations on geometry he derived the formulae of the theory of relativity by Lobachevski's geometry whereas the laws of classical physics are interpreted by Euclid's geometry. (edited)

**Primoratz, Igor**. Sexual Perversion. *Amer Phil Quart*, 34(2), 245-258, Ap 97.

After briefly describing the inconsistencies of ordinary use, the author discusses the main philosophical accounts of sexual perversion: the procreation account, R. Scruton's theory of sexual desire as characterized by "individualizing intentionality", the view of sex as a body language, the "plain sex" view, S.A. Ketchum's account of perverted sex as perversely bad sex and D. Levy's interpretation of sexual perversion as action that denies some basic human good for the sake of sexual pleasure involved in the denial. All these attempts at giving "sexual perversion" a clear meaning and deploying it to some useful purpose fail; accordingly, the term is best discarded.

**Prince, Alan** and Pinker, Steven. The Nature of Human Concepts/ Evidence from an Unusual Source. *Commun Cog*, 29(3/4), 307-362, 1996.

What kind of categories do human concepts represent? *Classical* categories are defined by necessary and sufficient criteria that determine whether an object is in a category or not in it. A popular contemporary view is that concepts correspond instead to *prototype* categories. *Prototype* categories lack necessary and sufficient conditions; their members need not be absolutely "in" or "out" of the category but can be members to greater or lesser degrees; their members display family resemblances in a number of characteristic properties rather than uniformly sharing a few defining properties; and they are organized around "prototypical" exemplars. This distinction raises several questions. Is one type of category psychologically real, the other an artifact? If both are psychologically real, do they serve different functions in cognition? Are they processed by the same kind of computational architecture? And do they correspond to fundamentally different kinds of things in the world? We suggest that some answers to these questions can be found in an unusual place: the English past tense system. (edited)

**Prior, William J** and Parent, William A. Thomson on the Moral Specification of Rights. *Phil Phenomenol Res*, 56(4), 837-845, D 96.

In this paper we offer a limited defense of the "moral specification" view of rights in response to criticisms of Judith Jarvis Thomson. The moral specification view states that moral rights embody principles of justice, so their meaning is specifiable by those principles. Our defense is limited in that we do not attempt to demonstrate the overall superiority of this view to others, including the view currently advocated by Thomson. We only attempt to show that the advocate of moral specifications (MS) has a plausible response to two objections she raises.

**Pritchard, Michael S**. Commentary on "Better Communication between Engineers and Managers". *Sci Eng Ethics*, 3(2), 213-214, Ap 97.

This paper addresses several concerns in teaching engineering ethics. First, there is the problem of finding space within already crowded engineering curricula for meaningful discussions of ethical dimensions in engineering. Some engineering programs may offer entire courses on engineering ethics; however, most do not at present and may not in the foreseeable future. A promising possibility is to weave ethics into already existing courses using case studies, but most current case studies are not well integrated with engineering technical analysis. There is a danger that case studies will be viewed by both instructors and students as departures from "business as usual"—interesting perhaps, but not essentially connected with "real" engineering. We offer a case study, inspired by the National Society of Professional Engineer's popular video *Gilbane Gold*, that can be used to make the connection. (edited)

**Pritchard, Michael S**. *Reasonable Children: Moral Education and Moral Learning*. Lawrence, Univ Pr Kansas, 1996.

Pritchard contends that children have a definite but frequently untapped capacity for reasonableness and that schools in a democratic society must

make the nurturing of that capacity one of their primary aims, as fundamental to learning as the development of reading, writing and math skills. Reasonableness itself, he shows, can be best cultivated through the practice of philosophical inquiry within a classroom community. In such an environment, children learn to work together, to listen to one another, to build on one another's ideas, to probe assumptions and different perspectives, and ultimately to think for themselves. (publisher, edited)

**Pritchard, Michael S** and Holtzapple, Mark. Responsible Engineering: *Gilbane Gold* Revisited. *Sci Eng Ethics*, 3(2), 217-230, Ap 97.

**Pritchard, Paul**. Metaphysics Delta 15 and Pre-Euclidean Mathematics. *Apeiron*, 30(1), 49-62, Mr 97.

The argument in the paper is that part of Aristotle's *Metaphysics* V ch.15 (1020b32-1021a8) has not been understood by commentators, all of whom seem to have been reduced to claiming that Aristotle is not here saying what he really meant. It turns out that when Aristotle's remarks at 1020b32-1021a8 are referred to the pre-Euclidean (or pre-Eudoxan) proportion theory based on alternate subtraction (*anthyphairesis*), the passage makes good sense as it stands. There is no need to suppose that Aristotle is failing to say what he means.

**Pritchett, Thomas K** (& others) and Chen, Henry C K and Allmon, Dean E. A Multicultural Examination of Business Ethics Perceptions. *J Bus Ethics*, 16(2), 183-188, F 97.

This study provides an evaluation of ethical business perception of business students from three countries: Australia, Taiwan and the United States. Although statistically significant differences do exist there is significant agreement with the way students perceive ethical/unethical practices in business. The findings of this paper indicate a universality of business ethical perceptions.

**Prokopijevic, Miroslav**. Regret, Trust, and Morality (in Serbo-Croatian). *Theoria (Yugoslavia)*, 38(2), 35-52, Je 95.

This article deals with economy of emotions by addressing the question "Is it reasonable to regret the wrong we have done?" The first part of the article brings about 1) whether it is reasonable to regret, and 2) why it is reasonable to regret. Regret is considered as a complex feeling (with cognitive and emotive elements), which plays the role of an insurance fund for encouraging mutual trust, what is stimulative for cooperation and individual benefits. The second part is devoted to discussion of other possible reasons for why it might be reasonable to regret things we did, and they are: a) because regret makes more possible that one will do better in the future; b) because regret obliterates wrongdoing; c) because without regret one fails to retain one's identity and character as a moral agent; d) because only in suffering do we recognize the wrongdoing. It seems that none of these reasons is able to justify the appearance of regret.

**Prosch, Michael**. "The Korporation in Hegel's Interpretation of Civil Society" in *Hegel, History, and Interpretation,* Gallagher, Shaun, 195-207. Albany, SUNY Pr, 1997.

**Protevi, John**. Egyptian Priests and German Professors: On the Alleged Difficulty of Philosophy. *Phil Today*, 41(1-4), 181-188, Spr 97.

This article develops the political and ontological consequences of Heidegger's reading, in his lectures on Plato's *Sophist*, of the opening section of Aristotle's *Metaphysics*. Heidegger reads the ascension from sensation through experience to technical knowledge, science, and wisdom, as a quasi-intellectual, quasi-spiritual struggle to achieve the proper, philosophical, temporality. He thus discounts Aristotle's acknowledgment that leisure—time free from bodily necessity, time given by the labor of others—is the political condition of philosophy. This overlooking of corporeal politics is consonant with Heidegger's effacing of the primacy of locomotion (*Bewegung*) in Aristotle in favor of the "motility" (*Bewegtheit*) of Dasein's temporality. (edited)

**Protevi, John**. Given Time and the Gift of Life. *Man World*, 30(1), 65-82, Ja 97.

"Given Time and the Gift of Life" explores the following nexus in Derrida's thought: the gift, the mother and life. The first section examines life within the trajectory of the gift, the excess of gift over return in the gift of life and the rewriting of Aristotelian generation in "differential species-being." The second section shows the "quasi-transcendental" nature of Derrida's thought. The conclusion sketches some of the political consequences of the gift of life thought as the quasi-transcendental gift of differential species-being.

**Protevi, John**. Violence and Authority in Kant. *Epoche*, 2(1), 65-89, 1994.

The German term *Gewalt* is used to investigate the political metaphorics of Kant's work. Meaning both "[private] violence" and "[state] authority," *Gewalt* is the key to Kant's social contract, the restriction of force to state authority. Kant's critical works negotiate a social contract for the cognitive and moral realms, a "commonwealth of reason" in which violent sensibility is submitted to rational authority. The legal regicide, however, as analyzed in the political writings, reveals the temporal torsion in the social contract, as any instituting force must presently work in the name of the future order it is to bring into being.

**Proudfoot, Diane**. On Wittgenstein on Cognitive Science. *Philosophy*, 72(280), 189-217, Ap 97.

This paper argues that there is considerable similarity—with respect, e.g., to the nature of the res cognitans, cognition and intentionality and to the problem of other minds—between the Cartesian and the contemporary view of the mind, despite the scientific sophistication of the latter and their differing metaphysical stances. This similarity allows much of Wittgenstein's attack on the old (Cartesian) paradigm to be remade against the new (computational) paradigm. The paper considers objections to this attack, including the ingenious claim that Wittgenstein himself foreshadowed the new paradigm. It suggests that

AUTHOR INDEX 855 Puntel, Lorenz

Wittgenstein's philosophical psychology offers an alternative way of naturalizing the mind.

**Proudfoot, Diane** and Copeland, B Jack. On Alan Turing's Anticipation of Connectionism. *Synthese*, 108(3), 361-377, S 96.

It is not widely realised that Turing was probably the first person to consider building computing machines out of simple, neuron-like elements connected together into networks in a largely random manner. Turing called his networks 'unorganised machines'. By the application of what he described as 'appropriate interference, mimicking education' an unorganised machine can be trained to perform any task that a Turing machine can carry out, provided the number of 'neurons' is sufficient. Turing proposed simulating both the behavior of the network and the training process by means of a computer program. We outline Turing's connectionist project of 1948.

**Provencal, Vernon**. Writing the Large Letter Small: the Analogy of State and Individual at *Republic V* 462c-d. *Apeiron*, 30(2), 73-88, Je 97.

The 'organic interpretation' of Plato's analogy of state and individual at Rep. 462c-d has led to its unfair dismissal as 'rhetorical symbolism'. An alternative reading in the manuscript tradition is defended as the basis of an alternative interpretation of the analogy. Rather than likening the state to an organism, the analogy likens the state to an individual in which the large letter of the state has already been writ small. Consequently, the analogy not only advocates *that* the state become one, but demonstrates *how* the state becomes one by means of the community of wives and children.

**Provost, C Antonio**. *The Reformation of Society Through Adequate Education*. Hanover, Christopher, 1997.

This unique treatise is presented in the hope that our society will understand the main causes of our nation being at risk of decline and total ruin. The author concludes that there must be a genuine reform in education and the curriculum if a proper reformation of society is to occur. (publisher, edited)

**Prucnal, Tadeusz** and Bugajska-Jaszczolt, Beata. Axiomatization of the Logic Determined by the System of Natural Numbers with Identity. *Rep Math Log*, 28, 61-71, 1994.

The notion of the first-order predicate logic determined by a relational system was introduced in [3]. In this paper we consider the pure first-order predicate logic determined by the system of natural numbers with identity. We show that this logic is axiomatizable.

**Prudovsky, Gad**. Can We Ascribe to Past Thinkers Concepts they had No Linguistic Means to Express?. *Hist Theor*, 36(1), 15-31, 1997.

This article takes a clear-cut case in which a historian (Alexander Koyré) ascribes to a writer (Galileo) a concept ("inertial mass") which neither the writer nor his contemporaries had the linguistic means to express. On the face of it the case may seem a violation of a basic methodological maxim in historiography: " avoid anachronistic ascriptions!" The aim of the article is to show that Koyré's ascription and others of its kind, are legitimate; and that the methodological maxim should not be given the strict reading which some writers recommend. More specifically, the conceptual repertoire of historical figures need not be reconstructed solely in terms of the social and linguistic conventions of their time and place.

**Prudovsky, Gad**. Counterexamples, Idealizations, and Intuitions: A Study in Philosophical Method. *Iyyun*, 46, 63-88, Ja 97.

**Prudovsky, Gad**. History of Science and the Historian's Self-Understanding. *J Value Inq*, 31(1), 73-76, Mr 97.

**Pruzhinin, Boris Isaevich**. Astrology: Science, Pseudoscience, Ideology. *Russian Stud Phil*, 34(1), 78-96, Sum 95.

Astrology outwardly meets the standards of the scientific reality. But its core element—interpretive hypotheses about "earth" meanings of "stars"—bases not upon rational arguments but traditional predilections. And that is the reason for modern astrologic boom in Russia. Astrology nowadays does not have pretensions to being a science—in the epoch of electronic clocks it's hardly possible to directly appeal to the traditions of life by star rhythms. But it successfully fulfills the functions of ideological expression of nostalgia for the lively rhythms of nature. And with all that, using the mechanisms of tradition makes it a strong mean for regulating human behavior (e.g., the effect of self-guiding to the result of prediction). And the main danger is that astrology can be easily turned into a powerful weapon for manipulating consciousness. Full text of the article—Voprosy Filosofi 1994, N 2.

**Przylebski, Andrzej**. War Rickert ein Fichteaner? Die Fichteschen Züge des badischen Neukantianismus. *Fichte-Studien*, 13, 131-141, 1997.

**Psarros, Nikos**. "Die Chemie als Gegendstand philosophischer Reflexion" in *Philosophie der Chemie: Bestandsaufnahme und Ausblick*, Schummer, Joachim (ed), 111-141. Wurzburg, Koenigshausen, 1996.

**Psarros, Nikos** (ed) and Schummer, Joachim (ed) and Ruthenberg, Klaus (ed). *Philosophie der Chemie: Bestandsaufnahme und Ausblick*. Wurzburg, Koenigshausen, 1996.

The German working group "Philosophy and Chemistry" (founded in 1993) has collected nine articles that provide a comprehensive survey of what have been done in the past and what should be done in a future philosophy of chemistry. Since many authors find a notorious neglect of chemistry in the past, they try to explain this neglect from various aspects among which reductionism seems to be the most important.

**Psillos, Stathis**. How not to Defend Constructive Empiricism: A Rejoinder. *Phil Quart*, 47(188), 369-372, Jl 97.

Douven, Horsten, Ladyman and van Fraassen have attempted to defend van Fraassen's critique of abductive reasoning against the arguments offered in a recent piece of mine. My short rejoinder shows two things. First, their counterarguments fail to refute my original arguments. Their arguments casually move from the actuality of "empirically equivalent theories" to the possibility of "equally good rivals". But pointing to the existence of the former would do nothing to establish that empirically equivalent alternatives are "equally good" or equally well-supported by the evidence. Second, I show that a central claim of their paper is very close to the conclusion of my original piece: if explanatory considerations are jettisoned, then even common sense existential claims are in danger of being unfounded.

**Psillos, Stathis**. Scientific Realism and the 'Pessimistic Induction'. *Proc Phil Sci Ass*, 3(Suppl), S306-S314, 1996.

Over the last two decades, the debate over scientific realism has been dominated by two arguments that pull in contrary directions: the 'no miracle' argument and the 'pessimistic induction'. The latter suggests that the historical record destroys the realist's belief in an explanatory connection between truthlikeness and genuine empirical success. This paper analyzes the structure of the 'pessimistic induction', presents a move—the *divine et impera* move—that neutralizes it and motivates a substantive yet realistic version of scientific realism. This move is also compared with Worrall's and Kitcher's recent reactions to the 'pessimistic induction'.

**Pstruzina, Karel**. The Temporal Nature of Thought and Concepts of Life (Czech). *Filosof Cas*, 45(1), 25-35, 1997.

Is the rhythm of life defined by the events and instants of choice or simply by the flow of experience of life? In either case the source of the rhythm can be clarified through analysis of ideas, since both the significance of events and the making of decisions are directly related with ideas. Life seen as the constant real experience of the world cannot be separated from thoughts. The rhythmic nature of thought can be deduced from the alternation of conscious thought processes, with sometimes unconsidered spontaneous meditations and from the regular alternation between waking and sleeping. The link between the temporal nature of life and events or instants of choice or in some cases the conscious action of the mind, is therefore an insufficient approach to the concept of the rhythmic nature of life.

**Pucci, Daniela**. "Vita, esistenza, storia nella filosofia di J. Ortega y Gasset" in *Lo Storicismo e la Sua Storia: Temi, Problemi, Prospettive*, Cacciatore, Giuseppe (ed), 486-495. Milano, Guerini, 1997.

**Puchala, Donald J**. The History of the Future of International Relations. *Ethics Int Affairs*, 8, 177-202, 1994.

**Puddifoot, John E**. The Processual Origins of Social Representations. *J Theor Soc Behav*, 27(1), 41-63, Mr 97.

Referring to some perceived difficulties in social representation theory, this paper offers an account of the genesis of social representations in a theory of valuing. Drawing on influential but previously largely unconnected ideas from interactionist theory, personal construct theory, and Rokeach's theory of values, it is suggested that a process of valuing can be presented as a crucial link between the individual and social levels of analysis, a present theoretical disjuncture that has been of concern to some commentators in social representations and widespread beliefs.

**Pugh, Matthew S**. Maritain, the Intuition of Being, and the Proper Starting Point for Thomistic Metaphysics. *Thomist*, 61(3), 405-424, Jl 97.

**Puig, Luis**. El *De Numeris Datis* de Jordanus Nemorarius como sistema matemático de signos. *Mathesis*, 10(1), 47-92, F 94.

The book *De Numeris Datis* by Jordanus Nemorarius is a precious text to examine the history of algebraic ideas due to its place in the Middle Ages, in the Christian Science, just after the translation of al-Khwârizmî's books and before the rediscovery of Diofanto's *Arithmetic*. In this paper I present a description of a part of *De Numeris Datis* from a semiotic theory of mathematics that attempts to show which are the characteristics of the mathematical sign system (MSS) in which it is written, how this MSS shapes the objects it allows to speak of and the kind of operativity the MSS has on the objects expressed in it. (edited)

**Pujia, Roberto** (ed) and Guetti, Carla (ed). *Momenti di Storia della Logica e di Storia della Filosofia*. Roma, Aracne Editrice, 1996.

**Pulman, Stephen G**. Higher Order Unification and the Interpretation of Focus. *Ling Phil*, 20(1), 73-115, F 97.

Higher order unification is a way of combining information (or equivalently, solving equations) expressed as terms of a typed higher order logic. A suitably restricted form of the notion has been used as a simple and perspicuous basis for the resolution of the meaning of elliptical expressions and for the interpretation of some noncompositional types of comparative construction also involving ellipsis. This paper explores another area of application for this concept in the interpretation of sentences containing intonationally marked 'focus', or various semantic constructs which are sensitive to focus. Similarities and differences between this approach and theories using 'alternative semantics', 'structured meanings', or flexible categorial grammars, are described. The paper argues that the higher order unification approach offers descriptive advantages over these alternatives, as well as the practical advantage of being capable of fairly direct computational implementation.

**Puntel, Lorenz**. Lässt sich der Begriff der Dialektik klären?. *J Gen Phil Sci*, 27(1), 131-165, 1996.

"Can the Concept of Dialectics Be Made Clear?" The present article purports to answer the old question of whether the concept (and the method) of Hegelian dialectic can be clarified. Three arguments are advanced in defence of the claim that Hegel's conception is not in fact intelligible. The first argument shows that dialectical negation leads to an infinite regress. The second argument analyses Hegel's claim that the dialectical method yields a positive result and demonstrates that this claim remains completely unsubstantiated and unsubstantiable. The third argument comes to the conclusion that Hegelian dialectic cannot pretend to be an acceptable explication of the "intuitive" understanding of negation. An *Appendix* examines critically a new attempt by D. Wandschneider of reconstructing the first steps of Hegelian dialectical logic by displaying "antinomic structures" and by employing (at least to a limited extent) the techniques of formal logic.

**Punzo, Vincent A**. Jacques Ellul on the Technical System and the Challenge of Christian Hope. *Amer Cath Phil Quart*, 70(Supp), 17-31, 1996.

**Puolimatka, Tapio**. "Democracy, Education and the Critical Citizen" in *Philosophy of Education (1996),* Margonis, Frank (ed), 329-338. Urbana, Phil Education Soc, 1997.

**Puolimatka, Tapio**. The Concept of Indoctrination. *Phil Reform*, 61(2), 109-134, 1996.

Indoctrination can be distinguished from educative teaching through the value orientation of the teaching-learning encounter. Educative teaching is distinguished from indoctrination by the activation and disclosure of the student's normative functions. Indoctrination is a misleading and one-sided way of teaching which employs speech-acts involving covert influence. It does not account for the metaphysical presuppositions inherent in the beliefs being taught, fosters the development of an uncritical mind, and involves a misuse of teacher authority since it employs teaching methods that imply structural untruth. It leaves the normative functions of the students in a closed, rigid state. (edited)

**Purcell, Michael**. For the Sake of Truth...The Demand of Discontinuity in Foucault, Blanchot and Levinas. *Amer Cath Phil Quart*, 71(2), 237-258, Spr 97.

This article argues that truth is not primarily to be considered as content and that the demand of continuity is secondary to the demand of discontinuity and fragment to which Maurice Blanchot draws attention. Signification is found outwith the totality (Levinas) and outwith serial classification (Foucault). Beyond the logic of contradiction, there is the possibility of noncompeting, noncontradictory understandings of theological 'truths' which might better accommodate the pastoral reality of divorce and remarriage and the theoretical truth of the Eucharist as a sign of unity. The truth of the Eucharist lies in the realm of justice before over it falls into the realm of theory, and at the level of justice, the coherent exclusion of the divorced and remarried from the Eucharist does not necessarily follow.

**Purcell, Michael**. Liturgy: Divine and Human Service. *Heythrop J*, 38 (2), 144-164, Ap 97.

Liturgy has been the forum for the enactment of a diverse range of theologies, at times stressing the human, at times the divine. Following Emmanuel Levinas, this article understands the meaning of liturgy as '*a movement of the Same towards the Other which never returns to the Same*'. Whether directed towards God, or expressive of human longing, the structure of liturgy is essentially '*for*-the-Other.' This movement out of self is seen when one considers liturgy as the 'work of the people,' where 'work' is understood as (*Euvre* rather than *travail*. (edited)

**Purcell, Michael**. Quasi-Formal Causality, or the Other-in-Me: Rahner and Lévinas. *Gregorianum*, 78(1), 79-93, 1997.

Le débat sur nature et grâce cherche à réconcilier théologiquement l'appel de la nature humaine à un accomplissement en Dieu sans compromettre en aucune façon la totale gratuité de la grâce. Rahner explique la relation entre les deux en termes de causalité quasi-formelle, par laquelle Dieu se communique à la créature tout en gardant sa transcendence et sa liberté. L'article présent tente d'unir la notion rahnérienne de la causalité formelle avec la compréhension qu'a Lévinas de la responsabilité. Pour autant que le soi est constitué comme le *pour* de la relation "un-pour-l'autre", on peut employer le langage de la causalité formelle pour exprimer la relation à l'autre, tout en employant la qualification *quasi* pour préserver à l'intérieur de cette relation l'absolue altérité de l'autre qui se détache de la relation et ne subit par elle aucune modification. (edited)

**Purdom, Judy**. "Postmodernity as a Spectre of the Future: The Force of Capital and the Unmasking of Difference" in *Deleuze and Philosophy: The Difference Engineer,* Ansell Pearson, Keith (ed), 115-129. New York, Routledge, 1997.

In this essay it is argued that Postmodernity is a force of radical material change, change which (de)forms its working images, the State and the subject. Ironically it is the 'progressive' reproduction of capitalism into an efficient virtual force that has brought it to crisis point and bifurcation into an untamed, anarchic and dissipative system, where collective identity is impossible and political and social breakdown ensue. This transmutation opens the possibility of new ontological levels, levels which breach historical or human limits. The challenge is to think change.

**Purdy, Laura M**. "Children's Liberation: A Blueprint for Disaster" in *The Liberation Debate: Rights at Issue,* Leahy, Michael (ed), 147-162. New York, Routledge, 1996.

This article objects to John Harris's arguments in favor of children's liberation. Harris believes that children are as autonomous as adults and hence ought to have the same right to determine how they shall live. I doubt that children are sufficiently autonomous to support this conclusion, even if autonomy were the only legitimate criterion for equal rights. Equally important, however, is moral sensitivity. There is little evidence in favor of the view that granting children equal rights would promote earlier development of these traits, and in their absence, equal rights would lead to significant harm both to children and to society as a whole.

**Purdy, Laura M**. "Good Bioethics Must Be Feminist Bioethics" in *Philosophical Perspectives on Bioethics,* Sumner, L W (ed), 143-162. Toronto, Univ of Toronto Pr, 1996.

This paper argues that bioethics must be feminist because otherwise it is biased toward men's interests. This position is justifiable when "core" feminism (the view that justice requires equal consideration of women's interests) is distinguished from "derived" feminism (constituted by a wide variety of more speculative positions not necessarily distinctive of, but compatible with, core feminism). The paper also deals with a variety of charges often levelled at feminist work.

**Purdy, Laura M**. What Can Progress in Reproductive Technology Mean for Women?. *J Med Phil*, 21(5), 499-514, O 96.

This article critically evaluates the central claims of the various feminist responses to new reproductive arrangements and technologies. Proponents of a "progressivism" object to naive technological optimism and raise questions about the control of such technology. Others, such as the FINRRAGE group, raise concerns about the potentially damaging consequences of the new technologies for women. While a central concern is whether these technologies reinforce harmful biologically determinist stereotypes of women, it may be that these critiques function with a devastating gender blindness that puts women at risk in other, heretofore unnoticed, ways.

**Pust, Joel**. Induction, Focused Sampling and the Law of Small Numbers. *Synthese*, 108(1), 89-104, Jl 96.

Hilary Kornblith (1993) has recently offered a reliabilist defense of the use of the Law of Small Numbers in inductive inference. In this paper I argue that Kornblith's defense of this inferential rule fails for a number of reasons. First, I argue that the sort of inferences that Kornblith seeks to justify are not really inductive inferences based on small samples. Instead, they are *knowledge-based* deductive inferences. Second, I address Kornblith's attempt to find support in the work of Dorrit Billman and I try to show that close attention to the workings of her computational model reveals that it does not support Kornblith's argument. While the knowledge required to ground the inferences in question is perhaps inductively derived, Billman's work does not support the notion that small samples provide a reliable basis for our generalizing inferences.

**Putallaz, François-Xavier**. Thomas de Sutton, ou la liberté controversée. *Rev Thomiste*, 97(1), 31-46, Ja-Mr 97.

Si l'on fait abstraction du tempérament et du génie propre du disciple de Thomas d'Aquin, il apparaît que dans le cas de la doctrine de la libre volonté chez Thomas de Sutton, deux points peuvent être soulignés, qui me serviront de conclusion. 1) Thomas de Sutton n'a pas rencontré Henri de Gand; il ne le connaît que par ses écrits (*ponitur in scriptis*, répète-t-il). Ce manque de sensibilité à d'autres formes théoriques tient, chez Sutton, au fait qu'il est obnubilé par Henri de Gand. (edited)

**Putman, Daniel**. Psychological Courage. *Phil Psychiat Psych*, 4(1), 1-11, Mr 97.

Beginning with Aristotle philosophers have analyzed physical courage and moral courage in great detail. However, philosophy has never addressed the type of courage involved in facing the fears generated by our habits and emotions. This essay introduces the concept of psychological courage and argues that it deserves to be recognized in ethics as a form of courage. I examine three broad areas of psychological problems: destructive habits; irrational anxieties; and psychological servitude in which one individual emotionally controls another. Psychological courage is the strength to confront and work through these problems. Such courage involves facing our deep-seated fear of psychological instability. I conclude that the development of psychological courage is essential to the well-being of many people.

**Putman, Daniel A**. The Intellectual Bias of Virtue Ethics. *Philosophy*, 72(280), 303-311, Ap 97.

Aristotle makes a useful distinction between virtues and skills that carries over to contemporary virtue ethics. However, in making this distinction, Aristotle conflates certain life styles or professions with the capability of being fully virtuous. Unfortunately, this confusion also carries over to modern virtue theory and is epitomized by MacIntyre's claim that bricklaying is not a practice but architecture is. Since only "practices" can fully model virtue, so much the worse for bricklayers. This paper attacks this confusion and clarifies the skill virtue distinction by arguing that skills and simple human activities can model virtue as fully as practices requiring education or abstract thinking.

**Putman, Daniel A**. What Exactly Is the Good of Self-Deception?. *Int J Applied Phil*, 10(2), 17-23, Wint-Spr 96.

Many arguments justifying self-deception have been made by philosophers, social scientists and biologists. This paper divides those arguments into four categories and examines the assumptions behind them. The evolutionary argument the utilitarian argument, the argument against truth as the primary value in life and the socialization argument all add to our understanding of self-deception. However, they all jump to conclusions about the "necessity" of self-deception which are not justified by their premises. Perhaps people are capable of greater courage than we admit into our reasoning.

**Putnam, Daniel**. Courage Alone. *Cont Phil*, 18(4 & 5), 46-49, Jl-Ag/S-O 96.

Courage is a virtue usually associated in the media with heroic efforts to help others. But individuals can and do act courageously when no one else is around. Such acts are often unrecognized and we are more skeptical about assigning courage to an act performed in order to save oneself. This paper examines what factors go into being courageous while alone and why we tend to overlook courage in such situations. The goal of the paper is to expand our understanding of how and when this virtue is practices.

**Putnam, Hilary**. "James's Theory of Truth" in *The Cambridge Companion to William James,* Putnam, Ruth Anna (ed), 166-185. New York, Cambridge Univ Pr, 1997.

**Putnam, Ruth Anna**. "Some of Life's Ideals" in *The Cambridge Companion to William James,* Putnam, Ruth Anna (ed), 282-299. New York, Cambridge Univ Pr, 1997.

This essay considers James in the role of moralist and public philosopher. It displays the pluralism of William James as it shows itself in the two essays "On a Certain Blindness in Human Beings" and "What Makes a Life Significant;" his point here is that no one point of view can take in the whole of reality and that many lives are worthwhile. The paper explores James's notion of an ideal that gives significance to a life and the associated idea of significance. James's opposition to war and imperialism are also noted.

**Putnam, Ruth Anna** (ed). *The Cambridge Companion to William James.* New York, Cambridge Univ Pr, 1997.

This Cambridge Companion is devoted primarily to the philosophical thought of its subject, although two articles deal with features of his psychology. All major aspects of James's philosophy are discussed, generally from more than one perspective; in addition James's relation to some of his contemporaries and to American culture are explored. The eighteen contributors include two professors of literature, two of religion/divinity, one of history and 13 philosophers. The book offers multiple interpretations of James's thought in an attempt to reflect James's own commitment to pluralism. It is a companion to, not a substitute for, reading James.

**Putney, David**. Some Problems in Interpretation: The Early and Late Writings of Dōgen. *Phil East West*, 46(4), 497-531, O 96.

There are inconsistencies in Dōgen's writing over his career, especially between the twelve-fascicle and the seventy-five-fascicle Shōbōgenzō. The nature of the twelve-fascicle edition, the hermeneutic of interpreting Dōgen's kōan style of writing, and the problems in relating the twelve-fascicle edition to the earlier kōan style of the seventy-five-fascicle edition are examined.

**Putsch, Robert W** and Kaufert, Joseph M. Communication through Interpreters in Health Care: Ethical Dilemmas Arising from Differences in Class, Culture, Language, and Power. *J Clin Ethics*, 8(1), 71-87, Spr 97.

This article considers the problems faced by medical interpreters as they facilitate communication in informed consent and end-of-life decisions. It examines power relationships between participants who hold different interpretations of illness and treatment, disparate values in relation to death and dying and use language or decision-making frameworks differently. Cases drawn from our ethnographic research on the health interpreters in Winnipeg, Canada and Seattle are used to examine the ethical dimension of the work of interpreters. The article considers the evolution and regulation of the role of the healthcare interpreter and their relationships with other healthcare providers.

**Pyysiäinen, Ilkka**. Jñānagarbha and the "God's-Eye View". *Asian Phil*, 6(3), 197-206, N 96.

In trying to define the difference between conventional and ultimate truth, the Mādyamika Buddhist author Jñānagarbha ends up in paradoxical formulations. Putnam's discussion of Nietzsche's remark that "as the circle of science grows larger it touches paradox at more places" is presented as an illustration for Jñānagarbha's case. No comparison of Putnam and Jñāgarbha is intended as regards the contents of their presentations, the focus being only on the logical form of their argumentation. The paradoxical nature of Jñānagarbha's doctrinal system is explained to derive from the logical incompleteness of formal systems. The paradox is also explained to work as a direction arrow pointing to what can only be realized in a mystical experience.

**Qizilbash, Mozaffar**. Well-Being and Despair: Dante's Ugolino. *Utilitas*, 9. (2), 227-240, Jl 97.

This paper considers three sorts of accounts of the quality of life. These are (1) capability views, due to Amartya Sen and Martha Nussbaum, (2) desire accounts, and (3) the prudential value list theory of James Griffin. Each approach is evaluated in the context of a tale of cannibalism and moral decay: the story of Count Ugolino in Dante's *The Divine Comedy.* It is argued that the example causes difficulties for Sen's version of the capability approach, as well as for desire accounts. Nussbaum's version of the capability approach deals with the example better than Sen's. However, it fails adequately to accommodate pluralism. I suggest that James Griffin's account of well-being deals well with this example and accommodates pluralism. I suggest that, of the views considered, Griffin's is the best account of the quality of life.

**Quante, Michael**. Absolutes Denken: Neuere Interpretationen der Hegelschen Logik. *Z Phil Forsch*, 50(4), 624-640, O-D 96.

Recent interpretations of Hegel's "Wissenschaft der Logik" and of the "Logik" (= Enzyklopädie, Tel I) are discussed. It is argued that Hegel tries to give an absolute foundation ("Letztbegründung") of the categories of thinking and being. So his logic has to be understood as an "onto-theo-logical" project. It is suggested that Hegel's logic can—at least partly—be justified if understood as a critique and an alternative to representationalism. His main thesis, that thinking and object are identical, is understood as a form of those versions of realism McDowell suggests in his "Mind and World". Understanding Hegel's logic this way doesn't allow to justify his theological interpretation of "idea", so his philosophical project can be made intelligible only in one of his central aspects.

**Quash, J B**. 'Between the Brutely Given, and the Brutally, Banally Free': Von Balthasar's Theology of Drama in Dialogue with Hegel. *Mod Theol*, 13(3), 293-318, Jl 97.

**Queiroz Guimaraes, Alexandre**. Algumas Notas sobre a Filosofia Política de Hobbes. *Educ Filosof*, 9(17), 113-137, Ja-Je 95.

The paper tries a particular interpretation of some aspects of Hobbes's political philosophy. It points to a specific way to read the author's principal work, reinforcing a transcendental reading of his political philosophy. The meaning of Hobbes's work would not be to take the utilitarian's motivations of political pact, but to show to a rational man (the universal subject) the reasons of obedience.(edited)

**Querido, René** (ed). *A Western Approach to Reincarnation and Karma: Selected Lectures and Writings by Rudolf Steiner.* Hudson, Anthroposophic Pr, 1997.

This book collects for the first time many of Steiner's major statements on reincarnation and karma. They have been selected and edited by René Querido, a lifelong student of Rudolf Steiner, as well as a Waldorf teacher and a past Secretary of the Anthroposophical Society in America. In his Introduction, Querido places Steiner's contribution within the context of the history of the idea of reincarnation and relates it to the needs and realities of the late twentieth century.(publisher)

**Quill, Timothy E** and Kimsma, Gerrit K. End-of-Life Care in the Netherlands and the United States: A Comparison of Values, Justifications, and Practices. *Cambridge Quart Healthcare Ethics*, 6(2), 189-204, Spr 97.

**Quine, Willard V**. Free Logic, Description, and Virtual Classes. *Dialogue (Canada)*, 36(1), 101-108, Wint 97.

On montre ici que la théorie des classes virtuelles constitue une application de la logique libre. Il s'agit de la théorie classique de la quantification qui ne fait usage que d'un prédicat à deux places: l'epsilon de Peano, et qui ne comporte qu'un axiome d'extensionnalité. Elle n'introduit aucune présupposition d'existence. Les individus y sont identifiés à leur singleton, et elle accommode les termes qui ne désignent rien. On montre aussi comment cette théorie peut fructifier et devenir une théorie des ensembles plus élaborée à l'aide de définitions et de conventions notationnelles.

**Quinn, J Kevin** and Reed, J David and Browne, M Neil (& others). Honesty, Individualism, and Pragmatic Business Ethics: Implications for Corporate Hierarchy. *J Bus Ethics*, 16(12-13), 1419-1430, S 97.

The boundaries of honesty are the focal point of this exploration of the individualistic origins of modernist ethics and the consequent need for a more pragmatic approach to business ethics. The tendency of modernist ethics to see honesty as an individual responsibility is described as a contextually naive approach, one that fails to account for the interactive effect between individual choices and corporate norms. By reviewing the empirical accounts of managerial struggles with ethical dilemmas, the article arrives at the contextual preconditions for encouraging the development of reflective moral agents in modern corporations.

**Quinn, John J**. Personal Ethics and Business Ethics: The Ethical Attitudes of Owner/Managers of Small Business. *J Bus Ethics*, 16(2), 119-127, F 97.

To date, the study of business ethics has been largely the study of the ethics of large companies. This paper is concerned with owner/managers of small firms and the link between the personal ethics of the owner/manager and his or her attitude to ethical problems in business. By using active membership of an organisation with an overt ethical dimension (for example, a church) as a surrogate for personal ethics the research provides some, though not unequivocal, support for the models of Trevino and others that suggest a link between personal ethics and business ethics.

**Quinn, Patrick**. "Being on the Boundary: Aquinas' Metaphor for Subject and Psyche" in *Critical Studies: Ethics and the Subject,* Simms, Karl (ed), 165-172. Amsterdam, Rodopi, 1997.

**Quintas, Avelino M**. El titular de la autoridad política en Santo Tomás y Rousseau. *Sapientia*, 51(200), 393-404, 1996.

**Quinton, Anthony**. The Trouble with Kant. *Philosophy*, 72(279), 5-18, Ja 97.

**Quitterer, Josef**. *Kant und die These vom Paradigmenwechsel: Eine Gegenüberstellung seiner Transzendentalphilosophie mit der Wissenschaftstheorie Thomas S. Kuhns.* New York, Lang, 1996.

The comparison between Kant's critical philosophy and the philosophy of science of Thomas S. Kuhn aims to answer the following question: Is Kant's transcendental philosophy obsolete because it depends on the scientific paradigm of classical mechanics? From a "Kuhnian" point of view central aspects of Kant's critical philosophy are closely analysed with a special emphasis on concepts like "revolution," "science," "scientific progress" etc. As a result of the analysis some nonparadigmatic principles of the Kantian philosophy are obtained and applied to a main problem of Kuhn's philosophy of science—the incommensurability-thesis.

**Qviller, Bjorn**. The Machiavellian Cosmos. *Hist Polit Thought*, 17(3), 326-353, Autumn 96.

Machiavelli's anthropology is based on the Manichean aspects of St. Augustine's doctrine of original sin. *Dell'Ambizione* and *Esortazione alla penitenza* are influenced by elements from Manichean theology which also appear in his other works. A letter by Machiavelli suggests that he is making a theory for survival in a state reminiscent of St. Augustine's concept of *civitas diaboli* which is of Manichena origin. Elements that betray an Augustinian and Manichean origin are the doctrine of scarcity, that human wants are insatiable (especially the desire for power), and his moral relativism and nihilism. Texts that exhibit similarity with Machiavelli are the parable on the unfaithful manager in *The Gospel according to St. Luke* and the Gnostic text called *The Teachings of Silvanus.*

**R-Toubes Muñiz, Joaquín**. Legal Principles and Legal Theory. *Ratio Juris*, 10(3), 267-287, S 97.

Current legal theory is concerned with the presence of principles in law partly because they are at the core of Dworkin's criticisms of Hart's rule of recognition.

**Raatzsch, Richard** 858 **AUTHOR INDEX**

Hart's theory is threatened by the possibility that the identification of some principles follows an extremely relaxed rule of recognition, or even no rule at all. Unfortunately, there is no conclusive test to ascertain what is the case in actual practice. On the other hand, the evaluative arguments which support Dworkin's proposal of principled adjudication are forceful but not conclusive. Moreover, since ultimate controversy over values is plausible, judicial discretion may sometimes be inevitable.

**Raatzsch, Richard**. Philosophical Investigations, Section 1—Setting the Stage. *Grazer Phil Stud*, 51, 47-84, 1996.

How much can and should be said about the beginning of Wittgenstein's *Philosophical Investigations (PI)* on the basis of its very first section alone? Is the only thing worth mentioning that it is designed to introduce the topic for the rest of the book—may this be a "prephilosophical", "pretheoretical", "Augustinian" picture of language (Baker/Hacker, Kenny, Katz, Canfield et al.) or a mentalistic picture of the use of language (Savigny)? These ways of interpreting leave too many aspects of the text untouched.(edited)

**Rábade, Ana Isabel**. La actualidad de Giordano Bruno en castellano. *Rev Filosof (Spain)*, 8(15), 219-225, 1996.

**Rábano Gutiérrez, Alberto**. "Actualidad de la interpretación epigenética del desarrollo de los seres vivos en la filosofía natural de Schelling" in *El inicio del Idealismo alemán,* Market, Oswaldo, 325-331. Madrid, Ed Complutense, 1996.

Nowadays, the understanding of the development of organisms gives rise to an internal division within biology that is homologous to the classical discussion between preformationists and epigenists that took place along the XVIIIth century, at the origin of biology as a science. It became then also a principal polemic topic in contemporary philosophy of nature. Kant took part in it with a profound criticism of preformationism based on his own concept of organism. Schelling criticized Kant's understanding of development from a radical epigenetist point of view based on the concept of freedom. The latter interpretation is still today highly suggestive against the utmost mechanistic and reductionistic interpretations of molecular biology.

**Rabben, Linda**. What Ethics?. *J Infor Ethics*, 6(1), 39-43, Spr 97.

**Rabel, Robert J**. Schema in Plato's Definition of Imitation. *Ancient Phil*, 16(2), 365-375, Fall 96.

In Book 3 of the *Republic*, Plato analyzes *mimesis* (imitation) in general and discusses, in particular, a poet's imitation or impersonation of his characters. I argue that the term *schema* in the definition of *mimesis* in Book 3 refers not only to the use of gestures and postures by actors, dancers, performing poets and other kinds of imitators as well, as commentators and translators commonly suppose, but also to the various "forms of speech" employed by poets in the act of narration. The use of the word *schema* to denote a form of speech. I argue, goes back at least to the rudimentary theory of speech-acts developed by Protagoras in the fifth century.

**Rabinowicz, Wlodzimierz** and Österberg, Jan. Value Based On Preferences: On Two Interpretations of Preference Utilitarianism. *Econ Phil*, 12(1), 1-27, Ap 96.

Does intrinsic value, as understood by preference utilitarians, reside in i) it being the case *that* our (intrinsic) desires and preferences are satisfied (the *satisfaction* interpretation), or rather in ii) those states that are the *objects* of our (intrinsic) preferences and desires (the *object* interpretation)? The paper is a dialogue between Österberg who pleads for the former view, and Rabinowicz who finds the latter interpretation more plausible, even though it leads to a very nonstandard (nonindividualistic and nonmonistic) form of preference utilitarianism. To these two interpretations correspond, respectively, two different ways of viewing utilitarianism: the *spectator* and the *participant* models. According to the former, the utilitarian attitude is embodied in a detached and impartial benevolent spectator, while the latter puts forward as a utilitarian ideal an attitude of sympathetic identification with other people and their desires: What it recommends is not a detachment from subjectivity but instead its universalization.

**Rabossi, Eduardo**. "Racionalidad dialógica: Falacia y retórica filosófica: El caso de la llamada 'falacia naturalista'" in *La racionalidad: su poder y sus límites,* Nudler, Oscar (ed), 461-470. Barcelona, Ed Paidos, 1996.

I evaluate the charge that naturalistic ethics is fallacious (hence, the naturalistic fallacy) in terms of a dialogic strategy. After a brief discussion of idealistic and realistic approaches to dialogue (Habermas and Schopenhauer's, respectively) I argue in favor of an ideal-type approach. I identify some basic canons of the rational (critical) dialogue typical of philosophical discussions. Finally, I argue that the charge made from Moore against naturalistic ethics involves a clear breaking off of those canons. I surmise that a similar strategy might be to appeal to deal with a host of the so-called "philosophical fallacies."

**Rabossi, Eduardo**. Nota sobre el no reduccionismo y la realizabilidad variable. *Analisis Filosof*, 15(1-2), 167-180, My-N 95.

In the first part of the paper I "reconstruct" the core thesis that makes a theory nonreductivist, elaborate on the motivation(s) that lead many philosophers to think that nonreductivism is a promising philosophical program and comment on two of the relations that have been posited to explain how psychological properties and physical properties "are made for each other": supervenience and realizability. In the rest of the paper I discuss the *argument of multiple realizability.* My main point is that the argument is far from having the know-down effect that most nonreductivist credit to it. I distinguish two versions of the argument: a factual one (Putnam, 1967) and a conceptual, a priori one (Fodor, 1974), I argue that the argument is refutable in the factual version and that may be counteracted in some respects in the conceptual one.

**Rabouin, Michelle**. Lyin' T(*)gers, and "Cares," Oh My: The Case for Feminist Integration of Business Ethics. *J Bus Ethics*, 16(3), 247-261, F 97.

In this revisioning, business ethics would integrate feminist theories and pedagogy which include the diversity of women in terms of race/ethnicity, class and sexual orientation, thereby expanding its coverage to include issues of power, gender cultural and theoretical conceptualizations, both in the conceptualization of morality, as well as in ethical constructs of analysis. My research indicates that the integration of feminist scholarship, ethics and pedagogy would make it possible to teach ethical decision making, and ultimately increase the likelihood of ethical behavior by showing students how to harness the multicultural ways of thinking needed to resolve ever more complex organizational problems. (edited)

**Radcliffe, Dana**. Scott-Kakures on Believing at Will. *Phil Phenomenol Res*, 57(1), 145-151, Mr 97.

Many philosophers hold that it is conceptually impossible to form a belief simply by willing it. Noting the failure of previous attempts to locate the presumed incoherence, Dion Scott-Kakures offers a version of the general line that voluntary believing is conceptually impossible because it could not qualify as a basic intentional action. This discussion analyzes his central argument, explaining how it turns on the assumption that a prospective voluntary believer must regard the desired belief as not justified, given her other beliefs. It then shows that this assumption is false and also that some initially plausible suggestions for weakening the assumption fail to secure Scott-Kakures's conclusion.

**Radcliffe, Elizabeth**. Kantian Tunes on a Humean Instrument: Why Hume is not *Really* a Skeptic About Practical Reasoning. *Can J Phil*, 27(2), 247-270, Je 97.

Some critics, among them Jean Hampton, Christine Korsgaard and Elijah Millgram, have argued that Hume has no theory of practical reasoning. This paper shows how their criticisms are based on false suppositions about the requirements of such a theory in an empiricist framework. In particular, it explains how an instrumentalist theory of practical reasoning such as Hume's is not the same as the system of hypothetical imperatives implied by a Kantian view of means/ends reasoning and it cannot be expected to meet the expectations of that system.

**Radcliffe Richards, Janet**. Nephrarious Goings On: Kidney Sales and Moral Arguments. *J Med Phil*, 21(4), 375-416, Ag 96.

From all points of the political compass, from widely different groups, have come indignant outcries against the trade in human organs from live vendors. Opponents contend that such practices constitute a morally outrageous and gross exploitation of the poor, inherently coercive and obviously intolerable in any civilized society. This article examines the arguments typically offered in defense of these claims and finds serious problems with all of them. The prohibition of organ sales is derived not from the principles and argument usually invoked in support of prohibition, but rather, from strong feelings of repugnance which exert an invisible but powerful influence on the debate, distorting the arguments [and working] to the detriment of the [very] people most in need of protection.

**Radden, Jennifer**. Commentary on "Psychopathy, Other-Regarding Moral Beliefs, and Responsibility". *Phil Psychiat Psych*, 3(4), 287-289, D 96.

**Radden, Jennifer**. Relational Individualism and Feminist Therapy. *Hypatia*, 11(3), 71-96, Sum 96.

My aim here is to clarify the honoring and validating the relational model of self which plays an important role in feminist therapy. This practice rests on a tangle of psychological claims, moral and political values, and mental health norms which require analysis. Also, severe pathology affects the relative "relationality" of the self. By understanding it we can better understand the senses of autonomy compatible with and even required for a desired relationality.

**Radermacher, Hans**. *Grundlegung eines Neorationalismus: Dekognition und Dissens.* New York, Lang, 1996.

Der vorgeschlagene Neorationalismus wird durch die Begriffe Dekognition und Dissens gekennzeichnet und impliziert skeptische Positionen. Der Begriffsrahmen ist durch das Dreieck Leibniz, Peirce und Nelson ausgemacht. Gegenüber transzendentalphilosophischen Ansätzen wird die Überlegenheit der skeptischen Position Kants betont. Im praktisch-politischen Teil ergibt sich eine Affinität zu den Themen von J. Berlin. Der Begriff *Konsens* wird verworfen. (publisher)

**Radford, Gary P** (ed) and Huspek, Michael (ed). *Transgressing Discourses: Communication and the Voice of Other.* Albany, SUNY Pr, 1997.

An essential theme running through this volume is the idea that our efforts to engage, as well as other's efforts to engage us, have been seriously impaired because of problems which are fundamentally communicative in nature. More specifically, there is general agreement among the contributors that the voice of others has not been sufficiently heard, and this on account of how discourses of the human sciences, as well as other dominant discourses (e.g., law) have structured our interaction with other. Each of the essays helps to clarify the nature of the communicative failing and to develop an appropriate corrective action. (publisher, edited)

**Radford, Luis**. La transformacion de una teoría matemática: el caso de los números poligonales. *Mathesis*, 11(3), 217-250, Ag 95.

This article deals with the study of conceptual *changes* in mathematics. We suggest that conceptual changes can be studied in terms of *epistemological ruptures.* These ruptures can lead to two kind of different conceptual changes: the first one is the *transformation* of an already existent theory; the second one is

AUTHOR INDEX 859 Rallapalli, Kumar C

the *emergence* of a new theory. In our approach, we suggest that the moments in the development of mathematical ideas during which an epistemological rupture occurs can be detected through a criterion stated by Glas (1993) related to the idea of progress in mathematical knowledge. Our article focuses its attention on the transformation phenomenon. Our general aim is to show that Dio-phantus theory of polygonal numbers achieves an epistemological rupture of transformational type in regards with the neo-Pythagorean theory of polygonal numbers. The specific aim of this article is to understand how this transformation took place. (edited)

**Radha, S**. The Special Features of Gandhian Ethics. *Darshana Int*, 36 (1/141), 18-24, Ja 96.

**Radic, Milanka**. Philosophy and Theology (in Serbo-Croatian). *Theoria (Yugoslavia)*, 38(4), 117-120, D 95.

**Radin, Margaret Jane**. *Contested Commodities*. Cambridge, Harvard Univ Pr, 1996.

Radin argues that many such areas of contested commodification reflect a persistent dilemma in liberal society: we value freedom of choice and simultaneously believe that choices ought to be restricted to protect the integrity of what it means to be a person. She views this tension as primarily the result of underlying social and economic inequalities, which need not reflect an irreconcilable conflict in the premises of liberal democracy. Conceiving of all human exchanges in terms of the market metaphor, Radin observes, creates the risk that we will become incapable of transcending that rhetoric's presuppositions about human nature and thus unable to inspire deeper, more humane visions of the good. (publisher, edited)

**Radnitzky, Gerard** (ed). *Values and the Social Order*. Brookfield, Avebury, 1997.

Every society has to rule out some acts as inadmissible. The mechanisms used to ensure conformity with the rules range from the informal (conventions, etc.) to the formal (eventually, penal sanctions). A social order is basically a set of institutions embodying such mechanisms. Two systems for describing social orders are outlined. One is based on crossing the distinction between voluntary and coercive with the distinction between spontaneous and constructed, another is based on degree or voluntariness, extent of state intervention, and degree of the rule of private law. Various types of orders, such as free society, welfare democracy, autocracy, and totalitarian state, are located within the descriptive systems. The prototype of coercive order is the state. Its origins and the changes it has brought about are examined. Tax-financed coercive orders have replaced voluntary orders. Can the state be legitimized? Contractarian legitimization of the state is discussed. Do we need the state? Overgovernment induces normally law-abiding citizens to take defensive measures; they try to escape from coercive to voluntary orders. The state—as a nation-state or as an association of states—responds by countermeasures. The European Union is briefly examined as an example.

**Radovan, Mario**. Mind and Metaphor. *Acta Analytica*, 215-227, 1995.

The paper examines the role of figurative speech within the scope of cognitive science. It is argued that our basic cognitive situation is intrinsically dualistic and that no metaphor can bridge the epistemic gap. Special attention is paid to the *computational metaphor* of the mind; it is argued that it suffers from serious limitations: it can serve as a paradigm for the simulation of the *functional* properties of mind, but not of the truly *mental* ones. Between the functional and the mental there is still a dark gap, and it seems that no appeal to mere computation will ever bridge it.

**Radrizzani, Ives**. Zur Geschichte der romantischen Ästhetik: Von Fichtes Transzendentalphilosophie zu Schlegels Transzendentalpoesie. *Fichte-Studien*, 12, 181-202, 1997.

**Räikkä, Juha**. On Disassociating Oneself from Collective Responsibility. *Soc Theor Pract*, 23(1), 93-108, Spr 97.

During the last twenty years or so philosophers have considered the issue of collective responsibility from many different perspectives. A common question is whether it is possible for every single member of a given ethnic, cultural, or national group to be responsible for the blameworthy practices of that group. Often it is assumed that as long as a member opposes such practices, he or she does not share responsibility for them. In this paper I challenge that assumption and argue that an individual's opposition to a practice does not, in principle at least, necessarily save him or her from blame for the practice.

**Räikkä, Juha**. Rawls and International Justice. *Philosophia (Israel)*, 25(1-4), 163-189, Ap 97.

I reconsider Rawls's original answer to the problem of whether boundaries between nation-states make moral difference. By reviewing and reconstruction the discussion I argue that both Rawls's solution and his critics' objections are problematic.

**Räikkä, Juha**. The Social Concept of Disease. *Theor Med*, 17(4), 353-361, D 96.

In the discussion of such social questions as "how should alcoholics be treated by society?" and "what kind of people are responsible in the face of the law?", is "disease" a value-free or value-laden notion, a natural or a normative one? It seems, for example, that by the utterance 'alcoholism should be classified as a disease' we mean something like the following: the condition called alcoholism is similar in morally relevant respects to conditions that we uncontroversially label diseases and, therefore, we have a moral obligation to consider alcoholism a disease. So there are grounds to think that, in the discussion of social questions, our concept of disease is strongly value-laden. However, it does not follow that the medical concept of disease is likewise value-laden. In this paper I distinguish between the medical and social concepts of disease, arguing that the naturalist-normativist debate is concerned with the former, but not the latter. Therefore, we need not settle the naturalist-normativist debate in order to conclude that the social concept of disease is value-laden.

**Ragghianti, Renzo**. Cousin e l''istituzionalizzazione' della filosofia. *G Crit Filosof Ital*, 17(1), 117-122, Ja-Ap 97.

**Railton, Peter** (ed) and Gibbard, Allan (ed) and Darwall, Stephen (ed). *Moral Discourse and Practice: Some Philosophical Approaches*. New York, Oxford Univ Pr, 1997.

The book is a unique anthology which collects important recent work, much of which is not easily available elsewhere, on core metaethical issues. Naturalist moral realism, once devastated by the charge of "naturalistic fallacy," has been reinvigorated, as have versions of moral realism that insist on the discontinuity between ethics and science. Irrealist, expressivist programs have also developed with great subtlety, encouraging the thought that a noncognitivist account may actually be able to explain ethical judgments' aspirations to objectivity. Neo-Kantian constructivist theories have flourished as well, offering hope that morality can be grounded in a plausible conception of reasonable conduct. (publisher,edited)

**Rainbolt, George**. Mercy: In Defense of Caprice. *Nous*, 31(2), 226-241, Je 97.

Six years ago I sketched an analysis of mercy. Since then, several well-taken criticisms of my analysis have appeared. I, therefore, offer a revised view. After a rather extensive review of the literature on mercy, I suggest that a person is merciful if and only if she, because of her compassion for others, has the disposition to do merciful acts. An act is merciful if and only if it is an act in which one person has a fairly strong reason to treat another harshly and intentionally does not do so.

**Rainbolt, George** and Reif, Alison F. Crime, Property, and Justice: The Ethics of Civil Forfeiture. *Pub Affairs Quart*, 11(1), 39-55, Ja 97.

This article explores the moral status of civil forfeiture law. It argues that many civil forfeitures are morally unproblematic and many have serious moral defects. Some civil forfeitures are morally defective because they result in punishments which do not fit the crime. Some civil forfeitures are morally defective because the procedures used are not proportional to the possible legal outcome. Recent U.S. Supreme Court civil forfeiture cases are examined in some detail. Possible modifications of civil forfeiture law are considered and it is argued that while modifications are necessary, elimination of civil forfeiture is not morally required.

**Raisner, Jack A**. Using the "Ethical Environment" Paradigm to Teach Business Ethics: The Case of the Maquiladoras. *J Bus Ethics*, 16(12-13), 1331-1346, S 97.

The "ethical environment of business" provides a constructive frame of reference for business ethics instruction. As illustrated by a suggested role play about foreign sweatshops, it provides a realistic, problem-solving context for the study of moral and ethical ideas. Once ethical behavior is viewed through this paradigm, students can better see how business policies are shaped by ethics and prepare themselves to react to their own ethical environment.

**Rajagopalan, Kanavillil**. Aesthetics vs. Ideology: The Case of Canon Formation. *Brit J Aes*, 37(1), 75-83, Ja 97.

The paper critically examines Willie van Peer's argument (cf. *British Journal of Aesthetics*, 36 (2), 97-108) that the politicized view of the literary canon will not hold water. I contend that van Peer fails to pay sufficient attention to the differences between politics and ideology. Furthermore, a full appreciation of what goes on can only be had if we take into account the actual process of transformation of well-entrenched canons rather than concentrate on the way those canons originally came into being. Finally I argue that the very idea of a disinterested aesthetics is an offspring of a certain ideology.

**Rakié, Natasa**. Past, Present, Future, and Special Relativity. *Brit J Phil Sci*, 48(2), 257-280, Je 97.

The open future view is the common-sense view that there is an ontological difference between the past, the present, and the future in the sense that the past and the present are real, whereas the future is not yet a part of reality. In this paper we develop a theory in which the open future view is consistently combined with special relativity. Technically, the heart of our contribution is a logical conservativity result showing that, although the open future view is not definible inside the causal geometry of Minkowski space-time, it can be conservatively added to it.

**Raley, Harold**. *A Watch Over Mortality: The Philosophical Story of Julián Marías*. Albany, SUNY Pr, 1997.

*A Watch Over Mortality* describes the premises, problem-set, and methodologies of the philosophy of Julián Marías, particularly in areas where he surpasses the final postures assumed by Ortega, Heidegger, and the phenomenologists as well as those of contemporary minimalist thinkers. Concrete problems are treated within the resulting dynamic matrix: the applicability of the generations to twentieth-century Spanish culture, the history of Spain understood through historical reason, the sexuate and personal nature of human life seen from the ground of metaphysical anthropology, and consideration of personal transcendency arising from the amorous condition of mortal life.

**Rallapalli, Kumar C** and Vitell, Scott J and Singhapakdi, Anusorn. The Perceived Role of Ethics and Social Responsibility: A Scale Development. *J Bus Ethics*, 15(11), 1131-1140, N 96.

Marketers must first perceive ethics and social responsibility to be important before their behaviors are likely to become more ethical and reflect greater social responsibility. However, little research has been conducted concerning marketers' perceptions regarding the importance of ethics and social responsibility as components of business decisions. The purpose of this study is to develop a reliable and valid scale for measuring marketers' perceptions regarding the importance of ethics and social responsibility. The authors develop an instrument for the measurement of the perceived role of ethics and social responsibility (PRESOR). Evidence that the scale is valid is presented through the assessment of scale reliability, as well as content and predictive validity. Finally, future research needs and the value of this construct to marketing are discussed.

**Ralón de Walton, Graciela**. La reversibilidad de silencio y lenguaje según Merleau-Ponty. *Agora (Spain)*, 15(1), 151-161, 1996.

This paper attempts to elucidate Merleau-Ponty's analysis of the transition from perceptual logos to spoken logos. This is initially pursued through an examination of the privileged status assigned to the perceived world and the body conceived as the condition of possibility for expression. Secondly, it is shown how the transition is accomplished through a paradoxically operation which attempts to convey, using as a basis existing meanings, a new meaning which transcends and transforms them. Finally, the paper focuses on how the relationship holding between perception and language is clarified in terms of Saussure's theory of linguistic sign.

**Ramachandran, Murali**. A Counterfactual Analysis of Causation. *Mind*, 106(422), 263-277, Ap 97.

On David Lewis's original analysis of causation, *c* causes *e only if c* is linked to *e* by a chain of distinct events such that each event in the chain (counter-factually) depends on the former one. But, this requirement precludes the possibility of late pre-emptive causation, of causation by fragile events and of indeterministic causation. Lewis proposes three different strategies for accommodating these three kinds of cases, but none of these turn out to be satisfactory. I offer a single analysis of causation that resolves these problems in one go but which respects Lewis's initial insights. One distinctive feature of my account is that it accommodates indeterministic causation without resorting to probabilities.

**Ramachandran, Murali**. Redundant Causation, Composite Events and M-sets. *Acta Analytica*, 147-156, 1996.

In this note, I wish to explore a problem facing David Lewis's original, counterfactual analysis of causation (Lewis 1973b). I hope (a) to show that both his and Michael McDermott's (1995) proposed solutions to the problem have unpalatable consequences; and (b) to identity what I take to be the Achille's heel of the approach Lewis and McDermott favour.

**Ramachandran, Murali**. The Ambiguity Thesis Versus Kripke's Defence of Russell. *Mind Lang*, 11(4), 371-387, D 96.

In his influential paper 'Speaker's Reference and Semantic Reference', Kripke defends Russell's theory of descriptions against the charge that the existence of *referential* and *attributive* uses of descriptions reflects a *semantic* ambiguity. He presents a purely defensive argument to show that Russell's theory in not refuted by the referential usage and a number of methodological considerations which apparently tell in favour of Russell's unitary theory over an ambiguity theory. In this paper, I put forward a case for the ambiguity theory that thwarts Kripke's defensive strategy and argue that it is not undermined by any of his methodological points.

**Ramachandran, Murali** and Noordhoof, Paul and Ganeri, Jonardon. Counterfactuals and Preemptive Causation. *Analysis*, 56(4), 219-225, O 96.

**Ramakrishnan, Lakshmi**. On Talk of Modes of Thought. *J Indian Counc Phil Res*, 13(2), 1-17, Ja-Ap 96.

**Rametta, Gaetano**. Satz und Grund: Der Anfang der Philosophie bei Fichte mit Bezugnahme auf die Werke BWL und GWL. *Fichte-Studien*, 9, 127-139, 1997.

**Ramírez, Mario Teodoro**. Muchas Culturas: Sobre el problema filosófico y práctico de la diversidad cultural. *Ideas Valores*, 74-93, D 96.

In this paper I propose to distinguish with precision two kinds of oppositions about the concept of culture. First, the opposition between abstract culture and concrete culture, second, the opposition between universal culture and particular culture (or particular cultures). I attempt to demonstrate that *culture* (and every culture) is necessarily a concrete reality and, therefore, a particular reality. From this point of view, I suggest that we can legitimize the necessity and value of cultural diversity, without restoring a universalistic position nor an abstract and trifling pluralism.

**Ramírez, Mario Teodoro**. Naturaleza/cultura: Un enfoque estético. *Rev Filosof (Costa Rica)*, 34(83-84), 265-273, D 96.

In this paper I introduce an aesthetic view of the relations between nature and culture. I hold that art operates as a dialectic mediator between those both dimensions. To base this proposal I do a brief analysis of the concept of art and I offer a phenomenological view of the problem of "aesthetic sense".

**Ramírez, Mario Teodoro**. No es una metáfora: Filosofía, lenguaje y hermenéutica en Merleau-Ponty. *Analogía*, 10(2), 55-71, 1996.

**Ramírez B, Edgar Roy**. La ética de los negocios. *Rev Filosof (Costa Rica)*, 34(83-84), 355-358, D 96.

In the context of applied ethics this paper deals with the possibility of business ethics and discusses mainly the notion of social responsibility.

**Ramos, Alberto Arvelo**. A Review of the Origins of the State (Spanish). *Rev Filosof (Venezuela)*, Supp(2-3), 241-250, 1996.

In this paper the author makes a historical review of the problem of the *state*, beginning with the classical conceptions (Aristotle) through Hegel and Marx. The relationship between ethics and politics is made based on the initial historical frame of reference.

**Ramos, Pedro**. El argumento fregeano de las oraciones aseverativas como nombres propios. *Rev Latin de Filosof*, 23(1), 35-54, O 97.

In this article I reconstruct Frege's argument that declarative sentences are singular terms denoting the *true* and the *false*. I try to show two things here: 1) That the argument's conclusion gets support from the semantic principles which

premises it and that, however, the validity of these principles is restricted to the semantics of Frege's system and 2), that from the argument's conclusion there follows as a way of illustration, innumerable ungrammatical consequences in natural language depending on some of its features which Frege did not take into account in the mentioned principles. These consequences call into question the unrestricted validity he seems to think his argument possesses. The conclusion following from 1) and 2) is, obviously, that declarative sentences are not and cannot be singular terms. (edited)

**Ramos, Pedro**. The Argument on Identity Statements and the Problem of Referring to Functions in Frege's Philosophy (Spanish). *Theoria (Spain)*, 12(29), 293-315, My 97.

In this paper, I relate two items not commonly related in the literature on Frege: Frege's argument on the interpretation of identity statements and his problem of referring to functions. First, I expound the argument and conclude that it is sound. Second, I characterize the semantical relations which the argument allows him to introduce. In what follows, I deal with the above-mentioned problem and show how it affects Frege's semantics: those semantical relations become unnamable and, therefore, his semantics turns out to be unexpressible. I consider a possible solution of this problem.

**Ramos Arenas, Jaime**. El Ejercicio de la Filosofía. *Ideas Valores*, 79-85, Ag 97.

**Ramose, Mogobe B**. "Specific African Thought Structures and Their Possible Contribution to World Peace" in *Kreativer Friede durch Begegnung der Weltkulturen,* Beck, Heinrich (ed), 227-251. New York, Lang, 1995.

In this essay we are concerned with specific African thought structures on the one hand and the problem of world peace on the other. This means that if there are any specific African thought structures at all, are these capable of contributing towards the construction and upkeep of peace in the world? Our first task then is to determine if there are any specific African thought structures. (edited)

**Ramsey, Jeffry L**. Molecular Shape, Reduction, Explanation and Approximate Concepts. *Synthese*, 111(3), 233-251, Je 97.

**Ramsey, William**. Do Connectionist Representations Earn Their Explanatory Keep?. *Mind Lang*, 12(1), 34-66, Mr 97.

In this paper I assess the explanatory role of internal representations in connectionist models of cognition. Focusing on both the internal 'hidden' units and the connection weights between units, I argue that the standard reasons for viewing these components as representations are inadequate to bestow an explanatory useful notion of representation. Hence, nothing would be lost from connectionist accounts of cognitive processes if we were to stop viewing the weights and hidden units as internal representations.

**Ramsey, William**. Rethinking Distributed Representation. *Acta Analytica*, 9-25, 1995.

It is argued that there are serious problems with connectionist accounts of fully distributed internal representations in feed forward networks. The standard reasons for viewing the activation patterns of the hidden units as representations are not sufficiently robust to differentiate the activation patterns from other types of nonintentional states. One possible solution exploits the recent work of Fred Dretske (1988, but this proposal ultimately fails too.

**Rancière, Jacques**. Democracy Means Equality. *Rad Phil*, 82, 29-36, Mr-Ap 97.

**Randall, Fiona** and Downie, Robin S. Parenting and the Best Interests of Minors. *J Med Phil*, 22(3), 219-231, Je 97.

The treatment decisions of competent adults, especially treatment refusals, are generally respected. In the case of minors something turns on their age, and older minors ought increasingly to make their own decisions. On the other hand, parents decide on behalf of infants and young children. Their right to do so can best be justified in terms of the importance of preserving intimate family relationships, rather than in terms of the child's best interests, although the child's best interests will most often follow from this arrangement. Nevertheless, there are and ought to be legal, ethical, and financial constraints on parental decision making.

**Rankin, Kenneth**. A Metaphysical Confirmation of "Folk" Psychology. *Maritain Stud*, 9, 135-143, 1993.

**Ransom, John S**. Forget Vitalism: Foucault and *Lebensphilosophie*. *Phil Soc Crit*, 23(1), 33-47, 1997.

Recent interpretations of Michel Foucault's work have leaned heavily on a reading that can be traced back to the 'vitalist/mechanist' debate in the philosophy of science from earlier in this century. Friends (Gilles Deleuze) and enemies (Jürgen Habermas) both read Foucault as a kind of vitalist, championing repressed and unrealized life-forces against a burdensome facticity. This reading of Foucault, however, comes with a prohibitively high cost: the giving up of Foucault's most trenchant insights regarding the nature of power. In fact, Foucault has a quite different relation to the history and philosophy of science than the one ascribed to him by critics.

**Ransom, John S**. *Foucault's Discipline: The Politics of Subjectivity*. Durham, Duke Univ Pr, 1997.

In *Foucault's Discipline*, John S. Ransom extracts a distinctive vision of the political world—and oppositional possibilities within it—from the welter of disparate topics and projects Michel Foucault pursued over his lifetime. Uniquely, Ransom presents Foucault as a political theorist in the tradition of Weber and Nietzsche, and specifically examines Foucault's work in relation to the political tradition of liberalism and the Frankfurt School. By concentrating primarily on *Discipline and Punish* and the later Foucauldian texts, Ransom provides a fresh interpretation of this controversial philosopher's perspectives on concepts such as freedom, right, truth, and power. (publisher, edited)

**Rantala, Veikko**. Metaphor and Conceptual Change. *Dan Yrbk Phil*, 31, 181-190, 1996.

A nonstandard notion of translation is defined which is called 'explanatory'. It is in many cases necessary to depart from the standard notion of translation and replace it by the requirement that there be syntactic and semantic transformations which correspond to each other. Due to the semantic transformation, such a nonstandard translation may involve a conceptual change. It is argued that the semantic and pragmatic import and the conceptual role of a metaphorical utterance can be understood by means of an explanatory translation. This theory of metaphor entails and explains some earlier theories.

**Rao, Spuma M** and Hamilton III, J Brooke. The Effect of Published Reports of Unethical Conduct on Stock Prices. *J Bus Ethics*, 15(12), 1321-1330, D 96.

This study adds to the empirical evidence supporting a significant connection between ethics and profitability by examining the connection between published reports of unethical behaviour by publicly traded U.S. and multinational firms and the performance of their stock. Using reports of unethical behaviour published in the Wall Street Journal from 1989 to 1993, the analysis shows that the actual stock performance for those companies was lower than the expected market adjusted returns. Unethical conduct by firms which is discovered and publicized does impact on the shareholders by lowering the value of their stock for an appreciable period of time. Whatever their views on whether ethical behaviour is profitable, managers should be able to see a definite connection between unethical behaviour and the worth of their firm's stock. Stockholders, the press and regulators should find this information important in pressing for greater corporate and managerial accountability.

**Rapaport, Herman**. *Is There Truth in Art?*. Ithaca, Cornell Univ Pr, 1997.

*Is There Truth in Art?* includes chapters on atonal music, environmental art, modern German and French poetry, contemporary French fiction, experimental French film, and a photograph taken by the National Socialists during the destruction of the Warsaw ghetto. Determining how truth can be said to occur in these examples, Rapaport maintains, requires analysis in each instance. He draws chiefly on the thinkers who have radically reformulated questions about truth—Nietzsche, Heidegger, Derrida, and Lévinas—and uses their writings to explore the works under analysis. (publisher,edited)

**Rapaport, William J**. "Understanding Understanding: Syntactic Semantics and Computational Cognition" in *AI, Connectionism and Philosophical Psychology, 1995*, Tomberlin, James E (ed), 49-88. Atascadero, Ridgeview, 1995.

John Searle once said: "The Chinese room shows what we knew all along: syntax by itself is not sufficient for semantics. (Does anyone actually deny this point, I mean straight out? Is anyone actually willing to say straight out, that they think that syntax, in the sense of formal symbols, is really the same as semantic content, in the sense of meanings, thought contents, understanding, etc.?)." I say: "Yes." Stuart C. Shapiro has said: "Does that make any sense? Yes: Everything makes sense. The question is: What sense does it make?" This essay explores what sense it makes to say that syntax by itself is sufficient for semantics.

**Rapp, Christof**. Aristoteles über die Rationalität rhetorischer Argumente. *Z Phil Forsch*, 50(1/2), 197-222, Ja-Je 96.

The paper is intended to examine, whether Aristotle did assume a specific rhetorical rationality. This task is essentially connected with the following three questions: 1) Is the enthymeme a syllogism in the technical sense of the *Prior Analytics*? (It is not.) 2) Did Aristotle allow for the possibility of relaxed inferences in the rhetorical domain? (He did.) 3. Can we conclude from this, that Aristotle neglects the difference between valid and fallacious arguments for rhetorical purposes? (We cannot.)

**Rappaport, Steven**. Relativism and Truth: A Rejoinder to Lynch. *Philosophia (Israel)*, 25(1-4), 423-428, Ap 97.

In a previous article appearing in *Philosophia*, I claimed that metaphysical relativism (the world does not come presorted but rather symbol users impose taxonomies on it) does not entail truth relativism (statements are true only relative to a framework). Michael Lynch has said that the *argument* I gave for this claim is defective. My argument uses the premise that truth relativism is inconsistent with the deflationary theory of truth. Lynch argues that this premise is false. However, I show that Lynch's argument misconstrues the deflationary theory. As a result, my premise remains unrefuted.

**Rapping, Elayne**. Textual Travel and Translation in an Age of Globalized Media. *J Soc Phil*, 28(2), 117-127, Fall 97.

**Rasinski Gregory, Dorothy**. Modern Medicine in a Multicultural Setting. *Bioethics Forum*, 11(2), 9-14, Sum 95.

In dealing with patients from other cultures, we often find that our "ethical" focus on autonomy, beneficence, nonmaleficence and justice fails to help solve a dilemma or answer a question. A broader view of autonomy, one that includes the person's culture—the values and belief system within which that person functions—is in order.

**Rasiowa, Helena**. Axiomatization and Completeness of Uncountably Valued Approximation Logic. *Stud Log*, 53(1), 137-160, F 94.

**Rasiowa, Helena**. Cecylia Rauszer. *Stud Log*, 53(4), 467-471, N 94.

**Rasmussen, Larry L**. *Earth Community: Earth Ethics*. Maryknoll, NY, Orbis, 1996.

In this important new book, social ethicist Larry Rasmussen lays the foundations for an approach to faith and ethics appropriate to a community of the earth, in all its peril and promise. *Earth Community, Earth Ethics* is a comprehensive treatment that synthesizes insights from religion, ethics, and environmentalism in a single vision for creating a sustainable community. The book is arranged in three parts. In the first, Rasmussen scans our global situation and brings into relief the extraordinary range of dangers threatening all life on our planet. In part two, he explores worlds of religion, ethics, and human symbolism to glean from them the resources for a necessary "conversion to earth." Finally, he sketches a constructive ethic that can guide us out of our present situation. (publisher, edited)

**Rasmussen, Stig Alstrup**. How Can a Metaphor Be Genuinely Illuminating?. *Dan Yrbk Phil*, 31, 191-200, 1996.

It is argued, on a broadly Aristotelian basis, that some metaphors are *dead* and, therefore, not cognitively illuminating. On the other hand, *ineradicable* metaphors are potentially illuminating, but ultimately incomprehensible. A third category of metaphor is introduced, the *replaceable* one. These have a chance of being illuminating, as well as correct. The discussion aims to throw some light on M. Dummett's views concerning the interrelationship between metaphysics and semantics. Substantive appeal is made to the efforts of H. Putnam, R. Fogelin, C. Wright, Jane Fonda, and Donald Sutherland.

**Rathjen, Michael** and Glass, Thomas and Schlüter, Andreas. On the Proof-Theoretic Strength of Monotone Induction in Explicit Mathematics. *Annals Pure Applied Log*, 85(1), 1-46, Ap 97.

We characterize the proof-theoretic strength of systems of explicit mathematics with a general principle (MID) asserting the existence of least fixed points for monotone inductive definitions, in terms of certain systems of analysis and set theory.... In the case of set theory, these are systems containing the Kripke-Platek axioms for a recursively inaccessible universe together with the existence of a stable ordinal. In all cases, the exact strength depends on what forms of induction are admitted in the respective systems. (edited)

**Ratté, Michel**. Christoph Menke: herméneutique, déconstruction et raison dans le problème de l'expérience esthétique. *Horiz Phil*, 7(2), 107-126, Spr 97.

**Ratto, Franco**. La *Scienza Nuova* (1725) en Nápoles: Testimonios e interpretaciones. *Cuad Vico*, 7/8, 167-179, 1997.

The author examines the testimonies to the 1725 edition of the *Scienza Nuova*, the Lipsian reception and the *Vici Vindicoe*. This examination, while bringing together the most influential interpretations, allows an analysis of the controversial question about the Vichian "isolation".

**Ratto, Franco**. Vico político antimoderno? (Breves observaciones sobre la reciente interpretación de Mark Lilla). *Cuad Vico*, 5/6, 283-292, 1995/96.

Nel volume *The Making of an Anti-Modern* (Harvard U.P., 1993) Mark Lilla sostiene che Giambattista Vico fu un "pensatore politico antimoderno": a suo dire, il napoletano avrebbe assunto una posizione "non tanto estranea alle maggiori correnti intellettuali del suo tempo, quanto ostinatamente contraria ad esse". Egli riassume una siffatta decisa opposizione nell'accusa di 'scetticismo' da Vico rivolta alla filosofia, in particolare a quella moderna, le cui conseguenze sarebbero state per il filosofo molto pericolose non solo per la "religione" e la "tradizione", ma anche nei confronti della "provvidenza divina" e del "diritto naturale". Lo studioso, come ulteriore conferma della propria tesi, ricorda: a) la concezione vichiana *anti-moderna* della natura umana, debole, ingannevole e bisognosa dell'opera provvidente di Dio; b) l'importanza attribuita dal filosofo alla "tradizione" e all'autorità contro la "ragione" e la "libertà", esaltate da Bacone, Cartesio, Hobbes ed altri; c) la convinzione del filosofo che il metodo usato dai moderni costituiva un'atto d'auto-affermazione dell'uomo contro Dio e la natura; d) la trasposizione da parte di Vico di presupposti e concetti "teologici" in ambito giuridico-storico-politico". (edited)

**Rauscher, Frederick**. How a Kantian Can Accept Evolutionary Metaethics. *Biol Phil*, 12(3), 303-326, Jl 97.

Contrary to widely held assumptions, an evolutionary metaethics need not be noncognitivist. I define evolutionary metaethics as the claim that certain phenotypic traits expressing certain genes are both necessary and sufficient for explanation of all other phenotypic traits we consider morally significant. A review of the influential cognitivist Immanuel Kant's metaethics shows that much of his ethical theory is independent of the antinaturalist metaphysics of transcendental idealism which itself is incompatible with evolutionary metaethics. By matching those independent aspects to an evolutionary metaethics a cognitivist Kantian evolutionary metaethical theory is a possibility for researchers to consider.

**Rauscher, Josef**. The Writing of History as Remembering the Future (in Serbo-Croatian). *Filozof Istraz*, 15(4), 655-672, 1995.

Der Autor versucht anhand von Nietzsches Bestimmung der Historie als interessengeleiteter Geschichtsschreibung, den bislang eher verstellten Blick auf Nation, Nationalismus, Geschichte und die Geschichten der Geschichte zu lenke.ı. In einer Umkehrung der üblichen Betrachtungsweise bewertet Nietzsche die Vergangenheit und den Umgang mit ihr in ihrer zukunftserschliessenden Relevanz, wodurch er den Raum zu einer ideologiekritischen Betrachtung öffnet und die Wertung der Tatsachen als Geschichtsentwurf kenntlich macht. Nietzsches eigenes Denken, das jenseits von Kriterien situiert werden möchte, hat in seiner Ausrichtung auf die Perspektivenvielfalt eine Strukturvorgabe. Dem auf die Vergangenheit sich berufenden Nationalismus kann von hierher der Vorwurf des Formalismus und der Vergangenheitsorientierung gemacht werden, wie, umgekehrt, der perspektivenöffnende Nationalismus in der Konsequenz seiner Betonung der Einzelperspektiven zu einer Selbstaufhebung tendiert.

**Rauszer, Cecylia** and Bartol, Wiktor. Helena Rasiowa and Cecylia Rauszer: Two Generations in Logic. *Bull Sec Log*, 25(3/4), 120-125, O-D 96.

**Rautenberg, Wolfgang**. On Reduced Matrices. *Stud Log*, 52(1), 63-72, F 93.

**Ravenscroft, Ian** and Currie, Gregory. Mental Simulation and Motor Imagery. *Phil Sci*, 64(1), 161-180, Mr 97.

Motor imagery typically involves an experience as of moving a body part. Recent studies reveal close parallels between the constraints on motor imagery and those on actual motor performance. How are these parallels to be explained? We advance a simulative theory of motor imagery, modeled on the idea that we predict and explain the decisions of others by simulating their decision-making processes. By proposing that motor imagery is essentially off-line motor action, we explain the tendency of motor imagery to mimic motor performance. We close by arguing that a simulative theory of motor imagery gives (modest) support to and illumination of the simulative theory of decision-prediction.

**Ravita, Tracienne** and Ellis, Ralph. Scientific Uncertainties, Environmental Policy, and Political Theory. *Phil Forum*, 28(3), 209-231, Spr 97.

Rights-based political theories neglect the problem of environmental destruction by demanding certainties that science cannot provide, resulting in the prevailing attitude that pollution is "innocent until proven guilty." We explore a consequentialist approach, using a *just distribution* principle to balance the competing outcomes of developers' rights, environmental preservation, and public health. Environmentalists fear that a crass consequentialism neglects environmental considerations, especially affecting small numbers; but if just distribution is another valued consequence, 'rights violations' simply become distributively unjust burdens. Because polluting interests can drive the government's interpretation of scientific findings, the solution proposed here also requires campaign finance reform.

**Rawes, Alan**. "Lord Byron: To Create, and in Creating Live a Being More Intense" in *Critical Studies: Ethics and the Subject,* Simms, Karl (ed), 237-243. Amsterdam, Rodopi, 1997.

**Rawling, Piers**. Expected Utility, Ordering, and Context Freedom. *Econ Phil*, 13(1), 79-86, Ap 97.

The context-free weak ordering principle (that rational preferences are weakly ordered, and that subtracting members from the domain of alternatives does not alter the ordering of the original domain) is viewed by many as a cornerstone of rational choice theory. But this principle is certainly not uncontroversial: there are examples of (putative) violations of it which do not appear irrational. This paper investigates the extent to which expected utility theory presupposes context freedom. I shall focus on the preference axiomatization for Savage's theory of decision, and argue that, whilst Savage's axiomatization requires ordering, it does not require context freedom.

**Rawlinson, Mary C**. "Perspectives and Horizons: Husserl on Seeing the Truth" in *Sites of Vision,* Levin, David Michael (ed), 265-292. Cambridge, MIT Pr, 1997.

This essay demonstrates how Husserl's transcendental method depends upon an metaphorical appropriation of visual perception. Aristotle defines a metaphor as the "ascription of an alien name". While using the terms ceaselessly, Husserl insists that transcendental *perception* or essential *seeing*, are "improper" expressions. Through the elaboration of a system of (dis)analogies Husserl attempts to invest transcendental reflection with certain perceptual values, while protecting it from the specificity and perspectivism of the body. By reconstructing human vision as "essential seeing", Husserl appropriates the other's body to the transcendental "sphere of my owness". The apodicticty of phenomenology's "absolute" or "transcendental" subjectivity is produced by this system of identifications and alienations with visual perception.

**Ray, Greg**. Logical Consequence: A Defense of Tarski. *J Phil Log*, 25(6), 617-677, D 96.

In this paper, I discuss the following four critical charges that Etchemendy makes against Tarski and his account of the logical properties: 1a) Tarski's account of logical consequence diverges from the standard model-theoretic account at points where the latter account gets it right. 1b) Tarski's account cannot be brought into line with the model-theoretic account, because the two are fundamentally incompatible. 2) There are simple counterexamples (enumerated by Etchemendy) which show that Tarski's account is wrong. 3) Tarski committed a modal fallacy when arguing that his account captures our pretheoretical concept of logical consequence and so obscured an essential weakness of the account. 4) Tarski's account depends on there being a distinction between the "logical terms" and the "nonlogical terms" of a language, but (according to Etchemendy) there are very simple (even first-order) languages for which no such distinction can be made. (edited)

**Rayburn, J Michael** and Rayburn, L Gayle. Relationship Between Machiavellianism and Type A Personality and Ethical-Orientation. *J Bus Ethics*, 15(11), 1209-1219, N 96.

Results of a study investigating the relation between personality traits and ethical-orientation indicate sex is not a good predictor for differences in Machiavellian-, Type A personality- or ethical-orientation. Intelligence is found to be positively associated with Machiavellian- and Type A personality-orientation but negatively associated with ethical-orientation. Machiavellians tend to have Type A personalities, but tend to be less ethically-oriented than non-Machiavellianians. Type A personalities are more ethically-oriented than Type B personalities.

**Rayburn, L Gayle** and Rayburn, J Michael. Relationship Between Machiavellianism and Type A Personality and Ethical-Orientation. *J Bus Ethics*, 15(11), 1209-1219, N 96.

Results of a study investigating the relation between personality traits and ethical-orientation indicate sex is not a good predictor for differences in Machiavellian-, Type A personality- or ethical-orientation. Intelligence is found to be positively associated with Machiavellian- and Type A personality-orientation

but negatively associated with ethical-orientation. Machiavellians tend to have Type A personalities, but tend to be less ethically-oriented than non-Machiavellianians. Type A personalities are more ethically-oriented than Type B personalities.

**Raz, Joseph**. Why Interpret?. *Ratio Juris*, 9(4), 349-363, D 96.

My article is about legal interpretation, but not about the question: how to interpret the law. Rather its aim is to make us consider seriously the question: Why is interpretation central to legal practices? After all not all normative practices assign interpretation such a central role. In this regard the law contrasts with morality. The reason for the contrast has to do with the status of sources in the law. There are no "moral sources" while legal sources are central to the law. Legal interpretations is primarily—I will suggest—the interpretation not of the law, but of its sources. To understand why interpretation is central to legal practices requires understanding the role of sources in the law: the reasons for having them, and hence also the ways in which they should be treated. I will show how reflections about these topics connect with some traditional jurisprudential puzzles, such as the relations between law and morality. Are there gaps in the law? Is the law or its interpretation objective or subjective?

**Raz, Joseph** and Ruben, David-Hillel. The Active and the Passive. *Aris Soc*, Supp(71), 211-246, 1997.

**Razavi, Mehdi Amin** (ed) and Ambuel, David (ed). *Philosophy, Religion, and the Question of Intolerance*. Albany, SUNY Pr, 1997.

The book begins with essays by three distinguished scholars, Robert Cummings Neville, J.B. Schneewind, and John McCumber. They assess the origins of intolerance, the genesis of our concept of toleration, and the outlook for the practice of tolerance in contemporary society. Beyond the opening essays, the collection is divided into three sections. The first concentrates on the relationship of religious faith and practice to toleration and inquires how religion might either impede or promote toleration. The second section deals primarily with questions regarding tolerance in the face of modern political realities. The final section discusses ethics, namely the philosophical analysis and definition of toleration as a virtue. (publisher, edited)

**Razzaque, Abdur**. The Theory of Meaning: An Impasse. *Phil Cont World*, 3(3), 24-28, Fall 96.

This paper endeavors to delineate the salient features of the theory of meaning and to show how meaning converges with metaphysics. For the British classical linguistic philosophers, meaning concerns only autonomous propositions, which allegedly in isolation clarify thought and facilitate understanding of language. But for the American philosophers W.V.O. Quino and Donald Davidson, meaning is inextricably related to human life and its problems. According to them, our experiences are interrelated and cannot be separated from one another. A statement cannot be meaningful in isolation; that is to say, it cannot have meaning without holistic connections and metaphysical presumptions.

**Rea, Michael C**. Supervenience and Co-Location. *Amer Phil Quart*, 34(3), 367-375, Jl 97.

It is widely believed that many (if not all) of the intrinsic qualitative properties of macrophysical objects supervene on the intrinsic properties and relations exemplified by its microphysical parts. An object's mass and shape seem to supervene in this way; its mental properties (if it has any) and its sortal properties seem to as well. If this is so, however, then, as several philosophers have pointed out, the possibility of collocation—the possibility of more than one material object filling the same region of space at the same time—raises a host of problems. My aim in this paper is to show how the collocationist can overcome these problems.

**Read, James H**. "Participation, Power, and Democracy" in *Political Dialogue: Theories and Practices,* Esquith, Stephen L (ed), 239-261. Amsterdam, Rodopi, 1996.

The purpose of this essay is to pursue the consequences of the premise that political participation requires a degree of actual *power* over an outcome—not merely an *attempt* (which might be unsuccessful) to shape outcomes. If participation requires power, then does more political participation for one individual or group necessarily entail less participation for another? Or is a multi-sided expansion of participation possible even where there are significant conflicts among participants? I argue that political participation (and political power itself) can be expanded for all even under conditions of conflict. Political outcomes are not like pies of fixed size but can themselves expand or contract. *Changes in the aims and perceptions of citizens,* not just laws passed or legislative seats gained and lost, must be included in our description of a political outcome. Better (or worse) political dialogue among citizens produces "greater" (or "lesser") political outcomes and thus expands (or shrinks) the pool of political power from which all must draw.

**Read, Rupert**. In What Sense is Kripke's Wittgensteinian Paradox a Scepticism? On the Opposition between its Epistemological and its Metaphysical Aspects. *De Phil*, 12, 117-132, 1995-1996.

Kripke's Wittgensteinian 'scepticism' has 'metaphysical' as well as epistemic aspects. This paper argues that these metaphysical aspects—for instance, the questioning of whether there is *any fact of the matter* at stake in attributions of meaning to utterances—unfortunately contravene the very (epistemic) devices through which the scepticism is initially rendered comprehensible. That is, the epistemic questions (about what our words mean) through which Kripke *enables* us to understand what he is talking about are rendered meaningless through the 'metaphysical' questions Kripke subsequently raises. Thus, we literally cannot understand what Kripke is talking about, unless he is wrong! His 'scepticism' is utterly unstatable.

**Read, Rupert**. On (Virtuous?) Circles of Concepts in Goodman—and Quine. *Dialogos*, 31(68), 23-28, Jl 96.

**Read, Stephen**. The Slingshot Argument. *Log Anal*, 36(144), 195-218, S-D 93.

The "slingshot argument" was produced by church to establish a claim of Frege's, that sentences designate truth-values. It was adapted by Quine to show that intensional logic is misconceived, for any context open to replacement of coextensive terms and logically equivalent sentences is truth-functional. The argument is invalid: if terms are treated in Russell's way, the term-replacement fails; if treated in Frege's way, the term-replacement succeeds but the sentence-replacement fails.

**Reader, Soran**. Principle Ethics, Particularism and Another Possibility. *Philosophy*, 72(280), 269-292, Ap 97.

**Reath, Andrews**. Agency and the Imputation of Consequences in Kant's Ethics. *Jahr Recht Ethik*, 2, 259-281, 1994.

Nach Kant werden dem Handelnden, der eine strikte moralische Pflicht verletzt, die schlechten Folgen dieses seines Verhaltens stets zugerechnet, und zwar unabhängig davon, ob diese Folgen nun vorhersehbar waren oder nicht. Umgekehrt: Schlechte Folgen, die aus einem pflichtgemässen Verhalten hervorgehen, sind nicht zurechenbar. Der Beitrag untersucht das Konzept, das diesen Kantischen Prinzipien für die moralische Zurechnung schlechter Folgen zugrunde liegt. (edited)

**Rebaglia, Alberta**. Modelli filosofici e interpretazione quantistica. *Epistemologia*, 19(2), 227-264, Jl-D 96.

The atypical behaviour of micro physical systems cannot be conceptually understood and linguistically described without applying it to some analogous models. Among the many analogies developed in the history of quantum mechanics, some useful suggestions have been introduced by Niels Bohr in accordance both with the ancient oriental yin-yang duality and the mathematical topological concept of Riemann surface. The most effective philosophical models, however, are those conceived by Bohr himself and by Werner Heisenberg. Such models allowed to reorganize both the methodological and the ontological perspectives deriving by the seemingly paradoxical quantum conceptual exigencies. These models seem partial and limited as philosophical tools. In order to improve our ability in understanding and explaining the new, nonclassical conceptual framework, it is necessary to work out deeper analogies, as a development of those previous ones. Here a new model is suggested, based on hermeneutic philosophy. (edited)

**Rebollo Espinosa, Maria José**. El educador viquiano. *Cuad Vico*, 7/8, 181-190, 1997.

This is a description and a commentary of a conception concerning the true educator's functions that Vico spread throughout his work. When shedding the light of the whole theory of his philosophy of education on these functions, one finds enough amazing gleams of modernity (communicative bidirectionality, no directivity, social utility, paido-centrism, humanism...) to acknowledge their actuality.

**Récanati, François**. Can We Believe What We Do Not Understand?. *Mind Lang*, 12(1), 84-100, Mr 97.

In a series of papers, Sperber provides the following analysis of the phenomenon of ill-understood belief (or 'quasi-belief', as I call it): I) the quasi-believer has a validating metabelief, to the effect that a certain representation is true; yet II) that representation does not give rise to a plain belief, because it is 'semipropositional'. In this paper I discuss several aspects of this treatment. In particular, I deny that the representation accepted by the quasi-believer is semantically indeterminate and I reject Sperber's claim that quasi-belief is a credal attitude distinct from plain belief.

**Rechenauer, Martin**. Individualism, Individuation and That-Clauses. *Erkenntnis*, 46(1), 49-67, Ja 97.

Brian Loar has argued that the well-known arguments against individualism in the philosophy of mind are insufficient because they rely on the assumption that that-clauses uniquely capture psychological content. He tried to show that this is not the use of that-clauses sometimes capture psychological content, if our system of mental ascription is to be workable at all. I argue further that individualism tends to be at odds with a requirement of intersubjective shareability of contents and that Loar is alternative conception of psychological content is beset with difficulties.

**Reck, Erich**. "Frege's Influence on Wittgenstein: Reversing Metaphysics via the Context Principle" in *Early Analytic Philosophy*, Tait, William W (ed), 123-185. Chicago, Open Court, 1997.

**Reckling, JoAnn Bell**. Who Plays What Role in Decisions about Withholding and Withdrawing Life-Sustaining Treatment?. *J Clin Ethics*, 8(1), 39-45, Spr 97.

**Reda, Clementina Gily**. *Temporalità e Comunicazione*. Napoli, Parresia, 1996.

**Rédei, Miklós**. Krylov's Proof that Statistical Mechanics Cannot Be Founded on Classical Mechanics and Interpretation of Classical Statistical Mechanical Probabilities. *Phil Natur*, 29(2), 268-284, 1992.

**Rédei, Miklós**. Why John Von Neumann Did Not Like the Hilbert Space Formalism of Quantum Mechanics (and What he Liked Instead). *Stud Hist Phil Mod Physics*, 27B(4), 493-510, D 96.

**Redekop, Benjamin W**. Thomas Abbt and the Formation of an Enlightened German "Public". *J Hist Ideas*, 58(1), 81-103, J 97.

**Redfield, Marc**. *Phantom Formations: Aesthetic Ideology and the Bildungsroman*. Ithaca, Cornell Univ Pr, 1996.

The author maintains that the literary genre of the *Bildungsroman* brings into sharp focus the contradictions of aesthetics, and also that aesthetics exemplifies what is called ideology. He combines a wide-ranging account of the history and theory of aesthetics with close readings of novels by Goethe, George Eliot, and Gustave Flaubert. For Redfield, these fictions of character formation demonstrate the paradoxical relation between aesthetics and literature: the notion of the *Bildungsroman* may be expanded to apply to any text that can be figured as a subject producing itself in history, which is to say any text whatsoever. At the same time, the category may be contracted to include only a handful of novels (or even none at all), a paradox that has led critics to denigrate the *Bildungsroman* as a phantom genre. (publisher, edited)

**Redhead, Michael**. *From Physics to Metaphysics*. New York, Cambridge Univ Pr, 1996.

The book is drawn from the Tarner Lectures delivered in Cambridge in 1993. It is concerned with the ultimate nature of reality and how this is revealed by modern physical theories such as relativity and quantum theory. The objectivity and rationality of science are defended against the views of relativists and social constructivists. This is a nontechnical discursive account of the interrelatedness of physics and metaphysics. (publisher,edited)

**Redhead, Michael**. Search for a Naturalistic World View by Abner Shimony, Volume I. *Synthese*, 110(2), 335-342, F 97.

In this article Abner Shimony's collected papers in the main fields of philosophy of physics, metaphysics and epistemology are reviewed. Shimony's seminal contributions to the interpretation of quantum mechanics are recognized in particular his discussion of nonlocality and the resulting putative conflict with the special theory of relativity. Shimony's emphasis on the role of potentiality in the philosophy of quantum mechanics is discussed. On epistemological issues Shimony is best known for the concept of tempered personalism in Bayesian confirmation theory. The article includes a new solution of the 'old evidence' problem, although this is not discussed by Shimony himself.

**Reding, Jean-Paul**. L'utilisation philosophique de la métaphore en Grèce et en Chine: Vers une métaphorologie comparée. *Rev Theol Phil*, 129(1), 1-30, 1997.

Everything leads us to believe that an *exotic* language produces exotic metaphors, which in turn condition those modes of thought different from our own. Comparative analysis of a metaphorical field common to Greece and China (light and the mirror) shows that the philosophical differences do not proceed from the various material of the metaphors used, but rather from the different attitudes to language. The hypothesis of linguistic relativism far from being either weakened or confirmed by this comparative analysis, appears itself to depend on the manner in which Greek and occidental thought conceived the relation of thought to language.

**Redpath, Peter A**. *Cartesian Nightmare: An Introduction to Transcendental Sophistry*. Amsterdam, Rodopi, 1997.

This book challenges the presupposition among professional philosophers that René Descartes is the Father of Modern Philosophy. It demonstrates by intensive textual analysis of Descartes's *Discourse* and *Meditations* that he inaugurated a new type of sophistry rather than a new way of conducting philosophy. Transcendental Sophistry is a synthesis of Renaissance humanism and Christian theology, especially the theology of creation. This striking re-evaluation of the achievement of Descartes opens the history of Western philosophy to radical reinterpretation. (publisher)

**Redpath, Peter A**. *Wisdom's Odyssey: From Philosophy to Transcendental Sophistry*. Amsterdam, Rodopi, 1997.

This book is a daring reappraisal of the history of Western philosophy through the Renaissance. It challenges the generally received view that what is called modern philosophy, beginning with Descartes, is philosophy. The thesis of this critical study is that the genuine philosophic tradition rooted in external sense experience as the measure of the intellect was obscured by a mythopoeic tradition based on inspiration. Mainly through the influence of St. Augustine, an apocryphal notion of philosophy, which conflated it with poetry and rhetoric, was transmitted through the Middle Ages to Renaissance humanists. (publisher, edited)

**Rée, Jonathan**. "Subjectivity in the Twentieth Century" in *Critical Studies: Ethics and the Subject*, Simms, Karl (ed), 17-28. Amsterdam, Rodopi, 1997.

Twentieth-century approaches to subjectivity are dominated by an anxiety not to be Descartes. This is often articulated by recommending an easy-going pluralism of "world-pictures," but this conception is incoherent—or so it is argued here, by reference to Heidegger and the early Wittgenstein. Doubts are then expressed at the idea that "subjectivity is constructed in language." At the beginning of the article, Virginia Woolf's idea that "human nature changed" in 1910 is likened to Jean-Paul Sartre's account of how the Husserlian phenomenology, by discrediting of the idea of an "inner life," called into existence a new kind of novel. But at the conclusion it is suggested that there is nothing more classically Cartesian than the idea of a break with Descartes.

**Rée, Jonathan**. Cosmopolitanism and the Experience of Nationality. *Phil Forum*, 28(1-2), 167-180, Fall-Wint 97.

This article is concerned with nationhood as a form of experience, rather than a principle of social and political organization. It argues that the experience of nationhood (or rather "internationality") is inherently delusive, ambiguous and contradictory. By reference to Kant, Russell, Hume and others, a number of "illusions of internationality" are identified, and divided into three classes: empirical, conceptual and dialectical. The third of these turns out to be particularly pernicious. It depends on the way in which the notion of "identity" oscillates between meaning an essential core of individuality, and a voluntary self-image. This illusion is linked in turn, it is argued, with the much-fetished concept of "politics." In conclusion, internationalism is sharply distinguished from cosmopolitanism, and it is argued that internationalism is tainted with the illusions of internationality, whereas cosmopolitanism is not.

**Rée, Jonathan**. Poor Bertie. *Rad Phil*, 81, 35-40, Ja-F 97.

This article is an assessment of the young Bertrand Russell (drawing on Philip Ironside, *The Social and Political Thought of Bertrand Russell* and Ray Monk, *Bertrand Russell: The Spirit of Solitude*), centered on Russell's attempt to reconstruct himself, around 1916, as an influential political thinker. In particular he was preoccupied by the contrast between "reason" and "instinct," in ways which are undoubtedly connected with his transient adoration for D.H. Lawrence. In conclusion, Russell's style as a politician is connected with his style as an amorist and as a thinker: in each case he was defeated by ambiguity.

**Reed, Edward S**. *From Soul to Mind: The Emergence of Psychology from Erasmus Darwin to William James*. New Haven, Yale Univ Pr, 1997.

*From Soul to Mind* introduces a cast that includes not only well-known scientists and philosophers (Kant, Reid, Darwin, James) but also figures important in their time who are largely forgotten today (R.H. Lotze in Germany, G.H. Lewes in Britain) and literary notables (Mary Shelley, E.T.A. Hoffmann, Edgar Allan Poe). Countering the widespread belief that psychology is the offspring of philosophy, Reed contends that modern philosophy arose when academic philosophers sought to distinguish themselves from psychologists. He places the histories of philosophy and psychology within a broad intellectual and social framework and offers a fresh perspective on the roots of the new psychology. (publisher, edited)

**Reed, J David** and Quinn, J Kevin and Browne, M Neil (& others). Honesty, Individualism, and Pragmatic Business Ethics: Implications for Corporate Hierarchy. *J Bus Ethics*, 16(12-13), 1419-1430, S 97.

The boundaries of honesty are the focal point of this exploration of the individualistic origins of modernist ethics and the consequent need for a more pragmatic approach to business ethics. The tendency of modernist ethics to see honesty as an individual responsibility is described as a contextually naive approach, one that fails to account for the interactive effect between individual choices and corporate norms. By reviewing the empirical accounts of managerial struggles with ethical dilemmas, the article arrives at the contextual preconditions for encouraging the development of reflective moral agents in modern corporations.

**Reed, Ronald**. Lost Times/Recovered Times. *Thinking*, 13(1), 34-36, 1997.

**Reese, Hayne W**. Spirituality, Belief, and Action. *J Mind Behav*, 18(1), 29-51, Wint 97.

Spirituality is only rule-governed behavior, regardless of the source of the rule and regardless of the content of the rule except that the rule must specify actually performable behavior so that consistency of the action with the belief can be assessed. The separation of action from belief is a form of alienation in a Marxian sense (which Skinner endorsed); to paraphrase Kant, beliefs without actions are empty and actions without beliefs are blind. That is, a belief that is not acted upon is literally useless and action that is not based on a belief is literally irrational. Alienation is resolved when action is based on "right" motives, which are motives based on a set of principles. Analogously, spirituality is a special kind of rule-governed behavior because the rules (beliefs) that govern this behavior (actions) are part of a coherent system that defines "rightness."(edited)

**Reese, William L**. *Dictionary of Philosophy and Religion: Eastern and Western Thought*. Atlantic Highlands, Humanities Pr, 1996.

First published in 1980, and now substantially revised and enlarged, *The Dictionary of Philosophy and Religion* presents a panorama of philosophic and religious thought, both ancient and modern, and provides access to the philosophers, their ideas, arguments, concepts, and development, and to the movements which supported and developed their thought. Not only a dictionary, the analytical and historical accounts on a vast range of topics, the select bibliographies attached to many of the entries, and the considerable cross-referencing turn the work into a true encyclopedia of philosophic endeavor. (publisher,edited)

**Reeve, C D C**. How Scientific is Aristotle's Ethics?. *Phil Inq*, 18(1-2), 77-87, Wint-Spr 96.

**Regan, Richard J** (trans). *The Human Constitution*. Cranbury, Univ of Scranton Pr, 1997.

The central position of St. Thomas Aquinas in the pantheon of Catholic thinkers along with St. Augustine of Hippo more than justifies ongoing attention to his thought and contributions to philosophy, theology and medieval culture. This volume is an anthology of the passages in his *Summa Theologiae* on human nature or the "Human Constitution" as he calls it. Richard Regan has carefully selected these passages and translated them in a way more accurate than the traditional Blackfriar's translation, especially in dealing with some of the absolutely key technical words like "esse."(publisher, edited)

**Regan, Thomas J**. Animating Rawls's Original Position. *Teach Phil*, 19(4), 357-370, D 96.

**Regan, Tom**. The Rights of Humans and Other Animals. *Ethics Behavior*, 7(2), 103-111, 1997.

Human moral rights place justified limits on what people are free to do to one another. Animals also have moral rights and arguments to support the use of animals in scientific research based on the benefits allegedly derived from animal model research are thus invalid. Animals do not belong in laboratories because placing them there, in the hope of benefits for others, violates their rights.

**Regazzini, Eugenio**. De Finetti's Reconstruction of the Bayes-Laplace Paradigm. *Erkenntnis*, 45(2 & 3), 159-176, Nov 96.

This paper includes a concise survey of the work done in compliance with de Finetti's reconstruction of the Bayes-Laplace paradigm. Section I explains that paradigm and Section 2 deals with de Finetti's criticism. Section 3 quotes some recent results connected with de Finetti's program and Section 4 provides an illustrative example.

**Regev, Motti**. Rock Aesthetics and Musics of the World. *Theor Cult Soc*, 14(3), 125-142, Ag 97.

**Reginster, Bernard**. Nietzsche on *Ressentiment* and Valuation. *Phil Phenomenol Res*, 57(2), 281-305, Je 97.

The paper examines Nietzsche's claim that valuations born out of a psychological condition he calls "*ressentiment*" are objectionable. It argues for a philosophically sound construal of this type of criticism, according to which the criticism is directed at the *agent* who holds values out of *ressentiment*, rather than at those values themselves. After presenting an analysis of *ressentiment*, the paper examines its impact on valuation and concludes with an inquiry into Nietzsche's reasons for claiming that *ressentiment* valuation is "corrupt." Specifically, the paper proposes that *ressentiment* valuation involves a form of self-deception, that such self-deception is objectionable because it undermines the integrity of the self and that the lack of such integrity ensnares the agent in a peculiar kind of practical inconsistency. The paper ends with a brief review of the problems and prospects of this interpretation.

**Regueira, José Blanco**. De cómo habitan los oscuros en lo claro. *Rev Filosof (Mexico)*, 29(87), 488-501, S-D 96.

**Reguera, Isidoro**. El Nietzsche práctico de Nolte: Nietzsche, profeta trágico de la guerra y organizador político de la aniquilación. *Rev Filosof (Spain)*, 8(15), 127-157, 1996.

Se trata de un comentario y presentación en España del controvertido libro sobre Nietzsche del Prof. Ernst Nolte. Una confrontación de Nietzsche con Marx, feminismo, socialismo, antisemitismo, etc. (edited)

**Reich, Rob**. "The Paradoxes of Education in Rorty's Liberal Utopia" in *Philosophy of Education (1996)*, Margonis, Frank (ed), 342-351. Urbana, Phil Education Soc, 1997.

Far from providing a safe haven for and exhortation to become ironic self-creators, Richard Rorty's vision of education within his liberal utopia describe a system in which only a select elite are afforded the opportunity at self-edification. Rorty's liberal utopia is riddled with inequity. Furthermore, because Rorty hopes to foster self-creating ironists who will likely have conflicting views, he needs to supplement his contingent notion of solidarity with a description of how citizens are educated to be liberals. Educating for self-edification is not enough.

**Reichlin, Massimo**. The Argument from Potential: A Reappraisal. *Bioethics*, 11(1), 1-23, Ja 97.

Several criticisms of the argument from potential are reported. It is noted that such criticisms are inspired by two similarly wrong interpretations of potentiality, one confusing it will possibility and another with probability. A brief analysis of the original Aristotelian context in which the concept emerged shows that potentiality cannot be thought of as indicating the provision of some empirical facts in the future, but must rather be referred to the inherent ontological structure of the being in question. It is then argued that such an Aristotelian concept can be useful to express the dynamic structure of the person, as it must be understood according to contemporary phenomenological personalism. In the light of this philosophical tradition, the embryo can be viewed as a being already possessing the human nature and actively developing its potential for personhood: it also follows that human nature must not be understood as a static and predetermined essence, but rather as the principle of becoming and movement toward further achievements.

**Reichlin, Massimo** and Cattorini, Paolo. Persistent Vegetative State: A Presumption to Treat. *Theor Med*, 18(3), 263-281, S 97.

The article briefly analyzes the concept of a person, arguing that personhood does not coincide with the actual enjoyment of certain intellectual capacities, but is coextensive with the embodiment of a human individual. Since in PVS patients we can observe a human individual functioning as a whole, we must conclude that these patients are still human persons, even if in a condition of extreme impairment. It is then argued that some forms of minimal treatment may not be futile for these patients; they may constitute a form of respect for their human dignity and benefit these patients, even if they are not aware of that. The best policy would be to provide, as a general rule, artificial nutrition and hydration to PVS patients: this treatment could be withdrawn, after a period of observation and reflection by the family and proxies, on the basis of the proxies' objection to the continuation or the patient's advance directives specifically referring to this situation. (edited)

**Reichling, Mary J**. Music, Imagination, and Play. *J Aes Educ*, 31(1), 41-55, Spr 97.

The association between play and music is long standing. A theoretical framework for the function of imagination in music is the basis for examining the extent to which musical experience bears the characteristics of play. Formal and functional likenesses are suggested between the real and make-believe in both play and music. Interpretation occurs along the continuum of imagination ranging from fantasy and making present the absent through figurative imagination, imagining X as Y, to literal imagination, perception and recognition. Each of these, as well as spatio-temporal considerations, are explored in the relation between play and musical experience.

**Reichling, Mary J**. On the Question of Method in Philosophical Research. *Phil Music Educ Rev*, 4(2), 117-127, Fall 96.

How should philosophical research method be defined and how does it impact research in the field of music? Method emerges from the context of a study as well as from a reading of the philosophical literature itself. While method cannot be articulated definitively for all instances, materials and tools of method include specific uses of language, analysis, criticism, and construction. It is suggested

AUTHOR INDEX 865 Reiss, Michael J

that the concept of method be re-envisioned as dynamic and propulsive rather than a static step-by-step model. Applications are offered for the teaching of philosophical method in music research classes.

**Reid, Jeffrey**. Hegel's Critique of Solger: The Problem of Scientific Communication (in French). *Arch Phil*, 60(2), 255-264, Ap-Je 97.

Solger's philosophical failure stems from the form of expression he applies to speculative content. Hegel's review of his works attempts to show that the only expression appropriate to speculative truth is a language which is itself the concrete expression of truth.

**Reid, Mark**. Narrative and Fission: A Review Essay of Marya Schechtman's *The Constitution of Selves*. *Phil Psych*, 10(2), 211-219, Je 97.

This book presents, in method, logical form and philosophical content, a counterproposal to mainstream personal identity theory. The latter's purported conflation of logical questions, i.e., reidentification with characterization, leads to an implausible reductionism about selves. A self-constituting narrative is the basis for identity and contra reductionism, the ontological primitive of a person. As a dynamic valuational and intentional system, the narrative meaningfully constructs the autobiographical past through memory and both causally directs and emotively anticipates the experiences and form of future selves. Schechtman's account, in contrast to mainstream theories, rightly connects identity to those four features that weigh heavily in our values, viz. survival, self-concern, responsibility and compensation. Though bold and original, the account dispels a couple of important issues along with its rejection of mainstream theory. These issues, encountered most notably through fission cases, are taken up in the evaluation with a "narrative split".

**Reif, Alison F** and Rainbolt, George. Crime, Property, and Justice: The Ethics of Civil Forfeiture. *Pub Affairs Quart*, 11(1), 39-55, Ja 97.

This article explores the moral status of civil forfeiture law. It argues that many civil forfeitures are morally unproblematic and many have serious moral defects. Some civil forfeitures are morally defective because they result in punishments which do not fit the crime. Some civil forfeitures are morally defective because the procedures used are not proportional to the possible legal outcome. Recent U.S. Supreme Court civil forfeiture cases are examined in some detail. Possible modifications of civil forfeiture law are considered and it is argued that while modifications are necessary, elimination of civil forfeiture is not morally required.

**Reiman, Jeffrey**. Abortion, Infanticide, and the Asymmetric Value of Human Life. *J Soc Phil*, 27(3), 181-200, Wint 96.

**Reimao, Cassiano**. Dialéctica e História em J.P. Sartre. *Rev Port Filosof*, 52(1-4), 713-735, Ja-D 96.

The present article sets out to illustrate Sartre's thought which, by placing the ethical primacy of man as subject of history, puts in evidence, as a supreme form of dialectic rationality, the way to articulate, in human history, liberty and necessity. Dialectic, as rationality, must occur as something related to whatever man realises; man cannot be a cosmic fatality; therefore, Sartre rejects nature's dialectic. However, the development of history is not merely an event with no mediation. There were only a dialectical as a rational reason for history if man undergoes the dialectic to the extent that he contributes to it and makes it as long as he suffers it. (edited)

**Reimer, Marga**. Could There Have Been Unicorns?. *Int J Phil Stud*, 5(1), 35-51, Mr 97.

Kripke and Dummett disagree over whether or not there could have been unicorns. Kripke thinks that there could not have been; Dummett thinks otherwise. I argue that Kripke is correct: there are no counterfactual situations properly describable as ones in which there would have been unicorns. In attempting to establish this claim, I argue that Dummett's critique of an argument (reminiscent of an argument of Kripke's) to the conclusion that there could not have been unicorns, is vitiated by a conflation of two superficially similar, though importantly different, claims. I then attempt to provide an account of the counter-intuitiveness of Kripke's position, arguing that the claim that there could not have been unicorns is best understood as a *semantic*, rather than *metaphysical*, claim. Finally, I provide a brief argument on behalf of the semantics of species terms that appears to underpin Kripke's position.

**Reimer, Marga**. Quotation Marks: Demonstratives or Demonstrations?. *Analysis*, 56(3), 131-141, Jl 96.

**Reimer, Marga**. What do Belief Ascribers Really Mean? A Reply to Stephen Schiffer. *Pac Phil Quart*, 77(4), 404-423, D 96.

Stephen Schiffer has recently claimed that the currently popular "hidden-indexical" theory of belief reports is an implausible theory of such reports. His central argument for this claim is based on what he refers to as the "meaning-intention" problem. In this paper, I claim that the meaning-intention problem is powerless against the hidden-indexical theory of belief reports. I further contend that the theory is in fact a plausible theory of such reports.

**Reinders, Hans S**. A Threat to Disabled Persons? On the Genetics Approach to Developmental Disabilities. *Bioethics Forum*, 12(3), 3-10, Fall 96.

This essay explores the claim that the genetics approach to intellectual disability does not imply a negative evaluation of disabled persons because there is a distinction between the person and the condition. Opponents of this claim deny the validity of the distinction. After identifying the presuppositions of the debate, the author discusses positive versions of the argument based on this distinction and suggests defenders of this distinction have committed the fallacy of genetization, which reduces personal identity to its biological basis.

**Reinders, Hans S**. The Ethics of Normalization. *Cambridge Quart Healthcare Ethics*, 6(4), 481-489, Fall 97.

Theoretical reflection on the normalization of mentally disabled persons has concentrated on the exchange between the disabled, their families and professional caregivers. Largely absent from this picture are members of the receiving community in which the disabled are supposed to participate. This essay explores the reason for this absence and explains why the normalization process is necessarily dependent on a positive commitment on the part of these members. Moreover, it explains how the failure to address this aspect in normalization philosophy may be related to the use of rights discourse in arguing for change on behalf of the disabled. The essay concludes by pointing to a serious limitation of the rights perspective in this connection and argues for a new orientation on the moral meaning of "community care".

**Reinhart, Tanya**. Quantifier Scope: How Labor is Divided between QR and Choice Functions. *Ling Phil*, 20(4), 335-397, Ag 97.

**Reinsmith, William**. A Brief Response to Jack Russell Weinstein. *Inquiry (USA)*, 15(3), 89-91, Spr 96.

The author responds to Weinstein's article, "Three Types of Critical Thinking about Religion: A Response to William Reinsmith" (*Inquiry*, XIV: 4 Summer, "95), which claimed that Reinsmith was guilty of oversimplification in regard to a religious framework and of ignoring the broader communitarian aspect of religion out of which all personal religious experience arises. Reinsmith notes that in speaking to readers on both sides of the issue he purposely took a perennialist perspective—a panoramic rather than a detailed look at religion for the sake of clarity. He also believes that Weinstein gives the specific religious community too large a role in personal development. Reinsmith maintains that a religious community is never more than a contextual factor in the individual's spiritual growth.

**Reinsmith, William**. Cultural Conditioning: The Dark Underside of Multiculturalism (Part Two: A Way Out). *Inquiry (USA)*, 14(2), 78-85, Wint 94.

Having pointed out in part one that in our enthusiasm for the overthrow of objectivity (the cultural project of the Enlightenment) little or no attention was given to cultural conditioning which forms the dark side of multiculturalism, Reinsmith states that there is a way out of this trap. He posits a transcultural liberation which represents a break with one's particular frame of reference into a spiritual dimension involving a new form of consciousness. Incorporating the insights of three Eastern thinkers (Aubrey Menen, Joseph Krishnamurti and Joseph Chilton Pierce) each of whom make use of *The Upanishads*, he elucidates the process by which one can reach a new kind of objectivity—or more properly—a fusion of subject and object, a realm of unbounded awareness.

**Reinsmith, William**. Religious Life and Critical Thought: Do They Need Each Other?. *Inquiry (USA)*, 14(4), 66-73, Sum 95.

The author attempts to make an accommodation between religious experience and critical thought. After defining in some detail the terms "critical thought" and "religion," Reinsmith suggests that there is a positive role for critical thinking within the religious domain other than the traditional adversarial one. Using Buddhist meditation practice as an example he shows how the activities of observation, mindfulness and, healthy doubt can work to foster authentic religious development in a sincere practitioner. Reinsmith concludes that to remain free of delusion, religious experience must incorporate critical thought as a cleansing tool, while critical thought needs religion to understand it's higher usefulness.

**Reinsmith, William**. Response to Richard Carrier. *Inquiry (USA)*, 16(3), 92-93, Spr 97.

The author responds to Carrier's claim (in "Do Religious Life and Critical Thought Need Each Other? A Reply to Reinsmith") that in singling out meditation as a key to the religious quest he has chosen a bad example since it is a behaviour rather than a religious state of belief. Reinsmith points out that he focused on "practice" because that is where the real dynamic of spiritual growth lies. He wanted to see if certain aspects of critical thought were compatible with this journey. He also defends his view that critical thought as a debunking device and as a cleansing tool for maintaining clarity are two different activities (against Carrier's claim that they are identical.) The former is purely destructive, the latter more positive.

**Reisch, George A**. How Postmodern was Neurath's Idea of Unity of Science?. *Stud Hist Phil Sci*, 28(3), 439-451, S 97.

**Reiser, Stanley Joel** and Bulger, Ruth Ellen. The Social Responsibilities of Biological Scientists. *Sci Eng Ethics*, 3(2), 137-143, Ap 97.

Biological scientists, like scientists in other disciplines, are uncertain about whether or how to use their knowledge and time to provide society with insight and guidance in handling the effects of inventions and discoveries. This article addresses this issue. It presents a typography of structures in which scientists may contribute to social understanding and decisions. It describes the different ways in which these contributions can be made. Finally it develops the ethical arguments that justify the view that biological scientists have social responsibilities.

**Reiss, Michael J**. Teaching about Homosexuality and Heterosexuality. *J Moral Educ*, 26(3), 343-352, S 97.

Should schools teach about homosexuality and heterosexuality and if so how? This paper outlines arguments both in favour of, and against, such teaching and concludes that, on balance, schools of 11-16/18-years-olds should teach about sexual orientation provided certain specified conditions are met. The author then defends the notion that to teach about sexual orientation is to teach about a controversial issue, but notes that few, if any, of the published approaches to teaching in this area treat it as such. He goes on to examine both the specific aims and possible approaches to teaching about homosexuality and heterosexuality. Good teaching in this area should enable 14-16-year-old students to become better informed about people's sexual orientations; it should help them better to understand each other's positions; and it should allow them to clarify their own values and attitudes.

**Reiss, Michael J**. The Value(s) of Sex Education. *J Moral Educ*, 26(3), 253-255, S 97.

This paper introduces a special issue of the *Journal of Moral Education* on 'Moral Values and Sex Education' which I edited. The issue explores the question as to what should be the ethical framework within which sex education takes place. Can a single framework be identified or do we need a multiplicity of frameworks? Some of the authors propose general solutions; others focus on particular questions—for example, teaching about sexual identity—and then use these to illuminate more general considerations. In addition to the main articles, there are a number of book reviews and reviews of curriculum materials.

**Reiss, Michael J** and Straughan, Roger. *Improving Nature?*. New York, Cambridge Univ Pr, 1996.

Little more than a decade ago the term 'genetic engineering' was hardly known outside research laboratories. By now, though, its use is widespread. Those in favour of genetic engineering—and those against it—tell us that it has the potential to change our lives perhaps more than any other scientific or technological advance. But what are the likely consequences of genetic engineering? Is it ethically acceptable? Should we be trying to improve on nature? The authors, a biologist and a moral philosopher, examine the implications of genetic engineering in every aspect of our lives. The underlying science is explained in a way easily understood by a general reader and the moral and ethical considerations that arise are fully discussed. Throughout, the authors clarify the issues involved so that readers can make up their own minds about these controversial issues. (publisher)

**Reiss, Timothy J**. Denying the Body? Memory and the Dilemmas of History in Descartes. *J Hist Ideas*, 57(4), 587-607, O 96.

**Reitan, Eric**. The Ethics of Community: The Ethical and Metaphysical Presuppositions of AVP. *Acorn*, 7(1), 19-28, Spr-Sum 92.

**Reitan, Eric A**. Thomistic Natural Philosophy and the Scientific Revolution. *Mod Sch*, 73(3), 265-282, Mr 96.

**Reitan, Eric H**. Deep Ecology and the Irrelevance of Morality. *Environ Ethics*, 18(4), 411-424, Winter 96.

Both Arne Naess and Warwick Fox have argued that deep ecology, in terms of "Self-realization," is essentially nonmoral. I argue that the attainment of the ecological Self does not render morality in the richest sense "superfluous," as Fox suggests. To the contrary, the achievement of the ecological Self is a *precondition* for being a truly moral person, both from the perspective of a robust Kantian moral framework and from the perspective of Aristotelian virtue ethics. The opposition between self-regard and morality is a false one. The two are the same. The ecological philosophy of Naess and Fox is an environmental ethic in the grand tradition of moral philosophy.

**Reitemeier, Paul J**. Perhaps We All Be Heroes. *J Clin Ethics*, 7(4), 307-309, Wint 96.

I argue that heroic acts in bioethics are difficult to identify objectively, but Freedman's examples of losing one's employment over a principled stand is too extreme to be a useful standard. On one analysis, the contextual nature of consultation in clinical settings may render all of bioethics "heroic" in a limited sense. Finally, the goals and processes of bioethics are themselves ill defined and persons with empirical experience of heroic acts by bioethicists have never been asked for their evaluative views, but perhaps should be.

**Reitemeier, Paul J** and Derse, Arthur R and Spike, Jeffrey. Retiring the Pacemaker. *Hastings Center Rep*, 27(1), 24-26, Ja-F 97.

**Remaud, Oliver**. Vico lector de Espinosa (Sobre la represión de la *Etica*, II, 7 en la *Scienza Nuova*, 1744, 238). *Cuad Vico*, 7/8, 191-206, 1997.

Vico's references to Spinoza are very scarce, but there is a conspicuous parallelism between *SN* paragraph 238 and *Etica*; II, 7. The lexical relationship, far from being an accident, is a very interpretative key for the *SN*. However, Vico's reprehension, by inserting time into the connection between the order of ideas and the order of things, involves a critic of Spinoza's axiom. This is something that allows the philosophical principles of the *Scienza Nuova* to be tested here again.

**Remmel, J B** and Knight, J F and Ash, C J. Quasi-Simple Relations in Copies of a given Recursive Structure. *Annals Pure Applied Log*, 86(3), 203-218, Jl 97.

**Remnant, Peter** (trans) and Bennett, Jonathan (trans). *New Essays on Human Understanding*. New York, Cambridge Univ Pr, 1996.

In the *New Essays on Human Understanding*, Leibniz argues chapter by chapter with John Locke's *Essay Concerning Human Understanding*, challenging his views about knowledge, personal identity, God, morality, mind and matter, nature versus nurture, logic and language, and a host of other topics. The work is a series of sharp, deep discussions by one great philosopher of the work of another. Leibniz's references to his contemporaries and his discussions of the ideas and institutions of the age make this a fascinating and valuable document in the history of ideas. (publisher,edited)

**Rempel, Richard A** and Russell, Bertrand. *Principles of Social Reconstruction*. New York, Routledge, 1997.

This book, originally entitled *Why Men Fight*, is generally seen as the fullest expression of Russell's political philosophy. Russell argues that after the experience of the great war the individualistic approach of traditional liberalism had reached its limits. Political theory must be based on the motivating forces of creativity and impulse, rather than on competition. Both are best fostered in the family, in education, and in religion—of each of which Russell proceeds to discuss. (publisher, edited)

**Remus, Harold**. Moses and the Thaumaturges: Philo's *De Vita Mosis* as a Rescue Operation. *Laval Theol Phil*, 52(3), 665-680, O 96.

Philo's extended treatment of Balaam in the *De Vita Mosis*, denigrating him as a mercenary technician, stands in sharp contrast to his portrait of Moses, the true prophet as well as philosopher-god-king, priest, thaumaturge and mystagogue—the answer to the longing of Philo's contemporaries for just such a figure. The writing thus serves to rescue Moses from possible misunderstandings of Moses as a mere thaumaturge or as a magician, a reputation attested in a variety of sources. Rather, Moses' command over nature derives from the revelation, received on the mountain, of the noetic reality—knowledge he employs for the benefaction of others. The *De Vita Mosis* thus sets the great leader apart from Balaam-like thaumaturges and magicians in Philo's Egypt, a land noted for such figures. The article situates the writing in a long tradition of rhetoric and biography employed as vehicles both of polemic and praise.

**Renaud, Michel**. A Universidade na Sociedade Actual. *Rev Port Filosof*, 52(1-4), 737-762, Ja-D 96.

**Rendón Rojas, Miguel Angel** and Okolova, Marina Dimitrieva. La re-presentación extrema del estetismo, del intelectualismo y del moralismo en política. *Analogia*, 10(2), 151-174, 1996.

The aestheticism with its cult for beauty, the intellectualism for truth, the moralism for goodness, can lead to political totalitarianism. This happens when one of these values (beauty, truth, goodness) becomes unlimited, without any kind of relation with the others, and on the other hand, when an excessive subjectivism takes a place and the leader's finite ego change to a transcendental ego representative or substitute of God. This political power legislates totally convinced that its special mission is to actualize the central value.

**Rensink, Arend**. Algebra and Theory of Order-Deterministic Pomsets. *Notre Dame J Form Log*, 37(2), 283-320, Spr 96.

This paper is about partially ordered multisets (pomsets for short). We investigate a particular class of pomsets that we call *order-deterministic*, properly including all partially ordered *sets*, which satisfies a number of interesting properties: among other things, it forms a *distributive lattice* under pomset prefix (hence prefix closed sets of order-deterministic pomsets are prime algebraic) and it constitutes a *reflective subcategory* of the category of all pomsets. For the order-deterministic pomsets we develop an algebra with a sound and ($w$-) complete equational theory. The operators in the algebra are *disjoint union* of pomsets. This theory is then extended in order to capture *refinement* of pomsets by incorporating homomorphisms between models as objects in the algebra and homomorphism application as a new operator.

**Rentto, Juha-Pekka**. Thomasian Natural Law and the Is-Ought Question. *Vera Lex*, 14(1-2), 41-46, 1994.

**Renz, David O** and Eddy, William B. Organizations, Ethics, and Health Care: Building an Ethics Infrastructure for a New Era. *Bioethics Forum*, 12(2), 29-39, Sum 96.

The changes occurring in today's health care environment, especially as driven by the emphasis on managed care strategies, focus attention on ethical questions, practices, and implications for all those involved in health care, including health care professionals, patients, administrators, and governing boards. These implications need to be studied and strategies developed to build an ethical infrastructure that will support health care organizations in this changing environment.

**Reppy, Judith** (ed) and Hampson, Fen Osler (ed). *Earthly Goods: Environmental Change and Social Justice*. Ithaca, Cornell Univ Pr, 1996.

The essays address the role of science in global change and argue that Western science does not provide morally disinterested solutions to environmental problems. They discuss the role of state and substate actors in the international politics of the environment and then use accounts of actual negotiations to argue for the centrality of social justice in reaching desirable and equitable agreements. They conclude that a framework for social justice under conditions of global environmental change must include community values and provide for participatory structures to arbitrate among competing interests. (publisher,edited)

**Requate, Angela**. R.G. Collingwood's Pragmatist Approach to Metaphysics. *Int Stud Phil*, 29(2), 57-71, 1997.

Collingwood suggests that metaphysical questions are absolute presuppositions, which can never be verified because they are never propounded or stated as propositions. He offers a pragmatic solution by saying that the use of absolute presuppositions in scientific inquiry consists in their "logical efficacy". Since their "being" is their functioning, absolute presuppositions allow for a pragmatic justification as a consequence metaphysics no longer establishes categorical universal propositions about Being but investigates singular propositions about what people of a certain time believed about the world's general nature. Thus Collingwood reforms metaphysics into a historical science by a pragmatic argument.

**Rescher, Nicholas**. "Progress and the Future" in *The Idea of Progress*, McLaughlin, Peter (ed), 103-119. Hawthorne, de Gruyter, 1997.

**Rescher, Nicholas**. Counterfactuals in Pragmatic Perspective. *Rev Metaph*, 50(1), 35-61, S 96.

**Rescher, Nicholas**. Leibniz on Possible Worlds. *Stud Leibniz*, 28(2), 129-162, 1996.

Leibniz' Theorie der möglichen Welten ist ein komplexes Ideengebäude, das er im Lauf der Jahre in verschiedenen Gelegenheitsschriften fortentwickelte. Hier wird diese Theorie systematisch dargestellt. Es werden sowohl die logischen Aspekte der Leibnizschen Möglichkeitstheorie erläutert als auch ihre Verbindungen mit Leibniz' Lehre von Raum und Zeit sowie ihre Beziehungen zu Leibniz' Theologie und insbesondere seiner Schöpfungslehre.

AUTHOR INDEX 867 Restall, Greg

**Rescher, Nicholas**. *Objectivity: The Obligations of Impersonal Reason.* Notre Dame, Univ Notre Dame Pr, 1997.

Rescher employs reasoned argumentation in making the case for restoring objectivity to a place of prominence in philosophic and social discourse. By tracing the source of objectivity back to the very core of rationality itself, Rescher is able to locate objectivity's reason for being deep in our nature as rational animals. His argument against the negativist and relativistic tendencies of contemporary times includes an examination of the flaws and fallacies at work in the deliberations of those who dismiss objectivity as obsolete and untenable. Rescher takes to task the cultural relativism of contemporary social science and social theory, as well as that of liberalistic political correctness and the postmodern aversion to the normative. (publisher, edited)

**Rescher, Nicholas**. Technological Escalation and the Exploration Model of Natural Science. *Sorites*, 6-17, My 96.

1) Our cognitive competence is well accounted for by our evolutionary niche in the world's scheme of things. 2) The development of inquiry in natural science is best understood on analogy with exploration—to be sure, not in the geographical mode 'but rather exploration' in nature's parametric space of such physical quantities as temperature, pressure and field strength. 3) The technology-mediated exploration at issue here involves an interaction between us humans and nature that becomes increasingly difficult (and expensive) as we move ever farther away from the home base of the accustomed environment of our evolutionary heritage. The course of scientific progress accordingly involves a *technological escalation*—an ascent to successively higher levels of technological sophistication that is unavoidably required for the production of the requisite observational data.

**Rescher, Nicholas**. The Promise of Process Philosophy. *Process Stud*, 25, 55-71, 1996.

**Resende Araújo, Cícero Romao**. Hume on Virtues and Rights. *Manuscrito*, 19(2), 145-164, O 96.

In this paper I explore how Hume's theory of justice brings "right" and "virtue" together and point out some problems that his approach creates. First, I briefly describe Hume's general moral theory. I then take up the difference between "virtue" and "right" and, finally, Hume's attempt to harmonize these two terms by means of the notion of "artificial virtue".

**Reshotko, Naomi**. A Bastard Kind of Reasoning: The Argument from the Sciences and the Introduction of the Receptacle in Plato's *Timaeus*. *Hist Phil Quart*, 14(1), 121-137, Ja 97.

At *Timaeus* 52b Plato says that the *Receptacle* is understood via a "bastard" form of reasoning. The reasoning to which Plato refers is importantly similar to the *Argument from the Sciences* which is considered to be Plato's strongest argument for the *Forms*. Although these two pieces of ontological reasoning are the same, Plato's use of the term bastard is not meant to impugn that reasoning in either case. Plato is using the term *descriptively* to capture a difference in the ontological presuppositions with which one launches the argument in each case. Plato might be asserting that ontological reasoning concerning the existence of abstract objects cannot be evaluated by the same criteria used to evaluate other kinds of reasoning, as the establishment of such criteria already assumes the existence of such objects and, so, is circular and *illegitimate*.

**Reshotko, Naomi**. Do Explanatory Desire Attributions Generate Opaque Contexts?. *Ratio*, 9(2), 153-170, S 96.

Many philosophers assert that psychological verbs generate opaque contexts and that the object of a psychological verb cannot be replaced with a coreferring expression *salva veritate* as the objects of nonpsychological verbs can be. I argue that the logical and linguistic concerns which govern this assertion do not transfer to observational and experimental situations because the criteria that we use in order to verify that an observed subject has one hypothesized desire rather than another provide inconclusive evidence when we don't allow for all regular substitutions in psychological contexts. This becomes more obvious when we contextualize intentional behavior within the appropriate framework by recognizing that, in order to make sense of any desire attribution, we must understand the subject experiencing the desire to be pursuing each desired situation as a means to a further overarching goals. I conclude that the object of desire should always be read *de re*.

**Reshotko, Naomi**. Plato's *Lysis*: A Socratic Treatise on Desire and Attraction. *Apeiron*, 30(1), 1-17, Mr 97.

In the *Lysis*, Socrates develops a general theory of attraction to which he refers using the word *philia*. Because he takes human friendship to be a special case of desire—which is itself a form of attraction—Socrates also uses the term *philia* to refer to human friendship. In order to appreciate what Socrates says about *philia* between humans, we must first understand what he says about *philia* generally.

**Resnick, David** and Fisher, Bonnie and Bennett, Stephen Earl. "Speaking of Politics in the United States: Who Talks to Whom, Why, and Why Not" in *Political Dialogue: Theories and Practices*, Esquith, Stephen L (ed), 263-293. Amsterdam, Rodopi, 1996.

Although normative political theorists have argued that citizens talking with other citizens about public affairs is essential in a democracy, empirically oriented political scientists have tended to ignore political discussions. This paper reviews what normative theories have said about political conversations and then draws on National Election Studies and Social Surveys to plumb the extent and breadth of political conversations in the United States. The paper also explores who talks about public affairs, with whom they speak and why some people discuss politics while others do not.

**Resnik, D** and Thomsen, Marshall. The Effectiveness of the Erratum in Avoiding Error Propagation in Physics. *Sci Eng Ethics*, 1(3), 231-240, Jl 95.

The propagation of errors in physics research is studied, with particular attention being paid to the effectiveness of the erratum in avoiding error propagation. We study the citation history of 17 physics papers which have significant errata associated with them. It would appear that the existence of an erratum does not significantly decrease the frequency with which a paper is cited and in most cases the erratum is *not* cited along with the original paper. The authors comment on implications for the responsibilities of authors.

**Resnik, David B**. A Proposal for a New System of Credit Allocation in Science. *Sci Eng Ethics*, 3(3), 237-243, Jl 97.

This essay discusses some of the problems with current authorship practices and puts forward a proposal for a new system of credit allocation: in published works, scientists should more clearly define the responsibilities and contributions of members of research teams and should distinguish between different roles, such as author, statistician, technician, grant writer, data collector, and so forth.

**Resnik, David B**. Adaptationism: Hypothesis or Heuristic?. *Biol Phil*, 12(1), 39-50, Ja 97.

Elliott Sober (1987, 1993) and Orzack and Sober (forthcoming) argue that adaptationism is a very general hypothesis that can be tested by testing various particular hypotheses that invoke natural selection to explain the presence of traits in populations of organisms. In this paper, I challenge Sober's claim that adaptationism is an hypothesis and I argue that it is best viewed as a heuristic (or research strategy). Biologists would still have good reasons for employing this research strategy even if it turns out that natural selection is not the most important cause of evolution.

**Resnik, David B**. Social Epistemology and the Ethics of Research. *Stud Hist Phil Sci*, 27(4), 565-586, D 96.

This essay explores the connections between social epistemology and the ethics of scientific research and defends twelve principles of research ethics. Ethical standards in science can be justified because 1) they are norms that promote cooperation and trust among scientists and therefore, play a key role in achieving science's aims, and 2) they follow from the application of general, ethical principles to science. Thus, fraud is unethical because it interferes with the acquisition of knowledge and because it is a form of lying, which is morally wrong.

**Resnik, David B**. The Morality of Human Gene Patents. *Kennedy Inst Ethics J*, 7(1), 43-61, Mr 97.

This paper discusses the morality of patenting human genes and genetic technologies. After examining arguments on different sides of the issue, the paper concludes that there are, at present, no compelling reasons to prohibit the extension of current patent laws to the realm of human genetics. However, since advances in genetics are likely to have profound social implications, the most prudent course of action demands a continual re-examination of genetics laws and policies in light of ongoing developments in science and technology.

**Resnik, Michael D**. "On Positing Mathematical Objects" in *Frege: Importance and Legacy*, Schirn, Matthias (ed), 45-69. Hawthorne, de Gruyter, 1996.

I discuss Frege's rejection of "creative definitions", his denigration of Dedekind's creating systems of new mathematical objects and his critique of Hilbert's postulationalism. I suggest that when mathematicians use axioms to introduce new objects they are positing the existence of objects having the structure required by the axioms and recognizing that evidence for the consistency of the axioms counts as evidence that objects of such a structure exist. I emphasize, however, that to posit an object is not create it but rather to hypothesize it. So the view combines Dedekind's structuralism and Hilbert's postulationalism while avoiding Frege's objections.

**Resta, Caterina**. "Il mito dell'autoctonia del pensiero (Note su Hegel, Fichte, Heidegger)" in *Geofilosofia*, Bonesio, Luisa (ed), 13-37. Sondrio, Lyasis, 1996.

Il lavoro intende decostruire il mito dell'autoctonia attraverso la filosofia della storia di Hegel, i discorsi all nazione tedesca di Fichte, la concezione del radicamento in Heidegger. In che modo è ancora possibile pensare l'essere-a-casa (*zu Hause sein*) nell'epoca dello sradicamento planetario, senza per questo ricadere nelle declinazioni *Blut und Boden* del nazionalsocialismo? Mentre per Hegel si tratte di un'autoctonia pensata come radicamento in un pensiero speculativo-autoriflessivo e per Fichte di un'autoctonia intesa come originaria appartenenza a una lingua (*Ursprache*), solo con Heidegger la rivendicazione del radicamento attinge non ad un pensiero dell'autoctonia, ma a quello di una *radicale* eteronomia.

**Resta, Caterina** (ed) and Baldino, Marco (ed) and Bonesio, Luisa (ed). *Geofilosofia*. Sondrio, Lyasis, 1996.

Primo tentativo italiano organico e ad ampio raggio, il volume *Geofilosofia* fornisce un'idea efficace del dialogo che si può intessere, da molteplici punti di osservazione, a partire dalla prospettiva geofilosofica: gli autori (Jacques Derrida, Jean-Luc Nancy, Otto Pöggeler, François Makowski, Vincenzo Vitiello, Pierluigi Cervellati, Guglielmo Scaramellini, Caterina Resta, Luisa Bonesio, Alessandro Marcenaro) si interrogano sul senso e le possibilità attuali dell'abitare sulla terra: riflessione sul senso del luogo, dell'identità, del paesaggio, dell'urbanistica, dell'Europa a venire; ma anche la rivendicazione dell'appartenenza, delle identità locali, il mondialismo, l'omologazione delle dimensioni culturali nella tecnoeconomia, la progettazione degli spazi tra salvaguardia e sfrenata urbanizzazione, le dimensioni di frontiera, l'emergenza ecologica, e il paesaggio, considerato come il risultato di una cooperazione complessa fra cultura e fisionomia naturale.

**Restall, Greg**. Display Logic and Gaggle Theory. *Rep Math Log*, 29, 133-146, 1995.

This paper is a revised version of a talk given at the *Logic and Logical Philosophy* conference in Poland in September 1995. In it, I sketch the connections between Nuel Belnap's *Display Logic* and J. Michael Dunn's *Gaggle Theory.*

**Restivo, Sal** and Bauchspies, Wenda K. Science, Social Theory, and Science Criticism. *Commun Cog*, 29(2), 249-272, 1996.

The popularization and public understanding of science must necessarily now deal with cultural and social studies of science and not simply 'science' in its traditional sense (that is, as a label for the methods, findings, and authority of the physical and natural sciences). At the same time, theories and criticisms of science must be alert to the implications of postmodernist and multicultural dimensions of science in/and society. This paper, then, is a contribution to the dialogue between science studies and science that we believe should inform discourse on the popularization and public understanding of science. (edited)

**Reuscher, Jay**. *A Concordance to the Critique of Pure Reason*. New York, Lang, 1996.

The Concordance is designed around units of philosophical sense whose limits in the text are indicated to the line. Unlike research tools based merely on the occurrence of key words (e.g., *cause*), it provides precise and complete information about not only the location but also the diversity of content in all the items covered by its survey. Furthermore it provides the capability for tracing the family of topics to which a particular text may belong. In short, the Concordance tells you as much as possible about a text before you look it up. (publisher, edited)

**Revelli, Marco**. La nuova destra. *Iride*, 9(18), 361-365, Ag 96.

Quella della quale si parla in questo articolo è la nuova destra. La sua fortuna è legata alla crisi della sinistra, che si è identificata con l'esistente. Se la modernità non viene più criticata dalla sinistra (che ha perso ogni differenza rispetto alla destra), si crea spazio per la critica antimoderna, tradizionalista, della modernità. Così, la nuova destra ha potuto svolgere il ruolo di unica opposizione culturale esistente, critica della cattiva modernità.

**Revilla, Carmen**. La recuperación de la palabra: Perspectivas hermenéuticas sobre la cuestión del lenguaje. *Convivium*, 10, 88-110, 1997.

The hermeneutic approach to language, in its Gadamerian version, constitutes an important contribution to the discussion between the various positions in which the thought of this century reflects the problem of the incapacity of language to articulate the experience of the world, in order to make possible the exercise of practical rationality. The aim of this paper is to present the perspective from which this intervention acquires particular protagonism in the philosophy of recent decades and to discuss some of the possibilities of development which have been proposed in the debate.

**Rey, Georges**. "A Not 'Merely Empirical' Argument for a Language of Thought" in *AI, Connectionism and Philosophical Psychology, 1995*, Tomberlin, James E (ed), 201-222. Atascadero, Ridgeview, 1995.

**Reyes Oribe, Beatriz Eugenia**. La finalidad de la naturaleza humana: Alcance y actualidad de la cuestión. *Sapientia*, 52(201), 159-173, 1997.

**Reymond, Bernard**. Jean Calvin et la triste richesse: Du travail, du loisir et du salut de l'âme. *Rev Theol Phil*, 129(1), 51-66, 1997.

The Calvinist quasi elimination of the spiritual significance of the day of the rest symbolizes well the opposition between active Protestant asceticism of monastic theology. Weber's great fresco of Protestantism, cradle of the spirit of capitalism, suggestive as it is in other respects, affirms continuity between the two ways of asceticism while completely neglecting their profound difference, even contrast. Far from being mere matter for historical and erudite research, this lively contrast is still at work in contemporary minds, as is shown by the debate between Weber and Scheler, which goes far beyond the limits of a controversy between historians. In effect, this debate opposes two fundamental attitudes of the mind and two ways of conceiving and practicing philosophy represented today in the respective inheritors of empiricism (and utilitarianism) and phenomenology.

**Reynolds, Andrew**. The Incongruity of Peirce's Tychism. *Trans Peirce Soc*, 33(3), 704-721, Sum 97.

Two distinct and irreducible notions of chance are identified in Peirce's thesis of indeterminism: a formal notion of independence and a metaphysical notion of spontaneous freedom from all law. The first appears in Peirce's invocation of statistical mechanics to explain temporal asymmetry. The second appears in his theory of a stochastic and irreversible principle of self-organization. The one involves a Bernoulli series of independent events, the other a chain of increasingly dependent events leading to correlated behaviour. Reasons are given for supposing that Peirce was unclear about the distinct and possibly incompatible natures of these two applications of the notion of chance.

**Reynolds, Don F**. Consultectonics: Ethics Committee Case Consultation as Mediation. *Bioethics Forum*, 10(4), 54-60, Fall 94.

Ethics committee case consultation is a trustworthy process and a safe place to handle health care impasses. Following appropriate rules and guidelines, such mediation forums provide a safe place for health care problems to be heard.

**Reynolds, Don F** and Flanigan, Rosemary and Emmott, Helen. Advance Directive Timeline and Case Study *Melinda's Story. Bioethics Forum*, 13(2), 40-43, Sum 97.

**Reynolds, Mark**. An Axiomatization for Until and Since over the Reals without the IRR Rule. *Stud Log*, 51(2), 165-193, 1992.

We give a Hilbert style axiomatization for the set of formulas in the temporal language with *Until* and *Since* which are valid over the real number flow of time. The axiomatization, which is orthodox in the sense of only having the usual temporal rules of inference, is complete with respect to single formulas.

**Reynolds, Mark**. Axiomatising First-Order Temporal Logic: Until and Since over Linear Time. *Stud Log*, 57(2-3), 279-302, O 96.

We present an axiomatisation for the first-order temporal logic with connectives Until and Since over the class of all linear flows of time. Completeness of the axiom system is proved. We also add a few axioms to find a sound and complete axiomatisation for the first-order temporal logic of Until and Since over rational numbers time.

**Reynolds, Sherrie** and Martin, Kathleen. Educational Reform: A Complex Matter. *J Thought*, 32(1), 77-86, Spr 97.

This research suggests an approach to educational reform which honors the complexity of classrooms and schools. The authors call for ways of thinking about change which are consonant with what is known about the behavior of complex systems. They discuss the initial conditions which facilitate the emergence of spontaneously self-organizing systems appropriate for learning and the conditions which permit the continued functioning of such systems in adaptive, dynamic ways.

**Rhees, Rush** and Phillips, D E (ed). Language as Emerging from Instinctive Behaviour. *Phil Invest*, 20(1), 1-14, Ja 97.

**Rheinwald, Rosemarie**. Causation and Intensionality: A Problem for Naturalism. *Euro J Phil*, 2(1), 41-64, Ap 94.

The concept of causation plays an essential part in all attempts to naturalize language and mind. In this paper it is argued that the concept of causation is intensional in the following sense: the answer to the question whether one event is a cause of another event depends not only on events in the world but also on their description. This view contradicts the realist idea that causation is a natural phenomenon existing independently of how we describe it. A possible way out of this difficulty lies in the claim that intensionality can be interpreted as part of nature.

**Rhode, Deborah L**. The Ideology and Biology of Gender Difference. *S J Phil*, 34(Supp), 73-98, 1996.

**Rhodes, Frank H T**. "The American University: National Treasure or Endangered Species?" in *The American University: National Treasure or Endangered Species?*, Ehrenberg, Ronald G (ed), 161-170. Ithaca, Cornell Univ Pr, 1997.

**Rhodes, Steven C** and Keyton, Joann. Sexual Harassment: A Matter of Individual Ethics, Legal Definitions, or Organizational Policy?. *J Bus Ethics*, 16(2), 129-146, F 97.

Although interest in business ethics has rapidly increased, little attention has been drawn to the relationship between ethics and sexual harassment. While most companies have addressed the problem of sexual harassment at the organizational level with corporate codes of ethics or sexual harassment policies, no research has examined the ethical ideology of individual employees. This study investigates the relationship between the ethical ideology of individual employees and their ability to identify social-sexual behaviors in superior-subordinate interactions. The results indicate that ethical ideology does have an effect on employees' ability to identify verbal sexually harassing behaviors. This effect, however, is not demonstrated on nonverbal sexually harassing behaviors.

**Riaza Molina, Carmen**. Crecimiento irrestricto y libertad en el pensamiento de Leonardo Polo. *Anu Filosof*, 29(2), 985-991, 1996.

Man is a being able to improve limitless as person. In Leonardo Polo's anthropology improvement and freedom are concepts fully related.

**Ribas Cezar, Cesar** (trans) and Scotus, John Duns. Do Princípio de Individuaçao. *Trans/Form/Acao*, 19, 241-253, 1996.

**Ribeiro de Barros, Alberto**. The Concept of Sovereignty in Jean Bodin's *Methodus* (in Spanish). *Discurso*, 27, 139-155, 1996.

The concept of sovereignty, which is dealt with (examined) systematically, for the first time in the *Six livres de la République* (1576), already stands as an issue for reflexion in the *Methodus ad Facilem Historiarum Cognitionem* (1566). The aim of this essay is to analyse this first approach which anticipates certain aspects of Bodin's theory.

**Ribeiro dos Santos, Leonel**. As Metamorfoses da Luz, ou a Retórica da Evidência na Filosofia Cartesiana. *Philosophica (Portugal)*, 17-36, 1996.

Pour beaucoup de commentateurs, la philosophie cartésienne de l'évidence rationnelle repousse la rhétorique et les métaphores hors du champ de la philosophie. En soulignant l'omniprésence des images de la lumière et de la vision dans l'oeuvre du philosophe du *cogito* et de la *mathesis*, nous essayons de montrer qu'il y a justement une rhétorique de l'évidence cartésienne et que c'est grâce à cette rhétorique que la philosophie de Descartes déploie toute sa puissance. La dominance du principe d'évidence et d'intuition ne va pas sans conséquences, notamment pour la théorie de la définition, mais aussi pour la pratique de l'argumentation philosophique et pour la conception du rôle de l'analogie et de la métaphore dans la philosophie et dans la science. Tout cela obéit à une économie d'intelligibilité qui s'exhibe comme poétique de la visibilité.

**Ribeiro dos Santos, Leonel**. O retorno ao mito, Nietzsche, a música e a tragédia. *Philosophica (Portugal)*, 89-111, 1993.

L'auteur essaie de montrer comment le projet nietzschéen déployé dans *La naissance de la tragédie* (1872) doit être compris à l'intérieur d'un mouvement spéculatif de retour au mythe, en cours dans la philosophie européenne depuis Kant. Ce mouvement se caractérise par le rôle qu'on attribue alors à l'art, comprise soit comme l'expression suprême de la subjectivité, de l'esprit (*Gemüt*) et de la volonté, soi comme la révélation même de l'Absolu, de l'Etre et de la Nature. Dans l'oeuvre de Nietzsche c'est la musique—l'art romantique par excellence qui, s'instituant d'abord comme "mythe et monde de symboles", mène la raison et la philosophie à la rencontre du sens du mythe tragique ancien et, par là, aussi à la rencontre de leur lieu d'origine, à la fois historique et essentiel, dans le mythe même.

**Ribeiro dos Santos, Leonel**. 'Ideia Poética' e 'Ideaia Filosófica': Sobre a Relaçao entre Poesia e Filosofia na Obra de Antero de Quental. *Philosophica (Portugal)*, 95-121, 1997.

Une relecture des idées de Antero de Quental concernant la nature de la poésie et de la philosophie nous montre que l'hybridisme de l'oeuvre du poète-philosophe portugais est solidaire d'une cohérente et suffisament dessinée conception de la poétique de l'esprit, laquelle, d'ailleurs, a été partagée par d'autres représentants de la culture poétique et philosophique du XIXe siècle. Le cas Antero illustre la condition de la pensée et de la littérature depuis le Romantisme, caractérisée par la crise des genres philosophique et poétique, par le changement du statut même de l'acte philosophique, et par la reconnaissance de l'originaire affinité et voisinage entre le philosophe et le poète.

**Ribeiro Ferreira, Maria Luísa**. Filosofia e História da Filosofia. *Philosophica (Portugal)*, 21-30, 1993.

Dans cet article—"Philosophie et Histoire de la Philosophie"—on relève la dimension historique dans l'enseignement/apprentissage philosophique en classes terminales. Le discours philosophique se croise avec le discours idéologique. Pour les élèves du secondaire la démarcation n'est pas très nette et la philosophie est considérée en tant que "opinion". Il faut contrarier cette conception, et présenter la philosophie comme une pratique intellectuelle où domine la rigueur. Le recours à l'histoire de la philosophie peut être une solution, répondant aussi à quelques doutes sur le statut de la discipline et du professeur de philosophie.

**Riccio, Monica**. "Mannheim e Bloch: storicismo e utopia" in *Lo Storicismo e la Sua Storia: Temi, Problemi, Prospettive*, Cacciatore, Giuseppe (ed), 443-454. Milano, Guerini, 1997.

**Rice, Lee** (ed) and Barbone, Steven (ed). *Spinoza Bibliography: 1991-1995*. Milwaukee, No Amer Spinoza Soc, 1997.

The 681 references comprising this bibliography were extracted from a larger bibliographical data base which we have maintained for several years: here you find the complete listings of the data base for works published between 1991 and 1995 (inclusive). Following our extraction of the data, we made every effort to verify doubtful entries and to update incomplete ones. In only a few cases, because of the tendency of European bibliographers to exclude publisher informations from listings, have we been unsuccessful. (edited)

**Rice, Lee C**. Spinoza's Relativistic Aesthetics. *Tijdschr Filosof*, 58(3), 476-489, S 96.

It is often claimed that Spinoza regards aesthetic values as inherently subjective and relative. I suggest in my opening section that this reading is derived from Leibniz's misconception of Spinoza's method, and go on to develop a Spinozistic account of aesthetic experience which is relational, but which sees it as rooted in human sensibility (imagination). In the closing section I take up the issue of intersubjective valuation, and the question how aesthetic values are shared within the human community. I suggest also that Spinoza's somewhat out-of-fashion approach to aesthetic valuation through the concepts of 'beauty' and 'well-being' are worthy of further attention and development by contemporary aestheticians.

**Rice, Suzanne**. "Dewey's Conception of "Virtue" and its Educational Implications" in *Philosophy of Education (1996)*, Margonis, Frank (ed), 356-364. Urbana, Phil Education Soc, 1997.

There has been much discussion about virtue as a moral concept and as educational ideal over the past ten years; and many schools have implemented, or are considering implementing, character education programs intended to foster virtue. Because different conceptions of virtue and how it develops will tend to recommend different educational practices, it is important to consider the merits of competing accounts. To this end, this paper tries to represent Dewey's particular conception of virtue, which has been largely overlooked, and then discusses some of the educational implications of this conception.

**Rice, Suzanne**. Dewey's Conception of "Virtue" and its Implications for Moral Education. *Educ Theor*, 46(3), 269-282, Sum 96.

Dewey's conception of "virtue" is closely linked to his conceptions of "habit" and "character"; and all three are conceived as "interactions" with the social and physical environment, and as existing in a state of "interpretation." The first part of this paper seeks to clarify Dewey's conception of "virtue" in relation to these and other related concepts. The second section discusses the implications of this conception for moral education. Dewey illuminates the conditions necessary for schools to become more conducive to virtue and good character and—arguably more important—the ways in which all our institutions are responsible for advancing this aim.

**Rich, Ben A**. Postmodern Personhood: A Matter of Consciousness. *Bioethics*, 11(3-4), 206-216, Jl 97.

The concept of person is integral to bioethical discourse because persons are the proper subject of the moral domain. Nevertheless, the concept of person has played no role in the prevailing formulation of human death because of a purported lack of consensus concerning the essential attributes of a person. Beginning with John Locke's fundamental proposition that person is a 'forensic term', I argue that in Western society we do have a consensus on at least one necessary condition for personhood, and that is the capacity for conscious experience. (edited)

**Rich, Ben A**. Prospective Autonomy and Critical Interests: A Narrative Defense of the Moral Authority of Advance Directives. *Cambridge Quart Healthcare Ethics*, 6(2), 138-147, Spr 97.

The moral and legal authority of advance directives has recently been challenged on the grounds that the loss of psychological continuity and connectedness between the competent person executing the directive and the incompetent person whose care it directs precludes the possibility that they could be the same person. I defend the authority of advance directives against this challenge by articulating a narrative view of the self and a Lockean perspective on personal identity and such exercises of prospective autonomy. On this view, both the competent and the later demented self are stages of the life of a single person.

**Rich, Paul** and De los Reyes, Guillermo. Volunteerism and Democracy: A Latin American Perspective. *Cont Phil*, 18(2-3), 59-65, Mr-Ap/My-Je 96.

The myriad number of voluntary organizations in the world are getting scholarly attention with regards to what they contribute to political culture. Nongovernmental associations are increasingly recognized as fundamental to democratization: "In the world of ideas, civil society is hot. It is almost impossible to read an article on foreign or domestic politics without coming across some mention of the concept.... At the heart of the concept of civil society lie 'intermediate institutions', private groups that thrive between the realm of the state and the family."

**Richard, Mark**. What Does Commonsense Psychology Tell Us about Meaning?. *Nous*, 31(1), 87-114, Mr 97.

**Richards, Diana** and Vanderschraaf, Peter. Joint Beliefs in Conflictual Coordination Games. *Theor Decis*, 42(3), 287-310, My 97.

The traditional solution concept for noncooperative game theory is the Nash equilibrium, which contains an implicit assumption that players' probability distributions satisfy *probabilistic independence*. However, in games with more than two players, relaxing this assumption results in a more general equilibrium concept based on *joint beliefs* (Vanderschraaf, 1995). This article explores the implications of this joint-beliefs equilibrium concept for two kinds of conflictual coordination games: crisis bargaining and public goods provision. We find that, using updating consistent with Bayes's rule, players' beliefs converge to equilibria in joint beliefs which do not satisfy probabilistic independence. In addition, joint beliefs greatly expand the set of mixed equilibria. On the face of it, allowing for joint beliefs might be expected to increase the prospects for coordination. However, we show that if players use joint beliefs, which may be more likely as the number of players increases, then the prospects for coordination in these games declines vis-à-vis independent beliefs.

**Richards, Jay Wesley**. Barth on the Divine 'Conscription' of Language. *Heythrop J*, 38(3), 247-266, Jl 97.

This essay analyzes and criticizes Karl Barth's claim that God *conscripts* human language in his revelation to make it *refer* to divine realities and to *assert* truth claims which such language would not otherwise do. Several problems beset Barth's conscription claim, including self-contradiction and errors over the notion of *meaning*, making it impossible to maintain. His errors also reflect a confusion over the notions of *knowledge* and *truth* and may result from a unresolved tension between Barth's *realism* and his *actualism*.

**Richards, Jay Wesley**. Truth and Meaning in George Lindbeck's *The Nature of Doctrine. Relig Stud*, 33(1), 33-53, Mr 97.

In this essay I analyze and criticize George Lindbeck's treatment of truth and meaning in his book *The Nature of Doctrine*. On truth, his theory is riddled with conceptual problems, fails as an adequate theoretical description of our pretheoretic intuition of truth, and is finally parasitic on this intuition. On meaning, his reduction of meaning (and sometimes truth) to *use* or usefulness leads him to an incorrect categorization of doctrines as (essentially) *performative utterances and second-order, nonassertive discourse*, rather than as *propositional attitude statements*. Finally, I suggest the inadequacy of his treatment of truth and meaning redounds to the failure of his theory of religion and doctrine as a whole.

**Richards, Jerald**. Gandhi's Qualified Acceptance of Violence. *Acorn*, 8(2), 5-16, Fall 95.

This paper examines the apparent contradiction in Mohandas K. Gandhi's thought between his advocacy of principled nonviolence and his acceptance of violence in certain situations. Key statements of Gandhi that justify violent action are identified and evaluated, with special attention being given to the necessary conditions of justifiable violent action. It is concluded that the tension in Gandhi's thought does not amount to a contradiction. Gandhi was a nonviolentist, but he was not an absolutist, so that a violent response to violence on the part of persons not capable of nonviolent action may be justifiable if certain stringent conditions are satisfied.

**Richards, Norvin**. Criminal Children. *Law Phil*, 16(1), 63-89, 97.

According to the conceptions embodied in the traditional Juvenile Court, young persons are insufficiently developed to do anything *very* bad. Specifically, they are incapable of committing a felony in such a way as to be culpable for it. The depressing flood of apparent counterexamples to this picture has produced a fall-back position, according to which adolescents are capable of culpability but are *less* culpable than adults who commit the same acts would be. I examine three forms of the lesser-culpability thesis, and argue that all of them fail. Adolescents may well differ from adults in what they know and in their susceptibility to certain pressures, but not in ways which support the lesser-culpability thesis, I contend. If adolescents are indeed capable of culpability, there is no principled basis for systematically taking them to be less so than adults.

**Richards, Richard A**. Darwin and the Inefficacy of Artificial Selection. *Stud Hist Phil Sci*, 28(1), 75-97, Mr 96.

Darwin is commonly understood to be making an analogical argument from domestic breeding to nature, in his *On the Origin of Species*, to establish the causal efficacy of natural selection. But if so, he would be making an argument that was understood by both critics and supporters to suggest the immutability of species. I argue that this standard reading of Darwin is mistaken and based partly on the assumption that Darwin's argument is fully stated in his *Origin*. His argument is instead found in his *Variation of Animals and Plants under Domestication*, where the nonanalogical character of it is more apparent.

**Richardson, Alan W**. "From Epistemology to the Logic of Science: Carnap's Philosophy of Empirical Knowledge in the 1930s" in *Origins of Logical Empiricism*, Giere, Ronald N (ed), 309-332. Minneapolis, Univ of Minnesota Pr, 1996.

**Richardson, Alan W**. "Introduction: Origins of Logical Empiricism" in *Origins of Logical Empiricism*, Giere, Ronald N (ed), 1-13. Minneapolis, Univ of Minnesota Pr, 1996.

**Richardson, Alan W** (ed) and Giere, Ronald N (ed). *Origins of Logical Empiricism*. Minneapolis, Univ of Minnesota Pr, 1996.

These articles challenge the idea that logical empiricism has its origins in traditional British empiricism, pointing instead to a movement of scientific philosophy that flourished in the German-speaking areas of Europe in the first four decades of the twentieth century. The intellectual refugees from the Third Reich who brought logical empiricism to North America did so in an environment influenced by Einstein's new physics, the ascension of modern logic, the birth of the social sciences as rivals to traditional humanistic philosophy, and other large-scale social, political, and cultural themes. (edited)

**Richardson, Brenda**. Teaching for Presence in the Democratic Classroom. *Thinking*, 13(1), 26-33, 1997.

**Richardson, Henry**. *Practical Reasoning about Final Ends*. New York, Cambridge Univ Pr, 1997.

How should we reason about what to do? The answer offered by most recent philosophy, as well as such disciplines as decision theory, welfare economics and political science, is that we should select efficient means to our ends. However, if we ask how we should decide which ends or goals to aim at, these standard theoretical approaches are silent. Henry Richardson argues that we can determine our ends rationally. He constructs a rich and original theory of how we can reason about what to seek for its own sake as a final end. Richardson defuses the counter-arguments for the limits of rational deliberation and develops interesting ideas about how his model might be extended to interpersonal deliberation of ends, taking him to the borders of political theory. Along the way Richardson offers illuminating discussions of, *inter alia*, Aristotle, Aquinas, Sidgwick and Dewey, as well as the work of several contemporary philosophers. This is a book of major importance to a broad swath of philosophers as well as social and political scientists. (publisher)

**Richardson, Jeff** and Kuhse, Helga and McKie, John. Allocating Healthcare By QALYs: The Relevance of Age. *Cambridge Quart Healthcare Ethics*, 5(4), 534-545, Fall 96.

The QALY method ranks health care programs according to the Quality-Adjusted Life-Years they are expected to produce for each available health care dollar. According to some critics, this involves a comprehensive bias against the aged, since the aged have fewer remaining life years than the young. Some ways of defending the QALY approach against the criticism—e.g., by arguing that the aged have already had a "fair innings"—are incompatible with the QALY approach. In contrast, the authors defend the QALY approach by placing it within the context of utilitarian ethics. If discriminating against the aged in the distribution of health care threatens to decrease utility overall, the QALYs of the aged can be given a greater weight in comparison with other groups.

**Richardson, Robert C**. The Prospects for an Evolutionary Psychology: Human Language and Human Reasoning. *Mind Mach*, 6(4), 541-557, N 96.

Evolutionary psychology purports to explain human capacities as adaptations to an ancestral environment. A complete explanation of human language or human reasoning as adaptations depends on assessing an historical claim, that these capacities evolved under the pressure of natural selection, and that they are prevalent because they provided systematic advantages to our ancestors. An outline of the character of the information needed in order to offer complete adaptation explanations is drawn from Robert Brandon (1990), and explanations offered for the evolution of language and reasoning within evolutionary psychology are evaluated. Pinker and Bloom's (1992) defense of human language as an adaptation for verbal communication, Robert Nozick's (1993) account of the evolutionary origin of rationality, and Cosmides and Tooby's (1992) explanation of human reasoning as an adaptation for social exchange, are discussed in light of what is known, and what is not known, about the history of human evolution. (edited)

**Richir, Marc**. Hyperbolic Doubt and "Machiavelism": The Modern Foundation of the Subject in Descartes (in French). *Arch Phil*, 60(1), 109-122, Ja-Mr 97.

Within the context of modernity, with its Machiavellian critique, in the realm of politics, of the classic distinction between truth and appearance, the complex movements of hyperbolic doubt in Descartes's *Méditations métaphysiques*, leaving aside their apparent resolution, reveal the modern foundation of the subject. This subject, as possessed facticity, proves capable of tricking the "trickster god" (an absolute despot). The cogito, in the Third Meditation, founds necessarily the experience of the sublime in order to found the objectivity of the objects of consciousness.

**Richli, Urs**. Das Wir in der späten Wissenschaftslehre. *Fichte-Studien*, 12, 351-363, 1997.

**Richman, Sam**. Resolving Discordant Results: Modern Solar Oblateness Experiments. *Stud Hist Phil Mod Physics*, 27B(1), 1-22, Mr 96.

We examine the history of the experimental refutation of the Brans-Dicke theory of gravitation, in particular the role of solar oblateness measurements. In this episode, the simple picture of unambiguous experimental results forcing a choice between different theories breaks down. The scientific community must make a decision on the validity of the different experiments themselves, as well as evidence from related experiments.

**Richmond, Catherine**. Preserving the Identity Crisis: Autonomy, System and Sovereignty in European Law. *Law Phil*, 16(4), 377-420, Jl 97.

This article uses Hans Kelsen's theory of a legal system to take a fresh look at European Community law and the relationship between the European Community, its member states and international law. It argues that the basis of the Community's legal legitimacy is indeterminate and offers a model to accommodate that indeterminacy. This model is founded on a constructivist approach suggested to be particularly useful in the EC context. Using this approach, it is argued that the concepts of system, autonomy and sovereignty in the Community can only be understood through the recognition of a plurality of viewpoints, and that it is crucial, in describing the Community, to distinguish between a concept *per se* and the choice to adopt that concept.

**Richmond, John W**. Ethics and the Philosophy of Music Education. *J Aes Educ*, 30(3), 3-22, Fall 96.

Music education philosophy has emerged largely from the field of aesthetics for most of this century. This article broadens this philosophical discourse by turning to ethics as an appropriate "lens" by which to inform professional practice. The author considers teleological, deontological, and rule utilitarian approaches in the abstract and then applies these approaches to a workplace case study regarding school music repertoire selection and the separation of church and state. The author closes with recommendations for the establishment of school ethics committees, modelled after those in medicine, as a way to build ethical expertise within the music teaching professions.

**Ricketts, Thomas**. "Carnap: From Logical Syntax to Semantics" in *Origins of Logical Empiricism*, Giere, Ronald N (ed), 231-250. Minneapolis, Univ of Minnesota Pr, 1996.

This paper reconciles Carnap's antipathy to semantics in *Logical Syntax of Language* with his enthusiastic adoption of Tarski's definition of truth. The paper concludes with a discussion of the vulnerabilities Carnap's adoption of semantics creates for his program of Wissenschaftslogik.

**Ricketts, Thomas**. "Pictures, Logic, and the Limits of Sense in Wittgenstein's *Tractatus*" in *The Cambridge Companion to Wittgenstein*, Sluga, Hans (ed), 59-99. Needham Heights, Cambridge, 1996.

Section 1 presents Wittgenstein's dissatisfactions with the Frege-Russell universalist conception of logic. Sections 2 and 3 chart the emergence of Wittgenstein's view of sentences as pictures against the backdrop of Russell's multiple relation theory of judgment. Section 4 links the view of sentences as pictures with the Tractarian conception of logic. Section 5 reflects on the self-thwarting character of the view of language and logic ostensibly espoused in the *Tractatus*.

**Ricketts, Thomas**. "Truth-Values and Courses-of-Value in Frege's *Grundgesetze*" in *Early Analytic Philosophy*, Tait, William W (ed), 187-211. Chicago, Open Court, 1997.

This paper argues that Frege's identification of the two truth-values with courses-of-value is put forward as a clarification of courses-of-value rather than to fix the ontological standing of the truth-values. The paper discusses Frege's motivations for introducing extensions in addition to concepts and presents a detailed alternative to model theoretic interpretations of *Grundgesetze* paragraph 10. The final section urges that, even apart from Russell's paradox, Frege's elucidation of courses-of-value is inadequate by Frege's own standards.

**Ricklin, Thomas**. L'image d'Albert le Grand et de Thomas d'Aquin chez Dante Alighieri. *Rev Thomiste*, 97(1), 129-142, Ja-Mr 97.

**Rickman, H P**. *Philosophy in Literature*. Madison, F Dickinson U Pr, 1996.

In this book scholar and author H. P. Rickman considers the entanglement of philosophy and literature, as felt by both philosophers and poets alike. Although the two fields are distinct because argumentation is an essential characteristic of the former and presentation is vital to the latter, the two disciplines share such features as a distance from practical, everyday life. They also supplement each other. While philosophers employ such literary devices as dialogue and metaphors, poets and novelists write about virtue and vice, truth and illusion, the passage of time, the vagaries of human nature and the workings of destiny, concepts which all receive helpful illumination in philosophy. (publisher, edited)

**Ricoeur, Paul**. "Is the Present Crisis a Specifically Modern Phenomenon?" in *The Ancients and the Moderns*, Lilly, Reginald (ed), 130-147. Bloomington, Indiana Univ Pr, 1996.

**Ricoeur, Paul**. Memory, Forgetfulness, and History. *Iyyun*, 45, 13-24, Jl 96.

**Ridley, Aaron**. Not Ideal: Collingwood's Expression Theory. *J Aes Art Crit*, 55(3), 263-272, Sum 97.

**Ridley, Aaron**. The Philosophy of Medium-Grade Art. *Brit J Aes*, 36(4), 413-423, O 96.

**Ridley, Aaron** and Madell, Geoffrey. Emotion and Feeling. *Aris Soc*, Supp(71), 147-176, 1997.

**Rieber, Arnulf**. "Grundtypen abendländischen Ganzheitsdenkens" in *Kreativer Friede durch Begegnung der Weltkulturen*, Beck, Heinrich (ed), 121-155. New York, Lang, 1995.

For Occidental thinking it is not a small challenge, when in the Kyoto-School, representative for modern Japanese philosophy, the Western philosophy of being is said to be overcome by Eastern philosophy of nothingness. This article explores and compares Western and Far-Eastern (esp. Buddhistic) worldviews.

AUTHOR INDEX 871 Riobó González, Manuel

The deliberations are centered especially upon Keiji Nishitani's book *Religion and Nothingness* (published in Japanese 1961, in English 1982). In a first step Nishitani's philosophy of nothingness (nihility/sunyata) is outlined, in a second step, in a critical reception of his understanding of selfhood, problematic terms ('Great Doubt', 'leap', 'breaking through', etc.) are discussed, furthermore a 'relative-dialectical' and a 'relational-dialogical' interpretation of opposites are contradistinguished. In a final note the onto-trinitarian implications of the 'egoteki' (i.e., circumincessional interpenetration) are explained.

**Rieber, Steven**. A Semiquotational Solution to Substitution Puzzles. *Phil Stud*, 86(3), 267-301, Je 97.

The solution to substitution puzzles involving synonyms or codesignative names in attitude reports is that the nonsubstitutable expression is being tacitly quoted. Unlike sentential theories of belief, the semiquotational approach does not claim that all belief reports are quotational or that the entire complement is being quoted. The semiquotational approach is supported by a test for quotation. It is shown to be superior to theories of interpreted logical forms.

**Rieber, Steven**. Conventional Implicatures as Tacit Performatives. *Ling Phil*, 20(1), 51-72, F 97.

The conventional implicatures carried by discourse connectives are analyzed in terms of parenthetical performatives. 'But', for example, means 'and (I suggest that this contrasts)'. The analysis explains why the implications of discourse connectives survive when embedded in conditionals. It also solves a problem for Grice's definition of what is said.

**Riedel, Manfred**. "In Search of a Civil Union: The Political Theme of European Democracy and Its Primordial Foundation in Greek Philosophy" in *The Ancients and the Moderns,* Lilly, Reginald (ed), 19-28. Bloomington, Indiana Univ Pr, 1996.

**Riedel, Manfred**. "Paradigm Evolution in Political Philosophy: Aristotle and Hobbes" in *The Ancients and the Moderns,* Lilly, Reginald (ed), 101-114. Bloomington, Indiana Univ Pr, 1996.

**Riedel, Manfred**. Für einen anderen Umgang mit Nietzsche. *Z Phil Forsch*, 50(1/2), 223-235, Ja-Je 96.

**Rieman, Fred**. On Subjectivity and Intersubjectivity. *Cont Phil*, 18(4 & 5), 11-16, Jl-Ag/S-O 96.

It is customary among both nonphilosophers and many philosophers to use or assume what I call an *objective* epistemology, one which builds the epistemology on a materialist ontology, so that the epistemology centers on methods of science. As to the human role it emphasizes neurology, perhaps in comparison to a computer. Thus it assumes materialism and works toward an epistemology. A serious problem with this approach is that so far it has been unable to provide a generally acceptable account of personal consciousness relegating it to the role of a 'ghost in the machine', or to an illusory, or at best cognitively unimportant, accompaniment to neurological events.

**Rif, Alan**. Strobos—On Issues of Origins, Development and Phenomenology in Some Areas of Science and Scholarship. *Cont Phil*, 18(4 & 5), 17-22, Jl-Ag/S-O 96.

The concept of a strobe, derived from Greek for "a whirling round" and used as a root or adjective in terms for various physical and biological phenomena, is offered as a defining image with a fundamental role in phenomenology and epistemology. The paper attempts to demonstrate its hypothesis by starting with the question of ultimate cosmic origins, in which the strobe manifests as echo-void. Echo-void is the reverberative paradox underlying cosmic reality and as, this universe, forms as infra-spherical space-time continuum. Such a universe, in terms of human experience, is described as a rippling edge 'tween nunc and null. All of the foregoing fulfill the paper's definition of a strobe. A strobe logistic is then described, offered as an analytical tool for strobic reality. The article concludes with briefly describing some direction of research implied by the strobe hypothesis, including cosmogony, history and temporal topology.

**Riggan, William**. Plagiarism and Reviewer/Editor Responsibility. *J Infor Ethics*, 6(1), 34-38, Spr 97.

In twenty years of assigning and editing (and writing) book reviews, I have encountered numerous small conflicts of interest but only two egregious instances of outright plagiarism. This essay recounts those two instances in some detail and assesses the propriety and the effects of the editorial decisions made at the time of each.

**Riggs, Peter**. The Principal Paradox of Time Travel. *Ratio*, 10(1), 48-64, Ap 97.

Most arguments against the possibility of time travel use the same old, familiar objection: If I could travel back in time, then I could kill my earlier (i.e., younger) self. Since I do exist such an action would result in a contradiction. Therefore time travel is impossible. This is a statement of the Principal Paradox of Time Travel. Some philosophers have argued that such actions as attempting to kill one's earlier self would always fail and that there is nothing especially strange about such failures. Despite these arguments, the problem generally is not viewed as being solved in favour of time travel. The above objection to time travel is also used to dismiss a particular class of cosmological models as being unphysical. This paper provides a solution to the Principal Paradox by exploring both the logical and causal implications of time travel.

**Riggs, Wayne D**. The Weakness of Strong Justification. *Austl J Phil*, 75(2), 179-189, Je 97.

Alvin Goldman's reliabilist theory of epistemic justification is a paradigm example of a truth-conducive conception of justification. Other philosophers (e.g., Stewart Cohen and Laurence BonJour, among others) have criticized his view for not satisfying the requirements of an alternative conception of justification often called "responsibilism." Goldman responds to these objections by trying to show that his view incorporates essential features of "responsibilism." This essay argues that Goldman fails in this attempt. Furthermore, the reasons for this failure highlight the tensions between the two conceptions of justification. It is precisely because his theory is truth-conducive that it cannot also be responsibilist.

**Rigo, Mirela** and Alarcón, Jesús and Waldegg, Guillermina. La ciencia analítica en la primera mitad del siglo XIX: el teorema del valor intermedio. *Mathesis*, 10(1), 93-113, F 94.

During the first half of the nineteenth century, the theories that presumed to be scientific described themselves as 'analytic'. From Lagrange's *Méchanique analytique* to Bolzano's *Purely analytic proof* of the intermediate value theorem, the high level of abstraction and generality reached by a theory was based on the 'analytic methods' used. However, the word 'analytic' did not have the same meaning for all the scientists of this period and remarkable differences can be detected in the assumptions underlying analytic methods in each author. In this article different approaches to the intermediate value theorem are analyzed, revealing the various conceptions of what being an 'analytic' theory entails.

**Rigobello, Armando**. "Il tempo in Bergson e nello spiritualismo francese" in *Il Concetto di Tempo: Atti del XXXII Congresso Nazionale della Società Filosofica Italiana,* Casertano, Giovanni (ed), 71-83. Napoli, Loffredo, 1997.

**Rigobello, Armando**. "La logica della vita morale in M. Blondel" in *Momenti di Storia della Logica e di Storia della Filosofia,* Guetti, Carla (ed), 131-145. Roma, Aracne Editrice, 1996.

**Rigotti, Francesca**. Dall'*albero del sovrano* all'*ulivo*: Simboli e metafore arboree nella politica lontana e vicina. *Iride*, 10(20), 68-87, Ap 97.

**Rigotti, Francesca**. Il velo e il fiume: Riflessioni sulle metafore dell'oblio. *Iride*, 8(14), 131-151, Ap 95.

**Riker, Stephen**. Al-Ghazali on Necessary Causality in *The Incoherence of the Philosophers*. *Monist*, 79(3), 315-324, Jl 96.

Many scholars of modern philosophy link the discussion of the necessary nature of causality inexorably with the name of the David Hume. Yet, long before Hume, the issue of necessary causality had been taken up by the Medieval Islamic philosopher Al-Ghazali. The purpose of this paper will be to examine Al-Ghazali's views concerning the necessary nature of causality in his work *The Incoherence of the Philosophers* with particular reference to the issue of whether there is a complete rejection of causality, and whether Ghazali's rejection of necessary causality entails that he holds to some sort of occasionalism.

**Riley, Patrick**. *Leibniz' Universal Jurisprudence: Justice as the Charity of the Wise*. Cambridge, Harvard Univ Pr, 1996.

For the first time Leibniz's political, moral, and legal thought are extensively discussed here in English. The text includes fragments of his work that have never before been translated. Riley shows that a justice based on both wisdom and love, "wise charity," has at least as much claim to be taken seriously as the familiar contractarian ideas of Hobbes and Locke. For Leibniz, nothing is more important than benevolence toward others, which he famously equates with justice and which he insists is morally crucial. (edited)

**Rinaldi, Giacomo**. Die Aktualität von Hegels Logik. *Jahr Hegelforschung*, 2, 27-54, 1996.

**Rinck, Christine** and Calkins, Carl F. Challenges Across the Life Span for Persons with Disabilities. *Bioethics Forum*, 12(3), 37-46, Fall 96.

Health care issues for persons with developmental disabilities have raised numerous bioethical dilemmas. These controversies bridge the life span from the prenatal period through old age. Some key discussions focus on the impact of genetic testing and amniocentesis on the birth of children with disabilities and the survival of very low birth weight babies. Other issues center on transplants for persons with disabilities, sexuality, and advance directives. With the movement away from institutionalization and toward independence, people with disabilities have more choice in all aspects of their lives. This choice can pose dilemmas for the individual and those who are care providers.

**Rinderle, Peter**. Gesellschaftsvertrag oder grösster Gesamtnutzen? Die Vertragstheorie von John Rawls und ihre neo-utilitaristischen Kritiker. *Z Phil Forsch*, 51(2), 193-215, Ap-Je 97.

**Ring, Jennifer**. *The Political Consequences of Thinking: Gender and Judaism in the Work of Hannah Arendt*. Albany, SUNY Pr, 1997.

In this book, Jennifer Ring offers a wholly new interpretation of Hannah Arendt's work, from *Eichmann in Jerusalem*, with its bitter reception by the Jewish community, to *The Life of the Mind*. Departing from previous scholarship, Ring applies the perspectives of gender and ethnicity to investigate the extent to which Arendt's identity as a Jewish woman influenced both her thought and its reception. (publisher, edited)

**Riobó González, Manuel**. "Observaciones críticas al Idealismo alemán en el bicentenario del "Fundamento de toda la Doctrina de la Ciencia" 1794, de J. G. Fichte" in *El inicio del Idealismo alemán,* Market, Oswaldo, 103-125. Madrid, Ed Complutense, 1996.

Estas *Observaciones críticas* al Idealismo alemán conlleban dos finalidades: conmemorar el bicentenario del "Fundamento de toda la Doctrina de la Ciencia" de Fichte y, a su vez, resaltar los puntos centrales de la misma, cuya correcta interpretación nunca puede hacerse desde el neoespinozismo schellingiano ni desde el idealismo absoluto de Hegel. Los "tres principios" de la *Doctrina de la Ciencia* excluyen cualquier tipo de monismo y nunca, por lo tanto, nos llevarán a considerar el sistema filosófico del Fichte como un "espinozismo invertido", como así lo intentaron Jacobi y Schelling y hasta algunos expositores modernos. La dirección trascendental Kant-Fichte implica siempre una dualidad entre el sujeto trascendental y la realidad extra-consciente en una "determinación recíproca"—especialmente en Fichte—, implicando por ello "una Fenomenología y una doctrina de la Verdad y de la Razón" (W-L/1804 Akad-Ausg. II, 8, 206).

**Riordan, Patrick**. *A Politics of the Common Good*. Dublin, Inst Public Admin, 1996.

*A Politics of the Common Good* attempts to show that a liberal democracy in a pluralist society needs a language of the common good. It argues that explanations of human behaviour in terms of self-interest are incomplete. The language of the social sciences, particularly that of liberal economics, dominates our thoughts and practices. We need a model that is richer, that explains how we accommodate and respect others' views. (edited)

**Ripstein, Arthur**. "Context, Continuity, and Fairness" in *The Morality of Nationalism,* McKim, Robert (ed), 209-226. New York, Oxford Univ Pr, 1997.

**Ripstein, Arthur** (ed) and Dyzenhaus, David (ed). *Law and Morality: Readings in Legal Philosophy*. Toronto, Univ of Toronto Pr, 1996.

This anthology fills a longstanding need for a contemporary Canadian textbook in the philosophy of law. It includes articles, readings, and cases in legal philosophy that give students the conceptual tools necessary to consider the general problems of jurisprudence. (publisher, edited)

**Risser, James**. *Hermeneutics and the Voice of the Other: Re-reading Gadamer's Philosophical Hermeneutics*. Albany, SUNY Pr, 1997.

Dealing extensively with Gadamer's later writings, *Hermeneutics and the Voice of the Other* shows neglected and widely misunderstood dimensions of Gadamer's hermeneutics: historicity, finitude, truth, the importance of the other and the eminence of the poetic text. (publisher)

**Risser, Rita**. Thick Paintings and the Logic of Things: The Non-Ultimate Nature of Particular Works of Art. *Ultim Real Mean*, 19(4), 292-297, D 96.

**Rist, John M**. On the Aims and Effects of Platonic Dialogues. *Iyyun*, 46, 29-46, Ja 97.

**Rittenburg, Terri** and Desai, Ashay B. Global Ethics: An Integrative Framework for MNEs. *J Bus Ethics*, 16(8), 791-800, Je 97.

Global ethics has recently emerged as a popular concept among researchers in the field of international management and is of immediate concern among managers of multinational enterprises (MNEs). This paper presents an integrative framework covering a range of factors and issues relevant to multinationals with respect to ethical decision making. The paper provides an overview of the existing literature on the topic, and framework is aimed at providing the managers of multinationals with a basis for relating and synthesizing the perspectives and prescriptions that are available for incorporating ethics into the strategic decision-making process.

**Rittenhouse, Cynthia D**. Survival Skills and Ethics Training for Graduate Students: A Graduate Student Perspective. *Sci Eng Ethics*, 2(3), 367-380, Jl 96.

Graduate students in the sciences must develop practical skills geared toward scientific survival and success. This is particularly true now, given the paucity of research funds and jobs. Along with more elementary skills, research ethics should be an integral part of students' scientific training. Survival skills include research skills, communication skills, general efficiency, and preparation for postgraduate work. Ethics training covers guidelines for use of animal and human subjects, data treatment, disclosure, credit issues, conflicts of interest, and response to misconduct. The objective of this paper is to describe, from a graduate student's perspective, the need for survival and ethics training in graduate programs and to raise both faculty and student awareness of the possibilities for explicit instruction of these skills. Many survival skills and ethical practices will be learned without explicit direction and some are already part of standard training; but, this is not the case for all students or for all skills, so specific instruction is a necessity. Research faculty can use their own experience to help students to develop the proficiencies they will need to succeed.

**Rivas Monroy, Uxía**. "El signo y el sentido de la realidad" in *Verdad: lógica, representación y mundo*, Villegas Forero, L, 421-430. Santiago de Compostela, Univ Santiago Comp, 1996.

The aim of this paper is to show the different arguments of some of the most representative philosophers of language-particularly, Frege, Russell and Strawson—in order to defend the "sense of reality". The conclusion of their arguments is that to preserve this sense of reality languages have to exclude of their expressions those whose referents don't exist. In this sense these philosophers stress the function of signs as instruments we have to know reality. But there are other authors, for instance Eco, who stress the contrary: languages don't need to obey the sense of reality, because a very important function of signs is that they can be used to create new worlds or to deform reality. In between this views, the semiosis proposed by Peirce shows how a sign functions, his thesis although closer to the position that defends the sense of reality, leaves a place to understand signs in these two ways, without doing any exclusion.

**Rivas Monroy, Uxía** and Martínez Vidal, C and Villegas Forero, L. *Verdad: lógica, representación y mundo*. Santiago de Compostela, Univ Santiago Comp, 1996.

This book corresponds to the Proceedings of the Symposium "Truth: Logic, Representation and World" (Santiago de Compostela, Spain, January 1996, from 17th to 20th). The volume is divided into the following sections: Truth Theories, Philosophy of Mathematics, Philosophy of Science, Philosophy of Language, Cognitive Sciences and Philosophy of Mind and Logic. The papers included in the different sections reflect the general and omnipresent character of the problem of truth in relation to research studies in semantics, representation and ontology.

**Rivenc, François** and Horák, Petr. The Heritage of Léon Brunschvicg (and Commentary by P. Horák) (in Czech). *Filosof Cas*, 45(2), 261-281, 1997.

G.-G. Granger's philosophical work is fully rooted in the tradition which the present paper proposes to identify as the *epistemology à la française*. This tradition goes back to the fundamental work by Léon Brunschvicg and as the author does suggest in his paper, its characteristic sings are some very topical philosophical categories like the object and the subject dialectics, the solidarity of the experiment and the theory, the discontinuity which does accompany the resolving of the problems by the means of the new conceptualizations. G.-G. Granger's work represents an attempt to give some substance to this dialectical categories with this result that the philosophy obtains a paradoxical status to be a knowledge without my object. The paper does suggest that this particular philosophical tradition represents a modern form of the idealism.

**Rivera, José A**. La creación de la nada: ¿apoteosis de la producción o misterio revelado?. *Dialogos*, 32(70), 123-146, Jl 97.

Thomas Prufer's criticism of the Heideggerian "destruction" of theology is unpacked. Heidegger does not distinguish sufficiently between the Aristotelian notion of being as actuality-in-the-world and Thomistic *esse* as being-taken-out-of-nothing. Hence, his application to theology of the same "destructive" analysis he applies to metaphysics is problematic. In making the appropriate distinctions between the metaphysical and theological contexts, underlining the differences between making *ex possibili* and creation *ex nihilo*, an exercise is made in what Robert Sokolowski has called the theology of disclosure.

**Rivera, José Luis** (ed). *Ensayos Aristotélicos*. Mexico, Univ Panamericana, 1996.

El presente volumen recoge cinco artículos de algunos miembros del cuerpo académico. Los hemos agrupado bajo el genérico título de *Ensayos aristotélicos*. Hemos titubeado al dar un nombre a esta colección, pero finalmente nos hemos decidido por llamarlos sencillamente "ensayos", pues este término indica el carácter sugerente, abierto, a la vez audaz y científico, de los artículos. Los hemos llamado "aristotélicos" porque todos tienen en común su referencia (tangencial o directa) al otrora "principe de los Filósofos".

**Rivera, Silvia**. Ludwig Wittgenstein: Matemáticas y ética. *Cuad Etica*, 21-22, 135-151, 1996.

This paper deals with the important role that the questioning of mathematical fundaments plays in the thought of Wittgenstein. Firstly, three different moments of his philosophy are examined in relation to this kind of problems. Secondly, Wittgenstein's reflections about mathematics and about ethics are closely related to that imperative which obliges a radical criticism of our linguistic forms.

**Rivera de Rosales, Jacinto**. "El primer principio en Fichte" in *El inicio del Idealismo alemán,* Market, Oswaldo, 63-102. Madrid, Ed Complutense, 1996.

En este artículo se aborda el punto de partida o primer principio de Fichte arrancando de las *Críticas* kantianas. El paso de la Apercepción transcendental a la intuición intelectual, de la cosa en sí al No-Yo, de la libertad moral como principio de acción real y de ordenación del mundo al primer principio de realidad, la Dialéctica transcendental y la imposibilidad de un primer principio cósico, más la necesidad de un sistema para una razón arquitectónica, sirven para ir desmontando algunos tópicos que velan la comprensión de estas filosofías que se apoyan en la subjetividad; a saber, que aquí no se parte de un sujeto *res*, aislado del mundo y de los otros, totalmente consciente de sí, ni creador del mundo, o meramente individual, arbitrario y dictatorial. Asimismo se critica la pretensión de prescindirse de la subjetividad en virtud de un determinismo seudocientífico o por quedarse en un mero análisis del lenguaje.

**Rivera de Rosales, Jacinto** and Market, Oswaldo. *El inicio del Idealismo alemán*. Madrid, Ed Complutense, 1996.

**Rivera de Ventosa, Enrique**. A los orígenes del pensamiento medieval español sobre la historia: Prudencio, Orosio, san Isidoro. *Rev Espan Filosof Med*, 4, 7-22, 1997.

At the source of the Hispanic thought about history are: Prudencius, Orosius and Isidore of Seville. The source of the Hispanic medieval thought comes out from the Roman-Hispanic writers: Prudentius, Orosius and Isidore of Seville. They are the starting point for a subsequent reflexion of the Hispanic historiography in the Middle Ages. The three writers present an important change of mentality. The historic perspective is not the same in Prudentius as it is in Isidore, while Orosius is rather intermediate. Everyone has his own way to know their mentality in order to penetrate into the secrets of our historic identity.

**Rivera García, Antonio**. La amenaza latente del vagabundo en la literatura política del siglo XVI. *Daimon Rev Filosof*, 10, 127-142, Ja-Je 95.

**Rivera López, Eduardo**. ¿Es el "trilema de Fishkin" un verdadero trilema?. *Analisis Filosof*, 16(1), 27-41, My 96.

Fishkin claims that the three liberal principles concerning assignment of social positions (family autonomy, merit and equal life chances) constitute a "trilemma"; the realization of any two of these principles precludes the realization of the third. In this paper, I try to prove that this is the case, only if these principles are interpreted in an extreme way. Liberalism, however, has strong reasons to reject such interpretation of each of these principles. Moreover, these reasons are independent from the question of whether their conjunction may be conflictive or not. If we assume moderate versions of the principles (as I claim liberalism would), the trilemma disappears or, at least, becomes much weaker.

**Rizk, Hadi**. Etre social et logique de l'impuissance. *Rev Phil Fr*, 3, 355-368, Jl-S 96.

AUTHOR INDEX 873 Robertson, Diana C

**Rizzacasa, Aurelio**. L'atteggiamento metafisico come espressione del trascendentale nella soggettività. *G Metaf*, 18(1-2), 281-286, Ja-Ag 96.

The purpose of our work is methodological; within this scope, we intend to restore the sense and the meaning of metaphysical investigation in present-day culture, which is called postmetaphysical in philosophy, thus referring to our times using a critical connotation. In this perspective, metaphysics becomes a philosophical position expressed as transcendental within an intentional consciousness structured as a universal feature of subjectivity. It is obvious, therefore, that our interpretation intends to surpass those conceptions which are philosophically weak and dissolve subjectivity.

**Roback Morse, Jennifer**. Who is Rational Economic Man?. *Soc Phil Pol*, 14(1), 179-206, Wint 97.

This paper expands the economists view of rational economic behavior. The paper models the human person as performing both a philosophical task and a calculation task. The philosophical task corresponds to choosing the utility function, which economists currently do not study. The paper shows how several commonly observed phenomena can be explained, using this expanded framework. These phenomena include the problem of disappointment, the problem of self-destructive behavior and the choice to renounce a large class of material goods.

**Robb, David**. The Properties of Mental Causation. *Phil Quart*, 47(187), 178-194, Ap 97.

If mental properties are not physical properties, how can they be causally relevant to what goes on in the causally closed physical world? I argue that this question can be answered by distinguishing two sorts of properties: types (i.e., universals or classes) and tropes (i.e., particularized properties). Although mental types are not physical types, every mental trope is a physical trope. And since tropes, not types, are causally relevant when one event causes another, mental tropes can be relevant to what goes on in the closed physical world.

**Robb, Fiona**. The Function of Repetition in Scholastic Theology of the Trinity. *Vivarium*, 34(1), 41-75, My 96.

**Robbeck, Johannes**. "Technik und symbolische Form bei Cassirer" in *Grenzen der kritischen Vernunft,* Schmid, Peter A, 197-212. Basel, Schwabe Verlag, 1997.

**Robenstine, Clark**. Confronting the Assumptions That Dominate Education Reform. *J Thought*, 32(3), 113-121, Fall 97.

One of the most striking aspects of the failure of contemporary education reform is that reform consistently accepts the system as it is. Few "reform" measures require fundamental alteration in the nature of the relationships among those who constitute the school system. By focusing on the system and the relationships within that system, the essay identifies and elaborates some of the ways that education reform is rooted in a set of systemic assumptions which constrains the very possibility of genuine reform. Left unchallenged, these assumptions have attained the formal status of inherent truth and will continue to delimit reform success.

**Roberts, Don D**. "A Decision Method for Existential Graphs" in *Studies in the Logic of Charles Sanders Peirce,* Houser, Nathan (ed), 387-401. Bloomington, Indiana Univ Pr, 1997.

By 1903 Charles Peirce had developed a decision procedure for his diagrammatic system of logic, the *Existential Graphs*(EG). It is clear from an examination of his manuscripts that he knew exactly what is meant by what is now called the decision problem, and it is also clear that he was confident his method could be extended to what we call first order logic. Though he was wrong about this extension, his procedure for the propositional logic part of EG is ingenious and is presented in detail in this essay.

**Roberts, Don D** (ed) and Houser, Nathan (ed) and Van Evra, James (ed). *Studies in the Logic of Charles Sanders Peirce.* Bloomington, Indiana Univ Pr, 1997.

This volume provides a comprehensive exploration of Charles Sanders Peirce's work in mathematics and formal logic, highlighting linkages between Peirce's work and present developments in the science and history of logic. The essays are collected from an internationally distinguished group of scholars who gathered at Harvard University in 1989 to commemorate Peirce's birth in 1839. Not just of historical interest, *Studies in the Logic of Charles Sanders Peirce* shows the considerable relevance of Peirce's work for current research. The stimulating depth and originality of Peirce's thought and the continuing importance and usefulness of his ideas are brought out by this major volume. (publisher)

**Roberts, Edwin A**. Liberalism as a Crisis in Democratic Theory: Three Critiques Reconsidered. *Nature Soc Thought*, 8(3), 275-308, 1995.

Ideologically dominant today is a resurgent classical liberalism that emphasizes the market-oriented values of possessive individualism and is often associated with democratization. This essay explores the degree to which this association should be seen as representing a crisis in democratic theory. Three key works by C. B. Macpherson, Benjamin Barber and Andrew Levine are reevaluated. Representing democratic liberalism, communitarianism and Marxism respectively, these three maintain that democratization of social and political life entails the downgrading, not expansion, of liberal values. After examining the contributions of these figures to democratic theory, the essay examines overlooked areas, specifically race and gender. The author argues that only by reinvigorating genuinely democratic thinking can an effective left political practice be developed for promoting a just, humane and progressive social order.

**Roberts, Lawrence D**. How Demonstrations Connect with Referential Intentions. *Austl J Phil*, 75(2), 190-200, Je 97.

David Kaplan switched from holding demonstrations to be sometimes required for the determination of demonstrative reference to holding that they are never so required and that only referential intentions are needed for determining such reference. I discuss Marga Reimer's and Kent Bach's arguments about this switch and I develop an account of reasonable referential intentions on the basis of some ideas from Donnellan. On this account, reasonable referential intentions are not merely in the head, but instead are *intentional actions* that require certain public and social mechanisms (including demonstrations sometimes) which enable an audience to pick out the referent.

**Roberts, Marcus**. Analytical Marxism—An Ex-Paradigm? The Odyssey of G.A. Cohen. *Rad Phil*, 82, 17-28, Mr-Ap 97.

This article examines G. A. Cohen's claim that the Marxist theory of exploitation relies upon a self-ownership principle inconsistent with socialist egalitarianism. It has two principal aims. 1) To examine Cohen's intellectual development and more generally that of analytical Marxism, from the 1970s onwards. 2) To provide a clear exposition of Cohen's position on exploitation and critical assessment of it. It is argued that, in spite of the power of Cohen's critique of Nozickian libertarianism, his position on exploitation is deeply problematic and that there is no longer any very informative sense in which he can be described as a Marxist (or semi-Marxist) philosopher.

**Roberts, Marcus**. *Analytical Marxism: A Critique.* New York, Verso, 1996.

Marcus Roberts's study serves as a lucid survey of the analytical Marxists' contributions to the understanding of historical materialism, exploitation, class structure, method, politics and ethics—a panoramic *tour de force* which he brings up to date with considerations on John Roemer's recent work on models of socialism. (publisher,edited)

**Roberts, Melinda A**. Human Cloning: A Case of No Harm Done?. *J Med Phil*, 21(5), 537-554, O 96.

Some have objected to the laboratory cloning of human pre-embryos on the grounds that the procedure would violate the dignity of and respect owed to human pre-embryos. Others have argued that human cloning ought be permitted if it will predictably benefit, or at least not burden, individuals who are, unlike the human pre-embryo, clearly entitled to our respect and concern. Taking this latter position, the legal theorist John A. Robertson has argued that, since cloning does not harm anyone who is clearly entitled to our respect and concern, it should be permitted. In particular, the offspring of cloning, he argues, cannot be genuinely harmed by cloning, since they owe their very existence to the cloning procedure. In this paper, I argue that cloning coupled with its related procedures does in fact place the flesh and blood human offspring of cloning at risk of genuine harm, I thus provide a basis for questioning the moral permissibility of cloning and its related technologies *without* implying that the human pre-embryo has dignity or is owed respect.

**Roberts, Peter**. Defending Freirean Intervention. *Educ Theor*, 46(3), 335-352, Sum 96.

While Paulo Freire's work has been widely admired, his pedagogy has also attracted strong criticism in some quarters. C.A. Bowers has mounted a comprehensive and sustained attack on the theory and practice of Freirean education. Bowers sees Freire as a "carrier" of a highly problematic Western mindset: one which has a "cultural bias" toward progressive change, critical reflection, and intervention. Bowers suggests that Freirean adult literacy programmes, in challenging traditional systems of authority and belief, are potentially invasive and hegemonic. This paper critiques Bowers's analysis and defends Freirean pedagogical intervention. The author argues that Bowers homogenizes Western modes of thought, romanticizes "traditional" cultures, and largely ignores the oppressive realities facing Freire in Brazil in the early 1960s. The paper develops the view that programmes of education are necessarily interventionist, and concludes that Freire's pedagogical approach in Brazil, while not devoid of difficulties and contradictions, was justified under the circumstances.

**Robertson, Chris** and Street, Marc D and Geiger, Scott W. Ethical Decision Making: The Effects of Escalating Commitment. *J Bus Ethics*, 16(11), 1153-1161, Ag 97.

In this paper a new variable is introduced into the ethical decision making literature. This variable, exposure to escalation situations, is posited to increase the likelihood that individuals will choose unethical decision alternatives. Further, it is proposed that escalation situations should be included as a variable in Jones's (1991) comprehensive model of ethical decision making. Finally, research propositions are provided based on the relationship between escalating commitment and the ethical decision making process.

**Robertson, Diana C** and Laufer, William S. Corporate Ethics Initiatives as Social Control. *J Bus Ethics*, 16(10), 1029-1048, Jl 97.

Efforts to institutionalize ethics in corporations have been discussed without first addressing the desirability of norm conformity or the possibility that the means used to elicit conformity will be coercive. This article presents a theoretical context, grounded in models of social control, within which ethics initiatives may be evaluated. Ethics initiatives are discussed in relation to variables that already exert control in the workplace, such as environmental controls, organizational controls and personal controls.

**Robertson, Diana C** and Nicholson, Nigel. Expressions of Corporate Social Responsibility in U.K. Firms. *J Bus Ethics*, 15(10), 1095-1106, O 96.

This study examines corporate publications of U.K. firms to investigate the nature of corporate social responsibility disclosure. Using a stakeholder approach to corporate social responsibility, our results suggest a hierarchical model of disclosure: from general rhetoric to specific endeavors to implementation and monitoring. Industry differences in attention to specific stakeholder groups are noted. These differences suggest the need to understand the effects on social responsibility disclosure of factors in a firm's immediate operating environment, such as the extent of government regulation and level of competitiveness in the industry.

**Robin, Richard S**. "Classical Pragmatism and Pragmatism's Proof" in *The Rule of Reason: The Philosophy of Charles Sanders Peirce,* Forster, Paul (ed), 139-152. Toronto, Univ of Toronto Pr, 1997.

**Robins, Michael H**. Is It Rational To Carry Out Strategic Intentions?. *Philosophia (Israel),* 25(1-4), 191-221, Ap 97.

Normally when we inform an intention to perform some act at a later time our practical reasoning begins with a consideration of the action and terminates with the intention. This is why we normally think that the reasons for so intending are the same for acting. This assumption, however, founders in a variety of cases in which the intentions produce "autonomous effects, i.e., effects independent of and at odds with the effects of the action. Such autonomous effects often generate reasons for intending to act that are reasons *not* to act accordingly. However, a better understanding of these "strategic paradoxes," as they have come to be known, suggests that, contrary to first appearances, the reasons for intending must be reasons for conformative action. This is because the information available at the time of intending does not change at the time of acting. The principle defended is that sameness of information *ex ante* to *ex post* is rationality-preserving, analogous to deductive validity's being truth-preserving.

**Robins, Michael H**. *Promising, Intending, and Moral Autonomy.* New York, Cambridge Univ Pr, 1984.

In Robin's view, however, there is much in the theory of action and particularly in the concept of intending, that is normative and can contribute to the foundations of ethics. He puts forward the novel and challenging thesis that a primitive notion of commitment is involved in the very notion of an intention and that this provides the basis on which the notions of a decision, a vow and finally the crucial notion of a voluntary obligation or a promise can be constructed. In this way, he argues, social acts like promising and contracting are built up from normative elements which are nonsocial and psychological. The link between action theory and ethics is further strengthened in that the same concept of commitment is also seen as vital to such fundamental, nonvoluntary obligations as veracity, respect for others and fair play. (publisher, edited)

**Robinson, Bambi E S**. "On a Woman's Obligation to Have an Abortion" in *Reproduction, Technology, and Rights: Biomedical Ethics Reviews,* Humber, James M (ed), 115-135. Clifton, Humana Pr, 1996.

I argue that when a woman learns she is pregnant with a fetus which has a serious problem which will result in a child that will know little other than pain and suffering until its death, she has an obligation to abort it. My argument consists of two parts: first, that it is wrong to deliberately inflict protracted suffering on a sentient being. In the case of a seriously impaired fetus, the judgment is made that life, itself, will be a harm to the child and thus not in its best interest. Second, the emotional and physical costs to the parents are less in the case of a second trimester abortion than in bringing such a seriously impaired child into the world. I consider, but reject, the justification that obligatory abortions in such cases serve the public good.

**Robinson, Bambi E S**. Birds Do It. Bees Do It. So Why Not Single Women and Lesbians?. *Bioethics,* 11(3-4), 217-227, Jl 97.

In this paper I will argue that marital status and sexual orientation should not serve as a barrier to accessing the world of reproductive medicine. I will base this conclusion on two arguments. First, that justice requires that we treat like cases alike. Just as we would not accept or reject patients for cardiac rehabilitation programs based on factors such as a history of poor eating habits, so too we should not look at nonmedical factors such as marital status when deciding whether to treat infertility. For the second justification for the conclusion of equal access to ART (assisted reproductive technologies), I will examine the concept of the family. I will argue that it is morally acceptable for single women and lesbian couples to have children and to head families. (edited)

**Robinson, Daniel N**. Commentary on "Autobiography, Narrative, and the Freudian Concept of Life History". *Phil Psychiat Psych,* 4(3), 205-207, S 97.

**Robinson, Daniel N** and Harré, Rom. What Makes Language Possible? Ethological Foundationalism in Reid and Wittgenstein. *Rev Metaph,* 50(3), 483-498, Mr 97.

Thomas Reid in the eighteenth century and Wittgenstein in the *Investigations* consider the necessary preconditions for language and arrive, by different paths, at a naturalistic point of origin. Reid's critique of (Lockean) conventionalist explanations of meaning is grounded in the proposition that conventions themselves presuppose the very linguistic resources needed for there to be compacts and convenants. This leads Reid to a theory of natural language on which artificial languages might then be constructed. Wittgenstein's concept of "natural expressions" are similar and lead to much the same theory. Both accounts successfully avoid the pitfalls of Chomskian "nativistic" theories while, at the same time, preserving the required foundationalism.

**Robinson, Hoke**. Kantian Appearances and Intentional Objects. *Kantstudien,* 87(4), 448-454, 1996.

A number of Kant scholars recently have explicated Kant's appearances as like the intentional object found in Husserlian phenomenology. This paper examines the notion of intentional object and tries to isolate the characteristics that make it appropriate for interpreting Kantian appearances, as opposed to things in themselves.

**Robinson, Howard**. "The Anti-Materialist Strategy and the 'Knowledge Argument'" in *Objections to Physicalism,* Robinson, Howard (ed), 159-183. New York, Clarendon/Oxford Pr, 1996.

**Robinson, Howard**. How to Give Analytical Rigour to 'Soupy' Metaphysics. *Inquiry,* 40(1), 95-113, Mr 97.

**Robinson, Howard** (ed). *Objections to Physicalism.* New York, Clarendon/Oxford Pr, 1996.

Physicalism has in recent years become almost an orthodoxy, especially in the philosophy of mind. Many philosophers, however, feel uneasy about this development, and this volume is intended as a collective response to it. Together these papers, written by philosophers from Britain, the USA, and Australasia, show that physicalism faces enormous problems in every area in which it is discussed. (publisher, edited)

**Robinson, Jenefer**. "Introduction: New Ways of Thinking about Musical Meaning" in *Music and Meaning,* Robinson, Jenefer (ed), 1-20. Ithaca, Cornell Univ Pr, 1997.

**Robinson, Jenefer** (ed). *Music and Meaning.* Ithaca, Cornell Univ Pr, 1997.

This volume focuses on the many and various kinds of meaning in music. Do musical meanings exist exclusively in internal, formal musical relations or might they also be found in the relationship between music and other areas of experience, such as action, emotion, ideas, and values? Also discussed is the vexed question why people listen to and apparently enjoy music that expresses unpleasant emotions, such as melancholy or despair. Among the particular pieces the writers discuss are Mahler's Ninth Symphony, Shostakovich's Tenth Symphony, and Schubert's last sonata. More broadly, they consider the relation of musical meaning and interpretation to language, storytelling, drama, imagination, metaphor, and emotion. (publisher, edited)

**Robinson, Jenefer**. Two Concepts of Expression. *J Aes Educ,* 31(2), 9-17, Sum 97.

**Robinson, Mark** and Moore, Mick. Can Foreign Aid Be Used to Promote Good Government in Developing Countries?. *Ethics Int Affairs,* 8, 142-158, 1994.

**Robinson, Mary Redner** and Thiel, Mary Martha. Physicians' Collaboration with Chaplains: Difficulties and Benefits. *J Clin Ethics,* 8(1), 94-103, Spr 97.

**Robinson, Thomas M**. "The *Dissoi Logoi* and Early Greek Scepticism" in *Scepticism in the History of Philosophy: A Pan-American Dialogue,* Popkin, Richard H (ed), 27-36. Dordrecht, Kluwer, 1996.

**Robinson, Timothy A** (ed). *God.* Indianapolis, Hackett, 1996.

*God* brings together philosophical and literary works representing the many ways—metaphysical, scientific, analytic, phenomenological—in which philosophers and others have attempted to address the question of the existence of God. (publisher, edited)

**Robinson, Walter**. Commentary on "Family Dynamics and Children in Medical Research". *J Clin Ethics,* 7(4), 362-364, Wint 96.

**Robinson, Walter** (& others) and Macklin, Ruth and Beer, Douglas A. Bad Night in the ER—Patients' Preferences and Reasonable Accommodation: Discussed by Douglas A. Beer, Ruth Macklin, Walter Robinson, and Philip Wang. *Ethics Behavior,* 6(4), 371-383, 1996.

**Robinson, William S**. Some Nonhuman Animals Can Have Pains in a Morally Relevant Sense. *Biol Phil,* 12(1), 51-71, Ja 97.

In a series of works, Peter Carruthers has argued for the denial of the title proposition. Here, I defend that proposition by offering direct support drawn from relevant sciences and by undercutting Carruthers's argument. In doing the latter, I distinguish an intrinsic theory of consciousness from Carruthers's relational theory of consciousness. This relational theory has two readings, one of which makes essential appeal to evolutionary theory. I argue that neither reading offers a successful view.

**Robles, José A**. "Berkeley: Scepticism, Matter and Infinite Divisibility" in *Scepticism in the History of Philosophy: A Pan-American Dialogue,* Popkin, Richard H (ed), 87-97. Dordrecht, Kluwer, 1996.

**Robles, José A** and Benítez, Laura. Ralph Cudworth (1617-1688) sobre la infinitud de Dios. *Mathesis,* 10(2), 129-152, My 94.

In this paper we put forth and discuss Cudworth's arguments for God's immensity (both temporal and spatial), which he presents in his thick book *The True Intellectual System of the Universe* [Cudworth 1678]. Cudworth, unlike his colleague Henry More (both from the Cambridge neo-Platonists group) argues for an infinite but unextended God. Cudworth in his discussion, makes clear that he follows the Aristotelian proposal with respect to the empirical infinite: if there is anything like that, it can only be a potential infinite; the only actual infinity is that of the divinity and it is not empirical. On the other hand, God's eternity *is not* a never ending temporal *process* and God's ubiquity is not in need of His being infinitely extended.

**Robles, Laureano**. Unamuno traductor de Th. Carlyle. *Daimon Rev Filosof,* 10, 7-22, Ja-Je 95.

This article points out Unamuno's period of time spent on the translation into Spanish of the book by T. Carlyle, "History of the French Revolution". At the same time it focused our attention on the influence that this task performed on Unamuno's work, since this author was considered, by means of it, a mixed synthesis of preacher, philosopher, poet and romantic historian.

**Roccaro, Giuseppe**. Metafisica tra scienza e sapienza: Tafsīr Lām 52-58 di Ibn Rusd. *G Metaf,* 18(3), 409-441, S-D 96.

**Rocha, Acílio da Silva**. Perspectivas da Prospectiva: Acerca da Obra de Lúcio Craveiro da Silva. *Rev Port Filosof,* 52(1-4), 1-26, Ja-D 96.

**Rocha, Ethel M**. Hobbes contra Descartes: A Questao da Substância Imaterial. *Cad Hist Filosof Cie*, 5(1-2), 73-85, Ja-D 95.

In this article the second objection proposed by Hobbes to Descartes will be analyzed. The aim of this analysis is to argue that this objection is only possible if, as does Hobbes but not Descartes, we take for granted two claims: 1) That there is a distinction between the proposition "I think" and the proposition "I exist"; and 2) That in the *Meditations* Descartes deals with the existence of things, that is, with the question of how things are, and not with the conditions of possibility of knowledge, that is, and not with the question of the access to things. The hypothesis sustained in this article is that it is possible to demonstrate that Descartes argues that the principle that passes through all the multiplicity of acts is an immaterial "I" in the sense that it is the condition of thought which, in its turn, is the condition of the idea of extension as the essence of any possible object and, therefore, is the condition of any external object.

**Rochlitz, Rainer**. L'esthétique et l'artistique. *Rev Int Phil*, 50(198), 651-667, 1996.

Kant's aesthetics contains three contradictory projects, all still decisive for actual aesthetic debates: romantical metaphysics—up to nowaday's negative ideals like *formlessness*—reads artworks as *true philosophy*; French empiricism (Genette, Schaeffer) defends objectivism of neutral description and relativism of *subjective appreciation*, due to causal effects of objects and works on individuals; 3) against these two (dominant) temptations, intersubjectivism develops the Kantian (pre-Wittgensteinian) idea of *not calling beautiful what you just like*: aesthetic qualities of objects are referred to by common predicates; identity and quality of artworks are objects of critical debates where we distinguish between preferences and pertinent verdicts.

**Rockmore, Tom**. "Hegel and the Social Function of Reason" in *Hegel, History, and Interpretation,* Gallagher, Shaun, 117-143. Albany, SUNY Pr, 1997.

**Rockmore, Tom**. Fichte, die sujektive Wende und der kartesianische Traum. *Fichte-Studien*, 9, 115-125, 1997.

**Rockmore, Tom**. *Heidegger and French Philosophy*. New York, Routledge, 1995.

**Rockmore, Tom**. Heidegger and Representationalism. *Hist Phil Quart*, 13(3), 363-374, Jl 96.

**Rockmore, Tom**. Margolis and the Historical Turn. *Man World*, 30(2), 145-149, Ap 97.

**Rockmore, Tom**. *On Heidegger's Nazism and Philosophy*. Berkeley, Univ of Calif Pr, 1992.

**Rockwell, Teed**. Awareness, Mental Phenomena and Consciousness: A Synthesis of Dennett and Rosenthal. *J Consciousness Stud*, 3(5-6), 463-476, 1996.

Both Dennett and his critics believe that the invalidity of the famed Stalinist-Orwellian distinction is a consequence of his multiple drafts model of consciousness (MDM). This is not so obvious, however, once we recognize that the question 'how do you get experience out of meat?' actually fragments into at least three different questions. How (out of meat) do we get: 1) a unified sense of *self*, 2) *awareness* and 3) *mental phenomena*? In the latter chapters of *Consciousness Explained*, Dennett shows how MDM has a radical and profound way of interrelating awareness and self. But the Stalinist-Orwellian distinction can be dissolved by analyzing the nature of mental phenomena, without making any reference to awareness or self or the MDM. This is because the Stalinist-Orwellian distinction rests on much the same category mistake (confusing of parts with wholes) which Ryle pointed out in his *Concept of Mind*. (edited)

**Rodes, Robert E** and Pospesel, Howard. *Premises and Conclusions: Symbolic Logic for Legal Analysis*. Englewood Cliffs, Prentice Hall, 1997.

This volume presents the elements of contemporary symbolic logic and applies that powerful instrument to reasoning in the law. Deductive logic is employed to illuminate the structure of legal reasoning and clarify various legal problems. Attention has been given to the clear and orderly presentation of concepts and techniques, and to their illustration with practical examples including many legal cases and problems. Numerous exercises are provided so that readers can check their mastery of the material. (publisher, edited)

**Rodetis, George A**. El Greco's Statements on Michelangelo the Painter. *J Aes Educ*, 31(3), 25-37, Fall 97.

**Rodman, Jeffrey**. "Defoe and the Psychotic Subject" in *Critical Studies: Ethics and the Subject,* Simms, Karl (ed), 245-251. Amsterdam, Rodopi, 1997.

**Rodrigo, Pierre**. Justice éthique et politique chez le jeune Aristote: la *Peri Dikaiosunes*. *Diotima*, 25, 136-141, 1997.

**Rodrigo Ewart, Luis**. Conocimiento del alma después de la muerte: Presentación de la doctrina de Santo Tomás de Aquino expuesta en las *Quaestiones disputatae de veritate q. 19 a. 1. Sapientia*, 51(200), 453-463, 1996.

**Rodrigues, Manuel J**. A Obra como Facto Comunicativo. *Philosophica (Portugal)*, 189-205, 1997.

Cet essai se présente comme une réflexion sur le processus historique de génération et de gestion des ressources artistiques (et culturelles), dans une perspective centrée dans l'activité communicative. Visée comme facteur de communication résistant aux usures de l'acte communicatif, elle est interprétée comme un trafic de sens canalisé par des intérets sociaux mais culturellement mobilisée par un intêret excentrique. Produisant l'estime, l'oeuvre d'art se présente comme une anticipation d'avenir, réussie dans la reconnaissance de la valeur de la présence et dans l'éxigence de "meilleur" par rapport au mode

de faire; ainsi, elle manifeste une intentionalité transsistémique qui prépare la sensibilité à sa supération en humanité et dessine un temps à venir qui refuse les idéaux directeurs, terminaux ou provisoires.

**Rodrigues Évora, Fátima Regina**. A Origem do Conceito do *Impetus. Cad Hist Filosof Cie*, 5(1-2), 281-305, Ja-D 95.

This article analyses the theory of imparted and incorporeal kinetic force introduced by John Philoponus in the sixth century, with the object of discovering whether, as Wohlwill claims, this theory can be considered the most ancient source of the theory of impetus. In the sequel we try to establish whether the theory of Philoponus had a determining role as part of the link connecting Aristotelian physics and modern mechanics. To this end we investigate the possible influence of Philoponus on the subsequent work of the Arab philosophers Avicenna and Avempace, through whom the theory of imparted and incorporeal kinetic force reappeared in Western Europe during the eleventh and twelfth centuries.

**Rodríguez, Amán Rosales**. Desarrollo técnico y evolución histórica: modelos metafísicos y antropológico-culturales. *Rev Filosof (Costa Rica)*, 34(83-84), 359-364, D 96.

Current research in history and philosophy of technology can tackle its subject-matter from two points of view. On the one hand there is an all-embracing, in a broad sense *metaphysical* perspective (Heidegger, Ellul, Schelsky). On the other hand there is a more sober, experience-oriented *anthropological-cultural* perspective (Landes, Basalla, Pacey). Both approaches will be presented and compared in this paper. The necessity of an integral, metaphysical-anthropological perspective will be stressed.

**Rodríguez, Ramón**. Reflexión y evidencia: Aspectos de la transformación hermenéutica de la fenomenología en la obra de Heidegger. *An Seminar Hist Filosof*, 13, 57-74, 1996.

The paper examines why Heidegger's "phenomenological hermeneutics of facticity" both rejects as a way of thinking unfit for its task and posits hermeneutic intuition as a logical consequence thereof. It is hypothesized that the inspiring model of this intuition is the idea of evidence analyzed by Husserl in the sixth *Logical Investigation*.

**Rodríguez, Víctor**. "Sobre la supuesta racionalidad de las reglas heurísticas" in *La racionalidad: su poder y sus límites,* Nudler, Oscar (ed), 399-406. Barcelona, Ed Paidos, 1996.

I maintain that the debate on Quine's metaethical views lacks a precise specification of the level in which the methodological comparison between science and ethics takes place and that this fact renders the debate endless and rather fruitless. I claim that it is possible to distinguish, at least, two different levels where the comparison between science and ethics can possibly take place. I also claim that the choice among these levels depends on our answer to a prior question: *why the epistemological comparison between science and ethics?* My answer is: *in order to know whether or not ethics can be defended from the sceptic as successfully as science.* (edited)

**Rodríguez Braun, Carlos**. Ilustración y Utilitarismo en Iberoamérica. *Telos (Spain)*, 1(3), 95-109, O 92.

**Rodríguez Braun, Carlos** and Schwartz, P. Las relaciones entre Jeremías Bentham y S. Bolívar. *Telos (Spain)*, 1(3), 45-68, O 92.

**Rodríguez Camarero, Luis**. Darwin: Evolution and Contingency (in Spanish). *Agora (Spain)*, 15(2), 153-163, 1996.

**Rodríguez Fouz, Marta**. Meditated History: An Approach to Karl Mannheim's Sociology of Knowledge through his Analysis of Mentalities (Spanish). *Rev Filosof (Venezuela)*, 24(2), 3-27, Jl-D 96.

This work stems from a steady attention to that area in Karl Mannheim's thought which deals with ideological and utopian thought. The analysis has been approached through an attempt to bring together Mannheim's reflections about these forms of collective mentality and his proposal concerning a sociology of knowledge segregated from distortions of the thinker's own historical settlement. The main focus has been placed on acknowledging the implications in theoretical reflections as well as individual historical actions stemming from Mannheim's radical call to an awareness of each one's present.

**Rodriguez Pereyra, Gonzalo**. Sobre una versión del nominalismo de semejanzas. *Rev Filosof (Argentina)*, 11(1-2), 35-41, N 96.

The concern of this paper is a version of *resemblance nominalism* according to which resemblance classes, i.e., classes of resembling things, are determined by paradigms. I show that the theory is false, since paradigms do not generally determine resemblance classes. Although I concentrate upon the version of the theory which was delineated by H.H. Price, my results apply to any other theory constructing resemblance classes out from paradigms.

**Rodríguez Ramírez, Carlos Alberto**. Algunos elementos para una deontología periodística. *Rev Filosof (Costa Rica)*, 34(83-84), 303-310, D 96.

From an ethical perspective, this paper analyzes the role of media and their reference to reality regarding specific topics such as violence, intimacy and privacy, indifference and passivity and, of course, the social role the communicator plays.

**Rodríguez Rodríguez, Rodolfo J**. Modelos cognoscitivos para la filosofía contemporánea de la mente. *Rev Filosof (Costa Rica)*, 34(83-84), 423-432, D 96.

This article examines models of the mind that have been developed from the cognitive science research. The first set are the information processing models such as the symbolic, the subsymbolic (connectionism) and the modularity. The second set are the cognitive neurobiology models such as the F. Crick and P.S. Churchland reauctionist models of mental processes, but specially the neural Darwinism of the Nobel Prize: G. Edelman. Finally the author suggests other kind of mental interpretations such as: the quantum thought of R. Penrose, the subjective ontology of J. Searle and the interpretation of the conscious mind of D. Dennett.

**Rodríguez Salas, Antonio Jesús** and Torrens, Antoni. Wajsberg Algebras and Post Algebras. *Stud Log*, 53(1), 1-19, F 94.

We give a presentation of Post algebras of order n + 1 (n "is equal to or greater than" 1) as n + 1 bounded Wajsberg algebras with an additional constant and we show that a Wajsberg algebra admits a P-algebra reduct if and only if it is n + 1 bounded. (edited)

**Rodríguez Sedano, Alfredo**. El trabajo como división de funciones. *Anu Filosof*, 29(2), 993-1001, 1996.

Work and its consequences in enterprise are studied. Family as an institution is the basic example of division of work, which is the situation where human being perfectionates himself. Perfection takes place working, as an integrating technique which has no limits.

**Rodríguez-Alcázar, Javier**. Naturalism Radicalized. *Metaphilosophy*, 27(4), 356-380, O 96.

In this paper I distinguish two ways of using the expression 'epistemological naturalism'. In one sense, naturalism amounts to a denial that epistemology should be understood as a kind of *first philosophy* providing the foundations for science from outside. In a second sense, naturalism holds that human knowledge is a *natural* phenomenon and that epistemology should be seen as a chapter of *natural* science. Finally, I argue for a conception of epistemology which is best described as a *radical antifoundationalism*. This conception sticks to the requirements that follow from naturalism when understood in the first sense above and takes the cluster of theses that give birth to the second as subsidiary and revisable. (edited)

**Rodríguez-Alcázar, Javier**. Naturalized Epistemology and the Is/Ought Gap. *Dialectica*, 50(2), 137-152, 1996.

This article discusses whether a naturalistic philosopher (e.g., Quine) should endorse the epistemological version of the "is/ought gap" thesis. Quine thinks that there is an epistemological gap between normative epistemology and normative ethics, but I claim that anybody holding his naturalistic and holistic views has good reasons to deny the existence of a gap separating either epistemology from ethics or descriptive discourse from normative discourse. I maintain that both gaps can be bridged if one adopts, like Quine, a holistic view of justification. Although justification in science, epistemology and ethics are different in certain respects, holism accounts for the justification of scientific, epistemological and ethical beliefs at a general level.

**Rodríguez-Campoamor, Hernán**. Monoteísmo, sacrificio, matadero: teodiceas y realidades históricas. *El Basilisco*, 22, 71-76, Jl-D 96.

**Rodríguez-Consuegra, Francisco**. Nominal Definitions and Logical Consequence in the Peano School. *Theoria (Spain)*, 12(28), 125-137, Ja 97.

This paper is devoted to show the development of some of the model-theoretic ideas which are clearly present in the main members of the Peano school (Peano himself, Burali-Forti, Pieri and Padoa) as a result of their conception of nominal definitions. Also, their semantic definition of logical consequence (Pieri, Padoa) is viewed as one of the outcomes of that conception. Some examples of their use of the expression "nominal definition" are presented first. Second, the main advantages of this kind of definition, as they saw them, are briefly explained, mainly in a philosophical context. Finally, already in the kernel of the paper, some of the details of the model-theoretic view itself are shown, first in Peano, then in Pieri and Padoa, including in both cases some study of their semantic definitions of logical consequence.

**Rodriguez-Pereyra, Gonzalo**. There might be Nothing: The Subtraction Argument Improved. *Analysis*, 57(3), 159-166, Jl 97.

The paper deals with Baldwin's *subtraction argument* for nihilism, the thesis that it is metaphysically possible that there are no concrete objects. Baldwin supports his premiss that there might be a world with a finite domain of concrete objects by making failure to satisfy the identity of indiscernibles the mark of concreteness. I argue that this fails to support the premise and then propose replacing it by one saying that there might be a world with a finite domain of concrete object, where a concrete object is any object that is concrete, memberless and a maximal occupant of a connected spatio-temporal region. The argument thus modified proves nihilism nicely.

**Roe, Emery**. Sustainable Development and the Local Justice Framework. *Phil Soc Crit*, 23(2), 97-114, Mr 97.

Jon Elster's notion of 'local justice systems' helps reconceive sustainable development in several fresh ways. Keeping options open for the future use of resources turns out to be a justice/injustice cycle: the more sustainable development becomes a global phenomenon, the more locally unjust its uniform application would necessarily be. The more uniform the application, the greater the local pressure for suitably varied alternatives. But the more varied the applications, the greater the chance of global injustice arising from the decentralization and lack of coordination on the ground. In this way, sustainable development must be seen as not ending when unjust global systems become more just, but rather as continuing through a set of iterations whose moments include a *rejection* of an overly globalized sustainable development.

**Roels, Shirley J**. The Business Ethics of Evangelicals. *Bus Ethics Quart*, 7(2), 109-122, Mr 97.

Understanding the evangelical framework for business ethics is important, since business evangelicals are well positioned to exercise considerable future influence. This article develops the context for understanding evangelical business ethics by examining their history, theology and culture. It then relates the findings to evangelical foundations for business ethics. The thesis is that business ethics, as practiced by those in the evangelical community, has developed inductively from a base of applied experience. As a result, emphases on piety, witnessing, tithing and neighborliness, important foundations in the evangelical model for business ethics, have resulted in a multitude of applied ethical strategies. (edited)

**Roemer, John E**. *Theories of Distributive Justice*. Cambridge, Harvard Univ Pr, 1996.

Roemer explores the major new philosophical concepts of the theory of distributive justice—primary goals, functionings and capability, responsibility in its various forms, procedural versus outcome justice, midfare—and shows how they can be sharpened and clarified with the aid of economic analysis. He critiques and extends the ideas of major contemporary theories of distributive justice, including those of Rawls, Sen, Nozick, and Dworkin. Beginning from the recent theories of Richard Arneson and G.A. Cohen, he constructs a theory of equality of opportunity. (edited)

**Römpp, Georg**. Pragmatismus redivivus? Eine Kritik an der Revitalisierung des pragmatistischen Grundgedankens. *Theol Phil*, 71(2), 187-204, 1996.

**Roeper, Peter**. Region-Based Topology. *J Phil Log*, 26(3), 251-309, Je 97.

A topological description of space is given, based on the relation of *connection* among regions and the property of being *limited*. A minimal set of 10 constraints is shown to permit definitions of points and of open and closed sets of points and to be characteristic of locally compact $T_2$ spaces. The effect of adding further constraints is investigated, especially those that characterize continua. Finally, the properties of mappings in region-based topology are studied. Not all such mappings correspond to point functions and those that do correspond to continuous functions.

**Roeper, Peter**. The Link between Probability Functions and Logical Consequence. *Dialogue (Canada)*, 36(1), 15-26, Wint 97.

On défend ici l'idée que la définition des notions sémantiques à l'aide des fonctions de probabilité devrait être vue non pas comme une généralisation (sous le nom de *sémantique probabiliste*) de la sémantique standard en termes d'assignations de valeurs de vérité, mais plutôt comme une généralisation aux degrés de conséquence logique, de la caractérisation de la relation de conséquence que l'on retrouve dans le calcul des séquents de Gentzen.

**Roeper, Peter** and Leblanc, Hughes. De *A* et *B*, de leur indépendance logique, et de ce qu'ils n'ont aucun contenu factuel commun. *Dialogue (Canada)*, 36(1), 137-155, Wint 97.

The logical independence of two statements is tantamount to their probabilistic independence, the latter understood in a sense that derives from stochastic independence. And analogous logical and probabilistic senses of having the same factual content similarly coincide. These results are extended to notions of nonsymmetrical independence and independence among more than two statements.

**Röttgers, Kurt**. Kant Zigeuner. *Kantstudien*, 88(1), 60-86, 1997.

Kant has had no special interest in the gipsies. But why should he have it? This question is examined here. And with regard to newly found and edited texts of his Königsberg colleague Chr. J. Krauss concerning linguistic and social studies about the gipsies, it is shown here how highly improbable for Kant it was to neglect these "strangers among us". It is furthermore argued that there are special reasons why Kant ignored the gipsies, reasons which have to do with the type of discourse of the transcendental philosophy.

**Roetti, Jorge Alfredo**. El finitismo metamatemático de Hilbert y la crítica de Oskar Becker. *Rev Filosof (Argentina)*, 11(1-2), 3-20, N 96.

This paper displays a short outline of Hilbert's finitistic tenets and afterwards the main objections that Oskar Becker proposes against them. Some of the Becker's objections against Hilbert's concept of metamathematics are the next ones: 1) Becker rejects the Hilbertian analogy between complex and transfinite numbers, for the complex numbers satisfy Hankel's principle, but transfinite ones don't obey it. 2) Hilbertian finitism fails inevitably because it cannot establish metamathematically the "weitere form" (*omega*-type) induction and his putative proof of the consistency of arithmetic is based on this questionable strategy (by means of the Hilbertian choice function *e*). Furthermore, Becker shows us a draft of his proof of the consistency of the arithmetic that suggests the later strictly constructive proof of Lorenzen (1955).

**Rötzer, Florian** and Aylesworth, Gary E (trans). *Conversations with French Philosophers*. Atlantic Highlands, Humanities Pr, 1995.

This volume consists of interviews with eight contemporary French philosophers. The main issue of discussion is how contemporary French philosophy is received in Germany, particularly by thinkers such as Jürgen Habermas, who tend to characterize the French as "irrationalists." The charge of irrationalism is provoked by two aspects of contemporary French thought: its preoccupation with the texts of Nietzsche and Heidegger (both of whom are tainted by an association with National Socialism), and the tendency to "aestheticize" philosophy by dissolving discursive identities into radical pluralities. The charge against the French is answered directly by the theorists interviewed here. They point out that the nonrational is not necessarily "irrational," and that the nonrational is discovered when reason seeks its own grounds or limits. The emergence of the nonrational in philosophy is thus a consequence of reason itself, whose destiny, as Kant says, is to find limit and definition in its other. (publisher)

**Rogers, G A J**. "Innate Ideas and the Ancient Philosophy in Cudworth's Epistemology" in *Mind Senior to the World*, Baldi, Marialuisa, 149-161. Milano, FrancoAngeli, 1996.

Cudworth's *Eternal and Immutable Morality* (1731) occupies an important place in the history of seventeenth-century epistemology which has been obscured because it was not published until about sixty years after it was written, by which time Locke's empiricism was all-dominant. It draws creatively on ancient sources to argue a sophisticated neo-Platonic epistemology in opposition to Hobbes and Gassendi. If published when written it would have constituted a significant contribution to the options available in epistemology in the second half of the seventeenth century, and would have presented a more robust challenge to Locke's young mind than was provided by any living thinker.

**Rogers, G A J** (ed). *Locke's Philosophy: Content and Context*. New York, Clarendon/Oxford Pr, 1996.

G.A.J. Rogers argues a unity for Locke's epistemology and politics: 'an epistemology of toleration'. J.R. Milton gives an account of Locke's early intellectual interests; Michael Ayers sees Locke as an empirical realist consciously opposed to Descartes; Martha Bolton examines Locke's answer to the Molyneux Question; Vere Chappell analyses Locke on free action; Michael Losonsky sees *Essay* III as the first modern treatise on philosophy of language; Peter Alexander analyses matter theory, especially the concept of solidity; James Tully examines Locke on political legitimacy and property rights; Ian Harris links Locke's politics and theology. Paschalis Kitromilides and Janina Rosicka explore Locke's influence in Greece and Poland.

**Rogers, James** and Backofen, Rolf and Vijay-Shanker, K. A First-Order Axiomatization of the Theory of Finite Trees. *J Log Lang Info*, 4(1), 5-39, 1995.

We provide first-order axioms for the theories of finite trees with bounded branching and finite trees with arbitrary (finite) branching. The signature is chosen to express, in a natural way, those properties of trees most relevant to linguistic theories. These axioms provide a foundation for results in linguistics that are based on reasoning formally about such properties. We include some observations on the expressive power of these theories relative to traditional language complexity classes.

**Rogers, Katherin A**. Omniscience, Eternity, and Freedom. *Int Phil Quart*, 36(4), 399-412, D 96.

God knows that I will do x tomorrow, so it is necessary that I do x tomorrow. How, then, can I be free? The Molinist and Ockhamist solutions are inadequate. Only the concomitance theory allows an explanation for *how* God foreknows my choices. That God is eternal does not change the fact that it is true *today* that He foreknows my choices and this does make my future choice "necessary." However, it is my actual choice which determines God's knowledge and hence renders itself "necessary." There is no contradiction between this necessity and libertarian freedom.

**Rogers, Katherin A**. *The Anselmian Approach to God and Creation*. Lewiston, Mellen Pr, 1997.

This collection of papers, more than half of which are previously unpublished, defends the traditional medieval approach to problems in the philosophy of religion. It is written largely in the contemporary analytic idiom, and focuses especially on Anselm because he explicitly adopts a libertarian view of freedom. Topics include divine simplicity, the necessity of creation, the problem of evil, God's causal omniscience, divine eternity, divine omniscience (there is *no* middle knowledge of the free choices of rational beings!) and Anselm's theistic idealism (the view that everything is God's idea is both innocuous and useful).

**Rogers, Katherin A**. *The Neoplatonic Metaphysics and Epistemology of Anselm of Canterbury*. Lewiston, Mellen Pr, 1997.

Anselm is famous for his "ontological" argument and his "proof" of the Incarnation. Scholars have been less concerned to study the systematic Augustinian neo-Platonism which underlies Anselm's work. Sticking close to the text, this book shows that Anselm adopted the Platonic theories of divine exemplars and participation, extreme realism with respect to universals, divine illumination, and univocal predication with respect to language about God. Interesting discussions along the way include Anselm's views on the necessity of creation, matter and individuation, and God's knowledge of colors. The book concludes by defending the *Proslogion* argument in the light of Anselm's neo-Platonism.

**Rogers, Kelly**. Beyond Self and Other. *Soc Phil Pol*, 14(1), 1-20, Wint 97.

Today there is a tendency to do ethics on the basis of what I should like to call the "self-other-model." On this view, an action has no moral worth unless it benefits others—and not even then, unless motivated by altruism rather than selfishness. Though aspects of the thesis that morality is "other-based" have been questioned by some, this paper attempts to develop a thoroughgoing critique of this idea, and drawing upon Aristotelian and American pragmatist sources, to make suggestions toward an alternative model for morality. The aim is to show that the "self" is not the basic problem in morality and the "other" is not the solution.

**Rogozinski, Jacob**. Desconstruir a Lei?. *Kriterion*, 34(87), 70-94, Ja-Jl 93.

This paper focuses the analysis on the Heideggerian interpretation of Kant, mainly in the Second Critique. The interpretation ultimately proposes a deconstruction of Kantian ethics as a consequence of the deconstruction of the metaphysics to which such an ethics is connected. According to the paper's author, there is a certain ambiguity in Heidegger's reading (filiation and disruption). This takes the author to ask whether the proposal of an ethics which is free from metaphysics and reconciled with the question about the being would not mean—for Heidegger himself—a kind of return to Kant.

**Rohatyn, Dennis**. *Philosophy History Sophistry*. Amsterdam, Rodopi, 1997.

This book is a provocative critique of chapters in the history of Western thought as well as a postmodernist thinking about historical understanding. With fresh scholarship and fresh wit, it exposes the sophistic games played in theory and interpretation. Descartes, Dostoyevsky, Richard Rorty and Allan Bloom are key authors dissected in these interconnected studies. (published)

**Rohrer, Patricia**. "Infinitely Interesting: Bloom, Kierkegaard, and the Educational Quest" in *Philosophy of Education (1996)*, Margonis, Frank (ed), 369-377. Urbana, Phil Education Soc, 1997.

**Roig, Arturo Andres**. La conducta humana y la naturaleza. *Cuad Etica*, 19-20, 117-131, 1995.

This paper retakes the idea of a "morality of emergency", asking to Latin-American peoples (with their claims for both the consolidation of their social, political and cultural autonomy and the questions concerning humanity's survival). In the present days of "ecological alarm", some forgotten spiritual experiences can be recovered. Thus, the loss of a possible *oikeiosis* as originary principle is analyzed and some *aporia* are posed which seem to be unavoidable in our world. The regaining of the stoic doctrine of *oikeiosis* should permit to reach new levels of understanding and should also permit to overrun a *narrow* vision of "human dignity".

**Rojcewicz, Richard** (trans) and Schuwer, André (trans). *Plato's Sophist*. Bloomington, Indiana Univ Pr, 1997.

In *Plato's Sophist*, Heidegger approaches Plato through Aristotle, devoting the first part of the lectures to an extended commentary on Book VI of the *Nichomachean Ethics*. In a line-by-line interpretation of Plato's later dialogue, the *Sophist*, Heidegger then takes up the relation of Being and nonbeing, the ontological problematic that forms the essential link between Greek philosophy and Heidegger's thought.

**Roland, Alan**. "How Universal is Psychoanalysis? The Self in India, Japan, and the United States" in *Culture and Self*, Allen, Douglas (ed), 27-39. Boulder, Westview Pr, 1997.

**Rollinger, Robin Daryl**. *Husserl's Position in the School of Brentano*. Utrecht, Utrecht, 1996.

**Rolston, III, Holmes**. Menschen ernähren oder Natur erhalten?. *Conceptus*, 29(74), 1-25, 1996.

Ought one feed people rather than save nature? People value many worthwhile things over feeding the hungry; they post national boundaries against the poor; there is unjust distribution of wealth; escalating birthrates offset gains in alleviating poverty; there is low productivity on domesticated lands; sacrificed wildlands are often low in productivity; and significant values may be at stake. Sometimes, one ought to save nature.

**Rolston, III, Holmes**. Nature, the Genesis of Value, and Human Understanding. *Environ Values*, 6(3), 361-364, Ag 97.

In reply to Emyr Vaughan Thomas, "Rolston, Naturogenic Value and Genuine Biocentrism" [*Environmental Values* 6 (1997):355-360], humans on Earth can and ought to examine and evaluate the world outside themselves sufficiently to discover and appreciate values that have been generated there objectively and independently of ourselves, in animals and in plants. Sometimes this will be by finding in nonhumans parallels and analogues of what we know in ourselves. Thomas complains that this is "assimilationist"; I interpret it rather as discovering what we have in common. At other times, humans will recognize achievements in which we take no part.

**Roman, Leslie**. Enesidemo: la recuperación de la tradición escéptica griega. *Pensamiento*, 204(52), 383-402, S-D 96.

Enesidemo es una de esas figuras de transición sin las cuales no puede entenderse posteriormente el significado y desarrollo de un movimiento filosófico. En este caso el escepticismo recibió un apoyo y un desarrollo técnico con el que modificaron las bases y objetivos de esta "doctrina". Con Enesidemo se recupera la verdadera y radical tradición griega, solapada y dulcificada por un escepticismo menos tajante como era el de la academia platónica. En este artículo no sólo se reconoce esta aportación de este singular autor, sino que se ponen en cuestión algunos tópicos que la tradición historiográfica ha venido defendiendo sobre la relación y condiciones que llevaron a Enesidemo a reconocerse como seguidor del pirronismo y a establecer esta corriente "pirrónica" como única plenamente legitimada para asumir el título de escéptica.

**Romanell, Patrick**. The Significance of American Philosophical Naturalism. *Free Inq*, 16(1), 42-44, Wint 95/96.

**Romano, Bruno**. Funzioni e senso del diritto nel moderno: Riconoscimento e ragione sistemica. *Riv Int Filosof Diritto*, 73(3), 512-525, Jl-S 96.

**Romera, Luis**. Ha ancora senso una domanda metafisica su Dio?. *Acta Phil*, 6(1), 117-135, 1997.

**Romerales Espinosa, Enrique**. Sobre el concepto trascendental de Dios en Kant. *Pensamiento*, 204(52), 337-360, S-D 96.

Se suele afirmar que Kant negó la teología especulativa y defendió la teología moral. Pero la existencia de una teología moral requiere y rehabilita a la vez la teología especulativa, al menos la llamada por Kant trascendental. Ahora bien, ¿cuál es el concepto trascendental de Dios según Kant? En principio tal concepto requiere predicados solamente ontológicos: uno, infinito y necesario. Pero la teología moral exige un concepto de Dios más determinado: un concepto teísta, no sólo deísta. Por eso, el concepto trascendental de Dios se desborda hasta convertirse en un concepto completo. (edited)

**Romerales Espinosa, Enrique**. Three Prospects for Theodicy: Some Anti-Leibnizian Approaches. *Sorites*, 7-25, Jl 95.

In focusing on the problem of evil from the viewpoint of theodicy, I argue that new conceptual regions are to be explored in order to get out of the permanent impasse. These possibilities respectively are: to reject the tenet that this world, if created by God, must be the best possible world; either to reject the tenet that human beings have had no previous existences to their present ones; or finally to reject causal determinism in the framework of the creation of the world and accept the idea that God proceeds with a margin of randomness in a nondeterministic universe. Since these three tenets are all embedded in the philosophical tradition and explicitly in Leibniz's theodicy (most remarkably the first one), my prospects are in this sense anti-Leibnizian.

**Romero Baró, José María**. Entrevista con Rhené Thom. *Convivium*, 9, 134-138, 1996.

**Romero R, María Margarita**. Ideas estéticas en Platón. *Analogia*, 11(1), 45-72, Ja-Je 97.

Para Platón el arte es un espejo, una imitación de una imitación, sentando las bases del criterio de la semejanza que se mantendrá vigente en la crítica de arte hasta el s. XIX. Considera que la belleza no es esencial en el arte y que éste no proporciona conocimiento, al tiempo que valora el producto artístico sobre el artista y su proceso creador, interesándose en su consumo y los efectos que ocasiona al espectador. Siendo testigo de innovaciones técnico-estilísticas que marcan una escisión entre las épocas arcaica y clásica del arte griego, asumirá una postura conservadora ante estos cambios.

**Romeyer Dherbey, Gilbert**. Cosmologie et Politique Chez Antiphon: Séance du 20 mai 1995 (Discussion avec: Gilbert Romeyer Dherbey, Bernard Bourgeois, Jean-Louis Bureau, Maurice de Gandillac, Solange Mericer Josa, Anne Souriau). *Bull Soc Fr Phil*, 89(4), 105-129, O-D 95.

The political thought of Antiphon, like that of other Sophists such as Hippias, is typified by the opposition between *law and nature* and by the questioning of the former. It is therefore necessary, in order to throw light on this central opposition, to consider the overall idea that Antiphon could have had of physis. It is usual to confront the Ionian thinkers or those of greater Greece, essentially 'physiologists', with the Sophists and Socrates, who were above all preoccupied by the 'city-dweller'. This judgement must be tempered insofar as one can find more than a trace of cosmological thinking in Antiphon. (edited)

**Rominger, Anna S** and Gupta, Umprakash K. Blind Man's Bluff: The Ethics of Quantity Surcharges. *J Bus Ethics*, 15(12), 1299-1312, D 96.

Empirical evidence, including a recent field study in Northwest Indiana, indicates that supermarkets and other retail merchants frequently incorporate quantity surcharges in their product pricing strategy. Retailers impose surcharges by charging higher unit prices for products packaged in a larger quantity than smaller quantity of the same goods and brand. The purpose of this article is to examine the business ethics of such pricing strategy in light of empirical findings, existing government regulations, factors that motivate quantity surcharges and prevailing consumer perceptions.

**Ronan, Laurence J** and Stoekle, John D and Emanuel, Linda L (& others). A Manual on Manners and Courtesies for the Shared Care of Patients. *J Clin Ethics*, 8(1), 22-33, Spr 97.

This paper is written by medical practitioners concerned with diminished *intraprofessional communication* as care becomes more corporate and commercialized while doctor-doctor communications is even more necessary with medicine's expanding specialization for the effective shared care of patients. Several cases and communication failures are illustrated from medical practice: in doctor-doctor, doctor-student, doctor-resident, doctor-nurse, and doctor-institutional relationships. Recommendations on standards of communication are made.

**Ronchi della Rocca, Simona** (& others) and Liquori, Luigi and Van Bakel, Steffen. Comparing Cubes of Typed and Type Assignment Systems. *Annals Pure Applied Log*, 86(3), 267-303, Jl 97.

We study the *cube of type assignment systems*, as introduced in Giannini et al. (Fund. Inform. 19 (1993) 87-126) and confront it with Barendregt's typed *Lambda*-cube (Barendregt, in: *Handbook of Logic in Computer Science*, Vol. 2, Clarenden Press, Oxford, 1992). The first is obtained from the latter through applying a natural type erasing function E to derivation rules, that erases type information from terms. In particular, we address the question whether a judgement, derivable in a type assignment system, is always an erasure of a derivable judgement in a corresponding typed system; we show that this property holds only for systems without polymorphism. The type assignment systems we consider satisfy the properties 'subject reduction' and 'strong normalization'. Moreover, we define a new type assignment cube that is isomorphic to the typed one.

**Rongione, Nicholas** and Duska, Ronald and Clarke, James. Codes of Ethics: Investment Company Money Managers Versus other Financial Professionals. *Bus Prof Ethics J*, 14(4), 43-55, Wint 95.

**Roochnik, David**. Of Art and Wisdom: Plato's Understanding of Techne. University Park, Pennsylvania Univ Pr, 1996.

This work offers a comprehensive analysis of the role that *techne*, typically translated as "art," "craft," "skill," "expertise," "technical knowledge," and sometimes even "science," plays in the early and middle Platonic dialogues. It includes a lengthy first chapter that traces the development of the word in pre-Platonic literature. Contrary to conventional wisdom, which has it that Plato conceived of *techne* as a positive theoretical model of moral knowledge, it concludes that in fact the purpose of the dialogues is to articulate a conception of nontechnical wisdom.

**Rood, Tina L** and McCampbell, Atefeh Sadri. Ethics in Government: A Survey of Misuse of Position for Personal Gain and Its Implications for Developing Acquisition Strategy. *J Bus Ethics*, 16(11), 1107-1116, Ag 97.

This study surveys one element of the government standards of conduct, named "Misuse of Position for Personal Gain", assesses the results and compares various acquisition strategies to identify high risk procurement where individual misuse of position for personal gain may be more pervasive. It also provides a valuable historical summary of government standards of conduct. The study concludes with an assessment of enforcement mechanisms, or lack thereof, to ensure that government procurement is conducted in a manner which gains public trust and confidence.

**Roodt, Vasti**. Nietzsche's Dynamite: The Biography of Modern Nihilism. *S Afr J Phil*, 16(2), 37-43, My 97.

This article explores Nietzsche's genealogical investigation into the mode of evaluation that sustains human society in modernity. I argue that this investigation takes the form of a subversive biography of how we moderns have become who we are, which both undermines the self-conceptions of our age and confronts us with alternative possibilities for action and evaluation in the future. The central focus is on Nietzsche's account of modern nihilism as a metaphysically inspired crisis of evaluation and authority which renders problematic the relations with others that make us into a society. In the later section of the article I deal with Nietzsche's own form of 'consummate' nihilism as an attempt to overcome the metaphysical logic of identity—an undertaking which also contains the possibility of rethinking and transforming the social order or modernity.

**Roorda, Jonathan**. Fallibilism, Ambivalence, and Belief. *J Phil*, 94(3), 126-155, Mr 97.

**Roorda, Jonathan**. Kitcher on Theory Choice. *Erkenntnis*, 46(2), 215-239, Mr 97.

**Roose, Marie-Clotilde**. Le sens du poétique: Approche phénoménologique. *Rev Phil Louvain*, 94(4), 646-676, N 96.

This article proposes a reading of poetics under the double horizon of signification and sense. How does the poem make sense? Is there a multiplicity of meanings and/or a global, original sense? Following certain phenomenologists (M. Dufrenne, G. Bachelard...), a first reflection is needed on the possibilities for approaching and understanding a poem. Then the following: 1) An analysis of the *poetical language* in all its forms (the word and its signification, the poetical image, lexis and grammar, musicality, ...). 2) The approach of the *poetical world* that is opened up by the poem (studied in the way it appears, in its relationship to the subject, with a view to letting the origin and sense reveal themselves). The study and confrontation of texts on poetics (Dufrenne, Heidegger...) lead the author to envisage *the desire of being* as the origin of the poem.

**Roqué, Xavier**. The Manufacture of the Positron. *Stud Hist Phil Mod Physics*, 28B(1), 73-129, Mr 97.

Chadwick and Blackett and Occhialini were the first to manufacture (if so crude a word may be permitted) the positive electron.

**Rorty, Amélie Oksenberg**. From Exasperating Virtues to Civic Virtues. *Amer Phil Quart*, 33(3), 303-314, Jl 96.

**Rorty, Amélie Oksenberg**. The Ethics of Reading: A Traveler's Guide. *Educ Theor*, 47(1), 85-89, Wint 97.

**Rorty, Amélie Oksenberg**. The Social and Political Sources of Akrasia. *Ethics*, 107(4), 644-657, Jl 97.

**Rorty, Richard**. "Religious Faith, Intellectual Responsibility, and Romance" in *The Cambridge Companion to William James*, Putnam, Ruth Anna (ed), 84-102. New York, Cambridge Univ Pr, 1997.

**Rorty, Richard**. "Remarks on Deconstruction and Pragmatism" in *Deconstruction and Pragmatism*, Mouffe, Chantal (ed), 13-18. New York, Routledge, 1996.

**Rorty, Richard**. "Response to Ernesto Laclau" in *Deconstruction and Pragmatism*, Mouffe, Chantal (ed), 69-76. New York, Routledge, 1996.

**Rorty, Richard**. "Response to Simon Critchley" in *Deconstruction and Pragmatism*, Mouffe, Chantal (ed), 41-46. New York, Routledge, 1996.

**Rorty, Richard**. Comments on Michael Williams' *Unnatural Doubts*. *J Phil Res*, 22, 1-10, Ap 97.

**Rorty, Richard**. Remembering John Dewey and Sidney Hook. *Free Inq*, 16(1), 40-42, Wint 95/96.

**Rorty, Richard**. The Ambiguity of 'Rationality'. *Constellations*, 3(1), 73-82, Ap 96.

**Rorty, Richard**. What Do You Do When They Call You a 'Relativist'. *Phil Phenomenol Res*, 57(1), 173-177, Mr 97.

**Ros, Arno**. Bemerkungen zum Verhältnis zwischen Neurophysiologie und Psychologie. *J Gen Phil Sci*, 27(1), 91-130, 1996.

"Remarks on the Relations between Neurophysiology and Psychology." In the last decades of analytical philosophy, contributions to the so-called mind-body-problem have been suffering by several serious methodological misunderstandings: they have failed, for instance, to distinguish between explanations of particular and strictly general ("necessary") properties and between two important senses of existential statements; and they have overlooked the role conceptual explanations play in the development of science. Changing our methodological premises, we should be able to put questions like that of the relation between (neuro)physiological and psychological phenomena in a new way—and we should be able to see that such newly understood questions allow answers which evade the pitfalls of both

**Ros, Arno**. Entwicklung von Erkenntnissen und Entwicklung von Erkenntnisfähigkeiten. *Phil Natur*, 26(1), 66-90, 1989.

reductionist and holistic positions. The paper tries to illustrate and to defend these contentions by reference to a very elementary example: the rational rebuilding of our concepts to identify behaviour by which a subject controls the position of his body in space.

**Rosa, Hartmut**. Cultural Relativism and Social Criticism from a Taylorian Perspective. *Constellations*, 3(1), 39-60, Ap 96.

**Rosa, Joaquim Coelho**. Razao e Cultura. *Rev Port Filosof*, 52(1-4), 763-767, Ja-D 96.

**Rosado Haddock, Guillermo E**. On Necessity and Existence. *Dialogos*, 31(68), 57-62, Jl 96.

**Rosales, José María**. "Sobre Política y Reformismo Cívico: A Partir de Ortega" in *Política y Sociedad en José Ortega y Gasset: En Torno a "Vieja y Nueva Política"*, Lopez de la Vieja, Maria Teresa (ed), 167-183. Barcelona, Anthropos, 1997.

The paper examines the reformist drive of Ortega's political thought and vindicates the modernizing role it played in the liberalism of his age, namely the first half of the twentieth century. Ortega's itinerary goes from a 'regenerationist' position, shared by the socialists of his generation (the generation of 1914), to a mature, politically engaged liberalism. This change proved to be crucial for the overcoming of the old politics. Besides, it provided a foundation for the emergence of modern liberalism in Spain. The alternative was, however, cut short by the civil war in 1936. This unfinished project represents Ortega's liberalism at its best.

**Rosas, Alejandro**. El grito de Libertad del Pensamiento. *Ideas Valores*, 96-98, Ag 97.

**Rosas, Alejandro**. Prometer en Falso: La Contradicción Práctica y el Imperativo Categórico. *Ideas Valores*, 86-93, Ap 97.

I argue that the contradiction by which the categorical imperative determines the (in)morality of a maxim is nothing more than a practical contradiction *between* two closely related rules of action understood prudentially. I discard an argument of Searle's that seems to back up the thesis of a "contradiction in thought", internal to the maxim. I note that this understanding of the categorical imperative explains Kant's appeal to authors such as Hare and Rawls, but that it is opposed to standard Kant-interpretation, specially Kant's idea that the categorical imperative requires an incompatibilist conception of human action.

**Rosas, Alejandro**. Universalización Moral y Prudencia en Kant. *Ideas Valores*, 104-111, D 96.

Kant's method for distinguishing maxims in relation to morality or immorality relies on the criteria of universalization and contradiction. Kant allows for two possible types of contradiction: contradiction in thought and contradiction in the will. I briefly show that in Kant's four examples in the *Groundwork* the operative contradiction is contradiction in the will and this requires viewing self-interest or prudence as essential to the application of the categorical imperative.

**Rose, Mary** and Fischer, Karla. Policies and Perspectives on Authorship. *Sci Eng Ethics*, 1(4), 361-370, O 95.

Authorship on publications has been described as a "meal ticket" for researchers in academic settings. Given the importance of authorship, inappropriate publication credit is a pertinent ethical issue. This paper presents an overview of authorship problems and policies intended to address them. Previous work has identified three types of inappropriate authorship practices: plagiarism, giving unwarranted credit and failure to give expected credit. Guidelines from universities, journals and professional organizations provide standards about requirements of authors and may describe inappropriate practices; to a lesser extent, they provide guidance for determining authorship order. While policies on authorship may be helpful in some circumstances, they are not panaceas. Formal guidelines may not address serious power imbalances in working relationships and may be difficult to enforce in the face of particular departmental or institutional cultures. In order to develop more effective and useful guidelines, we should gain more knowledge about how students and faculty members perceive policies as well as their understanding of how policies will best benefit collaborators.

**Rose, Nikolas** and Osborne, Thomas. In the Name of Society, or Three Theses on the History of Social Thought. *Hist Human Sci*, 10(3), 87-104, Ag 97.

This paper is something of a preview of a projected attempt on the part of the authors to capture the voice of social thought in rather different terms. Our three theses are: 1) that those who speak 'in the name of society' have just as frequently been doctors and bureaucrats as opposed to 'social philosophers' or professional sociologists; correlatively, 2) that the creative voice of social thought has more often been technical, problem-centred and tied up with particular rationalities of government as opposed to being either exclusively theoretical or merely responsive to 'objective problems' in society; and, 3) that if sociology today struggles for a voice in which to speak this may be in some part due to the ways in which the past history of social thought has typically been conceived. (edited)

**Rosebury, Brian**. Irrecoverable Intentions and Literary Interpretation. *Brit J Aes*, 37(1), 15-30, Ja 97.

Of the complete relevant set of intentions of an author in writing a text, some which would have been fulfilled by the intended text may not have been fulfilled by the text actually produced and may now be irrecoverable. The existence of irrecoverable relevant intentions (denied by Quentin Skinner, whose theory of interpretation founded on speech-act theory is otherwise largely accepted in this paper) is important because different conventions of discourse take account of it in different ways. Some types of discourse allow 'supplementary

explanation' of unfulfilled intentions in subsequent texts; this convention appears to be suspended when we are considering a text as an aesthetic object.

**Rosemann, Philipp W**. Penser l'Autre: De l'architectonique d'un système qui ne serait pas homogénéisant. *Rev Phil Louvain*, 94(2), 311-329, My 96.

Contemporary Continental philosophy is very suspicious of "systematic" philosophizing, in which it sees "totalizing" tendencies of the Hegelian type. Nevertheless, every philosophical discourse, in order to make sense, must in some fashion satisfy the exigencies of coherence and systematicity. My tentative claim in this paper is that the kind of "nontotalizing", "open" systems which contemporary thought is searching already exist in the buildings of postmodern architecture and in the creations of the couturier Gianni Versace. An analysis of the structure of these works of art can furnish us valuable indications for the construction of a "nonclosed" postmodern philosophical system.

**Rosemann, Philipp W** (ed) and LeJeune, Michel (ed). *Business Ethics in the African Context Today*. Kampala, Uganda, 1996.

This book brings together contributions from ten outstanding experts in business and ethics, combining theoretical with eminently practical perspectives. In the first part, it examines the possibility of founding business ethics theologically, in the principles of Christianity. In the second part, it analyses concrete problems of business ethics in contemporary Africa and, especially, Uganda: corruption and bribery, the ethics of banking, and, international finance, the role of women in the African business world.

**Rosemont, Henry**. "Classical Confucian and Contemporary Feminist Perspectives on the Self: Some Parallels and their Implications" in *Culture and Self*, Allen, Douglas (ed), 63-82. Boulder, Westview Pr, 1997.

**Rosen, C Martin** and Carr, Gabrielle M. Fares and Free Riders on the Information Highway. *J Bus Ethics*, 16(12-13), 1439-1445, S 97.

Public policy issues around access to networked information are explored and examined. Long viewed as the quintessential public good, information has evolved into a critically important market commodity in little more than a generation. New technologies and a political climate in which the meaning of universal access to information is no longer commonly understood and in which its importance is no longer taken for granted pose significant challenges for American society. Libraries, as information commons, offer the means of meeting those challenges. Historical, economical and professional factors that shape the conflict are described and discussed.

**Rosen, Eric**. Modal Logic over Finite Structures. *J Log Lang Info*, 6(4), 427-439, O 97.

We investigate properties of propositional modal logic over the class of finite structures. In particular, we show that certain known preservation theorems remain true over this class. We prove that a class of finite models is defined by a first-order sentence and closed under bisimulations if and only if it is definable by a modal formula. We also prove that a class of finite models defined by a modal formula is closed under extensions if and only if it is defined by a it-is-possible modal formula.

**Rosen, F**. Utilitarianism and the Punishment of the Innocent: The Origins of a False Doctrine. *Utilitas*, 9(1), 23-37, Mr 97.

This paper examines the commonplace assertion that utilitarianism allows for and even, at times, requires the punishment of the innocent. It traces the origins of this doctrine to the writings of the British idealists and the subsequent development of what is called the postutilitarian paradigm which posits various justifications for punishment such as retribution, deterrence and reform, finds all of them inadequate, and then, with the addition of other ideas, reconciles them. The idea of deterrence is falsely depicted as the utilitarian contribution to the theory of punishment, while deterrence in fact is one of several elements in the utilitarian theory. The mistake comes from ignoring the pain-pleasure dimension of Benthamite utilitarianism and from regarding the principle of utility itself as the sole criterion of action in a 'top-down' fashion.

**Rosen, Gideon**. Who Makes the Rules Around Here?. *Phil Phenomenol Res*, 57(1), 163-171, Mr 97.

In *Making It Explicit*, Brandom maintains that the normative is strictly prior to the intentional in the order of explanation, and also that normative facts are invariably "creatures of our practices," "imposed" by us. Brandom glosses the latter claim as the thesis that normative facts about the "normative statuses" of performances supervene on facts about our "practical attitudes" toward performances. The paper argues that this is not an adequate explication of the metaphors of "creation" and "imposition," and that any attempt to modify the account so as to sustain these metaphors involves rejecting the view that the normative is strictly prior to the intentional.

**Rosen, Gideon** and Burgess, John P. *A Subject with No Object: Strategies for Nominalistic Interpretation of Mathematics*. New York, Clarendon/ Oxford Pr, 1997.

*A Subject with No Object* cuts through a host of technicalities that have obscured previous discussions of these projects, and presents clear, concise accounts, with minimal prerequisites, of a dozen strategies for nominalistic interpretation of mathematics, thus equipping the reader to evaluate each and to compare different ones. The authors also offer critical discussion, rare in the literature, of the aims and claims of nominalistic interpretation, suggesting that it is significant in a very different way from that usually assumed. (publisher, edited)

**Rosenbaum, Stephen E**. Epicurean Moral Theory. *Hist Phil Quart*, 13(4), 389-410, O 96.

This paper interprets Epicurus's theory of justice in relation to his overall ethical theory. It shows how to combine coherently the aretaic, utilitarian, and

Rosenbaum, Stuart E 880 AUTHOR INDEX

contractarian aspects of Epicurean justice, and displays how the understanding of Epicurus's theory impinges on recent issues in moral theory.

**Rosenbaum, Stuart E**. Moral Theory and the Reflective Life. *SW Phil Rev*, 13(1), 211-221, Ja 97.

I endorse and reinforce a pragmatic and more specifically a Deweyan, account of the dim prospects of traditional moral theory. I further describe a role for moral philosophy that accepts the demise of moral theory, a role exemplified by Dewey himself in his insistence on the place of intelligence and reflection in a satisfactory life. Dewey's pervasive insistence on intelligence and reflection in a satisfactory life. Dewey's pervasive insistence on intelligence and reflection in the good life gives rise to a large-scale moral ideal, the ideal of the reflective life; I describe that ideal and contrast it with other ideals.

**Rosenbaum, Stuart E** (ed) and Baird, Robert M (ed). *Morality and the Law*. Amherst, Prometheus, 1993.

Law and morality spring from the same source: a fundamental social need for order and security. But what are we to do when the dictates of conscience conflict with the statute books? Which should be obeyed? Should the morality of some be visited upon all by giving it the force of law? Are there moral principles that go beyond legal jurisdiction to justify acts of civil disobedience? These and other important questions are addressed in this fascinating collection of essays by some of the most astute minds in law and philosophy: Hugo A. Bedau, Charles L. Black, Jr., Patrick Devlin, Joel Feinberg, Erich Fromm, H.L.A. Hart, Leon Jaworski, John Rawls, Peter Singer and Rudolph Weingartner. (publisher)

**Rosenberg, Alex**. Critical Review: Sober's *Philosophy of Biology* and His Philosophy of Biology. *Phil Sci*, 63(3), 452-464, S 96.

An examination of the foundations of Elliot Sober's philosophy of biology as reflected in his introductory textbook of that title reveals substantial and controversial philosophical commitments. Among these are the claim that all understanding is historical, the assertion that there are biological laws but they are necessary truths, the view that the fundamental theory in biology is a narrative, and the suggestion that biology adverts to ungrounded probabilistic propensities of the sort to be met with elsewhere only in quantum mechanics.

**Rosenberg, Esther** (& others) and Kaplan, Robert M and Schneiderman, Lawrence J. Do Physicians' Own Preferences for Life-Sustaining Treatment Influence Their Perceptions of Patients' Preferences? A Second Look. *Cambridge Quart Healthcare Ethics*, 6(2), 131-137, Spr 97.

Purpose: To follow up previous observations that physicians' predictions of their patients end-of-life treatment choices are closer to the choices they would make for themselves than to the choices expressed by their patients. Study: One hundred and eleven patients and 28 physicians completed two advance directive instruments—a procedure-oriented questionnaire and a quality of life questionnaire. The patients expressed their own preferences. Their physicians were asked to complete these instruments in terms of what they thought their patients would want and also what they would want for themselves, if they were in the same situation as their patient. Conclusion: The results show again that physicians perceptions of their patients wishes for treatment are influenced by what they would want for themselves.

**Rosenberg, Jay F**. Brandom's *Making It Explicit*: A First Encounter. *Phil Phenomenol Res*, 57(1), 179-187, Mr 97.

**Rosenberg, Sharon**. Intersecting Memories: Bearing Witness to the 1989 Massacre of Women in Montreal. *Hypatia*, 11(4), 119-129, Fall 96.

In this essay, I write memory across the public-private divide as a commemorative response to the Massacre of Women at École Polytechnique. Through five layers of remembering, I explore the creation of an analytic space that simultaneously considers traumatized subjectivity, bearing witness and feminist pedagogy.

**Rosenblatt, Helena**. *Rousseau and Geneva: From the First Discourse* to the *Social Contract*, 1749-1762. New York, Cambridge Univ Pr, 1997.

*Rousseau and Geneva* is an important contribution to the history of political thought, the history of Calvinism and the history of Geneva. Dr. Rosenblatt reconstructs the main aspects of Genevan socioeconomic, political and religious thought in the first half of the eighteenth century in order to contextualize the development of Rousseau's thought from the *First Discourse* to the *Social Contract*. Over time Rousseau has been adopted as a French thinker, but this adoption obscures his Genevan origin. Dr. Rosenblatt points out that he is, in fact, a Genevan thinker and illustrates for the first time that a knowledge of his Genevan roots, his relationship to Genevan politics and his continuing contacts with Geneva can help to elucidate Rousseau's concerns with civility, natural law, republican government and civil religion. The author persuasively argues that Rousseau's relationship with Geneva played an integral part in his development into an original political thinker. (publisher)

**Rosenblum, Nancy L**. "Democratic Sex: Reynolds v. U.S., Sexual Relations, and Community" in *Sex, Preference, and Family: Essays on Law and Nature*, Nussbaum, Martha C (ed), 63-85. New York, Oxford Univ Pr, 1997.

**Rosenfeld, Michel**. A Pluralist Look at Liberalism, Nationalism, and Democracy: Comments on Shapiro and Tamir. *Constellations*, 3(3), 326-339, Ja 97.

**Rosenfeld, Paul**. Impression Management, Fairness, and the Employment Interview. *J Bus Ethics*, 16(8), 801-808, Je 97.

This paper contends that impression management is not inherently a threat to fairness in employment interviews. Rather, regarding impression management as unfair is based on an outdated, narrow view of impression management as conscious, manipulative, and deceptive. A broader, expansive model of impression management is described which sees these behaviors as falling on a continuum from deceptive and manipulative on the one hand, to accurate, positive and beneficial on the other. (edited)

**Rosenfeld, Robert**. Can Animals Be Evil?: Kekes' Character-Morality, the Hard Reaction to Evil, and Animals. *Between Species*, 11(1-2), 33-41, Wint-Spr 95.

In arguing for a character-based conception of morality over a choice-based one, John Kekes makes a case for labeling *agents* of actions as evil, even when they lack choice over such actions, provided that such actions spring from their character. I argue that Kekes's standard would allow animals, particularly predators, to be labeled as "evil." However, I also argue that the consequences of this labeling will not necessarily justify abusive treatment of animals so labeled, since the pragmatic justifications that Kekes uses for labeling humans as evil do not necessarily apply to animals.

**Rosenfield, Denis**. La filosofía política y los problemas de nuestro tiempo. *Cuad Etica*, 15-16, 61-83, 1993.

Marx adds to the critics function of the raison a specific task: to reproduce in the thought the exploration mechanism of a type of social relation, which is not natural but historical. The consequence is that the politic can be a generating of the new man. However, the eschatological destiny of the Marxism contradicted its owns rational and critical grounds. Hegel, Strauss and, H. Arendt associated intimately politics philosophy and liberty, discussing the action, the human nature, the rule and in general the reason itself. Democracy pose paradoxes that demand a new perception of the political.

**Rosenkrantz, Carlos F**. El nuevo Rawls. *Rev Latin de Filosof*, 22(2), 223-249, 1996.

In this paper I try to show the direction in which Rawls has recently changed. I argue that Rawls in *Theory of Justice* offered a theory of the right characterized by philosophical foundations and wide scope while in *Political Liberalism* he articulates a theory of the right with political foundations which does not apply to all but only to those that with us are part of the same political community. I deal with two arguments that we may use to explain and justify this radical change of views. The first, a pragmatic argument that I call "the minimización of concesions" says that, given the fact of pluralism, it is easier to accept a political foundation of a theory of the right with narrow scope than a philosophical foundation. The second, a metaargument, claims that the task of justification is eminently political and therefore, philosophical argumentation is of no avail. I present objections to both arguments and conclude offering a different, philosophical strategy to justify a theory of the right.

**Rosenkrantz, Gary S** and Hoffman, Joshua. *Substance: Its Nature and Existence*. New York, Routledge, 1997.

Taking as their starting point the major philosophers in the historical debate—Aristotle, Descartes, Spinoza, Locke, and Hume—Joshua Hoffman and Gary S. Rosenkranz move on to a novel analysis of substance in terms of a kind of independence which insubstantial entities do not possess. The authors explore causal theories of the unity of the parts of inanimate objects and organisms; contemporary views about substance; the idea that the only existing physical substances are inanimate pieces of matter and living organisms, and that artifacts such as clocks, and natural formations like stars, do not really exist. (publisher,edited)

**Rosenmüller, Joachim**. Bargaining with Incomplete Information: An Axiomatic Approach. *Theor Decis*, 42(2), 105-146, Ja 97.

Within this paper we consider a model of Nash bargaining with incomplete information. In particular, we focus on fee games, which are a natural generalization of side payment games in the context of incomplete information. For a specific class of fee games we provide two axiomatic approaches in order to establish the *expected contract value*, which is a version of the Nash bargaining solution.

**Rosenthal, David M**. "Moore's Paradox and Consciousness" in *AI, Connectionism and Philosophical Psychology, 1995*, Tomberlin, James E (ed), 313-333. Atascadero, Ridgeview, 1995.

**Rosenthal, Sandra B**. "How Pragmatism *Is* and Environmental Ethic" in *Environmental Pragmatism*, Light, Andrew (ed), 38-49. New York, Routledge, 1996.

Several recent essays have criticized pragmatism's usefulness for the development of an environmental ethic. This essay provides a sketch of relevant pragmatic features to show that pragmatic ethics, properly understood, *is* by its very nature an environmental ethics and that it has implications for some of the dichotomies that appear over and over again in the literature—dichotomies such as anthropocentrism/biocentrism, individualism/holism and intrinsic/extrinsic values. The pragmatic perspective changes the nature of the issues and can provide an impetus for moving the debates beyond some of their current impasses caused by traditional dichotomies.

**Rosenthal, Sandra B**. "Pragmatic Experimentalism and the Derivation of the Categories" in *The Rule of Reason: The Philosophy of Charles Sanders Peirce*, Forster, Paul (ed), 120-138. Toronto, Univ of Toronto Pr, 1997.

It is generally held that Peirce's philosophy incorporates diverse methods for obtaining the categories, *a priori* deduction from mathematical principles and phenomenological inquiry. This paper first attempts to show that one method, the phenomenological method, is at work in Peirce's derivation of the categories, though he of course did not use this term until late in his career, and to decipher the distinctively pragmatic character of its dynamics with the implicit pluralism it involves. The remainder of the paper examines the significance of this view for interpreting his understanding of the nature of the metaphysical enterprise and the dynamics of its relation to his phenomenology.

**Rosenthal, Sandra B**. Classical American Pragmatism: The Other Naturalism. *Metaphilosophy*, 27(4), 399-407, O 96.

This essay compares and contrasts pragmatic naturalism with the more well known position of epistemological naturalism on several pivotal issues, in the process offering a pragmatic critique of the latter. It highlights their common rejection of both foundationalism and *a priori* methods and their positive claims that: what needs examination is not our concept of knowledge but knowledge itself; knowledge must be understood as tied to the world and as a natural phenomenon to be examined in its natural setting; the epistemic endeavor involves unifying its three traditional projects of giving an account of what knowledge is, explaining how knowledge is possible and providing useful epistemic advice, thus involving normative considerations; and the method of gaining knowledge in general is continuous with the method of science. Yet, there are very great divergences between the two naturalisms concerning the answers offered and these are explored and evaluated in the development of the essay.

**Rosenthal, Sandra B**. Continuity, Contingency, and Time: The Divergent Intuitions of Whitehead and Pragmatism. *Trans Peirce Soc*, 32(4), 542-567, Fall 96.

Whiteheadian and pragmatic process philosophies stand united in their rejections of substance philosophy and their endeavors to return to the full gamut of human experience in its emergence within and openness onto a rich, creatively advancing processive universe. Yet, there is a fundamental chasm between them because their respective attempts are founded in and pervaded by different intuitions of the nature of time, differences which are inextricably intertwined with diverse perceptions of the nature and interrelation of continuity, discreteness and contingency. This essay will, in necessarily broad strokes, first sketch the Whiteheadian view, highlighting what seem to be certain ongoing dilemmas and then characterize the alternative approach operative in the pragmatic position.

**Rosenthal, Sandra B**. Self, Community, and Time: A Shared Sociality. *Rev Metaph*, 50(1), 101-119, S 96.

Community and pluralism are often held to be at odds with each other, with a choice to be made between group conformity and individualism, community obligations or individual liberty and this dilemma in large part structures much contemporary debate. These tensions, which tend to dominate reflections on community, are rooted in incompatible understandings of the nature of the self and its relation to the communal order which it inhabits, understandings which are in turn inextricably intertwined with implicit temporal issues. This essay explores the way a pragmatic perspective offers the possibility for a novel understanding and interrelation of self, community and temporality which moves beyond some of the current problems and dilemmas.

**Roshwalb, Alan** and Mayer-Sommer, Alan P. An Examination of the Relationship Between Ethical Behavior, Espoused Ethical Values and Financial Performance in the U S Defense Industry: 1988-1992. *J Bus Ethics*, 15(12), 1249-1274, D 96.

This paper tests the ethics-is-good-for-profits as well as the ethics-and-profits-are-joint-outcomes-of-good-management hypotheses in the context of the U.S. defense industry in the 1988-1992 period. Both ethical behaviors are compared with measures of profitability for the defense-oriented business segments of sixty-two major U.S. defense contractors. We found statistically significant, positive correlations between 1) our two measures of espoused ethical values and 2) both measures of espoused ethical values and violative ethical acts. (edited)

**Rosner, Fay**. "Moral Dimensions of Classroom Discourse: A Deweyan Perspective" in *Philosophy of Education (1996),* Margonis, Frank (ed), 381-385. Urbana, Phil Education Soc, 1997.

**Rosner, Jennifer A**. Quine's Global Structuralism. *Dialectica*, 50(3), 235-242, 1996.

Quine's ontological relativity thesis requires that objects be treated as *neutral nodes* in the logical structure of our total theory of the world. It is by treating objects as neutral that we are able to vary ontology yet leave the evidential support of our theory undisturbed. In this article, I present arguments against the possibility of treating objects as *neutral.*

**Ross, Don**. Critical Notice of Ron McClamrock *Existential Cognition. Can J Phil*, 27(2), 271-284, Je 97.

McClamrock argues for a thesis he calls 'radical externalism' in the behavioral and cognitive sciences. In my paper, I contend that McClamrock's thesis, though true, is not radical. This is because he urges externalism with respect to cognitive task-individuation and task-explanation, both of which are standard practice in the relevant disciplines. Semantic externalism may remain contentious, I argue; but the sense in which philosophers continue to argue about it has little bearing on the actual conduct of cognitive science. I conclude with a diagnosis as to why externalism seems more contentious than it ought to.

**Ross, George MacDonald**. Socrates versus Plato: The Origins and Development of Socratic Thinking. *Thinking*, 12(4), 2-8, 1996.

The Socratic and Platonic approaches to philosophical education are contrasted. Socrates saw philosophy as an activity which involved questioning. It was inductive, concerned with language and essentially oral. It was open to all and applicable. For Plato, it was learned passively, and consisted of a deductive body of knowledge taught dogmatically. It involved concepts themselves rather than language and could be set down in writing. It was exclusive to an elite and other-worldly. The medieval universities struck a good balance, but subsequently the Platonic approach prevailed. Recent initiatives encouraged by the UK government have tended to reinstate the Socratic approach.

**Ross, Glenn**. Undefeated Naturalism. *Phil Stud*, 87(2), 159-184, Ag 97.

According to Alvin Plantinga, metaphysical naturalism cannot be rationally accepted, for it provides a defeater for the thesis that one's own faculties are reliable and thus a defeater for all of one's beliefs, including a belief in naturalism. I argue that there can be no universal defeaters; moreover, I contend that even if one's reasons for accepting defeaters of naturalism are as strong as one's reasons for accepting naturalism, a rational belief in naturalism can be sustained. I propose a new account of rational acceptance, an account that can make sense of the rational persistence of philosophical disagreement.

**Ross, Isobel A**. Practice Guidelines, Patient Interests, and Risky Procedures. *Bioethics*, 10(4), 310-322, O 96.

A clinical scenario is described where an anaesthetist is concerned about the seemingly high risk/benefit ration relating to laparoscopic versus standard inguinal hernia operations. Some options for further action by the anaesthetist are introduced. The remainder of the paper explores the question of who can legitimately assess the acceptability of risk/benefit ratios and defends the use of practice guidelines at the expense of so called clinical freedom. It is argued that respect for persons is not breached by limiting the treatment options offered to patients to those therapies which have a 'reasonable'risk/benefit ratio. This 'reasonableness' is context dependent and should be properly decided by those with expertise in the field.

**Ross, Judith Wilson**. Ethical Decision Making in Managed Care Environments. *Bioethics Forum*, 10(4), 22-26, Fall 94.

Ethics committee members need to look carefully at their frequently unarticulated beliefs about the value of health care and the role of health care institutions and professions before considering what constitutes an ethical response to changes in the way that health care is delivered.

**Ross, Lainie Friedman**. Arguments Against Health Care Autonomy for Minors. *Bioethics Forum*, 11(4), 22-26, Wint 95.

Competency is a necessary but not a sufficient condition on which to base respect for a minor's autonomy in health care decision making. The thesis is argued that parents' interest and responsibility in guiding children's moral and cognitive development and promoting life-time autonomy outweigh the costs of denying children decision-making authority.

**Ross, Stephen David**. *The Gift of Truth: Gathering the Good.* Albany, SUNY Pr, 1997.

This volume traces the history of the idea of truth as an ethical movement, exploring those developments in Western thought, from Plato and Aristotle through Kant and Hegel, when ethics was separated from science and philosophy. At the heart of the project is a reexamination of the good, found in Plato as that which makes being possible, which gives authority to knowledge and beckons to art, preserved in Levinas as infinite responsibility. The idea of the good is interpreted as nature's abundance, giving beauty and truth as gifts. It gives rise to an ethics of inclusion. (publisher)

**Ross, Thomas**. Adam Smith's Influence on James Madison. *Mod Sch*, 73(4), 283-294, M 96.

**Rossanno, Giovanna**. "La filosofia morale di Ludovico Limentani tra naturalismo e storicismo" in *Lo Storicismo e la Sua Storia: Temi, Problemi, Prospettive,* Cacciatore, Giuseppe (ed), 387-395. Milano, Guerini, 1997.

**Rossetti, Andrea**. Hans Kronning. Modalité, cognition et polysémie. sèmantique du verbe modal devoir. *Riv Int Filosof Diritto*, 74(1), 136-149, Ja-Mr 97.

**Rossetti, Livio**. El momento *epíkairos (Kairós* "espontáneo", *kairós* negativo, *kairós* inducido, contra-kairós). *Analogia*, 10(2), 3-30, 1996.

Hasta que uno no se concentra en las características de la ocasión, el concepto de *kairós* se revela no sólo refractario al análisis, sino también extraordinariamente genérico, ya que no existe una sola combinación de eventos y circunstancias que no dé lugar a *kairói* favorables (desde algunos puntos de vista y para alguno) y desfavorables (desde otros puntos de vista y en su caso para algún otro). En estas condiciones, la especificidad del concepto termina por desvanecerse. (edited)

**Rossetti, Livio**. Le tableau de Cléanthe. *Diotima*, 25, 118-124, 1997.

The stoic Cleanthes has been reported (by Cicero, *de finibus* II 21.69 and Augustine, *de civitate Dei* V 20) to have resorted to a rather vivid picture-in-words to explain his ideas about virtue and vice. Since the picture seems to open the avenue to an immediate retortion on the part of Epicureans, either Cleanthes has been unaware of it (unlikely), or he may have simply tried to examine whether even the rule of *voluptas* could possibly grant happiness, without adhering immediately to such an idea.

**Rossi, Osvaldo**. 'Gloria' e 'Essere': Heidegger nel pensiero di hans urs von Balthasar. *Aquinas*, 39(2), 395-407, My-Ag 96.

**Rossi, Paolo**. "Il tempo in Newton e in Leibniz" in *Il Concetto di Tempo: Atti del XXXII Congresso Nazionale della Società Filosofica Italiana,* Casertano, Giovanni (ed), 37-47. Napoli, Loffredo, 1997.

**Rossi, Paolo**. La scienza e la dimenticanza. *Iride*, 8(14), 152-159, Ap 95.

**Rossiter, Amy** and Prilleltensky, Isaac and Walsh-Bowers, Richard. Preventing Harm and Promoting Ethical Discourse in the Helping Professions: Conceptual, Research, Analytical, and Action Frameworks. *Ethics Behavior*, 6(4), 287-306, 1996.

The first in a series of four articles, this article provides an overview of the concepts and methods developed by a team of researchers concerned with preventing harm and promoting ethical discourse in the helping professions. In this article we introduce conceptual, research, analytical and action frameworks employed to promote the centrality of ethical discourse in mental health practice. We employ recursive processes whereby knowledge gained from case studies refines our emerging conceptual model of applied ethics. Our *participatory* conceptual framework differs markedly from the *restrictive* model typically used in applied ethics. (edited)

**Rossiter, Amy** and Walsh-Bowers, Richard and Prilleltensky, Isaac. Learning from Broken Rules: Individualism, Bureaucracy, and Ethics. *Ethics Behavior*, 6(4), 307-320, 1996.

The authors discuss findings from a qualitative research project concerning applied ethics that was undertaken at a general family counseling agency in southern Ontario. Interview data suggested that workers need to dialogue about ethical dilemmas, but that such dialogue demands a high level of risk taking that feels unsafe in the organization. This finding led the researchers to examine their own sense of "breaking rules" by suggesting an intersubjective view of ethics that requires a "safe space" for ethical dialogue. The authors critique the individualistic tendency of professional ethics as an effect of power that is tied to the history of professionalism and discuss the role of bureaucracies in diminishing a central role for ethics in helping services. (edited)

**Rossiter, Amy** and Walsh-Bowers, Richard and Prilleltensky, Isaac. The Personal Is the Organizational in the Ethics of Hospital Social Workers. *Ethics Behavior*, 6(4), 321-335, 1996.

Understanding the social context of clinical ethics is vital for making ethical discourse central in professional practice and for preventing harm. In this paper we present findings about clinical ethics from in-depth interviews and consultation with seven members of a hospital social work department. Workers gave different accounts of ethical dilemmas and resources for ethical decision making than did their managers, whereas workers and managers agreed on core-guiding ethical principles and on ideal situations for ethical discourse. We discuss the research team's initial interpretations, the relevance of the extant ethics literature to organizational structures and dynamics, and alternative perspectives on clinical ethics. (edited)

**Rossiter, Graham**. The Moral and Spiritual Dimension to Education: Some Reflections on the British Experience. *J Moral Educ*, 25(2), 201-214, Je 96.

In the United Kingdom and other Western countries, spiritual and moral development are being used increasingly with reference to general education—albeit with diverse and conflicting interpretations of what education to promote such development means in practice. Despite the similarities, there appears to be something distinctive about what is happening in Britain at education policy level. The first part of this paper looks into this question and in particular at some of the ambiguities relating to the inspection of schools' educational provisions for spiritual and moral development. The second part proposes a curriculum schema that might be used to give more coherence to a school's plans for promoting the spiritual and moral development of pupils. It includes reference to subjects whose content is directly concerned with the spiritual and moral; to the treatment of spiritual/moral issues in the general curriculum; and to the distinctive contribution that each learning area might be expected to contribute to students' personal development.

**Rossouw, Gedeon J**. Unbundling the Moral Dispute About Unbundling in South Africa. *J Bus Ethics*, 16(10), 1019-1028, Jl 97.

Unbundling—or the breaking up of conglomerates into smaller independent companies—normally has very little to do with morality because decisions to unbundle are usually taken on pure strategic business grounds. However, the way unbundling was introduced into the debate about the restructuring of the South African economy by the African National Congress (ANC), gave unbundling some very distinct moral undertones. In this paper the moral arguments in support of and in opposition to unbundling within the South African context are identified. It is then argued that these rival sets of arguments can be related back to two different sets of moral convictions about redistributive justice. (edited)

**Rota, Gian-Carlo**. The Phenomenology of Mathematical Beauty. *Synthese*, 111(2), 171-182, My 97.

It has been observed that whereas painters and musicians are likely to be embarrassed by references to the beauty in their work, mathematicians instead like to engage in discussions of the beauty of mathematics. Professional artists are more likely to stress the technical rather than the aesthetic aspects of their work. Mathematicians, instead, are fond of passing judgment on the beauty of their favored pieces of mathematics. Even a cursory observation shows that the characteristics of mathematical beauty are at variance with those of artistic beauty. For example, courses in "art appreciation" are fairly common; it is however unthinkable to find any "mathematical beauty appreciation" courses taught anywhere. The purpose of the present paper is to try to uncover the sense of the term "beauty" as it is currently used by mathematicians.

**Rota, Gian-Carlo**. The Phenomenology of Mathematical Proof. *Synthese*, 111(2), 183-196, My 97.

**Roth, Abraham Sesshu**. Hume's Psychology of Identity Ascriptions. *Hume Stud*, 22(2), 273-298, N 96.

Hume's remarks in the *Treatise* concerning object persistence occur in a *psychological* discussion about how we acquire such an idea. Metaphysical interpretations ignore this psychology, in particular Hume's contrast between vulgar as opposed to philosophical cognitive tendencies. This paper defends a new interpretation of Hume on identity, consistent with his psychology and making novel use of Hume's notion of "a distinction of reason" to interpret the idea of an "object existent at a time". An emphasis on psychology yields metaphysical dividends, allowing us to discern in Hume's thought an interesting alternative to the temporal parts view of identity over time.

**Roth, Robert J**. "Morality and Obligation" in *Reason, Experience, and God: John E. Smith in Dialogue*, Colapietro, Vincent M, 19-32. New York, Fordham Univ Pr, 1997.

**Rothenberg, David**. "Laws of Nature vs. Laws of Respect: Non-Violence in Practice in Norway" in *Environmental Pragmatism*, Light, Andrew (ed), 251-265. New York, Routledge, 1996.

**Rothenberg, L S** and Krimsky, Sheldon and Stott, P. Financial Interests of Authors in Scientific Journals: A Pilot Study of 14 Publications. *Sci Eng Ethics*, 2(4), 395-410, O 96.

This paper measures the frequency of selected financial interests held among authors of certain types of scientific publications and assesses disclosure

practices of authors. We examined 1105 university authors (first and last cited) from Massachusetts institutions whose 789 articles, published in 1992, appeared in 14 scientific and medical journals. (edited)

**Rotman, Brian**. Counting Information: A Note on Physicalized Numbers. *Mind Mach*, 6(2), 229-238, My 96.

Existing work on the ultimate limits of computation has urged that the apparatus of real numbers should be eschewed as an investigative tool and replaced by discrete mathematics. The present paper argues for a radical extension of this viewpoint: not only the continuum but all infinitary constructs including the rationals and the potential infinite sequence of whole numbers need to be eliminated if a self-consistent investigative framework is to be achieved.

**Rotondaro, Serafina**. "Tempo, uomo e memoria nella *Teogonia* di Esiodo" in *Il Concetto di Tempo: Atti del XXXII Congresso Nazionale della Società Filosofica Italiana*, Casertano, Giovanni (ed), 141-145. Napoli, Loffredo, 1997.

**Rottschaefer, William A**. Evolutionary Ethics: An Irresistible Temptation: Some Reflections on Paul Farber's The Temptation of Evolutionary Ethics. *Biol Phil*, 12(3), 369-384, Jl 97.

In his recent *The Temptation of Evolutionary Ethics*, Paul Farber has given a negative assessment of the last one hundred years of attempts in Anglo-American philosophy, beginning with Darwin, to develop an evolutionary ethics. Farber identifies some version of the naturalistic fallacy as one of the central sources for the failures of evolutionary ethics. For this reason and others, Farber urges that though it has its attraction, evolutionary ethics is a temptation to be resisted. In this discussion I identify three major, historically relevant forms of the naturalistic fallacy, the 1) the deductive, 2) genetic, and 3) open question forms and argue that none of them pose an intrinsic problem for evolutionary ethics. I conclude that on this score at least there is no reason to resist temptation.

**Rouquette, Michel-Louis**. Social Representations and Mass Communication Research. *J Theor Soc Behav*, 26(2), 221-231, Je 96.

It is argued that mass communication is basically a combination of social practices within a 'public space': opinion-leadership, roles in everyday conversations, decisions, etc. These practices are intrinsically bound to social representations. Two main points can serve as guidelines. First, insofar as social representations are specifically related to social groups, mass communication has to be studied in its specific relation to socially differentiated groups (see for instance, propaganda, propagation and diffusion, as defined by Moscovici). Another point, correlative in fact, would be to relate the specific characteristics of mass communications at a given moment to the structural properties of social representations. (edited)

**Rovaletti, María Lucrecia**. Alienación y libertad: La ética en la psicoterapia. *Cuad Etica*, 21-22, 153-166, 1996.

Each society, in a certain period, has its own criteria for the meanings of health and illness. Diagnosis and treatment are the results of a "professional construction" of illness. The present text points out that normality can be determined from different realms: statistics, axiology or pain and suggests that an answer should be given which considers both freedom and the historical dimension of the human self.

**Rovatti, Pier Aldo**. "Il Paiolo Bucato" in *Soggetto E Verità: La questione dell'uomo nella filosofia contemporanea*, Fagiuoli, Ettore, 71-76. 20136 Milano, Mimesis, 1996.

**Rovatti, Pier Aldo**. Il soggetto e l'etica del discorso. *Itinerari Filosof*, 3(5), 56-62, Ja-Ap 93.

**Rovira, Rogelio** and Palacios, Juan Miguel. Noticia sobre la edición de las *Obras Completas* de Manuel García Morente. *An Seminar Hist Filosof*, 13, 285-290, 1996.

**Rowan, Andrew N**. Ethics Education in Science and Engineering: The Case of Animal Research. *Sci Eng Ethics*, 1(2), 181-184, A 95.

**Rowan, John R**. Grounding Hypernorms: Towards a Contractarian Theory of Business Ethics. *Econ Phil*, 13(1), 107-112, Ap 97.

The *integrated social contracts theory* (ISCT), authored by Thomas Donaldson and Thomas Dunfee, is a promising framework for analyzing ethical issues which arise in business. In its current form, however, it suffers from a difficulty which greatly inhibits its practical applicability. While serious, the problem can be remedied by redescribing the theory so as to keep it more in line with the social contract tradition. This redescription entails providing a moral ground for "hypernorms," the "fundamental moral precepts of all human beings," which in ISCT serve to limit the freedom of individual business communities to develop their own moral codes.

**Rowe, M W**. Lamarque and Olsen on Literature and Truth. *Phil Quart*, 47(188), 322-341, Jl 97.

In *Fiction, Truth and Literature*, Lamarque and Olsen argue that if a critic claims or attempts to prove that the outlook of a work of literature is true or false, he is not engaging in literary or aesthetic appreciation. This paper argues against this position by adducing cases where literary critics discuss the truth or falsity of a work's view, when their opinions are obviously relevant to the work's aesthetic assessment. The paper considers in detail the way factual errors damage a work's aesthetic standing and shows that Lamarque and Olsen's alternative account of the role of propositional truths in literature only looks plausible because it considers a restricted range of examples. Finally, it considers the role *intention*, *date* and *genre* play in discussions of the aesthetic damage done by literal falsehood.

**Rowland, Robert C**. Why Rational Argument Needs Defending. *Phil Rhet*, 30(1), 82-88, 1997.

**Rowlands, Mark**. Teleological Semantics. *Mind*, 106(422), 279-303, Ap 97.

This paper argues that the teleological account is undermined by neither of these problems. Failure to appreciate this point stems from a conflation of two types of proper function—organismic and algorithmic—possessed by an evolved mechanism. These functions underwrite attributions of content to distinct objects. The algorithmic proper function of a mechanism underwrites attributions of content to the mechanism itself, while the organismic proper function of a mechanism underwrites attribution of content to the organism that possesses the mechanism. However, the problems of indeterminacy and transparency arise only if the attributions of content attach to the same object. (edited)

**Roy, Louis**. Kant's Reflections on the Sublime and the Infinite. *Kantstudien*, 88(1), 44-59, 1997.

The article tackles the issue of the compatibility between Kant's phenomenology of the sublime and his transcendental account of that experience. In disagreement with several commentators who have rejected his views on the human openness to the infinite, it is argued that, by bringing together the riches of aesthetics, epistemology and ethics, Kant's position is intellectually satisfying. We proceed in three steps and successively introduce: Kant's thesis regarding the mediation of the human mind; his dialectic of the logical and the aesthetic within the mathematically sublime; and the status he assigns to the concept of the infinite.

**Roy, Subrata**. Melody in Life: Some Reflections. *Darshana Int*, 36 (2/142), 46-52, Ap 96.

The purpose of the article—'Melody in Life...' is an attempt to study Raghunath Ghosh's book, *Sura, Man and Society: Philosophy of Harmony in Indian Tradition*, critically, in the way of appreciating its main thesis. It is also an attempt to add a few more dimensions to the concept of harmony (melody, *Sura*). In a way, it's an effort to show the hugeness of the concept of harmony, its principles and real nature, its relation with other concepts like 'one' and 'many', its existence in both the Indian and Western cultures and, finally, its basicness in respect of life and existence.

**Royakkers, Lambèr** and Dignum, Frank. "Defeasible Reasoning with Legal Rules" in *Deontic Logic, Agency and Normative Systems*, Brown, Mark A (ed), 174-193. New York, Springer-Verlag, 1996.

The last few years several defeasible deontic reasoning formalisms were developed as a way to solve the problem of deontic inconsistency. However, these formalisms are unable to deal with some very common forms of deontic reasoning, since, e.g., their expressiveness is restricted. In this paper we will establish a priority hierarchy of legal rules to solve the problem of deontic conflicts and we will give a mechanism to reason about nonmonotonicity of legal rules over the priority hierarchy. The theory presented here, based on default logic and a modification and extension of the argumentation framework of Prakken, properly deals with some shortcomings of other defeasible deontic reasoning approaches.

**Rozenberg, Jacques J**. Physiology, Embryology and Psychopathology: A Test Case for Hegelian Thought (in French). *Arch Phil*, 60(2), 243-253, Ap-Je 97.

The formulation of Hegelian philosophy was contemporaneous with the emergence of biology as a scientific discipline. However, beyond this merely historical convergence, there is the matter of locating the *traces of conceptual determinations* which, in spite of giving form to the thought patterns of biology, have never been recognized as such by the life sciences. In order to do this, it is necessary to analyse the examples which Hegel borrowed from the physiology and embryology of his time by resituating them within the history of these two disciplines. Finally, this article strongly attempts, in a *biopsychological* perspective, to articulate the concept of *living* within the domaine of pathology and more precisely in psychopathology.

**Rózsa, Erzsébet**. Explanations of Everyday Life: Georg Lukács and Agnes Heller (in Hungarian). *Magyar Filozof Szemle*, 4-5-6, 439-457, 1996.

Die bekannte Lukács-Schlülerin, Agnes Heller, hat eine Konzeption des alltaeglichen Lebens in den 60er und 70er Jahren ausgearbeitet, Diese Konzeption ist tief verwurzelt in der Lukács'schen Auffassung des Alltaeglichen, die er in seinem viel diskutierten Aesthaetik entworfen hatte. Gleichzeitig aber weicht das Hellersche Konzept vom Lukács'schen ab; ihre Auslegung ist sie in einer Monographie dargestellt, in der die Abweichungen leicht erkannt werden können. Waehrend Georg Lukács in seinem Werk nur einen Entwurf des Alltaeglichen gemacht hatte, hat Heller eine Theorie des Alltaeglichen ausgearbeitet. (edited)

**Ruben, David-Hillel**. John Searle's *The Construction of Social Reality*. *Phil Phenomenol Res*, 57(2), 443-447, Je 97.

A critical discussion of Searle's *The Construction of Social Reality*, focusing on his distinction between constitutive and regulative rules and arguing that the distinction can only be cashed out in a nonmetaphorical way as a rather uninteresting distinction between two different kinds of action descriptions.

**Ruben, David-Hillel** and Raz, Joseph. The Active and the Passive. *Aris Soc*, Supp(71), 211-246, 1997.

**Rubenstein, Eric M**. Colour as Simple: A Reply to Westphal. *Philosophy*, 71(278), 595-602, O 96.

In support of the thesis that colours are examples of metaphysical simples, this article critiques arguments to the contrary. It is shown that facts about colour resemblance do not entail the complexity of colour, for such facts may explained by recourse to acts of seeing-as. The logic of colour and colour terms is adumbrated in support of this and used in a positive argument for the claim that colours are simple.

**Rubin, Susan** and Zoloth-Dorfman, Laurie. She Said/He Said: Ethics Consultation and the Gendered Discourse. *J Clin Ethics*, 7(4), 321-332, Wint 96.

**Rubinoff, Lionel**. "The Autonomy of History: Collingwood's Critique of F.H. Bradley's Copernican Revolution in Historical Knowledge" in *Philosophy after F.H. Bradley*, Bradley, James (ed), 127-145. Bristol, Thoemmes, 1996.

Although Collingwood credits Bradley with accomplishing the Copernican Revolution in the philosophy of history Bradley is criticized for not taking the doctrine of historicity implied by his doctrine far enough. Rather than acknowledging that human nature and the principles of historical interpretation are part of a self-making process Bradley found himself still wedded to the enlightenment doctrines of human nature and scientific method. It was left for Collingwood to complete the Copernican revolution by working out the full implications of the doctrine of historicity as it applies to both human nature and the principles of historiography.

**Ruddick, William**. Do Doctors Undertreat Pain?. *Bioethics*, 11(3-4), 246-255, Jl 97.

Routinely, physicians discount patients' pain reports and provide too little analgesia too late. Critics call them callous, sadistic, and puritanical, but the causes of these clinical practices are different—namely, a psychological need to distance themselves from the pain they encounter and inflict, and more subtly, a peculiar concept of pain acquired in medical training. (edited)

**Rudeanu, Sergiu**. On Lukasiewicz-Moisil Algebras of Fuzzy Sets. *Stud Log*, 52(1), 95-111, F 93.

**Rudolph, Enno**. Naturgesetz und gegenständliche Realität. *Phil Natur*, 28(1), 12-16, 1991.

**Rudolph, Enno**. Wie definiert man einen physikalischen Gegenstand?. *Phil Natur*, 27(1), 99-110, 1990.

**Rudominer, Mitch**. Mouse Sets. *Annals Pure Applied Log*, 87(1), 1-100, Ag 97.

In this paper we explore a connection between descriptive set theory and inner model theory. From descriptive set theory, we will take a countable, definable set of reals, $A$. We will then show that $A = R$ intersection $M$, where $M$ is a canonical model from inner model theory. In technical terms, $M$ is a "mouse". Consequently, we say that $A$ is a mouse set. (edited)

**Rueger, Alexander**. Risk and Diversification in Theory Choice. *Synthese*, 109(2), 263-280, N 96.

How can it be rational to work on a new theory that does not yet meet the standards for good or acceptable theories? If diversity of approaches is a condition for scientific progress, how can a scientific community achieve such progress when each member does what it is rational to do, namely work on the best theory? These two methodological problems, the problem of pursuit and the problem of diversity, can be solved by taking into account the *cognitive risk* that is involved in theory choice. I compare this solution to other proposals, in particular T.S. Kuhn's and P. Kitcher's view that the two problems demonstrate the epistemic significance of the scientific community.

**Rühling, Frank**. Die Deduktion der Philosophie nach Fichte und Friedrich von Hardenberg. *Fichte-Studien*, 12, 91-110, 1997.

**Ruetsche, Laura**. Van Fraassen on Preparation and Measurement. *Proc Phil Sci Ass*, 3(Suppl), S338-S346, 1996.

Van Fraassen's 1991 modal interpretation of Quantum Mechanics offers accounts of measurement and state preparation. I argue that both accounts overlook a class of interactions I call General Unitary Measurements, or GUMs. Ironically, GUMs are significant for van Fraassen's account of measurement because they *challenge* it and significant for his account of preparation because they *simplify* it. Van Fraassen's oversight prompts a question about modal interpretations: developed to account for ideal measurement outcomes, can they consistently account as well for the whole horizon of laboratory practices by which we investigate QM?

**Ruf, Henry L**. "Radicalizing Liberalism and Modernity" in *Philosophy, Religion, and the Question of Intolerance*, Ambuel, David (ed), 170-185. Albany, SUNY Pr, 1997.

**Ruffman, Ted**. Do Children Understand the Mind by Means of Simulation or a Theory? Evidence from their Understanding of Inference. *Mind Lang*, 11(4), 388-414, D 96.

Three experiments investigating children's understanding of inference as a source of knowledge and beliefs were used to determine whether children use a theory in understanding the mind. The main finding was that children tended to say the doll would hold a false belief about the colour of the sweet whenever the doll had not looked in the box. This result is easily reconciled with the theory view as a drive for coherence within the different aspects (knowledge and belief predictions) of the child's theory of mind. The result is contrary to the simulation view. (edited)

**Rugási, Gyula**. "Gift of the Egyptians" (On the History of Christian Philosophy) (in Czech). *Magyar Filozof Szemle*, 1-2, 93-114, 1997.

En examinant un motif utilisé plusieurs fois par saint Augustin, l'auteur de l'article analyse les rapports originels de la théologie chrétienne et de la philosophie. Selon la comparaison augustinienne, la philosophie hellénique joue le même rôle dans l'histoire du christianisme primitif que les rapines dans l'histoire biblique des Juifs lors de l'Exode. La préhistoire du motif en question nous ramène à la *théologie* antérieure aux pères *alexandrins* et, d'une manière plus concrète, elle nous ramène à l'interprétation que les apologètes du IIe siècle, Irénée et Justin, avaient accordée à la notion de la philosophie. (edited)

**Ruhland, Sheila K** and Upchurch, Randall S. The Organizational Bases of Ethical Work Climates in Lodging Operations as Perceived by General Managers. *J Bus Ethics*, 15(10), 1083-1093, O 96.

The focus of this research concentrated on ascertaining the presence of ethical climate types and the level of analysis from which ethical decisions were based as perceived by lodging managers. In agreement with Victor and Cullen (1987, 1988), ethical work climates are multidimensional and multidetermined. The results of this study indicated that: a) benevolence is the predominate dimension of ethical climate present in the lodging organization as perceived by lodging managers, and b) the local level of analysis (e.g., immediate workplace norms and values) is the predominate determinant of ethical decisions in the organization. The implication of this study is that the knowledge gained from understanding that ethical decision making in an organization is multidimensional and multidetermined will foster understanding of ethical decision formation in the organizational context.

**Ruiz Manero, Juan** and Atienza, Manuel. Permissions, Principles and Rights: A Paper on Statements Expressing Constitutional Liberties. *Ratio Juris*, 9(3), 236-247, S 96.

In the first part of the paper the authors analyze how the distinction between mandatory rules, principles in the strict sense and policies can be understood in structural terms and in terms of reasons for action. In the second part, they attempt to clarify which kind of legal provisions embrace constitutional statements recognizing liberty rights are.

**Ruja, Harry**. Bertrand Russell's Life in Pictures. *Russell*, 15(2), 101-152, Wint 95-96.

Bertrand Russell (1872-1970), Fellow of the Royal Society, Order of Merit, Nobel Laureate, mathematician, philosopher, social critic, peace activist and author attracted widespread attention during his long lifetime, especially for his often controversial views and actions. As a consequence, he was frequently depicted in photographs, drawings, paintings, sculptures, cartoons and caricatures. This essay describes briefly certain key illustrations which throw light on some peak moments of his career and character and identifies their sources.

**Ruja, Harry** (ed) and Russell, Bertrand. *Mortals and Others: American Essays 1931-1935.* New York, Routledge, 1996.

From 1931 to 1935 Bertrand Russell was one of the regular contributors to the literary pages of the *New York American*, together with other distinguished authors such as Aldous Huxley and Vita Sackville-West. *Mortals and Others* presents a selection of his essays, ranging from the politically correct to the perfectly obscure: from *Is the World Going Mad?* to *Should Socialists Smoke Good Cigars?* Even though written in the politically heated climate of the 1930s, these essays are surprisingly topical and engaging for the present-day reader. *Mortals and Others* serves as a splendid, fresh introduction to the compassionate eclecticism of Bertrand Russell's mind. (publisher)

**Ruland, Robert G** and Lindblom, Cristi K. Functionalist and Conflict Views of AICPA Code of Conduct: Public Interest vs. Self Interest. *J Bus Ethics*, 16(5), 573-582, Ap 97.

The sociological model of functionalism and conflict are introduced and utilized to analyze professionalism in the accounting profession as it is manifest in the American Institute of Certified Public Accountant's Code of Conduct. Rule 203 of the code and provisions of the code related to the public interest are examined using semiotic analysis to determine if they are most consistent with the functionalist or conflict models. While the analysis does not address intent of the code, it is determined that the code contains semantic defects which result in different interpretations of the code to different readers. The defects found are most consistent with the conflict model of professionalism. This has implications for the public and for individuals within the profession, making the code less useful to both groups. The defects are seen as a potential battleground for the self-interest vs. the public interest orientation of the accounting profession.

**Rumbaugh, Duane M**. The Psychology of Harry F. Harlow: A Bridge from Radical to Rational Behaviorism. *Phil Psych*, 10(2), 197-210, Je 97.

Harry Harlow is credited with the discovery of learning set, a process whereby problem solving becomes essentially complete in a single trial of training. Harlow described that process as one that freed his primates from arduous trial-and-error learning. The capacity of the learner to acquire learning sets was in positive association with the complexity and maturation of their brains. It is here argued that Harlow's successful conveyance of learning-set phenomena is of historic significance to the philosophy of psychology. Learning set is said to reflect the affirmation or rejection of hypotheses. Hypotheses are generated by the learner's brain, not its muscles. Thus, learning-set research served to advance the perspective that even nonhuman primates think and that their thinking reflects the active processing of information accrued from efforts to solve problems. (edited)

**Rumfitt, Ian**. The Vagaries of Paraphrase: A Reply to Holton on the Counting Problem. *Analysis*, 56(4), 246-250, O 96.

**Rumsey, Jean P**. Justice, Care, and Questionable Dichotomies. *Hypatia*, 12(1), 99-113, Wint 97.

Throughout the development of an "ethic of care" different from an "ethic of justice," the relationship between the two has been problematic. Are they theories between which one must choose? Are they complementary? Are they domain-specific? In support of my view that neither is adequate by itself, I here examine the private domain of care of the dying by intimates and find there important issues both of care and of justice.

**Runggaldier, Edmund**. Analytische Religionsphilosophie: Zwischen Intersubjektivität und Esoterik. *Theol Phil*, 71(3), 410-418, 1996.

**Runggaldier, Edmund**. *Was sind Handlungen? Eine philosophische Auseinandersetzung mit dem Naturalismus.* Stuttgart, Kohlhammer, 1996.

The book is a critical assessment of the main contemporary naturalistic accounts of actions. It concentrates on: actions as ontological particulars; the "by-relation" of "action-trees"; intentions and intentionality; the causal explanation of actions; mental causation; agent causality; indexicality and the subjective perspective of the agents. The author defends the thesis that an adequate account of actions presupposes an ontology containing agents endowed with intentional capacities and understood as continuants: Actions have temporal parts but not agents.

**Rus Rufino, Salvador**. La justicia en el pensamiento jurídico anglo-americano contemporáneo: Acotaciones críticas. *Daimon Rev Filosof*, 12, 103-118, Ja-Je 96.

Since John Rawls wrote his acquaintance *A Theory of Justice*, in the English-speaking world an important fact took place: the justice was a fundamental topic in the studies and research of moral philosophy and politics, a question was continually debated. However, the jurists remained the margin this general concern. Only for about three lustrum began to elaborate a theory of the justice for the jurists, with the purpose of explaining fundamental questions which are concerned directly in the law system, the legal theory and the activity of lawyers. In the work are shown four different ways which the jurists have tried to give answer to the question of why and how to distribute and they also seek to justify an important fact: the assignment of goods and resources.

**Ruse, Michael E**. "Are Pictures Really Necessary? The Case of Sewall Wright's 'Adaptive Landscapes'" in *Picturing Knowledge,* Baigrie, Brian S (ed), 303-337. Toronto, Univ of Toronto Pr, 1996.

This article deals with the question of illustration in science, using the case study of Sewall Wright's "Adaptive Landscapes" it is argued that pictures are more than mere illustrations and of pedagogical value. They enter right into the science itself, both from an explanatory point of view and heuristically.

**Rushton, Cindy Hylton**. The Voices of Nurses on Ethics Committees. *Bioethics Forum*, 10(4), 30-35, Fall 94.

Nurses, the largest group of caregivers in hospitals, have been visibly absent from ethics committees. This situation is changing, with nurses becoming more educated and sophisticated in ethical discourse and ethical theory. However, more advances need to be made, with spaces on committees reserved for bedside nurses as well as those in managerial roles. Nurses, who focus on the patient's response to health problems rather than on the diagnosis and treatment of the disease, bring a unique and valuable perspective to ethics committees, one which enhances their efficacy.

**Russell, Bertrand**. *An Essay on the Foundations of Geometry*. New York, Routledge, 1996.

*The Foundations of Geometry* was first published in 1897 and is based on Russell's Cambridge dissertation as well as lectures given during a journey through the USA. This is the first reprint, complete with a new introduction by Professor John Slater. The book provides both an insight into Russell's earliest analytical and critical thought and an introduction to the philosophical and logical foundations of non-Euclidean geometry, a version of which is central to Einstein's theory of relativity. (edited)

**Russell, Bertrand**. *An Inquiry into Meaning and Truth: The William James Lectures for 1940 Delivered at Harvard University*. New York, Routledge, 1995.

In this volume, Bertrand Russell is concerned with the foundations of knowledge. Russell approaches his subject through a discussion of language, the relationships of truth to experience and an investigation into how knowledge of the structure of language helps our understanding of the structure of the world. This edition of *An Inquiry into Meaning and Truth* includes a new introduction by Thomas Baldwin, Clare College, Cambridge. (publisher)

**Russell, Bertrand**. *My Philosophical Development*. New York, Routledge, 1995.

*My Philosophical Development* is Russell's intellectual autobiography (whereas his *Autobiography* (1967) deals primarily with his personal life). It was published in 1959, when Russell was 87 years old, and internal evidence shows that some of it cannot have been written much before then. So it shows that Russell's extraordinary intellectual energy, which enabled him to write more than forty books, remained with him well past the age of 80—though it has to be added that Russell's critical discussions here of contemporary philosophy are not of the standard of his earlier work. (edited)

**Russell, Bertrand**. *Unpopular Essays*. New York, Routledge, 1995.

In this collection, Russell sets out to combat dogmatism, whether of the *right* or of the *left*. He ranges over a wide number of subjects with a serious purpose, but a lightness of touch. This edition includes a new introduction by Kirk Willis, University of Georgia. (publisher)

**Russell, Bertrand** and Rempel, Richard A. *Principles of Social Reconstruction*. New York, Routledge, 1997.

This book, originally entitled *Why Men Fight*, is generally seen as the fullest expression of Russell's political philosophy. Russell argues that after the experience of the great war the individualistic approach of traditional liberalism had reached its limits. Political theory must be based on the motivating forces of creativity and impulse, rather than on competition. Both are best fostered in the family, in education, and in religion—each of which Russell proceeds to discuss. (publisher, edited)

**Russell, Bertrand** and Ruja, Harry (ed). *Mortals and Others: American Essays 1931-1935*. New York, Routledge, 1996.

From 1931 to 1935 Bertrand Russell was one of the regular contributors to the literary pages of the *New York American*, together with other distinguished authors such as Aldous Huxley and Vita Sackville-West. *Mortals and Others* presents a selection of his essays, ranging from the politically correct to the

AUTHOR INDEX 885 Rychlak, Joseph F

perfectly obscure: from *Is the World Going Mad?* to *Should Socialists Smoke Good Cigars?* Even though written in the politically heated climate of the 1930s, these essays are surprisingly topical and engaging for the present-day reader. *Mortals and Others* serves as a splendid, fresh introduction to the compassionate eclecticism of Bertrand Russell's mind. (publisher)

**Russell, Robert** and Price, Thomas and Kennett, Stephen. Interview with A. J. Ayer. *Kinesis*, 23(1), 4-25, Sum 96.

**Russon, John**. "For Now We See Through a Glass Darkly": The Systematics of Hegel's Visual Imagery" in *Sites of Vision,* Levin, David Michael (ed), 197-239. Cambridge, MIT Pr, 1997.

Hegel's visual imagery mirrors his critique of the ego. Images of daylight, enlightenment and reflection show forth the tensions within rationalistic individualism. Images of night and darkness reveal the unconscious dialectic that drives human life. This dark motor of humanity is religion, the forum in which a society's commitment to images is at stake. The religious image of revelation provides a way into recognizing the philosophical import of images, and why the stance of ritualistic, traditional society cannot do justice to freedom. The imagery of speculation and *noesis* captures this philosophical vision that reconciles rationality and tradition within human society.

**Russon, John Edward**. Self-Consciousness and the Tradition in Aristotle's Psychology. *Laval Theol Phil*, 52(3), 777-803, O 96.

Aristotle's "historical method" in his approach to his predecessors is the one demanded by his psychology and epistemology. Aristotle's definition of soul in *De Anima* implies that all knowing is a unification of subject and object and is the animating of a body. The notion of habituation in *Posterior Analytics* II.19 shows how this applies to intellect. The mind's animating of its object (its body) in intellectual comprehension is only complete when the comprehending recognizes itself as the fulfillment for which its object has been asking. This very principle which justifies Aristotle's portrayal of himself as the fulfillment of his tradition requires that our comprehension of Aristotle's philosophy likewise recognize itself as the fulfillment of his texts.

**Russon, John Edward**. *The Self and Its Body in Hegel's Phenomenology of Spirit*. Toronto, Univ of Toronto Pr, 1997.

My project in this work, however, is not Hegel's project in the *Phenomenology of Spirit*. My intention is to proceed by rigorous argument to comprehend something else, namely, the human body. This will be a presentation not of the science of the experience of consciousness but of the science of the embodiment of consciousness. My argument is that such a phenomenology of the body is implicitly carried out in Hegel's *Phenomenology of Spirit* and the effort here will be directed to extracting from Hegel's text the philosophy of the body that is there implied and to showing how this is the rational comprehension of human embodiment. (publisher, edited)

**Russow, Lilly-Marlene**. Response: Language and Thought. *Between Species*, 12(1-2), 53-55, Wint-Spr 96.

**Ruthenberg, Klaus**. "Warum ist die Chemie ein Steifkind der Philosophie?" in *Philosophie der Chemie: Bestandsaufnahme und Ausblick,* Schummer, Joachim (ed), 27-35. Wurzburg, Koenigshausen, 1996.

**Ruthenberg, Klaus** (ed) and Psarros, Nikos (ed) and Schummer, Joachim (ed). *Philosophie der Chemie: Bestandsaufnahme und Ausblick*. Wurzburg, Koenigshausen, 1996.

The German working group "Philosophy and Chemistry" (founded in 1993) has collected nine articles that provide a comprehensive survey of what have been done in the past and what should be done in a future philosophy of chemistry. Since many authors find a notorious neglect of chemistry in the past, they try to explain this neglect from various aspects among which reductionism seems to be the most important.

**Rutherford, R B**. *The Art of Plato: Ten Essays in Platonic Interpretation*. Cambridge, Harvard Univ Pr, 1995.

This book is not a study of Plato's philosophy, but a contribution to the literary interpretation of the dialogues, through analysis of their formal structure, characterization, language and imagery. Among the dialogues considered in these interrelated essays are some of Plato's most admired and influential works, including the *Gorgias*, the *Symposium*, the *Republic* and the *Phaedrus*. Special attention is paid to the personality of Socrates, Plato's remarkable mentor, and to his interaction with the other characters in the dialogues. (publisher,edited)

**Ruttkamp, Emma**. A Model-Theoretic Interpretation of Science. *S Afr J Phil*, 16(1), 31-36, F 97.

I am arguing that it is only by concentrating on the role of models in theory construction, interpretation and change, that one can study the progress of science sensibly. I define the level at which these models operate as a level above the purely empirical (consisting of various systems in reality) but also indeed below that of the fundamental formal theories (expressed linguistically). (edited)

**Ruzsa, Imre**. *Introduction to Metalogic*. Budapest, Aron, 1997.

**Ryan, Frank X**. The "Extreme Heresy" of John Dewey and Arthur F. Bentley I: A Star Crossed Collaboration?. *Trans Peirce Soc*, 33(3), 774-794, Sum 97.

Despite a vigorous revival of Dewey scholarship in the past decade, little has appeared about his late collaboration with Arthur F. Bentley or the philosophy of "transaction" they developed. What has appeared has been mostly negative, with Bentley accused of coercing his aging friend into forsaking the basic tenets of his instrumentalism and naturalism. This essay, the first of two parts, argues that the collaboration was both genuine and faithful to Dewey's philosophy: Dewey profoundly influenced Bentley's intellectual development, an influence subsequently "borrowed back" in a sustained effort in which Dewey was an active and informed participant.

**Ryan, James A**. A Defence of Mencius' Ethical Naturalism. *Asian Phil*, 7(1), 23-36, Mr 97.

I argue that Mencius puts forth a defensible form of ethical naturalism, according to which moral properties, moral motivation, and moral deliberation can be accounted for within the parameters of a naturalistic worldview. On this position, moral properties are the subjectively real properties which acts have in virtue of their corresponding to our most coherent set of shared desires. I give a naturalistic definition of 'right' which, I argue, is implicit in Mencius's philosophy. I address the objection that some of the contemporary-sounding views which I attribute to Mencius are positions which are alien to the ancient thinker, and I argue that the version of Mencius given here is not only quite faithful to Mencius but also a true metaethical theory.

**Ryan, James A**. Taking the 'Error' Out of Ruse's Error Theory. *Biol Phil*, 12(3), 385-397, Jl 97.

Michael Ruse's Darwinian metaethics has come under just criticism from Peter Woolcock (1993). But with modification it remains defensible. Ruse (1986) holds that people ordinarily have a false belief that there are objective moral obligations. He argues that the evolutionary story should be taken as an error theory, i.e., as a theory which explains the belief that there are obligations as arising from nonrational causes, rather than from inference or evidential reasons. Woolcock quite rightly objects that this position entails moral nihilism. However, I argue here that people generally have justified true beliefs about which acts promote their most coherent set of moral values and hence, by definition, about which acts are right. (edited)

**Ryan, Mark** and Schobbens, Pierre-Yves. Counterfactuals and Updates as Inverse Modalities. *J Log Lang Info*, 6(2), 123-146, Ap 97.

We point out a simple but hitherto ignored link between the theory of *updates*, the theory of *counterfactuals* and classical modal logic: update is a classical existential modality, counterfactual is a classical universal modality and the accessibility relations corresponding to these modalities are inverses. The Ramsey Rule (often thought esoteric) is simply an axiomatisation of this inverse relationship. (edited)

**Ryan, Sharon**. The Epistemic Virtues of Consistency. *Synthese*, 109(2), 121-141, N 96.

The lottery paradox has been discussed widely. The standard solution to the lottery paradox is that a ticket holder is justified in believing each ticket will lose but the ticket holder is also justified in believing not all of the tickets will lose. If the standard solution is true, then we get the paradoxical result that it is possible for a person to have a justified set of beliefs that she knows is inconsistent. In this paper, I argue that the best solution to the paradox is that a ticket holder is not justified in believing any of the tickets are losers. My solution avoids the paradoxical result of the standard solution. The solution I defend has been hastily rejected by other philosophers because it appears to lead to skepticism. I defend my solution from the threat of skepticism and give two arguments in favor of my conclusion that the ticket holder in the original lottery case is not justified in believing that his ticket will lose.

**Ryan, William F** (ed) and Tyrrell, Bernard J (ed). *A Second Collection: Papers by Bernard J. F. Lonergan, S.J.*. Toronto, Univ of Toronto Pr, 1996.

This collection of essays, addresses, and one interview comes from the years 1966-73, a period during most of which Bernard Lonergan was at work completing his *Method in Theology*. The eighteen chapters cover a wide spectrum of interest, dealing with such general topics as 'The Absence of God in Modern Culture' and 'The Future of Christianity', and narrowing down through items such as 'Belief: Today's Issue' and more specialized theological and philosophical studies, to one on his own community in the church and the illuminating comment on his great work *Insight*. (edited)

**Rybakov, Vladimir V**. Criteria for Admissibility of Inference Rules: Modal and Intermediate Logics with the Branching Property. *Stud Log*, 53(2), 203-225, My 94.

The main result of this paper is the following theorem: each modal logic extending *K4* having the branching property below *m* and the effective M-drop point property is decidable with respect to admissibility. A similar result is obtained for intermediate intuitionistic logics with the branching property below *m* and the strong effective m-drop point property. Thus, general algorithmic criteria which allow to recognize the admissibility of inference rules for modal and intermediate logics of the above kind are found. (edited)

**Ryberg, Jesper**. Do Possible People have Moral Standing?. *Dan Yrbk Phil*, 30, 96-118, 1995.

**Ryberg, Jesper**. Is the Repugnant Conclusion Repugnant?. *Phil Papers*, 25(3), 161-177, N 96.

**Rychlak, Joseph F**. Memory: A Logical Learning Theory Account. *J Mind Behav*, 17(3), 229-250, Sum 96.

An interpretation of memory from the perspective of logical learning theory (LLT) is presented. In contrast to traditional associationistic theories of learning and memory, which rest on mediation modelling, LLT rests on a predication model. Predication draws on formal and final causation whereas mediation is limited to material and efficient causation. It is held in LLT that memory begins in predicate organization, where framing meanings are logically extended to targets. Passage of time is irrelevant in this meaning extension. The effectiveness of memory depends on the cohesiveness or "tightness" of meaningful organization as framed by a relevant context. Well-organized contexts facilitate memory and poorly organized contexts are detrimental to memory. Possible reasons for good or poor organization in memory are discussed and relevant research findings cited. The paper closes with a separate definition of memory as a content and as a process.

**Ryckman, T A**. "Einstein *Agonists*: Weyl and Reichenbach on Geometry and the General Theory of Relativity" in *Origins of Logical Empiricism,* Giere, Ronald N (ed), 165-209. Minneapolis, Univ of Minnesota Pr, 1996.

Weyl and Reichenbach give opposing epistemological analyses of space-time geometry after the advent of the "general theory of relativity" (GTR) (1915). Weyl's position is rooted in his "unified theory of gravitation and electromagnetism" (1918) in which comparisons of lengths at finite separations are no longer unambiguous. Reichenbach's *Axiomatik* (1924) explicitly counters Weyl by sharply distinguishing between empirical and conventional statements in the foundations of GTR. In so doing, it seeks to provide a principled basis for Einstein's own provisional defense of rods and clocks as chronogeometrical indicators. At the same time, it enshrines a factual/conventional distinction which will be a core position of logical empiricist philosophy of science.

**Ryder, John**. "The Use and Abuse of Modernity: Postmodernism and the American Philosophic Tradition" in *Philosophy in Experience: American Philosophy in Transition,* Hart, Richard (ed), 225-240. New York, Fordham Univ Pr, 1997.

**Ryder, John**. Yuri K. Melvil and American Pragmatism. *Trans Peirce Soc,* 32(4), 598-632, Fall 96

**Rygwelski, Janis** and Brody, Howard and Fetters, Michael D. Ethics at the Interface: Conventional Western and Complementary Medical Systems. *Bioethics Forum,* 12(4), 15-23, Wint 96.

Both conventional and complementary medicines have a duty to treat patients ethically. Problems arise in each system's relationships with the other. Recognizing one's assumptions, often unaddressed, and agreeing on common goals will go far to remove suspicion when the two schools meet in the treatment of the same patient.

**Rylander, Jason C** and Shanks, Roland E and Pimentel, David. Bioethics of Fish Production: Energy and the Environment. *J Agr Environ Ethics,* 9(2), 144-164, 1996.

Aquatic ecosystems are vital to the structure and function of all environments on earth. Worldwide, approximately 95 million metric tons of fishery products are harvested from marine and freshwater habitats. A major problem in fisheries around the world is the bioethics of overfishing. A wide range of management techniques exists for fishery, managers and policy-makers to improve fishery production in the future. The best approach to limit overfishing is to have an effective, federally regulated fishery, based on environmental standards and fishery carrying capacity. Soon, overfishing is more likely to cause fish scarcity than fossil fuel shortages and high energy prices for fish harvesting. However, oil and other fuel are projected to influence future fishery policies and the productive capacity of the fishery industry. Overall, small-scale fishing systems are more energy efficient than large-scale systems. Aquaculture is not the solution to wild fishery production. The energy input/output ratio of aquacultural fish is much higher than that of the harvest of wild populations. In addition, the energy ratios for aquaculture systems are higher than those for most livestock systems.

**Ryle, Martin**. Histories of Cultural Populism. *Rad Phil,* 78, 27-33, Jl-Ag 96.

The article discusses intellectuals' attitudes to, and investments in, the boundaries between 'high' and 'low' culture. Frankfurt school pessimism about mass culture has given way to a pluralist embrace of 'cultural production' in general: this can lead into an uncritical cultural populism. Recent feminist work has valuably acknowledged the personal dimensions of cultural judgement: these can be traced back to Wordsworth and earlier, in an unacknowledged ambivalence about the 'low'. Making this hidden affective dimension explicit should lead us to speak not of 'high' and 'low'. Making this hidden affective dimension explicit should lead us to speak not of 'high' and 'low' culture so much as of certain cultural *relations*.

**Ryn, Claes G**. *Will, Imagination & Reason: Babbitt, Croce and the Problem of Reality.* New Brunswick, Transaction Pub, 1997.

*Will, Imagination and Reason* sets forth a new understanding of reality and knowledge with far-reaching implications for the study of man and society. Employing a systematic approach, Claes Ryn goes to the philosophical depths to rethink and reconstitute the epistemology of the humanities and social sciences. He shows that will and imagination, together, shape our basic outlook on life and that reason derives its material and general orientation from their interaction. (publisher, edited)

**Rynasiewicz, Robert**. Is There a Syntactic Solution to the Hole Problem?. *Proc Phil Sci Ass,* 3(Suppl), S55-S62, 1996.

After some background setting in which it is shown how Maudlin's (1989, 1990) response to the hole argument of Earman and Norton (1987) is related to that of Rynasiewicz (1994), it is argued that the syntactic proposals of Mund (1992) and of Leeds (1995), which claim to dismiss the hole argument as an uninteresting blunder, are inadequate. This leads to a discussion of how the responses of Maudlin and Rynasiewicz relate to issues about gauge freedom and relativity principles.

**Ryue, Hisang**. Die Differenz zwischen 'Ich bin' und 'Ich bin Ich'. *Fichte-Studien,* 10, 143-156, 1997.

**Sá Pereira, Roberto Horácio**. Intentionality and Scepticism (in Spanish). *Discurso,* 27, 157-179, 1996.

The aim of this paper is a reflection about the possibility of the intentionality in the light of sceptical hypotheses as hypotheses to the effect that the causal origins of our beliefs and perceptions might be totally different from the way we take them to be. Against the sceptic I intend to defend the following naturalistic theses: our causal and epistemic position in the world as persons in the middle of material things do play an essential role in the ascription and identification of

intentional states. For this purpose, I shall consider three arguments here: Davidson's considerations about radical interpretation, Putnam's causal theory of intentional states and my own free reconstruction of Wittgenstein's private language argument.

**Sabatés, Marcelo H**. "Autoconocimiento, racionalidad y contenido mental" in *La racionalidad: su poder y sus límites,* Nudler, Oscar (ed), 239-259. Barcelona, Ed Paidos, 1996.

It has been argued that if mental contents (partly) depend on environmental and social circumstances of the thinker, we have to give up self-knowledge or at least the intuition that we have an epistemically privileged access to our own mental states. And without self-knowledge, some are willing to add, we could not be rational deliberators. The paper offers an account of self-knowledge that i) keeps the intuition of privileged access, ii) meets the requirements for rational deliberation, and iii) seems to solve the problems raised by the typical externalist arguments.

**Sabatés, Marcelo H**. Kim on the Metaphysics of Explanation. *Manuscrito,* 19(2), 93-110, O 96.

In a series of influential papers, Jaegwon Kim has argued for three substantive theses on the metaphysics of explanation, each of them having other prestigious defenders as well as independent intuitive appeal. They are: Explanatory Realism (ER): explanations are grounded in "world-cementing" objective relations between the events referred to by the explanandum and the explanans; Explanatory pluralism (EP): there are, in addition to causal explanations, explanations tied to noncausal dependence relations; Explanatory Exclusion (EE): there cannot be more than one complete and independent explanation of the same event. But the following puzzle arises: (ER) couples explanations with structural objective relations and causes are one kind among such relations. I suggest a way out of the puzzle that eschews one of the theses but preserves the intuitions behind it. (edited)

**Sabatés, Marcelo H** and Perez, Diana I. La noción de superveniencia en la visión estratificada del mundo. *Analisis Filosof,* 15(1-2), 181-199, My-N 95.

Arguably, the orthodox ontological doctrine of contemporary physicalism is the so-called "layered view of reality". According to this widespread but generally implicit or understated view, reality is hierarchically structured in a series of levels such that objects and properties characterizing higher layers depend on those that characterize lower layers. While the part-whole relation cements objects of different levels, supervenience is thought to be what ties properties of different strata. However, even though many alternative notions of supervenience have been proposed recently for diverse purposes, it is in no way clear whether any of these notions is apt to relate the properties of different layers. In this paper we: I) offer a brief but explicit statement of the layered view of reality, II) discuss the requirements a notion of supervenience has to meet in order to play a substantive role in such a view, and III) argue that a notion of supervenience that takes a particular side on issues such as strength, modal force, ontological import and composition of the supervenience base is a good starting point as the cementing relation between the properties of the different layers of reality.

**Sabete, Wagdi**. La méthodologie de la science constitutionnelle de la liberté. *Riv Int Filosof Diritto,* 74(4), 252-318, Ap-Je 97.

**Sabin, James E** and Neu, Carlos. Real World Resource Allocation: The Concept of "Good-Enough" Psychotherapy. *Bioethics Forum,* 12(1), 3-9, Spr 96.

Principles can be established within a managed care plan to assist clinicians in managing resources. The concept of "good enough psychotherapy" is illustrated as a principle by which resources in a managed mental health program can be allocated in an ethically justifiable manner.

**Sabini, John** and Silver, Maury. In Defense of Shame: Shame in the Context of Guilt and Embarrassment. *J Theor Soc Behav,* 27(1), 1-15, Mr 97.

We are interested in the relations among shame, guilt and embarrassment and especially in how each relates to judgments of character. We start by analyzing the distinction between being and feeling guilty and unearth the role of shame as a guilt feeling. We proceed to examine shame and guilt in relation to moral responsibility and flaws of character. (edited)

**Sabini, John** and Silver, Maury. On the Possible Non-Existence of Emotions: The Passions. *J Theor Soc Behav,* 26(4), 375-398, D 96.

This paper attempts to demonstrate, at least for the passions, that while emotions are important elements of common sense psychological thought, they are not psychological, neural, or mental entities. People talk of emotions, we claim, in two sorts of cases: Firstly, when it is believed that someone has done something that she shouldn't because she has been overwhelmed by desire (a motive) and secondly, when someone is found to be compelled to devote cognitive resources to an act she knows she will never carry out. In this case motivational states command attention and cognitive and physiological resources, distract us, even though they will not issue in action. In either case pointing to an emotion is pointing to a partial, aborted, or misdirected desire. We discuss why emotions are considered important in common sense and professional psychology though they do not exist.

**Sacadura, Carlos Alexandre B A**. Percursos da Filosofia Hermenêutica. *Rev Port Filosof,* 52(1-4), 769-784, Ja-D 96.

The purpose of this work is to reflect upon the history of modern and contemporary philosophical hermeneutics. This field of philosophical thinking deals with the problem of interpretation and many thinkers say that we live in an age of interpretation. The famous Thomas Kuhn's theory of paradigms helped us to understand the recent evolution of hermeneutics as an emergence of several paradigms of interpretation, such as the methodological (Dilthey), ontological (Heidegger) or phenomenological (Ricoeur) ones.

**Sacchi, Dario**. Alcuni rilievi sul nesso fra verità, libertà e temporalità nella filosofia di F. Nietzsche. *Riv Filosof Neo-Scolas*, 88(2), 223-243, Ap-Je 96.

**Sacchi, Mario Enrique**. La causalidad material de los elementos en la generación de los cuerpos mixtos. *Sapientia*, 52(201), 203-223, 1997.

**Sacchi, Mario Enrique**. La concepción del espacio en la física de Santo Tomás de Aquino. *Sapientia*, 51(200), 517-563, 1996.

**Sacchi, Mario Enrique**. Santo Tomás de Aquino y la Medicina. *Aquinas*, 39(3), 493-528, S-D 96.

**Sachidanand, Achayra John**. The Political Philosophy of the New Indian Renaissance. *J Dharma*, 22(1), 97-103, Ja-Mr 97.

**Sacks, Mark**. Transcendental Constraints and Transcendental Features. *Int J Phil Stud*, 5(2), 164-186, Je 97.

Transcendental idealism has been conceived of in philosophy as a position that aims to secure objectivity without traditional metaphysical underpinnings. This article contrasts two forms of transcendental idealism that have been identified: one in the work of Kant, the other in the later Wittgenstein. The distinction between these two positions is clarified by means of a distinction between *transcendental constraints* and *transcendental features*. It is argued that these conceptions provide the —fundamentally different—bases of the two positions under discussion. With the core of the positions identified, it is then suggested that neither form of transcendental idealism—the Kantian or the Wittgensteinian—manages to combine the twin aims of safeguarding objectivity and maintaining metaphysical parsimony. The Kantian form appears to succeed on the first score at the cost of failing on the second, while the Wittgensteinian form succeeds on the second and fails on the first.

**Sadler, John Z**. Epistemic Value Commitments in the Debate Over Categorical vs. Dimensional Personality Diagnosis. *Phil Psychiat Psych*, 3(3), 203-222, S 96.

The idea that values shape psychiatric classification is still a controversial one. This article addresses this controversy by 1) defining a particular domain or type of value commitment (epistemic values), 2) showing how they might be assumed in psychiatric classification, 3) developing a set of conceptual tools to analyze epistemic value content and 4) applying this set of tools to concretely illustrate how this type of value is "at work" in shaping classification. A classic paper on the dispute between categorical and dimensional models for personality disorders is systematically examined to illustrate this "epistemic value" rubric. (edited)

**Sadler, John Z** (ed). Recent and Classic References at the Interface of Philosophy, Psychiatry, and Psychology. *Phil Psychiat Psych*, 3(4), 309-311, D 96.

**Saez Rueda, Luis** and Milovic, Miroslav (trans). For Non-Relative Difference and Non-Coercive Dialogue (in Serbo-Croatian). *Theoria (Yugoslavia)*, 38(4), 7-21, D 95.

The aim of this article is to show that there are reasons for affirming the difference against the identity in a critical and nonrelative way. First, the author explains how the modern thinking of difference led to pluralism and relativism. Then he exposes Habermas's and Apel's thesis that "spiritual unity" cannot stem either from metaphysics nor from religion. He criticizes their "dialogical" solution and examines postmodern alternative. Finally, he defends his own, nonrelativistic view which relies on the so-called "tragic" conception of rationality.

**Saghafi, Kas**. The "Passion for the Outside": Foucault, Blanchot, and Exteriority. *Int Stud Phil*, 28(4), 79-92, 1996.

**Sagi, Avi**. Hume's Dilemma and the Defense of Interreligious Pluralism (in Hebrew_. *Iyyun*, 45, 419-442, O 96.

**Sagi, Avi**. Yeshayahu Leibowitz—A Breakthrough in Jewish Philosophy: Religion Without Metaphysics. *Relig Stud*, 33(2), 203-216, Je 97.

This article is an analysis of the theological-philosophical revolution that Leibowitz's thought represents in the philosophy of religion in general and in Jewish philosophy in particular. This revolution relies on a positivist viewpoint, which denies any possibility of making statements about God. In his approach, statements about God are interpreted as statements denoting the relationship between the individual and God. Conventional religious beliefs—such as the belief in the creation or in revelation—become meaningless. Leibowitz, therefore, suggests a new interpretation, both of theoretical religious beliefs and of the normative system—the Halakha. The belief in revelation is construed as a human judgment, which endows the halakhic system with divine validity. Halakha does not draw its meaning from its divine source but from its inner religious meaning, which Leibowitz sees in worship.

**Sagnotti, Simona C**. La relazione tra l'uomo e la natura: una prospettiva. *Riv Int Filosof Diritto*, 73(4), 729-733, O-D 96.

**Sagüillo, José M**. Logical Consequence Revisited. *Bull Sym Log*, 3(2), 216-241, Je 97.

Tarski's 1936 paper, "on the concept of logical consequence", is a rather philosophical, nontechnical paper that leaves room for conflicting interpretations. My purpose is to review some important issues that explicitly or implicitly constitute its themes. My discussion contains four sections: 1) terminological and conceptual preliminaries, 2) Tarski's definition of the concept of logical consequence, 3) Tarski's discussion of omega-incomplete theories, and 4) concluding remarks concerning the kind of conception that Tarski's definition was intended to explicate. The third section involves subsidiary issues, such as Tarski's discussion concerning the distinction between material

and formal consequence and the important question of the criterion for distinguishing between logical and nonlogical terms.

**Sahlin, Nils-Eric**. "He Is No Good for My Work" in *Knowledge and Inquiry: Essays on Jaakko Hintikka's Epistemology and Philosophy of Science,* Sintonen, Matti (ed), 61-84. Amsterdam, Rodopi, 1997.

This is a paper on the philosophical relations between F.P. Ramsey and Ludwig Wittgenstein. The key question of the paper is to what extent Frank Ramsey influenced the thinking of the later Wittgenstein. It is well known that Wittgenstein strongly influenced Frank Ramsey's philosophical thinking. But, what is less well known is that Ramsey came to change his view of philosophy and in doing so became a major force in Wittgenstein's upheaval of the Tractarian view. From 1929 and on one can clearly spot a remolded Ramsey in the work of Wittgenstein. Thus, it is argued that Wittgenstein probably was more influenced by Ramsey than Ramsey was influenced by Wittgenstein. The arguments are presented in three parts: 1) a few biographical glimpses are given; 2) Ramsey's British pragmatism is outlined and discussed; and 3) it is shown where this British pragmatism can be spotted in Wittgenstein's work after 1930.

**Sain, Ildikó** (& others) and Kurucz, Agnes and Németi, István. Decidable and Undecidable Logics with a Binary Modality. *J Log Lang Info*, 4(3), 191-206, 1995.

We give an overview of decidability results for modal logics having a binary modality. We put an emphasis on the demonstration of proof-techniques and hope that this will also help in finding the borderlines between decidable and undecidable fragments of usual first-order logic.

**Sainati, Vittorio**. Teologia e verità: Il problema della traduzione teologica. *Teoria*, 16(2), 7-20, 1996.

**Sainsbury, R M**. Crispin Wright: *Truth and Objectivity*. *Phil Phenomenol Res*, 56(4), 899-904, D 96.

This belongs to a symposium about Crispin Wright's *Truth and Objectivity*. Wright entertains the "possibility of a *pluralist* view of truth." I suggest that this should not entail ambiguity in the word "true." For truth to amount to different things for different kinds of subject matter no more entails ambiguity than does the fact that existence amounts to different things for different kinds of entity. Turning to *cognitive command*, I argue that it is trivially satisfied: if I judge that *p* and you disagree, then under suitable conditions I must take it that something is wrong with your cognitive mechanisms.

**Saint-Germain, Christian**. La fonction libératrice du désespoir chez Eugen Drewermann. *Laval Theol Phil*, 53(2), 385-393, Je 97.

This article intends to show the close relationship that exists between the thought of the philosopher Sören Kierkegaard and the ideas of the theologian Eugen Drewermann. In both works one finds a correlation between a complete surrender to God and a no less abysmal feeling of despair. Thus, both author reinstate the boundary situation of despair as a place for salvation and as a dimension of openness to the word of God.

**Saito, Akiko**. Social Origins of Cognition: Bartlett, Evolutionary Perspective and Embodied Mind Approach. *J Theor Soc Behav*, 26(4), 399-421, D 96.

This paper explores new avenues of research on social bases of cognition and a more adequate (than those extant) framework to conceive the phenomena of the human mind. It firstly examines Bartlett's work on social bases of cognition, from which three pertinent features are identified, namely multilevel analyses, evolutionary perspective and embodied mind approach. It then examines recent works on social origins of cognition in ethology and paleoanthropology, and various forms of the embodied mind approach recently proposed in neuroscience and cognitive science. The paper concludes that extending the embodied mind approach would provide the most potent framework to enable, amongst others, the conceptual integration of the biological, psychological and social bases of the human mind, which have in the past been treated mainly as competing alternatives.

**Saito, Naoko**. "Dewey's Idea of Sympathy and the Development of the Ethical Self: A Japanese Perspective" in *Philosophy of Education (1996)*, Margonis, Frank (ed), 389-396. Urbana, Phil Education Soc, 1997.

**Sakezles, Priscilla K**. Bringing Ancient Philosophy of Life: Teaching Aristotelian and Stoic Theories of Responsibility. *Teach Phil*, 20(1), 1-17, Mr 97.

Two problems involved in teaching ancient philosophy are that students find the material outdated and irrelevant and that teachers too often neglect Hellenistic philosophy in general and early Stoicism in particular. I detail a strategy for addressing these problems: teaching the Aristotelian and early Stoic theories about determinism and moral responsibility, focusing on the debate over whether "being able to do otherwise" is a necessary condition for being morally responsible for an action. In short, Aristotle says it is and the Stoics say it is not.

**Sakota, Jasna**. Ratio Indifferens (in Serbo-Croatian). *Theoria (Yugoslavia)*, 38(1), 7-27, Mr 95.

As a paradigm of certainty, *cogito* is the greatest burden for modern philosophy. As the sole irrefutable constituent of the subject, it is a barrier between the subject and knowledge, between the subject and reality. It has closed the subject into the world of ideas from which the subject cannot escape unless it proclaims arbitrarily its reflective thought at one moment as true and the next moment as false. However, the occurrence of this arbitrariness does not proceed only from the structure of the subject but primarily from endeavors of modernists to "conceal" that structure. The subject is not able to resist to the immediate content of *cogito* and for this powerlessness he compensates with the will for knowledge that invokes the concept of objective truth. (edited)

**Sakwa, Richard**. The Struggle for the Constitution in Russia and the Triumph of Ethical Individualism. *Stud East Euro Thought*, 48(2-4), 115-157, S 96.

The constitution of December 1993 both reproduces and repudiates elements of Russia's constitutional history. The document emerged out of competing visions for postcommunist Russia and in particular whether it should be a parliamentary or presidential republic and over the rights of federal subjects. The constitution incorporates the defence of individual rights while maintaining a concern for the ethical basis of social rights. The document is liberal in its overall conception, but its democratic procedures are flawed, above all in the dangerous concentration of powers granted the president. The problem is not so much the absence of the separation of powers but that the division is unbalanced.

**Salamatov, Vladimir** and Girnyk, Andryi and Milov, Yury P. The Chaos-Cosmos Transformation Cycle with Special Reference to the Chernobyl Disaster: Toward the Ultimate Reality and Meaning of the Ukraine. *Ultim Real Mean*, 20(2 & 3), 196-204, Je-S 97.

**Salaquarda, Jörg**. "Art is More Powerful Than Knowledge" (in Serbo-Croatian). *Filozof Istraz*, 15(4), 683-695, 1995.

Nietzsche hat schon als Student Kants Vernunftkritik zur Kenntnis genommen—vor allem in der ihr von Schopenhauer gegebenen Gestalt. Später hat er seine Kenntnis des transzendentalen Ansatzes und seiner Konsequenzen durch die Lektüre von Fr. A. Langes *Geschichte des Materialismus* vertieft. Nietzsche hat daraus gefolgert, dass die wesentlichen Fragen und Probleme von der Erkenntnis nicht beantwortet bzw. auch nur erfasst werden können. In seinen frühen Werken hat er deswegen die Kunst über die Erkenntnis gesetzt. Philosophisch war es ihm um eine Synthese von künstlerischem Schaffen und wissenschaftlichem Erkennen zu tun, wobei er einerseits an die Kultur der vorsokratischen Griechen, andererseits an Schopenhauer und Wagner anknüpfte. (edited)

**Salas, Mario**. La dialéctica de lo universal y lo particular y el ideal de la abolición del estado (Segunda parte). *Rev Filosof (Costa Rica)*, 34(83-84), 293-302, D 96.

This essay attempts to find, in the history of Western political philosophy, the roots of the Marxian ideal of the extinction of the state. It also shows the fundamental importance of this subject for Marx's thought and how it is left aside in the further development of Marxism and becomes only a ritual formula, without any practical significance.

**Salazar, Omar**. El concepto de "paradigma" en Thomas Kuhn y la filosofía. *Franciscanum*, 37(112), 103-139, Ja-Ap 96.

**Salazar P, Freddy**. "El Liberalismo como destino: A propósito de la obra de Francis Fukuyama" in *Liberalismo y Comunitarismo: Derechos Humanos y Democracia*, Monsalve Solórzano, Alfonso (ed), 265-297. 36-46003 València, Alfons el Magnànim, 1996.

**Sales, Bruce** and Morenz, Barry. Complexity of Ethical Decision Making in Psychiatry. *Ethics Behavior*, 7(1), 1-14, 1997.

Psychiatric residents and psychiatrists have little difficulty in making judgments about a clinical course of action to take with patients. However, making ethical clinical decisions is more challenging, because psychiatric residents are usually provided little formal training in ethics. Further, many ethical dilemmas are complex, requiring knowledge of the psychiatric profession's ethics code, moral principles, law and practice standards and of how they should be weighed in the decision-making process. The purpose of this article is to demonstrate this complexity in regard to the identification of potential ethical dilemmas, understanding the issues that these dilemmas raise and formulating potential solutions to them. Two common but important areas of treatment in which ethical dilemmas arise (informed consent and competence of care) are used as examples for our presentation. The article demonstrates that to successfully engage in ethical analysis in psychiatry is impossible without substantial formal training in the process.

**Salladay, Susan Anthony** and Shelley, Judith Allen. Spirituality in Nursing Theory and Practice: Dilemmas for Christian Bioethics. *Christian Bioethics*, 3(1), 20-38, Mr 97.

Moral strangerhood is due in part to competing worldviews. The profession of nursing is experiencing a paradigm shift which creates ethical dilemmas for both Christian nurses and Christian patients. Nursing's new focus on spirituality and spiritual care presents itself as broadly defining a desired state or patient outcome—spiritual integrity—supposed to be applicable to all patients of all faiths. Analysis of nursing's definition of spirituality reveals assumptions and values consistent with an Eastern/New Age worldview which may cause hostility towards Christian patients stereotyped as dogmatic or noncompliant.

**Sallis, John**. "The Politics of the *Chora*" in *The Ancients and the Moderns*, Lilly, Reginald (ed), 59-71. Bloomington, Indiana Univ Pr, 1996.

By way of a critique of Hannah Arendt's views on the relation of Greek thought to modern political theory, this paper attempts to develop the Platonic discourse on the *chora* in a way that would bear on the basic questions of political philosophy.

**Sallis, John**. Bread and Wine. *Phil Today*, 41(1-4), 219-228, Spr 97.

This paper, in memory of André Schuwer, discusses bread and wine in Hegel's account of the sacraments and in the poetic work of Hölderlin.

**Sallis, John**. Of the *Chora*. *Epoche*, 2(1), 1-12, 1994.

This essay is a response to Jacques Derrida's work on the *chora* in Plato's *Timaeus*. It underlines several significant issues developed in Derrida's interpretation and attempts to show the need, beyond Derrida's interpretation, to develop the question of the appearance of the *chora*, of how the *chora* becomes manifest.

**Sallis, John**. Platonism at the Limit of Metaphysics. *Grad Fac Phil J*, 19/20(2/1), 299-314, 1997.

This paper begins with a discussion of Reiner Schürmann's retrospective reading of Plotinian henology. On this basis and yet in distinction from Schürmann's reading, the paper then attempts a reading that, instead of returning from Heidegger to Plotinus, brings the resources of Plato's texts to bear on Plotinus. Attention is given especially to the way in which Plotinus's discourse on the One is set outside the discourse circulating between intelligible and sensible.

**Sallis, John** and Pasanen, Outi. Double Truths: An Interview with John Sallis. *Man World*, 30(1), 107-114, Ja 97.

This interview is devoted to such topics as the end of metaphysics, the role of imagination in addressing the limits of metaphysics and the implications for the concept of mimesis and for the understanding of art as mimesis. There are also discussions of John Sallis's current work on painting and on the *chora* in Plato's *Timaeus*.

**Salmon, J H M**. The Legacy of Jean Bodin: Absolutism, Populism or Constitutionalism?. *Hist Polit Thought*, 17(4), 500-522, Winter 96.

Bodin left a more ambiguous legacy in political thought than his theory of sovereignty as indivisible, unlimited, nonconsensual law-making authority would suggest. This was because he imposed the restrictions of divine and natural law (especially property rights) and fundamental constitutional law. In addition, he distinguished between the form of the state and the method of its administration, which could be shared between subordinate powers at the discretion of the sovereign. This essay traces his influence in Western Europe, concentrating on Germany, the Netherlands and England. It shows how Bodin was used to support monarchical absolutism, populist republicanism, the idea of double sovereignty, and constitutional doctrines of balance. Among theorists discussed are Althusius, Arnisaeus, Besold, Grotius, Pufendorf, Filmer, Prynne, Parker, Hunton, Lawson and Locke.

**Salmon, Merrilee H**. Landmarks in Critical Thinking Series: Machiavelli's *The Prince*. *Inquiry (USA)*, 15(1), 14-22, Fall 95.

This article presents Chapters XV-XVIII of Machiavelli's *The Prince* along with an introduction designed to show that the lessons Machiavelli offers to princes are lessons in critical thinking, not recipes for success. Rulers must learn how to make distinctions, how to consider alternative courses of action and evaluate their consequences, and how to assess conflicting advice. Machiavelli often presents these lessons in the form of dilemmas. He also shows that if rulers want to preserve and maintain their states, they need to know how to apply general information about human nature to particular circumstances before taking action.

**Salmon, Nathan**. Trans-World Identification and Stipulation. *Phil Stud*, 84(2-3), 203-223, D 96.

Kripke exposed the traditional "problem of trans-world identification" as a pseudo-problem with his doctrine, which is clarified here, that "possible worlds are not discovered, but stipulated." Kripke also presented another problem of transworld identification, which he takes to be a legitimate. On closer inspection, this bifurcates into separate alleged problems, one presupposing a version of reductionism and the other instead presupposing a version of essentialism. The former alleged problem (which appears to be the one Kripke intends) is rejected as yet another pseudo-problem similar to the traditional one, while the essentialist problem is endorsed as legitimate.

**Salmon, Wesley C**. La causalità. *Iride*, 8(14), 187-196, Ap 95.

**Salsbery, Kelly Joseph**. Van Inwagen and Gunk: A Response to Sider. *Sorites*, 21-27, N 96.

In a recent article, Theodore Sider raises an interesting objection to some of the ontological views of Peter van Inwagen. In van Inwagen's view, all material things are either mereological atoms or living things composed of such mereological atoms. Sider claims that it is possible for there to be worlds at which matter consists of atomless gunk. He argues that the possible existence of atomless gunk undermines van Inwagen's claims (along with any sort of atomism). I argue that the possible existence of atomless gunk does not undermine van Inwagen's position and that Sider's claims concerning gunk are unwarranted.

**Saltz, David Z**. The Art of Interaction: Interactivity, Performativity, and Computers. *J Aes Art Crit*, 55(2), 117-127, Spring 97.

Artists are using interactive technology to create works that cross traditional aesthetic categories. This paper considers the spectator's imaginative engagement with different types of interactive artworks, making use of Kendall Walton's theory of "games of make-believe." It focuses on the relationship between interactive computer art and the performing arts and the concepts of "interactivity" and "performativity." Most current criticism associates technological art with reproduction and simulacra. This paper argues that the fascination with interactive technologies represents a reaction *against* postmodern alienation, reviving the quest for presence and immediacy embodied by the happenings and environmental theater movement of the 1960s.

**Salvucci, Pasquale**. "Kant e la temporalità" in *Il Concetto di Tempo: Atti del XXXII Congresso Nazionale della Società Filosofica Italiana*, Casertano, Giovanni (ed), 49-69. Napoli, Loffredo, 1997.

**Salyards, Jane** and Siliceo-Roman, Laura and Kuehn, Glenn. Interview with Richard Rorty. *Kinesis*, 23(1), 51-64, Sum 96.

**Salzano, Giorgio**. Gli "ultimi uomini": a proposito di un libro su Max Weber. *Riv Int Filosof Diritto*, 73(4), 757-765, O-D 96.

**Salzberg, Aaron A**. Commentary on "The Social Responsibilities of Biological Scientists. *Sci Eng Ethics*, 3(2), 149-152, Ap 97.

In contrast to Reiser and Bulger's "The Responsibilities of Biological Scientists", I suggest that the exercise of socially responsible behaviour by biological scientists is primarily dependent upon the moral sensitivities of the individual researcher. This being the case, I propose that the public—and science—is better served by encouraging the development of qualities that increase the social awareness and sensitivity of the scientific community rather than defining rules or regulations that, without enforcement, fail to motivate ethical behavior.

**Salzberger, Ronald Paul**. Ethics Outside the Limits of Philosophy: Ethical Inquiry at Metropolitan State University. *Teach Phil*, 20(2), 169-191, Je 97.

**Sam, Mehran** (& others) and Kohut, Nitsa and Singer, Peter A. Stability of Treatment Preferences: Although Most Preferences Do Not Change, Most People Change Some of Their Preferences. *J Clin Ethics*, 8(2), 124-135, Sum 97.

**Samartha, S J**. Theologies of Religion and Theologies of Liberation: A Search for Relationship. *J Dharma*, 21(2), 188-197, Ap-Je 96.

**Samonà, Leonardo**. "Atto puro e pensiero nell'interpretazione di Hegel" in *Hegel e Aristotele,* Ferrarin, A, 203-252. Cagliari, Edizioni AV, 1997.

Hegel's Interpretation of the Aristotelian God is grounded in the idea that the Absolute must be thought not only as Substance, but also as Subject. The topic of this essay concerns Hegel's reconstruction of the passage from the Actus purus to the noesis noeseos, which remains unjustified in Aristotle. Hegel finds that the two aforementioned concepts are to be mediated by the teleological character of the movement in Aristotle. This character is speculatively grounded in the movement of the intelligence and inside of the latter, in the pure actuality of the divine thinking.

**Samonà, Leonardo**. Modernità e morte dell'arte: Büchner e Celan. *G Metaf*, 18(3), 349-367, S-D 96.

**Sample, Tex**. Where Is Will Rogers When We Need Him Most? Toward a Traditional Morality in Biomedical Ethics. *Bioethics Forum*, 11(2), 22-28, Sum 95.

A community ethic is needed to address issues in the biomedical field. To develop a community ethics, moral questions must be expressed in forms indigenous to various groups. A large number of Americans are more oral than literate. This paper details the ingredients of a traditional oral morality capable of engaging biomedical issues and indigenous to people who think in proverbs, stories and relationships.

**Samraj, Tennyson**. On Being Equally Free and Unequally Restricted. *Indian Phil Quart*, 23(3-4), 379-394, Jl-O 96.

Sartre's Claims on Freedom and Restriction is defined. Freedom is equated with choice, choice is related with change and change brings into focus the question of restriction in the context of a given situation. A slave is a slave only when one chooses not to be a slave—for when one chooses to change a given situation in the context of what *is not*—what *is* becomes restrictive. Only ontologically free beings can be practically *unfree*. Having to have to choose make us all equally free to choose, but choices made make us all unequally restricted in that what we choose to negate of situations is never the same.

**Samsonowicz, Henryk**. "Universities and Democracy" in *The Idea of University,* Brzezinski, Jerzy (ed), 77-81. Amsterdam, Rodopi, 1997.

The university, the scientific and teaching institution, and democracy, a form of social system, have long been regarded as the two concepts that do not appear to have much in common. The author maintains that the democratic transformations in history are impossible without the university, the centres for shaping public opinion and people who know how to think. (edited)

**Samuels, Jeffrey**. The Bodhisattva Ideal in Theravāda Buddhist Theory and Practice: A Reevaluation of the Bodhisattva-Srāvaka Opposition. *Phil East West*, 47(3), 399-415, Jl 97.

By illustrating the presence and scope of the bodhisattva ideal in Theravāda Buddhist theory and practice, this article shows that some of the distinctions used to separate Mahāyāna Buddhism from Hīnayāna Buddhism are problematic, and, in particular, calls into question the commonly held theoretical model that postulates that the goal of Mahāyāna practitioners is to become Buddhas by following the path of the bodhisattva (*bodhisattva-yā*na), whereas the goal of Hīnayāna practitioners is to become arahants by following the path of the hearers of Buddha's disciples (*srā*vaka-yāna).

**Samuelson, Norbert M**. Three Comparative Maps of the Human. *Zygon*, 31(4), 695-710, D 96.

This article is a response to the 1994 Star Island conference on the "Decade of the Brain" from a Jewish perspective. After a brief introduction about the logical function of models and maps, I compare and contrast three models of the human: Ezekiel's vision of the chariot in the Hebrew Scripture, Franz Rosenzweig's geometry of the human face in *Der Stern der Erlösung* (the Star of Redemption) and a standard anatomical picture of the human brain. Whereas Rosenzweig's face is seen to be compatible with Ezekiel's chariot, both are seen to be radically distinct from the implicit conception of what a human being is in modern medical science. I conclude with a suggestion that the differences are to be understood in terms of their different intended functions and express my hope for some new kind of model that will incorporate the functional advantages of both.

**San Juan Jr, E**. The Revolutionary Aesthetics of Frederick Engels. *Nature Soc Thought*, 8(4), 405-432, 1995.

**Sanabria, José Rubén**. Solo un dios puede salvarnos todavía. *Rev Filosof (Mexico)*, 29(87), 409-437, S-D 96.

El artículo *Sólo un Dios puede salvarnos todavía* pretende mostrar que Heidegger no fue ateo, como algunos creen. Ciertamente, por influjo de la teología protestante, cambió (no totalmente) su modo de pensar de la religión católica, pero nunca la negó. Al contrario, pensó que en la situación actual "sólo un Dios puede salvarnos todavía".

**Sánchez, Angel Martín**. Axiological Foundations of "Human Dignity" (Spanish). *Rev Filosof (Venezuela)*, Supp(2-3), 191-199, 1996.

*Human dignity* is not an essential attribute of the species, nor a quality common to every man. *Human dignity* can only be understood as a gift from or the grace of God, or a virtue acquired through *human acts*. Yet, the theological conception is restricted to faith's order. As a consequence, *human dignity* is defined as a just retribution for human moral conduct.

**Sánchez, Angel Martín**. Hierocracy either Sacredness of Authority (Spanish). *Fronesis*, 3(1), 1-10, Ap 96.

The problem now for us present has its origin in the "authority principle" and is manifest in the theo-philosophical and social-juridical order and in each of its meanings introduces us unfailingly in the ethical and moral contour. Until which extent the *Jus potestatis* is by itself consistent but not better a product of the sacredness, either of *taboo* conscience, or a determined imposition from the *might-authority*? Is it answering to any coherent conception instead to absolutist imperative of the religion or the state? Does it conduct us to an autonomist ethic, according to the "rationality ethics," or reduce us, subjugated, to the "ethic heteronomism?"

**Sánchez, Antonio**. Giovanni Botero y la *Razon de Estado. Cuad Vico*, 5/6, 339-343, 1995/96.

This is a review of *Botero e la 'Ragion di Stato',* proceedings of the convention in memory of Luigi Firpo (Torino 8-10, March 1990), edited by A. Enzo Baldini, Florence, Leo S. Olschki publisher, 1992, 581 pages. (edited)

**Sánchez, Clara Helena** (& others) and Charum, Jorge (ed) and Albis, Víctor S (ed). *Memorias Del Seminario En Conmemoración De Los 400 Anos Del Nacimiento De René Descartes.* Sankt Augustin, Academia, 1997.

Con este Seminario en commemoración de los 400 años del nacimiento de René Descartes promovido y organizado conjuntamente por la *Academia Colombiana de Ciencias* y la *Universidad Nacional de Colombia*, se busca relevar la obra de uno de los más grandes creadores del pensamiento científico moderno. (edited)

**Sánchez Huertas, María José**. La didáctica de la filosofía en Italia. *Dialogo Filosof*, 12(3), 431-454, S-D 96.

En un momento de tensión y polémica por la situación que tiene la enseñanza de la filosofía dentro de la L.O.G.S.E., es útil hacer una reflexión comparativa con el modo en el que se está dando respuesta a la didáctica de la filosofía en otro país europeo, en Italia.

**Sánchez Meca, Diego**. Comprensión e interpretación de las obras filosóficas. *Dialogo Filosof*, 13(1), 41-54, Ja-Ap.

Partiendo de la hermenéutica metódica de Schleiermacher y de la tipología de las concepciones del mundo de Dilthey, se reflexiona, sobre todo en compañía de Paul Ricoeur, acerca del método más adecuado de comprender e interpretar las obras filosóficas.

**Sánchez Meca, Diego**. La Historia de la Filosofía como Hermenéutica. Madrid, Univ Nacion Ed, 1996.

Cualquier aproximación del estudiante o del especialista al estudio de las obras filosóficas debería estar precedida o ir acompañada de una reflexión sobre el significado de esa tarea que proporcione las directrices teóricas y metodológicas necesarias y apropiadas. Lo que ofrece este libro es el desarrollo de una reflexión de estas características que tiene en cuenta, sobre todo, las transformaciones que se han producido en las disciplinas humanísticas, en general, bajo la influencia del giro lingüístico del pensamiento contemporáneo. Con ello se construye una perspectiva nueva desde la que se analizan críticamente, se releen y se reformulan las más importantes cuestiones de la historiografía filosófica. (publisher)

**Sánchez Palencia, Angel**. Cartesis en la *Poética* de Aristóteles. *An Seminar Hist Filosof*, 13, 127-147, 1996.

The article's purpose is the meaning of Aristotle's thought about the catharsis that tragedy accomplishes, through a critical study on the main concepts which involved the definition of tragedy in the *Poetics* (49b 28): imitation, action, and pity and fear; trying to show that the condition of this effect is the intellection, through the indirect way of the arts, of the human reality imitated by the poet.

**Sánchez Parodi, Horacio M**. Karl Popper y su crítica al verificacionismo de Freud. *Sapientia*, 51(200), 375-383, 1996.

**Sánchez Sánchez, Juana**. La lógica de la identidad en G. Frege. *Daimon Rev Filosof*, 10, 57-67, Ja-Je 95.

The aim of this paper is to show that Frege's concept of identity is closer to the relative identity thesis, than to a merely referencialist analysis based on the classical thesis of (absolute) identity. The reason is that according to Fregean analysis is possible to formulate a right relation between the sense, the identity criterium and the information we get from a nontrivial identity statement. So, following Frege, we can coherently maintain Leibniz's Law. And, according to the thesis of absolute identity, this law is the necessary and sufficient condition for the truth of an identity statement. But, as a previous condition to the application of that law, we have to take into account an identity criterium that, as a component of the sense of terms, points out which kind of things we are identifying. This would be close to the requirements of relative identity thesis, although this thesis implies that different identity criteria bring with them different identity relations.

Sanchez-Gonzalez, Miguel A 890 AUTHOR INDEX

**Sanchez-Gonzalez, Miguel A**. Advance Directives Outside the USA: Are They the Best Solution Everywhere?. *Theor Med*, 18(3), 283-301, S 97.

This article evaluates the potential role of advance directives outside of their original North American context. In order to do this, the article first analyses the historical process which has promoted advance directives in recent years. Next, it brings to light certain presuppositions which have given them force: atomistic individualism, contractualism, consumerism and entrepreneurialism, pluralism, proceduralism and "American moralism." The article next studies certain European cultural peculiarities which could affect advance directives: the importance of virtue versus rights, stoicism versus consumerist utilitarianism, rationalism versus empiricism, statism versus citizens' initiative and justice versus autonomy. (edited)

**Sancho García, Isabel**. "A Free Man's Worship," 1902 (El culto del hombre libre) El problema de la existencia humana en su relación con el destino y los ideales éticos. *Daimon Rev Filosof*, 12, 61-77, Ja-Je 96.

'The Free Man's Worship' is one of the *two* essential articles that precede the philosophical writings by Russell, or his philosophy. Written in difficult moments of his life, its content aims to find a new way of living, a new ethics, that may confront pain death, the past, and the irrational forces of the universe. In short, the question is that man should reach freedom of aspirations and thinking that escape from the blind advance of the universe; and confront death with the results of a "creative idealism", indestructible to it. The way to attain it has its beginning in the experience of the *beauty* of the tragedy of human life; and it is crossed renouncing to personal desires (freedom) and the practice of the possible good and human creation (wisdom), a support in friendship and the assimilation of the good (which is eternal) of the past. (edited)

**Sanders, Andy F**. Criticism, Contact with Reality and Truth. *Tradition Discovery*, 23(2), 24-37, 1996-97.

Partly in reply to D. Cannon's critique of my analytical reconstruction of Polanyi's postcritical theory of knowledge, I argue that there are good reasons for not appropriating Polanyi's programme of self-identification and the confessional rhetoric which may be derived from it. Arguing that "postcritical" should not be identified with an uncritical dogmatism, I then go on to suggest that the theory of tacit knowing had best be elaborated further by drawing on the work of J. Searle and M. Johnson. Finally, I make use of E. Meek's account of the notion of "contact with reality" to highlight the Polanyian criteria of truth.

**Sanders, John**. Why Simple Foreknowledge Offers No More Providential Control than the Openness of God. *Faith Phil*, 14(1), 26-40, Ja 97.

This paper examines the question of whether the theory of simply foreknowledge (SF) provides God with greater providential control than does the theory of present knowledge (PK). It is claimed by the proponents of SF that a deity lacking such knowledge would not be able to provide the sort of providential aid commonly thought by theists to be given by God. To see whether this is the case I first distinguish two different versions of how God's foreknowledge is accessed according to simple foreknowledge. These two versions are then utilized to examine seven different areas of divine providence to assess the utility of simple foreknowledge. I conclude that SF affords no greater providential control than PK.

**Sanders, John T** (ed) and Niznik, Jozef (ed). *Debating the State of Philosophy: Habermas, Rorty, and Kolakowski*. Westport, Praeger, 1996.

Habermas begins with a comprehensive account of contextualism. According to him, contextualism is a new form of historicism. What are the merits of an approach that takes into account both a historical and a cultural context? Is the pragmatism promoted by Richard Rorty an acceptable criticism of our Platonic heritage? If so, does this mean the end of rationality as a regulative ideal of the human universe? Rorty's answer is "Yes." This world-renowned American thinker recommends putting a full stop at the end of a narrative which was useful in pursuit of our ancestors' purposes but is no longer useful for ours. Leszek Kolakowski attempts to undermine the alleged pragmatic merits of pragmatism from the position of an analytic philosopher who continues to value classical elements of philosophical tradition. Ernest Gellner also turns against Rorty's pragmatism, which he denounces as a product of the Enlightenment roots of American culture and its centuries of political and economic stability. The future of Western culture may depend on the answers to the questions asked by these authors. (publisher, edited)

**Sanders, Lee M** (& others) and Marshall, Patricia A and Kelly, Susan E. Understanding the Practice of Ethics Consultation: Results of an Ethnographic Multi-Site Study. *J Clin Ethics*, 8(2), 136-149, Sum 97.

**Sanders, Lynn M**. Against Deliberation. *Polit Theory*, 25(3), 347-376, Je 97.

When democratic theorists suggest how to improve our politics, they now overwhelmingly recommend deliberation. "Against deliberation" argues against this focus. Deliberation cannot proceed in a way that democrats would approve, I claim, before preconditions of mutual respect and equal participation are met. Using evidence from juries in the United States, I show that patterns of inequality are reflected, even exacerbated, by deliberation. I urge theorists to delay their preoccupation with deliberation until a more important problem is addressed: that is, that those who are usually left out of discussions learn to speak whether their perspectives are common or not and those who usually dominate learn to hear the perspectives of others.

**Sanders, Theresa**. Rest for the Restless? Karl Rahner, Being, and the Evocation of Transcendence. *Phil Theol*, 8(4), 347-362, Sum 94.

In *Spirit in the World*, Karl Rahner contends that the existence of an Absolute Being is affirmed. However, such an affirmation is beyond the scope of his own methodology. Since the questions that characterize the philosophical theology of Rahner are also those that occupy postmodern thought (structures of knowing, the status of ontology, and the constitution of the subject), this essay attempts to read Rahner through the insights of philosophers such as Derrida and Taylor. The thesis is that Rahner's method does not lead to Absolute Being; rather, God can be understood as the restlessness that drives the human heart.

**Sanders Peirce, Charles** and Turrisi, Patricia Ann (ed). *Pragmatism as a Principle and Method of Right Thinking*. Albany, SUNY Pr, 1997.

This is a study edition of Charles Sanders Peirce's manuscripts for lectures on pragmatism given in spring 1903 at Harvard University. Excepts from these writings have been published elsewhere but in abbreviated form. Turrisi has edited the manuscripts for publication and has written a series of notes that illuminate the historical, scientific, and philosophical contexts of Peirce's references in the lectures. She has also written a Preface that describes the manner in which the lectures came to be given, including an account of Peirce's life and career pertinent to understanding the philosopher himself. Turrisi's introduction interprets Peirce's brand of pragmatism within his system of logic and philosophy of science as well as within general philosophical principles. (publisher, edited)

**Sandle, Mark**. Georgii Shakhnazarov and the Soviet Critique of Historical Materialism. *Stud East Euro Thought*, 49(2), 109-133, Je 97.

The emergence of ideological and political pluralism in the Soviet Union during 1990 led to a growing number of critiques of Marxism-Leninism. The development of the internal Soviet critique of orthodox Soviet Marxism-Leninism culminated in the publication of a two-part article by Georgii Shakhanzarov in *Kommunist* in 1991. In this article Shakhanzarov outlined a comprehensive critique of orthodox historical materialism and many of the ideas he developed became a central part of the Draft Party Programme of July/August 1991. This programme amounted to the virtual social-democratisation of Soviet Marxism-Leninism. The collapse of Soviet Marxism-Leninism can in part be explained by the internal critique of its basic tenets which developed in the period after 1988.

**Sandoe, Peter** and Holtug, Nils and Simonsen, H B. Ethical Limits to Domestication. *J Agr Environ Ethics*, 9(2), 114-122, 1996.

Through the process of domestication the genetic make-up of farm animals can be changed by means of either selective breeding or genetic engineering. This paper is about the ethical limits to such genetic changes. It is suggested that the ethical significance of domestication has become clear recently in the light of genetic engineering, but that the problem has been there all along. Two ethical approaches to domestication are presented, genetic integrity and animal welfare. It is argued that the welfare approach is superior. Finally, five ethical hypotheses based on the welfare approach are presented.

**Sandu, Gabriel**. On the Theory of Anaphor: Dynamic Predicate Logic vs. Game-Theoretical Semantics. *Ling Phil*, 20(2), 147-174, Ap 97.

In this paper I will examine critically the treatment of anaphora in dynamic logic and compare it with the game-theoretical treatment. Since the expositions of the former have been rather informal, one of the goals of the present paper is to give a technically precise description of the game-semantics and a precise analysis of text anaphora which will turn out to have clean advantages over the dynamic approach. Finally I will compare the game solution to anaphora to the Discourse Representation Theory of Kamp.

**Sanford, David H**. Temporal Parts, Temporal Portions, and Temporal Slices: An Exercise in Naive Mereology. *Acta Analytica*, 21-33, 1996.

Naive mereology studies ordinary conceptions of part and whole. Parts, unlike portions, have objective boundaries and many things, such as dances and sermons have temporal parts. In order to deal with Mark Heller's claim that temporal parts "are ontologically no more or less basic than the wholes that they compose," we retell the story of Laplace's Genius, here named "Swifty." Although Swifty processes lots of information very quickly, his conceptual repertoire need not extend beyond fundamental physics. So we attempt to follow Swifty's progress in the acquisition of ordinary concepts such as *table*. (Puzzles of precision and intrusion appear along the way.) Swifty has to understand what tables are before understanding what temporal portions of tables are. This is one reason for regarding tables as ontologically prior to table portions.

**Sanguineti, Juan José**. Aporías sobre el universo y su temporalidad a la luz de la filosofía de Leonardo Polo. *Anu Filosof*, 29(2), 1003-1017, 1996.

Some paradoxes emerging when the universe is thought of in terms of objectivity are considered in this article, in the light of the philosophy of L. Polo. Current metaphysical speculation on the basis of modern cosmology cannot easily avoid this risk. The author examines in particular the problem of the beginning of time, with a confrontation between Polo and Aquinas. It is argued that cosmological thought must be carefully controlled in order to be referred to a metaphysical perspective.

**Sanjeev, M P**. Rethinking the Social Contract. *Darshana Int*, 36(2/142), 32-39, Ap 96.

This article is the first part of the two articles on the theory of *social contract* which are written in order to assess it from our social and epistemological milieu. The theory of social contract which is formed in the medieval turmoils is a real progress in the history of political philosophy. Their considerations are antifeudal and based on reason. Though it may be helpful for geometrical explanation of the formation of state, Hobbes's concept of primitive society is fictitious and pessimistic. Locke's and Rousseau's concepts are different regarding this matter. However, all of them are treating the formation of state as a matter of mutual adjustment. (edited)

**Sankey, H** and Beed, Clive and Sawyer, K R. Underdetermination in Economics: The Duhem-Quine Thesis. *Econ Phil*, 13(1), 1-23, Ap 97.

AUTHOR INDEX 891 Sargent, Pauline


**Sankowski, Edward**. Racism, Human Rights, and Universities. *Soc Theor Pract*, 22(2), 225-249, Sum 96.

**Sanna, Manuela**. "Note sulla concezione leibniziana della storia" in *Lo Storicismo e la Sua Storia: Temi, Problemi, Prospettive,* Cacciatore, Giuseppe (ed), 39-49. Milano, Guerini, 1997.

**Sannino, Antonella**. La tradizione ermetica a Oxford nei secoli XIII e XIV: Ruggero Bacone e Tommaso Bradwardine. *Stud Filosofici*, 23-56, 1995.

My work follows the appeal of the hermetic tradition through a century (from 13th to 14th) in the Franciscan and Augustinian Oxford school. The diffusion of the hermetic philosophy goes in two directions: theology and natural philosophy. In this essay I have only examined the 'moral' and 'theological' meaning that Roger Bacon and Thomas Bradwardine assign to the hermetic philosophy by their speculations. In Oxford I have found the first hermetic testimonies beginning from the second half of the 13th century just in Bacon works. In Bacon's speculation the *Asclepius* has been widely quoted and Hermes is considered an authority 'maxime in moralibus'. The anonymous author of the *Summa Philosophiae*, Thomas of York in his *Sapientiale* shares the Baconian opinion on Hermes. A century later, in *De causa dei* Bradwardine reveals a profound knowledge of the hermetic philosophical texts. He cites and comments the theological anthropological and cosmological aspects (God and his attributes, man and his soul, fullness, void, eternity and necessity) through the comparison of *Asclepius, Liber XXIV philosophorum, Liber VI rerum principiis* theses.

**Sansubrino, Rosana**. Jean Piaget: razón y conflicto. *Cuad Etica*, 15-16, 85-102, 1993.

Man can reach early in his personal development moral autonomy. This achievement appears as presupposed in the resolution of conflicts among individuals. However, if we have a look over the societies, we can see that the rational practices find obstacles in the interindividual relationships. The couple moral autonomy-social equilibrium enclose in itself a conflicting nucleus. In this sense we explain some of the hypothesis that Piaget elaborated for an approach to the question of the construction of the social rationality and his relation with the conflict. (edited)

**Santas, Ari**. "The Environmental Value in G.H. Mead's Cosmology" in *Environmental Pragmatism,* Light, Andrew (ed), 73-83. New York, Routledge, 1996.

**Santas, Gerasimos**. Goodness: Aristotle and the Moderns: A Sketch. *Phil Inq*, 18(1-2), 43-60, Wint-Spr 96.

**Santas, Gerasimos**. The Structure of Aristotle's Ethical Theory: Is It Teleological or a Virtue Ethics?. *Topoi*, 15(1), 59-80, Mr 96.

**Santi, Giorgio**. Preghiera e Filosofia della Religione. *Aquinas*, 39(3), 475-492, S-D 96.

**Santiago de Carvalho, Mário A**. A Essência da Matéria Prima em Averróis Latino (Com uma Referência a Henrique de Gand). *Rev Port Filosof*, 52(1-4), 197-221, Ja-D 96.

Since his *Lectura Ordinaria Super Sacram Scripturam* and his first *Quodlibet* (qu. 9) Henry of Ghent quoted Averroes in order to give a kind of metaphysical being to prime matter. This procedure was correct. In fact, as far as the Latin Averroes is concerned, one read that prime matter is a substance. This paper intends to interpret Latin Averroes's main texts where prime matter is conceived as a substantial being and also explains why Henry of Ghent could not follow entirely Averroes's perspective: the core of the discrepancy lies on the distinction between *possibilitas in agente* (Henry's position) and *possibilitas in re* (Averroes's position).

**Santiago de Carvalho, Mário A**. Conspecto do Desenvolvimento da Filosofía em Portugal (Séculos XIII-XVI). *Rev Espan Filosof Med*, 4, 131-155, 1997.

The paper deals with some major figures of Portuguese medieval philosophers. One tries also to explain how to envisage what could be a characteristic Portuguese trend in his regional medieval thought.

**Santos, Filipe** and Carmo, José. "Indirect Action, Influence and Responsibility" in *Deontic Logic, Agency and Normative Systems,* Brown, Mark A (ed), 194-215. New York, Springer-Verlag, 1996.

The paper focuses on some concepts of agency relevant to the specification and analysis of organizations. It is argued that there is an important distinction to be drawn between a "direct" and an "indirect" agency concept, and that the latter allows an easy and abstract way of expressing the organizational notion of responsibility. An "influence" agency concept is also introduced in order to cope with interactions between different agents. The formal characterization of these concepts is given by means of modal logics, following the same tradition in the logical characterization of act descriptions as employed by Kanger and Pörn.

**Santos, Laura Ferreira dos**. A Nao-Violência no Pensamento de René Girard. *Rev Port Filosof*, 52(1-4), 785-795, Ja-D 96.

According to René Girard, the deconstruction of the victimarious and sacrificial mechanisms has put the occidental societies before a radical alternative: whether we reconcile ourselves among us without any help from sacrifice and that can only be arranged through nonviolence or evangelical love, or we will dye. Analysing the thought of Girard about nonviolence and confronting it with some texts from the psychoanalyst Marie Balmary and with others from J.-P. Dupuy, the article comes to the conclusion that there seems to be only one concern behind Girard's understanding of evangelical love: the renouncement to whatever may provoke a conflict.

**Santos López, Modesto**. Rivadeneira: la razón de Estado al servicio de la Contrarreforma. *Pensamiento*, 53(206), 243-262, My-Ag 97.

Pedro de Rivadeneira es consciente de dos peligros que acechan a la religión católica: la extensión de la herejía en el plano religioso y la falsa razón de Estado en el plano político. Su *Tratado* es una defensa de las ideas contrarreformistas y a la vez una crítica a las teorías de Maquiavelo.

**Santos-Escudero, Ceferino**. Bibliografía hispánica de filosofía: Elenco 1997. *Pensamiento*, 53(206), 271-327, My-Ag 97.

**Sanvisens Herreros, Alejandro**. Entidad y origen de la información. *Convivium*, 9, 117-133, 1996.

The information is defined as a communicative and optimizing cognitive content, showing its relations with the Popper's world 3, with the entropy and the probability. The concept of probability is also defined according to a new criterion based on the degree of set's homogeneity. The existence of laws of no statistical nature, based on the information is demonstrated and there also references to the brain-mind problem. It is considered that all information, including the genetic information, has his origin on some intelligent informer.

**Sanzgiri, Jyotsna** and Gottlieb, Jonathan Z. Towards an Ethical Dimension of Decision Making in Organizations. *J Bus Ethics*, 15(12), 1275-1285, D 96.

There is a growing need to increase our understanding of ethical decision making in U.S. based organizations. The authors examine the complexity of creating uniform ethical standards even when the meaning of ethical behavior is being debated. The nature of these controversies are considered, and three important dimensions for ethical decision making are discussed: leaders with integrity and a strong sense of social responsibility, organization cultures that foster dialogue and dissent, and organizations that are willing to reflect on and learn from their actions. (edited)

**Sapontzis, Steve F**. On Exploiting Inferiors. *Between Species*, 11(1-2), 1-24, Wint-Spr 95.

This article critiques the contentions a) that human life is more valuable than animal life because it has a quality lacking in animal life due to the greater richness of human life and b) that because it is inferior, animal life may be sacrificed to benefit humans. Conclusions: value of life does not depend solely on quality; quality of life does not depend solely on richness; comparisons of richness are arbitrary; we lack sufficient evidence to comparatively value the quality of human and animal lives; and superior value of life does not entail that inferiors may be sacrificed for it.

**Saporiti, Katia**. *Die Sprache des Geistes: Vergleich einer repräsentationalistischen und einer syntaktischen Theorie des Geistes.* Hawthorne, de Gruyter, 1997.

The author examines the language of thought hypothesis, contrasting a representational version of the thesis—as advanced by Jerry Fodor—and a syntactic version—as defended by Stephen Stich. The computational approach to the mind underlying both versions is criticized and it is argued that neither version can provide us with a satisfying account of cognition. While the representational theory fails to account for the semantics of the postulated language of thought, the syntactic theory draws an inadequate picture of cognitive psychology. Among the related topics also discussed are physicalism, individualism and the concept of narrow content.

**Saracino, Marilena**. Hobbes, Shakespeare and the Temptation to Skepticism. *Hobbes Stud*, 9, 36-50, 1996.

The aim of the paper is to show a kind of interrelationship between Hobbes and Shakespeare. I have tried to demonstrate their common epistemological roots especially in what concerns language, law and nature in the light of skepticism, a doctrine that has influenced both of them. My approach has been of the textual type and I have devoted more space to language than to law and nature because I think that it is the best case of knowledge which shows itself vulnerable to suspicion. It is generally agreed that in the seventeenth century a great effort was being made, by representative thinkers, to see things 'as in themselves they really are' and the ideas of *truth* and *fiction* which were then evolved seem to have exerted a decisive influence upon the poetic beliefs of succeeding times. It has been my aim to study this influence and to inquire what occurred when traditional beliefs, especially poetic beliefs, were exposed to the 'touch of cold philosophy'.

**Sarasohn, Lisa T**. *Gassendi's Ethics: Freedom in a Mechanistic Universe.* Ithaca, Cornell Univ Pr, 1996.

This is the first book to explore the ethical thought of Pierre Gassendi, the seventeenth-century French priest who rehabilitated Epicurean philosophy in the Western tradition. Lisa T. Sarasohn's discussion of the relationship between Gassendi's philosophy of nature and his ethics discloses the underlying unity of his philosophy and elucidates this critical figure in the intellectual revolution. Sarasohn demonstrates that Gassendi's ethics was an important part of his attempt to Christianize Epicureanism. (publisher, edited)

**Sardesai, Arundhati**. Epistemology of J. Krishnamurti. *Indian Phil Quart*, 23(3-4), 454-466, Jl-O 96.

To see how J. Krishnamurti's insistence on a radical transformation in human consciousness works when he refuses to confine himself to all methods and disciplines. To Krishnamurti Truth is ever-changing 'now' and cannot, therefore, be approached through a static and fixed path. He advocates a direct and simple approach that of intuitive discernment and action of intelligence, which is nondual and immediate. True knowledge needs clear mind, a mind that is capable of direct perception. It is penetration into the layers of consciousness and an expansion of its borders. This 'Choiceless Awareness' is the only means of awakening of intelligence. Knowledge is revelation not a creation, it is discovery not an achievement. Krishnamurti has the direct vision of Truth of the East with Western scepticism in it. Therefore, his refusal to definite solutions or methods has given a jolt to the age old thoughts, beliefs and values.

**Sargent, Pauline**. On the Use of Visualizations in the Practice of Science. *Proc Phil Sci Ass*, 3(Suppl), S230-S238, 1996.

Visualizations used in the practice of neuroscience, as one example of a scientific practice, can be sorted according to whether they represent A) actual

Sarkar, Anil K 892 AUTHOR INDEX

things, B) theoretical models, or C) some integration of these two. In this paper I hypothesize that an assessment of a chain of visual representations from (A) through (C) to (B) (and back again) is used, as part of the practice of scientific judgment, to assess the adequacy of the "working fit" between the theoretical model and the actual thing or process that the model is intended to explain.

**Sarkar, Anil K**. Prof. D. M. Dattai: As a Process-Philosopher from an Alternative Inter-Cultural Perspective. *Darshana Int*, 35(3/139), 27-38, Jl 95.

**Sarkar, Husain**. The Task of Group Rationality: The Subjectivist's View —Part I. *Stud Hist Phil Sci*, 28(2), 267-288, Je 97.

A subjectivist has claimed that a society of Hobbesian scientists interested in power, glory, and the like will produce diversity, multiplicity, or proliferation of theories whereas a society of Rousseauian scientists, interested in the dispassionate pursuit of truth, will not. This view fails because of the lack of focus on the question: What is the subject of group rationality? Philip Kitcher's view is discussed in detail. It is shown that his society of scientists who are ruthless egoists would fail to proliferate theories, too; several other serious problems—such as endemic irrationality—are outlined, topped with a paradox.

**Sarkar, Husain**. The Task of Group Rationality: The Subjectivist's View —Part II. *Stud Hist Phil Sci*, 28(3), 497-520, S 97.

In this part, Thomas Kuhn's theory is treated. The role of values in scientific decision making and their impact on a scientific group are examined; the transitions to various stages which are epistemically interesting are delineated; Kuhn's arguments about representative groups, value, and history are discussed and it is claimed that either Kuhn's view presupposes time-independent methods or he has failed to justify the study of history, at least for the normative problem of group rationality; finally, it is argued that a kind of society of scientists is entailed, on Kitcher's and Kuhn's views, which is fairly unappealing.

**Sarot, Marcel**. Why Trusting God Differs from All Other Forms of Trust. *Sophia (Australia)*, 35(1), 101-115, Mr-Ap 96.

I distinguish between four forms of trust (trusting things, trusting persons within a contractual agreement, trusting persons within a relation of fellowship and trusting God) by applying two criteria: the specifiability of the target of one's trust and the freedom (or lack of freedom) of the object of trust. With the help of this distinction, I argue that unconditional trust can be due to God, whereas it cannot be due to human beings.

**Sart, Frédéric**. Sémantique pour la Logique Déontique. *Log Anal*, 38(149), 89-106, Mr 95.

**Sartor, Giovanni** and Governatori, Guido and Artosi, Alberto. "Towards a Computational Treatment of Deontic Defeasibility" in *Deontic Logic, Agency and Normative Systems,* Brown, Mark A (ed), 27-46. New York, Springer-Verlag, 1996.

In this paper we describe an algorithmic framework for a multimodal logic arising from the combination of the system of modal (epistemic) logic devised by Meyer and van der Hoek for dealing with nonmonotonic reasoning with a deontic logic of the Jones and Pörn-type. The idea behind this (somewhat eclectic) formal set-up is to have a modal framework expressive enough to model certain kinds of deontic defeasibility, in particular by taking into account preferences on norms. The appropriate inference mechanism is provided by a tableau-like modal theorem proving system which supports a proof method closely related to the semantics of modal operators. We argue that this system is particularly well-suited for mechanizing nonmonotonic forms of inference in a monotonic multimodal setting.

**Sartre, Jean-Paul** and Sharpley-Whiting, T Denean (ed & trans). "Return from the United States" in *Existence in Black: An Anthology of Black Existential Philosophy,* Gordon, Lewis R (ed), 83-89. New York, Routledge, 1997.

The essay is an annotated translation of an article written by the philosopher after his return from the U.S. Its original title, "Retour des Etats Unis: Ce qui j'ai appris du problème noir" [Return from the United States: What I learned about the black problem"], was published by *Le Figaro* on June 15, 1945. While affirming his position as an outsider meddling in a family affair, Sartre nonetheless details the conflicts around race and racism in America, providing sociological and statistical data. The essay's translator offers commentary and comparative statistical data in notes on black existence in 1995.

**Sartwell, Crispin**. Bits of Broken Glass: Zora Neale Hurston's Conception of the Self. *Trans Peirce Soc*, 33(2), 358-391, Spr 97.

**Sasaki, Katsumi**. The Simple Substitution Property of the Intermediate Propositional Logics on Finite Slices. *Stud Log*, 52(1), 41-62, F 93.

The simple substitution property provides a systematic and easy method for proving a theorem by an axiomatic way. The notion of the property was introduced in Hosoi [4] but without a definite name and he showed three examples of the axioms with the property. Later, the property was given it's name as above in Sasaki [7]. Our main result here is that the necessary and sufficient condition for a logic L on a finite slice to have the simple substitution property is that L is finite. Here the necessity part is essentially new, for the sufficiency part has been proved in Hosoi and Sasaki [5]. Also the proof of sufficiency part is improved here. (edited)

**Sasso, Javier**. Some Skeptical Reflectiones on Renewed Ethics (Spanish). *Rev Filosof (Venezuela)*, Supp(2-3), 37-47, 1996.

This paper warns of the difficulties which threaten all attempts to construct a present day normative ethics. The philosophical ethics, especially in the area of analytical philosophy, has gone from the study of ethical language to a new philosophical enthusiasm, the elaboration of new substantive ethical doctrines with systematic structures, which propose the return to normative reflection or the restauration of ethics in their procedural or communitarian version. This new turn gives place to doubts both in the epistemological field as well as in the area of ideological self-consciousness. Clear examples of this are given by the reduction of the epistemic ambition of the work of Rawls on the *Theory of Justice* until reaching *Political Liberalism* or the description of actual *Sittlichkeit* in the work of communitarians.

**Sassoli, Bernardo** and Dessì, Paola and Sklar, Lawrence. Discutono *Il caso domato*, di Ian Hacking. *Iride*, 8(15), 483-494, Ag 95.

Il libro di I. Hacking ricostruisce nei tratti essenziali il clima intellettuale che nell'Ottocento veda la crisi del "determinismo" e la "rivoluzione probabilistica" e quindi permette l'affermazione di un nuovo "stile di ragionamento" che solleva il "caso" da "superstizione popolare" a evento assoggettabile a legge. P. Dessì discute l'idea dell'Autore che la pratica abbia anticipato la rivoluzione teorica; B. Sassoli si sofferma sull'epistemologia di Hacking e la sua nozione di "stile di ragionamento"; L. Sklar sottolinea il carattere illuminante che possiede la scoperta delle premesse sociali dell'idea di "legge statistica" indispensabile nella ricerca scientifica contemporanea.

**Sassower, Raphael**. Responsible Technoscience: The Haunting Reality of Auschwitz and Hiroshima. *Sci Eng Ethics*, 2(3), 277-290, Jl 96.

Auschwitz and Hiroshima stand out as two realities whose uniqueness must be reconciled with their inevitability as outcomes of highly rationalized processes of technoscientific progress. Contrary to Michael Walzer's notion of *double effect*, whereby unintended consequences and the particular uses to which warfare may lead remain outside the moral purview of scientists, this paper endorses the commitment of the Society for Social Responsibility in Science to argue that members of the technoscientific community are always responsible for their work and the eventual uses made of it. In what follows, four related views are outlined pertaining to modern situations within which the technoscientific community operates, so as to highlight the urgency of infusing a sense of responsibility for the products of their activities into this community. A provisional *code* is suggested that may serve as a guide for increased personal responsibility of individual technoscientists (academic scientists and industrial engineers).

**Sauer, James B**. "Discourse, Consensus, and Value: Conversations about the Intelligible Relation between the Private and Public Spheres" in *Political Dialogue: Theories and Practices,* Esquith, Stephen L (ed), 143-166. Amsterdam, Rodopi, 1996.

This paper examines how contributors to the dialogical turn in ethics understand the relationship between the private and public spheres of meaning and value; how, if at all, conflicts of values (or interests) can be resolved; and the significance of the notion of dialogical consensus that has come to the fore in applied ethics as an important criterion of ethical justification in the public sphere. I argue the positions can be schematized as two positions with four partners. I call the two positions proceduralism and contextualism. Proceduralists argue that the justification of normative judgments lies in the basis structure and form of moral argument such that the validity of ethical or value judgments is justified by the procedures of discourse. Contextualists argue that justification of normative judgments lies in the context of moral dialogue about substantive norms or values in or between traditions.

**Sauer, James B**. Economies, Technology, and the Structure of Human Living. *Phil Cont World*, 2(4), 22-28, Wint 95.

This paper argues that we need to rethink what the object of economic analysis is; that is, what the intelligible relations of an economy are. The paper starts by ackowledging that economies are a constitutive element of human habitats. It also agrees that modern economic analysis based on the price-auction market has provided substantial knowledge about the operation of economies. However, I argue that a more fruitful line of inquiry than the price-auction market is to focus on the schemes of personal and social meaning that set the context for economies. In developing this argument, I describe how such schemes function as a network of human relationships which provide the conditions of the possibilities of the emergence of economic technologies. That is, the explanandum of economy is not the classical price-auction market but the recurrent social cooperative structure (order) of economy in which markets are embedded.

**Sauer-Thompson, Gary** and Smith, Joseph Wayne. *Beyond Economics: Postmodernity, Globalization and National Sustainability.* Brookfield, Avebury, 1996.

**Saul, Jennifer M**. Reply to Forbes. *Analysis*, 57(2), 114-118, Ap 97.

Graeme Forbes has suggested a response to the problem cases posed in "Substitution and Simple Sentences" (*Analysis* 57(2), 102-108, Ap 97). In this paper, I argue that there are serious problems facing Forbes's response.

**Saul, Jennifer M**. Substitution and Simple Sentences. *Analysis*, 57(2), 102-108, Ap 97.

This paper argues that philosophers interested in substitution puzzle cases have been mistaken to focus so strongly on attitude-reporting sentences. Other sentences, which I call simple sentences, pose similar problems. (Examples include 'Clark Kent went into the phone booth and Superman came out' and 'Clark Kent went into the phone booth and Clark Kent came out'.) The paper explores the implications of such problem cases for theorists of various sets.

**Saul, Jennifer M**. What's Wrong with Metalinguistic Views. *Acta Analytica*, 81-94, 1996.

Metalinguistic accounts of belief-reporting are perennially popular. To some degree, this is to be expected, as they seem a natural and elegant solution to certain problems. On the other hand, the philosophical literature is filled with puzzle cases which pose devastating problems for such views. The force of these counterexamples, however, has not yet been sufficiently appreciated. The reason for this is that the cases which defeat metalinguistic views have not been gathered together in a systematic manner and applied to types of theories. Once this is done and a few other arguments and examples added in, such views do not look nearly so appealing.

**Saunders, Simon**. Naturalizing Metaphysics. *Monist*, 80(1), 44-69, Ja 97.

**Saunders, Simon**. Time, Quantum Mechanics, and Tense. *Synthese*, 107(1), 19-53, Ap 96.

The relational approach to tense holds that "the now", "passage" and "becoming" are to be understood in terms of relations between events. The debate over the adequacy of this framework is illustrated by a comparative study of the sense in which physical theories, (in) deterministic and (non) relativistic, can lend expression to the metaphysics at issue. The objective is not to settle the matter, but to clarify the nature of this metaphysics and to establish that the same issues are at stake in the relational approach to value-definiteness and probability in quantum mechanics. They concern the existence of a unique *present*, respectively *actuality* and a notion of identity over time that cannot be paraphrased in terms of relations.

**Sautter, Elise Truly** and Oretskin, Nancy A. Tobacco Targeting: The Ethical Complexity of Marketing to Minorities. *J Bus Ethics*, 16(10), 1011-1017, Jl 97.

In recent years, there has been heightened concern regarding the marketing of potentially harmful products (PHPs) to disadvantaged markets. Three issues which commonly dominate discussions in this controversy are: 1) the potential for exploitation of vulnerable markets, 2) the tradeoff between protection of disadvantaged consumers and their rights to make informed choices, and 3) the appropriateness of using the commercial speech doctrine to settle the issue of targeting minority markets with PHPs. This paper examines the arguments raised in this debate so that interested parties will better appreciate the ethical complexity of marketing PHPs to minority segments.

**Sauvé, Denis**. Interprétation, signification et "usage" chez Wittgenstein. *Dialogue (Canada)*, 35(4), 735-752, Fall 96.

**Savage, Gail**. "...Equality from the Masculine Point of View...": The 2nd Earl Russell and Divorce Law Reform in England. *Russell*, 16(1), 67-84, Sum 96.

**Savard, Nathalie**. Développement Moral et Jugement Moral: Réexamen de la Controverse Kohlberg-Gilligan. *Horiz Phil*, 7(1), 113-124, Fall 96.

This article's aim is to reconsider, from a philosophical standpoint, the controversy in moral philosophy opposing Kohlberg's theory to that of Gilligan. First, we demonstrate that each model refers to distinct parts of ethics (one, metaethical and formal, the other, normative and substantial) and, therefore, are not really in opposition. Furthermore, the sequence in the development of an ethics of care can be explained as the transition from a preconventional to a postconventional level of morality. So we conclude that because these two theories share their philosophical presuppositions, they are complementary and can be thought of as two specific parts of a general project for understanding morality.

**Savari Raj, L Anthony**. The Diatopical Hermeneutics: R. Panikkar's Response to the Scientific Study of Religions. *J Dharma*, 21(2), 198-203, Ap-Je 96.

**Savedoff, Barbara E**. Escaping Reality: Digital Imagery and the Resources of Photography. *J Aes Art Crit*, 55(2), 201-214, Spring 97.

**Savedoff, Barbara E**. Reconsidering Buster Keaton's Heroines. *Phil Lit*, 21(1), 77-90, Ap 97.

**Savignano, Armando**. Etica della responsabilità e impegno politico in Aranguren. *Aquinas*, 39(2), 381-394, My-Ag 96.

**Savignano, Armando**. Il Metodo della Filosofia della Religione di A. Sabatier. *Aquinas*, 39(3), 529-547, S-D 96.

**Savile, Anthony**. Instrumentalism and the Interpretation of Narrative. *Mind*, 105(420), 553-576, O 96.

This paper discusses the motivation underlying an instrumentalist conception of the retrieval of a literary narrative from the text that presents it. Focusing on the version of the doctrine recently advanced in Gregory Currie (1993), it argues that the advantages instrumentalism claims over the realism it seeks to displace are uncertainly based and cannot be made good. What would be needed to overcome obvious difficulties in its initial formulation would be a principled veil of ignorance occluding the actual author's mind from the competent reader. The imposition of such a veil cannot be adequately motivated. In consequence, the scepticism instrumentalism generates about criticism's traditional aspirations to objectivity in the form of uniquely correct reconstructions of its canonical narrative texts is found wanting. The literary nature of the narratives in which we have most interest itself imports an aesthetic norm of unity into their interpretation and it thereby privileges a notion of successful understanding that is committed to the goal of uniquely correct retrieval.

**Savitt, Steven F**. The Direction of Time. *Brit J Phil Sci*, 47(3), 347-370, S 96.

The aim of this essay is to introduce philosophers of science to some recent philosophical discussions of the nature and origin of the direction of time. The essay is organized around books by Hans Reichenbach, Paul Horwich, and Huw Price. I outline their major arguments and treat certain critical points in detail. I speculate at the end about the ways in which the subject may continue to develop and in which it may connect with other areas of philosophy: 1) Introduction, 2) Becoming, 3) Thermodynamics: Reichenbach, Sklar, and Earman, 4) Paul Horwich and the fork asymmetry, 5) Cosmology: Huw Price and 'The View from Nowhen', 6) Whither?

**Savorelli, Alessandro**. II) Teichmüller e gli amici napoletani. *G Crit Filosof Ital*, 17(1), 64-84, Ja-Ap 97.

Gustav Teichmüller (1832-1888), teacher at Dorpat University, is well-known mainly because of his studies on the history of ancient philosophy. His philosophical system represented a Spiritualistic attempt of answering to Positivism, quite relevant for its criticism of scientific rationality. For this reason his thought was esteemed and developed by Nietzsche. The second part of the essay is devoted to the relationship of Teichmüller with some Italian philosophers (the so-called "Neapolitan Hegelians": B. Spaventa, A. Vera, A. Labriola) and to his correspondence with them. Through these thinkers his ideas were introduced in the Italian culture.

**Savorelli, Alessandro**. L'astuzia della follia: Un'antologia di Lombroso. *G Crit Filosof Ital*, 16(2), 281-292, My-Ag 96.

**Savorelli, Mirella Brini**. Una lettura possibile: A proposito de "I boschi narrativi" di Umberto Eco. *Iride*, 8(14), 212-218, Ap 95.

**Savulescu, Julian**. Choosing the Best: Against Paternalistic Practice Guidelines. *Bioethics*, 10(4), 323-330, O 96.

Isobel Ross rightly points out that providing information is not enough to guarantee that patients will choose the best course of action. She argues that to adequately protect patients' interests, we need practice guidelines to 'ensure that dangerous and unnecessarily risky procedures are excluded from practice'. What constitutes an 'unnecessarily risky procedure' is to be determined by a group of reasonable doctors. At one point, Ross suggests that such guidelines are 'presumptive' rather than 'absolute'. But this is really a concession to patient variability. She intends that certain procedures are ruled out on paternalistic grounds. I will argue that practice guidelines are desirable but should not determine practice. We should not rule out procedures on paternalistic grounds.

**Savulescu, Julian**. Liberal Rationalism and Medical Decision-Making. *Bioethics*, 11(2), 115-129, Ap 97.

I contrast Robert Veatch's recent liberal vision of medical decision-making with a more rationalist liberal model. According to Veatch, physicians are biased in their determination of what is in their patient's overall interests in favor of their medical interests. I argue that if subjectivism about value and valuing is true, this move is plausible. However, if objectivism about value is true—that there really are states which are good for people regardless of whether they desire to be in them—then we should accept a more rationalist liberal alternative. According to this alternative, what is required to decide which course is best is rational dialogue between physicians and patients, both about the patient's circumstances and her values, and not the seeking out of people, physicians or others, who share the same values. Rational discussion requires that physicians be reasonable and empathic. I describe one possible account of a reasonable physician. (edited)

**Sawhney, Deepak Narang**. "Palimpsest: Towards a Minor Literature in Monstrosity" in *Deleuze and Philosophy: The Difference Engineer*, Ansell Pearson, Keith (ed), 130-146. New York, Routledge, 1997.

**Sawicki, Marianne**. Empathy before and after Husserl. *Phil Today*, 41(1-4), 123-127, Spr 97.

Husserl's transcendental phenomenology is indebted to Theodor Lipps's discussions of Einfühlung. That term is better translated "inner awareness" than "empathy." It stands for the only thing that can be shared among egos: a live following of motivated coherences. The possibility of perfect following is assumed in Husserl's account of the transcendental ego and of constitution. Husserl deferred formally treating the problem of other people until the 1930s; yet they are conspicuous by their suppression in his earlier texts, and they are figured into his writing practices. This observation subverts our accustomed authoritative, dogmatic reading of Husserl.

**Sawyer, K R** and Beed, Clive and Sankey, H. Underdetermination in Economics: The Duhem-Quine Thesis. *Econ Phil*, 13(1), 1-23, Ap 97.

**Sawyers, Roby B** and Chen, Al Y S and Williams, Paul F. Reinforcing Ethical Decision Making Through Corporate Culture. *J Bus Ethics*, 16(8), 855-865, Je 97.

Behaving ethically depends on the ability to recognize that ethical issues exist, to see from an ethical point of view. This ability to see and respond ethically may be related more to attributes of corporate culture than to attributes of individual employees. Efforts to increase ethical standards and decrease pressure to behave unethically should, therefore, concentrate on the organization and its culture. The purpose of this paper is to discuss how total quality (TQ) techniques can facilitate the development of a cooperative corporate culture that promotes and encourages ethical behavior throughout an organization.

**Saxlová, Tereza**. The Nature of the Common Concept in William of Ockham (in Czech). *Filosof Cas*, 45(2), 179-203, 1997.

The aim of this paper is to show systematical reasons which could have led William Ockham to his well-known change of mind as to the nature of general terms. In his *Ordinatio*, two questions can be found which seem to be closely connected with his later move from the theory of objective existence to the theory of intellection. (edited)

**Saxonhouse, Arlene W**. Diversity and Ancient Democracy: A Response to Schwartz. *Polit Theory*, 24(2), 321-325, My 96.

**Sayan, Erdinc**. A Mereological Look at Motion. *Phil Stud*, 84(1), 75-89, O 96.

**Sayre, Kenneth M**. *Parmenides' Lesson*. Notre Dame, Univ Notre Dame Pr, 1996.

Generally recognized as Plato's most difficult dialogue, the *Parmenides* has challenged interpreters through almost two thousand years of recorded commentary. In this book, Professor Sayre argues that the key to unlocking the puzzles of *Parmenides II* lies in the proper interpretive pairing of the eight hypotheses under which its arguments are grouped. Professor Sayre's commentary is prefaced by a full translation, including all the comments of the young respondent Aristoteles. Notice is taken throughout of other recent work on *Parmenides II*, with particular attention to alternative interpretations of pivotal passages. (publisher, edited)

**Scaltsas, Theodore**. Biological Matter and Perceptual Powers in Aristotle's *De Anima*. *Topoi*, 15(1), 25-37, Mr 96.

It has been claimed by Myles Burnyeat that Aristotle did not conceive of biological matter as inanimate, by contrast to our own Cartesian conception of matter, and that *perceptual powers* are *primitive properties* of biological matter. I argue that Aristotle's theory of perception in the *De Anima* (*On the Soul*) does not compel us to attribute this conception of biological matter to him. It allows, for example, that perceptual powers be *emergent* properties of matter; i.e., even if they are *irreducible* to physical properties, they need *not be primitive* powers of matter.

**Scaltsas, Theodore**. Metaphysical Models of the Mind in Aristotle. *Phil Inq*, 18(1-2), 31-42, Wint-Spr 96.

This article is about Aristotle's metaphysical account of the common sense, or the central consciousness; specifically, how we can compare and differentiate between the special objects of the senses, e.g., white and sweet. I examine several metaphysical models of the mind entertained by, or attributed to, Aristotle, in *De Anima* III.1-2, namely: the *multiple essences model*, the *multiple affections model*, the *multiple substrata model*, and the *multiple relations model*. I argue that Aristotle is not proposing any of the first three, but the fourth, because it secures for him, first, diversity—to incorporate forms that are incompatible; and unity—to secure a single act of awareness.

**Scannone, Juan Carlos**. Cultura mundial y mundos culturales. *Stromata*, 52. (1-2), 19-35, Ja-Je 96.

En primer lugar se aborda la cuestión semántica: cultura (en singular) y culturas (en plural). Luego se plantea el problema actual de la globalización cultural y los particularismos culturales en la postmodernidad. En tercer lugar se critican algunas respuestas ideológicas a dicho problema, que suponen una concepción inadecuada de la universalidad y particularidad de las culturas. Por último se indican caminos de solución como de hecho se están dando en América Latina, y se muestra que responden a una comprensión más ajustada de la contextualidad, dialogicidad y universabilidad de las culturas.

**Scaramellini, Guglielmo**. "Il pittoresco e il sublime nella natura e nel paesaggio" in *Geofilosofia*, Bonesio, Luisa (ed), 137-162. Sondrio, Lyasis, 1996.

**Scarcella, Attilio**. "Il concetto di tempo" in *Il Concetto di Tempo: Atti del XXXII Congresso Nazionale della Società Filosofica Italiana*, Casertano, Giovanni (ed), 351-356. Napoli, Loffredo, 1997.

**Scarelli, Antonino** and Venzi, Lorenzo. Nonparametric Statistics in Multicriteria Analysis. *Theor Decis*, 43(1), 89-105, Jl 97.

The paper deals with a method of hierarchization of alternatives in a multicriteria environment by means of statistical nonparametric procedures. For each criterion, alternatives are disposed on an ordinal scale. After that a procedure similar to ANOVA is activated on the data. The differences relating to the average ranks of each action are used to build the hierarchical algorithm. The concept of outranking, in a probabilistic meaning, is reached in this way. Thereafter, we arrive at the concept of dominance using pairwise comparisons. A case study is presented which implements the methodological suggestion.

**Scarlett, Brian**. "The Moral Uniqueness of the Human Animal" in *Human Lives: Critical Essays on Consequentialist Bioethics,* Oderberg, David S (ed), 77-95. New York, Macmillan, 1997.

This paper defends the 'common view' regarding animal welfare: that nonhuman animals are inferior forms of life compared to humans; that it is permissible to kill them for food and to use them for other human purposes; but that it is wrong to treat them cruelly. This is contrasted with Peter Singer's views, which are directly aimed at undermining the common view. It is argued that everything morally persuasive in Singer's approach is in complete conformity to the common view and consistent with the idea of a hierarchical ordering of forms of life. But it is Singer's concept of a 'person', in his special philosophical sense, that is radically at odds with the common view. This concept, which promotes animals and demotes humans, is subjected to criticism on several grounds, including that of potential, which Singer wrongly derides.

**Scarre, Geoffrey**. *Utilitarianism*. New York, Routledge, 1996.

This is the first general overview in many years of the history and the present condition of utilitarian ethics. Unlike other introductions to the subject, which narrowly focus on the Enlightenment and Victorian eras, *Utilitarianism* takes a wider view. Geoffrey Scarre introduces the major utilitarian philosophers from the Chinese sage Mo Tzu in the fifth century B.C. through to Richard Hare in the twentieth.(edited)

**Scedrov, Andre** and Mitchell, John C and Lincoln, Patrick D. Linear Logic Proof Games and Optimization. *Bull Sym Log*, 2(3), 322-338, S 96.

**Scerri, Eric R**. "Reduktion und Erklärung in der Chemie" in *Philosophie der Chemie: Bestandsaufnahme und Ausblick,* Schummer, Joachim (ed), 77-93. Wurzburg, Koenigshausen, 1996.

**Scerri, Eric R**. Bibliography on Philosophy of Chemistry. *Synthese*, 111(3), 305-324, Je 97.

This bibliography has been compiled in response to the recent rapid growth in interest in the field of philosophy of chemistry. It supersedes the only previous comprehensive bibliography produced in 1981 and includes articles which show overlap with the history of chemistry and chemical education as well as chemistry proper.

**Scerri, Eric R** and McIntyre, Lee. The Case for the Philosophy of Chemistry. *Synthese*, 111(3), 213-232, Je 97.

The philosophy of chemistry has been sadly neglected by most contemporary literature in the philosophy of science. This paper argues that this neglect has been unfortunate and that there is much to be learned from paying greater philosophical attention to the set of issues defined by the philosophy of chemistry. The potential contribution of this field to such current topics as reduction, laws, explanation and supervenience is explored, as are possible applications of insights gained by such study to the philosophy of mind and the philosophy of social science.

**Schachter, Jean-Pierre**. The Angel in the Machine. *J Phil Res*, 22, 445-460, Ap 97.

In "The Angel in the Machine" I argue that the substantial concept of mind is heir to a number of consequences not previously appreciated, included among which (but not limited to) are both *solipsism* and *atheism*. In addition, I suggest that the difficulties I indicate were to some extent already understood by Aristotle who seems to have laid the foundation for two concepts of mind, one associated with human beings, the other with *angels*. His distinction is recalled in the Middle Ages, but seems finally to be lost in Descartes who appears to have linked the angel mind-concept to human beings and dispensed entirely with the concept that Aristotle originally reserved for the human. Hence, "The Angel in the Machine."

**Schadel, Erwin**. "Das absolute Nichts als selbstloses Selbst; Nishitanis Erläuterungen der zen-buddhistischen Wirklichkeitsauffassung" in *Kreativer Friede durch Begegnung der Weltkulturen,* Beck, Heinrich (ed), 293-316. New York, Lang, 1995.

**Schadel, Erwin**. Monad as a Triadic Structure—Leibniz' Contribution to Post-Nihilistic Search for Identity. *J Indian Counc Phil Res*, 14(1), 17-33, S-D 96.

This paper deals with the common universal actuality of Leibnizian 'Monadology' and 'Theodicy' in three steps: The *first* one outlines the antitrinitarian "passion" of the subjectocentric Western rationality, which Leibniz has vehemently opposed. The *second* step explains the integrative structure of Leibniz's ontology, represented, for example, by the triad of '*power*', '*wisdom*' and '*goodness*'. Attention is given here to motivating influences that came from ancient and medieval philosophy to Leibniz. Finally, in a *third* step, is considered what might be the positive and innovative contribution of onto-triadic monadology with regard to the present-day identity crisis and to an ontically consistent forming of the future.

**Schaeffer, Jean-Marie**. Qu'est-ce qu'une conduite esthétique. *Rev Int Phil*, 50(198), 669-680, 1996.

**Schällibaum, Urs**. Reduktion und Ambivalenz: Zur Reflexionsstruktur von E. Lévinas' *Autrement qu'être*. *Frei Z Phil Theol*, 43(3), 335-349, 1996.

Levinas's ethics of responsibility does not say what we ought to do, but relies (contrary to Levinas's own statements) on "being", or rather—beyond ontology—on what occurs in every event of speech. Thus, we are not called upon to open up to "the other", but obliged by the fact that none of us will ever be the first to speak. This thesis is being developed through constant reduction up to the nucleus of subjectivity, within the ambivalence of "the saying" and "the said" and within the reflexivity of this ambivalence in Levinas' own text.

**Schall, James V**. Friendship and Political Philosophy. *Rev Metaph*, 50(1), 121-141, S 96.

Aristotle spends two books of his *Ethics* on friendship but only one on justice. In his *Politics*, friendship is more important to politics than justice. The classical tractates on friendship are reconsidered in the revelational tradition and make point of contact with it when the question of friendship with God is presented as a possibility. The modern treatises on friendship present the problem of the object of friendship and its place within reality, its relation to the polity and to the contemplative life.

**Schalow, Frank**. Textuality and Imagination: The Refracted Image of Hegelian Dialectic. *Res Phenomenol*, 26, 155-170, 1996.

This paper explores the interface between imagination and the deconstructive quest to uncover new meanings in a given text. As a source of innovation and play, imagination provides a more radical way to spawn new meanings than can be found in the organizational scheme of Hegelian dialectic. As an emissary of new meanings, imagination embodies the differentiating power of language in a more original way than dialectic can. Given its affinity with play, imagination then emerges as an indispensable facet of any deconstructive strategy.

**Schalow, Frank**. The Will as the Genuine Postscript of Modern Thought: At the Crossroads of an Anomaly. *Epoche*, 1(1), 77-104, 1993.

This paper examines the concept of will as marking a transition between a volitional expression in Nietzsche and a nonvolitional expression in Heidegger. In his hermeneutic phenomenology, Heidegger transforms the traditional concept of will into a decision-making process which entails the openness of truth, that is, *resoluteness*. It is argued, however, that Heidegger finds the seeds for this transformation in such German predecessors as Schelling and Nietzsche. Only by entering into dialogue with these two thinkers can Heidegger recover a more radical concept of freedom beyond the limits of modernity. Ultimately, the transformation of the concept of will into resolve provides the crucial step in arriving at a postmodern vision of freedom as "letting be."

**Schantz, Richard**. *Wahrheit, Referenz und Realismus: Eine Studie zur Sprachphilosophie und Metaphysik*. Hawthorne, de Gruyter, 1996.

**Schanze, Helmut**. Das *kleine Buch* und das *laute* Weltereignis: Fichtes *Wissenschaftslehre* als Paradigma und Problem der *Romantik*. *Fichte-Studien*, 12, 169-179, 1997.

AUTHOR INDEX 895 Schenkman, Bo

**Schatzki, Theodore R**. Practices and Actions: A Wittgensteinian Critique of Bourdieu and Giddens. *Phil Soc Sci*, 27(3), 283-308, S 97.

This article criticizes Bourdieu's and Giddens's overintellectualizing accounts of human activity on the basis of Wittgenstein's insights into practical understanding. Part 1 describes these two theorists' conceptions of a homology between the organization of practices (spatial-temporal manifolds of action) and the governance of individual actions. Part 2 draws on Wittgenstein's discussions of linguistic definition and following a rule to criticize these conceptions for ascribing content to the practical understanding they claim governs action. Part 3 then suggests an alternative, Wittgensteinian account of the homology between practices and actions that avoids this pitfall.

**Schauer, Frederick**. Generality and Equality. *Law Phil*, 16(3), 279-297, My 97.

Many people believe that racial inequality in particular and inequality in general, are special cases of the general moral error of over-generalizing, or stereotyping. Under this account, there is a moral mandate to treat all people as individuals and to attend to their own actual characteristics, rather than to assume that they have some trait or other because of the statistical presence of the trait in a group of which they are a part. I argue to the contrary that generalizing, even generalizing about people, is not for that reason alone morally problematic, even in those cases where such a method of actuarial decisionmaking attributes to people traits they do not in fact possess. The evil of racial and gender generalization (stereotyping), I argue, is in important ways about race and gender and not just an exemplar of a larger moral particularism.

**Schechtman, Marya**. The Brain/Body Problem. *Phil Psych*, 10(2), 149-164, Je 97.

It is a commonplace of contemporary thought that the mind is located in the brain. Although there have been some challenges to this view, it has remained mainstream outside of a few specialized discussions and plays a prominent role in a wide variety of philosophical arguments. It is further assumed that the source of this view is empirical. I argue it is not. Empirical discoveries show conclusively that the brain is the central organ of mental life, but do not show that it is the mind's location. The standard conception of the brain as the locus of mind stems, I claim, from the imposition of a Cartesian conception of the self on a materialist ontology. Recognizing that the empirical data do not justify such a move casts doubt on the foundations of a number of philosophical discussions and raises new questions about the nature of the psychological subject. (edited)

**Schechtman, Marya**. *The Constitution of Selves*. Ithaca, Cornell Univ Pr, 1996.

An amnesia victim who asks "Who am I?" means something different from a confused adolescent asking the same question. Marya Schechtman takes issue with analytic philosophy's emphasis on the first sort of question to the exclusion of the second. The problem of personal identity, she suggests, is usually understood to be a question about historical life. What she calls the "reidentification question" is taken to be the real metaphysical question of personal identity, whereas questions about beliefs or values and the actions they prompt—the "characterization question"—are often presented as merely metaphorical. Failure to recognize the philosophical importance of both, Schechtman argues, has undermined analytic philosophy's attempts to offer a satisfying account of personal identity. (publisher)

**Schechtman, Marya**. The Story of the Mind: Psychological and Biological Explanations of Human Behavior. *Zygon*, 31(4), 597-614, D 96.

Persons have a curious dual nature. On the one hand, they are subjects, whose actions must be explained in terms of beliefs, desires, plans and goals. At the same time, however, they also are physical objects, whose actions must be explicable in terms of physical laws. So far no satisfying account of this duality has been offered. Both Cartesian dualism and the modern materialist alternatives (reductionist and antireductionist) have failed to capture the full range of our experience of persons. I argue that an exciting new approach to this difficulty can be found by considering developments in clinical psychology. The clinical debate between those endorsing biological models of mental illness and those endorsing psychodynamic models mirrors broader debates in the philosophy of mind. The possible resolution of this debate through the development of integrated psychobiological models suggest a promising way to reconcile the dual nature of persons in a far more appealing way than any yet proposed.

**Scheer, Richard K**. What I Will Do and What I Intend To Do. *Philosophy*, 71(278), 531-539, O 96.

**Schefczyk, Michael** and Murmann, Sven. Bewusstes Leben und Metaphysik: Gespräch mit Dieter Henrich. *Z Phil Praxis*, 4-9, 1995.

In the interview mentioned above D. Henrich outlines ideas which are essential for his philosophical thinking. It becomes transparent that for Henrich genuine human self-understanding is based on nonmaterialist metaphysics. Towards the end of the interview he comes to a conclusion concerning *sense* and *non-sense* of philosophical counselling.

**Scheffler, Israel**. Moral Education and the Democratic Ideal. *Inquiry (USA)*, 16(3), 27-34, Spr 97.

The democratic ideal requires the institutionalization of reasoned procedures for the critical and public review of policy. To choose this ideal for society is to reject the idea of shaping or molding the mind of the pupil. The function of education in a democracy is rather to liberate the mind, strengthen its critical powers, inform it with knowledge, engage its human sympathies and illuminate its moral and practical choices. The challenge of moral education is the challenge to develop critical thought in the sphere of practice and it is continuous with the challenge to develop critical thought in all aspects and phases of schooling.

**Scheffler, Israel**. Replies. *Stud Phil Educ*, 16(1-2), 259-272, Ja-Ap 97.

This paper offers responses to each of the seventeen critical papers in *Reason and Education: Essays in Honor of Israel Scheffler*, edited by Harvey Siegel. These papers deal with various topics in the philosophy of education, including discussions of the aims of education, cognition and emotion, the analysis of teaching, the language of education, science education, moral and religious education and human potential.

**Scheffler, Samuel**. "Liberalism, Nationalism, and Egalitarianism" in *The Morality of Nationalism*, McKim, Robert (ed), 191-208. New York, Oxford Univ Pr, 1997.

**Scheibe, Erhard**. J. v. Neumanns und J.S. Bells Theorem: Ein Vergleich. *Phil Natur*, 28(1), 35-53, 1991.

**Scheibe, Erhard**. Lorenz Krüger. *Phil Natur*, 33(1), 177-186, 1996.

**Scheid, Don E**. Business Entities and the State: Who Should Provide Security from Crime?. *Pub Affairs Quart*, 11(2), 163-182, Ap 97.

The article explores the development in civil law of holding property owners liable to crime victims for crimes committed on their premises. After noting the "privatization of security" in the United States, I give a brief account of recent legal developments in premise liability for crime. I then argue against the claims that policing functions are traditionally the exclusive role of government and that this must be so to preserve state sovereignty. I argue, further, that premise owners are better placed than anyone else to provide security measures. Thus, the present trend is justified mainly on the basis of efficiency.

**Schelkshorn, Hans**. *Diskurs und Befreiung: Studien zur philosophischen Ethik von Karl-Otto Apel und Enrique Dussel*. Amsterdam, Rodopi, 1997.

Die europäische Diskursethik und die lateinamerikanische Philosophie der Befreiung artikulierten Anfang der 70er Jahre das weitverbreitete Bedürfnis nach grundlegenden gesellschaftlichen Veränderungen. Inzwischen stossen allerdings diskurstheoretische Vernunftmoralen und neomarxistische Befreiungsphilosophien nicht nur im postmodernen Denken auf tiefe Skepsis. Vor dem Hintergrund wachsender sozialer Ungleichheit in Nord und Süd und der zunehmenden Macht populistischer bzw. fundamentalistischer Strömungen scheint es gegenwärtig jedoch durchaus angebracht zu sein, mögliche Errungenschaften der Diskurs- und Befreiungsethik in einer präzisen and zugleich kritischen Auseinandersetzung mit ihren theoretischen Grundlagen zu rekonstruieren und damit vorschnellen Abschiedsreden nochmals ins Wort zufallen. In einer vorsichtigen, die universalistische Orientierung prinzipiell bewahrenden Rekontextualisierung der Moraltheorien von Karl-Otto Apel und Enrique Dussel werden einerseits Möglichkeiten für gegenseitige Korrekturen und Ergänzungen zwischen Diskurs- und Befreiungsethik, anderseits aber auch Perspektiven für eine interkulturell orientierte Ethik als Fundament einer Kritischen Theorie der globalen sozialen Frage analysiert.

**Schellenberg, J L**. Pluralism and Probability. *Relig Stud*, 33(2), 143-159, Je 97.

In this paper I discuss a neglected form of argument against religious belief-generically, 'the probabilistic argument from pluralism'. If the denial of a belief is equivalent to the disjunction of its alternatives and if we may gain some idea as to the probabilities of such disjunctions by adding the separate probabilities of their mutually exclusive disjuncts, and if, moreover, the denials of many religious beliefs are disjunctions known to have two or more mutually exclusive members each possessing a significant degree or probability, then at any rate in many such cases, the denial of a religious belief can be shown to be more probable than *it* is—which is to say that the belief can be shown to be improbable. I consider a large number of responses to arguments of this form, concluding that none suffices to overthrow it altogether. Indeed, the argument remains as a significant threat to any religious belief confronted by a plurality of alternatives.

**Schellenberg, J L**. Response to Howard-Snyder. *Can J Phil*, 26(3), 455-462, S 96.

In his "The Argument from Divine Hiddenness" (*Can J Phil*, 26(3), 433-453), Daniel Howard-Snyder takes on a "properly qualified" version of my argument in *Divine Hiddenness and Human Reason* (Cornell, 1993), concluding that it fails. In reply I argue 1) that Howard-Snyder's qualification is *not* proper, that my original version of the argument is stronger than the one he takes on and renders his seemingly most potent defeater (a skeptical argument of the sort used by Alston against Rowe's evidential argument from evil) irrelevant; and 2) that his other defeaters, new suggested reasons for Divine hiddenness, ultimately fail.

**Scheman, Naomi**. "Forms of Life: Mapping the Rough Ground" in *The Cambridge Companion to Wittgenstein*, Sluga, Hans (ed), 383-410. Needham Heights, Cambridge, 1996.

**Scheman, Naomi**. Reply to Louise Antony. *Hypatia*, 11(3), 150-153, Sum 96.

In her discussion of Naomi Scheman's "Individualism and the Objects of Psychology" Louise Antony misses the import of an unpublished paper of Scheman's that she cites. That paper argues against token identity theories on the grounds that only the sort of psycho-physical parallelisms that token identity theorists, such as Davidson and Fodor, reject could license the claim that each mental state or event is some particular state or event.

**Schenkman, Bo**. Computers, Radiation, and Ethics. *Ethics Behavior*, 6(2), 125-139, 1996.

The reduction of the levels of the electromagnetic fields surrounding and emanating from computer screens is discussed in relation to ethical issues of risk reduction, in particular where the factual basis for the actions taken is nonconclusive. The technical and scientific background is reviewed briefly. Some empirical approaches for determining risks, for example, the method of contingent valuations, are reviewed and their ethical implications are discussed. When both the risk level and the determination of the certainty of the risk level is unknown, it is not considered responsible to further the work on reduction of the levels of the electromagnetic fields. The present state of knowledge does not seem to warrant further action regarding these fields. It is suggested that the focus of endeavors be directed toward other concerns, in particular to image quality and the work situation.

**Schérer, René**. Powers of Desire: Deleuze and Mores. *Grad Fac Phil J*, 19(1), 113-117, 1996.

**Schervish, Mark J** and Kadane, Joseph B and Seidenfeld, Teddy. When Several Bayesians Agree That There Will Be No Reasoning to a Foregone Conclusion. *Proc Phil Sci Ass*, 3(Suppl), S281-S289, 1996.

When can a Bayesian investigator select an hypothesis H and design an experiment (or a sequence of experiments) to make certain that, given the experimental outcome(s), the posterior probability of H will be lower than its prior probability? We report an elementary result which establishes sufficient conditions under which this reasoning to a foregone conclusion cannot occur. Through an example, we discuss how this result extends to the perspective of an onlooker who agrees with the investigator about the statistical model for the data but who holds a different prior probability for the statistical parameters of that model. We consider, specifically, one-sided and two-sided statistical hypotheses involving i.i.d. normal data with conjugate priors. In a concluding section, using an "improper" prior, we illustrate how the preceding results depend upon the assumption that probability is countably additive.

**Scherzinger, Martin**. Max Black's "Interaction View" of Metaphor. *Conference*, 6(1), 89-97, Sum 95.

This article critically assesses Max Black's "interaction view" of metaphor. It argues against, or demands a fuller account of, the unparaphrasable cognitive content of metaphor on the "interaction view"; outlines the ways in which this view is beholden to the "substitution" and "comparison views" against which it has been distinguished; and contests the claim that metaphors remain unchanged in translation. By rendering the common distinction between the literal and the metaphorical less stable than Black, this article calls for a differently focused analysis of literal expressions and their relation to linguistic contexts—an analysis that would result in a different pertinence between literal and metaphoric language.

**Schiappa, Edward**. "Towards a Pragmatic Approach to Definition: 'Wetlands' and the Politics of Meaning" in *Environmental Pragmatism*, Light, Andrew (ed), 209-230. New York, Routledge, 1996.

**Schiappa, Edward**. Interpreting Gorgias's "Being" in *On Not-Being or On Nature*. *Phil Rhet*, 30(1), 13-30, 1997.

The essay describes the extant versions of Gorgias's *On Not Being* in order to identify difficulties facing the modern interpreter. The disciplinary assumptions made about the philosophical and rhetorical dimensions of *On Not Being* that have informed most past interpretations are discussed. In light of the different interpretive traditions associated with the texts of the *Eleatics*, the essay offers alternative approaches to interpreting the "being" in Gorgia's *On Not Being* that are less influenced by the philosophy/rhetoric framework through which the text is usually approached.

**Schick, Frederic**. *Making Choices: A Recasting of Decision Theory.* New York, Cambridge Univ Pr, 1997.

This book is a nonmathematical overview of decision theory. It presents the logic of rationality and the basis of the theory of games. It shows how social choice theory yields a parallel logic, a logic of choosing for others. It considers the part that is played by how people grasp or *see* their situations, how different *seeings* can make for ambiguity and for inner conflicts and value reversals—and how these can be dealt with. And it discusses some problems of time: problems of discounting, of value change, and of the contingency of our future values on what we do today. The author presents many examples from history and from literature, examples dealing with love, war, friendship and crime.

**Schick, Ida Critelli**. Personal Privacy and Confidentiality in an Electronic Environment. *Bioethics Forum*, 12(1), 25-30, Spr 96.

Information systems and technology are essential components in an efficient managed care organization. The question arises: Is it possible to develop an electronic system that is secure, that is, protects patient privacy and confidentiality? This question can be answered affirmatively if a proactive agenda based on sound ethical principles is developed and implemented.

**Schick, Theodore**. Morality Requires God...or Does It?: Bad News for Fundamentalists and Jean-Paul Sartre. *Free Inq*, 17(3), 32-34, Sum 97.

**Schilling, Kenneth** and Zivaljevic, Bosko. Louveau's Theorem for the Descriptive Set Theory of Internal Sets. *J Sym Log*, 62(2), 595-607, Je 97.

We give positive answers to two questions in the descriptive set theory of internal sets in countably saturated models of nonstandard analysis, both posed by Zivaljevic. 1) Every set countably determined over an algebra A of internal sets and Borel at level x (over the algebra of all internal sets) is in fact Borel at level x over A. 2) Every Borel subset of the product of two internal sets all of whose sections are Borel at level x can be represented as an intersection (or union) of Borel sets whose sections are Borel at level below x. We derive 2) from the analogous theorem of A. Louveau for Polish spaces.

**Schimmerling, E** and Mitchell, William J and Steel, J R. The Covering Lemma Up to a Woodin Cardinal. *Annals Pure Applied Log*, 84(2), 219-255, Mr 97.

It is proven that if there is no model with a Woodin cardinal and the Steel core model K exists, then the weak covering lemma holds at strong limit cardinals, that is, if lambda is a singular cardinal such that no smaller cardinal has lambda many countable subsets, then the successor of lambda is K is the same as the true successor of lambda.

**Schindler, Ronald Jeremiah**. *Applied Social Sciences in the Plutocratic Era of the United States: Dialectics of the Concrete.* Brookfield, Avebury, 1996.

The book posits a communicative competency to be within the capability of all scholars, properly educated, to perform public duties, no matter what the difficulty of the policy or research being universally discussed. Ideally, praxis supersedes theory-production, particularly as the latter has become reified in academic institutions. Theories in general, given their bureaucratic/power setting, can be an instrument to forge elite/mass differentiation and the will to power. Social scientists must give up their special claims to power and unilateral authority to speak to captured audiences. (edited)

**Schirn, Matthias**. "Frege über Widerspruchsfreiheit und die Schöpfung mathematischer Gegenstände" in *Das weite Spektrum der analytischen Philosophie*, Lenzen, Wolfgang, 274-289. Hawthorne, de Gruyter, 1997.

**Schirn, Matthias**. "Introduction: Frege on the Foundations of Arithmetic and Geometry" in *Frege: Importance and Legacy*, Schirn, Matthias (ed), 1-42. Hawthorne, de Gruyter, 1996.

**Schirn, Matthias**. "On Frege's Introduction of Cardinal Numbers as Logical Objects" in *Frege: Importance and Legacy*, Schirn, Matthias (ed), 114-173. Hawthorne, de Gruyter, 1996.

**Schirn, Matthias** (ed). *Frege: Importance and Legacy.* Hawthorne, de Gruyter, 1996.

Introduction: Frege on the foundations of arithmetic and geometry—M.D. Resnik: On positing mathematical objects—W.W. Tait: Frege versus Cantor and Dedekind: On the concept of number—M. Schirn: On Frege's introduction of cardinal numbers as logical objects—B. Hale and C. Wright: Nominalism and the contingency of abstract objects—R.G. Heck: Definition by induction in Frege's *Grundgesetze der Arithmetik*—G. Boolos: Whence the contradiction?—M.Dummett: Reply to Boolos—Chr. Thiel: On the structure of Frege's system of logic—P. Simmons: The horizontal—F.v. Kutschera: Frege and natural deduction—E. Picardi: Frege's antipsychologism—G. Gabriel: Frege's epistemology in disguise—T. Burge: Frege on knowing the third realm—T. Parsons: Definitions of truth and meaning in Fregean semantics—R. Mendelsohn: Frege's treatment of indirect reference—B. Hale: Singular terms. (publisher)

**Schirn, Matthias**. The Context Principle in Frege's *Grundgesetze* (in Spanish). *Theoria (Spain)*, 11(27), 177-201, S 96.

Taking course-of-values names as an example, I want to show that, contrary to what Michael Resnik and Michael Dummett claim, Frege never abandoned his context principle "Only in the context of a sentence do words have meaning." In particular, I want to show that Frege's attempted proof of referentiality for the formal language of *Grundgesetze der Arithmetik* rests on the context principle and that, consequently, course-of-values names have a reference only in the context of a sentence. It is only in the light of the context principle that Frege's theory of sense and reference can be understood appropriately.

**Schlecht, Ludwig F**. Re-Reading 'The Will to Believe'. *Relig Stud*, 33(2), 217-225, Je 97.

Since its first publication one hundred years ago, William James's essay 'The Will to Believe' has been criticized as providing 'an unrestricted license for wishful thinking' in religious matters. The criticism is based on the assumption that James is attempting to justify belief in traditional theism. A careful reading of this essay, and other works by James in which he addresses the issue of religious faith, reveals that the religious question for him is not whether a theistic God exists, but whether the universe offers us possibilities of meaning and fulfilment, whether life is worth living. James's argument is that we have a right to believe that this is so—an argument that is more cogent and convincing than it is often thought to be.

**Schlechta, Karl**. Completeness and Incompleteness for Plausibility Logic. *J Log Lang Info*, 5(2), 177-192, 1996.

Plausibility Logic was introduced by Daniel Lehmann. We show—among some other results—completeness of a subset of plausibility logic for preferential models and incompleteness of full plausibility logic for smooth preferential models.

**Schlee, Edward E**. The Sure Thing Principle and the Value of Information. *Theor Decis*, 42(1), 21-36, Ja 97.

This paper examines the relationship between Savage's sure thing principle and the value of information. We present two classes of results. First, we show that, under a consequentialist axiom, the sure thing principle is neither sufficient nor necessary for *perfect* information to be always desirable. Second, we demonstrate that, under consequentialism, the sure thing principle is necessary for a nonnegative value of possibly imperfect information (though of course the principle is still not sufficient). One implication of these results is that the sure thing principle, under consequentialism, plays a somewhat different role in ensuring dynamic consistency in decision making under certainty than does the independence axiom in decision making under risk. (edited)

**Schlesinger, George N**. Theological Necessity. *Relig Stud*, 33(1), 55-65, Mr 97.

The major objection to the *ontological argument* has been that 'existence' is not a predicate. Attempts to ground the argument on 'necessary existence' have not fared too well either. In this paper it is suggested that first we must inquire which worlds are, and which are not compatible with divine objectives. This leads us to the conclusion that the argument must be grounded in a proper subset of logically possible worlds, on 'theologically possible worlds'.

**Schlipphacke, Heidi** and Wilke, Sabine. "Construction of a Gendered Subject: A Feminist Reading of Adorno's *Aesthetic Theory*" in *The Semblance of Subjectivity*, Huhn, Tom (ed), 287-308. Cambridge, MIT Pr, 1997.

**Schlossberger, Eugene**. Technology and Civil Disobedience: Why Engineers Have a Special Duty to Obey the Law. *Sci Eng Ethics*, 1(2), 163-168, A 95.

The paper argues that, in the performance of their engineering duties, engineers are generally less free to engage in civil disobedience than are many other professionals. A general theory of civil disobedience is sketched. Two consequences of modern technology create special constraints for engineers working as engineers. Given the complexity of modern technology, it is argued, engineers have a special institutional duty to obey the law and so engineers can justify civil disobedience only in the most extreme of cases. However, since technology has increased the division of labor within engineering, the most extreme cases rarely arise for engineers.

**Schlüter, Andreas** and Glass, Thomas and Rathjen, Michael. On the Proof-Theoretic Strength of Monotone Induction in Explicit Mathematics. *Annals Pure Applied Log*, 85(1), 1-46, Ap 97.

We characterize the proof-theoretic strength of systems of explicit mathematics with a general principle (MID) asserting the existence of least fixed points for monotone inductive definitions, in terms of certain systems of analysis and set theory.... In the case of set theory, these are systems containing the Kripke-Platek axioms for a recursively inaccessible universe together with the existence of a stable ordinal. In all cases, the exact strength depends on what forms of induction are admitted in the respective systems. (edited)

**Schlup Sant'Anna, Adonai**. An Axiomatic Framework for Classical Particle Mechanics without Force. *Phil Natur*, 33(2), 187-203, 1996.

A set-theoretical predicate for nonrelativistic classical particle mechanics, inspired in Hertz's mechanics, is presented. We make some comparisons between Hertz's mechanics and our axiomatic framework. We discuss also other possible axiomatizations for physical theories inspired in Hertz's ideas about the coordinating relations of thoughts to facts.

**Schmaltz, Tad M**. *Malebranche's Theory of the Soul: A Cartesian Interpretation*. New York, Oxford Univ Pr, 1996.

The book is divided into two parts. In part one Tad Schmaltz assesses Malebranche's thesis that we know the modifications of the soul through a consciousness that is confused rather than through an idea that is clear. In part two he considers Malebranche's argument that this disputed thesis does not preclude the Cartesian project of constructing clear and evident demonstrations of the distinctive properties of the soul. The book concludes with a stimulating discussion of Malebranche's significance for contemporary debates in the philosophy of mind. (publisher, edited)

**Schmaus, Warren**. The Empirical Character of Methodological Rules. *Proc Phil Sci Ass*, 3(Suppl), S98-S106, 1996.

Critics of Laudan's normative naturalism have questioned whether methodological rules can be regarded as empirical hypotheses about relations between means and ends. Drawing on Laudan's defense that rules of method are contingent on assumptions about the world, I argue that even if such rules can be shown to be analytic in principle (Kaiser 1991), in practice the warrant for such rules will be empirical. Laudan's naturalism, however, acquires normative force only by construing both methods and epistemic goals as instrumental to practical concerns, and issues only in context-specific and not general methodological principles.

**Schmid, Dirk**. "Das Christentum als Verwirklichung des Religionsbegriffs in Fichtes Spätphilosophie 1813" in *Sein—Reflexion—Freiheit: Aspekte der Philosophie Johann Gottlieb Fichtes*, Asmuth, Christoph (ed), 221-236. Amsterdam, Gruner, 1997.

**Schmid, Michael**. *Rationalität und Theoriebildung: Studien zu Karl R. Poppers Methodologie der Sozialwissenschaften*. Amsterdam, Rodopi, 1996.

Der Band rekonstruiert und kritisiert die verstreuten Vorschläge, die Karl R. Popper zur Philosophie der Sozialwissenschaften gemacht hat. Dabei stehen drei Themenbereiche im Vordergrund: Zum einen wird der von Popper verteidigte Methodologische Individualismus in der Absicht untersucht, dessen begrenzte heuristische Fruchtbarkeit sichtbar zu machen; zum weiteren wird die von Popper favorisierte Logik von Handlungserklärungen einer nachhaltigen Revision unterzogen, was eine umfassendere handlungstheoretische Erklärungspraxis erlaubt, als sie Popper im Auge hatte; und zum dritten diskutiert der Autor die Frage, inwieweit Poppers Theorie des Wissensfortschritts für die sozialwissenschaftliche Theoriebildung verbindlich ist; auch in diesem Falle werden Mängel diagnostiziert und Wege zu deren Beseitigung erkundet. (publisher)

**Schmid, Peter A** and Zurbuchen, Simone. *Grenzen der kritischen Vernunft*. Basel, Schwabe Verlag, 1997.

Die Werke Kants und des Neukantianismus stehen exemplarisch für den Versuch, die Philosophie als Wissenschaft zu begründen. Diese konstruktive Arbeit hat ihre Grundlage in der kritischen Begrenzung der Vernunft, die ihrer Natur nach zu Grenzüberschreitungen verleitet und den Philosophen im metaphysischen Schein blendet. Die Grenzen der Vernunft repräsentieren die nüchterne Sachlichkeit der Wissenschaft, vor der die vielgestaltigen Wesen, welche die Metaphysik bevölkerten, zu weichen haben. (publisher, edited)

**Schmidig, Dominik**. Offene Intersubjektivität—nach Johann Gottlieb Fichte. *Perspekt Phil*, 22, 267-283, 1996.

Fichte will in seiner 'Wissenschaftslehre' die Prinzipien menschlichen Bewusstseins klären. Bei den abgeleiteten Prinzipien kommt er auch auf die menschliche Intersubjektivität zu sprechen und zog den Schluss: Der Mensch wird nur unter Menschen ein Mensch. Das hat Konsequenzen für vernünftiges Verhalten—bezüglich Natur, Mensch, Moral, Religion, Philosophie. Der Aufsatz handelt von Fichtes Offener Intersubjektivität, von seinen Ueberlegungen zu:

Bewusstseinsprinzipien, menschlicher Freiheit, Intersubjektivität, Begründung des Rechts; von Konsequenzen für Individuen, Gemeinschaften, menschliche Zukunft. Fichte erwartet, dass der Einfluss von Ideologien abnimmt und der Respekt vor Vernunft und Vernunftträgern wächst, also vor Freiheit, Wissen, Verantwortung, individuell und sozial.

**Schmidig, Dominik**. Sprachliche Vermittlung philosophischer Einsichten nach Fichtes Frühphilosophie. *Fichte-Studien*, 10, 1-15, 1997.

Fichtes Wissenschaftslehre will die 'Grundsätze' (Prinzipien) der von Kant begründeten Transzendentalphilosophie in einen inneren Zusammenhang bringen. Eine Besinnung auf das, was jeden Bewusstseinsakt notwendig, meist unbewusst prinzipiiert, führt auf 'Tathandlung' (reines Ich)—'Gegensetzen' (Nicht-Ich)—'Einschränken' (begrenztes Ich und Nicht-Ich). Solche und andere Einsichten lassen sich nur indirekt vermittel, und zwar indem Interessierte dazu gebracht werden, sie im eigenen Bewusstsein zu erzeugen und aufzufinden. Vermittlungsversuche haben zunächst performativen Charakter; erst nach gelungener Verständigung können Aussagen auch konstativen Charakter annehmen. Probleme: Einfluss der Freiheit, das Sich-Auswirken von Individualität, Darstellung in historisch gewachsenen Sprachformen (sinnliche Lebenspraxis, Kultur, Nationalität...).

**Schmidt, Burghart** and Moneti, Maria and Boella, Laura. Discutono *Il principio speranza*, di Ernst Bloch. *Iride*, 8(15), 466-482, Ag 95.

Il ritardo della traduzione italiana del capolavoro di E. Bloch, pubblicato in Germania alla fine degli anni cinquanta, probabilmente "offre oggi i vantaggi della maturazione tardiva o persino dell'inattualità permanente che tutti i grandi testi filosofici posseggono" (R. Bodei, *Introduzione*). I tre interventi che seguono rilevano e discutono aspetti essenziali del libro. L. Boella instaura un parallelo tra i "fantasmi" di Derrida e l'utopia di Bloch al fine di rilevare la stringente attualità della questione del presente in entrambi i pensatori; M. Moneti si sofferma su alcune nozioni centrali del *Principio speranza* sottolineandone una "certa debolezza teorica"; B. Schmidt, Presidente della *Ernst Bloch-Gesellschaft* a Ludwigshafen, approfondisce il nesso rintracciabile in Bloch tra ontologia e teoria critica della società.

**Schmidt, Catherine M**. Who Benefits? Music Education and the National Standards. *Phil Music Educ Rev*, 4(2), 71-82, Fall 96.

**Schmidt, Gerhart**. Eugen Finks Phänomenologie des Todes. *Perspekt Phil*, 22, 139-164, 1996.

Eugen Fink's philosophy follows distantly Heidegger by considering the intimacy of man and being. Fink insists that man needs above all a sensible interpretation of his life. Death is among the other principal phenomena of human being as working, struggle, love and play the most difficult to conceive. Death is the complete failure of metaphysical thinking. Fink, therefore, consults the Heraclitean interpretation of death and concludes, that human individuals death is the complete ruin of a living understanding of the universe. Finally he decides to a nonmetaphysical philosophy of the finiteness.

**Schmidt, James**. The Fool's Truth: Diderot, Goethe, and Hegel. *J Hist Ideas*, 57(4), 625-644, O 96.

Hegel's use of Diderot's *Rameau's Nephew* in the *Phenomenology of Spirit* must be understood against the background of Goethe's translation of the work. Goethe not only presented the dialogue for the first time, but also provided an extended commentary on the work that had a decisive influence on subsequent readings, including Hegel's. Hegel's appropriation of Diderot's work departs significantly from both Diderot's and Goethe's views on the relationship of morality, genius and society. Nevertheless, the narrative structure of the *Phenomenology* bears a remarkable affinity to Diderot's great dialogue.

**Schmidt, Josef**. Das philosophieimmanente Theodizeeproblem und seine theologische Radikalisierung. *Theol Phil*, 72(2), 247-256, 1997.

The problem of theodicy as question about the power of the good facing evil and suffering is already a philosophical, not only a religious problem. The option for the power of the good gives an implicit answer which was made explicit in theories of theodicy (Plato, Stoa, Leibniz and others). Within the Christian belief in a loving God, the same problem arises in an even more intensified way. Faith offers a solution to the problem which is no longer philosophical: God's compassion.

**Schmidt, Lawrence K**. Recalling the Hermeneutic Circle. *Phil Today*, 40(2), 263-272, Sum 96.

The hermeneutic circle should be retained. After distinguishing several senses of the circle, we claim that Hans-Georg Gadamer's concept of the preconception of completion is an essential advancement that may be added to Heidegger's understanding of the circle. This modified conception of the hermeneutic circle frees it from the language of metaphysics. Further, this analysis of the circle provides for an understanding of how the other and difference function in philosophical hermeneutics and opens an answer to Derrida's concern about the good will in hermeneutics.

**Schmidt, Thomas**. "Werte und Entscheidungen" in *Werte und Entscheidungen im Management*, Schmidt, Thomas, 29-82. Marburg, Metropolis, 1996.

The primary aim of the paper is to provide a brief introduction (addressed to nonphilosophers) into conceptions and questions related to the question of how values and decisions of individuals are interrelated. The author is concerned with the issue of how to integrate values into an appropriate framework for evaluating decisions as well as with the problem of interpreting individual behaviour with regard to possibly *underlying values*. The paper is part of the theoretical background work for a semiempirical project on *Values and Decisions in Management* which addresses the problem of how to develop an appropriate conceptual and methodological framework for describing and assessing business decisions with regard to their (often alleged) moral status.

**Schmidt, Thomas** and Lohmann, Karl R. *Werte und Entscheidungen im Management.* Marburg, Metropolis, 1996.

In der zeitgenössischen unternehmensethischen Debatte wird in erster Linie die Möglichkeit und der Sinn von Ethik-Programmen diskutiert. In der Untersuchung *Werte und Entscheidungen im Management* wurde ein anderer Ansatz gewählt. Die Autoren analysieren, wie Werte und moralische Überzeugungen von Personen in die Struktur individueller Entscheidungen integrierbar sind. In dem Buch werden der Verlauf der empirisch gestützten Studie, die verwendeten Instrumente und ihre Ergebnisse dargestellt. Die Ergebnisse sind für Theoretiker und Praktiker gleichermassen interessant. Zum einen muss in Theorie und Praxis der Organisationsentwicklung die Struktur individueller Entscheidungen berücksichtigt werden. Zum anderen bildet eben diese Struktur die Grundlage jeder Personalpolitik und jedes erfolgreichen Personaltrainings. (publisher, edited)

**Schmidt, Thomas** and Nida-Rümelin, Julian and Munk, Axel. Interpersonal Dependency of Preferences. *Theor Decis*, 41(3), 257-280, N 96.

Standard decision theoretic models disregard the phenomenon of interpersonal dependency of preferences. In this paper it is argued that interpersonal dependency of preferences is a serious challenge for standard utility theory. First we sketch the more philosophical aspects of the problem and then, using a simple, formal model for the two-person case, we show that interpersonal dependency of preferences generally results in indeterminacy of preferences (resp. of subjective utility).

**Schmidt-Biggemann, Wilhelm.** "Cassirers Renaissance-Auffassung" in *Grenzen der kritischen Vernunft,* Schmid, Peter A, 224-240. Basel, Schwabe Verlag, 1997.

**Schmidtz, David**. Guarantees. *Soc Phil Pol*, 14(2), 1-19, Sum 97.

The history of market society is a history of people flourishing under conditions of uncertainty. Do they flourish in spite of the uncertainty? Evidently they do, but more importantly, they flourish in response to the uncertainty. People respond to the lack of guarantees by taking responsibility for producing what they need. In this paper, I reject the distinction between individual and collective responsibility in favor of a distinction that I now consider more important: internalized versus externalized responsibility. I then discuss the history of mutual aid societies (a form of collective but internalized responsibility) prior to the emergence of the welfare state.

**Schmidtz, David**. *Rational Choice and Moral Agency.* Princeton, Princeton Univ Pr, 1995.

Schmidtz claims that being moral is rational, but he does not assume we have reasons to be rational. Instead, Schmidtz argues that being moral is rational in a particular way and that beings like us in situations like ours have reasons to be rational in just that way. This approach allows him to identify decisive reasons to be moral; at the same time, it explains why immorality is as prevalent as it is. This book thus offers a set of interesting and realistic conclusions about how morality fits into the lives of *humanly* rational agents operating in an institutional context like our own.

**Schmidtz, David**. Self-Interest: What's In It For Me?. *Soc Phil Pol*, 14(1), 107-121, Wint 97.

We have so much faith in the rationality of prudence that asking "why be prudent?" sounds like a joke. Yet, our reasons to be prudent are as contingent as our reasons to be moral. *Conflict* between morality and self-interest is contingent as well; the moral perspective does not require a universal regard for others and self-interest does not require a wholesale disregard for others. A third kind of contingency is involved in our reasons for failing to be moral. It is simplistic to use self-interest as an all-purpose scapegoat for our failures to be moral. Often, the problem lies elsewhere. We can be motivated to be moral even when being moral is not in our interest and we can be unmotivated to be moral even when morality and self-interest coincide.

**Schmidtz, David**. When Preservationism Doesn't Preserve. *Environ Values*, 6(3), 327-339, Ag 97.

According to conservationism, scarce and precious resources should be conserved and used wisely. According to preservation ethics, we should not think of wilderness as merely a resource. Wilderness commands reverence in a way mere resources do not. Each philosophy, I argue, can fail by its own lights, because trying to put the principles of conservationism or preservationism into institutional practice can have results that are the opposite of what the respective philosophies tell us we ought to be trying to achieve. For example, if the wisest use of South American rainforests is no use at all, then in that case conservationism by its own lights defers to preservationism. Analogously, if, when deprived of the option of preserving elephants as a resource, Africans respond by not preserving elephants at all, then in that case preservationism by its own lights defers to conservationism.

**Schmied-Kowarzik, Wolfdietrich**. Das Problem der Natur: Nähe und Differenz Fichtes und Schellings. *Fichte-Studien*, 12, 211-233, 1997.

1794 trat Fichte seine Professur in Jena an und legte sein Konzept *Über den Begriff der Wissenschaftslehre* vor. Ein Jahr später folgte ihm der noch ganz junge Schelling mit der Studie *Vom Ich als Prinzip der Philosophie* (1795). Blicken wir heute rückblickend auf ihre Gegnerschaft, so finden wir viele Missverständnisse auf beiden Seiten, aber auch Gemeinsamkeiten darin, dass wir über die Naturwissenschaften hinaus, die natur, in die wir sittlichpraktisch gestellt sind, philosophisch anders und grundsätzlich zu thematisieren haben. Dies ist angesichts unserer heutigen ökologischen Krise eine sogar noch dringlicher gewordene Aufgabe. (edited)

**Schmied-Kowarzik, Wolfdietrich**. O Futuro Ecológico como Tarefa da Filosofia. *Kriterion*, 34(87), 95-107, Ja-Jl 93.

Postulating that the current model of production leads necessarily to the destruction of nature—and of man as a part of it—the author seeks in classical pages of the history of philosophy (Kant, Hegel, Schelling and Marx) proposals as to how the problematic relation between man and nature could be worked out, contemplating the future emancipation of mankind. Special emphasis is placed on Marx's work, in which the ecological issue is brought into direct focus for the first time.

**Schmied-Kowarzik, Wolfdietrich**. Phänomenologische Versuche, sich den Grundlagen der gesellschaftlichen Praxis zu nähern. *Phil Rundsch*, 44(1), 74-80, Mr 97.

Der Artikel setzt sich mit zwei neueren Arbeiten auseinander: Heinrich Rombach versucht in seinem Buch "Phänomenologie des sozialen Lebens: Grundzüge einer phänomenologischen Soziologie" (Freiburg/München 1994) aufzuzeigen, dass alle Grundstrukturen des sozialen Lebens weder substanzontologisch von den Individuen noch systemtheoretisch vom gesellschaftlichen Ganzen her, sondern allein aus der "Konkreativität" der Individuen in der Gemeinschaft verstehbar sind. Diese Strukturen ist nichts Statisches, sondern sind als eine Sozialgenese des Zusichselberkommens der Individuen und der Gesellschaft phänomenologisch zu erschliessen. Diese Sozialgenese wird von Rombach nur als Entwicklung zum Guten hin gesehen. In seinem Buch "Phänomenologie und philosophische Theorie der Arbeit" (2 Bde., Freiburg/München 1994) setzt sich Severin Müller zunächst mit gegenwärtigen Phänomenen der Arbeitswelt und ihrer sozialen Implikation auseinander, um dann die Theorien der Arbeit von Karl Marx, John Locke und Immanuel Kant (in dieser Reihung) zu behandeln. Dabei schliesst er sich am stärksten an Locke an, übersetzt die theoretische Arbeit der Vernunft, wie sie Kant in seiner ersten Kritik praktiziert, auf die Arbeitswelt insgesamt und deutet Marx von einem anthropologischen Vorverständnis her, so dass ihm völlig entgeht, dass Marx im "Kapital" nicht eine phänomenologische Analyse des "Reichs der Notwendigkeit" in ihrer industriellen Gestalt gibt, sondern, dass es ihm um eine "Kritik" ihrer gegenwärtig verkehrten Formbestimmtheit geht, die es revolutionär aufzuheben gilt.

**Schminke, Marshall**. Gender Differences in Ethical Frameworks and Evaluation of Others' Choices in Ethical Dilemmas. *J Bus Ethics*, 16(1), 55-65, Ja 97.

This paper examines the relationship between gender and ethical decision models employed by managers. Subjects completed a survey that measured the extent to which they focused on actions or the outcomes of those actions in determining whether a behavior was ethical or not. The study also examined subjects' reactions to other managers' responses to ethical dilemmas. Results suggest that men and women do not differ in their underlying ethical models, that they do differ in the way in which they evaluate others in ethical situations and that ethical predispositions play an important role in those evaluations.

**Schminke, Marshall** and Ambrose, Maureen L. Asymmetric Perceptions of Ethical Frameworks of Men and Women in Business and Nonbusiness Settings. *J Bus Ethics*, 16(7), 719-729, My 97.

This paper examines the relationship between individuals' gender and their ethical decision models. The study seeks to identify asymmetries in men's and women's approaches to ethical decision making and differences in their perceptions of how same-sex and other-sex managers would likely act in business and nonbusiness situations that present an ethical dilemma. Results indicate that the models employed by men and women differ in both business and nonbusiness settings, that both sexes report changing models when leaving business settings, and that women were better predictors of both sex's likely ethical models.

**Schmirber, Gisela** (ed) and Beck, Heinrich (ed). *Kreativer Friede durch Begegnung der Weltkulturen.* New York, Lang, 1995.

Diese Veröffentlichung entstand aus einem gleichnamigen Projekt am Lehrstuhl für Philosophie I der Universität Bamberg in Zusammenarbeit mit der Hanns-Seidel-Stiftung. Ziel des Projektes ist es, mit den Mitteln philosophischer Reflexion die für die heutigen Kulturen prägenden geistig-religiösen Ursprünge zu erhellen. Der daraus entspringende Prozess der Selbst- und Fremdwahrnehmung intendiert wechselseitige Anerkennung und innovative interkulturelle Kooperation als Grundlage eines menschlich kreativen Friedens. Der Band lässt Repräsentanten verschiedener Fachgebiete und Weltreligionen zur Sprache kommen. Eine "philosophische Exposition" (H. Beck) legt dar, welchen Stellenwert die Abhandlungen "zur allgemeinen Problematik von Kulturbegegnung und Weltfrieden" sowie die Beiträge aus spezifischen Kulturbereichen (Europa—Afrika—Asien—(Latein-)Amerika) im "Dialog der Weltkulturen" besitzen.

**Schmitt, Richard**. *Introduction to Marx and Engels: A Critical Reconstruction.* Boulder, Westview Pr, 1997.

**Schmitt, Richard**. Marx's Concept of Alienation. *Topoi*, 15(2), 163-176, S 96.

Alienation in Marx is commonly interpreted as a characteristic of individuals whose human nature capitalism impairs. Open to question on purely philosophical grounds, this conception is later surrendered by Marx and replaced by a different concept of alienation. New alienation is said to prevail where a society does not have full control over its social life because important decisions are left to the automatic mechanisms of the market. Such a society, Marx believes, lack freedom. Alienation then is lack of freedom. This concept of freedom proves attractive but also difficult to understand.

**Schmitter, Amy M**. Formal Causation and the Explanation of Intentionality in Descartes. *Monist*, 79(3), 368-387, Jl 96.

Descartes's famous skeptical doubts are largely doubts about the explanatory value of then-prevailing causal theories of concept-formation and intentionality —doubts that extend to their underlying metaphysical framework. In place of matter and form, he offers modes and substances, touting their greater explanatory force for physics. Forms become mere modes of extension and formal causation a by-product of efficient agency. For this reason, the explanation of the intentionality of sense-perception provided by the theory of species is unavailable to Descartes; he can account for the causal origins of sensations readily enough, but needs additional resources from the intellect to explain intentionality.

**Schmitz, Kenneth L**. Created Receptivity and the Philosophy of the Concrete. *Thomist*, 61(3), 339-371, Jl 97.

**Schneewind, J B**. "Bayle, Locke, and the Concept of Toleration" in *Philosophy, Religion, and the Question of Intolerance,* Ambuel, David (ed), 3-15. Albany, SUNY Pr, 1997.

**Schneewind, J B** (ed) and Heath, Peter (ed & trans). *Lectures on Ethics.* New York, Cambridge Univ Pr, 1997.

The purpose of the Cambridge Edition is to offer translations of the best modern German edition of Kant's work in a uniform format suitable for Kant scholars. When complete (fourteen volumes are currently envisaged), the edition will include all of Kant's published writings and a generous selection of his unpublished writings such as the *Opus postumum, Handschriftliche Nachlass,* lectures, and correspondence. This volume contains four versions of the lecture notes taken by Kant's students in his university courses in ethics given regularly over a period of some thirty years. The notes are very comprehensive and expound not only Kant's views on ethics but many of his opinions on life and human nature as well. Much of this material has never before been translated into English. As in other volumes in the series, there are copious linguistic and explanatory notes and a glossary of key terms.

**Schneewind, J B** and Lecaldano, Eugenio and Vacatello, Marzio. I metodi dell'etica di Henry Sidgwick. *Iride*, 9(18), 495-511, Ag 96.

Dopo 120 anni dalla pubblicazione dei *Metodi dell'etica* di H. Sidgwick, risaltano con maggiore evidenza i nuclei più originali e significativi delle analisi che vi sono sviluppate. In particolare la presentazione di una dimostrazione razionale dell'utilitarismo che, oltre ad essere del tutto nuova a suo tempo, risulta tuttora come riconoscibile e inconfondibile nella storia di questa concezione normativa. Inoltre la delineazione di un programma di ricerca per la teoria etica che era allora del tutto nuovo, ma che alla fine del XX secolo possiamo riconoscere come fertile e operante malgrado alcuni suoi limiti. (edited)

**Schneider, Jennifer** and Potter, Robert Lyman. Bioethical Analysis of an Integrated Medicine Clinic. *Bioethics Forum*, 12(4), 30-38, Wint 96.

This paper considers the bioethical analysis of an alternative medicine project: first, it proposes a "bioethics analysis grid" constructed from the principles, virtues, and goals established by the discipline of bioethics; second, it describes the development of a public clinic that integrates conventional and natural medicine, and third, it supports the conclusion that this unique project has a core set of values that generally comply with the standards of bioethics.

**Schneider, Martin**. *Primeras Interpretaciones del Mundo en la Modernidad: Descartes y Leibniz.* Córdoba, Pub Univ Nac Córdoba, 1996.

**Schneiderman, Lawrence J** and Kaplan, Robert M and Rosenberg, Esther (& others). Do Physicians' Own Preferences for Life-Sustaining Treatment Influence Their Perceptions of Patients' Preferences? A Second Look. *Cambridge Quart Healthcare Ethics*, 6(2), 131-137, Spr 97.

Purpose: To follow up previous observations that physicians' predictions of their patients end-of-life treatment choices are closer to the choices they would make for themselves than to the choices expressed by their patients. Study: One hundred and eleven patients and 28 physicians completed two advance directive instruments—a procedure-oriented questionnaire and a quality of life questionnaire. The patients expressed their own preferences. Their physicians were asked to complete these instruments in terms of what they thought their patients would want and also what they would want for themselves, if they were in the same situation as their patient. Conclusion: The results show again that physicians perceptions of their patients wishes for treatment are influenced by what they would want for themselves.

**Schneiderman, Lawrence J** and Manning, Sharyn. The Baby K Case: A Search for the Elusive Standard of Medical Care. *Cambridge Quart Healthcare Ethics*, 6(1), 9-18, Winter 97.

A hospital resisted providing life-sustaining treatments for an anencephalic infant on the grounds that such treatment did not fall within the "prevailing standard of medical care." We conducted a phone survey of children's hospitals' physicians and reviewed guidelines and consensus statements by authoritative medical societies. Although there was universal condemnation of prolonged life support of an anencephalic baby, there was little evidence that the hospitals would resist such treatment if parents demanded it. Furthermore, guidelines by professional societies provide no grounds for refusing to treat an anencephalic infant on parental demand. There appears to be little to support the hospital's claim that in the face of parental demand for prolonged life support of an anencephalic infant a "prevailing standard of medical care" exists that rejects such treatment. Instead there appears to be a serious gap between the attitudes of the physicians interviewed as to what constitutes acceptable practice and the declarations of the professional leadership.

**Schneiders, Werner**. "Philosophie der Philosophie: Zur Frage nach dem Philosophiebegriff" in *Grenzen der kritischen Vernunft,* Schmid, Peter A, 32-42. Basel, Schwabe Verlag, 1997.

**Schobbens, Pierre-Yves** and Ryan, Mark. Counterfactuals and Updates as Inverse Modalities. *J Log Lang Info*, 6(2), 123-146, Ap 97.

We point out a simple but hitherto ignored link between the theory of *updates*, the theory of *counterfactuals* and classical modal logic: update is a classical existential modality, counterfactual is a classical universal modality and the accessibility relations corresponding to these modalities are inverses. The Ramsey Rule (often thought esoteric) is simply an axiomatisation of this inverse relationship. (edited)

**Schoen, Edward L**. Galileo and the Church: An Untidy Affair. *Phil Cont World*, 2(3), 23-28, Fall 95.

In his recent review of the Galileo affair, Pope John Paul II confidently proclaimed the intellectual autonomy of religion, comfortably affirming that the methods and ideas of religion are cleanly separable from those of the sciences. Unfortunately, a close review of the actual details of the Galilean controversy reveals that the lesson to be learned from that famous case is not one of sanitary intellectual compartmentalization, but one of entangling interdependencies among scientific, religious and philosophical thought.

**Schönbaumsfeld, Genia**. Wittgensteins Begriff der "Aesthetischen Erklärung" als Paradigma für die Philosophie. *Prima Philosophia*, 10(1), 23-42, 1997.

In *Culture and Value* Wittgenstein writes, *The queer resemblance between a philosophical investigation* and *an aesthetic one* and *Philosophy ought to be written only as a poetic composition.* It is the aim of this paper to elucidate these crucial remarks and to show that there is a striking resemblance between what Wittgenstein calls an "aesthetic explanation" in the *Lectures and Conversations on Aesthetics* and what he calls a "perspicuous representation" in the *Philosophical investigations.* In recognizing the "aesthetic explanation" to be the paradigm of Wittgenstein's conception of philosophy, misinterpretations of his work (such as his being "anti-realist") and of his famous quotation that philosophy must "do away with all explanation" can be avoided.

**Schöndorf, Harald**. God's Place in Descartes' Philosophy (in Spanish). *Univ Phil*, 14(27), 109-129, D 96.

In his *Discourse of Method,* Descartes asserts that God has given us the possibility to distinguish between right and false. This may be a preliminary positive condition for the search for truth in the *Meditations.* The fact that God is mentioned in the *First Meditation* in connection with truth and falsehood shows that for Descartes God has a well-defined function within the *Meditations:* to guarantee truth. This becomes clear in the *Third Meditation,* where the proof of God's existence is based on our experience of contingency as limitation, and this is only possible in relation to the infinite God whose image is our mind itself. On the other hand, the so-called ontological proof of the *Fifth Meditation* has no more validity than mathematical truths. (edited)

**Schöne-Seifert, Bettina**. "Medizinethik" in *Angewandte Ethik: Die Bereichsethiken und ihre theoretische Fundierung,* Nida-Rümelin, Julian (ed), 552-648. Stuttgart, Alfred Kröner, 1996.

**Schönecker, Dieter**. Zur Analytizität der *Grundlegung. Kantstudien*, 87(3), 348-354, 1996.

Without analyzing the terms 'analytic' and 'synthetic', I try to show that the *Grundlegung* as a whole is analytic. In the preface, Kant describes not only the *Grundlegung* but the whole project of the metaphysics of morals. It's first part, the *Grundlegung*, is analytic and only the second part, the later written *Metaphysik der Sitten,* is synthetic. At the end of chapter two, Kant confirms this strategy by saying that the synthetic use of pure practical reason may not be ventured in chapter three of the *Grundlegung.*

**Schoenig, Richard**. The Logical Status of Prayer. *S J Phil*, 35(1), 105-118, Spr 97.

Five common forms of prayer are distinguished. A definition of incoherence is formulated. On the basis of the definition of incoherence and the tenets and practices generally accepted within the Judeo-Christian-Islamic traditions, it is argued that the five forms of prayer are incoherent when directed to the Judeo-Christian-Islamic deity.

**Scholl, Ann**. Legally protecting Fetuses: A Study of the Legal Protections Afforded Organically United Individuals. *Pub Affairs Quart*, 11(2), 141-161, Ap 97.

**Scholz, Sally J**. Civil Disobedience in the Social Theory of Thomas Aquinas. *Thomist*, 60(3), 449-462, Jl 96.

In this article I define civil disobedience and classify it into four forms based on motive and extent of dissent. I then present Thomas Aquinas's account for justified civil disobedience. After first determining how a law or system of laws is unjust, the duty (virtue) of obedience to just and unjust laws is discussed. Finally, I argue that of the four possible forms of civil disobedience, Aquinas's natural Law Theory only clearly allows the fourth, i.e., altruistic disobedience of an unjust system of rule, while at times also apparently allowing the third, i.e., altruistic disobedience of an unjust law.

**Scholz, Sally J** and Groarke, Leo. Seven Principles for Better Practical Ethics. *Teach Phil*, 19(4), 337-355, D 96.

This paper identifies seven problems with traditional approaches to teaching practical (or "applied") ethics. These problems include an over emphasis on theory, intellectualism, formalism, an emphasis on moral disagreement, overspecialization, insularity and negativism. Alternative strategies for ethics courses are suggested, which include: making theory subservient to practice, engaging students in nonintellectual ways, recognizing the limits of formalism, teaching in ways that emphasize agreements, integrating ethics into wider curriculum and public programming, and providing positive examples of moral behavior. These strategies are designed to better assist the student, not only understanding moral theory, but also in being a moral person.

**Schonberg, Sue E** and Lee, Sandra S. Identifying the Real EAP Client: Ensuing Ethical Dilemmas. *Ethics Behavior*, 6(3), 203-212, 1996.

As employee assistance programs (EAPs) have evolved and expanded their scope in the past decade, many factors have contributed to meeting the

**Schoolman, Morton** 900 **AUTHOR INDEX**

demands of conflicting client constituencies in a multifaceted client environment. This article enumerates several of these factors, notes consequences of ensuing conflicts, and ultimately proposes some methods to counter some of these ethical dilemmas in the future. It is the hope that greater recognition and understanding of ethical conflicts in client loyalty within a host organization will foster increased sensitivity on the part of the EAP practitioner toward resolving these conflicts.

**Schoolman, Morton**. Toward a Politics of Darkness: Individuality and Its Politics in Adorno's Aesthetics. *Polit Theory*, 25(1), 57-92, F 97.

**Schopen, Gregory**. The Suppression of Nuns and the Ritual Murder of their Special Dead in Two Buddhist Monastic Texts. *J Indian Phil*, 24(6), 563-592, D 96.

**Schor, Juliet**. What's Wrong with Consumer Capitalism? *The Joyless Economy* after Twenty Years. *Crit Rev*, 10(4), 495-508, Fall 96.

*The Joyless Economy* seeks to explain the paradox of rising consumption and pervasive dissatisfaction, and is thus often cited as a critique of consumer society. Yet it is rather ambivalent as critique. A less ambivalent critique would be predicated on the existence of biases toward private consumption as against public consumption, savings, free time, and the environment. These biases result from two sources: the importance of social comparison and the nonexistence of a market in working hours. Because positional competitions occur far more readily around visible private consumer goods, these take a privileged place in expenditures. This process is compounded by the fact that employers systematically deny opportunities to trade income for leisure.

**Schotsmans, Paul**. Where is Truth? A Commentary from a Medical-Ethical and Personalistic Perspective (in Dutch). *Bijdragen*, 58(2), 153-163, 1997.

The author of this commentary shares with Merks his critique on procedural ethics, a critique which is crucial for medical ethics. Indeed, ethical decision-making procedures have invaded the most important institutes of medical ethics. Recently, this evolution has been criticized for neglecting to establish a foundational ethical culture for medicine. The author thinks personalist ethics can function as such a culture and as an answer to the need for a more comprehensive ethical approach. This leads him to his main critique on Merks's contribution: indeed, where Merks underlines the importance of "human rights" concepts as a tool for ethical reflection, the author warns for the abuses of this concept in the Anglo-American approach of medical ethics, where the concept functions as an instrument for individual self-determination and doesn't refer to the—more Germanic—interpretation of this concept in the lines of a foundation of human dignity. (edited)

**Schott, Robin May**. Gender and "Postmodern War". *Hypatia*, 11(4), 19-29, Fall 96.

In this essay I argue that war is not "above" gender analyses. I question in particular whether the concept of "postmodern war" is adequate to explain the intersections of gender with ethnicity and nationality, which underlie the sexual violence against women in wartime. The poststructuralist concept of the "fluidity" of the category of gender needs to be modified by an analysis of how "nonfluid" configurations of gender are entrenched in material conditions of existence.

**Schouls, Peter A**. Locke, "The Father of Modernity"?: A Discussion of Wolterstorff's *John Locke and the Ethics of Belief*. *Phil Reform*, 61(2), 175-195, 1996.

In this article the author comes to the conclusion that nursing science is a practical science and not an applied science. He tries to explain what a practical science is and denies that conceptual models of nursing are products of nursing science. To characterize the core of nursing science, he gives special attention to the technical and the moral aspect of nursing.

**Schouten, M K D** and De Jong, H Looren. Over Functies en Affordances. *Alg Ned Tijdschr Wijs*, 88(3), 216-228, Jl 96.

In this response to Meijering's (1996) article, we examine the concept of functional analysis. We argue that functional analysis should not be understood as resorting only to intrasystemic functions. Rather, an analysis of the functions of a natural (sub)system should take into account the (sub)system's extrasystemic relations with its environment. The relevance of the ecological niche in functional analysis is mirrored in a propensity view of functions. In addition, this view appears to rest comfortably with a view of science as a multitude of mutually constraining levels of analysis. Our approach is exemplified by Gibson's notion of affordances.

**Schrader, Wolfgang H**. Coscienza morale e realtà secondo J.G. Fichte. *Aquinas*, 39(2), 275-289, My-Ag 96.

**Schramme, Thomas**. Philosophie und Medizin: Ein Blick in aktuelle Veröffentlichungen. *Z Phil Forsch*, 51(1), 115-137, Ja-Mr 97.

This survey article on recent publications in the *Philosophy of Medicine* focuses on classificatory issues in psychiatry, the concepts of health and disease, and personal identity. The main aim is to point at the often neglected possible benefits which medicine provides for philosophy. Another goal is to show that health is not necessarily a value-laden concept (at least not in the way stated in the reviewed literature) since there are two different usages of "health," with only one of them obviously involving subjective values.

**Schrift, Alan D**. Foucault's Reconfiguration of the Subject: From Nietzsche to Butler, Laclau/Mouffe, and Beyond. *Phil Today*, 41(1-4), 153-159, Spr 97.

This paper examines Foucault's thinking on the question of the subject as it evolves from its Nietzschean beginnings to its final formulation in terms of a Self as a "*relation à soi*." Nietzsche's impact is shown in each phase of Foucault's thought: the "death of the subject," the genealogy of the modern, disciplined subject and the "ethical" reflection on subjectivation as the process by which the self relates to, acts upon and constructs itself. The paper concludes that while Foucault did not ultimately resolve the problem of agency, we see Foucaultian solutions in the recent work of Butler, Laclau and Mouffe.

**Schrift, Alan D** (ed). *The Logic of the Gift: Toward an Ethic of Generosity*. New York, Routledge, 1997.

What is a gift? In recent years, attacks upon fundamental notions of social welfare have spurred widespread discussion concerning the nature of gifts and gift giving. What assumptions about gift giving and generosity are at work in our society? Philosophers and anthropologists have established the terms for discussions of the subject. Marcel Mauss helped establish "the gift" as a key concept in anthropology. George Bataille articulated a general economy of expenditure. Martin Heidegger reflected on the *es gibt* of Being. Across disciplines of deconstruction, gender and feminist theory, ethics, philosophy, anthropology, and economics. (publisher, edited)

**Schroeder, Severin**. The Concept of Dreaming: On Three Theses by Malcolm. *Phil Invest*, 20(1), 15-38, Ja 97.

In his monograph *Dreaming*, Norman Malcolm puts forward the following theses: 1) The temporal location of dreams as taking place in one's sleep is not an empirical fact, but determined by grammar. 2) This grammatical determination does not allow dreams a precise date in physical time. 3) Dreams do not consist of mental occurrences. The author tries to give further reasons to believe that 1) is true; he tries to show that 2) is false; and that 3) is not borne out by Malcolm's verificationist main argument, although it can be shown to be largely true for other considerations.

**Schroeder, Steven**. No Goddess Was Your Mother: Western Philosophy's Abandonment of Its Multicultural Matrix. *Phil Cont World*, 2(1), 27-32, Spr 95.

This paper begins with three observations: 1) At what is generally believed to be its origin in ancient Greece, "Western" philosophy is not sharply distinguished from poetry, science, or theology; 2) At what is generally believed to be its origin, "Western" philosophy is not Western; it is born in a multicultural matrix consisting of African, Asian, Middle Eastern, and Southern European influences; 3) As philosophy comes to think of itself as "Western," it separates itself from poetry, science, and the rest of the world—particularly from its roots in Northern Africa. (edited)

**Schröder, Joachim**. A Simple Irredundance Test for Tautological Sequents. *Erkenntnis*, 46(2), 175-183, Mr 97.

From the standpoint of classical logic, irredundancy is a desirable, if not necessary property of valid inferences. Therefore, it would be useful to have a classically adequate calculus in which irredundancy is controlled by an additional notation. For an irredundancy criterion which goes back to Körner, such a notation is presented in this note. The calculus to which this notation is added is the propositional part of the Ketonen version of the classical sequent calculus. The open question of an axiomatization of Körner's criterion is discussed briefly. The connection between this criterion and condensed BCI logic is pointed out.

**Schröder, Jürgen**. Qualia und Physikalismus. *J Gen Phil Sci*, 28(1), 159-181, 1997.

*Qualia and Physicalism*. It is assumed that the following three relations exhaust the possibilities for a physicalist account of qualia: 1) determination, 2) identity, 3) realization. The first relation is immediately rejected because it does not exclude property dualism. The second faces the problem that it is probably impossible to discriminate *empirically* between the identity thesis and the epiphenomenalist position. The third cannot handle qualia adequately, for qualia are not functional properties and the realization relation is only plausible as a relation between physical realizers and functional properties. Finally, if one attempts to replace multiple realization by multiple identities it is shown that the notion of multiple *property* identities is unintelligible. The upshot is that if these three relations exhaust the possibilities of a physicalist construal of qualia then physicalism is wrong.

**Schröter, Joachim**. *Zur Meta-Theorie der Physik*. Hawthorne, de Gruyter, 1996.

Dieses Buch basiert auf Manuskripten zu Veranstaltungen, die der Autor über Grundlagenfragen der Physik an der Universität-Gesamthochschule Paderborn abgehalten hat und wendet sich gleichmassen an Wissenschaftstheoretiker wie interessierte Naturwissenschaftler. Das Thema wird im konzeptionellen Rahmen der auf G. Ludwig zurückgehende Meta-Theorie der Physik dargestellt. (publisher)

**Schubert, William H** and Thomas, Thomas P. Recent Curriculum Theory: Proposals for Understanding, Critical Praxis, Inquiry, and Expansion of Conversation. *Educ Theor*, 47(2), 261-285, Spr 97.

This article is a critical review and reflection of *Understanding Curriculum*, by William Pinar, William Reynolds, Patrick Slattery and Peter Taubman. The authors consider the contention of Pinar, et, al, that *curriculum development*, the primary language form for scholarly writing about the curriculum in past decades, has been superseded by efforts to *understand* curriculum. While finding this a valid portrait of current curriculum thought, Thomas and Schubert caution that the categorization of discourse provided by Pinal et, al. not be reified into opposing camps and question the value of focusing scholarly efforts primarily on "understanding" curriculum. Thomas and Schubert reflect on their efforts to engage the broader community of educators in conversations about curriculum across discourses, popularizing the conversations on the curriculum. (edited)

**Schües, Christina**. The Birth of Difference. *Human Stud*, 20(2), 243-252, Ap 97.

Although birth marks the entrance of a human being into the world and establishes the very possibility of experience, the philosophical implications of this event have been largely ignored in the history of thought. This is particularly troubling in phenomenology in general and in the work of Martin Heidegger in particular. While Heidegger raises the issue of birth he drops it very quickly on the path to defining *Dasein*'a existence as constituted from the standpoint of death, as being-towards-death. In this paper I argue, contra Heidegger, that intentional existence can only be understood from the standpoint of birth. I begin by showing that intentionality inheres in a double difference that is fundamentally dependent on birth insofar as birth is an original differentia*ting* from prenatal existence. I conclude with the argument that only a philosophy that regards *Dasein* from the standpoint of birth, as being-from-birth, can give an adequate account of humans as beings who *live* with others and who *can* initiate sence constitution and action.

**Schüklenk, Udo** and Stein, Edward and Kerin, Jacinta (& others). The Ethics of Genetic Research on Sexual Orientation. *Hastings Center Rep*, 27(4), 6-13, Jl-Ag 97.

Research into the genetic component of some complex behaviors often causes controversy, depending on the social meaning and significance of the behavior. Research into sexual orientation—simplistically referred to as "gay gene" research—is an example of research that provokes intense controversy. This research is worrisome for many reasons, including a long history of abuse against homosexuals. But there are other reasons to worry. The very motivation for seeking an "origin" of homosexuality reveals homophobia. Moreover, such research may lead to prenatal tests that claim to predict for homosexuality.

**Schueler, G F**. Why Modesty Is a Virtue. *Ethics*, 107(3), 467-485, Ap 97.

This article has two parts. In the first, I will examine some of the best-known recent accounts of modesty. I will argue that none of these accounts is successful in explaining the relevant sort of modesty in such a way as to both be plausible in itself and make sense of the idea that modesty might be a virtue. Roughly speaking, I will argue that Bennett's witticism points to a serious problem for all these accounts. In the second part of the article, I will propose and defend a different account of modesty against various sorts of attack. This account, I will argue, both avoids the difficulties of the other accounts and suggests an interesting answer to the question of why modesty is a virtue. (edited)

**Schürmann, Reiner**. How to Read Heidegger. *Grad Fac Phil J*, 19/20 (2/1), 3-8, 1997.

**Schürmann, Reiner**. Symbolic Difference. *Grad Fac Phil J*, 19/20(2/1), 9-38, 1997.

**Schürmann, Reiner**. Symbolic Praxis. *Grad Fac Phil J*, 19/20(2/1), 39-66, 1997.

**Schuhmann, Karl**. "Philosophy and Art in Munich Around the Turn of the Century" in *In Itinere* European Cities and the Birth of Modern Scientific Philosophy, Poli, Roberto (ed), 35-51. Amsterdam, Rodopi, 1997.

**Schulman, Charles Eric** and Shapiro, Daniel Edward. Ethical and Legal Issues in E-Mail Therapy. *Ethics Behavior*, 6(2), 107-124, 1996.

Psychologists and psychiatrists recently started using electronic mail (e-mail) to conduct therapy. This article explores relevant ethical and legal issues including, among others, the nature of the professional relationship, boundaries of competence, informed consent, treating minors, confidentiality and the duty to warn and protect. To illustrate these complex issues, two services currently operating are discussed. To address potential hazards to clients and the profession, a new ethical standard for e-main therapists is offered.

**Schulte, John M** and Cochrane, Donald B. *Ethics in School Counseling*. New York, Teachers College Pr, 1995.

The authors provide a set of principles that help guide school counselors through the ethical crises they face. Case histories are analyzed to illustrate the many kinds of problems that may arise in the relationships among counselors, students, parents and teachers. Larger issues of ethical reasoning and principles are related and developed and examples of typical dilemmas faced by school counselors are examined. One chapter critiques the professional ethics codes featured in the appendices: the standards of the American Counseling Association and the American School Counselor Association.

**Schulte, Oliver** and Bicchieri, Cristina. Common Reasoning about Admissibility. *Erkenntnis*, 45(2 & 3), 299-325, Nov 96.

We analyze common reasoning about admissibility in the strategic and extensive form of a game. We define a notion of sequential proper admissibility in the extensive form and show that, in finite extensive games with perfect recall, the strategies that are consistent with common reasoning about sequential proper admissibility in the extensive form are exactly those that are consistent with common reasoning about admissibility in the strategic form representation of the game. Thus in such games the solution given by common reasoning about admissibility does not depend on how the strategic situation is represented. We further explore the links between iterated admissibility and backward and forward induction.

**Schulthess, Daniel**. L'idée d'une doctrine cohérentiste de la justification épistémique. *Rev Theol Phil*, 129(2), 127-139, 1997.

Dans la tradition philosophique marquée par Descartes et l'empirisme, l'idée de justification épistémique a été vue le plus souvent en termes de construction sur des *fondements* qui seraient autant de points de départ immédiatement justifiés. L'article expose une tout autre approche de la question, due au philosophe Keith Lehrer (dont la *Revue* a publié récemment *L'unité de la raison théorique et de la raison pratique*, RThPh 127/4 (1995), p. 349-356), approche dans laquelle la justification épistémique découle d'un rapport de *cohérence* entre des croyances qui ne sont jamais des points de départ immédiatement justifiés. Ce qui est alors décisif pour la justification d'une croyance, c'est d'écarter ou de neutraliser toutes les objections qu'on peut élever contre elle. A partir d'un exemple, l'article présente cette approche de la justification épistémique et expose une difficulté que celle-ci rencontre.

**Schulthess, Peter**. Der Weg weg von der Metaphysik—ein Rundweg?. *Frei Z Phil Theol*, 44(1-2), 5-17, 1997.

**Schultz, Dawson S** and Carnevale, Franco A. Engagement and Suffering in Responsible Caregiving: On Overcoming Maleficience in Health Care. *Theor Med*, 17(3), 189-207, S 96.

The thesis of this article is that engagement and suffering are essential aspects of responsible caregiving. The sense of medical responsibility engendered by engaged caregiving is referred to herein as 'clinical *phronesis*', i.e., practical wisdom in health care, or, simply, practical health care wisdom. The idea of clinical phronesis calls to mind a *relational* or *communicative* sense of medical responsibility which can best be understood as a kind of 'virtue ethics', yet one that is informed by the exigencies of moral discourse and dialogue, as well as by the technical rigors of formal reasoning. The ideal of clinical phronesis is not (necessarily) contrary to the more common understandings of medical responsibility as either *beneficence* or *patient autonomy*—except, of course, when these notions are taken in their "disengaged" form (reflecting the malaise of "modern medicine"). (edited)

**Schultz, Margarita**. Violencia femenina y autorreferencia. *Cuad Etica*, 15-16, 147-153, 1993.

New criteria is looked at in order to examine female violence as a problem itself. Not all violence done by women should be called female violence. Historically, violence is associated with the male. There is a female stereotype that makes the woman be a passive, patient, peaceful and subordinated being. This stereotype is necessarily connected to the social roles. Are those characteristics virtues or faults? At least they are cause of discrimination. There is a "right to female badness". The increase of female violence may be a consciousness raising of this right. (edited)

**Schulz, Heiko**. Philosophie als Existenzwissenschaft: Empirismuskritik und Wissenschaftsklassifikation bei Soren Kierkegaard. *Theol Phil*, 71(2), 205-223, 1996.

The paper aims at clarifying Kierkegaard's classification of the sciences—especially his concept of an existential science. It starts with the so-called falsification-debate, which—in the fifties and sixties—focussed on the claim that religious utterances are meaningless. A Kierkegaard-inspired critique of empiricism in general, the falsification-criterion in particular leads to the distinction between sciences which operate within the realm of pure *ideality* (mathematics, formal ontology) and those which are directed towards *factual being* (all natural and historical sciences). Drawing on this distinction Kierkegaard's theory of subjectivity versus objectivity and its impact on the different kinds of science is being discussed, in order finally to explain his concept of an existential science.

**Schulz, Peter**. Il concetto di coscienza nella fenomenologia di E. Husserl e di E. Stein. *Aquinas*, 39(2), 291-305, My-Ag 96.

**Schulze, Hans-Joachim** and De Mey, Langha. Indoctrination and Moral Reasoning: A Comparison between Dutch and East German Students. *J Moral Educ*, 25(3), 309-323, S 96.

This contribution presents the results of an empirical study aiming to test Kohlberg's complexity hypothesis. It is assumed that in complex sociopolitical surroundings, individuals are stimulated into higher stages of moral judgments than in a less complicated environment. In order to test the hypothesis we compared the stages of moral judgments of Dutch and former German Democratic Republic (GDR) students belonging to two types of schools. The Dutch (Amsterdam) group was split into VWO (preuniversity) students and MAVO (low general secondary education) students. The East German students attend the "Gymnasium" (preuniversity) and the "Mittelschule" (low general secondary education). The mean age of the Dutch VWO-students was 16.33 and of the MAVO students, 15.39. The mean age of the East German "Gymnasium" students was 16.35 and that of the "Mittelschule" students was 16.00. The individuals of the Dutch and East German groups were asked to rate the moral problems in the Sociomoral Reflection Objective Measure. The scores were subjected to multivariate analyses of variance to detect differences between the groups. The results did not support Kohlberg's complexity hypothesis.

**Schumacher, Bernard**. ¿La filosofía como amor del saber o saber efectivo?. *Sapientia*, 51(200), 347-374, 1996.

The author critically discusses the nature of the philosophical act presented by the German contemporary philosopher, Josef Pieper. I) The different elements which constitute the philosophical act are presented and compared to scientific knowledge and to the world of *praxis*. II) Pieper's conception of theology is likewise exposed with reference to both Greek mythology and the whole of the Christian tradition. III) Finally, the problematic of the relationship between philosophy and theology is addressed from Pieper's perspective. Developing an original interpretation of Plato and of the concept of tradition, he argues that the philosophical act must integrate prephilosophical truths, including revelation, if philosophy is to be true to its orientation towards the whole of reality, which it seeks to understand under every knowable aspect. The philosopher—who belongs to a specific culture, religion (or lack thereof), historical time, etc.—necessarily has a particular "Weltanschauung" which is of the order of faith (including the choice not to believe) and which cannot be excluded from his philosophical reflection.

**Schumacher, Christian**. Acerca del Pensador Profesional. *Ideas Valores*, 20-28, Ag 97.

**Schumacher, Christian**. Sobre la Facticidad de la Memoria. *Ideas Valores*, 53-68, Ap 97.

How can we be sure about the facticity of our memories? Sceptical arguments abound and convincing answers are rare. In this essay, the main traditional answers to this problem are discussed and found unsatisfactory. Then, based on a detailed reading of Norman Malcolm's arguments from ordinary language, a "distributed" public form of justification for memory is proposed which effectively answers some of the doubts about the subject, even though the result is a somewhat weak form of justification.

**Schummer, Joachim**. "Philosophie der Stoffe, Bestandsaufnahme und Ausblicke" in *Philosophie der Chemie: Bestandsaufnahme und Ausblick*, Schummer, Joachim (ed), 143-164. Wurzburg, Koenigshausen, 1996.

The first part of this essay tells the story of an old struggle between philosophy of matter and philosophy of form in broad outline, from the pre-Socratics to analytical philosophy, leading to a philosophical and metaphorical "dematerialization" of the world (ontology), knowledge (epistemology) and language (mass terms). The second part argues, against the background of ecological crisis, for the need of sophisticating both our ordinary and scientific concepts of materials and it gives an outline of future philosophical contributions to these problems.

**Schummer, Joachim**. *Realismus und Chemie: Philosophische Untersuchungen der Wissenschaft von den Stoffen*. Wurzburg, Koenigshausen, 1996.

Against the background of recent concepts of scientific entity realism and experimentalism, especially those of Rom Harré, this book provides a nonphysicalistic philosophical approach to chemistry. Chemistry is considered to be the fundamental science of substances looking for a theoretically supported classification that enables to predict and create new substances. The development and methodological refinement of this scientific approach is dealt with along the whole history of chemistry, from Aristotle to modern synthetic chemistry. Fundamental concepts, classificatory approaches and theoretical reasoning of chemistry are shown to be inherently connected to experimental operations.

**Schummer, Joachim** (ed) and Psarros, Nikos (ed) and Ruthenberg, Klaus (ed). *Philosophie der Chemie: Bestandsaufnahme und Ausblick*. Wurzburg, Koenigshausen, 1996.

The German working group "Philosophy and Chemistry" (founded in 1993) has collected nine articles that provide a comprehensive survey of what have been done in the past and what should be done in a future philosophy of chemistry. Since many authors find a notorious neglect of chemistry in the past, they try to explain this neglect from various aspects among which reductionism seems to be the most important.

**Schurz, Gerhard**. "Die Goodman-Paradoxie: ein Invarianz—und Relevanzproblem" in *Das weite Spektrum der analytischen Philosophie*, Lenzen, Wolfgang, 290-306. Hawthorne, de Gruyter, 1997.

The deep problem behind Goodman's paradox is *linguistic relativism*: there exist *intertranslatable languages* L and L* such that an inductive relation (between theory and evidence) in L corresponds to an antiinductive relation in L*. This paper suggests a solution of Goodman's paradox which consists of two components. The first component is a *pragmatic criterion* for the *choice among intertranslatable languages*. The existence of such a criterion refutes the traditional view of the *cognitive equivalence* of intertranslatable languages. The second component is a criterion of *relevant observation pattern*, which tells us which statements are inductively projectable *within* a given language.

**Schurz, Gerhard**. Hume's Is-Ought Thesis in Logics with Alethic-Deontic Bridge Principles. *Log Anal*, 37(147-8), 265-293, S-D 94.

Various logical investigations of Hume's *is-ought* thesis have been performed in alethic-deontic logics (a.d.-logics) which do not contain is-ought bridge principles (BPs) among their axioms. After a brief overview of these investigations, the article turns to the question what happens if some of the following three BPs are added to standard a.d.-logics: the *ought-can* principle, the *means-end* principle, and the *must-ought* principle. It is proved that even in this case a 'weak' Hume thesis holds: every (categorial or conditional) obligation or permission derivable from purely descriptive premises will be trivial in a precise logical sense.

**Schurz, Gerhard** and Prendinger, Helmut. Reasoning about Action and Change. *J Log Lang Info*, 5(2), 209-245, 1996.

Reasoning about change is a central issue in research on human and robot planning. We study an approach to reasoning about action and change in a dynamic logic setting and provide a solution to problems which are related to the *frame problem*. Unlike most work on the frame problem the logic described in this paper is *monotonic*. It (implicitly) allows for the occurrence of actions of multiple agents by introducing nonstationary notions of waiting and test. The need to state a large number of "frame axioms" is alleviated by introducing a concept of *chronological preservation* to dynamic logic. As a side effect, this concept permits the encoding of *temporal* properties in a natural way. We compare the relative merits of our approach and nonmonotonic approaches as regards different aspects of the frame problem. Technically, we show that the resulting extended systems of propositional dynamic logic preserve (weak) completeness, finite model property and decidability.

**Schutte, Ofelia**. A Critique of Normative Heterosexuality: Identity, Embodiment, and Sexual Difference in Beauvoir and Irigaray. *Hypatia*, 12(1), 40-62, Wint 97.

The distinction between heterosexuality and homosexuality does not allow for sufficient attention to be given to the question of non-normative heterosexualities. This paper develops a feminist critique of normative sexuality, focusing on alternative readings of sex and/or gender offered by Beauvoir and Irigaray. Despite their differences, both accounts contribute significantly to dismantling the lure of normative sexuality in heterosexual relations—a dismantling necessary to the construction of a feminist social and political order.

**Schuwer, André** (trans) and Rojcewicz, Richard (trans). *Plato's Sophist*. Bloomington, Indiana Univ Pr, 1997.

In *Plato's Sophist*, Heidegger approaches Plato through Aristotle, devoting the first part of the lectures to an extended commentary on Book VI of the *Nichomachean Ethics*. In a line-by-line interpretation of Plato's later dialogue, the *Sophist*, Heidegger then takes up the relation of Being and nonbeing, the ontological problematic that forms the essential link between Greek philosophy and Heidegger's thought.

**Schwabsky, Barry**. Resistances: Meyer Schapiro's *Theory and Philosophy of Art*. *J Aes Art Crit*, 55(1), 1-5, Wint 97.

**Schwartz, David T**. The Limits of Self Interest: An Hegelian Critique of Gauthier's Compliance Problem. *SW Phil Rev*, 13(1), 137-146, Ja 97.

It is difficult to imagine two more disparate moral philosophers than G.W.F. Hegel and David Gauthier. Because of this, many would quickly dismiss Hegel's dialectical methods in the *Philosophy of Right* as at best irrelevant—and at worst antithetical—to the analytic project of Gauthier's *Morals by Agreement*. This is unfortunate, for a closer look reveals that the *Philosophy of Right* in fact offers both a principled description and a conceptual diagnosis of the fundamental difficulty facing contractarian accounts of moral obligation—the problem of moral compliance. Employing a nonmetaphysical interpretation of Hegel's dialectic, this paper seeks to demonstrate how Hegel's claims in the *Philosophy of Right*—specifically his critique of Civil Society—are indeed relevant to analyzing Gauthier's 'compliance problem.' Specifically, the paper seeks to establish 1) the historical claim that Hegel anticipated this primary difficulty of moral contractarianism and 2) the philosophical claim that Gauthier's own solution to the problem succeeds only to the extent that it incorporates essential aspects of Hegel's categorial critique.

**Schwartz, Gary**. "Toni Morrison at the Movies: Theorizing Race Through *Imitation of Life* (for Barbara Siegel)" in *Existence in Black: An Anthology of Black Existential Philosophy*, Gordon, Lewis R (ed), 111-128. New York, Routledge, 1997.

The focus of this essay is the initial version of the film *Imitation of Life* (1934) and its imbedded presence in, and interactivity with, the text of Toni Morrison's *Bluest Eye*. What is imitation of life? It is the state, condition, process or concatenation of phenomena in which one cannot lead one's life as one is naturally endowed; a prevalent and powerful imposition of bad faith. There is a barrier of denial which demarcates the genuine full life from imitation. *Imitation of Life* and *The Bluest Eye* atomize the problem's structure and its consequences.

**Schwartz, Michael Alan** and Wiggins, Osborne P. Edmund Husserl's Influence on Karl Jaspers's Phenomenology. *Phil Psychiat Psych*, 4(1), 15-36, Mr 97.

Karl Jaspers's phenomenology remains important today, not solely because of its continuing influence in some areas of psychiatry, but because, if fully understood, it can provide a method and set of concepts for making new progress in the science of psychopathology. In order to understand this method and set of concepts, it helps to recognize the significant influence that Edmund Husserl's early work, *Logical Investigations*, exercised on Jaspers's formulation of them. We trace the Husserlian influence while clarifying the main components of Jaspers's method. Jaspers adopted Husserl's notions of intuition, description, and presuppositionlessness, transforming them when necessary in order to serve the investigations of the psychopathologist. Jaspers also took over from Wilhelm Dilthey and others the tools of understanding (*Verstehen*) and self-transposal. The Diltheyian procedures were integrated into the Husserlian ones to produce a method that enables psychiatrists to define the basic kinds of psychopathological mental states.

**Schwartz, P** and Rodríguez Braun, Carlos. Las relaciones entre Jeremías Bentham y S. Bolívar. *Telos (Spain)*, 1(3), 45-68, O 92.

**Schwartz, Pedro**. ¿Importan los hechos para los juicios morales? Una defensa contra la navaja de Hume basada en la noción de coste de oportunidad. *Telos (Spain)*, 5(2), 87-113, D 96.

David Hume deplored the habit of philosophers to slide from propositions with *the usual copulations of propositions, is and is not* into propositions connected *with an ought and ought not*. G.E. Moore maintained that the good could not be reduced to other sensible qualities. The claims of natural law, the principle of utility and Pareto equivalence to solve the logical and metaphysical dichotomy of value and fact are thus disposed of. Hume's recommendation to give reasons for linking statements of fact with statements of value is obeyed in this essay with the help of Amartya Sen's distinction between basic and non basic values. (edited)

**Schwartz, Robert**. Symbols and Thought. *Synthese*, 106(3), 399-407, Mr 96.

No one need deny the importance of language to thought and cognition. At the same time, there is a tendency in studies of mind and mental functioning to assume that properties and principles of linguistic, or language-like, forms of representation must hold of forms of thought and representation in general. Consideration of a wider range of symbol systems shows that this is not so. In turn, various claims and arguments in cognitive theory that depend on assumptions applicable only to linguistic systems, do not go through or become difficult to state in a manner that makes them both interesting and plausible.

**Schwartz, Thomas**. *De Re* Language, *De Re* Eliminability, and the Essential Limits of Both. *J Phil Log*, 26(5), 521-544, O 97.

*De re* modality is eliminable if there is an effective translation of all wffs into non-*de re* equivalents. We cannot have logical equivalence unless 'logic' has odd theses, but we can have material equivalence by banning all essences, something the non-*de re* facts let us do, or by giving everything such humdrum essences as self-identity and banning the more interesting ones. Eliminability cannot be got from weaker assumptions, nor independent ones of even modest generality. The net philosophical import is that, quite apart from the merits of essentialism, *de re* language has scant utility.

**Schwartz, Yosef**. From Negation to Silence: Maimonides' Reception in the Latin West (in Hebrew). *Iyyun*, 45, 389-406, O 96.

**Schwarze, Maria G** and Mikenberg, Irene F and Lewin, Renato A. P1 Algebras. *Stud Log*, 53(1), 21-28, F 94.

In [3] the authors proved that the deductive system P1 introduced by Sette in [6] is algebraizable. In this paper we study the main features of the class of algebras thus obtained. The main results are a complete description of the free algebras in *n* generators and that this is not a congruence modular quasi-variety.

**Schwarzenbach, Sibyl A**. On Civic Friendship. *Ethics*, 107(1), 97-128, O 96.

The paper defends an Aristotelian conception of "civic friendship" as a necessary prerequisite for justice in the modern state. Part I presents Aristotle's idea of *politike philia* and distinguishes it from personal friendship, political patronage or a thick brotherhood. *Politike philia* is a form of reciprocal good will and practical agreement between citizens on constitutional essentials and works via the political process and public norms. I argue that neither the greater size of the modern state, nor the added new complexity of civil society, essentially compromises Aristotle's position. Finally, since mainly women have performed the friendship labor in modern society, their entry *en masse* into the public domain, provides the occasion for again acknowledging the importance of *philia* for political life.

**Schweickart, David**. Dr. Pangloss Goes to Market. *Crit Rev*, 10(3), 333-352, Sum 96.

David Ramsay Steele's *From Marx to Mises* argues correctly that the standard account of the economic calculation debate is a misrepresentation. Mises and Hayek were not bested by Lange and Taylor. However, it is not true, as Steele claims, that socialists have yet to face the Misesian challenge, nor that the debate over socialist calculation sheds much light on the recent collapse of communism. Steele's critiques of market socialism and worker self-management and his treatment of Marx are, moreover, deficient, as a consequence of his "Libertarian Panglossism."

**Schwepker, Jr, Charles H** and Ingram, Thomas N. Improving Sales Performance through Ethics: The Relationship Between Salesperson Moral Judgment and Job Performance. *J Bus Ethics*, 15(11), 1151-1160, N 96.

This study examines the relationship between salespeople's moral judgment and their job performance. Results indicate a positive relationship between moral judgment and job performance when certain characteristics are present. Implications for sales managers and sales researchers are provided. Additionally, directions for future research are given.

**Schwerin, Alan**. Some Thoughts on Thinking and Teaching Styles. *Inquiry (USA)*, 16(1), 48-54, Fall 96.

**Schwitzgebel, Eric**. Theories in Children and the Rest of Us. *Proc Phil Sci Ass*, 3(Suppl), S202-S210, 1996.

I offer an account of theories useful in addressing the question of whether children are young theoreticians whose development can be regarded as the product of theory change. I argue that to regard a set of propositions as a theory is to be committed to evaluating that set in terms of its explanatory power. If theory change is the substance of cognitive development, we should see patterns of affect and arousal consonant with the emergence and resolution of explanation-seeking curiosity. Affect has largely been ignored as a potential source of support or disconfirmation for the "theory theory" of development.

**Schwyzer, Hubert**. Subjectivity in Descartes and Kant. *Phil Quart*, 47(188), 342-357, Jl 97.

**Schyve, Paul M**. Patient Rights and Organization Ethics: The Joint Commission Perspective. *Bioethics Forum*, 12(2), 13-20, Sum 96.

A health care organization has an obligation to act in an ethical manner in clinical and business relationships with the public it serves. When examined closely, the boundary between these clinical relationships and business relationships is blurred, as is the boundary between clinical ethics and business ethics. Examples of ethical challenges that arise in a health care organization's business relationships are identified and a method for solving these challenges suggested. *Joint Commission* standards that address an organization's business ethics, with special reference to managed care, are reviewed. It is suggested that the function of current ethics mechanisms in health care organizations (e.g., ethics committees and consultation services) be expanded to encompass business ethics.

**Sciaccaluga, Nicoletta**. L'anticipazione nella scienza baconiana. *Teoria*, 16(2), 107-130, 1996.

**Scillitani, Lorenzo**. Fenomenologia del giuramento: un approccio antropologico. *Riv Int Filosof Diritto*, 73(4), 704-716, O-D 96.

**Scillitani, Lorenzo**. Un'introduzione all'antropologia giuridica. *Riv Int Filosof Diritto*, 74(4), 338-344, Ap-Je 97.

**Scitovsky, Tibor**. My Own Criticism of The Joyless Economy. *Crit Rev*, 10(4), 595-605, Fall 96.

*The Joyless Economy* focused on the boredom of the idle rich and neglected the boredom of the idle and idled poor. However, their boredom is much more serious than what the book dealt with, because it is chronic and often incurable. It usually begins with the neglect of destitute children who never learn how to concentrate on learning in school, become unruly and often end up unemployed, and have no better way than violence to release their energies.

**Scocozza, Antonio**. "Una polemica storiografica nel Cile del XIX secolo: Bello, Lastarria, Chacón" in *Lo Storicismo e la Sua Storia: Temi, Problemi, Prospettive*, Cacciatore, Giuseppe (ed), 218-232. Milano, Guerini, 1997.

**Scolnicov, Samuel**. The Private and Public Logos: Philosophy and the Other in Greek Thought until Socrates (in Hebrew). *Iyyun*, 45, 463-470, O 96.

There is in Greek thought no true subjectivity but only a 'generalized individuality'. For Heraclitus introspection yields not the idiosyncratic but the common logos, just as Parmenides is enjoined to decide for himself although his conclusion is foregone and inescapable. Protagoras accepts the necessity of personal persuasion but the expression of persuasion is now seen as political, placed in the interpersonal domain. For Socrates, as for Parmenides, the decision of the elenchus is given beforehand. But, whereas for the Eleatic shame plays no role, in the Socratic elenchus shame is an essential element. But this shame should not be confused with modern conscience. For Socrates, truth, even if attainable only by individual alone, remains always one for all.

**Scotland, Robert W** and Williams, David M and Humphries, Christopher J. Confusion in Philosophy: A Comment on Williams (1992). *Synthese*, 108(1), 127-136, Jl 96.

Patricia Williams made a number of claims concerning the methods and practice of cladistic analysis and classification. Her argument rests upon the distinction of two kinds of hierarchy: a 'divisional hierarchy' depicting 'evolutionary' descent and the Linnean hierarchy describing taxonomic groups in a classification. Williams goes on to outline five problems with cladistics that lead her to the conclusion that systematists should "eliminate cladism as a school of biological taxonomy and to replace it either with something that is philosophically coherent or to replace it with 'pure' methodology, untainted by theory" (Williams 1992, 151). Williams makes a number of points which she feels collectively add up to insurmountable problems for cladistics. We examine Williams's views concerning the 'two hierarchies' and consider what cladists currently understand about the status of ancestors. We will demonstrate that Williams has seriously misunderstood many modern commentators on this subject and all of her "five persistent problems" are derivable from this misunderstanding.

**Scott, Alexander D** and Scott, Michael. What's in the Two Envelope Paradox?. *Analysis*, 57(1), 34-41, Ja 97.

**Scott, Brian M**. Technical Notes on a Theory of Simplicity. *Synthese*, 109(2), 281-289, N 96.

Recently Samuel Richmond, generalizing Nelson Goodman, has proposed a measure of the simplicity of a theory that takes into account not only the polymorphicity of its models but also their internal homogeneity. By this measure a theory is simple if small subsets of its models exhibit only a few distinct (i.e., nonisomorphic) structures. Richmond shows that his measure, unlike that given by Goodman's theory of simplicity of predicates, orders the order relations in an intuitively satisfactory manner. In this note I formalize his presentation and suggest an improvement designed to overcome certain technical difficulties.

**Scott, Campbell L** and Stam, Henderikus J. The Psychological Subject and Harré's Social Psychology: An Analysis of a Constructionist Case. *J Theor Soc Behav*, 26(4), 327-352, D 96.

Taking Ron Harré's social constructionism as a focus we point to and discuss the issue of the *a priori* psychological subject in social constructionist theory. While Harré indicates that interacting, intending beings are necessary for conversation to occur, he assumes that the primary human reality is conversation and that psychological life emerges from this social domain. Nevertheless, we argue that a fundamental and agentive psychological subject is implicit to his constructionist works. Our critical analyses focus upon Harré's understandings of persons, human development and human agency. Our intention is neither to suggest that this latent entity must be understood in a Cartesian sense nor it is to ask for an explicit account of an autonomous agent. Rather, our claim is simply that psychological subjectivity is reflexively entailed in Harré's human psychology. We suggest that this pertains more generally to social constructionist theory.

**Scott, Charles E**. On Originating and Presenting Another Time. *Epoche*, 3(1 & 2), 25-42, 1995.

**Scott, Charles E**. Thinking Non-Interpretively: Heidegger on Technology and Heraclitus. *Epoche*, 1(1), 13-40, 1993.

**Scott, David**. Leibniz and the Two Clocks. *J Hist Ideas*, 58(3), 445-463, Jl 97.

Especially in his writings on occasionalism Leibniz often uses an example involving two clocks. The example illustrates a range of hypotheses that explain the connections between substances in the world. The most important of these hypotheses are Leibniz's own doctrine of the pre-established harmony and Malebranche's occasionalism. For Leibniz the two clocks' example illustrates the superiority of the hypothesis of the preestablished harmony. Whether the example succeeds in this regard is the primary question of this paper and the conclusion is that the example fails to illustrate Leibniz's point.

**Scott, David**. Malebranche on the Soul's Power. *Stud Leibniz*, 28(1), 37-57, 1996.

Dieser Aufsatz untersucht Malebranches Begriff der Macht oder Kraft des Willens, die für Malebranche eine notwendige Bedingung der Freiheit ist. Mein Ziel ist, festzustellen, welcher Art genau die Macht des Willens ist, indem ich Malebranches Hauptdarstellungen zu Freiheit, Sünde und Tugend untersuche. Der problematischste Zug dieser Lehre zeigt sich in Verbindung mit Malebranches Okkasionalismus, einer Lehre, die die kausale Ohnmacht aller spirituellen und materiellen Schöpfung zu benötigen scheint und innerhalb

Scott, Elizabeth 904 AUTHOR INDEX

derer Gott das einzige kausal wirkende Wesen ist. Wie wirkt sich dieser Grundsatz auf Malebranches Lehre von der Kraft der Seele aus? Welche Art Kraft ist innerhalb des okkasionalistischen Systems zulässig? Malebranches Antworten auf diese Fragen, die ich in diesem Aufsatz kurz darstelle, enthalten eine wichtige Unterscheidung zwischen dem 'Realen' und dem 'Moralischen' oder dem Ontologischen und dem Deontologischen. Ob diese Unterscheidung Malebranche weiterhilft, ist eine Frage, die ich offenlasse.

**Scott, Elizabeth** and Martin, Ursula. The Order Types of Termination Orderings on Monadic Terms, Strings and Multisets. *J Sym Log*, 62(2), 624-635, Je 97.

We consider total well-founded orderings on monadic terms satisfying the replacement and full invariance properties. We show that any such ordering on monadic terms in one variable and two unary function symbols must have order type *omega*, *omega*$^2$ or *omega*$^{omega}$. We show that a familiar construction gives rise to continuum many such orderings of order type *omega*. We construct a new family of such orderings of order type *omega*$^2$ and show that there are continuum many of these. We show that there are only four such orderings of order type *omega*$^{omega}$, the two familiar recursive path orderings and two closely related orderings. We consider also total well-founded orderings on $N^n$ which are preserved under vector addition. We show that any such ordering must have order type *omega*$^k$ for some 1 equal to or less then *k* equal to or less then *n*. We show that if *k* equal to *n* there are continuum many such orderings, and if $k = n$ there are only *n!*, the *n!* lexicographic orderings.

**Scott, Gary Alan**. Foucault's Analysis of Power's Methodologies. *Auslegung*, 21(2), 125-133, Sum 96.

This essay is an exposition and analysis of the contrast Michel Foucault draws in *The History of Sexuality Vol. 1*, between an outmoded conception of power as negatively restraining (which he terms "juridico-discursive") and his notion of power as productive, ubiquitous, and strategically dynamic. In *The Order of Things*, Foucault had already shown how the locus of sovereignty changes in the *classical age* without either its structure being called into question or its theoretical warrant being exhibited. But he shows this by utilizing the term *sovereignty* himself in all its richness and ambiguity. Contrasting his use of "sovereignty" with his more radical notion of fragmentary and inescapable "power," the essay concludes by arguing that at issue here is not the preemptive self-control of critical theory but normalizing interventions in the domain of everyday behaviors and practices.

**Scott, Gary Alan** and Welton, William A. An Overlooked Motive in Alcibiades' *Symposium* Speech. *Interpretation*, 24(1), 67-84, Fall 96.

The *Symposium's* infamous story of Alcibiades' attempt to seduce Socrates enacts a contrast between two kinds of Eros: the Eros of which Diotima speaks and the acquisitive Eros Alcibiades exhibits. This paper claims that Socrates resists Alcibiades' erotic advances not because he is incapable of love for particular persons and not because he champions an ascetic ideal, but rather because Alcibiades is attempting to dominate the philosopher by transacting an exchange with him, showing thereby that Socrates is corruptible. Most commentators have overlooked Alcibiades' motive—to gain an advantage (*pleonektein*) over Socrates in order to sully the philosopher and relieve his own sense of shame. We examine the evidence for this motive, and argue that it is chiefly to preserve his freedom that Socrates eschews the exchange.

**Scott, Michael** and Scott, Alexander D. What's in the Two Envelope Paradox?. *Analysis*, 57(1), 34-41, Ja 97.

**Scott-Kakures, Dion**. Self-Knowledge, Akrasia, and Self-Criticism. *Philosophia (Israel)*, 25(1-4), 267-295, Ap 97.

In the essay I characterize what I take to be a plausible account of akratic action. According to the account, akratic actions do not constitute a class of peculiarly irrational actions, and so do not constitute a difficulty for familiar belief/desire models of the explanation of action. Rather, I argue, akrasia is to understood by appeal to a failure of self-knowledge. Such a view offers a far simpler, more natural, and more elegant explanation of the phenomenon we term "akrasia." It explains what is puzzling about akrasia as well as displaying akrasia's kinship with an important form of self-criticism.

**Scotto, Carolina**. Cualidades Secundarias y autoconocimiento. *Analisis Filosof*, 17(1), 35-40, My 97.

This paper is a discussion about different models of self-knowledge: perceptual, inferential and "constitutive". I intend an evaluation of some criticisms to both the first and the second one. I discuss the C. Wright's view about the "constitutive" character of "self-knowledge", that's to say, as it were a nonepistemic model and its relationship with secondary qualities. I defend instead a Wittgensteinian view, by which I mean an analysis of the first personal psychological ordinary statements. Finally, I claim that it's not necessary neither possible to have only one model to reconstruct what we ordinary and philosophically call "self-knowledge".

**Scotto, Carolina**. Hay Problemas Filosóficos? Reflexiones Metafilosóficas Sobre Algunas Ideas Wittgensteineanas. *Cad Hist Filosof Cie*, 6(Spec), 179-199, Ja-D 96.

I argue in this paper for a positive answer to the title's question, understanding that more than philosophical problems, there are philosophical ways of dealing with problems. I assume the Wittgensteinian defense of this distinction, intending a revaluation of his approach. Even though Wittgenstein is one of the philosophers that have most influenced contemporary thinking, hardly anybody accepts nowadays the interest of his conception of philosophy. I intend to show that there is a lot of simplification at the origin of this by means of revision of Wittgenstein's metaphilosophical ideas. The character of these reflections is metaphilosophical, since my aim is to offer an up-to-date and perspectival vision of his achievement to the problem. (edited)

**Scotus, John Duns** and Ribas Cezar, Cesar (trans). Do Princípio de Individuaçao. *Trans/Form/Acao*, 19, 241-253, 1996.

**Scowcroft, Philip**. More on Imaginaries in *p*-ADIC Fields. *J Sym Log*, 62(1), 1-13, Mr 97.

This paper shows that a three-sorted theory of the *p*-adic field—with sorts for the field, for the value group, and for equivalence classes of the relation 'x-y is integral', as well as functions taking field elements to their values and to their equivalence classes—does not eliminate imaginaries. If one adds a new sort for the equivalence relation 'the ball with center x and radius given by y is the ball with center z and radius given by w', the resulting theory eliminates imaginaries corresponding to definable equivalence relations on the *p*-adic line.

**Scriven, Tal**. *Wrongness, Wisdom, and Wilderness: Toward a Libertarian Theory of Ethics and the Environment.* Albany, SUNY Pr, 1997.

The first part of the book articulates a libertarian approach to the ethics of social policy, arguing that the principle of utility should be understood, in judging social policy, through application of the principle of harm, or wrongness. Part II draws on Plato, Nietzsche, and Mill to give an account of ideas relevant to moral reflection on individual lives, analyzing various theories of prudential wisdom that apply to the private realm of purely personal action. Part III deals with our relationship, as individuals and societies, to nature. Scriven argues that nothing logically prevents a well-constructed libertarianism from supporting environmental-ethics positions at least as radical as biocentrism, although he finds deep problems with going as far as ecocentrism and its postmodern variants. (publisher, edited)

**Scruton, Roger**. "Gay Reservations" in *The Liberation Debate: Rights at Issue*, Leahy, Michael (ed), 108-124. New York, Routledge, 1996.

In considering the morality of homosexual conduct we should not confine our concern to those of rights. Rather we should see homosexuality in its full social context, and ask ourselves whether the feeling of revulsion traditionally directed towards it contributes a) to the well-being of society, and b) to the well-being of the individual. Various obnoxious and reactionary conclusions are drawn from this.

**Scruton, Roger**. "Perictione in Colophon" in *Verstehen and Humane Understanding*, O'Hear, Anthony (ed), 287-307. New York, Cambridge Univ Pr, 1996.

Imaginary dialogue between Xanthippe and Perictione, niece of Plato, on the topic of dancing, its metaphysical and spiritual significance, with reminiscences of Socrates' last dance on the kitchen table.

**Scruton, Roger**. *A Short History of Modern Philosophy: From Descartes to Wittgenstein.* New York, Routledge, 1995.

This book provides a synthetic vision of the history of modern philosophy, from an analytical perspective. It is necessarily selective, but I hope that I have identified the principal figures, and the principal intellectual preoccupations, that have formed Western philosophy since Descartes. It is, I believe, fruitful to approach these matters from the standpoint of analytical philosophy, which in recent years has become interested in the history which it had ignored for so long, and has sought to reestablish its connections with the Western intellectual tradition. (edited)

**Scutt, Tom** and O'Hara, Kieron. There Is No Hard Problem of Consciousness. *J Consciousness Stud*, 3(4), 290-302, 1996.

The paper attempts to establish the importance of addressing what Chalmers (1995) calls the 'easy problems' of consciousness, at the expense of the 'hard problem'. One pragmatic argument and two philosophical arguments are presented to defend this approach to consciousness and three major theories of consciousness are criticized in this light. Finally, it is shown that concentration on the easy problems does not lead to eliminativism with respect to consciousness.

**Seager, William**. Critical Notice of Fred Dretske *Naturalizing the Mind*. *Can J Phil*, 27(1), 83-109, Mr 97.

Dretske's representational theory of consciousness is a major advance in our understanding of consciousness, providing new approaches to the problems of qualia and conscious thought. It also raises a host of new difficulties. Some of these stem from tensions between the nature of consciousness and Dretske's favoured biofunctional theory of representation. The evident plasticity of function does not obviously match a corresponding plasticity in conscious experience. Other difficulties arise from the possibility of systems that lack functions altogether but are, intuitively, conscious. More general, problems also arise when we reflect on how it is possible at all for us to be conscious of the content of representations.

**Seamon, Roger**. From *The World is Beautiful* to *The Family of Man*: The Plight of Photography as a Modern Art. *J Aes Art Crit*, 55(3), 245-252, Sum 97.

From early on there were efforts to explain why photography had not "made it" as a fine art and it was only when photography abandoned its classical forms of expression—"straight" photography from, say, Paul Strand to Ansel Adams—that it succeeded in scaling the art-world heights. I reject the explanations for this phenomenon based on photography's mechanical nature and its transparency, the latter being the thesis advanced by Kendall Walton and Roger Scruton. Using some of Pierre Bourdieu's ideas, I argue instead that classic photography was the inheritor of a mimetic and morally normative aesthetic that was opposed to the principles of aesthetic modernism.

**Seamon, Roger**. Guided Rapid Unconscious Reconfiguration in Poetry and Art. *Phil Lit*, 20(2), 412-427, O 96.

Works of art appeal, in their aesthetic dimension, through a process I call guided unconscious rapid reconfiguration. Artists open gaps in meaning or perceptual logic which are filled by rapid unconscious inferences. If the gap is too large we are confused, and if it is too small we are bored. Pleasure is a function of "getting it" just right. This is a subjective version of the ancient formula of unity in variety.

The thesis can also help to account for a number of phenomena associated with art, for example, stylistic change and resistance to interpretation.

**Searle, John R**. Précis of *The Construction of Social Reality*. *Phil Phenomenol Res*, 57(2), 427-428, Je 97.

**Searle, John R**. Responses to Critics of *The Construction of Social Reality*. *Phil Phenomenol Res*, 57(2), 449-458, Je 97.

**Sears, James T**. Centering Culture: Teaching for Critical Sexual Literacy using the Sexual Diversity Wheel. *J Moral Educ*, 26(3), 273-283, S 97.

Expanding on the author's earlier work, this essay explicates the concept of critical sexual literacy within the context of four curricular models for multicultural sexuality education: tolerance, diversity, difference and *différance*. The *Sexual Diversity Wheel* is presented as a pedagogical tool to facilitate student inquiry into the multiple cross-cultural constructions and valuations of gender and sexuality. Illustrating these differences, the author describes his fieldwork activities in the central Philippines and explores the implications of these findings for those teaching about sexuality in Western societies.

**Sebestik, Jan**. "Prague Mosaic: Encounters with Prague Philosophers" in *In Itinere* European Cities and the Birth of Modern Scientific Philosophy, Poli, Roberto (ed), 125-144. Amsterdam, Rodopi, 1997.

**Secundy, Marian Gray**. An African American Looks at Death. *Bioethics Forum*, 13(1), 28-30, Spr 97.

**Seddon, Andrew M**. Predicting Our Health: Ethical Implications of Neural Networks and Outcome Potential Predictions. *Ethics Med*, 12(3), 53-55, 1996.

**Sedgwick, Sally**. Hegel's Critique of Kant's Empiricism and the Categorial Imperative. *Z Phil Forsch*, 50(4), 563-585, O-D 96.

**Sedgwick, Sally**. McDowell's Hegelianism. *Euro J Phil*, 5(1), 21-38, Ap 97.

The aims of this paper are, first, to draw attention to how closely John McDowell's treatment of Kant in *Mind and World* parallels Hegel's; and second, to use that parallel to present some features of Hegel's idealism in a charitable light. The author argues that Hegel's idealism implies neither a reduction of concepts to intuitions nor a reduction of intuitions to concepts. Like Kant, Hegel believes that experience for us requires both; like McDowell, he conceives of his form of idealism as committed to a denial of their separability. Hegel therefore subscribes neither to the "rampant Platonism" nor to the "bald naturalism" so often attributed to him.

**Sedivy, Sonia**. Must Conceptually Informed Perceptual Experience Involve Non-Conceptual Content?. *Can J Phil*, 26(3), 413-431, S 96.

**Seebass, Gottfried**. Handlungstheoretische Aspekte der Fahrlässigkeit. *Jahr Recht Ethik*, 2, 375-411, 1994.

Can the risks of the scientific technical world be sufficiently delimited in a normative (legal or moral) sense? The answer provided by this article is yes, assuming that the potentials of negligence liability are clarified and its principles consistently applied. An outline of the basic conditions for this endeavor proceeds from the distinctions drawn by the Analytical Theory of Action. "Negligence" is defined as taking risks beyond normative limits. It is treated on this basis (and not on the basis of "foreseeability") as the generic concept for "intention". A normative theoretical justification of "required care" is proffered. The care required is limited, however, on the one hand by its tie to the norm addressee's practical ability. (edited)

**Seel, Martin**. Well-Being: On a Fundamental Concept of Practical Philosophy. *Euro J Phil*, 5(1), 39-49, Ap 97.

With few exceptions modern practical philosophy has neglected a systematic explication of human well-being. But any philosophical account of moral and political issues—and especially any critical theory of modern society—has to rely on an a qualified understanding of the conditions and forms of a good life. Even thinkers such as Kant and Habermas, who explicitly refuse theories of the good (in the sense of good individual living), implicitly operate with assumptions about what is good for anyone. The article therefore argues that a formal conception of well-being is ethically unavoidable, theoretically possible and without alternative in social philosophy.

**Seeskin, Kenneth**. Of Dialogues and Seeds. *Phil Lit*, 21(1), 167-178, Ap 97.

**Segerberg, Krister**. Action Incompleteness. *Stud Log*, 51(3-4), 533-550, 1992.

The author has previously introduced an operator *delta* into dynamic logic which takes formulae to terms; the suggested reading of *delta* A was "the bringing about of A" or "the seeing to it that A". After criticism from S. K. Thomason and T. J. Surendonk the author now presents an improved version of his theory. The crucial feature is the introduction of an operator OK taking terms to formulae; the suggested reading of OK *alpha* is "*alpha* always terminates".

**Segerberg, Krister**. Getting Started: Beginnings in the Logic of Action. *Stud Log*, 51(3-4), 347-378, 1992.

A history of the logic of action is outlined, beginning with St Anselm. Five modern authors are discussed in some detail: von Wright, Fitch, Kanger, Chellas and Pratt.

**Segerstrale, Ullica**. Good to the Last Drop? Millikan Stories as "Canned" Pedagogy. *Sci Eng Ethics*, 1(3), 197-214, Jl 95.

Starting with the common source of all Millikan stories, historian of physics Gerald Holton's 1978 paper, I discuss recent "canned" versions of Millikan-as-misbehaver in books on scientific fraud. Then I examine some versions of Millikan-as-good-scientist, particularly the reconstruction by historian of physics Allan Franklin, and the views of some practicing physicists.

Finally, we have an instructive head-on collision between the two standard treatments of Millikan. The problem with canned stories is not only insufficient information; we also lack a realistic evaluation of the role of ethics in science. As a fundamentally knowledge-seeking enterprise, science may harbor an inherent perhaps irresolvable, conflict between scientific and ethical concerns. (edited)

**Sehon, Scott**. Deviant Causal Chains and the Irreducibility of Teleological Explanation. *Pac Phil Quart*, 78(2), 195-213, Je 97.

We typically explain human action teleologically, by citing the action's goal or purpose. However, a broad class of naturalistic projects within the philosophy of mind presuppose that teleological explanation is reducible to causal explanation. In this paper I argue that two recently suggested strategies—one suggested by Al Mele and the other proposed by John Bishop and Christopher Peacocke—fail to provide a successful causal analysis of teleological explanation. The persistent troubles encountered by the reductive project suggest that teleological explanations are irreducible and that the naturalistic accounts of mind and agency should be called into question.

**Sehon, Scott**. Natural-Kind Terms and the Status of Folk Psychology. *Amer Phil Quart*, 34(3), 333-344, Jl 97.

This paper argues that common sense psychological practices and beliefs do not embody a proto-scientific theory of human behavior. The first section discusses two features of folk psychology that make it look unlike a scientific theory: its normative character and its context sensitivity. The second section argues that mental state terms do not function semantically as natural-kind terms. If mental-state terms do not purport to denote natural kinds then folk psychology is not a theory in the strong sense maintained by many philosophers. This result in turn necessitates reopening several philosophical questions that have been viewed as settled in many circles.

**Sehon, Scott R**. Okin on Feminism and Rawls. *Phil Forum*, 27(4), 321-332, Sum 96.

**Seibt, Johanna**. The Myth of Substance and the Fallacy of Misplaced Concreteness. *Acta Analytica*, 119-139, 1996.

I investigate recent prototypical arguments for substance metaphysics and try to show that some explanatory functions of substance can also be fulfilled by other ontological categories. In particular, I argue against M. Ayers that there is no reason to think that all and only substances are discrete individuals, natural wholes and logical units. I conclude that the category of substance does not provide us with a uniquely powerful explanans for the notion of logical and physical unity. (edited)

**Seibt, Johanna**. The 'Umbau'—From Constitution Theory to Constructional Ontology. *Hist Phil Quart*, 14(3), 305-348, Jl 97.

The paper traces, historically and systematically, the influence of Carnap's philosophical program on the writings of Nelson Goodman, focusing on the relationship between Carnap's *Aufbau* and Goodman's *Structure of Appearance*. In particular, drawing on unpublished material from the Carnap Research Archives, I show that Carnap had already anticipated Goodman's criticism of the method of quasi-analysis and that Goodman misconstrued the status of this procedure on several counts. I also argue that Carnap's antimetaphysical stance left his approach with an explanatory deficit which Goodman's pragmatist pluralism is able to address.

**Seidel, George J**. Buddhism as Radical Religion. *Darshana Int*, 35 (3/139), 1-12, Jl 95.

The article describes Buddhism as a religion totally stripped down to the barest essentials, representing itself as the ultimate solution to the tangle that is sex, death, and religion. Along the way the author points out the meaning of those essentials, such as *anattâ* (no-self and no-Self), *samsâra*, *karma*, etc., within the context of a religion totally radicalized, so radicalized that its principal practitioners, in the Theravada tradition the monks, consider it "no-religion." Thus stripped down, it is a religion ready for travel. This advantage also has its disadvantages. With little in the way of cultural baggage of its own, Buddhism, at least in its popular form, tends to pick up the animistic beliefs, the gods and goddesses of the cultures where it settles. (edited)

**Seidenfeld, Teddy** and Kadane, Joseph B and Schervish, Mark J. When Several Bayesians Agree That There Will Be No Reasoning to a Foregone Conclusion. *Proc Phil Sci Ass*, 3(Suppl), S281-S289, 1996.

When can a Bayesian investigator select an hypothesis H and design an experiment (or a sequence of experiments) to make certain that, given the experimental outcome(s), the posterior probability of H will be lower than its prior probability? We report an elementary result which establishes sufficient conditions under which this reasoning to a foregone conclusion cannot occur. Through an example, we discuss how this result extends to the perspective of an onlooker who agrees with the investigator about the statistical model for the data but who holds a different prior probability for the statistical parameters of that model. We consider, specifically, one-sided and two-sided statistical hypotheses involving i.i.d. normal data with conjugate priors. In a concluding section, using an "improper" prior, we illustrate how the preceding results depend upon the assumption that probability is countably additive.

**Seidl, Horst**. "Temporalità e storicità" in *Il Concetto di Tempo: Atti del XXXII Congresso Nazionale della Società Filosofica Italiana,* Casertano, Giovanni (ed), 357-362. Napoli, Loffredo, 1997.

**Seidl, Horst**. Brevi Riflessioni Filosofiche sulla Storicità dell'Uomo. *Aquinas*, 39(3), 445-457, S-D 96.

**Seidl, Horst**. Sul duplice fine del matrimonio secondo la dottrina tomista. *Sapientia*, 51(200), 505-515, 1996.

**Seidl, Horst**. Sur l'origine de l'éthique de Zénon de Cittium. *Diotima*, 25, 37-47, 1997.

"The origin of Zeno's ethics is found in the ethical doctrines of his masters of the Platonic and cynic schools. But there is also an oriental religious impact (see E.

Zeller, A. Jagu, M. Wiersma) giving priority to ethics above physics and logic which have to serve as foundations of ethics. Hence there arises the problem of a vicious circle; for Zeno's ethics defines the good life as life according to reason and as according to the very nature of man, referring to the philosophy of nature, his physics. But in this discipline he defines the nature of all things ultimately as reason, referring thus to ethics. The solution seems to be that the reference between both disciplines is not circular, but complementary. (edited)

**Seidler, Michael J** and Carr, Craig L. Pufendorf, Sociality and the Modern State. *Hist Polit Thought*, 17(3), 354-378, Autumn 96.

This essay discusses the nature of Pufendorf's contribution to the history of political ideas. It is argued that his theory of sociality domesticates Hobbesian cynicism, systematizes Groatian visions, and establishes a moral foundation for the legitimacy of the modern state.

**Seifert, Josef**. La filosofia personalista di Dietrich von Hildebrand e la sua opposizione contro il nazionalsocialismo. *Acta Phil*, 6(1), 53-81, 1997.

This article recalls the chief points of the personalist philosophy of Dietrich von Hildebrand and his opposition to the foundations of the national-socialist ideology. His struggle was waged against relativism and positivism, from which arose national-socialism, which he considered radically anti-Christian. He defended an authentic personalism, which was based on the primacy of the spiritual dimension in relation to the vital dimension. Von Hildebrand strove against the ideological roots of racism and anti-Semitism and also against collectivism and the totalitarianism of the state and of the party.

**Seifert, Josef**. Philosophy as an Exact Science (in Czech). *Filosof Cas*, 44(6), 903-922, 1996.

As the title reveals, the author tries to sketch the main contributions of the realistic phenomenology to the new foundation of the classical realistic philosophy. In the present paper, he traces his own philosophical position as worked out in detail in his recently published papers on the background of a critical dialogue with the idea of philosophy as pure science which was developed by the father of phenomenology Edmund Husserl (esp. Husserl's *logos* article "Philosophie als strenge Wissenschaft"). The author chooses some of the most important theses of Husserl's article and examines them critically. Therefore, Seifert regards the answering of the above Kantian question as a significant, if not revolutionary contribution of the realistic phenomenology to the foundation of a strictly scientific philosophy. A carefully elaborated datum of the substantial necessity as a true primordial fact accessible to our mind, of its ontological foundation, as well as of its accurate distinction from other essentially different kinds of necessity makes it possible, according to Seifert, to get critically over the scepticism and relativism, both of them being immanent in the Kantian philosophy. At the same time, the foundation of the *a priori* cognition and of the synthetic one in the objective and absolute necessity overcomes the more radical immanentism and subjectivism of the later Husserl. Hence such a philosophy of substantial necessity and the simultaneous contribution of the realistic phenomenology to the new foundation of the scientific philosophy, a contribution that we owe to the realistic phenomenologists, namely Reinach and Hildebrand.

**Seiko, Goto**. The Influence of Chinese Philosophy on the English Style Garden: A Comparative Study of Wörlitz and Koishikawa Korakuen (in Japanese). *Bigaku*, 47(1), 61-72, Sum 96.

Wörlitzer Park and Koishikawa Korakuen were made for educational purposes based on Confucianism, the philosophy for ruling class. Both gardens are remarkable in that they were made not only enjoy natural scenery and poetic beauty but also to represent enlightened thought. This paper examines the influence of Chinese philosophy on Wörlitzer Park and Koishikawa Korakuen and stressed on the following points. 1) The importance of the influence of Chinese philosophy on the development of the enlightenment movement in 18th century Europe; 2) The role of Chinese philosophy on the English style garden; and 3) The similarity of forms between Wörlitzer Park and Koishikawa Korakuen stemming from the same underlying philosophy toward garden making.

**Seisaku, Yamamoto** (trans) and Carter, Robert E (trans). *Watsuji Tetsurō's* Rinrigaku. Albany, SUNY Pr, 1996.

Watsuji Tetsurō's *Rinrigaku* (literally, the principles that allow us to live in friendly community) has been regarded as the definitive study of Japanese ethics for half a century. In Japan, ethics is the study of human being or *ningen*. As an ethical being, one negates individuality by abandoning one's independence from others. This selflessness is the true meaning of goodness. (publisher)

**Seitz, Brian**. Power and the Constitution of Sartre's Identity. *Phil Today*, 40(3), 381-387, Fall 96.

**Seldin, Jonathan P**. On the Proof Theory of Coquand's Calculus of Constructions. *Annals Pure Applied Log*, 83(1), 23-101, Ja 97.

The calculus of constructions is formulated as a natural deduction system in which deductions follow the constructions of the terms to which types are assigned. Strong normalization is proved for deductions. This strong normalization result implies the consistency of the underlying systems, but it is still possible to make contradictory assumptions. A number of assumption sets useful in implementations are proved consistent, including certain sets of assumptions whose types are negations, negations of certain equations, arithmetic, classical logic, classical arithmetic and the existence of power sets. All results are given with complete proofs.

**Seligman, Jerry** and Blackburn, Patrick. Hybrid Languages. *J Log Lang Info*, 4(3), 251-272, 1995.

Hybrid languages have both modal and first-order characteristics: a Kripke semantics and explicit variable binding apparatus. This paper motivates the development of hybrid languages, sketches their history and examines the expressive power of three hybrid binders. We show that all three binders give rise to languages strictly weaker than the corresponding first-order language, that full first-order expressivity can be gained by adding the universal modality and that all three binders can force the existence of infinite models and have undecidable satisfiability problems.

**Sell, Annette**. "Aspekte des Lebens: Fichtes Wissenschaftslehre von 1804 und Hegels Phänomenologie des Geistes" in *Sein—Reflexion—Freiheit: Aspekte der Philosophie Johann Gottlieb Fichtes,* Asmuth, Christoph (ed), 79-94. Amsterdam, Gruner, 1997.

**Sellars, Wilfrid**. *Empiricism and the Philosophy of Mind*. Cambridge, Harvard Univ Pr, 1997.

The book is both the epitome of Wilfrid Sellars's entire philosophical system and a key document in the history of philosophy. First published in essay form in 1956, it helped bring about a sea change in analytic philosophy. It broke the link, which had bound Russell and Ayer to Locke and Hume—the doctrine of "knowledge by acquaintance." Sellars's attack on the Myth of the Given in *Empiricism and the Philosophy of Mind* was a decisive move in turning analytic philosophy away from the foundationalist motives of the logical empiricists and raised doubts about the very idea of "epistemology."(publisher, edited)

**Selleri, Franco**. Quantum Paradoxes and Physical Reality. *Phil Natur*, 27(1), 14-30, 1990.

Contemporary research in physics is in bad conditions and neglect of experimental evidence has become a mass phenomenon. This situation was recently pointed out by Oldershaw for elementary particle physics and by Arp for astrophysics and cosmology, but is shown here to exist also in the foundations of quantum physics. The tendency to resolve the Einstein-Podolsky-Rosen paradox by decree is, for example, far stronger than that to increment experimental activity. The usual formulation of quantum theory ("the Copenhagen interpretation") is hardly acceptable for a realist, because it rests on: 1) A strong limitation of the idea of causality; 2) A partial renunciation to describe phenomena in space and time; 3) A radical revision of the very idea of physical reality. The complete arbitrariness of this formulation is pointed out. The local realistic approach is shown to offer good hopes for future physics.

**Selleri, Franco**. The Weakest Local Realism Is still Incompatible with Quantum Theory. *Phil Natur*, 28(1), 17-34, 1991.

The existence of predictable probabilities in the microworld requires a reality tied to such a predictability. This is a very general form of realism, probably the weakest form that can be conceived. If we add the idea that single-particle probabilities are local (which is also true in quantum theory), then we can deduce Bell's type inequalities. In spite of its generality, our formulation of local realism is thus still incompatible with quantum theory.

**Sellés, Juan Fernando**. Los hábitos intelectuales según Polo. *Anu Filosof*, 29(2), 1017-1036, 1996.

After studying the historical background of the philosophical treatment or neglect of intellectual habits, this paper focuses on the research on the nature of habits and is divided into two essential parts: a) The research on the relationship that habits keep with the acts of knowing and the objects known by acts; b) The study of the existing relationship within habits themselves and the human being that is superior to them. All of this is based on the papers written by Prof. Polo.

**Selner-Wright, Susan C**. The Order of Charity in Thomas Aquinas. *Phil Theol*, 9(1-2), 13-27, 1995.

Thomas articulates the proper priority among charity's objects based on his understanding of charity as rooted in the fellowship of eternal happiness. God, as the source of the happiness, is our principal "fellow" in it and so first in the order of charity. The individual's fellowship with himself or herself, with the "inner man," is most intimate and so the individual comes next in the order. Then come our neighbors, all of whom are our fellows now and may be our fellows for eternity. Finally, the body is itself properly an object of charity, for it is by means of the acts we perform in the body that we may come to share in the fellowship of eternal happiness.

**Semin, Gün R** and Taris, Toon W. Passing on the Faith: How Mother-Child Communication Influences Transmission of Moral Values. *J Moral Educ*, 26(2), 211-221, Je 97.

This paper examines religious affiliation and commitment of teenagers as a function of the quality of mother-child interaction and the mothers' religious commitment, as an illustration of the principle that transmission of parental norms and values to their children is facilitated or inhibited by the quality of their interaction. We expected that in cases where mother-child interaction was good, parents would be better able to impose their own values upon their children, resulting in a lower disaffiliation and higher religious commitment in high quality of family-interaction families. This expectation was tested using data from 223 British adolescent-mother pairs, by means of logistic and ordinary regression analysis. The results largely supported the hypotheses, exemplifying how mothers in their role of moral agents may profit from good mother-child relationships.

**Semino, Ignazio**. Un convegno su *I filosofi e la genesi della coscienza culturale della "nuova Italia"*. *Riv Filosof Neo-Scolas*, 88(2), 325-327, Ap-Je 96.

**Sen, Amartya**. Economics, Business Principles and Moral Sentiments. *Bus Ethics Quart*, 7(3), 5-15, Jl 97.

The essay discusses the place of business principles and of moral sentiments in economic success, and examines the role of cultures in influencing norms of business behavior. Two presumptions held in standard economic analysis are disputed: the rudimentary nature of business principles (essentially restricted, directly or indirectly, to profit maximization), and the allegedly narrow reach of moral sentiments (often treated to be irrelevant to business and economics). In contrast, the author argues for the need to recognize the complex structure of business principles and the extensive reach of moral sentiments by using theoretical considerations, a thorough analysis of Adam Smith's work, and a careful interpretation of Japan's remarkable economic success. (edited)

**Sen, Amartya**. *On Economic Inequality.* New York, Clarendon/Oxford Pr, 1997.

This book, first published in 1973, presents a systematic treatment of the conceptual framework as well as the practical problems of measurement of inequality. Alternative approaches are evaluated in terms of their philosophical assumptions, economic content, and statistical requirements. In a new annex, Amartya Sen, jointly with James Foster, critically surveys the literature that followed the publication of this book, and evaluates the main analytical issues in the appraisal of economic inequality and poverty. (publisher, edited)

**Sen, Amartya K**. Desigualdades de Bienestar y axiomática rawlsiana. *Telos (Spain)*, 5(1), 79-102, Je 96.

**Sen, Amartya K**. Funciones de Bienestar social no lineales: una réplica al profesor Harsanyi. *Telos (Spain)*, 5(1), 107-112, Je 96.

**Sen, Amartya K**. On the Status of Equality. *Polit Theory*, 24(3), 394-400, Ag 96.

**Sen, Amartya K**. Rationality, Joy and Freedom. *Crit Rev*, 10(4), 481-494, Fall 96.

In *The Joyless Economy*, Tibor Scitovsky proposes a model of human behavior that differs substantially from that of standard economic theory. Scitovsky begins with a basic distinction between "comfort" and "stimulation." While stimulation is ultimately more satisfying and creative, we frequently fall for the bewitching attractions of comfort, which leads to impoverished lives. Scitovsky's analysis has far-reaching implications not only for the idea of rationality, but for the concept of utility (by making it plural in nature) and, perhaps most importantly, for the importance of freedom (including the freedom to change our preferences).

**Sen, Amit** (trans) and Lawlor, Leonard (trans) and Hyppolite, Jean. *Logic and Existence*. Albany, SUNY Pr, 1997.

*Logic and Existence*, which originally appeared in 1952, completes the project Hyppolite began with *Genesis and Structure of Hegel's "Phenomenology of Spirit."* Taking up successively the role of language, reflection, and categories in Hegel's *Science of Logic*, Hyppolite illuminates Hegelianism's most obscure dialectical synthesis: the relation between the phenomenology and the logic. (publisher, edited)

**Sen, Sanat Kumar**. Philosophy as Critical Reflection: The Philosophy of Rasvihary Das. *J Indian Counc Phil Res*, 13(2), 107-116, Ja-Ap 96.

**Sencik, Stefan**. Faith in God as Ultimate Strength: A Slovak Physician Who Resisted 'Brain Washing'. *Ultim Real Mean*, 20(2 & 3), 179-190, Je-S 97.

Dr. Silvester Krcméry, 1924, was a victim of Communist regime in Czecho-Slovakia. He spent 14 years in prisons and solitary confinement, persecuted for his faith in God. In his book "This Saved US" he describes the horrific experiences of the system of "Brain Washing". As a practical Christian he was well prepared for this persecution and as a physician he studied this system. His life in prison is a confirmation of Viktor Frankl's theory concerning value-based resistance to mental and physical coercion: "In the concentration camps we saw how ... one man degenerated while another attained saintliness". Krcméry's book has a spiritual message: it is possible to resist "Brain Washing" and other human suffering. The only weapon is faith in God and an authentic spiritual life.

**Senécal, Jacques**. La philosophie est un spectacle qu'on n'applaudit jamais mais qui tient l'affiche éternellement. *Philosopher*, 19, 73-80, 1996.

**Senigaglia, Cristiana**. Hegel und Weber im Vergleich: Die Bahnen der Rationalität. *Jahr Hegelforschung*, 2, 133-157, 1996.

**Senior, Matthew** (ed) and Ham, Jennifer (ed). *Animal Acts: Configuring the Human in Western History*. New York, Routledge, 1997.

*Animal Acts* records the history of the fluctuating boundary between animals and humans as expressed in literary, philosophical and scientific texts, as well as visual arts and historical practices such as dissections, the hunt, zoo construction and circus acts. Against a general background of the progressive exclusion of animals form human space and consciousness since the Enlightenment, the essays document a persistent return of animality. Essays on Marie de France, Boccaccio, Rabelais, La Fontaine, Schelling, Nietzsche, Flaubert, Kafka, Audubon, E.B. White, Levinas, Derrida, Heidegger, Dian Fossey and Gary Larson trace the lineage of those who have sought to enact the animal—to mime, tame, research, befriend and capture the beast within. (publisher)

**Senner, Walter**. Jean de Sterngassen et son commentaire des *Sentences*. *Rev Thomiste*, 97(1), 83-98, Ja-Mr 97.

**Sensat, Julius**. Marx's Inverted World. *Topoi*, 15(2), 177-188, S 96.

**Sensat, Julius**. Reification as Dependence of Extrinsic Information. *Synthese*, 109(3), 361-399, D 96.

Marx criticized political economy for propounding an inverted, mystical view of economic reality. But he went beyond asserting the falsity and apologetic character of the doctrine to characterize it as reflecting a social practice of inversion or mystification—an inverted social world—in which individuals incorporate their own actions into a process whose dynamic lies beyond their control. Caught up in this process, individuals confront aspects of their own agency in the alien or "reified" form of a given, determining reality. Marx leaves unclear exactly how the process exerts and maintains its hold on agents, the nature of the reasons they might have for wanting to free themselves of it and under what conditions they could do so. However, it is possible to abstract

somewhat from Marx's specific concerns and to model a self-reproducing practice of reification that works through the informational environment of decision. Though of wider interest, this more general conception can shed light on the nature and critique of Marx's inverted world. It draws on conceptual resources from decision theory, game theory and general equilibrium theory.

**Serequeberhan, Tsenay**. Eurocentrism in Philosophy: The Case of Immanuel Kant. *Phil Forum*, 27(4), 333-356, Sum 96.

**Sergeevich Pugachev, Oleg**. The Problem of Moral Absolutes in the Ethics of Vladimir Solov'ëv. *Stud East Euro Thought*, 48(2-4), 207-221, S 96.

The purpose of this work is the interpretation of the ethics of V. Solov'ëv in respect to moral absolutes and to determine in the field of ethics the absolute good. One of the most significant problems is the connection between the absolute and the relative and the elucidation of the manner acting on moral absolutes as the concretizations of the Supra-Real (God). Moral absolutes being attributes of the Supra-Real, may change their purely absolute status under "earthly" conditions. The conclusion is that moral absolutes may be presented as a system on two levels. On the first level, absolutes themselves function as transcendental essences and we note an element of hypostatization. On the second level, they function in the historical and social circumstances which transformed them. There is a major role in the insuring status of moral absolutes belonging to a rational belief. (edited)

**Serrano, Gonzalo**. "¿Qué nos importa Descartes todavía?" in *Memorias Del Seminario En Conmemoración De Los 400 Anos Del Nacimiento De René Descartes*, Albis, Víctor S (ed), 1-10. Sankt Augustin, Academia, 1997.

**Serrano, Vicente**. "Ontología y filosofía transcendental en el primer Schelling" in *El inicio del Idealismo alemán*, Market, Oswaldo, 299-306. Madrid, Ed Complutense, 1996.

Der Vortrag versucht herauszuarbeiten, dass Fichte und Schelling Anderes und sogar Gegensätzliches in Sinn haben. Der Vortrag analysiert die erste Fichte Rezeption Schellings, und zeigt wie zu diesem Zeitpunkt die Grundposition Schellings schon spinozistisch ist, weshalb sein Prinzip nicht das subjektive Prinzip Fichtes sein kann. Schelling macht sich dieses Prinzip trotzdem zu eigen, weil er nur über die "vorkritische" Fassung von Grundlage und Über den Begriff der Wissenschaftslehre verfügt, und Fichtes vorherige Entwicklung sowie die entscheidende Denkwerkstatt seines Gedankes, die Eigne Meditationen sind, nicht kennt.

**Serrano de Haro, Agustín**. Hannah Arendt y la cuestión del mal radical. *Dialogo Filosof*, 12(3), 421-430, S-D 96.

En la clasificación aristotélica de formas de gobierno no tendría encaje adecuado la forma de dominación política por la que será recordado nuestro siglo: el totalitarismo. Tal es la tesis de Hannah Arendt. Pero la pensadora judía ha querido mostrar ante todo que el análisis de los regímenes totalitarios y de su más peculiar realización—el campo de concentración—daba un sentido inesperado y desconcertante al concepto filosófico del mal radical.

**Serrano Marín, Vicente**. Sobre Hölderlin y los comienzos del Idealismo alemán. *An Seminar Hist Filosof*, 10, 173-194, 1993.

Seit der Publikation von "Urteil und Sein" hat sich die Forschung intensiv mit der Rolle Hölderlins im frühen Idealismus beschäftigt. Die Kritik an Fichte (1794-95) ist zweifellos ein wichtiger Punkt dieser Rolle. Dieser Aufsatzzeigt, dass die Voraussetzung für diese Kritik eine spinozistische Grundhaltung ist. Dafür spricht die inhaltliche Kontinuität in Hölderlins Schriften von der Spinoza Rezeption (1791) über den Brief an Hegel (26-II-1795) bis zu "Urteil und Sein".

**Serrapica, Salvatore**. Note napoletane alle *Passioni dell'anima*. *G Crit Filosof Ital*, 16(3), 476-494, S-D 96.

**Serres, Michel**. Meteore. *Iride*, 8(15), 373-393, Ag 95.

Nel Novecento l'esperienza del tempo subisce una profonda trasformazione. A partire dalle nuove dimensioni temporali delle categorie della contingenza e della libertà M. Serres, R. Berardi e G. Polizzi presentano una riflessione attorno alla nozione di tempo frammentato e contingente che interessa la filosofia, la scienza e il tempo-spazio della composizione umana.

**Servomaa, Sonia**. "Mountains of the Mind" in *East and West in Aesthetics*, Marchianò, Grazia (ed), 155-168. Pisa, Istituti Editoriali, 1997.

**Sesonske, Alexander**. Pre-Established Harmony and Other Comic Strategies. *J Aes Art Crit*, 55(3), 253-261, Sum 97.

**Seto, Belinda** and Baldwin, Wendy. Peer Review: Selecting the Best Science. *Sci Eng Ethics*, 3(1), 11-17, Ja 97.

The major challenge facing today's biomedical researchers is the increasing competition for available funds. The competitive review process, through which the National Institutes of Health (NIH) awards grants, is built upon review by a committee of expert scientists. The NIH is firmly committed to ensuring that its peer review system is fair and objective.

**Sette, A M** and Cifuentes, J C and Mundici, Daniele. Cauchy Completeness in Elementary Logic. *J Sym Log*, 61(4), 1153-1157, D 96.

**Seubold, Günter**. Der "Neuanfang" in der Ästhetik (J.-F. Lyotard). *Phil Rundsch*, 43(4), 297-317, D 96.

**Sevilla Fernández, José M**. Algo donoso pero no cortés: Una lectura diferencial del bifronte Marqués de Valdegamas a tenor de la modernidad de Vico. *Cuad Vico*, 7/8, 281-296, 1997.

This is a further step of the author's hermeneutical line that explores the reception of Vico in Spain. As a follow-up to his precedent article "Nuevos aportes (histórico y filosóficos) para la fortuna de Vico en el siglo XIX español" (*Cuadernos sobre Vico*, 5/6, 1995-96), it is presented a rereading of Vico's *modern image* through the reception of Juan Donoso Cortés. This image is reflected by Donoso: he first assumes Vico and then rejects him; such a thing corresponds with his *bifid* attitude towards his century: there is a "first" Donoso, enlightened, liberal and eclectic and there is a "second" Donoso, reactionary and traditionalist. Therefore, his reception of Vico is a master key for the interpretation of the Spanish 19th century as something that must be read with two languages: that of progress and that of tradition.

**Sevilla Fernández, José M**. La *Vía* Vico como pretexto en Isaiah Berlin: contracorriente, antimonismo y pluralismo. *Cuad Vico*, 5/6, 261-282, 1995/96.

This is a critical bibliographical study which traces the Vichian reception in Sir Isaiah Berlin's works and analyzes his particular interpretation of Vico's thought. The paper moves along his views according to which Vico is related with the "countercurrent" movement against the Enlightenment and tries to emphasize his efforts to comprise the Vichian doctrines in an antimonist and wider open conception which seems to be closely associated with Berlin's own concerns with cultural history.

**Sevilla Fernández, José M**. Maquiavelo y la episteme política. *Cuad Vico*, 5/6, 345-350, 1995/96.

This is a bibliographical and critical study of Miguel A. Pastor Pérez's work "El arte de la simulación. Estudio sobre ciencia y política en Nicolás Maquiavelo" (ORP. Colecc. Raigal n.2, Sevilla, 1944, pp. 198, ISBN 84-605-0651-1), in which Machiavelli's actuality turns out to be the seal issue today, particularly when politics is supposed to be seen connected with "Machiavelism" and is openly acknowledged in the acting principles as well as when the basic concepts purported by Machiavelli are incorporated both into the theory and the political enterprises of every day politics. (edited)

**Sevilla Fernández, José M**. Nuevos aportes (históricos y filosóficos) para la fortuna de Vico en el siglo XIX español (Fermín Gonzalo Morón, Ceferino González, Manuel Durán y Bas). *Cuad Vico*, 5/6, 217-236, 1995/96.

In his former paper on Vico's reception during the XIX century in Spain, the task of dislodging the thesis so frequently held that there is a Vico's "absence" in Spain was partially accomplished. This task is taken up again in a recent investigation where the author analyzes and assesses three further important cases related with the Spanish Vichian reception: that of eclectic historian Fermín Gonzalo Morón, the neoscholastic Ceferino González and finally the Catalan legal school founder Manuel Durán y Bas. With those examples the author aims to validate his claim that Vico was indeed acknowledged both as a modern and heterodox thinker by the positive as well as by the critical reception.

**Sevilla Fernández, José M**. Vico en Italia y en Alemania. *Cuad Vico*, 5/6, 357-366, 1995/96.

This is an outline of the *Bollettino del Centro di Studi Vichiani* (XXII-XIII, 1992-93) of Naples, a volume which includes the Congress's proceedings *Vico in Italia e in Germania* (Naples, March: 1-3, 1990). It contains also an assessment of J. Gebhardt's, M. Agrimi's, S. Otto's, G. Cantelli's, M. Papini's, E. Grassi's, B. Pinchard's, E. Di Magno's, F. Fellmann's, D. Di Cesare's, N. Badaloni's, O. Pöggeler's, C. Jermann's, A. Giuliani's, L. Geldsetzer's and A.M. Jacobelli Isoldi's studies. It is a compact volume in which is contained a sample of the interest which Germany has shown for the Vichian studies and at the same time it collects the interest which the Vichian scholars have exhibited for the Vico's German reception. (edited)

**Seymour, Michel**. "A Disquotational Theory of Truth" in *Verdad: lógica, representación y mundo*, Villegas Forero, L, 105-117. Santiago de Compostela, Univ Santiago Comp, 1996.

I shall be concerned with defending a sophisticated version of deflationism, one which can account for the occurrences of the truth predicate that do not apply to quoted sentences and for which a simple disquotational theory cannot provide an explanation. The preferred version is thus a sophisticated disquotational theory. I shall compare two versions: the Tarskian account and the substitutional account. I shall try to show that these two theories complete each other and that the best version exploits the semantic resources of a Tarskian language as well as those of a substitutional quantificational language. The result is a hybrid theory that countenances a certain number of the traditional criticisms formulated against disquotationalism. In particular, we are in a position to circumvent some of the difficulties mentioned recently in Marian David's *Correspondence and Disquotation*.

**Sfendoni-Mentzou, Demetra**. Peirce on Continuity and Laws of Nature. *Trans Peirce Soc*, 33(3), 646-678, Sum 97.

The object of my paper is to concentrate on the internal structure of the doctrine of continuity, so as to shed light on the role it plays in Peirce's account of laws of nature. My claim is that Peirce's fruitful synthesis of his logico-mathematical speculations and Aristotelean-scholastic realism with Synechism provide a most promising solution to the present day discussion on laws of nature viewed as universals. The key-concept in my analysis is that of potentiality, not only because of the central role it plays in Peirce's thought, but also because, as I argue, it is a *sine qua non* for a genuine realist account of laws of nature.

**Shafer-Landau, Russ**. Moral Rules. *Ethics*, 107(4), 584-611, Jl 97.

In this paper I defend a view of moral rules as universally quantified conditionals. I present three functions that moral rules can have: (I) that of identifying morally relevant features of situations, (II) that of delimiting the realm of morally valuable features, and (III) that of fixing the moral status of situations. I then explore the possibility of fulfilling these three functions for both prima facie and absolutist models of moral rules.

**Shaffer, Nancy E**. Understanding Bias in Scientific Practice. *Proc Phil Sci Ass*, 3(Suppl), S89-S97, 1996.

*Methodological objectivism* is a conception of bias which obscures the contingent and limited nature of methodological principles behind the guise of

fixed a priori standards. I suggest as an alternative a more flexible view of the operation of bias which I call *the attribution model*. The attribution model makes explicit the working principles of both parties to an actual charge of bias. It enables those involved to identify the issues in dispute between them, and is the basis for an approach to handling charges of bias within the process of discussion and negotiation which characterizes normal scientific decision-making.

**Shah, Sankiv**. Pessimism, Nihilism, and the Nietzschean Response. *Dialogue (PST)*, 39(2-3), 56-61, Ap 97.

**Shahrestani, S M A**. "The Islamic Perspective on Enlightenment: Principles and Implementation" in *Averroës and the Enlightenment*, Wahba, Mourad (ed), 203-219. Amherst, Prometheus, 1996.

**Shakespeare, Steven**. Stirring the Waters of Language: Kierkegaard on the Dangers of Doing Theology. *Heythrop J*, 37(4), 421-436, O 96.

**Shalkowski, Scott A**. Conventions, Cognitivism, and Necessity. *Amer Phil Quart*, 33(4), 375-392, O 96.

The major question of this paper is *Is there a viable reduction of necessity in terms of linguistic phenomena?* Substantival accounts, standard conventionalism and latter-day modal noncognitivism are examined. It is argued that all reductive approaches are deficient because they confront a fatal dilemma: either the reductive base is modally unconstrained and the proposal is arbitrary or the reductive base is modally constrained and the proposal is circular. Common mistakes about necessity, which make linguistic theories attractive and which hinder progress in the epistemology of modality, are noted and discussed.

**Shalkowski, Scott A**. Theoretical Virtues and Theological Construction. *Int J Phil Relig*, 41(2), 71-89, Ap 97.

Theist and critic alike typically assume rather traditional, medieval, understandings of God, thereby masking certain complexities in their disputes. Drawing on the practices of both scientific and theological theory construction, it is argued that traditional theologies should be seen as negotiable in certain ways. In the light of this, standard attempts at refutations of Christianity have significantly less force than is usually appreciated. Some pitfalls of both strong and weak commitments to any particular theological framework are discussed.

**Shanahan, Timothy**. Kitcher's Compromise: A Critical Examination of the Compromise Model of Scientific Closure, and its Implications for the Relationship Between History and Philosophy of Science. *Stud Hist Phil Sci*, 28(2), 319-338, Je 97.

I critically evaluate the compromise model by identifying its crucial assumptions and by attempting to apply the model to a major transition in the history of biology: the rejection of 'naive group selectionism' in the 1960s. (edited)

**Shand, John**. A Reply to Some Standard Objections to Euthanasia. *J Applied Phil*, 14(1), 43-47, 1997.

The purpose here is to cast doubt on some utilitarian non-rights-based arguments that are generally thought to be decisive objections to voluntary and nonvoluntary euthanasia. The aim is not to prove that euthanasia is morally vindicated (although I think rights-based arguments can do this) but rather to contend that such arguments, far from being decisively anti-euthanasia, can be made to point equally in the opposite direction.

**Shanks, Niall**. Genetics and Biomedicine: The Perils of Popularization. *Commun Cog*, 29(2), 185-214, 1996.

I want to explore the popularization of genetics and genetic engineering by studying the ways in which information in these fields of science have actually been popularized, and the purposes such popularizations have served. It turns out that the actual purposes served often differ from the lofty educational goals professed by many popularizers of science. I will then discuss a number of cases that illustrate what I take to be the perils of popularization. (edited)

**Shanks, Niall** and Gale, George. Methodology and the Birth of Modern Cosmological Inquiry. *Stud Hist Phil Mod Physics*, 27B(3), 279-296, S 96.

The central concern of this paper is with the ways in which issues, questions and debates in the domain of the *philosophy of science* can influence the birth and subsequent development of a science. The case study to be discussed is that of modern cosmology. We will argue that the study of events in the early history of modern cosmology affords ample evidence of the many ways in which philosophy of science and science are inextricably intertwined. (edited)

**Shanks, Niall** and LaFollette, Hugh. *Brute Science: Dilemmas of Animal Experimentation*. New York, Routledge, 1996.

Are humans morally justified in conducting sometimes painful experiments on animals in their search for a cure for cancer, heart disease and AIDS? Apologists for animal experimentation claim for practice is morally justified, because humans are more valuable than animals and scientifically justified, because the data derived from these experiments profoundly benefits humans. *Brute Science* investigates this standard defense of animal experimentation. The authors show, on methodological and empirical grounds, that defenders of animal experimentation seriously exaggerate its benefits. Consequently, we need to reassess, scientifically and morally, our use of animals in biomedical experimentation. (edited)

**Shanks, Roland E** and Pimentel, David and Rylander, Jason C. Bioethics of Fish Production: Energy and the Environment. *J Agr Environ Ethics*, 9(2), 144-164, 1996.

Aquatic ecosystems are vital to the structure and function of all environments on earth. Worldwide, approximately 95 million metric tons of fishery products are harvested from marine and freshwater habitats. A major problem in fisheries around the world is the bioethics of overfishing. A wide range of management techniques exists for fishery, managers and policy-makers to improve fishery

AUTHOR INDEX 909 Shapiro, Stewart

production in the future. The best approach to limit overfishing is to have an effective, federally regulated fishery, based on environmental standards and fishery carrying capacity. Soon, overfishing is more likely to cause fish scarcity than fossil fuel shortages and high energy prices for fish harvesting. However, oil and other fuel are projected to influence future fishery policies and the productive capacity of the fishery industry. Overall, small-scale fishing systems are more energy efficient than large-scale systems. Aquaculture is not the solution to wild fishery production. The energy input/output ratio of aquacultural fish is much higher than that of the harvest of wild populations. In addition, the energy ratios for aquaculture systems are higher than those for most livestock systems.

**Shanley, Brian J**. Eternal Knowledge of the Temporal in Aquinas. *Amer Cath Phil Quart*, 71(2), 197-224, Spr 97.

Aquinas's use of Boethian imagery to explain God's eternal knowledge of temporal events has engendered a persistent criticism, originated by Scotus, that such an account is incompatible with a dynamic view of time. This critique rests on a misinterpretation. Despite the apparently passive and static implications of the Boethian images, Aquinas's authentic position involves conceiving God's knowledge as active, practical and causal; it is the knowledge of the Creator of time, not the passive spectator of time. Once the causal view of knowledge is recognized, then the Scotistic critique dissolves and the dynamic view of time vindicated.

**Shanley, Mary Lyndon** (ed) and Narayan, Uma (ed). *Reconstructing Political Theory: Feminist Perspectives*. University Park, Pennsylvania Univ Pr, 1997.

While some of the chapters discuss traditional concepts such as rights, power, freedom, and citizenship, others argue that less frequently discussed topics in political theory—such as the family, childhood, dependency, compassion, and suffering—are just as significant for an understanding of political life. The opening chapter by Narayan and Shanley shows how this diverse set of topics can be linked together and how feminist political theory can be elaborated systematically if it takes notions of independence and dependancy, public and private, and power and empowerment as central to its agenda. (publisher, edited)

**Shanner, Laura**. "Bioethics through the Back Door: Phenomenology, Narratives, and Insights into Infertility" in *Philosophical Perspectives on Bioethics*, Sumner, L W (ed), 115-142. Toronto, Univ of Toronto Pr, 1996.

Unaddressed in most debates about normative bioethics theory is the process by which we determine the nature of the problem we are trying to resolve. The author promotes phenomenological, narrative and qualitative approaches as necessary steps to understand human experiences and the values at stake prior to seeking a normative resolution. Using infertility as an example, the phenomenological approach shows that traditional debates on embryo status, rights of access to treatment, etc. fail to address infertility's primary characteristic, which is psychosocial distress. The solutions generated in bioethics and clinical medicine are, therefore, incomplete moral responses to the needs of infertile individuals.

**Shannon, J Richard** and Berl, Robert L. Are We Teaching Ethics in Marketing?: A Survey of Students' Attitudes and Perceptions. *J Bus Ethics*, 16(10), 1059-1075, Jl 97.

This is a descriptive study which examined the attitudes and perceptions of 273 business students at eight universities across the U.S. towards ethics education. The results indicate that students perceive that the level of discussion of ethics and ethical issues ranges from less than adequate in some marketing courses to adequate in others. Sales/sales management courses received the highest ratings for coverage of ethical issues, while transportation/logistics courses scored the lowest. The study also finds that students believe, quite strongly, that the discussion of ethics and ethical issues is worthwhile and important. (edited)

**Shapiro, Daniel Edward** and Schulman, Charles Eric. Ethical and Legal Issues in E-Mail Therapy. *Ethics Behavior*, 6(2), 107-124, 1996.

Psychologists and psychiatrists recently started using electronic mail (e-mail) to conduct therapy. This article explores relevant ethical and legal issues including, among others, the nature of the professional relationship, boundaries of competence, informed consent, treating minors, confidentiality and the duty to warn and protect. To illustrate these complex issues, two services currently operating are discussed. To address potential hazards to clients and the profession, a new ethical standard for e-main therapists is offered.

**Shapiro, Daniel J**. Can Old-Age Social Insurance Be Justified. *Soc Phil Pol*, 14(2), 116-144, Sum 97.

I compare old-age social insurance (SI) to a system of compulsory private pensions (CP), such as Chile's, concerning 1) justice and fairness, 2) positive rights and security, 3) negative rights and freedom, and 4) public justification of basic political institutions. CP wins on all counts. 1. SI, but not CP, produces significant transfers from later to early generations, which harms the later generations, particularly its worst off members. 2. CP, but not SI, can ground a right to a pension based on prior contributions. 3. CP provides more freedom to decide how to invest one's contributions. 4. Reasonably accurate information about CP, but not SI, is widely accessible.

**Shapiro, Harold T**. "Cognition, Character, and Culture in Undergraduate Education: Rhetoric and Reality" in *The American University: National Treasure or Endangered Species?*, Ehrenberg, Ronald G (ed), 58-99. Ithaca, Cornell Univ Pr, 1997.

This paper discusses the evolution of undergraduate education in America within a broad historical framework. It focuses particularly on three topics: (1) the relationship of the university to the society that sustains it and the civic obligations thereby entailed, (2) the frequent discrepancy between the popular memory (of an earlier "golden age") and historical reality in considering the evolution of undergraduate education in America and (3) the nature of a liberal education and the necessity of recognizing an ethical dimension in higher education, which seeks to develop the moral imagination without inculcating a particular orthodoxy.

**Shapiro, Ian**. *Democracy's Place*. Ithaca, Cornell Univ Pr, 1996.

*Democracy's Place* includes seven essays in which Shapiro carefully integrates the theoretical and the applied. Four deal principally with democratic theory and its link to problems of social justice; the other three detail applications in the United States, the postcommunist world, and the author's native South Africa. All advance a view of democratic politics which rests on principled, yet nuanced, suspicion of hierarchical social arrangements and of political blueprints. Shapiro's writing is unified as well by a pervasive concern with the relations between the requirements of democracy and those of social justice. These themes, illuminated by complex yet accessible arguments, contribute to an attractive democratic perspective on contemporary debates about liberalism, communitarianism, and distributive justice. (publisher,edited)

**Shapiro, Ian**. Elements of Democratic Justice. *Polit Theory*, 24(4), 579-619, N 96.

A general argument for a democratic conception of social justice is developed and defended as an alternative to liberal, socialist, conservative and communitarian views. Drawing on the twin democratic commitments to universal participation in collective decisions and the right to oppose decisions that one rejects, the author explores the ways in which these commitments should influence the shape of civil institutions. Examples discussed include aspects of political institutions, family relations and the governance of work, education and religious practice. Several difficulties confronting the argument are anticipated and responded to, including potential tensions internal to democratic justice and tensions between it and other valuable goods. The last part of the essay deals with the role for the state implied by the general argument, with particular attention to problems of cumulative social injustice and the provision of public goods. A limited role for judicial review is defended as consistent with the spirit of the general argument.

**Shapiro, Ian**. Group Aspirations and Democratic Politics. *Constellations*, 3(3), 315-325, Ja 97.

Much of the philosophical literature on group rights evaluates their desirability, or lack of it, in general terms. Here, by contrast, I argue that because group rights are typically asserted by political parties and leaders with particular goals, their claims can be fairly evaluated only if those goals are taken into account. An appropriate criterion for evaluating demands for group rights concerns their likely impact on democratic politics, where this is understood to require inclusive participation of those affected by collective decisions and the toleration of "loyal" opposition within a democratic order. I explore this criterion by reference to a variety of recent competing demands for group rights in South Africa and the Middle East. This leads to a more general discussion of the foundations of politicized group identities and of institutional arrangements that are more and less likely to induce them to evolve in democratic directions.

**Shapiro, Joel**. Originary Pain: Animal Life Beyond the Pleasure Principle in Kant's *Anthropology*. *Epoche*, 3(1 & 2), 117-148, 1995.

Kant argues that we seek pleasure, which is the feeling of the enhancement of life and avoid pain, which is the feeling of the hindrance of life. He then defines (animal) life, however, as the continuous play of the antagonism of pleasure and pain. This situates pain (previously aligned with the hindrance of life) at the heart of life itself. Pleasure is then aligned with death in two different ways: contentment can become a kind of inertia or living death and uninhibited pleasure is said to issue an annihilating ecstasy. Finally, Kant privileges pain over pleasure, suggesting that it is the source, ground and motor or driving force of animal life.

**Shapiro, Kenneth J** and Gluck, John P. The Forum. *Ethics Behavior*, 7(2), 185-192, 1997.

**Shapiro, Lawrence A**. A Clearer Vision. *Phil Sci*, 64(1), 131-153, Mr 97.

Frances Egan argues that the states of computational theories of vision are individuated individualistically and, as far as the theory is concerned, are not intentional. Her argument depends on equating the goals and explanatory strategies of computational psychology with those of its algorithmic level. However, closer inspection of computational psychology reveals that the computational level plays an essential role in explaining visual processes and that explanations at this level are nonindividualistic and intentional. In conclusion, I sketch an account of content in which content does the sort of explanatory work that Egan denies is possible.

**Shapiro, Lawrence A**. Representation from Bottom and Top. *Can J Phil*, 26(4), 523-542, D 96.

Bottom-up strategies for naturalizing representational content seek to build representation up from nonrepresentational pieces. Dretske (1989) is such an attempt. I argue that such a strategy fails to provide scientifically acceptable ascriptions of representational content and that we are better off appealing to biological functions to ground these ascriptions. This conclusion is in keeping with Williams's (1966) advice that we distinguish that which a mechanism has the function to detect from that to which a mechanism is physically sensitive.

**Shapiro, Robyn S** and Klein, John P and Tym, Kristen A. Wisconsin Healthcare Ethics Committees. *Cambridge Quart Healthcare Ethics*, 6(3), 288-292, Sum 97.

**Shapiro, Stewart**. *Philosophy of Mathematics: Structure and Ontology*. New York, Oxford Univ Pr, 1997.

As Benacerraf first noted, we are confronted with the following powerful dilemma. The desired continuity between mathematical and, say, scientific language suggests realism, but realism in this context suggests seemingly intractable epistemic problems. As a way out of this dilemma, Shapiro articulates a structuralist approach. On this view, the subject matter of arithmetic, for example, is not a fixed domain of numbers independent of each other, but rather is the natural number structure, the pattern common to any system of objects that has an initial object and successor relation satisfying the induction principle. Using this framework, realism in mathematics can be preserved without troublesome epistemic consequences. (publisher, edited)

**Sharma, A D** and Shukla, S K. Pramāna Samplava and Pramāna Vyavasthā. *J Indian Counc Phil Res*, 14(2), 83-98, Ja-Ap 97.

**Sharma, Akshaya Kumar**. Gandhian Concept of Planned Society. *Darshana Int*, 36(2/142), 69-72, Ap 96.

**Sharma, Arun** and Jain, Sanjay. Characterizing Language Identification in Terms of Computable Numberings. *Annals Pure Applied Log*, 84(1), 51-72, Mr 97.

Identification of programs for computable functions from their graphs and identification of grammars (r.e., indices) for recursively enumerable languages from positive data are two extensively studied problems in the recursion theoretic framework of inductive inference. In the context of function identification, Freivalds et al. (1984) have shown that only those collections of functions, *L*, are identifiable in the limit for which there exists a 1-1 computable numbering Psi and a discrimination function *d* such that a) for each *f* "is an element of" *L*, the number of indices *i* such that Psi$_i$ = *f* is exactly one and b) for each *f* "is an element of" *L*, there are only finitely many indices *i* such that *f* and Psi$_i$ agree on the first *d(i)* arguments. A similar characterization for language identification in the limit has turned out to be difficult. A partial answer is provided in this paper. Several new techniques are introduced which have found use in other investigations on language identification. (edited)

**Sharma, M L**. Professor Date's New Light on the Vedanta of Samkara. *Darshana Int*, 35(3/139), 39-44, Jl 95.

**Sharma, Ramesh Kumar**. Nyāya Realism: Some Reflections. *J Indian Counc Phil Res*, 14(2), 138-155, Ja-Ap 97.

The essay defends the metaphysical realism of Nyāya (-Vaisesika) as against Daya Krishna's attempt to give it an idealist twist by comparing it with the Berkeleyean position; and explains the significance of the Nyāya theory of knowability of every existent by contrasting it with the Kantian doctrine of the unknowability of his 'things-in-themselves'. Then follows a rebuttal of the suggestion that Nyāya's postulation of isomorphism of structure between knowledge and reality amounts to conceiving (a la Hegel) the 'real' as 'rational'. The paper then seeks to show the mistakenness of some of the assumptions on which Arindam Chakraborty tries to uphold, rightly though, Nyāya realism. In the process I revisit the nirākāravāda-sāravāda controversy and attempt to make the respective doctrines further intelligible.

**Sharp, Ann Margaret**. Letter-Writing: A Tool in Feminist Inquiry. *Inquiry (USA)*, 14(3), 54-63, Spr 95.

**Sharp, Ann Margaret**. Self-transformation in the Community of Inquiry. *Inquiry (USA)*, 16(1), 36-47, Fall 96.

I propose in this paper that if we want to help students build a balanced self-esteem, that is a real regard for their personhood, they must be provided with an educational opportunity that allows participation in a classroom community of philosophical inquiry. Why? Because it is in such a classroom community that they are exposed to the *normative* disciplines of logic, ethics and aesthetics. Inquiry within these branches of philosophy are necessary tools in helping students not only to understand what is worthy of their esteem but also to come to understand the self as a process in relationship to all of nature, a process of endless transformation and self-correction. (edited)

**Sharpe, Kevin**. Sociobiology and Evil: Ultimate Reality and Meaning Through Biology. *Ultim Real Mean*, 19(3), 240-250, S 96.

Sociobiology provides insight into the problem of evil, first by suggesting that Ultimate Reality may not have the morality to which humans aspire. Ultimate Reality may not even have a morality at all. It is therefore inappropriate to think Ultimate Reality should abide by the highest human sense of love and justice. Second, sociobiology explains why humans plea for help from Ultimate Reality and are angry at Ultimate Reality if the suffering continues. Both the human understanding of Ultimate Reality and the pleading to Ultimate Reality are biological at root.

**Sharpe, Kevin**. The Origin of the Big Bang Universe in Ultimate Reality with Special Reference to the Cosmology of Stephen Hawking. *Ultim Real Mean*, 20(1), 61-71, Mr 97.

Theories on the origin of the universe—for example, Stephen Hawking's—assume the existence of something that generates the big bang and the existence of the universe. I call this "something" the subuniverse. It operates according to a form of logic and gives reality to the universe and its laws both at the big bang and throughout the life of the universe. These properties also characterize *ultimate reality*. I suggest that the subuniverse emerges directly from *ultimate reality*. Hawking's cosmology supposedly dispenses with the need for a creator. I show that, rather, it depends on the existence of something equivalent to *ultimate reality*.

**Sharpe, M E** (trans). On Human Rights. *Chin Stud Phil*, 28(1), 74-77, Fall 96.

**Sharpe, R A**. One Cheer for Simulation Theory. *Inquiry*, 40(1), 115-131, Mr 97.

The idea that our knowledge of others is a form of theoretical understanding, the theory-theory, is contrasted with this new rival, that our knowledge of others depends on simulation, essentially by putting ourselves in the position of others. I argue that neither is plausible as a general account of our knowledge of other

people, though both may play a role on occasion. However, unless the two theories are general accounts or make claims about what is primitive, they are of little interest. Finally, I suggest that much of the work offered here looks suspiciously like pseudoscience.

**Sharpe, Virginia A**. Why "Do No Harm?". *Theor Med*, 18(1-2), 197-215, Mr-Je 97.

Edmund Pellegrino has argued that the dramatic changes in American health care call for critical reflection on the traditional norms governing the therapeutic relationship. This paper offers such reflection on the obligation to "do no harm." Drawing on work by Beauchamp and Childress and Pellegrino and Thomasma, I argue that the libertarian model of medical ethics offered by Engelhardt cannot adequately sustain an obligation to "do no harm." Because the obligation to "do not harm" is not based simply on a negative duty of nonmaleficence but also on a positive duty of beneficence, I argue that it is best understood to derive from the fiduciary nature of the healing relationship.

**Sharpe, Virginia A** and Pellegrino, Edmund D. Medical Ethics in the Courtroom: A Reappraisal. *J Med Phil*, 22(4), 373-379, Ag 97.

Following up on a 1989 paper on the subject, this essay revisits the question of ethical expertise in the court room. Informed by recent developments in the use of ethics experts, the authors argue (1) that the adversarial nature of court proceedings challenges the integrity of the ethicist's pedagogical role; (2) that the use of ethics experts as normative authorities remains dubious; (3) that clarification of the State's interest in "protecting the ethical integrity of the medical profession" is urgently required; and (4) that the expertise of the ethicist may be more appropriately used in advising the legislature than in influencing the court.

**Sharples, Bob**. Aristotle and Others. *Phronesis*, 41(3), 351-360, 1996.

**Sharples, R W**. Stoics, Epicureans and Sceptics: An Introduction to Hellenistic Philosophy. New York, Routledge, 1996.

This study gives a comprehensive and readable account of the principal doctrines of the Stoics, Epicureans and various sceptical traditions from the death of Alexander the Great in 323 BC to about AD 200. The discussion is arranged according to topics, rather than schools, in order to bring out the underlying issues and make clear what the schools have in common and how they differ. At the same time, the coherence of each system as a whole is emphasised. (publisher, edited)

**Sharpley-Whiting, T Denean** (ed & trans) and Sartre, Jean-Paul. "Return from the United States" in *Existence in Black: An Anthology of Black Existential Philosophy*, Gordon, Lewis R (ed), 83-89. New York, Routledge, 1997.

The essay is an annotated translation of an article written by the philosopher after his return from the U.S. Its original title, "Retour des Etats Unis: Ce qui j'ai appris du problème noir" [Return from the United States: What I learned about the black problem"], was published by *Le Figaro* on June 15, 1945. While affirming his position as an outsider meddling in a family affair, Sartre nonetheless details the conflicts around race and racism in America, providing sociological and statistical data. The essay's translator offers commentary and comparative statistical data in notes on black existence in 1995.

**Shaskolsky Sheleff, Leon**. Social Cohesion and Legal Coercion: A Critique of Weber, Durkheim, and Marx. Amsterdam, Rodopi, 1997.

This book is a critical study of the work in the area of law of three classical social theorists: Max Weber, Emile Durkheim and Karl Marx. The critique focuses on the concept of rationality in Weber, the determination of law as repressive or restitutive in Durkheim and the idea of justice in society in Marx. The chapters deal with the themes of tradition, social control, equality, science, political authority, conflict resolution, ideology, community and altruism. The legal issues are examined with insights from philosophy, sociology, religion, anthropology, politics and economics. An extensive essay by Virginia Black, in the form of an Afterword, discusses the main theses of this multidisciplinary book. (publisher)

**Shatz, David**. Is Peer Review Overrated?. *Monist*, 79(4), 536-563, O 96.

**Shaver, Robert**. Sidgwick's False Friends. *Ethics*, 107(2), 314-320, Ja 97.

Many cite Sidgwick as holding a "full information" account of the good. Sidgwick does not, however, hold such a view. Instead, he offers a neglected criticism of full information accounts. In particular, he objects to the attempt to give a naturalistic account that relies on internalism.

**Shavrukov, V Yu**. Undecidability in Diagonalizable Algebras. *J Sym Log*, 62(1), 79-116, Mr 97.

**Shaw, Bill**. A Pragmatic Approach to Business Ethics. *Bus Ethics Quart*, 7(3), 159-167, Jl 97.

**Shaw, Bill**. A Virtue Ethics Approach to Aldo Leopold's Land Ethic. *Environ Ethics*, 19(1), 53-67, Spr 97.

I examine "The Land Ethic" by Aldo Leopold from a virtue ethics perspective. Following Leopold, I posit the "good" as the "integrity, stability, and beauty" of biotic communities and then develop "land virtues" that foster this good. I recommend and defend three land virtues: respect (or ecological sensitivity), prudence, and practical judgment.

**Shaw, Bill**. Sources of Virtue: The Market and the Community. *Bus Ethics Quart*, 7(1), 33-50, Ja 97.

Virtues are habits of character that advance excellence in all of ones endeavors. In the Aristotelian formulation, training in the virtues is driven by a sense of the "good," that is, by a widely shared agreement on the components of a good society and on the roles (and appropriate virtues or excellencies) of the "social animals" that energize that society. In the modern era, however, a strong sense of community has been much diminished. Freedom from the restraints of the church and other social institutions and an emphasis on individual autonomy has fostered a different ethical perspective, a perspective in which the market enters importantly into one's conception of the good. (edited)

**Shear, Jonathan** (ed). *Explaining Consciousness—The 'Hard Problem'*. Cambridge, MIT Pr, 1997.

In this book, philosophers, physicists, psychologists, neurophysiologists, computer scientists, and others—all the major participants in the debate—address this central topic in the growing discipline of consciousness studies. Some take issue with Chalmer's distinction, arguing that the hard problem is a nonproblem, or that the explanatory gap is too wide to be bridged. Others offer alternative suggestions as to how the problem might be solved, whether through cognitive science, fundamental physics, empirical phenomenology, or with theories that take consciousness as irreducible. (publisher, edited)

**Sheehan, Thomas**. Let a Hundred Translations Bloom! A Modest Proposal about *Being and Time*. *Man World*, 30(2), 227-238, Ap 97.

Joan Stambaugh's new translation of Heidegger's *Sein und Zeit* falls far short of the previous English rendering by Macquarrie and Robinson, both as an edition and as a translation. It is replete with mistranslations, omissions, syntactically incorrect translations, editorial errors, and incorrect transliterations of some forty Greek words. It fails to take into account hundreds of changes made in Heidegger's German text since 1963, it introduces more than a dozen of its own unannounced alterations to Heidegger's footnotes, and it makes numerous mistakes in translating Heidegger's marginal notes. The present article documents scores of these mistakes in detail.

**Sheets-Johnstone, Maxine**. Human Versus Nonhuman: Binary Opposition As an Ordering Principle of Western Human Thought. *Between Species*, 12(1-2), 57-63, Wint-Spr 96.

The human/nonhuman opposition is a fundamental binary opposition that in its mode of expression is endemic to Western culture. It subsumes other oppositions basic to Western ways of thinking—e.g., nature/culture—and subsumes also oppositions having to do with behavioral capability ascriptions such as learned/instinctual, future planning/immediate action. Following a brief historical introduction, this article shows how the subsumption works, how the fundamental binary opposition is an ordering principle of thought that is inconsistently applied and that disregards a basic tenet of evolutionary theory, and how the opposition is evidentially unsound, myopically self-serving, and for philosophers especially, a particularly thin justification for cherishing their species.

**Shein, David**. A Pragmatic Theory of Causal Analysis. *Conference*, 6(1), 15-30, Sum 95.

I distinguish between theories of causation—analysis of the causal relationship—and causal discourse. When we engage in causal discourse we bracket information—we make assumptions about what is and what is not the case. By respecting this distinction and making explicit this process of bracketing, we are able to reject certain sorts of problems which are regarded as reasons to reject counterfactual analyses of causation. Moreover, since what is bracketed depends on the context of causal analysis, we are led to a pragmatic theory of causal analysis on which what counts as a cause varies from context to context.

**Shekhawat, Virendra**. Problems of Formalization in Saṃvāda Sāstra. *J Indian Counc Phil Res*, 13(2), 77-95, Ja-Ap 96.

**Shekhawat, Virendra**. Research Monographs on the History of Science. *J Indian Counc Phil Res*, 14(1), 185-192, S-D 96.

**Shelah, S** and Gilchrist, M. Identities on Cardinals Less Than Aleph$_{omega}$. *J Sym Log*, 61(3), 780-787, S 96.

**Shelah, Saharon**. Colouring and Non-Productivity of Aleph$_2$-C.C.. *Annals Pure Applied Log*, 84(2), 153-174, Mr 97.

We prove that coloring of pairs from Aleph$_2$ with strong properties exists. The easiest to state (and quite a well-known) problem it solves is: there are two topological spaces with cellularity Aleph$_1$ whose product has cellularity Aleph$_2$; equivalently, we can speak of cellularity of Boolean algebras or of Boolean algebras satisfying the Aleph$_2$-c.c. whose product fails the Aleph$_2$-c.c. We also deal more with guessing of clubs.

**Shelah, Saharon**. If There is an Exactly Lambda-Free Abelian Group Then There is an Exactly Lambda-Separable One in Lambda. *J Sym Log*, 61(4), 1261-1278, D 96.

We give a solution stated in the title to problem 3 of part 1 of the problems listed in the book of Eklof and Mekler, p. 453. There, in pp. 241-242, this is discussed and proved in some cases. The existence of strongly *lambda*-free ones was proved earlier by the criteria. We can apply a similar proof to a large class of other varieties in particular to the variety of (noncommutative) groups.

**Shelah, Saharon**. In the random graph G($n$,$p$), $p = n^{a}$.... *Annals Pure Applied Log*, 82(1), 97-102, N 96.

**Shelah, Saharon** and Jech, Thomas. On Countably Closed Complete Boolean Algebras. *J Sym Log*, 61(4), 1380-1386, D 96.

It is unprovable that every complete subalgebra of a countably closed complete Boolean algebra is countably closed.

**Shelah, Saharon** and Jin, Renling. Can a Small Forcing Create Kurepa Trees. *Annals Pure Applied Log*, 85(1), 47-68, Ap 97.

In this paper we probe the possibilities of creating a Kurepa tree in a generic extension of a ground model of *CH* plus no Kurepa trees by an omega$_1$-preserving forcing notion of size at most omega$_1$. In Section I we show that in the Lévy model obtained by collapsing all cardinals between omega$_1$ and a strongly inaccessible cardinal by forcing with a countable support Lévy

collapsing order, many omega$_1$-preserving forcing notions of size at most omega$_1$ including all omega-proper forcing notions and some proper but not omega-proper forcing notions of size at most omega$_1$ do not create Kurepa trees. In Section 2 we construct a model of *CH* plus no Kurepa trees, in which there is an omega-distributive Aronszajn tree such that forcing with that Aronszajn tree does create a Kurepa tree in the generic extension. At the end of the paper we ask three questions.

**Shelah, Saharon** and Laskowski, Michael C. Forcing Isomorphism II. *J Sym Log*, 61(4), 1305-1320, D 96.

**Shelah, Saharon** and Lifsches, Shmuel. Uniformization, Choice Functions and Well Orders in the Class of Trees. *J Sym Log*, 61(4), 1206-1227, D 96.

The monadic second-order theory of trees allows quantification over elements and over arbitrary subsets. We classify the class of trees with respect to the question: does a tree *T* have a definable choice function (by a monadic formula with parameters)? A natural dichotomy arises where the trees that fall in the first class don't have a definable choice function and the trees in the second class have even a definable well ordering of their elements. This has a close connection to the uniformization problem.

**Shell, Susan Meld**. Bowling Alone: On the Saving Power of Kant's Perpetual Peace. *Ideal Stud*, 26(2), 153-173, Wint 96.

Kant's *Perpetual Peace* has a more complex rhetorical structure than has generally been noted. In this paper I examine that structure anew, with special attention to Kant's own efforts to successfully embody the role of the moral politician. I conclude that the work succeeds in the special task that it sets itself: namely, to combine, in the shear act of publicizing itself, the power of the sovereign with the wisdom of the philosopher.

**Shelley, Judith Allen** and Salladay, Susan Anthony. Spirituality in Nursing Theory and Practice: Dilemmas for Christian Bioethics. *Christian Bioethics*, 3(1), 20-38, Mr 97.

Moral strangerhood is due in part to competing worldviews. The profession of nursing is experiencing a paradigm shift which creates ethical dilemmas for both Christian nurses and Christian patients. Nursing's new focus on spirituality and spiritual care presents itself as broadly defining a desired state or patient outcome—spiritual integrity—supposed to be applicable to all patients of all faiths. Analysis of nursing's definition of spirituality reveals assumptions and values consistent with an Eastern/New Age worldview which may cause hostility towards Christian patients stereotyped as dogmatic or noncompliant.

**Shelton, Jo-Ann**. Contracts with Animals: Lucretius, *De Rerum Natura*. *Between Species*, 11(3-4), 115-121, Sum-Fall 95.

**Shepard, Jon M** and Betz, Michael and O'Connell, Lenahan. The Proactive Corporation: Its Nature and Causes. *J Bus Ethics*, 16(10), 1001-1010, Jl 97.

We argue that the stakeholder perspective on corporate social responsibility is in the process of being enlarged. Due to the process of institutional isomorphism, corporations are increasingly adopting organizational features designed to promote proactivity over mere reactivity in their stakeholder relationships. We identify two sources of pressure promoting the emergence of the proactive corporation—stakeholder activism and the recognition of the social embeddedness of the economy. The final section describes four organizational design dimensions being installed by the more proactive corporations today—cooperation, participation, negotiation, and direct anticipation.

**Shepard, Jon M** and Goldsby, Michael G and Gerde, Virginia W. Teaching Business Ethics Through Literature. *Teach Bus Ethics*, 1(1), 33-51, 1997.

America's economic ideology lacks a vocabulary of ethics. If, as we assume, an economic system requires a moral component for long-term survival, students in business schools must be exposed to a vocabulary of ethics that is consistent with the ideology of capitalism. We present a vocabulary of ethics and describe an approach to teaching business ethics based on business-related classic literature and moral philosophy.

**Shepard, Jon M** and Wimbush, James C and Markham, Steven E. An Empirical Examination of the Multi-Dimensionality of Ethical Climate in Organizations. *J Bus Ethics*, 16(1), 67-77, Ja 97.

The purpose of this study was to determine whether the ethical climate dimensions identified by Victor and Cullen (1987, 1988) could be replicated in the subunits of a multiunit organization and if so, were the dimensions associated with particular types of operating units. We identified three of the dimensions of ethical climate found by Victor and Cullen and also found a new dimension of ethical climate related to service. Partial support was found for Victor and Cullen's hypothesis that certain ethical climate dimensions are associated with particular forms of organizational governance and control.

**Shepard, Roger N** and Hut, Piet. Turning 'The Hard Problem' Upside Down & Sideways. *J Consciousness Stud*, 3(4), 313-329, 1996.

Instead of speaking of conscious experience as arising in a brain, we prefer to speak of a brain as arising in conscious experience. From an epistemological standpoint, starting from direct experiences strikes us as more justified. As a first option, we reconsider the 'hard problem' of the relation between conscious experience and the physical world by thus turning that problem upside down. We also consider a second option: turning the hard problem sideways. Rather than starting with the third-person approach used in physics, or the first-person approach of starting with individual conscious experience, we consider starting from an I-and-you basis, centered around the second-person. Finally, we present a candidate for what could be considered to underlie conscious experience: 'sense'. (edited)

Sheppard, Darren 912 AUTHOR INDEX

**Sheppard, Darren** (ed) and Sparks, Simon (ed) and Thomas, Colin (ed). *On Jean-Luc Nancy: The Sense of Philosophy.* New York, Routledge, 1997.

*On Jean-Luc Nancy* draws together a number of outstanding commentators to provide an invaluable companion to Nancy's own work. In addition to contributions by Howard Caygill, Rodolphe Gasché and Alphonso Lingis, there is a text by Nancy's renowned long-time co-author, Philippe Lacoue-Labarthe. These essays approach the main themes in Nancy's work. From Nancy the philosopher of the contemporary and of the disorientation in thinking today to Nancy and the significance of anger and sacrifice in philosophy, the recurrent themes of community, freedom, being and the divine in his work are brought out. (publisher, edited)

**Sher, G Y**. Partially-Ordered (Branching) Generalized Quantifiers: A General Definition. *J Phil Log*, 26(1), 1-43, F 97.

Following Henkin's discovery of partially-ordered (branching) quantification (POQ) with standard quantifiers in 1959, philosophers of language have attempted to extend his definition to POQ with generalized quantifiers. In this paper I propose a general definition of POQ with 1-place generalized quantifiers of the simplest kind: namely, predicative, or "cardinality" quantifiers, e.g., "most", "few", "finitely many", "exactly *alpha*, where *alpha* is any cardinal, etc. (edited)

**Sher, George**. *Beyond Neutrality: Perfectionism and Politics.* New York, Cambridge Univ Pr, 1997.

Many people, including many contemporary philosophers, believe that the state has no business trying to improve people's characters or elevating their tastes or preventing them from living degraded lives. They believe that governments should remain absolutely neutral when it comes to the consideration of competing conceptions of the good. One fundamental aim of George Sher's book is to show that this view is indefensible. A second complementary aim is to articulate a conception of the good that is worthy of promotion by the state. The first part of the book analyzes attempts to ground the neutrality thesis in the value of autonomy, respect for autonomy, the dangers of a nonneutral state, and skepticism about the good. The second part defends an objective conception of the good which remains sensitive to some of the considerations that make subjectivism attractive. According to this conception, the elements of a good life include (but are not exhausted by) knowledge, excellence, certain preferred modes of interaction among persons, and various familiar virtues. Lucidly written and structured, this book represents a major contribution to contemporary political theory. (publisher)

**Sher, George**. My Profession and Its Duties. *Monist*, 79(4), 471-487, O 96.

Much that is written about professional ethics concerns the requirements imposed by specific roles. We are often told what professionals such as doctors, lawyers, or teachers should do—or, alternatively, what a good doctor, lawyer, or teacher *will* do. This essay seeks to clarify such claims as they pertain to one particular role—that of a faculty member at a college or university—by asking 1) what special requirements the role imposes and 2) why faculty members are obligated to live up to those requirements. The thrust of the argument is that the most promising answer to each question leaves the other question unresolved. Thus, disturbingly, the moral status of the requirements imposed by the role of faculty member—and, by extension, other professional roles—remains unresolved.

**Sherblom, Stephen A** and Bier, Melinda C and Gallo, Michael A. Ethical Issues in a Study of Internet Use: Uncertainty, Responsibility, and the Spirit of Research Relationships. *Ethics Behavior*, 6(2), 141-151, 1996.

In this article we explore ethical issues arising in a study of home Internet use by low-income families. We consider questions of our responsibility as educational researchers and discuss the ethical implications of some unanticipated consequences of our study. We illustrate ways in which the principles of research ethics for use of human subjects can be ambiguous and possibly inadequate for anticipating potential harm in educational research. In this exploratory research of personal communication technologies, participants experienced changes that were personal and relational. These unanticipated changes in their way of being complicated our research relationships, testing the boundaries of our commitment to the principle of trustworthiness and forcing us to re-evaluate our responsibilities.

**Sherburne, Donald W**. "The Goldilocks Syndrome" in *The Recovery of Philosophy in America: Essays in Honor of John Edwin Smith,* Kasulis, Thomas P (ed), 167-181. Albany, SUNY Pr, 1997.

**Sherman, Nancy**. *Making a Necessity of Virtue.* Needham Heights, Cambridge, 1997.

This major collection of essays offers the first serious challenge to the traditional view that ancient and modern ethics are fundamentally opposed. It not only has important implications for contemporary ethical thought, but provides a significant reassessment of the work of Aristotle, Kant, and the Stoics. (publisher, edited)

**Sherry, David**. On Mathematical Error. *Stud Hist Phil Sci*, 28(3), 393-416, S 97.

Fallibilists point to the historical record as evidence of the fallible, corrigible and tentative nature of mathematics. I argue that errors implicating an entire community of mathematicians do not exist in any but a philosophically problematic sense. This is not a historical accident but a reflection of mathematics' nature.

**Sherwin, Susan**. "Theory versus Practice in Ethics: A Feminist Perspective on Justice in Health Care" in *Philosophical Perspectives on Bioethics,* Sumner, L W (ed), 187-209. Toronto, Univ of Toronto Pr, 1996.

This essay is aimed at dismantling the widely accepted distinction between conceptual and practical issues in ethics. I argue that the two sorts of ethics tasks are inextricably linked. In demonstration and support of this thesis, I explore the concept of justice to see how important it is to attend to the intimate interrelationship of conceptual and practical concerns when we invoke this central concept in health care discussions. I propose a methodology of "feminist reflective equilibrium" for ethics and bioethics as a means of ensuring that each dimension is considered in light of the other.

**Shevlin Edwards, Sue** and Orlowski, James P and Vinicky, Janicemarie K. Conflicts of Interest, Conflicting Interests, and Interesting Conflicts, Part 3. *J Clin Ethics*, 7(2), 184-186, Sum 96.

**Shibaike, Masami**. Esthétique de l'interprétation créatrice—Essai sur l'idée "interprétation" de Gisèle Brelet. *Bigaku*, 47(4), 58-67, Spr 97.

Dans "L'interprétation créatrice" (1951), Gisèle Brelet traite de l'interprétation musicale (au sens moderne) comme thème autonome de l'esthétique. Selon G. Brelet, la musique comprend la dualité entre l'oeuvre musicale (ou l'oeuvre écrite) et l'oeuvre exécutée, c'est-à-dire celle du temps objectif ordonné par le créateur et de la durée subjective de l'interprète. Or, dans l'art musical occidental, d'une part l'oeuvre écrite est l'être absolu, l'oeuvre où l'idée du créateur se condense; d'autre part elle comprend les possibles ou les virtuels aptes mêmes à se réaliser. Selon G. Brelet l'essence de l'interprétation musicale est *l'improvisation.* Elle en conclut que le respect du texte et la liberté de l'interprétation ne sont pas contraires, mais plutôt qu'ils se rejoignent sans contradiction. Et c'est un virtuose, en dépit de l'écriture stricte, qui joue complètement avec cette improvisation et qui réalise à la fois respect du texte et interprétation créatrice. Dans cet article, je tâcherai de répondre à ces questions. (edited)

**Shickle, Darren**. "Do 'All Men Desire to Know'? A Right of Society to Choose not to Know about the Genetics of Personality Traits" in *The Right to Know and the Right not to Know,* Chadwick, Ruth (ed), 69-77. Brookfield, Avebury, 1997.

**Shickle, Darren**. Public Preferences for Health Care: Prioritisation in the United Kingdom. *Bioethics*, 11(3-4), 277-290, Jl 97.

The government in the U.K. is encouraging consumerism within health care and is requiring health authorities to consult with the public on prioritization of resources. Public consultation within the National Health Service (NHS) has had limited success in the past. Many of the techniques used are flawed. Despite the limited scope of the public surveys conducted so far, a number of themes have emerged: 1) a willingness to pay for experimental, 'high-tech' life-saving treatments; 2) preference for treating the young rather than the old; 3) preference for treating patients with dependents (e.g., spouse, children) rather than those who have none; 4) a willingness to discriminate against those patients who were partially responsible for their illness due to choice of 'unhealthy lifestyle'. (edited)

**Shickle, Darren** (ed) and Levitt, Mairi (ed) and Chadwick, Ruth (ed). *The Right to Know and the Right not to Know.* Brookfield, Avebury, 1997.

Developments in genetics raise questions about the ability of traditional principles of biomedical ethics to deal with the complexity of the issues. Of central importance is the debate about the right to know versus the right not to know genetic information. Claims to a right *not* to know challenge the view that access to information is of value in facilitating choice and self-determination. This multidisciplinary collection of essays examines the issues from the perspectives of philosophy, sociology, history, law and public health. The volume goes beyond an examination of individual rights in considering the right of *society* not to know.

**Shields, George W**. Introduction: On the Interface of Analytic and Process Philosophy. *Process Stud*, 25, 34-54, 1996.

This essay introduces four articles comprising a special focus section of *Process Studies* devoted to the interface between contemporary analytic and process philosophy. The contributors include Nicholas Rescher, R. M. Gale, Leemon McHenry and George R. Lucas, Jr. Covering topics ranging from process semantics to disanalogies between space and time to analytic event theory to critical reactions to Lucas's effort at envisioning Whitehead as integral to early Cambridge analytic philosophy. The essay also contains a survey of the analytic/process literature with a focus on Hartshorne's contributions to the logic of future contingents and to the formal logic of asymmetry.

**Shields, Paul**. "Peirce's Axiomatization of Arithmetic" in *Studies in the Logic of Charles Sanders Peirce,* Houser, Nathan (ed), 43-52. Bloomington, Indiana Univ Pr, 1997.

**Shier, David**. Direct Reference for the Narrow Minded. *Pac Phil Quart*, 77(3), 225-248, S 96.

This paper develops a theory of belief and belief ascription which retains the core of the received *propositionalist theory* but which, unlike the propositionalist theory, is compatible with both direct reference and individualism about belief. The focus is on developing an alternative analysis of belief ascriptions, drawing out its implications and applying it to some standard problems. On that analysis, ascriptions involving directly referential embedded terms are seen as roughly characterizing, but not specifying, the contents of beliefs. This feature is what makes it possible to maintain both direct reference and individualism.

**Shier, David**. How Can Pictures Be Propositions?. *Ratio*, 10(1), 65-75, Ap 97.

Wittgenstein's picture theory of language holds that one fact can represent another and that propositions are pictures of states of affairs. What makes a fact into a picture of a given state of affairs are the correlations between picture elements and objects and the correlations between relations among picture elements and relations among objects. But a problem sometimes raised is that propositions can't be pictures, as pictures—unlike propositions—do not *say* anything. An interpretation (e.g., Anscombe's) holds that the above-mentioned correlations do make the picture into a proposition. But this neither handles the objection, nor is it Wittgenstein's view. Further, Wittgenstein's own account faces serious difficulties in addressing these issues and the Anscombe-type interpretation obscures this fact.

**Shier, David** and McGrew, Timothy J and Silverstein, Harry S. The Two-Envelope Paradox Resolved. *Analysis*, 57(1), 28-33, Ja 97.

The two envelope paradox, this paper contends, arises from an ambiguity as to whether the amount of money in the first envelope or the amount in the entire game is taken to be a fixed sum. In the former case, the conclusion that one should swap envelopes is correct and unparadoxical; in the latter, it is mathematically demonstrable that there is no advantage to swapping. This paper lays out the proof and then addresses three possible objections to this solution.

**Shigeki, Abe**. Ingres au milieu de l'école davidienne. *Bigaku*, 48(1), 13-24, Sum 97.

Notre étude tente d'éclairer les significations qu'avait le milieu davidien autour du jeune Ingres. Entre 1797 et 1801, le jeune artiste compléta sa formation artistique au milieu de l'école de David. L'atelier du maître au palais du Louvre fut entouré par d'autres ateliers des divers maîtres (fig.1). Ce lieu de travail permit donc à Ingres de rencontrer non seulement ses condisciples mais aussi les artistes de diverses tendances. De 1802 à 1806 Ingres travailla dans une pareille situation dans l'ancien couvent des Capucines (fig.2); ici Ingres avait des échanges artistiques étroits surtout avec les artistes davidiens: Bartolini, Bergeret, Girodet, Granet, etc. Durant cette période, et même après son départ à Rome, Ingres continua de s'inspirer des recherches effectuées par les davidiens, et de leurs oeuvres gravées, dessinées ou peintes; il s'agit des gravures dessinées par Wicar, Forbin et Girodet, des études préparatoires de Girodet et de Gérard et des portraits de ces mêmes artistes. Le milieu davidien eut ainsi une importance décisive sur la genèse de l'art très personnel de notre artiste.

**Shils, Edward** and Altbach, Philip G (ed). *The Order of Learning: Essays on the Contemporary University*. New Brunswick, Transaction Pub, 1997.

The book considers the problems facing higher education by focusing on some of the main underlying factors: the relationship of higher education to government, academic freedom, the responsibilities of the academic profession, among others. Edward Shils believes that higher education has a central role in modern society and that the distractions of the recent past, including undue pressures from government, the fads of some students and faculty, and increasing involvement of the postsecondary education with day-to-day questions, have damaged higher education by deflecting it from its essential commitment to teaching, learning, and research. (publisher, edited)

**Shimony, Abner**. A Bayesian Examination of Time-Symmetry in the Process of Measurement. *Erkenntnis*, 45(2 & 3), 337-348, Nov 96.

We investigate the thesis of Aharonov, Bergmann and Lebowitz that time-symmetry holds in ensembles defined by both an initial and a final condition, called "pre- and postselected ensembles". We distinguish two senses of time symmetry and show that the first one, concerning forward directed and time reversed measurements, holds if the measurement process is ideal, but fails if the measurement process is nonideal, i.e., violates Lüders's rule. The second kind of time symmetry, concerning the interchange of initial and final conditions, fails even in the case of ideal measurements. Bayes's theorem is used as a primary tool for calculating the relevant probabilities. We are critical of the concept that a pair of vectors in Hilbert space, characterizing the initial and final conditions, can be considered to constitute a generalized quantum state.

**Shimony, Abner** and Busch, Paul. Insolubility of the Quantum Measurement Problem for Unsharp Observables. *Stud Hist Phil Mod Physics*, 27B(4), 397-404, D 96.

The quantum mechanical measurement problem is the difficulty of dealing with the indefiniteness of the pointed observable at the conclusion of a measurement process governed by unitary quantum dynamics. There has been hope to solve this problem by eliminating idealizations from the characterization of measurement. We state and prove two 'insolubility theorems' that disappoint this hope. In both the initial state of the apparatus is taken to be mixed rather than pure, and the correlation of the object observable and the pointer observable is allowed to be imperfect. In the *insolubility theorem for sharp observables*, which is only a modest extension of previous results, the object observable is taken to be an arbitrary projection valued measure. (edited)

**Shimshon Rubin, Simon** and Dror, Omer. Professional Ethics of Psychologists and Physicians: Morality, Confidentiality, and Sexuality in Israel. *Ethics Behavior*, 6(3), 213-238, 1996.

Clinical psychologists' and nonpsychiatric physicians' attitudes and behaviors in sexual and confidentiality boundary violations were examined. The 171 participants' responses were analyzed by profession, sex, and status (student, resident, professional) on semantic differential, boundary violation vignettes, and a version of Pope, Tabachnick, and Keith-Spiegel's (1987) ethical scale. Psychologists rated sexual boundary violation as more unethical than did physicians (p001). Rationale (p01) and timing (p0001) influenced ratings. Psychologists reported fewer sexualized behaviors than physicians (p). Professional experience (p01) and sex (p05) were associated with confidence-violating behavior. Overall, 78% of the sample reported attitudes or behaviors associated with boundary violations. The behavior violations were correlated (r=.49). Actual violators rated vignette violators more leniently than did nonviolators (p01).

**Shimura, Tatsuya**. Kripke Completeness of Some Intermediate Predicate Logics with the Axiom of Constant Domain and a Variant of Canonical Formulas. *Stud Log*, 52(1), 23-40, F 93.

For each intermediate propositional logic J, J· denotes the least predicate extension of J. By the method of canonical models, the strongly Kripke completeness of... is shown in some cases including: 1) J is tabular; 2) J is a subframe logic. A variant of Zakharyashchev's canonical formulas for intermediate logics is introduced to prove the second case. (edited)

**Shin, Hyun Song** and Morris, Stephen. Approximate Common Knowledge and Co-Ordination: Recent Lessons from Game Theory. *J Log Lang Info*, 6(2), 171-190, Ap 97.

The importance of the notion of common knowledge in sustaining cooperative outcomes in strategic situations is well appreciated. However, the systematic analysis of the extent to which small departures from common knowledge affect equilibrium in games has only recently been attempted. We review the main themes in this literature, in particular, the notion of common p-belief. We outline both the analytical issues raised and the potential applicability of such ideas to game theory, computer science and the philosophy of language.

**Shiner, Roger A**. Causes and Tastes: A Response. *J Aes Art Crit*, 55(3), 320-324, Sum 97.

This article is a response to two criticisms in the same issue of the JAAC of my essay on Hume and the Causal Theory of Taste, in the JAAC last year. I reply to Mary Mothersill that her defence of causal theories assumes theses which it is the purpose of article to oppose and that her account of my rival view is prejudicial. I concede to John Bender and Richard Maning that gustatory is less 'internalist' than I made it out to be. But I stand by my position that aesthetic taste and gustatory taste are importantly distinct.

**Shiner, Roger A**. Sparshott and the Philosophy of Philosophy. *J Aes Educ*, 31(2), 3-8, Sum 97.

The article concentrates on the methodology of Francis Sparshott's enormous work, *The Theory of the Arts*. I try to show how the argument captures the essential dynamism of philosophical enquiry. It is not a static conceptual map. I also endorse and defend such a methodology.

**Shinoda, Juichi**. Strong Polynomial-Time Reducibility. *Annals Pure Applied Log*, 84(1), 97-117, Mr 97.

The degree structure of functions induced by a polynomial-time reducibility first introduced in G. Miller's work on the complexity of prime factorization is investigated. Several basic results are established including the facts that the degrees restricted to the sets do not form an upper semilattice and there is a minimal degree, as well as density for the low degrees, a weak form of the exact pair theorem, the existence of minimal pairs and the decidability of the $\Pi_2$ theory of the low degrees.

**Shiokawa, Tetsuya**. L'arc-en-ciel et les sacrements: de la sémiologie de la *Logique de Port-Royal* à la théorie pascalienne des figures. *Rev Int Phil*, 51(199), 77-99, 1997.

**Shlapentokh, Dmitry**. The Fedorovian Roots of Stalinism. *Phil Today*, 40(3), 388-404, Fall 96.

One of the essential aspects of Russian thought was belief in collectivised humanity's ability to harness the blind forces of nature and be ruler of the universe. For Russian nationalists, Russians as a chosen nation should be a leader of this process. Nikolai Fedorov, (d. 1903) was one of those Russian philosophers who better than anybody else propagandized these ideas. His teaching had been incorporated in the Soviet ideology where Russian nationalism and social millennialism were blended together. The end of Soviet Russia has led to the end of such thinking in the minds of Russian intellectuals.

**Shlapentokh, Vladimir**. Catastrophic Thinking in the Modern World: Russia and America. *Cont Phil*, 18(2-3), 34-46, Mr-Ap/My-Je 96.

The fear of the future has played an important and in some cases crucial role in the life of individuals and society. Trepidation concerning the unknown and unexplained is deeply rooted in the human mind, probably at the genetic level. Thus, it is not surprising that for a number of thinkers it is the most important (or one of the most important) elements in human life. As Andre Malraux once said, "fear is deeply rooted in each of us, to discover it is enough to see deeply in yourself."

**Shoaf, Richard**. Pascal's Wager Updated. *Teach Phil*, 19(4), 331-335, D 96.

Decision tree analysis, often used by modern businessmen, can be used in the classroom to give a new and interesting twist to Pascal's wager. This article explains how I use this method in my introductory philosophy classes. The logical diagramming of the problem intrigues the students and shows them that the wager is not a leap of blind faith but is based on sound logic. The decision tree is a great help in leading students to discover and analyze the usual criticisms of the wager (including the "many gods" argument, often difficult for beginning students) without much help from the instructor.

**Shoemaker, David**. Theoretical Persons and Practical Agents. *Phil Pub Affairs*, 25(4), 318-332, Fall 96.

My purpose in this paper is to dissolve the general Kantian objection that theoretical approaches to personal identity cannot account for certain crucial elements involved in the practical standpoint from which I view myself. Specifically, I deal with Christine Korsgaard's objection that Derek Parfit's Reductionism ignores the "authorial" nature of my relationship to my actions and thus misses an essential feature of what matters to me. I show that Parfit's more theoretical approach can indeed account for this feature of agency and also can better account for another feature of agency that Korsgaard herself ignores, what I call "authorial disconnectedness."

**Shoemaker, Sydney**. "Colors, Subjective Relations and Qualia" in *Perception*, Villanueva, Enrique (ed), 55-66. Atascadero, Ridgeview, 1996.

**Shore, Eleanor G**. Effectiveness of Research Guidelines in Prevention of Scientific Misconduct. *Sci Eng Ethics*, 1(4), 383-387, O 95.

The chief argument for adopting guidelines is to promote good science. There is no evidence that well-crafted guidelines have had any detrimental effect on creativity. This paper addresses a spectrum of causes of scientific misconduct or unacceptable scientific behavior and couples these with estimates of the potential for prevention if guidelines for scientific investigation are adopted. The conclusion is that clear and understandable guidelines should help to reduce the chance that flawed research will escape from our institutions. However, they cannot be relied upon alone to prevent all instances of scientific misconduct and should be regarded rather as one means of bolstering the integrity of the entire scientific enterprise. (edited)

**Shore, Richard A** and Nies, André and Slaman, Theodore A. Definability in the Recursively Enumerable Degrees. *Bull Sym Log*, 2(4), 392-404, D 96.

**Short, T L**. "Hypostatic Abstraction in Self-Consciousness" in *The Rule of Reason: The Philosophy of Charles Sanders Peirce,* Forster, Paul (ed), 289-308. Toronto, Univ of Toronto Pr, 1997.

Hypostatic abstraction posits an entity defined by its relation to something else: the self is posited, initially, as *that which* acts and is thwarted, speaks and is corrected. Thus the "inner" is defined by the "outer" and self by society, without the one being reduced to the other. But in this case abstraction creates rather than discloses its object. For self-representation makes self-control—the end-directed organization of actions, feelings, and thoughts—possible, constituting the ego. The immedicacy of self-consciousness lies in the feelings thus united, but self-conception and self-knowledge remain indirect and inferential.

**Short, T L**. Interpreting Peirce's Interpretant: A Response To Lalor, Liszka, and Meyers. *Trans Peirce Soc*, 32(4), 488-541, Fall 96.

In this response to three benighted souls who dared to question aspects of my earlier papers on Peirce's theory of signs, I marshall a mountain of evidence, its defiles threaded with brilliant argument, showing, according to Peirce's *later* theory: that signs are always interpretable but not always interpreted; that "interpretants" (whether potential, actual, or ideal) may be (as depends on the sign) feelings, actions, habits of action, or other signs; that each interpretant that is a sign is interpretable, ultimately, by a habit of action; and that this last grounds a Peircean analysis—teleological, not behavioristic—of intentionality.

**Short, T L**. Review Essay. *Synthese*, 106(3), 409-430, Mr 96.

This review of Volumes 1-5 of *Writings of Charles S Peirce* examines and criticizes editorial policies that guide the entire project, now one-quarter complete. But the heart of the review is a new interpretation of Peirce's philosophical development, based on previously unpublished materials made accessible in these volumes. Contrary to the prevailing view that Peirce progressed from nominalism to realism, I argue that it was the problem of accounting for individual existence that led Peirce from his early Kant-based realism to his later pragmatic realism. This exercise, it is hoped, illustrates the edition's potential value to Peirce scholarship.

**Shotter, John**. Dialogical Realities: The Ordinary, the Everyday, and Other Strange New Worlds. *J Theor Soc Behav*, 27(2-3), 345-357, Je-S 97.

We tend to seek theoretical explanations of our own human behavior, to understand everything we do as arising, computationally, from a systematic set of simple laws, principles, or rules. Here, influenced by the later Wittgenstein, I argue that the very possibility of the kind of talk we use in our theorizing arises out of the joint or dialogical activities in which we engage in our practical lives together and only has its meaning within the context of such activities—thus we cannot turn it around to explain its own genesis. We can, however, achieve a greater reflective awareness of our own structuring of our own activities through the new, nontheoretical methods Wittgenstein introduces into our intellectual practices. Here, I explore some of these methods and the strange nature of our dialogical activities when seen in their light.

**Shotter, John**. Living in a Wittgensteinian World: Beyond Theory to a Poetics of Practices. *J Theor Soc Behav*, 26(3), 293-311, S 96.

Wittgenstein's philosophy draws our attention to the details of our social practices, through the use, essentially, of poetic methods. Their function is not so much "to hunt out new facts...[as to] to understand something that is already in plain view" (PI, 1953, no. 89). They draw our attention to what we all 'see' but usually do not 'notice'. Unlike explanatory theories, intended to explain already perceived phenomena in terms of hidden, repeatable processes, a poetics of practices provides us with a first time acquaintance with, and elucidation of, the unique events in which we each express our own individual, unrepeatable, momentary being in the world.

**Shotter, John**. 'Now I Can Go On:' Wittgenstein and Our Embodied Embeddedness in the 'Hurly-Burly' of Life. *Human Stud*, 19(4), 385-407, O 96.

Wittgenstein is not primarily concerned with anything mysterious going on inside people's heads, but with us simply 'going on' with each other; that is, with us being able to interrelate our everyday, bodily activities in unproblematic ways in which those of others, in practice. Learning to communicate with clear and unequivocal meanings; to send messages; to fully understand each other; to be able to reach out, so to speak, from within language-game entwined forms of life, and to talk in theoretical terms of the contacts one has made, as an individual, with what is out there; and so on—all these abilities are, or can be, later developments. Wittgenstein's investigations into our preindividual, pretheoretical, embodied, compulsive activities are utterly revolutionary. They open up a vast new realm for empirical study to do with the detailed and subtle nature of the bodily activities in the 'background' to everything that we do. The *relational* character of such pretheoretical, Ur-linguisitic, spontaneous bodily activities—and the way in which they display us as 'seeing connections' from within a 'synopsis of trivialities'—is explored through the paradigm of currently fashionable 3-D random dot autostereograms.

**Shpet, G G**. A Work on Philosophy. *Russian Stud Phil*, 35(4), 43-59, Spr 97.

**Shrader-Frechette, Kristin**. Global Responsibility and Active Ethical Advocacy (No Apology for Academic Activism). *Phil Soc Act*, 22(3), 9-13, Jl-S 96.

One of the most difficult theoretical problems in normative ethics is understanding and resolving conflicts over collective responsibility. Apart from devising legal, governmental and institutional strategies for creatings and enforcing solutions to problems of the global environmental commons, the main strategy for environmental action (a noninstitutional strategy) is education and advocacy, especially through nongovernmental organizations. Advocacy of any kind, however, is viewed as inimical both to objectivity in general and to the academy in particular. In this essay I argue that environmental advocacy by scientists, philosophers and other intellectuals is not only permissible, but perhaps ethically mandatory. (edited)

**Shue, Henry**. "Eroding Sovereignty: The Advance of Principle" in *The Morality of Nationalism,* McKim, Robert (ed), 340-359. New York, Oxford Univ Pr, 1997.

**Shue, Henry**. *Basic Rights: Subsistence, Affluence, and U.S. Foreign Policy.* Princeton, Princeton Univ Pr, 1996.

Which human rights ought to be the first honored and the last sacrificed? In the first systematic attempt by an American philosopher to address the issue of human rights as it relates to U.S. foreign policy, Henry Shue proposes an original conception of basic rights that illuminates both the nature of moral rights generally and the determination of which specific rights are the *basic* ones.

**Shukla, S K** and Sharma, A D. Pramāna Samplava and Pramāna Vyavasthā. *J Indian Counc Phil Res*, 14(2), 83-98, Ja-Ap 97.

**Shulman, David**. Embracing the Subject: Harsa's Play within a Play. *J Indian Phil*, 25(1), 69-89, F 97.

**Shulman, George**. American Political Culture, Prophetic Narration, and Toni Morrison's *Beloved. Polit Theory*, 24(2), 295-314, My 96.

**Shun, Kwong-loi**. Mencius on *Jen-Hsing. Phil East West*, 47(1), 1-20, Ja 97.

The use of the term *hsing* in the *Meng-tzu* is discussed, along with Mencius's view on *jen-hsing.* It is argued that while the use of *hsing* need not connote something unlearned and shared, Mencius did view *jen-hsing* in terms of certain unlearned emotional predispositions shared by all *jen.* He regarded *jen* as a species distinguished from other animals by its capability of cultural accomplishment, and felt that it is the presence of the emotional predispositions that makes this possible.

**Shusterman, Richard**. *Practicing Philosophy: Pragmatism and the Philosophical Life.* New York, Routledge, 1997.

This book poses the question 'What does it mean to be a philosopher?' It also asks what the connection is between a so-called '*philosopher*' in a renowned university and say a rap musician who writes his own lyrics, or even a published poet. Members of religious orders may be some of the truest seekers of a contemplative philosophical style of living, but what can the rest of us do in our nonstop modern America; and does it really matter to us anyway? Shusterman writes with the knowledge of the academic, but in an accessible style which we can all understand. (publisher)

**Shusterman, Richard**. Putnam and Cavell on the Ethics of Democracy. *Polit Theory*, 25(2), 193-214, Ap 97.

**Shusterman, Richard**. The End of Aesthetic Experience. *J Aes Art Crit*, 55(1), 29-41, Wint 97.

The paper first survey's the twentieth-century critique of aesthetic experience in both Anglo-American philosophy (Dewey, Beardsley, Goodman, Danto, Dickie) and in continental theory (Heidegger, Gadamer, Adorno, Benjamin, Derrida, Bourdieu). In response to this critique, the paper distinguishes a variety of notions of aesthetic experience with different functional roles. In separating out what is problematic from what is still useful in this concept, it offers a way of redeeming the centrality of aesthetic experience for understanding art.

**Sichel, Betty A**. "Beyond Moral Stories" in *Philosophy of Education (1996),* Margonis, Frank (ed), 1-12. Urbana, Phil Education Soc, 1997.

**Siciliano, Julie I**. The Relationship of Board Member Diversity to Organizational Performance. *J Bus Ethics*, 15(12), 1313-1320, D 96.

Wider diversity in board member characteristics has been advocated as a means of improving organizational performance by providing boards with new insights and perspectives. With data from 240 YMCA organizations, a board diversity index was constructed and compared to multiple measures of board member diversity. Results revealed higher levels of social performance and fundraising results when board members had greater occupational diversity. Gender diversity compared favorably to the organization's level of social performance but a negative association surfaced for level of funds raised. The diversity in board member age groupings was linked to higher levels of donations.

**Sider, Theodore**. A New Grandfather Paradox?. *Phil Phenomenol Res*, 57(1), 139-144, Mr 97.

In a 1994 *Scientific American* article, physicist David Deutsch and philosopher Michael Lockwood give a defense of the possibility of time travel based on the "Many Worlds" interpretation of quantum mechanics. They motivate their appeal to the "Many Worlds" interpretation arguing that the standard formulation of the paradox of time travel in terms of ability is misguided, presenting their own version of the paradox based on "autonomy principle," and arguing that this paradox should be resolved by appeal to the "Many Worlds" interpretation. But whatever the merits of their solution, it is unmotivated, for their new version of the paradox turns out on closer scrutiny to be nothing more than the original ability version of the paradox in disguise.

**Sider, Theodore**. All the World's a Stage. *Austl J Phil*, 74(3), 433-453, S 96.

Most believers in temporal parts identify persons and other continuants with aggregates of temporal parts—"space time worms". I identify them instead with the instantaneous temporal parts themselves. Fortified with a temporal version of counterpart theory, this stage theory of persistence over time is the account best suited to solve the philosopher's repertoire of puzzles of identity over time. The stage theorist can agree that identity and psychological continuity are both what matters in survival, that a status is identical to the lump of matter from which it is made, and so on.

**Sider, Theodore**. On the Paradox of the Question. *Analysis*, 57(2), 97-101, Ap 97.

Ned Markosian has introduced the paradox of the question, involving an angel who agrees to answer any single question the human race chooses. Clever philosophers ask "what is the ordered pair of the best question and its answer?", but are thwarted by the useless answer they receive: "the ordered pair consisting of the question you have asked me and the answer I'm now giving." In answer to Markosian's question "what went wrong?", I place partial blame on the angel who can be shown to have answered incorrectly; but nevertheless there is a genuine (semantic?) paradox lurking in the neighborhood.

**Sidorkin, Alexander M**. "The Glass Bead Game" in *Philosophy of Education (1996)*, Margonis, Frank (ed), 315-317. Urbana, Phil Education Soc, 1997.

**Sidorkin, Alexander M**. Carnival and Domination: Pedagogies of Neither Care Nor Justice. *Educ Theor*, 47(2), 229-238, Spr 97.

**Sidorsky, David**. Value Neutrality and Ideological Commitment in Political Philosophy. *Iyyun*, 45, 125-152, Jl 96.

**Sie, Maureen**. Theoria and the Priority of the Practical (in Dutch). *Alg Ned Tijdschr Wijs*, 88(3), 173-191, Jl 96.

Richard Rorty's attack on *theoria* is based upon a misconception of the distinction between theory and practice. This twofold distinction should be replaced by a threefold distinction between participating, observing and theorizing. I argue that : 1) observation and theorizing are an indispensable part of our everyday practice, 2) theorizing can be understood as a quest for universally valid insights, and 3) theorizing is necessary to guarantee political, scientific and cultural progress. I conclude that Rorty's criticism should be aimed at the activity of observing, not at the activity of theorizing. His criticism, thus understood, however, has no practical significance.

**Siebel, Wigand**. *Systematische Wahrheitstheorie: Methodische und wissenschaftstheoretische Überlegungen zur Frage nach dem grundlegenden Einheitsprinzip*. New York, Lang, 1996.

In einer umfassenden Theorie der Wahrheit werden die Urteilswahrheit, die Begriffswahrheit und die Wahrheit als "das Ganze" in ihrem Zusammenhang beleuchtet. Die Wahrheitstheorien erhalten von hier aus ihren Platz. Der wissenschaftliche Forschungsprozess kann dann unter Berücksichtigung sozialer Perspektiven (Wahrheitsvermittlung) präziser erfasst werden. Ausgangspunkt ist das axiomatische Gefüge der Erkenntnisrelation. Gesucht wird das dem Erkenntnisvollzug zugrundeliegende materiale Einheitsprinzip. Dieses Prinzip muss selbst eine Erkenntnisrelation sein, Einfachheit u.a. aufweisen. Es muss aber auch als Gegenstand der Wahrheitsliebe begreifbar sein. Eine Lösung, die allen aufgestellten Forderungen genügt, wird als Ergebnis diskutiert. (publisher)

**Sieber, Joan E** and Trumbo, Bruce E. (Not) Giving Credit Where Credit Is Due: Citation of Data Sets. *Sci Eng Ethics*, 1(1), 11-20, J 95.

Adequate citation of data sets is crucial to the encouragement of data sharing, to the integrity and cost-effectiveness of science and to easy access to the work of others. The citation behavior of social scientists who have published based on shared data was examined and found to be inconsistent with important ideals of science. Insights gained from the social sciences, where data sharing is somewhat customary, suggest policies and incentives that would foster adequate citation by secondary users, and greater openness and sharing in other disciplines.

**Sieg, Wilfried**. Step by Recursive Step: Church's Analysis of Effective Calculability. *Bull Sym Log*, 3(2), 154-180, Je 97.

Alonzo Church's mathematical work on computability and undecidability is well-known indeed and we seem to have an excellent understanding of the context in which it arose. The approach Church took to the underlying conceptual issues, by contrast, is less well understood. A number of letters were exchanged between Church and Paul Bernays during the period from December 1934 to August 1937; they throw light on critical developments in Princeton during that period and reveal novel aspects of Church's distinctive contribution to the analysis of the informal notion of *effective calculability*. (edited)

**Siegel, Harvey**. "Can Reasons for Rationality be Redeemed?" in *Philosophy of Education (1996)*, Margonis, Frank (ed), 74-76. Urbana, Phil Education Soc, 1997.

In this reply to Alexander, I argue that reasons for rationality *can* be redeemed, in that one cannot both a) "call for a justification" of rationality, and yet b) *not* "care about reasons." The "paradox of rationality," which rests on embracing both a) and b), is thus overcome.

**Siegel, Harvey**. Instrumental Rationality and Naturalized Philosophy of Science. *Proc Phil Sci Ass*, 3(Suppl), S116-S124, 1996.

In two recent papers, I criticized Ronald N. Giere's and Larry Laudan's arguments for 'naturalizing' the philosophy of science (Siegel 1989, 1990). Both Giere and Laudan replied to my criticisms (Giere 1989, Laudan 1990b). The key issue arising in both interchanges is these naturalists' embrace of instrumental conceptions of rationality, and their concomitant rejection of noninstrumental conceptions of that key normative notion. In this reply I argue that their accounts of science's rationality as exclusively instrumental fail, and consequently that their cases for 'normatively naturalizing' the philosophy of science fail as well.

**Siegel, Harvey**. Israel Scheffler's "Moral Education and the Democratic Ideal". *Inquiry (USA)*, 16(3), 25-26, Spr 97.

This is a brief introduction to Scheffler's classic article, placing it in the broader context of his philosophy of education.

**Siegel, Harvey**. Naturalism, Instrumental Rationality, and the Normativity of Epistemology. *Protosoz*, 8/9, 97-110, 1996.

Advocates of naturalized epistemology who wish to secure epistemology's normativity want that normativity to be restricted to instrumental concerns, because these can be understood naturalistically. But epistemic normativity cannot be so limited; a 'categorical' sort of normativity must be acknowledged. Naturalism can neither account for nor do away with this sort of normativity. Hence, naturalism is at best a seriously incomplete and therefore inadequate metaepistemological position.

**Siegel, Harvey**. On Some Recent Challenges to the Ideal Reason. *Inquiry (USA)*, 15(4), 2-16, Sum 96.

Recent work in critical thinking and informal logic has depended heavily on the notions of *rationality* and *reasons*. Various authors in these areas have pointed to these notions as the basis for their scholarly and pedagogical efforts. As these notions are fundamentally epistemological, a general concern for the *epistemology* underlying critical thinking and informal logic has been manifest in the literature. But in the broader academic community, the epistemological ideal of rationality has been subjected to severe criticism. Postmodernists, feminists and many others have challenged the received "enlightenment" wisdom concerning the nature and value of rationality. In this paper I review some of these challenges, in order to determine whether or not critical thinking and informal logic can in good faith continue to rely upon the ideal of rationality. I argue that they can.

**Siegel, Harvey** (ed). *Reason and Education: Essays in Honor of Isreal Scheffler*. Dordrecht, Kluwer, 1997.

Israel Scheffler is the pre-eminent philosopher of education in the English-speaking world today. This volume collects seventeen original, invited papers on Scheffler's philosophy of education by scholars from around the world. The papers address the wide range of topics that Scheffler's work in philosophy of education has addressed, including the aims of education, cognition and emotion, teaching, the language of education, science education, moral education, religious education, and human potential. Each paper is followed by a response from Scheffler himself. (publisher, edited)

**Siegel, Harvey**. Why Should Educators Care about Argumentation?. *Inform Log*, 17(2), 159-176, Spr 95.

In this paper I will try to provide a defense and in doing so explain why educators should care about argumentation. The defense will be a moral one: I will argue that we are morally obliged to endeavour to foster the rationality of students because that is what is required to meet our obligations to treat students with respect as persons. I will also consider some general criticisms of the Enlightenment ideal of rationality, offered by feminist, multiculturalist and postmodernist scholars. If these criticisms are cogent, then both argumentation theory and the view that the aim of education is the fostering of rationality are threatened. I will argue that the criticisms, while important and instructive, are not so destructive of the ideal of rationality as some contemporary scholars suppose. (edited)

**Siegler, Mark** and Fletcher, John C. What Are the Goals of Ethics Consultation: A Consensus Statement. *J Clin Ethics*, 7(2), 122-126, Sum 96.

This article reports on the outcome of a consensus-development process to frame a statement of the goals of ethics case consultation, (ECC). ECC is a service provided by an individual consultant, team, or committee to address the ethical issues involved in a specific clinical case. The authors coled a Working Group on Goals that convened at the Conference on Evaluation of Ethics Case Consultation in Chicago, II, September 21-23, 1995. The overall goal of the conference was to explore the feasibility of a controlled study of the efficacy of ECC in several settings. Epidemiological study of evaluation of EEC is not possible without agreement about goals. Previously divided as to the main purpose and goals of ECC, the authors reconciled their differences prior to the meeting and went into the meeting united. Consequently, the Working Group was able to reach consensus on a goals statement of four parts: 1) on the outcome of ECC in maximizing benefit and minimizing harm to patients, families, clinicians and institutions and the process of ECC to foster fair and inclusive decision making, 2) on ECC as a conflict-resolution strategy, 3) on ECC's role in informing institutional efforts at policy development and 4) on the educational role of ECC.

**Siemek, Marek J**. "Sozialphilosophische Aspekte der Übersetzbarkeit" in *Epistemology and History*, Zeidler-Janiszewska, Anna (ed), 441-448. Amsterdam, Rodopi, 1996.

The paper is an attempt to analyse the concept of translatability from the standpoint of social philosophy and theory of communication. The main questions concern the relation between translating and understanding, the communicative functions of language, the connection of monological vs.

dialogical discourse form with two different kinds of human interests (symbolic vs. economic) and finally the dialogical roots of intersubjective rationality in the modern world.

**Siemek, Marek J**. Wissen und Tun: Zur Handlungsweise der transzendentalen Subjektivität in der ersten Wissenschaftslehre Fichtes. *Fichte-Studien*, 10, 241-252, 1997.

**Siena, Roberto Maria**. Hobbes e il cristianesimo dal De Cive al Leviatano. *Sapienza*, 49(3), 253-269, 1996.

**Siep, Ludwig**. Eine Skizze zur Grundlegung der Bioethik. *Z Phil Forsch*, 50(1/2), 236-253, Ja-Je 96.

The paper argues for a version of "cosmocentric" ethics. It refutes the usual anthropocentric criticism and argues for a normative concept of "cosmos" not susceptible to naturalistic fallacies. "Cosmos" is the idea of a just order of beings which allows individuals and species as much "flourishing" as possible. Approximations to such a good state of affairs may be temporarily achieved. Combined with a modern version of the "scala naturae," this idea can serve as a criterion for the solution of problems in medical and ecological ethics.

**Sierra, Guillermo Restrepo**. "¿René Descartes, cientifista?" in *Memorias Del Seminario En Conmemoración De Los 400 Anos Del Nacimiento De René Descartes*, Albis, Víctor S (ed), 171-206. Sankt Augustin, Academia, 1997.

**Sierra-Gutiérrez, Francisco** (trans) and Lonergan, Bernard J F. La filosofía y el fenómeno religioso. *Univ Phil*, 14(27), 131-158, D 96.

Shifting from a "metaphysics of objects" to a "theory of our conscious and intentional operations," Lonergan conceives a philosophy of religion as the foundational methodology of religious studies. Momentous to this heuristic structure is Lonergan's distinction between authenticity and inauthenticity, the level of symbolic operations, interpersonal relations and religious conversion. Also, his account and ordering of the various contexts in which religious living occurs and investigations of religious living are undertaken. This is a genuine approach to the academic integrity of religious studies; a very illumination of the function religions play out in various social and cultural contexts.

**Sihvola, Juha**. Emotional Animals: Do Aristotelian Emotions Require Beliefs?. *Apeiron*, 29(2), 105-144, Je 96.

**Sikka, Sonya**. *Forms of Transcendence: Heidegger and Medieval Mystical Theology*. Albany, SUNY Pr, 1997.

This book sets up a dialogue between Heidegger and four medieval authors: St. Bonaventure, Meister Eckhart, Johannes Tauler and Jan van Ruusbroec. Through a close reading of medieval and Heideggerian texts, the book brings to light elements that present possibilities for a revised appropriation of some traditional metaphysical and theological ideas, arguing that, in spite of Heidegger's critique of "ontotheology," many aspects of his thought make a positive and not exclusively critical, contribution. (publisher, edited)

**Sikula, Sr, Andrew**. Concepts of Moral Management and Moral Maximization. *Ethics Behavior*, 6(3), 181-188, 1996.

This article introduces two new concepts into the business ethics literature, *moral management* and *moral maximization*, and explains the ways to measure and implement these concepts using four major subcomponents of human rights, human freedoms, human equity, and human development. Each of these subcomponents is subdivided into eight factors or items, resulting in 32 specific and tangible measures of the morality of human behavior. Figures are provided to illustrate the relationships between moral management and moral maximization and their 32 submeasures.

**Siliceo-Roman, Laura** and Kuehn, Glenn and Salyards, Jane. Interview with Richard Rorty. *Kinesis*, 23(1), 51-64, Sum 96.

**Silk, Jonathan A**. The Composition of the *Guan Wuliangshoufo-Jing*: Some Buddhist and Jaina Parallels to its Narrative Frame. *J Indian Phil*, 25(2), 181-256, Ap 97.

**Silva, José R**. A Criticism of Leibniz's Views on the Ontological Argument. *Dialogos*, 31(68), 183-192, Jl 96.

**Silva de Choudens, José R**. Descartes según Leibniz. *Dialogos*, 32(69), 225-241, Ja 97.

**Silva Filho, Lauro de Barros**. A Educaçao no Imaginário Liberal. *Educ Filosof*, 9(17), 185-190, Ja-Je 95.

Este artigo pretende comunicar um breve entendimento sobre Imaginário e Educaçao. Discorre sobre a Educaçao no Imaginário Social, oferecendo uma análise reflexiva e crítica sobre o pensamento pedagógico brasileiro-aquele dominante do fazer educativo na perspectiva escolar, vista à luz do liberalismo.

**Silva-Sánchez, Jesús-Maria**. Probleme der Zurechnung bei impulsivem Handeln. *Jahr Recht Ethik*, 2, 505-526, 1994.

This article deals with the problem of "impulsive acts", trying to decide whether they are "acts" in the sense of the criminal law, or not. The author rejects the thesis that impulsive acts are not "voluntary acts" but rather "reflexes" or something similar. It is claimed that empirical arguments (voluntariness/involuntariness, consciousness/unconsciousness) cannot support the distinction between "acts" and mere bodily movements, which must be excluded from the field of criminal liability at the outset. Instead it is shown that a normative argument is needed. The preventive functions of the criminal law and its norms provide the criteria for drawing this distinction. The article concludes that treating impulsive acts as acts under the criminal law is compatible with the aims of criminal law policy.

**Silver, Maury** and Sabini, John. In Defense of Shame: Shame in the Context of Guilt and Embarrassment. *J Theor Soc Behav*, 27(1), 1-15, Mr 97.

We are interested in the relations among shame, guilt and embarrassment and especially in how each relates to judgments of character. We start by analyzing

the distinction between being and feeling guilty and unearth the role of shame as a guilt feeling. We proceed to examine shame and guilt in relation to moral responsibility and to flaws of character. (edited)

**Silver, Maury** and Sabini, John. On the Possible Non-Existence of Emotions: The Passions. *J Theor Soc Behav*, 26(4), 375-398, D 96.

This paper attempts to demonstrate, at least for the passions, that while emotions are important elements of common sense psychological thought, they are not psychological, neural, or mental entities. People talk of emotions, we claim, in two sorts of cases: Firstly, when it is believed that someone has done something that she shouldn't because she has been overwhelmed by desire (a motive) and secondly, when someone is found to be compelled to devote cognitive resources to an act she knows she will never carry out. In this case motivational states command attention and cognitive and physiological resources, distract us, even though they will not issue in action. In either case pointing to an emotion is pointing to a partial, aborted, or misdirected desire. We discuss why emotions are considered important in common sense and professional psychology though they do not exist.

**Silverman, Henry**. The Role of Emotions in Decisional Competence, Standards of Competency, and Altruistic Acts. *J Clin Ethics*, 8(2), 171-175, Sum 97.

**Silvers, Stuart**. Nonreductive Naturalism. *Theoria (Spain)*, 12(28), 163-184, Ja 97.

Nonreductive naturalism holds that we can preserve the (scientifically valued) metaphysical truth of physicalism while averting the methodological mistakes of reductionism. Acceptable scientific explanation need not (in some cases cannot and in many cases, should not) be formulated in the language of physical science. Persuasive arguments about the properties of phenomenal consciousness purport to show that physicalism is false, namely that phenomenal experience is a nonphysical fact. I examine two recent, comprehensive efforts to naturalize phenomenal consciousness and argue that nonreductive naturalism yields a dilemma of reductionism or panpsychism.

**Silverstein, Harry S** and Shier, David and McGrew, Timothy J. The Two-Envelope Paradox Resolved. *Analysis*, 57(1), 28-33, Ja 97.

The two envelope paradox, this paper contends, arises from an ambiguity as to whether the amount of money in the first envelope or the amount in the entire game is taken to be a fixed sum. In the former case, the conclusion that one should swap envelopes is correct and unparadoxical; in the latter, it is mathematically demonstrable that there is no advantage to swapping. This paper lays out the proof and then addresses three possible objections to this solution.

**Silvestre, Maria Luisa**. "Con Aristotele, otre Aristotele: Meyer e l'antropologia" in *Lo Storicismo e la Sua Storia: Temi, Problemi, Prospettive*, Cacciatore, Giuseppe (ed), 355-372. Milano, Guerini, 1997.

**Simao, Cristiana V**. Mens Sana in Corpore Sano? Reflexoes sobre o Enigma do Corpo. *Philosophica (Portugal)*, 207-223, 1997.

Au tour de plusieurs récits qui décrivent des situations, les unes vérdiques, d'autres fictionnelles, on s'interroge sur le statut et la signification du corps humain dans la vie et dans la culture contemporaine—d'un corps qui semble être devenu un simple objet d'usage, de manipulation, de commerce et d'expérimentation scientifique, et même un support matériel dont l'expérimentation artistique fait souvent une oeuvre d'art. On montre d'abord l'immense danger de cette méconnsaissance, pour aboutir à la reconnaissance de la valeur éthique, esthétique et anthropologique du corps, c'est-à-dire à la reconnaissance de notre humanité.

**Simeoni, Luca**. "Eudosso di Cnido e la misura del tempo nell'astrononmia greca" in *Il Concetto di Tempo: Atti del XXXII Congresso Nazionale della Società Filosofica Italiana*, Casertano, Giovanni (ed), 151-158. Napoli, Loffredo, 1997.

**Simester, A P**. Agency. *Law Phil*, 15(2), 159-181, 96.

In 1992, *Law and Philosophy* published an account of the paradigm case of intended action; one which gestured at, and did not pursue, an explanation of the requirement that a person be an agent in respect of her behaviour before that behaviour can constitute intended action. This paper completes that account by supplying an analysis of agency. The paper falls into three parts. It begins by casting doubt upon the possibility of specifying a causal account along the lines once envisaged by Davidson. An alternative approach is adopted: one that involves modifications to Frankfurt's depiction of action as behaviour under the agent's guidance, including a rejection of the view held by many writers that action requires intentional movement. Doubts about conventional wisdoms are also raised in the conclusion, which considers why philosophers and lawyers should be interested in the issue of agency at all.

**Simmonds, Nigel E** and Kramer, Matthew H. Reason Without Reasons: A Critique of Alan Gewirth's Moral Philosophy. *S J Phil*, 34(3), 301-315, Fall 96.

Alan Gewirth in numerous important writings has attempted to show that every purposive agent, simply by dint of being such an agent, is logically committed to a supreme moral principle—a principle which enjoins every agent to respect the fundamental well-being of every other agent. This essay refutes Gewirth's argument by exposing his repeated failure to attend to the distinction between not having a reason for action and not acknowledging a reason for action. When that distinction is properly heeded, Gewirth's derivation of a moral precept from the pre-moral posture of agency turns out to be untenable.

**Simmons, Howard**. Circumstances and the Truth of Words: A Reply to Travis. *Mind*, 106(421), 117-118, Ja 97.

Charles Travis has criticized the deflationist theory of truth for neglecting the fact that the truth of many descriptions depends on circumstances that determine how precisely they are to be understood on a given occasion. ("Meaning's Role in Truth," *Mind*, 105 (419), 451-466). I argue that it is possible to conceive of a linguistic community whose utterances do not depend in this way on circumstances, that such utterances could still meaningfully be described as true or false, and therefore that a general definition of truth need not in fact mention 'occasion sensitivity'.

**Simmons, I G**. Bach's Butterfly Effect: Culture, Environment and History. *Environ Values*, 6(2), 201-212, My 97.

The basic thesis that environmental values must spring from the economic relations of human societies is examined and it is suggested that although such connections are never absent, they do not account for the totality of values. Rather, they interact with other values in a kind of helical strand which is open-ended and self-organizing. In such a context, 'sustainability', for example, becomes a rather time-limited idea. Our present ways of describing such evolution and interactions are also briefly examined.

**Simmons, Lance**. "On Not Destroying the Health of One's Patients" in *Human Lives: Critical Essays on Consequentialist Bioethics,* Oderberg, David S (ed), 144-160. New York, Macmillan, 1997.

It is possible to show that certain kinds of reasoning and certain kinds of action are conceptually incompatible with medical practice, without presupposing that medicine has a primary end such as the promotion of health. This is done via an examination of recent accounts of virtue concepts by Bernard Williams and Alasdair MacIntyre. The former can be used to show that health is a 'thick' concept and can only be adequately explained in terms of virtue theory. The latter can be used to show that health is a good internal to the practice of medicine. From this it is concluded that good doctors do not attack the health of their patients, even to promote some other end such as enabling the patient to pursue a certain lifestyle.

**Simms, Karl**. "Introduction to Part I" in *Critical Studies: Ethics and the Subject,* Simms, Karl (ed), 3-15. Amsterdam, Rodopi, 1997.

This Introduction provides background to the articles assembled in the "From Phenomenology to Narrative Identity" section of the book. Beginning with a summary of Husserl's ontology in *Ideas I*, it proceeds to an explanation of the turn towards ethics in *Ideas II* and a consideration of the influence of that work on Levinas, Merleau-Ponty and Ricoeur. It argues that it is through acknowledgement of the Other that the solipsism of Descartes's dialectic of consciousness is escaped, so that in an ethical relation subjectivity is dependent on intersubjectivity. This kind of acknowledgement is the route to a "good life", whereby maintaining a constant character in the narrative of life becomes more ethically credible than the "timelessness" of the Cartesian *cogito*.

**Simms, Karl**. "Introduction to Part II" in *Critical Studies: Ethics and the Subject,* Simms, Karl (ed), 99-126. Amsterdam, Rodopi, 1997.

This Introduction provides background to the articles assembled in the "Genealogy, Agency and Psychoanalysis" section of the book. It begins with an explanation of Nietzschean genealogy as an alternative to historical method and the adoption of this by Foucault. The modification of Cartesian subjectivity which this implies is, like Lacanian psychoanalysis, a version of Thomist self-love as a basis for ethical interaction with others. This is demonstrated through readings of various cultural artifacts, including pornography, horror films, the novels of Charlotte Brontë and Daniel Defoe and the poetry of Wallace Stevens and Lord Byron.

**Simms, Karl** (ed). *Critical Studies: Ethics and the Subject.* Amsterdam, Rodopi, 1997.

This volume contains nineteen essays—eighteen here presented for the first time—exploring the question of subjectivity as seen from an ethical perspective. Part I concerns the phenomenological development of Cartesianism and the concept of *narrative identity*, with essays addressing Levinas's idea of the *Other*, Ricoeur's *Christianization of Levinas*, and Dennet's concept of folk psychology. Part II concerns the experience of reading ethically, as mediated through genealogy and psychoanalysis. The essays address the discourses of philosophy, psychoanalysis, film and literature, and are informed by Nietzsche, Freud, Foucault and Lacan among others. The volume will interest philosophers and critical theorists. Karl Simms provides comprehensive introductions to each of the parts, making the book accessible to informed general readers with an interest in cultural studies. (publisher)

**Simms, Karl** (ed). *Critical Studies: Language and the Subject.* Amsterdam, Rodopi, 1997.

This volume contains nineteen essays—eighteen here presented for the first time—exploring the question of subjectivity as seen from a linguistic perspective. Part I concerns the relationship between the linguistic subject, particularly the grammatical first person and the subject in more general sense of 'person'. Topics covered include deixis, verbal marking and temporalisation and performatives. Part II concerns the relationship of subjectivity to the experience of reading and as such considers the semiotics of both literary and nonliterary texts, intermodal representation, authorship and intertextuality. The essays in the volume are principally influenced by the thinking of Saussure, Jakobson, Guillaume, Benveniste, Wittgenstein, Barthes and Deleuze and the book will appeal to scholars with an interest in theoretical linguistics, semiotics, discourse, analysis and philosophy of language. Karl Simms provides comprehensive introductions to each of the parts, making the book accessible to inform general readers with an interest in cultural and communication studies. (publisher)

**Simoes Francisco, Maria de Fátima**. Thinking and Action in Hannah Arendt (in Portuguese). *Trans/Form/Acao*, 19, 163-175, 1996.

This paper intends to investigate in Hannah Arendt's last work *The Life of the Mind* the relationship between thinking and action, which is in the origin of the conflict between philosophy and politics and has influenced the whole philosophical tradition. Arendt aims to show that these two activities are not by themselves incompatible with each other, as this tradition made efforts to establish, but they have become so through the "professional" philosophical use of thinking.

**Simon, András** and Hodkinson, Ian. The *k*-Variable Property is Stronger than H-Dimension *k*. *J Phil Log*, 26(1), 81-101, F 97.

**Simon, Derek**. The *Sophist*, 246a-259e: *Ousia* and *to On* in Plato's Ontologies. *De Phil*, 12, 155-177, 1995-1996.

**Simon, Josef**. Zeichenmachende Phantasie: Zum systematischen Zusammenhang von Zeichen und Denken bei Hegel. *Z Phil Forsch*, 50(1/2), 254-270, Ja-Je 96.

**Simon, Rita J** and Altstein, Howard. The Relevance of Race in Adoption Law and Social Practice. *Notre Dame J Law Ethics*, 11(1), 171-195, 1997.

In summarizing the major research that has been conducted on transracial adoptees and their families, the authors emphasize that all of the empirical studies support transracial adoption. The studies show that transracial adoption serves the children's best interests. Simon & Altstein's twenty-year study of primarily black children who were adopted by white families and their recent study of adult Korean children who were adopted by white families show that the transracial adoptees grow up aware of their racial identity, committed to their adoptive families and sensitive to their community. The findings strongly support the 1996 federal statute that prohibits race to be used as a factor to delay or deny adoption.

**Simonetta, Patrick**. Une Correspondance entre Anneaux Partiels et Groupes. *J Sym Log*, 62(1), 60-78, Mr 97.

We study the extensions of the additive group of *A* by the group *S*, acting by right multiplication, and show that sometimes sigma($A_S$) is the unique extension of this type. We also give conditions allowing us to eliminate parameters appearing in interpretations. We emphasize the case where the domain is a division ring *K* and *S* is its multiplicative group $K^x$. Here, the interpretations can always be done without parameters. If the center of *K* contains more than two elements, then *sigma(K)* is the only extension of the additive group of *K* by its multiplicative group acting by right multiplication, and the class of all such *sigma(K)*'s is elementary and finitely axiomatizable. We give, in particular, an axiomatization for this class and for the class of *sigma(K*'s where *K* is an algebraically closed field of characteristic O. From these results it follows that some classical model-companion results about theories of fields can be translated and restated as results about theories of solvable groups of class 2. (edited)

**Simoni, Henry**. Omniscience and the Problem of Radical Particularity: Does God Know How to Ride a Bike?. *Int J Phil Relig*, 42(1), 1-22, Ag 97.

**Simons, Peter**. "The Horizontal" in *Frege: Importance and Legacy,* Schirn, Matthias (ed), 280-300. Hawthorne, de Gruyter, 1996.

The paper examines the history of the logical constant Frege initially called 'the content stroke' and later simply 'the horizontal', its logical properties in his earlier and later systems, and its interaction with his other primitives. It is shown how Frege's treatment of nontruth-values involves him in something very like a three-valued logic. Ringing the changes on the three-valued connectives definable shows two things: Frege's choice of primitives is very elegant and he could easily have defined other functions by cases.

**Simons, Peter**. "Vagueness, Many-Valued Logic, and Probability" in *Das weite Spektrum der analytischen Philosophie,* Lenzen, Wolfgang, 307-322. Hawthorne, de Gruyter, 1997.

The standard semantic approaches to vagueness are considered and rejected. An alternative framework is proposed in which the probabilistic notion of an expected truth-value is deployed. It is suggested that this offers a new way to understand the semantics of vagueness while explaining the attractions of other theories.

**Simons, Peter**. Lesniewski and Generalized Quantifiers. *Euro J Phil*, 2(1), 65-84, Ap 94.

The idea that higher-order quantitative functors form a family going beyond the usual quantifiers can be traced to the logical system of Stanislaw Lesniewski. It is shown that the freedom of definition Lesniewski allows enables conditions governing generalized quantifiers to be smoothly formulated in the object language rather than metalinguistically as is now usual.

**Simons, Peter**. Timothy Williamson *Vagueness*. *Int J Phil Stud*, 4(2), 321-327, S 96.

This essay review finds Williamson's criticisms of extant theories of vagueness to be cogent but finds his arguments for bivalence and for his own epistemic theory less than compelling. The conclusion is that a satisfactory theory of vagueness is till wanting.

**Simonsen, H B** and Holtug, Nils and Sandoe, Peter. Ethical Limits to Domestication. *J Agr Environ Ethics*, 9(2), 114-122, 1996.

Through the process of domestication the genetic make-up of farm animals can be changed by means of either selective breeding or genetic engineering. This paper is about the ethical limits to such genetic changes. It is suggested that the ethical significance of domestication has become clear recently in the light of genetic engineering, but that the problem has been there all along. Two ethical approaches to domestication are presented, genetic integrity and animal welfare. It is argued that the welfare approach is superior. Finally, five ethical hypotheses based on the welfare approach are presented.

**Simonutti, Luisa**. "John Howe: dissidente, neoplatonico e anti-spinozista" in *Mind Senior to the World,* Baldi, Marialuisa, 255-291. Milano, FrancoAngeli, 1996.

Attraverso le opere di Howe—che peraltro non mancano di una certa originalità—diventa possibile un'ulteriore verifica di quale e quanto dell'insegnamento platonico, stoico, origeniano, della filosofia rinascimentale e della filosofia dei neoplatonici di Cambridge abbia continuato a far parte e anzi sia stata oggetto di rinnovato interesse nella cultura inglese tra la fine del '600 e l'inizio del '700. Inoltre lo studio dell'opera di Howe ci permette di aggiungere un'ulteriore tessera alla storia della fortuna di Spinoza in Inghilterra. Infine, le sue opere politico-religiose possono fornire, da un lato, nuovi elementi nella rilettura della concezione della religione razionale all'epoca della Restaurazione avviata in questi ultimi anni e, dall'altro, contribuire a precisare meglio il significato della dissidenza religiosa e politica di fronte all'affermarsi del pensiero deista.

**Simonutti, Luisa**. Between Political Loyalty and Religious Liberty: Political Theory and Toleration in Huguenot Thought in the Epoch of Bayle. *Hist Polit Thought*, 17(4), 523-554, Winter 96.

**Simpson, David**. Administrative Lies and Philosopher-Kings. *Phil Inq*, 18(3-4), 45-65, Sum-Fall 96.

The question of whether lies by those who govern are acceptable receives a clear focus and an ideal case in the *Republic.*. Against C.D.C. Reeve and T.C. Brickhouse and N. D. Smith, I argue that the *Republic's* apparent recommendation of administrative lies is incoherent. While lies may be a necessary part of the City's administration, the process and practice of lying undermines that nature which is necessary for any suitable ruler—rendering the ideal impossible. I argue that this analysis, while concerned with an ideal case, also applies to the political realist's regrettable-but-necessary defence of such practices.

**Simpson, Evan**. "Forms of Political Thinking and the Persistence of Practical Philosophy" in *Political Dialogue: Theories and Practices,* Esquith, Stephen L (ed), 117-141. Amsterdam, Rodopi, 1996.

Many political disagreements are deeper than differences of opinion. People who simply differ in their opinions can understand and argue with one another, but between liberals and conservatives there is often a kind of mutual incomprehension. Employing different rules of relevance and inherence, they finds the views of their opponents to lack plausible grounds. By describing these forms of thinking in some detail, it is possible to better analyze intransigent problems of political dialogue and competing ideals of political association. The results of analysis also indicate that it is possible to describe further forms of thinking in addition to those that have enjoyed dominance in the past, in particular a form of democratic thinking that is distinct from the conservative and liberal forms. It is not possible to show that one form of thinking is inherently superior to the other, so that problems of dialogue will continue, but democratic thinking has resources that permit discussion to yield a former practical consensus than the alternatives.

**Simpson, Evan**. Rights Thinking. *Philosophy*, 72(279), 29-58, Ja 97.

The practice of rights thinking is desirable in modern societies but its scope is restricted by concern for utility and the demands of personal relationships. The result is a hybrid practice no part of which is a foundation for the others. Differences between pure rights thinking, theories of rights and rights talk support a moral pragmatism for which the objects of moral thinking are not decided a priori. The argument draws upon the historical context provided by Bentham, Burke, Locke and Marx. Contemporary views discussed include contributions by Richard Flathman and Beth Singer and Charles Taylor.

**Sims, Randi L** and Keon, Thomas L. Ethical Work Climate as a Factor in the Development of Person-Organization Fit. *J Bus Ethics*, 16(11), 1095-1105, Ag 97.

The purpose of this study was to determine if there is a relationship between the ethical climate of the organization and the development of person-organization fit. The relationship between an individual's stage of moral development and his/her perceived ethical work environment was examined using a sample of 86 working students. Results indicate that a match between individual preferences and present position proved most satisfying. Subjects expressing a match between their preferences for an ethical work climate and their present ethical work climate indicated that they were less likely to leave their positions.

**Sina, Mario**. "Origenismo e anti-agostinismo in Jean Le Clerc diffusore della cultura inglese" in *Mind Senior to the World,* Baldi, Marialuisa, 293-312. Milano, FrancoAngeli, 1996.

**Sina, Mario**. L'apologétique de Samuel Clarke. *Rev Phil Fr*, 1, 33-44, Ja-Mr 97.

**Sinemus, Kristina** and Platzer, Katrin and Bender, Wolfgang. On the Assessment of Genetic Technology: Reaching Ethical Judgments in the Light of Modern Technology. *Sci Eng Ethics*, 1(1), 21-32, J 95.

The "Model for Reaching Ethical Judgments in the Context of Modern Technologies—the Case of Genetic Technology," which is presented here, has arisen from the project "Ethical Criteria Bearing Upon Decisions Taken in the Field of Biotechnology." This project has been pursued since 1991 in the Zentrum für interdisziplinäre Technikforschung (ZIT) of the Technical University of Darmstadt, with the purpose of examining decision-making in selected activities involving the production of transgenic plants that have a useful application. The model is the basis of an outline for interviews to investigate how far decisions concerning the development of such plants with genetic techniques take ethical criteria into account. It was necessary to design this new model because other models for reaching judgments of this kind were not conceptually suited for concrete application. This model represents a problem related approach and combines methodological with substantive typology. In this it differs from comparable models for reaching ethical judgments.

**Singer, Alan E** and Singer, Ming S. Management-Science and Business-Ethics. *J Bus Ethics*, 16(4), 385-395, Mr 97.

Many leading management scientists have advocated ethicalism: the incorporation of social and ethical concerns into traditional "rational" OR-MS techniques and management decisions. In fact, elementary forms of decision analysis can readily be augmented, using ethical theory, in ways that sweep in ethical issues. In addition, alternative conceptual models of decision-analysis, game-theory and optimality are now available, all of which have brought OR-MS and business-ethics into a closer alignment.

**Singer, Alan E** and Singer, Ming S. Observer Judgements about Moral Agents' Ethical Decisions: The Role of Scope of Justice and Moral Intensity. *J Bus Ethics*, 16(5), 473-484, Ap 97.

The study ascertained 1) whether an observer's scope of justice with reference to either the moral agent or the target person of a moral act, would affect his/her judgments of the ethicality of the act, and 2) whether observer judgments of ethicality parallel the moral agent's decision processes in systematically evaluating the intensity of the moral issue. A scenario approach was used. Results affirmed both research questions. Discussions covered the implications of the findings for the underlying cognitive processes of moral judgments, for the link between judgments of fairness and ethicality, as well as for the debate of ethical absolutism versus relativism.

**Singer, M**. *Ethics and Justice in Organisations: A Normative-Empirical Dialogue.* Brookfield, Avebury, 1997.

**Singer, Marcus G** (ed) and Murphy, Arthur E. *Reason, Reality, and Speculative Philosophy.* Madison, Univ of Wisconsin Pr, 1996.

This book brings to publication the bulk of a previously unpublished manuscript which the author, who died in 1962, finished writing in 1940. In the course of his discussion of speculative philosophy and the main philosophical tendencies in the period 1890 to 1940, the author provides his own account of what a reasonable and sensible philosophy should be and do and what a reasonable philosophical method consists in. Among the topics discussed are Philosophy in the Contemporary World, The Rational Use of Ideas, The Standpoint of Philosophy, The Way Philosophies Work and The Life of Reason. The philosophies considered include idealism, Realism and the enterprise called Speculative Philosophy—its nature and character and major types and representatives. The author discusses, among other philosophers, Bradley, Bosanquet, Peirce, Russell, Whitehead, Alexander, R. W. Sellars, McTaggart, Gilson and Santayana, in the light of the ideas presented on what philosophy is and reasonably can accomplish. The book also presents an account of the nature of reason and reality and of critical philosophy as opposed to speculative philosophy and an argument for the method of operational or contextual analysis. The editor has provided a Preface, a Memoir of the author, an Introduction, Bibliographical Notes and explanatory comments where needed.

**Singer, Ming S** and Singer, Alan E. Management-Science and Business-Ethics. *J Bus Ethics*, 16(4), 385-395, Mr 97.

Many leading management scientists have advocated ethicalism: the incorporation of social and ethical concerns into traditional "rational" OR-MS techniques and management decisions. In fact, elementary forms of decision analysis can readily be augmented, using ethical theory, in ways that sweep in ethical issues. In addition, alternative conceptual models of decision-analysis, game-theory and optimality are now available, all of which have brought OR-MS and business-ethics into a closer alignment.

**Singer, Ming S** and Singer, Alan E. Observer Judgements about Moral Agents' Ethical Decisions: The Role of Scope of Justice and Moral Intensity. *J Bus Ethics*, 16(5), 473-484, Ap 97.

The study ascertained 1) whether an observer's scope of justice with reference to either the moral agent or the target person of a moral act, would affect his/her judgments of the ethicality of the act, and 2) whether observer judgments of ethicality parallel the moral agent's decision processes in systematically evaluating the intensity of the moral issue. A scenario approach was used. Results affirmed both research questions. Discussions covered the implications of the findings for the underlying cognitive processes of moral judgments, for the link between judgments of fairness and ethicality, as well as for the debate of ethical absolutism versus relativism.

**Singer, Peter A** and Kohut, Nitsa and Sam, Mehran (& others). Stability of Treatment Preferences: Although Most Preferences Do Not Change, Most People Change Some of Their Preferences. *J Clin Ethics*, 8(2), 124-135, Sum 97.

**Singh, Amita**. Proposing 'Project Mankind'. *Phil Soc Act*, 22(3), 15-23, Jl-S 96.

The constant threat to human survival from the militarist foundation of the global system has reduced mankind to a cog in the enormous 'military-industrial complex.' The multiplicity of socio-economic factors which now surround the questions of peace and war have started challenging the sovereignty of the state by exposing the link between arms and energy on one hand and human development on the other. The rising mass based movements today are psycho-political phenomenon projecting the need for human survival through the search for 'alternatives' in place of the state sponsored stereotyped militarization policies. (edited)

**Singh, Ramjee**. "Fundamentalism in India" in *Averroës and the Enlightenment,* Wahba, Mourad (ed), 189-201. Amherst, Prometheus, 1996.

**Singhapakdi, Anusorn** and Vitell, Scott J and Rallapalli, Kumar C. The Perceived Role of Ethics and Social Responsibility: A Scale Development. *J Bus Ethics*, 15(11), 1131-1140, N 96.

Marketers must first perceive ethics and social responsibility to be important before their behaviors are likely to become more ethical and reflect greater social responsibility. However, little research has been conducted concerning marketers' perceptions regarding the importance of ethics and social responsibility as components of business decisions. The purpose of this study is to develop a reliable and valid scale for measuring marketers' perceptions regarding the importance of ethics and social responsibility. The authors develop an instrument for the measurement of the perceived role of ethics and social responsibility (PRESOR). Evidence that the scale is valid is presented through the assessment of scale reliability, as well as content and predictive validity. Finally, future research needs and the value of this construct to marketing are discussed.

**Sinha, Rani Rupmati**. Relevance of Swami Vivekanand's Concept of Evil Today. *Darshana Int*, 35(3/139), 67-70, Jl 95.

**Sini, Carlo**. "Il segno e l'evento" in *Momenti di Storia della Logica e di Storia della Filosofia,* Guetti, Carla (ed), 113-130. Roma, Aracne Editrice, 1996.

**Sini, Carlo**. "Il Soggetto E La Verità" in *Soggetto E Verità: La questione dell'uomo nella filosofia contemporanea,* Fagiuoli, Ettore, 29-32. 20136 Milano, Mimesis, 1996.

**Sini, Carlo** and Cacciatore, Giuseppe. "Husserl e Heidegger: tempo e fenomenologia" in *Il Concetto di Tempo: Atti del XXXII Congresso Nazionale della Società Filosofica Italiana,* Casertano, Giovanni (ed), 85-90. Napoli, Loffredo, 1997.

**Sini, Carlo** and Grottanelli, Cristiano. Homo sacer, di Giorgio Agamben. *Iride*, 9(18), 485-494, Ag 96.

In *Homo sacer*, Agamben si interroga sui caratteri essenziali del politico e della democrazia moderni, rivelandone in particolare l'aspetto "biopolitico". Grottanelli si sofferma sull'ambiguità del concetto di sacro e sulla critica dell'ideologia sacrificale proposti da Agamben. Sini approfondisce alcuni concetti centrali delle analisi di Agamben, come quelli connessi al metodo biopolitico del potere, alla nozione di "bando" e di sovranità, per finire con quello di Stato.

**Sinnott-Armstrong, Walter** (ed) and Timmons, Mark (ed). *Moral Knowledge?: New Readings in Moral Epistemology.* New York, Oxford Univ Pr, 1996.

The book brings together eleven newly written essays by distinguished moral philosophers exploring the nature and possibility of moral knowledge. Each essay represents a major position within the exciting field of moral epistemology in which a proponent of the position presents and defends his or her view and locates it vis-à-vis competing views. (edited)

**Sintonen, Matti**. "Explanation: The Fifth Decade" in *Knowledge and Inquiry: Essays on Jaakko Hintikka's Epistemology and Philosophy of Science,* Sintonen, Matti (ed), 225-238. Amsterdam, Rodopi, 1997.

In his "Four Decades of Scientific Explanation" Wesley Salmon locates the roots of all three modern notions of explanation in Aristotle. Yet his account in which the so-called erotetic or question-answer-view is but one variant of the epistemic notion of explanation misses an important ecumenical message. This paper suggests that the erotetic or interrogative notion is best viewed as an umbrella notion under which all three rivals, the epistemic, modal and ontic notions of explanation, fit. This explains why there is a unitary notion—that of a satisfactory answer to a certain form of query—behind the various intuitions of explanation, although satisfactoriness can be cashed out differently in different cases. This view not just restores the angle which somehow got lost during the four decades but also shows that Aristotle was right in thinking that explanations, different kinds of answers to why-questions, fall into distinct types. This view also builds a bridge from the science of logic to the logic of science and hence does justice to the long interrogative tradition of inquiry.

**Sintonen, Matti** (ed). *Knowledge and Inquiry: Essays on Jaakko Hintikka's Epistemology and Philosophy of Science.* Amsterdam, Rodopi, 1997.

The volume consists of sixteen essays on Jaakko Hintikka's philosophy, as well as Hintikka's replies: Matti Sintonen: "From the Science of Logic to the Logic of Science"; Z. Bechler: "Hintikka on Plenitude in Aristotle"; M-L. Kakkuri-Knuuttila: "What Can the Sciences of Man Learn from Aristotle?"; M. Kusch: "Theories of Questions in German-Speaking Philosophy around the Turn of the Century"; N-E. Sahlin: "'He Is No Good for My Work': On the Philosophical Relations between Ramsey and Wittgenstein"; T. Kuipers: "The Carnap-Hintikka Programme in Inductive Logic"; I. Levi: "Caution and Nonmonotonic Inference"; I. Niiniluoto: "Inductive Logic, Atomism, and Observational Error"; A. Mutanen: "Theory of Identifiability"; S. Bromberger: "Natural Kinds and Questions"; S. Kleiner: "The Structure of Inquiry in Developmental Biology"; A. Wisniewski: "Some Foundational Concepts of Erotetic Semantics"; J. Wolenski: "Science and Games"; M. Sintonen: "Explanation—The Fifth Decade"; E. Weber: "Scientific Explanation and the Interrogative Model of Inquiry"; G. Gebhard: "Scientific Discovery, Induction, and the Multi-Level Character of Scientific Inquiry"; M. Kiikeri: "On the Logical Structure of Learning Models."

**Siorvanes, Lucas**. *Proclus: Neo-Platonic Philosophy and Science.* New Haven, Yale Univ Pr, 1996.

Siorvanes's extensive original research presents Proclus as much more than just a metaphysician. He surveys all of Proclus's philosophical interests—including religion, physics, astronomy, mathematics and poetry—revealing the philosopher's central concern with the problems of being and knowledge and relating the ideas of Proclus to those of such other major thinkers as Plato, Aristotle and Ptolemy. To help the newcomer, Siorvanes supplies more than 200 quotations from Proclus's works. He also traces the impact of Proclus's neo-Platonism across cultures, religions and centuries, in such diverse areas as Christian and Islamic theologies, Renaissance art, Kepler's astronomy, romantic poetry, Emerson's thought, modern philosophy and science and current popular phrases. (publisher, edited)

**Sismondo, Sergio**. Deflationary Metaphysics and the Construction of Laboratory Mice. *Metaphilosophy*, 28(3), 219-233, Jl 97.

The deflationist turn in recent philosophy of science has attracted attention, in part because it promises to end debates about scientific realism. In its recommendation that we leave metaphysics behind to look at practice, deflationism constructs itself as an end-of-philosophy philosophy, accepting knowledge and the evidence for it at face value. Meanwhile, recent work in philosophy, sociology and history of science that has focused on practice has underscored problems of such an acceptance: much scientific knowledge is not straightforwardly about the natural world and we would not want it to be. A concrete example from the history of comparative psychology illustrates this point and illustrates the value of interpretive work on scientific knowledge. A focus on practice, then, does not end metaphysical discussion, but rather regrounds and reshapes it.

**Skidmore, Arthur**. On Sartwell's Thesis that Knowledge is Merely True Belief. *SW Phil Rev*, 13(1), 123-127, Ja 97.

**Skillen, Tony**. Passing Likeness. *Phil Papers*, 25(2), 73-93, Ag 96.

This article argues for a 'likeness', 'resemblance' or 'similarity' view of pictures' relation to what they are pictures of. It defends their status as 'icons' (Peirce) against the claim of Goodman and other semiological theorists that they are 'symbols' conventionally tied to their subject. Modified 'natural generativity' views of Wollheim, Sheier and Peacocke are criticised. The 'likeness' view is tested and developed in relation to abstract, symbolic, expressive and formal aspects of pictures.

**Skirbekk, Gunnar**. The Discourse Principle and Those Affected. *Inquiry*, 40(1), 63-71, Mr 97.

Focusing on the terms 'possibly affected persons' and 'those affected' in the Habermasian 'discourse principle', I argue that we need a notion of *moral subjects* in addition to that of a *person* (in terms of *moral agents* and *moral discussants*) and that this notion of moral subjects implies a 'normative gradualism' which weakens the participatory and consensual aspect of discourse theory and strengthens the aspect of enlightened 'advocatory' deliberation in terms of needs and the good life. I argue that this notion of moral subjects ('those affected') represents a challenge for the discourse principle. Confronted with the huge number of (different kinds of) moral subjects and of (hypothetical) future persons, demanding various kinds of advocatory representation, the Habermasian discourse principle, as stated in *Between Facts and Norms*, becomes unsatisfactory.

**Sklar, Lawrence** and Sassoli, Bernardo and Dessì, Paola. Discutono *Il caso domato,* di Ian Hacking. *Iride*, 8(15), 483-494, Ag 95.

Il libro di I. Hacking ricostruisce nei tratti essenziali il clima intellettuale che nell'Ottocento veda la crisi del "determinismo" e la "rivoluzione probabilistica" e quindi permette l'affermazione di un nuovo "stile di ragionamento" che solleva il "caso" da "superstizione popolare" a evento assoggettabile a legge. P. Dessì discute l'idea dell'Autore che la pratica abbia anticipato la rivoluzione teorica; B. Sassoli si sofferma sull'epistemologia di Hacking e la sua nozione di "stile di ragionamento"; L. Sklar sottolinea il carattere illuminante che possiede la scoperta delle premesse sociali dell'idea di "legge statistica" indispensabile nella ricerca scientifica contemporanea.

**Skoble, Aeon James**. Two Errors in the Most Recent Edition of Peter of Spain's *Summulae Logicales. Mod Sch*, 74(3), 249-253, Mr 97.

**Skocpol, Theda**. The G.I. Bill and U.S. Social Policy, Past and Future. *Soc Phil Pol*, 14(2), 95-115, Sum 97.

**Skorpíková, Zuzana**. Veritas vincit (in Czech). *Filosof Cas*, 44(6), 923-936, 1996.

If we wish to take a serious philosophical interpretation of the slogan of the Czech reformation "*veritas vincit*" it seems at first sight somewhat surprising. The concept of "truth" as it is generally used today is essentially related to understanding rather than victory, struggle and destruction, as the slogan implies. Truth is something we must recognize and search for—not something to fight for (or even with?). Hus's exhortation to "stand by the known truth," which could imply the struggle to spread or enforce truth, only serves to obscure the problem. Truth is here subsumed to knowledge and the struggle is not essentially connected with it—"*veritas vincit*" would be just an effective battle cry. This work seeks to show that "*veritas vincit*" can fundamentally mean something different. This article looks at the conceptualization of Emanuel Rádl, the first Czech thinker to take a consistently philosophical approach to the idea of truth which wins, although his conceptualization remained unfinished. Rádl's starting point was that truth need not be primarily linked with knowledge, but that man can also come to it through his acts, which changes even the ontological determination of truth. The article tries to clarify Rádl's ideas and to show some of their consequences.

**Skorupski, John**. Why did Language Matter to Analytic Philosophy?. *Ratio*, 9(3), 269-283, D 96.

Language mattered to analytic philosophy because rules of language-use came to be seen as the primitive phenomenon in terms of which meaning, thought and the *a priori* could be understood. Behind this lay two ideas: that all assertoric content is factual and that no fact is intrinsically normative. I argue that reflection on what it is to apply a rule shows the first idea to be incoherent. There must be normative contents which are neither factual nor expressions of language-rules. The resulting view can retain the deflationary view of metaphysics which was influential in the analytic tradition.

**Skotnicki, Andrew**. Religion and Rehabilitation. *Crim Just Ethics*, 15(2), 34-43, Sum-Fall 96.

The article, "Religion and Rehabilitation", argues that current reinterest in rehabilitation as a goal of criminal justice labors under a set of misconceptions concerning the human person and religion that can be traced to late nineteenth century progressive ideology. Contemporary reformers have focused on rehabilitation with the same methodological limitations that guided earlier reforms which were later widely discredited. The article argues that to ignore conversion as a vehicle for personal transformation is not only to ignore what religion arguably does better than any therapeutic or medical mechanism but also to ignore the insights of noted cognitive psychologists.

**Skowron, Andrzej** and Pawlak, Zdzislaw. Helena Rasiowa and Cecylia Rauszer Research on Logical Foundations of Computer Science. *Bull Sec Log*, 25(3/4), 174-184, O-D 96.

It is an abstract of the talk presented on the session dedicated to the memory of Professor Helena Rasiowa and Professor Cecylia Rauszer on June 10, 1995 in the Faculty of Mathematics, Computer Science and Mechanics at Warsaw University, Poland. It presents the results received by Professor Rasiowa and Professor Rauszer on logical and algebraic foundations of computer science and the influence of Professor Rasiowa on the development of research on mathematical foundations of computer science in Poland and other countries.

**Skowron, Andrzej** and Polkowski, Lech T and Komorowski, Jan. Towards a Rough Mereology-Based Logic for Approximate Solution. *Stud Log*, 58(1), 143-184, 1997.

We are concerned with formal models of reasoning under uncertainty. Many approaches to this problem are known in the literature, e.g., Dempster-Shafer theory, Bayesian-based reasoning, belief networks, many-valued logics and fuzzy logics, nonmonotonic logics, neural network logics. We propose rough mereology developed by the last two authors as a foundation for approximate reasoning about complex objects. Our notion of a complex object includes, among others, proofs understood as schemes constructed in order to support within our knowledge assertions/hypotheses about reality described by our knowledge incompletely.

**Skultans, Vieda**. Looking for a Subject: Latvian Memory and Narrative. *Hist Human Sci*, 9(4), 65-80, N 96.

This paper is based on the narrativized memories of one Latvian who spent more than a decade in prison and labour camps in Siberia. Although given in the spirit of testimony and constructed around flashbulb memories, this account is no mere photographic record. Rather, the speaker seizes the narrative opportunity to select and organize the past around a number of shifting identities. Because the experiences recalled are at odds with the powerful and adventurous identity to which he aspires the narrative moves from one pronoun to another. It lies in tension between the singular and the collective, between the personal and the impersonal. There is no pronominal home, no owner for this narrative.

**Skura, Tomasz**. Some Aspects of Refutation Rules. *Rep Math Log*, 29, 109-116, 1995.

The purpose of the paper is to make a few remarks on the following aspects of refutation rules: a characteristic property of a logic, elegant and constructive completeness proofs. In particular a new constructive completeness proof for the provability logic G is given.

**Skutch, Alexander F**. Libertad básica. *Rev Filosof (Costa Rica)*, 34(83-84), 205-211, D 96.

This article examines an aspect of the conflict between mind and body. Invisible genes guide the growth and functioning of our body, in normal circumstances doing both very well without our conscious interference. While they control our internal relations, they endow us with intelligence to adjust our external relations in a world that is often confusing. Unfortunately, by the strong passions that they impose upon us, our genes too frequently confuse or oppose the rational control of our behavior. Especially in procreation, they often override judgment, impelling us to beget progeny without regard to circumstances. (edited)

**Skvortsov, D**. Non-Axiomatizable Second Order Intuitionistic Propositional Logic. *Annals Pure Applied Log*, 86(1), 33-46, Je 97.

The second order intuitionistic propositional logic characterized by the class of all "principal" Kripke frames (i.e., frames with the quantifiers ranging over all upward-closed sets) is nonrecursively axiomatizable, as well as any logic of a class of principal Kripke frames containing every finite frame.

**Skyrms, Brian**. The Structure of Radical Probabilism. *Erkenntnis*, 45(2 & 3), 285-297, Nov 96.

Does the philosophy of *radical probabilism* have enough structure to enable it to address fundamental epistemological questions? The requirement of dynamic coherence provides the structure for radical probabilist epistemology. This structure is sufficient to establish I) the value of knowledge and II) long run convergence of degrees of belief.

**Slade, Christina**. Reasoning and Children: The Wide Glare of the Children's Day. *Thinking*, 13(2), 2-7, 1997.

Robert Graves's 'children's day' has a 'wide glare', a vividness and intensity lost to adults who, to use a biblical image, see as through a glass darkly. The belief that the child's experience has characteristic lineaments, quite distinct from those of adults, is bound up in our conceptions of childhood. Children's perceptions are valued because they are distinctive, while at the same time adults are supposed to have a role in shaping those perceptions. There is an inherent tension between these two attitudes to children. This paper seeks to develop and question Matthews's views with a particular focus on children's reasoning as they create and react to art and literature. (edited)

**Slade, Christina**. Reflective Reasoning in Groups. *Inform Log*, 17(2), 223-234, Spr 95.

The conception of reflective reasoning, like that of higher order thinking, has been informed by a Cartesian view of the self. Reflection is conceived of as a solipsistic process, in which persons consider their own thoughts in isolation.

Higher order thinking has equally been represented as a single thinker considering thoughts at a metalevel. This paper proposes a different conception of reflection and higher order thinking, in which reflective dialogue is seen as the fundamental context in which reflection is possible and higher order thinking engendered. The very process of dialectic defines what it is to be reflective and to think critically. learning to reflect alone is a consequence of internalising the discourse.

**Slaman, Theodore A** and Calhoun, William C. The $Pi^0_2$ Enumeration Degrees are not Dense. *J Sym Log*, 61(4), 1364-1379, D 96.

We show that the $II^0_2$ enumeration degrees are not dense. This answers a question posed by Cooper.

**Slaman, Theodore A** and Groszek, Marcia J. $Pi^0_1$ Classes and Minimal Degrees. *Annals Pure Applied Log*, 87(2), 117-144, 15 S 97.

**Slaman, Theodore A** and Haught, Christine Ann. Automorphisms in the *PTIME*-Turing Degrees of Recursive Sets. *Annals Pure Applied Log*, 84(1), 139-152, Mr 97.

**Slaman, Theodore A** and Shore, Richard A and Nies, André. Definability in the Recursively Enumerable Degrees. *Bull Sym Log*, 2(4), 392-404, D 96.

**Slater, Hartley**. Art and Aesthetics. *Brit J Aes*, 37(3), 226-231, Jl 97.

This paper shows there is a thoroughgoing dualism in all the arts, which divides their production into more creative and more rule-bound stages. In Collingwood's terms, the arts are 'two-stage'. The dichotomy is shown to parallel Kant's distinction between independent and dependent beauty, Ryle's distinction between achievements and tasks and Best's distinction between purposive and nonpurposive sports. Goodman's 'Languages of Art' is discussed at length with respect to these matters and corrected in several places notably on what can and cannot be forged.

**Slatman, Jenny**. Seeing and Being: Merleau-Ponty's Ontology of Elusive Visibility (in Dutch). *Tijdschr Filosof*, 59(2), 276-303, Je 97.

The aim of this article is to demonstrate that a certain connection between 'seeing' and 'Being' can be traced within the later work of Merleau-Ponty. It is argued that a theory of seeing which is developed from a radical phenomenological point of view is not a confirmation, but rather a critique of Western representational ontology. The central principle of this critique is formed by the notion of reversibility. By means of the reversible relation between the seer and the seen and between the visible and the invisible—which is situated within seeing itself—, the traditional opposition between subject and object is abolished and 'Being' loses its alleged meaning of 'presence' and 'unity'. One could say that the meaning of 'seeing' evades the (traditional) philosophical discourse. Therefore, philosophy should consult the practice of the artist, particularly painting. Merleau-Ponty's analysis of painting embodies a profound critique of representational thought. (edited)

**Slatter, John**. P.A. Kropotkin on Legality and Ethics. *Stud East Euro Thought*, 48(2-4), 255-276, S 96.

This article shows how Kropotkin's ideas on ethics and legality stemmed from his study of Darwin and from his reaction to the Social Darwinism, in the person of Thomas Huxley. In articles written that year he mapped out a programme for his fight against these thinkers in which he proposed to show that the principal urge for human societies to act ethically—that is, altruistically—was not the urge to compete with and overcome individual opponents as the Social Darwinists' thought, but the urge to cooperate in order to overcome the problems set by the collective adversary, Nature. This led on to Kropotkin's major contribution to the subject, *Mutual Aid*, in which he sets out a historical approach, examining the development of cooperation in animals and in human history from the earliest communities through to modern humankind. After this, Kropotkin did amend his ideas on Darwinian evolutionary theory, coming to a position close to Lamarckianism, but his ideas on ethics were not much altered by this. (edited)

**Sleigh, Jr, Robert**. "Arnauld versus Leibniz and Malebranche on the Limits of Theological Knowledge" in *Scepticism in the History of Philosophy: A Pan-American Dialogue*, Popkin, Richard H (ed), 75-85. Dordrecht, Kluwer, 1996.

**Slingerland, Ted**. The Conception of *Ming* in Early Confucian Thought. *Phil East West*, 46(4), 567-581, O 96.

Various interpretations of the role that *ming* ("fate") plays in early Confucian thought are examined. An interpretation is advanced which argues that early Confucians saw reality as being bifurcated into two distinct realms—"inner" and "outer"—and that *ming* refers to unpredictable forces in the outside realm, which are beyond the bounds of proper human endeavor. The vagaries of *ming* are not the concern of the gentleman, whose efforts and worries are to be focused on the cultivation of the self: the inner realm where "seeking helps one to get it." It is argued that a sense of "interiority" is present in early Confucianism and an attempt is made to distinguish the world-view of Confucius and Mencius from that of later neo-Confucian interpreters.

**Slomczynska, Katarzyna**. Linear Equivalential Algebras. *Rep Math Log*, 29, 41-58, 1995.

**Sloop, John M** and Ono, Kent A. Out-Law Discourse: The Critical Politics of Material Judgment. *Phil Rhet*, 30(1), 50-69, 1997.

Drawing upon recent poststructural investigations of judgment and justice, we argue that judgment is most profitably investigated from a rhetorical perspective, investigating not what judgment "should be," but instead investigating judgments as practiced by people in the context of their own experiences and using these judgments to disrupt and alter existing dominant logics. Ultimately, we argue that the role of theorists and critics is to develop strategies to disrupt the logics of judgment of the center and to highlight, enhance and create new judgments; critical practice should produce what we

AUTHOR INDEX 921 Smith, David H

call "materialist conceptions of judgment," taking judgments made by (out)law communities in vernacular discourses and utilizing self-selected (out)law discourses as disruptive possibilities.

**Slote, Michael**. The Virtue in Self-Interest. *Soc Phil Pol*, 14(1), 264-285, Wint 97.

In modern times, attempts to understand the relation between virtue and self-interest or well-being have proceeded in two directions. They have either treated virtue and other "higher" values as reducible to ideas about "mere" well-being and pleasure, in the fashion of utilitarianism, or have, like Kant, been dualistic about the categories of virtue and well-being. But ancient ethics tended to understand well-being in terms of virtue, and this opposite sort of unification needn't be as implausible as those Stoic versions that regarded well-being as *nothing more* than virtue. (edited)

**Slote, Michael** (ed) and Crisp, Roger (ed). *Virtue Ethics*. New York, Oxford Univ Pr, 1997.

This volume brings together much of the strongest and most influential work undertaken in the field of virtue ethics over the last four decades. Divided into four sections, it includes articles critical of other traditions; early attempts to offer a positive vision of virtue ethics; some later criticisms of the revival of virtue ethics; and, finally, some recent, more theoretically ambitious essays in virtue ethics. (publisher)

**Sluga, Hans**. "Ludwig Wittgenstein: Life and work an Introduction" in *The Cambridge Companion to Wittgenstein*, Sluga, Hans (ed), 1-33. Needham Heights, Cambridge, 1996.

**Sluga, Hans**. "Whose House is That? Wittgenstein on the Self" in *The Cambridge Companion to Wittgenstein*, Sluga, Hans (ed), 320-353. Needham Heights, Cambridge, 1996.

**Sluga, Hans**. Frege on Meaning. *Ratio*, 9(3), 209-226, D 96.

**Sluga, Hans** (ed) and Stern, David G (ed). *The Cambridge Companion to Wittgenstein*. Needham Heights, Cambridge, 1996.

The essays in this volume address central themes in Wittgenstein's writings on the philosophy of mind, language, logic, and mathematics. They chart the development of his work and clarify the connections between its different stages. The authors illuminate the character of the whole body of work by keeping a tight focus on some key topics: the style of the philosophy, the conception of grammar contained in it, rule-following, convention, logical necessity, the self, and what Wittgenstein called in a famous phrase, "forms of life." An important final essay offers a fundamental reassessment of the status of the many posthumously published texts. (edited)

**Smajs, Josef**. The Evolutionary Ontological Foundation of the New Ethics? (in Czech). *Filosof Cas*, 45(3), 381-392, 1997.

The article considers the possibility of creating a morally constitutive ethics by using an evolutionary ontological concept of being. The author considers that traditional morality, which grew primarily out of experience is a failure in the current ecological crisis. The new ecological morality which is needed if we are to overcome this crisis will, through its ecological ethics, draw more heavily on the new philosophical image of the world.

**Small, Michael W**. Business Education, Values and Beliefs. *Teach Bus Ethics*, 1(1), 53-61, 1997.

The study was concerned with values, value systems and the beliefs of business students from a wide variety of cultural backgrounds. The study of values and values education in Western societies is clearly different from the approach to a study of Asian values advocated by Lee Kuan Yew. We talk about integrity, idealism, honesty, fairness, altruism, justice, equity, freedom, but can we expect overseas students from different cultural backgrounds to have the same understanding of these concepts as students who have been raised in Western society?

**Small, Robin**. Resentiment, Revenge, and Punishment: Origins of the Nietzschean Critique. *Utilitas*, 9(1), 39-58, Mr 97.

Nietzsche's thinking on justice and punishment explores the motives and forces which lie behind moral concepts and social institutions. His dialogue with several writers of his time is discussed here. Eugen Dühring had argued that a natural feeling of *ressentiment* against those who have harmed us is the source of the concept of injustice, so that punishment, even in its most impersonal form, is always a form of revenge. In attacking this theory, Nietzsche developed his own powerful critique of moral concepts such as responsibility and guilt. He borrowed his 'historical' approach to moral concepts from Paul Rée, who suggested that the utilitarian function of punishment had been obscured by its practice, which appears to be directly linked with moral guilt. Nietzsche responds that punishment has quite different purposes and meanings at different times, so that any single explanation or justification is inadequate. In this way, he rejects the presuppositions common to the retributivists and utilitarians of his time.

**Smilansky, Saul**. Egalitarian Justice and the Importance of the Free Will Problem. *Philosophia (Israel)*, 25(1-4), 153-161, Ap 97.

Recent political philosophy has tended to neglect and discount the free will issue and this attitude has had important consequences, since the implications of the free will issue have a profound significance for our understanding of issues such as distributive justice. By discussing what I take to be the most intuitively coherent form that egalitarianism has taken, G.A. Cohen's, I attempt to show the crucial importance of the free will issue for the egalitarian agenda.

**Smilansky, Saul**. Moral Accountancy and Moral Worth. *Metaphilosophy*, 28(1-2), 123-134, Ja-Ap 97.

People do good or bad things and get or do not get good or bad credit for their actions, depending (in part) on knowledge of their actions. I attempt to unfold some of the interconnections between these matters and between them and the achievement of moral worth. The main conclusion is that the heights of moral worth seem to appear in the oddest places.

**Smilansky, Saul**. Preferring not to have been Born. *Austl J Phil*, 75(2), 241-247, Je 97.

I discuss a paragraph appearing in Bernard Williams's recent essay, "Resenting One's Own Existence". I cast doubt on Williams's assimilation of the preference for not having been born into an evaluation that one's life is not worthwhile living. I attempt to show that there is conceptual and psychological space for the thought that one prefers not to have been born, while at the same time not believing that one's life is "not worth living".

**Smilansky, Saul**. Should I Be Grateful to You for Not Harming Me?. *Phil Phenomenol Res*, 57(3), 585-597, S 97.

Getting people not to harm others is a central goal of morality. But while it is commonly perceived that those who benefit others merit gratitude, those who do not harm others are not ordinarily thought to merit anything. I attempt to argue against this, claiming that all the arguments against gratitude to the nonmaleficent are unsuccessful. Finally, I explore the difference it would make if we thought that we owe gratitude to those who do not harm us.

**Smit, Dirk J**. Covenant and Ethics? Comments from a South African Perspective. *Annu Soc Christ Ethics*, 265-282, 1996.

According to popular perception, Calvinist covenant language dominated Afrikaner thought and apartheid society, making it improbable that covenant language could play a constructive role in post-apartheid South Africa. The author argues that this was not the case. Fundamental ideas undergirding the apartheid myth were covenantal, but the expression was absent. The article distinguishes four covenant discourses in South Africa, each with ethical implications: a doctrinal discourse leads to an ethics of responsibility, an ecclesiological discourse to an ethics of community, an ecumenical discourse to an ethics of liberative solidarity, and political-ethical discourse to an ethics for a public church in a civil society. However, it remains doubtful whether the covenant symbol could play a crucial role in South African ethics.

**Smith, A D**. "Non-Reductive Physicalism?" in *Objections to Physicalism*, Robinson, Howard (ed), 225-250. New York, Clarendon/Oxford Pr, 1996.

**Smith, Barbara Herrnstein**. *Belief and Resistance: Dynamics of Contemporary Intellectual Controversy*. Cambridge, Harvard Univ Pr, 1997.

Smith's analyses take her into important ongoing debates over the possibility of an objective grounding of legal and political judgments, the continuing value of enlightenment rationalism, significant challenges to dominant ideas of scientific truth, and proper responses to denials of the factuality of the holocaust. As she explores these and other controversies, Smith develops fresh ways to understand their motives and energies, and more positive ways to see the operations of intellectual conflict more generally, both in our individual lives and in the intellectual community at large. (publisher, edited)

**Smith, Barry**. On Substances, Accidents and Universals: In Defence of a Constituent Ontology. *Phil Papers*, 26(1), 105-127, Ap 97.

The essay constructs an ontological theory designed to capture the categories instantiated in those portions or levels of reality which are captured in our common sense conceptual scheme. It takes as its starting point an Aristotelian ontology of *substances* and *accidents*, which are treated via the instruments of mereology and topology. The theory recognizes not only individual parts of substances and accidents, including the internal and external boundaries of these, but also universal parts, such as the *humanity* which is an essential part of both Tom and Dick, and also *individual relations*, such as Tom's promise to Dick, or their current handshake.

**Smith, Barry** and Zelaniec, Wojciech. *The Recalcitrant Synthetic A Priori*. Lublin, Oficyna Wyda Artom, 1996.

This book poses the problem of the synthetic a priori thus: what is the nature of the obviousness enjoyed by sentences standardly cited as examples of the synthetic a priori? The author does not presuppose that this obviousness is a sure warrant that the sentences are true. He characterizes it rather by means of contrasts that synthetic a priori sentences have to other kinds of sentences which also appear obvious, including analytic sentences. The author demonstrates that in attempts to eliminate the differences between synthetic a priori and other sorts of sentences hitherto, synthetic a priori sentences are themselves used as surreptitious presuppositions. The whole category of the synthetic a priori thus turns out to be—to use a word dear to Quine—recalcitrant.

**Smith, Charles W**. The Ontological Status of Ideation: A Continuing Issue. *J Theor Soc Behav*, 27(2-3), 129-137, Je-S 97.

In this introductory paper, it is argued that the ontological status, or more correctly statuses, or ideations of varying sorts remains a central issue for the social sciences. The paper begins by tracing the central historical role played by ideations in accounting for human behavior and the inherent tension between ideations and the commonly assumed tenets of science. The central theme of the paper is that a naturalistic view of ideations must ground ideations in ongoing behavioral practices and other natural contexts. The variety of such contexts raises questions regarding the different forms and characteristics which ideations assume. Some of these alternatives are briefly introduced.

**Smith, David** and Greco, Michael A and Deleuze, Gilles. Literature and Life. *Crit Inquiry*, 23(2), 225-230, Wint 97.

**Smith, David H**. Religion and the Use of Animals in Research: Some First Thoughts. *Ethics Behavior*, 7(2), 137-147, 1997.

Religious traditions can be drawn on in a number of ways to illuminate discussions of the moral standing of animals and the ethical use of animals in scientific research. I begin with some general comments about relevant points in the history of major religions. I then briefly describe American civil religion, including the cult of health, and its relation to scientific research. Finally, I offer a critique of American civil religion from a Christian perspective.

**Smith, Douglas** (trans) and Nietzsche, Friedrich. *On the Genealogy of Morals.* New York, Oxford Univ Pr, 1996.

**Smith, Gregory Bruce.** Aristotle on Reason and its Limits. *Polis,* 14(1-2), 84-128, 1995.

**Smith, James K A.** "How to Avoid Not Speaking: Attestations" in *Knowing Other-Wise: Philosophy at the Threshold of Spirituality,* Olthuis, James H (ed), 217-234. New York, Fordham Univ Pr, 1997.

Engaging Derrida's "How to Avoid Speaking: Denials," this essay takes up the question of discourse about God in light of the deconstructive critique of language. Employing Derrida's metaphor of the 'postal system' for language and following an Augustinian schema, I sketch three interpretations of language: a fundamentalist/metaphysical model where the letter always arrives, a radical deconstructive model where the letter never arrives and a third model which suggests that the letter may not arrive, leaving open the possibility for communication. This third model is developed through an appropriation of the Heidegger's notion of 'formal indication' and its importance for theology.

**Smith, James K A.** The Art of Christian Atheism: Faith and Philosophy in Early Heidegger. *Faith Phil,* 14(1), 71-81, Ja 97.

In his early work, Martin Heidegger argues for a rigorous methodological atheism in philosophy, which is not opposed to a religious faith but only to the impact of faith when one is philosophizing. For the young Heidegger, the philosopher, even though possibly a religious person, must be an atheist when doing philosophy. Christian philosophy, then, is a round square. In this essay, I unpack Heidegger's methodological considerations and attempt to draw parallels with other traditions which argue for the possibility of a Christian philosophy but at root concede Heidegger's atheism. In conclusion, I propose that it is precisely Heidegger's work which points to the inescapability of and opens the door to religious philosophy.

**Smith, Janet E.** "The Pre-eminence of Autonomy in Bioethics" in *Human Lives: Critical Essays on Consequentialist Bioethics,* Oderberg, David S (ed), 182-195. New York, Macmillan, 1997.

The principle of respect for autonomy is at the heart of modern bioethics. Its elevation to such a central role is argued to derive from moral scepticism, in the form of pluralism about values and a denial of the view that it is even possible to reach a consensus. Examining some recent writings on bioethics, it can be seen that consequentialism also underpins most current thinking. Which poses the dilemma of how many modern bioethicists can be consequentialists while at the same time elevating autonomy to an absolute value and underlaying their theories with scepticism and relativism. Until these threads are disentangled, a large part of bioethics will be seen as an ad hoc device for justifying pre-formed ideas.

**Smith, John E.** "Enlarging the Scope of Reason: Response to Vincent Colapietro" in *Reason, Experience, and God: John E. Smith in Dialogue,* Colapietro, Vincent M, 117-130. New York, Fordham Univ Pr, 1997.

Colapietro has set forth in clear and concise fashion the distinction I draw between formal reason—argumentation, analysis and classification—and living reason—interpretation, deliberation and evaluation and the reasons for not confining our thinking to the former alone. Closely connected is the ancient distinction between the *analytic* and the *synoptic* roles of reason and, again, the error of confining it to the former alone. There is also a penetrating account of why the repeated emphasis on epistemology has led so many modern philosophers to postpone the discussion of first-order metaphysical issues.

**Smith, John E.** "Experience and Its Religious Dimension: Response to Vincent G. Potter" in *Reason, Experience, and God: John E. Smith in Dialogue,* Colapietro, Vincent M, 85-103. New York, Fordham Univ Pr, 1997.

The discussion revolves about the following topics: the nature of experience and its relation to cognition; my conception of the religious dimension of experience as distinct from the idea of "religious experience" set forth by James and others; the need for a natural knowledge of God as a condition for understanding any proposed revelation of God and the difference between the ontological and cosmological ways to God plus the possibility that the two may be brought into harmony.

**Smith, John E.** "Metaphysics, Experience, Being, and God: Response to Robert C. Neville" in *Reason, Experience, and God: John E. Smith in Dialogue,* Colapietro, Vincent M, 131-144. New York, Fordham Univ Pr, 1997.

Neville's main point is that my basic metaphysical position is one in which there emerges from my reinterpretation and reconstruction of experience a conception of being and of God. I express general agreement with Neville's account and I go on to supplement it with the position I developed in *The Analogy of Experience.* There I claimed that experience is a "firmament" for theology and functions in a way similar to the concept of Being in the tradition of philosophical theology in Western thought.

**Smith, John E.** "Morality, Religion, and the Force of Obligation: Response to Robert J. Roth, S.J." in *Reason, Experience, and God: John E. Smith in Dialogue,* Colapietro, Vincent M, 105-116. New York, Fordham Univ Pr, 1997.

I express agreement and appreciation for Roth's setting forth what I have written about the nature of morality and especially the problem of determining the relations between morality and religion. I take occasion to modify, under his prompting, an extreme position I took many years ago in which I claimed that there can be no morality without religion. I find most illuminating his idea that the injunction to love God carries with it the obligation to apprehend the intrinsic nature of God from which our love follows.

**Smith, John E.** "Philosophy in America: Recovery and Future Development" in *The Recovery of Philosophy in America: Essays in Honor of John Edwin Smith,* Kasulis, Thomas P (ed), 269-308. Albany, SUNY Pr, 1997.

My summary essay is a response to all the papers included in the volume. The emphasis falls for the most part on the resources to be found in the classical American philosophers for recovering systematic and constructive philosophy focused on current issues rather than on epistemological concerns inherited from the past. "Recovery" in this context does not mean merely repeating the ideas of Peirce, James, Dewey and Emerson, but reviving their spirit and approach to philosophical thinking in order to overcome the view that philosophy is at an end.

**Smith, John E.** "Responses" in *Reason, Experience, and God: John E. Smith in Dialogue,* Colapietro, Vincent M, 83. New York, Fordham Univ Pr, 1997.

These are responses by the author to papers presented by Vincent G. Potter, Robert J. Roth, S.J., Vincent Colapietro and Robert C. Neville, at a Conference held on December 13, 1993 at Fordham University and sponsored by the Department of Philosophy. The topics of these papers are indicated in the title of the volume.

**Smith, John H.** "Sighting the Spirit: The Rhetorical Visions of *Geist* in Hegel's *Encyclopedia*" in *Sites of Vision,* Levin, David Michael (ed), 241-264. Cambridge, MIT Pr, 1997.

**Smith, Jonathan M** (ed) and Light, Andrew (ed). *Philosophy and Geography I: Space, Place, and Environmental Ethics.* Lanham, Rowman & Littlefield, 1997.

The inaugural collection in an exciting new exchange between philosophers and geographers, this volume provides interdisciplinary approaches to the environment as space, place and idea. Never before have philosophers and geographers approached each other's subjects in such a strong spirit of mutual understanding. The result is one of the most concrete explorations of the human-nature relationship, eschewing esoterica, while embracing strong normative approaches to environmental problems. While grounded in philosophy and geography, the essays also will interest readers in political theory, environmental studies, public policy and other disciplines. (publisher)

**Smith, Joseph Wayne** and Sauer-Thompson, Gary. *Beyond Economics: Postmodernity, Globalization and National Sustainability.* Brookfield, Avebury, 1996.

**Smith, Ken** and Johnson, Phil and Cassell, Cathy. Opening the Black Box: Corporate Codes of Ethics in Their Organizational Context. *J Bus Ethics,* 16(10), 1077-1093, JI 97.

A review of the literature on Corporate Codes of Ethics suggests that while there exists an informative body of literature concerning the prevalence of such codes, their design, implementation and promulgation, it is also evident that there is a relative lack of consideration of their impact upon members' everyday organizational behaviour. By drawing upon organizational sociology and psychology this paper constructs a contextualist and interpretive model which seeks to enable an analysis and evaluation of their effects upon individual, group and organizational behaviour.

**Smith, Laurence D** and Freedman, Eric G. The Role of Data and Theory in Covariation Assessment: Implications for the Theory-Ladenness of Observation. *J Mind Behav,* 17(4), 321-344, Autumn 96.

The issue of the theory-ladenness of observation has long troubled philosophers of science, largely because it seems to threaten the objectivity of science. However, the way in which prior beliefs influence the perception of data is in part an empirical issue that can be investigated by cognitive psychology. This point is illustrated through an experimental analogue of scientific data-interpretation tasks in which subjects judging the covariation between personality variables based their judgments on a) pure data, b) their theoretical intuitions about the variables, or c) both data and prior theoretical beliefs. Results showed that the perceived magnitude of correlations was greatest when subjects relied solely on theoretical intuitions; that data-based judgments were drawn in the direction of those prior beliefs; but that exposure to data nonetheless moderated the strength of the prior theories. In addition, prior beliefs were found to influence judgments only after a brief priming interval, suggesting that subjects needed time to retrieve their theoretical intuitions from memory. These results suggest ways to investigate the processes mediating theory-laden observation, and contrary to the fears of positivist philosophers, imply that the theory-ladenness of observation does not entail that theoretical beliefs are immune to data.

**Smith, Michael.** Normative Reasons and Full Rationality: Reply to Swanton. *Analysis,* 56(3), 160-168, JI 96.

In *The Moral Problem* I develop an account of normative reasons in terms of what we would want if we were fully rational. Christine Swanton has a number of objections to this analysis. I show that each of these objections fails to undermine the analysis.

**Smith, Michael.** The Argument for Internalism: Reply to Miller. *Analysis,* 56(3), 175-184, JI 96.

Alexander Miller objects to the argument for moral judgement internalism that I provide in *The Moral Problem.* Miller's objection suggests a misunderstanding of the argument. In this reply I take the opportunity to restate the argument in slightly different terms, and to explain why Miller's objection betrays a misunderstanding.

**Smith, Michael** and Kennett, Jeanette. Synchronic Self-Control is Always Non-Actional. *Analysis,* 57(2), 123-131, Ap 97.

Self-control can be exercised at the very moment that agents are out of control (this is synchronic self-control), or it can be exercised prior to their losing control, so preventing the loss of control from ever arising (this is diachronic self-control). Though agents may exercise diachronic self-control by performing intentional actions, we argue that they never exercise synchronic self-control by performing intentional actions. Our paper is a reply to Alfred Mele's "Kennett and Smith on Frog and Toad" which appears in the same issue of *Analysis*.

**Smith, Michael B** (trans) and Levinas, Emmanuel. *Proper Names*. Stanford, Stanford Univ Pr, 1996.

Combining elements from Heidegger's philosophy of "being-in-the-world" and the tradition of Jewish theology, Levinas evolved a new type of ethics based on a concept of "the Other" in two different but complementary aspects. He describes his encounters with those philosophers and literary authors (most of them his contemporaries) whose writings have most significantly contributed to the construction of his own philosophy of "Otherness": Agnon, Buber, Celan, Delhomme, Derrida, Jabès, Kierkegaard, Lacroix, Laporte, Picard, Proust, Van Breda, Wahl and most notably Blanchor. (publisher)

**Smith, Michael Joseph**. Growing Up with *Just and Unjust Wars: An Appreciation*. *Ethics Int Affairs*, 11, 3-18, 1997.

After twenty years, Michael Walzer's *Just and Unjust Wars* continues to engage scholars in discussions of the moral realities of war. Smith provides a summary of Walzer's arguments, discussing in particular Walzer's method of moral argument. Walzer's argument focuses on moral norms or "practical morality," but ultimately, emphasizes the importance of moral judgment based on the principle of human rights rather than utilitarian calculations. Addressing realists' critiques of Walzer, David C. Hendrickson in particular, Smith reaffirms Walzer's call for the need to constrain the realist doctrine of necessity, which argues that moral considerations should be subordinate to the security of the state. Walzer's treatment of nuclear deterrence and intervention is discussed in light of the developments of the post-Cold War era. Smith concludes by paying tribute to *Just and Unjust Wars* as a continued reminder of the human capacity for hope and the will to change the world we live in.

**Smith, P Christopher**. "From Acoustics to Optics: The Rise of the Metaphysical and Demise of the Melodic in Aristotle's *Poetics*" in *Sites of Vision*, Levin, David Michael (ed), 69-91. Cambridge, MIT Pr, 1997.

**Smith, P Christopher**. "Hegel, Kierkegaard, and the Problem of Finitude" in *Hegel, History, and Interpretation*, Gallagher, Shaun, 209-226. Albany, SUNY Pr, 1997.

**Smith, Patricia L** and Oakley III, Elwood F. Gender-Related Differences in Ethical and Social Values of Business Students: Implications for Management. *J Bus Ethics*, 16(1), 37-45, Ja 97.

This study investigated gender-related differences in ethical attitudes of 318 graduate and undergraduate business students. Significant differences were observed in male and female responses to questions concerning ethics in social and personal relationships. No differences were noted for survey items concerning rules-based obligations. Implications for future management are discussed.

**Smith, Quentin**. Simplicity and Why the Universe Exists. *Philosophy*, 72(279), 125-132, Ja 97.

It may be that the universe came into being with the simplest thing in the simplest possible way. This hypothesis would be confirmed if the big bang singularity occurred uncaused.

**Smith, Quentin**. The Ontological Interpretation of the Wave Function of the Universe. *Monist*, 80(1), 160-185, Ja 97.

**Smith, Ralph A**. Concluding Observations. *J Aes Educ*, 30(4), 115-121, Wint 96.

The article summarizes the main features of articles printed in a special issue of the journal devoted to the topic "The Aesthetic Face of Leadership," a cooperative venture of the Center for Creative Leadership and the Getty Education Institute for the Arts. It uses the categories of thinking characteristic of aesthetics discussed in an article by Ronald Moore to bring out major points, e.g., the categories of instrumentalism, institutionalism, interpretivism and aspectivism.

**Smith, Ralph A**. Leadership as Aesthetic Process. *J Aes Educ*, 30(4), 39-52, Wint 96.

The article discusses the character of artistic and aesthetic processes and leadership skills and behavior in terms of background, aims, structure, limitations and values. The problems of interdisciplinary inquiry are also addressed as well as the uses of metaphor and the values of art. Points of similarity between the two sets of acting are acknowledged as well as differences. The article is part of a special issue supported by the Center for Creative Leadership and the Getty Education Institute for the Arts.

**Smith, Roger**. History and the History of the Human Sciences: What Voice?. *Hist Human Sci*, 10(3), 22-39, Ag 97.

This paper discusses the historical voice in the history of the human sciences. I address the question, 'Who speaks?', as a question about disciplinary identities and conventions of writing—identities and conventions which have the appearance of conditions of knowledge, in an area of activity where academic history and the history of science or intellectual history meet. If, as this paper contends, the subject-matter of the history of the human sciences is inherently contestable because of fundamental differences about the subject, man, how is the field to be shaped as if it were a whole?(edited)

**Smith, Stacy**. "Voluntary Segregation: Gender and Race as Legitimate Grounds for Differential Treatment and Freedom of Association" in *Philosophy of Education (1996)*, Margonis, Frank (ed), 48-57. Urbana, Phil Education Soc, 1997.

**Smith, Steven G**. Greatness in Theism and Atheism: The Anselm-Feuerbach Conversation. *Mod Theol*, 12(4), 385-403, O 96.

Anselm and Feuerbach both point to an inescapable conversation between theism and atheism. Each makes a pivotal analysis of the relation between the existence and the properties of beings; each interprets the existence-properties relation according to a greatness criterion; each understands greatness not as an abstract attribute of a possible being but as a function of a finite being's placement in a real encounter (for each is drawn by love toward the real as the extra-mental). Allowing each to speak in place of the dialectical foil already found in the other's argument, their positions become stronger together.

**Smith, Tara**. Reconsidering Zero-Sum Value: It's How You Play the Game. *J Soc Phil*, 28(2), 128-139, Fall 97.

Much moral philosophy proceeds on the assumption that the pursuit of value is a zero-sum game and that ethics is a means of adjudicating conflicting demands on value. This paper challenges the assumption that value is finite. Part I highlights two aspects of value that reveal its open-ended character. Value is *made* in that a person must adopt ends and act to achieve them in order to attain values. Value is *relational* insofar as anything's value depends on its relationship to a particular individual's purposes. Part II explains how the reason for pursuing value, *eudaimonia*, also refutes the zero-sum thesis. Whether a person achieves *eudaimonia* depends on how he leads his life rather than on beating others to a portion of readymade values.

**Smith, Tara**. Tolerance & Forgiveness: Virtues or Vices?. *J Applied Phil*, 14(1), 31-41, 1997.

This paper explores the relationship between tolerance, forgiveness and justice. Contrary to prevailing wisdom, it argues that tolerance and forgiveness are not independent virtues vying with justice for our allegiance, but that they fall under justice's imperative to judge other people objectively and treat them as they deserve. Misguided extensions of tolerance and forgiveness imperil the very values that ethics is designed to promote. Thus tolerance and forgiveness are *neither* virtues nor vices; they are appropriate only when authorised by justice. The paper clarifies the common confusion of tolerance with respect for individuals' rights and argues that forgiveness is not a supererogatory act of generosity, but is sometimes morally required.

**Smith, Thomas W**. Michael Oakeshott on History, Practice and Political Theory. *Hist Polit Thought*, 17(4), 591-614, Winter 96.

Michael Oakeshott's theory of history, rooted in the British idealist tradition, is best seen as a defense of the past from ideological and other practical abuses. Oakeshott's categorical precepts are meant to ensure the integrity of the "activity of the historian," yet his standards are too strictly posed, banishing moral questions and contemporary implications from the craft. Oakeshott concedes as much in his insistence that historical inquiry precede and contextualize traditionalist political thought. This is the case with his theory of the modern European polity in *On Human Conduct*. Oakeshott suggests in the end that political myths, such as that embodied in Hobbes's *Leviathan*, may foster the most coherent and solidaristic foundation for historical understanding.

**Smith, Timothy H**. "Dewey on Virtue" in *Philosophy of Education (1996)*, Margonis, Frank (ed), 365-368. Urbana, Phil Education Soc, 1997.

**Smith Churchland, Patricia**. The Hornswoggle Problem. *J Consciousness Stud*, 3(5-6), 402-408, 1996.

Beginning with Thomas Nagel, various philosophers have proposed setting conscious experience apart from all other problems of the mind as 'the most difficult problem'. When critically examined, the basis for this proposal reveals itself to be unconvincing and counter-productive. Use of our current ignorance as a premise to determine what we can never discover is one common logical flaw. Use of 'I-cannot-imagine' arguments is a related flaw. When not much is known about a domain of phenomena, our inability to imagine a mechanism is a rather uninteresting psychological fact about us, not an interesting metaphysical fact about the world. Rather than worrying too much about the metaproblem of whether or not consciousness is uniquely hard, I propose we get on with the task of seeing how far we get when we address neurobiologically the problems of mental phenomena.

**Smith Jr, Allyne L**. In the World but Not of It: Managing the Conflict between Christian and Institution. *Christian Bioethics*, 3(1), 74-84, Mr 97.

Christian physicians, nurses and other health care workers must manage a daily conflict of conscience between their Christian faith and predominantly secular health care institutions. This essay examines various efforts for managing these conflicts: a turn towards social justice or a seeking of holiness. Seeking social justice, however, is theologically empty. Traditionally, the Christian requirement that we be "in this world but not of it" requires a journey along a narrow path to holiness. Christian medical morality must, therefore, be understood within this light. However, just as there cannot be generic health care, but rather health care for a particular person's needs and problems, there cannot be generic holiness, but only a holiness grounded in worshipping God rightly. In so worshipping the Christian will be assisted in negotiating the inescapable and perilous vocation of being in the world but not of it.

**Smokrovic, Nenad**. Intentionalism and Rationality (A Criticism of Stich's Slippery Slope Argument). *Acta Analytica*, 101-111, 1995.

The author defends rationalist thesis by criticizing the attempt of Stephen Stich to decouple intentionality from rationality. Stich's Slippery Slope Argument that purports to do the decoupling is shown to rest on a mistaken view of what counts as accessible for a given cognizer.

**Smolkin, Doran**. HIV Infection, Risk Taking, and the Duty to Treat. *J Med Phil*, 22(1), 55-74, F 97.

The paper advances a consequence-based argument in support of the American Medical Association's policy that a physician may not ethically refuse to treat a person with HIV solely because the patient is seropositive. A limited number of alternative arguments, both in support of and in opposition to this policy are also considered, but are found wanting. The paper then concludes with a discussion of some of the other obstacles to quality health care that persons with HIV must often confront.

**Smythe, Thomas W**. Fawkes On Indicator Words. *Inquiry (USA)*, 16(1), 76-77, Fall 96.

**Smythe, Thomas W**. The Reliability of Premise and Conclusion Indicators. *Inquiry (USA)*, 16(3), 94-95, Spr 97.

The purpose of this paper is to give some reason for thinking that premise and conclusion indicators like "because" and "therefore" are, in fact, reliable indicators of premises and conclusions in spite of the many exceptions. I draw an analogy between such indicators and the philosophical discussion of the reliability of sense perception. Reference is made to some critical thinking and logic textbooks that warn students of the exceptions, such as their use in explanations. I conclude that indicator words are reliable indicators of premises and conclusions in arguments.

**Snauwaert, Dale T**. "The Relevance of the Anthropocentric-Ecocentric Debate" in *Philosophy of Education (1996)*, Margonis, Frank (ed), 264-267. Urbana, Phil Education Soc, 1997.

**Snik, Ger** and Van Haaften, Wouter. Critical Thinking and Foundational Development. *Stud Phil Educ*, 16(1-2), 19-41, Ja-Ap 97.

We elaborate on Israel Scheffler's claim that principles of rationality can be rationally evaluated, focusing on foundational development, by which we mean the evolution of principles which are constitutive of our conceptualization of a certain domain of rationality. How can claims that some such principles are better than prior ones be justified? We argue that Scheffler's metacriterion of overall systematic credibility is insufficient here. Two very different types of rational development are jointly involved, namely, development of general principles that are strictly constitutive of rationality as such, and development of specific principles determinative of our conceptualization of particular domains. (edited)

**Snodgrass, James** and Behling, Robert. Differences in Moral Reasoning Between College and University Business Majors and Non-Business Majors. *Bus Prof Ethics J*, 15(1), 79-84, Spr 94.

**Snoeck Henkemans, Francisca**. "Indicators of Independent and Interdependent Arguments: 'Anyway' and 'Even'" in *Logic and Argumentation*, Van Eemeren, Frans H (ed), 77-87. Amsterdam, North-Holland, 1994.

In this paper, a connection is established between the semantical descriptions of 'anyway' and 'even' given by linguists such as Ducrot and Anscombre, Bennett, Kay and others and the pragma-dialectical characterization of independent and interdependent arguments. By combining linguistic insights with insights from argumentation theory, a more systematic explanation of the indicative function of 'anyway' and 'even' can be given.

**Soare, Robert I**. Computability and Recursion. *Bull Sym Log*, 2(3), 284-321, S 96.

We consider the informal concept of "computability" or "effective calculability" and two of the formalisms commonly used to define it, "(*Turing*) *computability*" and "(*general*) *recursiveness*". We consider their origin, exact technical definition, concepts, history, general English meanings, how they became fixed in their present roles, how they were first and are now used, their impact on nonspecialists, how their use will affect the future content of the subject of computability theory and its connection to other related areas. After a careful historical and conceptual analysis of computability and recursion we make several recommendations in section paragraph 7 about preserving the *intensional* differences between the concepts of "computability" and "recursion."(edited)

**Sobel, David**. On the Subjectivity of Welfare. *Ethics*, 107(3), 501-508, Ap 97.

In "The Subjectivity of Welfare" L. W. Sumner hopes to, among other things, accomplish two important goals. First, he wants to "develop the appropriate interpretation of subjectivity (and objectivity)" (p. 765) in theories of well-being. Second, he wants to argue that subjective theories of well-being have decisive advantages over objective theories. Despite the many significant virtues of the article, I will, perhaps somewhat perversely, focus on arguing that each of these two goals has not been fully achieved. (edited)

**Sobel, Jordan Howard**. Cyclical Preferences and World Bayesianism. *Phil Sci*, 64(1), 42-73, Mr 97.

An example shows that 'pairwise preferences' (certain hypothetical choices) can cycle even when rational. General considerations entail that preferences *tout court* (certain relations of actual valuations) cannot cycle. A world-Bayesian theory is explained that accommodates these two kinds of preference and a theory for rational actions that would have them maximize and be objects of ratifiable choices. It is observed that choices can be unratifiable either because of troublesome credences or because of troublesome preferences. An appendix comments on a third way in which efforts to maximize can be frustrated.

**Sobel, Jordan Howard**. Hume's Utilitarian Theory of Right Action. *Phil Quart*, 47(186), 55-72, Ja 97.

A theory of right action is implicit in Hume's delineation of the virtues. It gives qualified priority to 'rules of justice' as Hume's remarks on 'that species of utility which attends this virtue' require. It is a useful actual-rule, not an ideal possible-rule, purely utilitarian theory that discounts rules of justice in 'extraordinary cases', has a problem when rules conflict and invites the question 'Why not hark directly to the supreme law of utility in every case?'. It does not

reflect contractarian considerations of mutuality of interests evident in Hume's texts, which while sometimes relevant to what is reasonable, are in his view never also relevant to what is moral. (publisher)

**Sobel, Jordan Howard**. On the Significance of Conditional Probabilities. *Synthese*, 109(3), 311-344, D 96.

The orthodoxy that conditional probabilities reflect what are for a subject evidential bearings is seconded. This significance suggests that there should be principles equating rationally revised probabilities on new information with probabilities reached by conditionalizing on this information. Several principles, two of which are endorsed, are considered. A 'book' is made against a violator of these and it is argued that there must be something wrong with a person against whom such books can be made. Appendices comment on Popper-functions, elaborate on bets and odds and relate Dutch books and strategies to conditions of inconsistency (Ramsey's idea) and imperfection.

**Sobel, Jordan Howard**. Pascalian Wagers. *Synthese*, 108(1), 11-61, Jl 96.

A person who does not have good intellectual reasons for believing in God can, depending on his probabilities and values for consequences of believing, have good practical reasons. Pascalian wagers founded on a variety of possible probability/value profiles are examined from a Bayesian perspective central to which is the idea that states and options are pragmatically reasonable only if they maximize subjective expected value. Attention is paid to problems posed by representations of values by Cantorian infinities. An appendix attends to Robinsonian hyperreals. Another appendix presents for comparison Newcomb's Problem and a problem in some ways like it suggested, I think, by ideas of John Calvin.

**Sobel, Reuven**. The Myth of the Control of Suffering. *J Med Human*, 17(4), 255-259, Wint 96.

Is it true that the suffering associated with chronic illness can be controlled in all but a few intractable cases? The bioethical literature gives the impression that suffering is primarily pain and that a competent physician should be able to control suffering. This perception jibes neither with my forty years of clinical experience nor with suffering as depicted in novels. Using Kenaz's novel *The Way to the Cats* as a starting point, I argue that, with regard to suffering and illness, fiction is closer to reality than professional literature, and suffering is far more than pain. I contend that the control of suffering is a modern myth. This argument applies equally well to the control of noninsulin dependent diabetes. Patient selection, duration of follow-up, remembering what we want to remember, bias, self-fulfilled prophecy, and asking the wrong questions are offered as partial explanation for the gap between perception and reality. The complexity of suffering and the elusiveness of its control should be honestly recognized.

**Sober, Elliott**. Some Comments on Rosenberg's Review. *Phil Sci*, 63(3), 465-469, S 96.

This article is a reply to Alexander Rosenberg's essay review of my book *Philosophy of Biology* (Westview Press, 1993). I try to correct what I think are Rosenberg's misinterpretations of my views concerning historicism, the existence of laws in biology, and the interpretation of probability in evolutionary biology.

**Soble, Alan**. "Union, Autonomy, and Concern" in *Love Analyzed*, Lamb, Roger E, 65-92. Boulder, Westview Pr, 1997.

"Union" accounts of love, in which two persons are claimed to merge into a single entity, are popular. This paper explores one defect of such accounts: they make it logically impossible that two persons who love each other show Aristotelian (or "robust") concern to the other. Union theorists discussed include Robert Nozick, Mark Fisher, Karol Wojtyla and, from the history of philosophy, Montaigne, Kant, and Hegel.

**Soble, Alan**. Antioch's "Sexual Offense Policy": A Philosophical Exploration. *J Soc Phil*, 28(1), 22-36, Spr 97.

After discussing analytic and practical proposals about rape made by the philosopher Raymond Belliotti and the legal scholar Susan Estrich, I turn to elucidating and criticizing Antioch University's "Sexual Offense Policy." I find the policy lacking in three areas: its insistence that verbal consent be obtained prior to any sexual activity is circular; it ignores the reliable ways that body language can convey consent; and its notion of consent makes it mysterious how consent could ever serve to justify sexual activity.

**Soble, Alan** (ed). *Sex, Love, and Friendship: Studies of the Society for the Philosophy of Sex and Love 1977-1992*. Amsterdam, Rodopi, 1997.

This book presents the work of the Society for Philosophy of Sex and Love during the 28 meetings of its first 15 years as a scholarly organization. The 60 chapters treat ethical and political issues (including homosexuality and abortion), conceptual matters (including friendship and sexual perversion), classical and historical figures (including Spinoza and Kierkegaard), and issues in feminist theory (including sexual objectification and the social construction of female sexuality). Extensive introductory material offers historical and intellectual connections for this work, while biographical information and copious illustrations give valuable testimony to the human dimensions of the society's enterprise. (publisher)

**Sobotka, Milan**. Descartes and Metaphysical Thought (in Czech). *Filosof Cas*, 44(5), 751-772, 1996.

The article discusses the paradigms of Descartes's philosophy as developed in his *Meditations*—the concepts of consciousness and of truth as certainty. It pays special attention to how these motifs relate to the metaphysical structure of the *Meditations*, i.e., the concept of the "first philosophy" as a knowledge of the principles of understanding. Referring to J.-L. Marion's book *Sur le prisme métaphysique de Descartes*, it starts from the idea that Descartes's teaching of the principles of knowledge is in accordance with metaphysics: the first philosophy moves beyond physics and mathematics and bases itself and its teaching on existence, as distinct from matter, using the example of consciousness. The path of thought follows the order of understanding rather than that of being. (edited)

**Sobotka, Milan**. Hegels Manuskripte aus der Berner Zeit: Kant—Rousseau—Herder—Schiller. *Jahr Hegelforschung*, 2, 165-189, 1996.

**Sobrevilla, David**. Reflexiones sobre la no violencia: Variedades, posibilidades y límites. *Cuad Etica*, 19-20, 133-148, 1995.

There are two possible views concerning nonviolence: the religious and the rational approach. This paper analyzes the sense of Christian love in Tolstoy, *ahimsa* and *satyagraha* in Gandhi and *agape* in Luther King. Religious approaches are founded in love, are born in under developed countries and tend to be wide, while rational views, instead, are founded in principles of justice and correspond to developed and well ordered societies. Among rationalists, the positions of Thoreau, H. Arendt, J. Rawls and N. Bobbio are also studied.

**Sobrino, Alejandro** and Manyà Serres, Felip and Escalda-Imaz, Gonzalo. Principles of Logic Programming with Uncertain Information: Description of Some of the Most Relevant Systems (in Spanish). *Theoria (Spain)*, 11(27), 123-148, S 96.

The purpose of this paper is to present the principles of the fuzzy logic programming, exemplifying them by a couple of proposals that we think are representatives of the advances in this field. We include also the description of another systems' programming with uncertain information that are based on other logics of uncertainty which are different from fuzzy logic. This article only presupposes an elementary knowledge of the classical first-order logic.

**Sockett, Hugh**. *The Moral Base for Teacher Professionalism*. New York, Teachers College Pr, 1993.

The central objective of this book is to provide a broad vision of the moral foundations of teacher professionalism by linking the professional role of the teacher, the men and women who occupy it, the moral demands it makes and the practical arts of teaching to the institution of education and its contemporary problems.

**Socorro Fernández, Maria**. La necesidad como totalidad de la posibilidad en Leibniz. *Anu Filosof*, 29(2), 527-537, 1996.

This article studies Polo's interpretation of the relation that Leibniz establishes between possibility and necessity. The necessity, understood as the totality of the possibility, allows Leibniz to reach the final formulation of the ontologic argument to demonstrate the existence of God, as well as to describe the essence of the Absolute.

**Sodibjo, Iman**. "Understanding Religion: The Contribution of Ibn Rushd" in *Averroës and the Enlightenment,* Wahba, Mourad (ed), 79-90. Amherst, Prometheus, 1996.

**Soeiro Chaimovich, Felipe**. Existe ou Nao uma Estética no Século XVII?. *Cad Hist Filosof Cie*, 5(1-2), 247-260, Ja-D 95.

Two important trends in aesthetic thought were elaborated during the seventeenth century in response to an initial problem, namely that of understanding the experience of the beautiful in terms of modern philosophy's concept of the subject. The first trend is set out in Boileau's *Art Pöetique*. Poetic composition and its appreciation are conceived from the point of view of an abstract, guided by reason. Boileau attempts to transfer the Cartesian method of knowledge to aesthetics. The second trend, found in the works of Shaftesbury, considers a personalized subject, both as concerns the composition and the appreciation of works of art. In this way, he succeeds in maintaining the tension, essential to any coherent theory of aesthetics, between the singularity of works of art and the universality of the instantiation of the beautiful.

**Söllner, Alfons**. Georg Lukács's *Destruction of Reason* and the Political Theories of the Western Emigration: Some Theses (in Hungarian). *Magyar Filozof Szemle*, 4-5-6, 363-372, 1996.

Ausgangspunkt meiner Überlegungen ist ein aktuelles und praktisches Interesse, nämlich die Frage, wie in Ostdeutschland bzw. in Osteuropa eine moderne Politikund Sozialwissenschaft aufgebaut werden kann, ohne in den Fehler zu verfallen, das westliche Modell—in der Form eines kulturellen Imperialismus—einfach überzustülpen. Eine Alternative dazu—oder besser eine Voraussetzung dafür—könnte darin bestehen, intellektuelle Entwicklungslinien so rekonstruieren, dass die verschiedenen Ergenisse von einem gemeinsamen Ausgangspunkt her verständlich werden. (edited)

**Soentgen, Jens**. Theorie als Gedächtniskunst. *J Gen Phil Sci*, 28(1), 183-203, 1997.

The essay develops the principles of the antique resp. Medieval *ars memorativa*, which was a skill of memorizing large amounts of varying informations. Then the Parsonian theory of society is analysed and it is shown, that it is constructed according to the same principles. Hence it follows the thesis, that at least special kinds of sociological (and psychological) theories can be considered as modernized forms of the old *ars memorativa*. The author defends this thesis against a set of nearby objections. It is not tried to prove the historical truth of thesis, i.e., to show, that the tradition of theoretical literature indeed roots in the tradition of antique resp. medieval *ars memorativa*. In any case an examination of this question might yield new insight in the prehistory of theoretical thought.

**Sörbom, Göran**. Art and Aesthetics in Scandinavia. *J Aes Educ*, 27(2), 85-97, Sum 93.

**Soffer, Walter**. Descartes' Secular Paradise: The Discourse on Method as Biblical Criticism. *Phil Theol*, 8(4), 309-346, Sum 94.

This paper attempts to show the way in which the *Discourse on Method* participates in the antitheological launching of the modern project—the securing of a secular paradise by the "universal instrument" of human reason. It is argued that the order of the presentation of the parts of the *Discourse* conceals the true architectonic order of the Cartesian edifice because the physics of Part Five is more foundational than the metaphysics which seemingly must ground it in Part Four.

**Sojka, Jacek**. Business Ethics and Computer Ethics: The View from Poland. *Sci Eng Ethics*, 2(2), 191-200, A 96.

An Aristotelian approach to understanding and teaching business ethics is presented and defended. The newly emerging field of computer ethics is also defined in an Aristotelian fashion and an argument is made that this new field should be called "information ethics". It is argued that values have their roots in the life and practices of a community; therefore, morality cannot be taught by training for a special way of reasoning. Transmission of values and norms occurs through socialization—the process by which an individual absorbs not only valued but also the whole way of life of his or her community. It follows that business ethics and information ethics can be considered kinds of socialization into a profession: role learning and acquiring a new self-identification. This way of understanding fields of applied ethics is especially important for their proper development in Central-Eastern Europe because of endemic factors which are the result of recent political developments there.

**Sójka, Jacek**. "Who is Afraid of Scientism?" in *Epistemology and History,* Zeidler-Janiszewska, Anna (ed), 113-131. Amsterdam, Rodopi, 1996.

This article describes the way Jerzy Kmita defines scientism and tries to avoid it within his own philosophy of science. He wants to overcome scientism not by simply rejecting it but by raising his own discourse above the level on which the scientism vs. antiscientism opposition takes place. Two objections are raised in this connection. First, the very definition of scientism is different than the one widely adopted among philosophers and social scientists. As a result J. Kmita opposes a phenomenon which is not very common and—the second objection—he seems to embrace another version of scientism, one which is much more popular: a belief in a strict and ahistorical separation of facts and values, the identification of rational knowledge with science and the ascription of the problem of the choice of values to the existential and irrational sphere of individual decisions.

**Sokal, Alan D**. Transgressing the Boundaries: An Afterword. *Phil Lit*, 20(2), 338-346, O 96.

I explain why I wrote the parody article, "Transgressing the Boundaries: Toward a Transformative Hermeneutics of Quantum Gravity," which appeared in the spring/summer 1996 issue of the cultural-studies journal *Social Text*. My principal aim is to combat a currently fashionable postmodernist/poststructuralist/social-constructivist discourse—and more generally a penchant for subjectivism—which is, I believe, inimical to the values and future of the American Left.

**Sokal, Michael M**. Baldwin, Cattell and the *Psychological Review*: A Collaboration and Its Discontents. *Hist Human Sci*, 10(1), 57-89, F 97.

This paper provides a detailed account of the origins of the *Psychological Review* in 1894, of the policies and practices of its editors (James Mark Baldwin and James McKeen Cattell) during its first decade, and of the public and private disagreements that led them to dissolve their collaboration in 1904. In doing so, it sheds light on the significant roles played by specialized scientific journals in the development of specific scientific specialties, and illustrates the value for historical exploration of a 'thick description' of the 'fine texture of the past'. It argues that personal factors such as luck and character and temperament often have a greater impact on the way in which science actually evolves than do intellectual interests and concerns. (edited)

**Sokolowski, William R**. Notes on Peirce's Objective Idealism. *Prima Philosophia*, 10(2), 149-156, 1997.

Charles Sanders Peirce's (1839-1914) preference for *objective idealism* is found in 6.33 in which he says that "the one intelligible theory of the universe is that of objective idealism, that matter is effete mind, inveterate habits becoming physical laws." The surface interpretation of this section is that Peirce was, without question and doubt, opting for an objective idealism as fundamental to this thought. The purpose of this article is to challenge that interpretation by considering the possible meanings of 'effete mind' and 'inveterate habits becoming physical laws'. The article concludes that Peirce is actually using 'mind' in a *Peircean* way. The idealist interpretation of 'mind' includes a preordained development which is directed and guided by mind. Peirce sees mind as subsequent to the *accidental* habit taking of matter. In this Peircean interpretation, mind is not the cause of matter being what it is. Rather, mind is concurrent with matter's possible development through accidental habit taking.

**Sokolowski, William R**. The Structure of Peirce's Realism. *Prima Philosophia*, 10(1), 77-88, 1997.

Statements considered as 'definitional' from Peirce's writings (5.384, 6.495, 8.41, 5.453) are analyzed to determine the elements of his realism. Peirce's rich concept of reality includes the external, the general, the vague and the possible. His position stands in contrast to that of nominalism and idealism, both of which are deficient and truncated intellectual positions.

**Sola Gutiérrez, Luis**. Relativismo filosófico contemporáneo: tres enfoques complementarios para dilucidar la génesis de un problema. *Euridice*, 153-164, 1995.

The problem of the philosophical relativism in its different types nowadays has an increasing importance in the field of the intellectual debate. Its study is, therefore, pertinent. This article intends to be a contribution toward a more adequate comprehension of the origin of relativism and it does it from three different but closely related perspectives. The first, from an epistemological point of view, makes relativism derive from the unstoppable process of "empirization" of the Kantian transcendental subject to which the philosophical discourse has been subjected for the last two hundred years. The second, from a more cultural point of view, places it in the context of the Enlightenment/Romanticism polemic. The third, of a sociological kind, expounds on the connection between relativism and the contemporary decline of totaling ideologies. (edited)

**Solberg, Mary M**. *Compelling Knowledge: A Feminist Proposal for an Epistemology of the Cross*. Albany, SUNY Pr, 1997.

Few feminist philosophers would expect to find a resonant dialogue partner in the sixteenth-century theologian and reformer Martin Luther. This book contends, however, that Luther's theology of the cross provides a solid theological and ethical basis for a surprisingly congenial conversation. The "epistemology of the cross" that emerges raises and responds to the essential epistemological questions of power, experience, objectivity and accountability. Solberg describes the movement from lived experience to "compelling knowledge": seeing what is the case, recognizing one's implication in it and responding accountably. (publisher)

**Soldati, Adriana**. Marc Augé e l'antropologia dei mondi contemporanei. *Iride*, 9(19), 773-779, S-D 96.

**Soldati, Gianfranco**. Antisoggettivismo e l'autorità della prima persona. *Iride*, 9(19), 667-683, S-D 96.

Most forms of externalism involve a rejection of the Cartesian view that the subject has a privileged access to the content of his own mental states. In recent publications, Donald Davidson has presented a *new antisubjectivism* based on externalist intuitions, which are compatible with a moderate form of first person authority. He claims that the crucial mistake of the Cartesian tradition lies in the confusion between the content and the object of a mental state. The present article provides an historical and theoretical background for that distinction. It appears that Husserl, who is generally considered as a prominent exponent of the Cartesian tradition, was fully aware of that distinction. Husserl's early philosophy inspires an alternative explanation of first person authority which does not involve acceptance of Davidson's antisubjectivism.

**Soldati, Gianfranco**. Bedeutungen und Gegenständlichkeiten: Zu Tugendhats sprachanalytischer Kritik von Husserls früher Phänomenologie. *Z Phil Forsch*, 50(3), 410-441, Jl-S 96.

In a number of articles and especially in his *Vorlesungen zur Einführung in die Sprachanalytische Philosophie* (1976), Ernst Tugendhat has vigorously criticized the theory of meaning developed by Husserl in his *Logical Investigations*. Tugendhat accuses Husserl of having construed meanings as objects that the subject stands in an intentional relation to. Soldati defends Husserl against this criticism. He shows that although understanding is an intentional act, this does not imply that the meaning we understand is the intentional object of the act. On the contrary, Husserl coherently distinguishes the object of an intentional act from its meaning, which, on Husserl's account, is instantiated by a real part of the act. Soldati clarifies this claim and examines some of its consequences. (edited)

**Solecki, Slawomir**. Analytic Ideals. *Bull Sym Log*, 2(3), 339-348, S 96.

**Solère, Jean-Luc**. Thomistes et antithomistes face à la question de l'infini créé. *Rev Thomiste*, 97(1), 219-244, Ja-Mr 97.

**Soles, Deborah Hansen**. *Strong Wits and Spider Webs: A Study in Hobbes's Philosophy of Language*. Brookfield, Avebury, 1996.

This work on Hobbes grows out of my conviction that much of twentieth century philosophy of language makes more sense when its historical roots are exposed. Certainly worries about the relationship between words and the world go back to Plato. But more interesting are the efforts to articulate these relationships which are found in the modern philosophers who have major and explicit epistemological concerns. It is in their works that one finds the epistemically motivated discussions of language which have in many ways, both positively and negatively, shaped the concerns of twentieth century figures. Frege's eviction of psychologism from logic and formal semantics has perhaps obscured these influences, but they are present in all the major philosophers of language in this century. (publisher, edited)

**Soller, Alois K**. Fichtes Lehre vom Anstoss, Nicht-Ich und Ding an sich in der GWL: Eine kritische Erörterung. *Fichte-Studien*, 10, 175-189, 1997.

The first purpose of the work is to explain the meaning of these expressions in Fichte's *Grundlage der gesamten Wissenschaftslehre*, by pointing out the philosophical motives, which induced Fichte to his position. In a second part Fichte's comprehension of "Anstoss" is immanently examined. It turns out that Fichte's mediation of idealism and realism has its own problems. Essential fields of our life, as, for example, communication between men, and acting, are inconceivable.

**Solomon, Graham** and DeVidi, David. "Box" in Intuitionistic Modal Logic. *Austl J Phil*, 75(2), 201-213, Je 97.

The box and diamond operators of classical modal logic are interdefinable, but the addition of interdefinable box and diamond to intuitionistic logic leads to intuitionistically implausible theorems, at least when intuitionistic logic and the modal operators are given their usual interpretations. The article discusses interpretations of intuitionistic logic and the modal operators on which the theorems in question are no longer implausible. In particular, the article includes a sketch of an interpretation in which intuitionistic logic is a logic of concepts suited to accounting for borderline cases, and the box operator is taken to be a "precisifier." Applied to a given concept, the box operator yields a concept for which all borderline cases between it and its opposite are resolved.

**Solomon, Mildred Z**. From What's Neutral to What's Meaningful: Reflections on a Study of Medical Interpreters. *J Clin Ethics*, 8(1), 88-93, Spr 97.

**Solomon, Miriam**. Commentary on Alison Gopnik's "The Scientist As Child". *Phil Sci*, 63(4), 547-551, D 96.

"The Scientist as Child" presents a theory about the nature of scientific change that is shown to be both incomplete and inaccurate. It is more productive to interpret the paper as presenting a heuristic (rather than a theory) for generating ideas about scientific change. So far, it has not generated much in the way of new ideas, although it shows promise.

**Solomon, Robert C**. Beyond Ontology: Ideation, Phenomenology and the Cross Cultural Study of Emotion. *J Theor Soc Behav*, 27(2-3), 289-303, Je-S 97.

In this essay, I want to raise certain questions about the nature of emotions, about the similarities and differences in human psychology ("human nature"), and about the relation of psychological inquiry to ethics (in particular, the relationship between emotions and ethics). The core of my thesis, which I have argued now for almost twenty-five years, is that emotions are (in part) a form of cognition, a matter of "ideas," or in the current lingo, *ideation*. David Hume, rather famously, analyzed several "passions," notably pride, in terms of "impressions" and "ideas." For Hume, in particular, morals are a matter not of reason but of "sentiment," thus bringing the understanding of emotions squarely into the arena of ethical discourse. (edited)

**Solomon, Robert C** and Higgins, Kathleen Marie. *A Passion for Wisdom: A Very Brief History of Philosophy*. New York, Oxford Univ Pr, 1997.

Without simplifying their subject, Solomon and Higgins tell the story of philosophy's development with great clarity and refreshing wit. They allow readers to see more clearly the connections and divergences between philosophers and their ideas as they change, reappear and evolve over time. They explore how, for example, the value of subjective experience is treated in Augustine, Luther, Descartes and Kierkegaard, how the idea of dynamic change appears in the work of Heraclitus, Darwin, Hegel and Nietzsche, and how the recurring dichotomies between faith and reason, belief and skepticism and mysticism and empiricism occupy philosophers from one generation to the next. (publisher, edited)

**Sols Lucia, José**. Filosofía y teología de Gaston Fessard acerca de la actualidad histórica en el período 1936-46. *Pensamiento*, 205(53), 65-88, Ja-Ap 97.

El estudio de algunos trabajos del filósofo-teólogo francés Gaston Fessard, insertos en la historia de Europa de los años treinta y cuarenta, permite descubrir una reintroducción de la reflexión teológica acerca de lo político en plena tradición de la Modernidad. Después de Voltaire parecía iluso intentar de nuevo ese tipo de reflexión y hacerlo podía suponer un discutible regreso a las grandes cosmovisiones teológicas de San Agustín o de Bossuet. Fessard muestra que la cuestión del sentido de la historia sólo puede ser abordada en el nivel de la "historicidad sobrenatural", al margen de si uno se considera cristiano, agnóstico o ateo, y que es la "dialéctica Pagano/Judío" la que permite engendrar al hombre a ese nivel de lo sobrenatural, cosa que no lograban las dialécticas Amo/Esclavo (Hegel) u Hombre/Mujer (Marx). La reflexión de Fessard nace de la urgencia de situaciones históricas y es en ese "aquí y ahora" donde su pensamiento quiere ser una articulación de lo lógico (Hegel), lo histórico (Marx) y lo existencial (Kierkegaard).

**Soltan, Karol Edward** (ed) and Elkin, Stephen L (ed). *The Constitution of Good Societies*. University Park, Pennsylvania Univ Pr, 1996.

The first part of the volume considers some of the boundaries of what is humanly possible in politico-economic designs and the role in them of deliberation and the processes of adapting to limits. The second part considers different ways of exercising constitutionalist judgment analyzing a variety of cases, including general visions of the good society. Looking at whole societies and at complexes of institutions, complements and informs the picture of the institutional microscale. Understanding the microscale, on the other hand, often makes the difference between empty slogans and realistic political proposals. (publisher,edited)

**Sommer, Andreas Urs**. Felix peccator? Kants geschichtsphilosophische Genesis-Exegese im *Muthmasslichen Anfang der Menschengeschichte* und die Theologie der Aufklärungszeit. *Kantstudien*, 88(2), 190-217, 1997.

Kant unternimmt in seiner kleinen Schrift "Der muthmassliche Anfang der Menschengeschichte" eine geschichtsphilosophische Deutung von Genesis 3-6. Diese Deutung eliminiert alle religiösen Ursprungsmythologien, nicht ohne aber selber mit sinnstiftendem Anspruch aufzutreten. Das Wichtigste sei, mit der Vorsehung zufrieden zu sein. Sommers Aufsatz zeigt die Gemeinsamkeiten und Differenzen zur zeitgenössischen theologischen Genesis-Auslegung auf und denkt über eine Philosophie nach, die im Gefolge und an Stelle der Religion mit Sinnstiftungsanspruch meint auftreten zu können. Weiter stellt der Beitrag die Frage, inwiefern sich Kants geschichtsphilosophische "Lustreise" mit seiner theoretischen und auch seiner praktischen Philosophie in ihrem kritischen Anspruch verträgt.

**Sommer, Manfred**. Abschattung. *Z Phil Forsch*, 50(1/2), 271-285, Ja-Je 96.

**Sommer, Richard** and Avigad, Jeremy. A Model-Theoretic Approach to Ordinal Analysis. *Bull Sym Log*, 3(1), 17-52, Mr 97.

We describe a model-theoretic approach to ordinal analysis via the finite combinatorial notion of an alpha-large set of natural numbers. In contrast to syntactic approaches that use cut elimination, this approach involves constructing finite sets of numbers with combinatorial properties that, in nonstandard instances, give rise to models of the theory being analyzed. This method is applied to obtain ordinal analyses of a number of interesting subsystems of first- and second-order arithmetic.

**Sommers, Fred**. Putnam's Born-Again Realism. *J Phil*, 94(9), 453-471, S 97.

**Sommers, Mary Catherine**. Useful Friendships: A Foundation for Business Ethics. *J Bus Ethics*, 16(12-13), 1453-1458, S 97.

All friendships tend to equality in the sense that they do not insist on 'what is due' as an ultimate end; friendship, like equity, surpasses justice in the fulfillment of what is owed. Because friendship fosters solidarity and justice it is politically important as a virtue-context, according to Aristotle. Is it possible that friendship can function as a virtue-context within economic life as well? Aristotle's notion of a type of useful friendship which functions through expectation of moral behavior will be shown to provide both motive and context for the performance of acts of virtue in a business setting. (edited)

**Somos, Róbert**. Alkinous: Explanation of Plato's Doctrines (in Hungarian). *Magyar Filozof Szemle*, 1-2, 242-280, 1997.

**Sonderegger, Erwin**. Considerations on the Plurality of the "Nothing-Speech" (in German). *Prima Philosophia*, 10(3), 341-357, 1997.

The variety and ambiguity of our use of negation has often been classified according to the classes of negated expressions. But if we take into account in addition to these, first, the negations of possibility and necessity, and second, the negations of questions and wishes, it seems, that not only negated expressions change, but the way to negate as well. If we consider that up to here every negation has only been a relative one, we may ask if it is possible to say "nothing" or "not" in an absolute manner. This attempt is not idle, since great principles, such as that of sufficient reason ("*ratio est in natura cur aliquid potius existat quam nihil*"), possibly make use of an absolute nothing. How to speak of an "absolute nothing?" Our negative speech is not exhausted by negation, since opposition, contradiction and difference contain some idea of the negative too. Certain remarks in Plato's *Sophistes* point to a prerogative position of difference within the whole just mentioned group of negative speech.

**Sonderegger, Ruth**. A Critique of Pure Meaning: Wittgenstein and Derrida. *Euro J Phil*, 5(2), 183-209, Ag 97.

The article argues that Derrida and Wittgenstein hold closely related views on linguistic meaning, both directed against varieties of objectivism and that it can be clearly shown how Derrida's attempt to represent speaking and understanding as interpretation constitutes an important advance beyond Wittgenstein. The main thesis of this paper is that it is important to reconstruct this advance beyond Wittgenstein, since only on the basis of such a reconstruction a productive confrontation of Wittgenstein and Derrida as philosophers of language, will be possible.

**Sonderen, Peter C**. Beauty and Desire: Frans Hemsterhuis' Aesthetic Experiments. *Brit J Hist Phil*, 4(2), 317-345, S 96.

**Sonenscher, Michael**. The Nation's Debt and the Birth of the Modern Republic: The French Fiscal Deficit and the Politics of the Revolution of 1789. *Hist Polit Thought*, 18(1), 64-103, Spr 97.

The aim of this article is to identify and explain the origins of the modern representative system as conceived of by the Abbé Sieyès at the beginning of the French Revolution. Sieyès's idea of the representative system was, it is claimed, a daring response to political problems generated by the growth of public credit during the eighteenth century. It involved adapting the idea of representation to face the problem of maintaining political and civil liberty when, for reasons of state, emergency conditions might force a government to default on the public debt.

**Sopher, Barry** and Gigliotti, Gary. Violations of Present-Value Maximization in Income Choice. *Theor Decis*, 43(1), 45-69, Jl 97.

We report results of an experiment testing for present-value maximization in intertemporal income choice. Two-thirds of subjects did not maximize present value. Through a series of experimental manipulations that impose costs on nonpresent value maximizers, we are able to reduce the level of violations substantially. We find, however, that a sizeable proportion of subjects continue to systematically violate present-value principles. Our interpretation is that these subjects either cannot or choose not to distinguish between *income* and *expenditure* in making their choices. Self-management, bounded rationality and sequence preference are suggested as possible explanations for such behavior.

**Sorabji, Richard**. The Ancient Greek Origins of the Western Debate on Animals. *J Indian Counc Phil Res*, 13(2), 69-76, Ja-Ap 96.

**Sorbi, Andrea** and Cooper, S Barry. Noncappable Enumeration Degrees Below O'e. *J Sym Log*, 61(4), 1347-1363, D 96.

We prove that there exists a noncappable enumeration degree strictly below $O'_e$.

**Sorbi, Andrea** and Cooper, S Barry and Yi, Xiaoding. Cupping and Noncupping in the Enumeration Degrees of Sigma$^0_2$ Sets [1]. *Annals Pure Applied Log*, 82(3), 317-342, D 96.

We prove the following three theorems on the enumeration degrees of Sigma$^0_2$ sets. Theorem A: There exists a nonzero noncuppable Sigma$^0_2$ enumeration degree. Theorem B: Every nonzero Delta$^0_2$ enumeration degree is cuppable to $O'_e$ by an incomplete total enumeration degree. Theorem C: There exists a nonzero low Delta$^0_2$ enumeration degree with the anticupping property. (edited)

**Sorensen, Roy A**. Modal Bloopers: Why Believable Impossibilities are Necessary. *Amer Phil Quart*, 33(3), 247-261, Jl 96.

A number of prominent philosophers argue that it is impossible to believe the impossible. They are refuted by the mere possibility that someone disagrees

with them. Since the author actually disagrees with them, it follows that it is possible to believe a proposition that it is necessarily false. The modal system S4 is all that is required to show the infallibility of the belief that it is possible to believe the impossible. This result is bad news for those who intimately link belief and possibility (such as Brian Ellis, Jaako Hintikka and Robert Stalnaker) and bad news for those who subscribe to a strong principle of charity (such as Donald Davidson and Daniel Dennett). However, it is good news for those seeking an explanation of the informativeness of deduction and analysis.

**Sorgi, Giuseppe**. At the Core of Hobbes' Thought. *Hobbes Stud*, 9, 3-10, 1996.

The efforts made by the scholars to direct their divergent and contrasting positions towards a univocal interpretation of Hobbes's work, do not mean underestimating the complexity of his thought, philosopher considered to be a 'many-minded thinker'. Hobbes is the political philosopher who most radically formulated the two essential questions on modern politics: why does the State exist? Under what conditions can it effectively function for the citizen's safety; yet his answer does not give us the recipe for solutions but shows that 'pluralism of minds', theoretical, methodological and empirical marking his speculative framework. The 'kernel' of his thought, is the endeavour to gather all man's existential contradictions and resolve them in an artificial political context, under the guidance of sure and efficacious sovereignty.

**Sorgi, Giuseppe**. Hobbes on "Bodies Politic". *Hobbes Stud*, 9, 71-87, 1996.

If absoluteness and uniqueness of sovereignty are fundamental requisites in Hobbes's theory, equally the 'bodies politic/subordinate bodies' question is very important. Political parties are inadmissible but to sovereign authority subordinated bodies, Hobbes reserves consideration both on principle and practical reasons. Three are the reasons connected to principles a natural human wish for power (participation): man's participation as fundamental requisite for State origins; in nature's state man has full sovereignty rights. The practical reasons refer to State running which necessarily needs politics-institutional bodies, but also social and economical, endowed with partial but all the same authorized and appointed (by the sovereign) autonomy. The 'subordinate bodies' reality finds its space in the framework's geometry and in the empirical interpretation of society.

**Soromenho-Marques, José Viriato**. Justiça e *Sentido da Terra*. *Philosophica (Portugal)*, 31-44, 1993.

Was bedeutet heute die Überlegung über das Problem der Gerechtigkeit? Dieser Vortrag versucht die Grundlage dieser Frage zur Klarheit bringen, nämlich durch die Feststellung der inneren Beziehung zwischen der riesigen Umweltpolitischproblemen unseres Jahrhunderts und die Hauptbestimmungen der Philosophie der Natur und der Philosophie der Politik in der Neuzeit.

**Sosa, David**. "Getting Acquainted with Perception" in *Perception*, Villanueva, Enrique (ed), 209-214. Atascadero, Ridgeview, 1996.

**Sosa, David**. "Irracionalidad en el externalismo" in *La racionalidad: su poder y sus límites*, Nudler, Oscar (ed), 261-269. Barcelona, Ed Paidos, 1996.

**Sosa, David**. "Reference from a Perspective *versus* Reference" in *Contents*, Villanueva, Enrique (ed), 79-89. Atascadero, Ridgeview, 1995.

**Sosa, David**. The Import of the Puzzle about Belief. *Phil Rev*, 105(3), 373-402, Jl 96.

Relocating Kripke's puzzle about belief, this paper investigates i) in what the puzzle consists, exactly; ii) the method used in its construction; and iii) relations between meaning and rationality. Essential to Kripke's puzzle is a normative notion of contradictory belief. Different positions about the meaning of names yield different views of what constitutes the attribution of contradictory belief; and Kripke's puzzle unwittingly *imports* a Millian assumption. Accordingly, the puzzle about belief is not independent of positions about the meaning of names.

**Sosa, Ernest**. "Fregean Reference Defended" in *Contents*, Villanueva, Enrique (ed), 91-99. Atascadero, Ridgeview, 1995.

**Sosa, Ernest**. "Is Color Psychological or Biological? Or Both?" in *Perception*, Villanueva, Enrique (ed), 67-74. Atascadero, Ridgeview, 1996.

**Sosa, Ernest**. "More on Fregean Reference" in *Contents*, Villanueva, Enrique (ed), 113-122. Atascadero, Ridgeview, 1995.

**Sosa, Ernest**. "Objetividad normativa" in *La racionalidad: su poder y sus límites*, Nudler, Oscar (ed), 213-227. Barcelona, Ed Paidos, 1996.

**Sosa, Ernest**. How to Resolve the Pyrrhonian Problematic: A Lesson from Descartes. *Phil Stud*, 85(2-3), 229-249, Mr 97.

Once placed in its proper Pyrrhonian context, Descartes's epistemology may be seen as a bilevel resolution which escapes viciousness in its circularity by giving its required due to foundational contact and reliability. Descartes has important lessons for contemporary epistemology.

**Sosa, Ernest**. Mythology of the Given. *Hist Phil Quart*, 14(3), 275-286, Jl 97.

Central European analytic philosophy in the first half of this century focused on the relation between science and experience. The issue of how experience relates to thought and language had two components: First, how does it relate to meaning? Second, how does it relate to knowledge? This controversy, though hardly novel with the Vienna Circle, much exercised them, and soon involved Rudolf Carnap and Carl Hempel and, eventually, Hans Reichenbach. With these it crossed the Atlantic, and with Karl Popper the Channel. In the second half of the century it has been a central issue in epistemology, where it has attracted Quine, Sellars, Chisholm, Davidson, Rescher, Rorty, and many others. It is this second issue that this article takes up: What is the epistemological bearing of sensory experience on our knowledge?

**Sosa, Ernest**. Reflective Knowledge in the Best Circles. *J Phil*, 94(8), 410-430, Ag 97.

The article proposes a defense of a form of virtue epistemology, following a strategy that it finds already in Descartes and one that would be available to Moore as well. Descartes's cogito and its place in Descartes's epistemology, are compared with Moore's conviction that he has two hands and its place in Moore's epistemology. The article tries to meet the circularity objections that have commonly been urged against Descartes and against Moore's proof of the external world, objections that can also be (and have been) urged against the form of virtue epistemology defended here.

**Sosa, Ernesto**. Cómo resolver la problemática pirrónica: lo que se aprende de Descartes. *Teorema*, 16(1), 7-26, 1996.

Descartes's epistemology is placed in the context of the Pyrrhonian problematic of the notorious triad: circle, regress, or foundations. It is argued that Descartes has been radically misinterpreted. His real focus is not the problem of the external world, nor is he a foundationalist. When we place his epistemology in its proper, Pyrrhonian, context, his views emerge as much more subtle and instructive to us today (and, I suspect, tomorrow). No Cartesian he, Descartes offers an epistemology whose architectural elegance survives the erosion of its individual stones.

**Sosa, Ernesto**. Objetividad Normativa. *Rev Filosof (Spain)*, 9(16), 171-185, 1996.

**Sosoé, Varus Atadi**. Droits naturels et devoir naturel chez Rawls. *De Phil*, 12, 91-115, 1995-1996.

**Soto, L G**. Readings of Barthes V. Hidden Philosophy? (in Portuguese). *Agora (Spain)*, 15(2), 125-142, 1996.

Monograph on reception of Barthes's work in the critical literature in English, French, Italian, Portuguese and Spanish, in which the very different approaches are studies in five main themes. In this fifth chapter books by J.M. Marinas and G. Rubino and articles by J.N. Andrade, J. Derrida, M. Dufrenne, J. Leenhardt, R. Lindekens, M. C. Mendes and M. Ferin, A. Ponzio and C. Reichler are commented. All of them pay attention to Barthes's philosophy, some noting the uses of philosophy in his texts and examining the philosophical questions that he suggests in them, while others outline a global philosophical characterization of his work, situating him in the line formed by historical philosophers and contemporary thinkers. Most of these authors coincide in focusing on Barthes's final texts.

**Soto, Maria Jesús**. Luz y opacidad: Una consideración de lo real desde el conocimiento humano. *Anu Filosof*, 29(2), 1037-1050, 1996.

Against the modern theory of representation, which makes the world opaque, Polo suggests revitalizing the classical theory of illumination. Intentionality of knowledge, according to Polo, makes possible the "deviling" of reality and shows its radical dependence from God. (edited)

**Soual, Philippe**. La moralité et le mal dans les *Principes de la Philosophie du Droit* de Hegel. *Rev Phil Fr*, 2, 223-264, Ap-Je 96.

On notera, enfin, le caractère et le statut nécessaires, du point de vue du concept, des figures du Mal mises au jour dans *La moralité*, et également le fait que celle-ci est une sphère nécessaire et justifiée de l'esprit dans l'histoire. Ces figures ne sont pas un destin pour l'homme, mais il ne peut pas ne pas y être exposé, selon les moments que l'on a vus. Le danger n'est pas extérieur à l'esprit, puisque la possibilité du Mal est constitutive de la vie morale de l'esprit libre. Il ne relève pas non plus d'une imperfection, mais de la manifestation de l'esprit, en tant qu'il est libre originairement. La liberté subjective se décidant au Mal accomplit l'auto-infirmation de sa liberté, qui se détruit dans son néant. La liberté subjective se décidant au Bien accomplit, au contraire, la *confirmation* de l'esprit libre en elle-même. Le problème du Mal est ainsi décisif, dans le système hégélien, qui montre en quel sens il l'est pour tout esprit fini, nul ne pouvant échapper au vertige de la liberté subjective. (edited)

**Soual, Philippe**. Person and Property in Hegel's *Philosophical Principles of Right* (in French). *Arch Phil*, 60(2), 217-241, Ap-Je 97.

With respect to the question of property, Hegel justifies both the concept and the institution in a manner which is rational rather than historical or empirical. He considers the principle and the right of the infinitely free person, which he both affirms and guarantees, by employing a conceptual hierarchy: first, as spirit's right to own its own interior (which constitutes it as a person) and, by extension, the right to own its own body and its life; then, the right to own exterior things. This right is the true principle of the world in its historical, moral and political aspects. Hegel affirms the absolute right of a human being to be a *person* which entails the inalienable character of personality in all its attributes.

**Souryal, Sam S** and McKay, Brian W. Personal Loyalty to Superiors in Public Service. *Crim Just Ethics*, 15(2), 44-62, Sum-Fall 96.

The purpose of this article is to expose the dangers of loyalty to the *person* of the superior. While one can and should be loyal to the organization, to the group, to authority, or to the profession, loyalty to the *person* of the superior in neither required nor is necessary. Two long arguments and six short ones are offered in support of this view. The arguments are philosophical in nature and attack the common, yet unsubstantiated, *belief* that loyalty to superiors is conducive to any good in public service. Indeed, it may lead to undesirable consequences.

**Sousedík, Stanislav**. E. Husserl and Descartes's Method of Doubt (in Czech). *Filosof Cas*, 44(5), 833-840, 1996.

Der Autor des Beitrags erläutert zunächst, dass der kartesische Zweifel von bestimmten Voraussertzungen der kartesischen Metaphysik abhängt. Weiter zeigt er dann auf, dass Husserl zwar Descartes' Metaphysik ablehnte, sich jedoch trotzdem zur Methode des Zweifels bekannte. Der Autor Schliesst, dass hierin ein Widerspruch besteht.

**Sousedík, Stanislav**. On the Problem of Collective Guilt (In Czech). *Filosof Cas*, 44(6), 1025-1028, 1996.

Der Verfasser unterscheidet die kollektive Schuld von der gemeinsamen, und verteidigt dann gegen die allgemein verbreite Meinung die These, dass der Begriff der kollektiven Schuld u.U. angewendet werden darf.

**Souza Araújo, José Carlos** and Gonçalves Neto, Wenceslau and Inácio Filho, Geraldo. Notícia sobre a Pesquisa de Fontes Histórico-educacionais no Triângulo Mineiro e Alto Paranaíba. *Educ Filosof*, 10(19), 115-127, Ja-Je 96.

A group of teachers at the Federal University of Uberlândia made, from 1994 to 1996, a survey and a catalogue of valuable primary and secondary sources for researchers dealing with the history of Brazilian education in the West region of the state of Minas Gerais, called Triângulo Mineiro. The same research program is now being developed in eighteen other regions of Brazil. This activity, included in a group of studies and research entitled *History, Education and Society in Brazil*, aims to, among other goals, give support to the research activities of the postgraduation program in education of the university, that focuses on Brazilian education.

**Sowa, John F**. "Matching Logical Structure to Linguistic Structure" in *Studies in the Logic of Charles Sanders Peirce*, Houser, Nathan (ed), 418-444. Bloomington, Indiana Univ Pr, 1997.

**Spaak, Torben** and Adams, Edward W. Fuzzifying the Natural Law-Legal Positivist Debate. *Vera Lex*, 14(1-2), 1-7, 1994.

**Spade, Paul Vincent**. Walter Burley on the Simple Supposition of Singular Terms. *Topoi*, 16(1), 7-13, Mr 97.

This paper argues that Burley's theory of simple supposition is not as it has usually been presented. Burley explicitly allows that some instances of simple supposition are for an individual and that in certain cases personal supposition and simple supposition coincide. The present paper explores Burley's theory on this topic and proposes a way of thinking about the metaphysics and the semantics that makes sense of what he says. (edited)

**Spade, Paul Vincent** (trans). Walter Burley, From the Beginning of His Treatise on the Kinds of Supposition (*De suppositionibus*). *Topoi*, 16(1), 95-102, Mr 97.

An annotated translation from the beginning of the fourteenth century logician Walter Burley's (or Burleigh's) early treatise on supposition or reference (dated 1302). The Translation is from Stephen Brown, ed., "Walter Burleigh's Treatise De Suppositionibus and Its Influence on William of Ockham," *Franciscan Studies* 32 (1972), 15-64. The translation is from pp. 31-43 (paragraph 1.1-2.425) of the edition, concerning the supposition of "absolute" terms. The remainder of Burley's treatise concerns the supposition of "respective" or "relative" terms and is not translated here. (edited)

**Spaemann, Robert**. Ahnlichkeit. *Z Phil Forsch*, 50(1/2), 286-290, Ja-Je 96.

**Spaemann, Robert**. Is Every Human Being a Person?. *Thomist*, 60(3), 463-474, Jl 96.

**Spangler, Al**. Landmarks in Critical Thinking Series: Plato's Euthyphro. *Inquiry (USA)*, 14(3), 1-12, Spr 95.

This piece contains an edited version of Plato's *Euthyphro* and some commentary indicating its importance for aspiring critical thinkers.

**Sparks, Simon** (ed) and Sheppard, Darren (ed) and Thomas, Colin (ed). *On Jean-Luc Nancy: The Sense of Philosophy*. New York, Routledge, 1997.

*On Jean-Luc Nancy* draws together a number of outstanding commentators to provide an invaluable companion to Nancy's own work. In addition to contributions by Howard Caygill, Rodolphe Gasché and Alphonso Lingis, there is a text by Nancy's renowned long-time co-author, Philippe Lacoue-Labarthe. These essays approach the main themes in Nancy's work. From Nancy the philosopher of the contemporary and of the disorientation in thinking today to Nancy and the significance of anger and sacrifice in philosophy, the recurrent themes of community, freedom, being and the divine in his work are brought out. (publisher, edited)

**Sparshott, Francis**. Art and Anthropology. *J Aes Art Crit*, 55(3), 239-243, Sum 97.

The article treats discursively of aspects of the relation between the practices of anthropology and art as a distinctive historical phenomenon of Western civilization.

**Sparshott, Francis**. Kant without Sade. *Phil Lit*, 21(1), 151-154, Ap 97.

The contention that Kant's moral theory strictly requires him to promote cruelty ignores the central place of the concept of a maxim in Kant's argument.

**Sparshott, Francis**. Reply to Commentators. *J Aes Educ*, 31(2), 61-69, Sum 97.

The author replies briefly to each of several articles in the same number of the journal devoted to various aspects of his work. The replies have no common theme.

**Sparshott, Francis**. Singing and Speaking. *Brit J Aes*, 37(3), 199-210, Jl 97.

This paper discusses the place of song in the philosophy of music. Aristotle's neglected distinction between "voice" and "language" as separate communication systems invites us to think of singing as a fusion of the two. But in a fully-fledged song both systems are subordinated to a third, the quasi-mathematical system of music itself. The meaning of a song is a matter of the interaction among these three systems, a relationship that remains to be fully worked out.

**Sparshott, Francis**. The View from Gadshill. *Phil Lit*, 20(2), 398-411, O 96.

Examination of Edward Said's treatment of texts by Jane Austen and Rudyard Kipling suggests that the use of marginalized and oppressed viewpoints to reinterpret literary texts may lead to misrepresentation of the very features on which new light is supposedly shed.

**Sparti, Davide** and Lecci, Bernardo. Scetticismo, riconoscimento, riscoperta dell'ordinario: La filosofia di Stanley Cavell. *Iride*, 10(20), 135-144, Ap 97.

**Spash, Clive L** and Clayton, M H. "The Maintenance of Natural Capital: Motivations and Methods" in *Philosophy and Geography I: Space, Place, and Environmental Ethics*, Light, Andrew (ed), 143-173. Lanham, Rowman & Littlefield, 1997.

This paper analyses the reasoning behind defining a class of inputs to production as natural capital as a response to environmental concerns. Two motivations are: ecological criticality and nonhuman intrinsic values. These justifications require the maintenance of resources which are excluded from exploitation, but free market systems cannot achieve this due to a basic assumption of trade-offs derived from utilitarianism and economic value. Three methods for the protection of natural capital are reviewed (compensating projects, cost-benefit analysis, scientifically designated limits) but a more interdisciplinary and inclusive approach is necessary and a type of systems analysis is suggested.

**Specht, Rainer**. Ideen von mehr oder weniger Süsse oder Licht: Zur Darstellung von Intensitäten bei Locke. *Z Phil Forsch*, 50(1/2), 291-308, Ja-Je 96.

**Spector, Horacio**. Relatividad agencial: Respuesta a Farrell. *Telos (Spain)*, 5(2), 115-123, D 96.

In a previous article Farrell suggested that Spector denies a moral distinction between duties and permissions. Farrell quoted a statement of Spector's *Autonomy and Rights* saying that, in trying to justify the agent-relative character of the moral duty not to harm, one should put aside the fact that it is a negative duty (as something different from a permission). Spector replies that Farrell misunderstands the statement. In the place where the statement appears he does not try to show there is a negative duty (this had been undertaken earlier in the book) but to determine whether it must be conceived as agent-relative or agent-neutral. To this effect the fact that it is a prohibition (rather than a permission) is irrelevant. This does not mean that Spector equates duties with permissions. (edited)

**Spelke, Elizabeth** and Carey, Susan. Science and Core Knowledge. *Phil Sci*, 63(4), 515-533, D 96.

While endorsing Gopnik's proposal that studies of the emergence and modification of scientific theories and studies of cognitive development in children are mutually illuminating, we offer a different picture of the beginning points of cognitive development from Gopnik's picture of "theories all the way down." Human infants are endowed with several distinct core systems of knowledge which are theory-like in some, but not all, important ways. The existence of these core systems of knowledge has implications for the joint research program between philosophers and psychologists that Gopnik advocates and we endorse. A few lessons already gained from this program of research are sketched.

**Spelman, Elizabeth V**. *Fruits of Sorrow*. Boston, Beacon Pr, 1997.

What are the hidden roots of the way we understand, use, and misuse human suffering? From the dialogues of Plato to representations of AIDS in present-day media, Elizabeth Spelman's book traces the immensely complex ways in which human beings try to redeem the pain we cause and witness. She shows in startling light the way our responses are often more than they seem: the way that compassion can mask condescension, that identifying with others' pain often slips into illicit appropriation. The author notes in the introduction that the book is not about types of suffering, or about how to deal with suffering in our individual lives, but a book about how we *think* about suffering, and how important thinkers and writers have done so in the past. (publisher, edited)

**Spencer, Edward M** (& others) and Fletcher, John C and Leeman, Cavin P. Quality Control for Hospitals' Clinical Ethics Services: Proposed Standards. *Cambridge Quart Healthcare Ethics*, 6(3), 257-268, Sum 97.

As hospital ethics committees have proliferated, problems in the way in which they operate have become increasingly apparent. In response, the authors propose two sets of standards. Standards for procedure and process are intended to help ensure that clinical ethics services are provided in ways which are fair, open, and procedurally consistent and predictable. Standards for education and training are designed to ensure that the people who provide clinical ethics services have the skills and expertise needed to do so competently, and to engender confidence in them. The standards are discussed, and examples of ways to meet them are offered.

**Sperber, Dan**. Intuitive and Reflective Beliefs. *Mind Lang*, 12(1), 67-83, Mr 97.

Humans have two kinds of beliefs, intuitive beliefs and reflective beliefs. Intuitive beliefs are a fundamental category of cognition, defined in the architecture of the mind. They are formulated in an intuitive mental lexicon. Humans are also capable of entertaining an indefinite variety of higher-order or 'reflective' propositional attitudes, many of which are of a credal sort. Reasons to hold reflective beliefs are provided by other beliefs that describe the source of the reflective belief as reliable, or that provide an explicit argument in favour of the reflective belief. The mental lexicon of reflective beliefs includes not only intuitive, but also reflective concepts.

**Spiecker, Ben** and Steutel, Jan. "Good Sex as the Aim of Sexual Education" in *Philosophy of Education (1996)*, Margonis, Frank (ed), 400-407. Urbana, Phil Education Soc, 1997.

This paper argues that sexual education should not be reduced to (an aspect of) moral education. Equally important are aims that relate to nonmorally good sex (i.e., sex that is satisfying or enjoyable) and the relative value of sex in a nonmorally good life. The nature of and the differences between these moral and nonmoral aims of sexual education are explained and some remarks are made on the central differences between the educational ways to achieve those aims.

**Spiecker, Ben** and Steutel, Jan. Paedophilia, Sexual Desire and Perversity. *J Moral Educ*, 26(3), 331-342, S 97.

In our society adults who are guilty of having sex with prepubescent children often have a paedophile disposition. This paper first criticizes the justifications that are given by paedophiles for having sex with children. Part of this criticism is a brief analysis of "sexual desire" and "erotic". Next, the question is raised whether paedophile activities can ever be morally permissible. Using the principles of mutual consent and nonexploitation as touchstone, the question is answered in the negative. Finally, it is examined whether paedophile desires can be regarded as perverse. In order to deal with this issue a moral conception of perversion is proposed.

**Spiecker, Ben** and Steutel, Jan. Rational Passions and Intellectual Virtues: A Conceptual Analysis. *Stud Phil Educ*, 16(1-2), 59-71, Ja-Ap 97.

Intellectual virtues, like open-mindedness, clarity, intellectual honesty and the willingness to participate in rational discussions, are conceived as important aims of education. In this paper an attempt is made to clarify the specific nature of intellectual virtues. Firstly, the intellectual virtues are systematically compared with more virtues. The upshot is that considering a trait of character to be an intellectual virtue implies assuming that such a trait can be derived from, or is a specification of, the cardinal virtue of concern and respect for truth. Secondly, several (possible) misconceptions of intellectual virtues are avoided by making the required distinctions. For example, it is argued that our concept of an intellectual virtue should not be confused with a normative conception of intellectual virtuousness.

**Spiegel, James S**. The Theological Orthodoxy of Berkeley's Immaterialism. *Faith Phil*, 13(2), 216-235, AP 96.

Ever since George Berkeley first published *Principles of Human Knowledge* his metaphysics has been opposed by, among others, some Christian philosophers who allege that his ideas fly in the face of orthodox Christian belief. The irony is that Berkeley's entire professional career is marked by an unwavering commitment to demonstrating the reasonableness of the Christian faith. In fact, Berkeley's immaterialist metaphysical system can be seen as an apologetic device. In this paper, I inquire into the question whether Berkeley's immaterialist metaphysics is congruent with the Christian scriptures. I conclude that not only are Berkeley's principles consistent with scripture, a case can be made for the claim that certain biblical passages actually recommend his brand of immaterialism.

**Spielman, Bethan J** and Agich, George J. Ethics Expert Testimony: Against the Skeptics. *J Med Phil*, 22(4), 381-403, Ag 97.

There is great skepticism about the admittance of expert normative ethics testimony into evidence. However, a practical analysis of the way ethics testimony has been used in courts of law reveals that the skeptical position is itself based on assumptions that are controversial. We argue for an alternative way to understand such expert testimony. This alternative understanding is based on the practice of clinical ethics.

**Spielman, Bethany** and Verhulst, Steve. Non-Heart-Beating Cadaver Procurement and the Work of Ethics Committees. *Cambridge Quart Healthcare Ethics*, 6(3), 282-287, Sum 97.

Recent ethics literature suggests that issues involved in nonheartbeating (NHB) organ procurement are both highly charged and rather urgent. Some fear that NHB is a public relations disaster waiting to happen or that it will create a backlash against organ donation. The purpose of the study described below was to assess ethics committees' current level of involvement and readiness for addressing the difficult issues that NHB organ retrieval raises—either proactively through policy development or concurrently through ethics consultation.

**Spier, Raymond**. Ethical Aspects of the University-Industry Interface. *Sci Eng Ethics*, 1(2), 151-162, A 95.

Following an examination of the missions of industry and the university there is a comparison of the 'wish-lists' of industry and the university. These 'wish-lists' have both similarities and differences. Some of the differences are expressed in a further section on the kinds of interactions that neither institution wants from the other. In the canonical university, the culture values features such as openness, individuality and the de-emphasis of monetary matters, whereas in the archetypal industry the prevailing ethos tends towards secrecy, teamwork and financial advancement. When two such cultures are juxtaposed under conditions where the survival of the university is dependent, in part, on receiving funds from industry, there is a danger of an erosion of academic standards as the university becomes more oriented to service the needs of industry as opposed to the development of its students and its independent scholastic and research activities. Industry, however, is in a position to derive benefit from the interaction without incurring an equivalent cost. These issues are discussed and some recommendations are made to improve the ethical nature of the interaction.

**Spier, Raymond**. Ethics as a Control System Component. *Sci Eng Ethics*, 2(3), 259-262, Jl 96.

**Spier, Raymond**. On the Acceptability of Biopharmaceuticals. *Sci Eng Ethics*, 2(3), 291-306, Jl 96.

The issues relating to the licensing of a biopharmaceutical are described. In particular, attention is focused on the mind of the regulator who has the responsibility of recommending licensure. There are two key factors which operate on the mind when confronted with such a task: psychology and ethics. The different factors which influence the psychological acceptability of a product for licensure are many and varied; they include perceived need, novelty, education, context and others. Also involved is the regulator's view of the ethicality of such products and the organisms which make them, with particular reference to those which are genetically engineered. These ethical views are in turn derived by reference to basic systems of ethics which provide guidelines for behavior. It is important for the manufacturers of biopharmaceuticals to be aware of both the psychological and ethical aspects of the regulator's mind when addressing such individuals with a view to obtaining a license to manufacture a particular biopharmaceutical.

**Spike, Jeffrey**. What's Love Got to Do with It? The Altruistic Giving of Organs. *J Clin Ethics*, 8(2), 165-170, Sum 97.

**Spike, Jeffrey** and Derse, Arthur R and Reitemeier, Paul J. Retiring the Pacemaker. *Hastings Center Rep*, 27(1), 24-26, Ja-F 97.

**Spinelli, Emidio**. "La corporeità del tempo: Ancora su Ensidemo e il suo eraclitismo" in *Il Concetto di Tempo: Atti del XXXII Congresso Nazionale della Società Filosofica Italiana*, Casertano, Giovanni (ed), 159-171. Napoli, Loffredo, 1997.

**Spinelli, Miguel**. Sobre a Ciência e o Magistério Filosófico de Pitágoras. *Rev Port Filosof*, 52(1-4), 889-917, Ja-D 96.

"On Pythagoras' Science and His Philosophical Teaching". The paper's central concern is to call attention to basic features of Pythagoras' science and of his ethical and philosophical teachings. It addresses theoretical foundations historically and philosophically, and proceeds by examining the doxographic testimonies of Plato, Aristotle and Pythagoras' disciples.

**Spini, Giorgio**. Secularization and Tolerance. *Ratio Juris*, 10(1), 9-12, Mr 97.

In this paper, starting from Condorcet's discussion on progress, the author analyzes the relationship between the decline of religions, the end of state paternalism and tolerance. The author underlines how history shows a different course with respect to illuminist previsions.

**Spinner, Helmut F**. "Wissensordnung, Ethik, Wissensethik" in *Angewandte Ethik: Die Bereichsethiken und ihre theoretische Fundierung*, Nida-Rümelin, Julian (ed), 718-749. Stuttgart, Alfred Kröner, 1996.

**Spinosa, Charles** and Dreyfus, Hubert L. Highway Bridges and Feasts: Heidegger and Borgmann on How to Affirm Technology. *Man World*, 30(2), 159-177, Ap 97.

Borgmann's views seem to clarify and elaborate Heidegger's. Both thinkers understand technology as a way of coping with people and things that reveals them, viz. make them intelligible. Both thinkers also claim that technological coping could devastate not only our environment and communal ties but more importantly the historical, world-opening being that has defined Westerners since the Greeks. Both think that this devastation can be prevented by attending to the practices for coping with simple things like family meals and footbridges. But, contrary to Borgmann, Heidegger claims further that, alongside simple things, we can affirm technological things such as autobahn bridges. For Borgmann, technological coping produces things like central heating that are so dispersed they inhibit skillful interaction with them and, therefore, prevent our being sensitive to ourselves as world-disclosers. For Heidegger, so long as we can still relate to nontechnological things, we can affirm relations with technological things because we can maintain both our technological and the nontechnological *ways of world-disclosing*. So Borgmann sees revealing as primarily directed to things while Heidegger sees it as directed to worlds. If Heidegger is right about us, we have more leeway to save ourselves from technological devastation than Borgmann sees.

**Spinosa, Charles** and Dreyfus, Hubert L. Single-World versus Plural-World Antiessentialism: A Reply to Tim Dean. *Crit Inquiry*, 23(4), 921-932, Sum 97.

**Spinosa, Charles** and Dreyfus, Hubert L. Two Kinds of Antiessentialism and Their Consequences. *Crit Inquiry*, 22(4), 735-763, Sum 96.

**Spitz, Jean-Fabien**. Apparence et fausseté: la double nature de l'ordre politique chez Pascal. *Rev Int Phil*, 51(199), 101-118, 1997.

**Splitter, Laurance**. Landmarks in Critical Thinking Series: John Passmore: On Teaching to be Critical. *Inquiry (USA)*, 15(3), 1-16, Spr 96.

This paper is a discussion of the views of one of the first philosophers to write explicitly about the nature of critical thinking and its importance in education. It endorses much of what Passmore offers—including the idea that critical thinking is as much an attitude or disposition as it is a skill, the insight that critical thinking and imagination are importantly related and the notion that when it comes to teaching someone to be critical, the role of the teacher in fostering a sympathetic classroom environment is crucial. However, in choosing to follow the "education as initiation" views of R. S. Peters, Passmore fails to take (what, for this author, is) the important pedagogic step of proclaiming philosophy as a discipline apt to the teaching of critical thinking. This failure renders Passmore's account less attractive than it would otherwise have been.

**Splitter, Laurance J**. On the Theme of "Teaching for Higher Order Thinking Skills". *Inquiry (USA)*, 14(4), 52-65, Sum 95.

**Spohn, Wolfgang**. "Begründungen a priori—oder: ein frischer Blick auf Dispositionsprädikate" in *Das weite Spektrum der analytischen Philosophie*, Lenzen, Wolfgang, 323-345. Hawthorne, de Gruyter, 1997.

More consequently than other attempts the paper analyzes the meaning of disposition predicates within the framework of Kaplan's character theory. It concludes that reduction sentences are a priori in two different senses, defines the epistemological role of the reference to normal conditions, explains the crucial role which the notion of a priori reasons (in the sense of positive relevance) plays in these considerations and finally discusses the extent to which dispositions are (metaphysically) identical with their bases. These issues turn out to be important for understanding the foundations of empirical knowledge and a refutation of skepticism.

**Spretnak, Charlene**. "Radical Nonduality in Ecofeminist Philosophy" in *Ecofeminism: Women, Culture, Nature*, Warren, Karen J (ed), 425-436. Bloomington, Indiana Univ Pr, 1997.

The ecofeminist rejection of dualism should logically lead to, at very least, consideration of nonduality, or even radical nonduality. The latter is defined as unitive dimensions of being, that is, manifestations of a subtle unitary field of form, motion, space and time. Resistance among both modern and deconstructive-postmodern feminist philosophers to acknowledge radical nonduality is examined. A phenomenological appreciation of experiential knowledge of unitive dimensions of being is then presented. Finally, the ontological implications of the orientation Spretnak calls "ecological postmodernism" are discussed with relation to ecofeminist philosophy and radical nonduality.

**Spretnak, Charlene**. The Spriritual Dimension of Gandhi's Activism. *Acorn*, 5-2 &(6-1), 5-12, S 90 - Mr 91.

Most of the scholarship on Gandhi's work has abided by modernity's prejudice against spirituality, focusing instead on his political strategy and tactics or his commitment to "ethics" or "morality." In fact, Gandhi was clear on the centrality of spiritual practice and guidance in his political work: "Religion is to morality what water is to the seed that is sown in the field." Numerous facets of this connection are presented, illuminating Gandhi's insistence that "The outward has no meaning to me at all except insofar as it helps the inward." Finally, a question is raised about the adequacy of Gandhi's choice of *karma yoga*, without *raga yoga*, to achieve the total inner transformation he sought for himself and India.

**Sprigge, T L S**. "James, Aboutness, and his British Critics" in *The Cambridge Companion to William James*, Putnam, Ruth Anna (ed), 125-144. New York, Cambridge Univ Pr, 1997.

Bertrand Russell and G. E. Moore suggested that according to James's pragmatism the two following propositions are compatible: It is true that God exists. God does not exist. James rightly thought that they were missing the point. A mental state is the belief that God exists if and only if it is such that it would usefully relate one to God should he exist, or somewhat differently, that God is that thing to whom if he exists the belief one expresses in those words would usefully relate one. Therefore, one's belief that God exists cannot be true unless he does.

**Sprigge, T L S**. Kerr-Lawson on Truth and Santayana. *Trans Peirce Soc*, 33(1), 113-130, Wint 97.

Santayana's realm of truth poses the problem that, since its members are those essences which are "illustrated" in the flux of events, it is a realm of predicates true of something, rather than of truths. Kerr-Lawson seeks to remove or reduce this problem by a discussion of the different types of truth Santayana distinguishes and of his concern to avoid a psychologistic account. He makes many good points about Santayana's position but does not altogether eliminate this problem. However, the general spirit of Santayana's treatment of truth is superbly right and sane, in spite of some inadequacies of detail.

**Sprigge, T L S**. Pantheism. *Monist*, 80(2), 191-217, Ap 97.

Pantheism is understood here as the doctrine that God and the universe are identical. Various forms of this claim are considered. Advaita Vedanta and Western absolute idealism are pantheisms of this kind. A brief case for such pantheism is presented and the charge, levelled especially against Vedanta by some critics, that it is inherently pessimistic is considered. The possibilities of pantheism as a living religion are then considered.

**Sprigge, T L S**. Spinoza and Indexicals. *Inquiry*, 40(1), 3-22, Mr 97.

Spinoza distinguishes between three grades of knowledge, i) sense perception and hearsay; ii) abstract scientific knowledge; iii) intuitive reason. It is implied that our intellectual ideal is to pass from the first to the second, and then from the second to the third. It is problematic, however, how such supresession of the first kind of knowledge is an intelligible ideal. For, on the face of it, it is this alone which can direct our attention on to those particulars (single individuals) a better understanding of which is the main value of the second and third types of knowledge. But perhaps the third (if not, the second) kind of knowledge targets particulars from its own resources. However, it is doubtful that this is quite Spinoza's position. So there is something of a problem as to how he conceives the clearest knowledge of particulars which it makes sense to strive for. (edited)

**Springborg, Patricia**. Review: The View from the 'Divell's Mountain'. *Hist Polit Thought*, 17(4), 615-622, Winter 96.

**Sprod, Tim**. Improving Scientific Reasoning through Philosophy for Children: An Empirical Study. *Thinking*, 13(2), 11-16, 1997.

Lipman's philosophy for children program claims to improve children's reasoning by promoting their ability to engage in philosophical inquiry. In this empirical study, the curriculum of a Year 7 science class was modified to make maximum use of philosophical inquiry on the Lipman model. Two types of measures of the effect were used: pre- and post-test quantitative measure of gains on the Science Reasoning Tasks against a control class and discourse analysis of discussion transcripts. The quantitative test showed significantly greater gains in reasoning by the experimental class, while discourse analysis provided evidence of how children's reasoning was improved.

**Spurlock, Jacqueline Bouchard** (trans) and Vandevelde, Pol (ed & trans) and Harris, Bond (trans). *Paul Ricoeur: A Key to Husserl's Ideas I*. Milwaukee, Marquette Univ Pr, 1996.

In 1950 Paul Ricoeur translated into French Husserl's major work *Ideen zu einer reinen Phänomenologie und phänomenologischen Philosophie*. In this French translation Ricoeur provided both a lengthy introductory chapter and a large running commentary in the form of notes. These notes were keyed to the beginning of many of Husserl's sections and to important places within the body of the text. The present translation brings at last this famous commentary into English. In undertaking this work the translators have benefited from the encouragement of Professor Ricoeur himself. (publisher, edited)

**Spurrett, David**. 'Beyond Determinism'. *S Afr J Phil*, 16(1), 14-22, F 97.

It is argued, following Bhaskar, that determinism can be shown to require conditions of atomism and reductionism, and further that these conditions can be shown to be unsatisfiable. The same arguments equally indicate the untenability of standard forms of indeterminism. The metaphysical position suggested by the denial of atomism and reductionism is not one where causality is problematized, and is referred to as nondeterminism. It is suggested that the nondeterminist position is independently worthy of further attention being particularly germane to the resurgent debates over causal emergence.

**Spychiger, Maria B**. Aesthetic and Praxial Philosophies of Music Education Compared: A Semiotic Consideration. *Phil Music Educ Rev*, 5(1), 33-41, Spr 97.

The author undertakes an analysis of aesthetic and praxial philosophy of music education in order to compare them and to determine whether the two philosophies are as opposed to each other as David Elliott has repeatedly stated. The semiotic framework (Peirce-based) of contemporary Swiss psychologist Alfred Lang is used as a method of analysis. The procedure reveals that both philosophies contain elements of each category in Lang's semiotic function circle (IntrO-semiosis, IntrA-semiosis, ExtrO-semiosis, ExtrA-semiosis) and the author concludes that aesthetic and praxial philosophies of music education are to be considered compatible rather than exclusive.

**Squadrito, Kathy**. Are Locke's Simple Ideas Abstract?. *Dialogos*, 31(68), 155-163, Jl 96.

**Squier, Susan**. Fetal Subjects and Maternal Objects: Reproductive Technology and the New Fetal/Maternal Relation. *J Med Phil*, 21(5), 515-535, O 96.

This essay examines three tendencies nurtured in the practices of reproductive technology—tendencies with profoundly disturbing implications for us as individuals and as social beings. They are: 1) the increasing subjectification of the fetus (that is, the increasing tendency to posit a fetal subject), 2) the increasing objectification of the gestating woman, leading to her representation as interchangeable object rather than unique subject, and 3) the increasing tendency to conceive of the fetus and the mother as social, medical, and legal antagonists. Considering the construction of fetus, mother, and the fetal/maternal relation in earlier (Western) historical periods, a contemporary work of literature, a government report, and the popular press, I argue that as the fetus is increasingly being understood as a subject, the mother is increasingly being reduced to an antagonist, an obstacle to fetal health, and an object. The essay concludes by offering some tentative conclusions about the general process of fetal subjectification in the United States and Europe.

**Srinivas, Kankanahalli** and Barnden, John A. Quantification without Variables in Connectionism. *Mind Mach*, 6(2), 173-201, My 96.

Connectionist attention to variables has been too restricted in two ways. First, it has not exploited certain ways of doing without variables in the *symbolic* arena. One variable-avoidance method, that of logical combinators, is particularly well established there. Secondly, the attention has been largely restricted to variables in long-term rules embodied in connection weight patterns. However, *short-lived* bodies of information, such as sentence interpretations or inference products, may involve quantification. Therefore, short-lived activation patterns may need to achieve the effect of variables. The paper is mainly a theoretical analysis of some benefits and drawbacks of using logical combinators to avoid variables in short-lived connectionist encodings without loss of expressive power. The paper also includes a brief survey of some possible methods for avoiding variables other than by using combinators.

**St Clair, Becky**. People with Developmental Disabilities Focusing on Their Own Health Care. *Bioethics Forum*, 12(3), 27-30, Fall 96.

People with developmental disabilities have often been denied the opportunity to participate in their own health care decision making. This paper describes how a group of adults with developmental disabilities began to correct this inequity. With support, seven individuals with cognitive limitations learned how to make choices and decisions about their own health, and then created a training program that enabled them to advocate for others like themselves on health care decision making.

**St. Denis, Paul** and Grim, Patrick. Fractal Images of Formal Systems. *J Phil Log*, 26(2), 181-222, Ap 97.

Here we outline a set of alternative and explicitly visual ways of envisaging and analyzing at least simple formal systems using fractal patterns of infinite depth. Progressively deeper dimensions of such a fractal can be used to map increasingly complex wffs or increasingly complex 'value spaces', with tautologies, contradictions, and various forms of contingency coded in terms of color. This and related approaches, it turns out, offer not only visually immediate

and geometrically intriguing representations of formal systems as a whole but also promising formal links 1) between standard systems and classical patterns in fractal geometry, 2) between quite different kinds of value spaces in classical and infinite-valued logics, and 3) between cellular automata and logic. It is hoped that pattern analysis of this kind may open possibilities for a geometrical approach to further questions within logic and metalogic. (edited)

**Stachniak, Zbigniew**. An Essay on Resolution Logics. *Stud Log*, 52(2), 309-322, My 93.

This paper discusses the resolution principle in the context of nonclassical logics.

**Stachniak, Zbigniew**. Nonmonotonic Theories and Their Axiomatic Varieties. *J Log Lang Info*, 4(4), 317-334, 1995.

The properties of monotonic inference systems and the properties of their theories are strongly linked. These links, however, are much weaker in nonmonotonic inference systems. In this paper we introduce the notion of an *axiomatic variety for a theory* and show how this notion, instead of the notion of a theory, can be used for the syntactic and semantic analysis of nonmonotonic inferences.

**Stachniak, Zbigniew**. On Minimal Resolution Proof Systems for Resolution Logics. *Bull Sec Log*, 26(2), 94-101, Je 97.

**Stackhouse, Max L**. The Moral Meanings of Covenant. *Annu Soc Christ Ethics*, 249-264, 1996.

The idea of "covenant," derived from Biblical roots, has been developed not only by Jewish, but by both Catholic and Protestant theologians, jurists, and social theorists in ways that give ethical fiber to faith communities and to the complex institutions of modern civil societies. "Covenant" joins several modes of moral discourse in ways that support pluralism, constitutional democracy, and human right in a global era. This overview traces key moments and themes in the history of the development of the term and points out why its structural and systematic implications are finding renewed support in contemporary ethics.

**Stadler, Christian M**. Die Hegelsche Fichte-Kritik und ihre Berechtigung. *Prima Philosophia*, 9(4), 399-417, 1996.

This paper elaborates the major points of the critique, that was leveled by Hegel against the 1794 version. In addition the paper explains, that these arguments did not at all take into account the parallel authentic self-interpretation of Fichte and his *novo methodo*-version of 1798. Against the main point of Hegel must be contended that he failed to take the essential changes in Fichte's system-conceptions into account. So, if there is something like Hegel's critique at all, one must wonder, whether Fichte's system was ever seriously affected by it. (edited)

**Stadler, Holly A** and Morrissey, John M and Tucker, Joycelyn E. Nurses' Perspectives of Hospital Ethics Committees. *Bioethics Forum*, 10(4), 61-65, Fall 94.

The Midwest Bioethics Center (MBC) commissioned a survey of nurses' attitudes and needs regarding Hospital Ethics Committees (HECs) to guide its Ethics Committee Consortium. The survey examined three areas related to nurse utilization of and participation on HECs: 1) perception of HEC role and function; 2) perception of HEC case consultation function; 3) nurses' ethics training and continuing education. Important findings include nurses' reported lack of knowledge regarding HEC policies; a perception that their training in clinical ethics was inadequate; and a strong indication that HECs should be accessible to a wide range of health care professionals.

**Stadler, Ingrid**. *Contemporary Art and Its Philosophical Problems*. Amherst, Prometheus, 1987.

*Contemporary Art and Its Philosophical Problems* makes the often bewildering art world seem understandable, as it examines the complex intersection where art and philosophy merge. The author and co-authors reveal a growing disaffection with an "anything goes" attitude toward the arts as they explore fascinating topics such as the criticism of Robert Hughes and Tom Wolfe, a retrospective gaze at the Minimalist sculpture of the Sixties, an intensive look at the metaphysics of photography, the aesthetics of performance art and an appreciation of the modernist works of Jackson Pollack and the architecture of Mies van der Rohe. There is also a critical look at why women have been denied entrance to the pantheon of great artists. Stadler and her coauthors offer lively and far-ranging observations that cause readers to pause and reflect on their own potential for creative, imaginative and sensitive responsiveness to art and encourages discussion that can result in original opinions or judgments. Ingrid Stadler is a professor of philosophy at Wellesley College. (publisher, edited)

**Stahl, Jürgen**. System und Methode—Zur methodologischen Begründung transzendentalen Philosophierens in Fichtes *Begriffsschrift*. *Fichte-Studien*, 10, 99-113, 1997.

**Stainton, Robert J**. What Assertion Is Not. *Phil Stud*, 85(1), 57-73, Ja 97.

Dummett's *Frege: Philosophy of Language* introduces a specific analysis of assertion—an analysis which is convention based. According to this specific analysis, assertion consists in the saying of assertoric sentences under conventionally specified conditions. I argue that his proposal flies in the face of actual linguistic practice, in that nonsentences—not elliptical sentences, mind you, but *non*-sentences—can be used literally to assert. I then consider some implications of this fact for the debate between "conventionalists" and "intentionalists" in the philosophy of language.

**Staley, Kent W**. Novelty, Severity, and History in the Testing of Hypotheses: The Case of the Top Quark. *Proc Phil Sci Ass*, 3(Suppl), S248-S255, 1996.

It is sometimes held that facts confirm a hypothesis only if they were not used in the construction of that hypothesis. This requirement of "use novelty" introduces a historical aspect into the assessment of evidence claims. I examine a methodological principle invoked by physicists in the experimental search for the top quark that bears a striking resemblance to this view. However, this principle is better understood, both historically and philosophically, in terms of the need to conduct a severe test than in terms of use novelty. Nevertheless, a historical factor remains in the assessment of some evidence claims.

**Stalley, R F**. The Unity of the State: Plato, Aristotle and Proclus. *Polis*, 14(1-2), 129-149, 1995.

This consists of a translation of Proclus's 'Examination of the objections made by Aristotle in the second book of the *Politics* against Plato's *Republic*', together with an introduction and notes. In this short work Proclus aims to defend Plato against Aristotle's charge that he goes astray in regarding unity as the goal of politics. Proclus argues that, providing we understand properly what is meant by 'unity' in this context, we should indeed seek to make the state as much of a unity as possible. In making this point he commits himself to an unashamedly organic view of the state.

**Stalnaker, Robert**. "On a Defense of the Hegemony of Representation" in *Perception,* Villanueva, Enrique (ed), 101-108. Atascadero, Ridgeview, 1996.

**Stalnaker, Robert**. Knowledge, Belief and Counterfactual Reasoning in Games. *Econ Phil*, 12(1), 133-163, Ap 96.

**Stam, Henderikus J** and Scott, Campbell L. The Psychological Subject and Harré's Social Psychology: An Analysis of a Constructionist Case. *J Theor Soc Behav*, 26(4), 327-352, D 96.

Taking Ron Harré's social constructionism as a focus we point to and discuss the issue of the *a priori* psychological subject in social constructionist theory. While Harré indicates that interacting, intending beings are necessary for conversation to occur, he assumes that the primary human reality is conversation and that psychological life emerges from this social domain. Nevertheless, we argue that a fundamental and agentive psychological subject is implicit to his constructionist works. Our critical analyses focus upon Harré's understandings of persons, human development and human agency. Our intention is neither to suggest that this latent entity must be understood in a Cartesian sense nor it is to ask for an explicit account of an autonomous agent. Rather, our claim is simply that psychological subjectivity is reflexively entailed in Harré's human psychology. We suggest that this pertains more generally to social constructionist theory.

**Stamatescu, Ion-Olimpiu**. Bemerkungen über die gegenwärtige Arbeit im Bereich der Naturphilosophie an der FEST und über die *Philosophy-and-Physics-Workshops*. *Phil Natur*, 27(1), 1-7, 1990.

Studies in philosophy of nature and the dialog between natural sciences and philosophy have always been an important branch in the interdisciplinary activity of FEST. A new project in natural philosophy has been started here with the "Philosophy and Physics Workshops" which aim at establishing a frame for the dialog between physics and philosophy. In the present article the basic questions for inquiries in natural philosophy are reviewed, starting from the modern developments in physics and their epistemological implications and the project "Philosophy and Physics Workshops" is described (this project finalized in the book *Philosophy, Mathematics and Modern Physics*, E. Rudolph and I.-O. Stamatescu eds., Springer, Heidelberg 1994).

**Stamatescu, Ion-Olimpiu**. Who Needs Reality?. *Phil Natur*, 28(1), 4-11, 1991.

Some points of view concerning the question of a "reality hypothesis" are briefly reviewed and commented upon, from "naive" realism to positivism. Then the question is raised again as a *physical question*, that is as a question concerning the interpretation of a physical theory and which can be put and answered by a physical analysis—the so-called Einstein-Podolsky-Rosen problem—thereby making explicit the interpretation problems of quantum mechanics.

**Stambaugh, Joan** and Stambaugh, Joan (trans). *Being and Time: A Translation of Sein und Zeit.* Albany, SUNY Pr, 1996.

**Stambaugh, Joan** (trans) and Stambaugh, Joan. *Being and Time: A Translation of Sein und Zeit.* Albany, SUNY Pr, 1996.

**Stambovsky, Phillip**. *Myth and the Limits of Reason.* Amsterdam, Rodopi, 1996.

This book explores the ways modernists in philosophy and literature have used the depictive rationality of myth to disclose, in self-reflective ways, the limits of discursive sense-making in various domains of human experience. It illustrates four widely diverse examples of this critical form of mythical thinking in works by Kierkegaard, Unamuno, Henry James and Margaret Atwood. The inquiry moves from classical conceptualizations of myth in Xenophanes and Plato to modern rationalist myth theory in Malinowski, Lévi-Strauss, Cassirer, Ricoeur and Blumenberg. This critical study will be of interest to scholars of myth theory in philosophy, religion, literature, and cultural anthropology. (publisher)

**Stamer, Gerhard**. Irrationalität und kritisches Bewusstsein. *Z Phil Praxis*, 13-18, 1996.

**Stamm, Marcelo**. Prinzipien und System: Rezeptionsmodelle der Wissenschaftslehre Fichtes 1794. *Fichte-Studien*, 9, 215-240, 1997.

**Stamos, David N**. A New Theory on Philo's Reversal. *Int Stud Phil*, 29 (2), 73-94, 1997.

By examining the interplay between Cleanthes and Philo in Hume's *Dialogues* I develop the suggestion of Norman Kemp Smith and Antony Flew that Hume was a Stratonician atheist. Strato of Lampsacus held that all so-called divine power is to be sought in nature as nonconscious and nonpurposive. In furtherance of this interpretation I introduce a new concept into Hume studies to complement the widely accepted concept of *natural beliefs*, namely *natural ideas*. Natural ideas are ideas that naturally come to mind (e.g., seeing faces in the clouds) given certain stimuli, but which lack the force and vivacity commonly associated with beliefs. I argue that for Hume the fact of order and means-ends relationships in nature (i.e., design) is sufficient to produce only a *natural idea,D of God and that conventions (education, rituals, scriptures, etc.) are necessary to raise that idea to the level of a belief.*

**Stamps III, Arthur E**. Advances in Peer Review Research: an Introduction. *Sci Eng Ethics*, 3(1), 3-10, Ja 97.

Peer review is a topic of considerable concern to many researchers and there is a correspondingly large body of research on the topic. This issue of *Science and Engineering Ethics* presents recent work on peer review that is both grounded in empirical science and is applicable to policy decisions. This research raises two basic questions; a) how does current peer review operate, and b) how can it be improved? Topics addressed include descriptions of how peer review is used in federal agencies, whether peer review leads to better manuscripts, demographic characteristics of authors or reviewers (status or institutional affiliation), blinding of reviewers, authors, or results, reliability and consistency of reviews, accepting a paper before the study is done, simultaneous submission, and use of dispute resolution procedures such as scientific dialectical and pleading protocols.

**Stamps III, Arthur E**. Using a Dialectical Scientific Brief in Peer Review. *Sci Eng Ethics*, 3(1), 85-98, Ja 97.

This paper presents a framework that editors, peer reviewers, and authors can use to identify and resolve efficiently disputes that arise during peer review in scientific journals. The framework is called a scientific dialectical brief. In this framework, differences among authors and reviewers are formatted into specific assertions and the support each party provides for its position. A literature review suggests that scientists use five main types of support: empirical data, reasoning, speculation, feelings and status. It is suggested that the scientific dialectical brief format can streamline the review process by facilitating rapid differentiation between stronger and weaker support, so that valuable time can be focused on the better-substantiated claims. The paper concludes with some suggestions for implementation.

**Stanley, Jason**. Truth and Metatheory in Frege. *Pac Phil Quart*, 77(1), 45-70, Mr 96.

In this paper it is contended, against a challenging recent interpretation of Frege, that Frege should be credited with the first semirigorous formulation of semantic theory. It is argued that the considerations advanced against this contention suffer from two kinds of error. The first involves the attribution to Frege of a skeptical attitude towards the truth-predicate. The second involves the sort of justification which these arguments assume a classical semantic theory attempts to provide. Finally, it is shown that Frege was in fact mindful of the need for the relevant sort of justification.

**Stanley, M C**. A Non-Generic Real Incompatible with $0^{\#}$. *Annals Pure Applied Log*, 85(2), 157-192, My 97.

**Stapp, Henry P**. The Hard Problem: A Quantum Approach. *J Consciousness Stud*, 3(3), 194-210, 1996.

The function of consciousness in a quantum mechanical theory of mind-brain dynamics is described. The conscious events are the basic realities of the theory: they are what the theory is about. The brain constitutes a field of deterministically evolving tendencies for the occurrence of these conscious events, each of which chooses from among alternative courses of action evolved by the brain. The experiential qualities themselves play an essential role of specifying the allowed possibilities for the events: the physical brain qualities are inadequate for this task. It is explained how the consciously experienced 'I' directs the course of mind-brain events. The questions posed by Chalmers in connection with the hard problem are answered within this framework.

**Stark, Andrew**. Don't Change the Subject: Interpreting Public Discourse over Quid Pro Quo. *Bus Ethics Quart*, 7(3), 93-116, Jl 97.

A *quid pro quo* is an exchange of value between a citizen or group—often a business person or organization—and an official; what the citizen or group offers can take either monetary or nonmonetary form and what the official supplies, in return, is some kind of public act. Despite the fact that instances of *quid pro quo* seem continually to compel public attention, very few rise to the level of bribery; i.e., the level in which they are resolved judicially. In part, *quid pro quo* eludes judicial forums for factual reasons: It is difficult to prove. And in part, the reasons are normative: The distinction between objectionable *quid pro quo* and acceptable democratic norms—on which citizens and groups ought to be able to support officials who are in turn responsive to them—is difficult to draw. Hence, a great gray area of *quid pro quo* finds itself resolved (or at least debated) in political forums. (edited)

**Stark, Andrew**. Limousine Liberals, Welfare Conservatives: On Belief, Interest, and Inconsistency in Democratic Discourse. *Polit Theory*, 25(4), 475-501, Ag 97.

**Stark, Cynthia A**. The Words We Love to Hate. *Law Phil*, 16(1), 107-114, 97.

The book discusses some of the most incendiary current issues around freedom of speech, including sexual harassment, flag burning, obscenity, hate speech and campus speech codes. The author compares the framing of free speech issues in the U.S. and Canada and considers the implications of the liberal-communitarian debate for free speech controversies. The combination of moments of detailed analysis with moments of superficiality makes the book somewhat uneven. Yet the author provides, in places, insightful and level-headed analyses of particular cases.

**Stark, Tracey**. Richard Kearney's Hermeneutic Imagination. *Phil Soc Crit*, 23(2), 115-130, Mr 97.

This article argues that Richard Kearney's most recent work, *Poetics of Modernity* (1995), addresses one of the most important issues in contemporary continental philosophy, namely, the cleavage of ethics and poetics. Through his studies of nineteenth and twentieth century continental thinkers, Kearney addresses the responses of European philosophy to the separation and possible reconciliation of these two poles. By explicitly addressing the links between ethics and the imagination in both modern and postmodern continental thought, Kearney gets to the heart of one of the most important contemporary debates, that between ethics and aesthetics.

**Starmans, Richard J C M.** "Argument Based Reasoning: Some Remarks on the Relation Between Argumentation Theory and Artificial Intelligence" in *Logic and Argumentation,* Van Eemeren, Frans H (ed), 209-225. Amsterdam, North-Holland, 1994.

In this paper, the relation is discussed between modern argumentation theory and formal theories of commonsense reasoning as they have been developed in artificial intelligence. On the one hand, argumentation theory can benefit from the concepts of inference developed in nonmonotonic logics, since logic plays a major role in argumentation and new concepts of logic and inference have been developed. Conversely, artificial intelligence has much to learn from modern argumentation theory. For example, ideas from dialectics, debate and the legal field can be welcome contributions to the work in defeasible logic.

**Starobinski, Jean.** Sulla nostalgia: La memoria tormentata. *Iride,* 8(14), 160-177, Ap 95.

A brief history of the medical concept of nostalgia.

**State, Stanley.** Speculations on Cosmology & God. *Cont Phil,* 17(6), 25-29, N-D 95.

The intent of this paper is strictly speculative. It proposes to stretch the concept of a relatively new science, Chaos, into a theory of Cosmology. The three major approaches to the God problem: Theism, Pantheism and Atheism are briefly described. Atheism is rejected from consideration by its own definition. Theism and Pantheism are found to be compatible with most of the attributes associates with the God concept. However, these attributes are not all found to be comfortable with the cosmology based on the Chaos theory. A fourth approach to the God question, Pannaturalism, is suggested. Pannaturalism is compatible with only some of the attributes of God and all of these are comfortable with a cosmology based on Chaos theory. It is not suggested that Pannaturalism will be immediately acceptable as a solution to the modern God problem. It is not suggested that Pannaturalism will be immediately acceptable as a solution to the modern God problem. (edited)

**Statman, Daniel.** Hard Cases and Moral Dilemmas. *Law Phil,* 15(2), 117-148, 96.

The purpose of this paper is to draw attention to the close connection that obtains between the problem of moral dilemmas in moral philosophy, on the one hand, and that of hard cases, in legal philosophy, on the other. I assume that comparing these two problems and in particular comparing the arguments offered to solve each of them might serve to advance our understanding of both. I go through the main arguments for and against the reality of moral dilemmas and see what can be learned from them with respect to the issue of hard cases, and the other way round too—what arguments about hard cases can teach us with respect to moral dilemmas.

**Statman, Daniel.** Hypocrisy and Self-Deception. *Phil Psych,* 10(1), 57-75, Mr 97.

Hypocrites are generally regarded as morally-corrupt, cynical egoists who consciously and deliberately deceive others in order to further their own interests. The purpose of my essay is to present a different view. I argue that hypocrisy typically involves or leads to self-deception and, therefore, that real hypocrites are hard to find. One reason for this merging of hypocrisy into self-deception is that a consistent and conscious deception of society is self-defeating from the point of view of egotistical hypocrites. The best way for them to achieve their ends would be to believe in the deception, thereby not only deceiving others but also themselves. If my thesis is sound, we ought to be more cautious in ascribing hypocrisy to people, and less harsh in our attitude toward hypocrites.

**Statman, Daniel.** The Time to Punish and the Problem of Moral Luck. *J Applied Phil,* 14(2), 129-135, 1997.

Christopher New recently argued for the seemingly paradoxical idea that there is no moral reason not to punish someone before she commits her crime ('prepunishment'), provided that we can be sure that she will, in fact, commit the crime in the future. I argue that the air of paradox dissolves if we understand the possibility of prepunishment as relying on an anti-moral-luck position. However, New does not draw the full conclusions from such a position, which would allow prepunishment even prior to the formation of a wrongful intention, on the basis of the idea that bad character is enough to entail blameworthiness. I conclude by examining a legal system which seems to use the idea of prepunishment, i.e., the Talmudic idea that we might punish a child who has not yet sinned in order to save him from sinning in the future.

**Statman, Richard** and Pfenning, Frank and Narendran, Paliath. On the Unification Problem for Cartesian Closed Categories. *J Sym Log,* 62(2), 636-647, Je 97.

Cartesian closed categories (CCCs) have played and continue to play an important role in the study of the semantics of programming languages. An axiomatization of the isomorphisms which hold in all Cartesian closed categories discovered independently by Soloviev and Bruce, Di Cosmo and Longo leads to seven equalities. We show that the unification problem for this theory is undecidable, thus settling an open question. We also show that an important subcase, namely unification modulo the *linear isomorphisms,* is NP-complete. Furthermore, the problem of matching in CCCs is NP-complete when the subject term is irreducible. (edited)

**Stavrakakis, Yannis.** Ambiguous Democracy and the Ethics of Psychoanalysis. *Phil Soc Crit,* 23(2), 79-96, Mr 97.

It is one of the paradoxes of our age that the 'success' of democracy in Eastern Europe and South Africa is coupled with grave disappointment in the 'birth places' of modern democracy. This disappointment is partly due to the irreducible ambiguity entailed in democratic institutional arrangements. Democracy, in fact, is founded on this ambiguity. It attempts to construct social unity on the basis of recognizing the lack around which the social field is always structured. In that sense the source of the disappointment caused by democracy is of an ethical status. It is the antithesis between the ambiguity of democracy and a still hegemonic ethics of harmony. Any aspiration, however, to eliminate the ambiguity of democracy ignores the innovative logic of democratic politics. If the ethics of harmony lead to a "de-democratization" of democracy, what a radical democratic project needs today is an ethical basis of a totally different nature. Here, the ethics of psychoanalysis, as formulated in the Lacanian tradition, can be of great help.

**Steadman, Lyle B** and Palmer, Craig T. Myths as Instructions from Ancestors: The Example of Oedipus. *Zygon,* 32(3), 341-350, S 97.

This essay proposes that traditional stories, or myths, can be seen as a way in which ancestors influence their descendant-leaving success by influencing the behavior of many generations of their descendants. The myth of Oedipus is used as an example of a traditional story aimed at promoting proper behavior and cooperation among kin. This interpretation of the Oedipus myth is contrasted with Freudian and structuralist interpretations. (edited)

**Stecker, Robert** and Fuller, Gary and Adams, Frederick. The Semantics of Fictional Names. *Pac Phil Quart,* 78(2), 128-148, Je 97.

In this paper we defend a direct reference theory of names. We maintain that the meaning of a name is its bearer. In the case of vacuous names, there is no bearer and they have no meaning. We develop a unified theory of names such that one theory applies to names whether they occur within or outside fiction. Hence, we apply our theory to sentences containing names within fiction, sentences about fiction or sentences making comparisons across fictions. We then defend our theory against objections and compare our view to the views of Currie, Walton and others.

**Stecker, Robert A.** *Artworks: Definition, Meaning, Value.* University Park, Pennsylvania Univ Pr, 1997.

Stecker defines art (roughly) as an item that is an art work at time *t* if and only if it is in one of the central art forms at *t* and is intended to fulfill a function art has at *t,* or it is an artifact that achieves excellence in fulfilling such a function. Further, he sees the standard of acceptability for interpretations of art works to be relative to their aim. Finally, he tries to understand the value of art works through an analysis of literature and the identification of the most important functions of literary works. (edited)

**Stecker, Robert A.** The Constructivist's Dilemma. *J Aes Art Crit,* 55(1), 43-52, Wint 97.

**Stecker, Robert A.** Two Conceptions of Artistic Value. *Iyyun,* 46, 51-62, Ja 97.

**Stecker, Robert A.** What is Literature?. *Rev Int Phil,* 50(198), 681-694, 1996.

**Steedman, Carolyn.** About Ends: On the Way in Which the End is Different from an Ending. *Hist Human Sci,* 9(4), 99-114, N 96.

**Steel, Daniel.** Bayesianism and the Value of Diverse Evidence. *Phil Sci,* 63(4), 666-674, D 96.

In a recent essay (1995), Andrew Wayne charges that Bayesian attempts to account for the rule that, *ceteris paribus,* diverse evidence confirms better than narrow evidence are inadequate. I reply to these criticisms and argue that, on the contrary, one of the Bayesian approaches considered by Wayne does an excellent job of explaining why and under what circumstances, diverse evidence is valuable.

**Steel, J R** and Andretta, Alessandro. How to Win Some Simple Iteration Games. *Annals Pure Applied Log,* 83(2), 103-164, Ja 97.

**Steel, J R** and Schimmerling, E and Mitchell, William J. The Covering Lemma Up to a Woodin Cardinal. *Annals Pure Applied Log,* 84(2), 219-255, Mr 97.

It is proven that if there is no model with a Woodin cardinal and the Steel core model K exists, then the weak covering lemma holds at strong limit cardinals, that is, if lambda is a singular cardinal such that no smaller cardinal has lambda many countable subsets, then the successor of lambda is K is the same as the true successor of lambda.

**Steele, David Ramsay.** Between Immorality and Unfeasibility: The Market Socialist Predicament. *Crit Rev,* 10(3), 307-331, Sum 96.

The recent proliferation of economically informed writings favoring market socialism exhibits dissonances in this evolving theoretical orientation. The ethical presuppositions of classical socialism have often been inherited by those who now embrace markets under socialism. But precisely because it accepts markets, market socialism may prove incompatible with these sentiments.

**Steelwater, Eliza.** "Mead and Heidegger: Exploring the Ethics and Theory of Space, Place, and Environment" in *Philosophy and Geography I: Space, Place, and Environmental Ethics,* Light, Andrew (ed), 189-207. Lanham, Rowman & Littlefield, 1997.

This study examines the spatial ontologies of Mead and Heidegger. Independently, both abrogated Cartesian subject-object dichotomy and portrayed space as socially constructed. Their analyses provide a basis in which geographers and other environmental scholars can ground theoretically, ethically adequate definitions of "human-environment relationship." Mead supplied a model of social process that includes spatially. Heidegger in *Being and Time* raised the ethical issue of authenticity and showed that, in spite of the ambiguity of human Being as spatially situated, intractable ties to the environment coupled with the potential for moral self-interrogation supply the ontology of an environmental ethic.

**Steenbakkers, Piet**. Spinozistic Delusions (in Dutch). *Tijdschr Filosof*, 59(1), 107-125, Mr 97.

W.N.A. Klever's claim that he has discovered new Spinoza texts is unfounded in every respect. The seventeenth-century manuscript annotations in a copy of Spinoza's *Opera posthuma*, kept in Leiden University Library (self mark 755 F32), do not originate in the circle of Spinoza's friends, nor do they contain any material that derives from the philosopher himself. They are an intelligent reader's comments, and as such they constitute an important document of the immediate reception of Spinoza's philosophy. So far, the author has not been identified. It was certainly not Spinoza's correspondent E.W. von Tschirnhaus, and Klever's attempt to attribute the annotations to Tschirnhaus is a dismal failure: the four arguments adduced to substantiate this claim are altogether spurious.

**Stegmaier, Werner** and Krochmalnik, Daniel. *Jüdischer Nietzscheanismus*. Hawthorne, de Gruyter, 1997.

Der Nationalsozialismus hat in Vergessenheit geraten lassen, dass es zum grossen Teil jüdische Intellektuelle waren, die sich zuerst für Nietzsche begeisterten; mit ihnen begann die Nietzsche-Rezeption überhaupt. Nietzsche hatte, gegen den verbreiteten Antisemitismus seiner Zeit, das Judentum hoch geschätzt, und viele Juden schätzten ihn dafür hoch. Sie erwarteten von seinem Denken starke Anstösse für die Erneuerung des Judentums selbst. Unter dem Begriff "Jüdischer Nietzscheanismus" werden jüdische Intellektuelle zusammengefasst, die sich mit Nietzsche im Blick auf ihr Judentum auseinandersetzten, von 1888 an bis zur Gegenwart. Der Band legt dabei das Schwergewicht auf die philosophische Auseinandersetzung mit Nietzsche.

**Steidlmeier, Paul**. Business Ethics and Politics in China. *Bus Ethics Quart*, 7(3), 131-143, Jl 97.

Business ethics in China is highly politicized, both within China as well as on the global scene. Over the past years many issues of business ethics have arisen. It turns out that the Chinese often have a different set of ethical priorities with respect to the economy than do their Western counterparts. China possesses rich and well-developed ethical traditions that provide a meaningful basis for evaluating its own problems. This article reviews China's ethical heritage, and at the same time, takes note of Western ethical concerns of human rights, property and so forth that have been injected into the debate. (edited)

**Steiger, Kornél**. Fragments from *Timon of Phleius* & Diogenes Laertius on Timon of Phleius (in Hungarian). *Magyar Filozof Szemle*, 1-2, 217-241, 1997.

**Steiger, Kornél**. Timon of Phleius and the *Silloi* (in Czech). *Magyar Filozof Szemle*, 1-2, 77-91, 1997.

Wenn man die doxographischen Quellen der *Fragmente der Vorsokratiker* betrachtet, findet man einen etwa zweihundert Jahre langen Hiatus zwischen Theophrastos (370-286) und Cicero (106-43). In demselben Zeitalter 3-2.Jh.) wurden die erheblichsten Biographien der vorsokratischen Philosophen geschrieben. Diese Umstände weisen darauf hin, dass der frühe Hellenismus sich nicht für die Lehre, sondern für die Figur der Vorsokratikern interessierte. Wir begegnen dieser Art der Rezeption in der fragmentarisch erhaltenen *Silloi* des Timon von Phleius. (edited)

**Steigerwald, Diane**. L'apport avicennien à la cosmologie à la lumière de la critique d'al-Shahrastānī. *Laval Theol Phil*, 52(3), 735-759, O 96.

This article tries to show that Avicenna was influenced by the Greeks for the elaboration of his cosmology and, in metaphysics, by al-Shahrastānī and Averroes, whose critical analyses enabled him to clarify certain problems in his conception of God, his division of being and his theory of creation.

**Steigleder, Klaus**. Gewirth und die Begründung der normativen Ethik. *Z Phil Forsch*, 51(2), 251-267, Ap-Je 97.

The aim of the paper is to show that Alan Gewirth's justification of a supreme moral principle is successful. The focus is on the highly disputed transition from necessary goods to necessary right claims. A reconstruction of the argument as a direct sequence of necessary judgments is offered. It is shown that the normative claims are not semantically entailed in the agent's judgment about necessary goods. But there is a necessary building up of normative claims in view of the agent's own vulnerability and of the dependence of her necessary goods on the conduct of the other agents.

**Stein, Christian**. Walker on the Voluntariness of Judgment. *Inquiry*, 40(2), 175-186, Je 97.

In this paper, "The Voluntariness of Judgment" Mark Thomas Walker claims that judgments are voluntary acts. According to Walker, theoretical reasoning can be seen as an instance of practical reasoning, and the outcomes of practical reasoning are actions. There are two reasons why Walker's argument does not establish this conclusion: i) There are nonreflective judgments which cannot reasonably be described as instances of practical reasoning; Walker's argument does not apply to these judgments. ii) If one judges that *p* as a result of deliberation, one has had no choice sincerely to judge as well that non-*p* instead of *p*, that is, one cannot judge contrary to one's evidence. Therefore, reflective judgements are not voluntary actions. Walker cannot show that reflective judgments are voluntary, because he fails to give a clear notion of voluntary action and the role of choice.

**Stein, Christian** and Müller, Vincent C. "Epistemic Theories of Truth: The Justifiability Paradox Investigated" in *Verdad: lógica, representación y mundo*, Villegas Forero, L, 95-104. Santiago de Compostela, Univ Santiago Comp, 1996.

Epistemic theories of truth, such as those presumed to be typical for antirealism, can be characterized as saying that what is true can be known in principle. Analysis of the nature of the paradox shows that such statements refute epistemic theories of truth only if the antirealist motivation for epistemic theories of truth is not taken into account. The motivation in a link of understandability and meaningfulness suggests to change the above principle and to restrict the theory to logically simple sentences, in which case the paradox does not arise. This suggestion also allows to see the deep philosophical problems for antirealism those counterexamples are pointing at. (edited)

**Stein, Edward**. Can We Be Justified in Believing that Humans Are Irrational?. *Phil Phenomenol Res*, 57(3), 545-565, S 97.

In this paper, the author considers an argument against the thesis that humans are irrational in the sense that we reason according to principles that differ from those we ought to follow. The argument begins by noting that if humans are irrational, we should not trust the results of our reasoning processes. If we are justified in believing that humans are irrational, then, since this belief results from a reasoning process, we should not accept this belief. The claim that humans are irrational is, thus, self-undermining. The author shows that this argument—and others like it—fails for several interesting reasons, in fact, there is nothing self-undermining about the claim that humans are irrational; empirical research to establish this claim does not face the sorts of a priori problems that some philosophers and psychologists have claimed it does.

**Stein, Edward** and Schüklenk, Udo and Kerin, Jacinta (& others). The Ethics of Genetic Research on Sexual Orientation. *Hastings Center Rep*, 27(4), 6-13, Jl-Ag 97.

Research into the genetic component of some complex behaviors often causes controversy, depending on the social meaning and significance of the behavior. Research into sexual orientation—simplistically referred to as "gay gene" research—is an example of research that provokes intense controversy. This research is worrisome for many reasons, including a long history of abuse against homosexuals. But there are other reasons to worry. The very motivation for seeking an "origin" of homosexuality reveals homophobia. Moreover, such research may lead to prenatal tests that claim to predict for homosexuality.

**Stein, Klaus**. Fichte, Schlegel, Nietzsche und die Moderne. *Fichte-Studien*, 13, 1-19, 1997.

**Stein, Stephen J** (ed). *Jonathan Edwards's Writings*: Text, Context, Interpretation. Bloomington, Indiana Univ Pr, 1996.

This collection of essays presents groundbreaking contemporary scholarship on the writings of the eighteenth-century American philosopher and theologian Jonathan Edwards. These essays range widely across the Edwardsian canon, including his most prominent and important published texts—*Religious Affections* and *The Nature of True Virtue*—as well as unfamiliar and unpublished treatises and sermons. They measure Edwards against significant Western religious and philosophical figures including Solomon Stoddard, Thomas Shepard, George Berkeley, and William James. The current debate concerning the nineteenth-century Edwardsian tradition is also featured in essays which show prominent American evangelicals, such as Nathanial William Taylor, Charles Grandison Finney, and Edwards Amasa Park, competing for the mantle of Edwards. A compact survey of current Edwards scholarship, this book engages the full range of Edwards's writings and shows their central importance for the history of American religion and culture. (publisher)

**Steinberg, Jonny**. The Burdens of Berlin's Modernity. *Hist Euro Ideas*, 22(5-6), 369-383, S-N 96.

**Steinberger, Peter J**. Was Socrates Guilty as Charged? *Apology* 24c-28a. *Ancient Phil*, 17(2), 13-29, Spr 97.

Reeve and Brickhouse/Smith agree that Socrates' arguments in the *Apology* are by no means as bad as has been traditionally thought; and they agree as well that the actual legal claims against Socrates were, at best, questionable. They suggest, therefore, that Socrates' defense against Meletus's indictment is intellectually sound and legally compelling and that his conviction was, therefore, a miscarriage of justice. I believe that this position, though argued with great care and acumen, cannot be sustained. Indeed, while Reeve and Brickhouse/Smith successfully and importantly criticize major features of the traditional interpretation of the *Apology*, the implications of their criticism seem to me quite different from what they themselves indicate.

**Steinberger, Peter J**. Who is Cephalus?. *Polit Theory*, 24(2), 172-199, My 96.

The treatment of Cephalus in Plato's *Republic* may be understood in terms of three distinct though not incompatible perspectives of a psychological, political and ethical nature. These perspectives reflect a diversity of important themes that resonate throughout the *Republic* and that lend the work a distinctive kind of aesthetic and argumentative unity. They also reflect certain important ideas and events external to the dialogue itself, hence characterize some of the relevant circumstances in which it was composed. By situating the problem of Cephalus within the larger parameters of text and context, we can better understand not only the meaning and function of the opening pages of the *Republic* but also the larger claims of the work in its entirety.

**Steinbock, Anthony J**. Back to the Things Themselves: Introduction. *Human Stud*, 20(2), 127-135, Ap 97.

**Steinbock, Anthony J**. The Origins and Crisis of Continental Philosophy. *Man World*, 30(2), 199-215, Ap 97.

When contemporary continental philosophy dismisses, with the discourse of postmodernism, the role of origin, teleology, foundation, etc., it is forsaking its

AUTHOR INDEX 935 Stephens, Christopher

own style of thinking and as a consequence is no longer able to discern crises of lived-meaning or to engage in the transformation of historical life. I address this crisis by characterizing continental philosophy as a particular style of thinking, generative thinking. I then examine the meaning and origins of philosophical thinking by drawing, for strategic reasons, on Jacques Derrida's essay "Cogito et histoire de la folie." For not only has the very question of "origins" come under fire through various postmodern readings of Derrida, but Derrida's own point of critique concerning Western metaphysics depends upon a specific understanding of origin that I call origin-originating. In the final section of this paper, I interpret the crisis within the generative structure of experience.

**Steiner, Daniel**. Competing Interests: The Need to Control Conflict of Interests in Biomedical Research. *Sci Eng Ethics*, 2(4), 457-468, O 96.

Individual and institutional conflict of interests in biomedical research have become matters of increasing concern in recent years. In the United States, the growth in relationships ™ sponsored research agreements, consultancies, memberships on boards, licensing agreements, and equity ownership ™ between for-profit corporations and research universities and their scientists has made the problem of conflicts, particularly financial conflicts, more acute. Conflicts can interfere with or compromise important principles and obligations of researchers and their institutions, e.g., adherence to accepted research norms, duty of care to patients, and open exchange of information. Disclosure is a key component of a successful conflict policy. Commitments which conflict with a faculty member's primary obligations to teaching, research, administrative responsibilities, or patient care also need attention. Institutional conflict of interests present different problems, some of which are discussed in an analysis of an actual problem posed by two proposed clinical trials.

**Steiner, Gary**. This Project is Mad: Descartes, Derrida, and the Notion of Philosophical Crisis. *Man World*, 30(2), 179-198, Ap 97.

In "Cogito and the History of Madness," Derrida maintains that crisis is endemic to philosophy rather than being, as Husserl forcefully argued, a temporary condition that can and must be overcome through the resources of reason. A reflection on the place of madness in Descartes's *Meditations* serves as the point of departure for demonstrating that Derrida has done an injustice to philosophy; and a comparison of Derrida's views with the thought of Husserl, Heidegger, and Nietzsche reveals that Derrida's position in "Cogito and the History of Madness" entails a sacrifice of the notion of responsibility that lies at the center of meaningful historical action.

**Steiner, Mark**. The Function of Ignorance in Scientific Discovery (in Hebrew). *Iyyun*, 45, 461-462, O 96.

Often the symmetries of nature are broken by perturbing forces. Discovery of the symmetries is therefore often dependent on our ignorance of these perturbing forces, an ignorance which enables us to see the "forest" rather than the "trees." As an example, had Newton taken account of the deviation of the actual planetary motions from Kepler's laws, he might never have discovered the symmetry embodied in his law of gravitation. Another example: the so-called "missing lines" of the hydrogen spectrum suggested to Bohr a new symmetry of nature. We are fortunate, then, that the human eye cannot detect the lines, which are actually not missing at all, only too faint to see. Thus, the shortcomings of the human race turn out in these cases actually to be assets.

**Steinhoff, Uwe**. Truth vs Rorty. *Phil Quart*, 47(188), 358-361, Jl 97.

**Steinitz, Yuval**. Kant, Frege, and the Ontological Proof (in Hebrew). *Iyyun*, 46, 155-166, Ap 97.

**Steinle, Friedrich**. Was ist Masse? Newtons Begriff der Materiemenge. *Phil Natur*, 29(1), 94-117, 1992.

In the paper I analyze Newton's concept of mass in his *Principia*. The focus is on how he actually makes use of the concept. The well-known problems of Newton's Definition I arise from his not clearly separating two different ideas: a dynamic idea of inertia and a specific notion of matter. I trace back the question to Newton's early manuscripts, in particular to his "de gravitatione..." in which he for the first time develops his mechanical concepts in a systematic manner. The roots of the later confusion lie in his metaphysical considerations, developed in explicit struggle with Cartesian concepts.

**Stekeler-Weithofer, Pirmin**. "Zu einer Interpretation von Platons Dialog "Parmenides" in *Das weite Spektrum der analytischen Philosophie,* Lenzen, Wolfgang, 346-363. Hawthorne, de Gruyter, 1997.

The main problem of the second part of Plato's *Parmenides* concerns the (logico-linguistic) process of nominalization by which we transform predicates into names of unified entities. By this process, Parmenides' own assumption that 'the one is' (almost ironically) leads to the consequence that the expressions "the one" and "existing" name different entities making a sentence like "manifold exists" true as well. Some implicit results are: a sentence of the form "N is P" cannot be read as "The N is the P" and sentences like "the one is" and "many are" only seem to contradict each other.

**Stekeler-Weithofer, Pirmin**. Hegel's Logic as a Theory of Meaning. *Phil Invest*, 19(4), 287-307, O 96.

The concepts of truth, reference and meaning depend heavily on accepted frameworks of representation. Hegel distinguishes in his "Science of Logic" different levels: The 'logic of being' analyses basis forms of our talk about perceptible and abstract things, sets, and other quantities. The 'logic of essence' shows what it means to claim that statements presented in a given form of representation (like, for example, in 'mythology' or 'folk psychology') are 'superficial' and that 'new' theories explain how things 'really' are. According to the 'logic of concept', knowledge, like any human institution, is relative to the 'contemporal' situation of cultural development.

**Stell, Lance K**. The Blessings of Injustice: Animals and the Right to Accept Medical Treatment. *Between Species*, 11(1-2), 42-53, Wint-Spr 95.

On principle, animal advocates oppose meat-eating and experimenting on animals in biomedical research. They argue that it is impermissible routinely to purchase and consume meat despite that one may have had no hand in the killing and suffering of the animals one would be eating, because is so doing, one would be supporting as well as benefitting from unjust socio-economic practices. Similarly, it is argued that it is wrong routinely to experiment on animals for purposes of gaining knowledge or for developing medical products and techniques. The question arises: what are the practical implications of animal advocates' principles for the permissibility of routinely consuming medical products and indeed, for having insurance to defray the expectable expenses involved? Remarkably, animal advocates have been silent on this question. Peter Singer's and Tom Regan's views are analyzed with an eye toward inferring their answers. It is argued that each must take the same position on the consumption of medical products as he takes on vegetarianism.

**Stellingwerff, J**. Onverenigbaarheid en evolutie-werkelijkheid. *Phil Reform*, 62(1), 75-98, 1997.

**Stelzner, Werner**. "Bestätigung und Relevanz" in *Das weite Spektrum der analytischen Philosophie,* Lenzen, Wolfgang, 364-382. Hawthorne, de Gruyter, 1997.

In the paper is shown that the lack of relevance connected with the Hempelian-like notions of deductive and reductive confirmation and their development given by Kutschera and Lenzen is not so much caused by these notions, but by the presupposed classical entailment relations. There are introduced different premise and conclusion relevant entailment relations, which are suitable for deductive and reductive confirmation. All these relations are closed under the fulfillment conditions that every partial fulfillment of the premises is a partial fulfillment of the conclusion (premise relevance) and vice versa (conclusion relevance).

**Stemich Huber, Martina**. *Heraklit: Der Werdegang des Weisen.* Amsterdam, J Benjamins, 1996.

This is a study of selected fragments of the writings of Heraclitus with emphasis on his understanding of philosophy as the search for wisdom. The author demonstrates how Heraclitus gives guidelines for practicing philosophy: ethical advice as well as instructions on how to become a wise man. Putting together relevant passages that have come down to us in the fragments, we can see how he taught the individual to look for the *logos* within and through that search, to attain the cosmic *logos* that governs reality. We can see that for Heraclitus philosophy meant starting from a new point of view. He did not create a new cosmology, however, but a new vision of the cosmos using a changed standpoint. In the context of the Ionian philosophy of nature, Heraclitus' search for the cosmic *logos* through one's inner *logos* represents an innovation.

**Stemmer, Peter**. Gutsein. *Z Phil Forsch*, 51(1), 65-92, Ja-Mr 97.

One of the major trends within the metaethics supposes that to say something is good means: it is *worthy* of desire, *worthy* of recommendation or *worthy* of preference, i.e., it is *right, rational* to have the respective proattitude, and that one *ought* to have this attitude. This thesis is proved with the result that it is incorrect. In the center of the inquiry there is particularly the thesis that "good" means "worthy of preference" and the claim implied by it that "good" has an implicitly comparative meaning and means "better than." Finally, the critical arguments are contracted to the positive result that who characterizes something as good says the thing in question has the descriptive properties by which it meets an underlying rational desire. (edited)

**Steneck, Nicholas H**. Role of the Institutional Animal Care and Use Committee in Monitoring Research. *Ethics Behavior*, 7(2), 173-184, 1997.

During the 1980s, federal regulations transferred significant portions of the responsibility for monitoring the care and use of research animals from animal care programs to Institutional Animal Care and Use Committees (IACUCs). After a brief review of the history of the regulation of the use of animals in research preceding and during the four decades following World War II, this article raises four problems associated with the role IACUCs currently play in monitoring the use of animals in research. (edited)

**Stenmark, Mikael**. What is Scientism?. *Relig Stud*, 33(1), 15-32, Mr 97.

In this article I try to define more precisely what scientism is and how it is related to a traditional religion such as Christianity. By first examining the writings of a number of contemporary natural scientists (Francis Crick, Richard Dawkins, Stephen Hawking, Carl Sagan and Edward O. Wilson), I show that the concept can be given numerous different meanings. I propose and defend a distinction between epistemic, rationalistic, ontological, axiological and redemptive scientism and it is also explained why we should not directly identify scientism with scientific materialism or scientific naturalism.

**Stenning, Keith**. "Embedding Logic in Communication: Lessons from the Logic Classroom" in *Logic and Argumentation,* Van Eemeren, Frans H (ed), 227-240. Amsterdam, North-Holland, 1994.

In this paper, a fresh approach is proposed to the tension between language as a formal structure and language as a social practice. Learning elementary logic can improve reasoning skills and therefore to characterise what it is that is being learnt in elementary logic classes can help to characterise what argumentation is and what relation it bears to logical theory.

**Stephens, Christopher**. Modelling Reciprocal Altruism. *Brit J Phil Sci*, 47(4), 533-551, D 96.

Biologists rely extensively on the iterated Prisoner's Dilemma game to model reciprocal altruism. After examining the informal conditions necessary for reciprocal altruism, I argue that formal games besides the standard iterated Prisoner's Dilemma meet these conditions. One alternate representation, the *modified* Prisoner's Dilemma game, removes a standard but unnecessary condition; the other game is what I call a *Cook's Dilemma.* We should explore these new models of reciprocal altruism because they predict different stability characteristics for various strategies; for instance, I show that strategies such as *Tit-for-Tat* have different stability dynamics in these alternate models. (edited)

**Stephens, William O**. Five Arguments for Vegetarianism. *Phil Cont World*, 1(4), 25-39, Wint 94.

Five different arguments for vegetarianism are discussed: the system of meat production deprives poor people of food to provide meat for the wealthy, thus violating the principle of distributive justice; the world livestock industry causes great and manifold ecological destruction; meat-eating cultures and societal oppression of women are intimately linked and so feminism and vegetarianism must both be embraced to transform our patriarchal culture; both utilitarian and rights-based reasoning lead to the conclusion that raising and slaughtering animals is immoral and so we ought to boycott meat; meat consumption causes many serious diseases and lowers life expectancy and so is unhealthy. Objections to each argument are examined. The conclusion reached is that the cumulative case successfully establishes vegetarianism as a virtuous goal.

**Stephens, William O** (trans) and Bonhöffer, Adolf Friedrich. *The Ethics of the Stoic Epictetus: An English Translation*. New York, Lang, 1996.

This work remains the most systematic and detailed study of Epictetus's ethics. The basis, content, and acquisition of virtue are methodically described, while important related points in Stoic ethics are discussed in an extensive appendix. Epictetus is compared throughout with the other late Stoics (Seneca, Marcus Aurelius), Cicero, the early Stoics (Zeno, Cleanthes, Chrysippus), and Christian moral thought. This approach shows that Stoic ethics continues to have great practical and pedagogical value. (publisher,edited)

**Stephenson, Wendell**. The Love of God and Neighbor in Simone Weil's Philosophy. *J Phil Res*, 22, 461-476, Ap 97.

Simone Weil recognized that there is a problem reconciling the love of God/good with the love of neighbor, and she probably believed that she never successfully resolved it. A quotation from her "New York Notebook" sets the problem nicely: "Only God is the good, therefore, only He is a worthy object of care, solicitude, anxiety, longing, and efforts of thought. Only He is a worthy object of all those movements of the soul which are related to some value." From this and other quotes, I construct various arguments showing that one cannot consistently both love God and one's neighbor. The bulk of the paper is taken up with a critical consideration of these arguments. The upshot of this is that there is no plausible way to reject all of these arguments; hence one must tentatively conclude that the love of God/good is irreconcilable with the love of neighbor in Weil's philosophy.

**Sterba, James P**. Progress in Reconciliation: Evidence from the Right and the Left. *J Soc Phil*, 28(2), 101-116, Fall 97.

**Sterba, James P**. Reconciliation Reaffirmed: A Reply to Steverson. *Environ Values*, 5(4), 363-368, N 96.

In this reply to Brian Steverson's objections to my reconciliationist argument, I have clarified the requirements that follow from my principles of environmental justice. I have also clarified the notion of intrinsic value that I am endorsing and the grounds on which my claim of greater intrinsic value for humans rests.

**Sterelny, Kim**. "Basic Minds" in *AI, Connectionism and Philosophical Psychology, 1995*, Tomberlin, James E (ed), 251-270. Atascadero, Ridgeview, 1995.

This paper has three main aims. First, it explains the distinction between organisms that merely respond to their environment and those whose behaviour is determined by their representations of that environment. The paper defends the idea that multiply ways of tracking a feature of the environment is the crucial difference between merely reactive organisms and those that represent their world. Second, within the class of representational systems, the paper explores the differences between subintentional organisms and intentional agents. Third, the paper uses the distinction between intentional and subintentional systems to analyse an important contemporary debate in the cognitive ethology literature, the "social intelligence hypothesis" and the associated idea that the higher primates represent not just their physical environment but also their social partners' representations of that environment; i.e., they have thoughts about thoughts. The paper argues that in the debate on this metarepresentational hypothesis, plausible intermediate positions have been overlooked.

**Sterelny, Kim**. Navigating the Social World: Simulation Versus Theory. *Phil Books*, 38(1), 11-29, Ja 97.

This is a critical notice of the two Davies and Stone collections, *Folk Psychology* and *Mental Simulation*. I defend a hybrid theory of our capacity to predict and explain the behaviour of human agents. I argue that the theory is in trouble on modularity. In many ways our capacity to predict and explain others has the classic features of a modular system, but in other and critical ways it cannot be modular. For the capacity to track other's behaviour is not one that an encapsulated mechanism could do with any reliability. (edited)

**Sterelny, Kim**. The Return of the Group. *Phil Sci*, 63(4), 562-584, D 96.

This paper discusses the recent revival of group selection within evolutionary theory. That revival depends on the ideas of "trait group" selection and the clearly seeing group selection as a theory of the vehicles of selection rather than evolutionary replicators. I discuss the response that group selection so understood is equivalent to "broad individualism", a version of organism-level selection which emphasizes the importance of an organism's social environment. I argue that the group selection debate has conflated two cases. For one of these, "population-structured selection", trait group selection and broad individualism are indeed equivalent. But population structured selection sometimes creates the preconditions for the evolution of high level vehicles. The paper concludes with some ideas about the nature of these high level vehicles and the circumstances in which they evolve.

**Stern, David G**. "Heidegger and Wittgenstein on the Subject of Kantian Philosophy" in *Figuring the Self: Subject, Absolute, and Others in Classical German Philosophy*, Zöller, Günter (ed), 245-259. Albany, SUNY Pr, 1997.

Kant's Copernican revolution left subsequent philosophers with the task of evaluating how much of his conception of the self as actively structuring our knowledge of the world should be retained. This paper explores the remarkably similar reasons that the early Heidegger and the later Wittgenstein give for rejecting Kant's conception of the subject of philosophy. I conclude that while neither is an orthodox Kantian, they do retain his fundamental insight into the role of human activity in structuring our knowledge of the world and so continue the "critical tradition" that Kant inaugurated.

**Stern, David G**. "The Availability of Wittgenstein's Philosophy" in *The Cambridge Companion to Wittgenstein*, Sluga, Hans (ed), 442-476. Needham Heights, Cambridge, 1996.

A discussion of the relationship between Wittgenstein's published work and the Wittgenstein papers which argues that attention to the way in which he wrote can cast light on the nature of his contribution to philosophy. Special attention is given to the editorial problems posed by Wittgenstein's repeated revision and rewriting of his remarks and the work on a complete electronic edition of his papers. Because the Wittgenstein papers are the product of such an extensive act of rewriting, they are not so much a collection of texts as a hypertext, an interconnected network of remarks.

**Stern, David G** (ed) and Sluga, Hans (ed). *The Cambridge Companion to Wittgenstein*. Needham Heights, Cambridge, 1996.

The essays in this volume address central themes in Wittgenstein's writings on the philosophy of mind, language, logic, and mathematics. They chart the development of his work and clarify the connections between its different stages. The authors illuminate the character of the whole body of work by keeping a tight focus on some key topics: the style of the philosophy, the conception of grammar contained in it, rule-following, convention, logical necessity, the self, and what Wittgenstein called in a famous phrase, "forms of life." An important final essay offers a fundamental reassessment of the status of the many posthumously published texts. (edited)

**Stern, Laurent**. Georg Lukács—A Spiritual Portrait (in Hungarian). *Magyar Filozof Szemle*, 4-5-6, 545-557, 1996.

This paper is the Hungarian translation of "Georg Lukács: An Intellectual Portrait," *Dissent*, Vol. V, pp. 162-73, 1958. It attempts to show the development of Lukács's intellectual views and of his political choices from his earliest essays to his last books.

**Stern-Gillet, Suzanne**. Plotinus and his Portrait. *Brit J Aes*, 37(3), 211-225, Jl 97.

**Sternstein, Wolfgang**. The Greens and the Lust for Power. *Acorn*, 5-2 &(6-1), 24-26, S 90 - Mr 91.

**Steup, Matthias**. Tidman On Critical Reflection. *Analysis*, 56(4), 277-281, O 96.

According to Paul Tidman, critical reflection can, under certain circumstances, mislead rational agents into thinking that they are justified in believing that p when in fact they are not. In this paper, I argue that the examples he describes for the purpose of supporting this claim are not conclusive and thus do not effectively undermine the view that, as long as their rational powers are unimpaired, rational agents can always find out, through critical reflection, whether they are, or would be, justified in believing that p.

**Steup, Matthias**. William Alston, *Perceiving God: The Epistemology of Religious Experience*. *Nous*, 31(3), 408-420, S 97.

In this critical study, I first present a synopsis of Alston's *Perceiving God*. In this book, Alston attempts to show that mystical perception is a source of epistemic justification for beliefs about God. His main claim is that, if sense perception in general and mystical perception in particular, take the form of an appropriately qualified doxastic practice, they can, respectively, justify sensory beliefs and beliefs about God. In the study's critical part, I raise doubts about Alston's strategy of deriving conclusions about the epistemic status of beliefs formed in a given doxastic practice from premises that ascribe rationality to that practice.

**Steutel, Jan**. On Emotion and Rationality: A Response to Barrett. *J Moral Educ*, 25(4), 395-400, D 96.

In a recent paper Richard Barrett criticizes Solomon (and the so-called cognitivists in general) for dismissing irrational emotions as marginal and atypical. This paper argues that Barrett's criticism is unwarranted. Two explanations are suggested for his misconception of Solomon's view (and, more generally, of the cognitive view) on irrational emotions. First, Barrett mistakenly conceives the reconciliation of emotion and reason as a conciliation of emotion and rationality in an evaluative or normative sense. Secondly, Barrett disregards the difference between the cognitive conception of (ir)rationality and his own definition of (ir)rationality in terms of coping. Some implications of the argument for the education of (moral) emotions are spelled out.

**Steutel, Jan** and Spiecker, Ben. "Good Sex as the Aim of Sexual Education" in *Philosophy of Education (1996)*, Margonis, Frank (ed), 400-407. Urbana, Phil Education Soc, 1997.

This paper argues that sexual education should not be reduced to (an aspect of) moral education. Equally important are aims that relate to nonmorally good sex (i.e., sex that is satisfying or enjoyable) and the relative value of sex in a nonmorally good life. The nature of and the differences between these moral and nonmoral aims of sexual education are explained and some remarks are made on the central differences between the educational ways to achieve those aims.

**Steutel, Jan** and Spiecker, Ben. Paedophilia, Sexual Desire and Perversity. *J Moral Educ*, 26(3), 331-342, S 97.

In our society adults who are guilty of having sex with prepubescent children often have a paedophile disposition. This paper first criticizes the justifications that are given by paedophiles for having sex with children. Part of this criticism is a brief analysis of "sexual desire" and "erotic". Next, the question is raised whether paedophile activities can ever be morally permissible. Using the principles of mutual consent and nonexploitation as touchstone, the question is answered in the negative. Finally, it is examined whether paedophile desires can be regarded as perverse. In order to deal with this issue a moral conception of perversion is proposed.

**Steutel, Jan** and Spiecker, Ben. Rational Passions and Intellectual Virtues: A Conceptual Analysis. *Stud Phil Educ*, 16(1-2), 59-71, Ja-Ap 97.

Intellectual virtues, like open-mindedness, clarity, intellectual honesty and the willingness to participate in rational discussions, are conceived as important aims of education. In this paper an attempt is made to clarify the specific nature of intellectual virtues. Firstly, the intellectual virtues are systematically compared with more virtues. The upshot is that considering a trait of character to be an intellectual virtue implies assuming that such a trait can be derived from, or is a specification of, the cardinal virtue of concern and respect for truth. Secondly, several (possible) misconceptions of intellectual virtues are avoided by making the required distinctions. For example, it is argued that our concept of an intellectual virtue should not be confused with a normative conception of intellectual virtuousness.

**Stevens, Jacqueline**. The Reasonableness of John Locke's Majority: Property Rights, Consent, and Resistance in the *Second Treatise*. *Polit Theory*, 24(3), 423-463, Ag 96.

**Stevens, Kevin T** and Thorley Hill, Nancy and Eynon, Gail. Factors that Influence the Moral Reasoning Abilities of Accountants: Implications for Universities and the Profession. *J Bus Ethics*, 16(12-13), 1297-1309, S 97.

The need to maintain the public trust in the integrity of the accounting profession has led to increased interest in research that examines the moral reasoning abilities (MRA) of Certified Public Accountants (CPAs). This study examines the MRA of CPAs practicing in small firms or as sole practitioners and the factors that affect MRA throughout their working careers. (edited)

**Stevenson, G W** and Hendrickson, John and Kloppenburg, Jr, Jack. Coming in to the Foodshed. *Agr Human Values*, 13(3), 33-42, Sum 96.

Bioregionalists have championed the utility of the concept of the watershed as an organizing framework for thought and action directed to understanding and implementing appropriate and respectful human interaction with particular pieces of land. In a creative analogue to the watershed, permaculturist Arthur Getz has recently introduced the term "foodshed" to facilitate critical thought about where our food is coming from and how it is getting to us. We find the "foodshed" to be a particularly rich and evocative metaphor; but it is much more than metaphor. Like its analogue the watershed, the foodshed can serve us as a conceptual and methodological unit of analysis that provides a frame for action as well as thought. (edited)

**Stevenson, Leslie F**. The Chance of a Singular Event?. *Philosophy*, 72(280), 312-316, Ap 97.

**Steverson, Brian K**. On the Reconciliation of Anthropocentric and Nonanthropocentric Environmental Ethics. *Environ Values*, 5(4), 349-361, N 96.

I argue that James Sterba's recent attempt to show that despite their foundational axiological differences regarding the relative value of humans and members of nonhuman species, anthropocentrists and nonanthropocentrists would accept the exact same principles of environmental justice fails. The failure to reconcile the two positions is a product of an underestimation of the divergence that occurs at the level of general principles and practical policy as a result of the initial value commitments which characterise each position. The upshot of this is that, contrary to those who argue that environmental ethicists ought to move beyond the traditional anthropocentric-nonanthropocentric debate, the foundational debate about interspecific egalitarianism will continue to issue in substantial debates about environmental policy formation.

**Steward, Helen**. On the Notion of Cause 'Philosophically Speaking'. *Proc Aris Soc*, 97, 125-140, 1997.

The paper argues that a conception of causation which the author calls the "network model of causation" is mistaken. Starting from the commonplace observation that there are always several different causal factors involved in the bringing about of any particular event, the network model goes on to represent causation as a process in which a number of causally efficacious particulars, usually conceived of as a mixture of events and states, combine together to produce a resultant consequence. The author argues that a proper appreciation of Davidson's distinction between particular causes and causes which are conditions renders the network model untenable.

**Steward, Helen**. The Ontology of Mind: Events, Processes, and States. New York, Clarendon/Oxford Pr, 1997.

The author contends that many current theories of mind are rendered unintelligible once it is seen how these explanations really work. A number of prominent features of contemporary philosophy of mind—token identity theories, the functionalist's conception of causal role, a common form of argument for eliminative materialism, and the structure of the debate about the efficacy of mental content—are impugned by her arguments. Steward concludes that the modern mind-body problem needs to be substantially rethought. (publisher, edited)

**Stewart, Earl** and Duran, Jane. Toward an Aesthetic of Black Musical Expression. *J Aes Educ*, 31(1), 73-85, Spr 97.

Various types of theories of musical expression, are presented by Kivy and others, are examined with the aim of the development of a Black theory. It is argued that such a theory can be developed, and the resemblance of much Western African music to speech patterns is noted. Several examples of African holdovers in Black American music are presented.

**Stewart, James B** (ed) and Bell, Bernard W (ed) and Grosholz, Emily (ed). *W.E.B. Du Bois on* Race and Culture. New York, Routledge, 1996.

W.E.B. Du Bois was one of the most profound and influential African-American intellectuals of the twentieth century. This volume addresses the complexities of Du Bois's legacy, showing how his work gets to the heart of today's theorizing about the color line. (publisher, edited)

**Stewart, Jon**. Borges and the Refutation of Idealism: A Study of "Tlön, Uqbar, Orbis Tertius". *Ideas Valores*, 64-99, Ag 96.

This paper tries to demonstrate that Borges's celebrated story, "Tlön, Uqbar, Orbis Tertius," contains a *reductio ad absurdum* argument of a form of subjective idealism usually associated with Berkeley. To show the incoherences that result from the idealism of Berkeley, Borges makes use of ideas which may be fruitfully illuminated by comparison with Kantian arguments against subjective idealism. He puts these arguments in the form of a *cuento* which illustrates the absurdities and contradictions of this idealist position. Specifically, he demonstrates that a radically subjective idealism is self-contradictory since it renders all objective experience indeterminate and incoherent.

**Stewart, Jon**. Die Beziehung zwischen der *Jenaer Metaphysik* von 1804/05 und der *Phänomenologie des Geistes*. *Jahr Hegelforschung*, 2, 99-132, 1996.

**Stewart, M A**. Hume's "Bellmen's Petition": The Original Text. *Hume Stud*, 23(1), 3-7, Ap 97.

David Hume's anonymous "Petition of the Grave and Venerable Bellmen" (1751) is a witty satire, directed at a target that merited greater sympathy than he spared for it. He aimed to undermine the principled case for increasing the outdated stipends of the Scottish clergy and schoolteachers, by an unfavorable comparison with the poverty of the bellringers or gravediggers. These he depicted as more universally useful than the clergy. Until recently, Hume's satire was known only through a seriously corrupt 19th century version. The correct text is here restored from a collation of three surviving copies of the original.

**Stewart, M A**. Hume's Philosophy of Religion: Part 2. *Phil Books*, 37(4), 225-235, O 96.

Seven monographs on Hume's philosophy of religion are surveyed, starting with two useful comprehensive studies by J. Gaskin and Keith Yandell. Beryl Logan's *A Religion without Talking* is the one serious contender in the literature for the view that Hume makes constructive use of the concepts of irregular argument and natural belief in his *Dialogues*, but this interpretation remains fundamentally flawed. Joseph Houston's *Reported Miracles* is outstanding as a study that is both philosophically challenging and theologically and historically informed. The dissertation, based studies by Delbert Hanson on fideism and Francis Beckwith and Michael Levine on miracles, are discounted.

**Stewart, Matthew**. *The Truth about Everything*. Amherst, Prometheus, 1997.

*The Truth about Everything* is an approach to the history of philosophy from well outside the modern institutional framework of knowledge. With an unusually frank and irreverent style, using parables, imaginary dialogues, and illustrations, Matthew Stewart picks apart the myths which make up widely accepted versions of the history of philosophy and offers in their place a realistic assessment of individual philosophers and schools and their contributions to the advance of human knowledge and happiness. (publisher, edited)

**Stieber, John** and Primeaux, Patrick. Managing Business Ethics and Opportunity Costs. *J Bus Ethics*, 16(8), 835-842, Je 97.

Economic profits differ from accounting profits. Accounting profits are usually defined as revenues minus costs and those costs as fixed and variable. Economic profits enlist a third cost, opportunity costs. While these costs are difficult to determine with mathematical precision, they are nonetheless significant, especially for decision making in business. They reflect social costs and benefits, tensions between individual and corporate interests, and all internal and external considerations which enter into decision making in business. It is precisely within opportunity cost decision making that Primeaux and Stieber situate business ethics.

**Stigol, Nora**. Cualidades secundarias y autoconocimiento. *Analisis Filosof*, 17(1), 41-48, My 97.

**Stile, Alessandro**. "Malebranche e la storia nella *Recherche de la Vérité*" in *Lo Storicismo e la Sua Storia: Temi, Problemi, Prospettive*, Cacciatore, Giuseppe (ed), 24-38. Milano, Guerini, 1997.

**Stile, Alessandro** and Cacciatore, Giuseppe. *L'Edizione Critica Di Vico: Bilanci E Prospettive*. Napoli, Guida, 1997.

**Still, Judith**. Homo Economicus in the 20th Century: *Écriture Masculine* and Women's Work. *Hist Human Sci*, 10(3), 105-121, Ag 97.

In this article I argue that the dominant discourse of our day is economic universalism. This has translated comfortably from modernity to postmodernity. Within this discourse real differences and inequalities are homogenized by narratives such as those of choice and diversity. I shall question this in two ways: first, by borrowing from French poststructuralism to rename the discourse a 'masculine economy' and thus to invoke a 'feminine economy' both as a philosophical structure of difference and as a deliberate introduction of the body; second, by analyzing economic narratives concerning women's work which tend to flatten out difference altogether or recast it as (well-advised) choice. (edited)

**Stjernfelt, Frederik** and Koppe, Simo and Emmeche, Claus. Explaining Emergence: Towards an Ontology of Levels. *J Gen Phil Sci*, 28(1), 83-119, 1997.

The vitalism/reductionism debate in the life sciences shows that the idea of emergence as something principally unexplainable will often be falsified by the development of science. Nevertheless, the concept of emergence keeps reappearing in various sciences and cannot easily be dispensed with in an evolutionary world-view. We argue that what is needed is an ontological nonreductionist theory of levels of reality which includes a concept of emergence and which can support an evolutionary account of the origin of levels. (edited)

**Stock, Brian**. *Augustine the Reader: Meditation, Self-Knowledge, and the Ethics of Interpretation*. Cambridge, Harvard Univ Pr, 1996.

Augustine was convinced that words and images play a mediating role in our perceptions of reality. In the union of philosophy, psychology, and literary insights that form the basis of his theory of reading, the reader emerges as the dominant model of the reflective self. Meditative reading, indeed the meditative act that constitutes reading itself, becomes the portal to inner being. At the same time, Augustine argues that the self-knowledge that reading brings is, of necessity, limited, since it is faith rather than interpretive reason that can translate reading into forms of understanding. (edited)

**Stocker, Michael**. Aristotelian *Akrasia* and Psychoanalytic Regression. *Phil Psychiat Psych*, 4(3), 231-241, S 97.

Many philosophers tell us that *akrasia*, weakness of the will, is not possible, thinking they are thus agreeing with Aristotle. I think it is possible and that Aristotle thought so, too. Many contemporaries (mis)understand Aristotelian akrasia in largely moral terms—e.g., in terms of knowingly not doing what one believes *best*. But he understood it in largely moral psychological terms—e.g., in terms of the nature of desire appropriate to people at different ages of their lives and the different ways different desires interact with judgment. (edited)

**Stocking, Carol B** and Tulsky, James A. Obstacles and Opportunities in the Design of Ethics Consultation Evaluation. *J Clin Ethics*, 7(2), 139-145, Sum 96.

Designing research to evaluate ethics consultation presents abundant methodological challenges. This article focuses on how to design studies that assess the important aspects of ethics consultation, avoid bias, are reproducible and can be generalized to a variety of health care settings. We propose a research agenda that includes developing a consortium of institutions to conduct coordinated research, creating a minimum standardized database, describing the range of activities called ethics consultation, developing and validating evaluative measures, enhancing models of ethics consultation through quality improvement methods, designing single site effectiveness studies using systematic consultation and considering multicentered randomized controlled trials.

**Stoeber, Michael** (ed) and Meynell, Hugo (ed). *Critical Reflections on the Paranormal*. Albany, SUNY Pr, 1996.

The book discusses various aspects of paranormal phenomena such as telepathy, psychokinesis, transmediumship, near death experiences, and past-life memories. It reflects on what is reasonable to believe about them and why; and it suggests what changes they might demand in our worldview if these phenomena are accepted as genuine. The collection includes essays, written by Susan Armstrong, Heather Botting, Stephen Braude, Don Evans, David Ray Griffin, James Horne, Terence Penelhum, and the editors. (publisher,edited)

**Stöckler, Manfred**. Materie in Raum und Zeit? Philosophische Aspekte der Raum-Zeit-Interpretation der Quantenfeldtheorie. *Phil Natur*, 27(1), 111-135, 1990.

**Stöckler, Manfred**. Was kann heute unter Naturphilosophie verstehen?. *Phil Natur*, 26(1), 1-18, 1989.

**Stoekle, John D** and Ronan, Laurence J and Emanuel, Linda L (& others). A Manual on Manners and Courtesies for the Shared Care of Patients. *J Clin Ethics*, 8(1), 22-33, Spr 97.

This paper is written by medical practitioners concerned with diminished *intraprofessional communication* as care becomes more corporate and commercialized while doctor-doctor communications is even more necessary with medicine's expanding specialization for the effective shared care of patients. Several cases and communication failures are illustrated from medical practice: in doctor-doctor, doctor-student, doctor-resident, doctor-nurse, and doctor-institutional relationships. Recommendations on standards of communication are made.

**Stokes, Geoff**. Karl Popper's Political Philosophy of Social Science. *Phil Soc Sci*, 27(1), 56-79, Mr 97.

This article examines critically Popper's arguments for a "unity of method" between natural science and social science. It discusses Popper's writings on the goals of science, the objects of scientific inquiry, the logic of scientific method, and the value of objectivity. The major argument is that, despite his unifying intention, Popper himself provides good reasons for treating the two sciences differently. Popper proposes that social scientists follow a number of rules that are *not* required for, and that have no direct equivalent in, natural science. It is argued further that Popper's accounts of the differences between natural and social science, and his call for moral responsibility, are based largely upon his understanding of the distinctive political threat that social science poses for the conduct of critical reason. (edited)

**Stokes, Karina**. Artificial Intelligence Modeling of Spontaneous Self Learning: An Application of Dialectical Philosophy. *Int J Applied Phil*, 10(2), 1-6, Wint-Spr 96.

**Stokes, W Ann**. Is Edwin Gordon's Learning Theory a Cognitive One?. *Phil Music Educ Rev*, 4(2), 96-106, Fall 96.

**Stolboushkin, Alexei** and Niwinski, Damian. $y = 2x$ VS. $y = 3x$. *J Sym Log*, 62(2), 661-672, Je 97.

We show that no formula of first order logic using linear ordering and the logical relation $y = 2x$ can define the property that the size of a finite model is divisible by 3. This answers a long-standing question which may be of relevance to certain open problems in circuit complexity.

**Stoljar, Daniel**. What What It's Like Isn't Like. *Analysis*, 56(4), 281-283, O 96.

**Stolz, Joachim**. The Research Program in Natural Philosophy from Gauss and Riemann to Einstein and Whitehead: From the Theory of Invariants to the Idea of a Field Theory of Cognition. *Prima Philosophia*, 10(2), 157-164, 1997.

The theoretical program of the *geometrization of nature* begins within the two generations between Descartes and Newton. The idea of generalized spaces of Gauss and the idea of generalized coordinates of Riemann incarnated the idea of the definition of mathematics as the theory of abstract structures. But it also initiated the research program for the theory of invariance in mathematics. Within physics this program was the background for Einstein's development from the *special theory of relativity* to the *general theory of relativity*. An analogous transition to the search for invariants in the description of natural processes in general is characteristic for the *natural philosophy* of Whitehead. The idea of a field theory of cognition is one result of this transition to the search for covariant representations of epistemic processes.

**Stolzenberg, Jürgen**. Absolutes Wissen und Sein: Zu Fichtes Wissenschaftslehre von 1801/02. *Fichte-Studien*, 12, 307-322, 1997.

In this paper an analysis is given of the work lines of the structure of Fichte's concept of absolute knowledge in his Doctrine of Science from 1801/02. It is shown what sort of negativity is underlying the relationship between the comments of this concept and the various are given which lead Fichte to his final thesis, that the absolute knowledge cannot be reconstructed without his relation to an absolute being.

**Stolzenberg, Jürgen**. Selbstbewusstsein: ein Problem der Philosophie nach Kant. *Rev Int Phil*, 50(197), 461-482, 1996.

In this paper it is shown that K. L. Reinhold was the first of the post-Kantian philosophers remarking a problem in the concept of self-consciousness and whose theory of consciousness and self-consciousness must be considered as the theoretical background of Hölderlin's Fichte-Critique in his famous paper on *Judgement and Being* from 1795. It is then shown, that there is an implicit answer of Fichte to Hölderlin's Critique in Fichte's *System of Morals* from 1798, where Fichte developed a new systematic interpretation of that concept of self-consciousness, which Reinhold and Hölderlin had in view.

**Stone, Lynda**. "A Rhetorical Revolution for Philosophy of Education" in *Philosophy of Education (1996)*, Margonis, Frank (ed), 412-420. Urbana, Phil Education Soc, 1997.

The purpose of this essay is to posit a new direction for philosophy of education building from the current resurgence of interest in rhetoric within literary criticism and the human sciences. Adoption and adaption of a rhetorical stance is revolutionary as a broad critique of the "reason" tradition of philosophy. Following a definitional section of the tradition, the writings on rhetoric, of ties to language, text, philosophy and culture from Paul DeMan and Hans Blumenberg are offered as inspirational exemplars. This is followed by a brief general characterization of rhetoric for philosophy and some implications for philosophy of education.

**Stott, P** and Rothenberg, L S and Krimsky, Sheldon. Financial Interests of Authors in Scientific Journals: A Pilot Study of 14 Publications. *Sci Eng Ethics*, 2(4), 395-410, O 96.

This paper measures the frequency of selected financial interests held among authors of certain types of scientific publications and assesses disclosure practices of authors. We examined 1105 university authors (first and last cited) from Massachusetts institutions whose 789 articles, published in 1992, appeared in 14 scientific and medical journals. (edited)

**Stout, Rowland**. Processes. *Philosophy*, 72(279), 19-27, Ja 97.

There is a linguistic distinction between sentences reporting events and sentences reporting processes based on the difference in aspect between "What was happening" and "What happened". A process is something that was happening, whereas an event is something that happened. The paper argues that there is a deep metaphysical distinction corresponding to this linguistic distinction. It is the distinction between things (events) which extend through time and things (processes) which persist in time as unified wholes. Processes, like objects, are continuants, present in their entirety at any one moment. Like objects and unlike events, they do not have temporal parts.

**Stout, Rowland**. *Things That Happen Because They Should: A Teleological Approach to Action*. New York, Oxford Univ Pr, 1996.

Philosophers have usually argued that the right way to explain people's actions is in terms of their beliefs and intentions rather than in terms of objective facts. Rowland Stout takes the opposite line in his account of action. Appeal to teleology is widely regarded with suspicion, but Dr. Stout argues that there are things in nature, namely actions, that can be teleologically explained: they happen because they serve some end. Moreover, this teleological explanation is externalist: it cites facts about the world, not beliefs and intentions which only represent the world. Such externalism about the explanation of action is a natural partner to externalism about knowledge and about reference, but has hardly ever been considered seriously before. One dramatic consequence of such a position is that it opens up the possibility of a behaviourist account of beliefs and intentions. (publisher)

AUTHOR INDEX 939 Ströker, Elisabeth

**Strahm, Thomas**. Polynomial Time Operations in Explicit Mathematics. *J Sym Log*, 62(2), 575-594, Je 97.

In this paper we study (self-)applicative theories of operations and binary words in the context of polynomial time computability. We propose a first order theory PTO which allows full self-application and whose provably total functions on *W*={0,1} are exactly the polynomial time computable functions. Our treatment of PTO is proof-theoretic and very much in the spirit of reductive proof theory.

**Strahm, Thomas** and Gerhard, Jäger. Some Theories with Positive Induction of Ordinal Strength *psi omega 0*. *J Sym Log*, 61(3), 818-842, S 96.

This paper deals with i) the theory $ID^{\#}_1$ which results from ID-hat-sub-one by restricting induction on the natural numbers to formulas which are positive in the fixed point constants, ii) the theory BON(mu) plus various forms of positive induction, and iii) a subtheory of Peano arithmetic with ordinals in which induction on the natural numbers is restricted to formulas which are Sigma in the ordinals. We show that these systems have proof-theoretic strength psi-omega-0. (edited)

**Strahm, Thomas** and Glass, Thomas. Systems of Explicit Mathematics with Non-Constructive Mu-Operator and Join. *Annals Pure Applied Log*, 82(2), 193-219, D 96.

The aim of this article is to give the proof-theoretic analysis of various subsystems of Feferman's theory $T_1$ for explicit mathematics which contain the nonconstructive mu-operator and join. We make use of standard proof-theoretic techniques such as cut-elimination of appropriate semi-formal systems and asymmetrical interpretations in standard structures for explicit mathematics.

**Straughan, Roger** and Reiss, Michael J. *Improving Nature?*. New York, Cambridge Univ Pr, 1996.

Little more than a decade ago the term 'genetic engineering' was hardly known outside research laboratories. By now, though, its use is widespread. Those in favour of genetic engineering—and those against it—tell us that it has the potential to change our lives perhaps more than any other scientific or technological advance. But what are the likely consequences of genetic engineering? Is it ethically acceptable? Should we be trying to improve on nature? The authors, a biologist and a moral philosopher, examine the implications of genetic engineering in every aspect of our lives. The underlying science is explained in a way easily understood by a general reader and the moral and ethical considerations that arise are fully discussed. Throughout, the authors clarify the issues involved so that readers can make up their own minds about these controversial issues. (publisher)

**Strauss, Leo** and Bolotin, David (ed) and Bruell, Christopher (& other eds). An Untitled Lecture on Plato's *Euthyphron*. *Interpretation*, 24(1), 3-23, Fall 96.

**Strauss, Misha** and Geller, Gail and Bernhardt, Barbara A (& others). "Decoding" Informed Consent: Insights from Women regarding Breast Cancer Susceptibility Testing. *Hastings Center Rep*, 27(2), 28-33, Mr-Ap 97.

Cancer susceptibility testing is likely to become routine in medical practice, despite many limitations and unanswered questions. These uncertainties greatly complicate the process of informed consent, creating an excellent opportunity to reconsider exactly how it should be conducted.

**Strawser, Michael**. *Both/And: Reading Kierkegaard from Irony to Edification*. New York, Fordham Univ Pr, 1997.

Strawser argues that Kierkegaard's place in the history of philosophy is well established; however, taking him "philosophically" has become the least common way of taking him. Strawser addresses the problematic but natural relationship between Kierkegaard and postmodernism and offers exciting possibilities. But Strawser urges a close reading of Kierkegaard to establish how, in a postmodernist light, he can be read. For this reason, Strawser believes that contemporary postmodern philosophical considerations aid a critical reading, but such a reading will not be overwhelmed by them. Strawser writes: "it is my view that one cannot adequately deal with interesting contemporary questions without first furnishing a comprehensive reading of the Kierkegaardian literature, because their answers need to be based on and preceded by such a reading. Any other method would be little more than intellectual guesswork." Such a comprehensive reading is what Strawser offers the reader in *Both/And*. (publisher, edited)

**Strawson, P F**. *Entity and Identity and Other Essays*. New York, Clarendon/Oxford Pr, 1997.

Gathered in this volume are selected essays by P.F. Strawson from the 1970s to the 1990s, in two areas of philosophy to which he has most notably contributed. The first twelve pieces concern the philosophy of language, a broad heading under which many controversial philosophical issues can be fruitfully approached. This volume is completed by four studies in Kantian metaphysics: these develop and strengthen Strawson's influential view of Kant's *Critique of Pure Reason* and bring out the implications of this view for current metaphysical debates. (publisher, edited)

**Streeck, Jürgen**. How to Do Things with Things: Objects trouvés and Symbolization. *Human Stud*, 19(4), 365-384, O 96.

J.L. Austin has demonstrated that people can "do things"—bring about social facts—with words. Here we describe how some people do things with things. This is a study of the symbolic use and situated history of material objects during a business negotiation between two German entrepreneurs: of the practical transformation of things-at-hand from objects of use into exemplars, or into forms-at-hand that can be used for the construction of transitory symbolic artifacts. Arranging boxes in a particular fashion can be the equivalent of an illocutionary act, but unlike words things remain on the scene as indexical monuments to prior interactional arrangements.

**Street, Marc D** and Robertson, Chris and Geiger, Scott W. Ethical Decision Making: The Effects of Escalating Commitment. *J Bus Ethics*, 16(11), 1153-1161, Ag 97.

In this paper a new variable is introduced into the ethical decision making literature. This variable, exposure to escalation situations, is posited to increase the likelihood that individuals will choose unethical decision alternatives. Further, it is proposed that escalation situations should be included as a variable in Jones's (1991) comprehensive model of ethical decision making. Finally, research propositions are provided based on the relationship between escalating commitment and the ethical decision making process.

**Strevens, Michael**. Quantum Mechanics and Frequentism: A Reply to Ismael. *Brit J Phil Sci*, 47(4), 575-577, D 96.

Ismael (BJPS, 196) has argued that frequentism is not a viable option for the interpretation of the probabilities of quantum mechanics. The argument assumes that the quantum probabilities are intrinsic properties of systems. I show that the formalism of quantum mechanics suggests no such fact.

**Strike, Kenneth A**. "Taylor, Equality, and the Metaphysics of Persons" in *Philosophy of Education (1996)*, Margonis, Frank (ed), 197-202. Urbana, Phil Education Soc, 1997.

**Strike, Kenneth A** (ed) and Ternasky, P Lance (ed). *Ethics for Professionals in Education: Perspectives for Preparation and Practice*. New York, Teachers College Pr, 1993.

This fifth volume in the Professional Ethics in Education Series delves into a relatively neglected area—the ethical principles governing the conduct of teachers, administrators and other education professionals—and provides a thoughtful starting-point for discussion in the field. The contributors' collective exploration of the subject, encompassing many different and sometimes conflicting vantage points, results in a unique overview of the many issues that define the place of ethics in professional preparation and practice. Part I lays out several alternative philosophical positions about teaching ethics to educational professionals. Parts II and III examine questions of how to include ethics in the preservice curriculum and how a concern for ethics can be institutionalized in the schools. (publisher, edited)

**Strikwerda, Robert** (ed) and May, Larry (ed) and Hopkins, Patrick D (ed). *Rethinking Masculinity: Philosophical Explorations in Light of Feminism*. Lanham, Rowman & Littlefield, 1996.

The new edition of this popular book is reorganized to present pairs of contrasting views on what it means to be a man in contemporary Western culture. Addressing such issues as sex differences, fatherhood, intimacy, homosexuality and oppression, the collection also includes new discussions of paternity, pornography, mixed race marriage, impotence and violence. Still the only philosophically-oriented collection on the subject, Rethinking Masculinity is an excellent text for gender studies, ethics and social philosophy courses. (publisher)

**Strncevic, Ljubica** and Gligorov, Vladimir. Rawls's "The Closed Society Assumption" (in Serbo-Croatian). *Theoria (Yugoslavia)*, 38(2), 53-64, Je 95.

The article analyzes "the closed society assumption" that Rawls introduces in his latest book *Political Liberalism*. It is shown that the assumption is i) new (it is stronger than the autarky assumption that is used in *A Theory of Justice*), ii) metaphysical and not political (contrary to Rawls's intentions), iii) contradictory, and iv) not necessary, as it does not have the political consequences.

**Strobach, Niko**. Die logische und die dialogische Form des Argumentes vom "Dritten Menschen" in Platons "Parmenides". *Prima Philosophia*, 10(2), 165-182, 1997.

In this article, the famous *third man argument* (TMA) in Plato's *Parmenides* 132 a/b is reconsidered in three steps. The first two steps are concerned with the *logical* form of the TMA, the third with its *diagonal* form hitherto neglected. 1) In a first step the two most detailed formal reconstructions of the TMA, by Fine (1993) and Sellars (1955), are discussed. Criticism of Fine's reconstruction leads to a step-by-step transformation of it whose final result is structurally analogous to Sellars's earlier reconstruction. 2) However, it may still be doubted that the result of the first step is what Plato had in mind. Doubts arise when Aristotle's version of the TMA is taken into account. This leads to a new reconstruction of the TMA differing from Sellars or the modified Fine version with respect of the premises of the TMA. 3) The way in which Fine's reconstruction had to be modified in the first step suggests paying some attention to the dialogical form of the TMA. In this sense I argue in a third step for the thesis that the TMA should be seen in close connection with the vision of the forms in *Symposion 209/11*. In this way, two central texts about the theory of forms can be shown to mutually explain each other.

**Strobach, Niko**. Einsteins Zug und logische Gesetze. *Phil Natur*, 34(1), 21-31, 1997.

The purpose of this article is (using the famous train example) to highlight two linked philosophical aspects of Albert Einstein's Special Theory of Relativity (SR), which seem to have received little attention: 1) The relativistic phenomenon called "length contraction" comprises more than is expressed by the word "contraction" in its ordinary use. 2) In SR, Leibniz's law of indiscernibility of identicals holds only in a more restricted version than one would expect. This is because of a feature this law shares with the Aristotelian principle of noncontradition. As a consequence, inertial frames should be considered as a new sort of contexts in a future intensional logic.

**Ströker, Elisabeth**. Krise der europäischen Kultur—ein Problemerbe der husserlschen Philosophie. *Z Phil Forsch*, 50(1/2), 309-322, Ja-Je 96.

This essay describes and interprets the analysis of the crisis of Western culture Husserl was engaged in for more than 20 years. It is based upon texts that have only been published in Husserliana XXVII in 1989 and have not gained public philosophical attention. My claim is to elucidate Husserl's early concern with problems of culture in general and especially his proposal to overcome its crisis, as it was caused by modern science as well as certain shortcomings of the preceding philosophy. But Husserl's conviction that his phenomenology could eventually master the crisis is also open to criticism.

**Stroll, Avrum**. "The Argument from Possibility" in *Scepticism in the History of Philosophy: A Pan-American Dialogue,* Popkin, Richard H (ed), 267-279. Dordrecht, Kluwer, 1996.

The paper argues that *The Argument from Possibility* underlies all forms of scepticism, including those which seem to be nonargumentative. This argument suffers from two defects: it rests on presuppositions that are inconsistent with the conclusion it draws; and it rests on a fallacious inference: a move from the admitted premise that it is always possible to be mistaken to the conclusion that in this or that particular case one is.

**Stromillo, Anna**. Osservazioni sulla dinamica strutturale della Promesa in quanto Atto linguistico. *Stud Filosofici*, 197-207, 1995.

**Strong, Carson**. Respecting the Health Care Decision-Making Capacity of Minors. *Bioethics Forum*, 11(4), 7-12, Wint 95.

The *Decision-Making Guidelines* document raises some unanswered questions and lacks arguments to support assertions made. This paper identifies and initiates discussion of these issues surrounding the decision-making capacity of minors.

**Strong, Carson** and Aiken, Margaret M and Muram, David. Children's Refusal of Gynecologic Examinations for Suspected Sexual Abuse. *J Clin Ethics*, 8(2), 158-164, Sum 97.

Cases are presented in which children refuse gynecologic examinations following suspected sexual abuse. Topics discussed include background concerning child sexual abuse, the purpose of the medical examination, and psychosocial aspects of such examinations. A framework for dealing with such refusals is presented that identifies relevant ethical values, distinguishes categories of decision-making capacity in children, and provides an interpretation of the principle of patient advocacy. Using this framework, the authors argue for proposed resolutions of the cases presented.

**Strong, Carson** and Wall, Hershel P and Jameson, Valerie. A Model Policy Addressing Mistreatment of Medical Students. *J Clin Ethics*, 7(4), 341-346, Wint 96.

The University of Tennessee College of Medicine developed a policy on student mistreatment that has three main components. First, a statement of standards of behavior was set forth that affirms the importance of mutual respect among teachers and students and asserts that the College will not condone mistreatment. Second, methods were developed for ongoing education of the college community concerning the standards of behavior and the process by which they are upheld. This educational process is directed toward preclinical and clinical students and faculty, residents, fellows and nurses. It attempts to promote a positive environment for learning by increasing sensitivity concerning the issue of mistreatment. It also informs persons who believe they have been mistreated that avenues for seeking redress are available. Third, a process for responding to allegations of mistreatment was established. This process, designed to be fair and to respect the rights of accuser and accused, involves use of a "mediator" and a "conflict-resolution council" to deal with alleged and actual mistreatment and promote reconciliation between conflicting parties. This approach has been implemented and its effectiveness will be assessed.

**Strong, Tracy B** and Miller, Ted. Meanings and Contexts: Mr. Skinner's Hobbes and the English Mode of Political Theory. *Inquiry*, 40(3), 323-356, S 97.

Skinner's approach to political theory, while important and interesting, rests on a particular thin version of his reading of Austin and Collingwood. In turn this affects both his analysis of rhetoric in the XVIIth century and his understanding of Hobbes's intentions for his various texts. Therewith, we argue against Skinner that Hobbes did not reverse himself on rhetoric. Instead, the differences between Hobbes's three iterations of his doctrine reflect efforts to prove its worth before distinct audiences: political opponents, potential students and the sovereign that might have made his doctrine the state's official teaching. Finally, Skinner's deficiencies on Hobbes show some of the problems of the "English Mode of Political Theory."

**Stroud, Barry**. "Hume's Scepticism: Natural Instincts and Philosophical Reflection" in *Scepticism in the History of Philosophy: A Pan-American Dialogue,* Popkin, Richard H (ed), 115-134. Dordrecht, Kluwer, 1996.

**Stroud, Barry**. "Mind, Meaning, and Practice" in *The Cambridge Companion to Wittgenstein,* Sluga, Hans (ed), 296-319. Needham Heights, Cambridge, 1996.

**Stroud, Barry**. Unpurged Pyrrhonism. *Phil Phenomenol Res*, 57(2), 411-416, Je 97.

**Stroumsa, Sarah**. Compassion for Wisdom: The Attitude of Some Medieval Arab Philosophers towards to Codification of Philosophy. *Bochumer Phil Jrbh*, 1, 39-55, 1996.

In studying the attitude of medieval philosophers toward the act of writing, scholars have tended to concentrate on their esoteric tendencies and their reluctance to commit philosophy to writing. The basic attitude of medieval philosophers to the decision to commit something to writing, whether it be that made by the prophets, the sages or the medieval philosophers themselves, however, is on the whole positive. This article examines the sources—both religious and philosophical—from which this positive attitude stems and then discusses its manifestations in the work of three medieval thinkers: Ab[u] Nasr al-F[a]r[a]b[i], Ab[u] al-Barak[a]t al-Baghd[a]d[i] and Moses Maimonides.

**Strózewski, Wladyslaw**. O. Profesor Józef Maria Bochenski (30. VIII. 1902—8. II. 1995) (in Polish). *Kwartalnik Filozof*, 23(1), 5-14, 1995.

**Strózewski, Wladyslaw**. Short Account of the Debates in the Higher Seminary of History of Philosophy, Catholic University in Lublin, in the Years 1953/54 to 1955/56 (in Polish). *Kwartalnik Filozof*, 25(1), 209-238, 1997.

**Strub, Christian** and Jacobi, Klaus and King, Peter. From *intellectus verus/falsus* to the *dictum propositionis*: The Semantics of Peter Abelard and his Circle. *Vivarium*, 34(1), 15-40, My 96.

**Strube, Claudius**. Heideggers Wende zum Deutschen Idealismus. *Fichte-Studien*, 13, 51-64, 1997.

**Strudler, Alan**. The Problem of Mass Torts. *Law Phil*, 16(1), 101-105, 97.

**Strutton, David** and Hamilton III, J Brooke and Lumpkin, James R. An Essay on When to Fully Disclose in Sales Relationships: Applying Two Practical Guidelines for Addressing Truth-Telling Problems. *J Bus Ethics*, 16(5), 545-560, Ap 97.

Salespeople have a moral obligation to prospect/customer, company and self. As such, they continually encounter truth-telling dilemmas. "Ignorance" and "conflict" often block the path to morally correct sales behaviors. Academics and practitioners agree that adoption of ethical codes is the most effective measure for encouraging ethical sales behaviors. Yet no ethical code has been offered which can be conveniently used to overcome the unique circumstances that contribute to the moral dilemmas often encountered in personal selling. An ethical code is developed that charts ethical paths across a variety of sales settings (addressing "ignorance") while illustrating why the cost associated with acting morally is generally reasonable (addressing "conflict"). (edited)

**Strutton, David** and Pelton, Lou E and Ferrell, O C. Ethical Behavior in Retail Settings: Is There a Generation Gap?. *J Bus Ethics*, 16(1), 87-105, Ja 97.

A new generation, earmarked the Thirteeners, is an emerging force in the marketplace. The Thirteener cohort group, so designated since they are the thirteenth generation to know the American flag and constitution, encompass over 62 million adult consumers. All the former "Mall Rats" have grown up. The normative structures that these Thirteeners employ in both acquisition and disposition retail settings is empirically assessed in this study through the use of a national sample. The findings suggest that Thirteeners are more likely to attempt to rationalize away unethical retailing consumption behaviors than their parent's generation. The managerial and theoretical implications for the practice of retailing in the 1990s associated with these observations are discussed.

**Struyker Boudier, C E M**. Ergo Cogito. *Tijdschr Filosof*, 59(1), 126-131, Mr 97.

**Struyker Boudier, C E M**. Van God los? Actuele godsdienstfilosofie in Nederland. *Tijdschr Filosof*, 59(2), 322-328, Je 97.

**Stuart, Matthew**. Locke's Geometrical Analogy. *Hist Phil Quart*, 13(4), 451-467, O 96.

Locke is widely construed as being officially committed to the view that if one had ideas of the real essences of bodies, the rest of physics could be demonstrated *a priori*. This interpretation, which gets much of its support from an analogy that Locke draws between bodies and geometrical figures, is at odds with its skepticism about a science of bodies. This prompts a more austere reading of the geometrical analogy; rather than suggesting the possibility of synthetic *a priori* knowledge in physics, Locke is merely endorsing deductivism about scientific explanation.

**Stubblefield, Anna**. Contraceptive Risk-Taking and Norms of Chastity. *J Soc Phil*, 27(3), 81-100, Wint 96.

One aspect of social group oppression is the double bind—situations in which options are reduced to a very few and all of them expose one to penalty, censure or deprivation. I explore the double bind faced by young American women in which neither (heterosexual) sexual activity nor inactivity is entirely acceptable. I use a case study of contraceptive risk-taking to show how norms of chastity contribute to this double bind, its implications for discussions of rationality and agency, and how it contributes to women's experience of gender oppression by affecting their perception of themselves as agents.

**Stueber, Karsten R**. "Indeterminacy and the First Person Perspective" in *Verdad: lógica, representación y mundo,* Villegas Forero, L, 333-341. Santiago de Compostela, Univ Santiago Comp, 1996.

In this paper, I will discuss Searle's main argument for the first person perspective in regard to meaning and intentionality. He claims that Quine's and Davidson's arguments for the indeterminacy of meaning and inscrutability of reference should be understood as a *reductio ad absurdum* of the third person methodology. I will defend the third person perspective by reevaluating the claims for the inscrutability thesis. It will be shown that Searle's argument for the first person perspective is not conclusive and that the inscrutability of reference does not follow from the analysis of radical interpretation.

**Stufflebeam, Robert**. Doing Without Concepts: An Interpretation of C.I. Lewis' Action-Oriented Foundationalism. *Sorites*, 4-20, Ag 96.

C.I. Lewis's action-oriented notion of cognition is consistent with a minimally representational picture of mind. I aim to show why. Toward this end, I explore some of the tensions between Lewis's theory of knowledge and his theory of mind. At face value, the former renders the latter implausible. Rehabilitation is possible, I argue, because I) Lewis isn't claiming that his epistemology describes *actual* justificatory practices, but rather what an agent *could* do; II) the social character of concepts [and meaning] considerably reduces the need for appealing to *internal* concepts when explaining why an agent does what she does; and III) among his paradigm cases of cognitive behavior are paradigm cases of nonreflective action. Here's the rub: not only do such actions account for most of our behavior [as Lewis himself notes], nonreflective actions, though cognitive, don't require conceptualization. (edited)

**Stuhlmann-Laeisz, Rainer**. "Die Theorie der Urteilsformen in der deutschen Schullogik des 19.Jahrhunderts" in *Das weite Spektrum der analytischen Philosophie,* Lenzen, Wolfgang, 383-400. Hawthorne, de Gruyter, 1997.

The notion of a judgment form plays a crucial role in German 18th and 19th centuries' textbooks on logic. The author of the present article is mainly concerned with the following claim of the traditional German logicians: Every judgment has a distinct logical form. However, according to the traditional view the characterization of the form of a judgment as, e.g., hypothetical is underdetermined, because every judgment can be subject to analysis with regard to four categories: quantity, quality, relation and modality, whereas from the point of view of modern logical syntax, it is not possible to combine different syntactical categories on the same level. The author presents a reconstruction of the traditional syntax with the intention to reconcile the uniqueness claim with the view that a judgment can be simultaneously characterized by different syntactical categories. A solution to this problem as to twelve kinds of judgment taken from the Kantian Urteilstafel—with exception of the title "modality"—is put forward.

**Stuhr, John J**. "Community, Identity, and Difference: Pragmatic Social Thought in Transition" in *Philosophy in Experience: American Philosophy in Transition,* Hart, Richard (ed), 106-126. New York, Fordham Univ Pr, 1997.

This essay develops a pragmatic notion of community and connects this notion to the concepts of identity and difference among community members. In doing so, I am concerned to bring pragmatic social theory to bear on contemporary concerns.

**Stump, Eleonore** and Kretzmann, Norman. An Objection to Swinburne's Argument for Dualism. *Faith Phil,* 13(3), 405-412, Jl 96.

In response to published objections, Swinburne has recently defended his 1984 argument for Cartesian dualism ("Dualism Intact," *Faith and Philosophy* 13 (1996)). We raise an objection that has not yet appeared in the literature and is fatal to the argument. We show that, viewed from more than one angle, the argument is either invalid, or unsound because the second of its three premises is false. We also emphasize that our criticisms don't constitute or even contribute to an argument against dualism generally.

**Sturdee, P G**. Commentary on "Aristotelian *Akrasia* and Psychoanalytic Regression". *Phil Psychiat Psych,* 4(3), 243-246, S 97.

**Sturm, Douglas**. The Idea of Human Rights: A Communitarian Perspective. *Process Stud,* 23(3-4), 238-253, Fall-Wint 94.

Given the current global crisis, we need to reconceive the underlying political ontology of the idea of human rights. Over against the individualism of classical Western liberalism, I propose a communitarian political ontology from whose perspective the central question of politics is: how might we so construct our lives together that all life flourishes? Within this setting, the point of human rights—including political/civil as well as economic/cultural rights—is to designate the kind of context most conducive to the self's agency.

**Suárez, Francisco** and Esposito, Costantino (ed & trans). *Disputazioni Metafisiche I-III.* Milano, Rusconi, 1996.

Quest'edizione—la prima in italiano—è curata da Costantino Esposito (Università di Bari), che si occupa di storia della metafisica con particolare riferimento a Kant e Heidegger. Dell'immensa mole delle 54 *Disputazioni* vengono tradotte qui le prime tre, per il fatto che esse si presentano, in maniera serrata e compiuta, come una vera e propria "introduzione alla metafisica", un'autentica monografia, in cui è presentata la natura, l'oggetto e il metodo di questa scienza. L'*introduzione* fornisce un primo approccio sintetico all'opera. Negli *apparati* è riportato l'indice completo di tutte le *Disputazioni;* l'indice delle fonti antiche, medioevali e rinascimentali discusse da Suárez; le *parole chiave* del testo e una *bibliografia* comprendente il prospetto degli *Opera omnia* di Suárez, l'elenco delle diverse edizioni delle *Disputazioni* e una raccolta esauriente degli studi sulle *Disputazioni* apparsi nel Novecento. (publisher, edited)

**Subler, Craig A** and Feagin, Susan L. Showing Pictures: Aesthetics and the Art Gallery. *J Aes Educ,* 27(3), 63-72, Fall 93.

Students often think that knowledge about technique, artist's intentions, or artistic or cultural context is irrelevant to understanding and appreciating art. Yet, students in an aesthetics class who were required to write a brief essay about an exhibit on campus complained that the gallery did not provide such information—no catalog, brochures, or explanatory wall labels. A newspaper review echoed these frustrations, highlighting questions about the educational functions of galleries, the relevance of artist's intentions to interpretation, how background information enriches one's experience and understanding, yet how viewers' experiences can be channeled by the selective presentation of background information.

**Subramaniam, Sharada**. Subjective, Not Objective, Truths. *J Indian Counc Phil Res,* 14(1), 1-16, S-D 96.

**Subrata, Roy**. Our Future in J. Krishnamurti. *Darshana Int,* 35(3/139), 58-62, Jl 95.

**Sucasas Peón, J Alberto**. Otra vuelta de tuerca: A propósito de *Espectros de Marx* de J. Derrida. *Daimon Rev Filosof,* 12, 131-135, Ja-Je 96.

**Such, Jan**. "Types of Determination vs. The Development of Science in Historical Epistemology" in *Epistemology and History,* Zeidler-Janiszewska, Anna (ed), 157-168. Amsterdam, Rodopi, 1996.

According to J. Kmita, the following types of determination take part in the development of science: functional, genetic and subjectively-rational which is a type of causal determination. The aim of this paper is to outline the role of these types of determination in the development of science in J. Kmita's formulation and to present a proposal considering the relation between functionally-genetic and subjectively-rational determination.

**Suchanek, Andreas**. "Verdirbt der *homo oeconomicus* die Moral?" in *Ökonomie und Moral: Beiträge zur Theorie ökonomischer Rationalität,* Lohmann, Karl Reinhard (ed), 65-84. München, Oldenbourg, 1997.

This paper examines two widely stated claims concerning the role of homo economicus. According to the first the assumption of self-interest is either empirically false or tautological. The second criticizes that the model of homo economicus cannot differentiate between particular and universalizable interests. As for the particular problem the model of homo economicus is used for both critiques are shown to be not valid.

**Suckiel, Ellen Kappy**. *Heaven's Champion: William James's Philosophy of Religion.* Notre Dame, Univ Notre Dame Pr, 1996.

Suckiel examines and extends James's insights and arguments, exhibiting their depth and contemporary relevance. Demonstrating how feelings and personal experiences may be used in justifying religious claims, she joins James in offering a model for assessing religion that is wider and deeper than that proposed by religion's "scientific rationalist" detractors. Suckiel challenges previous interpretations of James and answers longstanding objections to his position. In particular, she defends James against those philosophers who have interpreted his pragmatic justification of religion as being a disguised form of humanism, incongruous with the elevated domain of a genuine religious point of view. (publisher,edited)

**Süssmann, Georg**. Kennzeichnungen der Räume konstanter Krümmung. *Phil Natur,* 27(2), 206-233, 1990.

**Sugarman, Jeff** and Martin, Jack. Bridging Social Constructionism and Cognitive Constructivism: A Psychology of Human Possibility and Constraint. *J Mind Behav,* 17(4), 291-320, Autumn 96.

A theory intended to bridge social constructionist and cognitive constructivist thought is presented and some of its implications for psychotherapy and education are considered. The theory is mostly concerned with understanding the emergence and development of the psychological (mind, selfhood, intentionality, agency) from its biological and sociocultural origins. It is argued that the psychological is underdetermined by the biological and sociocultural, and possesses a shifting, dynamic ontology that emerges within a developmental context. Increasingly sophisticated capabilities of memory and imagination mediate and support the emergence of genuinely agentic psychological phenomena from appropriated sociocultural forms and practices.

**Sugarman, Jeremy** and Emanuel, Linda L. Relationships, Relationships, Relationships.... *J Clin Ethics,* 8(1), 6-10, Spr 97.

The network of relationships that exist within current medical practice extend well beyond the patient-physician relationship to include such people as healthcare providers, physician assistants, nurses, clergy, insurance representatives, technicians and others. Normative guidelines for these myriad professional roles are needed to enable appropriate responses to ethical difficulties that arise in the care of patients. Nevertheless, such guidelines have not yet been made explicit, and descriptive work related to these relationships, a necessary preliminary step, is just beginning. The authors review several manuscripts that comprise a special journal edition devoted to professional relationships and that provide such descriptions.

**Sugarman, Jeremy** and Kass, Nancy E and Faden, Ruth. Trust: The Fragile Foundation of Contemporary Biomedical Research. *Hastings Center Rep,* 26(5), 25-29, S-O 96.

It is widely assumed that informing prospective subjects about the risks and possible benefits of research not only protects their rights, but empowers them to protect their interests. Yet interviews with patient-subjects suggest this is not always the case. Patient-subjects often trust their physician to guide them through decisions.

**Sukla, Ananta C**. "Dhvani as a Pivot in Sanskrit Literary Aesthetics" in *East and West in Aesthetics,* Marchianò, Grazia (ed), 65-86. Pisa, Istituti Editoriali, 1997.

**Sullivan, Arthur**. Rorty and Davidson. *Dialogos,* 32(70), 7-26, Jl 97.

Rorty singles out Davidson as the champion of contemporary pragmatism. He calls himself a Davidsonian and argues that Davidson did for the study of language what Dewey did for epistemology. Davidson, however, rejects Rorty's characterization of him as a pragmatist. This paper is an investigation of the relationship between Davidson's thought and Rorty's pragmatism.

**Sullivan, Peter** and Potter, Michael. Hale on Caesar. *Phil Math,* 5, 135-152, Je 97.

Crispin Wright and Bob Hale have defended the strategy of defining the natural numbers contextually against the objection which led Frege himself to reject it, namely the so-called 'Julius Caesar problem'. To do this they have formulated principles (called sortal inclusion principles) designed to ensure that numbers are distinct from any objects, such as persons, a proper grasp of which could not be afforded by the contextual definition. We discuss whether either Hale or Wright has provided independent motivation for a defensible version of the sortal inclusion principle and whether they have succeeded in showing that numbers are *just* what the contextual definition says they are.

**Sullivan, Peter M**. The 'Truth' in Solipsism, and Wittgenstein's Rejection of the A Priori. *Euro J Phil,* 4(2), 195-219, Ag 96.

Sullivan, Philip R 942 AUTHOR INDEX

**Sullivan, Philip R**. Overriding the Natural Ought. *Behavior Phil*, 24(2), 129-135, Fall 96.

Natural selection favors not only more adaptive structural features but also more effective behavioral programs. Crucial for the prospering and very survival of an extremely sophisticated social species like *homo sapiens* is the biological/psychological program that might be conveniently labeled the human *sense of fairness*: a feeling often referred to in societies featuring supernaturalized explanations as one's "God given conscience." The sense of fairness and related programs derive a measure of their effectiveness from the fact that, in addition to the pleasure/pain mechanisms reinforcing their implementation, we are programmed *to want* to want the goals they introduce and to experience repugnance in the face of goals that strongly conflict.

**Sullivan, Shannon**. Democracy and the Individual: To What Extent is Dewey's Reconstruction Nietzsche's Self-Overcoming?. *Phil Today*, 41(2), 299-312, Sum 97.

This essay argues that Dewey's pragmatist philosophy of reconstruction is not opposed to, but rather complements Nietzsche's philosophy of self-overcoming. While Nietzsche and Dewey have similar concepts of the self as a bodily organism, their concepts of individuality differ greatly, which explains the clash between their different assessments of the desirability of democracy. After suggesting that the bodily nature of the self implies the need for democracy and for a catholic, instead of elitist approach to self-overcoming, the essay concludes that, despite their differences, Nietzscheans and Deweyan pragmatists should recognize in each other a kindred (free) spirit.

**Sullivan, Shannon**. Domination and Dialogue in Merleau-Ponty's *Phenomenology of Perception. Hypatia*, 12(1), 1-19, Wint 97.

Merleau-Ponty's claim in *Phenomenology of Perception* (1962) that the anonymous body guarantees an intersubjective world is problematic because it omits the particularities of bodies. This omission produces an account of "dialogue" with another in which I solipsistically hear only myself and dominate others with my intentionality. This essay develops an alternative to projective intentionality called "hypothetical construction," in which meaning is socially constructed through an appreciation of the differences of others.

**Sullivan, Shannon**. Fractured Passion in Kierkegaard's *Either/Or. Phil Today*, 41(1-4), 87-95, Spr 97.

By examining the role of ethical passion in Soren Kierkegaard's *Either/Or*, this essay demonstrates that as presented by Judge William, ethical passion disrupts the necessity of the unity of the person formed in passionate choice. While passion is responsible for the creation of the unified, continuous self that distinguishes ethical from aesthetic existence, it also creates the possibility of the disruption of the self's continuity. Thus instead of guaranteeing the unity of the self, ethical passion opens up the possibility for the creation of a person that is characterized not by her unity, but by a mosaic multiplicity of voices.

**Sullivan, Timothy**. Pandering. *J Thought*, 32(2), 75-84, Sum 97.

**Sulmasy, Daniel P**. Do the Bishops Have It Right On Health Care Reform?. *Christian Bioethics*, 2(3), 309-325, 1996.

The National Conference of Catholic Bishops has argued for significant government involvement in health care in order to assure respect for what they regard as the right to health care. Critics charge that the bishops are wrong because health care is not a right. In this article, it is argued that these critics are correct in their claim that health care is not a right. However, it is also argued that the premise that health care is not a right does not imply that the market is the most equitable and just system for providing health care natural law arguments in the tradition of Roman Catholic social teaching lead to the conclusion that a just and prosperous society has a moral obligation to provide health care even if there is no such right. (edited)

**Sulmasy, Daniel P**. Futility and the Varieties of Medical Judgment. *Theor Med*, 18(1-2), 63-78, Mr-Je 97.

Pellegrino has argued that end-of-life decisions should be based upon the physician's assessment of the effectiveness of the treatment and the patient's assessment of its benefits and burdens. This would seem to imply that conditions for medical futility could be met either if there were a judgment of ineffectiveness, or if the patient were in a state in which he or she were incapable of a subjective judgment of the benefits and burdens of the treatment. I argue that a theory of futility according to Pellegrino would deny that latter but would permit some cases of the former. I call this the "circumspect" view. I defend the circumspect view on the basis of a previously neglected aspect of the philosophy of medicine—an examination of varieties of medical judgment. I then offer some practical applications of this theory in clinical practice. (edited)

**Sumares, Manuel**. Mystics and Pragmatics in the Non-Philosophy of F. Laruelle: Lessons for Rorty's Metaphilosophizing. *Rev Port Filosof*, 53(1), 27-38, Ja-Mr 97.

Richard Rorty's recreation of pragmatism is a piece with his long and persistent practice of metaphilosophizing. The author of this essay proposes that something can be learned about the limits of Rorty's enterprise by comparing it with François Laruelle's transcendental approach to metaphilosophy, which coincides to a considerable degree with what Laruelle calls "nonphilosophy". Particular use of Laruelle's notions of "mystics" and "pragmatics" is made to bring out not only the lessons they might provide to Rorty's metaphilosophizing, but also aspects of Laruelle's original thinking.

**Summerell, Orrin F**. "Das Sich-Setzen der Freiheit: Zum Verhältnis Schelling-Fichte" in *Sein—Reflexion—Freiheit: Aspekte der Philosophie Johann Gottlieb Fichtes*, Asmuth, Christoph (ed), 69-78. Amsterdam, Gruner, 1997.

**Summerfield, Donna M**. "Fitting versus Tracking: Wittgenstein on Representation" in *The Cambridge Companion to Wittgenstein*, Sluga, Hans (ed), 100-138. Needham Heights, Cambridge, 1996.

Both fitting (shared feature) theories and tracking (covariance) theories may be proposed as explanations of how intentionality (aboutness) is possible. As the later Wittgenstein recognized, fitting theories fail to explain how signs can point to what is; tracking theories fail to explain how signs can point to what is not. I present Wittgenstein's *Tractatus* "picture theory" as a two-level theory which avoids central problems by combining elements of both theories. However, as the later Wittgenstein insisted, the *Tractatus* account is not correct. Recently, naturalists (Fred Dretske, Jerry Fodor) have revived tracking theory accounts of representation (in causal and/or nomological versions). And yet, the challenge they face (and have yet to meet) has not really changed substantially since Wittgenstein wrote his *Philosophical Investigations*: if there are no simple names and simple objects to provide the fixed backdrop against which signs can point to what is not there, how can they do so?

**Summers, Landon**. On the Education of Generalists: Religion, Public Schools, and Teacher Education. *Inquiry (USA)*, 14(1), 65-75, Fall 94.

**Sumner, David** and Gilmour, Peter. Response to Miller's 'Comment'. *Environ Values*, 6(1), 103-104, F 97.

**Sumner, L W**. *Welfare, Happiness, and Ethics*. New York, Clarendon/ Oxford Pr, 1996.

Moral philosophers agree that welfare matters. But they do not agree about what it is, or how much it matters. Wayne Sumner presents an original theory of welfare, investigating its nature and discussing its importance. He considers and rejects all notable rival theories, both objective and subjective, including hedonism and theories founded on desire or preference. His own theory connects welfare closely with happiness or life satisfaction. Professor Sumner then proceeds to defend welfarism, that is, to argue (against the value pluralism that currently dominates moral philosophy) that welfare is the only basic ethical value, the only thing which we have a moral reason to promote for its own sake. He concludes by discussing the implications of this thesis for ethical and political theory. (publisher)

**Sumner, L W** (ed) and Boyle, Joseph (ed). *Philosophical Perspectives on Bioethics*. Toronto, Univ of Toronto Pr, 1996.

How should we attempt to resolve concrete bioethical problems? How are we to understand the role of bioethics in the health care system, government, and academe? This collection of original essays raises these and other questions about the nature of bioethics as a discipline. The contributors to the volume discuss various approaches to bioethical thinking and the political and institutional context of bioethics, addressing underlying concerns about the purposes of its practice. Included are extended analyses of such important issues as the conduct of clinical trials, euthanasia, justice in health care, the care of children, cosmetic surgery, and reproductive technologies.

**Sundholm, Göran**. Implicit Epistemic Aspects of Constructive Logic. *J Log Lang Info*, 6(2), 191-212, Ap 97.

In the present paper I wish to regard constructive logic as a self-contained system for the treatment of epistemological issues; the explanations of the constructivist logical notions are cast in an epistemological mold already from the outset. The discussion offered here intends to make explicit this implicit epistemic character of constructivism. Particular attention will be given to the intended interpretation laid down by Heyting. This interpretation, especially as refined in the type-theoretical work of Per Martin-Löf, puts the system on par with the early efforts of Frege and Whitehead-Russell. This quite recent work, however, has proved valuable not only in the philosophy and foundations of mathematics, but has also found practical application in computer science, where the language of constructivism serves as an implementable programming language and within the philosophy of language. (edited)

**Sunstein, Cass R**. "Homosexuality and the Constitution" in *Sex, Preference, and Family: Essays on Law and Nature*, Nussbaum, Martha C (ed), 208-226. New York, Oxford Univ Pr, 1997.

**Supriya, K E**. Confessionals, Testimonials: Women's Speech in/and Contexts of Violence. *Hypatia*, 11(4), 92-106, Fall 96.

Theories of discursive genres provide the philosophical and theoretical framework for the empirical examination of the ways in which immigrant women construct their cultural identities in contexts of violence. The claim of the paper is that the analytical genres of confessional and testimonial discourse enable the examination of the particular ways by which immigrant women both reproduce and resist power and violence.

**Surber, Jere Paul**. Fichtes Sprachphilosophie und der Begriff einer Wissenschaftslehre. *Fichte-Studien*, 10, 35-49, 1997.

**Surendonk, Timothy J**. Canonicity for Intensional Logics without Iterative Axioms. *J Phil Log*, 26(4), 391-409, Ag 97.

David Lewis proved in 1974 that all logics without iterative axioms are weakly complete. In this paper we extend Lewis's ideas and provide a proof that such logics are canonical and so strongly complete. This paper also discusses the differences between rational and neighborhood frame semantics and poses a number of open questions about the latter.

**Surin, Ken**. The 'Epochality' of Deleuzean Thought. *Theor Cult Soc*, 14(2), 9-21, My 97.

**Susa, Oleg**. Environmental Responsibility: Individual Choice, Communication, Institutional Risks (in Czech). *Filosof Cas*, 45(3), 426-442, 1997.

After nearly three decades of environmental discourse, a comprehensive philosophical analysis of the environmental responsibility should avoid the danger of being too "generalist". The notion of environmental responsibility involves both individual and collective-social dimensions. The author of this contribution tries to offer the three-level approach in order to treat the matter more systematically: individual choice, communication, institutional risks are distinguished. Though the very institutional risks, which influence human individual as well as other natural beings, create urgent appeals to the environmental responsibility, given the complexity of modern social and technological forces transforming the ecological relationships. All the levels should be understood as mutually interconnected, so that individual choice, communication and institutional risks can be interpreted within the interactive sociocultural contexts. Individual choice could be more efficient in a framework of social action, when its sociopolitical context would enable the full participation in the critical challenge to the existing ways of discursive redesigns within the contemporary social institutions.

**Suster, Danilo**. Modality and Supervenience. *Acta Analytica*, 141-155, 1996.

According to the thesis of modal supervenience it is impossible that two objects be alike in their actual properties but differ in their modal properties. Some have argued that the concept of supervenience is inapplicable to the modal-actual case. Some have argued that the thesis of modal supervenience is trivially true. These arguments are refuted; a thesis of the supervenience of the modal on the actual is meaningful and nontrivial. The significance of the thesis is nevertheless limited by the problem of finding a nonmodal specification for the purported subvenient properties.

**Suttle, Bruce B**. "Can Hypocrites Be Good Teachers?" in *Philosophy of Education (1996)*, Margonis, Frank (ed), 326-328. Urbana, Phil Education Soc, 1997.

What is the relation between sincere teaching that honestly represents a teacher's conception of student learning and the achievement of quality student learning? Some claim it is analogous to a physician practicing the Hippocratic Oath and offering quality health care; that in both cases the former assures the latter. On the contrary, I argue the former is neither sufficient nor necessary for the latter, that those who devoutly follow their conception of student learning/who practice medicine according to the Hippocratic Oath can be poor teachers/physicians, just as hypocrites who teach or practice medicine can achieve quality student learning or offer quality health care.

**Sutton, Robert C**. Realism and Other Philosophical Mantras. *Inquiry (USA)*, 14(4), 36-41, Sum 95.

In the October 1992 issue of *Inquiry* there appeared an interesting article, "Epistemology and Pedagogy," by Donald Hatcher. This paper was followed in the February 1993 issue by my critical essay, "The Right Method?" Published in this issue of *Inquiry* is Dr. Hatcher's response to the questions and concerns which I raised in that paper. In responding to my concerns, Hatcher's latest effort is, in many ways, much clearer than his first. Nevertheless, his position is still a bit confusing to me, and, in an effort to examine the sources of that confusion, I would make a few observations.

**Suzuki, Nobu-Yuki**. Some Results on the Kripke Sheaf Semantics for Super-Intuitionistic Predicate Logics. *Stud Log*, 52(1), 73-94, F 93.

Some properties of Kripke-sheaf semantics for superintuitionistic predicate logics are shown. The concept of $p$-morphisms between Kripke sheaves is introduced. It is shown that if there exists a $p$-morphism from a Kripke sheaf $K_1$ into $K_2$ then the logic characterized by $K_1$ is contained in the logic characterized by $K_2$. Examples of Kripke-sheaf complete and finitely axiomatizable superintuitionistic (and intermediate) predicate logics each of which is Kripke-frame incomplete are given. (edited)

**Sverdlik, Steven**. Consistency Among Intentions and the 'Simple View'. *Can J Phil*, 26(4), 515-522, D 96.

**Swaine, Lucas A**. Blameless, Constructive, and Political Anger. *J Theor Soc Behav*, 26(3), 257-274, S 96.

Scholars of the emotions maintain that all anger requires an object of blame. In order to be angry, many writers argue, one must believe that an actor has done serious damage to something that one values. Yet an individual may be angered without blaming another. This kind of emotion, called *situational anger*, does not entail a corresponding object of blame. Situational anger can be a useful force in public life, enabling citizens to draw attention to the seriousness of social or political problems, without necessarily vilifying political officials.

**Swan, John**. Sharing and Stealing: Persistent Ambiguities. *J Infor Ethics*, 3(1), 42-47, Spr 94.

**Swanger, David**. The Metaphysics of Poetry: Subverting the "Ancient Quarrel" and Recasting the Problem. *J Aes Educ*, 31(3), 55-64, Fall 97.

The article reexamines the "ancient quarrel" between philosophy and poetry posited by Plato. The philosophic work of Wittgenstein and Bergson is invoked to lend credence to the view that poetry can extend understanding into a realm of meaning that philosophy unaided "must pass over in silence" (Wittgenstein). The author, who is also a poet, uses examples from his own work to explore how poetry may fill philosophy's silences and allow intelligence to enter "the mobile reality" of things (Bergson). The metaphysics of poetry is its linguistic method; and this method, the author suggests, abets, rather than subverts philosophy.

**Swanton, Christine**. Is the Moral Problem Solved?. *Analysis*, 56(3), 155-160, Jl 96.

**Swanton, Christine**. Virtue Ethics and the Problem of Indirection: A Pluralistic Value-Centred Approach. *Utilitas*, 9(2), 167-181, Jl 97.

Many forms of virtue ethics, like certain forms of utilitarianism, suffer from the problem of indirection. In those forms, the criterion for status of a trait as a virtue is not the same as the criterion for the status of an act as right. Furthermore, if the virtues, for example, are meant to promote the flourishing of the agent, the virtuous agent is not standardly supposed to be motivated by concern for her own flourishing in her activity. In this paper, I propose a virtue ethics which does not suffer from the problem. Traits are not virtues because their cultivation and manifestation promote a value such as agent flourishing. They are virtues in so

far as they are habits of appropriate response (which may be of various types) to various relevant values (valuable things, etc.). This means that there is a direct connection between the rationale of a virtue and what makes an action virtuous or right.

**Swart, H C M** and Perrick, M. Quantified Modal Logic, Reference and Essentialism. *Log Anal*, 36(144), 219-231, S-D 93.

After explaining in section 1 why modal contexts should be referentially transparent and extensionally opaque, we point out in section 2 that modal (necessity) contexts can only be referentially transparent if we take necessity as necessity de re, not de dicto. In section 3 we argue that quantified modal logic (as it appears in the literature) implies essentialism de dicto, in the sense that it limits the referring expressions to rigid designators. The arguments in the literature that "the Evening Star is the Morning Star" is a contingent truth are based on de dicto considerations and are not detrimental to the metaphysical (or de re) status of this sentence as a necessary truth. By making a distinction "de re—de dicto" we make it clear that essentialism (de re) and quantified modal logic (as conceived by Quine, Follesdal, Kripke and others) cannot be identified. Finally, we present two objections against the view that quantified modal logic presupposes that the referring terms are rigid designators.

**Swazey, Judith P** and Bird, Stephanie J. Teaching and Learning Research Ethics. *Prof Ethics*, 4(3-4), 155-178, Spr-Sum 95.

**Swazo, Norman K**. Planetary Politics and the Essence of Technology: A Heideggerian Analysis. *Dialogos*, 32(70), 147-179, Jl 97.

This essay explores the relationship between the "epoch" of technology (the planetary domination of technology) and the advent of "planetary" politics, including "world-order" thinking. Heidegger's rubric of closure to the Western tradition speaks of a "second" beginning: Our time is characterized by a precarious and ambiguous tension between the "first beginning" and the "second beginning"; metaphysical thinking and "essential thinking" (*wesentliche Denken*) inaugurating the second beginning are in tension. A precondition of essential thinking is to understand how the modern ontological commitment holds sway over contemporary politics. Technocratic conceptions of world order thereby become suspect as Heidegger's work calls us in the direction of "essential political thinking."

**Sweeney, Leo**. *Christian Philosophy: Greek, Medieval, Contemporary Reflections*. New York, Lang, 1997.

*Christian Philosophy* concerns the perennial paradox of reason/revelation and philosophy/theology by reflecting on: whether philosophy has ever been "pure," i.e., free of beliefs; how Plato, Aristotle, Plotinus helped prepare for Christian philosophy; how these practiced it: Bonaventure, Guerric, Albert, Aquinas, Maritain. As monists Marcel and Whitehead confirm that philosophy cannot be faith but must remain distinct and yet dependent on it if philosophy is to be Christian. This book closes by studying how Aquinas's positions are an antidote to current trends such as Sartre's existentialism, neo-Kantian self-centered epistemology and ethics, Derrida's deconstructionism. (publisher)

**Sweet, William**. "F.H. Bradley and Bernard Bosanquet" in *Philosophy after F.H. Bradley*, Bradley, James (ed), 31-56. Bristol, Thoemmes, 1996.

**Sweet, William**. Can There Be Moral Knowledge?. *Maritain Stud*, 11, 159-190, 1995.

**Sweet, William**. *Idealism and Rights: The Social Ontology of Human Rights in the Political Thought of Bernard Bosanquet*. Lanham, Univ Pr of America, 1997.

This volume presents and discusses the theory of rights of the British idealist political philosopher, Bernard Bosanquet. The political philosophy of the British idealists in general and of Bernard Bosanquet in particular, has been the subject of much misunderstanding and prejudice. Bosanquet's theory of rights proposes to provide a response to the utilitarianism of Jeremy Bentham and John Stuart Mill and the natural rights-based political philosophy of Herbert. The question addressed in this book then, is whether Bosanquet's theory is a plausible alternative to these 'individualist' views. The author believes that a complete statement of Bosanquet's theory of rights requires an elaboration of his "metaphysical theory of the nature of social reality"—his "social ontology."(publisher,edited)

**Sweet, William**. Jacques Maritain and the Nature of Religious Belief. *Maritain Stud*, 10, 142-155, 1994.

**Sweet, William**. Maritain's Criticisms of Natural Law Theories. *Maritain Stud*, 12, 33-49, 1996.

Jacques Maritain is widely recognized as one of the leading exponents of the natural law tradition of the 20th century. This essay deals with his analysis of 'rival' natural law theories, as presented in the recently published *La loi naturelle ou loi non-écrite*. Here, I begin by presenting Maritain's description of some rival theories of natural law. Next, I identify precisely what it is he criticizes in these theories. Finally, I consider some implications of these criticisms for Maritain's own natural law theory.

**Sweet, William**. Maritain, Post-Modern Epistemologies and the Rationality of Religious Belief. *Maritain Stud*, 9, 59-82, 1993.

**Swiderski, Edward**. "The Interpretational Paradigm in the Philosophy of the Human Sciences" in *Epistemology and History*, Zeidler-Janiszewska, Anna (ed), 237-266. Amsterdam, Rodopi, 1996.

Action theory, in the guise of the 'rational man' theory and theories of action explanation appealing to principles or assumptions of rationality, was the earliest topic which the Poznan theoreticians—Kmita and Nowak—investigated. In this essay I attempt to explore the parallels and differences between the mainstream, analytic philosophy of action, which has developed theories of rational action, and that of the Poznan theorists. I concentrate on two questions; "what does 'rationality' denote as regards the structure of action?" and "what follows as regards the nature of agency?" I suggest that the interpretational paradigm is incompatible with a 'realist' conception of action and is thus immune to the more scientistically minded programs for explanatory reduction. These results are then confronted with the theories of the Poznan school. The complicating factor in the latter case is the use made by the Poznan theoreticians of Marxist concepts. I conclude that the Poznan theory, while remaining in most respects within the framework of the interpretational paradigm, failed to combine it consistently with the Marxist conception of practice and the social ontology read into it.

**Swiezawski, Stefan** and Weksler-Waszkinel, R J. Freedom in Philosophy (in Polish). *Kwartalnik Filozof*, 25(1), 9-24, 1997.

**Swinburne, Richard**. Dualism Intact. *Faith Phil*, 13(1), 68-77, Ja 96.

I have argued in many places that a carefully articulated version of Descartes's argument to show that he is essentially an immaterial soul is sound. It is conceivable that I who am currently conscious continue to exist without my body, and that can only be if there is currently a nonbodily part of me which alone is essential for me. Recent counterarguments of Alston and Smythe, Moser and van der Nat, Zimmerman, and Shoemaker are rejected.

**Swinburne, Richard**. Reply to Stump and Kretzmann. *Faith Phil*, 13(3), 413-414, Jl 96.

Stump and Kretzmann object to my argument for substance dualism on the ground that its statement involves an implausibly stringent understanding of a hard fact about a time as one whose truth conditions lie solely at that time. I am, however, entitled to my own definitions and there is a simple reason why the "standard examples" of hard facts which they provide do not satisfy my definition—they all concern instants and not periods of time.

**Swinburne, Richard**. The Irreducibility of Causation. *Dialectica*, 51(1), 79-91, 1997.

Empiricists have sought to follow Hume in claiming that causality is a relation between events reducible to something more basic, e.g., regularities or counterfactuals. But all such attempts fail through their inability to distinguish cause from effect. The alternative is that causation is irreducible. Regularities are evidence of causation but do not constitute it. We understand what causation is through performing intentional actions which necessarily involve trying, which in turn just is exercising causal power.

**Swirydowicz, Kazimierz**. A Remark on the Maximal Extensions of the Relevant Logic *R*. *Rep Math Log*, 29, 19-33, 1995.

**Switala, Kristin**. Foucauldian Mutations of Language. *Phil Today*, 41(1-4), 166-173, Spr 97.

This paper examines two mutations of language in Foucault's discourse: the shift from classical to modern language and the shift from modern language to archaeology/genealogy. Three questions are addressed: a) does language function in archaeology or genealogy so differently from modern language that it has actually mutated? b) why does Foucault turn from the archaeological description of language to the genealogical? and c) since genealogy reintroduces 'the subject' into language, is it merely falling back into the modern episteme? The conclusion addresses whether or not Foucault's genealogical language remains trapped within the confines of modern thought.

**Swoyer, Chris**. Complex Predicates and Conversion Principles. *Phil Stud*, 87(1), 1-32, Jl 97.

Complex predicates allow us to ascribe complicated properties in an easy way and they afford a simple and perspicuous means of indicating scope. In cases where a conversion principle holds, such predicates can be introduced and eliminated in such a way that anything we can say with them can be said without them. The principle fails in various nonclassical settings, however, and my aim is to examine a range of cases to see where it fails, why it does and how to repair it.

**Sylvan, Richard**. Freedom without Determinism: Decent Logics of Relevance and Necessity Applied to Problems of Free-Will. *Acta Analytica*, 7-32, 1995.

Arguments for determinism do not enjoy the sound logical health that has been attributed to them. The main older argument is fallacious, indeed classically invalid, while a new "rectified" form is relevantly invalid (relying on modally covered form of Disjunctive Syllogism). What is more, there is no satisfactory way of repairing this form of argument so that it does yield a credible determinism. Other arguments for (nonvacuous) determinism are also dispatched, through a divide-and-dissolve technique, which operates by distinguishing types of determinism (such as logical determinism, which depends on another modal fallacy) and kinds of arguments for determinism (such as rational choice arguments, which inadmissibly assume maximization, and reductionistic arguments, which inadmissibly assume full reduction of choice and deliberation succeeds). In the largest of three appendices (the other two concern logical developments), a reasonable libertarianism is discerned and defended.

**Sylvan, Richard**. Process and Action: Relevant Theory and Logics. *Stud Log*, 51(3-4), 379-437, 1992.

Logical components from a properly expanded Humean model of action are supplied with relevant logics and semantics, in particular *doing*, *trying* and *striving*, *intention* and *motivation*. The difficult question of formalising practical inference is then addressed. Relevant dynamic logics, paralleling modal developments, are built up piece by piece, relevant theory change is considered within a dynamic framework and work on relevant temporal and process logics of programming cast, including functors such as *before*, *during* and *throughout*, is initiated. The present state of logical play is assessed. (edited)

**Szabados, Béla**. Wittgenstein's Women: The Philosophical Significance of Wittgenstein's Misogyny. *J Phil Res*, 22, 483-508, Ap 97.

While Wittgenstein commentators dismiss his remarks on women and femininity as trivial and unworthy of attention, I focus exactly on what they consider parenthetical and of no philosophical value. First, I document Wittgenstein's attitudes toward women and femininity and subject his remarks to critical analysis. Secondly, I retrieve and explore some aspects of Otto Weininger's influence on Wittgenstein. Thirdly, by introducing considerations of chronology and circumstance, I argue that while the early Wittgenstein of the *Tractatus* endorsed Weininger's views on women and sex, the mature Wittgenstein of the *Investigations* repudiated them without ceasing to admire his work or its spirit. Finally, I sketch crucial, unnoticed differences between Weininger and the mature Wittgenstein concerning femininity and philosophical method. The author's intention is to contribute to the project of challenging the supposed divide between the understanding of philosophical thought, on the one hand and sociocultural contexts and biography on the other.

**Szahaj, Andrzej**. "Between Modernism and Postmodernism: Jerzy Kmita's Epistemology" in *Epistemology and History*, Zeidler-Janiszewska, Anna (ed), 65-73. Amsterdam, Rodopi, 1996.

The main goal of the article is to place the epistemological views of Jerzy Kmita in the context of two different ways of thinking about cognition and science which can be found in a recent philosophy: the modernist and the postmodernist ones. The author is especially interested in the way in which Kmita treats the problems of reality, truth and cognitive progress as well as the way he tries to draw some ethical conclusions from the way science works. The author argues that Kmita keeps balance between modernism and postmodernism depriving science of all its myths and trying to stay faithful to its general ethical ethos.

**Szaniawksi, Klemens**. "The Ethics of Scientific Criticism" in *The Idea of University*, Brzezinski, Jerzy (ed), 129-137. Amsterdam, Rodopi, 1997.

**Szaniawski, Klemens**. "Plus Ratio Quam Vis" in *The Idea of University*, Brzezinski, Jerzy (ed), 105-113. Amsterdam, Rodopi, 1997.

**Szasz, Thomas**. *The Meaning of Mind: Language, Morality, and Neuroscience*. Westport, Praeger, 1996.

Only as a verb does the word "mind" name something in the real world, namely, the ability to pay attention and adapt to one's environment, mainly by using language to communicate with others and oneself. Viewing the mind as a potentially infinite variety of self-conversations is the key that unlocks many of the mysteries we associate with this concept. Modern neuroscience is a misdirected effort to explain "mind" in terms of brain functions. Its attraction lies in its discourse of brain-mind, which protects people from the dilemmas intrinsic to holding themselves responsible for their own actions and holding others responsible for their.

**Szatzscheider, Teresa Kwiatkowska**. From the Mexican Chiapas Crisis: A Different Perspective for Environmental Ethics. *Environ Ethics*, 19(3), 267-278, Fall 97.

The social unrest in Chiapas, a southern Mexican state, revealed the complexity of cultural and natural issues behind the idealized Western version of indigenous ecological ethics and its apparently universal perspective. In accordance with the conventional interpretation of traditional native beliefs, they are often pictured as alternative perspectives arising from challenges to the scientific worldview. In this paper, I point toward a more comprehensive account of human-environmental relation rooted in the particular type of social and natural conditions. I also discuss changes of place, changes of identity related to changes of place and respective changes in modes of environmental ethical insights: "openness" to the environment and respect for nonhuman living beings.

**Szécsi, Gábor**. Ontology, Realism and Instrumentalism: Comments on Lukács's Criticism of Logical Positivism (in Hungarian). *Magyar Filozof Szemle*, 4-5-6, 407-422, 1996.

In this essay I discuss the epistemological aspects of Lukács's Marxist criticism of logical positivism. In arguing for the approach taken to Lukács's criticism in my essay I attempt to clear up the nature of the epistemological confrontation that can be regarded as the very context of Lukács's objections to the logical positivist idea about the philosophical ignoration of ontology. It might seem, at first sight, that this epistemological confrontation is rooted in a realism-nominalism opposition. As I suggest, Lukács himself contributes to form such a conception of his criticism by regarding the logical positivist arguments against ontology as the manifestations of the sympathy with the nominalist tradition. (edited)

**Szolovits, Peter**. Sources of Error and Accountability in Computer Systems: Comments on "Accountability in a Computerized Society". *Sci Eng Ethics*, 2(1), 43-46, J 96.

**Taboada, M** and Marín, R. What's the Fuzzy Temporary Reasoning? (in Spanish). *Agora (Spain)*, 15(2), 83-96, 1996.

In this work we analyze the role of fuzzy logic in the field of temporal reasoning. The basic problems associated with the representation and management of time dependent information in expert systems are addressed and the basic strategies used to formally model temporal imprecision present in multiple domains are introduced. The foundations of time modelling through fuzzy temporal constraint networks are introduced and some examples are presented.

**Taborsky, Edwina**. *The Textual Society*. Toronto, Univ of Toronto Pr, 1997.

Taborsky looks at knowledge as a social construction involving two forces: stasis and variation, expressed within the group and the individual. These levels never merge, but exist in a state of continuous dialogical interaction, which transforms energy and permits meaning to exist. The unique, even tragic, nature of individuals is that they are the only means of expression for both realities, for the two opposing forces of energy—stasis and variation. Focusing on the nature of the dialogue between the two realities, Taborsky draws on key theoretical themes from the pragmatics and semiotics of Charles S. Peirce, the dialogues of Mikhail Bakhtin, and the fields of biology and quantum physics. As a whole, the book explores cognition as the social transformation of energy, and looks at different types of societies as differently organized forms of energy. (publisher, edited)

**Tabrizi, Firooz N**. *Life as Narcissism: A Unified Theory of Life*. New York, Vantage Pr, 1996.

In a sweeping overview that includes aspects of chemistry, physics and the evolution of man, author Firooz N. Tabrizi, M.D. presents a bold theory of the causative nature of the living organism in his book, *Life as Narcissism*. The author explores the common motivating principle that is evident from the subatomic level to that of world organizations. The topic of aggression is studied in all of its implications. In the service of self-interest, he asks, must it always lead to ultimate domination and chaos? Only by understanding its implications, he argues, can we create a just society. In addition, a nonaggression treaty is also proposed for and among men. A book that explores the factors affecting man's actions and the history of his social structures. (publisher)

**Tadashi, Kanai**. On Canova's Marble Sculptures (in Japanese). *Bigaku*, 47(1), 49-60, Sum 96.

Historically, the marble sculptures of Antonio Canova (1757-1822) have been criticized from two opposite standpoints. On the one hand, Canova's severely neoclassicist contemporaries were critical of the exquisitely finished surfaces and the quality of sensuality of his work. Modernist art historians, on the other hand, decried a cold academicism in Canova's work. In Quatremère de Quincy's (1755-1849) defense of Canova's work, however, we find a fluid approach to sculptural appreciation which is bound to neither of these fixed views. In some cases, Quatremère sought out sculptural outline and in others he strained his eyes to see the modulation of the surface. Although we should not limit Quatremère's attitudes merely to the issue of the criticism, we should recognize that it was only by being stimulated by the surfaces of canova's sculpture in the first place that Quatremère formulated his approach. (edited)

**Tännsjö, Torbjörn**. Doom Soon?. *Inquiry*, 40(2), 243-252, Je 97.

A critical notice of John Leslie, *The End of the World*. The notice is sympathetic with the main thrust of the argument of the book but critical on two points. The doomsday argument is not convincing and the author has neglected the repugnant conclusion.

**Tännsjö, Torbjörn**. Ought we to Sentence People to Psychiatric Treatment?. *Bioethics*, 11(3-4), 298-308, Jl 97.

In principle, there seem to be three main ways in which society can react when people commit crimes under influence of mental illness. 1) The standard model. We excuse them. If they are dangerous they are detained in the interest of safety of the rest of the citizens. 2) The Swedish model. We hold them responsible for their criminal offense, we convict them, but we do not sentence them to jail. Instead, we sentence them to psychiatric treatment. 3) My model. We sentence them to jail, but offer them (voluntary) psychiatric treatment. The advantages of my model are obvious. We get a clear delineation of roles. We allow the psychiatrist to be just a doctor, not a warden. We liberate psychiatry of the objective of deciding whether people who were mentally ill when they committed criminal offenses 'could have acted otherwise'—a hopeless task. We allow that psychiatrists live up to their professional ethical code (the Hawaii Declaration). We treat psychically ill persons as 'normal', we allow them to repent their crimes, which renders easier their recovery. (edited)

**Taft, Richard** (trans) and Heidegger, Martin. *Kant and the Problem of Metaphysics*. Bloomington, Indiana Univ Pr, 1997.

**Tagliacozzo, Giorgio**. La unidad del conocimiento: desde la especulación a la ciencia. (Introducción a la *Dendrognoseología*). *Cuad Vico*, 7/8, 207, 1997.

As a follow-up to his article "My Vichian Journey: A Chronology", the author gives us an introduction to a science of his invention: the *Dendrognoseology*. This science, whose main referent is the Vichian New Science, goes on with the immemorial human and scholarly preoccupation with the unity of knowledge. However, it does not consist any more of a *speculative* conception, but of a *science*, being—thanks to its unique and constant set of principles—a one-piece, unitary historical-taxonomic structure and being independent from any given worldview. *Dendrognoseology* amounts to a prototype valid throughout changing times and circumstances that encompasses and unifies all knowledge in a tree. Such a science, the cardinal basis of which is the concept of *symbolism* or of *imagination*, two most elementary philosophical concepts that are the respective points of departure of Cassirer's and Vico's philosophy, can help to improve the performance of an indefinite number of intellectual and para-intellectual tasks. (edited)

**Tagliaferri, Teodoro**. "Il compito dello storico nella lezione inaugurale di Richard Henry Tawney (1932)" in *Lo Storicismo e la Sua Storia: Temi, Problemi, Prospettive*, Cacciatore, Giuseppe (ed), 524-539. Milano, Guerini, 1997.

**Tagliavia, Grazia**. Essere e idea. *G Metaf*, 19(1), 75-100, Ja-Ap 97.

**Tagliavia, Grazia**. L'aporia del pensare fra scienza e storia. *G Metaf*, 18(1-2), 47-85, Ja-Ag 96.

**Tait, W W**. "Frege Versus Cantor and Dedekind: On the Concept of Number" in *Early Analytic Philosophy*, Tait, William W (ed), 213-248. Chicago, Open Court, 1997.

**Tait, William W**. "Frege versus Cantor and Dedekind: On the Concept of Number" in *Frege: Importance and Legacy*, Schirn, Matthias (ed), 70-113. Hawthorne, de Gruyter, 1996.

**Tait, William W** (ed). *Early Analytic Philosophy*. Chicago, Open Court, 1997.

These essays present new analyses of the central figures of analytic philosophy—Frege, Russell, Moore, Wittgenstein, and Carnap—from the beginnings of the analytic movement into the 1930s. The papers do not represent a single perspective, but rather express divergent interpretations of this controversial intellectual milieu. (publisher)

**Taitslin, Mikhail A** and Archangelsky, Dmitri A. A Logic for Information Systems. *Stud Log*, 58(1), 3-16, 1997.

A conception of an information system has been introduced by Pawlak. The study has been continued in works of Pawlak and Orlowska and in works of Vakarelov. They had proposed some basic relations and had constructed a formal system of a modal logic that describes the relations and some of their Boolean combinations. Our work is devoted to a generalization of this approach. A class of relation systems and a complete calculus construction method for these systems are proposed. As a corollary of our main result, our paper contains a solution of a Vakarelov's problem: how to construct a formal system that describes all the Boolean combinations of the basic relations.

**Taka, Iwao** and Dunfee, Thomas W. Japanese Moralogy as Business Ethics. *J Bus Ethics*, 16(5), 507-519, Ap 97.

Moralogy is an indigenous six-decade-old Japanese approach to business ethics which has been particularly influential among middle-sized business. The core themes of moralogy are 1) the inseparability of morality and economic activities, 2) the recognition of a difference between social justice and universal justice, and 3) an emphasis on identification of principles of supreme or universal morality. Moralogy recognizes moral liberty and a principle of "omni-directional fairness"; and may be best described as a virtue-based stakeholder approach to business ethics. It differs in significant ways, however, from Rawls's *theory of justice* and Donaldson and Dunfee's *integrative social contracts theory*.

**Takahashi, Akira**. Ethics in Developing Economies of Asia. *Bus Ethics Quart*, 7(3), 33-45, Jl 97.

This essay aims to deepen our comprehension of the economic ethics of different peoples in Asia, as well as realizing a degree of cultural relativism, in order to enhance amicable economic associations. It counterbalances the conventionally strong West-oriented views which regard exotic features of non-Western economies as backward and illogical elements that disturb smooth and orthodox development and, hence, should be eradicated. (edited)

**Takahashi, Yoshitomo** and Berger, Douglas and Fukunishi, Isao (& others). Japanese Psychiatrists' Attitudes toward Patients Wishing to Die in the General Hospital: A Cultural Perspective. *Cambridge Quart Healthcare Ethics*, 6(4), 470-479, Fall 97.

**Talaska, Richard A**. Philosophical Reasoning in Ethics and the Use of the History of Philosophy. *Teach Phil*, 20(2), 121-141, Je 97.

We need to study the history of philosophy to do ethics philosophically. We think within the horizon of our particular world views. If this horizon is not made thematic and questioned, we will be trying to do moral philosophy without unmasking our unquestioned moral assumptions. To make thematic and study the assumptions at the basis of our moral paradigm, we must study foundational moral texts of our own tradition and a tradition opposed to it, and then, by comparison and contrast, gradually bring to light and question the moral paradigm within which we think. Plato's *Republic*, compared and contrasted with fundamental tracts of Western liberalism, offers a tool to help Western students make thematic their own moral prejudices and begin to critique them.

**Tale, Camilo**. Examen del escepticismo moral y del relativismo moral. *Sapientia*, 52(201), 127-144, 1997.

**Taliaferro, Charles**. Possibilities in Philosophy of Mind. *Phil Phenomenol Res*, 57(1), 127-137, Mr 97.

This paper seeks to overturn the claim that Cartesian arguments for dualism based on the conceivable separation of person and body lack warrant, since it is just as conceivable that persons are identical with their bodies as it is that persons and their bodies are distinct. If the thesis of the paper is cogent, then it is not as easy to imagine person-body identity as many anti-Cartesians suppose.

**Taliaferro, Charles**. Saving our Souls: Hacking's Archaeology and Churchland's Neurology. *Inquiry*, 40(1), 73-94, Mr 97.

This is a critical comparison of Ian Hacking's work on memory and Paul Churchland's critique of folk psychology.

**Tallet, J A**. *The Possible Universe*. Lanham, Univ Pr of America, 1997.

**Tallon, Andrew**. *Head and Heart: Affection, Cognition, Volition as Triune Consciousness*. New York, Fordham Univ Pr, 1997.

*Head and Heart* proposes a theory of a triune consciousness formed by the heart and mind and composed of an equal partnership of reason, will and affection. Andrew Tallon sets out asking whether and how affective consciousness fits into this triad. By first defining affection in terms of intentionality (as the theory of a triune consciousness is possible only when affectivity has been shown to participate in intentionality), he argues that affection, in its full scope of passion, emotion and mood, earns a place equal to cognition and volition as a constituent of the human consciousness. Tallon proves the existence of affectivity as a distinct kind of consciousness but inseparable from the other two. He accomplishes this by showing precisely how affection works, how it operates in synthesis with reason and will and finally, by offering a new concept of a triune consciousness as paradigm for the human mind. (publisher)

**Talmage, Catherine J L**. Meaning and Triangulation. *Ling Phil*, 20(2), 139-145, Ap 97.

Is it essential that an individual has a *social* environment if she is to be able to produce utterances that are literally meaningful? If so, why? In this paper I first outline Donald Davidson's reason for rejecting the common view that it *is* essential that an individual has a social environment because it is *the conventions of an individual's linguistic community* that determines what that individual's utterances literally mean and then examines critically his own view concerning why an individual cannot be the speaker of a language in the absence of a social environment.

**Tamari, Meir**. The Challenge of Wealth: Jewish Business Ethics. *Bus Ethics Quart*, 7(2), 45-56, Mr 97.

Jewish business ethics in Israel addresses two major sources of economic immorality—unbounded desire and fear of economic uncertainty—through enforcement and spiritual education. Business is seen as a path to sanctity, when time is set apart for religious study, wealth is seen as originating from God, the vulnerable are protected against fraud and theft, charity is seen as an obligation and mercy towards debtors is tempered by justice.

**Tambini, Damian**. Explaining Monoculturalism: Beyond Gellner's Theory of Nationalism. *Crit Rev*, 10(2), 251-270, Spr 96.

For Ernest Gellner, nationalism occurs in the modern period because industrial societies, unlike agrarian ones, need homogeneous languages and cultures in order to work efficiently. Thus, states and intellectuals mobilize campaigns of assimilation through public education and the culture industries. Gellner's theory, however, fails to explain all forms of nationalism, is overly materialist and at times relies on dubious functionalist explanations. A more satisfactory theory would take into account the cultural content of nationalism—not only myths, but political culture—as well as phenomena of identity and collective action.

**Taminiaux, Jacques**. "Nothingness and the Professional Thinker: Arendt versus Heidegger" in *The Ancients and the Moderns,* Lilly, Reginald (ed), 196-210. Bloomington, Indiana Univ Pr, 1996.

**Taminiaux, Jacques** and Moran, Dermot (trans). *Bios politikos* and *bios theoretikos* in the Phenomenology of Hannah Arendt. *Int J Phil Stud*, 4(2), 215-232, S 96.

Hannah Arendt frequently referred to herself as a phenomenologist in that she wished to reveal how *action*, in the Greek sense of *praxis*, engenders a public space of appearances or of phenomenality. The life of the Greek city-state, of the *polis*, was made possible through this activity, this *bios politikos*. However, beginning with Plato and continuing right down to Hegel and Heidegger, there has been a sustained attempt to cover up and conceal the specific phenomenality of the *bios politikos* in favour of the *bio theoretikos*, involving the substitution of *poiesis* and *theoria* for the life of *praxis*. At the roots of this concealment of the active life is a misunderstanding of the true nature of the theoretical and its highest form, namely, thinking.

**Tamir, Yael**. "Pro Patria Mori!: Death and the State" in *The Morality of Nationalism,* McKim, Robert (ed), 227-241. New York, Oxford Univ Pr, 1997.

**Tamir, Yael**. The Land of the Fearful and the Free. *Constellations*, 3(3), 296-314, Ja 97.

**Tamminga, Allard M**. Logics of Rejection: Two Systems of Natural Deduction. *Log Anal*, 37(146), 169-208, Je 94.

**Tan, Kok-Chor**. Kantian Ethics and Global Justice. *Soc Theor Pract*, 23(1), 53-73, Spr 97.

Kant divides moral duties into duties of virtue and duties of justice. Duties of virtue are *imperfect duties*, the fulfilment of which is left to agent discretion and so cannot be externally demanded of one. Duties of justice, while *perfect*, seem to be restricted to negative duties (of nondeception and noncoercion). It may seem then that Kant's moral philosophy cannot meet the demands of global justice. I argue, however, that Kantian justice when applied to the social and historical realities of the world can generate positive duties to promote and provide for the well-being of others.

**Tan, Yao Hua** and Van den Akker, Johan. Paraconsistent Default Logic. *Log Anal*, 36(144), 311-328, S-D 93.

Pequeno and Buchsbaum presented a new default logic, *The Inconsistent Default Logic* (IDL), which is based on Da Costa's paraconsistent logic, in which the ex-falso rule does not hold. In this paper we present the *Question Marked Logic* (QML), a further development of IDL. We show that QML inherits the good behaviour of IDL on representing conflicts, and that in addition it can be used to model specificity between default rules in a very intuitive way.

**Tan, Yao-Hua**. Is Default Logic a Reinvention of Inductive-Statistical Reasoning?. *Synthese*, 110(3), 357-379, Mr 97.

Currently there is hardly any connection between philosophy of science and Artificial Intelligence research. We argue that both fields can benefit from each other. As an example of this mutual benefit we discuss the relation between *Inductive-Statistical Reasoning* and *Default Logic*. One of the main topics in AI research is the study of common-sense reasoning with incomplete information. Default logic is especially developed to formalise this type of reasoning. We show that there is a striking resemblance between inductive-statistical reasoning and default logic. A central theme in the logical positivist study of inductive-statistical reasoning such as Hempel's *Criterion of Maximal Specificity* turns out to be equally important in default logic. We also discuss to what extent the relevance of the results of Logical Positivism to AI research could contribute to a re-evaluation of Logical Positivism in general.

**Tan, Yao-Hua** and Van der Torre, Leendert W N. "How to Combine Ordering and Minimizing in a Deontic Logic Based on Preferences" in *Deontic Logic, Agency and Normative Systems,* Brown, Mark A (ed), 216-232. New York, Springer-Verlag, 1996.

In this paper we propose a semantics for dyadic deontic logic with an explicit preference ordering between worlds, representing different degrees of ideality. We argue that this ideality ordering can be used in two ways to evaluate formulas, which we call *ordering* and *minimizing*. Ordering uses all preference relations between relevant worlds, whereas minimizing uses the most preferred worlds only. We show that ordering corresponds to strengthening of the antecedent, and minimizing to weakening of the consequent. Moreover, we show that in some cases ordering and minimizing have to be combined to obtain certain desirable conclusions, and that this can only be done in a so-called two-phase deontic logic. In the first phase, the preference ordering is constructed, and in the second phase the ordering is used for minimization. If these two phases are not distinguished, then counterintuitive conclusions follow.

**Tanaka, Kazuyuki**. The Self-Embedding Theorem of $WKL_0$ and a Non-Standard Method. *Annals Pure Applied Log*, 84(1), 41-49, Mr 97.

We prove that every countable nonstandard model of $WKL_0$ has a proper initial part isomorphic to itself. This theorem enables us to carry out nonstandard arguments over $WKL_0$.

**Tannoch-Bland, Jennifer**. From Aperspectival Objectivity to Strong Objectivity: The Quest for Moral Objectivity. *Hypatia*, 12(1), 155-182, Wint 97.

Sandra Harding is working on the reconstruction of scientific objectivity. Lorraine Daston argues that objectivity is a concept that has historically evolved. Her account of the development of "aperspectival objectivity" provides an opportunity to see Harding's "strong objectivity" project as a stage in this evolution, to locate it in the history of migration of ideals from moral philosophy to natural science and to support Harding's desire to retain something of the ontological significance of objectivity.

**Tanovic, Predrag** and Loveys, James. Countable Model of Trivial Theories Which Admit Finite Coding. *J Sym Log*, 61(4), 1279-1286, D 96.

We prove: *Theorem.* A complete first order theory in a countable language which is strictly stable, trivial and which admits finite coding has $2^{\text{Aleph } 0}$ nonisomorphic countable models. Combined with the corresponding result or superstable theories from our result confirms the Vaught conjecture for trivial theories which admit finite coding.

**Tanovic, Predrag** and Loveys, James and Chowdhury, Ambar. A Definable Continuous Rank for Nonmultidimensional Superstable Theories. *J Sym Log*, 61(3), 967-984, S 96.

**Tappolet, Christine**. Mixed Inferences: A Problem for Pluralism about Truth Predicates. *Analysis*, 57(3), 209-210, Jl 97.

In reply to Geach's objection against expressivism, some have claimed that there is a plurality of truth predicates. I raise a difficulty for this claim: valid inferences can involve sentences assessible by any truth predicate, corresponding to 'lightweight' truth as well as to 'heavyweight' truth. To account for this, some unique truth predicate must apply to all sentences that can appear in inferences. Mixed inferences remind us of a central platitude about truth: truth is what is preserved in valid inferences. The question is why we should postulate truth predicates that do not satisfy this platitude.

**Taranto, Domenico**. L'esclusione dalla cittadinanza: Un casa limite: barbari e selvaggi. *Stud Filosofici*, 81-87, 1995.

Analysing the working of the category of barbarous in the Greek culture and that of savage in J. Ginés de Sepulveda, this essay shows the convergence of both the modalities for the exclusion of the citizenship on the political argument of the servitude as a feature of the racial inferiority. If the capability of autodetermination is a political value, the observation of its absence, acts as a political presupposition for enslavement.

**Tarcov, Nathan** (ed) and Grant, Ruth W (ed). *John Locke: Some Thoughts Concerning Education* and *Of the Conduct of the Understanding.* Indianapolis, Hackett, 1996.

This volume offers two contemporary works by John Locke, unabridged, in modernized, annotated texts—the only available edition priced for classroom use. Of interest to students and instructors of philosophy, political theory, and education, these important works shed light on conceptions of reason and freedom essential for understanding Locke's philosophy. With renewed interest in the relations between politics and education, Locke's epistemological and educational writings take on added significance. Read alongside Locke's political writings, these works allow the reader to develop a deeper appreciation of the various interconnected concerns at the core of Lockean liberalism. Grant and Tarcov provide a concise introduction, a note on the texts, and a select bibliography. (publisher)

**Tardiff, Andrew**. Simplifying the Case for Vegetarianism. *Soc Theor Pract*, 22(3), 299-314, Fall 96.

This article shows that a moral obligation to vegetarianism can be argued far more simply than it has been. The key principles can be derived from beliefs most people already hold and once identified the application of these principles to vegetarianism is straightforward. This alternative to the arguments of Regan and Singer better satisfies the former's five criteria of a good moral theory: consistency, scope, precision, conformity to reflective intuition and simplicity. It meets all of the above and is much simpler.

**Taris, Toon W** and Semin, Gün R. Passing on the Faith: How Mother-Child Communication Influences Transmission of Moral Values. *J Moral Educ*, 26(2), 211-221, Je 97.

This paper examines religious affiliation and commitment of teenagers as a function of the quality of mother-child interaction and the mothers' religious commitment, as an illustration of the principle that transmission of parental norms and values to their children is facilitated or inhibited by the quality of their interaction. We expected that in cases where mother-child interaction was good, parents would be better able to impose their own values upon their children, resulting in a lower disaffiliation and higher religious commitment in high quality

AUTHOR INDEX 947 Teixeira, António Braz

of family-interaction families. This expectation was tested using data from 223 British adolescent-mother pairs, by means of logistic and ordinary regression analysis. The results largely supported the hypotheses, exemplifying how mothers in their role of moral agents may profit from good mother-child relationships.

**Taroni, Paolo**. *Assoluto: Frammenti di misticismo nella filosofia di Francis Herbert Bradley.* Ravenna, Ed Coop Lib Inform, 1996.

Il pensiero di Francis Herbert Bradley (1846-1924) viene in questo saggio analizzato nel contesto dell'idealismo inglese e nei rapporti con Kant ed Hegel, per mostrarne le perculiarità che le caratterizzano. Attraverso un'analisi dei vari testi del filosofo di Oxford si evidenziano, infatti, gli elementi di novità e i legami con la tradizione presenti nella sua visione dell'Assoluto. Attraverso una critica serrata della logica occidentale, soprattutto con la precisa trattazione del concetto di relazione, Bradley viene a fondare in maniera unitaria la sua metafisica del Tutto. Tramite un originale scetticismo egli critica l'empirismo e il razionalismo classici, per cogliere l'Unità totale dell'Universo in un Assoluto di cui tutta la realtà fenomenica è parte espressiva. (publisher, edited)

**Tarr, Zoltan**. A Note on Weber and Lukács (in Hungarian). *Magyar Filozof Szemle*, 4-5-6, 574-582, 1996.

**Tarrant, Harold**. "Plato, Prejudice, and the Mature-Age Student in Antiquity" in *Dialogues with Plato,* Benitez, Eugenio (ed), 105-120. Edmonton, Academic, 1996.

The paper aims to assess the attitudes of Plato and Socrates to philosophical studies relatively late in life, and where, if at all, the two part company. The issue is examined in the light of Greek prejudices against the late-learner. Though Plato found the need to distinguish his late-learning from that associated with Euthydemus etc., Socrates himself clearly did study many subjects at an unexpectedly late age; the *Laches* demonstrates why. His own late learning can help to explain many familiar traits of the Platonic Socrates, such as irony.

**Tarrant, Harold**. Plato, Prejudice, and the Mature-Age Student in Antiquity. *Apeiron*, 29(4), 105-120, D 96.

The paper aims to assess the attitudes of Plato and Socrates to philosophical studies relatively late in life, and where, if at all, the two part company. The issue is examined in the light of Greek prejudices against the late-learner. Though Plato found the need to distinguish his late-learning from that associated with Euthydemus etc., Socrates himself clearly did study many subjects at an unexpectedly late age; the *Laches* demonstrates why. His own late learning can help to explain many familiar traits of the Platonic Socrates, such as irony.

**Tate, John W**. Dead or Alive? Reflective Versus Unreflective Traditions. *Phil Soc Crit*, 23(4), 71-91, Jl 97.

The Enlightenment heritage has meant that we have tended to conceive of *tradition* as inevitably opposed to reason and that the extension of one as a major constitutive element in social affairs, implies the retraction of the other. However, this paper attempts to conceive the relationship between tradition and reason in a more articulated context, suggesting that this dichotomy between reason and tradition may itself be what Hans-Georg Gadamer calls an 'Enlightenment prejudice'. By drawing on the work of thinkers within a broad *hermeneutic* tradition, this paper attempts to articulate an alternative means of thinking about the relationship between reason and tradition, which suggests that it is only when we adopt a particular Enlightenment perspective that we are hermeneutically confined to confirming Enlightenment presuppositions that there is such a dichotomy between reason and tradition.

**Taube, Daniel O** and Burkhardt, Susan. Ethical and Legal Risks Associated with Archival Research. *Ethics Behavior,* 7(1), 59-67, 1997.

Mental health facilities and practitioners commonly permit researchers to have direct access to patients' records for the purpose of archival research without the informed consent of patient-participants. Typically these researchers have access to all information in such records as long as they agree to maintain confidentiality and remove any identifying data from subsequent research reports. Changes in the American Psychological Association's Ethical Principles (American Psychological Association, 1992) raise ethical and legal issues that require consideration by practitioners, researchers, and facility Institutional Review Boards. This article addresses these issues and provides recommendations for changes in ethical standards as well as alternative avenues for conducting research using archival mental health records.

**Taube, Volkmar**. Exemplifikatorische Darstellung: Zu den Grundlagen einer kognitiven Ästhetik. *Protosoz*, 8/9, 68-80, 1996.

After having introduced Goodman's concept of exemplification I discuss his general argument that exemplification would be the best for comprehensible the expressive phenomena of art. But there will arise problems when making differences between features of works of art which are exemplified and which are not and when reconstructing the variable forms of autoreflexive expressions. I try to demonstrate that Goodman's concept of exemplification therefore is too limited: 1. Goodman doesn't take into account that the characteristics of works such as colours, form etc. also can be interpreted as materials of artistic expressions. 2. He doesn't give any idea to solve the question what would make an exemplification work effectively. Therefore, I suggest to reformulate the concept of exemplification.

**Tauer, Carol A**. Preimplantation Embryos, Research Ethics, and Public Policy. *Bioethics Forum*, 11(3), 30-37, Fall 95.

The NIH Human Embryo Panel, established in 1994, included members of various disciplines—science, ethics, law, medicine, public policy, as well as representatives of persons and groups that could be affected by the proposed research—all who worked together to recommend ethical guidelines for human embryo research. In this first-person account, the author describes the workings of such a panel, the method of deliberation, and the outcomes.

**Tauste Alcocer, Francisco**. El *Comentario* a la *Eneida* de Bernardo Silvestre. *Daimon Rev Filosof*, 10, 23-36, Ja-Je 95.

With this paper we display an analysis of *the Commentary on the Aeneid* attributed to Bernard Silvestris in which he explain the first six books of Vergil's work as a figuration of the pilgrimage of human life. Thus we attempt to prove that the more important topics of this work: integumentum's doctrine, intellectual and moral growth of the wise, naturalistic explication of the cosmos's genesis, role of the liberal arts in human education, are the typical of the *Thimaeus's* tradition present at Chartres School. Specially it could emphasize the integumentum's doctrine which confirms the relations between philosophy and literature in the XII century, accomplishing of the liberal arts's program: the union of Sapientia and Eloquentia.

**Tavares de Miranda, Maria Do Carmo**. Une philosophie de la "dynamique créative". *G Metaf*, 18(3), 443-446, S-D 96.

**Taylor, A E**. *Thomas Hobbes.* Bristol, Thoemmes, 1997.

This brief sketch has throughout been written directly from the original text of Hobbes himself and his contemporary biographers, though use has, of course, been made, especially in the first chapter, of the labors of such modern students as Professor Croom Robertson, Professor F. Tönnies, and Sir Leslie Stephen. (publisher, edited)

**Taylor, C C W** (trans). *Protagoras.* New York, Oxford Univ Pr, 1996.

**Taylor, Charles**. "Nationalism and Modernity" in *The Morality of Nationalism,* McKim, Robert (ed), 31-55. New York, Oxford Univ Pr, 1997.

**Taylor, John**. Kalam: A Swift Argument from Origins to First Cause?. *Relig Stud*, 33(2), 167-179, Je 97.

This paper contains a critique of the 'Kalam' Cosmological Argument for a first cause of the universe as a whole. I argue that one of its major premises (that the universe began to exist) cannot be justified *a priori* from the paradoxes of the actual infinite, nor by appeal to current cosmological theories. But those who wish to infer from cosmology to the nonexistence of a first cause also fail to make their case. I conclude with some morals for the project of natural theology.

**Taylor, John H** and Walker, Lawrence J. Moral Climate and the Development of Moral Reasoning: The Effects of Dyadic Discussions between Young Offenders. *J Moral Educ*, 26(1), 21-43, Mr 97.

Cognitive-developmental theory claims that moral reasoning can be developed through discussion with others, especially those at a higher stage. This study examined two social/contextual factors that may mediate such cognitive processes in moral development: sociometric status and moral climate. It was found that exposure to both higher-stage reasoning and higher peer status were essential elements within the developmental process. Implications for cognitive-developmental theory and moral education within correctional and school programmes are discussed. (edited)

**Taylor, Paul**. Intuitionistic Sets and Ordinals. *J Sym Log*, 61(3), 705-744, S 96.

Transitive extensional *well founded* relations provide an intuitionistic notion of *ordinals* which admits *transfinite induction*. However, these ordinals are not *directed* and their successor operation is poorly behaved, leading to problems of functoriality. We show how to make the successor monotone by introducing *plumpness*, which strengthens transitivity. This clarifies the traditional development of successors and unions, making it *intuitionistic*; even the (classical) proof of *trichotomy* is made simpler. The definition is, however, recursive and as their name suggests, the plump ordinals grow very rapidly. (edited)

**Taylor, Richard C**. "The Future Life" and Averroës's *Long Commentary on the De Anima of Aristotle*" in *Averroës and the Enlightenment,* Wahba, Mourad (ed), 263-277. Amherst, Prometheus, 1996.

**Teffo, Joe**. "The Averroistic Ethos Beyond the Enlightenment" in *Averroës and the Enlightenment,* Wahba, Mourad (ed), 93-98. Amherst, Prometheus, 1996.

**Tegtmeier, Erwin**. Meixner über Parmenides (Zu Uwe Meixner: Parmenides und die Logik der Existenz) *Grazer Philosophische Studien* 47, (1994). *Grazer Phil Stud*, 51, 253-257, 1996.

Meixner argues that Parmenides' refutation of becoming is logically defective, that the term "being" occurs in two senses in his inference, synonymously with "actual" and in a wider sense. This interpretation is rejected. In addition, it is pointed out that Meixner's concepts of actuality and potentiality are not relevant referring to facts rather than to things. Finally, Meixner's disproof of what he calls "actualism" is refuted.

**Teichert, Will**. "Journalistische Verantwortung: Medienethik als Qualitätsproblem" in *Angewandte Ethik: Die Bereichsethiken und ihre theoretische Fundierung,* Nida-Rümelin, Julian (ed), 750-776. Stuttgart, Alfred Kröner, 1996.

**Teichmann, Frank**. *Auferstehung im Denken: Der Christusimpuls in der "Philosophie der Freiheit" und in der Bewusstseinsgeschichte.* Stuttgart, Freies Geistesleben, 1996.

Was seit dem Beginn der griechischen Philosophie bei Sokrates und Plato bekannt war, was sich dann in der christlichen Philosophie seit Paulus bis hin zur Schule von Chartres fortsetzte und im deutschen Idealismus einen bewusstseinsgeschichtlichen Höhepunkt erlebte, wird durch die *Philosophie der Freiheit* Rudolf Steiners zu einem systematischen Schulungsweg des Denkens erweitert. Als ein wesentliches Ergebnis dieses Schulungsweges ergibt sich die Ausbildung eines neuen Organs für die Wahrnehmung des Geistes, ein Auferstehungserlebnis im Denken. (publisher, edited)

**Teixeira, António Braz**. Criacionismo e Evoluçao Criadora: Leonardo Coimbra Perante Henri Bergson. *Rev Port Filosof*, 52(1-4), 919-928, Ja-D 96.

**Tejera, Victorino**. *American Modern: The Path Not Taken*: Aesthetics, Metaphysics, and Intellectual History in Classic American Philosophy. Lanham, Rowman & Littlefield, 1996.

Written in the American tradition, the book describes how four major American thinkers practiced philosophy nonreductively by incorporating the arts and other human activities. Tejera provides a detailed analysis of Peirce, Dewey, Santayana, and Buchler, showing that the importance they placed on the human can cure what is missing in recent philosophy. (publisher, edited)

**Tejera, Victorino**. *Literature, Criticism, and the Theory of Signs*. Amsterdam, J Benjamins, 1996.

Following Peirce in his nonreductive understanding of the theory of signs as a branch of aesthetics, this book reconceptualizes the processes of literary creation, appreciation and reading in semiotic terms. Here is a carefully developed theory of what sort of criteria serve to distinguish apposite from inapposite readings of literary works-of-art. Given Peirce's triadic account of signification, it enlarges Aristotle's view of mimesis as expressive making into an understanding of literary works as deliberatively designed sign-systems belonging to Peirce's eighth class of signs. (publisher,edited)

**Tejera, Victorino**. On the Prelude to the *Timaeus*, and the Atlantis-Story. *Daimon Rev Filosof*, 12, 25-36, Ja-Je 96.

Does the *Timaeus* Identify Itself as a Sequel to the *Republic*? The Timaeus Version of the Atlantis Story. The Literalist Summary of "[Yesterday's"] State, & the Illusionism of 'Xthes'. The *Kritias* Version of the First Part of the Atlantis Story. Clumsy Prose in the Prelude to the *Timaeus*. Coopting Solon for Oligarchy. Scrutinizing the Ante-Cosmogonic Part of the *Timaeus*. Signs that the *Kritias* is a Children's Foundation-Story. The ideology behind the *Kritias*. Appendix of Key Words.

**Teles, Carlos**. O Objecto de Reflexao da Antropologia Filosófica desde uma Ontologia da Indeterminaçao Humana. *Rev Port Filosof*, 52(1-4), 929-934, Ja-D 96.

**Telfer, Elizabeth**. *Food for Thought: Philosophy and Food*. New York, Routledge, 1996.

*Food for Thought* brings together the work of philosophers from Plato to John Stuart Mill, Aristotle to Kant, to help us think about the issues surrounding food. How can we justify the recent explosion of attention given to gourmet food in a world where many are starving? Do we have a duty to be healthy? Are hospitableness and temperance moral virtues? Is the pleasure of good food illusory? *Food for Thought* is intended to make those who are involved in working with food think about some of the principles underpinning this field. For those studying philosophy, the book shows how traditional philosophy and some of its classic texts can illuminate an everyday subject. (publisher, edited)

**Teller, Paul**. *An Interpretive Introduction to Quantum Field Theory*. Princeton, Princeton Univ Pr, 1997.

In this provocative and thoughtful book, Paul Teller lays forth the basic ideas of quantum field theory in a way that is understandable to readers who are familiar with nonrelativistic quantum mechanics. He provides information about the physics of the theory without calculational detail, and he enlightens readers on how to think about the theory physically. *An Interpretive Introduction to Quantum Field Theory* challenges philosophers to extend their thinking beyond the realm of quantum mechanics and it challenges physicists to consider the philosophical issues that their explorations have encouraged. (publisher)

**Téllez Maqueo, David Ezequiel**. Immortalidad e Intelección según Tomás de Aquino. *Topicos*, 77-100, 1996.

After a brief discussion and some conclusions on the meaning of the eternity and immortality of the soul according to Aristotle, the paper tries to show some differences between Aristotle's and Aquinas's approaches to the subject.

**Tellkamp, Jörg Alejandro**. Actitudes proposicionales y conocimiento sensible en Tomás de Aquino. *Rev Espan Filosof Med*, 4, 87-102, 1997.

The traditional approach to Thomas Aquinas's theory of knowledge suggests that complex, intentional knowledge is only available to the intellect. Against this, there is strong evidence for an alternative view, which holds that the perceptual grasp of the sensible world renders a complex, however, different kind of knowledge. An analysis of Aquinas's theory of the sensibles reveals a stance which shows a striking resemblance to modern folk psychology, i.e., a strong commitment to describe animal and human perception and behavior in terms of daily life experience of singular objects.

**Temple, Dennis**. A Big Bang Cosmological Argument?. *Phil Cont World*, 2(2), 11-16, Sum 95.

William Lane Craig has defended a modern First Cause argument based on 1) a principle of universal causality and 2) the claim that the universe must have had a beginning. But 1) is susceptible to counter examples from quantum theory. Moreover, Craig's defense of 2) is open to serious question. He claims that an actual infinity (of time) is impossible; he also claims that 2) is in fact supported by big bang theory. I argue that both of these claims are mistaken, and that in consequence we have no particular reason to suppose that 2) is true. I conclude that the First Cause argument fails, but I suggest that a weaker inductive argument might be worth a try.

**Ten Have, Henk**. "Living with the Future: Genetic Information and Human Existence" in *The Right to Know and the Right not to Know*, Chadwick, Ruth (ed), 87-95. Brookfield, Avebury, 1997.

In the article the importance is acknowledged of media representations as part of the cultural context in which genetic discoveries are promulgated. Discussion of the right to know and not to know needs to take this into account and not simply concentrate on the individual. We live with the possibility of a 'geneticized' future, partly because of the tendency to link knowledge and its applications and partly because of a prevailing consensus about two ideals: nondirectiveness in counselling and individual responsibility for health, both of which encourage the idea that it is good to know as much as possible. What is required is prior discussion over the goals at which we should aim; the uses to which genetic knowledge should be put.

**Tenenbaum, Sergio**. Realists Without a Cause: Deflationary Theories of Truth and Ethical Realism. *Can J Phil*, 26(4), 561-590, D 96.

Boghossian argues that emotivism and deflationary theories of truth (DTTs) are incompatible. He also defends the stronger claim that DTTs are self-defeating. Thus, one might think that the incompatibility of emotivism and DTTs is only one aspect of the general failure of DTTs. In "Realist without a Cause," I argue that some DTTs withstand Boghossian's criticism. In fact, DTTs provide the background for a plausible version of moral realism. In particular, I argue that a defense of moral realism grounded upon DTTs is compatible with important features of an intuitive understanding of reality, truth, and of the differences between ethical and other kinds of knowledge.

**Tengelyi, Lászlo**. Lebensgeschichte als Selbstkonstitution bei Husserl. *Husserl Stud*, 13(2), 155-167, 1996-97.

The paper tries to show that Husserl's considerations on the relationship between *constitution of the self* and *the history of a life* (which are to be found in *Cartesian Meditations* and in manuscripts published under the title *Phenomenology of Intersubjectivity* in volume XV of the series *Husserliana*) are far from having lost their interest and actuality. This thesis is argued for by an analysis of the theory of narrative identity (whose main proponents are A. MacIntyre, P. Ricoeur, Ch. Taylor and D. Carr). It is made clear that this theory suffers from difficulties requiring a return to phenomenological investigations. It is not contended that these difficulties are surmounted by Husserl, but it is shown that they are treated in the phenomenology of intersubjectivity in a more promising way than in the theory of narrative identity. For the clue to their resolution is to be found in an inquiry into the relationship between *time* and *the other*. The first to undertake such an inquiry is, however, precisely the later Husserl.

**Tennant, Neil**. On the Necessary Existence of Numbers. *Nous*, 31(3), 307-336, S 97.

We examine the arguments on both sides of the recent debate (Hale and Wright v. Field) on the existence and modal status, of the natural numbers. We formulate precisely, with proper attention to denotational commitments, the analytic conditionals that link talk of numbers with talk of numerosity and with counting. These provide *conceptual controls* on the concept of number. We argue, against Field, that there is a serious disanalogy between the existence of God and the existence of numbers. We give stronger reasons than those advanced by Wright for resisting Field's analogy. We argue that the rules governing the basic numerical notions commit us to the natural numbers as *necessary* existents. We also show that the latest twist in the debate involving 'surdons' leaves both sides in a stalemate.

**Tennant, Neil**. *The Taming of the True*. New York, Clarendon/Oxford Pr, 1997.

*The Taming of the True* poses a broad challenge to the realist views of meaning and truth that have been prominent in recent philosophy. Neil Tennant starts with a careful critical survey of the realism debate, guiding the reader through its complexities; he then presents a sustained defence of the antirealist view that every truth is knowable in principle and that grasp of meaning must be able to be made manifest. Sceptical arguments for the indeterminacy or nonfactuality of meaning are countered; and the much-maligned notion of analyticity is reinvestigated and rehabilitated. Tennant goes on to show that an effective logical system can be based on his antirealist view; the logical system that he advocates is justified as a body of analytic truths and inferential principles. (publisher, edited)

**Terchek, Ronald J**. *Republican Paradoxes and Liberal Anxieties*. Lanham, Rowman & Littlefield, 1997.

Ronald J. Terchek offers insightful and original solutions to the intellectual rigidity and theoretical fragmentation that characterize much contemporary debate in political philosophy. Offering fresh interpretations of republicans such as Aristotle, Machiavelli and Rousseau and liberals share certain fundamental principles and ideals, despite their conflicting beliefs about the primacy of community, rights, citizenship, moral development and the roots of human behavior. This critical analysis of the modern state of political theory challenges political theorists to avoid contentious debates and to abandon the apolitical and inflexible construction of the liberal-communitarian paradigm. This is an important reading for anyone interested in political philosophy and theory. (publisher)

**Térézis, Christos**. The Ontological Relation "One-Many" according to the Neoplatonist Damascius. *Bochumer Phil Jrbh*, 1, 23-37, 1996.

In his commentary on the Platonic dialogue *Philebus*, the neo-Platonic philosopher Damascius investigates the ontological question of the relation between the *One* as the highest principle and the many sensible beings produced through it. Three points are emphasized: (1) Damascius attempts to situate movement in the metaphysical realm and avoid a static metaphysical model by propounding a connection between sensible beings and their productive archetype through what he conceives as metaphysical amplification. (2) His explication of the relation between the physical and the metaphysical indicates that he is not concerned with just a general description, but instead intends to specify the forms of their mutual communication. To a certain degree, physical beings are presented as developments of metaphysical states in terms of the relation of "appearance" to "being," in the sense that the appearance teleologically portrays that which is ontologically complete. (3) Because Damascius sets logic in analytic relation to ontology and defines the conditions of this coordination, it gains no independent status, even as its propriety becomes explicit, for he shows its principal determination by ontology. Hence, Damascius remains within the framework of a consistent ontological realism.

**Termini, Settimo**. Evolutionary Paradigms of Some New Scientific Disciplines (Two Examples: Cybernetics and Fuzzy Sets Theory) (in Spanish). *Agora (Spain)*, 15(2), 9-27, 1996.

The paper discusses some new methodological and conceptual problems posed by the development of some disciplines born in the last forty years. Another aim of the paper is to show that an analysis of the attempts at formalizing concepts that has recently entered the scene of the scientific discourse (as the one of vague predicates) is epistemologically related to the previous argument and can benefit from a discussion done in a more general setting.

**Ternasky, P Lance** (ed) and Strike, Kenneth A (ed). *Ethics for Professionals in Education: Perspectives for Preparation and Practice*. New York, Teachers College Pr, 1993.

This fifth volume in the Professional Ethics in Education Series delves into a relatively neglected area—the ethical principles governing the conduct of teachers, administrators and other education professionals—and provides a thoughtful starting-point for discussion in the field. The contributors' collective exploration of the subject, encompassing many different and sometimes conflicting vantage points, results in a unique overview of the many issues that define the place of ethics in professional preparation and practice. Part I lays out several alternative philosophical positions about teaching ethics to educational professionals. Parts II and III examine questions of how to include ethics in the preservice curriculum and how a concern for ethics can be institutionalized in the schools. (publisher, edited)

**Terry, Peter B**. Thoughts about the End-of-Life Decision-Making Process. *J Clin Ethics*, 8(1), 46-49, Spr 97.

**Tertulian, Nikolae**. The Thought of the Late Lukács (in Hungarian). *Magyar Filozof Szemle*, 4-5-6, 641-658, 1996.

**Teske, Roland J**. *Paradoxes of Time in Saint Augustine*. Milwaukee, Marquette Univ Pr, 1996.

Examining three paradoxes concerning time in book eleven of the *Confessions* of St. Augustine, I argue that in order to answer the Manichaean objection about what God was doing before he created the world, Augustine needed a concept of timeless eternity which he derived from Plotinus, that to find an extent of time to measure he exploited the Plotinian definition of time as a *distentio animi*, and that to avoid a purely subjective account of time he again followed Plotinus in maintaining that time was a distention of the universal or world soul, not merely of the individual soul.

**Tessin, Timothy**. The Frankfurt School. *Phil Invest*, 19(4), 329-336, O 96.

**Thagard, Paul**. Collaborative Knowledge. *Nous*, 31(2), 242-261, Je 97.

Collaboration is ubiquitous in the natural and social sciences. How collaboration contributes to the development of scientific knowledge can be assessed by considering four different kinds of collaboration in the light of Alvin Goldman's five standards for appraising epistemic practices. A sixth standard is proposed to help understand the importance of theoretical collaborations in cognitive science and other fields. I illustrate the application of these six standards by describing two recent scientific developments in which collaboration has been important, the bacterial theory of ulcers and the multiconstraint theory of analogy and by arguing that philosophy should become more collaborative.

**Thagard, Paul**. The Concept of Disease: Structure and Change. *Commun Cog*, 29(3/4), 445-478, 1996.

By contrasting Hippocratic and nineteenth century theories of disease, this paper describes important conceptual changes that have taken place in the history of medicine. Disease concepts are presented as causal networks that represent the relations among the symptoms, causes and treatment of a disease. The transition to the germ theory of disease produced dramatic conceptual changes as the result of a radically new view of disease causation. An analogy between disease and fermentation was important for two of the main developers of the germ theory of disease, Pasteur and Lister. Attention to the development of germ concepts shows the need for a referential account of conceptual change to complement a representational account. (edited)

**Thagard, Paul** and Eliasmith, Chris. Waves, Particles, and Explanatory Coherence. *Brit J Phil Sci*, 48(1), 1-19, Mr 97.

This paper discusses the nineteenth-century debate concerning the nature of light. We analyze the debate using a computational theory of coherence that models the acceptance of the wave theory of light and the rejection of the particle theory. We show how our analysis of the controversy avoids Achinstein's criticisms of Whewell's coherentist account, and argue that our interpretation in more computationally tractable and psychologically realistic than Achinstein's probabilistic account.

**Thagard, Paul** and Millgram, Elijah. Deliberative Coherence. *Synthese*, 108(1), 63-88, Jl 96.

Choosing the right plan is often choosing the more coherent plan: but what is coherence? We argue that coherence-directed practical inference ought to be represented computationally. To that end, we advance a theory of deliberative coherence and describe its implementation in a program modelled on Thagard's ECHO. We explain how the theory can be tested and extended and consider its bearing on instrumentalist accounts of practical rationality.

**Thalos, Mariam**. Conflict and Co-Ordination in the Aftermath of Oracular Statements. *Phil Quart*, 47(187), 212-226, Ap 97.

Can victims of the Oracle paradox—which is known primarily through its Unexpected Hanging and Surprise Examination versions—extricate themselves from their difficulties of reasoning? No. For they do not, contrary to

recent opinion, commit errors of fallacious elimination. As I shall argue, the difficulties of reasoning faced by these victims do not *originate* in the domain of concepts, propositions and their entailment relations; nor do they result from misapprehensions about limitations on what can be known. The difficulties of reasoning flow, instead, from conflicts that arise in the practical dimension of life. The Oracle paradox is in this way more evocative of problems faced in the theory of computation than it is like the celebrated Russell's paradox.

**Thalos, Mariam**. Self-Interest, Autonomy, and the Presuppositions of Decision Theory. *Amer Phil Quart*, 34(2), 287-297, Ap 97.

Certain critics of decision theory complain that its conclusions rest on illegitimate assumptions, such as that rational agents are purely self-interested, or that they are autonomous. The principal aim of this paper is to argue that the *maximization principle*, which is the central assumption of the theory of choice, does not presuppose autonomous decision makers. The thesis of the paper, then is that the *framework* of decision theory does not take for granted anything substantial about the decision procedures of rational individuals. Decision theory is, instead, a framework within which a variety of substantive models can be framed and subsequently put to the test against experience.

**Thau, Michael**. The omega-Rule. *Stud Log*, 51(2), 241-248, 1992.

We prove that all proofs in *Omega*-logic (a first order logic with *Omega*-rule added) in which *Omega*-rule is used finitely many times can be turned into proofs in which the *Omega*-rule is used at most one time. Next, we prove that the word "finitely" above cannot be changed by the word "infinitely".

**Thayer-Bacon, Barbara**. Doubting and Believing: Both are Important for Critical Thinking. *Inquiry (USA)*, 15(2), 59-66, Wint 95.

Relying on current philosophical work by feminists, postmodernists, and pragmatists, the author examines two recent theories on thinking to reconsider believing's role in critical thinking. Looking at Elbow's "Methodological Doubting and Believing: Contraries in Inquiry" and Belenky, et. al's "procedural knowing" helps us move away from the usual dichotomous views of critical thinking and toward the recognition that doubting and believing are complementary, not contrary, forms of thinking: both are needed to arrive at trustworthy knowledge. This article helps shift the focus in critical thinking theory from the current emphasis on doubting to a perspective that includes and values believing.

**Thayer-Bacon, Barbara J**. The Nurturing of a Relational Epistemology. *Educ Theor*, 47(2), 239-260, Spr 97.

The author uses the metaphor of relationships to take another look at knowledge. She begins redescribing epistemology in a relational manner, defining and distinguishing her theory, and examining the importance of nurturing through a discussion of self-development. She offers her description up for discussion, suggesting it has important advantages over others for this relational epistemological theory is more inclusive and less open to ideological abuse. It opens up possibilities for valuing contributions from all people. The author argues we need each other to nurture the constructing/deconstructing of knowledge. She concludes with suggested implications for education.

**Theis, Robert**. Die Vernunft innerhalb der Grenzen des Glaubens: Aspekte der anselmischen Methodologie in werkgenetischer Perspektive. *Theol Phil*, 72(2), 161-187, 1997.

The author reconstructs, from a *genetic* point of view, Anselm's thought regarding his methodological program *fides querens intellectum*. The author shows in what respect the Anselmian *intellectus* is always an *intellectus fidei* tending to make visible the necessary reasons that are already inherent in the statements of faith itself. It is thus limited in its semantic competence in as far as scripture eventually constitutes the true regulating and verifying authority of its conclusions. The author enhances a certain number of complementary aspects of this methodological program appearing throughout Anselm's literary output, such as the intermediate place of the *intellectus* within a global dynamic of faith, the presence of a minimal *intellectus* in subjective faith, the ecclesial and spiritual aspect of the intellectus.

**Theis, Robert**. En quel sens l'*Unique fondement possible d'une démonstration de l'existence de Dieu* de Kant est-il *unique* fondement *possible*?. *Rev Phil Louvain*, 95(1), 7-23, F 97.

The author examines the sting inherent in the title of Kant's work on the *Unique Possible Foundation of a Demonstration of the Existence of God*, published in 1762. In this work, Kant admits not wanting to establish a formal demonstration of the existence of God, but only the foundations of such a demonstration. In this way, he develops *less* than a proof, but at the same time *more*, i.e., the *unique possible* foundation of such a proof. The author critically analyses that in this formula, obviously to a different extent, both the Leibnizian proof starting from the possibles and the Wolffian, so-called a posteriori proof, at a critical moment of their respective articulations, resort to a second argumentation in order to prove the existence of the necessary being and that they are thus not auto-sufficient (unique).

**Thero, Daniel P**. Immortality of the Soul in Plato's Thought: The *Phaedo* Arguments and their Context. *Dialogue (PST)*, 39(1), 1-12, O 96.

I examine Plato's treatment in the *Phaedo* of the issue of immortality of the soul. I evaluate several interpretations and criticisms of the Platonic arguments from the recent literature. I support the position which holds that regardless of whether the arguments are formally valid, their soundness cannot ultimately be determined since Plato appears not to have defined "soul" adequately.

**Thibaud, Pierre**. Between Saying and Doing: Peirce's Propositional Space. *Trans Peirce Soc*, 33(2), 271-327, Spr 97.

**Thiebaut, Carlos**. The Logic of Autonomy and the Logic of Authenticity: A Two-Tiered Conception of Moral Subjectivity. *Phil Soc Crit*, 23(3), 93-108, My 97.

Moral subjectivity should not be considered only under the category of authenticity as late modern analyses suggest. The demands of recognition of authenticity operate with an assertive logic that requires the acceptance of the truthfulness of whatever moral predicates we may subscribe. On the other hand, the demands of recognition of autonomy are always presumptive, both in referring to others and taking them as autonomous and in postulation ourselves autonomous. These two logics intertwine in different social settings and contexts of interaction. The practical ability to operate with these logics sheds light on a reflection conception of the moral subject.

**Thiel, Christian**. "Der mathematische Hintergrund des Erweiterungsschrittes in Freges "Grundgesetzen der Arithmetik" in *Das weite Spektrum der analytischen Philosophie,* Lenzen, Wolfgang, 401-407. Hawthorne, de Gruyter, 1997.

The abstraction principle (basic law V) of Frege's "Basic Laws of Arithmetic" (vol. I, 1893) covers only equations between two names of courses-of-values, leaving equations between a name of a course-of-values and a name of a truth-value unexplained. Frege's amendment by identifying a truth-value with the extension (= course-of-values) of a concept under which exactly this truth-value falls, is elucidated by showing that this step is by no means arbitrary but follows an algebraic technique, well-known at Frege's time, of extending a domain B of numbers by "embedding" it into another domain E (its "extension") by exhibiting a subdomain of E isomorphic to B. Frege's procedure is nothing else but the extension of the domain T of the two truth-values by exhibiting, in the domain of all courses-of-values, a subdomain isomorphic to T.

**Thiel, Christian**. "On the Structure of Frege's System of Logic" in *Frege: Importance and Legacy,* Schirn, Matthias (ed), 261-279. Hawthorne, de Gruyter, 1996.

Some recent issues concerning the syntax and semantics of Frege's system of logic and set theory in "Grundgesetze der Arithmetik" (1893/1903) are analyzed with emphasis on the fact that this system is a term logic. The interplay between its syntactical and semantical rules, and in particular Frege's procedure of introducing names of courses-of-values is elucidated, and the origins of the Zermelo-Russell paradox in the system are laid open by locating the intrusion of impredicative concept-formations. Their avoidance seems to save Frege's abstraction principle in its unaltered form, but Frege's own theorem Chi (Grundgesetze II, 260) exhibits a more fundamental difficulty which remains even if courses-of-values are abandoned: the traditional conception of the extension of a concept (or, equivalently, the naive notion of set) cannot be upheld.

**Thiel, Mary Martha** and Robinson, Mary Redner. Physicians' Collaboration with Chaplains: Difficulties and Benefits. *J Clin Ethics*, 8(1), 94-103, Spr 97.

**Thijssen, J M M H**. 1277 Revisited: A New Interpretation of the Doctrinal Investigations of Thomas Aquinas and Giles of Rome. *Vivarium*, 35(1), 72-101, Mr 97.

**Thomä, Dieter**. Ethik und die Grenzen der Philosophie. *Phil Rundsch*, 44(2), 167-177, Je 97.

**Thomä, Dieter**. German Concord, German Discord: Two Concepts of a Nation and the Challenge of Multiculturalism. *Euro J Phil*, 4(3), 348-368, D 96.

The article offers a critical analysis of the philosophical debate on 'nation' in reunified Germany. The fixation on the controversy between 'people-nation' and 'citizen-nation' is leading to a misreading of the situation of Germany: the existing heterogeneity between East and West casts doubt on the integrative powers of the people-nation; but the current cultural conflict cannot be explained in the terms of a liberal 'citizen-nation' either. Instead, it should be interpreted as a manifestation of 'intra-German multiculturalism'. This idea is defended by reference to the debate between Taylor, Habermas, and others on a "politics of difference." The divergence between life-worlds is a challenge for political theory; the readiness for participation in a liberal society depends on its respect for cultural differences.

**Thomä, Dieter**. Selbstverwirklichung und Autorität: Philosophische Einwände gegen ein Begriffspaar aus der Debatte um Familie und Jugendgewalt. *Z Phil Praxis*, 19-25, 1995.

The author offers a critical analysis of the relationship between the concepts of "authority" and "self-realization" which are controversial topics in the philosophy of education. The concept of "self-realization" turns out to be implausible, because it refers to a purely potential "self"; it is symptomatic for an atomized society with defective social relations. "Authority," on the other hand, defines a special kind of social relationship between parents and children. Against Claus Leggewie the author argues that authority is not a remedy against individualized "self-realization," disorientation and violence, and develops—with Max Horkheimer—a concept of familial happiness as a paradigm of succeeding social life.

**Thomas, Alan**. Values, Reasons and Perspectives. *Proc Aris Soc*, 97, 61-80, 1997.

The paper focuses on an aspect of the problem of moral dilemmas. It explains how it is possible to combine the following three claims: we have moral knowledge, moral reasons are impartial, yet two judgers can judge both that a situation exemplified the same values and that the situation gives each judger different reasons for action. The hidden parameter explaining why this is not a paradox is the distinction between being "viewer" or "doer" of a given act. This terminology of Sen's is applied to different aspects of moral reasons, not, as in Sen's original proposal, to different kinds of value.

**Thomas, Bruce M**. Cartesian Epistemics and Descartes' *Regulae*. *Hist Phil Quart*, 13(4), 433-449, O 96.

A regulative theory of epistemic justification consists of a set of prescriptive, action-guiding norms. Richard Foley contends that every regulative theory is

"inevitably" misdirected or not sufficiently fundamental." This paper extracts a regulative theory from Descartes's *Regulae* and explores how Descartes might reply to Foley. It shows that Descartes did not attempt to provide absolutely fundamental cognitive advice and argues that adding second-order epistemic norms to the theory will enable it to remain aligned with the epistemic goals it is designed to serve.

**Thomas, Colin** (ed) and Sparks, Simon (ed) and Sheppard, Darren (ed). *On Jean-Luc Nancy: The Sense of Philosophy.* New York, Routledge, 1997.

*On Jean-Luc Nancy* draws together a number of outstanding commentators to provide an invaluable companion to Nancy's own work. In addition to contributions by Howard Caygill, Rodolphe Gasché and Alphonso Lingis, there is a text by Nancy's renowned long-time co-author, Philippe Lacoue-Labarthe. These essays approach the main themes in Nancy's work. From Nancy the philosopher of the contemporary and of the disorientation in thinking today to Nancy and the significance of anger and sacrifice in philosophy, the recurrent themes of community, freedom, being and the divine in his work are brought out. (publisher, edited)

**Thomas, Cornell**. The Impact of Culture on Education. *J Thought*, 32(2), 7-24, Sum 97.

This discussion is presented in three parts. Part one posits the notion of culture evolving as the environment transforms, therefore providing a need for people and society to accept change and difference. The second part of this discussion shares the comments of teachers. The third and final section emphasizes the need for a multidimensional teaching approach to adequately address student needs. (edited)

**Thomas, Douglas E**. Deconstruction and Rationality: A Response to Rowland, or Postmodernism 101. *Phil Rhet*, 30(1), 70-81, 1997.

**Thomas, Douglas E**. It's Not What You Say, It's *That* You Say It: Speech, Performance, and Sense in Austin and Deleuze. *Phil Rhet*, 29(4), 359-368, 1996.

**Thomas, Emyr Vaughan**. Rolston, Naturogenic Value and Genuine Biocentrism. *Environ Values*, 6(3), 355-360, Ag 97.

Holmes Rolston III attempts to get us to recognize nature as an objectively independent valuational sphere with its own activity of defending value. But in inspiring our '...psychological joining (with) on-going planetary natural history...' what his account ultimately does is assimilate nature to the human. The real depth to a biocentric viewpoint is to be found through a route other than the one taken by Rolston. It relates to seeing nature as other than the human (as illustrated with reference to Emerson), in a way that is genuinely unsullied by the claims of self—which, in the case of human beings, are the most elemental supports for a species perspective. (edited)

**Thomas, James**. Connatural Knowledge. *Maritain Stud*, 11, 191-201, 1995.

**Thomas, James**. The Inaccessible God. *Maritain Stud*, 10, 109-123, 1994.

**Thomas, John C**. Community of Inquiry and Differences of the Heart. *Thinking*, 13(1), 42-48, 1997.

**Thomas, John C**. The Hermeneutic Community and the Community of Inquiry. *Inquiry (USA)*, 16(4), 87-103, Sum 97.

**Thomas, Laurence**. Becoming an Evil Society: The Self and Strangers. *Polit Theory*, 24(2), 271-294, My 96.

**Thomas, Mark L**. Robert Adams and the Best Possible World. *Faith Phil*, 13(2), 252-259, AP 96.

Robert Merrihew Adams argues that it is permissible for a perfectly good moral agent to create a world less good than the best one she could create. He argues that God would exhibit the important virtue of grace in creating less than the best and that this virtue is incompatible with the merit considerations required by the standard of creating the best. In this paper I give three arguments for the compatibility of merit consideration and graciousness of God toward creation. I conclude that grace would not release a perfect agent from responsibility to create the best.

**Thomas, Nigel J T**. Imagery and the Coherence of Imagination: A Critique of White. *J Phil Res*, 22, 95-127, Ap 97.

Traditionally 'imagination' primarily denotes the faculty of mental imagery, other usages being derivative. However, contemporary philosophers commonly hold it to be a polysemous term, with several unrelated senses. This effectively eliminates this culturally important concept as an appropriate explanandum for science and paves the way for a thoroughgoing eliminative materialism. White challenges both these views of imagination, arguing that 'imagine' *never* means 'suppose,' 'believe,' 'pretend' or 'visualize,' that imagery may occur without imagination and that the true sense of 'imagine' is (roughly) 'think of as possibly being so.' I defend a version of the traditional view. (edited)

**Thomas, Stephen Naylor**. *Practical Reasoning in Natural Language.* Upper Saddle River, Prentice Hall, 1997.

This basic manual workbook uses natural language to analyze and evaluate inductive reasoning. Unlike many traditional texts, which depend on truthtables, Venn diagrams, and so forth, Stephen Naylor Thomas presents a method of "natural logic" that casts reasoning into a standard diagrammatic form without the need for symbolic notation and without commitments to selected informal fallacies or limited formal patterns. (publisher, edited)

**Thomas, Thomas P** and Schubert, William H. Recent Curriculum Theory: Proposals for Understanding, Critical Praxis, Inquiry, and Expansion of Conversation. *Educ Theor*, 47(2), 261-285, Spr 97.

This article is a critical review and reflection of *Understanding Curriculum*, by William Pinar, William Reynolds, Patrick Slattery and Peter Taubman. The authors consider the contention of Pinar, et, al, that *curriculum development*, the primary language form for scholarly writing about the curriculum in past decades, has been superseded by efforts to *understand* curriculum. While finding this a valid portrait of current curriculum thought, Thomas and Schubert caution that the categorization of discourse provided by Pinal et, al. not be reified into opposing camps and question the value of focusing scholarly efforts primarily on "understanding" curriculum. Thomas and Schubert reflect on their efforts to engage the broader community of educators in conversations about curriculum across discourses, popularizing the conversations on the curriculum. (edited)

**Thomas, Vernon G**. Attitudes and Issues Preventing Bans on Toxic Lead Shot and Sinkers in North America and Europe. *Environ Values*, 6(2), 185-199, My 97.

It is paradoxical that lead shot and fishing sinkers are still used widely, given society's understanding of lead contamination and avian lead toxicosis. The statutory action taken by governments varies from total bans on both lead products to no regulation of either shot or sinkers. Many government agencies and field sport organizations are reluctant to use the precautionary principle and the polluter pays principle and regulate use of available nontoxic substitutes. The attitudes of individuals towards their roles in environmental lead contamination and remediation reflect marked self-deception about the need for changes and the benefits to be derived from substitution. (edited)

**Thomasma, David C**. Antifoundationalism and the Possibility of a Moral Philosophy of Medicine. *Theor Med*, 18(1-2), 127-143, Mr-Je 97.

The problem of developing a moral philosophy of medicine is explored in this essay. Among the challenges posed to this development are the general mistrust of moral philosophy and philosophy in general created by post-modernist philosophical and even antiphilosophical thinking. This reaction to philosophical systematization is usually called antifoundationalism. I distinguish different forms of antifoundationalism, showing claims made about the certitude of moral thought. I conclude that we are correct to mistrust absolutist principles in a moral philosophy of medicine, but can find some center within the practice of medicine itself for a moral foundation.

**Thomasma, David C**. Edmund D. Pellegrino on the Future of Bioethics. *Cambridge Quart Healthcare Ethics*, 6(4), 373-375, Fall 97.

**Thomasma, David C**. Education of Ethics Committees. *Bioethics Forum*, 10(4), 12-18, Fall 94.

The education of ethics committee is explored as a process of gradual "education" from the experience of the committee members and the institution. In addition to updating oneself in ethical theory and practice, the committee must institute activities that help it ascertain what ethical issues occur in the institution and assist it in developing procedures for analyzing and resolving these issues. Sometimes these additional requirements lead the ethics committee down paths it did not anticipate.

**Thomasma, David C** and Jain, Renu. Discontinuing Life Support in an Infant of a Drug-Addicted Mother: Whose Decision Is It?. *Cambridge Quart Healthcare Ethics*, 6(1), 48-54, Winter 97.

**Thomasma, David C** and Loewy, Erich H. A Dialogue on Species-Specific Rights: Humans and Animals in Bioethics. *Cambridge Quart Healthcare Ethics*, 6(4), 435-444, Fall 97.

**Thomason, S K**. Relational Models for the Modal Syllogistic. *J Phil Log*, 26(2), 129-141, Ap 97.

An interpretation of Aristotle's modal syllogistic is proposed which is intuitively graspable, if only formally correct. The individuals to which a term applies and possibly applies, are supposed to be determined in a uniform way by the set of individuals to which the term necessarily applies.

**Thomasson, Amie L**. Fiction, Modality and Dependent Abstracta. *Phil Stud*, 84(2-3), 295-320, D 96.

I argue that three traditional views about the relationship between fictional characters and possible worlds are inadequate and develop the artifactual *theory of fiction*, according to which fictional characters are abstract artifacts existing in the actual world and some, but not all, other possible worlds. I argue that the *artifactual theory* provides a better understanding of fiction and better analyses of modal discourse about fiction. It also provides the basis for an alternative account of the place of other dependent abstracts such as literary works, universals, or the constructivist's mathematical entities, in a possible worlds ontology.

**Thomasson, Amie L**. Fictional Characters: Dependent or Abstract? A Reply to Reicher's Objections. *Conceptus*, 29(74), 119-144, 1996.

The dependentist theory of fiction and concomitant identity conditions which I laid out in "Die Identität fiktionaler Gegenstände" have come under attack by Maria Reicher who favors an abstractist conception of fictional characters. Here I address the problems she raises for my account, most notably those concerning the ontological status of texts and the role of the reader. I argue that her criticisms are either based on misunderstandings or may be dealt with readily without abandoning a dependentist view of fictional characters. Moreover, Reicher's abstractist account of fiction fails to overcome the major problem which has always plagued abstractist views: offering transtextual character identity conditions. This not only gives us reason for preferring a dependentist view of fiction, but also suggests the need to broaden our ontology beyond the narrow categories of mental and physical particulars and abstract entities.

**Thompson, Anthony P**. Relating the Psychological Literature to the American Psychological Association Ethical Standards. *Ethics Behavior*, 7(1), 79-88, 1997.

The psychological literature frequently elaborates ethical principles and standards and highlights the complexity of many ethical issues. The American

Psychological Association code of ethics (American Psychological Association, 1992) directs psychologists to become familiar with the code and its implications for their work. A computerized search strategy is described for identifying and organizing published articles dealing with ethical issues. Specifically, we report the development of a search strategy for use with the journal literature database contained on *PsycLIT* (CD-ROM). The search terms identify ethics articles and categorize them according to Ethical Standards 2 through 8 of the 1992 code.

**Thompson, Audrey**. "Political Pragmatism and Educational Inquiry" in *Philosophy of Education (1996)*, Margonis, Frank (ed), 425-434. Urbana, Phil Education Soc, 1997.

The distinctive contribution that pragmatism has to make to educational understanding is an emergent method of inquiry that avoids reifying prevailing conditions. Ironically, to the extent that classical pragmatism has employed a problem-centered method, it has tended to take up political inequities as departures from an idealized norm, thereby reifying prevailing conditions. Drawing primarily on African-American and feminist pragmatisms, the essay argues that, to avoid assuming the very social, political, and cultural conditions that pragmatism offers to interrogate, it must abandon its problem-centered approach in favor of an approach grounded in politicized experience.

**Thompson, Audrey**. Surrogate Family Values: The Refeminization of Teaching. *Educ Theor*, 47(3), 315-339, Sum 97.

**Thompson, Audrey**. When Manipulation Is Indispensable to Education: The Moral Work of Fiction. *J Thought*, 32(3), 27-52, Fall 97.

**Thompson, Caleb**. Wittgenstein, Tolstoy and the Meaning of Life. *Phil Invest*, 20(2), 97-116, Ap 97.

**Thompson, Christopher J**. Christian Identity and Augustine's *Confessions. Amer Cath Phil Quart*, 70(Supp), 249-258, 1996.

**Thompson, Dennis** and Gutmann, Amy. Deliberating about Bioethics. *Hastings Center Rep*, 27(3), 38-41, My-Je 97.

Bioethics was built on conflicts. Abortion, physician-assisted suicide, patients' demand for autonomy all are staple and contentious issues. What forum best serves such debates? A look at political theories of democracy is helpful: The most promising for bioethics debates are theories that ask citizens and officials to justify any demands for collective action by giving reasons that can be accepted by those who are bound by the action, otherwise known as deliberative democracy.

**Thompson, Dennis** and Gutmann, Amy. *Democracy and Disagreement*. Cambridge, Harvard Univ Pr, 1996.

Gutman and Thompson show how a deliberative democracy can address some of our most difficult controversies—from abortion and affirmative action to health care and welfare—and can allow diverse groups separated by class, race, religion, and gender to reason together. Their work goes beyond that of most political theorists and social scientists by exploring both the principles for reasonable argument and their application to actual cases. Not only do the authors suggest how deliberative democracy can work, they also show why improving our collective capacity for moral argument is better than referring all disagreements to procedural politics or judicial institutions. (edited)

**Thompson, Evan**. *Colour Vision: A Study in Cognitive Science and the Philosophy of Perception*. New York, Routledge, 1995.

*Colour Vision* provides an accessible view of the current scientific and philosophical discussions of colour vision. Evan Thompson steers clear of the extreme subjective and objective positions on colour, arguing instead for a relational explanation. His balanced account of colour vision also introduces a novel 'ecological' perspective to cognitive science and the philosophy of perception. (publisher, edited)

**Thompson, Garret**. "La dudas de Descartes y el lenguaje privado" in *Memorias Del Seminario En Conmemoración De Los 400 Anos Del Nacimiento De René Descartes*, Albis, Víctor S (ed), 207-217. Sankt Augustin, Academia, 1997.

**Thompson, Patricia J**. Re-Claiming Hestia: Goddess of Everyday Life. *Phil Cont World*, 3(4), 20-28, Wint 96.

The concepts of "hearth and home" and "keeping the home fire burning" can be traced back to ancient Greece and are associated with the *oikos*. Such metaphors remain pervasive (if often disregarded) expressions in contemporary life. The goddess Hestia, identified as the "goddess of the hearth," has been maligned in the patriarchal literature and ignored in feminist writing. This paper argues for revisiting and reclaiming Hestia as a unifying principle in meeting the quotidian demands of everyday life. It suggests a new perspective for further philosophical exploration of the "private sphere" with special relevance for practical reasoning in the ethics and aesthetics involved in contemporary life.

**Thompson, Paul B**. "Pragmatism and Policy: The Case of Water" in *Environmental Pragmatism*, Light, Andrew (ed), 187-208. New York, Routledge, 1996.

Landowners, developers and environmentalists disagree about water policy and their differences reflect classic lines of dispute between libertarian, utilitarian and ecocentric approaches to ethics. Classic applied ethics offers a poor model for compromise or for mediating disputes, but pragmatist principles derived from William James and John Dewey point toward procedural norms for community building and consensus formation. This pragmatist approach represents one of the most promising ways to integrate ethics and environmental philosophy into environmental policy.

**Thompson, Paul B**. Food Biotechnology's Challenge to Cultural Integrity and Individual Consent. *Hastings Center Rep*, 27(4), 34-38, Jl-Ag 97.

Consumer response to genetically altered foods has been mixed in the United

States. While transgenic crops have entered the food supply with little comment, other foods, such as the bioengineered tomato, have caused considerable controversy. As yet, there is no policy provision for informing consumers about the degree to which food has been genetically engineered.

**Thompson, Walter J** and Goerner, E A. Politics and Coercion. *Polit Theory*, 24(4), 620-652, N 96.

We compare communitarian and liberal approaches to coercion by comparing Aquinas's analysis of a hypothetical prelapsarian politics with Rawls's functionally similar, hypothetical, "strict compliance theory". We find 1) that coercion has a far less foundational role in Thomistic politics than in Rawlsian (and most liberal) politics; 2) that this general difference is reversed in a single, but historically crucial area: coercion to eradicate Christian heretics and 3) that this exception has tended to marginalize Thomistic contributions to the current communitarian-liberalism debates because it justifies the religious violence among Christians that historically led to the victory of liberal politics as a reactionary solution to that violence.

**Thomsen, Marshall** and Resnik, D. The Effectiveness of the Erratum in Avoiding Error Propagation in Physics. *Sci Eng Ethics*, 1(3), 231-240, Jl 95.

The propagation of errors in physics research is studied, with particular attention being paid to the effectiveness of the erratum in avoiding error propagation. We study the citation history of 17 physics papers which have significant errata associated with them. It would appear that the existence of an erratum does not significantly decrease the frequency with which a paper is cited and in most cases the erratum is *not* cited along with the original paper. The authors comment on implications for the responsibilities of authors.

**Thomson, Anne**. *Critical Reasoning: A Practical Introduction*. New York, Routledge, 1996.

Reasoning is the everyday process that we all use in order to draw conclusions from facts or evidence. To think critically about what you read and hear is a vital skill for everyone, whether you are a student or not. When we are faced with texts, news items or speeches, what is being said is often obscured by the words used, and we may be unsure whether our reasoning, or that of others, is in fact sound. By the end of this topical and exercise-based introduction to critical thinking, readers will be able to 1) identify flaws in arguments, 2) analyse the reasoning in newspaper articles, books or speeches and 3) approach any topic with the ability to reason clearly and to think critically. (publisher,edited)

**Thomson, Elizabeth J** and Meslin, Eric M and Boyer, Joy T. The Ethical, Legal, and Social Implications Research Program at the National Human Genome Research Institute. *Kennedy Inst Ethics J*, 7(3), 291-298, S 97.

**Thomson, Garret**. Problemas y Dilemas Éticos. *Ideas Valores*, 21-31, Ap 97.

I examine the conflict between the Utilitarian and Kantian elements in morality. Everyday morality comprises features from both types of theory and this is the source of many moral dilemmas. I characterize one aspect of this conflict: the tension between monism and pluralism regarding intrinsic values. After examining some solutions which do not work, I characterize the problem in terms of the failure of moral rules to adequately capture the content of morality.

**Thomson, Judith Jarvis**. The Right and the Good. *J Phil*, 94(6), 273-298, Je 97.

**Thomson, Rachel**. Diversity, Values and Social Change: Renegotiating a Consensus on Sex Education. *J Moral Educ*, 26(3), 257-271, S 97.

This paper explores three interrelated themes in order to contextualize and then propose a values framework for school sex education within a modern plural society. First, it outlines some of the social changes that have contributed to a growing uncertainty about values in British society in the area of sexuality and personal relationships. Secondly, it considers the ways in which policy changes in the area of sex education over the last 10 years have reflected competing claims over the moral legitimacy and content of this area of the curriculum. Thirdly, it describes the work of two related initiatives, that sought to renegotiate a consensus for values within school sex education. The paper suggests that it may not be possible to resolve what are fundamental conflicts of a plural society and argues that a moral agenda for sex education may be most appropriately realized as a pursuit of consistency between politics, policy and practice on the basis of confidence in the abilities of young people and a recognition of social change.

**Thoné, Astrid**. Eros without Perversion? (in Dutch). *Bijdragen*, 57(3), 281-304, 1996.

What are the essential features that a phenomenology of eros should take into account in order to do justice to the complexity of this reality? In order to put some light on this phenomenon, we have compared two contemporary French studies, that of Emmanuel Levinas in 'Totality and Infinity' and that of Sartre in 'Being and Nothingness'. We started by pointing at the new way in which subjectivity is experienced in eros. Sartre emphasizes the fact of feeling justified in one's life, Levinas accentuates the feeling of being liberated from the burden of oneself. In conclusion it can be stated that true love cannot be found in a relation without conflicts, but supposes lovers to learn to handle the tension proper to the erotic relation without ever being sure of the result. (edited)

**Thorley Hill, Nancy** and Eynon, Gail and Stevens, Kevin T. Factors that Influence the Moral Reasoning Abilities of Accountants: Implications for Universities and the Profession. *J Bus Ethics*, 16(12-13), 1297-1309, S 97.

The need to maintain the public trust in the integrity of the accounting profession has led to increased interest in research that examines the moral reasoning abilities (MRA) of Certified Public Accountants (CPAs). This study examines the MRA of CPAs practicing in small firms or as sole practitioners and the factors that affect MRA throughout their working careers. (edited)

**Thornbury, Robert**. Towards a Whole School or College Policy for a Pre-Philosophical and Higher Order Thinking 'Entitlement' Curriculum. *Inquiry (USA)*, 14(1), 59-63, Fall 94.

A teachers' group explored various notions of the *prephilosophical curriculum*, together with taxonomies and instruments helpful for designing a whole school or college policy and institutional development plan. Various justifications for teaching philosophy, critical and generalizable thinking were identified, together with conflicting philosophical stances among subject teacher concerning the 'ownership' of argument and critical thinking. Questions relating to teachers' initial and in service training and their philosophical 'careers and autobiographies' were addressed. Five approaches for timetabling critical thinking as a cross-curricular theme emerged. Strategies for institutionally launching a *prephilosophical curriculum* using in service, staff development and working party programs were compiled.

**Thorne, Debbie** and Everett, Linda and Danehower, Carol. Cognitive Moral Development and Attitudes Toward Women Executives. *J Bus Ethics*, 15(11), 1227-1235, N 96.

Research has shown that men and women are similar in their capabilities and management competence; however, there appears to be a "glass ceiling" which poses invisible barriers to their promotion to management positions. One explanation for the existence of these barriers lies in stereotyped, biased attitudes toward women in executive positions. This study supports earlier findings that attitudes of men toward women in executive positions are generally negative, while the attitudes of women are generally positive. Additionally, we found that an individual's level of cognitive moral development correlates significantly with attitudes toward women executives. Limitations of the present study and implications for ethics and diversity training in organizations are discussed.

**Thornton, Barbara C**. The Importance of Process in Ethical Decision Making. *Bioethics Forum*, 10(4), 41-45, Fall 94.

The field of bioethics is not only a normative field, but an applied one: one does ethics. Thus, committee members need to be familiar with two overlapping areas of bioethics: content and process and learn how to incorporate both in doing ethics effectively.

**Thornton, Tim**. "Intention, Rule Following and the Strategic Role of Wright's Order of Determination Test" in *Verdad: lógica, representación y mundo*, Villegas Forero, L, 343-354. Santiago de Compostela, Univ Santiago Comp, 1996.

I argue that Wright's constructivist account of intention is fundamentally flawed and that the source of its error can be diagnosed by locating it within its strategic context: Wright's response to Wittgenstein on rules. Wright deploys intentions as an analogy to disarm Kripkean scepticism. I raise a number of criticisms to show that constructivism fails to explain our knowledge of intentions. Finally I show that Wright's failure fits into a pattern anticipated by Wittgenstein. (edited)

**Thornton, Tim**. Intention, Rule Following and the Strategic Role of Wright's Order of Determination Test. *Phil Invest*, 20(2), 136-147, Ap 97.

Wright deploys intentions as an analogy to disarm Kripkean scepticism but goes on to argue that a substantial explanation should be given of first person access to their content using constructivism. The paper demonstrates that Wright's constructivist account of intentions is fundamentally flawed. Furthermore, Wright's failure fits a pattern anticipated by Wittgenstein. The ongoing judgments that are supposed to determine the content of intentions are like the interpretations of rules which need further interpretation. The real moral of the rule following considerations is that no substantial explanation can be given of the content of mental states.

**Thornton, W Laurence**. Commentary on "Primitive Mental Processes". *Phil Psychiat Psych*, 4(2), 151-158, Je 97.

**Thurston, Luke** (trans) and Laplanche, Jean. Psychoanalysis as Anti-Hermeneutics. *Rad Phil*, 79, 7-12, S-O 96.

**Tichtchenko, Pavel D** and Yudin, Boris. The Moral Status of Fetuses in Russia. *Cambridge Quart Healthcare Ethics*, 6(1), 31-38, Winter 97.

**Tidman, Paul**. Critical Reflection: An Alleged Epistemic Duty. *Analysis*, 56(4), 268-276, O 96.

**Tidwell, N L**. Holy Argument: Some Reflections on the Jewish Piety of Argument, Process Theology and the Philosophy of Religion. *Relig Stud*, 32(4), 477-488, D 96.

'Holy argument' is the most highly commended path to God in the Jewish tradition. The article seeks to draw out the nature, form and historical development of this Jewish piety of argument and to consider how it might be thought to work as a way to God and mode of spirituality. In the process certain parallels and contrasts between Jewish argument with God (one distinctive form of holy argument, particularly in the Chasidic tradition) and the enterprise of the philosophy of religion are examined and some elements of a Process Theology in the Jewish piety of argument tradition are drawn out.

**Tiedemann, Rolf**. "Concept, Image, Name: On Adorno's Utopia of Knowledge" in *The Semblance of Subjectivity*, Huhn, Tom (ed), 123-145. Cambridge, MIT Pr, 1997.

**Tiedemann, Rolf** (ed) and Adorno, Gretel (ed) and Hullot-Kentor, Robert (ed & trans). *Aesthetic Theory: Theodore W. Adorno*. Minneapolis, Univ of Minn Pr, 1997.

The culmination of a lifetime of aesthetic investigation, *Aesthetic Theory* is Adorno's major work, a defense of modernism that is paradoxical in its defense of illusion. In it, Adorno takes up the problem of art in a day when "it goes without saying that nothing concerning art goes without saying." In the course of Adorno's discussion, he revisits such concepts as the sublime, the ugly, and the beautiful, demonstrating that concepts such as these are reservoirs of human experience. These experiences ultimately underlie aesthetics, for in Adorno's formulation "art is the sedimented history of human misery."(publisher,edited)

**Tienson, John** and Horgan, Terence. "Connectionism and the Commitments of Folk Psychology" in *AI, Connectionism and Philosophical Psychology, 1995,* Tomberlin, James E (ed), 127-152. Atascadero, Ridgeview, 1995.

William Ramsey, Stephen Stich, and Joseph Garon argue that folk psychology (FP) is committed to a feature of mental states they call "modularity," that this feature is incompatible with certain connectionist models, and hence that those models support eliminativism. We offer three replies. First, FP is clearly committed only to a weak form of modularity that connectionism accommodates easily. Second, even if FP were committed to other forms of modularity not manifested in human cognition, this would not mean that FP is so radically false that there are no beliefs and desires. Third, connectionism actually can accommodate various other forms of modularity anyway.

**Tiercelin, Claudine**. Peirce on Norms, Evolution and Knowledge. *Trans Peirce Soc*, 33(1), 35-58, Wint 97.

**Tierney, William G** (ed) and Lincoln, Yvonna S (ed). *Representation and the Text: Re-Framing the Narrative Voice.* Albany, SUNY Pr, 1997.

This book focuses on representations of contested realities in qualitative research. The authors examine two separate, but interrelated, issues: criticisms of how researchers use "voice," and suggestions about how to develop experimental voices that expand the range of narrative strategies. (publisher, edited)

**Tierno, Joel Thomas**. Descartes on God and the Laws of Logic. *Int Stud Phil*, 28(4), 93-103, 1996.

**Tietz, John**. Truth and Thickness. *Dialogue (Canada)*, 36(2), 375-380, Spr 97.

A discussion of antirealism. Critical notice of Barry Allen's *Truth in Philosophy* (Cambridge, MA; Harvard, 1993).

**Tietz, Udo**. Lived Thought between Affirmation and Critique: Georg Lukács and Stalinism (in Hungarian). *Magyar Filozof Szemle*, 4-5-6, 590-609, Wint 96.

**Tijmes, Pieter**. Repliek op G. Vanheeswijck. *Tijdschr Filosof*, 59(1), 102-106, Mr 97.

The author articulates several statements against Vanheeswijck. 1) Vanheeswijck writes as if God, Christianity and Girard stand for the same cause. He goes too far in suggesting that it is God's metier to unmask mimetic desire, 2) One has to ask if Vanheeswijck following Girard does not make a category mistake, because mimesis and autonomy do not exclude each other. 3) One has to speak about two irreducible motives in Girard's work: a quasi-enlightenment motive and a religious one. a) As a son of *enlightenment* Girard unmasks modern ideologies on the basis of his mimetic hypothesis. b) The religious motive finds its expression in the words of Scheler 'one possesses either God or an idol'. From the mimetic theory one cannot conclude to the religious antithesis, and vice versa.

**Tiles, Mary** and Oberdiek, Hans. *Living in a Technological Culture: Human Tools and Human Values*. New York, Routledge, 1995.

This book is an introduction to the philosophy of technology, but assumes no background in philosophy. It explores the relations between science, technology and culture, and is designed to make us more mindful users of technology. It asks why is it that we are alternately dazzled by the prospect of apparently unlimited power that technological devices seems to offer, and threatened by the power that they have over our lives. In answering this question the book shows how our attitudes toward technology are intimately entangled with our aspirations as human beings and thus opens up a wider debate on whether or how we can shape the future.

**Tilliette, Xavier**. "El descubrimiento de la Doctrina de la Ciencia" in *El inicio del Idealismo alemán*, Market, Oswaldo, 51-62. Madrid, Ed Complutense, 1996.

Le point de départ thématique de la Doctrine de la Science est le Moi absolu qui se pose lui-même. Mais il n'est pas dit que le point de départ génétique et subjectif soit également l'absoluité du Moi, le sentiment vif interne de la liberté et de la conscience de soi. Bien plutôt la "decouverte" ou l'invention de la Doctrine de la Science chez Fichte reste-t-elle environnée de mystère. Le Moi est un sésame et une porte d'accès pour une intuition plus originelle qui est la Doctrine de la Science pour ainsi dire en personne. La découverte n'est pas antérieure ou extérieure à la philosophie comme Doctrine de la Science, elle est la Doctrine de la Science pluriface, *polifacética*, saisie par l'imagination, faculté merveilleuse, condensée en un système arbitraire et souple: un "pur inconcevable", un inconditionné, qui se donne à connaître et à concevoir dans une série d'injonctions transcendantales.

**Tilliette, Xavier**. Fichtes Erfindung der Wissenschaftslehre. *Fichte-Studien*, 9, 1-16, 1997.

**Tilliette, Xavier**. Nouveautés Schellingiennes. *Arch Phil*, 59(3), 463-477, Jl-S 96.

**Tilliette, Xavier**. Nouvelles réponses à Nunzio Incardona. *G Metaf*, 19(1), 131-136, Ja-Ap 97.

**Tilly, Charles**. The State of Nationalism. *Crit Rev*, 10(2), 299-306, Spr 96.

John Breuilly's *Nationalism and the State* provides an indispensable guide to the history of nationalist doctrines and practices since 1800. Yet it misses a crucial dynamic. Top-down nationalizing efforts by European rulers generated bottom-up demands for autonomy or independence by political entrepreneurs claiming to represent distinct nations. Those demands gained credibility and

strength when third parties such as great powers and international organizations validated them. This process established an evolving international procedure and an incentive structure that promote top-down suppression of minorities, bottom-up bids for recognition and violent struggles among the parties.

**Timmermans, Benoît**. L'analyse cartésienne et la construction de l'ordre des raisons. *Rev Phil Louvain*, 94(2), 205-215, My 96.

Descartes's method is related in some ways to the architectural model of analysis as developed by Galen, taken over by Hooke and indirectly commented upon by Kant. But if this relationship is stated without qualification, one runs up against a powerful objection by Vuillemin. Vuillemin emphasizes the asymmetrical nature of Cartesian order and recalls that this order cannot be traced forwards and backwards at the same time. The conclusion must be drawn that Descartes only uses analysis when a given order is confused and troubled and hence that it is necessary to *discover* and *construct* it. When order has finally been discovered and it appears fully in its asymmetry, analysis ceases and gives way to synthesis.

**Timmons, Brent D**. More Evidence Against Anti-Evidentialism. *Dialogue (PST)*, 39(2-3), Ap 97.

Alvin Plantinga is well-known, and much criticised, for his anti-evidentialist positions. In this paper I examine his latest treatment of evidentialism in *Warrant and Proper Function*. In this work Plantinga concludes that evidentialism fails to give an adequate account of justification. I argue that what Plantinga rejects in not the commonly accepted version of evidentialism he begins examining, but an altered and vastly less plausible version he subsequently introduces. The arguments he makes for rejecting the latter do not hold when applied to the former. I conclude that Plantinga has failed to show that evidentialism does not provide an adequate account of justification.

**Timmons, Mark**. Evil and Imputation in Kant's Ethics. *Jahr Recht Ethik*, 2, 113-141, 1994.

Für Kant manifestiert sich das moralisch Böse in allen seinen Varianten—das Böse nämlich, das im Charakter einer Person wurzelt—in Handlungen, die auf der einen Seite vom eigenen Standpunkt des Handelnden her explizit werden können und die deshalb zurechenbar sind, die aber auf der anderen Seite in einer gewissen Hinsicht als irrational bezeichnet werden müssen. Weil das Böse im Charakter der Person wurzelt, "verdirbt es den Grund aller Maximen" und verdient deshalb "das *radikal* Böse" genannt zu werden. Darüber hinaus sind menschliche Wesen nach Kant nicht nur für das Böse anfällig, es ist vielmehr unentrinnbar menschliches Schicksal, böse zu sein. (edited)

**Timmons, Mark** and Horgan, Terence. From Moral Realism to Moral Relativism in One Easy Step. *Critica*, 28(83), 3-39, Ag 96.

In recent years, defenses of moral realism have embraced what we call 'new wave moral semantics', which construes the semantic workings of moral terms like 'good' and 'right' as akin to the semantic workings of natural-kind terms in science and also takes inspiration from functionalist themes in the philosophy of mind. This sort of semantic view which we find in the metaethical views of David Brink, Richard Boyd, Peter Railton, is the crucial semantical underpinning of a naturalistic brand of moral realism that these philosophers favor—a view that promises to deliver a robust form of moral realism. We argue that new wave moral semantics leads, in one way or another, to moral relativism—a view that is incompatible with the kind of moral realism these philosophers aim to defend.

**Timmons, Mark** and Horgan, Terence. Troubles for Michael Smith's Metaethical Rationalism. *Phil Papers*, 25(3), 203-231, N 96.

In his recent book, *The Moral Problem*, Michael Smith defends as anti-Humean, rationalist account of normative reasons in terms of which he analyzes moral judgments of rightness. We argue that 1) if Smith's analysis of normative reasons is correct, then there is good reason to be skeptical about there being normative moral reasons, which would force one to accept an error theory of moral discourse; however we go on to argue that 2) there are serious problems with Smith's analysis of normative reasons and that 3) a kind of irrealist metaethical theory, not considered by Smith and not usually recognized as a metaethical option, has serious potential for solving what Smith call 'the moral problem'.

**Timmons, Mark** (ed) and Sinnott-Armstrong, Walter (ed). *Moral Knowledge?: New Readings in Moral Epistemology*. New York, Oxford Univ Pr, 1996.

The book brings together eleven newly written essays by distinguished moral philosophers exploring the nature and possibility of moral knowledge. Each essay represents a major position within the exciting field of moral epistemology in which a proponent of the position presents and defends his or her view and locates it vis-à-vis competing views. (edited)

**Tindale, Christopher W**. The Logic of Torture: A Critical Examination. *Soc Theor Pract*, 22(3), 349-374, Fall 96.

It is often assumed that no one would seriously argue for the practice of torture. Yet there have been and still are several justificatory arguments used to defend it. In this paper, the justification of torture is challenged through analyses of five of the clearest of such arguments. These include the philosophers' 'hard' case, against which it is most difficult to bring definitive arguments. Even in this case, and certainly in the others, the combined weight of different reasons against it raises serious doubts about whether torture in any of its manifestations can continue to be justified.

**Ting, Kathleen** and Brabeck, Mary M. Context, Politics and Moral Education: Comments on the Misgeld?Magendzo Conversation about Human Rights Education. *J Moral Educ*, 26(2), 147-149, Je 97.

We comment on Misgeld's and Magendzo's call for a political analysis of moral education, in which governmental, economic and social control goals are critically examined. We suggest character education programs overlook the necessity of engagement in historical analysis and critique of unjust systems and fail to recognize that politics are inevitable and inextricably involved in moral education. As a corrective to Kohlbergian theory, moral educators ought to stay close to the experience of people, so as not to get lost in immobilizing intellectual abstraction. Human rights education offers a corrective to both moral education and character education programs.

**Tinsley, Barbara Sher**. Sozzini's Ghost: Pierre Bayle and Socinian Toleration. *J Hist Ideas*, 57(4), 609-624, O 96.

**Tiscornia, Daniela**. A Methodology for the Representation of Legal Knowledge: Formal Ontology Applied to Law. *Sorites*, 26-43, Jl 95.

In this article, we shall describe the principles on which formal ontology is based, comparing its characteristics with those of legal domain and referring, as exemplification, to some models offered by legal theory which could lay the bases for a legal formal ontology. (edited)

**Titani, Satoko**. Completeness of Global Intuitionistic Set Theory. *J Sym Log*, 62(2), 506-528, Je 97.

Heyting valued universe is a model of intuitionistic set theory and constructed in ZFC that is the metatheory. The purpose of this work is to formulate the intuitionistic set theory in which the metatheory can be expressed. For that, we introduce a modal operator called *globalization*. We axiomatize the intuitionistic set theory with globalization, GIZF and prove the completeness in the sense that a sentence is provable in GIZF if and only if the validity of the sentence in any Heyting valued universe is provable in ZFC.

**Titiev, Robert**. Arbitrage and the Dutch Book Theorem. *J Phil Res*, 22, 477-482, Ap 97.

Philosophical writing on probability theory includes a great many articles discussing relationships between rational behavior and an agent's susceptibility to betting contexts where an overall loss is mathematically inevitable. What the Dutch book theorem establishes is that this kind of susceptibility is a consequence of having betting ratios that are in violation of the Kolmogorov probability axioms. In this article it is noted that a general result to rule out arbitrage can be shown to yield the Dutch book theorem as a special case. A formal framework is set forth to handle marketplace transactions involving contractual arrangements; and, within that framework, necessary and sufficient conditions are given for ruling out arbitrage. It is then shown that these conditions entail that pricing functions associated with particular kinds of betting contracts must turn out to be probability functions.

**Tittle, Peg**. Identity Politics as a Transposition of Fraser's Needs Politics. *Int J Applied Phil*, 11(1), 23-28, Sum-Fall 96.

By transposing Nancy Fraser's theory of needs politics to identity politics and exploring the transpositions, I broaden our understanding of identity claims. The three moments of Fraser's politics of needs are transposed to become a definition of identity politics: 1) the struggle to legitimate the identity; 2) the struggle to define the identity; and 3) the struggle to satisfy the identity. Three of Fraser's discourse questions are also transposed: 1) Why has identity-talk become so prominent? 2) What are the major varieties of identity-talk? 3) What opportunities and/or obstacles does the identity idiom pose for movements interested in social transformation?

**Tittle, Peg**. Sexual Activity, Consent, Mistaken Belief, and *Mens Rea*. *Phil Cont World*, 3(1), 19-23, Spr 96.

The gendered subcultures of our society may have different value systems. Consequently, sexual activity that involves members of these subcultures may be problematic, especially concerning the encoding and decoding of consent. This has serious consequences for labeling the activity as sex or sexual assault. Conceiving consent not as a mental act but as a behavioural act (that is, using a performative standard) would eliminate these problems. However, if we remove the mental element from one aspect, then to be consistent we must remove it from all; and, as a result, the "mistaken belief" defense would be eliminated and mens rea would become insignificant (in other words, if what the woman means is irrelevant, then what the man believes or intends should also be irrelevant). This consequence suggests major changes to our current conceptions of legal justice, which changes, if undesirable, prompt reconsideration of the initial proposal to use a performative standard for consent.

**Tiwari, D N**. Cognition, Being, and the Possibility of Expressions: A Bhartrharian Approach. *J Indian Counc Phil Res*, 14(1), 65-93, S-D 96.

**Tjong Tjin Tai, Eric**. Zelfbeheersing en democratie. *Alg Ned Tijdschr Wijs*, 89(3), 189-204, Jl 97.

Why are there no moral restraints on democratic citizenship in contemporary liberal states? In the classical view of Aristotle, temperance was a prerequisite for practical wisdom, having the consequence of an antiliberal state with strictly exclusive citizenship. A study of the early Stoa and Spinoza shows the reasons to reject this view. Stoic philosophy tightens the requirements for wisdom and *apatheia*, resulting in the practical equality of the vast majority of unwise people. Clear political consequences are, however, lacking. While assuming a similar position on the necessity of self-control, Spinoza does not make it a requirement for citizenship, nor does he recommend antiliberal measures since this would disturb peace among the unwise majority. He defends a liberal democracy because it is the best environment for the ideal of individual, autonomous development. Today this still is an important argument for caution against restraints on citizenship and personal life.

**Todd, Robert B** (trans). *Themistius: On Aristotle's On the Soul*. Ithaca, Cornell Univ Pr, 1996.

Themistius' paraphrase of Aristotle's *On the Soul* is his most important and influential work. It is also the first extant commentary on this work of Aristotle to survive from antiquity. A rival to that of Alexander of Aphrodisias, it represents one of the main interpretations of Aristotle's theory of the intellect, which was

debated throughout the Middle Ages and the Renaissance. It continues to be an important text for the reconstruction of Aristotle's philosophical psychology today. (publisher, edited)

**Toddington, Stuart**. Method, Morality and the Impossibility of Legal Positivism. *Ratio Juris*, 9(3), 283-299, S 96.

The dispute between legal positivists (e.g., Hart) and natural lawyers (e.g., Finnis) concerns the existence or otherwise of a necessary (conceptual) connection between law and morality. Legal positivists such as Hart deny this connection and assert the merely contingent relationship of law and morals. However, it can be demonstrated that implicit in the valid sociological method of concept formation of post-Austinian positivists are interpretative or ideal-typical models of the practical rationality of the legal enterprise which are not, and cannot possibly be, value-neutral. With particular attention to the work of John Finnis and his incorporation of Weberian and Aristotelian methodological principles, this paper exposes, if not the truth of Natural Law Theory, the impossibility of legal positivism.

**Todisco, Orlando**. Tragedia e cristianesimo: Agostino e il platonismo spezzato. *Sapienza*, 49(4), 373-396, 1996.

**Töllner, Uwe**. *Sartres Ontologie und die Frage einer Ethik: Zur Vereinbarkeit einer normativen Ethik und/oder Metaethik mit der Ontologie von "L'être et le néant"*. New York, Lang, 1996.

'Alle menschlichen Handlungen sind gleichwertig', so eine Aussage von Sartre in seinem ontologischen Hauptwerk *Das Sein und das Nichts*. Ist Sartres Ontologie überhaupt mit einer Ethik vereinbar? Diese Frage steht zudem im Kontext des Problems, wie Sartre nach dem Verlust der objektiven Werte seine politischen Handlungen legitimieren konnte. In einer detaillierten Analyse der Ontologie Sartres zeigt Töllner, dass diese Ontologie Ethik erlaubt, jedoch bestimmte Einschränkungen für die Ethik impliziert. Dadurch leistet das Buch auch einen Beitrag zur allgemeinen Ethik-Diskussion. Methodisch wurde Wert darauf gelegt, Sartre nicht—wie zumeist—nur mit seinen eigenen Worten zu wiederholen, sondern Bedeutungen und Analysen für unklare Begriffe und Aussagen zu finden. (publisher)

**Toepel, Friedrich**. Error in persona vel objecto und aberratio ictus. *Jahr Recht Ethik*, 2, 413-428, 1994.

An irrelevant error in *persona vel objecto* occurs when the following statement is true: "Concerning the object actually harmed, the actor at least thought it was possible and thus accepted that his action would result in the prohibited harm to this object." A relevant *aberratio ictus* occurs when this statement is false, since the actor did not at least think it possible and thus accept that his action would result in the prohibited harm to *this* object, but rather to *another* object. In the case of an irrelevant error in persona, the actor is in control of the objective violation of the norm of conduct at the time of that violation. Accordingly, this violation can be imputed to him directly as intentionally consummated. (edited)

**Tokarczyk, Roman A**. Principles of Lon Fuller's Conception of Natural Law. *Vera Lex*, 14(1-2), 24-29, 1994.

Fuller intended his doctrine as an empirical one, as a conception which derives specific norms of behavior from the scientific knowledge of the nature of man and society.... Human nature as the source of substantive natural law creates a certain kind of norm which...should be taken into account by everyone who deals with positive law.

**Tokarczyk, Roman A**. Why Positive Law Theory Makes a Big Difference: Editor's Commentary on "Principles of Lon Fuller's Conception of Natural Law". *Vera Lex*, 14(1-2), 30-31, 1994.

**Tokarz, Marek**. Non-Axiomatizability of Grice's Implicature. *Stud Log*, 53(2), 343-349, My 94.

The aim of this paper is to test Grice's theory of conversational implication [1], so-called *implicature*, by putting it into operation in the simplest possible formal language, that is, by constructing an adequate zero-order (sentential) logic. We are going to give a recursive formal description of Grice's maxims and show that the description cannot be made finite.

**Tola, Fernando** and Dragonetti, Carmen. Buddhist Conception of Reality. *J Indian Counc Phil Res*, 14(1), 35-64, S-D 96.

**Tollefsen, Christopher**. Donagan, Abortion, and Civil Rebellion. *Pub Affairs Quart*, 11(3), 303-312, Jl 97.

Violence at abortion clinics has brought to light a tension which exists in the Judeo-Christian tradition of moral teaching on abortion. Within that tradition, abortion is held to be the killing of the innocent. The same tradition holds that it is permissible, and sometimes obligatory, to defend innocent life with force. Yet most defenders of that tradition deny that force can be used in defense of the unborn. In this paper, I seek to resolve this tension by demonstrating that violence against abortion providers and clinics is best understood as an unjustified form of revolutionary activity.

**Tollefsen, Christopher**. Self-Assessing Emotions and Platonic Fear. *Int Phil Quart*, 37(3), 305-318, S 97.

Plato's account of courage in the *Republic* requires that fear play a motivating role in a courageous agent's actions. The danger which constitutes the intentional object of such fear is the damage to the soul which wrongful action causes. This view requires the agent to possess a normative conception of the best life as constituted by just acts and the worst by unjust acts. Plato's view of fear is situated within current discussion of self-assessing emotions, such as shame. It is argued that fear can play a more significant role than can shame in the preservation of one's character.

**Tomberlin, James E**. "Mental Causation: A Query for Kim" in *Contents*, Villanueva, Enrique (ed), 152-159. Atascadero, Ridgeview, 1995.

In the brief essay I sketch a *modal grade* view of causation. By this picture there is ample reason to believe that mental states participate in causal relations.

**Tomberlin, James E**. "Perception and Possibilia" in *Perception*, Villanueva, Enrique (ed), 109-115. Atascadero, Ridgeview, 1996.

This brief essay argues that *possibilia* are properly invoked in providing a correct account of a certain range of perception sentences.

**Tomberlin, James E**. Actualism or Possibilism?. *Phil Stud*, 84(2-3), 263-281, D 96.

Actualism is minimally the view that there are no objects that do not actually exist. According to the actualist, there are no philosophical problems whose solution calls for or requires an ontological commitment to nonactual objects. In the present essay I formulate a number of challenges against this ontological stance.

**Tomberlin, James E** (ed). *Philosophical Perspectives, 9, AI, Connectionism and Philosophical Psychology, 1995*. Atascadero, Ridgeview, 1995.

This volume, number 9 in the annual series *Philosophical Perspectives*, contains twenty-two original essays on a wide ranging spectrum of problems and issues in AI, connectionism and philosophical psychology.

**Tomek, Václav**. An Idea of Total Freedom? (in Czech). *Filosof Cas*, 45(2), 213-236, 1997.

The anarchists' distance from the violence with which late 19th-century anarchism was linked came from the idea of emancipation as being primarily cultivated through intellectual means. The *Manifesto* stated this priority in a call for an "intellectual revolution", as a necessary condition for a "material revolution". Future developments reversed this relationship, answering some of the movement's question, but at the same time deciding its fate. (edited)

**Tomin, Julius**. Plato's First Dialogue. *Ancient Phil*, 17(2), 31-45, Spr 97.

**Tommasi, Wanda**. Il re nudo: L'immaginario del potere in Simone Weil. *Iride*, 10(20), 88-101, Ap 97.

**Tomohiro, Takanashi**. Die Philosophie Nishidas als eine "Kunstlehre": Überlegungen zu Nishidas Beziehung zur Kunsttheorie Fiedlers (in Japanese). *Bigaku*, 47(2), 13-23, Autumn 96.

In dieser Abhandlung versuch ich das nachzuwiesen, indem ich die Beziehung der Nishida-Philosophie (*Nishida-Tetsugaku*) zur Kunsttheorie Konrad Fiedlers (1841-1895) untersuche, die Nishidas "Kunst"-auffassung entscheidend beeinflusste. Als Ergebnis dieses Versuchs lässt sich der Standpunkt vertreten, Nishida-Philosophie im Ganzen als "Kunstlehre" zu betrachten. Und diese "Kunstlehre" kann das Prinzip erhellen helfen, das den heute zunehmend vielgestaltigen künstlerischen Phänomenen oder Kunstschöpfungen zugrunde liegt. (edited)

**Tondl, Ladislav**. What is the Thematic Structure of Science? (Czech). *Filosof Cas*, 45(1), 51-71, 1997.

Attempts to justify a reliable system of classification criteria for the contemporary research activities were not connected with a general acceptance. Nevertheless, there exists a well-founded need of an acceptable "arrangement of knowledge" or "thematic structure" of science. The paper discusses some problems and tasks connected with establishing a thematic structure stressing, especially, integration tendencies and mutual dependencies. A system of criteria for justifying relative independence of a scientific discipline based on epistemological approaches is introduced.

**Tonelli, Mark**. Beyond Living Wills. *Bioethics Forum*, 13(2), 6-12, Sum 97.

Living wills are ineffective, primarily because they are too ambiguous to guide medical decision making and because the problem they were designed to address no longer exists to any significant degree. Attempts to reformulate instructive directives and make them more clinically relevant are unlikely to succeed. Responsibility for avoiding inappropriate care at the end of life not with patients, but with health care practitioners.

**Tong, Rosemarie**. *Feminist Approaches to Bioethics: Theoretical Reflections and Practical Applications*. Boulder, Westview Pr, 1997.

No other cluster of medical issues affects the genders as differently as those related to procreation—contraception, sterilization, abortion, artificial insemination, in vitro fertilization, surrogate motherhood, and genetic screening. Rosemarie Tong's approach to feminist bioethics serves as a catalyst to bring together different feminist voices in hope in actually *doing* something to make gender equity a present reality rather than a mere future possibility. (publisher,edited)

**Tong, Rosemarie**. Introduction: Feminist Approaches to Bioethics. *J Clin Ethics*, 7(2), 150, Sum 96.

In her *Introduction: Feminist Approaches to Bioethics*, Rosemarie Tong introduces the collaborative series related to feminist bioethics. In these articles, Tong, Anna Kirkland and Linda LeMoncheck discuss power relations between the sexes, specifically within the practices of reproductive technology and cosmetic surgery. As Tong states, these articles generally describe men's "empowerment" and women's "dispowerment," a cultural condition that makes it hard for women to make free choices even about their own bodies. Tong highlights the fact that in her article about reproductive technologies, LeMoncheck argues that it is possible for women to employ these technologies in an empowering way. In her article written with Anna Kirkland, Tong describes how certain women can likewise use cosmetic surgery for their own happiness, but that far too many women alter their bodies to suit others' desires rather than their own desires. Tong relates how each article in the series stresses that healthcare should be responsible for helping women make free and personally beneficial choices.

**Tong, Rosemarie**. Introduction: Feminist Approaches to Bioethics. *J Clin Ethics*, 7(4), 315-319, Wint 96.

**Tong, Rosemarie**. The Promises and Perils of Pragmatism: Commentary on Fins, Bacchetta, and Miller. *Kennedy Inst Ethics J*, 7(2), 147-152, Je 97.

In sum, there is within clinical pragmatism the potential for physicians to take back some of the power they ceded to patients during the height of the patients' rights and autonomy movement. Provided that clinicians guard against the temptation to use clinical pragmatism manipulatively, however, the method promises, more than most other methods of moral problem solving, to help increasingly diverse individuals make *good* moral decisions about patients' care under conditions of enormous uncertainty. (edited)

**Tong, Rosemarie** and Kirkland, Anna. Working within Contradiction: The Possibility of Feminist Cosmetic Surgery. *J Clin Ethics*, 7(2), 151-159, Sum 96.

**Tooley, Michael**. *Time, Tense, and Causation*. New York, Clarendon/Oxford Pr, 1997.

Michael Tooley presents a major new philosophical study of time and its relation to causation. The nature of time has always been one of the most fascinating and perplexing problems in philosophy. In recent years, it has become the focus of vigorous debate between advocates of rival theories, as traditional, 'tensed' accounts of time, which hold that time has a direction and that the flow of time is part of the nature of the universe, have been challenged by 'tenseless' accounts of time, according to which past, present, and future are merely subjective features of events, rather than objective properties of events. (publisher, edited)

**Toop, Richard**. The Aesthetics of a *Tabula Rasa*: Western Art Music's Avant-Garde from 1949-1953. *Lit Aes*, 6, 61-76, O 96.

**Topolski, Jerzy**. "Historians Look at Historical Truth" in *Epistemology and History*, Zeidler-Janiszewska, Anna (ed), 405-417. Amsterdam, Rodopi, 1996.

The notion of truth is one of the main categories of the historical profession. Historical truth is for historians not only a philosophical but also a moral category. It is not necessarily the classical truth presupposing metaphysical realism. The expectations of historians could possibly better satisfy other conceptions of truth like the conception of nonreferential truth proposed by Hilary Putnam. The notion of truth should be applied not only to singular sentences but also to whole narratives. This is indispensable insofar as historical narrative is composed not only of articulated but also of nonarticulated layers which carry informative, persuasive (rhetorical), ideological and theoretical content.

**Topolski, Jerzy**. "The Commonwealth of Scholars and New Conceptions of Truth" in *The Idea of University*, Brzezinski, Jerzy (ed), 83-103. Amsterdam, Rodopi, 1997.

The main aim of the article is to point to the growing responsibility of scholars in front of the new conceptions of truth. The "love of objective truth" (K. Twardowski) is now the love of argumentation because there is no truth independent of language. Nevertheless, one cannot give up truth, for above all, it is a moral value and by the same token, the fundamental regulator of human practices. In this striving for truth as a moral value the university plays an important role. The commonwealth of scholars is now facing new challenges.

**Topper, David**. "Towards an Epistemology of Scientific Illustration" in *Picturing Knowledge*, Baigrie, Brian S (ed), 215-249. Toronto, Univ of Toronto Pr, 1996.

This article is an overview of the literature on the epistemological status of scientific illustration, a topic relatively ignored by most art and science historians and philosophers until recently. A wide-range of sciences are covered (natural history, the life sciences, physics, geology and technology) as well as art artifacts themselves as a form of illustration. Matters pertaining to visual thinking, theory-ladenness, empiricism, pictures vs. text and demarcation of science, pseudo-science and art are also broached.

**Topuzian, Carlos Marcelo**. Acerca de "Una teoría de la textualidad". *Rev Latin de Filosof*, 23(1), 127-135, O 97.

In his book, Jorge Gracia does not admit the polemical substance in the discussion about textuality. He proposes a functional taxonomy of textual genres as the base of his theory, but it becomes difficult to verify it. He uses exclusively the "proper" idea of meaning, and that leads him to exclude from textual meaning the understanding caused by some interpretations (i.e., psychoanalytical). He speaks about the "hermeneutical circle" and proposes human behavior as a way to "get out" of it. He doesn't admit possible heterogeneities in textual meaning. He must refer to an essential human nature and tradition, in order to guarantee a correct textual understanding, but he does not argue adequately these instances.

**Toribio, Josefa**. "Ruritania and Ecology" in *Contents*, Villanueva, Enrique (ed), 188-195. Atascadero, Ridgeview, 1995.

Ned Block has argued that if there is such a thing as narrow content, it is holistic. He doesn't assume any particular theory of what narrow content actually *is*. Whatever it might be, the main restriction is that it plays a (causal) explanatory role in the agent's behavior. I argue, firstly, that the notion of narrow content is so seriously affected by this reasonable assumption that the only alternative is to give up on narrow content altogether. I argue, secondly, that there is a way of cashing an alternative notion of content, neither narrow nor wide, that is appropriate for psychological explanation and that doesn't have holism as a consequence. The way to do so, I suggest, is to locate this notion of content in a more *ecological* conceptual frame, one in which content is ascribed to an agent in virtue of her being embodied and embedded in a particular environment.

**Torralba Roselló, Francisco**. Sufrimiento y humildad ontológica: Kant y Schopenhauer. *Sapientia*, 51(200), 465-474, 1996.

**Torrell, Jean-Pierre**. Le savoir théologique chez les premiers thomistes. *Rev Thomiste*, 97(1), 9-30, Ja-Mr 97.

**Torrens, Antoni** and Rodríguez Salas, Antonio Jesús. Wajsberg Algebras and Post Algebras. *Stud Log*, 53(1), 1-19, F 94.

We give a presentation of Post algebras of order n + 1 (n "is equal to or greater than" 1) as n + 1 bounded Wajsberg algebras with an additional constant and we show that a Wajsberg algebra admits a P-algebra reduct if and only if it is n + 1 bounded. (edited)

**Torres, Amadeu**. Melo Bacelar, Filósofo da "Grammatica" na Lexicografia de Setecentos. *Rev Port Filosof*, 52(1-4), 935-943, Ja-D 96.

**Torres, Amadeu** (ed). *Mentoring the Mentor: A Critical Dialogue with Paulo Freire*. New York, Lang, 1997.

*Mentoring the Mentor* recreates a Freirian dialogue in a printed format. In this volume, sixteen distinguished scholars engage in a critical and thoughtful exchange with Paulo Freire. While some contributors voice appreciation for Freire's ideas and for what it means to "reinvent Freire" in a North American context, others offer sharp critiques of Freire's philosophy and, of equal importance, of the various interpretations of his work. A variety of chapters describe specific uses which have been made of Freire's ideas in diverse educational contexts, from the New York City public schools to the revolutions in Guinea Bissau and Eritrea. Finally, Paulo Freire himself responds to the major issues which are raised in the volume and invites readers to share in a continuing lively dialogue about the meaning of democratic and revolutionary education. (publisher)

**Torres, Juan Manuel**. Competing Research Programmes on the Origin of Life. *J Gen Phil Sci*, 27(2), 325-346, 1996.

During the course of its short history the discipline concerned with the origin of life has given birth to several scientific programmes in the Lakatosian sense, two of the most prominent and widespread being those initiated by Oparin (life began from protein entities) and Muller-Haldane (life began from genetic entities). The present paper sets down the bases for the rational reconstruction of both views by identifying their *hard core* and some of their successive *developments*. An assessment is made of the various stages in the evolution of these programmes with respect to the crucial Lakatosian notions of *progressivity* and *regressivity* and of how their arguments stand up against one another. This epistemological analysis also establishes the internal reasons why the RNA version of the *genotype programme* (developed in particular by L. Orgel and S. Spiegelman) has today taken one a progressive character and enjoys recognition by the international scientific community.

**Torres, Juan Manuel**. On the Limits of Enhancement in Human Gene Transfer: Drawing the Line. *J Med Phil*, 22(1), 43-53, F 97.

Enhancement-line human genetic engineering has recurrently been targeted for bioethical discussion and is usually (if not always) illustrated by examples alluding to a genetic technology that is far beyond our current possibilities. By discussing an ambitious project related to solid tumor cancers—multidrug resistance (MDR)—the present paper places the question on a more realistic plane and draws bioethical conclusions to serve as guidelines in the field. The paper also establishes the inadequacy of the prevalent concept of genetic medicine as one of substitution.

**Tortora, Roberto** and Gerla, Giangiacomo. Dissezioni e intersezioni di regioni in A.N. Whitehead. *Epistemologia*, 19(2), 289-308, Jl-D 96.

Here we take into account two interesting notions in [5], to which Whitehead devoted his Assumptions 13 to 18, namely the notion of *dissection* of a region and that of *intersection* of two regions. We discuss these two concepts in the framework of the general theory of ordered sets and extend the axiom system of [2] to a larger one. In the final section we prove the consistency of the system, constructing a "natural' model for it, which utilizes topological notions of the classical three-dimensional Euclidean space. (edited)

**Toshiyuki, Matsuzaki**. Musik und Sprache beim Frühen Nietzsche (in Japanese). *Bigaku*, 47(2), 1-12, Autumn 96.

Im vierten Abschnitt der "dionysischen Weltanschauung" (1870) betrachtet Nietzsche die Musik als eine Art von Sprache. Von diesem Standpunkt aus vergleicht er die Musik als Tonsprache mit der Begriffssprache als Sprache im engeren Sinn, und zwar in betreff ihrer Mitteilungsgegenstände und Mitteilungsweisen im Rahmen der Zweiweltenphilosophie Schopenhauers. In "Über Musik und Wörter" (1871) kritisiert Nietzsche hingegen die Zweiweltenphilosophie Schopenhauers und versucht, die Musik unter einer anderen Pro bemstellung zu behandeln. Die Entdifferenzierung der Musik und Sprache geht in "Ueber Wahrheit und Lüge im aussermoralischen Sinne" (1873) vorwärts, indem der Entstehungsprozess der Sprache ans Licht gebracht wird. Trotz der Verwandtschaften bleibt jedoch der unübersehbare, wesentliche Unterschied zwischen Musik und Begriffssprache übrig. Es ist die besondere Mitteilungsweise der Musik, die einen solchen Unterschied erzeugt.

**Totaro, Francesco**. Metafisica e trascendentalità: Confronto con l'epistemologia e l'ermeneutica. *G Metaf*, 18(1-2), 195-214, Ja-Ag 96.

**Totaro, Giuseppina**. "La fortuna del *Dictionnaire* in Italia in una lettera di Antonio Magliabechi" in *Pierre Bayle e l'Italia*, Bianchi, Lorenzo, 227-239. Napoli, Liguori Ed, 1996.

**Toumasis, Charalampos**. The NCTM Standards and the Philosophy of Mathematics. *Stud Phil Educ*, 16(3), 317-330, Jl 97.

It is argued that the philosophical and epistemological beliefs about the nature of mathematics have a significant influence on the way mathematics is taught at school. In this paper, the philosophy of mathematics of the NCTM's Standards is investigated by examining its explicit assumptions regarding the teaching and learning of school mathematics. The main conceptual tool used for this purpose is the model of two dichotomous philosophies of mathematics-absolutist versus-fallibilist and their relation to mathematics pedagogy. The main conclusion is that a fallibilist view of mathematics is assumed in the Standards and that most of its pedagogical assumptions and approaches are based on this philosophy.

**Tourpe, Emmanuel**. Le thomisme entre système et histoire. *Rev Phil Louvain*, 95(1), 144-158, F 97.

The present critical study's purpose is to compare a historical approach of Thomas's metaphysics with the latest book of L. Elders (entitled: *La métaphysique de saint Thomas d'Aquin dans une perspective historique*), and a systematic Thomism, with the work of Philipp W. Rosemann: *Omne ens est aliquid*. We suggest that both Elders and Rosemann compliment each other and achieve by their reciprocity the real way of development an integral Thomism is to aim.

**Tozzi, María Verónica**. El relato histórico: ¿hipótesis o ficción? Críticas al "narrativismo imposicionalista" de Hayden White. *Analisis Filosof*, 17(1), 75-94, My 97.

In the last years, both philosophers of history and historians have been concerned about the epistemological status of historical stories. The debate traces back to Hayden White, who rejected the idea that historical stories can be told from fictional ones on the basis of the real character of the facts referred to. In what follows, I will critically examine White's conception and I will show that the rejection of the thesis in question depends on three assumptions. The first one is a narrow characterization of the explanatory effect of the historical story conceived as a pictorial representation. Secondly, there is a narrow conception of historical reality, which allows for a continuity between the analytic philosophy of history and the imposicionalist narrativism. In third place, there is a reduction of the content of the historical text—namely, the past—to its form of expression. The upshot is a hypostatization of the literary aspects of the historical story with the consequent detriment to its ontological and evaluative commitments.

**Trachtenberg, Zev**. "Subject and Citizen: Hobbes and Rousseau on Sovereignty and the self" in *Jean-Jacques Rousseau and the Sources of the Self*, O'Hagan, Timothy (ed), 85-105. Brookfield, Avebury, 1997.

Following Hobbes, Rousseau holds that the self of the ideal citizen must be strongly disposed to obey the law. Hobbes argued that sovereigns must have the power to form their subjects' wills to absolute obedience. Rousseau takes up Hobbes's absolutism—but insists that sovereignty must be borne democratically by the community as a whole. Thus, for Rousseau, in addition to being obedient, citizens must be able to participate in the formation of society's general will. However, while the institutions Rousseau proposes for forming citizens' selves would indeed make them obedient, they would form selves incapable of participating in the sovereign authority.

**Trachtenberg, Zev**. "The Takings Clause and the Meanings of Land" in *Philosophy and Geography I: Space, Place, and Environmental Ethics*, Light, Andrew (ed), 63-90. Lanham, Rowman & Littlefield, 1997.

The takings problem can be conceived as a matter of distributing specific rights associated with land ownership between title-holders and the public. Following Walzer, we can look to the meanings of land to settle questions of distributive justice. This paper examines three meanings we associate with land, each of which supports a different distribution. None of these three meanings is preeminent, hence it is impossible to appeal to a single meaning to determine the single just distribution of rights. Rather, we must accept that the takings problem has a tragic dimension: however, we resolve it we are forced to sacrifice values we ought to hold dear.

**Trachtenberg, Zev**. Good Neighbors Make Good Fences: Frost's "Mending Wall". *Phil Lit*, 21(1), 114-122, Ap 97.

Frost's poem 'Mending Wall' dramatizes a confrontation between liberal and communitarian attitudes toward property. In the poem two neighbors repair the wall between their farms. One interprets this activity by saying "good fences make good neighbors," expressing the liberal view that property rights establish protected spheres of individual activity. The other understands the chore as an occasion to work together toward a common end, suggesting a communitarian vision that communal attachments sustain individual property rights.

**Tracy, James D**. *Erasmus of the Low Countries*. Berkeley, Univ of Calif Pr, 1996.

Erasmus of Rotterdam (1469-1536), frequently depicted by twentieth-century critics as the model of disengaged enlightenment, is portrayed by James Tracy as a passionately involved intellectual, who struggled to refashion in terms appropriate to his own age the traditional synthesis of Christian and classical values. Tracy shows that without understanding the context or background of Erasmus's life and ideas, we cannot appreciate the true originality of his program for the reform of Christian society. (publisher,edited)

**Traczyk, Tadeusz**. Post Algebras in Helena Rasiowa's Explorations. *Bull Sec Log*, 25(3/4), 159-160, O-D 96.

In her book *An Algebraic Approach to Non-Classical Logics* Helena Rasiowa gave a first full exposition of the up-to-date knowledge of Post algebras. There she added her own contribution; in particular a theory of D-filters. She extended to prime D-filters the well-known Rasiowa-Sikorski Lemma on existence of prime filters in Boolean algebras, preserving enumerable set of infinite joins and meets. It was applied in many ways in the theory of many-valued logics. A natural generalization of these results gave rise to her fruitful investigations in the theory of Post algebras of infinite order and its various applications.

**Trägårdh, Lars** and Breckman, Warren. Nationalism, Individualism, and Capitalism: Reply to Greenfield. *Crit Rev*, 10(3), 389-407, Sum 96.

Reversing the arguments of Anderson, Gellner, and Hobsbawm, Liah Greenfield contends that it is nationalism that produces economic development. Specifically, she claims that nationalism inspired three seminal economic

AUTHOR INDEX 957 Trillas, Enric


thinkers: Marx, List, and Smith. However, Greenfield's ideological preferences lead her to a problematic conception of individualism as nationalism, as well as to flawed treatments of Smith, List, and Marx. Nationalism is better understood as an attempt to address the deepening conflict between the imperative of community and the secular trends of the marketplace, which challenge national sovereignty and democracy.

**Trapp, Rainer**. "Sind moralische Aussagen objektiv wahr?" in *Das weite Spektrum der analytischen Philosophie,* Lenzen, Wolfgang, 408-428. Hawthorne, de Gruyter, 1997.

The paper argues for what I call metaethical "semicognitivism". This position adjudicates truth values to normative (= N) statements (and thus logical deductivity to moral reasoning), but at the same time rejects all cognitivistic objectivity claims for these values already for the reason that the "facts" in deontically perfect worlds that ground these values are only subject-relative mental facts. Consequently, the concept of a normal, exchangeable observer as a prerequisite for objectively testing general statements lacks an equivalent in N-matters. Several further points in favour of semicognitivism are made and defended against arguments to the contrary offered by moral realism and cognitivism.

**Trappenburg, Margo J**. Defining the Medical Sphere. *Cambridge Quart Healthcare Ethics*, 6(4), 416-434, Fall 97.

There are three major directions in the philosophical debate on the distribution of health care. (1) A Rawlsian health care distributional system, (2) a Nozickian market based approach, and (3) a communitarian strategy. Occasionally health care philosophers also refer to Walzer's *Spheres of Justice*. However, no one has undertaken the task to design a Walzerian health care system. Walzer argues that Americans ought to establish a health care system resembling the British NHS, because the concepts and categories in which they discuss the distribution of medical goods, as well as established institutions, such as Medicare and Medicaid, reveal that they have been committed to something akin to the NHS all along. Walzer's critics point out that a large part of medical goods in the United States is bought and sold on the market. Why shouldn't this be taken as evidence that a market system is what Americans really want? This controversy is based on a serious mistake in *Spheres of Justice*. Once this mistake has been rectified Walzer's theory of justice might be a fruitful approach to the discussion of cost containment in health care services.

**Traub, Hartmut**. "Natur, Vernunft-Natur und Absolutes" in *Sein—Reflexion—Freiheit: Aspekte der Philosophie Johann Gottlieb Fichtes,* Asmuth, Christoph (ed), 175-190. Amsterdam, Gruner, 1997.

Fichte's philosophy of nature has three periods. The first describes nature as irrational and to be cultivated. Nature is only the material of man's freedom. Secondly, Fichte develops the idea of the nature of reason itself. Phenomena like moral, esthetical and truth feelings have an heuristic function for science and research. Fichte's later theory of reason includes a complex conception of nature under the principles of materialism, legalism, moralism, religion and science. Nature can now be understood in different ways, as resource for materialistic needs, as the subject of human rights, as medium for art and moral ideas and as the appearance of divine creativity.

**Traub, Hartmut**. Wege zur Wahrheit: Zur Bedeutung von Fichtes wissenschaftlich- und populär-philosophischer Methode. *Fichte-Studien*, 10, 81-98, 1997.

**Travar, Dusan**. The Norm and History. *Filozof Istraz*, 16(3), 661-665, 1996.

The author starts by distinguishing between norms and imperatives, referring to the distinction made by *Kant*, and then notes that norm and imperative is equated in sociology. The problem of norms is viewed in the perspective of their historical determination with the content of each norm being historically conditioned. This has to do also with the chances of a given norm to spread and become implemented and accepted. The author stresses the purely philosophical search for the intellectual foundations of norms, taking into consideration the response of natural law and the response of utopia. The author shows that the former response is circular and the latter tautological. (edited)

**Travis, Charles**. Reply to Simmons. *Mind*, 106(421), 119-120, Ja 97.

**Treacy, Mary Jane**. Double Binds: Latin American Women's Prison Memories. *Hypatia*, 11(4), 130-145, Fall 96.

Scant attention given to gender in Latin American prison experiences implies that men and women suffer similarly and react according to their shared beliefs. This essay explores the prison memoirs of four Latin American women. Each account uses a standardized prison narrative adjusted to suit the narrator's own purpose and hints at how sexuality and motherhood, which shape women's experiences in prison, have been removed from sight.

**Trefousse, Hans L**. The Oates Case. *J Infor Ethics*, 3(1), 76-77, Spr 94.

**Treppiedi, Anna Maria**. L'esperienza del pensare: Indagine su un paradosso. *G Metaf*, 18(1-2), 113-130, Ja-Ag 96.

**Trevas, Robert** (ed) and Zucker, Arthur (ed) and Borchert, Donald (ed). *Philosophy of Sex and Love: A Reader.* Englewood Cliffs, Prentice Hall, 1997.

The human experience of sex and love has direct impact on our social well-being. By studying sexual philosophy, we allow ourselves, through exposure to a variety of alternative belief systems, to consider new possibilities and options as well as to develop a deeper understanding of the philosophy we already possess. This is the underlying principle behind the readings presented in the book. (publisher,edited)

**Treviño, A Javier** (ed) and Pound, Roscoe. *Social Control Through Law.* New Brunswick, Transaction Pub, 1997.

In *Social Control Through Law* Roscoe Pound formulates a list of social-ethical principles with a three-fold purpose. First, they are meant to identify and explain human claims, demands, or interests of a given social order. Second, they express what the majority of individuals in a given society want the law to do. Third, they are meant to guide the courts in applying the law. Pound distinguishes between individual interests, public interests, and social interests. He warns that these three types of interests are overlapping and interdependent and that most claims, demands, and desires can be placed in all three categories. Pound's theory of social interests is crucial to his thinking about law and lies at the conceptual core of sociological jurisprudence. In the new introduction, A. Javier Treviño outlines the principle aspects of Roscoe Pound's legal philosophy. (publisher, edited)

**Trías, Susana**. Reflexiones en torno a *Poema y Diálogo* de Gadamer. *Rev Filosof (Venezuela)*, 23(1), 79-91, 1996.

This paper discusses the interpretation validity's principle postulated by Gadamer in *Poem and Dialog* arguing that such criterion is inadmissible and also analyzes the relationship between Gadamer's practice of interpretation and the "Intentional Fallacy" debate.

**Trías, Susana**. The Ethics of Liberation and the Ethics of Discourse (Spanish). *Rev Filosof (Venezuela)*, Supp(2-3), 79-85, 1996.

This paper analyzes the relationship between the *Ethics of Liberation* (Dussel) and the *Ethics of Discourse* (Apel), centering on Dussel's texts from 1992 and 1995. Certain of Dussel's criticisms of the *Ethics of Discourse* are analyzed and a coming together of the *Ethics of Liberation* and moral sentiments is proposed.

**Trías Mercant, Sebastià**. Las claves hermenéuticas del pensamiento de Ramón Llull. *Rev Espan Filosof Med*, 4, 51-64, 1997.

One of the greatest difficulties to understand Ramon Llull's philosophy is its hermeneutic approach to his thought. Some have valued extremely his Latin scholastic studies, others have searched for his Arab background. This article gives a critical review of his bibliography with regard to the subject under discussion and takes into account that the scientific knowledge of Ramon Llull's thought was never part of the university world of his time. It is the result of the close union with the language and the Arab ideas during the postconquest days in Mallorca, the acquisition of first and second hand information of Latin texts and his presence at Montpellier's Medicine schools.

**Tricomi, Flavia**. "La dimensione del tempo nella psicanalisi di Freud" in *Il Concetto di Tempo: Atti del XXXII Congresso Nazionale della Società Filosofica Italiana,* Casertano, Giovanni (ed), 249-252. Napoli, Loffredo, 1997.

**Trifonas, Peter**. The Ends of Pedagogy: From the Dialectic of Memory to the Deconstruction of the Institution. *Educ Theor,* 46(3), 303-333, Sum 96.

The essay presents a reading of Jacques Derrida's "The Age of Hegel." It explores how the state of affairs that spawned the "ideology" of a report Hegel signs (in 1822) regarding the predicament of philosophy teaching can be reread through a deconstruction of the speculative presuppositions of the pedagogical memory of childhood the philosopher reveals. The question at hand is how the signature as a life-writing of the self stabilizes the pedagogical "truth" of a childhood memory to sanction the institutionalization of a speculative teaching-learning of philosophy. The deconstructive protocol of reading moves into the actual ethics and politics of the "scene of teaching" with a discussion of some recommendations Derrida makes to the GREPH for a critique of the institution of philosophy.

**Trigg, Roger**. The Inaugural Address: The Grounding of Reason. *Aris Soc*, Supp(71), 1-17, 1997.

The repudiation of the possibility of finding any certain foundations for our knowledge has led many into the self-contradictory paths of relativism. One response is to accept our language games on trust and in doing this Hilary Putnam makes use of the last work of Wittgenstein in 'On Certainty' to advocate a 'common sense realism'. Yet the view that justification can find no role beyond conceptual systems involves a grave diminution of the role of reason. It becomes powerless to deal with major areas of dispute. Instead, reasons must be seen to gain their force from the real world.

**Trigilio, Jo** and Alfonso, Rita. Surfing the Third Wave: A Dialogue Between Two Third Wave Feminists. *Hypatia*, 12(3), 7-16, Sum 97.

As third wave feminist philosophers attending graduate schools in different parts of the country, we decided to use our e-mail discussion as the format for presenting our thinking on the subject of third wave feminism. Our dialogue takes us through the subjects of postmodernism, the relationship between theory and practice, the generation gap, and the power relations associated with feminist philosophy as an established part of the academy.

**Trillas, Enric**. Menger's Trace in Fuzzy Logic. *Theoria (Spain)*, 11(27), 89-96, S 96.

This paper deals with the relation with fuzzy logic of some of the ideas of Karl Menger published between 1942 and 1966 and concerning what he called "hazy sets," probabilistic relations and statistical metric spaces. The author maintains the opinion that if Lofti A. Zadeh is actually the father of fuzzy logic, Menger not only was a forerunner of this field but that his ideas were and still are influential on it.

**Trillas, Enric** and De Soto, A R. What's an Approximate Conditional?. *Agora (Spain)*, 15(2), 71-81, 1996.

In any logic system, the representation of conditional information is a key element. The main inference rules habitually use propositions with a conditional form, i.e., conditionals, which facilitate an increase of the knowledge by means of making deductions. Fuzzy logic is not an exception, it needs conditionals to model fuzzy conditional statements. In this paper, after a brief discussion about classical conditionals, two forms to define fuzzy conditionals are given. Both of them are two different methods to obtain useful tools to make possible automatic process of approximate reasoning. Appropriate methods for approximate reasoning must necessarily be nonmonotonic because human beings think in a nonmonotonic manner. Several results in this field are also presented.

**Trilling, Leon**. Commentary: "On the Hazards of Whistleblowers and on Some Problems of Young Biomedical Scientists in our Time". *Sci Eng Ethics*, 1(4), 345-346, O 95.

**Trimiew, Darryl M** and Greene, Michael. How We Got Over: The Moral Teachings of The African-American Church on Business Ethics. *Bus Ethics Quart*, 7(2), 133-147, Mr 97.

An analysis of the business ethics of the African-American church during and after reconstruction reveals that it is a conflicted ethic, oscillating between two poles. The first is the sacralization of the business ethic of Booker T. Washington, in which self-help endeavors which valorize American capitalism but are preferentially oriented to the African-American community are advanced as the best and only options for economic uplift. The second is the "Blackwater" tradition, which rejects any racial discrimination and insists upon social justice. The inability of the Washingtonian business ethic to address the needs of the Black underclass are explored. (edited)

**Trindade Santos, José**. Platao, Heraclito e a estrutura metafórica do real. *Philosophica (Portugal)*, 45-68, 1993.

The author proposes an interpretation of the theory and practice of paradeigma, developed in conjunction with the method of diairesis in the *Sophist, Politicus* and *Philebus*. The conclusions reached are then balanced against the evidence of Plato's views on knowledge and language in the *Cratylus* and compared to the logos of Heraclitus, in order to explain the conception designated as the "metaphorical structure of reality". It is then suggested that the degradation and reevaluation of this structure in modern and contemporary thought was due to the attention paid, or not paid, to Aristotle's consideration of metaphor as a purely linguistic fact.

**Trindade Santos, José**. Platao, o Amor e a Retórica. *Philosophica (Portugal)*, 59-76, 1997.

I argue in favor of the unity of the *Phaedrus* following two parallel lines. First by establishing a meaningful relation between Phaedrus's and Socrates' two discourses I interpret them as steps in the search for that inner beauty which the philosopher asks the god Pan to grant him at the closing of the dialogue. Then the fact that both philosophical and "public" rhetoric join together under *psychagôgia* is shown to stress this link, revealing their common relation to love and desire for beauty. Thus despite being opposed in ends and means they are seen as stemming from the very same source and not as irreconcilable enemies.

**Trognon, Alain** and Grusenmeyer, Corinne. Structures of Natural Reasoning within Functional Dialogues. *Prag Cognition*, 4(2), 305-346, 1996.

The aim of this paper is to describe and characterize some structural features of natural reasoning by analyzing a number of conversations held by operators during shift changeovers. During this work phase the operators have to cooperate in order to carry out the same process. This need to cooperate leads to dialogues and joint elaboration of information, especially when involving the reporting of a malfunction. Three dialogues observed at this work phase on two study sites (a paper mill and a nuclear power plant) are analyzed. These analyses show that the step by step follow-up of the operators' collective reasoning is feasible. They highlight that these reasonings are complex experimental and hypothetico-deductive reasonings. They are reasonings for action, that are elaborated as the conversation unfolds and for which the operators do not always have the means of testing their hypotheses.

**Troisfontaines, Claude**. Présentation du professeur François Duchesneau. *Rev Phil Louvain*, 94(4), 564-567, N 96.

**Troncarelli, Barbara**. Diritti umani e dover essere. *Riv Int Filosof Diritto*, 73(4), 717-728, O-D 96.

**Trott, Elizabeth**. "Bradley and the Canadian Connection" in *Philosophy after F.H. Bradley,* Bradley, James (ed), 57-72. Bristol, Thoemmes, 1996.

**Trottmann, Christian**. Verbe mental et noétique thomiste dans le *De verbo* d'Hervé de Nédellec. *Rev Thomiste*, 97(1), 47-62, Ja-Mr 97.

Nous avons ainsi tenté de voir fonctionner le thomisme d'Hervé de Nédellec dans le *Tractatus de verbo*. Il ne cherche nullement à défendre un dogme établi. Au contraire, il est à l'oeuvre précisément sur un thème que Thomas d'Aquin n'avait guère développé pour lui-même. Son intérêt théologique allait plutôt à un verbe mental saisi dans l'émergence de son intellection, alors qu'il n'est pas encore traduit en mots, pour des raisons évidentes, car il permet l'analogie avec le Verbe divin qui ne saurait être discursif. Nédellec ne veut nullement défendre à tout prix l'existence d'un tel verbe en l'homme, au contraire il prend acte de la différence introduite entre Dieu et l'homme par la nécessaire médiation chez ce dernier de la discursivité, et il entend le penser philosophiquement. (edited)

**Trueba Atienza, Carmen**. Lógica filosófica medieval: San Anselmo y Guillermo de Occam. *Analogia*, 11(1), 151-166, Ja-Je 97.

**Truesdell, Sandra** and Moseley, Kathryn L. A Noncompliant Patient?. *J Clin Ethics*, 8(2), 176-177, Sum 97.

**Trujillo Pérez, Isabel**. Alle origini dei diritti dell'uomo: i diritti della comunicazione di Francisco de Vitoria. *Riv Int Filosof Diritto*, 74(1), 81-124, Ja-Mr 97.

**Trumbo, Bruce E** and Sieber, Joan E. (Not) Giving Credit Where Credit Is Due: Citation of Data Sets. *Sci Eng Ethics*, 1(1), 11-20, J 95.

Adequate citation of data sets is crucial to the encouragement of data sharing, to the integrity and cost-effectiveness of science and to easy access to the work of others. The citation behavior of social scientists who have published based on shared data was examined and found to be inconsistent with important

ideals of science. Insights gained from the social sciences, where data sharing is somewhat customary, suggest policies and incentives that would foster adequate citation by secondary users, and greater openness and sharing in other disciplines.

**Trundle, Robert**. Modalidades aristotélicas de san Agustín. *Augustinus*, 42(164-5), 13-40, Ja-Je 97.

Agustin complemento la epistemologia aristotelica mediante la nocion de que la omnipotente voluntad de Dios impide a la razon humana conocer la omnisciente razon de Dios. Ademas de adelantarse a la epistemologia de Tomas y de exponer elementos de la Escritura antes ignorados, las nociones de Agustin constan de interesantes intuiciones modales, que tienen que ver con las filosofias modernas de la logica y de la ciencia.

**Trundle, Jr, Robert C**. Thomas' Second Way: A Defense by Modal Scientific Reasoning. *Log Anal*, 37(146), 145-168, Je 94.

Among other things, it is argued that the controversial premise of Thomas's second way may be expressed "it is necessary that *not F* implies *not S*" where, when "*not S*" is expressed "*not S*$_m$" to designate current scientific modalities, $S_m$ not only entails the premise but, of course, comprises a second premise for deducing the conclusion *F* by way of Thomas's own modus-tollens form of argument. (edited)

**Truog, Robert D**. Is it Time to Abandon Brain Death?. *Hastings Center Rep*, 27(1), 29-37, Ja-F 97.

Despite its familiarity and widespread acceptance, the concept of "brain death" remains incoherent in theory and confused in practice. Moreover, the only purpose served by the concept is to facilitate the procurement of transplantable organs. By abandoning the concept of brain death and adopting different criteria for organ procurement, we may be able to increase both the supply of transplantable organs and clarity in our understanding of death.

**Tseng, Shian-Shyong** and Hong, Tzung-Pei and Chang, Kuo-Chin. Machine Learning by Imitating Human Learning. *Mind Mach*, 6(2), 203-228, My 96.

Learning general concepts in imperfect environments is difficult since training instances often include noisy data, inconclusive data, incomplete data, unknown attributes, unknown attribute values and other barriers to effective learning. It is well-known that people can learn effectively in imperfect environments and can manage to process very large amounts of data. Imitating human learning behavior, therefore, provides a useful model for machine learning in real-world applications. This paper proposes a new, more effective way to represent imperfect training instances and rules and based on the new representation, a Human-Like Learning (HULL) algorithm for incrementally learning concepts well in imperfect training environments. Several examples are given to make the algorithm clearer. Finally, experimental results are presented that show the proposed learning algorithm works well in imperfect learning environments

**Tsering, Khenpo Migmar**. Philosophy of Liberation According to Buddhism. *J Dharma*, 22(1), 86-96, Ja-Mr 97.

**Tsuzuki, Miho** and Asada, Yukiko and Akiyama, Shiro. High School Teaching of Bioethics in New Zealand, Australia and Japan. *J Moral Educ*, 25(4), 401-420, D 96.

This paper compares knowledge and teaching of 15 selected topics related to bioethics and biotechnology, with particular focus on the teaching of social, ethical and environmental issues of *in vitro* fertilization, prenatal diagnosis, biotechnology, nuclear power, pesticides and genetic engineering. The survey found that these issues were, generally, covered more in biology classes than in social science classes; and that there were differences in coverage among the three countries, with most coverage in Australia and least in Japan. Open questions looked at images of bioethics, and the reasons why about 90% of teachers thought bioethics was needed in education. Open questions on teaching materials, current and desired are also discussed. The data suggest a need for the development of more and higher quality materials, for the moral education that is conducted, especially in biology and social studies classes. (edited)

**Tuana, Nancy**. Fleshing Gender, Sexing the Body: Refiguring the Sex/Gender Distinction. *S J Phil*, 34(Supp), 53-73, 1996.

A critique of contemporary attempts to frame a dichotomy between sex and gender on the grounds that it and related binarisms, such as biology/culture, fail to acknowledge the complex nature of bodies as material-semiotic intra-actions. I argue that contemporary philosophies of the body must embrace a metaphysic that more adequately characterizes the processes of organisms and environments.

**Tuck, Donald R**. Lacuna in Sankara Studies: *A Thousand Teachings* (*Upadesasāhasrī*). *Asian Phil*, 6(3), 219-231, N 96.

In an important text, *A Thousand Teachings*, sometimes overlooked by scholars, Sankara expounds nondualist religion. This article analyses Sankara's thought for its theoretical and practical perspectives. First, the discussion views nonduality from the viewpoint of ignorance. This pluralistic/dualistic perspective obscures the unenlightened seeker's vision of the Ultimate Truth. Secondly, the study examines Sankara's introduction of a transitional idea, *Unevolved Name-and-Form* (avyākrte nāmarūpe). Such an idea assists the seeker's intellectual progress from the state of ignorance to a rational understanding leading toward nonduality (Advaita Vedānta). Finally, the exposition clarifies Sankara's expression of the "knowledge of Brahman." This fulfilling wisdom affects a transformation of the life experience of the unenlightened. Subsequently disciplined in meditation (parisamkhyāna), the persistent seeker develops into an experiencer of the nonduality (advaitavada).

**Tucker, Aviezer**. Jan Patocka's World Movement as Ultimate. *Ultim Real Mean*, 20(2 & 3), 107-122, Je-S 97.

Jam Patocka (1907-1977), the Czech phenomenologist and founder of the human rights movement *Charter 77*, understood human existence as a "movement," a dynamic reformulation of Heidegger's Being-in-the-World. This "movement" takes place between the "earth" and the "sky" and is divided into three submovements: taking root in the world, defence and self-extension and self-transcendence through care for the soul. The last is divided into: life in truth, authentic relation of the soul with the world; justice, social order that permits life in truth; and self-formation of the soul. Through following Socrates in holding that human essence is virtue and knowledge, Patocka joined a struggle for justice to enable virtuous life in truth.

**Tucker, John Allen**. Two Mencian Political Notions in Tokugawa Japan. *Phil East West*, 47(2), 233-253, Ap 97.

Two Mencian political notions are examined: rebellion against tyranny and righteous martyrdom, as explored theoretically by prominent Japanese scholars of the Tokugawa period (1603-1867). It is argued here generally that Confucianism, as represented by the *Mencius*, was more than a feudal ideology legitimizing the hegemony of Tokugawa shoguns, since these two Mencian notions were advocated and/or opposed by both supporters and opponents of the Tokugawa regime. In the development of this argument, it is also revealed that the two notions were important topics of Confucian debate among major Tokugawa scholars of all stripes throughout this period, and even in the early Meiji period. Without claiming that these two notions necessarily convey the central message of Mencius vis-à-vis political behavior, it is suggested that virtually all important Tokugawa scholars viewed them as crucial topics of debate, with most leaving a definitive statement or essay on them in their writings.

**Tucker, Joycelyn E** and Morrissey, John M and Stadler, Holly A. Nurses' Perspectives of Hospital Ethics Committees. *Bioethics Forum*, 10(4), 61-65, Fall 94.

The Midwest Bioethics Center (MBC) commissioned a survey of nurses' attitudes and needs regarding Hospital Ethics Committees (HECs) to guide its Ethics Committee Consortium. The survey examined three areas related to nurse utilization of and participation on HECs: 1) perception of HEC role and function; 2) perception of HEC case consultation function; 3) nurses' ethics training and continuing education. Important findings include nurses' reported lack of knowledge regarding HEC policies; a perception that their training in clinical ethics was inadequate; and a strong indication that HECs should be accessible to a wide range of health care professionals.

**Tucker, Robin** and Christensen, Kate T. Ethics without Walls: The Transformation of Ethics Committees in the New Healthcare Environment. *Cambridge Quart Healthcare Ethics*, 6(3), 299-301, Sum 97.

**Tugendhat, Ernst**. Gibt es eine moderne Moral?. *Z Phil Forsch*, 50(1/2), 323-338, Ja-Je 96.

**Tugendhat, Ernst**. Identidad Personal, Nacional y Universal. *Ideas Valores*, 3-18, Ap 96.

In the first section, personal identity is analysed as a type of qualitative, not individual indentity, including a reference to one's conception of life. This leads to a concept of happiness as concern for one's future. In the second section the question is raised whether in modernity the conception of one's identity can be satisfactory only if it is moral, that is universalistic and whether it can also be particularistic (national). The first question is left open, but it is maintained that universalism does not exclude particularism. Finally, pathological forms of modern identity are briefly sketched: worth mentioning is the attitude of indifference towards the poor, who are unable to even pose the question of identity.

**Tugendhat, Ernst**. Virtues. *Filosof Cas*, 44(3), 445-461, 1996.

**Tul'Chinskii, G L**. On a Mistake Made by Russian Philosophy. *Russian Stud Phil*, 35(2), 32-50, Fall 96.

**Tulsky, James A**. The Effect of Ethnicity on ICU Use and DNR Orders in Hospitalized AIDS Patients. *J Clin Ethics*, 8(2), 150-157, Sum 97.

We studied the effect of ethnicity on the use of intensive care (ICU) and do-not-resuscitate (DNR) orders in patients with AIDS. Among 1,376 patients hospitalized for pneumocystis carinii pneumonia in 63 urban hospitals, African-American ethnicity emerged as an independent predictor of admission to the ICU. Ethnicity did not predict the presence of a DNR order, yet African-American patients were less likely than white or Latino patients to have their DNR orders written during the first week of hospitalization. After adjusting for covariates, African-Americans remained more likely to have late DNR orders.

**Tulsky, James A** and Fox, Ellen. Evaluating Ethics Consultation: Framing the Questions. *J Clin Ethics*, 7(2), 109-115, Sum 96.

Case consultation in clinical ethics (ethics consultation) is a rapidly expanding health care service that, proponents argue, can improve patient care by resolving ethical dilemmas, ensuring quality ethical decision-making and mediating value conflicts among patients, families and health care providers. The rapid growth in the practice of ethics consultation has occurred, however, without either consensus about its goals or rigorous evaluation of the effectiveness of various approaches to its delivery. This article reviews the empirical literature in the field and reports on a conference that was held to initiate a process of evaluation for ethics consultation.

**Tulsky, James A** and Fox, Ellen. Evaluation Research and the Future of Ethics Consultation. *J Clin Ethics*, 7(2), 146-149, Sum 96.

**Tulsky, James A** and Stocking, Carol B. Obstacles and Opportunities in the Design of Ethics Consultation Evaluation. *J Clin Ethics*, 7(2), 139-145, Sum 96.

Designing research to evaluate ethics consultation presents abundant methodological challenges. This article focuses on how to design studies that assess the important aspects of ethics consultation, avoid bias, are reproducible and can be generalized to a variety of health care settings. We propose a research agenda that includes developing a consortium of institutions to conduct coordinated research, creating a minimum standardized database, describing the range of activities called ethics consultation, developing and validating evaluative measures, enhancing models of ethics consultation through quality improvement methods, designing single site effectiveness studies using systematic consultation and considering multicentered randomized controlled trials.

**Tunick, Mark**. Hegel's Nonfoundationalism: A Phenomenological Account of the Structure of Philosophy of Right. *Hist Phil Quart*, 11(3), 317-337, Jl 94.

The paper offers a nonfoundational interpretation of Hegel's *Philosophy of Right* that sees its structure determined by a phenomenological method in which the reader experiences deficiencies in the abstract account of right presented in earlier parts of the work and is driven to a richer, more concrete account of right as offered in the later sections of the book. The final account of right offered is justified, on this nonfoundational view, in providing a coherent account that will be experienced as entirely satisfying without appeal to external standards.

**Tuomela, Raimo**. Rational Cooperation and Collective Goals. *Protosoz*, 8/9, 260-291, 1996.

It is argued that full-blown cooperation needs collective goals in a strong sense satisfying the "Collectivity Condition". According to this condition, a collective goal is of the kind that necessarily, due to the goal-holders acceptance of the goal as their collective goal, if it is satisfied for one of the goal-holders it is satisfied for all the others. Not only collective goals but also other group-factors (such as possibly institutional "group-mode" preferences and utilities) are argued to be relevant to rational cooperative solutions of collective action dilemmas.

**Tuomela, Raimo**. Searle on Social Institutions. *Phil Phenomenol Res*, 57(2), 435-441, Je 97.

**Turchi, Athos**. L'Aurora degli Idoli: Una breva ricerca del senso dell'essere oltre Heidegger. *Sapienza*, 49(4), 417-434, 1996.

**Turcon, Sheila**. Recent Acquisitions: Manuscripts, Typescripts and Proofs. *Russell*, 16(1), 89-92, Sum 96.

**Turgeon, Wendy C**. Reviving Ophelia: A Role for Philosophy in Helping Young Women Achieve Selfhood. *Thinking*, 13(1), 2-4, 1997.

This article reviews the portrait of adolescent girls depicted by such contemporary observers as Mary Pipher, Peggy Orenstein and Carol Gilligan. They describe the psycho-social pressures on young women to define themselves according to externally derived models which limit self-construction instead of encouraging it. Current methodologies to promote a reflective building of self-determination are reviewed and found to be pedagogically unsound and substantively impoverished. The activity of philosophical reflection as developed in the philosophy for children methodology is examined as a more hopeful model of an education which supports adolescent women (and men) in the search for a creation of self-identity.

**Turner, Charles**. Holocaust Memories and History. *Hist Human Sci*, 9(4), 45-63, N 96.

This paper argues: that the issues of the holocaust's 'unrepresentability' and the difficulty of conceiving an individual life as a coherent narrative are part of a broader 'postmodern' concern; and that this must be linked to a decline in the state's capacity to make claims of loyalty and obligation on its members and a more general 'deinstitutionalization'. The kinds of collective belonging which, today, might sustain individuals in their efforts to conceive of their lives as a coherent narrative are discussed. It is argued that current concern with memory risks tying testimony exclusively to the psychological theory of trauma, a more which undermines recognition of the political nature of the offense. Finally, it is argued that the state may be rejected as a locus of history making but not as a collective support for the political identity of individuals.

**Turner, Charles**. Neo-Functionalist Critical Theory?. *Hist Human Sci*, 10(1), 135-146, F 97.

**Turner, Charles W** and Alexander, James F and Wilson, Carol A. Family Therapy Process and Outcome Research: Relationship to Treatment Ethics. *Ethics Behavior*, 6(4), 345-352, 1996.

We know from the research literature that psychotherapy is effective, but we also know that hundreds of diverse therapies are being practiced that have not been subjected to scientific scrutiny; thus, in some circumstances iatrogenic effects do occur. Therefore, it is crucial that we recognize and implement therapeutic interventions that are evidence-based rather than succumb to ethical dilemma, frustration and complacency. Recommendations for family therapists are discussed, including the need to a) keep abreast of research findings, b) translate research findings and developments as they apply to clinical practice, c) prioritize techniques and intervention models and b) reexamine funding priorities and research foci.

**Turner, Joia Lewis**. "Conceptual Knowledge and Intuitive Experience: Schlick's Dilemma" in *Origins of Logical Empiricism*, Giere, Ronald N (ed), 292-308. Minneapolis, Univ of Minnesota Pr, 1996.

**Turner, Norman**. The Semantic of Linear Perspective. *Phil Forum*, 27(4), 357-380, Sum 96.

**Turner, Stephanie S**. Toward a Feminist Revision of Research Protocols on the Etiology of Homosexuality. *Phil Cont World*, 3(2), 10-17, Sum 96.

Examining the language and paradigms of science as rhetorical, that is, arising from the sociocultural forces that shape ideology, reveals androcentric assumptions that tend to thwart democratic public policy as well as effective methodology. This paper applies some recent feminist critiques of the biological sciences to the current research on the possible hormonal and genetic factors contributing to homosexuality, clarifying how this research perpetuates hierarchical binaries and suggesting ways to reconceptualize human sexuality through revised research protocols.

**Turoldo, Fabrizio**. L'essere, il nulla e il divenire: Riprendendo le fila di una grande polemica. *Riv Filosof Neo-Scolas*, 88(2), 287-308, Ap-Je 96.

**Turrisi, Patricia Ann** (ed) and Sanders Peirce, Charles. *Pragmatism as a Principle and Method of Right Thinking*. Albany, SUNY Pr, 1997.

This is a study edition of Charles Sanders Peirce's manuscripts for lectures on pragmatism given in spring 1903 at Harvard University. Excepts from these writings have been published elsewhere but in abbreviated form. Turrisi has edited the manuscripts for publication and has written a series of notes that illuminate the historical, scientific, and philosophical contexts of Peirce's references in the lectures. She has also written a Preface that describes the manner in which the lectures came to be given, including an account of Peirce's life and career pertinent to understanding the philosopher himself. Turrisi's introduction interprets Peirce's brand of pragmatism within his system of logic and philosophy of science as well as within general philosophical principles. (publisher, edited)

**Tushnet, Mark**. *Plessy V. Ferguson* in Libertarian Perspective. *Law Phil*, 16(3), 245-258, My 97.

**Tuttle, Robert W**. Paul Ramsey and the Common Law Tradition. *Annu Soc Christ Ethics*, 171-201, 1996.

Despite a wealth of secondary literature on Paul Ramsey's ethics, one significant aspect of his work has gone unnoticed: the influence of the Anglo-American common law tradition. This essay explores four parallels between Ramsey's ethics and the common law: the authority of tradition; moral reasoning within a practice; the immanence of "higher law"; the institutional autonomy of the moral practice. The essay then illustrates the importance of these themes for Ramsey's ethics by examining Ramsey's debate with Richard McCormick over the use of children as research subjects.

**Twardowski, Kazimierz**. "The Majesty of the University" in *The Idea of University*, Brzezinski, Jerzy (ed), 9-17. Amsterdam, Rodopi, 1997.

**Tweedale, Martin M**. Saying What Aristotle Would Have Said. *Maritain Stud*, 11, 75-84, 1995.

**Twetten, David B**. Clearing a 'Way' for Aquinas: How the Proof from Motion Concludes to God. *Amer Cath Phil Quart*, 70(Supp), 259-278, 1996.

Contemporary scholars of Aquinas, most notably Fernand Van Steenberghen, have criticized Aquinas's proof of God's existence from motion for failing to conclude to the unique, provident, creative deity. But such criticisms, I maintain, are inspired by approaches to God that were developed after the condemnations of 1277. I argue that the first way of *Summa ttheologiae* 1.2.3 constitutes a legitimate proof given Aquinas's peculiar logic for existential arguments and given his consequent choice of a nonprescriptive nominal definition of God. Although the first way fails if interpreted as a physical argument, it succeeds when motion is understood in a universal 'metaphysical' sense, without needing to appeal to an 'existential' interpretation.

**Tweyman, Stanley** (ed). *Hume on Miracles*. Bristol, Thoemmes, 1996.

This is the first volume of a two-volume set containing the most important secondary literature on Hume on religion. Focusing on responses to the *Essay on Miracles*, the material included in this volume ranges from 1751 to 1882. Authors include: Thomas Rutherford, William Adams, Anthony Ellys, Reverend Samuel Vince, Joseph Napier and Thomas Huxley. (publisher, edited)

**Tye, Michael**. "A Representational Theory of Pains and Their Phenomenal Character" in *AI, Connectionism and Philosophical Psychology, 1995*, Tomberlin, James E (ed), 223-239. Atascadero, Ridgeview, 1995.

**Tye, Michael**. "Orgasms Again" in *Perception*, Villanueva, Enrique (ed), 51-54. Atascadero, Ridgeview, 1996.

This paper is a response to a demand made by Ned Block of those who hold that the phenomenal character of experience is representational to say in what the representational content of orgasm consists.

**Tye, Michael**. "Perceptual Experience Is a Many-Layered Thing" in *Perception*, Villanueva, Enrique (ed), 117-126. Atascadero, Ridgeview, 1996.

**Tye, Michael**. *Ten Problems of Consciousness: A Representational Theory of the Phenomenal Mind*. Cambridge, MIT Pr, 1996.

What is consciousness? Why do so many scientists and philosophers find it so puzzling? These are questions that Michael Tye addresses in this clear and lively book. Tye elaborates a new and enlightening theory about the phenomenal "what it feels like" aspect of consciousness. The test of any such theory, according to Tye, lies in how well it handles ten critical problems of consciousness. Tye argues that all experiences and all feelings represent things, and that their phenomenal aspects are to be understood in terms of what they represent. (publisher)

**Tye, Michael**. The Function of Consciousness. *Nous*, 30(3), 287-305, S 96.

What was consciousness selected for? What biological purpose or function does it serve? Not everyone finds these questions puzzling. To some, it is obvious in what the function of consciousness consists: there really is no room for serious disagreement. I argue that this unqualified assessment is jejune. Even so, in my view, answers are available for the above questions, and these

answers *are* obvious, once a certain theoretical framework is adopted. The purpose of this paper is to clarify the present debate, and to explain in what I take the function of consciousness to consist.

**Tym, Kristen A** and Klein, John P and Shapiro, Robyn S. Wisconsin Healthcare Ethics Committees. *Cambridge Quart Healthcare Ethics*, 6(3), 288-292, Sum 97.

**Tyman, Stephen**. The Concept of Act in the Naturalistic Idealism of John William Miller. *J Speculative Phil*, 10(3), 161-171, 1996.

**Tyron, Warren W**. Instrument Driven Theory. *J Mind Behav*, 17(1), 21-30, Wint 96.

Instruments are used primarily to provide data for testing theoretical predictions. However, sometimes instrument development sets the occasion for profound theoretical changes which are totally unanticipated. This article presents examples of instrument driven theory derived from biology and physics (astronomy) as well as discussing implications for psychology. The role of theory in the design of instruments is considered.

**Tyron, Warren W**. Measurement Units and Theory Construction. *J Mind Behav*, 17(3), 213-228, Sum 96.

The central thesis of this article is that measurement units are theoretical concepts because measurement presumes theoretical definition. New theoretical constructs can be defined in terms of algebraic combinations of previously defined measurement units. Physics has developed an impressive hierarchical knowledge structure on this basis. The unitless measures favored by psychology preclude the generation of such a knowledge hierarchy. It also leads to definitions of reliability and validity in correlational terms which can result in inaccurate measurement. Psychology has long used time as a fundamental unit. Adoption of a second measurement unit would enable construction of a psychological knowledge hierarchy to begin.

**Tyrrell, Bernard J** (ed) and Ryan, William F (ed). *A Second Collection: Papers by Bernard J. F. Lonergan, S.J.*. Toronto, Univ of Toronto Pr, 1996.

This collection of essays, addresses, and one interview comes from the years 1966-73, a period during most of which Bernard Lonergan was at work completing his *Method in Theology*. The eighteen chapters cover a wide spectrum of interest, dealing with such general topics as 'The Absence of God in Modern Culture' and 'The Future of Christianity', and narrowing down through items such as 'Belief: Today's Issue' and more specialized theological and philosophical studies, to one on his own community in the church and the illuminating comment on his great work *Insight*. (edited)

**Tyrrell, Martin**. Nation-States and States of Mind: Nationalism as Psychology. *Crit Rev*, 10(2), 233-250, Spr 96.

The rise of nationalism parallels that of the state, suggesting that the relationship between the two is symbiotic and that nations are neither natural nor spontaneous but rather are political constructions. Ernest Gellner's economically determinist account of the rise of the nation-state, however, understates the emotive and psychological appeal of nationalist ideology. The Social Identity Theory of Henri Tajfel, by contrast, suggests that nationalism benefits from possibly innate human tendencies to affiliate in social groups and to act in furtherance of these groups, while Serge Moscovici's social psychology of popular belief elucidates the means by which such tendencies can take the shape of nationalism in mass publics.

**Tzouvaras, Athanassios**. Aspects of Analytic Deduction. *J Phil Log*, 25(6), 581-596, D 96.

By "analytic inference rule" we understand here a rule *r* such that, if the sequent over the line is analytic, then so is the sequent under the line. We also discuss the notion of semantic relevance as contrasted to the previous syntactic one. We show that when introducing semantic sequents as axioms, i.e., when extending the pure logical axioms and rules by mathematical ones, the property of syntactic relevance is lost, since cut elimination no longer holds. We conclude that no purely syntactic notion of analytic deduction can ever replace successfully the complex semantico-syntactic deduction we already possess. (edited)

**U'Ren, Richard**. Psychiatry and Capitalism. *J Mind Behav*, 18(1), 1-11, Wint 97.

This paper seeks to show the relationship between psychiatry and capitalism and how psychiatry (and medical care) is being commodified to bring it into the capitalist circuit of accumulation. Capitalism extols the virtues of individualism, work and consumption and offers a rationalization for unlimited acquisition that blunts ethical challenge, themes that have a parallel in psychiatric thought and practice. In its incessant search for profit, capitalism is always seeking to enlarge its markets by, for example, commodifying various activities of daily life. Psychiatry creates and enlarges its market by expanding its diagnostic system: an increasing number of difficult or troubling experiences are labelled psychiatric, thus creating an ever-larger pool of potential customers, or patients, for psychiatric services. The relationship between capitalism and psychiatry has been obscured, in part, because psychiatry is a profession with different ideals than business. With the arrival of corporate capitalism in the health care arena, however, the boundaries between professionalism and business are eroding in favor of the latter. (edited)

**Ubeda Rives, José Pedro** and Lorente Tallada, Juan Manuel. "Representación de la relación de afianzamiento epistémico en *Prolog*" in *Verdad: lógica, representación y mundo*, Villegas Forero, L, 355-367. Santiago de Compostela, Univ Santiago Comp, 1996.

Within the framework of the model of belief change of Alchourrón, Gärdenfors, Makinson [1985], Gärdenfors [1988] proposes the relation of epistemic entrenchment between sentences as a procedure to uniquely determine the contraction and revision function for an arbitrary theory. In this paper this relation is analyzed when the language of sentences is PROLOG and a procedure is presented to represent this relation in PROLOG.

**Uduigwomen, Andrew F**. The Notion of African Philosophy. *Darshana Int*, 36(1/141), 48-53, Ja 96.

**Uebel, Thomas E**. "The Enlightenment Ambition of Epistemic Utopianism: Otto Neurath's Theory of Science in Historical Perspective" in *Origins of Logical Empiricism*, Giere, Ronald N (ed), 91-112. Minneapolis, Univ of Minnesota Pr, 1996.

Following a brief characterization of Neurath's mature epistemological naturalism, some important stages of its early development are reviewed, ending with a consideration of the political dimension of his attempt to refashion our image of scientific knowledge.

**Uebel, Thomas E**. Anti-Foundationalism and the Vienna Circle's Revolution in Philosophy. *Brit J Phil Sci*, 47(3), 415-440, S 96.

The tendency to attribute foundationalist ambitions to the Vienna Circle has long obscured our view of its attempted revolution in philosophy. The present paper makes the case for a consistently epistemologically antifoundationalist interpretation of all three of the Circle's main protagonists: Schlick, Carnap, and Neurath. Corresponding to the intellectual fault lines within the Circle, two ways of going about the radical reorientation of the pursuit of philosophy will then be distinguished and the contemporary potential of Carnap's and Neurath's project explored.

**Uebel, Thomas E**. Conventions in the *Aufbau*. *Brit J Hist Phil*, 4(2), 381-397, S 96.

Discussion of recent attempt to reinstate the foundationalist reading of Carnap's *Aufbau* dislodged by new Vienna Circle scholarship. It is argued that this attempt fails. Instead, attention is drawn to the conventionalist themes already in play in the *Aufbau*.

**Uemura, Hiroshi**. Théorie de la sensibilité dans le spritualisme français (in Japanese). *Bigaku*, 47(4), 13-24, Spr 97.

"La philosophie française" est devenue soi-consciente depuis que Cousin a instauré l'institution philosophique universitaire, où il a adopté pour principe le spiritualisme: en fait, c'est une sorte de biranisme à l'écossaise. Pour éviter et l'empirisme et l'idéalisme, il fonde sa philosophie sur l'abstraction immédiate, en tant que bon sens qui se tire lui-même des données primitives de la conscience. Rendant toute réalité au fait psychologique, il sensibilisa du même coup le vrai, le beau et le bien quoiqu'il distingue le rationnel et le sensible. Pour Cousin, la beauté n'est donc ni une forme rationnelle ni un phénomène physique. Elle est immédiatement abstraite des individus naturels, sous forme d'expérience psychologique. Dans le spiritualisme, notamment chez Ravaisson, la sensibilité s'est attribuée l'activité dans sa relation avec l'intelligence. (edited)

**Uffink, Jos**. Can the Maximum Entropy Principle Be Explained as a Consistency Requirement?. *Stud Hist Phil Mod Physics*, 26B(3), 223-261, D 96.

This paper reviews these consistency arguments and the surrounding controversy. It is shown that the uniqueness proofs are flawed, or rest on unreasonably strong assumptions. A more general class of inference rules, maximizing the so-called Rényi entropies, is exhibited which also fulfill the reasonable part of the consistency assumptions. (edited)

**Uffink, Jos**. The Constraint Rule of the Maximum Entropy Principle. *Stud Hist Phil Mod Physics*, 27B(1), 47-79, Mr 96.

The principle of maximum entropy is a method for assigning values to probability distributions on the basis of partial information. In usual formulations of this and related methods of inference one assumes that this partial information takes the form of a constraint on allowed probability distributions. In practical applications, however, the information consists of empirical data. A constraint rule is then employed to construct constraints on probability distributions out of these data. Usually one adopts the rule that equates the expectation values of certain functions with their empirical averages. There are, however, various other ways in which one can construct constraints from empirical data, which makes the maximum entropy principle lead to very different probability assignments. This paper shows that an argument by Jaynes to justify the usual constraint rule is unsatisfactory and investigates several alternative choices. The choice of a constraint rule is also shown to be of crucial importance to the debate on the question whether there is a conflict between the methods of inference based on maximum entropy and Bayesian conditionalization.

**Ugolini, Consuelo**. L'inconscio come finzione linguistica. *Iride*, 9(19), 733-743, S-D 96.

**Ulfig, Alexander**. Stufen der Rechtfertigung. *Protosoz*, 8/9, 197-209, 1996.

My starting point here is: there is a fundamental distinction between justifications in everyday-life and a theoretical level of justification (discoursive justifications). Thus, I discuss the hierarchy of justifications developed by Schnädelbach. Furthermore, I evaluate Schnädelbach's concept in a *semantic* perspective. I will show that Schnädelbach's pragmatical account requires a semantic analysis. Without recourse to such analysis, we cannot understand the universe of normative language. (edited)

**Umapathy, Ranjan**. The Mind-Body Problem: A Comparative Study. *J Indian Counc Phil Res*, 13(3), 25-51, My-Ag 96.

This paper discusses in outline dualism, identity theory, behaviorism, functionalism and Searle's position in his *Rediscovery of the Mind*. Weaknesses of all of these views are presented and Churchland is particularly singled out for attack. The doctrine of ancient Indian materialists called the "Carvakas" is presented and it is argued that Searle's theory is very similar to the Caravaka view. Some of Sankara's and Vacaspati Misra's arguments against materialism

are explained and it is suggested that these arguments might be directed against Searle as well. In the concluding section the Mandukya Upanisad's relevance to the problem is briefly sketched.

**Uña Juárez, Agustín**. San Agustín: la interioridad bella. *Pensamiento*, 205(53), 135-142, Ja-Ap 97.

Se indaga brevemente la relación entre belleza e interioridad, según Agustín, estudiando: 1) la belleza del *alma* y su mundo. 2) El *arte* como tránsito de la belleza desde el alma a las manos del artista (Plotino). 3) La belleza como *admonitio*, aviso para recuperar lo interior y lo superior 4) El *conocimiento* de la belleza, su juicio, sus "leyes" son propios del alma. El conocimiento estético es, pues, interior. 5) La *interioridad colectiva* del hombre, la historia, es calificada como bella, despliegue de belleza. Conclusión: hay una relación decisiva entre belleza e interioridad, a juicio de Agustín.

**Uniacke, Suzanne**. Replaceability and Infanticide. *J Value Inq*, 31(2), 153-166, Je 97.

The paper sets out elements of a nest of arguments invoked in recent utilitarian defenses of the replaceability of human infants. It argues that none of these arguments genuinely represent the claim that infants are replaceable. The paper highlights a range of controversial tenets and moves on which the various arguments for infant replaceability depend. They include elision of the relevant notion of replacement and rejection of its moral significance and the doubly indirect valuing of infants.

**Unnerstall, Thomas**. The Incompleteness of Quantum Mechanics as a Description of Physical Reality. *Phil Natur*, 29(2), 285-294, 1992.

It is shown that, in the framework of a certain ("realistic") philosophical viewpoint of nature and of science, the present theory of quantum mechanics cannot be considered to be a complete description of the objective physical reality of an individual quantum system. Emphasis is laid on conceptual clarity and on bringing out the logical structure of the argument.

**Upchurch, Randall S** and Ruhland, Sheila K. The Organizational Bases of Ethical Work Climates in Lodging Operations as Perceived by General Managers. *J Bus Ethics*, 15(10), 1083-1093, O 96.

The focus of this research concentrated on ascertaining the presence of ethical climate types and the level of analysis from which ethical decisions were based as perceived by lodging managers. In agreement with Victor and Cullen (1987, 1988), ethical work climates are multidimensional and multidetermined. The results of this study indicated that: a) benevolence is the predominate dimension of ethical climate present in the lodging organization as perceived by lodging managers, and b) the local level of analysis (e.g., immediate workplace norms and values) is the predominate determinant of ethical decisions in the organization. The implication of this study is that the knowledge gained from understanding that ethical decision making in an organization is multidimensional and multidetermined will foster understanding of ethical decision formation in the organizational context.

**Urabayen Pérez, Julia**. La esencia del hombre como disponer indisponible. *Anu Filosof*, 29(2), 1051-1059, 1996.

The purpose of this paper is to explain Polo's thought about human essence. Leonardo Polo proposes a new interpretation of the real difference of Thomas Aquinas and founded in it an ampliation transcendental. This is the sense of the transcendental anthropology.

**Urbas, Igor**. Dual-Intuitionistic Logic. *Notre Dame J Form Log*, 37(3), 440-451, Sum 96.

The sequent system LDJ is formulated using the same connectives as Gentzen's intuitionistic sequent system LJ, but is dual in the following sense: i) whereas LJ is singular in the consequent, LDJ is singular in the antecedent; ii) whereas LJ has the same sentential countertheorems as classical LK but not the same theorems, LDJ has the same sentential theorems as LK but not the same countertheorems. In particular, LDJ does not reject all contradictions and is accordingly paraconsistent. To obtain a more precise mapping, both LJ and LDJ are extended. (edited)

**Urchs, Max**. On the Logic of Event-Causation: Jaskowski-Style Systems of Causal Logic. *Stud Log*, 53(4), 551-578, N 94.

Causality is a concept which is sometimes claimed to be easy to illustrate, but hard to explain. It is not quite clear whether the former part of this claim is as obvious as the latter one. I will not present any specific theory of causation. Our aim is much less ambitious; to investigate the formal counterparts of causal relations between events, i.e., to propose a formal framework which enables us to construct metamathematical counterparts of causal relations between singular events. This should be a good starting point to define formal counterparts for concepts like "causal law", "causal explanation" and so on.

**Urdaneta Sandoval, Carlos Alberto**. Some Critical Considerations Regarding the Function of the Equity in the Law. *Fronesis*, 3(1), 49-69, Ap 96.

The purpose of this article is to discuss the principles and rules traditionally admitted in the jurisprudence regarding the equity or *epiqueya*, especially what refers to its sense, content and classification, in order to reflect on its real function as source of the law in the interpretation and integration of the rules system.

**Uriz Pemán, María Jesús**. Pragmatismo e interaccionismo simbólico. *Euridice*, 197-225, 1992.

The main objective of this paper is the analysis of the relation between pragmatism and social interactionism. American pragmatism's origin can be placed in James and Peirce's thought, and this theory to some European philosophers (Rousseau, Kant, Dilthey) and Mead's *Symbolic Interactionism*. The main connections between pragmatism and symbolic interactionism occur in the epistemological realm. Pragmatism argues that knowledge is the main guide to action; therefore, it is important to be able to anticipate the action's possible outcomes. Similarly, symbolic interactionism argues that knowledge has to be placed in conduct's domain, and that the social dimension of both—communication process and meaning—should be stressed.

**Uriz Pemán, María Jesús**. Un modelo de Filosofía Social y Política: la Filosofía de la Filantropía. *Euridice*, 165-181, 1995.

To understand a form of political and social philosophy it is necessary to study some basic concepts such as communication, social act, institutions, democracy, community.... In this article we analyze these concepts, trying to demonstrate that a society can operate much better if its members share interests and common objectives. The social progress implies that it is able to continually solve the problems that we find ourselves in our society. The achievement of this results from a greater utilization of the philosophy from the philanthropy, that is to say, to apply the "role-taking" mechanism to help other people and to work to obtain a new fairer social order. (edited)

**Urmson, J O** (trans). *Simplicius: On Aristotle's Physics 5*. Ithaca, Cornell Univ Pr, 1997.

In *Physics Book 5* Aristotle lays down some of the principles of his dynamics and theory of change. What does not count as a change: change of relation? the flux of time? There is no change of change, yet acceleration is recognized. Aristotle defines 'continuous', 'contact', and 'next', and uses these definitions in discussing when we can claim that the same change or event is still going on. (publisher, edited)

**Uroh, Chris Okechukwu**. In Defence of Philosophy Against the Endists. *Darshana Int*, 36(3/143), 16-24, Ap 96.

**Urquhart, Alasdair** and Fu, Xudong. Simplified Lower Bounds for Propositional Proofs. *Notre Dame J Form Log*, 37(4), 523-544, Fall 96.

This article presents a simplified proof of the result that bounded depth propositional proofs of the pigeonhole principle are exponentially large. The proof uses the new techniques for proving switching lemmas developed by Razborov and Beame. A similar result is also proved for some examples based on graphs.

**Urvoy, Dominique**. Chronique de philosophie arabe et islamique. *Rev Thomiste*, 97(2), 375-390, Ap-Je 97.

**Uyanne, Francis U**. "African Consensus Democracy Revisited" in *Philosophy and Democracy in Intercultural Perspective,* Kimmerle, Heinz (ed), 175-183. Amsterdam, Rodopi, 1997.

The focus on African consensus democracy is a search for how to overcome the basic weakness of the Western (liberal) majority rule democracy in Africa. A liberal one-, two- or multiparty: one person, one vote, democracy fails to account for the interests of all ethnic (other) groups in a country. Some must be winners, others losers. The latter often fight for their rights by other means. As an all-inclusive option, the consensus model is offered to enhance decision-making process. It accounts for the rights of both persons and groups. The igbo model is used for this analysis.

**Vacatello, Marzio**. Verità e prescrizione in etica. *Iride*, 8(15), 352-372, Ag 95.

I non congnitivisti (Ayer, Stevenson e Hare) hanno insistito su ciò che li divide da Moore. Respingono le sue tesi centrali: valori di verità degli enunciati morali, proprietà non naturali. Ma condividono varie conclusioni del peculiare intuizionismo di Moore: insistenza sui disaccordi morali, separazione tra certezza e verità, assenza di prove in etica, limiti del ragionamento morale. Alla radice delle inattese convergenze sta la comune difesa della legge di Hume.

**Vacatello, Marzio** and Schneewind, J B and Lecaldano, Eugenio. I metodi dell'etica di Henry Sidgwick. *Iride*, 9(18), 495-511, Ag 96.

Dopo 120 anni dalla pubblicazione dei *Metodi dell'etica* di H. Sidgwick, risaltano con maggiore evidenza i nuclei più originali e significativi delle analisi che vi sono sviluppate. In particolare la presentazione di una dimostrazione razionale dell'utilitarismo che, oltre ad essere del tutto nuova a suo tempo, risulta tuttora come riconoscibile e inconfondibile nella storia di questa concezione normativa. Inoltre la delineazione di un programma di ricerca per la teoria etica che era allora del tutto nuovo, ma che alla fine del XX secolo possiamo riconoscere come fertile e operante malgrado alcuni suoi limiti. (edited)

**Vaccaro, Andrea**. Dio parla in modo oscuro? Spunti filosofici e teologici sulle oscurità della Bibbia. *Sapienza*, 50(2), 163-171, 1997.

**Vaccaro, G Battista**. "Una Disavventura Della Differenza: Heidegger e i "francesi" in *Soggetto E Verità: La questione dell'uomo nella filosofia contemporanea,* Fagiuoli, Ettore, 119-136. 20136 Milano, Mimesis, 1996.

**Vacek, Edward C**. Love For God: Is It Obligatory?. *Annu Soc Christ Ethics*, 203-221, 1996.

In face of contemporary silence about a direct love of God, this essay argues that such love is ethically required. Love is first described as an emotional, affirming participation in the being of the beloved. Agapic, erotic, and philia loves are described. The essay then develops a natural law, basic-goods argument for the requirement of loving God. Without this love, there is a defect in essential humanity. Finally, exclusively anthropocentric and theocentric approaches to life are rejected in favor of a mutual love involvement with the world.

**Vadakumchery, Johnson**. Jharkhand: A Movement from Ethnicity to Empowerment of Autonomy. *J Dharma*, 22(1), 35-48, Ja-Mr 97.

Jharkhand is the home land of tribals like the Munda, Oraon, HO and Santal. They had an indigenous system of community ownership of land, democratic and decentralised administration, traditional ways of coping with their imrnediate ecology. When their autonomy was questioned by the British they

struggled against them as early as 1769. This struggle, after independence, led to the demand for a separate state in 1955. The benefit of the rich mineral and forest resources of the area goes to the nontribals. Therefore, the concept of DIKUS (Outsiders) play a great role in the worldview of the natives. From a tribal nucleus of ethnicity, the Jharkhand Movement has developed into a pan-tribal and nontribal phase incorporating the needs and aspirations of Jharkhandis for their liberation. Thus the article sketches the emergence of Jharkhand Movement and the struggle of the Jharkhandis for freedom.

**Väänänen, Jouko**. Unary Quantifiers on Finite Models. *J Log Lang Info*, 6(3), 275-304, Jl 97.

In this paper (except in Section 5) all quantifiers are assumed to be so-called simple unary quantifiers and all models are assumed to be finite. We give a necessary and sufficient condition for a quantifier to be definable in terms of monotone quantifiers. For a monotone quantifier we give a necessary and sufficient condition for being definable in terms of a given set of bounded monotone quantifiers. Finally, we give a necessary and sufficient condition for a monotone quantifier to be definable in terms of a given monotone quantifier. Our analysis shows that the quantifier "at least one half" and its relatives behave differently than other monotone quantifiers.

**Väänänen, Jouko** and Hella, Lauri and Westerståhl, Dag. Definability of Polyadic Lifts of Generalized Quantifiers. *J Log Lang Info*, 6(3), 305-335, Jl 97.

**Väänänen, Jouko** and Luosto, Kerkko and Hella, Lauri. The Hierarchy Theorem for Generalized Quantifiers. *J Sym Log*, 61(3), 802-817, S 96.

The concept of a generalized quantifier of a given similarity type was defined in [12]. Our main result says that on finite structures different similarity types give rise to different classes of generalized quantifiers. More exactly, for every similarity type $t$ there is a generalized quantifier of type $t$ which is not definable in the extension of first order logic by all generalized quantifiers of type smaller than $t$. This was proved for unary similarity types by Per Lindström [17] with a counting argument. We extend his method to arbitrary similarity types.

**Vaggione, Diego**. Definability of Directly Indecomposable Congruence Modular Algebras. *Stud Log*, 57(2-3), 239-241, O 96.

**Valady, Mohammad** (ed) and Hartshorne, Charles. *The Zero Fallacy and Other Essays in Neoclassical Philosophy*. Chicago, Open Court, 1997.

This collection of Charles Hartshorne's writings—many never before published—is an indispensible introduction to his rich and indelible contribution to contemporary philosophy. It covers the extraordinary range of Hartshorne's thought, including his reflection on the history of philosophy, philosophical psychology, philosophy of science, epistemology, ethics, aesthetics, literature, ornithology, and, above all, theology and metaphysics. (publisher, edited)

**Valdés, Sylvia**. Gaos y la religión. *Topicos*, 61-70, 1996.

At first sight, one may be confused when finds that José Gaos rejected the possibility of knowing something about God and at the same time insisted on Its necessity. Nevertheless, a deeper analysis on Gaos's thought about religion shows that this position is consistent with his vitalism.

**Valdivia, Lourdes**. "Can Peter Be Rational?" in *Contents,* Villanueva, Enrique (ed), 311-324. Atascadero, Ridgeview, 1995.

**Valentine, Jeremy**. Hobbes's Political Geometry. *Hist Human Sci,* 10(2), 23-40, My 97.

**Valentine, Timothy S**. "Moral Education and Inspiration Through Theatre" in *Philosophy of Education (1996),* Margonis, Frank (ed), 441-450. Urbana, Phil Education Soc, 1997.

**Vallentyne, Peter**. Self-Ownership and Equality: Brute Luck, Gifts, Universal Dominance, and Leximin. *Ethics*, 107(2), 321-343, Ja 97.

I criticize Philippe Van Parijs's theory of justice (in *Real Freedom for All*) from the perspective of a fellow liberal egalitarian. Like him, I hold that agents are self-owning in some sense, that natural resources are socially owned, and that socially-owned resources should be used to promote equality. I argue, however, that Van Parijs's theory does not respect a plausibly robust form of self-ownership, and that it does not promote equality in a plausible manner.

**Vallentyne, Peter** and Kagan, Shelly. Infinite Value and Finitely Additive Value Theory. *J Phil*, 94(1), 5-26, Ja 97.

Finitely additive value theories evaluate worlds containing a finite number of locations of value (people, times, etc.) by adding together the values at each location. A puzzle can arise when finitely additive value theories are applied to worlds involving an infinite number of locations. For in such cases the totals will often be infinite. The article develops and defends some principles for finitely additive value theories that imply that some worlds with infinite totals are better than other worlds with infinite totals.

**Vallicella, William**. Concurrentism or Occasionalism?. *Amer Cath Phil Quart*, 70(3), 339-359, Sum 96.

How deeply is God involved in nature? According to concurrentism, God not only maintains the universe in being, but also cooperates with nature causes in the production of natural effects. Concurrentism thus leaves room for genuine causal activity on the part of natural substances, which fact marks it off sharply from occasionalism, according to which God alone is a 'true' (productive) cause and natural causes are mere occasional causes. This paper aims to tilt the balance in favor of occasionalism, first by questioning the Aristotelian conception of natural causation that animates the concurrentist vision, and then by showing how a very plausible contemporary theory of causation can be pressed into occasionalism's service.

**Vallicella, William F**. Bundles and Indiscernibility: A Reply to O'Leary-Hawthorne. *Analysis*, 57(1), 91-94, Ja 97.

**Vallicella, William F**. On an Insufficient Argument against Sufficient Reason. *Ratio*, 10(1), 76-81, Ap 97.

The task of this article is to show that such maximal propositions pose no threat to the principle. According to what is perhaps the most 'popular' version of the principle to sufficient reason (PSR), every true proposition has a sufficient reason why it is true. Peter van Inwagen formulates the principle as follows: 'for every truth, for everything that is so, there is a sufficient reason for its being true or being so.' Like many contemporary philosophers, however, he rejects the principle. My purpose here is to show that the main philosophical argument against PSR rests on a mistaken assumption. There is also a 'scientific' argument against PSR that turns on considerations of quantum indeterminacy; but that argument lies beyond the scope of this discussion. (edited)

**Vallicella, William F**. The Hume-Edwards Objection to the Cosmo-logical Argument. *J Phil Res*, 22, 423-443, Ap 97.

The Hume-Edwards objection has recently come under attack by atheists and theists alike; if I am right, however, the real flaw in this objection lies deep and has yet to be isolated. This paper accordingly divides into two main parts. The first discusses three recent failed critiques of the objection. The second presents the beginnings of what I hope is a sound critique. I argue that there is no extant theory of causation according to which it could be true both that I) each state of the universe is caused by a preceding state and that II) each state is caused to exist by a preceding state. Here we go only part of the way in substantiating this ambitious thesis: we argue that no *nomological* theory of causation satisfied both I) and II). (edited)

**Vallota, Alfredo D**. Meta-Technics, Anthropocentrism and Evolution. *Epistemologia*, 19(2), 265-288, Jl-D 96.

In questo articolo ci occupiamo di due aspetti del *logos meta-tecnico*. Essi potrebbero apparire paradossali. Mostriamo che non sono tali, che si fondono insieme e che costituiscono parte di un tutto coerente e interrelato. Cerchiamo la ragione per cui la *meta-tecnica* risulta strettamente collegata agli incrementi della potenza umana anche se, come sostiene Mayz, essa non è antropocentrica o geocentrica. Tentiamo di comprendere ulteriormente questo nuovo *logos* in costante sviluppo chiedendoci se esso costituisce una svolta davvero rivoluzionaria o un semplice momento dell'evoluzione.

**Van Bakel, Steffen** and Liquori, Luigi and Ronchi della Rocca, Simona (& others). Comparing Cubes of Typed and Type Assignment Systems. *Annals Pure Applied Log*, 86(3), 267-303, Jl 97.

We study the *cube of type assignment systems*, as introduced in Giannini et al. (Fund. Inform. 19 (1993) 87-126) and confront it with Barendregt's typed *Lambda*-cube (Barendregt, in: *Handbook of Logic in Computer Science*, Vol. 2, Clarendon Press, Oxford, 1992). The first is obtained from the latter through applying a natural type erasing function *E* to derivation rules, that erases type information from terms. In particular, we address the question whether a judgement, derivable in a type assignment system, is always an erasure of a derivable judgement in a corresponding typed system; we show that this property holds only for systems without polymorphism. The type assignment systems we consider satisfy the properties 'subject reduction' and 'strong normalization'. Moreover, we define a new type assignment cube that is isomorphic to the typed one.

**Van Bendegem, Jean Paul**. The Popularization of Mathematics or The Pop-Music of the Spheres. *Commun Cog*, 29(2), 215-238, 1996.

In the first part of this paper, the present state of affairs concerning the popularization of mathematics is presented. In the second part, I raise the normative problem: what should it look like? The conclusion of the paper is that, rather than popularizing mathematics itself, it is the philosophy, sociology, psychology, politics, economics of mathematics—in short, not mathematics per se, but mathematics as a human, societal and cultural phenomenon—that needs to be brought to the attention of society at large.

**Van Benthem, Johan**. "Logic and Argumentation" in *Logic and Argumentation*, Van Eemeren, Frans H (ed), 27-41. Amsterdam, North-Holland, 1994.

Much has changed in modern conceptions of logic: logical tools and attitudes have matured and the initial tension found with Perelman and Toulmin seems unproductive by now. In this paper, some interfaces are discussed between current developments in logic and argumentation theory. Both logic and argumentation share a common concern with the variety and fine-structure of reasoning.

**Van Benthem, Johan** (ed) and Van Eemeren, Frans H (ed) and Grootendorst, Rob (ed). *Logic and Argumentation*. Amsterdam, North-Holland, 1994.

This volume aims at providing some insight into the connections between logic and argumentation. Van Eemeren and Grootendorst survey the state of the art in argumentation theory. Van Bentham describes the interfaces between developments in logic and argumentation theory. Pinto, Batens, and Starmans discuss the links between argumentation and logic, Finocchiaro the Oliver-Massey asymmetry, Jackson, Krabbe and Walton the fallacies. Woods pays attention to paradoxes. Zarefsky distinguishes between four forces that have shaped argumentation studies in the communication discipline. D. O'Keefe discusses interconnections between argumentation studies and persuasion effect research. Linguistic aspects are explored by Stenning, Van Rees, and Snoeck Henkemans.

**Van Binsbergen, Wim**. Black Athena and Africa's Contribution to Global Cultural History. *Quest*, 9(2), 100-137, D 96.

D'une façon initiale et constatante au même temps, cet article traite du projet de M. Martin Bernal comme effort de faire éclater le racisme inhérent aux conceptions qui dénient les antécédents de la civilisation grecque classique dans l'Égypte et l'Asie occidentale. L'auteur contraste la réception minimale du projet de Bernal aux Pays Bas et ailleurs, avec son appropriation et popularisation, aussi avides que distordues, dans les mains de savants africains et afriquaméricains: en termes du continent africain comme influence civilisatrice principale sur l'Europe. (edited)

**Van Brakel, Jaap**. "Über die Vernachlässigung der Philosophie der Chemie" in *Philosophie der Chemie: Bestandsaufnahme und Ausblick*, Schummer, Joachim (ed), 13-26. Wurzburg, Koenigshausen, 1996.

The paper investigates whether and to what extent the philosophy of chemistry is a neglected area. The emphasis is on ontological and methodological/epistemological themes, not on historical, social, or moral aspects.

**Van Brakel, Jaap**. Chemistry as the Science of the Transformation of Substances. *Synthese*, 111(3), 253-282, Je 97.

Reduction, either of chemistry to microphysics, or, more generally, of the manifest to the scientific does not work. Similarly, within chemistry (and physics) it is not the case that the microdescription will, in principle, always give a more complete description. If quantum mechanics turns out to be wrong, it would not affect all chemical knowledge. If molecular chemistry were wrong, it would not disqualify *all* knowledge about, say, water. In a very strong sense scientific substances supervene on manifest substances and not vice versa, and if there are any physical substances they supervene on chemical substances (and not vice versa).

**Van Buren, John**. What Does It All Come To? A Response to Reviews of *The Young Heidegger*. *Phil Today*, 41(2), 325-333, Sum 97.

**Van Camp, Julie**. Freedom of Expression at the National Endowment for the Arts: An Opportunity for Interdisciplinary Education. *J Aes Educ*, 30(3), 43-65, Fall 96.

Funding controversies at the National Endowment for the Arts have been discussed extensively in many forums, but the complexities of free speech in government-funded activities have been muddled in too much of this debate. I consider free speech for artists under the First Amendment of the U.S. Constitution, the appropriateness of government support for cultural activities, the role of Congress and the executive branch in carrying out these activities, the difficulties in judging aesthetic value both within and outside of government, and the philosophical and legal concerns surrounding the debate over free speech for artists.

**Van Cleve, James**. Minimal Truth is Realist Truth. *Phil Phenomenol Res*, 56(4), 869-875, D 96.

**Van de Putte, André** and Chaerle, Dries. Liberalism and Culture: Will Kymlicka on Multicultural Citizenship (in Dutch). *Tijdschr Filosof*, 59(2), 215-252, Je 97.

This study examines Will Kymlicka's liberal defense of minority rights. The starting point of his argument is provided by a particular conception of individual freedom, which stresses the need for a context of choice in which it can be exercised. This context of choice is conceived of as a societal culture, i.e., as "an intergenerational community, more or less institutionally complete, occupying a given territory or homeland, sharing a distinct language and history". As far as societal-cultural membership is constitutive for the freedom and identity of the individuals, it can be considered as a Rawlsian primary good. Confronted with the fact of multinational and polyethnic States, this consideration involves the need for an equal distribution and protection of this good for all (individuals of the) composing national or ethnic minorities. (edited)

**Van den Abbeele, Georges**. "Lost Horizons and Uncommon Grounds: For a Poetics of Finitude in the Work of Jean-Luc Nancy" in *On Jean-Luc Nancy: The Sense of Philosophy*, Sheppard, Darren (ed), 12-18. New York, Routledge, 1997.

**Van den Akker, Johan** and Tan, Yao Hua. Paraconsistent Default Logic. *Log Anal*, 36(144), 311-328, S-D 93.

Pequeno and Buchsbaum presented a new default logic, *The Inconsistent Default Logic* (IDL), which is based on Da Costa's paraconsistent logic, in which the ex-falso rule does not hold. In this paper we present the *Question Marked Logic* (QML), a further development of IDL. We show that QML inherits the good behaviour of IDL on representing conflicts, and that in addition it can be used to model specificity between default rules in a very intuitive way.

**Van den Beld, A**. Appropriate Guilt: Between Expansion and Limitations (in Dutch). *Tijdschr Filosof*, 58(4), 697-715, D 96.

According to the traditional (law) conception of morality one's feeling of guilt is appropriate if and only if one has culpably (knowingly, voluntarily) done wrong. The feeling must involve this propositional content. In recent literature, however, two opposite developments can be discerned. First there is a tendency to expand the range of things one can appropriately feel guilty about. This position is criticized on the ground that guilt is a painful emotion and should therefore be suffered only if it is deserved. On the other hand, there are also arguments in the literature to the effect 1) that agent regret should be substituted for guilt (Bernard Williams) and 2) that the range of appropriate guilt feelings should be limited (Allan Gibbard). (edited)

**Van den Dries, Lou**. T-Convexity and Tame Extensions II. *J Sym Log*, 62(1), 14-34, Mr 97.

**Van den Hengel, John**. Can There Be a Science of Action? Paul Ricoeur. *Phil Today*, 40(2), 235-250, Sum 96.

Human action as understood by analytic philosophy cannot have causal antecedents. Nor must human action be identified with events. How then is it possible to construct a science of human action as in psychology and sociology? In *Oneself as Another* Paul Ricoeur constructs both an ontology and epistemology of human action. At the epistemic level Ricoeur shifts the emphasis away from action explained through motives for action towards a

Van den Hoven, Jeroen 964 AUTHOR INDEX

recognition of action as the involvement or commitment of an agent. The quest for truth in human action accordingly is not toward a correspondence of action to a preexisting reality but toward the authenticity of human initiatives. The article explores the possibility for a science of human action within these parameters.

**Van den Hoven, Jeroen**. Computer Ethics and Moral Methodology. *Metaphilosophy*, 28(3), 234-248, Jl 97.

In computer ethics, as in other branches of applied ethics, the problem of the justification of moral judgment is still unresolved. I argue that the method which is referred to as "The Method of Wide Reflective Equilibrium" (WRE) offers the best solution to it. It does not fall victim to the false dilemma of having to choose either case-based particularist or principle-based universalist approaches to the problem of moral justification. I claim that WRE also provides the best model of practical moral reasoning available for computer ethics. It does not pretend to provide quasi-algorithmic procedures for moral decision making, but neither does it abandon the regulative ideal of communicative transparency in discursive public justification.

**Van der Burg, Wibren**. Bioethics and Law: A Developmental Perspective. *Bioethics*, 11(2), 91-114, Ap 97.

In most Western countries, health law bioethics are strongly intertwined. This strong connection is the result of some specific factors that, in the early years of these disciplines, facilitated a rapid development of both. In this paper, I analyze these factors and construe a development theory existing of three phases, or ideal-typical models. In the moralistic-paternalistic model, there is almost no health law of explicit medical ethics. In the liberal model, which is now dominant in most Western countries, law and ethics closely cooperate and converge, both disciplines use the same framework for analysis. In some countries, a third model is emerging. In this postliberal model, health law is more modest and acknowledge its inherent and normative limits, whereas ethics takes a richer and most ambitious self image. As a result health law and ethics will partly diverge again. (edited)

**Van der Burg, Wibren**. The Importance of Ideals. *J Value Inq*, 31(1), 23-37, Mr 97.

The central thesis is that we cannot fully understand, nor adequately guide normative practices without making references to ideals. Ideals should not be seen as the foundation of normative theories but as one element in a reflective equilibrium model, to be combined with other elements like principles, rules and concrete judgments. Recognition of ideals will result in better theories of law, morality and politics. Moreover, ideal-oriented approaches may also shed new lights on practical problems and on traditional theoretical controversies. Therefore, they will enrich our understanding of the reality of law, morality and politics and offer new perspectives for normative theory.

**Van der Does, Jaap** and Groeneveld, Willem and Veltman, Frank. An Update on "Might". *J Log Lang Info*, 6(4), 361-380, O 97.

This paper is on the update semantics for "might" of Veltman (1996). Three consequence relations are introduced and studied in an abstract setting. Next we present sequent-style systems for each of the consequence relations. We show the logics to be complete and decidable. The paper ends with a syntactic cut elimination result.

**Van der Dussen, Jan**. Collingwood's "Lost" Manuscript of *The Principles of History*. *Hist Theor*, 36(1), 32-62, 1997.

In his edition of *The Idea of History* Knox made use of parts of Collingwood's unfinished manuscript of *The Principles of History*, written during a voyage through the Dutch East Indies in 1938-1939. This manuscript, however, is not among Collingwood's manuscripts, available at the Bodleian Library at Oxford since 1978. It was therefore considered lost, but it has recently been discovered in the archives of Oxford University Press. Originally, it consisted of ninety pages containing finished chapters on "Evidence," "Action," and "nature and Action."(edited)

**Van der Hoeven, J**. Hartstocht en rede. *Phil Reform*, 62(1), 1-22, 1997.

**Van der Linden, Harry**. Marx's Political Universalism. *Topoi*, 15(2), 235-245, S 96.

Michael Walzer rejects Marx's view of a political ideal valid for all human beings as morally dangerous and based on the illusion of epistemic transcendence of one's location and particularity. The moral objections hold, however, against Marx's Hegelian conception of historical progress, not his political universalism as such. An epistemically plausible universal conception of the good society can be derived from Marx's anthropology, once it is elaborated by Martha Nussbaum's Aristotelian conception of human functioning. Progressive action in the global economy ("globalization from below") requires political universalism as a regulative ideal subject to continuous improvement rather than Walzer's pluralism.

**Van der Meer, Jitse M** (ed). *Facets of Faith and Science Volume 1: Historiography and Modes of Interaction*. Lanham, Univ Pr of America, 1996.

What role do religious beliefs play in the construction of scientific theories and how do religion and science interact? The first volume of *Facets of Faith and Science* explores these and other questions and addresses the specific roles of metaphysical and religious beliefs in explanation and theory construction in the natural sciences. The contributors survey modes of interaction between religion and science and use historical studies to construct models integrating the two. The volume offers reasons why religion and science should, or should not, interact. (publisher)

**Van der Meer, Jitse M** (ed). *Facets of Faith and Science Volume 2: The Role of Beliefs in Mathematics and the Natural Sciences—An Augustinian Perspective*. Lanham, Univ Pr of America, 1996.

This second volume in the Pascal Centre's series on faith and science examines if and how the content of science and mathematics has been affected by religious and metaphysical beliefs. Many of the essays present ideas in the context of the revival of the historic Reformation in the Netherlands and background studies on the philosophy and theology of the Reformation's major representatives, such as Kuyper, Bavinck, Dooyeweerd and Vollenhoven, are included. This volume is an invaluable companion for both specialists and nonspecialists. (publisher)

**Van der Meer, Jitse M** (ed). *Facets of Faith and Science Volume 3: The Role of Beliefs in the Natural Sciences*. Lanham, Univ Pr of America, 1996.

The third volume in the *Facets of Faith and Science* series, *The Role of Beliefs in the Natural Sciences*, explores the specific roles of metaphysical and religious beliefs in explanation and theory construction in the natural sciences. The contributors present numerous case studies culled from the fields of astronomy, biology, cosmology and physics to make their arguments. This volume is essential for anyone interested in the history of science and the theoretical frameworks of the natural sciences. (publisher)

**Van der Meer, Jitse M** (ed). *Facets of Faith and Science Volume 4: Interpreting God's Action in the World*. Lanham, Univ Pr of America, 1996.

This fourth volume of *Facets of Faith and Science* focuses on how to interpret God's action in nature, surveys recent thought on divine agency, proposes a new understanding of double agency and addresses the relation of divine action and omniscience to natural causation, randomness and Evolutionary theory. (publisher)

**Van der Scheer, Lieke**. The Rhetorical Force of Ambiguity: The No-Harm Argument in Medical Ethics (in Dutch). *Alg Ned Tijdschr Wijs*, 88(3), 192-207, Jl 96.

Several strategies have been proposed to formulate new ethical criteria which are being called for by developments in modern medical technology. H. Dupuis proposes to start from the primacy of the maxim that medical intervention must never be harmful and to justify this maxim on the basis of the principle of autonomy and that of the integrity of the body. It is argumented that this strategy is flawed by an ambiguous use of the concept of 'harming'. This concept takes on different meanings, depending on whether it is used within the context of the principle of the autonomy of the body or within that of the principle of bodily integrity. Moreover, it is shown that the arguments in which such flawed logic is to be found are used rhetorically to conceal the belief that, in some cases, the quality of life of some individuals is not worth sustaining.

**Van Der Schoot, Albert**. Schoonheid buiten proportie: Burkes afrekening met een klassiek ideaal. *Alg Ned Tijdschr Wijs*, 89(3), 177-188, Jl 97.

The status of proportion as an aesthetic ideal crumbles away quickly in the course of the 18th century. This must be understood in the light of the diminished authority, in that period, of mathematics when not in the service of mechanical purposes. During the 17th century, many authors still hailed mathematics as a methodological panacea for problems in any field (e.g., Spinoza, Craig, Vooght). In the 18th century, mathematics was ridiculed by philosophical opinion leaders (e.g., Diderot, Berkeley, Voltaire). It was Edmund Burke who dealt the final blow to the traditional conviction that beauty is, among other things, a matter of correct proportions.

**Van der Torre, Leendert W N** and Tan, Yao-Hua. "How to Combine Ordering and Minimizing in a Deontic Logic Based on Preferences" in *Deontic Logic, Agency and Normative Systems*, Brown, Mark A (ed), 216-232. New York, Springer-Verlag, 1996.

In this paper we propose a semantics for dyadic deontic logic with an explicit preference ordering between worlds, representing different degrees of ideality. We argue that this ideality ordering can be used in two ways to evaluate formulas, which we call *ordering* and *minimizing*. Ordering uses all preference relations between relevant worlds, whereas minimizing uses the most preferred worlds only. We show that ordering corresponds to strengthening of the antecedent, and minimizing to weakening of the consequent. Moreover, we show that in some cases ordering and minimizing have to be combined to obtain certain desirable conclusions, and that this can only be done in a so-called two-phase deontic logic. In the first phase, the preference ordering is constructed, and in the second phase the ordering is used for minimization. If these two phases are not distinguished, then counterintuitive conclusions follow.

**Van der Veken, Jan**. Particularity of Religion and Universality of Reason (in Dutch). *Bijdragen*, 58(2), 189-193, 1997.

Lieven Boeve seems to take it for granted that there is an opposition between the "modern" concern for universality and our "postmodern" awareness of invincible particularity. Christian religion, however, is according to Whitehead, "a religion seeking a metaphysics". Starting from its particular experience (the Exodus-experience; the Abba-experience of Jesus) it throws light upon our existence as a whole and even upon cosmic reality (interpreted as creation). If the God of Israel is the true God, He is also the God of heaven and earth. There is in Christian religion itself a unavoidable drive towards universality (and truth). L. Boeve agrees that religion should not be relegated to orthopraxis and revelational positivism. True religion cannot give up its claim "to be true". Religion focuses more on particularity; philosophy strives for a wider generality. But the two should not be opposed.

**Van der Zweerde, Evert**. Civil Society and Ideology: A Matter of Freedom. *Stud East Euro Thought*, 48(2-4), 171-205, S 96.

'Civil society' has been at the centre of discussions among Russian philosophers in recent years (1988-1992). Interesting cases are: discussions about civil society during perestrojka, reactions to Fukuyama's 'The End of History' by V.S. Nersesjants and others and N.V. Motroshilova's attempt to make the idea of civilization work. Those Russian theorists who try to replace Marxism with a new, positive doctrine, continue the Soviet conception of ideology as

AUTHOR INDEX 965 Van Inwagen, Peter

something coming from above and appreciate neither the fact that civil society comes from below, nor the formal character of its ideology, which allows for a plurality of contents.

**Van der Zweerde, Evert**. Philosophical Periodicals in Russia Today (mid-1995). *Stud East Euro Thought*, 49(1), 35-46, Mr 97.

The aim of this article is to present a survey of Russian philosophical journals today. Since 1988-1989, their number and variety have grown considerably, reflecting a philosophical culture that is much more interesting than the centralized Soviet situation. The main Soviet journal, *Voprosy filosofii* [Problems of Philosophy], is still leading and the only one that can claim a stable editorial policy. The variety in philosophical positions marking contemporary Russian philosophy is exemplified by many other, often more outspoken journals, like the phenomenological *Logos*, the religious-philosophical *Nachala* [Origins, or Beginnings], or the 'postmodern' *Volshebnaya Gora* [The Enchanting Mountain].

**Van Dijk, Paul**. Cor Dippel, denker op de grens van twee werelden. *Alg Ned Tijdschr Wijs*, 89(1), 6-25, Ja 97.

This article analyzes the views on science and technology held by the scientist and critic of culture Dr. C.J. Dippel, who as a professional chemist was extraordinarily widely read; not only the sciences but also philosophy, theology and politics were familiar to him. In Dippel's view, technology is not an autonomous cultural factor as science is. It has to be understood in its relation to society, being a response to demand of culture. This demand has the character of a need or a necessity, latent or public, essential or accidental. Every culture has the technology it deserves. Technology is the mirror of culture and never before we had such an adequate mirror. If the image reflected by the mirror does not please, it is utterly stupid to scold the mirror! Through technology science opens up new fields of reality for human action, without indicating how we have to act. Science teaches us what is possible and fulfills our material wishes through technology, but it does not tell us what we should strive for. That is the difficult freedom science presents to culture.

**Van Eemeren, Frans H**. A World of Difference: The Rich State of Argumentation Theory. *Inform Log*, 17(2), 144-158, Spr 95.

This paper surveys the contributions to the study of argumentation in the two decades since the work of Toulmin and Perelman. Developments include Radical Argumentativism (Anscombre and Ducot), Communication and Rhetoric (American Speech Communication Theory), Informal Logic (Johnson and Blair), Formal Analyses of Fallacies (Woods and Walton), Formal Dialectics (Barth and Krabbe) and Pragma-Dialectics (van Eemeren and Grootendorst). From the survey it is concluded that argumentation theory has been considerably enriched. If the contributions can be made to converge, a sound basis will be created for developing educational methods for producing, interpreting and evaluating argumentative discourse. Thus, argumentation theory may be instrumental in improving the quality of democracy by furthering a reasonable management of differences of opinion.

**Van Eemeren, Frans H** and Grootendorst, Rob. "Developments in Argumentation Theory" in *Logic and Argumentation,* Van Eemeren, Frans H (ed), 9-26. Amsterdam, North-Holland, 1994.

In this paper, a survey is provided of the state of the art in argumentation theory. Some of the most significant approaches of the past two decades are discussed: Informal logic, the formal theory of fallacies, formal dialectics, pragma-dialectics, radical argumentativism, and the modern revival of rhetoric. The survey is based not only on books, but also on papers published in professional journals or included in conference proceedings.

**Van Eemeren, Frans H** (ed) and Van Benthem, Johan (ed) and Grootendorst, Rob (ed). *Logic and Argumentation*. Amsterdam, North-Holland, 1994.

This volume aims at providing some insight into the connections between logic and argumentation. Van Eemeren and Grootendorst survey the state of the art in argumentation theory. Van Bentham describes the interfaces between developments in logic and argumentation theory. Pinto, Batens, and Starmans discuss the links between argumentation and logic, Finocchiaro the Oliver-Massey asymmetry, Jackson, Krabbe and Walton the fallacies. Woods pays attention to paradoxes. Zarefsky distinguishes between four forces that have shaped argumentation studies in the communication discipline. D. O'Keefe discusses interconnections between argumentation studies and persuasion effect research. Linguistic aspects are explored by Stenning, Van Rees, and Snoeck Henkemans.

**Van Evra, James**. "Logic and Mathematics in Charles Sanders Peirce's "Description of a Notation for the Logic of Relatives" in *Studies in the Logic of Charles Sanders Peirce,* Houser, Nathan (ed), 147-157. Bloomington, Indiana Univ Pr, 1997.

**Van Evra, James** (ed) and Roberts, Don D (ed) and Houser, Nathan (ed). *Studies in the Logic of Charles Sanders Peirce*. Bloomington, Indiana Univ Pr, 1997.

This volume provides a comprehensive exploration of Charles Sanders Peirce's work in mathematics and formal logic, highlighting linkages between Peirce's work and present developments in the science and history of logic. The essays are collected from an internationally distinguished group of scholars who gathered at Harvard University in 1989 to commemorate Peirce's birth in 1839. Not just of historical interest, *Studies in the Logic of Charles Sanders Peirce* shows the considerable relevance of Peirce's work for current research. The stimulating depth and originality of Peirce's thought and the continuing importance and usefulness of his ideas are brought out by this major volume. (publisher)

**Van Eyken, Albert**. Directed Evolution. *J Applied Phil*, 13(3), 251-258, 1996.

Though we humans are immensely more gifted than other animals, yet we are not the outcome of an inevitable selection of the 'fittest'. Nor on the other hand is our importance diminished by our evolutionary inheritance. Besides, we are already here! Faith in inevitable progress is a 'scientific', not a Christian, delusion. We realise that the universe has its own rules and complications which intrude on our lives and often thwart our choices. It is therefore legitimate to talk of chance, but we often fail to appreciate the real significance of this word. Chance is not a cause; in essence it refers to our own consciousness that we are immersed in circumstance and it has no reality without our own purposiveness. Thus chance is not some blind and indifferent or even hostile cosmic mystery; it is the occasion of our own responses and it even offers the opportunity of human growth. Just as we accept the laws (and dangers) of physics (e.g., gravitation), as the framework of our ordered existence, so also we may accept the surprises of chance without any despairing conclusion either from our latest researches in astronomy or from a fatal accident in the street.

**Van Fraassen, Bas C**. Comments on Peter Roeper's "The Link between Probability Functions and Logical Consequence". *Dialogue (Canada)*, 36(1), 27-31, Wint 97.

**Van Fraassen, Bas C**. Elgin on Lewis's Putnam's Paradox. *J Phil*, 94(2), 85-93, F 97.

**Van Fraassen, Bas C**. Probabilité conditionelle et certitude. *Dialogue (Canada)*, 36(1), 69-90, Wint 97.

Personal probability is now a familiar subject in epistemology, together with such more venerable notions as knowledge and belief. But there are severe strains between probability and belief; if either is taken as the more basic, the other may suffer. After explaining the difficulties of attempts to accommodate both, I shall propose a unified account which takes conditional personal probability as basic. Full belief is therefore a defined, derivative notion. Yet we will still be able to picture opinion as follows: my subjective probability is only a grading of the possibilities left open by my beliefs. My conditional probabilities generally derive—in a sense to be explicated—from the strongest belief I can maintain when admitting the relevant condition.

**Van Gigch, John P** and Dean, Burton V and Koenigsberg, Ernest. In Search of an Ethical Science: An Interview with C. West Churchman: An 80th Birthday Celebration. *J Bus Ethics*, 16(7), 731-744, My 97.

**Van Goubergen, Martine**. Concerning Lev Shestov's Conception of Ethics. *Stud East Euro Thought*, 48(2-4), 223-229, S 96.

The issue that is expounded in this essay is Chestov's hostility to ethics in general. An explanation for this attitude is sought by attempting to situate the role of ethics in the overall panorama of Chestov's thinking. From this it appears that the philosopher associates ethics with powerlessness and dependence before necessity. He attributes common values we usually ascribe to the concept of ethics, to the original and partly lost creative competence of man.

**Van Gulick, Robert**. "How Should We Understand the Relation between Intentionality and Phenomenal Consciousness?" in *AI, Connectionism and Philosophical Psychology, 1995,* Tomberlin, James E (ed), 271-289. Atascadero, Ridgeview, 1995.

**Van Haaften, Wouter** and Snik, Ger. Critical Thinking and Foundational Development. *Stud Phil Educ*, 16(1-2), 19-41, Ja-Ap 97.

We elaborate on Israel Scheffler's claim that principles of rationality can be rationally evaluated, focusing on foundational development, by which we mean the evolution of principles which are constitutive of our conceptualization of a certain domain of rationality. How can claims that some such principles are better than prior ones be justified? We argue that Scheffler's metacriterion of overall systematic credibility is insufficient here. Two very different types of rational development are jointly involved, namely, development of general principles that are strictly constitutive of rationality as such, and development of specific principles determinative of our conceptualization of particular domains. (edited)

**Van Heerden, Adriaan**. Foucault's Phallusy: Intimate Friendship as a Fundamental Ethic (Being a Reconstructive Reading of Foucault's *The Care of the Self*). *S Afr J Phil*, 16(1), 23-30, F 97.

The purpose of this essay is to render a reconstructive reading of the third volume of Foucault's *The History of Sexuality* (entitled *The Care of the Self*) and to ask what kind of ethic Foucault expounds in the subtext of the work. The absence of any explicit exposition of a (positive) ethic in the text seems to be due to Foucault's belief in the 'value-neutrality' of his methodology. (edited)

**Van Holthoon, Frederic L**. Hume and the 1763 Edition of His *History of England*: His Frame of Mind as a Revisionist. *Hume Stud*, 23(1), 133-152, Ap 97.

**Van Hooft, Stan**. Commitment and the Bond of Love. *Austl J Phil*, 74(3), 454-466, S 96.

I propose the hypothesis that much of what grounds love is hidden from the lovers and may only be uncovered with the greatest difficulty. My second hypothesis is that the constancy, exclusivity, and fidelity of love do not arise from the same sphere in our motivational fields as does moral duty. Rather, they are forms of commitment. And commitment is a constituent expression of the bond of love. It is distinguished from promises and intentions. One finds oneself with a commitment and this makes an ethical difference to one's comportment towards the beloved.

**Van Inwagen, Peter**. A Reply to Professor Hick. *Faith Phil*, 14(3), 299-302, Jl 97.

John Hick's "The Epistemological Challenge of Religious Pluralism" is in part a reply to my essay "Non Est Hick." Hick argues that since I do not claim to know what provisions have been made for non-Christians in the divine plan, I should not claim to know something I do claim to know: that God has established no instruments of salvation outside the church. In this rejoinder, I attempt to answer this point.

**Van Inwagen, Peter**. Fischer on Moral Responsibility. *Phil Quart*, 47(188), 373-381, Jl 97.

This essay is a critical study of John Martin Fischer's *The Metaphysics of Free Will*. In this book, Fischer argues that, although free will (the ability to act otherwise) may be incompatible with determinism, so-called Frankfurt examples demonstrate that moral responsibility does not require free will. In addition, he presents an account of the sort of "control" that, in his view is required for moral responsibility. This "control" is easily seen to be compatible with determinism. I argue that Fischer fails to establish the compatibility of moral responsibility and determinism.

**Van Kerckhoven, Guy**. Die Heimat Welt: Zur Deutung der Denkspur Martin Heideggers in Eugen Finks Frühwerk. *Perspekt Phil*, 22, 105-137, 1996.

"The origin of Zeno's ethics is found in the ethical doctrines of his masters of the Platonic and cynic schools. But there is also an oriental religious impact (see E. Zeller, A. Jagu, M. Wiersma) giving priority to ethics above physics and logic which have to serve as foundations of ethics. Hence there arises the problem of a vicious circle; for Zeno's ethics defines the good life as life according to reason and as according to the very nature of man, referring to the philosophy of nature, his physics. But in this discipline he defines the nature of all things ultimately as reason, referring thus to ethics. The solution seems to be that the reference between both disciplines is not circular, but complementary. (edited)

**Van Lambalgen, Michiel** and Alechina, Natasha. Generalized Quantification as Substructural Logic. *J Sym Log*, 61(3), 1006-1044, S 96.

We show how sequent calculi for some generalized quantifiers can be obtained by generalizing the Herbrand approach to ordinary first order proof theory. Typical of the Herbrand approach, as compared to plain sequent calculus, is increased control over relations of dependence between variables. In the case of generalized quantifiers, explicit attention to relations of dependence becomes indispensible for setting up proof systems. It is shown that this can be done by turning variables into structured objects, governed by various types of structural rules. These structured variables are interpreted semantically by means of a dependence relation. This relation is an analogue of the accessibility relation in modal logic. We then isolate a class of axioms for generalized quantifiers which correspond to first-order conditions on the dependence relation.

**Van Langevelde, A. P.**. Bilingualism in the Business World in West European Minority Language Regions: Profit or Loss?. *Phil Reform*, 61(2), 135-159, 1996.

The company framework developed in this paper is clearly helpful in formulating questions for empirical research. Yet that does not exhaust this framework's possibilities. It can also prove useful in connection with comparative studies between different West European minority language areas. Moreover, on the basis of the economic policy in the regions in question. Perhaps the bilingual situation can serve as a stimulus to regional authorities to foster an economic development more in harmony with the regional culture, in which the minority language plays so salient a role. Then bilingualism would form a point of profit in the economic development of West European minority language regions.

**Van Leeuwen, Evert** and Kimsma, Gerrit K. Philosophy of Medical Practice: A Discursive Approach. *Theor Med*, 18(1-2), 99-112, Mr-Je 97.

Medical practice is a discursive practice which is highly influenced by other discursive practices like science, law and economics. Philosophical analysis of those influences is needed to discern their effect on the goals of medicine and on the way in which the self-image of man may be changed. The nature of medical practice and discourse itself makes it necessary to include different philosophical disciplines, like philosophy of science, of law, ethics and epistemology. Possible scenario's of euthanasia and the human genome project in the USA and Europe are used to exemplify how philosophy of medicine can contribute to a realistic understanding of the problems which are related to the goals of medicine and health care. (edited)

**Van Loocke, Philip**. On the Properties of a Network that Associates Concepts on Basis of Share of Components and Its Relation with the Conceptual Memory of the Right Hemisphere. *Commun Cog*, 29(3/4), 363-392, 1996.

This paper considers two classes of connectionist units and it discusses the properties of representations for concepts that can be generated with them: More specifically, we differentiate between units that support an activation only and units that allow to represent bindings. The latter units are of importance for cognitive operations in which it matters at which place a concept appears in an n-ary relation. Units that have activations only are suited to control associations on basis of share of components. In a network that generates this type of associations, the representations of concepts are distributed and the patterns of activation are in general nonfocal. Such a network can provide quickly a large context with connotations when a concept is activated. It includes implicit information about the typicalities of concepts and it can generate associations during which large semantic distances are bridged. We consider evidence that relates our considerations with a functional network of the right hemisphere that memorizes concepts and we relate this evidence to a specific connectionist model.

**Van Megen, Freek** and Faccini, Giovanni and Borm, Peter (& others). Congestion Models and Weighted Bayesian Potential Games. *Theor Decis*, 42(2), 193-206, Ja 97.

Games associated with congestion situations à la Rosenthal (1973) have pure Nash equilibria. This result implicitly relies on the existence of a potential function. In this paper we provide a characterization of potential games in terms of coordination games and dummy games. Second, we extend Rosenthal's congestion model to an incomplete information setting and show that the related Bayesian games are potential games and therefore, have pure Bayesian equilibria.

**Van Niekerk, Anton A** and Van Zyl, Liezl. Embryo Experimentation, Personhood and Human Rights. *S Afr J Phil*, 15(4), 139-143, N 96.

This article deals with the ethics of embryo experimentation. Specific attention is paid to the argument that the embryo's potential for personhood endows it with a significant moral status. The question of whether we are obliged to fulfill this potential is approached first by determining whether it has a *right* to life and secondly by asking whether protection should be conferred to the embryo as a *benefit*.

**Van Nierop, Maarten**. Subjectivity and Illusion (in Dutch). *Tijdschr Filosof*, 58(4), 631-642, D 96.

According to a poet such as Gottfried Benn or a philosopher such as Arthur Schopenhauer, our experience of happiness is based on an illusion that doesn't agree with the gruesome facts of life. The crucial question is, then, whether such illusions can, as they seem to believe, ever be totally unmasked. Or are there illusions which are so deeply rooted in our psychological and anthropological economy that they are as incorrigible as optical illusions: delusions that can only be uncovered and explained but can never be removed definitively? The insight that such 'necessary illusions' exist may lead to the acceptance of a modest kind of subjectivity. (edited)

**Van Oosten, Jaap**. Extensional Realizability. *Annals Pure Applied Log*, 84(3), 317-349, Ap 97.

Two straightforward "extensionalizations" of Kleene's realizability are considered; denoted $r_e$-notion is (as a relation between numbers and sentences) a subset of Kleene's realizability, the e-notion is not. The problem of an axiomatization of e-realizability is attacked and one arrives at an axiomatization over a conservative extension of arithmetic, in a language with variables for finite sets. A derived rule for arithmetic is obtained by the use of a q-variant of e-realizability; this rule subsumes the well-known *Extended Church's Rule*. The second part of the paper focuses on toposes for these realizabilities. By a relaxation of the notion of partial combinatory algebra, a new class of realizability toposes emerges. Relationships between the various realizability toposes are given, and results analogous to Robinson and Rosolini's characterization of the effective topos, are obtained for a topos generalizing e-realizability.

**Van Patten, Jim**. Affirmative Action: Retrospect and Prospect. *Cont Phil*, 17(6), 2-7, N-D 95.

Providing opportunities for marginalized peoples—women, minorities, senior citizens—is an essential element in developing social networks so important in social stability. The pros and cons of one proactive governmental network, affirmative action, is examined in this paper.

**Van Ree, E**. Stalin and Marxism: A Research Note. *Stud East Euro Thought*, 49(1), 23-33, Mr 97.

This article concerns the research done by the author in Stalin's private library. The notes made in the works of Marx, Engels and Lenin suggest that until the end of his life Stalin felt himself in general agreement with these "classics." The choice of books and the notes support the thesis that, despite his historical interest and his identification with some of the tsars as powerful rulers, Stalin always continued to consider himself a Marxist and that he was unintereseted in other systems of thought, including those of traditional Russia.

**Van Rees, M Agnès**. "Accounting for Transformations in the Dialectical Reconstruction of Argumentative Discourse" in *Logic and Argumentation,* Van Eemeren, Frans H (ed), 89-99. Amsterdam, North-Holland, 1994.

In this paper, an argument is made for the importance of taking into account the social interactional aspect of argumentative discourse, when reconstructing such discourse as a critical discussion. The analysis of a particular problem-solving discussion shows how dialectical transformations can be accounted for by an appeal to social practices, especially with regard to the maintenance of a status balance between the participants.

**Van Roermund, Bert**. Jurisprudential Dilemmas of European Law. *Law Phil*, 16(4), 357-376, Jl 97.

Making a first sketch of philosophical issues arising from European Community law I want to present a series of more or less obvious and more or less interrelated dilemmas, or even 'double binds'. (I) Deepening the community becomes incompatible with widening membership. (II) National states seem both necessary for and obstructive in articulating transnational problems. (III) The more democracy is needed as a warrant for the public exercise of political power in Europe, the more the very concept of democracy on a European scale evades understanding. (IV) European unity presupposes a unifying rule of law, while member states have radically different conceptions of this principle. (V) Even the very core of European integration, the common market, is subject to two conflicting and, indeed, incompatible doctrines of competition. (edited)

**Van Roojen, Mark**. Affirmative Action, Non-Consequentialism, and Responsibility for the Effects of Past Discrimination. *Pub Affairs Quart*, 11(3), 281-301, Jl 97.

One popular criticism of affirmative action is that it discriminates against those who would otherwise have been offered jobs without it. This objection must rely on the nonconsequentialist distinction between what we do and what we merely allow to claim that doing nothing merely allows people to be harmed by the discrimination of others, while preferential programs actively harm those left out. It fails since the present effects of past discrimination result from social arrangements which result from actions of ours. We can be responsible for the effects of past discrimination, even without having discriminated, if we are responsible for that discrimination having those effects.

**Van Roojen, Mark**. Expressivism and Irrationality. *Phil Rev*, 105(3), 311-335, Jl 96.

Geach's problem of accounting for the fact that moral judgments function logically like other judgments plagues noncognitivism. Noncognitivists must offer interpretations of imbedded moral claim that also explains their logical interaction with straightforward moral assertions. Blackburn and Gibbard offer a series of accounts interpreting conditionals as expressing higher-order commitments. Each then invokes norms for the acceptance of attitudes to explain why certain combinations are inconsistent. I press two objections: 1) The norms needed to do the explanatory work cannot work without also ruling consistent attitudes inconsistent. 2) Norms of rational attitude acceptance do not track the distinction between consistent and inconsistent attitudes.

**Van Stigt, Walter P**. Introduction to *Life, Art, and Mysticism*. *Notre Dame J Form Log*, 37(3), 381-387, Sum 96.

**Van Stigt, Walter P**. Life, Art, and Mysticism. *Notre Dame J Form Log*, 37(3), 391-429, Sum 96.

**Van Tongeren, Paul**. Denken in trouw aan leven en geloof. *Tijdschr Filosof*, 59(1), 132-136, Mr 97.

The article reviews a book by the Dutch philosopher Theo de Boer in which he presents philosophy as the hermeneutics of life. For this hermeneutics he makes preferably use of poems, in which—more than in other narratives—a sense of transcendence can be found. That is important for De Boer, who as a Christian thinks that the bible should be a hermeneutical guide also for the philosopher. The question is asked whether the author does not turn out to be more a theologian than a philosopher in this book.

**Van Veuren, Pieter**. Does it Make Sense to Teach History Through Thinking Skills?. *Inquiry (USA)*, 14(3), 72-81, Spr 95.

**Van Woudenberg, René**. Theistic Arguments and the Crisis of Classical Foundationalism (in Dutch). *Bijdragen*, 58(1), 2-28, 1997.

This paper discusses some arguments against some traditional "proofs of God's existence." First, it is argued that it is not obvious that these arguments are fallacious. Secondly, I try to articulate why so many Protestant thinkers maintained a hostile attitude toward the traditional proofs. I argue their attitude was shaped by the conviction that belief in God is epistemically justified even when it is not based on argument or proof. I reconstruct Bavinck's treatment of the traditional proofs as a rejection of what has come to be called "classical foundationalism." Lastly, I try to show that even though Protestant thinkers were right in claiming that one does not need any traditional arguments in order to be epistemically justified in believing that God exists, this does not imply that such arguments are without *any* value (as some thinkers influenced by Wittgenstein maintain).

**Van Wymeersch, Brigitte**. L'esthétique musicale de Descartes et le cartésianisme. *Rev Phil Louvain*, 94(2), 271-293, My 96.

Descartes wrote no systematic on aesthetics, but expressed views on art and the beautiful on a number of occasions in several writings on music. From his first treatise in 1618—the *compendium musicae*—to the *traité des passions de l'âme*, he evolved from a philosophy of art with objective and intellectualist leanings towards a more subjective aesthetics in which the beautiful is a question of personal taste: the beauty of a piece of music becomes relative to the emotion felt. Such emotion pertains to the union of soul and body and cannot be directed by reason alone. It is because they did not grasp the precise place assigned by Descartes to aesthetic emotion that Cartesians, including Rameau, have betrayed his thought on the beautiful.

**Van Zyl, Liezl** and Van Niekerk, Anton A. Embryo Experimentation, Personhood and Human Rights. *S Afr J Phil*, 15(4), 139-143, N 96.

This article deals with the ethics of embryo experimentation. Specific attention is paid to the argument that the embryo's potential for personhood endows it with a significant moral status. The question of whether we are obliged to fulfill this potential is approached first by determining whether it has a *right* to life and secondly by asking whether protection should be conferred to the embryo as a *benefit*.

**Vance, Russell E**. Heroic Antireductionism and Genetics: A Tale of One Science. *Proc Phil Sci Ass*, 3(Suppl), S36-S45, 1996.

In this paper I provide a novel argument against the claim that classical genetics is being reduced to molecular genetics. Specifically, I demonstrate that reductionists must subscribe to the unargued and problematic thesis that molecular genetics is 'independent' of classical genetics. I also argue that several standard antireductionist positions can be faulted for unnecessarily conceding the Independence Thesis to the reductionists. In place of a 'tale of two sciences', I offer a 'heroic' stance that denies classical genetics is being reduced, yet sees classical and molecular genetics as fundamentally unified.

**Vandamme, F**. Letter of the Editor: On Knowledge Technology and its Relevance. *Commun Cog—AI*, 13(1), 3-11, 1996.

An overview of knowledge technology and artificial intelligence is given in a large and narrow sense. The main lines of the relevance of modern knowledge technology is looked at in view of solving the major cultural, social and commercial and industrial problems.

**Vanderschraaf, Peter** and Richards, Diana. Joint Beliefs in Conflictual Coordination Games. *Theor Decis*, 42(3), 287-310, My 97.

The traditional solution concept for noncooperative game theory is the Nash equilibrium, which contains an implicit assumption that players' probability distributions satisfy *probabilistic independence*. However, in games with more than two players, relaxing this assumption results in a more general equilibrium concept based on *joint beliefs* (Vanderschraaf, 1995). This article explores the implications of this joint-beliefs equilibrium concept for two kinds of conflictual coordination games: crisis bargaining and public goods provision. We find that,

using updating consistent with Bayes's rule, players' beliefs converge to equilibria in joint beliefs which do not satisfy probabilistic independence. In addition, joint beliefs greatly expand the set of mixed equilibria. On the face of it, allowing for joint beliefs might be expected to increase the prospects for coordination. However, we show that if players use joint beliefs, which may be more likely as the number of players increases, then the prospects for coordination in these games declines vis-à-vis independent beliefs.

**Vandevelde, Pol** (ed & trans) and Spurlock, Jacqueline Bouchard (trans) and Harris, Bond (trans). *Paul Ricoeur: A Key to Husserl's Ideas I*. Milwaukee, Marquette Univ Pr, 1996.

In 1950 Paul Ricoeur translated into French Husserl's major work *Ideen zu einer reinen Phänomenologie und phänomenologischen Philosophie*. In this French translation Ricoeur provided both a lengthy introductory chapter and a large running commentary in the form of notes. These notes were keyed to the beginning of many of Husserl's sections and to important places within the body of the text. The present translation brings at last this famous commentary into English. In undertaking this work the translators have benefited from the encouragement of Professor Ricoeur himself. (publisher, edited)

**Vanheeswijck, Guido**. De romaneske waarheid bij René Girard. *Tijdschr Filosof*, 59(1), 89-101, Mr 97.

In reaction to Tijmes's article 'De romaneske waarheid' (Tvf, 57/1995, 667-691) this article underlines the strong link between *Mensonge romantique et vérité romanesque* on the one hand and *Des Choses cachées depuis la fondation du monde* on the other. I work out my approach in three different steps. First, I start from the distinction internal-external mediation in order to elucidate Girard's interpretation of the distinction between the scapegoat's function in premodern societies and in modern ones. Secondly, starting from the same distinction internal-external mediation, I try to make clear the distinction between religion and Christianity in Girard's oeuvre. Against this background, I eventually try to elucidate the proper meaning of the concept 'romaneske waarheid' (vérité romanesque).

**Vanheeswijck, Guido**. Metaphysics as a "Science of Absolute Presuppositions": Another Look at R. G. Collingwood: A Reply to Rosemary Flanigan. *Mod Sch*, 73(4), 333-350, M 96.

**Vanheeswijck, Guido**. Self-Enlargement or Purification? On the Meaning of the Fragmentary Subject in René Girard's Early Writings (in Dutch). *Bijdragen*, 57(3), 242-263, 1996.

In this article I intend to focus on the interpretation of the so-called postmodern phenomenon of anthropological fragmentation/doubling. My starting-point is a comparison between the anthropological position of the American philosopher Richard Rorty on the one hand and that of the French-American anthropologist René Girard on the other. In the first section of this article, I shall go into Rorty's interpretation of the Freudian image of man. In the second section I shall present the Girardian image of man, which, to a certain extent, he has worked out in answer to the Freudian one. Eventually, in the third section, I shall confront both forms of current anthropology, situate Girard's early writings within the context of his entire oeuvre and put forward a few critical remarks with regard to his anthropological presuppositions. (edited)

**Vanheeswijck, Guido**. Where to Look for Truth: Focusing on the Symposium's Highlights. *Bijdragen*, 58(2), 206-209, 1997.

Particular traditions versus universal principles: a much too simplistic representation of the tension this symposium focused upon. The polarity here treated is a surfaced-phenomenon having deeper metaphysical roots, which themselves must be articulated. More specifically, the tension between particular traditions and universal principles is itself dependent on a number of fundamental nominalist premises which, from the start, direct our modern and postmodern culture. Does the main challenge of current philosophical thought not consist in precisely making explicit the central presuppositions of our culture? In other words, do we have to take the nominalist premises for granted as a starting point or do we have to take the opportunity to scrutinize them afresh? Of course, the latter approach can never aim at an integral return to different forms of premodern thought. Rather, it is the intention to find a middle course between an obstinate nominalism and an extreme realism.

**Varani, Giovanna**. Ramistische Spuren in Leibniz' Gestaltung der Begriffe ,dialectica', ,topica' und ,ars inveniendi'. *Stud Leibniz*, 27(2), 135-156, 1995.

Vers la fin du XVIe siècle, le ramisme se répandit en Allemagne, gagna un grand nombre de prosélytes et fit preuve d'une remarquable vitalité. L'histoire de ses effets constitue un intéressant, néanmoins peu recherché chapitre de l'historiographie de la philosophie, et la question portant sur les "dettes" éventuelles de Leibniz envers le ramisme se tiend au coeur de cet essai. En premier lieu, quelques caractères théoriques du ramisme allemand et surtout du philippo-ramisme sont mis en évidence, après cela on analyse l'emploi de Leibniz (jusqu'au 1680) des notion "dialectica", "topica" et "ars inveniendi" et l'on découvre une syntonisation conceptuelle entre cet emploi et la manière de penser des ramistes. Sans en tirer des conclusions hasardeuses, on peut comprendre le ramisme comme un ingrédient essentiel de l'univers leibnizien complexe et comme un thème de plus en plus important pour Leibniz.

**Vardi, Moshe Y**. Special Selection in Logic in Computer Science. *J Sym Log*, 62(2), 608, Je 97.

Over the last 25 years, logic proved to be a powerful tool in computer science and constitutes the primary analytical approach in many subfields of computer science. Logic in computer science is today a thriving, dynamic research area. In order to attract the attention of its readership to this research area, the *Journal of Symbolic Logic* has agreed to publish a *Special Selection in Logic in Computer Science*. (edited)

Vardi, Moshe Y 968 AUTHOR INDEX

**Vardi, Moshe Y** and Kolaitis, Phokion G and Grädel, Erich. On the Decision Problem for Two-Variable First-Order Logic. *Bull Sym Log*, 3(1), 53-69, Mr 97.

We identify the computational complexity of the satisfiability problem for $FO^2$, the fragment of first-order logic consisting of all relational first-order sentences with at most two distinct variables. Although this fragment was shown to be decidable a long time ago, the computational complexity of its decision problem has not been pinpointed so far. In 1975 Mortimer proved that $FO^2$ has the *finite-model property*, which means that if an $FO^2$-sentence is satisfiable, then it has a finite model. Moreover, Mortimer showed that every satisfiable $FO^2$-sentence has a model whose size is at most doubly exponential in the size of the sentence. In this paper, we improve Mortimer's bound by one exponential and show that every satisfiable $FO^2$-sentence has a model whose size is at most exponential in the size of the sentence. As a consequence, we establish that the satisfiability problem for $FO^2$ is NEXPTIME-complete.

**Varela, Charles R** and Harré, Rom. Conflicting Varieties of Realism: Causal Powers and the Problems of Social Structure. *J Theor Soc Behav*, 26(3), 313-325, S 96.

**Varela, Francisco J**. Neurophenomenology: A Methodological Remedy for the Hard Problem. *J Consciousness Stud*, 3(4), 330-349, 1996.

This paper starts with one of Chalmers's basic points: first-hand experience is an irreducible field of phenomena. I claim there is no 'theoretical fix' or 'extra ingredient' in nature that can possibly bridge this gap. Instead, the field of conscious phenomena requires a rigorous *method* and an explicit pragmatics for its exploration and analysis. My proposed approach, inspired by the style of inquiry of phenomenology, I have called neurophenomenology. It seeks articulations by *mutual constraints* between phenomena present in experience and the correlative field of phenomena established by the cognitive sciences. It needs to expand into a widening research community in which the method is cultivated further.

**Vargas, Celso** and Alfaro, Mario. Desarrollo sostenible y valoración de la vida humana. *Rev Filosof (Costa Rica)*, 34(83-84), 385-394, D 96.

In this paper we sketch an ethical approach called planetary ethics. Two fundamental values characterize the approach: the planet as the supporter of life and the life as a planetary value. Our approach is a nonanthropocentric one and it is compatible with the general guidelines of the United Nations Programme 21. An ethical system should incorporate the current knowledge on the human being, particularly that derived from biological sciences, including, of course, ecology. Concerning this requirement the paper draws some of the conclusions and remarks from the philosopher Gehlen as an important stage toward the conceptualization of the "essence" of human being and its place in the cosmos. After that, we sketch a general goal-oriented ethical model aim at allowing the discussion of general and specific questions, and implications of this planetary ethics. (edited)

**Vargas Bejarano, Julio César**. Fenomenología y Epistemología genética: revisión de la critica de Piaget a la fenomenología y algunas vías de convergencia. *Franciscanum*, 37(112), 89-102, Ja-Ap 96.

**Vargas Calvo, Jorge A**. Qué se sentiría ser Charlie Parker? (What is it like to be a bird?). *Rev Filosof (Costa Rica)*, 34(83-84), 433-443, D 96.

An important element in the literary work of the Argentine writer Julio Cortázar is the original philosophical research of the writer himself. Taking as a starting point the tale "El Perseguidor" ("The Pursuer"), we will show how the author made use of items of philosophy of mind, such as the accessibility of the personal point of view, nonverbal ways of knowing and the problem of having a private language. We like to show that this background forms a coherent whole and we will discuss it under the light of the current discussions in philosophy of mind. (edited)

**Varner, Gary E** and Gilbertz, Susan J and Peterson, Tarla Rai. "Teaching Environmental Ethics as a Method of Conflict Management" in *Environmental Pragmatism*, Light, Andrew (ed), 266-282. New York, Routledge, 1996.

Representatives of diverse interests in regional environmental disputes were brought together for two day workshops on environmental ethics. The workshops introduced participants to concepts and theories commonly discussed in college philosophy courses on the subject and presented them with opportunities to describe themselves and their perceived opponents in those terms. Content analysis of lengthy, unstructured interviews conducted months before and after suggest that such workshops affect participants' ways of framing environmental controversies and encourage related philosophical reflection.

**Varoufakis, Yanis**. Moral Rhetoric in the Face of Strategic Weakness: Emperimental Clues for an Ancient Puzzle. *Erkenntnis*, 46(1), 87-110, Ja 97.

Moralizing is a venerable last resort strategy. The ancient Melians presented the Athenian generals with a splendid example when in a particularly tight corner. In our Western philosophical tradition moral rhetoric is often couched in the form of reasons for action either external to preference and desire (e.g., Kant) or internal to the agent's calculus of desire (e.g., Hume, Gauthier). A third tradition dismisses such rhetoric as the last recourse of the weak (e.g., Aristotle, Nietzsche) whereas a fourth calls for an examination of the social context (e.g., Socrates, Marx, Wittgenstein, Habermas). This paper reports on an experiment which throws some empirical light on these debates and offers a surprising twist to the interpretation of the Melians's plea.

**Varwig, F R**. Éthique, physique, logique, champs d'investigation d'origine stoïcienne?. *Diotima*, 25, 31-36, 1997.

**Varzi, Achille C**. Boundaries, Continuity, and Contact. *Nous*, 31(1), 26-58, Mr 97.

There are conflicting intuitions concerning the status of a boundary separating two adjacent entities (or two parts of the same entity). The boundary cannot belong to both things, for adjacency excludes overlap; and it cannot belong to neither, for nothing lies between two adjacent things. Yet how can the dilemma be avoided without assigning the boundary to one or the other thing *at random*? Some philosophers regard this as a *reductio* of the very notion of a boundary, which should accordingly be treated a mere *façon de parler*. In this paper I resist this temptation and examine some ways of taking the puzzle at face value within a realist perspective—treating boundaries as ontologically on a par with (albeit parasitic upon) voluminous parts.

**Varzi, Achille C** and Casati, Roberto. *50 Years of Events: An Annotated Bibliography 1947 to 1997*. Bowling Green, Philosophy Doc Ctr, 1997.

This bibliography is concerned with recent literature on the nature of events and the place they occupy in our conceptual scheme. The subject has received extensive consideration in the philosophical debate over the last few decades, with ramifications reaching far into the domains of allied disciplines such as linguistics and the cognitive sciences. At the same time, the literature is so wide and widely scattered that it has become very difficult to keep track of every line of development. Our hope is that this work will prove useful to overcome that difficulty.

**Vásconez, Marcelo** and Peña, Lorenzo. What's a Gradual Ontology? (in Spanish). *Agora (Spain)*, 15(2), 29-48, 1996.

What makes fuzzy properties fuzzy is not vagueness but graduality. We argue that such graduality is objective, that there are degrees of truth which are as many degrees of existence of facts. We go on to uphold degrees of existence of other sorts of entities, such as artifacts and species. There is a thick fringe between what is and what is not at all, wherein entities both are and are not. Two different negations, *not* and *not... at all*, are distinguished. Disjunctive syllogism holds for the latter only. Thus, a gradualistic ontology successfully stops the disastrous final step of a sorites argument.

**Vasiliou, Iakovos**. The Role of Good Upbringing in Aristotle's *Ethics*. *Phil Phenomenol Res*, 56(4), 771-797, D 96.

It is argued that a proper appreciation of the passages in the *Nicomachean Ethics* where Aristotle requires the student of ethics to be well brought up implies that the *Ethics* is not attempting to justify the objective correctness of its substantive conception of happiness to someone who does not already appreciate its distinctive value. Reflection on the import of the good-upbringing restriction can lead us to see that Aristotle's conception of ethical objectivity is not only radically different from modern moral philosophy's appeal "to any rational agent", but philosophically important for contemporary ethical thought.

**Vasyukov, Vladimir L**. The Completeness of the Factor Semantics for Lukasiewicz's Infinite-Valued Logics. *Stud Log*, 52(1), 143-167, F 93.

In [12] it was shown that the factor semantics based on the notion of T-F-sequences is a correct model of the Lukasiewicz's infinite-valued logics. But we could not consider some important aspects of the structure of this model because of the short size of paper. In this paper we give a more complete study of this problem: A new proof of the completeness of the factor semantic for Lukasiewicz's logic using Wajsberg algebras [3] (and not MV-algebras in [1]) and Symmetrical Heyting monoids [7] is proposed. Some consequences of such an approach are investigated.

**Vatter, Miguel E**. Taking Exception to Liberalism: Heinrich Meier's *Carl Schmitt and Leo Strauss: The Hidden Dialogue*. *Grad Fac Phil J*, 19/20 (2/1), 323-344, 1997.

**Vattimo, Gianni**. Hermeneutics and Democracy. *Phil Soc Crit*, 23(4), 1-7, Jl 97.

**Vattimo, Gianni** and Webb, David (trans). *Beyond Interpretation: The Meaning of Hermeneutics for Philosophy*. Stanford, Stanford Univ Pr, 1997.

Vattimo argues that hermeneutics, understood in a general sense, has had a pervasive influence on contemporary philosophy and social thought. But its very generality is also a symptom of its malaise, for it threatens to leave hermeneutics empty of significance and wedded to a shallow relativism. Vattimo develops a new interpretation of hermeneutics that dispenses with the traditional bias toward aesthetic experience. His radical interpretation breaks the link between hermeneutics and metaphysical humanism, challenges the traditional opposition of the natural and human sciences, and opens up new perspectives on ethics, art and religion. (edited)

**Vaughn, Lewis**. What's Wrong with Relativism: Why Postmodernism's Most Radical Doctrine is Dead in the Water. *Free Inq*, 17(3), 40-42, Sum 97.

**Vaught, Carl G**. "Theft and Conversion: Two Augustinian Confessions" in *The Recovery of Philosophy in America: Essays in Honor of John Edwin Smith*, Kasulis, Thomas P (ed), 217-249. Albany, SUNY Pr, 1997.

This essay demonstrates that the pear-stealing episode in the orchard and the conversion in the garden are mirror images of one another. The first moves from finitude to fallenness, while the second moves from fallenness to existential transformation. As Augustine moves along the first path, he infinitizes himself. As he moves along the second, he becomes a finite-infinite reflection of God by putting a new garment called Jesus the Christ. In the theft, the community of adolescent companions splits apart into a collection of individuals; in the conversion, a community of individuals related to God is re-established.

**Vaux, Kenneth**. God is Great, God is Good: James Ashbrook's Contribution to Neuroethical Theology. *Zygon*, 31(3), 463-468, S 96.

James Ashbrook's work has not only clarified issues in brain and belief, it has offered intriguing suggestions for ethics. The relevance of neurotheology to ethics is evident if we assume that ethics entails, in part, concerns about character, responsibility and the art of living.

**Veatch, Robert M**. Single Payers and Multiple Lists: Must Everyone Get the Same Coverage in a Universal Health Plan?. *Kennedy Inst Ethics J*, 7(2), 153-169, Je 97.

In spite of recent political setbacks for the movement toward universal health insurance, considerable support remains for the idea. Among those supporting such plans, most assume that a universal insurance system, especially if it is a single-payer system, would offer a single list of basic covered services. This paper challenges that assumption and argues for the availability of multiple lists of services in a universal insurance system. The claim is made that multiple lists will be both more efficient and more fair. Fairness and efficiency require providing an entitlement to universal access to health insurance that could be purchased by typical consumers for a fixed price of perhaps $3500. By permitting everyone to pick their preferred list of services available at that price, each person will efficiently use his or her entitlement while getting more equal opportunity for benefits. (edited)

**Veatch, Robert M** (ed) and Beauchamp, Tom L (ed). *Ethical Issues in Death and Dying*. Englewood Cliffs, Prentice Hall, 1996.

Since the first edition of *Ethical Issues in Death and Dying* was published in 1978, enormous changes have transpired in the field of biomedical ethics. To give readers a more complete picture of historical developments and current thought, the *Second Edition* has thoroughly revised its coverage of: The Emergence of a Brain-Oriented Definition, Truthtelling with Dying Patients, Suicide, Physician-Assisted Suicide and Euthanasia, Forgoing Treatment and Causing Death, Decisions to Forgo Treatment Involving (once) Competent Patients, Decisions to Forgo Treatment Involving Never-Competent Patients, Futile Treatment and Terminal Care, Social Reasons for Limiting Terminal Care. (publisher)

**Veca, Salvatore**. La riforma del Welfare e un'idea di equità. *Iride*, 10(20), 5-15, Ap 97.

**Veca, Salvatore**. Sulla destra e i suoi principi. *Iride*, 9(18), 341-345, Ag 96.

Quali sono i principi della destra? Ma, prima ancora, che cosa sono i principi per una prospettiva di valore politico quale è la destra? La destra della quale si parla in questo articolo è definita da tre principi: 1. La libertà come assenza di vincoli: 2. l'appartenenza alla comunità morale: 3. la scelta democratica non vincolata. La metafora che la descrive meglio è quella della corsa nella quale vince il migliore.

**Vedder, Ben**. Schleiermacher's Idea of Hermeneutics and the Feeling of Absolute Dependence. *Epoche*, 2(1), 91-111, 1994.

**Vedo, Anne**. Asymptotic Probabilities for Second-Order Existential Kahr-Moore-Wang Sentences. *J Sym Log*, 62(1), 304-319, Mr 97.

We show that the 0-1 law does not hold for the class of second-order existential Kahr-Moore-Wang sentences *without* equality by finding a sentence in this class which almost surely expresses parity. We also show that every recursive real in the unit interval is the asymptotic probability of a sentence in this class. This extends a result by Lidia Tendera, who in 1994 proved that every *rational* number in the unit interval is the asymptotic probability of a sentence in the class of second-order existential Kahr-Moore-Wang sentences *with* equality.

**Vega, Gina**. Caveat Emptor. Ethical Chauvinism in the Global Economy. *J Bus Ethics*, 16(12-13), 1353-1362, S 97.

The tendency of American business schools to teach a "universal" set of ethical standards and managerial perspectives can have a serious impact on the business practices of new graduates as well as on the success of companies desiring to do business globally. We need to become more sensitive to other cultural/ethical approaches and to sensitize our business students to them early in their academic process in order to encourage the use of *common-norming* to attain mutual economic benefit. We can understand this process through the application of anthropological principles to ethical constructs.

**Vega, José Fernádez**. Un diálogo con la tradición: Foucault en su contexto. *Cuad Etica*, 17-18, 73-83, 1994.

Foucault has been a theoretical revolutionary who has transformed our vision upon institutions and power and also our political perspective. This paper ponders on the possibilities of the Foucaultian view about body, freedom and power, considered as fighting strategies. The conclusion tries to show that Foucault's thought is not close neither to postmodern demoralization nor to political resignation.

**Vega, Luis**. La demostración "more geometrico": notas para la historia de una exploración. *Mathesis*, 10(1), 25-45, F 94.

The motto "more geometrico" hints—specially from the XVIIth Century—at the systematic (axiomatic) arrangement of deductive proofs according to what it was supposed to be the paradigm of Euclid's *Elements*. But this label has been liable to common misunderstandings from the historical (and even historiographical) point of view. My aim in this paper is to introduce some suitable distinctions (second order extrapolation *vs* geometrization, weak *vs* strong sense or use of the "more geometrico" programs) and summarily review in this light three main historical moments in which this kind of program becomes apparent, paying special attention to its outstanding development in the XVIIth Century. Finally, some critical hints and problems are outlines.

**Vega Encabo, Jesús**. "Verdad y tecnología" in *Verdad: lógica, representación y mundo*, Villegas Forero, L, 119-134. Santiago de Compostela, Univ Santiago Comp, 1996.

In this paper, I discuss the need of truth as an epistemic value operating in technological development. I propose a new way to overcome the difficulties that a realist framework has to find an explanatory role for the concept of truth in technological activities.

**Vega Rodríguez, Margarita**. El soporte cognoscitivo de la filosofía en la postmodernidad. *Anu Filosof*, 29(2), 1061-1075, 1996.

The habitual knowledge offers the postmodernity philosophy the necessary cognitive support for its thematic opening. That is why the notion of habitual knowledge allows the continuation of the philosophy and, specifically, about metaphysics.

**Vegas González, Serafín**. La revisión neohistoricista del significado de la historia de la filosofía. *An Seminar Hist Filosof*, 10, 11-42, 1993.

La influencia del pensamiento analítico tradicional ha sido un factor determinante de que un amplio sector de filósofos acabara por desentenderse de la historia de la filosofía. Las vicisitudes sufridas en nuestros días por la filosofía analítica han conducido al movimiento postanalítico a acercarse a los problemas de la historia de la filosofía. La muestra más característica de ello acaso pueda ser el peculiar replanteamiento neohistoricista llevado a cabo, desde posiciones diferentes, por Macintyre y por Rorty. Este neohistoricismo se revela, sin embargo, insuficiente para solucionar el viejo problema de las relaciones entre la filosofía y su historia, incluyendo aquí la configuración del *historiador* que debe acompañar al *filósofo* cuando trata de adentrarse en el terreno de la historia de la filosofía.

**Vegas González, Serafín** and Klappenbach, Augusto and Núñez Tomás, Paloma. *Razón, Naturaleza y Libertad: En Torno a La Crítica de la Razón Práctica* Kantiana. X, Unknown, 1996.

**Vegetti, Mario** and Conant, James and Berti, Enrico. La fragilità del bene: Fortuna ed etica nella tragedia e nella filosofia greca di Martha C. Nussbaum. *Iride*, 10(20), 157-176, Ap 97.

For E. Berti the Aristotelian defended by Martha Nussbaum in her book *The Fragility of Goodness* is not conservative, because it conceives the human good as practicable in a society of "free and equal" citizens and because it proposes as method of philosophy the rational argumentation from the ways of thinking and speaking shared by the whole linguistic community (the *endoxa*). The only reserve advanced by the author to Nussbaum's thesis concerns the lack, in her book, of a clear distinction between the *endoxa* and the *phainomena*, which for Aristotle are all sort of opinions. J. Conant and M. Vegetti discuss other aspects of the book.

**Vegetti Finzi, Silvia**. Per la costruzione di un'autorità femminile. *Iride*, 8(15), 283-294, Ag 95.

Il saggio analizza l'enciclica *Evangelium vitae* da un punto di vista femminista e psicoanalitico, soffermandosi in particolare sul problema dell'aborto. L'Autrice propone di inserire la maternità negata, che nessuno persegue in quanto tale, nel processo generativo di cui rappresenta una crisi da interrogare e comprendere, prima che da condannare. Il Papa ha parole di vera sollecitudine nei confronti delle donne, ma non sembra aver fiducia nel lavoro che esse da tempo stanno compiendo su di sé e sulle relazioni fondamentali della loro vita: percorso indispensabile, secondo l'Autrice, per elaborare un'etica della maternità.

**Veit, E Theodore** and Baker, H Kent. Ethical Attitudes and Behavior of Investment Professionals in the United Kingdom. *Prof Ethics*, 5(1-2), 87-117, Spr-Sum 96.

**Veit, E Theodore** and Murphy, Michael R. Ethics Violations: A Survey of Investment Analysts. *J Bus Ethics*, 15(12), 1287-1297, D 96.

The authors analyze the responses to a mail survey of securities analysts who were asked about their ethical behavior and the ethical behavior of people with whom they work. The findings show the types of ethical violations that occur and the frequency with which they occur. The findings also show how respondents deal with observed violations of ethical behavior. All responses are analyzed to determine if differences exist between the responses of analysts having different characteristics (gender, age, years of employment, and education) and differences in employment circumstances (firm size, firm type, buy side/sell side, U.S./Canada)

**Velarde Lombraña, J**. "La Teoría Constructivista de la Verdad" in *Verdad: lógica, representación y mundo*, Villegas Forero, L, 135-141. Santiago de Compostela, Univ Santiago Comp, 1996.

The ground of this theory is the thesis of the identification of *knowledge* with *truth*. This thesis is essentially Platonic, but is generally present in the Greek classic philosophy, as well as in the principal philosophical systems: Thomism, Phenomenology,.... The thesis of the identification of *knowledge* with *truth* is reached from the notion of *gnoseologic field*: The knowledges (or truths) conform the gnoseologic fields, that is, disciplines, in function of the proper nature of the field's elements. (edited)

**Velasco, Mónica**. Language in Stories for Boys and Girls. *Thinking*, 13(2), 41-44, 1997.

**Velasco Gómez, Ambrosio**. "Racionalidad de las teorías políticas" in *La racionalidad: su poder y sus límites*, Nudler, Oscar (ed), 483-493. Barcelona, Ed Paidos, 1996.

**Velasquez, Manuel** and Brady, Neil. Natural Law and Business Ethics. *Bus Ethics Quart*, 7(2), 83-107, Mr 97.

We describe the Catholic natural law tradition by examining its origins in the medieval penitentials, the papal decretals, the writings of Thomas Aquinas and seventeenth century casuistry. Catholic natural law emerges as a flexible ethic that conceives of human nature as rational and as oriented to certain basic goods that ought to be pursued and whose pursuit is made possible by the virtues. We then identify four approaches to natural law that have evolved within the United States during the twentieth century, including the traditionalist, proportionalist, right reason and historicist approaches. (edited)

**Velásquez Delgado, Jorge**. Estado, soberanía y democracia. *Analogia*, 11(1), 73-85, Ja-Je 97.

**Velayos Castelo, Carmen**. Oikeiosis: la naturalización de lo moral en el estoicismo antiguo. *Pensamiento*, 204(52), 441-449, S-D 96.

**Velázquez, Héctor** and Gavito, Diana. El hombre como sistema libre, en el pensamiento de Leonardo Polo. *Anu Filosof*, 29(2), 651-663, 1996.

The only valid consideration of human being is what takes the person in his complexity. Human being is an *open system* in his relation with the medium. But, attending his rationality (deepest and most radical dimension), human being is *free system*. So, he is able to assert oneself ends according values.

**Velázquez Fernández, Héctor**. La generación absoluta, según la exposición aquiniana de Aristóteles. *Topicos*, 9-22, 1996.

The distinction between *absolute* and *relative generation* implies the difference between *substance* and *not-substance*, instead of that between *being* and *not-being*, according to Aristotle. This paper tries to explain how this distinction makes possible to talk about the *absolute not-being*, an avoidable concept when Aristotle tries to explain the *absolute* generation and corruption without appealing to *the nothing*.

**Veldman, Wim** and Waaldijk, Frank. Some Elementary Results in Intuitionistic Model Theory. *J Sym Log*, 61(3), 745-767, S 96.

We establish constructive refinements of several well-known theorems in elementary model theory. The additive group of the real numbers may be embedded elementarily into the additive group of pairs of real numbers, constructively as well as classically.

**Velek, Josef** and Honneth, Axel. Integrity and Disrespect (and J. Velek Commentary) (in Czech). *Filosof Cas*, 45(2), 297-309, 1997.

**Velema, Wyger R E**. Republican Readings of Montesquieu: *The Spirit of the Laws* in the Dutch Republic. *Hist Polit Thought*, 18(1), 43-63, Spr 97.

**Vélissaropoulos, D**. Hommage à Anastase Léventis. *Diotima*, 25, 133, 1997.

**Velkley, Richard L**. "Realizing Nature in the Self: Schelling on Art and Intellectual Intuition" in *Figuring the Self: Subject, Absolute, and Others in Classical German Philosophy,* Zöller, Günter (ed), 149-168. Albany, SUNY Pr, 1997.

**Velleman, J David**. How To Share An Intention. *Phil Phenomenol Res*, 57(1), 29-50, Mr 97.

Existing accounts of shared intention (by Bratman, Searle and others) do not claim that a single token of intention can be jointly framed and executed by multiple agents; rather, they claim that multiple agents can frame distinct, individual intentions in such a way as to qualify as jointly intending something. In this respect, the existing accounts do not show that intentions can be shared in any literal sense. This article argues that, in failing to show how intentions can be literally shared, these accounts fail to resolve what seems problematic in the notion of shared intention. It then offers an account in which the problem of shared intention is resolved, because intention can indeed be literally shared. This account is derived from Margaret Gilbert's notion of a "pool of wills," to which it applies Searle's definition of intention.

**Vellino, André**. The Relative Complexity of Analytic Tableaux and SL-Resolution. *Stud Log*, 52(2), 323-337, My 93.

In this paper we describe an improvement of Smullyan's analytic tableau method for the propositional calculus-Improved Parent Clash Restricted (IPCR) tableau and show that it is equivalent to SL-resolution in complexity.

**Veloso, Paulo A S**. Is Fork Set-Theoretical?. *Bull Sec Log*, 26(1), 20-30, Mr 97.

We examine the set-theoretical nature of fork algebras, namely to what extent fork algebras of relations are really set-based. We show that every fork algebra of relations (FAR, for short) can be represented by a Cartesian FAR by making use of the room provided by the neutral element *I* for relational composition. If one insists in taking *I* as the concrete identity (diagonal) relation, then such representation is not always possible: we show that there are many interesting FARs that cannot be represented by proper Cartesian FARs.

**Veltman, Frank** and Groeneveld, Willem and Van der Does, Jaap. An Update on "Might". *J Log Lang Info*, 6(4), 361-380, O 97.

This paper is on the update semantics for "might" of Veltman (1996). Three consequence relations are introduced and studied in an abstract setting. Next we present sequent-style systems for each of the consequence relations. We show the logics to be complete and decidable. The paper ends with a syntactic cut elimination result.

**Venema, Yde**. Tree Models and (Labeled) Categorial Grammar. *J Log Lang Info*, 5(3-4), 253-277, O 96.

This paper studies the relation between some extensions of the nonassociative Lambek Calculus *N L* and their interpretation in tree models (free groupoids). We give various examples of sequents that are valid in tree models, but not derivable in *N L*. We argue why tree models may not be axiomatizable if we add finitely many derivation rules to *N L*, and proceed to consider labeled calculi instead. We define two labeled categorial calculi, and prove soundness and completeness for interpretations that are 'almost' the intended one, namely for tree models where some branches of some trees may be responsible all branches of all trees must be infinitely extending. Extrapolating from the experiences in our quite simple systems, we briefly discuss some problems involved with the introduction of labels in categorial grammar, and argue that many of the basic questions are not yet understood.

**Venkat Rao, D**. The Ruptured Idiom: Of Dallmayr, Matilal and Ramanujan's 'Way of Thinking'. *J Indian Counc Phil Res*, 14(2), 99-121, Ja-Ap 97.

**Venkatalakshmi, M**. Epistemology of Mysticism. *Indian Phil Quart*, 23(3-4), 439-454, Jl-O 96.

The purpose of this article has been to provide epistemic justification for mystic experiences in general and Sri Aurobindo in particular since serious criticisms have been raised against its validity. The mystic claims have been questioned on the following grounds. 1) Lack of unanimity in mystic experience, 2) It is ineffable and unverifiable, 3) Does not fulfill the epistemic conditions for knowledge claim, 4) They are subjective experiences, and 5) It is unscientific. (edited)

**Venkatalakshmi, M**. Epistemology of Sri Aurobindo. *J Indian Counc Phil Res*, 14(1), 111-136, S-D 96.

There is a general misconceived notion that there is no epistemology in Sri Aurobindo's philosophy. But a deeper study of his works like, *The Life Divine, The Synthesis of Yoga,* and *Savitri,* reveals that his philosophy provides an epistemological substructure which forms the basis for its metaphysical superstructure. The author, by gathering the scattered ideas on epistemic problems, has formulated an organized theory of epistemology of Sri Aurobindo. The main objective of this article is not only to show that there is an epistemological theory in Sri Aurobindo, but also to show that it transcends the limitations of existing theories of epistemology and integral in nature. Sri Aurobindo gives a new dimension to epistemic approach by revising the existing standards of knowledge. Sri Aurobindo's concept of "supramental consciousness," "integral knowledge" and "logic of the infinite" are a unique contribution to epistemology. The whole epistemology of Sri Aurobindo is based upon three basic presuppositions: a) All experiences are real and worthy of philosophical interpretation; b) All possible knowledge is within the power of humanity; c) Knowledge must be integral.

**Venn, Couze**. Beyond Enlightenment? After the Subject of Foucault, Who Comes?. *Theor Cult Soc*, 14(3), 1-28, Ag 97.

**Venter, J J**. Mechanistic Individualism Versus Organismic Totalitarianism: Toward a Neo-Calvinist Perspective. *Ultim Real Mean*, 20(1), 41-60, Mr 97.

**Ventura, Antonino**. Pensiero e realtà nella gnoseologia di S. Tommaso D'Aquino. *Sapienza*, 50(1), 41-63, 1997.

**Venturelli, Domenico**. Etica e metafisica: Alcune riflessioni di Kant sulla filosofia di Platone. *G Metaf*, 18(1-2), 215-226, Ja-Ag 96.

**Venuti, Lawrence**. Translation, Philosophy, Materialism. *Rad Phil*, 79, 24-34, S-O 96.

**Venzi, Lorenzo** and Scarelli, Antonino. Nonparametric Statistics in Multicriteria Analysis. *Theor Decis*, 43(1), 89-105, Jl 97.

The paper deals with a method of hierarchization of alternatives in a multicriteria environment by means of statistical nonparametric procedures. For each criterion, alternatives are disposed on an ordinal scale. After that a procedure similar to ANOVA is activated on the data. The differences relating to the average ranks of each action are used to build the hierarchical algorithm. The concept of outranking, in a probabilistic meaning, is reached in this way. Thereafter, we arrive at the concept of dominance using pairwise comparisons. A case study is presented which implements the methodological suggestion.

**Verbeke, Willem** and Ouwerkerk, Cok and Peelen, Ed. Exploring the Contextual and Individual Factors on Ethical Decision Making of Salespeople. *J Bus Ethics*, 15(11), 1175-1187, N 96.

This paper studies how salespeople make ethical decisions. For this purpose a structural model has been developed which configures how the organization's environment, the organization's climate, and personality traits affect ethical decision making. Internal communication and the choice of a control system especially affect ethical decision making. Internal communication also affects the attraction of salespeople with unethical personality traits (Machiavellism), while the control system affects the ethical climate. Ethical climate and salespeople's personality traits also affect the ethical decision making. In fact the study shows that ethical decision making can be influenced by management.

**Verburg, Rudi M** and Wiegel, Vincent. On the Compatibility of Sustainability and Economic Growth. *Environ Ethics*, 19(3), 247-265, Fall 97.

It is generally assumed that sustainable development and economic growth are compatible objectives. Because this assumption has been left unspecified, the debate on sustainability and growth has remained vague and confusing. Attempts at specification not only involve clarification of the interrelation of the two concepts, but also, we argue, require a philosophical approach in which the concepts of sustainability and economic growth are analyzed in the context of our frame of reference. We suggest that if the notion of sustainability is to be taken seriously, the conflicting conceptual and normative orientations between the two concepts require the reconsideration of our frame of reference.

**Verdú, Ventura** and Font, Josep Maria. The Lattice of Distributive Closure Operators Over an Algebra. *Stud Log*, 52(1), 1-13, F 93.

In our previous paper "Algebraic Logic for Classical Conjunction and Disjunction", we studied some relations between the fragment L of classical logic having just conjunction and disjunction and the variety D of distributive lattices, within the context of algebraic logic. The central tool in that study was a class of closure operators which we called distributive and one of its main results was that for any algebra A of type (2,2) there is an isomorphism between the lattices of all D-congruences of A and of all distributive closure operators over A. In the present paper we study the lattice structure of this last set, give a description of its finite and infinite operations and obtain a topological representation. We also apply the mentioned isomorphism and other results to obtain proofs with a logical flavour for several new or well-known lattice-theoretical properties, like Hashimoto's characterization of distributive lattices and Priestley's topological representation of the congruence lattice of a bounded distributive lattice.

**Verdú Berganza, Ignacio**. Aspectos generales del pensamiento en el siglo XIV. *An Seminar Hist Filosof*, 10, 195-208, 1993.

What importance have the thought during the XIV century for the history? This period was a change in the way of facing the world, impelled by Petrarca, Boccaccio, Salutati, Giotto.... Science opened a new way of incomparable historical repercussions. In theology, with the mystic movement of Master Eckhart, we can detach Ockham, Bradwine, Gregory of Rimini, Wiclif of Hus, personalities that cannot be overlooked when you study the influences of the XIVth century in the Reformation. Without the study of the Ockhamist movement, the development of logic or the resurgence of the Augustianism, we couldn't understand the change of philosophy and general thought in that century.

**Verdú Berganza, Ignacio**. La estructura formal del *De causa Dei* de Thomas Bradwardine. *An Seminar Hist Filosof*, 13, 149-164, 1996.

The aims of this article are two. The first is to show what is the structure of the form in the more important book of Thomas Bradwardine's work: *De causa Dei contra Pelagium et de virtute causarum*. Bradwardine was a brilliant thinker of the XIV century, who had a prolific influence in that century and in later ones. The second is to study the method (that could be named "a mathematical method") he used in his work, trying to show why Bradwardine structured *De causa Dei* so, and its consequences.

**Verene, Donald Phillip**. Comentario a la *Reprensión de la metafísica de Renato Descartes, Benito Espinosa y Juan Locke*: Un añadido a la *Ciencia Nueva*. *Cuad Vico*, 5/6, 155-167, 1995/96.

Vico intended the "Reprehension" to be a short chapter added to the section on "Poetic Metaphysics" of Book 2 of the *New Science*. This commentary takes as starting point that it is Vico's most concise statement of his objections to all forms of modern metaphysics.

**Verene, Donald Phillip**. *Philosophy and the Return to Self-Knowledge*. New Haven, Yale Univ Pr, 1997.

Focusing in particular on the traditions of some of the late Greeks and the Romans, Renaissance humanism and the thought of Giambattista Vico, this book's concern is to revive the ancient Delphic injunction "know thyself," an idea of civil wisdom that Verene finds has been missing since Descartes. The author recovers the meaning of the vital relations that poetry, myth and rhetoric had with philosophy in thinkers like Cicero, Quintilian, Isocrates, Pico, Vives and Vico. He arrives at a conception of philosophy as a form of memory that requires both rhetoric and poetry to accomplish self-knowledge.

**Vergara, Eliseo Cruz**. Idealismo y materialismo: Max Horkheimer y la constitución del conocimiento en la ciencia social. *Dialogos*, 32(70), 53-108, Jl 97.

This essay describes the way Horkheimer develops in his early articles the opinion that in order to establish the foundations of critical social science, philosophy should follow the materialistic tradition. Metaphysics (Kant) and the idealistic identity of concept and reality in philosophy (Hegel) make impossible not only the critical knowledge of social reality but also the contribution of social theory to the possible transformation of the world. This conclusion assumes that social science *explains* theoretically the world. But if according to many others thinkers the social science in general shows likewise a dimension of self-knowledge of man in his world, may be the idealistic identity of concept and being should be reconsider in a more positive view. Until now the Marxist tradition that Horkheimer represents has been blind to this approach.

**Vergara, Julia**. Cualidades secundarias y autoconocimiento. *Analisis Filosof*, 17(1), 5-25, My 97.

Self-knowledge as a sort of knowledge can be justified through two kinds of paradigm: observational and inferential. This paper criticizes both epistemic lines and suggests instead that first-person statements exhibit the same logical structure as statements about secondary qualities, as proposed by Crispin Wright. The paper introduces a variant to this proposal: self-deception should not be seen as threatening the biconditional that expresses that self-knowledge is constitutive of intentionality. This is the constitutive thesis.

**Verharen, Charles**. Philosophy and Critical Thinking. *Inquiry (USA)*, 16(3), 64-75, Spr 97.

This essay criticizes contemporary canonical or rule-governed approaches to teaching logic or critical thinking as unphilosophical. Philosophy's interest is in the reasoning that leads to rules rather than in the rules themselves. Categorical syllogisms should be introduced to help students concentrate on the reasoning behind syllogistic definitions and rules rather than to double-check arguments. A philosophical introduction to logic should outline the history of the separation of syllogistic and symbolic logic rather than focusing on problem sets in elementary symbolic logic. Critical thinking courses ought to concentrate on "real-life" conditions for accepting scientific hypotheses rather than Mill's "rules" for induction.

**Verheggen, Claudine**. Davidson's Second Person. *Phil Quart*, 47 (188), 361-369, Jl 97.

I argue that Davidson has not succeeded in establishing the claim that only a person who has interacted linguistically with another could have a language, but that he has provided many of the materials out of which a successful argument could be built. Chief among these materials are the claims that some version of externalism about meaning is true, that possession of a language requires possession of the concept of objectivity, and hence that the issue here concerns the identity of the external event that makes possible possession of the concept of objectivity. I end by presenting some reasons for thinking that only interpersonal linguistic interaction could play this role.

**Verhulst, Steve** and Spielman, Bethany. Non-Heart-Beating Cadaver Procurement and the Work of Ethics Committees. *Cambridge Quart Healthcare Ethics*, 6(3), 282-287, Sum 97.

Recent ethics literature suggests that issues involved in nonheartbeating (NHB) organ procurement are both highly charged and rather urgent. Some fear that NHB is a public relations disaster waiting to happen or that it will create a backlash against organ donation. The purpose of the study described below was to assess ethics committees' current level of involvement in and readiness for addressing the difficult issues that NHB organ retrieval raises—either proactively through policy development or concurrently through ethics consultation.

**Veríssimo Serrao, Adriana**. A imagem de Ludwig Feuerbach na literatura mais recente (1988-1993). *Philosophica (Portugal)*, 123-142, 1993.

**Vermaas, Pieter E**. Unique Transition Probabilities in the Modal Interpretation. *Stud Hist Phil Mod Physics*, 27B(2), 133-159, Je 96.

The modal interpretation of quantum theory ascribes at each instant physical magnitudes with definite values to quantum systems. Starting from certain natural requirements, I determine unique solutions for the evolution of these possessed magnitudes in free systems and in special cases of interacting systems. The evolution is given in terms of transition probabilities that relate the values of the possessed magnitudes at one instant to the values at a second instant. I also determine a joint property ascription to a composite system and its separate subsystems. Finally, I give a proof that the predictions of the modal interpretation with respect to measurement outcomes agree with the predictions of the standard interpretation.

**Vermeulen, Kees** and Visser, Albert. Dynamic Bracketing and Discourse Representation. *Notre Dame J Form Log*, 37(2), 321-365, Spr 96.

In this paper we describe a framework for the construction of entities that can serve as interpretations of arbitrary contiguous chunks of text. An important part of the paper is devoted to describing stacking cells, or the proposed meanings for bracket-structures.

**Vernant, Denis**. Le statut de la vérité dans le calcul implicationnel de Russell en 1903. *Rev Int Phil*, 51(200), 221-229, Je 97.

**Verweyen, Hansjürgen**. Social Contract among Devils. *Ideal Stud*, 26(2), 189-202, Wint 96.

In his essay, "On Eternal Peace", Kant deals with the problem: "To organize a multitude of rational beings who demand universal laws for their preservation, but each of whom is secretly inclined to exempt himself from them". Kant's concept of a "social contract among devils" is no less radical in its abstraction from all presuppositions of morality than the political theories of Hobbes, Adam Smith, Machiavelli, or Glaucon (in Plato's *Republic*). What is the value of his theory of an automatic construction of a just society out of the free interplay of enlightened egotism, considered in itself? What is its place within a systematic conception of a universal moral order?

**Vescovini, Graziella Federici**. L'espressività del cielo di Marsilio Ficino, lo Zodiaco medievale e Plotino. *Bochumer Phil Jrbh*, 1, 111-125, 1996.

This essay provides an analysis of Marsilio Ficino's doctrine of the heavens, especially as this is developed in his commentary on Plotinus' *Enneads* with reference to contemporary debates in Florence concerning the legitimacy of astrology and in view of new interpretations of attendant problematic issues. Particular attention is given to Ficino's early works, such as the *Disputatio contra iudicium astrologorum*, as well as to his commentary on *Enneads* 4, 4-42 and his *De vita*. The leading interest of the essay consists in the attempt to clarify Ficino's reception of the medieval doctrine of the heavens, most pointedly the theory propounded by Peter of Abano in his *Lucidator dubitabililum astronomiae* of 1310.

**Veselinovic-Hofman, Mirjana**. The Nature of the Reception of European Musical Phenomena as a Paradigm of the Genuineness of Serbian Music—System of Values and Artistic Horizons. *Ultim Real Mean*, 20(2 & 3), 191-195, Je-S 97.

The purpose of the paper is to demonstrate an attempt to examine the *code of Serbian* music from the aspect of its reception of the musical phenomena which did not originate on its own soil. The conclusion reached is that the paradigm of the reception of new and alien phenomena in Serbian music reveals a system of values functioning in accordance with the following hierarchy: (1) genuineness as a basis, (2) insight into the relevant facts and their mastery, (3) ability to select them, (4) creative application based on a certain degree of elasticity and efficiency of the cause-effect relation between what is innate and acquired, and (5) the artistic genuineness of the achieved result. So, new horizons in Serbian music entail the span between two forms of authenticity.

**Vesilind, P Aarne**. There is No Such Thing as Environmental Ethics. *Sci Eng Ethics*, 2(3), 307-318, Jl 96.

Engineers and scientists, whose professional responsibilities often influence the natural environment, have sought to develop an environmental ethic that will be in tune with their attitudes toward the nonhuman environment, and that will assist them in decision making regarding questions of environmental quality. In this paper the classical traditions in normative ethics are explored in an attempt to formulate such an environmental ethic. I conclude, however, that because the discipline of ethics is directed at person-person interactions, ethics as a scholarly discipline does not help us understand how we ought to treat nonhuman nature. We, therefore, cannot look to ethics as a source for understanding our attitudes and for providing guidance to our actions with regard to the environment. To do so is to ask too much of ethics. If we are to find an acceptable environmental morality, it must come from a new paradigm. One approach might be to understand our attitudes on the basis of spirituality, modelled after animistic religions.

**Vest, Charles M**. "Research Universities: Overextended, Underfocused; Overstressed, Underfunded" in *The American University: National Treasure or Endangered Species?,* Ehrenberg, Ronald G (ed), 43-57. Ithaca, Cornell Univ Pr, 1997.

**Vetlesen, Arne J**. Worlds Apart? Habermas and Levinas. *Phil Soc Crit,* 23(1), 1-20, 1997.

Though doubtless two of the leading philosophers in ethics today, Habermas and Levinas have yet to be subjected to systematic comparison. This essay undertakes a first step. Differences of terminology aside, Habermas and Levinas can be seen to pursue, via separate routes, a similar core idea. I term this the idea of immanent normativity. While Habermas locates an unchosen normative pull in the medium of interpersonal communication, Levinas locates an unconditional ethical command in the Other as face. Hence, they unite in strongly opposing social contract theory's notion of morality as optional and of responsibility as conditional upon self-interest.

**Vetö, Miklos**. Etre et Apparition selon la doctrine de la science de 1812. *Fichte-Studien,* 12, 375-385, 1997.

**Vezjak, Boris**. Hegelianism in Slovenia: A Short Introduction. *Bull Hegel Soc Gt Brit,* 34, 1-12, Autumn-Wint 96.

The aim of this article is to outline the present philosophical situation in Slovenia, inasmuch as it is linked with the development of Hegelian thought and influenced by the work of Hegel. I briefly discuss some historical characteristics of its origin, and then introduce some aspects of Hegel's philosophy, as understood by Slovenian *lacaniens,* trying to summarize their reading of Hegel and consequently point out how deeply their work on Lacan is inspired by him.

**Viano, Carlo Augusto**. L'embrione è arrivato tra noi. *Iride,* 9(19), 541-553, S-D 96.

**Vianty, Bernard**. Pascal croyait-il en la loi naturelle?. *Maritain Stud,* 12, 67-76, 1996.

**Viau, Marcel**. La fonction argumentative dans les discours théologiques: L'exemple de la *Grammaire de l'assentiment* de Neuman. *Laval Theol Phil,* 52(3), 681-701, O 96.

This article intends to show that basic elements of rhetoric are to be found at the roots of many theological discourses. We will proceed here from a well-known example: Henry Newman's *Grammar of Assent.* Some maintain that Newman was a forerunner of what today is called "epistemic rhetoric", that is a rhetoric with a truth claim. One can indeed find something similar in Newman, in his assimilation of rhetorical judgments in aesthetics and ethics. Rhetoric may thus become an affective tool to solve epistemic problems related to theological discourses.

**Vicari, Dario**. "Il Luogo Della Filosofia: La paradossalità della *Seinsfrage* nel giovane Heidegger" in *Soggetto E Verità: La questione dell'uomo nella filosofia contemporanea,* Fagiuoli, Ettore, 33-50. 20136 Milano, Mimesis, 1996.

**Vicente Burgoa, Lorenzo**. Berkeley: Crítica de las ideas abstractas: La abstracción como simple semántica. *Daimon Rev Filosof,* 12, 49-60, Ja-Je 96.

Il ne manque pas des interprétations philosophiques, qui prétendent de se mettre a l'abri de la critique empiriste de la connaissance abstraite, comme s'il s'agissait d'une théorie sans aucun sense, désormais depuis long temps refutée. Pour tout cela nous pensons qu'il n'est pas inutile ou absurde de mettre attention, encore une fois, aux textes fondamentaux et de les soumettre à de nouveaux examens. Dans cet essai nous nous attachons spécialement à la critique de Berkeley, qui a porté sa recherche avec un indubitable sens de la sincérité. D'ailleurs, el est autant possible que sa critique soi plutôt efficiente en face d'une théorie de l'abstraction, celle-ci conçu comme une négation séparative; ce que n'est pas l'authentique conception des abstractionistes classiques. Pour tout cela il est bien possible que la conclusion de Berkeley à l'égard des idées abstraites doit être prise sous toute réserve

**Vico, Giambattista** and Visconti, Gian Galeazzo (ed). *Varia: Il De Mente Heroica* e gli Scritti Latini Minori. Napoli, Guida, 1996.

La rinnovata edizione delle opere di Vico, ispirata a rigorosi criteri di critica testuale, rispondendo alla richiesta di vecchi e nuovi lettori, consacra la realizzata familiarità con Vico, promossa e assicurata dall'impegno di filosofi, storici, filologi, convenuti a decifrare il problema Vico nei punti centrali e periferici, negli antecedenti e negli influssi del suo pensiero, liberando dall'antico, tradizionale timore dell'oscurità della pagina vichiana, ardua e superba. (publisher)

**Vidiella, Graciela** and Bertomeu, María Julia. Persona Moral y Justicia Distributiva. *Agora (Spain),* 14(2), 81-97, 1995.

**Vidricaure, André**. Problèmes de philosophie sociale au Québec: l'idée de pauvreté après 1840. *Maritain Stud,* 11, 98-145, 1995.

**Viegas, Pedro**. O tema da existência na *Nova Dilucidatio* de Kant. *Philosophica (Portugal),* 111-127, 1994.

The analysis of the existence theme in *Nova Dilucidatio* from Kant constitutes the aim of the article. After a brief introduction to the possible way of making the theme clear in the Kantian *corpus,* the analysis concentrates itself in the precritical text above mentioned and tries to prove its argumentative structure already indicts a surpass, in particular in its methodological premises, of the rationalistic ontology.

**Vieillard-Baron, Jean-Louis**. Bergson et Nabert, lecteurs de Fichte. *Fichte-Studien,* 13, 89-107, 1997.

**Vieira Silva, Maria**. Gerência da Qualidade Total: Conservaçao ou Superaçao do Processo de Alienaçao. *Educ Filosof,* 9(17), 209-225, Ja-Je 95.

**Vienne, Jean-Michel**. "*Assent* chez les Platoniciens de Cambridge" in *Mind Senior to the World,* Baldi, Marialuisa, 55-74. Milano, FrancoAngeli, 1996.

The neo-Platonist theory of assent has interesting epistemic implications. According to Cudworth, *Assent* is necessary only in probabilities (faith,...) where is judgment, and is useless in 'knowledge', where is evidence. This distinction is overcome by More and mainly by Norris, in relation with his introduction of the distinction between meaning and truth, parallel to the Malebranchist distinction between understanding and will: in order to know as well as to believe, you need first to understand the meaning and then to assent to the proposition and so to produce its truth.

**Vienne, Jean-Michel**. Les rapports entre raison et foi à la lumière de la métaphore de la vision. *Rev Phil Fr,* 1, 45-58, Ja-Mr 97.

Perceiving things is currently used as a metaphor for perceiving ideas. But the metaphor is misleading in that it makes it impossible to distinguish between the rationalist's intuition and the enthusiast's illuminism. This article evaluates three solutions given in the seventeenth and eighteenth centuries: a) through an external criteria (Locke), b) through the classical distinction between the external aspect of content and the internal aspect of assent (Malebranche, Norris, Collins and Berkeley), c) through the pure internal criterion of self-examination (Shaftesbury).

**Vieweg, Klaus**. El principio de reconocimiento en la teoría filosófica del derecho político externo de Hegel. *An Seminar Hist Filosof,* 13, 181-208, 1996.

Hier wird eine Aktualisierung des hegelschen Denkens in Hinsicht auf die politische Philosophie des äusseren Staatsrechts vorgeschlagen, die den Spuren von Kants *Zum ewigen Frieden* folgt und zwar mit der Absicht, eine "mittlere Bestimmung" zwischen leerem Liberalismus bzw. abstraktem Universalismus und Multikulturalismus bzw. Relativismus (welcher, auf dem Grund der unverwechselbaren Identität der Völker, jede Verteidigung der allgemeinen Würde der Person prinzipiell zerstört) zu finden. Dazu sieht man eine mögliche Lösung in der Idee einer interstaatlichen "inhaltlichsubstantiellen Anerkennung", die allmählich die Kriege durch "metaphorische Wettstreite" ersetzen soll.

**Vieweg, Klaus**. Man kannte mich, als man mich rufte: Die Berufung des Magister Fichte an die Gesamt-Akademie Jena im Jahre 1794. *Fichte-Studien,* 9, 47-57, 1997.

**Vigo, Alejandro G**. Temporalidad y trascendencia: La concepción heideggeriana de la trascendencia intencional en *Sein und Zeit. Acta Phil,* 6(1), 137-153, 1997.

"This paper deals with Heidegger's conception of the intentional transcendence of the Dasein, in so far as it is connected with temporality. The intentional transcendence of the Dasein is characterized by di-dimensionality and bi-horizontality. This intentional transcendence involves an ontological—opened through several forms of object-intentionality—as well as an ontic dimension, that is possible by the former. The 'horizon'—in Heidegger's jargon —of every form of intentional reference to objects are 'being' and 'time'. The paper finally deals with the connection of this conception referred to above with his theories about the matter and the method of ontology."

**Vijay-Shanker, K** and Rogers, James and Backofen, Rolf. A First-Order Axiomatization of the Theory of Finite Trees. *J Log Lang Info,* 4(1), 5-39, 1995.

We provide first-order axioms for the theories of finite trees with bounded branching and finite trees with arbitrary (finite) branching. The signature is chosen to express, in a natural way, those properties of trees most relevant to linguistic theories. These axioms provide a foundation for results in linguistics that are based on reasoning formally about such properties. We include some observations on the expressive power of these theories relative to traditional language complexity classes.

**Vijh, Ashok K**. Reflections on Peer Review Practices in Committees Selecting Laureates for Prestigious Awards and Prizes: Some Relevant and Irrelevant Criteria. *Sci Eng Ethics,* 2(4), 389-394, O 96.

An important function in all scholarly and academic activities is the publication in the peer review system. One aspect of this peer review evaluation is service on committees judging candidates for important awards, prizes and fellowships. Some reflective observations on this process are made in which a number of factors determining the final choice are identified. It is pointed out that the decisions of such committees are based not only on relevant and objective criteria but are also influenced by a number of irrelevant criteria; caution must be exercised to minimize the effect of the latter factors in order to maintain the highest ethical standards in the selection process. The ranking practices of awards committees, national academies and learned societies are briefly reviewed by pointing out some ethical pitfalls, anecdotal incidents, and the ways to avoid the tarnishing of the selection process.

**Vijh, Ashok K**. Some Remarks on Scientific Positivism and Constructivist Epistemology in Science. *Sci Eng Ethics,* 2(1), 5-8, J 96.

**Vila-Cha, Joao J**. Transcendental is the Difference: Derrida's Deconstruction of Husserl's Phenomenology of Language. *Rev Port Filosof,* 52(1-4), 967-988, Ja-D 96.

In this article an attempt is made to follow Derrida's *deconstruction* of Husserl's phenomenology, in particular of his philosophy of language. The aim is to detect the possibility of a new beginning on the path of thinking. First, we give attention to the problems associated with the nature of signification. Then we try to identify some of the wanderings and ambiguities inherent to the Husserlean description of meaning. And, finally, an effort is made to formulate the Derridean "position" in terms of a new, negative, transcendental dimension—the one abiding in *diffe(a)ence,* i.e., in the (non)principle of ontological *an-archy.*

**Vilanova Arias, Javier**. "Lógica condicional con múltiples operadores" in *Verdad: lógica, representación y mundo,* Villegas Forero, L, 219-229. Santiago de Compostela, Univ Santiago Comp, 1996.

The aim of this communication is to present and discuss a conditional logic, MCL, whose main novelty is the inclusion of a variety of conditional connectives, each one corresponding to a different degree of entailment of the consequent by the antecedent of the conditional sentence: conceptual, physical, actual and contingent implications. (edited)

**Vilanova Arias, Javier**. Enunciados causales de Burks y contra-fácticos substanciales. *Agora (Spain)*, 15(1), 163-171, 1996.

This article analyses Burks's *Logic of Causal Sentences* (Burks 1951, 1977) in the light of subsequent research on conditional logic. Two kinds of conditional sentence are used to test the expressiveness and conceptual validity of Burks's logic: accidental counterfactuals, in which the antecedent is contingently false in the actual world and substantive counterfactuals: gnomological sentences in which the antecedent is physically impossible in the actual world. The limitations hindering the formalization of these kinds of sentence in Burks's theory are diagnosed and are overcome by introducing additional conditional operators in the logic of causal sentences and by making use of the notion of similarity among possible worlds in the associated semantics.

**Villa, Vittorio**. Legal Theory and Value Judgments. *Law Phil*, 16(4), 447-477, Jl 97.

The aim of the paper is that of putting into question the dichotomy between fact-judgments and value judgments in the legal domain, with its epistemological presuppositions (descriptivist image of knowledge) and its methodological implications for legal knowledge (value freedom principle and neutrality thesis). The basic question that I will try to answer is whether and on what conditions strong ethical value-judgments belong within legal knowledge. (edited)

**Villacañas, José L**. Ethischer Neu-Fichteanismus und Geschichts-philosophie: Zur soziopolitischen Rezeption Fichtes im 20. Jahrhundert. *Fichte-Studien*, 13, 193-219, 1997.

**Villacañas Berlanga, José L**. "Hölderlin y Fichte o el sujeto descarriado en un mundo sin amor" in *El inicio del Idealismo alemán*, Market, Oswaldo, 343-363. Madrid, Ed Complutense, 1996.

Se parte de la afirmación fichteana: "Ich Bin Ausdruck einer Tathandlung" ("yo soy la expresión del ser de la suprema acción-hecho") para comprender el principio de la filosofía fichteana. En él se incluye el momento de la reflexión, gracias a la cual el Yo se constituye como acción propia, pero que introduce una escisión insalvable. A ello se contrapone la concepción de Hölderlin, que aboga por una reunificación intuitiva, estética y amorosa con lo Absoluto. Mientras que el Yo reflexivo de Fichte y de Kant están condenados a errar como cometas por un mundo sin amor, el poeta se lanza a la búsqueda del Ser ausente.

**Villacañas Berlanga, José L**. "Tönnies versus Weber: El debate Comunitarista desde la teoría social" in *Liberalismo y Comunitarismo: Derechos Humanos y Democracia*, Monsalve Solórzano, Alfonso (ed), 19-54. 36-46003 València, Alfons el Magnànim, 1996.

This essay hopes to throw light on the first episode of the controversy between liberalism and communitarianism through the work of Tönnies and Weber. It is important to analyze this from the positions reached by G. Simmel in that period. The basic conclusion reached is that Weber's work offers precise instruments by which to eliminate all ontological approaches to the theme of community. Therefore, there is no frontal clash with society as a structure put forward by liberalism. More than fixed entities, society and community are dynamic processes of greater or lesser intensity, degree and capacity of innovation.

**Villacañas Berlanga, José Luis**. De viajes y naufragios: Sobre el Libro de Santiago González Noriega *El Viaje a Siracusa: Ensayos de Filosofia y Teoría Social* Balsa de la Medusa 1994. *Daimon Rev Filosof*, 12, 121-129, Ja-Je 96.

This essay is a commentary on the aim of modern subjectivity to shape a new sense of the sacred. This is done through an analysis of the works of Molinos, S. Juan de la Cruz, Calvino, etc. Following the lines of disenchanted reality espoused by Max Weber, the author explains that all such essays are destined to fail. However, the certainty of that end does not replace the urgency or the temptation of attempting journey.

**Villalba de Tablón, Marisa**. Cuando las contradictorias son verdaderas. *Sapientia*, 52(201), 117-126, 1997.

**Villalobos, José**. Mathesis Universalis cartesiana. *Cuad Vico*, 5/6, 239-250, 1995/96.

Starting from the assumption that the dialogue with Descartes might appear to be an opportunity to think for himself, the author analyzes and disallows Descartes's recent and customary ("modern") image which has come down to us. It established the need to face up to the problem of thinking for himself within the frame of a new age, the so-called "radical age." In so doing, the author proposes to reclaim both a Descartes up-to-date image, not necessarily modern (since the modern age is already over) together with the notion of *mathesis universalis* without failing, however, to acknowledge that the rationalist reason has long collapsed and it can hardly be sustained in the very same way as Descartes did, though some of his claims might somehow be proven still valid. (edited)

**Villanueva, Enrique**. "Would More Acquaintance with the External World Relieve Epistemic Anxiety?" in *Perception*, Villanueva, Enrique (ed), 215-218. Atascadero, Ridgeview, 1996.

**Villanueva, Enrique** (ed). *Contents*. Atascadero, Ridgeview, 1995.

The papers in this volume are concerned with issues on content, concepts, holism, reference, *a priori* knowledge, computation, externalism, mental causation, realism and other subtopics. Those issues revolve on the frontiers of metaphysics, philosophy of mind and language and epistemology which have become prevalent in the volumes that form this *Philosophical Issues* series. It is good to remember one of the main aims of our society in organizing the conferences that give birth to these volumes, namely, to bring the main philosophers of our time to discuss the central issues of philosophy. Most of the papers in this volume were presented at the Seventh Annual Philosophy Conference of our Sociedad Filosófica Ibero Americana, SOFIA, held in Lisbon, Portugal. (edited)

**Villanueva, Enrique** (ed). *Perception*. Atascadero, Ridgeview, 1996.

The papers in this volume are concerned with issues on perceptual representation, functionalism, qualia, phenomenal externalism, acquaintance, realism, naturalism, rationality, shape and perceptual properties and other subtopics. Those issues spin on the frontiers of metaphysics, philosophy of mind and epistemology. The papers in this volume were presented at the Eighth Annual Philosophy Conference of our Sociedad Filosófica Ibero Americana, SOFIA, held in Cancún, México. (edited)

**Villegas, Luis**. Algunos Problemas de las Ciencias Reconstructivas. *Agora (Spain)*, 14(2), 31-39, 1995.

In this paper, the claim that Chomskian linguistics is a reconstructive science, in Habermas's sense is accepted. Then, assuming that metatheoretical position and in order to understand the Chomskian notion of "tacit knowledge of language", some of the problems put forward by the necessity to distinguish (propedeutically) among different types and levels of knowledge are discussed.

**Villegas Forero, L** and Martínez Vidal, C and Rivas Monroy, Uxía. *Verdad: lógica, representación y mundo*. Santiago de Compostela, Univ Santiago Comp, 1996.

This book corresponds to the Proceedings of the Symposium "Truth: Logic, Representation and World" (Santiago de Compostela, Spain, January 1996, from 17th to 20th). The volume is divided into the following sections: Truth Theories, Philosophy of Mathematics, Philosophy of Science, Philosophy of Language, Cognitive Sciences and Philosophy of Mind and Logic. The papers included in the different sections reflect the general and omnipresent character of the problem of truth in relation to research studies in semantics, representation and ontology.

**Vincent, Hubert**. Scepticisme et Usage du Monde. *Arch Phil*, 59(3), 403-425, Jl-S 96.

Perhaps one does injury to scepticism by classing it a critical theory of knowledge. Beyond this guide obvious aspect, it would probably be better to situate it in the broader context which Montaigne later would call the "use of the world". This article takes the second perspective, using a critique of the passion for glory as an introductory mechanism. Further, by means of an analysis of the sense of such expressions as "use of books", or the "use of the truth" and also through such experiences as sickness or rumor, we seek in the notion of exposition what seems to us an essential, aspect of this "use of the world".

**Vincent, Martínez Guzmán**. *Europa I El Progrés Sostingut*. Castelló, Univ Jaume I, 1993.

**Vine, Ian**. The Measure of Morality: Rethinking Moral Reasoning. *J Moral Educ*, 25(4), 455-466, D 96.

This critical notice examines themes highlighted by Peter E. Langford's book, *Approaches to the Development of Moral Reasoning* (Hove, Sussex: Lawrence Erlbaum Associates, 1995; ISSN 0959-3977). He presents a radical conceptual critique of Lawrence Kohlberg's highly influential psychological theory of stages in the acquisition of abstract and autonomous moral principles and an alternative to the 'strong interpretation' methodology used in assessing moral stages. Langford's data challenge the underlying Piagetian assumption that moral development equates with the conquest of egocentrism and of heteronomy.

**Vineberg, Susan**. Confirmation and the Indispensability of Mathematics to Science. *Proc Phil Sci Ass*, 3(Suppl), S256-S263, 1996.

Quine and Putnam argued for mathematical realism on the basis of the indispensability of mathematics to science. They claimed that the mathematics that is used in physical theories is confirmed along with those theories and that scientific realism entails mathematical realism. It is argued here that current theories of confirmation suggest that mathematics does not receive empirical support simply in virtue of being a part of well confirmed scientific theories and that the reasons for adopting a realist view of scientific theories do not support realism about mathematical entities, despite the use of mathematics in formulating scientific theory.

**Vineberg, Susan**. Dutch Books, Dutch Strategies and What They Show about Rationality. *Phil Stud*, 86(2), 185-201, My 97.

**Viney, Donald Wayne**. Jules Lequyer and the Openness of God. *Faith Phil*, 14(2), 212-235, Ap 97.

Until recently the most prominent defender of the openness of God was Charles Hartshorne. Evangelical thinkers are now defending similar ideas while being careful to distance themselves from the less orthodox dimensions of process theology. An overlooked figure in the debate is Jules Lequyer. Although process thinkers have praised Lequyer as anticipating their views, he may be closer in spirit to the evangelicals because of the foundational nature of his Catholicism. Lequyer's passionate defense of freedom conceived as a creative act as well as the theological implications he drew from this are examined for their relevance to the present discussion of the openness of God.

Viney, Donald Wayne 974 AUTHOR INDEX

**Viney, Donald Wayne**. Logic Crystallized. *Teach Phil*, 20(2), 143-154, Je 97.

This paper describes a three dimensional lattice structure, called the *Wachter crystal*, which presents, in a visually striking way, the fundamental relations of implication for elementary propositional logic. The crystal also provides a bridge to more advanced studies such as modal and multivalent logics and it helps one visualize distinctions between object language and metalanguage and between sentence connectives and predicates of sentences. The crystal is named for the nonacademic philosopher-logician who conceived it, Thomas C. Wachter (1942-1995).

**Viney, Donald Wayne**. William James on Free Will: The French Connection. *Hist Phil Quart*, 14(1), 29-52, Ja 97.

William James gave credit to Charles Renouvier (1815-1903) for providing him with "an intelligible and reasonable conception of freedom." By Renouvier's testimony, his own ideas on free will were borrowed from his friend Jules Lequyer (1814-1862). James too read and appreciated Lequyer, whom he called "a French philosopher of genius," although he never mentioned Lequyer by name in his published writings. These facts show, in R.B. Perry's words, an indirect influence of Lequyer on James through Renouvier. This paper provides evidence of a more direct influence of Lequyer on James. James used and expanded upon the basic ideas about free will that he learned from Renouvier, using Lequyer as a kind of palimpsest.

**Viney, Wayne**. Disunity in Psychology and Other Sciences: The Network or the Block Universe?. *J Mind Behav*, 17(1), 31-44, Wint 96.

The nineteenth-century metaphor of a block universe in which science is regarded as a structure consisting of basic building blocks resting on firm foundations is contrasted with the contemporary metaphor of science as a network of relations. The network metaphor challenges the view that one science is more foundational than others and raises questions about whether an all-pervasive unity is desirable or even possible. The unity-disunity issue in psychology and other sciences (with special reference to biology) is discussed with respect to the network and building block metaphors and with respect to three arenas: organizations, methodology and subject content areas. it is argued that in these three arenas, psychology is no more disunified than biology. There is no basis for the development of a disciplinary inferiority complex based on the belief that the other sciences are unified while psychology remains in the intellectual backwaters of plurality.

**Vinicky, Janicemarie K** and Orlowski, James P and Shevlin Edwards, Sue. Conflicts of Interest, Conflicting Interests, and Interesting Conflicts, Part 3. *J Clin Ethics*, 7(2), 184-186, Sum 96.

**Vintges, Karen**. *Philosophy as Passion: The Thinking of Simone de Beauvoir.* Bloomington, Indiana Univ Pr, 1996.

Vintges's *Philosophy as Passion* examines the philosophical merits of Simone de Beauvoir's total oeuvre. Beauvoir's philosophical treatises demonstrate how an existentialist ethics was created and developed by transforming Sartre's theory of emotion, reconciling his ontology with a phenomenological perspective. Beauvoir developed a concept of ethics as "art of living" and articulated this concept in philosophical novels. She developed and presented her own "art of living" in her autobiography, rejecting Freud's and other's perception of the creative and intellectual woman as a contradiction in terms. The heuristic background to this study is formed by Foucault's concept of ethics as the aesthetics of existence and Nussbaum's ideas on philosophical literature.

**Viola, Salvatore**. *"La volontéde puissance" n'existe pas*: A proposito dell'edizione francese di alcuni saggi di Mazzino Montinari. *G Crit Filosof Ital*, 17(1), 123-127, Ja-Ap 97.

**Virvidakis, Stelios**. Analytic Philosophy in Greece. *Dialectica*, 51(2), 135-142, 1997.

**Visconti, Gian Galeazzo** (ed) and Vico, Giambattista. *Varia: Il De Mente Heroica* e gli Scritti Latini Minori. Napoli, Guida, 1996.

La rinnovata edizione delle opere di Vico, ispirata a rigorosi criteri di critica testuale, rispondendo alla richiesta di vecchi e nuovi lettori, consacra la realizzata familiarità con Vico, promossa e assicurata dall'impegno di filosofi, storici, filologi, convenuti a decifrare il problema Vico nei punti centrali e periferici, negli antecedenti e negli influssi del suo pensiero, liberando dall'antico, tradizionale timore dell'oscurità della pagina vichiana, ardua e superba. (publisher)

**Vision, Gerald**. Believing Sentences. *Phil Stud*, 85(1), 75-93, Ja 97.

Can the contents or intentional objects of belief be identified by way of their purely syntactic properties (that is, as sentences) or do we need to appeal to semantic properties (that is, propositions) to identify them? I weigh in for semantic identification. First a case is discussed both to demonstrate and to illustrate the point. Next, a series of objections are considered along with my replies to them.

**Vision, Gerald**. *Problems of Vision: Rethinking the Causal Theory of Perception.* New York, Oxford Univ Pr, 1997.

At one time the causal theory of perception was regarded as our last best hope of reliably connecting the subjective contents of perception to external reality. With the decline of the view that perception consists of subjective contents, thinkers have had to reconceive the options for explaining perception/world relations. In this breakthrough study, Gerald Vision proposes a new causal theory, one that engages provocatively with a species of direct realism and makes no use of the now discredited subjectivism. (publisher,edited)

**Visker, Rudi**. Un-European Desires: Toward a Provincialism without Romanticism. *Epoche*, 2(1), 35-64, 1994.

**Visser, Albert**. Dynamic Relation Logic Is the Logic of DPL-Relations. *J Log Lang Info*, 6(4), 441-452, O 97.

In this paper we prove that the principles in the language with relation composition and dynamic implication, valid for all binary relations, are the same ones as the principles valid when we restrict ourselves to DPL-relations, i.e., relations generated from conditions (tests) and resettings.

**Visser, Albert** and Vermeulen, Kees. Dynamic Bracketing and Discourse Representation. *Notre Dame J Form Log*, 37(2), 321-365, Spr 96.

In this paper we describe a framework for the construction of entities that can serve as interpretations of arbitrary contiguous chunks of text. An important part of the paper is devoted to describing stacking cells, or the proposed meanings for bracket-structures.

**Viswesvaran, Chockalingam** and Deshpande, Satish P. Ethics, Success, and Job Satisfaction: A Test of Dissonance Theory in India. *J Bus Ethics*, 15(10), 1065-1069, O 96.

A survey of middle level managers in India showed that when respondents perceived that successful managers in their organization behaved unethically their levels of job satisfaction were reduced. Reduction in satisfaction with the facet of supervision was the most pronounced (than with pay or promotion or coworker or work). Results are interpreted within the framework of cognitive dissonance theory. Implications for ethics training programs (behavioral and cognitive) as well as international management are discussed. (edited)

**Vitell, Scott J** and Ho, Foo Nin. Ethical Decision Making in Marketing: A Synthesis and Evaluation of Scales Measuring the Various Components of Decision Making in Ethical Situations. *J Bus Ethics*, 16(7), 699-717, My 97.

The authors present a comprehensive synthesis and evaluation of the published scales measuring the components of the decision making process in ethical situations using the Hunt-Vitell (1993) theory of ethics as a framework to guide the research. Suggestions for future scale development are also provided.

**Vitell, Scott J** and Nwachukwu, Saviour L S. The Influence of Corporate Culture on Managerial Ethical Judgments. *J Bus Ethics*, 16(8), 757-776, Je 97.

The contention that organizational culture influences ethical decision making is not disputable. However, the extent to which it influences ethical decision making in the workplace is a topic for scholarly debate and investigation. There are scholars who argue that, though corporate values are a powerful force within organizations, these values are unperceived, unspoken, and taken for granted. However, there are others who argue that the formalization of corporate values facilitates job and role clarity and is the key to influencing employee behavior. The purpose of this study is to examine the extent of the influence of organizational codes of ethics. The findings suggest that, depending upon the particular situation, corporate culture and ethics may mitigate individual personal moral convictions about right and wrong.

**Vitell, Scott J** and Singhapakdi, Anusorn and Rallapalli, Kumar C. The Perceived Role of Ethics and Social Responsibility: A Scale Development. *J Bus Ethics*, 15(11), 1131-1140, N 96.

Marketers must first perceive ethics and social responsibility to be important before their behaviors are likely to become more ethical and reflect greater social responsibility. However, little research has been conducted concerning marketers' perceptions regarding the importance of ethics and social responsibility as components of business decisions. The purpose of this study is to develop a reliable and valid scale for measuring marketers' perceptions regarding the importance of ethics and social responsibility. The authors develop an instrument for the measurement of the perceived role of ethics and social responsibility (PRESOR). Evidence that the scale is valid is presented through the assessment of scale reliability, as well as content and predictive validity. Finally, future research needs and the value of this construct to marketing are discussed.

**Viti Cavaliere, Renata**. "M. Heidegger: Modernità, storia e destino dell'Essere" in *Lo Storicismo e la Sua Storia: Temi, Problemi, Prospettive*, Cacciatore, Giuseppe (ed), 506-515. Milano, Guerini, 1997.

The purpose of my work is to analyze Heidegger's relation to modernity. My point is: Heidegger is faithful to the spirit of "modernity" when he exercises his critic of the present and suggests to point towards an unassiomatic thought. Vice versa, he is contra modernity concerning the history of Being. He conceives human world dangerously cut from reflection in the unpredictable progress of history. But Dasein, ontologically opened to Being, has no ethical and practical weapons to choose with responsibility within the particular historical worlds.

**Vitiello, Vincenzo**. "Per una topologia dell'ego" in *Geofilosofia*, Bonesio, Luisa (ed), 77-97. Sondrio, Lyasis, 1996.

**Vitiello, Vincenzo**. Vico: entre historia y naturaleza. *Cuad Vico*, 5/6, 169-200, 1995/96.

Philosophy does not come out from philology (legislation), but rather it is philosophy itself which grounds the law. Correspondingly to Plato (Socrates), reason is embedded in law, the false into what is the true, reason in authority, *philosophy* finally into *philology*. This particular reading has certain consequences for the Vichian corpus, of which the author seems to be far away from the historic and philological interpretation. The *ordo rerum* is the essential feature in the Vichian principle related with the truth: according to doctrines of "order," philosophy and philology are just *one* thing altogether and not two separate things. From this hermeneutical view the author claims the *De antiquissima*'s importance and its central core along the Vico's work and sets forth a particular interpretation of history.

**Vitsaxis, V**. The Universality of Poetry. *Diotima*, 25, 153-162, 1997.

**Viviano, Benedict T**. The Spirit in John's Gospel: A Hegelian Perspective. *Frei Z Phil Theol*, 43(3), 368-387, 1996.

The article tries to show how Hegel derived some of his most important ideas from the Gospel According to John, and that Hegel's ideas in turn help the reader to understand some of the depth in John's gospel. For example, Hegel has the idea that neither the universal is worth much nor the particular by itself, but only the concrete universal. This is inspired by the incarnation of the Word in John 1:14. Another key idea of Hegel is the historicity of truth, that the completed historical process is necessary to an understanding of the whole of human reality. This is based on John 16:12-13; the disciples cannot understand everything at once. They need the guidance of the Spirit-Paraclete to accompany them along the path of historical experience in order to understand the unfolding of the plan of salvation.

**Vizguin, Vladimir P**. La 'revolución francesa' en la fisica: Nacimiento matemático de la fisica clásica en el primer tercio del siglo XIX. *Mathesis*, 10(4), 339-368, N 94.

This article examines the first stage of the formation of the classical physics in the beginning of the 20s of the XIX century connected with the origins of Fresnel's optics, Ampère's electrodynamics, Fourier's theory of thermal conductivity and Carnot's thermodynamics. The institutional (The Paris Polytechnic School) and conceptual (The Laplace-Berthollet program) premises of this 'French Revolution' in physics are emphasized. The particular constructive importance of mathematical analysis in the process of creation of the fundamentals of classical physics in shown.

**Vlasáková, Marta**. Dispositional Properties (Czech). *Filosof Cas*, 45(1), 37-49, 1997.

The article is intended to provide an overview of the main problems that arise for the analysis of the term "dispositional property", as well as some of the proposed solutions. The first part of the article deals with the definition of dispositional properties, the other part investigates the problem of the ontological status of dispositional properties. An explication of the concept of dispositional property which could in my opinion lead to solutions of some of the mentioned problems is suggested in the conclusion.

**Vlasáková, Marta** and Lhoták, Kamil. The Reflecting Symmetry of Subjective and Extra-Subjective Processes (and To Theme... M. Vlasáková) (in Czech). *Filosof Cas*, 45(2), 315-320, 1997.

**Vlot, Ad** and Haaksma, Hans W H. Henk van Riessen, pionier van de filosofie van de techniek. *Alg Ned Tijdschr Wijs*, 89(1), 26-43, Ja 97.

Van Riessen applied the philosophy of H. Dooyeweerd and D.T.H. Vollenhoven in an analysis of the structure of technology. This approach enabled him to differentiate between the characteristics of modern technology and those of traditional technology, and to clarify the usually blurred distinctions between technology, economical enterprise and science. According to Van Riessen, any discussion of the cultural impact of technology on society should be based on a philosophical analysis of technology itself. Without such an analysis, technology, is mistaken for an applied science only, and the technological artefact treated as a 'black box' without its own laws and structure.

**Voegelin, Eric** and Zanetti, Gianfrancesco (trans). *La Scienza Nuova* nella Storia del Pensiero Politico. Napoli, Guida, 1996.

Lo studio su Vico di Voegelin, che qui si presenta con l'introduzione di J. Gebhardt docente all'Università di Erlangen-Nürnberg—uno dei più importanti studiosi dell'opera del filosofo politico—costituisce un lungo capitolo della *History of Political Ideas*, rimasta inedita. Nell'approccio antignostico ed antiprogressivista proprio di Voegelin, Vico assume "una sua propria grandezza", con la quale non possono competere quei filosofi tedeschi che l'interpretazione crociana insiste nel sovrapporre al pensiero vichiano. "Difficilmente Vico può essere considerato pari a Kant come epistemologo, o pari a Hegel nella logica dello spirito, ma come filosofo della storia egli li supera entrambi, perché la sua consapevolezza cristiana dei problemi dello spirito lo protesse da quel deragliamento gnostico che esaurisce il significato della storia nella struttura della storia profana umanamente intellegibile". (edited)

**Völkel, Frank**. "Im Wechsel des Urteils und Seins: Zu Fichte und Hölderlin" in *Sein—Reflexion—Freiheit: Aspekte der Philosophie Johann Gottlieb Fichtes*, Asmuth, Christoph (ed), 95-111. Amsterdam, Gruner, 1997.

**Vogel, Jonathan**. Skepticism and Foundationalism: A Reply to Michael Williams. *J Phil Res*, 22, 11-28, Ap 97.

Michael Williams maintains that skepticism about the external world is vitiated by a commitment to *foundationalism* and *epistemological realism*. (The latter is, approximately, the view that there is such a thing as knowledge of the external world in general, which the skeptic can take as a target). I argue that skepticism is not encumbered in the ways Williams supposes. I find that Williams has offered no principled way to distinguish between ordinary challenges to knowledge and skeptical challenges which, supposedly, have no claim on our concern. (edited)

**Voigt, Uwe**. "Friede als Ziel der Geschichte? Drei europäische Positionen: Augustinus-Comenius-Kant" in *Kreativer Friede durch Begegnung der Weltkulturen*, Beck, Heinrich (ed), 157-177. New York, Lang, 1995.

This paper inquires into the occidental understanding of history as a way towards peace. For this purpose, peace-concepts of Augustine, John Amos Comenius and Kant are considered. Their comparison permits the conclusion that in Augustine history as "way" and peace as "aim" are strictly separated, while in Kant peace becomes an internal structuring element of history. According to the intermediary view of Comenius, history is a process which reaches its aim "peace" in a relative way, remaining open to transcendental perfection.

**Voizard, Alain**. Logiques et sémantiques non classiques. *Dialogue (Canada)*, 36(1), 3-13, Wint 97.

**Volf, Miroslav**. Truth and Community. *Filozof Istraz*, 16(3), 611-640, 1996.

This article consists of two parts (including some kind of introductory *Symposion*, in which *A Toast to the Past* and *A Counter Toast* are given as some prologue before developing the main theses of the text) and a conclusion of sorts. In the first part the author makes two *deconstructive* moves: one to discard a typically modern and the other to discard a poststructuralist construal of how truth relates to history. In the second part the author makes three *constructive* moves: one to suggest the rough outline of an alternative and the second to argue that the will to truth requires truthful life which in turn is inseparable from the will to embrace the other. The third move consists in showing that just as there can be no truth without the will to embrace the other, so there can be no genuine embrace without the will to truth. In conclusion the author sums up constructive as well as deconstructive moves about truth, deception, and difference by examining the encounter between Jesus and Pilate and drawing some implications for the relation between truth, freedom, and violence.

**Vollmer, Gerhard**. Der Evolutionsbegriff als Mittel zur Synthese: Leistung und Grenzen. *Phil Natur*, 26(1), 41-65, 1989.

For every real thing, we may sensibly ask how it evolves. This evolutionary question may be asked both on a descriptive and on an explanatory level. Thus it unites all empirical science. The most impressive part of our evolutionary outlook is—on both levels—the theory of organic evolution with Darwin's principle of natural selection. How far may it be extended to other parts of universal evolution? The "lower" limit is *self-replication*. There is, on the other side, *no "upper limit"* for this principle. It is, however, *incomplete* for the description and explanation of complex systems. Ignoring this incompleteness may be misleading and even dangerous.

**Vollmer, Gerhard**. Die vierte bis siebte Kränkung des Menschen—Gehirn, Evolution und Menschenbild. *Phil Natur*, 29(1), 118-134, 1992.

There is no doubt that science influences our view of world and man. According to Sigmund Freud, mankind has suffered three humiliations: 1) a cosmological one by Copernicus, 2) a biological one by Darwin and 3) a psychological one by Freud himself. Now and then, a *fourth* humiliation is stated; but, strangely enough, every author finds another one. Thus we seem to be left with humiliations by 4) ethology, 5) evolutionary epistemology, 6) sociobiology, 7) the computer model of mind, 8) ecology. We might even predict the next one by 9) neurobiology.

**Volpi, Franco**. Nietzsche e il nichilismo contemporaneo. *Teoria*, 16(1), 55-66, 1996.

**Voltolini, Alberto**. Are (Possible) Guises Internally Characterizable?. *Acta Analytica*, 65-90, 1995.

Castañeda's Guise Theory presents some ontological theses which are actually incompatible. The claims that an individual guise internally possesses the properties which characterize it and that an individual guise is a concrete object do not tally with the idea that a possible guise is a thought-of entity indifferent to existence. Besides, even the corresponding semantic theses of Guise Theory appear problematic. The claim that any definite description refers to an object which satisfies it may be legitimated only if an individual guise is taken to be the necessary denotation, in a Russellian way, of that description. But then such an entity cannot be a possible guise in Castañeda's sense.

**Von Bogdandy, Armin**. Supranationale und staatliche Herrschaft: Staatsphilosophische Aspekte einer neuen Form hoheitlicher Verfasstheit. *Z Phil Praxis*, 26-34, 1995.

**Von der Fehr, Drude**. From a Semiotic to a Neo-Pragmatic Understanding of Metaphor. *Dan Yrbk Phil*, 31, 39-48, 1996.

**Von der Pfordten, Dietmar**. "Rechtsethik" in *Angewandte Ethik: Die Bereichsethiken und ihre theoretische Fundierung*, Nida-Rümelin, Julian (ed), 200-289. Stuttgart, Alfred Kröner, 1996.

The article deals with the question of the ethical justification of law. It includes a discussion of more formal theories concerning the relation between law and ethics (e.g., Kelsen, Hart) and material approaches (Rawls, Hobbes, etc.).

**Von der Pfordten, Dietmar** and Nida-Rümelin, Julian. "Tierethik II: Zu den ethischen Grundlagen des Deutschen Tierschutzgesetzes" in *Angewandte Ethik: Die Bereichsethiken und ihre theoretische Fundierung*, Nida-Rümelin, Julian (ed), 484-509. Stuttgart, Alfred Kröner, 1996.

The article develops and criticizes the ethical foundations and implications of the German law regarding the treatment of animals. The original paper was presented at a hearing of the German National Parliament in October 1993.

**Von Eschenbach, Warren J**. Rational Self-Interest and Fear of Death: An Argument for an Agency Theory in Hobbes' *Leviathan*. *Dialogue (PST)*, 39(1), 13-20, O 96.

This paper examines the possibility of an agency theory of social contract in Hobbes by direct appeal to Hobbes's account of human psychology of rational self-interest and self-preservation. The author examines David Gauthier's article "Hobbes' Social Contract" and rejects his claim that an agency theory fails to sufficiently motivate individuals to provide active assistance to the sovereign. An alternative system is suggested that remains within the context of the agency theory and is based on Hobbesian individuals' fear of death and instinct for self-preservation.

**Von Hermann, Friedrich-Wilhelm**. Lógica y verdad en la Fenomenología de Heidegger y de Husserl. *An Seminar Hist Filosof*, 13, 39-55, 1996.

In einem ersten Abschnitt wird gezeigt, wie Heideggers fundamentalontologische Wesensbestimmung von Logik und Wahrheit ihren Ausgang nimmt von Husserls phänomenologischen Analysen in den *Logischen Untersuchungen*, in denen Heidegger wesentliche Ansätze zu einer von der

Von Herrmann, Friedrich-Wilhelm 976 AUTHOR INDEX

erstarrten traditionellen Logik sich abkehrend philosophierenden Logik sieht. Daran anschliessend zeichnet der zweite Abschnitt nach, wie im Übergang von der transzendental-horizontalen Fragebahn in die Blickbahn des Ereignis-Denkens Wahrheit und Logik nunmehr ihre gewandelte, seinsgeschichtliche Wesensbestimmung erfahren.

**Von Herrmann, Friedrich-Wilhelm** and Borges-Duarte, Irene (trans). *La "segunda mitad" de Ser y Tiempo.* Madrid, Ed Trotta, 1997.

Este libro constituye una aportación decisiva a la comprensión del proyecto heideggeriano que, bajo el título de *Ser y Tiempo. Primera Parte*, apareció sólo parcialmente desarrollado en la publicación de 1927. Partiendo de la anotación en la que Heidegger caracteriza el contenido de su curso de Marburgo de 1927 (*Los problemas fundamentales de la Fenomenología*) como una reelaboración de la temática de *Tiempo y ser*, con la que debía haberse iniciado la *segunda mitad* de *Ser y Tiempo*, el autor ofrece una interpretación fenomenológica de aquel proyector global, a la vez que una introducción a la lectura del texto del citado curso, con cuya publicación en 1975 se dio inicio a la de la *Edición integral*. (publisher, edited)

**Von Kempski, Jürgen**. Zur Typologie und Deontik von Privatrechts-instituten. *J Gen Phil Sci*, 27(2), 235-241, 1996.

In continuation of my treatise "Grundlegung zu einer Strukturtheorie des Rechts" part I of this paper develops a typology of the fundamental patterns of institutes of law belonging to the relations of persons to move (movable or fixed) assets. In Part II some reflections deal with the deontics of Gestalten of actions (in the sense of Part I) and related models in economics.

**Von Kutschera, Franz**. "Frege and Natural Deduction" in *Frege: Importance and Legacy,* Schirn, Matthias (ed), 301-304. Hawthorne, de Gruyter, 1996.

Gerhard Gentzen's calculus of sequents, as stated in his *Untersuchungen über das logische Schliessen* from 1934, surprisingly has a precursor in Gottlob Frege's system of the *Grundgesetze der Arithmetik* (vol.I, 1893). Gentzen certainly pursued other aims than Frege, who simply wanted to facilitate deductions, but the question remains whether he did not take a cue from Frege.

**Von Kutschera, Franz**. T x W Completeness. *J Phil Log*, 26(3), 241-250, Je 97.

T x W logic is a combination of tense and modal logic for worlds or histories with the same time order. It is the basis for logics of causation, agency and conditionals and, therefore, an important tool for philosophical logic. Semantically it has been defined, among others, by R.H. Thomason. Using an operator expressing truth in all worlds, first discussed by C.M. Di Maio and A. Zanardo, an axiomatization is given and its completeness proved via D. Gabbay's irreflexivity lemma. Given this lemma the proof is more or less straight forward. At the end an alternative axiomatization is sketched in which Di Maio's and Zanardo's operator is replaced by a version of "actually".

**Von Manz, Hans Georg**. Die Funktion praktischer Momente für Grundelemente der theoretischen Vernunft in Fichtes Manuskripten *Eigne Meditationen über Elementar Philosophie* und *Practische Philosophie* (1793/94). *Fichte-Studien*, 9, 83-99, 1997.

**Von Perger, Mischa** and Hoffmann, Michael. Ideen, Wissen und Wahrheit nach Platon: Neuere Monographien. *Phil Rundsch*, 44(2), 113-151, Je 97.

The review covers nine books on Plato that were published in the years 1987-1996: eight monographs (by Benitez, T. A. Blackson, L. Chen, Eming, Erler, v. Kutschera, Szaif) and one anthology (ed. by Kobusch & Mojsisch). Main issues are Plato's hypothesis that there exist "ideas", his supposed theory and teaching about them ("Ideenlehre") and the question what kind of knowledge could be elicited from them, especially knowledge concerning the ideas themselves. Statements about these matters turn out to be controversial even when restricted to single dialogues or to a group of works representing a certain state of Plato's thinking.

**Von Plato, Jan**. Formalization of Hilbert's Geometry of Incidence and Parallelism. *Synthese*, 110(1), 127-141, Ja 97.

Three things are presented: How Hilbert changed the original construction postulates of his geometry into existential axioms; In what sense he formalized geometry; How elementary geometry is formalized to present day's standards.

**Von Savigny, Eike**. "Die Lügner-Antinomie: eine pragmatische Lösung" in *Das weite Spektrum der analytischen Philosophie,* Lenzen, Wolfgang, 262-273. Hawthorne, de Gruyter, 1997.

Meanings of utterances being identified with their impact on the conventional set-up of the utterance situation, it is shown that utterances of liar sentences are meaningless in any language. Truth and falsity being considered as properties of meaningful utterances (rather than of well-formed sentences), utterances of liar sentences are neither true nor false and the antinomy vanishes. This solution is arrived at from a general speech act theoretical basis independently of any need to avoid the antinomy and it is generalizable for further supposed paradoxes. How utterance meaning rules of particular languages may avoid attributing meanings to such utterances is demonstrated on a rule for statements in German.

**Von Schönborn, Alexander**. Fichte und Reinhold über die Begrenzung der Philosophie. *Fichte-Studien*, 9, 241-255, 1997.

**Von Sivers, Kathrin**. Being—An Approach to the Beginning of Hegel's *Wissenschaft der Logik* (in German). *Prima Philosophia*, 10(3), 335-340, 1997.

Hegel himself often emphasized the simplicity and even triviality of the beginning of the *Science of Logic*. This seems to stand in strange contrast to the difficulties which the apparently cryptic opening parts of the *Logic of Being* do mean to the unbiased reader. This article is supposed to give an interpretation of this beginning and the contradiction which develops out of it. The interpretation is based on the contradiction in terms of the idea of *pure thought* (*reines Denken*). Considering this term more precisely, there arises the necessity of introducing a contrast-pair of reflection and abstract negation whose terms define each other as diametrically opposed. But on the other hand they indifferently coincide in the continuum of pure thought, or of Hegel's *Being* (*Sein*). Since they cannot be separately issued or stated, reflection and abstract negation are unindependent and on each other irreducible moments of one correlation. This correlation constitutes the actual logical primacy, the real beginning of logic—*becoming* (*Werden*). With the example of the derivation of *being determinate* (*Dasein*), the author then tries to evolve an argument that the term couple appearing in the logical beginning remains through all following derivations—as dialectical basic structure that always specifies itself whatever increase of the generated logical differentiations.

**Von Thülen, Bodil**. Bemerkungen zur musikalischen Künstlerästhetik des 20.Jahrhunderts. *Conceptus*, 29(74), 103-118, 1996.

What is the effect of the modern art to the philosophical science of aesthetics? Modern art gives us a lot of problems for the discussion in the philosophical science of aesthetics. What can we do? First of all we have to prove the new term of art. This term will give us a new form of communication between art and aesthetics. And this might be the first step to give answers in the difficult area of modern art and aesthetics.

**Von Wille, Dagmar**. Il Saggio sopra la Filosofia in genere di Lodovico Arnaldi: una traduzione settecentesca inedita del *Discursus praeliminaris* di Christian Wolff. *Stud Filosofici*, 89-126, 1995.

The article includes an introduction to the manuscript summarized Italian version of 1766 by Lodovico Arnaldi of the *Discursus praeliminaris* by Christian Wolff, preliminary to his *Philosophia rationalis sive Logica*, and the transcription of the text. Although Arnaldi's translation is explicitly meant for personal use only (along with his other handwritten translations of the major part of Wolff's Latin works), it is undoubtedly linked to the Italian Wolff reception in the sixties, based on historical and juridical interests, unlike the former in the thirties, more interested in the mathematical aspects of Wolff's philosophy.

**Von Wright, Georg Henrik**. "Progress: Fact and Fiction" in *The Idea of Progress,* McLaughlin, Peter (ed), 1-18. Hawthorne, de Gruyter, 1997.

The idea of "necessary and unending progress" is the belief that the advancement of science and technology will enhance the material well-being and eventually also the moral perfection of the human race. This belief, the author argues, is largely illusory. Acting on it has in our century conjured up threats to human survival in the form of overpopulation, draining of resources, pollution of the environment and impending climatological changes. Belief in progress is associated with a linear view of the course of history. In the writer's opinion, a cyclic perspective offers a deeper understanding of the historical process.

**Von Wright, Georg Henrik** (ed) and Malcolm, Norman. *Wittgensteinian Themes: Essays 1978-1989*. Ithaca, Cornell Univ Pr, 1995.

The book demonstrates the clarity and accessibility for which Malcolm's writing is renowned. Like most of his work, the essays examine basic issues in philosophy of language and philosophy of mind. Himself a noted philosopher, Georg Henrik von Wright has chosen the papers included here and appended to the volume his eloquent Memorial Address for Norman Malcolm, delivered at King's College, London, in November 1990. Professor von Wright has also supplied a brief preface. (publisher, edited)

**Vorobej, Mark**. Hybrid Arguments. *Inform Log*, 17(2), 289-296, Spr 95.

Sometimes logical support for a conclusion is provided exclusively by premises which are independently relevant to that conclusion. At other times, support is provided exclusively by independently irrelevant premises. On still other occasions, relevant and irrelevant premises may collectively offer a distinctive pattern of support. This paper provides a rigorous account of some of these differences in terms of a tripartite classification of convergent, linked and hybrid arguments. These various arguments are defined, diagrammed, and some of their logical properties are explored.

**Vorobej, Mark**. Monsters and the Paradox of Horror. *Dialogue (Canada)*, 36(2), 219-246, Spr 97.

L'horreur en art vise à effrayer, bouleverser, dégoûter et terroriser. Puisque nous ne sommes pas normalement attirés par de telles expériences, pourquoi quiconque s'exposerait-il délibérément à la fiction d'horreur? Noel Carroll soutient que le caractère constant du phénomène de l'horreur en art tient à certains plaisirs d'ordre cognitif, qui résultent de la satisfaction de notre curiosité naturelle à l'égard des monstres. Je soutiens, quant à moi, que la solution cognitive de Carroll au paradoxe de l'horreur est profondément erronée, étant donné la façon dont les monstres sont représentés dans la fiction d'horreur; j'explore brièvement une approche plus prometteuse, qui traite les monstres comme des moyens pour acquérir la connaissance de soi.

**Vorontsova, L M** and Filatov, S B. "The Russian Way" and Civil Society. *Russian Stud Phil*, 35(2), 6-20, Fall 96.

**Vuillemin, Jules**. De la paix perpétuelle et de l'espérance comme devoir. *Rev Theol Phil*, 128(4), 323-338, 1996.

After an analysis of Kant's concept of perpetual peace, it will be shown in its relation to a) positive law, by way of an immediately effective legal postulate and b) natural law, which imposes on perpetual peace the idea, as a goal, of a republican constitution to which it must indefinitely lean, obliging us to hope in spite of obstacles.

**Vukovic, Ivan**. Can One Lie for Moral Reasons? (in Serbo-Croatian). *Theoria (Yugoslavia)*, 38(2), 65-76, Je 95.

By analysing several examples that are usually used against Kant's interdiction of lying, the author is trying to show that this prohibition has a strong utilitarianistic justification and that Kant's system of morality is much more realistic than it is usually thought. At the same time, he wishes to suggest a general way to analyze and, when it is possible, resolve every conflict of duties.

**Waaldijk, Frank** and Veldman, Wim. Some Elementary Results in Intuitionistic Model Theory. *J Sym Log*, 61(3), 745-767, S 96.

We establish constructive refinements of several well-known theorems in elementary model theory. The additive group of the real numbers may be embedded elementarily into the additive group of pairs of real numbers, constructively as well as classically.

**Wackernagel, Wolfgang**. Maître Eckhart et le discernement mystique: A propos de la rencontre de Suso avec *la (chose) sauvage sans nom*. *Rev Theol Phil*, 129(2), 113-126, 1997.

Les commentateurs n'ont pas toujours reconnu que le dialogue de Henri Suso avec *la (chose) sauvage sans nom* pouvait être une glose allusive pour la réhabilitation de Maître Eckhart. Une comparaison de ce dialogue avec d'autres légendes (pseudo-)eckhartiennes, tend néanmoins à renforcer cette thèse. L'importance du discernement dans la vie spirituelle, ainsi que le problème de l'hérésie, sont aussi abordés dans cet article.

**Wagman, Morton**. *The General Unified Theory of Intelligence: Its Central Conceptions and Specific Application to Domains of Cognitive Science.* Westport, Praeger, 1997.

The general unified theory of intelligence addresses the cognitive functions of thinking, reasoning and problem solving. At an abstract level, this theory construes the intellective functions of humans and computers as, respectively, restricted and directed forms of the logic of implication. In other words, human intelligence operates according to production rules. Here, Wagman presents the central tenets and research elaboration of the general unified theory of intelligence that embraces both human and artificial intelligence across the cognitive domains of scientific discovery processes, inductive and deductive reasoning and the mechanisms basic to analogical thinking and problem solving. (publisher)

**Wagner, Joseph**. Incommensurable Differences: Cultural Relativism and Antirationalism Concerning Self and Other. *Phil Cont World*, 3(2), 18-26, Sum 96.

This paper is a defense of rationalism and a critique of what I call antirationalist themes in postmodernist, feminist and multiculturalist thought. The paper identifies central themes that reflect this antimodern and antirationalist temper and argues that each embodies a deep irresolvable philosophic confusion. In developing this critique, I try to show that the Enlightenment project, properly understood, provides the best and most comprehensive groundings for declaiming and remedying the faults of ethnocentrism and prejudice. (edited)

**Wagner, Paul A**. "Tolerance and Intolerance Gricean Intention and Doing Right by our Students" in *Philosophy of Education (1996)*, Margonis, Frank (ed), 224-227. Urbana, Phil Education Soc, 1997.

**Wagner, Paul A**. Total Quality Management: A Plan for Optimizing Human Potential?. *Stud Phil Educ*, 16(1-2), 241-258, Ja-Ap 97.

Israel Scheffler's ground-breaking essay, *On Human Potential*, deserves to be more widely known among educational policy analysts, especially in light of the popularity in educationists circles of W.E. Deming's organizational philosophy known as "Total Quality Management". In what follows, I argue that the heuristical value of Deming's prescriptions are entailed in Scheffler's *On Human Potential*. More importantly, I argue, where Deming's work falls short, especially in being naive about the human condition, Scheffler's analysis provides a foundation for management theory in education that insures the flourishing of an optimal number of contributing participants. In fashioning these ideas, Scheffler brings pioneering thinking to the emerging fields of management studies generally and educational policy specifically.

**Wagner, Stephen I**. Descartes on the Power of "Ideas". *Hist Phil Quart*, 13(3), 287-297, Jl 96.

This paper spells out the implications, for Descartes's theory of ideas, of my earlier paper, "Descartes's Wax: Discovering the Nature of Mind." I show that my reading of the wax investigation provides a number of clarifications of Descartes's *Meditation III* discussion of ideas. My reading of *Meditation III* provides a ground, internal to the *Meditations* for Descartes's claims about objective reality, the causal laws, material falsity and the idea of God. I show that Descartes's claims and conclusions regarding these issues is strengthened by the perspective I have provided.

**Wagner, Steven J**. "Truth, Physicalism, and Ultimate Theory" in *Objections to Physicalism,* Robinson, Howard (ed), 127-158. New York, Clarendon/Oxford Pr, 1996.

**Wagner, Wolfgang**. Queries about Social Representation and Construction. *J Theor Soc Behav*, 26(2), 95-120, Je 96.

Departing from the stated intent of the social representation approach to give a social constructionist account of social processes, this paper presents a critical analysis of language use within the realm of social representations research. Three questions are posed: a) Does a social representation represent an object? b) Can social representations be true or false? and c) Is social construction action? All three are answered negatively. It is shown that object-talk is inherent to social cognition and to the common-sensical view of social actors, but incompatible with a constructionist position; that truth-talk is part of collective discourse in the socio-genesis of representations, but senseless when talking about a representation; that a social representation is not a representation of an object, but ontologically identical with it; and that social construction *happens* rather than being *intended* by social actors. Consequently, social representations are interpreted as the significant meaning of constructive events and neither as entities in the minds of people nor floating above a collectivity. Their relationship with discourse analysis is discussed.

**Wagner de Reyna, Alberto**. Recordando a M. Heidegger. *Convivium*, 10, 111-129, 1997.

Three different memories are presented about the figure of M. Heidegger as teacher: (A) the academic atmosphere in Germany at 1935, (B) a letter from Heidegger and the explanation of the Spanish translation of *Über den Humanismus* in 1948, and (C) the description of a visit to Heidegger in 1962.

**Wahba, Mourad**. "The Politics of Logic" in *Averroës and the Enlightenment,* Wahba, Mourad (ed), 99-104. Amherst, Prometheus, 1996.

**Wahba, Mourad** (ed) and Abousenna, Mona (ed). *Averroës and the Enlightenment.* Amherst, Prometheus, 1996.

**Waibel, Violetta**. Hölderlins frühe Fichte-Kritik und ihre Wirkung auf den Gang der Ausarbeitung der Wissenschaftslehre. *Rev Int Phil*, 50 (197), 437-460, 1996.

In this article it is attempted to show that Hölderlin not only was the first critic of Fichte's theory of the Absolute Ego in the *Foundations of the Entire Science of Knowledge (Grundlage der gesammten Wissenschaftslehre)* of 1794, but also influenced the development of this theory in the foundation of the practical ego in Paragraph 5 of the *Science of Knowledge*. This new orientation leads finally to Fichtes *Foundations of Transcendental Philosophie (Wissenschaftslehre) nova methodo.*

**Waibel, Violetta**. Wechselbestimmung: Zum Verhältnis von Hölderlin, Schiller und Fichte in Jena. *Fichte-Studien*, 12, 43-69, 1997.

The concept of mutual determination (Wechselbestimmung) that Fichte introduced as central theorem in the theoretical part of his *Foundation of the Whole Doctrine of Science* (*Grundlage der gesammten Wissenschaftslehre*) of 1794 was accepted early by Schiller in his *On the Aesthetic Education of Man in a Series of Letters* (*Über die ästhetische Erziehung des Menschen in einer Reihe von Briefen*). Hölderlin soon followed and used the theorem in different ways in his theoretical sketches and in his poetry as is outlined in the inquiry. The concept of mutual determination became fundamental in Hölderlin's thinking and even in the discussion of Hölderlin with his friends in Jena and Homburg, Sinclair and Zwilling.

**Wain, Kenneth**. Foucault, Education, the Self and Modernity. *J Phil Educ*, 30(3), 345-360, N 96.

Michel Foucault is often criticised in English-speaking circles for being interested only in power as domination and of being uninterested in freedom and social reform. This paper shows, however, that Foucault's overarching concern was with the constitution of the self under conditions of modernity. It emphasises the significance of his interest in the Classical project of 'self-care' and of his countermodernist educational programme in which the skills of self-governance and the ethical (nondominating) governance of others, as well as the practice of freedom through self-creation, are the key ingredients.

**Wait, Eldon C**. Dissipating Illusions. *Human Stud*, 20(2), 221-242, Ap 97.

Perhaps the greatest challenge to an existential phenomenological account of perception is that posed by the argument from illusions. Recent developments in research on the behaviour of subjects suffering from illusions together with some seminal ideas found in Merleau-Ponty's writings enable us to develop and corroborate an account of the phenomenon of illusions, one, which unlike the empiricist account, does not undermine our conviction that in perception we "reach the things themselves". The traditional argument from illusions derives its force from an uncritical assumption that the process of experience takes place in time conceived as an infinite series of distinct moments. Once this assumption has been bracketed we are able to recognize the paradoxical truth that in the disillusion something can *become* that which it has always been and can *cease* to be that which it has never been. (edited)

**Wald, Berthold**. Abendländische Tugendlehre und moderne Moralphilosophie. *Prima Philosophia*, 9(4), 435-445, 1996.

Since the end of the 16th century moral obligation has been considered as a key term in political philosophy and moral universalization. One important critical review of this tradition began with Max Scheler's "Materiale Wertethik" and his attempt of a "Rehabilitierung der Tugend". Today, the philosophical importance of virtue ethics is even discussed by those, who like Habermas and Hare adhere to different concepts of universalization. The article deals with a rough survey about the philosophical debate on virtue and obligation and offers some perspectives on the presuppositions of the traditional view of the virtues formulated in the work of Josef Pieper.

**Waldegg, Guillermina** and Rigo, Mirela and Alarcón, Jesús. La ciencia analítica en la primera mitad del siglo XIX: el teorema del valor intermedio. *Mathesis*, 10(1), 93-113, F 94.

During the first half of the nineteenth century, the theories that presumed to be scientific described themselves as 'analytic'. From Lagrange's *Méchanique analytique* to Bolzano's *Purely analytic proof* of the intermediate value theorem, the high level of abstraction and generality reached by a theory was based on the 'analytic methods' used. However, the word 'analytic' did not have the same meaning for all the scientists of this period and remarkable differences can be detected in the assumptions underlying analytic methods in each author. In this article different approaches to the intermediate value theorem are analyzed, revealing the various conceptions of what being an 'analytic' theory entails.

**Waldenfels, Bernhard** and Parent, David J (trans). *Order in the Twilight.* Athens, Ohio Univ Pr, 1996.

Order in the twilight means that the idea of an all-encompassing or fundamental order comes to an end. Instead every order shows certain limits, selecting certain possibilities while excluding others. Closed orders are replaced by open-ended orders where interlocations and interactions take place, linking up and responding to the other's appeal or challenge in terms of responsive rationality. These events are no longer centered on a subject. New orders are inaugurated by deviation from existing orders, starting from certain key events. Finally, the ordinary continues to be perturbed by the extraordinary and the impossible. Possibility does not have the last word.

**Waldenfels, Bernhard** and Petrícek Jr, Miroslav. The Mine and That of Others (and M. Petrícek Commentary) (in Czech). *Filosof Cas*, 45(2), 283-295, 1997.

**Walhout, M D**. The Hermeneutical Turn in American Critical Theory, 1830-1860. *J Hist Ideas*, 57(4), 683-703, O 96.

**Walker, Lawrence J** and Taylor, John H. Moral Climate and the Development of Moral Reasoning: The Effects of Dyadic Discussions between Young Offenders. *J Moral Educ*, 26(1), 21-43, Mr 97.

Cognitive-developmental theory claims that moral reasoning can be developed through discussion with others, especially those at a higher stage. This study examined two social/contextual factors that may mediate such cognitive processes in moral development: sociometric status and moral climate. It was found that exposure to both higher-stage reasoning and higher peer status were essential elements within the developmental process. Implications for cognitive-developmental theory and moral education within correctional and school programmes are discussed. (edited)

**Walker, Margaret**. Geographies of Responsibility. *Hastings Center Rep*, 27(1), 38-44, Ja-F 97.

Most philosophical work on moral responsibility has taken up problems of freedom and determinism in their psychological or cosmological forms. I review here some recent philosophical work on the "geography" of responsibility, the complex and sometimes surprising ways responsibilities are distributed in everyday life, and for many more things than those we uncontroversially "do." Ranging over responsibility for consequences, individual contributions to outcomes, character, and commitments, I survey work by Claudia Card, Peter French, Robert Goodin, Christopher Gowans, Patricia Greenspan, Larry May, Michelle Moody-Adams, and Marion Smiley.

**Walker, Mary M**. Basanta Kumar Mallik and the Negative. *J Indian Counc Phil Res*, 14(1), 95-110, S-D 96.

**Walker, Nicholas** (trans) and Düttmann, Alexander García. The Culture of Polemic: Misrecognizing Recognition. *Rad Phil*, 81, 27-34, Ja-F 97.

**Walker, Ralph**. "Transcendental Arguments against Physicalism" in *Objections to Physicalism*, Robinson, Howard (ed), 61-80. New York, Clarendon/Oxford Pr, 1996.

**Walker, Ralph**. Sufficient Reason. *Proc Aris Soc*, 97, 109-123, 1997.

**Wall, Edmund** (ed). *Sexual Harassment: Confrontations and Decisions*. Amherst, Prometheus, 1992.

What exactly is sexual harassment? How and why does it occur? What, if anything, can be done to prevent it? The questions are obvious; the answers are not. Highlighting the work of social theorists, feminists, psychologists and legal scholars, this collection separates fact from emotion, focuses on opposing views and outlines the legal and moral complexity of a debate that is now taking shape in the public mind. (publisher, edited)

**Wall, Hershel P** and Strong, Carson and Jameson, Valerie. A Model Policy Addressing Mistreatment of Medical Students. *J Clin Ethics*, 7(4), 341-346, Wint 96.

The University of Tennessee College of Medicine developed a policy on student mistreatment that has three main components. First, a statement of standards of behavior was set forth that affirms the importance of mutual respect among teachers and students and asserts that the College will not condone mistreatment. Second, methods were developed for ongoing education of the college community concerning the standards of behavior and the process by which they are upheld. This educational process is directed toward preclinical and clinical students and faculty, residents, fellows and nurses. It attempts to promote a positive environment for learning by increasing sensitivity concerning the issue of mistreatment. It also informs persons who believe they have been mistreated that avenues for seeking redress are available. Third, a process for responding to allegations of mistreatment was established. This process, designed to be fair and to respect the rights of accuser and accused, involves use of a "mediator" and a "conflict-resolution council" to deal with alleged and actual mistreatment and promote reconciliation between conflicting parties. This approach has been implemented and its effectiveness will be assessed.

**Wall, Steven P**. Public Justification and the Transparency Argument. *Phil Quart*, 46(185), 501-507, O 96.

**Wallace, James D**. *Ethical Norms, Particular Cases*. Ithaca, Cornell Univ Pr, 1996.

The aim of this book is to present an account of ethics that emphasizes the similarities between moral and other kinds of practical knowledge. Morality is presented as a collection of disparate items of practical knowledge that have their origin and authority in the learned activities that are the substance of our lives. The result is a naturalistic account of ethics that understands moral knowledge as straightforwardly empirical. (publisher, edited)

**Wallace, Kathleen**. "Incarnation, Difference, and Identity: Materialism, Self, and the Life of Spirit" in *Philosophy in Experience: American Philosophy in Transition*, Hart, Richard (ed), 49-76. New York, Fordham Univ Pr, 1997.

Santayana gives a rich account of the self which is simultaneously bound by material conditions and circumstances and able to transcend those boundaries if not in material fact, at least in the life of spirit. In this essay I pursue the question, whether and how Santayana's view of "spirit" can be reconciled with his materialism. There is a tension between two of Santayana's claims about spirit: its inefficacy (required by his materialism) and its role in transforming human life from merely physical organic life to conscious, feeling life. What seems problematic to me is the account of "material" efficacy which Santayana commits himself to, and this problem in turn, I argue, has its origins in a limited notion of relation.

**Wallace, William A**. Thomism and the Quantum Enigma. *Thomist*, 61 (3), 455-467, Jl 97.

The first half of the article is a review of Wolfgang Smith's *The Quantum Enigma: Finding the Hidden Key* (Peru, Ill.: Sherwood Sugden & Co., 1995), the second half, a discussion of how the book relates to the author's *The Modeling of Nature: Philosophy of Science and Philosophy of Nature in Synthesis* (Washington, D.C.: Catholic U. P., 1996). Both reject Cartesian and Kantian eliminations of sensible qualities and natures from the physical world. Both urge, though in different ways, a return to the Aristotelian concept of *potentia*, along lines pioneered by Werner Heisenberg, as providing a key for the solution of quantum enigmas.

**Wallach, Alan**. Meyer Shapiro's Essay on Style: Falling into the Void. *J Aes Art Crit*, 55(1), 11-15, Wint 97.

In his well-known essay on style (1953), Meyer Schapiro examined and revealed the flaws of all major theories of style (Riegl, Wölfflin, Frankl) but offered nothing substantial in their place. Contemplating major scholars' failure to construct a convincing general theory, Schapiro argued that with the aid of Marxism it might be possible to develop a theory relating the social to the aesthetic. McCarthyism was at its height in 1953 and consequently a serious consideration of Marxist theory was almost unthinkable. Consequently, there was no direct response to Schapiro's essay and subsequent discussions of style failed to take up the issues Schapiro raised.

**Waller, Bruce N**. What Rationality Adds to Animal Morality. *Biol Phil*, 12(3), 341-356, Jl 97.

Philosophical tradition demands rational reflection as a condition for genuine moral acts. But the grounds for that requirement are untenable and when the requirement is dropped morality comes into clearer view as a naturally developing phenomenon that is not confined to human beings and does not require higher-level rational reflective processes. Rational consideration of rules and duties can enhance and extend moral behavior, but rationality is not necessary for morality and (contrary to the Kantian tradition represented by Thomas Nagel) morality cannot transcend its biological roots. Recognizing this helps forge a complementary rather than competitive relation between feminist care-based ethics and rationalistic duty-based ethics.

**Wallner, Fritz G**. "Interkulturelle Identität bzw: Variabilität und ihr möglicher Beitrag zum Frieden" in *Kreativer Friede durch Begegnung der Weltkulturen*, Beck, Heinrich (ed), 73-83. New York, Lang, 1995.

The paper wants to show a different procedure of intercultural cooperation instead of a leading culture by which other cultures are judged, we elaborate a model which enables equality of the cultures. This can be done by a new method: "strangification." It takes proposition systems into strange contexts (in our case: contexts of another culture) for revealing their presuppositions and borders. By this way the goal of intercultural cooperation is changed; it leads presumably to a better understanding of their own culture and in consequence to a better understanding of the human conditions. (edited)

**Walls, Jerry L**. As the Waters Cover the Sea: John Wesley on the Problem of Evil. *Faith Phil*, 13(4), 534-562, O 96.

John Wesley explained the existence of evil in moral rather than metaphysical terms. His understanding of the fall was fairly typical of Western theology and he also enthusiastically embraced a version of the *felix culpa* theme as essential for theodicy. Unlike many influential Western theologians, he also relied heavily on libertarian freedom to account for evil. His most striking proposal for theodicy involves his eschatological vision of the future in which he believed the entire world living then will be converted. I argue that his theodicy is implicitly universalist, especially in its eschatological speculations and show that this is in tension with his strong libertarian commitments.

**Walry, Jenny**. Een Reactie op Heleen Pott. *Alg Ned Tijdschr Wijs*, 89(2), 152-156, Ap 97.

**Walsh, Denis M**. Fitness and Function. *Brit J Phil Sci*, 47(4), 553-574, D 96.

According to historical theories of biological function, a trait's function is determined by natural selection in the past. I argue that, in addition to historical functions, a historical functions ought to be recognized. I propose a theory of biological function which accommodates both. The function of a trait is the way it contributes to fitness and fitness can only be determined relative to a selective regime. Therefore, the function of a trait can only be specified relative to a selective regime. Apart from its desirable pluralism, only this view of relational function can support the function/accident and function/malfunction distinctions commonly thought to be part of the concept of function. Furthermore, only relational function correctly characterizes the explanatory consequences of function attributions in evolutionary biology. (edited)

**Walsh, Denis M** and Ariew, André. A Taxonomy of Functions. *Can J Phil*, 26(4), 493-514, D 96.

We discuss the way in which a new theory of biological functions, the relational theory, illuminates the relationship between disparate conceptions of function: propensity, aetiological and causal role. According to the relational theory, evolutionary functions (including propensity and aetiological functions) are a type of causal role function—the typical causal contribution of a trait type to average individual fitness. We present a taxonomy showing the relationship between causal role, aetiological and propensity functions and discuss the distinctive explanatory roles played by each.

**Walsh, Marcia K**. One Woman's Journey. *Bioethics Forum*, 13(2), 35-37, Sum 97.

**Walsh, Michael**. "Brand Blanshard—A 'Student' of Bradley" in *Philosophy after F.H. Bradley*, Bradley, James (ed), 91-126. Bristol, Thoemmes, 1996.

**Walsh, W H**. *Kant's Criticism of Metaphysics*. Edinburgh, Edinburgh Univ Pr, 1997.

**Walsh-Bowers, Richard** and Rossiter, Amy and Prilleltensky, Isaac. Learning from Broken Rules: Individualism, Bureaucracy, and Ethics. *Ethics Behavior*, 6(4), 307-320, 1996.

The authors discuss findings from a qualitative research project concerning applied ethics that was undertaken at a general family counseling agency in southern Ontario. Interview data suggested that workers need to dialogue about ethical dilemmas, but that such dialogue demands a high level of risk taking that feels unsafe in the organization. This finding led the researchers to examine their own sense of "breaking rules" by suggesting an intersubjective view of ethics that requires a "safe space" for ethical dialogue. The authors critique the individualistic tendency of professional ethics as an effect of power that is tied to the history of professionalism and discuss the role of bureaucracies in diminishing a central role for ethics in helping services. (edited)

**Walsh-Bowers, Richard** and Rossiter, Amy and Prilleltensky, Isaac. Preventing Harm and Promoting Ethical Discourse in the Helping Professions: Conceptual, Research, Analytical, and Action Frameworks. *Ethics Behavior*, 6(4), 287-306, 1996.

The first in a series of four articles, this article provides an overview of the concepts and methods developed by a team of researchers concerned with preventing harm and promoting ethical discourse in the helping professions. In this article we introduce conceptual, research, analytical and action frameworks employed to promote the centrality of ethical discourse in mental health practice. We employ recursive processes whereby knowledge gained from case studies refines our emerging conceptual model of applied ethics. Our *participatory* conceptual framework differs markedly from the *restrictive* model typically used in applied ethics. (edited)

**Walsh-Bowers, Richard** and Rossiter, Amy and Prilleltensky, Isaac. The Personal Is the Organizational in the Ethics of Hospital Social Workers. *Ethics Behavior*, 6(4), 321-335, 1996.

Understanding the social context of clinical ethics is vital for making ethical discourse central in professional practice and for preventing harm. In this paper we present findings about clinical ethics from in-depth interviews and consultation with seven members of a hospital social work department. Workers gave different accounts of ethical dilemmas and resources for ethical decision making than did their managers, whereas workers and managers agreed on core-guiding ethical principles and on ideal situations for ethical discourse. We discuss the research team's initial interpretations, the relevance of the extant ethics literature to organizational structures and dynamics, and alternative perspectives on clinical ethics.

**Walt, Steven**. Practical Reason and the Ontology of Statutes. *Law Phil*, 15(3), 227-255, 96.

An adequate theory of statutory interpretation must contain epistemic and ontological components. It must both provide defensible evidentiary standards and an account of what a statute consists in—the item being interpreted. Practical reasoning accounts of statutory interpretation are popular in law. I argue that they provide epistemically defective because lacking defensible evidentiary standards and ontologically incomplete because omitting and ontological account of statutes. Ontological incompleteness is not by itself a defect. I defend practical reasoning accounts against an argument, based on metaphysical "oddness," that the object of statutory interpretation they presuppose is ontologically implausible.

**Walter, Edgar**. Intuition and Natural Law. *Vera Lex*, 14(1-2), 55-56, 1994.

**Walter, Henrik**. Authentische Entscheidungen und emotive Neurowissenschaft. *Phil Natur*, 34(1), 147-174, 1997.

**Walter, Henrik**. Die Freiheit des Deterministen: Chaos und Neurophilosophie. *Z Phil Forsch*, 50(3), 364-385, Jl-S 96.

According to Kant, free will is nonempirical. By applying the method of neurophilosophy to the "could-have-done-otherwise" condition it is argued that this is not necessarily true. Evidence comes from new results about the nonlinear, chaotic nature of neurodynamics. It is possible to construct a weaker, but falsifiable version of the aforementioned condition. Although this solution might not satisfy a strictly indeterministic account it guarantees flexibility and adaptivity of actions without loosing intelligibility; a problem that has never been solved by libertarians. Additionally, the neurophilosophical account has some surprising implications for the relation between responsibility and freedom.

**Walters, James W**. *What Is a Person? An Ethical Exploration*. Champaign, Univ of Illinois Pr, 1997.

For Walters the arguments lead in a logical progression to a set of conclusions. If terminally and seriously ill patients have the right to discontinue life-sustaining treatment, they should also have the right to donate organs, even if they are not yet dead (by current standards) but only permanently unconscious. If organs can be taken from those whose higher brain functions are irreversibly lost, then by logical extension, a surrogate should be able to implement the patient's wishes regarding organ donation. By further logical extension, a newborn infant whose higher brain is anatomically absent ought to be considered also a suitable organ donor if designated surrogates, such as parents, so decide.

**Walters, Kerry**. The Case of the Slain President: Teaching Critical Thinking in Context. *Teach Phil*, 20(1), 35-47, Mr 97.

**Walton, Douglas**. "The Straw Man Fallacy" in *Logic and Argumentation*, Van Eemeren, Frans H (ed), 115-128. Amsterdam, North-Holland, 1994.

In this paper, an analysis is given of the straw man fallacy as a misrepresentation of someone's commitments in order to refute that person's argument. With this analysis a distinction can be made between straw man and other closely related fallacies such as *ad hominem, secundum quid* and *ad verecundiam*. When alleged cases of the straw man fallacy are evaluated, the speaker's commitment should be conceived normatively in relation to the type of conversation the speaker was supposed to be engaged in.

**Walton, Douglas**. New Methods for Evaluating Arguments. *Inquiry (USA)*, 15(4), 44-65, Sum 96.

**Walton, Douglas N**. Practical Reasoning and the Structure of Fear Appeal Arguments. *Phil Rhet*, 29(4), 301-313, 1996.

**Walton, Kendall**. "Listening with Imagination: Is Music Representational?" in *Music and Meaning*, Robinson, Jenefer (ed), 57-82. Ithaca, Cornell Univ Pr, 1997.

Pictorial and literary representations establish fictional worlds, worlds consisting in what one is to imagine in appreciating them. Appreciating music also involves much imagining. Some is linked to fictional worlds established by the music, but imaginings which constitute appreciation of one important kind of musical expressiveness are not. Rather than imagining someone else, a fictional being in a world of the work, experiencing certain feelings, listeners imagine experiencing the feelings themselves. This accounts for the special *intimacy* listeners have with expressive qualities of music. And it justifies denying that music, insofar as it is expressive in this manner, is representational.

**Walukiewicz, Igor**. A Note on the Completeness of Kozen's Axiomatisation of the Propositional mu-Calculus. *Bull Sym Log*, 2(3), 349-366, S 96.

The propositional *Mu*-calculus is an extension of the modal system K with a least fixpoint operator. Kozen posed a question about completeness of the axiomatisation of the logic which is a small extension of the axiomatisation of the modal system K. It is shown that this axiomatisation is complete.

**Walzer, Michael**. "The Politics of Difference: Statehood and Toleration in a Multicultural World" in *The Morality of Nationalism*, McKim, Robert (ed), 245-257. New York, Oxford Univ Pr, 1997.

**Walzer, Michael**. A Response. *Ethics Int Affairs*, 11, 99-104, 1997.

Responding to the critiques of the four previous authors, Walzer opens with a statement of the inherent imperfection of any theory of war. He reminds us that theories are merely frameworks for decisions and cannot provide answers in and of themselves. Moral decisions in war are especially difficult, for it is often necessary to choose between equally valid claims. Walzer continues the discussion of sieges initiated by both Koontz and Boyle and concedes the validity of Koontz's criticism of inconsistency in his theory of noncombatant immunity. Addressing the different authors' moral doctrines—Hendrickson's consequentialism and Koontz's and Boyle's deontology—Walzer argues that it is better to judge each case individually, weighing both the consequences and principles, rather than strictly adhere to one moral doctrine, an approach that Smith had commended. Finally, in the search for a perfect just war theory, Walzer issues a realist reminder that there can be no such thing as a morally perfect war.

**Walzer, Michael**. The Politics of Difference: Statehood and Toleration in a Multicultural World. *Ratio Juris*, 10(2), 165-176, Je 97.

The author identifies four possible attitudes of tolerance toward groups with different ways of life: resignation, indifference, curiosity and enthusiasm. He explores the potential for these attitudes and concludes by discussing the role of boundaries within communities in modernism and postmodernism. The author is not going to focus on toleration of eccentric or dissident individuals in civil society; he is interested in individual rights primarily when they are exercised in common—in the course of voluntary association or religious worship or cultural elaboration—or when they are claimed by groups on behalf of their members.

**Walzer, Michael**. *Thick and Thin: Moral Argument at Home and Abroad*. Notre Dame, Univ Notre Dame Pr, 1994.

My aim in this book is twofold: first, to rehearse, revise and extend a set of arguments about justice, social criticism, and nationalist politics that I have been involved in making for some ten years. The revisions and extensions also represent so many responses to my critics. So I shall strengthen my arguments as best I can and wait for further criticism. Nothing in these pages is finished or done with. But I also want, second, to put my arguments to work in the new political world that has arisen since I first presented them. (edited)

**Walzer, Michael**. Three Paths in Moral Philosophy. *Filosof Cas*, 44(4), 641-674, 1996.

**Wamba dia Wamba, Ernest**. "Democracy *in* Africa and Democracy *for* Africa" in *Philosophy and Democracy in Intercultural Perspective*, Kimmerle, Heinz (ed), 129-131. Amsterdam, Rodopi, 1997.

**Wandschneider, Dieter**. Eine auch sich selbst missverstehende Kritik: Über das reflexionsdefizit formaler Explikationen. *J Gen Phil Sci*, 27(2), 347-352, 1996.

The criticism formulated by L. B. Puntel concerning the theory of dialectic proposed by the author is rejected. Puntel's attempt at explicating predication by means of (second order) predicate logic fails: It misjudges predication being already presupposed for the possibility of predicate logic, thus belonging to the transcendental conditions of formal predicate logic, so that predication itself cannot be further explicated by means of such logic. What is in fact criticized by Puntel is something like an artifact of formalization. The unreflected application of formal logic here generates problems instead of solving them.

**Wang, Youru**. An Inquiry into the Liminology in Language in the *Zhuangzi* and in Chan Buddhism. *Int Phil Quart*, 37(2), 161-178, Je 97.

**Wanjohi, Gerald J**. "Les éléments démocratiques dans des proverbes gikouyou" in *Philosophy and Democracy in Intercultural Perspective*, Kimmerle, Heinz (ed), 197-202. Amsterdam, Rodopi, 1997.

**Wanning, Berbeli**. Statt Nicht-Ich—Du! Die Umwendung der Fichteschen Wissenschaftslehre ins Dialogische durch Novalis (Friedrich von Hardenberg). *Fichte-Studien*, 12, 153-168, 1997.

**Wansing, Heinrich**. Strong Cut-Elimination in Display Logic. *Rep Math Log*, 29, 117-131, 1995.

It is shown that every displayable propositional logic enjoys strong cut-elimination. This result strengthens Belnap's general cut-elimination theorem for display logic.

**Warburton, Nigel**. Authentic Photographs. *Brit J Aes*, 37(2), 129-137, Ap 97.

What is to count as an authentic photographic print in the realm of photographic art? I argue that photographers typically confer the status of 'good enough print' on a subset of their output and that only prints which have been thus certified should be considered authentic. The act of conferring this status is an important element in the creation of an individual photographic style.

**Warburton, Nigel**. Individual Style in Photographic Art. *Brit J Aes*, 36(4), 389-397, O 96.

Roger Scruton claims that photography lacks 'all except the grossest features of style'. The standard response is that Scruton misrepresents the choices photographers make about what they photograph and how. This article presents a stronger response based on how individual style is actually achieved in photographic art. Photographers typically select a repertoire; within which particular images acquire new meaning in relation to each other. Individual style is achieved not only through the manner of representing subjects, but also through the selection of repertoire. This point has important consequences for the appreciation, interpretation and display of photographic art.

**Warburton, Nigel**. *Thinking from A to Z*. New York, Routledge, 1996.

Being able to spot poor reasoning and diversionary ploys like these will put more clout behind your arguments and sharpen your thinking. This brilliant book will give you the power to tell a good from a bad argument. Using witty and topical examples, Nigel Warburton will enable you to distinguish with confidence between a Red Herring and a Straw Man. For everyone who wants to refine their arguments, *Thinking from A to Z* is an indispensable reference tool, as well as being an irresistible guide to dip into. Honing your thinking skills might well help you win friends and influence people—it will certainly help you get your point across. (publisher)

**Ward Bynum, Terrell**. Symposium on Computer Ethics. *Metaphilosophy*, 28(3), 233, Jl 97.

**Ware, Robert B**. Hegel's Metaphilosophy and Historical Metamorphosis. *Hist Polit Thought*, 17(2), 253-279, Sum 96.

**Warfield, Ted A**. Divine Foreknowledge and Human Freedom Are Compatible. *Nous*, 31(1), 80-86, Mr 97.

**Wark, Gillian** and Denton, Kathy and Krebs, Dennis L. The Forms and Functions of Real-Life Moral Decision-Making. *J Moral Educ*, 26(2), 131-145, Je 97.

People rarely make the types of moral judgement evoked by Kohlberg's test when they make moral decisions in their everyday lives. The anticipated consequences of real-life moral decisions, to self and to others, may influence moral choices and the structure of moral reasoning. To understand real-life moral judgement we must attend to its functions, which, although they occasionally involve resolving hypothetical moral dilemmas like those on Kohlberg's test, more often involve promoting good social relations, upholding favourable self-concepts and justifying self-interested behaviour. We argue that a functional model of moral judgement and moral behaviour derived from evolutionary theory may supply a better account of real-life morality than the Kohlbergian model.

**Warner, C Terry** and Melby, Alan K. *The Possibility of Language: A Discussion of the Nature of Language, with Implications for Human and Machine Translation*. Amsterdam, J Benjamins, 1995.

We attempt to address several open issues by examining the intellectual tradition of mainstream linguistics and philosophy and to identify why this tradition has failed to provide an adequate theoretical framework for some of the goals of machine translation. In the course of this investigation, we present an alternative view of how human language is possible. We then trace some of the implications of this view for the shape of translation theories, the practice of human translation and the future of translation technology, including both machine translation and computer-based tools for human translators. (publisher, edited)

**Warner, Richard**. "Incorrigibility" in *Objections to Physicalism*, Robinson, Howard (ed), 185-205. New York, Clarendon/Oxford Pr, 1996.

**Warner, Richard**. Facing Ourselves: Incorrigibility and the Mind-Body Problem. *J Consciousness Stud*, 3(3), 217-230, 1996.

In the keynote essay, David Chalmers (1995) proposes that we explain consciousness by a nonreductive theory of experience which adds new basic principles to the laws of nature. This essay endorses Chalmers's proposal but argues—contrary to Chalmers—that the principles of such a theory interfere with purely physical laws, since the principles entail violations of physical conservation laws. The essay argues that the qualified incorrigibility of the mental nonetheless provides compelling reason to opt for a nonreductive theory.

**Warner, Stanley** and Feinstein, Mark and Coppinger, Raymond (& others). Global Population Growth and the Demise of Nature. *Environ Values*, 5(4), 285-301, N 96.

We suggest that current trends in population growth are unlikely to abate for three reasons: first, there are intrinsic biological pressures to reproduce regardless of social engineering; second, the character of the domestic alliance makes it a formidable competitor to wildlife; and third, the time-frame before population doubling is, from a biological perspective, virtually instantaneous. This paper draws from a wide body of research in the biological and social sciences. We neither condone nor endorse this picture of inexorable population increase. Rather, we appeal for a change in the nature of the discussion of population among environmentalists, to focus on the question of how best to manage what wildlife will be left on the margins of a domesticated world. (edited)

**Warnke, Camilla**. Wither Marxism?. *Phil Rundsch*, 44(1), 81-87, Mr 97.

**Warren, Dona**. Those Who Can, Do: A Response to Sidney Gendin's "Am I Wicked?". *Teach Phil*, 19(3), 275-279, S 96.

This paper examines the conceptual distinction between doing a thing and teaching that thing. It is argued that although the viability of the distinction normally depends upon the subject matter under discussion and upon what "teaching" and "doing" are taken to mean in a particular context, the nature of philosophy is such that this distinction should not be maintained with respect to it.

**Warren, Karen J**. "Taking Empirical Data Seriously: An Ecofeminist Philosophical Perspective" in *Ecofeminism: Women, Culture, Nature*, Warren, Karen J (ed), 3-20. Bloomington, Indiana Univ Pr, 1997.

**Warren, Karen J** (ed) and Erkal, Nisvan (ed). *Ecofeminism: Women, Culture, Nature*. Bloomington, Indiana Univ Pr, 1997.

The strengths and weaknesses of the growing ecofeminist movement are critically assessed by scholars in a variety of academic disciplines and vocations. Writers explore the real-life concerns that have motivated ecofeminism as a grassroots, women-initiated movement around the globe; the appropriateness of ecofeminism to academic and scientific research; and philosophical implications and underpinnings of the movement. (publisher)

**Warren, Mark E**. What Should We Expect From More Democracy? Radically Democratic Responses to Politics. *Polit Theory*, 24(2), 241-270, My 96.

**Warton, Pamela M** and Goodnow, Jacqueline J. Direct and Indirect Responsibility: Distributing Blame. *J Moral Educ*, 25(2), 173-184, Je 96.

This paper represents two studies exploring the distribution of blame in situations where one member of a family has asked a brother or sister to do a job normally done by the asker and the sibling fails to do the job. Study 1 samples 14- and 18-year olds. Study 2 samples 19-22-year-olds. The results bring out a) a preference for assigning blame to both parties rather than all to one or the other, b) a bias towards assigning less blame to the asker than to the person who has agreed, c) an effect from circumstances that reflect effort on the part of the asker (blame to the asker is reduced, for instance, if he or she has left a reminder) and d) a difference between the allocations made when subjects are in the role of the person asking against the person who has accepted (least blame to the asker when subjects are in the role of acceptor). Age and gender differences were not significant in either study. The results are discussed in terms of the need for an understanding of the circumstances encouraging the acceptance of indirect or vicarious responsibility.

**Waskan, Jonathan** and Bechtel, William. Directions in Connectionist Research: Tractable Computations without Syntactically Structured Representations. *Metaphilosophy*, 28(1-2), 31-62, Ja-Ap 97.

Should connectionists abandon the quest for tractably computable cognitive transition functions while retaining syntactically structured mental representations? We argue, in opposition to Horgan, that it should not. We argue that the case against tractably computable functions, based upon the claimed isotropic and Quinean character of cognition, fails since cognition is not as isotropic and Quinean as Fodor and Horgan contend. As to syntactically structured representations, we argue that they are unneeded for most cognitive tasks organisms confront and that when they are needed, they may be provided by external representational media such as natural language. (edited)

**Wasserman, David**. Let Them Eat Chances: Probability and Distributive Justice. *Econ Phil*, 12(1), 29-49, Ap 96.

**Wassermann, Gerhard D**. *From Occam's Razor to the Roots of Consciousness*. Brookfield, Avebury, 1997.

**Watkins, Eric** (ed & trans) and Brandt, Reinhard. *The Table of Judgments: Critique of Pure Reason* A 67-76; B 92-101. Atascadero, Ridgeview, 1995.

The "transcendental table of all moments of thought in judgments" (A73), generally called simply the "table of judgments," is located at the beginning of the Transcendental Logic and provides a systematic outline of the rest of the *Critique of Pure Reason's* philosophical development. According to Kant, the concepts of the understanding or categories can be derived from the table of judgments. In turn, the categories provide the plan for the Principles of Pure Understanding. The ideas of reason in the second part of the Transcendental Logic, that is, in the Dialectic, are both situated in the systematic plan justified by the table of judgments and grounded in the table of judgments. Our investigation will show that the Doctrine of Method, which follows upon the doctrines of the *concepts* of the understanding, *principles*, and *inferences*, will find its place in the table of judgments as well; it corresponds to the fourth heading, that of modality. (publisher, edited)

**Watkins, John**. "World 1, World 2 and the Theory of Evolution" in *The Significance of Popper's Thought,* Amsterdamski, Stefan (ed), 9-24. Amsterdam, Rodopi, 1996.

World 3 is set aside, not as nonexistent but as irrelevant to the mind-body problem. The article then considers the bearing of Popper's Darwinism on his Cartesian dualist interactionism. It focuses on the "Spearhead Model", which put in a brief appearance in *Objective Knowledge* and was then allowed to fall into neglect. The aim here is to revise and rehabilitate it, since it is of considerable interest and value. (edited)

**Watkins, Michael**. Colours and Causes: A Reply to Jackson and Pargetter. *Dialogue (Canada)*, 36(2), 281-285, Spr 97.

Frank Jackson et Robert Pargetter défendent l'idée que la couleur rouge est la propriété, quelle qu'elle soit, qui cause ou causerait l'apparition de rouge dans notre expérience visuelle. Ceci empêche la couleur rouge d'être une propriété dispositionnelle, soutiennent-ils, puisque les propriétés dispositionnelles sont causalement inertes. Pour des raisons similaires, ils concluent aussi que la couleur rouge ne peut pas être une propriété disjonctive. Mais, comme ils s'en rendent bien compte, plusieurs propriétés physiques différentes sont telles qu'elles causeraient l'apparition de rouge. Ils suggèrent donc de relativiser la couleur rouge aux observateurs, aux conditions d'observation et aux moments du temps. Je soutiens, contre Jackson et Pargetter, que leur solution se heurte aux mêmes objections que celles qu'ils adressent aux interprétations dispositionnelle et disjonctive.

**Watkins, Susan**. "Versions of the Feminine Subject in Charlotte Brontë's *Villette*" in *Critical Studies: Ethics and the Subject,* Simms, Karl (ed), 217-225. Amsterdam, Rodopi, 1997.

**Watson, Richard A**. "The Sceptical Epistemology on *Triste Tropiques*" in *Scepticism in the History of Philosophy: A Pan-American Dialogue,* Popkin, Richard H (ed), 197-203. Dordrecht, Kluwer, 1996.

Levi-Strauss lived the European dream of traveling to the New World to discover Rousseau's natural man. But—French, Rationalist, Cartesian, European—his essential journey was into the depths of his own mind. There he discovered universal laws of human thought that made the strangeness of the jungle people drop away "and one might as well have stayed in one's own village." He scorned Diderot's statement that natural *man* and artificial *man* are at war. Man means *language* means *society.* Man is the animal who puts things in order. But that order is mental, and this led Levi-Strauss to a profoundly pessimistic scepticism.

**Watson, Richard A**. The Ghost in the Machine—Fights—the Last Battle for the Human Soul. *Kriterion*, 37(94), 55-63, Jl-D 96.

The battle is between materialists and dualists. Descartes set the problem with his doctrines that mind and body are distinct substances, and that animals are machines. Dualists argue that the spiritual mind controls the body, but there is little evidence for this. Materialists claim that only bodies exist, that the brain is the mind and that thus human beings are machines. The more neuroscientists learn how the brain works and thus how to control thought, the more likely the materialists are to win.

**Watson, Stephen H**. Interpretation, Dialogue, and Friendship: On the Remainder of Community. *Res Phenomenol*, 26, 54-97, 1996.

**Watts, Fraser N**. Are Science and Religion in Conflict?. *Zygon*, 32(1), 125-138, Mr 97.

The widely held legend of historical conflict between science and religion cannot be sustained on the basis of research. Different sciences show different relationships to religion; the physical sciences show rapprochement, whereas the human sciences often are antagonistic to religion. Reconciling science and religion by regarding each as applicable to a different domain is rejected in favor of seeing them as complementary perspectives on the same phenomena. The science and theology of human nature represents a fruitful arena for the development of this approach. A key general requirement is the epistemological reconciliation of science and religion.

**Watts, Fraser N**. Psychological and Religious Perspectives on Emotion. *Zygon*, 32(2), 243-260, Je 97.

This article is devoted to examining theoretical issues on the interface of the psychology of religion and the psychology of emotion, something which recently has been surprisingly neglected. The broad range of psychological components involved in emotion and the importance of emotional processes in religion, make it a particularly relevant area of general psychology as far as religion is concerned. (edited)

**Waxman, Wayne**. Kant and the Imposition of Time and Space. *Grad Fac Phil J*, 19(1), 43-66, 1996.

**Waxse, David J**. The Role of Minors in Health Care Decision Making: Current Legal Issues. *Bioethics Forum*, 11(4), 17-21, Wint 95.

Legal guidelines have not kept pace with the ethical principles which serve as a basis for the *MBC Guidelines* document. Constitutional and statutory laws affecting children do not prohibit informed decision making and consent on the part of the minor provided the parent or guardian is also a part of this process.

**Wayman, Alex**. A Defense of Yogācāra Buddhism. *Phil East West*, 46(4), 447-476, O 96.

It is claimed that misrepresentations of Yogācāra Buddhism appeared in older and later works in India, and then in European and other scholarship. The thesis that Yogācāra denies external existence is rejected, the defense being this Buddhist system's own response. Two major sections divide the argument: 1) The Position of Yogācārins and 2) Three Clarifications of the Position.

**Wayne, Andrew**. Degrees of Freedom and the Interpretation of Quantum Field Theory. *Erkenntnis*, 46(2), 165-173, Mr 97.

Nick Huggett and Robert Weingard (1994) have recently proposed a novel approach to interpreting field theories in physics, one which makes central use of the fact that a field generally has an infinite number of degrees of freedom in any finite region of space it occupies. Their characterization, they argue, I) reproduces our intuitive categorizations of fields in the classical domain and thereby, II) provides a basis for arguing that the quantum field is a field. Furthermore, III) it accomplishes these tasks better than does a well-known rival approach due to Paul Teller (1990, 1995). This paper contends that all three of these claims are mistaken and suggests that Huggett and Weingard have not shown how counting degrees of freedom provides any insight into the interpretation or the formal properties of field theories in physics.

**Wear, Stephen** and Phillips, Benjamin. Clinical Ethics and the Suffering Christian. *Christian Bioethics*, 2(2), 239-252, Ag 96.

Contrary to the ecumenical spirit of our time, the differences among the Christian religions bring into question what one can say or do in common with fellow Christians. This issue, echoing the program of this journal, accentuates those differences, specifically when we focus on the Christian who is ill and suffering. At the bedside, it is the specifics of a religion, including not only its doctrines, but its informing and sustaining narratives, that must particularly be brought into play for the sake of the patient. Given this, our focus in this article regards what such a view implies for the clinician who is caring for a Christian patient whose religion he may or may not share, in general or in its specifics. Our basic conclusion is that the tendency for the clinician to act as both the patient's spiritual counselor, as well as his clinician, is generally neither prudent nor appropriate. Both hats should be worn concurrently. This view is advanced not only because of concerns regarding patient vulnerability and the possible abuse of power, but also because the two roles may collide with or undermine each other.

**Weatherall, Peter**. What Do Propositions Measure in Folk Psychology?. *Phil Psych*, 9(3), 365-380, S 96.

In this paper I examine the analogical argument that the use that is made of propositions in folk psychology in the characterization of propositional attitudes is no more puzzling than the use that is made of numbers in the physical sciences in the measurement of physical properties. It has been argued that the result of this analogy is that there is no need to postulate the existence of sentences in a language of thought which underpin the propositional characterisation of propositional attitudes in order to provide a naturalistic account of their use. I argue that a closer examination of the analogy implies rather than avoids the existence of structured representations constituting a language of thought and thus that it should be abandoned by those who wish to avoid the postulation of such internal representations.

**Weaver, George E**. Syntactic Features and Synonymy Relations: A Unified Treatment of Some Proofs of the Compactness and Interpolation Theorems. *Stud Log*, 53(2), 325-342, My 94.

This paper introduces the notion of syntactic feature to provide a unified treatment of earlier model theoretic proofs of both the compactness and interpolation theorems for a variety of two-valued logics including sentential logic, first-order logic, and a family of modal sentential logic including M, B, $S_4$, $S_5$. The compactness papers focused on providing a proof of the consequence formulation which exhibited the appropriate finite subset. A unified presentation of these proofs is given by isolating their essential feature and presenting it as an abstract principle about syntactic features. The interpolation papers focused on exhibiting the interpolant. A unified presentation of these proofs is given by isolating their essential feature and presenting it as a second abstract principle about syntactic features. This second principle reduces the problem of exhibiting the interpolant to that of establishing the existence of a family of syntactic features satisfying certain conditions. The existence of such features is established for a variety of logics (including those mentioned above) by purely combinatorial arguments.

**Weaver, Jace** (ed). *Defending Mother Earth: Native American Perspectives on Environmental Justice.* Maryknoll, NY, Orbis, 1996.

The book brings together important native voices to address urgent issues of environmental devastation as they affect the indigenous peoples throughout the Americas. The essays document a range of ecological disasters, including the devastating effects of mining, water pollution, nuclear power facilities, and toxic waste dumps. In an expression of "environmental racism," such hazards are commonly located on or near Indian lands. (publisher, edited)

**Webb, David** (trans) and Vattimo, Gianni. *Beyond Interpretation: The Meaning of Hermeneutics for Philosophy.* Stanford, Stanford Univ Pr, 1997.

Vattimo argues that hermeneutics, understood in a general sense, has had a pervasive influence on contemporary philosophy and social thought. But its very generality is also a symptom of its malaise, for it threatens to leave hermeneutics empty of significance and wedded to a shallow relativism. Vattimo develops a new interpretation of hermeneutics that dispenses with the traditional bias toward aesthetic experience. His radical interpretation breaks the link between hermeneutics and metaphysical humanism, challenges the traditional opposition of the natural and human sciences, and opens up new perspectives on ethics, art and religion. (edited)

**Webb, Judson C**. Hilbert's Formalism and Arithmetization of Mathematics. *Synthese*, 110(1), 1-14, Ja 97.

**Webb, Mark Owen**. The Legitimacy of Laws: A Puzzle for Hart. *Vera Lex*, 14(1-2), 57-59, 1994.

**Webb, Richard**. Terminology in the Salon Reviews of Charles Pierre Baudelaire. *J Aes Educ*, 27(2), 71-84, Sum 93.

**Weber, Erik**. "Scientific Explanation and the Interrogative Model of Inquiry" in *Knowledge and Inquiry: Essays on Jaakko Hintikka's Epistemology and Philosophy of Science,* Sintonen, Matti (ed), 239-259. Amsterdam, Rodopi, 1997.

The aim of the article is to analyze the nature of the construction process of scientific explanations. The search for scientific explanations is a type of inquiry which can be codified by means of Jaakko Hintikka's interrogative model of inquiry. But there is more to be said; the method for constructing scientific explanations which is developed is based on the interrogative model, but also takes into account the various forms of strategic knowledge we use when constructing scientific explanations.

**Weber, Erik**. Comment construit-on une explication déductive-nomologique?. *Dialectica*, 50(3), 183-203, 1996.

Comment devons-nous appliquer notre savoir scientifique (lois de la nature, théories, etc.) pour qu'il contribue à mieux comprendre les phénomènes (événements particuliers, régularités, etc.) que nous observons? Le modèle déductif-nomologique d'explication scientifique, dans lequel Carl Hempel construit le concept d'explication déductive-nomologique, ne procure pas une réponse complète à cette question. Un des problèmes est que Hempel nous dit ce que nous devons construire quand nous voulons comprendre un phénomène (une explication déductive-nomologique), mais ne nous dit pas comment une explication de ce type est construite. Afin de résoudre ce problème, une méthode pour construire des explications déductive-nomologiques est développée.

**Weber, Eugen**. What Rough Beast?. *Crit Rev*, 10(2), 285-298, Spr 96.

Eric Hobsbawm's *Nations and Nationalism since 1780* effectively describes the novelty and artificiality of the modern nation and nation-state, emphasizing the role that cultural and political elites have played in constructing nations, especially through nationally homogeneous schools and partly invented national traditions and histories. By defining nationalism as the congruence between nation and state, however, Hobsbawm gives insufficient attention to the sense in which nationalism goes beyond national patriotism to express chauvinism, xenophobia and paranoia. He is also too sanguine about the ethnic conflicts that will inevitably arise in the multilingual societies he endorses.

**Weber, James** and Green, Sharon. Influencing Ethical Development: Exposing Students to the AICPA Code of Conduct. *J Bus Ethics*, 16(8), 777-790, Je 97.

Although the AICPA code of professional conduct emphasizes the importance of education in ethics, very little is known about how and when the code and the topic of ethics can be presented to enhance the effectiveness of ethics-oriented education. The purpose of this research was to provide preliminary evidence about the ethical development of students prior to, and immediately following, such courses. (edited)

**Weber, Leonard J**. "In Vitro Fertilization and the Just Use of Health Care Resources" in *Reproduction, Technology, and Rights: Biomedical Ethics Reviews*, Humber, James M (ed), 75-109. Clifton, Humana Pr, 1996.

**Weber, Leonard J**. Ethics and the Political Activity of Business: Reviewing the Agenda. *Bus Ethics Quart*, 7(3), 71-79, Jl 97.

**Weber, Marcel**. Fitness Made Physical: The Supervenience of Biological Concepts Revisited. *Phil Sci*, 63(3), 411-431, S 96.

The supervenience and multiple realizability of biological properties have been invoked to support a disunified picture of the biological sciences. I argue that supervenience does not capture the relation between fitness and an organism's physical properties. The actual relation is one of causal dependence and is, therefore, amenable to causal explanation. A case from optimality theory is presented and interpreted as a microreductive explanation of fitness difference. Such microreductions can have considerable scope. Implications are discussed for reductive physicalism in evolutionary biology and for the unity of science.

**Weber, Martin** and Ahlbrecht, Martin. Preference for Gradual Resolution of Uncertainty. *Theor Decis*, 43(2), 167-185, S 97.

Analyzes of preference for the timing of uncertainty resolution usually assumes all uncertainty to resolve in one point in time. More realistically, uncertainty should be modelled to resolve gradually over time. Kreps and Porteus (1978) have introduced an axiomatically based model of time preference which can explain preferences for gradual uncertainty resolution. This paper presents an experimental test of the Kreps-Porteus model. We derive implications of the model relating preferences for gradual and one-time resolving lotteries. Our data do not support the Kreps-Porteus model but show that some of the behaviour observed may be explained by similarity heuristics.

**Weberman, David**. Heidegger and the Disclosive Character of the Emotions. *S J Phil*, 34(3), 379-410, Fall 96.

The purpose of this essay is two-fold: 1) to reconstruct and make more accessible to the non-specialist Heidegger's theory of the emotions; and 2) to put it forth as a promising alternative to current cognitivist accounts. Besides dealing with a number of original aspects of Heidegger's theory (e.g., moods and the ubiquity of affective states), I focus on his claim that emotions have a disclosive character because they tell us things about ourselves, other human beings and the world in general. I argue that such disclosure should not be misconstrued as subjective in nature.

**Weberman, David**. Sartre, Emotions, and Wallowing. *Amer Phil Quart*, 33(4), 393-407, O 96.

This paper clarifies and evaluates the central claim of Sartre's *The Emotions: Outline of a Theory*. That claim says that emotions are essentially modes of consciousness which apprehend the world so as to reduce inner conflicts and let individuals escape from having to take effective action. I argue that it is plausible only if limited to a certain range of emotions. I then show that Sartre's analysis of the *essence* of emotions is inadequate for any type of emotion whatsoever. The paper then explores some of the positive achievements of Sartre's theory and contrasts it with stoical views on emotions.

**Weberman, David**. The Nonfixity of the Historical Past. *Rev Metaph*, 50(4), 749-768, Je 97.

In *Analytical Philosophy of History*, Arthur Danto argued that the narrative structure of history entails that our description of past events will inevitably change as history unfolds. In this paper, I take Danto's insight one step further by showing that not only our descriptions of the past change, but the past events themselves. This is because past events come to have different relational properties as a result of later events. I defend this thesis from a realist, nonconstructivist position. I deal with such issues as the individuation of events, description versus ontology, and so-called Cambridge changes.

**Webster, Yehudi O**. Multiculturalism: An Unhappy Marriage of Multicultural Education and Postmodernism. *Inquiry (USA)*, 16(1), 22-35, Fall 96.

This paper presents arguments to the effect that the merging of postmodernist and multicultural educational tenets bears certain analytical and logical errors—an endorsement of racial and gender identities while at the same time criticizing their essentialist status, utilization of "Western" anthropologists' discovery of separates races and single cultures while protesting against Western "scientific" arrogance and appropriation of a Weberian-Foucauldian conception of power without considering its analytical incompleteness. By virtue of its analytical remissions, conceptual amorphousness, and strategic inconsistencies, multiculturalism self-deconstructs. It is not a revolutionary discourse on the relationships among capitalist commodity production, ideology and education. (edited)

**Webster, Yehudi O**. Thinking Critically About Identities. *Inquiry (USA)*, 16(2), 93-101, Wint 96.

**Wedde, Horst F** (ed). *CyberSpace Virtual Reality: Fortschritt und Gefahr einer innovativen Technologie*. Stuttgart, Urachhaus, 1996.

Virtual Reality—es ist unbestritten, dass diese Errungenschaft der Technik eine ganz neue Dimension eröffnen wird. Ungeahnte Möglichkeiten technischer Nutzung tun sich auf. Architekten, Ingenieure, Städteplaner und Mediziner können alles Beabsichtigte vor Augen haben und testen, ohne das Geringste im wirklichen Raum zu bewegen. Auf der anderen Seite wird Virtual Reality zweifellos tief in das Privatleben eingreifen und die Menschen zunehmend isolieren, wenn sie pseudosoziale Kommunikation und kommerzielle Nutzung in der Faszination der künstlichen Welten betreiben. Der massive Angriff auf die Ich-und Sinnesorganisation darf dabei nicht unterschätzt werden. (publisher,edited)

**Wedgwood, Ralph**. Non-Cognitivism, Truth and Logic. *Phil Stud*, 86(1), 73-91, Ap 97.

This paper provides a new argument for a position of Crispin Wright's: given that ethical statements can be embedded within all sorts of sentential operators and are subject to definite standards of warrantedness, they must have truth conditions. Allan Gibbard's 'normative logic' is the only noncognitivist logic that stands a chance of avoiding Geach's Fregean objection. But what, according to Gibbard, is the point of avoiding inconsistency in one's ethical statements? He must say that it is to ensure that one's ethical statements have a property that has certain features. But the only property that has those features is truth.

**Wedin, Michael V**. Aristotle on How to Define a Psychological State. *Topoi*, 15(1), 11-24, Mr 96.

**Wedlin, Attilio**. On the Notion of Second-Order Exchangeability. *Erkenntnis*, 45(2 & 3), 177-194, Nov 96.

In this paper we consider the conditions of second-order exchangeability and second-order partially exchangeability together with some applications. The first application concerns a general linear state-space model in which the noise process is assumed to be second-order partially exchangeable. Other applications of the second-order exchangeability condition regard statistical procedures in which imprecise prior probability assessments are employed.

**Weed, Douglas L**. Underdetermination and Incommensurability in Contemporary Epidemiology. *Kennedy Inst Ethics J*, 7(2), 107-127, Je 97.

The definitions and analyses provided by McMullin and by Veatch and Stempsey lay the foundation for the description of partial incommensurabilities in the current practice of assessing and interpreting epidemiologic evidence. This practice is called "causal inference" and is undertaken for the purpose of making causal conclusions and public health recommendations from population-based studies of exposures and diseases. Following the work of Bayley and Longino, several suggestions are examined for dealing with the partial incommensurabilities found in the general practice of causal inference in contemporary epidemiology. Two specific examples illustrate these ideas: studies on the relationship between induced abortion and breast cancer and those on the relationship between moderate alcohol consumption and breast cancer. (edited)

**Weeks, Peter**. Synchrony Lost, Synchrony Regained: The Achievement of Musical Co-ordination. *Human Stud*, 19(2), 199-228, Ap 96.

This paper analyzes three errors in a short passage and the ways in which they are 'corrected' either by the errant musician himself or by the other musician in response. In these cases, the restoration of synchrony and the routine performance of the piece thereafter are accomplished successfully in the sense that those listening to the tape of it generally fail to notice any problem! This contrasts to my detection of problems during both my participation in the performance and repeated listening of the resulting audio-tape, I argue that it is this systematic difference in possible hearings that musicians are oriented to when attempting to 'fake it'. Thus, the essential interest is in members' methods for *maintaining as well as restoring synchrony*. (edited)

**Wegner, Marion**. "Werte im Management: Eine empirische Untersuchung" in *Werte und Entscheidungen im Management*, Schmidt, Thomas, 83-135. Marburg, Metropolis, 1996.

AUTHOR INDEX 983 Weingarten, Michael

**Wehmeier, Kai F**. Classical and Intuitionistic Models of Arithmetic. *Notre Dame J Form Log*, 37(3), 452-461, Sum 96.

We will show that such models are in fact *PA*-normal, that is, they consist entirely of Peano nodes. These results are then applied to a somewhat larger class of frames. We close with some general considerations on properties of non-Peano nodes in arbitrary models of *HA*. (edited0

**Wei, Tan Tai**. Justice and Punishment Without Hell. *Sophia (Australia)*, 35(1), 62-72, Mr-Ap 96.

A theory of punishment is advanced that would rule out external hell. It combines the reformative and the retributive theories, retaining their strength and avoiding their pitfalls. It sees it as a means of teaching the injustice of rule-breaking, by which desert of punishment and its proportionality to the offense, are crucial.

**Weidemann, Hermann**. "Ein drittes modallogisches Argument für den Determinismus: Alexander von Aphrodisias" in *Das weite Spektrum der analytischen Philosophie,* Lenzen, Wolfgang, 429-446. Hawthorne, de Gruyter, 1997.

Alexander of Aphrodisias considers an argument for determinism which is based on Aristotle's definition of the possible as that which can be assumed to be realized without anything impossible following therefrom. According to this argument, the truth of a statement about the future and the possibility that what it predicts will not happen are incompatible. In the article it is shown that the argument in question is valid, but that its soundness depends on which sort of truth-conditions a statement about the future is taken to have.

**Weidhorn, Manfred**. Doing One's Own Thing: The Genealogy of a Slogan. *J Thought*, 31(4), 17-31, Wint 96.

The essay traces the evolution of the idea that individual autonomy rather than the welfare of the community is the supreme value. Plato suggests that self knowledge, i.e., awareness of the priority of the soul over the body, is a matter of nonconformity and individualism. 1500 years of the Judeo-Christian tradition see the triumph rather of the view that the individual is subordinate to the interests of the community. Martin Luther, Rabelais and Galileo in their different ways open the door to modern individualism. The idea blooms in the eighteenth and early nineteenth centuries and becomes the leading theme of the second half of the nineteenth century at the hands of men like Emerson, Thoreau, Whitman, Mill, Herzen, Nietzsche. It is dramatized in works like Huckleberry Finn and, especially, A Doll House.

**Weiermann, A** and Cichon, E A. Term Rewriting Theory for the Primitive Recursive Functions. *Annals Pure Applied Log*, 83(3), 199-223, F 97.

The termination of rewrite systems for parameter recursion, simple nested recursion and unnested multiple recursion is shown by using monotone interpretations both on the ordinals below the first primitive recursively closed ordinal and on the natural numbers. We show that the resulting derivation lengths are primitive recursive. As a corollary we obtain transparent and illuminating proofs of the facts that the schemata of parameter recursion, simple nested recursion and unnested multiple recursion lead from primitive recursive functions to primitive recursive functions.

**Weigand, Edda**. The State of the Art in Speech Act Theory. *Prag Cognition*, 4(2), 367-406, 1996.

The article represents a detailed review article on the book 'Foundations of Speech Act Theory. Philosophical and Linguistic Perspectives', edited by Savas L. Tsohatzidis, London/New York: Routledge, 1994. The contributions by well-known scholars (among them Alston, Vanderveken, Bird, Kasher, Dascal, Holdcroft, Sadock, Harnish) are judged according to the expectations raised by the ambitious title of the book. The review article comes to the conclusion that no foundation has been laid for speech act theory in the sense of a generally accepted consistent theory. Some positive aspects are appreciated. Speech act theory as presented in the book is a theory mainly dominated by truth-functional semantics and by Grice, i.e., a philosophical theory without an adequate linguistic basis.

**Weigert, Andrew J**. Definitional and Responsive Environmental Meanings: A Meadian Look at Landscapes and Drought. *J Theor Soc Behav*, 27(1), 65-91, Mr 97.

Current conceptual frameworks differ deeply on the meanings of human-natural environment relations. One is a monist social constructionist frame: meaning is only in human definitions and natural events are meaningless. The other offers dualist perspectives that locate meaning both in definitions and in realist indications of environmental events such as global environmental change. After discussing 'landscape' as a bridging concept, I suggest an ordering of the two perspectives through a metatheoretical distinction between definitional and responsive meanings with primacy in the response. Finally, I apply a metatheoretical schema based on the work of George H. Mead to meanings of natural environment implicated in a discussion of an official pronouncement, 'The drought is over'.

**Weil, Danny**. The Colonization of Subjectivity: The Privatized Curriculum and the Marketing of American Education in a Postmodern Era. *Inquiry (USA)*, 14(2), 70-77, Wint 94.

**Weil, Vivian** and Arzbaecher, Robert. Ethics and Relationships in Laboratories and Research Communities. *Prof Ethics*, 4(3-4), 83-125, Spr-Sum 95.

Scientific research is a highly decentralized enterprise. Research groups and laboratories are characterized by extreme disparities of power and they require cooperation and collaboration in a very competitive environment. Opportunities for unfair treatment, even exploitation, of the less powerful and for unchecked competition threaten the trust and responsible conduct on which the scientific enterprise relies. Seven vignettes of situations in research groups highlight important conflicts that arise. Commentary on the vignettes identifies issues of professional ethics and morality in those situations and explores defensible ways for the agents to deal with their situations and policies for their groups to adopt.

**Weiler, Kathleen**. Myths of Paulo Freire. *Educ Theor*, 46(3), 353-371, Sum 96.

This essay examines the ways in which Paulo Freire has been appropriated within educational theory. Focusing on five recent books on Freire, it highlights the ways in which Freire has been used as a kind of icon or sign by educational writers on the *left* to support a variety of progressive projects. It argues that the canonization of Freire and his use as a symbol without an active or critical engagement with her thought is a betrayal of the ideals he is calling for in his best work.

**Weinberger, Ota**. Information and Human Liberty. *Ratio Juris*, 9(3), 248-257, S 96.

Political and juristic enquiry must be conceived of as an action theoretical approach. On the basis of his formal and finalistic action theory as well as his neoinstitutionalist view, the author sketches the role of information in modern democracy. He holds the view that democratic institutions are always in danger of being misused. The complex role of mass media, party propaganda and the detrimental effects of state propaganda are analyzed. The author deals with some general features of information processes in the realm of political practice: Information has to be considered in relation to action; the message by itself does not show whether the information is true; there are two forms of reception of information, active and passive reception. Information processes have a deep influence on personal as well as on political liberty. The intrusion of marketing-methods of propaganda in political practice is a great danger for democratic life, particularly if realized by the state or central institutions. It can destroy intellectual freedom, which is a prerequisite of discursive democracy. Democracy and human liberty can flourish only in an open society.

**Weiner, Joan**. "Has Frege a Philosophy of Language?" in *Early Analytic Philosophy,* Tait, William W (ed), 249-272. Chicago, Open Court, 1997.

**Weinert, Friedel**. "Weber's Ideal Types as Models in the Social Sciences" in *Verstehen and Humane Understanding,* O'Hear, Anthony (ed), 73-93. New York, Cambridge Univ Pr, 1996.

The purpose of this paper is to link Weber's ideal types to a discussion of models in the natural sciences. Although there is a systematic ambiguity in Weber's characterization of ideal types, given the function of diverse types of models in the natural sciences, ideal types are best interpreted as hypothetical or *as if* models which abstract theoretical constructions from empirical data. But compared to hypothetical models in the natural sciences two problems remain: the degree of approximation of ideal types to empirical cases is often not specified and it remains unclear whether deviations from ideal types in the real world are due to accidental or lawful factors.

**Weinfeld, Irwin J** and Luckner, Kleia R. Informed Consent as a Parent Involvement Model in the NICU. *Bioethics Forum*, 11(1), 35-41, Spr 95.

The informed consent doctrine can be a viable model that ensures and enhances parental input in the decision-making process in the neonatal intensive care unit (NICU). Throughout medical history the purpose and practice of informed consent and patient disclosure has often been to encourage the patient to agree to what the physician wanted to do. A new understanding of this doctrine is necessary for both health care givers and patients, one that views informed consent as a process of mutual discovery, shared options and dialogue.

**Weingard, Robert** and Callender, Craig. Time, Bohm's Theory, and Quantum Cosmology. *Phil Sci*, 63(3), 470-474, S 96.

The so-called problem of time in canonical quantum gravity follows from the fact that the theory appears to describe a static universe, contrary to what we observe. As we have pointed out, Bohm's interpretation of quantum mechanics offers a neat solution to this problem: one can reintroduce time (and a coherent dynamics) through the Bohm equation of motion. However, a natural question to raise about this solution is how the 'Bohm time' is related to the time appearing in ordinary quantum mechanics. In this paper we explore a plausible way these two times can turn out to be the same.

**Weingard, Robert** and Callender, Craig. Trouble in Paradise? Problems for Bohm's Theory. *Monist*, 80(1), 24-43, Ja 97.

For good reason Bohm's interpretation of quantum mechanics recently has experienced a kind of renaissance. The theory provides us with a consistent, empirically adequate picture of the quantum world. However, it would be naive to think the theory is free of problems. In this essay we present some of the difficulties facing the theory and the prospects there are for solving them. In particular, we look at the problems of 1) its 'spoiled' symmetries, 2) extending it to field theory and quantum gravity, 3) the ontological status of the wavefunction, and 4) the justification of Born's rule.

**Weingard, Robert** and Huggett, Nick. Exposing the Machinery of Infinite Renormalization. *Proc Phil Sci Ass*, 3(Suppl), S159-S167, 1996.

This paper sets out the problem of renormalization in perturbative quantum field theory, and offers a transparent model as a clear counter example to the idea that the need for renormalization shows a theory to be inconsistent. The model is not of a quantum field but liquid diffusion through a porous medium: though the systems are physically dissimilar, their formal properties are identical, as we demonstrate. Since the model system is much easier to understand, we can see the meaning of renormalization much more clearly and, we claim, draw lessons about renormalization in field theory.

**Weingarten, Michael** and Gutmann, Wolfgang Friedrich. Maschinentheoretische Grundlagen der organismischen Konstruktionslehre. *Phil Natur*, 28(2), 231-256, 1991.

**Weinsheimer, Joel** (trans) and Gadamer, Hans-Georg and Grondin, Jean. *Introduction to Philosophical Hermeneutics*. New Haven, Yale Univ Pr, 1994.

In this wide-ranging historical introduction to philosophical hermeneutics, Jean Grondin discusses the major figures from Philo to Habermas, analyzes conflicts between various interpretive schools and provides a persuasive account and a critical appraisal of Gadamer's *Truth and Method*. (publisher)

**Weinstein, Jack Russell**. Critical Thinking and the Moral Sentiments: Adam Smith's Moral Psychology and Contemporary Debate in Critical Thinking and Informal Logic. *Inquiry (USA)*, 16(3), 76-91, Spr 97.

**Weinstein, Jack Russell**. Three Types of Critical Thinking about Religion: A Response to William Reinsmith. *Inquiry (USA)*, 15(3), 79-88, Spr 96.

**Weinstein, Mark**. "Decentering and Reasoning" in *Philosophy of Education (1996)*, Margonis, Frank (ed), 178-181. Urbana, Phil Education Soc, 1997.

The paper explores a possible solution to the tension between the need for objectivity and the postmodern sensitivity to contextual embeddedness offered by Endres. The solution is seen as lacking although the questions raised are well worth exploring.

**Weinstein, Mark**. Critical Thinking: Expanding the Paradigm. *Inquiry (USA)*, 15(1), 23-39, Fall 95.

Critical thinking at the college level needs a paradigm more deeply rooted in the social and moral requirements of thinking in a complex world, including a more critical look at prevailing practices across the disciplines. This requires, first that the normative force of educational reform through critical thinking be made transparent in its application to postsecondary education and that the theoretic weakness of prevailing conception of informal logic be exposed. The paper offers an analysis of critical thinking across the disciplinary as a framework available for post-secondary educational reform. Such a framework has theoretic consequences for informal logic adequate to the needs of a theory of inquiry.

**Weinstein, Mark**. Some Foundational Problems with Informal Logic and Their Solution. *Inquiry (USA)*, 15(4), 27-43, Sum 96.

Informal logic as currently conceived fails to successfully address essential concepts that underlie the four most vexing problems in informal logic theory today: premise acceptability; premise relevance; argument reconstruction; and argument cogency. The resolution of these problems seems unlikely given the unwillingness of informal logicians to examine the details of actual argumentation in the disciplines. The current conception of informal logic limited by the textbook trade, cannot adequately address the triad of concepts that support a useful logic; entailment, relevance and truth, whose analysis point away from concerns with fragmentary arguments in natural language and towards a project of another sort entirely.

**Weinstein, Michael A**. Civic Liberalism and Educational Reform. *Educ Theor*, 47(3), 411-425, Sum 97.

The predominant tendency in liberal thought in contemporary American social science is civic liberalism, which melds the traditions of John Locke and Jean-Jacques Rousseau to produce visions of the reconciliation of individuality and social responsibility that transcend the liberal/communitarian polemic in the name of civic virtue. Recent works by David Paris and John Witt define the parameters of civic liberalism in current educational theory. Paris's version of civic liberalism fails to reconcile liberal skepticism with communitarian affirmation, and falls into unconscious irony; whereas Watt's more critical version ends in an explicitly ironical stance.

**Weinstein, Steven**. Strange Couplings and Space-Time Structure. *Proc Phil Sci Ass*, 3(Suppl), S63-S70, 1996.

General relativity is commonly thought to imply the existence of a unique metric structure for space-time. A simple example is presented of a general relativistic theory with ambiguous metric structure. Brans-Dicke theory is then presented as a further example of a space-time theory in which the metric structure is ambiguous. Other examples of theories with ambiguous metrical structure are mentioned. Finally, it is suggested that several new and interesting philosophical questions arise from the sorts of theories discussed.

**Weinstock, Daniel M**. Making Sense of Mill. *Dialogue (Canada)*, 35(4), 791-804, Fall 96.

This critical review of Wendy Donner's *The Liberal Self* argues that the author fails to establish that Mill's utilitarianism can be seen as an objective decision procedure for ethics. The principal claim is that the "competent moral agents" whose judgments are meant to ground the objectivity of Mill's revised utilitarian theory are specified in a manner which fails to circumvent the circularity objection to which theories which refer to the judgments of ideal moral judges are particularly susceptible.

**Weinstock, Daniel M**. Natural Law and Public Reason in Kant's Political Philosophy. *Can J Phil*, 26(3), 389-411, S 96.

I argue that recent interpretations of Kant's political philosophy (e.g., Mulholland's) which stress its proximity to the natural law tradition, and which consequently downplay the justificatory relevance of his contractualist arguments, have tended to overlook the importance which the operation of fora of free public reason performs in the ability of legislators to satisfy Kant's hypothetical contractualist test.

**Weintraub, Ruth**. The Impossibility of Interpersonal Utility Comparisons: A Critical Note. *Mind*, 105(420), 661-665, O 96.

Hausman (1995) has recently provided an argument against identifying well-being with preference satisfaction: 1) The only way of comparing preferences is in terms of the so-called zero-one rule, assigning value 1 (0) to the top (bottom) of everybody's utility function; 2) The zero-one rule is unfair; 3) If a conception of well-being does not permit one to make ethically acceptable interpersonal comparisons, then that conception of well-being is untenable. I will focus on the first and third theses. Hausman's arguments for the first, I will suggest (II-III), fail. If the third thesis is correct, I shall then argue (IV), it can be used to undermine other plausible conceptions of the good.

**Weintraub, Ruth**. The Sceptical Life. *Dialectica*, 50(3), 225-233, 1996.

According to the radical sceptic we have no reason to believe anything, being unable even to distinguish the more probable from the less. I propose to consider the practical problems engendered by this stance. It seems to require that we suspend judgment, but it is not clear that we can acquiesce to this demand. Is it psychologically possible to suspend belief? And if it is, can the sceptic live and act without believing? The practical difficulties, I shall argue, are genuine (although not always properly understood), but do not absolve us from the need to contend with sceptical arguments.

**Weir, Alan**. On an Argument for Irrationalism. *Phil Papers*, 25(2), 95-114, Ag 96.

I present a dilemma which seems to force us to irrationalism. If we have no choice but to accept what purports to be reason's dictates then either there is no rationality or no significant difference between e.g., the persuader and the brainwasher. If we have a choice, in particular over which fundamental rational principles to adopt, rationality seems to rest ultimately on an arbitrary basis and there is no rationally significant asymmetry with an outright irrationalist acting and thinking on the merest whim. I argue that no currently popular epistemology can resolve this problem.

**Weir, Jack**. Poverty, Development, and Sustainability: The Hidden Moral Argument. *Acorn*, 8(2), 17-22, Fall 95.

Encouraged by the United Nations, the nations of the world have been quick to endorse sustainability. In this paper, I analyze the argument for sustainability. The concept of sustainability, I argue, is a euphemism for Westernization and capitalistic materialism and greed. Moreover, democratic political procedures will likely fail to prevent environmental collapse for two reasons: 1) the seductive nature of Westernization and 2) the philosophically controversial status of environmentally positive moral and political ideologies. Alternatively ways need to be found to encourage nations and individuals to adopt nonconsumptive values and lifestyles.

**Weiss, Andrea** and Katzner, James. Learning Philosophy Collaboratively with a Student. *Thinking*, 13(2), 23-26, 1997.

**Weiss, Bernhard**. Anti-Realism, Truth-Value Links and Tensed Truth Predicates. *Mind*, 105(420), 577-602, O 96.

Antirealism about the past is apparently in conflict with our acceptance of a set of systematic linkages between the truth-values of differently tensed sentences made at different times. Arguments based on acceptance of these so-called truth-value links seem to show that fully accounting for our use of the past and future tenses will involve use of a notion of truth which is not epistemically constrained and is thus antirealistically unacceptable. I elaborate these difficulties through an examination of work by Dummett and Wright. I agree with Wright's rejection of Dummett's proposal but go on to argue that Wright's account fares no better. Building on what I take to be the failure of Wright's account, I offer a solution for the antirealist which diagnoses the problem as stemming from an equivocation in the meanings assigned to the tensed truth predicates. I close by raising a different problem for antirealist accounts of the past, one which is, however, related to more general difficulties for antirealist theories of meaning.

**Weiss, Paul**. *Being and Other Realities*. Chicago, Open Court, 1995.

Paul Weiss maintains that "the primary, essential task of philosophy is to provide an account of the primary realities" and "to make evident their primary preconditions, interrelations and consequences." Accordingly, he subjects persons, humanized realities, nature and the cosmos to revolutionary examinations and opens up a new inquiry into the nature of the role of mediators. Weiss also provides original proofs for the existence of a primary, necessary reality—Being—and offers a new explanation of the existence of contingencies. At once daring and carefully defended, the book breaks new ground in its treatment of perception, evidence, passages from one domain to another, time, transcendents and hypotheses. (publisher, edited)

**Weiss, Thomas G**. UN Responses in the Former Yugoslavia: Moral and Operational Choices. *Ethics Int Affairs*, 8, 1-22, 1994.

In the former Yugoslavia, the West emphasized conciliation mixed with humanitarianism. Rather than a sensible moral choice, this approach constituted a palliative that served as a substitute for and may actually have impeded, more creative diplomacy and more vigorous military action. The sum of ad hoc operational decision can add up to a moral conclusion of significance—namely intervention on behalf of the aggressors.

**Weissberg, Robert**. The Real Marketplace of Ideas. *Crit Rev*, 10(1), 107-121, Wint 96.

"The marketplace of ideas" is a powerful legal and political metaphor—a bulwark of an open, liberal society—that suggests a positivistic debate utilizing reason and evidence. In reality, however, the marketplace of ideas often consists of illogic and bad evidence, producing clutter and confusion. The parallel with scientific research is misinformed. Evidence from collective decision-making and small group studies cast grave doubts on the "marketplace's" ability to maximize truth.

**Weissman, David**. Free Speech. *Metaphilosophy*, 27(4), 339-355, O 96.

Recognition of the harms done by free speech is a function of the social ontology presupposed. An atomist ontology implies that the harms suffered are

AUTHOR INDEX 985 Wenger, Neil S

restricted to individual people. This paper suggests an alternate ontology—one that describes systems established by the causal reciprocities of their proper parts. It proposes a consequentialist moral theory and considers the harms suffered by these systems a) when speech exposes their internal, otherwise private, behaviors or features, b) when speech is malicious and false and c) when speech is monopolistic. Does the proposed ontology have objectionable implications for public policy? Alternative answers are considered briefly.

**Weithman, Paul J**. "Natural Law, Morality, and Sexual Complementarity" in *Sex, Preference, and Family: Essays on Law and Nature,* Nussbaum, Martha C (ed), 227-246. New York, Oxford Univ Pr, 1997.

The author attempts to refute John Finnis's argument that homosexual activity is morally wrong and that its moral wrongness gives government good (though perhaps not conclusive) reason to discourage it.

**Weitzman, Leora**. Necessity, Apriority, and Logical Structure. *Erkenntnis,* 46(1), 33-47, Ja 97.

Logical structure may explain the necessity and *a priori* knowability of such truths as that if *A* is red then *A* is either red or green. But this explanation cannot be extended to sentences that, while necessary and knowable *a priori,* do not wear the appropriate logical structure on their sleeves—sentences like "if *A* is a point and *A* is red, then *A* is not green," or "if *A* is a sphere, then *A* is not a cube." The real origin of *these* sentences' necessity and *a priori* knowability is a relationship between the *meanings* of their component atomic sentences—a relationship which cannot be systematically reduced to logical structure by translating those atomic sentences into any kind of "ideal" language. Moreover, this kind of relationship is one to which *any* atomic sentences are susceptible if they have a classifying, or comparison-implying, content. Arguably, then, *all* atomic sentences are capable of being related to others in ways that are necessary and knowable *a priori.*

**Weksler-Waszkinel, R J** and Swiezawski, Stefan. Freedom in Philosophy (in Polish). *Kwartalnik Filozof,* 25(1), 9-24, 1997.

**Welch, David A**. Can We Think Systematically About Ethics and Statecraft?. *Ethics Int Affairs,* 8, 23-37, 1994.

To think systematically about ethics and statecraft is to draw logically-valid conclusions from ethical premises about the proper course of state action in such a way as to render like evaluations in like cases. Systematic ethical judgment is elusive in the modern world, partly because historically prominent (primarily foundational) ethical traditions dominate discourse on ethics and international affairs. Being parochial, these are incapable of extramural justification. Conventionalism offers a more promising long-term alternative basis for ethical deliberation and judgment.

**Welch, Edward J**. Business Ethics in Theory in Practice: Diagnostic Notes A: A Prescription for Value. *J Bus Ethics,* 16(3), 309-313, F 97.

A business ethics practitioner and a moral theologian discuss business ethics. Drawing from value-added accounting principles and extending them to include the company's stakeholders, especially its employees, Welch explains their significance for the origin, formation, and direction of his company's new ethics program. Primeaux responds to Welch from a perspective rooted in the economic theory of profit maximization and its ethical implications. Among the similarities in their thinking is a serious consideration of the role of profit for business and business ethics.

**Welchman, Alistair**. "Machinic Thinking" in *Deleuze and Philosophy: The Difference Engineer,* Ansell Pearson, Keith (ed), 211-229. New York, Routledge, 1997.

This paper argues that transcendence (most obviously theological) has skewed much of Western thinking by forcing material complexity to be interpreted as the intervention of something immaterial. Contemporary terms in the anglophone world that can play this role are: intentionality (privatized theology), representation and semantics. Deleuze launches a powerful critique of residually theological reasoning that has wide application in both philosophy and science. This critique converges with and deepens, perhaps surprisingly for a French philosopher, similar critiques that are being offered today in evolutionary biology and cognitive science.

**Welchman, Jennifer**. Dewey and Moore on the Science of Ethics. *Trans Peirce Soc,* 33(2), 392-409, Spr 97.

Differences in Dewey's and Moore's ethical theories are naturally but incorrectly attributed to differences in the epistemological and metaphysical positions they adopted after breaking with idealism. I trace the divergence to their respective reactions to debates among idealists about the nature and scope of ethical theory, the "science" of ethics.

**Welchman, Jennifer**. Kant and the Land Ethic. *Phil Cont World,* 2(2), 17-22, Sum 95.

Does Leopold's land ethic principle represent a break with traditional Western moral philosophies as some have argued? Or is it instead an extension of traditional Western moral ideas as Leopold believed? I argue that Leopold's principle is compatible with an ecologically-informed Kantianism.

**Welin, Stellan** and Munthe, Christian. The Morality of Scientific Openness. *Sci Eng Ethics,* 2(4), 411-428, O 96.

The ideal of scientific openness, i.e., the idea that scientific information should be freely accessible to interested parties, is strongly supported throughout the scientific community. At the same time, however, this ideal does not appear to be absolute in the everyday practice of science. In order to get the credit for new scientific advances, scientists often keep information to themselves. Also, it is common practice to withhold information obtained in commissioned research when the scientist has agreed with his or her employer to do so. The secrecy may be intended forever, as in the military area, but also temporarily until a patent application has been made. The paper explores to what extent such secrecy is undesirable, as seems to be suggested by the ideal of scientific openness. Should this ideal be interpreted as having certain exceptions which make the above-mentioned practices acceptable? Are there, on closer inspection, good arguments for the ideal of scientific openness, and for officially upholding it? Possible versions of the ideal of scientific openness are explored and the issue is found to be rather complex, allowing for wide variations depending on the acting parties, beneficiaries, types of information and moral requirements involved. We conclude that the arguments usually given in favor of this ideal are weaker than what seems to be generally believed, and that, on closer inspection, they have plenty of room for exceptions to it. These exceptions only partly cover the actual practice of withholding scientific information, and there may still be good reason to advocate, teach and enforce the ideal of scientific openness within the scientific community.

**Wellington, Alex**. Feminist Positions on Vegetarianism: Arguments For and Against and Otherwise. *Between Species,* 11(3-4), 98-104, Sum-Fall 95.

The paper explores purported connections between feminism and vegetarianism, the importance of which is evidenced by the large proportion of vegetarians who are women and recent proliferation of feminist theorizing about vegetarianism. I examine several versions of "care ethic" and antidomination" approaches to feminist morality. I find that although adherents of each approach claim that commitment to feminism requires vegetarianism, there are others who argue against that claim. I conclude that distinctive to feminist approaches to vegetarianism is style of moral reasoning, one which rejects exclusive reliance on rationality and which emphasizes emotional ties and political implications of moral choice.

**Wellmer, Albrecht**. The Conditions for Democratic Culture: (A. Bakesová): Commentary (Czech). *Filosof Cas,* 45(1), 89-111, 1997.

**Welsch, Wolfgang**. Vernunft heute. *Protosoz,* 8/9, 292-321, 1996.

What type of reason will work under the present conditions? To answer this question a meaningful conception of reason (as distinct from rationality) has to be developed, and is contemporary conditions (due to change in the field of rationality) have to be specified. In Part I of the paper, the radically altered structure of rationality is analysed; it turns out to be characterized by rational disorder. Part II offers a redefinition of reason; guided by the idea of justice reason operates in transition from one rationality to another. This new kind of reason—"transversal reason"—is further elaborated in Part III. It is regarded as a key-element of any type of reason.

**Welton, William A**. Divine Inspiration and the Origins of the Laws in Plato's *Laws. Polis,* 14(1-2), 53-83, 1995.

This paper investigates the theme of the divine inspiration of laws in Plato's *Laws*, examining evidence for and against the thesis that Plato endorses some conception of divine inspiration for laws. Various accounts of the origin of laws offered in the text are discussed in relation to the main question. It is argued that Plato's nontraditional conception of deity supports a notion of divine inspiration through participation in the rational order of the universe.

**Welton, William A** and Scott, Gary Alan. An Overlooked Motive in Alcibiades' *Symposium* Speech. *Interpretation,* 24(1), 67-84, Fall 96.

The *Symposium's* infamous story of Alcibiades' attempt to seduce Socrates enacts a contrast between two kinds of Eros: the Eros of which Diotima speaks and the acquisitive Eros Alcibiades exhibits. This paper claims that Socrates resists Alcibiades' erotic advances not because he is incapable of love for particular persons and not because he champions an ascetic ideal, but rather because Alcibiades is attempting to dominate the philosopher by transacting an exchange with him, showing thereby that Socrates is corruptible. Most commentators have overlooked Alcibiades' motive—to gain an advantage (*pleonektein*) over Socrates in order to sully the philosopher and relieve his own sense of shame. We examine the evidence for this motive, and argue that it is chiefly to preserve his freedom that Socrates eschews the exchange.

**Wendler, Dave**. Locke's Acceptance of Innate Concepts. *Austl J Phil,* 74(3), 467-483, S 96.

Jerry Fodor argues that, on Empiricist theories of concept acquisition, all of our concepts are innate. I analyze this argument by developing a Lockean account of innate concepts and comparing it to Fodor's analysis. I show that, for Locke at least, it is the arbitrariness, rather than the innateness, or the rationality, of the process of concept development that determines the innateness of the concepts thus developed. For this reason, Fodor is both right and wrong: Locke was committed to the innateness of our concepts of secondary qualities, but not our concepts of primary qualities.

**Wendling, Karen**. "Two Concepts of Rawls" in *A Question of Values: New Canadian Perspectives in Ethics and Political Philosophy,* Brennan, Samantha (ed), 135-153. Amsterdam, Rodopi, 1997.

I argue Rawls's contract focuses on a different form of social interaction than other models of the contract. Standardly, contracts focus on interactions between individuals. Rawls's contact, however, focuses on the major social institutions—government, economy and the family—that determine the acceptable boundaries of individual interactions. I trace the distinction between individual interactions and social institutions from Rawls's 1955 article "Two Concepts of Rules" to *Political Liberalism.* Shifting the focus from interactions to institutions requires the development of new contractual assumptions concerning value, rationality and interests and I suggest some alternative assumptions.

**Wenger, Neil S** and FitzGerald, John. The Invalid Advance Directive. *Bioethics Forum,* 13(2), 32-34, Sum 97.

Advance directives, when they stipulate that specific treatments be withdrawn or withheld, often fail to match the signer's more nuanced situation-based oral instructions. Nevertheless, they remain powerful documents that, when constructed and administered carefully, can direct decision making in end-of-life care.

**Wenkart, Henry**. Feminist Revaluation of the Mythical Triad, Lilith, Adam, Eve: A Contribution to Role Model Theory. *Phil Cont World*, 1(4), 40-44, Wint 94.

This essay inquires into the need for and power of role models and suggests some answers. The example it employs to study the issue is the contemporary Jewish feminist "role model," Lilith, first wife of Adam. Various and opposite forms of the Lilith-and-Adam myth through the ages are given, including new contributions from a Lilith anthology in preparation by the author and others. Those needs of women and men that the mythical "role model" is constructed to satisfy are suggested.

**Wennemann, Daryl J**. From Absurdity to Decision: The Challenge of Responsibility in a Technological Society. *Amer Cath Phil Quart*, 70(Supp), 105-120, 1996.

**Wenz, Peter S**. Philosophy Class as Commercial. *Environ Ethics*, 19(2), 205-216, Sum 97.

Because commercialism tends toward environmental degradation, selection and treatment of the philosophical canon are environmental matters. Environmentalists and others who teach early modern and modern philosophy should, I argue, alter typical pedagogical approaches that (usually unwittingly) reinforce common assumptions underlying commercialism and promote anti-environmental perspectives. Typical treatments of Hobbes, Locke, Descartes, Kant, Hume and Bentham focus on human selfishness, mind-body dualism, the subjectivity of values and the mathematical nature of reality, positions that are frequently identified as contributing causes both of the environmental crisis and of commercialism. The alternative, I argue, is to place canonical thinkers in historical perspective within a history of ideas that also includes such writers as Montaigne, Erasmus, Reid, Burke, Goethe and Emerson. Such courses can be historically accurate, pedagogically sound and environmentally benign.

**Werhane, Patricia** and Doering, Jeffrey. Conflicts of Interest and Conflicts of Commitment. *Prof Ethics*, 4(3-4), 47-81, Spr-Sum 95.

**Werpehowski, William**. "Do You Do Well to Be Angry?". *Annu Soc Christ Ethics*, 59-77, 1996.

I consider the role of anger in the moral life, and especially in the Christian moral life, by exploring three questions. 1) How should we describe the phenomenon of anger? 2) What virtues and/or vices properly account for the affection? 3) What theological assessments of the phenomenon are most fitting? I address the first two questions through an Aristotelian strategy that describes the mean rightly disposing us to be (both) good and angry, and move from there to theological assessments. I argue that the sin of pride deforms the creaturely self-respect that anger putatively protects and then present one sort of correction to that peril proposed within Christian tradition.

**Wertz, S K**. Moral Judgments in History: Hume's Position. *Hume Stud*, 22(2), 339-367, N 96.

This essay consists of four sections and a conclusion. The first section is a brief description of the problem of moral judgments in history from the standpoint of contemporary analytic philosophy of history. With this context, Hume is introduced into the debate and it is asked where he would stand on this issue. In this second section, his notion of history and conception of moral judgment are examined with an eye on illustrations (such as Hume's account of the fate of Montrose) from the *History of England*. Section three continues the argument with a look at various accounts of Cardinal Wolsey—including Hume's and Lord Action's. The fourth section analyzes Hume's crucial concepts of common experience, sympathy and presentation in light of later theories. The conclusion points to concerns other than those I have dealt with and how the subject could be further developed.

**Wescoat Jr, James L**. "Muslim Contributions to Geography and Environmental Ethics: The Challenges of Comparison and Pluralism" in *Philosophy and Geography I: Space, Place, and Environmental Ethics*, Light, Andrew (ed), 91-116. Lanham, Rowman & Littlefield, 1997.

**Wesling, Donald**. Michel Serres, Bruno Latour, and the Edges of Historical Periods. *Clio*, 26(2), 189-204, Wint 97.

**Wesselius, Janet Catherina**. "Points of Convergence Between Dooyeweerdian and Feminist Views of the Philosophic Self" in *Knowing Other-Wise: Philosophy at the Threshold of Spirituality*, Olthuis, James H (ed), 54-68. New York, Fordham Univ Pr, 1997.

This article examines how feminist and Dooyeweerdian critiques of the transcendental logical ego converge in the insistence that multifaceted persons are a better model for philosophy: Dooyeweerd's argument provides theoretical reasons for rejecting the transcendental logical ego, whereas feminist arguments are for new models of a philosophic self can concretely unfold the implications of Dooyeweerd's emphasis on integral human beings. First, Kant's transcendental logical ego is examined. Then, feminist arguments against the transcendental logical ego and alternative views are discussed. Then, Dooyeweerd's argument against the transcendental logical ego is examined. Finally, the convergent implications of Dooyeweerdian and feminist views are explored.

**Wessell, Leonard P**. Cómo he de criticar a Zubiri o "Much Ado about Nothing": Contrarréplica heterodoxa a Rafael Martínez Castro. *Agora (Spain)*, 15(1), 131-149, 1996.

**Westerståhl, Dag** and Väänänen, Jouko and Hella, Lauri. Definability of Polyadic Lifts of Generalized Quantifiers. *J Log Lang Info*, 6(3), 305-335, Jl 97.

**Westley, Robert St. Martin**. "White Normativity and the Rhetoric of Equal Protection" in *Existence in Black: An Anthology of Black Existential Philosophy*, Gordon, Lewis R (ed), 91-98. New York, Routledge, 1997.

The argument of this paper is that current hegemonic interpretations of equal protection have led to the racialization of white Americans in a historically unprecedented way. Thus, the equal protection rhetoric that places affirmative action in jeopardy and questions its constitutionality, concurrently displaces whiteness from a position of normativity by racializing it. In order to sustain the thesis of so-called "reverse (racial?) discrimination," white Americans must be seen as constituting a racial community in an analogous sense as, but the polar opposite of, the Black community. The rhetorical transformation of whiteness from a position of normativity to the racial margin, it is argued, is merely doctrinal. White normativity persists, rearticulated as a social ideal of colorblindness and equality of opportunity. Moreover, because of the persistence of even a racialized white normativity, state racial policy, under the banner of colorblindness and equality of opportunity, can now be formulated without appearing to be racial at all.

**Westmoreland, Robert** (ed) and Pojman, Louis (ed). *Equality: Selected Readings*. New York, Oxford Univ Pr, 1997.

The book collects the most representative material on the subject of equality, providing critical analyses of the egalitarian principles which underlie contemporary debate on issues such as welfare, civil and human rights, affirmative action, and immigration. This volume includes a broad range of readings, from the classical works of Aristotle, Hobbes, and Rousseau to contemporary selections by John Rawls, Thomas Nagel, R.M. Hare, Harry Frankfurt, Wallace Matson, Robert Nozick, Michael Walzer, and others. Several important topics are covered in depth, including the concept of equality; equal opportunity; welfare egalitarianism; resource egalitarianism; complex equality; and equal human worth and human rights. A comprehensive introduction and bibliography are also included. (publisher, edited)

**Weston, Anthony**. "Before Environmental Ethics" in *Environmental Pragmatism*, Light, Andrew (ed), 139-160. New York, Routledge, 1996.

Contemporary nonanthropocentric environmental ethics is profoundly shaped by the very anthropocentrism that it tries to transcend. New values only slowly struggle free of old contexts. Recognizing this struggle, however, opens a space for—indeed, necessitates—alternative models for contemporary environmental ethics. Rather than trying to unify or fine-tune our theories, we require more pluralistic and exploratory methods. We cannot reach theoretical finality; we can only coevolve an ethic with transformed practices.

**Weston, Anthony**. "Beyond Intrinsic Value: Pragmatism in Environmental Ethics" in *Environmental Pragmatism*, Light, Andrew (ed), 285-306. New York, Routledge, 1996.

In this essay I propose an environmental ethic in the pragmatic vein. I begin by suggesting that the contemporary debate in environmental ethics is forced into a familiar but highly restrictive set of distinctions and problems by the traditional notion of intrinsic value, particularly by its demands that intrinsic values be self-sufficient, abstract and justified in special ways. I criticize this notion and develop an alternative which stresses the interdependent structure of values, a structure which at once roots them deeply in our selves and at the same time opens them to critical challenge and change. Finally, I apply this alternative view back to environmental ethics. It becomes easy to justify respect for other life forms and concern for the natural environment and indeed many of the standard arguments only become stronger, once the demand to establish intrinsic values is removes.

**Weston, Anthony**. *A Practical Companion to Ethics*. New York, Oxford Univ Pr, 1997.

The book is a concise introduction to the basic attitudes and skills that make ethics work, like thinking for oneself, creative and integrative problem solving and keeping an open mind. This unique volume illuminates the broad kinds of practical intelligence required in moral judgment, complementing the narrower theoretical considerations that often dominate ethics courses. It offers practical instruction in problem solving by demonstrating how to frame an ethical problem and deal effectively with ethical disagreements. (publisher,edited)

**Weston, Anthony** and Katz, Eric. "Unfair to Swamps: A Reply to Katz Unfair to Foundations? A Reply to Weston" in *Environmental Pragmatism*, Light, Andrew (ed), 319-324. New York, Routledge, 1996.

**Westphal, Jonathan** (ed). *Justice*. Indianapolis, Hackett, 1996.

The readings in *Justice* include the central philosophical statements about justice in society organized to illustrate both the political vision of a good society and different attempts at an analysis of the concept of justice. (publisher, edited)

**Westphal, Kenneth R**. Affinity, Idealism, and Naturalism: The Stability of Cinnabar and the Possibility of Experience. *Kantstudien*, 88(2), 139-189, 1997.

Kant introduced both transcendental idealism and transcendental arguments into philosophy. Transcendental arguments aim to establish conditions necessary for our having self-conscious experience at all. Transcendental idealism holds that such conditions are satisfied only because they are generated by the structure or functioning of our cognitive capacities. Can only transcendental idealism fulfill such conditions? I show that: 1) The transcendental affinity of the manifold of intuition were vital to the second edition of the *Critique*. 2) Kant's link between transcendental idealism and transcendental arguments is substantive, not methodological. 3) Kant's views on transcendental affinity show that there are nonsubjective, transcendental *material* conditions for the possibility of unified self-conscious experience. 4) These conditions and Kant's arguments for them directly undermine Kant's own arguments for transcendental idealism. 5) These points reveal serious flaws in Allison's defense of Kant's idealism. 6) Realists, naturalists and pragmatists have much to learn and to borrow from Kant's transcendental analysis of the conditions of unified self-conscious experience.

**Westphal, Kenneth R**. Noumenal Causality Reconsidered: Affection, Agency, and Meaning in Kant. *Can J Phil*, 27(2), 209-245, Je 97.

Kant's theoretical philosophy has been interpreted by means of various antecedent verificationist, positivist, phenomenological, realist, or phenomenalist predilections of his expositors. Using Kant in this way can be and often has been a very fruitful enterprise philosophically. But treating Kant as a philosopher in himself requires taking seriously his theoretical aim to level the philosophical ground and render it sufficiently secure for majestical moral edifices (A319=B375-76), his claim that practical reason has primacy over theoretical reason and his claim that only the double-aspect metaphysics of transcendental idealism can reconcile theoretical and practical reason because it alone can reconcile autonomous rational action with natural determinism (B xxvi-xxx). If that requires countenancing noumenal causality, so be it. It is not an incoherent idea, and Kant was, after all, a very sophisticated kind of idealist.

**Westphal, Kenneth R** (ed) and Will, Frederick L and MacIntyre, Alasdair. *Pragmatism and Realism*. Lanham, Rowman & Littlefield, 1997.

Will demonstrates that a social account of human knowledge is consistent with, and ultimately requires, realism. The book culminates in a naturalistic account of the generation, assessment and revision of cognitive, moral and social norms. It is written clearly enough for undergraduates and makes a timely contribution to current debates. A critical introduction by the editor discusses the bearing of Will's views on current issues in analytic epistemology, philosophy of science, and moral theory. Will's work "is one of the more remarkable achievements of 20th-century North American philosophy."—Alasdair MacIntyre. (publisher)

**Westphal, Merold**. "Introduction" in *Reason, Experience, and God: John E. Smith in Dialogue*, Colapietro, Vincent M, 1-5. New York, Fordham Univ Pr, 1997.

A brief overview of John Smith's search for thicker, richer concepts of both reason and experience against a background of positivism.

**Westphal, Merold**. "Philosophy as Critique and as Vision" in *The Recovery of Philosophy in America: Essays in Honor of John Edwin Smith*, Kasulis, Thomas P (ed), 183-200. Albany, SUNY Pr, 1997.

Philosophy needs to be both Socratic and Platonic. Socrates teaches us philosophy as critique and Plato teaches us philosophy as vision. Critique without vision is nihilism, while vision without critique is despotism. So the two sides need to be simultaneous in spite of the radical difference between Socratic ignorance and irony on the one hand and Platonic myth and metaphysics on the other.

**Westphal, Merold**. *Becoming a Self: A Reading of Kierkegaard's Concluding Unscientific Postscript*. West Lafayette, Purdue Univ Pr, 1996.

This volume continues Westphal's attempt to show that the "individualism" and "irrationalism" that have for so long been associated with Kierkegaard's thought are not the abandonment of community and thoughtfulness but powerful protests against major pathologies of complacent modernity. In this light, Kierkegaard's thought can be seen as a non-Marxist form of ideology critique. (publisher, edited)

**Westphal, Merold**. Laughing at Hegel. *Owl Minerva*, 28(1), 39-58, Fall 96.

In Derrida's essay on Bataille we find the latter laughing at Hegel with a laughter that evokes Zen Buddhism. It is Bataille's response to what he takes to be Hegel's blind spot. His critique of immediacy is indeed a philosophy of difference. But in any dialectical *Aufhebung*, one meaning is lost, only to be replaced by another. It is the possibility that death signifies the loss of meaning altogether that Hegel ignores, his own political and religious themes presuppose meaning that is always disseminated but never wholly dissipated, possibly giving Hegel the last laugh.

**Westphal, Merold**. Nietzsche as a Theological Resource. *Mod Theol*, 13(2), 213-226, Ap 97.

Not every theology will find Nietzsche useful. But a theology which wants to transcend the onto-theological project of making God a means to our theoretical goals and the sociotheological project of making God a means to our practical goals will be able to find in Nietzsche a two-fold prophetic prophylaxis against telling its story badly. Nietzsche's perspectivism interrupts fundamentalisms of both the right and the left in their tendencies toward complacency and dogmatism; and his hermeneutics of suspicion compels every theology to ask not only about its content but about the uses to which that content is put in individual and social life.

**Westra, Laura**. Why Norton's Approach is Insufficient for Environmental Ethics. *Environ Ethics*, 19(3), 279-297, Fall 97.

There has been an ongoing debate about the best approach in environmental ethics. Bryan Norton believes that "weak anthropocentrism" will yield the best results for public policy and that it is the most defensible position. In contrast, I have argued that an ecocentric, holistic position is required to deal with the urgent environmental problems that face us and that position is complemented by the ecosystem approach and complex systems theory. I have called this approach "the ethics of integrity" and in this paper I show why this perspective suggests solutions to difficult cases, for which "weak anthropocentrism" fails to provide an answer.

**Wettersten, John**. Braucht die Wissenschaft methodologische Regeln?. *Conceptus*, 28(73), 255-270, 1995.

Gunnar Andersson has responded to criticisms of critical rationalism developed by Kuhn, Feyerabend and Lakatos. He disputes their claim that the use of ad hoc hypotheses shows that science is not critical. No special measures to ban ad hoc hypotheses from science are needed, he claims, as long as observation statements may be deduced from theories. If this thesis is correct, all efforts by critical rationalists to develop and improve theories of criticism have been

based on the false assumption that the philosophy of science must be prescriptive as well as descriptive. But this thesis is false. Various interesting normative-cum-descriptive problems concerning the admissible use of ad hoc hypotheses and the effective use of criticism still do exist for critical rationalists and offer promise of greater progress. (publisher,edited)

**Wettstein, R Harri**. *Leben-und Sterbenkönnen: Gedanken zur Sterbebegleitung und zur Selbstbestimmung der Person*. New York, Lang, 1997.

Die Arbeit entwirft einen wirklichkeitsnahen Gesetzesvorschlag und erforscht daraufhin aus der Praxis heraus fachübergreifend den ethischen Stellenwert der Selbstbestimmung. Der Umgang mit Schmerzen und Leiden ist ein fester Bestand der persönlichen Selbstbestimmung. Die sozialkritischen Nachforschungen über das gut Sterbenkönnen, in denen letztlich das gut Lebenkönnen auf dem Spiele steht, gehen in zwei Richtungen: Einmal schaffen sie eine gemeinsame Gesprächsebene für Medizin, Recht und Theologie. Dann schlagen sie eine kühne Brücke von allgemeinen ethischen Grundsätzen zu ganz konkreten Handlungsregeln. (publisher)

**Wetzel, Marc**. La religion de Pascal. *Rev Int Phil*, 51(199), 119-129, 1997.

**Whatmore, Richard**. Commerce, Constitutions, and the Manners of a Nation: Etienne Clavière's Revolutionary Political Economy, 1788-93. *Hist Euro Ideas*, 22(5-6), 351-368, S-N 96.

I would like to thank Professor Donald Winch for comments on an earlier draft of this paper and in addition Istran Hont, Michael Sonenscher, John Ramster, Ruth Woodfield and Brian Young.

**Wheeler, David L**. Universal Concerns and Concrete Commitments: In Response to Anderson. *Process Stud*, 23(3-4), 192-196, Fall-Wint 94.

C. Alan Anderson has criticized my description of God's redemptive activity in the world for remaining "so deeply committed to conservative Christianity" that it fails to produce "the most comprehensive understanding of the universally available grace." I respond that "universally available grace" is most fruitfully experienced through the relationships, rituals and actions of specific faith traditions. Living traditions constitute and promote concrete, communal expressions of religious intuitions which—when entertained only vaguely and generically—lack the power to transform and elicit commitment. At their most vigorous and focused, these concrete, communal religious expressions (doctrines) have both a norming function within their home communities and an ontological reference to generic human experience.

**Wheeler, John Archibald**. Wie kommt es zum Quantum?. *Phil Natur*, 27(2), 137-155, 1990.

**Wheeler, Wendy**. "Two Walks" in *Critical Studies: Ethics and the Subject*, Simms, Karl (ed), 157-163. Amsterdam, Rodopi, 1997.

**Wheeler III, Samuel C**. Plato's Enlightenment: The Good as the Sun. *Hist Phil Quart*, 14(2), 171-188, Ap 97.

In *Republic* VI, the Form of the Good is said to generate and make intelligible objects of knowledge just as the sun generates and makes visible sensory objects. This essay explains this simile. The passage is "mystical" only given unsound distinctions, such as the fact/value and analytic/synthetic distinctions. Absent those distinction Plato's ideas are metaphysically plausible. Briefly, "Good" is not homonymous. A Good proof is mathematically right. The One which makes mathematical objects is the Good. Mathematical structures are the Forms yielding intelligibility and being, because only the mathematically structured can be known and can be.

**Wheeler III, Samuel C**. Reparations Reconstructed. *Amer Phil Quart*, 34(3), 301-318, Jl 97.

Reparation is differential treatment of equally needy persons, i.e., discrimination. While there is no obligation to discriminate because of ancient wrongs, there can be reasons for the descendants of the wrong-doers to benefit descendants of those wronged. The first section argues that there is no obligation to discriminate. The second section shows that there can be reasons to discriminate. Partiality to descendants of those one's ancestors have wronged can be justified by partiality towards one's ancestors. The interests of one's ancestors are served by righting their ignorant wrongs. Discriminating in favor of descendants of those one's ancestors wronged benefits one's own ancestors.

**Wheeler III, Samuel C** and Peregrin, Jaroslav. The Extension of Deconstruction and Commentary (in Czech). *Filosof Cas*, 44(6), 943-967, 1996.

**Whelan, Timothy**. The Flesh and the Spirit: Anne Bradstreet and Seventeenth Century Dualism, Materialism, Vitalism and Reformed Theology. *Ultim Real Mean*, 19(4), 257-284, D 96.

This article uses the poem by the Puritan American Bradstreet as a focal point for a discussion of the materialist/immaterialist controversy of the seventeenth century, a controversy involving the atomistic materialism of Hobbes, the mechanistic dualism of Descartes, the spiritualistic dualism of Bradstreet and the Reformed theologians and the spiritualistic vitalism of John Smith, Henry More and the Cambridge Platonists. Her poem critiques the philosophical movement from Hobbes to More, a movement from ultimate reality as matter to ultimate reality as spirit, from reason as a mechanical function of man's senses and human cogitation to reason as an innate endowment of man's spirit and divine illumination.

**Whicher, Ian**. Nirodha, Yoga Praxis and the Transformation of the Mind. *J Indian Phil*, 25(1), 1-67, F 97.

This paper offers a reinterpretation of Patañjali's (second-third century CE) central definition of *yoga* and challenges and corrects misperceptions about *classical yoga* theory and practice drawn by traditional and modern interpretations of the "Yoga-Sūtras." A comprehensive epistemological perspective is developed in which the relation of identity and selfhood to the world is not severed due to a radical withdrawal from the world but is seen to be participatory in/with the world allowing the liberated "yogi" full access to the world. The author argues for an integral rather than isolationistic interpretation thereby contributing to our understanding of the meaning and practical relevance of *yoga*.

**Whitbeck, Caroline**. Comment: What We Can Learn from "Better Communication between Engineers and Managers" (M. Davis). *Sci Eng Ethics*, 3(3), 267-270, Jl 97.

**Whitbeck, Caroline**. Teaching Ethics to Scientists and Engineers: Moral Agents and Moral Problems. *Sci Eng Ethics*, 1(3), 299-308, Jl 95.

In this paper I outline an "agent-centered" approach to learning ethics. The approach is "agent-centered" in that its central aim is to prepare students to *act* wisely and responsibly when faced with moral problems. The methods characteristic of this approach are suitable for integrating material on professional and research ethics into technical courses, as well as for free-standing ethics courses. (edited)

**Whitbeck, Caroline**. Truth and Trustworthiness in Research. *Sci Eng Ethics*, 1(4), 403-416, O 95.

This paper develops an overview of the subject of trustworthiness among researchers. It illustrates and discusses various types of betrayal and defections in research conduct, and locates these in relation to many of the situations discussed elsewhere in this issue. Beginning with the breaches of trust that constitute major wrongdoing in research ("research misconduct"), I argue that these are more often examples of negligence or recklessness than they are of "fraud." Acts of negligence and recklessness figure not only in misconduct, narrowly defined, but in many lesser betrayals and defections that undermine trust. The presence or absence of an intentional deception is not a reliable indicator of the seriousness of some moral lapse. Such a lapse, where it does occur, may be simply a particularly poor response to perennially difficult research responsibility. Finally, I consider trust and trustworthiness among collaborating researchers and a range of intentional and unintentional behaviors that influence the character of these trust relationships. The supervisor-supervisee relationship is of particular significance because it is both a difficult area of responsibility for the supervisor and because this relationship is formative for a new researcher's subsequent expectations and behavior. (edited)

**White, F C**. *Schopenhauer's Early Fourfold Root*. Brookfield, Avebury, 1997.

**White, Hayden**. Commentary. *Hist Human Sci*, 9(4), 123-138, N 96.

**White, John**. Education and Nationality. *J Phil Educ*, 30(3), 327-343, N 96.

The paper argues that nationality and national sentiment have been, until recently, neglected concepts in liberal, as distinct from conservative, political and educational philosophy. It claims that, appropriately detached from nationalistic ideas associated with the political right, the promotion of national sentiment as an educational aim is not incompatible with liberalism and, more strongly, may be desirable for reasons of personal and cultural identity as well as for redistributive reasons. The paper then explores issues to do with British nationality in particular, arguing for a remodeled conception to replace the traditional one; and finally it looks at curricular implications, especially in the British context, of aiming at the cultivation of national sentiment within a liberal framework.

**White, John**. Education, Work and Well-Being. *J Phil Educ*, 31(2), 233-247, Jl 97.

The current crisis in the 'work-society' has implications for future educational policy. This paper explores some of the philosophical issues of relevance here. It starts with the meaning of 'work' and the claim that work should be central to our lives. It then examines the arguments that Richard Norman and Sean Sayers have provided for work as a basic human need, concluding that the case has not been made out. A section on the place of both autonomous and heteronomous work in personal well-being is followed by one on education and the future of work.

**White, Michael J**. Concepts of Space in Greek Thought. *Apeiron*, 29(2), 183-198, Je 96.

**White, Richard B**. A Consistent Theory of Attributes in a Logic without Contraction. *Stud Log*, 52(1), 113-142, F 93.

This essay demonstrates proof-theoretically the consistency of a type-free theory C with an unrestricted principle of comprehension and based on a predicate logic in which contraction (A implies (A implies B)) implies (A implies B), although it cannot holds in general, is provable for a wide range of A's. (edited)

**White, Richard J**. *Nietzsche and the Problem of Sovereignty*. Champaign, Univ of Illinois Pr, 1997.

From *The Birth of Tragedy* on, Nietzsche worked to comprehend the nature of the individual. Richard White shows how Nietzsche was inspired and guided by the question of personal "sovereignty" and how through his writings sought to provoke the very sovereignty he described. White argues that Nietzsche is a philosopher our contemporary age must therefore come to understand if we are ever to secure a genuinely meaningful direction for the future. Profoundly relevant to our era, Nietzsche's philosophy addresses a version of individuality that allows us to move beyond the self-dispossession of mass society and the alternative of selfish individualism—to fully understand how one becomes what one is. (publisher, edited)

**White, Richard J**. The Future of Romantic Love. *Int Stud Phil*, 29(2), 95-103, 1997.

Romantic love has a definite history and since we cannot treat it as an absolute given of all human experience, we can ask whether this kind of love may also have a future. The modern age sees an explosion in the popular themes of romantic love, celebrating excessive passion and fusion with the beloved; at the same time it brings with it the imperative of autonomy and the requirement that we should take command of our lives: given their emergence together, it is not unreasonable to regard these ideas as correlated to each other.

**White, Richard J**. The Sublime and the Other. *Heythrop J*, 38(2), 125-143, Ap 97.

In this essay, I explore the relationship between the concept of the sublime and the experience of alterity in the work of Otto, Burke and Kant. I argue that the sublime has become a major theme in postmodern theory, precisely because it gives us access to the "sacred" and that which is wholly "other."

**White, Stephen K**. Weak Ontology and Liberal Political Reflection. *Polit Theory*, 25(4), 502-523, Ag 97.

**White, V Alan**. Picturing Einstein's Train of Thought. *Philosophy*, 71 (278), 591-594, O 96.

This article attempts to finish a long-standing argument between Michael Cohen and me about the consistency and completeness of Einstein's train-and-lightning-bolts thought-experiment on the relativity of simultaneity. It includes a Minkowski space time diagram of the events of the thought-experiment, and attempts to show that Cohen may have mistaken argumentative asymmetry for physical asymmetry.

**Whitebook, Joel**. Response to Zizek. *Constellations*, 3(2), 157-163, O 96.

**Whitehead, Fred**. The Challenge of Explanation. *Nature Soc Thought*, 9(2), 135-157, 1996.

In the context of widespread contemporary religious wars and civil conflicts, the major Marxist concepts of religion are reviewed, including the contributions of scholars working in that tradition. Two recent theories of religion that concentrate on anthropomorphization and dissociation are discussed, evaluated and applied to the general outlines of U.S. intellectual history, to the persistence of market economics, and to problems of the USSR. A synthesis of Marxist and more recent psychological theories is called for to meet the challenges of present-day conflicts.

**Whitehead, Jack**. Living Educational Theories and Living Contra-dictions: A Response to Mike Newby. *J Phil Educ*, 30(3), 457-461, N 96.

I feel sure that Newby's review of Jean McNiff's (1993) book *Teaching as Learning* will help to stimulate philosophers of education to contribute to debate about the nature of the educational knowledge and the logic(s) of the educational theories being produced by educational action researchers. I share his commitment to clarity of thinking in education and to the value of philosophy in examining the grounds on which other discipline make their claims to knowledge. Let me take a number of criticisms that he explicitly makes of me in his review. (edited)

**Whitehouse, Peter J**. Readdressing Our Moral Relationship to Non-human Creatures. *Cambridge Quart Healthcare Ethics*, 6(4), 445-448, Fall 97.

**Whitehouse, Peter J** and Juengst, Eric T and Mehlman, Maxwell (& others). Enhancing Cognition in the Intellectually Intact. *Hastings Center Rep*, 27(3), 14-22, My-Je 97.

As science learns more about how the brain works and fails to work, the possibility for developing "cognition enhancers" becomes more plausible. The success of drugs like Ritalin points to an eager demand for drugs that can help us think faster, remember more and focus more keenly. Whether such drugs are good for individuals, or for society, is an open question, one that demands far more public discussion.

**Whitlock, Greg**. "Concerning Zelia Gregoriou's "Reading *Phaedrus* like a Girl" in *Philosophy of Education (1996)*, Margonis, Frank (ed), 214-217. Urbana, Phil Education Soc, 1997.

**Whitlock, Greg**. Reexamining Dr. King and Malcolm X On Violence. *Phil Forum*, 27(4), 289-320, Sum 96.

**Whitman, Glen**. Myth, Measurement, and the Minimum Wage: Sound and Fury Signifying What?. *Crit Rev*, 10(4), 607-619, Fall 96.

In *Myth & Measurement: The New Economics of the Minimum Wage*, David Card and Alan Krueger assemble a variety of evidence purporting to weaken the case that minimum wages lead to unemployment among low-wage workers. Although the authors succeed in casting doubt on some previous studies that supported the standard view, they fail to provide compelling evidence for their alternative model. The methodological errors in their showcase study of minimum wages in New Jersey and Pennsylvania render it nearly worthless and the remainder of the book's arguments are not weighty enough to reverse the conventional economic wisdom on minimum wages.

**Whittock, Trevor**. Dance Metaphors: A Reply to Julie Van Camp. *Brit J Aes*, 37(3), 274-282, Jl 97.

Responding to the criticism that there is no such thing as nonverbal metaphor and that it does not account for meaning in dance the paper argues that Van Camp, by defining metaphor as a verbal device only, presumes what she should prove. The paper claims that nonverbal categories do in fact play an important role in interpersonal behaviour and bodily communication, so bespeaking modes of awareness verbal languages do not adequately delineate. Further, it demonstrates through analysing specific dance examples that metaphorical interpretation is the only way to make sense of certain dance sequences and images.

**Whyte, J T**. Success Again: Replies to Brandom and Godfrey-Smith. *Analysis*, 57(1), 84-88, Ja 97.

**Whyte, Philip**. Did the Enlightenment Just Happen to Men?. *Z Phil Praxis*, 19-23, 1996.

**Widerker, David** and Katzoff, Charlotte. Avoidability and Libertarianism: A Response to Fischer. *Faith Phil*, 13(3), 415-421, Jl 96.

Recently, Widerker has attacked Fischer's contention that one could use Frankfurt-type counterexamples to the principle of alternative possibilities to show that even from a libertarian viewpoint an agent might be morally responsible for a decision that he could not have avoided. Fischer has responded by: a) arguing that Widerker's criticism presupposes the falsity of Molinism and b) presenting a version of libertarianism which avoids Widerker's criticism. Here we argue that : I) Fischer's first response is unconvincing and undermines Molinism itself; II) the version of libertarianism he presents is fallacious, and III) even on the version of libertarianism he proposes, avoidability remains a necessary condition for moral responsibility.

**Wiegel, Vincent** and Verburg, Rudi M. On the Compatibility of Sustainability and Economic Growth. *Environ Ethics*, 19(3), 247-265, Fall 97.

It is generally assumed that sustainable development and economic growth are compatible objectives. Because this assumption has been left unspecified, the debate on sustainability and growth has remained vague and confusing. Attempts at specification not only involve clarification of the interrelation of the two concepts, but also, we argue, require a philosophical approach in which the concepts of sustainability and economic growth are analyzed in the context of our frame of reference. We suggest that if the notion of sustainability is to be taken seriously, the conflicting conceptual and normative orientations between the two concepts require the reconsideration of our frame of reference.

**Wiehl, Reiner**. The History of Interpretation and the Interpretation of History in the History of Philosophy. *Filosof Cas*, 44(3), 413-429, 1996.

**Wiener, Neil I** and Wiesenthal, David L. Privacy and the Human Genome Project. *Ethics Behavior*, 6(3), 189-202, 1996.

The Human Genome Project has raised many issues regarding the contributions of genetics to a variety of diseases and societal conditions. With genetic testing now easily conducted with lowered costs in nonmedical domains, a variety of privacy issues must be considered. Such testing will result in the loss of significant privacy rights for the individual. Society must now consider such issues as the ownership of genetic data, confidentiality rights to such information, limits placed on genetic screening, and legislation to control genetic testing and its applications. There is often a conflict between individual rights to privacy and the need for societal protection.

**Wieringa, Roel J** (& others) and Meyer, John-Jules Ch and Dignum, Frank. "A Modal Approach to Intentions, Commitments and Obligations: Intention Plus Commitment Yields Obligation" in *Deontic Logic, Agency and Normative Systems*, Brown, Mark A (ed), 80-97. New York, Springer-Verlag, 1996.

In this paper we introduce some new operators into our framework that make it possible to reason about decisions and commitments to do actions. In our framework, a decision leads to an intention to do an action. The decision in itself does not change the state of the world, but only the relation to possible future worlds. A commitment to actually perform the intended action changes the deontic state of the world such that the intended action becomes obligated. Of course, the obligated action may never actually occur. In our semantic structure, we use static (ought-to-be) and dynamic (ought-to-do) obligation operators. The static operator resembles the classical conception of obligation as truth in ideal worlds, except that it takes the current state as well as the past history of the world into account. This is necessary because it allows us to compare the way a state is actually reached with the way we committed ourselves to reach it. We show that some situations that could formerly not be expressed easily in deontic logic can be described in a natural way using the extended logic described in this paper.

**Wiertz, Oliver**. Das Problem des Übels in Richard Swinburnes Religionsphilosophie: Über Sinn und Grenzen seines theistischen Antwortversuches auf das Problem des Übels und dessen Bedeutung für die Theologie. *Theol Phil*, 71(2), 224-256, 1996.

In several contributions Richard Swinburne has offered attempts to solve the logical and epistemic problem of evil. I summarize and systematize these, concentrating on Swinburne's natural law defence. I regard his solution, in spite of minor difficulties, as insightful, but criticize that Swinburne cannot justify alone on the basis of his theism the high value which he places on the concept of freedom in his defence. I try to solve this problem by taking account of the Christian review of the relationship between God and humans in a "God's love defence" which I defend in the last section against possible criticism. (edited)

**Wiesenthal, David L** and Wiener, Neil I. Privacy and the Human Genome Project. *Ethics Behavior*, 6(3), 189-202, 1996.

The Human Genome Project has raised many issues regarding the contributions of genetics to a variety of diseases and societal conditions. With genetic testing now easily conducted with lowered costs in nonmedical domains, a variety of privacy issues must be considered. Such testing will result in the loss of significant privacy rights for the individual. Society must now consider such issues as the ownership of genetic data, confidentiality rights to such information, limits placed on genetic screening, and legislation to control genetic testing and its applications. There is often a conflict between individual rights to privacy and the need for societal protection.

**Wiesing, Urban**. "Individual Rights and Genetics: The Historical Perspective" in *The Right to Know and the Right not to Know*, Chadwick, Ruth (ed), 23-27. Brookfield, Avebury, 1997.

**Wiggins, Osborne P** and Schwartz, Michael Alan. Edmund Husserl's Influence on Karl Jaspers's Phenomenology. *Phil Psychiat Psych*, 4(1), 15-36, Mr 97.

Karl Jaspers's phenomenology remains important today, not solely because of its continuing influence in some areas of psychiatry, but because, if fully understood, it can provide a method and set of concepts for making new progress in the science of psychopathology. In order to understand this method and set of concepts, it helps to recognize the significant influence that Edmund Husserl's early work, *Logical Investigations*, exercised on Jaspers's formulation of them. We trace the Husserlian influence while clarifying the main components of Jaspers's method. Jaspers adopted Husserl's notions of intuition, description, and presuppositionlessness, transforming them when necessary in order to serve the investigations of the psychopathologist. Jaspers also took over from Wilhelm Dilthey and others the tools of understanding (*Verstehen*) and self-transposal. The Diltheyian procedures were integrated into the Husserlian ones to produce a method that enables psychiatrists to define the basic kinds of psychopathological mental states.

**Wikler, Daniel**. Presidential Address: Bioethics and Social Responsibility. *Bioethics*, 11(3-4), 185-192, Jl 97.

**Wilber, Ken**. An Integral Theory of Consciousness. *J Consciousness Stud*, 4(1), 71-92, 1997.

There has recently been something of an explosion of interest in the development of a 'science of consciousness' and yet there are at present approximately a dozen major but conflicting schools of consciousness theory and research. My own approach to consciousness studies is based on the assumption that each of these schools has something irreplaceably important to offer and thus what is required is a general model sophisticated enough to incorporate the essentials of each of them. (edited)

**Wilburn, Ron**. Posits and Positing. *SW Phil Rev*, 13(1), 91-102, Ja 97.

After defending my attribution of full-blooded scientific realism and semantic antirealism to Quine, I argue that these two positions are incompatible. Referring to "Ontological Relativity," I argue that scientific realism presupposes semantic realism. I conclude by isolating and responding to, three aspects of Quine's account from which rejoinders to my objections might be thought to be forthcoming. These are: Quine's invocation of the use/mention distinction, Quine's recurrent claim that "structure is what matters to theory," and Quine's recent remarks on the nature of empirical evidence.

**Wild, Stefan**. "Between Ernest Renan and Ernst Bloch: Averroës Remembered, Discovered, and Invented. The European Reception Since the Nineteenth Century" in *Averroës and the Enlightenment*, Wahba, Mourad (ed), 155-170. Amherst, Prometheus, 1996.

Averroism is often seen as a Medieval forerunner of European enlightenment. Averroes (d. 1198) did not play a comparable role for Islamic philosophy. Today, he is claimed by Arab intellectuals as a model of an autochthonous Arab rationalism. This judgment is based on Ernest Renan (d. 1892) and his verdict, that Islamic philosophy had died with Averroes, or on a leftist version of Arabo-Islamic intellectual history which saw in Averroes a representative of an "Islamic materialism." This idea as developed by Ernest Bloch (d. 1965) was influential in the German Democratic Republic and found its way into Soviet philosophical encyclopedias.

**Wildenburg, Dorothea**. Aneinnander vorbei: Zum Horenstreit zwischen Fichte und Schiller. *Fichte-Studien*, 12, 27-41, 1997.

**Wildes, Kevin W**. Health Care, Equality, and Inequality: Christian Perspectives and Moral Disagreements. *Christian Bioethics*, 2(3), 271-279, 1996.

Equality is a concept that is often used in health care discussions about the allocation of resources and the design of health care systems. In secular discussions and debates the concept of equality is highly controverted and can take on many different specifications. One might think that Christians hold a common understanding of equality. A more careful study, though, makes it quite clear that equality is just as controversial among different Christian communities as it is in the secular world.

**Wildes, Kevin WM**. Healthy Skepticism: The Emperor Has Very Few Clothes. *J Med Phil*, 22(4), 365-371, Ag 97.

The role of an expert witness in ethics, as part of a legal proceeding, is examined in this essay. The essay argues that the use of such expertise rests on confusions about normative and nonnormative ethics compounded by misunderstandings about the challenges of moral argument in secular, morally pluralistic societies.

**Wildfeuer, Armin G**. Vernunft als Epiphänomen der Naturkausalität: Zu Herkunft und Bedeutung des ursprünglichen Determinismus J.G. Fichtes. *Fichte-Studien*, 9, 62-82, 1997.

**Wilke, Sabine** and Schlipphacke, Heidi. "Construction of a Gendered Subject: A Feminist Reading of Adorno's *Aesthetic Theory*" in *The Semblance of Subjectivity*, Huhn, Tom (ed), 287-308. Cambridge, MIT Pr, 1997.

**Wilkinson, T M**. Judging Our Own Good. *Austl J Phil*, 74(3), 488-494, S 96.

**Will, Frederick L** and Westphal, Kenneth R (ed) and MacIntyre, Alasdair. *Pragmatism and Realism*. Lanham, Rowman & Littlefield, 1997.

Will demonstrates that a social account of human knowledge is consistent with, and ultimately requires, realism. The book culminates in a naturalistic account of the generation, assessment and revision of cognitive, moral and social norms. It is written clearly enough for undergraduates and makes a timely contribution to current debates. A critical introduction by the editor discusses the bearing of

**Williams, A N** 990 **AUTHOR INDEX**

Will's views on current issues in analytic epistemology, philosophy of science, and moral theory. Will's work "is one of the more remarkable achievements of 20th-century North American philosophy."—Alasdair MacIntyre. (publisher)

**Williams, A N**. Deification in the *Summa Theologiae*: A Structural Interpretation of the *Prima Pars*. *Thomist*, 61(2), 219-255, Ap 97.

**Williams, Christopher**. Environmental Victims: Arguing the Costs. *Environ Values*, 6(1), 3-30, F 97.

The costs of anthropogenic environmental change are usually discussed in broad terms, for example embracing damage to the ecosystem or buildings. There has been little consideration of the direct human dimension—the cost to and of environmental victims—except in clinical terms. In order to prevent and minimize environmental victimization it seems necessary to present cost arguments to governments and commerce. This paper outlines the personal, social and cash costs of environmental victimization, using the psycho-social literature, and brief case studies of intellectual disability, road transport and cross-border pollution. It is proposed that governments and commerce might not respond in obvious ways to these cost arguments, but 'trust' is identified as a cost that both may recognize. It is concluded that the concept of *loss-costs* should be central to any analysis, and the paper provides a 'framework for comprehensive argument of the costs of environmental victimization', in the form of a simple matrix.

**Williams, David M** and Scotland, Robert W and Humphries, Christopher J. Confusion in Philosophy: A Comment on Williams (1992). *Synthese*, 108(1), 127-136, Jl 96.

Patricia Williams made a number of claims concerning the methods and practice of cladistic analysis and classification. Her argument rests upon the distinction of two kinds of hierarchy: a 'divisional hierarchy' depicting 'evolutionary' descent and the Linnean hierarchy describing taxonomic groups in a classification. Williams goes on to outline five problems with cladistics that lead her to the conclusion that systematists should "eliminate cladism as a school of biological taxonomy and to replace it either with something that is philosophically coherent or to replace it with 'pure' methodology, untainted by theory" (Williams 1992, 151). Williams makes a number of points which she feels collectively add up to insurmountable problems for cladistics. We examine Williams's views concerning the 'two hierarchies' and consider what cladists currently understand about the status of ancestors. We will demonstrate that Williams has seriously misunderstood many modern commentators on this subject and all of her "five persistent problems" are derivable from this misunderstanding.

**Williams, Hugh**. What is Good Forestry? An Ethical Examination of Forest Policy and Practice in New Brunswick. *Environ Ethics*, 18(4), 391-410, Winter 96.

I articulate a moral theory that affirms the existence of a public good that is understood teleologically as an objective purpose to be pursued. I argue that there is a connection between the philosophical and moral concept of creativity and the scientific concept of biological diversity. I suggest that these concepts are both linked to the political question of the public good. The maximization of the ethical good of creativity according to this theory is linked to the maximization of the public good. In forestry, the management of forest ecosystems in order to maximize their creative good is linked to the maximization of the public good and vice versa. (edited)

**Williams, James**. "Deleuze on J. M. W. Turner: Catastrophism in Philosophy?" in *Deleuze and Philosophy: The Difference Engineer,* Ansell Pearson, Keith (ed), 233-246. New York, Routledge, 1997.

It is argued here that Gilles Deleuze puts forward a world-view where catastrophe plays a positive role. This advocacy is most explicit in his studies of art, in particular, his work on Turner. There, the greatness of Turner's late paintings is seen to lie in their expression of catastrophe, that is, they allow catastrophe to become actual insofar as the works of art are catastrophes in themselves, as opposed to representations of catastrophes. The conclusion is that Deleuze's philosophy avoids a destructive nihilism by defending the expression of catastrophic changes in figures against mere chaos.

**Williams, Juliet**. On the Road Again: Hayek and the Rule of Law. *Crit Rev*, 11(1), 101-120, Wint 97.

In his political writings, F.A. Hayek faces a classic liberal dilemma: he opposes coercion but recognizes that sometimes the state can help to minimize it. Hayek attempts to resolve the dilemma of the limits of state power by offering a definition of the rule of law that does not depend on a controversial conception of rights. However, his effort to formalize the rule of law fails. Not only does Hayek implicitly rely on an undefended theory of rights, but his rule-of-law scheme is limited to the elaboration of general principles of good government, neglecting the need for reforms aimed directly at the political processes that result in the controversial forms of coercion he deplores.

**Williams, Michael**. Still Unnatural: A Reply to Vogel and Rorty. *J Phil Res*, 22, 29-39, Ap 97.

Professor Vogel claims that my responses to scepticism leave the traditional problems standing. I argue in reply that he fails to take sufficiently seriously the diagnostic character of my enterprise. My aim is not to offer direct refutations of sceptical arguments, taking such arguments at face value, but to undermine their plausibility by revealing their dependence on unacknowledged and contentious theoretical presuppositions. (edited)

**Williams, Paul F** and Sawyers, Roby B and Chen, Al Y S. Reinforcing Ethical Decision Making Through Corporate Culture. *J Bus Ethics*, 16(8), 855-865, Je 97.

Behaving ethically depends on the ability to recognize that ethical issues exist, to see from an ethical point of view. This ability to see and respond ethically may be related more to attributes of corporate culture than to attributes of individual employees. Efforts to increase ethical standards and decrease pressure to behave unethically should, therefore, concentrate on the organization and its culture. The purpose of this paper is to discuss how total quality (TQ) techniques can facilitate the development of a cooperative corporate culture that promotes and encourages ethical behavior throughout an organization.

**Williams, Rowan D**. Interiority and Epiphany: A Reading in New Testament Ethics. *Mod Theol*, 13(1), 29-51, Ja 97.

**Williams, Thomas**. Reason, Morality, and Voluntarism in Duns Scotus: A Pseudo-Problem Dissolved. *Mod Sch*, 74(2), 73-94, Ja 97.

Scotus sometimes seems to be a radical voluntarist about the moral law, but he also holds that reason plays an important role in morality. Interpreters have supposed that these two views are inconsistent and have, therefore, felt compelled to mitigate Scotus's apparent voluntarism. I argue that Scotus's voluntarism is perfectly consistent with the limited role he assigns to right reason as an element in the moral goodness of actions. I argue further that Scotus's brand of voluntarism entails that there can be no discursive natural knowledge of the moral law; Scotus, therefore, holds that we know the moral law nondiscursively.

**Williamson, Paul** and Asfour, Amal. Gainsborough's Wit. *J Hist Ideas*, 58(3), 479-501, Jl 97.

**Williamson, Timothy**. Cognitive Homelessness. *J Phil*, 93(11), 554-573, N 96.

The paper argues that any nontrivial condition can obtain when one is not in a position to know that it obtains. This includes conditions on one's mental state. The argument is related to sorites paradoxes, but is not itself a sorites paradox; it survives the removal of vagueness from the relevant terms. As an application, it is argued that Dummettian antirealist assertibility-conditional theories of meaning violate the constraint that Dummett criticizes realist truth-conditional theories of meaning for violating, because assertibility is a nontrivial condition.

**Williamson, Timothy**. Knowing and Asserting. *Phil Rev*, 105(4), 489-523, O 96.

The paper argues that the speech act of assertion is characterized by the rule "Assert that P only if you know that P". Alternative attempts to characterize assertion in terms of a rule of truth or justified belief are criticized. For example, the truth rule account makes false predictions about the Lottery Paradox. Applications are made to Moore's Paradox in the form "P and I do not know that P" and to mathematical assertions. The point of having a speech act governed by the knowledge rule in a community's repertoire is explained.

**Williamson, Timothy**. Self-Knowledge and Embedded Operators. *Analysis*, 56(4), 202-209, O 96.

A precise sense is defined in which two coextensive operators can satisfy different and even incompatible principles, if the latter involve self-embedding of the operators. This phenomenon is exemplified in several ways by the intensionality of self-knowledge. In particular, it is suggested that attempts by Lucas, Penrose and others to argue that we are not Turing machines by appeal to Gödel's incompleteness theorems neglect the phenomenon. The relevant operators are 'I can prove that...' and 'The Turing machine with state description T can prove that...', where I am the Turing machine with state description T.

**Williamson, Timothy**. Sense, Validity and Context. *Phil Phenomenol Res*, 57(3), 649-654, S 97.

The paper discusses John Campbell's book *Past, Space and Self.* Campbell defines sameness of sense in terms of the validity of inferences. The paper argues that, given an adequate logic of indexicals, this does not provide an account of sameness of sense across changes of context of the kind Campbell wants.

**Williamson, Timothy**. Unreflective Realism. *Phil Phenomenol Res*, 56(4), 905-909, D 96.

The paper critically discusses Crispin Wright's *Truth and Objectivity*, arguing that it overestimates the extent of the *a priori*, particularly in its discussion of the Euthyphro Contrast and Cognitive Command, and that it has no justification for imposing the burden of proof on realism. A view is sketched on which the default assumption is of a gap between truth and superassertibility.

**Williamson, Timothy**. *Vagueness*. New York, Routledge, 1996.

The author traces the history of the problem of vagueness from discussions of the heap-of-sand paradox in ancient Greece to modern formal approaches such as fuzzy logic. His is the first comprehensive treatment of this increasingly important topic in metaphysics and the philosophy of logic and language. (publisher, edited)

**Williamson, Timothy** and Pizzi, Claudio. Strong Boethius' Thesis and Consequential Implication. *J Phil Log*, 26(5), 569-588, O 97.

The paper studies the relation between systems of modal logic and systems of consequential implication, a nonmaterial form of implication satisfying "Aristotle's Thesis" (*p* does not imply not *p*) and "Weak Boethius' Thesis" (if *p* implies *q*, then *p* does not imply not *q*). Definitions are given of consequential implication in terms of modal operators and of modal operators in terms of consequential implication. The modal equivalent of "Strong Boethius' Thesis" (that *p* implies *q* implies that *p* does not imply not *q*) is identified.

**Willis, Clyde E**. The Phenomenology of Pornography: *A Comment on Catharine MacKinnon's* Only Words. *Law Phil*, 16(2), 177-199, 97.

Most people are familiar with Justice Stewart's now classic statement that while he cannot describe pornography, he certainly knows it when he sees it. We instantly identify with Justice Stewart. Pornography is not difficult to recognize, but it does elude description. This is because traditional attempts at description are attempts that seek to explain at either an abstract or empirical level rather than at the level that accounts for experience in its totality. Justice Stewart's lament represents the need to understand the subjective experience of pornography and cease trying to explain it in purely objective terms. Much feminist literature in general and Catharine MacKinnon's work in particular seeks to do just this. This essay suggests that MacKinnon's position not only needs the support of a nontraditional philosophical approach, but has one readily available in the phenomenology of philosopher Edmund Husserl. (edited)

**Willis, Kirk**. Russell and His Biographers. *Russell*, 16(2), 129-143, Wint 96-97.

**Williston, Byron**. Descartes on Love and/as Error. *J Hist Ideas*, 58(3), 429-444, Jl 97.

This paper examines Descartes's theory of love as laid out (chiefly) in *The Passions of the Soul*. I reveal a tension in Descartes thinking on this matter. On the one hand, he speaks repeatedly about the need to avoid moral judgements which rest on "bad foundations". On the other hand, he states that it is often difficult for us to appeal beyond our passions themselves in the formulation of our moral judgements. Therefore, as regards the love passion, I show that "error" is not a pressing worry for Descartes and that this passion itself may be the guarantor of the correctness of our judgements about beloved objects.

**Willmott, Robert**. Structure, Culture and Agency: Rejecting the Current Orthodoxy of Organisation Theory. *J Theor Soc Behav*, 27(1), 93-123, Mr 97.

The preoccupation with 'organizational culture' within organization theory continues to engage academia and the business world alike. This paper argues that not only has the decade-long emphasis on culture led to an unhelpful disregard for structure but more fundamentally involves an elision of structure and culture. In contradistinction, structure, culture and agency are held to be irreducible emergent strata of reality. It is maintained that Giddens's structuration theory—which commands considerable assent—conflates structure and agency, thereby precluding analysis of their relative interplay over time. Such conflationary premises are further evident in the literature on 'organizational culture'. Analytical dualism is held to be the methodological key to examining the relative interplay of structure, culture and agency and is predicated four-square on the reality of a stratified world.

**Wilshire, Bruce**. "The Breathtaking Intimacy of the Material World: William James's Last Thoughts" in *The Cambridge Companion to William James*, Putnam, Ruth Anna (ed), 103-124. New York, Cambridge Univ Pr, 1997.

The article traces James's development within the history of phenomenologies. His description of thought's *object* undermines the programmatic dualism of the ostensibly natural scientific *Principles of Psychology*. His radical empiricism opens up a level of prereflective experiencing anterior to the distinction between subject and object, knower and known. The body thinks and thinking is shot through with breathing. Belief, "the feeling of reality," is being open to the world: in the most arresting moments of intimacy and interfusion our breath is taken away. James reveals for Europeans a level of shamanic sacramental and healing experiencing. The article argues that most attempts to understand James's pragmatic theory of truth fail because failing to grasp the overall phenomenological-ontological drift of his thought.

**Wilson, Carol A** and Alexander, James F and Turner, Charles W. Family Therapy Process and Outcome Research: Relationship to Treatment Ethics. *Ethics Behavior*, 6(4), 345-352, 1996.

We know from the research literature that psychotherapy is effective, but we also know that hundreds of diverse therapies are being practiced that have not been subjected to scientific scrutiny; thus, in some circumstances iatrogenic effects do occur. Therefore, it is crucial that we recognize and implement therapeutic interventions that are evidence-based rather than succumb to ethical dilemma, frustration and complacency. Recommendations for family therapists are discussed, including the need to a) keep abreast of research findings, b) translate research findings and developments as they apply to clinical practice, c) prioritize techniques and intervention models and b) reexamine funding priorities and research foci.

**Wilson, Catherine**. "Discourses of Vision in Seventeenth-Century Metaphysics" in *Sites of Vision*, Levin, David Michael (ed), 117-138. Cambridge, MIT Pr, 1997.

The paper discusses visuality and the use of optical metaphors in Descartes, Malebranche, and Leibniz, and their hypothesized political and moral significance.

**Wilson, Catherine**. *The Invisible World: Early Modern Philosophy and the Invention of the Microscope*. Princeton, Princeton Univ Pr, 1995.

The invention of the microscope determined much of the evolution of 17th century epistemology, natural philosophy, and metaphysics. The book argues for the importance of the instrument and instrumentation generally in the Scientific Revolution and discusses the microscope's earliest usage and its applications to the study of generation and contagion. The origins of empiricism and the problems connected with experience, evidence and skepticism concerning unobservables are treated. Authors discussed include: Descartes, Leibniz, Malebranche, Locke and Berkeley.

**Wilson, Fred**. "Bradley's Impact on Empiricism" in *Philosophy after F.H. Bradley*, Bradley, James (ed), 251-281. Bristol, Thoemmes, 1996.

**Wilson, Gerald**. Transcendental Truth in Vico. *De Phil*, 11, 49-64, 1994-1995.

**Wilson, Holly L**. Kant's Integration of Morality and Anthropology. *Kantstudien*, 88(1), 87-104, 1997.

This essay is only a beginning attempt to show the integration of morality, teleological judgment and anthropology in Kant. First, it will establish that Kant's

theory of morality, as he laid it out in the *Grounding*, makes room for viewing morality as merely formal as well as both formal and concrete at the same time. Secondly, this essay will establish that Kant means to view human beings as sensible beings and the 'sensible world' by means of teleological judgment and not the determinative judgment of the first *Critique*. Thirdly, I will indicate how Kant construed human nature teleologically and worked out the details of this theory in his *Anthropology from a Pragmatic Point of View*. Finally, I will discuss two recent attempts, by Onora O'Neill and Allen Wood, to refute Kant's alleged formalism. (edited)

**Wilson, Holyn**. "Kant and Ecofeminism" in *Ecofeminism: Women, Culture, Nature*, Warren, Karen J (ed), 390-411. Bloomington, Indiana Univ Pr, 1997.

This essay poses the question of whether there is a theory of nature and specifically human nature in Kant that is consistent with ecofeminist views of nature and human nature. I make use of Kant's theory of teleological judgment and *anthropology* to articulate his ecological point of view and argue the development of that view from his early works. The feminist ethic of care is not inconsistent with Kant's view of moral responsibility. His view of moral responsibility does not entail a moral imperative to dominate animals and nature.

**Wilson, John**. "Some Procedural Problems" in *The Liberation Debate: Rights at Issue*, Leahy, Michael (ed), 227-240. New York, Routledge, 1996.

**Wilson, John**. Alertness and Determination: A Note on Moral Phenomenology. *J Moral Educ*, 25(2), 215-223, Je 96.

The ability and willingness to bring one's attention and determination to bear on moral situations are of central importance in moral education. Various ways in which a person may succeed or fail in doing this are considered, in the light of Aristotle's 'practical syllogism', and a rough classification is suggested. It is advocated a) that a fuller classification be attempted and b) that teachers and parents share with young people their understanding of typical practical syllogisms.

**Wilson, John Elbert**. *Schelling und Nietzsche: Zur Auslegung der frühen Werke Friedrich Nietzsches*. Hawthorne, de Gruyter, 1996.

A study of the German philosopher Schelling (1775-1854) and Nietzsche as a contribution to the interpretation of Nietzsche's early works. (publisher)

**Wilson, Liz**. Who is Authorized to Speak? Katherine Mayo and the Politics of Imperial Feminism in British India. *J Indian Phil*, 25(2), 139-151, Ap 97.

Katherine Mayo's *Mother India*, a journalistic exposé dealing with the plight of Hindu and Muslim women in India, raised a storm of controversy following its publication in 1927. Although the status of Indian women was a central topic of the debate that ensued upon the publication of Mayo's book, Indian women were in fact largely marginal to this discourse. Behind the Indian "woman question" lay the pressing issue of whether Indians were capable of governing themselves in a 'civilized' fashion. Thus the controversy over *Mother India* and the plight of Indian women quickly turned into a referendum on Indian *home rule*.

**Wilson, Mark**. Mechanism and Fracture in Cartesian Physics. *Topoi*, 16(2), 141-152, S 97.

Descartes's claims about impact and the relativity of motion in the *Principles* have puzzled many commentators. The present essay attempts to relate his thinking to natural principles governing the capacity of a closed mechanism to perform work. A clever approach to fracture forms an important addendum to this account.

**Wilson, Paul Eddy**. Sanity and Irresponsibility. *Phil Psychiat Psych*, 3(4), 293-302, D 96.

Taking up the idea that sanity is a necessary condition for responsibility, Susan Wolf sets forth two criteria for determining whether an actor is sane. I argue that the second criterion is inappropriate for this determination since it invokes some hidden axiological standard. I reexamine a case study that Wolf describes and arrive at a different judgment about the responsibility of the actor. I argue that the foremost criterion for determining whether an actor is sane is functional rather than axiological. The theory of responsibility, rather than the notion of sanity, must do the work of appraising the value of an actors' behavior and that must be done in light of the fact that responsible moral agents enjoy varying degrees of sanity.

**Wilson, W Kent**. Confession of a Weak Anti-Intentionalist: Exposing Myself. *J Aes Art Crit*, 55(3), 309-311, Sum 97.

This reply to Noel Carroll's "The Intentional Fallacy: Defending Myself" concedes a role for appeal to artist's intentions in interpreting art work where the goal of readers and interpreters is to communicate with the artist. This goal is not universal and no satisfactory argument has been advanced that it ought to be universal. Critical discussion is directed against a stronger intentionalist thesis that author's intentions must always determine a satisfactory interpretation.

**Wimalasiri, Jayantha S** and Pavri, Francis and Jalil, Abdul A K. An Empirical Study of Moral Reasoning Among Managers in Singapore. *J Bus Ethics*, 15(12), 1331-1341, D 96.

The study reported here sought to examine the ethical orientations of business managers and business students in Singapore. Data were obtained using Defining Issue Test. Analysis of Variance revealed that age, education and religious affiliation had influenced cognitive moral development stages of the respondents. Vocation, gender and ethnicity did not seem to have affected moral judgment of the subjects. Contrary to the general view both business students and business managers demonstrated the same level of sensitivity to ethical dimensions of decision-making. Implications of the findings and limitations of the study are discussed.

**Wimbush, James C** and Daily, Catherine M and Dalton, Dan R. Collecting "Sensitive" Data in Business Ethics Research: A Case for the Unmatched Count Technique (UCT). *J Bus Ethics*, 16(10), 1049-1057, Jl 97.

Some would argue that the more promising areas of business ethics research are "sensitive." In such areas, it would be expected that subjects, if inclined to respond at all, would be guarded in their responses, or respond inaccurately. We provide an introduction to an empirical approach—the unmatched block count (UCT)—for collecting these potentially sensitive data which provides absolute anonymity and confidentiality to subjects and "legal immunity" to the researcher. Interestingly, under UCT protocol researchers could not divulge subjects' responses even if they were inclined to do so. Beyond that, UCTs provide complete disclosure to subjects and there is no deception.

**Wimbush, James C** and Shepard, Jon M and Markham, Steven E. An Empirical Examination of the Multi-Dimensionality of Ethical Climate in Organizations. *J Bus Ethics*, 16(1), 67-77, Ja 97.

The purpose of this study was to determine whether the ethical climate dimensions identified by Victor and Cullen (1987, 1988) could be replicated in the subunits of a multiunit organization and if so, were the dimensions associated with particular types of operating units. We identified three of the dimensions of ethical climate found by Victor and Cullen and also found a new dimension of ethical climate related to service. Partial support was found for Victor and Cullen's hypothesis that certain ethical climate dimensions are associated with particular forms of organizational governance and control.

**Wimmer, Franz M** (ed) and Kimmerle, Heinz (ed). *Philosophy and Democracy in Intercultural Perspective*. Amsterdam, Rodopi, 1997.

**Winch, Christopher** and Gingell, John. Educational Assessment: Reply to Andrew Davis. *J Phil Educ*, 30(3), 377-388, N 96.

Assessment is at the heart of teaching as it provides a necessary condition for judging success or failure. It is also necessary to ensure that providers of education are accountable to users and providers of resources. Inferential hazard is an inescapable part of any assessment procedure but cannot be an argument against assessment as such. Rich knowledge may be the aim of education but it does not follow that it is the aim of every stage of education. Teaching to tests is the most natural way of ensuring that teaching matches assessment. Failure to assess places public education in jeopardy.

**Winch, Peter**. Can we Understand Ourselves?. *Phil Invest*, 20(3), 193-204, Jl 97.

**Winch, Peter**. Norman Malcolm, *Wittgensteinian Themes*. *Phil Invest*, 20 (1), 51-64, Ja 97.

**Winfield, Richard Dien**. Ethical Community Without Communitarianism. *Phil Today*, 40(2), 310-320, Sum 96.

Although the communitarian turn is motivated by due insight into the complementary difficulties of teleological and procedural justice, it distorts the idea of ethical community by 1) conceiving the latter as a formal context whose content is historically given and 2) by absolutizing ethical community as the sole locus of normativity in conduct. Ethical community, however, cannot have normativity, without 1) presupposing property right and moral accountability, neither of which is atomistic, and 2) comprising institutions of freedom whose structures are conceptually determinate. The logical possibilities of ethical association allow for three types of such institutions: the family, civil society and the state, each reconstituted as the framework of a specific form of self-determinism.

**Wingo, Ajume H**. Civic Education: A New Proposal. *Stud Phil Educ*, 16(3), 277-291, Jl 97.

**Wininger, Kathleen J**. On Nietzsche, *The Genealogy of Morals*. *J Value Inq*, 30(3), 453-470, S 96.

**Winkler, Earl**. "Moral Philosophy and Bioethics: Contextualism versus the Paradigm Theory" in *Philosophical Perspectives on Bioethics*, Sumner, L W (ed), 50-78. Toronto, Univ of Toronto Pr, 1996.

Relative to the field of bioethics, this paper discusses and defends contextualism as an alternative to the traditional "applied ethics" model for moral reasoning. Contextualism, as defended here, is a dominantly case-driven model of moral reasoning which disallows any decisive role for principle in the resolution of genuinely problematic moral issues. In important ways the present paper constitutes a further development of views advanced earlier in the authors' "From Kantianism to Contextualism: the Rise and Fall of the Paradigm Theory in Bioethics" (1993).

**Winkler, Kenneth P** (ed) and Locke, John. *John Locke: An Essay Concerning Human Understanding*. Indianapolis, Hackett, 1996.

Kenneth Winkler's abridgment of Locke's *Essay Concerning Human Understanding* includes generous selections from the *Essay*, topically arranged passages from the replies to Stillingfleet, a chronology, a bibliography, a glossary, and an index based on the entries that Locke himself devised. His introduction provides the reader with both a historical and a philosophical context in which to assess Locke's masterwork. (publisher, edited)

**Winslade, William J**. Irreconcilable Conflicts in Bioethics. *Bioethics Forum*, 11(3), 23-27, Fall 95.

Abortion, physician-assisted suicide, and euthanasia create irreconcilable conflicts in bioethics. These issues challenge our concepts of personhood and personal liberty. They also bring out underlying value conflicts that reveal uncertain sources of authority for resolving the conflicts. As a result, ambivalence about these practices is prevalent. This essay explores the reasons for the irreconcilable conflicts and how to negotiate solutions to the problems without resolving them in only one way.

**Winter, Michael**. Aristotle, *hos epi to polu* Relations, and a Demonstrative Science of Ethics. *Phronesis*, 42(2), 163-189, 1997.

**Winter, Yoad**. Choice Functions and the Scopal Semantics of Indefinites. *Ling Phil*, 20(4), 399-467, Ag 97.

This paper synthesizes two traditional approaches to indefinite descriptions: Russell's treatment using existential quantifiers and Hilbert and Bernays's analysis using epsilon terms. Following work by Reinhart, indefinites get interpreted using existential quantification over *choice functions*: functions that send any nonempty predicate to an individual in its extension. To overcome the problem of empty predicates, the entities picked up are not e-type but the corresponding generalized quantifiers. An empty predicate is mapped by a higher-order choice function to the null generalized quantifier. Linguistic evidence for this treatment is given from various scope effects. Especially: the scope of distributivity with plural indefinites.

**Wippel, John F**. Bishop Stephen Tempier and Thomas Aquinas: A Separate Process Against Aquinas?. *Frei Z Phil Theol*, 44(1-2), 117-136, 1997.

**Wiredu, Kwasi**. "The Need for Conceptual Decolonization in African Philosophy" in *Philosophy and Democracy in Intercultural Perspective*, Kimmerle, Heinz (ed), 11-22. Amsterdam, Rodopi, 1997.

**Wiredu, Kwasi**. *Cultural Universals and Particulars: An African Perspective*. Bloomington, Indiana Univ Pr, 1996.

The eminent Ghanaian philosopher Kwasi Wiredu confronts the paradox that while Western cultures recoil from claims of universality, previously colonized peoples, seeking to redefine their identities, insist on cultural particularities. Wiredu asserts that universals, rightly conceived on the basis of our common biological identity, are not incompatible with cultural particularities and, in fact, are what make intercultural communication possible. Drawing on aspects of Akan thought that appear to diverge from Western conceptions in the areas of ethics and metaphysics, Wiredu calls for a just reappraisal of these disparities, free of thought patterns corrupted by a colonial mentality. Wiredu's exposition of the principles of African traditional philosophy is not purely theoretical; he shows how certain aspects of African political thought may be applied to the practical resolution of some of Africa's most pressing problems. (publisher)

**Wischke, Mirko**. "The Conflict of Morality with Basic Life Instincts" (in Serbo-Croatian). *Filozof Istraz*, 15(4), 673-681, 1995.

Unter feministischen und kommunitarischen Vorzeichen bemüht man sich gegenwärtig um die Reaktualisierung einer Ethik, die im Kontext der frühromantischen Kritik an den Folgen der Moderne für das Leben der Personen entstanden ist. Im Anschluss an Friedrich Nietzsche hat es eine Reihe von Autoren unternommen, jene Ethik in Hinblick auf den Begriff der Person und ihre Lebensführung dezidiert individualistisch zu präzisieren und zum Bezugspunkt einer Ethik zusammenzufassen. Im Zentrum dieser Ethik steht die Vorstellung einer Selbstschaffung der Person—eine perspektivistische Selbstschaffung, die dem Schaffen des Künstlers gleicht, der unermüdlich um den Ausdruck seiner Originalität im Werke ringt. Auf die eine oder andere Weise relativieren diese Autoren den Umstand, dass die Privilegierung des Künstlers im Modell der Selbstschaffung von Nietzsche mit ambivalenten, ja widersprüchlichen Zügen versehen worden ist. Von den ambivalenten Zügen, ihren tragödientheoretischen und moralgenealogischen Denkmotiven und ihrem gegensätzlichen Bezug handelt der Beitrag.

**Wisner, David A**. Ernst Cassirer, Historian of the Will. *J Hist Ideas*, 58(1), 145-161, J 97.

An integral yet little studied dimension of Ernst Cassirer's philosophical work appears in his later essays on the history of culture. Cassirer sketches out a Kantian history of the will, according to which the task of Western philosophy has been to overcome a fundamental opposition between Greco-Roman rationalism and Judeo-Christian voluntarism and liberate the individual human will from all forms of servitude. The Enlightenment marked a brief victory for humanism, but modern forms of absolutism threatened to blur the fundamental ethical message of thinkers like Rousseau and Kant, whom Cassirer consciously emulates.

**Wisniewski, Andrzej**. "Some Foundational Concepts of Erotetic Semantics" in *Knowledge and Inquiry: Essays on Jaakko Hintikka's Epistemology and Philosophy of Science,* Sintonen, Matti (ed), 181-211. Amsterdam, Rodopi, 1997.

Some concepts which may be useful in the analysis of questions and questioning are defined in terms of model-theoretical semantics and multiple-conclusion entailment. In particular, the following concepts are defined: soundness of a question in an interpretation of a language, partial answerhood, normal question, regular question, proper question, relative soundness of a question, relative informativeness of a question, self-rhetoricity of a question, and various kinds of presuppositions. The connections between these concepts are examined in detail. In addition, a general overview of the existing logical theories of questions and answers is presented.

**Wisniewski, Andrzej**. The Logic of Questions as a Theory of Erotetic Arguments. *Synthese*, 109(1), 1-25, O 96.

This paper argues for the idea that the logic of questions should focus its attention on the analysis of arguments in which questions play the role of conclusions. The relevant concepts of validity are discussed and the concept of the logic of questions of a semantically interpreted formalized language is introduced.

**Wisser, Richard**. Karl Jaspers: The Person and His Cause, Not the Person or His Cause. *Int Phil Quart*, 36(4), 413-427, D 96.

**Wisser, Richard**. La visión de las "ideas" y la "verdad" de la verdad. *An Seminar Hist Filosof*, 10, 209-221, 1993.

Tomando como tema de reflexión la "tremenda confusión de ideas en el mundo actual", se pone de relieve el carácter histórico del "modo de ver" o de los juicios de valor que subyacen a tal designación y se intenta delimitar las diferentes situaciones hermenéuticas de las que parten. Desde esta perspectiva, se enfocan tanto el "nihilismo" nietzscheano como la experiencia griega del "caos" y la hebrea de "tohuwabohu", y se analiza, sin olvidar sus orígenes, aquella que ha servido de metáfora tradicional al fenómeno de la "confusión": la de la Torre de Babel.

**Wisser, Richard**. Three Judgments of Nietzsche's Demand for the *Übermensch* (in Serbo-Croatian). *Filozof Istraz*, 15(4), 717-737, 1995.

In Nietzsches Sicht des Übermenschen wird eine überanthropologische Philosophie formuliert, in der die Ontologie nicht auf Anthropologie reduziert werden kann. Die Kennzeichnung der "Stationen" Hans Prinzhorn, Heinz Heimsoeth und Martin Heidegger, die als Typen spezifischer Nietzsche-Interpretationen gefasst werden können, verdeutlicht, wie man mit diesem Problem bisher umgegangen ist. (edited)

**Witherall, Arthur**. The Value of Truth and the Care of the Soul. *J Applied Phil*, 13(2), 189-197, 1996.

Although the argument against the neo-Darwinian theory of evolution presented by Stephen R.L. Clark in *From Athens to Jerusalem* is based upon sound principles, it fails to provide an *a priori* refutation. If it did work, it would refute all objective scientific theories, since all of them make consciousness and subjectivity, as Clark characterises them, incomprehensible. Scientism, the thesis that science is the only source of truth, is Clark's real target, rather than science *per se*, but he does not diagnose this error as it is made by authors such as Jacques Monod and Richard Dawkins. Scientism is not essential to materialism in general, and a successful version of 'supervenience-materialism' could avoid both reductionism and scientism. However, Clark still has a reply. He may use his discussion of the value of truth to provide a more general critique of materialism, which in my view is far more effective.

**Witkowski, Lech**. "The Frankfurt School and Structuralism in Jerzy Kmita's Analysis" in *Epistemology and History*, Zeidler-Janiszewska, Anna (ed), 45-63. Amsterdam, Rodopi, 1996.

The author has identified a number of aspects of Jerzy Kmita's approach to the Frankfurt School and the structuralist tradition, including: I) the problem of criticism, II) the task of the humanities, III) legitimacy in the humanities and regularities in culture, IV) the advantages of structuralism, V) why is structuralism doomed to be pretheoretical? VI) cognitive interests and their logical status, VII) persuasion and ethical priority of interests. Quoting extensively from Kmita's texts the author reconstructs the basic critical synthetic evaluations proposed there in order to show their controversial, if not unverified status. The paper defends the view attributing to the Frankfurt School tradition and Habermas in particular, as well as to structuralism, a more profound and much less naive or incoherent approach. The axes of Kmita's criticism, however, are shown to be important lines of analysis.

**Witschen, Dieter**. All Human Rights for All: Zur Unteilbarkeit der Menschenrechte. *Frei Z Phil Theol*, 43(3), 350-367, 1996.

**Wittekind, Folkart**. Von der Religionsphilosophie zur Wissenschaftslehre: Die Religionsbegründung in Paragraph 2 der zweiten Auflage von Fichtes *Versuch einer Kritik aller Offenbarung*. *Fichte-Studien*, 9, 101-113, 1997.

**Wittwer, Roland** and Lanczkowski, Miroslaw. Les *Evidentiae contra Durandum* de Durandellus. *Rev Thomiste*, 97(1), 143-156, Ja-Mr 97.

**Wohlman, Avital**. Michel Serres (in Hebrew). *Iyyun*, 45, 443-460, O 96.

Serres, like Wittgenstein, believes that the correct method in philosophy is saying what can be said, i.e., sentences from various language games. Serres does not believe in a sharp distinction between the different activities constituting human culture. He searches for the origins of geometry in the writings of the first hundred years of Greek culture for one reason: thinkers of that period had no concept of the modern distinction between the humanities (nomos) and natural sciences (physis). Serres discovers not one but several origins of geometry. Ultimately, however, the origin is the *logos* (definition, concept), which is expressed in different ways in each domain, enabling discussion of the abstract.

**Wójtowicz, Anna**. The Interpolation, Halldén-Completeness, Robinson and Beth Properties in Modal Logics. *Bull Sec Log*, 26(2), 67-72, Je 97.

**Wojtylak, Piotr** and Kotas, Jerzy. Finite Distributive Lattices as Sums of Boolean Algebras. *Rep Math Log*, 29, 35-40, 1995.

**Wojtysiak, Jacek**. On Ingardenian and Thomistic Conceptions of Being (in Polish). *Kwartalnik Filozof*, 25(1), 145-174, 1997.

The purpose of this paper is the comparative analysis of two—Ingardenian and Thomistic—conceptions of being. The former is a three-factor conception (being as the unity of matter/qualities, form structure and mode of existence), the latter is a two-factor one (the unity of essence and existence/esse). For Ingarden the main factor in being is matter (ontological essentialism), for Thomists—existence (metaphysical existentialism). But both sides distinguish (in different terminology) the same following pairs of oppositions in beings: absolute (not produced)—contingent (produced), substantial (persisting, self-sufficient)—inherent, independent (spiritual)—dependent, real—intentional.

**Wokler, Robert**. "Deconstructing the Self on the Wild Side" in *Jean-Jacques Rousseau and the Sources of the Self*, O'Hagan, Timothy (ed), 106-119. Brookfield, Avebury, 1997.

**Wokler, Robert**. The French Revolutionary Roots of Political Modernity in Hegel's Philosophy, or the Enlightenment at Dusk. *Bull Hegel Soc Gt Brit*, 35, 71-89, Spr-Sum 97.

This essay addresses Hegel's treatment of the Enlightenment with respect to three themes. The first is his reading of "Rameau's Nephew" in the *Phenomenology*, as a manifestation of the *world spirit* of modernity. The second

considers his debt to the political economy of the Scottish Enlightenment with respect to his distinction between the state and civil society. The longest section considers Hegel's account of the genesis of the modern nation-state in the French Revolution. It argues that Hegel's perceptive reading of the ideological sources of *The Terror* is based largely on an inaccurate conflation of Rousseau, Sieyes and Robespierre.

**Wolenski, Jan**. "Lvov" in *In Itinere* European Cities and the Birth of Modern Scientific Philosophy, Poli, Roberto (ed), 161-176. Amsterdam, Rodopi, 1997.

This paper sketches a brief history of the city Lvov (before 1772—Poland, 1772-1918—Austria, 918-1939—Poland, 1939-1991—Soviet Union, since 1991—Ukraine), the Lvov University (1662) and philosophy at this university. A special attention is devoted to Kazimierz Twardowski and his activity as the professor of philosophy at the Lvov University (1895-1938). He established the Lvov-Warsaw School.

**Wolenski, Jan**. "Popper on Prophecies and Predictions" in *The Significance of Popper's Thought*, Amsterdamski, Stefan (ed), 87-97. Amsterdam, Rodopi, 1996.

Popper's distinction between prophecies and predictions has the double significance. Firstly, it is of interest for the philosophy of science. Secondly, it is inherently connected with Popper's criticism of historicism and enemies of open society. This second task is certainly more famous and important; it is not difficult to demonstrate that the diagnosis of a statement on the future as an element of historistic ideology disqualifies it or at least makes it very suspicious. This paper deals basically with prophecies as methodological category, although it also critically touches Popper's refutation of historicism. (edited)

**Wolenski, Jan**. "Science and Games" in *Knowledge and Inquiry: Essays on Jaakko Hintikka's Epistemology and Philosophy of Science*, Sintonen, Matti (ed), 213-221. Amsterdam, Rodopi, 1997.

This paper tries to combine ideas of Jaakko Hintikka and Jerzy Giedymin in order to achieve a general game-theoretical approach to science. The two players, *myself* and *nature*, taking part in a scientific game are as mutually dual. The same concerns their strategies. Following Giedymin, rational scientific games are defined as games without dictatorial strategies. Following Hintikka, game-theoretical semantics is used for describing the strategies of both players. In particular, strategies of nature are described by dual logic, that is, logic preserving falsity.

**Wolf, Jean-Claude**. Ein Pluralismus von prima-facie Pflichten als Alternative zu monistischen Theorien der Ethik. *Z Phil Forsch*, 50(4), 601-610, O-D 96.

David W. Ross anticipated many objections against a unifying moral theory. The principle of utility is one principle *entre autres*—not more and not less fundamental than the duty to keep promises. There are no moral absolutes and no rational procedures to grant the right moral answer in any case. Ethical theory has to take seriously the special *prima facie* duties which are irreducibly incorporated in personal relations. But Ross overestimated the epistemological status of our basic moral intuitions, and he overstated his case for intuitionism. Basic moral intuitions are not "knowledge from the start" (Ross), a catalogue of *prima facie* duties has to remain open for critical revisions.

**Wolf, Jean-Claude**. Moralischer Internalismus: Motivation durch Wünsche versus Motivation durch Überzeugungen. *Conceptus*, 29(74), 47-61, 1996.

A theory of practical reason as motivating reason is more plausibly defended in combination with a rich conception of rationality, which promotes the critical assessment of the content of desires. This theory is—in opposition to a neo-Humean approach of reason—best conceived as an inner dialogue between a fully rational self with the real self. The charming model of practical reason as a consultant guide and rational adviser lies at the heart of suggestions independently favored by Warren Quinn and Michael Smith.

**Wolf, Susan**. Happiness and Meaning: Two Aspects of the Good Life. *Soc Phil Pol*, 14(1), 207-225, Wint 97.

**Wolf, Susan**. Meaning and Morality. *Proc Aris Soc*, 97, 299-315, 1997.

**Wolf, Ursula**. "Gibt es moralische Probleme der Wirtschaft?" in *Ökonomie und Moral: Beiträge zur Theorie ökonomischer Rationalität*, Lohmann, Karl Reinhard (ed), 17-29. München, Oldenbourg, 1997.

The author asks, first, whether economics implies morality. The answer being negative, it is then asked whether economics is at all compatible with morality. Third, it is asked who is to solve conflicts between morality and economics. It is argued that economics by itself cannot do this job, that it's rather the job of the just state.

**Wolf II, David F**. Names, Nominata, the Forms and the *Cratylus*. *Phil Inq*, 18(3-4), 20-35, Sum-Fall 96.

Often interpreters of the *Cratylus* debate whether Plato sides with Cratylus or Hermogenes. Others argue that Plato does not take a position on language and naming, but demonstrates the problems with understanding language. I argue that all three of these positions are incorrect. Instead, Cratylus and Hermogenes parallel strong Heracliteanism and strong Protagoreanism with respect to language and knowledge. Socrates promotes a prescriptive theory of naming that contrasts with both positions. Further, Plato's superficial treatment of Heraclitean flux and meaning may imply that he was more interested in discrediting the common Greek conviction that names alone can ensure knowledge.

**Wolf II, David F**. Negative Procreative Liberties and Liberalism. *Phil Soc Act*, 23(1), 19-31, Ja-Mr 97.

Negative procreative liberties are the liberties that enable one to choose not to reproduce. I argue that a liberal theory of justice requires that a well-ordered society should have a basic structure that accommodates negative procreative liberties. First, the liberties are essential for promoting one's highest-order interests. These liberties allow citizens to autonomously decide what type of person they are and will become. Second, "negative procreative liberties" (NPLs) are necessary for meeting a formal requirement of equality of opportunity. For these reasons, a society should recognize the NPLs within the constitution of an institution. (edited)

**Wolf-Devine, Celia**. *Diversity and Community in the Academy: Affirmative Action in Faculty Appointments*. Lanham, Rowman & Littlefield, 1997.

In the wake of court rulings that have forced university administrators to re-evaluate affirmative action policies, this book examines three typical defenses of those policies: that affirmative action compensates for past discrimination; that it provides role models and ensures diversity; and that it corrects for systemic bias against women and racial minorities. While Wolf-Devine finds none of these arguments justifies adopting affirmative action across the board, she argues, contrary to most opponents of the policy, that some circumstances make affirmative action appropriate. (publisher, edited)

**Wolfe, Alan** and Klausen, Jytte. Identity Politics and the Welfare State. *Soc Phil Pol*, 14(2), 231-255, Sum 97.

**Wolfe, Charles T** (trans) and Granel, Gérard. Untameable Singularity (Some Remarks on *Broken Hegemonies*). *Grad Fac Phil J*, 19/20(2/1), 215-228, 1997.

**Wolff, Jonathan**. *An Essay on Rights* by Hillel Steiner. *Int J Phil Stud*, 5(2), 306-315, Je 97.

**Wolff, Jonathan**. Rational, Fair, and Reasonable. *Utilitas*, 8(3), 263-271, N 96.

Brian Barry's *Justice as Impartiality* (Oxford University Press, 1995) distinguishes and sets in competition three models of justice: mutual advantage; reciprocity; and impartiality (the 'rational', 'fair' and 'reasonable' of my title), arguing in favour of the last of these. I consider four questions. First, what is the nature of this competition? Second, has Barry adequately characterised the contenders? Third, can the competition be won on the grounds Barry suggests? Fourth, is it a competition that we should want to be won? By contrast I argue that there are advantages in retaining a pluralist perspective.

**Wolin, Richard**. "Benjamin, Adorno, Surrealism" in *The Semblance of Subjectivity*, Huhn, Tom (ed), 93-122. Cambridge, MIT Pr, 1997.

**Wollan, Jr, Laurin A**. Plagiarism and the Art of Copying. *J Infor Ethics*, 3(1), 58-64, Spr 94.

This article, with reference to the Thomas/Oates case, raises the question of what changes may be made in a passage in one text to avoid plagiarism in another. Judgments to be made of numerous types of changes are left to the reader. But the implications of these instances raise further—and more complex—questions of what constitutes plagiarism.

**Wollheim, Richard**. Due corsi della vita: la memoria e l'oblio. *Iride*, 8(14), 178-186, Ap 95.

**Wolpe, Paul Root**. If I Am Only My Genes, What Am I? Genetic Essentialism and a Jewish Response. *Kennedy Inst Ethics J*, 7(3), 213-230, S 97.

With the advent of the Genetic Age comes a unique new set of problems and ethical decisions. One example of the fallout of the Genetic Age is the development of a "genetic self," the idea that our essential selfhood lies in our genes. It is important to understand the assumptions of the Genetic Age, the development of genetic selfhood and the broader cultural trends and assumptions that underlie modern genetic thinking. It is equally important, however, to shape a reaction to the concept of a genetic self. Insights from Judaism may help to craft a reaction to the modern genetic self that incorporates the best of modern genetics as well as the integrity of a more transcendent selfhood. (edited)

**Wolter, Allan B** and Adams, Marilyn McCord. Memory and Intuition: A Focal Debate in Fourteenth Century Cognitive Psychology. *Fran Stud*, 53, 175-230, 1993.

**Wolter, Frank**. A Counterexample in Tense Logic. *Notre Dame J Form Log*, 37(2), 167-173, Spr 96.

We construct a normal extension of K4 with the finite model property whose minimal tense extension is not complete with respect to Kripke semantics.

**Wolter, Frank**. A Note on the Interpolation Property in Tense Logic. *J Phil Log*, 26(5), 545-551, O 97.

It is proved that all bimodal tense logics which contain the logic of the weak orderings and have unbounded depth do not have the interpolation property.

**Wolter, Frank**. Completeness and Decidability of Tense Logics Closely Related to Logics Above K4. *J Sym Log*, 62(1), 131-158, Mr 97.

Tense logics formulated in the bimodal propositional language are investigated with respect to Kripke-completeness (completeness) and decidability. It is proved that all minimal tense extensions of modal logics of finite width (in the sense of K. Kine) as well as all minimal tense extensions of cofinal subframe logics (in the sense of M. Zakharyaschev) are complete. The decidability of all finitely axiomatizable minimal tense extensions of cofinal subframe logics is shown. A number of variations and extensions of these results are also presented.

**Wolter, Frank**. Superintuitionistic Comparisons of Classical Modal Logics. *Stud Log*, 58(2), 229-259, Mr 97.

This paper investigates partitions of lattices of modal logics based on superintuitionistic logics which are defined by forming, for each superintuitionistic logic $L$ and classical modal logic Theta, the set $L$[Theta] of $L$-companions of Theta. Here $L$[Theta] consists of those modal logics whose

nonmodal fragments coincide with $L$ and which axiomatize Theta if the law of excluded middle is added. (edited)

**Wolter, Frank**. The Structure of Lattices of Subframe Logics. *Annals Pure Applied Log*, 86(1), 47-100, Je 97.

This paper investigates the structure of lattices of normal mono- and polymodal subframe logics, i.e., those modal logics whose frames are closed under a certain type of substructures. Nearly all basic modal logics belong to this class. The main lattice theoretic tool applied is the notion of a splitting of a complete lattice which turns out to be connected with the "geometry" and "topology" of frames, with Kripke completeness and with axiomatization problems. We investigate in detail subframe logics containing K4, those containing polymodal $alt_n$ and subframe logics which are tense logics.

**Wolter, Frank**. What Is the Upper Part of the Lattice of Bimodal Logics?. *Stud Log*, 53(2), 235-241, My 94.

We define an embedding from the lattice of extensions of $T$ into the lattice of extensions of the bimodal logic with two monomodal operators "it is necessary that sub1" and "it is necessary that sub2", whose "it is necessary that sub2"-fragment is $S_5$ and "it is necessary that sub1"-fragment is the logic of a two-element chain. This embedding reflects the fmp, decidability, completeness and compactness. It follows that the lattice of extension of a bimodal logic can be rather complicated even if the monomodal fragments of the logic belong to the upper part of the lattice of monomodal logics. (edited)

**Wolters, Gereon**. "The Idea of Progress in Evolutionary Biology: Philosophical Considerations" in *The Idea of Progress*, McLaughlin, Peter (ed), 201-217. Hawthorne, de Gruyter, 1997.

**Wolterstorff, Nicholas**. Barth on Evil. *Faith Phil*, 13(4), 584-608, O 96.

In this paper I offer an interpretation of Karl Barth's discussion of evil in volume III/3 of his *Church Dogmatics*. It is, I contend, an extraordinarily rich, imaginative and provocative discussion, philosophically informed, yet very different from the mainline philosophical treatments of the topic—and from the mainline theological treatments as well. I argue that though Barth's account is certainly subject to critique at various points, especially on onto-logical matters, nonetheless philosophers are well advised to take seriously what he says. It offers a powerful attack on many standard lines of thought.

**Wolz-Gottwald, Eckard**. Die Wendung nach Asien: Heideggers Ansatz interkultureller Philosophie. *Prima Philosophia*, 10(1), 89-107, 1997.

*The Turn to Asia: Heidegger's Attempt of Intercultural Philosophy* (by Eckard Wolz-Gottwald, Muenster, Germany). Heidegger on the one hand may be regarded as philosopher, who opened himself as hardly anyone else in recent occidental philosophy to Asian thinking. We owe him important impulses for the philosophical dialogue among East and West. In a first step this paper shows the essential moments of Heidegger's turn to Asian philosophy. On the other hand, we always find in Heidegger his return to his own, occidental tradition. A second step analyzes this restriction of him to the European and indeed German context. On the background of this paradoxical constellation we try to show thirdly the main lines of intercultural philosophy as projected by Heidegger. As a result, we find that not every paradox may be thought sensibly. Finally, the narrowing in Heidegger's thinking, his slipping back to the 'all-human', gets thematized.

**Wong, Kenman L**. Tobacco Advertising and Children: The Limits of First Amendment Protection. *J Bus Ethics*, 15(10), 1051-1064, O 96.

While I believe that commercial speech should be offered broad protection, I will argue that severe restrictions are morally justifiable and legally defensible when it comes to advertising to children, particularly with respect to harmful products. Since the free market of ideas model is premised upon a notion that there are "reasonable consumers" that can discern falsehood from truth, this model is invalidated when it comes to children since they cannot be expected to possess the same capacity for judgment as adults. (edited)

**Wood, David**. Much Obliged. *Phil Today*, 41(1-4), 135-140, Spr 97.

**Wood, David**. Reductivism, Retributivism, and the Civil Detention of Dangerous Offenders. *Utilitas*, 9(1), 131-146, Mr 97.

The paper examines one objection to the suggestion that, rather than being subjected to extended prison sentences on the one hand, or simply released on the other, dangerous offenders should be in principle liable to some form of civil detention on completion of their normal sentences. This objection raises the spectre of a 'social harm reduction system', pursuing various reductivist means outside the criminal justice system. The objection also threatens to undermine dualist theories of punishment, theories which combine reductivist and retributivist considerations. The paper attempts to refute the objection by holding that a wedge can be driven between incapacitation and other reductivist measures and hints at a possibly new version of dualism in the process.

**Wood, Forrest**. Averting Violence: Domestic, Social and Personal. *Cont Phil*, 18(2-3), 18-22, Mr-Ap/My-Je 96.

The purpose of this paper is to explore the nature and ways of averting domestic, social, and personal forms of violence. Our ability to avert violence, domestically, socially, and personally, depends upon our understanding of the nature of violence and our having insights as to its causes. Conclusions: Violence can be redirected (as in sacrifice or the courts) so as not to be unending. We may alleviate a source of violence by establishing community. The personal solution to violence lies in our willingness to accept ourselves.

**Wood, Michael**. Kafka's China and the Parable of Parables. *Phil Lit*, 20(2), 325-337, O 96.

This essay offers a reading of a well-known short work ('On parables') by Franz Kafka in the light of Kafka's presentation of China in his fiction. A theological discussion between Gershom Scholem and Walter Benjamin is considered in the light of the positions and arguments proposed by Kafka's parable. Kafka's China is described in some detail and seen as a paradigm for the location of interpreters caught between unusual clarity and unusual obscurity.

**Wood, Neal**. Avarice and Civil Unity: The Contribution of Sir Thomas Smith. *Hist Polit Thought*, 18(1), 24-42, Spr 97.

**Wood, Paul M**. Biodiversity as the Source of Biological Resources: A New Look at Biodiversity Values. *Environ Values*, 6(3), 251-268, Ag 97.

Biodiversity can be defined abstractly as the differences among biological entities. Using this definition, biodiversity can be seen more appropriately as: (a) a necessary precondition for the long term maintenance of biological resources and, therefore, (b) an essential environmental condition. Three values of biodiversity are identified and arranged in a hierarchy: (1) the self-augmenting phenomenon of biodiversity maintains (2) the conditions necessary for the adaptive evolution of species and higher taxa, which in turn is necessary for providing humans with (3) a range of biological resources in the long term. Two broad policy implications emerge: increments of biodiversity should not be traded off against biological resources as if they were the same and the conservation of biodiversity should be a constraint on the public interest, not a goal in service of the public interest. (edited)

**Wood, Rega**. Distinct Ideas and Perfect Solicitude: Alexander of Hales, Richard Rufus, and Odo Rigaldus. *Fran Stud*, 53, 7-46, 1993.

Does divine simplicity imply that God thinks only one thought? Anselm answered affirmatively; Augustine, negatively. In 1225, Alexander of Hales, agreed with Augustine; in 1245, with Anselm. By contrast, Richard Rufus believed there must be many divine ideas. He held that God's perfect solicitude required that each individual be known in virtue of its own proper idea. God knows individuals not confusedly in a single idea, but distinctly in potentially infinitely many ideas. Rufus's argument prompted Odo Rigaldus to modify the Halesian position, as we see in Odo's *Disputed Question on Ideas*, edited here from Toulouse.737 and Klosterneuberg.309.

**Wood, Rega** and Andrews, Robert. Causality and Demonstration: An Early Scholastic *Posterior Analytics* Commentary. *Monist*, 79(3), 325-356, Jl 96.

We introduce an early Western medieval posterior analytics commentary, written by Richard Rufus of Cornwall (d. c.1260), as well as an unfamiliar concept of cause: demonstrational cause. Demonstrational cause must be distinguished from metaphysical (explanatory), epistemological (evidentiary), and logical (validating) cause. Demonstrational cause is a concept employed by many medievals; Thomas Aquinas, for example, as well as Richard Rufus, presumes we understand it. So if we want to work with medieval philosophy, whose study is often rewarding precisely because of the extent to which it challenges current assumptions, we must try to comprehend a usage seldom considered today. A statement of the reasons for attributing this posterior analytics commentary to Richard Rufus and an excerpt from it completes our introduction to a puzzling concept in a newly discovered work.

**Wood, Robert**. Taking the Universal Viewpoint: A Descriptive Approach. *Rev Metaph*, 50(4), 769-781, Je 97.

**Wood, Robert E**. Architecture: The Confluence of Art, Technology, Politics and Nature. *Amer Cath Phil Quart*, 70(Supp), 79-93, 1996.

**Wood, Wallace A** and Glass, Richard S. Situational Determinants of Software Piracy: An Equity Theory Perspective. *J Bus Ethics*, 15(11), 1189-1198, N 96.

Software piracy has become recognized as a major problem for the software industry and for business. One research approach that has provided a theoretical framework for studying software piracy has been to place the illegal copying of software within the domain of ethical decision making and assumes that a person must be able to recognize software piracy as a moral issue. A person who fails to recognize a moral issue will fail to employ moral decision making schemata. There is substantial evidence that many individuals do not perceive software piracy to be an ethical problem. This paper applies social exchange theory, in particular equity theory, to predict the influence of situational factors on subjects' intentions to participate in software piracy. Consistent with the predictions of equity theory this study found that input and outcome situational variables significantly effect a person's intentions to commit software piracy.

**Woodford, Paul G**. Evaluating Edwin Gordon's Music Learning Theory from a Critical Thinking Perspective. *Phil Music Educ Rev*, 4(2), 83-95, Fall 96.

The argument is made that, from a critical thinking standpoint, Edwin E. Gordon's skills-based music learning theory is not so much a music learning theory as a set of preconditions for musical learning. Focusing on the development in children of certain musical skills and abilities coupled with the acquisition of an extended vocabulary of discrete and atomistic tonal and rhythm patterns, Gordon's formalistic theory does not adequately explain how students might be empowered to think musically, and thereby learn, for themselves. Nor does it take into account the social and cultural contexts in which musical thinking takes place.

**Woodruff, David M**. Creation and Discovery in Musical Works. *Pac Phil Quart*, 77(3), 249-261, S 96.

I argue that entities which best fill the role of musical works are discovered and not created. I begin by distinguishing two senses of 'create.' I then examine what our ordinary talk of musical works commits us to, paying special attention to this distinction. Finally, I look at Renée Cox's arguments for the creation view of musical works. One of her reasons actually supports the discovery position. Her other claims are consistent with the view that musical works are discovered. I conclude that though our ordinary talk concerning musical works is often ambiguous, the discovery view is superior.

**Woods, John**. "Semantic Intuitions: Conflict Resolution in the Formal Sciences" in *Logic and Argumentation*, Van Eemeren, Frans H (ed), 179-208. Amsterdam, North-Holland, 1994.

Thanks to Russell's Paradox, there is no intuitive concept of set. Thanks to the Liar Paradox, there is no intuitive concept of truth. Since truth enters into the definition of semantic consequence, there is no intuitive concept of it either. The loss of intuitive concepts is ruinous for a certain conception of how philosophical analysis is to be done. In Moore's hands, philosophical analysis is the decomposition of complex concepts into simple, intuitive concepts which reveal the basic structure of reality as it really is. Judged from this Moorean perspective, it ought to be philosophically impossible to produce theories of sets or of truths or of consequence. In the case of sets, this was precisely Frege's position. Russell soldiered on in *Principles of Mathematics*, he pleaded a distinction between analysis by way of philosophical definitions and analysis by way of mathematical definitions. Russell's mathematical analysis of sets was an undeclared return to idealism (in what was supposed to be his first analytic book).

**Woods, Richard**. Mysticism and Social Action: The Mystic's Calling, Development and Social Activity. *J Consciousness Stud*, 3(2), 158-171, 1996.

Relying on the philosophical analysis of Western religious mysticism by William Ernest Hocking and more recent writers, I propose that the connection between mystical experience and social action is not only a necessary one but manifests a reciprocal individual and social process by which communities recover, refine, and renew their primary ethical and religious goals and the appropriate means of achieving them. Although motivated by love, the mystic's calling, development, and subsequent activity constitute structurally integral phases of a social process involving a withdrawal from the world, a systematic reevaluation of the beliefs, goals, and values of the originating society, and the mystic's return to the world intent on and equipped to contribute significantly to social reform. (edited)

**Woods, Tim**. "The Ethical Subject: The Philosophy of Emmanuel Levinas" in *Critical Studies: Ethics and the Subject*, Simms, Karl (ed), 53-60. Amsterdam, Rodopi, 1997.

**Woodward, P A**. The Importance of the Proportionality Condition to the Doctrine of Double Effect: A Response to Fischer, Ravizza, and Copp. *J Soc Phil*, 28(2), 140-152, Fall 97.

**Woodward, Richard S**. Ethical Considerations in the Testing of Biopharmaceuticals for Adventitious Agents. *Sci Eng Ethics*, 1(3), 273-282, Jl 95.

Safety testing of biological pharmaceuticals is often carried out by contract testing laboratories which perform these tests on behalf of the drug's developer. These laboratories are confronted with a number of ethical issues related to selling their services, maintaining confidentiality, and the handling of results. This paper outlines these issues, and, by way of illustration, discusses how one such laboratory addresses them.

**Woollaston, Lin**. Counterpart Theory as a Semantics for Modal Logic. *Log Anal*, 37(147-8), 255-263, S-D 94.

In counterpart theory, unlike standard possible worlds, semantics, an object and its counterparts, are not identified with one another. Thus, an object need not have exactly one counterpart in any given world. I show that this results in the invalidity of some principles of regular modal logics. I also prove that such a semantics results in the invalidity of either universal instantiation or the necessity of the principle of excluded middle.

**Wootton, David** (ed). *Modern Political Thought: Readings from Machiavelli to Nietzsche*. Indianapolis, Hackett, 1996.

This reader provides an introduction to modern political philosophy from Machiavelli (1513) to Nietzsche (1887). Most of the works reprinted here have long been recognized as central to the history of political philosophy: Machiavelli, Hobbes, Locke, Rousseau, Mill. Like any such selection, this one also reflects contemporary interests and preoccupations: Nietzsche seems a much more important political philosopher now than he did thirty years ago, and Mill's *The Subjection of Women* seems a much more important text. Adding one text in a reader such as this means dropping another; Marxism is the obvious casualty of the last twenty years, and though I have included an extensive selection from Marx himself, I have excluded Luxembourg, Lenin, and Trotsky, to name three for whom space might once have been found. (edited)

**Worley, Joel K** (& others) and Aby, Carroll D and Fusilier, Marcelline R. Perceived Seriousness of Business Ethics Issues. *Bus Prof Ethics J*, 15(1), 67-78, Spr 96.

Respondents from over 900 businesses rated the seriousness of twenty major ethical issues. As representatives for their organizations, they also identified the issues that were most resolved and those that were least resolved. Workplace safety and employee theft had the two highest average ratings of seriousness. The issue most frequently rated as a) least resolved was theft, and b) most resolved was workplace safety. Results are discussed in the context of previous literature.

**Worley, Sara**. Belief and Consciousness. *Phil Psych*, 10(1), 41-55, Mr 97.

In this paper, I argue that we should not ascribe beliefs and desires to subjects like zombies or (present day) computers which do not have phenomenal consciousness. In order to ascribe beliefs, we must distinguish between personal and subpersonal content. There may be states in my brain which represent the array of light intensities on my retina, but these states are not beliefs, because they are merely subpersonal. I argue that we cannot distinguish between personal and subpersonal content without reference to phenomenal consciousness. I argue for this by examining two attempts to account for belief without reference to phenomenal consciousness, functionalism and Dennett's patterns of behavior theory, and showing that they both fail. In the course of the arguments that these attempts fail, I develop some positive reasons for believing that phenomenal consciousness is indeed necessary.

**Worley, Sara**. Counterfactuals, Causation, and Overdetermination. *Phil Papers*, 25(3), 189-202, N 96.

**Worsfold, Victor L**. "*Akrasia*: Irremediable but not Unapproachable" in *Philosophy of Education (1996)*, Margonis, Frank (ed), 139-141. Urbana, Phil Education Soc, 1997.

**Worsfold, Victor L**. Israel Scheffler's Ethics: Theory and Practice. *Stud Phil Educ*, 16(1-2), 189-200, Ja-Ap 97.

Evincing his not uncritical allegiance to pragmatic philosophy, Israel Scheffler's notion of ethics and its role in education is one which attempts to dissolve inherited distinctions in the field. For Scheffler's ethics, aimed always at justifiable conduct, is conduct guided by rationality, powered by emotion, responsible to the needs of it agents' community, learned through moral education, practiced habitually and ultimately justified by individual commitment to action. Scheffler's primary *desideratum* is to arrive at an ethics that is justifiable because it is reasonable and so can gain our commitment.

**Worsfold, Victor L**. Teaching Democracy Democratically. *Educ Theor*, 47(3), 395-410, Sum 97.

**Worth, Sarah E**. Wittgenstein's Musical Understanding. *Brit J Aes*, 37 (2), 158-167, Ap 97.

Although Wittgenstein is considered one of the greatest philosophers of the twentieth century, he may have left us with more questions than we started with. The questions he raises force us to re-examine the foundations that we once thought we had. In this paper, I elucidate some of his remarks, which are scattered throughout his writings, about the relation of music and understanding. Using music as a tool, Wittgenstein helps us comprehend how we understand the world. I focus on the examples of understanding a sentence and a musical theme and look at our resulting behavior when we claim to understand.

**Worth-Staten, Patricia A** and Poniatowski, Larry. Advance Directives and Patient Rights: A Joint Commission Perspective. *Bioethics Forum*, 13(2), 47-50, Sum 97.

Advance directives for health care are an inherent right from the perspective of the Joint Commission for the Accreditation of Healthcare's standards. Highlighting standards from the *Comprehensive Accreditation Manual of Hospitals: The Official Handbook*, the authors outline this right. They contrast barriers patients encounter to having their preferences respected.

**Woznicki, Andrew Nicholas**. *Metaphysical Animal: Divine and Human in Man*. New York, Lang, 1996.

The theantropic structure of man postulates a specific relationship between the Divine Immanence and the Divine Transcendence with respect to the divine/human composition of man's nature, thus establishing a synergetic union between God and man. Human nature so conceived, compels man to exist in an ambiguous situation and to live his life in a constant tension between his desire for eternity and his want for temporality. The author analyzes the traumatic conditions of theantropic consciousness of man as it is expressed by both the ancient and contemporary thinkers and how it is portrayed in the literary works of writers and poets, dramatists and film makers. (publisher, edited)

**Wright, Crispin**. "Can There Be a Rationally Compelling Argument for Anti-Realism about Ordinary ('Folk') Psychology?" in *Contents*, Villanueva, Enrique (ed), 197-221. Atascadero, Ridgeview, 1995.

**Wright, Crispin**. Human Nature?. *Euro J Phil*, 4(2), 235-254, Ag 96.

**Wright, Crispin**. Précis of *Truth and Objectivity*. *Phil Phenomenol Res*, 56(4), 863-868, D 96.

**Wright, Crispin**. Response to Commentators. *Phil Phenomenol Res*, 56(4), 911-941, D 96.

**Wright, Crispin** and Hale, Bob. "Nominalism and the Contingency of Abstract Objects" in *Frege: Importance and Legacy*, Schirn, Matthias (ed), 174-199. Hawthorne, de Gruyter, 1996.

An apparently serious difficulty for Hartry Field's unorthodox defense of nominalism in mathematics, pressed by both authors in earlier writings, is that it commits Field to an unpalatable contingency thesis: there are in fact no numbers, etc., but there might have been. Field's reply has been that the objection trades on an equivocation over the sense of 'contingent'. This paper attempts to explain why this response is ineffective and to provide a reformulation of the objection which captures its essential core whilst relying principles governing the notion of contingency which should command general assent.

**Wright, Ian** and Coombs, Jerrold. A Conception of Practical Reasoning. *Inquiry (USA)*, 14(2), 48-51, Wint 94.

**Wronski, Andrzej**. Gentzen-Style Calculi for Quasi-Identities of Finite Algebras. *Rep Math Log*, 28, 73-79, 1994.

Confirming a conjecture of K. Palasinska and D. Pigozzi we prove that the set of quasi-identities of a finite algebra can be finitely axiomatized by a Gentzen-style calculus which results from the calculus of Selman by adding one new inference rule.

**Wronski, Andrzej**. Transparent Unification Problem. *Rep Math Log*, 29, 105-107, 1995.

**Wu, Kuang-Ming**. "The Spirit of Pragmatism and the Pragmatic Spirit" in *The Recovery of Philosophy in America: Essays in Honor of John Edwin Smith*, Kasulis, Thomas P (ed), 59-91. Albany, SUNY Pr, 1997.

**Wuchterl, Kurt**. *Streitgespräche und Kontroversen in der Philosophie des 20.Jahrhunderts*. Berne, Haupt, 1997.

Among Kant scholars, it is a controversial question whether within the corpus of the extant Kantian manuscripts (the so-called "Opus postumum"), the textual form of the planned work is in such a condition so as to "need only redaction" before printing, as Hasse, one of Kant's contemporary biographers, held. The present edition works on the assumption that within the manuscripts of the "Opus postumum", we have a version of the "Übergang von den metaphysischen Anfangsgründen der Naturwissenschaft zur Physik" thoroughly prepared by Kant for printing. This edition is the first since 1936/38 and is based on Kant's original manuscripts in the "Opus postumum". (publisher, edited)

**Wüstehube, Axel**. Noch einmal: Rationalität und Normativität. *Protosoz*, 8/9, 149-169, 1996.

The ongoing discussion about a notion of pragmatic rationality has evolved in a variety of different approaches, mainly because every author tries to combine his genuine philosophical point of view with the interpretation of "rationality". Nevertheless there is an agreement of sorts that rationality cannot proceed merely descriptively but has also normative implications. The paper investigates the proposals of Nicholas Rescher and Herbert Schnädelbach concerning the question of a normativity of rationality. Moreover, it deals with the problem of "unity of reason" and its interconnectedness with the inherent normativity of rationality.

**Wurzer, Wilhelm S**. "Nancy and the Political Imaginary after Nature" in *On Jean-Luc Nancy: The Sense of Philosophy*, Sheppard, Darren (ed), 91-102. New York, Routledge, 1997.

**Wyld, David** and Jones, Coy A. The Importance of Context: The Ethical Work Climate Construct and Models of Ethical Decision Making—An Agenda for Research. *J Bus Ethics*, 16(4), 465-472, Mr 97.

This paper examines the role which organizational context factors play in individual ethical decision making. Two general propositions are set forth, examining the linkage between ethical work climate and decision making. An agenda for research and the potential implications of the study and practice of managerial ethics are then discussed.

**Wyller, Truls**. Das Verstehen singulärer Handlungen: Ein Kommentar zu Davidson und von Wright. *Grazer Phil Stud*, 51, 237-252, 1996.

Gegen *von Wright* und andere Anhänger nicht-kausaler Handlungs-erklärungen hat *Davidson* argumentiert, dass Handlungen nicht nur als sinnvolles Verhalten konzeptuell *verstanden*, sondern auch durch *singuläre Ursachen* als ihre "wahren" Motive *erklärt* werden. Dem entspricht auch der von *Perry* und anderen nachgewiesene *indexikalische* Charakter eines jeden Handlungsbewusstseins. Da jedoch ein singuläres Handlungsbewusstsein auch *zukunftsgerichtet* ist, hat das entsprechende, indexikalische Motiv keine von der erst zu realisierenden Handlung unabhängige Existenz. Die Handlung wird eher als eine "Wirkung von der Zukunft" verstanden, und so haben die Anti-Kausalisten recht, dass bei Handlungserklärungen nicht auf Humesche Ursachen hingewiesen wird.

**Wyller, Truls**. Kausalität und singuläre Referenz: Eine sprach-philosophische Rekonstruktion des empirischen Realismus bei Kant. *Kantstudien*, 88(1), 1-15, 1997.

Ich werde im folgenden den Versuch unternehmen, einige transzendental-philosophische Schlüsselbegriffe durch neuere sprachphilosophische Positionen zu beleuchten. Nach einer kurzen Beschreibung der Realismuskritik von Dummett und Putnam behaupte ich, dass Kants Theorie "realistisch" ist auf eine Weise, die eher Davidsons Position entspricht; dass man bei Kant jedoch einen Handlungsbegriff vorfindet, der menschlichen Verstehensbedingungen gemäss ist. Meine Argumentation für diese These besteht erstens in einem Aktualisieren der Kantischen Anschauungsformen durch die heutige Theorie der "singulären Referenz" sowie zweitens in einer Beschreibung der Kategorien der Substanz und der Kausalität aus der Sicht interventionistischer Theorien.

**Wyma, Keith D**. Moral Responsibility and Leeway for Action. *Amer Phil Quart*, 34(1), 57-70, Ja 97.

**Wynn, Mark**. Beauty, Providence and the Biophilia Hypothesis. *Heythrop J*, 38(3), 283-299, Jl 97.

The paper examines F.R. Tennant's argument for design from natural beauty. The argument is assessed in the light of i) social scientific studies of evaluative responses to nature in a variety of cultures, and ii) attempts to explain our aesthetic appreciation of nature in sociobiological terms. The paper argues that the first development ensures that the central premise of Tennant's argument can be given a sound empirical basis. It argues, moreover, that sociobiological explanations of aesthetic responses to nature, while partially successful, fail to account for all the data.

**Wynn, Mark**. Simplicity, Personhood, and Divinity. *Int J Phil Relig*, 41(2), 91-103, Ap 97.

The paper examines the religious rather than the metaphysical adequacy of the conception of God as an individual person who is passible and temporal. It argues that establishing the religious relevance of such a God will require some use of notions more commonly associated with a conception of God as 'simple'. Departing from Swinburne's account, the paper suggests that God conceived as an individual person would be worthy of worship not so much as the 'lord' of all, but as the integrated expression of the nature of existence.

**Wynn, Mark**. Trust-Relationships and the Moral Case for Religious Belief. *Int Phil Quart*, 37(2), 179-188, Je 97.

If there has been a deep exchange of trust between two people, then they have a moral reason for upholding beliefs which are required for the persistence of their relationship as a trust-relationship. The paper argues that a person's religious beliefs may contribute towards her participation in trust-relationships both in relation to other human beings and in relation to God. This suggests that there may be a moral argument for religious belief from trust-relationship considerations. The paper examines the strength of this case, and notes its consonance with the psychology of religious belief formation.

**Xenos, Nicholas**. Civic Nationalism: Oxymoron?. *Crit Rev*, 10(2), 213-231, Spr 96.

Recent attempts to distinguish a normatively acceptable "civic nationalism"—as distinct from an irrationally tainted "ethnic nationalism"—have failed to take seriously the implications of the transition from the city as the immediate spatial unit of the patria to the more abstract national state that replaced it. The nation-state has required a mythologizing naturalism to legitimate it, thus blurring the distinction between "civic" and "ethnic." The urban political experience of the patria is lost to us; cosmopolitan intellectuals should resist the comforting temptation to recover it in the nation and should recognize civic nationalism for the oxymoron it is.

**Xiyuan, Xiong**. A Preliminary Analysis of "National Consciousness". *Chin Stud Phil*, 28(2), 5-9, Wint 96-97.

**Xiyuan, Xiong**. A Tentative Discussion on the Common Mental Attributes of the Han Nationality. *Chin Stud Phil*, 28(2), 35-52, Wint 96-97.

**Xiyuan, Xiong**. A Tentative Discussion on the Common Mental Attributes of the Huihui Nationality. *Chin Stud Phil*, 28(2), 53-70, Wint 96-97.

**Xiyuan, Xiong**. National Consciousness and Motherland Consciousness. *Chin Stud Phil*, 28(2), 19-27, Wint 96-97.

**Xiyuan, Xiong**. National Consciousness and Nationalism. *Chin Stud Phil*, 28(2), 28-34, Wint 96-97.

**Xiyuan, Xiong**. Socialism and National Consciousness. *Chin Stud Phil*, 28(2), 10-18, Wint 96-97.

**Xiyuan, Xiong**. The Common Mental Attributes of the Dai Nationality Explored. *Chin Stud Phil*, 28(2), 71-87, Wint 96-97.

**Xu, Keqian**. The Unique Features of Hui Shi's Thought: A Comparative Study between Hui Shi and Other Pre-Qin Philosophers. *J Chin Phil*, 24(2), 231-253, Je 97.

The aim of this work is to find out the unique features of Hui Shi's thought in comparison with the other philosophers in pre-Qin China. The conclusion is that Hui Shi's scholarship was strongly oriented to material existence. And there is a tendency in his thought of tolerating, advocating and intentionally pursuing diversity, variety and unusual ideas. In judging the value of knowledge, Hui Shu's opinion embodied a sprout of scientific spirit which emphasized the truthfulness rather than usefulness of knowledge. All these features sharply contrast with those of the dominant Confucian and Taoist tradition of ancient China.

**Xu, Ming**. Decidability of *Stit* Theory with a Single Agent and *Refref* Equivalence. *Stud Log*, 53(2), 259-298, My 94.

The purpose of this paper is to prove the decidability of *stit* theory (a logic of "seeing to it that") with a single agent and *Refref Equivalence*. This result is obtained through an axiomatization of the theory and a proof that it has the *finite model property*. A notion of *companions to stit formulas* is introduced and extensively used in the proof.

**Yablo, Stephen**. "Singling Out Properties" in *AI, Connectionism and Philosophical Psychology, 1995*, Tomberlin, James E (ed), 477-502. Atascadero, Ridgeview, 1995.

**Yack, Bernard**. The Myth of the Civic Nation. *Crit Rev*, 10(2), 193-211, Spr 96.

The idea of a purely civic nationalism has attracted Western scholars, most of whom rightly disdain the myths that sustain ethnonationalist theories of political community. Civic nationalism is particularly attractive to many Americans, whose peculiar national heritage encourages the delusion that their mutual association is based solely on consciously chosen principles. But this idea misrepresents political reality as surely as the ethnonationalist myths it is designed to combat. And propagating a new political myth is an especially inappropriate way of defending the legacy of Enlightenment liberalism from the dangers posed by the growth of nationalist political passions.

**Yadira Martínez, Agustina**. A Modern Conception of the Human Rights (Spanish). *Fronesis*, 2(2), 133-153, D 95.

It has been tried to analyze the constant development of the human rights conception by determining their essential features as a result of the intervention of ideological, historical and political factors. This development has incidence in the advance of modern constitutionalism as means to strengthen the human rights consecration in the internal legislations. Obligations contracted by different countries are mentioned and the fundamental reasons for human rights indivisibility are presented, having as a result the acknowledgment of new categories to incorporate the human being as the center of the political and economical change, by challenging the traditional concepts. (edited)

**Yagisawa, Takashi**. Salmon Trapping. *Phil Phenomenol Res*, 57(2), 351-370, Je 97.

Call a sentential context *semantically transparent* if and only if all synonymous expressions are substitutable for one another in it *salva veritate*. Nathan Salmon has boldly advanced a refreshingly crisp semantic theory according to which belief contexts are semantically transparent. If he is right, belief contexts are much better behaved than widely suspected. Impressive as it is, this author does not believe that Salmon's theory is completely satisfactory. This article tries to show that Salmon's theory, in conjunction with a number of auxiliary but important claims he makes to buttress the theory, seems to lead to failure of semantic transparency of belief contexts.

**Yahot, Christophe**. La culture comme force. *Quest*, 9(2), 71-85, D 96.

**Yalowitz, Steven**. Rationality and the Argument for Anomalous Monism. *Phil Stud*, 87(3), 235-258, S 97.

Rationality plays a fundamental role in Donald Davidson's argument against the possibility of strict psychophysical and psychological laws. This paper argues that recent influential reconstructions of that argument, by Jaegwon Kim and William Child, fail to underwrite mental anomalism due to internal problems and controversial assumptions. Emphasis is put on the importance, within Davidson's framework, of the notion of strict laws, as well as his wider aim of using mental anomalism to argue for monism. A sketch is offered of an alternative argument for mental anomalism, based upon the causal nature of reasons and anomalism of causally defined concepts.

**Yamaji, Keizo**. A Global Perspective of Ethics in Business. *Bus Ethics Quart*, 7(3), 55-70, Jl 97.

Business ethics should not just be a corporate code, but be implemented in the line of business as a corporate philosophy. As an example of the above, I would like to present corporate activities of Canon, Inc. based on the "Kyosei" initiative which I directed, especially its global development. I would like to show that these activities are ahead of the times and result in great prosperity of a corporation, and to tell my dream to increase corporations which take the same types of actions based on the "Kyosei" initiative.

**Yamasaki, Toshiko**. The Changes of Painting Techniques in the Early Tang Wall Paintings of Dunhuang Mogao Grottos; The Relationship between "Pattern" and Pictorial Structure (in Japanese). *Bigaku*, 47(3), 12-23, Winter 96.

In this paper, I would like to focus on large and sophisticated scenes depicting different *Paradises of Buddha* in the early Tang period (618-781 A.D.), examining to what extent the wall paintings of Dunhuang Mogao grottos were technically drawn and how the changes in artistic techniques affected the pictorial structures. (edited)

**Yandell, David** and Moser, Paul K. Against Naturalizing Rationality. *Protosoz*, 8/9, 81-96, 1996.

Recent obituaries for traditional nonnaturalistic approaches to rationality are not just premature but demonstrably self-defeating. One such prominent obituary appears in the writings of W. V. Quine, whose pessimism about traditional epistemology stems from his scientism, the view that the natural sciences have a monopoly on legitimate theoretical explanation. Quine also offers an obituary for the a priori constraints on rationality found in "first philosophy", resting on his rejection of the "pernicious mentalism" of semantic theories of meaning. Quine's pronouncements of the death of traditional conceptions of rationality in epistemology and in the theory of meaning are, we contend, misguided wishes for their death, wishes that face severe problems of self-defeat. In addition, Quine's naturalistic epistemology is subject to damaging skeptical worries, the force of which one cannot escape by ignoring them. (edited)

**Yandell, Keith**. Persons (Real and Alleged) in Enlightenment Traditions: A Partial Look at Jainism and Buddhism. *Int J Phil Relig*, 42(1), 23-39, Ag 97.

**Yang, Yue** and Chong, C T. Sigma$_2$ Induction and Infinite Injury Priority Arguments: Part II: Tame Sigma$_2$ Coding and the Jump Operator. *Annals Pure Applied Log*, 87(2), 103-116, 15 S 97.

**Yanikoski, Charles S**. When the Trial *Is* the Punishment: The Ethics of Plagiarism Accusations. *J Infor Ethics*, 3(1), 83-88, Spr 94.

**Yao, Xinzhong**. Self-Construction and Identity: The Confucian Self in Relation to Some Western Perceptions. *Asian Phil*, 6(3), 179-195, N 96.

In contrast to the metaphysical, epistemological and psychological understandings of the self traditionally held and today still extensively considered in the West, the self in Confucianism is essentially an ethical concept, representing a holistic view of humanhood and a continuingly constructive process driven by self-cultivation and moral orientations. This paper first examines what is literally and philosophically meant by the self in these two traditions, then examines the contrasts or comparisons between the Confucian conception of the self and the self as perceived in some strands of Western philosophy; and finally, interprets and analyses the constructively organic theory of the Confucian self, which is clearly differentiated from the self perceived in mainstream philosophy in traditional Europe and yet is being echoed in the more recent developments of Western philosophy and in the strong current of postmodernism.

**Yarborough, Mark**. The Reluctant retained Witness: Alleged Sexual Misconduct in the Doctor/Patient Relationship. *J Med Phil*, 22(4), 345-364, Ag 97.

Testifying as an expert ethics witness raises a number of important issues. These include: the prospect of generating adverse publicity for oneself and one's institution, avoiding bias, giving testimony that is at odds with testimony given by colleagues, potential conflicts of interest introduced by reimbursement, the need of these who hear the testimony of bioethicists to appreciate the nature of moral expertise, the difficulty of assessing the quality of legal evidence which emerges from adversarial legal proceedings and the need to consider what weight should be assigned to expert ethics testimony. Along with these issues, what might constitute sexual misconduct is addressed in the essay so that readers can review the decision-making of the author in two cases.

**Yarbrough, Stephen R**. Force, Power, and Motive. *Phil Rhet*, 29(4), 344-358, 1996.

Poststructural explanations of changes in belief by means of the concepts of force and contingency do not acknowledge the effective difference between rhetorical force (the result of crediting a speaker with actual force) and rhetorical power (the result of crediting a speaker with rhetorical force). Force and power are generated differently and their exercise produces different effects. Although both are real, no necessary connection between the two obtains and so the difference between what we believe about a matter and what we believe others believe about it produces a space for rationally altering discursive grounds.

**Yarza, Ignacio**. Ética y dialéctica: Sócrates, Platón y Aristóteles. *Acta Phil*, 5(2), 293-315, 1996.

La tesi di questo articolo è che il fondamento ultimo e necessario della metodologia dialettica utilizzata da Aristotele nella sua etica sarebbe la sua dottrina metafisica, il suo personale pensiero sull'essere. La dialettica, dunque, non sarebbe un espediente messo in atto da Aristotele per distinguere il sapere pratico da quello teorico, ma piuttosto la sola razionalità capace di rispettare la visione aristotelica del reale. Tale conclusione viene raggiunta tenendo conto del precedente impiego e della teorizzazione della dialettica fatti da Socrate e da Platone, della tradizione cioè in cui nasce e si sviluppa la filosofia aristotelica.

**Yasenchuk, Ken**. Moral Realism and the Burden of Argument. *S J Phil*, 35(2), 247-264, Sum 97.

**Yeager, Daniel B**. Dangerous Games and the Criminal Law. *Crim Just Ethics*, 16(1), 3-12, Win-Spr 97.

**Yearwood, Stephen**. A Conception of Justice. *Cont Phil*, 18(2-3), 52-58, Mr-Ap/My-Je 96.

This article presents an approach to justice based on Warren Samuel's conception of social power (the ability to effect choices) and John Locke's emphasis on our being imbued with mutually independent and "equally valid" (my term) wills (or, "equal" wills). We use our equal wills and our social power (basically, the sum and substance of one's being) in effecting choices. (I submit) the various sources of social power are either innate or acquired. Justice is realized in respect for (at minimum, nonsubordination of) people's wills. Social justice refers to respect for people's wills in the structure and functioning of the "foundational institutions" of the community (institutions that as singular and integral entities are universal with respect to the members of the community). Social justice hinges on a just distribution (i.e., in accordance with a just principle, i.e., one which recognizes people's equality based on our equal wills) of those acquired sources of social power that are essential to participation in foundational institutions. Hence, rights of participation in the political system (the institution in which, borrowing from Samuels, choices are effected for the community as a whole) must be so distributed. (edited)

**Yeast, John D**. Prematernal Duty and the Resolution of Conflict. *Bioethics Forum*, 11(1), 3-8, Spr 95.

The national news media have recently highlighted several cases that demonstrate the conflict between maternal autonomy and fetal beneficence. The balance of these two ethical principles requires a complete understanding of the remarkable changes that have occurred in fetal diagnosis and therapy over the past thirty years. The recognition of the fetus as a patient has suggested prematernal duty not previously appreciated or understood. Application of preventive ethical analysis can minimize the actual occurrence of maternal-fetal conflict.

**Yepes, Ricardo**. Persona: Intimidad, don y libertad nativa: Hacia una antropología de los transcendentales personales. *Anu Filosof*, 29(2), 1077-1104, 1996.

Human person must be considered from the transcendental point of view, in order to discover his most deep dimensions of its being: intimacy or interiority, intellectual knowledge, giftness or love, liberty, incommunicability, filiation. The article offers an initial approach to these notions.

**Yepes Stork, Ricardo**. La persona como fuente de autenticidad. *Acta Phil*, 6(1), 83-100, 1997.

L'autenticità umana deve essere considerata in relazione alla libertà e al corso della vita. In tal modo, alla sua considerazione epistemologica e metafisica, si aggiungono in modo naturale la dimensione etica e politica, e la riflessione sulle sue radici profondamente radicate nella persona che, come gli elementi suddetti, ci conducono alla considerazione dell'identità personale e al modo in cui essa si raggiunge.

**Yi, Xiaoding**. A Non-Splitting Theorem for d.r.e. Sets. *Annals Pure Applied Log*, 82(1), 17-96, N 96.

A set of natural numbers is called d.r.e. (difference recursively enumerable) if it may be obtained from some recursively enumerable (r.e.) set by deleting the numbers belonging to another recursively enumerable set. Sacks showed that for each nonrecursive recursively enumerable set *A* there are disjoint recursively enumerable sets *B*, *C* which cover *A* such that *A* is recursive in neither the intersection of *A* and *B* nor the intersection of *A* and *C*. In this paper, we construct a counterexample which shows that Sacks's theorem is not in general true when *A* is d.r.e. rather than r.e. (edited)

**Yi, Xiaoding** and Sorbi, Andrea and Cooper, S Barry. Cupping and Noncupping in the Enumeration Degrees of Sigma$^0_2$ Sets [1]. *Annals Pure Applied Log*, 82(3), 317-342, D 96.

We prove the following three theorems on the enumeration degrees of Sigma$^0_2$ sets. Theorem A: There exists a nonzero noncuppable Sigma$^0_2$ enumeration degree. Theorem B: Every nonzero Delta$^0_2$ enumeration degree is cuppable to $O'_e$ by an incomplete total enumeration degree. Theorem C: There exists a nonzero low Delta$^0_2$ enumeration degree with the anticupping property. (edited)

**Yilmaz, M R**. In Defense of a Constructive, Information-Based Approach to Decision Theory. *Theor Decis*, 43(1), 21-44, Jl 97.

Since the middle of this century, the dominant prescriptive approach to decision theory has been a deductive viewpoint which is concerned with axioms of rational preference and their consequences. After summarizing important problems with the preference primitive, this paper argues for a constructive approach in which information is the foundation for decision-making. This approach poses comparability of uncertain acts as a question rather than an assumption. It is argued that, in general, neither preference nor subjective probability can be assumed given and that these need to be generated by using the relevant information available to the decision-agent in a given situation. A specific constructive model is discussed and illustrated with a real example from this viewpoint.

**Yob, Iris M**. "Can the Justification of Music Education be Justified?" in *Philosophy of Education (1996),* Margonis, Frank (ed), 237-240. Urbana, Phil Education Soc, 1997.

Estelle Jorgensen identifies the strengths and weaknesses inherent in traditional justifications for music education and proposes that these justifications can and should be held in dialectic tension in curriculum-building and educational policy-making. The historic difficulty of justifying music education raises the question of whether music can be justified in the curriculum. While music is disciplined by rational principles, it is not altogether a rational undertaking. The justifications that better speak for music and the other arts may not be rational ones at all but those that reflect the artistic enterprise itself: artistic, intuitive, emotional, a-rational.

**Yob, Iris M**. The Cognitive Emotions and Emotional Cognitions. *Stud Phil Educ*, 16(1-2), 43-57, Ja-Ap 97.

Israel Scheffler's *In Praise of the Cognitive Emotions* (1977, 1991) extends earlier analyses of the role of emotions in rational undertakings. It shows that some emotions—"rational passions," "perceptive feelings," "theoretical imagination," and "cognitive emotions"—are essentially cognitive in origin and may serve cognitive purposes. Though it analyzes the interplay of emotion and cognition, cognition is the focus and the emotions that are examined revolve about it. This prompts us to wonder about the effect of a "Copernican revolution." If emotion were to be put in the center, would there also be cognitions which are essentially emotional in origin and/or serve emotional purposes? Here we explore the possibility of "informed expression," "emotional cognizance" and "emotional cognitions," drawing primarily from aesthetic, religious, spiritual, and ethical experience.

**Yong, Patrick**. "Intellectualism and Moral Habituation in Plato's Earlier Dialogues" in *Dialogues with Plato,* Benitez, Eugenio (ed), 49-61. Edmonton, Academic, 1996.

Many historians of philosophy see Plato as an ethical intellectualist, whose primary concern is with an understanding of what the *good* itself is, rather than with the practical aspect of how one can become good. I call into question the correctness of such a reconstruction of Plato's ethical thought. Section I shows how such a mistaken reconstruction arises. Section II argues that moral habituation is just as basic to Plato's early moral theory as moral intellectualism. Section III considers one line of defence against an objection to the view that Plato thought moral habituation has a significant role in ethics.

**Yong, Patrick**. Intellectualism and Moral Habituation in Plato's Earlier Dialogues. *Apeiron*, 29(4), 49-61, D 96.

**Yoos, George**. Landmarks in Critical Thinking Series: Pragmatics and Critical Thinking. *Inquiry (USA)*, 14(4), 19-28, Sum 95.

**Yoshihara, Hideki** and Lee, Chung-Yeong. Business Ethics of Korean and Japanese Managers. *J Bus Ethics*, 16(1), 7-21, Ja 97.

This is a study of 288 Korean and 323 Japanese business executives. The result indicates that 1) the business executives believe basically in higher level business ethics, but 2) they occasionally have to make unethical business decisions which conflict with their personal values because of prevailing business practices. 3) However, they think higher ethical standards are useful for long-term profit and for improving workers' attitudes and the standards can be improved, and 4) to improve ethical standards, model setting by superiors is the most important and clear-cut company policies and code of ethics are essential.

**Yoshikawa, Elaine** and Leshowitz, Barry. An Instructional Model for Critical Thinking. *Inquiry (USA)*, 15(3), 17-37, Spr 96.

This paper describes a college-level instructional program in critical thinking emphasizing the practical application of scientific (methodological) reasoning to controversial, often emotional, everyday-life situations. Also included in the intervention is instruction on the role of cost/benefit analysis, personal values, and ethical and moral beliefs in optimizing decisions and taking effective action. The program was evaluated in a pre-post experimental design: Methodological reasoning and metacognitive processing were measured at the beginning and the end of the semester for a control group of students and for a treatment group enrolled in the critical thinking course. A statistical mediational model showed that the observed changes in metacognitive processing of the group participating in the instructional intervention were causally related to improvements in their methodological reasoning. A three-stage instructional model is introduced to provide a descriptive account of the changes in "ways of knowing" and decision making evinced by most students over the course of the intervention.

**Yoshimura, Noriko**. Aestheticism As Seen in British Tiles in the 1870s and 80s (in Japanese). *Bigaku*, 47(3), 24-35, Winter 96.

Aesthetic phenomenon spread in Britain in the 1870s and 80s. Aestheticism is the view that works of art should be judged by strictly aesthetic criteria and that their value has nothing to do with their moral, political, or religious utility. But aestheticism had another aspect which had a strong influence on people's lifestyle and taste, particularly of the middle classes. (edited)

**Young, B W**. Christianity, Commerce and the Canon: Josiah Tucker and Richard Woodward on Political Economy. *Hist Euro Ideas*, 22(5-6), 385-400, S-N 96.

**Young, Charles M**. The Doctrine of the Mean. *Topoi*, 15(1), 89-99, Mr 96.

**Young, Ernlé W D**. Ethics in the Outpatient Setting: New Challenges and Opportunities. *Cambridge Quart Healthcare Ethics*, 6(3), 293-298, Sum 97.

In managed care, cost-effectiveness considerations are causing more patients to be treated as outpatients rather than in hospitals. This is generating novel ethical issues for professionals and institutions. Five of these are explored: the issue of *patient autonomy* or *choice* (*how* and *where* to be treated); the "*care/compliance*" issue (the harm-benefit ratio for the same procedure may be worse in the outpatient setting); assuring *continuity* (of expressed patient preferences) across the various components of an integrated system; the looming issue of *genetic counseling* (testing will be done outside the hospital); and *compassionate aid-in-dying* (more likely in home care or hospice).

**Young, Iris Marion**. A Multicultural Continuum: A Critique of Will Kymlicka's Ethnic-Nation Dichotomy. *Constellations*, 4(1), 48-53, Ap 97.

This essay argues that Will Kymlicka's distinction between nation and ethnicity is too stark. It is better to theorize district peoples as on a continuism of distinctness.

**Young, Iris Marion**. Asymmetrical Reciprocity: On Moral Respect, Wonder, and Enlarged Thought. *Constellations*, 3(3), 340-363, Ja 97.

The essay argues that a moral theory should not endorse the idea that moral judgment involves taking the standpoint of others, reversing perspectives with them. It is both ontologically impossible and politically undesirable for people to imaginatively occupy one another's perspectives. I offer an account of moral respect instead as entailing an asymmetrical reciprocity where subjects are able to listen across the differences of temporality and social position. I draw on the writing of Benhabib, Levinas, Irigaray, Derrida and Habermas. I offer a different interpretation of Arendt's notion of "enlarged thought" based on the idea of asymmetrical reciprocity.

**Young, James O**. Aesthetic Antirealism. *S J Phil*, 35(1), 119-134, Spr 97.

Aesthetic realists hold that the aesthetic values of artworks are independent of anyone's beliefs, that when critics disagree about the aesthetic value of some artwork, at least one is mistaken, and that when artworks have identical primary qualities, they are alike in aesthetic value. Aesthetic antirealists disagree. Two arguments for aesthetic antirealism are presented. The first argument shows that some differences of opinion about the aesthetic values of artworks are not the results of errors. The second argument shows that artworks can have the same primary qualities but different aesthetic values.

**Young, James O**. Defining Art Responsibly. *Brit J Aes*, 37(1), 57-65, Ja 97.

An institutional definition of art has as a consequence that something can be a work of art even though it performs no valuable aesthetic function. A functionalist definition of art restricts the class of artworks to works which perform a valuable aesthetic function. Unfortunately, the institutional definition is the right one. Fortunately, the members of an art world can be responsible and accept as artworks only works which perform a valuable aesthetic function.

**Young, James O**. Relativism and the Evaluation of Art. *J Aes Educ*, 31(1), 9-22, Spr 97.

If the sole function of art is to make a certain sort of pleasure available, the evaluation of art will be plagued by a thorough-going relativism. Art can, however, be the source of knowledge as well as the source of pleasure. If so, some limits can be placed on relativism about aesthetic value, although a measure of relativism remains.

**Young, Julian**. *Heidegger, Philosophy, Nazism*. New York, Cambridge Univ Pr, 1997.

Since 1945, and particularly since 1987, when the facts of the 'Heidegger case' became widely known, an enormous number of words have been devoted to establishing, not only Heidegger's involvement with Nazism, but also, that his philosophy is thereby irredeemably discredited. This book denies neither the depth nor the seriousness of Heidegger's involvement. On the contrary, new aspects of it are disclosed. None the less, in opposition to the prevailing tide of opinion, Young argues that Heidegger's philosophy is not, in fact, compromised in any of its phases, and that the acceptance of it fully consistent with a deep commitment to liberal democracy. This striking and original thesis is grounded in an astute examination of Heidegger's thought that provides the reader with a clear and valuable exposition of one of the twentieth century's greatest thinkers.

**Young, Michele M**. Cognitive Reengineering: A Process for Cultivating Critical Thinking Skills in RNs. *Inquiry (USA)*, 14(1), 37-47, Fall 94.

**Young, Phillips E**. The Irony of Ironic Liberalism. *Int Stud Phil*, 29(1), 121-130, 1997.

This article critiques Rorty's ironic liberalism. Young presents Rorty's alternative to traditional philosophy in terms of Rorty's distinctions between objectivity and solidarity and between metaphysics and ironism. Fairness requires that Rorty's position not be judged by the criteria of the traditional model. However, commitment to solidarity as Rorty describes it entails commitment to open dialogue and Rorty's treatment of metaphysics amounts to a foreclosure of dialogue. This problematizes the ironic liberal's treatment of the marginalia more generally. Hence, despite sympathy with the aims of solidarity, Young finds that ironic liberalism fails on the criteria of its own model.

**Yourgrau, Palle**. What is Frege's Relativity Argument?. *Can J Phil*, 27(2), 137-171, Je 97.

In this paper I argue that Frege's famous *relativity argument*, that spans paragraph 21-25 of the *Foundations of Arithmetic*, the conclusion of which is that only a *concept* is assigned a number *non*relatively, does not succeed.

Concepts, as well as extensions of concepts, are as susceptible to the *relativity Argument* as are the packs of cards Frege discusses. As a consequence, Frege's definition of a number, as a 'set' of equinumerous concepts, also looses its force.

**Yovel, Jonathan**. Overruling Rules?. *Prag Cognition*, 4(2), 347-366, 1996.

This paper discusses issues relating to the normativity of prescriptive rules: what does it mean for a rule to be able to direct action, and what are the implications for the desirability of rule-based decision making? It is argued that: a) cognitively, one must allow for more than a single answer to the first question (the two interpretations of rules discussed here are based alternately on the concepts of exclusion and presumption); and b) normatively, these different structures typically serve for different purposes in allocation of power and discretion. The next issue is the connection between rule-based decision making and semantic theories of language. (edited)

**Yovel, Yirmiyahu**. History of Self-Interpretation: Jews and the Holocaust. *Iyyun*, 45, 55-70, Jl 96.

**Yovel, Yirmiyahu**. Tolerance as Grace and as Right (in Hebrew). *Iyyun*, 45, 482-487, O 96.

**Yrjönsuuri, Mikko**. Supposition and Truth in Ockham's Mental Language. *Topoi*, 16(1), 15-25, Mr 97.

In this paper, Ockham's theory of an ideal language of thought is used to illuminate problems of interpretation of his theory of truth. The twentieth century idea of logical form is used for finding out what kinds of atomic sentences there are in Ockham's mental language. It turns out that not only the theory of modes of supposition, but also the theory of supposition in general is insufficient as a full theory of truth. Rather, the theory of supposition is a theory of reference, which can help in the determination of truth values within the scope of simple predications. Outside this area, there are interesting types of sentences, whose truth does not depend on whether the terms supposit for the same things or not for the same things.

**Yturbe, Corina**. On Norberto Bobbio's "Theory of Democracy". *Polit Theory*, 25(3), 377-400, Je 97.

The "model of democracy" in Bobbio's work does more than describe the mechanisms of that form of government; it points to the developments that must take place in the social structure to set democracy in motion. Two aspects of Bobbio's discussion of democracy provide insights into his own understanding of democratic theory and practice: 1) Bobbio's examination of the relationship between liberal democracy and socialism. 2) His reflection on the "unfulfilled promises" of democracy. According to Bobbio, the promises of democracy have not been fulfilled, and the nature of this failure illuminates the continuous need to rethink, not only democratic theory in the light of the lessons of democratic practice itself.

**Yu, Jiyuan**. Aristotle's Criticism of the Subject Criterion. *Phil Inq*, 18(1-2), 119-142, Wint-Spr 96.

**Yuanhua, Wang**. On Imagination—A Correspondence with Prof. Zhang Longxi. *J Chin Phil*, 24(1), 123-128, Mr 97.

Some overseas sinologists are accustomed to judging Chinese culture by Western standards. Françoise Jullin , in *Far East and Far West*, questioned how the Chinese could have conceived in the 5th-6th centuries the concept of "inspired thinking" (*shen si*), similar to the theory of imagination by 19th c. romanticists? Works of Chinese literary criticism have since the 6th-2nd centuries B.C. emphasized "comparison and image" (*bi xing*), which is different from the Western theory of natural models exactly in that the Chinese stresses imagination. Liu Xie (465-532) was by far not the first one to theorize imagination.

**Yudin, Boris** and Tichtchenko, Pavel D. The Moral Status of Fetuses in Russia. *Cambridge Quart Healthcare Ethics*, 6(1), 31-38, Winter 97.

**Yujen Teng, Norman**. Sorensen on begging the Question. *Analysis*, 57(3), 220-222, Jl 97.

Richard Robinson denies that there is a fallacy of begging the question. Sorensen argues that Robinson's denial is not well grounded. He also argues that one cannot consistently deny that there is a fallacy of begging the question. I argue that Sorensen mistakes a number of points Robinson has made. And more critically, his argument presupposes that begging the question is fallacious. Without this presupposition, one can consistently say that an argument, in fact, begs the question without objecting that it is fallacious.

**Yutaka, Isshiki**. Understanding of Beauty and Incarnation in Quest: The Problem of Aesthetics in Plato's *Phaedrus* (in Japanese). *Bigaku*, 47(1), 13-24, Sum 96.

Beauty cannot be comprehended by definition. The proper way to understand beauty *per se* is self-knowledge. When one is asked 'what beauty is', one is asked at the same time 'what oneself is'. The most eminent beauty for Plato is that of virtue. The beauty of virtue is one of the strongest motivations of his philosophy. The task of 'Phaedrus' is to ask the possibility of understanding the rationality (logos) of this beauty by his method of philosophizing: dialektiké. Plato names the power to philosophize 'love' (erôs). (edited)

**Yuthas, Kristi** and Logsdon, Jeanne M. Corporate Social Performance, Stakeholder Orientation, and Organizational Moral Development. *J Bus Ethics*, 16(12-13), 1213-1226, S 97.

This article begins with an explanation of how moral development for organizations has parallels to Kohlberg's categorization of the levels of individual moral development. Then the levels of organizational moral development are integrated into the literature on corporate social performance by relating them to different stakeholder orientations. Finally, the authors propose a model of organizational moral development that emphasizes the role of top management in creating organizational processes that shape the

**Zabell, S L** 1000 **AUTHOR INDEX**

organizational and institutional components of corporate social performance. This article represents one approach to linking the distinct streams of business ethics and business-and-society research into a more complete understanding of how managers and firms address complex ethical and social issues.

**Zabell, S L**. Confirming Universal Generalizations. *Erkenntnis*, 45(2 & 3), 267-283, Nov 96.

The purpose of this paper is to make a simple observation regarding the Johnson-Carnap continuum of inductive methods (see Johnson 1932, Carnap 1952). From the outset, a common criticism of this continuum was its failure to permit the *confirmation of universal generalizations*: that is, if an event has unfailingly occurred in the past, the failure of the continuum to give some weight to the possibility that the event will continue to occur without fail in the future. The Johnson-Carnap continuum is the mathematical consequence of an axiom termed "Johnson's sufficientness postulate", the thesis of this paper is that, properly viewed, the failure of the Johnson-Carnap continuum to confirm universal generalizations is not a deep fact, but rather an *immediate* consequence of the sufficientness postulate; and that if this postulate is modified in the minimal manner necessary to eliminate such an entailment, then the result is a new continuum that differs from the old one in precisely one respect: it enjoys the desideratum of confirming universal generalizations.

**Zac, Sylvain**. The Relation between Life, *Conatus* and Virtue in Spinoza's Philosophy. *Grad Fac Phil J*, 19(1), 151-173, 1996.

**Zacares Pamblanco, Amparo**. El universo de la precisión: Galileo versus Vico: Del confuso conocimiento de la representación al transmundo antivital de la ciencia. *Cuad Vico*, 5/6, 201-213, 1995/96.

Science accomplishes with Galileus and Descartes the hermeneutical task of explaining chaos accordingly to mathematical reason. From this radical point of view, both aesthetics and fantasy found themselves outside the limits of knowledge. With the view of this particular conception, Vico writes precisely the *New Science*, where he ends by concluding that in front of the universal scientific truth there is also a supraindividual aesthetical truth. These two types of truth disclose the disturbing relationship between the eternal and the ephemeral, the stage set where the poetical reason seems to play.

**Zack, Naomi**. "Race, Life, Death, Identity, Tragedy and Good Faith" in *Existence in Black: An Anthology of Black Existential Philosophy,* Gordon, Lewis R (ed), 99-109. New York, Routledge, 1997.

Identity as a member of an oppressed nonwhite race does not affect the classic existentialist structures of life and death; neither is racialized death a form of tragedy in the first person. Good faith requires the rejection of both racist identification and unempirical concepts of race as grounds for the identity of free agents.

**Zagal, Héctor Arreguín**. "La argumentación aristotélica contra el socratismo" in *Ensayos Aristotélicos,* Rivera, José Luis (ed), 97-119. Mexico, Univ Panamericana, 1996.

Aristotle tries to state moral responsibility, and in doing so, he feels himself committed to refute the Socratic thesis of "badness as ignorance"; but the lack of a theory of will prevents him to escape from the nets of intellectualism.

**Zagal, Héctor Arreguín** and Aguilar-Alvarez, Sergio. *Límites de la Argumentación Ética en Aristóteles: Lógos, physis y éthos*. Mexico, Pub Cruz O, 1996.

Un texto documentado y bien escrito. Héctor Zagal y Sergio Aguilar-Alvarez dedican su atención al engranaje entre argumentación y ética. Los autores son honestos y abren su libro con una declaración de principios que es una declaración de modestia: "*Nuestro interés no es sistemático sino histórico*" nos dicen. Y tienen razón: el libro que vamos a leer consiste básicamente en una interpretación de algunos textos de Aristóteles. Sin embargo, ellos no poseen toda la razón en el siguiente sentido: en filosofía ninguna investigación histórica puede escapar de tener, en alguna medida, una dimensión sistemática. De lo contrario, nos encontraríamos ante una labor de anticuarios y no ante un repensar filosófico. Felizmente, como veremos, las repercusiones sistemáticas de este estudio son bien visibles. (publisher, edited)

**Zagwill, Nick**. Explaining Supervenience: Moral and Mental. *J Phil Res*, 22, 509-518, Ap 97.

I defend the view that supervenience relations need not be explained. My view is that some supervenience relations are brute, and explanatorily ultimate. I examine an argument of Terrence Horgan and Mark Timmons. They aim to rehabilitate John Mackie's metaphysical queerness argument. But the explanations of supervenience that Horgan and Timmons demand are *semantic* explanations. I criticize their attempt to explain psychophysical supervenience in this fashion. I then turn to their '*twin earth*' argument against naturalist moral realism. I reconstruct their argument in a charitable spirit. But then I show that the argument mutates into an epistemological argument. That is where the real problems for moral realism lie.

**Zahavi, Dan**. Beyond Realism and Idealism Husserl's Late Concept of Constitution. *Dan Yrbk Phil*, 29, 44-62, 1994.

Husserl's concept of constitution has often been interpreted either as being 1) a creative activity, 2) a matter of epistemic restoration, or 3) something pertaining exclusively to the dimension of *meaning*; not of *being*. The following paper will attempt to refute the above mentioned interpretations, presenting an alternative clarification by way of an explication of the late Husserl's view on the relationship between *world* and *subjectivity*. An explication making it apparent, that Husserl's concept of constitution entails reflections much more in line with the views espoused by later phenomenologists, such as Heidegger and Merleau-Ponty, than is normally assumed by his critics.

**Zahavi, Dan**. Horizontal Intentionality and Transcendental Intersubjectivity (in Dutch). *Tijdschr Filosof*, 59(2), 304-321, Je 97.

Through an investigation of Husserl's concept of horizontal intentionality, the article basically argues that the horizon is intrinsically intersubjective and that it entails an implicit reference to the intentions of possible Others. Against this background it is argued that our perceptual experience of an embodied Other, our factual encounter with the Other, is not the most basic and fundamental type of intersubjectivity. On the contrary, it presupposes a type of intersubjectivity which belongs *a priori* to the structure of constituting subjectivity.

**Zaid, Omar Abdullah**. Could Auditing Standards Be Based on Society's Values?. *J Bus Ethics*, 16(11), 1185-1200, Ag 97.

One of the criticisms directed at the accounting profession is that auditing and accounting standards are subjective in nature and do not represent the society's widespread interests and values. This paper examines whether a general consensus exists regarding the significance of incorporating society's values into auditing standards. The examination revealed the lack of such general agreement and further indicated that the perceptual differences are subjective in nature and not influenced by the participants qualifications, income, experience, gender or marital status.

**Zajaczkowski, Ryszard**. Cyprian Norwid—The Poet of Truth. *Ultim Real Mean*, 20(2 & 3), 146-156, Je-S 97.

Cyprian Norwid (1821-1883)—the favorite poet and thinker of John Paul II—is the representative of the second generation of Polish romantics. Reflections upon the truth are clearly dominating in his work. He wrote much about the ways of reaching the truth (through the dialogue, tradition and intuition) and about the sense and conditions of experiencing it. God was for Norwid the sower and the caretaker of the truth and its highest actualization. Norwid's works offer an area for research into the ultimate reality and meaning of the conscience of the Poles and is an example of an universal character of the Polish culture.

**Zajko, Vanda**. I May Be a Bit of a Jew: Trauma in Human Narrative. *Hist Human Sci*, 9(4), 21-26, N 96.

**Zakharyashchev, Michael** and Chagrov, Alexander. Modal Companions of Intermediate Propositional Logics. *Stud Log*, 51(1), 49-82, 1992.

This paper is a survey of results concerning embeddings of intuitionistic propositional logic and its extensions into various classical modal systems.

**Zalabardo, José L**. Predicates, Properties and the Goal of a Theory of Reference. *Grazer Phil Stud*, 51, 121-161, 1996.

An account of predicate reference is presented which attempts to steer a middle course between *reductionism*, which construes the notion in terms of speakers' inclinations and (*transcendent*) *realism*, which construes the notion in terms of properties. It is first introduced in the context of a discussion of the accounts of length (distance) advanced by Hans Reichenbach, Adolf Grünbaum and Hilary Putnam. A general account of predicate reference is then developed that explains the notion in terms of speakers' inclinations, while rejecting the idea that this explanation should take the form of a reduction. The view is presented as a vindication of extreme nominalism. (edited)

**Zalamea, Fernando**. Hipotesis del continuo, definibilidad y funciones recursivas: historia de un desencuentro (1925-1955). *Mathesis*, 10(2), 187-203, My 94.

En 1925 Hilbert intenta demostrar la hipótesis del continuo, usando definibilidad de funciones en la aritmética; introduce (sin llamarlos así) la recursión primitiva y los functionales recursivos. El intento no consigue el resultado deseado; sin embargo, rastreamos sus escondidas consecuencias en las tres décadas que siguen. En algunos momentos del período 1925-1955 se juntan esos dos enfoques a la hipótesis del continuo (definibilidad y recursión *versus* jerarquías proyectiva y analítica) pero, en realidad, la situación es la de un desencuentro. Estudiamos el porqué de ese desencuentro y tratamos de explicar algunos de los presupuestos epistemológicos en los que se basa la práctica matemática. Finalmente, en 1955, Kleene y Addison, siguiendo el camino abierto por Motowski, explican las honda conexiones entre las jerarquías de la recursión y los conjuntos analíticos. (edited)

**Zalamea, Fernando**. La filosofía de la matemática de Albert Lautman. *Mathesis*, 10(3), 273-289, Ag 94.

Albert Lautman (1908-1944) is one of the most original mathematical philosophers of the century. We draw attention on the philosophical insights that he elucidated in modern mathematical thinking (topology, differential geometry, analytic and algebraic number theory, modern algebra, etc.). We study Lautman's idiosyncratic concepts ('genetic schemes', 'structural schemes') and show how they are fully realized in what, later, would become crucial methodologies of model theory and category theory, Finally, following Lautman's philosophical critique, we draw a 'map' of 20th century work around the continuum hypothesis, showing how a blending of structural insights and Lautman's 'resolution of opposites' can be used to explain some trends in mathematical creativity.

**Zalta, Edward** and Linsky, Bernard. In Defense of the Contingently Nonconcrete. *Phil Stud*, 84(2-3), 283-294, D 96.

In our "In Defense of the Simplest Quantified Modal Logic" (*Philosophical Perspectives 8: Philosophy of Logic and Language*, Atascadero, CA: Ridgeview, pp. 431-458), we introduced the notion of contingently nonconcrete objects to provide an actualist interpretation of modal logic with the Barcan formulas. In "Actualism or Possibilism?" (this volume), James Tomberlin accepts that this work accounts for the truth of certain puzzling sentences, but objects to our understanding of essential properties and contingent existence. In this paper we respond to Tomberlin's objections. We first correct his account of our position by sharply distinguishing between possibilities and objects of intentional attitudes and then argue that our understanding of essential properties and contingent existence preserves ordinary intuitions about modal reality.

**Zambella, Domenico**. Notes on Polynomially Bounded Arithmetic. *J Sym Log*, 61(3), 942-966, S 96.

We characterize the collapse of Buss's bounded arithmetic in terms of the provable collapse of the polynomial time hierarchy. We include also some general model-theoretical investigations on fragments of bounded arithmetic.

**Zamiara, Krystyna**. "Jerzy Kmita's Social-Regulational Theory of Culture and the Category of Subject" in *Epistemology and History,* Zeidler-Janiszewska, Anna (ed), 339-349. Amsterdam, Rodopi, 1996.

Kmita's theory of culture presupposes some model notion of the human subject depending upon the description of the culture. The characterization of such a subject appears equivalent to some characterization of culture. Apart from the model notion of human subject Kmita also deals with real subjects being participants in a given culture. But here a problem emerges: what is the relation binding the model-subject to the real subjects entangled in the given culture? Such a relation is not defined in Kmita's works. In effect, the theory may be suspected of inconsistency and submitted to criticism.

**Zamora Bonilla, Jesús P**. "Neurophenomenalism and the Theories of Truth" in *Verdad: lógica, representación y mundo,* Villegas Forero, L, 369-374. Santiago de Compostela, Univ Santiago Comp, 1996.

The author argues that phenomena are identical to some kind of neuronal activity, but, against other approaches (esp. physicalism or materialism), he defends that the identification of the mental and the physical does not preclude to accept the phenomenological aspect of mental events (i.e., the existence of *qualia*). Assuming this "neurophenomenalism", a conception of truth as a kind of "regulative ideal" is also defended.

**Zaner, Richard M**. Justice and the Individual in the Hippocratic Tradition. *Cambridge Quart Healthcare Ethics*, 5(4), 511-518, Fall 96.

**Zaner, Richard M**. Listening or Telling? Thoughts on Responsibility in Clinical Ethics Consultation. *Theor Med*, 17(3), 255-277, S 96.

This article reviews the historical and current controversies about the nature of clinical ethics consultation, as a way to focus on the place and responsibility or ethics consultants within the context of clinical conversation—interpreted as a form of *dialogue*. These matters are approached through a particularly compelling instance of the controversy that involves several major figures in the field. The analysis serves to highlight very significant questions of the nature and constraints of clinical situations, and the moral responsibility and legal accountability that are especially important for clinical ethics consultants.

**Zanetti, Gianfrancesco** (trans) and Voegelin, Eric. *La Scienza Nuova* nella Storia del Pensiero Politico. Napoli, Guida, 1996.

Lo studio su Vico di Voegelin, che qui si presenta con l'introduzione di J. Gebhardt docente all'Università di Erlangen-Nürnberg—uno dei più importanti studiosi dell'opera del filosofo politico—costituisce un lungo capitolo della *History of Political Ideas*, rimasta inedita. Nell'approccio antignostico ed antiprogressivista proprio di Voegelin, Vico assume "una sua propria grandezza", con la quale non possono competere quei filosofi tedeschi che l'interpretazione crociana insiste nel sovrapporre al pensiero vichiano. "Difficilmente Vico può essere considerato pari a Kant come epistemologo, o pari a Hegel nella logica dello spirito, ma come filosofo della storia egli li supera entrambi, perché la sua consapevolezza cristiana dei problemi dello spirito lo protesse da quel deragliamento gnostico che esaurisce il significato della storia nella struttura della storia profana umanamente intellegibile". (edited)

**Zangrando, Robert L**. A Crying Need for Discourse. *J Infor Ethics*, 3 (1), 65-69, Spr 94.

The reluctance of the American Historical Association to publish its findings or even to allow members to write about the case, in its own newsletter, when an author is accused of plagiarism or other misuse of materials and the actions of a well-known historian in the early 1990s to deflect information about his case (except in releases prepared by him and his lawyers) serve to stifle inquiry among the Association's members and set a dreadful precedent for future controversies. Only open discourse should prevail among practicing scholars and their students.

**Zanini, Adelino**. "La Verità Come Tragedia: Immaginazione e immagine del Vero: Note sulla "civilizzazione" in *Soggetto E Verità: La questione dell'uomo nella filosofia contemporanea,* Fagiuoli, Ettore, 187-197. 20136 Milano, Mimesis, 1996.

**Zanini, Adelino**. Modi del dire, intenzioni ed immagini per la *Theory of Moral Sentiments* di Adam Smith. *Itinerari Filosof*, 3(5), 33-49, Ja-Ap 93.

**Zanotti, Gabriel J**. El problema de la "Theory Ladenness" de los juicios singulares en la epistemología contemporánea. *Acta Phil*, 5(2), 339-352, 1996.

This essay is a proposal in order to solve the problem of the theory-ladenness in the empirical basis. I try to establish a theory which is nor the positivism's naive realism neither the neo-Kantian Kuhn incommensurability thesis. I set forth an *hermeneutic realism*. Its principal thesis is that there is an "analogizing meaning" of a concept in each singular statement, which is the key in order to communicate different understanding-horizons. This analogizing meaning is the meaning of the essence in itself, which I propose to be considered from a nonscientific point of view, in order to communicate scientific conjectures which are in a close relation to the historical evolution of science. (edited)

**Zapletal, Jindrich**. Small Forcings and Cohen Reals. *J Sym Log*, 62(1), 280-284, Mr 97.

We show that all posits of uniform density *Aleph*$_1$ may have to add a Cohen real and develop some forcing machinery for obtaining this sort of result.

**Zapletal, Jindrich**. Splitting Number at Uncountable Cardinals. *J Sym Log*, 62(1), 35-42, Mr 97.

We study a generalization of the splitting number *s* to uncountable cardinals. We prove that *s(kappa)* "is greater than" *kappa*$^+$ for a regular uncountable cardinal *kappa* implies the existence of inner models with measurables of high Mitchell order. We prove that the assumption *s(Aleph*$_{omega}$*)* "is greater than" *aleph*$_{omega+1}$ has a considerable large cardinal strength as well.

**Zarefsky, David**. "Argumentation in the Tradition of Speech Communication Studies" in *Logic and Argumentation,* Van Eemeren, Frans H (ed), 43-59. Amsterdam, North-Holland, 1994.

In this paper, four broad forces are discussed that shape the nature of argumentation studies within the speech communication discipline: the evolution of competitive debate, the infusion of empirical perspectives and methods by the social sciences, the recovery of practical philosophy, and the growing interest in social and cultural critique. Unfortunately, the growth of the discipline of argumentation is not accompanied by a clear and common sense of what is being studied. To increase coherence, a root concept for argumentation studies is proposed and explicated: argumentation as the practice of justifying decisions under conditions of uncertainty.

**Zdrenka, Michael**. Die Seele in der Moderne: Therapie, Seelsorge, Philosophische Praxis. *Z Phil Praxis*, 30-33, 1996.

This article, which was written on the occasion of the "10. Kolloquium für Philosophische Praxis" in 1995 at Hanover, describes in what light practical philosophers nowadays are assessed by spiritual welfare workers and psychotherapists and to what extent *philosophical practice* is a useful supplement to those "helper's professions." It presents several lectures which criticize or support *philosophical practice* from a theological or psychotherapeutic standpoint. Finally, issues more distantly associated with practical philosophy are brought up, like for instance systemic management consulting and the debate on the death of the brain. Thus, the "Gesellschaft für Philosophische Praxis," which organized the colloquium, has for the first time in its history initiated a dialogue between neighboring professions.

**Zdrenka, Michael**. Zur Lage der Philosophischen Praxis. *Z Phil Praxis*, 26-29, 1996.

On the basis of a book by the author (*Philosophische Praxis. Konzeptionen und Probleme*, Cologne, 1997), this article outlines the present situation of philosophical practice on a global scale. It elucidates different conceptions of philosophical practice and their closeness to or dissociation from neighboring occupational groups such as psychotherapy and academic philosophy, but also homeotherapy, management consulting and spiritual welfare work. In a second section, typical problems from the field of philosophical practice are brought up, like for instance which are the prerequisites of philosophical practice and whether there can be a theory of philosophical practice. Also the article touches upon the issue that the press is lacking the ability to recognize what is new about philosophical practice.

**Zeh, Heinz-Dieter**. The 'Reality' of the Wave Function: Measurements, Entropy and Quantum Cosmology. *Phil Natur*, 28(1), 76-96, 1991.

The physical description of the information gained by an observer performing a process of measurement is investigated within the assumption of a universally valid quantum theory. It is compatible with a deterministically evolving wave function that may be assumed to be *real*, although any information gain requires a 'branching of the observer' experienced as an indeterministic evolution of the world. In a theory containing quantum gravity, the wave function does not depend on a time parameter. It 'evolves' with respect to the extension of the universe (thus rendering the latter's expansion a tautology), although causal connections are given by orbit-like (though in general branching) wave tubes through the locally Lorentzian configuration space 'superspace'. (edited)

**Zeidler, Kurt W**. Die Kopernikanische und die semiotische Wende der Philosophie. *Prima Philosophia*, 9(4), 377-398, 1996.

Nowadays, most philosophers consider all types of "idealism" or "transcendental philosophy" as obsolete mentalistic theorems that have been superseded by the linguistic turn and/or the pragmatic insights of 20th century-philosophy. In contrast to this view, the paper states that Kant's theory of cognition (despite its "mentalistic" terminology) should rather be understood as an attempt to overcome the shortcomings of the subject-object-dichotomy and the mentalistic approach. These shortcomings prevail—and therefore even prevail in "analytic" or "pragmatic" accounts—as long as Kant's question after the "synthetic a priori" is not answered by the means of a logic of relations, as it has been developed, from different points of view, but with similar results, by G.W.F. Hegel and Charles S. Peirce.

**Zeidler, Pawel**. "Some Issues of Historical Epistemology in the Light of the Structuralist Philosophy of Science" in *Epistemology and History,* Zeidler-Janiszewska, Anna (ed), 169-180. Amsterdam, Rodopi, 1996.

The paper refers to some issues which are considered by J. Kmita in his works in the field of historical epistemology. J. Kmita's account of the opposition of theory and experience, holism, the controversy between realists and instrumentalists, and the question of the relation among scientific theories is investigated in the light of J. Sneed's structuralistic approach to science. It is claimed that the application of J. Sneed's conceptual apparatus makes possible a better account of these issues than Kmita's.

**Zeidler-Janiszewska, Anna**. "The Problem of the Applicability of Humanistic Interpretation in the Light of Contemporary Artistic Practice" in *Epistemology and History,* Zeidler-Janiszewska, Anna (ed), 531-540. Amsterdam, Rodopi, 1996.

Historical and adaptive interpretations, one in artistic practice, are discussed (J Kmita, post-Heideggerian hermeneutics, Ricoeur, Gadamer). Various trends in the postmodern reflection accompanying artistic practice argue for rejection of both the category of work of art and interpretation as a proper "realization" of this work. Structuralism and hermeneutics are toughed upon in this context. There follows a discussion on idealizing and concrete/rationalizing models of humanistic interpretation, then on aesthetic thinking and aesthetic values.

**Zeidler-Janiszewska, Anna** (ed). *Epistemology and History: Humanities as a Philosophical Problem and Jerzy Kmita's Approach to It*. Amsterdam, Rodopi, 1996.

**Zeitlin, Irving M**. *Rulers and Ruled: An Introduction to Classical Political Theory from Plato to the Federalists*. Toronto, Univ of Toronto Pr, 1997.

This book illuminates several timeless principles of political philosophy that have come down to us through the ages in the writings of Plato, Aristotle, Machiavelli, Hobbes, Locke, Montesquieu, Rousseau and the authors of the Federalist Papers, Madison, Hamilton and Jay. Among these principles are the following: that a good society is based on law; that a good constitution balances social classes against each other; that a mixed constitution is best for this purpose; that popular sovereignty is the best foundation for a just and stable constitution; and that representative government is best for a large, complex society. (publisher)

**Zelaniec, Wojciech**. Red and Green after All These Years. *Acta Analytica*, 223-239, 1996.

This paper reexamines arguments employed in a discussion between Putnam and Pap concerning the analyticity or otherwise of this a priori proposition: "Nothing can be red and green all over." Putnam, who defended the analyticity of this proposition was, in contradistinction to many other champions of analyticity, right to see that this proposition is not a "meaning postulate" of either "red" or "green", as both terms are defined ostensively, but he did not see another, deeper-set trap, which was overlooked by Pap, too, whose defense of the syntheticity of the proposition in question was, consequently, rather weak. Morals are drawn and extrapolated on areas that may be of more interests than pure chromatology, to which the proposition belongs.

**Zelaniec, Wojciech** and Smith, Barry. *The Recalcitrant Synthetic A Priori*. Lublin, Oficyna Wyda Artom, 1996.

This book poses the problem of the synthetic a priori thus: what is the nature of the obviousness enjoyed by sentences standardly cited as examples of the synthetic a priori? The author does not presuppose that this obviousness is a sure warrant that the sentences are true. He characterizes it rather by means of contrasts that synthetic a priori sentences have to other kinds of sentences which also appear obvious, including analytic sentences. The author demonstrates that in attempts to eliminate the differences between synthetic a priori and other sorts of sentences hitherto, synthetic a priori sentences are themselves used as surreptitious presuppositions. The whole category of the synthetic a priori thus turns out to be—to use a word dear to Quine—recalcitrant.

**Zellweger, Shea**. "Untapped Potential in Peirce's Iconic Notation for the Sixteen Binary Connectives" in *Studies in the Logic of Charles Sanders Peirce*, Houser, Nathan (ed), 334-386. Bloomington, Indiana Univ Pr, 1997.

**Zemach, Eddy M**. A New Argument against Pascal (in Hebrew). *Iyyun*, 45, 407-408, O 96.

**Zemach, Eddy M**. *Real Beauty*. University Park, Pennsylvania Univ Pr, 1997.

By examining the opposing nonrealistic views of subjectivism, noncognitivism, and relativism, Zemach attempts to show how antirealistic interpretations of value generate absurd results and leave the realistic reading as the only cogent semantic interpretation of aesthetic statements. By discussing what inclines most people to hold nonrealistic views of aesthetics, such as the fluctuations of taste in fashion, Zemach argues that realism can account for these fluctuations. He proposes that the aesthetic value of some things is due to their relations to other things and that relation may be temporal, resulting in the need for a temporal point for the correct temporal angle from which to view things. Zemach concludes that great art reveals significant truths about reality and that significantly true statements are aesthetically valuable; hence truth is an aesthetic merit. (publisher,edited)

**Zeman, Jay**. "Peirce and Philo" in *Studies in the Logic of Charles Sanders Peirce*, Houser, Nathan (ed), 402-417. Bloomington, Indiana Univ Pr, 1997.

**Zeman, Jay**. "The Tinctures and Implicit Quantification over Worlds" in *The Rule of Reason: The Philosophy of Charles Sanders Peirce*, Forster, Paul (ed), 96-119. Toronto, Univ of Toronto Pr, 1997.

**Zhenbin, Sun**. Yan: A Dimension of Praxis and Its Philosophical Implications (A Chinese Perspective on Language). *J Chin Phil*, 24(2), 191-208, Je 97.

**Zheng, Yiwei**. Ontology and Ethics in Sartre's *Being and Nothingness*: On the Conditions of the Possibility of Bad Faith. *S J Phil*, 35(2), 265-287, Sum 97.

In this paper I reconstruct Sartre's theory of bad faith in *Being and Nothingness*, using the guiding thread of examining the conditions of the possibility of bad faith. On the basis of that, I argue that the link between the ontological characteristics and the ethical status of bad faith is not so tight and significant as many commentators claim, e.g., Ronald Santoni in his book, *Bad Faith, Good Faith, and Authenticity in Sartre's Early Philosophy*.

**Ziarek, Krzysztof**. After Aesthetics: Heidegger and Benjamin on Art and Experience. *Phil Today*, 41(1-4), 199-208, Spr 97.

**Ziche, Paul**. *Mathematische und naturwissenschaftliche Modelle in der Philosophie Schellings und Hegels*. Stuttgart, Frommann-Holzboog, 1996.

**Ziche, Paul**. Naturphilosophie zwischen Naturwissenschaft und Philosophie: Neue Sammelbände zur Naturphilosophie des deutschen Idealismus. *Z Phil Forsch*, 50(3), 473-491, Jl-S 96.

**Ziembinski, Zygmunt**. "Historical Interpretation vs. Adaptive Interpretation of a Legal Text" in *Epistemology and History*, Zeidler-Janiszewska, Anna (ed), 303-312. Amsterdam, Rodopi, 1996.

The use of the conception of humanistic interpretation (J. Kmita) in jurisprudence offers specific problems. They are presented and discussed in the article with special attention to the consequence of distinguishing between humanistic historical interpretation and humanistic adaptive interpretation. There follows a thorough discussion on the humanistic interpretation of legal texts, the rationality of the legislator (L. Nowak) and the tasks of a lawyer while formulating legal norms.

**Ziembinski, Zygmunt**. "What Can Be Saved of the Idea of the University?" in *The Idea of University*, Brzezinski, Jerzy (ed), 21-26. Amsterdam, Rodopi, 1997.

**Zieminski, Ireneusz**. Contingency of Being—Argument for the Existence of God: Attempt at Critical Analysis Part I (in Polish). *Kwartalnik Filozof*, 25(1), 129-144, 1997.

**Zika, Richard**. The Second Moment of the Inferences of Taste. *Filosof Cas*, 44(3), 492-494, 1996.

**Zimmerli, Walther Christoph** and Assländer, Michael. "Wirtschaftsethik" in *Angewandte Ethik: Die Bereichsethiken und ihre theoretische Fundierung*, Nida-Rümelin, Julian (ed), 290-344. Stuttgart, Alfred Kröner, 1996.

**Zimmerman, Dean W**. Coincident Objects: Could a 'Stuff Ontology' Help?. *Analysis*, 57(1), 19-27, Ja 97.

Michael Burke suggests that there is an ontological category somewhere between *mere plurality* and *individual physical object* and that the spatial coincidence of a physical object with a quantity of stuff would be unproblematic were the stuff to belong to this intermediate category [Burke, *Analysis* 56 (1996): 11-18]. I consider two ways of conceiving of the additional category of 'stuff' or 'matter'; but neither turns out to be particularly helpful for those seeking to avoid coincident objects.

**Zimmerman, Dean W**. Distinct Indiscernibles and the Bundle Theory. *Mind*, 106(422), 305-309, Ap 97.

In this dialogue—a minor sequel to Max Black's classic, "The Identity of Indiscernibles," *Mind* 61 (1952),—interlocutor A defends the bundle theory from B's objection that it renders impossible an evidently possible state of affairs: namely, that there be a symmetrical universe, such as Black's world consisting of nothing but two indiscernible spheres. A's strategy is that of John O'Leary-Hawthorne, "The Bundle Theory of Substance and the Identity of Indiscernibles," *Analysis* 55 (1995). B argues that, although A may have made room for symmetrical worlds, there are other evident possibilities ruled out by the bundle theory.

**Zimmerman, Dean W**. Persistence and Presentism. *Phil Papers*, 25(2), 115-126, Ag 96.

Ned Markosian alleges that David Lewis's account of the distinction between persisting by means of temporal parts and persisting without them ('perduring' vs. 'enduring') commits one to 'presentism'—the thesis that the only things that really exist are those that exist *now*. In the first half of this note, Lewis's distinction is defended against this charge. In the second half, the doctrine of temporal parts is so formulated as to be consistent with the views of Russell and Broad, who rejected absolutely instantaneous parts.

**Zimmerman, Dean W** and Chisholm, Roderick M. On the Logic of Intentional Help: Some Metaphysical Questions. *Faith Phil*, 13(3), 402-404, Jl 96.

In this note, we explore certain aspects of "the logic of helping", offer an account of the metaphysics of helping God, and suggest a way in which God's help differs from human help.

**Zimmerman, Dean W** and Chisholm, Roderick M. Theology and Tense. *Nous*, 31(2), 262-265, Je 97.

Should philosophers who "take tense seriously" also "take tenselessness seriously"? Are there truths expressible by tenseless statements that resist all paraphrase into a tensed idiom? Neither the tenselessness of statements made in the "historical present", nor that of the "eternal verities", justifies taking tenselessness seriously. And there is no philosophical motivation for saying that the Deity does not "exist in time", apart from a mistake about the nature of times.

**Zimmerman, Michael E**. The "Alien Abduction" Phenomenon: Forbidden Knowledge of Hidden Events. *Phil Today*, 41(2), 235-254, Sum 97.

In the process of evaluating claims (pro and con) about the "reality" status of the abduction phenomenon, the essay argues that it is no longer a hidden event, since descriptions of it have become widespread. Because of lingering fears about loss of professional credibility, however, academics remain hesitant to do research into this phenomenon. Such hesitation is regrettable, since the phenomenon is remarkably interesting and potentially enormously important. For philosophers, the abduction phenomenon is an ontological and epistemological gold mine.

**Zimmerman, Michael J**. A Plea for Accuses. *Amer Phil Quart*, 34(2), 229-243, Ap 97.

On the standard account, there is an excuse if there is reason or grounds for not imputing blameworthiness despite the presence of wrongdoing. There is an analogue to this that has been almost universally ignored and for which no common term is available. It may be called an "accuse" and defined as follows: the reason or grounds for imputing blameworthiness despite the absence of wrongdoing. This paper argues for the possibility that accuses exist and examines certain implications of this.

**Zimmerman, Michael J**. Moral Responsibility and Ignorance. *Ethics*, 107(3), 410-426, Ap 97.

This paper defends the view that moral responsibility for behavior of whose moral wrongness one is ignorant occurs less frequently than is commonly supposed. Its central argument is this. If one is culpable for ignorant behavior, then one is culpable for the ignorance to which this behavior may be traced. One is never in direct control of such ignorance. Hence one's culpability for it presupposes one's being culpable for something else. Whatever this something else is, it cannot be ignorant behavior, for then the argument would apply all over again. Hence all culpability for ignorant behavior can be traced to culpability that involves a lack of ignorance.

**Zimmermann, Rainer E**. Twistors and Self-Reference: On the Generic Non-Linearity of Nature. *Phil Natur*, 27(2), 272-297, 1990.

The twistor concept of Roger Penrose is discussed, with a view to recent developments in the theories of self-organization and the formation of structure. The spinor and twistor formalisms can be taken as example for methods which intrinsically characterize the interactions of the unfolding geometry of space-time and the evolutionary processes in the universe such that from the beginning on emphasis is laid on a pregeometric primordial structure from which space-time can be derived in first place. This concept points to a generically unified approach to physics. Implications of this concept are evaluated within the frame of the philosophy of nature.

**Zimmermann, Thomas Ede**. "Model Theory in the Analysis of Natural Language" in *Verdad: lógica, representación y mundo*, Villegas Forero, L, 431-440. Santiago de Compostela, Univ Santiago Comp, 1996.

This is a plea for an epistemic understanding of models in natural language semantics.

**Zimmermann-Acklin, Markus**. Tun und Unterlassen: Ein Beitrag von Dieter Birnbacher zu einem bedeutenden Problem ethischer Handlungstheorie. *Frei Z Phil Theol*, 43(3), 449-458, 1996.

This article is a commented and detailed book review from the important work "Tun und Unterlassen" written by the German philosopher Dieter Birnbacher (Düsseldorf). The idea of this interdisciplinary study, written out of a ethical viewpoint, derived firstly from the authors theoretical discussion with R. M. Hare and secondly from his practice to confront theoretical results with practical challenges (of the ecoethical or bioethical discussion, killing-letting die-distinction, euthanasia-debate). The central point of his work is the observation, that there is a daily tendency to make a more difference between doing and allowing, although the act of doing and the act of allowing don't differ in motives, intentions and consequences.

**Ziolkowski, Marek**. "The Functional Theory of Culture and Sociology" in *Epistemology and History*, Zeidler-Janiszewska, Anna (ed), 325-338. Amsterdam, Rodopi, 1996.

The article comments on Jerzy Kmita's functional theory of culture and its relations and application to sociology, particularly to the sociology of knowledge. The theory forms a general conceptual scheme involving various domains of social sciences and due to its sweeping scale—which includes philosophical and methodological considerations as well as social ones—it generalizes rather than explains in detail. Although the author accepts Kmita's idea of a functional-genetic explanation of social and cultural phenomena, he sees it rather as a starting point for concrete sociological investigation.

**Zivaljevic, Bosko** and Schilling, Kenneth. Louveau's Theorem for the Descriptive Set Theory of Internal Sets. *J Sym Log*, 62(2), 595-607, Je 97.

We give positive answers to two questions in the descriptive set theory of internal sets in countably saturated models of nonstandard analysis, both posed by Zivaljevic. 1) Every set countably determined over an algebra A of internal sets and Borel at level x (over the algebra of all internal sets) is in fact Borel at level x over A. 2) Every Borel subset of the product of two internal sets all of whose sections are Borel at level x can be represented as an intersection (or union) of Borel sets whose sections are Borel at level below x. We derive 2) from the analogous theorem of A. Louveau for Polish spaces.

**Zizek, Slavoj**. The Seven Veils of Paranoia, Or, Why Does the Paranoiac Need Two Fathers?. *Constellations*, 3(2), 139-156, O 96.

The psychoanalytic notion of paranoia, as it was elaborated by Lacan, enables us to elucidate some elementary features of the process of identification: every social identification involves 1) the gap between public symbolic rules and the obscene set of unwritten rules (i.e., the rules which, in order to be operative, must remain publicly unacknowledged); 2) the structure of the forced choice ("You are free to choose—on condition that you make the right choice!", or, "You are given the right to reject social order—on condition that you do not use it!"); 3) some fantasmatic support which answers the question of the Other's desire ("What am I for the Other? What does the Other want from me?").

**Zizi, Paolo**. "Il concetto metafisico di "intero" in *Aristotele e in Hegel*" in *Hegel e Aristotele*, Ferrarin, A, 103-109. Cagliari, Edizioni AV, 1997.

**Znoj, Milan**. Forms of Tolerance as Types of Democracy (in Czech). *Filosof Cas*, 45(3), 497-506, 1997.

The author points out the interconnection of the notions *tolerance* and *democracy*, drawing distinction among three types of tolerance: (a) the liberal conception allowing the plurality of the good and seeking conditions which make possible the just cooperation among the members of a society; (b) the monothematic conception issuing from the fundamental unity of the members of a society on the ground of the common moral good, not admitting tolerance but in details; (c) the instrumental conception assuming the nonexistence of a moral tie as prerequisite for the cooperation among the members of a society, admitting only the incompatible plurality of the good. These three types of tolerance are reflected in specific conceptions of democracy, the

characteristics of which are submitted by the author evidently arguing for the first one. He discusses next the three types of democracy as proposed by the Czech philosopher Emanuel Rádl, tracing some limits inherent in his idea of democracy.

**Zoë, K A**. Philosophical Counselling: Bridging the Narrative Rift. *Phil Cont World*, 2(2), 23-28, Sum 95.

Using the example of child sexual abuse, and drawing on the work of Bass, Spence, Schafer, and Guignon, I propose an examination of the nature of narrative fragmentation itself. Philosophical counselling may succeed where psychoanalysis might not: for where the latter has theoretical commitments to specific narratives, the former, through its reluctance to force epistemological or metaphysical assumptions on the narrator, may well facilitate a more comprehensive self-understanding. (edited)

**Zöller, Günter**. "An Eye for an I: Fichte's Transcendental Experiment" in *Figuring the Self: Subject, Absolute, and Others in Classical German Philosophy*, Zöller, Günter (ed), 73-95. Albany, SUNY Pr, 1997.

The essay places the substance of Fichte's transcendental theory or *Wissenschaftslehre*—his account of the pure *I* as the nonempirical ground of experience—into the context of his philosophical method. In particular, I explore Fichte's self-interpretation of the *Wissenschaftslehre* as a scientific experiment conducted by the philosopher upon himself or herself. The five sections address the overall nature of Fichte's philosophy, his peculiar brand of idealism, his manner of thinking about the absolute *I*, his actual basic account of the pure *I*, and the status of Fichte's philosophy of the *I* as a theory of human subjectivity.

**Zöller, Günter**. Geist oder Gespenst? Fichtes Noumenalismus in der *Wissenschaftslehre nova methodo*. *Fichte-Studien*, 12, 297-306, 1997.

The essay examines Fichte's transcendental theory of thinking in the lectures on the *Wissenschaftslehre nova methodo* (1796-99). The focus is on the role of the noumena or beings of thought in empirical thinking. Fichte's integration of the noumenal into the foundational structure of knowledge is contrasted with Kant's treatment of the noumenal as a limiting concept. Special attention is given to the close relation between thinking and willing and to the role of the noumenal in the foundation of interpersonality in Fichte. The conclusion of the essay points to the difficult relation between thinking and the absolute in Fichte's work after 1800.

**Zöller, Günter** (trans) and Henrich, Dieter. "Self-Consciousness and Speculative Thinking" in *Figuring the Self: Subject, Absolute, and Others in Classical German Philosophy*, Zöller, Günter (ed), 99-133. Albany, SUNY Pr, 1997.

**Zöller, Günter** (ed) and Klemm, David E (ed). *Figuring the Self: Subject, Absolute, and Others in Classical German Philosophy*. Albany, SUNY Pr, 1997.

The book consists of twelve essays which present, discuss and assess the principal accounts of the self in classical German philosophy, focusing on the period around 1800 and covering Kant, Fichte, Hölderlin, Novalis, Schelling, Schleiermacher and Hegel. (publisher)

**Zoglauer, Thomas**. Optimalität der Natur?. *Phil Natur*, 28(2), 193-215, 1991.

According to a common view in biology evolution is a kind of optimization process and organisms are regarded as optimized natural constructions. This view is criticized. Optimization is a goal directed process in which system parameters are varied in order to maximize or minimize a value function. In transferring this technical model to biology we carelessly project goals, purposes and values into nature. This model transfer is based on a teleological view of nature and is highly problematic.

**Zolo, Danilo**. La dottrina del "justum bellum" nell'etica militare di Michael Walzer. *Iride*, 8(15), 431-439, Ag 95.

D. Zolo considera il libro di Walzer *Just and Unjust Wars* come una duplice sfida al pacifismo e al realismo politico. Secondo Zolo la dottrina della "guerra giusta", che presupponeva il quadro politico della medievale *respublica christiana* e rimandava all'autorità giuridica e spirituale del papato, è divenuta obsoleta. Non solo: col ricorso all'idea della *supreme emergency* Walzer finisce per subordinare l'etica internazionale ad opzioni partigiane.

**Zolo, Danilo**. Positive Tolerance: An Ethical Oxymoron. *Ratio Juris*, 10 (2), 247-251, Je 97.

Analyzing Apel's proposal for positive tolerance in multicultural society, the author develops critical observations concerning: first, the distinction between negative and positive tolerance; second, the ethical foundation of positive tolerance; and finally, the semantic content of the notion.

**Zoloth-Dorfman, Laurie**. Audience and Authority: The Story in Front of the Story. *J Clin Ethics*, 7(4), 355-361, Wint 96.

**Zoloth-Dorfman, Laurie** and Rubin, Susan. She Said/He Said: Ethics Consultation and the Gendered Discourse. *J Clin Ethics*, 7(4), 321-332, Wint 96.

**Zuber, R**. On Negatively Restricting Boolean Algebras. *Bull Sec Log*, 26(1), 50-54, Mr 97.

The paper presents some properties of Boolean algebras formed by negatively restricting functions or by their particular subclass, negatively intersecting functions. Both these classes parallel the class of positively intersecting and positively restricting functions studied by Keenan. A function F from a Boolean algebra into itself is positively restricting if F(X) is less or equal than X. It is negatively restricting if F(X) is less or equal to the complement of X, for all X. All these functions have applications in formal semantics of natural languages. It is suggested that negatively restricting functions can be used to interpret higher order modifiers found in particular in quantifiers with exclusion clauses.

### Guidance on the Use of the Book Review Index

The Book Review Index lists, in alphabetical order, the authors of books reviewed in philosophy journals. Each entry includes the author's name, the title of the book, the publisher, and the place and date of publication. Under each entry is listed the name of the reviewer, the journal in which the review appeared, along with the volume, pagination and date.

**Aqvist, Lennart** and Mullock, Philip. *Causing Harm: A Logico-Legal Study.* Berlin, de Gruyter, 1989.
Van Hees, Martin. *Ratio Juris,* 10(3), 351-355, S 97.

**Aragues, J M**. *Volver a Sartre: 50 anos después de El ser y la nada.* Zaragoza, Mira Ed, 1994.
Bello, Eduardo. *Daimon Rev Filosof,* 12, 145-146, Ja-Je 96.

**Aramayo, R R**, Muguerza, J and Valdecantos, A. *El individuo y la historia.* Barcelona, Paidós, 1995.
Costa, María Victoria. *Rev Latin de Filosof,* 23(1), 183-185, O 97.

**Arcilla, René Vincent**. *For the Love of Perfection: Richard Rorty and Liberal Education.* New York, Routledge, 1995.
Standish, Paul. *J Phil Educ,* 30(3), 485-488, N 96.

**Arendt, Hannah**. *De la historia a la acción.* Barcelona, Paidós, 1995.
Hilb, Claudia. *Rev Latin de Filosof,* 23(1), 173-176, O 97.

**Arendt, Hannah**. *La condición humana.* Barcelona, Paidós, 1993.
Gotor Heras, Mercedes. *Daimon Rev Filosof,* 12, 147-148, Ja-Je 96.

**Ariew, Roger** (ed) and Greene, Marjorie (ed). *Descartes and His Contemporaries: Meditations, Objections and Replies.* Chicago, Univ of Chicago Pr, 1995.
Kane, Michael T. *Rev Metaph,* 50(2), 386-387, D 96.

**Aristotle**. *Analytica Posteriora.* Berlin, Akademie, 1993.
McKirahan, Richard. *Ancient Phil,* 17(2), 218-226, Spr 97.

**Aristotle**. *Uebersetzt und erläutert von Hermann Weidemann.* Berlin, Akademie, 1994.
De Rijk, L M. *Vivarium,* 34(2), 270-274, N 96.

**Aristotle** and Barnes, Jonathan (trans). *Posterior Analytics.* Oxford, Oxford Univ Pr, 1994.
McKirahan, Richard. *Ancient Phil,* 17(2), 210-217, Spr 97.

**Aristotle** and Bostock, David (trans). *Metaphysics: Books Z and H.* New York, Clarendon/Oxford Pr, 1994.
Graham, Daniel W. *Ancient Phil,* 16(2), 505-511, Fall 96.

**Aristotle** and Santos, Ricardo (ed & trans). *Categorias.* Porto, Porto Editora, 1995.
Mesquita, António Pedro. *Philosophica (Portugal),* 182-192, 1996.

**Armellini, Serenella**. *Le due mani della giustizia.* Turin, Giappichelli, 1996.
Baglioni, Emma. *Riv Int Filosof Diritto,* 73(3), 579-582, Jl-S 96.

**Armstrong, D M**, Martin, C B and Place, U T. *Dispositions: A Debate.* New York, Routledge, 1996.
Fantl, Jeremy. *Can Phil Rev,* 17(2), 80-82, Ap 97.

**Arnauld, Antoine**, Nicole, Pierre and Buroker, Jill Vance (ed & trans). *Logic or the Art of Thinking.* New York, Cambridge Univ Pr, 1996.
Van Evra, James. *Can Phil Rev,* 17(3), 153-155, Je 97.

**Arnold, Robert N** (ed), Youngner, Stuart J (ed) and Schapiro, Renie (ed). *Procuring Organs for Transplant: The Debate over Non-Heart-Beating Cadaver Protocols.* Baltimore, Johns Hopkins U Pr, 1995.
Annas, George J. *Bioethics,* 11(1), 77-80, Ja 97.

**Arnstine, Donald**. *Democracy and the Arts of Schooling.* Albany, SUNY Pr, 1995.
Swanger, David. *J Aes Educ,* 31(2), 112-113, Sum 97.

**Arrington, Robert L** (ed) and Glock, Hans-Johann (ed). *Wittgenstein and Quine.* London, Routledge, 1996.
Moore, A W. *Mind,* 106(422), 335-337, Ap 97.

**Arthur, John**. *Words That Bind: Judicial Review and the Grounds of Modern Constitutional Theory.* Boulder, Westview Pr, 1995.
Campbell, Tom D. *Phil Books,* 38(3), 212-214, Jl 97.
Ihlan, Amy. *Can Phil Rev,* 16(4), 238-240, Ag 96.

**Ash, Mitchell** and Söllner, Alfons. *Forced Migration and Scientific Change.* Washington, German Hist Inst, 1996.
Garrett, A C. *Hist Human Sci,* 9(4), 138-149, N 96.

**Assiter, Alison**. *Enlightened Women: Modernist Feminism in a Postmodern Age.* New York, Routledge, 1995.
Graham, Kevin M. *Can Phil Rev,* 16(6), 389-391, D 96.
Mendus, Susan. *Rad Phil,* 82, 50-51, Mr-Ap 97.

**Atlan, Henri**. *Enlightenment to Enlightenment: Intercritique of Science and Myth.* Albany, SUNY Pr, 1993.
Tauber, Alfred I. *Human Stud,* 19(2), 239-245, Apr 96.

**Attfield, Robin**. *Environmental Philosophy: Principles and Prospects.* Aldershot, Avebury, 1994.
Thompson, Janna. *Environ Values,* 6(2), 235-236, My 97.

**Attfield, Robin** (ed) and Belsey, Andrew (ed). *Philosophy and the Natural Environment.* New York, Cambridge Univ Pr, 1994.
Deane-Drummond, Celia. *Heythrop J,* 38(1), 103-105, Ja 97.

**Aubenque, Pierre** and Tordesillas, Alonso. *Aristote politique.* Paris, Pr Univ France, 1993.
Schütrumpf, Eckart E. *Ancient Phil,* 16(2), 511-521, Fall 96.

**Aubin, Paul**. *Plotin et le christianisme.* Paris, Beauchesne, 1992.
Narbonne, Jean-Marc. *Arch Phil,* 59(3), 480-482, Jl-S 96.

**Audi, Robert**. *Action, Intention and Reason.* Ithaca, Cornell Univ Pr, 1993.
Stoutland, Frederick. *Phil Quart,* 46(185), 537-541, O 96.

**Audi, Robert** (ed). *The Cambridge Dictionary of Philosophy.* New York, Cambridge Univ Pr, 1995.

Bates, Stanley. *Ethics,* 107(2), 381-383, Ja 97.
Fox, Rory. *Heythrop J,* 38(3), 357-358, Jl 97.

**Audi, Robert**. *The Structure of Justification.* New York, Cambridge Univ Pr, 1993.
Swain, Marshall. *Phil Phenomenol Res,* 56(4), 968-970, D 96.

**Aune, James Arnt**. *Rhetoric and Marxism.* Boulder, Westview Pr, 1994.
Hariman, Robert. *Phil Rhet,* 29(4), 462-467, 1996.

**Austin, David F**. *What's the Meaning of "This"? A Puzzle about Demonstrative Belief.* Ithaca, Cornell Univ Pr, 1990.
Braun, David. *Mind Mach,* 7(2), 297-302, My 97.

**Ayuso Torres, Miguel**. *La filosofía jurídica y política de Francisco Elías de Tejada.* Madrid, Unknown, 1994.
Sánchez Parodi, Horacio M. *Sapientia,* 52(201), 225-226, 1997.

**Azzouni, Jody**. *Metaphysical Myths, Mathematical Practice.* New York, Cambridge Univ Pr, 1994.
Banegas, Jesús Alcolea. *Mind,* 105(420), 683-688, O 96.
Moore, A W. *Brit J Phil Sci,* 47(4), 621-626, D 96.

**Babbitt, Susan E**. *Impossible Dreams: Rationality, Integrity, and Moral Imagination.* Boulder, Westview Pr, 1996.
Soifer, Eldon. *Can Phil Rev,* 16(5), 309-312, Oct 96.

**Babich, Babette E** (ed), Bergoffen, Debra B (ed) and Glynn, Simon V (ed). *Continental and Postmodern Perspectives in the Philosophy of Science.* Brookfield, Avebury, 1995.
Belsey, Andrew. *Brit J Phil Sci,* 48(2), 281-283, Je 97.

**Bacon, John**. *Ontology, Casuality and Mind: Essays in Honour of D M Armstrong.* Cambridge, Cambridge Univ Pr, 1995.
MacBride, Fraser. *Brit J Phil Sci,* 47(3), 463-466, S 96.

**Bacon, John**. *Universals and Property Instances: The Alphabet of Being.* Cambridge, Blackwell, 1995.
Daly, Chris. *Phil Books,* 37(4), 266-267, O 96.
Mertz, Donald W. *Mod Sch,* 74(1), 55-62, N 96.
Wolenski, Jan. *Austl J Phil,* 74(3), 510-511, S 96.

**Bacon, John** (ed), Campbell, Keith (ed) and Reinhardt, Lloyd (ed). *Ontology, Causality and Mind.* New York, Cambridge Univ Pr, 1993.
Brooks, David. *Phil Quart,* 46(185), 518-522, O 96.

**Badía Cabrera, Miguel A**. *La reflexión de David Hume en torno a la religión.* X, Unknown, 1996.
López Fernández, Alvaro. *Dialogos,* 32(70), 209-224, Jl 97.

**Badiou, Alain**. *Manifiesto por la filosofia.* Buenos Aires, Nueva Vision, 1990.
Vega, Jose Fernandez. *Cuad Etica,* 15-16, 170-174, 1993.

**Baier, Annette C**. *Moral Prejudices: Essays on Ethics.* Cambridge, Harvard Univ Pr, 1994.
Mendus, Susan. *Phil Invest,* 20(1), 76-81, J 97.

**Baier, Kurt**. *The Rational and the Moral Order.* La Salle, IL, Open Court, 1994.
McNaughton, David. *Philosophy,* 72(279), 154-158, Ja 97.

**Baker, Gordon** and Morris, Katherine J. *Descartes' Dualism.* New York, Routledge, 1966.
Burwood, Stephen. *Teorema,* 16(1), 112-114, 1996.

**Balasubramanian, R** (ed) and Mishra, Ramashanker (ed). *Man, Meaning and Morality.* New Delhi, Indian Coun Phil Res, 1995.
Pradhan, R C. *J Indian Counc Phil Res,* 13(2), 171-177, Ja-Ap 96.

**Baldwin, Anna** (ed) and Hutton, Sarah (ed). *Platonism and the English Imagination.* New York, Cambridge Univ Pr, 1994.
Howatson, M C. *Brit J Aes,* 37(2), 193-196, Ap 97.

**Balibar, Etienne** and Wallerstein, Immanuel. *Race, Nation, Class: Ambiguous Identities.* London, Verso, 1991.
James, Paul. *Phil Soc Sci,* 27(1), 130-135, Mr 97.

**Baltes, Matthias**. *Der Platonismus in der Antike Band 3-4.* Stuttgart, Frommann-Holzboog, 1996.
Bussanich, John. *Ancient Phil,* 16(2), 528-531, Fall 96.

**Bandyopadhyay, Tirthanath**. *In Search of a Moral Criterion.* Calcutta, Unknown, 1994.
Mehta, Ranju. *J Indian Counc Phil Res,* 14(2), 194-195, Ja-Ap 97.

**Bann, Stephen**. *Romanticism and the Rise of History.* New York, Twayne, 1995.
Baird, Andrew. *Hist Human Sci,* 9(3), 131-140, Ag 96.

**Barlow, Connie** (ed). *Evolution Extended: Biological Debates on the Meaning of Life.* Cambridge, MIT Pr, 1994.
Kraenzel, Frederick. *J Value Inq,* 30(3), 471-473, S 96.

**Barnes, Jonathan** (ed). *The Cambridge Companion to Aristotle.* Cambridge, Cambridge Univ Pr, 1995.
Carr, Jeffrey. *Phil Quart,* 47(187), 261-263, Ap 97.
D'Andrea, Thomas D. *Phil Books,* 38(3), 183-185, Jl 97.
Schomakers, Ben. *Tijdschr Filosof,* 59(1), 138-144, Mr 97.

**Baron, Marcia W**. *Kantian Ethics Almost Without Apology.* Ithaca, Cornell Univ Pr, 1995.
Richardson, Henry S. *Ethics,* 107(4), 746-749, Jl 97.
Sterling, Grant. *Can Phil Rev,* 16(5), 313-314, Oct 96.

**Baron, Marcia W**. *Kantian Ethics: Almost Without Apology.* Ithaca, Cornell Univ Pr, 1995.
Marshall, John. *Phil Books,* 38(2), 106-108, Ap 97.

**Brandom, Robert**. *Making it Explicit: Reasoning, Representation and Discursive Commitment*. Cambridge, Harvard Univ Pr, 1994.
Kroon, Frederick. *Austl J Phil*, 74(3), 511-513, S 96.
Halbig, Christoph. *Z Phil Forsch*, 51(1), 153-157, Ja-Mr 97.
Harrison, Bernard. *Phil Invest*, 19(4), 345-353, O 96.
Stout, Rowland. *Mind*, 106(422), 341-345, Ap 97.
Thomas, Alan. *Euro J Phil*, 4(3), 394-396, D 96.

**Brandon, Robert**. *Concepts and Methods in Evolutionary Biology*. Cambridge, Cambridge Univ Pr, 1996.
Dupré, John. *Brit J Phil Sci*, 48(2), 292-296, Je 97.

**Brandt, Reinhardt**. *Die Urteilstafel*. Hamburg, Meiner, 1991.
Hoffmann, Thomas Sören. *Kantstudien*, 87(4), 465-471, 1996.

**Braybrooke, David** (ed). *Social Rules: Origin; Character; Logic; Change*. Boulder, Westview Pr, 1996.
Mandle, Jon. *Ethics Behavior*, 6(3), 259-263, 1996.
Tuomela, Raimo. *Can Phil Rev*, 17(1), 3-5, F 97.

**Braybrooke, David**, Schotch, Peter and Brown, Bryson. *Logic on the Track of Social Change*. New York, Oxford Univ Pr, 1995.
Malachowski, Alan. *Phil Books*, 38(2), 140-142, Ap 97.
Vallentyne, Peter. *Can Phil Rev*, 16(5), 315-317, Oct 96.

**Breazeale, Daniel** (ed) and Rockmore, Tom (ed). *Fichte: Historical Contexts/Contemporary Controversies*. Atlantic Highlands, Humanities Pr, 1994.
Mather, Ronnie. *Bull Hegel Soc Gt Brit*, 34, 27-30, Autumn-Wint 96.

**Breger, H**. *G W Leibniz, Sämtliche Schriften und Briefe*. Berlin, Akademie, 1991.
Parmentier, Marc. *Leibniz Soc Rev*, 6, 141-144, D 96.

**Brena, Gian Luigi**. *Forme di verità: Introduzione all'epistemologia*. Torino, Ed San Paolo, 1995.
Buzzoni, Marco. *Epistemologia*, 19(2), 351-355, Jl-D 96.

**Brenner, William H**. *Logic and Philosophy: An Integrated Introduction*. Notre Dame, Univ Notre Dame Pr, 1993.
Wilson, Patrick A. *Amer Cath Phil Quart*, 70(3), 429-430, Sum 96.

**Breuer, Stefan**. *Asthetischer Fundamentalismus*. Darmstadt, Wiss Buchgesell, 1995.
Bothe, Henning. *Das Argument*, 217(5-6), 853-855, 1996.

**Brickhouse, Thomas C** and Smith, Nicholas D. *Plato's Socrates*. New York, Oxford Univ Pr, 1994.
Benitez, Eugenio. *Phil Books*, 38(1), 37-40, Ja 97.
Frank, Daniel H. *Int Stud Phil*, 29(2), 112-114, 1997.

**Brill, Susan**. *Wittgenstein and Critical Theory*. Athens, Ohio Univ Pr, 1995.
Hagberg, Garry L. *Phil Quart*, 47(186), 103-106, Ja 97.
Weston, Michael. *Phil Invest*, 20(2), 171-174, Ap 97.

**Brisson, Luc**. *Le Même et l'Autre dans la structure ontologique du Timée de Platon*. Sankt Augustin, Academia, 1994.
LaFrance, Yvon. *Dialogue (Canada)*, 36(2), 427-430, Spr 97.

**Broadie, Alexander**. *The Shadow of Scotus: Philosophy and Faith in Pre-Reformation Scotland*. Edinburgh, T & T Clark, 1995.
Sylwanowicz, M. *Heythrop J*, 38(3), 364-365, Jl 97.

**Brody, Celeste M** (ed) and Wallace, James (ed). *Ethical and Social Issues in Professional Education*. Albany, SUNY Pr, 1995.
Johnston, Marilyn. *J Moral Educ*, 26(2), 225-227, Je 97.

**Brogan, Walter** (trans), Warnek, Peter (trans) and Heidegger, Martin. *Aristotle's Metaphysics 1-3: On the Essence and Actuality of Force*. Bloomington, Indiana Univ Pr, 1995.
Groth, Miles. *Int Phil Quart*, 36(4), 492-493, D 96.

**Broncano, Fernando** (ed). *Enciclopedia Iberoamericana de Filosofía, Volume 8*. Madrid, Trotta, 1995.
Inés Pérez, Diana. *Rev Latin de Filosof*, 22(2), 353-355, 1996.

**Broncano, Fernando** (ed). *La mente humana*. Madrid, Trotta, 1995.
Garcia Rodríguez, Angel. *Teorema*, 16(2), 114-117, 1997.

**Bronner, Stephen Eric**. *Of Critical Theory and Its Theorists*. Cambridge, Blackwell, 1994.
Kingwell, Mark. *Polit Theory*, 24(2), 326-333, My 96.

**Brook, Andrew**. *Kant and the Mind*. New York, Cambridge Univ Pr, 1994.
Adair-Toteff, Christopher. *Brit J Hist Phil*, 5(1), 206-210, Mr 97.
Aquila, Richard E. *Int Stud Phil*, 28(4), 105-107, 1996.
Senderowicz, Yaron. *Prag Cognition*, 4(2), 409-416, 1996.

**Brooks, D H M**. *The Unity of the Mind*. New York, Macmillan, 1994.
Shute, Sara. *Int Stud Phil*, 29(2), 114-115, 1997.

**Brooks, Linda Marie**. *The Menace of the Sublime to the Individual Self*. Lewiston, Mellen Pr, 1996.
Harper, Albert W J. *Can Phil Rev*, 16(3), 159-160, Je 96.

**Brown, Hunter** (ed) and Hudecki, Dennis L (ed). *Images of the Human: The Philosophy of the Human Person in a Religious Context*. Chicago, Loyola Univ Pr, 1995.
Davies, Brian. *Int Phil Quart*, 37(2), 244-245, Je 97.

**Brown, Wendy**. *States of Injury: Power and Freedom in Late Modernity*. Princeton, Princeton Univ Pr, 1995.
Flathman, Richard E. *Polit Theory*, 24(4), 728-735, N 96.

**Bruner, Jerome**. *The Culture of Education*. Cambridge, Harvard Univ Pr, 1996.
Brown, Christine. *Phil Music Educ Rev*, 5(1), 59-60, Spr 97.

**Brunner, José**. *Freud and the Politics of Psychoanalysis*. Oxford, Blackwell, 1995.
Gardner, Sebastian. *Euro J Phil*, 5(2), 216-219, Ag 97.

**Brunschwig, Jacque**. *Papers in Hellenistic Philosophy*. New York, Cambridge Univ Pr, 1994.
Annas, Julia. *Euro J Phil*, 4(3), 369-373, D 96.
Rabel, Robert J. *Ancient Phil*, 17(2), 264-267, Spr 97.

**Brunschwig, Jacques**. *Études sur les philosophies hellénistiques*. Paris, Pr Univ France, 1995.
Annas, Julia. *Euro J Phil*, 4(3), 368-373, D 96.

**Brunschwig, Jacques** (ed) and Nussbaum, Martha (ed). *Passions and Perceptions*. Cambridge, Cambridge Univ Pr, 1993.
Dillon, John. *Int Stud Phil*, 29(2), 115-117, 1997.

**Bruter, Claude-Paul**. *Comprendre les mathématiques*. Paris, Odile Jacob, 1996.
Boutot, Alain. *Rev Phil Fr*, 2, 246-247, Ap-Je 97.

**Buchwald, Jed Z** (ed). *Scientific Practice: Theories and Stories of Doing Physics*. Chicago, Univ of Chicago Pr, 1995.
Chart, David. *Brit J Phil Sci*, 47(3), 479-482, S 96.
Sypel, Roland. *Can Phil Rev*, 17(1), 6-8, F 97.

**Buchwald, Jed Z**. *The Creation of Scientific Effects*. Chicago, Univ of Chicago Pr, 1994.
Hendry, Robin Findlay. *Brit J Phil Sci*, 48(1), 109-112, Mr 97.

**Buckle, Stephen**. *Natural Law and the Theory of Property*. New York, Clarendon/Oxford Pr, 1991.
Gregor, Mary. *Jahr Recht Ethik*, 2, 555-558, 1994.

**Budd, Malcolm**. *Values of Art: Pictures, Poetry and Music*. New York, Penguin USA, 1995.
Kieran, Matthew. *Phil Quart*, 47(187), 246-248, Ap 97.
Lamarque, Peter. *Brit J Aes*, 37(1), 84-86, Ja 97.

**Buddhist, Shin**. *International Association of Buddhist Culture*. X, Unknown, 1993.
Premur, Ksenija. *Filozof Istraz*, 15(4), 933-938, 1995.

**Bühler, Axel** (ed). *Unzeitgemässe Hermeneutik*. Frankfurt/M, Klostermann, 1994.
Thouard, Denis. *Arch Phil*, 59(4), 670-678, O-D 96.

**Buell, Lawrence**. *The Environmental Imagination*. Cambridge, Harvard Univ Pr, 1995.
Moore, Ronald. *J Aes Educ*, 31(2), 97-100, Sum 97.

**Buford, Thomas O**. *In Search of a Calling: The College's Role in Shaping Identity*. Macon, Mercer Univ Pr, 1995.
Preston, Robert A. *Rev Metaph*, 50(1), 147-148, S 96.

**Bugault, G**. *L'Inde pense-t-elle*. Paris, PUF, 1994.
Caramuta, Ersilia. *G Metaf*, 18(3), 473-476, S-D 96.

**Bunnin, Nicholas** (ed) and Tsui-James, E P (ed). *The Blackwell Companion to Philosophy*. Cambridge, Blackwell, 1996.
Foster, Stephen Paul. *Can Phil Rev*, 17(1), 8-10, F 97.

**Burchell, Graham** (trans). *What is Philosophy?*. New York, Verso, 1994.
Ferrell, Robyn. *Austl J Phil*, 74(3), 515-517, S 96.

**Burger, Hotimir**. *Filozofska antropologija*. Zagreb, Naprijed, 1993.
Zeman, Zdenko. *Filozof Istraz*, 16(3), 775-779, 1996.

**Burgess-Jackson, Keith**. *Rape: A Philosophical Investigation*. Brookfield, Dartmouth, 1996.
Archard, David. *Rad Phil*, 81, 44-45, Ja-F 97.

**Burgos, Juan Manuel**. *La inteligencia ética*. Bern, Lang, 1995.
Fernández, Francisco. *Acta Phil*, 5(2), 363-365, 1996.

**Burgos, Juan Manuel**. *La inteligencia ética, la propuesta de Jacques Maritain*. New York, Lang, 1995.
Velázquez Fernández, Héctor. *Topicos*, 11(2), 117-122, 1996.

**Burnod, Yves**. *An Adaptive Neural Network: The Cerebral Cortex*. London, Prentice Hall, 1990.
Duch, Wlodzislaw. *Mind Mach*, 7(1), 144-147, F 97.

**Burns, Timothy** (ed). *After History? Francis Fukuyama and His Critics*. Lanham, Rowman & Littlefield, 1994.
Grier, Philip T. *Owl Minerva*, 28(1), 94-97, Fall 96.

**Burrell, David B**. *Freedom and Creation in Three Traditions*. Notre Dame, Univ Notre Dame Pr, 1993.
Schwöbel, Christoph. *Relig Stud*, 33(1), 121-125, Mr 97.

**Burt, Sandra** (ed) and Code, Lorraine (ed). *Changing Methods: Feminists Transforming Practice*. Peterborough, Broadview Pr, 1995.
Andrew, Barbara S. *Can Phil Rev*, 16(5), 317-319, Oct 96.

**Busch, Elmar**. *Viele Subjekte, eine Person*. Würzburg, Koningshausen, 1993.
Faber, Roland. *Process Stud*, 24, 92-96, 1995.

**Bushnell, Dana E** (ed). *Nagging Questions: Feminist Ethics in Everyday Life*. Lanham, Rowman & Littlefield, 1995.
Sobstyl, Edrie. *Can Phil Rev*, 16(4), 247-249, Ag 96.

**Button, Graham**, Lee, John R E and Sharrock, Wes. *Computers, Minds, and Conduct*. Oxford, Polity Pr, 1995.
Gottfried, Gail M. *Mind Mach*, 7(1), 129-133, F 97.
Traiger, Saul. *Mind Mach*, 7(1), 129-133, F 97.

**Cacciari, Massimo**. *Desde Nietzsche: Tiempo, arte, política*. Buenos Aires, Ed Biblos, 1994.
Freixas, Javier. *Cuad Etica*, 17-18, 171-173, 1994.

**Cahill, Lisa Sowle**. *Sex, Gender and Christian Ethics*. New York, Cambridge Univ Pr, 1996.
Linnane, Brian. *Heythrop J*, 38(3), 331-333, Jl 97.

**Caldwell, Lynton Keith** and Shrader-Frechette, Kristen. *Policy for Land: Law and Ethics*. Lanham, Rowman & Littlefield, 1993.
Vadnjal, Dan T. *Environ Values*, 6(3), 365-366, Ag 97.

**Callahan, Joan C** (ed). *Reproduction, Ethics, and the Law: Feminist Perspectives*. Bloomington, Indiana Univ Pr, 1995.
Benkov, Laura. *Ethics Behavior*, 6(3), 265-267, 1996.

**Callicott, J Baird**. *Earth's Insights*. Berkeley, Univ of Calif Pr, 1994.
Palmer, Clare. *Environ Values*, 6(2), 236-239, My 97.

**Campanelli, Cosimo**. *Arte e poesia nella filosofia di Jacques Maritain*. Salerno, Palladio Ed, 1996.
Milano, Andrea. *Sapienza*, 50(1), 113-117, 1997.

**Campbell, James**. *Understanding John Dewey*. Chicago, Open Court, 1995.
Callaway, H G. *Phil Quart*, 47(187), 272-275, Ap 97.
Tiles, J E. *Int Stud Phil*, 29(2), 117-118, 1997.

**Canavan, Francis**. *The Pluralist Game: Pluralism, Liberalism and the Moral Conscience*. Lanham, Rowman & Littlefield, 1995.
Lynch, Edward A. *Int Phil Quart*, 37(1), 122-124, Mr 97.

**Canciani, D**. *Simone Weil: Il coraggio di pensare*. Rome, Ed Lavoro, 1996.
Tommasi, Wanda. *Iride*, 9(19), 811-813, D 96.

**Cantillo, Giuseppe**. *L'eccedenza del passato*. Napoli, Morano, 1993.
Colonnelo, Pio. *J Value Inq*, 31(2), 269-275, Je 97.

**Canziani, Guido** (ed) and Zarka, Yves Charles (ed). *L'interpretazione nei secoli XVI e XVII*. Milano, Franco Angeli, 1993.
Thouard, Denis. *Arch Phil*, 59(4), 670-678, O-D 96.

**Capitini, A**. *Scritti filosofici e religiosi*. Perugia, Protagon, 1994.
Rizzacasa, Aurelio. *Aquinas*, 39(2), 433-434, My-Ag 96.

**Caputo, John D**. *Against Ethics*. Bloomington, Indiana Univ Pr, 1993.
Westphal, Merold. *Phil Soc Crit*, 23(4), 93-97, Jl 97.

**Caputo, John D**. *Demythologizing Heidegger and Against Ethics*. Bloomington, Indiana Univ Pr, 1993.
Bourgeois, Patrick L. *Amer Cath Phil Quart*, 71(2), 259-264, Spr 97.

**Carabine, Deirdre**. *The Unknown God*. Leuven, Peeters, 1995.
Laird, Martin. *Heythrop J*, 38(3), 323-325, Jl 97.

**Caracciolo, A**. *Studi kantiani.*. Napoli, Ed Sci It, 1995.
Ulian, Alessandro. *G Metaf*, 19(1), 183-189, Ja-Ap 97.

**Carey, John**. *Hass auf die Massen*. Steidel, Gottingen, 1996.
Simanowski, Roberto. *Das Argument*, 217(5-6), 856-857, 1996.

**Carl, Wolfgang**. *Frege's Theory of Sense and Reference*. New York, Cambridge Univ Pr, 1994.
Beaney, Michael. *Int J Phil Stud*, 4(2), 328-330, S 96.
Holton, Richard. *Phil Quart*, 47(187), 275-278, Ap 97.
Valberg, J J. *Mind*, 106(422), 590-593, Ap 97.
Vassallo, Nicla. *Epistemologia*, 19(2), 349-351, Jl-D 96.

**Carlson, G C** (ed) and Pelletier, F J (ed). *The Generic Book*. Chicago, Univ of Chicago Pr, 1995.
Van Eijck, Jan. *J Log Lang Info*, 6(3), 339-341, Jl 97.

**Carpenter, Ronald H**. *History as Rhetoric: Style, Narrative, and Persuasion*. Columbia, Univ S Carolina Pr, 1995.
Aurand, Harold. *Phil Rhet*, 30(1), 94-97, 1997.
Smith, Jon. *Clio*, 26(1), 118-124, Fall 96.

**Carr, Craig L** (ed) and Seidler, Michael J (trans). *The Political Writings of Samuel Pufendorf*. New York, Oxford Univ Pr, 1994.
Masugi, Ken. *Phil Quart*, 47(187), 265-267, Ap 97.

**Carracedo, Rubio**. *José, Educación moral, postmodernidad y democracia*. Madrid, Ed Trotta, 1996.
Aznar, Hugo. *Agora (Spain)*, 15(2), 175-181, 1996.

**Carrier, David**. *The Aesthete in the City: The Philosophy and Practice of American Abstract Painting in the 1980's*. University Park, Penn St Univ Pr, 1994.
Krukowski, Lucian. *J Aes Art Crit*, 55(1), 82-84, Wint 97.

**Carroll, John W**. *Laws of Nature*. New York, Cambridge Univ Pr, 1994.
Zynda, Lyle. *Stud Hist Phil Sci*, 27(4), 587-592, D 96.

**Carruthers, Peter**. *Human Knowledge and Human Nature*. New York, Oxford Univ Pr, 1992.
Cowie, Fiona. *Phil Rev*, 105(4), 530-533, O 96.

**Carruthers, Peter**. *Language, Thought, and Consciousness: An Essay in Philosophical Psychology*. Cambridge, Cambridge Univ Pr, 1996.
Helm, Bennett W. *Rev Metaph*, 50(2), 391-392, D 96.
Manson, Neil. *Mind*, 106(423), 593-596, Jl 97.

**Carruthers, Peter** (ed) and Smith, Peter K (ed). *Theories of Theories of Mind*. New York, Cambridge Univ Pr, 1996.
Garrett, Brian Jonathan. *Can Phil Rev*, 16(5), 319-322, Oct 96.
Happé, Francesca. *Mind Lang*, 11(4), 447-451, D 96.
Rychlak, Joseph F. *J Mind Behav*, 18(1), 95-97, Wint 97.

**Cartwright, Nancy**, Cat, Jordi and Fleck, Lola. *Otto Neurath: Philosophy Between Science and Politics*. New York, Cambridge Univ Pr, 1996.
Mormann, Thomas. *Brit J Phil Sci*, 48(2), 306-309, Je 97.
Preston, John. *Can Phil Rev*, 16(5), 322-324, Oct 96.

**Carvalho, Maria Celília**. *A filosofia analítica no Brasil*. X, Unknown, 1995.
Itamar Borges, Bento. *Educ Filosof*, 10(19), 189-194, Ja-Je 96.
Lacey, Hugh. *Manuscrito*, 19(2), 253-258, O 96.

**Casati, Roberto** and Varzi, Achille C. *Holes and Other Superficialities*. Cambridge, MIT Pr, 1994.
Armstrong, D M. *J Phil*, 93(11), 585-586, Oct 96.

**Casey, Edward S**. *Getting Back Into Place*. Bloomington, Indiana Univ Pr, 1993.
Krell, David Farrell. *Res Phenomenol*, 26, 262-275, 1996.
May, Todd. *Human Stud*, 19(4), 433-439, O 96.

**Cassin, Barbara** (ed). *Nuestros griegos y sus modernos*. Paris, Ed du Seuil, 1992.
Medrano, Gregorio Luri. *Convivium*, 10, 130-134, 1997.

**Cassirer, E**. *Goethe e il mondo storico*. Brescia, Morcelliana, 1995.
Landi, Luca. *Iride*, 9(19), 813-814, D 96.

**Catapano, G**. *Epekeina tes philosophias*. Padova, Clueb, 1995.
Augello, Giuseppe. *G Metaf*, 18(3), 480-482, S-D 96.

**Catucci, Stefano**. *La filosofia critica di Husserl*. Milano, Guerini, 1995.
Frigerio, Aldo. *Riv Filosof Neo-Scolas*, 88(3), 526-532, Jl-S 96.

**Cavaciuti, Santino**. *Libertà e alterità nel pensiero di Louis Lavelle*. Genova, Barboni Editore, 1996.
Briganti, M Camilla. *Aquinas*, 39(3), 605-606, S-D 96.

**Cavarero, Adriana**. *In Spite of Plato: A Feminist Rewriting of Ancient Philosophy*. Cambridge, Polity Pr, 1995.
Sandford, Stella. *Rad Phil*, 81, 50-51, Ja-F 97.

**Cavazos, Edward A** and Morin, Gavino. *Cyberspace and the Law: Your Rights and Duties in the On-line World*. Cambridge, MIT Pr, 1994.
Behar, Joseph E. *J Infor Ethics*, 5(2), 87-90, Fall 96.

**Cavell, Marcia**. *The Psychoanalytic Mind: From Freud to Philosophy*. Cambridge, Harvard Univ Pr, 1993.
Watling, Christine P. *J Mind Behav*, 17(3), 287-290, Sum 96.

**Cavell, Stanley**. *Contesting Tears: The Hollywood Melodrama of the Unknown Woman*. Chicago, Univ of Chicago Pr, 1996.
Mulhall, Stephen. *Euro J Phil*, 5(2), 227-230, Ag 97.

**Caygill, Howard**. *A Kant Dictionary*. Oxford, Blackwell, 1995.
Lennon, Paul. *Int J Phil Stud*, 4(2), 331-333, S 96.
MacIntosh, J J. *Can Phil Rev*, 17(1), 10-12, F 97.

**Cesa, C**. *Introduzione a Fichte*. Bari, Laterza, 1995.
Di Tommaso, Giannino. *Teoria*, 16(1), 126-127, 1996.

**Ceynowa, Andrzej** (ed), Dziemidok, Bohdan (ed) and Janiak, Marek (ed). *The question of valuation in American twentieth-century philosophy and aesthetics*. X, Unknown, 1995.
Swiatek, Krzysztof. *Can Phil Rev*, 17(2), 82-85, Ap 97.

**Chakravarty, Nilima**. *Indian Philosophy: The Pathfinders and the System Builders*. New Delhi, Allied, 1995.
Panneerselvam, S. *J Indian Counc Phil Res*, 14(1), 201-206, S-D 96.

**Chalmers, David**. *The Conscious Mind: In Search of a Fundamental Theory*. New York, Oxford Univ Pr, 1996.
Hardcastle, Valerie Gray. *J Mind Behav*, 17(4), 391-398, Autumn 96.

**Chambers, Simone**. *Reasonable Democracy: Jürgen Habermas and the Politics of Discourse*. Ithaca, Cornell Univ Pr, 1996.
Boulad-Ayoub, Josiane. *Can Phil Rev*, 16(5), 327-328, Oct 96.

**Chambliss, Daniel F**. *Beyond Caring: Hospitals, Nurses, and the Social Organization of Ethics*. Chicago, Univ of Chicago Pr, 1996.
DeVries, Raymond. *Hastings Center Rep*, 27(4), 41-42, Jl-Ag 97.

**Chandrakala**. *Liberty and Social Transformation*. New Delhi, Heritage Publishers, 1992.
Greenspan, Louis. *J Aes Art Crit*, 54(4), 93-94, Fall 96.

**Chapell, T D J**. *Aristotle and Augustine on Freedom*. New York, St Martin's Pr, 1995.
Stone, M W F. *Relig Stud*, 33(1), 129-130, Mr 97.

**Chappell, Vere**. *The Cambridge Companion to Locke*. New York, Cambridge Univ Pr, 1994.
Losousky, Michael. *Int Stud Phil*, 29(2), 118-120, 1997.

**Chapple, Christopher Key**. *Nonviolence to Animals, Earth, and Self in Asian Traditions*. Albany, SUNY Pr, 1993.
Shrader, Douglas W. *Thomist*, 61(2), 274-279, Ap 97.

**Charvet, John**. *The Idea of an Ethical Community*. Ithaca, Cornell Univ Pr, 1995.
Milne, A J M. *Utilitas*, 9(1), 155-156, Mr 97.
Stratton-Lake, Philip. *Mind*, 106(421), 169-171, Ja 97.

**Chauviré, Christiane**. *Peirce et la signification*. Paris, Pr Univ France, 1995.
Trmblay, Robert. *Dialogue (Canada)*, 36(1), 200-202, Wint 97.

**Chazal, Gérard**. *Éléments de logique formelle*. Paris, Hermes, 1996.
Ginisti, Jean-Pierre. *Rev Phil Fr*, 2, 247-249, Ap-Je 97.

**Chierchia, Gennaro**. *Dynamics of Meaning: Anaphora, Presupposition, and the Theory of Grammar*. Chicago, Univ of Chicago Pr, 1995.
Slater, Hartley. *Austl J Phil*, 74(4), 687-689, D 96.

**Chow, Rey**. *Primitive Passions: Visuality, Sexuality, Ethnography, and Contemporary Chinese Cinema*. New York, Columbia Univ Pr, 1995.
Blum, Susan D. *Phil East West*, 47(3), 435-439, Jl 97.

**Christman, John**. *The Myth of Property: Toward an Egalitarian Theory of Ownership*. New York, Oxford Univ Pr, 1994.
Sterling Burnett, H. *Int Stud Phil*, 28(4), 107-108, 1996.

**Churchland, Paul M**. *The Engine of Reason, The Seat of the Soul*. Cambridge, MIT Pr, 1995.
French, Robert M. *Mind Mach*, 6(3), 416-421, O 96.
Haselager, W F G. *Phil Psych*, 9(3), 391-393, S 96.
Hooker, C A. *Austl J Phil*, 74(3), 513-515, S 96.
Horgan, Terence. *Phil Sci*, 63(3), 476-478, S 96.
Jones, Judith A. *Int Phil Quart*, 36(4), 496-498, D 96.
Manson, Neil. *Brit J Phil Sci*, 47(4), 633-635, D 96.

**Cirera, Ramón**. *Carnap and the Vienna Circle: Empiricism and Logical Syntax*. Amsterdam, Rodopi, 1994.
Tomasini Bassols, Alejandro. *Critica*, 28(83), 140-155, Ag 96.

**Cirera, Ramón** (ed), Ibarra, Andoni (ed) and Mormann, Thomas (ed). *El programa de Carnap: Ciencia, lenguaje, filosofía*. Barcelona, Ed Bronce, 1996.
Eizagirre, Xabier. *Critica*, 28(83), 137-140, Ag 96.

**Clair, André**. *Kierkegaard: Penser le singulier*. Paris, Ed du Cerf, 1993.
Politis, Hélène. *Rev Phil Fr*, 3, 426-428, Jl-S 96.

**Clancey, William J** (ed), Smoliar, Stephen W (ed) and Stefik, Mark J (ed). *Contemplating Minds: A Forum for Artificial Intelligence*. Cambridge, MIT Pr, 1994.
Slater, Carol W. *Phil Psych*, 9(3), 397-401, S 96.

**Clark, Kelly James** (ed). *Our Knowledge of God*. Dordrecht, Kluwer, 1992.
McLeod, Mark. *Faith Phil*, 14(1), 109-113, Ja 97.

**Clark, Peter** (ed) and Hale, Bob (ed). *Reading Putnam*. Cambridge, Blackwell, 1994.
Quante, Michael. *Protosoz*, 8/9, 346-351, 1996.

**Clark, Stephen R L**. *How to Live Forever: Science Fiction and Philosophy*. London, Routledge, 1995.
Morton, Adam. *Brit J Phil Sci*, 48(2), 310-312, Je 97.

**Clarke, J J**. *Jung and Eastern Thought: A Dialogue with the Orient*. New York, Routledge, 1994.
Parkes, Graham. *Phil East West*, 46(4), 588-589, O 96.
Pickering, J. *Asian Phil*, 6(3), 234-237, N 96.

**Clarke, W Norris**. *Person and Being*. Milwaukee, Marquette Univ Pr, 1993.
Cuddeback, Matthew. *Amer Cath Phil Quart*, 70(3), 434-438, Sum 96.

**Cleary, John J**. *Aristotle and Mathematics: Aporetic Method in Cosmology and Metaphysics*. Leiden, Brill, 1995.
Wilson, Malcolm. *Rev Metaph*, 50(1), 149-151, S 96.

**Coates, John**. *The Claims of Common Sense: Moore, Wittgenstein, Keynes and the Social Sciences*. Cambridge, Cambridge Univ Pr, 1996.
McManus, Denis. *Can Phil Rev*, 17(3), 157-159, Je 97.

**Cobben, Paul**. *Postdialectische zedelijkheid*. Kampen, Kok, 1996.
Griffioen, Sander. *Alg Ned Tijdschr Wijs*, 89(3), 243, Jl 97.

**Coffin, David R**. *The English Garden: Meditation and Memorial*. Princeton, Princeton Univ Pr, 1994.
Miller, Mara. *J Aes Art Crit*, 55(3), 333-335, Sum 97.

**Cohen, Carl**. *Naked Racial Preference: The Case against Affirmative Action*. Lanham, Madison Books, 1996.
Mack, Eric. *Ethics*, 107(2), 378-381, Ja 97.

**Cohen, Cynthia B**. *New Ways of Making Babies: The Case of Egg Donation*. Bloomington, Indiana Univ Pr, 1996.
Ryan, Kenneth J. *Ethics Behavior*, 6(4), 367-369, 1996.

**Cohen, G A**. *Self-Ownership, Freedom, and Equality*. Cambridge, Cambridge Univ Pr, 1995.
Mack, Eric. *Ethics*, 107(3), 517-520, Ap 97.

**Cohen, L Jonathan**. *An Essay on Belief and Acceptance*. New York, Clarendon/Oxford Pr, 1992.
Bezuidenhout, Anne. *Rev Metaph*, 50(2), 392-395, D 96.

**Cohen, Mitchell**. *The Wager of Lucien Goldmann: Tragedy, Dialectics and A Hidden God*. Princeton, Princeton Univ Pr, 1994.
Nielsen, Greg. *Constellations*, 3(2), 273-277, O 96.

**Cohen, Richard A**. *Elevations: The Height of the Good in Rosenzweig and Levinas*. Chicago, Univ of Chicago Pr, 1994.
Wyschogrod, Edith. *Int Stud Phil*, 28(4), 108-109, 1996.

**Cohen, Warren**. *Ethics in Thought and Action: Social and Professional Perspectives*. New York, Ardsley House, 1995.
Houlgate, Laurence D. *Teach Phil*, 20(1), 73-74, Mr 97.

**Cohn-Sherbok, Dan** (ed) and Lewis, Christopher (ed). *Beyond Death: Theological and Philosophical Reflections on Life After Death*. New York, St Martin's Pr, 1995.
Dilley, Frank B. *Int J Phil Relig*, 42(1), 65-67, Ag 97.

**Colapietro, Vincent M** (ed) and Olshewsky, Thomas M (ed). *Peirce's Doctrine of Signs: Theory, Applications and Connections*. New York, de Gruyter, 1996.
Ehrat, J. *Theol Phil*, 72(1), 119-123, 1997.

**Coleman, Jules** (ed) and Buchanan, Allen (ed). *In Harm's Way: Essays in Honor of Joel Feinberg*. New York, Cambridge Univ Pr, 1994.
Ripstein, Arthur. *Phil Books*, 38(1), 61-64, Ja 97.

**Colish, Marcia L**. *Peter Lombard*. Leiden, Brill, 1994.
Soule, W Becket. *Thomist*, 61(2), 317-320, Ap 97.

**Colli, Giorgio**. *Filosofía de la expresión*. X, Unknown, 1996.
Cifuentes Camacho, David. *Convivium*, 9, 142-144, 1996.

**Collier, Andrew**. *Critical Realism*. New York, Verso, 1994.
Harré, Rom. *Int Stud Phil*, 29(2), 120-122, 1997.

**Collier, John**. *Time's Arrow's Today: Recent Physical and Philosophical Work on the Direction of Time*. Cambridge, Cambridge Univ Pr, 1995.
Collier, John. *Brit J Phil Sci*, 48(2), 287-289, Je 97.

**Collin, Denis**. *La théorie de la connaissance chez Marx*. Paris, L'Harmattan, 1996.
Goffi, Jean-Yves. *Rev Theol Phil*, 129(2), 186-187, 1997.

**Collingwood, R G**. *Essays in Political Philosophy*. New York, Clarendon/Oxford Pr, 1989.
Ciocco, Gary. *Rev Metaph*, 50(2), 395-396, D 96.

**Collins, Ardis B** (ed). *Hegel on the Modern World*. Albany, SUNY Pr, 1995.
Hoffheimer, Michael H. *Clio*, 25(3), 321-329, Spr 96.

**Colombel, Jeannette**. *Michel Foucalt.*. Paris, Odile Jacob, 1994.
Verley, Xavier. *Rev Phil Fr*, 4, 568-571, O-D 96.

**Compagnoni, Francesco**. *Etica della vita*. Milan, Ed San Paolo, 1995.
Troncarelli, Barbara. *Riv Int Filosof Diritto*, 73(3), 586-589, Jl-S 96.

**Comte, Auguste**. *Discours sur l'esprit positif*. Paris, Vrin, 1995.
Seys, Pascale. *Rev Phil Louvain*, 94(2), 364-367, M 96.

**Comte, Auguste**. *Leçons sur la sociologie: Cours de philosophie positive*. Paris, Flammarion, 1995.
Seys, Pascale. *Rev Phil Louvain*, 94(2), 364-367, M 96.

**Concetti, Gino**. *Etica fiscale*. Casale Monferrato, Ed Piemme, 1995.
Gentile, Massimo. *Riv Int Filosof Diritto*, 74(4), 368-371, Ap-Je 97.

**Conche, Marcel**. *Pyrrhon ou l'apprence*. Paris, Pr Univ France, 1994.
Leroux, Georges. *Can Phil Rev*, 17(2), 85-86, Ap 97.

**Conforti, Joseph A**. *Jonathan Edwards, Religious Tradition and American Culture*. Chapel Hill, Univ N Carolina Pr, 1995.
Grange, Joseph. *Int Phil Quart*, 37(1), 120-122, Mr 97.

**Congdon, Lee**. *Exile and Social Thought*. Princeton, Princeton Univ Pr, 1991.
Gulick, Walter. *Tradition Discovery*, 23(2), 44-46, 1996-97.
Tamás, Demeter. *Magyar Filozof Szemle*, 4-5-6, 659-666, 1996.

**Conniff, James**. *The Useful Cobbler: Edmund Burke and the Politics of Progress*. Albany, SUNY Pr, 1994.
Bromwich, David. *Polit Theory*, 24(4), 739-746, N 96.

**Connolly, William E**. *The Ethos of Pluralization*. Minneapolis, Univ of Minnesota Pr, 1995.
Erickson, Chris. *Rad Phil*, 81, 53, Ja-F 97.
Kahane, David J. *Constellations*, 3(3), 428-431, Ja 97.

**Consarella, Bruna**. *La Rivoluzione e i suoi 'Miti'*. Paris, Flammarion, 1994.
Ratto, Franco. *Cuad Vico*, 7/8, 440-443, 1997.

**Consuegra, Francisco Rodriquez**. *Kurt Goedel: Ensayos inéditos*. Barcelona, Mondadori, 1994.
Alcaraz, Carlos Torre. *Mathesis*, 11(3), 251-283, Ag 95.

**Conti, Charles**. *Metaphysical Personalism*. New York, Clarendon/Oxford Pr, 1995.
Buford, Thomas O. *Rev Metaph*, 50(4), 873-874, Je 97.

**Conway, David**. *Classical Liberalism: The Unvanquished Ideal*. Basingstoke, Macmillan, 1995.
Archard, David. *Philosophy*, 71(278), 628-631, O 96.

**Cook, Daniel J** and Rosemont, Henry. *Gottfried Wilhelm Leibniz: Writings on China*. Peru, Open Court, 1994.
Parkinson, G H R. *Stud Leibniz*, 28(2), 226-228, 1997.

**Cook, Daniel J** (trans) and Rosemount, Jr., Henry (trans). *Writings on China*. Chicago, Open Court, 1994.
Saussy, Haun. *Phil East West*, 47(2), 263-271, Ap 97.

**Cook, Deborah**. *The Culture Industry Revisited: Theodor W. Adorno on Mass Culture*. Lanham, Rowman & Littlefield, 1996.
Fosl, Peter S. *Can Phil Rev*, 16(6), 13-15, D 96.

**Cook, John W**. *Wittgenstein's Metaphysics*. New York, Cambridge Univ Pr, 1994.
Ambrose, Alice. *Int Stud Phil*, 29(2), 122-124, 1997.

**Cook, Patricia** (ed). *Philosophical Imagination and Cultural Memory.* Durham, Duke Univ Pr, 1993.
Margolis, Joseph. *Phil Quart*, 46(185), 527-530, O 96.

**Cooper, David** (ed) and Palmer, Joy (ed). *Just Environments: Intergenerational, International and Interspecies Issues.* New York, Routledge, 1995.
De-Shalit, Avner. *Environ Values*, 6(1), 115-116, Mr 97.

**Cooper, David E**. *World Philosophies: An Historical Introduction.* Cambridge, Blackwell, 1996.
Sterling, Grant. *Can Phil Rev*, 16(6), 15-17, D 96.

**Cooper, Ron L**. *Heidegger and Whitehead.* Athens, Ohio Univ Pr, 1993.
Smith, Olav Bryant. *Process Stud*, 24, 99-102, 1995.

**Copeland, J**. *Artificial Intelligence: A Philosophical Introduction.* Cambridge, Blackwell, 1993.
Girle, Roderic A. *Austl J Phil*, 74(4), 689-691, D 96.

**Copjec, Joan**. *Read My Desire: Lacan Against the Historicists.* Cambridge, MIT Pr, 1994.
McWhorter, Ladelle. *Int Stud Phil*, 28(4), 110-111, 1996.

**Copp, David**. *Morality, Normativity, and Society.* New York, Oxford Univ Pr, 1995.
Hooker, Bradford. *Ethics*, 107(4), 749-752, Jl 97.
Isaacs, Tracy. *Can Phil Rev*, 17(1), 17-19, F 97.
Sinnott-Armstrong, Walter. *Phil Rev*, 105(4), 552-554, O 96.
Yelin, Lewis S. *Phil Quart*, 47(188), 411-413, Jl 97.

**Corbin, Henry**. *History of Islamic Philosophy.* London, Kegan Paul, 1993.
Cooper, David E. *Asian Phil*, 7(1), 59-61, Mr 97.

**Cornell, Drucilla**. *The Imaginary Domain: Abortion, Pornography and Sexual Harassment.* New York, Routledge, 1995.
Greschner, Donna. *Can Phil Rev*, 17(1), 19-21, F 97.

**Cortella, Lucio**. *Dopo il sapere assoluto.* Milano, Guerini, 1995.
Frigerio, Aldo. *Riv Filosof Neo-Scolas*, 88(3), 535-542, Jl-S 96.
Marzocchi, Virginio. *Iride*, 9(19), 815-816, D 96.

**Cortina, Adela**. *El quehacer ético.* Madrid, Santillana, 1996.
Binaburo Iturbide, J A. *Dialogo Filosof*, 13(1), 96-98, Ja-Ap 97.

**Cossutta, Frédéric** (ed). *Descartes et l'argumentation philosophique.* Paris, PUF, 1996.
Danblon, Emmanuelle. *Rev Int Phil*, 51(199), 161-166, 1997.

**Costa, Margarita**. *La filosofía británica en los siglos XVII y XVIII.* Buenos Aires, FUNDEC, 1995.
Ranea, Alberto Guillermo. *Rev Latin de Filosof*, 23(1), 178-179, O 97.

**Cotta, Sergio** and Di Brozolo, Luigi Radicati. *Il nuovo volto del l'universo.* Bari, Laterza, 1994.
Morchio, Renzo. *Epistemologia*, 19(1), 180-182, Ja-Je 96.

**Cottingham, John** (ed). *Reason, Will, and Sensation: Studies in Descartes' Metaphysics.* New York, Clarendon/Oxford Pr, 1994.
Anderson, Abraham. *Phil Quart*, 46(185), 547-550, O 96.
Ariew, Roger. *Phil Books*, 38(1), 46-48, Ja 97.
Simmons, Alison. *Phil Rev*, 105(4), 536-538, O 96.

**Coward, Harold** (ed) and Hurka, Thomas (ed). *Ethics and Climate Change: The Greenhouse Effect.* Waterloo, Wilfrid Laurier U Pr, 1993.
McDonald, Michael. *Dialogue (Canada)*, 35(4), 829-832, Fall 96.

**Cowley, Fraser**. *Metaphysical Delusion.* Buffalo, Prometheus, 1991.
Todd, D D. *Dialogue (Canada)*, 35(4), 852-854, Fall 96.

**Cox White, Becky**. *Competence to Consent.* Washington, Georgetown Univ Pr, 1994.
Crowdon, Andrew. *Bioethics*, 11(1), 88-89, Ja 97.

**Craig, Leon Harold**. *The War Lover: A Study of Plato's Republic.* Toronto, Univ of Toronto Pr, 1994.
Waterfield, Robin. *Heythrop J*, 37(4), 494-495, O 96.

**Craig, William Lane** and Smith, Quentin. *Theism, Atheism and Big Bang Cosmology.* New York, Clarendon/Oxford Pr, 1993.
Oppy, Graham. *Faith Phil*, 13(1), 125-133, Ja 96.

**Cramer-Naumann, Samuel**. *Gott als geschehende Geschichte.* Bochum, Unknown, 1993.
Summerell, Orrin F. *Bochumer Phil Jrbh*, 1, 239-242, 1996.

**Cranor, Carl F**. *Regulating Toxic Substances: A philosophy of science and the law.* Oxford, Oxford Univ Pr, 1993.
Parascandola, Mark. *J Applied Phil*, 13(2), 224-225, 1996.

**Credson, Joan**. *Christian Doctrine in the Light of Michael Polanyi's Theory of Personal Knowledge.* Lewiston, Mellen Pr, 1994.
Sullivan, John. *Heythrop J*, 37(4), 473-474, O 96.

**Cresswell, Max J**. *Language in the World.* New York, Cambridge Univ Pr, 1994.
Sual, Jennifer. *Phil Rev*, 105(2), 262-264, Ap 96.

**Crisp, Roger** (ed). *How Should One Live?: Essays on the Virtues.* Oxford, Oxford Univ Pr, 1996.
Swanton, Christine. *Mind*, 106(423), 596-598, Jl 97.

**Cristofolini, Paolo**. *Scienza Nuova: Introduzione alla lettura.* Roma, La Nuova Ital Sci, 1995.
Ratto, Franco. *Cuad Vico*, 7/8, 434-437, 1997.

**Cristofolini, Paolo**. *Vico et l'histoire.* Paris, PUF, 1995.
Remaud, Olivier. *Arch Phil*, 59(4), 664-667, O-D 96.
Remaud, Olivier. *Rev Phil Fr*, 3, 414-416, Jl-S 96.

**Critchley, Simon** (ed) and Dews, Peter (ed). *Deconstructive Subjectivities.* Albany, SUNY Pr, 1996.
Calder, Gideon. *Rad Phil*, 83, 51-52, My-J3 97.
Mooney, Timothy. *Int J Phil Stud*, 5(2), 323-326, Je 97.

**Croken, Robert** (ed), Crowe, Frederick (ed) and Doran, Robert (ed). *The Collected Works of Lonergan Volume Six: Philosophical and Theological Papers.* Toronto, Univ of Toronto Pr, 1996.
Sauer, James B. *Can Phil Rev*, 16(3), 189-192, Je 96.

**Crook, Paul**. *Darwinism, War and History.* New York, Cambridge Univ Pr, 1994.
Mitman, Gregg. *Biol Phil*, 12(2), 259-264, Ap 97.

**Cruz, Roberto**. *El hombre pregunta.* México, Univ Iberoamericana, 1994.
Gilbert, Paul. *Rev Filosof (Mexico)*, 29(87), 515-517, S-D 96.

**Cruz Cruz, Juan**. *Razones del corazón.* Pamplona, EUNSA, 1993.
Colomer, Eusebi. *Pensamiento*, 206(53), 346-348, My-Ag 97.

**Csirmaz, L** (ed), Gabbay, D (ed) and De Rijke, M (ed). *Logic Colloquium '92.* Menlo Park, CSLI, 1995.
Hodkinson, Ian. *J Log Lang Info*, 6(4), 453-457, O 97.

**Currie, Gregory**. *Image and Mind: Film, Philosophy and Cognitive Science.* New York, Cambridge Univ Pr, 1995.
Hopkins, Robert. *Mind*, 106(421), 172-176, Ja 97.
Davies, David. *Mind Mach*, 7(1), 138-142, F 97.
Mulhall, Stephen. *Philosophy*, 71(278), 617-622, O 96.

**Cushing, James T**. *Quantum Mechanics: Historical Contingency and the Copenhagen Hegemony.* Chicago, Univ of Chicago Pr, 1994.
MacCallum, David. *Phil Books*, 37(4), 280-282, O 96.
Wayne, Andrew. *Phil Sci*, 63(3), 478-480, S 96.

**Cutrofello, Andrew**. *The Owl at Dawn: A Sequel to Hegel's Phenomenology of Spirit.* Albany, SUNY Pr, 1995.
Schalow, Frank. *Owl Minerva*, 28(1), 108-121, Fall 96.

**Cytowic, Richard E**. *The Neurological Side of Neuropsychology.* Cambridge, MIT Pr, 1995.
Anderson, Jack R. *Behavior Phil*, 24(2), 191-194, Fall 96.

**Cziko, Gary**. *Without Miracles: Universal Selection Theory and the Second Darwinian Revolution.* Cambridge, MIT Pr, 1995.
Ogden, Dawn. *Can Phil Rev*, 17(3), 160-162, Je 97.

**d'Aquino, Tommaso**. *I vizi capitali.* Milan, Rizzoli, 1996.
Savino, Raffaella. *Riv Int Filosof Diritto*, 73(4), 789-791, O-D 96.

**D'Oyen, Fatima M**. *The Miracle of Life: a Guide on Islamic Family Life and Sex Education for Young People.* Leicester, Islamic Foundation, 1996.
Mabud, Shaikh Abdul. *J Moral Educ*, 26(3), 365-368, S 97.

**Dahlbom, B** (ed). *Dennett and his Critics.* Cambridge, Blackwell, 1995.
Hunter, Geoffrey. *Phil Invest*, 20(2), 174-179, Ap 97.

**Dahm, Helmut**. *Seid nüchtern und wachsam.* X, Unknown, 1991.
Ignatow, Assen. *Stud East Euro Thought*, 49(2), 135-139, Je 97.

**Dahms, Hans-Joachim**. *Positivismusstreit.* Frankfurt, Suhrkamp, 1994.
Eizagirre, Xabier. *Theoria (Spain)*, 12(28), 197-199, Ja 97.

**Dales, Richard C**. *The Problem of the Rational Soul in the Thirteenth Century.* Leiden, Brill, 1995.
Markowski, Mieczyslaw. *Kwartalnik Filozof*, 24(3), 203-206, 1996.

**Dalledonne, A** and Goglia, R. *Cornelio Fabro.* Frosinone, Pensatore Univ, 1996.
Perini, Giuseppe. *Aquinas*, 39(3), 640-643, S-D 96.

**Damasio, Antonio R**. *El error de Descartes.* Barcelona, Grijalbo, 1996.
Prades, J L. *Teorema*, 16(1), 107-109, 1996.

**Damisch, Hubert**. *The Origin of Perspective.* Cambridge, MIT Pr, 1994.
Maynard, Patrick. *J Aes Art Crit*, 55(1), 84-85, Wint 97.

**Danesi, Marcel**. *Giambattista Vico and the Cognitive Science Enterprise.* New York, Lang, 1995.
Haskell, Robert E. *J Mind Behav*, 17(1), 75-77, Winter 96.

**Danesi, Marcel**. *Vico, Metaphor, and the Origin of Language.* Bloomington, Indiana Univ Pr, 1993.
Haskell, Robert E. *J Mind Behav*, 17(1), 75-77, Winter 96.

**Daniel, Stephen H**. *The Philosophy of Jonathan Edwards: A Study in Divine Semiotics.* Bloomington, Indiana Univ Pr, 1994.
Edwards, Rem B. *Rev Metaph*, 50(2), 396-399, D 96.
Kuklick, Bruce. *Int Stud Phil*, 28(4), 111-112, 1996.

**Daniels, Norman**. *Seeking Fair Treatment, From the AIDS Epidemic to National Health Care Reform.* New York, Oxford Univ Pr, 1995.
Kuczewski, Mark. *Theor Med*, 18(3), 323-325, S 97.

**Daniels, Norman**. *Seeking Fair Treatment: From the AIDS Epidemic to National Health Care Reform.* New York, Oxford Univ Pr, 1995.
Flores, Albert. *Ethics*, 107(4), 731-733, Jl 97.

**Daniels, Norman**, Leight, Donald W and Kaplan, Ronald L. *Benchmarks of Fairness for Healthcare Reform.* New York, Oxford Univ Pr, 1996.
Dougherty, Charles J. *Hastings Center Rep*, 27(4), 39-41, Jl-Ag 97.

**Danto, Arthur C**. *Beyond the Brillo Box: The Visual Arts in Post-Historical Perspective.* New York, Farrar-Straus-Giroux, 1992.
Kulenkampff, Jens. *Euro J Phil*, 2(1), 97-101, Ap 94.

**Danto, Arthur C**. *Playing with the Edge: The Photographic Achievement of Robert Maplethorpe.* Berkeley, Univ of Calif Pr, 1996.
Feagin, Susan L. *J Aes Art Crit*, 55(1), 74-77, Wint 97.
Price, A W. *Brit J Aes*, 36(4), 439-441, O 96.

**Darwall, Stephen** (ed). *Equal Freedom: Selected Tanner Lectures on Human Values*. Ann Arbor, Univ of Michigan Pr, 1987.
McKerlie, Dennis. *Ethics*, 107(2), 353-356, Ja 97.

**Darwall, Stephen**. *The British Moralist and the Internal 'Ought': 1640-1740*. New York, Cambridge Univ Pr, 1995.
Mautner, Thomas. *Phil Books*, 38(2), 102-104, Ap 97.

**Darwall, Stephen L**. *The British Moralists and the Internal "Ought" 1640-1740*. Cambridge, Cambridge Univ Pr, 1995.
Lillehammer, Hallvard. *Mind*, 105(420), 691-694, O 96.

**David, Marian**. *Correspondence and Disquotation*. New York, Oxford Univ Pr, 1994.
Grover, Dorothy. *J Sym Log*, 62(1), 326-328, Mr 97.
Schiffer, Stephen. *Int Stud Phil*, 28(4), 112-113, 1996.

**Davidson, Herbert A**. *Alfarabi, Avicenna, and Averroes, on Intellect*. New York, Oxford Univ Pr, 1992.
Ivry, Alfred L. *Int Stud Phil*, 29(2), 124-125, 1997.

**Davies, Martin** and Stone, Tony. *Folk Psychology*. Cambridge, Blackwell, 1995.
Warmbrod, Ken. *Can Phil Rev*, 17(1), 21-25, F 97.

**Davies, Martin** and Stone, Tony. *Mental Simulation*. Cambridge, Blackwell, 1995.
Warmbrod, Ken. *Can Phil Rev*, 17(1), 21-25, F 97.

**Davies, Stephen**. *Musical Meaning and Expression*. Ithaca, Cornell Univ Pr, 1994.
Goldman, Alan H. *Phil Quart*, 46(185), 533-535, O 96.
Tappolet, Christine. *Phil Books*, 37(4), 275-277, O 96.

**Davis, Michael**. *The Politics of Philosophy: A Commentary on Aristotle's Politics*. Lanham, Rowman & Littlefield, 1996.
Dink, Michael. *Rev Metaph*, 50(4), 874-876, Je 97.

**Davis, Philip J**, Hersh, Reuben and Marchisotto, Elena Anne. *The Companion Guide to the Mathematical Experience Study Edition*. Basel, Birkhauser, 1995.
Burgess, John P. *Phil Math*, 5(2), 175-180, Je 97.
Ernest, Paul. *Phil Math*, 5(2), 181-188, Je 97.

**Davis, Philip J**, Hersh, Reuben and Marchisotto, Elena Anne. *The Mathematical Experience Study Guide*. Basel, Birkhauser, 1995.
Burgess, John P. *Phil Math*, 5(2), 175-180, Je 97.
Burgess, John P. *Phil Math*, 5(2), 181-188, Je 97.

**De Boer, N Theo** and Griffioen, Sander. *Pluralisme: cultuurfilosofische beschouwingen*. Meppel, Boom, 1995.
Hoogland, Jan. *Phil Reform*, 61(2), 211-218, 1996.

**De Duve, Christian**. *Vital Dust: Life as a Cosmic Imperative*. New York, Basic Books, 1995.
Peterson, Gregory R. *Zygon*, 32(3), 261-262, Je 97.

**De Gandt, François**. *Force and Geometry in Newton's Principia*. Princeton, Princeton Univ Pr, 1995.
Ellis, Brian. *Brit J Phil Sci*, 47(4), 636-639, D 96.
Malet, Antoni. *Mathesis*, 11(4), 395-399, Nov 95.

**De George, Richard T**. *Competing with Integrity in International Business*. New York, Oxford Univ Pr, 1993.
Brenkert, George G. *J Bus Ethics*, 16(1), 6,22,36, Ja 97.

**De Koninck, Thomas**. *De la dignité humaine*. Paris, Pr Univ France, 1995.
Deprex, Stanislas. *Rev Phil Louvain*, 94(4), 703-707, N 96.

**De Libera, Alain**. *La philosophie médiévale*. Paris, Pr Univ France, 1993.
Lafleur, Claude. *Dialogue (Canada)*, 35(3), 611-614, Sum 96.

**De Libera, Alain**. *La querelle des universaux: De Platon à la fin du Moyen Age*. Paris, Ed du Seuil, 1996.
Pasqua, Hervé. *Rev Phil Louvain*, 94(2), 346-354, M 96.

**De Libera, Alain**. *Storia della filosofia medievale*. Milano, Jaca Books, 1995.
Portalupi, Enzo. *Riv Filosof Neo-Scolas*, 88(2), 343-351, Ap-Ag 96.

**De Libera, Alain**. *Thomas d'Aquin contre Averroès*. Paris, Flammarion, 1994.
Pasqua, Hervé. *Rev Phil Louvain*, 94(2), 354-359, M 96.

**De Marzi, Giacomo**. *Piero Gobetti e Benedetto Croce*. Urbino, Quattroventi, 1996.
Recchi, Antonio. *Riv Int Filosof Diritto*, 74(4), 371-372, Ap-Je 97.

**De Muralt, André**. *Néoplatonisme et aristotélisme dans la métaphysique médiévale*. Paris, Vrin, 1995.
Pasqua, Hervé. *Rev Phil Louvain*, 94(2), 341-346, M 96.

**De Pisan, Christine** and Forham, Kate Langdon (ed & trans). *The Book of the Body Politic*. Cambridge, Cambridge Univ Pr, 1994.
Clark, Paul. *Rev Metaph*, 50(1), 148-149, S 96.

**De Regt, Herman**. *Representing the World by Scientific Theories: The Case for Scientific Realism*. Tilburg, Tilburg Univ Pr, 1994.
Ladyman, James. *Brit J Phil Sci*, 47(3), 487-490, S 96.

**De Romilly, Jacqueline** and Lloyd, Janet (trans). *The Great Sophists in Periclean Athens*. New York, Clarendon/Oxford Pr, 1992.
Schiappa, Edward. *Phil Rhet*, 29(4), 447-451, 1996.

**De S Camerson, Nigel M** (ed). *Death without Dignity: Euthanasia in Perspective*. Edinburgh, Rutherford House, 1990.
Sealey, Margaret M. *Ethics Med*, 12(3), 69-70, 1996.

**De Santis, M Gabriella**. *La politica scolastica dal fascismo al dopoguerra: dalla Riforma Gentile ai programmi del 1945*. X, Unknown, 1995.
Todisco, Orlando. *Sapienza*, 49(4), 472-475, 1996.

**De Tienne, André**. *L'analytique de la représentation chez Peirce*. Brussels, Pub Fac Un St Louis, 1996.
Poirier, Pierre. *Can Phil Rev*, 16(4), 251-253, Ag 96.

**De Vitiis, Pietro**. *Il problema religioso in Heidegger*. Rome, Bulzoni, 1995.
Monaco, Amalia. *G Metaf*, 18(3), 485-487, S-D 96.
Pellegrino, Antonia. *Teoria*, 16(1), 130-132, 1996.

**De-Shalit, Avner**. *Why Posterity Matters: Environmental Policies and Future Generations*. London, Routledge, 1995.
Roxbee Cox, Jeremy. *Phil Quart*, 47(186), 130-132, Ja 97.

**Dean, Thomas** (ed). *Religious Pluralism and Truth*. Albany, SUNY Pr, 1995.
Levine, Michael P. *Asian Phil*, 6(3), 238-241, N 96.
Sweet, William. *Can Phil Rev*, 16(4), 249-250, Ag 96.

**Dear, Peter**. *Discipline and Experience: The Mathematical Way in the Scientific Revolution*. Chicago, Univ of Chicago Pr, 1995.
Grene, Marjorie. *Brit J Phil Sci*, 48(1), 113-116, Mr 97.

**DeBellis, Mark**. *Music and Conceptualization*. New York, Cambridge Univ Pr, 1995.
Ridley, Aaron. *Brit J Aes*, 37(2), 187-189, Ap 97.
Skokowski, Paul. *Mind*, 106(423), 599-602, Jl 97.

**Debray, Régis**. *Media Manifestos: On the Technical Transmission of Cultural Forms*. New York, Verso, 1996.
Dauncey, Hugh. *Rad Phil*, 83, 50-51, My-J3 97.

**Deleuze, Gilles**. *Negotiations, 1972-1990*. New York, Columbia Univ Pr, 1995.
Stagoll, Cliff. *Brit J Aes*, 37(3), 290-291, Jl 97.

**Deleuze, Gilles** and Patton, Paul (trans). *Difference and Repetition*. New York, Columbia Univ Pr, 1994.
Colwell, C. *Int Stud Phil*, 29(1), 132-133, 1997.

**Delval, Juan** and Enesco, Ileana. *Moral, Desarrollo y Educación*. Madrid, Anaya, 1994.
Verde, Carmen. *Telos (Spain)*, 5(1), 165-169, Je 96.

**DeMarco, Joseph P**. *Moral Theory: A Contemporary Overview*. Boston, Jones & Bartlett, 1996.
Leever, Martin G. *Teach Phil*, 19(4), 410-412, D 96.

**Denkel, Arda**. *Object and Property*. Cambridge, Cambridge Univ Pr, 1996.
Fantl, Jeremy. *Can Phil Rev*, 17(3), 162-164, Je 97.
Merricks, Trenton. *Mind*, 105(420), 694-696, O 96.

**Dennett, Daniel**. *Kinds of minds*. New York, Basic Books, 1996.
Fetzer, James H. *Phil Psych*, 10(1), 113-115, Mr 97.

**Dennett, Daniel C**. *Darwin's Dangerous Idea*. New York, Simon & Schuster, 1995.
Cribbs, Henry. *Phil Psych*, 10(1), 115-117, Mr 97.
Gallagher, Kenneth T. *Int Phil Quart*, 36(4), 487-489, D 96.
Lennox, James G. *Rev Metaph*, 50(3), 652-654, Mr 97.
Thompson, Nicholas S. *Behavior Phil*, 24(2), 169-173, Fall 96.

**Dennett, Daniel D**. *Kinds of Minds*. X, Unknown, 1996.
Prades, J L. *Teorema*, 16(2), 117-120, 1997.

**Denning, Dorothy E** (ed) and Lin, Herbert S (ed). *Rights and Responsibilities of Participants in Networked Communities*. Washington, National Acad Pr, 1994.
Behar, Joseph E. *J Infor Ethics*, 5(2), 87-90, Fall 96.

**Dentone, Adriana**. *Fra conscio e inconscio*. X, Unknown, 1996.
Bracco, Michele. *Aquinas*, 39(3), 621-324, S-D 96.

**Denyer, Nicholas**. *Language, Thought and Falsehood in Ancient Greek Philosophy*. New York, Routledge, 1991.
White, Nicholas. *Mind*, 105(420), 696-699, O 96.

**DePaul, Michael R**. *Balance and Refinement*. New York, Routledge, 1993.
Copp, David. *Phil Phenomenol Res*, 56(4), 959-962, D 96.

**Depew, Daniel J** and Weber, Bruce H. *Darwinism Evolving: Systems Dynamics and the Genealogy of Natural Selection*. Cambridge, MIT Pr, 1995.
Griffiths, Paul E. *Biol Phil*, 12(3), 421-426, Jl 97.
Sterelny, Kim. *Brit J Phil Sci*, 47(4), 640-646, D 96.

**Derksen, Anthony A** (ed). *The Scientific Realism of Rom Harré*. Tilburg, Tilburg Univ Pr, 1994.
Hooker, C A. *Brit J Phil Sci*, 47(4), 647-653, D 96.

**Derksen, L D**. *Dialogues on Women, Images of Women in the History of Philosophy*. Amsterdam, Vandenhoeck, 1996.
Brüggemann-Kruijff, Atie. *Phil Reform*, 62(1), 112-117, 1997.

**Derrida, Jacques**. *Specters of Marx*. New York, Routledge, 1994.
Drydyk, Jay. *Can Phil Rev*, 16(5), 329-331, Oct 96.
Horowitz, Gregg. *Constellations*, 3(1), 120-124, Ap 96.

**Derrida, Jacques** and Dutoit, Thomas (trans). *Aporias*. Stanford, Stanford Univ Pr, 1993.
Thorp, Thomas R. *Int Stud Phil*, 29(1), 134, 1997.

**Des Chene, Dennis**. *Physiologia: Natural Philosophy in Late Aristotelian and Cartesian Thought*. Ithaca, Cornell Univ Pr, 1996.
Conley, John J. *Int Phil Quart*, 37(2), 231-232, Je 97.

**Descartes, René** and Quintás, Alianza. *Los principios de la filosofía*. Madrid, Alianza, 1995.
Martínez, José A. *Dialogo Filosof*, 12(3), 467-474, S-D 96.

**Descartes, René** and Ribeiro dos Santos, Leonel (trans). *Princípios da Filosofía*. Lisboa, Presenca, 1995.
Ribeiro Ferreira, Maria Luisa. *Philosophica (Portugal)*, 166-169, 1996.

**Descombes, Vincent** and Schwartz, Stephen Adam (trans). *The Barometer of Modern Reason*. New York, Oxford Univ Pr, 1993.
Baynes, Kenneth. *Constellations*, 2(1), 141-143, Ap 95.

**Desmond, William**. *Being and the Between*. Albany, SUNY Pr, 1995.
Martine, Brian. *Int J Phil Stud*, 5(1), 119-121, Mr 97.
Williamson, George E A. *Can Phil Rev*, 16(5), 331-333, Oct 96.

**Desmond, William**. *Perplexity and Ultimacy*. Albany, SUNY Pr, 1995.
Martine, Brian. *Int J Phil Stud*, 5(1), 119-121, Mr 97.

**Devaraja, N K**. *The Limits of Disagreement: An Essay on Reasoning in Humanistic Disciplines*. Delhi, Indian Inst Adv Stud, 1993.
Sinari, Ramakant. *J Indian Counc Phil Res*, 13(3), 175-178, My-Ag 96.
Singh, Manendra Pratap. *J Indian Counc Phil Res*, 13(3), 169-175, My-Ag 96.

**Devigne, Robert**. *Recasting Conservatism*. New Haven, Yale Univ Pr, 1995.
Johnson, Gregory R. *Rev Metaph*, 50(4), 876-878, Je 97.

**Dewey, John**. *Erfahrung und Natur*. Frankfurt, Suhrkamp, 1995.
Baltzer, Ulrich. *Phil Rundsch*, 44(2), 178-180, Je 97.

**Dews, Peter**. *The Limits of Disenchantment: Essays on Contemporary European Philosophy*. New York, Verso, 1995.
Saar, Martin. *Constellations*, 3(3), 417-420, Ja 97.
Smith, Nick. *Rad Phil*, 80, 40-42, N-D 96.

**Díaz, Esther**. *La producción de los conceptos científicos*. Buenos Aires, Ed Biblos, 1994.
Massa, Javier. *Convivium*, 9, 146-148, 1996.

**Dieterlen, Paulette**. *Marxismo analítico: explicaciones funcionales e intenciones*. Mexico, UNAM, 1995.
Jiménez Ramos, Omar. *Topicos*, 73-80, 1996.

**Dillon, Robin** (ed). *Dignity, Character, and Self-Respect*. New York, Routledge, 1995.
Paden, Roger. *Rev Metaph*, 50(4), 878-879, Je 97.

**Dilworth, Craig**. *Scientific Progress*. Dordrecht, Kluwer, 1986.
Oderberg, David S. *Ratio*, 10(2), 188-194, S 97.

**Dilworth, Craig**. *The Metaphysics of Science*. Dordrecht, Kluwer, 1996.
Bird, Alexander. *Brit J Phil Sci*, 48(2), 284-286, Je 97.
Oderberg, David S. *Ratio*, 10(2), 188-194, S 97.
Weinert, F. *Philosophy*, 72(280), 330-334, Apr 97.

**Dinwidy, John**. *Bentham*. New York, Oxford Univ Pr, 1989.
Martínez, Pilar. *Telos (Spain)*, 5(1), 125-134, Je 96.

**Diotima**. *La sapienza di partire da sé*. Napoli, Liguori Ed, 1996.
Tommasi, Wanda. *Iride*, 10(20), 179-181, Ap 97.

**Diprose, Rosalyn**. *The Bodies of Women: Ethics, embodiment and sexual difference*. London, Routledge, 1994.
Dhanda, Meena. *J Applied Phil*, 13(3), 327-328, 1996.

**Disch, Lisa Jane**. *Hannah Arendt and the Limits of Philosophy*. Ithaca, Cornell Univ Pr, 1995.
Stone-Mediatore, Shari. *Hypatia*, 11(3), 164-168, Sum 96.

**Dobson, Andrew**. *Jean-Paul Sartre and the Politics of Reason*. New York, Cambridge Univ Pr, 1993.
Catalano, Joseph S. *Int Stud Phil*, 29(1), 135, 1997.
Lee, Matthew. *Can Phil Rev*, 16(6), 394-396, D 96.

**Dolby Mugica, M**. *El hombre es imagen de Dios*. Pamplona, EUNSA, 1993.
Yépez, Mercedes Pinto. *Rev Filosof (Venezuela)*, Supp(2-3), 149-152, 1996.

**Dolby Mugica, M**. *Sócrates en el Siglo XX*. Barcelonas, Ed Universitaires, 1995.
Pinto Yépez, Mercedes. *Rev Filosof (Venezuela)*, 23(1), 128-130, 1996.

**Domanski, Juliusz**. *La philosophie, théorie ou manière de vivre?*. X, Unknown, 1996.
Kielbasa, Jan. *Kwartalnik Filozof*, 24(4), 217-222, 1996.

**Domínguez, A** (ed & trans). *Biografías de Spinoza*. Madrid, Alianza, 1995.
Lastra, Antonio. *Daimon Rev Filosof*, 12, 149-151, Ja-Je 96.

**Domínguez, Atilano** (ed). *Spinoza y España*. Castilla, Ed Univ Castilla, 1994.
Mármol Rodríguez, Purificación. *Daimon Rev Filosof*, 10, 156-158, Ja-Je 95.

**Dorato, Mauro**. *Time and Reality: Spacetime Physics and the Objectivity of Temporal Becoming*. Bologna, Clueb, 1995.
Callender, Craig. *Brit J Phil Sci*, 48(1), 117-120, Mr 97.

**Dorrien, Gary**. *Soul in Society: The Making and Renewal of Social Christianity*. Minneapolis, Fortress Pr, 1995.
Hauerwas, Stanley. *Mod Theol*, 13(3), 418-421, Jl 97.

**Dorter, Kenneth**. *Form and Good in Plato's Eleatic Dialogues*. Berkeley, Univ of Calif Pr, 1994.
Berman, Scott. *Ancient Phil*, 16(2), 487-491, Fall 96.
Malmsheimer, Arne. *Bochumer Phil Jrbh*, 1, 244-251, 1996.

**Douglass, R Bruce** and Hollenbach, David. *Catholicism and Liberalism*. Cambridge, Cambridge Univ Pr, 1994.
Weithman, Paul J. *Faith Phil*, 13(1), 140-146, Ja 96.

**Dowling, Linda**. *Hellenism and Homosexuality in Victorian Oxford*. Ithaca, Cornell Univ Pr, 1994.
Wald, Priscilla. *Clio*, 26(1), 124-132, Fall 96.

**Dowling, Linda**. *The Vulgarization of Art: The Victorians and Aesthetic Democracy*. Charlottesville, Univ Pr of Virginia, 1966.
Kirchhoff, Frederick. *Clio*, 26(2), 256-260, Wint 97.

**Downie, R S** (ed). *The Healing Arts*. New York, Oxford Univ Pr, 1994.
Gunderman, Richard. *Theor Med*, 18(3), 329-332, S 97.

**Dray, William H**. *History as Re-enactment: R.G. Collingwood's Idea of History*. New York, Oxford Univ Pr, 1995.
Pompa, Leon. *Phil Books*, 38(3), 194-196, Jl 97.
Tucker, Aviezer. *Phil Soc Sci*, 27(1), 102-129, Mr 97.
Van Gelder, Frederik. *Can Phil Rev*, 17(1), 25-27, F 97.

**Drees, Willem B**. *Religion, Science and Naturalism*. Cambridge, Cambridge Univ Pr, 1996.
Doede, Robert. *Relig Stud*, 33(1), 125-127, Mr 97.

**Dretske, Fred**. *Naturalizing the Mind*. Cambridge, MIT Pr, 1995.
Aizwa, Kenneth. *Mind Mach*, 6(3), 425-430, O 96.
Bach, Kent. *Phil Phenomenol Res*, 57(2), 459-468, Je 97.
Bailey, Andrew. *J Consciousness Stud*, 4(3), 274-277, 1997.
Browne, Derek. *Austl J Phil*, 75(1), 112-114, Mr 97.
José Acero, Juan. *Teorema*, 16(2), 111-114, 1997.
Macdonald, Cynthia. *Philosophy*, 72(279), 150-154, Ja 97.
Skokowski, Paul. *Mind Lang*, 11(4), 452-457, D 96.

**Dubarle, Dominique**. *L'ontologie de Thomas d'Aquin*. Paris, Ed du Cerf, 1990.
Tourpe, Emmanuel. *Rev Phil Louvain*, 94(4), 687-691, N 96.

**Dueso, José Solana**. *Los Sofistas: Testimonios y Fragmentos*. Barcelona, Cir de Lectores, 1996.
Gorri, Antonio Alegre. *Convivium*, 10, 141-145, 1997.

**Duff, Antony** (ed), Marshall, Sandra (ed) and Emerson Dobash, Rebecca (ed). *Penal Theory and Practice: Tradition and Innovation in Criminal Justice*. Manchester, Manchester Univ Pr, 1994.
Ellis, Anthony. *J Applied Phil*, 13(3), 323-325, 1996.

**Dummett, Michael**. *Frege: Philosophy of Mathematics*. Cambridge, Harvard Univ Pr, 1991.
Parsons, Charles. *Phil Rev*, 105(4), 540-547, O 96.
Simons, Peter. *J Sym Log*, 61(4), 1389-1391, D 96.

**Dummett, Michael**. *The Logical Basis of Metaphysics*. Cambridge, Harvard Univ Pr, 1991.
Clarke, D S. *Philosophia (Israel)*, 25(1-4), 453-459, Ap 97.

**Dummett, Michael**. *The Seas of Language*. New York, Clarendon/Oxford Pr, 1993.
Buekens, F. *Tijdschr Filosof*, 58(4), 781-782, D 96.

**Duns Scotus, John**. *Contingency and Freedom: Lectura I 39*. Dordrecht, Kluwer, 1994.
Noone, Timothy. *Thomist*, 60(3), 506-509, Jl 96.

**Dupré, Louis**. *Passage to Modernity: An Essay in the Hermeneutics of Nature and Culture*. New Haven, Yale Univ Pr, 1993.
Joy, Lynn S. *Faith Phil*, 13(3), 447-449, Jl 96.
Piercey, Robert. *Can Phil Rev*, 16(4), 253-254, Ag 96.

**Durkheim, Émile**. *Sociologia, educacao e moral*. X, Unknown, 1995.
Fonseca Vieira, Márcia Núbia. *Educ Filosof*, 10(19), 195-200, Ja-Je 96.

**Dussel, E**. *Las metáforas teológicas de Marx*. Navarra, Unknown, 1993.
Alvarez Pérez, Manuel. *Agora (Spain)*, 15(1), 192-195, 1996.

**Dussel, Enrique**. *The Underside of Modernity: Apel, Ricoeur, Rorty, Taylor, and the Philosophy of Liberation*. Atlantic Highlands, Humanities Pr, 1996.
Barber, Michael D. *Mod Sch*, 74(1), 67-69, N 96.

**Dworkin, Ronald**. *Freedom's Law: The Moral Reading of the American Constitution*. Cambridge, Harvard Univ Pr, 1996.
Kelbley, Charles. *Int Phil Quart*, 37(2), 232-235, Je 97.

**Dworkin, Ronald**. *Life's Dominion*. New York, HarperCollins, 1993.
Marquis, Don. *Phil Soc Crit*, 22(6), 127-131, 1996.
Salles, Arleen L F. *Rev Latin de Filosof*, 22(2), 364-366, 1996.

**Dybikowski, James**. *On Burning Ground: An Examination of the Ideas, Projects and Life of David Williams*. Oxford, Voltaire Taylor Inst, 1993.
Gunn, J A W. *Dialogue (Canada)*, 35(3), 639-641, Sum 96.

**Earman, John**. *Bangs, Crunches, Whimpers and Shrieks: Singularities and Acausalities in Relativistic Spacetimes*. Oxford, Oxford Univ Pr, 1995.
Hodgson, P E. *Int Phil Quart*, 36(4), 494-495, D 96.

**Earman, John**. *Bayes or Bust?*. Cambridge, MIT Pr, 1992.
Fahrbach, Ludwig. *Erkenntnis*, 46(1), 127-131, Ja 97.

**Earman, John** (ed), Janis, Allen I (ed) and Massey, J (ed). *Philosophical Problems of the Internal and External Worlds: Essays on the Philosophy of Adolf Grünbaum*. Pittsburgh, Univ of Pitt Pr, 1993.
Ellis, Brian. *Austl J Phil*, 74(3), 517-519, S 96.
Kilmister, Clive. *Stud Hist Phil Mod Physics*, 27B(4), 525-531, D 96.

**Ebbinghaus, Julius**. *Gesammelte Schriften*. X, Unknown, 1994.
Siep, Ludwig. *Z Phil Forsch*, 50(3), 495-502, Jl-S 96.

**Ebert, Theodor**. *Sokrates als Pythagoreer und die Anamnesis in Platons*. Stuttgart, Steiner Verlag, 1994.
Ferwerda, Rein. *Ancient Phil*, 17(2), 182-185, Spr 97.

**Echeverria, Javier** (ed), Ibarra, A (ed) and Mormann, T (ed). *The Space of Mathematics*. Hawthorne, de Gruyter, 1992.
Diederich, Werner. *Erkenntnis*, 45(1), 119-122, July 96.

**Edmundson, Mark**. *Literature Against Philosophy, Plato to Derrida: A Defense of Poetry*. New York, Cambridge Univ Pr, 1995.
Hedeen, Paul M. *Phil Lit*, 20(2), 538-540, O 96.
Reeves, Charles Eric. *J Aes Art Crit*, 55(1), 68-70, Wint 97.

**Edwards, Paul**. *Reincarnation: A Critical Examination*. Amherst, Prometheus, 1996.
Dilley, Frank B. *Int J Phil Relig*, 42(1), 61-63, Ag 97.

**Eells, Ellery** (ed) and Skyrms, Brian (ed). *Probability and Conditionals: Belief Revision and Rational Decision*. New York, Cambridge Univ Pr, 1994.
Koons, Robert C. *J Sym Log*, 62(1), 330-335, Mr 97.
Slater, Hartley. *Erkenntnis*, 46(2), 273-276, Mr 97.

**Ehman, Robert R**. *The Authentic Self*. Buffalo, Prometheus, 1994.
Halpern, Beth. *Int Stud Phil*, 28(4), 113-114, 1996.

**Eldridge, Richard** (ed). *Beyond Representation: Philosophy and Poetic Imagination*. New York, Cambridge Univ Pr, 1996.
Sharpe, R A. *Brit J Aes*, 37(3), 297-298, Jl 97.

**Elliott, Carl**. *The Rules of Insanity: Moral Responsibility and the Mentally Ill Offender*. Albany, SUNY Pr, 1996.
Clark, Michael. *Phil Books*, 38(3), 214-215, Jl 97.
Davie, Will. *J Applied Phil*, 14(2), 199-200, 1997.

**Elster, Jon**. *Lógica y Sociedad*. Barcelona, Gedisa, 1994.
Ambrosini, Cristina. *Cuad Etica*, 17-18, 174-178, 1994.

**Emberley, Peter C**. *Values, Education and Technology: The Ideology of Dispossession*. Toronto, Univ of Toronto Pr, 1995.
Wegierski, Mark. *Rev Metaph*, 50(4), 884-886, Je 97.

**Emery, Gilles**. *La Trinité Créatrice*. Paris, Vrin, 1995.
Houser, R E. *Thomist*, 60(3), 493-497, Jl 96.

**Emery, S W**. *Plato's Euthyphro, Apology and Crito*. Lanham, Univ Pr of America, 1995.
Crooks, James. *Can Phil Rev*, 16(4), 245-246, Ag 96.

**Empiricus, Sextus**. *Contro Gli Etici*. Naples, Bibliopolis, 1995.
Ferwerda, Rein. *Ancient Phil*, 16(2), 533-536, Fall 96.

**Engel, Pascal**. *Davidson et la philosophie du langage*. Paris, Pr Univ France, 1994.
Cayla, Fabien. *Rev Phil Fr*, 1, 65-67, Ja-Mr 97.

**Engel, Pascal**. *Philosophie et psychologie*. Paris, Gallimard, 1996.
Faucher, Luc. *Can Phil Rev*, 17(1), 28-30, F 97.
Leclercq, Bruno. *Rev Phil Louvain*, 94(4), 710-715, N 96.

**Engelhardt, H Tristam** (ed) and Pinkard, Terry (ed). *Hegel Reconsidered*. Dordrecht, Kluwer, 1994.
D'Oro, Josie. *Brit J Hist Phil*, 4(2), 441-443, S 96.

**Engelhardt, Hans-Tristan**. *Los fundamentos de la bioética*. Barcelona, Paidós, 1995.
Cecchetto, Sergio. *Cuad Etica*, 21-22, 183-185, 1996.

**Engstrom, Stephen** (ed) and Whiting, Jennifer (ed). *Aristotle, Kant, and the Stoics: Rethinking Happiness and Duty*. New York, Cambridge Univ Pr, 1996.
McKerlie, Dennis. *Can Phil Rev*, 17(3), 165-167, Je 97.

**Enos, Richard Leo**. *Roman Rhetoric: Revolution and the Greek Influence*. Prospect Heights, Waveland Pr, 1995.
Mifsud, Marilee. *Phil Rhet*, 30(1), 101-104, 1997.

**Erikson, Kai**. *A New Species of Trouble: Explorations in Disaster, Trauma, and Community*. New York, Norton, 1994.
Cohen, Maurie. *Environ Values*, 5(3), 276-278, Ag 96.

**Eriugena**. *De la division de la Nature*. Paris, Pr Univ France, 1995.
Dutton, Paul Edward. *Rev Metaph*, 50(3), 654-656, Mr 97.

**Erneling, Christina E**. *Understanding Language Acquisition: The Framework of Learning*. Albany, SUNY Pr, 1993.
Shute, Sara. *Int Stud Phil*, 29(2), 125-126, 1997.
Tilghman, Benjamin R. *Dialogue (Canada)*, 36(2), 425-427, Spr 97.

**Erwin, Edward** (ed). *Ethical Issues in Scientific Research: An Anthology*. New York, Garland, 1994.
Hites, Jeanne. *J Infor Ethics*, 5(2), 74-77, Fall 96.

**Etlin, Richard A**. *In Defense of Humanism: Value in the Arts and Letters*. New York, Cambridge Univ Pr, 1996.
Kieran, Matthew. *Brit J Aes*, 37(3), 292-294, Jl 97.

**Euler, Leonhard**. *Método de máximos y mínimos*. X, Unknown, 1993.
Hernández, Jesús. *Mathesis*, 11(4), 383-394, Nov 95.

**Everson, Stephen** (ed). *Companions to Ancient Thought 3: Language*. New York, Cambridge Univ Pr, 1994.
Carson, Scott. *Phil Books*, 37(4), 251-254, O 96.
Ketchum, Richard J. *Ancient Phil*, 16(2), 540-546, Fall 96.
Silverman, Allan. *Phil Rev*, 105(2), 241-243, Ap 96.

**Faerna, Angel Manuel**. *Introducción a la teoría pragmatista del conocimiento*. Madrid, Siglo Veintiuno, 1996.
Mendieta, Eduardo. *Trans Peirce Soc*, 33(3), 796-799, Sum 97.

**Fairbairn, Gavin**. *Contemplating Suicide: The language and ethics of self harm*. London, Routledge, 1995.
Campbell, Robert. *J Applied Phil*, 13(2), 225-226, 1996.
Mayo, David J. *Bioethics*, 10(4), 350-352, O 96.

**Fakhry, Majid**. *Philosophy, Dogma and the Impact of Greek Thought in Islam*. Brookfield, Variorum, 1994.
Bussanich, John. *Thomist*, 61(2), 282-283, Ap 97.

**Falcioni, Daniela**. *Natura e libertà in Kant*. Rome, Bulzoni, 1995.
Simari, Andrea. *Riv Int Filosof Diritto*, 74(4), 372-375, Ap-Je 97.

**Falco, Maria J**. *Feminist Interpretations of Mary Wollstonecraft*. University Park, Penn St Univ Pr, 1996.
Stanlick, Nancy A. *Hypatia*, 12(1), 179-182, Wint 97.

**Falkenstein, Lorne**. *Kant's Intuitionism: A Commentary on the Transcendental Aesthetic*. Toronto, Univ of Toronto Pr, 1996.
Adair-Toteff, Christopher. *Int J Phil Stud*, 5(1), 124-125, Mr 97.
Conard, Mark T. *Can Phil Rev*, 16(5), 333-335, Oct 96.

**Fankhauser, Samuel**. *Valuing Climate Change*. London, Earthscan, 1995.
Price, Colin. *Environ Values*, 6(3), 368-369, Ag 97.

**Farago, Claire** (ed). *Reframing the Renaissance*. New Haven, Yale Univ Pr, 1995.
Gash, John. *Brit J Aes*, 37(2), 179-180, Ap 97.

**Fauconnier, Gilles**. *Mental Spaces: Aspects of Meaning Construction in Natural Language*. Cambridge, Cambridge Univ Pr, 1994.
Abbott, Barbara. *Mind Mach*, 6(2), 239-242, My 96.

**Favrholdt, David**. *Niels Bohr's Philosophical Background*. Copenhagen, Royal Book, 1992.
Lacki, Jan. *Dialectica*, 50(4), 291-303, 1996.

**Feagin, Susan**. *Reading with Feeling*. Ithaca, Cornell Univ Pr, 1996.
Novitz, David. *Phil Lit*, 21(1), 201-204, Ap 97.

**Feinberg, Joel**. *Freedom and Fulfillment: Philosophical Essays*. Princeton, Princeton Univ Pr, 1992.
Wellman, Carl. *Phil Rev*, 105(3), 413-415, Jl 96.

**Feinberg, Joel** (ed) and Gross, Hyman (ed). *Philosophy of Law, 5th Edition*. Belmont, Wadsworth, 1995.
Gruber, David F. *Teach Phil*, 20(1), 75-77, Mr 97.

**Fellmann, Ferdinand**. *Phänomenologie als ästhetische Theorie*. Freiburg, Alber, 1989.
Volontè, Paolo. *Husserl Stud*, 13(2), 183-190, 1996-97.

**Felt, James W**. *Making Sense of Your Freedom*. Ithaca, Cornell Univ Pr, 1994.
Gunter, Pete A Y. *Int Phil Quart*, 37(1), 119-120, Mr 97.
Pols, Edward. *Faith Phil*, 14(2), 259-261, Ap 97.

**Fenner, David E W** (ed). *Ethics and the Arts: An Anthology*. New York, Garland, 1995.
Black, Sam. *Brit J Aes*, 37(2), 189-191, Ap 97.

**Ferguson, A**. *Essai sur l'histoire de la société civile*. Paris, PUF, 1992.
Lazzeri, Christian. *Arch Phil*, 59(3), 494-495, Jl-S 96.

**Ferraris, Maurizio**. *L'immaginazione*. Bologna, Il Mulino, 1996.
Desideri, Fabrizio. *Iride*, 10(20), 182-184, Ap 97.

**Ferré, Frederick**. *Being and Value: Toward a Constructive Postmodern Metaphysics*. Albany, SUNY Pr, 1996.
Allan, George. *Rev Metaph*, 50(3), 656-658, Mr 97.
Hargrove, Eugene C. *Can Phil Rev*, 16(5), 336-339, Oct 96.

**Ferré, Frederick**. *Hellfire and Lightening Rods: Liberating Science, Technology, and Religion*. Maryknoll, Orbis, 1993.
George, Allan. *Process Stud*, 25, 120-124, 1996.

**Ferry, Jean-Marc**. *L'éthique reconstructive*. Paris, Ed du Cerf, 1996.
Lemaire, Philippe. *Rev Phil Louvain*, 95(1), 174-176, 1997.

**Feyerabend, Paul**. *Killing Time*. Chicago, Univ of Chicago Pr, 1995.
McCarney, Joseph. *Rad Phil*, 79, 49-50, S-O 96.
Nola, Robert. *Brit J Phil Sci*, 47(3), 467-473, S 96.

**Fichte, Johann Gottlieb**. *Introductions to the Wissenschaftslehre and Other Writings (1797-1800)*. Indianapolis, Hackett, 1994.
Bowman, Curtis. *Owl Minerva*, 28(1), 81-88, Fall 96.

**Fichte, Johann Gottlieb** and Breazeale, Daniel (ed & trans). *Foundations of Transcendental Philosophy*. Ithaca, Cornell Univ Pr, 1992.
Bowman, Curtis. *Owl Minerva*, 28(1), 81-88, Fall 96.

**Fichte, Johann Gottlieb**, Lauth, Reinhard (ed) and Glivitzsky, Hans (ed). *Gesamtausgabe der Bayerischen Akademien der Wissenschaften*. X, Unknown, 1994.
Ameriks, Karl. *Rev Metaph*, 50(1), 151-153, S 96.

**Gaarder, J**. *El mundo de Sofía*. Madrid, Ed Siruela, 1995.
Pinto Yépez, Mercedes. *Rev Filosof (Venezuela)*, 23(1), 127-128, 1996.

**Gabbard, Krin** (ed). *Jazz Among the Discourses*. Durham, Duke Univ Pr, 1995.
Brown, Lee B. *J Aes Art Crit*, 55(3), 325-329, Sum 97.

**Gabbard, Krin** (ed). *Representing Jazz*. Durham, Duke Univ Pr, 1995.
Brown, Lee B. *J Aes Art Crit*, 55(3), 325-329, Sum 97.

**Gadamer, H G**. *La Philosophie herméneutique*. Paris, Pr Univ France, 1996.
Soussana, Gad. *Can Phil Rev*, 17(2), 87-90, Ap 97.

**Gadamer, Hans-Georg**. *La philosophie herméneutique*. Paris, Pr Univ France, 1996.
Bouckaert, Bertrand. *Rev Phil Louvain*, 94(4), 708-710, N 96.

**Gadamer, Hans-Georg**. *The Enigma of Health: The Art of Healing in a Scientific Age*. Stanford, Stanford Univ Pr, 1996.
Whelton, Beverly J. *Rev Metaph*, 50(4), 889-891, Je 97.

**Gaeta, G**, Bettinelli, C and Dal Lago, A. *Vite attive: Simone Weil, Edith Stein, Hannah Arendt*. Rome, Ed Lavoro, 1996.
Briganti, M Camilla. *Aquinas*, 39(3), 626-628, S-D 96.

**Galipeau, Claude J**. *Isaiah Berlin's Liberalism*. Oxford, Oxford Univ Pr, 1994.
Horton, John. *Hist Polit Thought*, 18(1), 164-169, Spr 97.

**Gallagher, David M**. *Thomas Aquinas and His Legacy*. Washington, Cath Univ Amer Pr, 1994.
Fox, Rory. *Heythrop J*, 38(1), 112-113, Ja 97.
Long, Steven A. *Thomist*, 61(1), 137-142, Ja 97.

**Garcí-Baró, Miguel**. *Categorías, intencionalidad y números*. Madrid, Tecnos, 1993.
Alvarez Pérez, Manuel. *Agora (Spain)*, 15(1), 195-198, 1996.

**García, J L**. *Prácticas paternalistas*. Barcelona, Ariel Pr, 1996.
Herrero, Nieves. *Agora (Spain)*, 15(2), 190-193, 1996.

**Garcia de la Sienra, Adolfo**. *The Logical Foundations of the Marxian Theory of Value*. Dordrecht, Kluwer, 1992.
Balzer, Wolfgang. *Erkenntnis*, 46(1), 133-135, Ja 97.

**García Manzano, Andrés**. *Filosofía natural de las cosmologías relativistas*. Salamanca, Pub Univ Pont Com, 1995.
Francesch, Valèria Gaillard. *Convivium*, 10, 139-141, 1997.

**García Marqués, Alfonso**. *Vico: Unidad y principio del saber*. Valencia, Nau Llibres, 1995.
De La Mora, J M G. *Convivium*, 9, 148-150, 1996.

**García Morente, Manuel**. *De la Metafísica de la Vida a una Teoría General de la Cultura*. X, Unknown, 1995.
De La Mora, J M G. *Convivium*, 9, 150-152, 1996.

**Gardies, Jean-Louis**. *Les fondements sémantiques du discours naturel*. Paris, Vrin, 1994.
Rivenc, François. *Dialogue (Canada)*, 36(1), 197-200, Wint 97.

**Gardner, Sebastian**. *Irrationality and the Philosophy of Psychoanalysis*. New York, Cambridge Univ Pr, 1993.
Cavell, Marcia. *Phil Rev*, 105(3), 405-408, Jl 96.
Cottingham, John. *Phil Quart*, 46(185), 544-546, O 96.

**Garrett, Don** (ed). *The Cambridge Companion to Spinoza*. New York, Cambridge Univ Pr, 1996.
Des Chene, Dennis. *Can Phil Rev*, 17(1), 33-35, F 97.

**Garritano, F**. *Questioni di legge*. Milano, Jaca Books, 1996.
Perrotta, Romolo. *G Metaf*, 19(1), 191-194, Ja-Ap 97.

**Garver, Eugene**. *Aristotle's Rhetoric: An Art of Character*. Chicago, Univ of Chicago Pr, 1994.
Casey, Ken. *Phil Rhet*, 29(4), 436-440, 1996.

**Gasché, Rodolphe**. *Inventions of Difference: On Jacques Derrida*. Cambridge, Harvard Univ Pr, 1994.
Mangiafico, James. *Res Phenomenol*, 26, 292-299, 1996.

**Gates, Brian** (ed). *Freedom and Authority in Religions and Religious Education*. London, Cassell, 1996.
Baumfield, Vivienne. *J Moral Educ*, 26(2), 231-233, Je 97.

**Gaukroger, Stephen**. *Descartes: An Intellectual Biography*. New York, Oxford Univ Pr, 1995.
Braddock, Louise. *Phil Invest*, 20(2), 148-152, Ap 97.
Buroker, Jill Vance. *Phil Books*, 38(2), 95-96, Ap 97.
Lloyd, Genevieve. *Austl J Phil*, 75(1), 114-115, Mr 97.
Milton, J R. *Brit J Phil Sci*, 48(2), 302-305, Je 97.

**Gaus, Gerald F**. *Justificatory Liberalism: An Essay on Epistemology and Political Theory*. New York, Oxford Univ Pr, 1996.
McMahon, Christopher. *Ethics*, 107(3), 515-517, Ap 97.

**Gauthier, Yvon**. *La philosophie des sciences*. Montréal, Pr Univ Montreal, 1995.
Tremblay, Frédérick. *Horiz Phil*, 7(1), 133-135, Autumn 96.

**Gavin, William Joseph**. *William James and the Reinstatement of the Vague*. Philadelphia, Temple Univ Pr, 1992.
Reck, Andrew J. *Int Stud Phil*, 28(4), 117-118, 1996.

**Gay, William** and Alekseeva, T A. *Capitalism with a Human Face: The Quest for a Middle Road in Russian Politics*. Lanham, Rowman & Littlefield, 1996.
McBride, William L. *Can Phil Rev*, 16(3), 162-164, Je 96.

**Gaziaux, Eric**. *Morale de la foi et morale autonome*. Leuven, Peeters, 1995.
Tourpe, Emmanuel. *Rev Phil Louvain*, 94(2), 369-371, M 96.

**Gazzaniga, Michael S** (ed). *The cognitive neurosciences*. Cambridge, MIT Pr, 1995.
Christiansen, Morten H. *Phil Psych*, 10(1), 117-122, Mr 97.
Grush, Rick. *Phil Sci*, 64(1), 188-190, Mr 97.

**Gebauer, Gunter** and Wulf, Christoph. *Mimesis: Culture, Art, Society*. Berkeley, Univ of Calif Pr, 1995.
Fendt, Gene. *Phil Lit*, 21(1), 199-201, Ap 97.

**Geertz, Clifford**. *After the Fact: Two Countries, Four Decades, One Anthropologist*. Cambridge, Harvard Univ Pr, 1995.
Inglis, Fred. *Hist Human Sci*, 9(4), 159-165, N 96.

**Geis, Robert J**. *Personal Existence After Death*. Toronto, Scholars Pr, 1995.
Hancock, Curtis L. *Rev Metaph*, 50(1), 154-156, S 96.
Marinoff, Louis. *Can Phil Rev*, 16(6), 396-397, D 96.

**Geison, Gerald L**. *The Private Science of Louis Pasteur*. Princeton, Princeton Univ Pr, 1995.
Slapin, Steven. *Phil Sci*, 63(3), 482-483, S 96.

**Geivett, R Douglas**. *Evil and the Evidence for God*. Philadelphia, Temple Univ Pr, 1993.
Bergmann, Michael. *Faith Phil*, 13(3), 436-441, Jl 96.

**Gellman, Jerome I**. *The Fear, the Trembling, and the Fire*. Lanham, Univ Pr of America, 1994.
Watkin, Julia. *Heythrop J*, 37(4), 500-501, O 96.

**Gellner, Ernest**. *Encounters with Nationalism*. Cambridge, Blackwell, 1994.
Archard, David. *Phil Quart*, 47(188), 415-417, Jl 97.
James, Paul. *Phil Soc Sci*, 27(1), 130-135, Mr 97.

**Gelven, Michael**. *The Quest for the Fine: A Philosophical Inquiry into Judgment, Worth and Existence*. Lanham, Rowman & Littlefield, 1996.
Wilkinson, Robert. *Brit J Aes*, 37(2), 191-193, Ap 97.

**Genova, Judith**. *Wittgenstein: A Way of Seeing*. New York, Routledge, 1995.
McGinn, Marie. *Philosophy*, 72(280), 327-330, Apr 97.
Poirier, Pierre. *Can Phil Rev*, 16(4), 257-259, Ag 96.

**Genovese, Rino**. *La tribù accidentale*. Torino, Bollati Boringhieri, 1995.
Carchia, Gianni. *Iride*, 9(19), 816-818, D 96.

**Gensler, Harry J**. *Formal Ethics*. New York, Routledge, 1996.
Clarke, D S. *Can Phil Rev*, 17(3), 167-169, Je 97.

**George, Robert P**. *Making Men Moral*. New York, Clarendon/Oxford Pr, 1993.
Correas, Carlos I Massini. *Sapientia*, 51(200), 573-578, 1996.
Lee, Patrick. *Rev Metaph*, 50(4), 891-893, Je 97.

**Geras, Norman**. *Solidarity in the Conversation of Humankind: The Ungroundable Liberalism of Richard Rorty*. New York, Verso, 1995.
Calder, Gideon. *Rad Phil*, 80, 47-48, N-D 96.
D'Agostino, Fred. *Austl J Phil*, 74(4), 691-692, D 96.

**Gerhardt, Volker**. *Immanuel Kants Entwurf 'Zum ewigen Frieden'*. Darmstadt, Wiss Buchgesell, 1995.
Mildenberger, Georg. *Z Phil Forsch*, 51(2), 336-339, Ap-Je 97.

**Gerlach, H M** and Sepp, H R (ed). *Husserl in Halle*. Frankfurt, Lang, 1994.
Gunturu, Vanamali. *Husserl Stud*, 13(1), 73-77, 1996.

**Gerson, Lloyd P**. *Plotinus*. New York, Routledge, 1994.
Corrigan, Kevin. *Heythrop J*, 37(4), 495-497, O 96.
Peri, Eric D. *Rev Metaph*, 50(2), 399-400, D 96.

**Gerson, Lloyd P** (trans) and Apostle, Hippocrates G (trans). *Aristotle: Selected Works Third Edition*. Grinnell, Peripatetic Pr, 1991.
Miller, Fred D. *Ancient Phil*, 17(2), 197-206, Spr 97.

**Gewirth, Alan**. *The Community of Rights*. Chicago, Univ of Chicago Pr, 1996.
Rainbolt, George. *Ethics*, 107(4), 733-735, Jl 97.
Upton, Hugh. *Phil Books*, 38(2), 134-136, Ap 97.

**Giannantoni, G** (& other eds). *La tradizione socratica*. Naples, Bibliopolis, 1995.
Ferwerda, Rein. *Ancient Phil*, 17(2), 164-167, Spr 97.

**Gibbon, Michael**, Limoges, Camille and Nowotny, Helga (& others). *The New Production of Knowledge: The Dynamics of Science and Research in Contemporary Societies*. London, Sage, 1994.
Agassi, Joseph. *Phil Soc Sci*, 27(3), 354-357, S 97.

**Gibbons, Sarah**. *Kant's Theory of Imagination*. New York, Oxford Univ Pr, 1994.
Adair-Toteff, Christopher. *Brit J Hist Phil*, 5(1), 206-210, Mr 97.
Guyer, Paul. *J Aes Art Crit*, 55(3), 337-340, Sum 97.

**Giere, Ronald N** (ed). *Cognitive Models of Science*. Minneapolis, Univ of Minn Pr, 1992.
Allwood, Carl Martin. *Stud Hist Phil Sci*, 27(4), 599-605, D 96.

**Gil, Marta Lopez**. *Obsesiones filosóficas de fin de siglo*. Buenos Aires, Ed Biblos, 1993.
Cohen, Ester. *Cuad Etica*, 15-16, 167-170, 1993.

**Gilbert, Margaret**. *On Social Facts*. New York, Routledge, 1989.
Betzler, Monika. *Phil Rundsch*, 43(4), 325-333, D 96.

**Gilbert, Paul**. *La simplicité du principe*. Namur, Verite, 1994.
Tournier, Francois. *Rev Metaph*, 50(2), 400-402, D 96.

**Gill, Christopher** (ed). *The Discourses of Epictetus*. London, Everyman, 1995.
Stephens, William O. *Ancient Phil*, 17(2), 268-273, Spr 97.

**Gill, Mary Louise** (trans) and Ryan, Paul (trans). *Plato: Parmenides*. Indianapolis, Hackett, 1996.
Ketchum, Richard J. *Can Phil Rev*, 16(6), 398-399, D 96.

**Gilmore, Grant**. *The Death of Contract 2nd Edition*. Columbus, Ohio St Univ Pr, 1995.
Shiner, Roger A. *Can Phil Rev*, 17(2), 90-92, Ap 97.

**Giner, Salvador**. *Carta sobre la democracia*. Barcelona, Ariel Pr, 1996.
Guisán, Esperanza. *Telos (Spain)*, 5(2), 127-128, D 96.

**Girard, Jean-Yves** (ed). *Advances in linear logic*. New York, Cambridge Univ Pr, 1995.
Miller, Dale. *J Sym Log*, 62(2), 678-680, Je 97.

**Giustiniani, Pasquale**. *Filosofia e religione.*. Napoli, Luciano Ed, 1996.
Colonnello, Pio. *Sapienza*, 50(2), 246-248, 1997.

**Givón, T**. *Functionalism and Grammar*. Amsterdam, J Benjamins, 1995.
Dor, Daniel. *Prag Cognition*, 4(2), 428-434, 1996.

**Glock, Hans-Johann**. *A Wittgenstein Dictionary*. Cambridge, Blackwell, 1996.
Morris, Katherine J. *Phil Books*, 38(2), 109-112, Ap 97.
Stern, David G. *Can Phil Rev*, 17(2), 93-95, Ap 97.

**Godfrey-Smith, Peter**. *Complexity and the Function of Mind in Nature*. New York, Cambridge Univ Pr, 1996.
Raymont, Paul. *Can Phil Rev*, 17(1), 35-38, F 97.

**Goetsch, James Robert**. *Vico's Axioms: The Geometry of the Human World*. New Haven, Yale Univ Pr, 1995.
Richardson, Brian. *Can Phil Rev*, 17(1), 38-39, F 97.

**Goetz, Hans**. *To Live is To Think: The Thought of Twentieth-Century German Philosopher Constantin Brunner*. Atlantic Highlands, Humanities Pr, 1995.
Westbrook, David. *Can Phil Rev*, 16(4), 259-260, Ag 96.

**Gold, Steven J** (ed). *Paradigms in Political Theory*. Ames, Iowa St Univ Pr, 1993.
Schultz, David A. *Int Stud Phil*, 29(2), 126-127, 1997.

**Goldaracena, C**. *Bataille y la filosofía*. X, Unknown, 1996.
Soto, L G. *Agora (Spain)*, 15(1), 188-190, 1996.

**Goldin, Owen**. *Explaining an Eclipse*. Ann Arbor, Univ of Michigan Pr, 1996.
Bell, Ian. *Rev Metaph*, 50(4), 893-894, Je 97.
Gerson, Lloyd P. *Can Phil Rev*, 17(1), 39-41, F 97.

**Goldman, Alan H**. *Aesthetic Value*. Boulder, Westview Pr, 1995.
Horvitz, Lee. *Teach Phil*, 19(4), 418-421, D 96.
Wymer, Rowland. *Brit J Aes*, 37(1), 98-101, Ja 97.

**Goldman, Alvin I**. *Liaisons: Philosophy Meets the Cognitive and Social Sciences*. Cambridge, MIT Pr, 1992.
Geirsson, Heimir. *Mind Mach*, 7(2), 306-312, My 97.
Losonsky, Michael. *Mind Mach*, 7(2), 306-312, My 97.

**Goldman, Alvin I**. *Philosophical Applications of Cognitive Science*. Boulder, Westview Pr, 1993.
Geirsson, Heimir. *Mind Mach*, 7(2), 306-312, My 97.
Losonsky, Michael. *Mind Mach*, 7(2), 306-312, My 97.

**Goldman, Alvin I**. *Readings in Philosophy and Cognitive Science*. Cambridge, MIT Pr, 1993.
Geirsson, Heimir. *Mind Mach*, 7(2), 306-312, My 97.
Losonsky, Michael. *Mind Mach*, 7(2), 306-312, My 97.

**Golomb, Jacob**. *In Search of Authenticity: From Kierkegaard to Camus*. New York, Routledge, 1995.
Dooley, Mark. *Int J Phil Stud*, 4(2), 334-336, S 96.

**Gómez, Ricardo**. *Neoliberalismo y seudociencia*. Buenos Aires, Lugar Ed, 1995.
Regnasco, Mario J. *Cuad Etica*, 21-22, 185-189, 1996.

**Gomez Pin, V**. *Descartes: La exigencia filosófica*. X, Unknown, 1996.
Martínez, José A. *Dialogo Filosof*, 12(3), 467-474, S-D 96.

**Gómez-Lobo, Alfonso**. *The Foundations of Socratic Ethics*. Indianapolis, Hackett, 1994.
Taylor, C C W. *Phil Quart*, 47(187), 257-260, Ap 97.
Young, Charles M. *Phil Rev*, 105(2), 233-235, Ap 96.

**González, Ana Marta**. *Naturaleza y dignidad: Un estudio desde Robert Spaemann*. Pamplona, EUNSA, 1996.
Correas, Carlos I Massini. *Sapientia*, 51(200), 578-580, 1996.
Massini Correas, Carlos I. *Analogia*, 10(2), 273-277, 1996.

**Gonzalez Wenceslao, J**. *Acción e Historia*. Coruna, Univ da Coruna, 1996.
Francisco Vázquez, G. *Telos (Spain)*, 5(2), 138-142, D 96.

**Goodell, Edward**. *The Noble Philosopher: Condorcet and the Enlightenment*. Amherst, Prometheus, 1994.
Pickering, Mary. *Int Stud Phil*, 29(2), 127-129, 1997.

**Goodin, Robert E**. *Utilitarianism as a Public Philosophy*. Cambridge, Cambridge Univ Pr, 1995.
Fairfield, Paul. *J Value Inq*, 31(1), 135-138, Mr 97.
McNaughton, David. *Euro J Phil*, 5(2), 224-227, Ag 97.

**Goodman, Dena**. *The Republic of Letters: A Cultural History of the French Enlightenment*. Ithaca, Cornell Univ Pr, 1996.
Kwasniewski, Peter A. *Rev Metaph*, 50(2), 402-403, D 96.

**Goodman, Robert F** (ed) and Ben-Ze'ev, Benjamin (ed). *Good Gossip*. Lawrence, Univ Pr Kansas, 1994.
Telfer, Elizabeth. *Phil Quart*, 46(185), 561-562, O 96.

**Gordillo, Lourdes**. *Trayectoria voluntarista de la libertad*. Valencia, Nau Llibres, 1996.
Dolby Múgica, Carmen. *Dialogo Filosof*, 13(1), 98-101, Ja-Ap 97.
Dolby Múgica, María del Carmen. *Rev Filosof (Venezuela)*, Supp(2-3), 153-157, 1996.

**Gordon, Lewis R**. *Bad Faith and Antiblack Racism*. Atlantic Highlands, Humanities Pr, 1995.
Gordon, Lewis. *Teach Phil*, 19(4), 403-406, D 96.
Martin Alcoff, Linda. *Can Phil Rev*, 17(2), 95-99, Ap 97.

**Gorlin, Rena A** (ed). *Codes of Professional Responsibility*. Washington, Natl Research Cncl, 1995.
Keith-Spiegel, Patricia. *Ethics Behavior*, 6(3), 257-258, 1996.

**Gormally, Luke** (ed). *Euthanasia: Clinical Practice and the Law*. London, Linacre Ctr, 1994.
Iozzio, M J. *Heythrop J*, 38(1), 106-107, Ja 97.

**Gormally, Luke** (ed). *Moral Truth and Moral Tradition*. Dublin, Four Courts Pr, 1994.
Edelman, John T. *Phil Invest*, 20(1), 81-84, J 97.
Johnson, Mark. *Thomist*, 61(3), 493-497, Jl 97.

**Gorman, Jonathan**. *Understanding History: An Introduction to Analytical Philosophy of History*. Ottawa, Univ of Ottawa Pr, 1992.
Tucker, Aviezer. *Phil Soc Sci*, 27(1), 102-129, Mr 97.

**Gosling, Justin**. *Weakness of the Will*. London, Routledge, 1990.
Georgedes, Kimberly. *Vivarium*, 34(2), 275-278, N 96.

**Gottsegen, Michael**. *The Political Thought of Hannah Arendt*. Albany, SUNY Pr, 1994.
Bar On, Bat-Ami. *Int Stud Phil*, 29(1), 136-137, 1997.

**Goyard-Fabre, Simone**. *La construction de la paix ou le travail de Sisyphe*. Paris, Vrin, 1994.
Nguyen, Vinh-De. *Dialogue (Canada)*, 35(3), 636-638, Sum 96.

**Goyard-Fabre, Simone**. *Montesquieu: La Nature, les Lois, la Liberté*. Paris, Pr Univ France, 1993.
Vienne, J M. *Brit J Hist Phil*, 4(2), 432-434, S 96.

**Goyne, G V** (ed), Heller, M (ed) and Zycinski, j (ed). *Newton and the New Direction in Science*. Vatican City, Vaticana, 1988.
Grabbe, Crockett L. *Process Stud*, 23(3-4), 285-288, Fall-Wint 94.
Grabbe, Crockett L. *Process Stud*, 23(3-4), 285-288, Winter 94.

**Graber, Mark A**. *Rethinking Abortion: Equal Choice, the Constitution and Reproductive Politics*. Princeton, Princeton Univ Pr, 1996.
Steinbock, Bonnie. *Ethics*, 107(4), 735-737, Jl 97.

**Gracia, Diego**. *Fundamentos de Bioética*. Madrid, Eudema Univ, 1989.
Pfeiffer, Maria Luisa. *Cuad Etica*, 15-16, 162-164, 1993.

**Gracia, Diego**. *Procedimientos de decisión en ética clínica*. Madrid, Eudema Univ, 1991.
Pfeiffer, Maria Luisa. *Cuad Etica*, 15-16, 164-165, 1993.

**Gracia, Jorge J E**. *A Theory of Textuality: The Logic and Epistemology*. Albany, SUNY Pr, 1995.
Patterson, Dennis. *Rev Metaph*, 50(4), 894-896, Je 97.

**Gracia, Jorge J E** (ed). *Individuation in Scholasticism*. Albany, SUNY Pr, 1994.
Blanchette, Oliva. *Rev Latin de Filosof*, 23(1), 185-187, O 97.

**Grant, George**. *Philosophy in the Mass Age*. Toronto, Univ of Toronto Pr, 1995.
Burns, Steven. *Can Phil Rev*, 16(3), 165-166, Je 96.

**Grant, George**. *Time as History*. Toronto, Univ of Toronto Pr, 1995.
Burns, Steven. *Can Phil Rev*, 16(3), 165-166, Je 96.

**Grassi, Ernesto**. *La filosofía del Humanismo*. Barcelona, Anthropos, 1993.
Damiani, Alberto M. *Cuad Vico*, 7/8, 423-424, 1997.

**Gray, John**. *Enlightenment's Wake: Politics and Culture at the Close of the Modern Age*. New York, Routledge, 1995.
Roberts, Marcus. *Rad Phil*, 79, 41-44, S-O 96.
Wegierski, Mark. *Rev Metaph*, 50(4), 896-898, Je 97.

**Gray, John**. *Isaiah Berlin*. Princeton, Princeton Univ Pr, 1996.
Capaldi, Nicholas. *Rev Metaph*, 50(2), 403-405, D 96.

**Gray, John**. *Mill on Liberty: A Defense, Second Edition*. New York, Routledge, 1996.
Barbanell, Edward M. *Can Phil Rev*, 17(3), 169-172, Je 97.

**Grayling, Anthony** (ed). *Philosophy: A Guide Through the Subject*. New York, Oxford Univ Pr, 1995.
Hamlyn, D W. *Phil Invest*, 20(2), 155-159, Ap 97.
Thomas, Janice. *Heythrop J*, 38(1), 109-110, Ja 97.
Warburton, Nigel. *Phil Quart*, 47(188), 421-422, Jl 97.

**Green, Donald P** and Shapiro, Ian. *Pathologies of Rational Choice Theory: A Critique of Applications in Political Science*. New Haven, Yale Univ Pr, 1994.
Monroe, Kristen Renwick. *Polit Theory*, 25(2), 289-295, Ap 97.

**Greenawalt, Kent**. *Fighting Words: Individuals, Communities, and Liberties of Speech*. Princeton, Princeton Univ Pr, 1995.
Brennan, Samantha. *Can Phil Rev*, 16(5), 348-350, Oct 96.

**Greenawalt, Kent**. *Private Consciences and Public Reasons*. New York, Oxford Univ Pr, 1995.
Estlund, David. *Ethics*, 107(2), 358-361, Ja 97.

**Greenspan, P S**. *Practical Guilt: Moral Dilemmas, Emotions, and Social Norms*. New York, Oxford Univ Pr, 1995.
Vallentyne, Peter. *Phil Rev*, 105(4), 550-552, O 96.

**Grene, Marjorie**. *A Philosophical Testament*. La Salle, Open Court, 1995.
Hull, David L. *Phil Sci*, 64(1), 187-188, Mr 97.

**Grewendorf, Günther**. *Sprache als Organ*. Frankfurt, Suhrkamp, 1995.
Pafel, Jürgen. *Z Phil Forsch*, 51(2), 323-327, Ap-Je 97.

**Griffin, Roger** (ed). *Fascism*. Oxford, Oxford Univ Pr, 1995.
Spektorowski, Alberto. *Hist Polit Thought*, 17(3), 460-462, Autumn 96.

**Griffioen, Sander** (ed) and Balk, Bert M (ed). *Christian Philosophy at the Close of the Twentieth Century*. X, Unknown, 1995.
Dengerink, J D. *Phil Reform*, 61(2), 196-205, 1996.

**Griffiths, A Phillips** (ed). *Philosophy, Psychology and Psychiatry*. Cambridge, Cambridge Univ Pr, 1994.
Bolton, Derek. *Brit J Phil Sci*, 47(3), 474-475, S 96.

**Griffiths, Morwenna**. *Feminisms and Self: The Web of Identity*. New York, Routledge, 1995.
Dhanda, Meena. *Rad Phil*, 81, 46-47, Ja-F 97.
Hogan, Pádraig. *J Phil Educ*, 31(2), 365-368, Jl 97.
Nadesan, Majia Holmer. *Can Phil Rev*, 16(6), 399-402, D 96.

**Griffiths, Morwenna** and Davies, Carol. *In Fairness to Children: working for social justice in the primary school*. London, David Fulton Pr, 1995.
Roth, Jean. *J Moral Educ*, 25(4), 475-476, D 96.

**Griffiths, Paul J**. *On Being Buddha*. Albany, SUNY Pr, 1994.
Phillips, Stephen H. *Int J Phil Relig*, 41(1), 66-69, F 97.

**Grodin, Michael A** (ed). *Meta-Medical Ethics: The Philosophical Foundations of Bioethics*. Dordrecht, Kluwer, 1995.
Schüklenk, Udo. *Bioethics*, 10(4), 341-344, O 96.

**Groethuysen, Bernard** and Dandois, Bernard (ed). *Philosophie Et Histoire*. Paris cedex 14, Albin Michel, 1995.
Gordon, Daniel. *Hist Theor*, 36(2), 289-311, 1997.

**Grondin, Jean**. *Introduction to Philosophical Hermeneutics*. New Haven, Yale Univ Pr, 1994.
Warnke, Georgia. *Phil Rev*, 105(3), 408-410, Jl 96.

**Gross, Paul R** and Levitt, Norman. *Higher Superstition: The Academic Left and Its Quarrels with Science*. Baltimore, Johns Hopkins U Pr, 1994.
Flew, Antony. *Phil Soc Sci*, 27(2), 256-260, Mr 97.

**Grosz, Elizabeth**. *Space, Time and Perversion*. London, Routledge, 1995.
Ainley, Alison. *J Applied Phil*, 14(2), 205-206, 1997.

**Grubb, Andrew** (ed) and Mehlman, Maxwell J (ed). *Justice and Health Care: Comparative Perspectives*. New York, Wiley & Sons, 1995.
Schüklenk, Udo. *Bioethics*, 11(1), 83-85, Ja 97.

**Grünbaum, Adolf**. *Validation in the Clinical Theory of Psychoanalysis*. Madison, Intl Univ Pr, 1993.
Church, Jennifer. *Int Stud Phil*, 29(2), 129-130, 1997.

**Grundmann, Thomas** (ed) and Stüber, Karsten (ed). *Philosophie der Skepsis*. Paderborn, Schoeningh, 1996.
Birke, Marcus. *Z Phil Forsch*, 51(2), 332-335, Ap-Je 97.

**Grundy, Peter**. *Doing Pragmatics*. London, Edward Arnold, 1995.
Mao, LuMing. *Prag Cognition*, 4(2), 416-423, 1996.

**Guagliardo, Vincent A**, Hess, Charles R and Taylor, Richard C. *Commentary on the Book of Causes of St. Thomas Aquinas*. Washington, Cath Univ Amer Pr, 1996.
Tomarchio, John. *Thomist*, 61(3), 477-480, Jl 97.

**Guariglia, Osvaldo**. *Universalismus und Neuaristotelismus in der zeitgenössischen Ethik*. Hildesheim, Olms, 1995.
Ferraro, Agustín E. *Rev Latin de Filosof*, 23(1), 187-190, O 97.

**Günther, Klaus**. *The Sense of Appropriateness: Application Discourses in Morality and Law*. Albany, SUNY Pr, 1993.
Lafont, Maria. *Constellations*, 3(2), 265-273, O 96.

**Gumbrecht, Hans Ulrich** (ed) and Pfeiffer, K Ludwig (ed). *Materialities of Communication*. Stanford, Stanford Univ Pr, 1994.
Buxton, William J. *Phil Soc Sci*, 27(2), 249-255, Je 97.

**Gupta, R K**. *Social Action and Non-Violence*. New Delhi, Indian Coun Phil Res, 1995.
Chopra, Yogendra. *J Indian Counc Phil Res*, 13(2), 200-203, Ja-Ap 96.

**Gustafson, James M**. *A Sense of the Divine: The Natural Environment from a Theocentric Perspective*. Cleveland, Pilgrim Pr, 1994.
Parker, Thomas D. *Zygon*, 32(3), 270-272, Je 97.

**Guthrie, Stewart Elliott**. *Faces in the Clouds: A New Theory of Religion*. New York, Oxford Univ Pr, 1993.
Levesque, Paul J. *Rev Metaph*, 50(3), 660-661, Mr 97.

**Gutmann, Amy** (ed). *Multiculturalism: Examining the Politics of Recognition*. Princeton, Princeton Univ Pr, 1994.
Outlaw, Lucius. *Constellations*, 3(1), 124-129, Ap 96.

**Gutmann, Amy** and Thompson, Dennis. *Democracy and Disagreement*. Cambridge, Harvard Univ Pr, 1996.
Soroski, John. *Can Phil Rev*, 17(2), 100-102, Ap 97.

**Gutowski, Piotr**. *Filozofia procesu i jej metafilozofia*. Lublin, Red Wyd Kato Uni Lub, 1995.
McHenry, Leemon. *Process Stud*, 24, 96-99, 1995.

**Guyer, Paul** (ed). *The Cambridge Companion to Kant*. New York, Cambridge Univ Pr, 1991.
Palmquist, Stephen. *Kantstudien*, 87(3), 369-374, 1996.

**Haac, Oscar A** (ed & trans). *The Correspondence of John Stuart Mill and Auguste Comte*. New Brunswick, Transaction Pub, 1995.
Hamilton, Andy. *Brit J Hist Phil*, 5(1), 211-214, Mr 97.

**Haack, Susan**. *Evidence and Inquiry: Towards Reconstruction in Epistemology*. Cambridge, Blackwell, 1993.
Biro, John. *Int J Phil Stud*, 5(1), 121-123, Mr 97.
Duica, William. *Ideas Valores*, 99-105, Ag 97.
Vassallo, Nicla. *Epistemologia*, 19(1), 184-186, Ja-Je 96.

**Haag, Rudolf**. *Local Quantum Physics*. Berlin, Springer-Verlag, 1992.
Landsman, N P. *Stud Hist Phil Mod Physics*, 27B(4), 511-524, D 96.

**Haas-Spohn, Ulrike**. *Versteckte Indexikalität und subjektive Bedeutung*. Berlin, Akademie, 1995.
Newen, Albert. *Z Phil Forsch*, 51(2), 327-332, Ap-Je 97.

**Habermas, Jürgen**. *La paix perpétuelle*. Paris, Ed du Cerf, 1996.
Lemaire, Philippe. *Rev Phil Louvain*, 95(1), 170-172, 1997.

**Habermas, Jürgen**. *Textes et contextes*. Paris, Ed du Cerf, 1994.
Trotignon, Pierre. *Rev Phil Fr*, 1, 70-72, Ja-Mr 97.

**Habermas, Jürgen**. *The Past as Future*. Lincoln, Univ of Nebraska Pr, 1994.
Gudmundsen, Sandra. *Phil Soc Sci*, 27(2), 265-272, Je 97.

**Habermas, Jürgen**. *Vom sinnlichen Eindruck zum symbolischen Ausdruck*. Frankfurt, Suhrkamp, 1997.
Sciacca, Fabrizio. *Riv Int Filosof Diritto*, 74(4), 375-377, Ap-Je 97.

**Habermas, Jürgen**, Nicholsen, Shierry Weber (trans) and Stark, Jerry A (trans). *On the Logic of the Social Sciences*. Cambridge, MIT Pr, 1988.
Gudmundsen, Sandra. *Phil Soc Sci*, 27(1), 139-146, Mr 97.

**Habermas, Jürgen** and Rawls, John. *Débat sur la justice sociale*. Paris, Ed du Cerf, 1997.
Poltier, Hugues. *Rev Theol Phil*, 129(2), 191-192, 1997.

**Hacking, Ian**. *Rewriting the Soul*. Princeton, Princeton Univ Pr, 1995.
Brook, Andrew. *Can Phil Rev*, 16(6), 402-405, D 96.
Schechtman, Marya. *Mind*, 105(420), 699-703, O 96.
Stephens, Lynn. *Phil Sci*, 64(1), 185-187, Mr 97.
Szawarski, Zbigniew. *Kwartalnik Filozof*, 24(3), 183-193, 1996.

**Hadot, P**. *Qu'est-ce que la philosophie antique?*. Parigi, Gallimard, 1995.
Imhoof, Stefan. *Rev Theol Phil*, 129(2), 173-174, 1997.

**Hadot, Pierre**. *Philosophy as a Way of Life*. Oxford, Blackwell, 1995.
Gerson, Lloyd P. *Phil Quart*, 47(188), 417-420, Jl 97.

**Hägler, Rudolf-Peter**. *Kritik des neuen Essentialismus*. Paderborn, Schoeningh, 1994.
Kober, Michael. *Phil Rundsch*, 43(4), 334-337, D 96.

**Hähnle, Reiner**. *Automated Deduction in Multiple-valued Logics*. Oxford, Clarendon/Oxford Pr, 1993.
Malinowski, Grzegorz. *Notre Dame J Form Log*, 37(4), 631-646, Fall 96.

**Hafner, Arthur W**. *Democracy and the Public Library: Essays on Fundamental Issues*. Westport, Greenwood Pr, 1993.
Stevens, Norman D. *Relig Stud*, 33(1), 80-82, Mr 97.

**Hagberg, G L**. *Art as Language: Wittgenstein, Meaning, and Aesthetic Theory*. Ithaca, Cornell Univ Pr, 1995.
Hamilton, Andy. *Brit J Aes*, 36(4), 451-452, O 96.
Haskins, Casey. *J Aes Art Crit*, 54(4), 388-389, Fall 96.
Hyman, John. *Phil Books*, 38(1), 71-73, Ja 97.
Sharpe, R A. *Phil Invest*, 20(3), 273-274, Jl 97.
Starr, Mark. *Rev Metaph*, 50(3), 661-663, Mr 97.

**Hagberg, G L**. *Meaning and Interpretation*. Ithaca, Cornell Univ Pr, 1994.
John, Eileen. *Phil Quart*, 47(186), 106-108, Ja 97.
Neill, Alex. *J Aes Art Crit*, 55(1), 81-82, Wint 97.

**Hager, P J**. *Continuity and Change in the Development of Russell's Philosophy*. Dordrecht, Kluwer, 1994.
Irvine, A D. *Phil Math*, 5(2), 166-172, Je 97.
Ryckman, Thomas. *Phil Quart*, 47(187), 278-280, Ap 97.
Wahl, Russell. *Russell*, 16(2), 177-181, Wint 96-97.

**Hahn, Lewis Edwin** (ed). *The Philosophy of Paul Ricoeur*. Peru, Open Court, 1995.
Dumphy-Blomfield, Jocelyn. *Austl J Phil*, 74(4), 693-695, D 96.

**Halévy, Elie**. *La formation du radicalisme philosophique*. Paris, PUF, 1995.
Verde, Carmen. *Telos (Spain)*, 5(1), 134-139, Je 96.

**Hall, David L**. *Richard Rorty: Prophet and Poet of the New Pragmatism*. Albany, SUNY Pr, 1994.
Calder, Gideon. *Rad Phil*, 80, 47-48, N-D 96.

**Honderich, Ted** (ed). *The Oxford Companion to Philosophy*. Oxford, Oxford Univ Pr, 1995.
Spurrett, David. *S Afr J Phil*, 15(4), 159-160, N 96.

**Honneth, Axel**. *The Fragmented World of the Social: Essays in Social and Political Philosophy*. Albany, SUNY Pr, 1995.
Hardimon, Michael O. *J Phil*, 94(1), 46-54, J 97.
Osborne, Peter. *Rad Phil*, 80, 34-37, N-D 96.
Thompson, Simon. *J Applied Phil*, 13(3), 325-327, 1996.

**Honneth, Axel**. *The Struggle For Recognition: The Moral Grammar of Social Conflicts*. Oxford, Polity Pr, 1995.
Osborne, Peter. *Rad Phil*, 80, 34-37, N-D 96.

**Hook, Sidney**. *John Dewey: An Intellectual Portrait*. New York, Prometheus, 1995.
Arnstine, Donald. *J Aes Educ*, 31(1), 120-123, Spr 97.

**Hook, Sidney**. *The Metaphysics of Pragmatism*. Amherst, Prometheus, 1996.
Callaway, H G. *Trans Peirce Soc*, 33(3), 799-808, Sum 97.

**Hooker, Brad**. *Truth in Ethics*. Cambridge, Blackwell, 1996.
Miller, Alexander. *Mind*, 106(423), 602-606, Jl 97.
Wolf, Jean-Claude. *Frei Z Phil Theol*, 43(3), 513-517, 1996.

**Hooker, C A**. *Reason, Regulation, and Realism: Towards a Regulatory Systems Theory of Reason and Evolutionary Epistemology*. Albany, SUNY Pr, 1995.
McLaughlin, Robert. *Austl J Phil*, 75(1), 117-119, Mr 97.
Siegel, Harvey. *Brit J Phil Sci*, 48(1), 121-125, Mr 97.

**Hooks, Bell**. *Art on My Mind: Visual Politics*. New York, New City Pr, 1995.
Winchester, James. *J Aes Art Crit*, 54(4), 389-391, Fall 96.

**Hookway, Christopher** (ed) and Peterson, Donald (ed). *Philosophy and Cognitive Science*.. Cambridge, Cambridge Univ Pr, 1993.
Kitts, Brendan J. *Mind Mach*, 6(2), 276-279, My 96.

**Horgan, John**. *The End of Science*. Reading, Addison-Wesley, 1996.
Harvey, Alex. *Interpretation*, 24(3), 371-375, Spr 97.

**Horgan, Terence** and Tienson, John. *Connectionism and the Philosophy of Psychology*. Cambridge, MIT Pr, 1996.
Stainton, Robert J. *Can Phil Rev*, 16(6), 413-414, D 96.

**Horowitz, Asher** (ed) and Maley, Terry (ed). *The Barbarism of Reason: Max Weber and the Twilight of Enlightenment*. Toronto, Univ of Toronto Pr, 1994.
Wegierski, Mark. *Rev Metaph*, 50(3), 666-668, Mr 97.

**Horton, John** (ed) and Mendus, Susan (ed). *After MacIntyre*. Oxford, Polity Pr, 1994.
Wolff, Jonathan. *Phil Books*, 38(1), 32-35, Ja 97.

**Horton, John** (ed) and Mendus, Susan (ed). *After MacIntyre: Critical Perspectives on the Work of Alasdair MacIntyre*. Oxford, Polity Pr, 1994.
Edelman, John T. *Phil Invest*, 19(4), 353-358, O 96.
Kent, Bonnie. *Phil Quart*, 46(185), 524-526, O 96.
Simmons, Lance. *Amer Cath Phil Quart*, 71(1), 117-120, 1997.

**Horwich, Paul**. *Truth*. Cambridge, Blackwell, 1990.
Grover, Dorothy. *J Sym Log*, 62(1), 326-328, Mr 97.

**Hosinski, Thomas E**. *Stubborn Fact and Creative Advance: An Introduction to the Metaphysics of Alfred North Whitehead*. Lanham, Rowman & Littlefield, 1993.
Ford, Lewis S. *Mod Sch*, 73(4), 353-355, May 96.

**Hottois, Gilbert**. *Entre symboles & technosciences*. Paris, PUF, 1996.
Damar Singh, Karine R. *Horiz Phil*, 7(2), 149-151, Spring 97.

**Houston, Joseph**. *Reported Miracles*. Cambridge, Cambridge Univ Pr, 1994.
Curd, Martin. *Mind*, 106(422), 349-353, Ap 97.
Durrant, Michael. *Phil Books*, 38(1), 66-67, Ja 97.
Keller, James A. *Faith Phil*, 13(2), 286-293, Ap 96.
Zagzebski, Linda. *Phil Rev*, 105(4), 538-540, O 96.

**Howard, Alex**. *Challenges to Counselling and Psychotherapy*. London, Macmillan, 1996.
Thorne, Brian. *J Applied Phil*, 14(2), 201-202, 1997.

**Howson, Colin** and Urbach, Peter. *Scientific Reasoning: The Bayesian Approach*. Peru, Open Court, 1993.
Gower, Barry. *Brit J Phil Sci*, 48(1), 126-131, Mr 97.

**Hoy, David Couzens** and McCarthy, Thomas. *Critical Theory*. Cambridge, Blackwell, 1994.
Kingwell, Mark. *Polit Theory*, 24(2), 326-333, My 96.
MacIntyre, Alasdair. *Phil Phenomenol Res*, 57(2), 485-487, Je 97.
Nuyen, A T. *Austl J Phil*, 74(3), 523-526, S 96.

**Hoyningen-Huene, Paul**. *Reconstructing Scientific Revolutions: Thomas S. Kuhn's Philosophy of Science*. Chicago, Univ of Chicago Pr, 1993.
Brown, Harold I. *Int Stud Phil*, 29(2), 132-133, 1997.

**Hudson, Deal W**. *Happiness and the Limits of Satisfaction*. Lanham, Rowman & Littlefield, 1996.
Hill, Susanne. *Amer Cath Phil Quart*, 71(2), 264-267, Spr 97.
Tadie, Andrew. *Int Phil Quart*, 37(3), 355-356, S 97.

**Hudson, Hud**. *Kant's Compatibilism*. Ithaca, Cornell Univ Pr, 1994.
Walker, Mark Thomas. *Phil Books*, 37(4), 256-258, O 96.

**Huff, Toby E**. *The Rise of Early Modern Science: Islam, China and the West*. New York, Cambridge Univ Pr, 1995.
Lloyd, Geoffrey. *Stud Hist Phil Sci*, 28(2), 363-368, Je 97.

**Huisnam, Bruno** and Ribes, Francois. *Les philosophes et le pouvoir*. Paris, Dunod, 1994.
Ambrosini, Cristina. *Cuad Etica*, 19-20, 191-193, 1995.

**Humber, James M** (ed) and Almeder, Robert F (ed). *Reproduction, Technology, and Rights*. Totowa, Humana Pr, 1996.
Boetzkes, Elisabeth. *Can Phil Rev*, 16(3), 171-173, Je 96.

**Hume, David**. *Diálogos Sobre La Religión Natural*. Madrid, Tecnos, 1994.
Montes Fuentes, José. *Telos (Spain)*, 5(1), 153-155, Je 96.

**Humphrey, Derek**. *Lawful Exit: The Limits of Freedom for Help in Dying*. Junction City, Norris Lane Pr, 1993.
Larue, Gerald. *Free Inq*, 16(1), 58, Wint 95/96.

**Hundert, Edward M**. *Lessons from an optical illusion*. Cambridge, Harvard Univ Pr, 1995.
DesAutels, Peggy. *Phil Psych*, 10(1), 122-124, Mr 97.

**Hunter, Michael** (ed). *Robert Boyle Reconsidered*. New York, Cambridge Univ Pr, 1994.
Golinski, Jan. *Stud Hist Phil Sci*, 28(1), 209-217, Mr 97.

**Hursthouse, Rosalind** (ed), Lawrence, Gavin (ed) and Quinn, Warren (ed). *Virtues and Reasons: Philippa Foot and Moral Theory*. New York, Clarendon/Oxford Pr, 1995.
Klagge, James C. *Ethics*, 107(4), 743-746, Jl 97.

**Hutchins, Edwin**. *Cognition in the Wild*. Cambridge, MIT Pr, 1995.
Clark, Andy. *Phil Psych*, 9(3), 393-395, S 96.
Solomon, Miriam. *Phil Sci*, 64(1), 181-182, Mr 97.

**Hyland, Drew A**. *Finitude and Transcendence in the Platonic Dialogues*. Albany, SUNY Pr, 1995.
Dybikowski, J. *Ancient Phil*, 16(2), 481-487, Fall 96.

**Hyland, James L**. *Democratic Theory: The Philosophical Foundations*. Manchester, Manchester Univ Pr, 1995.
Haugaard, Mark. *Int J Phil Stud*, 4(2), 338-340, S 96.

**Hyslop, Alec**. *Other Minds*. Dordrecht, Kluwer, 1995.
Sansom, Roger. *Mind Mach*, 6(3), 421-425, O 96.

**Ignasi Saranyana, Josep**, Martinez Ferrer, Luis and De Zaballa, Ana. *Historia de la Teología Latinoamericana*. Pamplona, EUNSA, 1996.
Fernández, Socorro. *Dialogo Filosof*, 13(1), 91-92, Ja-Ap 97.

**Ignatieff, Michael**. *Blood and Belonging: Journeys into the New Nationalism*. London, Vintage, 1994.
James, Paul. *Phil Soc Sci*, 27(1), 130-135, Mr 97.

**Ignatow, Assen**. *Anthropologische Geschichtsphilosophie*. Sankt Augustin, Academia, 1993.
Küenzlen, Gottfried. *Stud East Euro Thought*, 49(3), 227-230, S 97.

**Iheoma, Eugene O**. *Moral Education for Colleges and Universities*. X, Unknown, 1995.
Brown, Lalage. *J Moral Educ*, 25(4), 471-473, D 96.

**Illetterati, L**. *Natura e Ragione*. Trento, Verifiche, 1995.
Le Moli, Andrea. *G Metaf*, 18(3), 491-494, S-D 96.

**Illetterati, Luca**. *Natura e Ragione*. Trento, Verifiche, 1995.
Ranieri, Elena. *Riv Filosof Neo-Scolas*, 88(2), 354-357, Ap-Ag 96.

**Ineichen, Robert**. *Würfel und Wahrscheinlichkeit*. Heidelberg, Akademie, 1996.
Sommaruga-Rosolemos, G. *Frei Z Phil Theol*, 44(1-2), 204-207, 1997.

**Inglis, F**. *Raymond Williams*. New York, Routledge, 1995.
Chaney, David. *Hist Human Sci*, 9(4), 151-158, N 96.
Dawson, Graham. *Rad Phil*, 82, 40-42, Mr-Ap 97.

**Ingraffia, Brian D**. *Postmodern Theory and Biblical Theology: Vanquishing God's Shadow*. New York, Cambridge Univ Pr, 1995.
Hewitt, Marsha Aileen. *Can Phil Rev*, 17(2), 105-107, Ap 97.

**Ingram, Attracta**. *A Political Theory of Rights*. Clarendon, Oxford Univ Pr, 1994.
Mendus, Susan. *Int J Phil Stud*, 4(2), 340-342, S 96.

**Ingram, Catherine**. *In the Footsteps of Gandhi*. Berkeley, Parallax Pr, 1990.
Buffington, Kath. *Acorn*, 6(2), 32-33, Fall 91.

**Ingram, David**. *Reason, History, and Politics: The Communitarian Grounds of Legitimation in the Modern Age*. Albany, SUNY Pr, 1995.
Cronin, Ciaran. *Ethics*, 107(2), 366-368, Ja 97.
Fairfield, Paul. *Phil Books*, 38(2), 136-138, Ap 97.
Marsh, James L. *Int Phil Quart*, 37(2), 248-250, Je 97.

**Introvigne, Massimo**. *Il sacro postmoderno*. Milan, Gribaudi, 1996.
Vallanueva, Javier. *Acta Phil*, 6(1), 180-182, 1997.

**Invernizzi, G**. *Il pessimismo tedesco dell'Ottocento*. Firenze, La Nuova Italia, 1994.
Augello, Giuseppe. *G Metaf*, 18(3), 478-480, S-D 96.

**Irigaray, Luce**. *Thinking the Difference: For a Peaceful Revolution*. New York, Routledge, 1994.
O'Grady, Kathleen A. *Can Phil Rev*, 16(3), 174-176, Je 96.

**Irvine, A D** and Wedeking, G A. *Russell and Analytic Philosophy*. Toronto, Univ of Toronto Pr, 1993.
Hager, Paul. *Austl J Phil*, 74(3), 526-528, S 96.

**Kraus, Jody S**. *The Limits of Hobbesean Contractarianism*. New York, Cambridge Univ Pr, 1993.
Bertman, Martin A. *Int Stud Phil*, 29(2), 133-134, 1997.

**Krausz, Michael**. *Rightness and Reasons: Interpretation in Cultural Practices*. Ithaca, Cornell Univ Pr, 1993.
Schmitter, Amy Morgan. *Rev Metaph*, 50(1), 165-167, S 96.

**Krell, David Farrell**. *Nietzsche: A Novel*. Albany, SUNY Pr, 1996.
Canis, Laura Anders. *Can Phil Rev*, 17(2), 109-110, Ap 97.

**Kretzmann, Norman** (ed) and Stump, Eleonore (ed). *The Cambridge Companion to Aquinas*. New York, Cambridge Univ Pr, 1993.
Bos, E P. *Vivarium*, 34(2), 278-280, N 96.
Dell'Olio, Andrew J. *Faith Phil*, 14(1), 104-108, Ja 97.

**Kriegel, Blandine**. *The State and the Rule of Law*. Princeton, Princeton Univ Pr, 1995.
Hawkesworth, Mary. *Can Phil Rev*, 16(4), 260-262, Ag 96.

**Krieger, Murray**. *The Institution of Theory*. Baltimore, Johns Hopkins U Pr, 1994.
Youngerman, Mark. *Int Stud Phil*, 28(4), 119-121, 1996.

**Kristjánsson, Kristján**. *Social Freedom: The Responsibility View*. New York, Cambridge Univ Pr, 1996.
Bailey, Andrew. *Can Phil Rev*, 17(2), 111-113, Ap 97.

**Krondorfer, Bjorn**. *Remembrance and Reconciliation: encounters between young Jews and Germans*. New Haven, Yale Univ Pr, 1995.
Witherell, Carol S. *J Moral Educ*, 25(3), 364-366, S 96.

**Krueger, David**. *Keeping the Faith at Work: The Christian in the Workplace*. Nashville, Abingdon, 1994.
Jones, Donald. *Bus Ethics Quart*, 7(2), 149-150, Mr 97.

**Krynicky, M**, Mostowski, M and Szczerba, L W. *Quantifiers: Logic, Models and Computation*. Dordrecht, Kluwer, 1995.
Alechina, Natasha. *J Log Lang Info*, 6(3), 342-344, Jl 97.

**Kühn, Rolf**. *Existenz und Selbstaffektion in Therapie und Phänomenologie*. Wien, Passagen, 1994.
Dufour-Kowalska, Gabrielle. *Arch Phil*, 59(4), 692-694, O-D 96.

**Kultgen, John**. *Autonomy and Intervention: Parentalism in the Caring Life*. New York, Oxford Univ Pr, 1995.
Scarre, Geoffrey. *Phil Books*, 38(1), 57-58, Ja 97.
Spriggs, Merle. *Bioethics*, 10(4), 344-346, O 96.

**Kuran, Timur**. *Private Truths, Public Lies*. Cambridge, Harvard Univ Pr, 1995.
Campolo, Christian K. *Can Phil Rev*, 17(2), 113-115, Ap 97.

**Kuri Camacho, Ramón**. *Metafísica Medieval y Mundo Moderno*. Zacatecas, Univ Autónoma Zacat, 1996.
Pérez-Estévez, A. *Rev Filosof (Venezuela)*, 23(1), 134-137, 1996.

**Kvanvig, Jonathan L**. *The Problem of Hell*. New York, Oxford Univ Pr, 1993.
Reichenbach, Bruce R. *Int Stud Phil*, 29(2), 134-136, 1997.

**Kymlicka, Will**. *Multicultural Citizenship: A Liberal Theory of Minority Rights*. New York, Oxford Univ Pr, 1995.
Barclay, Linda. *Austl J Phil*, 75(1), 124-126, Mr 97.
Mason, Andrew. *Phil Quart*, 47(187), 250-253, Ap 97.
Thomas, D A Lloyd. *Phil Books*, 38(2), 139-140, Ap 97.

**Kymlikca, Will** (ed). *The Rights of Minority Culture*. New York, Oxford Univ Pr, 1995.
Goodin, Robert E. *Ethics*, 107(2), 356-358, Ja 97.

**La Mettrie, Julien**. *Machine Man and Other Writings*. New York, Cambridge Univ Pr, 1996.
Schachter, Jean-Pierre. *Can Phil Rev*, 17(3), 179-181, Je 97.

**Lacasta Zabalza, J I**. *Cultura y gramática del Leviatán portugués*. Zaragoza, Pr Univ Zaragoza, 1988.
Soto, L G. *Agora (Spain)*, 15(2), 184-187, 1996.

**Lacey, Nicola**. *State Punishment: Political Principles and Community Values*. London, Routledge, 1994.
Ellis, Anthony. *J Applied Phil*, 13(3), 323-325, 1996.

**Lachs, John**. *The Relevance of Philosophy to Life*. Nashville, Vanderbilt Univ Pr, 1995.
Bernstein, Jeffrey A. *Rev Metaph*, 50(1), 167-168, S 96.

**Lacombe, Dany**. *Blue Politics: Pornography and the Law in the Age of Feminism*. Toronto, Univ of Toronto Pr, 1994.
Arcand, Bernard. *Phil Soc Sci*, 27(1), 136-139, Mr 97.

**Lacrosse, Joachim**. *L'amour chez Plotin*. Brussells, Ed Ousia, 1994.
Leroux, Georges. *Can Phil Rev*, 17(2), 115-117, Ap 97.

**LaFollette, Hugh**. *Personal Relationships: Love, Identity and Morality*. Cambridge, Blackwell, 1996.
Gilbert, Paul. *Phil Books*, 38(2), 131-132, Ap 97.

**Lahav, Ran** (ed) and Da Venza Tillmanns, Maria (ed). *Essays on Philosophical Counseling*. Lanham, Univ Pr of America, 1995.
Tayler, Denise. *J Chin Phil*, 23(3), 353-367, S 96.

**Lamarque, Peter** and Haugom Olsen, Stein. *Truth, Fiction and Literature: A Philosophical Perspective*. New York, Clarendon/Oxford Pr, 1994.
Dammann, R M J. *Ratio*, 10(2), 184-188, S 97.
Neill, Alex. *Phil Quart*, 47(187), 241-243, Ap 97.

**Lamb, David**. *Therapy Abatement, Autonomy and Futility: Ethical Decisions at the Edge of Life*. Brookfield, Avebury, 1995.

Letts, Julie. *Bioethics*, 11(1), 86-88, Ja 97.

**Lamb, Sharon**. *The Trouble with Blame: Victims, Perpetrators, and Responsibility*. Cambridge, Harvard Univ Pr, 1995.
Blum, Lawrence. *Ethics*, 107(2), 376-378, Ja 97.

**Lampert, Laurence**. *Leo Strauss and Nietzsche*. Chicago, Univ of Chicago Pr, 1996.
Burch, Robert. *Can Phil Rev*, 16(3), 183-185, Je 96.

**Lampert, Lawrence**. *Nietzsche and Modern Times*. New Haven, Yale Univ Pr, 1993.
Balestra, Dominic J. *Int Phil Quart*, 37(2), 245-248, Je 97.

**Landman, Janet**. *Regret: The Persistence of the Possible*. New York, Oxford Univ Pr, 1993.
Farrell, Daniel M. *Phil Quart*, 47(188), 397-400, Jl 97.

**Langacker, Ronald W**. *Concept, Image, and Symbol*. Hawthorne, de Gruyter, 1990.
Herskovits, Annette. *Mind Mach*, 6(2), 242-248, My 96.

**Langford, Duncan**. *Practical Computer Ethics*. London, McGraw-Hill, 1995.
Lauer, Thomas W. *Ethics Behavior*, 6(2), 165-167, 1996.

**Langiulli, Nino**. *Possibility, Necessity, and Existence*. Philadelphia, Temple Univ Pr, 1993.
Hartle, Ann. *Thomist*, 60(3), 503-505, Jl 96.

**Langthaler, Rudolf**. *Organismus und Umwelt*. New York, Olms, 1992.
Kamaryt, J. *Filosof Cas*, 45(3), 513-516, 1997.

**Lapsley, Daniel**. *Moral Psychology*. Boulder, Westview Pr, 1996.
Brabeck, Mary M. *J Moral Educ*, 26(2), 223-225, Je 97.

**LaPuma, John** and Schiedermayer, David. *The Health Care Ethics Consultant*. Clifton, Humana Pr, 1994.
Tonti-Filippini, Nicholas. *Bioethics*, 10(4), 334-340, O 96.

**Larmore, Charles**. *The Morals of Modernity*. New York, Cambridge Univ Pr, 1996.
MacIntyre, Alasdair. *J Phil*, 94(9), 485-490, S 97.
Mills, Claudia. *Rev Metaph*, 50(3), 671-672, Mr 97.
Turner, Susan M. *Can Phil Rev*, 16(5), 357-360, Oct 96.

**Lasala, Malena**. *Sócrates y el arte de la fuga*. Buenos Aires, Ed Biblos, 1996.
Regnasco, Maria J. *Cuad Etica*, 21-22, 189-190, 1996.

**Lattis, James M**. *Between Copernicus and Galileo: Christoph Clavius and the Collapse of Ptolemeic Cosmology*. Chicago, Univ of Chicago Pr, 1994.
Pantin, Isabelle. *Stud Hist Phil Sci*, 27(4), 593-598, D 96.

**Lavine, Shaughan**. *Understanding the Infinite*. Cambridge, Harvard Univ Pr, 1994.
Liston, Michael. *Phil Sci*, 63(3), 480-482, S 96.
Shapiro, Stewart. *Phil Rev*, 105(2), 256-259, Ap 96.
Smircich, Mary Ellen. *Phil Rev*, 105(2), 256-259, Ap 96.

**Lawrence, Gavin** and Quinn, Warren. *Virtues and Reasons: Philippa Foot and Moral Theory*. New York, Clarendon/Oxford Pr, 1995.
Walker, Margaret Urban. *Int Phil Quart*, 37(2), 242-244, Je 97.

**Lazarus, Richard S** and Lazarus, Bernice N. *Passion and Reason: Making Sense of Our Emotions*. Oxford, Oxford Univ Pr, 1994.
Charland, Louis C. *Phil Psych*, 9(3), 401-404, S 96.

**Lazovic, Zivan**. *O prirodi epistemickog opravdanja*. Belgrade, Filozof Drustvo Sr, 1994.
Tomic, Taeda. *Theoria (Yugoslavia)*, 38(1), 115-130, Mr 95.

**Le Poidevin, Robin**. *Arguing for Atheism: An Introduction to the Philosophy of Religion*. New York, Routledge, 1996.
Meynell, Hugo. *Heythrop J*, 38(2), 198-200, Ap 97.

**Le Ru, Véronique**. *Jean Le Rond d'Alembert philosophe*. Paris, Vrin, 1994.
Boulad-Ayoub, Josiane. *Dialogue (Canada)*, 35(4), 821-823, Fall 96.

**Leahy, Michael** (ed) and Cohn-Sherbok, Dan (ed). *The Liberation Debate: Rights at Issue*. London, Routledge, 1996.
Walsh, Andrew. *J Applied Phil*, 14(1), 93-95, 1997.

**Leaman, Oliver**. *Evil and Suffering in Jewish Philosophy*. Cambridge, Cambridge Univ Pr, 1995.
Burrell, David B. *Int Phil Quart*, 37(3), 360-362, S 97.

**Lecaldano, Eugenio**. *Etica*. Torino, UTET, 1995.
Bergomi, Francesca. *Iride*, 9(18), 521-523, Ag 96.

**Lecercle, Jean-Jacques**. *Philosophy of Nonsense: The Intuitions of Victorian Nonsense Literature*. New York, Routledge, 1994.
Cowley, Julian. *Rad Phil*, 78, 51-52, Jl-Ag 96.

**Lederer, Susan E**. *Subjected to Science*. Baltimore, Johns Hopkins U Pr, 1995.
Reverby, Susan M. *Hastings Center Rep*, 26(5), 38-39, S-O 96.

**Leduc-Fayette, Denise**. *Fénelon et l'amour de Dieu*. Paris, Pr Univ France, 1996.
Tourpe, Emmanuel. *Rev Phil Louvain*, 94(2), 361-363, M 96.

**Leduc-Fayette, Denise**. *Fénelon: Philosophie et spiritualité*. Geneva, Droz, 1996.
Tourpe, Emmanuel. *Rev Phil Louvain*, 95(1), 168-170, 1997.

**Leduc-Fayette, Denise**. *Pascal et le mystère du mal*. Paris, Ed du Cerf, 1996.
Tourpe, Emmanuel. *Rev Phil Louvain*, 95(1), 164-168, 1997.

**Lee, Jung Young**. *Embracing Change: Postmodern Interpretations of the I Ching from a Christian Perspective*. Cranbury, Univ of Scranton Pr, 1994.
Berthrong, John. *Phil East West*, 46(4), 586-588, O 96.

**Lees, Susan**. *Carnal Knowledge: Rape on Trial*. London, Hamish Hamilton, 1996.
Archard, David. *Rad Phil*, 81, 44-45, Ja-F 97.

**Lehman, Hugh**. *Rationality and Ethics in Agriculture*. Moscow, Univ of Idaho Pr, 1995.
Thompson, Paul B. *Can Phil Rev*, 16(3), 185-187, Je 96.

**Lehmann, Hartmut** (ed) and Richter, Melvin (ed). *The Meaning of Historical Terms and Concepts: New Studies on Begriffsgeschichte*. Washington, German Hist Inst, 1996.
Burke, Peter. *Hist Euro Ideas*, 23(1), 55-58, Ja 97.

**Lembeck, Karl-Heinz**. *Einführung in die phänomenologische Philosophie*. Darmstadt, Wiss Buchgesell, 1994.
Schuhmann, Karl. *Husserl Stud*, 13(1), 79-83, 1996.

**Lemos, Noah M**. *Intrinsic Value: Concept and Warrant*. New York, Cambridge Univ Pr, 1994.
Brower, Bruce. *Phil Rev*, 105(2), 267-269, Ap 96.

**Lemos, Ramon M**. *The Nature of Value: Axiological Investigations*. Gainesville, Univ Pr of Florida, 1995.
Jacobs, Jonathan. *Rev Metaph*, 50(2), 410-411, D 96.

**Lenk, Hans** (ed). *Wissenschaft und Ethik*. Stuttgart, Reclam, 1991.
Lekka-Kowalik, Agnieszka. *J Value Inq*, 30(3), 479-483, S 96.

**Lennon, Thomas M**. *The Battle of the Gods and Giants*. Princeton, Princeton Univ Pr, 1993.
Baugh, David J. *Hist Polit Thought*, 17(3), 445-447, Autumn 96.

**Leonardi, Paolo** (ed) and Santambrogio, Marco (ed). *On Quine: New Essays*. New York, Cambridge Univ Pr, 1995.
Hookway, Christopher. *Rev Metaph*, 50(1), 168-170, S 96.
Richardson, Alan. *Phil Books*, 38(2), 112-113, Ap 97.
Stock, Guy. *Phil Invest*, 20(3), 257-265, Jl 97.

**Leppert, Richard**. *Art and the Committed Eye*. Boulder, Westview Pr, 1996.
Hueault, Kristina. *Brit J Aes*, 37(1), 102-104, Ja 97.

**Leslie, John**. *The End of the World: The Science and Ethics of Human Extinction*. New York, Routledge, 1996.
Flew, Antony. *Philosophy*, 72(279), 158-160, Ja 97.

**Lestienne, Remy**. *The Children of Time: Causality, Entropy, Becoming*. Champaign, Univ of Illinois Pr, 1995.
Mulhauser, Gregory R. *Can Phil Rev*, 16(4), 263-265, Ag 96.

**Levi, Albert William**. *The High Road of Humanity*. Amsterdam, Rodopi, 1995.
Marcus, Frederick R. *J Aes Educ*, 31(2), 106-108, Sum 97.

**Levi, Honor**. *Blaise Pascal: Pensées and Other Writings*. New York, Oxford Univ Pr, 1995.
Parish, Richard. *Heythrop J*, 38(1), 83-84, Ja 97.

**Levi, Isaac**. *For the Sake of the Argument*. New York, Cambridge Univ Pr, 1996.
Seager, William. *Can Phil Rev*, 17(3), 181-183, Je 97.

**Levinas, Emmanuel**. *L'intrigue de l'infini*. Paris, Flammarion, 1994.
Trotignon, Pierre. *Rev Phil Fr*, 1, 75-76, Ja-Mr 97.

**Levine, Barbara** (ed). *Works about John Dewey, 1886-1995*. Carbondale, So Illinois Univ Pr, 1996.
Browning, Douglas. *Can Phil Rev*, 16(3), 188-189, Je 96.

**Levine, Donald**. *Visions of the Sociological Tradition*. Chicago, Univ of Chicago Pr, 1995.
Levine, Donald N. *Hist Human Sci*, 10(2), 141-173, My 97.

**Levine, Michael P**. *Pantheism*. New York, Routledge, 1994.
Werner, Karel. *Asian Phil*, 7(1), 71-72, Mr 97.

**Levine, Peter**. *Nietzsche and the Modern Crisis of the Humanities*. Albany, SUNY Pr, 1995.
Cook, Deborah. *Clio*, 25(3), 329-333, Spr 96.

**Levine, Peter**. *Something To Hide*. New York, St Martin's Pr, 1996.
Butterworth, Charles E. *Interpretation*, 24(2), 239-242, Wint 97.

**Levinson, Jerrold**. *The Pleasures of Aesthetics*. Ithaca, Cornell Univ Pr, 1996.
Lyas, Colin. *Can Phil Rev*, 16(6), 416-418, D 96.
Matravers, Derek. *Brit J Aes*, 37(3), 286-288, Jl 97.

**Levy, David J**. *The Measure of Man*. Columbia, Univ of Missouri Pr, 1993.
Hancock, Curtis. *Int Phil Quart*, 37(3), 372-373, S 97.

**Lim, Richard**. *Public Disputation, Power, and Social Order in Late Antiquity*. Berkeley, Univ of Calif Pr, 1995.
Conley, Thomas M. *Phil Rhet*, 30(2), 207-210, 1997.

**Lindemann, Hilde**. *The Patient and the Family*. New York, Routledge, 1995.
LaFollette, Hugh. *Bioethics*, 11(2), 175-177, Ap 97.

**Lippard Lucy**. *The Pink Glass Swan: Selected Feminist Essays on Art*. New York, New City Pr, 1995.
Lauter, Estella. *J Aes Art Crit*, 55(1), 61-62, Wint 97.

**Liske, Michael-Thomas**. *Leibniz' Freiheitslehre*. Hamburg, Meiner, 1993.
Herbst, Jürgen. *Z Phil Forsch*, 50(3), 510-515, Jl-S 96.

**Lisska, Anthony J**. *Aquinas's Theory of Natural Law: An Analytic Reconstruction*. New York, Clarendon/Oxford Pr, 1996.
MacIntyre, Alasdair. *Int Phil Quart*, 37(1), 95-99, Mr 97.

**Little, Miles**. *Humane Medicine*. New York, Cambridge Univ Pr, 1995.
Joseph, Keith. *Can Phil Rev*, 16(4), 265-267, Ag 96.
Parker, Malcolm. *Bioethics*, 11(1), 80-83, Ja 97.

**Liyuan, Zhu** (ed) and Blocker, Gene (ed). *Asian Thought and Culture: Contemporary Chinese Aesthetics*. New York, Lang, 1995.
Pagenstecher, Garret. *Thomist*, 61(2), 272-274, Ap 97.

**Llavat, Boadas**. *Roger Bacon: subjectivitat i ètica*. Barcelona, Herder, 1996.
De La Mora, J M G. *Convivium*, 9, 139-142, 1996.

**Llewelyn, John**. *Emmanuel Levinas: The Genealogy of Ethics*. New York, Routledge, 1995.
Dalton, Stuart. *Man World*, 29(4), 441-444, O 96.
Sandford, Stella. *Rad Phil*, 80, 46-47, N-D 96.

**Llinás, Rodolfo** (ed) and Churchland, Patricia S (ed). *The Mind-Brain Continuum: Sensory Processes*. Cambridge, MIT Pr, 1996.
Scott, Alwyn. *J Consciousness Stud*, 4(3), 279-280, 1997.

**Lloyd, Genevieve**. *Part of Nature: Self-Knowledge in Spinoza's Ethics*. Ithaca, Cornell Univ Pr, 1994.
Cottingham, John. *Phil Books*, 38(1), 48-50, Ja 97.

**Lloyd Thomas, D A**. *Locke on Government*. New York, Routledge, 1995.
Knowles, Dudley. *Mind*, 106(421), 181-184, Ja 97.
Unwin, Nicholas. *Phil Books*, 38(2), 97-98, Ap 97.

**Lo Vuolo, Rueben**. *Contra la exclusión*. x, Unknown, 1995.
Verde, Carmen. *Telos (Spain)*, 5(1), 141-144, Je 96.

**Lobato, A** (ed), Forment, E (ed) and Segura, A (ed). *El pensamiento de santo Tomás de Aquino para el hombre de hoy*. Valencia, EDICEP, 1994.
Burgoa, L Vicente. *Daimon Rev Filosof*, 12, 151-153, Ja-Je 96.

**Longuenesse, Béatrice**. *Kant et le pouvoir de juger*. Paris, PUF, 1993.
Barthel, Georges. *Kantstudien*, 87(3), 374-378, 1996.
Langlois, Luc. *Dialogue (Canada)*, 35(4), 832-836, Fall 96.
Pippin, Robert B. *J Phil*, 94(6), 318-324, Je 97.

**Lopes, Dominic**. *Understanding Pictures*. New York, Oxford Univ Pr, 1996.
Hopkins, Robert. *Brit J Aes*, 37(3), 283-286, Jl 97.

**Lopez Gil, Marta** and Delgado, Liliana. *De camino a una ética empresarial*. Buenos Aires, Ed Biblos, 1996.
Abril, Ofelia. *Cuad Etica*, 21-22, 190-192, 1996.

**López Saenz, M Carmen**. *Investigaciones fenomenológicas sobre el origen del mundo social*. Zaragoza, Prensas Univ, 1994.
Blésin, Laurence. *Rev Phil Louvain*, 94(4), 715-717, N 96.

**Loptson, Peter**. *Theories of Human Nature.*. Peterborough, Broadview Pr, 1995.
Young, Julian. *Dialogue (Canada)*, 35(3), 620-623, Sum 96.

**Loraux, Nicole** and Levine, Caroline (trans). *The Children of Athena*. Princeton, Princeton Univ Pr, 1994.
Monoson, S Sara. *Polit Theory*, 25(2), 302-305, Ap 97.

**Lorite Mena, José**. *Sociedades sin Estado: El pensamiento de los otros*. Madrid, AKAL, 1995.
Fernández Arévalo, Antonio. *Daimon Rev Filosof*, 12, 154-156, Ja-Je 96.

**Loureiro, I M**. *Rosa Luxemburg: Os dilemas da acao revolucionária*. Sao Paulo, UNESP, 1995.
Musse, Ricardo. *Trans/Form/Acao*, 19, 260-262, 1996.

**Lowe, E J**. *Locke on Human Understanding*. New York, Routledge, 1995.
Hamlyn, D W. *Phil Invest*, 20(2), 155-159, Ap 97.
Maund, Barry. *Austl J Phil*, 74(3), 528-530, S 96.
Unwin, Nicholas. *Phil Books*, 38(2), 97-98, Ap 97.

**Lowe, E J**. *Subjects of Experience*. New York, Cambridge Univ Pr, 1966.
Madell, Geoffrey. *Philosophy*, 72(279), 147-150, Ja 97.
Paprzycka, Katarzyna. *Can Phil Rev*, 17(1), 45-47, F 97.

**Lubarsky, Sandra B** (ed) and Griffin, David Ray (ed). *Jewish Theology and Process Thought*. Albany, SUNY Pr, 1996.
Lane, M S. *Can Phil Rev*, 16(5), 360-362, Oct 96.

**Lucretuis** and Esolen, Anthony M (trans). *On the Nature of Things*. Baltimore, Johns Hopkins U Pr, 1995.
Stein, Gordon. *Free Inq*, 16(1), 57, Wint 95/96.

**Ludwig, Ralf**. *Kategorischer Imperativ und Metaphysik der Sitten*. New York, Lang, 1992.
Ruprecht, Thomas. *Kantstudien*, 87(3), 364-366, 1996.

**Luhmann, Niklas**. *Die Kunst der Gesellschaft*. Frankfurt, Suhrkamp, 1995.
Seel, Martin. *Euro J Phil*, 4(3), 390-393, D 96.

**Lumsdaine, David Holloran**. *Moral Vision in International Politics: The Aid Regime*. Princeton, Princeton Univ Pr, 1993.
Haggard, Stephan. *Ethics Int Affairs*, 8, 219, 1994.

**Lund, D H**. *Perception, Mind and Personal Identity*. Lanham, Univ Pr of America, 1994.
Madell, Geoffrey. *Mind*, 105(420), 708, O 96.

**Luzius, R** (ed), Rath, M (ed) and Schulz, P (ed). *Studien zur Philosophie von Edith Stein*. Freiburg, Alber, 1993.
Pavic, Zeljko. *Filozof Istraz*, 15(4), 922-927, 1995.

**Lycan, William G**. *Consciousness and Experience*. Cambridge, MIT Pr, 1996.
Delancey, Craig. *Phil Psych*, 10(2), 231-233, Je 97.

**Lynn, Richard John** (trans) and Bi, Wang. *The Classic of Changes*. New York, Columbia Univ Pr, 1994.
Schroeder, J Lee. *J Chin Phil*, 23(3), 369-380, S 96.

**Lyon, David**. *Postmodernidad*. Madrid, Alianza, 1996.
Aznar, Hugo. *Agora (Spain)*, 15(2), 175-181, 1996.

**Lyons, David**. *Rights, Welfare, and Mill's Moral Theory*. New York, Oxford Univ Pr, 1994.
Wallace, Gerry. *Phil Books*, 37(4), 269-271, O 96.

**Lyons, William**. *Approaches to Intentionality*. New York, Oxford Univ Pr, 1995.
Bickle, John. *Phil Books*, 38(1), 53-55, Ja 97.
Nichols, Shaun. *Rev Metaph*, 50(3), 672-673, Mr 97.
Palma, Adriano. *J Consciousness Stud*, 4(3), 280-281, 1997.

**MacCormae, Earl** (ed) and Stamenov, Maxim I (ed). *Fractals of Brain, Fractals of Mind: In Search of a Symmetry Bond*. Amsterdam, J Benjamins, 1996.
Nunn, Chris. *J Consciousness Stud*, 4(3), 281-282, 1997.

**Macer, Darryl R J**. *Bioethics for the People by the People*. X, Unknown, 1994.
Marshall, Mary Faith. *Bioethics*, 11(2), 172-175, Ap 97.

**Machan, Tibor R** (ed) and Rasmussen, Douglas B (ed). *Liberty for the 21st Century: Contemporary Libertarian Thought*. Lanham, Rowman & Littlefield, 1995.
Dobuzinskis, Laurent. *Can Phil Rev*, 16(3), 192-194, Je 96.
Miller, Fred D. *Rev Metaph*, 50(2), 411-413, D 96.

**Machiavelli, Niccolo**, Mansfield, Harvey C (trans) and Tarcov, Nathan (trans). *Discourses on Livy*. Chicago, Univ of Chicago Pr, 1996.
Mulvaney, Robert J. *Rev Metaph*, 50(4), 908-909, Je 97.

**MacIntyre, Alasdair**. *Quelle justice, quelle rationalité?*. Paris, PUF, 1993.
Lazzeri, Christian. *Arch Phil*, 59(4), 686-690, O-D 96.

**Mackey, James P**. *Power & Christian Ethics*. New York, Cambridge Univ Pr, 1994.
Sullivan, John. *Heythrop J*, 37(4), 513-514, O 96.

**MacKinnon, Catherine A**. *Only Words*. Cambridge, Harvard Univ Pr, 1993.
Stichler, Richard N. *J Infor Ethics*, 5(2), 79-83, Fall 96.

**Macnamara, John** (ed) and Reyes, Gonzalo E (ed). *The Logical Foundations of Cognition*. New York, Oxford Univ Pr, 1994.
Engel, Pascal. *Rev Phil Fr*, 2, 261-263, Ap-Je 97.
Harman, Gilbert. *Phil Quart*, 47(188), 385-386, Jl 97.

**Magalhaes, Joao Baptista**. *A Ideia de Progresso em Thomas Kuhn no contexto da "Nova Filosofia da Ciencia"*. Porto, Ed Contraponto, 1996.
Dinis, Alfredo. *Rev Port Filosof*, 53(1), 157-160, Ja-Mr 97.

**Magnavacca, Silvia**. *Cuatro aspectos de la crisis*. Buenos Aires, Patristica et Med, 1993.
Gesualdi, Carlos Rodrigues. *Rev Filosof (Argentina)*, 11(1-2), 91-94, N 96.

**Magnus, Bernd** (ed) and Cullenberg, Stephen (ed). *Whither Marxism?: Global Crises in International Perspective*. New York, Routledge, 1995.
Adams, Ian. *Can Phil Rev*, 17(2), 117-119, Ap 97.

**Magnus, Bernd** (ed) and Higgins, Kathleen M (ed). *The Cambridge Companion to Nietzsche*. New York, Cambridge Univ Pr, 1996.
Acampora, Christa Davis. *Can Phil Rev*, 17(1), 47-49, F 97.
Bates, Stanley. *Phil Books*, 38(3), 192-194, Jl 97.

**Mainzer, Klaus**. *Symmetrien der Natur, ein Handbuch zur Natur- und Wissenschaftsphilosophie*. Hawthorne, de Gruyter, 1988.
Klein, Carsten. *J Gen Phil Sci*, 27(1), 171-181, 1996.

**Maistre, Joseph**. *Considerations on France*. Cambridge, Cambridge Univ Pr, 1994.
Wegierski, Mark. *Rev Metaph*, 50(3), 674-675, Mr 97.

**Maker, William**. *Philosophy Without Foundations: Rethinking Hegel*. Albany, SUNY Pr, 1994.
Winfield, Richard Dien. *Owl Minerva*, 28(1), 100-108, Fall 96.

**Makin, Stephen**. *Indifference Arguments*. Cambridge, Blackwell, 1993.
Broadie, Sarah. *Mind*, 106(422), 353-355, Ap 97.

**Malcolm, Budd**. *Values of Art-Pictures, Poetry and Music*. New York, Penguin USA, 1995.
Sankowski, Edward. *J Aes Educ*, 31(2), 108-109, Sum 97.

**Malcolm, Norman**. *Wittgenstein: A Religious Point of View?*. Ithaca, Cornell Univ Pr, 1994.
Hustwit, Ronald E. *Faith Phil*, 13(1), 146-149, Ja 96.
Sweet, William. *Amer Cath Phil Quart*, 71(1), 127-130, 1997.

**Maliandi, Ricardo**. *Dejar la posmodernidad*. Buenos Aires, Almagesto, 1993.
Iribarne, Julia V. *Cuad Etica*, 15-16, 176-178, 1993.

**Malnes, Raino**. *Valuing the Environment*. Manchester, Manchester Univ Pr, 1995.
Spash, Clive L. *Environ Values*, 5(3), 270-273, Ag 96.

**Malpas, J E**. *The Philosophical Papers of Alan Donagan Volumes I and II*. Chicago, Univ of Chicago Pr, 1995.
Levesque, Paul J. *Rev Metaph*, 50(4), 879-884, Je 97.
Passmore, John A. *Ethics*, 107(4), 759-761, Jl 97.
Tessin, Timothy. *Phil Invest*, 20(1), 65-69, J 97.

**Mancosu, Paolo**. *Philosophy of Mathematics and Mathematical Practice in the Seventeenth Century*. New York, Oxford Univ Pr, 1996.
Bostock, David. *Int Phil Quart*, 37(3), 353-354, S 97.
Gaukroger, Stephen. *Phil Books*, 38(2), 93-94, Ap 97.

**Mandell, Nancy** (ed). *Feminist Issues: Race, Class, and Sexuality*. Ontario, Prentice Hall, 1995.
Gagnon, Carolle. *Teach Phil*, 19(3), 299-301, Sept 96.

**Mander, W J** (ed). *Perspectives on the Logic and Metaphysics of F H Bradley*. Herndon, Thoemmes, 1996.
King-Farlow, John. *Can Phil Rev*, 17(3), 183-185, Je 97.

**Mannila, Heikka** and Räihä, Kari-Jouko. *The Design of Relational Databases*. Reading, Addison-Wesley, 1992.
Makowsky, J A. *J Sym Log*, 62(1), 324-326, Mr 97.

**Mansfield, Harvey C**. *Machiavelli's Virtue*. Chicago, Univ of Chicago Pr, 1995.
Bradley, Michael P. *Can Phil Rev*, 17(3), 185-187, Je 97.
Masters, Roger D. *Ethics*, 107(4), 757-758, Jl 97.

**Marcos de Pinotti, Graciela E**. *Platón ante el problema del error*. Buenos Aires, FUNDEC, 1995.
Maceri, Sandra. *Rev Latin de Filosof*, 23(1), 176-178, O 97.

**Marcus, Ruth Barcan**. *Modalities: Philosophical Essays*. New York, Oxford Univ Pr, 1993.
Cresswell, M J. *Phil Phenomenol Res*, 56(4), 978-979, D 96.
Engel, Pascal. *Dialogue (Canada)*, 36(1), 157-169, Wint 97.
Ortiz Hill, Claire. *Rev Int Phil*, 51(200), 278-280, 1997.
Sinisi, Vito S. *Int Stud Phil*, 28(4), 121-122, 1996.

**Margalit, Avishai**. *The Decent Society*. Cambridge, Harvard Univ Pr, 1996.
Landesman, Bruce M. *Ethics*, 107(4), 729-731, Jl 97.

**Margolis, J**. *Life Without Principles*. Cambridge, Blackwell, 1996.
Schaber, Peter. *Phil Books*, 38(3), 208-210, Jl 97.

**Margolis, Joseph**. *The Flux of History and the Flux of Science*. Berkeley, Univ of Calif Pr, 1993.
Caws, Peter. *Int Stud Phil*, 28(4), 122-123, 1996.

**Marietta, Don E** (ed) and Embree, Lester (ed). *Environmental Philosophy and Environmental Activism*. Lanham, Rowman & Littlefield, 1995.
Teichman, Jenny. *J Applied Phil*, 14(1), 90-92, 1997.

**Marinho, José**. *Obras Volumes I and II*. Lisboa, Imprensa, 1995.
Esteves Borges, Paulo Alexandre. *Philosophica (Portugal)*, 176-182, 1996.

**Marino López, Antonio**. *Eros y hermenéutica platónica*. Mexico, UNAM, 1996.
Beuchot, Mauricio. *Analogia*, 10(2), 289-290, 1996.

**Marion, Mathieu** (ed) and Cohen, Robert S (ed). *Quebec Studies in the Philosophy of Science Part I*. Boston, Kluwer, 1995.
Falk, Arthur E. *Can Phil Rev*, 17(1), 50-51, F 97.

**Marion, Mathieu** (ed) and Cohen, Robert S (ed). *Quebec Studies in the Philosophy of Science Part II*. Boston, Kluwer, 1996.
Hardcastle, Valerie Gray. *Can Phil Rev*, 17(1), 52-54, F 97.

**Marmor, Andrei** (ed). *Law and Interpretation: Essays in Legal Philosophy*. New York, Oxford Univ Pr, 1995.
Wilcox, William H. *Ethics*, 107(4), 740-742, Jl 97.

**Marongiu, P** and Newman, G. *Vendetta*. Milan, Ed Giuffrè, 1995.
Gentile, Massimo. *Riv Int Filosof Diritto*, 74(1), 162-166, Ja-Mr 97.

**Marsh, James L**. *Critique, Action, and Liberation*. Albany, SUNY Pr, 1995.
Hendley, Steven. *Man World*, 30(1), 122-126, Ja 97.
Ingram, David. *Phil Soc Crit*, 23(5), 114-122, S 97.

**Marshall, John**. *John Locke: Resistance, Religion and Responsibility*. Cambridge, Cambridge Univ Pr, 1994.
Milton, J R. *Brit J Hist Phil*, 5(1), 189-191, Mr 97.

**Marsonet, Michele**. *Science, Reality, and Language*. Albany, SUNY Pr, 1995.
Psillos, Stathis. *Brit J Phil Sci*, 47(4), 663-668, D 96.

**Marsonet, Michele**. *The Primacy of Practical Reason: An Essay on Nicholas Rescher's Philosophy*. Lanham, Univ Pr of America, 1996.
Flichman, Eduardo H. *Rev Latin de Filosof*, 23(1), 169-173, O 97.
Skoble, Aeon James. *Can Phil Rev*, 17(1), 54-56, F 97.

**Martin, Bill**. *Humanism and its Aftermath*. Atlantic Highlands, Humanities Pr, 1995.
Calder, Gideon. *Rad Phil*, 81, 51-52, Ja-F 97.

**Martin, Jane Roland**. *Changing the Educational Landscape: philosophy, women and curriculum*. New York, Routledge, 1994.
Griffiths, Morwenna. *J Phil Educ*, 30(3), 463-470, N 96.

**Mehler, Jacques** (ed) and Franck, Susana (ed). *Cognition on Cognition.* Cambridge, MIT Pr, 1995.
Butler, Keith. *Mind Mach*, 7(2), 303-306, My 97.

**Mehuron, Kate** (ed) and Percesepe, Gary (ed). *Free Spirits: Feminist Philosophers on Culture.* Englewood Cliffs, Prentice Hall, 1995.
Shrage, Laurie. *Teach Phil*, 19(4), 417-418, D 96.

**Melchiorre, Virgilio**. *Analogia e analisi trascendentale.* Milano, Mursia, 1991.
Aportone, Anselmo. *Kantstudien*, 87(3), 360-364, 1996.

**Mele, Alfred R**. *Autonomous Agents: From Self-Control to Autonomy.* New York, Oxford Univ Pr, 1995.
Blumenfield, David. *Phil Psych*, 10(1), 133-137, Mr 97.
Cuypers, Stefaan E. *Phil Books*, 38(3), 205-208, Jl 97.
Guckes, Barbara. *Z Phil Forsch*, 51(1), 149-153, Ja-Mr 97.
McConnell, Terrance. *Ethics*, 107(2), 346-349, Ja 97.
Ranieri, John. *Rev Metaph*, 50(2), 416-418, D 96.

**Mellor, Hugh**. *The Facts of Causation.* New York, Routledge, 1995.
Katzav, Joel. *Int J Phil Stud*, 4(2), 344-347, S 96.
Urchs, Max. *Erkenntnis*, 46(2), 277-279, Mr 97.

**Melville, Andrei** (ed) and Lapidus, Gail W (ed). *The Glasnost Papers: Voices on Reform from Moscow.* Boulder, Westview Pr, 1990.
Scanlan, James P. *Stud East Euro Thought*, 49(1), 47-57, Mr 97.

**Melzer, Arthur M** (ed), Weinberger, Jerry (ed) and Zinman, M Richard (ed). *History and the Idea of Progress.* Ithaca, Cornell Univ Pr, 1995.
Tucker, Aviezer. *Phil Soc Sci*, 27(1), 102-129, Mr 97.

**Menn, Stephen**. *Plato on God as Nous.* Carbondale, So Illinois Univ Pr, 1995.
DeFilippo, Joseph G. *Ancient Phil*, 17(2), 189-196, Spr 97.

**Mepham, T B** (ed), Tucker, G A (ed) and Wiseman, J (ed). *Issues in Agricultural Bioethics.* Nottingham, Nottingham Univ Pr, 1995.
De Leij, Frans. *Sci Eng Ethics*, 3(1), 99-100, Ja 97.

**Merchant, Carolyn**. *Earthcare.* New York, Routledge, 1995.
Ebenreck, Sara. *Environ Ethics*, 19(3), 323-325, Fall 97.
Salleh, Ariel. *Environ Values*, 6(3), 372-373, Ag 97.

**Merrell, Floyd**. *Semiosis in the Postmodern Age.* West Lafayette, Purdue Univ Pr, 1995.
Taylor, Victor E. *Int J Phil Stud*, 4(2), 347-349, S 96.
Gullick, Mark. *Brit J Aes*, 36(4), 455-456, O 96.

**Mertz, D W**. *Moderate Realism and Its Logic.* New Haven, Yale Univ Pr, 1996.
Caruana, Louis. *Int J Phil Stud*, 5(2), 342-343, Je 97.

**Meyer, Leonard B**. *Music, the Arts, and Ideas.* Chicago, Univ of Chicago Pr, 1994.
Debellis, Mark. *J Aes Art Crit*, 55(3), 335-337, Sum 97.

**Meyer, Susan Sauvé**. *Aristotle on Moral Responsibility.* Cambridge, Blackwell, 1994.
Held, Dirk T D. *Ancient Phil*, 17(2), 250-254, Spr 97.
Young, Charles M. *Phil Invest*, 19(4), 372-375, O 96.

**Meynell, Hugo A**. *Is Christianity True?.* Washington, Cath Univ Amer Pr, 1994.
Burrell, David B. *Faith Phil*, 14(2), 265-266, Ap 97.

**Mézáros, István**. *Beyond Capital.* London, Merlin Pr, 1995.
Arthur, Chris. *Rad Phil*, 81, 41-43, Ja-F 97.

**Michael, Michaelis** (ed) and O'Leary-Hawthorne, John (ed). *Philosophy in Mind.* Dordrecht, Kluwer, 1994.
Guttenplan, Samuel. *Phil Quart*, 47(188), 386-389, Jl 97.

**Michelini, Dorando** (ed), San Martín, José (ed) and Wester, Jutta (ed). *Etica: Discurso, Conflictividad.* Río Cuarto, Univ Nac Rio Cuarto, 1995.
Ambrosini, Cristina. *Cuad Etica*, 21-22, 179-181, 1996.

**Midgley, Mary**. *The Ethical Primate: Humans, Freedom and Morality.* London, Routledge, 1994.
Carr, David. *Phil Books*, 37(4), 271-272, O 96.
Cottingham, John. *Phil Invest*, 20(1), 91-93, J 97.
Leiber, Justin. *Philosophia (Israel)*, 25(1-4), 467-471, Ap 97.

**Midgley, Mary**. *Utopias, Dolphins and Computers: Problems of Philosophical Plumbing.* London, Routledge, 1996.
Dance, John. *J Consciousness Stud*, 4(3), 283, 1997.

**Miller, Arnold W**. *Descriptive set theory and forcing.* New York, Springer, 1995.
Bartoszynski, Tomek. *J Sym Log*, 62(1), 320-321, Mr 97.

**Miller, Arthur I**. *Insights of Genius: Imagery and Creativity in Science and Art.* New York, Springer, 1996.
Arnheim, Rudolf. *J Aes Educ*, 31(2), 100-103, Sum 97.

**Miller, Cecilia**. *Giambattista Vico: Imagination and Historical Knowledge.* New York, St Martin's Pr, 1993.
Rosenthal, Michael. *Can Phil Rev*, 17(2), 120-122, Ap 97.

**Miller, David**. *Critical Rationalism.* Chicago, Open Court, 1994.
Cleland, Carol E. *Phil Quart*, 47(188), 400-404, Jl 97.
Kerszberg, Pierre. *Phil Books*, 38(1), 73-75, Ja 97.

**Miller, David**. *On Nationality.* Oxford, Clarendon/Oxford Pr, 1995.
Bellamy, Richard. *Rad Phil*, 80, 37-40, N-D 96.

Gans, Chaim. *Euro J Phil*, 5(2), 210-216, Ag 97.
Gilbert, Paul. *J Applied Phil*, 13(3), 319-321, 1996.

**Miller, Fred D**. *Nature, Justice, and Rights in Aristotle's Politics.* Oxford, Oxford Univ Pr, 1995.
Massini Correas, Carlos I. *Sapientia*, 52(201), 233-237, 1997.
Schütrumpf, Eckart E. *Ancient Phil*, 16(2), 511-521, Fall 96.
White, Michael J. *Teach Phil*, 19(4), 407-409, D 96.

**Miller, Mara**. *The Garden as an Art.* Albany, SUNY Pr, 1993.
Leddy, Thomas. *Int Stud Phil*, 28(4), 126-127, 1996.

**Minogue, Brendan**. *Bioethics: A Committee Approach.* Boston, Jones & Bartlett, 1996.
McDowell, J. *Teach Phil*, 19(3), 288-290, Sept 96.

**Minowitz, Peter**. *Profits, Priests, and Princes: Adam Smith's Emancipation of Economics from Politics and Religion.* Stanford, Stanford Univ Pr, 1993.
Velásquez, Eduardo A. *Interpretation*, 24(2), 233-238, Wint 97.

**Miranda, José Porfirio**. *Racionalidad y democracia.* Salamanca, Ed Sígueme, 1996.
Murillo, Ildefonso. *Dialogo Filosof*, 13(1), 102-103, Ja-Ap 97.

**Misak, C J**. *Verificationism: Its History and Prospects.* London, Routledge, 1995.
Cheyne, Colin. *Brit J Phil Sci*, 48(1), 140-142, Mr 97.
Hookway, Christopher. *Mind*, 105(420), 709-710, O 96.

**Mishra, Kamalakar**. *Kashmir Saivism: The Central Philosophy of Tantrism.* Cambridge, Rudra Pr, 1993.
Larson, Gerald James. *Phil East West*, 47(2), 259-263, Ap 97.

**Mishra, Vijay**. *The Gothic Sublime.* Albany, SUNY Pr, 1994.
Bernstein, Stephen. *Clio*, 25(3), 333-338, Spr 96.

**Misra, Vacaspati**. *Nyayavarttikatatparyatika.* New Delhi, Indian Coun Phil Res, 1995.
Dravid, N S. *J Indian Counc Phil Res*, 14(1), 200-201, S-D 96.

**Mitcham, Carl**. *Philosophy of Technology in Spanish Speaking Countries.* Dordrecht, Kluwer, 1993.
Huyke, Héctor José. *Int Stud Phil*, 28(4), 128-131, 1996.

**Mitcham, Carl**. *Thinking through Technology: The Path Between Engineering and Philosophy.* Chicago, Univ of Chicago Pr, 1994.
Durbin, Paul T. *Can Phil Rev*, 17(3), 190-193, Je 97.

**Mitchell, Basil**. *Faith and Criticism.* New York, Clarendon/Oxford Pr, 1994.
Alston, William P. *Faith Phil*, 14(2), 255-259, Ap 97.
Harrison, Victoria S. *Heythrop J*, 38(1), 97-99, Ja 97.

**Mitchell, Joshua**. *The Fragility of Freedom.* Chicago, Univ of Chicago Pr, 1995.
Mitchell, Harvey. *Hist Polit Thought*, 18(1), 182-186, Spr 97.

**Mitchell, William J**. *The Reconfigured Eye: Visual Truth in the Post-Photographic Era.* Cambridge, MIT Pr, 1992.
Anderson, Judy. *J Infor Ethics*, 5(2), 84-87, Fall 96.

**Mitias, Michael H** (ed). *Philosophy and Architecture.* Amsterdam, Rodopi, 1994.
Duncan, Elmer H. *J Aes Educ*, 31(1), 113-114, Spr 97.

**Möller, Hans-Georg**. *Laotse: Tao Te King.* Frankfurt, Fischer, 1995.
Kohn, Livia. *Phil East West*, 47(3), 441-444, Jl 97.

**Mojzes, Paul**. *Religious Liberty in Eastern Europe and the USSR.* New York, Columbia Univ Pr, 1992.
Colbert, James G. *Stud East Euro Thought*, 49(1), 57-70, Mr 97.

**Moll, Konrad**. *Der junge Leibniz III.* Stuttgart, Frommann-Holzboog, 1996.
Beeley, Philip. *Leibniz Soc Rev*, 6, 155-159, D 96.

**Mommsen, Wolfgang J**. *Bürgerliche Kultur und künstlerische Avantgarde 1870-1918.* X, Unknown, 1994.
Hoeres, Peter. *Protosoz*, 8/9, 351-356, 1996.

**Monateri, Pier Giuseppe**. *Pensare il diritto civile.* Turin, Giappichelli, 1995.
Andronico, Alberto. *Riv Int Filosof Diritto*, 73(4), 784-787, O-D 96.

**Monk, Ray**. *Bertrand Russell: The Spirit of Solitude.* London, Jonathan Cape, 1996.
Lugg, Andrew. *Can Phil Rev*, 16(4), 267-270, Ag 96.

**Montagu, Jennifer**. *The Expression of the Passions.* New Haven, Yale Univ Pr, 1994.
Schmitter, Amy M. *J Aes Art Crit*, 54(4), 384-386, Fall 96.

**Montague, Phillip**. *Punishment as Societal Defense.* Lanham, Rowman & Littlefield, 1995.
Davis, Michael. *Ethics*, 107(3), 532-534, Ap 97.

**Montmarquet, James**. *Epistemic Virture and Doxastic Responsibility.* Lanham, Rowman & Littlefield, 1993.
Kvanvig, Jonathan L. *Phil Phenomenol Res*, 56(4), 970-973, D 96.

**Moody, Todd C**. *Philosophy and Artificial Intelligence.* Englewood Cliffs, Prentice Hall, 1993.
Pelletier, Francis Jeffry. *Mind Mach*, 6(2), 266-273, My 96.

**Moonan, Lawrence**. *Divine Power.* New York, Clarendon/Oxford Pr, 1994.
Doig, James C. *Amer Cath Phil Quart*, 71(1), 130-133, 1997.
Gaskin, Richard. *Phil Quart*, 47(186), 111-112, Ja 97.

**Paetzold, Heinz**. *Ernst Cassirer: Von Marburg nach New York*. Darmstadt, Wiss Buchgesell, 1995.
Doyon, Stephanie. *Laval Theol Phil*, 52(3), 919-921, O 96.

**Page, Carl R**. *Philosophical Historicism and the Betrayal of First Philosophy*. University Park, Penn St Univ Pr, 1995.
Johnson, Gregory R. *Rev Metaph*, 50(4), 912-915, Je 97.

**Pailin, David A**. *Probing the Foundations*. Kampen, Kok Pharos, 1994.
Basinger, David. *Int J Phil Relig*, 40(3), 182-184, D 96.

**Palmarini, Massimo Piattelli**. *La réforme du jugement ou comment ne plus se tromper*. Paris, Odile Jacob, 1995.
Abraham, Luc-André. *Horiz Phil*, 7(1), 125-127, Autumn 96.

**Panda, N C**. *Mind and Beyond Mind*. New Delhi, D K Pub, 1996.
Mukherjee, Jugal Kishore. *J Indian Counc Phil Res*, 14(2), 165-177, Ja-Ap 97.

**Pande, Govind Chandra**. *Life and Thought of Sankaracarya*. Delhi, Motilal Banarsidass, 1994.
Nelson, Lance E. *Thomist*, 61(2), 279-282, Ap 97.

**Panofsky, Erwin** and Lavin, Irving (ed). *Three Essays on Style*. Cambridge, MIT Pr, 1995.
Herwitz, Daniel. *J Aes Art Crit*, 55(1), 66-68, Wint 97.

**Papadimitriou, Christos H**. *Computational Complexity*. Reading, Addison-Wesley, 1994.
Immerman, Neil. *J Sym Log*, 62(2), 677-678, Je 97.

**Papineau, David** (ed). *The Philosophy of Science.*. New York, Oxford Univ Pr, 1996.
Enfield, Patrick. *Int J Phil Stud*, 5(2), 334-336, Je 97.

**Pappas, Nicholas**. *Plato and the Republic*. New York, Routledge, 1995.
Cesarz, Gary L. *Ancient Phil*, 16(2), 471-474, Fall 96.
Hamlyn, D W. *Phil Invest*, 20(2), 155-159, Ap 97.

**Pappas, Nickolas**. *The Routledge Philosophy Guidebook to Plato and the Republic*. New York, Routledge, 1995.
Stalley, R F. *Phil Books*, 38(3), 181-183, Jl 97.

**Papworth, John**. *Small is Powerful*. Westport, Praeger, 1995.
Christie, Drew. *Can Phil Rev*, 16(4), 277-278, Ag 96.

**Paquin, Nycole**. *De l'interprétation en arts visuels*. Montréal, Triptyque, 1994.
Lauzon, Jean. *Horiz Phil*, 7(2), 141-145, Spring 97.

**Pareyson, L**. *Dostoevskij: Filosofia, romanzo ed esperienza religiosa*. Roma, Einaudi, 1993.
Necchi, Piercarlo. *Itinerari Filosof*, 3(5), 64-68, Ja-Ap 93.

**Parker, David**. *Ethics, Theory and the Novel*. New York, Cambridge Univ Pr, 1994.
Freadman, Richard. *Phil Lit*, 20(2), 519-522, O 96.

**Parkinson, G H R** (ed). *The Renaissance and Seventeenth-century Rationalism*. New York, Routledge, 1993.
Woolhouse, Roger S. *Stud Leibniz*, 27(1), 123-124, 1995.

**Parodi, Horacio M Sánchez**. *El liberalismo político*. Buenos Aires, Centro Bellarmino, 1993.
Tale, Camilo. *Sapientia*, 51(200), 586-588, 1996.

**Parrini, Paola** (ed). *Kant and Contemporary Epistemology*. Amsterdam, Kluwer, 1994.
Bird, Graham. *Brit J Hist Phil*, 4(2), 438-440, S 96.

**Parry, Richard D**. *Plato's Craft of Justice*. Albany, SUNY Pr, 1996.
Weiss, Roslyn. *Ancient Phil*, 17(2), 174-178, Spr 97.

**Parsons, Susan Frank**. *Feminism and Christian Ethics*. New York, Cambridge Univ Pr, 1996.
Craske, Jane. *Heythrop J*, 38(2), 204-205, Ap 97.

**Passerin d'Entreves, Maurizio**. *The Political Philosophy of Hannah Arendt*. New York, Routledge, 1994.
Flakne, April N. *Constellations*, 4(1), 144-147, Ap 97.
Forst, Rainer. *Phil Soc Crit*, 23(2), 115-124, Mr 97.

**Passmore, John**. *Serious Art*. Peru, Open Court, 1991.
Perricone, Christopher. *J Value Inq*, 31(1), 127-130, Mr 97.

**Patar, Benoît**. *Dictionnaire actuel de l'art d'écrire*. Montréal, Ed Fides, 1995.
Follon, Jacques. *Rev Phil Louvain*, 95(1), 159-163, 1997.
Leroux, François. *Horiz Phil*, 7(1), 141-146, Autumn 96.

**Paterson, R W K**. *Philosophy and the Belief in a Life after Death*. New York, Macmillan, 1995.
Schumacher, Bernard. *Rev Metaph*, 50(3), 679-682, Mr 97.

**Patnaik, Tandra**. *Sabda: A Study of Bhartrhari's Philosophy of Language*. New Delhi, D K Pub, 1994.
Kanthmani, A. *Indian Phil Quart*, 23(3-4), 491-497, Jl-O 96.

**Patterson, Dennis**. *Law and Truth*. New York, Oxford Univ Pr, 1996.
Culver, Keith. *Can Phil Rev*, 16(6), 431-432, D 96.

**Patterson, Richard**. *Aristotle's Modal Logic*. New York, Cambridge Univ Pr, 1995.
Bäck, Allan. *Can Phil Rev*, 16(4), 278-279, Ag 96.
Elders, Leo J. *Rev Metaph*, 50(4), 915, Je 97.

**Patton, Paul**. *Nietzsche, Feminism and Political Theory*. New York, Routledge, 1993.

Oliver, Kelly. *Int Stud Phil*, 28(4), 138-139, 1996.

**Paul, Ellen Frankel** (ed), Miller, Fred D (ed) and Paul, Jeffrey (ed). *The Good Life and the Human Good*. Cambridge, Cambridge Univ Pr, 1992.
Degnan, Michael J. *Zygon*, 32(3), 262-267, Je 97.

**Paul, Ellen Frankel** (ed), Miller, Jr, Fred D (ed) and Paul, Jeffrey (ed). *The Just Society*. New York, Cambridge Univ Pr, 1995.
Cunningham, Andrew. *Can Phil Rev*, 16(4), 280-282, Ag 96.

**Peacocke, Christopher** (ed). *Objectivity, Simulation and the Unity of Consciousness*. New York, Oxford Univ Pr, 1994.
Holton, Richard. *Phil Books*, 38(2), 125-128, Ap 97.
Wedgwood, Ralph. *Phil Quart*, 47(187), 255-257, Ap 97.

**Peden, W Creighton** (ed) and Axel, Larry E (ed). *New Essays in Religious Naturalism*. Macon, Mercer Univ Pr, 1993.
Mesle, C Robert. *Int J Phil Relig*, 40(3), 177-179, D 96.

**Pedro Mesquita, António**. *Reler Platao: Ensaio sobre a teoria das ideias*. Lisboa, Imprensa, 1995.
Vaz Pinto, Maria José. *Philosophica (Portugal)*, 156-165, 1996.

**Pegueroles, Juan**. *San Agustín: Un platonismo cristiano*. Barcelona, PPU, 1985.
Coutinho, Jorge. *Rev Port Filosof*, 53(1), 161-162, Ja-Mr 97.

**Pelikan, Jaroslav**. *Christianity and Classical Culture*. New Haven, Yale Univ Pr, 1993.
Voytko, Victoria Nichole. *Int J Phil Relig*, 41(3), 184-186, Je 97.

**Pellecchia, F**. *La libertà tentata: Margini dell'etica kantiana*. Gaeta, Bibliotheca, 1996.
Todisco, Orlando. *Sapienza*, 50(1), 117-119, 1997.

**Peltonen, Markku** (ed). *The Cambridge Companion to Bacon*. New York, Cambridge Univ Pr, 1996.
Kawalex, Pawel. *Can Phil Rev*, 17(3), 199-201, Je 97.

**Penelhum, Terence**. *Reason and Religious Faith*. Boulder, Westview Pr, 1996.
McGovern, Kenneth L. *Can Phil Rev*, 16(3), 197-201, Je 96.
Szabados, Béla. *Can Phil Rev*, 16(3), 197-201, Je 96.

**Pénisson, Pierre**. *Johann Gottfried Herder, la raison dans les peuples*. Paris, Ed du Cerf, 1992.
Thouard, Denis. *Arch Phil*, 59(3), 496-498, Jl-S 96.

**Penner, Peter**. *Die Aussenperspektive des Anderen. Eine formalpragmatische Interpretation zu Enrique Dussels Befreiungsethik*. Hamburg, Argument Verlag, 1996.
Barber, Michael D. *Mod Sch*, 74(1), 69-71, N 96.

**Penrose, Roger**. *Shadows of the mind: A search for the missing science of consciousness*. New York, Oxford Univ Pr, 1994.
Odifreddi, Piergiorgio. *J Sym Log*, 62(2), 673-675, Je 97.

**Penrose, Roger**. *The Large, the Small and the Human Mind*. Cambridge, Cambridge Univ Pr, 1997.
Josephson, Brian. *J Consciousness Stud*, 4(3), 271-274, 1997.

**Penslar, Robin Levin** (ed). *Research Ethics: Cases & Materials*. Bloomington, Indiana Univ Pr, 1995.
Wood, M Sandra. *J Infor Ethics*, 5(2), 77-79, Fall 96.

**Peperzak, Adriaan Theodoor**. *Hegels praktische Philosophie*. Stuttgart, Frommann-Holzboog, 1991.
Westphal, Kenneth R. *Jahr Recht Ethik*, 2, 565-573, 1994.

**Peres, Asher**. *Quantum Theory: Concepts and Methods*. Dordrecht, Kluwer, 1995.
Mermin, N David. *Stud Hist Phil Mod Physics*, 28B(1), 131-135, Mr 97.

**Pérez Haro, Eliecer**. *El misterio del ser*. Barcelona, Unknown, 1994.
Sacchi, Mario Enrique. *Sapientia*, 52(201), 243-245, 1997.

**Perkins, Mary Anne**. *Coleridge's Philosophy: The Logos as Unifying Principle*. Oxford, Clarendon/Oxford Pr, 1994.
Thomas, Sophie. *Bull Hegel Soc Gt Brit*, 34, 60-64, Autumn-Wint 96.

**Perkins, Ray**. *Logic and Mr. Limbaugh*. Chicago, Open Court, 1995.
Levi, Don. *Teach Phil*, 19(3), 296-299, Sept 96.

**Perkins, Robert L** (ed). *Fear and Trembling and Repetition*. Macon, Mercer Univ Pr, 1993.
Norris, John. *Heythrop J*, 37(4), 499-500, O 96.

**Perkins, Robert L** (ed). *International Kierkegaard Commentary*. Macon, Mercer Univ Pr, 1990.
Westphal, Merold. *Int Phil Quart*, 37(2), 241-242, Je 97.

**Perniola, Mario**. *Il pensiero neo-antico*. Milan, Mimesi, 1995.
Dalla Vigna, Pierre. *Iride*, 9(18), 523-525, Ag 96.

**Perone, U**. *Nonostante il soggetto*. Torino, Rosenberg Sellier, 1995.
Errante, Valentina. *G Metaf*, 19(1), 196-197, Ja-Ap 97.

**Perrotti, Gabriele**. *Il tempo e l'amore*. Naples, Bibliopolis, 1994.
Ghersi, Natalia. *Riv Filosof Neo-Scolas*, 88(2), 351-354, Ap-Ag 96.

**Pesek, Jiri**. *Changing Time in the Relation to Being and its Possible Significance*. Praha, Cesky, 1995.
Hála, V. *Filosof Cas*, 45(2), 325-328, 1997.

**Pessimenti, Rocco**. *La società aperta e i suoi amici*. Soveria Mannelli, Rubbettino, 1995.
Jellamo, Anna. *Riv Int Filosof Diritto*, 73(4), 787-789, O-D 96.

**Peters, Robert Henry**. *A Critique for Ecology*. Cambridge, Cambridge Univ Pr, 1991.
Haila, Yrjö. *Biol Phil*, 12(1), 109-118, Ja 97.

**Petrassi, Giovanni**. *Il problema della causalità in I. Kant*. Rome, Bulzoni, 1991.
Aportone, Anselmo. *Kantstudien*, 88(1), 119-123, 1997.

**Pettit, Philip**. *The Common Mind: An Essay on Psychology, Society and Politics*. New York, Oxford Univ Pr, 1993.
Gaus, Gerald F. *Ethics*, 107(4), 752-754, Jl 97.

**Philips, Michael**. *Between Universalism and Skepticism: Ethics as Social Artifact*. New York, Oxford Univ Pr, 1994.
Sullivan, Roger J. *Phil Books*, 37(4), 272-274, O 96.

**Phillips, Anne**. *The Politics of Presence*. Oxford, Oxford Univ Pr, 1995.
Held, Virginia. *Ethics*, 107(3), 530-532, Ap 97.

**Pichetto, Maria Teresa**. *Verso un nuovo liberalismo*. Milano, Franco Angeli, 1996.
Jellamo, Anna. *Riv Int Filosof Diritto*, 73(3), 595-597, Jl-S 96.

**Pickering, Andrew**. *The Mangle of Practice*. Chicago, Univ of Chicago Pr, 1995.
Chart, David. *Brit J Phil Sci*, 47(3), 479-482, S 96.

**Pickering, Mary**. *Auguste Comte: An Intellectual Biography (Volume I)*. New York, Cambridge Univ Pr, 1993.
Harrison, Ross. *Brit J Hist Phil*, 4(2), 444-446, S 96.

**Pinckaers, Servais**. *The Sources of Christian Ethics*. Washington, Cath Univ Amer Pr, 1995.
Hanink, James G. *Faith Phil*, 14(2), 252-255, Ap 97.

**Pink, Thomas**. *The Psychology of Freedom*. Cambridge, Cambridge Univ Pr, 1996.
Williams, Clifford. *Can Phil Rev*, 17(3), 201-203, Je 97.

**Pinkard, Terry**. *Hegel's Phenomenology: The Sociality of Reason*. New York, Cambridge Univ Pr, 1994.
Horstmann, Rolf-Peter. *Euro J Phil*, 5(2), 219-224, Ag 97.

**Pinnock, Clark** (ed). *The Openness of God*. Downers Grove, InterVarsity Pr, 1994.
Ford, Lewis S. *Int J Phil Relig*, 41(1), 59-63, F 97.
Wierenga, Edward. *Faith Phil*, 14(2), 248-252, Ap 97.

**Piquet, J Claude**. *Philosophie et musique*. Chene-Bourg, Georg, 1996.
Corbellari, Alain. *Rev Theol Phil*, 129(2), 194-195, 1997.

**Placher, William C**. *The Domestication of Transcendence: How Modern Thinking about God Went Wrong*. Louisville, Knox Pr, 1996.
Keating, James F. *Thomist*, 61(3), 469-473, Jl 97.

**Plato**. *Plato's Two Dialogues*. X, Unknown, 1994.
Joó, Mária. *Magyar Filozof Szemle*, 1-2, 425-431, 1997.

**Plato**, Nehamas, Alexander (ed) and Woodruff, Paul (ed). *Phaedrus*. Indianapolis, Hackett, 1995.
Carey, David H. *Teach Phil*, 20(1), 77-79, Mr 97.

**Plett, Heinrich F** (ed). *Renaissance Rhetoric*. Berlin, Walter de Gruyter, 1993.
Green, Lawrence D. *Phil Rhet*, 29(4), 451-458, 1996.

**Plotkin, Henry**. *Darwin Machines and the Nature of Knowledge*. New York, Penguin USA, 1994.
Allen, Barry. *Biol Phil*, 12(2), 233-241, Ap 97.

**Plumwood, V**. *Feminism and the Mastery of Nature*. New York, Routledge, 1993.
Cook, Julie. *Environ Values*, 6(2), 245-246, My 97.

**Pocock, J G A** (ed). *The Varieties of British Political Thought, 1500-1800*. Cambridge, Cambridge Univ Pr, 1993.
Clark, J C D. *Hist Polit Thought*, 17(2), 305-308, Sum 96.

**Poellner, Peter**. *Nietzsche and Metaphysics*. New York, Oxford Univ Pr, 1995.
Kerstein, Samuel. *Rev Metaph*, 50(3), 682-683, Mr 97.

**Poizat, Bruno**. *Les petits cailloux*. Lyon, Unknown, 1995.
De Rougemont, Michel. *J Sym Log*, 62(1), 323-324, Mr 97.

**Pojman, Louis P**. *What Can We Know?: An Introduction to the Theory of Knowledge*. Belmont, Wadsworth, 1995.
Vassallo, Nicla. *Epistemologia*, 19(2), 359-361, Jl-D 96.

**Poland, J**. *Physicalism: The Philosophical Foundations*. New York, Clarendon/Oxford Pr, 1994.
Campbell, Keith. *Phil Phenomenol Res*, 57(1), 223-226, Mr 97.
Daly, Chris. *Phil Quart*, 47(186), 115-118, Ja 97.

**Polkinghorne, John**. *The Faith of a Physicist: Reflections of a Bottom-Up Thinker*. Princeton, Princeton Univ Pr, 1994.
Vallicella, W F. *Int Stud Phil*, 28(4), 140-141, 1996.

**Pollock, John**. *Cognitive Carpentry: A Blueprint for How to Build a Person*. Cambridge, MIT Pr, 1995.
Munsat, Stanley. *Rev Metaph*, 50(2), 418-420, D 96.
Owens, David. *Mind*, 106(421), 192-195, Ja 97.

**Pols, Edward**. *Radical Realism, Direct Knowing in Science and Philosophy*. Ithaca, Cornell Univ Pr, 1992.
Felt, James W. *Int Phil Quart*, 36(4), 500-502, D 96.

**Poma, A**. *Impossibilità e necessità della teodicea*. Milano, Mursia, 1995.
Allegro, Giuseppe. *G Metaf*, 19(1), 194-195, Ja-Ap 97.

**Pontara, Giuliano**. *Ética y Generaciones Futuras*. Barcelona, Ariel Pr, 1996.
Pérez Sánchez, Elías. *Telos (Spain)*, 5(2), 136-138, D 96.

**Pope, Stephen J**. *The Evolution of Altruism and the Ordering of Love*. Washington, Georgetown Univ Pr, 1994.
Rousseau, Mary. *Amer Cath Phil Quart*, 71(1), 133-136, 1997.

**Popkorn, Sally**. *First Steps in Modal Logic*. Cambridge, Cambridge Univ Pr, 1995.
Goré, Rajeev. *J Sym Log*, 61(3), 1055-1056, S 96.

**Popper, Karl**. *Knowledge and the Body-Mind Problem*. New York, Routledge, 1994.
Lueken, G L. *Phil Invest*, 20(1), 69-76, J 97.

**Popper, Karl**. *The Myth of Framework*. New York, Routledge, 1994.
Koertge, Noretta. *Phil Sci*, 64(1), 182-184, Mr 97.
Lueken, G L. *Phil Invest*, 20(1), 69-76, J 97.

**Port, Robert** (ed) and Van Gelder, Timothy (ed). *Mind as Motion: Explorations in the Dynamics of Cognition*. Cambridge, MIT Pr, 1995.
Grush, Rick. *Phil Psych*, 10(2), 233-242, Je 97.

**Portelli, John P** (ed) and Reed, Ronald F (ed). *Children, Philosophy and Democracy*. Calgary, Detselig Enterprises, 1995.
Rowe, Don. *J Moral Educ*, 25(3), 360-362, S 96.

**Porter, Burton F**. *Philosophy: A Literary and Conceptual Approach*. New York, Harcourt Brace, 1995.
Horvitz, Lee. *Teach Phil*, 19(3), 293-296, Sept 96.

**Porter, Jean**. *Moral Action and Christian Ethics*. New York, Cambridge Univ Pr, 1995.
Meconi, David Vincent. *Rev Metaph*, 50(1), 173-174, S 96.
Thompson, Christopher J. *Thomist*, 61(3), 488-490, Jl 97.

**Possenti, Vittorio**. *Approssimazioni all'essere: Scritti di metafisica e morale*. Padua, Il Poligrafo, 1995.
Guietti, Paolo. *Rev Metaph*, 50(3), 683-686, Mr 97.

**Possenti, Vittorio**. *Razionalismo critico e metafísica*. Morcelliana, Brescia, 1994.
Crespo, Ricardo F. *Sapientia*, 52(201), 241-243, 1997.

**Post, Robert C**. *Constitutional Domains: Democracy, Community, Management*. Cambridge, Harvard Univ Pr, 1995.
Marshall, S E. *Phil Books*, 38(1), 64-65, Ja 97.

**Post, Stephen G**. *The Moral Challenge of Alzheimer Disease*. Baltimore, Johns Hopkins U Pr, 1995.
Young, Robert. *Bioethics*, 11(2), 177-178, Ap 97.

**Potkay, Adam**. *The Fate of Eloquence in the Age of Hume*. Ithaca, Cornell Univ Pr, 1994.
Bitzer, Lloyd F. *Phil Rhet*, 29(4), 472-475, 1996.

**Potter, Karl H** (ed). *The Encyclopaedia of Indian Philosophies: Bibliography*. Delhi, Motilal Banarsidass, 1995.
Krishna, Daya. *J Indian Counc Phil Res*, 13(3), 162-168, My-Ag 96.

**Potter, Vincent G** (ed) and Colapietro, Vincent M (ed). *Peirce's Philosophical Perspectives*. New York, Fordham Univ Pr, 1996.
Smith, John E. *Int Phil Quart*, 37(2), 225-230, Je 97.

**Potts, Timothy C**. *Structures and Categories for the Representation of Meaning*. Cambridge, Cambridge Univ Pr, 1994.
Rumfitt, Ian. *Phil Rev*, 105(2), 264-267, Ap 96.

**Pouivet, Roger**. *Esthétique et logique*. X, Unknown, 1996.
Cometti, Jean-Pierre. *Rev Int Phil*, 50(198), 697-699, 1996.

**Poulakos, John**. *Sophistical Rhetoric in Classical Greece*. Columbia, Univ S Carolina Pr, 1995.
Moss, Roger. *Phil Rhet*, 29(4), 444-447, 1996.

**Prado, C G**. *Starting with Foucault: An Introduction to Genealogy*. Boulder, Westview Pr, 1995.
Walsh, A J. *Austl J Phil*, 75(1), 126-128, Mr 97.

**Preterossi, Geminello**. *Carl Schmitt e la tradizione moderna*. Bari, Laterza, 1996.
Zolo, Danilo. *Iride*, 10(20), 189-191, Ap 97.

**Preyer, Gerhard** (ed), Siebelt, Frank (ed) and Ulfig, Alexander (ed). *Language, Mind and Epistemology: On Donald Davidson's Philosophy*. Dordrecht, Kluwer, 1994.
Marras, Ausonio. *Mind Mach*, 7(1), 133-138, F 97.
Peter, Georg. *Prima Philosophia*, 10(3), 387-391, 1997.
Stekeler-Weithofer, Pirmin. *Phil Invest*, 20(1), 85-90, J 97.

**Price, A W**. *Mental Conflict*. New York, Routledge, 1995.
Walker, A D M. *Phil Books*, 38(1), 40-42, Ja 97.

**Priest, Graham**. *Beyond the Limits of Thought*. Cambridge, Cambridge Univ Pr, 1995.
Thomas, Alan. *Bull Hegel Soc Gt Brit*, 34, 80-82, Autumn-Wint 96.

**Prigogine, Ilya**. *La fin des certitudes*. Paris, Odile Jacob, 1996.
Gauther, Yvon. *Horiz Phil*, 7(1), 129-131, Autumn 96.

**Prior, William** (ed). *Socrates: Critical Assessments*. New York, Routledge, 1996.
Waterfield, Robin. *Heythrop J*, 38(3), 360-361, Jl 97.

**Pritchard, Paul**. *Plato's Philosophy of Mathematics*. Sankt Augustin, Academia, 1995.
Sisson, Janet D. *Can Phil Rev*, 17(3), 203-205, Je 97.

**Protevi, John**. *Time and Exteriority: Aristotle, Heidegger, Derrida*. Lewisburg, Bucknell Univ Pr, 1994.
Richardson, Robert D. *Res Phenomenol*, 26, 283-291, 1996.

**Puleo, Alicia H**. *La Filosofía contemporánea desde una perspectiva no androcéntrica*. Madrid, M E C, 1993.
Cano López, Antonio José. *Daimon Rev Filosof*, 10, 164-166, Ja-Je 95.

**Pustejovsky, James**. *The Generative Lexicon*. Cambridge, MIT Pr, 1995.
Masuko, Mayumi. *J Log Lang Info*, 6(3), 350-353, Jl 97.

**Putnam, Hilary**. *Pragmatism*. Cambridge, Blackwell, 1995.
Corbí, Josep E. *Teorema*, 16(1), 114-118, 1996.
Macdonald, Cynthia. *Int J Phil Stud*, 4(2), 352-354, S 96.
Rorty, Richard. *Phil Rev*, 105(4), 560-561, O 96.

**Putnam, Hilary**. *Renewing Philosophy*. Cambridge, Harvard Univ Pr, 1992.
Balowitz, Victor. *Int Stud Phil*, 28(4), 141-142, 1996.
Biletzki, Anat. *Philosophia (Israel)*, 25(1-4), 437-451, Ap 97.

**Pyle, Andrew** (ed). *Agnosticism: Contemporary Responses to Spencer and Huxley*. Bristol, Thoemmes, 1995.
Flew, Antony. *Brit J Hist Phil*, 5(1), 218-220, Mr 97.

**Querido, A** (ed), Van Es, L A (ed) and Mandema, E (ed). *The Discipline of Medicine*. Amsterdam, North-Holland, 1994.
Caccamo, Leonard. *J Med Phil*, 21(4), 467-469, Aug 96.

**Quine, W V**. *From Stimulus to Science*. Cambridge, Harvard Univ Pr, 1995.
George, Alexander. *Mind*, 106(421), 195-201, Ja 97.
Kermode, Robert. *Can Phil Rev*, 16(5), 367-368, Oct 96.

**Quinn, Warren**. *Morality and Action*. Cambridge, Cambridge Univ Pr, 1993.
Kamm, F M. *J Phil*, 93(11), 578-584, Oct 96.
McNaughton, David. *Phil Books*, 38(1), 58-61, Ja 97.
Thompson, Michael. *Phil Rev*, 105(2), 270-272, Ap 96.

**Rabinow, Paul**. *Making PCR: A Story of Biotechnology*. Chicago, Univ of Chicago Pr, 1996.
Ankeny, Rachel. *Can Phil Rev*, 17(1), 67-69, F 97.

**Rachels, James**. *Created From Animals: The Moral Implications of Darwinism*. Oxford, Oxford Univ Pr, 1990.
Bradie, Michael. *Biol Phil*, 12(1), 73-88, Ja 97.

**Radcliffe, Elizabeth S** (ed) and White, Carol J (ed). *Faith in Theory and Practice: Essays on Justifying Religious Belief*. Peru, Open Court, 1993.
Garcia, Laura. *Faith Phil*, 14(1), 113-116, Ja 97.

**Radder, Hans**. *In and About the World: Philosophical Studies of Science and Technology*. Albany, SUNY Pr, 1996.
Wilkerson, T E. *Rev Metaph*, 50(4), 916-917, Je 97.

**Radin, Margaret Jane**. *Contested Commodities*. Cambridge, Harvard Univ Pr, 1996.
Penner, J E. *Can Phil Rev*, 17(3), 206-208, Je 97.

**Radnitzky, Gerard**. *Karl R. Popper*. X, Unknown, 1995.
Keuth, Herbert. *Z Phil Forsch*, 51(1), 167-168, Ja-Mr 97.

**Raio, G**. *Simbolismo tedesco*. Naples, Bibliopolis, 1995.
Lo Bue, Elisabetta. *G Metaf*, 19(1), 197-199, Ja-Ap 97.

**Rakovic, Dejan** (ed) and Koruga, Djuro (ed). *Consciousness: Scientific Challenge of the 21st Century*. Belgrade, Unknown, 1996.
Chakalov, Dimiter G. *J Consciousness Stud*, 4(3), 287-288, 1997.

**Ramamurthy, A**. *The Central Philosophy of the Rgveda*. Delhi, Ajanta, 1995.
Jayashanmukham, N. *J Indian Counc Phil Res*, 13(2), 182-190, Ja-Ap 96.

**Rametta, G**. *Le strutture speculative della Dottrina della Scienza*. Genova, Pantograf, 1995.
Augello, Giuseppe. *G Metaf*, 18(3), 477-478, S-D 96.

**Ramsey, F P** and Galavotti, Maria Carla (ed). *Notes on Philosophy, Probability and Mathematics*. Naples, Bibliopolis, 1991.
Lowe, E J. *Brit J Phil Sci*, 48(2), 300-301, Je 97.

**Rapp, Christof**. *Identität, Persistenz und Substantialität*. Freiburg, Alber, 1995.
Tuninetti, Luca F. *Acta Phil*, 5(2), 366-369, 1996.

**Rath, Matthias**. *Der Psychologismusstreit in der deutschen Philosophie*. Freiburg, Alber, 1994.
Rinofner-Kreidl, Sonja. *Grazer Phil Stud*, 51, 261-262, 1996.

**Raz, Joseph**. *Ethics in the Public Domain: Essays in the Morality of Law and Politics*. Oxford, Clarendon/Oxford Pr, 1994.
Martínez, Pilar. *Telos (Spain)*, 5(1), 144-146, Je 96.
Rosenblum, Nancy L. *Polit Theory*, 24(2), 333-338, My 96.

**Reale, Giovanni** and Bos, Abraham P. *Il trattato Sul cosmo per Alessandro attribuito ad Aristotele*. Milano, Vita Pensiero, 1995.
Cavagnaro, Elena. *Phil Reform*, 61(2), 206-210, 1996.

**Reboul, Olivier**. *Nietzsche, crítico de Kant*. Barcelona, Anthropos, 1993.

Romero López, José Ramón. *Daimon Rev Filosof*, 12, 159-161, Ja-Je 96.

**Recanati, Francois**. *Direct Reference*. Cambridge, Blackwell, 1993.
Kapitan, Tomis. *Phil Phenomenol Res*, 56(4), 953-956, D 96.
McCulloch, Gregory. *Euro J Phil*, 2(1), 101-104, Ap 94.

**Redding, Paul**. *Hegel's Hermeneutics*. Ithaca, Cornell Univ Pr, 1996.
Sherman, David. *Can Phil Rev*, 16(6), 433-435, D 96.

**Redhead, Michael**. *From Physics to Metaphysics*. New York, Cambridge Univ Pr, 1995.
Forrest, Peter. *Brit J Phil Sci*, 48(1), 149-150, Mr 97.
Lau, Joe. *Phil Books*, 38(1), 75-76, Ja 97.

**Rehg, William**. *Insight and Solidarity*. Berkeley, Univ of Calif Pr, 1994.
Benhabib, Seyla. *Phil Rev*, 105(4), 547-550, O 96.
Warnke, Georgia. *Int Stud Phil*, 28(4), 142-143, 1996.
Zurn, Christopher F. *Phil Soc Crit*, 22(6), 113-126, 1996.

**Reich, Klaus**, Kneller, Jane (trans) and Losonsky, Michael (trans). *The Completeness of Kant's Table of Judgments*. Stanford, Stanford Univ Pr, 1992.
Falkenstein, Lorne. *Kantstudien*, 87(4), 455-464, 1996.

**Reich, Warren T** (ed). *Encyclopedia of Bioethics*. New York, Macmillan, 1995.
Graber, Glenn C. *Hastings Center Rep*, 27(3), 42-43, My-Je 97.
Reynolds, Charles H. *Hastings Center Rep*, 27(3), 42-43, My-Je 97.

**Reinke, Edgar C** (trans), Briggs, Ward W (ed) and Kopff, E Christian (ed). *The Roosevelt Lectures of Paul Shorey 1913-14*. Hildesheim, Olms, 1995.
Sprague, Rosamond Kent. *Ancient Phil*, 17(2), 207-210, Spr 97.

**Reiss, Michael** and Straughan, Roger. *Improving Nature? The Science and Ethics of Genetic Engineering*. New York, Cambridge Univ Pr, 1996.
Spier, Raymond. *Sci Eng Ethics*, 3(1), 101-102, Ja 97.

**Renault, Laurence**. *Dieu et les créatures selon Thomas d'Aquin*. Paris, Pr Univ France, 1995.
Pasqua, Hervé. *Rev Phil Louvain*, 94(2), 359-361, M 96.

**Rescher, Nicholas**. *Pluralism: Against the Demand for Consensus*. New York, Clarendon/Oxford Pr, 1993.
Mau, Frank. *Erkenntnis*, 46(1), 137-142, Ja 97.

**Rescher, Nicholas**. *Process Metaphysics: An Introduction to Process Philosophy*. Albany, SUNY Pr, 1996.
Shields, George W. *Process Stud*, 25, 131-134, 1996.
Sorrell, Kory. *Int Phil Quart*, 37(2), 250-253, Je 97.

**Rescher, Nicholas**. *Public Concerns: Philosophical Studies of Social Issues*. Lanham, Rowman & Littlefield, 1995.
Skoble, Aeon James. *Can Phil Rev*, 17(1), 54-56, F 97.

**Reuscher, Jay**. *A Concordance to the 'Critique of Pure Reason'*. New York, Lang, 1996.
Ver Eecke, W. *Tijdschr Filosof*, 59(2), 351-352, Je 97.

**Rhonheimer, Martin**. *La prospettiva della morale*. Rome, Armando, 1994.
Vendemiati, Aldo. *Riv Filosof Neo-Scolas*, 88(2), 332-337, Ap-Ag 96.

**Richard, Mark**. *Propositional Attitudes*. New York, Cambridge Univ Pr, 1990.
Peterson, Philip L. *Mind Mach*, 6(2), 249-253, My 96.

**Richards, David**. *Masks of Difference: Cultural Representation in Literature, Anthropology and Art*. New York, Cambridge Univ Pr, 1994.
Eaglestone, Robert. *Brit J Aes*, 36(4), 456-458, O 96.

**Richardson, Henry**. *Practical Reasoning about Final Ends*. New York, Cambridge Univ Pr, 1994.
Kline, William. *Int Stud Phil*, 28(4), 144-145, 1996.
Schmidtz, David. *Int Stud Phil*, 28(4), 144-145, 1996.

**Richardson, John**. *Nietzsche's System*. Oxford, Oxford Univ Pr, 1996.
Conard, Mark T. *Rev Metaph*, 50(2), 420-421, D 96.

**Richmond, Sheldon**. *Aesthetic Criteria*. Milano, Rusconi, 1994.
Freeland, Cynthia A. *J Aes Art Crit*, 55(1), 79-80, Wint 97.

**Richter, Melvin**. *The History of Political and Social Concepts: A Critical Introduction*. New York, Oxford Univ Pr, 1995.
Burke, Peter. *Hist Euro Ideas*, 23(1), 55-58, Ja 97.

**Ricoeur, Paul**. *La critique et la conviction*. Paris, Calmann-Levy, 1995.
Chabot, Marc. *Horiz Phil*, 7(2), 146-147, Spring 97.

**Ridley, Aaron**. *Music, Value and the Passions*. Ithaca, Cornell Univ Pr, 1995.
Hagberg, Garry L. *Phil Music Educ Rev*, 4(2), 128-133, Fall 96.
Lorraine, Renée. *J Aes Art Crit*, 55(1), 64-66, Wint 97.
Sharpe, R A. *Phil Quart*, 47(187), 236-238, Ap 97.

**Rigotti, Francesca**. *La verità retorica: Etica, conoscenza e persuasione*. Milano, Feltrinelli, 1995.
Bergomi, Francesca. *Iride*, 9(18), 531-533, Ag 96.
Danblon, Emmanuelle. *Rev Int Phil*, 51(199), 166-170, 1997.

**Rippe, Klaus Peter**. *Ethischer Relativismus*. Paderborn, Ferdinand Schöningh, 1993.
Scarano, Nico. *Z Phil Forsch*, 50(3), 492-495, Jl-S 96.

**Rivera, Silvia**. *Ludwig Wittgenstein: Entre paradojas y aporías*. Buenos Aires, Almagesto, 1994.
Ambrosini, Cristina. *Cuad Etica*, 19-20, 184-186, 1995.

**Rothenberg, David** (ed). *Wild Ideas*. Minneapolis, Univ of Minn Pr, 1995.
Keller, David R. *Environ Ethics*, 19(3), 315-318, Fall 97.

**Rovaletti, Maria Lucrecia** (ed). *Etica y psicoterapia*. Buenos Aires, Ed Biblos, 1995.
Cohen, Ester. *Cuad Etica*, 19-20, 186-188, 1995.

**Rowe, Christopher J** (ed). *Reading the Statesman*. Sankt Augustin, Academia, 1995.
Di Camillo, Silvana. *Rev Latin de Filosof*, 23(1), 180-182, O 97.

**Rowlands, Mark**. *Supervenience and Materialism*. Aldershot, Avebury, 1995.
Smart, J J C. *Austl J Phil*, 75(1), 128-130, Mr 97.

**Rudd, A**. *Kierkegaard and the Limits of the Ethical*. New York, Oxford Univ Pr, 1993.
Green, Ronald M. *Int Stud Phil*, 28(4), 151-152, 1996.

**Rudder Baker, Lynne**. *Explaining Attitudes: A Practical Approach to the Mind*. New York, Cambridge Univ Pr, 1995.
Cheng, Kam-Yuen. *Phil Books*, 38(2), 121-123, Ap 97.
Child, William. *Mind Lang*, 11(3), 306-312, S 96.
Mackie, Penelope. *Philosophy*, 72(279), 143-147, Ja 97.
Sanford, David H. *Behavior Phil*, 24(2), 181-186, Fall 96.

**Rudolph, E** (ed) and Stamatescu, I O (ed). *Philosophy, Mathematics and Modern Physics: A Dialogue*. Heidelberg, Springer-Verlag, 1994.
Sanatani, Saurabh. *J Indian Counc Phil Res*, 13(3), 183-185, My-Ag 96.

**Ruler, J A Van**. *The Crisis of Causality: Voetius and Descartes on God, Nature and Change*. Leiden, Brill, 1995.
Ewbank, Michael. *Rev Metaph*, 50(1), 177-179, S 96.

**Runvos, C J**. *Filosofie van tijd en ruimte*. Utrecht, Uitgeverij Tijdstrm, 1996.
Debrock, Guy. *Alg Ned Tijdschr Wijs*, 89(3), 253-255, Jl 97.

**Ruse, Michael**. *Evolutionary Naturalism: Selected Essays*. New York, Routledge, 1995.
Grover, Stephen. *Phil Books*, 38(2), 114-115, Ap 97.

**Russell, Bertrand**. *My Philosophical Development*. New York, Routledge, 1995.
Lugg, Andrew. *Can Phil Rev*, 17(3), 209-211, Je 97.

**Russell, Paul**. *Freedom and Moral Sentiment: Hume's Way of Naturalizing Responsibility*. New York, Oxford Univ Pr, 1995.
Richman, Kenneth A. *Can Phil Rev*, 16(5), 371-373, Oct 96.

**Russo, Elena**. *Skeptical Selves: Empiricism and Modernity in the French Novel*. Stanford, Stanford Univ Pr, 1996.
Gordon, Daniel. *Phil Lit*, 21(1), 179-181, Ap 97.

**Rutherford, Donald**. *Leibniz and the Rational Order of Nature*. Cambridge, Cambridge Univ Pr, 1995.
Cover, J A. *Phil Books*, 38(3), 185-188, Jl 97.
Kelley, Andrew K. *Rev Metaph*, 50(2), 421-423, D 96.
Wilson, Catherine. *Can Phil Rev*, 16(4), 287-289, Ag 96.

**Rutherford, R B**. *The Art of Plato*. Cambridge, Harvard Univ Pr, 1995.
Bussanich, John. *Rev Metaph*, 50(1), 179-180, S 96.
Sprague, Rosamond Kent. *Ancient Phil*, 16(2), 474-477, Fall 96.

**Rychlak, Joseph F**. *Logical Learning Theory*. Lincoln, Univ of Nebraska Pr, 1994.
Viney, Wayne. *J Mind Behav*, 17(2), 207-211, Spr 96.

**Saatkamp, Herman J**. *Rorty and Pragmatism: The Philosopher Responds to his Critics*. Nashville, Vanderbilt Univ Pr, 1995.
Rumana, Richard. *Int J Phil Stud*, 5(1), 131-132, Mr 97.

**Sacchi, D**. *Necessità e oggettività nell'Analitica kantiana*. Milano, Vita Pensiero, 1995.
Cicatello, Angelo. *G Metaf*, 18(3), 494-497, S-D 96.

**Sachs, Joe**. *Aristotle's Physics: A Guided Study*. New Brunswick, Rutgers Univ Pr, 1995.
Carey, David H. *Teach Phil*, 19(3), 290-293, Sept 96.
Halper, Edward. *Rev Metaph*, 50(3), 687-689, Mr 97.

**Sacks, Oliver**. *An Anthropologist on Mars: Seven Paradoxical Tales*. New York, Knopf, 1995.
Indurkhya, Bipin. *Mind Mach*, 7(1), 115-119, F 97.

**Sadler, Ted**. *Nietzsche: Truth and Redemption*. London, Athlone, 1995.
Cauchi, Francesca. *Rad Phil*, 80, 48-49, N-D 96.
Sleinis, E E. *Austl J Phil*, 75(1), 130-131, Mr 97.

**Salas Astráin, R**. *Lo sagrado y lo humano*. Milan, Ed San Paolo, 1996.
Beuchot, Mauricio. *Analogia*, 11(1), 231-232, Ja-Je 97.

**Sallis, John**. *Double Truth*. Albany, SUNY Pr, 1995.
David, Stephen W. *Res Phenomenol*, 26, 276-283, 1996.

**Salmon, Wesley** (ed) and Wolters, Gereon (ed). *Logic, Language and the Structure of Scientific Theories*. Pittsburgh, Univ of Pitt Pr, 1994.
Clendinnen, F John. *Austl J Phil*, 75(1), 132-133, Mr 97.

**Salthe, Stanley N**. *Development and Evolution: Complexity and Change in Biology*. Cambridge, MIT Pr, 1993.
Depew, David J. *Biol Phil*, 12(3), 399-402, Jl 97.

**Samuelson, Norbert**. *Judaism and the Doctrine of Creation*. New York, Cambridge Univ Pr, 1995.
Batnitzky, Leora. *Mod Theol*, 13(3), 404-406, Jl 97.

**Sandel, Michael J**. *Democracy's Discontent: America in Search of a Public Philosophy*. Cambridge, Harvard Univ Pr, 1996.
Archard, David. *Rad Phil*, 83, 41-43, My-J3 97.
Galston, William A. *Ethics*, 107(3), 509-512, Ap 97.
Paden, Roger. *Rev Metaph*, 50(3), 689-690, Mr 97.

**Santoni, Ronald E**. *Bad Faith, Good Faith and Authenticity in Sartre's Early Philosophy*. Philadelphia, Temple Univ Pr, 1995.
McCulloch, Gregory. *Phil Quart*, 47(186), 99-101, Ja 97.
Morris, Phyllis Sutton. *Man World*, 30(1), 115-122, Ja 97.

**Sartre, Jean-Paul** and Lévy, Benny. *Hope Now: The 1980 Interviews*. Chicago, Univ of Chicago Pr, 1996.
Piercey, Robert. *Can Phil Rev*, 17(2), 132-133, Ap 97.

**Sartwell, Crispin**. *Obscenity, Anarchy, Reality*. Albany, SUNY Pr, 1996.
Timm, Jeffrey. *Phil East West*, 47(3), 447-448, Jl 97.

**Satchidananda Murty, K**. *Vedic Hermeneutics*. Delhi, Motilal Banarsidass, 1993.
Nath Jha, Kishor. *J Indian Counc Phil Res*, 13(2), 190-200, Ja-Ap 96.

**Savarese, Paolo**. *Schelling filosofo del diritto*. Turin, Giappichelli, 1996.
Troncarelli, Barbara. *Riv Int Filosof Diritto*, 74(1), 174-177, Ja-Mr 97.

**Savellos, E E** (ed) and Yalcin, U D (ed). *Supervenience: New Essays*. New York, Cambridge Univ Pr, 1995.
Garrett, Brian. *Mind*, 106(421), 201-202, Ja 97.
Ross, Don. *Can Phil Rev*, 17(2), 134-137, Ap 97.
Wilkerson, T E. *Phil Books*, 38(2), 116-117, Ap 97.

**Savignano, A**. *Introduzione a Ortega y Gasset*. Laterza, Roma-Bari, 1996.
Gorani, Fabio. *Aquinas*, 39(3), 631-640, S-D 96.
Tortorella, Luigi. *Sapienza*, 50(1), 119-123, 1997.

**Saxena, Sushil Kumar**. *Art and Philosophy: Seven Aestheticians*. New Delhi, Indian Coun Phil Res, 1994.
Farrelly-Jackson, Steven. *Brit J Aes*, 36(4), 441-443, O 96.

**Sayre, Kenneth M**. *Plato's Literary Garden: How to Read a Platonic Dialogue*. Notre Dame, Univ Notre Dame Pr, 1995.
Gerson, Lloyd P. *Rev Metaph*, 50(3), 690-691, Mr 97.

**Scalone, Antonio**. *Rappresentanza politica e rappresentanza degli interessi*. Milano, Franco Angeli, 1996.
Fracanzani, Marcello. *Riv Int Filosof Diritto*, 73(3), 603-605, Jl-S 96.

**Scaltsas, T**. *Substance and Universals in Aristotle's Metaphysics*. Ithaca, Cornell Univ Pr, 1994.
Mitchell, Dorothy. *Austl J Phil*, 74(3), 534, S 96.

**Scaltsas, Theodore**. *Substance and Universals in Aristotle's Metaphysics*. Ithaca, Cornell Univ Pr, 1994.
Wehrle, Walter E. *Ancient Phil*, 16(2), 495-505, Fall 96.

**Scarre, Geoffrey**. *Utilitarianism*. New York, Routledge, 1996.
Wolf, Jean-Claude. *Frei Z Phil Theol*, 43(3), 511-513, 1996.

**Schaberg, William H**. *The Nietzsche Canon: A Publication History and Bibliography*. Chicago, Univ of Chicago Pr, 1995.
Hatab, Lawrence J. *Can Phil Rev*, 16(3), 201-203, Je 96.

**Schacht, Richard**. *Making Sense of Nietzsche: Reflections Timely and Untimely*. Champaign, Univ of Illinois Pr, 1995.
Havas, Randall E. *Rev Metaph*, 50(1), 180-182, S 96.

**Schacht, Richard**. *The Future of Alienation*. Chicago, Univ of Illinois Pr, 1994.
Johnson, Peter. *Phil Invest*, 19(4), 366-369, O 96.

**Schäfer, Thomas**. *Reflektierte Vernunft*. Frankfurt, Suhrkamp, 1995.
Bertram, Georg W. *Das Argument*, 217(5-6), 843-845, 1996.

**Schaffner, Kenneth F**. *Discovery and Explanation in Biology and Medicine*. Chicago, Univ of Chicago Pr, 1993.
LaChapelle, Jean. *Biol Phil*, 12(2), 243-257, Ap 97.

**Schank, Roger C** and Cleary, Chip. *Engines for Education*. Hillsdale, Erlbaum, 1995.
Harvey, Brian. *Mind Mach*, 6(3), 403-407, O 96.

**Schaub, Diana J**. *Erotic Liberalism: Women and Revolution in Montesquieu's Persian Letters*. Lanham, Rowman & Littlefield, 1995.
Morrisey, Will. *Interpretation*, 24(1), 109-116, Fall 96.

**Schell, Susan Meld**. *The Embodiment of Reason*. Chicago, Univ of Chicago Pr, 1996.
Johnson, Gregory R. *Rev Metaph*, 50(4), 918-920, Je 97.

**Schelling, F W J**. *Idealism and the Endgame of Theory: Three Essays*. Albany, SUNY Pr, 1994.
Burbidge, John W. *Int Stud Phil*, 29(1), 145-146, 1997.

**Scherer, Irmgard**. *The Crisis of Judgment in Kant's Three Critiques*. New York, Lang, 1995.
Kerckhove, Lee. *Rev Metaph*, 50(4), 917-918, Je 97.

**Scheuerman, William E**. *Between the Norm and the Exception*. Cambridge, MIT Pr, 1994.
Jay, Martin. *Int Stud Phil*, 28(4), 153-154, 1996.

**Schlesinger, George N**. *Timely Topics*. New York, Macmillan, 1994.
Cockburn, David. *Phil Books*, 37(4), 268-269, O 96.

**Schmidtz, David**. *Rational Choice and Moral Agency*. Princeton, Princeton Univ Pr, 1995.
Farrell, Daniel M. *Ethics*, 107(3), 522-526, Ap 97.

**Shi, David E**. *Facing Facts: Realism in American Thought and Culture.* New York, Oxford Univ Pr, 1995.
Hobbs, Jack A. *J Aes Educ*, 31(1), 114-117, Spr 97.

**Shin, Sun-Joo**. *The Logical Status of Diagrams.* New York, Cambridge Univ Pr, 1995.
Corsi, Giovanna. *Brit J Phil Sci*, 48(2), 290-291, Je 97.
Peterson, Philip L. *Can Phil Rev*, 16(3), 208-210, Je 96.

**Shotter, John**. *Conversational Realities: Constructing Life through Language.* London, Sage, 1993.
Tracy, Karen. *Human Stud*, 20(1), 117-123, Ja 97.

**Shusterman, Richard**. *Pragmatist Aesthetics.* Cambridge, Blackwell, 1992.
Munitz, Charles. *Metaphilosophy*, 28(3), 276-283, Jl 97.

**Shute, Michael**. *The Origins of Lonergan's Notion of the Dialectic of History.* Lanham, Univ Pr of America, 1993.
Loptson, Peter. *Dialogue (Canada)*, 35(3), 633-636, Sum 96.

**Shuttleworth, Sally**. *Charlotte Brontë and Victorian Psychology.* Cambridge, Cambridge Univ Pr, 1996.
Lerner, Lawrence. *Hist Euro Ideas*, 23(1), 49-53, Ja 97.

**Sieg, Ulrich**. *Aufstieg und Niedergang des Marburger Neukantianismus.* Würzburg, Koningshausen, 1994.
Ollig, H L. *Theol Phil*, 72(1), 123-127, 1997.

**Siep, Ludwig**. *Praktische Philosophie im Deutschen Idealismus.* Frankfurt, Suhrkamp, 1992.
Stratton-Lake, Philip. *Bull Hegel Soc Gt Brit*, 34, 50-52, Autumn-Wint 96.

**Sierpinska, Anna**. *Understanding in Mathematics.* London, Falmer Pr, 1994.
Davis, Andrew. *J Phil Educ*, 31(2), 355-364, Jl 97.

**Sierra Mejía, Rubén**. *La época de la crisis.* Cali, Ed Univ del Valle, 1996.
Aurelio Díaz, Jorge. *Ideas Valores*, 106-109, Ag 97.

**Silva, Lúcio Craveiro**. *Novas Cartas Inéditas de Antero de Quental.* Braga, Pub Fac de Filosofia, 1996.
Borges, J F Pereira. *Rev Port Filosof*, 53(1), 160-161, Ja-Mr 97.

**Silverman, Hugh J**. *Textualities: Between Hermeneutics and Deconstruction.* New York, Routledge, 1994.
Stern, Laurent. *J Aes Art Crit*, 55(1), 70-72, Wint 97.

**Simon, Linda** (ed). *William James Remembered.* Lincoln, Univ of Nebraska Pr, 1996.
Kenny, Gayle. *Int J Phil Stud*, 5(2), 343-345, Je 97.

**Simons, Joe**. *Foucault and the Political.* New York, Routledge, 1995.
Haugaard, Mark. *Int J Phil Stud*, 5(2), 337-338, Je 97.

**Simons, Margaret A** (ed). *Feminist Interpretations of Simone de Beauvoir.* University Park, Penn St Univ Pr, 1995.
Bauer, Nancy. *Hypatia*, 11(3), 161-164, Sum 96.

**Sinaceur, Hourya**. *Corps et Modèles.* Paris, Vrin, 1991.
Gribomont, Pascal. *Rev Int Phil*, 51(200), 285-287, 1997.

**Singer, Peter**. *How Are We to Live?.* Amherst, Prometheus, 1995.
Crisp, Roger. *Ethics*, 107(2), 344-345, Ja 97.
Frazier, Robert L. *Mind*, 105(420), 720-722, O 96.

**Sinnot-Armstrong, Walter** (ed), Raffman, Diana (ed) and Asher, Nicholas (ed). *Modality, Morality and Belief: Essays in Honor of Ruth Barcan Marcus.* New York, Cambridge Univ Pr, 1995.
Bricker, Phillip. *J Sym Log*, 62(1), 328-330, Mr 97.

**Skinner, Quentin**. *Reason and Rhetoric in the Philosophy of Hobbes.* Cambridge, Cambridge Univ Pr, 1996.
Honohan, Iseult. *Int J Phil Stud*, 5(1), 116-119, Mr 97.
Vaughan, Geoffrey. *Hist Euro Ideas*, 23(1), 35-43, Ja 97.
Walker, William. *Phil Lit*, 21(1), 204-207, Ap 97.

**Sklar, Lawrence**. *Physics and Chance.* New York, Cambridge Univ Pr, 1993.
Folse, Henry J. *Int Stud Phil*, 29(1), 150-151, 1997.
Uffink, Jos. *Stud Hist Phil Mod Physics*, 27B(3), 373-387, S 96.

**Skovsmose, O**. *Towards a Philosophy of Critical Mathematics Education.* Dordrecht, Kluwer, 1994.
Ernest, Paul. *J Phil Educ*, 30(3), 488-493, N 96.

**Slater, John G**. *Bertrand Russell.* Bristol, Thoemmes, 1994.
Bruneau, William. *Russell*, 16(2), 187-190, Wint 96-97.
Linsky, Bernard. *Dialogue (Canada)*, 36(1), 207-208, Wint 97.

**Slife, Brent D**. *Time and Psychological Explanation.* Albany, SUNY Pr, 1993.
Jenkins, Adelbert. *J Theor Phil Psych*, 16(1), 67-72, Spr 96.

**Smart, J J C** and Haldane, J J. *Atheism and Theism..* Cambridge, Blackwell, 1996.
Baillie, James. *Phil Books*, 38(3), 215-218, Jl 97.

**Smith, Barry**. *Austrian Philosophy: The Legacy of Franz Brentano.* Chicago, Open Court, 1994.
Picardi, Eva. *Erkenntnis*, 45(1), 123-127, July 96.

**Smith, Barry** (ed). *European Philosophy and the American Academy.* LaSalle, Monist Library, 1994.
Jacobs, David C. *Teach Phil*, 19(3), 306-310, Sept 96.

**Smith, Barry** (ed) and Smith, David Woodruff (ed). *The Cambridge Companion to Husserl.* Cambridge, Cambridge Univ Pr, 1995.
Buckley, P. *Tijdschr Filosof*, 58(4), 768-769, D 96.
Buckley, R Philip. *Can Phil Rev*, 16(4), 294-296, Ag 96.
Inwood, M J. *Int Phil Quart*, 36(4), 490-492, D 96.

**Smith, George P**. *Bioethics and the Law.* Lanham, Univ Pr of America, 1993.
Belliotti, Raymond A. *Int Stud Phil*, 29(2), 142-143, 1997.

**Smith, Gregory Bruce**. *Nietzsche, Heidegger, and the Transition to Postmodernity.* Chicago, Univ of Chicago Pr, 1996.
Howey, Richard L. *Rev Metaph*, 50(3), 694-695, Mr 97.

**Smith, John E**. *America's Philosophical Vision.* Chicago, Univ of Chicago Pr, 1992.
Reck, Andrew J. *Int Stud Phil*, 29(1), 151-152, 1997.

**Smith, Laurence D** (ed) and Woodward, William R (ed). *B.F. Skinner and Behaviorism in American Culture.* London, Associated Univ Pr, 1996.
Epstein, Robert. *J Mind Behav*, 18(1), 99-102, Wint 97.

**Smith, Michael**. *The Moral Problem.* Cambridge, Blackwell, 1994.
Cooper, Neil. *Phil Invest*, 19(4), 359-362, O 96.

**Smith, Murray**. *Engaging Characters: Fiction, Emotion, and the Cinema.* New York, Clarendon/Oxford Pr, 1995.
Gaut, Berys. *Brit J Aes*, 37(1), 96-97, Ja 97.

**Smith, Norris Kelly**. *Here I Stand: Perspective from Another Point of View.* New York, Columbia Univ Pr, 1995.
Kemp, Martin. *Brit J Aes*, 37(2), 175-177, Ap 97.

**Smith, Quentin**. *Language and Time.* New York, Oxford Univ Pr, 1993.
Sklar, Lawrence. *Int Stud Phil*, 29(2), 143-144, 1997.

**Smith, Quentin** and Oaklander, L Nathan. *Time, Change and Freedom: An Introduction to Metaphysics.* New York, Routledge, 1995.
Huggett, Nick. *Can Phil Rev*, 16(4), 297-298, Ag 96.
Le Poidevin, Robin. *Phil Books*, 38(1), 77-79, Ja 97.

**Smith, Rowland**. *Julian's Gods.* New York, Routledge, 1995.
Von Dietze, Erich. *Can Phil Rev*, 17(1), 72-73, F 97.

**Smullyan, Raymond M**. *Diagonalization and self-reference.* Oxford, Oxford Univ Pr, 1994.
Beklemishev, Lev. *J Sym Log*, 61(3), 1052-1055, S 96.

**Sobel, Jordan Howard**. *Taking Chances.* New York, Cambridge Univ Pr, 1994.
Skyrms, Brian. *Phil Rev*, 105(3), 410-413, Jl 96.

**Sober, Elliot**. *Filosofía de la Biología.* Madrid, Alianza, 1996.
Massa Rincón, Francisco Javier. *Convivium*, 9, 158-160, 1996.

**Sober, Elliot**. *From a Biological Point of View.* Cambridge, Cambridge Univ Pr, 1994.
Griffiths, Paul E. *Biol Phil*, 12(3), 427-431, Jl 97.

**Sober, Elliott**. *From a Biological Point of View.* New York, Cambridge Univ Pr, 1994.
Godfrey-Smith, Peter. *J Phil*, 94(3), 160-164, Ma 97.

**Soble, Alan**. *Sexual Investigations.* New York, New York Univ Pr, 1996.
McMahan, Kerrin. *Can Phil Rev*, 17(2), 139-141, Ap 97.

**Soffer, Gail**. *Husserl and the Question of Relativism.* Dordrecht, Kluwer, 1991.
Cobb-Stevens, Richard. *Rev Metaph*, 50(1), 185-188, S 96.

**Soifer, Eldon** (ed). *Ethical Issues: Perspectives for Canadians.* Peterborough, Broadview Pr, 1996.
Welwood-Hreno, Travis. *Can Phil Rev*, 17(3), 214-215, Je 97.

**Solomon, Robert**. *About Love: Reinventing Romance for Our Times.* Lanham, Rowman & Littlefield, 1994.
Brown, Deborah. *Dialogue (Canada)*, 36(2), 430-435, Spr 97.

**Solomon, Robert C** and Higgins, Kathleen. *A Short History of Philosophy.* New York, Oxford Univ Pr, 1996.
Wilkerson, T E. *Phil Books*, 38(1), 35-37, Ja 97.

**Solomon, Robert C** (ed) and Higgins, Kathleen M (ed). *The Age of German Idealism.* London, Routledge, 1993.
Stone, Martin. *Heythrop J*, 37(4), 498-499, O 96.

**Solomon, Robert C** and Higgins, Kathleen M. *World Philosophy: A Text with Readings.* New York, McGraw-Hill, 1995.
Art, Brad. *Teach Phil*, 19(4), 399-403, D 96.

**Sommer, Susana E**. *Procreación: nuevas tecnologías.* Buenos Aires, Atuel, 1996.
Regnasco, Maria J. *Cuad Etica*, 21-22, 196-198, 1996.

**Somos, Róbert**. *Origin and Greek Philosophy.* X, Unknown, 1995.
Pesthy, Monika. *Magyar Filozof Szemle*, 1-2, 431-436, 1997.

**Sonderegger, Erwin**. *Aristoteles, Metaphysik Z 1-12.* Bern, Haupt, 1993.
Ambühl, Hans. *Frei Z Phil Theol*, 43(3), 498-501, 1996.

**Soneson, Jerome P**. *Pragmatism and Pluralism.* Minneapolis, Fortress Pr, 1992.
Robbins, J Wesley. *Zygon*, 32(3), 267-270, Je 97.

**Sontag, Frederick**. *Wittgenstein and the Mystical: Philosophy as an Ascetic Practice.* Atlanta, Scholars Pr, 1995.
Wildes, Kevin Wm. *Rev Metaph*, 50(1), 188-189, S 96.

**Sorabji, Richard**. *Animal Minds and Human Morals.* Ithaca, Cornell Univ Pr, 1993.
Nussbaum, Martha. *Phil Rev*, 105(3), 403-405, Jl 96.
Welch, John R. *Philosophia (Israel)*, 25(1-4), 473-480, Ap 97.

**Walters, Kerry S** (ed). *Re-Thinking Reason: New Perspectives in Critical Thinking*. Albany, SUNY Pr, 1994.
Glaser, Jen. *Austl J Phil*, 74(4), 704-707, D 96.

**Walters, LeRoy** and Palmer, Julie Gage. *The Ethics of Human Gene Therapy*. New York, Oxford Univ Pr, 1997.
Glassberg, Andrea E. *Cambridge Quart Healthcare Ethics*, 6(4), 494-496, Fall 97.

**Walton, Douglas N**. *Arguments from Ignorance*. University Park, Penn St Univ Pr, 1996.
Tindale, Christopher W. *Phil Rhet*, 30(1), 97-101, 1997.

**Walton, Douglas N**. *Begging the Question*. Westport, Greenwood Pr, 1991.
Woods, John. *Dialogue (Canada)*, 36(2), 435-440, Spr 97.

**Waluchow, W J** (ed). *Free Expression: Essays in Law and Philosophy*. New York, Oxford Univ Pr, 1994.
Campbell, Tom D. *Can Phil Rev*, 16(5), 382-384, Oct 96.
Reeder Bell, Karen. *Phil Quart*, 47(186), 132-135, Ja 97.

**Walzer, Michael**. *Thick and Thin*. Notre Dame, Univ Notre Dame Pr, 1994.
Donelan, Jed. *Constellations*, 3(1), 132-135, Ap 96.

**Wandschneider, Dieter**. *Grundzüge einer Theorie der Dialektik*. Stuttgart, Klett-Cotta, 1995.
Bondeli, Martin. *Frei Z Phil Theol*, 44(1-2), 207-211, 1997.

**Ward, Keith**. *God, Chance and Necessity*. Oxford, Oneworld Pub, 1996.
Meynell, Hugo. *Heythrop J*, 38(3), 330-331, Jl 97.

**Ward, Keith**. *Religion and Revelation*. Oxford, Clarendon/Oxford Pr, 1994.
Lamont, John. *Thomist*, 61(3), 491-493, Jl 97.

**Wardy, Robert**. *The Birth of Rhetoric: Gorgias, Plato and their successors*. London, Routledge, 1996.
Rowe, Christopher. *Phronesis*, 42(2), 228-235, 1997.

**Warehime, Nancy**. *To be one of us: Cultural conflict, creative democracy, and education*. Albany, SUNY Pr, 1993.
Gatenby, Bruce M. *J Value Inq*, 31(1), 131-134, Mr 97.

**Warnick, Barbara**. *The Sixth Canon: Belletristic Rhetorical Theory and Its French Antecedents*. Columbia, Univ S Carolina Pr, 1993.
Bormann, Dennis R. *Phil Rhet*, 29(4), 467-472, 1996.

**Warren, Karen J** (ed). *Ecological Feminism*. New York, Routledge, 1994.
Moitra, Shefali. *J Applied Phil*, 14(1), 87-88, 1997.
Twine, Richard. *Environ Values*, 6(3), 370-371, Ag 97.

**Warren, Karen J** (ed). *Ecological Feminist Philosophies*. Bloomington, Indiana Univ Pr, 1996.
Hare-Mustin, Rachel T. *Ethics Behavior*, 6(3), 269-271, 1996.

**Warren, Preston**. *Out of the Wilderness: Douglas Clyde Macintosh's Journeys through the Grounds and Claims of Modern Thought*. New York, Lang, 1989.
Fell, Joseph P. *Dialogue (Canada)*, 35(3), 628-631, Sum 96.

**Waszek, Norbert**. *The Scottish Enlightenment and Hegel's Account of 'Civil Society'*. Dordrecht, Kluwer, 1988.
Wokler, Robert. *Bull Hegel Soc Gt Brit*, 35, 90-91, Spr-Sum 97.

**Waxman, Wayne**. *Hume's Theory of Consciousness*. New York, Cambridge Univ Pr, 1994.
Broackes, Justin. *Phil Quart*, 47(187), 267-270, Ap 97.
Thiel, Udo. *Brit J Hist Phil*, 4(2), 435-437, S 96.

**Weber, Edouard-Henri**. *La personne humaine au XIII siècle*. Paris, Vrin, 1991.
Boulois, Olivier. *Arch Phil*, 59(3), 485-488, Jl-S 96.

**Webster, John**. *Barth's Ethics of Reconciliation*. Cambridge, Cambridge Univ Pr, 1995.
McCormack, Bruce L. *Mod Theol*, 13(2), 273-276, Ap 97.

**Weeks, Jeffrey**. *Invented Moralities: Sexual Values in an Age of Uncertainty*. Oxford, Polity Pr, 1995.
Roker, Debi. *J Moral Educ*, 26(3), 363-364, S 97.

**Weiner, Neil O**. *The Harmony of the Soul: Mental Health and Moral Virtue Reconsidered*. New York, New York Univ Pr, 1993.
Edwards, Rem B. *Int Stud Phil*, 29(2), 149-150, 1997.
Veatch, Henry. *J Value Inq*, 31(2), 277-279, Je 97.

**Weinert, Friedel** (ed). *Laws of Nature: Essays on the Philosophical, Scientific and Historical Dimensions*. Berlin, Walter de Gruyter, 1995.
Hinckuss, Ian. *Austl J Phil*, 74(4), 707-710, D 96.

**Weinreb, Lloyd**. *Oedipus at Fenway Park: What Rights There Are and Why There Are Any*. Cambridge, Harvard Univ Pr, 1994.
Lomasky, Loren. *Ethics*, 107(3), 534-536, Ap 97.

**Weinrib, Ernest**. *The Idea of Private Law*. Cambridge, Harvard Univ Pr, 1995.
Gray, C B. *Rev Metaph*, 50(1), 194-195, S 96.
Westerman, Pauline C. *Can Phil Rev*, 16(4), 302-303, Ag 96.

**Weinstein, Michael A**. *Culture/Flesh: Explorations of Postcivilized Modernity*. Lanham, Rowman & Littlefield, 1995.
Graham, Kevin M. *Can Phil Rev*, 16(4), 304-305, Ag 96.

**Weir, Allison**. *Sacrificial Logics: Feminist Theory and the Critique of Identity*. New York, Routledge, 1996.
Nagel, Mechthild. *Can Phil Rev*, 16(4), 305-307, Ag 96.

**Weiss, Paul**. *Being and Other Realities*. Peru, Open Court, 1995.
McTeigue, Robert. *Int Phil Quart*, 37(3), 349-350, S 97.

**Welsch, Wolfgang**. *Vernunft: Die zeitgenössische Vernunftkritik und das Konzept der transversalen Vernunft*. Frankfurt, Suhrkamp, 1995.
Kleimann, Bernd. *Z Phil Forsch*, 51(1), 145-149, Ja-Mr 97.

**Welsen, Peter**. *Schopenhauers Theorie des Subjekts*. Würzburg, Koningshausen, 1995.
Bonk, S. *Theol Phil*, 72(1), 116-119, 1997.

**Wendell, Susan**. *The Rejected Body*. New York, Routledge, 1996.
Lorraine, Renée Cox. *Can Phil Rev*, 17(2), 149-151, Ap 97.

**Wertheimer, Alan**. *Exploitation*. Princeton, Princeton Univ Pr, 1996.
McGrogor, Joan L. *Can Phil Rev*, 17(1), 73-75, F 97.

**Wesson, Robert**. *Beyond Natural Selection*. Cambridge, MIT Pr, 1993.
Collier, John. *Biol Phil*, 12(1), 89-99, Ja 97.

**West, Cornel**. *Keeping Faith*. New York, Routledge, 1993.
Bewaki, J A I. *Phil Soc Sci*, 27(2), 212-218, Je 97.

**West, Thomas H**. *Ultimate Hope Without God: The Atheistic Eschatology of Ernst Bloch*. New York, Lang, 1991.
Sponheim, Paul. *Process Stud*, 25, 137-140, 1996.

**Westberg, Daniel**. *Right Practical Reason*. New York, Oxford Univ Pr, 1994.
Gallagher, David M. *Phil Books*, 38(1), 42-44, Ja 97.
Hause, Jeffrey. *Phil Rev*, 105(2), 243-245, Ap 96.
Stone, Martin. *Phil Quart*, 47(187), 263-265, Ap 97.

**Weston, Michael**. *Kierkegaard and Modern Continental Philosophy*. New York, Routledge, 1994.
Norris, John. *Heythrop J*, 37(4), 501-502, O 96.

**Wetsel, David**. *Pascal and Disbelief: Catechesis and Conversion in the Pensées*. Washington, Cath Univ Amer Pr, 1994.
Levi, Anthony. *Heythrop J*, 38(1), 84-85, Ja 97.
Williams, Timothy J. *Rev Metaph*, 50(2), 428-429, D 96.

**Whitaker, Andrew**. *Einstein, Bohr and the Quantum Dilemma*. New York, Cambridge Univ Pr, 1995.
Squires, Euan J. *Stud Hist Phil Mod Physics*, 27B(3), 389-395, S 96.

**White, Patricia**. *Civic Virtues and Public Schooling*. New York, Teachers College Pr, 1996.
Carr, David. *J Phil Educ*, 31(2), 345-354, Jl 97.
Steutel, Jan W. *J Moral Educ*, 26(1), 107-109, Mr 97.

**White, Stephen K**. *Edmund Burke: Modernity, Politics, and Aesthetics*. Thousand Oaks, Sage, 1994.
Bromwich, David. *Polit Theory*, 24(4), 739-746, N 96.

**White, Stephen K** (ed). *The Cambridge Companion to Habermas*. New York, Cambridge Univ Pr, 1995.
McCarthy, Thomas. *Ethics*, 107(2), 369-372, Ja 97.
Papastephanou, Marianna. *Int Phil Quart*, 36(4), 498-500, D 96.

**Whitebook, Joel**. *Perversion and Utopia: A Study in Psychoanalysis and Critical Theory*. Cambridge, MIT Pr, 1995.
Ferrara, Alessandro. *Constellations*, 3(3), 425-428, Ja 97.

**Wians, William** (ed). *Aristotle's Philosophical Development: Problems and Prospects*. Lanham, Rowman & Littlefield, 1996.
Blair, George A. *Ancient Phil*, 17(2), 254-258, Spr 97.
Tress, Daryl M. *Int Phil Quart*, 37(2), 236-239, Je 97.

**Wiggershaus, Rolf**. *The Frankfurt School*. Cambridge, MIT Pr, 1994.
Bohman, James. *Polit Theory*, 25(4), 598-602, Ag 97.

**Wilkerson, T E**. *Natural Kinds*. Brookfield, Avebury, 1995.
Elder, Crawford L. *Phil Phenomenol Res*, 57(1), 239-241, Mr 97.
Ellis, Brian. *Austl J Phil*, 74(4), 710-711, D 96.

**Wilks, Yorick A**, Slater, Brian M and Guthrie, Lousie M. *Electric Words: Dictitionaries [sic], Computers, and Meanings*. Cambridge, MIT Pr, 1996.
Geirsson, Heimir. *Mind Mach*, 7(2), 312-315, My 97.

**Will, James E**. *The Universal God: Justice, Love and Peace in the Global Village*. Louisville, Knox Pr, 1994.
Lorenzen, Lynne F. *Process Stud*, 23(3-4), 202-203, Fall-Wint 94.

**Williams, B**. *Descartes: El proyecto de la investigación pura*. Madrid, Catedra, 1996.
García Rodríguez, Angel. *Teorema*, 16(1), 109-112, 1996.
Martínez, José A. *Dialogo Filosof*, 12(3), 467-474, S-D 96.

**Williams, Bernard**. *Making Sense of Humanity and Other Philosophical Papers*. New York, Cambridge Univ Pr, 1995.
Nussbaum, Martha. *Ethics*, 107(3), 526-529, Ap 97.
Porter, Jean. *Int Phil Quart*, 36(4), 489-490, D 96.
Slote, Michael. *Int J Phil Stud*, 4(2), 357-359, S 96.

**Williams, Bernard**. *Making Sense of Humanity and Other Philosophical Papers 1982-1993*. New York, Cambridge Univ Pr, 1995.
Glidden, David. *Can Phil Rev*, 16(4), 231-236, Ag 96.

**Williams, Patricia**. *The Rooster's Egg: On the Persistence of Prejudice*. Cambridge, Harvard Univ Pr, 1996.
Acorn, Annalise. *Can Phil Rev*, 16(3), 223-227, Je 96.

**Wilson, Catherine**. *The Invisible World: Early Modern Philosophy and the Invention of the Microscope*. Princeton, Princeton Univ Pr, 1995.
Gal, Ofer. *Leibniz Soc Rev*, 6, 144-148, D 96.

**Zuidervaart, Lambert**. *Adorno's Aesthetic Theory*. Cambridge, MIT Pr, 1991.
  Brown, Lee B. *J Aes Educ*, 27(2), 117-121, Sum 93.
**Zwicky, Jan**. *Lyric Philosophy*. Toronto, Univ of Toronto Pr, 1992.
  DeAngelis, William James. *Dialogue (Canada)*, 35(4), 847-851, Fall 96.